ISSN 0071-0202

ENCYCLOPEDIA OF ASSOCIATIONS®

AN ASSOCIATIONS UNLIMITED REFERENCE

A Guide to More Than 24,000 National and International Organizations, Including: Trade, Business, and Commercial; Environmental and Agricultural; Legal, Governmental, Public Administration, and Military; Engineering, Technological, and Natural and Social Sciences; Educational; Cultural; Social Welfare; Health and Medical; Public Affairs; Fraternal, Nationality, and Ethnic; Religious; Veterans', Hereditary, and Patriotic; Hobby and Avocational; Athletic and Sports; Labor Unions, Associations, and Federations; Chambers of Commerce and Trade and Tourism; Greek Letter and Related Organizations; and Fan Clubs.

56th EDITION

VOLUME 2
GEOGRAPHIC AND EXECUTIVE INDEXES

Tara E. Atterberry, Project Editor

GALE
A Cengage Company

Farmington Hills, Mich • San Francisco • New York • Waterville, Maine
Meriden, Conn • Mason, Ohio • Chicago

Encyclopedia of Associations, 56th Edition

Project Editor: Tara Atterberry

Composition and Electronic Capture: Gary Oudersluys

Manufacturing: Rita Wimberley

Gale
27500 Drake Rd.
Farmington Hills, MI 48331-3535

ISBN-13: 978-1-4144-8824-0 (vol. 1, 3-part set)
ISBN-13: 978-1-4144-8825-7 (vol. 1, part 1)
ISBN-13: 978-1-4144-8826-4 (vol. 1, part 2)
ISBN-13: 978-1-4144-8884-4 (vol. 1, part 3)
ISBN-13: 978-1-4144-8827-1 (vol. 2)

ISSN 0071-0202

Printed in the United States of America
2 3 4 5 6 7 21 20 19 18 17

Contents

Volume 2

The *Encyclopedia of Associations (EA)*, Volume 1, is the only comprehensive source of detailed information concerning more than 24,000 nonprofit American membership organizations of national scope. For nearly sixty years and through 55 earlier editions, *EA's* listing of associations and professional societies is unsurpassed as a 'switchboard' connecting persons needing information to highly qualified sources.

Frequently, a phone call, fax, or email to one of the thousands of organizations formed around a specific interest or objective produces more information faster than research in books, periodicals, and other printed materials.

Preparation of This Edition

The editorial objective for each edition of *EA* is complete verification or updating of existing entries and the identification and description of new or previously unlisted organizations. Information was compiled or confirmed through written correspondence, through the association's recently updated web site, by telephone or through email.

Scope of the Encyclopedia

The organizations described in *EA* fall into the following seven general categories:

National, nonprofit membership associations, which represent the largest number of organizations listed;

International associations, which are generally North American in scope and membership or binational, representing a direct link between the United States and another country or region; also includes American or North American sections, chapters, or divisions of associations headquartered outside of the United States;

Local and regional associations, only if their subjects or objectives are national in interest;

Nonmembership organizations, if they disseminate information to the public as well as to the researcher;

For-profit associations, if their names suggest that they are nonprofit organizations;

Available in Electronic Formats

Licensing. National Organizations of the U.S. is available for licensing. For more information, contact Gale's Business Development Group at 1-800-877-GALE.

This Directory is also available online as part of the Gale Directory Library. For more information, call 1-800-877-GALE.

Associations Unlimited. Associations Unlimited is a modular approach to the *Encyclopedia of Associations* database, allowing customers to select the pieces of the series that they want to purchase. The four modules include each of the *EA* series (national, international, and regional) as well as one module featuring U.S. government data on more than 450,000 nonprofit organizations. For more information, call 800-877-GALE.

Acknowledgments

The editors are grateful to the large number of organization officials in the United States and abroad who generously responded to our requests for updated information, provided additional data by telephone, fax, email or website and helped in the shaping of this edition with their comments and suggestions throughout the year.

Comments and Suggestions Welcome

Matters pertaining to specific listings in *EA,* as well as suggestions for new listings, should be directed to Tara Atterberry, Editor, *Encyclopedia of Associations.*

Please write or call:
Encyclopedia of Associations
Gale
27500 Drake Rd.
Farmington Hills, MI 48331-3535
Phone: (248) 699-8909
Toll-free: 800-347-GALE
Email: Tara.Atterberry@Cengage.com

Geographic Index

Entries in *EA*'s Geographic Index are listed according to the state in which the organization's headquarters are located. They are then sub-arranged by city and listed alphabetically according to the names of the organizations within each city.

A sample entry is shown below.

∎1∎ Amer. Soc. of Earth Sciences **∎2∎** [3348]
∎3∎ 123 Salina St.
PO Box 1992
Allen Park, NY 13201
∎4∎ Ph: (315)555-9500
∎5∎ Patsy Rachel, Pres.

Description of Numbered Elements

∎1∎ Organization Name. The formal name is given; 'The' and 'Inc.' are omitted in most listings, unless they are an integral part of the acronym used by the association.

∎2∎ Entry Number. Refers to the sequential entry number (rather than the page number) assigned to the organization's main entry in Volume 1, where other details concerning membership, objectives and activities, and publications can be found.

∎3∎ Address. The address is generally that of the permanent national headquarters, or of the chief official for groups that have no permanent offices. The city appears in **boldface.**

∎4∎ Telephone Number. A telephone number is listed when furnished by the organization.

∎5∎ Chief Official and Title. Lists the name of a full-time executive, an elected officer, or other contact person designated by the association.

Executive Index

Entries in *EA*'s Executive Index are listed alphabetically according to the surname of the chief executive of the organization. When an individual is listed as the chief executive of more than one organization, entries are arranged by organization name.

A sample entry is shown below.

∎1∎ Patsy, Mrs. Rachel, Pres.
∎2∎ Amer. Soc. of Earth Sciences **∎3∎** [3348]
∎4∎ 123 Salina St.
PO Box 1992
Allen Park, NY 13201
∎5∎ Ph: (315)555-9500

Description of Numbered Elements

∎1∎ Chief Official and Title. Lists the name of a full-time executive, an elected officer, or other contact person designated by the association.

∎2∎ Organization Name. The formal name is given; 'The' and 'Inc.' are omitted in most listings, unless they are an integral part of the acronym used by the association.

∎3∎ Entry Number. Refers to the sequential entry number (rather than the page number) assigned to the organization's main entry in Volume 1, where other details concerning membership, objectives and activities, and publications can be found.

∎4∎ Address. The address is generally that of the permanent national headquarters, or of the chief official for groups that have no permanent offices.

∎5∎ Telephone Number. A telephone number is listed when furnished by the organization.

Geographic Index

Entries in EA's Geographic Index are listed according to the state in which the organization's headquarters are located. They are then sub-arranged by city and listed alphabetically according to the names of the organizations within each city.

A sample entry is shown below.

Nat'l Assoc. of Basic Sciences #23 [23-4]
604 123 Sample St.
PO Box 1235
Anytown, NY 12301
607 Ph: (765)456-9890
123 Fancy Person, Pres.

Description of Numbered Elements

Organization Name. The formal name is given. *The* and *the* are omitted in most listings, unless they are an integral part of the acronym used by the association.

Entry Number. Refers to the sequential entry number (rather than the page number) assigned to the organization's main entry in Volume 1, where other details concerning membership, objectives and activities, and publications can be found.

Address. The address is generally that of the permanent national headquarters, or of the chief official for groups that have no permanent offices. The city appears in boldface.

Telephone Number. A telephone number is listed when furnished by the organization.

Chief Official and Title. Lists the name of a full-time executive, an elected officer, or other contact person designated by the association.

Executive Index

Entries in EA's Executive Index are listed alphabetically according to the surname of the chief executive of the organization. When an individual is listed as the chief executive of more than one organization, entries are arranged by organization name.

A sample entry is shown below.

114 Person, Mrs. Fancy, Pres.
123 Amer. Soc. of Gen'l Sciences #24 [23-4]
602 123 Sample St.
PO Box 1235
Anar Park, NY 12301
303 Ph: (765)456-9890

Description of Numbered Elements

Chief Official and Title. Lists the name of a full-time executive, an elected officer, or other contact person designated by the association.

Organization Name. The formal name is given. *The* and *the* are omitted in most listings, unless they are an integral part of the acronym used by the association.

Entry Number. Refers to the sequential entry number (rather than the page number) assigned to the organization's main entry in Volume 1, where other details concerning membership, objectives and activities, and publications can be found.

Address. The address is generally that of the permanent national headquarters, or of the chief official for groups that have no permanent offices.

Telephone Number. A telephone number is listed when furnished by the organization.

ix   Encyclopedia of Associations, 56th Edition

Abbreviations

Geographic Abbreviations

United States and U.S. Territories

AK	Alaska
AL	Alabama
AR	Arkansas
AZ	Arizona
CA	California
CO	Colorado
CT	Connecticut
DC	District of Columbia
DE	Delaware
FL	Florida
GA	Georgia
GU	Guam
HI	Hawaii
IA	Iowa
ID	Idaho
IL	Illinois
IN	Indiana
KS	Kansas
KY	Kentucky
LA	Louisiana
MA	Massachusetts
MD	Maryland
ME	Maine
MI	Michigan
MN	Minnesota
MO	Missouri
MS	Mississippi
MT	Montana
NC	North Carolina
ND	North Dakota
NE	Nebraska
NH	New Hampshire
NJ	New Jersey
NM	New Mexico
NV	Nevada
NY	New York
OH	Ohio
OK	Oklahoma
OR	Oregon
PA	Pennsylvania
PR	Puerto Rico
RI	Rhode Island
SC	South Carolina
SD	South Dakota
TN	Tennessee
TX	Texas
UT	Utah
VA	Virginia
VI	Virgin Islands
VT	Vermont
WA	Washington
WI	Wisconsin
WV	West Virginia
WY	Wyoming

Table of Abbreviations Used in Addresses and the Index

Acad	Academy
AFB	Air Force Base
Amer	American
APO	Army Post Office
Apt	Apartment
Assn	Association
Ave	Avenue
Bd	Board
Bldg	Building
Blvd	Boulevard
Br	Branch
Bur	Bureau
c/o	Care of
Co	Company
Coll	College
Comm	Committee
Commn	Commission
Conf	Conference
Confed	Confederation
Cong	Congress
Corp	Corporation
Coun	Council
Ct	Court
Dept	Department
Div	Division
Dr	Drive
E	East
Expy	Expressway
Fed	Federation
Fl	Floor
Found	Foundation
FPO	Fleet Post Office
Ft	Fort
Fwy	Freeway
Govt	Government
GPO	General Post Office
Hwy	Highway
Inc	Incorporated
Inst	Institute
Intl	International
Ln	Lane
Ltd	Limited
Mfrs	Manufacturers
Mgt	Management
Mt	Mount
N	North
Natl	National
NE	Northeast
No	Number
NW	Northwest
Pkwy	Parkway
Pl	Place
PO	Post Office
Prof	Professor
Rd	Road
RD	Rural Delivery
RFD	Rural Free Delivery
Rm	Room
RR	Rural Route
Rte	Route
S	South
SE	Southeast
Sect	Section
Soc	Society

Sq	Square	Subcommn	Subcommission	UN	United Nations
St	Saint, Street	SW	Southwest	Univ	University
Sta	Station	Terr	Terrace, Territory	U.S.	United States
Ste	Sainte, Suite	Tpke	Turnpike	U.S.A.	United States of America
Subcomm	Subcommittee	T.V.	Television	W	West

Currency Abbreviations and Definitions

Arranged by Currency Abbreviation

Abbr.	Currency Unit	Country
$	U.S. dollar	American Samoa, British Virgin Islands, Guam, Marshall Islands, Federated States of Micronesia, U.S.
$A	Australian dollar	Australia, Kiribati, Nauru, Norfolk Island, Tuvalu
$B	Belizean dollar	Belize
$b	boliviano	Bolivia
$F	Fijian dollar	Fiji
œ	pound sterling	England, Northern Ireland, Scotland, Wales
œC	Cyprus pound	Cyprus
œE	Egyptian pound	Egypt
œG	Gibraltar pound	Gibraltar
œS	Sudanese pound	Sudan
Syr	Syrian pound	Syria
A	Argentinian austral	Argentina
Af	afghani	Afghanistan
AF	Aruban florin	Aruba
AS	Austrian Schilling	Austria
B	balboa	Panama
B$	Bahamian dollar	Bahamas
BD	Bahraini dinar	Bahrain
BD$	Barbados dollar	Barbados
BFr	Belgian franc	Belgium
Bht	baht	Thailand
Bm$	Bermuda dollar	Bermuda
Br$	Brunei dollar	Brunei Darussalam
Bs	bolivar	Venezuela
C	colon	Costa Rica, El Salvador
Cd	cedi	Ghana
C$	Canadian dollar	Canada
C$	new cordoba	Nicaragua
CFP	Colonial Francs Pacifique	New Caledonia
ChP	Chilean peso	Chile
CI$	Cayman Island dollar	Cayman Islands
CoP	Colombian peso	Colombia
Cr$	cruzado	Brazil
CRs	Ceylon rupee	Sri Lanka
CuP	Cuban peso	Cuba
D	dalasi	Gambia
DA	dinar	Algeria
Db	dobra	Sao Tome and Principe
DFr	Djibouti franc	Djibouti
Dg	dong	Vietnam
Dh	dirham	Morocco
Din	dinar	Bosnia-Hercegovina, Croatia, Macedonia, Slovenia, Yugoslavia
DKr	Danish krone	Denmark, Faroe Islands, Greenland
DM	Deutsche Mark	Germany
DP	Dominican peso	Dominican Republic
Dr	drachma	Greece
Ec	escudo	Cape Verde
EC$	East Caribbean dollar	Antigua-Barbuda, Dominica, Grenada, Montserrat, St.Christopher-Nevis, St. Lucia, St. Vincent and the Grenadines
ECU	European currency unit	European Economic Community
E$	Ethiopian birr	Ethiopia
Eg	emalangeni	Swaziland
Esc	escudo	Portugal
EUR	Euro	Austria, Belgium, Finland, France, Germany, Greece, Ireland, Italy, Luxembourg, Netherlands, Portugal, Spain
f	florin	Netherlands
FM	Finnish mark	Finland
Fr	franc	Andorra, France, French Guiana, Guadeloupe, Martinique, Monaco, Reunion Island, St. Pierre and Miquelon
FrB	Burundi franc	Burundi
Fr CFA	Communaute Financiere Africaine franc	Benin, Burkina Faso, Cameroon, Central African Republic, Chad, Comoros, Congo, Cote d'Ivoire, Equatorial Guinea, Gabon, Mali, Niger, Senegal, Togo
Ft	forint	Hungary
G	gourde	Haiti
GBP	Guinea-Bissau peso	Guinea-Bissau
G$	Guyana dollar	Guyana
GFr	Guinea franc	Guinea
Gs	guarani	Paraguay
HK$	Hong Kong dollar	Hong Kong
ID	Iraqi dinar	Iraq
IKr	Icelandic krona	Iceland
IRœ	Irish pound	Republic of Ireland
IS	Israel shekel	Israel
It	inti	Peru
J$	Jamaican dollar	Jamaica
JD	Jordanian dinar	Jordan
K	kina	Papua New Guinea
K	new kip	Laos
Kcs	koruna	Czech Republic, Slovakia
KD	Kuwaiti dinar	Kuwait
KSh	Kenyan shilling	Kenya
Ky	kyat	Myanmar (Burma)
Kz	kwanza	Angola
L	leu	Romania
L$	Liberian dollar	Liberia
LD	Libyan dinar	Libya
Le	leone	Sierra Leone
LFr	Luxembourg franc	Luxembourg
Lk	lek	Albania
Lp	lempira	Honduras
L£	Lebanese pound	Lebanon
Lr	lira	Italy, San Marino
Lv	leva	Bulgaria
M$	Malaysian dollar	Malaysia
MFr	Malagasy franc	Madagascar
MKw	Malawi kwacha	Malawi
Ml	maloti	Lesotho
ML	Maltese lira	Malta

MP	Mexican peso	Mexico
MRs	Mauritius rupee	Mauritius
MRu	Maldivian rufiya	Maldives
Mt	metical	Mozambique
N	naira	Nigeria
NAf	Antillean florin	Netherlands Antilles
Ng	ngultrum	Bhutan
NKr	Norwegian krone	Norway
NP	nuevo peso	Uruguay
NRs	Nepalese rupee	Nepal
NTs	New Taiwanese dollar	Taiwan
NZ$	New Zealand dollar	Cook Islands, New Zealand, Niue
Og	ouguiya	Mauritania
P	pula	Botswana
PP	Philippine peso	Philippines
PRs	Pakistan rupee	Pakistan
Ptas	peseta	Spain
Ptcs	pataca	Macao
Q	quetzal	Guatemala
QRl	riyal	Qatar
R	rand	South Africa, Namibia
Rb	ruble	Armenia, Azerbaijan, Belarus, Estonia, Georgia, Kazakhstan, Kirgizstan, Latvia, Lithuania, Moldova, Russia, Tajikstan, Turkmenistan, Ukraine, Uzbekistan
RFr	Rwandan franc	Rwanda
riel	riel	Cambodia
Rl	Iranian rial	Iran
Rlo	rial Omani	Oman

Rp	rupiah	Indonesia
Rs	rupee	India
S	sucre	Ecuador
S$	Singapore dollar	Singapore
Sf	Suriname florin	Suriname
SFr	Swiss franc	Switzerland, Liechtenstein
SI$	Solomon Island dollar	Soloman Islands
SKr	Swedish krona	Sweden
SRl	Saudi riyal	Saudi Arabia
SRs	Seychelles rupee	Seychelles
SSh	Somali shilling	Somalia
T$	pa'anga	Tonga
TD	Tunisian dinar	Tunisia
Tg	tugrik	Mongolia
Tk	taka	Bangladesh
TL	Turkish lira	Turkey
TSh	Tanzanian shilling	Tanzania
TT$	Trinidad and Tobagoan dollar	Trinidad and Tobago
USh	Ugandan shilling	Uganda
V	vatu	Vanuatu
W	won	Democratic People's Republic of Korea, Republic of Korea
Y	yen	Japan
YRl	Yemen rial	Yemen
Yu	yuan	People's Republic of China
Z	Zaire	Zaire
Z$	Zimbabwe dollar	Zimbabwe
ZKw	Zambian kwacha	Zambia
Zl	zloty	Poland

ALABAMA

86th Chemical Mortar Battalion Association [21178]
c/o George Murray, Adjutant
818 W 62nd St.
Anniston, AL 36206
PH: (256)820-4415
Murray, George, Adj.

Mothers Against Methamphetamine [13154]
PO Box 8
Arab, AL 35016
PH: (256)498-6262
Toll free: 866-293-8901
Holley, Dr. Mary, Founder, President

We Care Program [11551]
3493 Highway 21
Atmore, AL 36502
PH: (251)368-8818
Fax: (251)368-0932
Metzler, Don, President

Association for Career and Technical Education Research [8734]
c/o Dr. Leane Skinner, President
Dept. of Curriculum and Teaching
Auburn University
5040 Haley
Auburn, AL 36849-5212
PH: (334)844-3823
Skinner, Dr. Leane, President

Black Entomologists [6608]
c/o Dept. of Entomology & Plant Pathology
301 Funchess Hall
Auburn, AL 36849
PH: (662)686-3646
    (334)844-5098
Fax: (662)686-5281
Riddick, Eric W., PhD, Officer

Comparative Nutrition Society [16215]
c/o Wendy Hood, President-Elect
315 Rouse Life Sciences Bldg.
Auburn University
Auburn, AL 36849
Hood, Wendy, President

Free Nation Foundation [18295]
c/o Robert T. Long, Director
Auburn University
6080 Haley Ctr.
Auburn, AL 36830
PH: (334)844-3782
Hammer, Richard O., Act. Pres., Founder

IEEE - Dielectrics and Electrical Insulation Society [6409]
Auburn University
Electrical and Computer Engineering
200 Broun Hall
Auburn, AL 36849-5201
PH: (334)844-1822
Fax: (334)844-1809
Lewin, Paul, VP

International Association of Astacology [6716]
c/o Jim Stoeckel, Secretary
203 Swingle Hall
Dept. of Fisheries and Allied Aquaculture
Auburn University
Auburn, AL 36849-5419
PH: (334)844-9249
Fax: (334)844-9208
Stoeckel, Jim, Secretary

University Aviation Association [7462]
2415 Moore's Mill Rd., Ste. 265-216
Auburn, AL 36830

PH: (334)528-0300
Kearns, Suzanne, President

Society for the History of Technology [9521]
Dept. of History
310 Thach Hall
Auburn University, AL 36849-5207
PH: (334)844-6770
Fax: (334)844-6673
Seely, Bruce, President

United States Aquaculture Society [3648]
c/o David Cline, President-Elect
203 Swingle Hall
Auburn University, AL 36849
PH: (334)844-2874
Fax: (334)844-0830
Flimlin, Gef, President

African Children's Mission [10837]
PO Box 26470
Birmingham, AL 35260
PH: (205)620-4937
Daniel, Mary, Founder

American Association of Nurse Attorneys [15526]
3416 Primm Ln.
Birmingham, AL 35216
PH: (205)824-7615
Toll free: 877-538-2262
Fax: (205)823-2760
Sanzio, RN, MPA, JD, Teressa M., President

American Association of Teachers of Arabic [8168]
3416 Primm Ln.
Birmingham, AL 35216
PH: (205)822-6800
Fax: (205)823-2760
    (205)978-3106
Attieh, Aman, Exec. Dir.

American Baseball Foundation [22542]
2660 10th Ave. S, Ste. 620
Birmingham, AL 35205
PH: (205)558-4235
Fax: (205)918-0800
Osinski, E. David, Exec. Dir.

American Nutraceutical Association [14977]
5120 Selkirk Dr., Ste. 100
Birmingham, AL 35242-4165
PH: (205)980-5710
Toll free: 800-566-3622
Fax: (205)991-9302
Montgomery, Allen, CEO, Exec. Dir., Founder

American Society for Reproductive Medicine [14753]
1209 Montgomery Hwy.
Birmingham, AL 35216-2809
PH: (205)978-5000
Fax: (205)978-5005
Reindollar, Richard H., MD, CEO

American Sports Medicine Institute [17278]
2660 10th Ave. S, Ste. 505
Birmingham, AL 35205
PH: (205)918-0000
Fax: (205)918-2177
Johnson, Lanier, Exec. Dir.

American Uveitis Society [16371]
700 18th St. S, Ste. 601
Birmingham, AL 35233
PH: (205)325-8507
Fax: (205)325-8200
Davis, Janet L., MD, Membership Chp.

American Wood Protection Association [1428]
100 Chase Park S, Ste. 116
Birmingham, AL 35236-1851

PH: (205)733-4077
Fax: (205)733-4075
McCown, Colin, Exec. VP

Association of Edison Illuminating Companies [3412]
600 N 18th St. N
Birmingham, AL 35203
PH: (205)257-3839
Fax: (205)257-2540
Boston, Terry W., Exec. Dir., Secretary, Treasurer

Association of Teachers of Maternal and Child Health [14168]
c/o Julie McDougal, Coordinator
1720 2nd Ave. S, Ryals 310G
Birmingham, AL 35294-0022
PH: (205)975-0531
Fax: (205)934-3347
Wingate, Martha, DrPH, Chairperson

Bass Anglers Sportsman Society [22841]
3500 Blue Lake Dr., Ste. 120
Birmingham, AL 35243
Toll free: 877-BAS-SUSA

Cancer Molecular Therapeutics Research Association [13926]
1670 University Blvd.
Birmingham, AL 35294
PH: (205)934-4569
Fax: (205)934-8240
Houghton, Peter, PhD, President

Cardiology Advocacy Alliance [14105]
PO Box 26588
Birmingham, AL 35260
PH: (202)505-2221
Fax: (205)978-3106
Attebery, Tim, President

Civitan International [12887]
PO Box 130744
Birmingham, AL 35213-0744
PH: (205)591-8910
Toll free: 800-CIVITAN
Capps, Duane, Officer

Council for Exceptional Children-Division on Visual Impairments [8581]
c/o Diane Pevsner, President
University of Alabama at Birmingham
School of Education
901 S 13th St. S
Birmingham, AL 35294
PH: (205)975-5351
Pevsner, Diane, President

Friends-in-Art of American Council of the Blind [8920]
c/o Lynn Hedl, President
521 Oxford Cir.
Birmingham, AL 35209
PH: (205)942-1987
Hedl, Lynn, President

Gold Star Wives of America [21040]
PO Box 361986
Birmingham, AL 35236
Toll free: 888-751-6350
Ellinger, Carol, Chmn. of the Bd.

International Andalusian and Lusitano Horse Association [4361]
101 Carnoustie N, No. 200
Birmingham, AL 35242
PH: (205)995-8900
Fax: (205)995-8966
Smith, Janita, President

International Association of Baptist Colleges and Universities [8709]
c/o Samford University
PO Box 293935

Birmingham, AL 35229
PH: (205)726-2036
Oliver, Samuel, President, Chmn. of the Bd.

International Association of Forensic and Security Metrology [7231]
3416 Primm Ln.
Birmingham, AL 35216
PH: (205)823-6106
Fax: (205)824-7700
Liscio, Eugene, President

International Bronchoesophagological Society [13861]
1720 2nd Ave. S, BDB 563
Birmingham, AL 35203
Chambers, Denise, Admin. Asst.

International Nurses Society on Addictions [16137]
3416 Primm Ln.
Birmingham, AL 35216
PH: (205)823-6106
Evans-Lombe, Monica, Exec. Dir.

International Society of Cardiovascular Ultrasound [14652]
4240 Kennesaw Dr.
Birmingham, AL 35213
PH: (205)934-8256
Fax: (205)934-6747
Nanda, Dr. Navin, MD, President

KampGround Owners Association [2911]
3416 Primm Ln.
Birmingham, AL 35216
PH: (205)824-0022
Toll free: 800-678-9976
Fax: (205)823-2760
Ranieri, William, Exec. Dir.

Manufacturers of Aerial Devices & Digger Derricks Council [1744]
c/o Dr. Joshua Chard, PhD, Chairman
33 Inverness Center Pky.
Birmingham, AL 35242
PH: (414)272-0943
Fax: (414)272-1170
Chard, Dr. Joshua, PhD, Chairman

Mitochondria Research and Medicine Society [14596]
PO Box 55322
Birmingham, AL 35255
PH: (205)934-2735
Fax: (205)934-2766
O'Brien, Prof. Thomas W., PhD, President

National Association of Abandoned Mine Land Programs [18700]
c/o Chuck Williams, President
Alabama Dept. of Labor
11 W Oxmoor Rd., Ste. 100
Birmingham, AL 35209
Scott, Bob, Comm. Chm.

National Association of Medical Education Companies [8330]
3416 Primm Ln.
Birmingham, AL 35216
PH: (205)824-7612
Fax: (205)823-2760
Kim, Joseph, President

National Association of Pipe Fabricators [2606]
2061 Brae Trl.
Birmingham, AL 35242
PH: (205)706-0886
Houghton, David, Legal Counsel

National Center for Sports Safety [17285]
2316 1st Ave. S
Birmingham, AL 35233

PH: (205)329-7535
Toll free: 866-508-6277
Fax: (205)329-7526
Lemak, Dr. Lawrence J., Founder

National CML Society **[15537]**
130 Inverness Plz., Ste. 307
Birmingham, AL 35242
Toll free: 877-431-2573
Stephens, Greg, Exec. Dir.

National Organization of Alternative
Programs **[17175]**
3416 Primm Ln.
Birmingham, AL 35216-5602
PH: (205)823-6106
Kinkle, Suzanne, Treasurer

Nuevas Esperanzas US **[11416]**
3517 Laurel View Rd.
Birmingham, AL 35216
PH: (507)205-7150
Woody, Kirstin, President

School Science and Mathematics
Association **[8556]**
School of Education, EB 246B
University of Alabama Birmingham
Birmingham, AL 35233
PH: (205)934-5067
Smith, Tommy, Exec. Dir.

Society for Academic Continuing
Medical Education **[8336]**
3416 Primm Ln.
Birmingham, AL 35216-5602
PH: (205)978-7990
Fax: (205)823-2760
Samuel, Deborah, MBA, Bd.
Member

Society for the Advancement of
American Philosophy **[10118]**
BSC Box 549013
Birmingham Southern College
Birmingham, AL 35254
PH: (205)226-4868
Myers, Dr. William T., Treasurer

Society for Assisted Reproductive
Technology **[17126]**
1209 Montgomery Hwy.
Birmingham, AL 35216-2809
PH: (205)978-5000
Fax: (205)978-5018
Jefferson, Kelley, M.D., Administrator

Society for Cardiovascular Pathology
[14143]
UAB Pathology
PD6A 175
Birmingham, AL 35294
Litovsky, Silvio H., MD, Treasurer

Society of Dance History Scholars
[9513]
3416 Primm Ln.
Birmingham, AL 35216
PH: (205)978-1404
Fax: (205)823-2760
Kowal, Rebekah J., VP

Society of Gynecologic Nurse
Oncologists **[16355]**
c/o Erica Lumpkin, Secretary-
Treasurer
5067 Skylar Way
Birmingham, AL 35235
Brown, Amy, RN, President

Society for Male Reproduction and
Urology **[17118]**
1209 Montgomery Hwy.
Birmingham, AL 35216
PH: (205)978-5000
Fax: (205)978-5005
Nangia, Ajay K., MD, Officer

Society for Reproductive Endocrinology and Infertility **[17128]**
1209 Montgomery Hwy.
Birmingham, AL 35216

PH: (205)978-5000
Fax: (205)978-5005
Price, Thomas M., M.D., VP

Society of Reproductive Surgeons
[17129]
1209 Montgomery Hwy.
Birmingham, AL 35216-2809
PH: (205)978-5000
Fax: (205)978-5005
Nezhat, Ceana H., M.D., VP

Southeastern Conference **[23254]**
2201 Richard Arrington Jr. Blvd. N
Birmingham, AL 35203-1103
PH: (205)458-3000
Slive, Mike, Commissioner

Southwestern Athletic Conference
[23255]
2101 6th Ave. N, Ste. 700
Birmingham, AL 35203-2761
Fax: (205)297-9820
Sharp, Duer, Commissioner

United States Racquet Stringers As-
sociation **[3166]**
310 Richard Arrington Jr. Blvd. N,
Ste. 400
Birmingham, AL 35203
PH: (760)536-1177
Fax: (760)536-1171
Bone, David, Exec. Dir.

Woman's Missionary Union **[19743]**
100 Missionary Ridge
Birmingham, AL 35283-0010
PH: (205)991-8100
Toll free: 800-968-7301
Fax: (888)422-7032
Akerman, Debby, President

Woven Wire Products Association
[1781]
PO Box 610280
Birmingham, AL 35261
Toll free: 800-529-6691
Fax: (517)542-2501

Marine Corps Aviation Reconnaissance Association **[5570]**
2404 Preston Ridge Dr.
Brownsboro, AL 35741
PH: (256)536-2694

Professional Armed Forces Rodeo
Association **[23102]**
c/o Rhonda Ellison, Treasurer
9370 Highway 25
Calera, AL 35040

Clan Campbell Society - North
America **[20800]**
118 Eagle Dr.
Daphne, AL 36526
PH: (251)621-0079
(910)864-4231
Campbell, Kenneth, Trustee

Santa America, Inc. **[11267]**
308 Belrose Ave., Ste. 200 E
Daphne, AL 36526
PH: (251)626-6609
Berger, Ernest, Founder, President

Hank Williams International Fan
Club **[24069]**
c/o Ed Kirby, President
103 Summit Cir.
Daphne, AL 36526
PH: (251)626-1645
Wise, John, Coord.

American Nystagmus Network
[17685]
303-D Beltline Pl., No. 321
Decatur, AL 35603
Cranmer, John D., Director

Clan Moncreiffe Society **[20833]**
1405 Plaza St. SE
Decatur, AL 35603-1521
Dawes, Robert V., President

Racking Horse Breeders' Association
of America **[4405]**
67 Horse Center Rd., Ste. B
Decatur, AL 35603
PH: (256)353-7225
Fax: (256)353-7266
Simmons, Bobby, President

National Lum and Abner Society
[22402]
81 Sharon Blvd.
Dora, AL 35062
Hollis, Tim, Secretary

American Obesity Treatment As-
sociation **[16247]**
117 Anderson Ct., Ste. 1
Dothan, AL 36301
PH: (334)651-0821
Cuneo, Cesar, President, Founder

Association of Fruit and Vegetable
Inspection and Standardization
Agencies **[4229]**
1557 Reeves St.
Dothan, AL 36302
PH: (334)792-5185
Fax: (334)671-7984
Jeffers, Jeff, Comm. Chm.

National Peanut Festival Association
[4510]
5622 Highway 231 S
Dothan, AL 36301
PH: (334)793-4323
Fax: (334)793-3247
Cavender, Carrie, Office Mgr.

East Coast Timing Association
[22398]
c/o Tonya Turk, President
206 Sylvan Dr.
Enterprise, AL 36330
PH: (334)806-5749
Turk, Tonya, President

National Council for Spirit Safety and
Education **[22726]**
c/o Debbie Bracewell, Executive
Director
PO Box 311192
Enterprise, AL 36331-1192
Toll free: 866-456-2773
Fax: (334)393-6799
Bracewell, Debbie, Exec. Dir.

Omicron Delta Epsilon **[23726]**
19 S Summit St., No. 9
Fairhope, AL 36532
PH: (251)928-0001
Fax: (251)928-0015
Niroomand, Farhang, Exec. Sec.,
Treasurer

Beta Beta Beta **[23683]**
University of North Alabama
Math Bldg. M1 - A
1 Harrison Plz.
Florence, AL 35632
PH: (256)765-6220
Fax: (256)765-6221
Roush, Kathy W., Secretary,
Treasurer

Cushing's Understanding Support
and Help Organization **[16769]**
PO Box 1424
Florence, AL 35631
Clemens, Lynne, President

Alabama Fan Club **[24021]**
101 Glenn Blvd. SW
Fort Payne, AL 35967-4963

PH: (256)845-1646

American Blonde d'Aquitaine Association **[3684]**
57 Friar Tuck Way
Fyffe, AL 35971
PH: (256)996-3142
(918)772-2844
Moss, Ed, President

National Christian Forensics and
Communications Association
[7998]
200 Broad St., 3rd Fl., Ste. B
Gadsden, AL 35901
PH: (205)500-0081
Hudson, Teresa, President, Chmn. of
the Bd.

Board of Certified Hazard Control
Management **[2992]**
173 Tucker Rd., Ste 202
Helena, AL 35080
PH: (205)664-8412
Fax: (205)663-9541
Tweedy, Jim, Exec. Dir.

International Board for Certification
of Safety Managers **[2996]**
173 Tucker Rd., Ste. 202
Helena, AL 35080
PH: (205)664-8412
Tweedy, Jim, Exec. Dir.

International Iridology Practitioners
Association **[16389]**
2100 Southbridge Pky., Ste. 650
Homewood, AL 35209
PH: (205)226-3522
Toll free: 888-682-2208
Fax: (205)226-3525
Norris, Kathy, President

International Society for Organ
Preservation **[16449]**
PO Box 590013
Homewood, AL 35259
McAfee, Amber, President

National Association of School
Resource Officers **[8523]**
2020 Valleydale Rd., Ste. 207A
Hoover, AL 35244-4803
PH: (205)739-6060
Toll free: 888-316-2776
Fax: (205)536-9255
Thornton, Jennifer, Mktg. Mgr.

National Roadside Vegetation
Management Association **[4288]**
c/o, John Reynolds, Executive Direc-
tor
5616 Lynchburg Cir.
Hueytown, AL 35023
PH: (205)491-7574
Fax: (205)491-2725
Smith, Michael, Exec.

Aircraft Engine Historical Society
[5855]
4608 Charles Dr. NW
Huntsville, AL 35816-1206
PH: (256)683-1458
McCutcheon, Kimble D., President

American Society for Engineering
Management **[6535]**
200 Sparkman Dr., Ste. 2
Huntsville, AL 35805
Daughton, Dr. William, Exec. Dir.

Armstrong Clan Society **[19636]**
2101 Mc Dowling Dr.
Huntsville, AL 35803-1225
Armstrong, Peter, President, Director

Christian Ophthalmology Society
[16381]
333 Whitesport Ctr., Ste. 101
Huntsville, AL 35801

PH: (616)439-4267
Pletcher, Stan, MD, President

Diabetes Education and Camping Association [14525]
PO Box 385
Huntsville, AL 35804
PH: (256)757-8114
Fax: (256)230-3171
Ackley, Terry, Exec. Dir.

Haiti Emergency Relief Organization [12666]
PO Box 5634
Huntsville, AL 35814
PH: (256)665-6151
Nerelus, Simeon S., Founder, Exec. Dir.

International Association of Educators for World Peace USA [18794]
Office of the President
2013 Orba Dr. NE
Huntsville, AL 35811-2414
PH: (256)534-5501
Fax: (256)536-1018
Mercieca, Dr. Charles, Founder, President

National Association for Rights Protection and Advocacy [17918]
c/o Ann Marshall, Administrator
PO Box 855
Huntsville, AL 35804
PH: (256)650-6311
Stewart, Bill, President

National Speleological Society [7228]
6001 Pulaski Pke.
Huntsville, AL 35810-1122
PH: (256)852-1300
Engel, Thom, Director

Von Braun Astronomical Society [6012]
PO Box 1142
Huntsville, AL 35807
PH: (256)539-0316
Schenck, Frank, Director

Martial Arts U.S.A. [23004]
c/o Patricia Hill, 1619 Fairway Dr., SW
1619 Fairway Dr. SW
Jacksonville, AL 36265
PH: (256)782-3045
    (256)714-8270
Chambers, John E., Founder

National Association of Federal Education Program Administrators [7435]
c/o Bobby Burns, Executive Director
PO Box 880
Jacksonville, AL 36265
PH: (256)310-9293
Toll free: 844-623-3721
Ling, Denise P., President

Dream Catchers USA [11593]
PO Box 701
Killen, AL 35645
PH: (256)272-0286
Fax: (256)272-0286
Copeland, Nancy J., President

League of the South [17908]
PO Box 760
Killen, AL 35645
PH: (256)757-6789
Toll free: 800-888-3163
Fax: (256)757-6768

Association for sTEm Teacher Education [8016]
1489 County Road 23
Lafayette, AL 36862

PH: (309)438-3502
Rogers, George E., EdD, President

Project Hope to Abolish the Death Penalty [17833]
c/o Esther Brown, Executive Director
PO Box 1362
Lanett, AL 36863
Brown, Esther, Exec. Dir.

Servants in Faith and Technology [17812]
2944 County Road 113
Lineville, AL 36266
PH: (256)396-2015
Fax: (256)396-2501
Corson, Tom, Exec. Dir.

Patriotic Education Inc. [7616]
107 Heritage Ln.
Madison, AL 35758-7974
PH: (256)461-0612
Toll free: 800-248-1787
Cahill, George F., Chairman

Rossica Society of Russian Philately [22358]
c/o Ray Pietruszka, President
211 Evalyn St.
Madison, AL 35758-2203
Pietruszka, Ray, President

Kappa Delta Epsilon [23729]
c/o Dr. Lesley Sheek, Vice President
302 Bibb St.
Marion, AL 36756
PH: (334)683-5133
Brown, Suzanne, Treasurer

Civil Air Patrol [5058]
105 S Hansell St., Bldg. 714
Maxwell AFB, AL 36112-6332
Toll free: 877-227-9142
Vazquez, Maj. Gen. Joseph R., Cmdr.

Autism Avenue [13745]
164 St. Francis St., Ste. 210
Mobile, AL 36602
PH: (251)432-0757
Toll free: 866-953-8644
Fax: (251)432-3999
Wilkins, Jeanie Guthans, Chairperson

Caring Now for Kids with Cystic Fibrosis [17136]
PO Box 851777
Mobile, AL 36685
PH: (251)623-3684
Werstler, Ronnie, Founder

Deep Draft Lubricant Association [2107]
PO Box 40788
Mobile, AL 36640
Jeremiah, Bill, President

Elevator Escalator Safety Foundation [1064]
356 Morgan Ave.
Mobile, AL 36606-1737
PH: (251)479-2199
Toll free: 800-949-6442
Fax: (251)479-7099
Sybert, Tom, Chairman

Errors, Freaks and Oddities Collectors' Club [22327]
3561 Country Ct. N
Mobile, AL 36619-5335

American College of Theriogenologists [17614]
PO Box 3065
Montgomery, AL 36109-3065
PH: (334)395-4666
Fax: (334)270-3399
Franz, Charles F., DVM, Contact

American Patriots Association [21078]
6701 Winton Blont Blvd.
Montgomery, AL 36124-1035
Lynch, Terry, Founder, President

Auburn University Montgomery Alumni Association [19306]
7400 East Dr.
Montgomery, AL 36117
PH: (334)244-3344
Fax: (334)394-5937
Golden, Carolyn C., Vice Chlr.

Child Welfare and Policy and Practice Group [10909]
428 E Jefferson St.
Montgomery, AL 36104
PH: (334)264-8300
Fax: (334)264-8310
Vincent, Paul, MSW, Director, Founder

Clan Macneil Association of America [20826]
PO Box 230693
Montgomery, AL 36123-0693
PH: (334)834-0612
Nimitz, Andrew MacNeely, Exec. VP

Equal Justice Initiative [18071]
122 Commerce St.
Montgomery, AL 36104
PH: (334)269-1803
Fax: (334)269-1806
Stevenson, Bryan, Exec. Dir.

F. Scott Fitzgerald Society [9050]
c/o Prof. Kirk Curnutt, Vice President
Troy University, Montgomery Campus
English Dept.
Montgomery, AL 36103-4419
Bryer, Jackson R., President

Intelligence Project [17902]
Southern Poverty Law Ctr.
400 Washington Ave.
Montgomery, AL 36104
PH: (334)956-8200
Toll free: 888-414-7752
Beirich, Heidi, Director

National Black Catholic Clergy Caucus [19873]
2815 Forbes Dr.
Montgomery, AL 36110
PH: (334)230-1910
    (505)234-8735
Bozeman, Rev. Anthony, President

National Square Dance Convention National Executive Committee [9269]
Montgomery, AL 36117
Ashwill, Barbi, President

National Young Farmer Educational Association [4164]
PO Box 20326
Montgomery, AL 36120
PH: (334)546-9951

Organization of Agreement States [5741]
201 Monroe St.
Montgomery, AL 36130-3017
PH: (334)396-9444
Shober, Megan, Secretary

Society for Theriogenology [17660]
PO Box 3007
Montgomery, AL 36109-3007
PH: (334)395-4666
Fax: (334)270-3399
Thompson, Dr. Mike, President

Southern Poverty Law Center [17932]
400 Washington Ave.
Montgomery, AL 36104-4344

PH: (334)956-8200
Fax: (334)956-8481
Cohen, Richard, President, CEO

Victims of Crime and Leniency [13267]
422 S Court St.
Montgomery, AL 36104-4102
PH: (334)262-7197
Toll free: 800-239-3219
Fax: (334)834-5645
Shehane, Miriam, Mgr.

Society of Classified Advertising Managers Association [110]
PO Box 531335
Mountain Brook, AL 35253
PH: (205)592-0389
Fax: (205)599-5598
Rushing, Hugh J., Exec. Ofc.

International Fertilizer Development Center [3568]
PO Box 2040
Muscle Shoals, AL 35662
PH: (256)381-6600
Fax: (256)381-7408
Cheek, Dr. Jimmy, Chmn. of the Bd.

Saleen Club of America [21488]
PO Box 274
Odenville, AL 35120
PH: (714)400-2121
Foley, Mike, VP

American Association of Bovine Practitioners [17592]
3320 Skyway Dr., Ste. 802
Opelika, AL 36801
PH: (334)821-0442
Fax: (334)821-9532
Riddell, M. Gatz, Exec. VP

Bullwhip Squadron Association [21113]
c/o Joe Bowen, President
5566 County Road 18
Ozark, AL 36360-5927
Wright, Larry, Membership Chp.

SmokEnders [17227]
3684 Highway 31 S, Ste. 263
Pelham, AL 35124
PH: (205)223-1982

American Association of Small Ruminant Practitioners [17600]
765 Tiger Oak Dr.
Pike Road, AL 36064-3060
PH: (334)517-1233
Fax: (334)270-3399
Scharko, Patty B., President

11th Airborne Division Association [20707]
c/o Charles J Magro, Treasurer
301 S Dabney Ln.
Rogersville, AL 35652
PH: (256)247-7390
Doshier, Joe, President

National Wheelchair Poolplayers Association [22791]
90 Flemons Dr.
Somerville, AL 35670
PH: (703)817-1215
Fax: (703)817-1215
Dolezal, Jeffrey, President

Kaiser-Frazer Owners Club International [21413]
PO Box 424
Thomasville, AL 36784
PH: (334)636-5873
Mueller, Jack, Hist.

International Boethius Society [10092]
c/o Noel Harold Kaylor Jr., Executive Director

Smith Hall 274
Dept. of English
Troy University
Troy, AL 36082
PH: (334)670-3519
Strawman, Dr. Tom, Dept. Chm.

Lambda Chi Alpha **[23907]**
404 Pell Ave.
Troy, AL 36081
Farkas, Bill, CEO

Casey's Cause **[13839]**
PO Box 1305
Trussville, AL 35173
PH: (205)281-3037
Grant, Christine, President

Machinery Information Management
  Open Systems Alliance **[2224]**
2200 Jack Warner Pky., Ste. 300
Tuscaloosa, AL 35406
PH: (949)625-8616
Fax: (949)625-8616
Johnston, Alan T., CEO, President

National Elementary Schools Press
  Association **[8455]**
c/o Meredith Cummings, CJE
Box 870172
Tuscaloosa, AL 35487-0172
PH: (205)348-2772
Levin, Mark, Managing Dir.

Trucker Buddy International **[7596]**
3200 Rice Mine Rd.
Tuscaloosa, AL 35406
PH: (205)248-1261
Toll free: 800-692-8339
Fax: (205)345-0958
Schwartzenburg, Randy, Exec. Dir.

Tuskegee Airmen Inc. **[20673]**
PO Box 830060
Tuskegee, AL 36083-0060
PH: (334)725-8200
Fax: (334)725-8205
Johnson, Leon A., President

World Detector Dog Organization
  [5523]
55 Kennel Dr.
Vincent, AL 35178
PH: (252)227-9227
Schonemann, Peter, President

Women's Army Corps Veterans' As-
  sociation **[20728]**
PO Box 663
Weaver, AL 36277
PH: (256)820-6824
LaRocca, Suzanne, President

ALASKA

Airlines Medical Directors Associa-
  tion **[13507]**
c/o Petra A. Illig, MD, Secretary
5011 Spenard Rd., No. 205
Anchorage, AK 99517
PH: (907)245-4359
Fax: (907)245-2212
Orford, Robert R., MD, President

Alaska Collectors' Club **[22296]**
c/o Eric Knapp, Secretary and
  Treasurer
4201 Folker St., Unit C102
Anchorage, AK 99508-5377
Zuelow, Jim, President

Center for Loss in Multiple Birth, Inc.
  [12409]
PO Box 91377
Anchorage, AK 99509
PH: (907)222-5321
Kollantai, Jean, Founder

Helping Hand for Nepal **[12673]**
2930 Brittany Dr.
Anchorage, AK 99504-3982
PH: (907)338-8128
Jackson, Linda, MFA, Exec. Dir.,
  Founder

Law Enforcement Bloodhound As-
  sociation **[5479]**
PO Box 190442
Anchorage, AK 99519
PH: (907)830-7431

Law Project for Psychiatric Rights
  [12049]
406 G St., Ste. 206
Anchorage, AK 99501
PH: (907)274-7686
Fax: (907)274-9493
Gottstein, James B., President, CEO

National Shelley China Club **[21699]**
591 W 67th Ave.
Anchorage, AK 99518-1555
Hart, Rochelle L, Treasurer

U.S.A. Powerlifting **[23074]**
1120 Huffman Rd., Ste. 24, No. 223
Anchorage, AK 99515
PH: (260)248-4889
Maile, Larry J., PhD, President

International Space Exploration and
  Colonization Co. **[5864]**
PO Box 60885
Fairbanks, AK 99706-0885
PH: (907)488-1001
Collins, Ray R., President

Native Movement **[19586]**
PO Box 83467
Fairbanks, AK 99708-3467
PH: (907)374-5950

United States Permafrost Associa-
  tion **[7195]**
PO Box 750141
Fairbanks, AK 99775-0141
PH: (302)831-0852
Fax: (302)831-6654
Waldrop, Mark, President

University of Alaska Fairbanks
  Alumni Association **[19354]**
201 Constitution Hall
Fairbanks, AK 99775
PH: (907)474-7081
Toll free: 800-770-2586
Fax: (907)474-6712
Ripley, Kate, Exec. Dir.

Western History Association **[8806]**
University of Alaska Fairbanks
Dept. of History
605 Gruening Bldg.
Fairbanks, AK 99775-6460
PH: (907)474-6509
   (907)474-6508
Fax: (435)797-3899
Szasz, Margaret Connell, Officer

International Bird Beer Label As-
  sociation **[21263]**
PO Box 2551
Homer, AK 99603
Field, Carmen, Founder

At-sea Processors Association
  [1297]
c/o Stephanie Madsen, Executive
  Director
222 Seward St., Ste. 201
Juneau, AK 99801
PH: (907)523-0970
   (206)285-5139
Fax: (907)523-0798
Madsen, Stephanie, Exec. Dir.

North American Levinas Society
  [10106]
c/o Sol Neely, President, 11120
  Glacier Hwy., SOB 1

11120 Glacier Hwy., SOB 1
Juneau, AK 99801
PH: (907)796-6411
Toll free: 877-465-4827
Fax: (907)796-6406
Neely, Sol, President

Oncology Association of Natur-
  opathic Physicians **[15865]**
c/o Corey Murphy, Executive Direc-
  tor
PO Box 20665
Juneau, AK 99802
Toll free: 800-908-5175
Murphy, Corey, Exec. Dir.

Pediatric Association of Naturopathic
  Physicians **[15866]**
PO Box 20665
Juneau, AK 99802
Barallon, Matthew, President

Maniilaq Association **[12377]**
733 2nd Ave.
Kotzebue, AK 99752
PH: (907)442-7660
   (907)442-3311
Toll free: 800-478-3312
Fax: (907)442-7830
Lincoln, John, Chmn. of the Bd.

North American Agricultural Market-
  ing Officials **[4481]**
c/o Amy Pettit, 1800 Glenn Hwy.,
  Ste. 12
1800 Glenn Hwy., Ste. 12
Palmer, AK 99645
PH: (907)761-3864
Borovilos, George, President

International Association for Aquatic
  Animal Medicine **[17648]**
c/o Pam Tuomi, President-elect
Alaska SeaLife Ctr.
301 Railway Ave.
Seward, AK 99664
PH: (907)229-5524
Murphy, Lisa A., VMD, DABT,
  President

ARIZONA

Harness Tracks of America **[22917]**
, AZ
PH: (520)529-2525
Fax: (520)529-3235
Fontaine, Paul, President

International Sonoran Desert Alli-
  ance **[4077]**
38 W Plz.
Ajo, AZ 85321
PH: (520)387-6823
Fax: (520)387-3005
Alegria, Mr. Eric, President

RVing Women **[22432]**
PO Box 1940
Apache Junction, AZ 85117-4074
PH: (480)671-6226
Fax: (480)671-6230
Brown, Linda, President

Superstition Mountain Historical
  Society **[8804]**
4087 N Apache Trl.
Apache Junction, AZ 85119
PH: (480)983-4888
Davis, Gregory E., President

South African Boerboel Breeders
  Association - U.S.A. and Canada
  [22820]
PO Box 353
Arivaca, AZ 85601
PH: (480)650-4406
Steffler, Ann, Bd. Member

High Twelve International Inc.
  [19561]
11404 W Olive Dr.
Avondale, AZ 85392-4210
Fax: (623)239-6170
Whistler, Donald M., Treasurer

National Association of Exclusive
  Buyer Agents **[2868]**
1481 N Eliseo C. Felix Jr. Way, Ste.
  110
Avondale, AZ 85323
PH: (623)932-0098
Toll free: 888-623-2299
Fax: (623)932-0212
Rae, Dawn, President

Afghanistan Zendabad **[10465]**
PO Box 1064
Bisbee, AZ 85603
PH: (520)366-7007
MacMakin, Mary, Founder

Bull Terrier Club of America **[21848]**
c/o Naomi Waynee, Executive
  Secretary
19135 W Taylor St.
Buckeye, AZ 85326-8506
Sharp, Claudia, President

U.S. Mexican Numismatic Associa-
  tion **[22289]**
PO Box 5270
Carefree, AZ 85377
PH: (480)921-2562
Fax: (480)575-1279
Frampton, Cory, Exec. Dir.

Aerobics and Fitness Association of
  America **[16691]**
1750 E Northrop Blvd., Ste. 200
Chandler, AZ 85286-1744
Toll free: 800-446-2322
Pfeffer, Linda D., RN, President

American Jewish Press Association
  [2650]
c/o KCA Association Management
107 S Southgate Dr.
Chandler, AZ 85226-3222
PH: (480)403-4602
Fax: (480)893-7775
Kestenbaum, Rick, President

American Sign Language Teachers
  Association **[15173]**
10413 E Spring Creek Rd.
Chandler, AZ 85248
Gunderson, Arlene, MEd, President

Association for Comparative
  Economic Studies **[6379]**
c/o Josef C. Brada, Executive
  Secretary
333 N Pennington Dr., No. 57
Chandler, AZ 85224-8269
Brada, Josef C., Exec. Sec.

British Universities North America
  Club **[8062]**
585 N Juniper Dr., Ste. 250
Chandler, AZ 85226
Toll free: 866-220-7771

Council on Chiropractic Practice
  [14267]
2950 N Dobson Rd., Ste. 1
Chandler, AZ 85224-1819
Sloane, William M., PhD, President

Digital Media Licensing Association
  [2577]
3165 S Alma School Rd., Ste. 18
Chandler, AZ 85248-3760
PH: (714)815-8427
Fax: (866)427-1464
Aron, Cathy, Exec. Dir.

Endocrine Nurses Society **[14704]**
c/o Molly Solares Yeardley,
  Treasurer

2991 E Beechnut Pl.
Chandler, AZ 85249
Gurel, Michelle, RN, President

The IMAGE Society, Inc. **[6248]**
PO Box 6221
Chandler, AZ 85246-6221

League for Innovation in the Com-
munity College **[7643]**
1333 S Spectrum Blvd., Ste. 210
Chandler, AZ 85286
PH: (480)705-8200
Fax: (480)705-8201
Wilson, Cynthia, VP

Manufacturing Enterprise Solutions
Association International **[2225]**
107 S Southgate Dr.
Chandler, AZ 85226
PH: (480)893-6883
   (952)548-5664
Fax: (480)893-7775
Sonnefeld, Ralf, Chairman

Musical Dog Sport Association
[22816]
PO Box 148
Chandler, AZ 85244-0148
Pirtle, Bridgette, President

National Odd Shoe Exchange
[11628]
PO Box 1120
Chandler, AZ 85244-1120
PH: (480)892-3484

Will2Walk Foundation **[17268]**
1909 E Ray Rd., No. 9-238
Chandler, AZ 85225
Fax: (480)634-7867
Hamill, Richard, Founder, President

National Association of Parents with
Children in Special Education
[8586]
3642 E Sunnydale Dr.
Chandler Heights, AZ 85142
Toll free: 800-754-4421
Fax: (800)424-0371
Giuliani, Dr. George, President

Creation Research Society **[20595]**
6801 N Highway 89
Chino Valley, AZ 86323
PH: (928)636-1153
Toll free: 877-277-2665
Fax: (928)636-8444
Chaffin, Eugene F., Chmn. of the Bd.

Music Teachers Association
International **[8377]**
11111 Maricopa Ln.
Dewey, AZ 86327
Evans-Richey, Elfriede, President,
Secretary, Treasurer

Amerind Foundation and Museum
[5904]
2100 N Amerind Rd.
Dragoon, AZ 85609
PH: (520)586-3666
Stansberry, Tammy, Coord.

Association for Business Simulation
and Experiential Learning **[7544]**
c/o Chris Scherpereel, President
WA Franke College of Business
Northern Arizona University
PO Box 15066
Flagstaff, AZ 86011
PH: (928)523-7831
Fekula, Mick, VP, Exec. Dir.

Association for the Study of
American Indian Literatures
[10035]
c/o Jeff Berglund, Treasurer
PO Box 6032

Flagstaff, AZ 86011-6032
Doerfler, Jill, President

Institute for Tribal Environmental
Professionals **[19580]**
PO Box 15004
Flagstaff, AZ 86011-5004
PH: (928)523-9555
Fax: (928)523-1266
Williams, Jennifer, Officer

Native American Fitness Council
[16711]
PO Box K
Flagstaff, AZ 86002
PH: (928)774-3048
Fax: (928)774-3049
Blievernicht, John A., Exec. Dir.

Native Public Media **[18661]**
PO Box 3955
Flagstaff, AZ 86003
PH: (602)820-4907
Taylor, Loris Ann, CEO, President

Naturopaths International **[15864]**
3011 N West St.
Flagstaff, AZ 86004
PH: (928)214-8793
Gowey, Dr. Brandie, NMD, Founder,
President

Western Social Science Association
[7174]
2307 Chof Trl.
Flagstaff, AZ 86005
Gould, Larry, Exec. Dir.

Wilderness Volunteers **[22294]**
PO Box 22292
Flagstaff, AZ 86002
PH: (928)255-1128
Fax: (928)222-1912
Leonard, Mike, Secretary

Military Intelligence Corps Associa-
tion **[4973]**
PO Box 13020
Fort Huachuca, AZ 85670-3020
Atkins, Charles, President

American-Israel Numismatic As-
sociation **[22255]**
PO Box 20255
Fountain Hills, AZ 85269-0255
PH: (818)225-1348
Wacks, Mr. Mel, President

Construction Industry CPAs/
Consultants Association **[21]**
15011 E Twilight View Dr.
Fountain Hills, AZ 85268
PH: (480)836-0300
Fax: (480)836-0400
Corcoran, John J., CPA, Exec. Dir.

United States Swim School Associa-
tion **[23289]**
13215 N Verde River Dr., Ste. 10
Fountain Hills, AZ 85268
PH: (480)837-5525
Fax: (480)836-8277
Mackie, Sue, Exec. Dir.

American Cavy Breeders Association
[3589]
1157 E San Angelo Ave.
Gilbert, AZ 85234
PH: (519)834-2110
   (831)630-0480
Buchanan, Sara, VP

American Waterslager Society
[21539]
556 S Cactus Wren St.
556 S Cactus Wren St.
Gilbert, AZ 85296
PH: (480)892-5464
Trujillo, Tom, President

Co-Anon Family Groups **[13130]**
PO Box 3664
Gilbert, AZ 85299
PH: (480)442-3869

Hope Arising **[11376]**
3604 E Leah Ct.
Gilbert, AZ 85234
PH: (480)313-6116
Fax: (480)654-1449
Sellers, Rochelle, Exec. Dir., Bd.
Member

International Society for
Cardiovascular Translational
Research **[14126]**
3104 E Camelback Rd., No. 564
Gilbert, AZ 85297
PH: (480)438-5015
Dib, Dr. Nabil, President

International Tuba-Euphonium As-
sociation **[9938]**
PO Box 1296
Gilbert, AZ 85299-1296
PH: (480)200-9765
Hanson, Scott, Exec. Dir.

Luscombe Endowment **[21238]**
2487 S Gilbert Rd., Ste. 106
Gilbert, AZ 85295
PH: (480)650-0883
   (480)917-0969
Fax: (484)762-6711

National Field Hockey Coaches As-
sociation **[22836]**
3352 E Virgil Dr.
Gilbert, AZ 85298
PH: (480)789-1136
Goodrich, Jennifer J., Exec. Dir.

North American Potbellied Pig As-
sociation **[3609]**
15525 E Via Del Palo
Gilbert, AZ 85298-9720
PH: (480)899-8941
Munici, Pam, President

United Association of Mobile
Contract Cleaners **[2144]**
PO Box 1914
Gilbert, AZ 85299
Toll free: 800-816-3240
Rucker, Doug, President

USA BMX **[22758]**
1645 W Sunrise Blvd.
Gilbert, AZ 85233
PH: (480)961-1903
Fax: (480)961-1842
Anderson, B.A., CEO

American Disc Jockey Association
[2416]
20118 N 67th Ave., Ste. 300-605
Glendale, AZ 85308
Toll free: 888-723-5776
Fax: (866)310-4676

Foundation for Children with Micro-
cephaly **[15933]**
PO Box 12134
Glendale, AZ 85318
PH: (623)476-7494
Toll free: 877-476-5503
Fax: (623)241-4543
Lewis, Jenniffer, Founder, CEO

National Association of Field Training
Officers **[5491]**
7942 W Bell Rd., Ste. C5, No. 463
Glendale, AZ 85308
Smith, Bob, President

National Law Enforcement Firearms
Instructors Association **[5501]**
6635 W Happy Valley Rd., Ste.
A104-108

Glendale, AZ 85310
Toll free: 800-930-2953
Fax: (623)225-7793
Wuestenberg, Jason, Exec. Dir.

Recovery Ministries **[13179]**
22015 N 64th Ave.
Glendale, AZ 85310
PH: (623)433-9643
Allbright, Jay, Founder

United Indian Missions International
[20471]
6419 W Maryland Ave.
Glendale, AZ 85301-3718
PH: (623)847-9227
Fax: (623)934-5996
Fredericks, Mr. Daniel P., Exec. Dir.

Parachute Industry Association
[23056]
6499 S Kings Ranch Rd., No. 6-1
Gold Canyon, AZ 85118
PH: (480)982-6125
Montanez, Roberto, President

Software Contractors' Guild **[980]**
7151 E US Highway 60, No. 704
Gold Canyon, AZ 85118-9769
Keeney, David, Administrator

Casting Industry Suppliers Associa-
tion **[1719]**
14175 W Indian School Rd., Ste.
B4-504
Goodyear, AZ 85395
PH: (623)547-0920
Fax: (623)536-1486
Bartol, Mike, 1st VP

Evangelical Lutheran Education As-
sociation **[8258]**
500 N Estrella Pky., Ste. 601
Goodyear, AZ 85338-4135
Toll free: 800-500-7644
Fax: (623)882-8770
Denny, Gayle, Exec. Dir.

United States Boxer Association
[21980]
c/o Jowhar Karim, Secretary
PO Box 5991
Goodyear, AZ 85338-0617
Chase, Mark, President

Black Pilots of America, Inc. **[360]**
c/o Les Morris, Treasurer
PO Box 1295
Green Valley, AZ 85622
PH: (520)625-4745
Hicks, John W., Jr., President

American Warmblood Society **[4332]**
PO Box 1561
Higley, AZ 85236
PH: (480)251-0348
Fax: (520)568-3318
Garcia, Nikki Atwell, Director

Asian-American Network Against
Abuse of Human Rights **[18375]**
PO Box 4324
Kingman, AZ 86402
PH: (928)550-0062

Arcosanti, A Project of the Cosanti
Foundation **[3988]**
13555 S Cross L Rd.
Mayer, AZ 86333
PH: (928)632-7135
Fax: (928)632-6229
Jeffries, Erin, Mgr. of Public Rel.

American Hydrogen Association
[6454]
PO Box 4205
Mesa, AZ 85211
PH: (480)234-5070
McAlister, Roy E., President

APA Division 29: The Society for the Advancement of Psychology [16879]
c/o Tracey Martin
6557 E Riverdale St.
Mesa, AZ 85215
PH: (602)363-9211
Fax: (480)854-8966
Stiles, William B., PhD, President

Armed Females of America [18246]
2702 E University Dr., Ste. 103
Mesa, AZ 85213
PH: (480)924-8202
Lewis, Carma, Exec. Dir.

Council on Library-Media Technicians [8231]
PO Box 42048
Mesa, AZ 85274-2048
PH: (202)231-3836
Fax: (202)231-3838

International Alliance for the Prevention of AIDS [13549]
1955 W Baseline Rd., Ste. 113-624
Mesa, AZ 85202
PH: (480)274-3561
Sinha, Sanjay, Director

International New Thought Alliance [10094]
5003 E Broadway Rd.
Mesa, AZ 85206
PH: (480)830-2461
Scherry, Rev. Jenny, Treasurer

Kids Need to Read [12247]
33 S Mesa Dr.
Mesa, AZ 85210
PH: (480)256-0115
Gary, Denise, Exec. Dir.

National Center for American Indian Enterprise Development [12378]
953 E Juanita Ave.
Mesa, AZ 85204
PH: (480)545-1298
Fax: (480)545-4208
Davis, Gary, President, CEO

Native American Fatherhood and Families Association [12420]
1215 E Brown Rd.
Mesa, AZ 85203
PH: (480)833-5007
Pooley, Mr. Albert M., Founder, President

Project GHB [13176]
2753 E Broadway Rd., Ste. 101
PMB 434
Mesa, AZ 85204
PH: (480)219-1180
Porrata, Trinka, President

Society for the Exploration of Psychotherapy Integration [16990]
c/o Tracey Martin, Administrative Officer
6557 E Riverdale St.
Mesa, AZ 85215
Martin, Tracey, Admin. Ofc.

Society of Forensic Toxicologists, Inc. [5253]
1 MacDonald Ctr., Ste. 15
1 N MacDonald St.
Mesa, AZ 85201
PH: (480)839-9106
Toll free: 888-866-7638

United National Indian Tribal Youth [10049]
1 N MacDonald Dr., Ste. 212
Mesa, AZ 85201
PH: (480)718-9793
Fax: (480)773-6369
Yazzie, Lynnann, Coord.

Visionledd USA [10555]
PO Box 20158
Mesa, AZ 85277
Toll free: 866-664-4673
Cantelon, Jim, President, Founder

Fresh Produce Association of the Americas [1330]
590 E Frontage Rd.
Nogales, AZ 85621-9753
PH: (520)287-2707
Fax: (520)287-2948
Jungmeyer, Mr. Lance, President

Hummingbird Monitoring Network [3663]
PO Box 115
Patagonia, AZ 85624
Wethington, Susan, Exec. Dir., Founder

Asatru Alliance [19707]
PO Box 961
Payson, AZ 85547
PH: (928)474-1010

Feed God's Hungry Children [10971]
16150 N Arrowhead Fountains Circle Dr., Ste. 195
Peoria, AZ 85382
PH: (602)499-1320
Toll free: 877-999-8322

Rural Rwanda Dental [15088]
14109 N 69th Dr.
Peoria, AZ 85381
PH: (623)258-5084
Reckmeyer, Dr. Richard, Exec. Dir., Team Ldr.

Society for Thai Philately [22368]
9379 W Escuda Dr.
Peoria, AZ 85382

Petrified Forest Museum Association [10064]
1 Park Rd.
Petrified Forest National Park, AZ 86028
PH: (928)524-6228
DoBell, Paul S., Exec. Dir.

Alport Syndrome Foundation [15868]
1608 E Briarwood Terr.
Phoenix, AZ 85048-9414
PH: (480)800-3510
Lagas, Sharon, President

Amalgamated Printers' Association [1553]
c/o Cindy Iverson
12236 S Tonalea Dr.
Phoenix, AZ 85044
Warren, Joe, President

American Academy of Dental Group Practice [14373]
2525 E Arizona Biltmore Cir., Ste. 127
Phoenix, AZ 85016
PH: (602)381-1185
Bernstein, Dr. Robert

American College of Medical Toxicology [17493]
10645 N Tatum Blvd., Ste. 200-111
Phoenix, AZ 85028
PH: (623)533-6340
Fax: (623)533-6520
Wax, Paul M., MD, Exec. Dir.

American Council on Alcoholism [13123]
1000 E Indian School Rd., Ste. B
Phoenix, AZ 85014
Toll free: 800-527-5344

American Dental Coders Association [14405]
3120 W Carefree Hwy., Ste. 1-511
Phoenix, AZ 85086
Toll free: 800-300-0239

APA Division 42: The Community for Psychologists in Independent Practice [16886]
919 W Marshall Ave.
Phoenix, AZ 85013
PH: (602)284-6219
Ching, June, President

Arizona Archaeological Society [5932]
PO Box 9665
Phoenix, AZ 85068
PH: (928)684-3251
    (928)284-9357
Simmons, Glenda, Chairman

Asian American Psychological Association [16898]
5025 N Central Ave.
Phoenix, AZ 85012-1520
Okazaki, Sumie, Officer

Association of Energy Services Professionals [6459]
15215 S 48th St., Ste. 170
Phoenix, AZ 85044
PH: (480)704-5900
Fax: (480)704-5905
Orfanedes, Laura

Association of Golf Merchandisers [3135]
PO Box 7247
Phoenix, AZ 85011-7247
PH: (602)604-8250
Fax: (602)604-8251
Blaney, Desane, Exec. Dir.

Association for Professional Basketball Research [22570]
PO Box 35771
Phoenix, AZ 85069-5771
LeBov, Mr. Ray, Exec. Dir.

Asthma Athletics [14169]
1928 E Highland, Ste. F-104
Phoenix, AZ 85016
PH: (602)999-3325
Yusin, Joseph S., MD, President, Founder

Black Family Genealogy and History Society [20960]
PO Box 8768
Phoenix, AZ 85066

Books for a Better World [7745]
PO Box 9053
Phoenix, AZ 85068
Gartell, Alice Finn, President

Charted Designers Association [22253]
c/o Designs with TLC
7310 W Roosevelt St., Ste. 6
Phoenix, AZ 85043
PH: (623)936-9900
Fax: (623)936-9981
Capps, Stew, President

Childhelp [10912]
Bldg. F250
4350 E Camelback Rd.
Phoenix, AZ 85018-2701
PH: (480)922-8212
Fax: (480)922-7061
O'Meara, Sara, Chairman, Founder, CEO

Co-Dependents Anonymous [12870]
PO Box 33577
Phoenix, AZ 85067-3577
PH: (602)277-7991
Toll free: 888-444-2359

Crosier Missions [20406]
4423 N 24th St., Ste. 400
Phoenix, AZ 85016-5584

PH: (602)443-7100

Desert Botanical Garden [6139]
1201 N Galvin Pkwy.
Phoenix, AZ 85008
PH: (480)941-1225
    (480)481-8133
Toll free: 888-314-9480
Fax: (480)481-8124
Sallot, John, Dir. of Mktg.

Desert German Shorthaired Pointer Club [21868]
2026 N 7th St.
Phoenix, AZ 85006
PH: (480)862-6896
Kulish, Tim, VP

Disciple Nations Alliance [20021]
1110 E Missouri Ave., No. 393
Phoenix, AZ 85014
PH: (602)386-4560
Fax: (602)386-4564
Allen, Scott, President

Dominican Advance, Inc. [19421]
PO Box 6354
Phoenix, AZ 85005
PH: (520)908-7324
Pensinger, Kim, President

Eating Disorders Anonymous [14636]
PO Box 55876
Phoenix, AZ 85078-5876
PH: (760)569-0800

The Milton H. Erickson Foundation [16972]
2632 E Thomas Rd., Ste. 200
Phoenix, AZ 85016
PH: (602)956-6196
Toll free: 877-212-6678
Fax: (602)956-0519
Zeig, Jeffrey K., PhD, Founder, CEO

Esperança [14999]
1911 W Earll Dr.
Phoenix, AZ 85015-6041
PH: (602)252-7772
Toll free: 888-701-5150
Fax: (602)340-9197
Hoyt, James, President, CEO

Evangelical Christian Publishers Association [2785]
9633 S 48th St., Ste. 195
Phoenix, AZ 85044
PH: (480)966-3998
Fax: (480)966-1944
Kuyper, Mark W., CEO, President

Feed My Hungry Children [10972]
PO Box 83775
Phoenix, AZ 85071-3775
PH: (602)241-2873
Taylor, Lon R., President

Food for the Hungry [12091]
1224 E Washington St.
Phoenix, AZ 85034-1102
PH: (480)998-3100
    (602)258-3750
Toll free: 800-248-6437
Meyers, Mike, Chief Dev. Ofc.

Friends of Namibian Children [10987]
PO Box 5572
Phoenix, AZ 85010
PH: (623)444-8171
Fax: (623)466-0688
Wenk, Janet, President, Founder

Fusion Architecture [5968]
PO Box 66853
Phoenix, AZ 85082-6853
Banning, Kobina, Founder, President

Gold Wing Road Riders Association
[22221]
21423 N 11th Ave.
Phoenix, AZ 85027-2813
PH: (623)581-2500
Toll free: 800-843-9460
Fax: (877)348-9416
Gallardo, Abel, President

Harvest [20364]
701 N 1st St.
Phoenix, AZ 85004
PH: (602)258-1083
Fax: (602)258-1318
Moffitt, Dr. Robert, Founder,
President

Health Industry Business Com-
munications Council [14362]
2525 E Arizona Biltmore Cir., Ste.
127
Phoenix, AZ 85016
PH: (602)381-1091
Fax: (602)381-1093
Hankin, Robert A., PhD, CEO,
President

Heroin Anonymous [13143]
5025 N Central Ave., No. 587
Phoenix, AZ 85012
S., Mike, Founder

Hispanic Women's Corporation
[9359]
PO Box 20725
Phoenix, AZ 85018-0725
PH: (602)954-7995
Fax: (602)954-7563
Guitierrez, Linda Mazon, President,
CEO

Intermarket Agency Network [2285]
c/o Alicia Wadas, President
LAVIDGE
2777 E Camelback Rd., Ste. 300
Phoenix, AZ 85016
Green, Cam, Contact

International Association of Duncan
Certified Ceramic Teachers
[21581]
3434 W Earll Dr., Ste. 101
Phoenix, AZ 85017
PH: (480)264-6982
Smith, Arlene, President

International Cruise Victims [19221]
4747 E Elliot Rd., No. 29598
Phoenix, AZ 85044
PH: (602)852-5896
(818)655-5711
Carver, Kendall, Chairman

International Intradiscal Therapy
Society [17256]
1635 E Myrtle Ave., Ste. 400
Phoenix, AZ 85020
PH: (310)279-3159
Fax: (602)944-0064
Choi, Gun, MD, PhD, President

Kids at Hope [11245]
2400 W Dunlap Ave., Ste. 135
Phoenix, AZ 85021-2885
PH: (602)674-0026
Toll free: 866-275-HOPE
Fax: (602)674-0034
Miller, Rick, President, Founder

Lambda Alpha International [23725]
PO Box 72720
Phoenix, AZ 85050
PH: (480)719-7404
Fax: (602)532-7865
Gragg, Steven, President

Let Hope Rise [12981]
4808 N 24th St., Ste. 902
Phoenix, AZ 85016

PH: (480)779-0530
Fax: (866)298-3607
Stringer, Daniel, President

Make-A-Wish Foundation of America
[11250]
4742 N 24th St., Ste. 400
Phoenix, AZ 85016
PH: (602)279-9474
Toll free: 800-722-9474
Fax: (602)279-0855
Williams, David A., CEO, President

Marketing Education Association
[8272]
1512 E Cambridge Ave.
Phoenix, AZ 85006-1128
Moore, Deb, President

Messianic Jewish Movement
International [20339]
PO Box 41071
Phoenix, AZ 85080
PH: (515)999-6564
Toll free: 800-493-7482
Geoffrey, Kevin, President

MISS Foundation [11919]
77 E Thomas Rd., No. 221
Phoenix, AZ 85012-3109
PH: (602)279-6477
Toll free: 888-455-6477
Soos, Jennifer, Coord.

Mission Africa [11402]
11002 S 48th St.
Phoenix, AZ 85044
PH: (480)788-3832
Fax: (480)893-8318
Jakpor, Viktor, Exec. Dir., Founder

Mothers Arms [12865]
4757 E Greenway Rd., No. 124
Phoenix, AZ 85032
Toll free: 800-464-4840
Wadas, Alicia A., Founder, President

National Association of Benefits and
Work Incentive Specialists [1074]
5025 E Washington St., Ste. 200
Phoenix, AZ 85034
PH: (602)443-0722
Cebula, Ray, VP

National Association of Campus
Card Users [3194]
2226 W Northern Ave., Ste C-120
Phoenix, AZ 85021
PH: (602)395-8989
Fax: (602)395-9090
Adkins, Lowell, Exec. Dir.

National Association of Early Childhood Specialists in State Departments of Education [7591]
c/o Amy Corriveau, Treasurer
Arizona Department of Education
1535 W Jefferson St., Bin 15
Phoenix, AZ 85007
PH: (602)364-1530
Adams, Deborah, President

National Association for Information
Destruction [1803]
3030 N 3rd St., Ste. 940
Phoenix, AZ 85012-3059
PH: (602)788-6243
Fax: (480)658-2088
Johnson, Robert, CEO

National Association of Railroad Trial
Counsel [5816]
1430 E Missouri Ave., Ste. B200
Phoenix, AZ 85014
PH: (602)265-2700
Fax: (602)265-2705

National Association of State
Contractors Licensing Agencies
[884]
Bldg. 1, Unit 110
23309 N 17th Dr.

Phoenix, AZ 85027
PH: (623)587-9354
Toll free: 866-948-3363
Fax: (623)587-9625
Whitaker, Angie, Exec. Dir.

National Bulk Vendors Association
[3432]
1202 E Maryland Ave., Ste. 1K
Phoenix, AZ 85014-1342
Toll free: 888-628-2872
Fax: (480)302-5108
Dumphy, Shawn, VP

National Day of the Cowboy [8802]
822 W Monte Way
Phoenix, AZ 85041
PH: (928)759-0951
Braley, Bethany, Chairperson, Exec.
Dir., Publisher

National Historical Fire Foundation
[22014]
c/o Hall of Flame Fire Museum
6101 E Van Buren St.
Phoenix, AZ 85008-3421
PH: (602)275-3473
Fax: (602)275-0896
Getz, George F., Jr., Founder

National Society for American Indian
Elderly [19585]
PO Box 50070
Phoenix, AZ 85076
PH: (602)424-0542
Wilson, Steve, Chairperson

Navy Carrier Society [22203]
c/o Ted Kraver, Secretary/Treasurer
225 W Orchid Ln.
Phoenix, AZ 85021
Perry, Dick, President

Organization Design Forum [2188]
5016 E Mulberry Dr.
Phoenix, AZ 85018-6525
PH: (602)510-9105
Spelts, Tanya, Administrator

Rubber Pavements Association
[576]
3420 W Danbury Dr.
Phoenix, AZ 85053
PH: (480)517-9944
Belshe, Mark, Exec. Dir.

Social Anxiety Association [13723]
2058 E Topeka Dr.
Phoenix, AZ 85024-2404
PH: (602)230-7316
Richards, Thomas, President

Society for American Baseball
Research [22567]
4455 E Camelback Rd., Ste. D140
Phoenix, AZ 85018-2847
PH: (602)343-6455
Toll free: 800-969-7227
Fax: (602)595-5690
Appleman, Marc, Exec. Dir.

Society of American Business Edi-
tors and Writers [2719]
c/o Walter Cronkite School of
Journalism and Mass Communica-
tion
555 N Central Ave., Ste. 406E
Phoenix, AZ 85004-1248
PH: (602)496-7862
Fax: (602)496-7041
Ossinger, Joanna, President

Society of Antique Modelers [21248]
c/o Walt Angus, Secretary
PO Box 73215
Phoenix, AZ 85050
PH: (707)255-3547
Angus, Walt, Treasurer, Secretary

Space Access Society [7221]
PO Box 16034
Phoenix, AZ 85011
Vanderbilt, Henry, Founder

Sports Financial Advisors Associa-
tion [1268]
10645 N Tatum Blvd., Ste. 200-608
Phoenix, AZ 85028
PH: (602)820-2220
Fax: (602)297-6608
Miller, Jonathan, President, CEO

Supima [3772]
4141 E Broadway Rd.
Phoenix, AZ 85040-8831
PH: (602)792-6002
Fax: (602)792-6004
Deputy, Keith B., Chairman

Transmission Rebuilders Network
International [331]
4757 E Greenway Rd., Ste. 107B-54
Phoenix, AZ 85032-8512
PH: (602)404-0299
Toll free: 888-582-8764
Fax: (602)404-7650
Fuller, Bill, Founder

United States Professional Poolplayers Association [22588]
4340 E Indian School Rd., Ste. 21-
115
Phoenix, AZ 85018
Alvarez, Frank, III, President

Association of Personal Computer
User Groups [6294]
PO Box 1384
Pine, AZ 85544-1384
Steward, David, Secretary

Self-Guided Hunting Association
[22168]
PO Box 2771
Pinetop, AZ 85935
Fax: (928)521-2063
Yorksmith, Bryan, Managing Ed.

Hope for Sderot [12675]
303 Gurley St., Ste. 240
Prescott, AZ 86301
PH: (530)918-4929
Ganulin, Stewart, Director

Meter Stamp Society [22343]
c/o Rick Stambaugh, President
100 Elder Ct.
Prescott, AZ 86303-5364
Effner, Harold, Secretary, Treasurer

Prescott College Alumni Association
[19345]
c/o Prescott College
220 Grove Ave.
Prescott, AZ 86301
Toll free: 877-350-2100
Smith, Marie, Director

White Mountain Education Associa-
tion [20620]
PO Box 11975
Prescott, AZ 86304
PH: (928)778-0638
DuBois, Rev. Joleen D., Founder,
President

International Submariners Associa-
tion/USA [21010]
7770 Loos Dr.
Prescott Valley, AZ 86314-5520
PH: (928)759-9544
Messersmith, Jack, President

Society of International Chinese in
Educational Technology [8676]
c/o Dr. Hong Zhan, Treasurer
7200 E Pioneer Ln.

Prescott Valley, AZ 86314
PH: (928)523-0408
Fax: (928)523-1929
Cheng, Dr. Jiangang, Officer

Hartz Club of America **[6959]**
1632 E Santa Fiore
Queen Creek, AZ 85140

National Alliance of Gang Investigators Associations **[5127]**
c/o Charles Schoville, President
PO Box 574
Queen Creek, AZ 85142
PH: (602)223-2569
Schoville, Charles, President

Association of Veterinary Hematology and Transfusion Medicine **[17639]**
PO Box 1234
Sahuarita, AZ 85629-1004
Toll free: 844-430-4300
Fax: (844)430-4300
Musulin, Sarah, President

Autism Angels Network **[13743]**
1693 E Desert Rose Trail
San Tan Valley, AZ 85143
Kent, Tanya, Contact.

Alcor Life Extension Foundation **[14354]**
7895 E Acoma Dr., Ste. 110
Scottsdale, AZ 85260-6916
PH: (480)905-1906
Toll free: 877-462-5267
Fax: (480)922-9027
More, Max, PhD, CEO, President

Alliance Defending Freedom **[18080]**
15100 N 90th St.
Scottsdale, AZ 85260-2769
PH: (480)444-0020
Toll free: 800-835-5233
Fax: (480)444-0025
Cox, Chapman B., Chairman

Alliance for Work-Life Progress **[2736]**
14040 N Northsight Blvd.
Scottsdale, AZ 85260-3601
PH: (480)951-9191
Toll free: 877-951-9191
Lingle, Kathie, Director

American Association of Cosmetology Schools **[7681]**
9927 E Bell Rd., Ste. 110
Scottsdale, AZ 85260
PH: (480)281-0431
Toll free: 800-831-1086
Fax: (480)905-0993
Cox, Jim, CEO

American Equestrian Alliance **[4305]**
PO Box 6230
Scottsdale, AZ 85261
Toll free: 800-874-9191
Fax: (602)992-8327
Allen, Brent, Exec. Dir.

Association for Learning Environments **[7825]**
11445 E Via Linda, Ste. 2-440
Scottsdale, AZ 85259
PH: (480)391-0840
Layne, Scott, Chairperson

Association of Retail Travel Agents **[3372]**
4320 N Miller Rd.
Scottsdale, AZ 85251-3606
Toll free: 866-369-8969
Fax: (866)743-8969
Funk, Pat, Editor

Brewmeisters Anonymous **[21260]**
20210 N 76th Way
Scottsdale, AZ 85255

PH: (480)319-2227
Nesbitt, Bill, President

Chances for Children **[10889]**
20343 N Hayden Rd., Ste. 105-114
Scottsdale, AZ 85255
PH: (480)513-3373
Fax: (480)323-2343
Juntunen, Kathi, President

Council on Chiropractic Education **[14264]**
8049 N 85th Way
Scottsdale, AZ 85258-4321
PH: (480)443-8877
Toll free: 888-443-3506
Fax: (480)483-7333
Little, Craig S., DC, President

Golf Fore Africa **[13512]**
32531 N Scottsdale Rd., Ste. 105
Scottsdale, AZ 85266-1519
PH: (480)284-5818
Fax: (480)292-8805
King, Betsy, President, CEO

Golf Tournament Association of America **[22881]**
16605 N, 56th Pl.
Scottsdale, AZ 85254
PH: (602)524-7034
Toll free: 888-810-4822
Immordino, Phil, President, Founder

Homeowners Against Deficient Dwellings **[11972]**
c/o Paula Schulman, National Treasurer
22393 N 76th Pl.
Scottsdale, AZ 85255
PH: (816)560-0030
Seats, Nancy, President

Independent Glass Association **[1505]**
14747 N Northsight Blvd., Ste. 111-387
Scottsdale, AZ 85260
PH: (480)535-8650
Fax: (480)522-3104
Bailey, Matt, President

Information Technology Alliance **[7272]**
23940 N 73rd Pl.
Scottsdale, AZ 85255
PH: (480)515-2003
Benzer, Jo Ann, Exec. Dir.

Institute for Health and Productivity Management **[2171]**
17470 N Pacesetter Way
Scottsdale, AZ 85255-5445
PH: (480)305-2100
Fax: (480)305-2189
Sullivan, Sean, JD, CEO, President, Founder

International Association of Law, Ethics and Science **[5428]**
c/o American University of Sovereign Nations
8840 E Chaparral Rd., Ste. 285
Scottsdale, AZ 85250-2611
PH: (602)396-5788
Byk, Prof. Christian, Sec. Gen.

International Guild of Realism **[8980]**
4400 N Scottsdale Rd., No. 9539
Scottsdale, AZ 85251-3331

International Society of Crime Prevention Practitioners **[11507]**
PO Box 15584
Scottsdale, AZ 85267
PH: (657)888-4277
Wall, Bruce, Treasurer

Mounted Archery Association of the Americas **[22501]**
c/o Joey Ogburn, Membership Officer

31711 N 164th St.
Scottsdale, AZ 85262
PH: (602)400-0826
Troyk, Diana, President

National Council for Prescription Drug Programs **[16678]**
9240 E Raintree Dr.
Scottsdale, AZ 85260
PH: (480)477-1000
Fax: (480)767-1042
Klimek, John, Sr. VP

National Dental EDI Council **[14461]**
9240 E Raintree Dr.
Scottsdale, AZ 85260-7518
PH: (480)734-2890
Fax: (480)734-2895
Rudnyk, Rebecca, Exec. Dir.

notMYkid **[13471]**
5230 E Shea Blvd.
Scottsdale, AZ 85254
PH: (602)652-0163
Morocco, Robert, Treasurer

Professional Beauty Association **[928]**
15825 N 71st St., No. 100
Scottsdale, AZ 85254
PH: (480)281-0424
Toll free: 800-468-2274
Fax: (480)905-0708
Sleeper, Steve, Exec. Dir.

Teleos Institute **[12016]**
7439 E Beryl Ave.
Scottsdale, AZ 85258
PH: (480)948-1800
Fax: (480)948-1870
Pike, Diane K., Director

United States Mangalarga Marchador Association **[4421]**
10487 E Rising Sun Dr.
Scottsdale, AZ 85262
PH: (480)595-2559
Kelley, John J., President

Wedding Industry Professionals Association **[448]**
8711 E Pinnacle Peak Rd., No. 227
Scottsdale, AZ 85255
PH: (844)444-9300
Fax: (480)513-3207
Davies, Rrivre, VP

WorldatWork **[1103]**
14040 N Northsight Blvd.
Scottsdale, AZ 85260
PH: (480)922-2020
(480)951-9191
Toll free: 866-816-2962
Fax: (480)483-8352
McAuley, Sara R., Chmn. of the Bd.

Frank Lloyd Wright Foundation **[7502]**
12621 N Frank Lloyd Wright Blvd.
Scottsdale, AZ 85259
PH: (480)860-2700
Graff, Stuart I., President, CEO

Hummingbird Society **[3664]**
6560 State Route 179, Ste. 124
Sedona, AZ 86351
PH: (928)284-2251
Toll free: 800-529-3699
Hawkins, Dr. Ross, Exec. Dir., Founder

World Research Foundation **[14968]**
PO Box 20828
Sedona, AZ 86341
PH: (928)284-3300
Boeckmann, Laverne, Founder

Fibonacci Association **[6820]**
c/o Ashley DeFazio, Subscription Manager

PO Box 1740
Sun City, AZ 85372
Dilcher, Karl, Mem.

Novelty Salt & Pepper Shakers Club **[21705]**
16468 W Juniper Ct.
Surprise, AZ 85387
PH: (623)975-6870
Yedlin, Barry, Editor

American Federation of Astrologers **[5987]**
6535 S Rural Rd.
Tempe, AZ 85283-3746
PH: (480)838-1751
Toll free: 888-301-7630
Fax: (480)838-8293
Arens, Christine, Director

American Matthay Association **[8359]**
c/o Mary Pendleton-Hoffer, President
405 E Hermosa Cir.
Tempe, AZ 85282
Razaq, Janice Larzon, VP

American Rainwater Catchment Systems Association **[7362]**
7650 S McClintock Dr., Ste. 103, No. 134
Tempe, AZ 85284-1673
PH: (512)617-6528
Crawford, David, President

American Society for Indexing **[9676]**
1628 E Southern Ave., No. 9-223
Tempe, AZ 85282
PH: (480)245-6750
Henson, Gwen, Exec. Dir.

Children with AIDS Project of America **[10447]**
PO Box 23778
Tempe, AZ 85285-3778
PH: (602)405-2196
Fax: (602)454-9092
Jenkins, Jim, Founder

Cross-Cultural Dance Resources **[9248]**
PO Box 872002
Tempe, AZ 85287-2002
PH: (480)727-9532
Fax: (480)965-2247
Vissicaro, Pegge, President

Do It Now Foundation **[13136]**
PO Box 27921
Tempe, AZ 85285
PH: (480)736-0599
Fax: (480)736-0771
Parker, Jim, Publisher

Edutechnia **[6741]**
4849 S Darrow Dr., No. L138
Tempe, AZ 85282
PH: (602)434-1778
Madrid, Jorge, Contact

Father Matters **[18765]**
PO Box 13575
Tempe, AZ 85284-3575
PH: (602)774-3298
Simms, Vance, CEO, Founder

Gamma Alpha Omega **[23873]**
PO Box 427
Tempe, AZ 85280
Galindo, Lorena, XI, President

Institute for Supply Management **[2817]**
2055 E Centennial Cir.
Tempe, AZ 85284
PH: (480)752-6276
Toll free: 800-888-6276
Fax: (480)752-7890
Barnes, Jim, Managing Dir.

International Association of Speakers Bureaus **[10175]**
4015 S McClintock Dr., Ste. 110
Tempe, AZ 85282
PH: (480)839-1423
Harris, Karen, President

International Association for World Englishs Inc. **[9283]**
c/o Aya Matsuda, Secretary/Treasurer
Arizona State University
Tempe, AZ 85280
Davis, Daniel R., Exec. Dir.

International Graphonomics Society **[10414]**
c/o Dr. Hans-Leo Teulings, Website Manager and Treasurer
NeuroScript
435 E Carson Dr.
Tempe, AZ 85282
Contreras-Vidal, Jose, President

National Association of Community College Teacher Education Programs **[8651]**
2323 W 14th St.
Tempe, AZ 85281-6942
Kelley, Cynthia S., Treasurer

National High School Baseball Coaches Association **[22561]**
PO Box 12843
Tempe, AZ 85284-0048
PH: (602)615-0571
Fax: (480)838-7133
Lowery, John, Sr., President

National Speakers Association **[10176]**
1500 S Priest Dr.
Tempe, AZ 85281
PH: (480)968-2552
Tetschner, Stacy, CAE, FASAE, CEO

National Stamp Dealers Association **[22350]**
430 E Southern Ave.
Tempe, AZ 85282-5216
PH: (248)709-8940
Toll free: 800-875-6633
Klein, Robert, President

Sigma Phi Beta Fraternity **[23929]**
PO Box 937
Tempe, AZ 85280-0937
Toll free: 888-744-2382
Thomas, Joshua, President, Chairman

TODOS: Mathematics for ALL **[8286]**
PO Box 25482
Tempe, AZ 85285-5482
Hakansson, Susie, President

Travel Journalists Guild **[2726]**
4701 S Lakeshore Dr., Ste. 1
Tempe, AZ 85282
PH: (480)897-3331
Fax: (480)897-3332
Finney, Mike, Exec. Dir.

United States Regional Association of the International Association for Landscape Ecology **[4017]**
c/o Janet Franklin, President
PO Box 875302
Tempe, AZ 85287-5302
PH: (480)965-9884
Hepinstall-Cymerman, Jeffrey, Secretary

University-Community Partnership for Social Action Research **[11454]**
PO Box 875402
Tempe, AZ 85287-5402
Wosinski, Marek, Facilitator, Exec. Ofc.

Aging Life Care Association **[16194]**
3275 W Ina Rd., Ste. 130
Tucson, AZ 85741-2198
PH: (520)881-8008
Fax: (520)325-7925
Boothroyd, Kaaren, CEO

American Association of Zoo Keepers **[7394]**
8476 E Speedway Blvd., Ste. 204
Tucson, AZ 85710-1728
PH: (520)298-9688
Hansen, Ed, CEO, CFO

The American Board of Radiology **[17039]**
5441 E Williams Cir.
Tucson, AZ 85711-7412
PH: (520)790-2900
Fax: (520)790-3200
Jackson, Valerie P., Exec. Dir.

American Fibromyalgia Syndrome Association **[14765]**
7371 E Tanque Verde Rd.
Tucson, AZ 85715-3475
PH: (520)733-1570
Fax: (520)290-5550
Thorson, Kristin, President

American First Day Cover Society **[22298]**
PO Box 16277
Tucson, AZ 85732-6277
PH: (520)321-0880
Ronnei, Todd, Chairman

American Institute for Maghrib Studies **[7464]**
Marshall Bldg., Rm. 470
Center for Middle Eastern Studies
845 N Park Ave.
Tucson, AZ 85719-4871
PH: (520)626-6498
Fax: (520)621-9257
Adams, Kerry, Exec. Dir.

American Society of Cosmetic Physicians **[14310]**
8040 S Kolb Rd.
Tucson, AZ 85756
PH: (520)574-1050
Fax: (520)545-1254
Petty, Sean Michael, President, Exec. Dir.

Arthritis Introspective **[17154]**
5217 E 26th St.
Tucson, AZ 85711
PH: (520)440-0771
Purcell, Kevin, Founder, President

Association of American Physicians and Surgeons **[16738]**
1601 N Tucson Blvd., No. 9
Tucson, AZ 85716
PH: (520)323-3110
Toll free: 800-635-1196
Fax: (520)326-3529
Madrigal-Dersch, Juliette, President

Association of University Research Parks **[8495]**
6262 N Swan Rd., Ste. 100
Tucson, AZ 85718
PH: (520)529-2521
Fax: (520)529-2499
D'Agostino, Charles, President

B-26 Marauder Historical Society **[21192]**
3900 E Timrod St.
Tucson, AZ 85711
PH: (520)322-6226
Gutt, Mr. Phillip, CAE, Exec. Dir.

The Biodiversity Group **[4795]**
10980 W Rudasill Rd.
Tucson, AZ 85743

PH: (520)647-1434
Hamilton, Paul, PhD, Founder, Exec. Dir.

Blue Marble Institute **[23219]**
3481 E Michigan St.
Tucson, AZ 85714-2221
PH: (520)382-4847
DeBernardis, Richard, Secretary, Director

Center for Electronic Packaging Research **[6967]**
Dept. of Electrical and Computer Engineering
University of Arizona
Tucson, AZ 85721-0104
PH: (520)621-6193
Fax: (520)621-8076
Dvorak, Prof. Steven L., Contact

Coalition to Protect America's National Parks **[4520]**
5625 N Wilmot Rd.
Tucson, AZ 85750-1216
PH: (520)615-9417
Fax: (520)615-9474
Finnerty, Maureen, Chairperson

ConserVentures **[3842]**
3400 E Speedway Blvd., Ste. 118-138
Tucson, AZ 85716
PH: (520)591-1410
Hanson, Roseann, Founder

Creative Play Project **[13440]**
3849 E Broadway Blvd., No. 293
Tucson, AZ 85716
Peiffer, Tim, President

Doctors for Disaster Preparedness **[14662]**
1601 N Tucson Blvd., Ste. 9
Tucson, AZ 85716
PH: (520)325-2680
Orient, Jane M., MD, President

Economic History Association **[7982]**
McClelland Hall, 401GG
Dept. of Economics
University of Arizona
Tucson, AZ 85721
PH: (520)621-4421
Fax: (520)621-8450
Fishback, Price, Exec. Dir.

Fibromyalgia Network **[14767]**
7371 E Tanque Verde Rd.
Tucson, AZ 85715
PH: (520)290-5508
Toll free: 800-853-2929
Fax: (520)290-5550

Freecycle Network **[4630]**
PO Box 294
Tucson, AZ 85702-0294
Beal, Deron, Exec. Dir., Founder, Chairperson

IEEE - Antennas and Propagation Society **[6423]**
c/o J. Scott Tyo, Secretary/Treasurer
University of Arizona
Meinel Bldg., Rm. 623
Tucson, AZ 85745
PH: (520)626-8183
Fax: (520)621-4358
Tyo, J. Scott, Secretary, Treasurer

Insurance and Financial Communicators Association **[96]**
PO Box 515 E Grant Rd., Ste. 141
Tucson, AZ 85705
PH: (602)350-0717
Fax: (866)402-7336
Niles, Jaimee, President

Integrative Touch for Kids **[14196]**
8340 N Thornydale Rd., No. 110-153
Tucson, AZ 85741

PH: (520)303-4992
Gold, Jeffrey, President

International Arid Lands Consortium **[4071]**
1955 E 6th St.
Tucson, AZ 85719
PH: (520)626-0329
Fax: (520)621-7196
Hutchinson, Dr. Barbara, Managing Dir.

International Association of Bloodstain Pattern Analysts **[5154]**
12139 E Makohoh Trl.
Tucson, AZ 85749-8179
PH: (520)760-6620
Fax: (520)760-5590
Reeves, Mr. Norman, Secretary, Treasurer, Membership Chp.

International Association of Chinese Linguistics **[8182]**
Dept. of East Asian Studies
University of Arizona
1512 1st St.
Tucson, AZ 85721-0105
Fax: (520)621-1149
Hu, Jianhua, Exec. Sec.

International Association for Creative Dance **[9257]**
PO Box 64213
Tucson, AZ 85728-4213
Victor, Douglas R., Founder

International Association of Fly Fishing Veterinarians **[22041]**
c/o Pantano Animal Clinic
8333 E 22nd St.
Tucson, AZ 85710
PH: (517)349-0454
       (520)572-6790
Sawyer, Donald C., DVM, President

International Child Amputee Network **[11606]**
PO Box 13812
Tucson, AZ 85732
Baughn, Joyce, Director

International Dark-Sky Association **[6004]**
3223 N 1st Ave.
Tucson, AZ 85719
PH: (520)293-3198
Fax: (520)293-3192
Hunter, Dr. Tim, Founder

International Foundation of Bio-Magnetics **[13634]**
5634 E Pima St.
Tucson, AZ 85712
PH: (520)751-7751
Toll free: 888-473-3812
McConico, Sylvia, President

International Science Writers Association **[2689]**
6666 N Mesa View Dr.
Tucson, AZ 85718
PH: (520)529-6835
Cornell, Mr. James, Consultant

International Society of Lymphology **[15542]**
PO Box 245200
Tucson, AZ 85724
PH: (520)626-6118
Fax: (520)626-0822
Witte, M.H., MD, Sec. Gen.

International Society for Vehicle Preservation **[21406]**
PO Box 50046
Tucson, AZ 85703-1046
Haessner, Elaine C., Exec. Dir.

Luz Social Services, Inc. **[13151]**
2797 N Cerrada de Beto Dr.
Tucson, AZ 85745-8617

PH: (520)882-6216
Fax: (520)623-9291
Barron, Dr. Pepe, Founder

Masonry Heater Association of North
America [1630]
2180 S Flying Q Ln.
Tucson, AZ 85713-6793
PH: (520)883-0191
Fax: (480)371-1139
Smith, Richard, Exec. Dir.

Medical Image Perception Society
[15691]
c/o Elizabeth Krupinski, PhD
Dept. of Radiology
University of Arizona
Tucson, AZ 85724
PH: (520)626-4498
Rolland, Jannick, PhD, Contact

Middle East Studies Association of
North America [18690]
University of Arizona
1219 N Santa Rita Ave.
Tucson, AZ 85721
PH: (520)621-5850
Fax: (520)626-9095
Newhall, Amy W., Exec. Dir.

National Association for Civilian
Oversight of Law Enforcement
[5489]
PO Box 87227
Tucson, AZ 85754-7227
PH: (317)721-8133
Buchner, Brian, President

National Association of Document
Examiners [5249]
c/o Heidi H. Harralson, President
PO Box 65095
Tucson, AZ 85728
Toll free: 866-569-0833
Harralson, Heidi H., President

National Association of Self-
Instructional Language Programs
[8188]
University of Arizona
1717 E Speedway Blvd., Ste. 3312
Tucson, AZ 85719-4514
PH: (520)621-3387
Fax: (520)626-8205
Arizumi, Koji, Exec. Dir.

National Business and Economics
Society [7562]
PO Box 65657
Tucson, AZ 85728
PH: (520)395-2622
Fax: (520)395-2622
Thorpe, Kenneth, President

National Shoe Retailers Association
[1401]
7386 N La Cholla Blvd.
Tucson, AZ 85741-2305
PH: (520)209-1710
Toll free: 800-673-8446
Schuyler, Chuck, President

Native American Indian Information
and Trade Center [23652]
PO Box 27626
Tucson, AZ 85726-7626
PH: (520)622-4900
Synder, Fred, Consultant, Director

Native Seeds/SEARCH [3912]
3584 E River Rd.
Tucson, AZ 85718
PH: (520)622-0830
   (520)622-5561
Fax: (520)622-0829
Anson, Cynthia, Chairman

New Parents Network [8404]
3760 N Bay Horse Loop, Ste. 210
Tucson, AZ 85719

PH: (520)461-6806
Storek, Ms. Karen, CEO, Exec. Dir.

No Child Dies Alone [11556]
7014 E Golf Links Rd.
PMB 126
Tucson, AZ 85730
Wrinn, Marie, CEO, Founder

North America Native American
Information and Trade Center
[10045]
PO Box 27626
Tucson, AZ 85726-7626
PH: (520)622-4900
Synder, Fred, Consultant, Director

North American Tang Shou Tao As-
sociation [13645]
PO Box 36235
Tucson, AZ 85740-6235
PH: (520)498-0678
Black, Dr. Vince, Founder

Nuclear Resister [18754]
PO Box 43383
Tucson, AZ 85733-3383
PH: (520)323-8697
Cohen-Joppa, Felice, Editor

Pan-African Education [11733]
PO Box 16653
Tucson, AZ 85732
PH: (520)465-0976
Ofori-Diallo, Jay, President

Pilatus Owners and Pilots Associa-
tion [155]
6890 E Sunrise Dr., Ste. 120
Tucson, AZ 85750
PH: (520)299-7485
Fax: (520)844-6161

Pilot Parents of Southern Arizona
[12332]
2600 N Wyatt Dr.
Tucson, AZ 85712
PH: (520)324-3150
Toll free: 877-365-7220
Fax: (520)324-3152
Kallis, Lynn, Exec. Dir.

Presidential Prayer Team [20300]
PO Box 69010
Tucson, AZ 85737-9010
Toll free: 866-433-7729
Fax: (480)347-2691
Graham, Franklin, Co-Ch.

Real Estate Educators Association
[2890]
7739 E Broadway, No. 337
Tucson, AZ 85710
PH: (520)609-2380
Lapp, Tina, Officer

Safari Club International [4879]
4800 W Gates Pass Rd.
Tucson, AZ 85745-9490
PH: (520)620-1220
Toll free: 888-486-8724
Fax: (520)622-1205
Kauffman, Craig L., Comm. Chm.

Sigma Phi Society [23931]
PO Box 57417
Tucson, AZ 85711-7417
PH: (520)777-3055
Solem, Marshall, Chairman

Special Needs Alliance [5552]
6341 E Brian Kent Dr.
Tucson, AZ 85710
PH: (520)546-1005
Toll free: 877-572-8472
Mayo, Pi-Yi, President

Student Organization of North
America [8630]
University Services Annex Bldg.
300A, Rm. 108

University of Arizona
220 W 6th St.
Tucson, AZ 85701
PH: (520)621-7761
Fax: (520)626-2675
Velazquez, Marianna, Coord.

Surgical Volunteers International
[17412]
65712 E Mesa Ridge Ct.
Tucson, AZ 85739
PH: (832)434-1593
Fax: (832)415-2814
Flood, Thomas W., Contact

United States Handball Association
[22904]
2333 N Tucson Blvd.
Tucson, AZ 85716
PH: (520)795-0434
Toll free: 800-289-8742
Fax: (520)795-0465
Martin, LeaAnn, President

Western National Parks Association
[6901]
12880 N Vistoso Village Dr.
Tucson, AZ 85755
PH: (520)622-1999

Wheelchair Athletes Worldwide
[11645]
7615 N Soledad Ave.
Tucson, AZ 85741
PH: (619)249-1885
Hughes, Peter, President

Women's Classical Caucus [9168]
c/o Prof. Alison Futrell, Secretary-
Treasurer
Dept. of History, Social Sciences
215
University of Arizona
1145 E South Campus Dr.
Tucson, AZ 85721
Futrell, Prof. Alison, Secretary,
Treasurer

World Care [11741]
Sam Levitz Warehouse
3430 E 36th St.
Tucson, AZ 85713
PH: (520)514-1588
Fax: (520)514-1589
Tierney, Bryn, President

Clan Menzies Society - North
American Branch [20831]
c/o Jerry Minnis
PO Box 397
Vernon, AZ 85940-0397
PH: (928)537-1902
Minnis, Jerry, Contact

Hope for Hypothalamic Hamartomas
[15941]
PO Box 721
Waddell, AZ 85355
Dunn Soeby, Lisa, President

National Police Canine Association
[5509]
PO Box 538
Waddell, AZ 85355
Toll free: 877-362-1219
Anderson, Terry, President

Peyote Way Church of God [20506]
30800 W Bonita Klondyke Rd.
Willcox, AZ 85643
PH: (928)828-3444

Navajo Code Talkers Association
[21198]
PO Box 1266
Window Rock, AZ 86515-1266
PH: (928)688-5202
Fax: (928)688-5204
Billison, Dr. Samuel, President

National Toggenburg Club [4279]
2100 Painted Desert Dr.
Winslow, AZ 86047
PH: (928)289-4868
Losey, Marshall, President

American Council for Accredited
Certification [4536]
PO Box 1000
Yarnell, AZ 85362
Toll free: 888-808-8381
Fax: (888)894-3590
Wiles, Charlie

Back to the Basics Please [13530]
10329 S Del Rey Dr.
Yuma, AZ 85367
PH: (928)550-3999
Bennett, Brandon, President

The Strong Family Association of
America, Inc. [20933]
c/o Helen M. Stoutnar, Corresponding Secretary
10667 South Ave. 10 E-71
Yuma, AZ 85365–7008
Stoutnar, Helen, Corr. Sec.

Welders Without Borders [7384]
PO Box 1597
Yuma, AZ 85364
PH: (928)344-7570
Colton, Prof. Samuel, Sr., Founder

ARKANSAS

Ouachita Baptist University Alumni
Association [19343]
410 Ouachita St.
Arkadelphia, AR 71998
PH: (870)245-5506
   (870)245-5111
Edwards, Shari, President

National Oil and Acrylic Painters'
Society [8875]
PO Box 5567
Bella Vista, AR 72714
PH: (479)899-4961
Pearson, Cathy, President

Owen Family Association [20910]
4190 Hurricane Shores Dr.
Benton, AR 72019
Owen, Cliff, President

International Defensive Pistol As-
sociation [23131]
2232 County Rd. 719
Berryville, AR 72616
PH: (870)545-3886
Fax: (870)545-3894
Wilson, Bill, President

National Water Center [7372]
5473 Highway 23 N
Eureka Springs, AR 72631
PH: (479)244-0985
Harmony, Barbara, Contact

Catalina 400 International Associa-
tion [22604]
PO Box 9207
Fayetteville, AR 72703
PH: (717)225-5325
Bliss, Martha, Secretary

Food Safety Consortium [1328]
University of Arkansas
110 Agriculture Bldg.
Fayetteville, AR 72701
PH: (479)575-5647
Fax: (479)575-7531
Edmark, Dave, Dir. of Comm.

International Conference of Funeral
Service Examining Boards of the
United States [2398]
1885 Shelby Ln.
Fayetteville, AR 72704

PH: (479)442-7076
Fax: (479)442-7090
Paull, Dalene, Exec. Dir.

International Weed Science Society
[3550]
c/o Dr. Nilda R. Burgos, Vice
President
Dept. of Crop, Soil, and
Environmental Sciences
University of Arkansas
1366 W Altheimer Dr.
Fayetteville, AR 72704
PH: (479)575-3984
    (479)575-3955
Fax: (479)575-3975
Burgos, Dr. Nilda R., VP

National Block and Bridle Club
[3619]
c/o Janeal Yancey, PhD, Editor
University of Arkansas
1120 W Maple St.
Fayetteville, AR 72701
PH: (479)575-4115
Fax: (479)575-7294
Yelich, Joel V., VP

North American Membrane Society
[6837]
Dept. of Chemical Engineering
University of Arkansas
3202 Bell Engineering Ctr.
Fayetteville, AR 72701-1201
PH: (479)575-3419
Fax: (479)575-7926
Bhattacharyya, Dibakar, President

Restore Humanity [12182]
1655 Woolsey Ave.
Fayetteville, AR 72703
PH: (479)841-2841
Fennel, Sarah, CEO, Founder

Per Diems Against Poverty [12106]
3315 Glen Flora Way
Fort Smith, AR 72908
Barker, Jennifer, Exec. Dir., Founder

National Taxidermists Association
[3203]
PO Box 549
Green Forest, AR 72638
PH: (855)772-8543
Fax: (870)438-4218
Thacker, Tim, Secretary

Hoo-Hoo International [1410]
207 Main St.
Gurdon, AR 71743
PH: (870)353-4997
Fax: (870)353-4151
O'Meara Moynihan, Mary, Chmn. of
the Bd.

Knights of the Ku Klux Klan [19239]
PO Box 2222
Harrison, AR 72601
PH: (870)427-3414
Pendergraft, Rachel, Coord.

Christian Motorcyclists Association
[22218]
4278 Highway 71 S
Hatfield, AR 71945-7119
PH: (870)389-6196
Ogden, John, Sr., Chairman

Aluminum Foil Container
Manufacturers Association [826]
10 Vecilla Ln.
Hot Springs Village, AR 71909
PH: (440)781-5819
Fax: (440)247-9053
Williams, Coke, Exec. Sec.,
Treasurer

Association of Army Dentistry
[14418]
10 Cordoba Way
Hot Springs Village, AR 71909
Lefler, Bill B., President

National Federation of State Poetry
Societies [10153]
c/o James Barton
PO Box 263
Huttig, AR 71747-0263
Barton, James, President, Coord.,
Member Svcs.

Falcon Club of America [21379]
PO Box 113
Jacksonville, AR 72078-0113
Nordboe, Jerry, Treasurer

Independent Professional Seed As-
sociation [3565]
Box 139
2504 Alexander Dr.
Jonesboro, AR 72401
PH: (870)336-0777
Toll free: 888-888-5058
Fax: (888)888-5058
Martin, Todd L., Exec. Dir., CEO

American College of Heraldry
[20952]
1818 N Taylor St., Ste. B, No. 312
Little Rock, AR 72207
Drake, Paul, Director

Association of Anglican Musicians
[20486]
PO Box 7530
Little Rock, AR 72217
PH: (501)661-9925
Fax: (501)661-9925
Garvey, James, President

The Benjamin Banneker Association,
Inc. [8278]
PO Box 55864
Little Rock, AR 72215
Walker, Margaret, President

Case Management Society of
America [15583]
6301 Ranch Dr.
Little Rock, AR 72223
PH: (501)225-2229
Toll free: 800-216-2672
Fax: (501)221-9068
Lattimer, Cheri A., RN, BSN, Exec.
Dir.

Change Bangladesh [17883]
505 Nan Cir.
Little Rock, AR 72211
PH: (501)255-2814

Communications Supply Service As-
sociation [3413]
5700 Murray St.
Little Rock, AR 72209
PH: (501)562-7666
Toll free: 800-252-2772
Brown, Mr. John, CEO, President

Heifer International [3727]
1 World Ave.
Little Rock, AR 72202
PH: (501)907-2902
Toll free: 855-948-6437
Haddigan, Hilary

Historic Iris Preservation Society
[22101]
c/o Linda Bell, Secretary
608 Beckwood
Little Rock, AR 72205
PH: (501)580-0183
Bell, Linda, Secretary

International Association of Yoga
Therapists [10421]
PO Box 251563
Little Rock, AR 72225
PH: (928)541-0004
Sarkar, Dilip, MD, President

International Goat Association [4277]
c/o Christian De Vries
12709 Grassy Dr.

Little Rock, AR 72210-2708
PH: (501)454-1641
Fax: (501)251-9391
Capote, Juan, Dr., President

International Society for the Study of
Vascular Anomalies [15948]
Arkansas Children's Hospital
1 Children's Way, Slot 836
Little Rock, AR 72202
PH: (501)364-2656
Fax: (501)364-4790
Fishman, Steven J., President

National Association of Hispanic
Nurses [16148]
6301 Ranch Dr.
Little Rock, AR 72223
PH: (501)367-8616
Fax: (501)227-5444
Suarez, MA, RN, Dan, President

National Institute for Case Manage-
ment [15590]
11701 W 36th St.
Little Rock, AR 72211
PH: (501)227-2262
Fax: (501)227-4247
Cunningham, L. Greg, CEO

National-Interstate Council of State
Boards of Cosmetology [926]
c/o Debra Norton, Coordinator
7622 Briarwood Cir.
Little Rock, AR 72205
PH: (501)227-8262
Helton, Bill, VP

Society for Commercial Archeology
[8905]
PO Box 2500
Little Rock, AR 72203
Hirsch, Michael, President

Trail of Tears Association [10048]
1100 N University Ave., Ste. 143
Little Rock, AR 72207
PH: (501)666-9032
Fax: (501)666-5875
Baker, Jack, President

William J. Clinton Foundation
[18506]
1200 President Clinton Ave.
Little Rock, AR 72201
PH: (501)748-0471
    (646)775-9175
Clinton, William J., Founder

Winrock International Institute for
Agricultural Development [17792]
2101 Riverfront Dr.
Little Rock, AR 72202
PH: (501)280-3000
Fax: (501)280-3090
Myers, Mike, CFO

Women in Endocrinology [14710]
c/o Dana Gaddy, PhD, President
University of Arkansas for Medical
Sciences
4301 W Markham St., Slot 505
Little Rock, AR 72205
PH: (501)686-5918
Fax: (501)686-8167
LAMBERT MESSERLIAN, GERA-
LYN, Secretary, Treasurer

Thunderbird and Cougar Club of
America [21501]
422 Cooper St.
Mountain Home, AR 72653
Wheeler, Bill, President

Ercoupe Owners Club [21224]
c/o Larry Snyder, Executive Director
PO Box 220
Pleasant Grove, AR 72567-0220

PH: (870)652-3925
Carden, Skip, Web Adm.

Knife Collectors Club [22175]
US 540 Exit 81
2900 S 26th St.
Rogers, AR 72758-8571
PH: (479)631-0130
Toll free: 800-255-9034
Fax: (479)631-8493

Alpha Chi [23773]
Alpha Chi National College Honor
Scholarship Society
915 E Market Ave.
Searcy, AR 72149
PH: (501)279-4443
Toll free: 800-477-4225
Fax: (501)279-4589
Yarbrough, Trisha, Exec. Dir.

National Center for Fathering
[12417]
1600 W Sunset Ave., Ste B
Springdale, AR 72762
Toll free: 800-593-3237
Paris, Leroy H., II, Chairman

American Water Buffalo Association
[4453]
2415 N Mosley Rd.
Texarkana, AR 71854
Popenoe, Dr. Hugh, Founder

Ford Galaxie Club of America
[21383]
PO Box 429
Valley Springs, AR 72682-0429
PH: (870)743-9757
Reynolds, Mark, Director

Society for the Study of Amphibians
and Reptiles [6708]
c/o Ann Paterson, Treasurer
60 W Fulbright Ave.
Walnut Ridge, AR 72476
Bauer, Aaron, President

Staffordshire Terrier Club of America
[21966]
c/o Stephanie Rogers, Secretary
70 Pamela Dr.
Ward, AR 72176
Conner, Frances, President

International Lawrence Durrell
Society [9057]
c/o Paul H. Lorenz, Secretary/
Treasurer
5601 W Barraque St.
White Hall, AR 71602
PH: (870)575-8618
Fax: (870)575-8040
Sligh, CharlesC

CALIFORNIA

Old English Sheepdog Club of
America [21937]
c/o Marilyn Marshall, Corresponding
Secretary
2541 Bent Spur Dr.
Acton, CA 93510-2105
PH: (661)269-5716
Carr, Sally, President

Coronado 15 National Association
[22609]
30025 Torrepines Pl.
Agoura Hills, CA 91301-4070
PH: (916)832-8015
Paternoster, Vincent, Secretary,
Treasurer

Conrad N. Hilton Foundation [13061]
30440 Agoura Rd.
Agoura Hills, CA 91301

PH: (818)851-3700
Laugham, Peter, President, CEO

Joni and Friends [11611]
30009 Ladyface Ct.
Agoura Hills, CA 91301
PH: (818)707-5664
Toll free: 800-736-4177
Fax: (818)707-2391
Tada, Joni Eareckson, CEO,
Founder

Lily of the Valley Endeavor [10546]
PO Box 1007
Agoura Hills, CA 91376-1007
PH: (805)277-1827
Clack, Sharon, Founder, President

Wheels for the World [11647]
PO Box 3333
Agoura Hills, CA 91376-3333
PH: (818)707-5664
Toll free: 800-736-4177
Fax: (818)707-2391
Tada, Joni Eareckson, CEO,
Founder

Alfa Romeo Association [21313]
PO Box 1458
Alameda, CA 94501
DeGolia, Bill, VP

American Primrose Society [22082]
c/o Jon Kawaguchi, Treasurer
3524 Bowman Ct.
Alameda, CA 94502-7607
Lawrence, Alan, President

**Association of Professional Humane
Educators [10591]**
c/o The Latham Foundation
Latham Plaza Bldg.
1826 Clement Ave.
Alameda, CA 94501

Center for Socialist History [9469]
PO Box 626
Alameda, CA 94501-8626
PH: (510)601-6460

**Institute for Women in Trades,
Technology and Science [3493]**
1150 Ballena Blvd., Ste. 102
Alameda, CA 94501-3682
PH: (510)749-0200
Fax: (510)749-0500
Milgram, Donna, Exec. Dir.

Latham Foundation [10658]
1320 Harbor Bay Pky., Ste. 200
Alameda, CA 94502
PH: (510)521-0920
Fax: (510)521-9861
Sternberg, Sue, Editor

**Parents and Teachers Against
Violence in Education [7721]**
PO Box 1033
Alamo, CA 94507-7033
PH: (925)831-1661
Riak, Jordan, Exec. Dir., Founder

ArchVoices [5960]
1014 Curtis St.
Albany, CA 94706
PH: (510)757-6213
Cary, John, Dir. of Operations,
Founder

**BioEnvironmental Polymer Society
[6192]**
Lead Scientist USDA-ARS
800 Buchanan St.
Albany, CA 94710
Kirwan, Kerry, President

**The ETHIC - The Essence of True
Humanity is Compassion [18718]**
PO Box 6640
Albany, CA 94706-0640
Toll free: 866-THE-ETHIC
Morlino, John, Director, Founder

**Global Strategies for HIV Prevention
[13543]**
828 San Pablo Ave., Ste. 260
Albany, CA 94706
PH: (415)451-1814
Bress, Joshua, President

**Information Services on Latin
America [18620]**
PO Box 6103
Albany, CA 94706
PH: (510)845-4922
Crump, Karen, Director

**Restoration Works International
[9431]**
PO Box 6803
Albany, CA 94706
Hintzke, Mark, Founder, Managing
Dir.

**Seismological Society of America
[7157]**
400 Evelyn Ave., Ste. 201
Albany, CA 94706-1375
PH: (510)525-5474
Fax: (510)525-7204
Mori, Jim, President

**American Association of Critical-
Care Nurses [16088]**
101 Columbia
Aliso Viejo, CA 92656-4109
PH: (949)362-2000
  (206)340-1275
Fax: (949)362-2020
Kiss, Teri Lynn, President

**The Communication Leadership
Exchange [762]**
65 Enterprise
Aliso Viejo, CA 92656
Toll free: 866-463-6226
Healy, Becky, President

Global Genes [14579]
28 Argonaut, Ste. 150
Aliso Viejo, CA 92656
PH: (949)248-7273
Boice, Nicole, Founder, CEO

**National Association of General
Merchandise Representatives
[2208]**
16 Journey, Ste. 200
Aliso Viejo, CA 92656-3317
PH: (847)380-7489
Perrone, David, President

Retina Global [17741]
2 Windflower
Aliso Viejo, CA 92656
PH: (626)737-1232
Trese, Michael T., MD, Chmn. of the
Bd.

**Women's Professional Billiard As-
sociation [22590]**
2710 Alpine Blvd., Ste. O-332
Alpine, CA 91901
Toll free: 855-367-9722
Rogers, Tamre, Contact

Art Aids Art [10486]
PO Box 6438
Altadena, CA 91003
Heath, Beverly, Contact

Coast Defense Study Group [9800]
1577 Braeburn Rd.
Altadena, CA 91001-2603

Mythopoeic Society [9762]
PO Box 6707
Altadena, CA 91003-6707
Oberhelman, David, Administrator

The Skeptics Society [7144]
PO Box 338
Altadena, CA 91001

PH: (626)794-3119
Fax: (626)794-1301
Shermer, Dr. Michael, Exec. Dir.,
Ed.-in-Chief

**United States Girls Wrestling As-
sociation [23373]**
3000 Newell Dr.
American Canyon, CA 94503
Fiske, Dan, Contact

**Upsilon Pi Epsilon Association
[23714]**
158 Wetlands Edge Rd.
American Canyon, CA 94503
PH: (530)518-8488
Fax: (707)647-3560
Madrigal, Orlando S., PhD, Exec.
Dir.

**American Holistic Health Association
[15263]**
PO Box 17400
Anaheim, CA 92817-7400
PH: (714)779-6152
Walter, Ms. Suzan, President

**Association of Woodworking and
Furnishings Suppliers [1475]**
2400 E Katella Ave., Ste. 340
Anaheim, CA 92806-5963
PH: (323)838-9440
Toll free: 800-946-2937
Fax: (323)838-9443
Gangone, Angelo, CEM, Exec. VP

**Engineering Contractors Association
[864]**
2190 S Towne Centre Pl., Ste. 310
Anaheim, CA 92806
PH: (714)937-5000
Fax: (714)937-5030
May, Wes, Exec. Dir.

**Fresh Produce and Floral Council
[1331]**
2400 E Katella Ave., Ste. 330
Anaheim, CA 92806
PH: (714)739-0177
Fax: (714)739-0226
Mace, Carissa, President

**International Society for Law and
Technology [5431]**
1811 W Katella Ave., Ste. 101
Anaheim, CA 92804-6657
PH: (714)778-3230
Fax: (714)778-5463
Lesavich, Stephen, PhD, President

Learn to be Foundation [8720]
1268 N Lakeview Ave., Ste. 201
Anaheim, CA 92807
Kapoor, Neeraj, Founder, CEO

Learning Light Foundation [9541]
1212 E Lincoln Ave.
Anaheim, CA 92805-4249
PH: (714)533-2311
Fax: (714)533-1458
Bates, Laura, Gen. Mgr.

**National Coalition of Healthcare
Recruiters [15589]**
1742 N Willow Woods Dr.
Anaheim, CA 92807
PH: (304)699-5426
Frey, John, Founder

**REFORMA: National Association to
Promote Library & Information
Services to Latinos and the Span-
ish Speaking [9725]**
PO Box 832
Anaheim, CA 92815-0832
Guevara, Beatriz, President

**Stucco Manufacturers Association
[587]**
5753 E Santa Ana Cyn Rd.
Anaheim, CA 92807

PH: (949)387-7611
Fax: (949)701-4476
Wensel, Kevin, President

**World Floor Covering Association
[2982]**
2211 E Howell Ave.
Anaheim, CA 92806
PH: (714)978-6440
Toll free: 800-624-6880
Fax: (714)978-6066
Humphrey, Scott, CEO

**American Institute of Engineers
[6532]**
5420 San Martin Way
Antioch, CA 94531-8506
PH: (510)758-6240
Fax: (510)758-6240
Gottlieb, Eng. Martin S., President

**Community Forestry International
[4197]**
1356 Mokelumne Dr.
Antioch, CA 94531
PH: (925)706-2906
Fax: (925)706-2906
Poffenberger, Mark, PhD, Exec. Dir.

Manos de Esperanza [13070]
PO Box 4604
Antioch, CA 94531
PH: (925)756-7029
Mendoza, David, President

International Banana Club [22162]
14012 Siesta Rd.
Apple Valley, CA 92307-5968

Liga International [12285]
19671 Lucaya Ct.
Apple Valley, CA 92308
PH: (714)257-9952
Fax: (714)257-9952
Parish, Winifred, President

**Sweet and Fortified Wine Associa-
tion [3481]**
PO Box 193
Applegate, CA 95703
PH: (916)258-7115
Prager, Peter, President

Electric Auto Association [6018]
323 Los Altos Dr.
Aptos, CA 95003
PH: (831)688-8669
Freund, Ron, Chairman

**Mixed Harmony Barbershop Quartet
Association [9956]**
c/o Kim Orloff, Coordinator
PO Box 1209
Aptos, CA 95001
Orloff, Kim, Coord., Founder

**Saving and Preserving Arts and
Cultural Environments [8887]**
9053 Soquel Dr., Ste. 205
Aptos, CA 95003
PH: (831)662-2907
Fax: (831)662-2918
Farb Hernandez, Prof. Jo, Director

**Burmese American Medical Associa-
tion [15719]**
339 Sharon Rd.
Arcadia, CA 91007
PH: (626)244-4744
Kyi, Sandar, MD, President

Dean Martin Fan Center [24014]
PO Box 660212
Arcadia, CA 91066-0212
Daniels, Neil T., Founder, President

**Choy Lee Fut Martial Arts Federation
of America [23000]**
500 1/2E Live Oak Ave.
Arcadia, CA 91006

PH: (626)574-1523
Hang, Sifu Ng Fu, Founder

Narramore Christian Foundation
[19994]
250 W Colorado Blvd., Ste. 100
Arcadia, CA 91007
PH: (626)821-8400
Fax: (626)821-8409
Narramore, Dr. Bruce, President

Central European History Society
[9470]
c/o Benjamin Marschke, Administrator
1 Harpst St.
Department of History
Humboldt State University
Arcata, CA 95521
Grossmann, Atina, VP of Admin.

Fertile Crescent Foundation [3862]
PO Box 4835
Arcata, CA 95521
Nichols, Pete, President

Internews Network [18655]
PO Box 4448
Arcata, CA 95518-4448
PH: (707)826-2030
Toll free: 877-247-8819
Fax: (707)826-2136
Hoffman, David, Founder

Mainstream Media Project [18656]
854 9th St., Ste. B
Arcata, CA 95521
PH: (707)826-9111
Fax: (707)826-9112
Durchslag, Jimmy, Exec. Dir.

Peace Resource Project [19114]
PO Box 1122
Arcata, CA 95518-1122
PH: (707)268-1106
Toll free: 888-822-7075
Fax: (707)268-8985

Redwood Alliance [18193]
PO Box 293
Arcata, CA 95518
PH: (707)822-7884
Welch, Michael, Contact

Servas International [18557]
1125 16th St., Ste. 201
Arcata, CA 95521-5585
PH: (707)825-1714
Fax: (707)825-1762
Såganger, Jonny, President

Seventh Generation Fund for
Indigenous Peoples [18713]
425 I St.
Arcata, CA 95518
PH: (707)825-7640
Fax: (707)825-7639
Peters, Tia Oros, Exec. Dir.

American Tax Token Society [22259]
c/o Jim Calvert, Secretary &
Treasurer
1984 B Lyn Rd.
Arroyo Grande, CA 93420
Ostendorf, John, President

American Society of Gas Engineers
[6455]
PO Box 66
Artesia, CA 90702
Moore, Jerry, CGE, Exec. Dir.

Golden Raspberry Award Foundation
[24018]
PO Box 835
Artesia, CA 90701-0835
Fax: (562)860-4136
Wilson, John, Founder

Western Society of Periodontology
[14474]
PO Box 458
Artesia, CA 90702-0458
PH: (562)493-4080
Toll free: 800-367-8386
Fax: (562)493-4340
Johnson, Deborah, Contact

Rescue Alliance of Hairless and
Other Breeds [10687]
PO Box 1135
Atascadero, CA 93423-1135
PH: (805)544-2480
Sweet, Debby, Founder

American Endurance Ride Conference [23319]
1373 Lincoln Way
Auburn, CA 95603
PH: (530)823-2260
Toll free: 866-271-2372
Fax: (530)823-7805
Henkel, Kathleen, Exec. Dir.

International Factoring Association
[1245]
6627 Bay Laurel Pl., Ste. C
Avila Beach, CA 93424
PH: (805)773-0011
Toll free: 800-563-1895
Fax: (805)773-0021
Capobianco, Tina, Bd. Member

Alternative Medicine International
[13585]
11800 Whippoorwill Ln.
Bakersfield, CA 93312

Bridal Association of America [443]
1901 Chester Ave., Ste. 201
Bakersfield, CA 93301-4477
PH: (661)633-9200
Toll free: 866-699-3334
Fax: (661)633-9199
Brown, Mr. Kyle, Exec. Dir.

Global Teams [20108]
3821 Mt. Vernon Ave.
Bakersfield, CA 93306
PH: (661)323-1214
Fax: (661)323-1252
Smith, Randy, Chmn. of the Bd.

MOVE International [11619]
5555 California Ave., Ste. 302
Bakersfield, CA 93309
Toll free: 800-397-6683
Bidabe, D. Linda, Founder

National Tree Society [4088]
PO Box 10808
Bakersfield, CA 93389
PH: (805)589-6912
Davis, Gregory W., Contact

Rock Out To Knock Out RSD
[15991]
PO Box 5332
Bakersfield, CA 93388-5332
PH: (661)399-0502
Goodall, Ashley, Founder, President

Stop Abuse for Everyone [11713]
4939 Calloway Dr., Ste. 104
Bakersfield, CA 93312
PH: (661)829-6848
Rubick, Jade, Founder

Cancer Federation [13922]
PO Box 1298
Banning, CA 92220-0009
PH: (951)849-4325
Cole, Lya, Contact

Friends of the Cassidys [24037]
1647 Crystal Downs St.
Banning, CA 92220
Corwin, Cheryl, President

National Organization of Injured
Workers [23539]
640 Bailey Rd., Ste. 129
Bay Point, CA 94565-4306
PH: (925)235-1115
Toll free: 866-755-2279

Help the Children [12671]
Bldg.1B
5600 Rickenbacker Rd.
Bell, CA 90201-6437
PH: (323)980-9870
Toll free: 888-818-4483
Fax: (323)980-9878
Lay, Andy, Chairman

National Association of Real Estate
Buyer Brokers [2875]
2704 Wemberly Dr.
Belmont, CA 94002
PH: (512)827-8323
Stoklosa, Raymond J., Exec. Dir.

North American Studio Alliance
[13644]
2313 Hastings Dr.
Belmont, CA 94002-3317
Toll free: 877-626-2782
Fax: (530)482-2311
Cunningham, Annalisa, Advisor

Society for the History of Discoveries
[9518]
c/o William Brandenburg, Treasurer
631 Masonic Way, Apt. 1
Belmont, CA 94002
PH: (650)591-1601
Matthews, Dr. James, President

International SalonSpa Business
Network [922]
4712 E 2nd St.
Belmont Shore, CA 90803
PH: (562)453-3995
Toll free: 866-444-4272
Volk, Jason, Officer

Committee to Bridge the Gap
[18743]
PO Box 4
Ben Lomond, CA 95005-0004
PH: (831)336-8003
Hirsch, Daniel, President

African Children's HIV/AIDS Relief
Global Alliance [13518]
PO Box 3115
Berkeley, CA 94703
PH: (510)520-1097
Fax: (510)530-8055
Sule, Abraham O., Exec. Dir., CEO

Americans for Nonsmokers' Rights
[17225]
2530 San Pablo Ave., Ste. J
Berkeley, CA 94702
PH: (510)841-3032
Fax: (510)841-3071
Callahan, Holly, Office Mgr.

Architects/Designers/Planners for
Social Responsibility [18741]
PO Box 9126
Berkeley, CA 94709
PH: (510)845-1000
Sperry, Raphael, President

Assyrian Aid Society of America
[12623]
350 Berkeley Park Blvd.
Berkeley, CA 94707
PH: (510)527-9997
Fax: (510)527-6633
David, Narsai M., Chairman

Avoided Deforestation Partners
[4196]
c/o Jeff Horowitz, Founding Partner
Avoided Deforestation Partners

134 The Uplands
Berkeley, CA 94705
Horowitz, Jeff, Founder, Partner

The Beatitudes Society [19946]
2345 Channing Way
Berkeley, CA 94704
Andreolli-Comstock, Rev. Lindsay,
Exec. Dir.

Bio-Integral Resource Center [4527]
PO Box 7414
Berkeley, CA 94707
PH: (510)524-2567
Fax: (510)524-1758
Quarles, William, Managing Ed.

Buddhist Peace Fellowship [18773]
PO Box 3470
Berkeley, CA 94703
PH: (510)239-3764
Haney, Dawn, Director

Catholic Association for Lesbian and
Gay Ministry [20176]
1798 Scenic Ave.
Berkeley, CA 94709
PH: (972)638-7648
Nelson, Sheila, VP

Center for Ecoliteracy [3994]
The David Brower Ctr.
2150 Allston Way, Ste. 270
Berkeley, CA 94704-1377
PH: (510)845-4595
Barlow, Zenobia, Exec. Dir.

Clan Rose Society of America
[20839]
c/o Patrice A. May, Membership
Director
1188 Cragmont Ave.
Berkeley, CA 94708-1613
PH: (510)848-1188
Rose, Greg, President

Diabetes Hands Foundation [14526]
1962 University Ave., No. 1
Berkeley, CA 94704
PH: (510)898-1301
Hernandez, Manny, Founder,
President

Disability Rights Education and
Defense Fund [11588]
3075 Adeline St., Ste. 210
Berkeley, CA 94703-2578
PH: (510)644-2555
Toll free: 800-348-4232
Fax: (510)841-8645
Henderson, Susan, Exec. Dir.

Doctor to Doctor [12272]
1749 MLK Jr. Way
Berkeley, CA 94709-2139
PH: (510)548-5200

Earth Island Institute [4051]
2150 Allston Way, Ste. 460
Berkeley, CA 94704-1375
PH: (510)859-9100
Fax: (510)859-9091
Knox, John A., Exec. Dir.

Earth Regeneration Society [4052]
c/o Glen Frendel, Executive Director
PO Box 2445
Berkeley, CA 94709
PH: (510)527-9716

Edu-Culture International [8069]
PO Box 2692
Berkeley, CA 94702
PH: (510)845-2230

Environmentalists Against War
[19234]
PO Box 27
Berkeley, CA 94701

PH: (650)223-3306
Smith, Mr. Gar, Editor

Federation of Philippine American Chambers of Commerce, Inc. [23585]
2625 Alcatraz Ave., No. 324
Berkeley, CA 94705
PH: (510)541-0964
Mercado, Ethel, Officer

Filipino/American Coalition for Environmental Solidarity [4140]
PO Box 566
Berkeley, CA 94701-0566
Suzara, Aileen, Director

Friends of Nigeria [19595]
c/o Warren Keller, Treasurer
PO Box 8032
Berkeley, CA 94707
PH: (319)466-3119
Jones, Greg, President

Global Alliance for Incinerator Alternatives [4742]
1958 University Ave.
Berkeley, CA 94704
PH: (510)883-9490
Fax: (510)883-9493
Larracas, Anne, Secretary

Global Healing [15452]
2140 Shattuck Ave., Ste. 203
Berkeley, CA 94704-1211
PH: (510)898-1859
Fax: (510)280-5365
Donnelly, John, President

Half the Sky [11011]
715 Hearst Ave., Ste. 200
Berkeley, CA 94710
PH: (510)525-3377
Fax: (510)525-3611
Bowen, Jenny, Founder, CEO

Hesperian Health Guides [15470]
1919 Addison St., Ste. 304
Berkeley, CA 94704-1143
PH: (510)845-1447
Toll free: 888-729-1796
Fax: (510)845-9141
Shannon, Sarah, Exec. Dir.

Human Rights Advocates [12040]
PO Box 5675
Berkeley, CA 94705
de la Vega, Connie, Director

Institute of Andean Studies [8808]
PO Box 9307
Berkeley, CA 94709
Owen, Bruce, Secretary, Treasurer

International Association for the Study of Dreams [17217]
1672 University Ave.
Berkeley, CA 94703
PH: (209)724-0889
Fax: (209)724-0889
Sparrow, G. Scott, Ed.D., Chmn. of the Bd.

International Building Performance Simulation Association [536]
c/o Michael Wetter, Treasurer
Lawrence Berkeley National Laboratory
1 Cyclotron Rd.
Berkeley, CA 94720
PH: (902)486-4000
Barnaby, Charles, President

International Child Resource Institute [11046]
2nd Fl., Southwest Ste.
125 University Ave.
Berkeley, CA 94710

PH: (510)644-1000
Fax: (510)644-1115
Jaffe, Kenneth, Exec. Dir., President

International Rivers [7369]
2054 University Ave., Ste. 300
Berkeley, CA 94704-2644
PH: (510)848-1155
Fax: (510)848-1008
Johnson, Chuck, Web Adm.

Interracial-InterCultural Pride [11823]
1581 LeRoy Ave.
Berkeley, CA 94708
PH: (510)644-1000
Fax: (510)525-4106
Fleming, Tarah, Director

Kroeber Anthropological Society [5915]
232 Kroeber Hall
Dept. of Anthropology
University of California - Berkeley
Berkeley, CA 94720-3710

Law of the Sea Institute [5575]
University of California, Berkeley
381 Boalt Hall
Berkeley, CA 94720-7200
PH: (510)643-5699
    (510)643-9788
Scheiber, Prof. Harry N., PhD, Prog. Dir.

The Life After Exoneration Program [18073]
760 Wildcat Canyon
Berkeley, CA 94708
PH: (510)292-6010
Vollen, Lola, MD, Exec. Dir., Founder

MBIRA [9952]
Box 7863
Berkeley, CA 94707-0863
PH: (510)548-6053
Azim, Erica, Director, President

Meiklejohn Civil Liberties Institute [12050]
PO Box 673
Berkeley, CA 94701-0673
PH: (510)848-0599
Ginger, Ann Fagan, Exec. Dir.

Middle East Children's Alliance [18424]
1101 8th St., Ste. 100
Berkeley, CA 94710
PH: (510)548-0542
Fax: (510)548-0543
Lubin, Barbara, Exec. Dir., Founder

Mujeres Activas en Letras Y Cambio Social [7973]
1404 66th St.
Berkeley, CA 94702
Hernandez, Lisa Justine, Treasurer

Multinational Exchange for Sustainable Agriculture [4698]
2362 Bancroft Way, No. 202
Berkeley, CA 94704
PH: (510)654-8858
Toll free: 888-834-7461
Augusta, Lauren, Exec. Dir., Founder

Mystery Readers International [24017]
PO Box 8116
Berkeley, CA 94707-8116
Rudolph, Janet A., Director, Editor

NARIKA [13386]
PO Box 14014
Berkeley, CA 94712
PH: (510)444-6068
Fax: (510)444-6025
Hiatt, Shobha, President, Founder

National Abandoned Infants Assistance Resource Center [11252]
University of California - Berkeley
1918 University Ave., Ste. 3D
Berkeley, CA 94704-7402
PH: (510)643-8390
Fax: (510)643-7019
Pietrzak, Jeanne, Mem.

National Association of Fellowships Advisors [8516]
c/o Alicia Hayes, Secretary
University of California, Berkeley
5 Durant Hall, No.2940
Berkeley, CA 94720-2940
Kuchem, Dana, President

National Association of Healthcare Advocacy Consultants [15040]
2625 Alcatraz Ave., Ste. 228
Berkeley, CA 94705
Hyslop, Marsha, RN, Secretary

National Association of Math Circles [8282]
c/o Mathematical Sciences Research Institute
17 Gauss Way
Berkeley, CA 94720-5070
PH: (510)642-0143
White, Diana, Director

National Association of Memoir Writers [10388]
1700 Solano Ave.
Berkeley, CA 94707
PH: (510)859-4718
Myers, Linda Joy, PhD, Founder, President

National Association of Science Writers [2698]
PO Box 7905
Berkeley, CA 94707
PH: (510)647-9500
Davis, Tinsley, Exec. Dir.

National Lymphedema Network [15546]
2288 Fulton St., Ste. 307
Berkeley, CA 94704
PH: (510)809-1660
Toll free: 800-541-3259
Fax: (510)809-1699
Thiadens, Saskia R.J., RN, Exec. Dir.

National Writing Project [8765]
University of California
2105 Bancroft Way, No. 1042
Berkeley, CA 94720-1042
PH: (510)642-0963
Fax: (510)642-4545
Eidman-Aadahl, Elyse, Exec. Dir.

Nautilus Institute [19094]
2342 Shattuck Ave., No. 300
Berkeley, CA 94704
PH: (510)423-0372
Hayes, Peter, PhD, Exec. Dir., Founder

Organization of Women Architects and Design Professionals [989]
PO Box 10078
Berkeley, CA 94709-5078
Crane, Janet, President

Ota Benga Alliance [10491]
PO Box 2847
Berkeley, CA 94702

Pacifica Foundation [10060]
1925 Martin Luther King Jr. Way
Berkeley, CA 94704-1037
PH: (510)849-2590
Argarwal, Sam, CFO

Plastic Pollution Coalition [4556]
2150 Allston Way, Ste. 460
Berkeley, CA 94704

PH: (323)936-3010
Russo, Daniella, Exec. Dir.

Preservation Institute [12987]
2140 Shattuck Ave., Ste. 2122
Berkeley, CA 94704

Prize4Life [15988]
2081 Center St.
Berkeley, CA 94704
PH: (617)545-4882
Shnider, Sara, Exec. Dir.

Seacology [3943]
1623 Solano Ave.
Berkeley, CA 94707
PH: (510)559-3505
Fax: (510)559-3506
Silverstein, Duane, Exec. Dir.

Section for Magnetic Resonance Technologists [15698]
2030 Addison St., 7th Fl.
Berkeley, CA 94704
PH: (510)841-1899
Fax: (510)841-2340
Jezzard, Peter, Ph.D, Mem.

Seva Foundation [12186]
1786 5th St.
Berkeley, CA 94710
PH: (510)845-7382
Fax: (510)845-7410
Blanks, Jack, Exec. Dir.

SHARE El Salvador [18178]
2425 College Ave.
Berkeley, CA 94704
PH: (510)848-8487
Artiga, Jose, Exec. Dir.

Substance Abuse Librarians and Information Specialists [9729]
PO Box 9513
Berkeley, CA 94709-0513
PH: (510)865-6225
Mitchell, Andrea, Exec. Dir.

Sustainable Agriculture Education [4702]
2150 Allston Way, Ste. 320
Berkeley, CA 94704-1381
PH: (510)526-1793
Fax: (510)524-7153
Kraus, Sibella, Founder, President

Sustainable World Coalition [3954]
c/o Earth Island Institute
2150 Allston Way, Ste. 460
Berkeley, CA 94704-1375
PH: (415)717-0422
Allen, Vinit, Founder, Exec. Dir.

Textile Society of America [3273]
PO Box 5617
Berkeley, CA 94705-0617
PH: (510)363-4541
Shaughnessy, Roxane, President

Tibetan Aid Project [12599]
2210 Harold Way
Berkeley, CA 94704-1425
PH: (510)848-4238
Toll free: 800-338-4238
Rasmussen, Judy, Exec. Dir.

United States Futsal Federation [23260]
PO Box 40077
Berkeley, CA 94704-4077
PH: (510)836-8733
Fax: (650)242-1036
Allen, Jeff, CFO

United States Snooker Association [22589]
PO Box 4000F
Berkeley, CA 94704

PH: (408)615-7479
Morris, Alan, Exec. Dir.

Urbanists International [5981]
134 The Uplands
Berkeley, CA 94705
PH: (510)547-5500
Fax: (510)654-5807
Horowitz, Jeffrey, Exec. Dir.,
Founder

USENIX Association [6306]
2560 9th St., Ste. 215
Berkeley, CA 94710
PH: (510)528-8649
Fax: (510)548-5738
Henderson, Casey, Exec. Dir.

Venture Strategies for Health and
Development [15068]
962 Arlington Ave.
Berkeley, CA 94707
PH: (510)524-4320
Campbell, Martha, PhD, Founder,
President

Women's Earth Alliance [3969]
2150 Allston Way, Ste. 460
Berkeley, CA 94704
PH: (510)859-9106
Kramer, Melinda, Director, Founder

Wood Machining Institute [3512]
PO Box 476
Berkeley, CA 94701
PH: (925)943-5240
Fax: (925)945-0947
Szymani, Dr. Ryszard, Director,
Founder

World Federation of Methodist and
Uniting Church Women North
America Area [20350]
c/o Dr. Sylvia Faulk
623 San Fernanco Ave.
Berkeley, CA 94707
Vanterpool, Brenda, VP

World Institute on Disability [11648]
3075 Adeline St., Ste. 155
Berkeley, CA 94703
PH: (510)225-6400
Fax: (510)225-0477
Bradley, Carol, Chairperson

The World War One Historical Association [9811]
2625 Alcatraz Ave. No. 237
Berkeley, CA 94705-2702
Suddaby, Steve, President

Youth for Environmental Sanity
[4120]
3240 King St.
Berkeley, CA 94703
PH: (510)922-8556
Herrera, J. Manuel, Chmn. of the
Bd.

Academy of Motion Picture Arts and
Sciences [1183]
8949 Wilshire Blvd.
Beverly Hills, CA 90211
PH: (310)247-3000
Fax: (310)859-9619
Mehr, Linda Harris, Director

Air Supply Fan Club [24020]
PO Box 3367
Beverly Hills, CA 90212-0367
PH: (310)535-6949

Alliance of Jamaican and American
Humanitarians [11313]
8549 Wilshire Blvd., Ste. 1004
Beverly Hills, CA 90211
PH: (424)249-8135
(909)851-9359
Crawford, Joan, President

American Association of Aesthetic
Medicine and Surgery [14303]
9478 W Olympic Blvd., Ste. 301
Beverly Hills, CA 90212
PH: (310)274-9955
Assassa, Dr. Sam B., President

American Screenwriters Association
[10358]
269 S Beverly Dr., Ste. 2600
Beverly Hills, CA 90212-3807
Kirwan, Steve, Exec. Dir.

Association for Astrological Network-
ing [5988]
8306 Wilshire Blvd., PMB 537
Beverly Hills, CA 90211
PH: (404)477-4121
Pride, Eric, Treasurer

Association of Film Commissioners
International [1188]
9595 Wilshire Blvd., Ste. 900
Beverly Hills, CA 90211
PH: (323)461-2324
Fax: (413)375-2903
Jennings, Kevin, Chairman

Aviation for Humanity [12624]
269 S Beverly Dr., No. 674
Beverly Hills, CA 90212
PH: (310)968-3503
Fax: (310)861-9041
Winter, Rymann, President

End Malaria Now [15396]
9461 Charleville Blvd., Ste. 558
Beverly Hills, CA 90212
PH: (310)860-6073
Fax: (310)773-1730
Harding, Richard, Chairman,
President

Entertainment Publicists Professional
Society [1135]
PO Box 5841
Beverly Hills, CA 90209
Pansky, Scott, VP

Face Forward [11701]
9735 Wilshire Blvd., Ste. 300
Beverly Hills, CA 90210
PH: (310)657-2253
Alessi, Dr. David, Founder

Fine Art Dealers Association [244]
9663 Santa Monica Blvd., Ste. 316
Beverly Hills, CA 90210
PH: (310)659-9888
Tasende, Ms. Betina, President

Girls Learn International, Inc. [7945]
433 S Beverly Dr.
Beverly Hills, CA 90212
PH: (310)556-2500
Fax: (310)556-2509
Steimer-King, Ashley, Prog. Dir.

Giving Vision [17702]
Box 206A
9663 Santa Monica Blvd.
Beverly Hills, CA 90210
PH: (310)860-1900
Fax: (310)860-1902
Boxer Wachler, Brian S., Founder,
Director

Global Neuroscience Initiative
Foundation [16047]
9776 Peavine Dr.
Beverly Hills, CA 90210
PH: (206)339-8274
Fax: (206)339-8274
Lakhan, Shaheen E., Exec. Dir.

Juvenile Arthritis Association [17160]
8549 Wilshire Blvd., Ste. 103
Beverly Hills, CA 90211
Rothman, Joel, Chairman

Mamburao-U.S.A. Association
[10072]
PO Box 17616
Beverly Hills, CA 90209-5616
PH: (310)286-2482
Fax: (310)286-9191

Music for Relief [12702]
8820 Wilshire Blvd., Ste. 300
Beverly Hills, CA 90211
PH: (310)358-0260
Showler, Whitney, Exec. Dir.

National Center for Women and
Policing [5497]
433 S Beverly Dr.
Beverly Hills, CA 90212
PH: (310)556-2500
Fax: (310)556-2509
Moore, Margaret, Director

National Congress of Inventor
Organizations [6771]
8306 Wilshire Blvd., Ste. 391
Beverly Hills, CA 90211
Toll free: 866-466-0253
Gnass, Stephen Paul, Exec. Dir.

Neuromuscular Disease Foundation
[15976]
269 S Beverly Dr., No. 1206
Beverly Hills, CA 90212
PH: (310)736-2978
Becher, Carolyn Yashari, Esq., Exec.
Dir.

PEN Center USA [10392]
PO Box 6037
Beverly Hills, CA 90212
PH: (323)424-4939
Fax: (323)424-4944
Vredenburg, Elliot, Prog. Dir.

Producers Guild of America [1203]
8530 Wilshire Blvd., Ste. 400
Beverly Hills, CA 90211
PH: (310)358-9020
Fax: (310)358-9520
Van Petten, Vance, Exec. Dir.

Surgical Friends [17410]
465 N Roxbury Dr., Ste. 1001
Beverly Hills, CA 90210
PH: (310)562-3631
Parsa, Kami, MD, President

TreePeople [3958]
12601 Mulholland Dr.
Beverly Hills, CA 90210
PH: (818)753-4600
(818)623-4848
Fax: (818)753-4635
Lipkis, Andy, President, Founder

Esalen Institute [9535]
55000 Highway 1
Big Sur, CA 93920-9546
PH: (831)667-3000
Toll free: 888-837-2536
Wheeler, Gordon, President

Desert Fishes Council [3845]
c/o Phil Pister, Executive Secretary
437 E South St.
Bishop, CA 93514
Pister, Phil, Exec. Sec.

Angels In Waiting [10855]
PO Box 1221
Blue Jay, CA 92317
Toll free: 800-974-4274
West-Conforti, Linda, CEO, Founder

Wellstart International [15070]
PO Box 602
Blue Jay, CA 92317-0602
PH: (714)724-1675
Fax: (802)985-8794
Naylor, Audrey, CEO

Western Society of Naturalists
[6902]
PO Box 247
Bodega Bay, CA 94923
Morgan, Steven, Secretary

Collaborative on Health and the
Environment [14714]
c/o Commonweal
PO Box 316
Bolinas, CA 94924
PH: (415)868-0970
Miller, Elise, MEd, Director

American Albacore Fishing Associa-
tion [1296]
4364 Bonita Rd.
Bonita, CA 91902
PH: (619)941-2307
Fax: (619)863-5046
Blocker, Bobby, Bd. Member

Afghanistan Water Polo [23359]
PO Box 438
Bonsall, CA 92003
PH: (760)451-1783
Piasecki, Jeremy, Exec. Dir.

Western Dredging Association
[2259]
c/o Thomas P. Cappellino, Executive
Director
PO Box 1393
Bonsall, CA 92003
PH: (949)422-8231
Cappellino, Thomas, Exec. Dir.

HeartMath Institute [9536]
14700 W Park Ave.
Boulder Creek, CA 95006
PH: (831)338-8500
Toll free: 800-711-6221
Fax: (831)338-8504
Childre, Sara, CEO, President

Bicycle Ride Directors' Association
of America [22745]
755 N Leafwood Ct.
Brea, CA 92821
PH: (562)690-9693
Lyons, Shiela, Contact

Canning Hunger [12079]
407 W Imperial Hwy., Ste. H-313
Brea, CA 92821
PH: (714)990-9234
Fax: (714)582-2452
Whan, Dr. Norm, Chairman,
President, Founder

International Automotive Technicians
Network [296]
640 W Lambert Rd.
Brea, CA 92821
PH: (714)257-1335
Buchholz, Monica, Contact

Telephone Collectors International
[22444]
3805 Spurr Cir.
Brea, CA 92823
PH: (714)528-3561
Mattingly, Chris, Editor

Together We Rise [11170]
580 W Lambert Rd., No. A
Brea, CA 92821
PH: (714)784-6760
Dahlia, Gianna, Exec. Dir.

Unlimited Scale Racing Association
[22207]
PO Box 819
Brea, CA 92822
PH: (214)649-8342
(714)255-7488
Powell, Jeff, Mem.

International Association of Home
Staging Professionals [1947]
2420 Sand Creek Rd. C-1, No. 263
Brentwood, CA 94513
Toll free: 800-392-7161
Schwarz, Barb, CEO, Founder

International Saw and Knife Associa-
tion [2066]
c/o Paul Muskat, President
200 Valley Dr. No. 34
Brisbane, CA 94005
PH: (949)480-1228
    (425)289-0125
Fax: (866)751-4979
Muskat, Paul, President

Giving Children Hope [10998]
8332 Commonwealth Ave.
Buena Park, CA 90621
PH: (714)523-4454
Fax: (714)523-4474
Barta, Bill, Chmn. of the Bd.

International Carotenoid Society
[6145]
c/o Kevin Gellenbeck, Secretary
Amway Corporation
Nutrilite Research Institute
5600 Beach Blvd.
Buena Park, CA 90621-2007
PH: (714)562-4875
Landrum, John T., President

NASCA International [12947]
PO Box 6978
Buena Park, CA 90622-6978
Lanzaratta, Tony, Exec. Dir.

American Auto Racing Writers and
Broadcasters Association [22520]
922 N Pass Ave.
Burbank, CA 91505-2703
PH: (818)842-7005
Fax: (818)842-7020
Brandel, Ms. Norma Dusty,
President

Assistance League [12884]
3100 W Burbank Blvd., Ste. 100
Burbank, CA 91505-2348
PH: (818)846-3777
Fax: (818)846-3535
Vispo, Carol, VP of Admin.

Association of Correctional Food
Service Affiliates [1386]
PO Box 10065
Burbank, CA 91510
PH: (818)843-6608
Fax: (818)843-7423
Nichols, Jon, Exec. Dir.

Blue Faery: The Adrienne Wilson
Liver Cancer Association [13905]
1135 N Valley St.
Burbank, CA 91505
PH: (818)636-5624
Wilson, Andrea J., President, Exec.
Dir.

Canadian Federation of Poets
[10149]
1248 E Elmwood Ave.
Burbank, CA 91501-1616
Repchuk, Tracy Lynn, Founder,
President

Caucus for Producers, Writers &
Directors [17938]
PO Box 11236
Burbank, CA 91510-1236
PH: (818)843-7572
Fax: (818)221-0347
Powell, Norman S., Chairman

Film Advisory Board, Inc. [9305]
263 W Olive Ave., No. 377
Burbank, CA 91502

PH: (323)461-6541
Fax: (323)469-8541
Stokes, Janet, Chairperson, CEO

Firefighter Cancer Support Network
[13969]
2600 W Olive Ave., 5th Fl., PMB 608
Burbank, CA 91505
PH: (866)994-3276
Frieders, Bryan, President

Immigrant Genealogical Society
[20973]
1310-B W Magnolia Blvd.
Burbank, CA 91506
PH: (818)848-3122
Fax: (818)716-6300
Grider, Mr. Ron, President

INCITE! Women of Color Against
Violence [19229]
2416 W Victory Blvd.
Burbank, CA 91506

Independent Visually Impaired
Entrepreneurs [17713]
2121 Scott Rd., No. 105
Burbank, CA 91504-2448
PH: (818)238-9321
Bazyn, Ardis, President

International Animated Film Society
[1194]
2114 W Burbank Blvd.
Burbank, CA 91506
PH: (818)842-8330
Gladstone, Frank, Exec. Dir.

Media Action Network for Asian
Americans [18658]
PO Box 6188
Burbank, CA 91510-6188
PH: (213)486-4433
Aleong, Aki, President

Mending Kids [14204]
2307 W Olive Ave., Ste. B
Burbank, CA 91506
PH: (818)843-6363
Fax: (818)843-6365
Sellers, Marchelle L., MBA, Exec.
Dir.

Society for Cinephiles/Cinecon
[9313]
3727 W Magnolia Blvd., No. 760
Burbank, CA 91505
Birchard, Bob, President

Supreme Lodge of the Danish
Sisterhood of America [9276]
c/o Aase Hansen, Trustee
2025 N Manning St.
Burbank, CA 91505
PH: (818)845-5726
    (707)545-6023
Morrison, Julie, VP

Themed Entertainment Association
[1161]
150 E Olive Ave., Ste. 306
Burbank, CA 91502
PH: (818)843-8497
Fax: (818)843-8477
Kerr, Christine, Exec.

American Association of Webmas-
ters [6307]
PO Box 1284
Burlingame, CA 94011
PH: (623)202-5613

Buddhist Text Translation Society
[19772]
International Translation Institute
1777 Murchison Dr.
Burlingame, CA 94010-4504
PH: (415)332-6221
Dzu, Heng, Master

Growing Planet [4204]
3133 Frontera Way, Ste. 113
Burlingame, CA 94010-5759
Toll free: 866-476-9873

Junior State of America [8196]
111 Anza Blvd., Ste. 109
Burlingame, CA 94010
PH: (650)347-1600
Toll free: 800-334-5353
Fax: (650)347-7200
Kaganoff Stern, Rachel, President

Junior Statesmen Foundation [8197]
111 Anza Blvd., Ste. 109
Burlingame, CA 94010
PH: (650)347-1600
Toll free: 800-334-5353
Fax: (650)347-7200
Kaganoff Stern, Rachel, President

MedLend [15035]
1820 Ogden Dr., 2nd Fl.
Burlingame, CA 94010
PH: (650)375-1800
Hamilton, Dr. Henry, Founder,
President

Moms Against Poverty [12554]
PO Box 4212
Burlingame, CA 94011
PH: (650)271-7178
Fanaie, Delfarib, Founder

Rebuilding Alliance [11990]
1818 Gilbreth Rd.
Burlingame, CA 94010
PH: (650)325-4663
    (650)651-7156
Baranski-Walker, Donna, Exec. Dir.,
Founder

Arthur Szyk Society [8945]
1200 Edgehill Dr.
Burlingame, CA 94010
PH: (650)343-9588
Ungar, Mr. Irvin, Curator

American Board of Clinical
Optometry [16420]
23679 Calabasas Rd., No. 1010
Calabasas, CA 91302
PH: (818)714-1350
Fax: (818)337-2226
Carter, Janet, Exec. Dir.

American Hair Loss Association
[14899]
23679 Calabasas Rd., No. 682
Calabasas, CA 91302-1502

Artists for Human Rights [18374]
23679 Calabasas Rd., Ste. 636
Calabasas, CA 91302
Toll free: 800-334-2802
Archer, Anne, Founder, Director

International Association of Media
Tie-in Writers [10378]
PO Box 8212
Calabasas, CA 91372
Collins, Max Allan, Founder,
President, VP

Society of Singers [12372]
26500 W Agoura Rd., No. 102-554
Calabasas, CA 91302
PH: (818)995-7100
Fax: (818)995-7466
Varley, Judy, Exec. Dir.

Community College Journalism As-
sociation [8153]
163 E Loop Dr.
Camarillo, CA 93010
PH: (805)389-3744
Fax: (520)438-4886
Ames, Dr. Steve, Exec. Sec.,
Treasurer

Heritage Roses Group [22100]
22 Gypsy Ln.
Camarillo, CA 93010
Jennings, Clay, Membership Chp.

Macrocosm USA [2799]
PO Box 185
Cambria, CA 93428
PH: (805)927-2515
Brockway, Sandi, Editor, President

American Yankee Association
[21214]
PO Box 1531
Cameron Park, CA 95682-1531
Wilson, Stew, Secretary, Treasurer

Society for Information Display
[6263]
1475 S Bascom Ave., Ste. 114
Campbell, CA 95008-0628
PH: (408)879-3901
Fax: (408)879-3833
Ghosh, Amal, President

Free Speech Coalition [17835]
PO Box 10480
Canoga Park, CA 91309
PH: (818)348-9373
Fax: (818)348-8893
Douglas, Jeffrey, Chmn. of the Bd.

Grandparents as Parents [11917]
22048 Sherman Way, Ste. 217
Canoga Park, CA 91303
PH: (818)264-0880
Fax: (818)264-0882
De Toledo, Sylvie, MSW, LCSW,
BCD, Founder

Na'amat U.S.A. [20267]
21515 Vanowen St., Ste. 102
Canoga Park, CA 91303
PH: (818)431-2200
Toll free: 844-777-5222
Fax: (818)937-6883
Schoenberg, Linda, Rec. Sec.

Zarathushtrian Assembly [20559]
6515 DeSoto Ave.
Canoga Park, CA 91303-2909
PH: (818)610-8610

Ninos de la Luz [11101]
PO Box 7686
Capistrano Beach, CA 92624
PH: (949)481-8355
Haslett, Jon, Founder

Academy for Peace Research
[18767]
600 Park Ave., Apt. 4D
Capitola, CA 95010
PH: (831)475-4250
Payne, Dr. Buryl, Founder, President

Ocean Champions [18018]
c/o David Wilmot, President and Co-
Founder
202 San Jose Ave.
Capitola, CA 95010
PH: (831)462-2539
Fax: (831)462-2542
Campbell, Samantha, Chairperson

1/87 Vehicle Club [22195]
PO Box 2701
Carlsbad, CA 92018-2701
PH: (760)721-3393
Fax: (760)721-3373

American College of Forensic
Psychiatry [5236]
PO Box 130458
Carlsbad, CA 92013-0458
PH: (760)929-9777
Fax: (760)929-9803
Miller, Debbie, Director

American College of Forensic
Psychology [16860]
PO Box 130458
Carlsbad, CA 92013-0458
PH: (760)929-9777
Fax: (760)929-9803
Miller, Debbie, Exec. Dir.

Cardiovascular Disease Foundation
[14151]
3088 Pio Pico Dr., Ste. 202
Carlsbad, CA 92008
PH: (760)730-1471
Toll free: 888-249-9575
Fax: (760)730-0165
Engerer, Malinda, MBA, Exec. Dir.

ConnectMed International [14992]
7040 Avenida Encinas, Ste. 104
Carlsbad, CA 92011
PH: (619)800-5349
Colburn, Sherry, Exec. Dir.

Gemological Institute of America
Alumni Association [19513]
The Robert Mouawad Campus
5345 Armada Dr.
Carlsbad, CA 92008
PH: (760)603-4000
    (760)603-4145
Toll free: 800-421-7250
Fax: (760)603-4080
Turner, Starla, Co-Pres.

Gemological Institute of America Inc.
[2047]
The Robert Mouawad Campus
5345 Armada Dr.
Carlsbad, CA 92008
PH: (760)603-4000
Toll free: 800-421-7250
Fax: (760)603-4080
Kimmel, Kathryn, Sr. VP, Chief Mktg.
Ofc.

Global Action International [12664]
7356 Altiva Pl.
Carlsbad, CA 92013
PH: (760)438-3979
Fax: (760)602-0383
Lee, Dwaine E., President

International Writing Centers As-
sociation [8764]
c/o Shareen Grogan, President
National University
705 Palomar Airport Rd.
Carlsbad, CA 92011
PH: (760)268-1567
Grogan, Shareen, President

Kids for Peace [18800]
1302 Pine Ave.
Carlsbad, CA 92008
PH: (760)730-3320
McManigal, Jill, Exec. Dir., Founder

NAMM Foundation [9962]
5790 Armada Dr.
Carlsbad, CA 92008
Lamond, Joe, CEO, President

NAMM, the International Music
Products Association [2431]
5790 Armada Dr.
Carlsbad, CA 92008
PH: (760)438-8001
Toll free: 800-767-6266
Fax: (760)438-7327
Lamond, Joe, CEO, President

Pearl Harbor Survivors Association
[21199]
PO Box 1816
Carlsbad, CA 92018-1816
PH: (760)727-9027
    (760)419-5878
Fax: (760)727-9087

Sustainable Surplus Exchange
[3953]
2647 Gateway Rd., Ste. 105-404
Carlsbad, CA 92009
PH: (760)736-4416
Prelozni, Sue, MA, Founder, Exec.
Dir.

Walking on Water [20012]
5928 Balfour Ct., Ste. C
Carlsbad, CA 92008
PH: (760)438-1111
Jennings, Bryan Scott, Director,
Founder

Child Empowerment International,
Inc. [10894]
225 Crossroads Blvd., No. 123
Carmel, CA 93923-8674
PH: (821)622-9094
Toll free: 800-725-8098
Salmon, Adam, Founder, President

Freedom Fields USA [11292]
PO Box 221820
Carmel, CA 93922
Ascher, Yvonne, Advisor

Friends of the Sea Otter [4820]
PO Box 223260
Carmel, CA 93922
PH: (831)915-3275
Reynolds, Frank, Director

Harry Singer Foundation [19005]
PO Box 223159
Carmel, CA 93922-3159
PH: (831)625-4223
Fax: (831)624-7994
Bohannon-Kaplan, Margaret, Direc-
tor, Founder

United Flying Octogenarians [21254]
24 Arboleda Ln.
Carmel Valley, CA 93924-9633
PH: (831)659-7523
Wood, Warren, President

Foundation for Chiropractic Educa-
tion [8322]
PO Box 560
Carmichael, CA 95609-0560
PH: (703)868-2420
Toll free: 866-901-3427
Greenawait, Kent S., President,
Chairman, Founder

Foundation for Chiropractic Progress
[14270]
PO Box 560
Carmichael, CA 95609-0560
PH: (703)868-2420
Toll free: 866-901-3427
Greenawalt, Kent S., Founder,
Chairman

Funk Aircraft Owners Association
[21228]
2836 California Ave.
Carmichael, CA 95608
PH: (916)971-3452
Shelnutt, Thad, Treasurer, Secretary

Neotropical Grassland Conservancy
[3916]
6274 Heathcliff Dr.
Carmichael, CA 95608
Langham, Gary, President

Rhythmical Massage Therapy Association of North America [15562]
c/o Kathy Strutz, Treasurer
3302 Parks Ln.
Carmichael, CA 95608
PH: (916)486-6127
Strutz, Kathy, Treasurer

United States Elite Coaches' Association for Women's Gymnastics
[22739]
c/o Natalie Duke
10 Quail Point Pl.

Carmichael, CA 95608
PH: (916)487-3559
Fax: (916)487-3706
Duke, Natalie, Secretary, Treasurer

Vietnamese Professionals Society
[19687]
5150 Fair Oaks Blvd., Ste. 101-128
Carmichael, CA 95608-5758
Tran, Nhan H., Contact

Association of Certified Adizes
Practitioners International [2151]
1212 Mark Ave.
Carpinteria, CA 93013
PH: (805)565-2901
Morgan, James C., Chairman

Blair Chiropractic Society [14258]
550 E Carson Plaza Dr., Ste. 122
Carson, CA 90746
Hall, Drew, DC, President

Contractors Pump Bureau [1721]
c/o Juan Quiros
Multiquip Inc.
18910 Wilmington Ave.
Carson, CA 90746
PH: (414)272-0943
Fax: (414)272-1170
Davis, Jeff, Chairman

National Association for the Study
and Performance of African-
American Music [8383]
c/o Martha C. Brown, Treasurer
809 E Gladwick St.
Carson, CA 90746-3818
McCarroll, Jesse C., President

Unrecognised States Numismatic
Society [22290]
PO Box 0534
Castaic, CA 91310-0534
Paz, Oded, Contact

The Aneurysm and AVM Foundation
[14561]
3636 Castro Valley Blvd., Ste. 3
Castro Valley, CA 94546
PH: (510)464-4540
Fax: (510)464-4540
Shing, Angela, Exec. Dir.

Walkaloosa Horse Association
[4423]
4055 Villa Creek Rd.
Cayucos, CA 93430
PH: (805)995-1894
Fax: (805)995-1252

Bet-Nahrain [10768]
3119 S Central Ave.
Ceres, CA 95307-3632
PH: (209)538-4130
    (209)538-9801
Yousip, Joe, VP

EarthSave International [3997]
20555 Devonshire St., Ste. 105
Chatsworth, CA 91311
PH: (415)234-0829
Fax: (818)337-1957
Nelson, Jeff, CEO

National Investigations Committee
on Unidentified Flying Objects
[7016]
PO Box 3847
Chatsworth, CA 91313-9998
PH: (818)882-0039
Fax: (818)998-6712
Stranges, Julie, Director

National Notary Association [5656]
9350 De Soto Ave.
Chatsworth, CA 91313-2402
Toll free: 800-876-6827
Valera, Milton G., President

Operation Gratitude [4975]
21100 Lassen St.
Chatsworth, CA 91311
PH: (818)469-0448
Blashek, Carolyn, President

National Police Bloodhound Association [5508]
c/o Coby Webb, Treasurer
38540 Alva Dr.
Cherry Valley, CA 92223
Lowry, Doug, President

The Animals Voice [10586]
1692 Mangrove Ave., No. 276
Chico, CA 95926
Moretti, Laura, Founder, President

Association Global View [7545]
PO Box 3324
Chico, CA 95927-3324
PH: (530)228-5886
    (530)892-9696
Hulsoor, Jean, Administrator

Gull Wing Group International
[21392]
776 Cessna Ave.
Chico, CA 95928-9571
PH: (949)364-6035
Bau, Tom, Director

Lambda Pi Alumni Association
[23758]
PO Box 36
Chico, CA 95927
Bates, Craig

MSPAlliance [6324]
1380 E Ave., Ste. 124-376
Chico, CA 95926-7349
PH: (530)891-1340
Fax: (530)433-5707
Weaver, Celia, President

Rat Assistance and Teaching Society
[22242]
857 Lindo Ln.
Chico, CA 95973
PH: (530)899-0605
Ducommun, Debbie, Contact

Rat Fan Club [22243]
857 Lindo Ln.
Chico, CA 95973-0914
PH: (530)899-0605
Ducommun, Debbie, Founder

Epiphyllum Society of America
[22093]
c/o Geneva Coats, Treasurer
13674 Geranium St.
Chino, CA 91710-5080
Schmidt, Maria, Secretary

Genesis International Orphanage
Foundation [10993]
PO Box 6458
Chula Vista, CA 91909-6458
PH: (619)977-7072

International Institute of
Photographic Arts [2584]
1690 Frontage Rd.
Chula Vista, CA 91911
PH: (619)628-1466
Barba, Martha M., Founder,
President

Los Ninos [11400]
717 3rd Ave.
Chula Vista, CA 91910
PH: (619)426-9110
Toll free: 866-922-8984
Fax: (619)426-6664
Hadley, Dr. Phillip, Chairman

National Image Inc. [19464]
374 E H St., Ste. A, PMB 419
Chula Vista, CA 91913
Chavez-Metoyer, Sylvia, Exec.,
CEO, President

Society of Hispanic Professional
Engineers [6592]
13181 Crossroads Pky. N, Ste. 450
City of Industry, CA 91746
PH: (323)725-3970
Fax: (323)725-0316
Cordero, Barry, Chairman

Taiwanese American Lawyers As-
sociation [5051]
1661 Hanover Rd., Ste. 215
City of Industry, CA 91748
PH: (626)839-3800
Chang, Cheryl S., Esq, President

All Our Children International
Outreach [10846]
PO Box 1807
Claremont, CA 91711
PH: (909)450-1177
Ranney, Rachael, Founder,
President

Association for Collaborative Leader-
ship [7953]
101 S Mills Ave.
Claremont, CA 91711
PH: (909)607-9870
Fax: (909)607-9837
Ramsbottom, Claire, President

Cactus and Succulent Society of
America [22090]
PO Box 1000
Claremont, CA 91711-1000
Meng, Clifford, Treasurer

Center for Process Studies [10083]
1325 N College Ave.
Claremont, CA 91711
PH: (909)621-5330
Fax: (909)621-2760
Hulbert, Steve, Dir. of Lib. Svcs.

International Society for the History,
Philosophy, and Social Studies of
Biology [7985]
c/o Laura Perini, Treasurer
Philosophy Dept.
130 Castleton Dr.
Claremont, CA 91711
Morange, Mitchel, President

Ottoman and Turkish Studies Association [10286]
c/o Heather Ferguson, Treasurer
850 Columbia Ave.
Claremont, CA 91711
Evered, Emine, Secretary

Parents Anonymous [11126]
250 W 1st St., Ste. 250
Claremont, CA 91711
PH: (909)621-6184
Fax: (909)621-0614
Notkin, Susan, Director

Scripps Association of Families
[7639]
Scripps College
1030 Columbia Ave., No. 2009
Claremont, CA 91711
PH: (909)621-8000
Marcus-Newhall, Amy, President

Society for Mathematical Biology
[6103]
c/o Lisette de Pillis, Treasurer
Department of Mathematics
Harvey Mudd College
Claremont, CA 91711
Pillis, Lisette de, Treasurer

Dales Pony Society of America
[4347]
4161 Leon Dr.
Clayton, CA 94517
PH: (925)788-0655
Raspotnik, Ken, President

American German Shepherd Rescue
Association, Inc. [10568]
c/o Linda Kury, President
PO Box 7113
Clearlake, CA 95422
PH: (707)994-5241
Kury, Linda, President

Association of Natural Biocontrol
Producers [4525]
PO Box 1609
Clovis, CA 93613-1609
PH: (559)360-7111
Ruiter, Rene, President

Association for Play Therapy
[17438]
401 Clovis Ave., Ste. 107
Clovis, CA 93612
PH: (559)298-3400
Fax: (559)238-3410
Burns, Bill, CAE

Consultants Association for the
Natural Products Industry [680]
PO Box 4014
Clovis, CA 93613-4014
PH: (559)325-7192
Dillon, Karena K., President

Association of Applied IPM Ecolo-
gists [4524]
PO Box 1119
Coarsegold, CA 93614
PH: (559)761-1064
Rothfuss, Bill, Contact

Kennedy's Disease Association
[15950]
PO Box 1105
Coarsegold, CA 93614-1105
Toll free: 855-532-7762
Tudor, Lou, President

Studebaker Driver's Club Inc.
[21496]
43306 Running Deer Dr.
Coarsegold, CA 93614-9662
Thomason, Carl, President

Center for Health Design [14986]
1850 Gateway Blvd., Ste. 1083
Concord, CA 94520
PH: (925)521-9404
Fax: (925)521-9405
Levin, Debra J., CEO, President

International Society for Magnetic
Resonance in Medicine [17058]
2300 Clayton Rd., Ste. 620
Concord, CA 94520
PH: (510)841-1899
Fax: (510)841-2340
Kravitz, Roberta A., Exec. Dir.

Lute Society of America, Inc. [9951]
PO Box 6499
Concord, CA 94524
PH: (925)686-5800
Rukavina, Phillip, President

National Association of Stock Plan
Professionals [1285]
PO Box 21639
Concord, CA 94521-0639
PH: (925)685-9271
Fax: (925)930-9284
Baksa, Barbara, Exec. Dir.

National Organization of Restoring
Men [11287]
3205 Northwood Dr., Ste. 209
Concord, CA 94520-4506
PH: (925)827-4077
Fax: (925)827-4119
Griffiths, R. Wayne, Contact

Pills Anonymous [13174]
2740 Grant St.
Concord, CA 94520

Death Valley '49ers Inc. [9386]
24601 Glen Ivy Rd., No. 39
Corona, CA 92883
Whipple, Robert, President

National Association Citizens on
Patrol [12828]
PO Box 727
Corona, CA 92878-0727
PH: (951)279-6893
Fax: (951)279-1915
Femister, Arthur, Founder, President

Society for Vector Ecology [4532]
1966 Compton Ave.
Corona, CA 92881
Fax: (951)340-2515

Vaseline Glass Collectors, Inc.
[21731]
14560 Schleisman Rd.
Corona, CA 92880

Bread and Roses [11794]
233 Tamalpais Dr., Ste. 100
Corte Madera, CA 94925-1415
PH: (415)945-7120
Fax: (415)945-7128
Nelson, Stacy, Chairperson

Give a Jumpstart [12036]
414 Redwood Ave.
Corte Madera, CA 94925
PH: (414)595-6757
Joyal, Suzanne, Exec. Dir.

The A21 Campaign [12021]
427 E 17th St., No. F223
Costa Mesa, CA 92627
PH: (949)202-4681
Fax: (949)612-0827
Caine, Christine, Founder

Associated Koi Clubs of America
[22030]
PO Box 10879
Costa Mesa, CA 92627
PH: (949)548-3690
Peterson, Kristine, Chairperson

CDMA Development Group [6730]
575 Anton Blvd., Ste. 440
Costa Mesa, CA 92626
PH: (714)545-5211
Toll free: 888-800-2362
Fax: (714)545-4601

International Prison Ministry [11533]
PO Box 2868
Costa Mesa, CA 92628-2868
Toll free: 800-527-1212
Fax: (714)972-0557
Hoekstra, Robert, Director

Knots of Love [13998]
2973 Harbor Blvd., No. 822
Costa Mesa, CA 92626
PH: (949)229-5668
Fabiani, Christine, Exec. Dir.

Krochet Kids International [12548]
1630 Superior Ave., Unit C
Costa Mesa, CA 92627
PH: (949)791-2560

National Association of Certified
Professionals of Equine Therapy
[13639]
711 W 17th St., No. A8
Costa Mesa, CA 92627
PH: (949)646-8010
Troxell, Mickey Kay, President,
Founder

National Bicycle Dealers Association
[3142]
3176 Pullman St., No. 117
Costa Mesa, CA 92626

PH: (949)722-6909
Clements, Fred, VP

National Pitching Association
[22563]
Vanguard University
55 Fair Dr.
Costa Mesa, CA 92626
House, Tom, Founder

Project Cuddle [11133]
2973 Harbor Blvd., No. 326
Costa Mesa, CA 92626
PH: (714)432-9681
Fax: (714)433-6815
Idell, Ed, President

Rewrite Beautiful [14651]
397 La Perle Ln., Ste. A
Costa Mesa, CA 92627
PH: (949)903-4784
Besch, Kate, President

Vizsla Club of America [21987]
379 Costa Mesa St.
Costa Mesa, CA 92627
Dutson, Greg, President

Animal Legal Defense Fund [10578]
525 E Cotati Ave.
Cotati, CA 94931
PH: (707)795-2533
Fax: (707)795-7280
Luick, Sarah, Chairwoman

InterAct Advocates for Intersex Youth
[17903]
PO Box 676
Cotati, CA 94931
PH: (707)793-1190
Dalke, Katie Baratz, President

Ryan's Reach [17350]
35 Augusta
Coto de Caza, CA 92679
PH: (949)733-0046
(949)246-4328
Michaelis, Mike, President

Reasons to Believe [20598]
818 S Oak Park Rd.
Covina, CA 91724
PH: (626)335-1480
Toll free: 855-732-7667
Fax: (626)852-0178
Ross, Dr. Hugh, Founder, President

Society for the Advancement of
Material and Process Engineering
[6587]
1161 Park View Dr., Ste. 200
Covina, CA 91724-3759
PH: (626)331-0616
Toll free: 800-562-7360
Fax: (626)332-8929
Balko, Gregg, Secretary

Anti-Racist Action-Los Angeles/
People Against Racist Terror
[17875]
PO Box 1055
Culver City, CA 90232
PH: (323)636-7388
Novick, Mr. Michael, Exec. Ofc.

Center for the Study of Political
Graphics [8849]
3916 Sepulveda Blvd., Ste. 103
Culver City, CA 90230
PH: (310)397-3100
Fax: (310)397-9305
Wells, Carol A., Exec. Dir., Founder

Ceramic Tile Institute of America
[860]
12061 Jefferson Blvd.
Culver City, CA 90230
PH: (310)574-7800
Fax: (310)821-4655
Brady, Thomas, Director

CHEER for Viet Nam [13269]
PO Box 341
Culver City, CA 90232
Nam-Hau, Doan Thi, EdD, Founder,
President

Coalition for Pulmonary Fibrosis
[17137]
10866 W Washington Blvd., No. 343
Culver City, CA 90232
Toll free: 888-222-8541
Michon, Mishka, CEO

Container Recycling Institute [4629]
4361 Keystone Ave.
Culver City, CA 90232
PH: (310)559-7451
Collins, Susan V., President

Helping Orphans Worldwide [11027]
10736 Jefferson Blvd., Ste. 808
Culver City, CA 90230
PH: (971)400-4100
Brown, Randy, Chmn. of the Bd.

Human Assistance and Development
International [12161]
PO Box 4598
Culver City, CA 90231
PH: (310)642-0006
Fax: (310)568-9533

International Education Research
Foundation [8102]
6133 Bristol Pky., Ste. 300
Culver City, CA 90230
PH: (310)258-9451
Fax: (310)342-7086
Bedil, Susan J., Exec. Dir.

International Forum for
Psychoanalytic Education [16847]
PO Box 961
Culver City, CA 90232-0961
PH: (310)694-3463
Ehrlich, Lois, Administrator

International Viola d'Amore Society
e.V [9939]
c/o Dr. Daniel Thomason, Co-
Director/Co-Founder
10917 Pickford Way
Culver City, CA 90230
PH: (310)838-5509
Thomason, Dr. Daniel, Director,
Founder

Journey to the Heart [9576]
10828 Whitburn St.
Culver City, CA 90230
Toll free: 800-540-0471
Langbecker, Kim, Exec. Dir.,
Founder

Kids With A Cause [11060]
10736 Jefferson Blvd., No. 401
Culver City, CA 90230
PH: (310)880-6780
Finnegan, Ms. Linda, Founder

Kidsave International [10457]
100 Corporate Pointe, Ste. 380
Culver City, CA 90230
PH: (310)642-7283
Fax: (310)641-7283
Thompson, Randi, CEO, Founder

National Association of Credential
Evaluation Services [7909]
PO Box 3665
Culver City, CA 90231-3665
PH: (310)258-9451
Fax: (310)342-7086

National Black Business Council
[652]
600 Corporate Pointe, Ste. 1010
Culver City, CA 90230

PH: (310)585-6222

National Coalition of Ethnic Minority
Nurse Associations [16158]
c/o Betty Smith Williams, President
6101 W Centinela Ave., Ste. 378
Culver City, CA 90230
PH: (310)258-9515
Fax: (310)258-9513
Williams, Dr. Betty Smith, RN,
President

No Limits [15207]
9801 Washington Blvd., 2nd Fl.
Culver City, CA 90232
PH: (310)280-0878
Fax: (310)280-0872
Christie, Michelle, Exec. Dir.,
Founder

Triage Cancer [14076]
c/o Navigating Cancer Survivorship
PO Box 4552
Culver City, CA 90231-4552
PH: (424)258-4628
Fax: (424)258-7064
Morales, Joanna Fawzy, Esq., CEO

World Molecular Imaging Society
[15752]
6162 Bristol Pky.
Culver City, CA 90230
PH: (310)215-9730
Fax: (310)215-9731
Baird, Lisa, Exec. Dir.

CompactFlash Association [6243]
PO Box 130
Cupertino, CA 95015-0130
PH: (650)843-1220
Fax: (650)644-0450

Fab Owners Association [1047]
19925 Stevens Creek Blvd., Ste.
100
Cupertino, CA 95014-2358
PH: (408)725-7127
Fax: (408)725-8885
Guttadauro, L.T., Contact

National Chinese Honor Society
[23706]
10100 Finch Ave.
Cupertino, CA 95014-3411
Mammone, Diane, Chairperson

ReformAMT [19162]
PO Box 915
Cupertino, CA 95015
PH: (408)482-2400
    (650)207-3940
Cena, Mr. Jay, Chairman

Shirley Family Association [20927]
10256 Glencoe Dr.
Cupertino, CA 95014
Scislaw, Ken, President

United States Floorball Association
[22535]
10037 Scenic Blvd.
Cupertino, CA 95014
Karlsson, Calle, President

International Human Powered
Vehicle Association [7349]
PO Box 357
Cutten, CA 95534-0357
PH: (707)443-8261
Toll free: 877-333-1029
Fax: (707)444-2579
Krause, Al, President

Afghanistan Relief Organization
[12607]
PO Box 866
Cypress, CA 90630
Toll free: 877-276-2440
Fax: (714)661-5932

American Association of Gynecologic
Laparoscopists [16268]
6757 Katella Ave.
Cypress, CA 90630-5105
PH: (714)503-6200
Toll free: 800-554-2245
Michels, Linda, Exec. Dir.

Morgan Plus Four Club [21443]
5073 Melbourne Dr.
Cypress, CA 90630
PH: (714)828-3127
Willburn, Gerry, Membership Chp.

Utility Industry Group [3426]
c/o Pat Howard, Secretary/Treasurer
5253 Vista Del Sol
Cypress, CA 90630
PH: (714)828-0698
Fax: (714)527-8986

International Shaolin Kenpo Associa-
tion [22995]
69 Washington St.
Daly City, CA 94014
PH: (650)755-8996
Castro, Ralph, Founder, President

Myanmar Community USA [11406]
1178 Southgate Ave.
Daly City, CA 94015
PH: (650)303-1800
Chin, Felix M., President, CEO

Underwater Society of America
[23347]
PO Box 628
Daly City, CA 94017
PH: (707)343-7132
Rose, Carol, President

Association for Medical Ethics
[17252]
14 Monarch Bay Plz., Ste. 405
Dana Point, CA 92629-3424
PH: (215)322-6643
Toll free: 800-497-0641
Rosen, Charles, MD, Founder, Bd.
Member

Community Managers International
Association [2163]
PO Box 848
Dana Point, CA 92629-0848
PH: (949)940-9263
Sibio, Mike, Director

United Association Manufacturers'
Representatives [2209]
PO Box 4216
Dana Point, CA 92629-9216
PH: (949)481-5214
Fax: (417)779-1576
Mazzola, Ms. Karen, Exec. Dir.

Big Little Book Collector's Club
[21627]
PO Box 1242
Danville, CA 94526
Lowery, Lawrence F., President

Children of Grace [10917]
PO Box 2394
Danville, CA 94526-7394
PH: (415)766-0981
McCoy, MaryAnn, Exec. Dir.,
Founder

FUNDaFIELD [10991]
20 Alamo Springs Ct.
Danville, CA 94526
Weiss, Mr. Kyle, Founder, Exec. Dir.

The Macedonian Outreach [20431]
PO Box 398
Danville, CA 94526-0398
PH: (925)820-4107
Thompson, Terry L., Chmn. of the
Bd.

Sikh Sports Association of USA
[23149]
4430 Deer Field Way
Danville, CA 94506
PH: (510)501-2263
Toll free: 866-499-0032
Dhaliwal, Harvinder S., Chairman

Solar for Peace [7210]
PO Box 764
Danville, CA 94526-0764
PH: (925)208-4989

Save the Waves Coalition [4773]
3500 Highway 1
Davenport, CA 95017
PH: (831)426-6169
Fax: (831)460-1256
Seelbach, Ryan, Secretary

American Romanian Academy of
Arts and Sciences [9014]
University of California Davis
1 Shields Ave.
Davis, CA 95616
Vidu, Prof. Ruxandra, President

American Society for Enology and
Viticulture [4923]
PO Box 1855
Davis, CA 95617-1855
PH: (530)753-3142
Fax: (530)753-3318
Boulton, Lyndie, Exec. Dir.

Association of National Park Rang-
ers [5662]
PO Box 984
Davis, CA 95617
Allen, Stacy, Bd. Member

Association for Spanish and
Portuguese Historical Studies
[9464]
c/o A. Katie Harris, General
Secretary
1 Shields Ave.
Department of History
University of California, Davis
Davis, CA 95616-8611
Holguín, Sandie, Gen. Sec.

Cognitive Neuroscience Society
[16045]
c/o Center for Mind and Brain
267 Cousteau Pl.
Davis, CA 95618
PH: (916)850-0837

Farmer-Veteran Coalition [21121]
4614 2nd St., Ste. 4
Davis, CA 95618
PH: (530)756-1395
O'Gorman, Michael, Exec. Dir.

Foundation for Teaching Economics
[7730]
260 Russell Blvd., Ste. B
Davis, CA 95616-3839
PH: (530)757-4630
Fax: (530)757-4636
Ream, Roger, President

Freedom from Hunger [12095]
1460 Drew Ave.; Ste. 300
Davis, CA 95618
PH: (530)758-6200
Toll free: 800-708-2555
Fax: (530)758-6241
Hollingworth, Steve, President, CEO

Geothermal Resources Council
[6690]
630 Pena Dr., Ste. 400
Davis, CA 95618
PH: (530)758-2360
Fax: (530)758-2839
Ponder, Steve, Exec. Dir.

Mind Justice [18425]
c/o Cheryl Welsh, Director
915 Zaragoza St.
Davis, CA 95618
Welsh, Cheryl, Director

Sahaya International [12184]
c/o Koen Van Rompay
1504 Portola St.
Davis, CA 95616-7306
PH: (530)756-9074
Yazdani, Dr. Ramin, Ph.D., President

Weight Loss Surgery Foundation of
America [17417]
417 Mace Blvd., Ste. J-236
Davis, CA 95618
PH: (657)229-5732
Namnath, Antonia, President

ZigBee Alliance [3250]
508 2nd St., Ste. 206
Davis, CA 95616
PH: (530)564-4565
Fax: (530)564-4721
Desbenoit, Jean-Pierre, V. Chmn. of
the Bd.

Extra Miler Club [22466]
PO Box 73
Death Valley, CA 92328
Bone, Sarah, Contact

Health Optimizing Institute [15265]
PO Box 1233
Del Mar, CA 92014
PH: (858)481-7751
Harris, David J., Founder

Mandala Society [12009]
c/o David J. Harris
PO Box 1233
Del Mar, CA 92014
PH: (858)481-7751
Harris, David J., Founder

National Association of Credit Union
Chairmen [952]
PO Box 160
Del Mar, CA 92014
PH: (858)792-3883
Toll free: 888-987-4247
Fax: (858)792-3884
Rangel, Rose, Chairperson

National Association of Credit Union
Supervisory and Auditing Commit-
tees [954]
PO Box 160
Del Mar, CA 92014
Toll free: 800-287-5949
Fax: (858)792-3884
Spindler, Bob, Assoc. Dir.

National Cage Bird Show [21541]
c/o Barbara Rosario, Membership
Chairman
715 Avocado Ct.
Del Mar, CA 92014-3911
PH: (858)259-0232
Morgan, Gary, President

National Council of Postal Credit
Unions [956]
PO Box 160
Del Mar, CA 92014
PH: (760)745-3883
Fax: (858)792-3884
Cuddy, Rebecca, Chairman

Nature and Culture International
[3915]
1400 Maiden Ln.
Del Mar, CA 92014
PH: (858)259-0374
Swift, Byron, President

Silver Age Yoga [10424]
PO Box 160
Del Mar, CA 92014

PH: (858)693-3110
Toll free: 877-313-3110
Iszak, Frank, Founder

Taking Control of Your Diabetes
[14543]
1110 Camino Del Mar, Ste. B
Del Mar, CA 92014-2649
PH: (858)755-5683
Toll free: 800-998-2693
Fax: (858)755-6854
Edelman, Steven V., MD, Director,
Founder

World Chiropractic Alliance [14285]
2683 Via de La Valle, Ste. G629
Del Mar, CA 92014-1911
Toll free: 800-347-1011
Fax: (866)789-8073
Rondberg, Dr. Terry A., President,
Founder

Association of Professors and
Scholars of Iranian Heritage [9592]
PO Box 4175
Diamond Bar, CA 91765-0175
PH: (909)869-2569
Fax: (909)869-2564
Fallah-Fini, Saeideh, Secretary

Light Truck Accessory Alliance [325]
1575 Valley Vista Dr.
Diamond Bar, CA 91765
White, Melanie, Chairperson

Specialty Equipment Market As-
sociation [329]
1575 S Valley Vista Dr.
Diamond Bar, CA 91765-0910
PH: (909)610-2030
Fax: (909)860-0184
Miller, William, Sr. VP of Operations

Afghan Education for a Better
Tomorrow [13022]
PO Box 2054
Discovery Bay, CA 94505
PH: (916)505-2364
Feda, Ghulam, President, Chairman

Athletic Success Institute [23075]
1933 Windward Pt.
Discovery Bay, CA 94514
PH: (925)516-8686

Bonus Families [11814]
PO Box 1238
Discovery Bay, CA 94505
PH: (925)516-2681
Fax: (925)308-4715
Blackstone, Jann, Founder

National Association of Settlement
Purchasers [1255]
720 Collier Dr.
Dixon, CA 95620
Laborde, Patricia, President

Luso-American Education Founda-
tion [10170]
7080 Donlon Way, Ste. 200
Dublin, CA 94568
PH: (925)828-4884
Toll free: 877-525-5876
Fax: (925)828-4554
Pio, Anthony, Treasurer

Luso-American Fraternal Federation
[19489]
c/o Luso-American Life Insurance
Society
7080 Donlon Way, Ste. 200
Dublin, CA 94568
PH: (925)828-4884
Toll free: 877-525-5876
Fax: (925)828-4554
Matos, Paulo, Chmn. of the Bd.

Luso-American Life Insurance
Society [19490]
7080 Donlon Way, Ste. 200
Dublin, CA 94568-2787

PH: (925)828-4884
Toll free: 877-525-5876
Fax: (925)828-4554
Vieira, Joseph B., Director

International Committee for the
Rescue of KAL 007 Survivors
[12743]
34 Blackbird St.
Edwards, CA 93523
PH: (661)475-4079
Schlossberg, Bert, Director

Evangelical Press Association
[20139]
PO Box 20198
El Cajon, CA 92021
Toll free: 888-311-1731
Maher, D'Arcy, Exec. Dir.

International Association of Dental
Traumatology [14447]
4425 Cass St., Ste. A
El Cajon, CA 92019
PH: (858)272-1018
Fax: (858)272-7687
Altay, Ayse Nil, Secretary

International Crime Free Association
[5125]
c/o Samantha Scheurn
El Cajon Police Dept.
100 Civic Center Way
El Cajon, CA 92020
PH: (619)579-4227
Fax: (619)441-5534
Noel, Becky, Exec. Dir.

National Social Science Association
[7169]
2020 Hills Lake Dr.
El Cajon, CA 92020
PH: (619)448-4709
Fax: (619)258-7636
Baydo, Jerry, Exec. Dir.

NBIA Disorders Association [15974]
2082 Monaco Ct.
El Cajon, CA 92019-4235
PH: (619)588-2315
Fax: (619)588-4093
Wood, Patricia V., Founder,
President

Red Cross of Constantine I United
Grand Imperial Council [19568]
PO Box 1606
El Cajon, CA 92022-1606
PH: (619)456-4652
Doan, David R, Officer

Unarius Academy of Science
[12018]
145 S Magnolia Ave.
El Cajon, CA 92020
PH: (619)444-7062
Toll free: 800-475-7062
Norman, Ruth E., Founder

World War II War Brides Association
[21047]
c/o Erin Craig
PO BOX 1812
El Centro, CA 92244-1812
PH: (928)237-1581
Reddy, Ms. Diane, President

Business Alliance for Commerce in
Hemp [18860]
PO Box 1716
El Cerrito, CA 94530
PH: (510)215-8326
Conrad, Chris, Director

Family Council on Drug Awareness
[13140]
PO Box 1716
El Cerrito, CA 94530

PH: (510)215-8326
Fax: (510)215-8326
Conrad, Chris, Director

Friends and Families of Cannabis
Consumers [18646]
PO Box 1716
El Cerrito, CA 94530
PH: (510)215-8326
Fax: (510)215-8326
Conrad, Chris, Director

Hydroponic Society of America
[4443]
PO Box 1183
El Cerrito, CA 94530
PH: (510)926-2908
Droll, Paul, Founder

National Association for Temple
Administration [20268]
3060 El Cerrito Plz., No. 331
El Cerrito, CA 94530
PH: (360)887-0464
Toll free: 800-966-NATA
Lauder, Ronald, Chairman

National Neigong Research Society
[9793]
3060 El Cerrito Plz., No. 237
El Cerrito, CA 94530
PH: (510)854-6374
Wong, Tony, Chairman, President

Solid Axle Corvette Club [21492]
c/o Noland Adams, Founding
President
PO Box 1134
El Dorado, CA 95623
PH: (916)991-7040
Fax: (916)991-7044
Adams, Noland, President, Founder

Asphalt Interlayer Association [494]
1811 Hampshire Pl.
El Dorado Hills, CA 95762
PH: (916)933-9140
Fax: (916)933-9473
Myers, Ray, Exec. Dir.

Day Sailer Association [22611]
c/o Mary Niederberger, Secretary
3840 Arrowhead Dr.
El Dorado Hills, CA 95762-4505
PH: (781)893-5030
Niederberger, Mary, Secretary

International Association of Financial
Crimes Investigators [5361]
1020 Suncast Ln., Ste. 102
El Dorado Hills, CA 95762
PH: (916)939-5000
Fax: (916)939-0395

Leadership Development Network
[17983]
3941 Park Dr., Ste. 20-311
El Dorado Hills, CA 95762-4549
PH: (916)514-7655
Fax: (916)514-8650
Camac, Clint, President

Multicore Association [6256]
PO Box 4794
El Dorado Hills, CA 95762
PH: (530)672-9113
Levy, Markus, President

Society for Social Neuroscience
[16056]
c/o TM Events, Inc.
2100 Valley View Pky., Ste. 1526
El Dorado Hills, CA 95762
Young, Larry, President

Yosemite Conservancy [6903]
PO Box 230
El Portal, CA 95318-0230

PH: (209)379-2317
Fax: (209)379-2486
Dean, Frank, President, CEO

Employers Group [2165]
4000 Continental Blvd., Ste. 300
El Segundo, CA 90245
PH: (213)765-3989
Toll free: 800-748-8484
Fax: (213)742-0301

Tree Musketeers [3957]
305 Richmond St.
El Segundo, CA 90245
PH: (310)322-0263
Fax: (310)322-4482
Church, Gail, Exec. Dir.

Chinese-American Environmental
Professionals Association [4040]
5237 Heavenly Ridge Ln.
El Sobrante, CA 94803
Wang, Danyun, President

Doberman Assistance Network
[11688]
c/o Heidi Merriman
3852 La Colina Rd.
El Sobrante, CA 94803
Brady, Vicki, President

Accellera Systems Initiative [6412]
8698 Elk Grove Blvd., Ste. 1, No.
114
Elk Grove, CA 95624
PH: (916)670-1056
Horobin, Lynn, Administrator

American Theatre Organ Society,
Inc. [9870]
7800 Laguna Vega Dr.
Elk Grove, CA 95758
PH: (503)372-6987
Double, Ken, CEO, President

Friends of Rwanda Association
[10988]
PO Box 1311
Elk Grove, CA 95759-1311
PH: (916)683-3356
Mukantabana, Mathilde, President

Gramma's Hugs International
[11009]
c/o Shirley J. King, Director/Founder
8652 Elk Way
Elk Grove, CA 95624
PH: (916)685-9660
King, Shirley J., Director, Founder

Grandmothers for Peace
International [18748]
PO Box 1292
Elk Grove, CA 95759-1292
PH: (916)730-6476
Krofchok, Lorraine, Director

Haiti Engineering [11664]
9384 Boulder River Way
Elk Grove, CA 95624
PH: (916)296-8586
Lissade, Herby, President

Junior Billboard Association [100]
PO Box 582096
Elk Grove, CA 95758
Osmus, Carla, Chairman

National Council on Teacher Retire-
ment [23410]
9370 Studio Ct., Ste. 100E
Elk Grove, CA 95758
PH: (916)897-9139
Fax: (916)897-9315
Williams, Meredith, Exec. Dir.

Team Success [13483]
5050 Laguna Blvd., Ste. 112-415
Elk Grove, CA 95758-4151

PH: (916)629-4229
Boyce, Aaron, Founder

U.S.A. Sanatan Sports and Cultural
Association [23198]
PO Box 5050
Elk Grove, CA 95758
Prakash, Suresh, President

Yuki Teikei Haiku Society [10162]
c/o Toni Homan, Membership
Secretary
9457 Mereoak Cir.
Elk Grove, CA 95758
Gallagher, Patrick, President

Passiflora Society International
[4440]
PO Box 350
Elmira, CA 95625
Boender, Ron, Founder

Center for Investigative Reporting
[17941]
1400 65th St., Ste. 200
Emeryville, CA 94608
PH: (510)809-3160
Fax: (510)849-6141
Scharfenberg, Christa, Officer

Esperanto-USA [9288]
1500 Park Ave., Ste. 134
Emeryville, CA 94608
PH: (510)653-0998
Toll free: 800-377-3726
Raola, Orlando, President

Green Yoga Association [10420]
2340 Powell St., No. 141
Emeryville, CA 94608
PH: (415)655-1081
Cornell, Laura, Founder

International Organization of Black
Security Executives [3061]
2340 Powell St., No. 327
Emeryville, CA 94608
PH: (510)648-4292
Baker, Will, Advisor

Pact, An Adoption Alliance [10463]
5515 Doyle St., Ste. 1
Emeryville, CA 94608-2510
PH: (510)243-9460
Toll free: 800-750-7590
Fax: (510)243-9970
Hall, Beth, Exec. Dir., Founder

American Bamboo Society [6126]
315 S Coast Highway 101, Ste. U
Encinitas, CA 92024-3555
Lucas, Susanne, President

CCHS Family Network [14568]
PO Box 230087
Encinitas, CA 92023-0087
Vanderlaan, Mary, Director, Founder

Children's PKU Network [15819]
3306 Bumann Rd.
Encinitas, CA 92024-5712
PH: (858)756-0079
Fax: (858)756-1059

Disorders of Chromosome 16
Foundation [14820]
PO Box 230448
Encinitas, CA 92023-0448
Hubbell, Samantha, CEO

Guitars in the Classroom [8369]
1911 Shady Acre Cir.
Encinitas, CA 92024
PH: (760)452-6123
Baron, Jessica, Exec. Dir.

Humanitarian Wave [13063]
649 Beach St.
Encinitas, CA 92024

PH: (760)436-6016
Fax: (760)230-6866
Muric, Maja, Founder, President

International Association of
Skateboard Companies [23089]
315 S Coast Highway 101, Ste.
U-253
Encinitas, CA 92024
PH: (949)455-1112
Fax: (949)455-1112
Friedberg, Josh, Exec. Dir.

MarineBio Conservation Society
[3899]
1995 Fairlee Dr.
Encinitas, CA 92024-4227
PH: (713)248-2576
Campbell, David, President, Founder

The New Violin Family Association,
Inc. [9983]
Hutchins Consort
701 3rd St.
Encinitas, CA 92024
PH: (760)632-0554
Hutchins, Dr. Carleen M., Exec. Dir.,
Founder

Orchid Conservation Alliance [3925]
564 Arden Dr.
Encinitas, CA 92024
PH: (720)518-5120
Tobias, Peter S., PhD, President,
Director

Saving Horses, Inc. [4407]
3224 Wildflower Valley Dr.
Encinitas, CA 92024
PH: (619)247-7237
Reynolds, Audrey, Founder

SurfAid International [11446]
345 S Coast Hwy. 101, Ste. K
Encinitas, CA 92024
PH: (760)753-1103
Fax: (760)487-1943
Jenkins, Dr. Dave, Founder, Director

Academy of Country Music [9845]
5500 Balboa Blvd.
Encino, CA 91316
PH: (818)788-8000
Fax: (818)788-0999
Romeo, Bob, CEO

Advancement of Research for Myo-
pathies [14802]
PO Box 261926
Encino, CA 91426-1926
Toll free: 800-276-2000
Fax: (818)609-7350
Darvish, Babak, MD, Founder,
President

Assyrian Medical Society [15716]
16055 Ventura Blvd., Ste. 1225
Encino, CA 91436-2625
PH: (818)501-8867
Davidoo, Albert, Chairman, Founder

Center for Surrogate Parenting, Inc.
[13203]
West Coast Office
15821 Ventura Blvd., Ste. 625
Encino, CA 91436
PH: (818)788-8288
Fax: (818)981-8287
Synesiou, Karen, CEO

Entertainment Merchants Association
[265]
16530 Ventura Blvd., Ste. 400
Encino, CA 91436-4551
PH: (818)385-1500
Fax: (818)933-0911
Andersen, Crossan, President, CEO

Hollywood Radio and Television
Society [462]
16530 Ventura Blvd.
Encino, CA 91436

PH: (818)789-1182
Fax: (818)789-1210
Gonzalez, Elvia, Mgr., Member Svcs.

Jewish World Watch [18309]
5551 Balboa Blvd.
Encino, CA 91316
PH: (818)501-1836
Fax: (818)501-1835
Brand, Mike, Dir. of Programs

Junior Hollywood Radio and Televi-
sion Society [465]
16530 Ventura Blvd., Ste. 411
Encino, CA 91436
PH: (818)789-1182
Perry, Sean, Partner, Dept. Head

National Association of Video
Distributors [1202]
16530 Ventura Blvd., Ste. 400
Encino, CA 91436
PH: (818)385-1500
Fax: (818)933-0911
Webb, Bob, President

National Risk Retention Association
[1909]
16133 Ventura Blvd., Ste. 1055
Encino, CA 91436
PH: (818)995-3274
Toll free: 800-421-5981
Fax: (818)995-6496
Deems, Joe, Exec. Dir.

New Civilization Network [12012]
PO Box 260433
Encino, CA 91316
PH: (818)725-3775
Funch, Flemming, Founder

Renew Our Minds and Hearts
Foundation [13017]
PO Box 18521
Encino, CA 91416
PH: (323)247-9581
Fax: (206)888-0328
Jardinaso, Ruth Ann, Founder,
President, CEO

Vital Options International [14080]
17328 Ventura Blvd., No. 161
Encino, CA 91316
PH: (818)508-5657
Duplay, David S., Chairman

Animal Behavior Management Alliance [7395]
c/o San Diego Zoo Safari Pk.
15500 San Pasqual Valley Rd.
Escondido, CA 92027
Boyd, Nicki, President

Center for Plant Conservation [3826]
15600 San Pasqual Valley Rd.
Escondido, CA 92027-7000
PH: (760)796-5686
Clark, John R., President, CEO

Friends of Neurosurgery
International [16064]
705 E Ohio Ave.
Escondido, CA 92025
PH: (760)489-9490
Fax: (760)489-7638
Stern, Mark S., MD, Founder

Tomiki Aikido of the Americas
[23015]
1835-A S Centre City Pky., Ste. 300
Escondido, CA 92025
PH: (510)459-4079
King, Bob, Director

U.S.-China Education Foundation
[8091]
970 W Valley Pky., No. 220
Escondido, CA 92025
Kennedy, Joseph, Chairman, CEO

Borderland Sciences Research
Foundation [7009]
PO Box 6250
Eureka, CA 95502
PH: (707)497-6911

International Thriller Writers [10382]
PO Box 311
Eureka, CA 95502
Child, Lee, Co-Pres.

Move to Amend [5072]
PO Box 610
Eureka, CA 95502
PH: (707)269-0984
Sopoci-Belknap, Kaitlin, Director

New Afghanistan Women Association [13390]
c/o Share Institute
8370 Sunset Ave.
Fair Oaks, CA 95628
PH: (916)966-7482
Fax: (916)863-0665

Living/Dying Project [13217]
PO Box 357
Fairfax, CA 94978-0357
PH: (415)456-3915
Borglum, Dale, PhD, Founder, Exec.
Dir.

Women's Mountain Bike and Tea
Society [22761]
PO Box 757
Fairfax, CA 94978
PH: (415)459-7093
Phelan, Jacquie, Founder

International Bird Rescue [4828]
4369 Cordelia Rd.
Fairfield, CA 94534
PH: (707)207-0380
Fax: (707)207-0395
Callahan, Barbara, Exec. Dir.

Punjabi-American Cultural Associa-
tion [9571]
5055 Business Center Dr., Ste. 108,
No. 165
Fairfield, CA 94534
Biring, Amarjot Singh, Contact

The Fiber Optic Association, Inc.
[8668]
1119 S Mission Rd., No. 355
Fallbrook, CA 92028
PH: (760)451-3655
Fax: (781)207-2421

Environmental Cleanup Coalition
[4544]
10507 E Zayante Rd.
Felton, CA 95018
PH: (808)563-9963
Owen, Richard Sundance, Exec.
Dir., Founder

Moderation Management [17315]
2795 E Bidwell St., Ste. 100-244
Folsom, CA 95630-6480
Wahlers, Larry, Exec. Dir.

National Coalition for Campus
Children's Centers [10811]
2036 Larkhall Cir.
Folsom, CA 95630
PH: (916)790-8261
Palla, Tonya, Exec. Dir.

North American Blueberry Council
[4246]
80 Iron Point Cir., Ste. 114
Folsom, CA 95630
PH: (616)399-2052
Villata, Mark, Exec. Dir.

Sufi Psychology Association [16946]
PO Box 681
Folsom, CA 95763

PH: (916)368-5530

God's Kids [11006]
11700 Industry Ave.
Fontana, CA 92337
Toll free: 877-246-3754
Quinn, Dion, Founder

Jensen Healey Preservation Society
[21410]
4 Estrade Ln.
Foothill Ranch, CA 92610
Fletcher, Greg, Contact

Cork Quality Council [1436]
Forestville, CA
PH: (707)887-0141
Weber, Peter, Exec. Dir.

Ethnobotanical Conservation
Organization for South East Asia
[3860]
PO Box 77
Fort Bragg, CA 95437
Fax: (815)331-0850
Pfeiffer, Jeanine, Exec. Dir.

National Title I Association [7441]
532 N Franklin St.
Fort Bragg, CA 95437
Toll free: 800-256-6452
Fax: (800)915-3291
Pauley, Gayle, Rep.

Diabetes Technology Society
[14531]
1157 Chess Dr., Ste. 100
Foster City, CA 94404
PH: (650)357-7140
Toll free: 800-397-7755
Fax: (650)349-6497
Klonoff, David C.

National Association to Advance Fat
Acceptance [12397]
PO Box 4662
Foster City, CA 94404-0662
PH: (916)558-6880
Howell, Darliene, Chmn. of the Bd.

Institute on Religion and Civic
Values [8124]
PO Box 20186
Fountain Valley, CA 92728-0186
PH: (714)839-2929
Fax: (714)839-2714
Shaikh, Munir A., Exec. Dir.

National Spasmodic Torticollis As-
sociation [15972]
9920 Talbert Ave.
Fountain Valley, CA 92708
PH: (714)378-9837
Toll free: 800-487-8385
Aquines, Justin G., Exec. Dir.

Retinoblastoma International [14056]
18030 Brookhurst St.
Fountain Valley, CA 92708
Dumm, Sue, Chmn. of the Bd.

Western Economic Association
International [6405]
18837 Brookhurst St., Ste. 304
Fountain Valley, CA 92708-7302
PH: (714)965-8800
Fax: (714)965-8829
Ashenfelter, Orley, VP

International Guild of Miniature
Artisans [21761]
PO Box 629
Freedom, CA 95019-0629
PH: (831)724-7974
Toll free: 800-711-4462
Hardy, Carol, Administrator

Six Seconds [7068]
PO Box 1985
Freedom, CA 95019

PH: (831)763-1800
Jensen, Anabel, PhD, President

Agami [7579]
PO Box 3178
Fremont, CA 94539
Rahman, Dr. Babu S., Bd. Member

Broadband Forum [1795]
48377 Fremont Blvd., Ste. 117
Fremont, CA 94538
PH: (510)492-4020
Fax: (510)492-4001
Corby, Christine, Exec. Dir.

CAMUS International [2216]
45738 Northport Loop W
Fremont, CA 94538
Lanza, Terri Glendon, President

DAST International Inc. [17389]
42611 Saratoga Park St.
Fremont, CA 94538
Marlow, Vicky, Founder

Gaming Standards Association
[22061]
48377 Fremont Blvd., Ste. 117
Fremont, CA 94538
PH: (510)492-4060
Olesiejuk, Michelle, Exec. Dir.

The Monorail Society [22461]
36193 Carnation Way
Fremont, CA 94536-2641
Pedersen, Kim, Founder, President

MulteFire Alliance [6886]
48377 Fremont Blvd., Ste. 117
Fremont, CA 94538
PH: (510)492-4026
Fax: (510)492-4001
Litjens, Stephan, Chmn. of the Bd.

Optical Internetworking Forum
[3212]
48377 Fremont Blvd., Ste. 117
Fremont, CA 94538
PH: (510)492-4040
Fax: (510)492-4001
Kosich, Andi, Exec. Dir.

Promise World Wide [12179]
46170 Paseo Padre Pky.
Fremont, CA 94539-6930
PH: (408)605-0495
Basu, Jaya, President

SailMail Association [6445]
39270 Paseo Padre Pky., No. 850
Fremont, CA 94538
PH: (619)980-6215
Toll free: 877-282-1485
Corenman, Jim, Director

Space Frontier Foundation [7222]
42354 Blacow Rd.
Fremont, CA 94538
Toll free: 800-787-7223
Watson, William, Contact

UHD Alliance [6015]
48377 Fremont Blvd., Ste. 117
Fremont, CA 94538
PH: (510)492-4025
Fax: (510)492-4001
Basse, Hanno, President, Chmn. of
the Bd.

Universal Ship Cancellation Society
[22379]
747 Shard Ct.
Fremont, CA 94539-7419

American Computer Barrel Racing
Association [22912]
PO Box 322
French Camp, CA 95231

PH: (209)481-8042
Cohn, Kendra, President

Alliance for the Separation of School
and State [7734]
1071 N Fulton St.
Fresno, CA 93728
PH: (559)499-1776
Toll free: 888-325-1776
Fax: (559)499-1703

Armenian Technology Group [3535]
550 E Shaw Ave.
Fresno, CA 93755-5969
PH: (559)224-1000
Fax: (559)224-1002
Der Simonian, Varoujan, MA, Exec.
Dir.

Association of Latina and Latino
Social Work Educators [8569]
California State University, Fresno
Department of Social Work Educa-
tion
5310 Campus Dr., M/S PH102
Fresno, CA 93740-8019
Hernandez, Virginia Rondero, PhD,
Contact

Association of Medicine and
Psychiatry [16826]
4747 N 1st St., Ste. 140
Fresno, CA 93726
Toll free: 800-544-6283
Fax: (559)227-1463
Onate, John, Treasurer

Breeder's Registry [22031]
5541 Columbia Dr. N
Fresno, CA 93727
Lang, Tom, President, CEO

California Table Grape Commission
[4230]
392 W Fallbrook Ave., Ste. 101
Fresno, CA 93711
PH: (559)447-8350
Fax: (559)447-9184
Marguleas, David, Chairman

Heart Bandits American Eskimo Dog
Rescue [10634]
PO Box 4322
Fresno, CA 93744-4322
PH: (559)787-2459
Davis, Bob, Founder

Mission Cataract USA [17727]
1233 E Brandywine Ln., PMB 211
Fresno, CA 93720
PH: (559)797-1629
Petree, Sheree, Exec. Dir.

National Council on Rehabilitation
Education [17093]
1099 E Champlain Dr., Ste. A, No.
137
Fresno, CA 93720
PH: (559)906-0787
Fax: (559)412-2550
Duncan, PhD, CRC, CPO, J. Chad,
Officer

National Truck & Heavy Equipment
Claims Council [1912]
c/o Richard Bruce, Executive Direc-
tor
PO Box 5928
Fresno, CA 93755-5928
PH: (559)431-3774
Fax: (559)436-4755
Bruce, Richard, Exec. Dir.

Raisin Bargaining Association [4249]
2444 Main St., No. 160
Fresno, CA 93721
PH: (559)221-1925
Fax: (559)221-0725
Goto, Glen S., CEO

Society for Armenian Studies [8827]
c/o Armenian Studies Program
California State University
5245 N Backer Ave., PB4
Fresno, CA 93740-8001
PH: (559)278-2669
Fax: (559)278-2129
Der Matossian, Bedross, VP

Specialty Crop Trade Council [4250]
8050 N Palm Ave., Ste. 300
Fresno, CA 93711
PH: (559)389-5895
    (559)287-1837
Keiper, Sam, CEO, President

Today's Children, Africa's Future
    [11168]
PO Box 28548
Fresno, CA 93729
PH: (559)433-6926
Shermer, Richard C., Sr., CEO,
    Founder

U.S. Board on Books for Young
    People [9137]
c/o V. Ellis Vance, Executive Director
5503 N El Adobe Dr.
Fresno, CA 93711-2373
PH: (559)351-6119
Vance, V. Ellis, Exec. Dir.

United States Entertainment Force
    [10763]
6504 N 7th St.
Fresno, CA 93710
PH: (559)981-5132
Payne, Jerry, Founder, President

Valley Fig Growers [4259]
2028 S 3rd St.
Fresno, CA 93702
PH: (559)237-3893
Fax: (559)237-3898
Cain, Linda, VP

Specialty Sleep Association [1488]
c/o Tambra Jones, Executive Direc-
    tor
46639 Jones Ranch Rd.
Friant, CA 93626
PH: (559)868-4187
Toll free: 888-220-6173
Read, Dale, President

Association of Vision Science Librar-
    ians [9692]
Marshall B. Ketchum University
2575 Yorba Linda Blvd.
Fullerton, CA 92831-1699
PH: (734)763-9468
Fax: (734)936-9050
Matthews, Ms. DJ, Chairperson

ChronoRecord Association [13810]
PO Box 3501
Fullerton, CA 92834
PH: (714)773-0301
Fax: (714)773-1037
Glenn, Tasha, President

Citrus Label Society [21637]
c/o Noel Gilbert, Secretary
131 Miramonte Dr.
Fullerton, CA 92835-3607
Spellman, Tom, President

Hope International University Alumni
    Association [19326]
2500 Nutwood Ave.
Fullerton, CA 92831
PH: (714)879-3901
Toll free: 888-352-HOPE
Fax: (714)681-7450
Derry, John, President

The Red Hat Society Inc. [10310]
431 S Acacia Ave.
Fullerton, CA 92831

PH: (714)738-0001
Toll free: 866-386-2850
Fax: (714)738-0005
Granich, Debra, CEO

Toy Train Operating Society [22192]
PO Box 6710
Fullerton, CA 92834-6710
PH: (714)449-9391
Fax: (714)449-9631
Giroux, Randy, President

Ancient Egyptian Order of Sciots
    [19553]
11597 Colony Rd.
Galt, CA 95632
PH: (916)687-0808

Performing Animal Welfare Society
    [10678]
PO Box 849
Galt, CA 95632
PH: (209)745-2606
Fax: (209)745-1809
Stewart, Ed, Founder, President

American Society for Aesthetic
    Plastic Surgery [14307]
11262 Monarch St.
Garden Grove, CA 92841
PH: (562)799-2356
Toll free: 800-364-2147
Fax: (562)799-1098
Dykema, Sue M., Exec. Dir.

National Alliance of Professional
    Psychology Providers [16926]
PO Box 6263
Garden Grove, CA 92846
Caccavale, John, PhD, Exec. Dir.

Physicians Coalition for Injectable
    Safety [14319]
11262 Monarch St.
Garden Grove, CA 92841
PH: (562)799-2356
Toll free: 800-364-2147
Fax: (562)799-1098
Jewell, Mark L., Mem.

Sindhi Association of North America
    [9235]
12881 Knott St., Ste. 219
Garden Grove, CA 92841-3925
PH: (714)271-9947
Fax: (714)373-3702
Daudi, Mr. Jamil, President

Society of Plastic Surgical Skin Care
    Specialists [14324]
11262 Monarch St.
Garden Grove, CA 92841
PH: (562)799-0466
Toll free: 800-486-0611
Fax: (562)799-1098
Erb, Donna, VP

Hispanic Scholarship Fund [7926]
1411 W 190th St., Ste. 700
Gardena, CA 90248
PH: (310)975-3700
Fax: (310)349-3328
Vargas, Fidel A., President, CEO

International Right of Way Associa-
    tion [5743]
19210 S Vermont Ave.
Bldg. A, Ste. 100
Gardena, CA 90248
PH: (310)538-0233
Toll free: 888-340-4792
Fax: (310)538-1471
Goss, Wayne L., President

A Minor Consideration [11494]
15003 S Denker Ave.
Gardena, CA 90247-3113
Petersen, Paul, Founder

Graham Owners Club International
    [21389]
c/o Gloria Reid, Treasurer, 4028
    Empire Creek Cir.
4028 Empire Creek Cir.
Georgetown, CA 95634
PH: (530)333-4105
Reid, Gloria, Treasurer

Auxiliary to Sons of Union Veterans
    of the Civil War [20739]
c/o Rachelle Campbell, Vice-
    President
9110 Avezan Way
Gilroy, CA 95020
PH: (408)489-0115
Mellor, Diane, President

United States of America
    Transactional Analysis Association
    [13806]
7881 Church St., Ste. F
Gilroy, CA 95020
PH: (408)848-2293
O'Brien, Catherine, Coord.

Jack London Research Center
    [9063]
PO Box 337
Glen Ellen, CA 95442-0337
PH: (707)996-2888
Kingman, Winnie, Director

AIR Commercial Real Estate As-
    sociation [2844]
500 N Brand Blvd., Ste. 900
Glendale, CA 91203-3315
PH: (213)687-8777
Fax: (213)687-8616
Lin, Joseph, Exec. Chmn. of the Bd.

American Association of
    Independent News Distributors
    [2648]
c/o Richard Mader, Secretary-
    Treasurer
Mader News, Inc.
913 Ruberta Ave.
Glendale, CA 91201-2346

Armenian American Chamber of
    Commerce [23557]
225 E Broadway, Ste. 313C
Glendale, CA 91205
PH: (818)247-0196
Fax: (818)247-7668

Armenian Educational Foundation
    [7829]
600 W Broadway, Ste. 130
Glendale, CA 91204
PH: (818)242-4154
Fax: (818)242-4913
Petrossian, Vahik, President

Armenian Engineers and Scientists
    of America [7120]
117 S Louise St., No. 306
Glendale, CA 91205-1076
PH: (818)547-3372
Gharakhanian, Razmik D., President

Armenian Professional Society
    [9203]
117 S Louise St.
Glendale, CA 91205
PH: (818)685-9946
Kazarians, Lily, President

Armenian Rugs Society [8838]
PO Box 21104
Glendale, CA 91201
PH: (650)343-8585
Fax: (650)343-0960
Bezdjian, Joseph, President

International Functional Electrical
    Stimulation Society [16019]
1854 Los Encinos Ave.
Glendale, CA 91208-2240
Davis, Glen, VP

National Council for Taekwondo
    Masters Certification [23006]
501 W Glenoaks Blvd., Ste. 336
Glendale, CA 91202
PH: (213)503-3302
Kim, Paul J., Founder, President

Never Again Campaign [18752]
Alpha Epsilon Omega Foundation
PO Box 9303
Glendale, CA 91226

The Protein Society [6060]
PO Box 9397
Glendale, CA 91226
Fax: (844)377-6834
Post, Carol, President

REACT International [5751]
PO Box 21064
Glendale, CA 91221
PH: (301)316-2900
Fax: (800)608-9755
Capodanno, John, Chmn. of the Bd.

Renal Support Network [15887]
1146 N Central Ave., No. 121
Glendale, CA 91202-2506
PH: (818)543-0896
Toll free: 866-903-1728
Fax: (818)244-9540
Hartwell, Lori, Founder, President

United Human Rights Council
    [18447]
104 N Belmont St., Ste. 313
Glendale, CA 91206
PH: (818)507-1933
Shirinian, Sanan, Chairperson

Ludwick Family Foundation [11860]
203 S Glendora Ave., Ste. B
Glendora, CA 91741
PH: (626)852-0092
Fax: (626)852-0776
Campbell, Ms. Trista, Officer

National Hot Rod Association
    [22528]
2035 Financial Way
Glendora, CA 91741
PH: (626)914-4761
Fax: (626)963-5360
Gardner, Dallas, Chmn. of the Bd.

Nonfiction Authors Association
    [9086]
11230 Gold Express Dr., Ste. 310-
    413
Gold River, CA 95670
Toll free: 877-800-1097
Chandler, Stephanie, Founder, CEO

Access Research Network [8543]
7668 Dartmoor Ave.
Goleta, CA 93117
PH: (805)448-9505
Ofwono, Juliet, Consultant

Americans for Medical Advancement
    [15639]
2251 Refugio Rd.
Goleta, CA 93117
PH: (805)685-6812
Greek, Dr. Ray, President, Founder

Cymbidium Society of America
    [22091]
c/o Stanley Fuelscher, Secretary
5710 Hollister Ave., No. 270
Goleta, CA 93117-3421

Ferrari Owners Club [21381]
PO Box 3671
Granada Hills, CA 91394-0671
PH: (714)213-4775
Fax: (714)960-4262
Adams, Richard, Chmn. of the Bd.,
    Treasurer

North American Collectors Inc. [22277]
10605 Balboa Blvd., No. 260
Granada Hills, CA 91344
Toll free: 800-370-4720
Fax: (818)488-8787
Simon, David, President

EcoLogical Mail Coalition [4056]
6886 Fallsbrook Ct.
Granite Bay, CA 95746-6510
Toll free: 800-620-3975
Fax: (925)397-3096
Moxley, Chuck, Founder, President

ImpactAVillage [11382]
5859 Wedgewood Dr.
Granite Bay, CA 95746
PH: (916)214-0579
Wade, Lisa, President

Open Voting Consortium [18186]
4941 Forest Creek Way
Granite Bay, CA 95746
PH: (916)209-6620
Dechert, Alan, CEO, President

Lutheran Historical Conference [20310]
c/o Richard O. Johnson, Treasurer
PO Box 235
Grass Valley, CA 95945
PH: (530)273-9631
Huggins, Marvin A., Secretary

Oceanic Preservation Society [3924]
336 Bon Air Ctr., No. 384
Greenbrae, CA 94904
PH: (303)444-2454
Fax: (303)545-9938
Psihoyos, Louie, Founder, CEO

American River Touring Association [3803]
24000 Casa Loma Rd.
Groveland, CA 95321
PH: (209)962-7873
Toll free: 800-323-2782
Fax: (209)962-4819

International Hyperbarics Association, Inc. [15343]
15810 E Gale Ave., No. 178
Hacienda Heights, CA 91745
Toll free: 877-442-8721
Heuser, Gunnar, PhD, Advisor

National Pigeon Association [21546]
C/o Lennie Mefferd, Secretary
17128 Colima Dr., Unit 603
Hacienda Heights, CA 91745
PH: (626)820-8080
DeCarlo, John, Jr., President

North America Christian Creative Association [20001]
PO Box 93027
Hacienda Heights, CA 91745-3027

Athena Alliance [18164]
231 Harvard Ave.
Half Moon Bay, CA 94019
PH: (202)547-7064
Jarboe, Kenan Patrick, President

Grassroots Alliance for Community Education [7646]
PO Box 185
Half Moon Bay, CA 94019
PH: (650)712-0561
Fax: (650)712-0562
Martin, Natasha, Founder

International Jet Sports Boating Association [23354]
330 Purissima St., Ste. C
Half Moon Bay, CA 94019
PH: (714)751-8695
Fax: (714)751-8609
Frazier, Scott, Contact

Friends of Patrick Henry [10326]
PO Box 1776
Hanford, CA 93232
PH: (559)584-5209
Fax: (559)584-4084
Smith, Bernadine, Founder

Second Amendment Committee [5220]
PO Box 1776
Hanford, CA 93232
PH: (559)584-5209
Fax: (559)584-4084
Smith, Bernadine, Founder

North American Taiwanese Medical Association [15130]
c/o Chao-Hsiung Hsu, M.D., President
790 E Latham Ave.
Hemet, CA 92543
PH: (951)658-3254
Fax: (951)766-7236
Hsu, Chao-Hsiung, President

Pacific Dragon Boat Association [22660]
c/o Diane McCabe, Treasurer
607 30th St.
Hermosa Beach, CA 90254
Skinner, Kathy, President

TeachingGreen [4119]
PO Box 754
Hermosa Beach, CA 90254
PH: (310)372-7484
Fax: (310)372-7484
Jacecko, Kathleen, Founder, Director

Home of Hope [11033]
190 Tobin Clark Dr.
Hillsborough, CA 94010
PH: (650)520-3204
Sabharwal, Dr. Nilima, Chairperson

Lawton Collector's Guild [22004]
PO Box 1227
Hilmar, CA 95324
PH: (209)632-3655
Fax: (209)632-6788
Lawton, Wendy, Founder

Association of Moving Image Archivists [9298]
1313 N Vine St.
Hollywood, CA 90028
PH: (323)463-1500
Fax: (323)463-1506
Kalas, Andrea, President, Director

Atheists United [19710]
4773 Hollywood Blvd.
Hollywood, CA 90027-5333
PH: (323)666-4258
Toll free: 866-GOD-LESS
Gulina, Gulnara, President

Bulgarian-American Chamber of Commerce [23569]
1427 N Wilcox Ave.
Hollywood, CA 90028-8123
PH: (323)962-2414
Fax: (323)962-2010
Page, Dr. Ogden C., Founder, President

Secular Organizations for Sobriety [13181]
4773 Hollywood Blvd.
Hollywood, CA 90027
PH: (323)666-4295
Fax: (323)666-4271
Christopher, Jim, Founder, Exec. Dir.

American Aviation Historical Society [21212]
15211 Springdale St.
Huntington Beach, CA 92649

PH: (714)549-4818
Bergen, Jerri, President

American Lebanese Medical Association [15707]
Pacifica Orthopedics
18800 Delaware St., Ste. 1100
Huntington Beach, CA 92648
Raad, Issam, President

Building Africa [11322]
5901 Warner Ave., Ste. 171
Huntington Beach, CA 92649
PH: (714)625-8172
Voorhees, Bob, President

Coalition for SafeMinds [15918]
PO Box 285
Huntington Beach, CA 92648
PH: (404)934-0777
     (202)780-9821
Bernard, Sallie, President

National Nurses in Business Association [657]
8941 Atlanta Ave., Ste. 202
Huntington Beach, CA 92646
Toll free: 877-353-8888
Podlesni, Michelle DeLizio, President, CEO

National Scholastic Surfing Association [23277]
17381 Nichols Ln., Ste. L
Huntington Beach, CA 92647
PH: (714)906-7423
Aragon, Janice, Exec. Dir.

Ocean Defenders Alliance [3921]
19744 Beach Blvd.
Huntington Beach, CA 92648
PH: (714)875-5881
Lieber, Kurt, Exec. Dir., Founder

United States Lifesaving Association [12750]
PO Box 366
Huntington Beach, CA 92648
Toll free: 866-367-8752
Williams, Rob, Treasurer

United States Water Polo [23352]
2124 Main St., Ste. 240
Huntington Beach, CA 92648-7456
PH: (714)500-5445
Fax: (714)960-2431
Ramsey, Christopher, CEO

USA Water Polo [23353]
2124 Main St., Ste. 240
Huntington Beach, CA 92648-7456
PH: (714)500-5445
Fax: (714)960-2431
Ramsey, Christopher, CEO

Women for World Health [15072]
16291 Fantasia Ln.
Huntington Beach, CA 92649
PH: (714)846-4524
Cucurny, Denise, Founder, President

Jin Shin Do Foundation for Bodymind Acupressure [16455]
PO Box 416
Idyllwild, CA 92549
PH: (951)767-3393
Fax: (951)767-2200
Teeguarden, Iona Marsaa, Exec. Dir.

Electrical Manufacturing and Coil Winding Association [1020]
PO Box 278
Imperial Beach, CA 91933
PH: (619)435-3629
Fax: (619)435-3639
Duke, Richard B., President

World Congress of Minimally Invasive Dentistry [14475]
865 11th St.
Imperial Beach, CA 91932
Toll free: 800-973-8003
Neish, Scott R., DMD, President

American Maritain Association [10075]
c/o James G. Hanink, President
Independent Scholar
443 W Hillsdale St.
Inglewood, CA 90302-1123
Hanink, James G., President

Caribbean Health Outreach, Inc. [15441]
PO Box 1092
Inglewood, CA 90308
PH: (323)403-3579
Fax: (323)291-7806
Miller, Hope, RN, President

American College of Trial Lawyers [5823]
19900 MacArthur Blvd., Ste. 530
Irvine, CA 92612
PH: (949)752-1801
Fax: (949)752-1674
Smith, Michael W., President

Angel Heart International [15213]
PO Box 17486
Irvine, CA 92623-7486
PH: (949)310-8181
Ding, Michelle, President

ATV Safety Institute [2990]
2 Jenner St., Ste. 150
Irvine, CA 92618-3806
PH: (949)727-3727
Toll free: 800-887-2887

Ayn Rand Institute [10081]
2121 Alton Pky., Ste. 250
Irvine, CA 92606
PH: (949)222-6550
Fax: (949)222-6558
Brook, Dr. Yaron, Exec. Dir., President

BEST Association [3116]
17701 Mitchell N
Irvine, CA 92614-6028
Toll free: 866-706-2225

Big West Conference [23218]
2 Corporate Pk., Ste. 206
Irvine, CA 92606
PH: (949)261-2525
Fax: (949)261-2528
Farrell, Dennis, Commissioner

Biotherapeutics, Education and Research Foundation [13611]
36 Urey Ct.
Irvine, CA 92617
PH: (949)246-1156
Fax: (949)679-3001
Sherman, Ronald A., MD, Chmn. of the Bd.

Cajal Club [16012]
c/o Charles E. Ribak, Secretary/Treasurer
Dept. of Anatomy & Neurobiology
School of Medicine
University Of California
Irvine, CA 92697-1275
Walsh, Christopher, President

Cargo of Dreams [12634]
17320 Red Hill Ave., Ste. 320
Irvine, CA 92614
PH: (949)340-6825
van der Colff, Marius, Exec. Dir., Founder

Comics Professional Retailers Organization [758]
PO Box 16804
Irvine, CA 92623-6804

Geographic Index

PH: (714)446-8871
Toll free: 866-457-2582
Field, Joe, Director

Crime Survivors [11504]
PO Box 54552
Irvine, CA 92619-4552
PH: (949)872-7895
Toll free: 844-853-4673
Fax: (775)245-4798
Wenskunas, Patricia, CEO, Founder

Disneyana Fan Club [24003]
PO Box 19212
Irvine, CA 92623-9212
PH: (714)731-4705
Rolls, Linda, President

Earthrise [6655]
2151 Michelson Dr., Ste. 258
Irvine, CA 92612
PH: (949)623-0980
Toll free: 800-949-7473
Fax: (949)623-0990

Free Wheelchair Mission [11598]
15279 Alton Pky., Ste. 300
Irvine, CA 92618
PH: (949)273-8470
Toll free: 800-733-0858
Fax: (949)453-0085
Schoendorfer, Don, PhD, Founder,
President

**Full Gospel Business Men's Fellow-
ship International [19982]**
18101 Von Karman Ave., No. 330
Irvine, CA 92612
PH: (949)529-4688
Shakarian, Richard, President

Guard a Heart [15216]
5405 Alton Pkwy., Ste. A-213
Irvine, CA 92604
Hancock, Ms. Rose, Chairman

**International Society for Children
with Cancer [13994]**
17155 Gillette Ave., Unit B
Irvine, CA 92614
PH: (949)679-9911
Fax: (949)679-3399
Tafazzoli, Mrs. Negin, President,
Director

**International Society for Productivity
Enhancement [6566]**
c/o CERA Institute
PO Box 60650
Irvine, CA 92602
PH: (714)396-9424
Curran, Prof. Ricky, Mem.

**Iranian American Society of
Engineers and Architects [6567]**
15333 Culver Dr., Ste. 340-402
Irvine, CA 92604
Yoosefi, Nooshin, President

Joint Forces Initiative [22062]
4 Montage
Irvine, CA 92614
PH: (818)371-1283
Zinone, Greg, Founder, President

The Latino Coalition [9663]
PO Box 55086
Irvine, CA 92619
Toll free: 855-852-1995
Fax: (866)496-1944
Barreto, Hector V., Chairman

Motorcycle Industry Council [22229]
2 Jenner St., Ste. 150
Irvine, CA 92618-3806
PH: (949)727-4211
Fax: (949)727-3313

Motorcycle Safety Foundation [3000]
2 Jenner St., Ste. 150
Irvine, CA 92618
Toll free: 866-441-9227
Buche, Tim, President, CEO

**Multi-Level Marketing International
Association [2293]**
119 Stanford Ct.
Irvine, CA 92612
PH: (949)257-0931
Wood, Doris, Chairperson, Founder

**National Association of Municipal
Advisors [1283]**
19900 MacArthur Blvd., Ste. 100
Irvine, CA 92612
PH: (703)395-4896
Toll free: 844-770-NAMA
Heaton, Terri, CIPMA, President

Nuru International [10729]
5405 Alton Pky., Ste. A-474
Irvine, CA 92604
PH: (949)667-0796
Harriman, Jake, CEO, Founder

Project Tomorrow [7813]
15707 Rockfield Blvd., Ste. 250
Irvine, CA 92618
PH: (949)609-4660
Fax: (949)609-4665
Evans, Julie, CEO

**Society for the Scientific Study of
Reading [8492]**
c/o Carol M. Connor, Treasurer
16 Coltrane Ct.
Irvine, CA 92617
Compton, Don, Officer

Supplier Excellence Alliance [1772]
6789 Quail Hill Pky., No. 733
Irvine, CA 92603
PH: (949)476-1144
Wiebe, Mickey, Exec. Dir.

Talk About Curing Autism [13780]
2222 Martin St., Ste. 140
Irvine, CA 92612
PH: (949)640-4401
Toll free: 855-726-7810
Fax: (949)640-4424
Ackerman, Glenn W., President,
Founder

UnitedAg [3532]
54 Corporate Pk.
Irvine, CA 92606-5105
PH: (949)975-1424
Toll free: 800-223-4590
Fax: (949)975-1573
DeMore, Mike, Managing Dir.

Western Growers Association [4260]
15525 Sand Canyon
Irvine, CA 92618-3114
PH: (949)863-1000
Toll free: 800-333-4942.
Fax: (949)863-9028
Simonds, Paul, Mgr., Comm.

Institute of Mentalphysics [20541]
59700 29 Palms Hwy.
Joshua Tree, CA 92252-4134
PH: (760)365-8371
Fax: (760)228-0626

**United Farm Workers of America
[23379]**
29700 Woodford-Tehachapi Rd.
Keene, CA 93531
PH: (661)823-6151
Rodriguez, Arturo S., President

**Federation of Petanque U.S.A.
[23058]**
PO Box 180
Kenwood, CA 95452
Porto, Ed, President

Haiti Communitere [13056]
PO Box 966
Kings Beach, CA 96143
PH: (530)563-8076
Bloch, Sam, Exec. Dir., Founder

Inventors Assistance League [6770]
PO Box 55
La Canada, CA 91011
PH: (818)246-6542
Toll free: 877-433-2246
Fax: (818)246-6546
Ruscetta, Rusty, CEO

Aid Africa [12525]
3916 Pennsylvania Ave.
La Crescenta, CA 91214
PH: (818)249-2398
Keller, Peter, Exec. Dir.

Opel Motorsports Club [21469]
c/o Dick Counsil, Treasurer
3824 Franklin St.
La Crescenta, CA 91214
Counsil, Dick, Treasurer

**National American Pit Bull Terrier
Association [21918]**
c/o Sherri Flosi, President
PO Box 296
La Grange, CA 95329
PH: (209)404-3077
Flosi, Sherri, President

**Association of Online Insurance
Agents [1839]**
501 S Idaho St., Ste. 210
La Habra, CA 90631
Toll free: 888-223-4773

Hope for a Cure Guild [14534]
PO Box 365
La Habra, CA 90633-0365
Toll free: 800-672-4673
Fax: (562)690-6091
Michaud, Lucy, President

**MIDI Manufacturers Association
[2226]**
PO Box 3173
La Habra, CA 90632-3173
PH: (714)736-9774
Billias, Athan, Contact

**Model A Ford Club of America
[21435]**
250 S Cypress St.
La Habra, CA 90631-5515
PH: (562)697-2712
Fax: (562)690-7452
Foulk, Dan, President

**American Historical Association -
Conference on Asian History
[9020]**
H&SS 4062
University of California San Diego
9500 Gilman Dr.
La Jolla, CA 92093
PH: (858)534-3401
Tanaka, Stefan, Chairman

**American Society for Genomic
Medicine [14876]**
1010 Pearl St.
La Jolla, CA 92038-2946

**Comision Interamericana del Atún
Tropical [1298]**
8901 La Jolla Shores Dr.
La Jolla, CA 92037-1509
PH: (858)546-7100
Fax: (858)546-7133
Bayliff, William H., Mem.

**Cooperative Association for Internet
Data Analysis [6765]**
9500 Gilman Dr.
La Jolla, CA 92093

PH: (858)534-5000
Huffaker, Bradley, Tech. Mgr.

International Golf Associates [22884]
1040 Genter St., No. 103
La Jolla, CA 92037-5550
PH: (858)546-4737
Fax: (619)615-2083
Austin, Scott, Contact

**International Society for
Computational Biology [1791]**
9500 Gilman Dr.
MC 0505
La Jolla, CA 92093-0505
PH: (858)534-0852
(858)822-0852
Fax: (619)374-2894
Rost, Burkhard, PhD, President

**International Surfing Association
[23276]**
5580 La Jolla Blvd., No. 145
La Jolla, CA 92037-7651
PH: (858)551-8580
Fax: (858)551-8563
Aguerre, Fernando, President

Peripheral Nerve Society [15667]
c/o Amber Millen, Executive Director
Basic Science Bldg., Rm. 5006
9500 Gilman Dr.
Department of Anesthesiology, MC
0629
University of California, San Diego
La Jolla, CA 92093-0629
PH: (858)534-3865
Fax: (858)534-1445

**Society for Marine Mammalogy
[4474]**
c/o Jay Barlow, President
8901 La Jolla Shores Dr.
La Jolla, CA 92037-1508
PH: (858)546-7178
Lunn, Nick, Chairman

**Border Patrol Supervisors' Associa-
tion [5459]**
3755 Avocado Blvd., No. 404
La Mesa, CA 91941
Haynes, Richard, President

**Empress Chinchilla Breeders
Cooperative [3600]**
5525 Heidi St.
La Mesa, CA 91942-2411
PH: (619)825-6204
Adcock, Mr. Gene, Director

Greyhound Adoption Center [10630]
PO Box 2433
La Mesa, CA 91943-2433
Toll free: 877-478-8364
Rigg, Darren, Founder, President

**Great Commission Research
Network [20024]**
13800 Biola Ave.
La Mirada, CA 90639
Cho, Rev. James, 1st VP

**Society of Professors in Christian
Education [7615]**
c/o Freddy Cardoza, Director
Biola University
Feinberg Ste. 119
13800 Biola Ave.
La Mirada, CA 90639
PH: (310)779-5224
(562)944-0351
Fax: (949)748-7006
Cardoza, Dr. Freddy, Director

**Performance Warehouse Association
[3440]**
79405 Highway 111, Ste. 9
La Quinta, CA 92253

PH: (760)346-5647
Ziozios, Dave, Treasurer

Professional Golf Teachers Associa-
tion of America [22891]
PO Box 912
La Quinta, CA 92247
PH: (760)777-1925
Toll free: 888-90-PGTAA
Fax: (760)406-9898
Lotz, Dr. Barry, President

Rousseau Association [9094]
c/o Jason Neidleman, Secretary-
Treasurer
University of La Verne
114 Founders Hall
1950 3rd St.
La Verne, CA 91750
Neidleman, Jason, Secretary,
Treasurer

Croatian American Bar Association
[5001]
6 Papette Cir.
Ladera Ranch, CA 92694-1090
PH: (949)274-5360
Valentina, Elizabeth, VP

International Board for Regression
Therapy [17448]
3746 Mount Diablo Blvd., Ste. 200
Lafayette, CA 94549
PH: (925)283-3941
Cunningham, Janet, PhD, President

Trust in Education [11453]
985 Moraga Rd., Ste. 207
Lafayette, CA 94549
PH: (925)299-2010
MacKenzie, Budd E., Founder

Western Cover Society [22380]
430 Ponderosa Ct.
Lafayette, CA 94549
Perlman, Michael, President

American Pathology Foundation
[16573]
1540 S Coast Hwy., No. 204
Laguna Beach, CA 92651
Toll free: 877-993-9935
Fax: (949)376-3456

ASSE International Student
Exchange Programs [8058]
228 N Coast Hwy.
Laguna Beach, CA 92651
PH: (949)494-4100
Toll free: 800-333-3802
Fax: (949)494-3579
Hayes, Mr. Pete, Exec. Dir.

Bowls USA [22702]
c/o Heather Stewart, President
Laguna Beach LBC
455 Cliff Dr.
Laguna Beach, CA 92651
Stewart, Heather, President

Heart of Sailing [22619]
PO Box 4776
Laguna Beach, CA 92652
PH: (949)236-7245
Fax: (866)609-0807
Saidah, George, Founder

The International Society for
Language Studies, Inc. [9654]
1968 S Coast Hwy., No. 142
Laguna Beach, CA 92651-3681
Miller, Paul Chamness, President

National Conference of Bankruptcy
Judges [5393]
c/o Jeanne Sleeper, Executive Director
954 La Mirada St.

Laguna Beach, CA 92651-3751
PH: (949)497-3673
Fax: (949)497-2523
Diehl, Mary Grace, President

Neuro-Developmental Treatment As-
sociation [16029]
1540 S Coast Hwy., Ste. 204
Laguna Beach, CA 92651
Toll free: 800-869-9295
Fax: (949)376-3456
Gutierrez, Teresa, President

Pacific Marine Mammal Center
[4863]
20612 Laguna Canyon Rd.
Laguna Beach, CA 92651
PH: (949)494-3050
Kinney, John, President

Sidelines National High-Risk
Pregnancy Support Network
[16303]
PO Box 1808
Laguna Beach, CA 92652
Toll free: 888-447-4754
Hurley, Candace, Exec. Dir.,
Founder

World Heritage [8092]
277 Lower Cliff Dr.
Laguna Beach, CA 92651
PH: (949)342-1777
Toll free: 800-888-9040
Fax: (949)419-1190

International Orphan Care [11050]
23201 Mill Creek Dr., Ste. 130
Laguna Hills, CA 92653-1692
PH: (949)939-1712
Whipple, Michael, Chmn. of the Bd.

Kids Konnected [11246]
26071 Merit Cir., Ste. 103
Laguna Hills, CA 92653
PH: (949)582-5443
DeFries, Michael, MBA, Chmn. of
the Bd.

Bicuspid Aortic Foundation [15214]
30100 Town Center Dr., Ste. O-299
Laguna Niguel, CA 92677
PH: (949)371-9223
Velebir, Ms. Arlys K., President

Iso and Bizzarrini Owners Club
[21408]
24042 Hillhurst Dr.
Laguna Niguel, CA 92677
Meluzio, Don, President

Serving Our World [11150]
30025 Alicia Pky., No. 179
Laguna Niguel, CA 92677
Thomforde, Michael, Founder,
President

TAALK: Talk About Abuse to Liberate
Kids [11279]
30251 Golden Lantern, E283
Laguna Niguel, CA 92677-5993
PH: (949)495-4553
Toll free: 888-808-6558
Cranley, Diane, President, Chmn. of
the Bd.

Ocean Conservation Research
[3920]
PO Box 559
Lagunitas, CA 94938-0559
PH: (415)488-0553
Stocker, Michael, Exec. Dir.

American Hatpin Society [21611]
c/o Jodi Lenocker, Vice President
PO Box 2672
Lake Arrowhead, CA 92352
Lenocker, Jodi, VP

National Historic Route 66 Federa-
tion [9419]
374 Klamath Dr.
Lake Arrowhead, CA 92352-1848
PH: (909)336-6131
Fax: (909)336-1039
Knudson, David, Founder

Center for Bio-Ethical Reform
[19056]
PO Box 219
Lake Forest, CA 92609
PH: (949)206-0600
Cunningham, Gregg, Esq., Exec. Dir.

Global Vaccine Awareness League
[14936]
25422 Trabuco Rd., Ste. 105-230
Lake Forest, CA 92630-2797
Helms-Gaddie, Ms. Michelle,
Founder

Hailey's Wish [14581]
25422 Trabuco Rd., Ste. 105-436
Lake Forest, CA 92630
PH: (949)878-2122
Cavlovic, Mike, Contact

National Labrador Retriever Club
[21923]
c/o Sandra Underhill, Secretary
12515 Woodside Ave., No. 1905
Lakeside, CA 92040
Willumsen, Sue, President

American Society of Questioned
Document Examiners [5239]
PO Box 6140
Lakewood, CA 90714
Nobles, Karen, Treasurer

Five P Minus Society [17340]
PO Box 268
Lakewood, CA 90714-0268
PH: (562)804-4506
Toll free: 888-970-0777
Fax: (562)920-5240
Castillo, Ms. Laura, Exec. Dir.

National Hydrocephalus Foundation
[14603]
12413 Centralia Rd.
Lakewood, CA 90715-1653
PH: (562)924-6666
Toll free: 888-857-3434
Fields, Debbi, Exec. Dir.

Academy of Forensic and Industrial
Chiropractic Consultants [14248]
1629 W Avenue J, Ste. 101
Lancaster, CA 93534-2850
PH: (661)942-2273
Fax: (661)274-1590
Gelfound, Craig, DC, President

Rat Terrier Club of America [21952]
47044 5th St. W
Lancaster, CA 93534-7501
PH: (661)945-5663

Society of Experimental Test Pilots
[5873]
44814 North Elm Ave.
Lancaster, CA 93534
PH: (661)942-9574
Fax: (661)940-0398
Morey, Timothy, President

Society of Flight Test Engineers
[5874]
44814 N Elm Ave.
Lancaster, CA 93534
PH: (817)320-1587
Fax: (817)320-1587
Scheidler, Peter, President

Conservation and Preservation
Charities of America [3840]
1100 Larkspur Landing Cir., Ste. 340
Larkspur, CA 94939

PH: (415)925-2654
Harte, Ms. Carri, Contact

Independent Charities of America
[1471]
1100 Larkspur Landing Cir., Ste. 340
Larkspur, CA 94939-1880
PH: (415)925-2600
Mead, Nancy Caldwell, President

Local Independent Charities of
America [12486]
1100 Larkspur Landing, Ste. 340
Larkspur, CA 94939
PH: (415)925-2663
Toll free: 800-876-0413
Fax: (415)925-2650
McPartland, Don, President

Military Family and Veterans Service
Organizations of America [21027]
1100 Larkspur Landing, Ste. 340
Larkspur, CA 94939
PH: (415)925-2673
Fax: (415)925-2650
Burke, Kathleen, President

Pathways to Peace [12439]
PO Box 1507
Larkspur, CA 94977
PH: (415)461-0500
Fax: (415)925-0330
Mattison, Avon, President, Founder

Project Coyote [4872]
PO Box 5007
Larkspur, CA 94977
PH: (415)945-3232
Fox, Camilla H., Founder, Exec. Dir.

Sports Charities U.S.A. [23256]
1100 Larkspur Landing Cir., Ste. 340
Larkspur, CA 94939
Fax: (415)925-2669

Wild Animals Worldwide [4901]
1100 Larkspur Landing Cir., Ste. 340
Larkspur, CA 94939
PH: (415)925-2675
Toll free: 877-999-8322

Women, Children and Family
Service Charities of America
[11864]
1100 Larkspur Landing Cir., Ste. 340
Larkspur, CA 94939
PH: (415)925-2662
Curry, Zanna, Contact

NextStep Fitness [17096]
4447 Redondo Beach Blvd.
Lawndale, CA 90260
PH: (310)546-5666
Fax: (310)542-8868
Kouri, Janne, Founder, Chmn. of the
Bd.

Price-Pottenger Nutrition Foundation
[16237]
7890 Broadway
Lemon Grove, CA 91945
PH: (619)462-7600
Toll free: 800-366-3748
Fax: (619)433-3136
Grinzi, Joan, RN, Exec. Dir.

Academy of Veterinary Homeopathy
[17587]
PO Box 232282
Leucadia, CA 92023-2282
Toll free: 866-652-1590
Fax: (866)652-1590
Brienen, Lisa, President

Air Brake Association, Inc. [2828]
PO Box 566
Lincoln, CA 95648-0566
PH: (916)434-8727
Fax: (916)645-1902

American Jeepster Club [21320]
PO Box 653
Lincoln, CA 95648
PH: (916)645-8761
Serr, Jim, President

Citizens for a Better America
[17885]
PO Box 1949
Littlerock, CA 93543-5949
PH: (818)574-8911
Colaco, Robert, Chairman, Founder

Greyhound Club of America [21891]
c/o Helen Hamilton
2443 Chardonnay Way
Livermore, CA 94550-6160
Edgerton, Dani, President

International Society on General
Relativity and Gravitation [6703]
PO Box 3388
Livermore, CA 94551-3388
PH: (805)893-2742
(925)371-8979
Horowitz, Prof. Gary, President

National Institute of Steel Detailing
[2362]
2600 Kitty Hawk Rd., Ste. 117
Livermore, CA 94551
PH: (925)294-9626
Fax: (925)294-9621
Hicks, Joel, President

Shakespeare Theatre Association
[10272]
c/o Lisa Tromovitch, President
PO Box 2616
Livermore, CA 94551-2616
Watkins, Jeff, Director

United States Rottweiler Club
[21985]
c/o Lucy Ang
Bay Area Rottweiler Klub
14724 W Sunset
Livingston, CA 95334-9627
PH: (608)825-9509
(209)394-8000
Wilson, Chuck, VP

Gaylord Family Organization [20869]
1910 S Church St.
Lodi, CA 95240
PH: (209)366-2773
Wood, Barry C., Contact

Adventist Health International
[15432]
11060 Anderson St.
Loma Linda, CA 92350
PH: (909)558-4540
Fax: (909)558-0242
Hart, Richard H., MD, President

Alumni Association, School of
Medicine of Loma Linda University
[7492]
11245 Anderson St., Ste. 200
Loma Linda, CA 92354
PH: (909)558-4633
Fax: (909)558-4638
Reeves, Mark, President

American Institute of Oral Biology
[14411]
PO Box 1338
Loma Linda, CA 92354
PH: (909)558-4671
Fax: (909)558-0285
Barrientos, June J., Exec. Sec.

National Association of Seventh-day
Adventist Dentists [14458]
PO Box 101
Loma Linda, CA 92354
PH: (909)558-8187
Fax: (909)558-0209
Libby, Landon, DDS, President

International Friesian Show Horse
Association [4365]
PO Box 2839
Lompoc, CA 93438
PH: (805)448-3027
Nathanson, Nancy, Exec. Dir.

Return to Freedom [10689]
PO Box 926
Lompoc, CA 93438
PH: (805)737-9246
Fax: (805)800-0868
DeMayo, Neda, Founder, President

Wildlife in Need [4916]
7651 Santos Rd.
Lompoc, CA 93436
PH: (805)737-3700
Fax: (805)737-3705

Academy of Managed Care Provid-
ers [15092]
1945 Palo Verde Ave., Ste. 202
Long Beach, CA 90815-3445
PH: (562)682-3559
Toll free: 800-297-2627
Fax: (562)799-3355
Russell, John K., PhD, President

American Microscopical Society
[6865]
Dept. of Biological Sciences
CSU, Long Beach
1250 Bellflower Blvd.
Long Beach, CA 90840
PH: (562)985-5378
Fax: (562)985-8878
Pilger, John, Treasurer

American Society for Mohs Surgery
[16336]
6475 E Pacific Coast Hwy.
Long Beach, CA 90803-4201
PH: (714)379-6262
Toll free: 800-616-2767
Fax: (714)379-6272
Rodgers, Novella M., MS, Exec. Dir.

Cambodian American Business As-
sociation [678]
1902 E Anaheim St.
Long Beach, CA 90813
PH: (424)226-2289
Kim, Anthony, President

Cambodian Health Professionals
Association of America [14985]
1025 Atlantic Ave.
Long Beach, CA 90813
PH: (562)491-9292
Fax: (562)495-1878
Tan, Song, MD, President

Cocaine Anonymous World Services
[13132]
21720 S Wilmington Ave., Ste. 304
Long Beach, CA 90810-1641
PH: (310)559-5833
Fax: (310)559-2554
Francisco, Ms. Linda, Dir. of Opera-
tions

Colored Pencil Society of America
[8851]
c/o Ruth Arthur, Membership Direc-
tor
PO Box 8638
Long Beach, CA 90808-0638
PH: (562)425-1609
Schmidt, Kay, VP

EndOil [6477]
c/o Gisele Fong, Executive Director
4000 Long Beach Blvd., Ste. 249
Long Beach, CA 90807
Fong, Gisele, PhD, Exec. Dir.

Federation for the American
Staffordshire Terrier [21282]
619 W 35th St.
Long Beach, CA 90806
Shoemaker, Calise A., President

Fellowship of Christian Released
Time Ministries [20079]
5722 Lime Ave.
Long Beach, CA 90805
PH: (562)428-7733
Toll free: 800-360-7943
Atkinson, John, President

Heinlein Society [9054]
3553 Atlantic Ave., No. 341
Long Beach, CA 90807-5606
Sheffield, Mike, Officer

Incest Survivors Anonymous [12925]
PO Box 17245
Long Beach, CA 90807
PH: (562)428-5599

Innes Clan Society [20885]
c/o Carole A. Innes, Membership
129 Ravenna Dr.
Long Beach, CA 90803
Innes, Diane D., Officer

International Coalition of Art Deco
Societies [8864]
c/o John Thomas, Treasurer
280 Molino Ave., No. 101
Long Beach, CA 90803
Thomas, John, Treasurer

Military Families Speak Out [19237]
1716 Clark Ave.
Long Beach, CA 90815
PH: (562)597-3980
Lessin, Nancy, Founder

Society of Allied Weight Engineers
[7236]
5734 E Lucia Walk
Long Beach, CA 90803-4015
PH: (562)596-2873
Fax: (562)596-2874
Fox, Ronald L., Exec. Dir.

Society for History Education [7990]
California State University, Long
Beach
1250 Bellflower Blvd.
Long Beach, CA 90840-0101
PH: (562)985-2573
Keirn, Tim, President

The Society for Human Performance
in Extreme Environments [6048]
790 E Willow St.
Long Beach, CA 90806

Western Association of Map Libraries [9734]
c/o Greg Armento
California State University
1250 Bellflower Blvd.
Long Beach, CA 90840-1901
Durante, Kim, President

Classic Jaguar Association [21358]
Reed Van Rozeboom, 11321 Loch
Lomond Rd., Rossmoor
11321 Loch Lomond Rd.
Los Alamitos, CA 90720
Becker, Don, President

National Fastener Distributors As-
sociation [1572]
10842 Noel St., No. 107
Los Alamitos, CA 90720
PH: (714)484-7858
Toll free: 877-487-6332
Fax: (562)684-0695

Signing Exact English Center for the
Advancement of Deaf Children
[15209]
PO Box 1181
Los Alamitos, CA 90720-1181
PH: (562)430-1467
Fax: (562)795-6614

Americare Neurosurgery
International [16061]
PO Box 4041
Los Altos, CA 94024
PH: (650)387-8647
Heit, Gary, PhD, Contact

HealthCare Volunteer [15018]
595 Loyola Dr.
Los Altos, CA 94024-5944
Patel, Neilesh, Founder

International Society for Quality
Electronic Design [6371]
PO Box 607
Los Altos, CA 94023-0607
PH: (408)573-0100
Fax: (408)573-0200
Iranmanesh, Dr. Ali A., Chairman,
Founder

National Association for Professional
Gerontologists [14896]
PO Box 1209
Los Altos, CA 94023
PH: (650)947-9132
Schafer, Donna, PhD, Exec. Dir.

Nepal and Tibet Philatelic Study
Circle [22351]
c/o Roger Skinner, Representative
1020 Covington Rd.
Los Altos, CA 94024-5003
Hepper, Colin, Secretary, Treasurer,
President

Saint Andrew's Ukrainian Orthodox
Society [19205]
c/o Vitali Vizir
1023 Yorkshire Dr.
Los Altos, CA 94024
PH: (440)582-1051
Mahlay, Rev. Ihor, President

US-China Green Energy Council
[6516]
1964 Deodara Dr.
Los Altos, CA 94024-7054
Wu, Robert S., Chairman, CEO

American Working Collie Association
[21829]
c/o Judy Cummings, Secretary
26695 Snell Ln.
Los Altos Hills, CA 94022
Cummings, Judy, Secretary

ABLE: Association for Better Living
and Education International
[11301]
7065 Hollywood Blvd.
Los Angeles, CA 90028
PH: (323)960-3530

Abolish Slavery Coalition [17860]
8620 W 3rd St.
Los Angeles, CA 90048
Toll free: 800-821-2009
Cohen, Aaron, Founder, President

Academy of Operative Dentistry
[14367]
PO Box 25637
Los Angeles, CA 90025
PH: (310)794-4387
Fax: (310)825-2536
Stevenson, Richard, Secretary

ACEing Autism [13736]
9064 Nemo St.
Los Angeles, CA 90069
PH: (617)901-7153
Spurling, Richard, Founder,
President

Aetherius Society [20604]
6202 Afton Pl.
Los Angeles, CA 90028-8205

PH: (323)465-9652
Toll free: 800-800-1354
Keneipp, Brian, Exec. Sec.

Affordable Shopping Destination [3190]
6255 W Sunset Blvd., 19th Fl.
Los Angeles, CA 90028
PH: (323)817-2200
Toll free: 800-421-4511
Fax: (310)481-1900
Candella, Camille, Dir. of Mktg.

African Kids In Need [10838]
Box 140
137 N Larchmont Blvd.
Los Angeles, CA 90020
Miller, Paul, Founder, Exec. Dir.

AIDS Healthcare Foundation [13523]
6255 W Sunset Blvd., Ste. 2100
Los Angeles, CA 90028
PH: (323)860-5200
(323)860-0173
Toll free: 877-274-2548
Fax: (323)962-8513
Weinstein, Michael, President

AIDS Research Alliance [13524]
1400 S Grand Ave., Ste. 701
Los Angeles, CA 90015-3011
PH: (310)358-2423
(310)358-2429
Fax: (310)358-2431
Hardy, David, MD, Chmn. of the Bd.

All Japan Ju-Jitsu International Federation [22979]
11677 San Vicente Blvd., Ste. 202
Los Angeles, CA 90049
Kunin, Gr. Mast. Alexey, Advisor

Alpha Mu Gamma Honor Society [23797]
855 N Vermont Ave.
Los Angeles, CA 90029
PH: (323)644-9752
Fax: (323)644-9752
Gomez-Acuña, Dr. Beatriz, President

American Amateur Karate Federation [22980]
1801 Century Park, 24th Fl.
Los Angeles, CA 90067
Toll free: 888-939-8882
Fax: (888)939-8555
Tong, Alex, President

American Association of Anger Management Providers [15756]
2300 Westridge Rd.
Los Angeles, CA 90049
PH: (310)476-0908
Fax: (310)476-6789
Anderson, George, Exec. Dir.

American Association of Endocrine Surgeons [14699]
11300 W Olympic Blvd., Ste. 600
Los Angeles, CA 90064
PH: (310)986-6452
Fax: (310)437-0585
Kent, Stacy, Exec. Dir.

American Association of Teachers of Slavic and East European Languages [8174]
c/o Elizabeth Durst, PhD, Executive Director
University of Southern California
3501 Trousdale Pky., THH 255L
Los Angeles, CA 90089
PH: (213)740-2734
Fax: (213)740-8550
Durst, Elizabeth, Ph.D., Exec. Dir.

American-Chinese CEO Society [3296]
World Trade Ctr., Ste. 425, 350 S Figueroa St.

350 S Figueroa St.
Los Angeles, CA 90071
Sun, Robert, President

American Film Institute [9294]
2021 N Western Ave.
Los Angeles, CA 90027-1657
PH: (323)856-7600
Toll free: 800-774-4234
Fax: (323)467-4578
Gazzale, Bob, CEO, President

American Foundation for Equal Rights [18371]
6565 Sunset Blvd., Ste. 400
Los Angeles, CA 90028
Cohen, Bruce, President

American Freedom Alliance [19023]
11500 W Olympic Blvd., Ste. 400
Los Angeles, CA 90064
PH: (310)444-3085
Fax: (310)444-3086
Davis, Avi, Exec. Dir.

American Head and Neck Society [16533]
11300 W Olympic Blvd., Ste. 600
Los Angeles, CA 90064
PH: (310)437-0559
Fax: (310)437-0585
Day, Terry, Contact

American International Chamber of Commerce [23553]
355 S Grand Ave., Ste. 2450
Los Angeles, CA 90071-1504
PH: (213)255-2066
Fax: (213)255-2077
Sawerthal, Inge, President

American Photographic Artists [2572]
5042 Wilshire Blvd., No. 321
Los Angeles, CA 90036
Toll free: 888-272-6264
White, Lee, VP

American Radium Society [16334]
11300 W Olympic Blvd., Ste. 600
Los Angeles, CA 90064
PH: (310)437-0581
Fax: (310)437-0585
Munoz, Diana, Admin. Asst.

American Russian Theatrical Alliance [10238]
1409 Midvale Ave., Ste. 105
Los Angeles, CA 90024
PH: (310)312-4989
Fax: (310)312-4989

American Sailing Association [22595]
5301 Beethoven St., Ste. No. 265
Los Angeles, CA 90066-7052
PH: (310)822-7171
Fax: (310)822-4741

American Society of Cinematographers [1186]
1782 N Orange Dr.
Los Angeles, CA 90078
PH: (323)969-4333
Toll free: 800-448-0145
Peterson, Lowell, VP

Anaerobe Society of the Americas [6074]
PO Box 452058
Los Angeles, CA 90045
PH: (310)216-9265
Fax: (310)216-9274
Goldman, Ronald, PhD, Exec. Dir.

Animal Defenders International U.S.A. [10573]
6100 Wilshire Blvd., No. 1150
Los Angeles, CA 90048

PH: (323)935-2234
Creamer, Jan, President, Founder, CEO

Animal Equality [10574]
8581 Santa Monica Blvd., Ste. 350
Los Angeles, CA 90069
PH: (424)400-2860
Moreno, Javier, Founder

Armenian Bar Association [4992]
c/o Lisa Boyadjian, Administrative Assistant
PO Box 29111
Los Angeles, CA 90029
PH: (626)584-0043
(818)905-6484
Boyadjian, Jacklin, Exec. Dir.

Armenian Bone Marrow Donor Registry [13844]
c/o Frieda Jordan, President
3111 Los Feliz Ave. No. 206
Los Angeles, CA 90039
PH: (323)663-3609
Fax: (323)662-3648
Kocharian, Bella, Chairperson

Artists for a New South Africa [18092]
2119 Kress St.
Los Angeles, CA 90064-4256

Artists United for Social Justice [19125]
5042 Wilshire Blvd., No.131
Los Angeles, CA 90036
Davis, Michael Cory, Founder

Asian American Advertising Federation [87]
6230 Wilshire Blvd., No. 1216
Los Angeles, CA 90048
Chang, Edward, President

Asian Pacific Americans for Progress [17819]
251 S Main St.
Los Angeles, CA 90012

Asians for Miracle Marrow Matches [17507]
244 S San Pedro St., No. 503
Los Angeles, CA 90012
Toll free: 888-236-4673
Fax: (213)625-2802
Choi, Susan, Exec. Dir.

Association for Academic Surgery [17377]
11300 W Olympic Blvd., Ste. 600
Los Angeles, CA 90064
PH: (310)437-1606
Fax: (310)437-0585
Kasendorf, Christina, Exec. Dir.

Association of Celebrity Personal Assistants [64]
907 Westwood Blvd., No. 363
Los Angeles, CA 90024-2905
McFarland, Kimberly, President

Association for Computing Machinery - Special Interest Group on Software Engineering [6271]
c/o Nenad Medvidovic, Chairperson
University of Southern California
941 Bloom Walk
Los Angeles, CA 90089-0134
PH: (213)740-5579
Fax: (213)740-4927
Medvidovic, Nenad, Chairman

Association of Latino Professionals in Finance and Accounting [15]
801 S Grand Ave., Ste. 650
Los Angeles, CA 90017
PH: (213)243-0004
Fax: (213)243-0006
Espinoza, Manny, Contact

Association of Sites Advocating Child Protection [10859]
5042 Wilshire Blvd., No. 540
Los Angeles, CA 90036-4305
PH: (323)908-7864
Henning, Tim, Exec. Dir.

Association of Talent Agents [162]
9255 Sunset Blvd., Ste. 930
Los Angeles, CA 90069
PH: (310)274-0628
Fax: (310)274-5063
Stuart, Karen, Exec. Dir.

Austrian Trade Commissions in the United States [23563]
11601 Wilshire Blvd., Ste. 2420
Los Angeles, CA 90025
PH: (310)477-9988
Fax: (310)477-1643
Thaler, Rudolf, Commissioner

Baltic American Freedom League [17822]
PO Box 65056
Los Angeles, CA 90065-0056
PH: (323)255-4215
Leitis, Imants, Director, Editor

Betty's Foundation for the Elimination of Alzheimer's Disease [13672]
PO Box 451477
Los Angeles, CA 90045
Woesner, Clint, Founder

Bilingual Foundation of the Arts [10243]
201 N Los Angeles St., Ste. 12
Los Angeles, CA 90012
PH: (213)437-0500
Jasso, Roy, Chmn. of the Exec. Committee

Black AIDS Institute [13533]
1833 W 8th St., No. 200
Los Angeles, CA 90057-4920
PH: (213)353-3610
Fax: (213)989-0181
Wilson, Phill, President, CEO

Boarding for Breast Cancer Foundation [13906]
1650 Mateo St.
Los Angeles, CA 90021
PH: (323)467-2663
Hudson, Lisa, Founder

Break the Cycle [11697]
PO Box 811334
Los Angeles, CA 90081
PH: (310)286-3383
Toll free: 888-988-TEEN
Fax: (310)286-3386
Kuhn, Jennifer, President

BrittiCares International [13912]
PO Box 43504
Los Angeles, CA 90043
PH: (323)393-0778
Fax: (323)292-8528
Henderson, Shirell, Founder

Brotherhood Organization of a New Destiny [19102]
6146 W Pico Blvd.
Los Angeles, CA 90035-0090
PH: (323)782-1980
Rooney, Patrick, Dir. of Dev.

Cancer Control Society [13919]
2043 N Berendo St.
Los Angeles, CA 90027-1906
PH: (323)663-7801
Fax: (323)663-7757
Cousineau, Frank, President

Career Transition For Dancers [11757]
5757 Wilshire Blvd., Ste. 400
Los Angeles, CA 90036

PH: (212)221-7300

Catholic Association of Latino Leaders [19808]
3424 Wilshire Blvd., 4th Fl.
Los Angeles, CA 90010
PH: (213)637-7400
Vela, Diana Richardson, President, CEO

Christian Pilots Association [20402]
PO Box 90452
Los Angeles, CA 90009
PH: (562)208-2912

The Climate Registry [4542]
601 W 5th St., Ste. 220
Los Angeles, CA 90071
Toll free: 866-523-0764
Rosenheim, David, Exec. Dir.

Clutterers Anonymous [12869]
PO Box 91413
Los Angeles, CA 90009-1413
Toll free: 866-402-6685

Coalition to Abolish Slavery and Trafficking [12029]
5042 Wilshire Blvd., No. 586
Los Angeles, CA 90036
PH: (213)365-1906
Toll free: 888-539-2373
Fax: (213)341-4439
Buck, Kay, Exec. Dir.

Coalition of Asian Pacifics in Entertainment [1134]
Los Angeles, CA
Fong, Wenda, Founder

Coalition for Economic Survival [13037]
514 Shatto Pl., Ste. 270
Los Angeles, CA 90020
PH: (213)252-4411
Fax: (213)252-4422
Gross, Larry, Exec. Dir.

College Athletic Business Management Association [23222]
PO Box 24044
PO Box 24044
Los Angeles, CA 90024-0044
PH: (310)825-2343
Fax: (310)267-2334
Vecchione, Bob, Mem.

Command Trust Network [17755]
11301 W Olympic Blvd., Ste. 332
Los Angeles, CA 90064
Goldrich, Sybil Niden, Founder, Exec. Dir.

Compulsive Eaters Anonymous-HOW [11851]
3371 Glendale Blvd., Ste. 104
Los Angeles, CA 90039
PH: (323)660-4333
Fax: (323)660-4334
K., Pamela, President

Concern Foundation [13950]
11111 W Olympic Blvd., Ste. 214
Los Angeles, CA 90064
PH: (310)360-6100
Fax: (310)473-8300
Brown, Jena, Dir. of Dev.

Constitutional Rights Foundation [18035]
601 S Kingsley Dr.
Los Angeles, CA 90005
PH: (213)487-5590
Fax: (213)386-0459
Paskach, Christopher H., Chairman

Consumer Action [18045]
11901 Santa Monica Blvd., PMB 563
Los Angeles, CA 90025

PH: (213)624-4631
Fax: (213)624-0574
Sturdevant, Patricia, President

Council of Chiropractic Physiological Therapeutics and Rehabilitation [14266]
11600 Wilshire Blvd., Ste. 412
Los Angeles, CA 90025
PH: (310)339-0442
Simon, Jerrold, President

Crystal Meth Anonymous [11716]
4470 W Sunset Blvd., Ste. 107
Los Angeles, CA 90027
Toll free: 855-638-4373
C., Bill, Founder

Cult Awareness Network [20046]
3055 Wilshire Blvd., Ste. 900
Los Angeles, CA 90010
Hayes, Steven, Owner

CuresNow [15684]
10100 Santa Monica Blvd., Ste. 1300
Los Angeles, CA 90067
Fisher, Lucy, Founder

D.A.R.E. America [13135]
PO Box 512090
Los Angeles, CA 90051-0090
PH: (310)215-0575
Toll free: 800-223-DARE
Fax: (310)215-0180
Hazelton, Thomas, President

DIGDEEP Water [13320]
3308 Descanso Dr.
Los Angeles, CA 90026
PH: (323)250-3844
McGraw, George, Founder, Exec. Dir.

Dinah Shore Memorial Fan Club [23991]
3552 Federal Ave.
Los Angeles, CA 90066
Daly, Kay, President

Directors Guild of America [1191]
7920 Sunset Blvd.
Los Angeles, CA 90046
PH: (310)289-2000
Toll free: 800-421-4173
Misiano, Vince, VP

Division for Early Childhood of the Council for Exceptional Children [8583]
3415 S Sepulveda Blvd., Ste. 1100
Los Angeles, CA 90034
PH: (310)428-7209
Fax: (855)678-1989
Barton, Erin, President

Carrie Estelle Doheny Foundation [13045]
707 Wilshire Blvd., Ste. 4960
Los Angeles, CA 90017
PH: (213)488-1122
Fax: (213)488-1544
Smith, Robert A., III, President

Joseph Drown Foundation [11726]
1999 Avenue of the Stars, Ste. 2330
Los Angeles, CA 90067
PH: (310)277-4488
Fax: (310)277-4573
Obrow, Norman C., Chairman

Educational Communications [7876]
PO Box 351419
Los Angeles, CA 90035-9119
PH: (310)559-9160
Pearlman, Nancy, Exec. Dir.

El Rescate [12588]
1501 W 8th St., Ste. 100
Los Angeles, CA 90017

PH: (213)387-3284
Fax: (213)387-9189
Sanabria, Salvador, Exec. Dir.

Every Mother is a Working Mother Network [19244]
PO Box 86681
Los Angeles, CA 90086-0681
PH: (323)276-9833

Famous Fone Friends [11229]
9101 Sawyer St.
Los Angeles, CA 90035
Howard, Randye, Director

Federal Court Clerks Association [5117]
c/o John Hermann, Treasurer
312 N Spring St., Rm. 815
Los Angeles, CA 90012-4701
PH: (213)894-5451
Fax: (213)894-3105
Fisher, Nicole Lennon, Secretary

Feral Cat Caretakers' Coalition [3624]
PO Box 491244
Los Angeles, CA 90049
PH: (310)820-4122
Baker, Dona Cosgrove, Founder, President

Film Music Society [9907]
1516 S Bundy Dr., Ste. 305
Los Angeles, CA 90025
PH: (310)820-1909
Fax: (310)820-1301
Newman, David, President

Florence Ballard Fan Club [24036]
PO Box 360502
Los Angeles, CA 90036
White, Alan, President

Gamblers Anonymous [11867]
PO Box 17173
Los Angeles, CA 90017-0173
PH: (626)960-3500
Fax: (626)960-3501

Gay Asian Pacific Support Network [11882]
PO Box 461104
Los Angeles, CA 90046
PH: (213)368-6488
(323)596-7574
Herbas, Ericson, Contact

Gay and Lesbian Association of Retiring Persons [10507]
10940 Wilshire Blvd., Ste. 1600
Los Angeles, CA 90024
PH: (310)722-1807
Fax: (310)477-0707
Thorndal, Mary, Founder

Gen Art [8857]
1617 Cosmo St. Ste., 412
Los Angeles, CA 90028
PH: (319)551-6157
Ingvarsson, Keri, CEO

GLAAD [11887]
5455 Wilshire Blvd., Ste. 1500
Los Angeles, CA 90036
PH: (212)629-3322
Ellis, Sarah Kate, CEO, President

Global Children's Organization [11234]
3580 Wilshire Blvd., Ste. 1800
Los Angeles, CA 90010
PH: (213)368-8385
Jenya, Judith, Founder

Global Inheritance [19272]
1855 Industrial St., Ste. 613
Los Angeles, CA 90021

PH: (213)626-0061
Ritz, Eric, Exec. Dir.

Global Physicians Corps [15462]
PO Box 25118
Los Angeles, CA 90025-0118
Alikakos, Dr. Maria, CEO, Founder

Global Possibilities [7200]
1955 Mandeville Canyon Rd.
Los Angeles, CA 90049-2200
Danson, Casey Coates, Founder, Director

Global Vision for Peace [18791]
5419 Hollywood Blvd., Ste. C208
Los Angeles, CA 90027
Rothman, Heathcliff, Co-Ch., Founder

The Grantsmanship Center [1470]
350 S Bixel St., Ste. 110
Los Angeles, CA 90017
PH: (213)482-9860
Toll free: 800-421-9512
Fax: (213)802-2240
Kiritz, Cathleen E., President

Healthy Child Healthy World [14193]
8383 Wilshire Blvd. Fl., 8
Los Angeles, CA 900211
PH: (424)343-0020
Chang, Gigi Lee, CEO

Herbalife Family Foundation [11030]
800 W Olympic Blvd., Ste. 406
Los Angeles, CA 90015
PH: (213)745-0569
Fax: (213)765-9812
Browning, Robyn M., CFRE, Exec. Dir.

Hero Initiative [9170]
11301 Olympic Blvd., No. 587
Los Angeles, CA 90064
PH: (626)676-6354
McLauchlin, Jim, President

Hispanas Organized for Political Equality [18337]
634 S Spring St., Ste. 920
Los Angeles, CA 90014-3903
PH: (213)622-0606
Fax: (213)622-0007
Torres, Helen Iris, Exec. Dir., CEO

Hispanic Public Relations Association [17948]
PO Box 86760
Los Angeles, CA 90086-0760
Hernandez, Antonio, President

Hollywood Sign Trust [9401]
PO Box 48361
Los Angeles, CA 90048-9998
PH: (213)300-0108
Baumgart, Chris, Chairman

Hollywood Unites For Haiti [11926]
5338 Hillcrest Dr., Ste. 2
Los Angeles, CA 90043
PH: (323)244-2712
Toll free: 866-533-1859
Fax: (323)290-9000
Jean-Louis, Jimmy, Founder, President

Humanity+ [9537]
5042 Wilshire Blvd., Ste. 14334
Los Angeles, CA 90036

Independent Film & Television Alliance [1192]
10850 Wilshire Blvd., 9th Fl.
Los Angeles, CA 90024-4321
PH: (310)446-1000
Fax: (310)446-1600
Prewitt, Jean M., President, CEO

Institute for Individual and World
Peace [12005]
3500 W Adams Blvd.
Los Angeles, CA 90018
PH: (323)328-1905
Roger, John, Founder, President

Interlaw [5109]
1900 Avenue of the Stars, 7th Fl.
Los Angeles, CA 90067
Siebold, Michael, Chmn. of the Bd.

International 3D and Advanced
Imaging Society [6719]
1801 Century Pk. E, Ste. 1040
Los Angeles, CA 90067
PH: (310)203-9733
Chabin, Jim, President

International Autoimmune Arthritis
Movement [17158]
646 S Barrington Ave.
Los Angeles, CA 90049
Toll free: 877-609-4226
Westrich, Tiffany, CEO, Founder

International Black Writers and Art-
ists, Inc. [10379]
PO Box 43576
Los Angeles, CA 90043
PH: (213)964-3721

International Criminal Court Alliance
[5149]
11835 W Olympic Blvd., Ste. 1090
Los Angeles, CA 90064
PH: (310)473-0777
Butler, Sean, Chairperson

International Documentary Associa-
tion [1197]
3470 Wilshire Blvd., Ste. 980
Los Angeles, CA 90010
PH: (213)232-1660
Fax: (213)232-1669
Kilmurry, Simon, Exec. Dir.

International Leptospirosis Society
[15405]
c/o David Haake, President
11301 Wilshire Blvd.
Los Angeles, CA 90073
PH: (310)268-3814
Fax: (310)268-4928
Haake, David, President

International Medical Corps [12684]
12400 Wilshire Blvd., Ste. 1500
Los Angeles, CA 90025
PH: (310)826-7800
Fax: (310)442-6622
Aossey, Nancy A., CEO, President,
Treasurer

International Pediatric Endosurgery
Group [16609]
11300 W Olympic Blvd., Ste. 600
Los Angeles, CA 90064
PH: (310)437-0553
Fax: (310)437-0585
Ponsky, Todd A., MD, Secretary

International Phonetic Association
[8423]
c/o Patricia Keating, President
3125 Campbell Hall
Dept. of Linguistics
University of California, Los Angeles
Los Angeles, CA 90095-1543
PH: (310)794-6316
Fax: (310)206-5743
Keating, Prof. Patricia A., PhD,
President

International Professional Surrogates
Association [17197]
3679 Motor Ave., Ste. 205
Los Angeles, CA 90034

PH: (413)247-4772

International Society of Filipinos in
Finance and Accounting [38]
801 S Grand Ave., Ste. 400
Los Angeles, CA 90017
Toll free: 800-375-2689
Padua, Maria Socorro, Chairperson

International Surgical Sleep Society
[17218]
c/o Mary Ellen Hernandez
Dept. of Otolaryngology - Head &
Neck Surgery
University of Southern California
1540 Alcazar St., Ste. 204-U
Los Angeles, CA 90089
Kezirian, Eric J., MD, President

International Traditional Karate
Federation [22997]
1930 Wilshire Blvd., Ste. 503
Los Angeles, CA 90057-3603
PH: (213)483-8262
Fax: (213)483-4060

International Volunteer Programs
Association [13301]
PO Box 811012
Los Angeles, CA 90081
PH: (646)505-8209
Brown, Genevieve, Exec. Dir.

Internet Corporation for Assigned
Names and Numbers [6321]
12025 Waterfront Dr., Ste. 300
Los Angeles, CA 90094-2536
PH: (310)301-5800
Fax: (310)823-8649
Burns, Duncan, VP

Iranian American Muslim Association
of North America [20498]
3376 Motor Ave.
Los Angeles, CA 90034-3712
PH: (310)202-8181
Fax: (310)202-0878

Jail Guitar Doors USA [12570]
840 N Fairfax Ave.
Los Angeles, CA 90046
Kramer, Wayne, Founder

Japanese American Bar Association
[5017]
PO Box 71961
Los Angeles, CA 90071
Tanaka, Kenneth, President

Howard Jarvis Taxpayers Association [19160]
621 S Westmoreland Ave., Ste. 202
Los Angeles, CA 90005-3903
PH: (213)384-9656
(916)444-9950
Vosburgh, Kris, Exec. Dir.

Jewish Free Loan Association
[20255]
6505 Wilshire Blvd., Ste. 715
Los Angeles, CA 90048
PH: (323)761-8830
Fax: (323)761-8841
Grose, Rachel, Assoc. Dir.

Jews for Judaism [20545]
PO Box 351235
Los Angeles, CA 90035-1235
PH: (310)556-3344
Toll free: 800-477-6631
Fax: (310)556-3304
Kravitz, Rabbi Bentzion, Exec. Dir.

Joseph and Edna Josephson
Institute of Ethics [11802]
9841 Airport Blvd., Ste. 300
Los Angeles, CA 90045
PH: (310)846-4800
Toll free: 800-711-2670
Fax: (310)846-4858
Rosenberg, David, Bd. Member

Just Detention International [11534]
3325 Wilshire Blvd., Ste. 340
Los Angeles, CA 90010
PH: (213)384-1400
Fax: (213)384-1411
Davison, Dawn M., Treasurer

W.M. Keck Foundation [15650]
550 S Hope St., Ste. 2500
Los Angeles, CA 90071
PH: (213)680-3833
Day, Robert A., Chairman

Kjaerulf Family Association [20892]
c/o Charles Taylor Kierulff
358 S Bentley Ave.
Los Angeles, CA 90049-3219
Kierulff, Charles Taylor, Contact

Organization of American Kodaly
Educators [8372]
10801 National Blvd., Ste. 590
Los Angeles, CA 90064
PH: (310)441-3555
Fax: (310)441-3577
Epstein, Mary, President

Kollaboration [13456]
1933 S Broadway, Ste. 745
Los Angeles, CA 90007
Chang, Christine Minji, Exec. Dir.

Konbit Mizik [13457]
2658 Griffith Park Blvd., Ste. 276
Los Angeles, CA 90039
PH: (917)450-2413
Evans, Ian, Founder

Korean American Coalition [18603]
3727 W 6th St., Ste. 305
Los Angeles, CA 90020
PH: (213)365-5999
Fax: (213)380-7990

Korean Churches for Community
Development [11394]
3550 Wilshire Blvd., Ste. 736
Los Angeles, CA 90010
PH: (213)985-1500
Im, Hyepin, President, CEO

Language Materials Project [8186]
1337 Rolfe Hall
University of California
Los Angeles, CA 90095-1487
PH: (310)267-4720
Fax: (310)206-5183
Hinnebusch, Thomas J., Project Mgr.

Last Chance for Animals [10656]
8033 Sunset Blvd., No. 835
Los Angeles, CA 90046
PH: (310)271-6096
Toll free: 888-882-6462
Fax: (310)271-1890
DeRose, Chris, President, Founder

Latin Business Association [648]
120 S San Pedro St., Ste. 530
Los Angeles, CA 90012
PH: (213)628-8510
Fax: (213)628-8519
Guerra, Ruben, Chmn. of the Bd.,
CEO

Law Enforcement Association of
Asian Pacifics [19536]
905 E 2nd St., Ste. 200
Los Angeles, CA 90012
Lee, Ben, President

Lay Mission-Helpers Association
[19853]
3435 Wilshire Blvd., Ste. 1940
Los Angeles, CA 90010
PH: (213)368-1870
Fax: (213)368-1871
England, Janice, Prog. Dir.

Leadership Education for Asian Pa-
cifics, Inc. [9027]
327 E 2nd St., Ste. 226
Los Angeles, CA 90012
PH: (213)485-1422
Akutagawa, Linda, President, CEO

Location Managers Guild
International [2180]
8033 Sunset Blvd., No. 1017
Los Angeles, CA 90046
PH: (310)967-2007
Fax: (310)967-2013
Haecker, Nancy, President

Clan Matheson Society [20896]
2880 W 15th St.
Los Angeles, CA 90006-4239
PH: (323)732-4737
Matheson, Malcolm, III, Lt.

MAZON [12101]
10495 Santa Monica Blvd., Ste. 100
Los Angeles, CA 90025
PH: (310)442-0020
Toll free: 800-813-0557
Fax: (310)442-0030
Leibman, Abby J., President

Mendez National Institute of
Transplantation Foundation
[17514]
2200 W 3rd St., Ste. 390
Los Angeles, CA 90057
PH: (213)457-7495
Mendez, Robert, MD, Founder

Mercy For Animals [10659]
8033 Sunset Blvd., Ste. 864
Los Angeles, CA 90046
Toll free: 866-632-6446
Runkle, Nathan, President, Founder

Metro Ethernet Forum [7282]
6033 W Century Blvd., Ste. 1107
Los Angeles, CA 90045
PH: (310)642-2800
Fax: (310)642-2808
Chen, Nan, Director, President

Mexican American Legal Defense
and Educational Fund [17911]
634 S Spring St.
Los Angeles, CA 90014
Saenz, Thomas, President, Gen.
Counsel

Michael Crawford International Fan
Association [23997]
2272 Colorado Blvd.
Los Angeles, CA 90041
Fax: (562)683-2677
Cline, Bobbee, Exec. Dir.

Minimally Invasive Robotic Associa-
tion [17394]
11300 W Olympic Blvd., Ste. 600
Los Angeles, CA 90064
PH: (310)424-3353
Fax: (310)437-0585
Kasendorf, Christina, Exec. Dir.

Mission Doctors Association [15607]
3435 Wilshire Blvd., Ste. 1940
Los Angeles, CA 90010
PH: (213)368-1872
Fax: (213)368-1871
Liautaud, Tom, President

mothers2mothers International
[13553]
7441 W Sunset Blvd., Ste. 205
Los Angeles, CA 90046
PH: (323)969-0445
Fax: (323)796-8152
Besser, Dr. Mitch, Founder, Medical
Dir.

Muslim Public Affairs Council
[18702]
3010 Wilshire Blvd., No. 217
Los Angeles, CA 90010

PH: (323)258-6722
Fax: (323)258-5879
Al-Marayati, Salam, President

National Academy of American
Scholars [7842]
601 Figuerroa St.
Los Angeles, CA 90017
Toll free: 888-504-2922

National Alliance of State Prostate
Cancer Coalitions [14018]
10250 Constellation Blvd., Ste. 2320
Los Angeles, CA 90067
Toll free: 877-627-7228
Fax: (310)525-3572
Nissenberg, Merel Grey, President

National Asian Pacific American
Families Against Substance Abuse
[13160]
340 E 2nd St., Ste. 409
Los Angeles, CA 90012
PH: (213)625-5795
   (231)625-5796
Shinn, Alan, Officer

National Association of Canine Scent
Work [22817]
7510 Sunset Blvd., No. 1180
Los Angeles, CA 90046
Gaunt, Ron, Founder

National Association of Composers
U.S.A. [9967]
PO Box 49256, Barrington Sta.
Los Angeles, CA 90049
PH: (541)765-2406
Steinke, Greg A., Ph.D, President,
Chairman, Coord., Member Svcs.

National Association of Latino
Elected and Appointed Officials
[18339]
1122 W Washington Blvd., 3rd Fl.
Los Angeles, CA 90015
PH: (213)747-7606
Fax: (213)747-7664
Shipley, Fernando, Treasurer

National Association of Latino
Independent Producers [1201]
3415 S Sepulveda Blvd., Ste. 1100
Los Angeles, CA 90034
PH: (310)470-1061
Fax: (310)470-1091
Caballero, Axel, Exec. Dir.

National Association of Record
Industry Professionals [2898]
PO Box 2446
Los Angeles, CA 90078-2446
PH: (818)769-7007
Taylor, Tess, President

National Association of Television
Program Executives [474]
5757 Wilshire Blvd., Penthouse 10
Los Angeles, CA 90036-3681
PH: (310)857-1621
Fax: (310)453-5258
Silverman, Pamela, Dir. of Opera-
tions

National Ayurvedic Medical Associa-
tion [13640]
8605 Santa Monica Blvd., No. 46789
Los Angeles, CA 90069-4109
Toll free: 800-669-8914
Fax: (949)743-5432
Nagano, Gwen, President

National Center for Research on
Evaluation, Standards, and
Student Testing [7788]
UCLA CSE/CRESST
GSE&IS Bldg., 3rd Fl.
300 Charles E. Young Dr. N

Los Angeles, CA 90095-1522
PH: (310)206-1101
Fax: (310)825-3883
Baker, Dr. Eva, Director

National Child Traumatic Stress
Network [17528]
11150 W Olympic Blvd., Ste. 650
Los Angeles, CA 90064
PH: (310)235-2633
Fax: (310)235-2612
Pynoos, Robert S., Director

National Day Laborer Organizing
Network [23460]
675 S Park View St., Ste. B
Los Angeles, CA 90057
PH: (213)380-2783
Fax: (213)380-2787
Loewe, B., Dir. of Comm.

National Health Law Program [5275]
3701 Wilshire Blvd., Ste. 750
Los Angeles, CA 90034
PH: (310)204-6010
Fax: (213)368-0774
Taylor, Elizabeth, Exec. Dir.

National Immigration Law Center
[18466]
PO Box 70067
Los Angeles, CA 90070
PH: (213)639-3900
Fax: (213)639-3911
Joaquin, Linton, Gen. Counsel

National Latina Business Women
Association [656]
1100 S Flower St., Ste. 3300
Los Angeles, CA 90015
Toll free: 888-696-5292
Covarrubias, Irene, Treasurer

Netting Nations [14607]
7119 W Sunset Blvd., Ste. 317
Los Angeles, CA 90046
Stranathan, Ike E., Founder

The Network for Social Work
Management [13114]
Special Service for Groups
905 E 8th St.
Los Angeles, CA 90021
PH: (213)553-1870
Fax: (213)553-1822
Flynn, Dr. Marilyn, President

NextAid [11099]
357 S Fairfax Ave., Ste. 267
Los Angeles, CA 90036
PH: (213)663-8638
Fax: (213)663-8638
Segal, Lauren, Founder, Exec. Dir.

Nkwen Cultural and Development
Association USA [19289]
7381 La Tijera Blvd.
Los Angeles, CA 90045
PH: (909)528-4904
Tamajong, Peter, President

North American Skull Base Society
[16033]
11300 W Olympic Blvd., Ste. 600
Los Angeles, CA 90064
PH: (310)424-3326
Fax: (310)437-0585
Berlant, Dan, Mgr.

OneKid OneWorld [11108]
1109 S Clark Dr.
Los Angeles, CA 90035
PH: (323)806-9294
Bycel, Josh, Founder, Exec. Dir.

Operation HOPE, Inc. [11420]
707 Wilshire Blvd., 30th Fl.
Los Angeles, CA 90017

PH: (213)891-2900
Fax: (213)489-7511
Bryant, John Hope, CEO, Founder,
Chairman

Operation U.S.A. [12296]
7421 Beverly Blvd.
Los Angeles, CA 90036
PH: (323)413-2353
Toll free: 800-678-7255
Fax: (323)931-5400
Walden, Richard M., CEO, President

Orangutan Conservancy [4860]
5001 Wilshire Blvd., No. 112
Los Angeles, CA 90036
Rosen, Norm, President

Organization of Black Screenwriters
[1157]
3010 Wilshire Blvd., No. 269
Los Angeles, CA 90010
PH: (323)735-2050
Allen, Kimberly, VP

Outfest [9309]
3470 Wilshire Blvd., Ste. 935
Los Angeles, CA 90010
PH: (213)480-7088
Fax: (213)480-7099
Mukerjee-Brown, Lucy, Officer

Pacific Council on International
Policy [18274]
725 S Figueroa St., Ste. 450
Los Angeles, CA 90017
PH: (213)221-2000
Fax: (213)221-2050
Green, Dr. Jerrold D., CEO,
President

Philosophical Research Society
[10111]
3910 Los Feliz Blvd.
Los Angeles, CA 90027
Toll free: 800-548-4062
Fax: (323)663-9443
Hall, Manly P., Founder

Point Foundation [4010]
5055 Wilshire Blvd., Ste. 501
Los Angeles, CA 90036
PH: (323)933-1234
Toll free: 866-337-6468
Valencia, Jorge, CEO, Exec. Dir.

POWER UP: Professional Organiza-
tion of Women in Entertainment
Reaching UP! [18302]
419 N Larchmont Blvd., No. 283
Los Angeles, CA 90004
PH: (323)463-3154
Codikow, Stacy, Exec. Dir., Founder

Prism Comics [759]
c/o Ted Abenheim, Pres.
3624 Westwood Blvd., No. 202
Los Angeles, CA 90034
PH: (714)258-6457
Madery, Tara Aveson, Treasurer

PROMAXBDA [478]
5700 Wilshire Blvd., Ste. 275
Los Angeles, CA 90036-3687
PH: (310)788-7600
Fax: (310)788-7616
Chastain, Scott, Chairman

Psychiatrists Global Training
Network [15802]
PO Box 480482
Los Angeles, CA 90048
PH: (310)954-1986
Smith, Pamela, Founder

Psychoneuroimmunology Research
Society [13802]
c/o Susan Keran Solomon, Executive Director

10724 Wilshire Blvd., No. 602
Los Angeles, CA 90024
Kavelaars, Annemieke, President

Purple Star Veterans and Families
[21137]
5042 Wilshire Blvd., No. 32196
Los Angeles, CA 90036
PH: (760)576-5649
Parker, John Henry, Founder

The Reason Foundation [5645]
5737 Mesmer Ave.
Los Angeles, CA 90230
PH: (310)391-2245
Fax: (310)391-4395
Beach, Thomas E., Chairman

Retina Vitreous Foundation [17742]
1127 Wilshire Blvd., Ste. 304
Los Angeles, CA 90017
PH: (310)644-3863
Boyer, David S., Bd. Member

Tomás Rivera Policy Institute
[19531]
Lewis Hall
Sol Price School of Public Policy
University of Southern California
650 Childs Way, Ste. 102
Los Angeles, CA 90089-0626
PH: (213)821-5615
Fax: (213)821-1976
Suro, Roberto, Director

Salvadoran American Leadership
and Educational Fund [18176]
1625 W Olympic Blvd., Ste. 718
Los Angeles, CA 90015
PH: (213)480-1052
Fax: (213)487-2530
Vaquerano, Carlos Antonio H., Exec.
Dir.

Salvadoran American National
Network [18177]
2845 W 7th St.
Los Angeles, CA 90005
Arias, Yanira, President

Saturn Awards [9311]
334 W 54th St.
Los Angeles, CA 90037
PH: (323)752-5811
Holguin, Robert, CEO, President

Save Africa's Children [11268]
3045 Crenshaw Blvd.
Los Angeles, CA 900016
PH: (323)733-1048
Fax: (323)778-8168
Blake, Bishop Charles E., CEO,
President

Save the Frogs! [3939]
PO Box 78758
Los Angeles, CA 90016
PH: (415)878-6525
Kriger, Dr. Kerry M., President

Screen Actors Guild - American
Federation of Television and Radio
Artists [23499]
5757 Wilshire Blvd., 7th Fl.
Los Angeles, CA 90036
PH: (323)954-1600
Toll free: 855-724-2387
Reardon, Roberta, Bd. Member

Self-Realization Fellowship [20655]
3880 San Rafael Ave.
Los Angeles, CA 90065-3219
PH: (818)549-5151
   (323)225-2471
Fax: (818)549-5100
Mata, Mrinalini, President

Shin Koyamada Foundation [13478]
5532 N Figueroa St., Ste. 220
Los Angeles, CA 90042

PH: (818)588-9754
Koyamada, Shin, Founder, Chairman

Shuttleworth Leadership Society
International [8204]
PO Box 27306
Los Angeles, CA 90027
PH: (323)663-5797
Shuttleworth, Mary, Founder

Simon Wiesenthal Center [18352]
1399 S Roxbury Dr.
Los Angeles, CA 90035
PH: (310)553-9036
Toll free: 800-900-9036
Fax: (310)553-4521
Mizel, Larry A., Chairman

Society of American Gastrointestinal
and Endoscopic Surgeons [14797]
11300 W Olympic Blvd., Ste. 600
Los Angeles, CA 90064
PH: (310)437-0544
Schwaitzberg, Steven D., M.D.,
President

Society for Calligraphy [10415]
PO Box 64174
Los Angeles, CA 90064-0174
Darwick, Kristi, President

Society of Children's Book Writers
and Illustrators [10400]
4727 Wilshire Blvd., Ste. 301
Los Angeles, CA 90010
PH: (323)782-1010
Fax: (323)782-1892
Mooser, Stephen, President

Society of Iranian Architects and
Planners [5979]
PO Box 643066
Los Angeles, CA 90064
Ziai, Abdi, President

Society for the Study of Japanese
Religions [20579]
USC School of Religion, ACB 233
Los Angeles, CA 90089-1481
Blair, Heather, Contact

Society of University Surgeons
[17408]
11300 W Olympic Blvd., Ste. 600
Los Angeles, CA 90064
PH: (310)986-6442
Fax: (310)437-0585
Minter, Rebecca M., President

Society of Young Philanthropists
[12496]
8322 Beverly Blvd., Ste. 301
Los Angeles, CA 90048
Ruzin, Francesca, VP

Solve ME/CFS Initiative [14613]
5455 Wilshire Blvd., Ste. 806
Los Angeles, CA 90036-0007
PH: (704)364-0016
Boies, Vicki, Chairman

Spirit of America [19015]
12021 Wilshire Blvd., No. 507
Los Angeles, CA 90025
PH: (310)230-5476
Fax: (310)826-4542
Hake, Jim, Founder

StandWithUs [18588]
PO Box 341069
Los Angeles, CA 90034-1069
PH: (310)836-6140
Fax: (310)836-6145
Rothstein, Roz, CEO

Starlight Children's Foundation
[11274]
2049 Century Pk. E, Ste. 4320
Los Angeles, CA 90067

PH: (310)479-1212
Shiffman, Roger, Director

Step Up [13399]
510 S Hewitt St., No. 111
Los Angeles, CA 90013-2268
PH: (213)382-9161
Luke, Jenni, CEO

Stroke Awareness for Everyone
[17298]
PO Box 36186
Los Angeles, CA 90036-6186
Manion, Bernadette, Treasurer

Support for International Change
[15499]
PO Box 25803
Los Angeles, CA 90025
Churchman, Emily, MPH, Chmn. of
the Bd.

Travelers' Century Club [22470]
8939 S Sepulveda Blvd., Ste. 102
Los Angeles, CA 90045
Toll free: 888-822-0228
Barrus, Pamela, Bd. Member

United Lodge of Theosophists
[20625]
245 W 33rd St.
Los Angeles, CA 90007
PH: (213)748-7244
Fax: (213)748-0634

United States Competitive Aerobics
Federation [22486]
8033 Sunset Blvd., No. 920
Los Angeles, CA 90046
Fax: (323)850-7795

U.S.A. for Africa [12734]
5670 Wilshire Blvd., Ste. 1740
Los Angeles, CA 90036
PH: (323)954-3124
Thomas, Marcia, Exec. Dir.

Unity-and-Diversity World Council
[18561]
PO Box 661401
Los Angeles, CA 90066-9201
PH: (424)228-2087
Fax: (310)827-9187
Stewart, Leland P., Founder, Coord.

Unity Fellowship Church Movement
[20191]
c/o Archbishop Carl Bean, DM,
Founder
PO Box 78342
Los Angeles, CA 90016-0342
PH: (323)938-8322
Bean, Arch. Carl, DM, Founder

University Film and Video Associa-
tion [9317]
3800 Barham Blvd.
Los Angeles, CA 90068
Toll free: 866-647-8382
Machiorlatti, Jennifer, Exec. VP

Variety - The Children's Charity
International [11178]
4601 Wilshire Blvd., Ste. 260
Los Angeles, CA 90010
PH: (323)934-4688
Fax: (323)658-8789
Small, David, Exec. Dir.

Western Center on Law and Poverty
[5555]
3701 Wilshire Blvd., Ste. 208
Los Angeles, CA 90010-2826
PH: (213)487-7211
Fax: (213)487-0242
Tepper, Paul, Exec. Dir.

Women Against Gun Violence
[19233]
8800 Venice Blvd., Ste. 304
Los Angeles, CA 90034

PH: (310)204-2348
Fax: (310)204-6643
Lane, Ann Reiss, Founder

Women Alive Coalition [13565]
1524 W 95th St.
Los Angeles, CA 90047-3914
PH: (323)965-1564
Thomas, Alfredia, President

Women in Animation [1211]
c/o Marine Hekimian
11400 W Olympic Blvd., No. 590
Los Angeles, CA 90064
Scanlan, Kristy, Co-Pres.

Women in Film [1212]
6100 Wilshire Blvd., Ste. 710
Los Angeles, CA 90048
PH: (323)935-2211
Fax: (323)935-2212
Schaffer, Kirsten, Exec. Dir.

Women in Photography International
[2598]
569 N Rossmore Ave., No. 604
Los Angeles, CA 90004
PH: (323)462-1444
Ferro, Jean, Exec. Dir., President

Women in Technology International
[7300]
11500 Olympic Blvd., Ste. 400
Los Angeles, CA 90064
PH: (818)788-9484
Fax: (818)788-9410
Leighton, Carolyn, Chairperson,
Founder, Chmn. of the Bd.

Women and Youth Supporting Each
Other [8760]
PO Box 712189
Los Angeles, CA 90071
PH: (714)390-8363
Kim, Linda, Chairperson

World Council of Comparative
Education Societies [7649]
Moore Hall 2018
405 Hilgard Ave.
Los Angeles, CA 90095-1521
Lamarra, Norberto Fernandez, VP

World Impact [20478]
2001 S Vermont Ave.
Los Angeles, CA 90007
PH: (323)735-1137
Fax: (323)735-2576
Davis, Don, Sr. VP, Director

Youth for Human Rights International
[12067]
1920 Hillhurst Ave., No. 416
Los Angeles, CA 90027-2712
PH: (323)663-5799
Shuttleworth, Dr. Mary, Founder,
President

Youth Policy Institute [19012]
634 S Spring St., 10th Fl.
Los Angeles, CA 90014
PH: (213)688-2802
Toll free: 800-999-6877
Slingerland, Dixon, VP

Project RACE [19431]
PO Box 2366
Los Banos, CA 93635
Fax: (209)826-2510
Graham, Susan, Exec. Dir.

2nd Chance 4 Pets [10557]
1484 Pollard Rd., No. 444
Los Gatos, CA 95032
PH: (408)871-1133
Toll free: 888-843-4040
Fax: (408)866-6659
Shever, Amy, Director, Founder

Shotcrete Concrete Contractors As-
sociation [796]
23565 Morrill Rd.
Los Gatos, CA 95033-9322
PH: (408)640-6219
Zynda, Christopher M., President

Finnish Spitz Club of America
[21878]
c/o Mary Ellis, Membership
Chairperson
317 Manzanita Dr.
Los Osos, CA 93402
PH: (805)528-3419
Pelland, Roland, President

American Tortoise Rescue [4784]
30745 Pacific Coast Hwy., Ste. 243
Malibu, CA 90265
Tellem, Ms. Susan, Founder

Cancer Schmancer Movement
[13929]
22837 Pacific Coast Hwy.
Malibu, CA 90265
Toll free: 888-621-2001
Holland, Susan, Exec. Dir.

Saving Wildlife International [4883]
PO Box 2626
Malibu, CA 90265
Toll free: 800-945-3794
Mehren, Steve, Exec. Dir., Founder

United States Apnea Association
[22813]
3642 Seahorn Dr.
Malibu, CA 90265
PH: (310)560-6104

Alpha Tau Delta [23837]
1904 Poinsettia Ave.
Manhattan Beach, CA 90266
Waltner, Aileen, Bd. Member

Center for the Study of Democratic
Societies [18093]
PO Box 475
Manhattan Beach, CA 90267-0475
George, Robley Evans, Director

Fertile Action [14755]
PO Box 3526
Manhattan Beach, CA 90266
Toll free: 877-276-5951
Crisci, Alice, Founder

Free Minds, Inc. [20047]
c/o Randall Watters, President
PO Box 3818
Manhattan Beach, CA 90266
PH: (310)545-7831
Watters, Randall, President, Founder

Independent Book Publishers As-
sociation [2788]
1020 Manhattan Beach Blvd., Ste.
204
Manhattan Beach, CA 90266
PH: (310)546-1818
Fax: (310)546-3939
Nathan, Terry, COO

Pancreatic Cancer Action Network
[14042]
1500 Rosecrans Ave., Ste. 200
Manhattan Beach, CA 90266
PH: (310)725-0025
Toll free: 877-272-6226
Fax: (310)725-0029
MacCaskill, Laurie, Chairman

The Cloth Diaper Foundation, Inc.
[11559]
511 W Center St.
Manteca, CA 95336
Toll free: 888-411-7151

American Association of Women
[18960]
337 Washington Blvd., Ste. 1
Marina del Rey, CA 90292

PH: (310)822-4449
Fax: (310)919-2890
Dutton, Leslie C., President

Association of Black Women Physicians **[16740]**
4712 Admiralty Way, Ste. 175
Marina del Rey, CA 90292
PH: (310)321-8688
Walker, Valencia, MD, President

Association of Independent Music Publishers **[2419]**
PO Box 10482
Marina del Rey, CA 90295
PH: (818)771-7301
Eames, Michael, President

Compassion into Action Network - Direct Outcome Organization **[11654]**
578 Washington Blvd., Ste. 390
Marina del Rey, CA 90292
Toll free: 877-226-3697
Klein, Eric, CEO, Founder

Digital Government Society **[5261]**
USC-ISI
4676 Admiralty Way
Marina del Rey, CA 90292
PH: (570)476-8006
Fax: (570)476-0860
Chun, Soon Ae, President

International Meta-Medicine Association **[13635]**
578 Washington Blvd., No. 716
Marina del Rey, CA 90292
PH: (310)906-0366
Fisslinger, Johannes R., Bookcrafter

International Society for Paranormal Research **[6986]**
4712 Admiralty Way, No. 541
Marina del Rey, CA 90292
PH: (323)644-8866
Montz, Dr. Larry, Founder

Dementia Advocacy and Support Network International **[15923]**
PO Box 1645
Mariposa, CA 95338
Friedell, Morris, Director, Treasurer

Association of Libertarian Feminists **[18639]**
1155C Arnold Dr., No. 418
Martinez, CA 94553
PH: (925)228-0565
Presley, Sharon, Exec. Dir.

North American Wensleydale Sheep Association **[4680]**
4589 Fruitland Rd.
Marysville, CA 95901
PH: (530)743-5262
Burrows, Barbara, Director

Home Garden Seed Association **[4642]**
PO Box 93
Maxwell, CA 95955
PH: (530)438-2126
Shepherd, Renee, President

Joshua's Journey of Hope **[14833]**
30141 Antelope Rd.
Menifee, CA 92584
PH: (951)719-5277
Clarke, David J., President

Alpha Omega Alpha Honor Medical Society **[23816]**
525 Middlefield Rd., Ste. 130
Menlo Park, CA 94025
PH: (650)329-0291
Fax: (650)329-1618
Atnip, Robert G., President

GeoHazards International **[4487]**
687 Bay Rd.
Menlo Park, CA 94025
PH: (650)614-9050
Fax: (650)614-9051
Tucker, Brian E., President

William and Flora Hewlett Foundation **[13060]**
2121 Sand Hill Rd.
Menlo Park, CA 94025
PH: (650)234-4500
Fax: (650)234-4501
Kramer, Larry D., President

Kaiser Family Foundation **[15028]**
2400 Sand Hill Rd.
Menlo Park, CA 94025
PH: (650)854-9400
Fax: (650)854-4800
Altman, Drew, PhD, CEO, President

Montenegrin Association of America **[9213]**
805 Magnolia St.
Menlo Park, CA 94025
Sredanovic, Blazo, President

People for Internet Responsibility **[18571]**
SRI International EL-243
333 Ravenswood Ave.
Menlo Park, CA 94025-3453
PH: (818)225-2800
   (650)859-2375
Weinstein, Lauren, Founder

Chen Qingzhou Martial Arts Association, USA **[23012]**
325M Sharon Park Dr., No. 729
Menlo Park, CA 94025
PH: (510)854-6374
Fax: (510)854-6374

Workaholics Anonymous **[12880]**
PO Box 289
Menlo Park, CA 94026-0289
PH: (510)273-9253

World Children's Initiative **[11189]**
1328 American Way
Menlo Park, CA 94025
PH: (408)554-4188
Daluvoy, Sanjay, MD, Founder, President

Eddy Family Association **[20860]**
c/o Elaine Darrah, Treasurer
3151 Erie Ave.
Merced, CA 95340-1408
White, Ward, President

National Staff Development and Training Association **[3132]**
2115 Wardrobe Ave.
Merced, CA 95341
PH: (209)385-3000
Fax: (209)354-2501
Schimmels, Karyn Corpron, President

National Staff Development and Training Association **[13076]**
2115 Wardrobe Ave.
Merced, CA 95341
PH: (209)385-3000
Fax: (209)354-2501
Schimmels, Karyn Corpron, President

Worldwide Aquatic Bodywork Association **[13668]**
PO Box 1817
Middletown, CA 95461
PH: (707)928-5860
Fax: (707)317-0052

American Sports Institute **[7742]**
PO Box 1837
Mill Valley, CA 94942

PH: (415)383-5750
Kirsch, Joel, President

Association for Cultural Evolution **[9225]**
PO Box 2382
Mill Valley, CA 94942
PH: (415)409-3220
Fax: (415)931-0948
Bray, Faustin, Events Coord.

CorStone **[15766]**
250 Camino Alto, Ste. 100A
Mill Valley, CA 94941
PH: (415)388-6161
Fax: (415)388-6165
Green, Tom, President

Forfeiture Endangers American Rights **[5086]**
20 Sunnyside Ave., Ste. A-419
Mill Valley, CA 94941
PH: (415)381-6105
Toll free: 888-332-7001
Grantland, Brenda, Esq., President

Foundation for Shamanic Studies **[20505]**
PO Box 1939
Mill Valley, CA 94942
PH: (415)897-6416
Fax: (415)897-4583
Mokelke, Susan, JD, President

Lewa Wildlife Conservancy U.S.A. **[4840]**
495 Miller Ave., Ste. 301
Mill Valley, CA 94941
PH: (415)627-8187
Joseph, Michael, Chairman

Muhyiddin Ibn 'Arabi Society **[20610]**
38 Miller Ave., No. 486
Mill Valley, CA 94941-1927
Collins, Grenville, Chairman

Sarcoma Alliance **[14059]**
775 E Blithedale, No. 334
Mill Valley, CA 94941
PH: (415)381-7236
Fax: (415)381-7235
Olig, Alison, Exec. Dir.

Trips for Kids **[7899]**
138 Sunnyside Ave.
Mill Valley, CA 94941
PH: (415)458-2986
Price, Marilyn, Director

Veterans2Work **[21153]**
95 Shelley Dr.
Mill Valley, CA 94941
PH: (415)925-1515
Reynolds, John, Exec. Dir., Founder

Women-Church Convergence **[20647]**
PO Box 806
Mill Valley, CA 94942
PH: (708)974-4220
Wojtan, Katherine, Coord.

Worldwide Forgiveness Alliance **[12449]**
20 Sunnyside Ave., Ste. A-268
Mill Valley, CA 94941
PH: (415)342-2650
Plath, Robert W., Exec. Dir., Founder

Federation of Jain Associations in North America **[20539]**
722 S Main St.
Milpitas, CA 95035
PH: (510)730-0204
Domadia, Ashok, 1st VP

Filipino American Real Estate Professionals Association **[2861]**
PO Box 261083
Milpitas, CA 95035

PH: (408)934-8202
Lamar, Judy, President

Fresh Lifelines for Youth **[13444]**
568 Valley Way
Milpitas, CA 95035
PH: (408)263-2630
Fax: (408)263-2631
Gannon, Christa, CEO, Founder

India Literacy Project **[8243]**
PO Box 361143
Milpitas, CA 95035-9998
Mani, Ravi, Trustee

International Children Assistance Network **[11047]**
532 Valley Way
Milpitas, CA 95035-4106
PH: (408)509-8788
   (408)509-1958
Fax: (408)935-9657
Ta, Hoai, Act. Chm.

Jeena, Inc. **[11608]**
1510 Centre Pointe Dr.
Milpitas, CA 95035
PH: (408)957-0481
Madan, Praveen, Founder

Mannlicher Collectors Association **[21683]**
1000 Jacklin Rd.
Milpitas, CA 95035
Levengood, Lynn, VP

North American Punjabi Association **[19478]**
1250 Ames Ave., Ste. 101
Milpitas, CA 95035
PH: (408)221-5732
Fax: (408)547-0522
Dhoot, Dalwinder Singh, Chairman

Society for Creative Anachronism, Inc. **[9789]**
PO Box 360789
Milpitas, CA 95036-0789
PH: (408)263-9305
Toll free: 800-789-7486
Fax: (408)263-0641
Anderson, Theresa, Admin. Asst.

Viet Dreams **[11180]**
PO Box 360624
Milpitas, CA 95036
PH: (408)410-4920
Nguyen, Khac-Quan, Founder, Exec. Dir.

Access to Empowerment International **[11720]**
12523 Limonite Ave., No. 440-222
Mira Loma, CA 91752
PH: (951)440-5542
Fax: (951)346-3897
Oduro, Erika, Exec. Dir.

Association of American Educators **[7847]**
27405 Puerta Real, Ste. 230
Mission Viejo, CA 92691
PH: (949)595-7979
Toll free: 800-704-7799
Fax: (949)595-7970
Beckner, Gary, Chairman, President

Continental Motosport Club **[23037]**
PO Box 3178
Mission Viejo, CA 92690-3178
PH: (949)367-1141

Everyone Needs a Hero **[11357]**
27596 Sweetbrier Ln.
Mission Viejo, CA 92691
PH: (619)807-0415
Walborn, Rachel, President

Gavel Clubs **[10173]**
PO Box 9052
Mission Viejo, CA 92690-9052

PH: (949)858-8255
Fax: (949)858-1207

International Map Industry Association [6167]
23052 Alicia Pky., Ste. H-602
Mission Viejo, CA 92692-1661
PH: (949)458-8200
Fax: (949)458-0300
Moe, Bennett, President

Almond Board of California [4505]
1150 9th St., Ste. 1500
Modesto, CA 95354
PH: (209)549-8262
Fax: (209)549-8267
Waycott, Richard, CEO

Association for Healthcare Documentation Integrity [15618]
4120 Dale Rd., Ste. J8-233
Modesto, CA 95356
PH: (209)527-9620
Toll free: 800-982-2182
Fax: (209)527-9633
Devrick, Jill, President

Nursing Network on Violence Against Women International [11712]
2401 E Orangeburg Ave., Ste. 675
Modesto, CA 95355-3379
Toll free: 800-933-6679
Ford-Gilboe, Marilyn, PhD, President

Reblooming Iris Society [22120]
c/o Riley Probst, President
2701 Fine Ave.
Modesto, CA 95355-9773
Landers, Jim, VP

International Association of Nanotechnology [7275]
NASA Ames Research Ctr.
PO Box 151
Moffett Field, CA 94035
PH: (408)280-6222
Toll free: 877-676-6266
Tran, Lloyd, President

Pacific Rocket Society [5870]
PO Box 662
Mojave, CA 93502-0662
PH: (661)824-1662
Milliron, Randa, Contact

Space Studies Institute [5875]
16922 Airport Blvd., No. 24
Mojave, CA 93501
PH: (661)750-2774
Hudson, Gary C., President, Trustee

Trans Lunar Research [5877]
PO Box 661
Mojave, CA 93502-0661
PH: (661)824-1662
    (661)965-0771

American Pet Society [10569]
135 W Lemon Ave.
135 W Lemon Ave.
Monrovia, CA 91016
PH: (626)447-2222
Toll free: 800-999-7295
Fax: (626)447-8350

Americanism Educational Leaders [18278]
610 W Foothill Blvd.
Monrovia, CA 91016
PH: (626)357-7733
Barbera, Robert J., Chmn. of the Bd., President

Aurora's Promise - 4 Kids [10860]
198 S Myrtle Ave.
Monrovia, CA 91016
PH: (626)233-9391
Baez, Aurora, President, Founder

National Health Federation [14956]
PO Box 688
Monrovia, CA 91017
PH: (626)357-2181
Tips, Scott, President

World Pet Association [2551]
135 W Lemon Ave.
Monrovia, CA 91016
PH: (626)447-2222
Fax: (626)447-8350
Guzman, Jessica, Dir. of Comm.

World Vision International [12740]
800 W Chestnut Ave.
Monrovia, CA 91016
PH: (626)303-8811
Fax: (626)301-7786
Jenkins, Kevin, CEO, President

Wired International [15507]
PO Box 371132
Montara, CA 94037-1132
Selnow, Gary, PhD, Exec. Dir.

Mexican American Opportunity Foundation [11944]
401 N Garfield Ave.
Montebello, CA 90640
PH: (323)890-9600
Fax: (323)890-9637
Castro, Martin, CEO, President

National Organization Taunting Safety and Fairness Everywhere [22164]
PO Box 5743
Montecito, CA 93150
Lowdermilk, Dale, Founder

International Health Emissaries [15148]
8 Sommerset Rise
Monterey, CA 93940
Bayless, J. Mark, DMD, Founder

Monterey County Vintners and Growers Association [4929]
PO Box 1793
Monterey, CA 93942
PH: (831)375-9400
Reade, Amanda, Dir. of Comm.

International Society for Business Education [7553]
c/o Ruth DiPieri, President
1301 Avenida Cesar Chavez
Monterey Park, CA 91754
PH: (619)469-5067
Peterson, Nancy, Secretary

Association for Peace and Understanding in the Middle East [18676]
2029 Verdugo Blvd.
Montrose, CA 91020
Lonstein, Avi, Exec. Dir.

Chiropractic Orthopedists of North America [14261]
2048 Montrose Ave.
Montrose, CA 91020-1605
PH: (818)249-8326
    (916)933-2707
Meltz, Lewis, DC, VP

Historic Motor Sports Association [21393]
2029 Verdugo Blvd., No. 1010
Montrose, CA 91020
PH: (818)249-3515
Fax: (818)249-4917
Vandagriff, Cris, President

American Cichlid Association [22027]
c/o Dr. Tim Hovanec, Tresurer
530 Los Angeles Ave., Ste. 115-243

Moorpark, CA 93021
PH: (631)668-5125
Wessel, Rusty, V. Chmn. of the Bd.

American Cryptogram Association [21790]
56 Sanders Ranch Rd.
Moraga, CA 94556-2806
Schretzmann, Charles, Treasurer

Association for Core Texts and Courses [7815]
St. Mary's College of California
1928 St. Marys Rd.
Moraga, CA 94556
PH: (925)631-8597
Lee, J. Scott, Exec. Dir.

Cystinosis Foundation [15820]
58 Miramonte Dr.
Moraga, CA 94556
PH: (925)631-1588
Toll free: 888-631-1588
Hotz, Jean, President

River of Words [4763]
1928 St. Mary's Rd.
Moraga, CA 94575
PH: (925)631-4289
Michael, Pamela, Exec. Dir., Founder

St. Mary's College of California Alumni Association [19347]
1928 St. Mary's Rd.
Moraga, CA 94575
PH: (925)631-4200
    (925)631-4803
Toll free: 800-800-ALUM
Fax: (925)631-0764
Lohmann, Courtney Carmignani, Director

Transferware Collectors Club [21862]
c/o Jo Anne Jones, Membership Chair
207 Paseo Bernal
Moraga, CA 94556
Jones, Jo Anne, Officer

BeachFront USA [10056]
PO Box 328
Moreno Valley, CA 92556
Roe, Bill, Director

CarCanMadCarLan Association U.S.A. [12631]
25564 Wedmore Dr.
Moreno Valley, CA 92553
PH: (951)880-5614
    (951)247-8522
Urbiztondo, Mario B., President

Energy Information Standards Alliance [1113]
275 Tennant Ave., Ste. 202
Morgan Hill, CA 95037
PH: (408)778-8370
    (614)657-6483
Fax: (408)852-3496
Kotting, Christopher, Exec. Dir.

Pacific Islanders' Cultural Association [10059]
409 Tenant Sta., No. 230
Morgan Hill, CA 95037
PH: (415)281-0221
Avilla, Shirley, Bd. Member

Nourish America [16231]
PO Box 1567
Morro Bay, CA 93443
PH: (805)715-2693
Larsen, Sarah, Secretary, Treasurer

Eureka Society [20654]
PO Box 222
Mount Shasta, CA 96067
Avenell, Bruce K., Director, Founder

Planetary Citizens [19264]
PO Box 1056
Mount Shasta, CA 96067
PH: (530)926-6424
Fax: (530)926-1245
Callahan, Sharon, Officer

Save the Rain [13336]
PO Box 1510
Mount Shasta, CA 96067
PH: (530)926-9999
Fax: (530)926-5050
Coleman, Kelly, Director

African Cradle, Inc. [11210]
2672 Bayshore Pky., Ste. 1000
Mountain View, CA 94043-1010
PH: (650)461-9192
Fax: (650)215-9897
Stime, Amber, MSW, Exec. Dir., Founder

HealthCare Tourism International [15017]
809B Cuesta Dr., Ste. 141
Mountain View, CA 94040
PH: (310)928-3611
Patel, Neilesh, Co-CEO

IEEE - Consumer Electronics Society [6425]
c/o Bill Orner, Secretary
1513 Meadow Ln.
Mountain View, CA 94040
Peng, Sharon, President

Indian Muslim Relief and Charities [12680]
849 Independence Ave., Ste. A
Mountain View, CA 94043
PH: (650)856-0440
Fax: (650)856-0444
Ahmed, Basheer, Secretary

International Society of Information Fusion [6744]
PO Box 4631
Mountain View, CA 94040
Dezert, Jean, President

International Society of Offshore and Polar Engineers [6565]
495 N Whisman Rd., Ste. 300
Mountain View, CA 94043-5711
PH: (650)254-1871
Fax: (650)254-2038
Chung, Prof. Jin S., PhD, Exec. Dir.

Libertarian Futurist Society [18641]
650 Castro St., Ste. 120-433
Mountain View, CA 94041
Grossberg, Michael, Secretary

National Council of Asian American Business Associations [684]
475 N Whisman Rd., Ste. 200
Mountain View, CA 94043
PH: (650)303-6164
Fax: (650)350-1545

National Fantasy Fan Federation [10204]
PO Box 1925
Mountain View, CA 94042
Speakman, David, Chairperson, Treasurer

North America Chinese Clean-tech & Semiconductor Association [1057]
809-B Cuesta Dr., Ste. 208
Mountain View, CA 94040-3666
Peng, Cheng, Chairman

Positive Coaching Alliance [22738]
1001 N Rengstorff Ave., Ste. 100
Mountain View, CA 94043-1766
Toll free: 866-725-0024
Fax: (650)969-1650
Thompson, Jim, CEO, Founder

Silicon Valley Chinese Engineers Association [6586]
PO Box 642
Mountain View, CA 94042
Luk, John, Chairman

Socialist Labor Party of America [18896]
PO Box 218
Mountain View, CA 94042-0218
PH: (650)938-8359
Fax: (650)938-8392
Bills, Robert, Secretary, Editor

Unicode Consortium [19154]
PO Box 391476
Mountain View, CA 94039-1476
PH: (650)693-2793
Fax: (650)693-3010
Davis, Dr. Mark, President, Founder

Web3D Consortium [6340]
650 Castro St., Ste. 120-490
Mountain View, CA 94041
PH: (248)342-7662
Fax: (844)768-6886
Havele, Anita, Exec. Dir.

International Food, Wine and Travel Writers Association [2685]
39252 Winchester Rd., Ste. 107, No. 418
Murrieta, CA 92563
Toll free: 877-439-8929
Fax: (877)439-8929
Kissam, Linda, President

National Animal Care and Control Association [10662]
40960 California Oaks Rd., No. 242
Murrieta, CA 92562
PH: (913)768-1319
Fax: (913)768-1378
Leinberger, Robert C., Jr., President

American Assisted Living Nurses Association [16087]
PO Box 10469
Napa, CA 94581
PH: (707)622-5628
Allen, Josh, RN, Director

American Vineyard Foundation [4924]
PO Box 5779
Napa, CA 94581
PH: (707)252-6911
Fax: (707)252-7672
Deitrick, Scott, Mgr. of Admin.

Association of African American Vintners [179]
4225 Solano Ave.
Napa, CA 94558
PH: (707)334-6048
Bryant, Daniel, Prop.

Association of Lighting and Mercury Recyclers [4624]
4139 Rhine Ct.
Napa, CA 94558
PH: (707)927-3844
Fax: (707)927-3936
Abernathy, Paul, Exec. Dir.

Free the Grapes! [4952]
2700 Napa Valley Corporate Dr., Ste. H
Napa, CA 94558
PH: (707)254-1107
Benson, Jeremy, Contact

Marine Corps Cryptologic Association [21013]
4486 Sandlewood St.
Napa, CA 94558-1766
Toll free: 877-856-9562
Adams, Jay, Exec. Dir.

Napa Valley Grapegrowers [4930]
1795 3rd St.
Napa, CA 94559
PH: (707)944-8311
Fax: (707)224-8644
Moulds, Steve, President

World Academy of Art and Science [9018]
4225 Solano Ave., Ste. 631
Napa, CA 94558
Jacobs, Garry, Chmn. of the Bd., CEO

Bilateral Safety Corridor Coalition [12025]
2050 Wilson Ave., Ste. C
National City, CA 91950
PH: (619)336-0770
    (619)666-2757
Fax: (619)336-0791
August, J. W., President

American College of Veterinary Dermatology [17616]
c/o Alexis Borich, Executive Secretary
11835 Forest Knolls Ct.
Nevada City, CA 95959
PH: (530)272-7334
Fax: (530)272-8518
Borich, Alexis, Exec. Sec.

American Herb Association [6131]
PO Box 1673
Nevada City, CA 95959
PH: (530)265-9552

Ananda Yoga Teachers Association [10418]
c/o The Expanding Light
14618 Tyler Foote Rd.
Nevada City, CA 95959
PH: (530)478-7518
Toll free: 800-346-5350
Fax: (530)478-7519

Flower Essence Society [13623]
PO Box 459
Nevada City, CA 95959
PH: (530)265-9163
Toll free: 800-736-9222
Fax: (530)265-0584
Kaminski, Patricia A., Director

Institute for the Development of the Harmonious Human Being, Inc. [12004]
PO Box 370
Nevada City, CA 95959
PH: (530)271-2239
Toll free: 800-869-0658
Fax: (530)687-0317
Gold, E.J., Founder

National Pediatrics AIDS Network [16611]
PO Box 1507
Nevada City, CA 95959

American Muslim Alliance [18701]
39675 Cedar Blvd., Ste. 220 E
Newark, CA 94560
PH: (510)252-9858
Fax: (510)252-9863
Saeed, Dr. Agha, Chairman

International Society for Minimal Intervention in Spinal Surgery [17257]
c/o John Chiu, Secretary-Treasurer
1001 Newbury Rd.
Newbury Park, CA 91320
Fax: (805)375-7975
Chiu, John C., MD, Secretary, Treasurer

American Society of Cosmetic Breast Surgery [14308]
1419 Superior Ave., Ste. 2
Newport Beach, CA 92663

PH: (949)645-6665
Fax: (949)645-6784
Tavoussi, Mohsen, MD, President

Americans for Free Choice in Medicine [15713]
1525 Superior Ave., Ste. 101
Newport Beach, CA 92663
Ralston, Richard E., Exec. Dir.

Association of Volleyball Professionals [23522]
1300 Quail St., No. 200
Newport Beach, CA 92660
PH: (949)679-3599

Coalition Duchenne [15917]
1300 Quail St., Ste. 100
Newport Beach, CA 92660
Fax: (949)721-9359
Jayasuriya, Catherine, Exec. Dir., Founder

CureDuchenne [14819]
1400 Quail St., Ste. 110
Newport Beach, CA 92660
PH: (949)872-2552
Miller, Debra, President, CEO

Down Syndrome Education USA [15814]
1451 Quail St., Ste. 104
Newport Beach, CA 92660-2747
PH: (949)757-1877
Fax: (949)757-1877
Medlen, Joan Guthrie, RD, VP

Egypt Cancer Network [13963]
20301 SW Birch St., No. 101
Newport Beach, CA 92660
PH: (617)942-7970
Toll free: 866-987-2869
Seify, Hisham, MD, President

First Fruit [20142]
14 Corporate Plz., Ste. 200
Newport Beach, CA 92660
Park, Paul, Exec. Dir.

Foundation for Retinal Regeneration [17701]
PO Box 10452
Newport Beach, CA 92658
PH: (714)551-6400
Klassen, Henry J., MD, Founder, Chairman

Institute for Historical Review [9446]
PO Box 2739
Newport Beach, CA 92659-1339
PH: (714)593-9725
Fax: (714)465-3176
Weber, Mark, Director

Lido 14 Class Association [22644]
PO Box 1252
Newport Beach, CA 92659-0252

Maritime Arbitration Association of the United States [4963]
PO Box 11466
Newport Beach, CA 92658
Toll free: 800-717-5750
Russell, Thomas A., Comm. Chm.

Mutual UFO Network [7015]
3822 Campus Dr., Ste. 201
Newport Beach, CA 92660
PH: (949)476-8366
Schuessler, John, Director

My Good Deed [13210]
503 32nd St., Ste. 120
Newport Beach, CA 92663
PH: (949)233-0050
Paine, David, Founder, President

National Association of Credit Union Services Organizations [953]
3419 Via Lido, PMB No. 135
Newport Beach, CA 92663

PH: (949)645-5296
Toll free: 888-462-2870
Fax: (949)645-5297
Antonini, Jack M., CEO, President

National Association of Service Dogs [11692]
2549 Eastbluff Dr., Ste. 430
Newport Beach, CA 92660
Toll free: 888-669-6273
Fax: (877)329-6273
Halverson, Julie, Exec. Dir.

National Cat Protection Society [10667]
6904 W Coast Hwy.
Newport Beach, CA 92663-1306
PH: (949)650-1232
Fax: (949)650-7367
Johnston, Denise, President

National Fibromyalgia Association [14768]
1000 Bristol St. N, Ste. 17-247
Newport Beach, CA 92660
Matallana, Lynne, Founder

Oral Cancer Foundation [14037]
3419 Via Lido, No. 205
Newport Beach, CA 92663
PH: (949)646-8000
Hill, Brian R., Founder, Exec. Dir.

Swedish-American Bar Association [5050]
5020 Campus Dr.
Newport Beach, CA 92660
PH: (949)706-9111
    (760)436-9600
Koltai, Mikael, Esq., Founder

U.S.A. Finn Association [22690]
1048 Irvine Ave., No. 227
Newport Beach, CA 92660

Friends of Debbie Reynolds Fan Club [23992]
5713 Rosario Blvd.
North Highlands, CA 95660
PH: (916)331-0247

Academy of Television Arts and Sciences [450]
5220 Lankershim Blvd.
North Hollywood, CA 91601
PH: (818)754-2800
Rosenblum, Bruce, Chairman, CEO

Actors and Others for Animals [10559]
11523 Burbank Blvd.
North Hollywood, CA 91601
PH: (818)755-6045
    (818)755-6323
Fax: (818)755-6048
Taylor, Susan, Exec. Dir.

Androgen Excess and PCOS Society [14700]
12520 Magnolia Blvd., Ste. 212
North Hollywood, CA 91607
Dokras, Anuja, MD, PhD, President

Heaven on Earth Society for Animals [10636]
7342 Fulton Ave.
North Hollywood, CA 91605
PH: (818)474-2700
Geisel, Ritchie, Chmn. of the Bd.

International Myeloma Foundation [13990]
12650 Riverside Dr., Ste. 206
North Hollywood, CA 91607-3421
PH: (818)487-7455
Toll free: 800-452-2873
Fax: (818)487-7454
Novis, Susie, President, Founder

Set Decorators Society of America
[1959]
7100 Tujunga Ave., Ste. A
North Hollywood, CA 91605-6216
PH: (818)255-2425
Fax: (818)982-8597
Starks, Shirley, President

Stuntmen's Association of Motion
Pictures **[1205]**
5200 Lankershim Blvd., Ste. 190
North Hollywood, CA 91601
PH: (818)766-4334
Fax: (818)766-5943

Association of VA Social Workers
[13105]
9451 Petit Ave.
Northridge, CA 91343
Bruce, LeAnn, President

English Springer Rescue America,
Inc. **[10616]**
19518 Nashville St.
Northridge, CA 91326-2240
Pola, Caryn, President, Chmn. of the
Bd.

International Perfume Bottle Associa-
tion **[21676]**
PO Box 7644
Northridge, CA 91327
Wirth, Teri, VP

Birzeit Society **[8815]**
PO Box 1822
Norwalk, CA 90651
PH: (714)991-1943
(510)786-8247
Kury, Nader, President

International Association of Sufism
[20218]
14 Commercial Blvd., Ste. 101
Novato, CA 94949
PH: (415)472-6959
(415)382-7834
Angha, Dr. Nahid, Founder

Somatics Society **[12015]**
1516 Grant Ave., Ste. 212
Novato, CA 94945
PH: (415)892-0617
(415)897-0336
Fax: (415)892-4388

Vision Sciences Society **[7151]**
19 Richardson Rd.
Novato, CA 94949
PH: (415)883-3301
Fax: (415)593-7606
Graham, Norma, Treasurer

Mini Lop Rabbit Club of America
[4601]
c/o Kassi Sieber-Laughlin, President
9684 Warnerville Rd.
Oakdale, CA 95361
PH: (209)480-1216
Sieber-Laughlin, Kassi, President

World Fast-Draw Association
[23146]
6000 Wilkins Ave.
Oakdale, CA 95361-9797
PH: (209)847-0483
Bright, Ron, Secretary

Adopt a Special Kid **[10436]**
8201 Edgewater Dr., Ste. 103
Oakland, CA 94621
Engle, Joe, Mgr.

Amazon Watch **[3797]**
2201 Broadway, Ste. 508
Oakland, CA 94612
PH: (510)281-9020
Fax: (510)281-9021
Soltani, Atossa, Founder

American Back Society **[16463]**
2648 International Blvd., Ste. 502
Oakland, CA 94601
PH: (510)536-9929
Fax: (510)536-1812
Simmons, James W., MD, President

American Bone Health **[13843]**
1814 Franklin St., Ste. 620
Oakland, CA 94612
PH: (510)832-2663
Toll free: 888-266-3015
Fax: (510)208-7174
Cody, Kathleen M., Exec. Dir.

As You Sow Foundation **[18064]**
1611 Telegraph Ave., Ste. 1450
Oakland, CA 94612
PH: (510)735-8158
Fax: (510)735-8143
Dyck, Thomas Van, Chairman,
Secretary

Asian Americans/Pacific Islanders in
Philanthropy **[12460]**
2201 Broadway, Ste. 720
Oakland, CA 94612
PH: (510)463-3155
Woo, Lillian, Chairman

Asian Pacific Institute on Gender-
Based Violence **[11696]**
500 12th St., Ste. 330
Oakland, CA 94607
PH: (415)568-3315
Fax: (415)954-9999
Dabby, Firoza Chic, Director

Asian and Pacific Islander American
Health Forum **[14927]**
1 Kaiser Plz., Ste. 850
Oakland, CA 94612
PH: (415)954-9988
Fax: (510)419-0263
Paloma, Diane

Asian Pacific Partners for Empowerment, Advocacy and Leadership
[11315]
424 3rd St., Ste. 220
Oakland, CA 94607
PH: (510)844-4147
Lew, Rod, MPH, Exec. Dir.

Association for Women in Comput-
ing **[6295]**
PO Box 2768
Oakland, CA 94602
Sweeney, Jill, President

Autism Answers **[13744]**
PO Box 2632
Oakland, CA 94619
PH: (510)749-7072
Fax: (510)749-0269
Pedraza, Linda, Founder

Backline **[11487]**
PO Box 28284
Oakland, CA 94604-8284
PH: (503)287-4344
(510)817-0781
Toll free: 888-493-0092
Dockray, J. Parker, President, Exec.
Dir.

Before Columbus Foundation **[9753]**
The Raymond House
655-13th St., Ste. 302
Oakland, CA 94612
PH: (510)268-9775

Breakthrough Collaborative **[7746]**
180 Grand Ave., Ste. 1225
Oakland, CA 94612
PH: (415)442-0600
Fax: (415)442-9371
Lachs, Joshua, Exec. Dir.

Business Alliance for Local Living
Economies **[11328]**
2323 Broadway
Oakland, CA 94612
PH: (510)587-9417
Long, Michelle, Exec. Dir.

California College of the Arts Alumni
Association **[19312]**
5212 Broadway
Oakland, CA 94618
PH: (510)594-3600
(415)703-9595
Toll free: 800-447-1ART
Fax: (415)703-9539
Malashock, Sarah, Director

Center for Third World Organizing
[17882]
900 Alice St., Ste. 300
Oakland, CA 94607
PH: (510)201-0080
Fax: (510)433-0908
Lewis, Karissa, Exec. Dir.

Children Now **[10920]**
1404 Franklin St., Ste. 700
Oakland, CA 94612-3232
PH: (510)763-2444
Fax: (510)763-1974
Lempert, Ted, President

Community Built Association **[11335]**
4217 Montgomery St.
Oakland, CA 94611
Donch, Tom Arie, President

Community Economics, Inc. **[11966]**
538 9th St., Ste. 200
Oakland, CA 94607
PH: (510)832-8300
Fax: (510)832-2227
Belzer, Dena, President

Compassionate Cooks **[17584]**
PO Box 16104
Oakland, CA 94610
PH: (510)550-5374
Patrick-Goudreau, Colleen, Founder

Cool Roof Rating Council **[518]**
449 15th St., Ste. 400
Oakland, CA 94612
Toll free: 866-465-2523
Fax: (510)482-4421
Ennis, Mike, Director

Critical Resistance **[18390]**
1904 Franklin St., Ste. 504
Oakland, CA 94612
PH: (510)444-0484
Fax: (510)444-2177
Heaney, Jess, Dir. of Dev.

DeafHope **[11939]**
470 27th St.
Oakland, CA 94612
PH: (510)267-8800
(510)735-8553
Fax: (510)740-0946
Rems-Smario, Julie, Director,
Founder

Earthquake Engineering Research
Institute **[7155]**
499 14th St., Ste. 320
Oakland, CA 94612-1934
PH: (510)451-0905
Fax: (510)451-5411
Berger, Jay, Exec. Dir.

Education Pioneers **[8614]**
360 22nd St., Ste. 220
Oakland, CA 94612
PH: (510)893-4374
Fax: (510)338-6517
Morgan, Scott, CEO, Founder

Electronics TakeBack Coalition
[6420]
4200 Park Blvd., No. 228
Oakland, CA 94602-1312

PH: (510)614-0110

Empowerment Works **[11352]**
1793 Northwood Ct.
Oakland, CA 94611-1167
PH: (415)967-1711
St. James, Melanie, MPA, Exec. Dir.,
Founder

Equal Justice Society **[5728]**
1999 Harrison St., Ste. 800
Oakland, CA 94612
PH: (415)288-8700
Fax: (510)338-3030
Paterson, Eva, President

Event Planners Association **[2326]**
4390 Piedmont Ave.
Oakland, CA 94611
PH: (510)426-5818
Dowd, Maria, VP, Exec. Dir.

Exhale **[10429]**
1714 Franklin St., No. 100-141
Oakland, CA 94612
PH: (510)446-7900
Fax: (309)410-1127
Baker, Aspen, Exec. Dir., Founder

EYH Network **[8280]**
5000 MacArthur Blvd., PMB 9968
Oakland, CA 94613-1301
PH: (510)277-0190
Willoughby, Ann, Liaison

Fair Trade USA **[3301]**
1500 Broadway, Ste. 400
Oakland, CA 94612-2079
PH: (510)663-5260
Fax: (510)663-5264
Rice, Paul, President, CEO

Filipino Advocates for Justice
[17896]
310 8th St., Ste. 308
Oakland, CA 94607
PH: (510)465-9876
Galedo, Lillian, Exec. Dir.

First Amendment Project **[18942]**
1736 Franklin St., 9th Fl.
Oakland, CA 94612-3442
PH: (510)208-7744
Fax: (510)208-4562
Greene, David, Counsel, Exec. Dir.
(Actg.)

Food First Books **[18455]**
398 60th St.
Oakland, CA 94618
PH: (510)654-4400
Fax: (510)654-4551
Borchardt, Ms. Marilyn, Dir. of Dev.

Forward Together **[12960]**
1440 Broadway, Ste. 301
Oakland, CA 94612
PH: (510)663-8300
Fax: (510)663-8301
Shen, Eveline, Exec. Dir.

Generation Five **[12922]**
1015 M.L.K. Jr. Way
Oakland, CA 94607
PH: (510)251-8552
Lymbertos, Chris, Director

Generation Green **[14190]**
c/o Center for Environmental Health
2201 Broadway, Ste. 302
Oakland, CA 94612
PH: (510)655-3900
Fax: (510)655-9100
Green, Michael, Exec. Dir.

Global Footprint Network **[4003]**
312 Clay St., Ste. 300
Oakland, CA 94607-3510

PH: (510)839-8879
Fax: (510)251-2410
Wackernagel, Mathis, President

Good World Solutions [12157]
1500 Broadway, Ste. 400
Oakland, CA 94612-2079
PH: (510)844-1693
Franzese, Heather, Exec. Dir.,
Founder

GreatSchools [7589]
1999 Harrison St., Ste. 1100
Oakland, CA 94612-4708
Jackson, Bill, CEO, Founder,
President

Green for All [17804]
1611 Telegraph Ave., Ste. 600
Oakland, CA 94612
PH: (510)663-6500
Jones, Van, President

Grid Alternatives' International
Program [7202]
1171 Ocean Ave., Ste. 200
Oakland, CA 94608
PH: (510)731-1310
Fax: (510)225-2585
Smith, Jenean, Director

Hands to Hearts International
[11013]
1611 Telegraph Ave., Ste. 1420
Oakland, CA 94612
PH: (510)763-7045
Fax: (510)763-6545
Peterson, Laura, MA, Exec. Dir.,
Founder

Health Outreach Partners [12339]
405 14th St., Ste. 909
Oakland, CA 94612
PH: (510)268-0091
Fax: (510)268-0093
Saborio, Rigoberto, Chairman

The Independent Institute [18983]
100 Swan Way
Oakland, CA 94621-1428
PH: (510)632-1366
Fax: (510)568-6040
Goodman, John, Officer

Insight Center for Community
Economic Development [18150]
1999 Harrison St., Ste. 1800
Oakland, CA 94612-4700
PH: (510)251-2600
Fax: (510)251-0600
Caftel, Brad, Chief Legal Ofc.

Institute for the Advanced Study of
Black Family Life and Culture
[8784]
1012 Linden St.
Oakland, CA 94607
PH: (510)836-3705
Nobles, Wade W., PhD, Exec. Dir.

Institute for Public Accuracy [18986]
1714 Franklin St., No. 100-133
Oakland, CA 94612-3409
PH: (510)788-4541
Solomon, Norman, Exec. Dir.

Integrative Clinics International
[15147]
3871 Piedmont Ave., No. 34
Oakland, CA 94611
Lewin, Bruno, MD, Founder

International Aid for Korean Animals
[10646]
PO Box 20600
Oakland, CA 94620
PH: (510)271-6795
Kum, Kyenan, Founder

International Society for Humor
Studies [9562]
c/o Martin Lampert, Ph.D., Executive
Secretary
Holy Names University
3500 Mountain Blvd.
Oakland, CA 94619
PH: (510)436-1532
Chiaro, Delia, President

International Unicycling Federation
[22749]
4100 Redwood Rd., No. 257
Oakland, CA 94619
Schlote, Olaf, President

International Volunteer Program
[13300]
7106 Sayre Dr.
Oakland, CA 94611
PH: (415)477-3667
Fax: (415)477-3669
Jewell, Rebecca, Dir. of Programs

Internet Sexuality Information
Services, Inc. [8563]
409 13th St., 14th Fl.
Oakland, CA 94612-2607
PH: (510)835-9400
Levine, Deb, MA, Founder

Italian Catholic Federation Central
Council [19506]
8393 Capwell Dr., Ste. 110
Oakland, CA 94621
PH: (510)633-9058
Toll free: 888-ICF-1924
Fax: (510)633-9758
Dianda, Jane, Officer

Jewish Voice for Peace [19520]
1611 Telegraph Ave., Ste. 1020
Oakland, CA 94612
PH: (510)465-1777
Fax: (510)465-1616
Vilkomerson, Rebecca, Exec. Dir.

Jobs for the Future [11767]
505 14th St., Ste. 900
Oakland, CA 94612
PH: (617)728-4446
Fax: (617)728-4857
Patton, Guy L., Chmn. of the Bd.

Karmann Ghia Club of North
America [21414]
4200 Park Blvd., No. 151
Oakland, CA 94602-1361
PH: (510)717-6942
Troy, Richard, Founder, President

Law Students for Reproductive
Justice [19033]
1730 Franklin St., Ste. 212
Oakland, CA 94612-3417
PH: (510)622-8134
Fax: (510)622-8138
Andrus, Sabrina, Exec. Dir.

Leonardo, The International Society
for the Arts, Sciences and Technology [9017]
1440 Broadway, Ste. 422
Oakland, CA 94612
Hebert, Marc, Chairman, President

Mayan Medical Aid [12288]
6988 Pinehaven Rd.
Oakland, CA 94611-1018
Sinkinson, Craig A., MD, President

Media Action Grassroots Network
[18657]
c/o Center for Media Justice
436 14th St., 5th Fl.
Oakland, CA 94612
PH: (510)698-3800
Cyril, Malkia, Exec. Dir.

Medical Education Cooperation with
Cuba [15625]
1814 Franklin St., Ste. 820
Oakland, CA 94612
PH: (678)904-8092
Bourne, Peter G., MD, Chairman

Medicine in Action [15736]
8101 Skyline Blvd.
Oakland, CA 94611
PH: (510)339-7579
Fax: (510)339-6012
Echols, Karolynn, MD, President

National Association of Asian
American Law Enforcement Com-
manders [5486]
PO Box 70581
Oakland, CA 94612
Balmaseda, Clarissa M., President

National Association of State and
Local Equity Funds [1256]
1970 Broadway, Ste. 250
Oakland, CA 94612
PH: (510)444-1101
Keller, Hal, VP

National Center for Employee
Ownership [1082]
1629 Telegraph Ave., Ste. 200
Oakland, CA 94612
PH: (510)208-1300
Fax: (510)272-9510
Rodgers, Loren, Exec. Dir.

National Center for Science Educa-
tion [8551]
1904 Franklin St., Ste. 600
Oakland, CA 94612-2922
PH: (510)601-7203
Fax: (510)788-7971
Newton, Steven, Dir. of Programs

National Center for Youth Law
[5190]
405 14th St., 15th Fl.
Oakland, CA 94612
PH: (510)835-8098
Fax: (510)835-8099
Edelman, Peter B., President

National Council on Crime and
Delinquency [11510]
1970 Broadway, Ste. 500
Oakland, CA 94612
Toll free: 800-306-6223
Hughes, Ronald, Chairman

National Employment Lawyers As-
sociation [5040]
2201 Broadway, Ste. 402
Oakland, CA 94612
PH: (415)296-7629
Toll free: 866-593-7521
Haynes, Alicia K., President

National Network for Immigrant and
Refugee Rights [18467]
310 8th St., Ste. 310
Oakland, CA 94607
PH: (510)465-1984
Fax: (510)465-1885
Tactaquin, Catherine, Exec. Dir.

National Organization for Lesbians
of Size [11902]
PO Box 5475
Oakland, CA 94605
Gino, Alex, Secretary

National Radio Project [18660]
1904 Franklin St., Ste. 405
Oakland, CA 94612
PH: (510)251-1332
(510)459-8558
Rudman, Lisa, Exec. Dir.

Neighborhood Funders Group
[12492]
436 14th St., Ste. 425
Oakland, CA 94612

PH: (510)444-6063
Ahuja, Sarita, Director

Network in Solidarity with the People
of Guatemala [18272]
PO Box 70494
Oakland, CA 94612-2728
PH: (510)763-1403
Van Slyke, Melinda, President

North American-Bulgarian Chamber
of Commerce [23608]
c/o Paul Andrews
6460 Leaona St.
Oakland, CA 94605
PH: (415)251-2322

Operation Rainbow [15610]
4200 Park Blvd., PMB 157
Oakland, CA 94602
PH: (510)273-2485
(510)655-4598
Escobosa, Laura, Exec. Dir.

Pacific Institute for Studies in
Development, Environment, and
Security [12958]
Preservation Pk.
654 13th St.
Oakland, CA 94612
PH: (510)251-1600
Fax: (510)251-2203
Gleick, Dr. Peter H., President

Peace and Freedom Party [18893]
PO Box 24764
Oakland, CA 94623
PH: (510)465-9414
Weber, C.T., Officer

Pesticide Action Network North
America Regional Center [13226]
1611 Telegraph Ave., Ste. 1200
Oakland, CA 94612-2130
PH: (510)788-9020
Hatcher, Judy, Exec. Dir.

Playworks [12507]
380 Washington St.
Oakland, CA 94607
PH: (510)893-4180
Fax: (510)893-4378
Wilson, Cindy

PolicyLink [11719]
1438 Webster St., Ste. 303
Oakland, CA 94612
PH: (510)663-2333
Fax: (510)663-9684
Blackwell, Angela Glover, CEO,
Founder

Polish Arts and Culture Foundation
[19606]
4077 Waterhouse Rd.
Oakland, CA 94602
PH: (510)599-2244
Tomczykowska, Caria, President

Prevention International: No Cervical
Cancer [14050]
PO Box 13081
Oakland, CA 94661
PH: (510)452-2542
Taylor, Kay, Founder, Exec. Dir.

Project Baobab [13476]
c/o Philanthropic Ventures Foundation
1222 Preservation Pky.
Oakland, CA 94612
Williams, Gee Gee, Founder

Race Forward: The Center for Racial
Justice Innovation [12989]
900 Alice St., Ste. 400
Oakland, CA 94607
PH: (510)653-3415
Fax: (510)986-1062
Iyer, Deepa, Chairman

Reach Global **[12990]**
1611 Telegraph Ave., Ste. 1420
Oakland, CA 94612
PH: (510)763-7045
Fax: (510)763-6545
Kline, Sean, Exec. Dir., Founder

Reconnecting America **[13234]**
436 14th St., Ste. 1005
Oakland, CA 94612
PH: (510)268-8602
Fax: (510)268-8673
Brooks, Allison, President, CEO

Redefining Progress **[18159]**
1904 Franklin St., Ste. 600
Oakland, CA 94612
PH: (510)444-3041
Fax: (510)444-3191
Barrett, James, Chairman

Responsible Purchasing Network **[4132]**
1440 Broadway, Ste. 901
Oakland, CA 94612
PH: (510)547-5475
Toll free: 866-776-1330
Culver, Alicia, Exec. Dir.

The Rock Poster Society **[8886]**
PO Box 20309
Oakland, CA 94620-0309
Hohn, Marty, President

Ruckus Society **[19130]**
PO Box 28741
Oakland, CA 94604
PH: (510)931-6339
Toll free: 866-778-6374
Gunn, Allen, Secretary

Sandtray Network **[16851]**
1946 Clemens Rd.
Oakland, CA 94602
PH: (510)530-1383

Sierra Club **[4012]**
2101 Webster St., Ste. 1300
Oakland, CA 94612
PH: (415)977-5500
Fax: (510)208-3140
Brune, Michael, Exec. Dir.

Socialist Action **[19144]**
PO Box 10328
Oakland, CA 94610
PH: (510)268-9429
Mackler, Jeff, Secretary

Society for the Eradication of Television **[17957]**
PO Box 10491
Oakland, CA 94610-0491
Wagner, Steve, Director

Society of Practitioners of Health Impact Assessment **[15065]**
304 12th St., Ste. 2B
Oakland, CA 94607
PH: (510)452-9442
Lin, Tatiana, President

Survivorship **[13274]**
Family Justice Center
470 27th St.
Oakland, CA 94612
Brick, Neil, President

Thrive Networks **[18502]**
1611 Telegraph Ave., Ste. 1420
Oakland, CA 94612
PH: (510)763-7045
Fax: (510)763-6545
Griffith, Melinda, CEO

Tibet Justice Center **[19192]**
440 Grand Ave., Ste. 425
Oakland, CA 94610

PH: (510)486-0588
Liddell, Iona, Exec. Dir.

Tradeswomen, Inc. **[11784]**
337 17th St., Ste. 204
Oakland, CA 94612-3356
PH: (510)891-8773
Fax: (510)891-8775
Vasey, Meg, Exec. Dir.

Ultra Marathon Cycling Association **[22755]**
c/o Paul Carpenter, President
7982 Hillmont Dr., Apt. B
Oakland, CA 94605
PH: (303)545-9566
Fax: (303)545-9619
Vander Linden, Merry, Mgr.

Union of American Physicians and Dentists **[23445]**
180 Grand Ave., Ste. 1380
Oakland, CA 94612
PH: (510)839-0193
Toll free: 800-622-0909
Fax: (510)763-8756
Bussey, Stuart A., President

United States Federation of Worker Cooperatives **[23538]**
1904 Franklin St., Ste. 400
Oakland, CA 94612
PH: (415)392-7277
Johnson, Amy, Exec. Dir.

Vote Solar Initiative **[7215]**
360 22nd St., Ste. 730
Oakland, CA 94612
PH: (415)817-5061
Browning, Adam, Exec. Dir.

We the People **[18738]**
200 Harrison St.
Oakland, CA 94607
PH: (510)836-3273
Fax: (510)836-3063
Brown, Edmund G., Jr., Leader

Western States Legal Foundation **[5657]**
c/o Jacqueline Cabasso, Executive Director
Preservation Pk.
655 13th St., Ste. 201
Oakland, CA 94612
PH: (510)839-5877
Fax: (510)839-5397
Cabasso, Jacqueline, Exec. Dir.

Women Organized to Respond to Life-Threatening Diseases **[13566]**
389 30th St.
Oakland, CA 94609-3402
PH: (510)986-0340
Fax: (510)986-0341
Carey-Grant, Cynthia, Exec. Dir.

Workers Solidarity Alliance **[19259]**
PO Box 3967
Oakland, CA 94609

International Scouting Collectors Association **[21678]**
c/o Craig Leighty, President
724 Kineo Ct.
Oakley, CA 94561-3541
PH: (925)548-9966
Leighty, Craig, President

Police Society for Problem Based Learning **[5516]**
PO Box 362
Oakley, CA 94561
Toll free: 800-862-6307
Buhlis, Roger, President

1st Marine Division Association **[21008]**
PO Box 9000
Oceanside, CA 92051

PH: (760)763-3268

Academy of American Franciscan History **[19786]**
4050 Mission Ave.
Oceanside, CA 92057
PH: (510)548-1755
Schwaller, Dr. John F., Mgr.

American Combat Veterans of War **[21105]**
3508 Seagate Way, Ste. 160
Oceanside, CA 92056-2686
PH: (706)696-0460
Rider, William, CEO, President

Church Growth Inc. **[20584]**
2530 Vista Way, Ste. F78
Oceanside, CA 92054
Arn, Dr. Charles, EdD, President

Love on a Leash **[17452]**
PO Box 4548
Oceanside, CA 92052-4548
PH: (760)740-2326
Edleman, Keith, Membership Chp.

National Public Employer Labor Relations Association **[5400]**
1012 S Coast Hwy., Ste. M
Oceanside, CA 92054
PH: (760)433-1686
Toll free: 877-673-5721
Fax: (760)433-1687
Kolb, Michael T., Exec. Dir.

Rosicrucian Fellowship **[19626]**
2222 Mission Ave.
Oceanside, CA 92058-2329
PH: (760)757-6600
Fax: (760)721-3806
Heindel, Max, Owner

Foundation for Grandparenting **[11916]**
108 Farnham Rd.
Ojai, CA 93023-1759
Kornhaber, Arthur, MD, Founder, President

Global Resource Alliance **[4492]**
963 Oso Rd.
Ojai, CA 93023
PH: (805)646-4439
Hebenstreit, Lyn, President

Green Burial Council **[2405]**
PO Box 851
Ojai, CA 93024-0851
Toll free: 888-966-3330
Currie, Candace, Secretary

Krishnamurti Foundation of America **[12008]**
1130 Mc Andrew Rd.
Ojai, CA 93023
PH: (805)646-2726
Sluijter, Jaap, Exec. Dir.

Lotus Outreach **[13013]**
c/o Patty Waltcher, President
1104 N Signal St.
Ojai, CA 93023
PH: (760)290-7190
Toll free: 888-831-9990
Norbu, Khyentse, Chairman

National Disaster Search Dog Foundation **[12746]**
501 E Ojai Ave.
Ojai, CA 93023
Toll free: 888-459-4376
Fax: (805)640-1848
Tosch, Debra, Exec. Dir.

Small Publishers, Artists and Writers Network **[2812]**
1129 Maricopa Highway 142
Ojai, CA 93023
Kaiser, Kathleen, President

Wild Burro Rescue and Preservation Project **[10715]**
PO Box 10
Olancha, CA 93549-0010
PH: (760)384-8523
Chontos, Ms. Diana, Founder, President

Society of Communications Technology Consultants International **[6352]**
PO Box 70
Old Station, CA 96071
PH: (530)335-7313
Toll free: 866-782-7670
Fax: (530)335-7370
Blythe, Patricia, Director

Society of Telecommunications Consultants **[3240]**
PO Box 70
Old Station, CA 96071
PH: (530)335-7313
Toll free: 800-782-7670
Fax: (800)859-3205
Swartz, Melissa, President

Turtle Island Restoration Network **[3961]**
9255 Sir Francis Drake Blvd.
Olema, CA 94950
PH: (415)663-8590
Toll free: 800-859-7283
Fax: (415)663-9534
Steiner, Todd, Exec. Dir.

Gospel Literature International **[20420]**
2940 Inland Empire Blvd., Ste. 101
Ontario, CA 91764-4898
PH: (909)481-5222
Fax: (909)481-5216
Wilkinson, Dr. Georgalyn, President

International Association of Plumbing and Mechanical Officials **[5067]**
4755 E Philadelphia St.
Ontario, CA 91761
PH: (909)472-4100
Fax: (909)472-4150
Pfeiffer, Bruce, President

International Kart Federation **[22970]**
1609 S Grove Ave., Ste. 105
Ontario, CA 91761
PH: (909)923-4999
Fax: (909)923-6940
Hilger, Bill, VP

Leathercraft Guild **[2085]**
c/o Robert Ambriz
PO Box 4603
Ontario, CA 91761-4603
PH: (909)983-9544
Ambriz, Robert, Contact

Afghan American Muslim Outreach **[19283]**
PO Box 5467
Orange, CA 92863

American Concrete Pressure Pipe Association **[2602]**
4122 E Chapman Ave., Ste. 27
Orange, CA 92869-4011
PH: (714)801-0298
Narcise, Alex, Chairperson

Child Vikaas International **[10816]**
6674 E Bonita Ct.
Orange, CA 92867
Rajagopalan, Dr. Sampath, President

Global Equity Organization **[1071]**
1442 E Lincoln Ave., No. 487
Orange, CA 92865
PH: (714)630-2908
Fax: (714)421-4900
Anderson, Danyle, Exec. Dir.

National Roof Certification and
Inspection Association **[560]**
2232 E Wilson Ave.
Orange, CA 92867
Toll free: 866-210-7464
Hogue, Bill, Director

USFN-America's Mortgage Banking
Attorneys **[5053]**
625 The City Dr., Ste. 310
Orange, CA 92868
PH: (714)838-7167
Toll free: 800-635-6128
Fax: (714)573-2650
Hultman, Ms. Alberta E., CAE, CEO,
Exec. Dir.

Greener Pastures Institute **[11970]**
PO Box 2916
Orcutt, CA 93457
Toll free: 800-688-6352
Fax: (805)938-1396
Seavey, William L., Director

Alliance for Water Education **[7883]**
120 Village Sq., Ste. 137
Orinda, CA 94563
PH: (925)386-0515
Fax: (925)386-0501
Jordan, Christie Batterman, Founder

Seventh Day Adventist Kinship
International **[20189]**
PO Box 244
Orinda, CA 94563-0244
Elliott, Yolanda, President

Automatic Transmission Rebuilders
Association **[306]**
2400 Latigo Ave.
Oxnard, CA 93030
PH: (805)604-2000
Toll free: 866-464-2872
Fax: (805)604-2003
Rodd, Jim, President

Olson 30 National Class Association
[22659]
3695 Via Pacifica Walk
Oxnard, CA 93035
Adamson, Jason, President

Surfer's Medical Association **[15747]**
PO Box 51881
Pacific Grove, CA 93950
Jones, Dr. Bill, Exec. Dir.

American Nordic Walking Associa-
tion **[16693]**
827 Via De La Paz
Pacific Palisades, CA 90272
PH: (323)244-2519
Fax: (310)459-2842

Center for Management Effective-
ness **[2160]**
PO Box 1202
Pacific Palisades, CA 90272-1202
PH: (310)459-6052
Herzog, Eric L., PhD, President

International Wildlife Conservation
Society **[4833]**
PO Box 34
Pacific Palisades, CA 90272
PH: (310)476-9305
Byrne, Peter, Founder

Parrot International **[3667]**
15332 Antioch Ave., No. 417
Pacific Palisades, CA 90272
Fax: (310)454-9915
Stafford, Dr. Mark L., Founder,
President

Pet Pride **[10680]**
PO Box 1055
Pacific Palisades, CA 90272-1055

PH: (310)836-5427

Protect Our Winters **[4096]**
PO Box 38
Pacific Palisades, CA 90272
PH: (310)909-7941
Jones, Jeremy, CEO, Founder

Reef Check **[4470]**
17575 Pacific Coast Hwy., Ste. B
Pacific Palisades, CA 90272-1057
PH: (310)230-2371
    (310)230-2360
Fax: (310)230-2376
Hodgson, Gregor, PhD, Exec. Dir.,
Founder

Humanities Education and Research
Association **[8005]**
PO Box 715
Pacifica, CA 94044-0715
Cannon, Sarita, Bd. Member

Melos Institute **[256]**
1071 Yosemite Dr.
Pacifica, CA 94044
PH: (650)355-4094
Fax: (650)359-3611
Hudson, Patricia A., President

Adelante Bolivia **[10782]**
41-990 Cook St., Ste. 501
Palm Desert, CA 92211
Armijo, Oscar Raziel, President,
Exec. Dir.

American Association of Franchisees
and Dealers **[1455]**
PO Box 10158
Palm Desert, CA 92255-0158
PH: (619)209-3775
Toll free: 800-733-9858
Purvin, Robert L., Jr., Chairman,
CEO

Mission America Coalition **[19993]**
PO Box 13930
Palm Desert, CA 92255
PH: (760)200-2707
Fax: (760)200-8837
Cedar, Dr. Paul A., Chairman, CEO

National Throws Coaches Associa-
tion **[22735]**
PO Box 14114
Palm Desert, CA 92255-4114
Toll free: 888-527-6772
Lasorsa, Rob, Contact

Parkinson's Resource Organization
[15983]
74-090 El Paseo, Ste. 104
Palm Desert, CA 92260
PH: (760)773-5628
Toll free: 877-775-4111
Rosen, Jo, President, Founder

American Forensic Nurses **[16105]**
255 N El Cielo Rd., Ste. 140-195
Palm Springs, CA 92262
PH: (760)322-9925
Fax: (760)322-9914
Otto, Faye Battiste, President

American Society for the Positive
Care of Children **[10852]**
777 E Tahquitz Canyon Way, Ste.
323
Palm Springs, CA 92262
PH: (760)990-2200
Toll free: 800-422-4453
O'Neal, Terry, President

Association of Construction Inspec-
tors **[1814]**
PO Box 879
Palm Springs, CA 92263-0879
Toll free: 877-743-6806
Merrell, Bill, Officer

Housing Inspection Foundation
[1816]
PO Box 879
Palm Springs, CA 92263-0879
Toll free: 877-743-6806
Merrell, Bill C., PhD, Dir. Ed.

International Real Estate Institute
[2866]
810 N Farrell Dr.
Palm Springs, CA 92262
Toll free: 877-327-5284
Fax: (760)327-5631
Jardosh, Snehal, Officer

International Society of Meeting
Planners **[2333]**
810 N Farell Dr.
Palm Springs, CA 92263
PH: (760)327-5284
Toll free: 877-743-6802
Fax: (760)327-5631
Merrell, Bill, Advisor

National Association of Real Estate
Appraisers **[229]**
PO Box 879
Palm Springs, CA 92263
Toll free: 877-743-6806
Fax: (760)327-5631
Merrell, Bill, Mem.

National Association of Review Ap-
praisers and Mortgage Underwrit-
ers **[2881]**
810 N Farrell Dr.
Palm Springs, CA 92262
PH: (760)327-5284
Toll free: 877-743-6805
Fax: (760)327-5631
Merrell, Dr. Bill, Advisor

One Voice of Peace **[8406]**
522 S Sunrise Way, Ste. 32
Palm Springs, CA 92264
PH: (760)424-8811
Chvany, Elena, Exec. Dir., Founder

World Water Rescue Foundation
[4776]
Airport Park Plz., Ste. 306
Palm Springs, CA 92262
Sauers, Philip E., Founder, Chair-
man

Desert Tortoise Council **[3847]**
4654 East Ave. S, No. 257B
Palmdale, CA 93552
MacDonald, Ken, Chairperson

Helping Orphans and Widows
[11026]
3413 Sungate Dr.
Palmdale, CA 93551
PH: (661)273-4249
Bayles, James, Director

Humanitarian Travels International
[13237]
37940 42nd St. E, Unit 133
Palmdale, CA 93552
PH: (661)285-3889

Scientists, Engineers, and Technicians Leadership Association
[6585]
2101 E Palmdale Blvd.
Palmdale, CA 93550
PH: (661)267-1505
Kartiala, Eero, Chmn. of the Bd.

American Business Association of
Russian-speaking Professionals
[2738]
555 Bryant St., Ste. 392
Palo Alto, CA 94301
PH: (650)278-0431
Fedorova, Tatiana, CEO

Ape Action Africa **[4786]**
555 Bryant St., No. 862
Palo Alto, CA 94301
Hogan, Rachel, Director

Asia America MultiTechnology As-
sociation **[7260]**
555 Bryant St., No. 332
Palo Alto, CA 94301-1704
PH: (650)773-2293
Lum, Lisa M., Exec. Dir.

Association for the Advancement of
Artificial Intelligence **[5983]**
2275 E Bayshore Rd., Ste. 160
Palo Alto, CA 94303
PH: (650)328-3123
Fax: (650)321-4457
Senator, Ted, Secretary, Treasurer

Association of French Schools in
North America **[8530]**
c/o Philippe Dietz, Treasurer
151 Laura Ln.
Palo Alto, CA 94303
Canadas, Frédéric, President

Association for Transpersonal
Psychology **[9532]**
PO Box 50187
Palo Alto, CA 94303
PH: (650)424-8764
Gaylinn, Daniel, Exec. Dir.

Anita Borg Institute for Women and
Technology **[12508]**
1501 Page Mill Rd., MS 1105
Palo Alto, CA 94304
PH: (212)897-2157
Beck, James, Treasurer, VP,
Secretary

Burmese American Democratic Alli-
ance **[17824]**
1952 Mcnair St.
Palo Alto, CA 94303
PH: (415)895-2232
Verma, Anil, Secretary

Canary Foundation **[13914]**
3155 Porer Dr.
Palo Alto, CA 94304
PH: (650)646-3200
Fax: (650)251-9758
Listwin, Don, Founder

CommerceNet **[7262]**
955A Alma St.
Palo Alto, CA 94301
PH: (650)289-4040
Fax: (650)289-4041
Rodin, Robert, Bd. Member

Electric Power Research Institute
[6474]
3420 Hillview Ave.
Palo Alto, CA 94304
PH: (650)855-2121
Toll free: 800-313-3774
Keefe, Pamela J., CFO, Sr. VP,
Treasurer

Foresight Institute **[7268]**
Box 61058
Palo Alto, CA 94306
PH: (650)289-0860
Fax: (650)289-0863
Morningstar, Chip, Secretary

Health Wrights **[17004]**
PO Box 1344
Palo Alto, CA 94302
PH: (650)325-7500
Fax: (650)325-1080
Werner, David, Director

Institute for Molecular Manufacturing
[6794]
555 Bryant St., Ste. 354
Palo Alto, CA 94301

PH: (650)917-1120
Fax: (650)917-1120
Jacobstein, Neil, Chairman

Mental Research Institute [13799]
555 Middlefield Rd.
Palo Alto, CA 94301
PH: (650)321-3055
(650)322-2252
Fax: (650)321-3785
Suberville, Sophie, Exec. Dir.

One Dollar for Life [12963]
783 Kendall Ave.
Palo Alto, CA 94306
PH: (661)203-8750
Fax: (650)856-1017
Freeman, Robert, Dir. of Admin.

One Million Lights [11298]
PO Box 444
Palo Alto, CA 94302
PH: (650)387-3150
Fax: (801)788-1420
Sidana, Anna, Founder, CEO, Bd.
Member

Open Networking Foundation [6911]
2275 E Bayshore Rd., Ste. 103
Palo Alto, CA 94303
PH: (510)492-4070
Pitt, Dan, Exec. Dir.

Rose Kushner Breast Cancer
Advisory Center [14000]
PO Box 757
Palos Verdes Estates, CA 90274

Guitar Foundation of America [9914]
PO Box 2900
Palos Verdes Peninsula, CA 90274
Toll free: 877-570-1651
Lane, Robert, VP, Secretary

Mission for Establishment of Human
Rights in Iran [18427]
PO Box 2037
Palos Verdes Peninsula, CA 90274
PH: (310)377-4590
Fax: (310)694-8039
Parvin, Dr. Mohammad, President

National Association for Asian and
Pacific American Education [8621]
PO Box 3471
Palos Verdes Peninsula, CA 90274
PH: (416)393-9400
Tsuchida, John N., President

Institute for Female Alternative
Medicine [17125]
14860 Roscoe Blvd., Ste. 200
Panorama City, CA 91402
PH: (818)997-5000
Toll free: 800-505-4326
Fax: (818)997-5005
del Junco, Dr. Tirso, Jr., Founder,
Medical Dir.

International Sex Worker Foundation
for Art, Culture and Education
[12945]
8801 Cedros Ave., No. 7
Panorama City, CA 91402
PH: (818)924-2776
Almodovar, Norma Jean,
Chairperson, President

American Fuchsia Society [22071]
c/o Judy Salome, Membership
Secretary
6979 Clark Rd.
Paradise, CA 95969-2210
PH: (530)876-8517
Bligh, Ms. Judy, President

Spirit Quilts [11156]
PO Box 3268
Paradise, CA 95967

PH: (530)873-2765
Gregory, JayaMae, CEO, Founder

American Construction Inspectors
Association [798]
530 S Lake Ave., No. 431
Pasadena, CA 91101
PH: (626)797-2242
Fax: (626)797-2214
Dooley, Dennis, RCI, VP

American Mindfulness Research Association [7061]
99 W California Blvd.
Pasadena, CA 91105
Black, David, Founder

American Seminar Leaders Associa-
tion [7667]
2405 E Washington Blvd.
Pasadena, CA 91104-2040
PH: (626)791-1211
Toll free: 800-801-1886
Fax: (626)791-0701
Davidson, June, Contact

American Vaulting Association
[23348]
1443 E Washington Blvd., No. 289
Pasadena, CA 91104
PH: (323)654-0800
Fax: (323)654-4306
Geisler, Connie, President

Bangladeshi American Charitable
Organization [10862]
155 N Lake Ave., Ste. 600
Pasadena, CA 91101
Islam, Dr. Saiful, President, Director

China Connection [12146]
458 S Pasadena Ave.
Pasadena, CA 91105-1838
PH: (626)793-3737
Fax: (626)793-3362
Call, Kathy, Exec. Dir., Founder

Evangelize China Fellowship
[20415]
PO Box 418
Pasadena, CA 91102-9969
Szeto, Dr. Paul C.C., Director,
President

Finlandia Foundation National [9320]
470 W Walnut St.
Pasadena, CA 91103
PH: (626)795-2081
Fax: (626)795-6533
Rahkonen, Ossi, President

Francis Bacon Foundation [9051]
100 Corson St.
Pasadena, CA 91103
Arensberg, Walter, Founder

Got Agua [13354]
23 E Colorado Blvd., Ste. 203
Pasadena, CA 91105
PH: (626)657-2255
Hickey, Connor, Founder

HEAR Center [15192]
301 E Del Mar Blvd.
Pasadena, CA 91101-2714
PH: (626)796-2016
Fax: (626)796-2320
Simon, Ellen, Exec. Dir.

HTML Writers Guild [6315]
119 E Union St., Ste. A
Pasadena, CA 91103
PH: (626)449-3709
Fax: (866)607-1773
Brinegar, Richard, Exec. Dir.

International Alliance of Hair
Restoration Surgeons [14901]
c/o Paul J. McAndrews, Senior
Medical Advisor

50 Alessandro Pl., Ste. 115
Pasadena, CA 91105
Fax: (626)449-4558
McAndrews, Paul J., MD, Advisor

International Christian Studies As-
sociation [19986]
1065 Pine Bluff Dr.
Pasadena, CA 91107-1751
PH: (626)351-0419
Gruenwald, Dr. Oskar, President

International String Figure Associa-
tion [21765]
PO Box 5134
Pasadena, CA 91117-0134
PH: (626)398-1057

International Webmasters Associa-
tion [6320]
119 E Union St., Ste. A
Pasadena, CA 91103
PH: (626)449-3709
Fax: (866)607-1773

National Association for Hispanic
Elderly [19462]
234 E Colorado Blvd., Ste. 300
Pasadena, CA 91101
PH: (626)564-1988
Lacayo, Dr. Carmela G., President,
CEO

National Hispanic Media Coalition
[17952]
55 S Grand Ave.
Pasadena, CA 91105
PH: (626)792-6462
Fax: (626)792-6051
Nogales, Alex, CEO, President

National Organization of Gay and
Lesbian Scientists and Technical
Professionals [7141]
PO Box 91803
Pasadena, CA 91109
PH: (626)791-7689
Fax: (626)791-7689
Diamond, Rochelle, Chairperson

North American Travel Journalists
Association [3388]
3579 E Foothill Blvd., No. 744
Pasadena, CA 91107
PH: (626)376-9754
Fax: (626)628-1854
Hernandez, Helen, CEO

Nutrition and Education International
[12105]
2500 E Foothill Blvd., Ste. 407
Pasadena, CA 91107
PH: (626)744-0270
Fax: (626)316-6067
Kwon, Steven, Founder, President

The Planetary Society [5871]
60 S Los Robles Ave.
Pasadena, CA 91101
PH: (626)793-5100
Fax: (626)793-5528
Nye, Bill, CEO

Population Communication [12513]
1250 E Walnut St., Ste. 160
Pasadena, CA 91106-1833
PH: (626)793-4750
Gillespie, Robert, President

Alisa Ann Ruch Burn Foundation
[13866]
50 N Hill Ave., Ste. 305
Pasadena, CA 91106
PH: (818)848-0223
Toll free: 800-242-BURN
Fax: (818)848-0296
Radics-Johnson, Jennifer, Exec. Dir.

Society for the Conservation of
Bighorn Sheep [4890]
PO Box 94182
Pasadena, CA 91109-4182

PH: (310)339-4677
Hybarger, John, Cmte. Mgmt. Ofc.

Spiritual Counterfeits Project [20050]
PO Box 40015
Pasadena, CA 91114-7015
PH: (510)540-0300
Fax: (510)540-1107
Brooke, Tal, President

Stand Up to Cancer [14066]
1801 W Olympic Blvd.
Pasadena, CA 91199-1224
Toll free: 888-204-5809
Couric, Katie, Founder

Tanka Society of America [10160]
c/o Kathabela Wilson, Secretary
439 S Catalina Ave., No. 306
Pasadena, CA 91106
Wilson, Kathabela, Secretary

Tournament of Roses Association
[9287]
391 S Orange Grove Blvd.
Pasadena, CA 91184
PH: (626)449-4100
Allen, Jeff, CFO

Association of Synthetic Grass
Installers [501]
17487 Penn Valley Dr., Ste. B103
Penn Valley, CA 95946
PH: (530)432-5851
Toll free: 888-378-4581
Fax: (530)432-1098
Costa, Annie, Exec. Dir.

Global Family [13008]
17756 Minnow Way
Penn Valley, CA 95946
PH: (530)277-2804
Anderson, Carolyn, Director,
Founder

The American Judo and Jujitsu
Federation [22965]
c/o Central Office Administrator
PO Box 596
Penryn, CA 95663-0596
Toll free: 800-850-AJJF
Fax: (415)457-9730
Pierre, Pete St., Comm. Chm.

Philalethes Society [19566]
PO Box 379
Penryn, CA 95663-0379
Tilton, Terry L., Exec. Sec.

American Silkie Bantam Club [4564]
c/o Carina Moncrief, Secretary/
Treasurer, 23754 Spenser Butte
Dr.
23754 Spenser Butte Dr.
Perris, CA 92570
PH: (951)240-2939
Gambill, Brenda, Director

American Small Business League
[3113]
3910 Cypress Dr., Ste. B
Petaluma, CA 94954
PH: (707)789-9575
Fax: (707)789-9580
Chapman, Lloyd, President

Chinese Christian Mission [20394]
1269 N McDowell Blvd.
Petaluma, CA 94954-1133
PH: (707)762-1314
Fax: (707)762-1713
Chiang, Rev. Samuel, Gen. Sec.

Inner Light Foundation [7092]
PO Box 750265
Petaluma, CA 94975
PH: (707)765-2200
Beyer, Marygale, Mgr.

Institute of Noetic Sciences [20606]
101 San Antonio Rd.
Petaluma, CA 94952
PH: (707)775-3500
Fax: (707)781-7420
Vieten, Cassandra, President, CEO

Polly Klaas Foundation [12357]
PO Box 800
Petaluma, CA 94953
Toll free: 800-587-4357
Fax: (707)769-4019
Fish, Lt. Dan, President

Project Censored [17838]
PO Box 750940
Petaluma, CA 94975
PH: (707)874-2695
Huff, Mickey, Director

Black Russian Terrier Club of
America [21842]
PO Box 291815
Phelan, CA 92329
Kellerman, Dana F., Secretary

Armenian Numismatic Society
[22262]
8511 Beverly Park Pl.
Pico Rivera, CA 90660-1920
PH: (562)695-0380
Nercessian, Y.T., Editor

African Scientific Institute [7114]
PO Box 20810
Piedmont, CA 94620
PH: (510)653-7027
Cherry, Mr. Lee O., CEO, President

International Jack Benny Fan Club
[24009]
PO Box 11288
Piedmont, CA 94611
Leff, Laura, President

Pionus Breeders Association [21549]
PO Box 150
Pilot Hill, CA 95664
PH: (530)885-7868

National Finch and Softbill Society
[21544]
c/o Sara Roberts, Treasurer
720 Live Oak Ln.
Pinole, CA 94564
Mikel, Rebecca, President

Southwest Bluegrass Association
[10014]
PO Box 720974
Pinon Hills, CA 92372-0974
Pritchett, Tony, Contact

International Society of Professional
Trackers [23325]
c/o Del Morris, Executive Director
PO Box 1162
Pioneer, CA 95666
Morris, Del, Exec. Dir.

International Association for Correctional and Forensic Psychology
[11530]
897 Oak Park Blvd., No. 124
Pismo Beach, CA 93449-3293
PH: (910)799-9107
Gannon, John L., Exec. Dir.

U.S. Deaf Cycling Association
[22800]
c/o Bobby Skedsmo, Secretary/
Treasurer
247 Jack London Ct.
Pittsburg, CA 94565-3661
PH: (925)203-1045
(925)203-1262
Osbrink, Rory, President

Association of Professional Ball
Players of America [22545]
101 S Kraemer Ave., Ste. 112
Placentia, CA 92870-6109

PH: (714)528-2012
Fax: (714)528-2037
Beverage, Dick, Secretary, Treasurer

United States Powerlifting Associa-
tion [23072]
PO Box 1090
Placentia, CA 92871
PH: (661)333-9800
Denison, Steve, President

World Access for the Blind [17749]
650 N Rose Dr., No. 208
Placentia, CA 92870
Toll free: 866-396-7035
Kish, Daniel, Founder, President

El Dorado Winery Association [184]
PO Box 1614
Placerville, CA 95667
Toll free: 800-306-3956

American Federation of Motorcyclists
[22209]
395 Taylor Blvd., No. 130
Pleasant Hill, CA 94523
PH: (510)833-7223
Woolridge, Berto, President

California Redwood Association
[1431]
818 Grayson Rd., Ste. 201
Pleasant Hill, CA 94523
PH: (925)935-1499
Toll free: 888-225-7339
Fax: (925)935-1496

Redwood Inspection Service [1418]
818 Grayson Rd., Ste. 201
Pleasant Hill, CA 94523
PH: (925)935-1499
Fax: (925)935-1496

Chinese American Cooperation
Council [12147]
PO Box 12028
Pleasanton, CA 94588
Xue, Jun, President

Ensaaf [19126]
PO Box 11682
Pleasanton, CA 94588-1682
PH: (206)866-5642
Fax: (270)916-7074
Dhami, Sukhman, Founder, Director

Go Green Initiative Association
[7891]
4307 Valley Ave., Ste. 2
Pleasanton, CA 94566
PH: (925)289-0145
Fax: (925)226-3942
Buck, Jill, Exec. Dir., Founder

Goodguys Rod and Custom Associa-
tion [21388]
PO Box 9132
Pleasanton, CA 94566
PH: (925)838-9876
Meadors, Marc, President

International Transactional Analysis
Association [16832]
2843 Hopyard Rd., Ste. 155
Pleasanton, CA 94588
PH: (925)600-8110
Fax: (925)600-8112

Q Users Experience [6753]
c/o Kathy Wetherell, Treasurer
4750 1st St.
Pleasanton, CA 94566
Hobbs, Chris, Web Adm.

Tremor Action Network [15996]
PO Box 5013
Pleasanton, CA 94566-0513
PH: (510)681-6565
Fax: (925)369-0485
Alcairo, Pet, Director

Zane Grey's West Society [9116]
c/o Sheryle Hodapp, Secretary-
Treasurer
15 Deer Oaks Dr.
Pleasanton, CA 94588-8236
PH: (925)485-1325
Bolinger, Terry, President, Web Adm.

Society of Air Force Clinical
Surgeons [17400]
1511 Paddington Way
Plumas Lake, CA 95961-9129
PH: (530)741-0680
Fax: (530)741-0680
Thomas, Rose, Exec. Dir.

Bethlehem Association [18677]
1192 N Garey Ave.
Pomona, CA 91767
PH: (610)353-2010
(650)740-3119
Elhihi, Maher, President

Organization for the Study of Sex
Differences [17201]
c/o Dr. Arbi Nazarian, Treasurer
College of Pharmacy
Western University of Health Sci-
ences
309 E 2nd St.
Pomona, CA 91766-1854
De Vries, Geert J., Contact

Jesse Cause Foundation [15388]
567 W Channel Islands Blvd., No.
235
Port Hueneme, CA 93041
PH: (805)228-2222
Pisciotta, Frank, Liaison

Moms in Prayer International
[20644]
13939 Poway Rd., Ste. 3
Poway, CA 92064
Toll free: 855-769-7729
Fax: (858)486-5132
Nichols, Fern, Founder, President

SFI Foundation [6021]
15708 Pomerado Rd., Ste. N208
Poway, CA 92064
PH: (858)451-8868
Fax: (858)451-9268

Pyrenean Mastiff Club of America
[21951]
4083 W Ave. L, No. 107
Quartz Hill, CA 93536
PH: (661)724-0268
Fax: (815)301-2908

National Button Society [21693]
c/o Susan Porter, Membership
Coordinator
1564 Wilson Rd.
Ramona, CA 92065-3539
Jordan, Susannah, President

United States Justice Foundation
[5726]
932 D St., Ste. 2
Ramona, CA 92065
PH: (760)788-6624
Fax: (760)788-6414
Connelly, Michael, Exec. Dir.

Rader Association [20918]
2633 Gilbert Way
Rancho Cordova, CA 95670-3513
Rader, Jim, Founder

Battery Recycling Association of
North America [4625]
12505 N Main St., Ste. 212
Rancho Cucamonga, CA 91739
Jorgensen, Daren E., President

International Institute of Municipal
Clerks [5639]
8331 Utica Ave., Ste. 200
Rancho Cucamonga, CA 91730

PH: (909)944-4162
Toll free: 800-251-1639
Fax: (909)944-8545
Simmons, Monica Martinez,
President

Skinner Family Association [20928]
c/o Gregg Legutki
PO Box 2594
Rancho Cucamonga, CA 91729
Legutki, Gregg, Contact

IMAHelps [15477]
PO Box 2727
Rancho Mirage, CA 92270
Allen, Ines, President

National Association of ADA
Coordinators [11622]
PO Box 958
Rancho Mirage, CA 92270
Toll free: 888-679-7227
Fax: (877)480-7858
Hagle, Paul D., Exec. Dir.

Silky Terrier Club of America [21962]
c/o Suzanne Detwiler
1 Clipper Rd., Unit A
Rancho Palos Verdes, CA 90275-
5956
Terrazas, Tarianne, President

Graves Disease and Thyroid
Foundation [17481]
PO Box 2793
Rancho Santa Fe, CA 92067
Toll free: 877-643-3123
Fax: (877)643-3123
Flynn, Steve, President, CEO

Women's International Center
[13410]
PO Box 669
Rancho Santa Fe, CA 92067-0669
PH: (858)759-3567
Fax: (619)296-1633
Lane, Gloria J., PhD, Founder

Xslaves.org [17934]
PO Box 2672
Rancho Santa Fe, CA 92067
Gloria, Soli Deo, Contact

Christian Comic Arts Society [8850]
c/o FrontGate Media
22342 Avenida Empresa, Ste. 260
Rancho Santa Margarita, CA 92688
Jansen, Eric, Coord.

Professional Association of Diving
Instructors [23345]
30151 Tomas St.
Rancho Santa Margarita, CA
92688-2125
PH: (949)858-7234
Toll free: 800-729-7234
Fax: (949)267-1267
Cronin, Brian, CEO

Toastmasters International [10177]
23182 Arroyo Vista
Rancho Santa Margarita, CA
92688-2620
PH: (949)858-8255
(949)835-1300
Fax: (949)858-1207
Storkey, Mike, DTM, President

DreamCatcher Wild Horse and Burro
Sanctuary [10612]
PO Box 9
Ravendale, CA 96123
PH: (530)260-0148
(530)260-0377
Fax: (530)625-3364
Clarke, Barbara, Director

Rock Detective Geoscience Education [7937]
14655 Betz Ln.
Red Bluff, CA 96080

PH: (530)529-4890
Fax: (530)529-6441
Deike, Ruth, Exec. Dir., Founder

American Trails [23321]
PO Box 491797
Redding, CA 96049-1797
PH: (530)605-4395
Fax: (530)547-2035
Gluck, Pam, Exec. Dir.

Contemporary Historical Vehicle Association [21361]
PO Box 493398
Redding, CA 96049-3398
Gorley, Jerry, President

Dwarf Athletic Association of America [22515]
1095 Hilltop Dr., No. 361
Redding, CA 96003
Toll free: 888-598-3222
Woika, Lucy, President

Philip Boileau Collectors' Society [21303]
1025 Redwood Blvd.
Redding, CA 96003-1905
Gamlin, Karen, Contact

AAA Charity Investment Fund [13020]
300 E State St., No. 531
Redlands, CA 92373
PH: (909)793-2009
Fax: (909)793-6880
Johnson, Fred M., President

American Retirees Association [21024]
700 E Redlands Bvld., Ste. U-307
Redlands, CA 92373-6152
PH: (909)557-0107
(703)527-3065
Fax: (909)335-2711
Egge, Dennis, President

Feeding Hungry Children International [12088]
300 E State St., Ste. 531
Redlands, CA 92373
PH: (909)793-2009
Fax: (909)793-6880
Phillips, Ken, Secretary

World-Wide Missions [20481]
300 E State St., Ste. 531
Redlands, CA 92373-5235
PH: (909)793-2009
Fax: (909)793-6880
Johnson, Fred M., President

Alliance of Area Business Publishers [2760]
2512 Artesia Blvd., Ste. 200
Redondo Beach, CA 90278
PH: (310)379-8261
Fax: (310)379-8283
Dowden, C. James, Exec. Dir.

American Academy of Medical Acupuncture [16452]
2512 Artesia Blvd., Ste. 200
Redondo Beach, CA 90278
PH: (310)379-8261
Fax: (310)379-8283
Kelly, Anna C., MD, FAAMA, VP

American Commission for Accreditation of Reflexology Education and Training [13592]
c/o Linda Chollar, President
515 N Juanita Ave., No. 4
Redondo Beach, CA 90277
PH: (310)318-3353

Asbestos Disease Awareness Organization [17486]
1525 Aviation Blvd., Ste. 318
Redondo Beach, CA 90278
Larkin, Douglas, Dir. of Comm.

City and Regional Magazine Association [2778]
2512 Artesia Blvd., Ste. 200
Redondo Beach, CA 90278
PH: (310)379-8261
Fax: (310)379-8283
Dowden, C. James, Exec. Dir.

Ancient Forest International [3807]
PO Box 1850
Redway, CA 95560
PH: (707)923-4475
Fax: (707)923-4475
Klein, Rick, Exec. Dir.

Applied Technology Council [6540]
201 Redwood Shores Pky., Ste. 240
Redwood City, CA 94065
PH: (650)595-1542
Fax: (650)593-2320
Rojahn, Christopher, Director

Association for Size Diversity and Health [16249]
PO Box 3093
Redwood City, CA 94064
Toll free: 877-576-1102
Ferguson, Fall, MA, President

Friends for Youth [13445]
1741 Broadway St.
Redwood City, CA 94063
PH: (650)368-4444
(650)368-4464
Fax: (650)368-4467
Cooper, Becky, Exec. Dir.

GlobalPlatform [7270]
544 Hillside Rd.
Redwood City, CA 94062
Gillick, Kevin, Exec. Dir.

Gorilla Foundation [5894]
1733 Woodside Rd., Ste. 330
Redwood City, CA 94061
Toll free: 800-634-6273
Sanford, Maizie, Secretary

HopeLab [15643]
1991 Broadway St., Ste. 136
Redwood City, CA 94063-1957
PH: (650)569-5900
Fax: (650)569-5901
Omidyar, Pamela, Chairman, Founder

International Earthlight Alliance [6856]
PO Box 620198
Redwood City, CA 94062

Internet Systems Consortium Inc. [6279]
950 Charter St.
Redwood City, CA 94063
PH: (650)423-1300
Fax: (650)423-1355
Morris, Stephen, Dir. of Engg.

Lifelong Fitness Alliance [23313]
2682 Middlefield Rd., Ste. Z
Redwood City, CA 94063
Toll free: 855-361-8282
Fax: (650)361-8885
Jackson, Victoria, Coord.

Malawi Children's Mission [11074]
274 Redwood Shores Pky., Box 313
Redwood City, CA 94065
Koffman, Steven, Director, Founder

Oracle Education Foundation [8117]
c/o Colleen Cassity, Executive Director
500 Oracle Pkwy., 5OP-8
Redwood City, CA 94065
Cassity, Colleen, Exec. Dir.

Raising a Reader [8488]
330 Twin Dolphin Dr., Ste. 147
Redwood City, CA 94065-1455

PH: (650)489-0550
Fax: (650)489-0551
Miller, Gabrielle E., EdD, Exec. Dir.

Singapore America Business Association [668]
3 Twin Dolphin Dr., Ste. 150
Redwood City, CA 94065
PH: (650)260-3388
Fax: (650)593-3276
Tan, Chek, CEO

Storage Performance Council [7238]
643 Bair Island Rd., Ste. 103
Redwood City, CA 94063
PH: (650)556-9384
Fax: (650)556-9385
Baker, Walter E., Administrator

Tanzania Health and Education Mission [11450]
151 Stratford St.
Redwood City, CA 94062
PH: (650)368-9454
Jones, Sarah, Founder

Vascular Cures [17583]
555 Price Ave., Ste. 180
Redwood City, CA 94063
PH: (650)358-6022
Stoney, Ronald J., Founder

House Rabbit Society [10640]
148 Broadway
Richmond, CA 94804
PH: (510)970-7575
Fax: (510)970-9820
DeMello, Margo, President

The Masquers Playhouse, Inc. [10260]
105 Park Pl.
Richmond, CA 94801-3922
PH: (510)232-3888
(510)232-4031
Cole, David, President

North American Catalysis Society [7143]
c/o C.Y. Chen, Treasurer
100 Chevron Way, Rm. 10-2320
Richmond, CA 94802
PH: (510)242-1860
Iglesia, Enrique, President

Randonneurs USA [22752]
c/o Rob Hawks, President
5630 Santa Cruz Ave.
Richmond, CA 94804
PH: (510)526-2653
Hawks, Rob, President

Tackett Family Association [20936]
260 Bella Vista Way
Rio Vista, CA 94571

Vagabundos Del Mar RV, Boat and Travel Club [22436]
190 Main St.
Rio Vista, CA 94571
PH: (707)374-5511
Toll free: 800-474-2252
Fax: (707)374-6843
Jones, Fred, Gen. Mgr., VP

129th Alumni and Heritage Association [21099]
c/o Col. John L. Ruppel, Jr., President
6718 Zerillo Dr.
Riverbank, CA 95367-2122
PH: (209)869-2879
Ruppel, Col. John L., Jr., President

American Fancy Rat and Mouse Association [22241]
9230 64th St.
Riverside, CA 92509-5924

PH: (626)626-0829
Robbins, Karen, Founder

Desert Tortoise Preserve Committee [3848]
4067 Mission Inn Ave.
Riverside, CA 92501
PH: (951)683-3872
Fax: (951)683-6949
Berger, Ron, President

International Organization of Citrus Virologists [6146]
University of California
900 University Ave.
Riverside, CA 92521
PH: (951)827-1012
Freitas-Astua, Juliana, Chairperson

International Society of Citriculture [4235]
University of California
Dept. of Botany and Plant Sciences
Riverside, CA 92521-0124
Lovatt, Dr. Carol, Secretary, Treasurer

North American Religious Liberty Association [20573]
PO Box 7505
Riverside, CA 92513
PH: (805)955-7683
Johnson, Orlan, President

American Chronic Pain Association [16550]
PO Box 850
Rocklin, CA 95677
Toll free: 800-533-3231
Fax: (916)652-8190
Cowan, Penney, CEO, Founder

Fiji Aid International [13049]
5800 Balfor Rd.
Rocklin, CA 95765
PH: (916)663-6578
Chandra, Damyenti, Founder

Karl Jaspers Society of North America [10099]
c/o Helmut Wautischer
Dept. of Philosophy
Sonoma State University
1801 E Cotati Ave.
Rohnert Park, CA 94928
PH: (707)664-2270
Fax: (707)644-4400
Burch, Ruth, Secretary, Treasurer

Women Educators [8758]
c/o Paula Lane, Treasurer
School of Education
Sonoma State University
1801 E Cotati
Rohnert Park, CA 94928
PH: (231)869-5939
Polnick, Barbara, Chairperson

Women's Voices Now [19257]
46-E Peninsula Ctr.
Rolling Hills Estates, CA 90274-3562
PH: (310)748-1929
Basch-Harod, Heidi, Exec. Dir.

Taiwanese American Citizens League [19670]
3001 Walnut Grove Ave., No. 7
Rosemead, CA 91770
PH: (626)551-0227
Wu, Jacqui, President

Association of Adventist Forums [20601]
AF 518 Riverside Ave.
Roseville, CA 95678-3126
PH: (916)774-1080
Fax: (916)791-4938
Scriven, Dr. Charles, President

Corporate Event Marketing Association [2275]
5098 Foothills Blvd., Ste. 3-386
Roseville, CA 95747
PH: (916)740-3623
Trost, Robb, Secretary

The Elongated Collectors [22269]
4010 Foothills Blvd., Ste. 103
Roseville, CA 95747-7241
Holbrook, Les, Secretary

High Technology Crime Investigation Association [5360]
140 Bogart Ct.
Roseville, CA 95747
PH: (916)408-1751
Fax: (916)384-2232
Quilty, Tom, 1st VP

Home Furnishings Association [1482]
500 Giuseppe Ct., Ste. 6
Roseville, CA 95678
Toll free: 800-422-3778
Fax: (916)784-7697
Bradley, Sharron, CEO, Exec. Dir.

House of Boyd Society [20882]
1609 Truscott Ct.
Roseville, CA 95661
McLachlan, Lauren Boyd, President

Maranatha Volunteers International [20153]
990 Reserve Dr., Ste. 100
Roseville, CA 95678-1387
PH: (916)774-7700
Fax: (916)774-7701
Noble, Don, Chairman, President

National Tax-Limitation Committee [19172]
1700 Eureka Rd., Ste. 150A
Roseville, CA 95661-7777
Uhler, Lewis K., Founder, President

Never Forget Our Fallen [10749]
PO Box 695
Roseville, CA 95661
PH: (916)223-6816
Getz, Deborah, Founder

The Oughtred Society [21708]
9 Stephens Ct.
Roseville, CA 95678
De Cesaris, Robert, President

Oceanic Society [6942]
PO Box 844
Ross, CA 94957
PH: (415)256-9604
Toll free: 800-326-7491
Hutchinson, Brian, Director

State of the World's Sea Turtles [4893]
30 Sir Francis Drake Blvd.
Ross, CA 94957
PH: (202)642-5830
Hutchinson, Brian, Officer

American Association of Japanese University Women [8741]
2164 Calmette Ave.
Rowland Heights, CA 91748

Mothers Against Pedophiles [11082]
PO Box 3426
Running Springs, CA 92382
Walsh, Chelsea M., President

American Association of Psychiatric Technicians [16814]
1220 S St., Ste. 100
Sacramento, CA 95811-7138
Toll free: 800-391-7589
Fax: (916)329-9145
Nolasco, Juan, President

American Civil Rights Institute [17868]
PO Box 188350
Sacramento, CA 95818-8350
PH: (916)444-2278
Connerly, Ward, Founder, President

American Criminal Justice Association - Lambda Alpha Epsilon [11518]
PO Box 601047
Sacramento, CA 95860-1047
PH: (916)484-6553
Fax: (916)488-2227
Koelling, Preston, President

American Escrow Association [1216]
1000 Q St., Ste. 205
Sacramento, CA 95811-6518
PH: (916)446-5165
Fax: (916)443-6719
Harris, AnDee, President

American Mule Racing Association [23078]
1600 Exposition Blvd.
Sacramento, CA 95815
Jacklin, Don, President

American Society of Dermatology [14486]
2721 Capital Ave.
Sacramento, CA 95816-8335
PH: (916)446-5054
Fax: (916)446-0500
Hanni, M. John, Jr., Exec. Dir.

Asian Resources [11755]
5709 Stockton Blvd.
Sacramento, CA 95824
PH: (916)454-1892
Fax: (916)454-1895
Lee, May O., Founder

Asphalt Sealcoat Manufacturers Association [497]
5431 Auburn Blvd., PMB 304
Sacramento, CA 95841-2801
PH: (916)373-1500

Association of Certified Fraud Specialists [1784]
4600 Northgate Blvd., Ste. 105
Sacramento, CA 95834-8777
PH: (916)419-6319
Toll free: 866-HEY-ACFS
Fax: (916)419-6318
Raborn, Charles W., Jr., Exec. Dir.

Association of Law Enforcement Intelligence Units [5455]
1825 Bell St., Ste. 205
Sacramento, CA 95825
PH: (916)263-1187
Fax: (916)263-1180
Godsey, Van, Chairperson

Association of Threat Assessment Professionals [3053]
700 R St., Ste. 200
Sacramento, CA 95811
PH: (916)231-2146
Fax: (916)231-2141
Tobin, Chuck, President

Association for Wedding Professionals International [1653]
PO Box 5598
Sacramento, CA 95817
PH: (916)392-5000
Fax: (916)392-5222
Markel, Richard, President

Center for Energy Efficiency and Renewable Technologies [4022]
1100 11th St., Ste. 311
Sacramento, CA 95814
PH: (916)442-7785
White, V. John, Exec. Dir.

Christians in Crisis [20602]
PO Box 293627
Sacramento, CA 95829-3627
PH: (916)682-0376
Magdangal, Pastor Wally, Founder, President

Council for Refractive Surgery Quality Assurance [17387]
8543 Everglade Dr.
Sacramento, CA 95826-3616
PH: (916)381-0769
Hagele, Glenn, Exec. Dir.

Criminal Justice Legal Foundation [5134]
2131 L St.
Sacramento, CA 95816
PH: (916)446-0345
Fax: (916)446-1194
Rushford, Michael D., CEO, President

DBA International [983]
1050 Fulton Ave., Ste. 120
Sacramento, CA 95825
PH: (916)482-2462
Fax: (916)482-2760
Stieger, Jan, Exec. Dir.

Delphi Foundation [23728]
c/o Lou Camera, Treasurer
1017 L St., PMB 274
Sacramento, CA 95814
Camera, Lou, Treasurer

Down Syndrome Information Alliance [14626]
400 Capitol Mall, 22nd Fl.
Sacramento, CA 95814
PH: (916)658-1686
Fax: (916)914-1875
Green, Heather, President

Foundation Aiding the Elderly [18048]
3430 American River Dr., Ste. 105
Sacramento, CA 95864
PH: (916)481-8558
Toll free: 877-481-8558
Fax: (916)481-2239
Herman, Carole, Chmn. of the Bd., President

Friends of the River [3871]
1418 20th St., Ste. 100
Sacramento, CA 95811
PH: (916)442-3155
Toll free: 888-464-2477
Fax: (916)442-3396
Philips, Corley, Chairman

Grooming Future World Leaders Inc. [13449]
2701 Del Paso Rd., No. 130-191
Sacramento, CA 95835
PH: (916)889-8195
Smith, Shirley F., CEO, Founder

International Association for the Advancement of Steam Power [7245]
Box 106
3323 Watt Ave.
Sacramento, CA 95821
PH: (916)473-1240
Dudzik, Dennis, Founder, President

International Association for Women of Color Day [18214]
3325 Northrop Ave.
Sacramento, CA 95864
PH: (916)483-9804
Fax: (916)483-9805
Brooks, Suzanne, MA, CEO, President, Founder

International Pemphigus and Pemphigoid Foundation [14588]
1331 Garden Hwy., Ste. 100
Sacramento, CA 95833-9773

PH: (916)922-1298
Toll free: 855-473-6744
Sirois, David A., PhD, Director

International Scientific Association for Probiotics and Prebiotics [16225]
3230 Arena Blvd., No. 245-172
Sacramento, CA 95834
PH: (303)793-9974
Sanders, Mary Ellen, PhD, Exec. Ofc.

International Society of Worldwide Stamp Collectors [22336]
c/o Joanne Berkowitz, Executive Director
PO Box 19006
Sacramento, CA 95819
Berkowitz, Joanne, Exec. Dir.

International Stinson Club [21234]
3005 6th St.
Sacramento, CA 95818
PH: (916)421-8942
Strumpf, Herk, President

Journalism Association of Community Colleges [8155]
2701 K St.
Sacramento, CA 95816
Fax: (916)288-6002
Cameron, Prof. Rich, Dir. of Comm.

LAM Health Project [17142]
1909 Capitol Ave., Ste. 203
Sacramento, CA 95811-4242
PH: (617)460-7339
Fax: (617)864-0614
Abrusci, Richard, COO

Marine Corps Veterans Association [21017]
2245 Park Towne Cir.
Sacramento, CA 95825-0415
PH: (916)979-1862
Marsh, George, Exec. Dir.

Mountain Lion Foundation [4844]
PO Box 1896
Sacramento, CA 95812
PH: (916)442-2666
Cooper, Toby, Chairman

Move America Forward [19185]
8795 Folsom Blvd., Ste. 103
Sacramento, CA 95826-3720
PH: (916)441-6197
Fax: (916)383-6608
Gonzalez, Danny, Dir. of Comm.

National Association of Motor Vehicle Boards and Commissions [5564]
1507 21st St., Ste. 330
Sacramento, CA 95811
PH: (916)445-1888
Christman, Ian, VP

National Association of Private Catholic and Independent Schools [7413]
2640 3rd Ave.
Sacramento, CA 95818
PH: (916)451-4963
Crotty, Francis, Trustee

National Association of Wine Retailers [3480]
621 Capitol Mall, Ste. 2500
Sacramento, CA 95814
PH: (707)266-1449
Fax: (916)442-0382
Wark, Tom, Exec. Dir.

National Plant Board [4950]
c/o Aurelio Posadas, Executive Secretary

10022 Calvine Rd.
Sacramento, CA 95829
PH: (916)709-3484
Fax: (916)689-2385
Cooper, Michael, Rep.

Portuguese Historical and Cultural
Society **[19620]**
PO Box 161990
Sacramento, CA 95816
PH: (916)391-7356
(530)662-8246
Fax: (916)427-3903
White, Terri, VP

Professional Football Writers of
America **[22867]**
c/o Howard Blazer, Secretary
The Sports Xchange
4632 Windsong St.
Sacramento, CA 95834
Ledbetter, D. Orlando, President

Real Diaper Industry Association
[991]
1017 L St., Ste. 338
Sacramento, CA 95814
PH: (678)224-1801
Cridland, Janelle, Exec. Dir.

RedRover **[10686]**
3800 J St., Ste. 100
Sacramento, CA 95816
PH: (916)429-2457
Fax: (916)378-5098
Forsyth, Ms. Nicole, CEO, President

Rise Up Belize! **[7814]**
PO Box 19841
Sacramento, CA 95819-0841
Garcia, Joey, President

Sacramento Food Bank & Family
Services **[12112]**
3333 3rd Ave.
Sacramento, CA 95817
PH: (916)456-1980
Fax: (916)451-5920
Young, Blake, President, CEO

SEARCH: The National Consortium
for Justice Information and
Statistics **[11547]**
7311 Greenhaven Dr., Ste. 270
Sacramento, CA 95831-3595
PH: (916)392-2550
Fax: (916)392-8440
Blumstein, Mr. Albert, Ph.D, Mem.

Solar Cookers International **[4104]**
2400 22nd St., Ste. 210
Sacramento, CA 95818
PH: (916)455-4499
Fax: (916)455-4497
Walters, Honey, President

TMJ and Orofacial Pain Society of
America **[15849]**
1020 12th St., Ste. 303
Sacramento, CA 95814
PH: (916)444-1985
Fax: (916)444-1501
Helms, Elizabeth, CEO, President

USS Nimitz (CVN-68) Association
[21071]
c/o Ed Deats, Secretary-Treasurer
8324 Triad Cir.
Sacramento, CA 95828-6642
PH: (630)575-7572
Deats, Edward, Secretary, Treasurer

Western Fairs Association **[1162]**
1776 Tribute Rd., Ste. 210
Sacramento, CA 95815
PH: (916)927-3100
Fax: (916)927-6397
Quaid, Barbara, President

Western Manufactured Housing
Communities Association **[2202]**
455 Capitol Mall, Ste. 800
Sacramento, CA 95814-4420
PH: (916)448-7002
Fax: (916)448-7085
Dey, Sheila, Exec. Dir., Gen.
Counsel

XP Family Support Group **[14869]**
8495 Folsom Blvd., No. 1
Sacramento, CA 95826
PH: (916)628-3814
(916)379-0741
Milota, Michele, Exec. Dir.

Napa Valley Vintners **[4931]**
1475 Library Ln.
Saint Helena, CA 94574
PH: (707)963-3388
Fax: (707)963-3488
Reiff, Linda, President, CEO

Napa Valley Wine Library Associa-
tion **[22476]**
PO Box 328
Saint Helena, CA 94574
PH: (707)963-5145
Martini, Carolyn, President

Nurturing Network **[13391]**
1241 Adam St., Ste. 1142
Saint Helena, CA 94574
PH: (509)493-4026
Fax: (509)493-4027
Agee, Mary Cunningham, Founder,
President

Medical Ambassadors International
[20372]
5012 Salida Blvd.
Salida, CA 95368
PH: (209)543-7500
Toll free: 888-403-0600
Fax: (209)543-7550
Payne, Dr. John C., MD, President

MedicAlert Foundation International
[14665]
5226 Pirrone Ct.
Salida, CA 95368
Toll free: 800-432-5378
Leslie, David, President, CEO

Agricultural Personnel Management
Association **[4147]**
512 Pajaro St., Ste. 7
Salinas, CA 93901
PH: (831)422-8023
Fax: (831)422-7318
Mallobox, Joseph, President

National Steinbeck Center **[9085]**
1 Main St.
Salinas, CA 93901
PH: (831)775-4721
Fax: (831)796-3828
Butler, David, Dir. of Fin. & Admin.

Partners for Peace **[18812]**
Bldg. H
855 E Laurel Dr.
Salinas, CA 93905
PH: (831)754-3888
Eastman, Brent, President

Pesticide Applicators Professional
Association **[2505]**
PO Box 80095
Salinas, CA 93912-0095
PH: (831)442-3536
Fax: (831)442-2351
Letterman, Judy, CEO

Joseph Campbell Foundation **[8645]**
PO Box 36
San Anselmo, CA 94979-0036

EcoMom Alliance **[13376]**
PO Box 2121
San Anselmo, CA 94979
Toll free: 866-506-9012
Pinkson, Kimberly Danek, Founder,
President

National Organization of Circumci-
sion Information Resource Centers
[11285]
PO Box 2512
San Anselmo, CA 94979-2512
PH: (415)488-9883
Fax: (415)488-9660

Phi Beta Delta **[23790]**
c/o Dr. Salaam Yousif, Interim PBD
Executive Director & CEO
Administration Bldg., Rms. 148 &
150
California State University
5500 University Pky.
San Bernardino, CA 92407
PH: (909)537-3250
Fax: (909)537-7458
Chuang, Rueyling, Ph.D., Exec. Dir.,
Reg.

Worldwide Marriage Encounter
[12261]
2210 E Highland Ave., Ste. 110
San Bernardino, CA 92404-4666
PH: (909)863-9963
Fax: (909)863-9986

Global Alliance for Preserving the
History of WW II in Asia **[21196]**
PO Box 1323
San Carlos, CA 94070-7323

Allergic To Hunger **[10847]**
244 Del Gado Rd.
San Clemente, CA 92672
Gallagher, Kevin, Founder

Answer Africa **[14563]**
203 E Avenida San Juan
San Clemente, CA 92672-2325
PH: (949)498-5274
Fax: (949)498-5280
Marangu, Makena, Founder

California Association of Tiger-
Owners **[21347]**
2950 Calle Grande Vista
San Clemente, CA 92672
Mueller, Rick, Treasurer

Christian Leadership Alliance
[20560]
635 Camino de los Mares, Ste. 216
San Clemente, CA 92673
PH: (949)487-0900
Fax: (949)487-0927
White, Jerry, Director

The Education Coalition **[7820]**
31 Segovia
San Clemente, CA 92672
PH: (949)369-3867
Fax: (949)369-3865
Lane, Dr. Carla, EdD, Exec. Dir.

Handicapped Scuba Association
[22781]
1104 El Prado
San Clemente, CA 92672-4637
PH: (949)498-4540
Gatacre, Jim, President

Petroleum Packaging Council **[2481]**
c/o ATD Management Inc.
1519 via Tulipan
San Clemente, CA 92673-3715
PH: (949)369-7102
Fax: (949)366-1057
Whittenhall, John, President

Surfrider Foundation **[3951]**
942 Calle Negocio, Ste. 350
San Clemente, CA 92673

PH: (949)492-8170
Fax: (949)492-8142
Fiedelholtz, Liisa Pierce, Chmn. of
the Bd.

Traditional Fine Arts Organization,
Inc. **[9005]**
90 Via Regalo
San Clemente, CA 92673

Academy of Neuroscience for
Architecture **[6913]**
1249 F St.
San Diego, CA 92101
PH: (619)235-0221
Albright, Tom, PhD, President

Accredited Gemologists Association
[2038]
3315 Juanita St.
San Diego, CA 92105
Toll free: 844-288-4367
Robertson, Stuart, GG, President

Advancement Via Individual
Determination **[7950]**
9246 Lightwave Ave., Ste. 200
San Diego, CA 92123
PH: (858)380-4800
Fax: (858)268-2265
Gira, Robert, Exec. VP

Alpha Pi Sigma **[23752]**
PO Box 15374
San Diego, CA 92175-0374
Vidales, Divina, Chairperson

American Academy of Estate Plan-
ning Attorneys **[4980]**
9444 Balboa Ave., Ste. 300
San Diego, CA 92123-1696
PH: (858)453-2128
Toll free: 877-679-6411
Fax: (858)874-5804
Armstrong, Robert, President

American Association of Teachers of
Persian **[8639]**
c/o Ramin Sarraf, President
3824 Creststone Pl.
San Diego, CA 92130
PH: (858)642-8580
Sarraf, Ramin, President

American Council on Exercise
[16692]
4851 Paramont Dr.
San Diego, CA 92123-1449
PH: (858)576-6500
Toll free: 888-825-3636
Fax: (858)576-6564
Goudeseune, Scott, CEO, President

American Council of Hypnotist
Examiners **[15357]**
3435 Camino del Rio S, Ste. 316
San Diego, CA 92108
PH: (619)280-7200
Boyne, Gil, Founder

American Personal and Private Chef
Association **[698]**
4572 Delaware St.
San Diego, CA 92116-1005
PH: (619)294-2436
Toll free: 800-644-8389
Wallace, Candy, Exec. Dir., Founder

American Professional Partnership
for Lithuanian Education **[9587]**
PO Box 179017
San Diego, CA 92177
Janowitz, Karl, President

American Society of Hispanic
Economists **[1011]**
c/o Catalina Amuedo-Dorantes,
President

Dept. of Economics
San Diego State University
5500 Campanile Dr.
San Diego, CA 92182
PH: (619)594-1663
Amuedo-Dorantes, Catalina,
President

America's Angel **[11813]**
PO Box 3124
San Diego, CA 92103
Rose, Morgan, MS, Exec. Dir.,
Founder

Amputees in Motion International
[11570]
PO Box 19236
San Diego, CA 92159
PH: (858)454-9300
Farmer, Gabby Penn, President, Edi-
tor

AngelCare Programs of Americans
Care & Share **[11213]**
3295 Meade Ave., Ste. 102
San Diego, CA 92116-4557
Toll free: 888-264-5227
Fax: (619)481-3089
Grosser, Dr. T.J., EdD, Bd. Member

Animal Charity Evaluators **[10572]**
PO Box 5482
San Diego, CA 92165
PH: (619)363-1402
Bockman, Jon, Exec. Dir.

Asian Real Estate Association of
America **[2850]**
3990 Old Town Ave., C304
San Diego, CA 92110
PH: (619)795-7873
Silvano, Vicky, Chairperson

Association for Collaborative Spine
Research **[15640]**
PO Box 420942
San Diego, CA 92142-0942
PH: (951)553-3556
Fax: (951)302-8629
Radcliff, Kris, MD, President

Autism Research Institute **[13752]**
4182 Adams Ave.
San Diego, CA 92116
PH: (619)281-7165
Toll free: 866-366-3361
Fax: (619)563-6840
Flynn, Chris, Treasurer

Burundi Friends International
[11327]
PO Box 927356
San Diego, CA 92192-7356
PH: (619)800-2340
Niyonzima-Aroian, Jeanine, Founder,
Chairperson

Center for Community Solutions
[18202]
4508 Mission Bay Dr.
San Diego, CA 92109-4919
PH: (858)272-5777
Rypins, Amy, President

Challenged America **[14548]**
c/o Disabled Businesspersons As-
sociation
SDSU - Interwork Institute
6367 Alvarado Ct., Ste. 350
San Diego, CA 92120
PH: (619)594-8805
Miyares, Urban, Founder, President

Children of Deaf Adults **[15181]**
7370 Formal Ct.
San Diego, CA 92120
Brother, Millie, Founder

Children's Corrective Surgery
Society **[17383]**
PO Box 500578
San Diego, CA 92150
Toll free: 800-803-9190
Martin, John C., CEO, President

Combatant Craft Crewmembers Asso-
ciation **[21052]**
PO Box 6912
San Diego, CA 92166
Lyons, Tom, VP

Committee Opposed to Militarism
and the Draft **[18136]**
PO Box 15195
San Diego, CA 92175-5195
PH: (760)753-7518

Contemporary Design Group **[1478]**
633 University Ave.
San Diego, CA 92103
Toll free: 888-588-4426
Mendez, Alicia, Exec. Dir.

Desert Protective Council **[3846]**
PO Box 3635
San Diego, CA 92163-1635
PH: (619)342-5524
    (619)228-6316
Anderson, Janet, President

Disability Management Employer
Coalition **[1089]**
5173 Waring Rd., Ste. 134
San Diego, CA 92120-2705
Toll free: 877-789-3632
Carruthers, Marcia, Chmn. of the Bd.

Disabled Businesspersons Associa-
tion **[11762]**
6367 Alvarado Ct., Ste. 350
San Diego, CA 92120
PH: (619)594-8805
Miyares, Mr. Urban, President

The Distinguished Flying Cross
Society **[20732]**
PO Box 502408
San Diego, CA 92150
Toll free: 866-332-6332
Sweeney, Chuck, President, CEO

Diving Equipment and Marketing As-
sociation **[3138]**
3750 Convoy St., Ste. 310
San Diego, CA 92111-3741
PH: (858)616-6408
Toll free: 800-862-3483
Fax: (858)616-6495
Ingram, Tom, Exec. Dir.

Fitness Industry Suppliers Associa-
tion - North America **[2599]**
3525 Del Mar Heights Rd.
San Diego, CA 92130
PH: (858)509-0034
Fax: (858)792-1251
Dinerman, David, Director

Forgotten Victims **[13259]**
1666 Garnet Ave., No. 108
San Diego, CA 92109-3116
Toll free: 877-668-4468

Foundation of Real Estate Apprais-
ers **[224]**
2645 Financial Ct., Ste. A
San Diego, CA 92117
Toll free: 888-820-5700
Fax: (858)273-8026

Freedom is Not Free **[12344]**
11760 Sorrento Valley Rd., Ste. G
San Diego, CA 92121
Frank, Carl, Founder, President

Freestyle Players Association
[22807]
San Diego, CA

Gerson Institute **[13625]**
4631 Viewridge Ave.
San Diego, CA 92123
PH: (858)694-0707
Toll free: 888-443-7766
Fax: (858)694-0757
Gerson, Charlotte, Founder

Give Clean Water **[13324]**
PO Box 720953
San Diego, CA 92172
Toll free: 888-429-6741
Fax: (775)923-7897
Mineer, Amanda L., Director,
Treasurer

Glamour Photographers International
[2579]
PO Box 84374
San Diego, CA 92138
PH: (619)575-0100

Global Autism Collaboration **[13766]**
Autism Research Institute
4182 Adams Ave.
San Diego, CA 92116
Toll free: 866-366-3361
Edelson, Stephen M., PhD,
President

The Governance Institute **[2168]**
9685 Via Excelencia, Ste. 100
San Diego, CA 92126
Toll free: 877-712-8778
Fax: (858)909-0813
Raasch, Jona, CEO

Growing Liberia's Children **[11203]**
PO Box 125065
San Diego, CA 92112
PH: (619)961-0287
Harris, Malia E., Founder, VP

Homeopathic Nurses Association
[15287]
c/o Margo Cohen, Membership
Secretary
3737 Moraga Ave., No. A-207
San Diego, CA 92117
Slonager, Kathleen, President

House of Palestine **[9212]**
6161 El Cajon Blvd., No. 149
San Diego, CA 92115
PH: (760)802-5255
Abukhalaf, Nadira, President

Humanitarian African Relief
Organization **[12677]**
6161 El Cajon Blvd., No. 912
San Diego, CA 92115
PH: (612)315-5691
    (619)741-9260
Fax: (612)315-5693
Abdinur, Ali Haji, President, CEO

IDEA Health and Fitness Association
[16701]
10190 Telesis Ct.
San Diego, CA 92121
PH: (858)535-8979
Toll free: 800-999-4332
Fax: (858)535-8234
Davis, Kathie, Exec. Dir.

Identity Theft Resource Center
[5533]
3625 Ruffin Rd., No. 204
San Diego, CA 92123
Toll free: 888-400-5530
Fergerson, Julie, Chairman

Information Storage Industry
Consortium **[6316]**
6920 Miramar Rd., Ste. 301
San Diego, CA 92121
PH: (619)392-0895
Frank, Dr. Paul D., Exec. Dir., CEO

Institute of Consumer Financial
Education **[7920]**
PO Box 34070
San Diego, CA 92163-4070
PH: (619)239-1401
Fax: (619)923-3284
Richard, Paul S., RFC, Exec. Dir.

International Association of Lesbian,
Gay, Bisexual and Transgender
Judges **[5386]**
PO Box 122724
San Diego, CA 92112-2724
Zeidler, D. Zeke, President

International Association for
Psychoanalytic Self Psychology
[16916]
4907 Morena Blvd., Ste. 1402
San Diego, CA 92117
PH: (858)270-3503
Toll free: 888-280-1476
Fax: (858)270-3513
Doctors, Shelley, PhD, President

International Bipolar Foundation
[15775]
8895 Town Centre Dr., Ste. 105-360
San Diego, CA 92122
PH: (858)764-2496
Fax: (858)764-2491
Walker, Muffy, Chairman

International College of Prosthodon-
tists **[14451]**
4425 Cass St., Ste. A
San Diego, CA 92109-4015
PH: (858)270-1814
Fax: (858)272-7687
Yancey, Mr. Eben, Exec. Dir.

International Council on Systems
Engineering **[6561]**
7670 Opportunity Rd., Ste. 220
San Diego, CA 92111-2222
PH: (858)541-1725
Toll free: 800-366-1164
Harding, Alan D., President

International Etchells Class Associa-
tion **[22629]**
2812 Canon St.
San Diego, CA 92106
PH: (619)222-0252
Gilbert, Gary, Chairman

International Foundation for Teleme-
tering **[7320]**
5665 Oberlin Dr., Ste. 200
San Diego, CA 92121
Moran, Ms. Lena, Coord.

International Laser Class Association
- North American Region **[22634]**
One Design Management
2812 Canon St.
San Diego, CA 92106
PH: (619)222-0252
Campbell, Sherri, Exec. Sec.

International Marine Animal Trainers
Association **[3617]**
1880 Harbor Island Dr.
San Diego, CA 92101
PH: (312)692-3193
Fax: (312)939-2216
Wolden, Bill, Bd. Member

International Naples Sabot Associa-
tion **[22637]**
2812 Canon St.
San Diego, CA 92106
PH: (949)275-2636
    (619)222-0252
Fax: (619)222-0528
Hallett, Jill, Secretary, Treasurer

International Relief Teams **[12686]**
4560 Alvarado Canyon Rd., Ste. 2G
San Diego, CA 92120

PH: (619)284-7979
Fax: (619)284-7938
La Forgia, Barry, Exec. Dir., Founder

International Society for Neoplatonic
Studies [10096]
c/o Michael Wagner, General
Secretary
Dept. of Philosophy
University of San Diego
5998 Alcala Park
San Diego, CA 92110-2492
PH: (619)260-4600
Fax: (619)260-4227
Gurtler, Gary Michael, President

International Sunfish Class Associa-
tion [22640]
2812 Canon St.
San Diego, CA 92106-2742
PH: (619)222-0252
Chapman, Richard F., President

Iraqi American Chamber of Com-
merce and Industry [23594]
15265 Maturin Dr., No. 184
San Diego, CA 92127-2323
PH: (858)613-9215
Toll free: 877-684-5162
Fax: (858)408-2624
Al-Hardan, Yousif, Exec. VP

Japan Karate-Do Organization
[22999]
3545 Midway Dr.
San Diego, CA 92110-4922
PH: (858)414-7361
Miki, Sherry, Inst.

Just Transition Alliance [23458]
2810 Camino Del Rio S, Ste. 116
San Diego, CA 92108-3819
PH: (619)573-4934
Fax: (619)546-9910
Bravo, Jose T., Exec. Dir.

Kids Korps USA [13302]
11526 Sorrento Valley Rd.
San Diego, CA 92121
PH: (858)500-8136
Fax: (858)847-9161
Wafer, Joani, Founder

Mega Society [9345]
c/o Jeff Ward, Administrator
13155 Wimberly Sq., No. 284
San Diego, CA 92128
Ward, Dr. Jeff, Administrator

Miniature Book Society [9131]
c/o Karen Nyman, Membership
Chair
702 Rosecrans St.
San Diego, CA 92106-3013
PH: (619)226-4441
Nyman, Karen, Membership Chp.,
Treasurer

Miracle Babies [14237]
8745 Aero Dr., Ste. 111
San Diego, CA 92123
PH: (858)633-8540
Robertson, Kevin, Exec. Dir.

Mountain Rescue Association
[12744]
PO Box 880868
San Diego, CA 92168-0868
Wessen, Doug, Comm. Chm.

National Association of Hispanic
Real Estate Professionals [2869]
591 Camino de la Reina, Ste. 720
San Diego, CA 92108
PH: (858)622-9046
Martinez, Juan, Director

National Association of Sports Nutrition [16229]
8898 Clsiremont Mesa Blvd., Ste. J
San Diego, CA 92111

PH: (858)694-0317
Kotterman, Mr. Jeff, LMSN, Director

National Association for Year-Round
Education [7785]
PO Box 711386
San Diego, CA 92171-1386
Hornak, David, Exec. Dir.

National Coalition for Men [18668]
932 C St., Ste. B
San Diego, CA 92101
PH: (619)231-1909
Toll free: 888-223-1280
Crouch, Harry, President

National Forensic Center [5250]
National Directory of Expert Wit-
nesses
PO Box 270529
San Diego, CA 92198-2529
Toll free: 800-735-6660
Fax: (858)487-7747

National Foundation for Autism
Research [13774]
PO Box 502177
San Diego, CA 92150-2177
PH: (858)679-8800
Leon, Sharon, Exec. Dir.

National Law Center for Children
and Families [5193]
501 W Broadway, Ste. 1310
San Diego, CA 92101
PH: (703)548-5522
Whidden, Richard R., Jr., Counsel,
Exec. Dir.

National Network of Youth Ministries
[20660]
PO Box 501748
San Diego, CA 92150-1748
PH: (858)451-1111
Fax: (858)451-6900
Nuss, Daryl, Exec. Dir., CEO

Natural High [13470]
6310 Greenwich Dr., Ste. 145
San Diego, CA 92122
PH: (858)551-7006
Fax: (858)551-1855
Sundt, Jon, Founder

Navy Anesthesia Society [13704]
Dept. of Anesthesiology
Naval Medical Ctr.
34800 Bob Wilson Dr.
San Diego, CA 92134-5000
PH: (619)532-8943
Fax: (619)532-8945
Elkins, Lt. Comdr. David G.,
Secretary

Network Professional Association
[6258]
3157 Carmino Del Rio S, Ste. 115
San Diego, CA 92108-4098
Toll free: 888-NPA-NPA0
Kelley, Richard Allan, Chairperson

North America Taiwanese Professors' Association [19669]
c/o Dr. Mao Lin, Membership Committee Chairperson
5250 Soledad Mountain Rd.
San Diego, CA 92109-1529
Dyson, Lily, Bd. Member

Oligonucleotide Therapeutics Society
[17458]
4377 Newport Ave.
San Diego, CA 92107
PH: (619)795-9458
Fax: (619)923-3230
Watts, Jonathan K., Secretary

Open Mobile Alliance [7318]
4330 La Jolla Village Dr., Ste. 110
San Diego, CA 92122
Fax: (858)623-0743
Newberry, Seth, Gen. Mgr.

Optometric Council on Refractive
Technology [16434]
8910 University Center Ln., Ste. 800
San Diego, CA
PH: (858)455-9950
Fax: (858)455-9954
Geffen, David I., OD, President

Parents Active for Vision Education
[17736]
4135 54th Pl.
San Diego, CA 92105
Nurisio, Robert, President

Pets America [12456]
1286 University Ave., Ste. 507
San Diego, CA 92103
PH: (512)497-7535

Plant With Purpose [18497]
4747 Morena Blvd., Ste. 100
San Diego, CA 92117-3466
Toll free: 800-633-5319
Fax: (858)274-3728
Sabin, Scott C., Exec. Dir.

Positive Discipline Association
[7067]
PO Box 9595
San Diego, CA 92169
Toll free: 866-767-3472
Fax: (855)415-2477
Rinehart, Kathy, Exec. Dir.

Postpartum Health Alliance [14240]
PO Box 927231
San Diego, CA 92192-7231
PH: (619)254-0023
Toll free: 800-479-3339
Heldman, Jessica, JD, President

Privacy Rights Clearinghouse [2734]
3033 5th Ave., Ste. 223
San Diego, CA 92103
PH: (619)298-3396
Fax: (619)298-5681
Givens, Beth, Director, Founder

Project Concern International
[15490]
5151 Murphy Canyon Rd., Ste. 320
San Diego, CA 92123-4339
PH: (858)279-9690
Toll free: 877-PCI-HOPE
Fax: (858)694-0294
Guimaraes, George, CEO, President

Real Diaper Association [11560]
3401 Adams Ave., Ste. A
San Diego, CA 92116-2490
Green, Mary, Exec. Dir.

Rebuild Global [5975]
241 14th Ave.
San Diego, CA 92101
PH: (619)796-4796
Plaza, Sandra, Exec. Dir.

Rock Cancer C.A.R.E [14058]
5402 Ruffin Rd., Ste. 205
San Diego, CA 92123
Toll free: 888-251-0620
Reed, Tamela A., Founder, CEO

Rolling Readers [12249]
2515 Camino del Rio S, Ste. 330
San Diego, CA 92108
PH: (619)516-4095
Fax: (619)516-4096
Quach, Hoa, President

Scouting For All [12860]
PO Box 600841
San Diego, CA 92120-0841
PH: (619)229-1612

Sepsis Alliance [15415]
1855 First Ave., Ste. 102
San Diego, CA 92101

PH: (619)232-0300
(813)874-2552
Flatley, Carl J., Chairman, Founder

Service Industry Association [3079]
2164 Historic Decatur Rd., Villa 19
San Diego, CA 92106
PH: (619)458-9063
Betzner, Claudia J., Exec. Dir.

Snipe Class International Racing
Association [22669]
2812 Canon St.
San Diego, CA 92106-2742
PH: (619)224-6998
Fax: (619)224-0528

The Society for Financial Awareness
[1265]
3914 Murphy Canyon Rd., Ste. A125
San Diego, CA 92123
Toll free: 800-689-4851
Chilton, Jim, Founder

Society for Minimally Invasive Spine
Surgery [16067]
8880 Rio San Diego Dr., Ste. 260
San Diego, CA 92108
PH: (619)265-5222
Fax: (619)265-5858
Anderson, D. Greg, MD, President

Society for Software Quality [6286]
PO Box 27634
San Diego, CA 92198
Hahn, Theodore, Contact

Spine Technology and Educational
Group Organization [17266]
PO Box 420942
San Diego, CA 92142-0942
PH: (858)279-9955
Fax: (858)279-1130
Curl, Pat, Coord.

Survivors of Torture International
[18444]
PO Box 151240
San Diego, CA 92175-1240
PH: (619)278-2400
Fax: (619)294-9405
Anderson, Kathi, Exec. Dir.,
President

Tailhook Association [5624]
9696 Businesspark Ave.
San Diego, CA 92131-1643
PH: (858)689-9223
Toll free: 800-322-4665
Nichols, Dave, Director

Technology Services Industry As-
sociation [3214]
17065 Camino San Bernadino, Ste.
200
San Diego, CA 92127-5737
PH: (858)674-5491
Fax: (858)946-0005
Wood, J.B., CEO, President

Tropical Forest Group [3959]
1125 Fort Stockton Dr.
San Diego, CA 92103
Cage, Patrick, Director

WAVES National [21075]
c/o Monica O'Hara, Treasurer
6383 Kimmy Ct.
San Diego, CA 92114-5631
Adamson, Jo, President

Wireless-Life Sciences Alliance
[17426]
6450 Lusk Blvd., Ste. E202
San Diego, CA 92121
PH: (858)227-9409
Mccray, Robert, CEO, President

Women's Empowerment
International [12568]
PO Box 501406
San Diego, CA 92150-1406

PH: (619)333-0026
Fenly, Leigh, Founder, President

World Council for Curriculum and Instruction [7697]
Hufstedler School of Education - HSOE 306
Alliant International University
10455 Pomerado Rd.
San Diego, CA 92131-1717
PH: (858)635-4718
Fax: (858)635-4714
Paed-Pedrajas, Teresita, President

WorldHope Corps [11465]
1984 Sunset Cliffs Blvd.
San Diego, CA 92167
PH: (619)886-7854
Christensen, Dr. Michael, Founder, CEO

Antique Barbed Wire Society [21618]
1475 Paseo Maravilla
San Dimas, CA 91773-3908

Avicultural Society of America [6955]
PO Box 3161
San Dimas, CA 91773

Pacific Railroad Society [10188]
210 W Bonita Ave.
San Dimas, CA 91773
PH: (909)394-0616
(714)637-4676
Grupp, Virginia, President

World Emergency Relief [12738]
425 W Allen Ave., No. 111
San Dimas, CA 91773-1485
PH: (909)593-7140
Toll free: 888-484-4543
Fax: (909)593-3100
Becks, Gary, Chairman

104th Infantry Division National Timberwolf Association [20716]
c/o National Timberwolf Pups Association
1749 9th Ave.
San Francisco, CA 94122
Lytle, Glen E., Contact

826 National [8762]
44 Gough St., Ste. 206
San Francisco, CA 94103
PH: (415)864-2098
Fax: (415)864-2388
Richards, Gerald, CEO

About-Face [13367]
PO Box 191145
San Francisco, CA 94119
PH: (415)839-6779
Berger, Jennifer, Exec. Dir.

Action for Nature, Inc. [4032]
2269 Chestnut St., No. 263
San Francisco, CA 94123
PH: (415)922-6155
Fax: (415)922-5717
Kay, Beryl, President

Afghan Friends Network [19284]
PO Box 170368
San Francisco, CA 94117
Toll free: 800-831-2339
Bortner, John, Chairman, Bd. Member

Aging Technology Alliance [7256]
3701 Sacramento St., No. 496
San Francisco, CA 94118
Radsliff, Peter, President

All of Us or None [17863]
c/o Legal Services for Prisoners with Children

1540 Market St., Ste. 490
San Francisco, CA 94102-6049
PH: (415)255-7036
Fax: (415)552-3150
Nunn, Dorsey, Exec. Dir.

Alliance for Smiles [14327]
2565 3rd St., Ste. 237
San Francisco, CA 94107-3160
PH: (415)647-4481
Fax: (415)647-7041
Brown, Kim, CEO, President

American Academy of Ophthalmology [16361]
655 Beach St.
San Francisco, CA 94109
PH: (415)561-8500
Fax: (415)561-8533
Parke, David W., II, CEO

American Association of Certified Orthoptists [16362]
655 Beach St.
San Francisco, CA 94109
PH: (415)561-8522
Fax: (415)561-8531
Galli, Marlo, C.O, Secretary

American Association of Ophthalmic Oncologists and Pathologists [16363]
655 Beach St.
San Francisco, CA 94109
PH: (415)561-8516
Fax: (415)561-8531
Chevez-Barrios, Patricia, President

American Association for Pediatric Ophthalmology and Strabismus [16364]
655 Beach St.
San Francisco, CA 94109
PH: (415)561-8505
Fax: (415)561-8531
Hull, Jennifer, Mgr.

American Asthma Foundation [17133]
4 Koret Way, LR-216
San Francisco, CA 94143-2218
PH: (415)514-0730
Fax: (415)514-0734
Seaman, William E., MD, Dir. of Res.

American Begonia Society [22065]
PO Box 471651
San Francisco, CA 94147-1651
Jens, Virginia, President

American Board of Foot and Ankle Surgery [16780]
445 Fillmore St.
San Francisco, CA 94117-3404
PH: (415)553-7800
Fax: (415)553-7801
Kreiter, Kathy, Exec. Dir.

American Conservatory Theater [10237]
30 Grant Ave., 7th Fl.
San Francisco, CA 94108-5834
PH: (415)834-3200
(415)439-2350
Livingston, Nancy, Chmn. of the Bd.

American Glaucoma Society [16366]
655 Beach St.
San Francisco, CA 94109
PH: (415)561-8587
Fax: (415)561-8531

American Muslims Intent on Learning and Activism [10028]
PO Box 420 614
San Francisco, CA 94142
Noor, Moina, Director

American Ophthalmological Society [16367]
655 Beach St.
San Francisco, CA 94109
PH: (415)561-8578
Fax: (415)561-8531
Moss, Mr. Stephen, Program Mgr.

American Qigong Association [13598]
117 Topaz Way
San Francisco, CA 94131
PH: (415)285-9400
Fax: (415)647-5745
Lahdenpera, V. Kay, RN, Exec. Dir.

American Rescue Team International [11948]
236 W Portal Ave.
San Francisco, CA 94127-1423
PH: (415)533-2231
Copp, Mr. Doug, Exec. Dir.

American Society on Aging [10498]
575 Market St., Ste. 2100
San Francisco, CA 94105-2938
PH: (415)974-9600
Toll free: 800-537-9728
Fax: (415)974-0300
Stein, Robert, President, CEO

American Society of Ophthalmic Registered Nurses [16112]
655 Beach St.
San Francisco, CA 94109
PH: (415)561-8513
Fax: (415)561-8531
Clouser, Sue F., RN, MSN, CRNO, Officer

Anti-Malware Testing Standards Organization [6269]
1 Ferry Bldg., Ste. 200
San Francisco, CA 94111-4213
PH: (415)963-3563
Edwards, Simon, Chairman

Antipsychiatry Coalition [16824]
2040 Polk St.
San Francisco, CA 94109
Drake, Carrie L., Contact

Apollo Alliance Project [6456]
155 Montgomery St., Ste. 1001
San Francisco, CA 94104
Angelides, Phil, Chairperson

Aquatic Animal Life Support Operators [6810]
1032 Irving St., No. 902
San Francisco, CA 94122
PH: (702)503-6472
(952)431-9539
Bajek, Mike, President

Asia Foundation [18936]
465 California St., 9th Fl.
San Francisco, CA 94104
PH: (415)982-4640
Fax: (415)392-8863
Siskel, Suzanne E., Exec. VP, COO

Asian American Architects and Engineers [5961]
1167 Mission St., 4th Fl.
San Francisco, CA 94103
PH: (415)392-9688
(415)777-2166
Young, Kendall, Director

Asian American Journalists Association [2656]
5 3rd St., Ste. 1108
San Francisco, CA 94103
PH: (415)346-2051
Fax: (415)346-6343
Cheung, Paul, President

Asian Business League of San Francisco [610]
PO Box 191345
San Francisco, CA 94119-1345
Chang, Claire

Asian Chefs Association [699]
3145 Geary Blvd., No. 112
San Francisco, CA 94118
PH: (408)634-9462

ASIAN, Inc. [9024]
1167 Mission St., 4th Fl.
San Francisco, CA 94103
PH: (415)928-5910
Fax: (415)921-0182
Lo, Robert, V. Chmn. of the Bd.

ASPECT Foundation [8057]
211 Sutter St., 10th Fl.
San Francisco, CA 94108
Toll free: 800-879-6884
Fax: (415)228-8051

Association of AE Business Leaders [2149]
PO Box 330152
San Francisco, CA 94133
PH: (415)659-9973
(415)350-9213
Cowdery, John, President

Association of Asian American Investment Managers [2018]
50 California St., Ste. 2320
San Francisco, CA 94111
Chan, Chris, President

Association of Chinese Finance Professionals [1222]
240 Hazelwood Ave.
San Francisco, CA 94127
Ren, Dr. William, President

Association for the Development of Pakistan [11317]
PO Box 2492
San Francisco, CA 94126
Zakaria, Anam, Director

Association of Moroccan Professionals in America [614]
PO Box 77254
San Francisco, CA 94107
Fax: (801)996-6334

Association of Pediatric Therapists [17437]
PO Box 194191
San Francisco, CA 94119-4191
Cowell, Karen, Co-Ch.

Association for the Study of Law, Culture and the Humanities [8046]
Dept. of Political Science
San Francisco State University
1600 Holloway Ave.
San Francisco, CA 94132
Higinbotham, Sarah, Treasurer

Association of University Anesthesiologists [13698]
44 Montgomery St., Ste. 1605
San Francisco, CA 94104-4703
PH: (415)296-6950
Fax: (415)296-6901
Fleisher, Lee A., MD, Contact

Association of University Professors of Ophthalmology [16376]
655 Beach St.
San Francisco, CA 94109
PH: (415)561-8548
Fax: (415)561-8531
Haller, MD, Julia A., President

Association of Veterans Affairs Ophthalmologists [16377]
655 Beach St.
San Francisco, CA 94109

PH: (415)561-8523
Fax: (415)561-8531
Vollman, David, Treasurer

Astronomical Society of the Pacific
[6002]
390 Ashton Ave.
San Francisco, CA 94112
PH: (415)337-1100
Toll free: 800-335-2624
Fax: (415)337-5205
Sowle, Michael, Dir. of Fin.

Autoinflammatory Alliance [14566]
PO Box 590354
San Francisco, CA 94159
PH: (415)831-8782
Durrant, Karen, President, Founder

Baraka Africa [10863]
425 1st St., Ste. 1103
San Francisco, CA 94105-4623
PH: (415)690-0601
     (415)425-5194
Fax: (415)520-0930
Esmail, Hafeez, Bd. Member

Basque Educational Organization
[9648]
PO Box 31861
San Francisco, CA 94131-0861
Sorhondo, Nicole, Secretary

Beta Pi Sigma Sorority [23690]
256 Waterville St.
San Francisco, CA 94124
PH: (415)467-0717
Farnum, Evayon, Bd. Member

A Better Course [16210]
30 Woodland Ave.
San Francisco, CA 94117
PH: (415)706-8094
Kavanagh, Colleen, Founder, Exec.
     Dir.

Biofuel Recycling [4626]
5758 Geary Blvd., No. 421
San Francisco, CA 94121
PH: (415)747-2771
Fax: (415)962-2372
Bowen, Eric, Bd. Member

Bioneers [4490]
1014 Torney Ave.
San Francisco, CA 94129
PH: (505)986-0366
Toll free: 877-246-6337
Fax: (505)986-1644
Ausubel, Kenny, CEO, Founder

Breast Cancer Action [13908]
657 Mission St., Ste. 302
San Francisco, CA 94105
PH: (415)243-9301
Toll free: 877-278-6722
Fax: (415)243-3996
Jaggar, Karuna, Exec. Dir.

Louise Brooks Society [23987]
1518 Church St.
San Francisco, CA 94131-2018
Gladysz, Thomas, Director

Buddhist Churches of America
[19771]
1710 Octavia St.
San Francisco, CA 94109
PH: (415)776-5600
Fax: (415)771-6293
Matsuda, Kent, President

Business Association Italy America
[1980]
625 2nd St., Ste. 280, 2nd Fl.
San Francisco, CA 94107
PH: (415)992-7454
Ghisini, Elisabetta, Director

Business for Social Responsibility
[618]
88 Kearny St., 12th Fl.
San Francisco, CA 94108
PH: (415)984-3200
Fax: (415)984-3201
Lederhausen, Mats, Founder

California Historical Radio Society
[3220]
PO Box 31659
San Francisco, CA 94131
PH: (415)203-2747

California Society of Printmakers
[1531]
PO Box 194202
San Francisco, CA 94119-4202
Ruiz, Luz Marina, President

Carrying Capacity Network [6367]
PO Box 457
San Francisco, CA 94104-0457

Center for Asian American Media
[17939]
145 9th St., Ste. 350
San Francisco, CA 94103-2641
PH: (415)863-0814
Fax: (415)863-7428
Gong, Stephen, Exec. Dir.

Center on Juvenile and Criminal
     Justice [5129]
40 Boardman Pl.
San Francisco, CA 94103
PH: (415)621-5661
Fax: (415)621-5466
Macallair, Daniel, MPA, Exec. Dir.

Center for Law and Justice
     International [5421]
c/o USF School of Law
Kendrick Hall, 342
2130 Fulton St.
San Francisco, CA 94117-1080
PH: (415)422-6280

Center for Sex and Culture [12942]
1349 Mission St.
San Francisco, CA 94103
PH: (415)902-2071
Queen, Dr. Carol, Founder, Exec.
     Dir.

Child Care Law Center [10806]
445 Church St.
San Francisco, CA 94114
PH: (415)558-8005
Stringer, Daniel, Chmn. of the Bd.

Child Family Health International
[14172]
995 Market St., Ste. 1104
San Francisco, CA 94103
PH: (415)957-9000
Toll free: 866-345-4674
Fax: (415)840-0486
Evert, Dr. Jessica, Exec. Dir.

China-U.S. Energy Efficiency Alli-
     ance [6465]
555 Mission St., Ste. 3300
San Francisco, CA 94105
PH: (415)951-8975
Schulberg, Fran, Exec. Dir.

Chinese for Affirmative Action
[17884]
17 Walter U. Lum Pl.
San Francisco, CA 94108
PH: (415)274-6750
Fax: (415)397-8770
Wong, Germaine Q., Chairman

Chinese American Biopharmaceuti-
     cal Society [16655]
268 Bush St., Ste. 1888
San Francisco, CA 94104
Pei, Zhonghua, PhD, President

Chinese American Citizens Alliance
[19413]
1044 Stockton St.
San Francisco, CA 94108
Gor, Edmond J., President

Chinese Culture Foundation of San
     Francisco [9153]
750 Kearny St., 3rd Fl.
San Francisco, CA 94108-1861
PH: (415)986-1822
Fax: (415)986-2825
Teng, Mabel, Exec. Dir.

Chinese Historical Society of
     America [9154]
965 Clay St.
San Francisco, CA 94108
PH: (415)391-1188
Fax: (415)391-1150
Lee, Sue, Exec. Dir.

Climate Policy Initiative [4127]
235 Montgomery St., 13th Fl.
San Francisco, CA 94104
PH: (415)202-5846
Heller, Thomas C., Exec. Dir.

Committee for Nuclear Responsibility
[18732]
PO Box 421993
San Francisco, CA 94142

Committees of Correspondence for
     Democracy and Socialism [5765]
522 Valencia St.
San Francisco, CA 94110
PH: (415)863-6637
Davidson, Carl, Co-Chmn. of the Bd.

Community Partners International
[11341]
225 Bush St., No. 590
San Francisco, CA 94104
PH: (415)217-7015
Sze, S., President

Community United Against Violence
[11879]
427 S Van Ness Ave.
San Francisco, CA 94103
PH: (415)777-5500
Fax: (415)777-5565
Schaudel, Stephanie, Chairman

Compton Foundation [12967]
101 Montgomery St., Ste. 850
San Francisco, CA 94104-4126
PH: (415)391-9001
Fax: (415)391-9005
Friedman, Ellen, Exec. Dir.

Congress of Russian Americans
[19630]
2460 Sutter St.
San Francisco, CA 94115
PH: (415)928-5841
Fax: (415)928-5831
Sabelnik, Natalie, President

CorpWatch [18389]
PO Box 29198
San Francisco, CA 94129
PH: (415)226-6226
Chatterjee, Pratap, Exec. Dir.

Cultural Conservancy [10039]
1016 Lincoln Blvd., Bldg. 1016, 1st
     Fl.
San Francisco, CA 94129
PH: (415)561-6594
Fax: (415)561-6482
Nelson, Dr. Melissa, President

Cultural Integration Fellowship
[9026]
2650 Fulton St.
San Francisco, CA 94118

PH: (415)668-1559
Pease, Rita Chaudhuri, President

Delancey Street Foundation [12872]
600 Embarcadero
San Francisco, CA 94107
PH: (415)957-9800
     (415)512-5104
Fax: (415)512-5141
Silbert, Mimi Halper, PhD, CEO,
     President

Dominican Mission Foundation
[20409]
2506 Pine St.
San Francisco, CA 94115
PH: (415)931-2183
Fax: (415)931-1772
Walsh, Fr. Martin de Porres, OP,
     Director

Dreamfly [18005]
1818 Great Hwy.
San Francisco, CA 94122
Mendhro, Umaimah, Founder

Earthjustice [5178]
50 California St., Ste. 500
San Francisco, CA 94111
Toll free: 800-584-6460
Fax: (510)217-2040
Noppen, Trip Van, President

East West Academy of Healing Arts
[16456]
117 Topaz Way
San Francisco, CA 94131
PH: (415)285-9401
Chow, Dr. Effie, Founder, President

Efficiency First [3854]
55 New Montgomery St., Ste. 802
San Francisco, CA 94105
PH: (415)449-0551
Fax: (415)449-0559
Thomas, Greg, Founder, CEO

Electronic Frontier Foundation
[7265]
815 Eddy St.
San Francisco, CA 94109-7701
PH: (415)436-9333
Fax: (415)436-9993
Steele, Shari, Director

Emerge America [19243]
44 Montgomery St., Ste. 2310
San Francisco, CA 94104-4711
PH: (415)344-0323
Fax: (415)500-4065
Pearl, Amy, Chairperson

Employment Law Alliance [5003]
505 Montgomery St., 13th Fl.
San Francisco, CA 94111-6529
PH: (415)835-9011
Fax: (415)834-0443
Hirschfeld, Stephen J., Esq., CEO,
     Founder

The Empowered Patient Coalition
[15637]
595 Buckingham Way, No. 305
San Francisco, CA 94132
Hallisy, Dr. Julia, Founder

Endangered Species International
[3855]
2112 Hayes St.
San Francisco, CA 94117
Fidenci, Pierre, Founder, President

Environmental Entrepreneurs [3857]
111 Sutter St., 21st Fl.
San Francisco, CA 94104-4540
Epstein, Bob, Founder

Equal Access [7902]
1212 Market St., Ste. 200
San Francisco, CA 94102

PH: (415)561-4884
Fax: (415)561-4885
Gunther, Mark, Officer

Equal Rights Advocates [5722]
1170 Market St., Ste. 700
San Francisco, CA 94102
PH: (415)621-0672
Toll free: 800-839-4372
Fax: (415)621-6744
Reisch, Jennifer, Dir. of Legal Svcs.

Federation of Chinese American and
Chinese Canadian Medical Societ-
ies [15723]
445 Grant Ave., 2nd Fl.
San Francisco, CA 94108-3208
PH: (415)677-2464
Fax: (415)677-2489
Chin, Warren W., MD, Chairman

Federation of Gay Games [23225]
584 Castro St., Ste. 343
San Francisco, CA 94114-2512
Toll free: 866-459-1261
Evans, Joanie, Co-Pres.

Filipina Women's Network [19245]
PO Box 192143
San Francisco, CA 94119
PH: (415)935-4396
Mondejar, Marily, Founder, CEO

Filipino-American Law Enforcement
Officers Association [5463]
PO Box 77086
San Francisco, CA 94107
Sylvester, Glenn, President

Forensic Expert Witness Association
[5245]
575 Market St., Ste. 2125
San Francisco, CA 94105
PH: (415)369-9614
Fax: (415)764-4933
McReynolds, John, President

The Forgotten International [12539]
PO Box 192066
San Francisco, CA 94119
PH: (415)517-6942
Nazario, Prof. Thomas, Founder,
President

Foundation for National Progress
[18977]
c/o Mother Jones
222 Sutter St., Ste. 600
San Francisco, CA 94108
PH: (415)321-1700
Fax: (415)321-1701
Straus, Phil, Chairman

Friends of Roman Cats [3678]
PO Box 12571
San Francisco, CA 94112
PH: (415)334-8036

The Future 500 [18006]
230 California St., Ste. 301
San Francisco, CA 94111
Toll free: 800-655-2020
Fax: (415)520-0830
Shireman, Bill, President, CEO

Futures Without Violence [11703]
The Presidio
100 Montgomery St.
San Francisco, CA 94129
PH: (415)678-5500
Fax: (415)529-2930
Soler, Esta, Founder, President

GalaxyGoo [7588]
4104 24th St., No. 349
San Francisco, CA 94114
Henry, Kristin F., President

Gay Asian Pacific Alliance Founda-
tion [11881]
PO Box 22482
San Francisco, CA 94142

PH: (415)857-4272
Lim, Ty, President

Gay, Lesbian, Bisexual, Transgender
Historical Society [9393]
4127 18th St.
San Francisco, CA 94114
PH: (415)621-1107
Beswick, Terry, Exec. Dir.

Gay, Lesbian, Bisexual, and Trans-
gender National Hotline [11883]
2261 Market St., No. 296
San Francisco, CA 94114
PH: (415)355-0003
Toll free: 888-843-4564

Genocide Education Project [18305]
51 Commonwealth Ave.
San Francisco, CA 94118
PH: (415)264-4203
Momjian, Raffi, Exec. Dir., Founder,
Chmn. of the Bd.

Glaucoma Research Foundation
[16384]
251 Post St., Ste. 600
San Francisco, CA 94108
PH: (415)986-3162
Toll free: 800-826-6693
Fax: (415)986-3763
Brunner, Thomas M., CEO,
President

Global Exchange [18098]
2017 Mission St., 2nd Fl.
San Francisco, CA 94110
PH: (415)255-7296
Toll free: 800-497-1994
Fax: (415)255-7498
Turner, Walter, President

Global Fund for Women [18210]
800 Market St., 7th Fl.
San Francisco, CA 94108-4456
PH: (415)248-4800
Fax: (415)248-4801
Kanyoro, Ms. Musimbi, CEO,
President

Global Options [18980]
PO Box 40601
San Francisco, CA 94140-0601
PH: (415)550-1703
Barak, Gregg, Editor

Global Pediatric Alliance [16607]
PO Box 640046
San Francisco, CA 94164
PH: (415)567-3698
Ramirez, Stacey, Exec. Dir.

Global Viral [15401]
1 Sutter St., Ste. 600
San Francisco, CA 94104
PH: (415)398-4712
Fax: (415)398-4716
Wolfe, Nathan, Founder

Grantmakers Without Borders
[12483]
Global Fund for Women
222 Sutter St., Ste. 500
San Francisco, CA 94129
PH: (415)248-4800
Fax: (415)248-4801
Stanga, Pete, Exec. Dir.

Greater Good Haiti [11369]
1230 Market St., No. 129
San Francisco, CA 94102
Kobza, Kelly, Founder

Greenaction for Health and
Environmental Justice [5274]
559 Ellis St.
San Francisco, CA 94109
PH: (415)447-3904
Fax: (415)447-3905
Angel, Bradley, Exec. Dir.

GSA Network [18402]
1550 Bryant St., Ste. 600
San Francisco, CA 94103
PH: (415)552-4229
Fax: (415)552-4729
Laub, Carolyn, Founder, Exec. Dir.

Haiku Society of America [10152]
c/o Fay Aoyagi, President
930 Pine St., No. 105
San Francisco, CA 94108
Aoyagi, Fay, President

Hearst Foundation [12976]
90 New Montgomery St., Ste. 1212
San Francisco, CA 94105
PH: (415)908-4500
Fax: (415)348-0887
Dinovitz, Paul, Exec. Dir.

Impact Carbon [4027]
582 Market St., Ste. 1204
San Francisco, CA 94104
PH: (415)968-9087
Haigler, Evan, Exec. Dir.

Independent Arts and Media [8860]
PO Box 420442
San Francisco, CA 94142-0442
PH: (415)738-4975
Burger, Lisa, President

Indus Women Leaders [18630]
236 W Portal Ave., No. 473
San Francisco, CA 94127

Institute for Global Communications
[7310]
PO Box 29047
San Francisco, CA 94129-0047
Strong, Shirley, Exec. Dir.

Institute for Medical Quality [17029]
180 Howard St., Ste. 210
San Francisco, CA 94105
PH: (415)882-5151
Fax: (415)882-5149
Silverman, Jill K., MSPH, CEO,
President

Interamerican Association for
Environmental Defense [4130]
50 California St., Ste. 500
San Francisco, CA 94111
PH: (415)217-2156
Fax: (415)217-2040
Cederstav, Anna, Exec. Dir.

International AIDS Society USA
[13547]
425 California St., Ste. 1450
San Francisco, CA 94104-2120
PH: (415)544-9400
Fax: (415)544-9401
Volberding, Paul A., MD, Chairman

International Anesthesia Research
Society [13702]
44 Montgomery St., Ste. 1605
San Francisco, CA 94104-4703
PH: (415)296-6900
Fax: (415)296-6901
Cooper, Thomas A., Exec. Dir.

International Association of Business
Communicators [770]
155 Montgomery St., Ste. 1210
San Francisco, CA 94104
PH: (415)544-4700
Toll free: 800-776-4222
Fax: (415)544-4747
Fulcher, Carlos, Exec. Dir.

International Association of Profes-
sional Security Consultants [3058]
575 Market St., Ste. 2125
San Francisco, CA 94105
PH: (415)536-0288
Fax: (415)764-4915
Gillens, Harold, President

International Computer Music As-
sociation [2425]
1819 Polk St., Ste. 330
San Francisco, CA 94109
Fax: (734)878-3031
Park, Tae Hong, VP

International Council of Ophthalmol-
ogy [16387]
711 Van Ness Ave., Ste. 445
San Francisco, CA 94102
PH: (415)521-1651
Fax: (415)521-1649
Gupta, Neeru, MD, PhD, MBA, VP

International Expressive Arts
Therapy Association [13730]
PO Box 40707
San Francisco, CA 94110-9991
PH: (415)522-8959
Decuire, Yasmin K., Treasurer

International Federation of Bike Mes-
senger Associations [3335]
PO Box 191443
San Francisco, CA 94119-1443
Hollinsworth, Leah, Contact

International Forum on Globalization
[18480]
1009 General Kennedy Ave., No. 2
San Francisco, CA 94129
PH: (415)561-7650
Fax: (415)561-7651
Menotti, Victor, Exec. Dir.

International Indian Treaty Council
[18474]
2940 16th St., Ste. 305
San Francisco, CA 94103-3664
PH: (415)641-4482
Fax: (415)641-1298
Cali, Francisco, President

International Latino Film Society
[9661]
984 Folsom St.
San Francisco, CA 94107-1007
PH: (415)513-5308
Fax: (415)512-7179

International Longshore and
Warehouse Union [23473]
1188 Franklin St., 4th Fl.
San Francisco, CA 94109-6800
PH: (415)775-0533
Fax: (415)775-1302
McEllrath, Robert, President

International Network of Boutique
Law Firms [5013]
c/o Spiegel Liao & Kagay, PC
388 Market St., Ste. 900
San Francisco, CA 94111
PH: (415)956-6062
Spielvogel, Steven, Esq., President

International Neuromodulation
Society [16021]
c/o Tia Sofatzis, Executive Director
2000 Van Ness Ave., Ste. 414
San Francisco, CA 94109-3019
PH: (415)683-3237
Fax: (415)683-3218
Sofatzis, Tia, Exec. Dir.

International Photographic Historical
Organization [10140]
PO Box 16074
San Francisco, CA 94116
PH: (415)681-4356
Silver, David F., President

International Society for Eye
Research [6092]
655 Beach St.
San Francisco, CA 94119
PH: (415)561-8569
Fax: (415)561-8531
Chan-Ling, Tailoi, Secretary

International Society for Individual Liberty **[18640]**
237 Kearny St., No. 120
San Francisco, CA 94108-4502
PH: (415)859-5174
Schoolland, Ken, President

International Tibet Network **[19190]**
1310 Fillmore St., Ste. 401
San Francisco, CA 94115

International Wizard of Oz Club **[9062]**
2443 Fillmore St., No. 347
San Francisco, CA 94115
Hedges, Ms. Carrie, President

International Women Fly Fishers **[22042]**
c/o Fanny Krieger, Founder
Krieger Enterprises
790 27th Ave.
San Francisco, CA 94121
PH: (415)752-0192
Brenner, Peggy, Mem.

Intrax Cultural Exchange **[7933]**
Intrax Global Headquarters
600 California St., 10th Fl.
San Francisco, CA 94108
PH: (415)434-1221
Diaz-Obregon, Emmanuel, Dir. of Operations

IP Justice **[5335]**
1192 Haight St.
San Francisco, CA 94117
PH: (415)553-6261
Fax: (415)462-6451
Gross, Robin D., Exec. Dir.

Iris Films **[10304]**
2443 Fillmore St., No. 380-3013
San Francisco, CA 94115
Reid, Frances, Director, Producer

Island Aid **[11673]**
450 Taraval St., No. 110
San Francisco, CA 94116-2530
PH: (415)992-7517
Cameron, Rick, President

Japanese American Citizens League **[19510]**
1765 Sutter St.
San Francisco, CA 94115
PH: (415)921-5225
   (415)345-1077
Abe, Toshi, VP of Member & Public Rel.

Jews for Jesus **[20337]**
60 Haight St.
San Francisco, CA 94102-5802
PH: (415)864-2600
Fax: (415)552-8325
Brickner, David, Director

KickStart International **[12547]**
123 10th St.
San Francisco, CA 94102
PH: (415)346-4820
Fax: (415)935-5116
Fisher, Martin, CEO

Legal Services for Children **[5541]**
1254 Market St., 3rd Fl.
San Francisco, CA 94102-4816
PH: (415)863-3762
Fax: (415)863-7708
Trillin, Abigail, Exec. Dir.

Legal Services for Prisoners with Children **[5287]**
1540 Market St., Ste. 490
San Francisco, CA 94102
PH: (415)255-7036
Fax: (415)552-3150
Nunn, Dorsey, Exec. Dir.

Lesbian, Gay, Bisexual, Transgender Returned Peace Corps Volunteers **[18846]**
PO Box 14332
San Francisco, CA 94114-0332
Toll free: 800-424-8580
Learned, Mike, Editor

Literate Nation **[8247]**
870 Market St., Ste. 962
San Francisco, CA 94102
PH: (415)789-5574
Coletti, Cinthia, Chmn. of the Bd., CEO

Mama Hope **[11401]**
582 Market St., Ste. 611
San Francisco, CA 94104-5307
PH: (415)986-3310
Rodgers, Nyla, Director, Founder

Media Alliance **[17949]**
2830 20th St., Ste. 102
San Francisco, CA 94110
PH: (415)746-9475
Fax: (510)238-8557
Rosenberg, Tracy, Exec. Dir.

Ms. JD **[5023]**
PO Box 77546
San Francisco, CA 94107
Tasher, Raychelle A., President

National Alliance for Filipino Concerns **[17814]**
4681 Mission St.
San Francisco, CA 94112
PH: (415)333-6267
Valen, Terry, President

National Alliance for Media Arts and Culture **[8986]**
145 9th St., Ste. 230
San Francisco, CA 94103
PH: (510)336-2555
De Michiel, Helen, Director

National Center for Lesbian Rights **[11899]**
870 Market St., Ste. 370
San Francisco, CA 94102
PH: (415)392-6257
Fax: (415)392-8442
Kendell, Kate, Esq., Exec. Dir.

National Council of Asian Pacific Islander Physicians **[16759]**
445 Grant Ave., Ste. 202
San Francisco, CA 94108
PH: (415)399-6565
Tran, Ho Luong, President, CEO

National Housing Law Project **[5283]**
703 Market St., Ste. 2000
San Francisco, CA 94103
PH: (415)546-7000
Fax: (415)546-7007
Pearman, Robert C., Jr., Chairperson

National Japanese American Historical Society **[9627]**
1684 Post St.
San Francisco, CA 94115-3604
PH: (415)921-5007
Fax: (415)921-5087
Tonai, Rosalyn, Exec. Dir.

National Network to End Violence Against Immigrant Women **[13389]**
Family Violence Prevention Fund
383 Rhode Island St., Ste. 304
San Francisco, CA 94103
PH: (415)252-8900
Fax: (415)252-8991

National Organization to Halt the Abuse and Routine Mutilation of Males **[11286]**
PO Box 460795
San Francisco, CA 94146

PH: (415)826-9351
Fax: (305)768-5967
Hammond, Tim, Founder, Exec. Dir.

National Society of Newspaper Columnists **[2706]**
PO Box 411532
San Francisco, CA 94141
PH: (415)488-6762
Fax: (484)297-0336
Molinari, Lisa Smith, President

National Women Law Students' Organization **[8222]**
PO Box 77546
San Francisco, CA 94107
Stern, Diana, Liaison

Native Daughters of the Golden West **[19393]**
543 Baker St.
San Francisco, CA 94117-1405
PH: (415)563-9091
Fax: (415)563-5230
Logan, Sharon D., Mem.

Native Sons of the Golden West **[19394]**
414 Mason St., Ste. 300
San Francisco, CA 94102
PH: (415)392-1223
Toll free: 800-337-1875
Dutschke, Dwight A., President

Nepal SEEDS: Social Educational Environmental Development Services in Nepal **[11411]**
800 Kansas St.
San Francisco, CA 94107-2607
PH: (415)813-3331
Kafle, KP, Exec. Dir., Founder

NESsT International **[12998]**
995 Market St., Ste. 1115
San Francisco, CA 94103
PH: (415)644-0509
Comolli, Loic, Co-CEO

Neurotechnology Industry Organization **[16032]**
2339 3rd St., Ste. 56
San Francisco, CA 94131
PH: (415)341-0193
Fax: (415)358-5888
Lynch, Zack, Exec. Dir., Founder

New America Media **[18662]**
209 9th St., Ste. 200
San Francisco, CA 94103
PH: (415)503-4170
Fax: (415)503-0970
Close, Sandy, Director, Editor

NewTithing Group **[18853]**
c/o Webster Systems, LLC dba Data360
1 Maritime Plz., Ste. 1545
San Francisco, CA 94111
PH: (415)733-9740
Anderson, Jamie, Administrator

North American Man/Boy Love Association **[12950]**
537 Jones St., No. 8418
San Francisco, CA 94102
PH: (347)269-0682
   (417)287-3427

Not For Sale **[12053]**
2225 3rd St.
San Francisco, CA 94107
PH: (650)560-9990
Batstone, Dave, Founder

OAfrica **[11103]**
268 Bush St., No. 3100
San Francisco, CA 94104
PH: (917)477-3822
Lovatt-Smith, Lisa, Founder

Occupational Knowledge International **[4555]**
4444 Geary Blvd., Ste. 208
San Francisco, CA 94118
PH: (415)221-8900
Fax: (415)221-8903
Gottesfeld, Mr. Perry, President

OmSpring **[13647]**
550 Wisconsin St.
San Francisco, CA 94107
PH: (415)206-9920
Navarro, Suteja, Specialist

One Warm Coat **[12556]**
2443 Fillmore St., No. 380-5363
San Francisco, CA 94115
Stockard, Jennifer, President, CEO

Online Policy Group **[17996]**
1800 Market St., No. 123
San Francisco, CA 94102-6227
Fax: (928)244-2347
Doherty, Will, Founder

Open Group **[1805]**
44 Montgomery St., Ste. 960
San Francisco, CA 94104-4704
PH: (415)374-8280
Fax: (415)374-8293
Nunn, Steve, CEO, President

Organization for Refuge Asylum and Migration **[12595]**
39 Drumm St., 4th Fl.
San Francisco, CA 94111
PH: (415)399-1701
Fax: (415)373-9191
Grungras, Neil, Founder, Exec. Dir.

Organize Training Center **[11473]**
442 Vicksburg St.
San Francisco, CA 94114-3831
PH: (415)648-6894
Miller, Mike, Exec. Dir.

Other Minds **[9993]**
55 Taylor St.
San Francisco, CA 94102-3916
PH: (415)934-8134
Fax: (415)934-8136
Amirkhanian, Charles, Exec. Dir.

Out and Equal Workplace Advocates **[11903]**
155 Sansome St., Ste. 450
San Francisco, CA 94104
PH: (415)694-6500
Berry, Selisse, Founder, CEO

Pachamama Alliance **[4614]**
Presidio Bldg., No. 1009
San Francisco, CA 94129
PH: (415)561-4522
Starr, Gordon, Chairman

Pacific Arts Association **[8879]**
c/o Christina Hellmich, Acting Treasurer
Fine Arts Museums of San Francisco
Golden Gate Pk.
Hagiwara Garden Tea Dr.
San Francisco, CA 94118
Hooper, Steven, President

Pacific Dermatologic Association **[14510]**
575 Market St., Ste. 2125
San Francisco, CA 94105
Toll free: 888-388-8815
Fax: (415)764-4915
Smith, Janellen, President

Pacific Research Institute for Public Policy **[18997]**
101 Montgomery St., Ste. 1300
San Francisco, CA 94111
PH: (415)989-0833
Fax: (415)989-2411
Pipes, Sally C., President, CEO

Papanicolaou Society of Cytopathology **[14360]**
2295 Vallejo St., No. 508
San Francisco, CA 94123
PH: (415)833-3871
Elsheikh, Tarik, President

Parents Education Network **[8405]**
6050 Geary Blvd., Ste. 101A
San Francisco, CA 94121
PH: (415)751-2237
Fax: (415)933-8772
Maloney, Laura, President

Peace Development Fund **[18816]**
3221 22nd St.
San Francisco, CA 94110-3006
PH: (415)642-0900
Fax: (415)642-8200
Juarez, Teresa, President

Peer Health Exchange **[8769]**
70 Gold St.
San Francisco, CA 94133
PH: (415)684-1234
Fax: (415)684-1222
Schneider, Martin, Chairman

Philippine American Writers and Artists, Inc. **[10394]**
PO Box 31928
San Francisco, CA 94131-0928
Lozada, Edwin Agustin, Director

Planet Drum Foundation **[17810]**
PO Box 31251
San Francisco, CA 94131-0251
PH: (415)285-6556
Fax: (415)285-6563
Berg, Mr. Peter, Director

Planetwork **[4009]**
29 Grove St., Ste. 517
San Francisco, CA 94102
PH: (415)721-1591
Fournier, Jim, Founder, President

Plug In America **[5889]**
2370 Market St., No. 419
San Francisco, CA 94114
PH: (415)323-3329
Kelly, Richard, Director

Population-Environment Balance **[12516]**
PO Box 268
San Francisco, CA 94104-0268

POWER: People Organized to Win Employment Rights **[11780]**
2145 Keith St.
San Francisco, CA 94124
PH: (415)864-8372
Fax: (415)864-8373
Lee, NTanya, Exec. Dir.

Print Council of America **[8882]**
Fine Arts Museums of San Francisco
Legion of Honor
100 34th Ave.
San Francisco, CA 94121-1677
Ganz, Jim, President

Project Inform **[13559]**
273 9th St.
San Francisco, CA 94103
PH: (415)558-8669
Toll free: 877-435-7443
Fax: (415)558-0684
Van Gorder, Dana, Exec. Dir.

Public Architecture **[235]**
1211 Folsom St., 4th Fl.
San Francisco, CA 94103
PH: (415)861-8200
Fax: (415)431-9695
Peterson, John, AIA, President, Founder

Radical Women **[18233]**
New Valencia Hall
747 Polk St.
San Francisco, CA 94109
PH: (415)864-1278

Rainforest Action Network **[3930]**
425 Bush St., Ste. 300
San Francisco, CA 94108
PH: (415)398-4404
Fax: (415)398-2732
Evans, Jodie, Bd. Member

Rebuild Sudan **[13084]**
2820 22nd St.
San Francisco, CA 94110
PH: (415)226-9879
De Kuany, Michael Ayuen, President, CEO

Red Panda Network **[4877]**
1859 Powell St., Ste. 100
San Francisco, CA 94133
PH: (541)228-1902
Boyd, Nicki, Chairperson

Rising Tide North America **[3933]**
268 Bush St., No. 3717
San Francisco, CA 94104-3503

RollerSoccer International Federation **[23253]**
PO Box 423318
San Francisco, CA 94142-3318
PH: (415)864-6879
Phillips, Zack, Founder, President

Room to Read **[11736]**
465 California St., Ste. 1000
San Francisco, CA 94104
PH: (415)839-4400
Fax: (415)591-0580
Wood, John, Founder

Rotaplast International **[14343]**
3317 26th St.
San Francisco, CA 94110
PH: (415)252-1111
Fax: (415)252-1211
Delaney, Anne, Chairperson

Sacred Dying Foundation **[11558]**
PO Box 210328
San Francisco, CA 94121
PH: (415)585-9455
Anderson, Dr. Megory, Founder, Exec. Dir.

Sailors' Union of the Pacific **[23476]**
450 Harrison St.
San Francisco, CA 94105
PH: (415)777-3400
(415)777-3616
Fax: (415)777-5088
Connolly, Dave, VP

Saluki Tree of Life Alliance, Inc. **[11694]**
3701 Sacramento St., No. 345
San Francisco, CA 94118-1705
Noll, Janet, President

San Francisco African American Historical and Cultural Society **[8787]**
762 Fulton St.
San Francisco, CA 94102
PH: (415)292-6172
Williams, Mr. Alfred W., President, Chmn. of the Bd.

San Francisco Camerawork **[9310]**
1011 Market St., 2nd Fl.
San Francisco, CA 94103
PH: (415)487-1011
Mobley, Chuck, Contact

The San Francisco Institute for Jewish Medical Ethics **[20280]**
645 14th Ave.
San Francisco, CA 94118

PH: (415)752-7333
Lipner, Rabbi Pinchas, Dean, Founder

San Francisco Maritime National Park Association **[9840]**
PO Box 470310
San Francisco, CA 94147-0310
PH: (415)561-6662
(415)775-1943
Fax: (415)561-6660
Bleicher, Robert A., President, Chairman

Save the Redwoods League **[3941]**
111 Sutter St., 11th Fl.
San Francisco, CA 94104
PH: (415)362-2352
Toll free: 888-836-0005
Thomas, Melinda, Chairperson

Scleroderma Research Foundation **[17182]**
220 Montgomery St., Ste. 1411
San Francisco, CA 94104
Toll free: 800-441-2873
Evnin, Luke, PhD, Chairman

SCSI Trade Association **[1807]**
Presidio of San Francisco
572-B Ruger St.
San Francisco, CA 94129
PH: (415)561-6273
Fax: (415)561-6120
Kutcipal, Rick, President

The Shanti Project Inc. **[11498]**
730 Polk St.
San Francisco, CA 94109
PH: (415)674-4700
(415)674-4722
Fax: (415)674-0373
Roy, Kaushik, Exec. Dir.

Shark Savers **[4887]**
744 Montgomery St., Ste. 300
San Francisco, CA 94111
PH: (415)834-3174
Fax: (415)834-1759
Benchley, Wendy W., President

Social Media Club **[2319]**
PO Box 14881
San Francisco, CA 94114-0881
Ashby, Golden, President

Social Venture Network **[669]**
Thoreau Center for Sustainability
1016 Torney Ave. 3
San Francisco, CA 94129
PH: (415)561-6501
Fax: (415)561-6435
Nelson, Deb, Contact

Society for Asian Art **[8890]**
Asian Art Museum
200 Larkin St.
San Francisco, CA 94102
PH: (415)581-3701
Fax: (415)861-2358
Kahn, Anne, VP

Society of California Pioneers **[21086]**
300 4th St.
San Francisco, CA 94107-1272
PH: (415)957-1849
Fax: (415)957-9858
Devine, Mercedes, Managing Dir.

Society of Critical Care Anesthesiologists **[13710]**
44 Montgomery St., Ste. 1605
San Francisco, CA 94104-4703
PH: (415)296-6952
Fax: (415)296-6901
Brown, Daniel R., Treasurer

Society for Orthomolecular Health Medicine **[13657]**
3637 Sacramento St., Ste. C
San Francisco, CA 94118-1726

PH: (415)922-6462
Fax: (415)346-2519
Kunin, Richard A., MD, President

Spanish Neuromodulation Society **[16037]**
c/o Tia Sofatzis, Executive Director
2000 Van Ness Ave., Ste. 414
San Francisco, CA 94109
PH: (415)683-3237
Fax: (415)683-3218
Pajuelo, Dr. Antonio, President

Stand **[4219]**
1 Haight St.
San Francisco, CA 94102
PH: (415)863-4563
Paglia, Todd J., Exec. Dir.

State of the World Forum **[19266]**
PO Box 29434
San Francisco, CA 94129
PH: (415)561-2345
Fax: (415)561-2323
Garrison, James, President

Swiss-American Chamber of Commerce **[23621]**
PO Box 26007
San Francisco, CA 94126-6007
PH: (415)433-6679
Jeker, Bjoern A., President

TechSoup Global **[6732]**
435 Brannan St., Ste. 100
San Francisco, CA 94107
PH: (415)633-9300
Ben-Horin, Daniel, Founder, Secretary

Transaction Processing Performance Council **[6266]**
572B Ruger St.
San Francisco, CA 94129-1770
PH: (415)561-6272
Fax: (415)561-6120
Serlin, Omri, Founder

Trauma Foundation at San Francisco General Hospital **[17532]**
San Francisco General Hospital
San Francisco, CA 94110
PH: (415)215-8980
Fax: (415)884-9230
McGuire, Mr. Andrew, Exec. Dir.

Trikone **[11910]**
60 29th St., No. 614
San Francisco, CA 94110
Toll free: 844-903-5663

Trust for Public Land **[3960]**
101 Montgomery St., Ste. 900
San Francisco, CA 94104
PH: (415)495-4014
Toll free: 800-714-LAND
Cowles, Page Knudsen, Chmn. of the Bd.

United Religions Initiative **[20567]**
1009 General Kennedy Ave.
San Francisco, CA 94129-1706
PH: (415)561-2300
Fax: (415)561-2313
Swing, Rev. William E., President, Founder

U.S./Japan Cultural Trade Network **[9217]**
1471 Guerrero St., Ste. 3
San Francisco, CA 94110-4371
PH: (415)867-7080
Yoshida, Kyoko, Exec. Dir.

UniversalGiving **[13309]**
901 Mission St., Ste. 205
San Francisco, CA 94103

PH: (415)296-9193
Fax: (415)296-9195
Hawley, Pamela, Founder, CEO

Upwardly Global [2745]
582 Market St., Ste. 1207
San Francisco, CA 94104
PH: (415)834-9901
Fax: (415)840-0334
Cicerani, Nikki, Exec. Dir., President

Vernacular Architecture Forum
[5982]
c/o William Littmann, Secretary
PO Box 225158
San Francisco, CA 94122
Buggeln, Gretchen, President

VIA [13310]
870 Market St., No. 656
San Francisco, CA 94102
PH: (415)904-8033
Brooke, Bryant, Dir. of Programs

Viet/American Cervical Cancer
Prevention Project [14079]
c/o Eric Suba, MD, President/Executive Director
350 St. Josephs Ave.
San Francisco, CA 94115
PH: (415)833-3870
Suba, Eric, MD, President, Exec. Dir.

ViviendasLeon [12388]
1585 Folsom St.
San Francisco, CA 94103
PH: (415)255-2920
Markiewicz, Evan, Exec. Dir.,
Founder

VolunteerMatch [13311]
550 Montgomery St., 8th Fl.
San Francisco, CA 94111
PH: (415)241-6868
Fax: (415)241-6869
Dixon, Jackie, Dir. of Admin., Dir. of
HR

We Interrupt This Message [18666]
1215 York St.
San Francisco, CA 94110
Bervera, Xochitl S., Director

Western Association for Art
Conservation [249]
c/o Denise Migdail, Secretary
200 Larkin St.
San Francisco, CA 94102
PH: (415)581-3544
Coueignoux, Catherine, President

Western Payments Alliance [1270]
300 Montgomery St., Ste.400
San Francisco, CA 94104
PH: (415)433-1230
Toll free: 800-977-0018
Fax: (415)433-1370
Schoch, William, CEO, President

WildAid [4906]
333 Pine St., Ste. 300
San Francisco, CA 94104
PH: (415)834-3174
Fax: (415)834-1759
Knights, Peter, Exec. Dir.

Wildflowers Institute [9158]
1144 Pacific Ave.
San Francisco, CA 94133
PH: (415)775-1151
Liu, Dr. Hanmin, CEO, President,
Founder

Wildlife Conservation Network
[4909]
209 Mississippi St.
San Francisco, CA 94107
PH: (415)202-6380
Fax: (415)202-6381
Knowles, Charles, President,
Founder, Chmn. of the Bd.

Wine Appreciation Guild [4935]
450 Taraval St., Ste. 201
San Francisco, CA 94116
PH: (650)866-3020
Toll free: 800-231-9463
MacKey, J., VP of Mktg.

Wine Institute [4936]
425 Market St., Ste. 1000
San Francisco, CA 94105
PH: (415)512-0151
Fax: (415)356-7569
Koch, Robert, CEO, President

Women Impacting Public Policy
[19009]
PO Box 31279
San Francisco, CA 94131
PH: (415)434-4314
Toll free: 888-488-9477
Fax: (415)434-4331
Kasoff, Barbara, President

Women's Funding Network [13408]
156 2nd St.
San Francisco, CA 94105
PH: (415)441-0706
Fax: (415)441-0827
Burow, Kirsty, Dir. of Comm.

World Peace Through Technology
Organization [12447]
San Francisco, CA 94105
Olsen, Brad, Exec. Dir.

World Savvy [8773]
917 Irving St., No. 4
San Francisco, CA 94122
PH: (415)292-7421
Fax: (888)452-0993
Hoven, Pat, Chairperson

World Wide Opportunities on
Organic Farms - USA [17794]
654 Fillmore St.
San Francisco, CA 94117
PH: (415)621-3276
Goldsmith, Ryan, President

Worldreader [8256]
120 Hickory St.
San Francisco, CA 94102
PH: (206)588-6057
Fax: (831)299-5366
Risher, David, Founder, President

Wrestlers WithOut Borders [23375]
63 Whitney St.
San Francisco, CA 94131
Lorefice, Chris, Chairman

YLEM: Artists Using Science and
Technology [8948]
PO Box 31923
San Francisco, CA 94131-0923
PH: (415)445-0196
Nommesen, Torrey, Contact

Young Women Social Entrepreneurs
[677]
1218 Green St.
San Francisco, CA 94109
PH: (707)272-0066
(415)716-6409
Conant, Sara Ellis, Contact

Youth Law Center [13488]
200 Pine St., Ste. 300
San Francisco, CA 94104
PH: (415)543-3379
Fax: (415)956-9022
Rodriguez, Jennifer, Exec. Dir.

Abrahamic Alliance International
[20213]
1930 Camden Ave., Ste. 3A
San Jose, CA 95124
PH: (408)728-8943
Fax: (408)641-7545
Cardoza, Rod, Exec. Dir., Founder

American Automobile Touring Alliance [3367]
PO Box 24980
San Jose, CA 95154
PH: (480)371-5635
Hedges, Arthur, President

American Beethoven Society [9175]
San Jose State University
Beethoven Ctr.
1 Washington Sq.
San Jose, CA 95192-0171
PH: (408)808-2058
Fax: (408)808-2060
Meredith, Dr. William, Exec. Dir.

American Indian Library Association
[9667]
c/o Heather Devine-Hardy, Membership Coordinator
PO Box 41296
San Jose, CA 95160
Poler, Omar, VP

American Lands Access Association
[22412]
PO Box 54398
San Jose, CA 95154
Leeson, Shirley, President

American Rock Art Research Association [5929]
c/o Jack Wedgwood, Treasurer
1884 The Alameda
San Jose, CA 95126-1733
Hamann, Diane, President

American Tapestry Alliance [8835]
PO Box 28600
San Jose, CA 95159-8600
PH: (360)438-5386
Rohde, Michael, Director

Ancient Mystical Order Rosae Crucis
[19625]
1342 Naglee Ave.
San Jose, CA 95191
PH: (408)947-3600
Toll free: 800-882-6672
Fax: (408)947-3677
Scott, Julie, Master, Director

Applied Voice Input/Output Society
[6235]
PO Box 20817
San Jose, CA 95160
PH: (408)323-1783
Fax: (408)323-1782
Scholz, K.W., President

Association of Certified Professional
Wedding Consultants [2306]
San Jose, CA
PH: (408)227-2792
Fax: (408)226-0697
Moody, Deborah, Director

Association of Kannada Kootas of
America [19472]
3174 Bourgogne Ct.
San Jose, CA 95135
Patil, Raj, President, Trustee

Automatic Musical Instrument Collectors' Association [9878]
416 Colfax Dr.
San Jose, CA 95123-3403
PH: (408)508-6019
Turner, Alan, President

Bigfoot Owners Club International
[21337]
PO Box 18282
San Jose, CA 95158
Dunn, Art, President

Bridges Cambodia International, Inc.
[10874]
2970 Almond Dr.
San Jose, CA 95148-2001

PH: (408)472-3489
(408)759-7902
Nayseap, Hong, Founder, President

Career Planning and Adult Development Network [11756]
PO Box 611930
San Jose, CA 95161-1930
PH: (408)828-3858
Knowdell, Richard, Contact

Child Quest International [10903]
1177 Branham Ln., No.280
San Jose, CA 95118-3766
Gonzalez, Mr. Anthony, Director

Chris LeDoux International Fan Club
[24029]
c/o Rob Fair, President
PO Box 41052
San Jose, CA 95160
Fair, Rob, President

CityTeam Ministries [12645]
2304 Zanker Rd.
San Jose, CA 95131
PH: (408)232-5600
Fax: (408)428-9505
Robertson, Mr. Patrick J., President

CMO Council [2274]
c/o Donovan Neale-May, Executive
Director
1494 Hamilton Way
San Jose, CA 95125
PH: (408)677-5300
Neale-May, Donovan, Exec. Dir.

Contemporary A Cappella Society
[9893]
1354 W Hedding St.
San Jose, CA 95126
PH: (415)358-8067
Sharon, Deke, Founder

Dance 4 Health [16698]
1072 S DeAnza Blvd., Ste. A107-
317
San Jose, CA 95129
PH: (408)253-4673
Fax: (408)253-4673
Dziekanowski, Alex, Founder, Exec.
Dir.

Divine Science Ministers Association
[20053]
1540 Hicks Ave.
San Jose, CA 95125
PH: (408)293-3838
Emmerling, Rev. Christine, President

Electronic System Design Alliance
[6419]
3081 Zanker Rd.
San Jose, CA 95134
PH: (408)287-3322
Smith, Robert, Exec. Dir.

Fistula Foundation [14229]
1922 The Alameda, Ste. 302
San Jose, CA 95126
PH: (408)249-9596
Toll free: 866-756-3700
Grant, Kate, CEO

FlexTech Alliance [3208]
3081 Zanker Rd.
San Jose, CA 95134
PH: (408)577-1300
Fax: (408)577-1301
Ciesinski, Michael, CEO, President

Girls for a Change [10995]
PO Box 1436
San Jose, CA 95109
PH: (866)738-4422
Williamson, Jennifer, VP

HandsNet Inc. [12390]
PO Box 90477
San Jose, CA 95109

PH: (408)291-5111
    (408)829-3342
Fax: (408)904-4874
Saunders, Michael, Exec. Ofc.

Immigration Voice [5291]
1177 Branham Ln., No. 321
San Jose, CA 95118
PH: (202)386-6250
Fax: (202)403-3853
Kapoor, Aman, Founder

International Disk Drive Equipment
   and Materials Association [6252]
1226 Lincoln Ave., Ste. 100
San Jose, CA 95125
PH: (408)294-0082
   (408)649-3415
Fax: (408)294-0087
Gressley, Trudy, Office Mgr.

International Mental Game Coaching
   Association [22731]
PO Box 8151
San Jose, CA 95155
PH: (408)440-2398
Toll free: 888-445-0291
Fax: (408)440-2339
Cole, Bill, MS, Founder, President

International Society for Self and
   Identity [7066]
c/o Camille Johnson, Secretary/
   Treasurer
San Jose State University
1 Washington Sq.
San Jose, CA 95192
PH: (520)621-7434
Fax: (520)621-9306
Sherman, David, President

Internet Keep Safe Coalition [18569]
97 S 2nd St., 100 No. 244
San Jose, CA 95113
PH: (703)717-9066
Fax: (703)852-7100
Hancock, Marsali S., President, CEO

Joint Venture: Silicon Valley Network
   [7280]
100 W San Fernando St., Ste. 310
San Jose, CA 95113
PH: (408)298-9330
Hancock, Russell, CEO, President

Korea IT Network [6255]
3003 N 1st St.
San Jose, CA 95134
PH: (408)232-5475
Kim, Baxon, Dir. of Bus. Dev.

Lending Promise [11396]
479 Tovar Dr.
San Jose, CA 95123
Taylor, Meg North, Founder

Litzenberger-Litzenberg Association
   [20895]
3233 Simberlan Dr.
San Jose, CA 95148-3128
PH: (408)270-7227
Litzenberg, Homer L., III, President

Military Law Task Force of the
   National Lawyers Guild [5603]
730 N 1st St.
San Jose, CA 95122
PH: (619)463-2369
Mayfield, Dan, Secretary

Monte Jade Science and Technology
   Association [7283]
2870 Zanker Rd., Ste. 140
San Jose, CA 95134
PH: (408)428-0388
Fax: (408)428-0378
Wang, Sean, Sec. Gen.

Mushroom Council [4240]
2880 Zanker Rd., Ste. 203
San Jose, CA 95134-2122

PH: (408)432-7210
Fax: (408)432-7213

National Association for Chicana and
   Chicano Studies [7974]
PO Box 720052
San Jose, CA 95172-0052
PH: (408)924-5310
Curry Rodriguez, Dr. Julia E., Exec.
   Dir.

National Association of Filipino
   Priests - USA [19869]
c/o Rev. Engelberto Gammad
1150 N First St.
San Jose, CA 95112
Gammad, Engelberto, President

National Compadres Network
   [18669]
1550 The Alameda, Ste. 303
San Jose, CA 95126-2304
PH: (408)676-8215
Sánchez-Flores, Héctor, Exec. Dir.

National DeSoto Club [21453]
c/o Dennis Pitchford, Treasurer
14947 Leigh Ave.
San Jose, CA 95124-4524
Taft, Barrett, Secretary

National Pet Alliance [10674]
PO Box 53385
San Jose, CA 95153
PH: (408)363-0700

North American South Asian Law
   Students Association [8223]
65 Rio Robles E, Unit 2311
San Jose, CA 95134

Pacific Coast Cichlid Association
   [22035]
PO Box 28145
San Jose, CA 95159-8145
PH: (408)243-0434
DiMeo, Sonny, VP

Resisting Defamation [17928]
San Jose, CA

Rose Family Association [20921]
761 Villa Teresa Way
San Jose, CA 95123
Rose, Seymour T., Owner

SEMI International [1061]
3081 Zanker Rd.
San Jose, CA 95134
PH: (408)943-6900
Toll free: 800-974-7364
Fax: (408)428-9600
McGuirk, Dennis P., President, CEO

Society for Cross-Cultural Research
   [9583]
c/o Lisa Oliver, Treasurer
Dept. of Counselor Education
San Jose State University
Sweeney Hall 420
San Jose, CA 95192
Ganapathy-Coleman, Hemalatha,
   President

United Postal Stationery Society
   [22375]
1659 Branham Ln., Ste. F-307
San Jose, CA 95118-2291
Starkey, Gary, President

United States Dental Tennis Associa-
   tion [23306]
1096 Wilmington Ave.
San Jose, CA 95129-3242
Toll free: 800-445-2524
Lee, Cori, RDH, Exec. Dir.

Video Electronics Standards Association [6440]
1754 Technology Dr., Ste. 238
San Jose, CA 95110

PH: (408)982-3850
Fax: (408)669-0976
Kobayashi, Alan, Chairman

Vietnam Village Health [12063]
PO Box 32973
San Jose, CA 95152
PH: (408)661-6751
   (408)923-7262
Pham, Trieu, Dir. of Operations

World Congress of Poets [10161]
4423 Pitch Pine Ct.
San Jose, CA 95136
Wang, Michelle, Treasurer

Homefront America [10745]
27375 Paseo La Serna
San Juan Capistrano, CA 92675
PH: (949)248-9468
Hasselbrink, Arthur R., Founder,
   President

International Chili Society [22148]
32244 Paseo Adelanto, Ste. D3
San Juan Capistrano, CA 92675
PH: (949)496-2651
Toll free: 877-777-4427
Fax: (949)496-7091
Hancock, Carol, CEO

International Coalition for the
   Advancement of Neurology
   [16018]
PO Box 1708
San Juan Capistrano, CA 92693
PH: (760)213-5320
Camarena, Fermin, Founder,
   President

North American Steel Alliance [2365]
30448 Rancho Viejo Rd., Ste. 250
San Juan Capistrano, CA 92675
PH: (949)240-0100
Fax: (949)240-0106
Terry, Lonnie, President, CEO

Traffic Directors Guild of America
   [483]
Bldg. 114
26000 Avenida Aeropuerto
San Juan Capistrano, CA 92675-
   4713
PH: (949)429-7063
Fax: (509)471-5765
Keene, Larry, CEO

American College of Phlebology
   [17569]
101 Callan Ave., Ste. 210
San Leandro, CA 94577-4558
PH: (510)346-6800
   (510)834-6500
Fax: (510)346-6808
Sanders, Bruce A., Exec. Dir.

Association of Asian Pacific Com-
   munity Health Organizations
   [15137]
101 Callan Ave., Ste. 400
San Leandro, CA 94577
PH: (510)272-9536
Fax: (510)272-0817
Caballero, Jeffrey B., Exec. Dir.

Divco Club of America [21649]
c/o Rich Ferguson, Secretary
309 Beverly Ave.
San Leandro, CA 94577
PH: (510)568-0887
Ferguson, Rich, Secretary

Foundation for Science and Dis-
   ability [11597]
c/o Angela Lee Foreman, Treasurer
PO Box 3384
San Leandro, CA 94578
Mankin, Richard, President

ActiveWater [13312]
PO Box 3131
San Luis Obispo, CA 93403
Toll free: 888-543-3426
Wendell, Daren, Exec. Dir., Founder

Cuban American Alliance Education
   Fund, Inc. [9195]
PO Box 5113
San Luis Obispo, CA 93403
PH: (805)627-1959
Fax: (805)627-1959
Castro Cortes, Raul, President

Lifewater International [13355]
PO Box 3131
San Luis Obispo, CA 93403
Toll free: 888-543-3426
Narducci, Justin, President

National Brussels Griffon Rescue,
   Inc. [10666]
c/o Betty Mundy
181 Bonetti Dr.
San Luis Obispo, CA 93401
Mundy, Betty, Contact

Seeds of Hope International Partner-
   ships [11428]
1023 Nipomo St., Ste. 110
San Luis Obispo, CA 93401
PH: (805)439-1489
Schauer, Kirk, Founder

Vitamin D Council [16242]
1241 Johnson Ave., No. 134
San Luis Obispo, CA 93401-3306
PH: (805)439-1075
Cannell, Dr. John Jacob, Medical
   Dir., Founder

American Association of Equine
   Veterinary Technicians and As-
   sistants [17594]
c/o Deborah B. Reeder, Executive
   Director
539 Wild Horse Ln.
San Marcos, CA 92078
Fax: (760)301-0349
Reeder, Deborah B., Exec. Dir.

Association for Prenatal and Perinatal Psychology and Health [16905]
420 N Twin Oaks Valley Rd., Ste.
   412
San Marcos, CA 92069
PH: (760)492-9048
Verny, Thomas R., Founder

Cal State San Marcos Alumni Association [19311]
333 S Twin Oaks Valley Rd.
San Marcos, CA 92096-0001
PH: (760)750-4406

North American Model Boating As-
   sociation [22204]
c/o Al Waters
162 Avenida Chapala
San Marcos, CA 92069
PH: (760)746-2408
Fax: (760)539-9009
Waters, Al, Exec. Sec.

Chronic Granulomatous Disease Association [14570]
c/o Mary Hurley
2616 Monterey Rd.
San Marino, CA 91108-1646
PH: (626)441-4118
Hurley, Mary, Contact

Asian America MultiTechnology As-
   sociation [1036]
3 W 37th Ave., Ste. 19
San Mateo, CA 94403
PH: (650)773-2293
Meek, Paige, Exec. Dir.

Global Workspace Association [70]
1900 S Norfolk St., Ste. 350
San Mateo, CA 94403
PH: (650)931-2588
Russo, Jamie, Exec. Dir.

Law Enforcement Technology
Information Exchange [5481]
155 Bovet Rd., Ste. 410
San Mateo, CA 94402
PH: (415)297-1226
Marshall, Charles, Chairman

National Association on Alcohol,
Drugs and Disability [17321]
2165 Bunker Hill Dr.
San Mateo, CA 94402-3801
PH: (650)578-8047
Fax: (650)286-9205
Larson, Deb, Bd. Member

Nursing Mothers Counsel [11257]
PO Box 5024
San Mateo, CA 94402-0024
PH: (650)327-6455
McBride, Ms. Lori, Chairperson

the Radiosurgery Society [17413]
PO Box 5631
San Mateo, CA 94402
PH: (408)385-9411
Gagliardi, Kristine, Corp. Dev. Ofc.

Zawaya [8818]
311 41st Ave.
San Mateo, CA 94403
PH: (650)504-5965
Mango, Nabila, Exec. Dir.

American Cetacean Society [6789]
PO Box 1391
San Pedro, CA 90733-1391
PH: (310)548-6279
Fax: (310)548-6950
Alps, Diane, President

Damfinos: The International Buster
Keaton Society [24008]
2222 S Mesa St., No. 27
San Pedro, CA 90731
PH: (310)547-2207
Tobias, Ms. Patricia Eliot, President

International Generic Horse Associa-
tion [4366]
PO Box 6778
San Pedro, CA 90734-6778
PH: (310)719-9094

Juvenile Scleroderma Network, Inc.
[17180]
1204 W 13th St.
San Pedro, CA 90731
PH: (310)519-9511
Toll free: 866-338-5892
Gaither, Kathy, Founder, President

National Watercolor Society [8876]
915 S Pacific Ave.
San Pedro, CA 90731
PH: (310)831-1099
    (424)225-4966
Goldman, Ken, President

U.S. Merchant Marine Veterans of
World War II [21202]
PO Box 629
San Pedro, CA 90733-0629
PH: (310)519-9545
Fax: (310)519-0265

Association of Natural Medicine
Pharmacists [15858]
PO Box 150727
San Rafael, CA 94915
PH: (415)847-8192
Grauds, Constance, RPh, President

Association for the Protection of
Afghan Archaeology [5933]
PO Box 6798
San Rafael, CA 94903-0798
Tarzi, Nadia, Exec. Dir., Founder

Beyond Hunger [14633]
PO Box 151148
San Rafael, CA 94915
PH: (415)459-2270
Adams, Vikki A., Contact

Center for Visionary Leadership
[18629]
369B 3rd St., No. 563
San Rafael, CA 94901-3581
PH: (415)472-2540
    (480)595-4709
Davidson, Gordon, President

Ecological Building Network [3676]
PO Box 6397
San Rafael, CA 94903
PH: (415)491-4802
King, Bruce, Director, Founder

Edutopia - The George Lucas
Educational Foundation [7766]
PO Box 3494
San Rafael, CA 94912-3494
Johanson, Ms. Cindy, Exec. Dir.

Global AIDS Interfaith Alliance
[13541]
2171 Francisco Blvd. E, Ste. 1
San Rafael, CA 94901
PH: (415)461-7196
Fax: (415)785-7389
Rankin, William, PhD, Founder

Guide Dogs for the Blind [17709]
350 Los Ranchitos Rd.
San Rafael, CA 94903
PH: (415)499-4000
Toll free: 800-295-4050
Fax: (415)499-4035
Ruppel, Brent, VP

Humane Farming Association
[10642]
PO Box 3577
San Rafael, CA 94912
PH: (415)485-1495
Fax: (415)485-0106
Miller, Bradley S., President

In Defense of Animals [10645]
3010 Kerner Blvd.
San Rafael, CA 94901
PH: (415)448-0048
Fax: (415)454-1031
Katz, Dr. Elliot M., DVM, Founder

Lawyers For One America [5538]
4136 Redwood Hwy., Ste. 9
San Rafael, CA 94903
PH: (415)479-3636
Fax: (415)479-3621
Barnes, Teveia Rose, Exec. Dir.,
President

National Alopecia Areata Foundation
[17177]
65 Mitchell Blvd., Ste. 200-B
San Rafael, CA 94903
PH: (415)472-3780
Fax: (415)480-1800
Smith, Maureen, Chief Dev. Ofc.

National Eczema Association
[14505]
4460 Redwood Hwy., Ste. 16-D
San Rafael, CA 94903-1953
PH: (415)499-3474
Toll free: 800-818-7546
Shenoy, Dinesh, CFO

Neighbors Without Borders [12172]
223 Mirada Ave.
San Rafael, CA 94903

PH: (415)497-8465
Shirley, Janet, Contact

Roots of Peace [18826]
990 A St., Ste. 402
San Rafael, CA 94901
PH: (415)455-8008
Toll free: 888-766-8731
Fax: (415)455-9086
Kuhn, Heidi, Chairperson, Founder

Shelter Animal Reiki Association
[17103]
369B 3rd St., No. 156
San Rafael, CA 94901
Prasad, Kathleen, President

Spine Intervention Society [17265]
161 Mitchell Blvd., Ste. 103
San Rafael, CA 94903
PH: (415)457-4747
Toll free: 888-255-0005
Fax: (415)457-3495
Smuck, Matthew, MD, Secretary

Turkish American Alliance for Fair-
ness [19675]
PO Box 6151
San Rafael, CA 94903
PH: (641)715-3900

ClimateTalk Alliance [5883]
2400 Camino Ramon, Ste. 375
San Ramon, CA 94583-4373
PH: (925)275-6641
Fax: (925)275-6691
Johnson, Craig, Chairman

EMerge Alliance [523]
2400 Camino Ramon, Ste. 375
San Ramon, CA 94583-4373
PH: (925)275-6617
Fax: (925)884-8668
Schader, Kevin, Exec. Dir.

International Peoplemedia Telecom-
munications Consortium [7313]
2400 Camino Ramon, Ste. 375
San Ramon, CA 94583
PH: (925)275-6600
Fax: (925)275-6691
Ehrig, John, Exec. Dir.

International Society of Arthroscopy,
Knee Surgery and Orthopaedic
Sports Medicine [16480]
2410 Camino Ramon, Ste. 215
San Ramon, CA 94583
PH: (925)807-1197
Fax: (925)807-1199
Johnson, Michele, Exec. Dir.

National Coalition Against Prescrip-
tion Drug Abuse [11717]
PO Box 87
San Ramon, CA 94583
PH: (925)480-7723
Fax: (925)901-1250
Rovero, April, CEO, Founder

The Eugene O'Neill Society [9087]
700 Hawthorn Ct.
San Ramon, CA 94582
Westgate, Chris, President

SD Association [6262]
2400 Camino Ramon, Ste. 375
San Ramon, CA 94583
PH: (925)275-6615
Fax: (925)886-4870

Tissue Engineering International and
Regenerative Medicine Society
[6115]
223 Park Pl.
San Ramon, CA 94583
PH: (925)362-0998
Fax: (925)362-0808
Williams, David, Comm. Chm.

WiMedia Alliance [6342]
2400 Camino Ramon, Ste. 375
San Ramon, CA 94583
PH: (925)275-6604
Fax: (925)886-3809
Crumb, Steve, Exec. Dir.

National Mini Rex Rabbit Club
[4606]
c/o Doug King, Secretary
2719 Terrace Ave.
Sanger, CA 93657
Charles, Mark, VP

Children's Hope International
Literacy and Development [10927]
1526 Brookhollow Dr., Ste. 82
Santa Ana, CA 92705
PH: (714)545-3050
Fax: (714)545-3030
Khatami, Haleh, President

Concern America [12650]
2015 N Broadway Ave.
Santa Ana, CA 92706
PH: (714)953-8575
Toll free: 800-266-2376
Fax: (714)953-1242
Straw, John, Exec. Dir.

Epilepsy Connection [14739]
1344 Cabrillo Park Dr., Unit H
Santa Ana, CA 92701
PH: (714)943-2567
Julian, David R., Founder

National Latino Peace Officers As-
sociation [19530]
PO Box 23116
Santa Ana, CA 92711
PH: (702)204-6383
Calderon, Vicente, Founder

Packards International Motor Car
Club [21473]
302 French St.
Santa Ana, CA 92701-4845
PH: (714)541-8431
Fax: (714)836-4014
Hull, Don, President

Peace Officers for Christ
International [20005]
3000 W MacArthur Blvd., Ste. 426
Santa Ana, CA 92704-6962
PH: (714)426-7632
Chase, Devin, President

Roasters Guild [751]
117 W 4th St., Ste. 300
Santa Ana, CA 92701
PH: (562)624-4100
Tellie, Mary, Chairperson

Society of Government Service
Urologists [17561]
c/o DeSantis Management Group
1950 Old Tustin Ave.
Santa Ana, CA 92705
PH: (714)550-9155
Fax: (714)550-9234
Frazier, Hal A., MD, President

Society for the Promotion of
Japanese Animation [8891]
1522 Brookhollow Dr., No. 1
Santa Ana, CA 92705
PH: (714)937-2994
Perez, Marc Houston, CEO

Specialty Coffee Association of
America [430]
117 W 4th St., Ste. 300
Santa Ana, CA 92701
Allen, Tracy, President

United Fathers of America [11687]
1651 E 4th St., Ste. 107
Santa Ana, CA 92701

PH: (714)558-7949
Chapman, Marvin, President

Web Wise Kids [11185]
PO Box 27203
Santa Ana, CA 92799
PH: (714)435-2885
Toll free: 866-WEB-WISE
Fax: (714)435-0523
Wolfe, Norman S., Chairman

World Spine Care [17269]
801 N Tustin Ave., Ste. 202
Santa Ana, CA 92705
Haldeman, Dr. Scott, President

Afghanistan Dental Relief Project
[14369]
PO Box 734
Santa Barbara, CA 93102
PH: (805)963-2329
(805)448-2812
Rolfe, James G., President, Founder

American Association of Teachers of
Esperanto [8169]
c/o Dorothy Holland, Corresponding
Secretary
5140 San Lorenzo Dr.
Santa Barbara, CA 93111-2521
Anderson, Gary, Secretary

American Institute of Commemora-
tive Art [2399]
3 N Milpas St.
Santa Barbara, CA 93103
PH: (805)886-8384
Fax: (805)564-8296
Hendrickson, Jed, Exec. Dir.

American Support for Afghanistan
[10467]
3905 State St., Ste. 7-177
Santa Barbara, CA 93105
PH: (805)455-4066
Zahir, Homaira, Founder, President

Association of Commercial Diving
Educators [23341]
c/o Santa Barbara City College
721 Cliff Dr.
Santa Barbara, CA 93109
PH: (805)965-0581
Fax: (805)560-6059
Barthelmess, Don, Treasurer

Child Hope International [10898]
1225 Coast Village Rd., Ste. C
Santa Barbara, CA 93108
PH: (805)845-1946
Bohlinger, Peter, Contact

Classical Music Lovers' Exchange
[9890]
PO Box 275
Santa Barbara, CA 93102-0275

Community Environmental Council
[4739]
26 W Anapamu St., 2nd Fl.
Santa Barbara, CA 93101
PH: (805)963-0583
Wright, Sigrid, CEO, Exec. Dir.

DeLorean Owners Association
[21369]
879 Randolph Rd.
Santa Barbara, CA 93111
PH: (805)964-5296
Powell, Linda, Secretary

Exploring Solutions Past: The Maya
Forest Alliance [5938]
PO Box 3962
Santa Barbara, CA 93130
PH: (805)893-8191
Ford, Dr. Anabel, President

Get Oil Out! [4548]
PO Box 23625
Santa Barbara, CA 93121

PH: (805)963-1622
Fax: (805)962-3152

IEEE - Control Systems Society
[6556]
c/o Francis J. Doyle III, President
Dept. of Chemical Engineering
University of California - Santa
Barbara
333 Engineering II
Santa Barbara, CA 93106
Doyle, Francis J., III, President

International Chiari Association
[15944]
27 W Anapamu St., No. 340
Santa Barbara, CA 93101
PH: (805)570-0484
Fax: (815)301-6541
Dal Bello, Pete, President, Founder

International Qajar Studies Associa-
tion [9594]
PO Box 31107
Santa Barbara, CA 93130
PH: (805)687-1148
Fax: (805)687-1148
Eskandari-Qajar, Dr. Manoutchehr
M., Founder, President

Inventors Workshop International
[5334]
PO Box 285
Santa Barbara, CA 93102-0285
PH: (805)735-7261
Tratner, Alan A., President

I.T. Financial Management Associa-
tion [1247]
PO Box 30188
Santa Barbara, CA 93130
PH: (805)687-7390
Fax: (805)687-7382
Quinlan, Terence, Director

Legion of Valor of the United States
of America [20736]
c/o Philip J. Conran, Adjutant
4704 Calle Reina
Santa Barbara, CA 93110-2018
PH: (805)692-2244

Nuclear Age Peace Foundation
[18811]
1622 Anacapa St.
Santa Barbara, CA 93101
PH: (805)965-3443
Krieger, David, President

Ocean Futures Society [4771]
513 De La Vina St.
Santa Barbara, CA 93101
PH: (805)899-8899
Earle, Sylvia, Bd. Member

Society for the Psychological Study
of Ethnic Minority Issues [16940]
c/o J. Manuel Casas, President
317 E Padre St.
Santa Barbara, CA 93105-3609
PH: (805)983-3375
Fax: (805)983-7264
Casas, J. Manuel, President

Surgical Eye Expeditions
International [17747]
5638 Hollister Ave., Ste. 210
Santa Barbara, CA 93117
PH: (805)963-3303
Toll free: 877-937-3133
Fax: (805)965-3564
Groff, Scott W., Chmn. of the Bd.

Turn the Page Uganda [12250]
3723 Dixon St.
Santa Barbara, CA 93105
PH: (805)569-0709
Harbison, Victoria, President

Vitamin Angel Alliance, Inc. [16241]
111 W Micheltorena St., Ste. 300
Santa Barbara, CA 93101
PH: (805)564-8400
Fax: (805)564-8400
Schiffer, Howard, Founder, President

Worldhealer, Inc. [12201]
PO Box 62121
Santa Barbara, CA 93160
PH: (805)253-2324
Bonderson, Roxana, Founder,
Developer, Exec. Dir.

The Holiday Project [13298]
c/o Melinda Sedlacek, Treasurer
2632 Tartan Dr.
Santa Clara, CA 95051
PH: (408)984-6555
Anderson, Bobby, VP

Japan Art History Forum [8900]
Santa Clara University
Dept. of Art and Art History
500 El Camino Real
Santa Clara, CA 95053
Wu, Xiaojin, VP

Legal Immigrant Association [5292]
PO Box 2082
Santa Clara, CA 95055
Toll free: 800-556-7065

LonMark International [3193]
2901 Patrick Henry Dr.
Santa Clara, CA 95054
PH: (408)938-5266
Fax: (408)790-3838
Markie, Tracy, Chairman

Maitri [13382]
PO Box 697
Santa Clara, CA 95052
PH: (408)436-8393
Toll free: 888-862-4874
Fax: (408)503-0887
Sharangpani, Mukta, President

Media Ecology Association [8289]
Communication Dept.
Santa Clara University
500 El Camino Real
Santa Clara, CA 95053-0277
PH: (408)554-4022
Fax: (408)554-4913
Strate, Lance, Advisor

Mercy Beyond Borders [12552]
1885 De La Cruz Blvd., Ste. 101
Santa Clara, CA 95050-3000
PH: (650)815-1554
Lacey, Marilyn, Chairperson, Exec.
Dir.

Optical Storage Technology Associa-
tion [2457]
65 Washington St.
Santa Clara, CA 95050
PH: (650)938-6945
Zollo, Bob, Chairman

Physical Security Interoperability Alli-
ance [6581]
65 Washington St., Ste. 170
Santa Clara, CA 95050
PH: (650)938-6945
Fax: (408)516-3950
Bunzel, David, Exec. Dir.

Professional and Technical
Consultants Association [822]
PO Box 2261
Santa Clara, CA 95055
PH: (408)971-5902
Toll free: 800-747-2822
Forbus, Tonia, Exec. Dir.

Society for Philosophy and Technology [10128]
c/o Shannon Vallor, President
500 El Vamino Real

Santa Clara, CA 95053
PH: (408)554-5190
Sullins, John, Secretary, Treasurer

Triple Nine Society [9346]
c/o Dr. Ina Bendis, Membership Officer
3129 Barkley Ave.
Santa Clara, CA 95051
Zimmermann, Eric, Reg.

Turkish American Business Connec-
tion [670]
2784 Homestead Rd., No. 118
Santa Clara, CA 95051
PH: (408)404-5208
Fax: (408)404-5208
Orhun, Efe, Founder

Vision New America [19008]
100 N Winchester Blvd., Ste. 368
Santa Clara, CA 95050
PH: (408)260-0116
Fax: (408)260-0180
Li, Liliana, Exec. Dir.

1in6, Inc. [12917]
PO Box 222033
Santa Clarita, CA 91322
Lisak, David, President

Association of Professional Animal
Waste Specialists [3445]
c/o Timothy Stone, Treasurer/
Founder
PO Box 2325
Santa Clarita, CA 91386-2325
PH: (409)422-7297
Levy, Deb, President, Founder

African Family Film Foundation
[8775]
PO Box 630
Santa Cruz, CA 95061-0630
Rosellini, Taale Laafi, MFA, Exec.
Dir., Founder

Community Agroecology Network
[4695]
PO Box 7653
Santa Cruz, CA 95061-7653
PH: (831)459-3619
Gliessman, Stephen, Chairman

Everybody Solar [7198]
3129 Branciforte Dr.
Santa Cruz, CA 95065
PH: (978)310-1042
Tempchin, Robert, Chairman

Gonstead Clinical Studies Society
[14271]
1280 17th Ave., Ste. 101
Santa Cruz, CA 95062
PH: (831)476-1873
Toll free: 888-556-4277
Perugini, Rocco, President

International Association of Seismol-
ogy and Physics of the Earth's
Interior [7156]
Earth and Marine Science Bldg.
Dept. of Earth and Planetary Sci-
ence
University of California - Santa Cruz
Santa Cruz, CA 95064
PH: (831)459-3164
Fax: (831)459-3074
Lay, Prof. Thorne, President

Island Conservation [3889]
2161 Delaware Ave., Ste. A
Santa Cruz, CA 95060
PH: (831)359-4787
Hartwell, David, Chairman

Kidpower Teenpower Fullpower
International **[12825]**
PO Box 1212
Santa Cruz, CA 95061
Toll free: 800-467-6997
van der Zande, Irene, Exec. Dir.,
Founder

Media Watch **[17951]**
PO Box 618
Santa Cruz, CA 95061-0618
PH: (831)423-6355
Simonton, Ann, Director, Founder,
Coord.

Monterey Bay International Trade
Association **[1987]**
PO Box 523
Santa Cruz, CA 95061
PH: (831)335-4780
Fax: (831)335-4822

Multidisciplinary Association for
Psychedelic Studies **[16671]**
1115 Mission St.
Santa Cruz, CA 95060-3528
PH: (831)429-6362
Fax: (831)429-6370
Doblin, Rick, PhD, Founder, Exec.
Dir.

National Coalition of Associations of
7-Eleven Franchisees **[1462]**
740 Front St., Ste. 170
Santa Cruz, CA 95060
PH: (831)426-4711
Fax: (831)426-4713
Galea, Joe, Chairman

New Teacher Center **[7855]**
725 Front St., Ste. 400
Santa Cruz, CA 95060
PH: (831)600-2200
Fax: (861)427-9017
Moir, Ellen, Founder, CEO

Resource Center for Nonviolence
[18726]
612 Ocean St.
Santa Cruz, CA 95060-4006
PH: (831)423-1626
Chamberlin, Peter Klotz, Coord.

Rising International **[10732]**
300 Potrero St.
Santa Cruz, CA 95060-2769
PH: (831)429-7473
Toll free: 888-574-7464
Brose, Judy, Chairperson

Santa Cruz Mountains Winegrowers
Association **[4932]**
101 Cooper St.
Santa Cruz, CA 95060
PH: (831)685-8463
Metz, Megan, Exec. Dir.

Society for Advancement of
Chicanos/Hispanics and Native
Americans in Science **[7145]**
1121 Pacific Ave.
Santa Cruz, CA 95060
PH: (831)459-0170
Toll free: 877-722-6271
Fax: (831)459-0194
Franco, Antonia O., Ed.D, Exec. Dir.

Sustainable Fishery Advocates
[4188]
PO Box 233
Santa Cruz, CA 95061-0233
PH: (831)427-1707
Fax: (309)213-4688
Aguirre, Tobias, Exec. Dir.

The TLC Foundation for Body-
Focused Repetitive Behaviors
[15809]
716 Soquel Ave., Ste. A
Santa Cruz, CA 95062

PH: (831)457-1004
Fax: (831)427-5541
Pearson, Christina, Founder

Cessna Pilots Association **[21218]**
3409 Corsair Cir.
Santa Maria, CA 93455
PH: (805)934-0493
Toll free: 800-343-6416
Frank, John M., Jr., Exec. Dir.,
Founder

Aid Still Required **[11650]**
PO Box 7353
Santa Monica, CA 90406
PH: (310)454-4646
Toll free: 888-363-GIVE
Payne, Andrea Herz, Chairperson,
Founder

Angel Flight West **[12264]**
3161 Donald Douglas Loop S
Santa Monica, CA 90405
PH: (310)390-2958
Toll free: 888-426-2643
Fax: (310)397-9636
Wood, Geoff, Treasurer

Beauty Bus Foundation **[13208]**
2716 Ocean Park Blvd., Ste. 1062
Santa Monica, CA 90405
PH: (310)392-0900
Fax: (310)392-0907
Liotta, Alicia Marantz, CEO, Founder

Find the Children **[10973]**
2656 29th St., Ste. 203
Santa Monica, CA 90405-2984
PH: (310)314-3213
Toll free: 888-477-6721
Fax: (310)314-3169
Otto, Linda, Founder

Global Association for Interpersonal
Neurobiology Studies **[6915]**
PO Box 3605
Santa Monica, CA 90408
McCall, Debra Pearce, Editor

Global Green U.S.A. **[4063]**
2218 Main St., 2nd Fl.
Santa Monica, CA 90405
PH: (310)581-2700
Fax: (310)581-2702
Petersen, Matt, Bd. Member

GRAMMY Foundation **[9912]**
3030 Olympic Blvd.
Santa Monica, CA 90404
PH: (310)392-3777
Fax: (310)392-2188
Portnow, Neil, President, CEO

Human Factors and Ergonomics
Society **[6709]**
1124 Montana Ave., Ste. B
Santa Monica, CA 90403-1617
PH: (310)394-1811
Fax: (310)394-2410

International Society for
Phylogenetic Nomenclature **[6669]**
c/o Michael Keesey, Treasurer
2450 Colorado Ave., Ste. 3000 W
Santa Monica, CA 90404
Cantino, Philip, President

National Academy of Recording Arts
and Sciences **[2903]**
3030 Olympic Blvd.
Santa Monica, CA 90404
PH: (310)392-3777
Fax: (310)392-2188
Albert, Christine, Chairperson

New Zealand Tourism Board **[23607]**
501 Santa Monica Blvd., Ste. 300
Santa Monica, CA 90401

PH: (310)395-7480
Fax: (310)395-5453
Bowler, Kevin, CEO

Office of the Americas **[17843]**
2016 Hill St.
Santa Monica, CA 90405
PH: (310)450-1185
Lafferty, James, President

Pediatric Brain Foundation **[15985]**
1223 Wilshire Blvd., No. 937
Santa Monica, CA 90403
PH: (310)889-8611
Fax: (866)267-5580
Richmond, Fia, Founder, President

Seventh Generation Advisors **[4103]**
3435 Ocean Park Blvd., Ste. 203
Santa Monica, CA 90405
PH: (310)664-0300
Fax: (310)664-0305
Tamminen, Terry, President, Founder

Skate Park Association of the United
States of America **[23155]**
2118 Wilshire Blvd., No. 622
Santa Monica, CA 90403
PH: (310)495-7112
　　(310)261-2816

Soka Gakkai International-United
States of America **[19783]**
606 Wilshire Blvd.
Santa Monica, CA 90401
PH: (310)260-8900
Fax: (310)260-8917
Ikeda, Mr. Daisaku, President

Whole Child International **[11187]**
610 Santa Monica Blvd., No. 215
Santa Monica, CA 90401
PH: (310)394-1000
Spencer, Karen, Founder, CEO

World Surf League **[23280]**
149 Bay St.
Santa Monica, CA 90405
PH: (310)450-1212
Bernardo, Meg, Gen. Mgr.

American Glovebox Society **[6925]**
526 S East St.
Santa Rosa, CA 95404
Toll free: 800-530-1022
Fax: (707)578-4406
Levene, Nate, Secretary, Treasurer

American Merchant Marine Veterans
[21190]
2722 Maynes Ct.
Santa Rosa, CA 95405
Harvey, Morris, VP

American Society of Church History
[20202]
PO Box 2793
Santa Rosa, CA 95405-2793
PH: (707)538-6005
Fax: (707)538-2166
Francis, Keith A., Contact

Assistance Dogs International
[11574]
PO Box 5174
Santa Rosa, CA 95402
Lord, Richard, President

Brotherhood of the Knights of the
Vine **[4928]**
3343 Industrial Dr., Ste. 2
Santa Rosa, CA 95403-2060
PH: (707)579-3781
Fax: (707)579-3996
Bade, Donald D., Treasurer

Canine Companions for
Independence **[11577]**
2965 Dutton Ave.
Santa Rosa, CA 95407

PH: (707)577-1700
Toll free: 866-224-3647
Miller, John, Chairman

Clan Macpherson Association
[20827]
c/o Jean Macpherson Duffy, Chairman
6438 Stone Bridge Rd.
Santa Rosa, CA 95409
Duffy, Jean Macpherson, Chairman

Compassion Without Borders
[10607]
537 4th St., Ste. F
Santa Rosa, CA 95401
PH: (707)474-3345
Camblor, Dr. Christi, Director

Dodge Pilothouse Era Truck Club of
America **[22474]**
3778 Hoen Ave.
Santa Rosa, CA 95405
Koch, Robert, Treasurer

Institute for the Advancement of Hu-
man Behavior **[13796]**
PO Box 5527
Santa Rosa, CA 95402
PH: (650)851-8411
Toll free: 800-258-8411
Fax: (707)755-3133
Piaget, Gerry, President

International Maledicta Society
[9742]
PO Box 14123
Santa Rosa, CA 95402-6123
PH: (707)795-8178
Aman, Reinhold A., PhD, Editor,
Publisher

National Association of County
Surveyors **[5116]**
526 S East St.
Santa Rosa, CA 95404
PH: (707)578-1130
Fax: (707)578-4406
Demman, Reid, Mem.

National Indian Justice Center
[19584]
5250 Aero Dr.
Santa Rosa, CA 95403
PH: (707)579-5507
Toll free: 800-966-0662
Fax: (707)579-9019
Myers, Joseph A., Exec. Dir.

National Women's History Project
[10308]
730 2nd St., Ste. 469
Santa Rosa, CA 95402
PH: (707)636-2888
Fax: (707)636-2909
MacGregor, Ms. Molly Murphy, Exec.
Dir., Founder

North American Peruvian Horse As-
sociation **[4394]**
PO Box 2187
Santa Rosa, CA 95405
PH: (707)544-5807
Gandy, Edith, 1st VP

Russian Numismatic Society **[22285]**
PO Box 3684
Santa Rosa, CA 95402
PH: (707)527-1007
Fax: (707)527-1204
Elmen, Jim, Editor

Save the Turtles **[4881]**
5114 Parkhurst Dr.
Santa Rosa, CA 95409
PH: (707)579-8084
Sherman, Debbie, Exec. Dir.

Sonoma County Vintners **[4933]**
400 Aviation Blvd., Ste. 500
Santa Rosa, CA 95403

PH: (707)522-5840
Fax: (707)573-3942
Sessions, Jean Arnold, Exec. Dir.

Sonoma County Winegrape Commission **[4934]**
400 Aviation Blvd., Ste. 500
Santa Rosa, CA 95403
PH: (707)522-5860
Kruse, Karissa, President

United Silver and Golden Fanciers **[21575]**
c/o Sally Daniels, Treasurer
5242 Vista Grande Dr.
Santa Rosa, CA 95403
PH: (707)545-8927
Reichle, Janice, President

Floodplain Management Association **[4486]**
PO Box 712080
Santee, CA 92072
PH: (760)936-3676
Seits, Mark, Chairman

Renault Owners Club of North America **[21482]**
c/o Sharon Desplaines, Secretary
7467 Mission Gorge Rd., No. 81
Santee, CA 92071
PH: (619)334-1711
Desplaines, Sharon, Secretary

International Society for Mannosidosis and Related Diseases **[14832]**
c/o The International Advocate for Glycoprotein Storage Diseases
20880 Canyon View Dr.
Saratoga, CA 95070
Forman, Mr. John, VP of Res.

Myelin Repair Foundation **[15961]**
18809 Cox Ave., Ste. 190
Saratoga, CA 95070
PH: (408)871-2410
Toll free: 877-863-4967
Fax: (408)871-2409
Johnson, Scott, President, CEO, Founder

Our Developing World **[18553]**
13004 Paseo Presada
Saratoga, CA 95070-4125
PH: (408)379-4431
Ahlquist, Roberta, President

United Stuntwomen's Association **[1208]**
26893 Bouquet Cyn Rd., Ste. C
Saugus, CA 91350
PH: (818)508-4651
Happy, Bonnie, President

El Toro International Yacht Racing Association **[22612]**
91 Waldo Point S 40
Sausalito, CA 94965
PH: (415)332-7269
Nash, Gordon, President

PlanetQuest **[6009]**
PO Box 211
Sausalito, CA 94966
Doyle, Dr. Laurance, President

US Sailing-One-Design Class Council **[22691]**
3001 Bridgeway Blvd., Ste. K-255
Sausalito, CA 94965
PH: (415)315-9622

Venezuelan Tourism Association **[3407]**
PO Box 3010
Sausalito, CA 94966-3010
PH: (415)331-0100
Benus, John, Director, Founder

American Herbal Pharmacopoeia **[13594]**
PO Box 66809
Scotts Valley, CA 95067
PH: (831)461-6318
Fax: (831)438-2196
Upton, Roy, RH, President, CEO

Assist International **[12265]**
230 Mt. Hermon Rd., Ste. 206
Scotts Valley, CA 95066-4034
PH: (831)438-4582
Fax: (831)439-9602
Pagett, Robert J., Founder, CEO

Education, Training and Research Associates **[8028]**
100 Enterprise Way, Ste. G300
Scotts Valley, CA 95066
PH: (831)438-4284
Toll free: 800-620-8884
Lanfronza, Vincent, MS, EdD, Chmn. of the Bd.

National Service-Learning Clearinghouse **[8541]**
4 Carbonero Way
Scotts Valley, CA 95066
PH: (831)461-0205
Toll free: 866-245-7378
Fax: (831)430-9471
Snow, Deborah, Contact

Responsible Hospitality Institute **[11635]**
4200 Scotts Valley Dr., Ste. B
Scotts Valley, CA 95066
PH: (831)469-3396
    (831)438-1404
Peters, Jim, President

Danish/Swedish Farmdog Club of America **[21867]**
PO Box 819
Seal Beach, CA 90740
Lemmon, Brita, President

National Coalition of Creative Arts Therapies Associations **[16984]**
PO Box 3403
Seal Beach, CA 90740
Mulder, Randy, Treasurer

Save the Whales **[4882]**
1192 Waring St.
Seaside, CA 93955
PH: (831)899-9957
Fax: (831)394-5555
Sidenstecker, Maris, Exec. Dir.

Children's Humanitarian International **[10929]**
PO Box 1735
Sebastopol, CA 95473
PH: (707)596-8398
Burns, Jordan, President

New Ways to Work **[11777]**
555 S Main St., No. 1
Sebastopol, CA 95472
PH: (707)824-4000
Trippe, Steve, President, Exec. Dir.

Surface Design Association **[3271]**
PO Box 360
Sebastopol, CA 95473-0360
PH: (707)829-3110
Fax: (707)829-3285
Reis, Jennifer, VP

Transition United States **[4146]**
970 Gravenstein Hwy. S
Sebastopol, CA 95472
PH: (707)824-1554
Heckman, Trathen, President

Alliance of Motion Picture and Television Producers **[1184]**
Bldg. E
15301 Ventura Blvd.

Sherman Oaks, CA 91403
PH: (818)935-5938
Lombardini, Carol, President

Alliance for Safety Awareness for Patients **[15391]**
14622 Ventura Blvd., No. 102-827
Sherman Oaks, CA 91403
PH: (818)379-9679
Cole, Alicia, Founder

American Academy of Husband-Coached Childbirth **[16266]**
PO Box 5224
Sherman Oaks, CA 91413-5224
PH: (818)788-6662
Toll free: 800-422-4784
Fax: (818)788-1580
Hathaway, Marjie, Exec. Dir.

Athgo International **[13428]**
13636 Ventura Blvd., Ste. 222
Sherman Oaks, CA 91423
PH: (818)345-6734
Fax: (818)345-0955
Orujyan, Armen, PhD, CEO, Founder, President

Bruce Boxleitner's Official Fan Club **[23988]**
PO Box 5513
Sherman Oaks, CA 91413-5513

Concerned United Birthparents, Inc. **[10450]**
PO Box 5538
Sherman Oaks, CA 91413
Toll free: 800-822-2777
Fax: (858)712-3317
Collings, Patty, President

Enrichment Educational Experiences, Inc. **[9534]**
13425 Ventura Blvd., Ste. 304
Sherman Oaks, CA 91423
PH: (818)989-7509
Fax: (818)989-1763
McManus, M. Linda, President

Generation Rescue **[13765]**
13636 Ventura Blvd., No. 259
Sherman Oaks, CA 91423
Toll free: 877-98-AUTISM
McDonald, Candace, Exec. Dir.

International Federation of Festival Organizations **[1141]**
4230 Stansbury Ave., Ste. 105
Sherman Oaks, CA 91423
PH: (818)789-7596
Fax: (818)784-9141
Moreno, Prof. Armando, President

Linda Gray's Official Fan Club **[23996]**
PO Box 5064
Sherman Oaks, CA 91413-5064
Gray, Linda, Director

National Honors Society of Sports Medicine **[17286]**
13636 Ventura Blvd., No. 387
Sherman Oaks, CA 91423
PH: (641)715-3900
Hallak, Eli, Founder, President

Stefanie Powers' Official Fan Club **[24000]**
PO Box 5087
Sherman Oaks, CA 91413-5087

Stunts Unlimited **[19662]**
15233 Ventura Blvd., Ste. 425
Sherman Oaks, CA 91403
PH: (818)501-1970
Romano, Pat, President

US Doctors for Africa **[15505]**
14945 Ventura Blvd., Ste. 224
Sherman Oaks, CA 91403

PH: (818)728-6629
Alemayhu, Ted M., Chairman, Founder

Visual Effects Society **[1209]**
5805 Sepulveda Blvd., Ste. 620
Sherman Oaks, CA 91411
PH: (818)981-7861
Fax: (818)981-0179
Roth, Mr. Eric, Exec. Dir.

Lindsay Wagner's Official Fan Club **[24001]**
PO Box 5002
Sherman Oaks, CA 91403

We Love Lucy/International Lucille Ball Fan Club **[24002]**
c/o Thomas J. Watson
PO Box 56234
Sherman Oaks, CA 91413
PH: (818)981-0752
Fax: (818)981-0757

Wild Horse Sanctuary **[10716]**
5796 Wilson Hill Rd.
Shingletown, CA 96088-0030
PH: (530)474-5770
Fax: (530)474-1384
Nelson, Dianne, Founder, President

Classic Thunderbird Club International **[21359]**
1308 E 29th St.
Signal Hill, CA 90755-1842
PH: (562)426-2709
Toll free: 800-488-2709
Fax: (562)426-7023
Long, Bill, President

National Lighting Contractors Association of America **[6786]**
3301 E Hill St., Ste. 406-408
Signal Hill, CA 90755
PH: (310)890-0878
Fax: (562)976-7648
Scalzo, Michael, President

Dalmatian Club of America **[21865]**
864 Ettin Ave.
Simi Valley, CA 93065-4209
PH: (805)583-5914
Hennesey, Meg, President

Forever Found **[10979]**
2321 Tapo St., Ste. C
Simi Valley, CA 93063
PH: (805)306-8018
Sergey, Shannon, Founder, President, CEO

NepalAama **[7593]**
PO Box 1565
Simi Valley, CA 93062-1565
Rajbhandari, Sarju, Director

Redbird **[19589]**
PO Box 702
Simi Valley, CA 93062-0702
PH: (805)217-0364
Roberts, Corina, Founder

Insulindependence, Inc. **[14536]**
249 S Hwy. 101, No. 8000
Solana Beach, CA 92075
Toll free: 888-912-3837
Nerothin, Peter H., President, Founder

U.S. Green Chamber of Commerce **[23630]**
249 S Highway 101, No. 420
Solana Beach, CA 92075
Thatcher, Michelle, CEO

Water for Life International **[13342]**
514 Via de la Valle, Ste. 207
Solana Beach, CA 92075-2717

PH: (858)509-9445
Fax: (858)509-0708
George, David, Exec. Dir.

F-14 Tomcat Association [21527]
PO Box 1347
Somis, CA 93066
Rabens, Capt. Mike, President

Bread Bakers Guild of America [373]
670 W Napa St., Ste. B
Sonoma, CA 95476
PH: (707)935-1468
Fax: (707)935-1672
Yankellow, Jeff, Chmn. of the Bd.

Energy Kinesiology Awareness
Council [13621]
c/o Adam H. Lehman, TNP,
President
Institute of BioEnergetic Arts and
Sciences
19210 Sonoma Hwy.
Sonoma, CA 95476
Lehman, Adam H., TNP, President

The Hope of Survivors [12924]
843 Broadway
Sonoma, CA 95476
Toll free: 866-260-8958
Nelson, Ms. Samantha, CEO, VP

Oyate [19587]
330 E Thomson Ave.
Sonoma, CA 95476-3957
PH: (707)996-6700
Fax: (707)935-9961
Dias, Robette, President

American Academy of Pain Manage-
ment [16546]
975 Morning Star Dr., Ste. A
Sonora, CA 95370-9249
PH: (209)533-9744
Fax: (209)533-9750
Coneghen, Cathleen, Asst. Dir.

American Board of Vocational
Experts [8732]
3121 Park Ave., Ste. C
Soquel, CA 95073
PH: (831)464-4890
Fax: (831)576-1417
Hutchinson, Estelle, President

Association of International Graduate
Admissions Consultants [7446]
3121 Park Ave., Ste. C
Soquel, CA 95073
PH: (831)464-4892
Sparrey, Andrea, President

Ecological Farming Association
[3548]
2901 Park Ave., Ste. D-2
Soquel, CA 95073
PH: (831)763-2111
Dickerson, Ken, Exec. Dir.

Protected Harvest [4700]
2901 Park Ave., Ste. A2
Soquel, CA 95073
PH: (831)477-7797
    (530)601-0740
Vandine, Jane, Administrator

Women for Winesense [22479]
3121 Park Ave., Ste. C
Soquel, CA 95073
PH: (831)464-4893
Barber, Karla R., President

American Institute of Inspectors
[1813]
PO Box 7243
South Lake Tahoe, CA 96158
PH: (530)577-1407
Toll free: 800-877-4770
Hawkins, Perry, Chairman

League to Save Lake Tahoe [3895]
2608 Lake Tahoe Blvd.
South Lake Tahoe, CA 96150
PH: (530)541-5388
Fax: (530)541-5454
Goodman-Collins, Darcie, PhD,
    Exec. Dir.

United States of America Snowboard
and Freeski Association [23177]
PO Box 15500
South Lake Tahoe, CA 96151
Toll free: 800-404-9213
Schaal, John, President

Episcopal Women's Caucus [20103]
1103 Magnolia St.
South Pasadena, CA 91030
Mackey, Chris, Bus. Mgr.

Global Solutions for Infectious
Diseases [15400]
830 Dubuque Ave.
South San Francisco, CA 94080
PH: (650)228-7900
Fax: (650)228-7901
Francis, Donald P., MD, Exec. Dir.,
    Founder

National Association of Casino Party
Operators [1149]
PO Box 5626
South San Francisco, CA 94083-
5626
Toll free: 888-922-0777
Miller, Mike, Director

Carnegie Foundation for the
Advancement of Teaching [8646]
51 Vista Ln.
Stanford, CA 94305-8703
PH: (650)566-5100
Fax: (650)326-0278
Gomez, Kimberley, Mem.

Hoover Institution on War, Revolu-
tion and Peace [19262]
434 Galvez Mall
Stanford University
Stanford, CA 94305
PH: (650)723-1754
Schieron, Laureen, Asst. Dir.

North American Specialized
Coagulation Laboratory Association
[15520]
c/o James L. Zehnder, President
Dept. of Pathology
Stanford University
Stanford, CA 94305
PH: (650)723-9232
Fax: (650)736-1476
Zehnder, James L., President

Organization of Biological Field Sta-
tions [6094]
PO Box 20492
Stanford, CA 94309
Cohen, Philippe S., Treasurer

Stanford Chicano/Latino Alumni As-
sociation [19350]
c/o Frances C. Arrillaga Alumni
Center
326 Galvez St.
Stanford, CA 94305-6105
PH: (650)723-2021
Toll free: 800-786-2586
Vasquez, Mario, Contact

American Darts Organization
[22766]
PO Box 209
Stanton, CA 90680-0209
Toll free: 844-883-2787
Hascup, David, President

Official Betty Boop Fan Club [24004]
10550 Western Ave., No. 133
Stanton, CA 90680-6909

A More Balanced World [11729]
25149 Smokewood Way
Stevenson Ranch, CA 91381
PH: (805)587-1897
Fazeli, Mandy, President, Founder

American Handwriting Analysis
Foundation [10410]
1011 S Tuxedo Ave.
Stockton, CA 95204-6219
PH: (209)518-6886
    (805)658-0109
Otto, Tim, Treasurer

Architects of Peace Foundation
[12431]
119 E Weber Ave.
Stockton, CA 95219
PH: (209)608-5455
Collopy, Michael, Founder

Ariel Motorcycle Club North America
[22213]
c/o Tom Voss, Treasurer
PO Box 77737
Stockton, CA 95267-1037
Voss, Tom, Treasurer

Friends Outside [11527]
7272 Murray Dr.
Stockton, CA 95210-3339
PH: (209)955-0701
Fax: (209)955-0735
Davis, David D., Jr., Director

Wide Smiles [17354]
PO Box 5153
Stockton, CA 95205-0153
PH: (209)942-2812
Fax: (209)464-1497
Green, Joanne, Director

Alliance of Special Effects and
Pyrotechnic Operators [2820]
12522 Moorpark St.
Studio City, CA 91604-1355
PH: (818)506-8173
Fax: (818)769-9438
Streett, J.D., President

Art Directors Guild [9296]
11969 Ventura Blvd., 2nd Fl.
Studio City, CA 91604-2630
PH: (818)762-9995
Fax: (818)762-9997
Roth, Scott, Exec. Dir.

Richard Burgi Fan Club [23989]
c/o Kathleen Cole, President
11155 Aqua Vista St., No. 302
Studio City, CA 91602-3700
Cole, Kathleen, President

Costume Designers Guild [23407]
11969 Ventura Blvd., 1st Fl.
Studio City, CA 91604-2630
PH: (818)752-2400
Fax: (818)752-2402
Perez, Salvador, President

Digital Cinema Society [1190]
PO Box 1973
Studio City, CA 91614-0973
PH: (818)762-2214
Mathers, James, Founder, President

For Grace [16555]
PO Box 1724
Studio City, CA 91614
PH: (818)760-7635
Fax: (818)760-7635
Toussaint, Cynthia, Founder

The Mr. Holland's Opus Foundation
[8374]
4370 Tujunga Ave., Ste. 330
Studio City, CA 91604
PH: (818)762-4328
Fax: (818)643-2463
Ringer-Ross, Doreen, V. Ch.

National Organization for Renal
Disease [15883]
11018 Aqua Vista St., No. 19
Studio City, CA 91602
Jackson, Mamie V., Founder

RADD [12840]
4370 Tujunga Ave., Ste. 212
Studio City, CA 91604-2763
PH: (818)752-7799
Fax: (818)752-7792
Meluso, Erin, President

Shatner and Friends International
[23999]
PO Box 1345
Studio City, CA 91604

Society of American Indian Dentists
[14469]
3940 Laurel Canyon Blvd., No. 1068
Studio City, CA 91604
Preston, Drew, DDS, President

Stuntwomen's Association of Motion
Pictures [1206]
3760 Cahuenga Blvd., Ste. 104
Studio City, CA 91604
PH: (818)588-8888

WordTheatre [10228]
PO Box 1981
Studio City, CA 91614
PH: (323)822-0823
Fox, Cedering, Art Dir.

Hemp Industries Association [3258]
PO Box 575
Summerland, CA 93067
PH: (707)874-3648
Steenstra, Eric, Exec. Dir.

American Cryonics Society [14355]
510 S Mathilda Ave., Ste. 8
Sunnyvale, CA 94086
PH: (408)530-9001
Toll free: 800-523-2001
Swank, Edgar, President

Chemists Without Borders [12269]
745 S Bernardo Ave., No. A121
Sunnyvale, CA 94087-1051
PH: (707)750-5945
Gerber, Bego, Founder, Chairman

Chinese American Semiconductor
Professional Association [1038]
1159 Sonora Ct., Ste. 105
Sunnyvale, CA 94086
PH: (408)940-4600
Qi, Xiaoning, Chairman, President

Friends of the Western Philatelic
Library [10071]
PO Box 2219
Sunnyvale, CA 94087-0219
PH: (408)733-0336
Leven, Stuart, Chairperson

Graphics Philately Association
[22331]
1030 E El Camino Real, Ste. 107
Sunnyvale, CA 94087-3759
Winnegrad, Mark H., President

Innovative Support to Emergencies
Diseases and Disasters [11672]
955 Benecia Ave.
Sunnyvale, CA 94085
PH: (408)471-5758
Jezierski, Eduardo, CEO, Bd.
Member

North America Taiwanese Engineers'
Association [6579]
PO Box 2772
Sunnyvale, CA 94087-0772
Wu, Ming-chi, Sec. Gen.

ReSurge International [14322]
145 N Wolfe Rd.
Sunnyvale, CA 94086
PH: (408)737-8743
Fax: (408)737-8000
Chang, Jim, Officer

Twirly Birds [21253]
c/o Steve Sullivan, President
PO Box 70158
Sunnyvale, CA 94086-0158
Sullivan, Steve, President

Vibha [11179]
1030 E El Camino Real, No. 424
Sunnyvale, CA 94087
PH: (408)997-9992
Fax: (775)593-1061
Victor, Ron, President

The National Jersey Wooly Rabbit
Club [4604]
c/o Angel LeSage, President
PO Box 663
Sutter Creek, CA 95685
Wright, Sandra, VP

Guide Dogs of America [17708]
13445 Glenoaks Blvd.
Sylmar, CA 91342-2049
PH: (818)362-5834
Hartford, Mr. Dale E., Director,
President

Demeter Biodynamic Trade Associa-
tion [4152]
PO Box 264
Talmage, CA 95481-0264
Nonini, Gena, President

American Hypnosis Association
[15359]
18607 Ventura Blvd., Ste. 310
Tarzana, CA 91356-4158
PH: (818)758-2730
Kappas, George J., Director

Fluorescent Mineral Society [6874]
PO Box 572694
Tarzana, CA 91357-2694
PH: (862)259-2367
Wittenberg, Jan, Membership Chp.

Bomber Legends [21193]
PO Box 1479
Tehachapi, CA 93581
McGuire, Robert E., Founder

United Pegasus Foundation [18356]
20411 Pegasus Rd.
Tehachapi, CA 93561
PH: (661)823-9672
Fax: (626)452-8620
Meredith, Helen, Founder, President

Caring for Orphans - Mozambique
[10886]
45895 Piute St.
Temecula, CA 92592
PH: (714)632-9972
Zimmerman, David W., President

Foundation for a Course in Miracles
[20605]
41397 Buecking Dr.
Temecula, CA 92590-5668
PH: (951)296-6261
Fax: (951)296-9117
Wapnick, Kenneth, PhD, President

Gold Prospectors Association of
America [22392]
43445 Business Park Dr., Ste. 113
Temecula, CA 92590-3671
PH: (951)699-4749
Toll free: 800-551-9707
Fax: (951)699-4062
Johnson, Brandon, Contact

Gospel Recordings Network [20421]
41823 Enterprise Cir. N, Ste. 200
Temecula, CA 92590-5682
PH: (951)719-1650
Toll free: 888-444-7872
Fax: (951)719-1651
Stott, Colin, Exec. Dir.

The Havana Silk Dog Association of
America [21892]
35394 Linda Rosea Rd.
Temecula, CA 92592
O'Day, Mary, Contact

Native American Environmental
Protection Coalition [3909]
EDGE-SCI Bldg.
27368 Via Industria, Ste. 105
Temecula, CA 92590
PH: (951)296-5595
Toll free: 877-739-9243
Fax: (951)926-5109
Sherman-Warne, Jill, Exec. Dir.

Professional Numismatists Guild
[22283]
28441 Rancho California Rd., Ste.
106
Temecula, CA 92590-3618
PH: (951)587-8300
Samuelson, Dana, President

National Association of Buyers'
Agents [298]
4040 Civic Center Dr., Ste. 200
Terra Linda, CA 94903
PH: (415)721-7741
Toll free: 800-517-2277
Goldberg, Linda Lee, Exec. Dir.,
Founder

146th Alumni Association [19297]
1534 N Moorpark Rd., No. 365
Thousand Oaks, CA 91360
Romanisky, Andy, President

Achieve in Africa [10829]
1104 Woodridge Ave.
Thousand Oaks, CA 91362
Callahan, Brendan, Founder,
President

Armenian Film Foundation [8825]
2219 E Thousand Oaks Blvd., Ste.
292
Thousand Oaks, CA 91362
PH: (805)495-0717
Fax: (805)379-0667
Papazian, Gerald S., Esq., Chairman

Guild of Temple Musicians [20491]
2420 E Hillcrest Dr.
Thousand Oaks, CA 91362
Mason, Alan, President

Pituitary Network Association
[16771]
PO Box 1958
Thousand Oaks, CA 91358-1958
PH: (805)499-9973
Fax: (805)480-0633
Knutzen, Robert, Chairman, CEO

World Hapkido Association [23026]
1789 Thousand Oaks Blvd.
Thousand Oaks, CA 91362
PH: (805)495-9622
Fax: (805)494-4554
Jung, Tae, President

Urban Art International [1559]
PO Box 868
Tiburon, CA 94920-0868
PH: (415)435-5767
Fax: (415)435-4240

Gay and Lesbian Rowing Federation
[23109]
10153 Riverside Dr., Ste. 698
Toluca Lake, CA 91602

PH: (323)774-1903
Fax: (208)977-2045
Todd, Brian, Exec. Dir.

Motion Picture Sound Editors [1200]
10061 Riverside Dr.
Toluca Lake, CA 91602-2550
PH: (818)506-7731
Fax: (818)506-7732
McCarthy, Tom C., President

Society of Camera Operators [3434]
PO Box 2006
Toluca Lake, CA 91610
PH: (818)563-9110
Fax: (818)563-9117
Billinger, George, President

Talent Managers Association [1160]
10061 Riverside Dr., Ste. 582
Toluca Lake, CA 91602-2560
PH: (818)487-5556
Simons, Daryn, President

Center for Critical Thinking [7694]
PO Box 196
Tomales, CA 94971
Toll free: 800-833-3645
Fax: (707)878-9111
Elder, Dr. Linda, Exec. Dir.

U.S. Blind Tandem Cycling Connec-
tion [22757]
21063 Winfield Rd.
Topanga, CA 90290
PH: (310)455-1954
Tinberg, Christine, Founder,
President

Adult Children of Alcoholics World
Service Organization Inc. [12866]
PO Box 3216
Torrance, CA 90510
PH: (310)534-1815
A., Larry, Chairman

American Board of Podiatric
Medicine [16779]
3812 Sepulveda Blvd., Ste. 530
Torrance, CA 90505
PH: (310)375-0700
Fax: (310)375-1386
Benard, Marc A., DPM, Exec. Dir.

American Youth Soccer Organization
[23185]
19750 S Vermont Ave., Ste. 200
Torrance, CA 90502
Toll free: 800-USA-AYSO
Fax: (310)525-1155
Stewart, Mark, President

Arthur Rackham Society [8843]
20705 Wood Ave.
Torrance, CA 90503-2755
Swinson, Mary Ann, Exec.

Association for Women in
Architecture + Design [233]
1315 Storm Pky.
Torrance, CA 90501
PH: (310)534-8466
Fax: (310)257-1942
Silva, Kishani De, President

Bowfishing Association of America
[22842]
c/o MemberPlanet Inc.
23224 Crenshaw Blvd.
Torrance, CA 90505
PH: (501)730-3169
Acosta, Jody, VP

International Association of Law
Enforcement Planners [5136]
PO Box 11437
Torrance, CA 90510-1437
PH: (310)225-5148
Carpenter, Mark, President

Japanese American Living Legacy
[9626]
PO Box 10179
Torrance, CA 905050
PH: (424)230-7723
Uyemura, Ray, COO

Liberty in North Korea [18605]
1751 Torrance Blvd., Ste. L
Torrance, CA 90501
PH: (310)212-7190
Fax: (202)315-3748
Song, Hannah, President, CEO

National Collegiate Roller Hockey
Association [22910]
4733 Torrance Blvd., No. 618
Torrance, CA 90503
PH: (310)753-7285
Fax: (310)347-4001
Edwards, Brennan, Exec. Dir.

National Hormone and Pituitary
Program [16770]
Harbor - UCLA Medical Ctr.
1000 W Carson St.
Torrance, CA 90509
PH: (310)222-3537
    (310)415-2994
Fax: (310)222-3432
Parlow, Dr. A. F., Science Dir.

Pakistani American Business Execu-
tives Association [664]
23105 Kashiwa Ct.
Torrance, CA 90505
PH: (310)534-1505
Fax: (310)534-1424
Lodhie, Pervaiz, Chairman

SafetyBeltSafe U.S.A. [19083]
L A BioMed
Bldg. B-1 W
1124 W Carson St.
Torrance, CA 90502
PH: (310)222-6860
Toll free: 800-745-SAFE
Fax: (310)222-6862
Tombrello, Stephanie M., Exec. Dir.

Clan MacAlpine Society [20818]
32682 Rosemont Dr.
Trabuco Canyon, CA 92679-3386
McAlpin, Michael T., President

National Association of Independent
Insurance Adjusters [1894]
1880 Radcliff Ct.
Tracy, CA 95376-2330
PH: (209)832-6962
Fax: (209)832-6964
Reisinger, Brenda, Exec. Dir.

Subaru 360 Drivers' Club [21498]
c/o Brian Kliment
23251 Hansen Rd.
Tracy, CA 95304
Kliment, Brian, Contact

Missionary Gospel Fellowship
[20440]
PO Box 1535
Turlock, CA 95381-1535
PH: (209)634-8575
Hyatt, Jay, Director

Chiropractic Diplomatic Corps
[14260]
17602 17th St., Ste. 102
Tustin, CA 92780
Tetrault, Dr. Michel, Exec. Dir.

Hands for Africa [12668]
14511 Myford Rd., Ste. 250
Tustin, CA 92780
PH: (714)426-2245
    (714)249-4773
Harding, Alton, Founder, President

Little People of America [12955]
250 El Camino Real, Ste. 218
Tustin, CA 92780
PH: (714)368-3689
Toll free: 888-LPA-2001
Fax: (714)368-3367
Brazier, April, Sr. VP

American Civil War Association
[9454]
298 Warren Dr.
Ukiah, CA 95482
Aguirre, Stephen, President

Dharma Realm Buddhist Association
[19776]
2001 Talmage Rd.
Ukiah, CA 95482
PH: (707)462-0939
Fax: (707)462-0949
Hua, Hsuan, Founder

American Cinema Editors, Inc.
[1185]
Bldg. 9128, Ste. 260
100 Universal City Plz.
Universal City, CA 91608
PH: (818)777-2900
Heim, Alan, President

American Alliance Drug Testing
[13121]
326 N Euclid Ave.
Upland, CA 91786-6031
PH: (909)982-8409
Toll free: 800-820-9314
Medina, Sandy, Customer Svc.

Claremont Institute [17854]
1317 W Foothill Blvd., Ste. 120
Upland, CA 91786
PH: (909)981-2200
Fax: (909)981-1616
Kennedy, Brian T., Director

Stearman Restorers Association
[21250]
1456 Lemon Grove Dr.
Upland, CA 91786-2533

Llama Association of North America
[3603]
3966 Estate Dr.
Vacaville, CA 95688
PH: (707)447-5046
Fax: (707)471-4020
Mogler, Chene, President

National Morgan Reining Horse Association [4382]
c/o Barb Elfers
7701 Olivas Ln.
Vacaville, CA 95688
Elfers, Barb, Contact

SISTAS [13397]
PO Box 2845
Vacaville, CA 95687-9998
PH: (707)317-9478
Toll free: 888-SISTAS-8
Gainey, Cheryl A., Exec. Dir.,
Founder

Children's Liver Association for Support Services [15253]
25379 Wayne Mills Pl., Ste. 143
Valencia, CA 91355
PH: (661)263-9099
Toll free: 877-679-8256
Fax: (661)263-9099
Sumner, Diane, Founder

Narcotic Educational Foundation of
America [13156]
28245 Avenue Crocker, Ste. 230
Valencia, CA 91355-1201
PH: (661)775-6960
Stewart, Joe, Exec. Dir.

Neuro-Optometric Rehabilitation Association International, Inc. [16030]
28514 Costellation Rd.
Valencia, CA 91355
PH: (949)250-0176
    (253)661-6005
Durham, Susan, VP

Veteran's Association of the USS
Iowa [21074]
24307 Magic Mountain Pky., No. 342
Valencia, CA 91355
Schultz, John, Web Adm.

Chalcedon Foundation [20583]
3900 Highway 4
Vallecito, CA 95251
PH: (209)736-4365
Fax: (209)736-0536
Rushdoony, Rev. Mark R., President

Comic Book Collecting Association
[21734]
PO Box 655
Valley Center, CA 92082
Zarelli, Steve, President

National Animal Supplement Council
[3618]
PO Box 2568
Valley Center, CA 92082
PH: (760)751-3360
Bookout, Bill, President, Chmn. of
the Bd.

Equine Guided Education Association [4348]
PO Box 415
Valley Ford, CA 94972
PH: (707)876-1908
Fax: (707)876-1908

Real Estate Staging Association
[2893]
2274 Partridge Dr.
Valley Springs, CA 95252
Toll free: 888-201-8687
Fax: (916)273-7736
Brodnax, Shell, CEO

Resources for Independent Thinking
[10116]
39 California St., No. 153
Valley Springs, CA 95252-8777
PH: (209)772-2721
Fax: (925)391-3515
Presley, Sharon, PhD, Exec. Dir.

Elysia Skye Breast Cancer
Organization [13964]
5805 Whitsett Ave., No. 211
Valley Village, CA 91607
PH: (310)255-0460
Skye, Elysia, Founder

American Society of Music Arrangers
and Composers [9869]
5903 Noble Ave.
Van Nuys, CA 91411
PH: (818)994-4661
Pool, Jeannie, Secretary

Children of the Night [12792]
14530 Sylvan St.
Van Nuys, CA 91411-2324
PH: (818)908-4474
Toll free: 800-551-1300
Fax: (818)908-1468
Lee, Dr. Lois, Founder, President

International Bowling Media Association [2683]
c/o Joan Romero, President
6544 Gloria Ave.
Van Nuys, CA 91406
PH: (818)787-2310
Romeo, Joan, President

International Utilities Revenue
Protection Association [5832]
c/o Wayne Wohler, Chairperson,
    14401 Saticoy St., Bldg. 3

14404 Saticoy St., Bldg. 3
Van Nuys, CA 91405
PH: (818)771-2151
Fax: (818)771-2060

Motion Picture Pilots Association
[364]
7641 Densmore Ave.
Van Nuys, CA 91406
PH: (818)947-5454
Patlin, Mike, Director

Narcotics Anonymous [13157]
PO Box 9999
Van Nuys, CA 91409
PH: (818)773-9999
Fax: (818)700-0700
Gershoff, Jeff, Coord.

National Black Public Relations
Society [2754]
14636 Runnymede St.
Van Nuys, CA 91405
Toll free: 888-976-0005
Foote, Neil, President

Spondylitis Association of America
[17168]
16360 Roscoe Blvd., Ste. 100
Van Nuys, CA 91406
PH: (818)892-1616
Toll free: 800-777-8189
Fax: (818)892-1611
Savage, Laurie, Exec. Dir.

Beyond Baroque Literary/Arts Center
[8968]
681 Venice Blvd.
Venice, CA 90291
PH: (310)822-3006
Fax: (310)821-0256
Modiano, Richard, Director

Code Pink Women's Pre-Emptive
Strike for Peace [18778]
2010 Linden Ave.
Venice, CA 90291
PH: (310)827-4320
Fax: (310)827-4547
Evans, Jodie, Founder, Director

I'll Be the One Organization [4631]
659A Sunset Ave.
Venice, CA 90291
PH: (310)392-1370
Tickell, Joshua, Founder

Oneworld Works [12176]
2138 Penmar Ave., Ste. 3
Venice, CA 90291
PH: (310)572-1090
Simmons, Ira, CEO, President

United States Water and Power
[5892]
1179 Nelrose Ave.
Venice, CA 90291
Leddy, John C., Founder, President

A Window Between Worlds [11715]
710 4th Ave., Ste. 5
Venice, CA 90291
PH: (310)396-0317
Fax: (310)396-9698
Salser, Cathy, Founder

Alliance for Education and Community Development [11721]
9452 Telephone Rd., No. 274
Ventura, CA 93004-2600
PH: (805)861-0010
Fax: (805)477-9883
Beller, Floyd O., President, CEO

Artists for a Better World
International [8960]
PO Box 1872
Ventura, CA 93002
Alger, George, President

Association for Advanced Training in
the Behavioral Sciences [8467]
5126 Ralston St.
Ventura, CA 93003
PH: (805)676-3030
Toll free: 800-472-1931
Fax: (805)676-3033
Ables, Scott, President

International Association of Infant
Massage [15559]
PO Box 2447
Ventura, CA 93002
PH: (805)644-8524
Fax: (805)299-4563
Kelly, Andrea M., CEO

Los Californianos [19392]
PO Box 1633
Ventura, CA 93002-1633
Haywood, Arleene, Treasurer

The Old Appliance Club [21294]
PO Box 65
Ventura, CA 93002-0065
PH: (805)643-3532
Santoro, Jack, Founder

Pantera International [21474]
PO Box 920
Ventura, CA 93002
PH: (805)648-6464
Fax: (805)648-8074
Pence, George, President

Paso Pacifico [3928]
PO Box 1244
Ventura, CA 93002-1244
PH: (805)643-7044
Otterstrom, Sarah, PhD, Exec. Dir.

Professional Accounting Society of
America [56]
986 Colina Vista
Ventura, CA 93003

Public Safety Writers Association
[3518]
PO Box 4825
Ventura, CA 93007-0825
Olsen, Marilyn, President

Risley Family Association [20993]
29 Dana Point Ave.
Ventura, CA 93004-1656
Risley, Clark, Secretary, Treasurer

Society of Aviation and Flight Educators [7528]
PO Box 4283
Ventura, CA 93007
PH: (901)687-5217
Wilt, Donna, Chairperson

Celebration U.S.A. [8444]
18482 Valley Dr.
Villa Park, CA 92861-2849
PH: (714)974-3691
Fax: (714)974-3691
Burton, Paula, Chmn. of the Bd.,
Founder

American Association of Veterinary
Laboratory Diagnosticians [17604]
PO Box 6396
Visalia, CA 93290-6396
PH: (559)781-8900
Fax: (559)781-8989
Baldwin, Tom, President

Beirut Veterans of America [21111]
3320 W Modoc Ave.
Visalia, CA 93291-8087

Travel China Roads [7604]
1719 E Feemster Ct.
Visalia, CA 93292
PH: (559)636-6026
Vance, Josh, Director, President

Universal Pantheist Society [20616]
PO Box 3499
Visalia, CA 93278
Pearlman, Nancy, VP

Society for Modeling & Simulation
International [6264]
2598 Fortune Way, Ste. I
Vista, CA 92081
PH: (858)277-3888
Fax: (858)277-3930
Darensburg, Oletha, Secretary,
Exec. Dir.

Abyssinian Cat Club of America
[21563]
23700 Stagecoach Rd.
Volcano, CA 95689-9663
PH: (716)839-5919
Reilly, Beth, President

International Footprint Association
[5473]
PO Box 1652
Walnut, CA 91788
Partlow, Doug, VP

Marijuana Anonymous World
Services [12875]
340 S Lemon Ave., No. 9420
Walnut, CA 91789-2706
Toll free: 800-766-6779
W., Tom, Office Mgr.

Union of North American
Vietnamese Student Associations
[19686]
340 S Lemon Ave., No. 8246
Walnut, CA 91789
Tran, Lucy, VP

American Academy of Gnathologic
Orthopedics [14377]
2651 Oak Grove Rd.
Walnut Creek, CA 94598
Toll free: 800-510-2246
Fax: (925)934-4531

Books for the Barrios [11723]
1125 Wiget Ln.
Walnut Creek, CA 94598
PH: (925)934-6718
Harrington, Nancy, Founder

Children's Skin Disease Foundation
[14490]
1600 S Main St., Ste. 192B
Walnut Creek, CA 94596
PH: (925)947-3825
Fax: (866)236-6474
Tenconi, Francesca, Founder

Construction Employers' Association
[515]
2175 N California Blvd., Ste. 420
Walnut Creek, CA 94596
PH: (925)930-8184
Fax: (925)930-9014
Dumesnil, Robert, Jr., Trustee

Help Aid Africa [11375]
1132 Corrie Ln.
Walnut Creek, CA 94597-1804

Infrared Data Association [6363]
PO Box 3883
Walnut Creek, CA 94598
Terrell, Daphne, Exec. Dir.,
Secretary

International Carnivorous Plant
Society [22105]
2121 N California Blvd., Ste. 290
Walnut Creek, CA 94596-7351
van de Broek, Marcel, President

Mount Diablo Peace and Justice
Center [18805]
55 Eckley Ln.
Walnut Creek, CA 94596

PH: (925)933-7850
Reynolds, Daniel, Chmn. of the Bd.

National Safety Management Society
[12836]
PO Box 4460
Walnut Creek, CA 94596-0460
PH: (925)944-7094
Chung, Jeffrey, Exec. Dir.

Riva Club USA [22664]
2528 Ptarmigan Dr., No. 4
Walnut Creek, CA 94595-3254
PH: (530)277-7507
    (954)609-6485
Reed, Dirk, President

Sandplay Therapists of America
[17462]
PO Box 4847
Walnut Creek, CA 94596
PH: (925)820-2109
Tatum, Janet, President

Society of Medical Friends of Wine
[22477]
511 Jones Pl.
Walnut Creek, CA 94597
PH: (925)933-9691
Fax: (925)933-9691
Rosenberg, Mark, M.D., President

Council of American Master Mariners
Inc. [2240]
30623 Chihuahua Valley Rd.
Warner Springs, CA 92086-9220
Klein, Capt. Richard, President

Blue Dolphin Alliance [4465]
PO Box 312
Watsonville, CA 95077
PH: (831)761-1477
Toll free: 888-694-2537
Godley, Alan, Director

REG - The International Roger
Waters Fan Club [24060]
c/o Michael Simone, President, 128
onyx dr.
128 Onyx Dr.
Watsonville, CA 95076
Simone, Michael, President

Wild Farm Alliance [4172]
406 Main St., Ste. 316
Watsonville, CA 95076
PH: (831)761-8408
Fax: (831)761-8103
Baumgartner, Jo Ann, Exec. Dir.

Caring Hand for Children [11199]
6901 McLaren Ave.
West Hills, CA 91307-2527
PH: (818)620-1206
Basin, Geetu, Dir. of Public Rel.

Family Health Alliance [17105]
6520 Platt Ave., Ste. 433
West Hills, CA 91307-3218
PH: (818)610-7278
Salke, Taraneh R., Founder,
President

Knightsbridge International [12691]
PO Box 4394
West Hills, CA 91308-4394
PH: (818)372-6902
Fax: (818)716-9494
Artis, Edward A., PhD, Chairman,
Founder

United Shoe Retailers Association
[1405]
PO Box 4931
West Hills, CA 91308
PH: (818)703-6062
Fax: (866)929-6068
Hauss, Linda, Exec. Dir.

Unmarried Equality [12260]
7149 Rivol Rd.
West Hills, CA 91307
PH: (347)987-1068
Butler, Cindy, Exec. Dir.

Hollywood Foreign Press Association
[2682]
646 N Robertson Blvd.
West Hollywood, CA 90069

Homosexual Information Center
[11891]
8721 Santa Monica Blvd., Ste. 37
West Hollywood, CA 90069
PH: (818)527-5442
Schneider, Jim, Founder

KiteChild [11064]
8252 1/2 Santa Monica Blvd., Ste. A
West Hollywood, CA 90046
Salas-Uruena, Pollyanna, President,
Founder

March Forth Kenya Kids [11075]
PO Box 69A92
West Hollywood, CA 90069
Rossetto, Lynn, President, Exec. Dir.

Society for Brain Mapping and
Therapeutics [16035]
8159 Santa Monica Blvd., Ste. 200
West Hollywood, CA 90046
PH: (310)500-6196
Fax: (323)654-3511
Kateb, Babak, Chairman, CEO

Tribal Court Clearinghouse [5448]
8235 Santa Monica Blvd., Ste. 211
West Hollywood, CA 90046
PH: (323)650-5467
Fax: (323)650-8149
Gardner, Jerry, Exec. Dir.

Health Education Council [14938]
3950 Industrial Blvd., Ste. 600
West Sacramento, CA 95691
PH: (916)556-3344
Toll free: 888-442-2836
Fax: (916)446-0427
Oto-Kent, Debra, Exec. Dir.

Miyamoto Global Disaster Relief
[11674]
1450 Halyard Dr., Ste. 1
West Sacramento, CA 95691
PH: (916)373-1995
Fax: (916)373-1466
Miyamoto, H. Kit, President

Public Agency Risk Managers Association [5319]
c/o Kim Hunt, President
707 3rd St. 1-330
West Sacramento, CA 95605
PH: (916)376-5271
Hunt, Kim, President

American Association for Long-Term
Care Insurance [1826]
3835 E Thousand Oaks Blvd., Ste.
336
Westlake Village, CA 91362-3637
PH: (818)597-3227
    (818)597-3205
Fax: (818)597-3206
Slome, Jesse, Contact

American Association for Medicare
Supplement Insurance [15418]
3835 E Thousand Oaks Blvd., Ste.
336
Westlake Village, CA 91362
PH: (818)597-3205
Slome, Jesse, Exec. Dir.

American Board of Oriental
Reproductive Medicine [17124]
910 Hampshire Rd., Ste. A
Westlake Village, CA 91361

PH: (805)497-1335
Cridennda, Diane, Secretary

Christian Solidarity International
[20571]
870 Hampshire Rd., Ste. T
Westlake Village, CA 91361-6038
PH: (805)777-7107
Toll free: 888-676-5700
Fax: (805)777-7508
Eibner, Dr. John, CEO

Cure Research Foundation [13955]
PO Box 3782
Westlake Village, CA 91359
PH: (805)498-0185
Toll free: 800-282-2873
Fax: (805)498-4868
Griffin, G. Edward, Founder,
President

Devil Pups [21009]
PO Box 6607
Westlake Village, CA 91359
PH: (805)470-8340
Fax: (805)435-1767
Linsday, Richard, President

Foundation for Airway and Maxillofa-
cial Surgery [16446]
696 Hampshire Rd., Ste. 110
Westlake Village, CA 91361
PH: (805)230-1111
Kerner, Marc, MD, Founder,
President, CEO

Haiti Healthcare Partners [15464]
4607 Lakeview Canyon Ave., No.
640
Westlake Village, CA 91361

International Biogeography Society
[6672]
2133 Basswood Ct.
Westlake Village, CA 91361
Field, Richard, Secretary

National School Safety Center
[8525]
141 Duesenberg Dr., Ste. 7B
Westlake Village, CA 91362-3472
PH: (805)373-9977
Stephens, Dr. Ronald D., Exec. Dir.

Hugh O'Brian Youth Leadership
[8203]
31255 Cedar Valley Dr., Ste. 327
Westlake Village, CA 91362-7140
PH: (818)851-3980
Fax: (818)851-3999
LaFianza, Javier, CEO

FAMILIA Ancestral Research As-
sociation [20966]
PO Box 10425
Westminster, CA 92685
PH: (714)687-0390
Schmal, John P., Mem.

Rat and Mouse Club of America
[22244]
6082 Modoc Rd.
Westminster, CA 92683

Vietnam Human Rights Network
[12062]
8971 Colchester Ave.
Westminster, CA 92683-5416
PH: (714)657-9488
Tung, Dr. Nguyen Ba, DPA,
President

Association of Medical Directors of
Information Systems [6737]
682 Peninsula Dr.
Westwood, CA 96137
PH: (719)548-9360
Bria, William, MD, Chairman

National Shiba Club of America **[21924]**
c/o Lisa Sakashita, Corresponding
Secretary
15508 Janine Dr.
Whittier, CA 90603
Pendergast, Lori, President

North American Danish Warmblood
Association **[4391]**
c/o Jane Hayes, Treasurer
32781 Chadlyn Ct.
Wildomar, CA 92595
PH: (951)609-3787
Fernandez, Bonney, President

North American Radio Archives
[22403]
33888 The Farm Rd.
Wildomar, CA 92595-9107
PH: (951)244-5242
Fax: (951)244-5242

Help Hospitalized Veterans **[13240]**
36585 Penfield Ln.
Winchester, CA 92596
PH: (951)926-4500
Egan, Nora, Director

Science Fiction Poetry Association
[10205]
PO Box 907
Winchester, CA 92596
Lindow, Sandra J., VP

Afghan Association for Women and
Children **[13021]**
20033 Blythe St.
Winnetka, CA 91306
PH: (818)709-6359
Zaman, Mariam, Founder

Because I Love You: The Parent
Support Group **[13201]**
PO Box 2062
Winnetka, CA 91396-2062
PH: (818)884-8242
Poncher, Dennis, Founder

International Alliance for Animal
Therapy and Healing **[17446]**
PO Box 1255
Winters, CA 95694
PH: (530)795-5040

National Forest Recreation Associa-
tion **[2913]**
PO Box 488
Woodlake, CA 93286
PH: (559)564-2365
Fax: (559)564-2048
Reese, Marily, Exec. Dir.

International Okinawa Kobudo As-
sociation **[22993]**
2354 Ackley Pl.
Woodland, CA 95776
PH: (707)428-7266
Bolz, Shihan Mary H., VP

Moulding and Millwork Producers
Association **[548]**
507 1st St.
Woodland, CA 95695
PH: (530)661-9591
Toll free: 800-550-7889
Fax: (530)661-9586
Schroeder, Kellie A., CEO, Exec. VP

American Canary Fanciers Associa-
tion **[21534]**
5349 Overing Dr.
Woodland Hills, CA 91367
PH: (818)884-6338
Mena, Rey, President

Association Promoting Education
and Conservation in Amazonia
[4788]
21338 Dumetz Rd.
Woodland Hills, CA 91364
Low, Gina, Contact

Autism Care and Treatment Today!
[13746]
21600 Oxnard St., Ste. 1800
Woodland Hills, CA 91367
PH: (818)340-4010
Toll free: 877-922-8863
Granpeesheh, Dr. Doreen, President

Celiac Disease Foundation **[14784]**
20350 Ventura Blvd., Ste. 240
Woodland Hills, CA 91364
PH: (818)716-1513
Fax: (818)267-5577
Geller, Marilyn Grunzweig, CEO

German Shepherd Dog Club of
America-Working Dog Association
[21883]
PO Box 5021
Woodland Hills, CA 91365
PH: (747)900-6805
Fax: (747)200-2560
Torres, Richard, Secretary

International Commission of Peace
[18007]
20669 Martinez St.
Woodland Hills, CA 91364
Bachmann, Mr. Brett, CEO, Exec.
Dir.

League for Earth & Animal Protec-
tion **[3894]**
21781 Ventura Blvd., Ste. 633
Woodland Hills, CA 91364
PH: (818)346-5280
Laws, Charlotte Anne, Chairperson,
President

Motion Picture and Television Fund
[11795]
23388 Mulholland Dr.
Woodland Hills, CA 91364-2733
PH: (818)876-1977
    (818)876-1900
Toll free: 855-760-6783
Pisano, Robert A., Chairman

Retinitis Pigmentosa International
[17743]
PO Box 900
Woodland Hills, CA 91365-0900
Toll free: 800-344-4877
Fax: (818)992-3265
Harris, Helen, Founder, President

Watering Seeds Organization
[22804]
6303 Owensmouth Ave., 10th Fl.
Woodland Hills, CA 91367-2262
PH: (818)936-3476
Mazzola, Brady, CEO, Founder

Refugee Relief International **[12299]**
2995 Woodside Rd., No. 400-244
Woodside, CA 94062
Chan-Padgett, Vicki, Treasurer

World Community Chaplains **[12737]**
PO Box 3112
Wrightwood, CA 92397-3112
PH: (714)980-1709

526th Armored Infantry Battalion As-
sociation **[21187]**
PO Box 456
Yolo, CA 95697-0456
PH: (530)662-8160
Morrison, Sherrie, Secretary,
Treasurer

Cobra Owners Club of America
[21360]
4676 Lakeview Ave., Ste. 109G
Yorba Linda, CA 92886
PH: (714)546-5670
Stockwell, Bob, President

Evangelical Friends International -
North American Region **[20167]**
18639 Yorba Linda Blvd.
Yorba Linda, CA 92886

PH: (714)779-7662
Toll free: 888-704-9393
Fax: (714)779-7740
Williams, Dr. John P., Jr., Reg. Dir.

National Organization for Disorders
of the Corpus Callosum **[15969]**
18032-C Lemon Dr., PMB 363
Yorba Linda, CA 92886
PH: (714)747-0063
Fax: (714)693-0808
Rumberg, Steve, President

Salisbury Sound Association **[21061]**
c/o Maurice Medland, President
19842 Villager Cir.
Yorba Linda, CA 92886
PH: (505)293-3841
    (714)970-2288
Medland, Maurice, President

Strategic Energy, Environmental and
Transportation Alternatives **[7898]**
c/o Cynthia Verdugo-Peralta,
President/Chief Executive Officer
18340 Yorba Linda Blvd., Ste. 107-
509
Yorba Linda, CA 92886
PH: (714)777-7729
Fax: (714)777-7728
Verdugo-Peralta, Cynthia, CEO,
President

Sunsweet Growers **[4251]**
901 N Walton Ave.
Yuba City, CA 95993
PH: (530)674-5010
Toll free: 800-417-2253
Fax: (530)751-5395
Braun, Sharon, VP

Lutheran Braille Workers **[17724]**
13471 California St.
Yucaipa, CA 92399
PH: (909)795-8977
Toll free: 800-925-6092
Fax: (909)795-8970
Pledger, Rev. Phil, President

COLORADO

Hope for Children of Africa **[10478]**
PO Box 399
Alma, CO 80420
PH: (303)902-9276
Wood, Nancy, Founder, Director

Biofeedback Certification
International Alliance **[13817]**
5310 Ward Rd., Ste. 201
Arvada, CO 80002
PH: (720)502-5829
    (303)420-2902
Fax: (303)422-8894
Shaffer, Dr. Fred, PhD, Chairman

Heroes Forever **[13981]**
PO Box 1872
Arvada, CO 80001
PH: (303)428-6171
Sternicki, Vicki, Founder, President

Horse Protection League **[4359]**
17999 W 60th Ave.
Arvada, CO 80403
PH: (303)216-0141
Millet, Bev, Director

Manufacturers' Representatives
Educational Research Foundation
[2207]
5460 Ward Rd., Ste. 125
Arvada, CO 80002
PH: (303)463-1801
Fax: (303)379-6024
Brusacoram, Gary, Contact

National Translator Association **[477]**
6868 Vivian St.
Arvada, CO 80004

PH: (303)378-8209
Fax: (303)465-4067
Mcdonald, Jim, President

PeaceJam **[8408]**
11200 Ralston Rd.
Arvada, CO 80004
PH: (303)455-2099
Fax: (303)455-3921
Keene, Beverly, Chairperson

Second Bombardment Association
[20685]
c/o Matt R. Bryner, Treasurer
8386 Fenton Way
Arvada, CO 80003
Nelson, Karen, President

Thirst-Aid **[13357]**
12478 W 70th Pl.
Arvada, CO 80004
Bradner, Curt, Founder

Veterinary Institute of Integrative
Medicine **[17671]**
PO Box 740053
Arvada, CO 80006
PH: (303)277-8227
Abdallah, Bobbie, Contact

Climb for Conservation **[3833]**
PO Box 4971
Aspen, CO 81612
PH: (970)948-2991
Fax: (757)548-2345
Kelly, Ginna, Founder

EcoFlight **[3998]**
307 L Aspen Airport Business Ctr.
Aspen, CO 81611
PH: (970)429-1110
Fax: (970)429-1110
Gordon, Bruce, Founder, Exec. Dir.

Accountants Global Network **[1]**
2851 S Parker Rd., Ste. 850
Aurora, CO 80014
PH: (303)743-7880
Toll free: 800-782-2272
Fax: (303)743-7660
Hood, Rita J., Reg. Dir.

AGN International **[5]**
2851 S Parker Rd., Ste. 850
Aurora, CO 80014
PH: (303)743-7880
Fax: (303)743-7660
Ward, Malcolm, CEO

AGN North America **[6]**
2851 S Parker Rd., Ste. 850
Aurora, CO 80014
PH: (303)743-7880
Fax: (303)743-7660
Hood, Rita, Exec. Dir.

Air and Surface Transport Nurses
Association **[16081]**
13918 E Mississippi Ave., Ste. 215
Aurora, CO 80012
PH: (303)344-0457
Toll free: 800-897-6362
Fax: (800)937-9890
Good, Nikole, Exec. Dir.

Aircraft Mechanics Fraternal As-
sociation **[23382]**
14001 E Iliff Ave., Ste. 217
Aurora, CO 80014
PH: (303)752-2632
Fax: (303)362-7736
Key, Louie, Director

American Association of Paranormal
Investigators **[6979]**
13973 E Utah Cir.
Aurora, CO 80012
PH: (720)432-2746
Weidner, Stephen, Founder

American Society for Stereotactic
and Functional Neurosurgery
[16060]
c/o Aviva Abosch, President
Dept. of Neurosurgery
University Colorado
12631 E 17th Ave., C307
Aurora, CO 80045
PH: (303)724-2204
Fax: (303)724-2300
Abosch, Aviva, President

Arabian Horse Association [4336]
10805 E Bethany Dr.
Aurora, CO 80014
PH: (303)696-4500
Fax: (303)696-4599
Harvey, Nancy A., VP

Arabian Jockey Club [22913]
10805 E Bethany Dr.
Aurora, CO 80014
PH: (303)696-4523
Fax: (303)696-4599
Smoke, Kathryn, Chairperson

Association of Postdoctoral
Programs in Clinical Neuropsychol-
ogy [16904]
Dept. of Neurosurgery
12631 E 17th Ave., C307
Aurora, CO 80045
PH: (303)724-5957
Grote, Christopher, PhD, President

Association for Repetitive Motion
Syndromes [16318]
PO Box 471973
Aurora, CO 80047
PH: (303)369-0803

Auburn-Cord-Duesenberg Club
[21330]
24218 E Arapahoe Pl.
Aurora, CO 80016
PH: (303)748-3579
Givner, Joel, President

International Association for the
Study of Lung Cancer [13989]
13100 E Colfax Ave., Unit 10
Aurora, CO 80011
Toll free: 855-464-2752
Fax: (720)505-2176
Bunn, Paul A., Jr., Mem.

International Gay Rodeo Association
[23095]
PO Box 460504
Aurora, CO 80046-0504
Channel, Tommy, Mem.

International Society for Prevention
of Child Abuse and Neglect
[11051]
13123 E 16th Ave. B390
Aurora, CO 80045
PH: (303)864-5220
Fax: (303)964-5222
Niekerk, Joan Van, President

Kempe Center for the Prevention
and Treatment of Child Abuse and
Neglect [11055]
13123 E 16th Ave., Ste. B390
Aurora, CO 80045-7106
PH: (303)864-5300
Smith, Mark, Bd. Member

National Association of Counsel for
Children [11254]
13123 E 16th Ave. No. B390
Aurora, CO 80045
Toll free: 888-828-NACC
Marlowe, Kendall, Exec. Dir.

National Center for American Indian
and Alaska Native Mental Health
Research [15792]
c/o Colorado School of Public Health
13001 E 17th Pl.

Aurora, CO 80045
PH: (303)724-4585
Floersch, Ms. Natasha, Officer

National Council of Supervisors of
Mathematics [8283]
2851 S Parker Rd., No. 1210
Aurora, CO 80014
PH: (303)758-9611
Fax: (303)200-7099
Matsumoto, Carol, Chairman

National Leather Association -
International [12949]
PO Box 470395
Aurora, CO 80047
PH: (780)454-1992
Shafer, CandiAnne, President

National Resource Center for Health
and Safety in Child Care and Early
Education [10812]
13120 E 19th Ave., Mail Stop F541
Aurora, CO 80045
Toll free: 800-598-5437
Fax: (303)724-0960
Krajicek, Marilyn J., EdD, Director

Renewal 4 Haiti [12300]
18625 E Dorado Dr.
Aurora, CO 80015
PH: (720)530-6975
Charles, Jodel Stanley, Founder

The Retired Enlisted Association
[21139]
1111 S Abilene Ct.
Aurora, CO 80012
PH: (303)752-0660
Toll free: 800-338-9337
Fax: (303)752-0835
Davis, Michael, VP

United Doberman Club [21974]
c/o Bonnie Guzman, Membership
Secretary
367 Chickadee Ln.
Bailey, CO 80421
PH: (303)733-4220
Bishop, Beth, VP

Rocky Mountain Institute [4499]
22830 Two Rivers Rd.
Basalt, CO 81621
PH: (970)927-3851
Fax: (970)927-3420
Kortenhorst, Jules, CEO

Birthing the Future [14223]
PO Box 1040
Bayfield, CO 81122
PH: (970)884-4005
Arms, Suzanne, Founder, Director

Suenos International [10699]
255 McKinley Dr.
Bennett, CO 80102
PH: (720)350-2199
Atwater, Danielle, DVM, Contact

North American Gun Dog Associa-
tion [21928]
1404 Willow Dr.
Berthoud, CO 80513
PH: (719)342-0776
Gish, Bob, Chairman

Norwegian Fjord Horse Registry
[4397]
1801 W County Road 4
Berthoud, CO 80513
PH: (303)684-6466
Fax: (888)646-5613
Newport, Nancy, Exec. Dir.

Shibumi International Reiki Associa-
tion [17104]
PO Box 1776
Berthoud, CO 80513
Edwards, Trish, Director

Society of Animal Artists [8942]
5451 Sedona Hills Dr.
Berthoud, CO 80513-8987
PH: (970)532-3127
Fax: (970)532-2537
Bemis, Reneé, President

American Saddle Makers Association, Inc. [2081]
12155 Donovan Ln.
Black Forest, CO 80908
PH: (719)494-2848

Access Fund [23208]
207 Canyon, Ste. 201
Boulder, CO 80302
PH: (303)545-6772
Fax: (303)545-6774
Robinson, Brady, Exec. Dir.

Adventures in Preservation [9364]
1557 North St.
Boulder, CO 80304
PH: (303)444-0128
Broeker, Judith, Founder, President,
Prog. Dir.

Afghans4Tomorrow [11306]
4699 Apple Way
Boulder, CO 80301
Barikzai, M. Ilias, Director

Alliance for Climate Education [4111]
4696 Broadway St., Ste. 2
Boulder, CO 80304
PH: (510)251-5990
Fax: (510)419-0383
Haas, Michael, Chmn. of the Bd.,
Founder

American Association of Teachers of
Japanese [8173]
366 University of Colorado
1424 Broadway
Boulder, CO 80309-0366
PH: (303)492-5487
Fax: (303)492-5856
Schmidt, Susan, Exec. Dir.

American Homebrewers Association
[177]
1327 Spruce St.
Boulder, CO 80302
PH: (303)447-0816
Toll free: 888-822-6273
Ruud, Susan, Secretary

American Literacy Council [8233]
1441 Mariposa Ave.
Boulder, CO 80302
PH: (303)440-7385
Campbell, Jim, Director

American Mountain Guides Associa-
tion [21595]
207 Canyon Blvd., Ste. 201N
Boulder, CO 80302-4932
PH: (303)271-0984
Fax: (303)271-1377
Kosseff, Alex, Exec. Dir.

American Safe Climbing Association
[21596]
PO Box 3691
Boulder, CO 80307
Barnes, Greg, Director

American Solar Energy Society
[7197]
2525 Arapahoe Ave., Ste. E4-253
Boulder, CO 80302
PH: (303)443-3130
Hebert, Elaine, Chairman

Association for Experiential Education [7910]
1435 Yarmouth Ave., Ste. 104
Boulder, CO 80304

PH: (303)440-8844
Toll free: 866-522-8337
Beale, Bobbi, President

Association for Social Anthropology
in Oceania [5910]
c/o Jerry Jacka, Secretary
Dept. of Anthropology
University of Colorado - Boulder
CB 233
Boulder, CO 80309-0233
Muru-Lanning, Marama, Chmn. of
the Bd.

Behavior Genetics Association
[14878]
Dept. of Psychology and Neurosci-
ence
University of Colorado
Boulder, CO 80309
Prescott, Carol, Exec.

Bicycle Product Suppliers Associa-
tion [3136]
740 34th St.
Boulder, CO 80303
PH: (303)442-2466
Fax: (303)552-2060
Gierhart, Roger, President

BMW Vintage and Classic Car Club
of America [21339]
4862 Silver Sage Ct.
Boulder, CO 80301
PH: (303)300-9946
    (303)808-9135
Fax: (303)575-3234
Pfafflin, Goetz E., President

Brewers Association [181]
1327 Spruce St.
Boulder, CO 80302-5006
PH: (303)447-0816
Toll free: 888-822-6273
Fax: (303)447-2825
Papazian, Charlie, Founder

CancerClimber Association [13933]
Boulder, CO
Swarmer, Sean, Bd. Member

Conscious Alliance [11345]
2525 Arapahoe Ave., Ste. E4 - 182
Boulder, CO 80302
PH: (720)406-7871
Toll free: 866-259-9455
Levy, Justin, Exec. Dir.

Developing Opportunities for
Orphans and Residents of
Cameroon [11346]
PO Box 1439
Boulder, CO 80306
Wingo, Ajume, Founder

Environment for the Americas [3660]
5171 Eldorado Springs Dr., Ste. N
Boulder, CO 80303-9672
PH: (303)499-1950
Toll free: 866-334-3330
Fax: (303)499-9567
Bonfield, Susan, Exec. Dir.

Food Family Farming Foundation
[15090]
PO Box 20708
Boulder, CO 80308
Collins, Beth, Exec. Dir.

Geological Society of America
[6680]
3300 Penrose Pl.
Boulder, CO 80301
PH: (303)357-1000
Fax: (303)357-1070
Mora, Claudia I., President

Girls Education International [8748]
PO Box 537
Boulder, CO 80306-0537
Thompson, Ms. Therese, Dir. of Dev.

Hands and Voices [15191]
PO Box 3093
Boulder, CO 80307
PH: (303)492-6283
Toll free: 866-422-0422
Johnson, Harold, Director

Herb Research Foundation [6141]
5589 Arapahoe Ave., Ste. 205
Boulder, CO 80303
PH: (303)449-2265
Fax: (303)449-7849
McCaleb, Robert S., President

Inliners International [21398]
c/o Linda Henry, Membership Chair
6558 Red Hill Rd.
Boulder, CO 80302-3400
PH: (303)443-8185
Fax: (303)449-7937
Willis, Will, President

International Association of Certified
Home Inspectors [1817]
1750 30th St., Ste. 301
Boulder, CO 80301
PH: (303)502-6214
Toll free: 877-346-3467
Fax: (650)429-2057
Endza, Lisa, Dir. of Comm.

International Midwife Assistance
[16289]
PO Box 916
Boulder, CO 80306
PH: (303)241-1355
    (303)588-1663
Wyrick, Claudia, M.D., President

International Mountain Bicycling As-
sociation [22748]
4888 Pearl East Cir., Ste. 200E
Boulder, CO 80301
PH: (303)545-9011
Toll free: 888-442-4622
Fax: (303)545-9026
Abel, Mike Van, Exec. Dir., President

International Society for
Environmental Ethics [4072]
c/o Ben Hale, Vice President
University of Colorado, Boulder
1333 Grandview, UCB 0488
Boulder, CO 80309
PH: (303)735-3624
    (970)491-2061
Fax: (303)735-1576
Thompson, Allen, VP

International Veterinarians Dedicated
to Animal Health [17651]
PO Box 20246
Boulder, CO 80308-3246
Parkin, Ruth, DVM, President

Japanese National Honor Society
[23793]
c/o American Association of Teachers of Japanese
1424 Broadway
Boulder, CO 80309-0366
PH: (303)492-5487
Fax: (303)492-5856
Fujimoto, Junko, Director

JILA [7027]
440 UCB
Boulder, CO 80309-5004
PH: (303)492-7789
Fax: (303)492-5235
Bachinski, Julia, Admin. Ofc.

The Kitchen Community [8400]
1980 8th St.
Boulder, CO 80302
PH: (720)263-0501
Musk, Kimbal, Founder, CEO

LENA Research Foundation [17242]
5525 Central Ave., Ste. 100
Boulder, CO 80301
Toll free: 866-503-9918
Fax: (305)545-2166
Paul, Judith, Founder

Mali Assistance Project [10482]
c/o Karen Marx, Executive Director
Box 221
3601 Arapahoe Ave.
Boulder, CO 80303
PH: (303)449-4464
Marx, Karen, Exec. Dir.

Mediators Without Borders [4965]
885 Arapahoe Ave.
Boulder, CO 80302
PH: (720)565-4055
Toll free: 877-268-5337
Ries, Shauna, President, Founder

Mesoamerican Ecotourism Alliance
[3383]
c/o Mark Willuhn, Director
4076 Crystal Ct.
Boulder, CO 80304
PH: (303)440-3362
Toll free: 800-682-0584
Fax: (303)447-0815
Willuhn, Mark, Exec. Dir.

Mining and Metallurgical Society of
America [6881]
PO Box 810
Boulder, CO 80306-0810
PH: (303)444-6032
Blois, Michael, VP

Musical Missions of Peace [18806]
1930 Central Ave., Ste. E
Boulder, CO 80301
PH: (303)449-4196
Fax: (303)440-9592
Jacobs, Pete, President

National American Indian Court
Judges Association [5388]
1942 Broadway, Ste. 215
Boulder, CO 80302
PH: (303)449-4112
Fax: (303)449-4038
Blake, Richard, President

National Center for Higher Education
Management Systems [7438]
3035 Center Green Dr., Ste. 150
Boulder, CO 80301-2205
PH: (303)497-0301
Fax: (303)497-0338
Roberts, Clara, Mgr., Dir. of Admin.

National Council on Education for
the Ceramic Arts [21773]
4845 Pearl East Cir., Ste. 101
Boulder, CO 80301
PH: (303)828-2811
Toll free: 866-266-2322
Fax: (303)828-0911
Staley, Chris, President

National Institute for Trial Advocacy
[5828]
1685 38th St., Ste. 200
Boulder, CO 80301-2735
PH: (303)953-6845
    (720)890-4860
Toll free: 800-225-6482
Fax: (720)890-7069
Lockwood, Karen, Exec. Dir.

National Scholarship Providers As-
sociation [8517]
2222 14th St.
Boulder, CO 80302
Fax: (303)443-5098
Weinstein, Amy, Contact

Native American Rights Fund
[18711]
1506 Broadway
Boulder, CO 80302-6296

PH: (303)447-8760
Fax: (303)443-7776
O'Brien, Morgan, Dir. of Dev.

NCSL International [7233]
2995 Wilderness Pl., Ste. 107
Boulder, CO 80301-5404
PH: (303)440-3339
Fax: (303)440-3384
Harris, Georgia L., President

Organic Reactions Catalysis Society
[6211]
c/o Will Medlin, Chairman
University of Colorado, Boulder
596 UCB
Boulder, CO 80309-0596
Medlin, Will, Chairman

Organization for Professional Astrology [5994]
c/o Sarah Leigh Serio, Treasurer
574 Linden Park Ct.
Boulder, CO 80304
Mulligan, Bob, Contact

Outdoor Industries Women's Coali-
tion [2468]
PO Box 7203
Boulder, CO 80306
PH: (513)202-6492
Toll free: 877-686-6492
Buck, Deanne, Exec. Dir.

Outdoor Industry Association [2469]
4909 Pearl E Cir., Ste. 300
Boulder, CO 80301
PH: (303)444-3353
Fax: (303)444-3284
Roberts, Amy, Exec. Dir.

Paleontological Society [6973]
PO Box 9044
Boulder, CO 80301
Toll free: 855-357-1032
Fax: (303)357-1070
Yacobucci, Margaret, Secretary

Partners in Parenting Haiti [11128]
3970 Newport Ln.
Boulder, CO 80304
Arney, Jan, Director

Partners for Rural Improvement and
Development in Ethiopia [12806]
2828 Kenyon Cir.
Boulder, CO 80305
PH: (303)543-0515
Gebre-Mariam, Zewge, Founder

PeopleForBikes [10781]
1966 13th St., Ste. 250
Boulder, CO 80302
PH: (303)449-4893
Clements, Fred, Treasurer

Positive Music Association [9997]
c/o Scott Johnson
4593 Maple Ct.
Boulder, CO 80301-5829
Johnson, Scott, Leader

Potters for Peace [21778]
c/o Abby Silver, Director
PO Box 2214
Boulder, CO 80306
PH: (303)442-1253
Silver, Abby, Director

Public Media Company [2825]
5277 Manhattan Cir., Ste. 210
Boulder, CO 80303-8201
PH: (720)304-7274
Fax: (720)304-8923
Hand, Marc, CEO, Founder

Recycling for Charities [4635]
5541 Central Ave., Ste. 125
Boulder, CO 80301
Toll free: 866-630-7557
Fax: (248)543-7677
Zahringer, Dwight, Founder

River Network [3935]
2400 Spruce St., Ste. 200
Boulder, CO 80302
PH: (503)241-3506
Fax: (503)241-9256
Brown, Chris, Secretary

Rolf Institute of Structural Integration
[13654]
5055 Chaparral Ct., Ste. 103
Boulder, CO 80301
PH: (303)449-5903
Fax: (303)449-5978
McCoy, Kevin, Chmn. of the Bd.

Slow Money Alliance [4701]
PO Box 2231
Boulder, CO 80306
PH: (303)443-1154
Tasch, Woody, Founder, Chairman

Sound Healers Association [13658]
PO Box 2240
Boulder, CO 80306
PH: (303)443-8181
Fax: (303)443-6023
Goldman, Jonathan, Director,
Founder

State Higher Education Executive
Officers [8443]
3035 Center Green Dr., Ste. 100
Boulder, CO 80301-2205
PH: (303)541-1600
Fax: (303)541-1639
Whitfield, Christina, Assoc. VP

Suzuki Association of the Americas
[8390]
PO Box 17310
Boulder, CO 80308
PH: (303)444-0948
Toll free: 888-378-9854
Fax: (303)444-0984
Brasch, Pamela, Exec. Dir., CEO

Thorne Nature Experience [4016]
1466 N 63rd St.
Boulder, CO 80303
PH: (303)499-3647
Fax: (720)565-3873
Desrosiers, Keith, Exec. Dir.

U.S.A. Climbing [21600]
4909 Pearl East Cir., Ste. 102
Boulder, CO 80301-2498
PH: (303)499-0715
Fax: (561)423-0715
Pair, Daron, President

University of Colorado at Boulder I
Natural Hazards Center [6890]
1440 15th St.
Boulder, CO 80309
PH: (303)492-6818
Fax: (303)492-2151
Smith, Diane, Office Mgr.

University Corporation for
Atmospheric Research [6860]
3090 Center Green Dr.
Boulder, CO 80301
PH: (303)497-1000
Bogdan, Thomas J., President

Women Work Together [11747]
3232 6th St.
Boulder, CO 80304
PH: (303)444-8193
Dvorin, Diane, Managing Dir.,
Founder

World Council of Elders [9223]
PO Box 7915
Boulder, CO 80306
PH: (303)444-9263
Johnson, Catie, Exec. Dir.

Association of Air Force Missileers
[20683]
PO Box 5693
Breckenridge, CO 80424-5693

PH: (970)453-0500
Fax: (970)453-0500
Lord, Gen. (Ret.) Lance, President

Mountain2Mountain [11404]
PO Box 7399
Breckenridge, CO 80424
PH: (970)376-0754
Galpin, Shannon, President,
Founder

American Highland Cattle Association [3695]
Historic City Hall
22 S 4th Ave., Ste. 201
Brighton, CO 80601-2042
PH: (303)659-2399
Fax: (303)659-2241
Nelson, Deborah, President

American Military Family [21038]
PO Box 1101
Brighton, CO 80601
PH: (303)746-8195
Quackenbush, Debbie, Founder,
CEO

North American Parrot Society [21548]
c/o Gary Morgan, Chairman/
President
15341 Kingston St.
Brighton, CO 80602-7439
PH: (303)659-9544
Morgan, Gary, Chairman, President

Wheat Quality Council [3776]
5231 Tall Spruce St.
Brighton, CO 80601
PH: (303)558-0101
Fax: (303)558-0100
Handcock, Ben, Exec. VP

Angel Covers [10853]
PO Box 6891
Broomfield, CO 80021
PH: (303)947-5215
    (303)552-6129
Fillmore, Kari, Exec. Dir.

Billiard Congress of America [22584]
10900 W 120th Ave., Ste. B7
Broomfield, CO 80021
PH: (303)243-5070
Johnson, Rob, CEO

Birds of Prey Foundation [4797]
2290 S 104th St.
Broomfield, CO 80020
PH: (303)460-0674
Bucknam, Heidi, Exec. Dir.

North American Working Bouvier Association [21933]
1677 Dexter St.
Broomfield, CO 80020
Toll free: 866-457-2582
vanDuyvenbode, Carla, President

Youth in Model Railroading [22194]
12990 Prince Ct.
Broomfield, CO 80020-5419
PH: (303)466-2857
Averhoff, Shad, Officer

Nichiren Buddhist Association of America [19782]
PO Box 5156
Buena Vista, CO 81211-5156
Heimburg, Shannon, President

Fellowship of Christian Cowboys [19976]
PO Box 1210
Canon City, CO 81215
PH: (719)275-7636
Shay, Reese, President

Mining History Association [9494]
323 Daniels Pl.
Canon City, CO 81212

PH: (573)290-2453
Culver, Bill, President

Solar Energy International [7208]
520 S 3rd St., Rm. 16
Carbondale, CO 81623
PH: (970)963-8855
Fax: (970)963-8866
Weiss, Johnny, Advisor, Founder

Spellbinders [10226]
520 S 3rd St.
Carbondale, CO 81623
PH: (970)544-2389
Johnson, Catherine, Exec. Dir.

Amateur Baseball Umpires' Association [22539]
200 S Wilcox St., No. 508
Castle Rock, CO 80104
PH: (303)290-7411
Toll free: 866-332-3492

International Network of Children's Ministry [19990]
PO Box 190
Castle Rock, CO 80104
Toll free: 855-933-6466
Guevara, Matt, Exec. Dir.

National Carousel Association [21562]
c/o Norma Pankratz, Executive
Secretary
PO Box 1256
Castle Rock, CO 80104-1256
Largent, Bette, President

World Orphans [11190]
PO Box 1840
Castle Rock, CO 80104
Toll free: 888-677-4267
Vair, Scott, President

Allied Beauty Experts [918]
6551 S Revere Pky., Ste. 120
Centennial, CO 80111-6410
PH: (303)662-9075
Toll free: 800-444-7546
Fax: (303)662-9845
Callison, Kenneth P., Contact

AlloSource [17500]
6278 S Troy Cir.
Centennial, CO 80111
PH: (720)873-0213
Toll free: 800-557-3587
Fax: (720)873-0212
Cycyota, Thomas A., CEO,
President

American Galvanizers Association [743]
6881 S Holy Cir., Ste. 108
Centennial, CO 80112
PH: (720)554-0900
Fax: (720)554-0909
Rahrig, Philip G., BS, Exec. Dir.

American Institute of Timber Construction [1425]
7012 S Revere Pky., Ste. 140
Centennial, CO 80112
PH: (503)639-0651
Fax: (503)684-8928
DeVisser, Don, PE, Exec. VP

Cattlemen's Beef Promotion and Research Board [3725]
9000 E Nichols Ave., Ste. 215
Centennial, CO 80112
PH: (303)220-9890
Fax: (303)220-9280
Ruhland, Polly, CEO

FOOTPRINTS in the Sky [12275]
7375 S Peoria St., Ste. 209, B-10
Centennial, CO 80112-4157

PH: (303)799-0461
Fax: (303)799-8020
Langland, Johnny, Founder,
President

Gamma Phi Beta [23955]
12737 E Euclid Dr.
Centennial, CO 80111
PH: (303)799-1874
Fax: (303)799-1876
Velhuizen, Laurie, Exec. Dir.

International Christian Cycling Club [22747]
6834 S University, No. 232
Centennial, CO 80122
PH: (720)870-3707
Wade, Drew, Exec. Dir.

International Society for British Genealogy and Family History [20975]
PO Box 3345
Centennial, CO 80161
Pearson, Ann Lisa, President

National Association of RV Parks & Campgrounds [2912]
9085 E Mineral Cir., Ste. 200
Centennial, CO 80112
PH: (303)681-0401
Fax: (303)681-0426
Littman, Karl, CPO, OHC, Chairman

National Cattlemen's Beef Association [3736]
9110 E Nichols Ave., No. 300
Centennial, CO 80112
PH: (303)694-0305
Fax: (303)694-2851

National Cattlemen's Foundation [3737]
9110 E Nichols Ave., Ste. 300
Centennial, CO 80112
PH: (303)694-0305
Wilkinson, Barb, Exec. Dir.

National Stroke Association [17297]
9707 E Easter Ln., Ste. B
Centennial, CO 80112
Toll free: 800-787-6537
Lopez, Matt, CEO

Now I Lay Me Down to Sleep [12505]
7500 E Arapahoe Rd., Ste. 101
Centennial, CO 80112
PH: (720)283-3339
Toll free: 877-834-5667
Fax: (720)283-8998
Erickson, Robbyn, President

Outpatient Ophthalmic Surgery Society [16404]
c/o Kent L. Jackson, Executive
Director
4671 E Phillips Pl.
Centennial, CO 80122
PH: (720)550-7667
Jackson, Kent L., PhD, Exec. Dir.

Prostate Conditions Education Council [17555]
7009 S Potomac St., Ste. 125
Centennial, CO 80112
PH: (303)316-4685
Toll free: 866-477-6788
Fax: (303)320-3835
Poage, Wendy L., President

Gary Morris Fan Club [24039]
PO Box 187
Chromo, CO 81128
PH: (615)777-6995

International Society of Neuro-Semantics [17187]
PO Box 8
Clifton, CO 81520-0008

PH: (970)523-7877
Hall, L. Michael, PhD, Founder

Miniature Hereford Breeders Association [3735]
c/o Fran MacKenzie, Treasurer
60885 Salt Creek Rd.
Collbran, CO 81624
PH: (970)487-3182
Grady, Justin, President

About Books [2759]
1001 Taurus Dr.
Colorado Springs, CO 80906
PH: (719)632-8226
Fax: (719)213-2602
Flora, Debi, President, Owner

Adopt-a-Village International [11305]
PO Box 26599
Colorado Springs, CO 80936
PH: (719)492-8736
Ruckman, Dave, Bd. Member

American Board of Forensic Odontology [14772]
Forensic Sciences Foundation, Inc.
410 N 21st St.
Colorado Springs, CO 80904-2798
PH: (734)697-4400
Golden, Dr. Gregory S., Contact

American Numismatic Association [22256]
818 N Cascade Ave.
Colorado Springs, CO 80903-3208
Toll free: 800-367-9723
Fax: (719)634-4085
Miller, Brian, Mgr.

Angels of America's Fallen [10854]
10010 Devonwood Ct.
Colorado Springs, CO 80920
PH: (719)377-7352
Lewis, Joe, President

Association of Christian Schools International [7607]
731 Chapel Hills Dr.
Colorado Springs, CO 80920-3949
PH: (719)528-6906
Toll free: 866-793-8162
Fax: (719)531-0631
Egeler, Dr. Dan, President

Association of Gospel Rescue Missions [13032]
7222 Commerce Center Dr., Ste.
120
Colorado Springs, CO 80919
PH: (719)266-8300
Toll free: 800-473-7283
Fax: (719)266-6600
Ashmen, John, President, CEO

Association of Peyronie's Disease Advocates [17194]
PO Box 62865
Colorado Springs, CO 80962
Hardin, Stan, President

Association of Publishers for Special Sales [2772]
PO Box 9725
Colorado Springs, CO 80932-0725
PH: (719)924-5534
Fax: (719)213-2602
Flora, Scott, Consultant

Austrian Studies Association [9031]
c/o Robert von Dassanowsky,
President
1420 Austin Bluffs Pky.
Department of Visual and Performing Arts
University of Colorado at Colorado
Springs
Colorado Springs, CO 80918
Meyer, Imke, President

Bibles For The World [20388]
1105 Garden of the Gods Rd.
Colorado Springs, CO 80949-9759
PH: (719)630-7733
Toll free: 888-382-4253
Pudaite, Dr. Lalrimawii, Founder,
President

Biblica [19755]
1820 Jet Stream Dr.
Colorado Springs, CO 80921
PH: (719)488-9200
Toll free: 800-524-1588
Moo, Dr. Douglas, Chairman

CBA: The Association for Christian
Retail [2950]
1365 Garden of the Gods Rd., Ste.
105
Colorado Springs, CO 80907
PH: (719)265-9895
Toll free: 800-252-1950
Fax: (719)272-3510
Riskey, Curtis, President

Center for Organizational and
Ministry Development [19950]
PO Box 49488
Colorado Springs, CO 80949-9488
PH: (719)590-8808
Graham, Thomas M., PhD, Founder,
President

Children's HopeChest [10928]
PO Box 63842
Colorado Springs, CO 80962-3842
PH: (719)487-7800
Fax: (719)487-7799
Wilson, Steve, Secretary

Christian Camp and Conference As-
sociation [22719]
405 W Rockrimmon Blvd.
Colorado Springs, CO 80919
PH: (719)260-9400
Hunter, Gregg, President

ChristianTrade Association
International [19968]
9240 Explorer Dr., No. 200
Colorado Springs, CO 80920
PH: (719)265-9895
Pettit, Ms. Kim, Exec. Dir.

Civil Censorship Study Group
[22320]
c/o Charles J. LaBlonde, Secretary
15091 Ridgefield Ln.
Colorado Springs, CO 80921
LaBlonde, Charles J., Secretary

Delta Sigma Rho - Tau Kappa Alpha
[23980]
c/o Mike Edmonds, Treasurer
Colorado College
14 E Cache La Poudre
Colorado Springs, CO 80903
Martinelli, Amy, VP

Engineering Ministries International
[19974]
130 E Kiowa St., Ste. 200
Colorado Springs, CO 80903-1722
PH: (719)633-2078
Fax: (719)633-2970
Gresham, Robert, Chairman

Family Research Institute [18327]
PO Box 62640
Colorado Springs, CO 80962-2640
PH: (303)681-3113
Cameron, Dr. Paul, Chairman

Finding Refuge [10974]
5390 Academy Bldg.
Colorado Springs, CO 80918
PH: (480)442-6219
Fax: (719)227-0238
Kurica, Ken, Founder

Focus on the Family [11820]
8605 Explorer Dr.
Colorado Springs, CO 80920
Toll free: 800-232-6459
Fax: (719)548-5947
Rosati, Kelly, VP

Food for Orphans [12093]
PO Box 26123
Colorado Springs, CO 80936
PH: (719)591-7777
Vandyke, Gary, President

Forensic Sciences Foundation
[5246]
410 N 21st St.
Colorado Springs, CO 80904
PH: (719)636-1100
Fax: (719)636-1993
Baker, Andrew M., Chairman

Global Market Development Center
[3470]
1275 Lake Plaza Dr.
Colorado Springs, CO 80906
PH: (719)576-4260
Fax: (719)576-2661
Davis, Stephen, Chairman

HEARTBEAT Grief Support Follow-
ing Suicide [13193]
PO Box 16985
Colorado Springs, CO 80935-6985
PH: (719)596-2575
Archibald, LaRita, Director, Founder

Help Desk Institute [3074]
121 S Tejon, Ste. 1100
Colorado Springs, CO 80903-2254
PH: (719)955-8146
    (719)955-8180
Toll free: 800-248-5667
Fax: (719)955-8114
Frilow-Steenhoek, Michelle, CMP,
Director

International Christian Technologists
Association [20369]
5555 Erindale Dr., Ste. 205
Colorado Springs, CO 80918-6965
PH: (719)785-0120
Holzmann, Pete, Exec. Dir., Founder

International Council of Iranian
Christians [19989]
PO Box 25607
Colorado Springs, CO 80936
PH: (719)596-0010
Fax: (719)574-1141

International Project Management
Association [2178]
6547 N Academy, No. 404
Colorado Springs, CO 80918-8342
PH: (719)488-3850
Goff, Stacy, Dir. of Mktg.

International Racquetball Federation
[23087]
1631 Mesa Ave.
Colorado Springs, CO 80906
PH: (719)433-2017
Maggi, Osvaldo, President

International Society for Organization
Development and Change [2462]
PO Box 50827
Colorado Springs, CO 80949
Preston, Joanne C., Editor

International Students Inc. [20148]
PO Box C
Colorado Springs, CO 80901
PH: (719)576-2700
Fax: (719)576-5363
Shaw, Dr. Douglas, CEO, President

Junior Achievement [7554]
1 Education Way
Colorado Springs, CO 80906

PH: (719)540-8000
Kosakowski, Jack E., President,
CEO

Kinder Goat Breeders Association
[4278]
PO Box 63406
Colorado Springs, CO 80962
LaRose, Lisa, Treasurer

Major League Baseball Players
Alumni Association [22553]
Copper Bldg., Ste. D
1631 Mesa Ave.
Colorado Springs, CO 80906
PH: (719)477-1870
Fax: (727)898-8911
Robinson, Brooks, President

Mercedes-Benz Club of America
[21429]
1907 Lelaray St.
Colorado Springs, CO 80909-2872
PH: (719)633-6427
Toll free: 800-637-2360
Fax: (719)633-9283
Dierks, Steve, Director

Message! Products [19134]
8245 N Union Blvd.
Colorado Springs, CO 80920-4456
Toll free: 866-460-0099

National Alliance Against Christian
Discrimination, Inc. [19995]
c/o Rev. Thomas L. Pedigo, Founder
and Executive Director
PO Box 62685
Colorado Springs, CO 80962
Pedigo, Rev. Thomas L., Exec. Dir.,
Founder

National Archery Association of the
United States [22502]
4065 Sinton Rd., Ste. 110
Colorado Springs, CO 80907-5093
PH: (719)866-4576
Fax: (719)632-4733
Corbin, Bill, Chairman

National Association of Marine
Services [2251]
5458 Wagon Master Dr.
Colorado Springs, CO 80917-2235
PH: (719)573-5946
Fax: (719)573-5952
Goldberg, Max, President

National Institute for Animal
Agriculture [4460]
13570 Meadowgrass Dr., Ste. 201
Colorado Springs, CO 80921
PH: (719)538-8843
Fax: (719)538-8847
Stuart, R. Scott, CEO

National Junior College Athletic As-
sociation [23245]
1631 Mesa Ave., Ste. B
Colorado Springs, CO 80906-2956
PH: (719)590-9788
Fax: (719)590-7324
Leicht, Mary Ellen, Exec. Dir.

National Little Britches Rodeo As-
sociation [23101]
5050 Edison Ave., Ste. 105
Colorado Springs, CO 80915
PH: (719)389-0333
Toll free: 800-763-3694
Fax: (719)578-1367

National Livestock Producers As-
sociation [4480]
13570 Meadowgrass Dr., Ste. 201
Colorado Springs, CO 80921
PH: (719)538-8843
Toll free: 800-237-7193
Fax: (719)538-8447
Stuart, Scott, President

National Organization for Rivers
[23093]
212 W Cheyenne Mountain Blvd.
Colorado Springs, CO 80906
PH: (719)579-8759
Leaper, Eric, President, Exec. Dir.

National Strength and Conditioning
Association [23337]
1885 Bob Johnson Dr.
Colorado Springs, CO 80906
PH: (719)632-6722
Toll free: 800-815-6826
Fax: (719)632-6367
Haff, G. Gregory, President

National Swimming Pool Foundation
[2914]
4775 Granby Cir.
Colorado Springs, CO 80919
PH: (719)540-9119
Fax: (719)540-2787
Dunn, Bruce, President

National Uterine Fibroids Foundation
[17112]
PO Box 9688
Colorado Springs, CO 80932
PH: (719)633-3454
Dionne, Carla, Founder, Exec. Dir.

National Versatility Ranch Horse As-
sociation [22946]
5925 Omaha Blvd.
Colorado Springs, CO 80915
PH: (719)550-0189
Fax: (719)550-0194
Henson, Jay, President

National Wheelchair Basketball As-
sociation [22790]
1130 Elkton St., Ste. C
Colorado Springs, CO 80907
PH: (719)266-4082
Fax: (719)266-4876
McCoy, Pat, Bd. Member

Native American Sports Council
[23045]
1235 Lake Plaza Dr., Ste. 221
Colorado Springs, CO 80906
PH: (719)632-5282

The Navigators [19999]
3820 N 30th St.
Colorado Springs, CO 80904-5001
PH: (719)598-1212
Fax: (719)260-0479
Elmore, DG, Chmn. of the Bd.

New Hope International [20445]
5550 Tech Center Dr., Ste. 307
Colorado Springs, CO 80919
PH: (719)577-4450
Toll free: 877-874-3264
Paulson, Hank, Founder

Michael Oakeshott Association
[10110]
Political Sciences Dept.
Colorado College
14 E Cache La Poudre St.
Colorado Springs, CO 80903
Kos, Eric, President, Secretary,
Treasurer

One Challenge International [20451]
PO Box 36900
Colorado Springs, CO 80936
PH: (719)592-9292
Toll free: 800-676-7837
Fax: (719)592-0693
Micetic, Dale, Chmn. of the Bd.

One Child Matters [12555]
15475 Gleneagle Dr.
Colorado Springs, CO 80921
Toll free: 800-864-0200
Fax: (719)481-4649
Pluimer, Mark, President

Orphan Coalition [11115]
1880 Office Club Pointe, Ste. 1000
Colorado Springs, CO 80920
PH: (719)481-3700
Fax: (303)253-8972
Harp, Becky, Contact

Over the Hill Gang, International
[23249]
2121 N Weber St.
Colorado Springs, CO 80907
PH: (719)471-0222
Fax: (719)389-0024
Lofland, Doug, President

Paraclete [20453]
PO Box 63450
Colorado Springs, CO 80962
PH: (719)302-2500
Ginter, Gary, Chairman, Founder

Professional Rodeo Cowboys Association [23103]
101 Pro Rodeo Dr.
Colorado Springs, CO 80919
PH: (719)593-8840
Fax: (719)548-4876
Stressman, Karl, Commissioner

Smile for a Lifetime Foundation
[15160]
4565 Hilton Pkwy., Ste. 203
Colorado Springs, CO 80907
Von Fange, Michelle, Exec. Dir.

Space Foundation [7460]
4425 Arrowswest Dr.
Colorado Springs, CO 80907
PH: (719)576-8000
Toll free: 800-691-4000
Pulham, Mr. Elliot Holokauahi, CEO

Storage Networking Industry Association [6265]
4360 ArrowsWest Dr.
Colorado Springs, CO 80907-3444
PH: (719)694-1380
   (415)402-0006
Fax: (719)694-1389
Zmyslowski, Allan, Treasurer

Sustainable Communities Worldwide
[12072]
PO Box 50347
Colorado Springs, CO 80949
McCausland, Mike, Exec. Dir.

U.S. Association for Blind Athletes
[22798]
1 Olympic Plz.
Colorado Springs, CO 80909
PH: (719)866-3224
Fax: (719)866-3400
Lucas, Mark A., Exec. Dir.

United States Fencing Association
[22834]
4065 Sinton Rd., Ste. 140
Colorado Springs, CO 80907
PH: (719)866-4511
Fax: (719)632-5737
Anthony, Donald K., Jr., President

U.S. Field Hockey Association
[22837]
5540 N Academy Blvd., Ste. 100
Colorado Springs, CO 80918
PH: (719)866-4567
Fax: (719)632-0979
Hindy, Shawn, Chairman

United States Figure Skating Association [23157]
20 1st St.
Colorado Springs, CO 80906
PH: (719)635-5200
Fax: (719)635-9548
Auxier, Sam, President

United States Hang Gliding and
   Paragliding Association [22492]
1685 W Uintah St.
Colorado Springs, CO 80904
PH: (719)632-8300
Toll free: 800-616-6888
Fax: (719)632-6417
Palmaz, Martin, Exec. Dir.

United States Modern Pentathlon
Association [23314]
1 Olympic Plz.
Colorado Springs, CO 80909
PH: (305)332-8148
Matchett, Barry, Chairman

United States Olympic Committee
[23049]
1 Olympic Plz.
Colorado Springs, CO 80909
PH: (719)632-5551
   (719)866-4618
Toll free: 888-222-2313
Probst, Lawrence F., III, Chmn. of
   the Bd.

U.S. Taekwondo [23022]
1 Olympic Plz.
Colorado Springs, CO 80909
PH: (719)866-4632
Fax: (719)866-4642
Harris, Bruce, CEO

U.S.A. Badminton [22531]
1 Olympic Plz.
Colorado Springs, CO 80909
PH: (719)866-4808
Fax: (719)866-4507
Cloppas, Dan, CEO, Sec. Gen.

U.S.A. Basketball [22578]
5465 Mark Dabling Blvd.
Colorado Springs, CO 80918-3842
PH: (719)590-4800
Fax: (719)590-4811
Tooley, Jim, CEO, Exec. Dir.

U.S.A. Boxing [22717]
1 Olympic Plz.
Colorado Springs, CO 80909
PH: (719)866-2300
Toll free: 888-222-2313
Fax: (719)866-2132
Martino, Mike, Exec. Dir.

U.S.A. Swimming [23290]
1 Olympic Plz.
Colorado Springs, CO 80909
PH: (719)866-4578
Wielgus, Chuck, Exec. Dir.

U.S.A. Table Tennis [23294]
4065 Sinton Rd., Ste 120
Colorado Springs, CO 80907-5093
PH: (719)866-4583
Fax: (719)632-6071
Scudner, Peter D., Director

U.S.A Team Handball [22538]
1 Olympic Plz.
Colorado Springs, CO 80909-5780
PH: (719)866-2203
Gascon, Dave, Director

U.S.A. Triathlon [23339]
5825 Delmonico Dr., Ste. 200
Colorado Springs, CO 80919
PH: (719)597-9090
   (719)955-2807
Fax: (719)597-2121
Siff, Barry, President

U.S.A. Ultimate [22809]
5825 Delmonico Dr., Ste. 350
Colorado Springs, CO 80919
PH: (719)219-8322
Toll free: 800-872-4384
Crawford, Tom, CEO

U.S.A. Wrestling [23374]
6155 Lehman Dr.
Colorado Springs, CO 80918-3456
PH: (719)598-8181
Fax: (719)598-9440
Bender, Rich, Exec. Dir.

USA Cycling [22759]
210 USA Cycling Pt., Ste. 100
Colorado Springs, CO 80919
PH: (719)434-4200
Johnson, Steve, CEO, President

USA Hockey [22911]
1775 Bob Johnson Dr.
Colorado Springs, CO 80906-4090
PH: (719)576-8724
Fax: (719)538-1160
Ogrean, Dave, Exec. Dir.

USA National Karate-do Federation
[23025]
1631 Mesa Ave., Ste. A1
Colorado Springs, CO 80906-2956
PH: (719)477-6925
DiPasquale, John, Chairman,
   President

USA Racquetball [23088]
2812 W Colorado Ave., Ste. 200
Colorado Springs, CO 80904-2906
PH: (719)635-5396
Fax: (719)635-0685
Haemmerle, Larry, President

USA Shooting [23145]
1 Olympic Plz.
Colorado Springs, CO 80909
PH: (719)866-4670
Mitchell, Robert, Exec. Dir.

USA Volleyball [23350]
4065 Sinton Rd., Ste. 200
Colorado Springs, CO 80907
PH: (719)228-6800
Fax: (719)228-6899
Beal, Doug, CEO

USA Weightlifting [23368]
1 Olympic Plz.
Colorado Springs, CO 80909
PH: (719)866-4508
Fax: (719)866-4741
Massik, Michael, Gen. Sec.

White Bison [10050]
5585 Erindale Dr., Ste. 203
Colorado Springs, CO 80918
PH: (877)871-1495
Toll free: 877-871-1495
Fax: (719)548-9407
Coyhis, Don, Founder, President

Women's Professional Rodeo Association [23105]
431 S Cascade Ave.
Colorado Springs, CO 80903
PH: (719)447-4627
Fax: (719)447-4631
Vietor, Carolynn, President

World Confederation of Billiard
   Sports [22591]
4345 Beverly St., Ste. D
Colorado Springs, CO 80918
PH: (719)264-8300
Fax: (719)264-0900
Dupont, Jean-Claude, President

Young Life [20664]
PO Box 520
Colorado Springs, CO 80901
Fax: (719)332-6732
Nilsen, Scott, Director

Our Family Orphan Communities,
   Inc. [11259]
PO Box 158
Conifer, CO 80433-0158

PH: (303)514-6858
Fax: (435)228-2298
Miller, Robert E., President, CEO

National Federation of Community
   Broadcasters [476]
1308 Clear Fork Rd.
Crawford, CO 81415-8501
PH: (970)279-3411
Green, Sonya, President

Western Public Radio [2827]
1308 Clear Fork Rd.
Crawford, CO 81415
PH: (970)279-3411
Freeman, Lakisha, VP

Spiritual Life Institute [20611]
c/o NADA Hermitage
PO Box 219
Crestone, CO 81131
PH: (719)256-4778

International Miniature Donkey
   Registry [4456]
PO Box 982
Cripple Creek, CO 80813
PH: (719)689-2904

AIDS Treatment Activists Coalition
[10533]
PO Box 9153
Denver, CO 80209-0153
Dorosh, Michael, Bd. Member

American Association of Nurse Assessment Coordination [14975]
400 S Colorado Blvd., Ste. 600
Denver, CO 80246
PH: (303)758-7647
Toll free: 800-768-1880
Fax: (303)758-3588
Carter, Diane, RN, CEO, President

American Board of Obesity Medicine
[16246]
2696 S Colorado Blvd., St.e 340
Denver, CO 80222
PH: (303)770-9100
Fax: (303)770-9104
Brittan, Dana Rasis, MBA, Exec. Dir.

American Cheese Society [969]
2696 S Colorado Blvd., Ste. 570
Denver, CO 80222-5954
PH: (720)328-2788
Fax: (720)328-2786
Weiser, Nora, Exec. Dir.

American Chiropractic Association
   Council on Sports Injuries and
   Physical Fitness [14251]
c/o Carly May, Secretary
1720 S Bellaire St., Ste. 406
Denver, CO 80222
PH: (303)758-1100
Hastad, Nick, VP

American Disabled for Attendant
   Programs Today [11569]
1208 S Logan St.
Denver, CO 80210
DeRusso, Dean, Contact

American Grassfed Association
[4451]
469 S Cherry St., Ste. 220
Denver, CO 80246
Toll free: 877-774-7277
Harris, Will, President

American Hernia Society [17368]
4582 S Ulster St., Ste. 201
Denver, CO 80237
Toll free: 866-798-5406
Fax: (303)771-2550
Goddard, Carol A., Exec. Dir.

American Indian College Fund
[8512]
8333 Greenwood Blvd.
Denver, CO 80221-4488

PH: (303)426-8900
Toll free: 800-776-3863
Fax: (303)426-1200
Guy, Elmer, Chairman

American Orthopsychiatric Association [16821]
PO Box 202798
Denver, CO 80220
PH: (720)708-0187
Fax: (303)366-3471
Kimbrough-Melton, Robin, Exec. Ofc.

American Society of Farm Managers and Rural Appraisers [217]
950 S Cherry St., Ste. 508
Denver, CO 80246-2664
PH: (303)758-3513
Fax: (303)758-0190
Stockman, Brian, Exec. VP, CEO

American Society of General Surgeons [17372]
4582 S Ulster St., Ste 201
Denver, CO 80237-2633
PH: (303)771-5948
Toll free: 800-998-8322
Fax: (303)771-2550
Shearburn, Web, MD, Officer

American Society of Sugar Beet Technologists [6640]
800 Grant St., Ste. 300
Denver, CO 80203
PH: (303)832-4460
Hatch, Robert, President

American Water Works Association [3457]
6666 W Quincy Ave.
Denver, CO 80235
PH: (303)794-7711
Toll free: 800-926-7337
Fax: (303)347-0804
LaFrance, David B., Secretary, CEO

Association of Liberian Lawyers in the Americas [5418]
1582 S Parker Rd., Ste. 110
Denver, CO 80231
PH: (720)535-5237
Fax: (720)535-4681
Jayweh, Frederick A.B., Exec. Dir.

Association of PeriOperative Registered Nurses [16123]
2170 S Parker Rd., Ste. 400
Denver, CO 80231
PH: (303)755-6300
Toll free: 800-755-2676
Fax: (800)847-0045
Davis, Stephanie S., Treasurer

Association of State and Territorial Local Health Liaison Officials [5715]
PO Box 260451
Denver, CO 80226
McCarthy, JoBeth, VP

Bridges to Prosperity [12798]
1031 33rd St., Ste. 170
Denver, CO 80205
PH: (757)784-5071
Bang, Avery Louise, CEO

Build Change [11964]
535 16th St., Ste. 605
Denver, CO 80202
PH: (303)953-2563
Hausler, Dr. Elizabeth, CEO, Founder

Building Bridges [13435]
PO Box 101958
Denver, CO 80250
PH: (303)691-2393
Fax: (303)691-2394
Breeze, Erin, Bd. Member

Building Bridges: Middle East-US [8097]
PO Box 101958
Denver, CO 80250
PH: (303)691-2393
Fax: (303)691-2394
Treas, Emily

CAD Society [6273]
Strategic Reach PR
7100 N Broadway, Bldg. 2, Ste. 2LPH
Denver, CO 80221
PH: (303)487-7406
Toll free: 888-750-0839
Stavanja, Rick, President

Cartography and Geographic Information Society [6166]
c/o Michael P. Finn, President
Box 25046, MS 510
Denver, CO 80225-0046
Anderson, Eric, Exec. Dir.

Chamber of the Americas [23571]
720 Kipling St., Ste. 13
Denver, CO 80215
PH: (303)462-1275
Fax: (303)462-1560
Cisneros, Gilbert M., Chairman, CEO

Children's Future International [10926]
1031 33rd St., Ste. 174
Denver, CO 80205
PH: (720)295-3312
Wolf, Andrew, Exec. Dir., Founder

A Christian Ministry in the National Parks [19963]
9185 E Kenyon Ave., Ste. 230
Denver, CO 80237
PH: (303)220-2808
Toll free: 800-786-3450
Fax: (303)220-0128
Lundgaard, Rev. Spencer L., Exec. Dir.

Coalition of Visionary Resources [2951]
PO Box 100866
Denver, CO 80250
PH: (303)758-0007
Baumann, Micki, Officer

Compassion and Choices [11805]
PO Box 101810
Denver, CO 80250-1810
Toll free: 800-247-7421
Klee, Susie, Info. Technology Mgr.

Competency and Credentialing Institute [15322]
2170 S Parker Rd., Ste. 120
Denver, CO 80231
PH: (303)369-9566
Toll free: 888-257-2667
Fax: (303)695-8464
Carter, Shannon S., MA, CEO

An Comunn Gaidhealach Ameireaganach [19638]
PO Box 103069
Denver, CO 80250
Mackay, Mike, President

DanceSafe [13134]
800 Grant St., Ste. 110
Denver, CO 80203
Toll free: 888-MDMA-411
Karas, Kristin, Coord.

Deaf Overcoming Violence through Empowerment [11937]
PO Box 150449
Denver, CO 80215
PH: (303)831-7932
Fax: (303)831-4092
Frederickson, Sara, President

Dental Lifeline Network [14430]
1800 15th St., Ste. 100
Denver, CO 80202-7134
PH: (303)534-5360
Fax: (303)534-5290
Coffee, Larry, DDS, Founder, CEO

Dreams InDeed International [12959]
PO Box 211006
Denver, CO 80221
PH: (303)953-0426
Haskell, David, CEO

Earth Force [4050]
35 Park Ave. W
Denver, CO 80205
PH: (303)433-0016
Fax: (888)899-5324
Meldrum, Vince, President, CEO

Education Commission of the States [7763]
700 N Broadway, Ste. 810
Denver, CO 80203-3442
PH: (303)299-3600
Anderson, Jeremy, President

Elephant Energy [6476]
1031 33rd St., Ste. 174
Denver, CO 80205
PH: (720)446-8609
Alvarez, Julia, Exec. Dir.

Engineers Without Borders-U.S.A. [6553]
1031 33rd St., Ste. 210
Denver, CO 80205
PH: (303)772-2723
Fax: (303)772-2699
Leslie, Catherine A., Exec. Dir.

Environmental and Engineering Geophysical Society [6686]
1720 S Bellaire St., Ste. 110
Denver, CO 80222-4308
PH: (303)531-7517
Fax: (303)820-3844
Barstnar, Kathie A., Exec. Dir.

Experiential Learning International [7912]
1557 Ogden St., Ste. 5
Denver, CO 80218
PH: (303)321-8278
O'Neill, Dr. Kevin, Director

Financial Planning Association [1236]
7535 E Hampden Ave., Ste. 600
Denver, CO 80231
PH: (303)759-4900
Toll free: 800-322-4237

Fire Museum Network [9324]
c/o Bob Vallero, Treasurer
2912 S Otis St.
Denver, CO 80227-3530
Hall, Bill, President

Free Speech TV [19109]
PO Box 44099
Denver, CO 80201
PH: (303)442-8445
Williams, Ron, Exec. Dir.

Geoscience Information Society [6689]
Emily Wild, President
US Geological Survey, Denver Library
Denver Federal Ctr.
Denver, CO 80225-0046
PH: (303)236-1003
    (303)357-1020
Hudson, Matt, President

Global Dental Relief [14437]
4105 E Florida Ave., Ste. 200
Denver, CO 80222

PH: (303)858-8857
Toll free: 800-543-1171
Melcher, Melanie, Chairman

Gray Line Sightseeing Association [3329]
1835 Gaylord St.
Denver, CO 80206
PH: (303)539-8502
Toll free: 800-472-9546
Fax: (303)484-2185
Weber, Brad, CEO, President

Independence Institute [17901]
727 E 16th Ave.
Denver, CO 80203
PH: (303)279-6536
Fax: (303)279-4176
Caldara, Jon, President

International Association of Gay Square Dance Clubs [9259]
PO Box 9176
Denver, CO 80209-0176
Hazen, Bob, Mem.

International Erosion Control Association [3887]
3401 Quebec St., Ste. 3500
Denver, CO 80207
PH: (303)640-7554
Toll free: 800-455-4322
Peters, Brock, President

International Hunter Education Association [22961]
800 E 73rd Ave., Unit 2
Denver, CO 80229
PH: (303)430-7233
Fax: (303)430-7236
Hall, Steve, Exec. Dir.

International Society for Biomedical Research on Alcoholism [17314]
PO Box 202332
Denver, CO 80220-8332
PH: (303)355-6420
Fax: (303)355-1207
Sung-Gon, Kim, Secretary

Jewish Children's Adoption Network [10455]
PO Box 147016
Denver, CO 80214-7016
PH: (303)573-8113
Fax: (303)893-1447
Krausz, Dr. Steve, PhD, Asst. Dir.

Laboratory to Combat Human Trafficking [18421]
3455 Ringsby Ct., No. 101
Denver, CO 80216
PH: (303)295-0451
Finger, Amanda, MA, Exec. Dir.

Latin American Educational Foundation [7972]
561 Santa Fe Dr.
Denver, CO 80204
PH: (303)446-0541
Fax: (303)446-0526
Chavez, Jim, Exec. Dir.

Mending Faces [14341]
422 Humboldt St.
Denver, CO 80218
Charles, David, MD, Chairman

Mexico-Elmhurst Philatelic Society International [22345]
PO Box 29040
Denver, CO 80229-0040
Bland, Bubba, President

Missions Door [19733]
2530 Washington St.
Denver, CO 80205-3142
PH: (303)308-1818
Fax: (303)295-9090
Miller, Rick, President

Morris Animal Foundation **[10661]**
720 S Colorado Blvd., Ste. 174A
Denver, CO 80246
PH: (303)790-2345
Toll free: 800-243-2345
Fax: (303)790-4066
Reddington, John, President, CEO

Museum Store Association **[2962]**
789 Sherman St., Ste. 600
Denver, CO 80203
PH: (303)504-9223
Anderson, Jennifer, Mgr.

National Academy of Neuropsychology **[16925]**
7555 E Hampden Ave., Ste. 525
Denver, CO 80231- 4836
PH: (303)691-3694
Fax: (303)691-5983
Lacritz, Laura, Ph.D., President

National Asian American Pacific Islander Mental Health Association **[15787]**
1215 19th St., Ste. A
Denver, CO 80202
PH: (303)298-7910
Fax: (303)298-8081
Ida, DJ, PhD, Exec. Dir.

National Association of Addiction Treatment Providers **[13161]**
PO Box 6693
Denver, CO 80206
Toll free: 888-574-1008
Fax: (888)574-1008
Ventrell, Marvin, JD, Exec. Dir.

National Association for Premenstrual Dysphoric Disorder **[16296]**
PO Box 102361
Denver, CO 80250
Toll free: 800-609-7633
LaFleur, Amanda, Exec. Dir.

National Civic League **[5643]**
6000 E Evans Ave., Ste. 3-012
Denver, CO 80222
PH: (303)571-4343
Sander, David, Chairman

National Coalition Against Domestic Violence **[11706]**
1 Broadway, Ste. B210
Denver, CO 80203
PH: (303)839-1852
Fax: (303)831-9251
Garrity, Rose, President

National Conference of State Legislatures **[5783]**
7700 E 1st Pl.
Denver, CO 80230
PH: (303)364-7700
Fax: (303)364-7800
Bramble, Sen. Curt, President

National Conference of State Transportation Specialists **[5818]**
c/o Larry Herold, Treasurer
1560 Broadway, Ste. 250
Denver, CO 80202
PH: (303)894-2859
Hoeme, Mike, VP

National Council of State Legislatures **[18330]**
7700 E 1st Pl.
Denver, CO 80230
PH: (303)364-7700
Fax: (303)364-7800
Pound, William T., Exec. Dir.

National Environmental Health Association **[14719]**
720 S Colorado Blvd., Ste. 1000-N
Denver, CO 80246

PH: (303)756-9090
Fax: (303)691-9490
Osner, Terry, Coord., Admin.

National High School Rodeo Association **[23099]**
12011 Tejon St., Ste. 900
Denver, CO 80234
PH: (303)452-0820
Toll free: 800-466-4772
Fax: (303)452-0912
Dechant, Bobbie, Officer

National Hydrologic Warning Council **[7370]**
2480 W 26th Ave., Ste. 156-B
Denver, CO 80211-5304
PH: (303)455-6277
Fax: (303)455-7880
Fitzgerald, Steve, President

National Jewish Health **[17145]**
1400 Jackson St.
Denver, CO 80206
PH: (303)388-4461
Toll free: 877-225-5654
Salem, Michael, MD, FACS, CEO, President

National Lawyers Association **[5041]**
3801 E Florida Ave., Ste. 400
Denver, CO 80210
Toll free: 800-471-2994
McCaig, Joshua, President

National Native American AIDS Prevention Center **[10549]**
1031 33rd St.
Denver, CO 80205
PH: (720)382-2244
Fax: (720)382-2248
Feather, Alexander White Tail, Exec. Dir.

National Network for Oral Health Access **[14467]**
181 E 56th Ave., Ste. 501
Denver, CO 80216
PH: (303)957-0635
Fax: (866)316-4995
Bozzone, Janet, DMD, President

National Organization for Men Against Sexism **[18432]**
3500 E 17th Ave.
Denver, CO 80206
PH: (720)466-3882
Corben, Allen, Co-Ch.

National Victims' Constitutional Amendment Passage **[19222]**
90 Galapago St.
Denver, CO 80223
PH: (303)861-1160
Fax: (303)861-1265

Native American Cancer Research Corporation **[14031]**
PO Box 27494
Denver, CO 80227
PH: (303)838-9359
Toll free: 800-537-8295
Clark, Rick, Founder, VP

North American Transportation Management Institute **[7725]**
2460 W 26th Ave., Ste. 245-C
Denver, CO 80211
PH: (303)952-4013
Fax: (775)370-4055
Penner, Rob, Chairman

Obesity Medicine Association **[16262]**
101 University Blvd., Ste. 330
Denver, CO 80206
PH: (303)770-2526
Fax: (303)779-4834
Horn, Deborah Bade, DO, President

Pioneers **[11861]**
1801 California St., Ste. 225
Denver, CO 80202
PH: (303)571-1200
Toll free: 800-872-5995
Fax: (303)572-0520
Wirtzfeld, Carey, President

Portuguese Podengo Club of America **[21946]**
2051 Elm St.
Denver, CO 80207
Brawders, Bob, Director

Professional Association of Therapeutic Horsemanship International **[22795]**
PO Box 33150
Denver, CO 80221-6920
PH: (303)452-1212
Toll free: 800-369-7433
Fax: (303)252-4610
Alm, Kathy, CEO

Professional Dancers Federation **[22764]**
6830 N Broadway, Ste. D
Denver, CO 80221
PH: (858)560-4372
Vargas, Yolanda, President

Professional Decorative Painters Association **[2488]**
PO Box 13427
Denver, CO 80201
Martinez, Andre, President

Promise Keepers **[20006]**
PO Box 11798
Denver, CO 80211-0798
Toll free: 866-776-6473
Fax: (303)433-1036
Washington, Dr. Raleigh, President

Raptor Education Foundation **[4875]**
PO Box 200400
Denver, CO 80220
PH: (303)680-8500
   (720)685-8100
Fax: (720)685-9988
Reshetniak, Mr. Peter, President

Riviera Owners Association **[21484]**
PO Box 261218
Denver, CO 80226-9218
PH: (303)233-2987
Fax: (303)984-0909
Knott, Ray, Director, Editor

Rock the Earth **[4099]**
1536 Wynkoop St., Ste. B200
Denver, CO 80202
PH: (303)454-3304
Fax: (303)454-3306
Ross, Marc, Exec. Dir.

Rocky Mountain Cichlid Association **[22036]**
PO Box 172403
Denver, CO 80217-2403
PH: (303)915-4992
Schumacher, Jesse, President

Society for Asian and Comparative Philosophy **[10121]**
c/o Geoffrey Ashton, Treasurer
University of Colorado
1800 Grant St., Ste. 800
Denver, CO 80203
Wang, Robin R., President

Society for Shamanic Practitioners **[20507]**
PO Box 100007
Denver, CO 80250
PH: (303)757-0908
Johnston, Sara, Exec. Dir.

Society for the Study of Psychiatry and Culture **[16838]**
c/o Dan Savin, Treasurer
6737 E 5th Ave.

Denver, CO 80220
PH: (717)848-2978
Kramer, Liz, Exec. Dir.

TechAssure Association **[3213]**
c/o Mark Ware, Chairman Elect
IMA
1705 17th St., Ste 100
Denver, CO 80202
PH: (888)208-8670
Lewis, Bill, Mem.

ThinkImpact **[12190]**
50 S Steele St., No. 328
Denver, CO 80209
PH: (303)377-3776
Garlick, Saul, Founder

U.S. Committee on Irrigation and Drainage **[7376]**
1616 17th St., No. 483
Denver, CO 80202
PH: (303)628-5430
Fax: (303)628-5431
Stephens, Larry D., Exec. VP

U.S. Meat Export Federation **[2312]**
1660 Lincoln St., Ste. 2800
Denver, CO 80264
PH: (303)623-6328
Fax: (303)623-0297
Nelson, Conley, Secretary, Treasurer

United States Potato Board **[4257]**
4949 S Syracuse St., Ste. 400
Denver, CO 80237
PH: (303)369-7783
Fax: (303)369-7718
Richardson, Blair, President, CEO

United States Society on Dams **[7377]**
1616 17th St., Ste. 483
Denver, CO 80202-1277
PH: (303)628-5430
Fax: (303)628-5431
Stephens, Larry D., Exec. Dir.

Up With People **[7804]**
6800 Broadway, Unit 106
Denver, CO 80221-2848
PH: (303)460-7100
Fax: (303)225-4649
Penny, Dale, President, CEO

Uplift Internationale **[16448]**
PO Box 181658
Denver, CO 80218
PH: (303)707-1361
Yrastorza, Jaime, DMD, Founder

Water for People **[12198]**
100 E Tennessee Ave.
Denver, CO 80209
PH: (720)488-4590
Allen, Eleanor, CEO, Secretary

WINGS Foundation **[12941]**
7550 W Yale Ave., Ste. B-201
Denver, CO 80227
PH: (303)238-8660
Fax: (303)238-4739
Stith, Jennifer, MAT, MA, Exec. Dir.

Women in Engineering ProActive Network **[3504]**
1901 E Asbury St., Ste. 220
Denver, CO 80210
PH: (303)871-4642
Matt, C. Diane, CAE, Exec. Dir.

Work for Progress **[12394]**
1543 Wazee St., Ste. 440
Denver, CO 80202-1450
PH: (303)801-0570

Combat Helicopter Pilots Association **[20668]**
PO Box 42
Divide, CO 80814-0042
Toll free: 800-832-5144
Brown, Mr. Jay, Exec. Dir.

Giant Schnauzer Club of America
[21886]
c/o Cindy Wallace, Membership
Chairperson
PO Box 967
Divide, CO 80814
Demchak, Kimberly, President

International Hedgehog Association
[10649]
PO Box 1060
Divide, CO 80814

Adaptive Sports Association [22769]
125 E 32nd St.
Durango, CO 81301
PH: (970)259-0374
Meighan, Ann Marie, Exec. Dir.

American Brush Manufacturers As-
sociation [1680]
736 Main Ave., Ste. 7
Durango, CO 81301
PH: (720)392-2262
Fax: (866)837-8450
Fultz, D. Mark, President

American Wilderness Coalition
[4785]
PO Box 2622
Durango, CO 81302-2622
PH: (202)266-0455
Watson, Melyssa, Chairperson

Distributed Wind Energy Association
[7387]
c/o Jennifer Jenkins, Executive
Director
1065 Main Ave., No. 209
Durango, CO 81301-5297
PH: (928)380-6012
Jenkins, Jennifer, Exec. Dir.

World Wide Association of Treasure
Seekers [22393]
361 S Camino Del Rio, Ste. 241
Durango, CO 81303-7997
Armstrong, Larry, Director

Society of Asian Scientists and
Engineers [6589]
PO Box 147139
Edgewater, CO 80214
Mitra, Shekhar, Founder, President

SOS Outreach [23176]
450 Miller Ranch Rd.
Edwards, CO 81632
PH: (970)926-9292
Fax: (970)306-0269
Merconi, Arn, Exec. Dir., Founder

American Fuzzy Lop Rabbit Club
[22397]
c/o Paula Grady, Secretary
PO Box 267
Elbert, CO 80106
Green, Carol, President

American Cut Glass Association
[22131]
c/o Bill Evans, Executive Secretary
PO Box 1147
Elizabeth, CO 80107-1147
Evans, Bill, Exec. Sec.

American College of Medical
Practice Executives [15574]
c/o Medical Group Management As-
sociation
104 Inverness Ter. E
Englewood, CO 80112-5306
PH: (303)799-1111
Toll free: 877-275-6462

American Institute of Mining, Metallurgical, and Petroleum Engineers
[6878]
12999 E Adam Aircraft Cir.
Englewood, CO 80112

PH: (303)325-5185
Fax: (888)702-0049
Lawrie-Munro, L. Michele, Exec. Dir.

American Sheep Industry Associa-
tion [4663]
9785 Maroon Cir., Ste. 360
Englewood, CO 80112
PH: (303)771-3500
Orwick, Peter, Exec. Dir.

Case for MS [15911]
4588 S Acoma St.
Englewood, CO 80110
PH: (303)781-0475
Storey, Linda, President

Christian Military Fellowship [19962]
PO Box 1207
Englewood, CO 80150-1207
PH: (303)761-1959
Toll free: 800-798-7875
Fax: (303)761-4577
Flynn, Bob, CEO, President

Good Sam Recreational Vehicle
Club [22424]
PO Box 6888
Englewood, CO 80155-6888
Toll free: 866-205-7451

Integrated Family Community
Services [12546]
3370 S Irving St.
Englewood, CO 80110-1816
PH: (303)789-0501
Fax: (303)789-3808
Blythe-Perry, Sandra, Exec. Dir.

Medical Group Management As-
sociation [15585]
104 Inverness Ter. E
Englewood, CO 80112-5306
PH: (303)799-1111
Toll free: 877-275-6462

National Costumers Association
[207]
PO Box 3406
Englewood, CO 80155
PH: (303)758-9611
Toll free: 800-NCA-1321
Fax: (303)758-9616
Grizzard, Karen, President

North American Limousin Foundation
[3745]
6 Inverness Ct. E, Ste. 260
Englewood, CO 80112-5595
PH: (303)220-1693
Toll free: 888-320-8747
Fax: (303)220-1884
Begert, Bret, President

North American Limousin Junior As-
sociation [3746]
N American Limousin Foundation
6 Inverness Ct. E, Ste. 260
Englewood, CO 80112-5595
PH: (303)220-1693
Fax: (303)220-1884
Corns, Randee, President

Officers' Christian Fellowship of the
U.S.A. [20002]
3784 S Inca St.
Englewood, CO 80110-3405
PH: (303)761-1984
Toll free: 800-424-1984
Warner, Brig. Gen. (Ret.) David B.,
Exec. Dir.

Performing Arts Medicine Associa-
tion [16932]
PO Box 117
Englewood, CO 80151
PH: (303)808-5643
Toll free: 866-408-7069
Massaro, Julie, Exec. Dir.

PSC Partners Seeking a Cure
[13790]
5237 S Kenton Way
Englewood, CO 80111
PH: (303)771-5227
Safer, Ms. Ricky, President

Society for Mining, Metallurgy, and
Exploration [6884]
12999 E Adam Aircraft Cir.
Englewood, CO 80112
PH: (303)948-4200
Toll free: 800-763-3132
Fax: (303)973-3845
Kanagy, David, Exec. Dir.

Truckers Against Trafficking [12017]
PO Box 816
Englewood, CO 80151
Paris, Kendis, Director

Western Athletic Conference [23264]
9250 E Costilla Ave., Ste. 300
Englewood, CO 80112
PH: (303)799-9221
Fax: (303)799-3888
Hurd, Jeff, Commissioner

World Sport Stacking Association
[23267]
11 Inverness Way S
Englewood, CO 80112
PH: (303)962-5667
Washburn, Roger, Contact

Youth for Christ/U.S.A. [20665]
7670 S Vaughn Ct.
Englewood, CO 80112
PH: (303)843-9000
Arkills, Bobby, Exec. Dir.

Alpaca Breeders of the Rockies
[3584]
PO Box 1965
Estes Park, CO 80517
PH: (970)586-5589
Toll free: 888-993-9898
Danielson, Ann, President

American Association for Horseman-
ship Safety [22954]
4125 Fish Creek Rd.
Estes Park, CO 80517
Toll free: 866-485-6800
Dawson, Jan, President

North American Study Group on Eth-
nomathematics [6825]
c/o Fredrick L. Silverman, Treasurer
1459 S St. Vrain Ave.
Estes Park, CO 80517-7318
Engblom-Bradley, Claudette,
Secretary

Story Circle Network [10227]
PO Box 1670
Estes Park, CO 80517-1670
PH: (970)235-1477
Moody, Ms. Peggy, Exec. Dir.

Alpha Gamma Omega [23707]
28000 Meadow Dr., Ste. 104
Evergreen, CO 80439

Association of Energy and
Environmental Real Estate Profes-
sionals [7884]
PO Box 1985
Evergreen, CO 80437
PH: (303)674-7770
Fax: (303)674-6599
Seiter, Doug, Advisor

Into Your Hands [8508]
PO Box 3981
Evergreen, CO 80437
PH: (720)491-1901
King, Julie, President

National Honey Board [1359]
11409 Business Park Cir., Ste. No.
210
Firestone, CO 80504-9200
PH: (303)776-2337
Barkman, Brent, Chairperson

American Hippotherapy Association,
Inc. [17432]
PO Box 2014
Fort Collins, CO 80522
PH: (970)818-1322
Toll free: 877-851-4592
Fax: (877)700-3498
McKenzie, Steve, President

Association of Collegiate Conference
and Events Directors International
[2322]
2900 S College Ave., Ste. 3B
Fort Collins, CO 80525
PH: (970)449-4960
Fax: (970)449-4965
Ebrahimi, Sharifa, CCEP, Treasurer

Association of Fraternal Leadership
& Values [23753]
PO Box 1576
Fort Collins, CO 80522-1576
PH: (970)372-1174
Koepsell, Mark, Exec. Dir.

Association of Fraternity/Sorority
Advisors [23754]
PO Box 1369
Fort Collins, CO 80522-1369
PH: (970)797-4361
Toll free: 888-855-8670
Kirk, Justin, Treasurer

Christian Chiropractors Association
Inc. [19953]
2550 Stover B-102
Fort Collins, CO 80525
PH: (970)482-1404
Toll free: 800-999-1970
Fax: (970)482-1538
Scharf, Brian K., President

Council for the Advancement of
Standards in Higher Education
[8613]
PO Box 1369
Fort Collins, CO 80522
PH: (202)862-1400
Garrett, Deborah, President

Envirofit International [4137]
109 N College Ave., Ste. 200
Fort Collins, CO 80524
PH: (970)372-2874
Fax: (970)221-1550
Bills, Ron, Chmn. of the Bd., CEO

Epsilon Sigma Alpha [23872]
363 W Drake Rd.
Fort Collins, CO 80526
PH: (970)223-2824
Fax: (970)223-4456
Price, Barbara, Secretary

A Face to Reframe [11997]
PO Box 273112
Fort Collins, CO 80527
PH: (970)213-9457
Bruno, Beth, MA, Exec. Dir.

Hospital-Based Massage Network
[15556]
612 S College Ave., No. 1
Fort Collins, CO 80524
PH: (970)407-9232
Toll free: 800-754-9790
Koch, Laura, Editor, Founder

International Integrative
Psychotherapy Association [16978]
c/o Wayne Carpenter, Trustee
5900 Greenwalt Ln.

Fort Collins, CO 80524-9508
Zavin, Joshua, PhD, President

International Union of Radio
Science-United States National
Committee **[7315]**
Colorado State University
Electrical and Computer Engineering
Dept.
1373 Campus Delivery
Fort Collins, CO 80523-1373
PH: (970)491-2228
Fax: (970)491-2249
Reising, Steven C., Chairman

International Veterinary Acupuncture
Society **[17652]**
1730 S College Ave., Ste. 301
Fort Collins, CO 80525
PH: (970)266-0666
Fax: (970)266-0777
Prevratil, Deborah, Exec. Dir.

Jacob Sheep Breeders Association
[4671]
c/o Mickey Ramirez, Liaison
2540 W Mulberry
Fort Collins, CO 80521
PH: (970)491-9750
Anderson, Gary, President

Life and Liberty for Women **[10430]**
PO Box 271778
Fort Collins, CO 80527-1778
PH: (970)217-7577
Loonan, Peggy, Exec. Dir., Founder

Mu Phi Epsilon International **[23829]**
PO Box 1369
Fort Collins, CO 80522-1369
Toll free: 888-259-1471
Debatin, Gloria, Contact

National Association for Interpreta-
tion **[6897]**
230 Cherry St., Ste. 200
Fort Collins, CO 80521
PH: (970)484-8283
Toll free: 888-900-8283
Fax: (970)484-8179
Caputo, Paul, Dep. Dir.

National Association of Veterans
Program Administrators **[21131]**
c/o Marc Barker, President
Colorado State University
Asst. Registrar, Military & Veterans
Benefits
1063 Campus Delivery
Fort Collins, CO 80523-1063
PH: (970)491-1342
Fax: (970)491-2283
Barker, Marc, President

National Earth Science Teachers
Association **[8552]**
PO Box 2716521
Fort Collins, CO 80527
PH: (201)519-1071
Manning, Cheryl, President

Neighbor to Neighbor **[17842]**
1550 Blue Spruce Dr.
Fort Collins, CO 80524
PH: (970)484-7498
Hallauer, Jake, Secretary

No Barriers Youth **[8718]**
224 Canyon Ave., Unit 207
Fort Collins, CO 80521
PH: (970)484-3633
Shurna, David, Exec. Dir., Founder

Open Water Foundation **[6282]**
320 E Vine Dr., Ste. 315
Fort Collins, CO 80524
PH: (970)286-7439
Fax: (970)286-7439
Malers, Steve, Founder

Sigma Iota Epsilon **[23809]**
c/o Dr. G. James Francis, President
Colorado State University
213 Rockwell Hall
Fort Collins, CO 80521
PH: (970)491-6265
(970)491-7200
Fax: (970)491-3522
Francis, Dr. G. James, President

The Spa Association **[2979]**
1001 E Harmony Rd., Ste. A 167
Fort Collins, CO 80525
PH: (970)682-6045
Minton, Melinda, Founder, Exec. Dir.

Trees, Water and People **[4106]**
633 Remington St.
Fort Collins, CO 80524
Toll free: 877-606-4TWP
Fax: (970)224-1726
Conway, Stuart, President

Village Earth: CSVBD **[11456]**
PO Box 797
Fort Collins, CO 80522
PH: (970)237-3002
Fax: (970)237-3026
Bartecchi, David, MA, Exec. Dir.

International Federation for Home
Economics USA **[7991]**
c/o Luann Boyer, Director of Finance
238 County Road 21
Fort Morgan, CO 80701-9337
Boyer, Luann, Dir. of Fin.

Professional Chef's Association, Inc.
[701]
PO Box 453
Frederick, CO 80530
PH: (720)379-8759
Neuhold, Walter, Founder

Association of Equipment Manage-
ment Professionals **[1713]**
823 Grand Ave.Ste. 300
Glenwood Springs, CO 81601
PH: (970)384-0510
Fax: (970)384-0512
Orr, Stan, President, Chief Sales
Ofc.

International Association of Natural
Resource Pilots **[3651]**
222 7 Oaks Rd.
Glenwood Springs, CO 81601
PH: (701)220-7248
(970)618-9483
Anderson, Paul, President

Alaskan Malamute Assistance
League **[10562]**
PO Box 7161
Golden, CO 80403
Ulman, Mike, Secretary

American Alpine Club **[22727]**
710 10th St., Ste. 100
Golden, CO 80401
PH: (303)384-0110
(303)384-0112
Fax: (303)384-0111
Buck, Deanne, Secretary

Applied Computational Electromag-
netics Society **[6414]**
Colorado School of Mines
310D Brown Bldg.
1610 Illinois St.
Golden, CO 80401
PH: (408)646-1111
Fax: (408)646-0300
Mohammed, Osama, Treasurer

Associated Bodywork & Massage
Professionals **[15554]**
25188 Genesee Trail Rd., Ste. 200
Golden, CO 80401

PH: (303)674-8478
Toll free: 800-667-8260

CCSVI Alliance **[15912]**
5019 Gladiola Way
Golden, CO 80403
Richardson, Sharon, Chairperson

Colorado School of Mines Alumni
Association **[23675]**
PO Box 1410
Golden, CO 80402
PH: (303)273-3295
Toll free: 800-446-9488
Fax: (303)273-3583
Priestley, Raymond, President

Ductile Iron Pipe Research Associa-
tion **[2604]**
PO Box 19206
Golden, CO 80402-6053
PH: (205)402-8700
Watson, Lynn, Dir. of Comm.

Energy Efficiency Business Coalition
[1111]
Bldg. 52, 3rd Fl.
14062 Denver West Pky.
Golden, CO 80401
PH: (720)274-9764
Detsky, Mark, Officer

Healing Waters International **[13327]**
15000 W 6th Ave., Ste. 404
Golden, CO 80401
PH: (303)526-7278
Toll free: 866-913-8522
Anderson, Ed, CEO

Highpointers Club **[22467]**
PO Box 1496
Golden, CO 80402
Comstack, Mark, VP

National Association of Professional
Martial Artists **[23005]**
14143 Denver West Pky., Ste. 100
Golden, CO 80401
PH: (727)540-0500
Fax: (727)683-9581
Oliver, Stephen, CEO

Outward Bound **[13206]**
910 Jackson St., Ste. 150
Golden, CO 80401-1977
Toll free: 866-467-7651
Skold, Lee, Chairman

Peruvian Hearts **[11130]**
24918 Genesee Trail Rd.
Golden, CO 80401
PH: (303)526-2756
Dodson, Judi, President

Pipeline Association for Public
Awareness **[2612]**
16361 Table Mountain Pky.
Golden, CO 80403-1826
PH: (719)375-3873
(248)205-7604
Snyder, Val, Director

Operation Interdependence **[12347]**
2695 Patterson, No. 2-147
Grand Junction, CO 81506
PH: (760)468-8001
Carley, Karon, CEO, President

Testicular Cancer Awareness
Foundation **[14073]**
202 North Ave., No. 305
Grand Junction, CO 81501
Toll free: 888-610-8223
Jones, Kim, Founder, CEO

Intercollegiate Women's Lacrosse
Coaches Association **[22973]**
PO Box 1124
Grand Lake, CO 80447

PH: (443)951-9611
Fax: (970)432-7058
Caro, Danie, Dir. of Comm.

Catholic Psychotherapy Association
[16967]
7251 W 20th St., M-2
Greeley, CO 80634
PH: (402)885-9272
Baars, Suzanne, President

Collegiate Soaring Association
[22487]
PO Box 337081
Greeley, CO 80633

Federation of Chiropractic Licensing
Boards **[14269]**
5401 W 10th St., Ste. 101
Greeley, CO 80634-4468
PH: (970)356-3500
Fax: (970)356-3599
Winkler, Carol, Reg. Dir.,
Chairperson

James A. Michener Society **[9064]**
c/o Kay A. Ferrell, Treasurer
1536 - 12th Ave.
Greeley, CO 80631-4734
Gambs, Edwin P., President

National Board of Chiropractic
Examiners **[14278]**
901 54th Ave.
Greeley, CO 80634
Toll free: 800-964-6223
Colucci, Margaret, Officer

National Onion Association **[4242]**
822 7th St., No. 510
Greeley, CO 80631
PH: (970)353-5895
Fax: (970)353-5897
Meyer, Mike, Trustee

Investment Management
Consultants Association **[2025]**
5619 DTC Pky., Ste. 500
Greenwood Village, CO 80111
PH: (303)770-3377
Fax: (303)770-1812
Walters, Sean, CAE, CEO, Exec.
Dir.

Women Writing the West **[3521]**
8547 E Arapahoe Rd., No. J-541
Greenwood Village, CO 80112-
1436
Baker, Doris, President

461st Bombardment Group Associa-
tion **[20680]**
c/o Hughes J. Glantzberg, President
PO Box 926
Gunnison, CO 81230
Glantzberg, Hughes, President

International Hearing Dog **[15197]**
5901 E 89th Ave.
Henderson, CO 80640
PH: (303)287-3277
Fax: (303)287-3425
Foss-Brugger, Valerie, Exec. Dir.,
President

Berger Picard Club of America
[21839]
1071 S Lakeside Dr.
Hesperus, CO 81326
PH: (970)749-5540
Black, Valerie, VP

Great Britain Collectors Club **[21658]**
10309 Brookhollow Cir.
Highlands Ranch, CO 80129-1800

Pro Athletes Outreach **[20160]**
640 Plaza Dr., Ste. 110
Highlands Ranch, CO 80129
Fax: (408)674-6161
Stenstrom, Steve, President

Cushman Club of America [22219]
c/o Patty Dart, Treasurer
PO Box 102
Indian Hills, CO 80454
PH: (303)697-4436
Dart, Patty, Treasurer

Order of the Indian Wars [9806]
PO Box 1650
Johnstown, CO 80534-1650
Koury, Mike, Chairman

Keystone Policy Center [6731]
1628 St. John Rd.
Keystone, CO 80435
PH: (970)513-5800
Fax: (970)262-0152
Alexander, Sarah Stokes, VP

Souvenir Wholesale Distributors Association [2978]
32770 Arapahoe Rd., No. 132-155
Lafayette, CO 80026
Toll free: 888-599-4474
Fax: (888)589-7610
Rohnke, Angie, President

USA Rugby [23115]
2655 Crescent Dr., Unit A
Lafayette, CO 80026
PH: (303)539-0300
Fax: (303)539-0311
Melville, Nigel, CEO

52 Plus Joker [21604]
12290 W 18th Dr.
Lakewood, CO 80215
Dawson, Tom, President

American Animal Hospital Association [17590]
12575 W Bayaud Ave.
Lakewood, CO 80228-2021
PH: (303)986-2800
Toll free: 800-252-2242
Fax: (303)986-1700
Knutson, Kate S., President

American Bail Coalition [5063]
225 Union Blvd., Ste. 150
Lakewood, CO 80228
PH: (303)885-5872
Toll free: 855-718-3006
Clayton, Jeffrey J., Director

American College of Veterinary Internal Medicine [17618]
1997 Wadsworth Blvd.
Lakewood, CO 80214-5293
PH: (303)231-9933
Toll free: 800-245-9081
Fax: (303)231-0880
Herman, Roberta, CEO

Colorado Christian University Alumni Association [19318]
8787 W Alameda Ave.
Lakewood, CO 80226
PH: (303)963-3330
Toll free: 800-44F-AITH
Seatvet, Daniel, President

Council of Petroleum Accountants Societies [22]
445 Union Blvd., Ste. 207
Lakewood, CO 80228
PH: (303)300-1131
Toll free: 877-992-6727
Fax: (303)300-3733
Wright, Jeff, President

Dodge Family Association [20855]
10105 W 17th Pl.
Lakewood, CO 80215-2863
PH: (303)237-4947
Dodge, Norman E., President

Federal Employee Education and Assistance Fund [19574]
3333 S Wadsworth Blvd., Ste. 300
Lakewood, CO 80227

PH: (303)933-7580
Toll free: 800-323-4140
Fax: (303)933-7587
Bauer, Steve, Exec. Dir.

Healing Beyond Borders [15007]
445 Union Blvd., Ste. 105
Lakewood, CO 80228
PH: (303)989-7982
Anselme, Lisa, Exec. Dir.

International Mine Water Association [6880]
c/o Itasca Denver, Inc.
143 Union Blvd., Ste. 525
Lakewood, CO 80228
PH: (303)969-8033
Geroni, Dr. Jennifer, Treasurer

Jeffco Schools Foundation [18037]
Bldg. No. 1
809 Quail St.
Lakewood, CO 80215
PH: (303)982-2210
Inman, Sam, President

Lighthouse Stamp Society [22383]
c/o Dalene Thomas
1805 S Balsam St., Apt. 106
Lakewood, CO 80232
Thomas, Dalene, Contact

Mars Society [7218]
11111 W 8th Ave., Unit A
Lakewood, CO 80215-5516
PH: (303)980-0890
Zubrin, Dr. Robert, Founder, President

Ministry Architecture, Inc. [5971]
1904 S Union Pl.
Lakewood, CO 80228-5704
PH: (303)989-4870
Fax: (303)989-0884
Rosenberg, Leonard C., AIA, Exec. Dir.

Namlo International [12171]
8790 W Colfax Ave., Ste. 100
Lakewood, CO 80215
PH: (303)399-3649
Fax: (303)399-1995
Frausto, Keith, Exec. Dir.

National Ski Areas Association [1674]
133 S Van Gordon St., Ste. 300
Lakewood, CO 80228
PH: (303)987-1111
Fax: (303)986-2345
Berry, Michael, President

National Ski Patrol System [23166]
133 S Van Gordon St., Ste. 100
Lakewood, CO 80228
PH: (303)988-1111
Fax: (303)988-3005
McMahon, John, Exec. Dir.

Professional Ski Instructors of America and American Association of Snowboard Instructors [23167]
133 S Van Gordon St., Ste. 200
Lakewood, CO 80228
Toll free: 844-340-7669
Dorsey, Mark, Exec. Dir., CEO

StreetSchool Network [8772]
1380 Ammons St.
Lakewood, CO 80214
PH: (720)299-3420
   (720)425-1642
Tillapaugh, Mr. Tom, Founder, President

Village Science [11471]
10707 W Center Ave.
Lakewood, CO 80226
Spelman, Justin, Exec. Dir.

Women in Mining [2390]
PO Box 260246
Lakewood, CO 80226
Toll free: 866-537-9694
Bray, Darlene, President

Complex Weavers [243]
PO Box 1237
Laporte, CO 80535-1237
Spangler, Kathi, VP, Director

Accreditation Review Council on Education in Surgical Technology and Surgical Assisting [15670]
6 W Dry Creek Cir., Ste. 110
Littleton, CO 80120
PH: (303)694-9262
Fax: (303)741-3655
Orloff, Keith, Exec. Dir.

Alliance of International Aromatherapists [13584]
9956 W Remington Pl., Unit A10, Ste. 323
Littleton, CO 80128-6733
PH: (303)531-6377
Toll free: 877-531-6377
Fax: (303)979-7135
d'Angelo, Raphael, M.D., President

American Association for Crystal Growth [6358]
10922 Main Range Trl.
Littleton, CO 801287
PH: (303)539-6907
Fax: (303)600-5144
Schunemann, Peter, Officer

American Association of Neuro-pathologists [16569]
5575 S Sycamore St., Ste. 235
Littleton, CO 80120
PH: (440)793-6565
   (720)372-0888
Fax: (303)568-0406
Montine, Thomas J., President

Association of Surgical Technologists [15682]
6 W Dry Creek Cir., Ste. 200
Littleton, CO 80120-8031
PH: (303)694-9130
Toll free: 800-637-7433
Fax: (303)694-9169
Zacharias, Roy, President

Automobile Competition Committee for the United States FIA [22522]
7800 S Elati St., Ste. 303
Littleton, CO 80120-4456
PH: (303)730-8100
Fax: (303)730-8108
Jones, Robyn A., Contact

BACCHUS Network [13127]
PO Box 938
Littleton, CO 80160
PH: (303)871-0901
Fax: (202)379-7704

Care 4 Kids Worldwide [10883]
PO Box 630704
Littleton, CO 80163
Thompson, Nara, Founder

Community Aid Relief and Development [12647]
PO Box 632162
Littleton, CO 80163
PH: (720)432-7027
Neill, Steve, Exec. Dir., President

Indigo Threads [11383]
1601 W Canal Ct.
Littleton, CO 80120
PH: (760)564-2679
Meyer, Mary D., Project Mgr., Founder, President

Murray Clan Society of North America [20903]
c/o Steve Murray-Wolf, President
5764 S Kline St.
Littleton, CO 80127
Murray, Evelyn M.E., FSA, Mem.

National Adult Baseball Association [22554]
5944 S Kipling St., Ste. 200
Littleton, CO 80127
Toll free: 800-621-6479
Fugita, Shane, Director, President

National Board of Surgical Technology and Surgical Assisting [13497]
6 W Dry Creek Cir., Ste. 100
Littleton, CO 80120
Toll free: 800-707-0057
Fax: (303)325-2536
Fisher, Crit, President

National Coal Transportation Association [739]
4 W Meadow Lark Ln., Ste. 100
Littleton, CO 80127-5718
Canter, Thomas C., Exec. Dir.

National Coalition Against Violent Athletes [22511]
PO Box 620453
Littleton, CO 80162
PH: (303)524-9853
Redmond, Katherine, Founder

National Public Safety Telecom-munications Council [3235]
8191 Southpark Ln., Unit 205
Littleton, CO 80120-4641
Toll free: 866-807-4755
Fax: (303)649-1844
Battalion, John Lenihan, Comm. Chm.

OMF International U.S. [20450]
10 W Dry Creek Cir.
Littleton, CO 80120-4413
PH: (303)730-4165
Toll free: 800-422-5330
Potter, Barry, VP of Personnel

Pandas International [4867]
PO Box 620335
Littleton, CO 80162
PH: (303)933-2365
Braden, Suzanne, Director

Pura Vida [11209]
9609 S University Blvd.
Littleton, CO 80163
PH: (303)215-0994
Toll free: 888-845-8963
Fax: (303)215-0995
Ely, Mark, Founder, Exec. Dir.

Road to Hope [11141]
PO Box 210
Littleton, CO 80160
Harris, Richard, Founder

Society of American Magicians [22179]
c/o Manon Rodriguez, Administrator
4927 S Oak Ct.
Littleton, CO 80127
PH: (303)362-0575
Rodriguez, Manon, Administrator

Society of Economic Geologists [6682]
7811 Shaffer Pky.
Littleton, CO 80127-3732
PH: (720)981-7882
Fax: (720)981-7874
Hoal, Brian G., Exec. Dir.

Society for Range Management [4620]
6901 S Pierce St., Ste. 225
Littleton, CO 80128

PH: (303)986-3309
Fax: (303)986-3892
Howery, Larry D., 1st VP

Wheelchair and Ambulatory Sports, USA [22805]
PO Box 621023
Littleton, CO 80162
PH: (720)412-7979
Toll free: 866-204-8018

World Cultural Heritage Voices [9238]
PO Box 3584
Littleton, CO 80161
PH: (720)352-5092
Chamanara, Soudy, Chairperson

WorldVenture [19745]
1501 W Mineral Ave.
Littleton, CO 80120
PH: (720)283-2000
Fax: (720)283-9383
Macfarland, Randy, Chmn. of the Bd.

Aquatic & Fitness Professional Association International [23062]
547 WCR 18
Longmont, CO 80504
Fax: (303)678-9989
Holcomb Krafft, Ms. Cynthia, PhD, President

Association of Waldorf Schools of North America [8002]
515 Kimbark, Ste. 106
Longmont, CO 80501
PH: (612)870-8310
Bertelsen, Val, III, VP

Conservative Baptist Association of America [19727]
3686 Stagecoach Rd., Ste. F
Longmont, CO 80504
PH: (720)283-3030
Russell, Rev. Allen, Director

First Nations Development Institute [12375]
2432 Main St., 2nd Fl.
Longmont, CO 80501
PH: (303)774-7836
Fax: (303)774-7841
Roberts, Michael, President

International Association for Disaster Preparedness and Response [14663]
PO Box 797
Longmont, CO 80502-0797
Wilson, Bascombe J., Exec. Dir.

Lalmba Association [12693]
1000 Corey St.
Longmont, CO 80501
PH: (303)485-1810
Downey, Hugh, Founder

The Masonry Society [6812]
105 S Sunset St., Ste. Q
Longmont, CO 80501-6172
PH: (303)939-9700
Fax: (303)541-9215
Samblanet, Phillip J., Exec. Dir.

Native American Fish and Wildlife Society [4089]
1055 17th Ave., Ste. 91
Longmont, CO 80501
PH: (303)466-1725
Toll free: 866-890-7258
Fax: (303)466-5414
Matt, D. Fred, Exec. Dir.

North American Boxing Federation [22716]
911 Kimbark St.
Longmont, CO 80501

PH: (303)442-0258
Fax: (303)442-0380
Ford, Duane B., President

Western Winter Sports Representatives Association [3167]
726 Tenacity Dr., Unit B
Longmont, CO 80504
PH: (303)532-4002
Fax: (866)929-4572
Morton, Linda, Rep.

Cable Television Laboratories, Inc. [691]
858 Coal Creek Cir.
Louisville, CO 80027-9750
PH: (303)661-9100
Fax: (303)661-9199
McKinney, Phil, CEO, President

EDUCAUSE [8029]
282 Century Pl., Ste. 5000
Louisville, CO 80027
PH: (303)449-4430
Fax: (303)440-0461
Hogue, Bill, Treasurer

Gottscheer Heritage and Genealogy Association [19447]
PO Box 725
Louisville, CO 80027-0725
Rees, Mary ', Membership Chp.

International Association for Public Participation Practitioners [5733]
PO Box 270723
Louisville, CO 80027-5012
Cochrane, Kylie, Secretary

International Cryogenic Materials Conference [6357]
908 Main St., Ste. 230
Louisville, CO 80027
PH: (303)499-2299
Fax: (303)499-2599
Goldacker, Wilfried, President

Louis and Harold Price Foundation [13069]
1371 E Hecla Dr., Ste. B-1
Louisville, CO 80027
PH: (303)665-9201
Fax: (303)665-1027
Leuthauser, Kishawn, VP, Director

National Association of Psychometrists [16927]
275 Century Circle, Ste 203
275 Century Cir., Ste. 203
Louisville, CO 80027
Porter, Pamela, MA, President

Attunement Guild [13608]
c/o Bob Ewing, Practitioner
100 Sunrise Ranch Rd.
Loveland, CO 80538
Ewing, Bob, Contact

Loving More [12946]
PO Box 1658
Loveland, CO 80539
PH: (970)667-5683
Trask, Robyn, Exec. Dir.

Motorcycle Touring Association [23040]
PO Box 2394
Loveland, CO 80539
PH: (970)663-2044
Jarrow, Paul, President

Operation Kid-To-Kid [11111]
1515 Cascade Ave.
Loveland, CO 80538
Toll free: 800-385-4545

Tree-Ring Society [4220]
4624 Foothills Dr.
Loveland, CO 80537
Kennedy-Sutherland, Elaine, President

Biomagnetic Therapy Association [17439]
PO Box 394
Lyons, CO 80540
PH: (303)823-0307
Balliett, Suzy, Founder

Christian Anti-Communism Crusade [17802]
PO Box 129
Manitou Springs, CO 80829-0129
PH: (719)685-9043
Noebel, Dr. David, President

National Association for Legal Support of Alternative Schools [7490]
c/o Ed Nagel, Coordinator/Chairman
1 Alceda Ct.
Moffat, CO 81143-9792
PH: (719)298-3020
Nagel, Ed, Coord., Chairman, CEO

Wild Felid Research and Management Association [4903]
PO Box 3335
Montrose, CO 81402-3335
PH: (970)252-1928
Sweanor, Linda, Officer

American Custom Gunmakers Guild [1292]
445 Harness Way
Monument, CO 80132
Ullman, Michael D., President

American National CattleWomen [3706]
15954 Jackson Creek Pky., Ste. B 225
Monument, CO 80132
PH: (303)850-3441
Fax: (303)694-2390
Bowen, Shelia, Rec. Sec.

North American Corriente Association [3744]
PO Box 2698
Monument, CO 80132
PH: (719)425-9151
Mara, Ricky L., President

Energy Services Coalition [6481]
5590 Crestbrook Dr.
Morrison, CO 80465
Arwood, Jim, Exec. Dir.

United States Peruvian Horse Association [4422]
PO Box 249
Morrison, CO 80465
PH: (303)697-9567

Professional and Organizational Development Network in Higher Education [7970]
PO Box 3318
Nederland, CO 80466
PH: (303)258-9521
Fax: (303)258-7377
Barry, Kevin, President

APA Division 12: Society of Clinical Psychology [16870]
PO Box 1082
Niwot, CO 80544-1082
PH: (303)652-3126
Fax: (303)652-2723
Sobell, Mark, PhD, Rep.

IVI Foundation [6322]
PO Box 1016
Niwot, CO 80544-1016
PH: (303)652-2585
Fax: (303)652-1444
Helsel, Bob, Director

PXI Systems Alliance [6331]
PO Box 1016
Niwot, CO 80544-1016

PH: (303)652-2585
Fax: (303)652-1444
Helsel, Bob, Exec. Dir.

Society for a Science of Clinical Psychology [16944]
PO Box 1082
Niwot, CO 80544
PH: (303)652-3126
Fax: (303)652-2723
Smith, Dave, Liaison

VXIbus Consortium [7329]
PO Box 1016
Niwot, CO 80544-1016
PH: (303)652-2585
Fax: (303)652-1444
Helsel, Bob, Exec. Dir.

American Treibball Association [22532]
PO Box 33780
Northglenn, CO 80233-0780
PH: (303)718-7705
Lane, Hilary, Secretary, Treasurer

International Titanium Association [2352]
11674 Huron St., Ste. 100
Northglenn, CO 80234
PH: (303)404-2221
Fax: (303)404-9111
Stager, Chad, Rep.

Search and Rescue Dogs of the United States [11695]
46848 Highway 61
Otis, CO 80743
Hiebert, Jeff, President

Laughter Therapy Enterprises [17451]
c/o Enda Junkins
PO Box 684
Ouray, CO 81427
PH: (970)325-0050
Funt, Peter, President

Mission Training International [20439]
421 Highway 105
Palmer Lake, CO 80133
PH: (719)487-0111
Toll free: 800-896-3710
Fax: (719)487-9350
Wilhelm, Carl, Chmn. of the Bd.

American Association for Emergency Psychiatry [16812]
PO Box 3948
Parker, CO 80134
Toll free: 877-749-0737
Fax: (720)496-4974
Nordstrom, Kimberly D., MD, President

American Salers Association [3710]
19590 E Main St., Ste. 202
Parker, CO 80138
PH: (303)770-9292
Fax: (303)770-9302
Doubet, Sherry, Exec. VP

American Salers Junior Association [3711]
American Salers Association
19590 E Main St., No. 104
Parker, CO 80138
PH: (303)770-9292
Fax: (303)770-9302
Leibhart, Allison, President

Association of Deans and Directors of University Colleges & Undergraduate Studies [7624]
PO Box 3948
Parker, CO 80134-1443
PH: (720)496-4974
Toll free: 844-705-3293
Hood, David S., President

Association of Dental Support Organizations [14420]
19751 E Mainstreet, Ste. 340
Parker, CO 80138
PH: (720)379-5342
Fax: (720)379-5409
Dufurrena, Dr. Quinn, Exec. Dir.

Gamma Sigma Alpha [19434]
PO Box 3948
Parker, CO 80134
Toll free: 866-793-5406
Smithhisler, Peter, President

Invisible Disabilities Association [14551]
PO Box 4067
Parker, CO 80134
Connell, Wayne, Founder, President

National Writers Association [2709]
10940 S Parker Rd., No. 508
Parker, CO 80134
PH: (303)841-0246
Fax: (303)841-2607
Whelchel, Sandy, Editor

North American South Devon Association [3749]
19590 E Main St., Ste. 104
Parker, CO 80138
PH: (303)770-3130
Fax: (303)770-9302
Giess, Dar, President

Pregnancy Loss and Infant Death Alliance [10776]
PO Box 658
Parker, CO 80134
Toll free: 888-693-1435
Fax: (866)705-9251
Lammert, Catherine, RN, President

Veterinary Orthopedic Society [17674]
PO Box 665
Parker, CO 80134
PH: (720)335-6051
Probst, Maralyn R., Exec. Sec.

National Mill Dog Rescue [10672]
5335 JD Johnson Rd.
Peyton, CO 80831
PH: (719)445-6787
Toll free: 888-495-DOGS
Fax: (866)718-1185
Strader, Theresa, RN, Founder, Exec. Dir.

Pro Players Association [13306]
PO Box 396
Peyton, CO 80831
PH: (720)327-9207
Adler, Gary R., CEO, Founder, President

Fairy Lamp Club [21652]
PO Box 438
Pine, CO 80470-0438
Brown, Dee, President, Curator

Genealogical Society of Hispanic America [20970]
PO Box 3040
Pueblo, CO 81005-3040
Craig, Bob, President

National Major Gang Task Force [5144]
PO Box 3689
Pueblo, CO 81005
PH: (719)226-4915
Vigil, Daryl A., Exec. Dir.

North American Piedmontese Cattle Association [3748]
1740 County Road 185
Ramah, CO 80832

PH: (306)329-8600
Johnson, Vicki, Exec. Dir.

American Association of Orthopedic Medicine [16462]
555 Waterview Ln.
Ridgway, CO 81432
Toll free: 888-687-1920
Fax: (970)626-5033
Trister, Jon, MD, Fac. Memb.

Wheat Foods Council [1525]
51 Red Fox Ln., Unit D
Ridgway, CO 81432
PH: (970)275-4440
O'Connor, Tim, President

International Communications Agency Network [771]
PO Box 490
Rollinsville, CO 80474
PH: (808)965-8240
Fax: (303)484-4087
Burandt, Mr. Gary, Contact

Erosion Control Technology Council [4685]
8357 N Rampart Range Rd., Unit 106, PMB 154
Roxborough, CO 80125-9365
PH: (720)353-4977
Fax: (612)235-8454
Honnigford, Laurie L., Exec. Dir.

International Association of Geosynthetic Installers [869]
8357 N Rampart Range Rd., Unit 106
Roxborough, CO 80125
PH: (720)353-4977
Fax: (612)235-6484
Honnigford, Laurie, Managing Dir.

North American Trail Ride Conference [23330]
PO Box 224
Sedalia, CO 80135
PH: (303)688-1677
Fax: (303)688-3022
Cowart, Kim, President

IMS Forum [7309]
PO Box 10000
Silverthorne, CO 80498-1000
PH: (970)262-6100
Fax: (407)641-9595
Khalilian, Michael, Chairman, President

Challenge Aspen at Snowmass [22779]
PO Box 6639
Snowmass Village, CO 81615
PH: (970)923-0578
Fax: (970)923-7338
Cowan, Houston, CEO, Founder

International Brotherhood of Motorcycle Campers [23038]
PO Box 24
South Fork, CO 81154
PH: (435)650-3290
(719)873-5466
Goldsmith, Michelle, Director

International Federation for Biblio/Poetry Therapy [16977]
1625 Mid Valley Dr., No. 1, Ste. 126
Steamboat Springs, CO 80487
de Wardt, Susan, Treasurer, Secretary, Comm. Chm.

International M-100 Group [21403]
c/o Francis Abate
PO Box 880283
Steamboat Springs, CO 80488
Love, Arthur, Mem.

World Footbag Association [23266]
2673 Jacob Cir., Unit 400
Steamboat Springs, CO 80487

PH: (970)870-9898
Toll free: 800-878-8797
Guettich, Bruce, Founder

LightHawk [3896]
PO Box 2710
Telluride, CO 81435
PH: (970)797-9355
Ryan, Emilie, CFO

American Institute of Professional Geologists [6677]
12000 Washington St.
Thornton, CO 80241
PH: (303)412-6205
Fax: (303)253-9220

Association for Women Geoscientists [6685]
12000 N Washington St., Ste. 285
Thornton, CO 80241-3134
PH: (303)412-6219
Fax: (303)253-9220

Carbon Monoxide Safety Association [17495]
12500 1st St., Ste. 5
Thornton, CO 80241
Toll free: 800-394-5253
Fax: (800)546-3726
Dwyer, Bob, Contact

Developing Hands [10955]
1602 E 100th Pl.
Thornton, CO 80229
PH: (303)949-2363
Carr, Jim, VP

American Academy of Veterinary Pharmacology and Therapeutics [17589]
PO Box 103
Timnath, CO 80547-0103
Gehring, Ronette, President

GTO Association of America [21390]
PO Box 213
Timnath, CO 80547
Oxler, Thomas, President

Association of Graduates of the United States Air Force Academy [19305]
3116 Academy Dr.
USAF Academy, CO 80840-4475
PH: (719)472-0300
Fax: (719)333-4194
Thompson, William T., CEO, President

International Association of Correctional Training Personnel [11531]
PO Box 274
Walsenburg, CO 81089
PH: (719)738-9969
Fax: (719)744-9561
Perdue, Randy, Bd. Member

Galgo Rescue International Network [10627]
17784 N County Road 15
Wellington, CO 80549-2030
Christman, Abigail, CVT, Director

Mission: Wolf [4843]
PO Box 1211
Westcliffe, CO 81252
PH: (719)859-2157
Gaarde, Mike, Officer

Alliance of Marine Mammal Parks and Aquariums [4462]
2850 Ranch Reserve Ln.
Westminster, CO 80234
PH: (720)887-5921

American Gelbvieh Association [3692]
10900 Dover St.
Westminster, CO 80021

PH: (303)465-2333
Goes, Mark, President

Association of Blauvelt Descendants [20781]
3367 W 113th Ave.
Westminster, CO 80031
Blauvelt, George A., President

Children's Grief Education Association [10773]
6883 Wyman Way
Westminster, CO 80030
PH: (303)246-3826
Lyles, Mary M., PhD, Exec. Dir.

International Association of Biblical Counselors [20042]
11500 Sheridan Blvd.
Westminster, CO 80020
Toll free: 844-843-4222
Bulkley, Dr. Ed, President

National Alliance for Drug Endangered Children [13159]
9101 Harlan St., Ste. 245
Westminster, CO 80031
PH: (612)860-1599
Noerenberg, Chuck, President, Bd. Member

National Bison Association [4479]
8690 Wolff Ct., No. 200
Westminster, CO 80031
PH: (303)292-2833
Fax: (303)845-9081
Anderson, Bruce, President

National Hearing Conservation Association [15205]
12011 Tejon St., Ste. 700
Westminster, CO 80234
PH: (303)224-9022
Fax: (303)458-0002
Wojcik, Nancy, MS, Dir. of Comm.

North American Hazardous Materials Management Association [6705]
12011 Tejon St., Ste. 700
Westminster, CO 80234
PH: (303)451-5945
Toll free: 877-292-1403
Fax: (303)458-0002
Hodge, Victoria L., President

Scrum Alliance, Inc. [6334]
7401 Church Ranch Blvd., No. 210
Westminster, CO 80021-5539
Gonzalez, Manny, CEO

World Senior Golf Federation [22899]
PO Box 350667
Westminster, CO 80035-0667
PH: (303)920-4206
Fax: (303)920-8206
Clark, Sherry, Exec. Dir.

WSA Fraternal Life [19503]
11265 Decatur St., Ste. 100
Westminster, CO 80234
PH: (303)451-1494
Toll free: 800-451-7528
Fax: (303)451-5112
Kogovsek, John, Chmn. of the Bd.

American Association for the History of Nursing [9450]
10200 W 44th Ave., Ste. 304
Wheat Ridge, CO 80033
PH: (303)422-2685
Fax: (720)881-6101
Whelan, Jean, President

American Right To Life [12761]
PO Box 1145
Wheat Ridge, CO 80034
PH: (303)753-9341
Toll free: 888-888-2785
Hanks, Leslie, President

Association for Applied Psychophysiology and Biofeedback [13816]
10200 W 44th Ave., Ste. 304
Wheat Ridge, CO 80033-2840
PH: (303)422-8436
Toll free: 800-477-8892
Stumph, David, Exec. Dir.

Association of Community Health Nursing Educators [16119]
10200 W 44th Ave., Ste. 304
Wheat Ridge, CO 80033
PH: (303)422-0769
     (720)881-6044
Fax: (303)422-8894
Stanhope, Marcia, Ph.D, VP

Association of Healthcare Internal Auditors [15580]
10200 W 44th Ave., Ste. 304
Wheat Ridge, CO 80033
PH: (303)327-7546
Toll free: 888-ASK-AHIA
Fax: (720)881-6101
Richstone, David, Chairman

Association of Professional Genealogists [20957]
PO Box 535
Wheat Ridge, CO 80034-0535
PH: (303)465-6980
Powell, Kimberly T., President

Cognitive Science Society [5985]
10200 W 44th Ave., Ste. 304
Wheat Ridge, CO 80033-2840
PH: (303)327-7547
Fax: (720)881-6101
Newcombe, Nora, Chairperson

Council of Science Editors [2675]
10200 W 44th Ave., Ste. 304
Wheat Ridge, CO 80033
PH: (720)881-6046
Fax: (720)881-6101
Cochran, Angela, President

International Food Service Executives Association [1390]
4955 Miller St., Ste. 107
Wheat Ridge, CO 80033
Toll free: 800-893-5499
Wright, Fred, Chairman

Professional Electrical Apparatus Recyclers League [1033]
10200 W 44th Ave., Ste. 304
Wheat Ridge, CO 80033
PH: (720)881-6043
Fax: (720)881-6101
Powell, Doug, President, Chairperson

Professional Society of Forensic Mapping [5251]
4964 Ward Rd.
Wheat Ridge, CO 80033
Boots, Kent E., President

Society for Scholarly Publishing [2813]
10200 W 44th Ave., Ste. 304
Wheat Ridge, CO 80033
PH: (303)422-3914
Fax: (720)881-6101
Crosse, Ann Mehan, CAE, Exec. Dir.

Alpines International Club [3586]
10447 Weld County Road 70
Windsor, CO 80550
PH: (970)686-6672

Associated Schools of Construction [7664]
PO Box 29
Windsor, CO 80550-0029
PH: (970)988-1130
Fax: (970)282-0396
Brown, Lori A., President

His Little Feet [11032]
1555 Main St., Ste. A3-290
Windsor, CO 80550
Toll free: 866-252-3988
Hahn, Mike, Founder, President

Bertrand Russell Society [9095]
c/o Michael Berumen, Treasurer
37155 Dickerson Run
Windsor, CO 80550
PH: (802)295-9058
Trainer, Chad, Chmn. of the Bd.

Soil and Plant Analysis Council [7193]
347 N Shores Cir.
Windsor, CO 80550
PH: (970)686-5702
     (352)392-1951
Mikkelsen, Robert, VP

U.S. Metric Association [7239]
PO Box 471
Windsor, CO 80550-0471
PH: (310)832-3763
Trusten, Paul, Editor

CONNECTICUT

Cornelia de Lange Syndrome Foundation [13828]
302 W Main St., No. 100
Avon, CT 06001
PH: (860)676-8166
     (860)676-8255
Toll free: 800-223-8355
Fax: (860)676-8337

Fermata Arts Foundation [8854]
24 Brentwood Dr.
Avon, CT 06001
PH: (860)404-1781
Fax: (860)404-1781
Cummings, Sean, President

North American Cockatiel Society [21547]
PO Box 143
Bethel, CT 06801-0143
Kiesewetter, Cynthia, President

Society for Experimental Mechanics [7247]
7 School St.
Bethel, CT 06801-1405
PH: (203)790-6373
Fax: (203)790-4472
Zimmermann, Kristin, Exec. Dir., Secretary

Society of Plastics Engineers [6597]
6 Berkshire Blvd., Ste. 306
Bethel, CT 06801
PH: (203)775-0471
Fax: (203)775-8490
Al-Zu'bi, Dr. Raed, President

American Academy of Psychiatry and the Law [5270]
1 Regency Dr.
Bloomfield, CT 06002-2310
PH: (860)242-5450
Toll free: 800-331-1389
Fax: (860)286-0787
Coleman, Jacquelyn T., Exec. Dir.

American Academy of Psychoanalysis and Dynamic Psychiatry [16840]
1 Regency Dr.
Bloomfield, CT 06002
Toll free: 888-691-8281
Fax: (860)286-0787
Coleman, Jacquelyn T., CAE, Exec. Dir.

Builders Exchange Network [858]
c/o Kristin Loney, Executive Director
1 Regency Dr.

Bloomfield, CT 06002
PH: (860)243-3977
Fax: (860)286-0787
Cowan, Daniel, Mem.

Fidelco Guide Dog Foundation [17699]
103 Vision Way
Bloomfield, CT 06002
PH: (860)243-5200
     (860)243-4044
Fax: (860)769-0567
Nelson, Doug, VP, Dir. of Dev.

Health Horizons International [15468]
1 Regency Dr.
Bloomfield, CT 06002
PH: (860)243-3977
Fax: (860)286-0787
Geier, Elizabeth, Exec. Dir.

North American Association of Christians in Social Work [13115]
PO Box 121
Botsford, CT 06404-0121
Toll free: 888-426-4712
Chamiec-Case, Rick, PhD, Exec. Dir.

Food Allergy Education Network [13576]
1 Wildwood Dr.
Branford, CT 06405
PH: (203)206-3141
Lee, Gina Mennett, MEd, Founder, President

Haiti Works! [12159]
PO Box 55483
Bridgeport, CT 06610-5483
PH: (203)526-3542
     (203)908-4007
d'Haiti, Pierre F., MBS, President

Service for Peace [18829]
360 Fairfield Ave.
Bridgeport, CT 06604
PH: (203)339-0064
Fax: (203)339-0874
Lenaghan, Michael J., Chmn. of the Bd.

Citizens for Legitimate Government [18311]
PO Box 1142
Bristol, CT 06011-1142
Rectenwald, Michael, PhD, Chairman, Founder

Hearts Around the World [14117]
PO Box 5336
Brookfield, CT 06804
PH: (203)733-3222
Jarrett, Robert M., MD, President

Republican Liberty Caucus [19047]
PO Box 64
Brookfield, CT 06804
PH: (202)524-9581
Toll free: 866-752-5423
Nalle, Mr. Dave, Reg. Dir.

MG Vintage Racers [22400]
c/o Chris Meyers, President
55 Belden Rd.
Burlington, CT 06013
Meyers, Chris, Editor, President

National Organization of Sisters of Color Ending Sexual Assault [12929]
PO Box 625
Canton, CT 06019
Brade, Condencia, Exec. Dir.

Distressed Children and Infants International [10956]
195 S Main St.
Cheshire, CT 06410

PH: (203)272-3869
Toll free: 866-516-7495
Fax: (203)272-3869
DeBroff, Dr. Brian M., President

National Society of Compliance Professionals [1515]
22 Kent Rd.
Cornwall Bridge, CT 06754
PH: (860)672-0843
Fax: (860)672-3005
Crossley, Lisa, Exec. Dir.

National Association of Milk Bottle Collectors [21690]
18 Pond Pl.
Cos Cob, CT 06807-2220
Weller, Tom, President

Little Hearts [14199]
PO Box 171
Cromwell, CT 06416
PH: (860)635-0006
Toll free: 866-435-HOPE
Cameron, Tim, Director

Alpha Epsilon Phi [23942]
11 Lake Avenue Ext., Ste. 1A
Danbury, CT 06811
PH: (203)748-0029
Fax: (203)748-0039
Wunsch, Bonnie, Exec. Dir.

Eastern Association of Rowing Colleges [23108]
39 Old Ridgebury Rd., Ste. 22
Matrix Conference Ctr.
39 Old Ridgebury Rd.
Danbury, CT 06810
PH: (203)745-0440
Fax: (203)745-0434

Eastern College Athletic Conference [22908]
39 Old Ridgebury Rd.
Danbury, CT 06810
PH: (203)745-0434
Fax: (203)745-0440
Mcginniss, Kevin, President, CEO

Intercollegiate Association of Amateur Athletes of America [23228]
39 Old Ridgebury Rd.
Matrix Corporate Ctr.
39 Old Ridgebury Rd.
Danbury, CT 06810
Doris, Gene, Comm. Chm.

Intercollegiate Fencing Association [22832]
Eastern College Athletic Conference
9 Old Ridgebury Rd.
Danbury, CT 06810
PH: (203)745-0434
Fax: (203)745-0440

National Organization for Rare Disorders [14605]
55 Kenosia Ave.
Danbury, CT 06810
PH: (203)744-0100
Fax: (203)798-2291
Scott, E. Michael D., Director

Pi Lambda Phi Fraternity, Inc. [23922]
60 Newtown Rd., No. 118
Danbury, CT 06810
PH: (203)740-1044
Fax: (203)740-1644
Buhler, Jeff, President

Society for Biological Engineering [6096]
100 Mill Plain Rd., 3rd Fl.
Danbury, CT 06811
Toll free: 800-242-4363
Fax: (203)775-5177
Wispelwey, June C., Exec. Dir.

**World Economic Processing Zones
Association [3307]**
3 Bullet Hill Rd.
Danbury, CT 06811-2906
PH: (203)798-9394
Fax: (203)798-9394
Gauthier, Jean-Paul, Sec. Gen.

Friends of Animals [10624]
777 Post Rd., Ste. 205
Darien, CT 06820
PH: (203)656-1522
Fax: (203)656-0267
Feral, Priscilla, President

**National Veterans Services Fund
[13246]**
PO Box 2465
Darien, CT 06820-0465
Toll free: 800-521-0198
Kraft, Phillip R., President, Treasurer

**Rasmussen's Encephalitis Children's
Project [15989]**
79 Christie Hill Rd.
Darien, CT 06820
Wohlberg, Seth, Contact

Planetree [14961]
130 Division St.
Derby, CT 06418
PH: (203)732-1365
Frampton, Susan, PhD, President

Matchbox U.S.A. [21685]
62 Saw Mill Rd.
Durham, CT 06422
PH: (860)349-1655
Fax: (860)349-3256
Mack, Charles, Editor, Owner

**Chinese Shar-Pei Club of America
[21855]**
c/o Bob Calltharp, Membership
Chairman
44 Mt. Parnasus Rd.
East Haddam, CT 06423
PH: (860)873-2572
Stewart, Cate, President

**National Federation of Democratic
Women [18115]**
c/o Joanne Sullivan, President
4 Gorman Pl.
East Hartford, CT 06108
Sullivan, Joanne, President

**Elder William Brewster Society
[20789]**
17 David Dr.
East Haven, CT 06512
Thompson, Gregory E, Hist.,
Membership Chp.

Healing Hands of Gambia [15601]
PO Box 638
East Lyme, CT 06333
Sidibeh, Dr. Ingrid Feder, CEO,
President

**Mailer's Postmark Permit Club
[22340]**
c/o Robert Johnston, Secretary
PO Box 902
East Windsor, CT 06088-0902
French, Dan, Act. Pres., Editor

**National Aviation and Space Educa-
tion Alliance [7526]**
23 Nutmeg Dr.
Enfield, CT 06082
PH: (505)774-0029
Murtari, Joseph, President

**Science Fiction and Fantasy Writers
of America [10397]**
PO Box 3238
Enfield, CT 06083-3238
Rambo, Cat, President

**National Marine Distributors Associa-
tion [2252]**
37 Pratt St.
Essex, CT 06426
PH: (860)767-7898
Fax: (860)767-7932
Staehle, Bob, Director

**Outdoor Power Equipment and
Engine Service Association [1127]**
37 Pratt St.
Essex, CT 06426-1159
PH: (860)767-1770
Fax: (860)767-7932
Cueroni, Nancy, Exec. Dir.

**Society of Daughters of Holland
Dames [20762]**
PO Box 536
Essex, CT 06426
Kimmelman, Elbrun E., Dir. Gen.

**Center for Christian and Jewish
Understanding [20057]**
5151 Park Ave.
Fairfield, CT 06825-1000
PH: (203)371-7999
(203)371-7912
Ciorra, Anthony, Officer

**The Educational Foundation of
America [3853]**
55 Walls Dr., Ste. 302
Fairfield, CT 06824
PH: (845)765-2670
Toll free: 800-839-1821
Beck, Melissa, Exec. Dir.

Friends of Christ in India [19981]
1045 Old Academy Rd.
Fairfield, CT 06824
PH: (203)259-1790
Ward, Rev. Alida, Contact

Haiti Lumiere de Demain [11204]
PO Box 1114
Fairfield, CT 06825
PH: (203)612-7860
Elneus, Louis, Founder, President

**Making a Difference in Infectious
Diseases Pharmacotherapy
[16669]**
PO Box 1604
Fairfield, CT 06825
PH: (203)373-0599
Toll free: 866-373-0599
Gorman, Alicia, Contact

**North American Association of
Subway Franchisees [1464]**
PO Box 320955
Fairfield, CT 06825
PH: (203)579-7779
Toll free: 866-590-9865
Berecz, Ms. Illya, Exec. Dir.

**Nuclear Information and Records
Management Association [6932]**
c/o Julie Hannum, Administrator
245 Sunnyridge Ave., No. 34
Fairfield, CT 06824
PH: (203)388-8795
Hoerber, Janice, Treasurer

**Professional Jamaicans for Jamaica
[12216]**
PO Box 320058
Fairfield, CT 06825
Toll free: 866-285-9312
Daley, Horace A., Founder,
President, CEO

Save the Children US [11147]
501 Kings Hwy. E, Ste. 400
Fairfield, CT 06825
PH: (203)221-4000
Toll free: 800-728-3843
Miles, Carolyn S., President, CEO

**National Alliance of Advocates for
Buprenorphine Treatment [17319]**
PO Box 333
Farmington, CT 06034
Fax: (860)269-4391

**Cetacean Society International
[4802]**
65 Redding Road 0953
Georgetown, CT 06829-0953
PH: (203)770-8615
Fax: (860)561-0187
Kaplan, David, President

**Golf Range Association of America
[3158]**
PO Box 240
Georgetown, CT 06829-0240
PH: (610)745-0862
Toll free: 800-541-1123
Summers, Rick, CEO, Chairman

**American Academy of Clinical
Psychiatrists [16808]**
PO Box 458
Glastonbury, CT 06033
PH: (860)633-6023
Toll free: 866-668-9858
Black, Donald W., MD, President

American Nuclear Insurers [1833]
95 Glastonbury Blvd., Ste. 300
Glastonbury, CT 06033-4412
Turner, George, CEO, President

Milan Cultural Association [9568]
75 Ruff Cir.
Glastonbury, CT 06033
PH: (860)657-4271
Sharma, Suresh, President

**Tai Chi for Health Community
[17423]**
PO Box 481
Glastonbury, CT 06033
McBrien, Bob, President

**TPG International Health Academy
[15594]**
160 Oak St.
Glastonbury, CT 06033
Schmidt, Dave, President

Hidden Choices [12770]
PO Box 194
Greens Farms, CT 06838
Toll free: 877-488-9537
Hatchett-Teske, Rivers, President,
Founder

**American Pet Products Association
[2540]**
255 Glenville Rd.
Greenwich, CT 06831
PH: (203)532-0000
Toll free: 800-452-1225
Fax: (203)532-0551
Darmohraj, Andrew, Exec. VP, COO

**Committee to Reduce Infection
Deaths [15321]**
c/o Betsy McCaughey, PhD,
Founder and Chairperson
5 Partridge Hollow Rd.
Greenwich, CT 06831
PH: (212)369-3329
McCaughey, Betsy, PhD,
Chairperson, Founder

**Friendship Ambassadors Foundation
[18541]**
299 Greenwich Ave.
Greenwich, CT 06830
PH: (203)542-0652
(203)622-7420
Toll free: 800-526-2908
Fax: (203)542-0661
Babay, Karim, Chairman

Heart Care International [14112]
139 E Putnam Ave.
Greenwich, CT 06830-5612
PH: (203)552-5343
Fax: (203)552-5344
Michler, Robert, MD, Chairman,
Founder

Stand for the Troops [20706]
PO Box 11179
Greenwich, CT 06831
PH: (203)629-0288
Hackworth, Eilhys England,
Chairperson

Ubuntu Africa [11175]
PO Box 7906
Greenwich, CT 06836-7906
Gillman, Theodore J., Chairman

Junkins Family Association [20889]
c/o Ann H. Cheney, Vice President,
46 Sibicky Rd.
46 Sibicky Rd.
Griswold, CT 06351
PH: (215)295-4279

**PRIDE Foundation - Promote Real
Independence for the Disabled and
Elderly [11633]**
c/o Sewtique, Inc.
391 Long Hill Rd.
Groton, CT 06340-1293
PH: (860)445-7320
Toll free: 800-332-9122
Fax: (860)445-1448
Kennedy, Evelyn S., Founder,
President

**National Middle Level Science
Teachers Association [8553]**
c/o Kathy Brooks, Membership
Chairperson
258 River St.
Guilford, CT 06437
Cost, Diana, President

**Spanish Water Dog Club of America
[21965]**
308 Granite Rd.
Guilford, CT 06437-4318
Gaines, Sheryl, President

**Association for Psychological Astrol-
ogy [5989]**
133 Injun Hollow Rd.
Haddam Neck, CT 06424
PH: (860)467-6919
Perry, Glenn, PhD, Director

**EMDR Humanitarian Assistance
Programs [12522]**
2911 Dixwell Ave., Ste. 201
Hamden, CT 06518
PH: (203)288-4450
Fax: (203)288-4060
Martin, Carol, Exec. Dir.

**Gray is Green: The National Senior
Conservation Corps [3879]**
PO Box 6055
Hamden, CT 06517
Schomaker, Kath, Exec. Dir.

**National Gypsy Moth Management
Board [4531]**
Northeastern Center for Forest
Health Research
51 Mill Pond Rd.
Hamden, CT 06514-1703
PH: (203)230-4321
Fax: (203)230-4315
Johnson, Nancy, Secretary,
Treasurer

**New England Theatre Conference
[10267]**
215 Knob Hill Dr.
Hamden, CT 06518

PH: (617)851-8535
Klein, Sabine, President

Delta Psi [23896]
Trinity College, St. Anthony Hall
300 Summit St.
Hartford, CT 06106
PH: (607)533-9200

Everyday Democracy [19657]
75 Charter Oak Ave., Ste. 2-300
Hartford, CT 06106
PH: (860)928-2616
Fax: (860)928-3713
McCoy, Martha L., Exec. Dir.

Hartford Whalers Booster Club
[24074]
PO Box 273
Hartford, CT 06141
PH: (860)956-3839
Wysocki, Joe, VP

International Society for Ecological
Psychology [7064]
c/o William M. Mace
Dept. of Psychology
Trinity College
300 Summit St.
Hartford, CT 06106-3100
PH: (860)297-2343
Fax: (860)297-2538
Mace, William M., Officer

International Society of Sustainability
Professionals [4143]
1429 Park St., Ste. 114
Hartford, CT 06106
PH: (860)231-9197
Willard, Marsha, Exec. Dir.,
Secretary

Lawyers for Children America [5536]
151 Farmington Ave., RW61
Hartford, CT 06156-3124
PH: (860)273-0441
Fax: (860)273-8340
Harris, Richard, President

Mark Twain Memorial [9076]
351 Farmington Ave.
Hartford, CT 06105-6400
PH: (860)247-0998
    (860)280-3127
Fax: (860)278-8148
Lovell, Cindy, Exec. Dir.

National Association of Public Affairs
Networks [472]
21 Oak St., Ste. 605
Hartford, CT 06106
PH: (860)246-1553
Fax: (860)246-1547
Giguere, Paul, Bd. Member

National Labor Alliance of Health
Care Coalitions [23444]
942 Main St.
Hartford, CT 06123
PH: (860)249-6100

National Working Positive Coalition
[10550]
c/o ACT, 110 Bartholomew Ave., Ste
3050
110 Bartholomew Ave., Ste. 3050
Hartford, CT 06106-2251
Misrok, Mark, President

Pension Real Estate Association
[2886]
100 Pearl St., 13th Fl.
Hartford, CT 06103
PH: (860)692-6341
Fax: (860)692-6351
Lang, Eric, Chairman

The Society for the Increase of the
Ministry [20376]
120 Sigourney St.
Hartford, CT 06105

PH: (860)233-1732
Fax: (860)233-2644
Cobb, Rev. David C., Chairman

Harriet Beecher Stowe Center
[10403]
77 Forest St.
Hartford, CT 06105
PH: (860)522-9258
Fax: (860)522-9259
Kane, Katherine, Exec. Dir.

Wire Reinforcement Institute [602]
942 Main St.
Hartford, CT 06103
PH: (860)240-9545

CONTACT USA [20040]
165 Nedobity Rd.
Higganum, CT 06441
Toll free: 800-273-8255
Reading, Michael, Chmn. of the Bd.

International Society of Differentia-
tion [6090]
PO Box 55
Higganum, CT 06441
Fax: (860)838-4242
Wylie, Christopher, President

Company of Fifers and Drummers
[9891]
62 N Main St.
Ivoryton, CT 06442-0277
PH: (860)767-2237
Fax: (860)767-9765
Brown, Sara, Secretary

Arica Institute [9531]
27 N Main St., Ste. 6
Kent, CT 06757-1512
PH: (860)927-1006
Fax: (860)201-1003
Ichazo, Oscar, Founder, Owner

American Association of Cat
Enthusiasts [21564]
PO Box 321
Ledyard, CT 06339-0321
PH: (973)658-5198
Fax: (866)890-2223
Andruscavage, Willam, President

American Lyme Disease Foundation
[14558]
PO Box 466
Lyme, CT 06371
Baker, Dr. Phillip J., Exec. Dir.

Association of Independent School
Admission Professionals [7445]
PO Box 709
Madison, CT 06443
PH: (203)421-7051
Crampton, Janice, Exec. Dir.

Call to Care Uganda [10879]
PO Box 1075
Madison, CT 06443
PH: (203)245-3932
Hoffman, Martha, President

Friction Materials Standards Institute
[319]
23 Woodland Rd., Apt. B3
Madison, CT 06443
PH: (203)245-8425
Fax: (203)245-8537
Healey, Patrick, President

Lynch Syndrome International
[14839]
PO Box 19
Madison, CT 06443-0019
PH: (203)779-5034
Lynch, Henry T., MD, Founder

The Wire Association International,
Inc. [6852]
71 Bradley Rd., Ste. 9
Madison, CT 06443-2662

PH: (203)453-2777
Fax: (203)453-8384
Fetteroll, Steven J., Exec. Dir.

Books to Dreams [12243]
312 Ferguson Rd.
Manchester, CT 06040
PH: (860)646-5934
Epstein, Miriam Stannard, Director,
Founder

Nepal Public Health Network
[17014]
872 Vernon St.
Manchester, CT 06042
PH: (903)407-0387
Shrestha, Roman, Director

North American Sundial Society
[8712]
27 Ninas Way - Humpton Run
Manchester, CT 06040-6388
Sawyer, Frederick W., III, Editor,
President

Society of American Period Furniture
Makers [1487]
c/o Connecticut Valley School of
Woodworking, 249 Spencer St.,
249 Spencer St.
Manchester, CT 06040
Johnson, Ken, Mem.

National Institute for the Clinical Ap-
plication of Behavioral Medicine
[13801]
PO Box 523
Mansfield Center, CT 06250-0523
PH: (860)456-1153
Fax: (860)477-1454
Buczynski, Ruth, PhD, President

North American Grappling Associa-
tion [23372]
36 Saner Rd.
Marlborough, CT 06447
PH: (860)295-0403
Fax: (860)295-0447
Kollar, Kipp, President

Generations of Hope, Haiti [13053]
210 Dogwood Ln.
Meriden, CT 06450
PH: (305)458-1098
Jean-Louis, Dr. Franco, President,
Founder

The Maryheart Crusaders [19860]
531 W Main St.
Meriden, CT 06451
PH: (203)238-9735
Toll free: 800-879-1957
Fax: (203)235-0059
D'Angelo, Michael, Director

Artists for World Peace [12432]
PO Box 95
Middletown, CT 06457
PH: (860)685-1789
Black-Nasta, Wendy, Founder, Exec.
Dir.

International Society for Clinical
Densitometry [16499]
Bldg. C
955 S Main St.
Middletown, CT 06457-5153
PH: (860)259-1000
Fax: (860)259-1030
Leslie, William D., MD, MSc,
President

Lily's Kids [15218]
589 East St.
Middletown, CT 06457
Gagliardi, Lily, Founder, CEO

National Organization of Forensic
Social Work [8573]
460 Smith St., Ste. K
Middletown, CT 06457

PH: (860)613-0254
Toll free: 866-668-9858
Brady, Mr. Paul W., Exec. Dir.

Environmental Alliance for Senior
Involvement [3856]
PO Box 250
Milford, CT 06460-0250
PH: (203)779-0024
Fax: (203)779-0025

Reflex Sympathetic Dystrophy
Syndrome Association [15990]
99 Cherry St.
Milford, CT 06460
PH: (203)877-3790
Toll free: 877-662-7737
Fax: (203)882-8362
Broatch, James W., MSW, Exec. VP,
Director

American Society for Scleroderma
Research [17178]
31 Patmar Terr.
Monroe, CT 06468
PH: (203)273-2034
LoSchiavo, Joe, President

Army Aviation Association of
America [5592]
593 Main St.
Monroe, CT 06468-2830
PH: (203)268-2450
Fax: (203)268-5870
McCann, Barbara, Exec. Asst.

Comicbook Artists' Guild [9169]
PO Box 38
Moodus, CT 06469
Buchner, Chris, President

Denison Homestead [20853]
120 Pequotsepos Rd.
Mystic, CT 06355-3043
PH: (860)536-9248
Solley, Steve, President

International Congress of Maritime
Museums [9831]
c/o Stephen C. White, President
Mystic Seaport
75 Greenmanville Ave.
Mystic, CT 06355-1946
White, Stephen C., President

Mystic Seaport [9775]
75 Greenmanville Ave.
Mystic, CT 06355-0990
PH: (860)572-0711
    (860)572-5367
Toll free: 888-973-2767
Fax: (860)572-5395
White, Stephen C., President

Traditional Small Craft Association
[22676]
PO Box 350
Mystic, CT 06355-0350
Allen, Roger, VP

Polish American Historical Associa-
tion [10166]
Central Connecticut State University
1615 Stanley St.
New Britain, CT 06050
PH: (860)832-3010
Fax: (248)738-6736
Versteegh, Dr. Pien, Exec. Dir.

Pura Vida for Children [11136]
PO Box 1692
New Canaan, CT 06840
PH: (203)644-4404
Knechtle, Sharon, Founder

Silvermine Arts Center [8888]
1037 Silvermine Rd.
New Canaan, CT 06840-4398

PH: (203)966-9700
Mudre, Roger, Bd. Member

Voices of September 11th [19188]
161 Cherry St.
New Canaan, CT 06840
PH: (203)966-3911
Toll free: 866-505-3911
Fax: (203)966-5701
Fetchet, Mary, Founder

Alpha Delta Phi [23881]
21 Byron Pl.
New Haven, CT 06515
PH: (508)226-1832
Fax: (508)226-4456
Starnes, Stephen, President

American Law and Economics As-
sociation [5413]
127 Wall St.
New Haven, CT 06511-8918
PH: (203)432-7801
Fax: (203)432-7225
Spier, Kathyrn, President

AMISTAD America [7979]
Westville Station
Bldg. 12, Ste. 208
60 Connolly Pkwy.
New Haven, CT 06514-2519
PH: (203)387-0370

Belgian American Educational
Foundation [9118]
195 Church St.
New Haven, CT 06510
PH: (203)777-5765
(203)785-4055
Fax: (203)777-5765
Boulpaep, Prof. Emile L., CEO,
President

Cents of Relief [12635]
109 Church St., No. 202
New Haven, CT 06510
PH: (860)251-9004
Patel, Rina, Founder

Changing Children's Lives [15442]
136 Sherman Ave., Ste. 407
New Haven, CT 06511
PH: (203)907-0040
Fax: (203)907-4593
Weinstein, Mark H., MD, Director,
Founder

Chinese American Ophthalmological
Society [16380]
c/o Christopher C. Teng, Secretary
PO Box 208061
New Haven, CT 06520-8061

ClearWater Initiative [13353]
PO Box 1684
New Haven, CT 06507
Toll free: 866-585-6078
Freedman, Brett D., President

Daughters of Isabella, International
Circle [19406]
PO Box 9585
New Haven, CT 06535
PH: (203)865-2570
Chagnon, Christiane, Mem.

Endangered Language Fund [9650]
300 George St., Ste. 900
New Haven, CT 06511-6660
PH: (203)865-6163
Fax: (203)865-8963
Whalen, Douglas H., Founder, Chair-
man

Green Parking Council [4519]
55 Church St., 7th Fl.
New Haven, CT 06510
PH: (203)672-5892
Wessel, Paul, Exec. Dir.

Human Relations Area Files, Inc.
[9549]
755 Prospect St.
New Haven, CT 06511-1225
PH: (203)764-9401
Toll free: 800-520-4723
Fax: (203)764-9404
Andreucci, Patricia, Mgr., Coord.

Innovations for Poverty Action
[17805]
101 Whitney Ave.
New Haven, CT 06510-1256
PH: (203)772-2216
Fax: (203)772-2428
Karlan, Prof. Dean, President,
Founder

International Conference for the
Study of Political Thought [7046]
Dept. of Political Science
Yale University
115 Prospect St.
New Haven, CT 06520
McClure, Kristie, Assoc. Prof.

International Society for Industrial
Ecology [4075]
Yale School of Forestry and
Environmental Studies
Yale University
195 Prospect St.
New Haven, CT 06511-2189
PH: (203)432-6953
Fax: (203)432-5556
Clift, Roland, CBE, FREng,
FIChemE, HonFCIWEM, FRSA,
Comm. Chm.

Knights of Columbus [19409]
1 Columbus Plz.
New Haven, CT 06510
PH: (203)752-4000
Toll free: 800-380-9995
Brosnan, Susan H., Arch., Librarian

Lawyers Without Borders, Inc.
[5539]
59 Elm St.
New Haven, CT 06510
PH: (203)823-9397
Fax: (203)823-9438
Storm, Christina M., Esq., Exec. Dir.,
Founder

Lithuanian-American Community Inc.
[19541]
43 Anthony St.
New Haven, CT 06515
PH: (203)415-7776
Fax: (703)773-1257
Rosen, Sigita Simkuviene, President

Love146 [11072]
PO Box 8266
New Haven, CT 06530
PH: (203)772-4420
Morris, Rob, President, Founder

Promoting Enduring Peace [18824]
323 Temple St.
New Haven, CT 06511-6602
PH: (203)584-5224
Hodel, Paul L., President

Psychodynamic Psychoanalytic
Research Society [16850]
Yale Child Study Center
230 S Frontage Rd.
New Haven, CT 06519
PH: (203)785-7205
Fax: (203)785-7926
Mayes, Linda, MD, Bd. Member

Recovered Medical Equipment for
the Developing World [15613]
333 Cedar St.
New Haven, CT 06520-8051

PH: (203)737-5356
(203)785-6750
Fax: (203)785-5241
Rosenblatt, William H., MD,
President

Religious Education Association: An
Association of Professors,
Practitioners, and Researchers in
Religious Education [20089]
Yale Divinity School
409 Prospect St.
New Haven, CT 06511
PH: (765)225-8836
Fax: (203)432-5356
Horell, Harold (Bud), President

Southern Connecticut State
University Alumni Association
[19348]
501 Crescent St.
New Haven, CT 06515
PH: (203)392-6500
(203)392-8824
Parker, Bob, President

The Thomas Hardy Association
[9103]
c/o Rosemarie Morgan, President
124 Bishop St.
New Haven, CT 06511
Morgan, Rosemarie, Editor,
President

Unite for Sight [13279]
234 Church St., 15th Fl.
New Haven, CT 06510
PH: (203)404-4900
Staple-Clark, Jennifer, CEO,
Founder

Yale-China Association [8095]
442 Temple St.
New Haven, CT 06520
PH: (203)432-0884
Fax: (203)432-7246
Youtz, David, Exec. Dir.

Association of Bridal Consultants
[442]
56 Danbury Rd., Ste. 11
New Milford, CT 06776
PH: (860)355-7000
Fax: (860)354-1404
Grannis, Renee, Director

ARRL [21265]
225 Main St.
Newington, CT 06111-1494
PH: (860)594-0200
Toll free: 888-277-5289
Fax: (860)594-0259
Harrison, Joel, President

ARRL Foundation [21266]
225 Main St.
Newington, CT 06111-1494
PH: (860)594-0200
Fax: (860)594-0259
Niswander, Rick, Treasurer

International Amateur Radio Union
[21268]
PO Box 310905
Newington, CT 06131
Stafford, Rod, Secretary

National Association of Professional
Mortgage Women [410]
c/o Agility Resources Group LLC
705 N Mountain Business Ctr., Ste.
E-104
Newington, CT 06111
Toll free: 800-827-3034
Hendricks, Kelly, President

National Association of Shooting
Ranges [23133]
11 Mile Hill Rd.
Newtown, CT 06470-2359

PH: (203)426-1320
Fax: (203)426-1087
Kriss, Holden, President

National Shooting Sports Foundation
[1294]
Flintlock Ridge Office Ctr.
11 Mile Hill Rd.
Newtown, CT 06470
PH: (203)462-1320
Fax: (203)426-1087
Scott, Robert L., Chairman

Société de Chimie Industrielle -
American Section [6213]
10 Winton Farm Rd.
Newtown, CT 06470
PH: (212)725-9539
Young, Peter, Chairman

Sporting Arms and Ammunition
Manufacturers' Institute Inc. [1295]
11 Mile Hill Rd.
Newtown, CT 06470-2359
PH: (203)426-4358
Fax: (203)426-3592

American Revolution Round Table of
New York [8793]
8 Spencer Ave.
Niantic, CT 06357-3015
PH: (860)739-5505
Jacobs, Mr. David W., Chairman

Colonial Rottweiler Club [21860]
c/o Sue Chodorov
61 Sea View Ave.
Niantic, CT 06357
Sims, Karen L., President

Environment and Human Health, Inc.
[14715]
1191 Ridge Rd.
North Haven, CT 06473-4437
PH: (203)248-6582
Fax: (203)288-7571
Addiss, Susan S., MPH, MUrS, Bd.
Member

National Rowing Foundation [23111]
67 Mystic Rd.
North Stonington, CT 06359
PH: (860)535-0634
Meehan, Michael J., President

American Accordionists' Association
[9850]
c/o Mary J. Tokarski, President
15 Maplewood Ln.
Northford, CT 06472
PH: (203)484-5095
Fax: (203)484-5095
Reed, Linda Soley, VP

Association for the Promotion of
Tourism to Africa [3289]
Norwalk, CT
PH: (203)858-0444
De Vries, Yvette, President

Courage International [20177]
8 Leonard St.
Norwalk, CT 06850
PH: (203)803-1564
Check, Fr. Paul N., Exec. Dir.

Financial Accounting Standards
Board [27]
401 Merritt 7
Norwalk, CT 06856-5116
PH: (203)847-0700
Fax: (203)849-9714
Golden, Russell G., Chairman

Governmental Accounting Standards
Board [4939]
401 Merritt 7
Norwalk, CT 06856-5116

PH: (203)847-0700
Fax: (203)849-9714
Vaudt, David A., Chairman

Multiple Myeloma Research Foundation [14017]
383 Main Ave., 5th Fl.
Norwalk, CT 06851
PH: (203)229-0464
Fax: (203)229-0572
Giusti, Kathy, Chairman, Founder

National Emphysema Foundation [14135]
128 East Ave.
Norwalk, CT 06851
PH: (203)866-5000
Nair, Sreedhar, MD, President

Parenting Media Association [2808]
287 Richards Ave.
Norwalk, CT 06850
PH: (310)364-0193
Fax: (310)364-0196
Taylor, Sarah, President

Shatterproof [13182]
101 Merritt 7 Corporate Pk., 1st Fl.
Norwalk, CT 06851
Toll free: 800-597-2557
Mendell, Gary, Founder, CEO

World Health Clinicians [13567]
618 West Ave.
Norwalk, CT 06850-4008
PH: (203)852-9525
Toll free: 855-205-7535
Fax: (203)854-0371
Blick, Dr. Gary, Founder

Society of the Founders and Friends
of Norwich, Connecticut [9435]
348 Washington St.
Norwich, CT 06360
PH: (860)889-9440
Deming, Austin Jay

Children of Tanzania [10719]
3 Little Cove Pl.
Old Greenwich, CT 06870-2137
PH: (203)570-0337
Rohrer, Susan, Chairperson

International Blue Jay Class Association [22626]
12 Sandpiper Pt. Rd.
12 Sandpiper Point Rd.
Old Lyme, CT 06371
PH: (860)434-5125
Dunbar, William K., Exec., Officer

Lambda Psi Delta Sorority, Inc. [23975]
PO Box 734
Old Saybrook, CT 06475
Ladd, Paula Arputhasamy, Esq.,
President

Marketing Executives Networking
Group [2290]
3 Anchorage Ln.
Old Saybrook, CT 06475
PH: (860)984-6186
Fax: (860)510-0249
Sullivan, Jay, Treasurer

North American Steam Boat Association [22657]
165 Jacks Hill Rd.
Oxford, CT 06478
PH: (203)463-8288

Wreck and Crash Mail Society [22381]
c/o Ken Sanford
613 Championship Dr.
Oxford, CT 06478-128
PH: (203)888-9237
Fax: (203)888-9237
Berlin, Dr. Steven, Treasurer

Clan Maxwell Society of the USA [20829]
54 Pawcatuck Ave.
Pawcatuck, CT 06379-2417
Maxwell, James A., President

Post Mark Collectors Club [22355]
c/o Andy Mitchell
PO Box 265
Poquonock, CT 06064
Milligan, Robert J., Mgr., Member
Svcs.

International Association for Contract
& Commercial Management [682]
90 Grove St.
Ridgefield, CT 06877
PH: (203)431-8741
Cummins, Tim, CEO, President

New England M.G. "T" Register
Limited [21460]
PO Box 1028
Ridgefield, CT 06877-9028
PH: (802)434-8418
Fax: (203)261-9131
Sander, David, Chairman

Gasoline and Automotive Service
Dealers Association [343]
29 Thornhill Rd.
Riverside, CT 06878-1322
PH: (203)327-4773
Fax: (203)323-6935
Fox, Michael J., Exec. Dir.

Association for Long Term Care
Financial Managers [15581]
c/o Jaclyn Farnham, Administrator
95 West St.
Rocky Hill, CT 06067-3546
PH: (860)721-7400
Fax: (860)721-7406
McCarthy, Maureen, President, CEO

Give2TheTroops [12345]
1275 Cromwell Ave.
Rocky Hill, CT 06067
Toll free: 888-876-6775

Inyana - League for Rwandan
Children and Youth [11241]
c/o Thomas Kainamura, Treasurer/
Co-Founder
230 Sunset Ridge
Rocky Hill, CT 06067
Murekeyisoni, Juliette, President

North American Bar-Related Title
Insurers [1914]
101 Corporate Pl.
Rocky Hill, CT 06067
PH: (860)257-0606
Fax: (860)563-4833
Csuka, Anne G., Exec. VP

Shelby American Automobile Club [21489]
PO Box 788
Sharon, CT 06069
Talbott, Jay, Dir. of Member Svcs.

BPA Worldwide [91]
100 Beard Sawmill Rd., 6th Fl.
Shelton, CT 06484
PH: (203)447-2800
Fax: (203)447-2900
Hansen, Glenn J., CEO, President

Friends of Peace Pilgrim [10327]
PO Box 2207
Shelton, CT 06484-1841
PH: (203)926-1581
Nichols, Bruce, Bd. Member

NanoBusiness Commercialization
Association [7284]
4 Research Dr., Ste. 402
Shelton, CT 06484

PH: (203)733-1949
Caprio, Vincent, Chairman

Tom Jones "Tom Terrific" Fan Club [24067]
136 Kyle's Way
Shelton, CT 06484-6614
Mariotti, Margaret, President

Water Innovations Alliance [7379]
4 Research Dr., Ste. 402
Shelton, CT 06484-6242
PH: (203)733-1949
Caprio, Vincent, Founder, Exec. Dir.

AMC Rambler Club [21315]
77 County Rd.
Simsbury, CT 06070
PH: (860)923-0485
     (860)658-0027
Yacino, Brian, President

Nonverbal Learning Disorders Association [12240]
507 Hopmeadow St.
Simsbury, CT 06070
PH: (860)658-5522
Fax: (860)658-6688
Carrin, Patricia, President

North American Maple Syrup Council [1364]
PO Box 581
Simsbury, CT 06070

Worldwide Television-FM DX Association [21274]
PO Box 501
Somersville, CT 06072
Bugaj, Mike, Editor, Publisher

Eastern Coast Breweriana Association [21261]
PO Box 826
South Windsor, CT 06074-0826
Pawlowski, Steve, Agent

International Remote Viewing Association [6227]
PO Box 1471
South Windsor, CT 06074
PH: (860)882-1210
Toll free: 866-374-4782
Fax: (860)648-4005
Smith, Paul H., Ph.D., President

Laboratory Animal Welfare Training
Exchange [3629]
885 Strongtown Rd.
Southbury, CT 06488
Kelly, Lisa, President

Musical Instrument Technicians Association, International [2430]
c/o Fran Hellmann, Treasurer
376 Old Woodbury Rd.
Southbury, CT 06488
PH: (203)264-1828
Fax: (203)264-9304

Hands Across the Water [11012]
29 Deacon Cir.
Southington, CT 06489
PH: (860)620-3735
     (860)620-3705
Fax: (860)620-3700
Hession, David M., Founder,
President

Independent Jewelers Organization [2048]
136 Old Post Rd.
Southport, CT 06890-1302
Toll free: 800-624-9252
Fax: (203)254-7429

Alliance for Cancer Gene Therapy [14871]
96 Cummings Point Rd.
Stamford, CT 06902

PH: (203)358-8000
Netter, Barbara, President, Founder

American Homeowners Association [2123]
3001 Summer St.
Stamford, CT 06905
PH: (203)323-7715
Toll free: 800-470-2242
Roll, Richard J., Founder, President

American Institute for Foreign Study [8108]
1 High Ridge Pk.
Stamford, CT 06905
PH: (203)399-5000
Toll free: 866-906-2437
Fax: (203)399-5590
Taylor, Sir Cyril, Founder, Chairman

American Institute for Foreign Study
Foundation [8109]
1 High Ridge Pk.
Stamford, CT 06905
PH: (203)399-5414
Toll free: 800-322-4678
Fax: (203)724-1536
French, Ms. Melanie, Exec. Dir.

AmeriCares Foundation Inc. [12620]
88 Hamilton Ave.
Stamford, CT 06902-3111
PH: (203)658-9500
Toll free: 800-486-4357
Fax: (203)327-5200
Maglaris, Dean C., CEO

Au Pair in America [8059]
1 High Ridge Pk.
Stamford, CT 06905
PH: (203)399-5000
Toll free: 800-928-7247
Ferry, Ruth, Director, Sr. VP

buildOn [11325]
PO Box 16741
Stamford, CT 06905
Ziolkowski, Jim, CEO

Father Josef's Method of Reflexology [13622]
1441 High Ridge Rd.
Stamford, CT 06903-4906
PH: (203)968-6824
Eugster, Fr. Josef, Chairman

International Association of Employment Web Sites [1093]
2052 Shippan Ave.
Stamford, CT 06902
Weddle, Peter, Exec. Dir.

Keep America Beautiful [4078]
1010 Washington Blvd.
Stamford, CT 06901
PH: (203)659-3000
Rogers, Mike, Chief Dev. Ofc.

Lyme Research Alliance [15408]
2001 W Main St., Ste. 280
Stamford, CT 06902
PH: (203)969-1333
Siciliano, Deborah, Co-Pres.

PASSION: Pursuing A Successful
Seed In-spite of Negativity [13473]
110 Lenox Ave., Ste. D
Stamford, CT 06911-2069
PH: (203)577-5744
James, Rolita, Exec. Dir.

Sonar Class Association [22670]
123 Harbor Dr., Ste. 209
200 Rowayton Ave.
Stamford, CT 06902
PH: (203)655-6665

Puppeteers of America [22394]
336 Chestnut Hill Rd.
Stevenson, CT 06491

PH: (860)462-8072
Zapletal, Peter, Trustee

Association for Tropical Biology and
  Conservation [6076]
c/o Robin L. Chazdon, Executive
  Director
Dept. of Ecology and Evolutionary
  Biology, U-3043
75 N Eagleville Rd.
Storrs, CT 06269-3042
Chazdon, Dr. Robin L., Exec. Dir.

Cell Stress Society International
  [17290]
91 N Eagleville Rd.
Storrs, CT 06269-3125
PH: (860)486-6304
Fax: (860)486-5709
Wu, Tangchun, President

International Federation of Societies
  for Microscopy [6866]
c/o C. Barry Carter, Vice President
Chemical, Materials & Biomolecular
  Engineering Department, Unit 3222
University of Connecticut
191 Auditorium Rd.
Storrs, CT 06269-3222
PH: (860)486-4020
Fax: (860)486-2959
Carter, Prof. C. Barry, VP

International Society for
  Interpersonal Acceptance-Rejection
  [9550]
348 Mansfield Rd., U-1058
Storrs, CT 06269-1058
PH: (860)486-0073
Rohner, Ronald P., Exec. Dir.

International Studies Association
  [8115]
337 Mansfield Rd., Unit 1013
Storrs, CT 06269-1013
PH: (860)486-5850
Paul, T. V., President

Pi Tau Sigma [23742]
c/o Mun Young Choi, President
University of Connecticut
352 Mansfield Rd., Unit 1086
Storrs, CT 06269
PH: (860)486-6399
Choi, Dr. Mun Young, President

Studio Art Quilt Associates [9002]
PO Box 572
Storrs, CT 06268-0572
PH: (860)487-4199
Sielman, Martha, Exec. Dir.

Ethiopian Geophysical Union -
  International [6687]
261 Glenbrook Rd., Unit 2037
Storrs Mansfield, CT 06269-2037
PH: (204)989-2254
Demisse, Dr. Yonas, President

Pearl Harbor History Associates, Inc.
  [9505]
PO Box 1007
Stratford, CT 06615

Lock Museum of America [21769]
230 Main St.
Terryville, CT 06786
PH: (860)480-4408
Fax: (860)589-6359
Hennessy, Thomas F., Jr., Asst. Cur.,
  President

Pocketful of Joy [11131]
24 Goose Ln.
Tolland, CT 06084
PH: (860)875-3379

Society Farsarotul [9236]
PO Box 753
Trumbull, CT 06611
Nicola, Robert J., President

International Wooden Bow Tie Club
  [206]
5112 Ashlar Village
Wallingford, CT 06492
PH: (203)265-3001
Burch, Peter, MD, President

Soul Friends [17464]
300 Church St., Ste. 105
Wallingford, CT 06492
PH: (203)679-0849
Fax: (203)679-0348
Nicoll, Kate, LCSW, Exec. Dir.,
  Founder

Historians of American Communism
  [7984]
PO Box 1216
Washington, CT 06793
Leab, Daniel, Gen. Sec.

Eugene O'Neill Theater Center
  [10250]
305 Great Neck Rd.
Waterford, CT 06385
PH: (860)443-5378
Fax: (860)443-9653
Whiteway, Preston, Exec. Dir.

National Theater Institute at the
  Eugene O'Neill Theater Center
  [8700]
Eugene O'Neill Theater Ctr.
305 Great Neck Rd.
Waterford, CT 06385
PH: (860)443-7139
Fax: (860)444-1212
Whiteway, Preston, Exec. Dir.

American Board of Prosthodontics
  [14400]
PO Box 271894
West Hartford, CT 06127-1894
Fax: (860)206-1169
Taylor, Dr. Thomas D., Exec. Dir.

American Council for Polish Culture
  [19601]
c/o Florence Langrige, Membership
  Chair
78 Meadow Ln.
West Hartford, CT 06107
PH: (860)521-4034
Langrige, Florence, Membership
  Chp.

American Epilepsy Society [14737]
342 N Main St., Ste. 301
West Hartford, CT 06117-2507
PH: (860)586-7505
Fax: (860)586-7550
Murray, Eileen, Exec. Dir.

American Society for Experimental
  Neuro Therapeutics [16005]
342 N Main St.
West Hartford, CT 06117
PH: (860)586-7570
Fax: (860)586-7550
Federoff, Howard J., MD, President

Bridge2Peace [7747]
1574 Asylum Ave.
West Hartford, CT 06117
Anderson, Bernadine, Exec. Dir.

Endocrine Fellows Foundation
  [14703]
342 N Main St., Ste. 301
West Hartford, CT 06117-2507
Fax: (860)586-7500
Bilezikian, John P., MD, Chairman

International Association of Black
  Actuaries [1873]
PO Box 270701
West Hartford, CT 06127
PH: (860)906-1286
Fax: (860)906-1369
Murray, Jamala, VP, Director

International Association of Campus
  Law Enforcement Administrators
  [5467]
342 N Main St.
West Hartford, CT 06117-2507
PH: (860)586-7517
Fax: (860)586-7550
Leonard, John, Jr., Dir. of Accred.

International Society for Autism
  Research [13771]
342 N Main St.
West Hartford, CT 06117-2507
PH: (860)586-7575
Fax: (860)586-7550
Newschaffer, Craig, VP

International Society for Ayurveda
  and Health [13636]
PO Box 271737
West Hartford, CT 06127-1737
PH: (860)561-4857
Guha, Dr. Amala, Director

Medical Aid to Haiti [12289]
80 S Main St.
West Hartford, CT 06107
PH: (860)760-7009
Thibadeau, Richard, Founder,
  President

National Association of Long Term
  Hospitals [15333]
342 N Main St.
West Hartford, CT 06117-2507
PH: (860)586-7579
Burzynski, Cherri, RN, President

Noah Webster House [9424]
227 S Main St.
West Hartford, CT 06107
PH: (860)521-5362
Fax: (860)521-4036
Daley, Sheila, Director, Curator

Peace History Society [9504]
c/o Kevin J. Callahan, President
University of Saint Joseph
1678 Asylum Ave.
West Hartford, CT 06117
Callahan, Kevin J., President

Professional Association of Athlete
  Development Specialists [22517]
41 Crossroads Plz., No. 127
West Hartford, CT 06117
Galloway, Libba, Exec. Dir.

World Kouk Sun Do Society [18844]
45 S Main St., Ste. 90
West Hartford, CT 06107-2402
PH: (860)523-5260
Lee, Anne, Coord.

Drums No Guns [18250]
193 Lamson St.
West Haven, CT 06516
PH: (203)675-4827
  (203)931-8750
Mills, Michael, Exec. Dir., Founder

Navy Seabee Veterans of America
  [21059]
c/o Charles Coffin, Secretary
16 Graham Ave.
West Haven, CT 06516
PH: (203)843-5513
Toll free: 800-SEA-BEE5
Coffin, Charles, Secretary

The Financial Executives Networking
  Group [1234]
32 Gray's Farm Rd.
Weston, CT 06883
PH: (203)227-8965
Fax: (203)227-8984
Bud, Matthew R., Chairman

National Institute of American Doll
  Artists [22006]
c/o Donna May Robinson
109 Ladder Hill N

Weston, CT 06883
PH: (203)557-3169
Marriott, Tanya, President

Coalition to Cure Calpain 3 [15847]
15 Compo Pkwy.
Westport, CT 06880
Boslego, Jordan, President

Exhibit Designers and Producers
  Association [1171]
19 Compo Rd. S
Westport, CT 06880
PH: (203)557-6321
Fax: (203)557-6324
Provost, Jeff, Exec. Dir.

Guinea Fowl Breeders Association
  [3661]
4 Coach Ln.
Westport, CT 06880

Interaction Design Association
  [6370]
PO Box 2833
Westport, CT 06880
Sanderson, Brenda, Exec. Dir.

Never Surrender to Parkinson's
  [15977]
15 Old Mill Rd.
Westport, CT 06880
PH: (203)227-6500
Fax: (203)227-6500
Green, Paul, Founder

SeriousFun Children's Network
  [11149]
228 Saugatuck Ave.
Westport, CT 06880
PH: (203)562-1203
Fax: (203)341-8707
Powers, Mary Beth, CEO

Smart Kids with Learning Disabilities
  [12241]
38 Kings Hwy. N
Westport, CT 06880
PH: (203)226-6831
Fax: (203)226-6708
Ross, Jane B., Exec. Dir., Founder

Victims of Chiropractic Abuse
  [14284]
PO Box 3278
Westville, CT 06515

1970 Dart Swinger 340s Registry
  [21311]
PO Box 9
Wethersfield, CT 06129-0009
PH: (860)257-8434
Cooper, Joel, Founder

DARTS Club [21367]
PO Box 9
Wethersfield, CT 06129-0009
PH: (860)257-8434
Cooper, Joel, Editor, Founder

Center for Medicare Advocacy
  [15096]
PO Box 350
Willimantic, CT 06226
PH: (860)456-7790
Fax: (860)456-2614
Stein, Judith A., JD, Exec. Dir.

Entertainment Consumers Associa-
  tion [18047]
64 Danbury Rd., Ste. 700
Wilton, CT 06897-4406
PH: (203)761-6183
Halpin, Hal, Founder, President

Norman Mailer Society [10389]
c/o David Light, Treasurer
75 Jennings Ln.

Windham, CT 06280
Lennon, J. Michael, President

Charette/Charest Family Association
[20794]
c/o Ray Thomas, Treasurer
22 Ludlow Rd.
Windsor, CT 06095
Charette, Everett, President

LIMRA International [1882]
300 Day Hill Rd.
Windsor, CT 06095
PH: (860)688-3358
    (860)285-7789
Toll free: 800-235-4672
Fax: (860)298-9555
Kerzner, Robert A., CEO, President

American Board of Neurological
  Surgery [16059]
245 Amity Rd., Ste. 208
Woodbridge, CT 06525
PH: (203)397-2267
Fax: (203)392-0400
Bruce, Jeffrey N., Chairman

American Teilhard Association
[9036]
c/o John Grim, Director
29 Spoke Dr.
Woodbridge, CT 06525
Grim, Dr. John A., Director

Guild of Fine Craftsmen and Artisans
[8858]
17 Vernon Ct.
Woodbridge, CT 06525
PH: (203)397-8505
Fax: (203)389-7516

Spanish-Norman Horse Registry
[4412]
c/o Linda Osterman Hamid,
  Registrar
PO Box 985
Woodbury, CT 06798
PH: (203)266-4048
Fax: (203)263-3306
Hamid, Allan H., Founder

Richard III Society - American
  Branch [10347]
c/o Sally Keil, Membership Chair
1219 Route 171
Woodstock, CT 06281-2126
Fax: (504)822-7599
Hayes, Jonathan, ChairmanD

DELAWARE

Saving Soles Foundation [12564]
PO Box 1475
Bear, DE 19701-7475
PH: (708)218-8945
Johnson, Dwain Anthony, Founder

Alpha Phi Delta Fraternity [23885]
257 E Camden Wyoming Ave., Unit
  A
Camden, DE 19934
PH: (302)531-7854
Lentini, Rev. James, Secretary

Orders and Medals Society of
  America [22184]
PO Box 540
Claymont, DE 19703-0540
Borch, Colonel (Retired) Fred,
  President

American Birding Association [6952]
PO Box 744
Delaware City, DE 19706
PH: (302)838-3660
Toll free: 800-850-2473
Fax: (302)838-3651
Pilger, LeAnn, Coord.

Ecological Research and Develop-
  ment Group [3851]
190 Main St.
Dover, DE 19901-4801
PH: (302)236-5383
Gauvry, Glenn, President

Hof Reunion Association [20704]
232 Green View Dr.
Dover, DE 19901-5748
Riverkamp, Don, Secretary

International Association for Teach-
  ers of Chinese to Speakers of
  Other Languages [7602]
9 E Loockerman St., Ste. 3A
Dover, DE 19901-7316
Yang, Mr. Vincent C.S., President

National Council on Agricultural Life
  and Labor Research Fund [11979]
363 Saulsbury Rd.
Dover, DE 19904
PH: (302)678-9400
Fax: (302)678-9058
Kunkle, Randall, VP

Operation Shooting Star [13788]
32711 Fisher Pl.
Frankford, DE 19945
PH: (302)542-2393
Killen, Audrey Fisher, Exec. Dir.

DuBois Family Association [20856]
c/o Pamela Bailey, Treasurer
726 Loveville Rd., Cottage 60
Hockessin, DE 19707
DuBois, David, President

National Society of Pershing Rifles
[23823]
2 Spring Meadow Ln.
Hockessin, DE 19707
PH: (605)390-3001
Whisenand, Tymothy, Cmdr.

International Association of CPAs,
  Attorneys, and Management
[5686]
16192 Coastal Hwy.
Lewes, DE 19958
Toll free: 800-518-0950
Ninivaggi, Michele, Advisor

United States Ultralight Association
[21255]
16192 Coastal Hwy.
Lewes, DE 19958
PH: (717)339-0200
Comperini, Bob, Inst.

American Osteopathic Association of
  Prolotherapy Regenerative
  Medicine [16510]
303 S Ingram Ct.
Middletown, DE 19709
PH: (302)530-2489
Toll free: 800-889-9898
Pavina, Linda J., Exec. Dir.

Association of American Pesticide
  Control Officials [4523]
PO Box 466
Milford, DE 19963
PH: (302)422-8152
Alessandri, Gina, Mem.

International League of Antiquarian
  Booksellers [2957]
310 Delaware St.
New Castle, DE 19720-5038
Donhofer, Norbert, President

80-20 Initiative [17818]
5 Farm House Rd.
Newark, DE 19711
PH: (858)472-5558
Chaudhary, Ved, Advisor

American Philosophical Association
[10076]
University of Delaware
31 Amstel Ave.
Newark, DE 19716
PH: (302)831-1112
Fax: (302)831-8690
Ferrer, Amy, Exec. Dir.

Association of Field Ornithologists
[6954]
c/o Gregory Shriver, Treasurer
257 Townsend Hall
University of Delaware
Newark, DE 19717-2160
PH: (302)831-1300
Shriver, W. Gregory, Treasurer

Cancer Care Connection [13918]
1 Innovation Way, Ste. 400
Newark, DE 19711
PH: (302)266-8050
Toll free: 866-266-7008
Fax: (302)266-9687
Walker, Clint, Chairman

Council of Writing Program
  Administrators [8763]
c/o Michael McCamley, Secretary
212 Memorial Hall
University of Delaware
Newark, DE 19716
Miller-Cochran, Susan, President

Cyclone Montego Torino Registry
[21366]
19 Glyn Dr.
Newark, DE 19713-4016
PH: (302)737-4252
Day, Robert, Contact

Institute of Public Administration
  USA [5695]
University of Delaware
180 Graham Hall
Newark, DE 19716
PH: (302)831-8971
Fax: (302)831-3488
Lewis, Jerome R., Director

International Literacy Association
[8485]
800 Barksdale Rd.
Newark, DE 19711-3204
PH: (302)731-1600
Toll free: 800-336-7323
Fax: (302)731-1057
Barone, Diane, President

Patent Information Users Group, Inc.
[5337]
40 E Main St., No. 1438
Newark, DE 19711
PH: (302)660-3275
Fax: (302)660-3276
Yates, Martha, Chairperson

Society for Seventeenth-Century
  Music [10011]
c/o Maria Anne Purciello, Treasurer
University of Delaware
Department of Music
317 Amy E. du Pont Music Bldg.
Newark, DE 19716
PH: (319)335-1622
Purciello, Maria Anne, Treasurer

Eskridge Family Association [20864]
PO Box 102
Ocean View, DE 19970
PH: (804)270-7841
Brown, Betty, VP

Global Urban Development [11368]
PO Box 1510
Rehoboth Beach, DE 19971
Weiss, Marc, Chairman, CEO

National Organization of Professional Hispanic Natural Resources
  Conservation Service Employees
[3906]
7098 Atlanta Cir.
Seaford, DE 19973
Martinez, Astrid, President

American Alliance of Paralegals, Inc.
[5658]
4023 Kennett Pke., Ste. 146
Wilmington, DE 19807-2018
Goudie, John C., President

American Amputee Soccer Associa-
  tion [23184]
1033 Creekside Dr.
Wilmington, DE 19804
PH: (302)683-0997
Hofmann, Rick, President

American Association of Electronic
  Reporters and Transcribers [2737]
PO Box 9826
Wilmington, DE 19809
PH: (302)765-3510
Toll free: 800-233-5306
Fax: (302)241-2177
Hunt, Geoffrey, Secretary

American Heartworm Society
[17623]
PO Box 8266
Wilmington, DE 19803-8266
Jones, Dr. Stephen, President

American Society of Cytopathology
[14357]
100 W 10th St., Ste. 605
Wilmington, DE 19801-6604
PH: (302)543-6583
Fax: (302)543-6597
Jenkins, Elizabeth, Exec. Dir.

Business History Conference [9468]
c/o Hagley Museum and Library
PO Box 3630
Wilmington, DE 19807-0630
PH: (302)658-2400
Fax: (302)655-3188
Horowitz, Roger, Secretary,
  Treasurer

Collegiate Network [8152]
3901 Centerville Rd.
Wilmington, DE 19807
PH: (302)652-4600
Toll free: 800-526-7022
Fax: (302)652-1760
Lane, Jacob, Director

Greyhound Racing Association of
  America [22825]
2207 Concord Pike, No. 335
Wilmington, DE 19803
PH: (717)274-3097
Hevener, Ron, CEO, Founder,
  President

Intercollegiate Studies Institute
[18026]
3901 Centerville Rd.
Wilmington, DE 19807-1938
PH: (302)652-4600
Toll free: 800-526-7022
Fax: (302)652-1760
Donahue, Jed, Ed.-in-Chief

International Association of
  Corporate Entertainment Produc-
  ers [1139]
PO Box 9826
Wilmington, DE 19809-9826
PH: (312)285-0227
Tannen, Michael F., CESP, Exec. Dir.

International Association of Used
  Equipment Dealers [2625]
214 Edgewood Dr., Ste. 100
Wilmington, DE 19809-3255

The International Ecotourism Society **[3292]**
427 N Tatnall St.
Wilmington, DE 19801-2230
PH: (202)506-5033
Fax: (202)789-7279
Bricker, Dr. Kelly S., Chairperson

International Phalaenopsis Alliance **[4434]**
c/o Lynn Fuller, Membership Secretary
1401 Pennsylvania Ave., No. 1604
Wilmington, DE 19806
Fax: (302)425-4660
Fighetti, Carlos, President

International Society of African Scientists **[7137]**
c/o Senyo Opong, Secretary
PO Box 9209
Wilmington, DE 19809
Opong, Senyo, Secretary

National Association of State Agencies of the Deaf and Hard of Hearing **[11942]**
c/o Delaware Office for the Deaf and Hard of Hearing
4425 N Market St.
Wilmington, DE 19802-1307
Withers, Jan, Secretary

North American Simulation and Gaming Association **[22063]**
4023 Kennett Pke., No. 530
Wilmington, DE 19807
PH: (980)224-2637
Saeger, Chris, Exec. Dir.

Raskob Foundation for Catholic Activities, Inc. **[19899]**
10 Montchanin Rd.
Wilmington, DE 19807
PH: (302)655-4440
Fax: (302)655-3223
Fracyon, Noelle M., President

Small Business Council of America **[18063]**
1523 Concord Pke., Ste. 300
Brandywine E
Wilmington, DE 19803
PH: (302)691-7222
Redstone, Leanne H., Exec. Dir., Secretary

DISTRICT OF COLUMBIA

Georgian Association in the United States of America **[19439]**
2200 Pennsylvania Ave. NW, 4th Fl.
Washington, DC 20037
PH: (202)234-2441
Tsereteli, Mamuka, President

National Committee for a Human Life Amendment Inc. **[19062]**
PO Box 34116
Washingon, DC 20043
PH: (202)393-0703
Taylor, Michael A., Exec. Dir.

2Seeds Network **[3533]**
920 U St. NW
Washington, DC 20001
PH: (202)697-9565
Baker, Amy, Exec. Dir.

21st Century Democrats **[18107]**
2120 L St. NW, Ste. 305
Washington, DC 20037
PH: (202)768-9222
Plati, Crystal, Exec. Dir.

100% Recycled Paperboard Alliance **[2490]**
1601 K St. NW
Washington, DC 20006

PH: (202)347-8000
Toll free: 877-772-6200
Schutes, Paul J., Exec. Dir.

A. Philip Randolph Institute **[19100]**
815 16th St. NW, 4th Fl.
Washington, DC 20006-4101
PH: (202)508-3710
Fax: (202)508-3711
Brown, Clayola, President

AAA Foundation for Traffic Safety **[12810]**
607 14th St. NW, Ste. 201
Washington, DC 20005
PH: (202)638-5944
Fax: (202)638-5943
Kissinger, J. Peter, CEO, President

AARP **[12752]**
601 E St. NW
Washington, DC 20049-0001
PH: (202)434-3525
Toll free: 888-687-2277
Raphael, Carol, Chairperson

AAUW Legal Advocacy Fund **[5403]**
1111 16th St. NW
Washington, DC 20036
PH: (202)785-7700
Toll free: 800-326-2289
Fax: (202)872-1425
Hallman, Linda D., CAE, CEO

AcademyHealth **[14921]**
1666 K St. NW, Ste. 1100
Washington, DC 20036
PH: (202)292-6700
Fax: (202)292-6800
Wallace, Paul, CEO

Access to Benefits Coalition **[18325]**
1901 L St. NW, 4th Fl.
Washington, DC 20036
PH: (202)479-6670
Fax: (202)479-0735
Parkin, Scott, Contact

ACCORD Network **[12602]**
PO Box 15815
Washington, DC 20003
Hayward, Chad, Exec. Dir.

Accrediting Council for Continuing Education and Training **[7665]**
1722 N St. NW
Washington, DC 20036
PH: (202)955-1113
Fax: (202)955-1118
Williams, Roger J.

Accrediting Council for Independent Colleges and Schools **[7411]**
750 1st St. NE, Ste. 980
Washington, DC 20002-4241
PH: (202)336-6780
Fax: (202)842-2593
Gray, Albert C., PhD, CEO, Exec. Dir.

ACCSES **[17965]**
1501 M St. NW, 7th Fl.
Washington, DC 20005
PH: (202)349-4259
Fax: (202)785-1756
Goosman, Gary, Dir. of Comm.

ACDI/VOCA **[3976]**
50 F St. NW, Ste. 1000
Washington, DC 20001
PH: (202)469-6000
Toll free: 800-929-8622
Fax: (202)469-6257
Guenette, Paul, Sr. VP

Acrylonitrile Group **[705]**
1250 Connecticut Ave. NW, Ste. 700
Washington, DC 20036

PH: (202)419-1500
Fensterheim, Robert, Contact

Act Now to Stop War and End Racism Coalition **[18768]**
617 Florida Ave. NW, Lower Level
Washington, DC 20001
PH: (202)265-1948

ACTION **[17131]**
RESULTS Educational Fund
1101 15th St. NW, Ste. 1200
Washington, DC 20005
PH: (202)783-4800
Fax: (202)783-2818
Bouchane, Kolleen, Director

Action Africa **[17769]**
2903 Mills Ave. NE
Washington, DC 20018
PH: (202)529-8350
Fax: (202)529-1912
Egbulem, Fatmata, Officer

Action on Smoking and Health **[17224]**
701 4th St. NW
Washington, DC 20001
PH: (202)659-4310
Fax: (202)289-7166
Huber, Laurent, Exec. Dir.

ActionAid International USA **[12133]**
1420 K St. NW, Ste. 900
Washington, DC 20005
PH: (202)835-1240
Natarajan, Mohan, Chairperson

Active Minds **[15754]**
2001 S St. NW, Ste. 450
Washington, DC 20009
PH: (202)332-9595
Toll free: 800-273-TALK
Malmon, Alison, Exec. Dir., Founder

ADAP Advocacy Association **[13516]**
PO Box 15275
Washington, DC 20003
Rose, Gary R., Bd. Member

Adult Vaccine Access Coalition **[15368]**
1150 17th St. NW, Ste. 400
Washington, DC 20036
PH: (202)540-1070
Hanen, Laura, Chairperson

Advanced Biofuels Association **[1465]**
800 17th St. NW, Ste. 1100
Washington, DC 20006-3962
PH: (202)469-5140
McAdams, Michael J., President

Advanced Energy Management Alliance **[1105]**
1155 15th St. NW, Ste. 500
Washington, DC 20005
PH: (202)524-8832
Hamilton, Katherine, Exec. Dir.

Advanced Initiatives in Medical Simulation **[15672]**
1500 K St. NW, Ste. 1100
Washington, DC 20005-3317
PH: (202)230-5091
Fax: (202)842-8465
Dawson, Steve, MD, Chairman

Advanced Medical Technology Association **[15075]**
701 Pennsylvania Ave. NW, Ste. 800
Washington, DC 20004-2654
PH: (202)783-8700
Fax: (202)783-8750
Mendez, Kenneth, Sr. VP

Advanced Television Systems Committee **[451]**
1776 K St. NW, 8th Fl.
Washington, DC 20006-2304

PH: (202)872-9160
Fax: (202)872-9161
Reitmeier, Glenn, Bd. Member

Advancing Girls' Education in Africa **[7944]**
PO Box 15298
Washington, DC 20003
PH: (202)760-4299
Sidle, Aubryn Allyn, Exec. Dir.

Advisory Council for Bosnia and Herzegovina **[18475]**
1510 H St. NW, Ste. 900
Washington, DC 20005
PH: (202)347-6742
Deumic, Vehid, VP

Advisory Council on Historic Preservation **[9365]**
401 F St. NW, Ste. 308
Washington, DC 20001-2637
PH: (202)517-0200
Hauser, Valerie, Director

Advocates for Better Children's Diets **[16199]**
1050 17th St. NW, Ste. 600
Washington, DC 20036
PH: (202)659-1858
Fax: (202)659-3522
Chapman, Nancy, MPH, RD, Principal

Advocates for Highway and Auto Safety **[12811]**
750 1st St. NE, Ste. 1130
Washington, DC 20002
PH: (202)408-1711
Fax: (202)408-1699
Gillan, Jackie, President

Advocates for Youth **[11834]**
2000 M St. NW, Ste. 750
Washington, DC 20036
PH: (202)419-3420
Fax: (202)419-1448
Wagoner, James, President

Affordable Housing Tax Credit Coalition **[486]**
1909 K St. NW, 12th Fl.
Washington, DC 20006
PH: (202)661-7698
Fax: (202)661-2299
Spielman, Victoria E., Exec. Dir.

AFL-CIO **[23450]**
815 16th St. NW
Washington, DC 20006
PH: (202)637-5010
(202)637-5000
Trumka, Richard L., President

AFL-CIO-Building and Construction Trades Department **[23451]**
815 16th St., 6th Fl.
Washington, DC 20006
PH: (202)347-1461
McGarvey, Sean, President

AFL-CIO- Department Professional Employees **[23452]**
815 16th St. NW, 7th Fl.
Washington, DC 20006
PH: (202)638-0320
Almeida, Paul E., President

AFL-CIO-Maritime Trades Department **[23472]**
815 16th St. NW
Washington, DC 20006-4101
PH: (202)628-6300
Sacco, Michael, President

AFL-CIO - Metal Trades Department **[23479]**
815 16th St. NW
Washington, DC 20006

PH: (202)508-3705
Fax: (202)508-3706
Ault, Ron, President

AFL-CIO-Union Label and Service
Trades Department [23528]
815 16th St. NW
Washington, DC 20006
PH: (202)508-3700
Kline, Richard, President

Africa Development Corps [12134]
2710 Ontario Rd. NW
Washington, DC 20009
PH: (301)944-3370
Skelton, Shaun, PhD, Director,
Founder

Africa Faith and Justice Network
[17771]
3025 4th St. NE, Ste. 122
Washington, DC 20017
PH: (202)817-3670
Fax: (202)817-3671
Okure, Aniedi, Exec. Dir.

Africa Travel Association [3366]
1100 17th St. NW, Ste. 1000
Washington, DC 20036
PH: (202)835-1115
Toll free: 888-439-0478
Fax: (202)835-1117
Bergman, Edward, Exec. Dir.

African Aid Organization Inc. [10531]
1325 G St. NE, Ste. 500
Washington, DC 20005
PH: (202)449-7708

African American Environmentalist
Association [4033]
1629 K St. NW, Ste. 300
Washington, DC 20006-1631
McDonald, Norris, President

African Wildlife Foundation [4779]
1400 16th St. NW, Ste. 120
Washington, DC 20036
PH: (202)939-3333
Toll free: 888-494-5354
Fax: (202)939-3332
Sebunya, Kaddu, President

Africare [11309]
440 R St. NW
Washington, DC 20001
PH: (202)462-3614
Fax: (202)464-0867
Francis, Peter, Treasurer

Afro-American Historical and
Genealogical Society [20950]
PO Box 73067
Washington, DC 20056-3067
PH: (202)234-5350
Camp, Sherri, President

AFT Nurses and Health Profession-
als [23442]
555 New Jersey Ave. NW
Washington, DC 20001
PH: (202)879-4400
Weingarten, Randi, President

Afterschool Alliance [10801]
1616 H St. NW, Ste. 820
Washington, DC 20006
PH: (202)347-2030
Toll free: 866-543-7863
Fax: (202)347-2092
Grant, Jodi, Exec. Dir.

Agri-Energy Roundtable [18482]
PO Box 5565
Washington, DC 20016
PH: (202)887-0528
Hollis, Nicholas E., Exec. Dir.

Agribusiness Council [3522]
PO Box 5565
Washington, DC 20016

PH: (202)296-4563
Hollis, Nicholas E., CEO, President

Agricultural Retailers Association
[2943]
1156 15th St. NW, Ste. 500
Washington, DC 20005
PH: (202)457-0825
Fax: (202)457-0864
Coppock, Daren, CEO, President

Agriculture Transportation Coalition
[3317]
1120 G St. NW, Ste. 1020
Washington, DC 20005
PH: (202)783-3333
Fax: (202)783-4422
Friedmann, Peter, Exec. Dir.

Aid to Artisans [12136]
5225 Wisconsin Ave. NW, Ste. 104
Washington, DC 20015
PH: (202)572-2628
Mandelbaum, Carola, Managing Dir.

AIDS Alliance for Children, Youth
and Families [13520]
1705 DeSales St. NW, Ste. 700
Washington, DC 20036
PH: (202)754-1858
Ruppal, Michael, Exec. Dir.

AIDS Global Action [13522]
5185 MacArthur Blvd. NW, No. 607
Washington, DC 20016
PH: (202)716-4000
Fax: (347)841-3126
Mehta, Rajan, Director

AIDS United [18856]
1424 K St. NW, Ste. 200
Washington, DC 20005-2411
PH: (202)408-4848
Fax: (202)408-1818
Kaplan, Michael, CEO, President

Air Line Pilots Association
International [23381]
1625 Massachusetts Ave. NW
Washington, DC 20036
PH: (703)689-2270
Canoll, Tim, President

Aircraft Carrier Industrial Base Coali-
tion [985]
700 13th St. NW
Washington, DC 20005
PH: (202)585-2141
Fax: (202)383-0079
Giannini, Richard A., Chairperson

Aircraft Fleet Recycling Association
[12579]
529 14th St. NW, Ste. 750
Washington, DC 20045
PH: (202)591-2478
Fax: (202)223-9741
Hitchcock, Reed, Exec. Dir.

Airforwarders Association [2112]
750 National Press Bldg.
529 14th St. NW, Ste. 750
Washington, DC 20045
PH: (202)591-2456
Fax: (202)591-2445
Fried, Brandon, Exec. Dir.

Airline Ambassadors International
[13024]
1500 Massachusetts Ave., No. 648
Washington, DC 20005
PH: (415)359-8006
Toll free: 866-264-3586
Rivard, Nancy, Founder, President

Airlines for America [125]
Communications Dept.
1301 Pennsylvania Ave. NW, Ste.
1100

Washington, DC 20004-7017
PH: (202)626-4000
Calio, Nicholas E., CEO, President

Airports Council International - North
America [126]
1615 L St. NW, Ste. 300
Washington, DC 20036
PH: (202)293-8500
Toll free: 888-424-7767
Fax: (202)331-1362
Principato, Greg, President

Alaska Coalition [3791]
122 C St. NW, Ste. 240
Washington, DC 20001
PH: (505)438-4245
VanDenzen, Liz, Director

Alexander Graham Bell Association
for the Deaf and Hard of Hearing
[15166]
3417 Volta Pl. NW
Washington, DC 20007
PH: (202)337-5220
Sugar, Meredith K., Director

The Alexander Hamilton Society
[5679]
11 Dupont Cir. NW, Ste. 325
Washington, DC 20036
PH: (202)559-7389
Friedberg, Aaron L., Founder,
President

Alkylphenols and Ethoxylates
Research Council [706]
1250 Connecticut Ave. NW, Ste. 700
Washington, DC 20036
PH: (202)419-1500

Alliance for the Adoption of Innova-
tions in Medicine [14971]
1000 Potomac St. NW, Ste. 150-A
Washington, DC 20007
PH: (202)559-0380
Fax: (202)459-9611
Ginnan, Shannon, MD, Director

The Alliance for Advancing Nonprofit
Health Care [14972]
PO Box 41015
Washington, DC 20018
Toll free: 877-299-6497
McPherson, Bruce, CEO, President

Alliance for Aging Research [10497]
1700 K St. NW, Ste. 740
Washington, DC 20006
PH: (202)293-2856
Fax: (202)955-8394
Williams, Jackie, Administrator

Alliance for American Manufacturing
[2210]
711 D St. NW, 3rd Fl.
Washington, DC 20004
PH: (202)393-3430
Paul, Scott, President

Alliance of Automobile Manufactur-
ers [305]
803 7th St. NW, Ste. 300
Washington, DC 20001
PH: (202)326-5500
Bainwol, Mitch, President, CEO

Alliance for Aviation Across America
[6025]
1025 Connecticut Ave. NW, Ste.
1000
Washington, DC 20036
PH: (202)223-9523
Shilad, Selena, Exec. Dir.

Alliance for Balanced Pain Manage-
ment [16544]
Washington, DC
PH: (202)499-4114
Cowan, Penney, Contact

Alliance for Biking and Walking
[19194]
PO Box 65150
Washington, DC 20035
PH: (202)449-9692
(202)621-5442
Ford-Wagner, Amy, V. Chmn. of the
Bd.

Alliance of Business Immigration
Lawyers [5071]
11 Dupont Cir. NW, Ste. 775
Washington, DC 20036
PH: (404)949-8150
Fax: (404)816-8615
Wolfsdorf, Bernard, Mem.

Alliance of Community Health Plans
[15093]
1825 Eye St. NW, Ste. 401
Washington, DC 20006
PH: (202)785-2247
Fax: (202)785-4060
Cropp, Michael, M.D., Officer

Alliance for Community Trees [4192]
6856 Eastern Ave. NW, Ste. 150
Washington, DC 20012
PH: (202)291-8733
Fax: (202)291-1433

Alliance for Consumer Education
[4121]
1667 K St. NW, Ste. 300
Washington, DC 20006
PH: (202)862-3902
Fax: (202)872-8114
Creighton, Colleen, Exec. Dir.

Alliance for Continuing Education in
the Health Professions [8300]
2025 M St. NW, Ste. 800
Washington, DC 20036
PH: (202)367-1151
Fax: (202)367-2151
Sulkes, Destry J., MD, MBA, Mem.

Alliance to End Hunger [12076]
425 3rd St. SW, Ste. 1200
Washington, DC 20024
PH: (202)688-1157
Hall, Tony P., Exec. Dir.

Alliance to End Slavery and Traffick-
ing [18367]
1700 Pennsylvania Ave. NW, Ste.
520
Washington, DC 20006
PH: (202)503-3200
Fax: (202)503-3201
Brown, Ann, Comm. Spec.

Alliance for Environmental Technol-
ogy [1424]
1250 24th St. NW, Ste. 300
Washington, DC 20037-1186
PH: (519)217-5162
Pryke, Douglas C., Exec. Dir.

Alliance for Excellent Education
[8558]
1201 Connecticut Ave. NW, Ste. 901
Washington, DC 20036
PH: (202)828-0828
Fax: (202)828-0821
Wise, Bob, President

Alliance to Feed the Future [3557]
1100 Connecticut Ave. NW
Washington, DC 20036
Raymond, Matt, Contact

Alliance for Health Reform [18326]
1444 Eye St. NW, Ste. 910
Washington, DC 20005-6573
PH: (202)789-2300
Fax: (202)789-2233
Graham, Robert, MD, Chairman

Alliance for Home Health Quality
and Innovation **[15274]**
PO Box 7319
Washington, DC 20044
PH: (202)239-3983
Borne, Bill, President, Chairman

Alliance for International Educational
and Cultural Exchange **[8052]**
1828 L St. NW, Ste. 1150
Washington, DC 20036
PH: (202)293-6141
Fax: (202)293-6144
Zherka, Ilir, Exec. Dir.

Alliance for Justice **[5720]**
11 Dupont Cir. NW, 2nd Fl.
Washington, DC 20036
PH: (202)822-6070
Fax: (202)822-6068
Aron, Nan, President

Alliance for a New Transportation
Charter **[5807]**
Surface Transportation Policy Project
1100 17th St. NW, 10 Fl.
Washington, DC 20036
PH: (202)466-2636
Fax: (202)466-2247
Canby, Anne P., President

Alliance of Nonprofit Mailers **[2113]**
1211 Connecticut Ave. NW, Ste. 610
Washington, DC 20036-2705
PH: (202)462-5132
Fax: (202)462-0423
Kearney, Stephen, Exec. Dir.

Alliance for Patient Advocacy
[14973]
1747 Pennsylvania Ave. NW, Ste.
470
Washington, DC 20006
PH: (202)775-9110
Toll free: 877-775-9110
Fax: (202)775-2074
Vogel, Michelle, MPA, Founder,
Exec. Dir.

Alliance for Peacebuilding **[18769]**
1800 Massachusetts Ave. NW, Ste.
401
Washington, DC 20036
PH: (202)822-2047
Fax: (202)822-2049
Greenberg, Melanie, President, CEO

Alliance for Quality Nursing Home
Care **[16082]**
1350 Connecticut Ave. NW, Ste. 900
Washington, DC 20036
PH: (202)459-6313
Fax: (202)459-6308
Rosenbloom, Alan, President

Alliance for Rail Competition **[2829]**
412 1st St. SE, Ste. 1
Washington, DC 20003
PH: (202)484-7133
Fax: (202)484-0770
Whiteside, Terry, Chairman

Alliance for Retired Americans
[12753]
815 16th St. NW, 4th Fl.
Washington, DC 20006
PH: (202)637-5399
    (202)637-5275
Toll free: 800-333-7212
Fiesta, Richard, Exec. Dir.

Alliance to Save Energy **[6449]**
1850 M St. NW, Ste. 610
Washington, DC 20036
PH: (202)857-0666
Fax: (202)331-9588
Callahan, Kateri, President

Alliance for School Choice **[8527]**
1660 L St. NW, Ste. 1000
Washington, DC 20036

PH: (202)280-1990
Fax: (202)280-1989
Brock, Greg, Exec. Dir.

Alliance for Strong Families and
Communities **[11809]**
1020 19th St. NW, Ste. 500
Washington, DC 20036
PH: (414)359-1040
Toll free: 800-221-3726
Dreyfus, Susan, President, CEO

Alliance in Support of the Afghan
People **[10466]**
1225 Eye St. NW
Washington, DC 20005
Crocker, Amb. Ryan, Co-Ch.

Alliance in Support of Independent
Research **[2016]**
1990 M St. NW, Ste. 660
Washington, DC 20036-3417
PH: (202)223-4418
Pickard, Lee A., Counsel

Alliance for Telecommunications
Industry Solutions **[3215]**
1200 G St. NW, Ste. 500
Washington, DC 20005
PH: (202)628-6380
Miller, Susan, CEO, President

Alliance for Women in Media **[452]**
1250 24th St. NW, Ste. 300
Washington, DC 20037
PH: (202)750-3664
Brooks, Becky, Exec. Dir.

Allies Building Community **[9019]**
PO Box 57250
Washington, DC 20037-0250
PH: (202)496-1555
Tai, Dr. Dwan, Founder, Chairperson

Amazon Conservation Association
[3796]
1012 14th St. NW, Ste. 625
Washington, DC 20005
PH: (202)234-2356
    (202)234-2357
Fax: (202)234-2358
Cacciatore, Dr. Joanne, Founder,
President

America Abroad Media **[18651]**
1701 Pennsylvania Ave. NW, Ste.
300
Washington, DC 20006
PH: (202)249-7380
Albright, Madeleine K., Chairman

America-Georgia Business Council
[1975]
2200 Pennsylvania Ave. NW, 4th Fl.
E
Washington, DC 20037
PH: (202)416-1606
Tsereteli, Mamuka, President

America-MidEast Educational and
Training Services **[18671]**
2025 M St. NW, Ste. 600
Washington, DC 20036-3363
PH: (202)776-9600
Fax: (202)776-7000
Gray, Mary W., Chairwoman

American Academy of Actuaries
[1822]
1850 M St. NW, Ste. 300
Washington, DC 20036
PH: (202)223-8196
Fax: (202)872-1948
Hanna, Craig, Dir. Pub. Aff.

American Academy of Adoption At-
torneys **[4978]**
PO Box 33053
Washington, DC 20033-0053

PH: (202)832-2222
Fairfax, Jennifer, VP

American Academy of Child and
Adolescent Psychiatry **[16807]**
3615 Wisconsin Ave. NW
Washington, DC 20016-3007
PH: (202)966-7300
Fax: (202)966-2891
Joshi, Paramjit T., M.D., President

American Academy of Diplomacy
[5228]
1200 18th St. NW, Ste. 902
Washington, DC 20036
PH: (202)331-3721
Fax: (202)833-4555
Courtney, William, Director

American Academy of HIV Medicine
[13527]
1705 DeSales St. NW, Ste. 700
Washington, DC 20036
PH: (202)659-0699
Fax: (202)659-0976
Friedman, James M., MD, Exec. Dir.

American Academy for Liberal
Education **[8225]**
1200 G St. NW, Ste. 883
Washington, DC 20005
PH: (202)434-8971
Butterworth, Prof. Charles E.,
Secretary

American Academy of Microbiology
[6066]
1752 N St. NW
Washington, DC 20036
PH: (202)737-3600
Swanson, Michele S., Chairperson

American Academy of Nursing
[16085]
1000 Vermont Ave. NW, Ste. 910
Washington, DC 20005-4903
PH: (202)777-1170
Sullivan, Cheryl G., MSES, CEO

American Academy of Orthotists and
Prosthetists **[16492]**
1331 H St. NW, Ste. 501
Washington, DC 20005
PH: (202)380-3663
Fax: (202)380-3447
Middleton, Lydia, Exec. Dir.

American Adoption Congress
[10443]
PO Box 7601
Washington, DC 20004
PH: (202)483-3399
McGuigan, Cindy, Treasurer

American Advertising Federation
[84]
1101 Vermont Ave. NW, Ste. 500
Washington, DC 20005-6306
PH: (202)898-0089
Datri, James Edmund, CEO,
President

American-Arab Anti-Discrimination
Committee **[17864]**
1990 M St. NW, Ste. 610
Washington, DC 20036
PH: (202)244-2990
Fax: (202)333-3980
Rifka, Safa, MD, Chairman

American Architectural Foundation
[5951]
740 15th St. NW, Ste. 225
Washington, DC 20005
PH: (202)787-1001
Fax: (202)787-1002
Bogle, Hon. Ronald, CEO, President

American Association for Access,
Equity and Diversity **[11751]**
1701 Pennsylvania Ave. NW, Ste.
206

Washington, DC 20006
PH: (202)349-9855
Fax: (202)355-1399
Rose, Marshall, President

American Association of
Acupuncture and Oriental Medicine
[16453]
PO Box 96503, No. 44144
Washington, DC 20090-6503
Toll free: 866-455-7999
Fax: (866)455-7999
Lee, Don, President

American Association of Acupuncture
and Oriental Medicine **[13502]**
PO Box 96503
Washington, DC 20090-6503
PH: (916)451-6950
Toll free: 866-455-7999
Fax: (916)451-6952
Biris, Anne, LAc, President

American Association for the
Advancement of Science **[7116]**
1200 New York Ave. NW
Washington, DC 20005
PH: (202)326-6400
Fedoroff, Nina V., Chairperson

American Association for the
Advancement of Science - Science
and Human Rights Coalition
[18369]
1200 New York Ave. NW
Washington, DC 20005-3928
PH: (202)326-6400
Gran, Brian, Mem.

American Association of Bank Direc-
tors **[377]**
1250 24th St. NW, Ste. 700
Washington, DC 20037-1222
PH: (202)463-4888
Fax: (202)349-8080
Baris, David H., Esq., President

American Association of Blacks in
Energy **[6451]**
1625 K St. NW, Ste. 405
Washington, DC 20006
PH: (202)371-9530
Fax: (202)371-9218
Williams, George, Chairman

American Association for Clinical
Chemistry **[6178]**
900 7th St., NW, Ste. 400
Washington, DC 20006
Toll free: 800-892-5093
Fax: (202)887-0717
Wong, Steven H., PhD, President

American Association of Colleges of
Nursing **[8301]**
1 Dupont Cir. NW, Ste. 530
Washington, DC 20036
PH: (202)463-6930
Fax: (202)785-8320
Trautman, Deborah, CEO

American Association of Colleges for
Teacher Education **[8635]**
1307 New York Ave. NW, Ste. 300
Washington, DC 20005-4721
PH: (202)293-2450
Fax: (202)457-8095
LaCelle-Peterson, Mark, Sr. VP

American Association of Collegiate
Registrars and Admissions Officers
[7443]
1 Dupont Cir. NW, Ste. 520
Washington, DC 20036
PH: (202)293-9161
    (301)490-7651
Fax: (202)872-8857
Rooker, LeRoy, Exec. Dir.

American Association of Community
Colleges **[7640]**
1 Dupont Cir. NW, Ste. 410
Washington, DC 20036-1145
PH: (202)728-0200
Fax: (202)833-2467
Royal, Angel, Chief of Staff

American Association of Crop Insur-
ers **[1823]**
1 Massachusetts Ave. NW, Ste. 800
Washington, DC 20001
PH: (202)789-4100
Fax: (202)408-7763
Weber, Tim, Chairman

American Association of Exporters
and Importers **[1976]**
1717 K St. NW, Ste. 1120
Washington, DC 20006
PH: (202)857-8009
Fax: (202)857-7843
Wigginton, Phyliss, Chairman

American Association of
Geographers **[6670]**
1710 16th St. NW
Washington, DC 20009
PH: (202)234-1450
Fax: (202)234-2744

American Association for Higher
Education and Accreditation **[7737]**
2020 Pennsylvania Ave. NW 975
Washington, DC 20006
PH: (202)293-6440
Fax: (855)252-7622
Rabac, Ken, Director

American Association for Homecare
[15076]
1707 L St. NW, Ste. 350
Washington, DC 20036
PH: (202)372-0107
Fax: (202)835-8306
Letizia, John J., Chairman

American Association on Intellectual
and Developmental Disabilities
[15812]
501 3rd St. NW, Ste. 200
Washington, DC 20001
PH: (202)387-1968
Fax: (202)387-2193
Nygren, Margaret A., Exec. Dir.,
CEO

American Association for Justice
[5821]
777 6th St. NW, Ste. 200
Washington, DC 20001
PH: (202)965-3500
Toll free: 800-424-2725
Tawwater, Larry A., President

The American Association of
Language Specialists **[3310]**
PO Box 27306
Washington, DC 20038-7306

American Association for Museum
Volunteers **[9816]**
PO Box 9494
Washington, DC 20016-9494
PH: (215)299-1029
Kuter, Lois, President

American Association of Natur-
opathic Physicians **[15855]**
818 18th St., Ste. 250
Washington, DC 20006
PH: (202)237-8150
Toll free: 866-538-2267
Fax: (202)237-8152
Chasse, Jaclyn, ND, President

American Association of People with
Disabilities **[11568]**
2013 H St. NW, 5th Fl.
Washington, DC 20006

PH: (202)521-4316
Toll free: 800-840-8844
Berger, Helena, President, CEO

American Association of Sexuality
Educators, Counselors and
Therapists **[17190]**
1444 I St. NW, Ste. 700
Washington, DC 20005-6542
PH: (202)449-1099
Fax: (202)216-9646
McCaffree, Konnie, President

American Association of State Col-
leges and Universities **[7619]**
1307 New York Ave. NW, 5th Fl.
Washington, DC 20005-4701
PH: (202)293-7070
   (202)478-4647
Fax: (202)296-5819
Dockett, Shirley, Associate

American Association of State
Highway and Transportation Of-
ficials **[5808]**
444 N Capitol St. NW, Ste. 249
Washington, DC 20001
PH: (202)624-5800
Fax: (202)624-5806
Adem, Jenet, Dir. of Fin. & Admin.

American Association of State
Service Commissions **[5692]**
455 Massachusetts Ave. NW, Ste.
153
1625 K St. NW, 5th Fl.
Washington, DC 20001
PH: (202)729-8179
Branen, Tom, Exec. Dir.

American Association of Suicidology
[13191]
5221 Wisconsin Ave. NW
Washington, DC 20015
PH: (202)237-2280
Fax: (202)237-2282
Miller, David, PhD, President

American Association of University
Professors **[8464]**
1133 19th St. NW, Ste. 200
Washington, DC 20036
PH: (202)737-5900
Fax: (202)737-5526
Fichtenbaum, Rudy H., President

American Association of University
Women **[8742]**
1111 16th St. NW
Washington, DC 20036-4809
PH: (202)785-7700
   (202)728-7602
Toll free: 800-326-2289
Fax: (202)872-1425
Hallman, Ms. Linda D., Exec. Dir.

American Association of University
Women - Women Educational
Foundation **[8743]**
1111 16th St. NW
Washington, DC 20036
PH: (202)785-7700
Toll free: 800-326-2289
Fax: (202)785-7777
Ho, Patricia Fae, President

American Astronomical Society
[5997]
2000 Florida Ave. NW, Ste. 400
Washington, DC 20009-1231
PH: (202)328-2010
Fax: (202)234-2560
Marvel, Kevin B., Exec. Ofc.

American Automotive Policy Council
[276]
1401 H St. NW, Ste. 780
Washington, DC 20005

PH: (202)789-0030
Fax: (202)789-0054
Blunt, Matt, President

American Bahraini Friendship
Society **[18509]**
3502 International Dr. NW
Washington, DC 20008-3035
PH: (202)342-1111
Habiby, Mrs. Nadira F., Dir. of
Admin.

American Bakers Association **[367]**
601 Pennsylvania Ave. NW, Ste. 230
Washington, DC 20004
PH: (202)789-0300
Fax: (202)898-1164
MacKie, Robb, CEO, President

American Bankers Association **[378]**
1120 Connecticut Ave. NW
Washington, DC 20036
PH: (202)663-5071
Toll free: 800-226-5377
Fax: (202)828-4540
Blanton, R. Daniel, Chairman

American Bar Association Center on
Children and the Law **[10849]**
1050 Connecticut Ave. NW, Ste. 400
Washington, DC 20036
PH: (202)662-1720
Toll free: 800-285-2221
Fax: (202)662-1755
Rives, Jack L.

American Bar Association - Commis-
sion on Disability Rights **[5271]**
1050 Connecticut Ave. NW, Ste. 400
Washington, DC 20036
PH: (202)662-1570
Fax: (202)442-3439
Allbright, Amy, Director

American Bar Association Commis-
sion on Homelessness and
Poverty **[11947]**
1050 Connecticut Ave. NW, Ste. 400
Washington, DC 20036
PH: (202)662-1693
Fax: (202)638-3844
Small, Theodore W., Jr., Chairman

American Bar Association Commis-
sion on Law and Aging **[5405]**
1050 Connecticut Ave. NW, Ste. 400
Washington, DC 20036
PH: (202)662-8690
Fax: (202)662-8698
Sabatino, Charles P., Director

American Bar Association Criminal
Justice Section **[5407]**
1050 Connecticut Ave. NW, Ste. 400
Washington, DC 20036
PH: (202)662-1500
Fax: (202)662-1501
Scruggs, Kevin, Director

American Bar Association Section of
Civil Rights and Social Justice
[17865]
1050 Connecticut Ave. NW, Ste. 400
Washington, DC 20036
PH: (202)662-1030
Toll free: 800-285-2221
Fax: (202)662-1031
Walters, Caroline, Asst. Dir.

American Bar Association - Section
of Dispute Resolution **[4956]**
1050 Connecticut NW, Ste. 400
Washington, DC 20036
PH: (202)662-1680
Fax: (202)662-1683
Herman, Howard, Chairman

American Bearing Manufacturers
Association **[1704]**
2025 M St. NW, Ste. 800
Washington, DC 20036-3309

PH: (202)367-1155
Caulfield, Cheryl, President

American Benefits Council **[5677]**
1501 M St. NW, Ste. 600
Washington, DC 20005-1775
PH: (202)289-6700
Fax: (202)289-4582
Klein, James A., President

American Beverage Association
[421]
1275 Pennsylvania Ave. NW, Ste.
1100
Washington, DC 20004
PH: (202)463-6732
   (202)463-6770
Fax: (202)659-5349
Hancock, Amy E., Secretary

American Beverage Institute **[422]**
Washington, DC 20005
PH: (202)463-7110
Longwell, Sarah, Managing Dir.

American Biogas Council **[5881]**
1211 Connecticut Ave. NW, Ste. 650
Washington, DC 20036-2701
PH: (202)640-6595
   (202)904-0220
Serfass, Patrick, Exec. Dir.

American Board of Clinical
Chemistry **[6179]**
900 17th St. NW, Ste. 400
Washington, DC 20006
PH: (202)835-8717
Fax: (202)833-4576
Abadie, Jude, President

American Board of Examiners of
Psychodrama, Sociometry, and
Group Psychotherapy **[16958]**
PO Box 15572
Washington, DC 20003
PH: (202)483-0514
Swallow, Judith A., Treasurer

American Board of Forensic
Anthropology **[14771]**
c/o Joan E. Baker, Secretary
Defense POW/MIA Accounting
Agency
2600 Defence Pentagon
Washington, DC 20301-2600
PH: (703)699-1428
Bartelink, Eric J., President

American Board of Wound Manage-
ment **[17524]**
1800 M St. NW, Ste. 400S
Washington, DC 20036
PH: (202)457-8408
Fax: (202)530-0659
Murphy, Christopher M., Exec. Dir.

American Bus Association **[3320]**
111 K St. NE, 9th Fl.
Washington, DC 20002
PH: (202)842-1645
Toll free: 800-283-2877
Fax: (202)842-0850
Lewis, Roderick, Director

American Business Conference
[1977]
1828 L St. NW, Ste. 280
Washington, DC 20036-5114
PH: (202)822-9300
Fax: (202)467-4070
Endean, John, President

American Cancer Society Cancer
Action Network **[13883]**
555 11th St. NW, Ste. 300
Washington, DC 20004
PH: (202)661-5700
Seffrin, John R., PhD, CEO

American Center for Law and
Justice [12759]
PO Box 90555
Washington, DC 20090-0555
PH: (757)226-2489
Toll free: 800-342-2255
Fax: (757)226-2836
Sekulow, Jay Alan, Chief Counsel

American Chemical Society [708]
1155 16th St. NW
Washington, DC 20036
PH: (202)872-4600
Toll free: 800-227-5558
Mitchem, Kathy, Administrator

American Chemistry Council [709]
700 2nd St. NE
Washington, DC 20002
PH: (202)249-7000
    (202)249-6623
Fax: (202)249-6100
Dooley, Calvin M., CEO, President

American Chemistry Council-
Chlorine Chemistry Division [6181]
700 2nd St. NE
Washington, DC 20002
PH: (202)249-7000
Fax: (202)249-6100
Simon, Robert J., VP

American Civil Liberties Union
National Prison Project [11516]
915 15th St. NW, 7th Fl.
Washington, DC 20005
PH: (202)393-4930
Fax: (202)393-4931
Herman, Susan N., President

American Cleaning Institute [710]
1331 L St. NW, Ste. 650
Washington, DC 20005
PH: (202)347-2900
Fax: (202)347-4110
Rosenberg, Ernie, President, CEO

American Clergy Leadership Confer-
ence [20532]
3224 16th St. NW
Washington, DC 20010
PH: (202)319-3200
Jenkins, Michael W., Chairman

American Clinical Laboratory As-
sociation [15515]
1100 New York Ave. NW, Ste. 725
W
Washington, DC 20005
PH: (202)637-9466
Mertz, Alan, President

American Coal Council [734]
1101 Pennsylvania Ave. NW, Ste.
600
Washington, DC 20004
PH: (202)756-4540
Fax: (202)756-7323
Monseu, Betsy, CEO

American Coal Foundation [735]
101 Constitution Ave. NW, Ste. 500
E
Washington, DC 20001-2133
PH: (202)463-9875
Fax: (202)463-9786

American Coalition for Clean Coal
Electricity [6406]
1152 15th St. NW, Ste. 400
Washington, DC 20005
PH: (202)459-4800

American Coalition for Fathers and
Children [12407]
1718 M St. NW, No. 1187
Washington, DC 20036
PH: (202)330-3248
Toll free: 800-978-3237
Roberts, David A., Chairman

American Coatings Association
[2487]
1500 Rhode Island Ave. NW
Washington, DC 20005
PH: (202)462-6272
Fax: (202)462-8549
Doyle, J. Andrew, Officer

American Coke and Coal Chemicals
Institute [736]
25 Massachusetts Ave. NW, Ste.
800
Washington, DC 20001
PH: (724)772-1167
Toll free: 866-422-7794
Owens, Richard, Chairman

American College of Cardiology
[14089]
2400 N St. NW
Washington, DC 20037
PH: (202)375-6000
Toll free: 800-253-4636
Fax: (202)375-7000
Holmes, David R., MD

American College of Environmental
Lawyers [5175]
1730 M St. NW Ste. 700
Washington, DC 20036
PH: (617)832-1203
Fax: (617)832-7000
Farer, David B., President

American College of Health Care
Administrators [16196]
1101 Connecticut Ave. NW, Ste. 450
Washington, DC 20036
PH: (202)536-5120
Fax: (866)874-1585
Sepp, Cecilia, CAE, President, CEO

American College of Obstetricians
and Gynecologists - Council on
Resident Education in Obstetrics
and Gynecology [16270]
409 12th St. SW
Washington, DC 20024-2188
PH: (202)638-5577
Toll free: 800-673-8444
Graves, Mark, Web Adm.

American College of Oral and Maxil-
lofacial Surgeons [16443]
2025 M St. NW, Ste. 800
Washington, DC 20036
PH: (202)367-1182
Fax: (202)367-2182
Franco, Pedro F., DDS, President

American College Personnel As-
sociation [8413]
1 Dupont Cir. NW, Ste. 300
Washington, DC 20036-1137
PH: (202)835-2272
Fax: (202)296-3286
Lee, Donna A., President

American College of Preventive
Medicine [16798]
455 Massachusetts Ave. NW, Ste.
200
Washington, DC 20001
PH: (202)466-2044
Fax: (202)466-2662
Barry, Michael, CAE, Exec. Dir.

American College of Trust and
Estate Counsel [5684]
901 15th St. NW, Ste. 525
Washington, DC 20005
PH: (202)684-8460
Fax: (202)684-8459
Fox, Charles D., IV, VP

American Committee for Peace in
the Caucasus [18770]
1301 Connecticut Ave. NW, 6th Fl.
Washington, DC 20036

PH: (202)296-5101
Howard, Glen, President

American Conference of Academic
Deans [7419]
1818 R St. NW
Washington, DC 20009
PH: (202)884-7419
Fax: (202)265-9532
Meyer, Thomas, Chairman

American Congress of Obstetricians
and Gynecologists [16272]
409 12th St. SW
Washington, DC 20024-2188
PH: (202)638-5577
Toll free: 800-673-8444
Lawrence, Hal C, III, MD, Exec. VP,
CEO

American Conservative Union
[18019]
1331 H St. NW, Ste. 500
Washington, DC 20005
PH: (202)347-9388
Fax: (202)347-9389
Schneider, Dan, Exec. Dir.

American Constitution Society for
Law and Policy [5100]
1333 H St. NW, 11th Fl.
Washington, DC 20005
PH: (202)393-6181
Fax: (202)393-6189
Lyle, David, Counsel

American Council for Capital Forma-
tion [18062]
1001 Connecticut Ave. NW, Ste. 620
Washington, DC 20036
PH: (202)293-5811
Fax: (202)785-8165
Bloomfield, Mr. Mark A., CEO,
President

American Council on Education
[7738]
1 Dupont Cir. NW
Washington, DC 20036
PH: (202)939-9300
Sirianni, Jim, Director

American Council on Education-
Center for Lifelong Learning [7908]
1 Dupont Cir. NW
Washington, DC 20036
PH: (202)939-9300

American Council on Education -
Inclusive Excellence Group [8745]
1 Dupont Cir. NW
Washington, DC 20036
PH: (202)939-9390
Gangone, Lynn, VP

American Council for an Energy-
Efficient Economy [6452]
529 14th St. NW, Ste. 600
Washington, DC 20045
PH: (202)507-4000
Fax: (202)429-2248
Nadel, Steven, Exec. Dir.

American Council of Engineering
Companies [6528]
1015 15th St. NW, 8th Fl.
Washington, DC 20005-2605
PH: (202)347-7474
Fax: (202)898-0068
Raymond, David A., CEO, President

American Council of Independent
Laboratories [6775]
1875 I St. NW, Ste. 500
Washington, DC 20006
PH: (202)887-5872
Fax: (202)887-0021
Bush, Milton, CEO

American Council for Kosovo
[18607]
PO Box 14522
Washington, DC 20044
O'Donnell, Patrick E., Chairman

American Council of Life Insurers
[1829]
101 Constitution Ave. NW, Ste. 700
Washington, DC 20001-2133
PH: (202)624-2000
Toll free: 877-674-4659
Kempthorne, Dirk, CEO, President

American Council on Renewable
Energy [6453]
1600 K St. NW, Ste. 650
Washington, DC 20006
PH: (202)393-0001
Fax: (202)393-0606
Wetstone, Gregory, President, CEO

American Council of State Savings
Supervisors [379]
1129 20th St. NW, 9th Fl.
Washington, DC 20036
PH: (512)475-1038
Fax: (512)475-1505
Jones, Caroline, Chairman

American Council of Trustees and
Alumni [7405]
1730 M St. NW, Ste. 600
Washington, DC 20036-4525
PH: (202)467-6787
Fax: (202)467-6784
Poliakoff, Michael B., President

American Council of Young Political
Leaders [18626]
2131 K St. NW, Ste. 400
Washington, DC 20037-1870
PH: (202)857-0999
Fax: (202)857-0027
Fujii, Stacie, Founder, President

American Councils for International
Education [7739]
1828 L St. NW, Ste. 1200
Washington, DC 20036-5136
PH: (202)833-7522
Fax: (202)833-7523
Davidson, Dr. Dan E., President

American Cultural Resources As-
sociation [8951]
2101 L St. NW, Ste. 800
Washington, DC 20037
PH: (202)367-9094
Toll free: 866-875-6492
Burrow, Ian, VP of Government Rel.

American Dental Education Associa-
tion [7707]
655 K St. NW, Ste. 800
Washington, DC 20001
PH: (202)289-7201
Fax: (202)289-7204
Valachovic, Richard, President, CEO

American Educational Research As-
sociation [8494]
1430 K St. NW, Ste. 1200
Washington, DC 20005-2504
PH: (202)238-3200
Fax: (202)238-3250
Levine, Felice J., PhD, Exec. Dir.

American Educational Trust [18672]
1902 18th St. NW
Washington, DC 20009
PH: (202)939-6050
Toll free: 800-368-5788
Fax: (202)265-4574
Hanley, Delinda C., Dir. of Advertis-
ing, Editor

American Energy Alliance [18189]
1155 15th St. NW, Ste. 900
Washington, DC 20005-2706

PH: (202)621-2940
Fax: (202)741-9170
Pyle, Thomas J., President

American Evaluation Association
[6622]
2025 M St. NW, Ste. 800
Washington, DC 20036
PH: (202)367-1166
Fax: (202)367-2166
Roosendaal, Denise, Exec. Dir.

American Exploration & Production
Council [2508]
101 Constitution Ave. NW, Ste. 700
Washington, DC 20001
PH: (202)742-4540
Thompson, V. Bruce, President

American Farm Bureau Federation
[4149]
600 Maryland Ave. SW, Ste. 1000W
Washington, DC 20024
PH: (202)406-3600
    (202)406-3614
Stallman, Bob, President

American Farm Bureau Foundation
for Agriculture [3543]
600 Maryland Ave. SW, Ste. 1000W
Washington, DC 20024
Toll free: 800-443-8456
Fax: (202)314-5121
Duvall, Zippy, Chairman

American Farmland Trust [17786]
1150 Connecticut Ave. NW, Ste. 600
Washington, DC 20036
Toll free: 800-431-1499
Larson, John, Exec. Dir.

American Federation for Children
[11722]
1660 L St. NW, Ste. 1000
Washington, DC 20036
PH: (202)280-1990
Fax: (202)280-1989
Brock, Greg, Exec. Dir.

American Federation of Government
Employees [23424]
80 F St. NW
Washington, DC 20001
PH: (202)737-8700
Hudson Jr., Eugene, Secretary,
Treasurer

American Federation of School
Administrators [7420]
1101 17th St. NW, Ste. 408
Washington, DC 20036
PH: (202)986-4209
Fax: (202)986-4211
Woodard, Diann, President

American Federation of State,
County and Municipal Employees
[23425]
1625 L St. NW
Washington, DC 20036-5687
PH: (202)429-1000
Fax: (202)429-1293
Saunders, Lee, President

American Federation of Teachers
[23408]
555 New Jersey Ave. NW
Washington, DC 20001
PH: (202)879-4400
Weingarten, Randi, President

American Financial Services Association [2089]
919 18th St. NW, Ste. 300
Washington, DC 20006
Stinebert, Chris, President, CEO

American Foreign Service Association [23426]
2101 E St. NW
Washington, DC 20037

PH: (202)338-4045
Fax: (202)338-6820
Bradley, Patrick, Specialist

American Foreign Service Protective
Association [19480]
1620 L St. NW, Ste. 800
Washington, DC 20036-2902
PH: (202)833-4910
Fax: (202)833-4918
Jakub, Paula S., Exec. VP, CEO

American Forest and Paper Associa-
tion [4193]
1101 K St., NW, Ste. 700
Washington, DC 20005
PH: (202)463-2700
Fax: (202)463-2785
Kowlzan, Mark W., Chmn. of the Bd.

American Forests [3799]
1220 L St. NW, Ste. 750
Washington, DC 20005
PH: (202)737-1944
Steen, Scott, CEO

American Friends of the Czech
Republic [19416]
4410 Massachusetts Ave. NW, No.
391
Washington, DC 20016-5572
PH: (202)413-5528
Malek, Fred, Chairman

American Friends of "For Survival"
[13205]
5333 42nd St. NW
Washington, DC 20015
Fox, Katie, President

American Friends of St. David's
Cathedral [9370]
c/o St. David's Episcopal Church
5150 Macomb St. NW
Washington, DC 20016
Dodge, Rev. Robin, President

American Friends of Turkey [19202]
1025 Connecticut Ave. NW, Ste.
1000
Washington, DC 20036
PH: (202)327-5450
Lukens, Amb. Alan W., Bd. Member

American Fuel and Petrochemical
Manufacturers [2509]
1667 K St. NW, Ste. 700
Washington, DC 20006
PH: (202)457-0480
Fax: (202)457-0486
Williams, Brendan E., Exec. VP

American Gaming Association
[22059]
799 9th St. NW, Ste. 700
Washington, DC 20001
PH: (202)552-2675
Fax: (202)552-2676
Freeman, Geoff, President, CEO

American Gas Association [4262]
400 N Capitol St. NW
Washington, DC 20001
PH: (202)824-7000
McCurdy, Dave, President, CEO

American Geophysical Union [6684]
2000 Florida Ave. NW
Washington, DC 20009-1277
PH: (202)462-6900
Toll free: 800-966-2481
Fax: (202)328-0566
Leinen, Margaret, President

American Gold Star Mothers [21036]
2128 Leroy Pl. NW
Washington, DC 20008-1847
PH: (202)265-0991
Jackman, Jennifer, Officer

American Health Care Association
[14924]
1201 L St. NW
Washington, DC 20005
PH: (202)842-4444
Fax: (202)842-3860

American Health Lawyers Associa-
tion [5273]
1620 Eye St. NW, 6th Fl.
Washington, DC 20006-4010
PH: (202)833-1100
Fax: (202)833-1105
Cornell, Lois Dehls, President

American Hellenic Educational
Progressive Association [19450]
1909 Q St. NW, Ste. 500
Washington, DC 20009-1050
PH: (202)232-6300
Fax: (202)232-2140
Karacostas, Nicholas A., Chairman

American Hellenic Institute [23642]
1220 16th St. NW
Washington, DC 20036
PH: (202)785-8430
Fax: (202)785-5178
Larigakis, Nick, President

American Heraldry Society [20954]
PO Box 96503
Washington, DC 20090-6503
McMillan, Joseph, President

American Highway Users Alliance
[12814]
1920 L St. NW, Ste. 525
Washington, DC 20036
PH: (202)857-1200
Fax: (202)857-1220
Cohen, Greg, President, CEO

American Historical Association
[9455]
400 A St. SE
Washington, DC 20003-3889
PH: (202)544-2422
Fax: (202)544-8307
Grossman, Jim, Exec. Dir.

American Horse Council [4312]
1616 H St. NW, 7th Fl.
Washington, DC 20006
PH: (202)296-4031
Shoemake, Jim, Chairman

American Hotel and Lodging As-
sociation [1647]
1250 I St. NW, Ste. 1100
Washington, DC 20005
PH: (202)289-3100
Fax: (202)289-3199
Lugar, Katherine, President, CEO

American Hotel & Lodging
Educational Foundation [1648]
1250 I St. NW, Ste. 1100
Washington, DC 20005-3931
PH: (202)289-3180
Fax: (202)289-3199
Abji, Minaz, Chairman

American Humane Association
[13028]
1400 16th St. NW, Ste. 360
Washington, DC 20036
PH: (818)501-0123
Toll free: 800-227-4645
Rose, Clifford, CFO

American Humanist Association
[20208]
1777 T St. NW
Washington, DC 20009-7102
PH: (202)238-9088
Toll free: 800-837-3792
Fax: (202)238-9003
Speckhardt, Mr. Roy, Exec. Dir.

American Immigration Council
[5288]
1331.G St. NW, Ste. 200
Washington, DC 20005-3141
PH: (202)507-7500
Fax: (202)742-5619
Juceam, Robert E., Secretary

American Immigration Lawyers As-
sociation [5289]
1331 G St. NW, Ste. 300
Washington, DC 20005-3142
PH: (202)507-7600
Fax: (202)783-7853
Nieblas, Victor D., President

American Immunization Registry As-
sociation [15371]
1155 F St. NW, Ste. 1050
Washington, DC 20004
PH: (202)552-0208
Coyle, Rebecca, Exec. Dir.

American Institute of Architects
[5953]
1735 New York Ave. NW
Washington, DC 20006
Toll free: 800-AIA-3837
Fax: (202)626-7547
Davidson, Russell A., President

American Institute of Architecture
Students [230]
1735 New York Ave. NW, Ste. 300
Washington, DC 20006-5209
PH: (202)626-7472
Fax: (202)626-7414
Caulfield, Joshua, Liaison, CEO

American Institute of Building Design
[5954]
7059 Blair Rd. NW, Ste. 400
Washington, DC 20012
PH: (202)750-4900
Toll free: 800-366-2423
Fax: (866)204-0293
Pillsbury, David, President

American Institute for Cancer
Research [13886]
1759 R St. NW
Washington, DC 20009
PH: (202)328-7744
Toll free: 800-843-8114
Fax: (202)328-7226
Gentry, Marilyn, President

American Institute of Certified Plan-
ners [5094]
American Planning Association
1030 15th St. NW, Ste. 750 W
Washington, DC 20005-1503
PH: (202)872-0611
Fax: (202)872-0643

American Institute for Conservation
of Historic & Artistic Works [9371]
1156 15th St. NW, Ste. 320
Washington, DC 20005
PH: (202)452-9545
Fax: (202)452-9328
Winfield, Ryan, Coord.

American Institute for Contemporary
German Studies [9338]
1755 Massachusetts Ave. NW, Ste.
700
Washington, DC 20036-2121
PH: (202)332-9312
Fax: (866)307-6691
Dieper, Ms. Susanne, Dir. of Admin.

American Institute for Medical and
Biological Engineering [6665]
1400 I St. NW, Ste. 235
Washington, DC 20005
PH: (202)496-9660
Bellamkonda, Ravi V., PhD,
President

American Institutes for Research in the Behavioral Sciences **[6027]**
1000 Thomas Jefferson St. NW
Washington, DC 20007
PH: (202)403-5000
Fax: (202)403-5001
Myers, David, CEO, President

American Insurance Association **[1831]**
2101 L St. NW, Ste. 400
Washington, DC 20037
PH: (202)828-7100
Fax: (202)293-1219
Pusey, Leigh Ann, CEO, President

American International Health Alliance **[15134]**
1225 Eye St. NW, Ste. 205
Washington, DC 20005
PH: (202)789-1136
Fax: (202)789-1277
Smith, James P., MA, Exec. Dir.

American Iron and Steel Institute **[2343]**
25 Massachusetts Ave. NW, Ste. 800
Washington, DC 20001
PH: (202)452-7100
Bell, David E., VP of Fin. Admin.

American Israel Public Affairs Committee **[18673]**
251 H St. NW
Washington, DC 20001
PH: (202)639-5200
Kohr, Howard, CEO

American Kurdish Information Network **[19525]**
2722 Connecticut Ave. NW, No. 42
Washington, DC 20008
PH: (202)483-6444
Xulam, Kani, Director

American-Kuwaiti Alliance **[1978]**
2550 M St. NW
Washington, DC 20037
PH: (202)429-4999
Dawkins, Brig. Gen. Peter, Chairman

American Land Title Association **[2845]**
1800 M St. NW, Ste. 300S
Washington, DC 20036-5828
PH: (202)296-3671
Toll free: 800-787-ALTA
Fax: (202)223-5843
Korsmo, Michelle L., CEO

American Legal Finance Association **[1219]**
818 Connecticut Ave. NW, Ste. 1100
Washington, DC 20006
PH: (202)552-2793
Gilroy, Kelly, Exec. Dir.

American-Lithuanian Business Council **[609]**
701 8th St. NW, Ste. 500
Washington, DC 20001
PH: (202)973-5975
Fax: (202)659-5249
Stewart, Eric, President

American Logistics Association **[5588]**
1101 Vermont Ave. NW, Ste. 1002
Washington, DC 20005
PH: (202)466-2520
Fax: (240)823-9181
Hall, Kurt, V. Chmn. of the Bd.

American Lung Association in the District of Columbia **[17134]**
1301 Pennsylvania Ave. NW
Washington, DC 20004

PH: (202)785-3355
    (202)747-5541
Toll free: 800-548-8252
Fax: (202)452-1805
Forbes, Kathryn A., Chmn. of the Bd.

American Maritime Congress **[5578]**
444 N Capitol St. NW, Ste. 800
Washington, DC 20001
PH: (202)347-8020
Fax: (202)347-1550
Ainley, Marshall, Chmn. of the Bd.

American Masters of Laws Association **[4991]**
PO Box 5466
Washington, DC 20016
Mancebo, Mr. Christian, LLM, President

American Medical Political Action Committee **[18857]**
25 Massachusetts Ave. NW, Ste. 600
Washington, DC 20001-7400
PH: (202)789-7400
Puchalski, Dr. Robert, Chairman

American Medical Rehabilitation Providers Association **[17081]**
c/o Carolyn C. Zollar, Vice President of Government Relations
1710 N St. NW
Washington, DC 20036
PH: (202)223-1920
Toll free: 888-346-4624
Fax: (202)223-1925
Zollar, Carolyn C., VP of Government Rel.

American Military Partner Association **[5589]**
1725 I St. NW, Ste. 300
Washington, DC 20006
PH: (202)695-2672
Broadway, Ashley, President

American Military Society **[5590]**
PO Box 90740
Washington, DC 20090-0740
Toll free: 800-379-6128
Fax: (301)583-8717

American Mothers **[11812]**
1701 K St. NW, Ste. 650
Washington, DC 20006
Toll free: 877-242-4264
Ball, Andrea, Exec. Dir.

American National Red Cross **[12616]**
2025 E St. NW
Washington, DC 20006
PH: (202)303-5214
    (202)303-4498
Toll free: 800-733-2767
McGovern, Gail J., CEO, President

American National Standards Institute **[5770]**
1899 L St. NW, 11th Fl.
Washington, DC 20036
PH: (202)293-8020
Fax: (202)293-9287
Lawlor, Kevan P., Chmn. of the Bd.

American Near East Refugee Aid **[12583]**
1111 14th St. NW, Ste. 400
Washington, DC 20005-5604
PH: (202)266-9700
Fax: (202)266-9701
Corcoran, William, President, CEO

American News Women's Club **[2652]**
1607 22nd St. NW
Washington, DC 20008

PH: (202)332-6770
Fax: (202)265-6092
Roncevic, Janina, Officer

American Oil and Gas Historical Society **[2510]**
c/o Bruce A. Wells, Executive Director
1201 15th St. NW, Ste. 300
Washington, DC 20005
PH: (202)387-6996
Fax: (202)857-4799
Wells, Bruce, Exec. Dir., Founder

American Organization of Nurse Executives **[16109]**
Two City Ctr., Ste. 400
800 10th St. NW
Washington, DC 20001
PH: (202)626-2240
Fax: (202)638-5499
Thompson, Pamela A., RN, CEO

American Petroleum Institute **[2511]**
1220 L St. NW
Washington, DC 20005
PH: (202)682-8000
Gerard, Jack, President, CEO

American Pharmacists Association **[16641]**
2215 Constitution Ave. NW
Washington, DC 20037
PH: (202)628-4410
Toll free: 800-237-2742
Fax: (202)783-2351
Menighan, Thomas E., CEO

American Pilots' Association **[128]**
Fairchild Bldg.
499 S Capitol St. SW, Ste. 409
Washington, DC 20003
PH: (202)484-0700
Fax: (202)484-9320
Watson, Michael R., President

American Political Science Association **[7042]**
1527 New Hampshire Ave. NW
Washington, DC 20036-1206
PH: (202)483-2512
Fax: (202)483-2657
Hochschild, Jennifer, President

American Postal Workers Union **[23504]**
1300 L St. NW
Washington, DC 20005
PH: (202)842-4250
Dimondstein, Mark, President

American Psychological Association **[16861]**
750 1st St. NE
Washington, DC 20002-4242
PH: (202)336-5500
Toll free: 800-374-2721
Beebe, Linda, Director

American Psychological Association Committee on International Relations in Psychology **[16862]**
Office of International Affairs
750 1st St. NE
Washington, DC 20002-4242
PH: (202)336-6025
Fax: (202)312-6499
Consoli, Melissa Morgan, Chairperson

American Psychological Association Education Directorate **[16863]**
750 1st St. NE
Washington, DC 20002-4242
PH: (202)336-5970
Toll free: 800-374-2721
Diaz-Granados, Jim, Exec. Dir.

American Psychological Association of Graduate Students **[16864]**
750 1st St. NE
Washington, DC 20002-4242

PH: (202)336-5500
Toll free: 800-374-2721
Fax: (202)336-5997
Belar, Cynthia D., CEO

American Psychological Association Practice Organization **[13808]**
750 1st St. NE
Washington, DC 20002-4241
Toll free: 800-374-2723
Fax: (202)336-5797
Nordal, Katherine C., PhD, Exec. Dir.

American Psychological Association Science Directorate **[16865]**
750 1st St. NE
Washington, DC 20002-4242
PH: (202)336-6000
Fax: (202)336-5953
Thornton, Kymberly, Mgr.

American Psychology-Law Society **[16866]**
750 1st St. NE
Washington, DC 20002-4242
PH: (202)336-5500
Woolard, Jennifer, President

American Public Gas Association **[3411]**
201 Massachusetts Ave. NE, Ste. C-4
Washington, DC 20002
PH: (202)464-2742
Toll free: 800-927-4204
Fax: (202)464-0246
Schryver, Dave, Exec. VP

American Public Health Association **[16993]**
800 I St. NW
Washington, DC 20001
PH: (202)777-2742
Fax: (202)777-2534
Cohen, Richard J., Treasurer

American Public Human Services Association **[13029]**
1133 19th St. NW, Ste. 400
Washington, DC 20036-3631
PH: (202)682-0100
Fax: (202)289-6555
Bicha, Reggie, Exec.

American Public Transportation Association **[3321]**
1300 I St. NW, Ste. 1200 E
Washington, DC 20005
PH: (202)496-4800
Fax: (202)496-4324
White, Richard A., Act. Pres., Acting CEO

American Public Works Association **[5730]**
1275 K St. NW, Ste. 750
Washington, DC 20005
PH: (202)408-9541
Fax: (202)408-9542
LaViolet, Raye, Dir. of Fin.

American Railway Car Institute **[2832]**
c/o Railway Supply Institute, Inc., 425 Third St., SW, Ste. 920
425 3rd St. SW, Ste. 920
Washington, DC 20024
PH: (202)347-4664
    (202)347-0047
Whalen, Edward, Chairman

American Recreation Coalition **[12574]**
1200 G St. NW, Ste. 650
Washington, DC 20005-3832
PH: (202)682-9530
Fax: (202)682-9529
Crandall, Derrick A., President, CEO

American Resort Development Association **[2848]**
1201 15th St. NW, Ste. 400
Washington, DC 20005
PH: (202)371-6700
Fax: (202)289-8544
Lacey, Catherine, VP

American Rivers **[3804]**
1101 14th St. NW, Ste. 1400
Washington, DC 20005
PH: (202)347-7550
Toll free: 877-347-7550
Fax: (202)347-9240
Taylor, Alex, Chairman

American Road & Transportation Builders Association **[5809]**
1219 28th St. NW
Washington, DC 20007
PH: (202)289-4434
Ruane, Pete, President, CEO

American Savings Education Council **[7931]**
1100 13th St. NW, Ste. 878
Washington, DC 20005-4204
PH: (202)659-0670
Fax: (202)775-6312
Adams, Nevin E., Director

American Security Council Foundation **[19086]**
1250 24th St. NW, Ste. 300
Washington, DC 20037
PH: (202)263-3661
Fax: (202)263-3662
Smith, Brig. Gen. (Ret.) Donald B., Chairman

American Seniors Housing Association **[11960]**
5225 Wisconsin Ave. NW, Ste. 502
Washington, DC 20015
PH: (202)237-0900
Fax: (202)237-1616
Cohen, Larry, Chairman

American Short Line and Regional Railroad Association **[2834]**
50 F St. NW, Ste. 7020
Washington, DC 20001
PH: (202)628-4500
   (202)585-3442
Fax: (202)628-6430
Borman, Keith T., VP, Gen. Counsel

American Sleep Apnea Association **[17212]**
1717 Pennsylvania Ave. NW, Ste. 1025
Washington, DC 20006
Toll free: 888-293-3650
Fax: (888)293-3650
Drobnich, Darrel, President

American Small Manufacturers Coalition **[2212]**
PO Box 15289
Washington, DC 20003
PH: (202)341-7066
Fax: (202)315-3906
Hines, Carrie, President, CEO

American Society of Access Professionals **[5299]**
1444 I St. NW, Ste. 700
Washington, DC 20005
PH: (202)712-9054
Fax: (202)216-9646
Bennett, Amy, President

American Society for the Advancement of Pharmacotherapy **[16867]**
750 1st St. NE
Washington, DC 20002

American Society for Bone and Mineral Research **[16498]**
2025 M St. NW, Ste. 800
Washington, DC 20036-3309

PH: (202)367-1161
Fax: (202)367-2161
Fesler, Douglas, Assoc. Exec.

American Society of Cost Segregation Professionals **[3200]**
1101 Pennsylvania Ave. NW, 6th Fl.
Washington, DC 20004
PH: (203)671-7372
Fax: (203)745-0724
Caputo, Peter, Act. Pres.

American Society for Cybernetics **[6234]**
c/o Stuart A. Umpleby, Professor
204 Funger Hall
Dept. of Management
The George Washington University
2201 G St. NW
Washington, DC 20052
PH: (617)475-0514
Lissack, Michael, President

American Society for Deaf Children **[15174]**
800 Florida Ave. NE, No. 2047
Washington, DC 20002-3695
Toll free: 800-942-2732
Fax: (410)795-0965
Benedict, Beth, Ph.D., President

American Society for Engineering Education **[7857]**
1818 N St. NW, Ste. 600
Washington, DC 20036-2479
PH: (202)331-3500
   (202)331-3511
Fortenberry, Norman, Exec. Dir.

American Society of Health Economists **[1010]**
725 15th St. NW, Ste. 600
Washington, DC 20005
PH: (202)737-6608
Fax: (202)737-7308
Ellis, Randall, President

American Society of Hematology **[15220]**
2021 L St. NW, Ste. 900
Washington, DC 20036-4929
PH: (202)776-0544
Fax: (202)776-0545
Liggett, Martha, Esq., Exec. Dir.

American Society of Interior Designers **[1938]**
1152 15th St. NW, Ste. 910
Washington, DC 20005
PH: (202)546-3480
Fax: (202)546-3240
Fiser, Randy, CEO

American Society of International Law **[5349]**
2223 Massachusetts Ave. NW
Washington, DC 20008
PH: (202)939-6000
Fax: (202)797-7133
Damrosch, Prof. Lori, VP

American Society of Landscape Architects **[5956]**
636 Eye St. NW
Washington, DC 20001-3736
PH: (202)898-2444
Toll free: 888-999-2752
Fax: (202)898-1185
Somerville, Nancy C., Exec. VP

American Society for Microbiology **[6071]**
1752 N St. NW
Washington, DC 20036-2904
PH: (202)942-9207
   (202)737-3600
Fax: (202)942-9333
Campos, Joseph M., Secretary

American Society for Nanomedicine **[15712]**
Georgetown University Medical Ctr.
3970 Reservoir Rd. NW
Washington, DC 20057
PH: (202)687-8418
Chang, Esther, PhD, Act. Pres.

American Society of Nephrology **[15873]**
1510 H St. NW, Ste. 800
Washington, DC 20005
PH: (202)640-4660
Fax: (202)637-9793
Ibrahim, Mr. Tod, Exec. Dir.

American Society for Public Administration **[5693]**
1370 Rhode Island Ave. NW, Ste. 500
Washington, DC 20036
PH: (202)393-7878
Fax: (202)638-4952
Lachance, Janice, VP

American Sociological Association **[7176]**
1430 K St. NW, Ste. 600
Washington, DC 20005
PH: (202)383-9005
Fax: (202)638-0882
Risman, Barbara, VP

American Sociological Association - Status of Women in Sociology **[7177]**
1430 K St. NW, Ste. 600
Washington, DC 20005-2529
PH: (202)383-9005
Fax: (202)638-0882
Hillsman, Sally, Exec. Ofc.

American Spice Trade Association **[1314]**
1101 17th St. NW, Ste. 700
Washington, DC 20036
PH: (202)331-2460
Fax: (202)463-8998
Bewley, Kirk, Bd. Member

American Studies Association **[8788]**
1120 19th St. NW, Ste. 301
Washington, DC 20036
PH: (202)467-4783
Fax: (202)467-4786
Stephens, John F., Exec. Dir.

American Sugarbeet Growers Association **[4694]**
1156 15th St. NW, Ste. 1101
Washington, DC 20005
PH: (202)833-2398
Fax: (240)235-4291
Gerstenberger, Richard, VP

American Sustainable Business Council **[1002]**
1401 New York Ave. NW, Ste. 1225
Washington, DC 20005
PH: (202)595-9302
Levine, David, Founder, CEO

American Task Force for Lebanon **[18634]**
1100 Connecticut Ave. NW, Ste. 1250
Washington, DC 20036
PH: (202)223-9333
Fax: (202)223-1399
Touma, Leslie, Exec. Dir.

American Task Force on Palestine **[18514]**
1634 Eye St. NW, Ste. 725
Washington, DC 20006
PH: (202)887-0177
Fax: (202)887-1920
Asali, Ziad J., President

American Tax Policy Institute **[19164]**
c/o Ms. Charmaine Wright, Director
National Tax Association
725 15th St. NW, Ste. 600
Washington, DC 20005-2109
PH: (202)737-3325
Fax: (202)737-7308
Shay, Steven, President

American Telemedicine Association **[17425]**
1100 Connecticut Ave. NW, Ste. 540
Washington, DC 20036
PH: (202)223-3333
Fax: (202)223-2787
Linkous, Jonathan, CEO

American Tort Reform Association **[5415]**
1101 Connecticut Ave. NW, Ste. 400
Washington, DC 20036
PH: (202)682-1163
Fax: (202)682-1022
Joyce, Sherman, President

American-Turkish Council **[19203]**
1111 14th St. NW, Ste. 1050
Washington, DC 20005
PH: (202)783-0483
Fax: (202)783-0511
Jones, James L., Chairman

American University in Moscow **[8056]**
1800 Connecticut Ave. NW
Washington, DC 20009-5704
PH: (202)364-0200
Fax: (240)554-1650

American Urogynecologic Society **[17548]**
2025 M St. NW, Ste. 800
Washington, DC 20036-2422
PH: (301)273-0570
Fax: (301)273-0778
Zinnert, Michelle, Exec. Dir.

American-Uzbekistan Chamber of Commerce **[23555]**
1030 15th St. NW, Ste. 555W
Washington, DC 20005
PH: (202)223-1770
   (202)509-3744
Lamm, Carolyn B., Chmn. of the Bd.

American Veterinary Medical Law Association **[5416]**
1701 K St. NW, Ste. 650
Washington, DC 20006
PH: (202)449-3818
Fax: (202)449-8560
Owens, John, Esq., Director

American Wind Energy Association **[7386]**
1501 M St. NW, Ste. 1000
Washington, DC 20005
PH: (202)383-2500
Fax: (202)383-2505
Alonso, Gabriel, Director

American Wine Alliance for Research and Education **[4925]**
PO Box 765
Washington, DC 20004-0765
Toll free: 800-700-4050
Juergens, Dr. John P., Chairman

American Youth Policy Forum **[13425]**
1836 Jefferson Pl. NW
Washington, DC 20036
PH: (202)775-9731
Fax: (202)775-9733
Brand, Betsy, Exec. Dir., Treasurer

AmericanHort **[4501]**
525 9th St. NW, Ste. 800
Washington, DC 20004

PH: (202)789-2900
Fax: (202)789-1893
Regelbrugge, Craig J., VP

Americans for the Arts [8957]
1000 Vermont Ave. NW, 6th Fl.
Washington, DC 20005
PH: (202)371-2830
Fax: (202)371-0424
Lynch, Robert L., President, CEO

Americans to Ban Cloning [17871]
1100 H St. NW, Ste. 700
Washington, DC 20005
PH: (202)347-6840
Fax: (202)347-6849
Tarne, Gene, Contact

Americans for Democratic Action
[18636]
1629 K St. NW, Ste. 300
Washington, DC 20006
PH: (202)600-7762
Fax: (202)204-8637
Woolsey, Lynn, President

Americans for Fair Electronic Com-
merce Transactions [995]
111 G St. NW
Washington, DC 20001
PH: (202)662-9200
Baish, Mary Alice, Contact

Americans for Financial Reform
[18242]
1629 K St. NW, 10th Fl.
Washington, DC 20006
PH: (202)466-1885
Donner, Lisa, Exec. Dir.

Americans for Informed Democracy
[18091]
1220 L St. NW, Ste. 100-161
Washington, DC 20005
PH: (202)709-6172
Green, Seth, Founder

Americans for Medical Progress
[13716]
444 N Capitol St. NW, Ste. 417
Washington, DC 20001
PH: (202)624-8810
Calnan, Jacqueline, MPA, President

Americans for Peace Now [18583]
2100 M St. NW, Ste. 619
Washington, DC 20037
PH: (202)408-9898
Fax: (202)408-9899
Klutznick, James, Chairman

Americans for Peace Prosperity and
Security [18263]
707 8th St. SE, Ste. 100
Washington, DC 20003
Rogers, Mike, Chairman

Americans for Responsible Solutions
[18245]
PO Box 15642
Washington, DC 20003
Giffords, Gabrielle, Founder

Americans for Safe Access [18645]
1806 Vernon St. NW
Washington, DC 20009
PH: (202)857-4272
Sherer, Steph, Exec. Dir.

Americans for Tax Reform [19165]
722 12th St. NW, Ste. 400
Washington, DC 20005
PH: (202)785-0266
Fax: (202)785-0261
Norquist, Grover G., President

Americans for Transit [19195]
1616 P St. NW, Ste. 210
Washington, DC 20036

PH: (202)232-1616
LeRoy, Greg, Exec. Dir. (Actg.)

Americans for Transportation Mobil-
ity [5810]
US Chamber of Commerce
1615 H St. NW
Washington, DC 20062-2000
PH: (202)463-5600
Kavinoky, Janet, VP

Americans United for Life [12762]
655 15th St. NW, Ste. 410
Washington, DC 20005
PH: (202)289-1478
    (202)696-4632
Harrison, Donna, Dir. of Res.

Americans United for Separation of
Church and State [20013]
1901 L St. NW, Ste. 400
Washington, DC 20036-3564
PH: (202)466-3234
Fax: (202)466-2587
Lynn, Barry W., Exec. Dir.

Americans Well-informed on
Automobile Retailing Economics
[279]
919 18th St. NW, Ste. 300
Washington, DC 20006
PH: (202)585-2808
Toll free: 888-400-7577
Hoffman, Eric, Contact

America's Essential Hospitals
[15301]
401 9th St. NW, Ste. 900
Washington, DC 20004-1712
PH: (202)585-0100
Walker, MD, William B., Contact

America's Blood Centers [13837]
725 15th St. NW, Ste. 700
Washington, DC 20005
PH: (202)393-5725
Fax: (202)393-1282
Rossman, Susan, President

America's Health Insurance Plans
[15095]
South Bldg., Ste. 500
601 Pennsylvania Ave. NW
Washington, DC 20004
PH: (202)778-3200
Fax: (202)331-7487
Khalid, Aryana, Exec. VP of Fin.,
    Exec. VP of HR

America's Heroes of Freedom
[20702]
PO Box 18984
Washington, DC 20036-8984
Brewer, Susan, Founder, President

America's Natural Gas Alliance
[2512]
701 8th St. NW, Ste. 800
Washington, DC 20001
PH: (202)789-2642
Parker, Karen, Exec. Asst.

America's Promise - The Alliance for
Youth [13426]
1110 Vermont Ave. NW, Ste. 900
Washington, DC 20005
PH: (202)657-0600
Fax: (202)657-0601
Tucker, Tanya, Sr. VP

AmeriCorps VISTA [13280]
250 E St. SW
Washington, DC 20005
PH: (202)606-5000
Toll free: 800-942-2677
Strasser, Mary, Director

Amyotrophic Lateral Sclerosis Association [13682]
1275 K St. NW, Ste. 250
Washington, DC 20005

PH: (202)407-8580
Toll free: 800-782-4747
Fax: (202)289-6801
Newhouse, Barbara, President, CEO

Anahata International [13603]
c/o Anahata International
1450 P St. NW
Washington, DC 20005
Parell, Shawn, Prog. Dir.

Ancient and Accepted Scottish Rite
of Free Masonry - Southern
Jurisdiction [19550]
1733 16th St. NW
Washington, DC 20009-3103
PH: (202)232-3579
Fax: (202)464-0487
Seale, Ronald A., Cmdr.

Animal Health Institute [2553]
1325 G St. NW, Ste. 700
Washington, DC 20005-3127
PH: (202)637-2440

Animal Welfare Institute [10583]
900 Pennsylvania Ave. SE
Washington, DC 20003-2140
PH: (202)337-2332
Fax: (202)446-2131
Millward, Susan, Exec. Dir.

Antarctic and Southern Ocean Coali-
tion [7039]
1320 19th St. NW, 5th Fl.
Washington, DC 20036
PH: (202)234-2480
Bauman, Mark, Chairman

APA Division 7: Developmental
Psychology [16868]
750 1st St. NE
Washington, DC 20002-4242
PH: (202)336-5500
Goodman, Gail S., President

APA Division 10: Society for the
Psychology of Aesthetics, Creativ-
ity and the Arts [16869]
750 1st St. NE
Washington, DC 20002-4241
PH: (202)336-6013
Fax: (202)218-3599
Reiter-Palmon, Dr. Roni, Secretary

APA Division 16: School Psychology
[16871]
750 1st St. NE
Washington, DC 20002-4242
PH: (202)336-5500
DiPerna, James C., PhD, President

APA Division 17: Society of Counseling Psychology [16872]
c/o Ashley Randall, PhD, Membership Chair
APA Membership Department
750 1st St. NE
Washington, DC 20002-4242
Toll free: 800-374-2721
Lichtenberg, James, President

APA Division 19: Society for Military
Psychology [16873]
c/o APA Division Services
750 1st St. NE
Washington, DC 20002-4242
PH: (202)216-7602
    (202)336-6013
Landes, Ann, President

APA Division 22: Rehabilitation
Psychology [16874]
c/o American Psychological Associa-
tion
750 1st St. NE
Washington, DC 20002-4242
PH: (202)216-7602
    (202)218-3599
Fax: (202)820-0291
Brown, Kathleen S., PhD, President

APA Division 25: Behavioral Analysis
[16877]
750 1st St. NE
Washington, DC 20002-4242
PH: (202)336-5500
Reilly, Mark, President

APA Division 30: Society of
Psychological Hypnosis [16880]
750 1st St. NE
Washington, DC 20002-4242
PH: (202)336-5500
Schilder, Steffanie, President

APA Division 31: State, Provincial
and Territorial Affairs [16881]
750 1st St. NE
Washington, DC 20002-4241
PH: (202)336-5500
Rosa, Dinelia, PhD, President

APA Division 35: Society for the
Psychology of Women [16882]
c/o APA Division Services
750 1st St. NE
Washington, DC 20002-4242
PH: (202)336-6013
Fax: (202)218-3599
Garrett-Akinsanya, BraVada, PhD,
President

APA Division 37: Society for Child
and Family Policy and Practice
[16883]
750 1st St. NE
Washington, DC 20002-4242
PH: (202)336-5500
McCabe, Mary Ann, PhD, President

APA Division 43: Society for Couple
and Family Psychology [16887]
750 1st St. NE
Washington, DC 20002-4242
PH: (202)336-6013
    (202)336-5500

APA Division 43: Society for Family
Psychology [16888]
Division Services Office
750 1st St. NE
Washington, DC 20002
PH: (202)336-6013
Chambers, Anthony, President

APA Division 46: Society for Media
Psychology and Technology
[16889]
750 1st St. NE
Washington, DC 20002-4242
PH: (202)336-5500
Gregerson, Mary, Div. Pres.

APA Division 47: Exercise and Sport
Psychology [16890]
c/o American Psychological Associa-
tion
750 1st St. NE
Washington, DC 20002-4242
PH: (202)336-6121
Fax: (202)218-3599
Kantos, Anthony P., President

APA Division 49: Society of Group
Psychology and Group
Psychotherapy [16892]
750 1st St. NE
Washington, DC 20002-4242
PH: (202)336-6013
Fax: (202)218-3599
Riva, Maria T., PhD, Mem.

APA Division 50: Society of Addiction
Psychology [16893]
750 1st St. NE
Washington, DC 20002-4242
PH: (202)216-7602
McKee, Sherry, President

APA Division 51: Society for the Psychological Study of Men and Masculinity **[16894]**
750 1st St. NE
Washington, DC 20002-4241
Toll free: 800-336-6013
Remer, Randa, Treasurer

APA Division 52: International Psychology **[16895]**
750 1st St. NE
Washington, DC 20002-4242
PH: (202)336-6013
   (202)336-5500
Toll free: 800-374-2721
Carey, Martha Ann, Treasurer

APA Division 56: Trauma Psychology **[16897]**
750 1st St. NE
Washington, DC 20002-4242
PH: (607)722-5857
Toll free: 800-429-6784
Cook, Joan, President

APhA Academy of Pharmaceutical Research and Science **[16648]**
2215 Constitution Ave. NW
Washington, DC 20037
PH: (202)628-4410
Toll free: 800-237-2742
Fax: (202)783-2351
Osterhaus, Matthew C., President

APhA Academy of Pharmacy Practice and Management **[16649]**
2215 Constitution Ave. NW
Washington, DC 20037
PH: (202)628-4410
Toll free: 800-237-2742
Fax: (202)783-2351
Menighan, Thomas E., CEO, Exec. VP

APhA Academy of Student Pharmacists **[16650]**
American Pharmacists Association
2215 Constitution Ave. NW
Washington, DC 20037
PH: (202)628-4410
Toll free: 800-237-2742
Fax: (202)783-2351
Capote, Nicholas, President

Appendiceal Cancer Advocacy Network **[13888]**
2825 McKinley Pl. NW
Washington, DC 20015
PH: (301)512-0708
Fax: (301)654-8508
Rurka, Steve, Founder, Exec. Dir.

Apple Processors Association **[4228]**
1701 K St. NW, Ste. 650
Washington, DC 20006
PH: (202)785-6715
Fax: (202)331-4212
Weller, Paul S., Jr., President

Arab American Institute **[18903]**
1600 K St. NW, Ste. 601
Washington, DC 20006
PH: (202)429-9210
Fax: (202)429-9214
Berry, Maya, Exec. Dir.

Arab American Leadership Council **[18628]**
1600 K St. NW, Ste. 601
Washington, DC 20006
PH: (202)429-9210
Fax: (202)429-9214
Zogby, Dr. James J., Treasurer

The Arc **[12315]**
1825 K St. NW, Ste. 1200
Washington, DC 20006-1266
PH: (202)534-3700
Toll free: 800-433-5255
Fax: (202)534-3731
Berns, Peter V., CEO

Armenian Assembly of America **[8824]**
734 15th St. NW, Ste. 500
Washington, DC 20005
PH: (202)393-3434
Fax: (202)638-4904
Ardouny, Bryan, Exec. Dir.

Armenian National Committee of America **[19386]**
1711 N St. NW
Washington, DC 20036-2801
PH: (202)775-1918
Fax: (202)223-7964
Hamparian, Aram S., Exec. Dir.

Arms Control Association **[18121]**
1313 L St. NW, Ste. 130
Washington, DC 20005
PH: (202)463-8270
Fax: (202)463-8273
Walker, Paul, V. Chmn. of the Bd.

Arts Education Partnership **[7506]**
1 Massachusetts Ave. NW, Ste. 700
Washington, DC 20001-1431
PH: (202)326-8693
Fax: (202)408-8081
Best, Jane R., PhD, Director

ASAE: The Center for Association Leadership **[254]**
1575 I St. NW
Washington, DC 20005-1103
PH: (202)371-0940
Toll free: 888-950-ASAE
Fax: (202)371-8315
Neely, Ms. Susan K., Chairperson

Asia America Initiative **[11314]**
1523 16th St. NW
Washington, DC 20036
PH: (202)232-7020
Fax: (202)232-7023
Santoli, Albert, Founder, Director

Asia Policy Point **[9621]**
1730 Rhode Island Ave. NW, Ste. 414
Washington, DC 20036
PH: (202)822-6040
Fax: (202)822-6044
Kotler, Mindy L., Director

Asian American Government Executives Network **[5260]**
1001 Connecticut Ave. NW, Ste. 320
Washington, DC 20036
PH: (202)930-2024
Fax: (202)296-9236
Milton, Marina, Treasurer

Asian Pacific American Advocates **[17847]**
1322 18th St. NW
Washington, DC 20036-1803
PH: (202)223-5500
Fax: (202)296-0540
Lee, Ken, CEO

Asian Pacific American Labor Alliance **[23453]**
815 16th St. NW
Washington, DC 20009
PH: (202)508-3733
Cendana, Gregory A., Exec. Dir.

Asian and Pacific Islander American Vote **[18904]**
1612 K St. NW, Ste. 510
Washington, DC 20006
PH: (202)223-9170
Chen, Christine, Exec. Dir.

Asian & Pacific Islander Americans in Historic Preservation **[9375]**
1628 16th St. NW, Ste. 4
Washington, DC 20009
Magalong, Michelle, Chairperson

Aspen Institute **[20209]**
1 Dupont Cir. NW, Ste. 700
Washington, DC 20036-1133
PH: (202)736-5800
Fax: (202)467-0790
Isaacson, Walter, CEO, President

Asphalt Roofing Manufacturers Association **[496]**
750 National Press Bldg.
529 14th St. NW
Washington, DC 20045
PH: (202)591-2450
Fax: (202)591-2445
Hitchcock, Reed, Exec. VP, Director

ASPIRA Association **[7743]**
1444 I St. NW, Ste. 800
Washington, DC 20005
PH: (202)835-3600
Fax: (202)853-3613
Blackburn-Moreno, Ronald, President, CEO

Assembly of Turkish American Associations **[19673]**
1526 18th St. NW
Washington, DC 20036
PH: (202)483-9090
Fax: (202)483-9092
Celebi, Mehmet, Bd. Member

Associated Air Balance Council **[498]**
1518 K St. NW, Ste. 503
Washington, DC 20005
PH: (202)737-0202
Fax: (202)638-4833
Sufka, Kenneth M., Exec. Dir.

Associated Builders and Contractors **[853]**
440 1st St. NW, Ste. 200
Washington, DC 20001
Bellaman, Michael D., CEO, President

Association of Academic Health Centers **[14928]**
1400 16th St. NW, Ste. 720
Washington, DC 20036
PH: (202)265-9600
Fax: (202)265-7514
Wartman, Mr. Steven, MD, CEO, President

Association for the Accreditation of Human Research Protection Programs **[7085]**
2301 M St. NW, Ste. 500
Washington, DC 20037-1427
PH: (202)783-1112
Toll free: 888-601-1112
Fax: (202)783-1113
Wendel, Jeffrey, Chairman

Association of Accredited Naturopathic Medical Colleges **[15857]**
818 18th St. NW, Ste. 250
Washington, DC 20006
Toll free: 800-345-7454
Guiltinan, Jane, President

Association of Administrators of the Interstate Compact on Adoption and Medical Assistance **[10445]**
1133 19th St. NW
Washington, DC 20036
PH: (202)682-0100
Fax: (202)289-6555
Savage, Diane, V. Ch.

Association of Administrators of the Interstate Compact on the Placement of Children **[10858]**
American Public Human Services Association
1133 19th St. NW, Ste. 400

Washington, DC 20036
PH: (202)682-0100
Fax: (202)289-6555
Peterson, Mical Anne, President

Association of African American Museums **[9820]**
PO Box 23698
Washington, DC 20026
PH: (202)633-1134
Black, Samuel W., President

Association of American Chambers of Commerce in Latin America and the Caribbean **[23560]**
1615 H St. NW
Washington, DC 20062-0001
PH: (202)463-5485
Smith-Vaughan, Reuben, Exec. Dir.

Association of American Colleges and Universities **[7621]**
1818 R St. NW
Washington, DC 20009
PH: (202)387-3760
Decatur, Sean, Treasurer

Association of American Law Schools **[8209]**
1614 20th St. NW
Washington, DC 20009-1001
PH: (202)296-8851
Fax: (202)296-8869
Thomas, Tracie L., Mgr.

Association of American Law Schools - Section on Sexual Orientation and Gender Identity Issues **[8210]**
1614 20th St. NW
Washington, DC 20009-1001
Macias, Steven J., Chairman

Association of American Medical Colleges **[8307]**
655 K St. NW, Ste. 100
Washington, DC 20001-2399
PH: (202)828-0400
Kirch, Darrell G., MD, CEO, President

Association of American Railroads **[2835]**
425 3rd St. SW
Washington, DC 20024
PH: (202)639-2100
Gray, John, Sr. VP

Association of American Universities **[7622]**
1200 New York Ave. NW, Ste. 550
Washington, DC 20005-6122
PH: (202)408-7500
Fax: (202)408-8184
Rawlings, Hunter R., President

Association of American Veterinary Medical Colleges **[17633]**
1101 Vermont Ave. NW, Ste. 301
Washington, DC 20005
PH: (202)371-9195
Fax: (202)842-0773
Green, Eleanor M., President

Association for Behavioral Health and Wellness **[14979]**
1325 G St. NW, Ste. 500
Washington, DC 20005-3136
PH: (202)449-7660
Fax: (202)449-7659
Greenberg, Pamela, MPP, CEO, President

Association for Canadian Studies in the United States **[9206]**
1740 Massachusetts Ave. NW, Nitze 516
Washington, DC 20036

PH: (202)670-1424
Fax: (202)663-5717
Holland, Kenneth, President

Association of Cancer Executives [13891]
1025 Thomas Jefferson St. NW, Ste. 500 E
Washington, DC 20007
PH: (202)521-1886
Fax: (202)833-3636
Mandrier, Brian J., Exec. Dir.

Association of Catholic Colleges and Universities [7573]
1 Dupont Cir. NW, Ste. 650
Washington, DC 20036
PH: (202)457-0650
Fax: (202)728-0977
Galligan-Stierle, Michael, PhD, CEO, President

Association for Childhood Education International [7581]
1200 18th St. NW, Ste. 700
Washington, DC 20036
PH: (202)372-9986
Toll free: 800-423-3563
Fax: (202)372-9989
Chen, Christine, President

Association of Clean Water Administrators [5176]
1634 Eye St. NW, Ste. No. 750
Washington, DC 20006
PH: (202)756-0605
Fax: (202)756-0600
LaFlamme, Pete, VP

Association of Climate Change Officers [4035]
1921 Florida Ave. NW
Washington, DC 20009
PH: (202)496-7390
Kreeger, Daniel, Exec. Dir.

Association of Clinical Research Organizations [14289]
915 15th St. NW, 2nd Fl.
Washington, DC 20005
PH: (202)464-9340
Peddicord, Douglas, PhD, Exec. Dir.

Association for Clinical and Translational Science [14291]
2025 M St. NW, Ste. 800
Washington, DC 20036
PH: (202)367-1119
Fax: (202)367-2119
Lichtenstein, Dr. Michael, Comm. Chm.

Association of Club Executives [1650]
601 Pennsylvania Ave. NW, Ste. 900 S
Washington, DC 20004-3647
PH: (202)220-3019
Spencer, Angelina, Exec. Dir.

Association of Collegiate Schools of Architecture [7497]
1735 New York Ave. NW, 3rd Fl.
Washington, DC 20006
PH: (202)785-2324
Fax: (202)628-0448
Monti, Michael J., PhD, Exec. Dir.

Association for Community Affiliated Plans [14981]
1015 15th St. NW, Ste. 950
Washington, DC 20005
PH: (202)204-7508
Fax: (202)204-7517
MacFarlane, Glenn, President, CEO

Association of Community College Trustees [7641]
1101 17th St. NW, Ste. 300
Washington, DC 20036

PH: (202)775-4667
Fax: (202)223-1297
Zarate, Roberto, Chairman

Association for Competitive Technology [3207]
1401 K St. NW, Ste. 501
Washington, DC 20005
PH: (202)331-2130
Fax: (202)331-2139
Zuck, Jonathan, President

Association of Corporate Counsel [5108]
1025 Connecticut Ave. NW, Ste. 200
Washington, DC 20036
PH: (202)293-4103
Fax: (202)293-4701
Benjamin, Renee, Director

Association of Defense Communities [5296]
2020 K St. NW, Ste. 650
Washington, DC 20006
PH: (202)822-5256
Fax: (202)289-8326
Ford, Tim, CEO

Association for Demand Response and Smart Grid [6415]
1220 19th St. NW
Washington, DC 20036
PH: (202)857-0898
Covino, Susan, Officer

Association of Dermatology Administrators and Managers [14489]
1120 G St. NW, Ste. 1000
Washington, DC 20005
Toll free: 866-480-3573
Fax: (800)671-3763
Turpin, Diane, Exec. Dir.

Association for Enterprise Opportunity [3115]
1310 L St NW, Ste. 830
Washington, DC 20005
PH: (202)650-5580
Evans, Connie, CEO, President

Association of Environmental Engineering & Science Professors [8465]
1211 Connecticut Ave. NW, Ste. 650
Washington, DC 20036
PH: (202)640-6591
Characklis, Gregory W., President

Association of Environmental and Resource Economists [3812]
c/o Dr. Alan J. Krupnick, President
1616 P St. NW, Ste. 600
Washington, DC 20036
PH: (202)328-5125
Fax: (202)939-3460
Adamowicz, W.L., President

Association for Environmental Studies and Sciences [7885]
1101 17th St. NW, Ste. 250
Washington, DC 20036
Fax: (202)628-4311
Laitner, John, President

Association of Farmworker Opportunity Programs [12335]
1120 20th St. NW, Ste 300 S
Washington, DC 20036
PH: (202)828-6006
Flores, Ernie, President

Association of Federal Communications Consulting Engineers [7305]
PO Box 19333
Washington, DC 20036-0333
Wandel, Eric, President

Association of Fish and Wildlife Agencies [3813]
444 N Capitol St. NW, Ste. 725
Washington, DC 20001

PH: (202)624-7890
Fax: (202)624-7891
Regan, Ron, Exec. Dir.

Association of Flight Attendants - CWA [23385]
501 3rd St. NW
Washington, DC 20001
PH: (202)434-1300
Toll free: 800-424-2401
Nelson, Sara, President

Association of Foreign Investors in Real Estate [2019]
1300 Pennsylvania Ave. NW
Washington, DC 20004
PH: (202)312-1400
Fetgatter, James A., CEO

Association for Gerontology in Higher Education [7940]
1220 L St. NW, Ste. 901
Washington, DC 20005-4001
PH: (202)289-9806
Fax: (202)289-9824
Baker, Ms. M. Angela, Director

Association of Governing Boards of Universities and Colleges [7424]
1133 20th St. NW, Ste. 300
Washington, DC 20036
PH: (202)296-8400
Fax: (202)223-7053
Jackson, Yvonne R., Chmn. of the Bd.

Association of Home Appliance Manufacturers [212]
1111 19th St. NW, Ste. 402
Washington, DC 20036
PH: (202)872-5955
Fax: (202)872-9354
Cook, Melanie K., Chmn. of the Bd.

Association of Home Office Underwriters [1838]
1155 15th St. NW, Ste. 500
Washington, DC 20005
PH: (202)962-0167
Fax: (202)530-0659
Leblond, Norm, FALU, President

Association for Interdisciplinary Research in Values and Social Change [12764]
512 10th St. NW
Washington, DC 20004
PH: (202)626-8800
Hagan, Marie, Exec. Sec.

Association of International Photography Art Dealers [10136]
2025 M St. NW, Ste. 800
Washington, DC 20036
PH: (202)367-1158
Fax: (202)367-2158
Edelman, Catherine, President

Association of Jesuit Colleges and Universities [7574]
1 Dupont Cir., Ste. 405
Washington, DC 20036
PH: (202)862-9893
Sheeran, Rev. Michael J., SJ, President

Association of Jewish Aging Services [10500]
2519 Connecticut Ave. NW
Washington, DC 20008
PH: (202)543-7500
Cohen, Jeff, Chmn. of the Bd.

Association of Labor Relations Agencies [23465]
National Labor Relations Board
1099 14th St. NW
Washington, DC 20570-0001

PH: (202)273-1067
Fax: (202)273-4270
Sims, Pat, President

Association of Latino Administrators and Superintendents [7426]
PO Box 65204
Washington, DC 20035
PH: (202)466-0808
Rivera, Veronica, Exec. Dir.

Association of Literary Scholars, Critics, and Writers [9751]
Marist Hall
The Catholic University of America
620 Michigan Ave. NE
Washington, DC 20064
PH: (202)319-5650
Fax: (202)319-5650
Briggs, John, President

Association of Maternal and Child Health Programs [14167]
2030 M St. NW, Ste. 350
Washington, DC 20036
PH: (202)775-0436
Fax: (202)775-0061
Jones, Millie, Bd. Member

Association of Medical Device Reprocessors [15715]
429 R St. NW
Washington, DC 20001
PH: (202)747-6566
Vukelich, Daniel J., Esq., President, CEO

Association of Medical Diagnostics Manufacturers [3025]
c/o Leif Olsen, Director
Columbia Sq.
555 13th St. NW
Washington, DC 20004
Smith, Judi, VP

Association of Meeting Professionals [1651]
2025 M St. NW, Ste. 800
Washington, DC 20036-2422
PH: (202)973-8686
Fax: (202)973-8722
Oxendine-Medley, Jill, CHSE, Chmn. of the Bd.

Association of Metropolitan Planning Organizations [17966]
444 N Capitol St. NW, Ste. 345
Washington, DC 20001
PH: (202)624-3680
Fax: (202)624-3685

Association of Metropolitan Water Agencies [5650]
1620 I St. NW, Ste. 500
Washington, DC 20006
PH: (202)331-2820
Fax: (202)785-1845
VanDe Hei, Diane, CEO

Association for NeuroPsychoEconomics [6382]
c/o Catherine Wattenberg
750 1st St. NE
Washington, DC 20002
Reimann, Martin

Association of Occupational and Environmental Clinics [16316]
1010 Vermont Ave. NW, Ste. 513
Washington, DC 20005
PH: (202)347-4976
Toll free: 888-347-2632
Fax: (202)347-4950
Kirkland, Katherine H., Exec. Dir.

Association of Official Seed Analysts [4945]
653 Constitution Ave. NE
Washington, DC 20002

PH: (202)870-2412
Reed, Susan, President

Association of Oil Pipe Lines [2514]
1808 Eye St. NW, Ste. 300
Washington, DC 20006
PH: (202)408-7970
Fax: (202)280-1949
Black, Andrew J., President, CEO

**Association of Performing Arts
Presenters [7508]**
1211 Connecticut Ave. NW, Ste. 200
Washington, DC 20036-2716
PH: (202)833-2787
Toll free: 888-820-2787
Fax: (202)833-1543
Durham, Mario Garcia, President,
CEO

**Association of Postconsumer Plastic
Recyclers [2619]**
1001 G St. NW, Ste. 500 W
Washington, DC 20001
PH: (202)316-3046
Alexander, Steve, Exec. Dir.

**Association for Prevention Teaching
and Research [16800]**
1001 Connecticut Ave. NW, Ste. 610
Washington, DC 20036
PH: (202)463-0550
Toll free: 866-520-2787
Fax: (202)463-0555
Lewis, Allison L., Exec. Dir.

**Association of Private Sector Col-
leges and Universities [8735]**
1101 Connecticut Ave. NW, Ste. 900
Washington, DC 20036
PH: (202)336-6700
Toll free: 866-711-8574
Fax: (202)336-6828
Dakduk, Michael, Exec. VP

**Association of Professional Schools
of International Affairs [8110]**
1615 L St., NW 8th Flt.
Washington, DC 20036
PH: (202)559-5831
Iezzi Mezzera, Carmen, Exec. Dir.

**Association for Professionals in
Infection Control and Epidemiology
[15393]**
1275 K St. NW, Ste. 1000
Washington, DC 20005-4006
PH: (202)789-1890
Fax: (202)789-1899
Manning, PhD, CRNP, CIC, FAAN,
Mary Lou, President

**Association of Professors of Cardiol-
ogy [14101]**
2400 N St. NW
Washington, DC 20037
PH: (202)375-6191
Taylor, Robert, Secretary, Treasurer

**Association of Program Directors in
Endocrinology, Diabetes and
Metabolism [14701]**
2055 L St. NW, Ste. 600
Washington, DC 20036
PH: (202)971-3706
Fax: (202)736-9705
Gopalakrishnan, Geetha, MD,
President

**Association of Proposal Manage-
ment Professionals [2156]**
c/o Rick Harris, Executive Director
20 F St. NW, 7th Fl.
Washington, DC 20001
PH: (240)646-7075
Toll free: 866-466-APMP
Harris, Rick, Exec. Dir.

**Association of Prosecuting Attorneys
[4999]**
1615 L St. NW, Ste. 1100
Washington, DC 20036

PH: (202)861-2480
Fax: (202)223-4688
LaBahn, David, President, CEO

**Association for Psychological Sci-
ence [16906]**
1800 Massachusetts Ave. NW, Ste.
402
Washington, DC 20036
PH: (202)293-9300
Fax: (202)293-9350

**Association of Public and Land-
Grant Universities [7627]**
1307 New York Ave. NW, Ste. 400
Washington, DC 20005-4722
PH: (202)478-6040
Fax: (202)478-6046
McPherson, Peter, President

**Association of Public and Land
Grant Universities - Commission
on International Programs [18483]**
1307 New York Ave. NW, Ste. 400
Washington, DC 20005-4722
PH: (202)478-6040
Fax: (202)478-6046
McPherson, M. Peter, President

**Association for Public Policy
Analysis and Management [18962]**
1100 Vermont Ave. NW, Ste. 650
Washington, DC 20005
PH: (202)496-0134
Fax: (202)496-0134
Sheehan, Tara, Exec. Dir.

**Association for Quality Imaging
[15681]**
1629 K St. NW, Ste. 300
Washington, DC 20006
PH: (202)355-6406
Fax: (202)355-6407
Winkle, C. Christian, Chairman

**Association of Reproductive Health
Professionals [11836]**
1300 19th St. NW, Ste. 200
Washington, DC 20036
PH: (202)466-3825
Fax: (202)466-3826
Shields, Wayne C., President, CEO

**Association of Research Libraries
[9689]**
21 Dupont Cir. NW, Ste. 800
Washington, DC 20036-1543
PH: (202)296-2296
Fax: (202)872-0884
Shore, Elliott, Exec. Dir.

**Association for Retail Technology
Standards [2947]**
1101 New York Ave. NW
Washington, DC 20005
PH: (202)783-7971
Toll free: 800-673-4692
Fax: (202)737-2849

**Association of Schools of Allied
Health Professions [8313]**
122 C St. NW, Ste. 650
Washington, DC 20001
PH: (202)237-6481
Petrosino, Linda, PhD, President

**Association of Schools and
Programs of Public Health [16998]**
1900 M St. NW, Ste. 710
Washington, DC 20036
PH: (202)296-1099
Fax: (202)296-1252
Foster, Allison, Exec. Dir.

**Association of Science-Technology
Centers [9826]**
818 Connecticut Ave. NW, 7th Fl.
Washington, DC 20006

PH: (202)783-7200
Fax: (202)783-7207
Rock, Anthony, CEO, President

**Association of Securities and
Exchange Commission Alumni
[3039]**
PO Box 5767
Washington, DC 20016
PH: (202)462-1211
Riesenberg, Thomas, President

**Association of State and Territorial
Solid Waste Management Officials
[5844]**
1101 17th St. NW, Ste. 707
Washington, DC 20036
PH: (202)640-1060
Fax: (202)331-3254
Buthker, Bonnie, President

**Association for the Study of African-
American Life and History [8783]**
Howard Ctr.
2225 Georgia Ave. NW, Ste. 331
Washington, DC 20059
PH: (202)238-5910
Fax: (202)986-1506
Cyrus, Sylvia, Exec. Dir.

**Association for the Study of the
Middle East and Africa [8339]**
2100 M St. NW, No. 170-291
Washington, DC 20037
PH: (202)429-8860
Clark, Prof. Mark T., President

**Association for the Study of Peak Oil
and Gas U.S.A. [6999]**
1725 Eye St. NW, Ste. 300
Washington, DC 20006
PH: (202)470-4809
Baldauf, Jim, Founder

**Association of Test Publishers
[2773]**
South Bldg., Ste. 900
601 Pennsylvania Ave. NW
Washington, DC 20004-3647
PH: (717)755-9747
Toll free: 866-240-7909
Harris, William G., PhD, CEO

**Association on Third World Affairs,
Inc. [18484]**
c/o Dr. Lorna Hahn
1717 K St. NW, Ste. 600
Washington, DC 20036
PH: (202)973-0157
Fax: (202)775-7465
Hahn, Dr. Lorna, Exec. Dir.

**Association of Universities for
Research in Astronomy [6000]**
1212 New York Ave. NW, Ste. 450
Washington, DC 20005
PH: (202)483-2101
Fax: (202)483-2106
Mountain, Matt, President

**Association of University Programs
in Health Administration [8315]**
1730 M St. NW, Ste. 407
Washington, DC 20036
PH: (202)763-7283
Fax: (202)894-0941
Glandon, Gerald, PhD, President,
CEO

**Association of Women's Business
Centers [3488]**
1629 K St. NW, Ste. 300
Washington, DC 20006
PH: (202)552-8732
Bailey, Marsha, Chairperson

**Association of Women's Health,
Obstetric and Neonatal Nurses
[16125]**
2000 L St. NW, Ste. 740
Washington, DC 20036-4912

PH: (202)261-2400
Toll free: 800-673-8499
Fax: (202)728-0575
Erdman, Lynn, CEO

Atatürk Society of America [18905]
4731 Massachusetts Ave. NW
Washington, DC 20016
PH: (202)362-7173
Yavalar, Hudai, Chairman, Founder

Atheist Alliance International [19709]
1777 T St. NW
Washington, DC 20009-7102
Hamill, John, Secretary

**Atlantic Council of the United States
[19087]**
1030 15th St. NW, 12th Fl.
Washington, DC 20005
PH: (202)463-7226
Fax: (202)463-7241
Huntsman, Jon M., Jr., Chairman

Atlas Network [6384]
1201 L St. NW
Washington, DC 20005
PH: (202)449-8449
Fax: (202)280-1259
López, Rómulo, Dir. of Fin.

**Australian New Zealand American
Chambers of Commerce [23562]**
c/o Embassy of Australia
1601 Massachusetts Ave. NW
Washington, DC 20036
PH: (202)797-3000
Fax: (202)797-3168

**Austrian Press and Information
Service [23542]**
3524 International Ct. NW
Washington, DC 20008
PH: (202)895-6700
Fax: (202)895-6750
Irvin, Ms. Alice, Ed.-in-Chief

**Autistic Self Advocacy Network
[13758]**
PO Box 66122
Washington, DC 20035
PH: (202)596-1056
Ne'eman, Ari, Founder, President

**Automotive Aftermarket Suppliers
Association | Brake Manufacturers
Council [307]**
1030 15th St. NW, Ste. 500 E
Washington, DC 20005
PH: (919)406-8856
Fax: (919)549-4824
Oliveto, Frank, Officer

**Automotive Specialty Products Alli-
ance [285]**
1667 K St. NW, Ste. 300
Washington, DC 20006
PH: (202)833-7308
Fax: (202)223-2636
Power, Kristin, Contact

**Aviation Suppliers Association
[2215]**
2233 Wisconsin Ave. NW, Ste. 503
Washington, DC 20007-4124
PH: (202)347-6899
Fax: (202)347-6894
Dickstein, Michele L., President

Bank Information Center [386]
1023 15th St. NW, 10th Fl.
Washington, DC 20005
PH: (202)737-7752
Fax: (202)737-1155
Redford, Katie, Chmn. of the Bd.

**Bank Insurance and Securities As-
sociation [1842]**
2025 M St. NW, Ste. 800
Washington, DC 20036-2422

PH: (202)367-1111
Fax: (202)367-2111
Consalo, Frank A., VP

Banker Association for Foreign and
Trade [387]
1120 Connecticut Ave. NW
Washington, DC 20036
PH: (202)663-7575
Fax: (202)663-5538
Burwell, Tod, President, CEO

Bankers Association for Finance and
Trade [388]
1120 Connecticut Ave. NW
Washington, DC 20036
PH: (202)663-7575
Fax: (202)663-5538
Ahearn, John, Chairman

Baptist Joint Committee for Religious
Liberty [19723]
200 Maryland Ave. NE
Washington, DC 20002
PH: (202)544-4226
Fax: (202)544-2094
Jordan, Edwards, Officer

Basic Education Coalition [8234]
1400 16th St. NW, Ste. 210
Washington, DC 20036
PH: (202)729-6712
Fax: (202)729-6713
Gillies, John, Co-Ch.

Judge David L. Bazelon Center for
Mental Health Law [17878]
1101 15th St. NW, Ste. 1212
Washington, DC 20005
PH: (202)467-5730
Fax: (202)223-0409
Smith, Karen, Exec. Asst.

BBYO, Inc. [20235]
800 8th St. NW
Washington, DC 20001
PH: (202)857-6633
(202)857-6580
Fax: (202)857-6568
Grossman, Mr. Matthew, CEO

Becket Fund for Religious Liberty
[19025]
1200 New Hampshire Ave. NW, Ste.
700
Washington, DC 20036
PH: (202)955-0095
(202)349-7220
Fax: (202)955-0090
Arriaga, Kristina, Exec. Dir.

Beer Institute [180]
440 1st. NW, Ste. 350
Washington, DC 20001
PH: (202)737-2337
Fax: (202)737-7004
Dubost, Joy, Officer

Better Hearing Institute [15178]
1444 I St. NW, Ste. 700
Washington, DC 20005
PH: (202)449-1100
Fax: (202)216-9646
Kochkin, Sergei, PhD, Exec. Dir.

Beyond Borders [12143]
5016 Connecticut Ave. NW
Washington, DC 20008
PH: (202)686-2088
Diggs, David, Exec. Dir.

Beyond Pesticides [13220]
701 E St. SE, Ste. 200
Washington, DC 20003
PH: (202)543-5450
Fax: (202)543-4791
Feldman, Jay, Exec. Dir.

Biblical Archaeology Society [5934]
4710 41st. NW
Washington, DC 20016

PH: (202)364-3300
Toll free: 800-221-4644
Singer, Suzanne F., Editor

Biblical Institute for Social Change
[20534]
1400 Shepherd Street Ne Ste. 264 &
266
Cain Hope Felder, PhD
Washington, DC 20017
PH: (202)269-4311
Fax: (202)269-0051
Felder, Dr. Cain Hope, Chairman,
CEO, Founder

Bio-Process Systems Alliance [2554]
1850 M St. NW, Ste. 700
Washington, DC 20036
PH: (212)721-4100
Fax: (212)296-8120
Boehm, John, Chmn. of the Bd.

Biomass Energy Research Associa-
tion [6461]
901 D St. SW, Ste. 100
Washington, DC 20024
PH: (410)953-6202
Fax: (410)290-0377
Pellegrino, Joan, President,
Treasurer

Biomass Thermal Energy Council
[6462]
1211 Connecticut Ave. NW, Ste. 650
Washington, DC 20036-2701
PH: (202)596-3974
Fax: (202)223-5537
Serfass, Jeff, Exec. Dir.

Biotechnology Industry Organization
[6120]
1201 Maryland Ave. SW, Ste. 900
Washington, DC 20024
PH: (202)962-9200
Fax: (202)488-6301
Cohen, Ron, Chairman

Black Alliance for Educational Op-
tions [7817]
1001 G St. NW, Ste. 800
Washington, DC 20001
PH: (202)429-2236
Fuller, Howard, Bd. Member

Black Americans for Life [12765]
512 10th St. NW
Washington, DC 20004
PH: (202)378-8855
James, Kay, Founder

Black Community Crusade for
Children [10867]
c/o Children's Defense Fund
25 E St. NW
Washington, DC 20001-1522
Toll free: 800-233-1200
Edelman, Mrs. Marian Wright,
Founder, President

Black Theatre Network [10244]
2609 Douglas Rd. SE, Ste. 102
Washington, DC 20020
PH: (202)274-5667
Fax: (202)806-6708
Saine, KB, President

Black Women in Sisterhood for Ac-
tion [13371]
PO Box 1592
Washington, DC 20013
PH: (301)460-1565

Black Women's Health Imperative
[17753]
55 M St. SE, Ste. 940
Washington, DC 20003
PH: (202)548-4000
Winston, Carol, Asst. to the Pres.

Black Women's Roundtable on Voter
Participation [18906]
c/o National Coalition on Black Civic
Participation
1050 Connecticut Ave. NW, 10th Fl.,
Ste. No. 1000
Washington, DC 20036
PH: (202)659-4929
Fax: (202)659-5025
Campbell, Melanie L., President,
CEO

Blinded American Veterans Founda-
tion [20765]
PO Box 65900
Washington, DC 20035-5900
PH: (202)257-5446
Fax: (301)622-3330
Fales, Sgt. John, Jr., President

Blinded Veterans Association
[17692]
477 H St. NW
Washington, DC 20001-2694
PH: (202)371-8880
Toll free: 800-669-7079
Fax: (202)371-8258
Stamper, Robert Dale, President

Blue Frontier Campaign [4134]
PO Box 19367
Washington, DC 20036
PH: (202)387-8030
Fax: (202)234-5176
Helvarg, David, Exec. Dir.

B'nai B'rith International [20237]
1120 20th St. NW, Ste. 300 N
Washington, DC 20036
PH: (202)857-6600
Toll free: 888-388-4224
Saltzman, Gary P., President

B'nai B'rith International's Center for
Jewish Identity [8137]
1120 20th St. NW, Ste. 300 N
Washington, DC 20036
PH: (212)490-3290
(202)857-6600
Toll free: 888-388-4224
Love, Rhonda, VP

Board for Certification of Genealo-
gists [20962]
PO Box 14291
Washington, DC 20044
McDonald, David, Secretary

BoardSource [12400]
750 9th St. NW, Ste. 650
Washington, DC 20001
PH: (202)349-2500
Toll free: 877-892-6273
Fax: (202)349-2599
Griswold, John, Chairman

Bonobo Conservation Initiative
[4798]
2701 Connecticut Ave. NW, No. 702
Washington, DC 20008
PH: (202)332-1014
Coxe, Sally, President, Founder

Born Free USA [10595]
PO Box 32160
Washington, DC 20007
PH: (202)450-3168
Travers, Will, Secretary

Bound4LIFE [19055]
205 3rd St. SE
Washington, DC 20003
PH: (202)681-7729
Lockett, Matt, Director

Brady Campaign to Prevent Gun
Violence [18247]
840 1st St. NE, Ste. 400
Washington, DC 20002

PH: (202)370-8100
Gross, Daniel, President

Brady Center to Prevent Gun
Violence [18248]
840 1st St. NE, Ste. 400
Washington, DC 20002
PH: (202)370-8101
Gross, Dan, President

Brave Kids [14170]
c/o United Cerebral Palsy
1825 K St. NW, Ste. 600
Washington, DC 20006
PH: (202)776-0406
Toll free: 800-872-5827
Fitzgerald, Kristen, Founder,
President

Brazil Industries Coalition [1979]
818 18th St. NW, Ste. 630
Washington, DC 20006
PH: (202)471-4020
Fax: (202)471-4024
Abijaodi, Carlos Eduardo, Chmn. of
the Bd.

Brazil-U.S. Business Council [23566]
1615 H St. NW
Washington, DC 20062
PH: (202)463-5729
Carvalho, Cassia, Exec. Dir.

Bread for the World [18453]
425 3rd St. SW, Ste. 1200
Washington, DC 20024
PH: (202)639-9400
Toll free: 800-822-7323
Fax: (202)639-9401
Beckmann, David, President

Bretton Woods Committee [18144]
1701 K St. NW, Ste. 950
Washington, DC 20006
PH: (202)331-1616
Rodgers, Randy, Exec. Dir.

Brewery and Soft Drink Conference
[23394]
25 Louisiana Ave., NW
25 Louisiana Ave. NW
Washington, DC 20001
PH: (202)624-6800
Hall, Ken, Gen. Sec., Treasurer

Bridging Nations Foundation [18517]
1779 Massachusetts Ave. NW, Ste.
715
Washington, DC 20036
PH: (202)518-1247
Ambegaonkar, Dr. Prakash, CEO,
Founder

Bridging Refugee Youth and
Children's Services [11217]
United States Conference of
Catholic Bishops
3211 4th St. NE
Washington, DC 20017
Toll free: 888-572-6500
Morland, Lyn, MSW, Director

British American Security Information
Council [18082]
1725 DeSales St. NW, Ste. 600
Washington, DC 20036
PH: (202)546-8055
Ingram, Paul, Exec. Dir.

Broadcast Education Association
[7535]
1771 N St. NW
Washington, DC 20036-2800
PH: (202)602-0584
Fax: (202)609-9940
Birks, Heather, Exec. Dir.

Brookings Institution [18963]
1775 Massachusetts Ave. NW
Washington, DC 20036

PH: (202)797-6210
Fax: (202)797-6133
Bennett, Steven, COO, VP

Building Enclosure Council -
National [6162]
c/o Philip J. Schneider, Program
Director
1090 Vermont Ave. NW, Ste. 700
Washington, DC 20005
PH: (202)289-7800
Fax: (202)289-1092
Stoik, Brian M., Chairman

Building Enclosure Technology and
Environment Council [506]
c/o National Institute of Building Sci-
ences
1090 Vermont Ave. NW, Ste. 700
Washington, DC 20005
PH: (202)289-7800
Fax: (202)289-1092
Anis, Wagdy, Bd. Member

Building Owners and Managers As-
sociation International [2852]
1101 15th St. NW, Ste. 800
Washington, DC 20005
PH: (202)408-2662
Fax: (202)326-6377
Chamberlain, Henry, COO, President

BuildingSMART Alliance [6348]
National Institute of Building Sci-
ences
1090 Vermont Ave. NW, Ste. 700
Washington, DC 20005
PH: (202)289-7800
Fax: (202)289-1092
Green, Henry L., AIA, President

Business Council [18951]
1901 Pennsylvania Ave. NW, Ste.
701
Washington, DC 20006
PH: (202)298-7650
Fax: (202)785-0296
Colucci, Marlene M., Exec. Dir.

Business Council for Sustainable
Energy [1107]
805 15th St., NW Ste. 708
Washington, DC 20005
PH: (202)785-0507
Fax: (202)785-0514
Jacobson, Lisa, President

Business Executives for National
Security [19088]
1030 15th St. NW, Ste. 200 E
Washington, DC 20005-1505
PH: (202)296-2125
Fax: (202)296-2490
Jackson, Lisa, Chief Adm. Ofc.

Business-Higher Education Forum
[7547]
2025 M St. NW, Ste. 800
Washington, DC 20036
PH: (202)367-1189
Fitzgerald, Brian K., Officer

Business-Industry Political Action
Committee [18861]
888 16th St. NW, Ste. 305
Washington, DC 20006-4103
PH: (202)833-1880
Fax: (202)833-2338
Pallat, John, Chairman

Business and Professional Women/
U.S.A. [18201]
1620 Eye St. NW, Ste. 210
Washington, DC 20006
PH: (202)293-1100
Toll free: 888-491-8833
Fax: (202)861-0298
Frett, Deborah L., CEO

Business and Professional Women's
Foundation [3489]
1030 15th St., NW, Ste. B1, No. 148
Washington, DC 20005
PH: (202)293-1100
Fax: (202)861-0298
Ridgeway, Roslyn, Chmn. of the Bd.

Business Roundtable [18952]
300 New Jersey Ave. NW, Ste. 800
Washington, DC 20001
PH: (202)872-1260
Engler, John, President

Business Software Alliance [5324]
20 F St. NW, Ste. 800
Washington, DC 20001
PH: (202)872-5500
Fax: (202)872-5501
Albright, Craig, VP

C-Change [13913]
2445 L St., NW, Ste. 601
Washington, DC 20037
PH: (202)753-9791
Fax: (708)430-1191
Smith, Alison, Advisor

Campaign for America's Future
[18937]
1825 K St. NW, Ste. 400
Washington, DC 20006-1254
PH: (202)955-5665
Fax: (202)955-5606
Hickey, Roger, Director

Campaign to End Obesity [16250]
805 15th St. NW, Ste. 650
Washington, DC 20005
PH: (202)466-8100
Licitra, Karen, Chairwoman

Campaign for High School Equity
[8532]
1015 18th St. NW, Ste. 300
Washington, DC 20036

Can Manufacturers Institute [829]
1730 Rhode Island Ave. NW, Ste.
1000
Washington, DC 20036
PH: (202)232-4677
Fax: (202)232-5756

Canadian-American Business
Council [619]
1900 K St. NW, Ste. 100
Washington, DC 20006
PH: (202)496-7255
Slack, David, Chmn. of the Bd.

Cancer Leadership Council [13925]
2446 39th St. NW
Washington, DC 20007
PH: (202)333-4041
Fax: (202)333-4081
Goss, Elizabeth, Contact

Cancer Support Community [13931]
1050 17th St. NW, Ste. 500
Washington, DC 20036
PH: (202)659-9709
Toll free: 888-793-9355
Fax: (202)974-7999
Thiboldeaux, Kim, CEO

Canon Law Society of America
[19806]
The Hecker Ctr., Ste. 111
415 Michigan Ave. NE
Washington, DC 20017-1102
PH: (202)832-2350
Fax: (202)832-2331
Viera, Rev. Manuel, President

Capital Press Club [2669]
PO Box 75114
Washington, DC 20013-5114
Arnwine, Barbara, President

Capitol Hill Restoration Society
[9379]
420 10th St. SE
Washington, DC 20003-0264
PH: (202)543-0425
Jones, Lisa Dale, President

Caregiver Action Network [15276]
1130 Connecticut Ave. NW, Ste. 300
Washington, DC 20036-3981
PH: (202)454-3970
Shanfield, Jon, Chairman

Cargo Airline Association [132]
1620 L St. NW, Ste. 610
Washington, DC 20036
PH: (202)293-1030
Alterman, Stephen A., President

Caribbean - Central American Action
[12144]
1625 K St. NW, Ste. 200
Washington, DC 20006
PH: (202)464-2031
Edmunds, Anton E., Consultant

Carnegie Endowment for
International Peace [18519]
1779 Massachusetts Ave. NW
Washington, DC 20036-2103
PH: (202)483-7600
Fax: (202)483-1840
Giordano, Richard, Trustee

Carnegie Institution for Science
[7088]
1530 P St. NW
Washington, DC 20005
PH: (202)387-6400
Fax: (202)387-8092
Barrett, Craig, Chairman

Catholic Biblical Association of
America [8706]
Catholic University of America
433 Caldwell Hall
Washington, DC 20064
PH: (202)319-5519
Fax: (202)319-4799
Tarker, Lisa, Asst.

Catholic Campaign for Human
Development [12466]
c/o United States Conference of
Catholic Bishops
3211 4th St., NE
Washington, DC 20017
PH: (202)541-3210
Toll free: 800-946-4-CHD
Fax: (202)541-3329
McCloud, Ralph, Director

Catholic Climate Covenant [3824]
415 Michigan Ave. NE, Ste. 260
Washington, DC 20017
PH: (202)756-5545
Misleh, Mr. Dan, Exec. Dir.

Catholic News Service [2670]
3211 4th St. NE
Washington, DC 20017
PH: (202)541-3250
Fax: (202)541-3255
Smith, Gladys, Admin. Asst.

Catholics in Alliance for the Common
Good [19819]
1612 K St., Ste. 400
Washington, DC 20006
PH: (202)499-4968
Rotondaro, Alfred M., Chairman

Catholics for Choice [19031]
1436 U St. NW, Ste. 301
Washington, DC 20009-3997
PH: (202)986-6093
Fax: (202)332-7995
O'Brien, Jon, President

Cato Institute [18964]
1000 Massachusetts Ave. NW
Washington, DC 20001-5403
PH: (202)842-0200
Fax: (202)842-3490
Levy, Robert A., Chairman

CECA Solutions [18190]
2737 Devonshire Pl. NW, Ste. 102
Washington, DC 20008
Berman, Ellen, CEO

Center for Applied Linguistics [9739]
4646 40th St. NW
Washington, DC 20016-1859
PH: (202)362-0700
Fax: (202)362-3740
Christian, Donna, Associate

Center for Audit Quality [19]
1155 F St. NW, Ste. 450
Washington, DC 20004
PH: (202)609-8120
Fornelli, Cynthia M., Exec. Dir.

Center for Auto Safety [12817]
1825 Connecticut Ave. NW, Ste. 330
Washington, DC 20009-5708
PH: (202)328-7700
Ditlow, Clarence, Exec. Dir.

Center for Aviation Research and
Education [5057]
Washington National Airport
Hangar 7, Ste. 218
Washington, DC 20001
PH: (703)417-1883
Ogrodzinski, Henry M., President,
CEO

Center for the Book in the Library of
Congress [9754]
101 Independence Ave. SE
Washington, DC 20540-4920
PH: (202)707-5221
Fax: (202)707-0269
Cole, John Y., Director

Center on Budget and Policy Priorities [18953]
820 1st St. NE, Ste. 510
Washington, DC 20002
PH: (202)408-1080
Fax: (202)408-1056
de Ferranti, David, President

Center for the Child Care Workforce
[11758]
American Federation of Teachers,
AFL-CIO
555 New Jersey Ave. NW
Washington, DC 20001
PH: (202)879-4400
Young, Marci P., Director

Center for Civilians in Conflict
[17999]
1210 18th St. NW, 4th Fl.
Washington, DC 20036
PH: (202)558-6958
Borello, Federico, Exec. Dir.

Center for Clean Air Policy [4537]
750 1st St. NE, Ste. 940
Washington, DC 20002
PH: (202)408-9260
Fax: (202)408-8896
Helme, Ned, Advisor

Center for Community Action of
B'Nai B'rith International [11330]
1120 20th St. NW, Ste. 300N
Washington, DC 20036
PH: (212)490-3290
Bartfield, Ira, VP

Center for Community Change
[12532]
1536 U St. NW
Washington, DC 20009

PH: (202)339-9300
Bhargava, Deepak, Exec. Dir.

Center of Concern [18382]
1225 Otis St. NE
Washington, DC 20017
PH: (202)635-2757
Fax: (202)832-9494
Caliari, Aldo, Director

Center on Conscience and War [18135]
1830 Connecticut Ave. NW
Washington, DC 20009-5732
Toll free: 800-379-2679
Fax: (202)483-1246
Santelli, Maria, Exec. Dir.

Center for Democracy and Human Rights in Saudi Arabia [12027]
1050 17th St. NW, Ste. 1000
Washington, DC 20036
PH: (202)558-5552
Fax: (202)536-5210

Center for Democracy and Technology [17940]
1401 K St. NW, Ste. 200
Washington, DC 20005
PH: (202)637-9800
Fax: (202)637-0968
O'Connor, Nuala, President, CEO

Center for Dispute Settlement [4958]
1666 Connecticut Ave. NW, Ste. 525
Washington, DC 20009-1039
PH: (202)265-9572
Fax: (202)332-3951
Singer, Linda R., Founder, President

Center for Economic and Policy Research [18165]
1611 Connecticut Ave. NW, Ste. 400
Washington, DC 20009
PH: (202)293-5380
Fax: (202)588-1356
Baker, Dean, Director

Center for Economic and Social Justice [18166]
PO Box 40711
Washington, DC 20016
PH: (703)243-5155
Fax: (703)243-5935
Kurland, Norman G., President

Center for Effective Government [18314]
2040 S St. NW, 2nd Fl.
Washington, DC 20009
PH: (202)234-8494
Fax: (202)234-8584
McFate, Katherine, President, CEO

Center for Food Safety [6643]
660 Pennsylvania Ave. SE, Ste. 302
Washington, DC 20003
PH: (202)547-9359
Fax: (202)547-9429
Douglass, Adele, President

Center For Black Equity [11876]
PO Box 77313
Washington, DC 20013
PH: (202)641-8527
Fowlkes, Earl D., Jr., CEO, President

Center for Immigration Studies [18462]
1629 K St. NW, Ste. 600
Washington, DC 20006
PH: (202)466-8185
Fax: (202)466-8076
Krikorian, Mark, Exec. Dir.

Center for International Disaster Information [11652]
529 14th St. NW, Ste. 700W
Washington, DC 20045-1000

PH: (202)821-1999
(202)821-4040
Rilling, Ms. Juanita, Director

Center for International Environmental Law [5177]
1350 Connecticut Ave. NW, Ste. 1100
Washington, DC 20036
PH: (202)785-8700
Fax: (202)785-8701
Muffett, Carroll, CEO, President

Center for International Policy [18383]
2000 M St. NW, Ste. 720
Washington, DC 20036
PH: (202)232-3317
Fax: (202)232-3440
Goodfellow, Bill, Exec. Dir.

Center for International Private Enterprise [620]
1211 Connecticut Ave. NW, Ste. 700
Washington, DC 20036
PH: (202)721-9200
Fax: (202)721-9250
Donohue, Thomas J., President

Center for Internationalization and Global Engagement [8193]
American Council on Education
1 Dupont Cir. NW
Washington, DC 20036
PH: (202)939-9300
Farnsworth, Brad, Asst. VP

Center for Law and Education [5161]
1875 Connecticut Ave. NW, Ste. 510
Washington, DC 20009
PH: (202)986-3000
Weckstein, Paul, Director

Center for National Security Studies [19089]
1730 Pennsylvania Ave. NW, 7th Fl.
Washington, DC 20006
PH: (202)721-5650
Fax: (202)530-0128
Martin, Kate, Director

Center for Neighborhood Enterprise [17968]
1625 K St. NW, Ste. 1200
Washington, DC 20006
PH: (202)518-6500
Fax: (202)588-0314

Center for the Polyurethanes Industry of the American Chemistry Council [2621]
700 2nd St. NE
Washington, DC 20002
PH: (202)249-7000
Salamone, Lee, Director

Center for Public Integrity [18315]
910 17th St. NW, Ste. 700
Washington, DC 20006
PH: (202)466-1300
(202)481-1232
Bale, Peter, CEO

Center for Public Justice [18967]
1115 Massachusetts Ave. NW
Washington, DC 20005
PH: (202)695-2667
Toll free: 866-275-8784
Summers, Stephanie, CEO

Center for Respect of Life & Environment [4112]
2100 L St. NW
Washington, DC 20037
PH: (202)778-6133
Fax: (202)778-6138
Clugston, Richard M., Exec. Dir.

Center for Responsive Politics [18907]
1101 14th St. NW, Ste. 1030
Washington, DC 20005-5635
PH: (202)857-0044
Fax: (202)857-7809
Krumholz, Sheila, Exec. Dir.

Center for Security Policy [7152]
1901 Pennsylvania Ave. NW, Ste. 201
Washington, DC 20006
PH: (202)835-9077
Prentice, E. Miles, III, Chmn. of the Bd.

Center for Spiritual and Ethical Education [8009]
910 M St. NW, No.722
Washington, DC 20001
PH: (202)838-1099
Toll free: 800-298-4599
Fax: (678)623-5634
Mattingly, Bob, Exec. Dir.

Center for Strategic and Budgetary Assessments [18694]
1667 K St. NW, Ste. 900
Washington, DC 20006
PH: (202)331-7990
Fax: (202)331-8019
Ford, Nelson M., Chairman

Center for Strategic and International Studies [18939]
1616 Rhode Island Ave. NW
Washington, DC 20036
PH: (202)887-0200
(202)775-3242
Fax: (202)775-3199
Hamre, John J., CEO, President

Center for the Study of the Presidency and Congress [17852]
601 13th St., NW Ste. 1050N
Washington, DC 20005
PH: (202)872-9800
Fax: (202)872-9811
Perch, Elizabeth, CFO, COO

Center for Study of Responsive Law [18043]
PO Box 19367
Washington, DC 20036
Nader, Ralph, Founder

Center for the Study of Social Policy [18968]
1575 Eye St. NW, Ste. 500
Washington, DC 20005
PH: (202)371-1565
Fax: (202)371-1472
Spigner, Carol Wilson, Chairperson

Center for Worker Freedom [23537]
722 12th St. NW, Ste. 400
Washington, DC 20005
PH: (202)785-0266
Fax: (202)785-0261
Patterson, Matt, Exec. Dir.

Center for Workers with Disabilities [11579]
1133 19th St. NW, Ste. 400
Washington, DC 20036
PH: (202)682-0100
Fax: (202)204-0071
Relave, Nanette, Director

Central American Resource Center [19016]
1460 Columbia Rd. NW, Ste. C-1
Washington, DC 20009
PH: (202)328-9799
Fax: (202)328-7894
Nuñez, Abel, Exec. Dir.

Centre for Development and Population Activities [12145]
1255 23rd St. NW, Ste. 300
Washington, DC 20037

PH: (202)617-2300
Fax: (202)332-4496
Van Dusen, Dr. Ann, Chairwoman

Certified Automotive Parts Association [290]
1000 Vermont Ave. NW, Ste. 1010
Washington, DC 20005-4908
PH: (202)737-2212
Fax: (202)737-2214
Northup, Chris, Distributor

Certified Financial Planner Board of Standards [1277]
1425 K St. NW, No. 800
Washington, DC 20005
PH: (202)379-2200
Toll free: 800-487-1497
Fax: (202)379-2299
Myers, Roger, CFO

Chamber of Shipping of America [5579]
1730 Rhode Island Ave., Ste. 702
Washington, DC 20036
PH: (202)775-4399
Fax: (202)659-3795
Metcalf, Kathy J., President, CEO

Champions for America's Future [10815]
1212 New York Ave. NW, Ste. 300
Washington, DC 20005
PH: (202)684-8865
Cernich, Andrea, Director

Change to Win [23529]
1900 L St. NW, Ste. 900
Washington, DC 20036
PH: (202)721-0660
Fax: (202)721-0661
Hoffa, James P., Chairperson

character.org [11724]
1634 I St. NW, Ste. 550
Washington, DC 20036
PH: (202)296-7743
Keating, Frank, V. Chmn. of the Bd.

Check Payment Systems Association [3170]
2025 M St. NW, Ste. 800
Washington, DC 20036-3309
PH: (202)367-1144
Fax: (202)367-2144
Antolick, Steven, Exec. Dir.

Cheese Importers Association of America [972]
204 E St. NE
Washington, DC 20002
PH: (202)547-0899
Fax: (202)547-6348
Summers, Annette, Exec. Dir.

Chi Eta Phi Sorority [23838]
3029 13th St. NW
Washington, DC 20009
PH: (202)232-3858
Fax: (202)232-3460
Murphy, Priscilla, 1st VP

Chief Executives Organization [621]
1825 K St. NW, Ste. 1450
Washington, DC 20006
PH: (201)813-1880
Fax: (201)296-2821

Chief Warrant and Warrant Officers Association [5595]
12 Brookley Ave. SW
Washington, DC 20032
PH: (202)554-7753
Light, Brent A., Secretary

Child Labor Coalition [10900]
National Consumers League
1701 K St. NW, Ste. 1200

Washington, DC 20006
Greenberg, Sally, Co-Ch.

**Child Welfare League of America
[10908]**
1726 M St. NW, Ste. 500
Washington, DC 20036-4522
PH: (202)688-4200
Fax: (202)833-1689
James-Brown, Christine, President,
CEO

Childbirth Connection [16280]
1875 Connecticut Ave. NW, Ste. 650
Washington, DC 20009
PH: (202)986-2600
Fax: (202)986-2539
Corry, Maureen P., MPH, Advisor

**Children's AIDS Fund International
[10536]**
PO Box 16433
Washington, DC 20041
PH: (703)433-1560
Fax: (703)433-1561
Smith, Anita M., President

**Children's Cause for Cancer
Advocacy [13940]**
122 C St. NW, Ste. 240
Washington, DC 20001-2109
PH: (202)304-1850
Weiner, Susan L., PhD, Founder

Children's Defense Fund [11223]
25 E St. NW
Washington, DC 20001
Toll free: 800-233-1200
Edelman, Marian Wright, President

**Children's Environmental Health
Network [14713]**
110 Maryland Ave. NE, Ste. 402
Washington, DC 20002
PH: (202)543-4033
Fax: (202)543-8797
Robert, James, MD, MPH,
Chairperson

**Children's Hospital Association
[15319]**
600 13th St. NW, Ste. 500
Washington, DC 20005
PH: (202)753-5500
Fax: (202)347-5147
Wietecha, Mark, President, CEO

The Children's Partnership [10932]
2013 H St. NW, 6th Fl.
Washington, DC 20036
PH: (202)429-0033
Fax: (202)429-0974
Lipper, Laurie, Founder, President

**Chlorinated Paraffins Industry As-
sociation [713]**
1250 Connecticut Ave. NW, Ste. 700
Washington, DC 20036
PH: (202)419-1500
Fensterheim, Robert J., Exec. Dir.

Chorus America [9889]
1156 15th St. NW, Ste. 310
Washington, DC 20005-1747
PH: (202)331-7577
Fax: (202)331-7599
Tagg, Barbara, Contact

Chow Chow Club [21856]
c/p Dr. Joyce A. Dandridge, Cor-
responding Secretary
8132 Eastern Ave. NW
Washington, DC 20012-1312
PH: (202)726-9155
Fax: (202)726-9155
Dandridge, Dr. Joyce A., Corr. Sec.

CHP Association [7355]
718 7th St. NW, 2nd Fl.
Washington, DC 20001

PH: (202)888-0708
Louda, Dale, Exec. Dir.

**Christian Coalition of America
[18034]**
PO Box 37030
Washington, DC 20013
PH: (202)479-6900
Combs, Roberta, President, CEO

**Christians' Israel Public Action
Campaign [18584]**
1300 Pennsylvania Ave. NW, Ste.
700
Washington, DC 20004
PH: (202)234-3600
Hellman, Richard A., Founder,
President

**Cigar Association of America, Inc.
[3284]**
1100 G St. NW, Ste. 1050
Washington, DC 20005-7405
PH: (202)223-8204
Fax: (202)833-0379
Estades, Javier, Chairman

Citizen Advocacy Center [18331]
1400 16th St. NW, Ste. 101
Washington, DC 20036
PH: (202)462-1174
Fax: (202)354-5372
Swankin, David A., CEO, President

Citizen Works [17853]
PO Box 18478
Washington, DC 20036
PH: (202)265-6164
Nader, Ralph, Founder

**Citizens Against Government Waste
[18316]**
1301 Pensylvania Ave. NW, Ste.
1075
Washington, DC 20004
PH: (202)467-5300
Fax: (202)467-4253
Sweeney, Ariane E., VP, Comm.

Citizens for Global Solutions [18776]
420 7th St. SE
Washington, DC 20003-2707
PH: (202)546-3950
Bankhead, Jordan, Chairman

Citizens for Health [13614]
1400 16th St., NW Ste.101
Washington, DC 20036
PH: (202)462-8800
McCormack, Michael, President

**Citizens for Responsibility and Ethics
in Washington [18195]**
1400 Eye St. NW, Ste. 450
Washington, DC 20005
PH: (202)408-5565
Sloan, Melanie, Exec. Dir.

**Citizens' Stamp Advisory Committee
[22319]**
475 L'Enfant Plz. SW, Rm. 3300
Washington, DC 20260
Anderson, Gail, Mem.

Citizens for Tax Justice [5721]
1616 P St. NW, Ste. 200
Washington, DC 20036
PH: (202)299-1066
Fax: (202)299-1065
Robinson, Jenice, Dir. of Comm.

Citizens United [18312]
1006 Pennsylvania Ave. SE
Washington, DC 20003
PH: (202)547-5420
Fax: (202)547-5421
Robinson, Ron, Director

**Citizens United for Rehabilitation of
Errants [11522]**
PO Box 2310
Washington, DC 20013-2310

PH: (202)789-2126
Sullivan, Mr. Charles, Founder

City Parks Alliance [17971]
2121 Ward Ct. NW, 5th Fl.
Washington, DC 20037
PH: (202)974-5120
Fax: (202)223-9257
Nagel, Catherine, Exec. Dir.

Civil War Trust [9381]
1156 15th St. NW, Ste. 900
Washington, DC 20005
PH: (202)367-1861
Fax: (202)367-1865
Lighthizer, James, President

Classification Society [6994]
c/o Beth Ayers, Secretary/ Treasurer
American Institutes for Research
1000 Thomas Jefferson St. NW
Washington, DC 20007
Nugent, Rebecca, Contact

Clean Air Watch [4540]
1250 Connecticut Ave. NW, Ste. 200
Washington, DC 20036-2643
PH: (202)558-3527
O'Donnell, Frank, President

Clean Beaches Coalition [4041]
Washington, DC

**Clean and Safe Energy Coalition
[6470]**
607 14th St. NW, Ste. 300
Washington, DC 20005
PH: (202)338-2273
Whitman, Christine Todd, Co-Ch.

Clean Water Action [4750]
1444 Eye St. NW, Ste. 400
Washington, DC 20005-6538
PH: (202)895-0420
Fax: (202)895-0438
Tykulsker, David, Chairman

Clean Water Fund [4753]
1444 Eye St. NW, Ste. 400
Washington, DC 20005
PH: (202)895-0420
Fax: (202)895-0438
Lockwood, Peter, President

**Clearinghouse on Women's Issues
[18203]**
700 7th St. SW, Ste. 3
Washington, DC 20024-2469
PH: (202)232-8173
Stonehill, Harriett, Co-Pres.

**Laurent Clerc National Deaf Educa-
tion Center [11933]**
800 Florida Ave. NE
Washington, DC 20002-3695
PH: (202)651-5051
Nussbaum, Debra, Mgr.

Climate Institute [4043]
1400 16th St. NW, Ste. 430
Washington, DC 20036
PH: (202)552-0163
Topping, John C., Jr., CEO,
President

Clinicians for Choice [10427]
1660 L St. NW, Ste. 450
1660 L St. NW, Ste. 450
Washington, DC 20036
PH: (202)667-5881
Fax: (202)667-5890

Club for Growth [18281]
2001 L St. NW, Ste. 600
Washington, DC 20036
PH: (202)955-5500
Toll free: 855-432-0899
McIntosh, David, President

**Coalition Against Counterfeiting and
Piracy [5325]**
US Chamber of Commerce
Global Intellectual Property Ctr.
1615 H St. NW
Washington, DC 20062-0001
PH: (202)463-5601
Fax: (202)463-3114
Hirschmann, David, CEO, President

**Coalition Against Domain Name
Abuse [6764]**
1000 Potomac St. NW, Ste. 350
Washington, DC 20007
PH: (202)503-8649
Beauchere, Jacqueline, President

**Coalition Against Insurance Fraud
[1846]**
1012 14th St. NW, Ste. 200
Washington, DC 20005
PH: (202)393-7330
Jay, Dennis, Exec. Dir.

Coalition Against Landmines [18123]
1516 Crittenden St. NW
Washington, DC 20011
PH: (202)465-5213
Fax: (270)747-0935
Arnall, Gail, PhD, President

**Coalition on Agricultural Greenhouse
Gases [6660]**
c/o New Venture Fund
1201 Connecticut Ave. NW, Ste. 300
Washington, DC 20036
PH: (202)701-4298
Reed, Debbie, Exec. Dir.

**Coalition for Anabolic Steroid Precur-
sor and Ephedra Regulation
[17281]**
2099 Pennsylvania Ave. NW, Ste.
850
Washington, DC 20006
PH: (202)419-2521
Smeallie, Shawn, Exec. Dir.

**Coalition of Asian American Busi-
ness Organizations [679]**
Ronald Reagan Bldg. & International
Trade Ctr.
1300 Pennsylvania Ave. NW, No.
700
Washington, DC 20004
PH: (202)204-3019
Lam, Shau-Wai, Co-Chmn. of the
Bd.

**Coalition of Black Trade Unionists
[23530]**
1150 17th St. NW, Ste. 300
Washington, DC 20036
PH: (202)778-3318
Fax: (202)419-1486
Melvin, Terry L., President

**Coalition for Community Schools
[8535]**
c/o Institute for Educational Leadership
4301 Connecticut Ave. NW, Ste. 100
Washington, DC 20008-2304
PH: (202)822-8405
Fax: (202)872-4050
Villarreal, Lisa, Chairperson

**Coalition for Employment through
Exports [1982]**
1625 K St. NW, Ste. 200
Washington, DC 20006
PH: (202)296-6107
Fax: (202)296-9709
Hardy, John, Jr., President

**Coalition on the Environment and
Jewish Life [20242]**
1775 K St. NW
Washington, DC 20006

PH: (202)579-6800
Gutow, Rabbi Steve, Bd. Member

Coalition of Franchisee Associations,
Inc. **[1457]**
1750 K St. NW, Ste. 200
Washington, DC 20006
PH: (202)416-0277
Fax: (202)416-0269
Miller, Keith, Chairman

Coalition for Genetic Fairness
[17887]
4301 Connecticut Ave. NW, No. 404
Washington, DC 20008-2369
PH: (202)966-5557
Fax: (202)966-8553
Terry, Sharon F., Chairperson

Coalition for Government Procure-
ment **[1513]**
1990 M St. NW, Ste. 450
Washington, DC 20036
PH: (202)331-0975
Fax: (202)521-3533
Waldron, Roger, President

Coalition for Health Funding **[16999]**
c/o Cavarocchi Ruscio Dennis As-
sociates, L.L.C.
600 Maryland Ave. SW, Ste. 835W
Washington, DC 20024
PH: (202)484-1100
Fax: (202)484-1244
Hoppert, Don, President

Coalition for Heritable Disorders of
Connective Tissue **[14816]**
4301 Connecticut Ave. NW, Ste. 404
Washington, DC 20008
PH: (202)362-9599
Fax: (202)966-8553
Ciccariello, Priscilla, MA, Co-Pres.

Coalition of Higher Education As-
sistance Organizations **[7831]**
1101 Vermont Ave. NW, Ste. 400
Washington, DC 20005-3521
PH: (202)289-3910
Fax: (202)371-0197
Wadsworth, Harrison M., Exec. Dir.

Coalition on Human Needs **[13038]**
1120 Connecticut Ave. NW, Ste. 312
Washington, DC 20036
PH: (202)223-2532
Fax: (202)223-2538
Teller, Ellen, Chairwoman

Coalition for Imaging and
Bioengineering Research **[13819]**
1001 Connecticut Ave. NW, Ste. 601
Washington, DC 20036
PH: (202)347-5872
Fax: (202)347-5876
Seltzer, Steven E., MD, Chairman

Coalition to Insure Against Terrorism
[1847]
1875 I St. NW, Ste. 600
Washington, DC 20006-5413
PH: (202)739-9454
Kuykendall, Ron, Contact

Coalition for Intellectual Property
Rights **[5326]**
c/o Tom Thompson
607 14th St. NW, Ste. 500
Washington, DC 20036
PH: (202)466-6210
Thomson, Tom, Exec. Dir.

Coalition for Juvenile Justice **[5132]**
1319 F St. NW, Ste. 402
Washington, DC 20004
PH: (202)467-0864
Fax: (202)887-0738
Palmer, Edward L., Sr., Chairperson

Coalition of Labor Union Women
[23531]
815 16th St. NW
Washington, DC 20006
PH: (313)926-5415
See, Karen J., Coord., Member
Svcs.

Coalition for Networked Information
[6739]
21 Dupont Cir., Ste. 800
Washington, DC 20036
PH: (202)296-5098
Fax: (202)872-0884
Lynch, Clifford A., Exec. Dir.

Coalition for a Realistic Foreign
Policy **[18264]**
1220 L St. NW, Ste. 100-221
Washington, DC 20005-4018
Preble, Christopher, PhD, Exec. Dir.,
Founder

Coalition of Service Industries **[3071]**
1707 L St. NW, Ste. 1000
Washington, DC 20036
PH: (202)289-7460
Bliss, Christine, President

Coalition to Stop Gun Violence
[18249]
805 15th St. NW, Ste. 700
Washington, DC 20005
PH: (202)408-0061
Beard, Mike, President

Cold Finished Steel Bar Institute
[2345]
Washington, DC
PH: (708)735-8000
Toll free: 800-323-2750
Fax: (708)735-8100
Geary, Bill, Chairman

Collections and Stories of American
Muslims **[10029]**
2524 Elvans Rd. SE
Washington, DC 20020

College Consortium for International
Studies **[7631]**
2000 P St. NW, Ste. 408
Washington, DC 20036-6921
PH: (202)223-0330
Toll free: 800-453-6956
Fax: (202)223-0999

College Democrats of America
[18109]
c/o Democratic National Committee
430 S Capitol St. SE
Washington, DC 20003
Bissett, Jennifer, Exec. Dir.

College Republican National Com-
mittee **[19037]**
1500 K St. NW, Ste. 325
Washington, DC 20005-1265
PH: (202)608-1411
Fax: (202)608-1429
Smith, Alex, Chairman

College Summit **[7958]**
1763 Columbia Rd. NW, 2nd Fl.
Washington, DC 20009-2834
PH: (202)319-1763
Fax: (202)319-1233
Schramm, J. B., CEO, Founder

Color Pigments Manufacturers As-
sociation, Inc. **[754]**
1850 M St. NW, Ste. 730
Washington, DC 20036
PH: (202)465-4900
Fax: (202)296-8120

Commercial Alert **[18940]**
1600 20th St. NW
Washington, DC 20009-1001

PH: (202)588-7741
Weissman, Robert, Managing Ed.

Commercial Spaceflight Federation
[133]
500 New Jersey Ave. NW, Ste. 400
Washington, DC 20001
PH: (202)715-2928
Stallmer, Eric W., President

Commission on Collegiate Nursing
Education **[8318]**
1 Dupont Cir. NW, Ste. 530
Washington, DC 20036
PH: (202)887-6791
Fax: (202)887-8476
Butlin, Jennifer, Exec. Dir.

Commission on Presidential Debates
[18908]
Box 445
1200 New Hampshire Ave. NW
Washington, DC 20036
PH: (202)872-1020
Brown, Janet H., Exec. Dir.

Commission on Professionals in Sci-
ence and Technology **[7128]**
1200 New York Ave. NW, Ste. 113
Washington, DC 20005
Fortenberry, Norman L., ScD, Exec.
Dir.

Commission for Social Justice
[17888]
219 E St. NE
Washington, DC 20002-4922
PH: (202)547-2900
Fax: (202)546-8168
Piccigallo, Philip R., PhD, Exec. Dir.,
CEO

Committee of Annuity Insurers
[1848]
c/o Davis & Harman, LLP
1455 Pennsylvania Ave. NW, Ste.
1200
Washington, DC 20004
PH: (202)347-2230
Fax: (202)393-3310

Committee for a Constructive Tomor-
row **[18044]**
PO Box 65722
Washington, DC 20035-5722
PH: (202)429-2737
Rucker, Craig, Exec. Dir., Founder

Committee for Education Funding
[7832]
1341 G St. NW, 5th Fl.
Washington, DC 20005
PH: (202)383-0083
Fax: (202)463-4803
Packer, Joel, Exec. Dir., Secretary

Committee on Human Rights of
National Academies of Sciences,
Engineering and Medicine **[18387]**
500 5th St. NW
Washington, DC 20001
PH: (202)334-3043
Fax: (202)334-2225
Chalfie, Martin, Chairman

Committee for Human Rights in
North Korea **[18388]**
1001 Connecticut Ave. NW, Ste. 435
Washington, DC 20036
PH: (202)499-7970
Fax: (202)758-2348
Scarlatoiu, Greg, Exec. Dir.

Committee for the Promotion and
Advancement of Cooperatives
[18486]
c/o International Co-operative Alliance

1401 New York Ave.
Washington, DC 20005
McCrae, Fran, Coord.

Committee for a Responsible
Federal Budget **[18954]**
1900 M St. NW, Ste. 850
Washington, DC 20036
PH: (202)596-3597
Fax: (202)478-0681
MacGuineas, Maya, President

Committee in Solidarity With the
People of El Salvador **[18175]**
1525 Newton St. NW
Washington, DC 20010
PH: (202)521-2510
Fax: (202)332-3339
Stoumbelis, Alexis, Coord.

Committee of Ten Thousand **[13537]**
236 Massachusetts Ave. NE, Ste.
609
Washington, DC 20002-4971
PH: (202)543-0988
    (202)681-2351
Toll free: 800-488-2688
Dubin, Corey S., President

Commodity Markets Council **[1517]**
1300 L St. NW, Ste. 1020
Washington, DC 20005
PH: (202)842-0400
Doud, Gregg, President

Common Cause **[18863]**
805 15th St. NW, 11th Fl.
Washington, DC 20005
PH: (202)833-1200
Rapoport, Miles, President

Common Sense about Kids and
Guns **[5216]**
1225 I St. NW, Ste. 1100
Washington, DC 20005-3914
PH: (202)546-0200
Toll free: 877-955-KIDS
Kennedy, Victoria Reggie, President

Communications Workers of America
[23405]
501 3rd St. NW
Washington, DC 20001-2797
PH: (202)434-1100
Shelton, Chris, President

Communitarian Network **[18971]**
1922 F St. NW, Rm. 413
Washington, DC 20052
PH: (202)994-8190
Fax: (202)994-1606
Etzioni, Dr. Amitai, Director, Founder

Communities Against Violence
Network **[13271]**
2711 Ordway St. NW, No. 111
Washington, DC 20008
PH: (305)896-3000
Dubin, Marc, Exec. Dir., Founder

Community Action Partnership
[12534]
1140 Connecticut Ave. NW, Ste.
1210
Washington, DC 20036
PH: (202)265-7546
Fax: (202)265-5048
Duncan, Bryan, V. Chmn. of the Bd.

Community for Creative Non-
Violence **[11949]**
425 2nd St. NW
Washington, DC 20001
PH: (202)393-1909
Fax: (202)783-3254
Harris, Rico E., Exec. Dir.

Community Development Bankers
Association **[390]**
1444 Eye St., Ste. 201
Washington, DC 20005

PH: (202)689-8935
Reiling, David, Director

Community Oncology Alliance
[16341]
1101 Pennsylvania Ave. NW, Ste.
700
Washington, DC 20004
PH: (202)756-2258
Okon, Ted, Exec. Dir.

Community Transportation Associa-
tion of America [11343]
1341 G St. NW, 10th Fl.
Washington, DC 20005
Toll free: 800-891-0590
Fax: (202)737-9197
McDonald, Bill, VP

Compassion Over Killing [10606]
PO Box 9773
Washington, DC 20016
PH: (301)891-2458
Meier, Erica, Exec. Dir.

Compete America [11760]
1615 H St. NW
Washington, DC 20062
Corley, Scott, Exec. Dir.

Competitive Carriers Association
[3222]
805 15th St. NW, Ste. 401
Washington, DC 20005
Toll free: 800-722-1872
Fax: (866)436-1080
Smith, Ron, Director

Composite Lumber Manufacturers
Association [1433]
750 National Press Bldg.
529 14th St. NW
Washington, DC 20045
PH: (202)591-2451
Fax: (202)591-2445
Kotiadis, Peter, President

Computer and Communications
Industry Association [3223]
900 17th St. NW, Ste. 1100
Washington, DC 20006
PH: (202)783-0070
Fax: (202)783-0534
Black, Edward J., President, CEO

Computer Ethics Institute [8496]
1775 Massachusetts Ave. NW
Washington, DC 20036
PH: (202)797-6183
Barquin, Ramon, President

Computing Research Association
[6245]
1828 L St. NW, Ste. 800
Washington, DC 20036-5104
PH: (202)234-2111
Fax: (202)667-1066
Drobnis, Ann, Director

Concern, Inc. [4045]
PO Box 5892
Washington, DC 20016

Concerned Women for America
[19970]
1015 15th St. NW, Ste. 1100
Washington, DC 20005
PH: (202)488-7000
Nance, Penny Young, President,
CEO

Confederate Memorial Association
[8789]
PO Box 6010
Washington, DC 20005
PH: (202)483-5700

Conference on Asian Pacific
American Leadership [19391]
PO Box 65073
Washington, DC 20035
Toll free: 877-892-5427
Thompson, Elizabeth, Mgr. Dir.

Conference Board of the Mathemati-
cal Sciences [6819]
1529 18th St.
Washington, DC 20036
PH: (202)293-1170
Fax: (202)293-3412
Rosier, Ronald C., Director

Conference of Minority Public
Administrators [5694]
1120 G St. NW, Ste. 700
Washington, DC 20005
Tillery, Loretta, VP

Conference of Minority Transporta-
tion Officials [3326]
1875 I St. NW, Ste. 500
Washington, DC 20006
PH: (703)234-4072
Fax: (202)318-0364
Moses, Mioshi J., President, CEO

Conference of State Bank Supervi-
sors [391]
1129 20th St. NW, 9th Fl.
Washington, DC 20036
PH: (202)296-2840
Fax: (202)296-1928
Ryan, Mr. John, President, CEO

Conflict Solutions International
[18004]
1629 K St. NW, Ste. 300
Washington, DC 20006
d'Angelo, George, President

Congressional Automotive Caucus
[18011]
Longworth House Office Bldg., Rm.
1519
15 Independence Ave. SE
Washington, DC 20515
PH: (202)225-5406
Fax: (202)225-3103
Kildee, Dale, Co-Ch.

Congressional Black Caucus
[18012]
2305 Rayburn House Office Bldg.
Washington, DC 20515
PH: (202)226-9776
Butterfield, G. K., Chairman

Congressional Club [19690]
2001 New Hampshire Ave. NW
Washington, DC 20009
PH: (202)332-1155
Fax: (202)797-0698

Congressional Hispanic Caucus
[18336]
2329 Rayburn House Office Bldg.
Washington, DC 20515
PH: (202)225-2410
Fax: (202)226-1012

Congressional Management Founda-
tion [18013]
710 East St. SE
Washington, DC 20003
PH: (202)546-0100
Fax: (202)547-0936
Fitch, Bradford, President, CEO

Consortia of Administrators for Na-
tive American Rehabilitation
[19577]
1775 Eye Street NW, Ste. 1150
Washington, DC 20006
PH: (202)587-2741
Toll free: 877-260-8098
Slikkers, Randall G., Exec. Dir.

Consortium for Citizens with Dis-
abilities [11582]
1825 K St. NW, Ste. 1200
Washington, DC 20006
PH: (202)783-2229
Fax: (202)783-8250
Musheno, Kim, Chairman

Consortium for School Networking
[8027]
1025 Vermont Ave. NW, Ste. 1010
Washington, DC 20005-3599
PH: (202)861-2676
Toll free: 800-727-1227
Fax: (202)393-2011
Krueger, Keith R., CEO

Consortium of Social Science As-
sociations [7165]
1701 K St. NW, Ste. 1150
Washington, DC 20006
PH: (202)842-3525
Fax: (202)842-2788
Levine, Felice, Chmn. of the Bd.

Constituency for Africa [17775]
1350 Connecticut Ave., NW, Ste.
850
Washington, DC 20036
PH: (202)255-8893
Fax: (202)371-9017
Foote, Melvin P., President

Consultative Group to Assist the
Poor [18487]
1825 I Street, NW 7th Fl.
Washington, DC 20006
PH: (202)473-9594
Tsuji, Kazuto, Chairman

Consultative Group on International
Agricultural Research [12148]
900 19th St. NW, 6th Fl.
Washington, DC 20433
PH: (202)473-8951
Fax: (202)473-8110
Wadsworth, Jonathan, Sec. Gen.,
Exec. Sec.

Consumer Bankers Association
[392]
1225 Eye St. NW, Ste. 550
Washington, DC 20005
Hunt, Richard, President, CEO

Consumer Coalition for Quality
Health Care [14993]
1612 K St. NW, Ste. 400
Washington, DC 20006
PH: (202)789-3606
Fax: (202)898-2389
Lindberg, Brian W., Exec. Dir.

Consumer Data Industry Association
[1228]
1090 Vermont Ave. NW, Ste. 200
Washington, DC 20005-4905
PH: (202)371-0910
Fax: (202)371-0134
Byrnes, Betty, Contact

Consumer Federation of America
[18046]
1620 I St. NW, Ste. 200
Washington, DC 20006
PH: (202)387-6121
(202)737-0766
Leech, Irene, President

Consumer Healthcare Products As-
sociation [2556]
1625 Eye St. NW, Ste. 600
Washington, DC 20006
PH: (202)429-9260
Fax: (202)223-6835
Melville, Scott, President, CEO

Consumer Specialty Products Association [715]
1667 K St. NW, Ste. 300
Washington, DC 20006

PH: (202)872-8110
Fax: (202)223-2636
Cathcart, Christopher, CEO,
President

Consumers for Dental Choice
[14425]
316 F St. NE, Ste. 210
Washington, DC 20002
PH: (202)544-6333
Fax: (202)544-6331
Duffy, Sandy, Contact

Copyright Alliance [5327]
1224 M St. NW, Ste. 101
Washington, DC 20005
PH: (202)540-2243
Hart, Terry, Dir. of Legal Svcs.

CORE: Coalition for Residential
Education [8536]
1001 G St. NW, Ste. 800
Washington, DC 20001
PH: (202)627-6832
Fax: (240)510-9456
Forrester, Don, Chairman

Corn Refiners Association [1323]
1701 Pennsylvania Ave. NW, Ste.
950
Washington, DC 20006
PH: (202)331-1634
Fax: (202)331-2054
Erickson, Audrae, President

Corporate Council on Africa [625]
1100 17th St. NW, Ste. 1000
Washington, DC 20036
PH: (202)835-1115
Fax: (202)835-1117
Hayes, Stephen, CEO, President

Corporate Voices for Working
Families [18065]
1020 19th St. NW, Ste. 750
Washington, DC 20036
PH: (202)467-8130
Fax: (202)467-8140
Klein, Donna M., Chairman, CEO

Corporation for Enterprise Develop-
ment [18148]
1200 G St. NW, Ste. 400
Washington, DC 20005
PH: (202)408-9788
Fax: (202)408-9793
Friedman, Robert, Chmn. of the Bd.,
Founder, Gen. Counsel

Corporation for National & Community Service I Senior Corps
[13290]
250 E St. SW
Washington, DC 20525
Eitel, Maria, CEO

Corporation for Public Broadcasting
[9142]
401 9th St. NW
Washington, DC 20004-2129
PH: (202)879-9600
Toll free: 800-272-2190
Tayman, William P., Jr., CFO,
Treasurer

The Corps Network [13438]
1275 K St. NW, Ste. 1050
Washington, DC 20005
PH: (202)737-6272
Fax: (202)737-6277
Holtrop, Joel, Chmn. of the Bd.

Cosmetic Ingredient Review [1585]
1620 L St. NW, Ste. 1200
Washington, DC 20036
PH: (202)331-0651
Fax: (202)331-0088
Bergfeld, Wilma F., MD, Chairperson

Cosmic Baseball Association **[22548]**
907 6th St. SW, Ste. 214
Washington, DC 20024
Stein, Eileen Pollock, Chairperson

Cotton Council International **[932]**
1521 New Hampshire Ave. NW
Washington, DC 20036
PH: (202)745-7805
Fax: (202)483-4040
Hancock, Dahlen K., President

Cotton Warehouse Association of
America **[935]**
316 Pennsylvania Ave. SE, Ste. 401
Washington, DC 20003
PH: (202)544-5875
Fax: (202)544-5874
Underwood, Brett, Comm. Chm.

The Council for the Advancement of
Nursing Science **[16128]**
c/o American Academy of Nursing
1000 Vermont Ave. NW, Ste. 910
Washington, DC 20005
PH: (202)777-1166
DeVon, Holli, RN, Chairperson

Council for Advancement and Sup-
port of Education **[7754]**
1307 New York Ave. NW, Ste. 1000
Washington, DC 20005-4701
PH: (202)328-2273
Toll free: 800-554-8536
Lippincott, John, President

Council for Affordable Health Cover-
age **[15097]**
1101 14th St. NW, Ste. 700
Washington, DC 20005
PH: (202)559-0205
White, Joel, President

Council for Affordable Quality
Healthcare **[14994]**
1900 K St. NW, Ste. 650
Washington, DC 20006-1110
PH: (202)517-0400
Thomashauer, Robin J., Exec. Dir.

Council on American-Islamic Rela-
tions **[9604]**
453 New Jersey Ave. SE
Washington, DC 20003
PH: (202)488-8787
Fax: (202)488-0833
Awad, Nihad, Exec. Dir., Bd.
Member

Council of American Overseas
Research Centers **[7089]**
PO Box 37012
Washington, DC 20013-7012
PH: (202)633-1599
Fax: (202)633-3141
Tuttle, Christopher A., PhD, Exec.
Dir.

Council of Chief State School Of-
ficers **[7755]**
1 Massachusetts Ave. NW, Ste. 700
Washington, DC 20001-1431
PH: (202)336-7000
Fax: (202)408-8072
Luna, Thomas R., President

Council for Christian Colleges and
Universities **[7610]**
321 8th St. NE
Washington, DC 20002
PH: (202)546-8713
Fax: (202)546-8913
Zigler, Christina, Exec. Asst.

Council for a Community of
Democracies **[18094]**
1801 F St. NW, Ste. 308
Washington, DC 20006

PH: (202)789-9771
Fax: (202)789-9764

Council on Competitiveness **[3300]**
900 17th St. NW, Ste. 700
Washington, DC 20006
PH: (202)682-4292
Fax: (202)682-5150
Allen, Samuel R., Chairman

Council for Court Excellence **[5380]**
1111 14th St. NW, Ste. 500
Washington, DC 20005
PH: (202)785-5917
Johns, Marie C., Chairman

Council on Education of the Deaf
[15185]
Gallaudet University
800 Florida Ave. NE
Washington, DC 20002
Fischgrund, Joseph E., Exec. Dir.

Council on Employee Benefits
[1066]
1501 M St. NW, Ste. 620
Washington, DC 20005
PH: (202)861-6025
Fax: (202)861-6027
Sheehy, Julie R., President

Council of Environmental Deans and
Directors **[7886]**
National Council for Science and the
Environment
1101 17th St. NW, Ste. 250
Washington, DC 20036
PH: (202)530-5810
Fax: (202)628-4311
Geidel, Gwen, Secretary, Treasurer

The Council on Food, Agricultural
and Resource Economics **[3560]**
c/o Caron Gala, Executive Director
502 C St. NE
Washington, DC 20002
PH: (202)408-8522
Fax: (202)408-5385
Ahearn, Mary, V. Ch.

Council on Governmental Relations
[8498]
1200 New York Ave. NW, Ste. 460
Washington, DC 20005
PH: (202)289-6655
Fax: (202)289-6698
Decrappeo, Tony, President

Council of Graduate Schools **[7959]**
1 Dupont Cir. NW, Ste. 230
Washington, DC 20036
PH: (202)223-3791
Fax: (202)331-7157
Ortega, Suzanne, President

Council of the Great City Schools
[8727]
1301 Pennsylvania Ave. NW, Ste.
702
Washington, DC 20004
PH: (202)393-2427
Fax: (202)393-2400
Casserly, Michael D., Exec. Dir.

Council on Hemispheric Affairs
[17796]
1250 Connecticut Ave. NW, Ste. 1C
Washington, DC 20036
PH: (202)223-4975
Fax: (202)223-4979
Birns, Larry, Director

Council for Higher Education Ac-
creditation **[7756]**
1 Dupont Cir. NW, Ste. 510
Washington, DC 20036
PH: (202)955-6126
Fax: (202)955-6129
Gaudino, James L., Chairman

Council of Independent Colleges
[8010]
1 Dupont Cir. NW, Ste. 320
Washington, DC 20036-1142
PH: (202)466-7230
Fax: (202)466-7238
Moore, Ned, Exec. Dir., VP

Council of Infrastructure Financing
Authorities **[5731]**
316 Pennsylvania Ave. SE, Ste. 201
Washington, DC 20003
PH: (202)547-7886
Fax: (202)547-1867
Beary, Lori, President

Council of Institutional Investors
[3041]
888 17th St. NW, Ste. 500
Washington, DC 20006
PH: (202)822-0800
Fax: (202)822-0801
Johnson, Dale, Treasurer

Council of Insurance Agents and
Brokers **[1852]**
701 Pennsylvania Ave. NW, Ste. 750
Washington, DC 20004-2608
PH: (202)783-4400
Fax: (202)783-4410
Crerar, Ken A., President

Council on Intellectual and
Developmental Disability **[20137]**
415 Michigan Ave. NE, Ste. 95
Washington, DC 20017-4501
PH: (202)529-2933
Fax: (202)529-4678
Benton, Janice, Exec. Dir.

Council for International Exchange of
Scholars **[8065]**
1400 K St. NW, Ste. 700
Washington, DC 20005
PH: (202)686-4000
Fax: (202)686-4029
Crummett, Maria de los Angeles,
Exec. Dir.

Council on International Nontheatri-
cal Events **[9304]**
1003 K St. NW, Ste. 208
Washington, DC 20001
PH: (507)400-2463
Gardner, Bill, President

Council of Large Public Housing
Authorities **[5277]**
455 Massachusetts Ave. NW, Ste.
425
Washington, DC 20001
PH: (202)638-1300
Fax: (202)638-2364
Zaterman, Sunia, Exec. Dir.

Council on Library and Information
Resources **[9702]**
1707 NW L St., Ste. 650
Washington, DC 20036
PH: (202)939-4750
Fax: (202)939-4765
Cohen, Dan

Council for a Livable World **[18124]**
322 4th St. NE
Washington, DC 20002-5824
PH: (202)543-4100
Isaacs, John, Officer

Council for a Livable World Educa-
tion Fund **[18125]**
322 4th St. NE
Washington, DC 20002
PH: (202)543-4100
Musil, Robert K., Chmn. of the Bd.

Council of Manufacturing Associations **[2219]**
733 10th St. NW, Ste. 700
Washington, DC 20001

PH: (202)637-3000
Toll free: 800-814-8468
Fax: (202)637-3182
Muse, Tonya, Exec. Dir.

Council for the National Register of
Health Service Providers in
Psychology, Inc. **[16913]**
1200 New York Ave. NW, Ste. 800
Washington, DC 20005
PH: (202)783-7663
Fax: (202)347-0550
Sammons, Morgan T., PhD, ABPP,
Exec. Ofc.

Council On State Taxation **[19169]**
122 C St. NW, Ste. 330
Washington, DC 20001-2109
PH: (202)484-5222
Fax: (202)484-5229
Lindholm, Douglas L., Esq., Exec.
Dir., President

Council for Opportunity in Education
[7819]
1025 Vermont Ave. NW, Ste. 900
Washington, DC 20005-3516
PH: (202)347-7430
Fax: (202)347-0786
Ball, Trent, Chairman

Council of Producers & Distributors
of Agrotechnology **[716]**
1730 Rhode Island Ave. NW, Ste.
812
Washington, DC 20036
PH: (202)386-7407
Fax: (202)386-7409
Ferenc, Dr. Susan, President

Council of Professional Associations
on Federal Statistics **[5301]**
20 F St. NW, Ste. 700
Washington, DC 20001
PH: (202)507-6254
Jacobsen, Linda, Chairperson

Council for Professional Recognition
[10807]
2460 16th St. NW
Washington, DC 20009-3547
PH: (202)265-9090
Toll free: 800-424-4310
Fax: (202)265-9161
Washington, Valora, President, CEO

Council of Professional Surveyors
[7250]
American Council of Engineering
Companies
1015 15th St. NW, 8th Fl.
Washington, DC 20005-2605
PH: (202)347-7474
Fax: (202)898-0068
Schneider, John k., President

Council for Research in Values and
Philosophy **[10085]**
Gibbons Hall, B-20
620 Michigan Ave. NE
Washington, DC 20064-0001
PH: (202)319-6089
McLean, George F., President

Council for Responsible Nutrition
[16216]
1828 L St. NW, Ste. 510
Washington, DC 20036-5114
PH: (202)204-7700
Fax: (202)204-7701
Mister, Steven M., Esq., CEO,
President

Council of Scientific Society
Presidents **[7130]**
1155 16th St. NW
Washington, DC 20036
PH: (202)872-6230
Downing, John, Chairman

Council for Social and Economic
Studies [18972]
1133 13th St. NW
Washington, DC 20005
PH: (202)371-2700
Fax: (202)371-1523
Pearson, Dr. Roger, Editor

Council of State Community
Development Agencies [5774]
1825 K St. NW, Ste. 515
Washington, DC 20006
PH: (202)293-5820
Fax: (202)293-2820
Thompson, Linda, Director

Council of State Restaurant Associa-
tions [2936]
2055 L St. NW
Washington, DC 20036
PH: (410)931-8100
    (202)973-5377
Fax: (410)931-8111
Harris, Stan, President

Council for a Strong America
[19269]
1212 New York Ave. NW, Ste. 300
Washington, DC 20005
PH: (202)464-7005
Seip, Norman R., General, Chmn. of
the Bd.

Council on Undergraduate Research
[8499]
734 15th St. NW, Ste. 550
Washington, DC 20005-1013
PH: (202)783-4810
Fax: (202)783-4811
Ambos, Elizabeth, Exec. Ofc.

CRE Finance Council [2857]
900 7th St. NW, Ste. 501
Washington, DC 20001
PH: (202)448-0850
Fax: (202)448-0865
Durning, David, President, CEO

Credit Builders Alliance [942]
1701 K St. NW, Ste. 1000
Washington, DC 20006
PH: (202)730-9390
Fax: (202)350-9430
Lass, Carmina, Director

Crime Prevention Coalition of
America [11503]
1201 Connecticut Ave. NW, Ste. 200
Washington, DC 20036
PH: (202)466-6272
Desrosiers, Chuck, Contact

Crop Insurance Professionals As-
sociation [1854]
316 Pennsylvania Ave. SE, Ste. 401
Washington, DC 20003
PH: (202)544-5873
Fax: (202)544-5874
Cole, William, Chairman

Crop Insurance and Reinsurance
Bureau [1855]
440 1st St. NW, Ste. 500
Washington, DC 20002
PH: (202)544-0067
Torrey, Mike, Exec. VP

CropLife America [717]
1156 15th St. NW
Washington, DC 20005
PH: (202)296-1585
Fax: (202)463-0474
Vroom, Jay J., CEO, President

Cruise Lines International Association [3376]
1201 F St. NW, Ste. 250
Washington, DC 20004

PH: (202)759-9370
Fax: (202)759-9344
Darr, Bud, Sr. VP

CTIA - The Wireless Association
[3225]
1400 16th St. NW, Ste. 600
Washington, DC 20036-2225
PH: (202)785-0081
Miller, Jeff, Secretary

Cultivating New Frontiers in
Agriculture [18522]
1828 L St. NW, Ste. 710
Washington, DC 20036
PH: (202)296-3920
Fax: (202)296-3948
Roy, Sylvain, President, CEO

Cushman Foundation for Foramin-
iferal Research [6970]
PO Box 37012
Washington, DC 20560-0121
PH: (202)633-1333
Fax: (202)786-2832
Lipps, Jere H., President

Customized Logistics and Delivery
Association [3083]
750 National Press Bldg.
529 14th St. NW
Washington, DC 20045
PH: (202)591-2460
Fax: (202)591-2445
DeCaprio, Bob, Exec. Dir.

Customs and International Trade Bar
Association [5156]
204 E St. NE
Washington, DC 20002
PH: (212)549-0149
Fax: (212)883-0068
Friedman, Lawrence, President

DACOR [5229]
1801 F St. NW
Washington, DC 20006
PH: (202)682-0500
Fax: (202)842-3295
Cleveland, Paul M., Trustee

Dam Safety Coalition [13319]
101 Constitution Ave. NW, Ste. 375
E
Washington, DC 20001-2133
PH: (202)789-7850
Toll free: 800-548-2723
Pallasch, Brian, Co-Ch.

Damien Ministries [20041]
2200 Rhode Island Ave. NE
Washington, DC 20018
PH: (202)526-3020

Dance Heritage Coalition [9252]
1111 16th St. NW, Ste. 300
Washington, DC 20036
PH: (202)223-8392
Fax: (202)833-2686
Smigel, Libby, PhD, Advisor

Dance USA [9254]
1029 Vermont Ave. NW, Ste. 400
Washington, DC 20005
PH: (202)833-1717
Fax: (202)833-2686
Fitterer, Amy, Exec. Dir.

Daughters of Penelope [19452]
1909 Q St. NW, Ste. 500
Washington, DC 20009
PH: (202)234-9741
Fax: (202)483-6983
Saltas, Joanne, Mem.

Deadliest Cancers Coalition [13959]
c/o Megan Gordon Don
Pancreatic Cancer Action Network

Government Affairs & Advocacy Of-
fice
1050 Connecticut Ave. NW, Ste. 500
Washington, DC 20036
PH: (202)742-6776
Don, Megan Gordon, Contact

Deaf in Government [5276]
PO Box 76087
Washington, DC 20013
PH: (202)618-3009
Rice, David, President

Deaf-REACH [15186]
3521 12th St. NE
Washington, DC 20017
PH: (202)832-6681
Tomar, Jon, President

Death Penalty Information Center
[17829]
1015 18th St. NW, Ste. 704
Washington, DC 20036
PH: (202)289-2275
Dunham, Robert, Exec. Dir.

Defenders of Wildlife [4805]
1130 17th St. NW
Washington, DC 20036
PH: (202)682-9400
Toll free: 800-385-9712
Clark, Jamie Rappaport, President,
CEO

Defense Credit Union Council [950]
South Bldg., Ste. 600
601 Pennsylvania Ave. NW
Washington, DC 20004
PH: (202)638-3950
Fax: (202)638-3410
Arteaga, Roland A., Officer

Delta Lambda Phi National Social
Fraternity [23895]
2020 Pennsylvania Ave. NW, No.
355
Washington, DC 20006-1811
PH: (202)558-2801
Fax: (202)318-2277
Strickland, Vernon L., III, Founder

Delta Omega [23857]
1900 M St. NW, Ste. 710
Washington, DC 20036
Hurwitz, Eric L., President

Delta Phi Epsilon, Professional
Foreign Service Fraternity [23748]
3401 Prospect St. NW
Washington, DC 20007
PH: (202)337-9702
von Stroebel, James-Michael,
President

Delta Phi Epsilon Professional
Foreign Service Sorority [23749]
3401 Prospect St. NW
Washington, DC 20007
McCoy, Kalli, President

Delta Sigma Theta Sorority, Inc.
[23871]
1707 New Hampshire Ave. NW
Washington, DC 20009
PH: (202)986-2400
Fax: (202)986-2513
Walker, Paulette C., President

Democratic Congressional
Campaign Committee [18110]
430 S Capitol St. SE
Washington, DC 20003-4024
PH: (202)863-1500
Pelosi, Rep. Nancy, Leader

Democratic Governors Association
[5775]
1401 K St. NW, Ste. 200
Washington, DC 20005-3497

PH: (202)772-5600
Fax: (202)772-5602
Pearson, Elisabeth, Exec. Dir.

Democratic National Committee
[18111]
430 S Capitol St. SE
Washington, DC 20003-4024
PH: (202)863-8000
Toll free: 877-336-7200
Schultz, Debbie Wasserman,
Chairperson

Democratic Senatorial Campaign
Committee [18112]
120 Maryland Ave. NE
Washington, DC 20002
PH: (202)224-2447
Fax: (202)969-0354

Democrats Abroad [18113]
PO Box 15130
Washington, DC 20003
PH: (202)621-2085
Solon, Kathryn, Chairperson

Democrats for Education Reform
[18172]
840 1st St. NE, 3rd Fl.
Washington, DC 20002
PH: (212)614-3213
Williams, Joe, Exec. Dir.

Design-Build Institute of America
[520]
1331 Pennsylvania Ave. NW, 4th Fl.
Washington, DC 20004-1721
PH: (202)682-0110
Fax: (202)682-5877
Washington, Lisa, Exec. Dir., CEO

Destination Marketing Association
International [2325]
2025 M St. NW, Ste. 500
Washington, DC 20036
PH: (202)296-7888
Fax: (202)296-7889
Rosquist, Elaine, Director

Development Group for Alternative
Policies [18488]
3179 18th St. NW
Washington, DC 20010
PH: (202)321-0822
Hellinger, Douglas, Exec. Dir.,
Founder

DFK International/USA [26]
1025 Thomas Jefferson St. NW, Ste.
500 E
Washington, DC 20007
PH: (202)452-1588
Fax: (202)833-3636
Hauck, Graham, Exec. Dir.

Dialogue on Diversity [8346]
1629 K St. NW, Ste. 300
Washington, DC 20006
PH: (703)631-0650
Fax: (703)631-0617
Caballero, Ma. Cristina C., CEO,
President

Dialysis Patient Citizens [15877]
1012 14th St. NW, Ste. No. 905
Washington, DC 20005-3403
Toll free: 866-877-4242
Fax: (888)423-5002
Jamgochian, Hrant, CEO

Digestive Disease National Coalition
[14788]
507 Capitol Ct. NE, Ste. 200
Washington, DC 20002
PH: (202)544-7497
Fax: (202)546-7105
DeGerome, James, MD, Officer

Digital Library Federation [9703]
1707 L St. NW, Ste. 650
Washington, DC 20036-4228

PH: (202)939-4758
Frick, Rachel L., Director

Digital Promise [7302]
1001 Connecticut Ave. NW, Ste. 830
Washington, DC 20036
PH: (202)450-3675
Cator, Karen, President

Direct Selling Association [3010]
1667 K St. NW, Ste. 1100
Washington, DC 20006
PH: (202)452-8866
Fax: (202)452-9010
Burke, Nancy M., VP

Direct Selling Education Foundation
[3011]
1667 K St. NW, Ste. 1100
Washington, DC 20006-1660
PH: (202)452-8866
Fax: (202)452-9015
Parker, John P., Chairperson

Directors of Health Promotion and
Education [5716]
1432 K St. NW, Ste. 400
Washington, DC 20005-2539
PH: (202)659-2230
Fax: (202)478-0884
Girard, Karen, Chairman

Disability Rights International
[12322]
1666 Connecticut Ave. NW, Ste. 325
Washington, DC 20009
PH: (202)296-0800
Fax: (202)697-5422
Rosenthal, Eric, Exec. Dir., Founder

Disabled Veterans National Founda-
tion [20768]
1020 19th St. NW, Ste. 475
Washington, DC 20036
PH: (202)737-0522
Wilkewitz, Precilla Landry, President

Disaster Management Alliance
[11657]
Pan American Development Founda-
tion
1889 F St. NW, 2nd Fl.
Washington, DC 20006
PH: (202)458-3969
Toll free: 877-572-4484
Valero, Caterina, Prog. Dir.

Distance Education Accrediting
Commission [7994]
1101 17th St. NW, Ste. 808
Washington, DC 20036
PH: (202)234-5100
Fax: (202)332-1386
Baldwin, Charles, CFO

Distilled Spirits Council of the United
States [183]
1250 Eye St. NW, Ste. 400
Washington, DC 20005
PH: (202)628-3544
Fax: (202)682-8888

DMA Nonprofit Federation [255]
1615 L St. NW, Ste. 1100
Washington, DC 20036
PH: (202)861-2427
(202)861-2498
Boone, Xenia, Exec. Dir.

Document Security Alliance [5302]
204 E St. NE
Washington, DC 20002
PH: (202)543-5552
Fax: (202)547-6348
Poole, Tony, President

Dominican American National
Roundtable [19422]
PO Box 472
Washington, DC 20044
Toll free: 800-647-1083
Martinez-Marmolejos, Claribel,
President

Doris Day Animal League [10611]
2100 L St. NW
Washington, DC 20037
PH: (202)452-1100
Coupe, Anita W., Director

Dredging Contractors of America
[2241]
503 D St. NW, Ste. 150
Washington, DC 20001
PH: (202)737-2674
Fax: (202)737-2677
Holliday, Barry, Exec. Dir.

Driver Employer Council of America
[3327]
815 Connecticut Ave. NW, Ste. 400
Washington, DC 20006-4046
PH: (202)842-3400
Fax: (202)842-0011
Broome, Mr. David, Chairman

Drug & Alcohol Testing Industry As-
sociation [13137]
1325 G St. NW, Ste. 500, No. 5001
Washington, DC 20005
Toll free: 800-355-1257
Fax: (202)315-3579
Shelton, Laura, Exec. Dir.

Drug Policy Alliance [17892]
925 15th St. NW, 2nd Fl.
Washington, DC 20005
PH: (202)683-2030
Fax: (202)216-0803
Nadelmann, Ethan, Exec. Dir.,
Founder

Earth Council Alliance [18717]
1250 24th St. NW, Ste. 300
Washington, DC 20037
PH: (202)467-2786
Vaidya, Shilpa, Secretary

Earth Day Network [4049]
1616 P St. NW, Ste. 340
Washington, DC 20036
PH: (202)518-0044
Fax: (202)518-8794
Rogers, Kathleen, President

EarthEcho International [3849]
2101 L St. NW, Ste. 800
Washington, DC 20037
PH: (202)350-3190
Fax: (202)857-3977
Cousteau, Philippe, Jr., Founder,
President

EarthRights International [18394]
1612 K St. NW, Ste. 401
Washington, DC 20006
PH: (202)466-5188
Redford, Katie, Director, Founder

EarthSpark International [4024]
1616 H St. NW, Ste. 900
Washington, DC 20006
Schnitzer, Dan, Exec. Dir., Founder

Earthworks [5633]
1612 K St. NW, Ste. 808
Washington, DC 20006
PH: (202)887-1872
Fax: (202)887-1875
Krill, Jennifer, Exec. Dir.

Eating Disorders Coalition for
Research, Policy and Action
[14637]
PO Box 96503-98807
Washington, DC 20090

PH: (202)543-9570
Schoenbach, Gail R., Secretary

Eco-Justice Working Group [19105]
110 Maryland Ave. NE, Ste. 203
Washington, DC 20002
PH: (202)827-3975
Alonso, Shantha Ready, Exec. Dir.

Ecoagriculture Partners [4696]
1100 17th St. NW, Ste. 600
Washington, DC 20036
PH: (202)393-5315
Fax: (202)393-2424
Scherr, Sara J., PhD, CEO,
President

ecoAmerica [3850]
1730 Rhode Island Ave. NW, Ste.
200
Washington, DC 20036-3120
PH: (202)457-1900
Fax: (509)351-1900
Perkowitz, Bob, Founder, President

Ecological Society of America [4000]
1990 M St. NW, Ste. 700
Washington, DC 20036
PH: (202)833-8773
Fax: (202)833-8775
Davis, Frank, VP of Public Affairs

Economic Policy Institute [18973]
1225 Eye St. NW, Ste. 600
Washington, DC 20005
PH: (202)775-8810
Toll free: 800-374-4844
Fax: (202)775-0819
Eisenbrey, Ross, VP

Economic Success Clearinghouse
[12535]
The Finance Project
1150 18th St. NW, Ste. 325
Washington, DC 20036
PH: (202)628-4200
Fax: (202)628-1293
Massinga, Ruth, Co-Ch.

Edison Electric Institute [3414]
701 Pennsylvania Ave. NW
Washington, DC 20004-2696
PH: (202)508-5000
Toll free: 800-334-5453
Akins, Nick, Chairman

Education for Peace in Iraq Center
[18396]
900 2nd St. NE, Ste. 216
Washington, DC 20002
PH: (202)682-0208
Gustafson, Erik, Exec. Dir.

Education Writers Association [2679]
3516 Connecticut Ave. NW
Washington, DC 20008
PH: (202)452-9830
Elliott, Scott, President

Educational Fund to Stop Gun
Violence [18251]
805 15th St. NW, Ste. 700
Washington, DC 20005
PH: (202)408-7560
Horwitz, Joshua, Exec. Dir.

eHealth Initiative [14997]
818 Connecticut Ave. NW, Ste. 500
Washington, DC 20006
PH: (202)624-3270
Fax: (202)429-5553
Bordenick, Jennifer Covich, CEO

Elder Justice Coalition [11748]
1612 K St. NW, Ste. 400
Washington, DC 20006
PH: (202)682-4140
Fax: (202)223-2099
Blancato, Robert B., Coord.

Electric Drive Transportation As-
sociation [6019]
1250 Eye St. NW, Ste. 902
Washington, DC 20005
PH: (202)408-0774
Spann, Christine, Dir. of Comm.

Electric Power Supply Association
[6475]
1401 New York Ave. NW, Ste. 1230
Washington, DC 20005-2110
PH: (202)628-8200
Fax: (202)628-8260
Shelk, John E., CEO, President

Electricity Consumers Resource
Council [1021]
1101 K St. NW, Ste. 700
Washington, DC 20005
PH: (202)682-1390
Fax: (202)289-6370
Acquard, Charles, VP of Gvt. Affairs

Electrification Coalition [3328]
1111 19th St. NW, Ste. 406
Washington, DC 20036-3627
PH: (202)448-9300
Fax: (202)461-2379
Diamond, Robbie, President, CEO

Electronic Privacy Information
Center [6742]
1718 Connecticut Ave. NW, Ste. 200
Washington, DC 20009
PH: (202)483-1140
Rotenberg, Marc, President, Exec.
Dir.

Electronic Retailing Association
[2280]
607 14th St. NW, Ste. 530
Washington, DC 20005
PH: (703)841-1751
Toll free: 800-987-6462
Fax: (425)977-1036
Sater, Gregory, Chmn. of the Bd.

Electronic Transactions Association
[394]
1101 16th St. NW, No. 402
Washington, DC 20036
PH: (202)828-2635
Toll free: 800-695-5509
Cohen, Greg, President

Email Experience Council [6443]
1615 L St. NW
Washington, DC 20036
Mullen, Jeanniey, Founder

Emergency Coalition for U.S.
Financial Support of the United
Nations [19210]
110 Maryland Ave. NE, Ste. 409
Washington, DC 20002
PH: (202)546-1572
Fax: (202)543-6297

Emergency Committee for American
Trade [1983]
900 17th St. NW, Ste. 1150
Washington, DC 20006
PH: (202)659-5147
Fax: (202)659-1347

Emerging Markets Private Equity
Association [1232]
1077 30th St. NW, Ste. 100
Washington, DC 20007
PH: (202)333-8171
Van Zwieten, Robert W., President,
CEO

EMILY's List [18867]
1800 M St. NW, Ste. 375N
Washington, DC 20036
PH: (202)326-1400
Toll free: 800-683-6459
Malcolm, Ellen R., Chmn. of the Bd.,
Founder

Employee Benefit Research Institute [1067]
1100 13th St. NW, Ste. 878
Washington, DC 20005-4051
PH: (202)659-0670
Fax: (202)775-6312
Salisbury, Dallas L., President, CEO

Employers Council on Flexible Compensation [1069]
1444 I St. NW, Ste. 700
Washington, DC 20005-2210
PH: (202)659-4300
Fax: (202)216-9646
Rankin, Natasha, Exec. Dir.

End Slavery Now [17893]
PO Box 65007
Washington, DC 20035
Taylor, Lauren, Founder, President

Endangered Species Coalition [4813]
PO Box 65195
Washington, DC 20035
PH: (240)353-2765
Fax: (202)
Huta, Leda, Exec. Dir.

Endocrine Society [14705]
2055 L St. NW, Ste. 600
Washington, DC 20036
PH: (202)971-3636
Toll free: 888-363-6274
Fax: (202)736-9705
Kronenberg, Henry H., MD, President

Energy Action Coalition [6478]
1875 Connecticut Ave. NW, 10th Fl.
Washington, DC 20009-5728
Avila, Lydia, Exec. Dir.

Energy Bar Association [5169]
2000 M St. NW, Ste. 715
Washington, DC 20036
PH: (202)223-5625
Fax: (202)833-5596
Meyer, Richard, President

Energy Communities Alliance [4025]
1101 Connecticut Ave. NW, Ste. 1000
Washington, DC 20036-4374
PH: (202)828-2317
Fax: (202)828-2488
Young, Steve, V. Chmn. of the Bd.

Energy Equipment and Infrastructure Alliance [1112]
601 Pennsylvania Ave. NW, Ste. 900
Washington, DC 20004
PH: (202)870-7715

Energy Frontiers International [4026]
1425 K St. NW
Washington, DC 20005
PH: (202)587-5780
Mart, Charles, V. Ch.

Energy Future Coalition [6480]
1750 Pennsylvania Ave. NW, Ste. 300
Washington, DC 20006
PH: (202)463-1947
Detchon, Reid, Exec. Dir.

Energy Policy Research Foundation, Inc. [7000]
1031 31st St. NW
Washington, DC 20007-4401
PH: (202)944-3339
Fax: (202)944-9830
Pugliaresi, Lucian (Lou), President

Energy Storage Association [3416]
1800 M St. NW, No. 400S
Washington, DC 20036
PH: (202)293-0537
Roberts, Matt, Exec. Dir.

Eno Transportation Foundation [7347]
1710 Rhode Island Ave. NW, Ste. 500
Washington, DC 20036
PH: (202)879-4700
Lewis, Paul, VP of Fin.

Enough Project [18304]
1333 H St. NW, 10th Fl.
Washington, DC 20005
PH: (202)682-1611
Fax: (202)682-6140
Prendergast, John, Director

Enroll America [14998]
1001 G St. NW, 8th Fl.
Washington, DC 20001
PH: (202)737-6340
Filipic, Anne, President

EnterpriseWorks/VITA [17807]
818 Connecticut Ave. NW, Ste. 600
Washington, DC 20006
PH: (202)639-8660
Fax: (202)639-8664
Levengood, Paul, Chmn. of the Bd.

Entertainment Software Association [6274]
575 7th St. NW, Ste. 300
Washington, DC 20004
Gallagher, Michael D., President, CEO

The Entomological Collections Network [6611]
c/o Floyd W. Shockley, President
PO Box 37012, MRC 165
Washington, DC 20013-7012
PH: (202)633-0982
Fax: (202)786-2894
Shockley, Floyd W., President

The Environmental Council of the States [4138]
50 F St. NW, Ste. 350
Washington, DC 20001
PH: (202)266-4920
Fax: (202)266-4937
Dunn, Alexandra Dapolito, Officer

Environmental and Energy Study Institute [4001]
1112 16th St. NW, Ste. 300
Washington, DC 20036
PH: (202)628-1400
Fax: (202)204-5244
Werner, Carol, Exec. Dir.

Environmental Law Institute [5180]
2000 L St. NW, Ste. 620
Washington, DC 20036
PH: (202)939-3824
Cruden, John, President

Environmental Working Group [4061]
1436 U St. NW, Ste. 100
Washington, DC 20009
PH: (202)667-6982
Fax: (202)232-2592
Faber, Scott, VP of Gvt. Affairs

Enzyme Technical Association [1167]
1111 Pennsylvania Ave. NW
Washington, DC 20004-2541
PH: (202)739-5613
Fax: (202)739-3001
Begley, Ann M., Secretary, Gen. Counsel

EPDM Roofing Association [526]
529 14th St. NW, Ste. 750
Washington, DC 20045
PH: (202)591-2474
Fax: (202)591-2474
Thorp, Ellen, Exec. Dir.

Equal Employment Advisory Council [11763]
1501 M St. NW, Ste. 400
Washington, DC 20005
PH: (202)629-5650
Fax: (202)629-5651
Siansky, Cory, VP of Operations

Equal Justice Works [5381]
1730 M St. NW, Ste. 1010
Washington, DC 20036-4511
PH: (202)466-3686
Stern, David, Exec. Dir.

Equal Visibility Everywhere [12032]
1400 Church St. NW, No. 201
Washington, DC 20005
Long, Dr. Lynette, President

Equipment Leasing and Finance Association [2927]
1825 K St. NW, Ste. 900
Washington, DC 20006
PH: (202)238-3400
Fax: (202)238-3401
Choi, Bill, VP of Res.

ERISA Industry Committee [1070]
1400 L St. NW, Ste. 350
Washington, DC 20005
PH: (202)789-1400
Fax: (202)789-1120
Young, Gretchen, Sr. VP

ESOP Association [1080]
1200 18th St. NW, Ste. 1125
Washington, DC 20036-2506
PH: (202)293-2971
Toll free: 866-366-3832
Fax: (202)293-7568
Keeling, J. Michael, President

Essential Information [17944]
PO Box 19405
Washington, DC 20036
PH: (202)387-8030
Nader, Ralph, Founder

ETAD: Ecological and Toxicological Association of Dyes and Organic Pigments Manufacturers [4545]
1850 M St. NW, Ste. 700
Washington, DC 20036
PH: (202)721-4154
Fax: (202)296-8120

Ethics and Public Policy Center [18975]
1730 M St. NW, Ste. 910
Washington, DC 20036
PH: (202)682-1200
Fax: (202)408-0632
Burleigh, William R., Chmn. of the Bd.

Ethylene Oxide Sterilization Association, Inc. [718]
PO Box 33361
Washington, DC 20033-0361
Toll free: 866-235-5030
Fax: (202)557-3836
Bull, Jonathan, President

European Union Delegation to the United States [18320]
2175 K St. NW
Washington, DC 20037
PH: (202)862-9500
Fax: (202)429-1766
O'Sullivan, David, Amb.

Every Child By Two [14188]
1233 20th St. NW, Ste. 403
Washington, DC 20036-2304
PH: (202)783-7034
Fax: (202)783-7042
Hannan, Claire, MPH, Treasurer

Every Voice Center [18941]
1211 Connecticut Ave. NW, Ste. 600
Washington, DC 20036

PH: (202)640-5600
Fax: (202)521-0605
Donnelly, David, President, CEO

Everybody Wins! USA [7587]
1920 N St. NW
Washington, DC 20036
PH: (202)216-9467
Fax: (202)216-9552
Director, Mark, Chairman

Excelencia in Education [8347]
1156 5th St. NW, Ste. 1001
Washington, DC 20005
PH: (202)785-7350
Fax: (202)785-7351
Brown, Sarita E., President

Executive Women in Government [5194]
PO Box 4233
Washington, DC 20044-9233
PH: (202)496-1293
Fax: (202)466-3226
Mullen-Roth, Barbara, President

Experience Corps [7850]
601 E St. NW
Washington, DC 20049-0001
Toll free: 800-687-2277
Fax: (202)434-6480
Strong, Lester, CEO, VP

Exponent Philanthropy [18852]
1720 N St. NW
Washington, DC 20036
PH: (202)580-6560
Toll free: 888-212-9922
Fax: (202)580-6579
Berman, Henry L., CEO

Eye Bank Association of America [14618]
1015 18th St. NW, Ste. 1010
Washington, DC 20036
PH: (202)775-4999
Fax: (202)429-6036
Corcoran, Kevin P., President, CEO

Faces and Voices of Recovery [19157]
840 1st St., NE, 3rd Fl.
Washington, DC 20002
PH: (202)737-0690
Fax: (202)737-0695
Metcalf, Patty McCarthy, Exec. Dir.

Fair Elections Legal Network [5004]
1825 K St. NW, Ste. 450
Washington, DC 20006
PH: (202)331-1550
Brandon, Robert M., Founder, President

Families Against Mandatory Minimums Foundation [11524]
1100 H St. NW, Ste. 1000
Washington, DC 20005
PH: (202)822-6700
Fax: (202)822-6704
Stewart, Julie, Founder, President

Families for Private Adoption [10452]
PO Box 6375
Washington, DC 20015-0375
Ayer, Lynsay, President

Families U.S.A. Foundation [10506]
1201 New York Ave. NW, Ste. 1100
Washington, DC 20005
PH: (202)628-3030
Fax: (202)347-2417
Pollack, Ron, Exec. Dir.

Families USA [15001]
1201 New York Ave. NW, Ste. 1100
Washington, DC 20005

PH: (202)628-3030
Fax: (202)347-2417
Pollack, Ron, Exec. Dir.

Family Business Coalition **[17826]**
PO Box 722
Washington, DC 20044
PH: (202)393-8959
Schoening, Palmer, Chairman

Family Research Council **[11818]**
801 G St. NW
Washington, DC 20001
Toll free: 800-225-4008
Perkins, Tony, President

Farm Credit Council **[396]**
50 F St. NW, No. 900
Washington, DC 20001
PH: (202)626-8710
   (202)879-0843
Fax: (202)626-8718
Hancock, Curtis, President

Farmworker Justice **[12337]**
1126 16th St. NW, Ste. 270
Washington, DC 20036
PH: (202)293-5420
Goldstein, Bruce, President

Federacion Interamericana de
   Abogados **[5423]**
1889 F St. NW, Ste. 335, 3rd Fl.
Washington, DC 20036
PH: (202)466-5944
Fax: (202)466-5946
López, Carlos, President

Federal Administrative Law Judges
   Conference **[5382]**
PO Box 1772
Washington, DC 20013
PH: (202)523-5750
Fax: (202)566-0042
Farley, Judge William, VP

Federal Circuit Bar Association
   [5006]
1620 I St. NW, Ste. 801
Washington, DC 20006-4033
PH: (202)466-3923
   (202)558-2421
Fax: (202)833-1061
Brookshire, James E., Esq., Exec.
   Dir.

Federal Communications Bar As-
   sociation **[5090]**
1020 19th St. NW, Ste. 325
Washington, DC 20036-6101
PH: (202)293-4000
Fax: (202)293-4317
Wright, Christopher J., President

Federal Education Association
   [23409]
1201 16th St. NW, Ste. 117
Washington, DC 20036-3201
PH: (202)822-7850
Fax: (202)822-7867
Priser, Michael, VP, Secretary,
   Treasurer

Federal Facilities Council **[5195]**
National Academy of Sciences
500 5th St. NW, Keck 912
Washington, DC 20001
Oskvig, Cameron, Director

Federalist Society for Law and
   Public Policy Studies **[5383]**
1776 I St. NW, Ste. 300
Washington, DC 20006
PH: (202)822-8138
Fax: (202)296-8061
Meyer, Eugene B., President

Federally Employed Women **[18206]**
455 Massachusetts Ave. NW
Washington, DC 20001

PH: (202)898-0994
Crockett, Michelle, President

Federation of American Hospitals
   [15325]
750 9th St. NW, Ste. 600
Washington, DC 20001-4524
PH: (202)624-1500
Fax: (202)737-6462
Speil, Steven, Sr. VP

Federation for American Immigration
   Reform **[18464]**
25 Massachusetts Ave. NW, Ste.
   330
Washington, DC 20001
PH: (202)328-7004
Toll free: 877-627-3247
Fax: (202)387-3447
Stein, Daniel, President

Federation of American Scientists
   [18976]
1725 DeSales St. NW, 6th Fl.
Washington, DC 20036
PH: (202)546-3300
Ferguson, Charles D., President

Federation of Associations in
   Behavioral and Brain Sciences
   [6037]
1001 Connecticut Ave. NW, Ste.
   1100
Washington, DC 20036
PH: (202)888-3949
Skedsvold, Paula, Exec. Dir.

Federation of Diocesan Liturgical
   Commissions **[19833]**
415 Michigan Ave. NE
Washington, DC 20017-4503
PH: (202)635-6990
Fax: (202)529-2452
Tarker, Lisa, Exec. Dir.

Federation of Materials Societies
   [6813]
910 17th St. NW, Ste. 800
Washington, DC 20006-2606
PH: (301)325-2494
Houston, Betsy, Exec. Dir.

Federation of Tax Administrators
   [5791]
444 N Capitol St. NW
Washington, DC 20001
PH: (202)624-5890
Garriott, Gale, Exec. Dir.

The Fellowship of Catholic Scholars
   [19834]
c/o William L. Saunders, Esq.,
   President
655 15th St., Ste. 410
Washington, DC 20005-5709
PH: (202)289-1478
Saunders, William L., Esq.,
   President

Fellowship of Concerned Churchmen
   [19703]
1215 Independence Ave. SE
Washington, DC 20003-1445
PH: (202)621-6729
Spaulding, Wallace H., President

The Fertilizer Institute **[1182]**
425 3rd St. SW, Ste. 950
Washington, DC 20024
PH: (202)962-0490
Fax: (202)962-0577
Conway, Monica, Exec. Asst.

FIABCI-USA **[2860]**
1050 Connecticut Ave. NW, Ste.
   1000
Washington, DC 20036
PH: (202)772-3308
Kruger, Ruth, President

Fight Crime: Invest in Kids **[17845]**
1212 New York Ave. NW, Ste. 300
Washington, DC 20005
PH: (202)776-0027
Fax: (202)776-0110
Baca, Leroy, Chmn. of the Bd.

The Finance Project **[18243]**
1150 18th St. NW, Ste. 325
Washington, DC 20036
PH: (202)628-4200
Fax: (202)628-1293
Hayes, Cheryl D., Contact

Financial Industry Regulatory Author-
   ity **[3043]**
1735 K St.
Washington, DC 20006
PH: (301)590-6500
Ketchum, Richard G., Chairman,
   CEO, Chmn. of the Bd.

Financial Markets Association **[1235]**
333 2nd St. NE, No. 104
Washington, DC 20002
PH: (202)544-6327
Pearce, Dorcas, Managing Dir.

Financial Services Roundtable **[398]**
600 13th St. NW, Ste. 400
Washington, DC 20005
PH: (202)289-4322
Fax: (202)628-2507
Banga, Ajaypal S., Chairman

Financial Services Technology
   Consortium **[7267]**
600 13th St., NW, Ste. 400
Washington, DC 20005
Schutzer, Dan, Exec. Dir.

First Book **[8241]**
1319 F St. NW, Ste. 1000
Washington, DC 20004
PH: (202)393-1222
Toll free: 866-732-3669
Zimmer, Kyle, CEO, President

First Star **[10976]**
901 K St. NW, Ste. 700
Washington, DC 20001
PH: (202)293-3703
Samuelson, Mr. Peter, Founder,
   President, Chairman

Flavor and Extract Manufacturers
   Association of the United States
   [1325]
1101 17th St. NW, Ste. 700
Washington, DC 20036
PH: (202)293-5800
Fax: (202)463-8998
Cox, John H., Exec. Dir.

Flex Your Rights **[18398]**
PO Box 21497
Washington, DC 20009
Silverman, Steve, Exec. Dir.

Food and Drug Law Institute **[5223]**
1155 15th St. NW, Ste. 910
Washington, DC 20005-2706
PH: (202)371-1420
Toll free: 800-956-6293
Fax: (202)371-0649
Cohen, Marsha, Comm. Chm.

Food and Nutrition Board **[16220]**
Keck Ctr., W700
500 5th St. NW
Washington, DC 20001
PH: (202)334-1732
Fax: (202)334-2316
Behney, Clyde J., Exec. Dir.

Food Research and Action Center
   [12094]
1200 18th St. NW, Ste. 400
Washington, DC 20036

PH: (202)986-2200
Fax: (202)986-2525
Weill, James D. (Jim), President

Food Waste Reduction Alliance
   [4191]
1350 Eye I St. NW, Ste. 300
Washington, DC 20005
Stasz, Meghan, Contact

Food and Water Watch **[18262]**
1616 P St. NW, Ste. 300
Washington, DC 20036
PH: (202)683-2500
Fax: (202)683-2501
Hauter, Wenonah, Exec. Dir.

Footwear Distributors and Retailers
   of America **[1400]**
1319 F St. NW, Ste. 700
Washington, DC 20004
PH: (202)737-5660
Fax: (202)645-0789
Tunney, Greg, Director

Thomas B. Fordham Institute
   [11727]
1016 16th St. NW, 8th Fl.
Washington, DC 20036
PH: (202)223-5452
Fax: (202)223-9226
Petrilli, Michael J., President

Ford's Theatre Society **[10251]**
511 10th St. NW
Washington, DC 20004
PH: (202)638-2941
   (202)434-9545
Fax: (202)347-6269
Tetreault, Paul R., Director

Foreign Policy in Focus **[18267]**
1112 16th St. NW, Ste. 600
Washington, DC 20036
PH: (202)787-5271
Feffer, John, Director

Forest Resources Association, Inc.
   [1409]
1901 Pennsylvania Ave. NW, Ste.
   303
Washington, DC 20006
PH: (202)296-3937
Fax: (202)296-0562
Reed, Thomas M., Chairman

Forest Trends **[3866]**
1203 19th St. NW, 4th Fl.
Washington, DC 20036
PH: (202)298-3000
Fax: (202)298-3014
Jenkins, Michael, CEO, President

Formosan Association for Public Af-
   fairs **[18400]**
552 7th St. SE
Washington, DC 20003
PH: (202)547-3686
Fax: (202)543-7891
Kao, Mark L., PhD, President

Forum of Regional Associations of
   Grantmakers **[12474]**
1020 19th St. NW, Ste. 360
Washington, DC 20036
PH: (202)888-7533
   (202)457-8784
Toll free: 888-391-3235
Biemesderfer, David, CEO,
   President

Foundation for Afghanistan **[10468]**
1212 New York Ave. NW, Ste. 825
Washington, DC 20005
PH: (202)289-2515
Fax: (202)289-2516
Jawad, Said Tayeb, President

Foundation for BioMedical Research
   [13717]
1100 Vermont Ave. NW, Ste. 1100
Washington, DC 20005

PH: (202)457-0654
Fax: (202)457-0659
Trull, Ms. Frankie L., President, Founder

Foundation for International Community Assistance [17976]
1201 15th St. NW, 8th Fl.
Washington, DC 20005
PH: (202)682-1510
Fax: (202)682-1535
Hatch, Robert W., Chmn. of the Bd.

Foundation for Middle East Peace [18681]
1761 N St. NW
Washington, DC 20036
PH: (202)835-3650
Fax: (202)835-3651
Duss, Matthew, President

Foundation for Public Affairs [18978]
2121 K St. NW, Ste. 900
Washington, DC 20037
PH: (202)787-5970
Fax: (202)787-5942
Pinkham, Douglas G., President

Foundations and Donors Interested in Catholic Activities [19836]
4201 Connecticut Ave. NW, Ste. 505
Washington, DC 20008
PH: (202)223-3550
Jenkins, Forrest (Joe) N, V. Chmn. of the Bd., Treasurer

Fraud.org [18049]
1701 K St. NW, Ste. 1200
Washington, DC 20006
PH: (202)835-3323
Fax: (202)835-0747
Breyault, John, Director

Free Muslims Coalition [18096]
1050 17th St. NW, Ste. 1000
Washington, DC 20036
PH: (202)776-7190
   (202)907-5724
Nawash, Kamal, President

Free the Slaves [12034]
1320 19th St. NW, Ste. 600
Washington, DC 20036
PH: (202)775-7480
Fax: (202)775-7485
Bales, Kevin, Founder, President

Freedom House [18097]
1850 M St. NW, 11th Fl.
Washington, DC 20036
PH: (202)296-5101
Fax: (212)293-2840
Nguyen, Quoc, CFO

Freedom of Information Clearinghouse [18957]
1600 20th St. NW
Washington, DC 20009
PH: (202)588-7741
Bradbery, Angela, Dir. of Comm.

FreedomWorks [18869]
400 N Capitol St. NW, Ste. 765
Washington, DC 20001
PH: (202)783-3870
Toll free: 888-564-6273
Brandon, Adam, President, CEO

Freight Rail Customer Alliance [18870]
300 New Jersey Ave. NW, Ste. 900
Washington, DC 20001
PH: (202)469-3471
Fax: (202)347-0130
Jackson, Steve, VP

Friends Committee on National Legislation [20168]
245 2nd St. NE
Washington, DC 20002-5761

PH: (202)547-6000
Toll free: 800-630-1330
Fax: (202)547-6019
Randall, Diane, Exec. Sec.

Friends of the Earth [3869]
1101 15th St. NW, 11th Fl.
Washington, DC 20005
PH: (202)783-7400
Fax: (202)783-0444
Moore, Charles, Director

Friends of the Global Fight Against AIDS, Tuberculosis and Malaria [15399]
1730 Rhode Island Ave. NW, Ste. 912
Washington, DC 20036
PH: (202)789-0801
Fax: (202)789-0802
Derrick, Deb, President

Friends of the Kennedy Center [8974]
2700 F St. NW
Washington, DC 20566
PH: (202)467-4600
Toll free: 800-444-1324
Rubenstein, David M., Chairman

Friends of Mali [18786]
PO Box 27417
Washington, DC 20038-7417
Qamruddin, Jumana, President

Friends of Morocco [19572]
PO Box 2579
Washington, DC 20013-2579
PH: (703)470-3166
Birch, Tom, Rep.

Friends of the National Arboretum [6140]
3501 New York Ave. NE
Washington, DC 20002
PH: (202)544-8733
Fax: (202)544-5398
Horan, Kathy, Director

Friends of the National Zoo [7401]
3001 Connecticut Ave. NW
Washington, DC 20008
PH: (202)633-3038
   (202)633-4888
Mento, Lynn, Exec. Dir.

Fulbright Association [8073]
1900 L St. NW, Ste. 302
Washington, DC 20036-5016
PH: (202)775-0725
Fax: (202)775-0727
Schmider, Mary Ellen Heian, Secretary

Fund for American Studies [8194]
1706 New Hampshire Ave. NW
Washington, DC 20009
PH: (202)986-0384
Fax: (202)986-0390
Ream, Roger R., President

Fund for Constitutional Government [18317]
122 Maryland Ave. NE
Washington, DC 20002
PH: (202)546-3799
Fax: (202)543-3156
Cavanagh, John, Chairperson

Fund for Investigative Journalism [17946]
529 14th St. NW, 13th Fl.
Washington, DC 20045
PH: (202)662-7564
Palos, Ricardo Sandoval, President

Fund for Peace [19260]
1101 14th St. NW, Ste. 1020
Washington, DC 20005

PH: (202)223-7940
Hendry, Krista, Mem.

Futures Industry Association [1493]
2001 Pennsylvania Ave. NW, Ste. 600
Washington, DC 20006
PH: (202)466-5460
Lukken, Walter L., President, CEO

Gallaudet University Alumni Association [19325]
c/o Gallaudet University
800 Florida Ave. NE
Washington, DC 20002
PH: (202)651-5060
Fax: (202)651-5062
Sonnenstrahl, Mr. Sam, Exec. Dir.

GAVI Alliance [15142]
1776 I St. NW, Ste. 600
Washington, DC 20006
PH: (202)478-1050
Fax: (202)478-1060
Berkley, Seth, CEO

Gay and Lesbian Medical Association [14800]
1326 18th St., Ste. 22
Washington, DC 20036
PH: (202)600-8037
Fax: (202)478-1500
Vargas, Hector, Exec. Dir.

Gaylactic Network [10202]
PO Box 7587
Washington, DC 20044-7587
PH: (612)387-8265
Bertke, Andrew, Web Adm.

Gays and Lesbians in Foreign Affairs Agencies USA [23431]
PO Box 18774
Washington, DC 20036-8774
Ariturk, Selim, Officer

Geekcorps [3209]
1900 M St. NW, Ste. 500
Washington, DC 20036
PH: (202)589-2600
Fax: (202)326-0289
Miller, Thomas, President, CEO

Gender Action [19254]
925 H St. NW, Ste. 410
Washington, DC 20001-4978
PH: (202)234-7722
Hellinger, Douglas, Founder, Exec. Dir.

General Aviation Manufacturers Association [136]
1400 K St. NW, Ste. 801
Washington, DC 20005-2485
PH: (202)393-1500
Fax: (202)842-4063
Bunce, Peter J., CEO, President

General Federation of Women's Clubs [19691]
1734 N St. NW
Washington, DC 20036-2990
PH: (202)347-3168
Fax: (202)835-0246
Laister, Mary Ellen, Mem.

General Grand Chapter, Order of the Eastern Star [19555]
1618 New Hampshire Ave. NW
Washington, DC 20009-2549
PH: (202)667-4737
Fax: (202)462-5162
Berry, Michael, Treasurer, Trustee

Generation Engage [19270]
2800 Calvert St. NW
Washington, DC 20008

Generations United [13054]
25 E St. NW, 3rd Fl.
Washington, DC 20001

PH: (202)289-3979
Minnix, William L., Jr., Officer

Generic Pharmaceutical Association [2558]
777 6th St. NW, Ste. 510
Washington, DC 20001-4498
PH: (202)249-7100
Fax: (202)249-7105
Davis, Chester, Jr., President, CEO

Genetic Alliance [17342]
4301 Connecticut Ave. NW, Ste. 404
Washington, DC 20008-2369
PH: (202)966-5557
Fax: (202)966-8553
Terry, Sharon, CEO, President

Genocide Watch [18306]
PO Box 809
Washington, DC 20044
PH: (703)448-0222
Stanton, Dr. Gregory H., President

Geochemical Society [6688]
5241 Broad Branch Rd. NW
Washington, DC 20015-1305
PH: (202)545-6946
Johnson, Kevin, COO

German Foods North America [4476]
719 6th St. NW
Washington, DC 20001
Toll free: 800-881-6419
von Friedeburg, Arnim, Managing Dir.

German Historical Institute [9479]
1607 New Hampshire Ave. NW
Washington, DC 20009-2562
PH: (202)387-3355
Fax: (202)387-6437
Lässig, Prof. Simone, PhD, Director

German Marshall Fund of the United States [18543]
1744 R St. NW
Washington, DC 20009
PH: (202)683-2650
Fax: (202)265-1662
Budak, Taylor, Asst.

Gerontological Society of America [14892]
1220 L St. NW, Ste. 901
Washington, DC 20005-4001
PH: (202)842-1275
Appleby, James, Exec. Dir., CEO

Gettysburg College | Eisenhower Institute [18979]
818 Connecticut Ave. NW, Ste. 800
Washington, DC 20006
PH: (202)628-4444
Fax: (202)628-4445
Eisenhower, Susan, Chairman

Elizabeth Glaser Pediatric AIDS Foundation [13540]
1140 Connecticut Ave. NW, Ste. 200
Washington, DC 20036
PH: (202)296-9165
Fax: (202)296-9185
Lyons, Charles, CEO, President

Global Automakers [292]
1050 K St. NW, Ste. 650
Washington, DC 20001
PH: (202)650-5555
Mendel, John, Chairman

Global Environment Facility [4062]
1818 H St. NW
Washington, DC 20433
PH: (202)473-0508
Fax: (202)522-3240
Ishii, Dr. Naoko, Chairperson, CEO

Global Environmental Management
Initiative **[4128]**
1156 15th St. NW, Ste. 800
Washington, DC 20005
PH: (202)296-7449
Hellem, Steve, Exec. Dir.

Global Facility for Disaster Reduc-
tion and Recovery **[11662]**
1818 H St. NW
Washington, DC 20433
PH: (202)473-6253
Fax: (202)522-3227
Ghesquiere, Francis, Exec. Dir.

Global Federation of Animal
Sanctuaries **[10628]**
PO Box 32294
Washington, DC 20007
PH: (928)472-1173
  (623)252-5122
Robinson, Ian, Secretary

Global Forest Watch **[4203]**
10 G St. NE, Ste. 800
Washington, DC 20002
PH: (202)729-7600
Fax: (202)729-7610
Hanson, Craig, Director

Global Health Technologies Coalition
[15460]
455 Massachusetts Ave. NW, Ste.
1000
Washington, DC 20001
PH: (202)822-0033
Morton, Erin Will, Director

Global Integrity **[916]**
1110 Vermont Ave. NW, Ste. 500
Washington, DC 20005
PH: (202)449-4100
Fax: (202)888-3172
Davies, Mark, Chairman

Global Network for Neglected Tropical Diseases **[14580]**
2000 Pennsylvania Ave. NW, Ste.
7100
Washington, DC 20006
PH: (202)842-5025
Brooks, Michelle, Director

Global Offset and Countertrade As-
sociation **[1984]**
818 Connecticut Ave. NW, 12th Fl.
Washington, DC 20006
PH: (202)887-9011
Fax: (202)872-8324
Fromyer, Mary O., Exec. Dir.

Global Peace Services **[18790]**
PO Box 27922
Washington, DC 20038-7922
PH: (202)216-9886
Eriksson, John, President

Global Solar Council **[7201]**
1717 K St. NW, Ste. 1120
Washington, DC 20006
Smirnow, John P., Sec. Gen.

Global Ties U.S. **[18545]**
1250 H St. NW, Ste. 305
Washington, DC 20005
PH: (202)842-1414
Fax: (202)289-4625
Durtka, Alexander, Jr., Counsel

GoodWeave International **[11008]**
1111 14th St. NW, Ste. 820
Washington, DC 20005
PH: (202)234-9050
Fax: (202)234-9056
Smith, Nina, Exec. Dir.

Government Accountability Project
[18318]
1612 K St. NW, Ste. 1100
Washington, DC 20006

PH: (202)457-0034
Edwards, Beatrice, Prog. Dir.

Governors Highway Safety Associa-
tion **[5812]**
444 N Capitol St. NW, Ste. 722
Washington, DC 20001
PH: (202)789-0942
Fax: (202)789-0946
Simpler, Jana, Chairman

Grantmakers in Health **[17003]**
1100 Connecticut Ave. NW, Ste.
1200
Washington, DC 20036
PH: (202)452-8331
Fax: (202)452-8340
Mockenhaupt, Robin, Ph.D, Chair-
man

Graphic Communications Conference of the International Brotherhood of Teamsters **[23440]**
25 Louisiana Ave. NW
Washington, DC 20001
PH: (202)624-6800
Tedeschi, George, President

Gray Panthers **[10508]**
10 G St. NE, Ste. 600
Washington, DC 20002
PH: (202)737-6637
Toll free: 800-280-5362
BenDor, Jan, Chairman

Green America **[907]**
1612 K St. NW, Ste. 600
Washington, DC 20006-2810
Toll free: 800-584-7336
Fax: (202)331-8166
Gravitz, Alisa, CEO

Green Party of the United States
[18890]
PO Box 75075
Washington, DC 20013
PH: (202)319-7191
Clement, Audrey, Co-Ch.

Green Schools Alliance **[7894]**
1875 Connecticut Ave. NW, 10th Fl.
Washington, DC 20009
PH: (860)468-5289
Watson, Margaret Howard, Founder,
President

Green Seal **[18050]**
1001 Connecticut Ave. NW, Ste. 827
Washington, DC 20036-5525
PH: (202)872-6400
Fax: (202)872-4324
Bateman, Paul, Secretary

Greenpeace U.S.A. **[4068]**
702 H St. NW, Ste. 300
Washington, DC 20001
PH: (202)462-1177
Toll free: 800-722-6995
Fax: (202)462-4507
Topakian, Karen, Chairperson

Greeting Card Association **[3173]**
1444 I St. NW, Ste. 700
Washington, DC 20005
PH: (202)216-9627
Fax: (202)216-9646
Rankin, Natasha, Exec. Dir.

GridWise Alliance, Inc. **[6487]**
1800 M St. NW, Ste. 400S
Washington, DC 20036
PH: (202)530-5910
Fax: (202)530-0659
Prochazka, Scott, Chairman

Grocery Manufacturers Association
[1334]
1350 I St. NW
Washington, DC 20005

PH: (202)639-5900
Fax: (202)639-5932
Bailey, Pamela G., President, CEO

Group of Thirty **[1013]**
1701 K St. NW, Ste. 950
Washington, DC 20006
PH: (202)331-2472
Mackintosh, Stuart P.M., Exec. Dir.

Growth Energy **[6488]**
777 N Capitol St. NE, Ste. 805
Washington, DC 20002
PH: (202)545-4000
Fax: (202)545-4001
Skor, Emily, CEO

Guatemala Human Rights Commis-
sion USA **[18403]**
3321 12th St. NE
Washington, DC 20017-4008
PH: (202)529-6599
Fax: (202)526-4611
Alford-Jones, Ms. Kelsey, Exec. Dir.

Guild of Natural Science Illustrators
[6698]
Ben Franklin Sta.
Washington, DC 20044-0652
PH: (301)309-1514
Fax: (301)309-1514
Kayama, Ikumi, Secretary

HALO Trust **[18001]**
1730 Rhode Island Ave. NW, Ste.
403
Washington, DC 20036
PH: (202)331-1266
Fax: (202)331-1277
Pullinger, Amanda, Chairperson

Hands Across the Mideast Support
Alliance **[18683]**
American Islamic Congress
1718 M St. NW, No. 243
Washington, DC 20036
PH: (202)595-3160
Fax: (202)621-6005
Al-Suwaij, Zainab, Exec. Dir.

Hardwood Federation **[1439]**
1101 K St. NW, Ste. 100
Washington, DC 20005
PH: (202)463-2705
  (202)463-2452
Fax: (202)463-4702
Cole, Dana Lee, Exec. Dir.

Health Care for America Now
[18333]
1825 K St. NW, Ste. 400
Washington, DC 20006
PH: (202)454-6200
Goldstein, Avram, Dir. of Comm., Dir.
of Res.

Health Coalition on Liability and Ac-
cess **[15010]**
PO Box 78096
Washington, DC 20013-9096

Health Volunteers Overseas **[12282]**
1900 L St. NW, No. 310
Washington, DC 20036
PH: (202)296-0928
Fax: (202)296-8018
Kelly, Nancy, Exec. Dir.

Healthcare Billing and Management
Association **[15727]**
2025 M St. NW, Ste. 800
Washington, DC 20036
Toll free: 877-640-4262
Fax: (202)367-2177
Williams, Andre, Exec. Dir.

Healthcare Leadership Council
[15145]
750 9th St. NW, Ste. 500
Washington, DC 20001

PH: (202)452-8700
Fax: (202)296-9561
DeVore, Susan, President

Healthcare Supply Chain Association
[15078]
1341 G Street NW, 6th Fl.
Washington, DC 20005
PH: (202)629-5833
Fax: (202)466-9666
Perlman, Lee, Chairman

Healthy Building Network **[4129]**
1710 Connecticut Ave.
Washington, DC 20009
PH: (202)741-5717
Toll free: 877-974-2767
Walsh, Bill, Founder, Exec. Dir.

Hearing Industries Association
[1602]
1444 I St. NW, Ste. 700
Washington, DC 20005
PH: (202)449-1090
Fax: (202)216-9646

Heart Rhythm Society **[14115]**
1325 G St. NW, Ste. 400
Washington, DC 20005
PH: (202)464-3400
Fax: (202)464-3401
Youngblood, James, CEO

HEATH Resource Center at the
National Youth Transitions Center
[7717]
2134 G St. NW
Washington, DC 20052-0001
Knapp, Steven, President

Hellenic American National Council
[9353]
1220 16th St. NW
Washington, DC 20036
PH: (610)446-1463
Fax: (610)446-3189
Antonakakis, Stavros, Officer

Help Abolish Legal Tyranny **[18599]**
1612 K St. NW, Ste. 1102
Washington, DC 20006
PH: (202)887-8255
Martin, Conrad, Co-Ch.

Hemophilia Federation of America
[15231]
820 1st St. NE, Ste. 720
Washington, DC 20002
PH: (202)675-6984
Toll free: 800-230-9797
Fax: (202)675-6983
Cleghorn, Tracy, President

The Heritage Foundation **[18285]**
214 Massachusetts Ave. NE
Washington, DC 20002-4999
PH: (202)546-4400
  (202)675-1761
Toll free: 800-544-4843
Truluck, Phillip N., Chairman

High Temperature Insulation Wool
Coalition **[695]**
1200 17th St. NW, Rm. 07-54
Washington, DC 20036-3006
PH: (202)663-9188
Fax: (202)354-4982

Hillel: The Foundation for Jewish
Campus Life **[20251]**
800 8th St. NW
Washington, DC 20001-3724
PH: (202)449-6500
Fax: (202)449-6600
Blumberg, Thomas A., Gov.

Hindu American Foundation **[20201]**
910 17th St. NW, Ste. 316A
Washington, DC 20006

PH: (202)223-8222
Fax: (202)223-8004

Hispanic American Police Command
Officers Association [5464]
PO Box 29626
Washington, DC 20017
PH: (202)664-4461
Chapa, Anthony, Exec. Dir.

Hispanic Association on Corporate
Responsibility [18066]
1220 L St. NW, Ste. 701
Washington, DC 20005-6502
PH: (202)682-4012
Fax: (202)682-0086
Orta, Carlos F., Mem.

Hispanic Elected Local Officials
[5637]
c/o National League of Cities
1301 Pennsylvania Ave. NW, Ste.
550
Washington, DC 20004-1747
PH: (202)626-3169
Martinez, Lydia N., VP

Hispanic National Bar Association
[5008]
1020 19th St. NW, Ste. 505
Washington, DC 20036
PH: (202)223-4777
Maldonado, Robert, President

Hispanic-Serving Health Professions
Schools [8324]
2639 Connecticut Ave. NW, Ste. 203
Washington, DC 20008
PH: (202)290-1186
Fax: (202)290-1339
Pérez, Norma A., MD, VP

Hmong National Development
[18473]
1628 16th St. NW
Washington, DC 20009
PH: (202)588-1661
Vang, Bao, President, CEO

Home Builders Institute [535]
1201 15th St. NW, Ste. 600
Washington, DC 20005
PH: (202)371-0600
Toll free: 800-795-7955
Courson, John A., President, CEO

Home Care Technology Association
of America [15277]
228 7th St. SE
Washington, DC 20003
PH: (202)547-2871
Fax: (202)547-3540
Brennan, Richard, Exec. Dir.

Home Healthcare Nurses Associa-
tion [16134]
228 7th St. SE
Washington, DC 20003
PH: (202)547-7424
Fax: (202)547-3540
Stephens, Elaine D., Director

Home Performance Coalition [3883]
1620 Eye St. NW, Ste. 501
Washington, DC 20006
PH: (202)463-2005
Rinaldi, Kara Saul, Exec. Dir.

Homeland Security and Defense
Business Council [3055]
1990 M St., Ste. 760
Washington, DC 20036
PH: (202)470-6440
Pearl, Marc, President, CEO

Hope for Children in Vietnam
[11037]
3900A Watson Pl. NW, Apt. 2B
Washington, DC 20016
Tran, Diana Phuong My, Chmn. of
the Bd.

Hope for Tomorrow [11378]
901 New Jersey Ave. NW, Ste. 101
Washington, DC 20001
PH: (202)705-8547
Segero, Rosemary, Chairperson

Horticultural Research Institute
[4503]
525 9th St. NW, Ste. 800
Washington, DC 20004
PH: (202)789-2900
Fax: (202)789-1893
Coulter, John, President

Hospice Association of America
[15278]
228 7th St. SE
Washington, DC 20003
PH: (202)546-4759
Fax: (202)547-9559
Levine, Susan Goldwater, Exec. Dir.

Hospice Foundation of America
[15295]
1707 L St. NW, Ste. 220
Washington, DC 20036-3123
PH: (202)457-5811
Toll free: 800-854-3402
Doka, Kenneth J., Consultant

Hotel Electronic Distribution Network
Association [1660]
750 National Press Bldg.
529 14th St. NW
Washington, DC 20045
PH: (202)204-8400
Fax: (202)591-2445
Hitchcock, Reed, Exec. Dir.

House Plan Marketing Alliance [988]
529 14th St. NW, Ste. 750
Washington, DC 20045
Toll free: 800-366-2423
Fax: (866)204-0293

Housing Assistance Council [11973]
1025 Vermont Ave. NW, Ste. 606
Washington, DC 20005
PH: (202)842-8600
Fax: (202)347-3441
Loza, Moises, Exec. Dir.

HR Policy Association [18609]
1100 13th St. NW, Ste. 850
Washington, DC 20005
PH: (202)789-8670
Fax: (202)789-0064

Hudson Institute [18982]
1201 Pennsylvania Ave. NW, Ste.
400
Washington, DC 20004
PH: (202)974-2400
Fax: (202)974-2410
Austria, Thereza, Dir. of Fin.

Human Rights Campaign [11893]
1640 Rhode Island Ave. NW
Washington, DC 20036-3278
PH: (202)628-4160
Toll free: 800-777-4723
Fax: (202)347-5323
Griffin, Chad, President

The Humane Society of the United
States [10643]
1255 23rd St., NW, Ste. 450
Washington, DC 20037
PH: (202)452-1100
Toll free: 866-720-2676
Pacelle, Wayne, President, CEO

Hungarian American Coalition
[18524]
2400 N St. NW, Ste. 603
Washington, DC 20037
PH: (202)296-9505
Fax: (202)775-5175
Teleki, Mr. Maximilian, President

Hungarian Freedom Fighters
Federation, Inc. [18297]
PO Box 42048
Washington, DC 20015
PH: (571)594-1961

IEEE - Computer Society [6246]
2001 L St. NW, Ste. 700
Washington, DC 20036-4928
PH: (202)371-0101
Toll free: 800-678-4333
Fax: (202)728-9614
Burgess, Angela R., Exec. Dir.

IMA World Health [15476]
1730 M St. NW, Ste. 1100
Washington, DC 20036
PH: (202)888-6200
Fax: (202)470-3370
Rothenberger, Lisa, Chairman

Impact Alliance [12162]
1350 610 8th St. NE
Washington, DC 20002
PH: (202)470-5566
Kwaterski, Mr. Jeffrey, Director

INCOMPAS [3417]
1200 G St. NW, Ste. 350
Washington, DC 20005
PH: (202)296-6650
Fax: (202)296-7585
Smith, Amy, Contact

Independent Bakers Association
[374]
PO Box 3731
Washington, DC 20027-0231
PH: (202)333-8190
Barth, Scott, Chairman

Independent Community Bankers of
America [400]
1615 L St. NW, Ste. 900
Washington, DC 20036
PH: (202)659-8111
Toll free: 800-422-8439
Fax: (202)659-3604
Meyer, John, Director

Independent Laboratories Institute
[6778]
1875 I St. NW, Ste. 500
Washington, DC 20006
PH: (202)887-5872
Fax: (202)887-0021
Bush, Milton, CEO

Independent Petroleum Association
of America [2524]
1201 15th St. NW, Ste. 300
Washington, DC 20005
PH: (202)857-4722
Fax: (202)857-4799
Russell, Barry, President, CEO

Independent Sector [12484]
1602 L St. NW, Ste. 900
Washington, DC 20036
PH: (202)467-6100
(202)467-6161
Fax: (202)467-6101
Aviv, Diana, CEO, President

Independent Women's Forum
[18879]
1875 I St. NW, Ste. 500
Washington, DC 20006
PH: (202)857-3293
Fax: (202)429-9574
Schaeffer, Sabrina L., Exec. Dir.

The India Study Circle for Philately
[22333]
PO Box 7326
Washington, DC 20044-7326
PH: (202)564-6876
Fax: (202)565-2441
Warren, John, Secretary

Industrial Energy Consumers of
America [1114]
1776 K St. NW, Ste. 720
Washington, DC 20006
PH: (202)223-1661
(202)223-1420
Fax: (202)530-0659
Cicio, Paul N., President

Industrial Minerals Association-North
America [2380]
2011 Pennsylvania Ave. NW, Ste.
301
Washington, DC 20006
PH: (202)457-0200
Fax: (202)457-0287
Ellis, Mark, President

Industrial Truck Association [322]
1750 K St. NW, Ste. 460
Washington, DC 20006
PH: (202)296-9880
Fax: (202)296-9884
Feehan, Brian J., President

Industry Council for Emergency
Response Technologies [768]
PO Box 42563
Washington, DC 20015-2604
PH: (240)398-3065
Brittingham, Don, V. Chmn. of the
Bd.

Information Technology Industry
Council [6317]
1101 K St. NW, Ste. 610
Washington, DC 20005
PH: (202)737-8888
Fax: (202)638-4922
Garfield, Dean, CEO, President

Initiative for Global Development
[12545]
1101 Pennsylvania Ave. NW, 6th Fl.
Washington, DC 20004
PH: (202)454-3972
Nedelcovych, Dr. Mima S.,
President, CEO

Innocents at Risk [12043]
1101 30th St. NW, Ste. 500
Washington, DC 20007
PH: (202)625-4338
Fax: (202)625-4363
Sigmund, Deborah, Founder

Innovation Network [6759]
1625 K St. NW, Ste. 1050
Washington, DC 20006
PH: (202)728-0727
Fax: (202)728-0136
Pankaj, Veena, Director

Innovations in Civic Participation
[17859]
PO Box 39222
Washington, DC 20016
PH: (202)775-0290
Stroud, Susan, Exec. Dir., Founder

Institute for America's Future
[18910]
1825 K St. NW, Ste. 400
Washington, DC 20006-1254
PH: (202)955-5665
Fax: (202)955-5606
Hickey, Roger, Director

Institute of Caribbean Studies
[12163]
1629 K St. NW, Ste. 300
Washington, DC 20001
PH: (202)638-0460
Masters, Amb. Carl, Chmn. of the
Bd.

Institute for Community Economics
[17981]
1101 30th St. NW, Ste. 100A
Washington, DC 20007

PH: (202)333-8931
Bodaken, Michael, Exec. Dir.

Institute for Credentialing Excellence
[14941]
2025 M St. NW, Ste. 800
Washington, DC 20036
PH: (202)367-1165
Fax: (202)367-2165
Zacharias, Claudia, MBA, CAE,
  Chairperson

Institute of Current World Affairs
[19263]
1779 Massachusetts Ave. NW, Ste.
  615
Washington, DC 20036
PH: (202)364-4068
Barlow, Julie, Trustee

Institute for Democracy in Eastern
  Europe [18139]
1718 M St. NW, No. 147
Washington, DC 20036
PH: (202)361-9346
Lasota, Irena, Director, Founder

Institute for Distribution Excellence
[3471]
1325 G St. NW, Ste. 1000
Washington, DC 20005-3100
PH: (202)872-0885
Fax: (202)785-0586
Schreibman, Ron, Exec. Dir.

Institute of Education Sciences |
  National Center for Education
  Statistics | National Assessment of
  Educational Progress [8686]
Assessment Division, 8th Fl.
1990 K St. NW
Washington, DC 20006
PH: (202)502-7400
Fax: (202)502-7440
Carr, Peggy G., PhD, Commissioner

Institute for Educational Leadership
[7772]
4301 Connecticut Ave. NW, Ste. 100
Washington, DC 20008-2304
PH: (202)822-8405
Fax: (202)872-4050
Blank, Martin J., President

Institute of Electrical and Electronics
  Engineers USA [6557]
2001 L St. NW, Ste. 700
Washington, DC 20036-4910
PH: (202)785-0017
Fax: (202)785-0835
Eckstein, Peter A., President

Institute for Health Policy Solutions
[15098]
1444 Eye St. NW, Ste. 900
Washington, DC 20005
PH: (202)789-1491
Fax: (202)789-1879
Curtis, Richard E., President

Institute of International Container
  Lessors [836]
1120 Connecticut Ave. NW, Ste. 440
Washington, DC 20036-3946
PH: (202)223-9800
Fax: (202)223-9810
Vernon, Simon, Chairman

Institute of International Finance
[402]
1333 H St. NW, Ste. 800E
Washington, DC 20005-4770
PH: (202)857-3600
Fax: (202)775-1430
Flint, Douglas J., Chairman

Institute for Local Self-Reliance
[11384]
1710 Connecticut Ave. NW, 4th Fl.
Washington, DC 20009

PH: (202)898-1610
Seldman, Neil, President

Institute of Makers of Explosives
[6626]
1120 19th St. NW, Ste. 310
Washington, DC 20036-3605
PH: (202)429-9280
Fax: (202)293-2420
Lopez, Cindy, Office Mgr.

Institute for Palestine Studies [8817]
3501 M St. NW
Washington, DC 20007
PH: (202)342-3990
Fax: (202)342-3927
Mitri, Tarek, Chairman

Institute for Policy Studies [18985]
1301 Connecticut Ave. NW, Ste. 600
Washington, DC 20036
PH: (202)234-9382
Anderson, Sarah, Secretary

Institute for Polyacrylate Absorbents
[720]
1850 M St. NW, Ste. 700
Washington, DC 20036-5810
PH: (202)721-4100
Fax: (202)296-8120
Helmes, Tucker C., PhD, Exec. Dir.

Institute on Religion and Democracy
[18099]
1023 15th St. NW, Ste. 601
Washington, DC 20005-2601
PH: (202)682-4131
    (202)413-5639
Fax: (202)682-4136
Tooley, Dr. Mark, President

Institute for Responsible Housing
  Preservation [5278]
799 9th St., NW Ste. 500
Washington, DC 20001
PH: (202)737-0019
Fax: (202)737-0021
Poulin, Brian, President

Institute for Science and
  International Security [7133]
440 1st St. NW, Ste. 800
Washington, DC 20001
PH: (202)547-3633
Fax: (202)547-3634
Albright, David, Founder, President,
  Chairman

Institute of Scrap Recycling
  Industries [4632]
1615 L St. NW, Ste. 600
Washington, DC 20036-5610
PH: (202)662-8500
Fax: (202)626-0900
Wiener, Robin K., Liaison

Institute of Shortening and Edible
  Oils [2449]
1319 F St. NW, Ste. 600
Washington, DC 20004
PH: (202)783-7960
Fax: (202)393-1367
Collette, Robert L., President

Institute for the Study of Man [5913]
1133 13th St. NW, Ste. C2
Washington, DC 20005
PH: (202)371-2700
Fax: (202)371-1523
Adams, Douglas Q., Editor

Institute on Taxation and Economic
  Policy [18167]
Washington Office
1616 P St. NW, Ste. 200
Washington, DC 20036
PH: (202)299-1066
Fax: (202)299-1065
Johnson, Nicholas, President

Institute of Transportation Engineers
[7348]
1627 Eye St. NW, Ste. 600
Washington, DC 20006
PH: (202)785-0060
Fax: (202)785-0609
Flores, Paula, President

Institute of Turkish Studies [10285]
Georgetown University
Intercultural Ctr. 305R
Washington, DC 20057-1033
PH: (202)687-0292
Fax: (202)687-3780
Erickson, Edward, Treasurer

Institute for War and Peace
  Reporting-U.S. [18653]
729 15th St. NW, Ste. 500
Washington, DC 20005
PH: (202)393-5641

Institute for Women's Policy
  Research [18212]
1200 18th St. NW, Ste. 301
Washington, DC 20036
PH: (202)785-5100
Fax: (202)833-4362
Mullen, Janet, Dir. of Fin. & Admin.

Institute of World Affairs [8119]
1255 23rd St. NW, Ste. 275
Washington, DC 20037
PH: (202)944-2300
Fax: (202)338-1264
Gregorian, Dr. Hrach, President

Instructional Technology Council
[8033]
426 C St. NE
Washington, DC 20002-5839
PH: (202)293-3110
    (202)293-3132
Spalding, Carol, Treasurer

Intellectual Property Owners As-
  sociation [5330]
1501 M St. NW, Ste. 1150
Washington, DC 20005
PH: (202)507-4500
Fax: (202)507-4501
Landacre, Jessica K., Deputy

Intelligent Transportation Society of
  America [3331]
1100 New Jersey Ave. SE, Ste. 850
Washington, DC 20003
PH: (202)484-4847
Toll free: 800-374-8472
Hopper, Regina, President, CEO

Inter-American Commission on Hu-
  man Rights [18411]
1889 F St. NW
Washington, DC 20006-4401
PH: (202)370-9000
Fax: (202)458-3992
Icaza, Emilio Alvarez, Exec. Sec.

Inter-American Commission of
  Women [18213]
17th St. & Constitution Ave. NW
Washington, DC 20006-4499
PH: (202)370-5000
Fax: (202)458-3967
Moreno, Carmen, Exec. Sec.

Inter-American Development Bank
[18151]
1300 New York Ave. NW
Washington, DC 20577
PH: (202)623-1000
Fax: (202)623-3096
Palomino, Norma, Libn., Access
  Svcs.

Inter-American Foundation [19075]
1331 Pennsylvania Ave. NW, Ste.
  1200 N

Washington, DC 20004-1766
PH: (202)360-4530
    (703)306-4301
Fax: (703)306-4365
Kaplan, Robert N., President, CEO

Inter-American Health Alliance
[15022]
PO Box 5518
Washington, DC 20016
Savoie, Brent, Founder, VP of
  Strategic Planning

Inter-American Telecommunication
  Commission [3228]
1889 F St. NW, 6th Fl.
Washington, DC 20006
PH: (202)370-4713
    (202)370-4953
León, Oscar, Exec. Sec.

InterAction [12165]
1400 16th St. NW, Ste. 210
Washington, DC 20036
PH: (202)667-8227
Keny-Guyer, Neal, Chairman

Interfaith Alliance [20542]
1250 24th St. NW, Ste. 300
Washington, DC 20037
PH: (202)466-0567
    (202)466-0520
Garcia, Helio Fred, Chairman

International Action [13329]
PO Box 15188
Washington, DC 20003
PH: (202)488-0735
Fax: (202)488-0736
Mattison, Lindsay, Bd. Member

The International Alliance for Women
[637]
1101 Pennsylvania Ave. NW, 6th Fl.
Washington, DC 20004-2544
Toll free: 888-712-5200
Westaway, Maxine, Exec. Dir.

International Allied Printing Trades
  Association [23441]
6210 N Capitol St. NW
Washington, DC 20011
PH: (202)882-3000
Fax: (202)291-8951
Williams, Edward, Sr., President

International Anticounterfeiting Coali-
  tion [18052]
1730 M St. NW, Ste. 1020
Washington, DC 20036
PH: (202)223-6667
Barchiesi, Robert C., President

International Arts and Artists [8978]
9 Hillyer Ct. NW
Washington, DC 20008
PH: (202)338-0680
Furchgott, David, President

International Association of Airport
  Duty Free Stores [2955]
2025 M St. NW, Ste. 800
Washington, DC 20036-3309
PH: (202)367-1184
Fax: (202)429-5154
Antolick, Steven, Assoc. Dir.

International Association of Black
  Professional Fire Fighters [5206]
1200 G St. NW, Ste. 800
Washington, DC 20005
PH: (202)434-4526
Toll free: 877-213-2170
Fax: (202)434-8707
Hill, James, President

International Association of Bridge,
  Structural, Ornamental and
  Reinforcing Iron Workers [23480]
1750 New York Ave. NW, Ste. 400
Washington, DC 20006

PH: (202)383-4800
Fax: (202)638-4856
Dean, Eric, Gen., President

International Association of Color
Manufacturers [756]
1101 17th St. NW, Ste. 700
Washington, DC 20036
PH: (202)293-5800
Fax: (202)463-8998
Carpenter, David R., Director

International Association of Fire
Fighters [23416]
1750 New York Ave. NW, Ste. 300
Washington, DC 20006-5395
PH: (202)737-8484
Fax: (202)737-8418
Schaitberger, Harold A., President

International Association of Homes
and Services for the Ageing
[10510]
2519 Connecticut Ave. NW
Washington, DC 20008-1520
PH: (202)508-9468
(202)508-9472
Sloan, Katie Smith, Exec. Dir.

International Association for Human
Values [12007]
2401 15th St. NW
Washington, DC 20009
Shankar, Sri Sri Ravi, Founder

International Association of Official
Human Rights Agencies [12045]
444 N Capitol St. NW, Ste. 536
Washington, DC 20001
PH: (202)624-5410
Toma, Robin S., VP

International Association of Political
Consultants [18100]
c/o Goddard Gunster
701 8th St. NW, Ste. 400
Washington, DC 20001
PH: (202)659-4300
Fax: (202)371-1467
Noguera, Felipe, Chairman

International Association of Providers
of AIDS Care [16752]
2200 Pennsylvania Ave., NW, 4th Fl.
E
Washington, DC 20037
PH: (202)507-5899
Fax: (202)315-3651
Zuniga, Jose M., Ph.D,MPH, CEO,
President

International Association of Sheet
Metal, Air, Rail and Transportation
Workers [23481]
1750 New York Ave. NW, 6th Fl.
Washington, DC 20006
PH: (202)783-5880
(202)662-0858
Nigro, Joseph J., President

International Association for the
Study of Forced Migration [9797]
c/o Institute for the Study of
International Migration
Georgetown University
3300 Whitehaven St. NW, Ste. 3100
Washington, DC 20007
PH: (202)687-2258
Fax: (202)687-2541
Banerjee, Paula, President

International Association for the
Study of Organized Crime [11506]
1919 Connecticut Ave. NW
Washington, DC 20009
Melzer, Sharon, Exec. Dir.

International Association for the
Study of Pain [16558]
1510 H St. NW, Ste. 600
Washington, DC 20005-1020

PH: (202)524-5300
Fax: (202)524-5301
Goldberg, Joan R., Exec. Dir. (Actg.)

International Association for Suicide
Prevention [13194]
5221 Washington Ave. NW
Washington, DC 20015
Khan, Dr. Murad, VP

International Association for
Volunteer Effort [13299]
c/o Civil Society Consulting Group
LLC
805 15th St. NW, Ste. 100
Washington, DC 20005
PH: (202)628-4360
Fax: (202)330-4597
Ripley, Mary, Founder, President

International Association of Women
Judges [5387]
1901 L St. NW, Ste. 640
Washington, DC 20036
PH: (202)223-4455
Fax: (202)223-4480
Winship, Ms. Joan, Exec. Dir.

International Biometric Identification
Association [7277]
1090 Vermount Ave. NW, 6th Fl.
Washington, DC 20005
PH: (202)789-4452
Fax: (202)289-7097
Bergman, Christer, Secretary

International Biometric Society
[7243]
1444 I St. NW, Ste. 700
Washington, DC 20005
PH: (202)712-9049
Fax: (202)216-9646
Thompson, Elizabeth, President

International Bridge, Tunnel and
Turnpike Association [5813]
1146 19th St. NW, Ste. 600
Washington, DC 20036
PH: (202)659-4620
Fax: (202)659-0500
Croft, Earl J., III, President

International Brotherhood of Electri-
cal Workers [23413]
900 Seventh St. NW
Washington, DC 20001-3886
PH: (202)833-7000
Fax: (202)728-7676
Hill, Edwin D., President

International Budget Partnership [36]
820 1st St. NE, Ste. 510
Washington, DC 20002
PH: (202)408-1080
Fax: (202)408-8173
Krafchik, Warren, Exec. Dir.

International Campaign for Tibet
[19189]
1825 Jefferson Pl. NW
Washington, DC 20036
PH: (202)785-1515
Fax: (202)785-4343
Gere, Richard, Chairman

International Center for Alcohol Poli-
cies [186]
The Jefferson Bldg., Ste. 500
1225 19th St. NW
Washington, DC 20036
PH: (202)986-1159
Fax: (202)986-2080
Grant, Marcus, President

International Center for Journalists
[2684]
2000 M St., Ste. 250
Washington, DC 20036

PH: (202)737-3700
(202)349-7636
Golden, Michael, Chairman

International Center for Not-for-Profit
Law [5429]
1126 16th St. NW, Ste. 400
Washington, DC 20036-4837
PH: (202)452-8600
Fax: (202)452-8555
Rutzen, Douglas, President

International Center for Research on
Women [18216]
1120 20th St. NW, Ste. 500 N
Washington, DC 20036-3491
PH: (202)797-0007
Fax: (202)797-0020
Warner, Jeanne L., Bd. Member

International Centre for Settlement of
Investment Disputes [4961]
1818 H St. NW
Washington, DC 20433
PH: (202)458-1534
Fax: (202)522-2615
Kinnear, Meg, Sec. Gen.

International Christian Concern
[19985]
2020 Pennsylvania Ave. NW, No.
941
Washington, DC 20006-1846
PH: (301)585-5915
Toll free: 800-ICC-5441
Fax: (301)585-5918
Schnabel, J., Chairman

International City/County Manage-
ment Association [5638]
777 N Capitol St. NE, Ste. 500
Washington, DC 20002-4201
PH: (202)289-4262
Toll free: 800-745-8780
Fax: (202)962-3500
Feldman, Lee, President

International Claim Association
[1877]
1155 15th St. NW, Ste. 500
Washington, DC 20005
PH: (202)452-0143
Fax: (202)530-0659
Grannan, David W., President

International Coalition for Religious
Freedom [19028]
3600 New York Ave. NE, 3rd Fl.
Washington, DC 20002
PH: (202)558-5462
Fefferman, Mr. Dan, President

International Code Council [5068]
500 New Jersey Ave. NW, 6th Fl.
Washington, DC 20001
PH: (202)370-1800
Toll free: 888-422-7233
Fax: (202)783-2348
Olszowy, Alex, III, President

International Commission for Dalit
Rights [18414]
PO Box 11191
Washington, DC 20008
PH: (202)538-1435
Bishwakarma, Dil, President,
Founder

International Committee for Informa-
tion Technology Standards [7278]
Information Technology Industry
Council
1101 K St. NW, Ste. 610
Washington, DC 20005
PH: (202)737-8888
Fax: (202)638-4922
Morris, Patrick, Exec. Dir.

International Committee of the Red
Cross-United States and Canada
[12682]
1100 Connecticut Ave. NW, Ste. 500
Washington, DC 20036
PH: (202)587-4600
Fax: (202)587-4696

International Committee of Sports for
the Deaf [22782]
PO Box 91267
Washington, DC 20090
Fax: (499)255-0436
Valery, Rukhledev, President

International Communication As-
sociation [3230]
1500 21st St. NW
Washington, DC 20036
PH: (202)955-1444
Fax: (202)955-1448
Sawyer, Laura, Exec. Dir.

International Contrast Ultrasound
Society [17539]
East Tower, Ste. 600
1301 K St. NW
Washington, DC 20005
PH: (202)408-6199
Feinstein, Steven B., MD, Co-Pres.

International Cooperative and Mutual
Insurance Federation/Regional As-
sociation for The Americas [1878]
1775 Eye St., NW 8th Fl.
Washington, DC 20006-2402
PH: (202)442-2305
Fax: (202)318-0753
Potter, Mr. Edward, CAE, Director

International Cotton Advisory Com-
mittee [3763]
1629 K St. NW, Ste. 702
Washington, DC 20006-1636
PH: (202)463-6660
Fax: (202)463-6950
Johnson, James, Chairman

International Council on Clean
Transportation [3334]
1225 I St. NW, Ste. 900
Washington, DC 20005
PH: (202)534-1600
Kodjak, Drew, Exec. Dir.

International Council of Grocery
Manufacturer Associations [1339]
1350 I St. NW, Ste. 300
Washington, DC 20005
PH: (202)337-9400
Fax: (202)337-4508
Jack, Maia, Secretary

International Council for Middle East
Studies [18684]
The Old Foundry Bldg., Ste. M100
1055 Thomas Jefferson St. NW
Washington, DC 20007-5219
PH: (212)758-3817
Wallace, Don, Chairman

International Council on Monuments
and Sites - United States National
Committee [9404]
1307 New Hampshire Ave. NW
Washington, DC 20036-1531
PH: (202)463-1291
Fax: (202)463-1299
Comer, Douglas C., V. Chmn. of the
Bd.

International Council of Museums -
U.S. National Committee [9832]
1025 Thomas Jefferson St. NW, Ste.
500 E
Washington, DC 20007
PH: (202)452-1200
Fax: (202)833-3636
Duggal, Elizabeth, Co-Chmn. of the
Bd.

International Council for Small Business [3119]
Funger Hall, Ste. 315
2201 G St. NW
Washington, DC 20052
PH: (202)994-0704
Fax: (202)994-4930
Kim, Dr. Ki-Chan, President

International Crisis Group -
Washington Office [18002]
1629 K St. NW, Ste. 450
Washington, DC 20006
PH: (202)785-1601
Fax: (202)785-1630
Schneider, Mark, Sr. VP

International Dairy Foods Association [975]
1250 H St. NW, Ste. 900
Washington, DC 20005
PH: (202)737-4332
Fax: (202)331-7820
Davis, Jon, Bd. Member

International Development Association [18492]
The World Bank
1818 H St. NW
Washington, DC 20433
PH: (202)473-1000
Fax: (202)477-6391
Kim, Jim Yong, Ph.D, President

International DME Association [5886]
1425 K St. NW, Ste. 350
Washington, DC 20005
PH: (202)587-5760
Taupy, Jean-Alain, Officer

International Downtown Association [640]
910 17th St. NW, Ste. 1050
Washington, DC 20006
PH: (202)204-1385
Fax: (202)393-6869
Downey, David T., CAE, President,
CEO

International Economic Development Council [5297]
734 15th St. NW, Ste. 900
Washington, DC 20005
PH: (202)223-7800
Fax: (202)223-4745
Kitts, Tracy, Chief Adm. Ofc.

International Executive Service Corps. [641]
1900 M St. NW, Ste. 500
Washington, DC 20036
PH: (202)589-2600
Fax: (202)326-0289
Miller, Thomas J., President, CEO

International Federation of Professional and Technical Engineers [6562]
501 3rd St. NW, Ste. 701
Washington, DC 20001
PH: (202)239-4880
Fax: (202)239-4881
Junemann, Gregory J., President

International Finance Corporation [18152]
2121 Pennsylvania Ave. NW
Washington, DC 20433
PH: (202)473-1000
   (202)473-3800
Fax: (202)974-4384
Hua, Jingdong, VP

International Food and Agribusiness Management Association [1342]
1010 Vermont Ave. NW, Ste. 201
Washington, DC 20005

PH: (202)429-1610
Fax: (202)628-9044
Braga, Francesco, CEO

International Food Information Council [1343]
1100 Connecticut Ave. NW, Ste. 430
Washington, DC 20036
PH: (202)296-6540
Reed, Kimberly, JD, CAE, President

International Food Policy Research Institute [18457]
2033 K St. NW
Washington, DC 20006-1002
PH: (202)862-5600
Fax: (202)467-4439
Fan, Shenggen, Dir. Gen.

International Franchise Association [1461]
1900 K St., NW Ste. 700
Washington, DC 20006
PH: (202)628-8000
Fax: (202)628-0812
Taylor, Elizabeth, VP

International Furniture Rental Association [1485]
c/o Alston & Bird LLP
950 F St. NW, 10th Fl.
Washington, DC 20004
PH: (202)239-3818
Fax: (202)654-4818
Anaya, Bill, Exec. Dir.

International Green Energy Council [5887]
1701 Pennsylvania Ave. NW, Ste. 300
Washington, DC 20006
PH: (202)349-7138
Avallone, Ralph, President

International Hajji Baba Society [8867]
1105 D St. SE
Washington, DC 20003-2231
Webb, Kelvin, Treasurer

International Imaging Industry Association [2583]
2001 L St., NW Ste. 700
Washington, DC 20036
PH: (202)371-0101
Toll free: 800-272-6657
Fax: (202)728-9614
Burgess, Angela, Exec. Dir.

International Institute for Strategic Studies - Americas [18945]
2121 K St., Ste. 801
Washington, DC 20037
PH: (202)659-1490
Fax: (202)296-1499
Chipman, John, Dir. Gen., CEO

International Intellectual Property Alliance [5331]
1818 N St. NW, 18th Fl.
Washington, DC 20036
PH: (202)355-7900
Fax: (202)355-7899
Metalitz, Steven J., Counsel

International Joint Commission [4494]
2000 L St. NW, Ste. 615
Washington, DC 20036-4930
PH: (202)736-9000
Fax: (202)632-2006
Bevacqua, Frank, Officer

International Justice Mission [12046]
PO Box 58147
Washington, DC 20037
PH: (703)465-5495
Fax: (703)465-5499
Haugen, Gary A., CEO, President

International Labor Communications Association [2792]
815 16th St. NW
Washington, DC 20006
PH: (202)637-5068
Fax: (202)637-3931
Cummings, Kathy, President

International Labor Rights Forum [18610]
1634 I St. NW, No. 1001
Washington, DC 20006
PH: (202)347-4100
Fax: (202)347-4885
Gearhart, Judy, Exec. Dir.

International Law Institute [5350]
1055 Thomas Jefferson St. NW, Ste. M-100
Washington, DC 20007
PH: (202)247-6006
Fax: (202)247-6010
Wallace, Prof. Don, Jr., Chairman

International Law Students Association [5351]
701 13th St. NW, 6th Fl.
Washington, DC 20005
PH: (202)729-2470
Fax: (202)639-9355
Schneebaum, Steven, Chairman

International League of Conservation Photographers [10139]
1003 K St. NW, Ste. 404
Washington, DC 20001
PH: (202)347-5695
Plummer, Shari Sant, Director

International Microelectronic and Packaging Society [6437]
611 2nd St. NE
Washington, DC 20002-4909
PH: (202)548-4001
   (202)548-8707
Toll free: 888-464-1066
Fax: (202)548-6115
Bell, Ann, Mktg. Mgr., Mgr., Comm.

International Monetary Fund [18153]
700 19th St. NW
Washington, DC 20431
PH: (202)623-7000
Fax: (202)623-4661
Allen, Mark, Director

International Oromo Women's Organization [12047]
PO Box 34144
Washington, DC 20043-4144
Kitila, Dinknesh, Director

International Oxygen Manufacturers Association [1498]
1025 Thomas Jefferson St. NW, Ste. 500 E
Washington, DC 20007
PH: (202)521-9300
Fax: (202)833-3636
Saunders, David A., Exec. Dir.

International Republican Institute USA [18102]
1225 Eye St. NW, Ste. 700
Washington, DC 20005-5962
PH: (202)408-9450
Fax: (202)408-9462
McCain, John, Chairman

International Research and Exchanges Board [8081]
1275 K St. NW, Ste. 600
Washington, DC 20005
PH: (202)628-8188
Fax: (202)628-8189
Evans, Kathy, Officer

International Rights Advocates [18417]
1156 15th St. NW, Ste. 502
Washington, DC 20005

PH: (202)527-7997
Toll free: 866-594-4001
Collingsworth, Terry, Exec. Dir.

International Seafood Sustainability Association [1301]
805 15th St. NW, Ste. 708
Washington, DC 20005
PH: (703)226-8101

International Society for Biosafety Research [6089]
c/o ILSI Research Foundation
1156 15th St. NW, Ste. 200
Washington, DC 20005-1743
Garcia-Alonso, Monica, Secretary

International Stability Operations Association [18796]
2025 M St. NW, Ste. 800
Washington, DC 20036
PH: (202)367-1153
Fax: (202)367-2153
Lariviere, James, Exec. Dir.

International Stevia Council [1347]
750 National Press Bldg.
529 14th St. NW
Washington, DC 20045-1000
PH: (202)591-2467
Scardigli, Ms. Maria Teresa, Exec. Dir.

International Sugar Trade Coalition [3189]
401 9th St. NW, Ste. 640
Washington, DC 20004
PH: (202)531-4028
Johnson, Robert W., II, VP

International Telecommunications Satellite Organization [7314]
4400 Jenifer St. NW, Ste. 332
Washington, DC 20015
PH: (202)243-5096
Fax: (202)243-5018
Toscano, Jose, CEO, Dir. Gen.

International Union of Bricklayers and Allied Craftworkers [23397]
620 F St. NW
Washington, DC 20004
PH: (202)783-3788
Toll free: 888-880-8222
Thompson, Tim, Regional VP

International Union for Conservation of Nature [3888]
1630 Connecticut Ave. NW, 3rd Fl.
Washington, DC 20009
PH: (202)387-4826
Fax: (202)387-4823
Robinson, John, VP

International Union of Operating Engineers [23398]
1125 17th St. NW
Washington, DC 20036
PH: (202)429-9100
Brown, Kuba J., Chairman

International Women's Forum [13380]
2120 L St. NW, Ste. 460
Washington, DC 20037
PH: (202)387-1010
Fax: (202)387-1009
Amin, Shahira, Officer

International Women's Media Foundation [3494]
1625 K St. NW, Ste. 1275
Washington, DC 20006
PH: (202)496-1992
Munoz, Elisa Lees, Exec. Dir.

Internet Alliance [645]
1615 L St. NW, Ste. 1100
Washington, DC 20036-5624

PH: (202)861-2407
(802)279-3534
Cota, Tammy, Exec. Dir.

Internet Commerce Association
[2007]
1155 F St. NW
Washington, DC 20004-1312
PH: (202)255-6172
Johnston, Jeremiah, Bd. Member

Interstate Migrant Education Council
[12340]
1 Massachusetts Ave., Ste. 700
Washington, DC 20001
PH: (202)336-7078
Fax: (202)336-7078
Wiehe, Ms. Nancy, Associate

Interstate Natural Gas Association of
America [4264]
20 F St. NW, Ste. 450
Washington, DC 20001
PH: (202)216-5900
Hoffmann, Richard R., Exec. Dir.

Investment Adviser Association
[3044]
1050 17th St. NW, Ste. 725
Washington, DC 20036-5514
PH: (202)293-4222
Fax: (202)293-4223
Aderton, Alex, Dir. of Mktg.

Investment Company Institute [3045]
1401 H St. NW, Ste. 1200
Washington, DC 20005
PH: (202)326-5800
Beck, Matthew, Contact

Invisible Children [17846]
641 S St. NW
Washington, DC 20001-5196
PH: (619)562-2799
Keesey, Ben, Chmn. of the Bd.

Iota Phi Lambda [23696]
1325 G St. NW, Ste. 500
Washington, DC 20005
PH: (202)462-4682
Fax: (202)234-4682
Dilworth, Stephanie, President

Iran Policy Committee [18576]
Alban Towers
3700 Massachusetts Ave. NW, Ste.
L34
Washington, DC 20016-5807
PH: (202)333-7346
Tanter, Prof. Raymond, Founder,
President

Iranian American Bar Association
[5016]
5185 MacArthur Blvd. NW, Ste. 624
Washington, DC 20016
Babayi, Robert, Founder

Iraq Foundation [12048]
1012 14th St. NW, Ste. 1110
Washington, DC 20005
PH: (202)347-4662
Fax: (202)347-7897
Al-Rahim, Rend, President

Irish American Unity Conference
[18580]
PO Box 55573
Washington, DC 20040
Toll free: 888-295-5077
Burke, Thomas J., President

Irish National Caucus [18581]
PO Box 15128
Washington, DC 20003-0849
PH: (202)544-0568
Fax: (202)488-7537
McManus, Fr. Sean, President,
Founder

Irob Relief and Rehabilitation Operations Brotherhood [12689]
620 Keefer Pl. NW
Washington, DC 20010
Toll free: 877-722-5430

Island Resources Foundation [4495]
1718 P St. NW, Ste. T-4
Washington, DC 20036
PH: (202)265-9712
Fax: (202)232-0748
Potter, Bruce, President

The Israel Project [18585]
2020 K St. NW, Ste. 7600
Washington, DC 20006
PH: (202)857-6644
Fax: (202)540-4567
Myer, Allan A., Chmn. of the Bd.

ISRI [1053]
1615 L St. NW, Ste. 600
Washington, DC 20036-5664
PH: (202)662-8500
Fax: (202)626-0900
Greene, Maryann, Exec. Asst.

ITC Trial Lawyers Association [5826]
Benjamin Franklin Sta.
Washington, DC 20044
Odom, Linda C., President

ITEM Coalition [15099]
1501 M St., NW, 7th Fl.
Washington, DC 20005-1700
PH: (202)446-6550
Fax: (202)785-1756
Rosta, Sara, Coord.

Jack and Jill of America, Inc. [11242]
1930 17th St. NW
Washington, DC 20009
PH: (202)667-7010
Fax: (202)667-6133
Cooper-Nelson, Joli, VP

Jack and Jill Foundation [11243]
1930 17th St. NW
Washington, DC 20009
PH: (202)232-5290
Fax: (202)232-1747
Cooper, Shelley B., President

Jamestown Foundation [18140]
1111 16th St. NW, Ste. 320
Washington, DC 20036
PH: (202)483-8888
Fax: (202)483-8337
de Vogel, Willem, Chairman

Japan-America Society of
Washington, D.C. [9622]
1819 L St. NW, B2
Washington, DC 20036
PH: (202)833-2210
Fax: (202)833-2456
Hitzig, Marc, Exec. Dir.

Japan-America Student Conference
[8082]
International Student Conferences
1211 Connecticut Ave. NW, Ste. 420
Washington, DC 20036
PH: (202)289-9088
Jeon, Danny, Chairperson

Japan Automobile Manufacturers
Association, Washington Office
[324]
1050 17th St. NW, Ste. 410
Washington, DC 20036
PH: (202)296-8537
Fax: (202)872-1212

The Jerusalem Fund | Palestine
Center [8083]
2425 Virginia Ave. NW
Washington, DC 20037

PH: (202)338-1958
Fax: (202)333-7742
Ali, Subhi D., MD, Chairman

Jesuit Association of Student
Personnel Administrators [7429]
1 Dupont Cir. NW, Ste. 405
Washington, DC 20036
Rosenberger, Jeanne, President

Jesuit Conference [19847]
1016 16th St. NW, Ste. 400
Washington, DC 20036
PH: (202)462-0400
Smolich, Fr. Thomas H., SJ,
President

Jesuit Refugee Service/U.S.A.
[12592]
1016 16th St. NW, Ste. 500
Washington, DC 20036
PH: (202)629-5939
Borja, Armando, Director

Jewish Institute for National Security
Affairs [18085]
1101 14th St. NW, Ste. 1110
Washington, DC 20005
PH: (202)667-3900
Fax: (202)667-0601
Steinmann, David P., Chairman

Jewish War Veterans of the United
States of America [21128]
1811 R St. NW
Washington, DC 20009
PH: (202)265-6280
Fax: (202)234-5662
Rosenbleeth, Herb, Exec. Dir.

Jewish Women International [20261]
1129 20th St. NW, Ste. 801
Washington, DC 20036
PH: (202)857-1300
Toll free: 800-343-2823
Fax: (202)857-1380
Weinstein, Loribeth, Exec. Dir.

Jobs With Justice [19258]
1616 P St. NW, Ste. 150
Washington, DC 20036-1427
PH: (202)393-1044
Fax: (202)822-2168
Gupta, Sarita, Exec. Dir.

John F. Kennedy Center for the
Performing Arts - Department of
VSA and Accessibility [11610]
2700 F St. NW
Washington, DC 20566-0002
PH: (202)467-4600
Toll free: 800-444-1324
Rutter, Deborah F., President

Joint Center for Political and
Economic Studies [7047]
2000 H St. NW, Ste. 422
Washington, DC 20052
PH: (202)789-3500
Fax: (202)789-6390
Johnson, Barbara L., Chairman

Joint National Committee for
Languages and the National
Council for Languages and
International Studies [9655]
4646 40th St. NW, No. 310
Washington, DC 20016
PH: (202)580-8684
Rivers, Dr. William P., Exec. Dir.

Jordan Information Bureau [23647]
c/o Embassy of the Hashemite
Kingdom of Jordan
3504 International Dr. NW
Washington, DC 20008
PH: (202)265-1606
Fax: (202)966-3110
Daoud, Dana Zureikat, Director

Jubilee U.S.A. Network [18244]
212 E Capitol St. NE
Washington, DC 20003
PH: (202)783-3566
Fax: (202)546-4468
Okure, Aniedi, Treasurer

Judge Advocates Association [5602]
c/o The Army Navy Club
901 17th St.
Washington, DC 20006
Jenkins, John, Exec. Dir.

Juice Products Association [427]
529 14th St. NW
Washington, DC 20045
PH: (202)591-2438
Freysinger, Carol, Exec. Dir.

JumpStart Coalition for Personal
Financial Literacy [7921]
919 18th St. NW, Ste. 300
Washington, DC 20006
Toll free: 888-45-EDUCATE
Fax: (202)223-0321
Levine, Laura, CEO, President

Junior American Citizens [8795]
1776 D St. NW
Washington, DC 20006-5303
PH: (202)628-1776
Young, Lynn Forney, President

Junta Interamericana de Defensa
[18086]
2600 NW 16th St.
Washington, DC 20441
PH: (202)939-6041
Fax: (202)319-2791
Polastri, Gonzalo Nicolás Ríos,
Chairman

Just Vision [18008]
1616 P St. NW, Ste. 340
Washington, DC 20036
Avni, Ronit, Founder

Justice in Aging [10511]
1444 Eye St. NW, Ste. 1100
Washington, DC 20005
PH: (202)289-6976
Litt, Barrett S., Chmn. of the Bd.

Justice Research and Statistics As-
sociation [11535]
720 7th St. NW, 3rd Fl.
Washington, DC 20001
PH: (202)842-9330
Fax: (202)448-1723
Michel, Nancy, Pub. Dir.

Justice at Stake [19128]
717 D St. NW, Ste. 203
Washington, DC 20004
PH: (202)588-9700
Fax: (202)588-9485
Brandenburg, Bert, Exec. Dir.

KaBOOM! [12506]
4301 Connecticut Ave. NW, Ste.
ML-1
Washington, DC 20008
PH: (202)659-0215
Fax: (202)659-0210
Hammond, Mr. Darrell, Founder

Keeping IDentities Safe [19091]
1300 Pennsylvania Ave. NW, Ste.
880
Washington, DC 20004-3020
PH: (202)312-1540

Kennedy Center Alliance for Arts
Education Network [7513]
John F. Kennedy Center for the
Performing Arts
2700 F St. NW
Washington, DC 20566

PH: (202)416-8843
Toll free: 800-444-1324
Fax: (202)416-4844
Shepherd, Barbara, Director

Robert F. Kennedy Center for
Justice and Human Rights [13455]
1300 19th St. NW, Ste. 750
Washington, DC 20036
PH: (202)463-7575
Fax: (202)463-6606
Kennedy, Kerry, President

Joseph P. and Rose F. Kennedy
Institute of Ethics [11803]
Healy Hall, 4th Fl.
Georgetown University
37th & O Sts. NW
Washington, DC 20057
PH: (202)687-8099
Little, Margaret Olivia, Ph.D., Direc-
tor

Joseph P. Kennedy, Jr. Foundation
[12325]
1133 19th St. NW, 12th Fl.
Washington, DC 20036-3604
PH: (202)393-1250
Eidelman, Steven M., Exec. Dir.

Kid Support [10790]
The Wellness Community
919 18th St. NW
Washington, DC 20006
PH: (202)659-9709
Fax: (202)659-9703
Speltz, Ann, PhD, President,
Founder

Kidney Care Partners [15878]
601 13th St. NW, 11th Fl.
Washington, DC 20005
PH: (703)830-9192
Murdock, Susan, Dir. of Operations,
Dir. of Member Svcs.

Kids Enjoy Exercise Now [14552]
1301 K St. NW, Ste. 600
Washington, DC 20005
Toll free: 866-903-5336
Fax: (866)597-5336
Portnoy, Elliott I., President

Kids in Need of Defense [5535]
1300 L St. NW, Ste. 1100
Washington, DC 20005
PH: (202)824-8680
Smith, Brad, Chairman

Knowledge Alliance [8502]
20 F St. NW, Ste. 700
Washington, DC 20001
PH: (202)507-6370
McLaughlin, Michele, President

Knowledge Ecology International
[7281]
1621 Connecticut Ave. NW, Ste. 500
Washington, DC 20009
PH: (202)332-2670
Fax: (202)332-2673
Love, James, Director

Korea Economic Institute [18601]
1800 K St. NW, Ste. 1010
Washington, DC 20006
PH: (202)464-1982
Fax: (202)464-1987
Manzullo, Donald, President, CEO

Labor Council for Latin American
Advancement [23459]
815 16th St. NW, 4th Fl.
Washington, DC 20006
PH: (202)508-6919
Fax: (202)508-6922
Rosado, Milton, President

Labor Heritage Foundation [8983]
815 16th St. NW
Washington, DC 20006

PH: (202)639-6204
Fax: (202)639-6204
Schniderman, Saul, Director, Chair-
man, Founder

Labor Project for Working Families
[23469]
1101 15th St. NW, Ste., 1212
Washington, DC 20005
PH: (202)288-4762
Joyner, Carolyn, Director

Laborers' International Union of
North America [23399]
905 16th St. NW
Washington, DC 20006
PH: (202)737-8320
Sabitoni, Armand, Treasurer, Tax
Ofc.

Lamaze International [16292]
2025 M St. NW, Ste. 800
Washington, DC 20036-3309
PH: (202)367-1128
Toll free: 800-368-4404
Fax: (202)367-2128
Harmon, Linda L., MPH, CEO, Exec.
Dir.

Land Trust Alliance [3892]
1660 L St. NW, Ste. 1100
Washington, DC 20036
PH: (202)638-4725
Fax: (202)638-4730
Bates, Sylvia, Dir. of Res.

Landscape Architecture Foundation
[5970]
1129 20th St. NW, Ste. 202
Washington, DC 20036
PH: (202)331-7070
Fax: (202)331-7079
Sanders, Lucinda R., FASLA, VP

Laogai Research Foundation
[18422]
1734 20th St. NW
Washington, DC 20009
Wu, Harry, Exec. Dir., Founder

Laotian American National Alliance,
Inc. [19527]
1628 16th St. NW
Washington, DC 20009
PH: (202)370-7841
(415)680-4027
Fax: (202)462-2774
Chanthyasack, Sirch, CEO

Large Public Power Council [5171]
c/o Van Ness Feldman
1050 Thomas Jefferson St. NW, 5th
Fl.
Washington, DC 20007-3877
PH: (202)430-0101
Fax: (843)278-8351
Mandell, Missy, Exec. Dir.

Lasallian Volunteers [20429]
415 Michigan Ave. NE, 3rd Fl.
Washington, DC 20017
PH: (202)529-0047
Fax: (202)529-0775
Wagner, Bro. Jolleen, Director

Latin America Trade Coalition [1985]
1615 H St. NW
Washington, DC 20062-2000
PH: (202)463-5485
Fax: (202)463-3126
Smith-Vaughan, Reuben, Contact

Latin America Working Group
[18621]
2029 P St. NW, Ste. 301
Washington, DC 20036
PH: (202)546-7010
Haugaard, Lisa, Exec. Dir.

Lawyers for Civil Justice [18600]
1140 Connecticut Ave. NW, Ste. 503
Washington, DC 20036
PH: (202)429-0045
Fax: (202)429-6982
Campbell, James, VP

Lawyers' Committee for Civil Rights
Under Law [5537]
1401 New York Ave. NW, Ste. 400
Washington, DC 20005
PH: (202)662-8600
Toll free: 888-299-5227
Fax: (202)783-0857
Joseph, James, Co-Chmn. of the
Bd.

Lawyers' Committee for Cultural
Heritage Preservation [9232]
2600 Virginia Ave. NW, Ste. 1000
Washington, DC 20037
Edelman, Diane Penneys, President

Leadership Conference on Civil and
Human Rights [17906]
1629 K St. NW, 10th Fl.
Washington, DC 20006-1602
PH: (202)466-3311
Fax: (202)466-3434
Henderson, Wade, Esq., CEO,
President

Leadership Conference Education
Fund [17907]
1629 K St. NW, 10th Fl.
Washington, DC 20006
PH: (202)466-3311
(202)466-3434
Henderson, Wade, CEO, President

Leadership Council of Aging
Organizations [10513]
10 G St. NE
Washington, DC 20002
PH: (202)216-8387
Fax: (202)787-3726
Richtman, Max, Chairman

Leading Builders of America [541]
1455 Pennsylvania Ave. NW, Ste.
400
Washington, DC 20004
PH: (202)621-1815
Traylor, Clayton, Officer

LeadingAge [10514]
2519 Connecticut Ave. NW
Washington, DC 20008-1520
PH: (202)783-2242
Fax: (202)783-2255
Elliott, Carol Silver, Secretary

League of American Bicyclists
[22750]
1612 K St. NW, Ste. 308
Washington, DC 20006-2849
PH: (202)822-1333
Clarke, Andy D., President

League of Conservation Voters
[18880]
1920 L St. NW, Ste. 800
Washington, DC 20036-5045
PH: (202)785-8683
Fax: (202)835-0491
Noppen, Trip Van, Treasurer

League of United Latin American
Citizens [19461]
1133 19th St. NW, Ste. 1000
Washington, DC 20036
PH: (202)833-6130
Fax: (202)833-6135
Wilkes, Brent A., Exec. Dir.

League of Women Voters Education
Fund [18988]
1730 M St. NW, Ste. 1000
Washington, DC 20036-4508

PH: (202)429-1965
Fax: (202)429-0854
MacNamara, Elisabeth, President

League of Women Voters of the
United States [18911]
1730 M St. NW, Ste. 1000
Washington, DC 20036-4570
PH: (202)429-1965
Fax: (202)429-0854
MacNamara, Elisabeth, President

Leapfrog Group [15029]
1660 L St. NW, Ste. 308
Washington, DC 20036
PH: (202)292-6713
Fax: (202)292-6813
Binder, Leah, MA, CEO, President

LearnServe International [8538]
PO Box 6203
Washington, DC 20015
PH: (202)370-1865
Fax: (202)355-0993
Rechler, Scott, CEO, Director

Leather Industries of America [2084]
3050 K St. NW, Ste. 400
Washington, DC 20007
PH: (202)342-8497
Fax: (202)342-8583

Lebanese Information Center
[18686]
1101 Pennsylvania Ave. NW, Ste.
600
Washington, DC 20004
PH: (202)505-4542
Fax: (202)318-8409
Gebeily, Joseph, MD, President

Legacies of War [7986]
1312 9th St. NW
Washington, DC 20001
PH: (202)841-7841
Khamvongsa, Channapha, Exec. Dir.

Lesbian and Gay Band Association
[9947]
1718 M St. NW, No. 500
Washington, DC 20036-4504
PH: (202)656-5422
Smith, Betsy, President

Lex Mundi Pro Bono Foundation
[5543]
2001 K St. NW, Ste. 400
Washington, DC 20006-1040
PH: (202)429-1630
(925)962-0115
Anduri, Carl E., Jr., President

Libraries Without Borders [9712]
1875 Connecticut Ave. NW
Washington, DC 20009
Weil, Patrick, Chairman

LIFT [10724]
1620 I St. NW, Ste. 820
Washington, DC 20006
PH: (202)289-1151
Lodal, Kirsten, CEO, Founder

Lighter Association [1571]
5614 Connecticut Ave. NW, No. 292
Washington, DC 20015
PH: (202)253-4347
Fax: (202)330-5092
Baker, David H., Gen. Counsel

Linguistic Society of America [9746]
Archibald A. Hill
522 21st St. NW, Ste. 120
Washington, DC 20006-5012
PH: (202)835-1714
Fax: (202)835-1717
Harris, Alice, President

Links Foundation, Incorporated
[12896]
1200 Massachusetts Ave. NW
Washington, DC 20005-4501

PH: (202)842-8686
Fax: (202)842-4020
Sims, Eris T., Exec. Dir.

Log Cabin Republicans [19038]
1090 Vermont Ave. NW, Ste. 850
Washington, DC 20005
PH: (202)420-7873
Longwell, Sarah, V. Chmn. of the
Bd.

LULAC National Educational Service
Centers [7779]
1133 19th St. NW, Ste. 1000
Washington, DC 20036
PH: (202)835-9646
Fax: (202)835-9685
Roybal, Richard, Exec. Dir.

Lung Cancer Alliance [14004]
1700 K St. NW, Ste. 660
Washington, DC 20006
PH: (202)463-2080
Toll free: 800-298-2436
Ambrose, Laurie Fenton, CEO,
President

Lupus Foundation of America
[15541]
2000 L St. NW, Ste. 410
Washington, DC 20036-4952
Fax: (202)349-1156
Raymond, Sandra C., CEO,
President

Lutheran Services in America
[20312]
100 Maryland Ave. NE, Ste. 500
Washington, DC 20002
PH: (202)499-5836
Toll free: 800-664-3848
Fax: (202)544-0890
Haberaecker, Charlotte, President,
CEO

Lutheran Volunteer Corps [20313]
1226 Vermont Ave. NW
Washington, DC 20005
PH: (202)387-3222
Fax: (202)667-0037
Albright, Bruce, Director

Magis Americas [10726]
1016 16th NW, Ste. 400
Washington, DC 20036
PH: (212)777-8930
Fassett, Edward, Chairman

Maids of Athena [19455]
1909 Q St. NW, Ste. 500
Washington, DC 20009
PH: (202)232-6300
Fax: (202)232-2145
Armstrong, Angela, Mem.

Maktab Tarighat Oveyssi Shahmagh-
soudi [20608]
PO Box 3620
Washington, DC 20027
Toll free: 800-820-2180
Fax: (703)430-6530

MANA, A National Latina Organiza-
tion [18218]
1140 19th St. NW, Ste. 550
Washington, DC 20036
PH: (202)525-5113
Padilla, Veronica, Bd. Member

Managed Funds Association [2028]
600 14th St. NW, Ste. 900
Washington, DC 20005
PH: (202)730-2600
Haley, David C., President

Management Assistance Group
[12403]
1155 F St. NW, Ste. 1050
Washington, DC 20004

PH: (202)659-1963
Fax: (866)403-6080
Plati, Crystal, Chmn. of the Bd.

MarbleRoad [15152]
PO Box 34176
Washington, DC 20043-4176
PH: (415)562-7253
Liebers, Howard, Founder, CEO

March for Life Education and
Defense Fund [19061]
1317 8th St. NW
Washington, DC 20001
PH: (202)234-3300
Fax: (202)234-3350
Monahan, Jeanne F., President

Marijuana Policy Project [18647]
PO Box 77492
Washington, DC 20013
PH: (202)462-5747
Kampia, Rob, Exec. Dir.

Marine Board [6802]
c/o Transportation Research Board
500 5th St. NW
Washington, DC 20001
Card, Vice Adm. James C., Chairman

Marine Engineers' Beneficial As-
sociation [6803]
444 N Capitol St. NW, Ste. 800
Washington, DC 20001-1570
PH: (202)257-2825
Fax: (202)638-5369
Ainley, Marshall, President

Marine Fish Conservation Network
[3898]
Washington, DC
Tinning, Matt, Exec. Dir.

Marine Technology Society [6804]
1100 H St. NW, Ste. LL100
Washington, DC 20005
PH: (202)717-8705
Fax: (202)347-4302
Lawson, Richard, Exec. Dir., Director

Marketing Research Association
[2291]
1156 15th St. NW, Ste. 302
Washington, DC 20005
PH: (202)800-2545
Toll free: 888-512-1050
Fax: (888)512-1050
Brownell, Larry, CEO

Mathematical Association of America
[6823]
1529 18th St. NW
Washington, DC 20036-1358
PH: (202)387-5200
Toll free: 800-741-9415
Fax: (202)265-2384
Faires, Barbara, Secretary

Mauritius-U.S. Business Association,
Inc. [1986]
401 9th St. NW, Ste. 640
Washington, DC 20004
PH: (202)531-4028
Ryberg, Paul, President

Meat Import Council of America
[2310]
1150 Connecticut Ave. NW, 12th Fl.
Washington, DC 20036
PH: (703)522-1910
Fax: (703)524-6039

Medicaid-CHIP State Dental As-
sociation [14455]
4411 Connecticut Ave. NW, No. 104
Washington, DC 20008
PH: (202)248-3993
Fax: (202)248-2315
Foley, Mary E., Exec. Dir.

Medicaid Health Plans of America
[15100]
1150 18th St. NW, Ste. 1010
Washington, DC 20036
PH: (202)857-5720
Fax: (202)857-5731
Myers, Jeff, President, CEO

Medical Device Manufacturers As-
sociation [3029]
1333 H St. NW, Ste. 400 W
Washington, DC 20005
PH: (202)354-7171
Leahey, Mark B., CEO, President

Medicine for Peace [17006]
2732 Unicorn Ln. NW
Washington, DC 20015
PH: (202)441-4545
Fax: (301)571-0769
Viola, Dr. Michael V., Director

Melanoma Research Alliance
[14011]
1101 New York Ave. NW, Ste. 620
Washington, DC 20005
Selig, Wendy K.D., President, CEO

Melanoma Research Foundation
[14012]
1411 K St. NW, Ste. 800
Washington, DC 20005
PH: (202)347-9675
Toll free: 800-673-1290
Fax: (202)347-9678
Turnham, Tim, PhD, Exec. Dir.

Men's Health Network [14946]
PO Box 75972
Washington, DC 20013
PH: (202)543-6461
Henry, Ronald, Founder

Merchants Payment Coalition [2960]
325 7th St. NW, Ste. 1100
Washington, DC 20004
Flagg, Michael, Contact

Merck Childhood Asthma Network,
Inc. [17143]
North Bldg., Ste. 1200
601 Pennsylvania Ave. NW
Washington, DC 20004
PH: (202)326-5200
Malveaux, Floyd J., MD, Exec. VP,
Exec. Dir.

Meridian International Center
[18550]
1630 Crescent Pl. NW
Washington, DC 20009
PH: (202)667-6800
Toll free: 800-424-2974
Fax: (202)667-1475
Holliday, Stuart W., CEO, President

Meridian International Center
Programming Division [18551]
1630 Crescent Pl. NW
Washington, DC 20009
PH: (202)667-6800
Toll free: 800-424-2974
Fax: (202)667-1475
Holliday, Stuart W., CEO, President

Methodist Federation for Social Ac-
tion [20345]
212 E Capitol St. NE
Washington, DC 20003
PH: (202)546-8806
Fax: (202)546-6811
Wright, Rev. Christina, Co-Pres.

mHealth Alliance [15486]
1800 Massachusetts Ave. NW, Ste.
400
Washington, DC 20036
Mechael, Patricia, Exec. Dir.

Middle East Institute [18687]
1761 N St. NW
Washington, DC 20036
PH: (202)785-1141
     (202)785-1141
Fax: (202)331-8861
Chamberlin, Wendy J., President

Middle East Investment Initiative
[1251]
500 Eighth St. NW
Washington, DC 20004
PH: (202)799-4345
Fax: (202)799-5000
Bernhard, Berl, V. Chmn. of the Bd.

Middle East Policy Council [18688]
1730 M St. NW, Ste. 512
Washington, DC 20036
PH: (202)296-6767
Fax: (202)296-5791
Fraker, Hon. Ford M., President

Middle East Research and Informa-
tion Project [18689]
1344 T St. NW, No. 1
Washington, DC 20009
PH: (202)223-3677
Fax: (202)223-3604
Toensing, Chris, Exec. Dir.

Migrant Legal Action Program [5544]
1001 Connecticut Ave. NW, Ste. 915
Washington, DC 20036-5524
PH: (202)775-7780
Fax: (202)775-7784

Miles Value Foundation [6723]
5505 Connecticut Ave. NW, No. 149
Washington, DC 20015-2601
PH: (202)253-5550
Kirk, Stephen J., VP

Military Reporters and Editors [5683]
Medill School of Journalism
1325 G St. NW, Ste. 730
Washington, DC 20005
Preston, Stephen W., Gen. Counsel

Millenium Water Alliance [13330]
1001 Connecticut Ave. NW, Ste. 710
Washington, DC 20036
PH: (202)296-1832
Fax: (202)296-1786
Sparks, John D., Dir. of Comm.

Millennium Institute [18495]
1634 Eye St. NW, Ste. 300
Washington, DC 20006
PH: (202)383-6200
Fax: (202)383-6209
Herren, Dr. Hans R., President

Millennium Water Alliance [13331]
1001 Connecticut Ave. NW, Ste. 710
Washington, DC 20036
PH: (202)296-1832
Fax: (202)296-1786
Callejas, Rafael, Exec. Dir.

Million Mom March [18252]
c/o The Brady Campaign to Prevent
Gun Violence, 840 First St. NE,
Ste. 400
840 1st St. NE, Ste. 400
Washington, DC 20002
PH: (202)370-8100
Pletcher, Valerie Mullen, Chief Dev.
Ofc.

Milton S. Eisenhower Foundation
[11508]
1875 Connecticut Ave. NW, Ste. 410
Washington, DC 20009
PH: (202)234-8104
Fax: (202)234-8484
Austin, Charles P., Sr., Chairman

Minority Corporate Counsel Association [5110]
1111 Pennsylvania Ave. NW
Washington, DC 20004

PH: (202)739-5901
Fax: (202)739-5999
Lee, Jean, President, CEO

Mission: Readiness [5756]
1212 New York Ave. NW, Ste. 300
Washington, DC 20005
PH: (202)464-5224
Fax: (202)464-5357
Dawson Taggart, Amy, Director

Modification and Replacement Parts
Association [173]
2233 Wisconsin Ave., NW, Ste. 503
Washington, DC 20007
PH: (202)628-6777
Fax: (202)628-8948
Dickstein, Jason, President

William Morris Society in the United
States [9082]
PO Box 53263
Washington, DC 20009
Frederick, Margaretta, Secretary

Mortgage Bankers Association [405]
1919 M St. NW, 5th Fl.
Washington, DC 20036
PH: (202)557-2700
Toll free: 800-793-6222
Davies, Marcia, COO

Motion Picture Association of
America, Inc. [1199]
1600 Eye St. NW
Washington, DC 20006
PH: (202)293-1966
Fax: (202)296-7410
Dodd, Christopher J., CEO, Chairman

Motorcycle Riders Foundation
[22230]
1325 G St. NW, Ste. 500
Washington, DC 20005
PH: (202)546-0983
Fax: (202)546-0986
Korte, Paulette, Secretary

Mountain Institute [9329]
3000 Connecticut Ave. NW, Ste. 101
Washington, DC 20008
PH: (202)234-4050
Fax: (202)234-4054
Taber, Andrew, Exec. Dir.

MultiState Tax Commission [5796]
444 N Capitol St. NW, Ste. 425
Washington, DC 20001
PH: (202)650-0300
Jackson, Rich, V. Chmn. of the Bd.

Municipal Waste Management As-
sociation [5845]
United States Conference of Mayors
1620 Eye St. NW
Washington, DC 20006
Gonaver, Chris, President

Museum Education Roundtable
[9835]
PO Box 15727
Washington, DC 20003
Evans, Brooke DiGiovanni, President

Museum Small Craft Association
[9836]
Heritage Documentation Programs
US National Park Service
1849 C St. NW
Washington, DC 20240
PH: (202)208-6843

NAEM [4082]
1612 K St. NW, Ste. 1002
Washington, DC 20006-2843
PH: (202)986-6616
Toll free: 800-391-NAEM
Fax: (202)530-4408
Neuvelt, Carol Singer, Mem.

NAFSA: Association of International
Educators [7934]
1307 New York Ave. NW, 8th Fl.
Washington, DC 20005-4701
PH: (202)737-3699
Fax: (202)737-3657
Aw, Fanta, President, Chmn. of the
Bd.

NAHB Leading Suppliers Council
[549]
1201 15th St. NW
Washington, DC 20005
PH: (202)266-8247
McLarty, Christopher, Contact

NAHB Log Homes and Timber
Council [2200]
1201 15th St. NW
Washington, DC 20005
Toll free: 800-368-5242
Fax: (202)266-8400
Parsons, Doug, Chairman

NARAL Pro-Choice America [19034]
1156 15th St. NW, Ste. 700
Washington, DC 20005
PH: (202)973-3000
(202)973-3032
Fax: (202)973-3096
Bruce, Sasha, Sr. VP

NASPA - Student Affairs Administra-
tors in Higher Education [7431]
111 K St. NE, 10th Fl.
Washington, DC 20002
PH: (202)265-7500
Kruger, Kevin, President

National Abortion Federation [10431]
1660 L St. NW, Ste. 450
Washington, DC 20036
PH: (202)667-5881
Toll free: 800-772-9100
Fax: (202)667-5890
Saporta, Vicki, CEO, President

National Abstinence Education As-
sociation [8564]
1701 Pennsylvania Ave. NW, Ste.
300
Washington, DC 20006
PH: (202)248-5420
Toll free: 866-935-4850
Huber, Valerie, President, CEO

The National Academies | National
Research Council [7139]
500 5th St. NW
Washington, DC 20001
PH: (202)334-2000
McNutt, Marcia K., President

The National Academies of Sci-
ences, Engineering, Medicine |
Division on Earth and Life Studies
| Institute for Laboratory Animal
Research [13719]
500 5th St. NW
Washington, DC 20001
PH: (202)334-2590
Fax: (202)334-1687
Sharples, Fran, PhD, Dir. (Actg.)

National Academies of Sciences,
Engineering, and Medicine | Divi-
sion on Engineering and Physical
Sciences | Space Studies Board
[7220]
500 5th St. NW
Washington, DC 20001
PH: (202)334-3477
Fax: (202)334-3701
Moloney, Michael, Director

National Academies of Sciences,
Engineering, and Medicine |
Institute of Medicine [15737]
500 5th St. NW
Washington, DC 20001

PH: (202)334-2352
Fax: (202)334-1694
Behney, Clyde J., Exec. Dir.

National Academy of Clinical
Biochemistry [13813]
American Association for Clinical
Chemistry
900 7th St. NW, Ste. 400
Washington, DC 20001
PH: (202)857-0717
Toll free: 800-892-1400
Fax: (202)887-5093
Langman, Loralie, PhD, FACB,
President

National Academy of Education
[7783]
500 5th St. NW
Washington, DC 20001
White, Gregory, Exec. Dir.

National Academy of Engineering
[6572]
500 5th St. NW
Washington, DC 20001
PH: (202)334-3200
Fax: (202)334-2290
Romig, Alton D., Jr., Exec. Ofc.

National Academy of Public
Administration [5696]
1600 K St. NW, Ste. 400
Washington, DC 20006
PH: (202)347-3190
Fax: (202)223-0823
Blair, Dan G., President, CEO

National Academy of Sciences
National Research Council |
Transportation Research Board
[7350]
The National Academies, 500 Fifth
St. NW
500 5th St. NW
Washington, DC 20001-2736
PH: (202)334-2934
(202)334-2000
Pedersen, Neil, Exec. Dir.

National Academy of Social Insur-
ance [19136]
1200 New Hampshire Ave. NW, Ste.
830
Washington, DC 20036
PH: (202)452-8097
Fax: (202)452-8111
Arnone, William J., Chmn. of the Bd.

National Action Alliance for Suicide
Prevention [13195]
1025 Thomas Jefferson St. NW, Ste.
700
Washington, DC 20007
PH: (202)572-3784
Litts, David, OD, Exec. Sec.

National Adult Education Profes-
sional Development Consortium
[7455]
c/o Lennox McLendon, Executive
Director
444 N Capitol St. NW, Ste. 422
Washington, DC 20001
PH: (202)624-5250
Fax: (202)624-1497
McLendon, Dr. Lennox L., Exec. Dir.

National Aeronautic Association
[145]
Reagan Washington National Airport
Hangar 7, Ste. 202
Washington, DC 20001-6015
PH: (703)416-4888
Toll free: 800-644-9777
Fax: (703)416-4877
Gaffney, Jonathan, President, CEO

National African American Drug
Policy Coalition [13158]
2900 Van Ness St. NW
Washington, DC 20008

PH: (202)577-8365
Price, Winston, MD, President,
Chairman

National African-American Insurance
Association [1886]
1718 M St. NW
Washington, DC 20036-4504
Toll free: 866-56-NAAIA
Fax: (513)563-9743
Redd, Margaret, Exec. Dir.

National AIDS Housing Coalition
[11976]
727 15th St. NW, 11th Fl.
Washington, DC 20005
PH: (202)347-0333
Fax: (202)347-3411
Bennett, Russell, Exec. Dir.

National Air Disaster Alliance
[17821]
2020 Pennsylvania Ave., No. 315
Washington, DC 20006-1846
Toll free: 888-444-6232
Fax: (336)643-1394
Ziemkiewicz, Matt, President

National Air Traffic Controllers As-
sociation [23389]
1325 Massachusetts Ave. NW
Washington, DC 20005
PH: (202)628-5451
Toll free: 800-266-0895
Fax: (202)628-5767
Rinaldi, Paul, President

National Air Transportation Associa-
tion [147]
818 Connecticut Ave. NW, Ste. 900
Washington, DC 20006
PH: (202)774-1535
Toll free: 800-808-6282
Fax: (202)452-0837
Priester, Andy, Chairman

National Alliance of Black School
Educators [8649]
310 Pennsylvania Ave. SE
Washington, DC 20003
PH: (202)608-6310
Toll free: 800-221-2654
Fax: (202)608-6319
English, Marietta, President

National Alliance of Community
Economic Development Associa-
tions [18154]
1660 L St. NW, Ste. 306
Washington, DC 20036
PH: (202)518-2660
Woodruff, Frank, Exec. Dir.

National Alliance to End Homeless-
ness [11955]
1518 K St. NW, 2nd Fl.
Washington, DC 20005
PH: (202)638-1526
Fax: (202)638-4664
Roman, Nan, CEO, President

National Alliance for Fair Contracting
[23400]
905 16th St. NW
Washington, DC 20006-1703
Toll free: 866-523-6232
Fax: (202)942-2228
Davis, Rocco, Chairman

National Alliance of Forest Owners
[4208]
122 C St. NW, Ste. 630
Washington, DC 20001
PH: (202)747-0750
Fax: (202)824-0770
Murray, William, VP

National Alliance for Hispanic Health
[13072]
1501 16th St. NW
Washington, DC 20036-1401

PH: (202)387-5000
Delgado, Dr. Jane L., President,
CEO

**National Alliance of Postal and
Federal Employees [23505]**
1628 11th St. NW
Washington, DC 20001-5008
PH: (202)939-6325
Fax: (202)939-6392
McGee, James M., President

**National Alliance for Prisoners'
Rights [18430]**
Penal Reform International
2100 M St. NW, Ste. 170-350
Washington, DC 20037
Spikes, Bonnita, Director

**National Alliance for Public Charter
Schools [8477]**
1101 15th St. NW, Ste. 1010
Washington, DC 20005
PH: (202)289-2700
Rees, Nina, President, CEO

**National Alliance of Sentencing
Advocates and Mitigation Specialists [5138]**
c/o Edwin A. Burnette
1140 Connecticut Ave. NW, Ste. 900
Washington, DC 20036
PH: (202)452-0620
James-Townes, Lori, MSW, Chairman

**National Alliance of State and Ter-
ritorial AIDS Directors [10547]**
444 N Capitol St. NW, Ste. 339
Washington, DC 20001
PH: (202)434-8090
Fax: (202)434-8092
Gorman, Christelle, Exec. Asst.

**National American Indian Housing
Council [5279]**
900 2nd St. NE, Ste. 107
Washington, DC 20002
PH: (202)789-1754
Toll free: 800-284-9165
Fax: (202)789-1758
Silas, Pamala M., Exec. Dir.

**National Architectural Accrediting
Board [7500]**
1101 Connecticut Ave. NW, Ste. 410
Washington, DC 20036
PH: (202)783-2007
Fax: (202)783-2822
Rutledge, Andrea S., CAE, Exec.
Dir.

**National Asian Pacific American Bar
Association [5434]**
1612 K St. NW, Ste. 1400
Washington, DC 20006
PH: (202)775-9555
Fax: (202)775-9333
Matsuoka, Tina R., Exec. Dir.

**National Asian Peace Officers' As-
sociation [5485]**
1776 I St. NW, Ste. 900
Washington, DC 20006
PH: (202)632-5384
Fax: (202)756-1301
Ng, Sgt. James, President

**National Assembly of State Arts
Agencies [8988]**
1200 18th St. NW, Ste. 1100
Washington, DC 20036
PH: (202)347-6352
Fax: (202)737-0526
Gibbs, Gary, President

**National Association for the
Advancement of Orthotics and
Prosthetics [16496]**
1501 M St. NW, 7th Fl.
Washington, DC 20005-1700

PH: (202)624-0064
Toll free: 800-622-6740
Fax: (202)785-1756
Breece, George W., Exec. Dir.

**National Association of Affordable
Housing Lenders [407]**
1667 K St. NW, Ste. 210
Washington, DC 20006
PH: (202)293-9850
Fax: (202)293-9852
Haaland, Paul, COO

**National Association for Alternative
Certification [7853]**
PO Box 5750
Washington, DC 20016
PH: (202)277-3600
Fax: (202)403-3545
Corcillo, Judy, Exec. Dir.

**National Association of Area Agen-
cies on Aging [10518]**
1730 Rhode Island Ave. NW, Ste.
1200
Washington, DC 20036
PH: (202)872-0888
Fax: (202)872-0057
Markwood, Sandy, CEO

**National Association of Attorneys
General [5776]**
2030 M St. NW, 8th Fl.
Washington, DC 20036
PH: (202)326-6000
Jackley, Marty, President

**National Association of Beverage
Importers Inc. [187]**
National Press Bldg.
529 14th St. NW, Ste. 1183
Washington, DC 20045
PH: (202)393-6224
Toll free: 877-393-6224
Fax: (202)393-6595
Earle, William T., President

**National Association for Biomedical
Research [13720]**
1100 Vermont Ave. NW, Ste. 1100
Washington, DC 20006-2733
PH: (202)857-0540
Fax: (202)659-1902
Bailey, Matthew R., Exec. VP

**National Association of Black County
Officials [5112]**
25 Massachusetts Ave. NW, Ste.
500
Washington, DC 20001
PH: (202)350-6696
Williams, Arlanda J., Treasurer

**National Association of Black Owned
Broadcasters [469]**
1201 Connecticut Ave. NW, Ste. 200
Washington, DC 20036
PH: (202)463-8970
Fax: (202)429-0657
Carter, Michael L., VP

**National Association of Black Scuba
Divers [23362]**
PO Box 91630
Washington, DC 20090
Toll free: 800-521-NABS
Dooley, Jeffrey, President

**National Association of Black Social
Workers [13111]**
2305 Martin Luther King, Jr. Ave. SE
Washington, DC 20020-5813
PH: (202)678-4570
Fax: (202)678-4572
Benton, Joe, Mem.

**National Association of Bond
Lawyers [5437]**
601 13th St. NW, Ste. 800 S
Washington, DC 20005-3807

PH: (202)503-3300
Fax: (202)637-0217
MacLennan, Alexandra M., Treasurer

**National Association Broadcast
Employees and Technicians
[23396]**
501 3rd St. NW
Washington, DC 20001
PH: (202)434-1254
Fax: (202)434-1426
Braico, Charlie, President

**National Association of Broadcasters
[470]**
1771 N St. NW
Washington, DC 20036
PH: (202)429-5300
(202)429-5490
Smith, Gordon H., President, CEO

**National Association for Business
Economics [6396]**
1920 L St. NW, Ste. 300
Washington, DC 20036
PH: (202)463-6223
Fax: (202)463-6239
Beers, Tom, Exec. Dir.

**National Association of Business
Political Action Committees
[18872]**
101 Constitution Ave. NW, Ste.
L-110
Washington, DC 20001-2115
PH: (202)341-3780
Fax: (202)478-0342
Reiter, Scott, President

**National Association of Catholic
Youth Ministry Leaders [19867]**
415 Michigan Ave. NE, Ste. 40
Washington, DC 20017
PH: (202)636-3825
Fax: (202)526-7544
McCorquodale, Charlotte, Chairman

**National Association for Children's
Behavioral Health [16833]**
1025 Connecticut Ave. NW, Ste.
1012
Washington, DC 20036-5417
PH: (202)857-9735
Fax: (202)362-5145
Johnston, Pat, Exec. Dir.

**National Association of Clean Air
Agencies [5183]**
444 N Capitol St. NW, Ste. 307
Washington, DC 20001
PH: (202)624-7864
Fax: (202)624-7863
Kruger, Nancy, Dep. Dir.

**National Association of Clean Water
Agencies [5735]**
1816 Jefferson Pl. NW
Washington, DC 20036
PH: (202)833-2672
Fax: (888)267-9505
Marshall, Raymond J., VP

**National Association of College and
University Attorneys [5163]**
1 Dupont Cir., Ste. 620
Washington, DC 20036
PH: (202)833-8390
Fax: (202)296-8379
Parsons, Paul L., Dep. Chief

**National Association of College and
University Business Officers [7432]**
1110 Vermont Ave. NW, Ste. 800
Washington, DC 20005
PH: (202)861-2500
(202)861-2517
Toll free: 800-462-4916
Fax: (202)861-2583
Walda, John, CEO, President

**National Association of Colored
Women's Clubs [12898]**
1601 R St. NW
Washington, DC 20009
PH: (202)667-4080
Fax: (202)667-2574
Hansbury, Vivien, Chairwoman

**National Association of Conservation
Districts [3901]**
509 Capitol Ct. NE
Washington, DC 20002
PH: (202)547-6223
Fax: (202)547-6450
Larson, John, CEO

**National Association of Consumer
Advocates [18053]**
1215 17th St. NW, 5th Fl.
Washington, DC 20036-3021
PH: (202)452-1989
Fax: (202)452-0099
Bardo, Stacy, Co-Chmn. of the Bd.

**National Association of Consumer
Bankruptcy Attorneys [5028]**
2200 Pennsylvania Ave. NW, 4th Fl.
Washington, DC 20037
Toll free: 800-499-9040
Fax: (866)408-9515
LaBert, Dan, Exec. Dir.

**National Association of Corporate
Directors [2183]**
2001 Pennsylvania Ave. NW, Ste.
500
Washington, DC 20006
PH: (202)775-0509
Fax: (202)775-4857
Daly, Kenneth, CEO

**National Association of Councils on
Developmental Disabilities [12328]**
1825 K St. NW, Ste. 600
Washington, DC 20006
PH: (202)506-5813
Mantonya, Claire, MA, President

**National Association of Counties
[5113]**
25 Massachusetts Ave. NW, Ste.
500
Washington, DC 20001
PH: (202)393-6226
Toll free: 888-407-6226
Fax: (202)393-2630
Clark, Sallie, President

**National Association of County
Behavioral Health and
Developmental Disability Directors
[15127]**
25 Massachusetts Ave. NW, Ste.
500
Washington, DC 20001
PH: (202)661-8816
Fax: (202)478-1659
Evans, Leon, Bd. Member

**National Association of County and
City Health Officials [5717]**
1100 17th St. NW, 7th Fl.
Washington, DC 20036
PH: (202)783-5550
Fax: (202)783-1583
Hasbrouck, LaMar, Exec. Dir.

**National Association for County
Community and Economic
Development [17986]**
2025 M St. NW, Ste. 800
Washington, DC 20036-3309
PH: (202)367-1149
Fax: (202)367-2149
Agliata, Tony, President

**National Association of County
Engineers [6573]**
25 Massachusetts Ave. NW, Ste.
580

Washington, DC 20001
PH: (202)393-5041
Fax: (202)393-2630
Roberts, Brian C., Exec. Dir.

National Association of County
Veterans Service Officers **[21130]**
25 Massachusetts Ave. NW, Ste.
500
Washington, DC 20001
Golgart, Jim, President

National Association of Criminal
Defense Lawyers **[5150]**
1660 L St. NW, 12th Fl.
Washington, DC 20036
PH: (202)872-8600
Fax: (202)872-8690
Adams, Chris, Director

National Association of Dealer
Counsel **[299]**
1800 M St. NW, Ste. 400 S
Washington, DC 20036
PH: (202)293-1454
Fax: (202)530-0659
Tasini, Oren, Officer

National Association of Development
Companies **[2092]**
1725 Desales St. NW, Ste. 504
Washington, DC 20036
PH: (202)349-0070
Fax: (202)349-0071
Mansfield, Mary, Chairperson

National Association of Development
Organizations **[11408]**
400 N Capitol St. NW, Ste. 390
Washington, DC 20001
PH: (202)624-7806
Fax: (202)624-8813
McKinney, Joe, Exec. Dir.

National Association of Development
Organizations Research Founda-
tion **[17987]**
400 N Capitol St. NW, Ste. 390
Washington, DC 20001
PH: (202)624-7806
Fax: (202)624-8813
McKinney, Joe, Exec. Dir.

National Association of Disability
Representatives **[19137]**
PO Box 96503
Washington, DC 20090-6503
PH: (202)822-2155
Fax: (972)245-6701
Sirman, Eva, Mgr.

National Association for the Educa-
tion of Young Children **[7592]**
1313 L St. NW, Ste. 500
Washington, DC 20005
PH: (202)232-8777
Toll free: 800-424-2460
Fax: (202)328-1846
Allvin, Rhian Evans, Exec. Dir.

National Association of Energy
Service Companies **[6496]**
1615 M St. NW, Ste. 800
Washington, DC 20036
PH: (202)822-0950
Fax: (202)822-0955
McGinnis, Charles, Secretary

National Association of Enrolled
Agents **[5798]**
1730 Rhode Island Ave., NW, Ste.
400
Washington, DC 20036-3953
PH: (202)822-6232
Toll free: 855-880-6232
Fax: (202)822-6270
Ziegler, Laurie, Secretary, Treasurer

National Association for Equal Op-
portunity in Higher Education
[7637]
209 3rd St. SE
Washington, DC 20003
PH: (202)552-3300
Fax: (202)552-3330
Baskerville, Dr. Lezli, CEO,
President

National Association of Evangelicals
[20156]
PO Box 23269
Washington, DC 20026
PH: (202)479-0815
Taylor, L. Roy, Bd. Member

National Association of Federal
Veterinarians **[17654]**
1910 Sunderland Pl. NW
Washington, DC 20036-1608
PH: (202)223-4878
Angel, Dr. Ken, President

National Association of Federally
Impacted Schools **[7835]**
444 N Capitol St. NW, Ste. 419
Washington, DC 20001
PH: (202)624-5455
Fax: (202)624-5468
Doebert, Sandra, President

National Association for Fixed Annui-
ties **[1891]**
1155 F St. NW, Ste. 1050
Washington, DC 20004
PH: (414)332-9306
Fax: (888)946-3532
O'Brien, Kim, MBA, President, CEO

National Association of Flood and
Stormwater Management Agencies
[5654]
PO Box 56764
Washington, DC 20040
PH: (202)289-8625
Fax: (202)530-3389
Williams, Dusty, President

National Association of Foreign-
Trade Zones **[1988]**
National Press Bldg.
529 14th St. NW, Ste. 1071
Washington, DC 20045
PH: (202)331-1950
Fax: (202)331-1994
Williams, Rebecca, Treasurer

National Association for Gifted
Children **[7943]**
1331 H St. NW, Ste. 1001
Washington, DC 20005
PH: (202)785-4268
Fax: (202)785-4248
Betts, George, President

National Association of Government
Archives and Records Administra-
tors **[5305]**
444 N Capitol St. NW, Ste. 237
Washington, DC 20001
PH: (202)508-3800
Fax: (202)508-3801
Swift, Pari, President

National Association of Graduate-
Professional Students **[8622]**
1050 K St. NW, No. 400
Washington, DC 20001-4448
PH: (202)643-8043
Johnson, M. Scout, VP

National Association of Health
Services Executives **[14950]**
1050 Connecticut Ave. NW, 10th Fl.
Washington, DC 20036
PH: (202)772-1030
Fax: (202)772-1072
Garland, Tracy, Secretary

National Association of Health
Underwriters **[1893]**
1212 New York Ave. NW, Ste. 1100
Washington, DC 20005
PH: (202)552-5060
Fax: (202)747-6820
Trautwein, Janet, CEO, Exec. VP

National Association of Healthcare
Access Management **[15332]**
2025 M St. NW, Ste. 800
Washington, DC 20036-2422
PH: (202)367-1125
Fax: (202)367-2125
Kemp, Steven C., CAE

National Association of Hispanic
Federal Executives **[5198]**
PO Box 23270
Washington, DC 20026
PH: (202)315-3942
Gallegos, Mr. Al, President

National Association of Hispanic
Journalists **[2694]**
1050 Connecticut Ave. NW, 5th Fl.
Washington, DC 20036
PH: (202)853-7700
Fax: (202)662-7144
Mendoza, Alberto B., Exec. Dir.

National Association of Hispanic
Publications, Inc. **[2803]**
National Press Bldg.
529 14th St. NW, Ste. 923
Washington, DC 20045
PH: (202)662-7250
Bush, Robert D., Secretary

National Association of Home Build-
ers **[554]**
1201 15th St. NW
Washington, DC 20005
Toll free: 800-268-5242
Woods, Tom, Chmn. of the Bd.

National Association for Home Care
and Hospice **[15280]**
228 7th St. SE
Washington, DC 20003
PH: (202)547-7424
Fax: (202)547-3540
Devoti, Andrea, Chairperson

National Association of Housing
Cooperatives **[11977]**
1444 I St. NW, Ste. 700
Washington, DC 20005-6542
PH: (202)737-0797
Fax: (202)216-9646
Wilder, Ruthie, Director

National Association of Housing and
Redevelopment Officials **[5280]**
630 Eye St. NW
Washington, DC 20001-3736
PH: (202)289-3500
Toll free: 877-866-2476
Fax: (202)289-8181
Ramirez, Saul N., Jr., CEO

National Association of Independent
Colleges and Universities **[8012]**
1025 Connecticut Ave. NW, Ste. 700
Washington, DC 20036
PH: (202)785-8866
Fax: (202)835-0003
Warren, Dr. David L., President

National Association of Independent
Schools **[8013]**
1129 20th St. NW, Ste. 800
Washington, DC 20036-3425
PH: (202)973-9700
Fax: (888)316-3862
McGovern, Myra, Officer

National Association of Japan-
America Societies **[19511]**
1819 L St. NW, Ste. 800
Washington, DC 20036

PH: (202)429-5545
Fax: (202)429-0027
Kelley, Mr. Peter, President

National Association for Law Place-
ment **[8217]**
1220 19th St. NW, Ste. 401
Washington, DC 20036-2405
PH: (202)835-1001
Fax: (202)835-1112
Quirk, Lisa, Dir. of MIS

National Association of Law
Students With Disabilities **[8218]**
Washington, DC
Ruvalcaba, Jovan, President

National Association of Letter Carri-
ers **[23506]**
100 Indiana Ave. NW
Washington, DC 20001-2144
PH: (202)393-4695
Rolando, Fredric V., President

National Association of Local
Government Environmental Profes-
sionals **[5640]**
1001 Connecticut Ave., Ste. 405
Washington, DC 20036
PH: (202)337-4503
Fax: (202)429-5290
Brown, Ken, Exec. Dir.

National Association of Local Hous-
ing Finance Agencies **[5281]**
2025 M St. NW, Ste. 800
Washington, DC 20036
PH: (202)367-1197
Williams, Ron, President

National Association Long Term
Care Administrator Boards **[16197]**
1444 I St. NW
Washington, DC 20005-6542
PH: (202)712-9040
Lindner, Randy, President, CEO

National Association of Manufactur-
ers **[2227]**
733 10th St. NW, Ste. 700
Washington, DC 20001
PH: (202)637-3000
Toll free: 800-814-8468
Fax: (202)637-3182
Andringa, Mary Vermeer, Exec. Ofc.

National Association of Margarine
Manufacturers **[2451]**
1156 15th St. NW, Ste. 900
Washington, DC 20005
PH: (202)785-3232

National Association of Medicaid
Directors **[15102]**
444 N Capitol St. NW, Ste. 524
Washington, DC 20001
PH: (202)403-8620
Salo, Matt, Exec. Dir.

National Association Medical Staff
Services **[15588]**
2025 M St. NW, Ste. 800
Washington, DC 20036
PH: (202)367-1196
Fax: (202)367-2196
Boyd, Lynn, Exec. Dir.

National Association of Minority
Contractors **[878]**
The Barr Bldg.
910 17th St. NW, Ste. 413
Washington, DC 20006
PH: (202)296-1600
Fax: (202)296-1644
Stemley, Wendell, President

National Association of Minority
Government Contractors **[879]**
PO Box 44609
Washington, DC 20026
Roberts, Alpha, Founder, President

National Association of Mortgage
Processors [409]
1250 Connecticut Ave. NW, Ste. 200
Washington, DC 20036
PH: (202)261-6505
Toll free: 800-977-1197
Fax: (202)318-0655
Wilt-Hild, Bonnie, Contact

National Association for Multicultural
Education [8045]
2100 M St., Ste. 170-245
Washington, DC 20037
PH: (202)679-6263
Duhon-Sells, Rose, Founder

National Association of Negro Busi-
ness and Professional Women's
Clubs, Inc. [12900]
1806 New Hampshire Ave. NW
Washington, DC 20009-3206
PH: (202)483-4206
Fax: (202)462-7253
Bryant, Jennifer, Exec. Dir.

National Association of Neighbor-
hoods [11295]
1300 Pennsylvania Ave. NW, Ste.
700
Washington, DC 20004
PH: (202)332-7766
Winslow, Hon. Cleta, Director

National Association of Nurse
Practitioners in Women's Health
[16151]
505 C St. NE
Washington, DC 20002
PH: (202)543-9693
Johnson, Gay, CEO

National Association of Nutrition and
Aging Services Programs [16228]
1612 K St. NW, Ste. 400
Washington, DC 20006
PH: (202)682-6899
Fax: (202)223-2099
Blancato, Robert, Exec. Dir.

National Association for Olmsted
Parks [5098]
1200 18th St. NW, Ste. 330
Washington, DC 20036
PH: (202)223-9113
Fax: (202)223-9112
Addonizio, Lane, Assoc. VP

National Association of Patent
Practitioners [5675]
1629 K St. NW, Ste. 300
Washington, DC 20006
PH: (919)230-9635
Grossman, David, President

National Association of Pharmaceuti-
cal Sales Representatives [2561]
2020 Pennsylvania Ave., Ste. 5050
Washington, DC 20006
Toll free: 800-672-9104
Neece, Steven, COO

National Association of Private
Special Education Centers [8587]
South Bldg.
601 Pennsylvania Ave. NW, Ste. 900
Washington, DC 20004
PH: (202)434-8225
Fax: (202)434-8224
Collins, Dr. Richard, Director

National Association of Pro-Life
Nurses [12782]
2200 Pennsylvania Ave., 4th Fl. E
Washington, DC 20037
PH: (202)556-1240
Fax: (202)556-1240
Meyers, Susan, RN, President

National Association for Proton
Therapy [16347]
1155 15th Street NW, Ste. 500
Washington, DC 20005

PH: (202)495-3133
Fax: (202)530-0659
Arzt, Leonard, Mem.

National Association of Psychiatric
Health Systems [16834]
900 17th St. NW, Ste. 420
Washington, DC 20006-2507
PH: (202)393-6700
Fax: (202)783-6041
Covall, Mark J., CEO, President

National Association of Public Child
Welfare Administrators [11087]
c/o American Public Human Services
Association
1133 19th St. NW, Ste. 400
Washington, DC 20036
PH: (202)682-0100
Fax: (202)204-0071
Krow, Julie, President

National Association of Railroad
Passengers [2837]
505 Capitol Ct. NE, Ste. 300
Washington, DC 20002-7706
PH: (202)408-8362
Fax: (202)408-8287
LeCody, Peter J., Chairman

National Association of Real Estate
Investment Trusts [2879]
1875 I St. NW, Ste. 600
Washington, DC 20006-5413
PH: (202)739-9400
Fax: (202)739-9401
Dristas, Victor, VP of Operations

National Association of Regulatory
Utility Commissioners [5833]
1101 Vermont Ave. NW, Ste. 200
Washington, DC 20005
PH: (202)898-2200
Fax: (202)898-2213
White, Greg, Exec. Dir.

National Association of Rehabilitation
Providers and Agencies [17091]
701 8th St. NW, Ste. 500
Washington, DC 20001
Toll free: 866-839-7710
Fax: (800)716-1847
Hunter, Stephen, President

National Association of Resource
Conservation and Development
Councils [3902]
444 N Capitol St. NW, Ste. 618
Washington, DC 20001
PH: (202)434-4780
Fax: (202)434-4783
Walter, Olga, President

National Association for Rural Mental
Health [15789]
25 Massachusetts Ave. NW, Ste.
500
Washington, DC 20001
PH: (202)942-4276
Irvine, Lori, Chairman

National Association of Rural
Rehabilitation Corporations
[12804]
c/o Mike Hinton
USDA-FSA, Loan Servicing Division
1400 Independence Ave. SW, Stop
0522
Washington, DC 20250-0522
PH: (202)720-1472
Hinton, Mike, Contact

National Association of Secretaries
of State [5777]
444 N Capitol St. NW, Ste. 401
Washington, DC 20001
PH: (202)624-3525
Schedler, Tom, President

National Association of Securities
Professionals [3047]
1000 Vermont Ave. NW, Ste. 810
Washington, DC 20005
PH: (202)371-5535
Fax: (202)371-5536
Bond, Leslie, Jr., CEO

National Association of Security
Companies [3063]
444 N Capitol St. NW, Ste. 345
Washington, DC 20001
PH: (202)347-3257
Fax: (202)393-7006
McNulty, Jim, Chairman

National Association of Small Busi-
ness Contractors [883]
700 12th St. NW, Ste. 700
Washington, DC 20005
Toll free: 888-861-9290
Young, Cris, President

National Association of Social Work-
ers [13113]
750 1st St. NE, Ste. 800
Washington, DC 20002-4241
PH: (202)408-8600
Toll free: 800-742-4089
Fax: (202)336-8313
Joyner, Mildred C., VP

National Association of Social Work-
ers I National Committee on
Lesbian, Gay and Bisexual Issues
[11897]
750 1st St. NE, Ste. 700
Washington, DC 20002
PH: (202)408-8600
Toll free: 800-742-4089
Wheeler, Darrell P., PhD, MPH,
President

National Association of Special
Education Teachers [8588]
1250 Connecticut Ave. NW, Ste. 200
Washington, DC 20036
Toll free: 800-754-4421
Pierangelo, Dr. Roger, Exec. Dir.

National Association of State Alcohol
and Drug Abuse Directors [13165]
1025 Connecticut Ave. NW, Ste. 605
Washington, DC 20036
PH: (202)293-0090
Fax: (202)293-1250
Morrison, Robert, Exec. Dir.

National Association of State Budget
Officers [5709]
Hall of the States Bldg.
444 N Capitol St. NW, Ste. 642
Washington, DC 20001
PH: (202)624-5382
Fax: (202)624-7745
Mullaney, Tom, President

National Association for State Community Services Programs [5779]
111 K St. NE, Ste. 300
Washington, DC 20001-1569
PH: (202)624-5866
(202)624-5850
Bjelland, Jenae, Exec. Dir.

National Association of State Directors of Migrant Education [12342]
1001 Connecticut Ave. NW, Ste. 915
Washington, DC 20036
Coultress, Susie, President

National Association of State Direc-
tors of Teacher Education and
Certification [8663]
1629 K St. NW, Ste. 300
Washington, DC 20006
PH: (202)204-2208
Fax: (202)204-2210
Rogers, Dr. Phillip, Exec. Dir.

National Association of State Forest-
ers [4209]
444 N Capitol St. NW, Ste. 540
Washington, DC 20001
PH: (202)624-5415
Fax: (202)624-5407
Maisch, Chris, President

National Association of State
Workforce Agencies [5166]
444 N Capitol St. NW, Ste. 142
Washington, DC 20001
PH: (202)434-8020
Fax: (202)434-8033
Cotter, James, Project Mgr.

National Association of States United
for Aging and Disabilities [10519]
1201 15th St. NW, Ste. 350
Washington, DC 20005
PH: (202)898-2578
Fax: (202)898-2583
Jessee, Gary, President

National Association of Student
Financial Aid Administrators [7836]
1101 Connecticut Ave. NW, Ste.
1100
Washington, DC 20036-4303
PH: (202)785-0453
Fax: (202)785-1487
Draeger, Justin, CEO, President

National Association for the Support
of Long Term Care [15044]
1050 17th St. NW, Ste. 500
Washington, DC 20036-5558
PH: (202)803-2385
Morton, Cynthia, Exec. VP

National Association of Surety Bond
Producers [1904]
1140 19th St., Ste. 800
Washington, DC 20036-5104
PH: (202)686-3700
Fax: (202)686-3656
McCallum, Mark, CEO

National Association for Surface
Finishing [1288]
1155 15th St. NW, Ste. 500
Washington, DC 20005
PH: (202)457-8404
Fax: (202)530-0659

National Association of Theatre
Owners [1151]
750 1st St. NE, Ste. 1130
Washington, DC 20002
PH: (202)962-0054
Fax: (202)962-0370
Conroy, Kathy, VP, COO

National Association of Towns and
Townships [5641]
1130 Connecticut Ave. NW, Ste. 300
Washington, DC 20036
PH: (202)454-3954
Toll free: 866-830-0008
Fax: (202)331-1598
DeTemple, Matthew, President

National Association of Tribal
Historic Preservation Officers
[9413]
1320 18th St. NW, 2nd Fl.
Washington, DC 20036
PH: (202)628-8476
Fax: (202)628-2241
Kraus, D. Bambi, President

National Association of University
Women [8750]
1001 E St. SE
Washington, DC 20003
PH: (202)547-3967
Fax: (202)547-5226
Wright, Evelyn L., President

National Association of Vision Professionals **[16395]**
1775 Church St. NW
Washington, DC 20036
PH: (202)234-1010
Fax: (202)234-1020
Oberbeck, Tamara, President

National Association of Water Companies **[3459]**
2001 L St. NW, Ste. 850
Washington, DC 20036
PH: (202)833-8383
Fax: (202)331-7442
Sparrow, Lisa A., Bd. Member

National Association of Waterfront Employers **[2263]**
1200 19th St., Flr. 3
Washington, DC 20036
PH: (202)587-4800
Fax: (202)587-4888
Stritmatter, Claude, President

National Association of Wheat Growers **[3765]**
415 2nd St. NE, Ste. 300
Washington, DC 20002
PH: (202)547-7800
Palmer, Jim, CEO

National Association of Wholesaler-Distributors **[3474]**
1325 G St. NW, Ste. 1000
Washington, DC 20005
PH: (202)872-0885
Fax: (202)785-0586
Anderson, James A., Jr., VP

National Association of Women Business Owners **[651]**
South Bldg., Ste. 900
601 Pennsylvania Ave. NW
Washington, DC 20004
Toll free: 800-556-2926
Fax: (202)403-3788
Arredondo, Crystal, Chairperson

National Association of Women Judges **[5391]**
1001 Connecticut Ave. NW, Ste. 1138
Washington, DC 20036
PH: (202)393-0222
Fax: (202)393-0125
Komisar, Marie, Exec. Dir.

National Association of Workforce Boards **[11769]**
1155 15th St. NW, Ste. 350
Washington, DC 20005
PH: (202)857-7900
Fax: (202)857-7955
Painter, Ron, CEO

National Association of Workforce Development Professionals **[11770]**
1155 15th St. NW, Ste. 350
Washington, DC 20005
PH: (202)589-1790
Fax: (202)589-1799
Brown, Bridget, Exec. Dir.

National Association of Youth Clubs **[13463]**
National Association of Colored Women's Clubs
1601 R St. NW
Washington, DC 20009-6420
PH: (202)667-4080
Fax: (202)667-2574
Myles, Mrs. Peggie, Supervisor

National Bankers Association **[412]**
1513 P St. NW
Washington, DC 20005
PH: (202)588-5432
Fax: (202)588-5443
Pinkett, Preston, III, Chairman, CEO

National Bar Association **[5032]**
1225 11th St. NW
Washington, DC 20001
PH: (202)842-3900
Fax: (202)289-6170
Richardson, Jonathan, Secretary

National Barley Growers Association **[4177]**
c/o Dale Thorenson
600 Pennsylvania Ave. SE, Ste. 320
Washington, DC 20003
PH: (202)548-0734
Fax: (202)969-7036
Thorenson, Dale, Contact

National Beauty Culturists' League, Inc. **[924]**
25 Logan Cir. NW
Washington, DC 20005-3725
PH: (202)332-2695
Fax: (202)223-0940
Catalon, Dr. Katie B., President

National Black Caucus of Local Elected Officials **[5642]**
National League of Cities
1301 Pennsylvania Ave. NW, Ste. 550
Washington, DC 20004
Toll free: 877-827-2385
Tyson, Priscilla, President

National Black Caucus of State Legislators **[5781]**
444 N Capitol St. NW, Ste. 622
Washington, DC 20001
PH: (202)624-5457
Fax: (202)508-3826
Hunter, Gilda Cobb, VP

National Black Chamber of Commerce **[23603]**
4400 Jenifer St. NW, Ste. 331
Washington, DC 20015-2133
PH: (202)466-6888
Fax: (202)466-4918
Alford, Harry C., CEO, President

National Black Child Development Institute **[10820]**
1313 L St. NW, Ste. 110
Washington, DC 20005-4110
PH: (202)833-2220
Toll free: 800-556-2234
Fax: (202)833-8222
Hutcherson, Dimitrius, Chairman

National Black Environmental Justice Network **[4084]**
PO Box 15845
Washington, DC 20003
PH: (202)265-4919
Fax: (202)326-3357
Wilkins, Donele, Co-Ch.

National Black Gay Men's Advocacy Coalition **[11898]**
3636 Georgia Ave. NW
Washington, DC 20010-1646
PH: (202)455-8441
Hopkins, Ernest, Chairman

National Black Graduate Student Association **[19294]**
MSC 590507
Washington, DC 20059
Toll free: 800-471-4102
Nwosu, John, President

National Black Justice Coalition **[19129]**
PO Box 71395
Washington, DC 20024
PH: (202)319-1552
Fax: (202)319-7365
Lettman-Hicks, Sharon J., CEO, Exec. Dir.

National Black Law Students Association **[8220]**
1225 11th St. NW
Washington, DC 20001-4217
PH: (202)618-2572
Dailey, Derick, Chairperson

National Black Sisters' Conference **[19875]**
1200 Varnum St. NE
Washington, DC 20017
PH: (202)529-9250
Fax: (202)529-9370
Dual, Patricia, Secretary

National Breast Cancer Coalition **[14020]**
1010 Vermont Ave. NW, Ste. 900
Washington, DC 20005
PH: (202)296-7477
Toll free: 800-622-2838
Fax: (202)265-6854
Visco, Frances M., President

National Building Granite Quarries Association, Inc. **[3187]**
1220 L St. NW, Ste. 100-167
Washington, DC 20005
Toll free: 800-557-2848

National Building Museum **[5972]**
401 F St. NW
Washington, DC 20001
PH: (202)272-2448
Fax: (202)272-2564
Rynd, Chase W., Exec. Dir.

National Bus Traffic Association **[3342]**
111 K St. NE, 9th Fl.
Washington, DC 20002-8110
PH: (202)898-2700
Fax: (202)842-0850

National Business Aviation Association **[151]**
1200 G St. NW, Ste. 1100
Washington, DC 20005
PH: (202)783-9000
Fax: (202)331-8364
Anderson, Paul, Chairman

National Business Coalition on Health **[14953]**
1015 18th St. NW, Ste. 730
Washington, DC 20036-5207
PH: (202)775-9300
Fax: (202)775-1569
Thompson, Michael, President, CEO

National Business Officers Association **[7564]**
1400 I St. NW, Ste. 850
Washington, DC 20005
PH: (202)407-7140
Fax: (202)354-4944
Shields, Jeffrey N., President, CEO

National Cable and Telecommunications Association **[475]**
25 Massachusetts Ave. NW, Ste. 100
Washington, DC 20001
PH: (202)222-2300
Fax: (202)222-2514
Powell, Michael, President, CEO

National Campaign for a Peace Tax Fund **[19171]**
2121 Decatur Pl. NW
Washington, DC 20008
PH: (202)483-3751
Woodard, Richard N., Chairman

National Campaign to Prevent Teen and Unplanned Pregnancy **[13464]**
1776 Massachusetts Ave. NW, Ste. 200

Washington, DC 20036
PH: (202)478-8500
Fax: (202)478-8588
Kean, Thomas H., Chairman

National Candle Association **[1953]**
529 14th St. NW, Ste. 750
Washington, DC 20045
PH: (202)591-2455

National Cannabis Industry Association **[18648]**
PO Box 78062
Washington, DC 20013
Toll free: 888-683-5650
Fax: (888)683-5670
Smith, F. Aaron, Exec. Dir.

National Cathedral Association **[20068]**
3101 Wisconsin Ave. NW
Washington, DC 20016-5015
PH: (202)537-6200
Fax: (202)364-6600
Cox, Kathleen, Exec. Dir., COO

National Catholic Development Conference **[19878]**
734 15th St. NW Ste.,700
Washington, DC 20005-1013
PH: (202)637-0470
Fax: (202)637-0471
Lehmuth, Sr. Georgette, CEO, President

National Catholic Partnership on Disability **[19880]**
415 Michigan Ave. NE, Ste. 95
Washington, DC 20017-4501
PH: (202)529-2933
Fax: (202)529-4678
Benton, Janice, Exec. Dir.

National Caucus and Center on Black Aging, Inc. **[10520]**
1220 L St. NW, Ste. 800
Washington, DC 20005
PH: (202)637-8400
Fax: (202)347-0895
Jones, Karyne, CEO, President

National Center for Bicycling and Walking **[22751]**
1612 K St. NW, Ste. 802
Washington, DC 20006
PH: (202)223-3621
Plotz, Mark, Program Mgr.

National Center for Charitable Statistics **[12489]**
Urban Institute
2100 M St. NW, 5th Fl.
Washington, DC 20037
Toll free: 866-518-3874
Fax: (202)833-6231
Pollak, Thomas H., Prog. Dir.

National Center on Education and the Economy **[7786]**
2121 K St. NW, Ste. 700
Washington, DC 20037
PH: (202)379-1800
Fax: (202)293-1560
Tucker, Marc S., CEO, President

National Center for Education Statistics **[7787]**
Institute of Education Sciences
550 12th St. SW
Washington, DC 20202
PH: (202)245-6940
Hussar, William J., Economist

National Center for Public Policy Research **[18991]**
20 F St. NW, Ste. 700
Washington, DC 20001
PH: (202)507-6398
Ridenour, Amy Moritz, Chairman

National Center on Sexual Exploitation **[18927]**
1100 G St. NW, No. 1030
Washington, DC 20005
PH: (202)393-7245
Trueman, Patrick A., CEO, President

National Center for Tobacco-Free Kids **[17226]**
1400 Eye St. NW, Ste. 1200
Washington, DC 20005
PH: (202)296-5469
Fax: (202)296-5427
Myers, Matthew L., President

National Center for Transgender Equality **[13227]**
1325 Massachusetts Ave. NW, Ste. 700
Washington, DC 20005
PH: (202)903-0112
Keisling, Mara, Exec. Dir.

National Center for Victims of Crime **[13263]**
2000 M St. NW, Ste. 480
Washington, DC 20036
PH: (202)467-8700
Fax: (202)467-8701
Fernandez, Mai, Exec. Dir.

National Chicken Council **[4568]**
1152 15th St. NW, Ste. 430
Washington, DC 20005-2622
PH: (202)296-2622
Fax: (202)293-4005
Brown, Michael J., President

National Child Care Association **[10810]**
1325 G St. NW, Ste. 500
Washington, DC 20005-3136
Toll free: 800-543-7161
Darstein, Marie W., Exec. Dir.

National Children's Alliance **[11090]**
516 C St. NE
Washington, DC 20002
PH: (202)548-0090
Huizar, Teresa, Exec. Dir.

National Civic Art Society **[8873]**
300 New Jersey Ave. NW, Ste. 900
Washington, DC 20001
PH: (202)670-1776
Fax: (202)543-3311
Shubow, Justin, President

National Club Association **[733]**
1201 15th St. NW, Ste. 450
Washington, DC 20005
PH: (202)822-9822
Toll free: 800-625-6221
Fax: (202)822-9808
Wallmeyer, Henry, President, CEO

National Club Industry Association of America **[1155]**
1090 Vermont Ave. NW, No. 910
Washington, DC 20005
Toll free: 866-266-6526

National Coalition of 100 Black Women Inc. **[18221]**
300 New Jersey, NW, Ste. 900
Washington, DC 20001
PH: (212)222-5660
Fax: (212)222-5675
McNeill-Emery, Michele, President

National Coalition to Abolish the Death Penalty **[17831]**
1620 L St., NW, Ste. 250
Washington, DC 20036-5698
PH: (202)331-4090
Rust-Tierney, Diann, Exec. Dir.

National Coalition for Asian Pacific American Community Development **[11409]**
1628 16th St. NW, 4th Fl.
Washington, DC 20009

PH: (202)223-2442
Fax: (202)223-4144
Hasegawa, Lisa, Exec. Dir.

National Coalition on Black Civic Participation **[18913]**
1050 Connecticut Ave. NW, 5th Fl., Ste. 500
Washington, DC 20036
PH: (202)659-4929
Fax: (202)659-5025
Campbell, Melanie L., President, CEO

National Coalition of Blacks for Reparations in America **[17782]**
PO Box 90604
Washington, DC 20090
PH: (202)291-8400
Fax: (202)291-4600

National Coalition for Capital **[1006]**
1028 33rd St. NW, Ste. 200
Washington, DC 20007
PH: (202)337-1661
McIlvaine, Greg, President

National Coalition on Health Care **[18335]**
1825 K St. NW, Ste. 411
Washington, DC 20006
PH: (202)638-7151
Rother, John C., President, CEO

National Coalition for History **[9498]**
400 A St. SE
Washington, DC 20003
PH: (202)544-2422
White, Lee, Exec. Dir.

National Coalition for the Homeless **[11957]**
2201 P St. NW
Washington, DC 20037-1033
PH: (202)462-4822
Fax: (202)462-4823
Jones, Jerry, Exec. Dir.

National Coalition for Homeless Veterans **[21132]**
333 1/2 Pennsylvania Ave. SE
Washington, DC 20003-1148
PH: (202)546-1969
Toll free: 800-233-8582
Fax: (202)546-2063
Brown, Randy, Dir. of Comm.

National Coalition for Infant Health **[16622]**
1275 Pennsylvania Ave. NW, Ste. 1100
Washington, DC 20004
PH: (202)499-4114
Goldstein, Mitchell, MD, Medical Dir.

National Coalition for LGBT Health **[11900]**
2000 S St. NW
Washington, DC 20009
PH: (202)232-6749
Fax: (202)232-6750

National Coalition for Literacy **[8250]**
PO Box 2932
Washington, DC 20013-2932
Fax: (866)738-3757
Finsterbusch, Marty, Treasurer

National Coalition for Mental Health Recovery **[15794]**
611 Pennsylvania Ave. SE, No. 133
Washington, DC 20003
Toll free: 877-246-9058
Marsh, Valerie L., Exec. Dir.

National Coalition of Pro-Democracy Advocates **[18103]**
2020 Pennsylvania Ave. NW, Ste. 235

Washington, DC 20006-1811
PH: (202)595-1823
Fax: (202)318-8152

National Coalition for Promoting Physical Activity **[23063]**
1150 Connecticut Ave. NW, Ste. 300
Washington, DC 20036
Merson, Melissa, Exec. Dir.

National Coalition of STD Directors **[17200]**
1029 Vermont Ave. NW, Ste. 500
Washington, DC 20005
PH: (202)842-4660
Fax: (202)842-4542
Smith, William A., Exec. Dir.

National Coalition Supporting Eurasian Jewry **[18141]**
1120 20th St. NW, Ste. 300N
Washington, DC 20036
PH: (202)898-2500
Fax: (202)898-0822
Levin, Mark B., Exec. Dir.

National Coalition for Women and Girls in Education **[8751]**
American Association of University Women
1111 16th St. NW
Washington, DC 20036
PH: (202)785-7793
Maatz, Lisa, Chairperson

National Colorectal Cancer Roundtable **[14026]**
901 E St. NW, Ste. 500
Washington, DC 20004
PH: (202)661-5729
Fax: (202)661-5750
Wender, Dr. Richard, Chairman

National Commission for the Accreditation of Special Education Services **[8590]**
South Bldg., Ste. 900
601 Pennsylvania Ave. NW
Washington, DC 20004
PH: (202)434-8225
Fax: (202)434-8224
Dempsey, Tom, President

National Committee for an Effective Congress **[18014]**
218 D St. SE, 3rd Fl.
Washington, DC 20003
PH: (202)639-8300
Roosevelt, Eleanor, Founder

National Committee on Pay Equity **[18222]**
c/o AFT
555 New Jersey Ave. NW
Washington, DC 20001-2029
PH: (703)920-2010
Fax: (703)979-6372
Leber, Michele, Chairman

National Committee to Preserve Social Security and Medicare **[19138]**
10 G St. NE, Ste. 600
Washington, DC 20002
PH: (202)216-0420
Toll free: 800-966-1935
Fax: (202)216-0446
Richtman, Mr. Max, JD, CEO, President

National Committee for the Prevention of Elder Abuse **[10521]**
1730 Rhode Island Ave. NW, Ste. 1200
Washington, DC 20036-3109
PH: (202)464-9481
(855)500-3537
Toll free: 800-677-1116
Fax: (202)872-0057
Brownwell, Patricia, PhD, President

National Committee for Quality Assurance **[17031]**
1100 13th St., Ste. 1000
Washington, DC 20005
PH: (202)955-3500
Toll free: 888-275-7585
Fax: (202)955-3599
O'Kane, Margaret E., President

National Committee for Responsive Philanthropy **[12490]**
1331 H St. NW, Ste. 200
Washington, DC 20005-4706
PH: (202)387-9177
Fax: (202)332-5084
Feeney, Diane, Bd. Member

National Communication Association **[8597]**
1765 N St. NW
Washington, DC 20036
PH: (202)464-4622
Fax: (202)464-4600
Brumskine, Winifred, Accountant

National Community Action Foundation **[11296]**
PO Box 78214
Washington, DC 20013
PH: (202)842-2092
Fax: (202)842-2095
Bradley, David, Exec. Dir.

National Community Development Association **[17989]**
1825 K St. NW, Ste. 515
Washington, DC 20006
PH: (202)587-2772
Fax: (202)887-5546
Watson, Vicki, Exec. Dir.

National Community Reinvestment Coalition **[17990]**
727 15th St. NW, Ste. 900
Washington, DC 20005
PH: (202)628-8866
Fax: (202)628-9800
Dickerson, Bob, Chairman

National Confectioners Association **[1355]**
1101 30th St. NW, Ste. 200
Washington, DC 20007
PH: (202)534-1440
Fax: (202)337-0637
Downs Jr., John H., President, CEO

National Conference for Catechetical Leadership **[20087]**
415 Michigan Ave., Ste. 110
Washington, DC 20017
PH: (202)756-5512
Fax: (202)756-5519
Matijasevic, Margaret, Exec. Dir.

National Conference on Citizenship **[17857]**
1100 17th St. NW, 12th Fl.
Washington, DC 20036
PH: (202)601-7096
Weiser, Michael, Chairman

National Conference of Executives of the Arc **[2185]**
1825 K St. NW, Ste. 1200
Washington, DC 20006
PH: (202)534-3700
Toll free: 800-433-5255
Fax: (202)534-3731
Berns, Peter V., CEO

National Conference on Public Employee Retirement Systems **[5079]**
444 N Capitol St. NW, Ste. 630
Washington, DC 20001
PH: (202)624-1456
Toll free: 877-202-5706
Fax: (202)624-1439
Aaronson, Mel, President

National Conference of Puerto Rican
  Women **[18223]**
1220 L St. NW, Ste. 100-177
Washington, DC 20005
PH: (773)405-3535
Gordils, Wanda, President

National Conference of State
  Historic Preservation Officers
  [9417]
Hall of States
444 N Capitol St. NW, Ste. 342
Washington, DC 20001
PH: (202)624-5465
Fax: (202)624-5419
Wolfe, Mark, VP

National Conference of State Societ-
  ies **[19660]**
PO Box 70175
Washington, DC 20024
Christian, Bill, President

National Conferences on
  Undergraduate Research **[8503]**
734 15th St. NW, Ste. 550
Washington, DC 20005
PH: (202)783-4810
Fax: (202)783-4811
Rowlett, Prof. Roger S., President

National Congress of American
  Indians **[18709]**
1516 P St. NW
Washington, DC 20005-1910
PH: (202)466-7767
Fax: (202)466-7797
Cladoosbys, Brian, President

National Congress of Black Women
  [18914]
1250 4th St. SW, Ste. WG-1
Washington, DC 20024
PH: (202)678-6788
Williams, Dr. E. Faye, President,
  CEO

National Conservation District
  Employees Association **[23535]**
c/o Rich Duesterhaus, Executive
  Director
509 Capitol Ct. NE
Washington, DC 20002-4937
PH: (202)547-6223
Fax: (202)547-6450
Riley, Tim, President

National Consumer Voice for Quality
  Long-Term Care **[18054]**
1001 Connecticut Ave. NW, Ste. 632
Washington, DC 20036
PH: (202)332-2275
Fax: (866)230-9789
Celentano, Amanda, Associate

National Consumers League **[18055]**
1701 K St. NW, Ste. 1200
Washington, DC 20006
PH: (202)835-3323
Fax: (202)835-0747
Greenberg, Sally, Exec. Dir.

National Cooperative Business As-
  sociation **[909]**
1401 New York Ave. NW, Ste. 1100
Washington, DC 20005
PH: (202)638-6222
Fax: (202)638-1374

National Coordinating Committee for
  Multi-employer Plans **[1075]**
815 16th St. NW
Washington, DC 20006
PH: (202)737-5315
Fax: (202)737-1308
DeFrehn, Randy G., Exec. Dir.

National Council for Accreditation of
  Teacher Education **[7414]**
1140 19th St., Ste. 400
Washington, DC 20036

PH: (202)223-0077
Fax: (202)296-6620
Cibulka, James G., President

National Council for Advanced
  Manufacturing **[2229]**
2025 M St. NW, Ste. 800
Washington, DC 20036
PH: (202)367-1178
Patterson, Rusty, Chairman, CEO

National Council of Agricultural
  Employers **[3528]**
525 9th St. NW, Ste. 800
Washington, DC 20004
PH: (202)629-9320
Leitz, Fred, President

National Council of Architectural
  Registration Boards **[5973]**
1801 K St. NW, Ste. 700K
Washington, DC 20006-1301
PH: (202)879-0520
Fax: (202)783-0290
Armstrong, Michael J., CEO

National Council of Asian Pacific
  Americans **[17820]**
1629 K St. NW, Ste. 400
Washington, DC 20006
PH: (202)706-6768
Dinh, Quyên, Chairman

National Council for Behavioral
  Health **[15795]**
1400 K St. NW, Ste. 400
Washington, DC 20005
PH: (202)684-7457
Rosenberg, Ms. Linda, MSW, CEO,
  President

National Council on Child Abuse and
  Family Violence **[11707]**
1025 Connecticut Ave. NW, Ste.
  1000
Washington, DC 20036
PH: (202)429-6695
Fax: (202)521-3479
Davis, Alan, Chairman

National Council of the Churches of
  Christ in the USA **[20069]**
110 Maryland Ave. NE, Ste. 108
Washington, DC 20002-5603
PH: (202)544-2350
Toll free: 800-379-7729
Fax: (212)543-1297
Winkler, Jim, President, Gen. Sec.

National Council for Eurasian and
  East European Research **[10218]**
1828 L St. NW, Ste. 1200
Washington, DC 20036
PH: (202)572-9095
    (202)572-9125
Fax: (866)937-9872
Patton, David, President

National Council of Farmer Coopera-
  tives **[3977]**
50 F St. NW, Ste. 900
Washington, DC 20001
PH: (202)626-8700
Fax: (202)626-8722
Natz, Kevin, VP

National Council on Fireworks Safety
  [6628]
1701 Pennsylvania Ave. NW, Ste.
  300
Washington, DC 20006
Blogin, Nancy, Director, President

National Council on Folic Acid
  [16230]
4590 MacArthur Blvd. NW, Ste. 250
Washington, DC 20007
Toll free: 800-621-3141
Austin, Robin, Comm. Spec.

National Council for GeoCosmic
  Research **[6353]**
c/o Alvin Burns, Executive Secretary
1351 Maryland Ave. NE, Apt. B
Washington, DC 20002-4439
Marchesella, John, Chairman

National Council for Geographic
  Education **[7935]**
1775 Eye St. NW, Ste. 1150
Washington, DC 20006-2435
PH: (202)587-5727
Fax: (202)618-6249
Dulli, Zachary R., CEO

National Council of Higher Education
  Resources **[7837]**
1100 Connecticut Ave. NW, Ste.
  1200
Washington, DC 20036-4110
PH: (202)822-2106
Fax: (202)822-2143
Wilson, Quentin, Chairman

National Council on Independent
  Living **[11624]**
2013 H St. NW, 6th Fl.
Washington, DC 20006
PH: (202)207-0334
Toll free: 877-525-3400
Fax: (202)207-0341
Buckland, Kelly, Exec. Dir.

National Council for Interior Design
  Qualification **[1954]**
1602 L St. NW, Ste. 200
Washington, DC 20036-2581
Hanson, David, President

National Council on International
  Trade Development **[1970]**
1901 Pennsylvania Ave. NW, Ste.
  804
Washington, DC 20006-3438
PH: (202)872-9280
Fax: (202)293-0495
Prior, E. J., Treasurer

National Council on Interpreting in
  Health Care **[1592]**
5614 Connecticut Ave. NW, Ste. 119
Washington, DC 20015-2604
Ardemagni, Enrica, PhD, President

National Council of La Raza **[17919]**
1126 16th St. NW, Ste. 600
Washington, DC 20036-4845
PH: (202)785-1670
Fax: (202)776-1792
Soto, Renata, Chairman

National Council of Minorities in
  Energy **[1116]**
1725 I St. NW, Ste. 300
Washington, DC 20006
Toll free: 866-663-9045
Fax: (866)663-8007
Patten, Ezekiel, Chairman

National Council of Negro Women,
  Inc. **[18224]**
633 Pennsylvania Ave. NW
Washington, DC 20004-2605
PH: (202)737-0120
Fax: (202)737-0476
Mathis, Janice L., Exec. Dir.

National Council of Nonprofits **[257]**
1001 G St. NW, Ste. 700E
Washington, DC 20001
PH: (202)962-0322
Fax: (202)962-0321
Delaney, Tim, CEO, President

National Council on Problem
  Gambling **[11868]**
730 11th St. NW, Ste. 601
Washington, DC 20001

PH: (202)547-9204
Toll free: 800-522-4700
Fax: (202)547-9206
Feeney, Don, Bd. Member

National Council for Public-Private
  Partnerships **[18287]**
2020 K St. NW, Ste. 650
Washington, DC 20006
PH: (202)962-0555
Fax: (202)289-7499
Smith, Arthur, Chairman

National Council for Science and the
  Environment **[4085]**
1101 17th St. NW, Ste. 250
Washington, DC 20036
PH: (202)530-5810
Fax: (202)628-4311
Saundry, Peter, Exec. Dir.

National Council on Skin Cancer
  Prevention **[14028]**
c/o John Antonishak, Executive
  Director
1875 I St. NW, Ste. 500
Washington, DC 20006
PH: (301)801-4422
Fax: (301)831-5062
Antonishak, John, Exec. Dir.

National Council of State Directors
  of Community Colleges **[7644]**
1 Dupont Cir. NW, Ste. 410
Washington, DC 20036
PH: (202)728-0200
Fax: (202)833-2467
Cech, John, Dep. Comm.

National Council of State Housing
  Agencies **[5282]**
444 N Capitol St. NW, Ste. 438
Washington, DC 20001
PH: (202)624-7710
Fax: (202)624-5899
Gleason, Thomas R., President

National Council of State Tourism
  Directors **[23662]**
c/o US Travel Association
1100 New York Ave. NW, Ste. 450
Washington, DC 20005-3934
Beauvois, Nan Marchand, VP

National Council on Teacher Quality
  [8655]
1120 G St. NW, Ste. 800
Washington, DC 20005
PH: (202)393-0020
Fax: (202)393-0095
Walsh, Kate, President

National Council of Textile Organiza-
  tions **[3265]**
1701 K St. NW, Ste. 625
Washington, DC 20006
PH: (202)822-8028
Fax: (202)822-8029
Tantillo, Auggie, President

National Council on U.S.-Arab Rela-
  tions **[18691]**
1730 M St. NW, Ste. 503
Washington, DC 20036
PH: (202)293-6466
Fax: (202)293-7770
Anthony, Dr. John Duke, CEO,
  Founder, President

National Council of University
  Research Administrators **[8504]**
1015 18th St. NW, Ste. 901
Washington, DC 20036-5273
PH: (202)466-3894
Fax: (202)223-5573
Larmett, Kathleen, Exec. Dir.

National Council of Urban Education
  Associations **[8728]**
1201 16th St. NW, Ste. 410
Washington, DC 20036

PH: (202)822-7155
Underwood, Katherine, President

National Council of Urban Indian
Health [18710]
924 Pennsylvania Ave. SE
Washington, DC 20003
PH: (202)544-0344
Fax: (202)544-9394
Eaglefeathers, Moke, Exec. Dir., Bd.
Member

National Council of Women's
Organizations [18225]
1050 17th St. NW, Ste. 250
Washington, DC 20036
PH: (202)293-4505
Fax: (202)293-4507
Cha, Susan Scanlan, Contact

National Crime Prevention Council
[11511]
1201 Connecticut Ave. NW, Ste. 200
Washington, DC 20036
PH: (202)466-6272
Fax: (202)296-1356
Harkins, Ann M., President, CEO

National Crime Victim Bar Associa-
tion [5843]
National Center for Victims of Crime
2000 M St. NW, Ste. 480
Washington, DC 20036
PH: (202)467-8700
     (202)467-8753
Fax: (202)467-8701
Dion, Jeffrey R., Director

National Criminal Justice Association
[11540]
720 7th St. NW, 3rd Fl.
Washington, DC 20001
PH: (202)628-8550
Fax: (202)448-1723
Smith, Jeanne, President

National Cued Speech Association
[17245]
1300 Pennsylvania Ave. NW, Ste.
190-713
Washington, DC 20004
Toll free: 800-459-3529
Huffman, Anne, President

National Customs Brokers and
Forwarders Association of America,
Inc. [1989]
1200 18th St. NW, No. 901
Washington, DC 20036
PH: (202)466-0222
Fax: (202)466-0226
Powell, Geoffrey, President

National Cyber Security Alliance
[7153]
1101 Pennsylvania Ave. NW, Ste.
600
Washington, DC 20004
PH: (756)756-2278
Kaiser, Michael, Exec. Dir.

National Democratic Club [18114]
30 Ivy St. SE
Washington, DC 20003-4006
PH: (202)543-2035
Fax: (202)479-4273
Richards, Terry, President

National Democratic Institute for
International Affairs [18525]
455 Massachusetts Ave. NW, 8th Fl.
Washington, DC 20001-2783
PH: (202)728-5500
Toll free: 888-875-2887
Albright, Madeleine K., Chairman

National Demolition Association
[886]
2025 M St. NW, Ste. 800
Washington, DC 20036

PH: (202)367-1152
Toll free: 800-541-2412
Fax: (202)367-2152
Caulfield, Cheryl, Exec. Dir.

National Dental Association [14460]
3517 16th St. NW
Washington, DC 20010
PH: (202)588-1697
Fax: (202)588-1244
Perry, Dr. Kim B., VP

National Disability Rights Network
[11626]
820 1st St. NE, Ste. 740
Washington, DC 20002
PH: (202)408-9514
Fax: (202)408-9520
Moody, Kim, VP

National Economists Club [6399]
PO Box 33511
Washington, DC 20033-3511
PH: (703)493-8824
Tomasi, Corinne, Secretary

National Education Association
[23411]
1201 16th St. NW
Washington, DC 20036-3290
PH: (202)833-4000
Fax: (202)822-7974
Stocks, John C., Exec. Dir.

National Endangered Species Act
Reform Coalition [5185]
1050 Thomas Jefferson St. NW, 6th
Fl.
Washington, DC 20007-3837
PH: (202)333-7481
Fax: (202)338-2416
McNally, Nancy Macan, Exec. Dir.

National Endowment for Democracy
[18104]
1025 F St. NW, Ste. 800
Washington, DC 20004-1432
PH: (202)378-9700
Fax: (202)378-9407
Gershman, Carl, President

National Endowment for the Humani-
ties [8006]
400 7th St. SW
Washington, DC 20506
PH: (202)606-8400
     (202)606-8244
Toll free: 800-634-1121
Voyatzis, Lisette, Cmte. Mgmt. Ofc.

National Energy Assistance Directors' Association [1702]
c/o Mark Wolfe, Executive Director
1350 Connecticut Ave. NW, No.
1100
Washington, DC 20007
PH: (202)237-5199
Wolfe, Mark, Exec. Dir.

National Energy Marketers Associa-
tion [1117]
3333 K St. NW, Ste. 110
Washington, DC 20007
PH: (202)333-3288
Fax: (202)333-3266
Goodman, Craig, President

National Environmental Education
Foundation [7896]
4301 Connecticut Ave. NW, Ste. 160
Washington, DC 20008
PH: (202)833-2933
Wood, Diane W., President

National Fabry Disease Foundation
[15966]
4301 Connecticut Ave. NW, Ste. 404
Washington, DC 20008
Toll free: 800-651-9131
Fax: (919)932-7786
Walter, Mr. Jerry, President, CEO

National Fair Housing Alliance
[18359]
1101 Vermont Ave. NW, Ste. 710
Washington, DC 20005
PH: (202)898-1661
Fax: (202)371-9744
McCarthy, Jim, Chairman

National Family Farm Coalition
[17790]
110 Maryland Ave. NE, Ste. 307
Washington, DC 20002
PH: (202)543-5675
Fax: (202)543-0978
Ozer, Katherine, Exec. Dir.

National Family Planning and
Reproductive Health Association
[11845]
1627 K St. NW, 12th Fl.
Washington, DC 20006
PH: (202)293-3114
Coleman, Clare, President, CEO

National Farmers Union [4162]
20 F St. NW, Ste. 300
Washington, DC 20001
PH: (202)554-1600
Fax: (202)554-1654
Teske, Donn, VP

National Federation for Catholic
Youth Ministry [19886]
415 Michigan Ave. NE, Ste. 40
Washington, DC 20017-4503
PH: (202)636-3825
Fax: (202)526-7544
McCarty, Dr. Robert J., Exec. Dir.

National Federation of Federal
Employees [23435]
1225 New York Ave., Ste. 450
Washington, DC 20005
PH: (202)216-4420
Fax: (202)898-1861
Dougan, William R., President

National Federation of Filipino
American Associations [10073]
1322 18th St. NW
Washington, DC 20036-1803
PH: (347)669-8764
Flores, Brendan, Chairman

National Federation of Humane
Societies [10669]
c/o Washington Humane Society
7319 Georgia Ave. NW
Washington, DC 20012
PH: (202)723-5730

The National Flossing Council
[14464]
533 4th St. SE
Washington, DC 20003
PH: (202)544-0711
Lione, Armand, PhD, President

National Foreign Trade Council
[1971]
1625 K St. NW, Ste. 200
Washington, DC 20006
PH: (202)887-0278
Fax: (202)452-8160
Reinsch, William A., President

National Forum for Black Public
Administrators [5698]
777 N Capitol St. NE, Ste. 550
Washington, DC 20002
PH: (202)408-9300
Fax: (202)408-8558
Williams-Gates, Regina V.K., Exec.
Dir. (Actg.)

National Forum for Heart Disease
and Stroke Prevention [17010]
1150 Connecticut Ave. NW, Ste. 300
Washington, DC 20036
Toll free: 866-894-3500
Fax: (202)330-5080
Moffatt, Sharon, RN, Chairperson

National Foster Care Coalition
[11094]
1220 L St. NW, Ste. 100-241
Washington, DC 20005
Pai-Espinosa, Jeannette, Chmn. of
the Exec. Committee

National Foundation for Credit
Counseling [2094]
2000 M St. NW, Ste. 505
Washington, DC 20036
PH: (202)677-4300
Toll free: 800-388-2227
Fax: (202)677-4333
Diaz, Nelson, Chairman

National Foundation for Unemploy-
ment Compensation and Workers
Compensation [5167]
910 17th St., Ste. 1070
Washington, DC 20006
PH: (202)223-8902
     (202)223-8904
Fax: (202)783-1616
Holmes, Douglas J., President

National Fragile X Foundation
[14846]
2100 M St. NW, Ste. 170
Washington, DC 20037-1233
Toll free: 800-688-8765
Fax: (202)747-6208
Ferlenda, Tony, CEO

National Gay and Lesbian Chamber
of Commerce [23604]
729 15th St. NW, 9th Fl.
Washington, DC 20005
PH: (202)234-9181
Fax: (202)234-9185
Nelson, Justin G., Founder,
President

National Geographic Society [6673]
1145 17th St. NW
Washington, DC 20036-4688
PH: (202)862-8638
Toll free: 800-373-1717
Kelly, Tim T., President

National Governors' Association
[5784]
Hall of the States
444 N Capitol St. NW, Ste. 267
Washington, DC 20001-1512
PH: (202)624-5300
Fax: (202)624-5313
Thornburg, John, CFO

National Grain and Feed Association
[4178]
1250 I St. NW, Ste. 1003
Washington, DC 20005
PH: (202)289-0873
Fax: (202)289-5388
Gordon, Randall C., President

National Grange [4163]
1616 H St. NW
Washington, DC 20006
PH: (202)628-3507
Toll free: 888-447-2643
Fax: (202)347-1091
Luttrell, Ed, President

National Grants Management As-
sociation [2186]
2100 M St. NW, Ste. 170
Washington, DC 20037
PH: (202)308-9443
Javornik, Emy Neuman, President

National Guard Association of the
United States [5609]
1 Massachusetts Ave. NW
Washington, DC 20001
PH: (202)789-0031
Fax: (202)682-9358
Ashenhurst, Maj. Gen. Deborah A.,
Chairman

National Health Care Anti-Fraud Association [15422]
1220 L St. NW, Ste. 600
Washington, DC 20005
PH: (202)659-5955
Fax: (202)785-6764
Messuri, Nicholas, Chairman

National Health Council [14955]
1730 M St. NW, Ste. 500
Washington, DC 20036-4561
PH: (202)785-3910
Fax: (202)785-5923
Collura, Barbara, Director

National Healthy Start Association [16298]
1325 G St. NW, Ste. 500
Washington, DC 20005
PH: (202)296-2195
Toll free: 877-437-8126
Fax: (202)296-2197
Derrick, Lisa L., President

National Hispana Leadership Institute [18340]
PO Box 70061
Washington, DC 20024
PH: (703)527-6007
Espenoza, Cecelia M., Chairperson

National Hispanic Coalition of Federal Aviation Employees [5062]
PO Box 23276
Washington, DC 20026-3276

National Hispanic Corporate Council [655]
1050 Connecticut Ave. NW, 5 Fl.
Washington, DC 20036
PH: (202)772-1100
Fax: (202)772-3101
Martinez, Pat, CEO, President

National Hispanic Council on Aging [10523]
734 15th St. NW, Ste. 1050
Washington, DC 20005
PH: (202)347-9733
Fax: (202)347-9735
Cruz, Ms. Yanira L., MPH, CEO, President

National Hispanic Foundation for the Arts [19463]
1010 Wisconsin Ave. NW, Ste. 650
Washington, DC 20007
PH: (202)293-8330
Fax: (202)772-3101
Rodriguez, Richard, Exec. Dir.

National Hispanic Institute of Liturgy [19888]
620 Michigan Ave. NE
Washington, DC 20064
PH: (305)274-6333
Fax: (305)274-6337
Sosa, Rev. Juan J., President

National Hispanic Medical Association [15739]
1920 L St. NW, Ste. 725
Washington, DC 20036-5050
PH: (202)628-5895
Fax: (202)628-5898
Rios, Elena, MD, CEO, President

National Housing Conference [11980]
1900 M St. NW, Ste. 200
Washington, DC 20036
PH: (202)466-2121
Fax: (202)466-2122
Estes, Chris, President, CEO

National Housing Endowment [558]
1201 15th St. NW
Washington, DC 20005
Toll free: 800-368-5242
Silver, Bruce S., CEO, President

National Housing and Rehabilitation Association [11982]
1400 16th St. NW, Ste. 420
Washington, DC 20036-2244
PH: (202)939-1750
Fax: (202)265-4435
Bell, Peter, President, CEO

National Human Services Assembly [13304]
1101 14th St. NW, Ste. 600
Washington, DC 20005-5639
PH: (202)347-2080
Katz, Irv, CEO, President

National Humanities Alliance [9555]
21 Dupont Cir. NW, Ste. 800
Washington, DC 20036
PH: (202)296-4994
Fax: (202)872-0884
Yu, Pauline, Secretary

National Hydropower Association [6499]
25 Massachusetts Ave. NW, Ste. 450
Washington, DC 20001
PH: (202)682-1700
Fax: (202)682-9478
Ciocci, Linda Church, Exec. Dir.

National Immigration Forum [18465]
50 F St. NW, Ste. 300
Washington, DC 20001-1552
PH: (202)347-0040
Fax: (202)347-0058
Noorani, Ali, Exec. Dir.

National Indian Education Association [8397]
1514 P St. NW, Ste. B
Washington, DC 20005
PH: (202)544-7290
Fax: (202)544-7293
Whitefoot, Patricia, President

National Indian Gaming Association [5257]
224 2nd St. SE
Washington, DC 20003-1943
PH: (202)546-7711
Stevens, Ernest L., Chairman

National Indian Health Board [12380]
926 Pennsylvania Ave. SE
Washington, DC 20003
PH: (202)507-4085
Bohlen, Stacy A., Exec. Dir.

National Industrial Sand Association [2381]
2011 Pennsylvania Ave. NW, Ste. 301
Washington, DC 20006
PH: (202)457-0200
Fax: (202)457-0287
Ellis, Mark, President

National Initiative for a Networked Cultural Heritage [9233]
21 Dupont Cir. NW
Washington, DC 20036-1109
PH: (202)296-5346
Fax: (202)872-0886
Henry, Charles, President

National Institute of Building Sciences [6350]
1090 Vermont Ave. NW, Ste. 700
Washington, DC 20005
PH: (202)289-7800
Fax: (202)289-1092
Green, Henry L., President

National Institute for Health Care Management Research and Educational Foundation [15048]
1225 19th St. NW, Ste. 710
Washington, DC 20036-2454

PH: (202)296-4426
Fax: (202)296-4319
Chockley, Nancy, CEO, President

National Institute of Oilseed Products [2453]
750 National Press Bldg.
529 14th St. NW
Washington, DC 20045
PH: (202)591-2461
Fax: (202)223-9741
LeMunyan Newberry, Lauren, Exec. Dir.

National Institute for Science, Law and Public Policy [3552]
1400 16th St. NW, Ste. 101
Washington, DC 20036
PH: (202)462-8800
Fax: (202)265-6564
Turner, James S., Founder, Principal

National Institute of Senior Housing [11983]
National Council on Aging
1901 L St. NW, 4th Fl.
Washington, DC 20036
PH: (202)479-1200
Fax: (202)479-0735
Firman, James, President

National Iranian American Council [9596]
1411 K St. NW, Ste. 250
Washington, DC 20005
PH: (202)386-6325
Parsi, Dr. Trita, President

National Italian American Bar Association [5442]
2020 Pennsylvania Ave. NW, PMB 932
Washington, DC 20006-1846
PH: (414)750-4404
Fax: (414)255-3615
Mazzone, Dino, Officer

National Italian American Foundation [9619]
1860 19th St. NW
Washington, DC 20009
PH: (202)387-0600
Fax: (202)387-0800
Aspromonte, Kenneth J, Exec. VP

National Jewish Democratic Council [18916]
PO Box 65683
Washington, DC 20035
Rosenbaum, Greg, Chairman

National Job Corps Association [11775]
1023 15th St. NW, Ste. 200
Washington, DC 20005
PH: (202)216-0217
Fax: (202)289-7499

National Juvenile Justice Network [5143]
1319 F St. NW, Ste. 402
Washington, DC 20004
PH: (202)467-0864
Owens, Jody, Co-Ch.

National Ladies Auxiliary of the Jewish War Veterans of the United States of America Inc. [21041]
1811 R St. NW
Washington, DC 20009-1603
PH: (202)667-9061
Kaatz, Petra C., President

National Latino Tobacco Control Network [17485]
Indiana Latino Institute
1869 Park Rd. NW
Washington, DC 20010

PH: (202)328-1313
Fax: (202)797-9856
Noltenius, Jeannette, MA, Director

National Law Center on Homelessness and Poverty [11958]
2000 M St. NW, Ste. 210
Washington, DC 20036-3382
PH: (202)638-2535
Fax: (202)628-2737
Foscarinis, Maria, Exec. Dir., Founder

National Law Enforcement Officers Memorial Fund [5502]
901 E St. NW, Ste. 100
Washington, DC 20004-2025
PH: (202)737-3400
Fax: (202)737-3405
Floyd, Craig W., President, CEO

National Law Enforcement Partnership to Prevent Gun Violence [5219]
c/o Police Foundation
1201 Connecticut Ave. NW, No. 200
Washington, DC 20036
PH: (202)833-1460
Johnson, Chief Jim, Chairperson

National League of American Pen Women [8990]
1300 17th St. NW
Washington, DC 20036
PH: (202)785-1997
Fax: (202)452-8868
Long, Candace, President

National League of Cities [5644]
1301 Pennsylvania Ave. NW, Ste. 550
Washington, DC 20004
Toll free: 877-827-2385
Anthony, Clarence E., Exec. Dir.

National League for Nursing [16162]
2600 Virginia Ave. NW, 8th Fl.
Washington, DC 20037
PH: (212)812-0300
Toll free: 800-669-1656
Fax: (212)812-0391

National Leased Housing Association [11984]
1900 L St. NW, Ste. 300
Washington, DC 20036-5027
PH: (202)785-8888
Fax: (202)785-2008
Muha, Denise B., Exec. Dir.

National Legal Aid and Defender Association [5547]
1901 Pennsylvania Ave. NW, Ste. 500
Washington, DC 20006
PH: (202)452-0620
Fax: (202)872-1031
Wallace, Jo-Ann, CEO, President

National Lesbian and Gay Journalists Association [2701]
2120 L St. NW, Ste. 850
Washington, DC 20037
PH: (202)588-9888
Stuckey, Rick, Secretary

National LGBT Bar Association [5043]
1875 I St. NW, Ste. 1100
Washington, DC 20006
PH: (202)637-7661
Kemnitz, D'Arcy, Exec. Dir.

National LGBTQ Task Force [11901]
1325 Massachusetts Ave. NW, Ste. 600
Washington, DC 20005-4164
PH: (202)393-5177
Fax: (202)393-2241
David, Pam, Exec. Dir.

National Low Income Housing Coalition [11985]
1000 Vermont Ave., Ste. 500
Washington, DC 20005
PH: (202)662-1530
Fax: (202)393-1973
Kealey, Paul, COO

National Lumber and Building Material Dealers Association [1444]
2025 M St. NW, Ste. 800
Washington, DC 20036-3309
PH: (202)367-1169
Fax: (202)367-2169
Yates, Scott, Chmn. of the Bd.

National Mining Association [740]
101 Constitution Ave. NW, Ste. 500 E
Washington, DC 20001
PH: (202)463-2600
    (202)463-2639
Fax: (202)463-2666
Crutchfield, Kevin, Chairman

National Minority AIDS Council [13556]
1000 Vermont Ave., NW, Ste. 200
Washington, DC 20005-4903
PH: (202)853-1846
Kawata, Paul A., Exec. Dir.

National Multi Housing Council [2883]
1850 M St. NW, Ste. 540
Washington, DC 20036-5803
PH: (202)974-2300
Fax: (202)775-0112
DeWitt, Robert E., Chairman

National Museum of American Jewish Military History [21134]
1811 R St. NW
Washington, DC 20009
PH: (202)265-6280
Fax: (202)462-3192
Rosenshein, Norman, President

National Music Publishers' Association [2434]
975 F St. NW, Ste. 375
Washington, DC 20004
PH: (202)393-6672
Israelite, David M., CEO, President

National Native American Law Enforcement Association [5505]
1300 Pennsylvania Ave. NW
Washington, DC 20004
PH: (202)204-3065
Fax: (866)506-7631

National Network to End Domestic Violence [11710]
1400 16th St. NW, Ste. 330
Washington, DC 20036
PH: (202)543-5566
Fax: (202)543-5626
Gandy, Kim A., President, CEO

National Network for Youth [12793]
741 8th St. SE
Washington, DC 20003
PH: (202)783-7949
Harper, Jane, President, CEO

National New Play Network [10263]
641 D St. NW
Washington, DC 20004
PH: (202)312-5270
Fax: (202)289-2446
Suilebhan, Gwydion, Director

National Ocean Industries Association [6941]
1120 G St. NW, Ste. 900
Washington, DC 20005
PH: (202)347-6900
Fax: (202)347-8650
Luthi, Randall, President

National Oilseed Processors Association [2454]
1300 L St. NW, Ste. 1020
Washington, DC 20005
PH: (202)842-0463
Fax: (202)842-9126
Stonacek, Mark, Chairman

National Organization of Blacks in Government [5080]
3005 Georgia Ave. NW
Washington, DC 20001-3807
PH: (202)667-3280
Fax: (202)667-3705
Stewart, Faye, Chairperson

National Organization on Fetal Alcohol Syndrome [17324]
1200 Eton Court NW, 3rd Flr.
Washington, DC 20007
PH: (202)785-4585
Toll free: 800-66N-OFAS
Fax: (202)466-6456
Donaldson, Tom, President

National Organization for Marriage [12258]
2029 K St. NW, Ste. 300
Washington, DC 20006
Toll free: 888-894-3604
Brown, Brian S., President

National Organization of Minority Architects [5974]
1735 New York Ave. NW, No. 357
Washington, DC 20006
PH: (202)586-6682
Henmi, Rod, VP

National Organization of Nurse Practitioners Faculties [16164]
1615 M St. NW, Ste. 270
Washington, DC 20036
PH: (202)289-8044
Fax: (202)289-8046
Thomas, Anne, President

National Organization for People of Color Against Suicide [13196]
PO Box 75571
Washington, DC 20013-0571
PH: (202)549-6039
    (202)806-7706
Holland Barnes, Donna, PhD, President, Founder, Exec. Dir.

National Organization for the Reform of Marijuana Laws [17921]
1100 H St. NW, Ste. 830
Washington, DC 20005-5485
PH: (202)483-5500
Fax: (202)483-0057
Kent, Norman Elliott, V. Ch.

National Organization of Veterans' Advocates [5841]
1425 K St. NW, Ste. 350
Washington, DC 20005-3514
PH: (202)587-5708
Hobson, David, Exec. Dir.

National Organization for Women [18227]
1100 H St. NW, Ste 300
Washington, DC 20005-5488
PH: (202)628-8669
O'Neill, Terry, President

National Park Foundation [5665]
1110 Vermont Ave. NW, Ste. 200
Washington, DC 20005
PH: (202)796-2500
Fax: (202)796-2509
Jewell, Sally, Chairman

National Park Hospitality Association [1156]
1200 G St. NW, Ste. 650
Washington, DC 20005

PH: (202)682-9530
Fax: (202)682-9529
Belland, Chris, CEO

National Parking Association [2497]
1112 16th St. NW, Ste. 840
Washington, DC 20036
PH: (202)296-4336
Toll free: 800-647-7275
Fax: (202)296-3102
Muglich, Mark, Chairman

National Parks Conservation Association [5666]
777 6th St. NW, Ste. 700
Washington, DC 20036
PH: (202)223-6722
Toll free: 800-628-7275
Fax: (202)454-3333
McKenna, Robin Martin, Exec. VP

National Partnership for Community Leadership [11478]
1629 K St. NW, Ste. 300
Washington, DC 20006
Johnson, Jeffery M., PhD, CEO, President

National Partnership for Women & Families [18228]
1875 Connecticut Ave. NW, Ste. 650
Washington, DC 20009
PH: (202)986-2600
Fax: (202)986-2539
Malcolm, Ellen R., Chairperson

National Pasta Association [1361]
750 National Press Bldg.
529 14th St. NW
Washington, DC 20045
PH: (202)591-2459
Fax: (202)591-2445
Pearson, Greg, Chairman

National Peace Corps Association [18848]
1900 L St. NW, Ste. 610
Washington, DC 20036
PH: (202)293-7728
Fax: (202)293-7554
Barclay, Tony, Treasurer

National Petroleum Council [5173]
1625 K St. NW, Ste. 600
Washington, DC 20006
PH: (202)393-6100
Fax: (202)331-8539
Hackett, James T., Chairman

National Pharmaceutical Council [2563]
1717 Pennsylvania Ave. NW, Ste. 800
Washington, DC 20006
PH: (202)827-2100
Fax: (202)827-0314
Leonard, Dan, President

National Physicians Alliance [16760]
1001 G St. NW, Ste. 800
Washington, DC 20001
PH: (202)420-7896
    (202)753-0428
Fax: (202)747-2969
Silver-Isenstadt, Dr. Jean, Exec. Dir.

National Pollution Prevention Roundtable [4554]
50 F St. NW, Ste. 350
Washington, DC 20001-1770
PH: (202)299-9701
Brown, Landon, Chairman

National Pork Producers Council [4713]
122 C St. NW, Ste. 875
Washington, DC 20001
PH: (202)347-3600
Fax: (202)347-5265
Dierks, Neil, CEO

National Postal Mail Handlers Union [23509]
1101 Connecticut Ave. NW, Ste. 500
Washington, DC 20036
PH: (202)833-9095
Hegarty, John F., President

National Postdoctoral Association [8505]
1200 New York Ave. NW, Ste. 610
Washington, DC 20005
PH: (202)326-6424
Fax: (202)371-9489
Wilson, Amy, Exec. Dir.

National Potato Council [4244]
1300 L St. NW, Ste. 910
Washington, DC 20005
PH: (202)682-9456
Fax: (202)682-0333
Tiede, Jim, President

The National Press Club [2704]
529 14th St. NW, 13th Fl.
Washington, DC 20045
PH: (202)662-7500
    (202)662-7505
Morton, Joseph, Secretary

National Press Foundation [2705]
1211 Connecticut Ave. NW, Ste. 310
Washington, DC 20036
PH: (202)663-7280
Adams, Chris, Director

National Pressure Ulcer Advisory Panel [15050]
1000 Potomac St. NW, Ste. 108
Washington, DC 20007
PH: (202)521-6789
Fax: (202)833-3636
Saunders, David A., Exec. Dir.

National Propane Gas Association [4265]
1899 L St. NW, Ste. 350
Washington, DC 20036-4623
PH: (202)466-7200
Fax: (202)466-7205
O'Dell, Mollie, VP, Comm.

National Public Radio [9145]
1111 N Capitol St. NE
Washington, DC 20002
Fax: (202)513-3329
Carrasco, Emma, Chief Mktg. Ofc.

National Puerto Rican Coalition [9234]
1220 L St. NW, Ste. 701
Washington, DC 20005
PH: (202)223-3915
Fantauzzi, Rafael A., CEO, President

National Quality Forum [15051]
1030 15th St. NW, Ste. 800
Washington, DC 20005
PH: (202)783-1300
Fax: (202)783-3434
Darling, Helen, President, CEO

National Railroad Construction and Maintenance Association, Inc. [2839]
500 New Jersey Ave. NW, Ste. 400
Washington, DC 20001
PH: (202)715-1264
Fax: (202)318-0867
Baker, Chuck, President

National Recycling Coalition [3453]
1220 L St. NW, Ste. 100-155
Washington, DC 20005
PH: (202)618-2107
Cooper, Jeff, Bd. Member

National Register of Health Service Psychologists [16929]
1200 New York Ave. NW, Ste. 800
Washington, DC 20005

PH: (202)783-7663
Fax: (202)347-0550
Folen, Raymond A., PhD, Chairman,
President

National Religious Affairs Association
[20548]
712 18th St. NE
Washington, DC 20002
Dolphus, Rev. Warren H., Founder

National Republican Club of Capitol
Hill **[19042]**
300 1st St. SE
Washington, DC 20003
PH: (202)484-4590
Fax: (202)479-9110
Rodriguez, Gilbert, Exec.

National Republican Congressional
Committee **[19043]**
320 1st St. SE
Washington, DC 20003
PH: (202)479-7000
Walden, Greg, Chairman

National Republican Senatorial Com-
mittee **[19044]**
425 2nd St. NE
Washington, DC 20002
PH: (202)675-6000
Wicker, Roger F., Senator, Chairman

National Resident Matching Program
[8334]
2121 K St. NW, Ste. 1000
Washington, DC 20037
PH: (202)400-2233
Toll free: 866-653-6767
Signer, Mona M., MPH, President,
CEO

National Restaurant Association
[1672]
2055 L St. NW, Ste. 700
Washington, DC 20036
PH: (202)331-5900
Toll free: 800-424-5156
Fax: (202)331-2429
Kadow, Joe, Chairman

National Restaurant Association
Educational Foundation **[1673]**
2055 L St. NW
Washington, DC 20036
Toll free: 800-424-5156

National Retail Federation **[2970]**
1101 New York Ave. NW
Washington, DC 20005
PH: (202)783-7971
(202)347-1932
Toll free: 800-673-4692
Fax: (202)737-2849
Tindell, Kip, Chmn. of the Bd.

National Retired Teachers Associa-
tion **[8506]**
American Association of Retired
Persons
601 E St. NW
Washington, DC 20049
Toll free: 888-687-2277

National Retiree Legislative Network
[12751]
South Bldg., Ste. 900
601 Pennsylvania Ave. NW
Washington, DC 20004-2601
PH: (202)220-3172
Toll free: 866-360-7197
Kadereit, Bill, President

National Reverse Mortgage Lenders
Association **[2096]**
1400 16th St. NW, Ste. 420
Washington, DC 20036
PH: (202)939-1760
Fax: (202)265-4435
Bell, Peter H., President, CEO

National Right to Life Committee
[12784]
512 10th St. NW
Washington, DC 20004-1401
PH: (202)626-8800
Tobias, Carol, President

National Right to Life Educational
Trust Fund **[19065]**
512 10th St. NW
Washington, DC 20004
PH: (202)626-8829
Tobias, Carol, President

National Rural Housing Coalition
[11986]
1331 G St. NW, 10th Fl.
Washington, DC 20005
PH: (202)393-5229
Fax: (202)393-3034
McGahee, Selvin, Bd. Member

National Security and Law Society
[5757]
c/o American University Washington
College of Law
4801 Massachusetts Ave. NW
Washington, DC 20016
PH: (202)274-4000
Creedon, James, President

National Skills Coalition **[11776]**
1730 Rhode Island Ave. NW, Ste.
712
Washington, DC 20036
PH: (202)223-8991
Fax: (202)318-2609
Kleunen, Andy Van, Exec. Dir.

National Small Business Association
[3124]
1156 15th St. NW, Ste. 502
Washington, DC 20005
Toll free: 800-345-6728
McCracken, Todd, President, CEO

National Society of the Children of
the American Revolution **[20693]**
1776 D St. NW, Rm. 224
Washington, DC 20006-5303
PH: (202)638-3153
Fax: (202)737-3162

National Society of Collegiate
Scholars **[8518]**
2000 M St. NW, Ste. 600
Washington, DC 20036
PH: (202)265-9000
Fax: (202)265-9200
Loflin, Stephen E., Founder, CEO

National Society Colonial Dames
XVII Century **[20754]**
1300 New Hampshire Ave. NW
Washington, DC 20036-1502
PH: (202)293-1700
Miller, Felisia, Office Mgr.

National Society of the Colonial
Dames of America **[20755]**
2715 Q St. NW
Washington, DC 20007-3071
PH: (202)337-2288
(202)372-7836
Fax: (202)337-0348

National Society, Daughters of the
American Colonists **[20756]**
2205 Massachusetts Ave. NW
Washington, DC 20008-2813
PH: (202)667-3076

National Society, Daughters of the
American Revolution **[20694]**
1776 D St. NW
Washington, DC 20006
PH: (202)628-1776
Wright, Merry Ann T., President

National Society Sons of Colonial
New England **[20758]**
c/o Paul Melvin Hays, Registrar
General
147 12th St. SE
Washington, DC 20003-1420
Hay, Paul Melvin, Registrar

National Society, United States
Daughters of 1812 **[21176]**
1461 Rhode Island Ave. NW
Washington, DC 20005-5402
PH: (202)745-1812

National Space Club and Foundation
[5865]
204 E St. NE
Washington, DC 20002
PH: (202)547-0060
Emmons, Debra Lynn, President

National Space Society **[5866]**
PO Box 98106
Washington, DC 20090-8106
PH: (202)429-1600
Fax: (703)435-4390
Money, Ken, President

National Star Route Mail Contractors
Association **[2120]**
324 E Capitol St.
Washington, DC 20003-3897
PH: (202)543-1661
Fax: (202)543-8863
Sheehy, John, President

National Structured Settlements
Trade Association **[5548]**
1100 New York Ave. NW, Ste. 750W
Washington, DC 20005
PH: (202)289-4004
Fax: (202)289-4002
Vaughn, Eric, Exec. Dir.

National Sudden and Unexpected
Infant/Child Death and Pregnancy
Loss Resource Center **[17334]**
Georgetown University, Box 571272
2115 Wisconsin Ave. NW, Ste. 601
Washington, DC 20007-2292
PH: (202)687-7466
(202)784-9552
Toll free: 866-866-7437
Fax: (202)784-9777
Mayer, Rochelle, EdD, Director

National Surgical Assistant Associa-
tion **[17396]**
1775 Eye St. NW, Ste. 1150
Washington, DC 20006
PH: (206)266-9951
Toll free: 855-270-6722
Fax: (202)587-5610
Baird, Daniel D., Chmn. of the Bd.

National Sustainable Agriculture
Coalition **[4699]**
110 Maryland Ave. NE, Ste. 209
Washington, DC 20002
PH: (202)547-5754
Charney, Alyssa, Specialist

National Symphony Orchestra
[9979]
John F. Kennedy Center for the
Performing Arts
2700 F St. NW
Washington, DC 20566
PH: (202)416-8100
Fax: (202)416-8105
Shapiro, Rita, Exec. Dir.

National Tax Association **[5801]**
725 15th St. NW, No. 600
Washington, DC 20005-2109
PH: (202)737-3325
Fax: (202)737-7308
Brady, Peter, President

National Taxpayers Union **[19173]**
25 Massachusetts Ave. NW, Ste.
140
Washington, DC 20001
PH: (703)683-5700
Fax: (703)683-5722
Sepp, Pete, President

National Technical Association
[7286]
2705 Bladensburg Rd. NE
Washington, DC 20018
Artis, Claude, Treasurer

National Teens for Life **[12785]**
c/o Derrick Jones, Advisor
512 10th St. NW
Washington, DC 20004
PH: (202)626-8800
(202)626-8825
Little, Joleigh, Advisor

National Traffic Incident Management Coalition **[5806]**
c/o American Association of State
Highway and Transportation Officials
444 N Capitol St. NW, Ste. 249
Washington, DC 20001
PH: (608)266-0459
Corbin, John, Chairman

National Transitions of Care Coali-
tion **[15052]**
10 G St. NE, Ste. 605
Washington, DC 20002
Toll free: 888-562-9267
Lattimer, Cheri A., RN, BSN, Exec.
Dir.

National Treasury Employees Union
[23437]
1750 H St. NW
Washington, DC 20006
PH: (202)572-5500
Kelley, Colleen M., President

National Trust for Historic Preserva-
tion **[9422]**
2600 Virginia Ave. NW, Ste. 1100
Washington, DC 20037
PH: (202)588-6000
Toll free: 800-944-6847
Fax: (202)588-6038
Meeks, Stephanie, President, CEO

National Turkey Federation **[4569]**
1225 New York Ave., Ste. 400
Washington, DC 20005
PH: (202)898-0100
Fax: (202)898-0203
Brandenberger, Joel, President

National United States-Arab
Chamber of Commerce **[23605]**
1101 17th St., NW, Ste. 1220
Washington, DC 20036
PH: (202)289-5920
Fax: (202)289-5938
Hamod, Mr. David, CEO, President

National Venture Capital Association
[2035]
25 Massachusetts Avenue NW, Ste.
730
Washington, DC 20001
PH: (202)864-5920
Fax: (202)864-5930
Haque, Maryam, VP of Res.

National Veterans Legal Services
Program **[21136]**
PO Box 65762
Washington, DC 20035
PH: (202)265-8305
Flagg, Ronald S., Chairman

National Vietnam and Gulf War
Veterans Coalition **[19223]**
2020 Pennsylvania Ave., No. 961
Washington, DC 20006
Molloy, Mr. John J., Chairman

National Waste and Recycling Association [3454]
4301 Connecticut Ave. NW, Ste. 300
Washington, DC 20008-2304
PH: (202)244-4700
Toll free: 800-424-2869
Fax: (202)966-4824
Parker, Bruce, CEO, President

National Water Resources Association [7373]
4 E St. SE
Washington, DC 20003
PH: (202)698-0693
Lyle, Ian, Director

National Weather Service Employees Organization [6858]
601 Pennsylvania Ave. NW, Ste. 900
Washington, DC 20004
PH: (202)907-3036
Sobien, Daniel A., President

National Whistleblower Center [12838]
PO Box 25074
Washington, DC 20027
PH: (202)342-1903
Kohn, Stephen M., Exec. Dir., Chairman

National WIC Association [5763]
2001 S St. NW, Ste. 580
Washington, DC 20009-1165
PH: (202)232-5492
Fax: (202)387-5281
Greenaway, Rev. Douglas A., CEO, President

National Wildlife Refuge Association [4848]
1001 Connecticut Ave. NW, Ste. 905
Washington, DC 20036
PH: (202)417-3803
Watson, Stuart, Chairman

National Woman's Party [18229]
Sewall-Belmont House and Museum
144 Constitution Ave. NE
Washington, DC 20002-5608
PH: (202)546-1210
Harrington, Page, Exec. Dir.

National Women's Business Council [3498]
409 3rd St. SW, 5th Fl.
Washington, DC 20416
PH: (202)205-3850
Fax: (202)205-6825
Borja, Anie, Exec. Dir.

National Women's Health Network [17763]
1413 K St. NW, 4th Fl.
Washington, DC 20005
PH: (202)682-2640
    (202)682-2646
Fax: (202)682-2648
Pearson, Cynthia, Exec. Dir.

National Women's Law Center [18230]
11 Dupont Cir. NW, No. 800
Washington, DC 20036
PH: (202)588-5180
Fax: (202)588-5185
Campbell, Nancy Duff, Co-Pres.

National Women's Political Caucus [18231]
PO Box 50476
Washington, DC 20091
PH: (202)785-1100
Fax: (202)370-6306
Lent, Donna, President

National Workforce Association [5263]
1 Massachusetts Ave. NW, Ste. 310
Washington, DC 20001

PH: (202)842-2092
Bradley, David A., CEO

National Youth Employment Coalition [13469]
115 15th St. NW, Ste. 350
Washington, DC 20036
PH: (202)780-5928
Martinez, John, Chairman, Dep. Dir.

Native American Contractors Association [895]
750 1st St. NE, Ste. 950
Washington, DC 20002
PH: (202)758-2676
Fax: (202)758-2699
Anderson, Michael G., Exec. Dir.

Native American Finance Officers Association [1259]
1101 30th St. NW, Ste. 500
Washington, DC 20007
PH: (202)631-2003
Lomax, William, President

Native American Leadership Alliance [20511]
3600 New York Ave. NE, 3rd Fl.
Washington, DC 20002
PH: (202)841-9061
Joseph, Dr. Robert, Chairman

Natural Gas Supply Association [4266]
1620 Eye St. NW, Ste. 700
Washington, DC 20006
PH: (202)326-9300
Wiggins, Dena, President

Natural Gas Vehicles for America [6020]
400 N Capitol St. NW
Washington, DC 20001
PH: (202)824-7360
Godlewski, Matthew, President

Natural Products Association [2972]
1773 T St. NW
Washington, DC 20009
PH: (202)223-0101
Toll free: 800-966-6632
Fax: (202)223-0250
Fabricant, Dr. Daniel, Exec. Dir., CEO

Naval Historical Foundation [9804]
Washington Navy Yard
1306 Dahlgren Ave. SE
Washington, DC 20374-5109
PH: (202)678-4333
Toll free: 888-880-0102
Fax: (703)580-5280
Fallon, William J., Chairman

NEA Foundation [7793]
1201 16th St. NW
Washington, DC 20036-3201
PH: (202)822-7840
Fax: (202)822-7779
Brown, Crystal, Chairperson

NEA Healthy Futures [15086]
1201 16th St. NW, No. 216
Washington, DC 20036
PH: (202)822-7570
Fax: (202)822-7775
Newberry, Jerald, Director

Neighborhood Reinvestment Corp. [11988]
999 N Capitol St. NE, Ste. 900
Washington, DC 20002
PH: (202)760-4000
Fax: (202)376-2600
Wehrwein, Chuck, CEO, Act. Pres.

Network of Sacred Heart Schools [8014]
821 Varnum St. NE
Washington, DC 20017

PH: (202)636-9300
Fax: (202)636-9306
Humphreys, Ian, Director

Network of Schools of Public Policy, Affairs, and Administration [5699]
1029 Vermont Ave. NW, Ste. 1100
Washington, DC 20005-3517
PH: (202)628-8965
Fax: (202)626-4978
McFarland, Laurel, Exec. Dir.

New America Alliance [1007]
c/o Maria del Pilar Avila, Chief Executive Officer
1050 Connecticut Ave. NW, 10th Fl.
Washington, DC 20036
PH: (202)772-1044
Fax: (214)466-6415
Avila, Maria del Pilar, CEO

New America Foundation [18994]
740 15th St. NW, Ste. 900
Washington, DC 20005
PH: (202)986-2700
Fax: (202)986-3696
Coll, Steve, Contact

New Perimeter [5549]
500 8th St. NW
Washington, DC 20004
PH: (202)799-4505
Dewey, Elizabeth, Director

New Rules for Global Finance Coalition [18156]
2000 M St. NW, Ste. 720
Washington, DC 20036-3327
PH: (202)277-9390
Fax: (202)280-1141
Coplin, Nathan, Program Mgr., Coord.

New Water Supply Coalition [7374]
1750 H St. NW, Ste. 600
Washington, DC 20006
PH: (202)737-0700
Fax: (202)737-0455

Newborn Coalition [14208]
750 9th St. NW, Ste. 750
Washington, DC 20001
PH: (858)353-3581
Fax: (858)353-3581
Bialick, Jim, Exec. Dir., Founder

The Newspaper Guild [23485]
501 3rd St. NW
Washington, DC 20001-2797
PH: (202)434-7177
Fax: (202)434-1472
Waggoner, Martha, Chairperson

Nixon Center [18273]
1025 NW Connecticut Ave., Ste. 1200
Washington, DC 20036
PH: (202)887-1000
Fax: (202)887-5222
Simes, Dimitri K., CEO, President

Non-Ferrous Metals Producers Committee [2364]
2030 M St. NW, Ste. 800
Washington, DC 20036-3379
PH: (202)466-7720
Fax: (202)466-2710

Nonviolence International [18724]
4000 Albemarle St. NW, Ste. 401
Washington, DC 20016
PH: (202)244-0951
Fax: (202)244-6396
Beer, Michael, Exec. Dir.

North American Association for Environmental Education [7882]
2000 P St. NW, Ste. 540
Washington, DC 20036

PH: (202)419-0412
Braus, Judy, Exec. Dir.

North American Export Grain Association [1521]
1250 I St. NW, Ste. 1003
Washington, DC 20005
PH: (202)682-4030
Fax: (202)682-4033
Martin, Gary C., President, CEO

North American Importers Association [1992]
1250 Connecticut Ave. NW, Ste. 200
Washington, DC 20036-2643
Toll free: 888-483-5777
Fax: (209)436-3820

North American Laminate Flooring Association [569]
1747 Pennsylvania Ave. NW, Ste. 1000
Washington, DC 20006-4636
PH: (202)785-9500
Fax: (202)835-0243
Dearing, Bill, President

North American Meat Institute [2311]
1150 Connecticut Ave. NW, 12th Fl.
Washington, DC 20036
PH: (202)587-4200
Fax: (202)587-4300
Carpenter, Barry, President, CEO

North American Millers' Association [2378]
600 Maryland Ave. SW, Ste. 825 W
Washington, DC 20024
PH: (202)484-2200
Fax: (202)488-7416
McCarthy, James A., President, CEO

North American Securities Administrators Association [3049]
750 1st St. NE, Ste. 1140
Washington, DC 20002
PH: (202)737-0900
Fax: (202)783-3571
Rome, Gerald, Treasurer

North American Security Products Organization [3066]
204 E St. NE
Washington, DC 20002
PH: (202)608-1322
Fax: (202)547-6348
O'Neil, Mike, President

Nuclear Control Institute [18753]
1000 Connecticut Ave. NW, Ste. 400
Washington, DC 20036-5302
PH: (202)822-8444
Fax: (202)452-0892
Tanzer, Sharon, VP

Nuclear Energy Institute [6505]
1201 F St. NW, Ste. 1100
Washington, DC 20004-1218
PH: (202)739-8000
Fax: (202)785-4019
Fertel, Marvin S., CEO, President

Nuclear Threat Initiative [18755]
1747 Pennsylvania Ave. NW, 7th Fl.
Washington, DC 20006
PH: (202)296-4810
Fax: (202)296-4811
Browne, Des, V. Ch.

OAS Staff Association [23487]
1889 F St. NW, No. 622
Washington, DC 20006
PH: (202)370-4643
    (202)370-4645
Garicoche, Tamara, Administrator

Ocean Conservancy [3919]
1300 19th St. NW, 8th Fl.
Washington, DC 20036

PH: (202)429-5609
Toll free: 800-519-1541
Fax: (202)872-0619
Merkl, Andreas, CEO

Ocean Doctor [3922]
PO Box 53090
Washington, DC 20009
PH: (202)695-2550
Fax: (202)888-3329
Guggenheim, Dr. David E., President

Oceana [4772]
1350 Connecticut Ave. NW, 5th Fl.
Washington, DC 20036
PH: (202)833-3900
Toll free: 877-7-OCEANA
Fax: (202)833-2070
Sharpless, Andrew, CEO

Oil Change International [4029]
714 G St. SE, No. 202
Washington, DC 20003
PH: (202)518-9029
Kretzmann, Stephen, Exec. Dir.,
Founder

One Common Unity [11417]
Josephine Butler Parks Ctr.
2437 15th St NW
Washington, DC 20009
PH: (202)765-3757
Fax: (240)331-5897
Hawah, Exec. Dir.

One World Education [8628]
1752 Columbia Rd. NW, 3rd Fl.
Washington, DC 20009
Goldstein, Eric, Exec. Dir., Founder

Online News Association [2713]
1111 N Capitol St. NE, 6th Fl.
Washington, DC 20002
PH: (646)290-7900
McDonnell, Jane, Exec. Dir.

**Opportunities Industrialization
Centers International [13080]**
1875 Connecticut Ave. NW, 10th Fl.
Washington, DC 20009
PH: (202)499-2380
Fax: (202)499-2382
Scotland, Lynton, VP

Optical Society of America [6948]
2010 Massachusetts Ave. NW
Washington, DC 20036
PH: (202)223-8130
Fax: (202)223-1096
Willner, Alan, President

**Optical Society of America Founda-
tion [6949]**
2010 Massachusetts Ave. NW
Washington, DC 20036
PH: (202)416-1985
Fax: (202)416-6130
Sawchuk, Alexander, Chairman

**Optoelectronics Industry Develop-
ment Association [2458]**
2010 Massachusetts Ave. NW
Washington, DC 20036
PH: (202)416-1982
Fax: (202)416-1408
Mazzali, Claudio, Chairman

**ORACLE Religious Association
[20551]**
6101 New Hampshire Ave. NE
Washington, DC 20011

**Order Sons of Italy in America
[19508]**
219 E St. NE
Washington, DC 20002
PH: (202)547-2900
    (202)547-8115
Toll free: 800-552-OSIA
Fax: (202)546-8168
Longo, Daniel J., President

Organic Trade Association [4483]
444 N Capitol St. NW, Ste. 445A
Washington, DC 20001
PH: (202)403-8520
Batcha, Laura, CEO, Exec. Dir.

**Organization of American States
[17798]**
17th St. & Constitution Ave. NW
Washington, DC 20006
PH: (202)370-5000
Fax: (202)458-3967
Robert, Maryse, Director

**Organization of Black Designers
[9279]**
300 M St. SW, Ste. N110
Washington, DC 20024
PH: (202)489-4822
Rice, David H., Chairman, Founder

**Organization Development Network
[2464]**
2025 M St. NW, Ste. 800
Washington, DC 20036
PH: (202)367-1127
Fax: (202)367-2127
Duda, Sherry, Chairperson

**Organization for Economic Coopera-
tion and Development [18157]**
1776 Eye St. NW, Ste. 450
Washington, DC 20006
PH: (202)785-6323
Fax: (202)315-2508
Guthrie, Carol, Officer

**Organization for International Invest-
ment [18996]**
1225 19th St. NW, Ste. 501
Washington, DC 20036
PH: (202)659-1903
Fax: (202)659-2293
McLernon, Nancy, CEO, President

**Organization of Professional
Employees of the United States
Department of Agriculture [4951]**
PO Box 23762
Washington, DC 20026-3762
PH: (202)720-4898
Dickerhoof, Edward, Exec. VP

Orphanages for Africa [11118]
PO Box 44294
Washington, DC 20026
Evans, Catherine, President,
Founder

Orthopaedics Overseas [16489]
1900 L St. NW, No. 310
Washington, DC 20036
PH: (202)296-0928
Fax: (202)296-8018
Kelly, Nancy, Exec. Dir.

OSA Conservation [3926]
1012 14th St. NW, Ste. 625
Washington, DC 20005
PH: (202)765-2266
Fax: (202)765-2228
Madrigal, Liliana, President

**Outdoor Advertising Association of
America, Inc. [106]**
1850 M St. NW, Ste. 1040
Washington, DC 20036
PH: (202)833-5566
Fax: (202)833-1522
O'Donnell, Patrick, Comm. Chm.

OutServe-SLDN [5620]
PO Box 65301
Washington, DC 20035-5301
Toll free: 800-538-7418
Thorn, Matt, Exec. Dir. (Actg.)

**Ovarian Cancer National Alliance
[14038]**
1101 14th St. NW, Ste. 850
Washington, DC 20005

PH: (202)331-1332
Toll free: 866-399-6262
Fax: (202)331-2292
Balas, Calaneet H., CEO

**OWL - The Voice of Midlife and
Older Women [13392]**
1627 K St. NW, Ste. 600
Washington, DC 20006
Fax: (202)450-8986
Huyck, Margaret Hellie, President

Paleoanthropology Society [6971]
810 E St. SE
Washington, DC 20003
Yellen, Dr. John, President

Palliative Care Policy Center [11557]
2000 M St. NW, Ste. 400
Washington, DC 20036
Wilkinson, Anne, PhD, Director

**PALTEX-Expanded Textbook and
Instructional Materials Program
[8694]**
525 23rd St. NW
Washington, DC 20037
PH: (202)974-3000
Fax: (202)974-3663
Periago, Dr. Mirta Roses, Director

**Pan American Development Founda-
tion [17799]**
1889 F St. NW, 2nd Fl.
Washington, DC 20006
PH: (202)458-3969
Toll free: 877-572-4484
Fax: (202)458-6316
Sanbrailo, John, Exec. Dir.

**Pan American Health Organization
Foundation [15611]**
1889 F St. NW, Ste. 312
Washington, DC 20006
PH: (202)974-3416
    (202)974-3000
Fax: (202)974-3636
Etienne, Dr. Carissa, Director

**Panelized Building Systems Council
[2201]**
National Association of Home Build-
ers
1201 15th St. NW
Washington, DC 20005
PH: (202)266-8200
Toll free: 800-368-5242
Fax: (202)266-8400
Beaton, Dianne, Chairman

Panos Institute [12178]
Webster House
1718 P St. NW, Ste. T-6
Washington, DC 20036
PH: (202)429-0730
    (202)429-0731
Fax: (202)483-3059
Oliviero, Melanie Beth, Exec. Dir.

**Paralyzed Veterans of America
[20772]**
801 18th St. NW
Washington, DC 20006-3517
Toll free: 800-424-8200
Townsend, Homer S., Jr., Exec. Dir.

**Parent Cooperative Preschools
International [7594]**
National Cooperative Business Ctr.
1401 New York Ave. NW, Ste. 1100
Washington, DC 20005
Ems, Kathy, VP of Fin.

**Parents, Families and Friends of
Lesbians and Gays, Inc. [11905]**
1828 L St. NW, Ste. 660
Washington, DC 20036
PH: (202)467-8180
Fax: (202)467-8194
Hodges, Jean, President

Parkinson's Action Network [14610]
1025 Vermont Ave. NW, Ste. 1120
Washington, DC 20005
PH: (202)638-4101
Toll free: 800-850-4726
Thompson, Ted, JD, President, CEO

Partners of the Americas [17800]
1424 K St. NW, Ste. 700
Washington, DC 20005
PH: (202)628-3300
Vetter, Stephen G., President, CEO

**Partners for Democratic Change
[18496]**
1800 Massachusetts Ave. NW, Ste.
401
Washington, DC 20036-2131
PH: (202)942-2166
Fax: (202)939-0606
Roig, Julia, President

**Partnership for Advancing the
Transition to Hydrogen [6506]**
1211 Connecticut Ave. NW, Ste. 650
Washington, DC 20036-2701
PH: (202)457-0076
Fax: (202)223-5537
Serfass, Jeff, Gen. Mgr.

**Partnership to Cut Hunger and
Poverty in Africa [12559]**
1100 New Jersey Ave. SE, Ste. 735
Washington, DC 20003
PH: (202)678-4000
Fax: (202)488-0590
McPherson, Peter, Chairman

Partnership for Prevention [14959]
1015 18th St. NW, Ste. 300
Washington, DC 20036
PH: (202)833-0009
Fax: (202)833-0113
Howse, Jennifer L., PhD, Comm.
Chm.

**Partnership for Public Service
[18947]**
Office Bldg.
1100 New York Ave. NW
Washington, DC 20005
PH: (202)775-9111
Fax: (202)775-8885
Stier, Max, CEO, President

**Partnership for a Secure America
[5758]**
2000 P St. NW, Ste. 505
Washington, DC 20036
PH: (202)293-8580
Semmel, Andrew K., Exec. Dir.

Pathways to College Network [7969]
c/o American Institute for Research
1000 Thomas Jefferson St. NW
Washington, DC 20007
Brand, Betsy, Exec. Dir.

**Paulist Evangelization Ministries
[19895]**
3031 4th St. NE
Washington, DC 20017
PH: (202)832-5022
Fax: (202)269-0209
DeSiano, Fr. Frank, CSP, President

Pax Christi U.S.A. [18725]
415 Michigan Ave. NE, Ste. 240
Washington, DC 20017-4503
PH: (202)635-2741
Chappell, Patricia, Exec. Dir.

Peace Alliance [18814]
1616 P St. NW, Ste. 100
Washington, DC 20036
PH: (202)684-2553
Fax: (202)204-5712
Baskin, Bob, President

Peace Brigades International -
U.S.A. **[18815]**
PO Box 75880
Washington, DC 20013
PH: (202)232-0142
Fax: (202)232-0143
Parker, Amelia, Exec. Dir.

Peace and Justice Studies Association **[18818]**
1421 37th St. NW, Ste. 130
Washington, DC 20057
Amster, Randall, Exec. Dir.

Peace Pac **[18760]**
322 4th St. NE
Washington, DC 20002
PH: (202)543-4100

Peace X Peace **[18820]**
1776 I St. NW, 9th Fl.
Washington, DC 20006
Toll free: 877-684-3770
Weichel, Kimberly, CEO

William Penn House **[18275]**
515 E Capitol St. SE
Washington, DC 20003
PH: (202)543-5560
Fax: (202)543-3814
Sandford, Byron, Exec. Dir.

Pension Rights Center **[12451]**
1350 Connecticut Ave. NW, Ste. 206
Washington, DC 20036-1739
PH: (202)296-3776
Toll free: 888-420-6550
Ferguson, Karen, Director

People for the American Way
[17924]
1101 15th St. NW, Ste. 600
Washington, DC 20005
PH: (202)467-4999
Baker, Margery F., Exec. VP

People-Animals-Love **[17459]**
731 8th St. SE, Ste. 202
Washington, DC 20003
PH: (202)966-2171
Fax: (202)966-2172
Young, Autumn, Exec. Dir.

Performing Arts Alliance **[8996]**
1211 Connecticut Ave. NW, Ste. 200
Washington, DC 20036
PH: (202)207-3850
Fax: (202)833-1543
Durham, Mario Garcia, Chairman

Personal Care Product Council
[1587]
1620 L St. NW, Ste. 1200
Washington, DC 20036
PH: (202)331-1770
Fax: (202)331-1969
Westine, Lezlee, President, CEO

Personal Watercraft Industry Association **[2919]**
650 Massachusetts Ave. NW, Ste.
520
Washington, DC 20001
Dickerson, Dave, VP

Personalized Medicine Coalition
[15743]
1710 Rhode Island Ave. NW, Ste.
700
Washington, DC 20036
PH: (202)589-1770
Abrahams, Edward, PhD, President

Pet Food Institute **[2547]**
1020 19th St. NW, Ste. 225
Washington, DC 20036
PH: (202)791-9440
Enright, Cathleen, President, CEO

Pet Industry Joint Advisory Council
[2549]
1146 19th St. NW, Ste. 350
Washington, DC 20036-3746
PH: (202)452-1525
Reid, Laura, Chairperson

Pharmaceutical Care Management
Association **[16681]**
325 7th St. NW
Washington, DC 20004
PH: (202)756-5700
Fax: (202)756-5708
Merritt, Mark, President, CEO

Pharmaceutical Research and
Manufacturers of America **[2570]**
950 F St. NW, Ste. 300
Washington, DC 20004
PH: (202)835-3400
Ubl, Steve, President, CEO

The Phi Beta Kappa Society **[23681]**
1606 New Hampshire Ave. NW
Washington, DC 20009
PH: (202)265-3808
Fax: (202)986-1601
Churchill, John, Secretary

Phi Beta Sigma Fraternity **[23867]**
145 Kennedy St. NW
Washington, DC 20011-5294
PH: (202)726-5434
Fax: (202)882-1681
Anderson, Daryl, Exec. Dir.

Philanthropy Roundtable **[12493]**
1730 M St. NW, Ste. 601
Washington, DC 20036
PH: (202)822-8333
Fax: (202)822-8325
Meyerson, Adam, President

Philippine American Chamber of
Commerce **[23613]**
Washington, DC
Cabrera, John P., Contact

Philosophy Education Society
[10113]
The Catholic University of America
223 Aquinas Hall
Washington, DC 20064
PH: (202)635-8778
Toll free: 800-255-5924
Fax: (202)319-4484
Ellrod, Dr. Frederick, III, Chairman

Physician Assistant Education As-
sociation **[16724]**
655 K St. NW, Ste. 700
Washington, DC 20001-2385
PH: (703)548-5538
Barwick, Timi Agar, CEO

Physician Hospitals of America
[15744]
2025 M St. NW, Ste. 800
Washington, DC 20036
PH: (202)367-1113
Fax: (202)367-2113
Richardson, John, Exec. Dir.

Physicians Committee for
Responsible Medicine **[14960]**
5100 Wisconsin Ave. NW, Ste. 400
Washington, DC 20016
PH: (202)686-2210
Toll free: 866-416-PCRM
Fax: (202)686-2216
Barnard, Neal D., MD, President

Physicians for Social Responsibility
[18822]
1111 14th St. NW, Ste. 700
Washington, DC 20005-5603
PH: (202)667-4260
Fax: (202)667-4201
Thomasson, Catherine, MD, Exec.
Dir.

Pi Alpha Alpha **[23856]**
1029 Vermont Ave. NW, Ste. 1100
Washington, DC 20005
PH: (202)628-8965
Fax: (202)626-4978
Tschirhart, Mary, President

Pi Sigma Alpha **[23851]**
1527 New Hampshire Ave. NW
Washington, DC 20036
PH: (202)349-9285
Twombly, Sean, Exec. Dir.

Pickle Packers International, Inc.
[1367]
1101 17th St. NW, Ste. 700
Washington, DC 20036
PH: (202)331-2456

Planting Empowerment **[4214]**
Washington, DC 20009
Croston, Damion, Dir. of Operations

Plastic Shipping Container Institute
[841]
5614 Connecticut Ave. NW, No. 284
Washington, DC 20015
PH: (202)253-4347
Fax: (202)330-5092
Baker, David H., Gen. Counsel

Plastics Division of the American
Plastics Council **[2629]**
700 2nd St. NE
Washington, DC 20002
PH: (202)249-7000
   (202)249-6100
Dooley, Calvin M., President, CEO

Plastics Foodservice Packaging
Group **[2482]**
American Chemistry Council
700 2nd St. NE
Washington, DC 20002
PH: (202)249-7000
Fax: (202)249-6100
Levy, Michael H., Contact

Poker Players Alliance **[22388]**
705 8th St. SE, Ste. 300
Washington, DC 20003
PH: (202)621-6936
D'Amato, Alfonse, Chmn. of the Bd.

Polaris Project **[18437]**
PO Box 65323
Washington, DC 20035
PH: (202)745-1001
Fax: (202)745-1119
Myles, Bradley, CEO

Police Executive Research Forum
[5514]
1120 Connecticut Ave. NW, Ste. 930
Washington, DC 20036
PH: (202)466-7820
Wexler, Chuck, Exec. Dir.

Police Foundation **[5515]**
1201 Connecticut Ave. NW, Ste. 200
Washington, DC 20036-2636
PH: (202)833-1460
Fax: (202)659-9149
Norton, Blake, VP, COO

Policy Studies Organization **[19000]**
1527 New Hampshire Ave. NW
Washington, DC 20036
Fax: (202)483-2657
Kallembach, Rex, Treasurer

Policy and Taxation Group **[19161]**
1775 Pennsylvania Ave. NW, Ste.
350
Washington, DC 20006
PH: (202)505-4255
Hiden, Taylor, Advisor

Polish American Congress **[19605]**
1612 K St. NW, Ste. 1200
Washington, DC 20006

PH: (202)296-6955
Fax: (202)835-1565
Spula, Frank J., President

Polyisocyanurate Insulation
Manufacturers Association **[570]**
529 14th St. NW, Ste. 750
Washington, DC 20045
PH: (202)591-2473
Blum, Jared O., President

Population Action International
[12512]
1300 19th St. NW, Ste. 200
Washington, DC 20036-1624
PH: (202)557-3400
Fax: (202)728-4177
Ehlers, Suzanne, CEO, President

Population Connection **[12514]**
2120 L St. NW, Ste. 500
Washington, DC 20037
PH: (202)332-2200
Toll free: 800-767-1956
Fax: (202)332-2302
Gabel, Marianne, Contact

Population Institute **[12517]**
107 2nd St. NE
Washington, DC 20002
PH: (202)544-3300
Fax: (202)544-0068
Ryerson, William, Chmn. of the Bd.,
CEO

Population Reference Bureau **[6369]**
1875 Connecticut Ave. NW, Ste. 520
Washington, DC 20009-5728
Toll free: 800-877-9881
Fax: (202)328-3937
Desai, Viresh, CFO

Population Resource Center **[12519]**
1725 K St. NW
Washington, DC 20006
PH: (202)467-5030
Mitchell, Faith M., Ph.D., Chairman

Postsecondary Electronic Standards
Council **[7235]**
1250 Connecticut Ave. NW, Ste. 200
Washington, DC 20036
PH: (202)261-6514
   (202)261-6516
Fax: (202)261-6517
Sessa, Michael, CEO, President

Pound Civil Justice Institute **[5829]**
777 6th St. NW, Ste. 200
Washington, DC 20001
PH: (202)944-2841
Fax: (202)298-6390
Malone, Patrick A., Treasurer

Poverty and Race Research Action
Council **[12561]**
1200 18th St. NW, No. 200
Washington, DC 20036-2529
PH: (202)906-8023
Fax: (202)842-2885
Hartman, Chester, Dir. of Res.

Prairie Dog Coalition **[10683]**
c/o Humane Society of the United
States
2100 L St. NW
Washington, DC 20037
PH: (301)258-8276
Krank, Lindsey Sterling, Director

Praxis Project **[11299]**
7731 Alaska Ave. NW
Washington, DC 20012
PH: (202)234-5921
Fax: (202)234-2689
Themba, Makani, Exec. Dir.

PRBA - The Rechargeable Battery
Association **[1059]**
1776 K St., 4th Fl.
Washington, DC 20006

PH: (202)719-4978
Smith, Douglas, Director

Preservation Action **[9427]**
1307 New Hampshire Ave. NW, 3rd
Fl.
Washington, DC 20036-1531
PH: (202)463-0970
Fax: (202)463-1299
Miller, Shanon, Chairman

Prevent Human Trafficking **[12056]**
4410 Massachusetts Ave. NW, No.
210
Washington, DC 20016
PH: (202)330-2800
Arnold, Christina, Founder, Exec.
Dir.

Weston A. Price Foundation **[16236]**
4200 Wisconsin Ave. NW, PMB 106-
380
Washington, DC 20016
PH: (202)363-4394
Fax: (202)363-4396
Morell, Sally Fallon, President,
Treasurer

Prison Fellowship International
[11543]
PO Box 17434
Washington, DC 20041
PH: (703)481-0000
Lofaro, Frank, CEO

Private Agencies Collaborating
Together **[5445]**
1828 L St. NW, Ste. 300
Washington, DC 20036-5104
PH: (202)466-5666
Fax: (202)466-5665
Viso, Mark, CEO, President

Private Duty Homecare Association
[15282]
228 7th St. SE
Washington, DC 20003
PH: (202)547-7424
Fax: (202)547-3660
Drea, Patricia, Chairman

Process Gas Consumers Group
[18056]
1909 K St. NW, 12th Fl.
Washington, DC 20006
PH: (202)661-7607
Chambers, Andrea, Contact

ProEnglish **[9284]**
20 F St. NW, 7th Fl.
Washington, DC 20001
PH: (202)507-6203
Fax: (571)527-2813
Vandervoort, Robert, Exec. Dir.

Professional Aviation Safety Special-
ists **[23390]**
1150 17th St. NW, Ste. 702
Washington, DC 20036
PH: (202)293-7277
Fax: (202)293-7727
Perrone, Mike, President

Professional Managers Association
[5199]
PO Box 77235
Washington, DC 20013
PH: (202)803-9597
Fax: (202)803-9044
Leszcz, Michael, President

Professional Women Controllers,
Inc. **[1263]**
PO Box 23924
Washington, DC 20024
Wilson, Patti, President

Progressive Policy Institute **[19001]**
1200 New Hampshire Ave. NW, Ste.
575

Washington, DC 20036
PH: (202)525-3926
Fax: (202)525-3941
Marshall, Will, III, Founder, President

Project on Defense Alternatives
[18089]
Center for International Policy
2000 M St. NW, Ste. 720
Washington, DC 20036-3327
PH: (202)232-3317
Conetta, Carl, Director

Project on Government Oversight
[18698]
1100 G St. NW, Ste. 500
Washington, DC 20005-3806
PH: (202)347-1122
Fax: (202)347-1116
Hunter, David, Chairman

Project on Technology, Work and
Character **[6712]**
c/o The Maccoby Group
4825 Linnean Ave. NW
Washington, DC 20008
PH: (202)895-8922
Fax: (202)895-8923
Margolies, Richard, VP

Project Vote! **[18920]**
1420 K St., Ste. 700
Washington, DC 20005
PH: (202)546-4173
Fax: (202)733-4762
Slater, Michael, President, Exec. Dir.

Property Rights Alliance **[5691]**
722 12th St. NW, 4th Fl.
Washington, DC 20005
PH: (202)785-0266
Montanari, Lorenzo, Exec. Dir.

Protection Project **[12057]**
1717 Massachusetts Ave. NW
Washington, DC 20036
PH: (202)256-7520
Mattar, Dr. Mohammed Y., Exec. Dir.

Psychotherapy Networker **[16988]**
5135 MacArthur Blvd. NW
Washington, DC 20016
PH: (202)537-8950
Toll free: 888-851-9498
Fax: (202)537-6869
Simon, Richard, Editor

Public Affairs Alliance of Iranian
Americans **[18577]**
1001 Connecticut Ave. NW
Washington, DC 20036-5504
PH: (202)828-8370
Fax: (202)828-8371
Austin, Leila Golestaneh, Dr., Exec.
Dir.

Public Affairs Council **[18068]**
2121 K St. NW, Ste. 900
Washington, DC 20037
PH: (202)787-5950
Fax: (202)787-5942
Ring, Rusty, Chairman

Public Citizen **[18057]**
1600 20th St. NW
Washington, DC 20009-1001
PH: (202)588-1000
Toll free: 800-289-3787
Fax: (202)588-7798
Weissman, Robert, President

Public Citizen Health Research
Group **[17016]**
1600 20th St. NW
Washington, DC 20009
PH: (202)588-1000
Wolfe, Sidney M., MD, Founder,
Advisor

Public Citizen Litigation Group
[18058]
1600 20th St. NW
Washington, DC 20009-1001
PH: (202)588-1000
Weissman, Robert, President

Public Citizen's Congress Watch
[18059]
215 Pennsylvania Ave. SE
Washington, DC 20003
PH: (202)546-4996
Gilbert, Lisa, Director

Public Education Center **[18948]**
1830 Connecticut Ave. NW
Washington, DC 20009
PH: (202)466-4310
Fax: (202)466-4344
Clifford, Garry, Director

Public Employees Roundtable
[5081]
500 N Capitol St., Ste. 1204
Washington, DC 20001
PH: (202)927-4926
Fax: (202)927-4920
Bratton, Adam, COO

Public Health Foundation **[17017]**
1300 L St. NW, Ste. 800
Washington, DC 20005
PH: (202)218-4400
    (202)218-4420
Fax: (202)218-4409
Stefanak, Matthew, Secretary,
Treasurer

Public Housing Authorities Directors
Association **[5285]**
511 Capitol Ct. NE
Washington, DC 20002-4937
PH: (202)546-5445
Fax: (202)546-2280
Kaiser, Timothy G., Exec. Dir.

Public Interest Intellectual Property
Advisors **[5340]**
PO Box 65245
Washington, DC 20035
Lyfoung, Pacyinz, Prog. Dir.

Public Justice **[5724]**
1620 L St. NW, Ste. 630
Washington, DC 20006-1220
PH: (202)797-8600
Fax: (202)232-7203
Bland, F. Paul, Jr., Exec. Dir.

Public Lands Council **[4581]**
1301 Pennsylvania Ave. NW, Ste.
300
Washington, DC 20004
PH: (202)347-0228
Richards, Brenda, President

Public Leadership Education
Network **[8754]**
1875 Connecticut Ave. NW, 10th Fl.
Washington, DC 20009
PH: (202)872-1585
Bruno, Sarah, Exec. Dir.

Public Welfare Foundation **[12988]**
1200 U St. NW
Washington, DC 20009-4443
PH: (202)965-1800
McClymont, Mary E., President

PublicSchoolOptions.org **[8480]**
2100 M St. NW, Ste. 170-257
Washington, DC 20037-1233
Toll free: 866-558-2874
Elvrum, Tillie, President

Puerto Rico U.S.A. Citizenship
Foundation **[18158]**
600 13th St. NW
Washington, DC 20005-3005

Pugwash Conferences on Science
and World Affairs **[18003]**
Washington Office
1211 Connecticut Ave. NW, Ste. 800
Washington, DC 20036
PH: (202)478-3440
Fax: (202)238-9604
Miller, Steve, Chairman

PXE International **[14855]**
4301 Connecticut Ave. NW, Ste. 404
Washington, DC 20008-2369
PH: (202)362-9599
Fax: (202)966-8553
Terry, Patrick F., President

PYXERA Global **[18498]**
1030 15th St. NW, Ste. 730 E
Washington, DC 20005
PH: (202)872-0933
Fax: (202)872-0923
White, Deirdre, CEO, President

Quality Education for Minorities
Network **[7798]**
1818 N St. NW, Ste. 350
Washington, DC 20036
PH: (202)659-1818
Fax: (202)659-5408
McBay, Shirley, President

Quota International **[12905]**
1420 21st St. NW
Washington, DC 20036-5901
PH: (202)331-9694
Fax: (202)331-4395
Murphy, Karen, President

Radio Free Europe/Radio Liberty
[17954]
1201 Connecticut Ave. NW
Washington, DC 20036
PH: (202)457-6900
Fax: (202)457-6962
Shell, Jeffrey, Chmn. of the Bd.

Radio-Television Digital News As-
sociation **[481]**
529 14th St. NW, Ste. 1240
Washington, DC 20045
Fax: (202)223-4007
Cavender, Mike, Exec. Dir.

Rails-to-Trails Conservancy **[23331]**
Duke Ellington Bldg., 5th Fl.
2121 Ward Ct. NW
Washington, DC 20037
PH: (202)331-9696
Fax: (202)223-9257
Laughlin, Keith, President

Railway Engineering-Maintenance
Suppliers Association **[2840]**
500 New Jersey Ave. NW, Ste. 400
Washington, DC 20001
PH: (202)715-2921
Fax: (202)204-5753
Soucie, Urszula M., Dir. of Opera-
tions

Railway Supply Institute **[2841]**
425 3rd St. SW, Ste. 920
Washington, DC 20024
PH: (202)347-4664
Fax: (202)347-0047
Simpson, Thomas D., President

Rape, Abuse and Incest National
Network **[12571]**
1220 L St. NW, Ste. 505
Washington, DC 20005
PH: (202)544-3064
    (202)544-1034
Toll free: 800-656-4673
Berkowitz, Scott, Founder, President

Reading Is Fundamental **[8490]**
1730 Rhode Island Ave. NW, 11th
Fl.

Washington, DC 20036
PH: (202)536-3400
Toll free: 877-743-7323
Rasco, Carol H., CEO, President

ReadyNation **[18173]**
1212 New York Ave. NW, Ste. 300
Washington, DC 20005-3988
PH: (202)408-9282
Fax: (202)776-0110
Watson, Sara, Director

The Real Estate Roundtable **[2891]**
801 Pennsylvania Ave. NW, Ste. 720
Washington, DC 20004
PH: (202)639-8400
Fax: (202)639-8442
Reid, Michelle M., Dir. of Mtgs.,
Exec. Asst.

Real Estate Services Providers
Council **[2892]**
2101 L St. NW, Ste. 800
Washington, DC 20037
PH: (202)862-2051
Fax: (202)862-2052
Johnson, Susan E., President

Rebuilding Together **[11991]**
1899 L St. NW, Ste. 1000
Washington, DC 20036-3810
Toll free: 800-473-4229
Carr, Tom, Bd. Member

Recording Industry Association of
America **[2904]**
1025 F St. NW, 10th Fl.
Washington, DC 20004
PH: (202)775-0101
Sherman, Cary, Chairman, CEO

Reform Judaism **[20279]**
2027 Massachusetts Ave. NW
Washington, DC 20036
PH: (202)387-2800
Weinstein, Barbara, Assoc. Dir.

Refugee Council USA **[19019]**
1628 16th St. NW
Washington, DC 20009-3064
PH: (202)319-2102
Fax: (202)319-2104
Nezer, Melanie, Chairman

Refugees International **[12597]**
2001 S St. NW, Ste. 700
Washington, DC 20009
PH: (202)828-0110
   (202)361-6131
Toll free: 800-733-8433
Fax: (202)828-0819
Gabaudan, Michel, President

Regional Airline Association **[157]**
2025 M St. NW, Ste. 800
Washington, DC 20036-3309
PH: (202)367-1170
Fax: (202)367-2170
Black, Faye Malarkey, President

Regional Reporters Association
[2716]
PO Box 254, Ben Franklin Sta.
Washington, DC 20005
Jackson, Herb, Treasurer

Reinsurance Association of America
[1922]
1445 New York Ave., 7th Fl.
Washington, DC 20005
PH: (202)638-3690
Fax: (202)638-0936
Nutter, Franklin W., President

Relief International **[12719]**
1101 14th St. NW, Ste. 1100
Washington, DC 20006
PH: (202)639-8660
Fax: (202)639-8664
Wilson, Nancy, CEO, President

Religion News Service **[2717]**
National Press Bldg.
529 14th St. NW
Washington, DC 20045
PH: (202)463-8777
Toll free: 888-707-3755
Fax: (202)662-7154
Southworth, Don, Treasurer

Religious Action Center of Reform
Judaism **[18594]**
2027 Massachusetts Ave. NW
Washington, DC 20036
PH: (202)387-2800
Fax: (202)667-9070
Pesner, Jonah, Rabbi, Director

Religious Coalition for Reproductive
Choice **[19035]**
1413 K St. NW, 14th Fl.
Washington, DC 20005
PH: (202)628-7700
Fax: (202)628-7716
Zeh, Katey, Chairman

Religious Formation Conference
[19901]
3025 4th St. NE, Ste. 124
Washington, DC 20017-1101
PH: (202)827-4562
Fax: (202)827-4564
Regan, Carol, Assoc. Dir.

Religious Freedom Coalition **[12721]**
601 Pennsylvania Ave. NW, Ste. 900
Washington, DC 20004-3647
Murray, William J., Chairman

Renewable Energy Markets Associa-
tion **[1121]**
1211 Connecticut Ave. NW, Ste. 600
Washington, DC 20036-2701
PH: (202)640-6597
Fax: (202)223-5537
Anderson, Richard, President

Renewable Fuels Association **[6507]**
425 3rd St. SW, Ste. 1150
Washington, DC 20024
PH: (202)289-3835
Fax: (202)289-7519
Dinneen, Bob, CEO, President

Reporters Committee for Freedom of
the Press **[17955]**
1156 15th St. NW, Ste. 1250
Washington, DC 20005-1779
PH: (202)795-9300
Toll free: 800-336-4243
Brown, Bruce D., Exec. Dir.

Reporters Without Borders **[18441]**
Southern Railway Bldg., Ste. 600
15th & K St. NW
Washington, DC 20005
Chol, Eric, VP

Representative of German Industry
and Trade **[667]**
1130 Connecticut Ave. NW, Ste.
1200
Washington, DC 20006
PH: (202)659-4777
Fax: (202)659-4779
Zielke, Dr. Thomas, President

Reproductive Toxicology Center
[14763]
2737 Devonshire Pl. NW, No. 120
Washington, DC 20008-3479
PH: (703)203-6040
Fax: (202)249-0111

Republican Governors Association
[5786]
1747 Pennsylvania Ave. NW, Ste.
250
Washington, DC 20006-4643

PH: (202)662-4140
Adams, Mike, Gen. Counsel, Dep.
Dir.

Republican Jewish Coalition **[19046]**
50 F St. NW, Ste. 100
Washington, DC 20001
PH: (202)638-6688
Fax: (202)638-6694
Adelson, Sheldon G., Chairman

Republican National Committee
[19049]
310 1st St. SE
Washington, DC 20003
PH: (202)863-8500
Priebus, Reince, Chairman

Republicans Abroad International
[18895]
2445 M St. NW, Ste. 3103
Washington, DC 20037-1435

Reserve Officers Association of the
United States **[5622]**
1 Constitution Ave. NE
Washington, DC 20002
PH: (202)479-2200
Toll free: 800-809-9448
Fax: (202)547-1641
Sweeney, Col. James R., President

RESOLVE **[19003]**
1255 23rd St. NW, Ste. 275
Washington, DC 20037
PH: (202)944-2300
Fax: (202)338-1264
D'Esposito, Stephen, President

Responsible Industry for a Sound
Environment **[2506]**
1156 15th St. NW, Ste. 400
Washington, DC 20005
PH: (202)872-3860

Restoration Industry Association
[2140]
2025 M St. NW, Ste. 800
Washington, DC 20036
PH: (202)367-1180
Fax: (202)367-2180
White, Jack, Secretary

RESULTS **[18458]**
1101 15th St. NW, Ste. 1200
Washington, DC 20005
PH: (202)783-7100
Fax: (202)466-1397
Carter, Joanne, Exec. Dir.

Retail Advertising and Marketing As-
sociation **[109]**
325 7th St. NW, Ste. 1100
Washington, DC 20004-2818
PH: (202)783-7971
Toll free: 800-673-4692
Fax: (202)737-2849
Gatti, Mike, Exec. Dir.

Rights and Resources Initiative
[4215]
1238 Wisconsin Ave. NW, Ste. 300
Washington, DC 20007
PH: (202)470-3900
   (202)470-3890
Fax: (202)944-3315
White, Andy, Coord.

Ripon Society **[19051]**
1155 15th St. NW, Ste. 550
Washington, DC 20005
PH: (202)216-1008
Jackson, Stephen, Pol. Dir.

The Road Information Program
[3356]
3000 Connecticut Ave. NW, Ste. 208
Washington, DC 20008

PH: (202)466-6706
Wilkins, William M., Exec. Dir.

Roadway Safety Foundation **[12842]**
1101 14th St. NW, Ste. 750
Washington, DC 20005
PH: (202)857-1208
Fax: (202)857-1220
Gillen, Cathy, Managing Dir.

Rock the Vote **[17839]**
1875 Connecticut Ave. NW, 10th Fl.
Washington, DC 20009
PH: (202)719-9910
Rubin, Jon, Chairman

Roof Coatings Manufacturers As-
sociation **[748]**
750 National Press Bldg.
529 14th St. NW
Washington, DC 20045
PH: (202)591-2452
Fax: (202)591-2445
Ritchie, Chelsea, Coord.

Roots of Development **[12808]**
1325 18th St. NW, Unit 303
Washington, DC 20036-6505
PH: (202)466-0805
Bissonnette, Chad W., Exec. Dir.,
Founder

Roundtable Association of Catholic
Diocesan Social Action Directors
[20566]
415 Michigan Ave. NE, Ste. 210B
Washington, DC 20017
PH: (202)635-5858
   (202)635-5828
Orr, Catherine, Co-Ch.

Rubber Manufacturers Association
[2986]
1400 K St. NW, Ste. 900
Washington, DC 20005
PH: (202)682-4800
Luke, Anne Forristall, President,
CEO

Rumi Forum **[18827]**
750 1st St. NE, Ste. 1120
Washington, DC 20002-8013
PH: (202)429-1690
Fax: (202)747-2919
Celik, Emre, President

Rural Coalition **[19078]**
1029 Vermont Ave. NW, Ste. 601
Washington, DC 20005
PH: (202)628-7160
Fax: (202)393-1816
Zippert, John, Chmn. of the Bd.

Rural Community Assistance
Partnership **[7375]**
1701 K St. NW, Ste. 700
Washington, DC 20006
PH: (202)408-1273
Toll free: 800-321-7227
Fax: (202)408-8165
Stewart, Robert, Exec. Dir.

Rural School and Community Trust
[8511]
4301 Connecticut Ave. NW, Ste. 100
Washington, DC 20008
PH: (202)822-3919
Fax: (202)872-4050
Guajardo, Francisco J., PhD, V. Ch.

Rwandan International Network As-
sociation **[11426]**
901 15th St. NW
Washington, DC 20005
PH: (301)259-1792
Kayinamura, Yohani, PhD, President

Safe Kids Worldwide **[11144]**
1301 Pennsylvania Ave. NW, Ste.
1000

Washington, DC 20004-1707
PH: (202)662-0600
Fax: (202)393-2072
Carr, Kate S., President, CEO

Safer Chemicals, Healthy Families **[17019]**
641 S St. NW, 3rd Fl.
Washington, DC 20001
Igrejas, Andy, Director

Safety Net Hospitals for Pharmaceutical Access **[16684]**
1101 15th St. NW, Ste. 910
Washington, DC 20005
PH: (202)552-5850
Fax: (202)552-5868
Slafsky, Ted, President, CEO

Salam Institute for Peace and Justice **[18010]**
1628 16th St. NW
Washington, DC 20009
PH: (202)360-4955
Abu-Niber, Mohammed, Founder, President

Salzburg Global Seminar **[9582]**
1250 H St., NW, Ste. 1150
Washington, DC 20005
PH: (202)637-7683
Fax: (202)637-7699
Salyer, Stephen, President, CEO

Satellite Broadcasting and Communications Association **[3238]**
1100 17th St. NW, Ste. 1150
Washington, DC 20036
PH: (202)349-3620
Toll free: 800-541-5981
Fax: (202)318-2618
Reinsdorf, Andrew, V. Chmn. of the Bd.

Satellite Industry Association **[776]**
1200 18th St. NW, Ste. 1001
Washington, DC 20036
PH: (202)503-1560
Fax: (202)503-1590
Cooper, Patricia, V. Ch.

Save America's Forests **[3938]**
4 Library Ct. SE
Washington, DC 20003
PH: (202)544-9219
Ross, Carl, Director, Founder

Scenic America **[4102]**
1307 New Hampshire Ave. NW
Washington, DC 20036-1351
PH: (202)463-1294
Fax: (202)463-1299
Tracy, Mary, President

Scholarly Publishing and Academic Resources Coalition **[2811]**
21 Dupont Cir. NW, Ste. 800
Washington, DC 20036
PH: (202)296-2296
Fax: (202)872-0884
Joseph, Heather, Exec. Dir.

School of the Americas Watch **[18949]**
5525 Illinois Ave. NW
Washington, DC 20011-2937
PH: (202)234-3440
Fax: (202)636-4505
Bourgeois, Fr. Roy, Founder

School-Based Health Alliance **[15063]**
1010 Vermont Ave. NW, Ste. 600
Washington, DC 20005
PH: (202)638-5872
Fax: (202)638-5879
Schlitt, John, President

Schools Interoperability Framework Association **[6261]**
1090 Vermont Ave. NW, 6th Fl.
Washington, DC 20005

PH: (202)789-4460
Fax: (202)289-7097
Fruth, Dr. Larry L., II, CEO, Exec. Dir.

Scottish Rite Research Society **[19570]**
c/o House of the Temple
1733 16th St. NW
Washington, DC 20009
PH: (202)232-3579

SEA Professional Development League **[5200]**
Senior Executives Association
77 K St. NE, Ste. 2600
Washington, DC 20002
PH: (202)971-3300
Fax: (202)971-3317
Bonosaro, Carol A., President

Seafood Harvesters of America **[1303]**
PO Box 66365
Washington, DC 20035
PH: (202)888-2733
Brown, Christopher, President

Search for Common Ground **[18528]**
1601 Connecticut Ave. NW, Ste. 200
Washington, DC 20009-1035
PH: (202)265-4300
Fax: (202)232-6718
Idriss, Shamil, President, CEO

Secular Coalition for America **[20599]**
1012 14th St. NW, Ste. 205
Washington, DC 20005-3429
PH: (202)299-1091
Fax: (202)293-0922
Silverman, Herb, President

Securing America's Future Energy **[6512]**
1111 19th St. NW, Ste. 406
Washington, DC 20036
PH: (202)461-2360
Fax: (202)461-2379
Diamond, Robbie, CEO, President, Founder

Semiconductor Industry Association **[1062]**
1101 K St. NW, Ste. 450
Washington, DC 20005
PH: (202)446-1700
Toll free: 866-756-0715
Fax: (202)216-9745
Neuffer, John, President, CEO

Senior Executives Association **[5201]**
77 K St. NE, Ste. 2600
Washington, DC 20002
PH: (202)971-3300
Fax: (202)971-3317
Bonosaro, Carol A., President

The Seniors Coalition **[10529]**
1250 Connecticut Ave. NW, Ste. 200
Washington, DC 20036-2643
PH: (202)261-3594
Bridges, Dr. Joseph L., CEO, President

Sentencing Project **[11548]**
1705 DeSales St. NW, 8th Fl.
Washington, DC 20036
PH: (202)628-0871
Fax: (202)628-1091
Mauer, Marc, Exec. Dir.

Service Employees International Union **[23461]**
1800 Massachusetts Ave. NW
Washington, DC 20036
PH: (202)730-7000
(202)730-7684
Toll free: 800-424-8592
Henry, Mary Kay, President

Sexuality Information and Education Council of the U.S. **[17203]**
1012 14th St. NW, Ste. 1108
Washington, DC 20005-3424
PH: (202)265-2405
Fax: (202)462-2340
Rodriguez, Monica, President, CEO

Share Our Strength **[12114]**
1030 15th St. NW, Ste. 1100 W
Washington, DC 20005
PH: (202)393-2925
Toll free: 800-969-4767
Fax: (202)347-5868
Shore, Bill, CEO, Founder

Shea Yeleen International **[1588]**
733 Euclid St. NW, 2nd Fl.
Washington, DC 20001
PH: (202)285-3435
Adu-Gyamfi, Yaw, Founder, Exec. Dir.

Shia Rights Watch **[18442]**
1050 17th St. NW, Ste. 800
Washington, DC 20036
PH: (202)350-4302
Akhwand, Mustafa, Founder, Exec. Dir.

Shipbuilders Council of America **[2257]**
20 F St. NW, Ste. 500
Washington, DC 20001
PH: (202)737-3234
Fax: (202)737-0264
Paxton, Matt, President

Short Span Steel Bridge Alliance **[6159]**
25 Massachusetts Ave. NW, Ste. 800
Washington, DC 20001
PH: (301)367-6179
Snyder, Dan, Mgr.

Sierra Student Coalition **[4013]**
50 F St. NW, 8th Fl.
Washington, DC 20001
PH: (202)547-1141
Fax: (202)547-6009
Gerhke, Karissa, Director

Sikh American Legal Defense and Education Fund **[19098]**
1012 14th St. NW, Ste. 450
Washington, DC 20005
PH: (202)393-2700
Fax: (202)318-4433
Singh, Jasjit, Exec. Dir.

Silicones Environmental, Health and Safety Council **[726]**
700 2nd St. NE
Washington, DC 20002
PH: (703)249-7000
Fax: (703)249-6100
Thomas, Karluss, Contact

Silver Institute **[2370]**
1400 I St. NW, Ste. 550
Washington, DC 20005
PH: (202)835-0185
Fax: (202)835-0155
Krebs, Mitchell, President

Sister Cities International **[18558]**
915 15th St. NW, 4th Fl.
Washington, DC 20005
PH: (202)347-8630
Fax: (202)393-6524
Kane, Mary D., President, CEO

Small Business Exporters Association of the United States **[1993]**
1156 15th St. NW, Ste. 1100
Washington, DC 20005
PH: (202)552-2903
(202)552-2904
Toll free: 800-345-6728
Milanese, Jody, VP of Government Rel.

Small Business Investor Alliance **[3127]**
1100 H St. NW, Ste. 1200
Washington, DC 20005
PH: (202)628-5055
Palmer, Brett, President

Smart Growth America **[11438]**
1707 L St. NW, Ste. 250
Washington, DC 20036
PH: (202)207-3355
Anderson, Geoffrey, CEO, President

SmartPower **[4030]**
1120 Connecticut Ave. NW, Ste. 1040
Washington, DC 20036
PH: (202)775-2040
Fax: (202)775-2045
Rosoff, Lyn, Dir. of Comm.

Smithsonian Institution Archives of American Art **[8889]**
750 9th St. NW
Victor Bldg., Ste. 2200
Washington, DC 20013-7012
PH: (202)633-7940
Fax: (202)633-7994
Kirwin, Liza, Dep. Dir.

Smoke Free Alternatives Trade Association **[3131]**
1155 F St. NW, Ste. 1050
Washington, DC 20004
PH: (202)251-1661
Cabrera, Cynthia, President

Society for American Archaeology **[5947]**
1111 14th St. NW, Ste. 800
Washington, DC 20005-5622
PH: (202)789-8200
Fax: (202)789-0284
Brimsek, Tobi, Exec. Dir.

Society of American Indian Government Employees **[23438]**
PO Box 7715
Washington, DC 20044
PH: (202)564-0375
Fax: (202)564-7899
Sappier, Brian, V. Chmn. of the Bd.

Society for Cardiovascular Angiography and Interventions **[14142]**
1100 17th St. NW, Ste. 330
Washington, DC 20036
PH: (202)741-9854
Toll free: 800-992-7224
Fax: (800)863-5202
Cox, David A., Treasurer

Society of Chemical Manufacturers and Affiliates **[728]**
1850 M St. NW, Ste. 700
Washington, DC 20036-5810
PH: (202)721-4100
Fax: (202)296-8120
Helmes, C. Tucker, PhD, Managing Dir.

Society of the Cincinnati **[20696]**
2118 Massachusetts Ave. NW
Washington, DC 20008-2810
PH: (202)785-2040

Society of Commercial Seed Technologists **[4646]**
653 Constitution Ave. NE
Washington, DC 20002
PH: (202)870-2412
(605)688-4606
Cleave, Barbara, President

Society for Conservation Biology **[6097]**
1133 15th St. NW, Ste. 300
Washington, DC 20001

PH: (202)234-4133
Fax: (703)995-4633
Unger, Geri, Exec. Dir.

Society for Ecological Restoration
International [4014]
1133 15th St. NW, Ste. 300
Washington, DC 20005
PH: (202)299-9518
Fax: (270)626-5485
Walder, Bethanie, Exec. Dir.

Society for Economic Anthropology
[5922]
c/o Dolores Koenig, President
Hamilton - 202A
College of Arts and Sciences -
Anthropology
American University
Washington, DC 20016
Wallace, Richard, Treasurer

Society for Environmental Graphic
Design [1557]
1900 L St. NW, Ste. 710
Washington, DC 20036
PH: (202)638-5555
Ayers, Jill, President

Society for Experimental Biology and
Medicine [6100]
3220 N St. NW, No. 179
Washington, DC 20007-2829
PH: (201)962-3519
Fax: (201)962-3522
Gaskins, H. Rex, PhD, Officer

Society of Government Economists
[5160]
PO Box 23010
Washington, DC 20026-3010
PH: (202)643-1743
Constant, Amelie F., President

Society for History in the Federal
Government [9519]
PO Box 14139
Washington, DC 20044
Charles, Elizabeth C., Secretary

Society of Industrial and Office Real-
tors [2895]
1201 New York Ave. NW, Ste. 350
Washington, DC 20005-6126
PH: (202)449-8200
Fax: (202)216-9325
Hollander, Richard, Exec. VP

Society for International Develop-
ment - USA [18499]
1101 15th St. NW, 3rd Fl.
Washington, DC 20005
PH: (202)331-1317
Raphaelson, Katherine, President

Society for Maternal-Fetal Medicine
[16627]
409 12th St. SW
Washington, DC 20024
PH: (202)863-2476
Fax: (202)554-1132
Stahr, Patricia D., Exec. Dir.

Society of Missionaries of Africa
[19908]
1622 21st St. NW
Washington, DC 20009-1089
PH: (202)232-5995
Toll free: 877-523-4662
Fax: (303)232-0120
Lynch, Fr. John P., Director

Society for Neuroscience [6921]
1121 14th St. NW, Ste. 1010
Washington, DC 20005
PH: (202)962-4000
Gonzalez, Elvia, Asst. Dir.

Society for Occupational and
Environmental Health [16321]
1010 Vermont Ave. NW, No. 513
Washington, DC 20005

PH: (202)347-4976
Dobbin, Ronald, President

Society for Personality and Social
Psychology [7075]
1660 L St. NW, No. 1000
Washington, DC 20036
PH: (202)524-6545
Rummel, Chad, Exec. Dir.

Society of the Plastics Industry, Flex-
ible Film and Bag Division [844]
1667 K St. NW, Ste. 1000
Washington, DC 20006
PH: (202)974-5216
Henagan, Mr. Mike, Chairman

Society for the Preservation of the
Greek Heritage [9355]
PO Box 53341
Washington, DC 20009
PH: (757)692-4701
Koliatsos, Dr. Vassilis, Chairperson

Society of Professors of Child and
Adolescent Psychiatry [16837]
3615 Wisconsin Ave. NW
Washington, DC 20016
PH: (202)966-1994
Fax: (202)966-2037
Magee, Mr. Earl, Exec. Dir.

Society for the Psychological Study
of Social Issues [16942]
208 I St. NE
Washington, DC 20002-4340
PH: (202)675-6956
Toll free: 877-310-7778
Fax: (202)675-6902
Dudley, Dr. Susan, Exec. Dir.

Society for Public Health Education
[17022]
10 G St. NE, Ste. 605
Washington, DC 20002-4242
PH: (202)408-9804
Fax: (202)408-9815
Auld, Elaine, CEO

Society for Science and the Public
[7146]
1719 N St. NW
Washington, DC 20036
PH: (202)785-2255
Toll free: 800-552-4412
Marincola, Elizabeth, President

Society for Simulation in Healthcare
[15700]
2021 L St. NW, Ste. 400
Washington, DC 20036
Toll free: 866-730-6127
Epps, Chad, President

Society of State Leaders of Health
and Physical Education [8435]
1432 K St. NW, Ste. 400
Washington, DC 20005
Stewart, Patricia, President

Society for the Study of Religion and
Spirituality [16945]
750 1st St. NE
Washington, DC 20002-4242
PH: (202)336-6013
Fax: (202)218-3599

Society of Wine Educators [22478]
1612 K St. NW, Ste. 700
Washington, DC 20006
PH: (202)408-8777
Fax: (202)408-8677
Lembeck, William, Director

Society of Woman Geographers
[6674]
415 E Capitol St. SE
Washington, DC 20003-3810

PH: (202)546-9228
Nichols, Sandra, President

Society for Women's Health
Research [17766]
1025 Connecticut Ave. NW, Ste. 601
Washington, DC 20036
PH: (202)223-8224
Fax: (202)833-3472
Greenberger, Phyllis, MSW, CEO,
President

Software and Information Industry
Association [5341]
1090 Vermont Ave. NW, 6th Fl.
Washington, DC 20005-4095
PH: (202)289-7442
Fax: (202)289-7097
Wasch, Ken, President

Sojourners [20008]
3333 14th St. NW, Ste. 200
Washington, DC 20010
PH: (202)328-8842
    (917)288-9529
Toll free: 800-714-7474
Fax: (202)328-8757
Wallis, Jim, President, Founder

Solar Electric Power Association
[7206]
1220 19th St. NW, Ste. 800
Washington, DC 20036-2405
PH: (202)857-0898
Hamm, Julia, CEO, President

Solar Energy Industries Association
[7207]
600 14th St. NW, Ste. 400
Washington, DC 20005
PH: (202)682-0556
Resch, Rhone, President, CEO

Solar Household Energy [7209]
3327 18th St. NW
Washington, DC 20010
Curtis, Darwin, Director, Founder

Solar Rating and Certification
Corporation [7211]
500 New Jersey Ave., 6th Fl. NW
Washington, DC 20001
PH: (321)213-6037
Toll free: 888-422-7233
Fax: (321)821-0910
Prado, Eileen, Exec. Dir.

Sons of Pericles [19458]
1909 Q St. NW, Ste. 500
Washington, DC 20009-1050
PH: (202)232-6300
Fax: (202)232-2140
Christou, Andreas, VP

Sorptive Minerals Institute [2383]
1800 M St, Ste. 400S
Washington, DC 20036
PH: (202)289-2760
Fax: (202)530-0659
Nicholson, Bryan, Exec. Dir.

SOS Children's Villages-USA
[11153]
1620 I St. NW, Ste. 900
Washington, DC 20006
Toll free: 888-767-4543
Croneberger, Lynn M., CEO

SoundExchange [2439]
733 10th St. NW, 10th Fl.
Washington, DC 20001
PH: (202)640-5858
Huppe, Michael J., President, CEO

Southeast Asia Resource Action
Center [12598]
1628 16th St. NW
Washington, DC 20009-3064

PH: (202)601-2960
Fax: (202)667-6449
Kith, Sarah R., Contact

Southern Governors' Association
[5787]
Hall of the States
444 N Capitol St. NW, Ste. 200
Washington, DC 20001
PH: (202)624-5897
Fax: (202)624-7797
Duff, Ms. Diane, Exec. Dir.

Soyfoods Association of North
America [3771]
1050 17th St. NW, Ste. 600
Washington, DC 20036
PH: (202)659-3520
Leavitt, Kate, President

Special Olympics [22797]
1133 19th St. NW
Washington, DC 20036-3604
PH: (202)628-3630
Toll free: 800-700-8585
Fax: (202)824-0200
Shriver, Timothy P., PhD, Chairman,
CEO

Specialty Steel Industry of North
America [2371]
3050 K St. NW
Washington, DC 20007
PH: (202)342-8630
Toll free: 800-982-0355
Fax: (202)342-8451

SPI: The Plastics Industry Trade As-
sociation [2632]
1425 K St. NW, Ste. 500
Washington, DC 20005
PH: (202)974-5200
Fax: (202)296-7005
Carteaux, William R., President,
CEO

Springboard Enterprises [3500]
2100 Foxhall Rd. NW
Washington, DC 20007
PH: (202)242-6282
Fax: (202)242-6284
Koplovitz, Kay, Chairperson

Stable Value Investment Association
[2037]
1025 Connecticut Ave. NW, Ste.
1000
Washington, DC 20036-5417
PH: (202)580-7620
Fax: (202)580-7621
King, James, Chairman

State Department Watch [18276]
PO Box 65398
Washington, DC 20035
Eichler, Steve, JD, President

Steel Framing Alliance [2372]
25 Massachusetts Ave. NW, Ste.
800
Washington, DC 20001-7400
PH: (202)452-1039
Fax: (202)452-1039
Nowak, Mark, President

Steel Manufacturers Association
[2373]
1150 Connecticut Ave. NW, Ste. 715
Washington, DC 20036-4131
PH: (202)296-1515
Fax: (202)296-2506
Wittenborn, John, Gen. Counsel

Henry L. Stimson Center [18481]
1211 Connecticut Ave. NW, 8th Fl.
Washington, DC 20036
PH: (202)223-5956
Fax: (202)238-9604
Bloomfield, Lincoln, Jr., Chmn. of the
Bd.

Stop Predatory Gambling Foundation [11869]
100 Maryland Ave. NE, Rm. 310
Washington, DC 20002
PH: (202)567-6996
Clark, Guy C., DDS, Chairman

Strategies for International Development [12189]
330 Pennsylvania Ave. SE, Ste. 304
Washington, DC 20003
PH: (202)544-1115
Fax: (202)543-5288
Moorehead, Paul, President

Strategies to Overcome and Prevent Obesity Alliance [16264]
George Washington University
School of Public Health and Health Services
2021 K St. NW, Ste. 850
Washington, DC 20006
PH: (202)609-6003
Carmona, Richard H., Chairperson

Student National Dental Association [7711]
3517 16th St. NW
Washington, DC 20010
PH: (202)806-0065
    (202)588-1697
Fax: (202)518-7471
Cathey, Christopher D., President

Student National Medical Association [8338]
5113 Georgia Ave. NW
Washington, DC 20011-3921
PH: (202)882-2881
Fax: (202)882-2886
Kulukulualani, Anthony, President

Student Peace Alliance [18830]
1616 P St. NW, Ste. 100
Washington, DC 20036
PH: (202)684-2553
Kaplan, Sally, Coord.

Student Press Law Center [17958]
1608 Rhode Island Ave. NW, Ste. 211
Washington, DC 20036
PH: (202)785-5450
Fax: (202)822-5045
LoMonte, Frank, Exec. Dir.

Student Veterans of America [21140]
1012 14th St. NW, 2nd Fl.
Washington, DC 20005
PH: (202)223-4710
Garcia, Rodrigo, Chmn. of the Bd.

Students for Sensible Drug Policy [19158]
1317 F St. NW, Ste. 501
Washington, DC 20004
PH: (202)393-5280
Houston, Aaron, Exec. Dir.

Styrene Information and Research Center [729]
910 17th St. NW, 5th Fl.
Washington, DC 20006
PH: (202)787-5996
Snyder, Jack, Exec. Dir.

Submarine Industrial Base Council [986]
1825 Eye St. NW, Ste. 600
Washington, DC 20006-5415
PH: (202)207-3633
Fax: (202)575-3400
Jelinek, James, Co-Ch.

Sudden Cardiac Arrest Association [14148]
910 17th St. NW, Ste. 800
Washington, DC 20006

PH: (202)441-5982
Tappe, Mary, Chairman

Sugar Association [1374]
1300 L St. NW, Ste. 1001
Washington, DC 20005
PH: (202)785-1122
Fax: (202)785-5019
Gaine, P. Courtney, Act. Pres., CEO

The Sulphur Institute [730]
1020 19th St. NW, Ste. 520
Washington, DC 20036
PH: (202)331-9660
Fax: (202)293-2940
McBride, Robert W., President, CEO

Support Our Aging Religious [10530]
3025 4th St. NE
Washington, DC 20017
PH: (202)529-7627
Fax: (202)529-7633
Lunsmann, Sr. Kathleen, IHM, President

Supreme Court Historical Society [9522]
Opperman House
224 E Capitol St. NE
Washington, DC 20003
PH: (202)543-0400
Toll free: 888-539-4438
Fax: (202)547-7730
Joseph, Gregory P., President

Surety & Fidelity Association of America [1934]
1101 Connecticut Ave. NW, Ste. 800
Washington, DC 20036
PH: (202)463-0600
Fax: (202)463-0606
Schubert, Lynn M., President

Surface Transportation Policy Partnership [19199]
750 1st St. NE, Ste. 901
Washington, DC 20002
PH: (202)466-6251
Wilkinson, Bill, Exec. Dir.

Surviving Parents Coalition [11278]
1414 22nd St. NW, Ste. 4
Washington, DC 20037
Toll free: 888-301-4343
Moulton, Mika, President

Sustainable Buildings Industry Council [7214]
1090 Vermont Ave. NW, Ste. 700
Washington, DC 20005-4950
PH: (202)289-7800
Fax: (202)289-1092
Green, Henry L., AIA, President

Sustainable Nanotechnology Organization [7296]
2020 Pennsylvania Ave. NW, Ste. 200
Washington, DC 20006
Sadik, Wunmi, President, Founder

SustainUS [13482]
1718 21st St. NW
Washington, DC 20009
Gracey, Kyle, Chmn. of the Bd.

Swedish-American Chambers of Commerce, U.S.A. [23620]
2900 K St. NW, Ste. 403
Washington, DC 20007
PH: (202)536-1520
Linde, Therese, Contact

Syrian-American Council [18529]
1875 I St. NW, No. 500
Washington, DC 20006
PH: (202)429-2099
Fax: (202)429-9574
Barq, Mirna, President

TASH [11642]
2013 H St. NW
Washington, DC 20006
PH: (202)540-9020
Fax: (202)540-9019
Trader, Barbara, Exec. Dir.

Tau Alpha Pi [23744]
c/o ASEE
1818 North St. NW, Ste. 600
Washington, DC 20036
PH: (202)350-5764
Fax: (202)265-8504
Fortenberry, Norman, Exec. Dir.

The Tax Council [5802]
600 13th St. NW, Ste. 1000
Washington, DC 20005
PH: (202)822-8062
Fax: (202)315-3413
Brown, Robert, Director

Tax Executives Institute [5803]
1200 G St. NW, Ste. 300
Washington, DC 20005
PH: (202)638-5601
Dicker, Eli J., Exec. Dir.

Tax Foundation [5804]
1325 G St. NW, Ste. 950
Washington, DC 20005
PH: (202)464-6200
    (202)464-5120
Fax: (202)464-6201
Lewis, David P., Chairman

Taxpayers Against Fraud Education Fund [19176]
1220 19th St. NW, Ste. 501
Washington, DC 20036-2497
PH: (202)296-4826
Garner, Takeia, Dir. of Member Svcs.

Taxpayers for Common Sense [19163]
651 Pennsylvania Ave. SE
Washington, DC 20003
PH: (202)546-8500
Smith, Mark, Chairman

Teaching for Change [7846]
1832 11th St. NW
Washington, DC 20009-4436
PH: (202)588-7204
Toll free: 800-763-9131
Fax: (202)238-0109
Brown, Allyson Criner, Project Mgr.

TechnoServe Inc. [18501]
1120 19th St. NW, 8th Fl.
Washington, DC 20036
PH: (202)785-4515
Toll free: 800-999-6757
Fax: (202)785-4544
Winter, Simon, Sr. VP

Telework Advisory Group of WorldatWork [3243]
1100 13th Street, NW
Suite 800
Washington, DC 20005
Rhodes, Marcia, Contact

Telework Coalition [3244]
204 E St. NE
Washington, DC 20002
Wilsker, Chuck, CEO, President, Founder

Terror Free Tomorrow [19187]
5335 Wisconsin Ave. NW, Ste. 440
Washington, DC 20015-2052
PH: (202)274-1800
Fax: (202)274-1821
Ballen, Kenneth, President

Theodore Roosevelt Conservation Partnership [3956]
1660 L St. NW, Ste. 208
Washington, DC 20036

PH: (202)639-8727
Fax: (202)639-8728
Fosburgh, Whit, CEO, President

THIS for Diplomats [18559]
1630 Crescent Pl. NW
Washington, DC 20009
PH: (202)232-3002
Regis, Nicolette, Administrator

Thurgood Marshall College Fund [7469]
901 F St. NW, Ste. 300
Washington, DC 20004
PH: (202)507-4851
Fax: (202)652-2934
Taylor, Johnny C., Jr., CEO, President

TimeBanks USA [13219]
5500 39th St. NW
Washington, DC 20015
PH: (202)686-5200
Fax: (202)537-5033
Cahn, Edgar, Founder, CEO, Chmn. of the Bd.

Torture Abolition and Survivors Support Coalition International [18445]
4121 Harewood Rd. NE, Ste. B
Washington, DC 20017
PH: (202)529-2991
Emiru, Gizachew, Esq, Exec. Dir.

Tostan-U.S. [12059]
2121 Decatur Pl. NW
Washington, DC 20008
PH: (202)818-8851
Mbacke, Dr. Cheikh, Chmn. of the Bd.

Total Family Care Coalition [11833]
1214 I St. SE, Ste. 11
Washington, DC 20003
PH: (202)758-3281
Avent, Gail, Founder, Exec. Dir.

Towing and Recovery Association of America, Inc. [355]
700 12th St. NW, Ste. 700
Washington, DC 20005
Toll free: 888-392-9300
Fax: (888)392-9300
Martineau, Cynthia J., Exec. Dir.

Traffic North America [4894]
c/o WWF-US
1250 24th St. NW
Washington, DC 20037
PH: (202)293-4800
Fax: (202)775-8287
Broad, Steven, Exec. Dir.

Trans-Atlantic Business Council [23622]
919 18th St. NW, Ste. 220
Washington, DC 20006
PH: (202)828-9104
Fax: (202)828-9106
Paemen, Amb. Hugo, Chmn. of the Bd.

Transport Workers Union of America [23527]
501 3rd St. NW, 9th Fl.
Washington, DC 20001
PH: (202)719-3900
Fax: (202)347-0454
Garcia, Alex, Secretary, Treasurer

Transportation for America [19200]
1707 L St. NW, Ste. 250
Washington, DC 20036
PH: (202)955-5543
Corless, James, Director

Treasury Historical Association [9524]
PO Box 28118
Washington, DC 20038-8118

PH: (202)298-0550
Grippo, Gary, VP

Treated Wood Council [594]
1101 K St. NW, Ste. 700
Washington, DC 20005
PH: (202)641-5427
Fax: (202)463-2059
Miller, Jeff, President, Exec. Dir.

Treatment Communities of America
[13186]
1875 I St. NW, Rm. 574
Washington, DC 20006
PH: (202)296-3503
Carlson, Ed, 1st VP

Trekking for Kids Inc. [23332]
PO Box 25493
Washington, DC 20027
PH: (202)651-1387
Montero, Jose, Jr., Chairman,
President

Triangle Club [13187]
2030 P St. NW
Washington, DC 20036
PH: (202)659-8641
Terry A-R., President

Trilateral Commission [18530]
1156 15th St. NW
Washington, DC 20005
PH: (202)467-5410
Fax: (202)467-5415
Nye, Joseph S., Jr., Chairman

Tropical Forest and Climate Coali-
tion [4618]
1616 P St. NW, Ste. 403
Washington, DC 20036
PH: (202)552-1828
Hurowitz, Glenn, Director

True Food Network [6651]
660 Pennsylvania Ave. SE, No. 302
Washington, DC 20003
PH: (202)547-9359
Fax: (202)547-9429
Kimbrell, Andrew, Exec. Dir.

Truman Center for National Policy
[19006]
1250 I St. NW, Ste. 500
Washington, DC 20005
PH: (202)216-9723
Fax: (202)682-1818
Breen, Michael, President, CEO

Harry S. Truman Scholarship
Foundation [7928]
712 Jackson Pl. NW
Washington, DC 20006
PH: (202)395-4831
Rich, Andrew, Exec. Sec.

Trust for America's Health [17025]
1730 M St. NW, Ste. 900
Washington, DC 20036
PH: (202)223-9870
Fax: (202)223-9871
Levi, Jeffrey, PhD, Exec. Dir.

Truth Initiative [19159]
900 G St. NW, 4th Fl.
Washington, DC 20001
PH: (202)454-5555
Moore, Mike, Treasurer

Turkish American Scientists and
Scholars Association [7149]
1526 18th St. NW
Washington, DC 20036
Toll free: 855-827-7204
Unal, Haluk, President, Chmn. of the
Bd.

Turkish Coalition of America [19204]
1510 H St. NW, Ste. 900
Washington, DC 20005

PH: (202)370-1399
Fax: (202)370-1398
McCurdy, G. Lincoln, President

Turkish Coalition U.S.A. Political Action Committee [18875]
1025 Connecticut Ave. NW, Ste.
1000
Washington, DC 20036-5417
Fax: (866)314-7977
McCurdy, G. Lincoln, Treasurer

Ugbajo Itsekiri USA [18079]
PO Box 11465
Washington, DC 20008-0665
Iwere, Dr. Fabian, President

ULI Foundation [19219]
1025 Thomas Jefferson St. NW, Ste.
500 W
Washington, DC 20007
PH: (202)624-7000
Fax: (855)442-6702
Abbott, Corinne, Sr. VP

Union of Councils for Jews in the
Former Soviet Union [18142]
East Tower, 4th Fl.
2200 Pennsylvania Ave. NW
Washington, DC 20037
PH: (202)567-7572
Fax: (888)825-8314
Lerner, Lawrence, President

United Black Fund [11862]
2500 Martin Luther King, Jr. Ave. SE
Washington, DC 20020
PH: (202)783-9300
Fax: (202)347-2564
LeNoir, Barry, President

United Brotherhood of Carpenters
and Joiners of America [23402]
101 Constituition Ave. NW
Washington, DC 20001
PH: (202)546-6206
Fax: (202)547-8979
McCarron, Douglas J., President

United Cerebral Palsy [14158]
1825 K St. NW, Ste. 600
Washington, DC 20006
PH: (202)776-0406
Toll free: 800-872-5827
Bennett, Stephen, CEO, President

United to End Genocide [18310]
1010 Vermont Ave. NW, Ste. 1100
Washington, DC 20005
PH: (202)556-2100
Andrews, Tom, President, CEO

United Food and Commercial Workers International Union [23419]
1775 K St. NW
Washington, DC 20006
Hansen, Joseph T., President

United Fresh Produce Association
[4253]
1901 Pennsylvania Ave. NW, Ste.
1100
Washington, DC 20006
PH: (202)303-3400
Fax: (202)303-3433
Tillar, Tressie, Mgr. of Admin.

United Inventors Association of the
United States of America [6772]
1025 Connecticut Ave., Ste. 1000
Washington, DC 20036-5417
Tuttle, Warren, President

United Methodist Church | General
Board of Church and Society
[20348]
100 Maryland Ave. NE
Washington, DC 20002

PH: (202)488-5600
Henry-Crowe, Rev. Susan, Gen.
Sec.

United Negro College Fund [7929]
1805 7th St. NW
Washington, DC 20001
Toll free: 800-331-2244
Lomax, Michael L., PhD, CEO,
President

United Negro College Fund -
National Alumni Council [19353]
1805 7th St. NW
Washington, DC 20001
Toll free: 800-331-2244
Colson, Dorothy, President

United Press International, Inc.
[2728]
1133 19th St. NW, Ste. 800
Washington, DC 20036-3655
PH: (202)898-8000
Chiaia, Nicholas, President

United States African Development
Foundation [18505]
1400 I St. NW, Ste. 1000
Washington, DC 20005-2248
PH: (202)673-3916
Fax: (202)673-3810
Berenbach, Shari, CEO, President

U.S.- Angola Chamber of Commerce
[23625]
1100 17th St. NW, Ste. 1000
Washington, DC 20036
PH: (202)857-0789
Fax: (202)223-0551
da Cruz, Maria, Exec. Dir.

U.S. ASEAN Business Council
[3306]
1101 17th St. NW, Ste. 411
Washington, DC 20036-4720
PH: (202)289-1911
Feldman, Alexander C., President,
CEO

U.S.-Asia Institute [17815]
232 E Capitol St. NE
Washington, DC 20003
PH: (202)544-3181
Fax: (202)747-5889
Bissell, Mary Sue, VP, Trustee,
Exec. Dir.

United States Association of Former
Members of Congress [18015]
1401 K St. NW, Ste. 503
Washington, DC 20005
PH: (202)222-0972
Fax: (202)222-0977
Kennelly, Barbara, President

United States - Azerbaijan Chamber
of Commerce [18532]
1212 Potomac St. NW
Washington, DC 20007
PH: (202)333-8702
Fax: (202)333-8703
Sadigova, Susan, Exec. Dir.

United States-Azerbaijan Chamber
of Commerce [23627]
1212 Potomac St. NW
Washington, DC 20007
PH: (202)333-8702
Fax: (202)333-8703
Koten, Mustafa, Program Mgr.

U.S.-Bahrain Business Council
[1997]
1615 H St. NW
Washington, DC 20062
Fax: (202)463-3114
Miel, Jennifer, Exec. Dir.

United States Beet Sugar Association [1378]
1156 15th St. NW, Ste. 1019
Washington, DC 20005

PH: (202)296-4820
Fax: (202)331-2065
Johnson, James, President

U.S. Border Control [18468]
PO Box 97115
Washington, DC 20090

United States Business and Industry
Council [18290]
512 C St. NE
Washington, DC 20002-5810
PH: (202)266-3980
Fax: (202)266-3981
Kearns, Kevin L., President, Ed.-in-
Chief

United States Campaign for Burma
[18448]
1444 N St. NW, Ste. A2
Washington, DC 20005
PH: (202)234-8022
Din, Aung, Exec. Dir., Founder

U.S. Canola Association [1379]
600 Pennsylvania Ave. SE, Ste. 320
Washington, DC 20003
PH: (202)969-8113
Fax: (202)969-7036
Gordley, John, Exec. Dir.

U.S. Capitol Historical Society
[9525]
200 Maryland Ave. NE
Washington, DC 20002
Toll free: 800-887-9318
Fax: (202)544-8244
Sarasin, Hon. Ronald A., President

United States Catholic Mission As-
sociation [19916]
415 Michigan Ave. NE, Ste. 102
Washington, DC 20017
PH: (202)832-3112
Fax: (202)832-3688
Nuelle, Fr. John, Exec. Dir.

U.S. Chamber of Commerce [23628]
1615 H St. NW
Washington, DC 20062-2000
PH: (202)659-6000
Toll free: 800-638-6582
Fax: (202)463-3190
Donohue, Thomas J., President

U.S. Chamber of Commerce
Foundation [19007]
1615 H St. NW
Washington, DC 20062
PH: (202)463-5500
Eversole, Eric, President, Advisor

U.S. Chamber Litigation Center
[5725]
1615 H St. NW
Washington, DC 20062
PH: (202)463-5337
Fax: (202)463-5346
Leitch, David G., Director

U.S.-China Business Council [1998]
1818 N St. NW, Ste. 200
Washington, DC 20036
PH: (202)429-0340
Fax: (202)775-2476
Luk, Joseph, Director

U.S. Committee of the Blue Shield
[9237]
1025 Thomas Jefferson St. NW, Ste.
500 E
Washington, DC 20007
PH: (507)222-4231
Wilkie, Nancy C., President

United States Conference of
Catholic Bishops [19917]
3211 4th St. NE
Washington, DC 20017

PH: (202)541-3000
Kurtz, Rev. Joseph, President

United States Conference of
Catholic Bishops - Committee on
Divine Worship **[19918]**
3211 4th St. NE
Washington, DC 20017-1104
PH: (202)541-3000
Serratelli, Bishop Arthur, Comm.
Chm.

U.S. Conference of Catholic Bishops
- Ecumenical and Interreligious
Affairs **[19919]**
3211 4th St. NE
Washington, DC 20017-1104
PH: (202)541-3000
Madden, Rev. Denis J., Mem.

United States Conference of
Catholic Bishops Migration and
Refugee Services **[12600]**
3211 4th St. NE
Washington, DC 20017-1194
PH: (202)541-3352
Canny, William, Exec. Dir.

United States Conference of City
Human Services Officials **[5764]**
United States Conference of Mayors
1620 Eye St. NW, 4th Fl.
Washington, DC 20006
PH: (202)861-6707
Fax: (202)293-2352
Swann, Crystal D., Asst. Dir.

United States Conference of Mayors
[5647]
1620 Eye St. NW
Washington, DC 20006
PH: (202)293-7330
Fax: (202)293-2352
Cochran, Tom, CEO, Exec. Dir.

United States Court of Federal
Claims Bar Association **[5449]**
Ben Franklin Sta.
Washington, DC 20044-7614
PH: (202)220-8638
  (202)357-6400
Maglio, Altom M., President

U.S.-Cuba Trade Association **[1999]**
2300 M St. NW, Ste. 800
Washington, DC 20037

United States Department of
Agriculture - Forest Service
Volunteers Program **[4222]**
1400 Independence Ave. SW
Washington, DC 20250-1111
Toll free: 800-832-1355
DeCoster, Tim, Chief of Staff

U.S. Department of the Interior |
Bureau of Land Management |
National Wild Horse and Burro
Program **[4417]**
BLM Washington Office
1849 C St. NW, Rm. 5665
Washington, DC 20240
PH: (202)208-3801
Fax: (202)208-5242
Lin, Janet, Chief of Staff

United States Department of Labor |
Employment and Training
Administration | Senior Community
Service Employment Program
[11785]
Frances Perkins Bldg.
200 Constitution Ave. NW
Washington, DC 20210
Toll free: 877-872-5627

United States Energy Association
[6515]
1300 Pennsylvania Ave. NW, Ste.
550

Mailbox 142
Washington, DC 20004-3022
PH: (202)312-1230
Fax: (202)682-1682
Bailey, Vicky A., Chairman

U.S. English **[18877]**
5335 Wisconsin Ave. NW, Ste. 930
Washington, DC 20015
PH: (202)833-0100
Toll free: 800-787-8216
Fax: (202)833-0108
Mujica, Mr. Mauro E., Chairman,
CEO

U.S. Equal Employment Opportunity
Commission **[5168]**
131 M St. NE, 4th Fl., Ste. 4NWO2F
Washington, DC 20507
Toll free: 800-669-4000
Fax: (202)419-0739
Yang, Jenny R., Chairman

United States Fashion Industry As-
sociation **[3275]**
1140 Connecticut Ave., Ste. 950
Washington, DC 20036
PH: (202)419-0444
Fax: (202)783-0727
Hughes, Julia, President

U.S. Grains Council **[4180]**
20 F St. NW, Ste. 600
Washington, DC 20001
PH: (202)789-0789
Fax: (202)898-0522
Gray, Ron, Chairman

U.S. Green Building Council **[596]**
2101 L St. NW, Ste. 500
Washington, DC 20037-1599
PH: (202)742-3792
Toll free: 800-795-1747
Fedrizzi, S. Richard, Chairman,
CEO, Founder

United States Healthful Food Council
[15091]
1200 18th St. NW, Ste. 700
Washington, DC 20036
PH: (202)503-9122
Williams, Lawrence, Chairman, CEO

U.S. Hide, Skin and Leather As-
sociation **[2088]**
1150 Connecticut Ave. NW, 12th Fl.
Washington, DC 20036
PH: (202)587-4250
Sothmann, Stephen, President

United States Hispanic Advocacy
Association **[18342]**
601 Pennsylvania Ave. NW, Ste. 900
Washington, DC 20004
Diaz, Luis J., Esq., CEO, President

United States Hispanic Chamber of
Commerce **[23631]**
1424 K St. NW, Ste. 401
Washington, DC 20005
PH: (202)842-1212
Fax: (202)842-3221
Palomarez, Javier, CEO, President

U.S. Holocaust Memorial Council
[18353]
100 Raoul Wallenberg Pl. SW
Washington, DC 20024-2126
PH: (202)488-0400
Bernstein, Tom A., Chairman

U.S.-Hungary Business Council
[673]
701 8th St. NW, Ste. 500
Washington, DC 20001
PH: (202)659-8201
Toll free: 800-638-6582
Donohue, Thomas J., CEO,
President

United States-Indonesia Society
[687]
1625 Massachusetts Ave. NW, Ste.
550
Washington, DC 20036-2260
PH: (202)232-1400
Fax: (202)232-7300
Merrill, David, President

United States Institute of Peace
[18835]
2301 Constitution Ave. NW
Washington, DC 20037-2900
PH: (202)457-1700
Fax: (202)429-6063
Lindborg, Nancy, President, CEO

United States International Council
on Disabilities **[11643]**
1012 14th St. NW, Ste. 105
Washington, DC 20005-3429
PH: (202)347-0102
Fax: (202)347-0351
Bristo, Marca, President

U.S. Internet Service Provider Association **[6337]**
700 12th St. NW, Ste. 700E
Washington, DC 20005
PH: (202)904-2351

U.S.-Japan Business Council
[23646]
1615 H St. NW
Washington, DC 20062
PH: (202)463-5772
Fatheree, James W., President,
COO

U.S.-Japan Council **[18534]**
1819 L St. NW, Ste. 200
Washington, DC 20036
PH: (202)223-6840
Fax: (202)280-1235
Hirano, Irene, President

U.S.-Kazakhstan Business Associa-
tion **[2000]**
1625 K St. NW, Ste. 200
Washington, DC 20006
PH: (202)464-2034
Courtney, William, President

U.S. Labor Education in the
Americas Project **[18614]**
1634 I St. NW, Ste. 1001
Washington, DC 20006
PH: (202)347-4100
Fax: (202)347-4885
Cavanagh, John, Director

United States Lactation Consultant
Association **[13859]**
4410 Massachusetts Ave. NW, No.
406
Washington, DC 20016
PH: (202)738-1125
Ferrarello, Debi Page, President

U.S. Letter Carriers Mutual Benefit
Association **[19497]**
100 Indiana Ave. NW, Ste. 510
Washington, DC 20001-2144
PH: (202)638-4318
Toll free: 800-424-5184
Rolando, Fredric V., President

U.S.-Libya Business Association
[2001]
1625 K St. NW, Ste. 200
Washington, DC 20006
PH: (202)464-2038
Dittrich, Charles, Exec. Dir.

U.S. Lumber Coalition **[1445]**
1750 K St. NW, Ste. 800
Washington, DC 20006
PH: (703)597-8651
van Heyningen, Zoltan, Exec. Dir.

United States-Mexico Chamber of
Commerce **[23633]**
PO Box 14414
Washington, DC 20044
PH: (703)752-4751
Fax: (703)642-1088
Zapanta, Al, CEO, President

United States National Committee
for Pacific Economic Cooperation
[18162]
1819 L St. NW, 6th Fl.
Washington, DC 20036
PH: (202)293-3995
Fax: (202)293-1402
Borthwick, Dr. Mark, Exec. Dir.

U.S. National Committee on
Theoretical and Applied Mechanics
[6833]
Board on International Scientific
Organizations
The National Academies
500 5th St.
Washington, DC 20001
PH: (202)334-2807
Fax: (202)334-2231
Liu, Wing Kam, Chairman

U.S. National Committee for World
Food Day **[12119]**
2121 K St. NW, Ste. 800-B
Washington, DC 20037-1896
Young, Patricia, Coord.

United States Navy Memorial
Foundation **[21064]**
701 Pennsylvania Ave. NW
Washington, DC 20004
PH: (202)380-0710
  (202)380-0714
Totushek, John, President, CEO

United States-New Zealand Council
[2002]
DACOR Bacon House
1801 F St. NW, 3rd Fl.
Washington, DC 20006
PH: (202)638-8601
Farrell, Edward J, Chairman

U.S. Office on Colombia **[18449]**
1350 Connecticut Ave. NW, Ste.
1100
Washington, DC 20036
PH: (202)232-8090
Fax: (202)232-7530
Melo, Diego, Officer

U.S.-Pakistan Business Council
[674]
1615 H St. NW
Washington, DC 20062
PH: (202)463-5732
Fax: (202)822-2491
Gomez-Jelalian, Esperanza,
President

U.S. Pan Asian American Chamber
of Commerce **[23634]**
1329 18th St. NW
Washington, DC 20036
PH: (202)296-5221
Toll free: 800-696-7818
Fax: (202)296-5225
Au Allen, Susan, CEO, President

United States Peace Corps **[18850]**
1111 20th St. NW
Washington, DC 20526
Toll free: 855-855-1961
Hessler-Radelet, Carrie, Director

U.S. Poland Business Council
[23635]
701 8th St, NW Ste. 500
Washington, DC 20062-2000
PH: (202)973-5979
Fax: (202)659-5249

U.S.-Russia Business Council [2003]
1110 Vermont Ave. NW, Ste. 350
Washington, DC 20005
PH: (202)739-9180
Fax: (202)659-5920
Levinas, Randi, Exec. VP

U.S. Senate Press Photographers'
Gallery [2595]
S-317, United States Capitol
Washington, DC 20510
PH: (202)224-6548
Kent, Jeffrey S., Director

United States Student Association
[8631]
1211 Connecticut Ave. NW, Ste. 406
Washington, DC 20036
PH: (202)640-6570
Fax: (202)223-4005
Flores-Quilty, Alexandra, President

United States Table Soccer Federa-
tion [22058]
PO Box 14455
Washington, DC 20044
Nardoci, Bruce, VP

United States Tamil Political Action
Council [19151]
PO Box 35536
Washington, DC 20033-5536
PH: (202)595-3123
Jeyarajah, Dr. Elias, President

United States Telecom Association
[3424]
607 14th St. NW, Ste. 400
Washington, DC 20005
PH: (202)326-7300
Fax: (202)326-7333
Hunt, Robert A., Chmn. of the Bd.

U.S. Travel Association [3405]
1100 New York Ave. NW, Ste. 450
Washington, DC 20005-3934
PH: (202)408-8422
Fax: (202)408-1255
Tratt, Noah, Secretary

U.S.-U.A.E. Business Council [2006]
505 9th St. NW, Ste. 6010
Washington, DC 20004
PH: (202)863-7285
Sebright, Danny E., President

U.S.-Ukraine Business Council [688]
1030 15th St. NW, Ste. 555 W
Washington, DC 20005
PH: (202)216-0995
    (202)437-4707
Fax: (202)216-0997
Williams, Mr. Morgan, CEO,
    President, Chairman

U.S. - Ukraine Foundation [19207]
1660 L St. NW, Ste. 1000
Washington, DC 20036-5634
PH: (202)524-6555
Fax: (202)280-1989
McConnell, Nadia K., President

U.S.-Vietnam Trade Council [17816]
737 8th St. SE, Ste. 202
Washington, DC 20003
PH: (202)464-9380
Fax: (202)544-4065
Foote, Virginia B., President

U.S.-Vietnam WTO Coalition [18536]
1101 17th St. NW, Ste. 411
Washington, DC 20036
PH: (202)289-1912
Fax: (202)289-0519
Foote, Virginia B., President

U.S. Water Alliance [4765]
1816 Jefferson Pl. NW
Washington, DC 20036

PH: (202)263-3677
    (202)263-3671
Fox, Radhika, CEO

U.S. Women in Nuclear [6936]
c/o Nuclear Energy Institute
1201 F St. NW, Ste. 1100
Washington, DC 20004-1218
PH: (202)739-8000
Fax: (202)785-4019
Maxwell, Kim, President

U.S. Women's Chamber of Com-
    merce [23636]
700 12th St. NW, Ste. 700
Washington, DC 20005
Toll free: 888-418-7922
Dorfman, Margot, CEO

United Union of Roofers Waterproof-
    ers and Allied Workers [23403]
1660 L St. NW, Ste. 800
Washington, DC 20036-5646
PH: (202)463-7663
Fax: (202)463-6906
Danley, Robert J., Secretary,
    Treasurer

Universal Muslim Association of
    America [20502]
1701 Pennsylvania Ave. NW
Washington, DC 20004
PH: (202)559-9123
Abidi, Syed E., President

Universities Allied for Essential
    Medicines [15503]
641 S St. NW
Washington, DC 20001
PH: (510)868-1159
Tavera, Gloria, President

Universities Research Association
[7098]
1111 19th St. NW, Ste. 400
Washington, DC 20036
PH: (202)293-1382
Fax: (202)293-5012

University Faculty for Life [8657]
Georgetown University
120 New North
Washington, DC 20057
PH: (718)817-3291
Fax: (718)817-3300
Hayden-Lemmons, R. Mary, PhD,
    President

University Professional and Continu-
    ing Education Association [7675]
1 Dupont Cir., Ste. 615
Washington, DC 20036
PH: (202)659-3130
Fax: (202)785-0374
Hansen, Robert, CEO

Unwanted Horse Coalition [10711]
1616 H St. NW, 7th Fl.
Washington, DC 20006
PH: (202)296-4031
Fax: (202)296-1970
Purcell, Jennifer, Director

URAC [13498]
1220 L St. NW, Ste. 400
Washington, DC 20005
PH: (202)216-9010
Fax: (202)216-9006
Green, Kylanne, President, CEO

Urban-Brookings Tax Policy Center
[19177]
2100 M St. NW
Washington, DC 20037
PH: (202)797-6000
    (202)833-7200
Greenstein, Bob, Founder, President

Urban Ed, Inc. [8730]
2041 Martin Luther King, Jr. Ave.
    SE, Ste. M-2

Washington, DC 20020
PH: (202)610-2344
Fax: (202)610-2355
Williams, Roxanne J., President

Urban Financial Services Coalition
[418]
1200 G St. NW, Ste. 800
Washington, DC 20005
PH: (202)434-8970
Fax: (202)434-8704
Brown, Walter, Jr., Bd. Member

Urban Institute [19220]
2100 M St. NW
Washington, DC 20037
PH: (202)833-7200
Wartell, Sarah Rosen, President

Urban Land Institute [5099]
2001 L St. NW
Washington, DC 20036
PH: (202)624-7000
Fax: (202)624-7140
Campbell, Joan

Urban Libraries Council [9733]
1333 H St. NW, Ste. 1000W
Washington, DC 20005
PH: (202)750-8650
Benton, Susan, President, CEO

US Council of Muslim Organizations
[20503]
1155 F St. NW, Ste. 1050
Washington, DC 20004
PH: (202)683-6557
Jammal, Oussama, Sec. Gen.

US-Qatar Business Council [23638]
1341 Connecticut Ave. NW, Ste. 4A
Washington, DC 20036
PH: (202)457-8555
Fax: (202)457-1919
Theros, Amb. Patrick N., President

US SIF: The Forum for Sustainable
    and Responsible Investment
[19135]
1660 L St. NW, Ste. 306
Washington, DC 20036
PH: (202)872-5361
Fax: (202)775-8686
Woll, Lisa, CEO

USA Coal Exports [741]
c/o National Mining Association
101 Constitution Ave. NW, Ste. 500
    E
Washington, DC 20001

USA Engage [18163]
1625 K St. NW, Ste. 200
Washington, DC 20006
PH: (202)887-0278
    (202)822-9491
Fax: (202)452-8160
Sawaya, Richard, Director

USA for the United Nations High
    Commissioner for Refugees
[12601]
1775 K St. NW, Ste. 580
Washington, DC 20006
PH: (202)296-1081
Toll free: 855-808-6427
DeSantis, Charles, Chairperson

USAction [19121]
1825 K St. NW, Ste. 210
Washington, DC 20006-1220
PH: (202)263-4520
Fax: (202)263-4530
Booth, Heather, Chairman

USO World Headquarters [19384]
PO Box 96860
Washington, DC 20077-7677

PH: (703)908-6400
Toll free: 888-484-3876
Casey, George, Chairman

USSA Foundation [8632]
United States Student Association
1211 Connecticut Ave. NW, Ste. 406
Washington, DC 20036
PH: (202)640-6570
Fax: (202)223-4005
Wasserman, Becky, Chairperson

Utilities Telecom Council [3245]
1129 20th St. NW, Ste. 350
Washington, DC 20036
PH: (202)872-0030
Fax: (202)872-1331
Taylor, Ron, Chairman

Utility Workers Union of America
[23464]
1300 L St. NW No. 1200
Washington, DC 20005
PH: (202)899-2851
Fax: (202)974-8201
Langford, Michael, President

UWC: Strategic Services on
    Unemployment and Workers'
    Compensation [13239]
910 17th St. NW, Ste. 1070
Washington, DC 20006
PH: (202)223-8904
Fax: (202)783-1616
Holmes, Douglas J., President

Uyghur American Association
[18451]
1420 K St. NW, Ste. 350
Washington, DC 20005
PH: (202)478-1920
Fax: (202)478-1910
Hassan, Ilshat, President

Vacation Rental Managers Associa-
    tion [2896]
2025 M St. NW, Ste. 800
Washington, DC 20036
PH: (202)367-1179
    (202)321-5138
Fax: (202)367-2179
Copps, Mike, Exec. Dir.

Valve Manufacturers Association of
    America [1579]
1050 17th St. NW, Ste. 280
Washington, DC 20036-5521
PH: (202)331-8105
Fax: (202)296-0378
Pasternak, Marc, VP, Exec. Dir.

Valve Repair Council [1580]
1050 17th St. NW, Ste. 280
Washington, DC 20036
PH: (202)331-8105
Fax: (202)296-0378
Pasternak, Marc, Exec. Dir., VP

Vanadium Producers and Reclaim-
    ers Association [2375]
1001 G St. NW, Ste. 500 W
Washington, DC 20001-4545
PH: (202)251-3200
    (202)842-3203
Hilbert, John W., III, President

Veterans for Common Sense
[21148]
900 2nd St. NE, Ste. 216
Washington, DC 20002
PH: (202)558-4553
Fahey, Dan, Leader

Veterans and Military Families for
    Progress [21151]
PO Box 66353
Washington, DC 20035
PH: (202)841-1687
    (563)451-9919
Krueger, Jack, President

Veterans of Modern Warfare **[21152]**
PO Box 96503
Washington, DC 20090
Toll free: 888-273-8255
Morgan, Joseph, President

Vinyl Building Council **[597]**
1747 Pennsylvania Ave. NW, Ste.
825
Washington, DC 20006
PH: (202)765-2200
Koonce, Kevin, Exec. Dir.

The Vinyl Institute **[2633]**
1747 Pennsylvania Ave. NW, Ste.
825
Washington, DC 20006
PH: (202)765-2200
Fax: (202)765-2275
Barcan, Cristian, VP

Vinyl Siding Institute, Inc. **[598]**
National Housing Ctr.
1201 15th St. NW, Ste. 220
Washington, DC 20005
PH: (202)587-5100
Fax: (202)587-5127
Offringa, Kate, President

Violence Policy Center **[19231]**
1730 Rhode Island Ave. NW, Ste.
1014
Washington, DC 20036
PH: (202)822-8200
    (202)822-8200
Sugarmann, Josh, Exec. Dir.

Vital Voices Global Partnership
[13402]
1625 Massachusetts Ave. NW, Ste.
300
Washington, DC 20036
PH: (202)861-2625
Nelson, Alyse, President, CEO

VON Coalition **[2008]**
c/o Pillsbury Winthrop Shaw Pittman
LLP
1200 17th St. NW
Washington, DC 20036-3006
PH: (202)663-8215
Fax: (202)513-8006
Richards, Glenn S., Exec. Dir.

Voter Participation Center **[19246]**
1707 L St. NW, Ste. 300
Washington, DC 20036
PH: (202)659-9570
Fax: (202)659-9585
Gardner, Page S., Founder,
President

Wallace Genetic Foundation **[3581]**
4910 Massachusetts Ave. NW, Ste.
221
Washington, DC 20016
PH: (202)966-2932
Fax: (202)966-3370
Lee, Patricia M., Exec. Dir.

WAM International: Women Advancing Microfinance **[1269]**
402 Constitution Ave. NE
Washington, DC 20002-5924
PH: (202)547-4546

Washington Buddhist Vihara **[19784]**
5017 16th St. NW
Washington, DC 20011
PH: (202)723-0773
Dhammasiri, Venerable Maha-
ragama, President, Founder

The Washington Group **[19683]**
Washington, DC
Bihun, Andrew, President

Washington Journalism Center
[8162]
331 8th St. NE
Washington, DC 20002
Mattingly, Terry, Director

Washington Legal Foundation **[5727]**
2009 Massachusetts Ave. NW
Washington, DC 20036
PH: (202)588-0302
Thornburgh, Dick, Chairman

Washington Office on Latin America
[18624]
1666 Connecticut Ave. NW, Ste. 400
Washington, DC 20009
PH: (202)797-2171
Fax: (202)797-2172
Olson, Joy, Exec. Dir.

Water Resources Coalition **[7380]**
c/o American Society of Civil
Engineers
101 Constitution Ave. NW
Washington, DC 20001
PH: (202)789-7850
Pallasch, Brian T., CAE, Co-Ch.

Water Systems Council **[3463]**
1101 30th St. NW, Ste. 500
Washington, DC 20007
PH: (202)625-4387
Fax: (202)625-4363
Mest, Richard, VP

Water and Wastewater Equipment
Manufacturers Association **[1777]**
PO Box 17402
Washington, DC 20041
PH: (703)444-1777
Fax: (703)444-1779
Champney, Dawn Kristof, President

The Waterfront Center **[11460]**
PO Box 53351
Washington, DC 20009-5351
PH: (202)337-0356
Rigby, Dick, Director

Waterways Council **[19201]**
499 S Capitol St. SW, Ste. 401
Washington, DC 20003
PH: (202)765-2166
Fax: (202)765-2167
Toohey, Mike, President, CEO

Weather Risk Management Associa-
tion **[6862]**
529 14th St. NW, Ste. 750
Washington, DC 20045
PH: (202)289-3800
Fax: (202)591-2445
Hoggatt, Brad, VP

Wendt Center for Loss and Healing
[13218]
4201 Connecticut Ave. NW, Ste. 300
Washington, DC 20008
PH: (202)624-0010
Fax: (202)624-0062
Pearson, Cynthia, Officer

White House Correspondents' As-
sociation **[2732]**
600 New Hampshire Ave., Ste. 800
Washington, DC 20037
PH: (202)266-7453
Fax: (202)266-7454
Whiston, Julia, Exec. Dir.

White House Historical Association
[9527]
1610 H St. NW
Washington, DC 20006-4907
PH: (202)218-4337
    (202)737-8292
McLaurin, Stewart, President

White House News Photographers
Association **[2597]**
7119 Ben Franklin Sta.
Washington, DC 20044-7119
Shefte, Whitney, President

White Ribbon Alliance **[11198]**
1120 20th St. NW, 500 N
Washington, DC 20036

PH: (202)742-1214
Shaver, Theresa, Founder, President

Who's Positive **[10556]**
c/o Tom Donohue, Executive Director
2200 Prout St. SE, Ste. 1
Washington, DC 20020
Donohue, Mr. Tom, Exec. Dir.,
Founder

Wider Opportunities for Women
[11788]
1001 Connecticut Ave. NW, Ste. 930
Washington, DC 20036-5565
PH: (202)464-1596
Fax: (202)354-4638
Andere, Amanda, President, CEO

WildCat Conservation Legal Aid
Society **[4907]**
1725 I St. NW, Ste. 300
Washington, DC 20006
PH: (202)349-3760
Tekancic, Lisa Ann, President,
Chmn. of the Bd., CEO

The Wilderness Society **[3966]**
1615 M St. NW
Washington, DC 20036
PH: (202)833-2300
Toll free: 800-843-9453
Williams, Jamie, President

Woodrow Wilson International
Center for Scholars **[9559]**
1 Woodrow Wilson Plz.
1300 Pennsylvania Ave. NW
Washington, DC 20004-3027
PH: (202)691-4000
Fax: (202)691-4001
Harman, Jane, CEO, President,
Director

Win Without War **[18730]**
2000 M St. NW, Ste. 720
Washington, DC 20036
PH: (202)232-3317

Windmill Class Association **[22692]**
1200 14th St. NW, Apt. 1104
Washington, DC 20005
PH: (336)414-2327
Sponar, Ralph, President

Wine Scholar Guild **[3482]**
1777 Church St. NW, Ste. B
Washington, DC 20036
PH: (202)600-8022
Fax: (202)449-8331
Camus, Julien, President

Wine and Spirits Wholesalers of
America **[194]**
805 15th St. NW, Ste. 430
Washington, DC 20005
PH: (202)371-9792
Fax: (202)789-2405
Wolf, Craig, CEO, President

WineAmerica: The National Associa-
tion of American Wineries **[3483]**
818 Connecticut Ave. NW, Ste. 1006
Washington, DC 20006
PH: (202)783-2756
    (202)223-5172
Kaiser, Michael, Dir. Pub. Aff.

Wireless Communications Associa-
tion International **[3247]**
1333 H St. NW, Ste. 700 W
Washington, DC 20005
PH: (202)452-7823
Fax: (202)452-0041
Sandri, Joseph M., Sr. VP

Witness for Peace **[18840]**
1616 P St. NW, Ste. 100
Washington, DC 20036

PH: (202)547-6112
Fax: (202)536-4708
Brown, Dana, Exec. Dir.

Woman's National Democratic Club
[18118]
1526 New Hampshire Ave. NW
Washington, DC 20036
PH: (202)232-7363
Fax: (202)328-8772
Currier, Nuchhi, VP of Admin.

Women in Aerospace **[5879]**
204 E St. NE
Washington, DC 20002
PH: (202)547-0229
Fax: (202)547-6348
Brunswick, Shelli, Chairperson

Women Against Prostate Cancer
[14081]
1220 L St. NW, Ste. 100-271
Washington, DC 20005-4018
PH: (202)805-3266
Fax: (202)543-2727
Morrow, Theresa, VP

Women in Cable Telecommunica-
tions **[484]**
2000 K St. NW, Ste. 350
Washington, DC 20006
PH: (202)827-4794
Fax: (202)450-5596
Meduski, Mary

Women in Film & Television
International **[3506]**
c/o WIFV-DC
4000 Albemarle St. NW
Washington, DC 20016
Hoeter, Eileen, Chmn. of the Bd.

Women in Film and Video **[1213]**
4000 Albemarle St. NW, Ste. 305
Washington, DC 20016
PH: (202)429-9438
Fax: (202)429-9440
Houghton, Melissa, Exec. Dir.

Women in Government **[5648]**
1319 F St. NW, Ste. 710
Washington, DC 20004
PH: (202)333-0825
Fax: (202)333-0875
Wolf, Kay, Chairman

Women in International Security
[19097]
1779 Massachusetts Ave. NW, Ste.
510
Washington, DC 20036
Stedman, Brooke, Dep. Dir.

Women in Military Service for
America Memorial Foundation
[5850]
Dept. 560
Washington, DC 20042-0560
PH: (703)533-1155
Toll free: 800-222-2294
Fax: (703)931-4208
Vaught, Brig. Gen. (Ret.) Wilma L.,
President

Women in Municipal Government
[5649]
c/o National League of Cities
1301 Pennsylvania Ave. NW, Ste.
550
Washington, DC 20004-1747
PH: (202)626-3169
LaMarche, Mary, President

Women Organizing for Change in
Agriculture & Natural Resource
Management **[3583]**
1775 K St. NW, Ste. 410
Washington, DC 20006

PH: (202)331-9099
Gurung, Jeannette, PhD, Exec. Dir.

Women for Women International [13407]
2000 M St. NW, Ste. 200
Washington, DC 20036
PH: (202)737-7705
    (202)521-0016
Fax: (202)737-7709
Salbi, Zainab, Founder

WomenHeart: National Coalition for Women with Heart Disease [14150]
1100 17th St. NW, Ste. 500
Washington, DC 20036
PH: (202)728-7199
Fax: (202)728-7238
Webster, Kathy, Chairman

Women's Business Enterprise National Council [3508]
1120 Connecticut Ave. NW, Ste. 1000
Washington, DC 20036
PH: (202)872-5515
Fax: (202)872-5505
Taylor, Laura K., Officer

Women's Campaign Fund [18237]
718 7th St. NW, 2nd Fl.
Washington, DC 20001
PH: (202)796-8259
Mullins, Betsy, President, CEO

Women's Council on Energy and the Environment [6518]
816 Connecticut Ave. NW, Ste. 200
Washington, DC 20006
PH: (202)997-4512
Fax: (202)478-2098
Chandran, Joyce, Exec. Dir.

Women's Foreign Policy Group [19249]
1615 M St. NW, Ste. 210
Washington, DC 20036-3235
PH: (202)429-2692
Fax: (202)429-2630
Ellis, Patricia, President

Women's High Tech Coalition [7301]
100 M St. SE, No. 500
Washington, DC 20003
PH: (202)479-7141
Fitzgerald, MaryClare, CEO, President

Women's Institute for Freedom of the Press [17961]
1940 Calvert St. NW
Washington, DC 20009-1502
PH: (202)656-0893
Allen, Martha Leslie, PhD, Director

Women's Leadership Forum [18119]
Democratic National Committee
430 S Capitol St. SE
Washington, DC 20003-4024
PH: (202)863-8000
Toll free: 877-336-7200
Olszewski, Claire, Dir. of Fin.

Women's Media Center [19250]
1825 K St. NW, Ste. 400
Washington, DC 20006
PH: (212)563-0680
Fax: (212)563-0688
Embrey, Lauren, Chmn. of the Bd.

Women's Missionary Society, AME Church [20649]
1134 11th St. NW
Washington, DC 20001
PH: (202)371-8886
Fax: (202)371-8820
Cason-Reed, Dr. Shirley, President

Women's Ordination Conference [19922]
PO Box 15057
Washington, DC 20003
PH: (202)675-1006
Fax: (202)675-1008
Philipson, Katherine, Office Mgr.

Women's Policy, Inc. [19251]
409 12th St. SW, Ste. 310
Washington, DC 20024
PH: (202)554-2323
Plaster, Amy, Chairman

Women's Research and Education Institute [18241]
714 G St. SE, Ste. 200
Washington, DC 20003
PH: (202)506-9804
    (703)837-1977
Scanlan, Susan, President

Women's Transportation Seminar [3363]
1701 K St. NW, Ste. 800
Washington, DC 20006
PH: (202)955-5085
Fax: (202)955-5088
Swaim-Staley, Beverly, Chairperson

WomensLaw.org [19252]
c/o National Network to End Domestic Violence
1400 16th St. NW, Ste. 330
Washington, DC 20036
Martin, Elizabeth, Exec. Dir.

Workers' Injury Law and Advocacy Group [5752]
1701 Pennsylvania Ave. NW, Ste. 300
Washington, DC 20006
PH: (202)349-7150
Fax: (202)249-4191
Boyd, John R., President

Working for America Institute [11791]
815 16th St. NW
Washington, DC 20005
PH: (202)509-3717
Mills, Nancy, Exec. Dir.

Workplace Fairness [11792]
920 U St. NW
Washington, DC 20001
PH: (202)683-6114
Fax: (240)282-8801
Brantner, Paula, Exec. Dir.

World Affairs Councils of America [19267]
1200 18th St. NW, Ste. 902
Washington, DC 20036
PH: (202)833-4557
Fax: (202)833-4555
Anderson, Dixie, V. Ch.

World Alliance for Decentralized Energy [6520]
1513 16th St. NW
Washington, DC 20036
PH: (202)667-5600
Fax: (202)315-3719
Zilonis, Stephen A., Chairman

World Bank Group [18507]
1818 H St. NW
Washington, DC 20433
PH: (202)473-1000
    (202)477-1234
Toll free: 800-831-0463
Fax: (202)477-6391
Kim, Dr. Jim Yong, President

World Cocoa Foundation [4173]
1411 K St. NW, Ste. 500
Washington, DC 20005

PH: (202)737-7870
Fax: (202)737-7832
Guyton, Bill, President

World Congress of Gay, Lesbian, Bisexual, and Transgender Jews [20192]
PO Box 23379
Washington, DC 20026-3379
Ga'avah, Keshet, Treasurer

World Council of Enterostomal Therapists [16529]
1000 Potomac St. NW, Ste. 108
Washington, DC 20007
PH: (202)567-3030
Fax: (202)833-3636
Stelton, Susan, President

World Environment Center [3970]
734 15th St. NW, Ste. 720
Washington, DC 20005
PH: (202)312-1370
Fax: (202)637-2411
Yosie, Dr. Terry F., President, CEO

World Environmental Organization [3971]
2020 Pennsylvania Ave. NW, Ste. 2001
Washington, DC 20006
Toll free: 800-800-2099
Fax: (202)351-6867
Gold, Jeff, Founder

World Federation of Direct Selling Associations [3020]
1667 K St. NW, Ste. 1100
Washington, DC 20006
PH: (202)452-8866
Fax: (202)452-9010

World Food Program USA [12120]
1725 I St. NW, Ste. 510
Washington, DC 20006
PH: (202)627-3737
Fax: (202)530-1698
Leach, Richard, CEO, President

World Health Partners [15508]
1875 Connecticut Ave. NW
Washington, DC 20008
Gopalakrishnan, Gopi, Founder, President

World Heart Foundation [17420]
1828 L St. NW, Ste. 1100
Washington, DC 20036
PH: (502)222-9003
Fax: (502)222-9555
Cox, James L., MD, President, CEO

World Homecare and Hospice Organization [15284]
228 7th St. SE
Washington, DC 20003
PH: (202)547-7424
Fax: (202)547-3540
Halamandaris, Val J., President

World Hunger Education Service [18460]
PO Box 29015
Washington, DC 20017
PH: (202)269-6322
Morris, Margie Ferris, Chairperson

World Nature Coalition [4920]
601 Pennsylvania Ave. NW, South Bldg., Ste. 900
Washington, DC 20004
PH: (865)300-3232
Stockdale, Dan, Founder, CEO

World Organization for Human Rights USA [12066]
2029 P St. NW, Ste. 202
Washington, DC 20036

World Resources Institute [3973]
10 G St. NE, Ste. 800
Washington, DC 20002
PH: (202)729-7600
    (202)729-7602
Fax: (202)729-7610
Bapna, Manish, Exec. VP, Managing Dir.

World Service Authority [18884]
5 Thomas Cir. NW
Washington, DC 20005-4104
PH: (202)638-2662
Fax: (202)638-0638
Davis, Garry, Coord., Founder

World Wildlife Fund [3975]
1250 24th St. NW
Washington, DC 20037
PH: (202)293-4800
Toll free: 800-960-0993
Roberts, Mr. Carter S., President, CEO

Worldwatch Institute [19268]
1400 16th St. NW, Ste. 430
Washington, DC 20036-2239
PH: (202)745-8092
Engelman, Robert, Contact

Writing Instrument Manufacturers Association [3179]
1701 Pennsylvania Ave. NW, Ste. 300
Washington, DC 20006
Baker, David H., Exec. Dir.

Young Democrats of America [18120]
PO Box 77496
Washington, DC 20013-8496
Elrod, Louis, President

Young Invincibles [19282]
1411 K St. NW, 4th Fl.
Washington, DC 20005
PH: (202)734-6519
Matusiak, Ari A., Founder, Chairman

Young Professionals in Transportation [3364]
PO Box 77783
Washington, DC 20013
Kortum, Katherine, Chairperson

Young Republican National Federation [19053]
PO Box 15293
Washington, DC 20003-0293
Cook, Dennis, Chairman

Youth Advocate Program International [11194]
4000 Albemarle St. NW, Ste. 401
Washington, DC 20016
PH: (202)224-6410
Fax: (202)244-6396

Youth For Understanding USA [8096]
641 South St. NW, Ste. 200
Washington, DC 20001
PH: (202)774-5200
Toll free: 800-833-6243
Hill, Michael E., President, CEO

Youth Pride Alliance [11913]
PO Box 12196
Washington, DC 20005
Cendana, Gregory A., VP

Youth Service America [12912]
1101 15th St. NW, No. 200
Washington, DC 20005
PH: (202)296-2992
Culbertson, Steven A., President, CEO

YWCA U.S.A. [13493]
2025 M St. NW, Ste. 550
Washington, DC 20036

PH: (202)467-0801
Fax: (202)467-0802
Henderson, Marsha B., Chairperson

Zero to Three: National Center for Infants, Toddlers and Families [14162]
1255 23rd St. NW, Ste. 350
Washington, DC 20037
PH: (202)638-1144
Fax: (202)638-0851
Melmed, Matthew E., JD, Exec. Dir.

Zeta Phi Beta Sorority, Inc. [23877]
1734 New Hampshire Ave. NW
Washington, DC 20009
PH: (202)387-3103
Fax: (202)232-4593
Montez, Stacye, Exec. Dir.F

FLORIDA

Yamaha 650 Society [22240]
, FL
Lawson, Don, Dir. (Actg.)

National Center for Construction Education and Research [18286]
13614 Progress Blvd.
Alachua, FL 32615-9407
PH: (386)518-6500
Toll free: 888-622-3720
Fax: (386)518-6303
Whyte, Don, President, CEO

Society to Preserve and Encourage Radio Drama, Variety and Comedy [22405]
PO Box 7
Alachua, FL 32616
Gassman, Larry, President

Tyler's Hope for a Dystonia Cure [16038]
13351 Progress Blvd.
Alachua, FL 32615
PH: (386)462-5220
Staab, Richard A., President

Veterinary Hospital Managers Association [17670]
PO Box 2280
Alachua, FL 32616-2280
PH: (518)433-8911
Toll free: 888-795-4520
Nash, James, VP

American Association for Paralegal Education [8206]
222 S Westmonte Dr., Ste. 101
Altamonte Springs, FL 32714
PH: (407)774-7880
Fax: (407)774-6440
Davis, Bruce, Treasurer

Association of Standardized Patient Educators [15623]
222 S Westmonte Dr., Ste. 101
Altamonte Springs, FL 32714
PH: (407)774-7880
Fax: (407)774-6440
Gliva-McConvey, Gayle, Comm. Chm.

Association of TeleServices International [3218]
222 S Westmonte Dr., Ste. 101
Altamonte Springs, FL 32714
Toll free: 866-896-ATSI
Fax: (407)774-6440
Edwards, Gary, Chairman

HeartStrong [11888]
478 E Altamonte Dr., Ste. 108, No. 714
Altamonte Springs, FL 32701
PH: (206)388-3894
Adams, Marc, Exec. Dir.

Institute of Internal Auditors [32]
247 Maitland Ave.
Altamonte Springs, FL 32701-4201
PH: (407)937-1111
Fax: (407)937-1101
Chambers, Richard F., CIA, CGAP, CCSA, CRMA, President, CEO

Literacy Research Association [8486]
222 S Westmonte Dr., Ste. 101
Altamonte Springs, FL 32714
PH: (407)774-7880
Fax: (407)774-6440
Almasi, Janice, President

National Association of Locum Tenens Organizations [16755]
222 S Westmonte Dr., Ste. 101
Altamonte Springs, FL 32714
PH: (407)774-7880
Fax: (407)774-6440
Anderson, Anne, Director

National Association of Physician Recruiters [16757]
222 S Westmonte Dr., Ste. 101
Altamonte Springs, FL 32714
PH: (407)774-7880
Toll free: 800-726-5613
Fax: (407)774-6440
Fowler, Craig, President

Society for the Technological Advancement of Reporting [5122]
222 S Westmonte Dr., Ste. 101
Altamonte Springs, FL 32714-4268
Toll free: 800-565-6054
Fax: (407)774-6440
Hunter, Shelly, President

United People in Christ, Inc. [20010]
789 Douglas Ave., Ste. 137
Altamonte Springs, FL 32714
PH: (407)862-0107
Fax: (407)862-1283
Habib, Amid, MD, Founder, President

American Pre-Veterinary Medical Association [17625]
c/o Alexa Brandsetter
2183 Wyandotte Ave.
Alva, FL 32920
Strait, Kimberly, President

Society of the 3rd Infantry Division [21030]
c/o Kathleen M. Daddato, Membership Chairperson
22511 N River Rd.
Alva, FL 33920-3358
PH: (239)728-2475
Mills, David, President

Girl Power 2 Cure [15935]
1881 S 14th St., No. 1
Amelia Island, FL 32034
PH: (904)277-2628
Fax: (904)212-0587
Harding, Ingrid, Founder, Exec. Dir.

Haiti Help Med Plus, Inc. [11921]
3145 Cecelia Dr.
Apopka, FL 32703
PH: (407)928-8317
Fax: (407)964-1189
Gousse, Ralph, MD, President

Christian Disaster Response International [11653]
209 Bridgers Ave.
Auburndale, FL 33823
PH: (863)967-4357
Patterson, Dr. Ron, Exec. Dir.

Legatus [19856]
5072 Annunciation Cir., Ste. 202
Ave Maria, FL 34142

PH: (239)867-4900
Fax: (239)867-4198
Hunt, John, Exec. Dir.

Association of Fertilizer and Phosphate Chemists [6190]
PO Box 1645
Bartow, FL 33831-1645
Jones, Greg, Secretary

Operation ShoeBox [10755]
8360 E Highway 25
Belleview, FL 34420
PH: (352)307-6723
Harper, Mary, Contact

American Academy of Anti-Aging Medicine [15673]
1801 N Military Trail, Ste. 200
Boca Raton, FL 33431
PH: (561)997-0112
Toll free: 888-997-0112
Fax: (561)997-0287
Goldman, Robert, Founder, Chmn. of the Bd.

American Association of Caregiving Youth [13423]
1515 N Federal Hwy., No. 218
Boca Raton, FL 33432
PH: (561)391-7401
Toll free: 800-725-2512
Siskowski, Connie, PhD, President

American Boxer Club [21799]
c/o Jeri Poller, Membership Chairperson
6013 SW 23rd Ave.
Boca Raton, FL 33496-3504
PH: (561)350-0889
Wyerman, Barry, President

ASAIO [13732]
7700 Congress Ave., Ste. 3107
Boca Raton, FL 33487-1356
PH: (561)999-8969
Fax: (561)999-8972
Fissell, William, MD, President

Chromosome Disorder Outreach [14815]
PO Box 724
Boca Raton, FL 33429-0724
PH: (561)395-4252
Sorg, Linda, President

Connected Warriors [13617]
900 Broken Sound Pky., Ste. 125
Boca Raton, FL 33487
PH: (954)278-3764
Greenfield, William, Chairman

Electrical Generating Systems Association [1019]
1650 S Dixie Hwy., Ste. 400
Boca Raton, FL 33432
PH: (561)750-5575
Fax: (561)395-8557
Pope, Michael, Dir. Ed.

Green Business Alliance [4066]
925 S Federal Hwy., Ste. 750
Boca Raton, FL 33432
PH: (561)361-6766
Fax: (561)431-7835
Kusel, Hilary, Exec. Dir.

International Association for the Fantastic in the Arts [10203]
1279 W Palmetto Park Rd., Unit 272285
Boca Raton, FL 33427
Attebery, Stina, Rep.

International Association for Marriage and Family Counselors [11491]
c/o Dr. Paul Peluso, President
Bldg. 47, Rm. 270

Dept. of Counselor Education
Florida Atlantic University
777 Glades Rd.
Boca Raton, FL 33431-0991
PH: (561)297-3625
Peluso, Dr. Paul, President

International Schools Association [8104]
1033 Diego Dr. S
Boca Raton, FL 33428
PH: (561)883-3854
Fax: (561)483-2004
Martinez, Mr. Luis, Chairman

International Underwater Spearfishing Association [22847]
2515 NW 29th Dr.
Boca Raton, FL 33434
Daye, Sheri, President

Lymphangiomatosis and Gorham's Disease Alliance [15543]
19919 Villa Lante Pl.
Boca Raton, FL 33434
Toll free: 844-588-5771
Kelly, John F., President

National Association of Real Estate Editors [2697]
1003 NW 6th Ter.
Boca Raton, FL 33486-3455
PH: (561)391-3599
Fax: (561)391-0099
Doyle-Kimball, Mary, Exec. Dir.

National Council on Compensation Insurance [1905]
901 Peninsula Corporate Cir.
Boca Raton, FL 33487
PH: (561)893-1000
Toll free: 800-622-4123
Fax: (561)893-1191
Klingel, Stephen J., CEO, President

Prepare Tomorrow's Parents [13475]
454 NE 3rd St.
Boca Raton, FL 33432
PH: (561)620-0256
Fax: (561)391-9711
Garfinkle, Suzy, President, Founder

Puresa Humanitarian [18439]
5970 SW 18th St., Ste. 102
Boca Raton, FL 33433
PH: (561)826-7527
Meza, Giselle, Founder, President

Salt Therapy Association [13655]
120 NW 11th St.
Boca Raton, FL 33432
Toll free: 844-STA-INFO
Tonkin, Leo M., Founder

Scoliosis Association, Inc. [17185]
PO Box 811705
Boca Raton, FL 33481
Toll free: 800-800-0669

Spirit of Women [15337]
Spirit Health Group
2424 N Federal Hwy., Ste. 100
Boca Raton, FL 33431
PH: (561)544-0755
Abreu, Tanya, President

Stand Among Friends [11640]
777 Glades Rd., Bldg. NU84, Ste. 120
Boca Raton, FL 33431
PH: (561)297-4400
Fax: (561)297-4405
Hicks, Dawn Alexandra, Exec. Dir.

Visionary Alternatives, Inc. [13666]
7725 Kenway Pl. E
Boca Raton, FL 33433-3323
PH: (561)750-4551
Toll free: 866-750-4551
Fax: (561)750-4541
Tobal, Jane, President, Founder

American Riding Instructors Association **[22939]**
28801 Trenton Ct.
Bonita Springs, FL 34134-3337
PH: (239)948-3232
Fax: (239)948-5053
Kneeland, Charlotte, Director

Community College Baccalaureate Association **[7642]**
25216 Pelican Creek Cir., No. 103
Bonita Springs, FL 34134-1979
PH: (239)947-8085
Fax: (239)947-8870
Hagan, Beth, Exec. Dir.

International Cultic Studies Association **[20048]**
PO Box 2265
Bonita Springs, FL 34133
PH: (239)514-3081
Fax: (305)393-8193
Eichel, Steve K. D., PhD, ABPP, President

Contemporary Ceramic Studios Association **[694]**
217 N Seacrest Blvd., No. 295
Boynton Beach, FL 33425-0295
Toll free: 888-291-2272
Pearlman, Dena, Exec. Dir.

Dance Educators of America **[7700]**
PO Box 740387
Boynton Beach, FL 33474
PH: (914)636-3200
Ball, Stephen, Coord.

Deaf Seniors of America **[15187]**
5619 Ainsley Ct.
Boynton Beach, FL 33437-1503
Kensicki, Nancy E.

Smart Women Securities **[7568]**
1530 W Boynton Beach Blvd., Ste. 3834
Boynton Beach, FL 33436
Hsiao, Teresa, Founder

United States Water Fitness Association **[23067]**
PO Box 243279
Boynton Beach, FL 33424-3279
PH: (561)732-9908
Fax: (561)732-0950
Spannuth, John R., CEO, President

National Association of Home Inspectors **[1819]**
4426 5th St. W
Bradenton, FL 34207
PH: (941)462-4265
Toll free: 800-448-3942
Fax: (941)896-3187
Allen, Charles, Director

Sigma Alpha Lambda **[23792]**
501 Village Green Pky., Ste. 1
Bradenton, FL 34209
PH: (941)866-5614
Fax: (941)827-2924
Pickhardt, D. Mark, Exec. Dir.

Herocare **[13010]**
235 W Brandon Blvd., Ste. 241
Brandon, FL 33511
Toll free: 877-437-6411
Fax: (877)437-6411
Houk, Lane, Founder, Exec. Dir.

National Association of Amusement Ride Safety Officials **[1147]**
PO Box 638
Brandon, FL 33509-0638
PH: (813)661-2779
Toll free: 800-669-9053
Fax: (813)685-5117
Smith, Rick, VP

National Independent Concessionaires Association, Inc. **[1395]**
1043 E Brandon Blvd.
Brandon, FL 33511-5515
PH: (813)438-8926
Fax: (813)438-8928
Keene, Paulette, President

30th Infantry Division Veterans of WWII **[20698]**
2915 W State Rd. 235
Brooker, FL 32622-5167
PH: (352)485-1173
Fax: (352)485-2763
Towers, Mr. Frank W., Hist., President

National Cockatiel Society **[21542]**
c/o Deb Dollar, Treasurer
PO Box 12058
Brooksville, FL 34603-2058
Dollar, Deb, Treasurer

American Contact Dermatitis Society **[14480]**
2323 N State St., Unit 30
Bunnell, FL 32110-4395
PH: (386)437-4405
    (386)206-8215
Fax: (386)437-4427
Brod, Bruce, President

Gospel Association for the Blind **[17705]**
PO Box 1162
Bunnell, FL 32110-1162
PH: (386)586-5885
Fax: (386)586-5886
Montanus, George, President

International Society of Dermatology **[14499]**
2323 N State St., No. 30
Bunnell, FL 32110
PH: (386)437-4405
Fax: (386)437-4427
Kerdel, Francisco, MD, Bd. Member

All the Children are Children **[10845]**
PO Box 153012
Cape Coral, FL 33915
PH: (239)878-2104
Desir, Mr. Philocles, Founder

Genealogical Speakers Guild **[10174]**
PO Box 152987
Cape Coral, FL 33915
Smith, Gary M., President

U.S.A. Dance **[9272]**
PO Box 152988
Cape Coral, FL 33915-2988
Toll free: 800-447-9047
Fax: (239)573-0946
Pover, Peter, President

International Fibrodysplasia Ossificans Progressiva Association **[14831]**
101 Sunnytown Rd., Ste. 208
Casselberry, FL 32707
PH: (407)365-4194
Fax: (407)365-3213
Peeper, Jeannie, Founder, President

National Coalition of Ministries to Men **[19998]**
180 Wilshire Blvd.
Casselberry, FL 32707
PH: (407)472-2188
Fax: (407)331-7839
Billups, Darrel, Exec. Dir.

International Academy of Oral Medicine and Toxicology **[14444]**
8297 Champions Gate Blvd., No. 193

Champions Gate, FL 33896
PH: (863)420-6373
Fax: (863)419-8136
Haley, Boyd, PhD, Director

African Good Samaritan Mission **[13000]**
6700 150th Ave. N, Unit No. 705
Clearwater, FL 33764
Olade, Dr. Rosaline, President

American College of Nutrition **[16203]**
300 S Duncan Ave., Ste. 225
Clearwater, FL 33755
PH: (727)446-6086
Fax: (727)446-6202
Teter, Beverly, PhD, MACN, CNS, President

Circus Historical Society **[9162]**
c/o Les Smout CHS Treasurer
PO Box 15742
Clearwater, FL 33766
Cline, Robert, Secretary

Commission on Accreditation of Allied Health Education Programs **[8293]**
25400 US Highway 19 N, Ste. 158
Clearwater, FL 33763
PH: (727)210-2350
Fax: (727)210-2354
Fuchs, Susan, Secretary

Conference on Consumer Finance Law **[5104]**
PO Box 17981
Clearwater, FL 33762
PH: (405)208-5198
Ropiequet, John L., Chairman

Garden Centers of America **[4502]**
2873 Saber Dr.
Clearwater, FL 33759
Toll free: 800-721-0024
Morey, Jeff, Director

International Information Systems Security Certification Consortium **[6318]**
311 Park Place Blvd., Ste. 400
Clearwater, FL 33759
PH: (727)785-0189
Shearer, David, Exec. Dir.

National Association of Community Development Extension Professionals **[11407]**
600 Cleveland St., Ste 780
Clearwater, FL 33755
PH: (561)477-8100
Fox, Julie M., Secretary

World Union of Deists **[20581]**
PO Box 4052
Clearwater, FL 33758
Johnson, Bob, Contact

Communications Media Management Association **[264]**
140 Island Way, Ste. 316
Clearwater Beach, FL 33767
PH: (561)477-8100
Moss, Gregg, President

Martial Arts Teachers' Association **[23003]**
800 S Gulfview Blvd., Ste. 804
Clearwater Beach, FL 33767
Graden, John, Founder, Exec. Dir.

National Extension Association of Family and Consumer Sciences **[5107]**
140 Island Way, Ste. 316
Clearwater Beach, FL 33767
PH: (561)477-8100
Fax: (561)910-0896
Atkins, Jody Rosen, Exec. Dir.

Transported Asset Protection Association **[7154]**
140 Island Way, Ste. 316
Clearwater Beach, FL 33767
PH: (561)206-0344
Wilt, David, Director

International Brugmansia and Datura Society **[1309]**
PO Box 121236
Clermont, FL 34712-1236

Sugar Industry Technologists **[6650]**
201 Cypress Ave.
Clewiston, FL 33440
PH: (863)983-3637
Fax: (863)983-7855

Clan Munro Association **[20835]**
6895 Hundred Acre Dr.
Cocoa, FL 32927-2981
PH: (321)632-2118
Hoffman, Fred G., Treasurer

Rheumatoid Patient Foundation **[17164]**
PO Box 236251
Cocoa, FL 32923

Grind for Life **[10788]**
81 N Atlantic Ave.
Cocoa Beach, FL 32931
PH: (561)252-3839
Rogers, Mike, Founder

Hands of Mercy **[11951]**
163 Minutemen Cswy.
Cocoa Beach, FL 32931
PH: (321)799-9445

Ataxia Telangiectasia Children's Project **[14565]**
5300 W Hillsboro Blvd., Ste. 105
Coconut Creek, FL 33073-4395
PH: (954)481-6611
Toll free: 800-543-5728
Fax: (954)725-1153
Thornton, Jennifer, Exec. Dir.

Food for the Poor **[12538]**
6401 Lyons Rd.
Coconut Creek, FL 33073
PH: (954)427-2222
Toll free: 800-427-9104
Aloma, Angel, Exec. Dir.

Hudson Family Association **[20884]**
c/o Joan Hudson, President
3570 Coco Lake Dr.
Coconut Creek, FL 33073-4145

National Gym Association **[23064]**
PO Box 970579
Coconut Creek, FL 33097-0579
PH: (954)344-8410
Fax: (954)344-8412
Bostinto, Mr. Andrew, Founder, President

Alpha-1 Foundation **[14804]**
3300 Ponce de Leon Blvd.
Coral Gables, FL 33134
PH: (305)567-9888
Toll free: 877-228-7321
Fax: (305)567-1317
Erven, Marlene, Exec. Dir.

American Orchid Society **[6132]**
10901 Old Cutler Rd.
Coral Gables, FL 33156
PH: (305)740-2010
Fax: (305)740-2011
Smith, Frank, President

Caribbean Hotel and Tourism Association **[3374]**
2655 Le Jeune Rd., Ste. 910
Coral Gables, FL 33134

PH: (305)443-3040
Fax: (305)675-7977
Doumeng, Richard, Chairman

Cuban American Veterans Association [21120]
PO Box 140305
Coral Gables, FL 33114-0305
Santelices, Armando, Treasurer

Footprints Foundation [12274]
4000 Ponce Deleon Blvd., Ste. 470
Coral Gables, FL 33146
PH: (305)573-8423
Fax: (305)854-2980
Owens, Lorna, Founder, Exec. Dir.

Funders' Network for Smart Growth
and Livable Communities [11361]
1500 San Remo Ave., Ste. 249
Coral Gables, FL 33146
PH: (305)667-6350
Fax: (305)667-6355
Starrett, Ben, Exec. Dir., Founder

Give To Colombia [12476]
6705 Red Rd., Ste. 502
Coral Gables, FL 33143
PH: (305)669-4630
Fax: (305)675-2946
Tafur, Angela M., President, Founder

Holistic Dental Association [14440]
1825 Ponce de Leon Blvd., No. 148
Coral Gables, FL 33134
PH: (305)356-7338
Fax: (305)468-6359
Glasser, Roberta, Exec. Dir.

International Association for Housing
Science [11974]
PO Box 340254
Coral Gables, FL 33134
Ural, Prof. Oktay, President, Founder

International Association for the
Management of Technology [7274]
248294 College of Engineering
University of Miami
Coral Gables, FL 33124-0623
PH: (305)284-2344
Fax: (305)284-4040
Hosni, Yasser, President

International SeaKeepers Society
[4468]
355 Alhambra Cir., Ste. 1100
Coral Gables, FL 33134
PH: (305)448-7089
Snow, Richard, CEO, President

National Council on Strength and
Fitness [23335]
5915 Ponce de Leon Blvd., Ste. 60
Coral Gables, FL 33146
Toll free: 800-772-NCSF
Fax: (305)666-3482

Organ Donation and Transplantation
Alliance [17518]
PO Box 140027
Coral Gables, FL 33114
PH: (757)818-1205
Swanson, LeAnn N., Exec. Dir.

Tropical Flowering Tree Society
[4442]
Fairchild Tropical Botanical Garden
10901 Old Cutler Rd.
Coral Gables, FL 33156
Cabrera, Jessica, Contact

Venezuelan-American Chamber of
Commerce [23639]
1600 Ponce de Leon Blvd., 10th Fl.,
Ste. 1033
Coral Gables, FL 33134
PH: (786)350-1190
Fax: (786)350-1191
Santiago, Juan, President

Academy of Laser Dentistry [14366]
9900 W Sample Rd., Ste. 400
Coral Springs, FL 33065-4079
PH: (954)346-3776
Toll free: 877-527-3776
Fax: (954)757-2598
Siminovsky, Gail S., Officer

One Village Planet [11418]
1440 Coral Ridge Dr., Ste. 104
Coral Springs, FL 33071
PH: (954)290-9147
Warren, Dan, Founder

International Game Fish Association
[22846]
IGFA Fishing Hall of Fame and
Museum
300 Gulf Stream Way
Dania Beach, FL 33004
PH: (954)927-2628
Fax: (954)924-4299
Kramer, Rob, President

American Dermatological Association
[14481]
PO Box 551301
Davie, FL 33355
PH: (954)452-1113
Fax: (954)252-2093
Pariser, David M., Hist.

Association for International
Agricultural and Extension Educa-
tion [7472]
c/o Anita Zavodska, Treasurer
School of Professional and Career
Education
Barry University
4900 S University Dr., Ste. 203-205
Davie, FL 33328
Pardello, Renee, President

I Care I Cure Childhood Cancer
Foundation [13986]
PO Box 291386
Davie, FL 33329
Toll free: 800-807-8013
Krimsky, Beth-Ann, President

Whooping Crane Conservation Association [4900]
11411 SW 49th Pl.
Davie, FL 33330
Johns, Brian, President

Association of Public-Safety Com-
munications Officials International
[5744]
351 N Williamson Blvd.
Daytona Beach, FL 32114-1112
PH: (386)322-2500
Toll free: 888-272-6911
Fax: (386)322-2501
Smith, Georggina, President

Bethune-Cookman University
National Alumni Association
[19308]
PO Box 11646
Daytona Beach, FL 32120
PH: (386)226-2131
Fax: (386)226-2131
Brinson, Mr. A. Ray, Exec. Ofc.

International Motor Sports Associa-
tion [22526]
International Motorsports Ctr.
1 Daytona Blvd.
Daytona Beach, FL 32114
PH: (386)310-6500
Fax: (386)310-6505
Elkins, Scot, VP

Ladies Professional Golf Association
[22885]
100 International Golf Dr.
Daytona Beach, FL 32124-1092

PH: (386)274-6200
Fax: (386)274-1099
Whan, Michael, Commissioner

National Association for Stock Car
Auto Racing [22527]
PO Box 2875
Daytona Beach, FL 32120
Toll free: 800-CARCASH
France, Brian, Chairman, CEO

Support Our Troops [10761]
PO Box 70
Daytona Beach, FL 32115-0070
PH: (386)767-8882
Boire, Martin C., Chairman

American Iris Society [22078]
c/o Tom Gormley, Membership
Secretary
PO Box 177
De Leon Springs, FL 32130
PH: (386)277-2057
Fax: (386)277-2057
Gormley, Tom, Mgr.

Fraternal Order Orioles [19433]
PO Box 530447
Debary, FL 32753
Parnell, Steve, President

The National Association of Railway
Business Women [2838]
367 Hinsdale Dr.
Debary, FL 32713-4555
McKim, Melanie, Membership Chp.

American Professional Practice Association [15111]
550 Fairway Dr., Ste. 107
Deerfield Beach, FL 33441-1834
Toll free: 800-221-2168

Children's Relief Network [10934]
PO Box 668
Deerfield Beach, FL 33443
PH: (561)620-2970
Toll free: 800-326-6500
Fax: (561)393-3151
Thomson, Angie, Founder, President

International Society of Sports Nutri-
tion [16226]
c/o Jose Antonio, Founder
4511 NW 7th St.
Deerfield Beach, FL 33442
Fax: (561)239-1754
Antonio, Dr. Jose, PhD, CEO,
Founder

National Association of Residents
and Interns [15738]
350 Fairway Dr., Ste. 200
Deerfield Beach, FL 33441
Fax: (954)571-1877

Parents of Galactosemic Children
[15833]
PO Box 1512
Deerfield Beach, FL 33443
Toll free: 866-900-7421
Saylor, Scott, VP

American Warmblood Registry
[4331]
PO Box 1332
DeLeon Springs, FL 32130
PH: (561)693-5516
Fax: (775)667-0516

American Association of Food
Hygiene Veterinarians [17596]
1730 S Federal Highway 205
Delray Beach, FL 33483
Willinghan, Eric, Exec. VP

Fire Safe North America [1289]
200 NE 2nd Ave., Unit 309
Delray Beach, FL 33444

PH: (561)278-8776
Fax: (561)771-1701
Scott, John, VP

International Anaplastology Associa-
tion [14338]
PO Box 8685
Delray Beach, FL 33482
PH: (202)642-2053
Brooke, Rachel, Exec. Dir.

The National Special Needs
Network, Inc. [14556]
6424 Overland Dr.
Delray Beach, FL 33484
PH: (561)447-4152
Minde, Jeffrey H., President

World Association of Natural
Disaster Awareness and Assistance [12386]
1865 SW 4th Ave., Ste. D5-A
Delray Beach, FL 33444

International Conference of Police
Chaplains [19929]
PO Box 5590
Destin, FL 32540
PH: (850)654-9736
Fax: (850)654-9742
Neal, Pam, VP

America Developing Smiles [13026]
8300 NW 53rd St., Ste. 350
Doral, FL 33166
PH: (305)742-2136
Fax: (305)742-2161
Penalosa, Carmen, President

Chile-U.S. Chamber of Commerce
[23572]
8600 NW 17th St., Ste. 110
Doral, FL 33126-1034
PH: (786)400-1748
Fax: (305)599-2992
Sepulveda, Patricio, President

Peruvian American Chamber of
Commerce [23612]
1948 NW 82nd Ave.
Doral, FL 33126
PH: (305)599-1057
Alvarado, Nelson, President

Resistance Welding Manufacturing
Alliance [1765]
c/o Adrian Bustillo
8669 Doral Blvd., Ste. 130
Doral, FL 33166
PH: (305)443-9353
Snow, Tom, V. Chmn. of the Exec.
Committee

Clan Ramsay Association of North
America [20838]
434 Skinner Blvd., Ste. 105
Dunedin, FL 34698
PH: (727)409-4639
Fax: (775)781-3812
Ramsay, John, Jr., President

Pekingese Club of America [21942]
c/o Elizabeth Tilley-Poole, Treasurer
9455 SW 140th Ave.
Dunnellon, FL 34432-3973
PH: (352)465-1628
Shephard, Susan, Act. Pres.

Silk Painters International [8940]
PO Box 1074
Eastpoint, FL 32328
Steward, Kaki, President

Face Autism, Inc. [13763]
5610 74th Pl. E
Ellenton, FL 34222-4058

Clowns of America International
[21601]
PO Box 122
Eustis, FL 32727-0122

PH: (352)357-1676
Toll free: 877-816-6941
Cox, Mike, President

Nissan Infiniti Car Owners Club [21461]
237 Fernwood Blvd., Ste. 111
Fern Park, FL 32730-2116
PH: (407)828-8908
Childs, Greg, CEO

Federation of Dining Room Professionals [2938]
1417 Sadler Rd., No. 100
Fernandina Beach, FL 32034
PH: (904)491-6690
Fax: (904)491-6689
Martinage, Bernard, Chairman, Founder, President

Pine Chemicals Association [725]
PO Box 17136
Fernandina Beach, FL 32035
PH: (404)994-6267
Morris, Charles W., Sr. VP

Resort and Commercial Recreation Association [2915]
PO Box 16449
Fernandina Beach, FL 32035
Boliver, Bruce, President

Alpha Phi Sigma [23751]
3301 College Ave.
Fort Lauderdale, FL 33314
PH: (954)262-7004
Fax: (954)262-3646
Shearn, Regina, Exec. Dir.

American Academy of Medical Esthetic Professionals [16084]
2000 S Andrews Ave.
Fort Lauderdale, FL 33316
PH: (954)463-5594
Fax: (954)653-2499
Parker, Ms. Sasha S., President

American Boat Builders & Repairers Association [2233]
1075 SE 17th St.
Fort Lauderdale, FL 33316
PH: (954)654-7821
Fax: (954)239-2600
Wright, Graham, President

American Fair Credit Council [1217]
100 W Cypress Creek Rd., Ste. 700
Fort Lauderdale, FL 33309
Toll free: 888-657-8272
Fax: (954)343-6960
Birnbaum, Robby H., President

American Swimming Coaches Association [23281]
5101 NW 21st Ave., Ste. 530
Fort Lauderdale, FL 33309
PH: (954)563-4930
Toll free: 800-356-2722
Fax: (954)563-9813
Heidary, Don, President

Association for the Advancement of International Education [8100]
Maliman Hollywood Bldg. No. 314
3301 College Ave.
Fort Lauderdale, FL 33314-7721
PH: (954)262-6937
Duevel, Linda, President

The Association of American Editorial Cartoonists [2659]
PO Box 460673
Fort Lauderdale, FL 33346
Zyglis, Adam, President

The Billfish Foundation [4794]
5100 N Federal Hwy., Ste. 200
Fort Lauderdale, FL 33308

PH: (954)938-0150
Toll free: 800-438-8247
Fax: (954)938-5311
MacMillan, Sandra, Bd. Member

Bridal Show Producers International [444]
1510 SE 17th St., Ste. 200
Fort Lauderdale, FL 33316
Toll free: 800-573-6070
Thiebauth, Bruce, Treasurer

Bright Steps Forward [10875]
4026 N Ocean Blvd.
Fort Lauderdale, FL 33308
PH: (954)491-6611
Toll free: 877-NOW-ICAN
Castellano, John, President

CenterLink [11476]
PO Box 24490
Fort Lauderdale, FL 33307-4490
PH: (954)765-6024
Fax: (954)206-0469
Stone, Mr. Terry, Exec. Dir.

Deliver the Dream, Inc. [12873]
3223 NW 10th Terr., Ste. 602
Fort Lauderdale, FL 33309-5940
PH: (954)564-3512
Toll free: 888-687-3732
Fax: (954)564-4385
Withrow, Paul, Exec. Dir.

Ferrari Club of America [21380]
PO Box 2488
Fort Lauderdale, FL 33303-2488
Toll free: 800-328-0444
DeLauro, Al, Chmn. of the Bd.

Goldfish Society of America [22032]
PO Box 551373
Fort Lauderdale, FL 33355-1373
Cusick, Terry, Chairman

Great Commission Alliance [11663]
4700 SW 188th Ave.
Fort Lauderdale, FL 33332
PH: (954)434-4500
Kelso, Brian, Exec. Dir.

Haiti Needs My Help [13057]
1131 Alabama Ave.
Fort Lauderdale, FL 33312
PH: (954)302-7422
Fax: (954)302-2041
Hyppolite, Francinor, President

International Gay and Lesbian Travel Association [3381]
1201 NE 26th St., Ste. 103
Fort Lauderdale, FL 33305
PH: (954)630-1637
Fax: (954)630-1652
Tanzella, John, President

International Superyacht Society [435]
757 SE 17th St., No. 744
Fort Lauderdale, FL 33316
PH: (954)525-6625
Fax: (954)525-5325
Wagner, Derik, President

International Swimming Hall of Fame [23285]
1 Hall of Fame Dr.
Fort Lauderdale, FL 33316
PH: (954)462-6536
Fax: (954)525-4031
Wigo, Bruce, CEO, President

Kids Ecology Corps [4118]
3299 SW 4th Ave.
Fort Lauderdale, FL 33315
PH: (954)524-0366
Starr, Joan, CEO

Multiple Sclerosis Foundation [15957]
6520 N Andrews Ave.
Fort Lauderdale, FL 33309-2130

PH: (954)776-6805
Toll free: 800-225-6495
Fax: (954)938-8708
Schenck, Eric, President, Director

National Association of Black Hotel Owners, Operators and Developers [1667]
3520 W Broward Blvd., Ste. 119
Fort Lauderdale, FL 33312
PH: (954)797-7102
Fax: (954)337-2877
Roberts, Michael, Chairman

National Drowning Prevention Alliance [12831]
1 Hall of Fame Dr.
Fort Lauderdale, FL 33316
PH: (951)659-8600
   (209)323-5438
Paterson, Jim, President

North American Maritime Ministry Association [12861]
PO Box 460158
Fort Lauderdale, FL 33346-0158
PH: (514)993-6528
Zuidema, Dr. Jason, Exec. Dir.

Phi Delta Phi International Legal Fraternity [23806]
PO Box 11570
Fort Lauderdale, FL 33339
PH: (202)223-6801
Fax: (202)223-6808
Wheat, Tim, Exec. Dir.

Prison Pen Pals [21739]
PO Box 120997
Fort Lauderdale, FL 33312
PH: (954)583-6958
   (828)765-2461
Perry, Joy, CEO

Seven Seas Cruising Association [22667]
2501 E Commercial Blvd., Ste. 203
Fort Lauderdale, FL 33308
PH: (954)771-5660
Fax: (954)771-5662
Mkam, Ms. Judith, Assoc. Dir.

Share a Pet [12457]
2881 E Oakland Park Blvd., Ste. 204
Fort Lauderdale, FL 33309-6302
PH: (954)630-8763
Mayi, Dr. Bindu, Chmn. of the Bd.

Structural Insulated Panel Association [586]
PO Box 39848
Fort Lauderdale, FL 33339
PH: (253)858-7472
Cobb, Al, Bd. Member

Swedish Women's Educational Association International, Inc. [19665]
PO Box 4128
Fort Lauderdale, FL 33338
Ahlquist, Margaret Sikkens, Officer

Tattoo-a-Pet [10701]
6571 SW 20th Ct.
Fort Lauderdale, FL 33317
PH: (954)581-5834
Toll free: 800-828-8667

U.S. Superyacht Association [440]
757 SE 17th St., No. 662
Fort Lauderdale, FL 33316
PH: (954)792-8666
Toll free: 800-208-5801
Fax: (954)523-0607
McGowan, Ms. Kitty, President

WECAI Network [1001]
PO Box 550856
Fort Lauderdale, FL 33355-0856

PH: (954)625-6606
Toll free: 877-947-3337
Richards Mooney, Heidi, MS, CEO, Founder

Women's International Shipping and Trading Association [3110]
Total Marine Solutions Inc.
4350 Oakes Rd., Ste. 502
Fort Lauderdale, FL 33314
Haines, Kathleen, Treasurer

American Canine Sports Medicine Association [17612]
PO Box 07412
Fort Myers, FL 33919

American Shore & Beach Preservation Association [3805]
5460 Beaujolais Ln.
Fort Myers, FL 33919
PH: (239)489-2616
Fax: (239)362-9771
Pratt, Anthony P., President

Light Electric Vehicle Association [3338]
6900-29 Daniels Pky., No. 209
Fort Myers, FL 33912
Munjal, Naveen, Director

National Meningitis Association [14604]
PO Box 60143
Fort Myers, FL 33906
Toll free: 866-366-3662
Bozof, Lynn, President

SeniorNet [8674]
5237 Summerlin Commons Blvd., Ste. 314
Fort Myers, FL 33907
PH: (239)275-2202
Fax: (239)275-2501
Smith, Leslie M., Chmn. of the Bd.

The Tanygnathus Society [3672]
4510 Buckingham Rd.
Fort Myers, FL 33905
Dinger, June, President

U.S. Surveyors Association [7254]
13430 McGregor Blvd.
Fort Myers, FL 33919-5924
PH: (239)481-5150
Toll free: 800-245-4425
Harper, Virginia, Director, Founder

Alliance for Addiction Solutions [15892]
PO Box 13375
Fort Pierce, FL 34979-3375
PH: (424)256-8227
Reuben, Carolyn, Bd. Member, Founder

Alliance for Massage Therapy Education [8274]
1232 Bonefish Ct.
Fort Pierce, FL 34949-2901
Toll free: 855-236-8331
Fax: (786)522-2440
Sohnen-Moe, Cherie, President

Loving Hands for the Needy, Inc. [11073]
LHFN, Unit 2163
3170 Airmans Dr.
Fort Pierce, FL 34946
PH: (561)305-5268
Miller, Rev. John Henry, Founder

National Teen Anglers [22043]
1177 Bayshore Dr., No. 207
Fort Pierce, FL 34949
PH: (772)519-0482
Bernetti, Capt. Al, President

Ocean Research & Conservation Association, Inc. [3923]
Duerr Laboratory for Marine Conservation

1420 Seaway Dr.
Fort Pierce, FL 34949
PH: (772)467-1600
Fax: (772)467-1602
Widder, Edie, PhD, CEO

Save the Chimps **[10693]**
PO Box 12220
Fort Pierce, FL 34979-2220
PH: (772)429-0403
Fax: (772)461-7147
North, Jason, Chmn. of the Bd.

Conservative Majority for Citizen's
  Rights **[18023]**
c/o Jim Harkins, Sr.
American Gospel Ministries
302 Briarwood Cir. NW
Fort Walton Beach, FL 32548-3904
PH: (850)862-6211
    (850)862-4429
Harkins, James Stanley, Sr.,
  President

American Association of Traditional
  Chinese Veterinary Medicine
  [13590]
PO Box 141324
Gainesville, FL 32614
PH: (352)672-6400
Ferguson, Bruce, President, Asst.
  Ed.

American Board of Veterinary
  Practitioners **[17609]**
5003 SW 41st Blvd.
Gainesville, FL 32608-4930
PH: (352)431-2843
Toll free: 800-697-3583
Fax: (352)354-9046
French, Dennis, Comm. Chm.

American Dream Coalition **[17870]**
3711 NW 59th Pl.
Gainesville, FL 32653
PH: (352)281-5817
Fax: (352)381-7026
Bruskewitz, Eileen, Exec. Dir.

American Society for Metabolic and
  Bariatric Surgery **[17374]**
100 SW 75th St., Ste. 201
Gainesville, FL 32607-5776
PH: (352)331-4900
Fax: (352)331-4975
Mallory, Georgeann, RD, Exec. Dir.

American Student Government As-
  sociation **[8612]**
412 NW 16th Ave.
Gainesville, FL 32602-4203
PH: (352)373-8120
Fax: (352)373-8120
Oxendine, Mr. W.H., Jr., Exec. Dir.

Aquatic Plant Management Society,
  Inc. **[6137]**
7922 NW 71st St.
Gainesville, FL 32653
PH: (662)617-4571
Fax: (352)392-3462
Richardson, Rob, President

Association for Tropical Lepidoptera
  [6607]
PO Box 141210
Gainesville, FL 32614-1210
Fax: (352)373-3249
Turner, Dr. Jon D., Exec. Dir.

Association for Young Astrologers
  [5990]
2019 NW 31st Ter.
Gainesville, FL 32605
Brennan, Chris, President

Center for Applications of
  Psychological Type **[16910]**
2815 NW 13th St., Ste. 401
Gainesville, FL 32609-2878

PH: (352)375-0160
Toll free: 800-777-2278
Fax: (352)378-0503
Kummerow, Jean M.

CPAmerica International **[25]**
104 N Main St., 5th Flr.
Gainesville, FL 32601-5320
PH: (352)727-4070
Fax: (352)727-4031
Malthouse, Brian, Director

Equestrian Medical Safety Associa-
  tion **[17283]**
PO Box 100236
Gainesville, FL 32610-0236
Stanitski, Debbie, MD, President

Facial Pain Association **[15930]**
408 W University Ave., Ste. 602
Gainesville, FL 32601
PH: (352)384-3600
Toll free: 800-923-3608
Fax: (352)384-3606
Bodington, Jeffrey, Chairman

Fight Slavery **[12033]**
PO Box 358531
Gainesville, FL 32635-8531
Tovar, Richard M., President

Institute for Public Relations **[8470]**
2096 Weimer Hall
Gainesville, FL 32611-8400
PH: (352)392-0280
Fax: (352)846-1122
McCorkindale, Dr. Tina, President,
  CEO

Insulin for Life USA **[14535]**
5745 SW 75th St., No. 116
Gainesville, FL 32608
PH: (352)327-8649
Atkinson, Carol, Coord.

International Society for Astrological
  Research **[5993]**
PO Box 358945
Gainesville, FL 32635-8945
PH: (805)525-0461
Toll free: 800-731-9456
Perry, Glenn, Director

International Society for Cow Protec-
  tion **[10652]**
7016 SE 92 Ter.
Gainesville, FL 32641
PH: (352)792-6777
Dove, William E., President

International Society for the Study of
  Religion, Nature and Culture
  [8044]
107 Anderson Hall
Gainesville, FL 32611-7410
PH: (352)392-1625
Pike, Sarah, President

Modern Greek Studies Association
  [9354]
c/o Gonda Van Steen, Executive
  Director
PO Box 117435
Gainesville, FL 32611-7435
PH: (352)273-3796
Karakatsanis, Neovi, President

National Association for Cave Diving
  [23342]
PO Box 14492
Gainesville, FL 32604
Syme, Don, Secretary, Treasurer,
  Director

Organization of Nematologists of
  Tropical America **[6909]**
1911 SW 34th St.
Nematology Section

Division of Plant Industry, DPI-
  FDACS
1911 SW 34th St.
Gainesville, FL 32614
PH: (352)395-4752
Fax: (352)395-4714
Brito, Janete A., Director

Pet Nutrition Alliance **[16235]**
5003 SW 41st Blvd.
Gainesville, FL 32608
Aspros, Douglas G., DVM, President

Sea Turtle Conservancy **[4885]**
4424 NW 13th St., Ste. B-11
Gainesville, FL 32609
PH: (352)373-6441
Toll free: 800-678-7853
Fax: (352)375-2449
Clay, Landon T., Chairman

Society for Exact Philosophy **[10123]**
Dept. of Philosophy
University of Florida
330 Griffin-Floyd Hall
Gainesville, FL 32611-8545
PH: (352)392-2084
Fax: (352)392-5577
Ray, Greg, Secretary

Society for the Study of Human
  Development **[9543]**
c/o Monika Ardelt, Executive
  Secretary
University of Florida
PO Box 117330
Gainesville, FL 32611-7330
Overton, Willis, Officer

Society for Utopian Studies **[10132]**
c/o Dr. Phillip E. Wegner, Member-
  ship Chairman
Dept. of English
University of Florida
Gainesville, FL 32611-7310
PH: (352)392-6650
Wegner, Dr. Phillip E., Membership
  Chp.

Spinal Health International **[17264]**
2221 NW 3rd Pl.
Gainesville, FL 32603-1406
Gregory, Mindy, Bd. Member

Sustainable Cambodia **[11447]**
101 SE 2nd Pl., Ste. 201-B
Gainesville, FL 32601
PH: (352)371-2075
Phang, Polin, Exec. Dir.

University of Florida Alumni Associa-
  tion **[19355]**
1938 W University Ave.
Gainesville, FL 32603
PH: (352)392-1905
Toll free: 888-352-5866
Fax: (352)846-3636
Nias, Danita, Exec. Dir.

All Navy Women's National Alliance
  [5587]
PO Box 147
Goldenrod, FL 32733-0147
Breece, Sharon L., President

Baromedical Nurses Association
  [16126]
PO Box 53
Gotha, FL 34734
PH: (407)361-4715
Evenson, Becky, VP

American Association of Public
  Health Physicians **[16992]**
1605 Pebble Beach Blvd.
Green Cove Springs, FL 32043-
  8077
Toll free: 888-447-7281
Fax: (202)333-5016
Rhodes, Katrina, President

RV Manufacturers' Clubs Association
  [22431]
413 Walnut St.
Green Cove Springs, FL 32043
PH: (904)529-6575
Toll free: 866-467-8622
Fax: (904)284-4472

Suntanning Association for Educa-
  tion **[2916]**
c/o Paul Germek
PO Box 1181
Gulf Breeze, FL 32562
PH: (850)939-3388
Toll free: 800-536-8255
Fax: (801)348-9571
Germek, Paul, Contact

Basically Bats Wildlife Conservation
  Society **[4790]**
106 Spooner Rd.
Hawthorne, FL 32640
PH: (352)481-2913

Sharkhunters International, Inc.
  [9808]
PO Box 1539
Hernando, FL 34442
PH: (352)637-2917
Toll free: 866-258-2188
Fax: (352)637-6289
Cooper, Harry, Founder, President

Global Underwater Explorers **[4466]**
18487 High Springs Main St.
High Springs, FL 32643
PH: (386)454-0820
Toll free: 800-762-3483
Fax: (386)454-0654
Jablonski, Jarrod, Founder,
  President, Chairman

International Society for Vascular
  Surgery **[17392]**
10062 SE Osprey Point Dr.
Hobe Sound, FL 33455
PH: (631)993-4321
Dardik, Alan, MD, PhD, President

International Street Painting Society
  [8869]
9285 SE Delafield St.
Hobe Sound, FL 33455
PH: (561)315-0243
Chaparro, Jennifer, Founder, Director

World Bulldog Alliance **[21996]**
1700 Ridgewood Ave., Ste. D
Holly Hill, FL 32117-1782
PH: (386)437-4762
Giacobbe, Ray, President

Diabetes Research Institute Founda-
  tion **[14529]**
200 S Park Rd., Ste. 100
Hollywood, FL 33021
PH: (954)964-4040
Toll free: 800-321-3437
Fax: (954)964-7036
Beber, Diane, Director

Gases and Welding Distributors As-
  sociation **[1731]**
1 Oakwood Blvd., Ste. 195
Hollywood, FL 33020
PH: (954)367-7728
Toll free: 844-251-3219
Fax: (954)367-7790
Lane, Ned, 1st VP

The Holocaust Documentation and
  Education Center, Inc. **[18347]**
2031 Harrison St.
Hollywood, FL 33020
PH: (954)929-5690
Kenigsberg, Rositta E., President

International Association for
  Identification **[5247]**
2131 Hollywood Blvd., Ste. 403
Hollywood, FL 33020

PH: (954)589-0628
Fax: (954)589-0657
Calhoun, Glen, COO

International Autograph Dealer Alliance & Collectors Club [21667]
11435 Lake Shore Dr.
Hollywood, FL 33026-1120
Frost, Michael, Founder

Phi Delta Epsilon International Medical Fraternity [23819]
1005 N Northlake Dr.
Hollywood, FL 33019
PH: (786)302-1120
Fax: (786)472-7133
Katz, Karen, CEO

Planning and Visual Education Partnership [2974]
4651 Sheridan St., Ste. 470
Hollywood, FL 33021-3437
PH: (954)893-7225
Fax: (954)893-8375
Goddu, Bill, VP

World Flower Council [1312]
1608 Tyler St.
Hollywood, FL 33020
PH: (954)444-6445
Fax: (888)506-7808
Hoffman, R. Lynn, Chairman

World Salt Foundation [20479]
6810 Lee St.
Hollywood, FL 33024
PH: (954)600-6381
Bening, Stephen L., Chairman

International Barter Alliance USA [419]
7801 W Rosedale Dr.
Homosassa, FL 34448
PH: (727)489-2634
Toll free: 866-205-8554
Fax: (630)604-6177

New Frontiers Health Force [12706]
PO Box 1059
Indian Rocks Beach, FL 33785
PH: (727)544-3555
Fax: (727)546-0106
Hawthorne, Dr. Tonya, Founder, President

Preferred Funeral Directors International [2414]
PO Box 335
Indian Rocks Beach, FL 33785
Toll free: 888-655-1566
Perotto, Michael, President

77th Artillery Association [21164]
PO Box 8621
Jacksonville, FL 32239-8621
PH: (904)236-4856
Toll free: 877-220-0393
Taylor, Fred, Treasurer

Academy of Physicians in Clinical Research [8299]
6816 Southpoint Pky., Ste. 1000
jacksonville, FL 32216
PH: (703)254-8100
   (904)309-6271
Fax: (703)254-8101
Kilkenny, Sara, Director

Alliance for the Lost Boys of Sudan [12024]
8241 Wallingford Hills Ln.
Jacksonville, FL 32256
PH: (904)363-9821
Hecht, Joan, President, Founder

American Association of Avian Pathologists [17591]
12627 San Jose Blvd., Ste. 202
Jacksonville, FL 32223-8638

PH: (904)425-5735
Fax: (281)664-4744
Hofacre, Charles, Exec. VP

American Association of Clinical Endocrinologists [14698]
245 Riverside Ave., Ste. 200
Jacksonville, FL 32202
PH: (904)353-7878
Fax: (904)353-8185
Grunberger, George, MD, FACP, President

American Cutaneous Oncology Society [16331]
6816 Southpoint Pky., No. 1000
Jacksonville, FL 32216
Nestor, Mark S., MD, President

American Society for Preventive Cardiology [14095]
6816 Southpoint Pky., Ste. 1000
Jacksonville, FL 32216
PH: (904)309-6235
Fax: (904)998-0855
Sperling, Laurence S., MD, President

Jessie Ball duPont Fund [12462]
40 E Adams St. E, Ste. 300
Jacksonville, FL 32202-3302
PH: (904)353-0890
Toll free: 800-252-3452
Fax: (904)353-3879
Magill, Sherry P., PhD, President

Be The Change International [12142]
1131 N Laura St.
Jacksonville, FL 32206
PH: (904)355-0000
Lee, Dr. Robert V., III, Chairman, CEO, Founder

Care Through Education International [11218]
13810 Sutton Park Dr. N, No. 137
Jacksonville, FL 32224
PH: (904)992-0977
Herrmann, Dr. Siegfried, Founder

Certified Claims Professional Accreditation Council [3324]
PO Box 550922
Jacksonville, FL 32255-0922
O'Dell, John, HCCP, Exec. Dir.

Commercial Vehicle Solutions Network [316]
3943-2 Baymeadows Rd.
Jacksonville, FL 32217
PH: (904)737-2900
Fax: (904)636-9881
Neeley, Edward, President

Arthur Vining Davis Foundations [11725]
225 Water St., Ste. 1510
Jacksonville, FL 32202-5185
PH: (904)359-0670
Fax: (904)359-0675
Cable, Nancy J., PhD, President

From Us With Love [12035]
2000 Corporate Square Blvd., Ste. 101
Jacksonville, FL 32216
Toll free: 800-392-8717
Smith, Michael, Director, Founder

International Herb Association [4294]
PO Box 5667
Jacksonville, FL 32247-5667
Reisen, Matthias, President, Trustee

International Messianic Jewish Alliance [20147]
c/o Paul Wilbur, Executive Director
Jacksonville, FL
Fischer, John, President

International Society for Comparative Studies of Chinese and Western Philosophy [8421]
c/o Sarah Mattice, Secretary & Treasurer
Philosophy & Religious Studies
College of Arts & Sciences
University of North Florida
1 UNF Dr.
Jacksonville, FL 32224
Mattice, Sarah, Secretary, Treasurer

International Society of Ocular Toxicology [17497]
c/o K.V. Chalam, Secretary-Treasurer
653 W 8th St.
Department of Ophthalmology
University of Florida Jacksonville
Jacksonville, FL 32209
PH: (904)244-9301
Fax: (904)244-9391

Metal Treating Institute [2358]
8825 Perimeter Park Blvd., No. 501
Jacksonville, FL 32216
PH: (904)249-0448
Fax: (904)249-0459
Morrison, Tom, CEO

National Association of Teachers of Singing [8384]
9957 Moorings Dr., Ste. 401
Jacksonville, FL 32257
PH: (904)992-9101
Fax: (904)262-2587
Henderson, Allen, Exec. Dir.

National ATM Council [411]
9802-12 Baymeadows Rd., No. 196
Jacksonville, FL 32256
PH: (904)683-6533
Fax: (904)425-6010
Braddock, David, VP, Treasurer

National Board of Fitness Examiners [16707]
1650 Margaret St., Ste. 302-342
Jacksonville, FL 32204-3869
Arria, Dr. Sal, President

National Certification Commission for Acupuncture and Oriental Medicine [16457]
76 S Laura St., Ste. 1290
Jacksonville, FL 32202
PH: (904)598-1005
Fax: (904)598-5001
Ward-Cook, Dr. Kory, CEO

National Fastdance Association [9268]
c/o Bill Maddox, President
3371 Debussy Rd.
Jacksonville, FL 32277
PH: (904)744-2424
Toll free: 877-632-2582
Maddox, Bill, President, Founder

National Lipid Association [13814]
6816 Southpoint Pky., Ste. 1000
Jacksonville, FL 32216
PH: (904)998-0854
Fax: (904)998-0855
Seymour, Christopher, MBA, Liaison

PBR Forces Veterans Association [21168]
14015 Spanish Point Rd.
Jacksonville, FL 32225
PH: (812)636-4343
Fax: (812)636-4343
Myers, Bruce D., VP

Railway Systems Suppliers, Inc. [2842]
13133 Professional Dr., Ste. 100
Jacksonville, FL 32225-4178

PH: (904)379-3366
Fax: (904)379-3941
Drudy, Michael A., Exec. Dir., Secretary, Treasurer

Recreational Scuba Training Council [23346]
PO Box 11083
Jacksonville, FL 32239-1083

The Rhinoplasty Society [14323]
PO Box 441745
Jacksonville, FL 32222
PH: (904)786-1377
Fax: (904)786-9939
Gryskiewicz, Joe, MD, President

Society of Accredited Marine Surveyors, Inc. [7253]
7855 Argyle Forest Blvd., No. 203
Jacksonville, FL 32244-5598
PH: (904)384-1494
Toll free: 800-344-9077
Fax: (904)388-3958
Lobley, Joseph B., VP

Society for the Advancement of Geriatric Anesthesia [13706]
c/o Michael Lewis, MD
University of Florida
College of Medicine
655 W 8th St.
Jacksonville, FL 32209
PH: (904)244-5431
Lewis, Michael, MD, President

Society of Biological Psychiatry [16836]
Mayo Clinic of Jacksonville
Research-Birdsall 310
4500 San Pablo Rd.
Jacksonville, FL 32224
PH: (904)953-2842
Fax: (904)953-7117
Peterson, Maggie, MBA, Exec. Dir.

Supervised Visitation Network [11162]
3955 Riverside Ave.
Jacksonville, FL 32205
PH: (904)419-7861
Fax: (904)239-5888
Nullet, Joe, Exec. Dir.

Wildlife Conservation Global Inc. [4908]
1615 Riverside Ave.
Jacksonville, FL 32204

World Head of Family Sokeship Council [23027]
6035 Ft. Caroline Rd., Ste. 22
Jacksonville, FL 32277-1883
PH: (904)361-9218
Fax: (904)744-4625
Sanchez, Frank E., Exec. Dir., Founder

Wounded Warrior Project [21157]
4899 Belfort Rd., Ste. 300
Jacksonville, FL 32256
PH: (904)296-7350
Toll free: 877-832-6997
Fax: (904)296-7347
Nardizzi, Steven, ESQ, CEO

World Solutions Against Infectious Diseases [15417]
PO Box 49042
Jacksonville Beach, FL 32240-9042
Fax: (786)513-5762
Delgado, Jairo, CEO

Spinal Cord Tumor Association, Inc. [17263]
PO Box 461
Jay, FL 32565

PH: (850)675-6663
Toll free: 866-893-1689
Mandell, Missy, Secretary, Director

Apostolic Association of Churches, Ministers & Leaders International [20016]
810 Saturn St., Ste. 16
Jupiter, FL 33477
PH: (954)309-7388
Neuhaus, Dr. John, Founder

CrimeWatch USA [11505]
6671 W Indiantown Rd.
Jupiter, FL 33458-3991
PH: (561)247-5113
Lopilato, Mike, Exec. Dir.

DES Action USA [13960]
PO Box 7296
Jupiter, FL 33468-7296
Toll free: 800-337-9288
Howell, Fran, Contact

Edna Hibel Society [9829]
c/o Hibel Museum of Art
5353 Parkside Dr.
Jupiter, FL 33458
PH: (561)622-5560
Plotkin, Andrew, President

International Geosynthetics Society [6223]
1934 Commerce Ln., Ste. 4
Jupiter, FL 33458
PH: (561)768-9489
Fax: (561)828-7618
Zornberg, Jorge G., Mem.

Karma Krew [10423]
4300 S US Highway 1, Ste. 203-144
Jupiter, FL 33477
Feinberg, Scott, Exec. Dir.

National Association of Police Athletic/Activities Leagues, Inc. [13462]
1662 N US Highway 1, Ste. C
Jupiter, FL 33469
PH: (561)745-5535
Fax: (561)745-3147
Dillhyon, Michael D., Exec. Dir.

National Golf Foundation [3162]
501 N Highway A1A
Jupiter, FL 33477
PH: (561)744-6006
Toll free: 888-275-4643
Fax: (561)744-6107
Brewer, Chip, Chairman

Bonefish & Tarpon Trust [4184]
24 Dockside Ln.
Key Largo, FL 33037
PH: (321)674-7758
Adams, Aaron, PhD, Science Dir.

Island Dolphin Care [11607]
150 Lorelane Pl.
Key Largo, FL 33037
PH: (305)451-5884
Fax: (305)453-5399
Hoagland, Deena, LCSW, Exec. Dir.

Marine Mammal Conservancy [4841]
102200 Overseas Hwy.
Key Largo, FL 33037
PH: (405)451-4774
Fax: (405)451-4730
Cooper, Arthur G., Chairman

Art Schools Network [7505]
c/o Kristy Callaway, Executive Director
PO Box 5534
Key West, FL 33045
PH: (970)300-4650
Fax: (970)797-9116
Callaway, Kristy, Exec. Dir.

International Women's Flag Football Association [22859]
25 A 7th Ave.
Key West, FL 33040
PH: (305)293-9315
Toll free: 888-464-9332
Fax: (305)293-9315
Beruldsen, Diane, President

Reef Relief [4471]
631 Greene St.
Key West, FL 33040
PH: (305)294-3100
Fax: (305)294-9515
Stafford, Mimi, Secretary, Treasurer

American Association for Nude Recreation [10054]
1703 N Main St., Ste. E
Kissimmee, FL 34744
PH: (407)933-2064
Toll free: 800-879-6833
Fax: (407)933-7577

ASGM [19748]
7862 W Irlo Bronson Hwy., PMB 240
Kissimmee, FL 34747
PH: (321)251-8494
Toll free: 877-873-2746

Give Kids the World Village [11233]
210 S Bass Rd.
Kissimmee, FL 34746
PH: (407)396-1114
Fax: (407)396-1207
Belden, John, Bd. Member

International Jugglers' Association [22968]
PO Box 580005
Kissimmee, FL 34758
PH: (714)584-4533
Wakefield, Nathan, Chairman, Coord.

United States Specialty Sports Association [23261]
611 Line Dr.
Kissimmee, FL 34744
Toll free: 800-741-3014
DeDonatis, Don, Chairman, CEO, Exec. Dir.

Professional Association of Health Care Office Management [15592]
1576 Bella Cruz Dr., Ste. 360
Lady Lake, FL 32159
Toll free: 800-451-9311
Fax: (407)386-7006
Blanchette, Karen, Director

International Federation of Nematology Societies [6908]
c/o Larry Duncan, President
Citrus Research and Education Ctr.
University of Florida, IFAS
700 Experiment Station Rd.
Lake Alfred, FL 33850
PH: (863)956-8821
Fax: (863)956-4631
San-Blas, Dr. Ernesto, VP

Amateur Athletic Union [23209]
PO Box 22409
Lake Buena Vista, FL 32830-2409
PH: (407)934-7200
Toll free: 800-AAU-4USA
Fax: (407)934-7242
Dodd, Bobby, CEO, President

American Reiki Master Association [13600]
PO Box 130
Lake City, FL 32056-0130
PH: (904)755-9638

International Association of Nitrox and Technical Divers [22812]
119 NW Ethan Pl., Ste. 101
Lake City, FL 32055

PH: (386)438-8312
Fax: (509)355-1297
Mount, Tom, PhD, CEO, President

American Hemochromatosis Society [14926]
PO Box 950871
Lake Mary, FL 32795-0871
PH: (407)829-4488
Toll free: 888-655-4766
Fax: (407)333-1284
Thomas, Sandra, Founder, President

Combined Organizations of Numismatic Error Collectors of America [22266]
c/o Mark Lighterman, President
PO Box 471518
Lake Monroe, FL 32747-1518
PH: (407)688-7006
Lighterman, Mark, President

American Society for the Support of Injured Survivors of Terrorism [13256]
c/o Mr. Worley Lee Reed, Chairperson
4371 Dinner Lake Blvd.
Lake Wales, FL 33859-2135
PH: (863)223-1818
Fax: (863)582-9318
Reed, Mr. Worley Lee, Chairperson

American Polo Horse Association, Inc. [23069]
4095 State Road 7, Ste. L
Lake Worth, FL 33449
Hale, Sunny, Founder, President

Association for Counselor Education and Supervision [7685]
PO Box 862
Lake Worth, FL 33460
Toll free: 800-347-6647
Lawson, Gerard, PhD, Rep.

Association of Haitians Living Abroad for Development [12140]
10 S Dixie Hwy.
Lake Worth, FL 33460
PH: (561)935-4545
Simon, Pauline Jean, President, CEO

Bringing Relief Internationally Through Education [10876]
1520 N K St.
Lake Worth, FL 33460
PH: (561)384-8474
Odjo, Nadia, President

The Cycad Society [3844]
c/o Larry Kraus, Membership Director
3355 Blanchette Trl.
Lake Worth, FL 33467-1130
Schutzman, Dr. Bart, Editor

Forgotten Soldiers Outreach [10741]
3550 23rd Ave. S, Ste. 7
Lake Worth, FL 33461
PH: (561)369-2933
Fax: (561)493-9819
Zelnar, Lynelle Chauncey, Exec. Dir., Founder

Solace International [13398]
629 S K St.
Lake Worth, FL 33460
PH: (520)270-5916
Azizi, Ayub, Director

United States Polo Association [23070]
9011 Lake Worth Rd.
Lake Worth, FL 33467
Toll free: 800-232-8772
Rizzo, Peter, CEO

U.S.A. Cricket Association [23262]
8461 Lake Worth Rd., Ste. B-1-185
Lake Worth, FL 33467
PH: (561)839-1888
Dainty, Gladstone, President, Chairman

International Association of Medical Thermographers [17468]
5120 S Florida Ave., Ste. 301
Lakeland, FL 33813
PH: (863)646-1599
Allen, Teresa, DO, President

International Association of Silver Art Collectors [21666]
PO Box 5202
Lakeland, FL 33807-5202
Jennings, Doug, President

Mining Electrical Maintenance and Safety Association [2387]
PO Box 7163
Lakeland, FL 33807
Collins, Bill, Director

Morse Society [20984]
PO Box 984
Lakeland, FL 33802
Mullins, Marcia Morse, President

National Tutoring Association [8721]
PO Box 6840
Lakeland, FL 33807
PH: (863)529-5206
Fax: (863)937-3390
Ayaz, Dr. Sandi, Exec. Dir.

National Watermelon Association [4245]
190 Fitzgerald Rd., Ste. 3
Lakeland, FL 33813
PH: (813)619-7575
Fax: (813)619-7577
Schmidt, Jim, Bd. Member

Seaplane Pilots Association [158]
3859 Laird Blvd.
Lakeland, FL 33811
PH: (863)701-7979
McCaughey, Steve, Exec. Dir.

ShelterBox USA [11679]
8374 Market St., No. 203
Lakewood Ranch, FL 34202
PH: (941)907-6036
Fax: (941)907-6970
Sperling, Emily, President

American Asperger's Association [15896]
1301 Seminole Blvd., Ste. B-112
Largo, FL 33770
PH: (727)518-7294
Knaus, Dr. Ron, Founder

American Grant Writers' Association [12459]
13801 Walsingham Rd., No. A-410
Largo, FL 33774
PH: (727)596-5150
Fax: (727)596-5192
Porter, Dr. John, Exec. Dir.

USS Wainwright Veterans Association [21145]
210 Greenwood Ave.
Lehigh Acres, FL 33936
Cookenham, Edward, President

Waterbirth International [14243]
PO Box 5578
Lighthouse Point, FL 33074-5578
PH: (954)821-9125
Harper, Barbara, Founder

Fuling Kids International [10990]
6110 Kestrel Park Dr.
Lithia, FL 33547
Postma, Kathlene, Chairwoman

The Chatlos Foundation, Inc. **[20622]**
PO Box 915048
Longwood, FL 32791-5048
PH: (407)862-5077
Chatlos, Mr. William J., Founder

Academy of Religion and Psychical
Research **[6982]**
PO Box 84
Loxahatchee, FL 33470
PH: (561)714-1423
Batey, Mr. Boyce, Exec. Dir.

Sword Swallowers Association
International **[10069]**
18842 Maisons Dr.
Lutz, FL 33558-2878
PH: (615)969-2568
Meyer, Dan, President

Xplor International **[1552]**
24156 State Rd., Ste. 4
Lutz, FL 33559
PH: (813)949-6170
Fax: (813)949-9977
Henk, Skip, CEO, President

American Marinelife Dealers As-
sociation **[4463]**
PO Box 1052
Madison, FL 32341
PH: (850)973-3488
Patrick, Burton, President

Green Parent Association, Inc.
[3881]
2601 Westhall Ln.
Maitland, FL 32751
PH: (407)493-1372
    (321)331-7456
Ashlock, Joy Austin, Founder,
President

National Association of Christian
Financial Consultants **[1281]**
1055 Maitland Center Commons
Blvd.
Maitland, FL 32751-7205
Toll free: 877-966-2232
Fax: (716)204-0904
Sanders, Jim, VP

Save the Manatee Club **[4880]**
500 N Maitland Ave.
Maitland, FL 32751
PH: (407)539-0990
Toll free: 800-432-JOIN
Fax: (407)539-0871
Rose, Patrick, Exec. Dir.

National Order of Trench Rats
[20770]
PO Box 500208
Malabar, FL 32950-0208
PH: (321)507-0702

Dolphin Research Center **[6792]**
58901 Overseas Hwy.
Marathon, FL 33050-6019
PH: (305)289-1121
Fax: (305)743-7627
Zimmerman, Joanne, Chmn. of the
Bd.

Gulf and Caribbean Fisheries
Institute **[4185]**
Florida Fish and Wildlife Conserva-
tion Commission
Marine Research Institute
2796 Overseas Hwy., Ste. 119
Marathon, FL 33050
PH: (305)289-2330
Fax: (305)289-2334
Glazer, Bob, Exec. Dir.

Association of Internal Management
Consultants **[2153]**
720 N Collier Blvd., Unit 201
Marco Island, FL 34145

PH: (239)642-0580
Fax: (239)642-1119
Kamath, Janine, President

Textile Bag and Packaging Associa-
tion **[847]**
3000 Royal Marco Way PH-N
Marco Island, FL 34145
PH: (616)481-4739
Stout, Bill, President

Yachting Club of America **[22694]**
Box 1040
Marco Island, FL 34146

National Association of Cruise-
Oriented Agencies Inc. **[3385]**
7378 W Atlantic Blvd., Ste. 115
Margate, FL 33063
PH: (305)663-5626
Fax: (866)816-7143
Esposito, Donna Kaye, MCC,
President

Air Commando Association **[21101]**
PO Box 7
Mary Esther, FL 32569
PH: (850)581-0099
Fax: (850)581-8988
Rossel, Eugene D., Contact

Republican National Hispanic As-
sembly **[19050]**
247 Boca Ciega Rd.
Mascotte, FL 34753-9275
PH: (202)800-8334
Remirez, Felix, Treasurer

American Model Yachting Associa-
tion **[22196]**
c/o Michelle Dannenhoffer, Secretary
PO Box 360374
Melbourne, FL 32936-0374
Toll free: 888-237-9524
Dannenhoffer, Michelle, Secretary

Bondurant Family Association
[20786]
c/o Amy B. Sanders
2143 Lansing St.
Melbourne, FL 32935-2176
Hoffman, Marcelle, President

Future Problem Solving Program
International **[7678]**
2015 Grant Pl.
Melbourne, FL 32901
PH: (321)768-0074
Solomon, Ms. Marianne, Exec. Dir.

International Association for Cross-
Cultural Psychology **[16915]**
c/o William Gabrenya, Secretary
General
Florida Institute of Technology
School of Psychology
150 W University Blvd.
Melbourne, FL 32901
PH: (310)825-7526
    (310)825-2961
Gabrenya, William, Sec. Gen.

Life Coalition International **[12777]**
PO Box 360221
Melbourne, FL 32936-0221
PH: (321)726-0444
Tucci, Keith, Founder

M.O.R.G.A.N. Project **[15953]**
4241 N Hwy. 1
Melbourne, FL 32935
PH: (321)506-2707
Malfara, Robert, President, Founder

National Organization for Human
Services **[13075]**
1600 Sarno Rd., Ste. 16
Melbourne, FL 32935-4993
Toll free: 800-597-2306
Rother, Franklyn, President

North American Society for the
Study of Hypertension in
Pregnancy **[17114]**
c/o Sara Gauthier
6905 N Wickham Rd., Ste. 302
Melbourne, FL 32940
PH: (321)421-6699
Fax: (321)821-0450
Rana, Sarosh, MD, MPH, Secretary,
Treasurer

The Patriots **[18756]**
1494 Patriot Dr.
Melbourne, FL 32940
PH: (321)752-5955
Katz, Dave, Chief of Staff

Preeclampsia Foundation **[14241]**
6767 N Wickham Rd., Ste. 400
Melbourne, FL 32940-2025
PH: (321)421-6957
Toll free: 800-665-9341
Fax: (321)821-0450
Tsigas, Eleni Z., Exec. Dir.

Solar Light for Africa **[11441]**
PO Box 361752
Melbourne, FL 32936
Turner, Charlene, Exec. Dir.

Space Coast Writers' Guild **[10402]**
7900 Greenboro Dr.
Melbourne, FL 32902-0262
PH: (321)723-7345
Tilley, Scott, President

Teen Missions International **[20468]**
885 E Hall Rd.
Merritt Island, FL 32953
PH: (321)453-0350
Fax: (321)452-7988
Bland, Robert M., Founder, Director

American Institute of Polish Culture
[10163]
1440 79th St. Causeway, Ste. 117
Miami, FL 33141
PH: (305)864-2349
Fax: (305)865-5150
Rosenstiel, Blanka A., Contact

American Veterans Alliance **[21108]**
13899 Biscayne Blvd.
Miami, FL 33181
PH: (305)200-7492
Humes, Kevin, Exec. Dir.

American Welding Society **[7382]**
8669 NW 36th St., Ste. 130
Miami, FL 33166-6672
PH: (305)443-9353
Toll free: 800-443-9353
McQuaid, David L., President

Asociacion Filatelica Salvadorena
[22310]
c/o Pierre Cahen
PO Box 02-5364
Miami, FL 33102
Yudice, Santiago, President

Asociacion de Ingenieros Cubano-
Americanos **[6542]**
PO Box 941436
Miami, FL 33194-1436
Solo-Gabriele, Dr. Helena, Contact

Association of Certified Anti-Money
Laundering Specialists **[381]**
Brickell City Twr.
80 SW 8th St., Ste. 2350
Miami, FL 33130
PH: (305)373-0020
Fax: (305)373-7788
Weissberg, Ted, CEO

Be Healthy, Inc **[13609]**
4588 NE 2nd Ave.
Miami, FL 33137

PH: (305)538-8998
Fax: (305)538-1255

Bees for Life **[13610]**
PO Box 65-0707
Miami, FL 33265-0707
Asis, Moises, Contact

Best Buddies International **[12318]**
100 SE 2nd St., Ste. 2200
Miami, FL 33131-2151
PH: (305)374-2233
Toll free: 800-892-8339
Fax: (305)374-5305
Shriver, Anthony K., Chairman,
Founder

Chopin Foundation of the United
States **[9888]**
1440 79th Street Cswy., Ste. 117
Miami, FL 33141
PH: (305)868-0624
Fax: (305)865-5150
Gewert, Jadwiga, Exec. Dir.

Colombian-American Chamber of
Commerce of Greater Miami
[23575]
2305 NW 107 Ave., Ste. 1M14, Box
No. 105
Miami, FL 33172
PH: (305)446-2542
Borrero, Francisco, President

The Cormac McCarthy Society
[10368]
13850 SW 100th Ave.
Miami, FL 33176-6717
Frye, Steven, President

Cuban American Association of Civil
Engineers **[6220]**
2191 NW 97th Ave.
Miami, FL 33172
Acosta, Jose, President

Cuban American National Council
[13044]
1223 SW 4th St.
Miami, FL 33135
PH: (305)642-3484
Fax: (305)642-9122
Claro, Maria Cristina, Asst. VP of
Fin.

Cuban American National Founda-
tion **[18075]**
2147 SW 8th St.
Miami, FL 33135
PH: (305)592-7768
Hernández, Dr. Francisco José
(Pepe), President

Directorio Democratico Cubano
[18076]
730 NW 170 Ave., Ste. 177
Miami, FL 33155
PH: (305)220-2713
Cespedes, Javier de, Founder,
President

Ecuadorian-American Chamber of
Commerce of Miami **[23582]**
3403 NW 82 Ave., Ste. 310
Miami, FL 33122
PH: (305)591-0058
    (305)539-0010
Fax: (305)591-0868

Educate Tomorrow **[8767]**
1717 N Bayshore Dr., No. 203
Miami, FL 33132
PH: (305)374-3751
Floyd, Devin, Director

Fighting Infectious Diseases in
Emerging Countries **[15398]**
2050 Coral Way, Ste. 407
Miami, FL 33145

PH: (305)854-0075
Fax: (305)856-7847
Stamboulian, Dr. Daniel, Founder,
President

Forest Bird Society [3864]
10969 SW 47th Ter.
Miami, FL 33165
PH: (305)223-2680
Sevilla, Francisco T., Exec. Dir.,
President

Fotokonbit [13051]
12555 Biscayne Blvd., No. 926
Miami, FL 33181
PH: (305)962-8568
Arago, Marie, Exec. Dir.

Friends of the Everglades [3870]
11767 S Dixie Hwy., No. 232
Miami, FL 33156
PH: (305)669-0858
Fax: (305)479-2893
Washburn, Connie, VP

Give a Child Hope [10996]
12021 SW 97th Terr.
Miami, FL 33186
Canal, Adolfo, President

**Haitian American Association Against
Cancer, Inc. [13980]**
225 NE 34th St., Ste. 208
Miami, FL 33137-3800
PH: (305)572-1825
Fax: (305)572-1827
Calixte, Mr. Jacques Albert,
President

**Haitian American Professionals
Coalition [11373]**
PO Box 693118
Miami, FL 33269
PH: (305)771-3585
Fax: (954)728-8660
Seraphin, Barbara G., MS, Exec. Dir.

**Hemispheric Congress of Latin
Chambers of Commerce [23590]**
Latin Chamber of Commerce of USA
1401 W Flagler St.
Miami, FL 33135
PH: (305)642-3870
Fax: (305)642-3961

**Interamerican Accounting Associa-
tion [34]**
275 Fountainebleau Blvd., Ste. 245
Miami, FL 33172-4576
PH: (305)225-1991
Fax: (305)225-2011
Abreu Paez, Victor Manuel, Exec.
Dir.

**InterAmerican Society for Tropical
Horticulture [4433]**
Fairchild Tropical Garden Research
Ctr.
11935 Old Cutler Rd.
Miami, FL 33156
PH: (305)667-1651
Fax: (305)665-8032
Morales-Payan, Jose Pablo,
President

International Agro Alliance [4697]
173 NW 89th St.
Miami, FL 33150
PH: (844)422-7333
Toll free: 877-292-3921
Fax: (844)422-7333
Abdoulaye, Kone, Founder,
President

**The International Air Cargo Associa-
tion [3333]**
5600 NW 36th St., Ste. 620
Miami, FL 33166

PH: (786)265-7011
Fax: (786)265-7012
Edward, Sanjiv, Chairman

**International Association for
Hydrogen Energy [6492]**
5794 SW 40 St., No. 303
Miami, FL 33155

**International Association for the
Study of Attachment [15773]**
c/o Patricia M. Crittenden, PhD,
Honorary and Founding President
Family Relations Institute
9481 SW 147th St.
Miami, FL 33176
PH: (305)256-9110
Fax: (305)251-0806
Crittenden, Patricia M., PhD,
President

**International Economics and Finance
Society [6395]**
c/o Florida International University
Dept. of Economics
11200 SW 8th St.
Miami, FL 33199-2516
PH: (305)348-2316
Fax: (305)348-1524
Bergstrand, Jeffrey, President

**International Society of Hospitality
Purchasers [1665]**
c/o Mitchell Parker, President
Parker Company
6205 Blue Lagoon Dr., Ste. 300
Miami, FL 33126
PH: (305)421-6900
Parker, Mitchell, President

Jamaica Tourist Board [23661]
5201 Blue Lagoon Dr., Ste. 670
Miami, FL 33126
PH: (305)665-0557
Fax: (305)666-7239
Morrison, Dennis, Chairman

**Jamaica USA Chamber of Com-
merce [23598]**
4770 Biscayne Blvd., Ste. 1050
Miami, FL 33137-3247
PH: (305)573-3235
Toll free: 866-577-3236
Fax: (305)576-0089
Gill, Ms. Marie, President, CEO

**Latin Chamber of Commerce of
U.S.A. [23650]**
1401 W Flagler St.
Miami, FL 33135
PH: (305)642-3870
Fax: (305)642-3961
Arias, Patricia, Managing Dir.

**Marine Animal Rescue Society
[3897]**
PO Box 833356
Miami, FL 33283
PH: (305)546-1111

**Miami Rare Fruit Council
International [4239]**
14735 SW 48 Ter.
Miami, FL 33185-4066
PH: (305)554-1333
Snow, Dr. Matthew, President

Mission to Haiti [11927]
PO Box 523157
Miami, FL 33152-3157
PH: (305)823-7516
Nealey, William J., Jr., Exec. Dir.

**National Art Exhibitions of the
Mentally Ill [8987]**
PO Box 350891
Miami, FL 33135
PH: (954)922-8692
Salazar, Christian, Web Adm.

**National Association of Shortwave
Broadcasters [473]**
175 Fontainebleau Blvd., Ste. 1N4
Miami, FL 33172
PH: (305)559-9764
Fax: (305)559-8186
White, Jeff, Secretary, Treasurer

**National Coalition of Pharmaceutical
Distributors [2562]**
20101 NE 16th Pl.
Miami, FL 33179
PH: (305)690-4233
Fax: (305)760-7227
Moody, Karen, President

National Family Partnership [13170]
2490 Coral Way
Miami, FL 33145-3430
Toll free: 888-474-0008
Sapp, Peggy B., CEO, President

**National Parkinson Foundation
[15970]**
200 SE 1st St., Ste. 800
Miami, FL 33131
Toll free: 800-473-4636
Fax: (305)537-9901
Schmidt, Peter, Sr. VP

**National YoungArts Foundation
[8991]**
2100 Biscayne Blvd.
Miami, FL 33137
PH: (305)377-1140
Toll free: 800-970-2787
Fax: (305)377-1149
Kohan, Richard, Chairman

One Laptop Per Child [11481]
848 Brickell Ave., Ste. 307
Miami, FL 33131-2943
PH: (305)971-3755
Negroponte, Nicholas, Chairman,
Founder

**Optometric Glaucoma Society
[16402]**
900 NW 17th St.
Miami, FL 33136
Toll free: 800-329-7000
Fax: (305)326-6113
Gaddie, Ben, President

**Peace Education Foundation
[18009]**
1900 Biscayne Blvd.
Miami, FL 33132
PH: (305)576-5075
Toll free: 800-749-8838
Fax: (305)576-3106
Van Bylevett, Lloyd, President

Project YES [8770]
5275 Sunset Dr.
Miami, FL 33143-5914
PH: (305)663-7195
Fax: (305)663-7197
Logvin, Rachel Sottile, Exec. Dir.

**Sociedad Interamericana de Prensa
[17956]**
Jules Dubois Bldg.
1801 SW 3rd Ave.
Miami, FL 33129
PH: (305)634-2465
Fax: (305)635-2272
Correa, Juan Luis, 1st VP

**Society of Laparoendoscopic
Surgeons [17403]**
7330 SW 62nd Pl., Ste. 410
Miami, FL 33143-4825
PH: (305)665-9959
Wetter, Paul Alan, MD, Chairman

**Society for Research on Identity
Formation [8412]**
College of Arts and Science
Florida International University

University Pk., DM 269-F
11200 SW 8th St.
Miami, FL 33199
PH: (305)348-3941
Pittman, Joe, President

Vision Earth Society [4019]
c/o David Haylock, Director
1825 NE 149 St.
Miami, FL 33181
PH: (305)945-2727
Fax: (305)945-0300
Haylock, David, Founder, Director

World Salsa Federation [9274]
8080 SW 81 Dr.
Miami, FL 33143
PH: (305)746-1282
Altman, Isaac, CEO

Yoga Research Foundation [20656]
6111 SW 74th Ave.
Miami, FL 33143
PH: (305)666-2006
Fax: (305)666-4443
Jyotirmayananda, Swami, Founder

**American Youth Football and Cheer
[22855]**
1000 S Point Dr., TH-9
Miami Beach, FL 33139
Toll free: 800-622-7370
Galat, Joe, President

**Association of Booksellers for
Children [2767]**
6538 Collin Ave., No. 168
Miami Beach, FL 33141
PH: (617)390-7759
Fax: (617)344-0540

**Association of Research Institutes in
Art History [8896]**
The Wolfsonian-Florida International
University
1001 Washington Ave.
Miami Beach, FL 33139
PH: (305)535-2613
Fax: (305)531-2133
Mogul, Jonathan, Chairperson

**Czech Collector's Association
[21647]**
c/o Davin Fein
810 - 11th St., Ste. 201
Miami Beach, FL 33139-4834
Fein, David, Contact

**United States Sommelier Associa-
tion, Inc. [192]**
1111 Lincoln Rd., Ste. 400
Miami Beach, FL 33139
PH: (786)497-1854
(954)437-0449
Garced, Rick, DVS, CEO, President

**Disabled Drummers Association
[11592]**
18901 NW 19th Ave.
Miami Gardens, FL 33056-2808
PH: (305)621-9022
Katz, Steve, Contact

**Beach Education Advocates for
Culture, Health, Environment and
Safety Foundation Institute [10055]**
PO Box 530702
Miami Shores, FL 33153
PH: (305)620-7090
Mason, Shirley, Exec. Dir.,
Secretary, Founder

Marmon Club [21424]
c/o George Bradley, Membership
Chairman
PO Box 530759
Miami Shores, FL 33153-0759
PH: (786)457-3400

American Bell Association
International [21607]
26 Hunting Lodge Dr.
Miami Springs, FL 33166-5100
Davenport, Jane, President

Creative Floral Arrangers of the
Americas [1307]
PO Box 237
Mims, FL 32754-0237
Decker, Penny, Advisor

Brave International [17967]
5338 SW 183rd Ave.
Miramar, FL 33029
PH: (954)964-2362
(786)486-0897
Jean-Jacques, Vasquez, CEO

Seventh Day Baptist World Federa-
tion [19740]
2612 Arcadia Dr.
Miramar, FL 33023
PH: (954)684-4961
Thorngate, Rev. Dale, President

Shelter Alliance [11434]
2201 SW 145th Ave., No. 209
Miramar, FL 33027
Toll free: 866-744-1003
Badcock, Tracy A., Act. Pres.

Universal Autograph Collectors Club
[21730]
PO Box 1392
Mount Dora, FL 32756
Hecht, Michael, President

American Sudden Infant Death
Syndrome Institute [17331]
528 Raven Way
Naples, FL 34110
PH: (239)431-5425
Fax: (239)431-5536
Peterzell, Marc, JD, Chairman

Center for Reduction of Religious-
Based Conflict [19026]
649 5th Ave. S, Ste. 201
Naples, FL 34102-6601
PH: (239)821-4850
Fax: (239)263-2824
Trowbridge, Terry O., Director,
Founder

Conveyor Equipment Manufacturers
Association [1723]
5672 Strand Ct., Ste. 2
Naples, FL 34110
PH: (239)514-3441
Fax: (239)514-3470
Abraham, Garry, President

International Foundation for Protec-
tion Officers [3059]
1250 Tamiami Trl. N, Ste. 206
Naples, FL 34102
PH: (239)430-0534
Fax: (239)430-0533
Davies, Sandi, Exec. Dir.

Laity for Life [19850]
PO Box 111478
Naples, FL 34108
PH: (239)352-6333
Bucalo, Patricia, Founder, President

Mechanical Power Transmission As-
sociation [1750]
5672 Strand Ct., Ste. 2
Naples, FL 34110
PH: (239)514-3441
Fax: (239)514-3470

Miracles in Action [12553]
241 Countryside Dr.
Naples, FL 34104
PH: (239)348-0815
Rambacher, Penny, Chairperson,
President

Movers and Shakers [15954]
880 Grand Rapids Blvd.
Naples, FL 34120
PH: (239)919-8287
Church, Michael, Exec. Dir.

National Association for Males with
Eating Disorders [14647]
164 Palm Dr., No. 2
Naples, FL 34112
Walen, Andrew, President

No-Scalpel Vasectomy International
[17113]
3579 Midas Pl.
Naples, FL 34105
PH: (813)787-6809
Suarez, Ramon, MD, Founder,
President

People for Guatemala Inc. [12807]
400 5th Ave. S, Ste. 304
Naples, FL 34102
PH: (941)244-8692
Werner, Lois, Founder

Salt Institute [2382]
405 5th Ave. S, Ste. 7G
Naples, FL 34102
PH: (703)549-4648
Fax: (703)548-2194
Amselle, Jorge, Dir. of Comm.

Spring Research Institute [330]
422 Kings Way
Naples, FL 34104
PH: (239)643-7769
Thomson, John D., President

USS Leyte CV32 Association
[21068]
c/o Angelo R. Maisi, Treasurer
127 Glen Eagle Cir.
Naples, FL 34104-5714
PH: (239)348-0085
Mitchell, John E., VP

American Board of Quality Assur-
ance and Utilization Review Physi-
cians [17026]
6640 Congress St.
New Port Richey, FL 34653
PH: (727)569-0195
Toll free: 800-998-6030
Fax: (727)569-0195
Broder, Arthur I., MD, Chairman

Association of Defense Trial At-
torneys [5310]
4135 Topsail Trail
New Port Richey, FL 34652
PH: (727)859-0350
Schultz, Peggy L., Exec. Dir.

C Diff Foundation [15395]
6931 Ian Ct., Ste. 14
New Port Richey, FL 34653
PH: (919)201-1512
Caralla, Nancy C., Founder, Exec.
Dir., President

Psi Beta [23854]
c/o Kathleen Hughes, President
Pasco-Hernando State College
10230 Ridge Rd.
New Port Richey, FL 34654
PH: (727)816-3330
Rudmann, Jerry, PhD, Exec. Dir.

American Senior Fitness Association
[16694]
PO Box 2575
New Smyrna Beach, FL 32170
PH: (386)423-6634
Toll free: 888-689-6791
Fax: (877)365-3048
Clark, Janie, MA, President

Infant and Children Sleep Apnea
Awareness Foundation [17216]
PO Box 2328
New Smyrna Beach, FL 32170

PH: (386)423-5430
Fax: (386)428-2001
Ellis-Brearey, Terri Lynn, Founder,
CEO

Society of Otorhinolaryngology and
Head-Neck Nurses [16184]
207 Downing St.
New Smyrna Beach, FL 32168
PH: (386)428-1695
Fax: (386)423-7566
Schwartz, Ms. Sandra, Exec. Dir.

Little Bighorn History Alliance
[10337]
PO Box 1752
Niceville, FL 32588
Merkel, Mrs. Diane, Founder

Aquatic Exercise Association
[23061]
201 Tamiami Trl. S, Ste. 3
Nokomis, FL 34275-3198
PH: (941)486-8600
Toll free: 888-232-9283
Fax: (941)486-8820
See, Julie, President, Dir. Ed.

Pilates Method Alliance [16712]
1666 Kennedy Cswy., Ste. 402
North Bay Village, FL 33141
PH: (305)573-4946
Toll free: 866-573-4945
Fax: (305)573-4461
Anderson, Elizabeth, Exec. Dir.

Society for Worldwide Medical
Exchange [15497]
1666 Kennedy Cswy., Ste. 71
North Bay Village, FL 33141
PH: (305)407-9222
Fax: (305)433-7128
Musch, Bruno, Chmn. of the Bd.

Educational Concerns for Hunger
Organization [12082]
17391 Durrance Rd.
North Fort Myers, FL 33917
PH: (239)543-3246
Erickson, David, President, CEO

Pan American Indian Association
[10046]
8355 Sevigny Dr.
North Fort Myers, FL 33917
PH: (707)725-9627
Ojala, Dr. Rosalind Skyhawk, Dir. of
Admin., Founder

Health through Walls [15469]
12555 Biscayne Blvd., No. 955
North Miami, FL 33181
May, John P., MD, President,
Founder

International Solidarity for Human
Rights [18419]
12555 Biscayne Blvd., No. 915
North Miami, FL 33181
Vega, Elizabeth Sanchez, Founder,
President

National Alliance to Nurture the Aged
and the Youth [12011]
659 NE 125th St.
North Miami, FL 33161-5503
PH: (305)981-3232
Bruce, Dr. Joy, Chairperson,
President

Christ for the Poor [12638]
PO Box 601181
North Miami Beach, FL 33160
PH: (305)891-2242
Torres, Mr. Alejandro, CEO,
President

National Association of The
Bahamas [19396]
Parish Hall
16711 W Dixie Hwy.

North Miami Beach, FL 33160
PH: (954)673-0980
Fax: (954)673-0980
Gomez, Rosamon, President

Institute of Management Consultants
USA [2173]
631 US Highway 1, Ste. 400
North Palm Beach, FL 33408
PH: (561)570-0833
Toll free: 800-837-7321
Norman, David, Bd. Member

Society of Consulting Psychology
[16935]
c/o Debra Nolan, CAE
631 US Highway 1, Ste., 400
North Palm Beach, FL 33408
Toll free: 800-440-4066
Buford, Brian, PhD, Treasurer

Undersea and Hyperbaric Medical
Society [17542]
631 US Highway 1, Ste. 307
North Palm Beach, FL 33408
PH: (919)490-5140
Toll free: 877-533-8467
Fax: (919)490-5149
Peters, John, Exec. Dir.

United Rheumor Arthritis Society
[17170]
PO Box 6874
North Port, FL 34290
PH: (941)564-9443
Toll free: 855-355-8727
Shearer, Mika R., Founder, CEO

A Chance for Kids [10888]
601 W Oakland Park Blvd., No. 14
Oakland Park, FL 33311
PH: (954)326-0513
Octavien, Nixon, President

American Academy of Podiatric
Sports Medicine [17273]
3121 NE 26th St.
Ocala, FL 34470
PH: (352)620-8562
Fax: (352)620-8765
Yates, Rita J., Exec. Dir.

Front Range Equine Rescue [4352]
PO Box 458
Ocala, FL 34478
PH: (352)209-7510
Wood, Hilary, President

Leopold Stokowski Club [9187]
3900 SE 33 Ave.
Ocala, FL 34480
Stumpf, Robert M., II, President

America Sings! [9848]
PO Box 990
Ocoee, FL 34761
PH: (321)209-0097
Jacobson, John, Founder, President

World Airline Historical Society
[21257]
PO Box 489
Ocoee, FL 34761
Fax: (407)522-9352
Levine, Don, VP

Grateful American Coin [10743]
15207 Hammock Chase Ct.
Odessa, FL 33556
PH: (813)404-2568
Benson, Deborah, Officer

International Association of Human
Trafficking Investigators [5286]
PO Box 2185
Oldsmar, FL 34677
PH: (727)504-7203
Fax: (865)851-9141
Lewis, Jeremy, Exec. Dir.

National Association of Photoshop Professionals [1556]
333 Douglas Rd. E
Oldsmar, FL 34677-2922
PH: (813)433-5005
Toll free: 800-738-8513
Fax: (813)433-5015

Silver Wings Fraternity [21247]
PO Box 1694
Oldsmar, FL 34677
McCarthy, James, Director

Pile Driving Contractors Association [897]
33 Knight Boxx Rd., Ste. 1
Orange Park, FL 32065
PH: (904)215-4771
Toll free: 888-311-7322
Fax: (904)215-2977
Hall, Stevan A., Exec. Dir.

Alliance of Supplier Diversity Professionals [2815]
PO Box 782049
Orlando, FL 32878-2049
Toll free: 877-405-6565
Davidson, Joan, President

American Academy of Optometry [16419]
2909 Fairgreen St.
Orlando, FL 32803
PH: (321)710-3937
Toll free: 800-969-4226
Fax: (407)893-9890
Schoenbrun, Lois, CAE, FAAO, Exec. Dir.

American Academy of Urgent Care Medicine [13675]
2813 S Hiawassee Rd., Ste. 206
Orlando, FL 32835
PH: (407)521-5789
Fax: (407)521-5790
Rogers, Brian, Director

American Association of Safety Councils [12812]
United/Florida Safety Council
1505 E Colonial Dr.
Orlando, FL 32803
PH: (407)896-1894
Toll free: 800-372-3335
Fax: (407)897-8945
Meade, Jim, President

American Optometric Foundation [16423]
2909 Fairgreen St.
Orlando, FL 32803
PH: (321)710-3936
Toll free: 800-368-6263
Fax: (407)893-9890
Kirschen, OD, PhD, FAAO, David G., President

Asian Pacific American Librarians Association [9681]
PO Box 677593
Orlando, FL 32867-7593
Basco, Buenaventura, Exec. Dir.

Asociacion para la Educacion Teologica Hispana [8703]
PO Box 677848
Orlando, FL 32867-7848
PH: (407)482-7598
   (407)482-7599
Fax: (407)641-9198
Adorno, Wilfredo Estrada, Secretary

Association for Biblical Higher Education [7606]
5850 T.G. Lee Blvd., Ste. 130
Orlando, FL 32822
PH: (407)207-0808
Fax: (407)207-0840
Moore, Steve, Exec. Dir.

Association of Refrigerant and Desuperheating Manufacturing [1615]
7050 Overland Rd.
Orlando, FL 32810
PH: (407)292-4400
Fax: (407)299-6178

Augustan Society [20958]
PO Box 771267
Orlando, FL 32877-1267
PH: (407)745-0848
Fax: (321)206-6313
Hartwell, Jessica, Chairman

Birth Defect Research for Children [13825]
976 Lake Baldwin Ln., Ste. 104
Orlando, FL 32814
PH: (407)895-0802
Mekdeci, Betty, Exec. Dir.

Campus Crusade for Christ International [20131]
100 Lake Hart Dr.
Orlando, FL 32832
Toll free: 888-278-7233
Douglass, Stephen B., President, Chmn. of the Bd.

Pierre Chastain Family Association [20795]
c/o David Long, Vice President
2796 Vine St.
Orlando, FL 32806
PH: (407)894-8454
   (931)388-9289
Long, David, VP

Child Watch of North America [10906]
PO Box 691782
Orlando, FL 32869-1782
PH: (407)290-5100
Toll free: 888-CHILDWATCH
Wood, Don, Founder

Children Beyond Our Borders [17844]
PO Box 568411
Orlando, FL 32856
Lipkin, John, President

Clean the World [4628]
28 W Central Blvd., Ste. 280
Orlando, FL 32801-1408
PH: (407)574-8353
Fax: (732)847-5446
Seipler, Shawn, Chairman, Founder

Exercise Safety Association [16699]
PO Box 547916
Orlando, FL 32854-7916
PH: (407)246-5090
Foy, Sharon, Director

Futon Association International [1480]
PO Box 593730
Orlando, FL 32824
PH: (407)447-1706

Global Hope Network International [12665]
934 N Magnolia Ave.
Orlando, FL 32801
PH: (407)207-3256
Jones, Hal, CEO, President

Honduras Relief Effort [12674]
4400 Cranston Pl.
Orlando, FL 32812
PH: (407)277-9920
Fax: (407)277-9920
Holbrook, Anna Maria, VP, Director

In Need of Diagnosis [15549]
PO Box 536456
Orlando, FL 32853-6456

PH: (407)894-9190
Toll free: 888-894-9190
Fax: (407)898-4234
Genetti, Marianne, Exec. Dir., Founder

The Institute of Financial Operations [6301]
149 Terra Mango Loop, Ste. B
Orlando, FL 32835
PH: (407)351-3322
Fax: (407)895-5031
Mallon, Michael, Bd. Member

International Business Innovation Association [638]
12703 Research Pky., Ste. 100
Orlando, FL 32826
PH: (407)965-5653
Chadwick, Kirstie, President, CEO

International Commission for Optics [6947]
c/o Angela M. Guzman, Secretary
College of Optics and Photonics
University of Central Florida
4000 Central Florida Blvd.
Orlando, FL 32816-2700
PH: (561)313-8204
Guzman, Angela M., Secretary

International Fitness Association [16703]
12472 Lake Underhill Rd., No. 341
Orlando, FL 32828-7144
PH: (407)579-8610
Toll free: 800-227-1976
Krautblatt, Chuck, CEO, President

International Geriatric Fracture Society [16478]
1215 E Robinson St.
Orlando, FL 32801
PH: (813)909-0450
Fax: (813)949-8994
Suk, Michael, MD, President

International Laser Display Association [1143]
7062 Edgeworth Dr.
Orlando, FL 32819
PH: (407)797-7654
Murphy, Mr. Patrick, Exec. Dir.

International Society for the Social Studies [8565]
PO Box 161250
Orlando, FL 32816-1250
Russell, William B., III, Director

International Songwriters Guild [2426]
5108 Louvre Ave.
Orlando, FL 32812-1028
PH: (407)760-2153
Robinson, Russ, President

Laser Institute of America [6782]
13501 Ingenuity Dr., Ste. 128
Orlando, FL 32826
PH: (407)380-1553
Toll free: 800-345-2737
Fax: (407)380-5588
Capp, Stephen, Treasurer

National Association of Naval Photography [5678]
1435 Lake Baldwin Ln.
Orlando, FL 32814
White, John, Secretary, Treasurer

National Business Incubation Association [653]
12703 Research Pky., Ste. 100
Orlando, FL 32826
PH: (407)965-5653
Chadwick, Kirstie, President, CEO

National Cartoonists Society [8931]
PO Box 592927
Orlando, FL 32859-2927

PH: (407)994-6703
Fax: (407)442-0786
Lynch, Mike, Mem.

Pediatric Chaplains Network [19937]
PO Box 561071
Orlando, FL 32856
Brown, Mark, President

Professional Bail Agents of the United States [5064]
801 N Magnolia Ave., Ste. 418
Orlando, FL 32803
PH: (202)783-4120
Toll free: 800-883-7287
Fax: (202)783-4125
Chapman, Mrs. Beth, Chmn. of the Bd., President

Simulation Interoperability Standards Organization [7292]
3100 Technology Pkwy.
Orlando, FL 32826
PH: (407)882-1378
Fax: (407)882-1304
Coolahan, James, President

Society for News Design [2722]
424 E Central Blvd., Ste. 406
Orlando, FL 32801
PH: (407)420-7748
Fax: (407)420-7697
Komives, Stephen, Exec. Dir.

SolarUnited [1123]
PO Box 771507
Orlando, FL 32877
PH: (747)777-2081
Ekus, Bryan, Exec. Dir.

Speaking Out About Rape [12572]
3208 E Colonial Dr., Unit 243
Orlando, FL 32803
PH: (321)278-5246
Greene, Kellie, Founder

United States Personal Chef Association [702]
7680 Universal Blvd., Ste. 550
Orlando, FL 32819-8959
Toll free: 800-995-2138
Lynch, Robert, VP

United States Windsurfing Association [22688]
8211 Sun Spring Cir., Apt. 73
Orlando, FL 32825
Toll free: 877-386-8708
Bauer, Scotia, Exec. Dir.

Water is Life International [13343]
PO Box 540318
Orlando, FL 32854-0318
PH: (407)716-4214
Stuart, Betty, CFO, Dir. of Dev.

Water Sports Industry Association [3149]
PO Box 568512
Orlando, FL 32856-8512
PH: (407)251-9039
   (407)835-1363
Emmons, Jim, President

Worldwide Camaro Club [21523]
8235 N Orange Blossom Trl.
Orlando, FL 32810
Toll free: 800-456-1957
Fax: (407)299-3341

Wycliffe Bible Translators [19767]
11221 John Wycliffe Blvd.
Orlando, FL 32832
PH: (407)852-3600
Toll free: 800-992-5433
Fax: (407)852-3601
Jones, Larry, Mem.

Aviation Crime Prevention Institute [359]
PO Box 730118
Ormond Beach, FL 32173

PH: (386)843-2274
Toll free: 800-969-5473
Sychak, Les, Chmn. of the Bd.

Book Manufacturers' Institute [1530]
PO Box 731388
Ormond Beach, FL 32173
PH: (386)986-4552
Fax: (386)986-4553
Garner, Jac B., Director

Helping Ugandans Grow Stronger
[11029]
PO Box 731312
Ormond Beach, FL 32173
PH: (386)492-7624
Gibson, Victoria, BSN, Founder,
President, Chmn. of the Bd.

National Employment Counseling
Association [11773]
c/o Seneka Arrington, President
Adapt Behavioral Services, Inc.
1000 St. Georges Rd.
Ormond Beach, FL 32174
PH: (386)259-0154
Hakemian, John, Exec. Dir.

National Token Collectors Associa-
tion [22276]
PO Box 281
Ormond Beach, FL 32175
PH: (386)677-4206
Avila, Merle, VP

Fly By Night: The Bat Specialists
[4817]
PO Box 562
Osteen, FL 32764-0562
PH: (407)414-2142
Finn, Laura Seckbach, Founder

Associated Church Press [2764]
924 Woodcrest Way
Oviedo, FL 32762-1001
PH: (407)341-6615
Fax: (407)386-3236
Medley, Carlos, Treasurer

American Christian Fiction Writers
[10356]
PO Box 101066
Palm Bay, FL 32910-1066
Coble, Dave, Dir. of Member Svcs.

Association of Israel's Decorative
Arts [8965]
c/o Dale & Doug Anderson
100 Worth Ave., Apt. 713
Palm Beach, FL 33480
Ben-Sira, Aviva, Director

U.S. Term Limits Foundation [18883]
c/o US Term Limits - Palm Beach
Office
2875 S Ocean Blvd., No. 200
Palm Beach, FL 33480-5593
PH: (561)578-8636
Fax: (561)578-8660
Blumel, Philip, President

Whitehall Foundation [6922]
125 Worth Ave., Ste. 220
Palm Beach, FL 33480
PH: (561)655-4474
Fax: (561)655-1296

American College of Addiction Treat-
ment Administrators [13122]
11380 Prosperity Farms Rd., Ste.
209A
Palm Beach Gardens, FL 33410
PH: (561)429-4527
Fax: (561)429-4650
Kasper, Nate, Dir. of Operations

American CranioSacral Therapy Association [15261]
c/o The Upledger Institute
International, Inc.

11211 Prosperity Farms Rd., Ste.
D-325
Palm Beach Gardens, FL 33410
PH: (561)622-4334
Toll free: 800-233-5880
Fax: (561)622-4771
Upledger, John E., President

Executive Women's Golf Association
[22879]
8895 N Military Trl., Ste. 102e
Palm Beach Gardens, FL 33410
PH: (561)691-0096
Swensen, Pam, CEO

Financial Publishers Association
[2786]
4400 Northcorp Pky.
Palm Beach Gardens, FL 33410
PH: (561)515-8555
Fax: (561)282-4509

Global Flying Hospitals [15004]
4440 PGA Blvd., Ste. 600
Palm Beach Gardens, FL 33410
Toll free: 855-434-4747
Newton, Neill F., Chairman, Founder

International Association of Health-
care Practitioners [15023]
11211 Prosperity Farms Rd., Ste.
D-325
Palm Beach Gardens, FL 33410
PH: (561)622-8273
Toll free: 800-311-9204
Fax: (561)622-4771

International Topical Steroid Addiction Network [14500]
11380 Prosperity Farms Rd., No.
221E
Palm Beach Gardens, FL 33410
VanDyke, JoAnne, President

International Women's Fishing As-
sociation [22848]
PO Box 31507
Palm Beach Gardens, FL 33420-
1507
Everett, Lisa O., President

Library Binding Council [1540]
4440 PGA Blvd., Ste. 600
Palm Beach Gardens, FL 33410
PH: (561)745-6821
Toll free: 800-837-7321
Campbell, Duncan, President

National Association of Diversity Of-
ficers in Higher Education [7963]
4440 PGA Blvd., Ste. 600
Palm Beach Gardens, FL 33410
PH: (561)472-8479
Fax: (561)472-8401
Reese, Benjamin D., Jr., President

Professional Golfers' Association of
America [22892]
100 Avenue of the Champions
Palm Beach Gardens, FL 33418-
3653
PH: (561)624-8400
Levy, Paul, VP

Upledger Institute [13665]
11211 Prosperity Farms Rd., Ste.
D-325
Palm Beach Gardens, FL 33410
PH: (561)622-4334
Toll free: 800-233-5880
Fax: (561)622-4771
Upledger, John Matthew, President

Vintage Drivers Club of America
[21514]
13505 Running Water Rd.
Palm Beach Gardens, FL 33418-
7933

PH: (561)622-7554
Fax: (561)228-0552
Meis, Doug, Director

American College of Eye Surgeons
[17366]
334 E Lake Rd., No. 135
Palm Harbor, FL 34685-2427
PH: (727)366-1487
Fax: (727)836-9783
Hollingshead, Mark, Secretary,
Treasurer

American Wheelchair Bowling Association [22775]
c/o Wayne Webber
1533 Pelican Pl.
Palm Harbor, FL 34683
PH: (727)728-1342
Ryan, Gary, Secretary

Association of Thai Professionals in
America and Canada [19671]
4398 Ellinwood Blvd.
Palm Harbor, FL 34685
Changchit, Chuleeporn, VP

Audubon Lifestyles [3992]
35246 US Highway 19 N, No. 299
Palm Harbor, FL 34684
PH: (727)733-0762
Fax: (727)683-9153
Dodson, Eric, CEO

Healing Heroes Network [21123]
31640 US Hwy. 19 N, Ste. 2
Palm Harbor, FL 34684
PH: (727)781-4376
Toll free: 877-470-4376
Spiegel, Dr. Allan, Founder

International Sustainability Council
[4007]
35246 US Highway 19, No. 299
Palm Harbor, FL 34684
PH: (727)733-0762
Fax: (727)683-9153
Dodson, Ronald, Chairman

Outpost for Hope [12364]
3438 E Lake Rd., Ste. 14
Palm Harbor, FL 34685
Phillips, Libba, CEO, Founder

Whirly-Girls International Women
Helicopter Pilots [21256]
c/o Deb Sawyer, Membership
Coordinator
4617 Gilronan Ct.
Palm Harbor, FL 34685-2655
Sawyer, Deborah, Membership Chp.

American Board of Criminalistics
[5233]
PO Box 1358
Palmetto, FL 34220
PH: (941)729-9050
Aceves, Margaret, President

American Standard Chinchilla Rabbit
Breeders Association [4594]
c/o Patricia Gest, Secretary/
Treasurer
1607 9th St. W
Palmetto, FL 34221
PH: (941)729-1184
Pappas, Stephen, President

American Hot Rod Association
[22521]
c/o Rod Saint, Chief Executive
Offcer
PO Box 10278
Panama City, FL 32404
PH: (850)215-1019
Saint, Rod, CEO

International Doll Makers Association
[22002]
515 Harrison Ave.
Panama City Beach, FL 32401
Andersen, Anne, President

United States Fastpitch Association
[23207]
7814 Laird St.
Panama City Beach, FL 32408
PH: (850)234-2839
Cain, John, Director

Water Planet USA [4475]
203 Greenwood Dr.
Panama City Beach, FL 32407
PH: (850)230-6030
Toll free: 866-449-5591
Richard, Denis, President

Pen Collectors of America [21711]
PO Box 705
Parrish, FL 34219
PH: (920)809-5182
Anderson, Lisa, Mem.

Association of American Schools in
South America [8101]
1911 NW 150 Ave., Ste. 101
Pembroke Pines, FL 33028
PH: (954)436-4034
Fax: (954)436-4092
Poore, Mr. Paul, Exec. Dir.

National Association of Black
Women in Construction, Inc. [809]
c/o Gladys Keith, Member
1910 NW 105th Ave.
Pembroke Pines, FL 33026-2365
PH: (954)323-3587
Toll free: 866-364-4998
Fax: (954)437-4998
McNeill, Ann, Founder, President

Rebati Sante Mentale [15803]
18503 Pines Blvd., Ste. 214
Pembroke Pines, FL 33029
PH: (954)432-3800
Rigaud, Marie-Claude, MPH, Exec.
Chmn. of the Bd.

American Association of Women
Dentists [14394]
7794 Grow Dr.
Pensacola, FL 32514
Toll free: 800-920-2293
Fax: (850)484-8762
Martin, Mary, President

Doll Artisan Guild [22000]
233 Cherokee Trl.
Pensacola, FL 32506-3513
PH: (607)432-4977
Fax: (607)441-0460
Grzymkowski, Karlyn, VP

International Precious Metals
Institute [6847]
5101 N 12th Ave., Ste. C
Pensacola, FL 32504
PH: (850)476-1156
Fax: (850)476-1548
Cook, Brad, Bd. Member

Mustang Club of America [21446]
4051 Barrancas Ave.
Pensacola, FL 32507
PH: (850)438-0626
Prewitt, Steve, President

Organization for Associate Degree
Nursing [16177]
7794 Grow Dr.
Pensacola, FL 32514
Toll free: 877-966-6236
Fax: (850)484-8762
Meyer, Donna, CEO

Society of Environmental Toxicology
and Chemistry [14724]
229 S Baylen St., 2nd Fl.
Pensacola, FL 32502
PH: (850)469-1500
Fax: (888)296-4136
Van den Brink, Paul, President

Southern Pine Inspection Bureau
[1420]
PO Box 10915
Pensacola, FL 32524-0915
PH: (850)434-2611
Fax: (850)434-1290
Browder, Bob, Div. Dir.

Special Military Active Recreational
Travelers **[21033]**
600 University Office Blvd., Ste. 1A
Pensacola, FL 32504-6238
PH: (850)478-1986
Toll free: 800-354-7681
Wade, Melissa, Mgr.

U.S. Naval Cryptologic Veterans As-
sociation **[21143]**
PO Box 16009
Pensacola, FL 32507-6009
PH: (850)452-6990
Hickey, Bill, Exec. Dir.

International Softball Federation
[23202]
1900 S Park Rd.
Plant City, FL 33563
PH: (813)864-0100
Fax: (813)864-0105
McMann, Dale, President

Angel's Pediatric Heart House
[14096]
151 N Nob Hill Rd., Ste. 139
Plantation, FL 33324
PH: (954)318-2020
Perez, Sonia, Founder

Association of Certified Green
Technology Auditors **[6457]**
1802 N University Dr., Ste. 112
Plantation, FL 33322
PH: (954)594-3584
Fax: (754)551-5354
Graham, David W., Chairman,
Founder

Bringing U Maternal Paternal Suc-
cess **[14754]**
7744 Peters Rd., Ste. 305
Plantation, FL 33324
PH: (954)472-2867
Minkowitz, Lior Levy, Esq.,
President, Founder

Claims and Litigation Management
Alliance **[5528]**
4100 S Hospital Dr., Ste. 209
Plantation, FL 33317
PH: (954)587-2488
Potter, Adam, Exec. Dir.

End Childhood Hunger **[12083]**
c/o Michael Farver, President and
Founder
1080 W Tropical Way
Plantation, FL 33317-3358
PH: (954)792-3852
Fax: (954)678-3004
Farver, Michael, President, Founder

National Association for Continuing
Education **[7671]**
300 NW 70th Ave., Ste. 102
Plantation, FL 33317
PH: (954)723-0057
Toll free: 866-266-6223
Fax: (954)723-0353
Graham, Sharon, Consultant

No More Tears **[11711]**
10097 Clearly Blvd., Ste. 150
Plantation, FL 33324
PH: (954)324-7669
Ali, Somy, Founder, President

Salvadoran American Medical
Society **[15626]**
2080 SW 59th Ave.
Plantation, FL 33317

PH: (713)864-1150
    (954)583-9995
Toll free: 800-360-SAMS
Fax: (713)864-1150
Mendez, Dr. Hermann, Contact

National Collegiate Water Ski As-
sociation **[23355]**
1251 Holy Cow Rd.
Polk City, FL 33868
PH: (863)324-4341
Fax: (863)325-8259
Surdej, Jeff, Chairman

U.S.A. Water Ski **[23357]**
1251 Holy Cow Rd.
Polk City, FL 33868
PH: (863)324-4341
Toll free: 800-533-2972
Fax: (863)325-8259
Crowley, Bob, Exec. Dir.

USA Water Ski Foundation **[23358]**
1251 Holy Cow Rd.
Polk City, FL 33868-8200
PH: (863)324-2472
Fax: (863)324-3996
Mattes, Tracy, Exec. Dir.

Marine Corps Interrogator Translator
Teams Association **[19548]**
1900 S Ocean Blvd., Apt. 14L
Pompano Beach, FL 33062-8030
Burdelski, Vince, Chmn. of the Bd.

National Dance Teachers Associa-
tion of America **[22763]**
2309 E Atlantic Blvd.
Pompano Beach, FL 33062
PH: (954)782-7760
Fox, Lee, President

Patti Page Appreciation Society
[24057]
c/o Rene Paquette, President
4565 S Atlantic Ave., Ste. 5103
Ponce Inlet, FL 32127
PH: (386)756-6682
Paquette, Rene, President

Imagine World Health **[14940]**
105 E Dolphin Blvd.
Ponte Vedra Beach, FL 32082-1714
PH: (904)285-0240
Stearns, David, Founder

International MotherBaby Childbirth
Organization **[14234]**
PO Box 2346
Ponte Vedra Beach, FL 32004
PH: (904)285-0028
Davies, Rae, Dir. of Admin.

Saving Animals Via Education
[10694]
PO Box 2961
Ponte Vedra Beach, FL 32004
PH: (904)476-7532
Pichot, Delphine S., President

American Himalayan Rabbit Associa-
tion **[4590]**
c/o Errean Kratochvil, Secretary-
Treasurer
2159 Bendway Dr.
Port Charlotte, FL 33948
PH: (727)686-9075
Kratochvil, Errean, Secretary,
Treasurer

Park Law Enforcement Association
[5668]
4397 McCullough St.
Port Charlotte, FL 33948
PH: (941)286-7410
Westerfield, William, President

Bromeliad Society International
[22089]
c/o Jay Thurrott, President
713 Breckenridge Dr.

Port Orange, FL 32127
Thurrott, Jay, President

Light Aircraft Manufacturers Associa-
tion **[363]**
2001 Steamboat Ridge Ct.
Port Orange, FL 32128-6918
PH: (651)592-7565
    (651)226-1825
Johnson, Dan, Chmn. of the Bd.,
President

Christian Action and Relief for Haiti
[12639]
PO Box 880145
Port Saint Lucie, FL 34988-0145
PH: (901)412-1829
    (772)882-1125
Septembre, Djumy, Director

Diabetes National Research Group
[14527]
11350 SW Vilage Pkwy.
Port Saint Lucie, FL 34987
PH: (858)597-3816
Toll free: 800-877-3457
Fax: (858)597-3804
Richey, Daniel, President

Food Addicts Anonymous **[11852]**
529 NW Prima Vista Blvd., Ste.
301A
Port Saint Lucie, FL 34983
PH: (772)878-9657
Ambrosio, Kathy, Treasurer

Project Lifesaver International
[12748]
201 SW Port St. Lucie Blvd. S
Port Saint Lucie, FL 34984
PH: (772)446-1271
Saunders, Gene, CEO, Founder

Society for Marketing Advances
[2302]
c/o Cynthia Rodriguez Cano,
Treasurer, 836 SW Munjack Cir.
Northwood University
836 SW Munjack Cir.
Port Saint Lucie, FL 34986-3459
PH: (772)380-2667
Kalamas, Maria, Exec. Dir.

United States Golf Teachers Federa-
tion **[22896]**
1295 SE Port St. Lucie Blvd.
Port Saint Lucie, FL 34952
PH: (772)335-3216
Toll free: 888-346-3290
Fax: (772)335-3822
Bryant, Geoff, President, Founder

World Association of Traditional
Chinese Veterinary Medicine
[17676]
9700 W Highway 318
Reddick, FL 32686
Toll free: 844-422-8286
Memon, Mushtaq, Exec. Dir., Bd.
Member

Antique Reloading Tool Collector's
Association **[22016]**
c/o Bruce Dow, Treasurer
6048 Fairway Dr.
Ridge Manor, FL 33523

National Association of Underwater
Instructors **[23343]**
9030 Camden Field Pky.
Riverview, FL 33578
PH: (813)628-6284
Toll free: 800-553-6284
Fax: (813)628-8253
Bram, Jim, President

National Professional Science
Master's Association **[7967]**
PO Box 3455
Riverview, FL 33568-3455

PH: (508)471-4487
Strausbaugh, Linda, PhD, Director

International Municipal Signal As-
sociation **[5748]**
597 Haverty Ct., Ste. 100
Rockledge, FL 32955
PH: (321)392-0500
Toll free: 800-723-4672
Fax: (321)806-1400
Kristensen, Hans, President

Clan McAlister of America **[20830]**
c/o Robert W. McAlister, Membership Chairman
208 Annapolis Ln.
Rotonda West, FL 33947
PH: (941)698-1112
Bresson, Cindy McAlister, President

American Culinary Federation **[697]**
180 Center Place Way
Saint Augustine, FL 32095
Toll free: 800-624-9458
Fax: (904)824-4468
Cramb, Heidi, Exec. Dir.

BlueVoice.org **[3821]**
10 Sunfish Dr.
Saint Augustine, FL 32080-6386
Jones, Hardy, Exec. Dir.

Clearer Vision Ministries **[13276]**
251B San Marco Ave.
Saint Augustine, FL 32084
PH: (904)201-1358
Thompson, Rev. Sam, Founder,
President

Conference of Educational
Administrators of Schools and
Programs for the Deaf **[15183]**
PO Box 1778
Saint Augustine, FL 32085-1778
PH: (904)810-5200
Fax: (904)810-5525
Finnegan, Joseph P., Jr., Exec. Dir.

International Fancy Guppy Association **[22034]**
c/o Ramino Carbonell, Treasurer,
744 Flowers St.
744 Flowers St.
Saint Augustine, FL 32092
PH: (561)414-0057
Lewis, Bob, President

Made By Survivors **[12070]**
PO Box 3403
Saint Augustine, FL 32085
Toll free: 800-831-6089
Symons, Sarah, Founder, Exec. Dir.

National Alliance for Accessible Golf
[22785]
1 World Golf Pl.
Saint Augustine, FL 32092-2724
PH: (904)940-4204
Low, Ms. Melissa, VP

Saint Photios Foundation **[20196]**
41 St. George St.
Saint Augustine, FL 32085-1960
PH: (904)829-8205
Toll free: 800-222-6727
Fax: (904)829-8707
Hillier, Polexeni Maouris, Director

Hunting Retriever Club **[21895]**
c/o Tracy Stubbs, President
850 Hennecy Ln.
Saint Cloud, FL 34773-9119
PH: (407)744-2797
Stubbs, Tracy, President

International Association of Project
and Program Management **[2176]**
2220 County Rd. 210 W, Ste. 108,
No. 418

Saint Johns, FL 32259
Toll free: 800-571-0470

US Navy Beach Jumpers Association **[21065]**
450-106 State Road 13N, No. 407
Saint Johns, FL 32259-3860
PH: (727)487-6252
Markaverich, Larry, President

American Neurotology Society **[17236]**
c/o Kristen Bordignon, Administrator
4960 Dover St. NE
Saint Petersburg, FL 33703
PH: (217)638-0801
Fax: (217)679-1677
Bordignon, Kristen, Administrator

American Otological Society **[16536]**
c/o Kristen Bordignon, Administrator
4960 Dover St. NE
Saint Petersburg, FL 33703
PH: (217)638-0801
Fax: (727)800-9428
Welling, Bradley, Officer

Association of Opinion Journalists **[2665]**
c/o The Poynter Institute
801 3rd St. S
Saint Petersburg, FL 33701
Haynes, David, President

Concrete Sawing and Drilling Association **[786]**
100 2nd Ave. S, Ste. 402N
Saint Petersburg, FL 33701
PH: (727)577-5004
Fax: (727)577-5012
O'Brien, Patrick, Exec. Dir.

Global Technology Distribution Council **[3210]**
141 Bay Point Dr. NE
Saint Petersburg, FL 33704-3805
PH: (813)412-1148
Curran, Tim, CEO

Institute on Global Drug Policy **[13145]**
Journal of Global Drug Policy and Practice
2600 9th St. N, Ste. 200
Saint Petersburg, FL 33704-2744
PH: (727)828-0211
Fax: (727)828-0210
Voth, Eric, Chairman

International Butterfly Breeders Association **[3677]**
c/o Dale McClung
3025 70th Ln. N
Saint Petersburg, FL 33710
PH: (727)381-1932
Fax: (727)381-5046
Brons, Gloria J., Officer

International Institute of Reflexology, Inc. **[17450]**
5650 1st Ave. N
Saint Petersburg, FL 33710
PH: (727)343-4811
Fax: (727)381-2807
Byers, Gail, Dept. Mgr.

International Plastic Modelers Society - United States Branch **[22199]**
PO Box 56023
Saint Petersburg, FL 33732-6023
PH: (727)537-6886
Bell, Ron, President

Motorcycle Events Association **[22228]**
3221 Tyrone Blvd. N
Saint Petersburg, FL 33710

PH: (727)343-1049
Toll free: 866-203-4485
Fax: (727)344-0327
Kessler, Ryan, Contact

National Association of Professional Baseball Leagues **[22557]**
9550 16th St. N
Saint Petersburg, FL 33716
PH: (727)822-6937
Fax: (727)821-5819
O'Conner, Pat, CEO, President

North American Trailer Dealers Association **[3352]**
111 2nd Ave. NE, Unit 1405
Saint Petersburg, FL 33701
PH: (727)360-0304
Fax: (727)231-8356
Ackerman, Andy, President

Professional Association of Resume Writers and Career Coaches **[11781]**
1388 Brightwaters Blvd. NE
Saint Petersburg, FL 33704
PH: (727)821-2274
Toll free: 800-822-7279
Fax: (727)894-1277
Fox, Frank, Exec. Dir.

The Radiance Technique International Association **[13651]**
PO Box 40570
Saint Petersburg, FL 33743
PH: (727)347-2106
Fax: (727)347-2106

Save Our Society From Drugs **[11718]**
5999 Central Ave., Ste. 301
Saint Petersburg, FL 33710
PH: (727)828-0211
Fay, Calvina L., Exec. Dir.

Society of Saint Mary Magdalene **[19912]**
PO Box 28423
Saint Petersburg, FL 33709
Filliette, Edith, Founder

United States Optimist Dinghy Association **[22682]**
PO Box 506
Saint Petersburg, FL 33731
PH: (609)510-0798
Toll free: 866-410-7456
Shanahan, Brendan, President

Williams Syndrome Changing Lives Foundation **[14867]**
PO Box 76021
Saint Petersburg, FL 33734
PH: (727)557-7177
Perez, Penny, CEO, Founder

World Aquatic Babies and Children Network **[23292]**
838 20th Ave. N
Saint Petersburg, FL 33704
PH: (727)804-3399
Graves, Steve, President

WTA Tour Players Association **[23311]**
100 2nd Ave. S, Ste. 1100S
Saint Petersburg, FL 33701
PH: (727)895-5000
Fax: (727)894-1982
Allaster, Stacey, Chairman

Heart of Romania's Children Foundation **[11016]**
399 Fairfield Dr.
Sanford, FL 32771
PH: (407)392-6817
Fax: (407)964-1693
Pauna, Zamfira, President, Founder

New Tribes Mission **[20446]**
1000 E 1st St.
Sanford, FL 32771-1441
PH: (407)323-3430
Burnham, Gracia, Rep.

Open Door Haiti **[13079]**
5070 Orange Blvd.
Sanford, FL 32771
PH: (407)221-4386
Holliday, Doug, President

The International Osprey Foundation **[4830]**
PO Box 250
Sanibel, FL 33957
Glissman, Inge, Treasurer, Secretary

Academy of Parish Clergy **[20353]**
2249 Florinda St.
Sarasota, FL 34231
PH: (941)922-8633
Moore, David Moffett, President

American Accounting Association **[9]**
5717 Bessie Dr.
Sarasota, FL 34233-2399
PH: (941)921-7747
Fax: (941)923-4093
Sutherland, Tracey, Exec. Dir.

American Board of Professional Neuropsychology **[16858]**
c/o Geoffrey Kanter, Executive Director
1090 S Tamiami Trl.
Sarasota, FL 34239
PH: (941)363-0878
Wilhelm, Karen L., Ph.D., President

American Elasmobranch Society **[6809]**
c/o Cathy J. Walsh, Treasurer
1600 Ken Thompson Pkwy.
Sarasota, FL 34236
Lowe, Christopher, President

American Pointer Club **[21816]**
c/o Paul Wessberg, Membership Chairman
4485 N Lake Dr.
Sarasota, FL 34232
PH: (412)343-9169
Harper, Deborah, President

American Society of Dentist Anesthesiologists **[14415]**
4411 Bee Ridge Rd., No. 172
Sarasota, FL 34233
PH: (312)624-9591
Fax: (773)304-9894
Sarno, Amy L, MBA, Exec. Dir.

American Yoga Association **[10417]**
PO Box 19986
Sarasota, FL 34276
Christensen, Alice, Founder, Director

Brides Against Breast Cancer **[13911]**
6279 Lake Osprey Dr.
Sarasota, FL 34240
PH: (941)907-9350
Toll free: 877-721-4673
Fax: (877)471-8353
Paulishak, Amy, VP of Bus. Dev.

Flyersrights.org **[19197]**
4411 Bee Ridge Rd., No. 274
Sarasota, FL 34233-2514
Toll free: 800-662-1859
Hudsont, Paul, President

International Union of Police Associations **[23471]**
1549 Ringling Blvd., Ste. 600
Sarasota, FL 34236
Toll free: 800-247-4872
Fax: (941)487-2570
Cabral, Samuel A., President

Macular Degeneration Association **[17725]**
PO Box 20256
Sarasota, FL 34276
PH: (941)870-4399
Fax: (866)317-0593
Hoffheimer, Lawrence S., Chairman, Founder

Metropolitan Community Churches **[20185]**
PO Box 50488
Sarasota, FL 34232-0304
PH: (310)360-8640
Fax: (310)388-1252
Crabtree, Barbara, Dir. of Operations

National Association of Fire Investigators **[1890]**
857 Tallevast Rd.
Sarasota, FL 34243-3257
PH: (941)359-2800
Toll free: 877-506-NAFI
Fax: (941)351-5849
Hopkins, Ronald L., President

National Association of Youth Courts **[19275]**
PO Box 48927
Sarasota, FL 34230
PH: (410)528-0143
Fax: (410)528-0170
Albert-Konecky, Lisa, VP

National Black Republican Association **[19040]**
4594 Chase Oaks Dr.
Sarasota, FL 34241-9183
Rice, Frances, Chairperson

Prader-Willi Syndrome Association USA **[14852]**
8588 Potter Park Dr., Ste. 500
Sarasota, FL 34238
PH: (941)312-0400
Toll free: 800-926-4797
Fax: (941)312-0142
Torbert, Michelle, Chairperson

Retirement Industry Trust Association **[415]**
c/o Mary L. Mohr, MBA, JD, Executive Director
4251 Pasadena Cir.
Sarasota, FL 34233
PH: (941)724-0900
Mohr, Mary, Exec. Dir.

Rheumatology Nurses Society **[16183]**
8437 Tuttle Ave., Ste. 404
Sarasota, FL 34243
Toll free: 800-380-7081
Fax: (410)384-4222
Ruffing, Victoria, RN, CCRP, Founder

SafeChildrenUSA **[12936]**
1935 S Tamiami Trail
Sarasota, FL 34239
PH: (941)600-3262
Fax: (941)375-0506
Stimpert, Ryan, Chairman, Founder

United States Masters Swimming **[23288]**
1751 Mound St., Ste. 201
Sarasota, FL 34236
PH: (941)256-8767
Toll free: 800-550-7946
Fax: (941)556-7946
Grilli, Tracy, Mgr., Member Svcs.

Wedding and Event Videographers Association International **[1210]**
8499 S Tamiami Trl., No. 208
Sarasota, FL 34238
PH: (941)923-5334
Fax: (941)921-3836

Anglers for Conservation **[3808]**
PO Box 372423
Satellite Beach, FL 32937
Wnek, Warren E., Bd. Member

American Association of Surgical
Physician Assistants **[17361]**
PO Box 781688
Sebastian, FL 32978
PH: (772)388-0498
Fax: (772)388-3457
Biedenbach, Amy, Rep.

Association of Former Customs
Special Agents **[5267]**
PO Box 781214
Sebastian, FL 32978-1214
Toll free: 877-954-7646

National Association of Independent
Artists **[8929]**
1125 US Highway 1
Sebastian, FL 32958
Swayze, Carroll, Chairperson

River Fund **[10551]**
11155 Roseland Rd., Unit 16
Sebastian, FL 32958
PH: (772)589-5076
Canterbury-Counts, Jaya, MEd,
Exec. Dir.

American Association for Teaching
and Curriculum **[8640]**
c/o Lynne Bailey, Executive
Secretary
5640 Seminole Blvd.
Seminole, FL 33772
Bohan, Chara Haeussler, President

American Society of Orthopedic
Professionals **[16468]**
PO Box 7440
Seminole, FL 33775
PH: (727)394-1700
Barocas, Charles, Exec. Dir.

L'Athletique d'Haiti **[13429]**
13799 Park Blvd. N, No. 284
Seminole, FL 33776
Duval, Robert, Director

Brazilian Dimensional Embroidery
International Guild, Inc. **[21300]**
13013 89th Ave. N
Seminole, FL 33776-2706
PH: (727)391-9207
Goff, Debbie, Membership Chp.

Flying Dentists Association **[14434]**
8850 Lynwood Dr.
Seminole, FL 33772
PH: (727)391-1750
(716)913-4036

Papillon Club of America **[21939]**
c/o Lori Landis, Secretary
8697 134th St.
Seminole, FL 33776
Wright, Anita, President

Association of Companion Animal
Behavior Counselors **[7398]**
PO Box 104
Seville, FL 32190-0104
Toll free: 866-224-2728
Abrantes, Roger, PhD, President

1956 Studebaker Golden Hawk
Owners Register **[21310]**
31654 Wekiva River Rd.
Sorrento, FL 32776-9233
Ambrogio, Frank, Contact

American Horse Publications **[2763]**
49 Spinnaker Cir.
South Daytona, FL 32119-8552
PH: (386)760-7743
Fax: (386)760-7728
Brune, Christine W., Exec. Dir.

International Auto Sound Challenge
Association **[1050]**
2200 S Ridgewood Ave.
South Daytona, FL 32119
PH: (386)322-1551
Papadeas, Paul, President

International Aroid Society **[22104]**
PO Box 43-1853
South Miami, FL 33143
DuFran, Zac, Mem.

American Venous Forum **[17570]**
6800 Gulfport Blvd., Ste. 201-212
South Pasadena, FL 33707-2163
PH: (414)918-9880
(727)202-6213
Fax: (414)276-3349
Kabnick, Lowell S., President

American Membrane Technology
Association **[7361]**
2409 SE Dixie Hwy.
Stuart, FL 34996
PH: (772)463-0820
Fax: (772)463-0860
Freeman, Scott, President

Caribbean Desalination Association
[7365]
2409 SE Dixie Hwy.
Stuart, FL 34996
PH: (772)781-8507
Fax: (772)463-0860
Thompson, John david, President

Certified Interior Decorators
International **[1942]**
649 SE Central Pky.
Stuart, FL 34994
PH: (772)287-1855
Toll free: 800-624-0093
Fax: (772)287-0398
Renner, Ron, President, Founder

Criminal Defense Investigation Train-
ing Council **[5147]**
416 SE Balboa Ave., Ste. 2
Stuart, FL 34994
Toll free: 800-465-5233
Perron, Brandon A., Director

National Alliance for Grieving
Children **[11253]**
900 SE Ocean Blvd., Ste. 130D
Stuart, FL 34994
Toll free: 866-432-1542
McNiel, Andy, CFO

National Council of Youth Sports
[23242]
7185 SE Seagate Ln.
Stuart, FL 34997-2160
PH: (772)781-1452
Fax: (772)781-7298
Johnson, Sally S., CSA, Exec. Dir.

Southeast Desalting Association
[4774]
2409 SE Dixie Hwy.
Stuart, FL 34996
PH: (772)781-7698
Fax: (772)463-0860
Bailey, Michael, Secretary

Claims Support Professional Association **[1845]**
10001 W Oakland Park Blvd., Ste.
301
Sunrise, FL 33351
PH: (954)530-0715
Fax: (954)537-4942

Humans in Crisis International
Corporation **[12678]**
9417 NW 39th Pl.
Sunrise, FL 33351
PH: (615)305-5796
Garbharran, Hari, Founder, Chair-
man

National Association of Forensic Accountants **[47]**
10001 W Oakland Park Blvd., Ste.
301
Sunrise, FL 33351

American Association for Geodetic
Surveying **[7249]**
c/o Ronnie Taylor
2905 Carnaby Ct.
Tallahassee, FL 32309-2537
PH: (850)933-9155
Taylor, Ronnie, President

American Association of State
Troopers **[5453]**
1949 Raymond Diehl Rd.
Tallahassee, FL 32308
Toll free: 800-765-5456
Fax: (850)385-8697
Barbier, Keith, President

American Real Estate and Urban
Economics Association **[2847]**
The Center for Real State Education
and Research
821 Academic Way, 223 RBB
Tallahassee, FL 32306-1110
PH: (850)644-7898
Toll free: 866-273-8321
Fax: (850)644-4077
Riddiough, Timothy, Bd. Member

American Society of Cosmetic
Dermatology and Aesthetic
Surgery **[14309]**
1876-B Eider Ct.
Tallahassee, FL 32308
PH: (850)531-8330
Toll free: 888-531-8330
Fax: (850)531-8344
Bodkin, Larry E., Jr., Exec. Dir.

American Society of Notaries **[5655]**
PO Box 5707
Tallahassee, FL 32314-5707
PH: (850)671-5164
Fax: (850)671-5165
Butler, Kathleen, Exec. Dir.

Architectural Precast Association
[782]
325 John Knox Rd., Ste. L103
Tallahassee, FL 32303
PH: (850)205-5637
Fax: (850)222-3019
Cox, Chris, President

Association of American State
Geologists **[6678]**
903 W Tennessee St.
Tallahassee, FL 32304-7716
PH: (850)617-0320
(701)328-8000
Cobb, James C., Rep.

Association of Collegiate Schools of
Planning **[8722]**
6311 Mallard Trace Dr.
Tallahassee, FL 32312
PH: (850)385-2054
Fax: (850)385-2084
Dodd, Donna, Mgr., Dir. of Conf.

Association for Institutional Research
[8440]
1435 E Piedmont Dr., Ste. 211
Tallahassee, FL 32308
PH: (850)385-4155
Fax: (850)385-5180
Lewis, Jason, Exec. Dir. (Actg.),
CFO

Association of Osteopathic State
Executive Directors **[16521]**
2544 Blairstone Pines Dr.
Tallahassee, FL 32301-5925
PH: (850)878-7364

Association of Plastic Surgery Physi-
cian Assistants **[14314]**
5790 Farnsworth Dr.
Tallahassee, FL 32312-4881
PH: (850)385-4596
Fax: (585)383-4051
Charno, Chrysa, Director

Barbara Bush Foundation for Family
Literacy **[8236]**
516 N Adams St.
Tallahassee, FL 32301
PH: (850)562-5300
Bush, Barbara, Founder

College Language Association
[8180]
c/o Yakini B. Kemp, Treasurer
PO Box 38515
Tallahassee, FL 32315
PH: (850)599-3737
(850)561-2608
Fax: (850)561-2976
McIntosh, Yvonne, Asst. Sec.

Corrections Technology Association
[18070]
c/o Conference Management Solutions, Inc.
1732 Copperfield Cir.
Tallahassee, FL 32312
Garner, Aaron, Exec. Dir.

Dragonfly Society of the Americas
[6610]
c/o Jerrell Daigle, Treasurer
2067 Little River Ln.
Tallahassee, FL 32311
Daigle, Jerrell, Treasurer

Dyslexia Research Institute **[14629]**
5746 Centerville Rd.
Tallahassee, FL 32309
PH: (850)893-2216
Fax: (850)893-2440
Hardman, Patricia K., PhD, Director

Federal Alliance For Safe Homes
[14693]
1427 E Piedmont Dr., Ste. 2
Tallahassee, FL 32308
Toll free: 877-221-7233
Fax: (850)201-1067
Chapman-Henderson, Leslie, CEO,
President

Latino Medical Student Association
[8326]
113 S Monroe St., 1st Fl.
Tallahassee, FL 32301
PH: (904)999-4690
Homan-Sandoval, Elizabeth, MD,
Exec. Dir.

Mental Health Corporations of
America **[13798]**
1876 Eider Ct., Ste. A
Tallahassee, FL 32308
PH: (850)942-4900
Fax: (850)942-0560
Klatzker, Dale K., PH.D., Chairman

National Aquaculture Association
[3644]
PO Box 12759
Tallahassee, FL 32317
PH: (850)216-2400
Fax: (850)216-2480
Parsons, Jim, VP

National Association of Dental
Laboratories **[14457]**
325 John Knox Rd., No. L103
Tallahassee, FL 32303
Toll free: 800-950-1150
Fax: (850)222-0053
Lanier, Dena, President

National Association for Relationship and Marriage Education **[12256]**
PO Box 14946
Tallahassee, FL 32317
Mackenzie, Joneen, V. Ch.

National Association of State Directors of Pupil Transportation Services **[3341]**
c/o Charlie Hood, Executive Director
8205 Bristol Ct.
Tallahassee, FL 32311
PH: (850)274-4308
Langley, Leon, President

National Board for Certification in Dental Laboratory Technology **[14459]**
325 John Knox Rd., No. L103
Tallahassee, FL 32303
PH: (850)205-5627
Toll free: 800-684-5310
Fax: (850)222-0053
Wester, Thomas, Chairman

Pediatric Sunshine Academics **[16616]**
PO Box 3208
Tallahassee, FL 32315-3208
PH: (805)708-3270
Toll free: 800-890-2454

Portrait Society of America **[8881]**
1349 E Lafayette St.
Tallahassee, FL 32301
Toll free: 877-772-4321
Fax: (850)222-7890
Egnoski, Christine, Exec. Dir.

Project Food, Land and People **[3575]**
7023 Alhambra Dr.
Tallahassee, FL 32317
PH: (850)219-1175
Wolanyk, Betty, Chairperson

Service Contract Industry Council **[3078]**
PO Box 11247
Tallahassee, FL 32302
PH: (850)681-1058
Fax: (850)425-4001
Meenan, Timothy J., Exec. Dir., Gen. Counsel

Society for Judgment and Decision Making **[7569]**
c/o Bud Fennema, Secretary-Treasurer
College of Business
Florida State University
Tallahassee, FL 32306-1110
PH: (850)644-8231
Fax: (850)644-8234
Fennema, Bud, Secretary, Treasurer

Striped Bass Growers Association **[4187]**
PO Box 12759
Tallahassee, FL 32317
PH: (850)216-2400
Fax: (850)216-2480
Zajicek, Paul W., Dir. of Dev.

Tall Timbers Land Conservancy **[3955]**
Tall Timbers Research Sta.
13093 Henry Beadel Dr.
Tallahassee, FL 32312-0918
PH: (850)893-4153
Fax: (850)668-7781
Roberts, Jennifer, Admin. Asst.

Selective Mutism Foundation **[15806]**
c/o Sue Newman
PO Box 25972
Tamarac, FL 33320
Miller, Carolyn, Director, Founder

Advocates for World Health **[15595]**
13650 N 12th St.
Tampa, FL 33613
Kania, Ryan, Founder

American Association of Kidney Patients **[15869]**
1440 Bruce B. Downs Blvd.
Tampa, FL 33613
Toll free: 800-749-2257
Fax: (813)636-8122
Green, Gary, Exec. Dir.

American Association for Physician Leadership **[15572]**
400 N Ashley Dr., Ste. 400
Tampa, FL 33602
Toll free: 800-562-8088
Fax: (813)287-8993
Angood, Peter, CEO

American Association of Physician Specialists, Inc. **[16503]**
5550 W Executive Dr., Ste. 400
Tampa, FL 33609
PH: (813)433-2277
Fax: (813)830-6599
Carbone, William J., CEO

American Association of Spanish Timbrado Breeders **[21532]**
c/o Orlando Perez, President
4100 N Tampania Ave.
Tampa, FL 33607
PH: (813)781-4153
Crespo, Orlando Perez, President

American Board of Oral and Maxillo-facial Pathology **[16571]**
One Urban Ctr., Ste. 690
4830 W Kennedy Blvd.
Tampa, FL 33609-2571
PH: (813)286-2444
Fax: (813)289-5279
Scioscia, Mrs. Clarita, Exec. Dir.

American Board of Pathology **[16572]**
4830 W Kennedy Blvd., Ste. 690
Tampa, FL 33609-2571
PH: (813)286-2444
Fax: (813)289-5279
Johnson, Rebecca L., MD, CEO

American Society of Hypothermic Medicine **[15711]**
901 S Oregon Ave.
Tampa, FL 33606
PH: (813)323-5448
Fax: (813)875-4149
Melton, William, Exec. Dir.

American Society for Neural Therapy and Repair **[16006]**
c/o Paul R. Sanberg, Executive Director
MDC-78
12901 Bruce B. Downs Blvd.
Tampa, FL 33612
PH: (813)974-3154
Fax: (813)974-3078
Dunbar, Dr. Gary L., President

Asian American Convenience Stores Association **[2945]**
14502 N Dale Mabry Hwy., Ste. 306
Tampa, FL 33618-2072

Association to Advance Collegiate Schools of Business **[7542]**
777 S Harbour Island Blvd., Ste. 750
Tampa, FL 33602
PH: (813)769-6500
Fax: (813)769-6559
Fernandes, John J., President, CEO

Association of Nepalese Mathematicians in America **[8276]**
4106 Skipper Rd., Apt. 221
Tampa, FL 33613
Khanal, Dr. Netra, President

Association of Neurosurgical Physician Assistants **[16722]**
PO Box 17781
Tampa, FL 33682
PH: (813)799-8807
Fax: (813)856-3533
Damm, Paul, PA-C, President

Association of Physician Assistants in Oncology **[16338]**
30658 USF Holly Dr.
Tampa, FL 33620-3065
PH: (813)988-7795
Fax: (813)988-7796.
Wei, Steven, President

Association for the Sociology of Religion **[7182]**
University of South Florida
Dept. of Sociology
4202 E Fowler Ave.
Tampa, FL 33620
PH: (813)974-2758
Fax: (813)974-6455
Cavendish, James C., Exec. Ofc.

BICSI **[3219]**
8610 Hidden River Pky.
Tampa, FL 33637-1000
PH: (813)979-1991
Toll free: 800-242-7405
Fax: (813)971-4311
Clark, John D., Jr., CEO, Exec. Dir.

Big Brothers Big Sisters of America **[11216]**
2202 N Westshore Blvd., Ste. 455
Tampa, FL 33607
PH: (469)351-3100
    (813)720-8778
Fax: (972)717-6507
Iorio, Pam, President

Clinical Magnetic Resonance Society **[14292]**
5620 W Sligh Ave.
Tampa, FL 33634-4490
PH: (813)806-1080
Toll free: 888-350-CMRS
Fax: (813)806-1081
Awh, Mark H., MD, President

Coalition for a Healthy and Active America **[16256]**
301 W Platt St.
Tampa, FL 33606
Toll free: 866-881-7666
Fax: (561)746-4023
Weidenfeller, Tara, Exec. Dir.

Cuban Numismatic Association **[22267]**
c/o Joseph A. Crespo, Treasurer
PO Box 47304
Tampa, FL 33646
Pino, Joseph Algazi, President

Dentistry from the Heart **[14431]**
8313 W Hillsborough Ave.
Tampa, FL 33615
PH: (727)849-2002
Monticciolo, Dr. Vincent, Founder

Enable America, Inc. **[11595]**
101 E Kennedy Blvd.
Tampa, FL 33602-5179
Toll free: 877-362-2533
Fax: (813)221-8811
Salem, Richard J., CEO, Founder

Facing Our Risk of Cancer Empowered **[13966]**
16057 Tampa Palms Blvd. W
Tampa, FL 33647
Toll free: 866-288-7475
Fax: (954)827-2200

Federation of Defense and Corporate Counsel **[5313]**
11812 N 56th St.
Tampa, FL 33617

PH: (813)983-0022
Fax: (813)988-5837
Streeper, Martha J., Exec. Dir.

Financial Management Association International **[1278]**
College of Business Administration
University of South Florida
4202 E Fowler Ave., BSN 3416
Tampa, FL 33620-5500
PH: (813)974-2084
Fax: (813)974-3318
Denis, David, President

Gastroenterology Physician Assistants **[14790]**
PO Box 82511
Tampa, FL 33682
PH: (813)766-8807
Fax: (813)856-3533
Abramov, Frida, Contact

Hands4Africa **[12280]**
13046 Race Track Rd., Ste. 242
Tampa, FL 33626
PH: (813)343-8899
Logan, Brad, Director

Hispanic Professional Women's Association **[3492]**
PO Box 152344
Tampa, FL 33684-2344
PH: (813)877-5880
Nichols, Marggie, President

Home Improvement Research Institute **[825]**
10117 Princess Palm Ave., Ste. 575
Tampa, FL 33610
PH: (813)627-6750
Miller, Fred, Managing Dir.

Hoola for Happiness **[13062]**
3225 S MacDill Ave., Ste. 129-343
Tampa, FL 33629
Caricato, Carissa, Founder

Inflatable Advertising Dealers Association **[95]**
c/o Bruce Cohen, President
Skyline International
PO Box 152641
Tampa, FL 33684-2641
Toll free: 888-923-8652
Hansen, Josh, Director

Insurance Advertising Compliance Association **[1863]**
PO Box 26364
Tampa, FL 33623
PH: (813)288-7492
Vassar, Murray, President

Insurance Institute for Business & Home Safety **[1867]**
4775 E Fowler Ave.
Tampa, FL 33617
PH: (813)286-3400
Fax: (813)286-9960
Rochman, Julie, CEO, President

International Aesthetic and Laser Association **[15523]**
4830 W Kennedy Blvd., Ste. 440
Tampa, FL 33609
PH: (813)676-7704
Strothman, Nicole, President

International Association of Avian Trainers and Educators **[21540]**
301 E Hollywood St.
Tampa, FL 33604
Shewokis, Robin, President

International Bossons Collectors Society **[21669]**
8316 Woodlake Pl.
Tampa, FL 33615-1728

PH: (813)885-2038
McLernon, Donna, Exec. Dir., President

International Cardioncology Society, North America [14121]
602 S Audubon Ave., Ste. B
Tampa, FL 33609
Lenihan, Daniel J., MD, President

International Federation of Nonlinear Analysts [7135]
c/o Dr. Rebecca Wooten, Vice President/Treasurer
University of South Florida, CMC 319
4202 E Fowler Ave.
Tampa, FL 33620
Tsokos, Chris P., President

International Federation of Sephardic and Ashkenazi Jews [20336]
PO Box 271708
Tampa, FL 33688-1708

International Fitness Professionals Association [16704]
14509 University Point Pl.
Tampa, FL 33613
PH: (813)979-1925
Toll free: 800-785-1924
Fax: (813)979-1978

International Homicide Investigators Association [5363]
2310 Falkenburg Rd. N
Tampa, FL 33619
PH: (540)898-7898
Holmes, James, President

International Packaged Ice Association [1629]
238 E Davis Blvd., Ste. 213
Tampa, FL 33606
PH: (813)258-1690
Sedler, Tommy, Chairman

International Society for Pharmaceutical Engineering [7006]
600 N Westshore Blvd., Ste. 900
Tampa, FL 33609-1114
PH: (813)960-2105
Fax: (813)264-2816
Berg, Nancy S., CEO, President

International Society of Phonetic Sciences [9743]
c/o Prof. Ruth Huntley Bahr, PhD
University of South Florida
4202 E Fowler Ave., PCD 1017
Tampa, FL 33647
PH: (813)974-3182
Fax: (813)974-0822
Bahr, Prof. Ruth Huntley, PhD, President

International Zoo Educators Association [7852]
3605 E Bougainvillea Ave.
Tampa, FL 33612
Lowry, Rachel, President

Kidney Community Emergency Response Coalition [15879]
3000 Bayport Dr., Ste. 300
Tampa, FL 33607
Toll free: 866-901-3773
Gore, Sally, Director

National Academy of Dermatology Nurse Practitioners [14503]
17427-B Bridge Hill Ct., Ste. J
Tampa, FL 33647
Shelby, Debra, PhD, President, Founder

National Association of Media Brokers [2873]
c/o Glenn Serafin, President
Serafin Bros.

PO Box 262888
Tampa, FL 33685
Serafin, Glenn, President

National Mobility Equipment Dealers Association [11627]
3327 W Bearss Ave.
Tampa, FL 33618
PH: (813)264-2697
Toll free: 866-948-8341
Fax: (813)962-8970
Blake, Chad, President

Neurotech Network [16053]
PO Box 27386
Tampa, FL 33623
PH: (727)321-0150
French, Jennifer, Founder, Exec. Dir.

North American Academy of Ecumenists [20070]
3838 W Cypress St.
Tampa, FL 33607
PH: (813)435-5335
Best, Rev. Thomas F, VP

Obesity Action Coalition [16261]
4511 N Himes Ave., Ste. 250
Tampa, FL 33614
Toll free: 800-717-3117
Nadglowski, Joseph, Jr., CEO, President

Paws for Friendship [13305]
PO Box 341378
Tampa, FL 33694
PH: (813)969-1954
(913)957-6829
Fax: (813)968-2848
Schmidt, Jan, President

People for Haiti [12711]
12157 W Linebaugh Ave., No. 357
Tampa, FL 33626
PH: (813)750-7346
Vieira, Guiga, President

Phi Alpha Theta [23770]
University of South Florida
4202 E Fowler Ave., SOC107
Tampa, FL 33620-8100
Toll free: 800-394-8195
Fax: (813)974-8215
Tunstall, Graydon A., Jr., Exec. Dir.

Renew Haiti [12722]
821 South Dale Mabry Hwy.
Tampa, FL 33609
PH: (813)876-5841
Eddy, Patricia, Founder

Reusable Packaging Association [4636]
PO Box 25078
Tampa, FL 33622
PH: (813)358-5327
Welcome, Jerry, President, CEO

Rexx Language Association [7058]
7028 W Waters Ave.
Tampa, FL 33634-2292
Jansen, Rene, President

Shriners Hospitals for Children [14214]
2900 N Rocky Point Dr.
Tampa, FL 33607
PH: (813)281-0300
Toll free: 800-237-5055
Molnar, Louis A., CEO

Society for the Scientific Study of Psychopathy [15808]
University of South Florida
Louis de la Parte Florida Mental Health Institute
13301 Bruce B. Downs Blvd., MHC 2639

Tampa, FL 33612
PH: (813)974-8612
Fax: (813)974-6411
Kosson, David, PhD, President

Sociologists Without Borders [7190]
c/o Bruce K. Friesen, President
401 W Kennedy Blvd.
University of Tampa
Tampa, FL 33606

The Witches' Voice [20638]
PO Box 341018
Tampa, FL 33694-1018
Walker, Wren, Founder

American Council on Consumer Interests [18039]
PO Box 2528
Tarpon Springs, FL 34688-2528
PH: (727)940-2658
Phillips, Ginger, Exec. Dir.

International Lightning Class Association [22635]
1528 Big Bass Dr.
Tarpon Springs, FL 34689-5604
PH: (727)942-7969
Fax: (727)942-0173
Ruhlman, Robert, VP

Wheelchairs 4 Kids [11646]
1406 Stonehaven Way
Tarpon Springs, FL 34689
PH: (727)946-0963
Robinson, Madeline, President

Christian Boaters Association [20135]
c/o Earlene Nelson, Membership Coordinator
193 Plantation Dr.
Tavernier, FL 33070
PH: (305)852-4799
Simon, Marlin, Act. Pres.

Cancer Cure Coalition [13920]
325 Beach Rd., Ste. 204
Tequesta, FL 33469
PH: (561)747-2174
Fax: (561)747-2174
Reinwald, Charles, Jr., President

Citizens United for Alternatives to the Death Penalty [5130]
177 US Highway No. 1
Tequesta, FL 33469
Toll free: 800-973-6548
Bonowitz, Abraham J., Director, Founder

The Curtis/s Family Society [20851]
c/o Cheryl Behrend, Secretary
17924 SE 89th Rothway Ct.
The Villages, FL 32162-4840
Behrend, Cheryl, Secretary

Dachshund Rescue of North America [10610]
c/o Elieen Pratt
1197 Allaire Loop
The Villages, FL 32163
Pratt, Elieen, Contact

Episcopal Conference of the Deaf [20101]
1804 Hollow Branch Way
The Villages, FL 32162-2350
PH: (352)350-5357
Stuart, Rev. Marianne, President

National Pedigreed Livestock Council [3605]
177 Palermo Pl.
177 Palermo Pl.
The Villages, FL 32159-0094
PH: (352)259-6005
Taylor, Steve, President

American Federation of Police and Concerned Citizens [5454]
6350 Horizon Dr.
Titusville, FL 32780
PH: (321)264-0911
Shepherd, Barry, CEO

Astronaut Scholars Honor Society [23858]
Astronaut Scholarship Foundation
Kennedy Space Center, SR 405
Titusville, FL 32780
PH: (321)449-4876
Fax: (321)264-9176
Brandenstein, Daniel, Chairman

Classic Chevy International [21357]
5200 S Washington Ave.
Titusville, FL 32780-7316
Toll free: 800-284-4096
Fax: (321)383-2059

National Association of Chiefs of Police [5488]
6350 Horizon Dr.
Titusville, FL 32780
PH: (321)264-0911
Shepherd, Brent, COO

Alternative Religions Educational Network [20512]
PO Box 1893
Trenton, FL 32693
PH: (352)363-0637

National Creditors Bar Association [5038]
8043 Cooper Creek Blvd., Ste. 206
University Park, FL 34201
PH: (202)861-0706
Dobosz, Mark, Exec. Dir.

Episcopalians for Global Reconciliation [20104]
2202 Wildwood Hollow Dr.
Valrico, FL 33594
PH: (813)333-1832
Hammock, Dr. John, Co-Chmn. of the Bd.

American Hibiscus Society [22074]
PO Box 1580
Venice, FL 34284-1580
PH: (941)627-1332
Veach, Damon, VP

Imaging Supplies Coalition [5329]
MBN 249
1435 E Venice Ave., No. 104
Venice, FL 34292-3074
PH: (941)961-7897
Westerfield, Allen D., President

Venus Project [19122]
21 Valley Ln.
Venus, FL 33960-2327
PH: (863)465-0321
Fresco, Jacque, Founder

Goff/Gough Family Association [20871]
5704 Riverboat Cir. SW
Vero Beach, FL 32968
Goff, Phil, President

Council on Law in Higher Education [5162]
9386 Via Classico W
Wellington, FL 33411
PH: (561)792-4440
Fax: (561)792-4441

Hispanic Council for Reform and Educational Options [7770]
Ste. L, No. 151
4095 State Road 7
Wellington, FL 33449
Fuentes, Julio A., CEO, President

JustWorld International [11054]
11924 W Forest Hill Blvd., Ste. 22-396
Wellington, FL 33414
PH: (561)333-9391
Fax: (561)792-0757
Newman, Jessica, Exec. Dir.

Norwegian Lundehund Association
of America, Inc. [21935]
c/o Leon Hustad, President/Membership Chairperson
744 Via Toscana
Wellington, FL 33414-7984
PH: (561)385-4642
Hustad, Leon, President, Membership Chp.

Regenerative Medicine Foundation
[14885]
9314 Forest Hill Blvd., Ste. 2
2875 S Ocean Blvd.
Wellington, FL 33411
Toll free: 888-238-1423
Fax: (561)791-3889
Siegel, Bernard, JD, Exec. Dir.,
Founder

Angels for Hope [13031]
708 Falls Creek Dr.
West Melbourne, FL 32904
Gabner, Cindy, President

Alliance for Eating Disorders Awareness [14632]
1649 Forum Pl., No. 2
West Palm Beach, FL 33401
PH: (561)841-0900
Toll free: 866-662-1235
Wypych, Leah, Chmn. of the Bd.

American Greyhound Track Operators Association [22824]
Palm Beach Kennel Club
1111 N Congress Ave.
West Palm Beach, FL 33409
PH: (561)688-5799
Fax: (801)751-2404
Fra, Juan, President

American Jewish League for Israel
[20228]
400 N Flagler Drive, PH D4
West Palm Beach, FL 33401
PH: (212)371-1583
Fax: (561)659-0402
Kalmanson, Dr. Martin L., President

American Miniature Schnauzer Club
[21815]
c/o Jacquelyn Ebersbach
424 45th St.
West Palm Beach, FL 33407
Constantine, John, President

Croquet Foundation of America
[22740]
700 Florida Mango Rd.
West Palm Beach, FL 33406-4461
PH: (561)315-5226
Fax: (561)478-0709
McCoy, W. David, President

Fondation Hopital Bon Samaritain
[15141]
PO Box 32446
West Palm Beach, FL 33420
PH: (561)246-3360
Hodges, Joanna, Founder

International Alliance for Youth
Sports [23376]
2050 Vista Pky.
West Palm Beach, FL 33411
Toll free: 800-688-KIDS
Fax: (561)712-9887
Engh, Fred C., CEO, President

International Council of Fine Arts
Deans [7512]
PO Box 331
West Palm Beach, FL 33402

PH: (561)514-0810
Crawford-Spinelli, John R., President

Iron Overload Diseases Association
[15826]
525 Mayflower Rd.
West Palm Beach, FL 33405
PH: (561)586-8246
Barfield, Steve, Editor

Israel Cancer Association USA
[13996]
2751 S Dixie Hwy., Ste. 3A
West Palm Beach, FL 33405
PH: (561)832-9277
Fax: (561)832-9337
Cooper, Jill, Exec. Dir.

Locks of Love [14200]
234 Southern Blvd.
West Palm Beach, FL 33405-2701
PH: (561)833-7332
Toll free: 888-896-1588
Fax: (561)833-7962
Coffman, Madonna W., President

Medical Tourism Association [15735]
10130 Northlake Blvd., Ste. 214-315
West Palm Beach, FL 33412
PH: (561)791-2000
Edelheit, Jonathan, CEO

National Alliance for Youth Sports
[22733]
2050 Vista Pky.
West Palm Beach, FL 33411
PH: (561)684-1141
Toll free: 800-729-2057
Fax: (561)684-2546
Engh, Fred, Founder

Quarter Century Wireless Association [21273]
12967 N Normandy Way
West Palm Beach, FL 33410-1412
PH: (352)425-1097
Oelke, Ken, President

United States Croquet Association
[22741]
700 Florida Mango Rd.
West Palm Beach, FL 33406-4461
PH: (561)478-0760
Fax: (561)686-5507
Mitchell, Johnny, Jr., President

J/80 Class Association [22642]
c/o Chris Chadwick, President
433 Fairmont Ln.
Weston, FL 33326
PH: (860)539-3938
Bannura, Ramzi, Treasurer

National Association of Legal Search
Consultants [2013]
1525 N Park Dr., Ste. 102
Weston, FL 33326-3225
PH: (954)349-8081
Toll free: 866-902-6587
Fax: (954)349-1979
Binstock, Dan, Director

United States Marine Corps Combat
Correspondents Association [2730]
110 Fox Ct.
Wildwood, FL 34785
Paxton, John, Exec. Dir.

Tomato Genetics Cooperative [4252]
Gulf Coast Research and Education
Center
University of Florida
14625 County Road 672
Wimauma, FL 33598
PH: (813)633-4135
Scott, J.W., PhD, Managing Ed.

American Society for Neurochemistry [6914]
9037 Ron Den Ln.
Windermere, FL 34786

PH: (407)909-9064
Fax: (407)876-0750
Hewett, Sandra, Phd, Secretary

GDE Haiti [10992]
5119 Butler Ridge Dr.
Windermere, FL 34786
PH: (407)929-7205
Severe, Jodi, Founder, Director

National Neurotrauma Society
[16028]
9037 Ron Den Ln.
Windermere, FL 34786
PH: (407)876-0750
Lifshitz, Jonathan, Ph.D, VP

Women in Neurotrauma Research
[16042]
c/o National Neurotrauma Society
9037 Ron Den Ln.
Windermere, FL 34786
PH: (407)876-0750
Noble, Linda, PhD, President

Lift Disability Network [11615]
PO Box 770607
Winter Garden, FL 34777
PH: (407)228-8343
Fax: (407)403-6528
Hukill, Jim, Exec. Dir.

National Association of Birth Centers
of Color [14238]
213 S Dillard St., Ste. 340
Winter Garden, FL 34787
PH: (706)901-7508
Bailey, Rolinda, Secretary, Treasurer

The Cairn Terrier Club of America
[21849]
c/o Pauli Christy
226 Kilmer Ln.
Winter Haven, FL 33884-2314
Quarles, Tom, President

Sigma Phi Alpha [23721]
c/o Cindy Sensabaug, Vice
President
2208 Edmonton St.
Winter Haven, FL 33881
PH: (919)537-3464
Sensabaugh, Cindy, VP

American Board of Sexology [17191]
PO Box 1166
Winter Park, FL 32790-1166
PH: (407)645-1641
Walker, James, PhD, President

CAUCUS - The Association of
Technology Acquisition Professionals [7261]
PO Box 2970
Winter Park, FL 32790-2970
PH: (407)740-5600
Schleiden, Roy, Chmn. of the Exec.
Committee

Colombia ChildCare International
[10943]
Calvary Assembly
1199 Clay St.
Winter Park, FL 32789
PH: (407)644-1199
Taylor, David, Founder, President

Global Culinary Innovators Association [962]
PO Box 2005
Winter Park, FL 32790-2005
PH: (407)539-1459
Fax: (407)985-4538
McMillin, Matt, VP

Hemingway Foundation and Society
[9055]
c/o Gail Sinclair
Rollins College

1000 Holt Ave. 2770
Winter Park, FL 32789
Stoneback, Harry R., President

International Corporate Chefs Association [700]
PO Box 2005
Winter Park, FL 32790-2005
PH: (407)539-1459
Fax: (407)985-4538
Smith, Amy, Secretary

Life Insurance Settlement Association [1880]
280 W Canton Ave., Ste. 430
Winter Park, FL 32789
PH: (407)894-3797
Bayston, Darwin, CEO, President

Outdoor Amusement Business Association [1158]
1035 S Semoran Blvd., Ste. 1045A
Winter Park, FL 32792
PH: (407)681-9444
Toll free: 800-517-OABA
Fax: (407)681-9445
Johnson, Robert W., President

United Amputee Services Association, Inc. [15614]
PO Box 4277
Winter Park, FL 32793-4277
PH: (407)359-5500
Fax: (407)359-8855

Coalition to Defeat Childhood
Obesity [16254]
600 Northern Way, Ste. 1803
Winter Springs, FL 32708
PH: (407)542-3150
Agostini, Augusto, Founder, CEO

American Association of Zoo
Veterinarians [17608]
581705 White Oak Rd.
Yulee, FL 32097
PH: (904)225-3275
Fax: (904)225-3289
Hilsenroth, Dr. Robert, Exec. Dir.

Association of Zoo Veterinary
Technicians [17641]
c/o Marcie Oliva, CVT, Executive
Director
White Oak Conservation Center
581705 White Oak Rd.
Yulee, FL 32097-2169
Oliva, Marcie, Exec. Dir.G

GEORGIA

Veterinary Botanical Medicine Association [17667]
c/o Jasmine C. Lyon, Executive
Director
6410 Highway 92
Acworth, GA 30102
Lyon, Jasmine C., Exec. Dir.

American Peanut Shellers Association [4508]
2336 Lake Park Dr.
Albany, GA 31707
PH: (229)888-2508
Fax: (229)888-5150
Gray, John, President

American Rehabilitation Counseling
Association [17082]
c/o Quiteya Walker, President
Albany State University
504 College Dr.
Albany, GA 31705
PH: (229)430-4783
Walker, Quiteya, President

National Association of Student Affairs Professionals [7437]
c/o Gwinetta L. Trice, Recording
Secretary

504 College Drive
Albany, GA 31705
PH: (540)831-6297
(229)903-3606
Chanay, Dr. Marcus A., President

Peanut Institute **[4513]**
PO Box 70157
Albany, GA 31708-0157
PH: (229)888-0216
Toll free: 888-873-2688
Fax: (229)888-5150

Pedorthic Footcare Association
[1402]
PO Box 72184
Albany, GA 31708-2184
PH: (229)389-3440
Fax: (888)563-0954
Sobel, Robert, President

AdvancED **[8526]**
9115 Westside Pky.
Alpharetta, GA 30009
Toll free: 888-413-3669
Borders, Denise, Chairman

American Guild of Judaic Art **[8833]**
135 Shaker Hollow
Alpharetta, GA 30022
PH: (404)981-2308
Schloss, Lawrence Mark, MA, Prog.
Dir.

Association for Catechumenal
Ministry **[20354]**
990 Reece Rd.
Alpharetta, GA 30004
PH: (513)301-4826
Norris, Gary, Chmn. of the Bd.

Attachment Parenting International
[12408]
PO Box 4615
Alpharetta, GA 30023
Fax: (800)850-8320
Parker, Lysa, MS, Director, Founder

Auto Haulers Association of America
[3409]
Bldg. 500, Ste. 503
4080 McGinnis Ferry Rd.
Alpharetta, GA 30005
PH: (678)264-8610
Hansen, Steve, Chairman

Cell Phones for Soldiers **[10740]**
5665 N Commerce Ct.
Alpharetta, GA 30004
PH: (678)580-1976
Bergquist, Robbie, Founder,
President

Children Without a Voice, USA
[10925]
PO Box 4351
Alpharetta, GA 30023
Toll free: 800-799-7233
Seahorn, Lin, President

Coordinating Research Council
[2517]
5755 N Point Pky., Ste. 265
Alpharetta, GA 30022-1175
PH: (678)795-0506
Fax: (678)795-0509
Bailey, Brent, Exec. Dir.

Electronic Components Industry Association **[1043]**
1111 Alderman Dr., Ste. 400
Alpharetta, GA 30005
PH: (678)393-9990
Fax: (678)393-9998
Willis, Robert, President

Insulated Cable Engineers Association **[6559]**
PO Box 2694
Alpharetta, GA 30023

PH: (770)830-0369
Fax: (770)830-8501
Nuckles, K., President

The IPA Association of America
[16753]
12850 Highway 9, No. 600-334
Alpharetta, GA 30004
PH: (510)967-7305
Fax: (510)217-2241
Holloway, Albert, CEO, Founder,
President

Old Reel Collectors Association
[21706]
160 Shoreline Walk
Alpharetta, GA 30022
Schulz, Roger, Secretary, Treasurer

Postpartum Progress Inc. **[16626]**
4920 Atlanta Hwy., No. 316
Alpharetta, GA 30004
Toll free: 877-470-4877
Stone, Katherine, Founder, Exec.
Dir.

Reaching for the Stars **[14157]**
3000 Old Alabama Rd., Ste. 119-300
Alpharetta, GA 30022
Toll free: 855-240-RFTS
Frisina, Cynthia, Founder, Exec. Dir.

Reverse Logistics Association **[685]**
2300 Lakeview Pky., Ste. 700
Alpharetta, GA 30009
PH: (801)331-8949
Fax: (801)206-0090
Sciarrotta, Tony, Exec. Dir.

Tile Partners for Humanity **[11993]**
505 Sable Ct.
Alpharetta, GA 30004
PH: (678)366-1815
Fax: (678)366-1816

United Egg Processors **[4572]**
1720 Windwind Concourse, Ste. 230
Alpharetta, GA 30005
PH: (770)360-9220
Fax: (770)360-7058
Gregory, Chad, President, CEO

United Egg Producers **[4573]**
1720 Windward Concourse, Ste. 230
Alpharetta, GA 30005
PH: (770)360-9220
Fax: (770)360-7058
Gregory, Chad, President

World Association for Vedic Studies
[9222]
c/o Dhirenda A. Shah, Treasurer
780 Ullswater Cove
Alpharetta, GA 30022-6661
PH: (770)664-8779
Fax: (770)664-8780
Shah, Dhirendra A., Dr., Treasurer

Association of Third World Studies
[18485]
PO Box 1232
Americus, GA 31709
PH: (318)797-5349
(318)797-5158
Fax: (318)795-4203
Pederson, Dr. William D., Exec. Dir.

Habitat for Humanity International
[11971]
121 Habitat St.
Americus, GA 31709-3498
PH: (229)924-6935
Toll free: 800-422-4828
Reckford, Jonathan, CEO

Professional Disc Golf Association
[22808]
International Disc Golf Ctr.
3828 Dogwood Ln.

Appling, GA 30802-3012
PH: (706)261-6342
Toll free: 888-840-7342
Fax: (706)261-6347
Duffy, Rebecca, President

International Cuemakers Association
[22586]
444 Flint Hill Rd.
Aragon, GA 30104
PH: (770)684-7004
Hightower, Chris, Director

Association of Natural Resource
Extension Professionals **[4489]**
c/o Bill Hubbard, Executive
Secretary
4-402 Forest Resources Bldg.
Warnell School of Forestry & Natural
Resources
University of Georgia
Athens, GA 30602-2152
PH: (706)542-7813
Fax: (706)542-3342
Hubbard, Bill, Exec. Sec.

Citizens for Midwifery **[14226]**
PO Box 82227
Athens, GA 30608-2227
Toll free: 888-CFM-4880
Pfaffl, Nasima, President, Sec.
(Actg.)

Council on Governmental Ethics
Laws **[5772]**
PO Box 81237
Athens, GA 30608
PH: (706)548-7758
Fax: (706)548-7079
Sullivan, Michael, President

Edsel Club **[21374]**
255 Roberts Dr.
Athens, GA 30606-1225

National Press Photographers Association **[2587]**
120 Hooper St.
Athens, GA 30602
Kenniff, Thomas, Director

Natural Fitness Trainers Association
[23066]
PO Box 49874
Athens, GA 30606-9998
PH: (706)623-3671

Southern Historical Association
[8799]
c/o Stephen Berry, Secretary-
Treasurer
LeConte Hall, Rm. 111A
Dept. of History
University of Georgia
Athens, GA 30602-1602
PH: (706)542-8848
Clinton, Catherine, President

100 Black Men of America **[19292]**
141 Auburn Ave.
Atlanta, GA 30303
PH: (404)688-5100
Fax: (404)522-5652
Dossman, Mr. Curley M., Jr., Chmn.
of the Exec. Committee

Alliance for Digital Equality **[6729]**
Piedmont Ctr.
3525 Piedmont Rd.
Atlanta, GA 30305
PH: (404)262-0188
Bradford, Brian, Secretary

Alliance for International Reforestation **[3793]**
4514 Chamblee Dunwoody Rd., Unit
496
Atlanta, GA 30338

PH: (770)543-9529
Hallum, Anne, Founder, President

Alliance for Natural Health USA
[16795]
Bldg. 6, Ste. 110
3525 Piedmont Rd. NE
Atlanta, GA 30305
PH: (202)803-5123
Toll free: 800-230-2762
Fax: (202)315-5837
Lewis, Hunter, President

Alpha Delta Pi **[23882]**
1386 Ponce de Leon Ave. NE
Atlanta, GA 30306
PH: (404)378-3164
Ablard, Linda Welch, CEO

American Academy of Anesthesiologist Assistants **[13690]**
1231 Collier Rd. NW, Ste. J
Atlanta, GA 30318-2322
PH: (678)222-4221
Fax: (404)249-8831
Dunipace, David, Director

American Academy of Religion
[7736]
825 Houston Mill Rd. NE, Ste. 300
Atlanta, GA 30329-4205
PH: (404)727-3049
Fitzmier, John R., Exec. Dir.

American Association of adapted-
SPORTS Programs **[22770]**
PO Box 451047
Atlanta, GA 31145
PH: (404)294-0070
Vaughn, Ben, CEO

American Association for Adult and
Continuing Education **[7666]**
Bldg. 14, Ste. 100
1827 Powers Ferry Rd.
Atlanta, GA 30339
PH: (678)271-4319
Fax: (678)229-2777
Eggleston, Margaret, PhD, President

American Association for Applied
Linguistics **[9735]**
Bldg. 14, Ste. 100
1827 Powers Ferry Rd.
Atlanta, GA 30339
PH: (678)229-2892
Toll free: 866-821-7700
Fax: (678)229-2777
Bailey, Kathleen M., President

American Association of Intensive
English Programs **[7864]**
PO Box 170128
Atlanta, GA 30317
PH: (415)926-1975
Szasz, Patricia, President

American Association of Wildlife
Veterinarians **[17607]**
c/o Dr. Megin Nichols, Treasurer
1616 Piedmont Ave. NE, Apt. S5
Atlanta, GA 30324
Gillin, Dr. Colin, Chairman, Web
Adm.

American Baptist Historical Society
[19712]
3001 Mercer University Dr.,
Atlanta, GA 30341
PH: (678)547-6680
(610)768-2269
Toll free: 800-222-3872
Fax: (678)547-6682
Fair, Shirley, Treasurer

American Beekeeping Federation
[3632]
3525 Piedmont Rd., Bldg. 5, Ste.
300

Atlanta, GA 30305
PH: (404)760-2875
Fax: (404)240-0998
Tucker, Tim, President

American Black Chiropractic Association [14249]
3915 Cascade Rd., Ste. 220
Atlanta, GA 30331
PH: (404)647-2225
Fax: (404)699-0988
Carhee, Winston, President

American Board of Dental Public Health [14395]
827 Brookridge Dr. NE
Atlanta, GA 30306-3618
PH: (404)876-3530
Alderman, E. Joseph, DDS, Exec. Dir.

American Board of Professional Liability Attorneys [5558]
4355 Cobb Pky., Ste. J-208
Atlanta, GA 30339
PH: (404)919-4009
Fax: (866)531-9643
Callaham, William C., President

American Bridge Association [21557]
c/o Willetta Phipps, Secretary
2828 Lakewood Ave. SW
Atlanta, GA 30315-5804
PH: (404)768-5517
Phipps, Willetta, Secretary

American Cancer Society [13882]
250 Williams St. NW
Atlanta, GA 30303-1002
Toll free: 800-227-2345
Reedy, Gary, CEO

American College of Rheumatology [17152]
2200 Lake Blvd. NE
Atlanta, GA 30319
PH: (404)633-3777
Fax: (404)633-1870
Schlenk, Elizabeth A., President

American Council for Judaism [20225]
PO Box 888484
Atlanta, GA 30356-0484
PH: (904)280-3131
Naman, Stephen L., President

American Hydrangea Society [22077]
PO Box 53234
Atlanta, GA 30355-1234
Felton, Cheri, Treasurer

American Industrial Extension Alliance [2211]
Georgia Institute of Technology
Enterprise Innovation Institute
75 5th St. NW, Ste. 300
Atlanta, GA 30308-2272
PH: (404)894-2272
Fax: (404)894-1192
Israel, Tim, President

American Partnership for Eosinophilic Disorders [14780]
PO Box 29545
Atlanta, GA 30359-0545
PH: (713)493-7749
Mays, Elizabeth, Founder

American Society of Digital Forensics and eDiscovery [6652]
2451 Cumberland Pky., Ste. 3382
Atlanta, GA 30339-6157
Toll free: 866-534-9734
Dampier, David, PhD, Director

American Society of Heating, Refrigerating and Air-Conditioning Engineers [6536]
1791 Tullie Cir. NE
Atlanta, GA 30329

PH: (404)636-8400
Toll free: 800-527-4723
Fax: (404)321-5478
Littleton, Jeff H., Exec. VP

American Track Racing Association [22744]
PO Box 93245
Atlanta, GA 30377
Antonvich, Pete, President

American Turkish Friendship Council [18515]
1266 W Paces Ferry Rd., No. 257
Atlanta, GA 30327-2306
PH: (404)884-8666
Fax: (404)393-9301
Eroglu, Dogan, PhD, President

Americas Apparel Producers' Network [199]
PO Box 720693
Atlanta, GA 30358
PH: (404)843-3171
Fax: (404)671-9456
Strickland, Sue C., Exec. Dir.

Aniz, Inc. [12068]
236 Forsyth St., Ste. 300
Atlanta, GA 30303
PH: (404)521-2410
Toll free: 866-521-2410
Fax: (404)521-2499
Age, Zina, CEO, Founder

Ape Conservation Effort [4787]
800 Cherokee Ave. SE
Atlanta, GA 30315-1470
Mayer Todd, Donna, President

Arthritis Foundation [17153]
1330 Peachtree St. NE, 6th Fl.
Atlanta, GA 30309
PH: (404)872-7100
Ortman, Michael V., Chairman

Asian American Hotel Owners Association [1649]
1100 Abernathy Rd., Ste. 1100
Atlanta, GA 30328-6707
PH: (404)816-5759
Toll free: 888-692-2462
Fax: (404)816-6260
Patel, Alkesh R., Contact

Association for Dressings and Sauces [1317]
1100 Johnson Ferry Rd., Ste. 300
Atlanta, GA 30342
PH: (678)298-1181
Fax: (404)591-6811

Association of Energy Engineers [6458]
3168 Mercer University Dr.
Atlanta, GA 30341
PH: (770)447-5083
Thumann, Albert, PE, Exec. Dir.

Association of Fund-Raising Distributors and Suppliers [1467]
1100 Johnson Ferry Rd., Ste. 300
Atlanta, GA 30342
PH: (404)252-3663
Fax: (404)252-0774
Krueger, Jon, Exec. Dir.

Association for Information Systems [6242]
Computer Information Systems Dept.
J. Mack Robinson College of Business
Georgia State University
35 Broad St., Ste. 917
Atlanta, GA 30303
PH: (404)413-7445
Lee, Jae Kyu, President

Association of Rheumatology Health Professionals [17155]
2200 Lake Blvd. NE
Atlanta, GA 30319

PH: (404)633-3777
Fax: (404)633-1870

Association for Specialists in Group Work [11485]
c/o Nikki Carol Elston, President
Georgia State University
Atlanta, GA 30302-3980
PH: (202)491-9561
Elston, Nikki Carol, President

Baptist Women in Ministry [19725]
3001 Mercer University Dr.
Atlanta, GA 30341-4115
PH: (404)513-6022
Durso, Pam, Exec. Dir.

Black Methodists for Church Renewal [20340]
653 Beckwith St. SW
Atlanta, GA 30314
PH: (470)428-2251
Fax: (470)428-3353
Dangerfield, Deborah, Chairperson

Boys and Girls Clubs of America [13430]
1275 Peachtree St. NE
Atlanta, GA 30309-3506
PH: (404)487-5700
Clark, James, President, CEO

Calorie Control Council [1319]
1100 Johnson Ferry Rd., Ste. 300
Atlanta, GA 30342
PH: (404)252-3663

CARE USA [12633]
151 Ellis St. NE
Atlanta, GA 30303-2440
PH: (404)681-2552
(202)595-2800
Toll free: 800-422-7385
Nunn, Michelle, President, CEO

Carter Center [18938]
1 Copenhill
453 Freedom Pkwy.
Atlanta, GA 30307
PH: (404)420-5100
Toll free: 800-550-3560
Fax: (404)331-0283
Hochman, Steven H., PhD, Dir. of Res.

CEO Netweavers [914]
3535 Peachtree Rd. NE, Ste. 520-231
Atlanta, GA 30326
PH: (773)914-1735
Horton, Mackie, Contact

Children's Cross Connection International [14178]
2192 Greencliff Dr.
Atlanta, GA 30345
PH: (404)358-7960
Fax: (770)234-4147
Rundle, Pamela M., CEO, President

Children's Wish Foundation International [11224]
8615 Roswell Rd.
Atlanta, GA 30350
PH: (770)393-9474
Toll free: 800-323-9474
Fax: (770)393-0683
Dozoretz, Linda, Exec. Dir., Founder

Childspring International [14184]
1328 Peachtree St. NE
Atlanta, GA 30309-3209
PH: (404)228-7770
(404)228-7744
Fussell, Alison, Exec. Dir.

Chinese-American Professors in Environmental Engineering and Science [6550]
c/o Baoxia Mi, Secretary
623 Davis Hall

Dept. of Civil and Environmental Engineering
University of California, Berkeley
Atlanta, GA 30332
PH: (510)664-7446
Zhang, Huichun, President

Clearing the Fog About Autism [13761]
3695F Cascade Rd., No. 2172
Atlanta, GA 30331
Toll free: 888-803-6046
Fax: (404)585-5687
Barry, Ms. Alethia, Chairperson

College Athletic Trainers' Society [23333]
c/o Robert Murphy, Treasurer/ Secretary
PO Box 250325
Atlanta, GA 30325
Anderson, Scott, President

Community Voices: Healthcare for the Underserved [11344]
c/o National Center for Primary Care
Morehouse School of Medicine
720 Westview Dr. SW
Atlanta, GA 30310
PH: (404)756-8914
Fax: (404)752-1198
Graves, Whitney C., Asst.

Concord Grape Association [4232]
1100 Johnson Ferry Rd., Ste. 300
Atlanta, GA 30342
PH: (404)252-3663
Fax: (404)252-0774

Construction History Society of America [802]
PO Box 93461
Atlanta, GA 30377
PH: (404)378-3779
Beard, Jeffrey, Chairperson

Consumer Credit Industry Association [1851]
6300 Powers Ferry Rd., Ste. 600-286
Atlanta, GA 30339
PH: (678)858-4001
Euwema, John, VP

CoreNet Global [2854]
133 Peachtree St. NE, Ste. 3000
Atlanta, GA 30303-1815
PH: (404)589-3200
Toll free: 800-726-8111
Fax: (404)589-3201
Davis, John, Controller

Council on Occupational Education [7757]
Bldg. 300, Ste. 325
7840 Roswell Rd.
Atlanta, GA 30350
PH: (770)396-3898
Toll free: 800-917-2081
Fax: (770)396-3790
Puckett, Gary, Exec. Dir., President

Council of State and Territorial Epidemiologists [14729]
2872 Woodcock Blvd., Ste. 250
Atlanta, GA 30341
PH: (770)458-3811
Fax: (770)458-8516
DeMaria, Alfred, VP

Daisy Alliance [18780]
990 Hammond Dr., Ste. 830
Atlanta, GA 30328
PH: (770)261-4274
Fax: (770)804-5631
Roth, Bruce, Exec. Dir., Founder

Dian Fossey Gorilla Fund International [4807]
800 Cherokee Ave. SE
Atlanta, GA 30315

PH: (404)624-5881
Toll free: 800-851-0203
Stoinski, Tara, PhD, President, CEO

Early Music Network Inc. **[9903]**
PO Box 854
Atlanta, GA 30301-0854
PH: (770)638-7574
Gosta, Predrag, PGCE, Founder,
President

Educational Center for Applied Ekis-
tics **[9581]**
1900 DeKalb Ave. NE
Atlanta, GA 30307
PH: (404)378-2219
Fax: (404)378-8946

Environmental Bankers Association
[395]
Bldg. 14, Ste. 100
1827 Powers Ferry Rd.
Atlanta, GA 30339
PH: (678)619-5045
Fax: (678)229-2777
Lambert, David, Treasurer

Evidence Photographers
International Council **[5244]**
229 Peachtree St. NE, No. 2200
Atlanta, GA 30303
Toll free: 866-868-3742
Fax: (404)614-6406
White, Claire, Director

Fellowship of Companies for Christ
International **[19979]**
4201 N Peachtree Rd., Ste. 200
Atlanta, GA 30341
PH: (770)685-6000
Fax: (770)685-6001
Mitchell, Bobby, Chmn. of the Bd.,
Founder

Forest Landowners Association
[4200]
900 Circle 75 Pky., Ste. 205
Atlanta, GA 30339
PH: (404)325-2954
Toll free: 800-325-2954
Fax: (404)325-2955
Hopkins, Joe, President

Foundation for Economic Education
[18955]
1718 Peachtree Rd. NE, Ste. 300
Atlanta, GA 30309
PH: (404)554-9980
Toll free: 800-960-4333
Fax: (404)393-3142
Ream, Roger, Chairman

Friendship Force International
[18542]
127 Peachtree St., Ste. 501
Atlanta, GA 30303
PH: (404)522-9490
Snook, Jeremi, President, CEO

Global Health Action **[15453]**
1190 W Druid Hills, Ste. 145
Atlanta, GA 30329
PH: (404)634-5748
Fax: (404)634-9685
Davis, Robin C., RN, Officer

Golden Key International Honour
Society **[23781]**
1040 Crown Pointe Pky., Ste. 900
Atlanta, GA 30338
PH: (678)689-2200
Toll free: 800-377-2401
Fax: (678)689-2297
Rainey, Brad, Exec. Dir.

Green Meeting Industry Council
[2330]
Bldg. 14, Ste. 100
1827 Powers Ferry Rd.

Atlanta, GA 30339
PH: (571)527-3116
Nardone, Natalie, CMP, Exec. Dir.

Green Spa Network **[2907]**
PO Box 15428
Atlanta, GA 30333
Toll free: 800-275-3045
Stusser, Michael, Bd. Member

HandsOn Network **[13296]**
600 Means St., Ste. 210
Atlanta, GA 30318
PH: (404)979-2900
Fax: (404)979-2901
Smith, Amy, President

Helping Our Teen Girls in Real Life
Situations **[11028]**
3645 Marketplace Blvd., Ste. 130-
190
Atlanta, GA 30344
Stokes, Carla, PhD, CEO, Founder

IHG Owners Association **[1662]**
3 Ravinia Dr., Ste. 100
Atlanta, GA 30346
PH: (770)604-5555
Fax: (770)604-5684
Berg, Don, CEO

Indoor Air Quality Association **[4550]**
1791 Tullie Cir. NE
Atlanta, GA 30329
Toll free: 844-802-4103
Sears, Stephanie, Exec. Dir.

Institute of Nuclear Power Operations **[6929]**
700 Galleria Pky. SE, Ste. 100
Atlanta, GA 30339-5943

Institute for Professionals in Taxation
[5793]
600 Northpark Town Ctr.
1200 Abernathy Rd., Ste. L-2
Atlanta, GA 30328-1040
PH: (404)240-2300
Fax: (404)240-2315
Wilson, Margaret C., President

International Association of Insur-
ance Professionals **[1874]**
Bldg. 5, Ste. 300
3525 Piedmont Rd.
Atlanta, GA 30305
PH: (404)789-3153
Toll free: 800-766-6249
Fax: (404)240-0998
McColloch, John C., Dir. of Member
Svcs.

International Association of Larynge-
ctomees **[11605]**
925B Peachtree St. NE, Ste. 316
Atlanta, GA 30309
Toll free: 866-425-3678
Herbst, Bob, President

International Association for Music &
Medicine **[16976]**
c/o Dr. Fred Schwartz, Treasurer
314 Woodward Way NW
Atlanta, GA 30305-4039
Edwards, Jane, PhD, President

International Association of National
Public Health Institutes **[17005]**
Emory University
Global Health Institute
1599 Clifton Rd. NE
Atlanta, GA 30322
PH: (404)727-1416
Koplan, Jeffrey P., President

International Atlantic Economic
Society **[6392]**
229 Peachtree St. NE, Ste. 650
Atlanta, GA 30303

PH: (404)965-1555
Fax: (404)965-1556
Mokyr, Joel, President

International Coalition of Library
Consortia **[9710]**
1438 W Peachtree St. NW, Ste. 200
Atlanta, GA 30309
PH: (404)892-0943
Sanville, Tom, Contact

International Flight Services Associa-
tion **[1389]**
1100 Johnson Ferry Rd., Ste. 300
Atlanta, GA 30342
PH: (678)298-1187
Fax: (404)591-6811
McLendon, Kelly, Program Mgr.

International Food Additives Council
[1341]
1100 Johnson Ferry Rd., Ste. 300
Atlanta, GA 30342-1733
PH: (404)252-3663
Rogers, Judy, Contact

International Janitorial Cleaning
Services Association **[2131]**
34 Peachtree St. NW, Ste. 2200
Atlanta, GA 30303
PH: (678)653-5065

International Jelly and Preserve As-
sociation **[1345]**
5775 Peachtree-Dunwoody Rd., Ste.
500-G
Atlanta, GA 30342
PH: (404)252-3663
Fax: (404)252-0774
Chumley, Pamela A, Exec. Dir.

International League of Associations
for Rheumatology **[17159]**
c/o Mark Andrejeski, Secretary
2200 Lake Blvd. NE
Atlanta, GA 30319
Andrejeski, Mark, Secretary

International Practice Management
Association **[5430]**
Bldg. 5, Ste. 300
3525 Piedmont Rd. NE
Atlanta, GA 30305
PH: (404)467-6757
Bibb, Marcia M., President

International Society for Restorative
Neurology **[16027]**
2020 Peachtree Rd. NW
Atlanta, GA 30309
Tang, Simon F.T., MD, President

International Spenser Society **[9058]**
Dept. of English
Emory University
Callaway Ste. N302
537 Kilgo Cir.
Atlanta, GA 30322
Grogan, Jane, President

JumpStart International **[11391]**
112 Krog St., Ste. 17
Atlanta, GA 30307
PH: (678)383-9618
Latimer, Megan, Exec. Dir.

Kappa Theta Epsilon Sorority
[23767]
Atlanta, GA

KIDSCOPE **[10791]**
2045 Peachtree Rd., Ste. 150
Atlanta, GA 30309
King, H. Elizabeth, PhD, Bd.
Member

Laughing at Leukemia **[15536]**
260 Peachtree St., Ste. 2200
Atlanta, GA 30303

PH: (404)784-1839
Aliniece, Pamala Gail, Founder,
CEO

Life Insurers Council **[1881]**
6190 Powers Ferry Rd., Ste. 600
Atlanta, GA 30339-8443
PH: (770)951-1770
Kerzner, Robert A., CLU, CEO,
President

LOMA **[1883]**
6190 Powers Ferry Rd., Ste. 600
Atlanta, GA 30339
PH: (770)951-1770
     (770)984-3720
Toll free: 800-ASK-LOMA
Fax: (770)984-6422
Kerzner, Robert A., CEO, President

Lord's Day Alliance of the United
States **[20593]**
2715 Peachtree Rd. NE
Atlanta, GA 30305
PH: (404)693-5530
Petersen, Rev. Rodney L., Exec. Dir.

Manufacturers' Agents Association
for the Foodservice Industry **[1384]**
1199 Euclid Ave.
Atlanta, GA 30307
PH: (404)214-9474
Fax: (404)522-0133
Cody, Alison, Exec. Dir.

Marine Aquarium Societies of North
America **[3642]**
PO Box 105603
Atlanta, GA 30348-5603
Mougey, Rob, VP

Martin Luther King, Jr. Center for
Nonviolent Social Change **[18722]**
449 Auburn Ave. NE
Atlanta, GA 30312
PH: (404)526-8900
     (404)526-8983
King, Mr. Martin Luther, III, President

Men's Collegiate Lacrosse Associa-
tion **[22974]**
PO Box 93531
Atlanta, GA 30377
Coyne, Jac, Director

Mike's Angels **[11077]**
2090 Dunwoody Club Dr., Ste. 106-
120
Atlanta, GA 30350-5424
PH: (770)396-7858
Sheeran, Patricia Marcucci,
President

Minorities in Agriculture, Natural
Resources and Related Sciences
[3572]
1720 Peachtree Rd. NW, Ste. 776 S
Atlanta, GA 30309-2449
PH: (404)347-2975
Fax: (404)892-9405
Patterson, Koni, President

Names Project Foundation I AIDS
Memorial Quilt **[13554]**
204 14th St. NW
Atlanta, GA 30318
PH: (404)688-5500
Fax: (404)688-5552
Rhoad, Julie, Exec. Dir.

National Association of African
Americans in Human Resources
[1696]
PO Box 311395
Atlanta, GA 31131
PH: (404)346-1542
Fax: (866)571-0533
Rolack, William T., Sr., CEO

National Association of Chronic
  Disease Directors **[14597]**
2200 Century Pky., Ste. 250
Atlanta, GA 30345
PH: (770)458-7400
Robitscher, John W., CEO

National Association of Judiciary
  Interpreters and Translators **[5119]**
2002 Summit Blvd., Ste. 300
Atlanta, GA 30319
PH: (404)566-4705
Fax: (404)566-2301
De La Cruz, Jennifer, Treasurer

National Association State Agencies
  for Surplus Property **[5687]**
c/o Steve Ekin, President
200 Piedmont Ave. SE, Ste. 1802 W
Atlanta, GA 30334-9030
PH: (405)657-8544
Pepperman, Scott E., Exec. Dir.

National Basketball Athletic Trainers
  Association **[22575]**
c/o Rollin Mallernee
400 Colony Sq. NE, Ste. 1750
Atlanta, GA 30361
Mallernee, Rollin, Gen. Counsel

National Black Coalition of Federal
  Aviation Employees **[5061]**
PO Box 87216
Atlanta, GA 30337
Bradley, Paquita, Officer

National Black Herstory Task Force
  [10307]
PO Box 55021
Atlanta, GA 30308
PH: (404)749-6994
Galloway, Mozella, Founder,
  President

National Conference of State Social
  Security Administrators **[5759]**
61 Forsyth St. SW, Ste. 22T64
Atlanta, GA 30303
PH: (404)562-1315
Fax: (404)562-1313
Motza, Maryann, President

National Families in Action **[13169]**
PO Box 133136
Atlanta, GA 30333-3136
PH: (404)248-9676
Rusche, Sue, CEO, President

National Pecan Shellers Association
  [4511]
1100 Johnson Ferry Rd., Ste. 300
Atlanta, GA 30342
PH: (678)298-1189

National Physical Activity Society
  [16709]
1100 Peachtree St., Ste. 200
Atlanta, GA 30309
PH: (404)692-5396
Eidson, Pam, MEd, Exec. Dir.

National Property Management As-
  sociation **[2749]**
Bldg. 5, Ste. 300
3525 Piedmont Rd.
Atlanta, GA 30305
PH: (404)477-5811
Fax: (404)240-0998

National Society of High School
  Scholars **[8519]**
1936 N Druid Hills Rd.
Atlanta, GA 30319
PH: (404)235-5500
Toll free: 866-343-1800
Nobel, Mr. Claes, Chairman

National Society of Madison Family
  Descendants **[20987]**
c/o Frederick Madison Smith,
  President

1180 Peachtree St., Ste. 1700
Atlanta, GA 30309-7525
PH: (404)572-4714
Smith, Frederick Madison, President

North American Electric Reliability
  Corporation **[1032]**
North Twr., Ste. 600
3353 Peachtree Rd. NE
Atlanta, GA 30326
PH: (404)446-2560
Fax: (404)446-2595
Cauley, Gerry W., CEO, President

North American Football League
  [22863]
5775 Glenridge Dr. NE
Atlanta, GA 30328
Williams, Robin, Commissioner

The Office of Black Women in
  Church and Society **[20645]**
700 Martin Luther King Jr. Dr.
Atlanta, GA 30314
PH: (404)527-5710
Fax: (404)525-5715
Grant, Jacquelyn, PhD, Director,
  Founder

One Body Village **[11104]**
PO Box 162933
Atlanta, GA 30321
PH: (706)825-3032
Ba Thong, Martino Nguyen, Founder

One Hundred Days **[14958]**
PO Box 29715
Atlanta, GA 30359
Sasser, Scott, President, Founder

Oracle Applications Users Group
  [6284]
Bldg. 5, Ste. 300
3525 Piedmont Rd. NE
Atlanta, GA 30305-1509
PH: (404)240-0897
Fax: (404)240-0998
Hughes, Steven R., Exec. Dir.

Oral History Association **[9502]**
c/o Gayle Knight, Program Associate
Dept. of History
Georgia State University
Atlanta, GA 30302-4117
PH: (404)413-5751
Fax: (404)413-6384
Valk, Anne M., President

Organization for Safety, Asepsis and
  Prevention **[14468]**
Bldg. 5, Ste. 300
3525 Piedmont Rd.
Atlanta, GA 30305
PH: (410)571-0003
Toll free: 800-298-6727
Fax: (404)264-1956
Long, Therese M., MBA, Exec. Dir.

Osteoarthritis Action Alliance **[17162]**
PO Box 7669
Atlanta, GA 30357-0669
PH: (202)887-2916
Jordan, Heather, Contact

Pediatric Brain Tumor Foundation -
  Georgia **[14210]**
6065 Roswell Rd. NE, Ste. 505
Atlanta, GA 30328
PH: (404)252-4107
Fax: (404)252-4108
Bates, Tammy, Liaison

Professional Baseball Athletic Trainers Society **[22566]**
400 Colony Sq., Ste. 1750
1201 Peachtree St.
Atlanta, GA 30361
O'Neal, Mark, President

Project South: Institute for the
  Elimination of Poverty and
  Genocide **[18527]**
9 Gammon Ave. SE
Atlanta, GA 30315-2773
Fax: (404)622-4137

Red Nose Response **[12074]**
2660 Peachtree Rd., Ste. 25F
Atlanta, GA 30305
Kleinberger, Paul, President

Renewable Bioproducts Institute
  [6978]
500 10th St. NW
Atlanta, GA 30332-0620
PH: (404)894-5700
Fax: (404)894-4778
Hakovirta, Marko, Assoc. Dir.

Research Chefs Association **[964]**
1100 Johnson Ferry Rd., Ste. 300
Atlanta, GA 30342
PH: (678)298-1178
Bohle, Suzanne, Exec. Dir.

Safe States Alliance **[19082]**
2200 Century Pkwy., Ste. 700
Atlanta, GA 30345
PH: (770)690-9000
Fax: (770)690-8996
Williams, Amber, Exec. Dir.

Sales Management Association
  [3018]
1440 Dutch Valley Pl. NE, Ste. 990
Atlanta, GA 30324
PH: (404)963-7992
Kelly, Robert J., Chairman

Scattering Resources **[12726]**
PO Box 725215
Atlanta, GA 31139
PH: (678)729-7228

ServeHAITI **[11432]**
999 Peachtree St. NE, Ste. 2300
Atlanta, GA 30309
PH: (404)407-5023
Book, Dr. Wayne J., Chairman

Sober Living America **[13183]**
2530 Peachwood Cir.
Atlanta, GA 30345
Toll free: 877-430-0086
Fax: (404)639-9887
Devarennes, Jim, Founder,
  President

Soccer in the Streets **[11439]**
236 Auburn Ave., Ste. 207
Atlanta, GA 30303
Toll free: 888-436-5833
Robbins, Jill, COO

Society of Biblical Literature **[19765]**
Luce Ctr.
825 Houston Mill Rd.
Atlanta, GA 30329
PH: (404)727-3100
Fax: (404)727-3101
Kutsko, John, Exec. Dir.

Society of Independent Show
  Organizers **[1178]**
2700 Cumberland Pky. SE, Ste. 580
Atlanta, GA 30339
PH: (310)450-8831
Toll free: 877-937-7476
Fax: (310)450-9305
Audrain, David, Exec. Dir.

Society of International Business
  Fellows **[1972]**
Peachtree Ctr., Ste. 1410
South Twr.
225 Peachtree St. NE
Atlanta, GA 30303

PH: (404)525-7423
Fax: (404)525-5331
West, John, Chairman

Society of Jewish Ethics **[20283]**
1531 Dickey Dr.
Atlanta, GA 30322
PH: (404)712-8550
Fax: (404)727-7399
Johnson, Kristina, Program Mgr.

Society for Maintenance and Reli-
  ability Professionals **[2143]**
1100 Johnson Ferry Rd., Ste. 300
Atlanta, GA 30342
Toll free: 800-950-7354
Fax: (404)591-6811
Kazar, Bob, Chmn. of the Bd.

Southern Center for Human Rights
  [17834]
83 Poplar St. NW
Atlanta, GA 30303
PH: (404)688-1202
Fax: (404)688-9440
Bright, Stephen B., President

Southern Christian Leadership
  Conference **[17931]**
320 Auburn Ave. NE
Atlanta, GA 30303
PH: (404)522-1420
Steele, Charles, Jr., President, CEO

Southern Newspaper Publishers As-
  sociation **[2814]**
3680 N Peachtree Rd., Ste. 300
Atlanta, GA 30341
PH: (404)256-0444
Fax: (404)252-9135
VanHorn, Edward, Exec. Dir.

Southface Energy Institute **[6513]**
241 Pine St. NE
Atlanta, GA 30308
PH: (404)872-3549
Fax: (404)872-5009
Creech, Dennis, Exec. Dir.

StandUp for Kids **[11157]**
83 Walton St. NW, Ste. 500
Atlanta, GA 30303
Toll free: 800-365-4KID
Fax: (404)954-6610
Meuter, Jeffrey, Treasurer

Struggling Kids **[13117]**
227 Sandy Springs Pl., Ste.
  G-28416
Atlanta, GA 30358
PH: (770)953-0437
Stillwagon, Gary B., MD, CEO,
  President

Student Photographic Society
  [10146]
229 Peachtree St. NE, Ste. 2200
Atlanta, GA 30303
Toll free: 888-722-1334

TheConference of Black Mayors
  [5646]
200 Peachtree St., Ste. 206
Atlanta, GA 30303
PH: (404)931-2059

Tree Climbers International **[21598]**
PO Box 5588
Atlanta, GA 31107
PH: (404)377-3150
  (404)458-4303
Jenkins, Peter, Founder

Turner Foundation, Inc. **[4107]**
133 Luckie St. NW, 2nd Fl.
Atlanta, GA 30303
PH: (404)681-9900
Fax: (404)681-0172
Finley, Michael, President, Treasurer

Union Internationale de la Marion-
nette **[22395]**
1404 Spring St. NW
Atlanta, GA 30309
PH: (404)881-5110
Fax: (404)873-9907
Morán, Manuel, President

UniPro Foodservice **[1377]**
2500 Cumberland Pky. SE, Ste. 600
Atlanta, GA 30339
PH: (770)952-0871
Stewart, Bob, CEO

US Human Rights Network **[18450]**
250 Georgia Ave. SE, Ste. 330
Atlanta, GA 30312
PH: (404)588-9761
Fax: (404)588-9763
Dike, Ejim, Exec. Dir.

Village Empowerment **[11457]**
PO Box 720004
Atlanta, GA 30358
PH: (404)290-1354
Smith, Don, Founder, Director

Vinegar Institute **[1380]**
1100 Johnson Ferry Rd. NE, Ste.
300
Atlanta, GA 30342
PH: (404)252-3663
Fax: (404)252-0774

Women's Entrepreneurial Op-
portunity Project, Inc. **[19248]**
250 Georgia Ave., Ste. 213
Atlanta, GA 30312
PH: (404)681-2497
Fax: (404)681-2499
Ball, Antionette, CEO, Founder

World Alliance for Retail Excellence
& Standards **[2981]**
1100 Johnson Ferry Rd. NE
Atlanta, GA 30342
PH: (678)303-2959
Fax: (404)591-6811
Donzelli, Steve, Chairman

World Chamber of Commerce
[23641]
2870 Peachtree Rd., No. 435
Atlanta, GA 30305
Toll free: 800-590-9227
Warner, Solange, Founder, Co-
Chmn. of the Bd.

World Water Relief **[13352]**
931 Monroe Dr., Ste. 102-593
Atlanta, GA 30308
PH: (678)661-9982
Fax: (770)993-9770
Fusell, Kevin, MD, President

National Barrel Horse Association
[22922]
725 Broad St.
Augusta, GA 30901
PH: (706)722-7223
Fulmer, Sherry, Exec. Dir.

Construction Owners Association of
America **[516]**
5000 Austell Powder Springs Rd.,
Ste. 217
Austell, GA 30106
PH: (770)433-0820
Toll free: 800-994-2622
Fax: (404)577-3551
McCormick, Dean, President

Break Away: The Alternative Break
Connection **[12575]**
112 N Avodale Rd., Ste. 280
Avondale Estates, GA 30002
PH: (404)919-7482
Giacobozzi, Samantha, Exec. Dir.

Women Watch Afrika **[19247]**
PO Box 208
Avondale Estates, GA 30002
PH: (404)759-6419
Fax: (404)300-3505
Kilanko, Glory, Director, Founder,
CEO

Youth Media Minds of America
[8680]
206 N Clarendon Ave.
Avondale Estates, GA 30002
PH: (404)292-1265
(404)848-5000
Gipson, Roy, CEO, Founder

National Investment Banking As-
sociation **[413]**
422 Chesterfield Rd.
Bogart, GA 30622
PH: (706)208-9620
Fax: (706)993-3342
Foshee, Emily, Exec. Dir.

American Junior Golf Association
[22873]
1980 Sports Club Dr.
Braselton, GA 30517
PH: (770)868-4200
Toll free: 877-373-2542
Fax: (770)868-4211
Hamblin, Stephen A., Exec. Dir.

American Vision **[19943]**
PO Box 611
Braselton, GA 30517
PH: (770)222-7266
Toll free: 800-628-9460
Fax: (770)222-7269
DeMar, Dr. Gary, Sr. Partner

Society for the Preservation of
English Language and Literature
[7870]
PO Box 321
Braselton, GA 30517
PH: (770)586-0184
Wallace, James, Exec. Dir.,
President

Association of Natural Health
[13607]
108 Buchanan St. N
Bremen, GA 30110
PH: (202)505-2664
Abukittah, Sam, Founder, Bd.
Member

International Association of
Undercover Officers **[5472]**
142 Banks Dr.
Brunswick, GA 31523
Toll free: 800-876-5943
Fax: (800)876-5912
Sallee, Brian, President

MAP International **[15151]**
4700 Glynco Pky.
Brunswick, GA 31525-6800
Toll free: 800-225-8550
Stirling, Steve, President, CEO

Amigos for Christ **[12387]**
1845 S Lee Ct., Ste. A
Buford, GA 30518
PH: (770)614-9250
Fax: (770)614-9850
Curling, Michael, VP

Unlocking Autism **[13782]**
Byron, GA
Toll free: 866-366-3361
Reynolds, Shelley Hendrix, Founder,
President

Association of Marine Technicians
[2238]
513 River Estates Pky.
Canton, GA 30115-3019

PH: (770)720-4324
Toll free: 800-467-0982
Fax: (770)720-4329
DeMarco, Joseph J., Exec. Dir.,
Founder, President

Southern Peanut Growers **[4514]**
1025 Sugar Pike Way
Canton, GA 30115
PH: (770)751-6615
Wagner, Leslie, Exec. Dir.

WERA Motorcycle Roadracing
[23041]
2555 Marietta Hwy., No. 104
Canton, GA 30114
PH: (770)720-5010
Fax: (770)720-5015

Bikers Battling Breast Cancer
[13901]
2035 N Hwy. 113
Carrollton, GA 30117
PH: (678)378-5653
Herman, Lisa Redding, Contact

International Society for the Study of
Pilgrimage Art **[8868]**
324 Humanities Hall
Art Dept.
University of West Georgia
Carrollton, GA 30118
PH: (770)836-4532
(740)427-5347
Fax: (770)836-4392
Tekippe, Rita, Editor

Charles S. Peirce Society **[9088]**
University of West Georgia
Philosophy Program
1601 Maple St.
Carrollton, GA 30118
Ibri, Ivo, President

Society of Professors of Education
[7800]
c/o Dr. Robert C. Morris, Secretary/
Treasurer
College of Education
University of West Georgia
1601 Maple St.
Carrollton, GA 30118-0001
PH: (678)839-6132
Morris, Robert C., Secretary,
Treasurer

Advocates for Self-Government
[18638]
405 Massachusetts Ave.
Cartersville, GA 30120-8528
PH: (770)386-8372
Toll free: 800-932-1776
Fax: (770)386-8373
Bittner, Brett, Exec. Dir.

Christian Ladies All together Stand-
ing against Social Injustice
Corporation **[13373]**
PO Box 3795
Cartersville, GA 30120
PH: (404)326-8619
Lounds-Brooks, Ashley, President,
Founder

Options for Animals International
[17658]
PO Box 3682
Cartersville, GA 30120
PH: (309)658-2920
Hroza, Robbie, VP of Operations

Utility Technology Association **[7358]**
PO Box 695
Clermont, GA 30527
PH: (770)519-1676
Powell, Suzanne, Contact

American Community Gardening Association **[22069]**
3271 Main St.
College Park, GA 30337
Toll free: 877-275-2242

United States Hapki Hae **[23018]**
4826 Old National Hwy.
College Park, GA 30337
Moreland, Master Shelton R., Director, Founder

American Association of Private
Railroad Car Owners, Inc. **[2830]**
PO Box 6307
Columbus, GA 31917-6307
PH: (706)326-6262
Black, Borden, Exec. Dir.

Army Sniper Association **[20718]**
2525 Auburn Ave.
Columbus, GA 31906
James, Adam, Secretary

Association for Conflict Resolution
[4957]
c/o Cheryl L. Jamison, J.D., Executive Director
1639 Bradley Park Dr., Ste. 500-142
Columbus, GA 31904
PH: (202)780-5999
Fax: (703)435-4390
Robinson, Donzell, President

Brent Schoening Strike Out
Leukemia Foundation **[15533]**
2525 Auburn Ave.
Columbus, GA 31906
PH: (706)536-1933
Pearson, Lauren B., President

The Carson McCullers Society
[10367]
Dept. of English
Columbus State University
4225 University Ave.
Columbus, GA 31907-5679
Kayser, Casey, President

Costume Society of America **[9189]**
PO Box 852
Columbus, GA 31902-0852
PH: (706)615-2851
Toll free: 800-CSA-9447
Campbell, Robin, President

High School Band Directors National
Association **[8370]**
4166 Will Rhodes Dr.
Columbus, GA 31909
PH: (706)568-0760
Boone, Dr. Oliver C., Founder, Exec.
Dir.

House of Heroes **[13242]**
4709 Milgen Rd.
Columbus, GA 31907
PH: (706)562-1032
Anthony, Wayne, President

Independent Automotive Damage
Appraisers Association **[225]**
PO Box 12291
Columbus, GA 31917-2291
Toll free: 800-369-IADA
Nathan, Mark, President

International Premium Cigar & Pipe
Retailers Association **[2959]**
513 Capital Ct. NE
Columbus, GA 31904-3637
PH: (202)621-8064
Cass, Craig, President

Modern Free and Accepted Masons
of the World **[19564]**
627 5th Ave.
Columbus, GA 31901
PH: (706)322-3326
Fax: (706)322-3805
Richardson, Wayne, Master

National High School Band Directors
Hall of Fame **[8386]**
4166 Will Rhoades Dr.
Columbus, GA 31909
Boone, Dr. Oliver C., Exec. Dir.

U.S. Calvary and Armor Association
[5626]
3100 Gentian Blvd., Ste. 17B
Columbus, GA 31907
PH: (706)563-5714

U.S. Cavalry & Armor Association
[5627]
3100 Gentian Blvd., Ste. 17B
Columbus, GA 31907
PH: (706)563-5714
Gavula, Mark S., Exec. Dir.

Clan Forrester Society **[20810]**
c/o Ben Forrester, Membership
Director
1034 Blue Heron Dr.
Commerce, GA 30529-4210
Forrester, Ben, Membership Chp.

Global Environmental Relief **[11661]**
PO Box 81628
Conyers, GA 30013
PH: (770)679-0942
Smith, Dr. Darrell, Exec. Dir.

International Association of Accident
Reconstruction Specialists **[5465]**
c/o Ralph Cunningham, Secretary
1804 Thornhill Pass, SE
Conyers, GA 30013-6321
PH: (770)918-0973
Cunningham, Ralph, Secretary

Miracle League Association **[22783]**
1506 Klondike Rd., Ste. 105
Conyers, GA 30094
PH: (770)760-1933
Fax: (770)483-1223
Alford, Diane, Exec. Dir.

National Alliance of Black Interpret-
ers **[3315]**
PO Box 82646
Conyers, GA 30013

National Association of Elevator
Contractors **[877]**
1298 Wellbrook Cir.
Conyers, GA 30012
PH: (770)760-9660
Toll free: 800-900-6232
Fax: (770)760-9714
Bell, Kathy, Coord., Ed. Resources

Paisley Family Society **[20912]**
c/o Martha Pasley M. Brown, USA
Commissioner
2205 Pine Knoll Cir.
Conyers, GA 30013
PH: (770)483-6949
Mone, Rev. John A., President

Tobacconists' Association of America
[3288]
PO Box 81152
Conyers, GA 30013
PH: (770)597-6264
Koebel, George, President

Association of Tourist Railroads and
Railway Museums **[2836]**
PO Box 1189
Covington, GA 30015
PH: (770)278-0088
Ray, G. Mark, President

2D Reconnaissance Battalion As-
sociation **[4970]**
PO Box 3383
Cumming, GA 30028-6520

Acoustic Neuroma Association
[16530]
600 Peachtree Pky., Ste. 108
Cumming, GA 30041-6899
PH: (770)205-8211
Toll free: 877-200-8211
Fax: (770)205-0239
Feldman, Allison, CEO

Big Smiles Big Hearts **[14422]**
PO Box 3388
Cumming, GA 30028-6520
Elliott, Jennifer, RDH, President

Montessori Institute of America
[7782]
3482 Keith Bridge Rd., No. 340
Cumming, GA 30041
Toll free: 844-642-9675
Munn, Christine, President

National Credit Union Management
Association **[957]**
1220 Crestbrook Dr.
Cumming, GA 30040
Fax: (770)406-0289

New Hope in Africa **[13356]**
PO Box 3092
Cumming, GA 30028
PH: (770)888-9269
Vanderhoff, Mike, Director

Africa Hope, Inc. **[10836]**
PO Box 127
Dacula, GA 30019
PH: (770)573-0676
Fax: (678)528-3025
Tshimanga, Felix, MD, President,
Chairman

National Clogging Organization Inc.
[9267]
2986 Mill Park Ct.
Dacula, GA 30019
PH: (678)889-4355
Fax: (603)925-0967
Phillips, David, Exec. Dir.

Antique Telescope Society **[21287]**
c/o Walter Breyer, PhD, Secretary
1878 Robinson Rd.
Dahlonega, GA 30533
Breyer, Dr. Walter H., Secretary

Association for Renaissance Martial
Arts **[22986]**
105 Gainesborough Walk
Dallas, GA 30157
Clements, John, Director

American Floorcovering Alliance
[1937]
210 W Cuyler St.
Dalton, GA 30720
PH: (706)278-4101
Toll free: 800-288-4101
Fax: (706)278-5323
Ellis, Wanda J., Exec. Dir.

Carpet and Rug Institute **[1941]**
100 S Hamilton St.
Dalton, GA 30720
PH: (706)278-3176
Fax: (706)278-8835
Kirkpatrick, Jim, Treasurer

Eller Family Association **[20861]**
c/o Edward K. Eller, Secretay/
Treasurer
3009 E Walnut Ave.
Dalton, GA 30721
Liggett, Lauren, President

National Association of Personnel
Services **[1097]**
78 Dawson Village Way, Ste. 410-
201
Dawsonville, GA 30534
PH: (706)531-0060
Fax: (866)739-4750
Carlson, Mark, Chairman

Tree Climber's Coalition **[21597]**
6625 Highway 53 E, Ste. 410
Dawsonville, GA 30534
PH: (706)216-1679
(706)216-2402

Asperger Spirit **[15904]**
PO Box 360207
Decatur, GA 30036
PH: (404)626-2403
Richardson-Atubeh, Carolyn, Exec.
Dir., Founder

Association for Clinical Pastoral
Education **[20073]**
1 W Court Sq., Ste. 325
Decatur, GA 30030-2576
PH: (404)320-1472
Fax: (404)320-0849
Johnson, David C, President

Association of Presbyterian Colleges
and Universities **[20520]**
Agnes Scott College
141 E College Ave.
Decatur, GA 30030
PH: (470)443-1948
Arnold, Jeffrey, Exec. Dir.

Children Without Worms **[14176]**
c/o The Task Force for Global Health
325 Swanton Way
Decatur, GA 30030
PH: (404)371-0466
Addiss, David, MD, Director

Christian Lesbians Out **[19961]**
3653-F Flakes Mill Rd., No. 306
Decatur, GA 30034-5255
MacDonald, Shawn, Coord.

International Trachoma Initiative
[17716]
325 Swanton Way
Decatur, GA 30030
PH: (404)371-0466
Toll free: 800-765-7173
Fax: (404)371-1087
Haddad, Danny, MD, Director

MedShare International **[12292]**
3240 Clifton Springs Rd.
Decatur, GA 30034-4608
PH: (770)323-5858
Fax: (770)323-4301
Redding, Charles, President, CEO

Men Stopping Violence **[18723]**
2785 Lawrenceville Hwy., Ste. 112
Decatur, GA 30033
PH: (404)270-9894
Toll free: 866-717-9317
Fax: (404)270-9895
Douglas, Ulester, Exec. Dir.

National Pan-Hellenic Council
[23761]
3951 Snapfinger Pky., Ste. 218
Decatur, GA 30035
PH: (404)942-3257
Fax: (404)806-9943
Jones, Jennifer M., President

Omega Psi Phi Fraternity **[23909]**
3951 Snapfinger Pky.
Decatur, GA 30035
PH: (404)284-5533
Fax: (404)284-0333
Barnes, Kenneth, Exec. Dir.

Ray of Hope **[13197]**
2778 Snapfinger Rd.
Decatur, GA 30034
PH: (770)696-5100
Fax: (770)696-5111
Hale, Dr. Cynthia L., Pastor

Refugee Women's Network **[13396]**
1431-A McLendon Dr., Ste. A
Decatur, GA 30033
PH: (404)437-7767
Fax: (404)806-1440
Luttrell, Barbara Ann, President

Society for the Analysis of African-
American Public Health Issues
[17021]
PO Box 360350
Decatur, GA 30036
Amutah, Dr. Ndidi, President

Task Force for Global Health
[12302]
325 Swanton Way
Decatur, GA 30030
PH: (404)371-0466
Toll free: 800-765-7173
Fax: (404)371-1087
Rosenberg, Mark L., MD, CEO,
President

Voices for Vaccines **[14217]**
325 Swanton Way
Decatur, GA 30030
Ernst, Karen, Administrator

Welcoming America **[18469]**
PO Box 2554
Decatur, GA 30031
PH: (404)631-6593
Lubell, David, Exec. Dir.

Women's College Coalition **[8761]**
PO Box 3983
Decatur, GA 30031
PH: (404)913-9492
Gangone, Lynn, Director

World Crafts Council North America
[9191]
c/o Cindy Bowden, President
1246 Fork Creek Trl.
Decatur, GA 30033
PH: (404)213-1864
Bowden, Cindy, President

Golden Threads **[21737]**
PO Box 1688
Demorest, GA 30535-1688

Red Devon USA **[3753]**
c/o Sarah Wilkerson, Administrative
Secretary
2983 US Hwy. 84
Dixie, GA 31629
PH: (229)516-0394
Colucci, Paul, Treasurer

Clan Douglas Society of North
America **[20807]**
4115 Bent Oak Ct.
Douglasville, GA 30135-3658
Peterson, Mark A., President

INTERTEL **[9344]**
c/o Linda Woodhead, Acting
Secretary
PO Box 5518
Douglasville, GA 30154
PH: (678)426-8379
Keay, Lou Carter, President

National Association of State Boards
of Geology **[6681]**
PO Box 5219
Douglasville, GA 30154
PH: (678)713-1251
Fax: (678)839-4071
Weiland, Eric, Treasurer

Accreditation Review Commission
on Education for the Physician As-
sistant **[16720]**
12000 Findley Rd., Ste. 150
Duluth, GA 30097
PH: (770)476-1224
Fax: (770)476-1738
McCarty, John E., Exec. Dir.

African Business Alliance **[1974]**
5805 State Bridge Rd., Ste. G255
Duluth, GA 30097

PH: (770)409-8780
Fax: (678)605-0271

American Association of Veterinary
Parasitologists [17605]
c/o Doug Carithers, Secretary-
Treasurer
Merial Limited
3239 Satellite Blvd.
Duluth, GA 30096
PH: (678)638-3837
Carithers, Doug, Secretary,
Treasurer

Human Development Resource
Council [12771]
655 Sugarloaf Pky., Ste. 307
Duluth, GA 30097-4934
PH: (770)513-0060

Kenyan Americans Community
Organization, Inc. [10489]
PO Box 1701
Duluth, GA 30096
PH: (404)219-2098
Mutunga, Charles, Chairman

PrimeGlobal [55]
Bldg. 400, Ste. 300
3235 Satellite Blvd.
Duluth, GA 30096
PH: (678)417-7730
Fax: (678)999-3959
Mead, Kevin, CEO, President

Workplace Benefits Association
[1078]
1770 Breckenridge Pky., Ste. 500
Duluth, GA 30096
PH: (770)381-2511
Toll free: 800-221-1809
Fax: (770)935-9484
Podgurski, Walt, CLU, Publisher

International Society of Travel
Medicine [15731]
1200 Ashwood Pky., Ste. 310
Dunwoody, GA 30338-4767
PH: (404)373-8282
Fax: (404)373-8283
Wilder-Smith, Annelies, President

Federation of Southern Cooperatives
[12801]
2769 Church St.
East Point, GA 30344-3258
PH: (404)765-0991
Fax: (404)765-9178
Blakely, Shirley Williams,
Chairperson

Uncle Remus Museum [9107]
Turner Pk., Highway 441
Eatonton, GA 31024
PH: (706)485-6856

Elberton Granite Association [3183]
1 Granite Plz.
Elberton, GA 30635
PH: (706)283-2551
Fax: (706)283-6380
Pruitt, Matthew, Contact

United States and Canadian
Academy of Pathology [16596]
404 Town Park Blvd., Ste. 201
Evans, GA 30809
PH: (706)733-7550
Fax: (706)733-8033
Adsay, N. Volkan, MD, President

Fellowship of Christian Airline
Personnel [20140]
136 Providence Rd.
Fayetteville, GA 30215
PH: (770)461-9320
Curtas, Paul M., Director

Railway Tie Association [2843]
115 Commerce Dr., Ste. C
Fayetteville, GA 30214-7335

PH: (770)460-5553
Fax: (770)460-5573
Gauntt, Jim, Exec. Dir.

Tree Climbing USA [21599]
PO Box 142062
Fayetteville, GA 30214
PH: (770)487-6929
Winters, Abe, Contact

Childbirth and Postpartum Profes-
sional Association [14224]
PO Box 547
Flowery Branch, GA 30542
PH: (770)965-9777
Toll free: 888-688-5241
Peters, Tracy Wilson, CEO

U.S. Army Ranger Association
[20727]
PO Box 52126
Fort Benning, GA 31995-2126
PH: (608)561-1779
West, Travis, President

American Camellia Society [22068]
Massee Lane Gardens
100 Massee Ln.
Fort Valley, GA 31030
PH: (478)967-2358
Toll free: 877-422-6355
Fax: (478)967-2083
Richard, Celeste, Exec. Dir.

Independent Textile Rental Associa-
tion [3260]
202 Commerce St.
Hogansville, GA 30230-1120
PH: (706)637-6552
    (706)637-8875
Evans, Ron, Exec. Dir.

American Bandmasters Association
[9851]
c/o Thomas V. Fraschillo, Secretary-
Treasurer
11738 Big Canoe
209 Cherokee Trl.
Jasper, GA 30143
Rhea, Dr. Timothy, President

Clan Fergusson Society of North
America [20809]
c/o Billy J. Ferguson, President
192 Hawthorne Hill Rd.
Jasper, GA 30143
Ferguson, Billy J., President

International Society of Mine Safety
Professionals [16325]
PO Box 772
Jasper, GA 30143
PH: (706)253-3675

Society of Typographic Aficionados
[1549]
PO Box 457
Jefferson, GA 30549
Summerour, Neil, Chairman

National Commission on Certification
of Physician Assistants [16723]
12000 Findley Rd., Ste. 100
Johns Creek, GA 30097
PH: (678)417-8100
Fax: (678)417-8135
Woodmansee, Denni J., Chairman

The Tube Council [2485]
114 S Tamie Cir.
Kathleen, GA 31047
Hoard, Michael G., President

Africa America Crisis Assistance
Network [12608]
PO Box 440151
Kennesaw, GA 30160
PH: (678)467-7202
Fax: (770)529-5026

Archery Shooters Association
[22499]
PO Box 399
Kennesaw, GA 30156-0399
PH: (770)795-0232
Fax: (770)795-0953
Falks, Laval D., Director

Center Helping Obesity in Children
End Successfully [16251]
1275 Shiloh Rd., Ste. 2660
Kennesaw, GA 30144
PH: (678)819-3663
Fax: (770)850-1236
Keyes, Vanetta S., Exec. Dir.,
President, Founder

Clan Keith Society [20816]
c/o Dorothy G. Keith, Treasurer
1256 Tinderbox Ln. NW
Kennesaw, GA 30144-3038
PH: (404)539-5222
Taylor, Paul, VP

Georgia Writers Association [10372]
440 Bartow Ave.
Kennesaw, GA 30144
Walters, Dr. Margaret, Exec. Dir.

National Franchisee Association
[1463]
1701 Barrett Lakes Blvd. NW, Ste.
180
Kennesaw, GA 30144
PH: (678)797-5160
Fax: (678)797-5170
Reynolds, Jeff, CMCA, AMS, Comm.
Chm.

Southern Society for Philosophy and
Psychology [10133]
c/o Lauren A. Taglialatela, Treasurer
Dept. of Psychology
Kennesaw State University
1000 Chastain Rd. NW
Kennesaw, GA 30144-5588
Kind, Amy, Co-Pres.

Brotherhood of Working Farriers As-
sociation [1179]
14013 E Highway 136
La Fayette, GA 30728-5660
PH: (706)397-8047
Fax: (706)397-8047
Casey, Ralph, Exec. Dir.

American Association of Clinical
Anatomists [13688]
c/o Caitlin Hyatt, Executive Director
PO Box 2945
LaGrange, GA 30241-0061
PH: (706)298-0287
Fax: (706)883-8215
Norton, Neil S., Ph.D., President

Direct Gardening Association [2952]
PO Box 429
Lagrange, GA 30241-0008
PH: (706)298-0022
Toll free: 888-820-6646
Fax: (706)883-8215
Zuckermandel, Mike, Officer

Human Anatomy and Physiology
Society [13689]
251 SL White Blvd.
LaGrange, GA 30241-9417
PH: (706)845-8204
Toll free: 800-448-4277
Fax: (706)883-8215
Ott, Betsy, President

Resilient Floor Covering Institute
[574]
115 Broad St., Ste. 201
LaGrange, GA 30240-2757
PH: (706)882-3833
Fax: (706)882-3880
Thompson, Dean, President

Personal Ponies Ltd. [11631]
c/o Cindy Pullen, National Director
368 River Rd.
Lakeland, GA 31635
PH: (229)503-9964
Chasin, Denise, Director

Administrative Personnel Association
of the Presbyterian Church (U.S.
A.) [20015]
c/o Rose Miller, Treasurer
First Presbyterian Church
PO Box 765
Lawrenceville, GA 30046
PH: (770)963-9498
Miller, Rose, Treasurer

Adoption Information Services
[10439]
1840 Old Nocross Rd., Ste. 400
Lawrenceville, GA 30044
PH: (770)339-7236
Fax: (770)456-5961
Barker, Marcia S., Exec. Dir.,
Founder

Allinial Global [7]
1745 N Brown Rd., Ste. 350
Lawrenceville, GA 30043
PH: (770)279-4560
Fax: (770)279-4566
Snyder, Terry, President, CEO

American Academy of Sanitarians,
Inc. [17176]
c/o Gary Noonan, Executive
Secretary/Treasurer
1568 LeGrand Cir.
Lawrenceville, GA 30043-8191
PH: (678)518-4028
Noonan, Gary, Exec. Sec., Treasurer

Biblical Ministries Worldwide [20128]
1595 Herrington Rd.
Lawrenceville, GA 30043
PH: (770)339-3500
Fax: (770)513-1254
Grubbs, Richard, President

Clan Anderson Society [20796]
360 Silver Creek Run
Lawrenceville, GA 30044-4800
Anderson, Jim, Treasurer

Clan MacKay Society [20822]
c/o Doug McCoy, President
1898 Prince Dr.
Lawrenceville, GA 30043
PH: (972)424-3304
McCoy, Doug, President

Committee for Missing Children
[12356]
934 Stone Mill Run
Lawrenceville, GA 30046
PH: (678)376-6265
Toll free: 800-525-8204
Fax: (678)376-6268
Thelen, David C., CEO, Founder

Mission to the World [20523]
1600 N Brown Rd.
Lawrenceville, GA 30043-8141
PH: (678)823-0004
Toll free: 866-373-6133
Fax: (678)823-0027

National Association of Asian
American Professionals [9029]
4850 Sugarloaf Pky., Ste. 209-289
Lawrenceville, GA 30044
PH: (404)409-2471
De Rozario, Fabian, President, CEO

National Association of Volunteer
Programs in Local Government
[13303]
c/o Kay Sibetta, President
75 Langley Dr.

Lawrenceville, GA 30046
Price, Yolanda

National Ornamental & Miscellaneous Metals Association **[2363]**
PO Box 492167
Lawrenceville, GA 30049
Toll free: 888-516-8585
Fax: (888)279-7994
Moseley, Allyn, President

Rotarian Action Group for Population and Development **[12520]**
344 W Pike St.
Lawrenceville, GA 30046
PH: (770)407-5633
Fax: (770)822-9492
Brueggemann, Ingar, Chairman

Ford Owners' Association **[21384]**
3875 Thornhill Dr.
Lilburn, GA 30047
Gardner, Tim, Chmn. of the Bd.

International Sand Collectors Society **[21677]**
PO Box 1786
Lilburn, GA 30048-1786
Hopen, Thomas, Advisor

Lewy Body Dementia Association, Inc. **[15951]**
912 Killian Hill Rd. SW
Lilburn, GA 30047-3110
PH: (404)935-6444
Toll free: 800-539-9767
Fax: (480)422-5434
Wall, Mark, VP

North American Registry of Midwives **[14239]**
5257 Rosestone Dr.
Lilburn, GA 30047
PH: (770)381-9051
Toll free: 888-842-4784
Pulley, Debbie, Secretary

Society for the Education of Pharmacy Technicians **[16687]**
PO Box 1176
Lyons, GA 30436
Toll free: 800-811-7214
Fax: (800)811-7214
Davis, Karen, CPhT, President

Global Civic Preservation **[12154]**
PO Box 1820
Mableton, GA 30126
PH: (770)217-0717
Toll free: 800-206-8224
Fax: (404)393-9675

Alpha Lambda Delta **[23750]**
328 Orange St.
Macon, GA 31201
Toll free: 800-9AL-7491
Fax: (478)744-9924
Merberg, Eileen, Exec. Dir.

Baptist History and Heritage Society **[19722]**
c/o Jackie Riley, Office Manager
151 Broadleaf Dr.
Macon, GA 31210
PH: (406)600-7433
Weaver, Doug, VP

China Clay Producers Association **[2386]**
113 Arkwright Landing
Macon, GA 31210
PH: (478)757-1211
Fax: (478)757-1949
Lemke, Lee, Exec. VP

International Association of Ministers Wives and Ministers Widows **[20064]**
105 River Knoll
Macon, GA 31211

PH: (478)743-5126
Fax: (478)745-5504
Glover, Dr. Beverly W., President

National Alpha Lambda Delta **[23784]**
328 Orange St.
Macon, GA 31201
Toll free: 800-925-7421
Earwood, Dr. Glenda, Exec. Dir.

National Criminal Defense College **[5151]**
Mercer Law School
343 Orange St.
Macon, GA 31207
PH: (478)746-4151
Flanigan, Rosie, Exec. Dir.

Pilot International Founders Fund **[12904]**
102 Preston Ct.
Macon, GA 31210-5768
PH: (478)477-1208
Fax: (478)477-6978
Davidson, Peggy, Exec. Dir.

Society for Community Research and Action **[7071]**
PO Box 6560
Macon, GA 31208
PH: (770)545-6448
Moritsugu, John, President

Wingfield Family Society **[20943]**
c/o John D. Wingfield
5300 Zebulon Rd., Unit 32
Macon, GA 31210
PH: (478)957-5974
Wingfield, John D., President

American Association of Rehabilitation Veterinarians **[17599]**
1230 Johnson Ferry Rd.
Marietta, GA 30068
PH: (678)803-2626
Orenbuch, Dr. Evelyn, President

American Salvage Pool Association **[277]**
2900 Delk Rd., Ste. 700
Marietta, GA 30067
PH: (678)560-6678
Fax: (678)229-2777
Vannuccini, Robert, President

Association for Aviation Psychology **[5859]**
PO Box 671393
Marietta, GA 30066
Beringer, Dennis, President, Exec. Sec., Treasurer

Association for Catholic Chiropractors **[14255]**
2049 Kolb Ridge Ct. SW
Marietta, GA 30008

Baptist Communicators Association **[19721]**
c/o Margaret Colson, Executive Director
4519 Lashley Ct.
Marietta, GA 30068
PH: (678)641-4457
Veneman, Jim, Mem.

Clan Colquhoun of North America **[20803]**
2984 Mike Dr.
Marietta, GA 30064

Foundation for Hospital Art **[13729]**
4238 Highborne Dr.
Marietta, GA 30066
PH: (678)324-1705
Feight, Scott, Exec. Dir.

Gift and Home Trade Association **[3014]**
Box 214
2550 Sandy Plains Rd., Ste. 225

Marietta, GA 30066
Toll free: 877-600-4872
Kacic, George, Secretary

Health and Education Relief Organization **[12160]**
PO Box 670804
Marietta, GA 30066
PH: (678)494-5595
Fax: (678)494-5533
Waldbart, Ted, CEO, President

Network of Ingredient Marketing Specialists **[1363]**
PO Box 681864
Marietta, GA 30068-0032
PH: (770)971-8116
Fax: (770)971-1094

Open Applications Group **[6280]**
PO Box 4897
Marietta, GA 30061-4897
PH: (404)402-1962
Fax: (801)740-0100
Connelly, David, CEO

Operation Stars and Stripes **[10756]**
483 Old Canton Rd., Ste. 100
Marietta, GA 30068
PH: (770)509-1156
Smith, Rosalyn-Sue, CEO

Ouderkerk Family Genealogical Association **[20909]**
700 Atlanta Country Club Dr.
Marietta, GA 30067

Professional Pricing Society **[930]**
3535 Roswell Rd., Ste. 59
Marietta, GA 30062
PH: (770)509-9933
Mitchell, Kevin, President

Refrigerated Foods Association **[1370]**
3823 Roswell Rd., Ste. 208
Marietta, GA 30062
PH: (770)303-9905
(770)303-9906
Fax: (678)550-4504
Loehndorf, Steve, President

Southeastern Legal Foundation **[5447]**
2255 Sewell Mill Rd., Ste. 320
Marietta, GA 30062-7218
PH: (770)977-2131
Fax: (770)977-2134
Goessling, Shannon L., Counsel, Exec. Dir.

USS Liberty Veterans Association **[21069]**
PO Box 680275
Marietta, GA 30068
Gallo, Ernie, President

Signal Corps Regimental Association **[20724]**
4570 Dewey Dr.
Martinez, GA 30907
Tuschen, Bryan, Mgr.

Antique and Amusement Photographers International **[2575]**
PO Box 3094
McDonough, GA 30253
PH: (860)578-2274
Fax: (877)865-1052
Gillikin, Derrick, President

Association of Technical and Supervisory Professionals **[5222]**
c/o Larry Hortert, Treasurer
153 Nettie Ln.
McDonough, GA 30252
Bridgeman, Pete, Contact

CID Agents Association **[21048]**
c/o Warren L. Cox, Membership Chairperson

165 Birch Creek Cir.
McDonough, GA 30253-7253
PH: (770)363-1188
Cox, Warren L., Membership Chp.

National Alliance for the Primary Prevention of Sharps Injuries **[17174]**
PO Box 10
Milner, GA 30257
PH: (770)358-7860
Fax: (770)358-6793
Bierman, Steve, MD, Founder, President

Canine Assistants **[11576]**
3160 Francis Rd.
Milton, GA 30004
PH: (770)664-7178
Toll free: 800-771-7221
Fax: (770)664-7820
Scott, David, Chairman

National Association of Black Military Women **[21028]**
5695 Pine Meadows Ct.
Morrow, GA 30260-1053
PH: (404)675-0195
Dawson, Stephanie A., President

American Cavalier King Charles Spaniel Club **[21804]**
c/o Lun Dunham, Corresponding Secretary
2 Bud Davis Rd.
Newnan, GA 30263
Dunham, Luanne K., Corr. Sec.

Health Industry Representatives Association **[2281]**
8 The Meadows
Newnan, GA 30265
PH: (303)756-8115
Fax: (770)683-4648
Pruitt, Tom, President

Association for Women in Sports Media **[2666]**
7742 Spalding Dr., No. 377
Norcross, GA 30092
Overman, Jennifer, President

BlazeSports America **[22777]**
1670 Oakbrook Dr., Ste. 331
Norcross, GA 30093
PH: (404)270-2000
Fax: (404)270-2039
Holland, Daniel J., Chairman

Children's Network International **[10931]**
5449 Robin Hill Ct.
Norcross, GA 30093
PH: (404)259-8818
Fax: (770)925-0580
Matthew, Thampy, Contact

Enamelist Society **[21756]**
PO Box 920220
Norcross, GA 30010
PH: (770)807-0142
Fax: (770)409-7280
Shepps, Averill, VP

Institute of Industrial and Systems Engineers **[6558]**
3577 Parkway Ln., Ste. 200
Norcross, GA 30092
PH: (770)449-0460
(770)449-0461
Toll free: 800-494-0460
Fax: (770)441-3295
Calvert, Donna, Mem.

International Gas Turbine Institute **[6563]**
6525 The Corners Pky., Ste. 115
Norcross, GA 30092

PH: (404)847-0072
Fax: (404)847-0151
Ireland, Michael, Mem.

International Plant Nutrition Institute
    [4686]
3500 Parkway Ln., Ste. 550
Norcross, GA 30092-2844
PH: (770)447-0335
Fax: (770)448-0439
Couch, Steve, VP of Admin.

The Mission Society [20346]
6234 Crooked Creek Rd.
Norcross, GA 30092-3106
PH: (770)446-1381
Toll free: 800-478-8963
Fax: (770)446-3044
Wilkins, Max, President, CEO

Paper Industry Management As-
    sociation [2494]
15 Technology Pkwy. S
Norcross, GA 30092
PH: (770)209-7230
Fax: (770)209-7359
Konkel, Joseph L., President

Porcelain Enamel Institute [571]
PO Box 920220
Norcross, GA 30010
PH: (770)676-9366
Fax: (770)409-7280
Coursin, Kevin, Chmn. of the Bd.

United with Hope [11177]
PO Box 1086
Palmetto, GA 30268
Millar, Nancy, Director

Africa Inland Mission International
    [20379]
PO Box 3611
Peachtree City, GA 30269-7611
PH: (845)735-4014
Toll free: 800-254-0010
Fax: (770)631-3213
Ewing, Wade, Director

American Print Alliance [8954]
302 Larkspur Turn
Peachtree City, GA 30269-2210
Pulin, Dr. Carol, Director

Civil Aviation Medical Association
    [13509]
PO Box 2382
Peachtree City, GA 30269-2382
PH: (770)487-0100
Fax: (770)487-0080
Millett, David P., MD, Exec. VP

Guitars Not Guns [18721]
PO Box 3562
Peachtree City, GA 30269
PH: (770)861-2443
Nelson, Ray, CEO, Founder

HeroBox [10744]
237 Senoia Rd.
Peachtree City, GA 30269
Toll free: 866-999-4376
Housley, Ryan, Exec. Dir.

Phi Mu Fraternity [23960]
400 Westpark Dr.
Peachtree City, GA 30269
PH: (770)632-2090
Fax: (770)632-2136
Reyes, Darlene, Exec. Dir.

Association of Suppliers to the
    Paper Industry [1715]
15 Technology Pky. S
Peachtree Corners, GA 30092
PH: (770)209-7521
Fax: (770)209-7581
Fletty, Eric, Exec. Dir.

Forest Products Society [4201]
15 Technology Pky. S, Ste. 115
Peachtree Corners, GA 30092
Toll free: 855-475-0291
Puettmann, Maureen, President

Industrial Asset Management
    Council [2863]
6625 The Corners Pky., Ste. 200
Peachtree Corners, GA 30092
PH: (770)325-3461
Fax: (770)263-8825
Turner, Samantha, Chairman

National Association of Printing Ink
    Manufacturers [1542]
15 Technology Pky. S
Peachtree Corners, GA 30092
PH: (770)209-7289
Fax: (678)680-4920

Pulp and Paper Safety Association
    [6977]
15 Technology Pky. S
Peachtree Corners, GA 30092-8200
PH: (770)209-7300
Kanneberg, Matthew, Chairman

Technical Association of the Pulp
    and Paper Industry [2495]
15 Technology Pky. S, Ste. 115
Peachtree Corners, GA 30092
PH: (770)446-1400
Luettgen, Chris, Chairperson

American Society for Aesthetics
    [8956]
PO Box 915
Pooler, GA 31322
PH: (912)748-9524
Freeland, Cynthia, President

Eighth Air Force Historical Society
    [21194]
PO Box 956
Pooler, GA 31322
PH: (912)748-8884
Nowack, David, President

African American Wine Tasting
    Society [174]
PO Box 681
Powder Springs, GA 30127
PH: (770)437-1753
Toll free: 888-437-1753

Brantley Association of America
    [20788]
4750 Oakleigh Manor Dr.
Powder Springs, GA 30127
PH: (770)428-4402
Brantley, John Kenneth, President

WebWhispers, Inc. [17416]
PO Box 1275
Powder Springs, GA 30127
Whitworth, Tom, President

Adult Higher Education Alliance
    [7452]
c/o Fred Prasuhn, Treasurer
350 Will Wynne Rd.
Rayle, GA 30660-2515
Cox, Thomas D., President

National Alliance of Burmese Breed-
    ers [3681]
c/o Janice Lancaster, Secretary
91 Maner Rd.
Rockmart, GA 30153
Lancaster, Janice, Secretary

Online Imperial Club [21467]
c/o Elijah Scott, Treasurer
70 Boyd Rd. SW
Rome, GA 30161
Scott, Elijah, Treasurer

American Academy of Medical
    Management [15620]
560 W Crossville Rd., Ste. 104
Roswell, GA 30075

PH: (770)649-7150
Fax: (770)649-7552
Bonds, Roger G., Exec. Dir.

Heart for Africa [11015]
PO Box 1308
Roswell, GA 30077
PH: (678)566-1589
Toll free: 800-901-7585
Maxwell, Ian, CEO, Founder

National Down Syndrome Congress
    [12330]
30 Mansell Ct., Ste. 108
Roswell, GA 30076-4858
PH: (770)604-9500
Toll free: 800-232-6372
Fax: (770)604-9898
Tolbert, Marilyn, President

North American Reggio Emilia Alli-
    ance [11102]
1131 Canton St.
Roswell, GA 30075
PH: (770)552-0179
Fax: (770)552-0767
Curling, Lauren Lynn, Coord.,
    Admin.

Restaurant Loss Prevention and
    Security Association [2942]
885 Woodstock Rd., Ste. 430
Roswell, GA 30075-2274
PH: (240)252-5542
Brown, Robert, Div. Mgr.

National Poultry and Food Distribu-
    tors Association [1362]
2014 Osborne Rd.
Saint Marys, GA 31558
PH: (678)850-9311
    (770)535-9901
Fax: (770)535-7385
Wilson, Lee, President

Conexx: America Israel Business
    Connector [23576]
400 Northridge Rd., No. 250
Sandy Springs, GA 30350
PH: (404)843-9426
Fax: (404)843-1416
Swartz, Barry, VP

Rally Foundation [14054]
5775 Glenridge Dr., Bldg. B, Ste.
    370
Sandy Springs, GA 30328
PH: (404)847-1270
Fax: (678)251-4067
Crowe, Dean, Founder, CEO

Utility Communicators International
    [778]
150 Mark Trl.
Sandy Springs, GA 30328
PH: (970)368-2021
Phillips, Brian, President

BP Amoco Marketers Association
    [2515]
4 Skidaway Village Sq., Ste. 201
Savannah, GA 31411
PH: (912)598-7939
Fax: (912)598-7949
Mancini, Pete, Chairman

Confraternity of the Blessed Sacra-
    ment [20098]
224 E 34th St.
Savannah, GA 31401
Willoughby, Rev. William, III, Gen.
    Sec.

Horizon International Medical Mis-
    sion [15474]
111 Lions Gate Rd.
Savannah, GA 31419
PH: (912)308-8799

Intercollegiate Horse Shows As-
    sociation [22943]
c/o Eddie Federswich, Director
Savannah College of Art & Design
342 Bull St.
Savannah, GA 31402
PH: (315)682-1933
Fax: (315)682-9416
Cacchione, Robert, Exec. Dir.

Negro Airmen International [5868]
PO Box 23911
Savannah, GA 31403
PH: (912)232-7524
Jones, Sam Louis, Jr., President

Smocking Arts Guild of America
    [21783]
PO Box 5828
Savannah, GA 31414-5828
PH: (817)350-4883
Toll free: 855-350-7242
Fax: (817)886-0393
Perch, Liz, Receptionist

Women in Bio [6125]
PO Box 31493
Sea Island, GA 31561-1493
PH: (240)204-0719
Dillinger, Phyllis, Bd. Member

Go Eat Give [9210]
2366 Oberon Walk SE
Smyrna, GA 30080
PH: (678)744-8306
Rawal, Sucheta, Founder, Exec. Dir.

India American Cultural Association
    [9566]
1281 Cooper Lake Rd.
Smyrna, GA 30082
PH: (770)436-3719
Fax: (770)436-4272
Gupta, Rina, President

National Tuberculosis Controllers
    Association [14606]
2452 Spring Rd. SE
Smyrna, GA 30080-3828
PH: (678)503-0503
    (678)503-0804
Toll free: 877-503-0806
Fax: (678)503-0805
Belknap, Robert, President

International Association of Flight
    and Critical Care Paramedics
    [14682]
c/o Monica Newman, Executive
    Director
4835 Riveredge Cove
Snellville, GA 30039
PH: (770)979-6372
Fax: (770)979-6500
Newman, Ms. Monica, Exec. Dir.

Society of Chiropractic Orthospinol-
    ogy [14283]
c/o Dr. Steve Humber, Treasurer
Humber Clinic, P.C.
2336 Wisteria Dr., Ste. 110
Snellville, GA 30078-6162
PH: (770)979-8327
Fax: (770)979-8338
Hunt, Julie Mayer, DC, President

American Dove Association [21536]
7334 Highway 15
Sparta, GA 31087-3567
Kell, James, President

Caring for Haitian Orphans with
    AIDS [10885]
PO Box 145
Statesboro, GA 30459-0145
PH: (813)843-0038
Denis-Luque, Marie F., Founder

Knifemakers' Guild [21767]
121 Mount Pisgah Church Rd.
Statesboro, GA 30458

PH: (912)682-8103
Hensley, Wayne, VP

Human Ecology Action League
[14717]
PO Box 509
Stockbridge, GA 30281
PH: (770)389-4519
Fax: (770)389-4520

Used Truck Association [357]
325 Country Club Dr., Ste. A
Stockbridge, GA 30281
Toll free: 877-438-7882
Clark, Rick, President

Missio Nexus [20436]
655 Village Square Dr., Ste. A
Stone Mountain, GA 30083
PH: (770)457-6677
    (630)682-9270
Janzen, Warren, Chairman

U.S.A. Poultry and Egg Export
Council [4575]
2300 W Park Place Blvd., Ste. 100
Stone Mountain, GA 30087
PH: (770)413-0006
Fax: (770)413-0007
Sumner, James H., President

Chi Phi [23892]
1160 Satellite Blvd.
Suwanee, GA 30024
PH: (404)231-1824
Toll free: 800-849-1824
Azarian, Michael, Exec. Dir.

Handweavers Guild of America, Inc.
[21760]
1255 Buford Hwy., Ste. 211
Suwanee, GA 30024-8421
PH: (678)730-0010
Fax: (678)730-0836
Bowles, Sandra, Ed.-in-Chief, Exec.
Dir.

Laotian American Society [19528]
PO Box 1558
Suwanee, GA 30024
Arounnarath, Meiling, President

National Association of Exotic Pest
Plant Councils [4530]
University of Georgia
Center for Invasive Species and
Ecosystem Health
2360 Rainwater Rd.
Tifton, GA 31793
PH: (229)386-3298
Fax: (229)386-3352
Johnson, Doug, Chmn. of the Bd.

National Peanut Buying Points As-
sociation [4509]
115 W 2nd St.
Tifton, GA 31793-0314
PH: (229)386-1716
Fax: (229)386-8757
Brownlee, Kenny, Treasurer

Our Journey [11122]
15617 US Hwy. 17
Townsend, GA 31331
PH: (912)832-2809
Ahern, Maureen, President

Global Initiative for the Advancement
of Nutritional Therapy, Inc. [17442]
4426 Hugh Howell Rd., Ste. B-333
Tucker, GA 30084
PH: (770)491-8667
Fax: (770)491-8655
Oladele, Dr. Alawode, Bd. Member

Honduras Outreach, Inc. [17979]
1990 Lakeside Pky., Ste. 140
Tucker, GA 30084

PH: (404)327-5770
Willing, Laurie, Exec. Dir.

North American Alliances for Social
Relief [12174]
PO Box 468
Tucker, GA 30085
PH: (770)330-3897
Khan, Awal, PhD, President

Nuclear Medicine Technology
Certification Board [16076]
Bldg. I
3558 Habersham at Northlake
Tucker, GA 30084-4009
PH: (404)315-1739
Toll free: 800-659-3953
Fax: (404)315-6502
Perry, Dave, CNMT, PET, Exec. Dir.

U.S. Poultry and Egg Association
[4574]
1530 Cooledge Rd.
Tucker, GA 30084-7303
PH: (770)493-9401
Fax: (770)493-9257
Starkey, John, President

Association of State and Provincial
Psychology Boards [16909]
215 Market Rd.
Tyrone, GA 30290
PH: (678)216-1175
Toll free: 800-513-6910
Fax: (678)216-1176
Rallo, Joseph S., PhD, Director

National Funeral Directors and Morti-
cians Association [2413]
6290 Shannon Pky.
Union City, GA 30291
PH: (770)969-0064
Toll free: 800-434-0958
Fax: (770)969-0505
Wynn, Alexander C., III, President

Buick GS Club of America [21345]
625 Pine Point Cir.
Valdosta, GA 31602
PH: (229)244-0577

Council of Administrators of Special
Education [8578]
Osigian Office Ctre.
101 Katelyn Cir., Ste. E
Warner Robins, GA 31088
PH: (478)333-6892
Fax: (478)333-2453
Purcell, Dr. Luann L., Exec. Dir.

National Association of Lively
Families [20904]
c/o Polly Lively, Treasurer
411 Claxton-Lively Rd.
Waynesboro, GA 30830
Lively, John, President

American Association for Vocational
Instructional Materials [8731]
220 Smithonia Rd.
Winterville, GA 30683-9527
PH: (706)742-5355
Fax: (706)742-7005

German Wirehaired Pointer Club of
America [21885]
c/o Erika Brown, Treasurer
236 Park Ave.
Woodstock, GA 30188-4274
PH: (770)591-4329
Braddock, Mike, Director

International Professional Pond
Companies Association [3641]
4045 N Arnold Mill Rd.
Woodstock, GA 30188
PH: (770)592-9790
Fax: (770)924-9589
Jones, Gloria, Secretary

Order of the Daughters of the King
[20113]
101 Weatherstone Dr., Ste. 870
Woodstock, GA 30188
PH: (770)517-8552
Fax: (770)517-8066
Fletcher, Mary, AdministratorH

HAWAII

Association for Marine Exploration
[4464]
91-1056 A'awa Dr.
Ewa Beach, HI 96706
PH: (858)337-9418
Dituri, Joseph, MS, CEO

Parson Russell Terrier Association of
America [21940]
c/o Lance Nobriga, Secretary
91-1650 Laupai St.
Ewa Beach, HI 96706-4902
PH: (808)652-7877
Koeppel, Gary, Delegate

International Rainwater Catchment
Systems Association [7368]
875 Komohana St.
Hilo, HI 96720
Crawford, David, Treasurer

Japanese Chamber of Commerce
and Industry of Hawaii [23599]
714 Kanoelehua Ave.
Hilo, HI 96720
PH: (808)934-0177
Fax: (808)934-0178

Pele Defense Fund [3929]
PO Box 4969
Hilo, HI 96720

Advocates for Africa's Children
[10833]
PO Box 283233
Honolulu, HI 96828
PH: (808)391-9777
Lum, Heidi, President

Apollo Society [20667]
PO Box 61206
Honolulu, HI 96839-61206
Smith, Gregory A., Chairman,
President

Association of State Supervisor of
Mathematics [8277]
c/o Dewey Gottlieb, Vice President
475 22nd Ave., Rm. 116
Honolulu, HI 96816
Kasbaum, Diana, Coord.

Carol Burnett Fund for Responsible
Journalism [8150]
c/o Prof. Tom Brislin, Administrator
School of Communications
University of Hawaii
2550 Campus Rd.
Honolulu, HI 96822-2250
Brislin, Prof. Tom, Administrator

Chinese Chamber of Commerce of
Hawaii [23574]
8 S King St., Ste. 201
Honolulu, HI 96813
PH: (808)533-3181
Fax: (808)537-6767
Yu, Robert, President

East-West Center [18538]
1601 E West Rd.
Honolulu, HI 96848-1601
PH: (808)944-7111
Fax: (808)944-7376
Morrison, Charles E., President

Emerging Humanity [12151]
2279 Makanani Dr.
Honolulu, HI 96817
Abbott, Bart, President

Hawaii Heptachlor Research and
Education Foundation [13222]
PO Box 3735
Honolulu, HI 96812
Mori, Art, PhD, President, Director

Hawaiian International Billfish
Tournament [22040]
PO Box 29638
Honolulu, HI 96820
PH: (808)836-3422
    (808)383-6701
Fax: (808)833-7756
Fithian, Peter, Founder

Historic Hawaii Foundation [9397]
Dole Office Building Twr.
680 Iwilei Rd., Ste. 690
Honolulu, HI 96817
PH: (808)523-2900
Fax: (808)523-0800
Faulkner, Kiersten, Exec. Dir.

Honolulu Japanese Chamber of
Commerce [23591]
2454 S Beretania St., Ste. 201
Honolulu, HI 96826
PH: (808)949-5531
Fax: (808)949-3020
Ishihara, Wayne, President

Indo-Pacific Conservation Alliance
[3884]
1525 Bernice St.
Honolulu, HI 96817
PH: (808)848-4124
Fax: (808)847-8252
Allison, Allen, PhD, Chmn. of the Bd.

International Marine Minerals Society
[4467]
c/o Karynne Morgan
University of Hawaii
1000 Pope Rd., MSB 303
Honolulu, HI 96822
PH: (808)956-6036
Fax: (808)956-9772
Hein, James R., Officer

National Association for the Educa-
tion and Advancement of
Cambodian, Laotian, and
Vietnamese Americans [19684]
c/o Dr. Chhany Sak-Humphry,
President
University of Hawaii
Dept. of Indo-Pacific Languages and
Literatures
Spalding Hall 255
2540 Maile Way
Honolulu, HI 96822
PH: (808)956-8070
Fax: (808)956-5978
Sak-Humphry, Dr. Chhany, President

Pacific Islanders in Communications
[9785]
615 Pikoii St., Ste. 1504
Honolulu, HI 96814
PH: (808)591-0059
Fax: (808)591-1114
Ferrer, Leanne, Exec. Dir.

Pacific Seabird Group [4864]
PO Box 61493
Honolulu, HI 96839-1493
Kuletz, Kathy, Chairman

PACON International [4469]
Oceanography Mail Room
MSB 2nd Fl.
1000 Pope Rd.
Honolulu, HI 96822
PH: (808)956-6163
Fax: (808)956-2580
Kohno, Hikedi, President

Polynesian Voyaging Society [5945]
10 Sand Island Pky.
Honolulu, HI 96819-4355

PH: (808)842-1101
Thompson, Nainoa, President

Scientific Association of Forensic
Examiners [5252]
c/o Reed Hayes, Membership
Chairperson
PO Box 235213
Honolulu, HI 96823
Hayes, Reed, Membership Chp.

Sustainable Fisheries Partnership
[3647]
4348 Waialae Ave., No. 692
Honolulu, HI 96816-5767
PH: (202)580-8187
Cannon, Jim, CEO, Founder,
President

United Nations Educational,
Scientific and Cultural Organization
l Intergovernmental Oceanographic
Commission [7158]
Bldg. 176
1845 Wasp Blvd.
Honolulu, HI 96818
PH: (808)725-6050
Fax: (808)725-6055
Kong, Dr. Laura S.L., Director

United States Hereditary An-
gioedema Association [14863]
500 Ala Moana Blvd., Ste. 400
7 Waterfront Plz.
Honolulu, HI 96813
Toll free: 866-798-5598
Fax: (508)437-0303
Castaldo, Anthony, President

World Ocean Council [4775]
3035 Hibiscus Dr., Ste. 1
Honolulu, HI 96815
PH: (808)277-9008
Holthus, Paul, President, CEO

Sustainable Biodiesel Alliance [4268]
PO Box 1677
Kahului, HI 96732
PH: (512)410-7841
Fax: (512)410-7841
Plowman, Jeff, V. Chmn. of the Bd.

Association of Vision Educators
[16378]
c/o Kate Keilman
111 Hekili St., Ste. A206
Kailua, HI 96734-2800
PH: (631)563-5007

Direct Selling Women's Alliance
[3012]
111 Hekili St., Ste. A-139
Kailua, HI 96734
PH: (808)230-2427
Toll free: 888-417-0743
Keohohou, Nicki, CEO, Founder

Earthtrust [4809]
1118 Maunawili Rd.
Kailua, HI 96734
PH: (415)662-3264
Fax: (206)202-3893
White, DJ, CEO, President, Founder

Oikonos [4008]
PO Box 1918
Kailua, HI 96734
PH: (808)228-4463
Hester, Michelle, President

Association for Integrative Psychol-
ogy, Inc. [16903]
75-6099 Kuakini Hwy.
Kailua Kona, HI 96740
PH: (808)930-8707
Toll free: 877-935-0247
Fax: (808)930-8701
James, Matthew B., MA, Founder

Pacific Ocean Research Foundation
[6718]
74-381 Kealakehe Pkwy., Ste. C
Kailua Kona, HI 96740
PH: (808)329-6105

Youth With a Mission [20484]
c/o Darlene Cunningham, Founder
75-5851 Kuakini Hwy.
Kailua Kona, HI 96740
PH: (808)326-7228
    (808)326-4400
Cunningham, Darlene, Founder

Heliconia Society International
[4432]
3530 Papalina Rd.
Kalaheo, HI 96741-9599
PH: (808)332-7324
Kress, W. John, Director

International Lunar Observatory As-
sociation [6005]
65-1230 Mamalahoa Highway D20
Kamuela, HI 96743
PH: (808)885-3474
Fax: (808)885-3475
Durst, Steve, Founder, Director

FORCES International [18399]
PO Box 4267
Kaneohe, HI 96744
PH: (808)721-8384
Tenn, Jolyn, Treasurer

International Organisation for
Biological Control [4529]
c/o Dr. Russell Messing, Secretary
General
University of Hawaii at Manoa
Kauai Agricultural Research Center
7370 Kuamoo Rd.
Kapaa, HI 96746
PH: (808)822-4984
Fax: (808)822-2190
Messing, Russell, Sec. Gen.

American Reef Coalition [3802]
PO Box 844
Kihei, HI 96753
PH: (808)870-5817
Hunt, Capt. Terry, Contact

Friends of Health [13624]
Box 906
Kula, HI 96790
PH: (808)878-6762
Baz, Chris, President, Owner

Polynesian Cultural Center [9215]
55-370 Kamehameha Hwy.
Laie, HI 96762
PH: (808)293-3333
Toll free: 844-572-2347
Fax: (808)293-3339
Orgill, Von, CEO, President

International Horn Society [9929]
c/o Heidi Vogel, Executive Secretary
PO Box 630158
Lanai City, HI 96763-0158
PH: (808)565-7273
Fax: (808)565-7273
Vogel, Heidi, Exec. Sec.

National Association of Mammogra-
phers [17060]
PO Box 792011
Paia, HI 96779
Comer, Lisa, Dir. (Actg.)

Professional Windsurfers Association
[22661]
PO Box 791656
Paia, HI 96779
Diaz, Jimmy, Chairman

Save Our Seas [3940]
PO Box 223508
Princeville, HI 96722

PH: (808)651-3452
Clark, Capt. Paul, President

Surfing Medicine International
[13659]
PO Box 548
Waialua, HI 96791
PH: (518)635-0899
Ragosta, Dr. Summer, Founder

Rocky Mountain Llama and Alpaca
Association [3612]
c/o Lougene Baird, President
PO Box 385403
Waikoloa, HI 96738
PH: (808)747-5023
Williams, Dick, VP

Pacific Whale Foundation [4865]
300 Ma'alaea Rd.
Wailuku, HI 96793
PH: (808)249-8811
Toll free: 800-942-5311
Fax: (808)243-9021
Vough, Kelly, Program Mgr., Coord.l

IDAHO

Pembroke Welsh Corgi Club of
America [21943]
c/o Patty Gailey, Secretary
94 South 250 East
Blackfoot, ID 83221-5982
PH: (208)782-2510
Gailey, Patty, Corr. Sec.

Jane Austen Society of North
America [9039]
c/o Carole Stokes, Membership
Secretary
3140 S Temperance Way
Boise, ID 83706
Toll free: 800-836-3911
Bellanti, Claire, President

International Festivals & Events As-
sociation [1142]
2603 W Eastover Ter.
Boise, ID 83706
PH: (208)433-0950
Fax: (208)433-9812
Schmader, Mr. Steven Wood, CEO,
President

The National Institutes for Water
Resources [7371]
c/o Dr. John C. Tracy, Secretary-
Treasurer
Idaho Water Resources Institute
322 E Front St.
Boise, ID 83702
Tracy, John, Secretary, Treasurer

North American Packgoat Associa-
tion [4281]
PO Box 170166
Boise, ID 83717
PH: (208)331-0772
Fax: (208)331-0772
Robinson, Larry, Treasurer

Organization of Wildlife Planners
[4862]
c/o Michele Beucler
600 S Walnut St.
Boise, ID 83707
PH: (208)287-2856
Forstchen, Ann, President

The Peregrine Fund [4869]
5668 W Flying Hawk Ln.
Boise, ID 83709
PH: (208)362-3716
Fax: (208)362-2376
Jenny, J. Peter, President

Raptor Research Foundation [4876]
c/o Rick Watson, Conservation Committee Co-Chairman

5668 W Flying Hawk Ln.
Boise, ID 83709
PH: (208)362-8272
Boal, Clint, President

North American Lily Society [22117]
PO Box W
Bonners Ferry, ID 83805-1287
Diehl, Larry, Director

National Family Preservation
Network [11828]
3971 North 1400 East
Buhl, ID 83316
Toll free: 888-498-9047
Martens, Priscilla, Exec. Dir.

American Wagyu Association [3715]
PO Box 3235
Coeur d Alene, ID 83816
PH: (208)262-8100
Fax: (208)292-2670
Beattie, Michael, Exec. Dir.

Flying Doctors of America [12273]
212 W Ironwood Dr., Ste. D-129
Coeur d Alene, ID 83814
PH: (404)273-8348
Gathercoal, Allan, DD, Founder,
President

Alliance to Stabilize Our Population
[13025]
PO Box 515
Eagle, ID 83616
PH: (208)994-2094

World Wins International [11464]
5812 W Cavendale Dr.
Eagle, ID 83616
PH: (208)585-7370
Houck, Amy, Director, Founder

National Lutheran Outdoors Ministry
Association [20317]
PO Box 1965
Hailey, ID 83333
PH: (208)720-4371
White, Signe, President

Wild Gift [4904]
PO Box 1151
Hailey, ID 83333
PH: (208)471-5091
Jonas, Bob, Founder

Samoyed Club of America [21956]
c/o Darlene Rautio, Membership
Chairperson
1759 E Garwood Rd.
Hayden, ID 83835-5129
Sencenbaugh, Bob, President

Hypoparathyroidism Association, Inc.
[14706]
PO Box 2258
Idaho Falls, ID 83403
PH: (208)524-3857
Toll free: 866-213-0394
Sanders, James, President

North American Brewers' Association
[189]
2845 Holly Pl.
Idaho Falls, ID 83402

Sacro Occipital Research Society
International [14281]
2184 Channing Way, No. 460
Idaho Falls, ID 83404
PH: (913)239-0228
Fax: (913)239-0305
Unger, Joe, President

Curly Sporthorse International [4346]
17829 Hubbard Gulch
Juliaetta, ID 83535
PH: (208)276-7540
VavRosky, Linda, Director, President

Helping Hands Rescue, Inc. [10637]
PO Box 1975
Lewiston, ID 83501
PH: (208)743-3157

National Association of Real Estate
Consultants [2877]
404 4th Ave.
Lewiston, ID 83501
PH: (208)746-7963
Toll free: 800-445-8543
Fax: (208)746-4760
Garton-Good, Julie, Founder,
President

Society of Mineral Analysts [6876]
Lewiston, ID 83501
PH: (775)313-4229
Braun, Patrick, Contact

National Center for Constitutional
Studies [18038]
37777 W Juniper Rd.
Malta, ID 83342
PH: (208)645-2625
Toll free: 800-388-4512
Fax: (208)645-2667
Nelson, Zeldon, Chmn. of the Bd.,
CEO

American College of Veterinary
Ophthalmologists [17619]
PO Box 1311
Meridian, ID 83680
PH: (208)466-7624
Fax: (208)895-7872
Daniel, Stacee, Exec. Dir.

Flair Bartenders' Association [185]
104 E Fairview Ave., No. 283
Meridian, ID 83642-1733
PH: (208)888-3146
Toll free: 877-794-9446
Fax: (208)887-1505
Allison, James, CEO, President

Horseless Carriage Club of America
[21394]
1301 N Manship Pl.
Meridian, ID 83642-5072
PH: (626)287-4222
Darby, Karl, Chmn. of the Bd.

Humanity Corps [11379]
PO Box 1543
Meridian, ID 83680
PH: (720)239-2858
Heywood, Nicole, President

International Association of Directors
of Law Enforcement Standards
and Training [5469]
1330 N Manship Pl.
Meridian, ID 83642
PH: (517)857-3828
    (208)288-5491
Becar, Michael N., Exec. Dir.

Appaloosa Horse Club [4335]
2720 W Pullman Rd.
Moscow, ID 83843
PH: (208)882-5578
Fax: (208)882-8150
Taylor, Steve, CEO

Association of Classical and
Christian Schools [8529]
205 E 5th St.
Moscow, ID 83843
PH: (208)882-6101
Fax: (208)882-9097
Blakey, Patch, Exec. Dir.

Building Technology Educators'
Society [7498]
c/o Dept. of Architecture and Interior
Design
University of Idaho

207 AAS
Moscow, ID 83844-2451
Trubiano, Franca, President

The International Society for
Research in Human Milk and
Lactation [13856]
c/o Dr. Shelley McGuire, Secretary-
Treasurer
1908 E D St.
Moscow, ID 83843
Bode, Lars, President

USA Dry Pea & Lentil Council [3580]
2780 W Pullman Rd.
Moscow, ID 83843
PH: (208)882-3023
Fax: (208)882-6406
McGreevy, Tim D., CEO

National Challenged Homeschoolers
Associated Network [7997]
PO Box 310
Moyie Springs, ID 83845
PH: (208)267-6246
Toll free: 800-266-9837
Bushnell, Tom, Director

American Blazer Horse Association
[4299]
16114 Idaho Center Blvd., Ste. 3
Nampa, ID 83687
PH: (208)461-1055

Because International [12527]
216 12th Ave. N
Nampa, ID 83686
PH: (208)697-4417
Lee, Kenton, CEO, President,
Founder

Mission Aviation Fellowship [20437]
112 N Pilatus Ln.
Nampa, ID 83687
PH: (208)498-0800
Toll free: 800-359-7623
Fax: (208)498-0801
Boyd, John, President, CEO

Northwest Nazarene University
Alumni Association [19339]
Office of Alumni Relations
524 E Dewey St.
Nampa, ID 83686
PH: (208)467-8841
Toll free: 800-654-2411
Fax: (208)467-8838
Bruner, Darl, Director

BlueRibbon Coalition [23090]
4555 Burley Dr., Ste. A
Pocatello, ID 83202-1945
PH: (208)237-1008
Fax: (208)237-9424
Mogstad, Joni, Treasurer

Councils on Chiropractic Education
International [14268]
PO Box 4943
Pocatello, ID 83205
PH: (208)241-4855
Woolcock, Kylie, Exec. Sec.

Hands4Uganda [11014]
2900 Summit Dr.
Pocatello, ID 83201
Reynolds, Karla, Chairman

North American Colleges and Teach-
ers of Agriculture [7481]
c/o Marilyn Parker, Secretary and
Treasurer
151 West 100 South
Rupert, ID 83350
PH: (208)957-7001
Fax: (208)436-1384
Parker, Marilyn B., Secretary,
Treasurer

Traditional Cowboy Arts Association
[8805]
PO Box 2002
Salmon, ID 83467
PH: (208)865-2006
Bellamy, Don, Contact

American Society of Agricultural Ap-
praisers [214]
1126 Eastland Dr. N, Ste. 100
Twin Falls, ID 83303-0186
Toll free: 800-704-7020
Fax: (208)733-2326
Proost, Jay, Exec. Dir.

American Society of Farm Equip-
ment Appraisers [216]
1126 Eastland Dr. N, Ste. 100
Twin Falls, ID 83303-0186
PH: (208)733-2323
Toll free: 800-488-7570
Fax: (208)733-2326
Proost, Jay, Exec. Dir.

Austin Bantam Society [21331]
1050 Trotter Dr.
Twin Falls, ID 83301

Epsilon Sigma Phi [23715]
c/o Bob Ohlensehlen, Executive
Director
450 Falls Ave., Ste. 106
Twin Falls, ID 83301
PH: (208)736-4495
Fax: (208)736-6081
Ohlensehlen, Bob, Exec. Dir.

American Avalanche Association
[12813]
c/o Jaime Musnicki, Executive Direc-
tor
PO Box 248
Victor, ID 83455
PH: (307)699-2049
Musnicki, Jaime, Exec. Dir.

Camp To Belong [10880]
PO Box 1147
Victor, ID 83455
PH: (520)413-1395
    (208)390-0950
Toll free: 855-500-RIDE
Patterson, Carrie, Chairperson

Laptops to Lesotho [11066]
55 Eagle Creek Rd.
Wayan, ID 83285
PH: (208)574-2990
Balcomb, Janissa, President

National Oldtime Fiddlers' Associa-
tion, Inc. [9975]
PO Box 447
Weiser, ID 83672
PH: (208)414-0255
Fax: (208)414-0256
Cooper, Sandra, Director

ILLINOIS

United Hellenic Voters of America
[19459]
861 W Lake St.
Addison, IL 60101
PH: (630)628-1721
Sypolt, Arika, President

National Hereford Hog Record Association [4711]
c/o Becky Hyett, Secretary
2056 50th Ave.
Aledo, IL 61231
PH: (309)299-5122
Hyett, Becky, Secretary

Mason Contractors Association of
America [875]
1481 Merchant Dr.
Algonquin, IL 60102

PH: (224)678-9709
Toll free: 800-536-2225
Fax: (224)678-9714
Kemp, Mark, Comm. Chm.

World Bocce League [22696]
14 Tiverton Ct.
Algonquin, IL 60102-6290
PH: (847)669-9444
Toll free: 855-652-6223
Fax: (847)669-2613
Ferrari, Philip, President

North American Nature Photography
Association [2588]
6382 Charleston Rd.
Alma, IL 62807-2026
PH: (618)547-7616
Fax: (618)547-7438
Salazar, Gabby, Bd. Member

Callmakers and Collectors Associa-
tion of America [21630]
2925 Ethel Ave.
Alton, IL 62002
PH: (216)978-8589
Taylor, Troy, Secretary

NSU Enthusiasts U.S.A. [21463]
2909 Utah Pl.
Alton, IL 62002
PH: (618)462-9195
Stuchlik, Terry, Contact

Republican National Coalition for
Life [19070]
PO Box 618
Alton, IL 62002
PH: (618)462-5415
Fax: (618)462-8909
Edmondson, Dianne, Exec. Dir.

Academy of Osseointegration
[14368]
85 W Algonquin Rd., Ste. 550
Arlington Heights, IL 60005
PH: (847)439-1919
Toll free: 800-656-7736
Fax: (847)427-9656
Smith, Kevin P., Exec. Dir.

Air Movement and Control Associa-
tion International, Inc. [1614]
30 W University Dr.
Arlington Heights, IL 60004
PH: (847)394-0150
Fax: (847)253-0088
Smith, Wade, Exec. Dir.

Alliance for Audited Media [115]
48 W Seegers Rd.
Arlington Heights, IL 60005-3913
PH: (224)366-6939
Toll free: 800-285-2220
Fax: (224)366-6949
Meringolo, Christina, Chairman

American Board of Pain Medicine
[16549]
85 W Algonquin Rd., No. 550
Arlington Heights, IL 60005
PH: (847)981-8905
Fax: (847)427-9656
Lincer, James D., MD, President

American College of Allergy, Asthma
and Immunology [13572]
85 W Algonquin Rd., Ste. 550
Arlington Heights, IL 60005-4460
PH: (847)427-1200
Fax: (847)427-1294
Foggs, Michael B., MD, President

American College of Osteopathic
Family Physicians [16504]
330 E Algonquin Rd., Ste. 1
Arlington Heights, IL 60005
PH: (847)952-5100
    (847)952-5108
Toll free: 800-323-0794
Fax: (847)228-9755
Schmelzer, Peter L., CAE, Exec. Dir.

American Copy Editors Society **[2649]**
c/o Teresa Schmedding, President
155 E Algonquin Rd.
Arlington Heights, IL 60005-4617
Sullivan, David, VP

American Osteopathic Board of
Family Physicians **[16511]**
330 E Algonquin Rd., Ste. 6
Arlington Heights, IL 60005
PH: (847)640-8477
Thoma, Carol A., MBA, Exec. Dir.

American Society for Blood and Mar-
row Transplantation **[17503]**
85 W Algonquin Rd., Ste. 550
Arlington Heights, IL 60005-4460
PH: (847)427-0224
Fax: (847)427-9656
Luurs, Ken, Exec. Dir.

American Society of Colon and
Rectal Surgeons **[16804]**
85 W Algonquin Rd., Ste. 550
Arlington Heights, IL 60005
PH: (847)290-9184
Fax: (847)290-9203
Wexner, Steven D., MD,PhD,
President

American Society of Plastic
Surgeons **[14312]**
444 E Algonquin Rd.
Arlington Heights, IL 60005
PH: (847)228-9900
Toll free: 800-514-5058
Song, David H., MD, President

Automotive Maintenance and Repair
Association **[338]**
725 E Dundee Rd., Ste. 206
Arlington Heights, IL 60004-1538
PH: (847)947-2650
Fax: (202)318-0378
Henmueller, Joseph M., President,
COO

General Association of Regular
Baptist Churches **[19731]**
3715 N Ventura Dr.
Arlington Heights, IL 60004-7678
PH: (847)843-1600
Toll free: 888-588-1600
Fax: (847)843-3757
Greening, Rev. John, Rep.

Heartland Institute **[12977]**
3939 N Wilke Rd.
Arlington Heights, IL 60004
PH: (312)377-4000
Fax: (312)377-5000
Bast, Joseph L., CEO, President

Institute of Environmental Sciences
and Technology **[7093]**
2340 S Arlington Heights Rd., Ste.
620
Arlington Heights, IL 60005-4510
PH: (847)981-0100
Fax: (847)981-4130
Burrows, Roberta, Exec. Dir.

Malayalee Engineers Association in
North America **[6570]**
c/o Abraham Joseph, President
2214 N Williamsburg St.
Arlington Heights, IL 60004
John, Tony, VP

National Certification Board for
Diabetes Educators **[14540]**
330 E Algonquin Rd., Ste. 4
Arlington Heights, IL 60005
PH: (847)228-9795
Toll free: 877-239-3233
Fax: (847)228-8469
Johnson, John, Ph.D, Chairman

National Shared Housing Resource
Center **[11987]**
c/o Pam Reed
2004 E Sherwood Rd.
Arlington Heights, IL 60004
PH: (847)823-0453
Dunn, Kirby, President

North American Die Casting Associa-
tion **[1757]**
3250 N Arlington Heights Rd., Ste.
101
Arlington Heights, IL 60004
PH: (847)279-0001
Fax: (847)279-0002
Twarog, Daniel L., President

The Plastic Surgery Foundation
[14320]
444 E Algonquin Rd.
Arlington Heights, IL 60005-4664
PH: (847)228-9900
Toll free: 800-766-4955
Butler, Charles E., President

American Purchasing Society **[2816]**
8 E Galena Blvd., Ste. 203
Aurora, IL 60506
PH: (630)859-0250
Fax: (630)859-0270
Hough, Richard H., Exec. VP

Angelman Syndrome Foundation
[17335]
75 Executive Dr., Ste. 327
Aurora, IL 60504
PH: (630)978-4245
Toll free: 800-432-6435
Fax: (630)978-7408
Braun, Eileen, Exec. Dir.

Association for Individual Develop-
ment **[11562]**
309 New Indian Trail Ct.
Aurora, IL 60506
PH: (630)966-4000
Fax: (630)844-2065
O'Shea, Lynn, President

Construction and Demolition
Recycling Association **[514]**
1585 Beverly Ct., Ste. 112
Aurora, IL 60502-8725
PH: (630)585-7530
Turley, William, Exec. Dir.

Ewing Family Association **[19640]**
1330 Vaughn Ct.
Aurora, IL 60504
Ewing, Wallace K., Chancellor

International Society for the
Advancement of Spine Surgery
[16065]
2397 Waterbury Cir., Ste. 1
Aurora, IL 60504
PH: (630)375-1432
Wong, Hee Kit, President

National Barn Alliance **[9414]**
55 S Commonwealth Ave.
Aurora, IL 60506
Truax, Don, President

IPC - Association Connecting
Electronics Industries **[1052]**
3000 Lakeside Dr., 105 N
Bannockburn, IL 60015
PH: (847)615-7100
Fax: (847)615-7105
Mitchell, John W., President, CEO

National Rosacea Society **[14507]**
196 James St.
Barrington, IL 60010
Toll free: 888-662-5874
Huff, Samuel, Exec. Dir., President

Allied Finance Adjusters **[606]**
956 S Bartlett Rd., Ste. 321
Bartlett, IL 60103
Toll free: 800-843-1232
Fax: (888)949-8520
Osselburn, James, President

Salmon Unlimited Inc. **[22852]**
c/o Massard Foot and Ankle Clinic
321 W Railroad Ave.
Bartlett, IL 60103
Nelligan, Jim, President

Christian Association for Psychologi-
cal Studies **[16912]**
PO Box 365
Batavia, IL 60510-0365
PH: (630)639-9478
Fax: (630)454-3799
Buhrow, William C., Jr., President

Institute for Food Safety and Health
[1338]
Illinois Institute of Technology
Moffett Campus
6502 S Archer Rd.
Bedford Park, IL 60501-1957
PH: (708)563-1576
    (708)563-8175
Fax: (708)563-1873
Brackett, Robert E., PhD, VP

American Chain of Warehouses
[3436]
156 Flamingo Dr.
Beecher, IL 60401
PH: (708)946-9792
Fax: (708)946-9793
Jurus, William L., Rep.

Beta Sigma Psi **[23890]**
2408 Lebanon Ave.
Belleville, IL 62221-2529
PH: (618)235-0014
Fax: (618)235-0051

San Juan 21 Class Association
[22665]
6 Stately Oaks Ln.
Belleville, IL 62220
Abelin, Bob, Commodore

North American Deutsch Kurzhaar
Club **[21927]**
c/o Rick Medina, Membership
Coordinator
17W050 Woodland Ave.
Bensenville, IL 60106
Kaltenegger, Jörg, VP

Bishop Hill Heritage Association
[20959]
103 Bishop Hill St.
Bishop Hill, IL 61419-0092
PH: (309)927-3899
DeDecker, Todd, Administrator

American Dental Assistants Associa-
tion **[14403]**
140 N Bloomingdale Rd.
Bloomingdale, IL 60108-1017
PH: (630)994-4247
Toll free: 877-874-3785
Fax: (630)351-8490
Kasper, John, Exec. Dir.

American Society of Clinical
Hypnosis **[15360]**
140 N Bloomingdale Rd.
Bloomingdale, IL 60108-1017
PH: (630)980-4740
Fax: (630)351-8490
Erickson, Milton H., Founder

User Experience Professionals Association **[1808]**
140 N Bloomingdale Rd.
Bloomingdale, IL 60108-1017

PH: (630)980-4997
    (470)333-8972
Fox, Jean, Treasurer

American Rabbit Breeders Associa-
tion **[4592]**
PO Box 5667
Bloomington, IL 61702
PH: (309)664-7500
Fax: (309)664-0941
Stewart, Eric, Exec. Dir.

Cervantes Society of America **[9048]**
c/o Carolyn Nadeau, Managing
Director
Illinois Wesleyan University
Dept. of Hispanic Studies
Bloomington, IL 61702
Nadeau, Carolyn, Managing Dir.

Chinese American Educational
Research and Development As-
sociation **[7599]**
PO Box 355
Bloomington, IL 61702
Rui, Bai, Bd. Member

Corporate Alliance to End Partner
Violence **[11698]**
2416 E Washington St., Ste. E
Bloomington, IL 61704
PH: (309)664-0667
Fax: (309)664-0747

Project Linus **[11134]**
PO Box 5621
Bloomington, IL 61702-5621
PH: (309)585-0686
Fax: (309)585-0745
Babbitt, Carol, Chairperson, Exec.
Dir.

Evangelical Church Alliance **[20119]**
205 W Broadway St.
Bradley, IL 60915
PH: (815)937-0720
Toll free: 888-855-6060
Fax: (815)937-0001
Turrill, Rev. Robert, President, CEO

Friends of Shelter Children in Kenya
[10989]
PO Box 2206
Bridgeview, IL 60455
McLaughlin, Willie, President

United States Adult Soccer Associa-
tion **[23192]**
7000 S Harlem Ave.
Bridgeview, IL 60455-1160
PH: (708)496-6870
Fax: (708)496-6879
Riddle, Duncan, Exec. Dir.

American Sokol Organization
[19417]
9126 Ogden Ave.
Brookfield, IL 60513-1943
PH: (708)255-5397
Cushing, Mary, Advisor

Delta Mu Delta Honor Society
[23691]
9217 Broadway Ave.
Brookfield, IL 60513-1251
PH: (708)485-8494
Toll free: 866-789-7067
Fax: (708)221-6183
Arnold, Jeffrey, Exec. Dir.

International Association of Jazz
Record Collectors **[22249]**
c/o Ian Tiele, Treasurer
PO Box 524
Brookfield, IL 60513-0524
Wheeler, Geoff, President

Association of Christian Truckers
[20355]
1366 US Highway 40
Brownstown, IL 62418

PH: (618)427-3737
Weaver, Pastor Mel, VP

Fur Takers of America [4723]
PO Box 3
Buckley, IL 60918
PH: (217)394-2577
Andres, Charles, President

American Board of Psychiatry and
Neurology [16817]
2150 E Lake Cook Rd., Ste. 900
Buffalo Grove, IL 60089
PH: (847)229-6500
Fax: (847)229-6600
Faulkner, Larry R., MD, CEO,
President

Chinese American Food Society
[6644]
c/o Zachary Zheng, Treasurer
2390 Chambound Dr.
Buffalo Grove, IL 60089
Wu, Vivian, President

Haviland Collectors International
Foundation [21580]
PO Box 5163
Buffalo Grove, IL 60089
Daniels, Fred, President

National Certification Board for
Therapeutic Massage & Bodywork
[15561]
1333 Burr Ridge Pky., Ste. 200
Burr Ridge, IL 60527
PH: (630)627-8000
Toll free: 800-296-0664
Watts, Dr. Stuart, Treasurer

North American Spine Society
[16034]
7075 Veterans Blvd.
Burr Ridge, IL 60527
PH: (630)230-3600
Toll free: 866-960-6277
Fax: (630)230-3700
Muehlbauer, Eric, Exec. Dir.

Professional Reactor Operator
Society [6935]
PO Box 484
Byron, IL 61010-0484
PH: (815)234-8140

National Association of Farm Busi-
ness Analysis Specialists [3526]
c/o Bob Rhea, Executive Director
PO Box 467
Camp Point, IL 62320
Rhea, Bob, Exec. Dir.

American Institute of Hydrology
[7360]
Southern Illinois University Carbon-
dale
1230 Lincoln Dr.
Carbondale, IL 62901
PH: (618)453-7809
(651)484-8169
Fax: (651)484-8357
Suro, Thomas P., Secretary

Center for Teaching About China
[8024]
c/o Kathleen Trescott, Manager
1214 W Schwartz St.
Carbondale, IL 62901
PH: (618)549-1555
Greer, Diana, President

Universities Council on Water
Resources [7378]
Southern Illinois University Carbon-
dale
1231 Lincoln Dr.
Carbondale, IL 62901
PH: (618)536-7571
Fax: (618)453-2671
Williard, Karl, Exec. Dir.

Adopt A Husky, Inc. [10560]
PO Box 87226
Carol Stream, IL 60188-7226
PH: (262)909-2244
Toll free: 866-232-6882

Dietetics in Health Care Communi-
ties [16217]
c/o Academy of Nutrition and Dietet-
ics
PO Box 4489
Carol Stream, IL 60197-4489
PH: (319)235-0991
Toll free: 800-877-1600
Fax: (319)235-7224
Weigand, Kathy, Comm. Chm.

The Evangelical Alliance Mission
[20411]
400 S Main Pl.
Carol Stream, IL 60188
PH: (630)653-5300
Toll free: 800-343-3144
Fax: (630)653-1826
Kowalenko, Don, Chairman

Media Associates International
[20121]
351 S Main Pl., Ste. 230
Carol Stream, IL 60188-2455
PH: (630)260-9063
Fax: (630)260-9265
Maust, John D., President

Q Place [19763]
25W560 Geneva Rd.
Carol Stream, IL 60188
PH: (630)668-4399
Toll free: 800-369-0307
Fax: (630)668-4363
Schaller, Mary, President

American Topical Association
[22306]
100 N Division St., Fl. 2
Carterville, IL 62918
PH: (618)985-5100
(817)274-1181
Fax: (618)985-5100
Felts, Vera, Exec. Dir., Director

Create A Smile Dental Foundation
[14426]
607 W Idaho Ave.
Carterville, IL 62918
PH: (618)925-2140
Flora, John, Founder, President

American Dairy Science Association
[3979]
1880 S Oak St., Ste. 100
Champaign, IL 61820-6974
PH: (217)356-5146
Fax: (217)398-4119
Studney, Peter, Exec. Dir.

American Embryo Transfer Associa-
tion [3613]
1800 S Oak St., Ste. 100
Champaign, IL 61820-6974
PH: (217)398-2217
Fax: (217)398-4119
Schmidt, Jon, President

American Meat Science Association
[6639]
1 E Main St., Ste. 200
Champaign, IL 61820
PH: (217)356-5370
Toll free: 800-517-AMSA
Fax: (217)356-5370
Powell, Thomas, Exec. Dir.

American Registry of Professional
Animal Scientists [3614]
1800 S Oak St., Ste. 100
Champaign, IL 61820-6974
PH: (217)356-5390
Fax: (217)398-4119
Wettemann, Robert P., President

American Society of Animal Science
[3615]
PO Box 7410
Champaign, IL 61826-7410
PH: (217)356-9050
Fax: (217)568-6070
Aaron, Dr. Debra K., President

American Society of Mining and
Reclamation [5632]
1305 Weathervane
Champaign, IL 61821
PH: (217)333-9489
Darmody, Robert, Exec. Sec.

Association of American Feed
Control Officials [4942]
1800 S Oak St., Ste. 100
Champaign, IL 61820-6974
PH: (217)356-4221
Fax: (217)398-4119
Kashani, Ali, Secretary, Treasurer

Board of Certified Safety Profession-
als [7107]
2301 W Bradley Ave.
Champaign, IL 61821
PH: (217)359-9263
Fax: (217)359-0055
Turnbeaugh, Treasa M., Ph.D.,
CEO, Secretary

Committee on Institutional Coopera-
tion [7632]
1819 S Neil St., Ste. D
Champaign, IL 61820-7271
PH: (217)333-8475
(217)244-9240
Fax: (217)244-7127
McFadden-Allen, Barbara, Exec. Dir.

Council for Research in Music
Education [8365]
University of Illinois Press
1325 S Oak St.
Champaign, IL 61820
PH: (217)244-0626
Toll free: 866-244-0626
Fax: (217)244-9910
Barrett, Dr. Janet R., Editor

Federation of Animal Science Societ-
ies [3616]
1800 S Oak St., Ste. 100
Champaign, IL 61820-6974
PH: (217)356-3182
Fax: (217)398-4119
Rankin, Scott, President

IEEE - Ultrasonics, Ferroelectrics,
and Frequency Control Society
[5854]
1800 S Oak St., Ste 100
Champaign, IL 61820
PH: (217)356-3182
Lu, Jian-yu, President

International Coalition for Aging and
Physical Activity [16702]
1607 N Market St.
Champaign, IL 61820-2220

International Embryo Transfer
Society [17649]
1800 S Oak St., Ste. 100
Champaign, IL 61820-6974
PH: (217)398-4697
Fax: (217)398-4119
Blondin, Patrick, President

International Society of Arboriculture
[4731]
2101 W Park Ct.
Champaign, IL 61821
PH: (217)355-9411
Toll free: 888-472-8733
Fax: (217)355-9516
Roberts, Mark, President

Labor and Employment Relations
Association [23467]
c/o Emily Smith, Interim Executive
Director
121 Labor & Employment Relations
Bldg.
School of Labor & Employment
Relations
University of Illinois at Urbana-
Champaign
504 E Armory Ave.
Champaign, IL 61820
PH: (217)333-0072
Fax: (217)265-5130
Smith, Emily, Exec. Dir. (Actg.)

National Academy of Kinesiology
[8429]
PO Box 5076
Champaign, IL 61825-5076
Fax: (217)351-1549
Ennis, Catherine D., PhD,
Chairperson

National Association of Advisors for
the Health Professions, Inc. [8328]
108 Hessel Blvd., Ste. 101
Champaign, IL 61820-6574
PH: (217)355-0063
Fax: (217)355-1287
Maxwell, Susan A., Exec. Dir.

National Coalition for Food and
Agricultural Research [3551]
1800 S Oak St., Ste. 100
Champaign, IL 61820-6974
PH: (217)356-3182
Fax: (217)398-4119
LaVigne, Andrew W., VP

Orthopterists' Society [6616]
c/o Pamm Mihm, Treasurer
2417 Fields South Dr.
Champaign, IL 61822
Hunter, David, Exec. Dir.

Poultry Science Association [4571]
1800 S Oak St., Ste. 100
Champaign, IL 61820-6974
PH: (217)356-5285
Fax: (217)398-4119
Koenig, Stephen E., Exec. Dir.

Society of Municipal Arborists [4217]
PO Box 3129
Champaign, IL 61826-3129
Lefcourt, David, President

Vietnam Veterans Against the War
[19225]
PO Box 355
Champaign, IL 61824-0355
PH: (773)569-3520
Branson, Bill, Coord.

Korean War Veterans Association
[21007]
430 W Lincoln Ave.
Charleston, IL 61920-3021
PH: (863)859-1384
(682)518-1040
Mac Swain, William F., Officer

AACM Chicago [9844]
Chicago, IL
PH: (312)555-5555
Bowden, Mwata, Chairman

Academy of General Dentistry
[14365]
560 W Lake St., 6th Fl.
Chicago, IL 60661-6600
Toll free: 888-243-DENT
Buksa, Daniel, Assoc. Dir.

Academy of Nutrition and Dietetics
[16198]
120 S Riverside Plz, Ste. 2000
Chicago, IL 60606-6995

PH: (312)899-0040
Toll free: 800-877-1600
Babjak, Patricia M., CEO

Accessibility Interoperability Alliance [6733]
330 N Wabash Ave., Ste. 2000
Chicago, IL 60611
PH: (312)321-5172
Toll free: 877-687-2842
Fax: (312)673-6659
Dikter, David, CEO

Accreditation Council for Continuing Medical Education [15701]
515 N State St., Ste. 1801
Chicago, IL 60654
PH: (312)527-9200
LeBlanc, Kim Edward, MD, Exec. Dir.

Accreditation Council for Graduate Medical Education [7409]
515 N State St., Ste. 2000
Chicago, IL 60654
PH: (312)755-5000
Fax: (312)755-7498
Meyer, Lynne, PhD, Exec. Dir.

Accreditation Council for Pharmacy Education [16630]
135 S LaSalle St., Ste. 4100
Chicago, IL 60603-4810
PH: (312)664-3575
Fax: (312)664-4652
Rouse, Michael J., Director

Action for Healthy Kids [14163]
600 W Van Buren St., Ste. 720
Chicago, IL 60607
Toll free: 800-416-5136
Fax: (312)212-0098
Bisceglie, Rob, CEO

Advocates for the American Osteopathic Association [16500]
142 E Ontario St.
Chicago, IL 60611-2864
PH: (303)617-5310
    (312)202-8192
Toll free: 800-621-1773

AFL-CIO/ALA Joint Committee on Library Service to Labor Groups [9665]
50 E Huron St.
Chicago, IL 60611
Toll free: 800-545-2433

Aikido Association of America [22494]
1016 W Belmont Ave.
Chicago, IL 60657
PH: (773)525-3141
Toyoda, Fumio, Founder

Alianza Americas [11312]
1638 S Blue Island Ave.
Chicago, IL 60608
Toll free: 877-683-2908
Sanbrano, Angela, President

Alliance of the American Dental Association [14370]
211 E Chicago Ave., Ste. 730
Chicago, IL 60611-2616
Toll free: 800-621-8099
Fax: (312)440-2587
Rubik-Rothstein, Trish, Director

Alliance of Independent Academic Medical Centers [15619]
401 N Michigan Ave., Ste. 1200
Chicago, IL 60611-4264
PH: (312)836-3712
Pierce-Boggs, Kimberly, Exec. Dir.

Alliance of Merger and Acquisition Advisors [605]
222 N LaSalle St., Ste. 300
Chicago, IL 60601

PH: (312)856-9590
Toll free: 877-844-2535
Nall, Michael, Founder

Alliance for Water Efficiency [4749]
33 N LaSalle St., Ste. 2275
Chicago, IL 60602
PH: (773)360-5100
Toll free: 866-730-A4WE
Fax: (773)345-3636
Dickinson, Mary Ann, CEO, President

Alpha Kappa Alpha [23869]
5656 S Stony Island Ave.
Chicago, IL 60637
PH: (773)684-1282
Howell, Cynthia D., Exec. Dir.

Alpha Psi Lambda National [23886]
PO Box 804835
Chicago, IL 60680
PH: (847)361-4378
Maday, Michelle L., President

Altrusa International, Inc. [12882]
1 N LaSalle St., Ste. 1955
Chicago, IL 60602-4006
PH: (312)427-4410
Silverman, Silvia, President

Alzheimer's Association [13669]
225 N Michigan Ave., 17th Fl.
Chicago, IL 60601-7633
PH: (312)335-8700
    (312)335-5886
Toll free: 866-699-1246
Urbashich, Mary Ann

Alzheimer's Impact Movement [13671]
225 N Michigan Ave., 17th Fl.
Chicago, IL 60601-7633
Thompson, Evan, Chairman

American Academy of Cosmetic Surgery [14300]
225 W Wacker Dr., Ste. 650
Chicago, IL 60606
PH: (312)981-6760
Fax: (312)265-2908
Shumway, Robert A., President

American Academy of Esthetic Dentistry [14375]
225 W Wacker Dr., Ste. 650
Chicago, IL 60606
PH: (312)981-6770
Jackson, Mr. Joseph M., CAE, Exec. Dir.

American Academy of Home Care Medicine [15275]
8735 W Higgins Rd., Ste. 300
Chicago, IL 60631
PH: (847)375-4719
Fax: (847)375-6395
Simons, Suzanne, Exec. Dir.

American Academy of Hospice and Palliative Medicine [16733]
8735 W Higgins Rd., Ste. 300
Chicago, IL 60631
PH: (847)375-4712
Fax: (847)375-6475
Smith, Steve R., CAE, CEO, Exec. Dir.

American Academy of Implant Dentistry [14380]
211 E Chicago Ave., Ste. 750
Chicago, IL 60611
PH: (312)335-1550
Toll free: 877-335-2243
Bennett, Sharon, Exec. Dir.

American Academy of Matrimonial Lawyers [5187]
150 N Michigan Ave., Ste. 1420
Chicago, IL 60601

PH: (312)263-6477
Fax: (312)263-7682
Davis, Joslin, President

American Academy of Medical Administrators [15566]
330 N Wabash 2000
Chicago, IL 60611
Baliozian, Kevin, Exec. Dir.

American Academy of Medical Administrators Research and Educational Foundation [15567]
330 N Wabash Ave., Ste. 2000
Chicago, IL 60611
PH: (312)321-6815
Fax: (312)673-6705
Conde, Eric, MSA, CFAAMA, Bd. Member

American Academy of Neurological and Orthopaedic Surgeons [16057]
1516 N Lakeshore Dr.
Chicago, IL 60610
PH: (312)787-1608
Fax: (312)787-9289

American Academy of Pain Medicine [16547]
8735 W Higgins Rd., Ste. 3000
Chicago, IL 60631-2738
PH: (847)375-4731
Fax: (847)375-6477
McCarberg, Bill H., M.D., Director

American Academy of Pain Medicine Foundation [16548]
8735 W Higgins Rd., Ste. 300
Chicago, IL 60631
PH: (847)375-4731
Saigh, Phil, Exec. Dir.

American Academy of Pediatric Dentistry [14386]
211 E Chicago Ave., Ste. 1600
Chicago, IL 60611-2637
PH: (312)337-2169
Fax: (312)337-6329
Rutkauskas, John S., CEO

American Academy of Periodontology [14387]
737 N Michigan Ave., Ste. 800
Chicago, IL 60611-6660
PH: (312)787-5518
Newhouse, Nancy L.

American Aid Society of German Descendants [19440]
6540 N Milwaukee Ave.
Chicago, IL 60631-1750
Henz, Siegfried, President

American Anthropological Association - Archeology Division [5928]
c/o Jane Eva Baxter, Secretary
DePaul University
2343 N Racine Ave.
Chicago, IL 60614
PH: (773)325-4757
Fax: (773)325-4761
McAnany, Patricia, President

American Association of Cardiovascular and Pulmonary Rehabilitation [14087]
330 N Wabash Ave., Ste. 200
Chicago, IL 60611
PH: (312)321-5146
Fax: (312)673-6924
Cohen, Megan, Exec. Dir.

American Association of Dental Boards [14389]
211 E Chicago Ave., Ste. 760
Chicago, IL 60611
PH: (312)440-7464
Fax: (312)440-3525
Hetke, Richard, Exec. Dir.

American Association of Diabetes Educators [14517]
200 W Madison St., Ste. 800
Chicago, IL 60606
Toll free: 800-338-3633
Fax: (312)424-2427
D'Hondt, Nancy, Officer

American Association of Endodontists [14391]
211 E Chicago Ave., Ste. 1100
Chicago, IL 60611-2691
PH: (312)266-7255
Toll free: 800-872-3636
Fax: (312)266-9867
Hannen, Margie, Exec. Sec.

American Association of Individual Investors [7918]
625 N Michigan Ave.
Chicago, IL 60611
PH: (312)280-0170
Toll free: 800-428-2244
Fax: (312)280-9883
Cloonan, James B., PhD, Founder, Chairman

American Association of Law Libraries [5562]
105 W Adams St., Ste. 3300
Chicago, IL 60603
PH: (312)939-4764
Fax: (312)431-1097
Hagan, Kate, Exec. Dir.

American Association of Legal Nurse Consultants [15525]
330 N Wabash Ste. 2000
Chicago, IL 60611-4267
Toll free: 877-402-2562
Fax: (312)673-6655
Sussex, Mary K., MBA, Secretary, Treasurer

American Association of Medical Assistants [15615]
20 N Wacker Dr., Ste. 1575
Chicago, IL 60606
PH: (312)899-1500
Toll free: 800-228-2262
Fax: (312)899-1259
Watson, Nina, CMA (AAMA), CPC, President

American Association of Neuroscience Nurses [16093]
8735 W Higgins Rd., Ste. 300
Chicago, IL 60631
PH: (847)375-4733
Fax: (847)375-6430
Kram, Joan, Exec. Dir.

American Association of Occupational Health Nurses [16097]
330 N Wabash Ave., Ste. 2000
Chicago, IL 60611
PH: (312)321-5173
Fax: (312)673-6719
Tomlinson, Jeannie, President

American Association of School Librarians [9666]
50 E Huron St.
Chicago, IL 60611-2729
PH: (312)280-4382
Toll free: 800-545-2433
Fax: (312)280-5276
Cline, Allison, Dep. Dir.

American Association for the Surgery of Trauma [17523]
633 N St. Clair St., Ste. 2600
Chicago, IL 60611
Toll free: 800-789-4006
Fax: (312)202-5064
Gautschy, Ms. Sharon, Exec. Dir.

American Bar Association [4981]
321 N Clark St.
Chicago, IL 60654

PH: (312)988-5000
Toll free: 800-285-2221
Brown, Paulette, President

American Bar Association Center for
Professional Responsibility [4982]
321 N Clark St.
Chicago, IL 60654
PH: (312)988-5000
Toll free: 800-988-2221
Garwin, Arthur H., Director

American Bar Association - Commis-
sion on Women in the Profession
[5406]
321 N Clark St., 18th Fl.
Chicago, IL 60654
PH: (312)988-5715
Fax: (312)988-5790
Brown, Paulette, President

American Bar Association - Health
Law Section [5272]
321 N Clark St.
Chicago, IL 60654-7598
Fax: (312)988-5814
Clark, Michael E., Chairman

American Bar Association - Law
Student Division [8207]
321 N Clark St.
Chicago, IL 60654
PH: (312)988-5624
Toll free: 800-285-2221
Fax: (312)988-6033
Groothuis, Austin, Director

American Bar Association National
Conference of the Administrative
Law Judiciary [5408]
321 N Clark St.
Chicago, IL 60654
Toll free: 800-285-2221
Mann, Hon. Julian, III, Chairman

American Bar Association - Section
of International Law [5346]
321 N Clark St.
Chicago, IL 60654
PH: (312)988-5000
Pfautz, Leanne, Director

American Bar Association - Section
of Science and Technology Law
[5409]
321 N Clark St., 18th Fl.
Chicago, IL 60654-4740
PH: (312)988-5599
Fax: (312)988-6797
Hawk, Caryn, Director

American Bar Association - Young
Lawyers Division [4983]
321 N Clark St., 18th Fl.
Chicago, IL 60654-7598
PH: (312)988-5611
Toll free: 800-285-2221
Fax: (312)988-6231
Rone, Robin, Director

American Bar Foundation [5410]
750 N Lake Shore Dr.
Chicago, IL 60611-4403
PH: (312)988-6500
Fax: (312)988-6579
Flannery, Ellen J., VP

American Board of Certification for
Gastroenterology Nurses [16098]
330 N Wabash Ave., Ste. 2000
Chicago, IL 60611
Toll free: 855-252-2246
Fax: (312)673-6723
Buffington, Kathy

American Board of Endodontics
[14396]
211 E Chicago Ave., Ste. 1100
Chicago, IL 60611-2691

PH: (312)266-7255
Toll free: 800-872-3636
Fax: (312)266-9867
Johnson, Dr. James D., President

American Board of Medical Special-
ties [15661]
353 N Clark St., Ste. 1400
Chicago, IL 60654
PH: (312)436-2600
Parisi, Valerie M., MD, Chairperson

American Board of Neuroscience
Nursing [16100]
8735 W Higgins Rd., Ste. 300
Chicago, IL 60631
PH: (847)375-4733
Toll free: 888-557-2266
Fax: (847)375-6430
Kram, Joan, Exec. Dir.

American Board of Oral and Maxillo-
facial Surgery [16442]
625 N Michigan Ave., Ste. 1820
Chicago, IL 60611-3177
PH: (312)642-0070
Hoxie, Lance O., Contact

American Board of Preventive
Medicine [16796]
111 W Jackson Blvd., Ste. 1340
Chicago, IL 60604
PH: (312)939-2276
Fax: (312)939-2218
Greaves, William W., MD, Exec. Dir.

American Board of Thoracic Surgery
[17470]
633 N St. Clair St., Ste. 2320
Chicago, IL 60611
PH: (312)202-5900
Fax: (312)202-5960
Baumgartner, William A., MD, Exec.
Dir.

American Brain Tumor Association
[13880]
8550 W Bryn Mawr Ave., Ste. 550
Chicago, IL 60631
PH: (773)577-8750
Toll free: 800-886-2282
Fax: (773)577-8738
Wilson, Elizabeth M., President,
CEO

American Broncho-Esophagological
Association [13860]
c/o American College of Surgeons
633 N St. Clair St., 27th Fl.
Chicago, IL 60611
Toll free: 855-876-2232
Fax: (312)278-0793
Grillone, Gregory A., President

American Burn Association [13862]
311 S Wacker Dr., Ste. 4150
Chicago, IL 60606-6671
PH: (312)642-9260
Fax: (312)642-9130
Krichbaum, John A., JD, Exec. Dir.,
CEO

American College of Cardiovascular
Administrators [15573]
American Academy of Medical
Administrators
330 N Wabash Ave., Ste. 200
Chicago, IL 60611
PH: (312)321-6815
Fax: (312)673-6705
Steaban, Robin, President

American College of Correctional
Physicians [16735]
1145 W Diversey Pky.
Chicago, IL 60614-1318
Toll free: 800-229-7380
Fax: (773)880-2424
Wilcox, Todd, President

American College of Foot and Ankle
Surgeons [16782]
8725 W Higgins Rd., Ste. 555
Chicago, IL 60631-2724
PH: (773)693-9300
Toll free: 800-421-2237
Fax: (773)693-9304
Mahaffey, J.C., CAE, Exec. Dir.

American College of Healthcare
Executives [15304]
1 N Franklin St., Ste. 1700
Chicago, IL 60606-3529
PH: (312)424-2800
 (312)424-9400
Fax: (312)424-0023
Bowen, Deborah J., CEO, President

American College of Osteopathic
Emergency Physicians [14674]
142 E Ontario St., Ste. 1500
Chicago, IL 60611-5277
PH: (312)587-3709
Toll free: 800-521-3709
Fax: (312)587-9951
Wachtler, Janice, Exec. Dir.

American College of Prosthodontists
[14402]
211 E Chicago Ave., Ste. 1000
Chicago, IL 60611
PH: (312)573-1260
Driscoll, Carl F., President

American College of Psychiatrists
[16818]
122 S Michigan Ave., Ste. 1360
Chicago, IL 60603
PH: (312)662-1020
Fax: (312)662-1025
Samuels, Craig, Exec. Dir.

American College of Surgeons
[17367]
633 N St. Clair St.
Chicago, IL 60611-3211
PH: (312)202-5000
Toll free: 800-621-4111
Fax: (312)202-5001
Hoyt, David B., MD, Exec. Dir.

American College of Surgeons Com-
mission on Cancer [13885]
633 N St. Clair St.
Chicago, IL 60611-3211
PH: (312)202-5085
Fax: (312)202-5009
Watt, Lynda, Admin. Asst.

American Collegiate Hockey As-
sociation [22905]
7638 Solution Ctr.
Chicago, IL 60677-7006
PH: (330)221-4411
Hebert, Paul, President

American Contract Compliance As-
sociation [11753]
17 E Monroe St., No. 150
Chicago, IL 60603
Toll free: 866-222-2298
Fax: (510)287-2158
Alexander, Lisa, President

American Council for Southern Asian
Art [8831]
Dept. of Art History
University of Illinois at Chicago
211A Henry Hall
935 W Harrison St.
Chicago, IL 60607
PH: (312)996-3303
Fax: (312)413-2460
Becker, Catherine, Secretary

American Dental Association [14404]
211 E Chicago Ave.
Chicago, IL 60611-2678

PH: (312)440-2500
Toll free: 800-947-4746
Fax: (312)440-3542
Berry, James H., Assoc. Pub.

American Dental Hygienists' Association [14406]
444 N Michigan Ave., Ste. 3400
Chicago, IL 60611
PH: (312)440-8900
 (312)440-8913
Battrell, Ann, Exec. Dir.

American Dental Hygienists' Association Institute for Oral Health
[14407]
444 N Michigan Ave., Ste. 3400
Chicago, IL 60611
PH: (312)440-8900

American Dental Society of
Anesthesiology [14408]
211 E Chicago Ave.
Chicago, IL 60611
PH: (312)664-8270
Fax: (312)224-8624
Charlton, Mr. Knight, Exec. Dir.

American Equilibration Society
[14410]
207 E Ohio St., Ste. 399
Chicago, IL 60611
PH: (847)965-2888
Fax: (609)573-5064
Peters, Dr. Kenneth S., Exec.

American Foundation for Surgery of
the Hand [14906]
822 W Washington Blvd.
Chicago, IL 60607
PH: (312)880-1900
Fax: (847)384-1435
Anderson, Mark C., CAE, CEO,
Exec. VP

American Franchisee Association
[1456]
53 W Jackson Blvd., Ste. 1256
Chicago, IL 60604
PH: (312)431-0545
Fax: (312)431-1469
Kezios, Susan P., President

American Gynecological and
Obstetrical Society [16273]
230 W Monroe St., Ste. 710
Chicago, IL 60606
PH: (312)676-3920
Fax: (312)235-4059
Ocampo, Jennifer, Exec. Dir.

American Health and Beauty Aids
Institute [1582]
PO Box 19510
Chicago, IL 60619-0510
PH: (708)633-6328
Fax: (708)633-6329
Hammond, Clyde, Chairman

American Health Information
Management Association [15633]
233 N Michigan Ave., 21st Fl.
Chicago, IL 60601-5809
PH: (312)233-1100
Toll free: 800-335-5535
Fax: (312)233-1090
Martin, Melissa M., President,
Chairperson

American Hospital Association
[15305]
155 N Wacker Dr.
Chicago, IL 60606
PH: (312)422-3000
Evans, John, Sr. VP, CFO

American Hospital Association - Section for Long-Term Care and
Rehabilitation [15306]
155 N Wacker Dr., Ste. 400
Chicago, IL 60606

PH: (312)422-3000
Sonik, Susanne, Director

American Hospital Association - Section for Metropolitan Hospitals [15307]
155 N Wacker Dr., Ste. 400
Chicago, IL 60606
PH: (312)422-3000
   (312)422-3317
Coopwood, Reginald, Chairman

American Hospital Association Section for Psychiatric and Substance Abuse Services [16819]
155 N Wacker Dr.
Chicago, IL 60606
PH: (312)422-3000
Toll free: 800-424-4301
Fax: (312)422-4796
Perlin, MD, PhD, Jonathan B., Chairman

American Institute of Indian Studies [9564]
1130 E 59th St.
Chicago, IL 60637
PH: (773)702-8638
Lutgendorf, Philip, President

American Institute of Steel Construction [6346]
1 E Wacker Dr., Ste. 700
Chicago, IL 60601-1802
PH: (312)670-2400
Fax: (312)670-5403
Melnick, Scott, VP of Corp. Comm.

American Joint Committee on Cancer [16332]
633 N St. Clair St.
Chicago, IL 60611-3211
PH: (312)202-5205
Fax: (312)202-5009
Winchester, David P., MD, Exec. Dir.

American Ladder Institute [1564]
330 N Wabash Ave., Ste. 2000
Chicago, IL 60611
PH: (202)367-1136
Fax: (312)673-6929
Moss, Ryan, President

American Library Association [9668]
50 E Huron St.
Chicago, IL 60611-2795
PH: (312)944-6780
Toll free: 800-545-2433
Fax: (312)440-9374
Fiels, Keith Michael, Exec. Dir.

American Library Association - Alternatives Media Task Force [9669]
Alternatives Media Task Force
50 E Huron St.
Chicago, IL 60611
Toll free: 800-545-2433
Gulyas, Carol, Coord.

American Library Association - Gay, Lesbian, Bisexual and Transgender Round Table [9670]
50 E Huron St.
Chicago, IL 60611-2795
PH: (312)944-6780
Toll free: 800-545-2433
Hansen, Roland C., Officer

American Library Association Learning Round Table [9671]
50 E Huron St.
Chicago, IL 60611-2729
PH: (312)944-6780
Toll free: 800-545-2433
Fax: (312)440-9374
Moen, Caitlin, President

American Library Association - Office for Intellectual Freedom [9672]
50 E Huron St.
Chicago, IL 60611

PH: (312)280-4220
Toll free: 800-545-2433
Fax: (312)280-4227
LaRue, James, Director

American Library Association Office for Research and Statistics [9673]
50 E Huron St.
Chicago, IL 60611
PH: (312)280-4283
Toll free: 800-545-2433
Rosa, Kathy, Director

American Library Association Public Awareness Office [9674]
50 E Huron St.
Chicago, IL 60611
PH: (312)280-4393
   (312)280-1546
Gould, Mark R., Director

American Library Association Young Adult Library Services Association [9675]
50 E Huron St.
Chicago, IL 60611
PH: (312)280-4390
Toll free: 800-545-2433
Fax: (312)280-5276
Yoke, Beth, Exec. Dir.

American Marketing Association [2264]
311 S Wacker Dr., Ste. 5800
Chicago, IL 60606
PH: (312)542-9000
Toll free: 800-AMA-1150
Fax: (312)542-9001
Sweeney, Ric, Chairperson

American Medical Association [15708]
AMA Plaza
330 N Wabash Ave.
Chicago, IL 60611
PH: (312)464-4430
Toll free: 800-621-8335
Fax: (312)464-5226
Gierhahn, Rebecca, Director

American Medical Association Council on Medical Education [8291]
AMA Plz.
330 N Wabash Ave.
Chicago, IL 60611-5885
Menscer, Darlyne, Chairperson

American Medical Association Foundation [8302]
AMA Plz.
330 N Wabash Ave., Ste. 39300
Chicago, IL 60611-5885
PH: (312)464-4200
Fax: (312)464-4142
Kobler, William, MD, President

American Medical Association - Liaison Committee on Medical Education [8292]
330 N Wabash Ave., Ste. 39300
Chicago, IL 60611-5885
PH: (312)464-4933
Barzansky, Barbara, PhD, MHPE, Secretary

American MGB Association [21321]
PO Box 11401
Chicago, IL 60611
PH: (773)769-7084
Fax: (773)769-3240
Ochal, Frank J., President

American Naprapathic Association [15851]
2731 N Lincoln Ave.
Chicago, IL 60614
PH: (312)698-9855
Fax: (312)380-4637
Varanauski, Daniel E, DN, President

American Osteopathic Association [16508]
142 E Ontario St.
Chicago, IL 60611-2864
PH: (312)202-8000
Toll free: 800-621-1773
Fax: (312)202-8200
Becher, John W., President

American Osteopathic Association of Medical Informatics [16509]
142 E Ontario St.
Chicago, IL 60611-2864
PH: (312)202-8142
Toll free: 800-621-1773
Fax: (312)202-8449
Gippe, Annette, Exec. Dir.

American Osteopathic Board of Emergency Medicine [14675]
c/o Jennifer Hausman, Certification Director
142 E Ontario
Chicago, IL 60611
PH: (312)202-8293
Fax: (312)202-8402
Janssen, Alan, Chairman

American Osteopathic Board of Pediatrics [16512]
142 E Ontario St., 4th Fl.
Chicago, IL 60611
Toll free: 800-621-1773
Fax: (312)202-8441
Woods, Ellen, MSC, Exec. Dir.

American Osteopathic Board of Preventive Medicine [16513]
142 E Ontario St., 4th Fl.
Chicago, IL 60611
Toll free: 800-621-1773
Fax: (312)202-8319
Woods, Ellen, MSC, Contact

American Osteopathic College of Pathologists [16515]
142 E Ontario St.
Chicago, IL 60611-8224
PH: (312)202-8197
Fax: (312)202-8224
Nelson, Donald, President

American Osteopathic Foundation [16518]
142 E Ontario St., Ste. 1450
Chicago, IL 60611
PH: (312)202-8234
Toll free: 866-455-9383
Fax: (312)202-8216
Downey, Stephen S., Exec. Dir.

American Pain Society [16551]
8735 W Higgins, Ste. 300
Chicago, IL 60631-2738
PH: (847)375-4715
Inturrisi, Charles E., Ph.D., President

American Planning Association [5095]
205 N Michigan Ave., Ste. 1200
Chicago, IL 60601
PH: (312)431-9100
Fax: (312)786-6700
Simms, Ann, CFO, COO

American Prosthodontic Society [14413]
225 W Wacker Dr., Ste. 650
Chicago, IL 60606
PH: (312)981-6780
Fax: (312)265-2908
Bello, Antonio, Officer

American-Russian Chamber of Commerce & Industry [23554]
Aon Ctr.
200 E Randolph St., Ste. 2200
Chicago, IL 60601

PH: (312)494-6562
Fax: (312)494-9840
Jones, Thomas M., Chairman

American Schools Association [7684]
PO Box 577820
Chicago, IL 60657-7820
Toll free: 800-230-2263
Fax: (773)782-0113

American Singers Club [21538]
c/o Ed Medrano, Secretary & Treasurer
8908 S Yates Blvd.
Chicago, IL 60617-3863
PH: (773)717-6506
Ferguson, Paul, President

American Society for Bioethics and Humanities [8305]
O'Hare Plz. Office Complex
8735 W Higgins Rd., Ste. 300
Chicago, IL 60631
PH: (847)375-4745
Fax: (847)375-6482
Cohn, Felicia, PhD, MA, President

American Society for Clinical Pathology [16574]
33 W Monroe St., Ste. 1600
Chicago, IL 60603
PH: (312)541-4999
Fax: (312)541-4998
Lewin, David N.B., President

American Society of ExtraCorporeal Technology [15678]
330 N Wabash Ave., Ste. 2000
Chicago, IL 60611
PH: (312)321-5156
Fax: (312)673-6656
Hinckley, Stewart, Exec. Dir.

American Society for Healthcare Engineering [15308]
155 N Wacker Dr., Ste. 400
Chicago, IL 60606-1719
PH: (312)422-3800
Fax: (312)422-4571
Woodin, Mr. Dale, Exec. Dir.

American Society for Healthcare Human Resources Administration [15309]
155 N Wacker Dr., Ste. 400
Chicago, IL 60606
PH: (312)422-3720
Fax: (312)422-4577
Rubens, Deborah, President

American Society for Healthcare Risk Management [15310]
155 N Wacker Dr., Ste. 400
Chicago, IL 60606
PH: (312)422-3980
Fax: (312)422-4580
Hoarle, Kimberly, MBA, Exec. Dir.

American Society of Lipo-Suction Surgery [17373]
American Academy of Cosmetic Surgery
225 W Wacker Dr., Ste. 650
Chicago, IL 60606
PH: (312)981-6760

American Society of Naturalists [6893]
PO Box 37005
Chicago, IL 60637-0005
PH: (773)753-3347
Toll free: 877-705-1878
Lau, Jennifer, Secretary

American Society of Pediatric Hematology/Oncology [15221]
8735 W Higgins Rd., Ste. 300
Chicago, IL 60631-2738

PH: (847)375-4716
Fax: (847)375-6483
Biddle, Steve, Consultant

American Society for Reconstructive
Microsurgery [17375]
20 N Michigan Ave., Ste. 700
Chicago, IL 60602-4822
PH: (312)456-9579
Fax: (312)782-0553
Greco, Krista A., Contact

American Society of Retina Special-
ists [16370]
20 N Wacker Dr., Ste. 2030
Chicago, IL 60606
PH: (312)578-8760
Fax: (312)578-8763

American Society for Surgery of the
Hand [14908]
822 W Washington Blvd.
Chicago, IL 60607
PH: (312)880-1900
Fax: (847)384-1435
Anderson, Mark C., CAE, CEO,
Exec. VP

American Specialty Toy Retailing
Association [2063]
432 N Clark St., Ste. 305
Chicago, IL 60654
PH: (312)222-0984
Fax: (312)222-0986
May, Dean, Chairman

American Student Dental Association
[7708]
211 E Chicago Ave., Ste. 700
Chicago, IL 60611-2663
PH: (312)440-2795
Toll free: 800-621-8099
Fax: (312)440-2820
Honeycutt, Nancy, Exec. Dir.

American Theological Library As-
sociation [9677]
300 S Wacker Dr., Ste. 2100
Chicago, IL 60606-6701
PH: (312)454-5100
Toll free: 888-665-2852
Fax: (312)454-5505
Bailey-Hainer, Brenda, Exec. Dir.

American Transplant Association
[17506]
980 N Michigan Ave., Ste. 1400
Chicago, IL 60611
Toll free: 800-494-4527

American Working Malinois Associa-
tion [21281]
c/o Angie Stark, Membership Chair
PO Box 9183
Chicago, IL 60609
PH: (708)359-4113
Camper, Anne, President

Americans for Effective Law
Enforcement [5146]
PO Box 75401
Chicago, IL 60675-5401
PH: (847)685-0700
Fax: (847)685-9700
Hales, Daniel B., Director

Anti-Cruelty Society [10588]
157 W Grand Ave.
Chicago, IL 60654
PH: (312)644-8338
Fax: (312)644-3878
Barbieri, Robyn, President

Appliance Parts Distributors Associa-
tion [211]
3621 N Oakley Ave.
Chicago, IL 60618
PH: (773)230-9851
Fax: (888)308-1423
Orazietti, Phil F., President

Appraisal Institute [218]
200 W Madison St., Ste. 1500
Chicago, IL 60606
PH: (312)335-4401
(312)335-4111
Toll free: 888-756-4624
Fax: (312)335-4415
Grubbe, Fred, CEO

Arab American Association of
Engineers and Architects [5957]
PO Box 1536
Chicago, IL 60690
PH: (312)409-8560
Najib, Rabih, President

Art Therapy Connection [13728]
PO Box 146462
Chicago, IL 60614
PH: (773)791-7865
Collins, Carolyn, President

Asian Health Care Leaders Association [15577]
566 W Adams St., Ste. 750
Chicago, IL 60661
Elgarico, David, MHA, Officer

Associated Colleges of the Midwest
[7620]
11 E Adams St., Ste. 800
Chicago, IL 60603
PH: (312)263-5000
Fax: (312)263-5879
Welna, Christopher, President

Association for the Advancement of
Automotive Medicine [12815]
35 E Wacker Dr., Ste. 850
Chicago, IL 60601
PH: (847)844-3880
Fax: (312)644-8557
Pintar, Frank A., PhD, President

Association of Architecture Organiza-
tions [5962]
224 S Michigan Ave., Ste. 116
Chicago, IL 60604
PH: (312)561-2159
Fax: (312)922-2607
Wood, Michael, Exec. Dir.

Association of Black Sociologists
[7180]
3473 S Martin Luther King Dr.
Chicago, IL 60616-4108
PH: (312)342-7618
Fax: (773)955-8890
Darity, William, President

Association of Clinical Scientists
[14290]
33 W Monroe St., Ste. 1600
Chicago, IL 60603
Toll free: 800-267-2727
Fax: (312)541-4998
Valdes, Roland, Jr., PhD, Officer

Association of College and Research
Libraries [9684]
50 E Huron St.
Chicago, IL 60611
PH: (312)280-2523
Toll free: 800-545-2433
Fax: (312)280-2520
Davis, Mary Ellen K., Exec. Dir.

Association for Community Health
Improvement [16995]
155 N Wacker Dr., Ste. 400
Chicago, IL 60606
Fax: (312)422-2609
Griffin, Berna, Specialist

Association for Corporate Growth
[612]
125 S Wacker Dr., Ste. 3100
Chicago, IL 60606
Toll free: 877-358-2220
Jaffe, Richard P., Chmn. of the Bd.

Association of Directors of Anatomic
and Surgical Pathology [16576]
c/o Nilda Barrett
American Society for Clinical Pathol-
ogy
33 W Monroe St., Ste. 1600
Chicago, IL
Toll free: 800-267-2727
Fax: (312)541-4998
DeYoung, Barry R., MD, President

Association for the Healthcare
Environment [15312]
155 N Wacker Dr., Ste. 400
Chicago, IL 60606
PH: (312)422-3860
Fax: (312)422-4578
Costello, Patti, Exec. Dir.

Association for Healthcare Resource
and Materials Management
[15315]
155 N Wacker Dr., Ste. 400
Chicago, IL 60606
PH: (312)422-3840
Fax: (312)422-4573
Petty, CMRP, Brent, Chairman

Association for Healthcare Volunteer
Resource Professionals [13283]
155 N Wacker Dr., Ste. 400
Chicago, IL 60606-1725
PH: (312)422-3939
Fax: (312)278-0884
Miller, Joan M., Exec. Dir.

Association Internationale pour
l'Etude du Foie [15251]
230 S Clark St., No. 315
Chicago, IL 60604-1406
Jia, Ji-Dong, President

Association of Legal Administrators
[5417]
Presidents Plz.
8700 W Bryn Mawr Ave., Ste. 110S
Chicago, IL 60631-3512
PH: (847)267-1252
Fax: (847)267-1329
Walker, Teresa, President

Association for Library Collections &
Technical Services [9686]
50 E Huron St.
Chicago, IL 60611-2795
PH: (312)280-5037
Toll free: 800-545-2433
Fax: (312)280-5033
Sipe, Vicki L., Secretary

Association for Library Service to
Children [9687]
50 E Huron St.
Chicago, IL 60611-2795
Toll free: 800-545-2433
Fax: (312)280-5271
Striitmatter, Aimee, Exec. Dir.

Association for Nursing Professional
Development [16120]
330 N Wabash Ave., Ste. 2000
Chicago, IL 60611
PH: (312)673-5135
Fax: (312)673-6835
Warren, Joan, President

Association of Osteopathic Directors
and Medical Educators [16520]
142 E Ontario St., 4th Fl.
Chicago, IL 60611-2874
PH: (312)202-8211
Toll free: 800-621-1773
Bulger, John B., DO, Comm. Chm.

Association of Pediatric Hematology/
Oncology Nurses [16122]
8735 W Higgins Ave., Ste. 300
Chicago, IL 60631

PH: (847)375-4724
(855)202-9760
Fax: (847)375-6478
Bergeson, Dave, Exec. Dir.

Association of Printing and Data
Solutions Professionals [1528]
PO Box 13347
Chicago, IL 60613
PH: (708)218-7755
(708)571-4685
Toll free: 800-325-5165
Fax: (708)571-4731
Militano, Tony, President

Association of Professional Design
Firms [1554]
1448 E 52nd St., No. 201
Chicago, IL 60615
PH: (773)643-7052
Brownlee, Cathy, Exec. Dir.

Association of Professional
Researchers for Advancement
[11857]
330 N Wabash Ave., Ste. 2000
Chicago, IL 60611
PH: (312)321-5196
Fax: (312)673-6966
Rapp, Janet, Exec. Dir.

Association of Professional
Responsibility Lawyers [4998]
2 1st National Plz.
20 S Clark St., Ste. 1050
Chicago, IL 60603
PH: (312)782-4396
Fax: (312)782-4725
Shely, Lynda C., President

Association of Professors of Human
and Medical Genetics [14877]
c/o Darrel Waggoner, President
5841 S Maryland Ave., Rm. L161
Chicago, IL 60637
PH: (773)834-0555
Fax: (773)834-0556
Waggoner, Darrel, MD, President

Association of Program Directors in
Vascular Surgery [17379]
633 N St. Clair St., 22nd Fl.
Chicago, IL 60611
Toll free: 800-258-7188
Fax: (312)334-2320
Jordan, William, President

Association of Pulmonary and Criti-
cal Care Medicine Program Direc-
tors [14350]
559 W Diversey Pky.
Chicago, IL 60614
Toll free: 877-301-6800
Bruno-Reitzner, Joyce, MBA, Exec.
Dir.

Association of Real Estate License
Law Officials [5742]
150 N Wacker Dr., Ste. 920
Chicago, IL 60606-1682
PH: (312)300-4800
(312)300-4807
Coffee, Craig F., President

Association of Rehabilitation Nurses
[16124]
8735 W Higgins Rd., Ste. 300
Chicago, IL 60631-2738
Toll free: 800-229-7530
Lehman, Cheryl A., PhD, RN,
President

Association of Specialized and
Cooperative Library Agencies
[9691]
50 E Huron St.
Chicago, IL 60611-2729
PH: (312)280-4395
Hornung, Susan, Exec. Dir.

Association of Specialized and
  Professional Accreditors [1012]
3304 N Broadway St., No. 214
Chicago, IL 60657
PH: (773)857-7900
Fax: (888)859-4932
Vibert, Joseph, Exec. Dir.

Association of Welcoming & Affirm-
  ing Baptists [19718]
PO Box 60008
Chicago, IL 60660
PH: (240)242-9220
Lunn, Rev. Robin R., Exec. Dir.

Association of Women Surgeons
  [17381]
35 E Wacker Dr., Ste. 850
Chicago, IL 60601
PH: (312)224-2575
Fax: (312)644-8557
Cochran, Amalia, MD, FACS, FCCM,
  President

Automotive Oil Change Association
  [339]
330 N Wabash Ave., Ste. 2000
Chicago, IL 60611
PH: (312)321-5132
Toll free: 800-230-0702
Fax: (312)673-6832
White, Bryan, Exec. Dir.

Auxiliaries of Our Lady of the Ce-
  nacle [19802]
513 W Fullerton Pky.
Chicago, IL 60614-6428
PH: (773)528-6300
Fax: (773)549-0554
Rennert, James R., Director

Awards and Personalization Associa-
  tion [20730]
8735 W Higgins Rd., Ste. 300
Chicago, IL 60631
PH: (847)375-4800
Fax: (847)375-6480
Scarano, Mario, President

Bank Administration Institute [385]
115 S La Salle St., Ste. 3300
Chicago, IL 60603-3801
Toll free: 800-224-9889
Fax: (312)683-2373
Nagarkatte, Ajay, Managing Dir.

Battery Council International [315]
330 N Wabash Ave., Ste. 2000
Chicago, IL 60611
PH: (312)245-1074
Fax: (312)527-6640

Benevolent and Protective Order of
  Elks [19425]
2750 N Lakeview Ave.
Chicago, IL 60614-1889
PH: (773)755-4700
Fax: (773)755-4790
Klatt, Bryan, Secretary

Better Boys Foundation [11215]
1512 S Pulaski Rd.
Chicago, IL 60623
PH: (773)542-7300
Fax: (773)521-4153
Kellman, Jack, President

Better Government Association
  [18859]
223 W Jackson Blvd., Ste. 900
Chicago, IL 60606
PH: (312)427-8330
Herguth, Robert, Director

Beyondmedia Education [8288]
6119 N Hermitage Ave.
Chicago, IL 60660-2305
PH: (773)216-5556

Bioelectromagnetics Society [6062]
c/o James C. Lin. Editor-in-Chief
University of Illinois
851 S Morgan St.
Chicago, IL 60607-7053
Fax: (312)413-0024
Chadwick, Phil, President

Black on Black Love Campaign
  [11501]
1000 E 87th St.
Chicago, IL 60619-6397
PH: (773)978-0868
Fax: (773)978-7345
Wright, Mrs. Frances, CEO,
  President

Blind Service Association [17691]
17 N State St., Ste. 1050
Chicago, IL 60602-3510
PH: (312)236-0808
Grossman, Debbie, Exec. Dir.

BLOOM Africa [10870]
PO Box 4646
Chicago, IL 60680-4646
PH: (856)905-8779
Steele, Andrew, Exec. Dir., Founder,
  Chmn. of the Bd.

Blue Cross and Blue Shield Associa-
  tion [15419]
225 N Michigan Ave.
Chicago, IL 60601
Toll free: 888-630-2583
Serota, Scott P., CEO, President

Blues Heaven Foundation [9882]
2120 S Michigan Ave.
Chicago, IL 60616
PH: (312)808-1286

Bright Pink [17754]
670 N Clark St., Ste. 2
Chicago, IL 60654
PH: (312)787-4412
Avner, Lindsay, Founder, CEO

Building Materials Reuse Association
  [508]
PO Box 47776
Chicago, IL 60647
PH: (773)340-2672
Kingfisher, Alli, President

Building Service Contractors As-
  sociation International [2125]
330 N Wabash Ave., Ste. 2000
Chicago, IL 60611
PH: (312)321-5167
Toll free: 800-368-3414
Fax: (312)673-6735
Diamond, Michael, Treasurer

Bulletin of the Atomic Scientists
  [7125]
1155 E 60th St.
Chicago, IL 60637
PH: (707)481-9372
McCabe, Lisa, Officer

Bureau of Osteopathic Specialists
  [16522]
142 E Ontario St.
Chicago, IL 60611
Toll free: 800-621-1773

Business Sweden [3298]
150 N Michigan Ave., Ste. 1950
Chicago, IL 60601-7550
PH: (312)781-6222
Fax: (312)276-8606
Armstrong, James, Consultant

Cabinet Makers Association [1477]
47 W Polk St., Ste. 100-145
Chicago, IL 60605-2085
Toll free: 866-562-2512
Fax: (866)645-0468
Krig, Matt, President

Cameroon America AIDS Alliance
  [13534]
25 E Superior St., No. 3702
Chicago, IL 60611
PH: (847)963-1664
Ntowe, Dr. Francis, Exec. Dir.

Campaign to End the Death Penalty
  [17828]
PO Box 25730
Chicago, IL 60625
PH: (773)955-4841
Hughes, Lily, Director

Cancer Prevention Coalition [13927]
1735 W Harrison St., Ste. 206
School of Public Health
2121 W Taylor St.
MC 922
Chicago, IL 60612
Epstein, Dr. Samuel S., MD, Chair-
  man, Founder

Capuchin-Franciscans [19807]
3407 S Archer Ave.
Chicago, IL 60608
PH: (773)475-6206
Hugo, Fr. Bill, Director

Catholic Church Extension Society
  of the U.S.A. [19810]
150 S Wacker Dr., Ste. 2000
Chicago, IL 60606
PH: (312)795-5109
Toll free: 800-842-7804
Fax: (312)236-5276
Wall, Rev. John J., President, CEO

Catholic Library Association [9696]
205 W Monroe St., Ste. 314
Chicago, IL 60606-5061
PH: (312)739-1776
Toll free: 855-739-1776
Fax: (312)739-1778
Kokolus, Cait C., Bd. Member

Catholic Press Association [2775]
205 W Monroe St., Ste. 470
Chicago, IL 60606
PH: (312)380-6789
Fax: (312)361-0256
Schiller, Matthew, President

CCIM Institute [2853]
430 N Michigan Ave., Ste. 800
Chicago, IL 60611
PH: (312)321-4460
Toll free: 800-621-7027
Fax: (312)321-4530
Landreneau, Karl, CCIM, President

Center for Community and Organiza-
  tion Development [11291]
DePaul University
1 E Jackson Blvd.
Chicago, IL 60604
PH: (773)325-4250
   (312)362-8000
Fax: (773)325-4249
Cellar, Dr. Doug, Contact

Center for Computer-Assisted Legal
  Instruction [6297]
565 W Adams St., Rm. 542
Chicago, IL 60661-3652
PH: (312)906-5307
Mayer, John, Exec. Dir.

Center for Neighborhood Technology
  [17969]
2125 W North Ave.
Chicago, IL 60647
PH: (773)278-4800
Fax: (773)278-3840
Bernstein, Scott, President, Founder

Center for New Community [17970]
47 W Division St., No. 514
Chicago, IL 60610

PH: (312)266-0319
Fax: (312)266-0278
Johnson, Terri, Exec. Dir.

Center for Research Libraries [9697]
6050 S Kenwood Ave.
Chicago, IL 60637-2804
PH: (773)955-4545
Toll free: 800-621-6044
Fax: (773)955-4339
Waugh, Scott, Chairman

Center for the Study of Multiple Birth
  [15845]
333 E Superior St., Ste. 464
Chicago, IL 60611
PH: (312)695-1677
Fax: (312)908-8777
Keith, Dr. Louis G., Founder

Central Electric Railfans' Association
  [22408]
PO Box 503
Chicago, IL 60690-0503
PH: (312)987-4391
Walbrun, Mark, Director

Certification of Disability Manage-
  ment Specialists Commission
  [13495]
8735 W Higgins Rd., Ste. 300
Chicago, IL 60631
PH: (847)375-6380
Fax: (847)375-6379
Sochacki, Stacy, MS, Exec. Dir.

CharityWatch [12468]
3450 N Lake Shore Dr., Ste. 2802
Chicago, IL 60657-2862
PH: (773)529-2300
Fax: (773)529-0024
Borochoff, Mr. Daniel, Founder,
  President

Chemical Development and Market-
  ing Association [6194]
c/o Product Development and
  Management Association
401 N Michigan Ave., Ste. 2200
Chicago, IL 60611
PH: (312)321-5145
Toll free: 800-232-5241
Fax: (312)673-6885
Goldman, Theodore D., President,
  Treasurer

Chevy Club [21352]
5433 N Ashland Ave.
Chicago, IL 60640
PH: (773)769-7458
Fax: (773)769-3240
Ochal, Frank, President

Child Welfare Institute [10907]
111 E Wacker Dr., Ste. 325
Chicago, IL 60601
PH: (312)949-5640
Fax: (312)922-6736
Morton, Thomas D., President

Christian Community Development
  Association [20362]
3851 W Ogden Ave.
Chicago, IL 60623
PH: (773)475-7370
Fax: (773)475-6303
Castellanos, Noel, CEO

Christian Peacemaker Teams
  [12435]
PO Box 6508
Chicago, IL 60680-6508
PH: (773)376-0550
Fax: (773)376-0549
Thompson, Sarah, Exec. Dir.

Churchill Centre [10319]
c/o Lee Pollock, Executive Director
131 S Dearborn St., Ste. 1700

Chicago, IL 60603
PH: (312)263-5637
Geller, Laurence S., Chairman

Citizens United for Research in
Epilepsy **[14738]**
430 W Erie St., Ste. 210
Chicago, IL 60654
PH: (312)255-1801
Toll free: 800-765-7118
Axelrod, Susan, Chairperson,
Founder

The Claretian Initiative **[19824]**
205 W Monroe St.
Chicago, IL 60606
PH: (312)236-7782

Classic Car Club of America **[21356]**
PO Box 346160
Chicago, IL 60634
PH: (847)390-0443
Fax: (847)916-2674
Johnson, David, President

Clinical Laboratory Management As-
sociation **[15517]**
330 N Wabash Ave., Ste. 2000
Chicago, IL 60611
PH: (312)321-5111
Forsman, Rodney W., Treasurer

Clinical Robotic Surgery Association
[17385]
2 Prudential Plz.
180 N Stetson Ave., Ste. 3500
Chicago, IL 60601
PH: (312)268-5754
    (312)355-2494
Fax: (312)355-1987
Pigazzi, Alessio, President

Cognitive Development Society
[13811]
c/o Amanda Woodward, President
5801 S Ellis Ave.
Chicago, IL 60637
Toll free: 800-354-1420
Fax: (215)625-8914
Uttal, David, President

Colon Cancer Alliance for Research
and Education for Lynch Syndrome
[14818]
127 W Oak St., Unit C
Chicago, IL 60610
PH: (312)725-9769
Fax: (847)267-0746
Perlman, Sharon, President

Commission on Dietetic Registration
[16213]
120 S Riverside Plz., Ste. 2000
Chicago, IL 60606-6995
PH: (312)899-0040
Toll free: 800-877-1600
Fax: (312)899-4772
Reidy, Christine, Exec. Dir.

Committee of 200 **[624]**
980 N Michigan Ave., Ste. 1575
Chicago, IL 60611
PH: (312)255-0296
Fax: (312)255-0789
Gaddis, Gay, Chairperson

COMMON **[6298]**
8770 W Bryn Mawr Ave., Ste. 1350
Chicago, IL 60631
PH: (312)279-0192
Toll free: 800-777-6734
Fax: (312)279-0227
Dufault, Randy, Director

Communities First Association
[11334]
PO Box 6104
Chicago, IL 60680
Washington, Ressheda N, Exec. Dir.

Community Banking Advisory
Network **[20]**
111 E Wacker Dr.
Chicago, IL 60601
PH: (312)729-9900
Pruett, Patrick, Exec. Dir.

Congress for the New Urbanism
[19217]
PO Box A3104
Chicago, IL 60690
PH: (312)551-7300
Fax: (312)346-3323
Sheridan, Abigail, Dep. Dir.

Construction Writers Association
[2672]
PO Box 14784
Chicago, IL 60614-0784
PH: (773)687-8726
Fax: (773)687-8627
Hodges, Deborah J., Exec. Dir.

Consumers Advancing Patient
Safety **[17172]**
405 N Wabash Ave., Ste. P2W
Chicago, IL 60611
PH: (312)464-0602
Fax: (312)277-3307
Washington, Knitasha, Exec. Dir.

Council for Adult and Experiential
Learning **[7911]**
55 E Monroe St., Ste. 2710
Chicago, IL 60603
PH: (312)499-2600
Campbell, Scott, VP

Council of Medical Specialty Societ-
ies **[15664]**
35 E Wacker Dr., Ste. 850
Chicago, IL 60601-2106
PH: (312)224-2585
Fax: (312)644-8557
Dvorak, Mitchell L.

Council for a Parliament of the
World's Religions **[20536]**
70 E Lake St., Ste. 205
Chicago, IL 60601
PH: (312)629-2990
Fax: (312)629-2991
Savage, Brian, Dir. of Logistics

Council of Residential Specialists
[2855]
430 N Michigan Ave., 3rd Fl.
Chicago, IL 60611
PH: (312)321-4400
Toll free: 800-462-8841
Fax: (312)329-8551
Priore, Anthony, VP of Mktg., VP,
Comm.

Council on Surgical and Perioperan-
tive Safety **[17388]**
633 N St. Clair
Chicago, IL 60611
PH: (312)202-5700
Fax: (312)267-1782
Hannenburg, Alexander A., MD,
Chairman

Council on Tall Buildings and Urban
Habitat **[5966]**
c/o Patti Thurmond, Manager of
Operations
SR Crown Hall
Illinois Institute of Technology
3360 S State St.
Chicago, IL 60616
PH: (312)567-3487
Fax: (312)567-3820
Wood, Antony, Exec. Dir.

Counselors of Real Estate **[2856]**
430 N Michigan Ave.
Chicago, IL 60611-4089

PH: (312)329-8427
Haack, Susan, Dir. of Member Svcs.

Covenant World Relief **[12653]**
8303 W Higgins Rd.
Chicago, IL 60631
PH: (773)907-3301

Crane Certification Association of
America **[805]**
1608 S Ashland Ave., No. 83408
Chicago, IL 60608
Toll free: 800-447-3402
Fax: (407)598-2902
Ludwig, Andy, VP

Croatian American Association
[18521]
6607 W Archer Ave.
Chicago, IL 60638-2407
Raguz, Stan, President

CTSNet: Cardiothoracic Surgery
Network **[17472]**
633 N St. Clair St., 23rd Fl.
Chicago, IL 60611-3658
PH: (312)202-5848
Fax: (312)202-5801
Rush, Grahame, Exec. Dir.

Decalogue Society of Lawyers
[5002]
134 N LaSalle St., Ste. 1430
Chicago, IL 60602
PH: (312)263-6493
Goldberg, Mitchell B., VP

Defense Research Institute **[5559]**
55 W Monroe St., Ste. 2000
Chicago, IL 60603
PH: (312)795-1101
    (312)698-6218
Fax: (312)795-0749
Burrell, Douglas K., Director

Dental Assisting National Board, Inc.
[14429]
444 N Michigan Ave., Ste. 900
Chicago, IL 60611
PH: (312)642-3368
Toll free: 800-367-3262
Fax: (312)642-8507
Durley, Cynthia C., Exec. Dir.

Depression and Bipolar Support Alli-
ance **[15768]**
55 E Jackson Blvd., Ste. 490
Chicago, IL 60604
Toll free: 800-826-3632
Fax: (312)642-7243
Jewell, Lucinda, V. Chmn. of the Bd.

Designs for Change **[8475]**
29 East Madison, Ste. 950
Chicago, IL 60602
PH: (312)236-7252
Fax: (312)236-7927
Moore, Donald R., Exec. Dir.

DOCARE International **[12271]**
142 E Ontario St., 18th Fl.
Chicago, IL 60611
PH: (312)202-8163
Fax: (312)202-8316
Glaser, Kelli, President

Dominican Volunteers USA **[20410]**
1914 S Ashland Ave.
Chicago, IL 60608
PH: (312)226-0919
Fax: (312)226-0919
Cotterman, Col. JoAnn, OP,
President

DONA International **[16282]**
35 E Wacker Dr., Ste. 850
Chicago, IL 60601-2106
PH: (312)224-2595
Toll free: 888-788-3662
Fax: (312)644-8557
Rokeby-Mayeux, Jennifer, Mem.

Dystonia Medical Research Founda-
tion **[15929]**
1 E Wacker Dr., Ste. 2810
Chicago, IL 60601-1905
PH: (312)755-0198
Toll free: 800-377-3978
Fax: (312)803-0138
Hieshetter, Janet, Exec. Dir.

Educating Africa's Children **[11200]**
2633 N Wilton Ave., Unit 1
Chicago, IL 60614
PH: (773)991-2812
Dusek, Robin, President, Exec. Dir.

Electrical and Computer Engineering
Department Heads Association
[6552]
Two Prudential Plz.
180 N Stetson, Ste. 3500
Chicago, IL 60601
PH: (312)559-3724
Fax: (312)559-4111
Najafi, Khalil, VP

Electronics Representatives Associa-
tion **[1045]**
309 W Washington St., Ste. 500
Chicago, IL 60606
PH: (312)419-1432
Fax: (312)419-1660
Tobin, Walter, CEO

Ethnic and Multicultural Information
Exchange Round Table of the
American Library Association
[9704]
50 E Huron St.
Chicago, IL 60611
Toll free: 800-545-5433
Hime, Dr. Leslie Campbell,
Chairperson

Expanded Shale, Clay and Slate
Institute **[527]**
35 E Wacker Dr., Ste. 850
Chicago, IL 60601
PH: (801)272-7070
Fax: (312)644-8557

Family Resource Center on Dis-
abilities **[7716]**
11 E Adams St., Ste. 1002
Chicago, IL 60603
PH: (312)939-3513
Fax: (312)854-8980

Fantasy Sports Trade Association
[3155]
600 N Lake Shore Dr.
Chicago, IL 60611
PH: (312)771-7019
Charchian, Paul, President

Fathers' Rights **[11685]**
19 S LaSalle St., Ste. 450
Chicago, IL 60603
PH: (312)807-3990

Federation Des Grandes Tours Du
Monde **[7499]**
PO Box 11278
Chicago, IL 60611
PH: (312)363-7093
Sun, Lei, Exec.

Feeding America **[12086]**
35 E Whacker Dr., Ste. 2000
Chicago, IL 60601
PH: (312)263-2303
Fax: (312)263-5626
Aviv, Diana, CEO

Fellows of the American Bar
Foundation **[5007]**
750 N Lake Shore Dr., 4th Fl.
Chicago, IL 60611
Toll free: 800-292-5065
Fax: (312)564-8910
Neville, Cara Lee T., Chairman

Fellowship of Saint James [19980]
PO Box 410788
Chicago, IL 60641
PH: (773)481-1090
Kushiner, James M., Exec. Ed.

Financial & Insurance Conference
Planners [2329]
330 N Wabash Ave., Ste. 2000
Chicago, IL 60611-7621
PH: (312)245-1023
Bova, Steve, Exec. Dir.

Financial Managers Society [2167]
1 N La Salle St., Ste. 3100
Chicago, IL 60602-4003
PH: (312)578-1300
Toll free: 800-275-4367
Fax: (312)578-1308
Yingst, Dick, CEO, President

First Amendment Lawyers Associa-
tion [5103]
c/o Wayne B. Giampietro
123 W Madison St., Ste. 1300
Chicago, IL 60602
PH: (312)236-0606
Fax: (312)236-9264
Giampietro, Mr. Wayne, Gen.
Counsel

Food Animal Concerns Trust [4454]
3525 W Peterson Ave., Ste. 213
Chicago, IL 60659-3314
PH: (773)525-4952
Brown, Robert, Founder

Foundation for Women's Cancer
[13972]
230 W Monroe St., Ste. 2528
Chicago, IL 60606-4902
PH: (312)578-1439
Fax: (312)235-4059
Carlson, Karen J., Exec. Dir.

Freedom to Read Foundation
[17836]
50 E Huron St.
Chicago, IL 60611
PH: (312)280-4226
Toll free: 800-545-2433
Garnar, Martin, VP

Freedom Road Socialist Organiza-
tion [5766]
PO Box 87613
Chicago, IL 60680-0613

Friends of Astrology Inc. [5992]
5122 S May St.
Chicago, IL 60609-5009
PH: (630)654-4742
Arens, Christine, President

GAIA Movement USA [3873]
8918 S Green St.
Chicago, IL 60620
PH: (773)651-7870
Toll free: 877-787-4242
Nielsen, Eva, President

Gamma Rho Lambda National
Sorority [23766]
PO Box 3201
Chicago, IL 60654

Gastro-Intestinal Research Founda-
tion [14789]
70 E Lake St.
Chicago, IL 60601
PH: (312)332-1350
Grill, Howard A., VP of Fin.

General Commission on the Status
and Role of Women [18209]
77 W Washington St., Ste. 1500
Chicago, IL 60602
PH: (312)346-4900
Toll free: 800-523-8390
Fax: (312)346-3986
Wallace-Padgett, Bishop Debra,
President

German-American National
Congress [19444]
4740 N Western Ave., Ste. 206
Chicago, IL 60625-2013
PH: (773)275-1100
Toll free: 888-872-3265
Fax: (773)275-4010
Pochatko, Beverly, Secretary

The Giving Institute [1469]
225 W Wacker Dr., Ste. 650
Chicago, IL 60606-3396
PH: (312)981-6794
Fax: (312)265-2908
Berggren, Erin, Exec. Dir.

Giving U.S.A. Foundation [12477]
225 W Wacker Dr., Ste. 650
Chicago, IL 60606
PH: (312)981-6794
Byrne, Jeffrey, Chairman

Global Alliance for Africa [17776]
703 W Monroe St.
Chicago, IL 60661
PH: (312)382-0607
Fax: (312)382-8850
Kayler, J. Allan, Treasurer

Global Alliance of Artists [8921]
2405 N Sheffield Ave., No. 14199
Chicago, IL 60614
Rabadi, Dina, Exec. Dir., Founder,
President

Global FoodBanking Network
[12097]
203 N LaSalle St., Ste. 1900
Chicago, IL 60601-1263
PH: (312)782-4560
Fax: (312)782-4580
Moon, Lisa, President, CEO

Global Studies Association North
America [8043]
1250 N Wood St.
Chicago, IL 60622
Harris, Jerry, Secretary

Goals 4 Ghana [11003]
5830 N Glenwood Ave.
Chicago, IL 60660
PH: (773)307-8848
Eckerle, Mark, President

Gold and Silver Plate Society
[20733]
c/o Jenniefer Tarulis
180 N Stetson Ave., Ste. 850
Chicago, IL 60601
PH: (312)540-4400
Tarulis, Jennifer, Contact

Government Finance Officers As-
sociation of United States and
Canada [5706]
203 N LaSalle St., Ste. 2700
Chicago, IL 60601-1210
PH: (312)977-9700
Fax: (312)977-4806
Esser, Jeffrey L., CEO, Exec. Dir.

Graham Foundation [234]
Madlener House
4 W Burton Pl.
Chicago, IL 60610-1416
PH: (312)787-4071
Wimer, Ross, President

Great Books Foundation [9127]
35 E Wacker Dr., Ste. 400
Chicago, IL 60601-2105
PH: (312)332-5870
Toll free: 800-222-5870
Fax: (312)407-0224
Pollock, Alex J., Director

Group Legal Services Association
[5532]
321 N Clark St., 19th Fl.
Chicago, IL 60610

PH: (312)988-5751
Fax: (312)932-6436
Schippers, Nicolle, President

Harmony House for Cats [10633]
2914 N Elston Ave.
Chicago, IL 60618
PH: (773)293-6103

Health Research and Educational
Trust [15327]
155 N Wacker, Ste. 400
Chicago, IL 60606
PH: (312)422-2600
Fax: (312)422-4568
Combes, John R., President

Healthcare Information and Manage-
ment Systems Society [1646]
33 W Monroe St., Ste. 1700
Chicago, IL 60603-5616
PH: (312)664-4467
Fax: (312)664-6143
Melling, Jon, Chairman

HELPSudan [11205]
5255 N Ashland Ave.
Chicago, IL 60640-2001
PH: (773)353-1919
Wel, Jok Kuol, Founder, President

Hematology/Oncology Pharmacy
Association [16663]
8735 W Higgins Rd., Ste.300
Chicago, IL 60631
Toll free: 877-467-2791
Scarpace, Sarah, President

Heshima Kenya, Inc. [11031]
1111 N Wells St., Ste. 306
Chicago, IL 60610
PH: (312)985-5667
Laatsch, Ann, Chairperson

HIMSS Electronic Health Record
Association [15634]
33 W Monroe St., Ste. 1700
Chicago, IL 60603-5616
PH: (312)664-4467
Fax: (312)664-6143
Burchell, Leigh, Chairperson

Hispanic Alliance for Career
Enhancement [18338]
29 E Madison
Chicago, IL 60606
PH: (312)435-0498
Fax: (312)454-7448
Beckmann, Derek, Secretary

Historic Pullman Foundation [9399]
614 E 113th St.
Chicago, IL 60628
PH: (773)785-8181
Fax: (773)785-8182
Shymanski, Michael, President

HOPOS, The International Society
for the History of Philosophy of
Science [8546]
c/o The University of Chicago Press
Journals Division
PO Box 37005
Chicago, IL 60637
Richardson, Alan, President

John Howard Association of Illinois
[11529]
PO Box 10042
Chicago, IL 60610-0042
PH: (312)291-9183
Fax: (312)526-3714
Hoffman, Daniel, Office Mgr.

J. Allen Hynek Center for UFO Stud-
ies [7012]
PO Box 31335
Chicago, IL 60631

PH: (773)271-3611
Rodeghier, Mark, Science Dir.

Imerman Angels [13987]
205 W Randolph, 19th Fl.
Chicago, IL 60606
PH: (312)274-5529
Toll free: 877-274-5529
Fax: (312)274-5530
May, John, Chairman, Founder

Independent Grocers Alliance [1337]
8745 W Higgins Rd., Ste. 350
Chicago, IL 60631
PH: (773)693-4520
Fax: (773)693-4533
Bennett, Dave, Sr. VP

Independent Order of Svithiod
[10200]
5518 W Lawrence Ave.
Chicago, IL 60630
PH: (773)736-1191
Pearson, Barbro, Chairman

Independent Schools Association of
the Central States [8011]
55 W Wacker Dr., Ste. 701
Chicago, IL 60601
PH: (312)750-1190
Fax: (312)750-1193
Dagget, Claudia, President

India Development Service [19074]
PO Box 980
Chicago, IL 60690
Muppidi, Dr. Uma, VP

Industrial Areas Foundation [17980]
Chicago, IL

Industrial Workers of the World
[23446]
PO Box 180195
Chicago, IL 60618
PH: (773)728-0996

Infectious Diseases Society for
Obstetrics and Gynecology
[15404]
230 W Monroe St., Ste. 710
Chicago, IL 60606
PH: (312)676-3928
Beigi, Richard, MD, President

Institute of Cultural Affairs in the
U.S.A. [12003]
4750 N Sheridan Rd.
Chicago, IL 60640
PH: (773)769-6363
Fax: (773)944-1582
Bergdall, Terry, PhD, CEO

Institute for Diversity in Health
Management [15120]
155 N Wacker Ave.
Chicago, IL 60606
PH: (312)422-2630
Mallett, Jetaun, CAE, Operations
Mgr., Bus. Dev. Mgr.

Institute of Food Technologists
[6648]
525 W Van Buren St., Ste. 1000
Chicago, IL 60607
PH: (312)782-8424
Toll free: 800-438-3663
Fax: (312)782-8348
Gravani, Robert, Treasurer

Institute for the International Educa-
tion of Students [8616]
33 W Monroe St., Ste. 2300
Chicago, IL 60603-5405
PH: (312)944-1750
Toll free: 800-995-2300
Fax: (312)944-1448
Dwyer, Mary M., PhD, CEO,
President

Institute of Lithuanian Studies [19539]
5600 S Claremont Ave.
Chicago, IL 60636-1039
PH: (773)434-4545
Fax: (773)434-9363
Rackauskas, Jonas, PhD, President

Institute of Real Estate Management [2864]
430 N Michigan Ave.
Chicago, IL 60611
Toll free: 800-837-0706
Fax: (800)338-4736
Coneset, Phyllis M., VP

Institute on Religion in an Age of Science [20597]
c/o Dan Solomon, Membership Coordinator
6434 N Mozart St.
Chicago, IL 60645
Solomon, Dan, Coord.

Institute of Women Today [18211]
7315 S Yale Ave.
Chicago, IL 60621
PH: (773)651-8372
Fax: (773)783-2673
Hibbs, Maria, Chmn. of the Bd.

Inter-University Program for Latino Research [19429]
College of Liberal Arts and Sciences
University of Illinois at Chicago
412 S Peoria St., 3rd Fl.
Chicago, IL 60607
PH: (312)413-7871
Villafranca, Nancy, Director

Inter-University Seminar on Armed Forces and Society [5600]
Dept. of Political Science
Loyola University Chicago
1032 W Sheridan Rd.
Chicago, IL 60660
PH: (773)508-2930
Fax: (773)508-2929
Vitas, Robert A., Exec. Dir., Treasurer

Interfaith Worker Justice [20214]
1020 W Bryn Mawr Ave.
Chicago, IL 60660
PH: (773)728-8400
Hubbard, Bishop Howard, VP

International Association of Bryologists [6143]
c/o Matt von Konrat, Secretary-Treasurer
1400 S Lake Shore Dr.
Chicago, IL 60605
PH: (312)665-7864
Goffinet, Bernard, President

International Association of Conference Centres [2320]
35 E Wacker Dr., Ste. 850
Chicago, IL 60601-2106
PH: (312)224-2580
Fax: (312)644-8557
Cabañas, Alex, President

International Association of Defense Counsel [5011]
303 W Madison St., Ste. 925
Chicago, IL 60606
PH: (312)368-1494
Fax: (312)368-1854
Kurzak, Mary Beth, Exec. Dir.

International Association for Dialogue Analysis [8183]
Northeastern Illinois University
5500 N St. Louis Ave.
Chicago, IL 60625

International Association of Healthcare Central Service Materiel Management [15329]
55 W Wacker Dr., Ste. 501
Chicago, IL 60601
PH: (312)440-0078
Toll free: 800-962-8274
Fax: (312)440-9474
Hanna, Betty

International Association of Lighting Designers [1948]
440 N Wells St., Ste. 210
Chicago, IL 60654
PH: (312)527-3677
Fax: (312)527-3680
Turner, Marsha L., CEO

International Association of Oral and Maxillofacial Surgeons [16447]
8618 W Catalpa Ave., Ste. 1116
Chicago, IL 60656
PH: (224)232-8737
Fax: (224)735-2965
Dvorak, Mitchell, Exec. Dir.

International Avaya Users Group [3229]
330 N Wabash Ave.
Chicago, IL 60611
PH: (312)321-5126
Bohnert, Victor, Exec. Dir.

International Carwash Association [345]
230 E Ohio St.
Chicago, IL 60611
Toll free: 888-422-8422
Wulf, Eric, CEO

International Certification Accreditation Board [59]
6263 N McCormick Rd., Ste. 318
Chicago, IL 60659
PH: (847)724-6631
Fax: (847)724-4223
McDaniels, Lon, Bd. Member

International College of Surgeons [17390]
1516 N Lakeshore Dr.
Chicago, IL 60610
PH: (312)642-3555
Fax: (312)787-1624
Downham, Max C., Exec. Dir.

International Consumer Product Health and Safety Organization [2997]
c/o Nancy A. Cowles, President
Kids in Danger
116 W Illinois St., Ste. 4E
Chicago, IL 60654
PH: (312)595-0649
Cowles, Nancy A., President

International DB2 Users Group [6364]
330 N Wabash, Ste. 2000
Chicago, IL 60611-4267
PH: (312)321-6881
Fax: (312)673-6688
Turpin, Paul, Treasurer

International Engineering Consortium [6436]
180 N Stetson Ave., Ste. 3500
Chicago, IL 60601
PH: (312)559-3724
Fax: (312)559-4111

International Federation for Choral Music [9928]
c/o Dr. Michael J. Anderson, President
1040 W Harrison St., Rm. L216
Chicago, IL 60607-7130
Wickström, Håkan, Treasurer

International Fellowship of Christians and Jews [20543]
30 N LaSalle St., Ste. 4300
Chicago, IL 60602
Toll free: 800-486-8844
Eckstein, Rabbi Yechiel Z., Founder, President

International Foodservice Manufacturers Association [1344]
2 Prudential Plz.
180 N Stetson Ave., Ste. 850
Chicago, IL 60601
PH: (312)540-4400
Oberkfell, Larry, CEO, President

International Foundation for Ethical Research [10647]
53 W Jackson Blvd., Ste. 1552
Chicago, IL 60604
PH: (312)427-6025
Fax: (312)427-6524
O'Donovan, Peter, Exec. Dir.

International Interior Design Association [1951]
222 Merchandise Mart, Ste. 567
Chicago, IL 60654
PH: (312)467-1950
Toll free: 888-799-4432
Braga, Julio, VP

International Kennel Club of Chicago [21900]
20 S Clark, Ste. 1830
Chicago, IL 60603
PH: (773)237-5100
Fax: (773)237-5126
Auslander, Mr. Louis, President

International Network for Urban Agriculture [3569]
Chicago, IL
Fager, Hayley, Dir. of Programs, Dir. of Operations

International Oracle Users Group [6302]
330 N Wabash Ave., Ste. 2000
Chicago, IL 60611
PH: (312)245-1579
Anderson, Maria, President

International Organization for Adolescents [11049]
53 W Jackson Blvd., Ste. 857
Chicago, IL 60604
PH: (773)404-8831
Fax: (773)257-9128
Boak, Alison, MPH, Founder, Exec. Dir.

International Polka Association [9930]
4608 S Archer Ave.
Chicago, IL 60632
Toll free: 800-867-6552
Rzeszutko, Rick, President

International Society of Appraisers [227]
225 W Wacker Dr., Ste. 650
Chicago, IL 60606
PH: (312)981-6778
Fax: (312)265-2908
Jackson, Joseph M., Exec. Dir.

International Society for Experimental Hematology [15237]
330 N Wabash Ave., Ste. 2000
Chicago, IL 60611
PH: (312)321-5114
Fax: (312)673-6923
Travers, David, President

International Society for Gesture Studies [6228]
c/o David McNeill
Dept. of Psychology

International Fellowship of Christians and Jews
University of Chicago
5848 S University Ave.
Chicago, IL 60637
PH: (773)702-8833
Fax: (773)702-4186
Mcneill, David, Co-Pres.

International Society of Hospitality Consultants [821]
c/o David Neff, President
131 S Dearborn St., Ste.1700
Chicago, IL
PH: (312)324-8689
Fax: (312)324-9689
Belfanti, Andrea, Exec. Dir.

International Society of Transport Aircraft Trading [143]
330 N Wabash Ave., Ste. 2000
Chicago, IL 60611
PH: (312)321-5169
Fax: (312)673-6579
Allinson, Marc, President

International Special Events Society [1145]
330 N Wabash Ave., Ste. 2000
Chicago, IL 60611
PH: (312)321-6853
Toll free: 800-688-4737
Fax: (312)673-6953
Collen, Jodi, President

International Staple, Nail and Tool Association [1570]
8735 W Higgins Rd., Ste. 300
Chicago, IL 60631
PH: (847)375-6454
Fax: (847)375-6455
Henry, Jeff, Exec. Dir.

International Tactical Training Association [5601]
PO Box 59833
Chicago, IL 60659
PH: (872)221-4882
Fax: (872)221-5882
Cunningham, Aaron, President

International Trade Club of Chicago [1968]
134 N LaSalle St., Ste. 1300
Chicago, IL 60602
PH: (312)423-5250
Bonvoisin, Fabrice, President

International Transplant Nurses Society [16141]
8735 W Higgins Rd., Ste. 300
Chicago, IL 60631
PH: (847)375-6340
(847)375-4877
Fax: (847)375-6341
Kram, Joan, Exec. Dir.

Islamic Texts Society [8127]
c/o Independent Publishers Group
814 N Franklin St.
Chicago, IL 60610
PH: (312)337-0747
Fax: (312)337-5985

Italian-American Chamber of Commerce [23596]
500 N Michigan Ave., Ste. 506
Chicago, IL 60611
Calcinardi, Fulvio, Exec. Dir.

It's Nice to be Nice International [11389]
2715 W 85th Pl.
Chicago, IL 60652
PH: (773)673-7528
Blakey, Victoria D., Exec. Dir.

Jeanette MacDonald International Fan Club [23995]
PO Box 180172
Chicago, IL 60618-0172
Williams, Tessa, President

Joint Council on Thoracic Surgery
Education **[17473]**
633 N St. Clair St., Ste. 2320
Chicago, IL 60611
PH: (312)202-5890
Fax: (312)202-5801

Joint Review Committee on Educa-
tion in Radiologic Technology
[8298]
20 N Wacker Dr., Ste. 2850
Chicago, IL 60606-3182
PH: (312)704-5300
Fax: (312)704-5304
Winter, Leslie F., RT, CEO

Kidney Cancer Association **[13997]**
PO Box 803338, No. 38269
Chicago, IL 60680-3338
PH: (847)332-1051
(503)215-7921
Toll free: 800-850-9132
Konosky, Carolyn, Co-CEO,
Secretary

Kids In Danger **[11058]**
116 W Illinois St., Ste. 4E
Chicago, IL 60654
PH: (312)595-0649
Fax: (312)595-0939
Cowles, Nancy, Exec. Dir.

Komedyplast **[14340]**
222 N Columbus Dr., Ste. 4702
Chicago, IL 60601
PH: (617)530-0250
Fax: (312)276-4452
Weinzweig, Dr. Jeffrey, Founder,
Exec. Dir.

La Leche League International
[11249]
35 E Wacker Dr., Ste. 850
Chicago, IL 60601
PH: (312)646-6260
Toll free: 800-525-3243
Fax: (312)644-8557
de Raad, Lydia, Co-Chmn. of the
Bd.

League of Revolutionaries for a New
America **[18871]**
PO Box 477113
Chicago, IL 60647
PH: (773)486-0028
Heagerty, Brooke, Editor

Legal Marketing Association **[2288]**
330 N Wabash Ave., Ste. 2000
Chicago, IL 60611
PH: (312)321-6898
Fax: (312)673-6894
Whitaker, Kathryn, Secretary

Legion of Young Polish Women
[19603]
PO Box 56-110
Chicago, IL 60656
Anselmo, Mary Sendra, President

Letter Writers Alliance **[21738]**
PO Box 221168
Chicago, IL 60622
Zadrozny, Kathy, Founder

Library and Information Technology
Association **[9713]**
50 E Huron St.
Chicago, IL 60611-2795
PH: (312)944-6780
Toll free: 800-545-2433
Fax: (312)280-3257
Levine, Jenny, Exec. Dir.

Library Leadership and Management
Association **[9714]**
50 E Huron St.
Chicago, IL 60611-2729
Toll free: 800-545-2433
Fax: (312)280-2169
Ward, Kerry, Exec. Dir.

Lithuanian American Council **[19542]**
6500 S Pulaski Rd., Ste. 200
Chicago, IL 60629
PH: (773)735-6677
Fax: (773)735-3946
Kuprys, Saulius V., Esq., President

Lithuanian Catholic Press Society
[19543]
4545 W 63rd St.
Chicago, IL 60629-5532
PH: (773)585-9500
Fax: (773)585-8284
Stanevičius, Vytas, President

Lituanus Foundation, Inc. **[19544]**
47 W Polk St., Ste. 100-300
Chicago, IL 60605
PH: (312)341-9396
Armanaviciute, Vaida, Managing Ed.

A Long Walk Home **[13731]**
1658 N Milwaukee, Ste. 104
Chicago, IL 60647
Toll free: 877-571-1751
Fax: (877)571-1751
Tillet, Salamishah, PhD, President

Lutheran Men in Mission **[20311]**
8765 W Higgins Rd.
Chicago, IL 60631
Toll free: 800-638-3522
Fax: (773)380-2632
White, Rich, President

Maghreb Association of North
America **[19287]**
4346 N Pulaski Rd.
Chicago, IL 60641
PH: (773)459-7710
(773)517-8058

Manufacturing Renaissance **[18611]**
3411 W Diversey Ave., Ste. 10
Chicago, IL 60647
PH: (773)278-5418
Fax: (773)278-5918
Swinney, Dan, Exec. Dir.

Mazda Club **[21428]**
5433 N Ashland Ave.
Chicago, IL 60640
PH: (773)769-7396
Fax: (773)769-3240
Ochal, Frank, President

Medical Library Association **[9716]**
65 E Wacker Pl., Ste. 1900
Chicago, IL 60601-7246
PH: (312)419-9094
Fax: (312)419-8950
Baliozian, Kevin, Exec. Dir.

Medical Wings International **[15034]**
PO Box 16812
Chicago, IL 60616
PH: (817)800-0080
Johnson, Glenda, Founder,
President

Metal Construction Association **[546]**
8735 W Higgins Rd., Ste. 300
Chicago, IL 60631
PH: (847)375-4718
Fax: (847)375-6488
Nelson, Dale, Chairman

Metal Framing Manufacturers As-
sociation **[547]**
330 N Wabash Ave.
Chicago, IL 60611
PH: (312)644-6610
Thorsby, Mark, Exec. Dir.

Midwest Academy **[11294]**
27 E Monroe St., 11th Fl.
Chicago, IL 60603
PH: (312)427-2304
Fax: (312)379-0313
Booth, Heather, President

Mindful Medicine Worldwide **[13638]**
1011 W Wellington Ave., Ste. 220
Chicago, IL 60657
McKeown, Grainne, Exec. Dir.,
Founder

Muscular Dystrophy Association
[15959]
222 S Riverside Plz., Ste. 1500
Chicago, IL 60606
Toll free: 800-572-1717
Derks, Steven M., President, CEO

Napoleonic Historical Society
[10342]
6000A W Irving Park Rd.
Chicago, IL 60634
PH: (773)794-1804
Fax: (773)794-1769
Fisher, Todd, Exec. Dir.

National Alliance for Advanced
Technology Batteries **[1115]**
122 S Michigan Ave., Ste. 1700
Chicago, IL 60603
PH: (312)588-0477
Greenberger, Jim, Exec. Dir.

National Alliance Against Racist and
Political Repression **[17914]**
1325 S Wabash Ave., Ste. 105
Chicago, IL 60614
PH: (312)939-2750
Durham, Clarice, Co-Ch.

National Anti-Vivisection Society
[10664]
53 W Jackson Blvd., Ste. 1552
Chicago, IL 60604
PH: (312)427-6065
Toll free: 800-888-NAVS
Fax: (312)427-6524
Kandaras, Kenneth, President

National Association of Bar Execu-
tives **[5436]**
321 N Clark St.
Chicago, IL 60654
PH: (312)988-6008
Roberson, Nancy, President

National Association of Charter
School Authorizers **[7784]**
105 W Adams St., Ste. 1900
Chicago, IL 60603-6253
PH: (312)376-2300
Fax: (312)376-2400
Richmond, Greg, CEO, President

National Association of Conces-
sionaires **[1394]**
180 N Michigan Ave., Ste. 2215
Chicago, IL 60601
PH: (312)236-3858
Fax: (312)236-7809
Borschke, Dan, Exec. VP

National Association of County Park
and Recreation Officials **[5663]**
c/o Daniel Betts, President
69 W Washington, Ste. 290
Chicago, IL 60602
PH: (312)603-0310
Fax: (312)603-9971
Cardin, RJ, Director

National Association of Executive
Recruiters **[1095]**
1 E Wacker Dr., Ste. 2600
Chicago, IL 60601
PH: (618)398-6027
Schneider, Jim, President

National Association of Fire Equip-
ment Distributors **[3001]**
180 N Wabash Ave., Ste. 401
Chicago, IL 60603
PH: (312)461-9600
Fax: (312)461-0777
Harris, Danny, CAE, Exec. Dir., CEO

National Association for Healthcare
Quality **[17030]**
8735 W Higgins Rd., Ste. 300
Chicago, IL 60631
PH: (847)375-4720
Toll free: 800-966-9392
Fax: (847)375-6320
Mercado, Stephanie, Exec. Dir.

National Association of Independent
Fee Appraisers **[228]**
330 N Wabash Ave., Ste. 2000
Chicago, IL 60611
PH: (312)321-6830
Fax: (312)673-6652
Hacke, Kevin, VP

National Association for Lay Ministry
[20295]
5401 S Cornell, Rm. 210
Chicago, IL 60615
PH: (773)595-4042
Fax: (773)595-4020
Walters, Carol A., Chmn. of the Bd.

National Association of Legal Fee
Analysis **[5438]**
1712 W Greeanleaf Ave., No. 2
Chicago, IL 60626
PH: (312)907-7275
Jesse, Terry, Exec. Dir.

National Association of Minority and
Women Owned Law Firms **[5029]**
150 N Michigan Ave., Ste. 800
Chicago, IL 60601
PH: (312)733-7780
Wofford, Robin, Chmn. of the Bd.

National Association of Neonatal
Nurses **[16149]**
8735 W Higgins Rd., Ste. 300
Chicago, IL 60631
PH: (847)375-3660
Fax: (866)927-5321
Grazel, Regina, President

National Association of Orthopaedic
Nurses **[16152]**
330 N Wabash Ave., Ste.2000
Chicago, IL 60611
Toll free: 800-289-6266
Fax: (312)673-6941
Twiss, Julie, RN, Officer

National Association of Personal
Financial Advisors **[1284]**
8700 W Bryn Mawr Ave., Ste. 700N
Chicago, IL 60630
PH: (847)483-5400
Toll free: 888-333-6659
Fax: (847)483-5415
Brown, Geoffrey, CEO

National Association of Real Estate
Companies **[2876]**
6348 N Milwaukee Ave., No. 103
Chicago, IL 60646
PH: (773)283-6362
Troiani, Sheryl, President

National Association of Real Estate
Investment Managers **[2878]**
410 N Michigan Ave., Ste. 330
Chicago, IL 60611
PH: (312)884-5180
Gibson, Patricia, Chmn. of the Bd.

National Association of Realtors
[2880]
430 N Michigan Ave.
Chicago, IL 60611-4087
Toll free: 800-874-6500
Brown, Bill, President

National Association of Urban
Debate Leagues **[8595]**
200 S Michigan Ave., Ste. 1040
Chicago, IL 60604-2421

PH: (312)427-0175
Fax: (312)427-6130
Haynes, Rhonda, Dep. Dir.

National Association of Women
Lawyers [5031]
American Bar Ctr., MS 19.1
321 N Clark St.
Chicago, IL 60654
PH: (312)988-6186
Fax: (312)932-6450
Anastasia, Marsha L., President

National Association of Worksite
Health Centers [16326]
125 S Wacker Dr., Ste. 1350
Chicago, IL 60606
PH: (312)372-9090
Fax: (312)372-9091
Sheeran, James, Chmn. of the Bd.

National Automatic Merchandising
Association [3431]
20 N Wacker Dr., Ste. 3500
Chicago, IL 60606
PH: (312)346-0370
Fax: (312)704-4140
Balakgie, Carla, President, CEO

National Black MBA Association
[7561]
1 E Wacker Dr., Ste. 3500
Chicago, IL 60601
Tyson, Jesse J., President, CEO

National Board on Certification and
Recertification for Nurse
Anesthetists [16157]
8725 W Higgins Rd., Ste. 525
Chicago, IL 60631
Toll free: 855-285-4658
Fax: (708)669-7636
Plaus, Karen, CEO

National Board of Osteopathic Medi-
cal Examiners [16523]
8765 W Higgins Rd., Ste. 200
Chicago, IL 60631-4174
PH: (773)714-0622
Toll free: 866-479-6828
Fax: (773)714-0631
Gimpel, John R., President, CEO

National Brotherhood of Skiers
[23164]
1525 E 53rd St., Ste. 418
Chicago, IL 60615
PH: (773)955-4100

National Catholic Forensic League
[8596]
c/o Michael Colletti, Executive
Secretary-Treasurer
PO Box 31785
Chicago, IL 60631
Hyland, Roberta, 1st VP

National Coalition for Telecommunications Education and Learning [7317]
c/o Council for Adult and Experiential
Learning
55 E Monroe St., Ste. 2710
Chicago, IL 60603
Kannel, Susan, Exec. Dir.

National Commission on Cor-
rectional Health Care [15157]
1145 W Diversey Pky.
Chicago, IL 60614
PH: (773)880-1460
Fax: (773)880-2424
Alvarez, Jeffrey J., MD, CCHP,
Director

National Conference of Bar Foundations [5441]
Division for Bar Services
321 N Clark St., Ste. 1600

Chicago, IL 60654
PH: (312)988-5344
Fax: (312)988-5492
Barineau, Leslie, Secretary

National Conference of Bar
Presidents [5034]
Division for Bar Services
321 N Clark St., 16th Fl.
Chicago, IL 60654
PH: (803)227-4248
Fax: (803)400-1523
Lambert, Lanneau W., Jr., President

National Conference of Catholic
Airport Chaplains [19935]
PO Box 66353
Chicago, IL 60666-0353
PH: (773)686-2636
Fax: (773)686-0130
Zaniolo, Fr. Michael G., President

National Conference of Commission-
ers on Uniform State Laws [5782]
111 N Wabash Ave., Ste. 1010
Chicago, IL 60602
PH: (312)450-6600
Cassidy, Richard T., President

National Conference of Federal Trial
Judges [5394]
American Bar Association, Judicial
Division
321 N Clark St., 19th Fl.
Chicago, IL 60654
Toll free: 800-238-2667
Baker, Hon. Nannette A.,
Chairperson

National Conference of Specialized
Court Judges [5395]
c/o American Bar Association
321 N Clark St., 19th Fl.
Chicago, IL 60654
Toll free: 800-238-2667
Fax: (321)988-5709
Brown, Pamila, Chairman

National Council of Real Estate
Investment Fiduciaries [2031]
Aon Ctr.
200 E Randolph St., Ste. 5135
Chicago, IL 60601
PH: (312)819-5890
Fax: (312)819-5891
Steil, Peter, CEO

National Council of State Boards of
Nursing [16160]
111 E Wacker Dr., Ste. 2900
Chicago, IL 60601-4277
PH: (312)525-3600
Fax: (312)279-1032
Brekken, MS, RN, Shirley, President

National Council of Structural
Engineers Associations [6575]
645 N Michigan Ave., Ste. 540
Chicago, IL 60611
PH: (312)649-4600
Fax: (312)649-5840
Vogelzang, Jeanne M., Exec. Dir.

National Farm to School Network
[3541]
8770 W Bryn Mawr Ave., Ste. 1300
Chicago, IL 60631
PH: (847)917-7292
Joshi, Anupama, Exec. Dir., Founder

National Federation of Priests'
Councils [19887]
333 N Michigan Ave., Ste. 1114
Chicago, IL 60601-4001
PH: (312)442-9700
Toll free: 888-271-6372
Cutcher, Rev. Anthony, President

National Firebird and Trans Am Club
[21454]
5433 N Ashland Ave.
Chicago, IL 60640

PH: (773)769-7166
Fax: (773)769-3240
Ochal, Frank, President

National Flute Association [9973]
70 E Lake St., No. 200
Chicago, IL 60601
PH: (312)332-6682
Fax: (312)332-6684
Jocius, Kelly, Exec. Dir.

National Frame Builders Association
[889]
8735 W Higgins Rd., Ste. 300
Chicago, IL 60631
Toll free: 800-557-6957
Fax: (847)375-6495
Giseke, Ken, Chairman

National Futures Association [1494]
300 S Riverside Plz., Ste. 1800
Chicago, IL 60606-6615
PH: (312)781-1300
Toll free: 800-621-3570
Fax: (312)781-1467
Roth, Daniel J., President, CEO

National Gun Victims Action Council
[18253]
PO Box 10657
Chicago, IL 60610-0657
Fineman, Elliot, President, CEO

National Headache Foundation
[14919]
820 N Orleans St., Ste. 411
Chicago, IL 60610
PH: (312)274-2650
Toll free: 888-NHF-5552
Elkind, Arthur H., MD, President

National Hook-Up of Black Women
[18226]
1809 E 71st St., Ste. 205
Chicago, IL 60649-2000
PH: (773)667-7061
Fax: (773)667-7064
Summers, Deborah, President

National Independent Flag Dealers
Association [20948]
7984 S South Chicago Ave.
Chicago, IL 60617-1010
PH: (961)798-5730
Griebling, Kim, President

National Institute of Pension
Administrators [1076]
330 N Wabash Ave., Ste. 2000
Chicago, IL 60611-7621
Toll free: 800-999-6472
Fax: (312)673-6609
Rudzinski, Laura J., Exec. Dir.

National Introducing Brokers As-
sociation [1495]
55 W Monroe St., Ste. 3600
Chicago, IL 60603
PH: (312)977-0598
Fax: (312)977-0733
Schramm, Melinda, Chairperson,
Founder

National Marine Manufacturers As-
sociation [437]
231 S LaSalle St., Ste. 2050
Chicago, IL 60604
PH: (312)946-6200
Dammrich, Thomas, President

National Organization of Nurses with
Disabilities [16165]
1640 W Roosevelt Rd., Rm. 736
Chicago, IL 60608
Arora, Parul, RN, BSN, Director

National People's Action [11297]
810 N Milwaukee Ave.
Chicago, IL 60642

PH: (312)243-3035
Goehl, George, Exec. Dir.

National Podiatric Medical Associa-
tion [16791]
1706 E 87th St.
Chicago, IL 60617
PH: (773)374-5300
Fax: (773)374-5860
Burton, Debby, Exec. Dir.

National Poetry Foundation [10154]
61 W Superior St.
Chicago, IL 60654
PH: (312)787-7070
Fax: (312)787-6650
Sapiel, Gail, Bus. Mgr., Bus. Dev.
Mgr.

National Religious Vocation Confer-
ence [19889]
5401 S Cornell Ave., Ste. 207
Chicago, IL 60615
PH: (773)363-5454
Fax: (773)363-5530
Bednarczyk, Bro. Paul, CSC, Exec.
Dir.

National Runaway Safeline [12794]
3141B N Lincoln
Chicago, IL 60657
PH: (773)880-9860
Toll free: 800-344-2785
Fax: (773)929-5150
Philbin, Jack, Bd. Member

National Shippers Strategic
Transportation Council [3096]
330 N Wabash Ave., Ste. 2000
Chicago, IL 60611
PH: (202)367-1174
Fax: (952)442-3941
Cutler Jr., John M.

National Society of Genetic
Counselors [14883]
330 N Wabash Ave., Ste. 2000
Chicago, IL 60611
PH: (312)321-6834
Fax: (312)673-6972
Carey, Meghan, Exec. Dir.

National Society of Hispanic
Physicists [7029]
c/o Jesus Pando, President
Dept. of Physics
2219 N Kenmore Ave., Ste. 211
Chicago, IL 60614-3504
PH: (773)325-4942
Cid, Ximena, Secretary

National Sorority of Phi Delta Kappa
[23732]
8233 S King Dr.
Chicago, IL 60619-4932
PH: (773)783-7379
Fax: (773)783-7354

National Steel Bridge Alliance [6158]
1 E Wacker Dr., Ste. 700
Chicago, IL 60601-1802
PH: (312)670-2400
Fax: (312)670-5403
Ferch, Roger E., President

News and Letters Committee
[19143]
228 S Wabash, Ste. 230
Chicago, IL 60604-2383
PH: (312)431-8242
Fax: (312)431-8252
Moon, Terry, Managing Ed.

North American Association of Floor
Covering Distributors [565]
330 N Wabash Ave., Ste. 2000
Chicago, IL 60611-4267
PH: (312)321-6836
Toll free: 800-383-3091
Fax: (312)673-6962
Gammonley, Kevin, Exec. VP

North American Association of Food
    Equipment Manufacturers [1385]
161 N Clark St., Ste. 2020
Chicago, IL 60601
PH: (312)821-0201
Fax: (312)821-0202
Flynn, Deirdre, Exec. VP

North American Building Material
    Distribution Association [566]
330 N Wabash Ave., Ste. 2000
Chicago, IL 60611
PH: (312)321-6845
Toll free: 888-747-7862
Fax: (312)644-0310
Gammonley, Kevin, Executive Vice
    President

North American Neuromodulation
    Society [16562]
8735 W Higgins Rd., Ste. 300
Chicago, IL 60631
PH: (847)375-4714
Fax: (847)375-6424
Welber, Chris, Exec. Dir.

North American Retail Dealers As-
    sociation [1058]
222 S Riverside Plz., Ste. 2100
Chicago, IL 60606
PH: (312)648-0649
Toll free: 800-621-0298
Fax: (312)648-1212
Papasadero, Otto, Exec. Dir.

North American Students of
    Cooperation [8627]
330 S Wells St., Ste. 618-F
Chicago, IL 60606
PH: (773)404-2667
Fax: (331)223-9727
Scott, Jennifer, President

North American Wholesale Lumber
    Association [1413]
330 N Wabash, Ste. 2000
Chicago, IL 60611
PH: (312)321-5133
Toll free: 800-527-8258
Fax: (312)673-6838
Ekstein, Rick

Note Karacel Uganda [11415]
3338 S Aberdeen St.
Chicago, IL 60608
Billups, Christie, Founder

NPTA Alliance [2493]
330 N Wabash Ave., Ste. 2000
Chicago, IL 60611
PH: (312)321-4092
Fax: (312)673-6736
Tynes, Bayard, Chairman

Nuclear Energy Information Service
    [18733]
3411 W Diversey Ave., No. 16
Chicago, IL 60647
PH: (773)342-7650
Kraft, Dave, Director

Nuestros Pequenos Hermanos
    International [20449]
134 N La Salle St., Ste. 500
Chicago, IL 60602-1036
PH: (312)386-7499
Toll free: 888-201-8880
Fax: (312)658-0040
Wasson, Fr. William B., Founder

Nutrient Rich Foods Coalition
    [16232]
328 S Jefferson St., Ste. 750
Chicago, IL 60661
PH: (312)258-9500
Fax: (312)258-9501

Operation Homelink [10751]
25 E Washington St., Ste. 1501
Chicago, IL 60602

PH: (312)863-6336
Fax: (312)863-6206
Shannon, Dan, Founder, President

Opportunity International [12071]
550 W Van Buren, Ste. 200
Chicago, IL 60607
PH: (312)487-5000
Toll free: 800-793-9455
Fax: (312)487-5656
Murdoch, Chris, Dir. of Programs

Oral Health America [7710]
180 N Michigan Ave., Ste. 1150
Chicago, IL 60601
PH: (312)836-9900
Fax: (312)836-9986
Truett, Beth, CEO, President

Order of Kush [19290]
559 W Diversey Pky., No. 315
Chicago, IL 60614-7640
PH: (773)572-4632
Fax: (773)353-2763

Osteopathic International Alliance
    [16525]
142 E Ontario St.
Chicago, IL 60611
Carreiro, Jane, Chairman

Ovarian Cancer Symptom Aware-
    ness [14039]
875 N Michigan Ave., No. 1525
Chicago, IL 60611
PH: (312)280-0457
Harvill, Denise E., Chmn. of the Bd.

Parents Across America [8479]
c/o Siegel and Assoc.
53 W Jackson Blvd., Ste. 405
Chicago, IL 60604
Taylor, Dora, President

Partnership for Patient Safety
    [15053]
405 N Wabash Ave., Ste. P2W
Chicago, IL 60611
PH: (312)464-0600
Fax: (312)277-3307
Hatlie, Martin J., JD, CEO, President

People's Lobby [18918]
810 N Milwaukee Ave.
Chicago, IL 60642
PH: (312)676-2805
Berg, Jim, President

Physicians for a National Health
    Program [18881]
29 E Madison St., Ste. 1412
Chicago, IL 60602-4406
PH: (312)782-6006
Fax: (312)782-6007
Zarr, Robert, President

Plan Sponsor Council of America
    [1101]
200 S Wacker Dr., Ste. 3164
Chicago, IL 60606
PH: (312)419-1863
Fax: (312)419-1864
McCaffrey, Stephen, Chairperson

Play for Peace [12441]
500 N Michigan Ave., Ste. 600
Chicago, IL 60611-3754
PH: (312)675-8568
Guarrine, John, Chairperson

The Poetry Foundation [10156]
61 W Superior St.
Chicago, IL 60654
PH: (312)787-7070
Fax: (312)787-6650
Polito, Robert, President

Polish American Chamber of Com-
    merce [23614]
5214 W Lawrence Ave., Ste. 1
Chicago, IL 60630

PH: (773)205-1998
Morzy, Anna, President

Polish Genealogical Society of
    America [20992]
984 N Milwaukee Ave.
Chicago, IL 60642-4101
Carter, Terry, VP

Polish Museum of America [10168]
984 N Milwaukee Ave.
Chicago, IL 60622-4101
PH: (773)384-3352
Fax: (773)384-3799
Ciesla, Maria, President

Polish National Alliance of the United
    States of North America [19610]
6100 N Cicero Ave.
Chicago, IL 60646
PH: (773)286-0500
Toll free: 800-621-3723
Milcinovic, David, VP

Polish Roman Catholic Union of
    America [19613]
984 N Milwaukee Ave.
Chicago, IL 60642-4101
PH: (773)782-2600
Toll free: 800-772-8632
Fax: (773)278-4595
Drobot, Joseph A., Jr., President

Polish Women's Alliance of America
    [19616]
6643 N Northwest Hwy., 2nd Fl.
Chicago, IL 60631-1300
PH: (847)384-1200
Toll free: 888-522-1898
Fax: (847)384-1494
Huneycutt, Delphine, Mem.

Popcorn Board [1368]
330 N Wabash Ave., Ste. 2000
Chicago, IL 60611
PH: (312)644-6610

Power Transmission Distributors As-
    sociation [1760]
230 W Monroe St., Ste. 1410
Chicago, IL 60606-4703
PH: (312)516-2100
Fax: (312)516-2101
Burcroff, LeRoy, President

Power for Women [13393]
401 S LaSalle St., Ste. 801-U
Chicago, IL 60605
PH: (312)957-0195

Precast/Prestressed Concrete
    Institute [795]
200 W Adams St., No. 2100
Chicago, IL 60606
PH: (312)786-0300
Risser, Robert, President

Prevent Blindness [17738]
211 W Wacker Dr., Ste. 1700
Chicago, IL 60606
Toll free: 800-331-2020
Parry, Hugh R., CEO, President

Prevent Child Abuse America
    [11132]
228 S Wabash Ave., 10th Fl.
Chicago, IL 60604
PH: (312)663-3520
Toll free: 800-244-5373
Fax: (312)939-8962
Hmurovich, James M., CEO,
    President

Print Services and Distribution As-
    sociation [3177]
330 N Wabash Ave., Ste. 2000
Chicago, IL 60611
Toll free: 800-230-0175
Fax: (312)673-6880
Barbarone, Toni, Officer

PRISM International [1806]
8735 W Higgins Rd., Ste. 300
Chicago, IL 60631
PH: (847)375-6344
Toll free: 800-336-9793
Fax: (847)375-3643
Bergeson, Dave, Exec. Dir.

Pro-Life Action League [19069]
6160 N Cicero Ave., Ste. 600
Chicago, IL 60646
PH: (773)777-2900
    (773)777-2525
Fax: (773)777-3061
Scheidler, Joseph M., Exec.

Product Development and Manage-
    ment Association [2189]
330 N Wabash Ave., Ste. 2000
Chicago, IL 60611
PH: (312)321-5145
Toll free: 800-232-5241
Fax: (312)673-6885
Mundschenk, Chris, Exec. Dir.

Professional Association for SQL
    Server [6330]
203 N LaSalle St., Ste. 2100
Chicago, IL 60601
PH: (604)899-6009
Fax: (604)899-1269
Jorgensen, Adam, President

Professional Bowlers Association of
    America [22708]
55 E Jackson Blvd., Ste. 401
Chicago, IL 60604
PH: (206)332-9688
Fax: (312)341-1469

Professional Convention Manage-
    ment Association [2336]
35 E Wacker Dr., Ste. 500
Chicago, IL 60601-2105
PH: (312)423-7262
Toll free: 877-827-7262
Fax: (312)423-7222
Reed, William, Chairman

Professional Insurance Marketing
    Association [1917]
35 E Wacker Dr., Ste. 850
Chicago, IL 60601-2106
PH: (817)569-7462
Fax: (312)644-8557
Buckley, Mona F., MPA, CEO

Property Casualty Insurers Associa-
    tion of America [1920]
8700 W Bryn Mawr Ave., Ste. 1200S
Chicago, IL 60631-3512
PH: (847)297-7800
Fax: (847)297-5064
Sampson, David A., President, CEO

ProSkaters [23152]
1844 N Larrabee St.
Chicago, IL 60614-5208
PH: (312)296-7864
Fax: (312)896-9119
Heath, Craig, President

Psychologists for Social Responsibil-
    ity [18761]
c/o Brad Olson, Treasurer
National Louis University
122 S Michigan Ave.
Chicago, IL 60603
PH: (707)797-7016
Fax: (312)261-3464
Lee, Gordon, President

Public Library Association [9723]
50 E Huron St.
Chicago, IL 60611
PH: (312)280-5752
    (312)280-5047
Toll free: 800-545-2433
Fax: (312)280-5029
Macikas, Barb, Exec. Dir.

Radical Art Caucus [8884]
Dept. of Art and Art History
Depaul University
1150 W Fullerton Ave.
Chicago, IL 60614
PH: (773)325-4890
Gardner-Huggett, Joanna, Secretary

Rafiki Collaborative [13560]
PO Box 14825
Chicago, IL 60614
Riplinger, Andrew, Exec. Dir.

Rainbow/PUSH Coalition [13083]
930 E 50th St.
Chicago, IL 60615
PH: (773)373-3366
Fax: (773)373-3571
Ellis, Mark, COO

Real Estate Business Institute
[2888]
430 N Michigan Ave.
Chicago, IL 60611
PH: (312)321-4414
Toll free: 800-621-8738
Fax: (312)329-8882
Thompson, Michelle, Director

Real Estate Buyer's Agent Council
[2889]
430 N Michigan Ave.
Chicago, IL 60611
PH: (312)329-8656
Toll free: 800-648-6224
Fax: (312)329-8632
Gould, Marc, Exec. Dir.

Realtors Land Institute [2894]
430 N Michigan Ave., 11th Fl.
Chicago, IL 60611
Toll free: 800-441-5263
Fax: (312)329-8633
Friedrich, Jessa, Specialist

Reconciling Ministries Network
[20187]
123 W Madison St., Ste. 2150
Chicago, IL 60602
PH: (773)736-5526
Berryman, Matt, Exec. Dir.

Red Tag News Publications Associa-
tion [2122]
1415 N Dayton St.
Chicago, IL 60622
PH: (312)274-2215
Fax: (312)266-3363
Franklin, Jim, Exec. Dir.

Reference and User Services As-
sociation of the American Library
Association [9724]
50 E Huron St.
Chicago, IL 60611
PH: (312)280-4395
Toll free: 800-545-2433
Fax: (312)280-5273
Hornung, Susan, Exec. Dir.

Religious Brothers Conference
[19900]
233 S Wacker Dr., 84th Fl.
Chicago, IL 60606
Toll free: 866-339-0371
Fax: (866)339-0371
Henn, Jack, President

Research Council on Structural Con-
nections [7246]
1 E Wacker Dr., Ste. 700
Chicago, IL 60601
PH: (312)670-5414
Carter, Charlie, Officer

Retirement Research Foundation
[10528]
8765 W Higgins Rd., Ste. 430
Chicago, IL 60631-4172

PH: (773)714-8080
Fax: (773)714-8089
Frye, Irene, Exec. Dir.

St. Jude League [19903]
205 W Monroe St.
Chicago, IL 60606
PH: (312)544-8230
Brummel, Fr. Mark, CMF, Director

Sargent Shriver National Center on
Poverty Law [5551]
50 E Washington St., Ste. 500
Chicago, IL 60602
PH: (312)263-3830
Fax: (312)263-3846
Zuckerberg, Elizabeth Ring, COO

Save the Patient [14964]
260 E Chestnut St., No. 1712
Chicago, IL 60611
PH: (312)440-0630
Fax: (312)440-0631
Janecek, Lenore, CEO, President

Screen Manufacturers Association
[1575]
c/o Kathryn R. Fitzgerald
10526 S Ave. J
Chicago, IL 60617
Fax: (801)469-9727
White, Michael, President

Scribes - The American Society of
Legal Writers [5093]
c/o Michael B. Hyman, President
50 W Washington St., Chambers
415
Chicago, IL 60602
PH: (312)603-7582
Hyman, Michael B., President

Selfreliance Association of American
Ukrainians [19677]
2332 W Chicago Ave.
Chicago, IL 60622
PH: (773)328-7500
Toll free: 888-222-8571
Fax: (773)328-7501
Watral, Bohdan, President, CEO

Serbian-American Chamber of Com-
merce [23616]
448 W Barry Ave.
Chicago, IL 60657
Toll free: 877-686-7222
Golubovich, Zoran, Director

Serbian Bar Association of America
[5048]
20 S Clark St., Ste. 700
Chicago, IL 60603
PH: (312)782-8500
Duric, Marko, President

Serra International [19905]
333 W Wacker Dr., Ste. 500
Chicago, IL 60606-2218
PH: (312)419-7411
Woodward, John W., Mem.

Showmen's League of America
[1159]
1023 W Fulton Market
Chicago, IL 60607
PH: (312)733-9533
Fax: (312)733-9534
Porter, Ron, President

Sibling Leadership Network [11564]
332 S Michigan Ave., Ste. 1032-
S240
Chicago, IL 60604-4434
Arnold, Katie, Exec. Dir.

Social Responsibilities Round Table
of American Library Association
[9726]
50 E Huron St.
Chicago, IL 60611
Toll free: 800-545-2433

Society for Advancing the History of
South Asia [9510]
c/o John Pincince, President
Crown Center, Rm. 527
1032 W Sheridan Rd.
Department of History
Loyola University
Chicago, IL 60660-1537

Society for Ambulatory Anesthesia
[13707]
330 N Wabash Ave., Ste. 2000
Chicago, IL 60611
PH: (312)321-6872
Fax: (312)673-6620
Desai, Meena, President

Society of American Archivists
[8822]
17 N State St., Ste. 1425
Chicago, IL 60602-4061
PH: (312)606-0722
Toll free: 866-722-7858
Fax: (312)606-0728
Banks, Brenda, President

Society of Architectural Historians
[9511]
1365 N Astor St.
Chicago, IL 60610-2144
PH: (312)573-1365
Saliga, Pauline, Exec. Dir.

Society for Business Ethics [5186]
820 N Michigan Ave.
Chicago, IL 60611
Elm, Dawn, Exec. Dir.

Society of Cardiovascular
Anesthesiologists [13709]
8735 W Higgins Rd., Ste. 300
Chicago, IL 60631
Toll free: 855-658-2828
Fax: (847)375-6323
Reeves, Scott, Contact

Society of Gastroenterology Nurses
and Associates [14798]
330 N Wabash Ave., Ste. 2000
Chicago, IL 60611-7621
PH: (312)321-5165
Toll free: 800-245-7462
Fax: (312)673-6694
Fonkalsrud, Lisa, President

Society of Gynecologic Oncology
[16356]
230 W Monroe St., Ste. 710
Chicago, IL 60606-4703
PH: (312)235-4060
Fax: (312)235-4059
Eiken, Mary C., MS, RN, Exec. Dir.

Society for Healthcare Strategy and
Market Development [15335]
155 N Wacker Dr., Ste. 400
Chicago, IL 60606
PH: (312)422-3888
Fax: (312)278-0883
Barnett, Lauren

Society for Hematopathology
[16592]
33 W Monroe, Ste. 1600
Chicago, IL 60603-5617
PH: (312)541-4853
     (312)541-4944
Fax: (312)541-4998
Perkins, MD, PhD, Sherrie L.,
President

Society for Incentive Travel Excel-
lence [3394]
330 N Wabash Ave.
Chicago, IL 60611
PH: (312)321-5148
Fax: (312)527-6783
Hinton, Kevin M., CIS, CEO

Society of Incentive and Travel
Executives [3395]
330 N Wabash
Chicago, IL 60611
PH: (312)321-5148
Hinton, Kevin M., CIS, CEO

Society of Midland Authors [3520]
PO Box 10419
Chicago, IL 60610
Frisbie, Thomas, President

Society for Music Theory [10009]
Dept. of Music
University of Chicago
1010 E 59th St.
Chicago, IL 60637
PH: (773)834-3821
Long, Victoria L., Exec. Dir.

Society of Pediatric Nurses [16185]
330 N Wabash Ave., Ste. 2000
Chicago, IL 60611-7621
PH: (312)321-5154
Fax: (312)673-6754
Huth, Myra Martz, PhD, Comm.
Chm.

Society of Surgical Chairs [17407]
c/o Ellen Waller, Administrator
633 N St. Clair St.
Chicago, IL 60611
PH: (312)202-5447
Kent, Kenneth Craig, MD, President

Society of Thoracic Surgeons
[17474]
633 N St. Clair St., 23rd Fl.
Chicago, IL 60611
PH: (312)202-5800
Fax: (312)202-5801

Society for Vascular Surgery [17581]
633 N St. Clair St., 22nd Fl.
Chicago, IL 60611-5098
PH: (312)334-2300
Toll free: 800-258-7188
Fax: (312)334-2320
Fairman, Ronald M., President

Society of Women Engineers [6601]
203 N La Salle St., Ste. 1675
Chicago, IL 60601
Toll free: 877-793-4636
Layman, Colleen M., President

South-East Asia Center [19021]
5120 N Broadway St.
Chicago, IL 60640
PH: (773)989-6927
Fax: (888)831-5471
Wong, Fanny, Exec. Dir.

Spark Ventures [11154]
134 N LaSalle St., 5th Fl.
Chicago, IL 60602
PH: (773)293-6710
Fax: (773)293-6920
Johnson, Richard, CEO

Special Care Dentistry Association
[14471]
330 N Wabash Ave., Ste. 2000
Chicago, IL 60611
PH: (312)527-6764
Fax: (312)673-6663
Dougherty, Ms. Nancy J., President

Spencer Foundation [11737]
625 N Michigan Ave., Ste. 1600
Chicago, IL 60611
PH: (312)337-7000
Fax: (312)337-0282
McPherson, Michael S., President

States Organization for Boating Access [439]
231 S LaSalle St., Ste. 2050
Chicago, IL 60604

PH: (312)946-6283
Fax: (312)946-0388
Adams, James, VP

Straight Spouse Network [12259]
PO Box 4985
Chicago, IL 60680
PH: (773)413-8213
Callori, Kathy, Mem.

Strategic Account Management Association [2304]
10 N Dearborn St., 2nd Fl.
Chicago, IL 60602
PH: (312)251-3131
Fax: (312)251-3132
Quancard, Bernard, CEO, President

Strategic Management Society [2194]
Rice Bldg., Ste. 215
815 W Van Burren St.
Chicago, IL 60607-3567
PH: (312)492-6224
Fax: (312)492-6223
Lyles, Marjorie, President

Structural Stability Research Council [7248]
c/o Janet T. Cummins, Coordinator
1 E Wacker Dr., Ste. 700
Chicago, IL 60601
Ziemian, Ronald, Treasurer

Student Osteopathic Medical Association [16526]
142 E Ontario St.
Chicago, IL 60611-2864
PH: (312)202-8193
Toll free: 800-621-1773
Fax: (312)202-8200
Smith, Alex, President

SURGE [13338]
1254 W Jackson Blvd., No. 4W
Chicago, IL 60607
Yamani, Ummul Banin, Founder

Survivors Network of Those Abused by Priests [13266]
PO Box 6416
Chicago, IL 60680-6416
PH: (312)455-1499
Toll free: 877-762-7432
Fax: (312)455-1498
Blaine, Barbara, President

Swedish-American Historical Society [10231]
3225 W Foster Ave.
Chicago, IL 60625
PH: (773)583-5722
    (773)244-6224
Noren, Carol, Secretary

Swedish American Museum Association of Chicago [20998]
5211 N Clark St.
Chicago, IL 60640
PH: (773)728-8111
Abercrombie, Karin Moen, Exec. Dir.

Swiss-American Business Council [1995]
PO Box 64975
Chicago, IL 60664-0975
PH: (312)508-3340
Kouidri, David, Exec. Dir.

Tang Center for Herbal Medicine Research [15500]
Pritzker School of Medicine
University of Chicago
5841 S Maryland Ave., MC 4028
Chicago, IL 60637·
PH: (773)834-2399
    (773)702-4055
Fax: (773)834-0601
Yuan, Dr. Chun-Su, Director

Theatre for Young Audiences USA [10278]
c/o Theatre School at DePaul University
2350 N Racine Ave.
Chicago, IL 60614
PH: (773)325-7981
Fax: (773)325-7920
Van Kerckhove, Michael, Exec. Dir.

Thoracic Surgery Directors Association [17476]
633 N St. Clair St., 23rd Fl.
Chicago, IL 60611
PH: (312)202-5854
Fax: (773)289-0871
Iannettoni, Mark, MD, President

Thoracic Surgery Foundation for Research and Education [17477]
633 N St. Clair St., 23rd Fl.
Chicago, IL 60611
PH: (312)202-5868
Fax: (773)289-0871
Calhoon, John H., MD, President

Thoracic Surgery Residents Association [17478]
633 N St. Clair St., 23rd Fl.
Chicago, IL 60611-3234
PH: (312)202-5854
Fax: (773)289-0871
Walters, Dustin, President

Tithing and Stewardship Foundation [20626]
1100 E 55th St.
Chicago, IL 60615-5112
PH: (773)256-0679
Fax: (773)256-0692
Landahl, Rev. Paul R., Director

Tree House Humane Society [10703]
1212 W Carmen Ave.
Chicago, IL 60640
PH: (773)784-5488
Fax: (773)784-2332
De Funiak, David, Exec. Dir.

Truck and Engine Manufacturers Association [332]
333 W Wacker Dr., Ste. 810
Chicago, IL 60606-1249
PH: (312)929-1970
Fax: (312)929-1975
Mandel, Jed R., President

Truth Wins Out [11911]
5315 N Clark St., No. 634
Chicago, IL 60640
Besen, Wayne, Exec. Dir., Founder

Turnaround Management Association [2195]
150 N Wacker Dr., Ste. 1900
Chicago, IL 60606
PH: (312)578-6900
Fax: (312)578-8336
Victor, J. Scott, Chairman

Ukrainian Medical Association of North America [15748]
2247 W Chicago Ave.
Chicago, IL 60622-8957
PH: (773)278-6262
Fax: (773)278-6962
Hrycelak, George, MD, Exec. Dir.

United Dance Merchants of America [979]
PO Box 57086
Chicago, IL 60657
Toll free: 800-304-8362
Fax: (800)517-6070
Stone, Ashley, President

United States of America-China Chamber of Commerce [23624]
55 W Monroe St., Ste. 630
Chicago, IL 60603

PH: (312)368-9911
Fax: (312)368-9922
Yam, Siva, President

United States Artists [8946]
980 N Michigan Ave., Ste. 1300
Chicago, IL 60611-4513
PH: (312)470-6325
Fax: (312)470-6335
Leary, Meg, Dir. of Programs

United States Breastfeeding Committee [13858]
4044 N Lincoln Ave., No. 288
Chicago, IL 60618
PH: (773)359-1549
Fax: (773)313-3498
Renner, Megan, Exec. Dir.

United States Pacifist Party [18898]
5729 S Dorchester Ave.
Chicago, IL 60637
PH: (773)324-0654
Fax: (773)324-6426
Lyttle, Bradford, Founder

U.S. Powerlifting Federation [23073]
c/o Lance Carabel, President
Lance's Gym
3636 S Iron St.
Chicago, IL 60609
PH: (773)927-0009
Karabel, Lance, President

U.S. Soccer Federation [23196]
1801 S Prairie Ave.
Chicago, IL 60616
PH: (312)808-1300
Fax: (312)808-1301
Cordeiro, Carlos, Exec. VP

URANTIA Association of the United States [20557]
533 Diversey Pky.
Chicago, IL 60614
PH: (773)525-3319
Fax: (773)525-7739
Brown, Bruce, Treasurer

Urantia Foundation [20617]
533 Diversey Pky.
Chicago, IL 60614
PH: (773)525-3319
Fax: (773)525-7739
Siegel, Mo, President

Urban Teacher Residency United [8658]
1332 N Halsted St., Ste. 304
Chicago, IL 60642-2694
PH: (312)397-8878
Listak, Anissa, Exec. Dir.

Voices in the Wilderness [18838]
1460 W Carmen Ave.
Chicago, IL 60640
PH: (773)784-8065
Fax: (773)784-8837

Wallcoverings Association [1961]
330 N Wabash Ave., Ste. 2000
Chicago, IL 60611
PH: (312)321-5166
Fax: (312)673-6928

Window and Door Manufacturers Association [601]
330 N Wabash Ave., Ste. 2000
Chicago, IL 60611
PH: (312)321-6802
    (202)367-1157
O'Brien, Michael, CEO, President

Women Employed [11790]
65 E Wacker Pl., Ste. 1500
Chicago, IL 60601
PH: (312)782-3902
Fax: (312)782-5249
Thorne, Deborah L., V. Chmn. of the Bd.

Women in Real Estate [8759]
c/o Larissa Herczeg, Board Member
Oak Street Real Estate Capital
55 W Monroe St., Ste. 2825
Chicago, IL 60603

Women in Thoracic Surgery [17479]
633 N Saint Clair St., 23rd Fl.
Chicago, IL 60611
PH: (312)202-5835
Fax: (773)289-0871
Lawton, Jennifer S., MD, President

Women's Council of Realtors [2897]
430 N Michigan Ave.
Chicago, IL 60611
Toll free: 800-245-8512
Fax: (312)329-3290
Zimbelman, Melissa, PMN, Chairman, President

Word of Mouth Marketing Association [2305]
200 E Randolph St., Ste. 5100
Chicago, IL 60601
PH: (312)577-7610
Fanning, Suzanne, President

World Bicycle Relief [12736]
1000 W Fulton Market, 4th Fl.
Chicago, IL 60607
PH: (312)664-3836
Benzer, Brian, Chairman

World Council of Hellenes Abroad [19460]
801 W Adams St., Ste. 235
Chicago, IL 60607
PH: (312)627-1821
Fax: (312)627-1943
Tamvakis, Stefanos, President

World Future Society [6658]
333 N Lasalle St.
Chicago, IL 60654
Toll free: 800-989-8274
Steele, Julie Friedman, Chairperson

World Society for Reconstructive Microsurgery [17421]
20 N Michigan Ave., Ste. 700
Chicago, IL 60602
PH: (312)263-7150
Fax: (312)782-0553
Chang, David, MD, Sec. Gen.

Frank Lloyd Wright Trust [9445]
209 S LaSalle St., Ste. 118
Chicago, IL 60604
PH: (312)994-4000
Rafkin, John M., Chmn. of the Bd.

YMCA of the U.S.A. [13421]
101 N Wacker Dr.
Chicago, IL 60606
PH: (312)977-0031
Toll free: 800-872-9622
Allen, Sharon L., Chmn. of the Bd.

Delta Xi Phi Multicultural Sorority, Inc. [23953]
PO Box 151
Chicago Ridge, IL 60415-0151
Nelson, Vicki, President

CUSA: An Apostolate of Persons with Chronic Illness or Disability [19830]
4856 W 29th St.
Cicero, IL 60804-3611
Jagdfeld, Fr. Lawrence, Administrator

American Corriedale Association [4650]
c/o Marcia Craig, Executive Secretary
PO Box 391

Clay City, IL 62824
PH: (618)676-1046
Fax: (618)676-1133
Craig, Ryan, President

Angels of Hope **[11196]**
1043 Ferrari Dr.
Coal City, IL 60416
Holsinger, Russelle, Contact

Gaited Morgan Horse Organization **[4354]**
c/o Janet Hunter, Secretary
337 Hess Ln.
Cobden, IL 62920
PH: (618)833-3728
Suddarth, Jim, President

William Glasser Institute **[16991]**
4053 W 183rd St., No. 2666
Country Club Hills, IL 60478
PH: (708)957-6048
Olver, Kim, Exec. Dir.

National Association of Catholic Nurses-U.S.A. **[16145]**
c/o Diocese of Joliet
Blanchette Catholic Center
16555 Weber Rd.
Crest Hill, IL 60403
PH: (774)413-5084
Albuelouf, Alma, BSN, RN, FCN, Bd. Member

American Electrology Association **[14657]**
c/o Pearl G. Warner, President
4711 Midlothian Tpke. 13
Crestwood, IL 60445
PH: (708)293-1400
Fax: (708)293-1405
Ludwig, Deborah, Treasurer

Bible League International **[19753]**
3801 Eagle Nest Dr.
Crete, IL 60417
Toll free: 866-825-4636
Fax: (708)367-8600
Frank, Rob, CEO, President

A to Z Literacy Movement **[10827]**
PO Box 2483
Crystal Lake, IL 60039
PH: (815)477-8187
Keenan, Mal, Founder

Automotive Engine Rebuilders Association **[311]**
500 Coventry Ln., Ste. 180
Crystal Lake, IL 60014
PH: (815)526-7600
Toll free: 888-326-2372
Fax: (815)526-7601
Crumpton, Rex B., Chairman

International Association of Diecutting and Diemaking **[1736]**
651 W Terra Cotta Ave., Ste. 132
Crystal Lake, IL 60014-3406
PH: (815)455-7519
Toll free: 800-828-4233
Fax: (815)455-7510
Crouse, Cindy C., CEO

National Institute of Red Orange Canaries and All Other Cage Birds **[21545]**
c/o Chuck Eggenseammer, Membership Secretary
3318 Wirth Trl.
Crystal Lake, IL 60012
PH: (815)455-4439
Eggensammer, Chuck, Secretary

Oil Painters of America **[8936]**
PO Box 2488
Crystal Lake, IL 60039-2488
PH: (815)356-5987
Fax: (815)356-5987
Cadwallader, Ken, President

Steel Founders' Society of America **[1770]**
780 McArdle Dr., Unit G
Crystal Lake, IL 60014
PH: (815)455-8240
Fax: (815)455-8241
Monroe, Raymond W., Exec. VP

Ukrainian Children's Aid and Relief Effort, Inc. **[11176]**
6123 Hidden Oak Dr.
Crystal Lake, IL 60012
Kosogof, Alexandra, VP

U.S. Psychotronics Association **[6992]**
525 Juanita Vista
Crystal Lake, IL 60014
PH: (815)355-8030
Beutlich, Scott, Secretary, Treasurer

International Shrine Clown Association **[21602]**
c/o Lon Burke, President
19859 Country Road 200 E
Dahlgren, IL 62828
PH: (618)736-2763
Burke, Lon, President

American Academy of Dental Sleep Medicine **[17207]**
2510 N Frontage Rd.
Darien, IL 60561
PH: (630)737-9755
      (630)737-9705
Fax: (630)737-9790
Bennett, Kathleen, President

American Academy of Sleep Medicine **[17208]**
2510 N Frontage Rd.
Darien, IL 60561
PH: (630)737-9700
Fax: (630)737-9790
Chervin, Ronald, President

American Association of Sleep Technologists **[17210]**
2510 N Frontage Rd.
Darien, IL 60561
PH: (630)737-9704
Fax: (630)737-9788
Linley, Laura, President

American Board of Sleep Medicine **[17211]**
2510 N Frontage Rd.
Darien, IL 60561
PH: (630)737-9701
Fax: (630)737-9790
Carden, Kelly, MD, President

Associated Professional Sleep Societies **[17213]**
2510 N Frontage Rd.
Darien, IL 60561
PH: (630)737-9700
Fax: (630)737-9789

Lay Carmelite Order of the Blessed Virgin Mary **[19852]**
8501 Bailey Rd.
Darien, IL 60561-8417
PH: (630)969-5050

Sleep Research Society **[17221]**
2510 N Frontage Rd.
Darien, IL 60561
PH: (630)737-9702
Fax: (630)737-9790
Barrett, Jerome A., Exec. Dir.

Society of the Little Flower **[19907]**
1313 Frontage Rd.
Darien, IL 60561
PH: (630)968-9400
Toll free: 800-621-2806
Fax: (630)968-9542
Colaresi, Fr. Robert E., Mem.

High Standard Collectors' Association **[22019]**
PO Box 1578
Decatur, IL 62525

Independent Cosmetic Manufacturers and Distributors **[919]**
21925 W Field Pky., Ste. 205
Deer Park, IL 60010
Toll free: 800-334-2623
Fax: (847)991-8161
Busiek, Pam, President, CEO

American Thrombosis and Hemostasis Network **[15222]**
72 Treasure Ln.
Deerfield, IL 60015
Toll free: 800-360-2846
Fax: (847)572-0967
Recht, Michael, MD, PhD, Chairman

Association for Challenge Course Technology **[2467]**
PO Box 47
Deerfield, IL 60015
PH: (773)966-2503
Toll free: 800-991-0286
Fax: (800)991-0287
Borishade, James, Exec. Dir.

The Gospel Coalition **[19983]**
2065 Half Day Rd.
Deerfield, IL 60015
Peays, Ben, PhD, Exec. Dir.

Selected Independent Funeral Homes **[2415]**
500 Lake Cook Rd., Ste. 205
Deerfield, IL 60015
Toll free: 800-323-4219
Fax: (847)236-9968
Zoephel, Denise, Asst. CEO

Society for Adolescent Health and Medicine **[14215]**
1 Parkview Pl., Ste. 800
Deerfield, IL 60015-4943
PH: (847)753-5226
Fax: (847)480-9282
Ford, Carol, Bd. Member

Association for Black Culture Centers **[9196]**
c/o Dr. Fred Hord, Founder and Executive Director
312 Altgeld Hall
Northern Illinois University
DeKalb, IL 60115
PH: (815)753-5275
Hord, Dr. Fred, Founder, Exec. Dir.

Global Economic Education Alliance **[7731]**
307 Lowden Hall
Northern Illinois University
DeKalb, IL 60115
Brock, John, PhD, President

Sigma Tau Delta **[23747]**
711 N 1st St.
DeKalb, IL 60115
PH: (815)981-9974
Johnson, Dr. William C., Exec. Dir.

United Leukodystrophy Foundation **[15998]**
224 N 2nd St., Ste. 2
DeKalb, IL 60115
PH: (815)748-3211
Toll free: 800-728-5483
Fax: (815)748-0844
Rauner, Robert, President

American Society of Home Inspectors **[490]**
932 Lee St., Ste. 101
Des Plaines, IL 60016
PH: (847)759-2820
Fax: (847)759-1620
Lesh, Frank, Exec. Dir.

American Women for International Understanding **[12203]**
2100 S Wolf Rd.
Des Plaines, IL 60018-1932
PH: (847)298-0442
Rubio, Barbara, VP

Association for Redevelopment Initiatives **[4577]**
2200 E Devon Ave., Ste. 354
Des Plaines, IL 60018
PH: (312)987-1050
Rasher, Bruce, Chairman, Treasurer

Emergency Nurses Association **[14860]**
915 Lee St.
Des Plaines, IL 60016-6569
PH: (847)460-4123
Toll free: 800-900-9659
Hohenhaus, Susan M., Exec. Dir.

Families Anonymous **[13139]**
701 Lee St., Ste. 670
Des Plaines, IL 60016-4508
PH: (847)294-5877
Toll free: 800-736-9805
Fax: (847)294-5837

Gas Technology Institute **[4263]**
1700 S Mount Prospect Rd.
Des Plaines, IL 60018-1804
PH: (847)768-0500
Toll free: 866-484-5227
Fax: (847)768-0501
Chromek, Paul, Secretary, Gen. Counsel

GISCorps **[13292]**
701 Lee St., Ste. 680
Des Plaines, IL 60016
PH: (847)824-6300
Fax: (847)824-6363
Haley, Dianne, Chairperson

Inland Press Association **[2791]**
701 Lee St., Ste. 925
Des Plaines, IL 60016
PH: (847)795-0380
Fax: (847)795-0385
Campbell, Scott, Director

Institute for Certification of Computing Professionals **[7655]**
2400 E Devon Ave., Ste. 281
Des Plaines, IL 60018
PH: (847)299-4227

International Warehouse Logistics Association **[3438]**
2800 S River Rd., Ste. 260
Des Plaines, IL 60018
PH: (847)813-4699
Fax: (847)813-0115
Strother, Jay, VP

Islamic Information Center of America **[20221]**
PO Box 4052
Des Plaines, IL 60016
PH: (847)541-8141
Fax: (847)824-8436

MTM Association for Standards and Research **[6710]**
1111 E Touhy Ave.
Des Plaines, IL 60018
PH: (847)299-1111
Toll free: 844-300-5355

National Association of the Remodeling Industry **[555]**
PO Box 4250
Des Plaines, IL 60016
PH: (847)298-9200
Fax: (847)298-9225
Mozen, Judy, President

National Insurance Crime Bureau **[1908]**
1111 E Touhy Ave., Ste. 400
Des Plaines, IL 60018

PH: (847)544-7000
Toll free: 800-447-6282
Fax: (847)544-7100
Wehrle, Joseph H., Jr., CEO,
President

Society for Academic Emergency
Medicine [14690]
2340 S River Rd., Ste. 208
Des Plaines, IL 60018
PH: (847)813-9823
Fax: (847)813-5450
Jones, Alan E., MD, President

Society of Permanent Cosmetic
Professionals [929]
69 N Broadway St.
Des Plaines, IL 60016
PH: (847)635-1330
Fax: (847)635-1326
Ferriola, Melissa ', Secretary

Urban and Regional Information
Systems Association [6756]
701 Lee St., Ste. 680
Des Plaines, IL 60016
PH: (847)824-6300
Fax: (847)824-6363
Nelson, Wendy, Exec. Dir.

Us TOO International [14078]
2720 S River Rd., Ste. 112
Des Plaines, IL 60018
PH: (630)795-1002
Fax: (630)795-1602
Rieder, James L., Chairman

Ronald Reagan Home Preservation
Foundation [10345]
816 S Hennepin Ave.
Dixon, IL 61021
PH: (815)288-5176
Fax: (815)288-3642
Lewis, Ann, President

English Springer Spaniel Field Trial
Association [21874]
c/o Danelle Oliver, Secretary
8312 Old Moro Rd.
Dorsey, IL 62021
Haglin, Mark, President

American Society for Gastrointestinal
Endoscopy [14781]
3300 Woodcreek Dr.
Downers Grove, IL 60515
PH: (630)573-0600
    (630)570-5605
Toll free: 866-353-2743
Fax: (630)963-8332
Faigel, Douglas O., President

Computing Technology Industry As-
sociation [6312]
3500 Lacey Rd., Ste. 100
Downers Grove, IL 60515
PH: (630)678-8300
Fax: (630)678-8384
Harris, George, VP of Bus. Dev.

Foundation for Angelman Syndrome
Therapeutics [15932]
PO Box 608
Downers Grove, IL 60515-0608
PH: (630)852-3278
Toll free: 866-783-0078
Fax: (630)852-3270
Evans, Paula M., Chairman

National Garden Bureau [4437]
1311 Butterfield Rd., Ste. 310
Downers Grove, IL 60515-5625
PH: (630)963-0770
Fax: (630)963-8864
Kieft, Janis, President

Property and Liability Resource
Bureau [1921]
3025 Highland Pky., Ste. 800
Downers Grove, IL 60515-1291

PH: (630)724-2200
Fax: (630)724-2260
Kelley, Bruce, EMC, Chairman

Technology Councils of North
America [6755]
3500 Lacey Rd., Ste. 100
Downers Grove, IL 60515-5439
Zylstra, Steve, Chairman

Inland Rivers Ports and Terminals,
Inc. [2242]
1 Confluence Way
East Alton, IL 62024
PH: (618)468-3010
Costello, Jerry, Contact

Xi Psi Phi [23722]
160 S Bellwood Dr., Ste. Z
East Alton, IL 62024
PH: (618)307-5433
Fax: (618)307-5430
Parmlee, Dr. Randy A., President

Anheuser-Busch Collectors Club
[21617]
1070 Dundee Ave., Ste. A
East Dundee, IL 60118
PH: (847)428-3150
Toll free: 800-498-3215
Fax: (847)428-3170
Steffen, Tony, Owner

The Lawn Institute [4283]
2 E Main St.
East Dundee, IL 60118
PH: (847)649-5555
Toll free: 800-405-8873
Fax: (847)649-5678

Turfgrass Producers International
[4285]
2 E Main St.
East Dundee, IL 60118
PH: (847)649-5555
Toll free: 800-405-8873
Fax: (847)649-5678
Hall, Susan, Mktg. Mgr.

Mass Finishing Job Shops Associa-
tion [1287]
808 13th St.
East Moline, IL 61244
PH: (309)755-1101
Fax: (309)755-1121
Williams, Jack, Exec. Dir.

Federation of American Consumers
and Travelers [13236]
318 Hillsboro Ave.
Edwardsville, IL 62025
Toll free: 800-872-3228
Fax: (618)656-5369
Rolens, Vicki, Managing Dir.

Bernese Mountain Dog Club of
America [21840]
c/o Dee McDuffee, Membership
Chairperson
4N156 Country View Ln.
Elburn, IL 60119
PH: (630)365-0190
Latterell, Julie, President

American Academy of Disability
Evaluating Physicians [14297]
2575 Northwest Pky.
Elgin, IL 60124
PH: (312)663-1171
Toll free: 800-456-6095
Fax: (312)663-1175
Yost, Sandra L., MBA, Director

Brethren Volunteer Service [13286]
1451 Dundee Ave.
Elgin, IL 60120-1674
PH: (847)742-5100
Toll free: 800-323-8039
Fax: (847)429-4394
McFadden, Dan, Director

Church of the Brethren's Caring
Ministries [10504]
1451 Dundee Ave.
Elgin, IL 60120
Toll free: 800-323-8039

Council of Religious Volunteer Agen-
cies [13291]
Brethren Volunteer Service
1451 Dundee Ave.
Elgin, IL 60120
Doty, Ed, Chairman

Foodservice Equipment Distributors
Association [1383]
2250 Point Blvd., Ste. 200
Elgin, IL 60123
PH: (224)293-6500
Fax: (224)293-6505
Schmitt, Joe, President

Recycled Paperboard Technical As-
sociation [842]
PO Box 5774
Elgin, IL 60121-5774
PH: (847)622-2544
Schaffer, Amy, Exec. Dir.

Society of Skeletal Radiology
[17073]
2575 Northwest Pky.
Elgin, IL 60124
PH: (847)752-6249
Fax: (847)960-3861
Sonin, Andrew, MD, President

Women in Management Fox Valley
[2196]
PO Box 6690
Elgin, IL 60121-6690
Groeper, Michelle, Secretary

World Professional Association for
Transgender Health [12953]
2575 Northwest Pky.
Elgin, IL 60124
PH: (612)624-9397
Fax: (612)624-9541
Robinson, Bean, PhD, Exec. Dir.

American Academy of Pediatrics
[16598]
141 NW Point Blvd.
Elk Grove Village, IL 60007-1098
PH: (847)434-4000
Toll free: 800-433-9016
Fax: (847)434-8000
Perrin, James M., MD, President

American Amusement Machine As-
sociation [1131]
450 E Higgins Rd., Ste. 201
Elk Grove Village, IL 60007
PH: (847)290-9088
Felix, Chris, President

American College of Occupational
and Environmental Medicine
[16312]
25 NW Point Blvd., Ste. 700
Elk Grove Village, IL 60007-1030
PH: (847)818-1800
Fax: (847)818-9266
Tacci, James A., Officer

Cure SMA [15921]
925 Busse Rd.
Elk Grove Village, IL 60007
Toll free: 800-886-1762
Hobby, Kenneth, President

National Ice Cream Retailers As-
sociation [976]
1028 W Devon Ave.
Elk Grove Village, IL 60007
PH: (847)301-7500
Toll free: 866-303-6960
Fax: (847)301-8402
Oden, Jim, President

VOR [12333]
836 S Arlington Heights Rd., No.
351
Elk Grove Village, IL 60007
Toll free: 877-399-4867
Fax: (605)399-1631
Innis, Larry, Treasurer

The Caspian Horse Society of the
Americas [4341]
29056 East 1200 North Rd.
Ellsworth, IL 61737
PH: (309)724-8373
Harrison, Mary, Secretary

American Dairy Products Institute
[971]
126 N Addison Ave.
Elmhurst, IL 60126
PH: (630)530-8700
Fax: (630)530-8707
Thomas, David, CEO

American Hearing Research
Foundation [15172]
275 N York St., Ste. 401
Elmhurst, IL 60126
PH: (630)617-5079
Fax: (630)563-9181
Muench, Richard G., Chairman

American Society of Neurophysi-
ological Monitoring [16007]
275 N York St., Ste. 401
Elmhurst, IL 60126
PH: (630)832-1300
Lee, George, President

Association of Technology, Management and Applied Engineering
[8017]
275 N York St., Ste. 401
Elmhurst, IL 60126
PH: (630)433-4514
Wyatt, John, Chairperson

Council of International Investigators
[2009]
PO Box 565
Elmhurst, IL 60126-0565
PH: (630)501-1880
Toll free: 888-759-8884
Kumar, Sachit, President

International Society of Managing
and Technical Editors [2794]
275 N York St., Ste. 401
Elmhurst, IL 60126-2752
PH: (630)433-4513
Fax: (630)563-9181
Higgins, Jan, VP

Medical Dental Hospital Business
Associates [41]
350 Poplar Ave.
Elmhurst, IL 60126
PH: (630)359-4273
Fax: (630)359-4274
Nixon, Jon, President

National Alliance of Medicare Set-
Aside Professionals [18334]
275 N York St., Ste. 401
Elmhurst, IL 60126
PH: (630)617-5047
Patureau, Gary, President

National Organization of Bar
Counsel [5444]
275 N York St., Ste. 401
Elmhurst, IL 60126
PH: (630)617-5153
    (215)560-6296
Burgoyne, Paul J., President

Pan Arcadian Federation of America
[19456]
880 N York Rd.
Elmhurst, IL 60126

PH: (630)833-1900
Potakis, Mr. Evangelos, Trustee

The Ray E. Helfer Society [14211]
350 Poplar Ave.
Elmhurst, IL 60126
PH: (630)359-4273
Fax: (630)359-4274
Leventhal, John, President

Blue & White Pottery & Old Sleepy
Eye Collectors Club [21577]
c/o Susie Reicheneker
402 N Laurel St.
Elmwood, IL 61529
Eakin, Max, Co-Pres.

Working-Class Studies Association
[8167]
PO Box 264
Emden, IL 62635

Affirmation: United Methodists for
Lesbian, Gay, Bisexual, Transgen-
der and Queer Concerns [20174]
PO Box 1021
Evanston, IL 60204
Ellis, Lynn, Rep.

Alliance of Hope for Suicide Loss
Survivors [13190]
PO Box 7005
Evanston, IL 60201
PH: (847)868-3313
Walker, Ronnie, Founder, CEO

Alpha Phi International Fraternity
[23945]
1930 Sherman Ave.
Evanston, IL 60201
PH: (847)475-0663
     (847)475-4786
Fax: (847)475-6820
Kahangi, Linda, Exec. Dir.

American Board of Lower Extremity
Surgery [16777]
PO Box 5373
Evanston, IL 60204-5373
PH: (248)855-7740
Fax: (248)855-7743
Gimbel, Joseph B., DPM, President,
Treasurer

American Massage Therapy As-
sociation [15551]
500 Davis St., Ste. 900
Evanston, IL 60201-4695
Toll free: 877-905-0577
Johnson, Shelly

Benton Foundation [11318]
1560 Sherman Ave., Ste. 440
Evanston, IL 60201
PH: (847)328-3049
Fax: (847)328-3046
Smith, Michael, Treasurer

Common Ground - U.S.A. [19167]
PO Box 57
Evanston, IL 60204
PH: (847)475-0391
Stoner, Nadine, President

Council of Georgist Organizations
[19168]
c/o Sue Walton, Administrator
PO Box 57
Evanston, IL 60204
PH: (847)209-0047
Walton, Sue, Administrator

Dermatology Foundation [14492]
1560 Sherman Ave., Ste. 870
Evanston, IL 60201-4808
PH: (847)328-2256
Fax: (847)328-0509
Wintroub, Bruce U., Chairman

GlobeMed [15463]
Scott Hall, Rm. 14, 16, 16A
601 University Pl.
Evanston, IL 60208
PH: (847)786-5716
Hanson, Brian, Chairman

National Spiritual Assembly of the
Baha'is of the U.S. [20549]
1233 Central St.
Evanston, IL 60201
PH: (847)733-3400
Fullmer, Glen, Dir. of Comm.

Prevention Through Education
[13557]
1007 Church St., Ste. 302
Evanston, IL 60201
Suk, Gabriel, Founder

Rainbows for All Children [11264]
1007 Church St., Ste. 408
Evanston, IL 60201
PH: (847)952-1770
Fax: (847)952-1774
Thomas, Bob, CEO

Rotary International [12906]
1 Rotary Ctr.
1560 Sherman Ave.
Evanston, IL 60201-3698
Toll free: 866-976-8279
Klinginsmith, Ray, Trustee

Sigma Alpha Epsilon [23924]
1856 Sheridan Rd.
Evanston, IL 60201-3837
PH: (847)475-1856
Fax: (847)475-2250
Ayers, Blaine, Exec. Dir.

Sigma Chi Fraternity [23927]
1714 Hinman Ave.
Evanston, IL 60201
PH: (847)869-3655
Fax: (847)869-4906
Church, Michael, Exec. Dir.

Society for Research on Educational
Effectiveness [7801]
2040 Sheridan Rd.
Evanston, IL 60208
PH: (202)495-0920
Fax: (202)640-4401
Hedges, Larry V., PhD, President

U.S.A. Toy Library Association
[10824]
2719 Broadway Ave.
Evanston, IL 60201-1503
PH: (847)612-6966
Fax: (847)864-8473
Iacuzzi, Judith Q., Exec. Dir.

Woman's Christian Temperance
Union [13188]
1730 Chicago Ave.
Evanston, IL 60201-4585
PH: (847)864-1397
Toll free: 800-755-1321
Olsen, Janet, Arch.

National Association of Bench and
Bar Spouses Inc. [5027]
7422 Lonewolf Ct.
Fairview Heights, IL 62208
PH: (618)741-3589
Meanes, Willam M., Sr., President

National Foundation for Ectodermal
Dysplasias [14845]
6 Executive Dr., Ste. 2
Fairview Heights, IL 62208-1360
PH: (618)566-2020
Fete, Mary, MSN,RN,CCM, Exec.
Dir.

Academy for Sports Dentistry
[17272]
PO Box 364
Farmersville, IL 62533

PH: (217)227-3431
Fax: (217)227-3438
Lovelace, James, President

Historical Diving Society U.S.A.
[22811]
c/o Greg Platt, Treasurer
PO Box 453
Fox River Grove, IL 60021-0453
PH: (805)934-1660
Orr, Dan, Chairman

America Against Malaria [15392]
PO Box 4
Frankfort, IL 60423
PH: (815)693-1657
     (773)640-1347
Fax: (815)464-3531
Dubsky, Dawn, President

International Council of Community
Churches [20026]
21116 Washington Pky.
Frankfort, IL 60423
PH: (815)464-5690
Griffith, Richard O., President

Lincoln Highway Association [9407]
136 N Elm St.
Franklin Grove, IL 61031
PH: (815)456-3030
Dieterich, Bob, Advisor

National Association of Baby
Boomer Women [13387]
9672 W US Highway 20
Galena, IL 61036
Toll free: 877-266-6379
Holmes, Anne, Chairperson

International Formalwear Association
[205]
244 E Main St.
Galesburg, IL 61401
PH: (309)721-5450
Fax: (309)342-5921
Benbrook, Rod, President

National Association for the
Exchange of Industrial Resources
[7826]
560 McClure St.
Galesburg, IL 61401
Toll free: 800-562-0955
Smith, Mr. Gary C., CEO, President

Tea Leaf Club International [21585]
21275 E 900 St.
Geneseo, IL 61254
Birch, Woody, President

Cord Blood Association [13840]
211 Garfield St.
Geneva, IL 60134-2313
PH: (630)463-9040
Kurtzberg, Joanne, MD, President

International Society for Cutaneous
Lymphomas [14498]
303 W State St.
Geneva, IL 60134
PH: (630)578-3991
Fax: (630)262-1520
Vermeer, Dr. Maarten H., Ph.D.,
President

International Society of Hair Restora-
tion Surgery [14902]
303 W State St.
Geneva, IL 60134
PH: (630)262-5399
Toll free: 800-444-2737
Fax: (630)262-1520
Yagyu, Kuniyoshi, MD, President

North American Hair Research
Society [14903]
303 W State St.
Geneva, IL 60134-2156

PH: (630)578-3991
Fax: (630)262-1520
Bergfeld, Wilma F., MD, Officer

Skin of Color Society [14512]
303 W State St.
Geneva, IL 60134
PH: (630)578-3991
Fax: (630)262-1520
McMichael, Amy, MD, President

Society of Registered Professional
Adjusters [1931]
PO Box 512
Geneva, IL 60134
PH: (630)262-2270
Toll free: 800-949-5272
Fax: (630)262-2274
Mehren, Dave, Exec. Dir.

American Bugatti Club [21317]
c/o Paul Simms, Secretary
600 Lakeview Terr.
Glen Ellyn, IL 60137
PH: (630)469-4920
Mullin, Peter, President

American Endodontic Society
[14409]
PO Box 545
Glen Ellyn, IL 60138-0545
PH: (773)519-4879
Fax: (630)858-0525
Dreslin, John E., DMD, MAES,
Chairman

Association of Independent
Manufacturers'/Representatives,
Inc. [2203]
800 Roosevelt Rd., Suite C-312
Glen Ellyn, IL 60137
PH: (630)942-6581
Fax: (630)790-3095
Fleming, Steve, CPMR, Chairman

Association of Rotational Molders
[2620]
800 Roosevelt Rd., Ste. C-312
Glen Ellyn, IL 60137
PH: (630)942-6589
Fax: (630)790-3095
Church, Rick, Exec. Dir.

Bearing Specialists Association
[1718]
Bldg. C, Ste. 312
800 Roosevelt Rd.
Glen Ellyn, IL 60137
PH: (630)858-3838
Fax: (630)790-3095
Negri, Brian, Director

Ceramic Tile Distributors Association
[511]
800 Roosevelt Rd., Bldg. C, Ste.
312
Glen Ellyn, IL 60137
PH: (630)545-9415
Fax: (630)790-3095
Church, Rick, Exec. Dir.

Evangelical Church Library Associa-
tion [9705]
PO Box 353
Glen Ellyn, IL 60138
PH: (630)474-1080
Waln, Donna, Conferences Coord.

National Association of Alternative
Benefits Consultants [1608]
435 Pennsylvania Ave.
Glen Ellyn, IL 60137
Toll free: 800-627-0552
Randecker, Harvey, President

National Association of Architectural
Metal Manufacturers [2360]
800 Roosevelt Rd., Bldg. C, Ste.
312

Glen Ellyn, IL 60137
PH: (630)942-6591
Fax: (630)790-3095

National Association of Container
Distributors [838]
800 Roosevelt Rd., Bldg. C-312
Glen Ellyn, IL 60137
PH: (630)942-6585
Fax: (630)790-3095
Burns, Gary, President

National Church Goods Association
[20582]
Bldg. C, Ste. 312
800 Roosevelt Rd.
Glen Ellyn, IL 60137
PH: (630)942-6599
Fax: (630)790-3095
Tally, P.J., President

Plastic Pipe and Fittings Association
[2613]
Bldg. C, Ste. 312
800 Roosevelt Rd.
Glen Ellyn, IL 60137
PH: (630)858-6540
Fax: (630)790-3095

Pressure Vessel Manufacturers As-
sociation [1761]
Bldg. C, Ste. 312
800 Roosevelt Rd.
Glen Ellyn, IL 60137
PH: (630)942-6590
Fax: (630)790-3095
Church, Jeff, Exec. Dir.

Thermoset Resin Formulators As-
sociation [750]
Bldg. C, Ste. 312
800 Roosevelt Rd.
Glen Ellyn, IL 60137
PH: (630)942-6596
Fax: (630)790-3095
Church, Jerilyn J., CAE, Exec. Dir.

Botanic Gardens Conservation
International U.S. [3674]
c/o Kate Sackman, Executive Direc-
tor
Chicago Botanic Garden
1000 Lake Cook Rd.
Glencoe, IL 60022
PH: (847)835-6928
Affolter, James, President

Pickard Collectors Club [21714]
PO Box 317
Glencoe, IL 60022
Poulos, Harry, Treasurer

International Association for Health-
care Security and Safety [15330]
PO Box 5038
Glendale Heights, IL 60139
PH: (630)529-3913
Fax: (630)529-4139
LaRose, CHPA,CPP, David,
President

American College of Chest Physi-
cians [14090]
2595 Patriot Blvd.
Glenview, IL 60026
PH: (224)521-9800
Toll free: 800-343-2227
Fax: (224)521-9801
Welch, Stephen J., Sr. VP, Publisher

Animal Behavior Society [7396]
2111 Chestnut Ave., Ste. 145
Glenview, IL 60025
PH: (312)893-6585
Fax: (312)896-5619
Bertram, Susan, Secretary

Association of Visual Packaging
Manufacturers [2473]
PO Box 758
Glenview, IL 60025-0758

PH: (224)330-7470
Garvin, Peter, President

Commission on Accreditation of
Ambulance Services [13496]
1926 Waukegan Rd., Ste. 300
Glenview, IL 60025-1770
PH: (847)657-6828
Toll free: 877-457-2227
Fax: (847)657-6825
McEntee, Ms. Sarah, Exec. Dir.

Fat Disorders Research Society
[15822]
2305 Robincrest Ln.
Glenview, IL 60025
PH: (847)331-6874

Feed the Dream Guatemala [10970]
PO Box 2642
Glenview, IL 60025
Haggart, Sandy, Founder

Hellenic American Dental Society
[14438]
PO Box 2505
Glenview, IL 60025-2505
Karras, Dr. Louis, Exec. Dir.

International Association of
Rehabilitation Professionals
[17088]
1926 Waukegan Rd., Ste. 1
Glenview, IL 60025-1770
PH: (847)657-6964
Toll free: 888-427-7722
Fax: (847)657-6963
Wangman, Carl, CAE, Exec. Dir.

International Clinical Cytometry
Society [16584]
2111 Chestnut Ave., Ste. 145
Glenview, IL 60025
PH: (847)550-3080
Fax: (312)896-5614
Craig, Fiona, President

International Penguin Class Dinghy
Association [22638]
1812 Highland Terr.
Glenview, IL 60025
Krafft, Charles, President

International Society for Laboratory
Hematology [15238]
2111 Chestnut Ave., Ste. 145
Glenview, IL 60025
PH: (847)737-1584
Fax: (312)896-5614
Hayward, Catherine, President

Iraqi Christian Relief Council [12688]
PO Box 3021
Glenview, IL 60025
PH: (847)401-8846
Taimoorazy, Juliana, Founder,
President

Little By Little [15031]
PO Box 934
Glenview, IL 60025-0934
Walsh, Sue, Founder, President

National Luggage Dealers Associa-
tion [2086]
1817 Elmdale Ave.
Glenview, IL 60026-1355
PH: (847)998-6869
Fax: (847)998-6884

National Registry of Environmental
Professionals [4087]
PO Box 2099
Glenview, IL 60025-6099
PH: (847)724-6631
Fax: (847)724-4223
Young, Richard A., PhD, Exec. Dir.

Society for the Study of Ingestive
Behavior [13805]
2111 Chestnut Ave., Ste. 145
Glenview, IL 60025

PH: (847)807-4924
Fax: (312)896-5614
Watts, Alan, President

Steel Tube Institute of North America
[846]
2516 Waukegan Rd., Ste. 172
Glenview, IL 60025
PH: (847)461-1701
Fax: (847)660-7981
Werner, Richard, Exec.

Thrombosis and Hemostasis Societ-
ies of North America [15246]
2111 Chestnut Ave., Ste. 145
Glenview, IL 60025
PH: (847)978-2001
Grabowski, Eric, President

United States Bridge Federation
[21561]
c/o Stan Subeck
106 Penn Ct.
Glenview, IL 60026
Weinstein, Howard, President

Colonial Coverlet Guild of America
[21639]
536 Arizona Ave.
Glenwood, IL 60425-1006
Coolidge, Laurie, Contact

Keeshond Club of America [21908]
c/o Donna Smith, President
652 Grafton Hills Dr.
Grafton, IL 62037
Smith, Donna, President

American Association for Accredita-
tion of Ambulatory Surgery Facili-
ties [17359]
5101 Washington St., Ste. 2F
Gurnee, IL 60031
PH: (847)775-1970
Toll free: 888-545-5222
Fax: (847)775-1985
Griffin-Rossi, Theresa, Exec. Dir.

Green Builder Coalition [532]
PO Box 7507
Gurnee, IL 60031-7000
Blissard, Laureen, Tech. Dir.

National Conference of State Liquor
Administrators [4954]
543 Long Hill Rd.
Gurnee, IL 60031
PH: (847)721-6410
Waters, Jerry W., Sr., President

National Marine Representatives As-
sociation [2254]
PO Box 360
Gurnee, IL 60031
PH: (847)662-3167
Fax: (847)336-7126
Flack, Brandon, President

National Snaffle Bit Association
[4388]
1391 St. Paul Ave.
Gurnee, IL 60031
PH: (847)623-6722
Fax: (847)625-7435

Organization of Parents Through
Surrogacy [13204]
PO Box 611
Gurnee, IL 60031
PH: (847)782-0224

Pharmaceutical Printed Literature
Association [2569]
c/o Nosco, Inc.
2199 N Delany Rd.
Gurnee, IL 60031
Hace, Gerald, V. Chmn. of the Bd.

Polish Tatra Sheepdog Club of
America [21944]
c/o Donna Gnuechtel, Secretary
110 Jack Dylan Dr.

Hampshire, IL 60140
PH: (414)329-1373
Williams, Jill, Director

Circus Model Builders International
[22197]
c/o Armando Ortiz, Membership
Secretary
1649 Park Ave.
Hanover Park, IL 60133-3610
Butash, Mike, President

Elevator U [522]
4751 N Olcott Ave.
Harwood Heights, IL 60706
Flint, Terri, President

Blood and Marrow Transplant
Information Network [17508]
1548 Old Skokie Rd., Ste. 1
Highland Park, IL 60035
PH: (847)433-3313
Toll free: 888-597-7674
Fax: (847)433-4599
Stewart, Susan K., Exec. Dir.

International Housewares
Representatives Association [1684]
1755 Lake Cook Rd., No. 318
Highland Park, IL 60035
PH: (847)748-8269
Fax: (847)748-8273
Grob, John, Chairperson

Submersible Wastewater Pump As-
sociation [588]
1866 Sheridan Rd., Ste. 212
Highland Park, IL 60035
PH: (847)681-1868
Fax: (847)681-1869
Stolberg, Adam, Exec. Dir.

Dyspraxia Foundation USA [15928]
84 Westover Rd.
Highwood, IL 60040
PH: (847)780-3311
Fried, Warren, Exec. Dir., Founder

Air Distribution Institute [1613]
4415 Harrison St., Ste. 426
Hillside, IL 60162
Tuggle, Peter, President

Catholic Cemetery Conference
[2401]
Bldg. No. 3
1400 S Wolf Rd.
Hillside, IL 60162-2197
PH: (708)202-1242
Toll free: 888-850-8131
Fax: (708)202-1255
Bittner, Stephen E., VP

Firestop Contractors International
Association [807]
4415 W Harrison St., Ste. 436
Hillside, IL 60162-1906
PH: (708)202-1108
Fax: (708)449-0837
McHugh, Bill, Exec. Dir.

National Fireproofing Contractors
Association [1291]
4415 W Harrison St., No. 436
Hillside, IL 60162
PH: (708)236-3411
Fax: (708)449-0837
Taglienti, John, President

Dalit Solidarity, Inc. [18392]
PO Box 112
Hines, IL 60141-0112
PH: (708)612-4248
Chinnappan, Benjamin, President

American Board for Occupational
Health Nurses [16102]
201 E Ogden Ave., Ste. 114
Hinsdale, IL 60521-3652

PH: (630)789-5799
Toll free: 888-842-2646
Fax: (630)789-8901
Niebuhr, Bonnie, RN, MS, CAE, CEO

MRSA Survivors Network [17007]
PO Box 241
Hinsdale, IL 60522
PH: (630)325-4354
Thomas, Jeanine, Founder

National Association of Senior Move
Managers [2184]
PO Box 209
Hinsdale, IL 60522
Toll free: 877-606-2766
Fax: (630)230-3594
Stieger, Carolyn, Mgr.

Active 20-30 U.S. & Canada [12881]
2800 W Higgins Rd., Ste. 440
Hoffman Estates, IL 60169-7286
PH: (847)852-5206
Fax: (847)885-8393
Sternberg, Dana Von, President

Bright Hope International [12531]
2060 Stonington Ave.
Hoffman Estates, IL 60169
PH: (224)520-6100
Fax: (866)530-3489
Dyer, C.H., President, CEO

Canaan Dog Club of America
[21850]
565 Illinois Blvd.
Hoffman Estates, IL 60169-3360
Comsky, Bryna, Rec. Sec.

Coalition on Abortion/Breast Cancer
[13494]
PO Box 957133
Hoffman Estates, IL 60195
PH: (847)421-4000
Toll free: 877-803-0102
Malec, Karen, Founder, President

Inter-Industry Conference on Auto
Collision Repair [344]
5125 Trillium Blvd.
Hoffman Estates, IL 60192
PH: (847)590-1198
Toll free: 800-590-1215
Van Alstyne, John S., President, CEO

National Association of Publishers'
Representatives, Inc. [2805]
2800 W Higgins Rd., Ste. 440
Hoffman Estates, IL 60169
Toll free: 877-263-9640
Fax: (847)885-8393
Dunay, Darren, President

National Association of Wastewater
Technicians [3452]
2800 W Higgins Rd., Ste. 440
Hoffman Estates, IL 60169
Toll free: 800-236-NAWT
Fax: (866)220-1055
Bassett, Gene, President

Neuroblastoma Children's Cancer
Society [14032]
PO Box 957672
Hoffman Estates, IL 60195
PH: (847)605-0700
Toll free: 800-532-5162
Fax: (847)605-0705

Global Spine Outreach [17255]
12701 W 143rd St., Ste. 110
Homer Glen, IL 60491
Toll free: 866-GSO-0880
Rinella, Anthony S., MD, President

Matanya's Hope [12551]
PO Box 562
Homewood, IL 60430

PH: (708)822-4673
Stark, Michelle, Founder, President

Progressive Health Partnership
[15489]
3040 Fresno Ln.
Homewood, IL 60430
PH: (708)365-9747
Greenberg, Josh, CEO

Cultural Studies Association [9230]
3333 York Ln.
Island Lake, IL 60042
PH: (630)999-1711
Toll free: 800-519-6057
Aksikas, Jaafar, President

American Supply Association [2634]
1200 N Arlington Heights Rd., Ste. 150
Itasca, IL 60143
PH: (630)467-0000
Fax: (630)467-0001
Black, Amy, Exec. Dir.

Corrugated Packaging Alliance
[2475]
500 Park Blvd., Ste. 985
Itasca, IL 60143
PH: (847)364-9600
Fax: (847)364-9739
Schmidt, Dwight, Contact

Fibre Box Association [2491]
500 Park Blvd., Ste. 985
Itasca, IL 60143
PH: (847)364-9600
Fax: (847)364-9639
Colley, Dennis, President

International Corrugated Case As-
sociation [837]
500 Park Blvd., Ste. 985
Itasca, IL 60143
PH: (847)364-9600
Fax: (847)364-9639
Bohm, Mr. Carl, President

National Safety Council [12835]
1121 Spring Lake Dr.
Itasca, IL 60143-3201
PH: (630)285-1121
Toll free: 800-621-7615
Phelan, Patrick, CFO

National Spasmodic Dysphonia As-
sociation [15971]
300 Park Blvd., Ste. 335
Itasca, IL 60143
Toll free: 800-795-6732
Fax: (630)250-4505
Reavis, Mr. Charlie, President

Wheat Ridge Ministries [20321]
1 Pierce Pl., Ste. 250E
Itasca, IL 60143-2634
PH: (630)766-9066
Toll free: 800-762-6748
Fax: (630)766-9622
Miles, Paul, President

Slovenian Union of America [19654]
431 N Chicago St.
Joliet, IL 60432-1703
PH: (815)727-1926
Deyak Voelk, Mary Lou, President

Center for American Archeology
[5935]
PO Box 366
Kampsville, IL 62053
PH: (618)653-4316
Buikstra, Dr. Jane, President

Hull Pottery Association [21663]
c/o Gloria Giese
4806 W Hilltop Dr.
Kankakee, IL 60901

Society of Environmental
Understanding and Sustainability
[4764]
716 Kent Rd.
Kenilworth, IL 60043
PH: (847)251-2079
Davis, Mr. Kenneth, Director

Treasures for Little Children [22451]
20581 E CR 1100 N
Kilbourne, IL 62655-6529
Curtis, Graham, Treasurer

Lifeline to Africa [15482]
407 N Hebard St.
Knoxville, IL 61448
PH: (845)661-8465
Carstens, Peter, Founder

American Nuclear Society [6926]
555 N Kensington Ave.
La Grange Park, IL 60526
PH: (708)352-6611
Toll free: 800-323-3044
Fax: (708)352-0499
Fine, Robert C, Exec. Dir.

American Association of Railroad
Superintendents [2831]
PO Box 200
Lafox, IL 60147-0200
Foor, Carrie, Exec. Dir.

Casket and Funeral Supply Associa-
tion of America [2400]
49 Sherwood Ter., Ste. Y
Lake Bluff, IL 60044
PH: (847)295-6630
Fax: (847)295-6647
Galletly, Pete, President

American Pie Council [368]
PO Box 368
Lake Forest, IL 60045
PH: (847)371-0170
Fax: (847)371-0199
Hoskins, Linda, Exec. Dir.

Beef4Hunger [12077]
PO Box 464
Lake Forest, IL 60045
Barnum, Greg, Chairman, President

Benny's World [13898]
PO Box 372
Lake Forest, IL 60045
PH: (847)612-5567
Fax: (847)810-7400
Watters, Lisa, Founder

Cystinosis Research Network
[15821]
302 Whytegate Ct.
Lake Forest, IL 60045-4705
PH: (847)735-0471
Toll free: 866-276-3669
Fax: (847)235-2773
Greeley, Christy, Exec. Dir.

Glass Paperweight Foundation
[22295]
644 E Deerpath Rd.
Lake Forest, IL 60045
PH: (312)419-0403
Clark, Wes, Contact

Insurance Consumer Affairs
Exchange [1864]
PO Box 746
Lake Zurich, IL 60047
PH: (847)991-8454
Brebner, Nancy, Exec. Dir.

Steel Tank Institute and Steel Plate
Fabricators Association [845]
944 Donata Ct.
Lake Zurich, IL 60047
PH: (847)438-8265
Fax: (847)438-8766
Watson, David, President

Life in Messiah International [20151]
PO Box 5470
Lansing, IL 60438-5470
PH: (708)418-0020

The Henry Nyberg Society [21465]
17822 Chicago Ave.
Lansing, IL 60438
PH: (708)474-3416
Fax: (708)474-3416
Youngberg, Bob, Contact

North American Wildlife Enforcement
Officers Association [4859]
c/o Steve Beltran, Treasurer
PO Box 7
Leaf River, IL 61047
PH: (815)243-7777
(250)442-5643
Fax: (250)442-4312
Huddleston, Lew, VP

Corvair Society of America [21362]
PO Box 607
Lemont, IL 60439-0607
PH: (630)257-6530
Sergeant, Paul, President

Neutron Scattering Society of
America [7030]
c/o Stephan Rosenkranz, President,
Materials Science Division, Ar-
gonne National Laboratory
Argonne National Laboratory
Materials Science Div.
9700 S Cass Ave.
Lemont, IL 60439
PH: (630)252-5475
Rosenkranz, Stephan, PhD,
President

Vintage Chevrolet Club of America
[21513]
PO Box 609
Lemont, IL 60439-0609
PH: (708)455-8222
Miner, Dave, Director

Health Information Resource Center
[14939]
328 W Lincoln Ave., Ste. 10
Libertyville, IL 60048-2725
Toll free: 800-828-8225
Fax: (847)816-8662

Iraqi Medical Sciences Association
[15481]
PO Box 1154
Libertyville, IL 60048-1154
Sabri, Mazin, President

Militia of the Immaculata Movement
[19862]
1600 W Park Ave.
Libertyville, IL 60048
PH: (847)367-7800
Galignano, Fr. Eugenio, President

United Lightning Protection Associa-
tion [3008]
426 North Ave.
Libertyville, IL 60048
Toll free: 800-668-8572
Fax: (847)362-6443
Harger, Justin, President

International Federation for Secular
and Humanistic Judaism [20211]
175 Olde Half Day Rd., Ste. 123
Lincolnshire, IL 60069
PH: (847)383-6330
Master, Lynne, President

Save-A-Vet [10692]
387 Northgate Rd.
Lindenhurst, IL 60046-8541
PH: (815)349-9647
Fax: (815)349-9648

Tucker Automobile Club of America
[21506]
PO Box 6177
Lindenhurst, IL 60046
Donaldson, Martyn, Director

American Association of Insurance
Services [1825]
701 Warrenville Rd.
Lisle, IL 60532
PH: (630)681-8347
Toll free: 800-564-AAIS
Fax: (630)681-8356
Kelly, Edmund, CEO, President

Association of Black Nursing Faculty
[8308]
c/o Dr. Sallie Tucker Allen, Founder
PO Box 580
Lisle, IL 60532
PH: (630)969-0221
Fax: (630)969-3895
Smith, Patsy, Secretary

Land Improvement Contractors of
America [3891]
3080 Ogden Ave., Ste. 300
Lisle, IL 60532
PH: (630)548-1984
Fax: (630)548-9189
Anderson, Steve, President

Original Hobo Nickel Society [22281]
c/o Becky Jirka, Secretary
5111 Illinois Ave.
Lisle, IL 60532-2015
Bastable, Caroline, President

Quality Chekd Dairies [978]
901 Warrenville Rd., Ste. 405
Lisle, IL 60532
Toll free: 800-222-6455
Fax: (630)717-1126
Horvath, Peter W., President

Society for Academic Specialists in
General Obstetrics and Gynecol-
ogy [16304]
817 Ogden Ave., No. 4537
Lisle, IL 60532
Toll free: 844-472-7464
Gaba, Nancy, MD, President

Water Quality Association [3462]
4151 Naperville Rd.
Lisle, IL 60532-3696
PH: (630)505-0160
Fax: (630)505-9637
Haataja, Dave, Exec. Dir.

Council of Supply Chain Manage-
ment Professionals [3468]
333 E Butterfield Rd., Ste. 140
Lombard, IL 60148
PH: (630)574-0985
Fax: (630)574-0989
Smith, Kevin, President, CEO

CSA Fraternal Life [19418]
2050 Finley Rd., Ste. 70
Lombard, IL 60148
PH: (630)472-0500
Toll free: 800-543-3272
Fax: (630)472-1100
Kielczewski, John J., President

International Academy of Aquatic Art
[23283]
803 E Washington Blvd.
Lombard, IL 60148
Pietrantoni, Nadine, VP

International Consortium for
Organizational Resilience [2177]
PO Box 1171
Lombard, IL 60148
PH: (630)705-0910
Toll free: 866-765-8321
Nelson, James, Chairman

Islamic Medical Association of North
America [16754]
101 W 22nd St., Ste. 104
Lombard, IL 60148
PH: (630)932-0000
Fax: (630)932-0005
Zahir, Khalique, MD, Chairman

National Amusement Park Historical
Association [21277]
PO Box 871
Lombard, IL 60148-0871
Abbate, Jim, Director

Prairie Club [12578]
12 E Willow St., Unit A
Lombard, IL 60148-2681
PH: (630)620-9334
Fax: (630)620-9335
Krusack, Sue, President

Conference of Consulting Actuaries
[1850]
3880 Salem Lake Dr., Ste. H
Long Grove, IL 60047-5292
PH: (847)719-6500
Segal, Donald J., President

Professional Ropes Course Associa-
tion [2470]
6260 E Riverside Blvd., No. 104
Loves Park, IL 61111
PH: (815)986-7776
Fax: (815)637-2964
Barker, Mike, President

Slavic Gospel Association [20462]
6151 Commonwealth Dr.
Loves Park, IL 61111
PH: (815)282-8900
Toll free: 800-242-5350
Fax: (815)282-8901
Provost, Dr. Robert W., President

Association for Community
Organization and Social
Administration [13102]
20560 Bensley Ave.
Lynwood, IL 60411
PH: (708)757-4187
Fax: (708)757-4234
Coconis, Michel, Chairman

National Reamer Collectors Association [22171]
c/o Joan Ellen Nawrocki
8019 W 45th Pl.
Lyons, IL 60534
PH: (708)447-6978

American Lhasa Apso Club [21812]
c/o Joyce Johanson, Membership
Chair, 126 W Kurlene Dr.
126 W Kurlene Dr.
Macomb, IL 61455
PH: (309)837-1665
Worlton, Tom, President

Association for the Advancement of
Industrial Crops [3558]
c/o Winthrop Phippen, Treasurer
Western Illinois University
1 University Cir.
Macomb, IL 61455
Phippen, Winthrop, Treasurer

Association of Ancient Historians
[9459]
c/o Lee Brice, President
Morgan Hall 438
Western Illinois University
1 University Cir.
Macomb, IL 61455-1390
Brice, Lee, President

Rural Sociological Society [7188]
Western Illinois University
1 University Cir.

Macomb, IL 61455-1367
PH: (309)298-3518
Rudel, Tom, President

Society for the Study of Symbolic
Interaction [7189]
c/o Patrick McGinty, Vice President
Morgan Hall 404
1 University Cir.
Macomb, IL 61455
Waskul, Dennis, President

Soil Science Society of America -
Consulting Soil Scientists Division
[4689]
c/o Matthew Duncan, Chair
10379 E 1000th St.
Macomb, IL 61455-8111
PH: (309)333-0535
   (406)581-5066
Duncan, Matthew, Chairman

International Flying Farmers [4156]
PO Box 309
Mansfield, IL 61854
PH: (217)489-9300
Fax: (217)489-9280
Wilderman, Wayne, President

Chihuahua Club of America [21854]
c/o Craig Eugene, Membership
Chairman
24515 Anthony Rd.
Marengo, IL 60152
PH: (815)568-6450
Potts, Kyle, President

American Association of Teachers of
French [8170]
302 N Granite St.
Marion, IL 62959
PH: (815)310-0490
Fax: (815)310-5754
Abrate, Jayne, Exec. Dir.

National Association of County
Agricultural Agents [4948]
6584 W Duroc Rd.
Maroa, IL 61756
PH: (217)794-3700
Fax: (217)794-5901
Galloway, Alan, VP

American Association of
Genitourinary Surgeons [17544]
Fahey Bldg. 54, Rm. 267
2160 S 1st Ave.
Maywood, IL 60153
PH: (708)216-5100
Fax: (708)216-8991
Sufrin, Gerald, President

National Antique Tractor Pullers Association [22457]
c/o Brad Begeman, President
1863 E 1000th St.
Mendon, IL 62351-2213
PH: (217)242-4634
Alexander, Dan, Chmn. of the Bd.

Hudson Essex Terraplane Historical
Society [21396]
c/o Cheri Holz
13270 McKanna Rd.
Minooka, IL 60447
PH: (815)263-3827
Buchanan, Calvin, President

American Society of Sanitary
Engineering [7111]
18927 Hickory Creek Dr., Ste. 220
Mokena, IL 60448
PH: (708)995-3019
Fax: (708)479-6139
Hamilton, Scott, Exec. Dir.

Radiant Professionals Alliance
[1635]
18927 Hickory Creek Dr., Ste. 220
Mokena, IL 60448
Toll free: 877-427-6601
Fax: (708)479-6023
Chaffee, Mark J., Chairman

American Rental Association [2925]
1900 19th St.
Moline, IL 61265-4179
PH: (309)764-2475
Toll free: 800-334-2177
Fax: (309)764-1533
Wehrman, Christine, CEO

Association of Official Seed Certify-
ing Agencies [4946]
1601 52nd Ave., Ste. 1
Moline, IL 61265
PH: (309)736-0120
Fax: (309)736-0115
Galbreth, Alan, President

National Clearinghouse for Com-
muter Programs [8625]
Western Illinois University - Quad
Cities
3300 River Dr.
Moline, IL 61265
PH: (309)762-8843
Mahan, Dr. Melissa, Director

Currier and Ives Dinnerware Collectors [21646]
c/o Carol Hasse, Treasurer
922 East 1st Ave.
Monmouth, IL 61462
Titkemeier, Pat, Secretary

Wire Fabricators Association [1581]
PO Box 304
Montgomery, IL 60538-0304
PH: (630)896-1469
Fax: (209)633-6265
Hoban, Roseanne, Exec. Dir.

International Society of Precision
Agriculture [3571]
107 S State St., Ste. 300
Monticello, IL 61856-1968
PH: (217)762-7955
Sudduth, Ken, Dr., President

National Conference on Interstate
Milk Shipments [3980]
PO Box 108
Monticello, IL 61856
PH: (217)762-2656
Beam, Dr. Stephen, Chairman

Moose International [19435]
155 S International Dr.
Mooseheart, IL 60539-1169
PH: (630)906-3658
Hart, Scott D., CEO, Dir. Gen.

Transparent Watercolor Society of
America [8894]
249 E US Route 6, No. 209
Morris, IL 60450
Rodell, Pat, President

American Shetland Pony Club |
American Miniature Horse Registry
[4327]
81 B Queenwood Rd.
Morton, IL 61550
PH: (309)263-4044
Fax: (309)263-5113
Sanders, Patrick, President

Insurance Loss Control Association
[1868]
PO Box 346
Morton, IL 61550
PH: (309)696-2551

Indian American Muslim Council
[19475]
6321 W Dempster St., Ste. 295
Morton Grove, IL 60053-2848
Toll free: 800-839-7270
Khateeb, Mr. Shaheen, President

Manufacturers' Agents National As-
sociation [2206]
6321 W Dempster St., Ste. 110
Morton Grove, IL 60053
PH: (949)859-4040
Toll free: 877-626-2776
Fax: (949)855-2973
Cohon, Charles, President

Bright Stars of Bethlehem [20514]
PO Box 185
Mount Morris, IL 61054
PH: (815)315-0682
Raheb, Mitri, CEO, President,
Founder

Feeding Children Worldwide [12087]
PO Box 883
Mount Prospect, IL 60056
Tracy, Eldon L., President

Foreign Pharmacy Graduate
Examination Committee [16660]
National Association of Boards of
Pharmacy
1600 Feehanville Dr.
Mount Prospect, IL 60056
PH: (847)391-4406
Fax: (847)391-4502
Catizone, Carmen A., MS, RPh,
DPh, Exec. Dir., Secretary

Green Mechanical Council [6554]
PO Box 521
Mount Prospect, IL 60056
PH: (847)342-0049
Toll free: 800-726-9696
Allen, Steven H., Exec. Dir.

National Association of Boards of
Pharmacy [16673]
1600 Feehanville Dr.
Mount Prospect, IL 60056
PH: (847)391-4406
Fax: (847)391-4502
Adams, Joseph L., Chairperson

National Association to Stop Guard-
ian Abuse [11749]
PO Box 886
Mount Prospect, IL 60056
Rudek, Sylvia, Director

National Catholic Society of Forest-
ers [19410]
320 S School St.
Mount Prospect, IL 60056
PH: (847)342-4500
Toll free: 800-344-6273
Fax: (847)342-4556
Schmitt, Margaret, President

National Ski and Snowboard Retail-
ers Association [3143]
1601 Feehanville Dr., Ste. 300
Mount Prospect, IL 60056
PH: (847)391-9825
Toll free: 888-257-1168
Fax: (847)391-9827
Weindruch, Larry, President

National Sporting Goods Association
[3144]
1601 Feehanville Dr., Ste. 300
Mount Prospect, IL 60056
PH: (847)296-6742
Toll free: 800-815-5422
Fax: (847)391-9827
Carlson, Matt, CEO, President

Society of Critical Care Medicine
[14353]
500 Midway Dr.
Mount Prospect, IL 60056

PH: (847)827-6869
Fax: (847)827-6886
Dorman, Todd, President

Clan Irwin Association [20814]
226 1750th Ave.
Mount Pulaski, IL 62548-6635
PH: (217)792-5226
Irvin, Guy C., Chairman

ABSA International [2987]
1200 Allanson Rd.
Mundelein, IL 60060-3808
PH: (847)949-1517
Toll free: 866-425-1385
Fax: (847)566-4580
Downing, RBP, CBSP, SM, Marian
M., Officer

Cast Iron Soil Pipe Institute [2603]
2401 Fieldcrest Dr.
Mundelein, IL 60060
PH: (224)864-2910

American Telugu Association [9202]
PO Box 4496
Naperville, IL 60567
PH: (630)783-2250
Fax: (630)783-2251
Madhavaram, Karunakar R.,
President

Cable and Telecommunications Hu-
man Resources Association [1694]
1717 N Naper Blvd., Ste. 102
Naperville, IL 60563
PH: (630)416-1166
Fax: (630)416-9798
Williams, Pamela V., Exec. Dir.

Catholic Order of Foresters [19403]
355 Shuman Blvd.
Naperville, IL 60563
PH: (630)983-4900
Toll free: 800-552-0145
James, Judith M, Asst. VP

Equine Welfare Alliance [10619]
PO Box 6161
Naperville, IL 60567
PH: (630)961-9292
Holland, John, President

Flow Blue International Collectors
Club [21655]
PO Box 5427
Naperville, IL 60567-5427
Meyer, Brenda, President

Gait and Clinical Movement Analysis
Society [14934]
Naperville, IL
Chapin, Krissane, PhD, President

Global Warming International Center
[4065]
22W381, 75th St.
Naperville, IL 60565-9245
PH: (630)910-1551
Fax: (630)910-1561
Shen, Dr. Sinyan, Director

Illinois Physical Therapy Association
[17444]
905 N Main St.
Naperville, IL 60563
PH: (630)904-0101
Fax: (630)904-0102
Riley, Michael, President

Institute of Packaging Professionals
[6968]
1 Parkview Plz., Ste. 800
Naperville, IL 60563
PH: (630)544-5050
Fax: (630)544-5055
Farrey, Patrick, Exec. Dir.

Institutional Locksmiths' Association
[994]
PO Box 9560
Naperville, IL 60567-9560
Piper, Kevin, President

Miscarriage Matters Inc. [12353]
PO Box 9614
Naperville, IL 60567
Toll free: 888-520-7743
Stanard, Esther, Founder

National Association of Anorexia
Nervosa and Associated Disorders
[14646]
750 E Diehl Rd., No. 127
Naperville, IL 60563
PH: (630)577-1330
(630)577-1333
Discipio, Laura, LCSW, Exec. Dir.

National Barbecue Association
[1354]
PO Box 9686
Naperville, IL 60567-9686
PH: (331)444-7347
Orrison, Linda, President

National School Foundation Associa-
tion [8540]
509 Aurora Ave., Ste. 406
Naperville, IL 60540
Toll free: 866-824-8513
Dzwonkowski, Megan, Exec. Dir.

North American Ohara Teachers As-
sociation [8878]
c/o E-Ling Lou, President
717 Chesterfield Ave.
Naperville, IL 60540
PH: (630)527-0663
Fax: (630)527-0663
Melton, Dr. Judy, Director

Operation Support Our Troops -
America [10757]
1807 S Washington St., No. 100
Naperville, IL 60565
PH: (630)971-1150
Gulit, Nadine, Founder

Private Citizen [17926]
PO Box 233
Naperville, IL 60566-0233
PH: (630)393-2370
Bulmash, Robert, President

ThinkFirst National Injury Prevention
Foundation [17267]
1801 N Mill St., Ste. F
Naperville, IL 60563-4869
PH: (630)961-1400
Toll free: 800-844-6556
Fax: (630)961-1401
Spatola, Mark, Chairman

Turbine Inlet Cooling Association
[1130]
427 Prairie Knoll Dr., Ste. 102
Naperville, IL 60565
PH: (630)357-3960
Fax: (630)357-1004
Mincey, Christopher, President

Urgent Care Association of America
[13679]
387 Shuman Blvd., Ste. 235W
Naperville, IL 60563
PH: (331)472-3739
Toll free: 877-698-2262
Fax: (331)457-5439
Newman, Nathan, Officer

World Packaging Organisation
[2486]
1833 Centre Point Cir., Ste. 123
Naperville, IL 60563
PH: (630)596-9007
Fax: (630)544-5055
Pearson, Keith, Gen. Sec.

Californian Rabbit Specialty Club
[4595]
c/o Jerry Hicks, Secretary/Treasurer
10698 Prairie Creek Rd.
New Berlin, IL 62670
PH: (217)626-1811
Klindt, Sara, Director

National Association of Qualified
Developmental Disability Profes-
sionals [15815]
301 Veterans Pky.
New Lenox, IL 60451
PH: (815)320-7301
(815)485-4781
Fax: (815)320-7357
Schaefer, Kevin, Assoc. Dir.

National Association of Government
Web Professionals, Inc. [6325]
6311 W Gross Point Rd.
Niles, IL 60714
PH: (847)647-7226
Belli, Barbara, Secretary

Society for Sex Therapy and
Research [17205]
6311 W Gross Point Rd.
Niles, IL 60714
PH: (847)647-8832
Fax: (847)647-8940
Watter, Daniel N., EdD, President

Step Out USA [12242]
8926 Greenwood Ave.
Niles, IL 60714
PH: (847)289-4480
Coy, Patricia, MS, Exec. Dir.

Hungarian Horse Association of
America [4360]
281 Ruby Rd.
Noble, IL 62868
PH: (618)752-7181
Rudolphi, Linda, Registrar

Association of Overseas Chinese
Agricultural, Biological and Food
Engineers [6547]
c/o Dr. Liangcheng Yang
Illinois State University
Dept. of Health Sciences
324 Felmley Hall Annex
Normal, IL 61790
PH: (309)438-7133
Ge, Yufeng, Treasurer

Coalition of National Health Educa-
tion Organizations [8316]
Illinois Station University
Campus Mail 5220
Normal, IL 61790-5220
PH: (309)438-2324
Fax: (309)438-2450
Wilson, Kelly L., Coord.

National Association of Professional
Band Instrument Repair Techni-
cians, Inc. [2432]
2026 Eagle Rd.
Normal, IL 61761
PH: (309)452-4257
Fax: (309)452-4825
Matthews, Bill, Exec. Dir.

Pull-thru Network [14796]
c/o Lori Parker, Executive Director
1705 Wintergreen Pky.
Normal, IL 61761-5642
Mihalic, Tricia, Director

Volkswagen Club of America [21519]
PO Box 154
North Aurora, IL 60542

Mail Systems Management Associa-
tion [2118]
PO Box 1145
North Riverside, IL 60546-1145
Toll free: 800-714-6762
Fahy, Barbara, President

American Society of Pharmacognosy
[16646]
3149 Dundee Rd., No. 260
Northbrook, IL 60062-2402
PH: (773)995-3748
Fax: (847)656-2800
Kennelly, Ed, President

Collision Industry Electronic Com-
merce Association [996]
c/o Fred Iantorno, Executive Director
3149 Dundee Rd., No. 181
Northbrook, IL 60062-2402
PH: (847)498-6945
Fax: (847)897-2094
Muller, Eugene, Chairperson

Federation of Associations of
Regulatory Boards [14933]
1466 Techny Rd.
Northbrook, IL 60062
PH: (847)559-3272
Fax: (847)714-9796
Atkinson, Dale J., Exec. Dir.

Glenkirk [11599]
3504 Commercial Ave.
Northbrook, IL 60062
PH: (847)272-5111
Fax: (847)272-7350
Bentz, Brian, Officer

Group Underwriters Association of
America [1858]
PO Box 735
Northbrook, IL 60065-0735
PH: (205)427-2638
Fax: (205)981-2901
Corcillo, Libby, President

International Mercury Owners As-
sociation [21404]
PO Box 1245
Northbrook, IL 60065-1245
PH: (847)997-8624
Fax: (847)272-1850
Robbin, Jerry, President

International Sanitary Supply As-
sociation [2133]
3300 Dundee Rd.
Northbrook, IL 60062
PH: (847)982-0800
Toll free: 800-225-4772
Fax: (847)982-1012
Barrett, John, Exec. Dir.

National Equipment Finance As-
sociation [2929]
PO Box 69
Northbrook, IL 60065
PH: (847)380-5050
Fax: (847)380-5055
Hall, Stephanie, President, Chmn. of
the Bd.

Preimplantation Genetic Diagnosis
International Society [14884]
2910 MacArthur Blvd.
Northbrook, IL 60062
PH: (773)472-4900
   (847)400-1515
Fax: (773)871-5221
Kahraman, Semra, President

United States Lawn Mower Racing
Association [23086]
PO Box 628
Northbrook, IL 60065
PH: (847)272-2120
   (251)645-2942
Fax: (847)272-2120
Kaufman, Bruce, President, Founder

Broadcast Cable Credit Association
[456]
550 W Frontage Rd., Ste. 3600
Northfield, IL 60093

PH: (847)881-8757
Fax: (847)784-8059
Collins, Mary, President, CEO

College of American Pathologists
[16581]
325 Waukegan Rd.
Northfield, IL 60093-2750
PH: (847)832-7000
Toll free: 800-323-4040
Fax: (847)832-8000
Friedberg, Richard C., MD, PhD,
President

Media Financial Management As-
sociation [1250]
550 W Frontage Rd., Ste. 3600
Northfield, IL 60093
PH: (847)716-7000
Fax: (847)716-7004
Collins, Mary M., President, CEO

American Association of Physicians
of Indian Origin [16734]
600 Enterprise Dr., Ste. 108
Oak Brook, IL 60523
PH: (630)990-2277
Fax: (630)990-2281
Samadder, Gautam, MD, VP

American Fraternal Alliance [19481]
1301 W 22nd St., Ste. 700
Oak Brook, IL 60523
PH: (630)522-6322
Fax: (630)522-6326
Annotti, Mr. Joseph J., CEO,
President

American Osteopathic Academy of
Addiction Medicine [17306]
PO Box 3278
Oak Brook, IL 60522
PH: (708)338-0760
Fax: (708)401-0360
Vidmer, Nina Albano, Exec. Dir.

American Society of Functional Neu-
roradiology [17045]
800 Enterprise Dr., Ste. 205
Oak Brook, IL 60523
PH: (630)574-0220
Fax: (630)574-0661
Barboriak, Daniel P., MD, President

American Society of Head and Neck
Radiology [17046]
800 Enterprise Dr., Ste. 205
Oak Brook, IL 60523-4216
PH: (630)574-0220
Fax: (630)574-0661
Michel, Michelle A., MD, Officer

American Society of Neuroradiology
[17048]
800 Enterprise Dr., Ste. 205
Oak Brook, IL 60523
PH: (630)574-0220
Fax: (630)574-0661
Gantenberg, James B., Exec. Dir.,
CEO

American Society of Pediatric Neuroradiology [17049]
c/o Kristine Kulpaka, Coordinator
800 Enterprise Dr., Ste. 205
Oak Brook, IL 60523-4216
PH: (630)574-0220
Palasis, Susan, MD

American Society of Spine Radiol-
ogy [17051]
800 Enterprise Dr., Ste. 205
Oak Brook, IL 60523-4216
PH: (630)574-0220
Fax: (630)574-0661
Hirsch, Joshua A., MD, President

Associated Equipment Distributors
[1711]
600 22nd St., Ste. 220
Oak Brook, IL 60523

PH: (630)574-0650
Johnson, Steve, Exec. Dir.

Association of Program Coordinators
in Radiology [17053]
820 Jorie Blvd.
Oak Brook, IL 60523
PH: (630)368-3737
Fax: (630)571-2198
Reede, Deborah L., President

Association of Program Directors in
Radiology [15622]
820 Jorie Blvd.
Oak Brook, IL 60523
PH: (630)368-3737
Reede, Deborah L., President

Association of University Radiolo-
gists [17055]
820 Jorie Blvd.
Oak Brook, IL 60523
PH: (630)368-3730
Fax: (630)571-7837
Taylor, Stephanie, Account Exec.

Ceilings and Interior Systems
Construction Association [859]
1010 Jorie Blvd., Ste. 30
Oak Brook, IL 60523
PH: (630)584-1919
Fax: (866)560-8537
Gordon, Jason, President

Children's Literature Association
[9755]
1301 W 22nd St., Ste. 202
Oak Brook, IL 60523
PH: (630)571-4520
Fax: (708)876-5598
Keeling, Kara, President

Compassionate Friends [12410]
1000 Jorie Blvd., Ste. 140
Oak Brook, IL 60523-4494
PH: (630)990-0010
Toll free: 877-969-0010
Fax: (630)990-0246
Allen, Barbara, VP

Farm Foundation [3549]
1301 W 22nd St., Ste. 906
Oak Brook, IL 60523-2197
PH: (630)571-9393
Fax: (630)571-9580
Jones, Sheldon R., VP

Hand in Hand USA [12667]
710 St. Josephs Dr.
Oak Brook, IL 60523
Chunduri, Durga, President

Institute in Basic Life Principles
[13452]
Box 1
Oak Brook, IL 60522-3001
PH: (630)323-9800
Gothard, Bill, Founder, President

Justinian Society of Lawyers [5018]
PO Box 3217
Oak Brook, IL 60522
PH: (708)338-0760
Fax: (708)401-0360
DePinto, Jessica, President

Lions Clubs International [12897]
300 W 22nd St.
Oak Brook, IL 60523-8842
PH: (630)571-5466
Scruggs, Sid L., III, Contact

Lions-Quest [7712]
Lions Clubs International Foundation
300 W 22nd St.
Oak Brook, IL 60523-8842
Toll free: 844-567-8378
Kiefer, Matthew, Mgr.

North American Islamic Trust [9608]
721 Enterprise Dr.
Oak Brook, IL 60523
PH: (630)789-9191
Fax: (630)789-9455
Siddiqi, Dr. Muzammil, Bd. Member

R2P Coalition [13273]
c/o General Welfare Group LLC
611 Enterprise Dr.
Oak Brook, IL 60523
PH: (630)573-4403
Fax: (630)573-0652

Radiological Society of North
America [17061]
820 Jorie Blvd.
Oak Brook, IL 60523-2251
PH: (630)571-2670
Toll free: 800-381-6660
Fax: (630)571-7837
Drayer, Burton P., MD, Chairman

Society of Chairs of Academic
Radiology Departments [17065]
820 Jorie Blvd.
Oak Brook, IL 60523
PH: (630)368-3731
Fax: (630)590-7709
Taylor, Ms. Stephanie, Account
Exec.

Spring Manufacturers Institute
[1577]
2001 Midwest Rd., Ste. 106
Oak Brook, IL 60523-1335
PH: (630)495-8588
Fax: (630)495-8595
Betts, Mike, President

Vibration Institute [6834]
2625 Butterfield Rd., Ste. 128 N
Oak Brook, IL 60523-3415
PH: (630)654-2254
Fax: (630)654-2271
Corelli, Dave, President

Warehousing Education and
Research Council [3442]
1100 Jorie Blvd., Ste. 170
Oak Brook, IL 60523-4413
PH: (630)990-0001
Fax: (630)990-0256
Mikitka, Michael J., CEO

World Federation of Neuroradiologi-
cal Societies [17075]
c/o James B Gantenberg, Executive
Director
800 Enterprise Dr., Ste. 205
Oak Brook, IL 60523
PH: (630)574-0220
Fax: (630)574-0661
Gantenberg, James, Exec. Dir.

Zonta International [12913]
1211 W 22nd St., Ste. 900
Oak Brook, IL 60523-3384
PH: (630)928-1400
Fax: (630)928-1559
Summers, Allison, Exec. Dir.

American Edge Collectors Association [21610]
9401 Oak Park Ave.
Oak Lawn, IL 60453

Ghost Research Society [7011]
PO Box 205
Oak Lawn, IL 60454-0205
PH: (708)425-5163
Hauck, Dennis William, Coord.

Cryogenic Society of America [6355]
c/o Laurie Huget, Executive Director
218 Lake St.
Oak Park, IL 60302-2609
PH: (708)383-6220
Fax: (708)383-9337
Weisend, John, II, Chairman

Hope for Grieving Children Africa
[11038]
1011 Lake St., Ste. 404
Oak Park, IL 60301
PH: (708)445-8678
Stephens, Anthony T., Chairman

International Association of Sickle
Cell Nurses and Physician As-
sistants [15121]
c/o Patricia Bailey, RN
PO Box 3235
Oak Park, IL 60303
Jones, Susan, Director

MAGIC Foundation [14201]
6645 W North Ave.
Oak Park, IL 60302
PH: (708)383-0808
Toll free: 800-362-4423
Andrews, Mary, CEO

Seven Generations Ahead [11433]
1049 Lake St., Ste. 200
Oak Park, IL 60301
PH: (708)660-9909
Fax: (708)660-9913
Ledogar, Mark, President

American Association for Public
Opinion Research [18922]
1 Parkview Plz., Ste. 800
Oakbrook Terrace, IL 60181
PH: (847)686-2230
Fax: (847)686-2251
Schweinzger, Jacky, Mgr.

American Pediatric Surgical Associa-
tion [16601]
1 Parkview Plz., Ste. 800
Oakbrook Terrace, IL 60181
PH: (847)686-2237
Fax: (847)686-2253
Clark, Lee Ann, Exec. Dir.

American Pediatric Surgical Nurses
Association [16110]
1 Parkview Plz., Ste. 800
Oakbrook Terrace, IL 60181
PH: (605)376-4742
Toll free: 855-984-1609
Pasarón, Raquel

American Society of Dermatopathol-
ogy [14487]
1 Parkview Plz., Ste. 800
Oakbrook Terrace, IL 60181
PH: (847)686-2231
Fax: (847)686-2251
McCrackin, Leah, Exec. Dir.

American Society of Tropical
Medicine and Hygiene [17534]
1 Parkview Plz., Ste. 800
Oakbrook Terrace, IL 60181
PH: (847)480-9592
  (847)686-2238
Fax: (847)480-9282
Rosenthal, Philip, Ed.-in-Chief

Association for Death Education and
Counseling [11555]
1 Parkview Plz., Ste. 800
Oakbrook Terrace, IL 60181
PH: (847)686-2240
Fax: (847)686-2251
McCord, Janet, PhD, FT, President

Association of Oncology Social Work
[13103]
1 Parkview Plz., Ste. 800
Oakbrook Terrace, IL 60181
PH: (847)686-2233
Fax: (847)686-2253
Mayer Sachs, Alison, President

Association of University Technology
Managers [5323]
1 Parkview Plz., Ste. 800
Oakbrook Terrace, IL 60181

PH: (847)686-2244
Fax: (847)686-2253
Susalka, Stephen J., Exec. Dir.

Coin Laundry Association [2076]
1 S 660 Midwest Rd., Ste. 205
Oakbrook Terrace, IL 60181
Toll free: 800-570-5629
Fax: (630)953-7925
Wallace, Brian, CEO, President

Contract Packaging Association
[2474]
1 Parkview Plz., Ste. 800
Oakbrook Terrace, IL 60181
PH: (630)544-5053
Fax: (630)544-5055
Smitley, Vicky, President

Finishing Contractors Association
International [528]
1 Parkview Plz., Ste. 610
Oakbrook Terrace, IL 60181
PH: (630)537-1042
Toll free: 866-322-3477
Fax: (630)590-5272
Clerkin, Tom, V. Chmn. of the Bd.

Institute of Nuclear Materials
Management [6928]
1 Parkview Plz., Ste. 800
Oakbrook Terrace, IL 60181
PH: (847)686-2236
Fax: (847)686-2253
Satkowiak, Larry, President

Interior Design Educators Council
[8050]
1 Parkview Plz., Ste. 800
Oakbrook Terrace, IL 60181
PH: (630)544-5057
Washburn, Sarah, Exec. Dir.

International Ombudsman Associa-
tion [644]
1 Parkview Plz., Ste. 800
17W110 22nd St.
Oakbrook Terrace, IL 60181
PH: (847)686-2242
Fax: (847)686-2253
Koepke, Rick, Exec. Dir.

International Society for Traumatic
Stress Studies [17292]
1 Parkview Plz., Ste. 800
Oakbrook Terrace, IL 60181
PH: (847)686-2234
Fax: (847)686-2251
Koepke, Rick, Exec. Dir.

Joint Commission [15331]
1515 W 22nd St., Ste. 1300W
Oakbrook Terrace, IL 60181-4294
PH: (630)792-5000
Toll free: 800-746-6578
Fax: (630)792-5005
Loeb, Jerod M.

Maple Flooring Manufacturers As-
sociation [542]
1 Parkview Plz., Ste. 800
Oakbrook Terrace, IL 60181
PH: (847)480-9138
Toll free: 888-480-9138
Fax: (847)686-2251
Heney, Daniel F., Exec. Dir.

National Association of Sporting
Goods Wholesalers [3141]
1 Parkview Plz.
Oakbrook Terrace, IL 60181
PH: (630)596-9006
Fax: (630)544-5055
Brownell, Peter, Chairman

National Federation of Paralegal Associations [5660]
1 Parkview Plz., Ste. 800
Oakbrook Terrace, IL 60181

PH: (847)686-2247
Fax: (847)686-2251
Vessels, Lisa, President

Pressure Sensitive Tape Council
[61]
1 Parkview Plz., Ste. 800
Oakbrook Terrace, IL 60181
PH: (630)544-5048
Fax: (630)544-5055
Miller, Michelle, Exec. VP

Recreational Vehicle Aftermarket As-
sociation [2922]
One ParkView Plaza, Ste. 800
Oakbrook Terrace, IL 60181
PH: (630)596-9004
Fax: (630)544-5055
Krueger, Jon, Exec. Dir.

Society of American Travel Writers
[2720]
1 Parkview Plz.
Oakbrook Terrace, IL 60181
Schrager, Marla, Exec. Dir.

Society for Vascular Medicine
[17580]
One ParkView Plz., Ste. 100
Oakbrook Terrace, IL 60181
PH: (847)686-2232
Fax: (847)686-2251
Bartholomew, John R., MD, MSVM,
President

International Crime Scene Investiga-
tors Association [5248]
PMB 385
15774 S LaGrange Rd.
Orland Park, IL 60462
PH: (708)460-8082
Baldwin, Hayden B., Exec. Dir.

National Arab American Journalists
Association [2692]
c/o Ray Hanania
PO Box 2127
Orland Park, IL 60462
Fax: (708)575-9078
Hanania, Ray, Contact

Still Bank Collectors Club of America
[21726]
13239 Bundoran Ct.
Orland Park, IL 60462
Harold, Elliotte, Membership Chp.

American Emu Association [4450]
510 W Madison St.
Ottawa, IL 61350
PH: (541)332-0675
Citrhyn, Tony, President

Handicapped Travel Club [22425]
c/o Mark Neurohr
1465 N 32nd Rd.
Ottawa, IL 61350
PH: (815)252-1868
Neurohr, Mark, President

American Academy of Dental
Practice Administration [14374]
c/o Kathleen Uebel, Executive Direc-
tor
1063 Whippoorwill Ln.
Palatine, IL 60067
PH: (847)934-4404
Uebel, Kathleen S., Exec. Dir.

American Chiropractic Registry of
Radiologic Technologists [17040]
52 W Colfax St.
Palatine, IL 60067
PH: (847)705-1178
Fax: (847)705-1178
Pyzik, Dr. Larry, Exec. Dir.

American Plate Number Single
Society [22303]
PO Box 1023
Palatine, IL 60078-1023
Chaulsett, Eric, Director

American Society of Artists [8910]
PO Box 1326
Palatine, IL 60078
PH: (312)751-2500
  (847)991-4748

Association of Licensed Architects
[232]
1 E Northwest Hwy., Ste. 200
Palatine, IL 60067
PH: (847)382-0630
Fax: (847)382-8380
Budgell, Jeffrey, President

Joint Council of Allergy, Asthma and
Immunology [13578]
50 N Brockway
Palatine, IL 60067
PH: (847)934-1918
Sublett, James, MD, Director

Little City Foundation [12327]
1760 W Algonquin Rd.
Palatine, IL 60067-4799
PH: (847)358-5510
Fax: (847)358-3291
Schubert, Matthew B., President

SuperSibs! [11277]
660 N 1st Bank Dr.
Palatine, IL 60067
PH: (847)462-4742
Fax: (847)984-9292
Skala, Suzanne, Exec. Dir.

Collegiate and Professional Sports
Dietitians Association [16212]
38 E Lucas Dr.
Palos Hills, IL 60465
PH: (708)974-3153
Fax: (708)974-3174
Bragg, Amy F., RD, President

University Photographers Association of America [8427]
c/o Glenn Carpenter, President
Moraine Valley Community College
9000 W College Pky.
Palos Hills, IL 60465
Carpenter, Glenn, President

Women Band Directors International
[8392]
c/o Carol Nendza, Treasurer
10611 Ridgewood Dr.
Palos Park, IL 60464
Bennet, Marilyn, President

AACTION Autism [13735]
1861 Manor Ln.
Park Ridge, IL 60068
PH: (773)456-3655
Flint, Christopher, President

American Association of Nurse
Anesthetists [16094]
222 S Prospect Ave.
Park Ridge, IL 60068-4001
PH: (847)692-7050
  (847)655-1106
Toll free: 855-526-2262
Fax: (847)692-6968
Wilson, Wanda, Exec. Dir.

American Egg Board [4561]
1460 Renaissance Dr., Ste. 301
Park Ridge, IL 60068
PH: (847)296-7043
Fax: (847)296-7007
Ivy, Joanne, President, CEO

American Society of Safety
Engineers [7106]
520 N Northwest Hwy.
Park Ridge, IL 60068
PH: (847)699-2929
Fax: (847)768-3434

The Association of Bone and Joint
Surgeons [16470]
300 S Northwest Hwy., Ste. 203
Park Ridge, IL 60068

PH: (847)720-4186
Fax: (847)720-4013
Hohimer, Colette Iocca, Exec. Dir.

Council on Accreditation of Nurse
Anesthesia Educational Programs
[8296]
222 S Prospect Ave.
Park Ridge, IL 60068-4001
PH: (847)655-1160
Fax: (847)692-7137
Gerbasi, Francis, PhD, Exec. Dir.

Education Industry Association
[8647]
c/o Jim Giovannini, Executive Director
120 Main St., Ste. 202
Park Ridge, IL 60068
PH: (703)938-2429
Olchefske, Joseph, Act. Pres.

Egg Nutrition Center [16218]
PO Box 738
Park Ridge, IL 60068
PH: (847)296-7055
Fax: (847)768-7973
Kanter, Mitch, PhD, Exec. Dir.

Foundation for International
Cooperation [8072]
1237 S Western Ave.
Park Ridge, IL 60068
Horst, Irene B., Exec. Dir.

Islamic Food and Nutrition Council of
America [1349]
777 Busse Hwy.
Park Ridge, IL 60068
PH: (847)993-0034
Fax: (847)993-0038
Chaudry, Dr. Muhammad Munir,
President

Million Dollar Round Table [1885]
325 W Touhy Ave.
Park Ridge, IL 60068-4265
PH: (847)692-6378
Fax: (847)518-8921
Banks, Caroline, President

National Association for Down
Syndrome [14627]
1460 Renaissance Dr., Ste. 405
Park Ridge, IL 60068
PH: (630)325-9112
Fax: (847)376-8908
Urhausen, Diane, Exec. Dir.

Non-Ferrous Founders' Society
[1756]
1480 Renaissance Dr., Ste. 310
Park Ridge, IL 60068
PH: (847)299-0950
Fax: (847)299-3598

Society of Academic Anesthesiology
Associations [13705]
520 N Northwest Hwy.
Park Ridge, IL 60068
PH: (847)825-5586
Fitch, Jane C.K., MD, President

Society of Tribologists and Lubrica-
tion Engineers [6599]
840 Busse Hwy.
Park Ridge, IL 60068-2302
PH: (847)825-5536
Astrene, Tom, Exec. Dir.

Clydesdale Breeders of the U.S.A.
[4344]
17346 Kelley Rd.
Pecatonica, IL 61063
PH: (815)247-8780
Fax: (815)247-8337
Harmon-Dodge, Linda, VP

International Association of Eating
Disorders Professionals [14641]
PO Box 1295
Pekin, IL 61555-1295
Toll free: 800-800-8126
Harken, Bonnie, Managing Dir.

Antique Caterpillar Machinery Own-
ers Club [21619]
7501 N University St., Ste. 117
Peoria, IL 61614
PH: (309)691-5002
Fax: (309)296-4518
Potts, Tricia, Exec. Dir.

Chester White Swine Record As-
sociation [4709]
Box 9758
Peoria, IL 61612-9758
PH: (309)691-0151
Fax: (309)691-0168

Creative Musicians Coalition [2422]
PO Box 6205
Peoria, IL 61601-6205
PH: (309)685-4843
Toll free: 800-882-4262
Fax: (309)685-4879
Wallace, Ronald A., President

International Pediatric Specialists
Alliance for the Children of
Vietnam [16610]
1425 W Forrest Hill Ave.
Peoria, IL 61604
Holterman, Ai-Xuan, MD, President

National Spotted Swine Record
[4714]
PO Box 9758
Peoria, IL 61612-9758
PH: (309)691-0151
Fax: (309)691-0168

North American Association of Sum-
mer Sessions [8634]
Bradley University
Continuing Education
1501 W Bradley Ave.
Peoria, IL 61625
PH: (309)677-2523
Toll free: 866-880-9607
Fax: (309)677-3321
Lange, Janet, Exec. Sec.

Poland China Record Association
[4717]
Box 9758
Peoria, IL 61612-9758
PH: (309)691-0151
Fax: (309)691-0168

Lionel Collectors Club of America
[22185]
PO Box 529
Peru, IL 61354-0529
Fax: (815)223-0791
DeVito, Dennis, President

American Chiropractic College of
Radiology [14252]
PO Box 986
Plainfield, IL 60544
Schultz, Gary, DC, President

Healthcare Laundry Accreditation
Council [2078]
PO Box 1306
Plainfield, IL 60544
PH: (815)436-1404
Toll free: 855-277-4522
Fax: (815)436-1403
Baras, Regina, Exec. Dir.

Institute for Biblical Research
[19758]
PO Box 305
Princeton, IL 61356
Longman, Tremper, III, President

Dermatologic and Aesthetic Surgery
International League [14491]
453 Williamsburg Ln.
Prospect Heights, IL 60070
PH: (847)577-6543
Fax: (847)577-6583
Roscher, Marc B., MD, President

Pierre Robin Network [14850]
3604 Biscayne St.
Quincy, IL 62305-4740
Barry, Nancy, Founder, President

Western Catholic Union [19411]
510 Maine St.
Quincy, IL 62301
PH: (217)223-9721
Toll free: 800-223-4928
Fax: (217)223-9726
Player, Roger W., Chairman

American Educational Studies Association [7741]
c/o Pamela J. Konkol, Secretary
Concordia University Chicago
7400 Augusta St.
River Forest, IL 60305
Taliaferro-Baszile, Denise, President

Clan Ross America [20840]
PO Box 6341
River Forest, IL 60305
Ross, Liz, President

Lutheran Education Association
[20308]
7400 Augusta St.
River Forest, IL 60305
PH: (708)209-3343
Fax: (708)209-3458
Laabs, Jonathan C., EdD, Exec. Dir.

James Jones Literary Society
[10384]
PO Box 68
Robinson, IL 62454-0068
Wood, Thomas J., Editor

Cochlear Implant Awareness
Foundation [15182]
130 S John St.
Rochester, IL 62563
PH: (202)895-2781
Fax: (202)895-2782
Tjelmeland, Michelle, Founder,
Chairman

Association for the History of
Chiropractic [14257]
4430 8th St.
Rock Island, IL 61201-6608
PH: (309)788-0799
    (309)781-9903
Callender, Alana, EdD, Exec. Dir.

Fraternal Field Managers' Associa-
tion [1856]
c/o Patrick J. Barnes, FLMI
Modern Woodmen of America
1701 1st Ave.
Rock Island, IL 61201-8724
PH: (309)786-6481
Barnes, Patrick J., FLMI, President

Integrity: Arts & Culture Association
[8862]
PO Box 6491
Rock Island, IL 61204-6491
PH: (309)721-6155
Brown, Kristina, Exec. Dir.

Modern Woodmen of America
[19693]
1701 1st Ave.
Rock Island, IL 61201-8724
Toll free: 800-447-9811
Fax: (309)793-5547
Massey, Mr. W. Kenny, CEO,
President

Royal Neighbors of America [19493]
230 16th St.
Rock Island, IL 61201-8645
Toll free: 800-627-4762
Elam, Joyce, Director

Associated Mail and Business
Centers [2114]
5411 E State St., No. 599
Rockford, IL 61108
PH: (815)316-8255
Fax: (866)314-2672
Buford, Bryan, Exec. Dir.

Association for Applied and
Therapeutic Humor [17436]
220 E State St., Fl. G
Rockford, IL 61104
PH: (815)708-6587
Morrison, Mary Kay, President

Association of Late-Deafened Adults
[15176]
8038 MacIntosh Ln., Ste. 2
Rockford, IL 61107
PH: (815)332-1515
Toll free: 866-402-2532
Littlewood, Chris, VP

Association of Steel Distributors
[2344]
833 Featherstone Rd.
Rockford, IL 61107
PH: (312)673-5793
    (815)227-8227
Fax: (312)527-6705
Warren, Jim, Exec. Dir.

Fabricators and Manufacturers As-
sociation, International [1727]
833 Featherstone Rd.
Rockford, IL 61107
PH: (815)399-8700
Toll free: 888-394-4362
Zelt, Al, Chairman

National Association of Health Unit
Coordinators [14951]
1947 Madron Rd.
Rockford, IL 61107-1716
PH: (815)633-4351
Toll free: 888-226-2482
Fax: (815)633-4438
Olsen, Juliann, President

Tube and Pipe Association,
International [2616]
833 Featherstone Rd.
Rockford, IL 61107-6301
PH: (815)399-8700
Toll free: 888-394-4362
Zelt, Al, Chairman

United Square Dancers of America
[9271]
c/o Jerry Robey, President
2702 Aldersgate Dr.
Rockford, IL 61103
PH: (815)977-5763
Robey, Jerry, President

VietNow National [13254]
1835 Broadway
Rockford, IL 61104
PH: (815)227-5100
Toll free: 800-837-8669
Lewis, Joe, President

Vision Surgery Rehab Network
[17415]
1643 N Alpine Rd., Ste. 104
PMB 180
Rockford, IL 61107
Toll free: 877-666-8776
Hartzok, David, OD, Exec. Dir.

American Belgian Hare Club [4584]
c/o Jeanne Walton, President
15330 Sharp Rd.

Rockton, IL 61072
PH: (815)629-2465
Walton, Jeanne, President

Inland Bird Banding Association
[6962]
c/o Mike Eickman, Treasurer/
Membership Secretary
11114 Harrison Rd.
Rockton, IL 61072
Kleen, Vernon, President

American Association of Neurologi-
cal Surgeons [16058]
5550 Meadowbrook Dr.
Rolling Meadows, IL 60008-3852
PH: (847)378-0500
Toll free: 888-566-2267
Fax: (847)378-0600
Benzil, Deborah L., VP

American Muslim Health Professionals [15438]
2118 Plum Grove Rd., No. 201
Rolling Meadows, IL 60008
Pless, Albert W., President

American Society for Dermatologic
Surgery [14485]
5550 Meadowbrook Dr., Ste. 120
Rolling Meadows, IL 60008
PH: (847)956-0900
Fax: (847)956-0999
Goldman, Mitchel P., MD, Bd.
Member

Association for Manufacturing Excel-
lence [2213]
3701 Algonquin Rd., Ste. 225
Rolling Meadows, IL 60008-3150
PH: (224)232-5980
Fax: (224)232-5981
Morrison, Barbara, President, CEO

Diabetes Scholars Foundation
[14530]
2118 Plum Grove Rd., No. 356
Rolling Meadows, IL 60008
PH: (312)215-9861
Fax: (847)991-8739
Podjasek, Mary, President

Information Systems Audit and
Control Association [71]
3701 Algonquin Rd., Ste. 1010
Rolling Meadows, IL 60008
PH: (847)253-1545
Fax: (847)253-1443
Stroud, Robert E., Bd. Member

International Catholic Deaf Association United States Section [19845]
c/o T.K. Hill, Treasurer
5608 Lavender Ct.
Rolling Meadows, IL 60008
Cox, Jean, President

Kinship United [11248]
5105 Tollview Dr., Ste. 155
Rolling Meadows, IL 60008
PH: (847)577-1070
Toll free: 877-577-1070
Fax: (877)577-1080
Muller, Craig, CEO, President

Metals Service Center Institute
[2359]
4201 Euclid Ave.
Rolling Meadows, IL 60008-2025
PH: (847)485-3000
Fax: (847)485-3001
Robinson, Richard, Chairman

North American Fiberboard Associa-
tion [567]
2118 Plum Grove Rd., No. 283
Rolling Meadows, IL 60008
PH: (434)797-1321
Fax: (434)799-5714

Plumbing Manufacturers
International [2640]
1921 Rohlwing Rd., Unit G
Rolling Meadows, IL 60008
PH: (847)481-5500
Fax: (847)481-5501
Higgens, Barbara C., CEO, Exec.
Dir.

Refrigeration Service Engineers
Society [1636]
1911 Rohlwing Rd., Ste. A
Rolling Meadows, IL 60008-1397
PH: (847)297-6464
Toll free: 800-297-5660
Fax: (547)297-5038
Thompson, Michael, Comm. Chm.

Women in Neurosurgery [16072]
5550 Meadowbrook Dr.
Rolling Meadows, IL 60008-3852
PH: (847)378-0500
Toll free: 888-566-2267
Parr, Ann M., Secretary

National Consumer Reporting As-
sociation [944]
701 E Irving Park Rd., Ste. 306
Roselle, IL 60172-2358
PH: (630)539-1525
Fax: (630)539-1526
Clemans, Terry, Exec. Dir.

American Academy of Orthopaedic
Surgeons [16460]
9400 W Higgins Rd.
Rosemont, IL 60018-4262
PH: (847)823-7186
Toll free: 800-346-2267
Fax: (847)823-8125
Azar, Frederick M., VP

American Academy of Physical
Medicine and Rehabilitation
[17076]
9700 W Bryn Mawr Ave., Ste. 200
Rosemont, IL 60018-5706
PH: (847)737-6000
Toll free: 877-227-6799
Fax: (847)737-6001
Stautzenbach, Thomas E., Exec.
Dir., CEO

American Association of Hip and
Knee Surgeons [17360]
9400 W Higgins Rd.
Rosemont, IL 60018-4976
PH: (847)698-1200
Parsley, Brian S., MD, Bd. Member

American Association of Oral and
Maxillofacial Surgeons [16441]
9700 W Bryn Mawr Ave.
Rosemont, IL 60018-5701
PH: (847)678-6200
Toll free: 800-822-6637
Fax: (847)678-6286
Rinaldi, Dr. Robert, Exec. Dir.

American College of Legal Medicine
[15527]
9700 W Bryn Mawr Ave., Ste. 210
Rosemont, IL 60018
PH: (847)447-1713
Fax: (847)447-1150
Green, Victoria L., Counsel

American Concrete Pavement As-
sociation [779]
9450 W Bryn Mawr, Ste. 150
Rosemont, IL 60018
PH: (847)966-2272
Jackson, Steve, Chairman

American Medical Technologists
[15676]
10700 W Higgins Rd., Ste. 150
Rosemont, IL 60018

PH: (847)823-5169
Toll free: 800-275-1268
Fax: (847)823-0458
Anderson, Edna, Exec. Ofc.

The American Orthopaedic Associa-
tion [16465]
9400 W Higgins Rd., Ste. 205
Rosemont, IL 60018-4975
PH: (847)318-7330
Fax: (847)318-7339
Black, Kevin P., President

American Orthopaedic Society for
Sports Medicine [17276]
9400 W Higgins Rd., Ste. 300
Rosemont, IL 60018
PH: (847)292-4900
Toll free: 877-321-3500
Fax: (847)292-4905
Bomberger, Irvin E., Exec. Dir.

American Orthopedic Foot and Ankle
Society [16466]
9400 W Higgins Rd., Ste. 220
Rosemont, IL 60018-3315
PH: (847)698-4654
Toll free: 800-235-4855
Fax: (847)692-3315
Oster, Susan M., Exec. Dir.

American Shoulder and Elbow
Surgeons [17369]
9400 W Higgins Rd., Ste. 500
Rosemont, IL 60018
PH: (847)698-1629
Fax: (847)268-9499
Jupiter, Jesse, MD, President

American Society of Plumbing
Engineers [6538]
6400 Shafer Ct., Ste. 350
Rosemont, IL 60018-4914
PH: (847)296-0002
Fax: (847)296-2963
Thurner, Donald, Dir. of Fin. &
Admin.

Arthroscopy Association of North
America [16469]
9400 W Higgins Rd., Ste. 200
Rosemont, IL 60018
PH: (847)292-2262
Fax: (847)292-2268
Richmond, John C., MD, President

Association of Children's Prosthetic-
Orthotic Clinics [16494]
9400 W Higgins Rd., Ste. 500
Rosemont, IL 60018-4976
PH: (847)698-1637
Fax: (847)268-9560
Shannon, Susan, Mgr.

Big Ten Conference [23217]
5440 Park Pl.
Rosemont, IL 60018-3732
PH: (847)696-1010
Fax: (847)696-1150
Delany, James E., Commissioner

Board of Specialty Societies [15846]
9400 W Higgins Rd.
Rosemont, IL 60018
PH: (847)823-7186
Fax: (847)823-8125
Williams, Gerald R., Jr., MD,
President

Cervical Spine Research Society
[17253]
9400 W Higgins Rd., Ste. 500
Rosemont, IL 60018-4976
PH: (847)698-1628
Fax: (847)268-9699
Heary, Robert F., MD, President

Dairy Management, Inc. [973]
10255 W Higgins Rd., Ste. 900
Rosemont, IL 60018-5616
Toll free: 800-853-2479
Fax: (847)627-2077
O'Brien, Barbara, Officer

J. Robert Gladden Orthopaedic
Society [16475]
9400 W Higgins Rd., Ste. 500
Rosemont, IL 60018-4238
PH: (847)698-1633
Fax: (847)823-4921
Crawford, Alvin H., MD, President

Hip Society [16476]
9400 W Higgins Rd., Ste. 500
Rosemont, IL 60018-4976
PH: (847)698-1638
Fax: (847)823-0536
Rubash, Harry E., MD, President

International Federation of Foot and
Ankle Societies [16789]
6300 N River Rd., Ste. 510
Rosemont, IL 60018-4235
PH: (847)698-4654
Fax: (847)692-3315
Saltzman, Charles L., MD, President

International Housewares Associa-
tion [1683]
6400 Shafer Ct., Ste. 650
Rosemont, IL 60018
PH: (847)292-4200
Fax: (847)292-4211
Schatz, Sharon, Mgr. of Fin. &
Admin.

Ruth Jackson Orthopaedic Society
[16482]
9400 W Higgins Rd., Ste. 500
Rosemont, IL 60018
PH: (847)698-1626
Fax: (847)268-9461
Weber, MD, Kristy, President

Musculoskeletal Tumor Society
[15848]
9400 W Higgins Rd., Ste. 500
Rosemont, IL 60018
PH: (847)698-1625
Fax: (847)823-0536
Parsons, Theodore W., III, MD,
FACS, President

National Accrediting Agency for Clini-
cal Laboratory Sciences [15692]
5600 N River Rd., Ste. 720
Rosemont, IL 60018-5119
PH: (773)714-8880
    (847)939-3597
Fax: (773)714-8886
Simonian, Yasmin, MLS, CM,
FASAPH, President

National Roofing Contractors As-
sociation [891]
10255 W Higgins Rd., Ste. 600
Rosemont, IL 60018-5607
PH: (847)299-9070
Fax: (847)299-1183
Good, William, Exec. VP

Orthopaedic Research and Educa-
tion Foundation [16486]
9400 W Higgins Rd., Ste. 215
Rosemont, IL 60018-4975
PH: (847)698-9980
Fax: (847)698-7806
Lewallen, David G., MD, President

Orthopaedic Research Society
[16487]
9400 W Higgins Rd., Ste. 225
Rosemont, IL 60018-4976
PH: (847)823-5770
    (847)430-5020
Fax: (847)823-5772
Frederick, Brenda, Exec. Dir.

Orthopaedic Trauma Association [16488]
9400 W Higgins Rd., Ste. 305
Rosemont, IL 60018-4226
PH: (847)698-1631
Fax: (847)430-5140
Caswell, Kathleen, Exec. Dir.

Pediatric Orthopedic Society of North America [16491]
9400 W Higgins Rd., Ste. 500
Rosemont, IL 60018-4976
PH: (847)698-1692
Fax: (847)268-9684
McCarthy, James, President

Roofing Industry Alliance for Progress [811]
10255 W Higgins, Ste. 600
10255 W Higgins Rd., Ste. 600
Rosemont, IL 60018-5607
Toll free: 800-323-9545
Fax: (847)493-7959
Judson, Bennett, Exec. Dir.

Society of Surgical Oncology [16358]
9525 W Bryn Mawr Ave., Ste. 870
Rosemont, IL 60018
PH: (847)427-1400
Fax: (847)427-1411
Weigel, Ronald J., MD, President

Association of Nutrition and Food-service Professionals [16209]
406 Surrey Woods Dr.
Saint Charles, IL 60174
PH: (630)587-6336
Toll free: 800-323-1908
Fax: (630)587-6308
Gilbert, Joyce, President

Healthcare Caterers International [1335]
c/o William St. John, Executive Director
3045 Meadow Dr.
Saint Charles, IL 60175
PH: (630)878-0724
St. John, William, CAE, Exec. Dir.

Leading Edge Alliance [39]
621 Cedar St.
Saint Charles, IL 60174
PH: (630)513-9814
Fax: (630)524-9014
Kehl-Rose, Karen, President

North American Rail Shippers Association [3349]
40W815 S Bridle Creek Dr.
Saint Charles, IL 60175
PH: (630)386-1366
Foor, Carrie, Exec. Dir.

Society for Laboratory Automation and Screening [6217]
100 Illinois St., Ste. 242
Saint Charles, IL 60174
PH: (630)256-7527
Toll free: 877-990-SLAS
Fax: (630)741-7527
Dummer, Greg, CAE, CEO

Blue/White Pottery Club [21288]
C/o Priscilla Lindstrom, Treasurer
PO Box 297
Saint Joseph, IL 61873
Eakin, Max, President

Air Diffusion Council [1612]
1901 N Roselle Rd., Ste. 800
Schaumburg, IL 60195
PH: (847)706-6750
Fax: (847)706-6751
Lamborn, Jason, Comm. Chm.

American Academy of Dermatology [14477]
930 E Woodfield Rd.
Schaumburg, IL 60173

PH: (847)240-1280
(202)842-3555
Toll free: 866-503-7546
Fax: (847)240-1859
Lebwohl, Mark, President

American Architectural Manufactur-ers Association [488]
1827 Walden Office Sq., Ste. 550
Schaumburg, IL 60173
PH: (847)303-5664
Fax: (847)303-5774
Fronek, Steve, Chairman

American Association of Clinical Urologists, Inc. [17543]
1100 E Woodfield Rd., Ste. 350
Schaumburg, IL 60173
PH: (847)517-1050
Fax: (847)517-7229
Dineen, Martin K., President

American Blind Skiing Foundation [22772]
609 Crandell Ln.
Schaumburg, IL 60193
PH: (312)409-1605
Ferrick, Joe, President

American Board of Veterinary Specialties [17610]
American Veterinary Medical Assn.
1931 N Meacham Rd., Ste. 100
Schaumburg, IL 60173-4360
PH: (847)925-8070
Toll free: 800-248-2862
Fax: (847)285-5732

American Conference of Cantors [20224]
1375 Remington Rd., Ste. M
Schaumburg, IL 60173-4844
PH: (847)781-7800
Fax: (847)781-7801
Goldman, Mark, President

American Foundry Society [8659]
1695 N Penny Ln.
Schaumburg, IL 60173
PH: (847)824-0181
Toll free: 800-537-4237
Fax: (847)824-7848
Call, Jerry, CEO

American Hardware Manufacturers Association [1563]
The William P. Farrell Bldg.
10 N Martingale Rd., Ste. 400
Schaumburg, IL 60173
PH: (847)605-1025
Fax: (847)466-1311

American Society of Andrology [17547]
1100 E Woodfield Rd., Ste. 350
Schaumburg, IL 60173-5125
PH: (847)619-4909
Fax: (847)517-7229
Lee, Mary M., MD, President

American Society of Anesthesiolo-gists [13694]
1061 American Ln.
Schaumburg, IL 60173-4973
PH: (847)825-5586
Fax: (847)825-1692
Bieterman, Karen, Mgr.

American Veterinary Medical Association [17630]
1931 N Meacham Rd., Ste. 100
Schaumburg, IL 60173-4360
Toll free: 800-248-2862
Fax: (847)925-1329
Schmidt, Barbara A., Treasurer

Association of Chinese Scientists and Engineers U.S.A. [6543]
PO Box 59715
Schaumburg, IL 60159
Guidong, Zhu, VP

Association of Professional Chaplains [19925]
2800 W Higgins Rd., Ste. 295
Schaumburg, IL 60173
PH: (847)240-1014
Fax: (847)240-1015
Atkinson, Mary-Margaret, President

Coalition of State Rheumatology Organizations [17157]
1100 E Woodfield Rd., Ste. 350
Schaumburg, IL 60173
PH: (847)517-7225
Schweitz, Michael, MD, President

Commission on Rehabilitation Counselor Certification [11488]
1699 E Woodfield Rd., Ste. 300
Schaumburg, IL 60173-4957
PH: (847)944-1325
Fax: (847)944-1346
Chapman, Cindy, Exec. Dir.

Concrete Reinforcing Steel Institute [513]
933 N Plum Grove Rd.
Schaumburg, IL 60173-4758
PH: (847)517-1200
Fax: (847)517-1206
Risser, Robert J., Jr., CEO, President

Congress of Neurological Surgeons [16063]
10 N Martingale Rd., Ste. 190
Schaumburg, IL 60173
PH: (847)240-2500
Toll free: 877-517-1CNS
Fax: (847)240-0804
Lonser, Russell R., President

Council on Rehabilitation Education [17086]
1699 E Woodfield Rd., Ste. 300
Schaumburg, IL 60173
PH: (847)944-1345
Fax: (847)944-1346
Andre, Kristine, Admin. Asst.

Hotel Technology Next Generation [1661]
650 E Algonquin Rd., Ste. 207
Schaumburg, IL 60173
PH: (847)303-5560
Rice, Mr. Douglas, Contact

International BioIron Society [14585]
Two Woodfield Lake
1100 E Woodfield Rd., Ste. 350
Schaumburg, IL 60173-5121
PH: (847)517-7225
Fax: (847)517-7229
Fleming, Robert E., MD, President

International Pelvic Pain Society [16560]
1100 E Woodfield Rd., Ste. 350
Schaumburg, IL 60173
PH: (847)517-8712
Fax: (847)517-7229
Echeverri, Juan Diego Villegas, MD, President

International Skeletal Society [17057]
1100 E Woodfield Rd., Ste. 350
Schaumburg, IL 60173
PH: (847)517-7225
Fax: (847)517-7229
White, Lawrence M., Secretary

Large Urology Group Practice Association [17552]
1100 E Woodfield Rd., Ste. 350
Schaumburg, IL 60173
PH: (847)517-7225
Kirschner, Celeste, CEO

National Amateur Dodgeball Association [22533]
c/o Schaumburg Park District
220 E Weathersfield Way

Schaumburg, IL 60193
PH: (847)985-2120
Fax: (847)985-2461

Society of Actuaries [1928]
475 N Martingale Rd., Ste. 600
Schaumburg, IL 60173
PH: (847)706-3500
Fax: (847)706-3599
Heidrich, Greg, Exec. Dir.

Society for Behavioral Neuroendocri-nology [13804]
1100 E Woodfield Rd., Ste. 350
Schaumburg, IL 60173-5121
PH: (847)517-7225
Fax: (847)517-7229
Weiser, Wendy J., Exec. Dir.

Society of Robotic Surgery [17405]
WJ Weiser and Associates, Inc.
Two Woodfield Lake
1100 E Woodfield Rd., Ste. 520
Schaumburg, IL 60173
PH: (847)517-7225
Fax: (847)517-7229
Advincula, Arnold P., President

Society for the Study of Male Reproduction, Inc. [17119]
1100 E Woodfield Rd., Ste. 350
Schaumburg, IL 60173
PH: (847)517-7225
Fax: (847)517-7229
Swanson, Heather, Exec. Dir.

Society of University Urologists [17563]
1100 E Woodfield Rd., Ste. 350
Schaumburg, IL 60173
PH: (847)517-7225
Fax: (847)517-7229
Kogan, Barry Allan, MD, President

Society of Urodynamics, Female Pelvic Medicine and Urogenital Reconstruction [17564]
1100 E Woodfield Rd., Ste. 350
Schaumburg, IL 60173
PH: (847)517-7225
Fax: (847)517-7229
Rovner, Eric Scott, MD, President

Society of Urology Chairpersons and Program Directors [17565]
Two Woodfield Lake
1100 E Woodfield Rd., Ste. 350
Schaumburg, IL 60173
PH: (847)517-7225
Fax: (847)517-7229
Thrasher, J. Brantley, MD, President

Society of Women in Urology [17566]
1100 E Woodfield Rd., Ste. 520
Schaumburg, IL 60173
PH: (847)517-7225
Fax: (847)517-7229
Williams, Elizabeth Anne, MD, President

Student American Veterinary Medical Association [17664]
1931 N Meacham Rd., Ste. 100
Schaumburg, IL 60173
Toll free: 800-248-2862
Fax: (847)925-1329

Technology and Manufacturing As-sociation [2232]
1651 Wilkening Rd.
Schaumburg, IL 60173
PH: (847)825-1120
Fax: (847)825-0041
Carr, Jim, Chairman

Urological Association of Physician Assistants [17567]
Two Woodfield Lake
1100 E Woodfield Rd., Ste. 350

Schaumburg, IL 60173
Kreiensieck, Charlene, President

Women's Energy Network **[6519]**
Two Woodfield Lake
1100 E Woodfield Rd., Ste. 350
Schaumburg, IL 60173
Toll free: 855-390-0650
Fax: (847)517-7229
Lawson, Karyl McCurdy, Founder

Worldwide Fistula Fund **[14244]**
1100 E Woodfield Rd., Ste. 350
Schaumburg, IL 60173
PH: (847)592-2438
Wittek, Michael R., Chmn. of the Bd.

Gift from the Heart Foundation
[14191]
3860 25th Ave.
Schiller Park, IL 60176
PH: (847)671-2711
Fax: (847)671-2713
Wolosewicz, Andrzej, Treasurer

Echo Dogs White Shepherd Rescue
[10613]
PO Box 63
Sherman, IL 62684
Cox, Laura, Contact

American Brussels Griffon Association **[21801]**
c/o Linda G. Vance, Secretary
PO Box 11
Shirley, IL 61772-0011
PH: (309)453-1674
Stants, Heather, President

Academy of Aphasia **[13724]**
5130 W Suffield Ter.
Skokie, IL 60077
Martin, Randi, Bd. Member

Accreditation Association for
Ambulatory Health Care **[13674]**
5250 Old Orchard Rd., Ste. 200
Skokie, IL 60077-4461
PH: (847)853-6060
Fax: (847)853-9028
Burke, John, PhD, President, CEO

Assyrian Academic Society **[9647]**
8324 Lincoln Ave.
Skokie, IL 60077-2436
Neesan, Ramsen, Secretary

International Society for Stem Cell
Research **[14882]**
5215 Old Orchard Rd., Ste. 270
Skokie, IL 60077
PH: (224)592-5700
Fax: (224)365-0004
Witty, Nancy, CEO

Portland Cement Association **[794]**
5420 Old Orchard Rd.
Skokie, IL 60077-1083
PH: (847)966-6200
Fax: (847)966-8389
Stull, John, Chairman

United States Court Reporters Association **[5123]**
8430 Gross Point Rd., Ste. 115
Skokie, IL 60077-2036
PH: (847)470-9500
Toll free: 800-628-2730
Fax: (847)470-9505
Mousseau, Kristine, President

Polish-American Engineers Association **[6582]**
1 Watergate Dr.
South Barrington, IL 60010
Pawlowski, Andrzej, President

Willow Creek Association **[20030]**
67 E Algonquin Rd.
South Barrington, IL 60010-6132
Toll free: 800-570-9812
Gogis, Mike, CFO

Amateur Trapshooting Association
[23124]
1105 E Broadway
Sparta, IL 62286
PH: (618)449-2224
Toll free: 866-454-5198
Burke, John, President

Academy of Spinal Cord Injury
Nurses Section **[16080]**
Academy of Spinal Cord Injury
Professionals
206 S 6th St.
Springfield, IL 62701
PH: (217)753-1190
Fax: (217)525-1271
Beck, Lisa, RN, President

American Academy of Oral and Maxillofacial Radiology **[14382]**
3085 Stevenson Dr., Ste. 200
Springfield, IL 62703
Williamson, Gail, Assoc. Exec.

American Association of Public
Health Dentistry **[14393]**
3085 Stevenson Dr., Ste. 200
Springfield, IL 62703
PH: (217)529-6941
Fax: (217)529-9120
Tolson, Pamela J., CAE, Contact

American Board of Registration of
EEG and EP Technologists
[14654]
2908 Greenbriar Dr., Ste. A
Springfield, IL 62704
PH: (217)726-7980
Fax: (217)726-7989
Padilla, Erik, President

American Commodity Distribution
Association **[3760]**
3085 Stevenson Dr., Ste. 200
Springfield, IL 62703
PH: (217)241-6747
Fax: (217)529-9120
Herrera, Ed, President

American Osteopathic College of
Anesthesiologists **[13692]**
3085 Stevenson Dr., Ste. 200
Springfield, IL 62703
PH: (217)529-6503
Toll free: 800-842-2622
Fax: (217)529-9120
Sohn, Raymond G., DO, Bd.
Member

American Society for Pharmacy Law
[15529]
3085 Stevenson Dr., Ste. 200
Springfield, IL 62703-4270
PH: (217)529-6948
Fax: (217)529-9120
Chatara, Nathela, CAE, Exec. Dir.

Association of Assistive Technology
Act Programs **[14546]**
1020 S Spring St.
Springfield, IL 62704
Knue, Alan, Chairman

Association of Business Process
Management Professionals **[2150]**
100 East Washington St.
Springfield, IL 62701
PH: (217)753-4007
Fax: (217)528-6545
Benedict, Tony, President

Association of Lunar and Planetary
Observers **[21306]**
c/o Matthew L. Will, Secretary
PO Box 13456
Springfield, IL 62791
Benton, Julius L., Jr., Director

Association for Preservation
Technology International **[9377]**
3085 Stevenson Dr., Ste. 200
Springfield, IL 62703

PH: (217)529-9039
Fax: (888)723-4242
Chatara, Nathela, Dir. of Admin.

Association of Science Museum
Directors **[9825]**
Illinois State Museum
502 S Spring St.
Springfield, IL 62706-5000
PH: (217)782-5969
Fax: (217)557-9226
Jones, Douglas S., PhD, President

Association for Surgical Education
[8314]
3085 Stevenson Dr., Ste. 200
Springfield, IL 62703
PH: (217)529-6503
Kepner, Susan, MEd, Exec. Dir.

Association of Veterinary Technician
Educators **[17640]**
206 S 6th St.
Springfield, IL 62701
PH: (701)231-7531
Tighe, Monica, Chairman

Daughters of Union Veterans of the
Civil War, 1861-1865 **[20740]**
503 S Walnut St.
Springfield, IL 62705
PH: (217)544-0616
Redinger, Sally, President

Elliot Institute **[10428]**
PO Box 7348
Springfield, IL 62791-7348
PH: (217)525-8202
Toll free: 888-412-2676
Fax: (217)525-8212
Reardon, David C., PhD, Director

Federated Funeral Directors of
America **[2403]**
1622 S MacArthur Blvd.
Springfield, IL 62704
Toll free: 800-877-3332
Fax: (217)525-2104
Rodenburg, John R., President

Herpetologists' League **[6707]**
c/o Meredith Mahoney, Treasurer
ISM Research and Collections Ctr.
1011 E Ash St.
Springfield, IL 62703
PH: (217)785-4843
(215)895-2627
Mahoney, Meredith, Treasurer

Independent Order of Vikings
[19487]
5250 S 6th St.
Springfield, IL 62705-5147
Toll free: 877-241-6006
Beck, Ralph S., President

International Health and Development Network **[15480]**
3950 Mill Stone Dr.
Springfield, IL 62711
PH: (217)787-6530
Agamah, Dr. Edem, President

Abraham Lincoln Association
[10336]
1 Old State Capitol Plz.
Springfield, IL 62701-1507
Toll free: 866-865-8500
Harris, Kathryn M., VP

National Newspaper Association
[2703]
900 Community Dr.
Springfield, IL 62703
PH: (217)241-1400
Fax: (217)241-1301
Edgecombe, John, Jr., Officer

North American Association of
Central Cancer Registries **[14035]**
2050 W Iles, Ste. A
Springfield, IL 62704-7412

PH: (217)698-0800
Fax: (217)698-0188
Kohler, Betsy, Exec. Dir.

Radical Psychology Network **[16934]**
c/o Roberta F. Sprague, Co-Moderator
University of Illinois at Springfield
1 William Maxwell Ln.
Springfield, IL 62703
Fox, Dennis, Arch., Founder

Vachel Lindsay Association **[9108]**
PO Box 9356
Springfield, IL 62791-9356

Awana Clubs International **[20658]**
1 E Bode Rd.
Streamwood, IL 60107-6658
PH: (630)213-2000
Toll free: 866-292-6227
Fax: (877)292-6232
Bell, Valerie, CEO

Corson/Colson Family History Association **[20849]**
c/o Brian Corson
105 Diane Dr.
Streamwood, IL 60107
Corson, Dr. Michael, President

Immigration and Ethnic History
Society **[9489]**
Div. of Social Science and Education
Waubonsee Community College
Waubonsee Dr., Route 47
Sugar Grove, IL 60554-9454
PH: (630)466-7900
Draper, Timothy D., Secretary

American Society of Check Collectors **[22258]**
c/o Lyman Hensley, Secretary
473 E Elm St.
Sycamore, IL 60178-1934
Hensley, Lyman, Secretary .

International Sporthorse Registry,
Inc. **[4371]**
517 DeKalb Ave.
Sycamore, IL 60178
PH: (815)899-7803
Fax: (815)899-7823

Oldenburg Registry North America
[4398]
517 DeKalb Ave.
Sycamore, IL 60178
PH: (815)899-7803
Fax: (815)899-7823

American Bicycle Racing **[23077]**
PO Box 487
Tinley Park, IL 60477-0487

Retail Bakers of America **[376]**
15941 Harlem Ave., No. 347
Tinley Park, IL 60477
Toll free: 800-638-0924
Shanahan-Haas, Bernadette, Dir. of
Operations

American Killifish Association
[22028]
c/o Bob Meyer
733 County Road 600 E
Tolono, IL 61880
PH: (508)643-4603
(717)266-3453
Harrison, Charles, Trustee

T-34 Association Inc. **[21528]**
880 N County Rd., 900-E
Tuscola, IL 61953
Clark, Julie, Director

National Association of Multicultural
Rehabilitation Concerns **[17089]**
c/o Robin Washington, PhD,
President

Governors State University
Department of Physical Therapy
University Park, IL
PH: (708)534-3147
Mundis, Cindy, M.A, CRC, LPC, Bd.
Member

Academy of Leisure Sciences [7161]
1807 N Federal Dr.
Urbana, IL 61801
PH: (217)819-5994
Fax: (217)359-5975
Parr, Mary, President

American Oil Chemists' Society
[6185]
2710 S Boulder Dr.
Urbana, IL 61802-6996
PH: (217)359-2344
Fax: (217)351-8091
Trautmann, M., President

Conference on College Composition
and Communication [7867]
1111 W Kenyon Rd.
Urbana, IL 61801-1010
PH: (217)328-3870
Toll free: 877-369-6283
Carter, Joyce, Chairperson

Conference on English Education
[7868]
National Council of Teachers of
English
1111 W Kenyon Rd.
Urbana, IL 61801-1010
PH: (217)328-3870
Toll free: 877-369-6283
Reid, Louann, Chairperson

Conference on English Leadership
[7848]
National Council of Teachers of
English
1111 W Kenyon Rd.
Urbana, IL 61801-1096
PH: (217)328-3870
Toll free: 877-369-6283
Fax: (217)328-9645
Rocco, Heather, Chairman

International Guild of Musicians in
Dance [23497]
c/o John Toenjes, Administrator
University of Illinois
Dance Administration Bldg.
907 1/2 W Nevada St.
Urbana, IL 61801
Knosp, Suzanne, Contact

International Society for Fat
Research [6945]
c/o AOCS
2710 S Boulder
Urbana, IL 61802-6996
PH: (217)359-2344
Fax: (217)351-8091
Newman, Mr. Jeffry, Secretary

National Association of Plant Breed-
ers [4436]
c/o Dr. Rita Mumm, Awards Panel
Chairperson
University of Illinois
1102 S Goodwin Ave.
Urbana, IL 61801
PH: (217)244-9497
Francis, David, President

National Council of Teachers of
English [7869]
1111 W Kenyon Rd.
Urbana, IL 61801-1010
PH: (217)328-3870
Toll free: 877-369-6283
Fax: (217)328-9645
Houser, Susan, Officer

North American Nietzsche Society
[10107]
105 Gregory Hall
Dept. of Philosophy

University of Illinois
810 S Wright St.
Urbana, IL 61801
PH: (217)333-1939
Schacht, Prof. Richard, Exec. Dir.

University of Illinois Alumni Associa-
tion [19356]
Alice Campbell Alumni Ctr.
601 S Lincoln Ave.
Urbana, IL 61801
PH: (217)333-1471
Toll free: 800-355-2586
Stratton, William, Chairman

Writers Workshop [10407]
208 English Bldg.
608 S Wright St.
Urbana, IL 61801
PH: (217)333-8796
Wisniewski, Carolyn, Director

Material Handling Equipment
Distributors Association [1747]
201 US Highway 45
Vernon Hills, IL 60061
PH: (847)680-3500
Fax: (847)362-6989
Richards, Liz, CEO

Stuff for the Poor [11445]
PO Box 6477
Villa Park, IL 60181
PH: (630)401-4719
Toll free: 877-579-7387
Rubingisa, Providence, President,
Exec. Dir.

BueLingo Beef Cattle Society [3723]
15904 W Warren Rd.
Warren, IL 61087-9601
PH: (815)745-2147
Smith, Rick, President

Corn Items Collectors Association
[21642]
9288 Poland Rd.
Warrensburg, IL 62573
PH: (217)674-3334
Chamberlain, Robert S., Secretary,
Treasurer

World Organization of Webmasters
[1809]
PO Box 584
Washington, IL 61571
PH: (916)989-2933
Fax: (916)989-2933
Cullifer, Bill, Exec. Dir.

International Association of R.S.
Prussia Collectors [21665]
PO Box 64
Waterman, IL 60556

Aluminum Anodizers Council [742]
1000 N Rand Rd., No. 214
Wauconda, IL 60084
PH: (847)526-2010
Fax: (847)526-3993
Molenda, Nancy, Contact

Aluminum Extruders Council [2340]
1000 N Rand Rd., Ste. 214
Wauconda, IL 60084
PH: (847)526-2010
Fax: (847)526-3993
McMahon, Matt, President

Commercial Law League of America
[5085]
1000 N Rand Rd., Ste. 214
Wauconda, IL 60084
PH: (312)240-1400
Fax: (847)526-3993
Bernstein, Robert, President

National Plasterers Council, Inc.
[2618]
1000 N Rand Rd., Ste. 214
Wauconda, IL 60084

PH: (847)416-7272
Fax: (847)526-3993
Schilling, Dave, Chmn. of the Bd.

Rebuilding Haiti Now [12716]
2314 Alamance Dr.
West Chicago, IL 60185-6447
Rocourt, Gladys Doebeli, Founder

Amusement & Music Operators As-
sociation [1133]
600 Spring Hill Ring Rd., Ste. 111
West Dundee, IL 60118
PH: (847)428-7699
Toll free: 800-937-2662
Fax: (847)428-7719
Butler, Gaines, President

Healthcare Financial Management
Association [15016]
3 Westbrook Corporate Ctr., Ste.
600
Westchester, IL 60154
PH: (708)531-9600
Toll free: 800-252-HFMA
Fifer, Joseph J., FHFMA, CEO,
President

Joni James International Fan Club
[24015]
PO Box 7207
Westchester, IL 60154-7207

Organization of Black Aerospace
Professionals [154]
1 Westbrook Corporate Ctr., Ste.
300
Westchester, IL 60154
Toll free: 800-JET-OBAP
Glenn, Capt. Albert, Advisor

Professional Currency Dealers As-
sociation [22282]
c/o James A. Simek, Secretary
PO Box 7157
Westchester, IL 60154
PH: (414)807-0116
Fax: (414)423-0343
Simek, James A., Secretary

American Nutrition Association
[16204]
PO Box 262
Western Springs, IL 60558
PH: (708)246-3663
Fax: (708)246-3663

Friends of Fiber Art International
[8856]
PO Box 468
Western Springs, IL 60558
PH: (708)710-0644
Herman, Lloyd E., Director

USA Professional Platform Tennis
Association [23310]
4143 Woodland Ave.
Western Springs, IL 60558-1666
PH: (708)261-5779

Wilderness Classroom [8401]
4605 Grand Ave.
Western Springs, IL 60558
PH: (312)505-9973
Frost, Eric, Bd. Member

Association of Physicians of
Pakistani Descent of North
America [16743]
6414 S Cass Ave.
Westmont, IL 60559-3209
PH: (630)968-8585
Fax: (630)968-8677
Qureshi, M. Nasar, President

Nautical Research Guild [22656]
237 S Lincoln St.
Westmont, IL 60559-1917

PH: (585)968-8111
Draper, Mike, Secretary

American Academy of Oral and Max-
illofacial Pathology [16568]
214 N Hale St.
Wheaton, IL 60187
PH: (630)510-4552
Toll free: 888-552-2667
Fax: (630)510-4501
Svazas, Ms. Janet, Exec. Dir.

American Liszt Society [9179]
c/o Alexander Djordjevic, Member-
ship Secretary
PO Box 1020
Wheaton, IL 60187-6777
PH: (845)586-4457
Kolb, Justin, Exec. Sec.

American Society of Business
Publication Editors [2653]
214 N Hale St.
Wheaton, IL 60187
PH: (630)510-4588
Fax: (630)510-4501
Zemler, Jessica, President

American Tract Society [20125]
1300 Crescent St.
Wheaton, IL 60187
PH: (630)682-4300
Toll free: 800-543-1659
Dennis, Lane T., President,
Publisher

Association of Christians in the
Mathematical Sciences [19945]
Dept. of Mathematics
Wheaton College
501 College Ave.
Wheaton, IL 60187
PH: (630)752-5869
Brabenec, Robert, Exec. Sec.

Calendar Marketing Association, Inc.
[2271]
214 N Hale St.
Wheaton, IL 60187
PH: (630)510-4564
Fax: (630)510-4501

Center for Applied Christian Ethics
[19948]
501 College Ave.
Wheaton, IL 60187-5593
PH: (630)752-5890
Bacote, Dr. Vincent, Director

Conference on Christianity and
Literature [9756]
Wheaton College
501 College Ave.
Wheaton, IL 60187
Tippens, Darryl, President

Evangelical Training Association
[20078]
PO Box 327
Wheaton, IL 60187-0327
Toll free: 800-369-8291

Help Congo Network [12672]
PO Box 650
Wheaton, IL 60187
Buthidi, Willie, President

Kuza Project [13012]
PO Box 529
Wheaton, IL 60187
PH: (630)220-0101
Birch, J., Officer

National Association of Ticket
Brokers [1152]
214 N Hale St.
Wheaton, IL 60187
PH: (630)510-4594
Fax: (630)510-4501
Berger, Jason, Director

National Retail Hobby Stores Association [658]
214 N Hale St.
Wheaton, IL 60187
PH: (630)510-4596
Fax: (630)510-4501
Svazas, Janet, Exec. Dir.

Neurofibromatosis Network [14847]
213 S Wheaton Ave.
Wheaton, IL 60187
PH: (630)510-1115
Toll free: 800-942-6825
Fax: (630)510-8508
Stewart, Cheri, President

Pioneer Clubs [20661]
PO Box 788
Wheaton, IL 60187-0788
Toll free: 800-694-2582
Cedar, Dr. Paul A., Chairman, CEO

Romanian Missionary Society [20457]
PO Box 527
Wheaton, IL 60187
PH: (630)665-6503
Fax: (630)665-6538
Percy, Dr. Livius T., President

Sotos Syndrome Support Association [14858]
PO Box 4626
Wheaton, IL 60189
Toll free: 888-246-7772

Theosophical Society in America [20624]
1926 N Main St.
Wheaton, IL 60187
PH: (630)668-1571
Toll free: 800-669-9425
Boyd, Tim, President

Cremation Association of North America [2402]
499 Northgate Pky.
Wheeling, IL 60090-2646
PH: (312)245-1077
Fax: (312)321-4098
Stahl, Sheri, President

International Council on Education for Teaching [8648]
1000 Capitol Dr.
Wheeling, IL 60090-7201
PH: (847)947-5881
Fax: (847)947-5881
O'Meara, James, President

90th Division Association [21098]
c/o James R. Reid, Executive Secretary/Treasurer
17 Lake Shore Dr.
Willowbrook, IL 60527-2221
PH: (630)789-0204
Fax: (630)789-0499
Reid, James R., Secretary, Treasurer

American Association of Police Polygraphists [5232]
3223 Lake Ave., Unit 15c-168
Wilmette, IL 60091-1069
PH: (847)635-3980
Clark, Karen, Chairman

American Committee for Kiyosato Educational Experiment Project [12138]
825 Green Bay Rd., Ste. 122
Wilmette, IL 60091-2500
PH: (847)853-2500
Fax: (847)853-8901
Corwin, Jennifer, Exec. Dir.

Boating Writers International [2668]
108 9th St.
Wilmette, IL 60091

PH: (847)736-4142
Wendt, Alan, President

Liturgical Conference [20066]
c/o First Congregational Church UCC
1125 Wilmette Ave.
Wilmette, IL 60091
Toll free: 800-354-1420
Anderson, E. Byron, Bd. Member

Simon Foundation for Continence [17556]
PO Box 815
Wilmette, IL 60091
PH: (847)864-3913
Toll free: 800-237-4666
Fax: (847)864-9758
Gartley, Cheryle B., President, Founder

Basenji Club of America [21835]
c/o Janet Ketz, Secretary
34025 W River Rd.
Wilmington, IL 60481-9599
Gregory, Bryan, President

American Academy of Medical Hypnoanalysts [15352]
PO Box 365
Winfield, IL 60190-0365
PH: (720)975-4485
Toll free: 888-454-9766
Hardy-Holley, Don, President

Amyloidosis Support Groups [14560]
232 Orchard Dr.
Wood Dale, IL 60191
PH: (630)350-7539
Toll free: 866-404-7539
Finkel, Muriel, President

Chinese Music Society of North America [9887]
PO Box 5275
Woodridge, IL 60517
Lee, Dr. Yuan Yuan, Contact

Northwest Territory Alliance [8796]
c/o Jane Whiteside, Adjutant General
8417 Adbeth Ave.
Woodridge, IL 60517
PH: (630)985-1124
Whiteside, Jane, Adj. Gen., Secretary

Our World-Underwater Scholarship Society [23344]
PO Box 6157
Woodridge, IL 60517
PH: (630)969-6690
Fax: (630)969-6690
Leech, Elvin W. D., Chmn. of the Bd.

Society of Chinese American Professors and Scientists [8466]
c/o Dr. Zuotao Zeng, Treasurer
PO Box 5735
Woodridge, IL 60517

Hooved Animal Humane Society [10638]
10804 McConnell Rd.
Woodstock, IL 60098
PH: (815)337-5563
Fax: (815)337-5569
McGonigle, Dr. Tracy, Exec. Dir.

Zakat Foundation of America [11467]
PO Box 639
Worth, IL 60482
PH: (708)233-0555
 (773)363-4230
Toll free: 888-925-2887
Demir, Khalil, Exec. Dir.

Aftermath: Surviving Psychopathy Foundation [16949]
PO Box 267
Yorkville, IL 60560
Kosson, David, PhD, President

INDIANA

Christian Women Connection [20019]
PO Box 2328
Anderson, IN 46018
PH: (765)648-2102
Toll free: 866-778-0804
Fax: (765)608-3094
Bryant, Naomi, President

Dogs Against Drugs/Dogs Against Crime [11690]
3320 Main St., Ste. G
Anderson, IN 46013
PH: (765)642-9447
Toll free: 888-323-3227
Fax: (765)642-4899
Sparks, Darron, President

Starfleet Command [24082]
PO Box 348
Anderson, IN 46015
Williams, Mark, CEO

Wesleyan/Holiness Women Clergy [20377]
305 W 10th St.
Anderson, IN 46016-1323
PH: (260)241-2993
Gonlag, Mari, VP

Hunters Helping Hunters, Inc. [22166]
1695 N Main St.
Auburn, IN 46706

International Trotting and Pacing Association [22919]
5140 County Road 56
Auburn, IN 46706
PH: (260)337-5808
Fax: (260)337-5808

National Association of Automobile Museums [9838]
PO Box 271
Auburn, IN 46706
PH: (260)925-1444
Fax: (260)925-6266
Ernest, Terry, President

National Automotive and Truck Museum of United States [9839]
1000 Gordon M. Buehrig Pl.
Auburn, IN 46706
PH: (260)925-9100

International Association of Dive Rescue Specialists [2097]
8103 E US Highway 36
Avon, IN 46123
PH: (317)464-9787
Fax: (317)641-0730
Robinson, Blades, Exec. Dir.

Antique Small Engine Collectors Club [22010]
5655 US Highway 50 E
Bedford, IN 47421-8688
Crane, Dale, President

Evangelistic Faith Missions [20414]
PO Box 609
Bedford, IN 47421
PH: (812)275-7531
Manley, Rev. J. Stevan, President

Fur Information Council of America [204]
1921 Stevens Ave., No. 210
Bedford, IN 47421

PH: (323)782-1700
Fax: (323)651-1417
Kaplan, Keith, Exec. Dir.

Indiana Limestone Institute of America, Inc. [3184]
1502 I St., Ste. 400
Bedford, IN 47421
PH: (812)275-4426
Schnatzmeyer, Todd, Exec. Dir.

National Trappers Association [4724]
2815 Washington Ave.
Bedford, IN 47421
PH: (812)277-9670
Toll free: 866-680-8727
Fax: (812)277-9672
Kaatz, Kraig, Rep.

African Language Teachers Association [8637]
708 Eigennmann Hall
Indiana University
1900 E 10th St.
Bloomington, IN 47406
PH: (812)856-4185
Fax: (812)856-4189
Schleicher, Dr. Antonia, Exec. Dir.

Agency for Instructional Technology [8020]
8111 Lee Paul Rd.
Bloomington, IN 47404-7916
PH: (812)339-2203
Toll free: 800-457-4509
Fax: (812)333-4218
Wilson, Chuck, Exec. Dir.

American Association of Teachers of Italian [8172]
c/o Colleen M. Ryan
626 Ballantine Hall
Department of French and Italian
Indiana University
Bloomington, IN 47405
PH: (815)855-1429
Bancheri, Salvatore, President

American Folklore Society [9325]
Indiana University
1900 E 10th St.
Bloomington, IN 47406
PH: (812)856-2379
Fax: (812)856-2483
Lloyd, Timothy, Exec. Dir.

American Literary Translators Association [8713]
900 E 7th St
Bloomington, IN 47405-3201
PH: (415)735-4546
Daw, Paul, Treasurer

Association of College Unions International [8603]
1 City Centre Ste. 200
120 W 7th St.
Bloomington, IN 47404-3925
PH: (812)245-2284
Fax: (812)245-6710
Herman-Betzen, Marsha, Exec. Dir.

Association for Educational Communications and Technology [8023]
320 W 8th St., Ste. 101
Bloomington, IN 47404-3745
PH: (812)335-7675
Toll free: 877-677-2328
Donaldson, Ana, Comm. Chm.

Association for Practical and Professional Ethics [8420]
Indiana University
618 E 3rd St.
Bloomington, IN 47405-3602
PH: (812)855-6450
Fax: (812)856-4969
Yoak, Dr. Stuart, Exec. Dir.

Association for Women in Slavic
Studies [10216]
c/o Sarah D. Phillips, Treasur-
er,Bloomington
Student Bldg. 130
Dept. of Anthropology
Indiana University
701 E Kirkwood Ave.
Bloomington, IN 47405
PH: (812)855-0216
Chatterjee, Choi, President

Campus Safety, Health and
Environmental Management As-
sociation [4125]
One City Centre, Ste. 204
120 W 7th St.
Bloomington, IN 47404
PH: (812)245-8084
Fax: (812)245-6710
Brakensiek, Jay, Treasurer

Center for the Study of the College
Fraternity [23755]
900 E 7th St., Ste. 371
Bloomington, IN 47405
PH: (812)855-1235
Veldkamp, Steve, Exec. Dir.

Children's Organ Transplant As-
sociation [14183]
2501 W COTA Dr.
Bloomington, IN 47403
Toll free: 800-366-2682
Fax: (812)336-8885
Porter, Rod

Consortium of College and
University Media Centers [8026]
Indiana University
306 N Union St.
Bloomington, IN 47405-3888
PH: (812)855-6049
Scales, Aileen, Exec. Dir.

First Issues Collectors Club [22328]
c/o Kurt Streepy, Secretary and
Treasurer
3128 Mattatha Dr.
Bloomington, IN 47401
Laflamme, Louis, President

Ibsen Society of America [9056]
c/o Gergana May, Treasurer
Germanic Studies Dept.
Indiana University
Bloomington, IN 47405
Sandberg, Mark, President

International Association for the
Study of the Commons [3886]
513 N Park Ave.
Bloomington, IN 47408-3895
PH: (317)608-3067
de Moor, Tine, President

International Collegiate Licensing
Association [2286]
c/o Robin Cooper, President
400 E. 7th St., Poplars Rm. No. 410
Bloomington, IN 47405
PH: (440)892-4000
(440)788-7466
Fax: (440)892-4007
Virtue, Ryan, Asst. Treas., Asst. Sec.

Mongolia Society [9813]
703 Eigenmann Hall
1900 E 10th St.
Indiana University
Bloomington, IN 47406-7512
PH: (812)855-4078
Fax: (812)855-4078
Campi, Dr. Alicia, President

National Association of Student
Anthropologists [7494]
c/o Suzanne Marie Barber, President
Indiana University

107 S Indiana Ave.
Bloomington, IN 47405
Goodman, Julie, Comm. Chm.

National Council of Less Commonly
Taught Languages [8189]
Eigenmann Hall, Rm. 708
1900 E 10th St.
Bloomington, IN 47406
PH: (812)856-4185
Fax: (812)856-4189
Schleicher, Antonia Folarin, PhD,
Exec. Dir.

National Intercollegiate Running
Club Association [23118]
121 N College Ave.
Bloomington, IN 47404
Bartley, Ben, Exec. Dir.

North American Bluebird Society
[4855]
PO Box 7844
Bloomington, IN 47407
PH: (812)200-5700
Linn, Sherry, Cmte. Mgmt. Ofc.

Norwegian Researchers and Teach-
ers Association of North America
[8398]
c/o Gergana May, Treasurer
Global and International Studies
Bldg., No. 3111
Indiana University
Bloomington, IN 47405-1105
Gjellstad, Melissa, President

Organization of American Historians
[9503]
112 N Bryan Ave.
Bloomington, IN 47408-4141
PH: (812)855-7311
Fax: (812)855-0696
Finley, Katherine, Exec. Dir.

Phi Delta Kappa [23853]
320 W 8th St., Ste. 216
Bloomington, IN 47404
PH: (812)339-1156
Toll free: 800-766-1156
Fax: (812)339-0018
Starr, Joshua P., CEO

Pi Lambda Theta [23734]
320 W 8th St., Ste. 216
Bloomington, IN 47404
PH: (812)339-1156
Toll free: 800-766-1156
Fax: (812)339-0018
Chen, Albert, COO

School Project Foundation [7904]
349 S Walnut St.
Bloomington, IN 47401
PH: (812)558-0041
Baron, Daniel, Exec. Dir.

Society for Ethnomusicology [10007]
Indiana University
800 E 3rd St.
Bloomington, IN 47405-3700
PH: (812)855-6672
Fax: (812)855-6673
Rasmussen, Anne K., President

Society for the Experimental
Analysis of Behavior [6047]
Indiana University
Psychological and Brain Sciences
1101 E 10th St.
Bloomington, IN 47405-7007
PH: (812)336-1257
Fax: (812)855-4691
Bonner, Monica, Contact

University Risk Management and
Insurance Association [8040]
PO Box 1027
Bloomington, IN 47402-1027

PH: (812)727-7130
Fax: (812)727-7129
Whittington, Ms. Jenny, Exec. Dir.

Thomas Wolfe Society [9115]
PO Box 1146
Bloomington, IN 47402-1146
Strange, David, Director

World Communication Association
[7538]
Dept. of Communication and Culture
Indiana University
800 E 3rd St.
Bloomington, IN 47405-3657
PH: (812)855-0524
Fax: (812)855-6014
Del Villar, Dr. Carmencita, Bd.
Member

Forgotten Children Worldwide
[10980]
650 N Main St.
Bluffton, IN 46714
PH: (260)353-1580
Toll free: 888-353-1580
Fax: (260)824-1955
Hartsell, Matt, Founder, Exec. Dir.

Irish Wolfhound Club of America
[21904]
c/o Kathy Welling, Secretary
180 W 3rd St.
Campbellsburg, IN 47108
PH: (317)727-4954
Stolpe, Birgitta, PhD, President

Alpha Kappa Lambda [23884]
354 Gradle Dr.
Carmel, IN 46032
PH: (317)564-8003
Toll free: 866-556-8719
Slivinski, Jeremy, Secretary

Alpha Sigma Phi [23887]
710 Adams St.
Carmel, IN 46032
PH: (317)843-1911
Heminger, Gordon F., CEO,
President

American Boxer Rescue Association
[10567]
PO Box 184
Carmel, IN 46082
PH: (334)272-2590
Lombard, Gail, President

Association for Management
Information in Financial Services
[382]
14247 Saffron Cir.
Carmel, IN 46032
PH: (317)815-5857
Nathasingh, Jeff, President

Gift of Water [13323]
1025 Pine Hill Way
Carmel, IN 46032-7701
PH: (317)371-1656
Moehling, Laura, Bd. Member

National Antique Doll Dealers Association [22005]
c/o Lynette Gross, Secretary
13710 Smokey Ridge Trace
Carmel, IN 46033-9297
PH: (623)266-2926
Kolibaba, Sharon, Mem.

National Association of Miniature
Enthusiasts [21691]
130 N Rangeline Rd.
Carmel, IN 46032
PH: (317)571-8094
Fax: (317)571-8105

National Precast Concrete Association [792]
1320 City Center Dr., Ste. 200
Carmel, IN 46032

PH: (317)571-0041
Toll free: 800-366-7731
Fax: (317)571-0041
Wieser, Andy, Chairman

National Renewables Cooperative
Organization [6500]
4140 W 99th St.
Carmel, IN 46032-7731
PH: (317)344-7900
Fax: (317)344-7901
Fall, Amadou, CEO

Police and Firemen's Insurance As-
sociation [19492]
101 E 116th St.
Carmel, IN 46032
PH: (317)581-1913
Toll free: 800-221-7342
Fax: (317)571-5946
Kemp, Mark, President

Sigma Delta Tau [23962]
714 Adams St.
Carmel, IN 46032
PH: (317)846-7747
Carlson, Michelle, President

Sigma Kappa Foundation [23963]
695 Pro Med Ln., Ste. 300
Carmel, IN 46032
PH: (317)381-5531
Fax: (317)872-0716
Swiontek, Lisa Fedler, Exec. Dir.

Sigma Kappa Sorority [23964]
695 Pro-Med Ln., Ste. 300
Carmel, IN 46032-5323
PH: (317)872-3275
Fax: (317)872-0716
DeJong, Cheri Morrell, President

Theta Chi Fraternity [23936]
PO Box 503
Carmel, IN 46082
PH: (317)848-1856
Fax: (317)824-1908
Elder, Richard D., President

U.S.A. Defenders of Greyhounds
[10709]
PO Box 1256
Carmel, IN 46082
PH: (317)244-0113
Allen, Ms. Sally, President

Women's Oncology Research and
Dialogue [14082]
828 Hickory Dr.
Carmel, IN 46032
PH: (317)489-4187
Manahan, Nathan, Exec. Dir.

Model T Ford Club of America
[21438]
119 W Main St.
Centerville, IN 47330
PH: (765)855-5248
Fax: (765)855-3428
Miles, Tom, Director

International Association of Civil
Aviation Chaplains [19928]
c/o Beverly McNeely, Treasurer
2571 Oak Dr.
Clayton, IN 46118
PH: (317)491-5089
Fax: (317)244-9362
Lane, George, President

North American Powerlifting Federa-
tion [23071]
c/o Lawrence Maile, President
PO Box 668
Columbia City, IN 46725
PH: (907)334-9977
Maile, Dr. Lawrence, President

North American Shagya-Arabian
Society [4395]
c/o Beverly Thompson, Treasurer
2345 S Washington Rd.

Columbia City, IN 46725
Michaud, Arlene, President

Association for General and Liberal
Studies **[8226]**
c/o Joyce Lucke, Executive Director
428 5th St.
Columbus, IN 47201
PH: (812)376-7468
Mulrooney, Margaret, President

Fellowship of American Baptist Musi-
cians **[20490]**
3300 Fairlawn Dr.
Columbus, IN 47203-2731
PH: (317)635-3552
Fax: (317)635-3554
Newman, Steve, President

Society of the Descendants of
Washington's Army at Valley Forge
[20697]
908 Washington St.
Columbus, IN 47201
PH: (432)393-5790
Rynerson, Jan Stone, Contact

Delta Psi Omega **[23724]**
Wabash College
Theater Dept.
Crawfordsville, IN 47933-2484
PH: (765)361-6394

Veitch Historical Society **[20941]**
909 W Oak Hill Rd.
Crawfordsville, IN 47933
PH: (765)362-2503
Arnold, Bud, President

OASIS @ MAPP **[15979]**
950 S Court St.
Crown Point, IN 46307
PH: (219)662-1311
Moreno, Susan J., Editor

Society for Intercultural Education,
Training and Research U.S.A.
[8122]
PO Box 1382
Crown Point, IN 46308
Toll free: 877-796-9700
Coleman, Patricia M., President

Gypsy Cob and Drum Horse Association **[4356]**
1812 10th St.
Danville, IN 46122
PH: (317)417-2943

American Association of Pesticide
Safety Educators **[4123]**
PO Box 580
Delphi, IN 46923
PH: (765)494-4567
Fax: (765)496-1556
Renchie, Don, President

International Harvester Collectors
[22455]
c/o Emmett Webb, Membership
Chairperson
PO Box 35
Dublin, IN 47335-0035
PH: (765)478-6179
Buxton, Robert, President

National American Eskimo Dog Association **[21917]**
c/o Diana Allen, President
8767 S Edinburgh Rd.
Edinburgh, IN 46124
PH: (812)526-6682
Strong, Renee, Secretary

Church World Service **[12643]**
28606 Phillips St.
Elkhart, IN 46514-1239
PH: (574)264-3102
Toll free: 800-297-1516
Fax: (574)262-0966
McCullough, Rev. John L., CEO,
President

Holiday Rambler Recreational
Vehicle Club **[22427]**
PO Box 3028
Elkhart, IN 46515
PH: (574)295-9800
Toll free: 877-702-5415
Cline, Phil, Officer

Mennonite Education Agency
[20330]
3145 Benham Ave., Ste. 2
Elkhart, IN 46517
PH: (574)642-3164
Toll free: 866-866-2872
Romero, Carlos, Exec. Dir.

Mennonite Voluntary Service **[20332]**
3145 Benham Ave., Ste. 3
Elkhart, IN 46517
PH: (574)523-3000
Toll free: 866-866-2872
Fax: (316)283-0454
Cook, Diana, Coord.

National American Semi-Professional
Baseball Association **[22556]**
4609 Saybrook Dr.
Evansville, IN 47711-7771
PH: (812)430-2725
Turpin, Tim, Director

Phi Mu Alpha Sinfonia Fraternity of
America **[23831]**
10600 Old State Rd.
Evansville, IN 47711
PH: (812)867-2433
Toll free: 800-473-2649
Lichtenberg, Mark R., President

Recent Past Preservation Network
[9430]
PO Box 383
Evansville, IN 47703-0383
PH: (765)387-7776
Marcavitch, Aaron, President

Unchartered International **[12195]**
400 S Green River Rd.
Evansville, IN 47715
PH: (812)402-1886
Kerney, Brian, Exec. Dir.

Youth Evangelism Association
[20166]
13000 US Highway 41 N
Evansville, IN 47725
PH: (812)867-2418
Fax: (812)867-8933
Dooms, Tami, President, CEO

Feingold Association of the United
States **[16219]**
11849 Suncatcher Dr.
Fishers, IN 46037
PH: (631)369-9340
Hersey, Jane, Director

Phi Chi Medical Fraternity **[23818]**
2039 Ridgeview Dr.
Floyds Knobs, IN 47119
PH: (812)923-7270
Toll free: 800-800-7442
LeBlond, Lawrence, Secretary,
Treasurer

Abbott and Costello International
Fan Club **[24007]**
PO Box 5566
Fort Wayne, IN 46895-5566
Honor, Bill, Administrator

Confraternity of Penitents **[19826]**
1702 Lumbard St.
Fort Wayne, IN 46803
PH: (260)739-6882
Nugent, Ms. Madeline Pecora, Min.

Family Literacy Alliance **[12246]**
801 E Wayne St.
Fort Wayne, IN 46802
Landram, Mike, Exec. Dir.

The Frank Norris Society **[10371]**
c/o Dr. Eric Carl Link, President
Liberal Arts Bldg., Rm. 153D
College of Arts and Sciences
Indiana University-Purdue University
Fort Wayne
2101 E Coliseum Blvd.
Fort Wayne, IN 46805-1499
PH: (260)481-5750
Link, Dr. Eric Carl, President

Friends of the Third World **[12541]**
611 W Wayne St.
Fort Wayne, IN 46802-2167
PH: (260)422-6821
Fax: (260)422-1650
Goetsch, Jim, Administrator

Gordon Setter Club of America
[21888]
c/o Sharon Hultquist, Membership
Chairperson
13332 Redding Dr.
Fort Wayne, IN 46814-9773
PH: (260)672-3338
Rosskamp, Alison, Mem.

Lissencephaly Network **[15952]**
10408 Bitterroot Ct.
Fort Wayne, IN 46804
PH: (260)432-4310
Fax: (260)432-4310

Macedonian Patriotic Organization of
United States and Canada **[9772]**
124 W Wayne St.
Fort Wayne, IN 46802-2500
PH: (260)422-5900
Fax: (260)422-1348
Lebamoff, Jordan, President

National Association of Forensic
Counselors **[5140]**
PO Box 8827
Fort Wayne, IN 46898
PH: (260)426-7234
Fax: (260)426-7431
Taylor, Ms. Karla, MS, CEO,
President

National Student Exchange **[8608]**
4656 W Jefferson Blvd., Ste. 140
Fort Wayne, IN 46804
PH: (260)436-2634
Fax: (260)436-5676
Worley, Ms. Bette, President

North American Society of Adlerian
Psychology **[16930]**
429 E Dupont Rd., No. 276
Fort Wayne, IN 46825
PH: (260)267-8807
Fax: (260)818-2098

American Red Poll Association
[3709]
PO Box 847
Frankton, IN 46044
PH: (765)425-4515
Rager, John, President

National Muzzle Loading Rifle As-
sociation **[23136]**
State Road 62 Maxine Moss Dr.
Friendship, IN 47021
PH: (812)667-5131
Toll free: 800-745-1493
Fax: (812)667-5136
Voegele, Robert, President

Fourth Freedom Forum **[18719]**
129 S Main St., Ste. 1
Goshen, IN 46526
PH: (574)534-3402

Jacob Hochstetler Family Associa-
tion **[20881]**
PO Box 154
Goshen, IN 46527-0154
Hochstetler, Daniel E., VP

Hovercraft Club of America **[22159]**
PO Box 389
Goshen, IN 46527
Songer, Marquis, President

Mennonite Church USA Historical
Committee **[20328]**
1700 S Main St.
Goshen, IN 46526-4794
PH: (574)523-3080
Toll free: 866-866-2872
Fax: (574)535-7756
McFarland, Colleen, Director

Mennonite Historical Society **[20331]**
1700 Main St.
Goshen, IN 46526
PH: (574)535-7433
Nofziger, Joel, Dir. of Comm.

North American Spotted Draft Horse
Association **[4396]**
17594 US Highway 20
Goshen, IN 46528
PH: (574)821-4226
Douglas, Cindy, President

Electronics Technicians Association
International **[1046]**
5 Depot St.
Greencastle, IN 46135
PH: (765)653-8262
Toll free: 800-288-3824
Fax: (765)653-4287
Maher, Teresa, President

International Wood Collectors
Society **[22480]**
2300 W Rangeline Rd.
Greencastle, IN 46135-7875
PH: (765)653-6483
Hunt, Elaine, President

General Grand Chapter of Royal
Arch Masons International **[19556]**
PO Box 128
Greenfield, IN 46140-0128
PH: (317)467-3600
Fax: (317)467-3899
Gray, Larry, Gen. Sec., Principal

Native American Recreation and
Sport Institute **[23044]**
116 W Osage St.
Greenfield, IN 46140-2429
PH: (317)604-1649
Fax: (317)462-4245
Shepherd, Judith G., Founder

American Association of Dental
Consultants **[1824]**
10032 Wind Hill Dr.
Greenville, IN 47124
PH: (812)923-2600
Toll free: 800-896-0707
Fax: (812)923-2900
Weisenfeld, Dr. Michael D.,
President

College Sports Information Directors
of America **[23223]**
PO Box 7818
Greenwood, IN 46142-6427
PH: (785)691-7708
Poe, Shelly, Director

International Association of Animal
Hospice and Palliative Care
[17647]
2143 Cheviot Ct.
Greenwood, IN 46143
PH: (317)966-0096
Kesnow, Robyn, RVT, President

International Police Work Dog As-
sociation **[5476]**
PO Box 7455
Greenwood, IN 46142-6424
McQueary, Richard L., President

Men for Missions International
[20435]
PO Box A
Greenwood, IN 46142-6599
PH: (317)881-6752
Fax: (317)865-1076
Ellert, Kent, Director

National Federation of Music Clubs
[9972]
1646 Smith Valley Rd.
Greenwood, IN 46142
PH: (317)882-4003
Fax: (317)882-4019
Edwards, Michael, President

One Mission Society [20452]
941 Fry Rd.
Greenwood, IN 46142-1821
PH: (317)888-3333
Fax: (317)888-5275
Long, David, President

Organization of Facial Plastic
Surgery Assistants [14318]
c/o Debbie Carlisle, President
533 E County Line Rd., Ste. 104
Greenwood, IN 46143
PH: (317)859-3810
Fax: (317)851-3817
Carlisle, Debbie, President

National Philosophical Counseling
Association [16985]
c/o Samuel Zinaich, President
Purdue University Calumet
2200 169th St.
Hammond, IN 46323-2094
Zinaich, Samuel, President,
Secretary, Treasurer

American College of Chiropractic
Consultants [14253]
c/o David Cox, Secretary/Treasurer
8219 Kennedy Ave.
Highland, IN 46322
PH: (219)838-3141
Fax: (708)895-2268
Tellin, William, Mem.

Any Soldier [10736]
PO Box 15187
Hoagland, IN 46745-0029

Acres Land Trust [3785]
1802 Chapman Rd.
Huntertown, IN 46748
PH: (260)637-2273
Fax: (260)637-2273
Hammer, Steven, President

North American Coalition for
Christian Admissions Professionals
[7451]
PO Box 5211
Huntington, IN 46750-5211
Toll free: 888-423-2477
Thompson, Mr. Chant, Exec. Dir.

Acacia Fraternity [23878]
8777 Purdue Rd., Ste. 225
Indianapolis, IN 46268
PH: (317)872-8210
Fax: (317)872-8213
Davis, Jeremy, President

African University Foundation [7463]
545 Edgemere Dr.
Indianapolis, IN 46260
PH: (317)252-0123
Toll free: 855-252-0432
Fax: (317)252-0124
Agbor-Baiyee, Baiyee-Mbi, PhD,
CEO, President

Alpha Chi Omega [23941]
5939 Castle Creek Pky.
North Dr.

Indianapolis, IN 46250
PH: (317)579-5050
Fax: (317)579-5051
Fox, Gina, Assoc. Dir.

Alpha Chi Sigma Fraternity, Inc.
[23703]
6296 Rucker Rd., Ste. B
Indianapolis, IN 46220
PH: (317)357-5944
Toll free: 800-252-4369
Fax: (317)351-9702
Johanns, Patrick J., Leader

Alpha Epsilon Pi [19663]
8815 Wesleyan Rd.
Indianapolis, IN 46268-1185
PH: (317)876-1913
Fax: (317)876-1057
Borans, Mr. Andrew S., Exec. Dir.

Alpha Epsilon Pi [23883]
8815 Wesleyan Rd.
Indianapolis, IN 46268-1185
PH: (317)876-1913
Fax: (317)876-1057
Borans, Mr. Andrew S., Exec. Dir.

Alpha Gamma Delta [23943]
8710 N Meridian St.
Indianapolis, IN 46260
PH: (317)663-4200
Fax: (317)663-4210
Bright Faust, Wendy, Exec. Dir.

Alpha Kappa Psi [23687]
7801 E 88th St.
Indianapolis, IN 46256-1233
PH: (317)872-1553
Fax: (317)872-1567
Sultan, Alexander T., President

Alpha Sigma Alpha [23946]
9002 Vincennes Cir.
Indianapolis, IN 46268-3018
PH: (317)871-2920
Fax: (317)871-2924
Slivinski, Krystal Geyer, Exec. Dir.

Alpha Sigma Tau [23947]
3334 Founders Rd.
Indianapolis, IN 46268
PH: (317)613-7575
Toll free: 877-505-1899
Fax: (317)613-7111
Covington, Chris, President

Alpha Tau Omega [23888]
1 N Pennsylvania St., 12th Fl.
Indianapolis, IN 46204
PH: (317)684-1865
Fax: (317)684-1862
Smiley, Wynn R., CEO

Alpha Xi Delta Women's Fraternity
[23948]
8702 Founders Rd.
Indianapolis, IN 46268
PH: (317)872-3500
Fax: (317)872-2947
Gallivan, Elysia Balster, Exec. Dir.

Alternative & Direct Investment
Securities Association [1688]
Two Meridian Plz.
10401 N Meridian St., Ste. 202
Indianapolis, IN 46290
Toll free: 866-353-8422
Harrison, John, Exec. Dir., CEO

American Academy of Osteopathy
[16501]
3500 DePauw Blvd., Ste. 1100
Indianapolis, IN 46268-1138
PH: (317)879-1881
Fax: (317)879-0563
Quarles, Sherri, Exec. Dir.

American Association of Directors of
Psychiatric Residency Training
[16811]
c/o Sara Brewer, Administrative
Director
PO Box 30618
Indianapolis, IN 46230
PH: (317)407-1173
Boland, Bob, President

American Association of Orthopaedic
Executives [16461]
6602 E 17th St., Ste. 112
Indianapolis, IN 46250
Toll free: 800-247-9699
Fax: (317)805-0340
Kidd, Jim, President

American College of Sports
Medicine [17274]
401 W Michigan St.
Indianapolis, IN 46202-3233
PH: (317)637-9200
Toll free: 800-486-5643
Fax: (317)634-7817
Armstrong, Lawrence E., President

American Legion [20687]
700 N Pennsylvania St.
Indianapolis, IN 46206
PH: (317)630-1200
Fax: (317)630-1223
Bozella, Ralph, Chairman

American Legion Auxiliary [21037]
8945 N Meridian St., Ste. 200
Indianapolis, IN 46260
PH: (317)569-4500
Fax: (317)569-4502
Davis, Mary, VP

American Legion Auxiliary Girls Na-
tion [17851]
8945 N Meridian St., Ste. 200
Indianapolis, IN 46260
PH: (317)569-4500
Fax: (317)569-4502
Jefford, Janet, President

American Legion Baseball [22543]
700 N Pennsylvania St.
Indianapolis, IN 46204-1129
PH: (317)630-1200
Fax: (317)630-1223

American Mold Builders Association
[1707]
7321 Shadeland Station Way, No.
285
Indianapolis, IN 46256
PH: (317)436-3102
Fax: (317)913-2445
Mcphee, Justin, VP

American Pianists Association
[22245]
4603 Clarendon Rd., Ste. 030
Indianapolis, IN 46208
PH: (317)940-9945
Harrison, Joel, Art Dir., CEO,
President

American World War II Orphans
Network [10444]
5745 Lee Rd.
Indianapolis, IN 46216-2063
PH: (540)310-0750
Mix, Ann Bennett, Founder

American Y-Flyer Yacht Racing As-
sociation [22596]
7349 Scarborough Blvd., E Dr.
Indianapolis, IN 46256-2052
PH: (518)831-1321
Haile, Dan, President

AMOA National Dart Association
[22767]
9100 Purdue Rd., Ste. 200
Indianapolis, IN 46268
Toll free: 800-808-9884
Gerlach, Alvin, President

Anesthesia Patient Safety Founda-
tion [13697]
Bldg. 1, Ste. 2
8007 S Meridian St.
Indianapolis, IN 46217-2922
Fax: (317)888-1482
Stoeolting, Robert K., MD, President

Anti-Poverty Initiative [17803]
10444 Kensington Way
Indianapolis, IN 46234
PH: (317)504-4528
Ujereh, Sebastine, Director, Founder

Association of African Women
Scholars [8513]
c/o Obioma Nnaemeka, President
Cavanaugh Hall, Rm. 001C
Indiana University
425 University Blvd.
Indianapolis, IN 46202
PH: (317)278-2038
(317)274-0062
Fax: (317)274-2347
Nnaemeka, Dr. Obioma, President

Association for Applied Sport
Psychology [17279]
8365 Keystone Crossing, Ste. 107
Indianapolis, IN 46240
PH: (317)205-9225
Fax: (317)205-9481
Lindeman, Kent, Exec. Dir.

Association of Disciple Musicians
[9876]
c/o Brenda Tyler
Disciples Home Missions
PO Box 1986
Indianapolis, IN 46206
PH: (317)713-2652
Showalter, Jeanette, President

Association for Humanist Sociology
[7181]
Esch Hall, Rm. 230
University of Indianapolis
1400 E Hanna Ave.
Indianapolis, IN 46227
PH: (317)788-3365
Koeber, Chuck, President

Association for Research on
Nonprofit Organizations and
Voluntary Action [13285]
550 W North St., Ste. 301
Indianapolis, IN 46202
PH: (317)684-2120
Fax: (317)684-2128
Siddiqui, Shariq, Exec. Dir.

Association of Retired Americans
[12755]
6505 E 82nd St., No. 130
Indianapolis, IN 46250
Toll free: 800-806-6160
Fax: (317)915-2510
Smith, John K., President, CEO

Association for University and College Counseling Center Directors
[7686]
1101 N Delaware St., Ste. 200
Indianapolis, IN 46202
PH: (317)635-4755
Sharma, Micky M., President

Beta Chi Theta National Fraternity,
Inc. [23889]
5868 E 71st St., Ste. E-120
Indianapolis, IN 46220-4081
PH: (847)238-2244
Patel, Sheevum, President

Building Tomorrow [12464]
407 Fulton St.
Indianapolis, IN 46202
PH: (317)632-3545
Srour, George, Exec. Dir., Founder

Christian Feminism Today [20118]
PO Box 78171
Indianapolis, IN 46278
Weddle Irons, Kendra, Coord.

Christian Missionary Fellowship
[20400]
5525 E 82nd St.
Indianapolis, IN 46250
PH: (317)578-2700
Fax: (317)578-2827
Priest, Doug, PhD, Exec. Dir.

Circle K International [12886]
3636 Woodview Trace
Indianapolis, IN 46268
PH: (317)875-8755
(317)879-0204
Toll free: 800-KIWANIS
Fax: (317)879-0204
Stewart, Jason, President

Citizens Flag Alliance [5102]
PO Box 7197
Indianapolis, IN 46207-7197
PH: (317)630-1384
Fax: (317)630-1369

Clinica Esperanza [15138]
PO Box 44510
Indianapolis, IN 46244
Stranges, Peggy, Founder

Clinical Exercise Physiology Association [16767]
401 W Michigan St.
Indianapolis, IN 46202
Coyne, Brian, President

Combined Council of America's
Credit Unions [947]
7101 E 56th St.
Indianapolis, IN 46226
Garmon, Ann, President

Congo Helping Hands [10475]
8170 Hague Rd.
Indianapolis, IN 46256-1649
Collins, Woody M., President

Cornea Research Foundation of
America [15642]
9002 N Meridian St., Ste. 212
Indianapolis, IN 46260
PH: (317)814-2993
Fax: (317)814-2806
Price, Dr. Francis, Jr., President,
Founder

Council on Christian Unity [20059]
PO Box 1986
Indianapolis, IN 46206
PH: (317)635-3100
(317)713-2585
Welsh, Rev. Robert K., President

Custom Electronic Design Installa-
tion Association [987]
7150 Winton Dr., Ste. 300
Indianapolis, IN 46268
PH: (317)328-4336
Toll free: 800-669-5329
Pexton, Larry, Exec. Ofc.

The Dameron-Damron Family Association [20852]
1326 N Audubon Rd.
Indianapolis, IN 46219
Guthrie, Davonna, Treasurer

Delta Upsilon [23898]
8705 Founders Rd.
Indianapolis, IN 46268
PH: (317)875-8900
Fax: (317)876-1629
Taylor, Richard, Chairman

Diagnostic Marketing Association
[2278]
10293 N Meridian St., Ste. 175
Indianapolis, IN 46290

PH: (201)653-2420
Fax: (201)653-5705
Robinson, Peggy, President

Digital Pathology Association
[16582]
10293 N Meridian St., Ste. 175
Indianapolis, IN 46290
PH: (317)816-1630
Toll free: 877-824-4085
Fax: (317)816-1633
Chlipala, Liz, Treasurer

Disciples Ecumenical Consultative
Council [20023]
c/o Council on Christian Unity
PO Box 1986
Indianapolis, IN 46206
PH: (317)713-2585
Welsh, Dr. Robert K., Gen. Sec.

Disciples Peace Fellowship [18781]
PO Box 1986
Indianapolis, IN 46206-1986
PH: (317)713-2666
Brock, John, Treasurer

Drum Corps International, Inc.
[9901]
110 W Washington St., Ste. C
Indianapolis, IN 46204
PH: (317)275-1212
Acheson, Daniel E., CEO, Exec. Dir.

Federation of American Aquarium
Societies [6715]
c/o Hedy Padgett, Membership Chair
4816 E 64th St.
Indianapolis, IN 46220-4728
PH: (847)478-8110
(847)732-0526
Borstein, Rick, President

Fellowship of Associates of Medical
Evangelism [20324]
4545 Southeastern Ave.
Indianapolis, IN 46203
PH: (317)358-2480
Warren, Bill, Exec. Dir.

Firehawk Association of America
[21382]
6446 Bonneville Dr.
Indianapolis, IN 46237
Thomas, Wayne E.A., Founder

Forty and Eight [20688]
250 E 38th St.
Indianapolis, IN 46205
PH: (317)639-1879
(317)634-1804
Fax: (317)632-9365
Taylor, Terri, Exec. Sec.

Fraternity Communications Association [23712]
c/o KB Parrish
6840 Eagle Highlands Way
Indianapolis, IN 46254
Lyons, Jesse, President

Fraternity Executives Association
[23756]
3201 E 56th St.
Indianapolis, IN 46220
PH: (317)490-1924
Smiley, Wynn R., President

Friends of Honduran Children
[10985]
PO Box 501213
Indianapolis, IN 46250
Stevens, John, Chairman

Give Hope, Fight Poverty [10997]
2436 N Alabama St.
Indianapolis, IN 46205
Todt, Annie Elble, PhD, Founder,
Exec. Dir.

GLAD Alliance [20181]
PO Box 44400
Indianapolis, IN 46244-0400
PH: (317)721-5230
Adolphson, Rev. Dan, Officer

Honda Sport Touring Association
[22224]
4040 E 82nd St., Ste. C9
PMB 331
Indianapolis, IN 46250-4209
PH: (317)890-8858
(615)758-3734
Fax: (317)841-0111
Brickner, David W., President

The International Bengal Cat Society
[3679]
7915 S Emerson Ave., Ste. B 142
Indianapolis, IN 46237
Prince, Nancy, VP

International Disciples Women's
Ministries [20643]
1099 N Meridian St., Ste. 700
Indianapolis, IN 46206-1986
PH: (317)635-3100
Jacobs, Mary, President

International Society for Frontotemporal Dementias [15947]
1124 Frederick Dr. S
Indianapolis, IN 46260
Ghetti, Bernardino, MD, President

International Strabismological As-
sociation [17288]
1160 W Michigan St., No. 220
Indianapolis, IN 46202-5209
Fax: (317)328-8864
Ozkan, Seyhan, President

International Ticketing Association
[1146]
5868 E 71st St., Ste. E-367
Indianapolis, IN 46290
PH: (212)629-4036
Ballentine, Debbie, Director

ION Inc. [2011]
5235 Decatur Blvd.
Indianapolis, IN 46241
Toll free: 800-338-3463
Sandlin, Jack, Officer

Just Plain Folks Music Organization
[2427]
5327 Kit Dr.
Indianapolis, IN 46237
Whitney, Brian Austin, Founder

Kappa Alpha Theta [23956]
8740 Founders Rd.
Indianapolis, IN 46268
Toll free: 800-526-1870
Fax: (317)876-1925
Corridan, Betsy Sierk, Exec. Dir.

Kappa Delta Pi [23730]
3707 Woodview Trace
Indianapolis, IN 46268
PH: (317)871-4900
Toll free: 800-284-3167
Fax: (317)704-2323
Snodgress, Faye, Exec. Dir.

Key Club International [12893]
3636 Woodview Trace
Indianapolis, IN 46268-3196
PH: (317)875-8755
Toll free: 800-KIW-ANIS
Fax: (317)879-0204
Spice, Amanda, Director

Kiwanis International [12894]
3636 Woodview Trace
Indianapolis, IN 46268-3196
PH: (317)875-8755
Toll free: 800-549-2647
Fax: (317)879-0204
Erickson, Jane, Officer

The Malawi Project, Inc. [10481]
3314 Van Tassel Dr.
Indianapolis, IN 46240-3555
Bhagwandin, Bryon, Chmn. of the
Bd.

Milestone Car Society [21433]
626 N Park Ave.
Indianapolis, IN 46204
PH: (317)636-9900
Miller, Shawn, Contact

Music for All, Inc. [9958]
39 W Jackson Pl., Ste. 150
Indianapolis, IN 46225
PH: (317)636-2263
Toll free: 800-848-2263
Fax: (317)524-6200
Martin, Eric, CEO, President

National Art Museum of Sport [8872]
PO Box 441155
Indianapolis, IN 46244
PH: (317)931-8600
McNeely, Kathleen, Treasurer

National Association of Independent
Real Estate Brokers [2870]
7102 Mardyke Ln.
Indianapolis, IN 46226
PH: (317)547-4679
Conner, Gary, Exec. Dir.

National Association of Institutional
Agribusiness [3527]
c/o Lin Paul, Secretary
PO Box 338
Indianapolis, IN 46201
PH: (317)796-2588

National Association of Mutual Insur-
ance Cos [1898]
3601 Vincennes Rd.
Indianapolis, IN 46268
PH: (317)875-5250
Fax: (317)879-8408
Chamness, Charles, President

National Association of Orthopaedic
Technologists [15693]
8365 Keystone Crossing, Ste. 107
Indianapolis, IN 46240
PH: (317)205-9484
Fax: (317)205-9481
Davis, Bruce, Exec. Dir.

National Collegiate Athletic Associa-
tion [23241]
700 W Washington St.
Indianapolis, IN 46206
PH: (317)917-6222
Fax: (317)917-6888
Emmert, Dr. Mark A., President

National Council of Acoustical
Consultants [556]
9100 Purdue Rd., Ste. 200
Indianapolis, IN 46268
PH: (317)328-0642
Fax: (317)328-4629
Williams, Jackie, CPA, Exec. Dir.

National Council on Educating Black
Children [7468]
3737 N Meridian St., Ste. 102
Indianapolis, IN 46208
PH: (317)283-9081
Daniels, Diana, Exec. Dir.

National Council on Public History
[9499]
127 Cavanaugh Hall
425 University Blvd.
Indianapolis, IN 46202
PH: (317)274-2716
Moore, Patrick, President

National Episcopal AIDS Coalition **[10548]**
6050 N Meridian St.
Indianapolis, IN 46208-1549
Toll free: 800-588-6628
Ellis, Mr. Matthew, Exec. Dir.

National Federation of State High
School Associations **[23244]**
PO Box 690
Indianapolis, IN 46206-0690
PH: (317)972-6900
Fax: (317)822-5700
Wulkow, Rick, President

National FFA Organization **[7479]**
6060 FFA Dr.
Indianapolis, IN 46278-1370
PH: (317)802-6060
Toll free: 888-332-2668
Brown, Steve A., Advisor, Chmn. of
the Bd.

National Guard Executive Directors
Association **[5610]**
Bldg. 8
2002 S Holt Rd.
indianapolis, IN 46241
PH: (317)247-3301
Sturm, Mike, President

National Interscholastic Athletic
Administrators Association **[8432]**
9100 Keystone Xing, Ste. 650
Indianapolis, IN 46240
PH: (317)587-1450
Fax: (317)587-1451
Whitehead, Bruce, CMAA, Exec. Dir.

National Network of Estate Planning
Attorneys **[5044]**
3500 DePauw Blvd., Ste. 2090
Indianapolis, IN 46268-6139
Toll free: 800-638-8681

National Panhellenic Conference
[23762]
3901 W 86th St., Ste. 398
Indianapolis, IN 46268
PH: (317)872-3185
Fax: (317)872-3192
Weatherford, Dani, Exec. Dir.

NFHS Coaches Association **[22736]**
c/o National Federation of State
High Schools
PO Box 690
Indianapolis, IN 46206
PH: (317)972-6900
Fax: (317)822-5700
Musselman, Gary, President

NFHS Music Association **[8388]**
c/o National Federation of State
High School Associations
PO Box 690
Indianapolis, IN 46206-0690
PH: (317)972-6900
Fax: (317)822-5700
Summers, Kent, Asst. Dir.

NFHS Officials Association **[23271]**
PO Box 690
Indianapolis, IN 46206
PH: (317)972-6900
Fax: (317)822-5700
Mezzanotte, Tom, President

NFHS Speech, Debate and Theatre
Association **[8601]**
PO Box 690
Indianapolis, IN 46206
PH: (317)972-6900
Fax: (317)822-5700
Gardner, Bob, Exec. Dir.

NFHS Spirit Association **[22737]**
National Federation of State High
School Associations

PO Box 690
Indianapolis, IN 46206
PH: (317)972-6900
Fax: (317)822-5700
Gardner, Bob, Exec. Dir.

The Noah Worcester Dermatological
Society **[14509]**
8365 Keystone Crossing, Ste. 107
Indianapolis, IN 46240
PH: (317)257-5907
Fax: (317)205-9481
Davis, Bruce, Exec. Dir.

North-American Interfraternity
Conference **[23763]**
3901 W 86th St., Ste. 390
Indianapolis, IN 46268
PH: (317)872-1112
Fax: (317)872-1134
Horras, Jud, President, CEO

North American Retail Hardware As-
sociation **[1573]**
136 N Delaware St.
Indianapolis, IN 46204
PH: (317)275-9400
Toll free: 800-772-4424
Fax: (317)275-9403

Nurses for a Healthier Tomorrow
[16169]
Honor Society of Nursing, Sigma
Theta Tau International
550 W North St.
Indianapolis, IN 46202
Johnson, Luci Baines, Chairperson

The Osteopathic Cranial Academy
[16524]
3535 E 96th St., Ste. 101
Indianapolis, IN 46240
PH: (317)581-0411
Fax: (317)580-9299
Dunn, Sidney N., Exec. Dir.

Partnership for Philanthropic Plan-
ning **[1472]**
233 McCrea St., Ste. 300
Indianapolis, IN 46225
PH: (317)269-6274
Fax: (317)269-6268
Kenyon, Michael, President, CEO

Pentecostal Assemblies of the World
[20517]
3939 N Meadows Dr.
Indianapolis, IN 46205-3113
PH: (317)547-9541
Fax: (317)543-0513
Ellis, Bishop Charles H., III, Bishop

Percussive Arts Society **[9995]**
110 W Washington St., Ste. A
Indianapolis, IN 46204
PH: (317)974-4488
Fax: (317)974-4499
Sircy, Otice, Curator, Librarian

Phi Epsilon Kappa **[23848]**
901 W New York St.
Indianapolis, IN 46202
PH: (317)627-8745
Fax: (317)278-2041

Phi Kappa Theta National Fraternity
[23914]
3901 W 86th St., Ste. 360
Indianapolis, IN 46268
PH: (317)872-9934
    (317)536-4747
Riggs, Robert, Exec. VP

Phi Rho Sigma Medical Society
[23820]
PO Box 90264
Indianapolis, IN 46290
Righter, Elisabeth, President

Phi Sigma Kappa **[23916]**
2925 E 96th St.
Indianapolis, IN 46240
PH: (317)573-5420
Toll free: 888-846-6851
Fax: (317)573-5430
Carey, Michael, Exec. VP

Pony of the Americas Club **[4402]**
3828 S Emerson Ave.
Indianapolis, IN 46203
PH: (317)788-0107
Fax: (317)788-8974
Peaton, Diana, President

Professional Association for
Customer Engagement **[2299]**
8500 Keystone Crossing, Ste. 480
Indianapolis, IN 46240-2460
PH: (317)816-9336
Grudzinski, Phil, CEO, President

Professional Insurance Communica-
tors of America Inc. **[775]**
PO Box 68700
Indianapolis, IN 46268-0700
PH: (317)446-9367
Wright, Janet E.H., APR, Asst. Sec.,
Asst. Treas.

Psi Upsilon **[23923]**
3003 E 96th St.
Indianapolis, IN 46240
PH: (317)571-1833
Fox, Thomas J., Exec. Dir.

Religious Conference Management
Association **[2337]**
7702 Woodland Dr., Ste. 120
Indianapolis, IN 46278
PH: (317)632-1888
Fax: (317)632-7909
Schmidt, Harry, President, CEO

Roller Skating Association
International **[23153]**
6905 Corporate Dr.
Indianapolis, IN 46278
PH: (317)347-2626
Fax: (317)347-2636
Bentley, Robert, President

Safe Sitter **[10813]**
8604 Allisonville Rd., Ste. 248
Indianapolis, IN 46250-1597
PH: (317)596-5001
Fax: (317)596-5008
Keener, Dr. Patricia A., Founder

Sigma Alpha Mu **[23925]**
8701 Founders Rd.
Indianapolis, IN 46268
PH: (317)789-8338
Fax: (317)824-1505
Huston, Andy, Exec. Dir.

Sigma Delta Chi Foundation **[23796]**
3909 N Meridian St.
Indianapolis, IN 46208
PH: (317)927-8000
Fax: (317)920-4789
Skeel, Mr. Joe, Exec. Dir.

Sigma Theta Tau International
[23839]
550 W North St.
Indianapolis, IN 46202
PH: (317)634-8171
Toll free: 888-634-7575
Thompson, Patricia E., RN, CEO

Society of Broadcast Engineers
[482]
9102 N Meridian St., Ste. 150
Indianapolis, IN 46260
PH: (317)846-9000
Fax: (317)846-9120
Scherer, Chriss, President, Div. Dir.

Society for Free Radical Biology and
Medicine **[6118]**
8365 Keystone Crossing, Ste. 107
Indianapolis, IN 46240-2685
PH: (317)205-9482
Fax: (317)205-9481
Lindeman, Kent, Exec. Dir.

Society of Indiana Pioneers **[21087]**
140 N Senate Ave.
Indianapolis, IN 46204-2207
PH: (317)233-6588
Miller, Michael H., President

Society of Neurological Surgeons
[16068]
c/o Nicholas M. Barbaro, MD,
Secretary
Dept. of Neurosurgery
Goodman Campbell Brain & Spine
Indiana University
355 W 16th St., GH 5100
Indianapolis, IN 46202
PH: (317)396-1234
Harbaugh, Dr. Robert E., President

Society for Nutrition Education and
Behavior **[16239]**
9100 Purdue Rd., Ste. 200
Indianapolis, IN 46268
PH: (317)328-4627
Toll free: 800-235-6690
Fax: (317)280-8527
Williams, Jackie, CPA, Exec. Dir.

Society of Ortho-Bionomy
International **[13656]**
5335 N Tacoma St., Ste. 21G
Indianapolis, IN 46220
PH: (317)536-0064
Fax: (317)536-0065

Society for Pediatric Dermatology
[14514]
8365 Keystone Crossing, Ste. 107
Indianapolis, IN 46240
PH: (317)202-0224
Fax: (317)205-9481
Lindeman, Kent, Exec. Dir.

Society of Professional Journalists
[2723]
Eugene Pulliam National Journalism
Ctr.
3909 N Meridian St.
Indianapolis, IN 46208
PH: (317)927-8000
Fax: (317)920-4789
Skeel, Joe, Exec. Dir.

Society for the Scientific Study of
Religion **[20553]**
Indiana University - Purdue
University Indianapolis
Cavanaugh Hall 417
425 University Blvd.
Indianapolis, IN 46202-5148
PH: (317)278-6491
Yang, Fenggang, President

Sociologists' AIDS Network **[13561]**
c/o Neal Carnes, Treasurer
3813 Cooper Ln.
Indianapolis, IN 46228
Labov, Teresa G.

Software in the Public Interest
[6287]
PO Box 501248
Indianapolis, IN 46250-6248
Michlmayr, Martin, Secretary

Sons of the American Legion
[21044]
700 N Pennsylvania St.
Indianapolis, IN 46206
PH: (317)630-1205
Fax: (317)630-1223
Collier, Kevin L., Cmdr.

Sump and Sewage Pump
  Manufacturers Association **[589]**
c/o Blake Jeffery, Managing Director
PO Box 44071
Indianapolis, IN 46244
PH: (317)636-0278
Stayton, Scott, VP

Tau Kappa Epsilon **[23935]**
7439 Woodland Dr., Ste. 100
Indianapolis, IN 46278
PH: (317)872-6533
Fax: (317)875-8353
Baker, Alex, CIO

Teen Association of Model Railroaders **[22190]**
3645 Toronto Ct.
Indianapolis, IN 46268

United Council of Corvette Clubs
  [21508]
PO Box 532605
Indianapolis, IN 46253
Tunstall, Larry, President

United Methodist Association of
  Ministers with Disabilities **[20347]**
3645 Toronto Ct.
Indianapolis, IN 46268
Edwards, Greg, Treasurer

United States Magnetic Materials
  Association **[6877]**
c/o Ed Richardson, President
1120 E 23rd St.
Indianapolis, IN 46206
PH: (317)418-0137
Richardson, Ed, President

U.S.A. Track and Field **[23315]**
132 E Washington St., Ste. 800
Indianapolis, IN 46204
PH: (317)261-0500
Fax: (317)261-0481
Hightower, Stephanie, V. Chmn. of
  the Bd., President

USA Diving **[22814]**
1060 N Capitol Ave., Ste. E-310
Indianapolis, IN 46204
PH: (317)237-5252
Fax: (317)237-5257
Paul, Linda, President, CEO

USA Football **[22871]**
45 N Pennsylvania St., Ste. 700
Indianapolis, IN 46204
PH: (317)614-7750
Toll free: 877-536-6822
Hallenbeck, Scott, Exec. Dir.

USA Gymnastics **[22903]**
132 E Washington St., Ste. 700
Indianapolis, IN 46204-3674
PH: (317)237-5050
    (317)829-5667
Toll free: 800-345-4719
Laughon, Carisa, Director

USA Synchro **[23291]**
132 E Washington St., Ste. 820
Indianapolis, IN 46204
PH: (317)237-5700
Fax: (317)237-5705
McGowan, Judy, President

Women's Philanthropy Institute
  [12501]
c/o Lilly Family School of
  Philanthropy, Indiana University
University Hall, Ste. 3000
301 N University Blvd.
Indianapolis, IN
PH: (317)274-4200
    (317)278-8990
Fax: (317)684-8900
Rooney, Patrick, PhD, Assoc. Dean

Zeta Beta Tau **[23939]**
3905 Vincennes Rd., Ste. 100
Indianapolis, IN 46268
PH: (317)334-1898
Fax: (317)334-1899
Bolotin, Laurence A., Exec. Dir.

Zeta Tau Alpha **[23967]**
3450 Founders Rd.
Indianapolis, IN 46268
PH: (317)872-0540
Fax: (317)876-3948
Carpenter, Carolyn Hoff, President

American Gourd Society **[22072]**
PO Box 2186
Kokomo, IN 46904-2186
Sandgren, Hudi, President

National Association of Breweriana
  Advertising **[21689]**
1585 W Tiffany Woods Dr.
La Porte, IN 46350-7599
PH: (219)325-8811
Ferguson, John, President

International Society for Quality-of-
  Life Studies **[6042]**
c/o Rhonda Phillips, President
Windsor Halls, Duhme Rm. 134
205 N Russell St. W
Lafayette, IN 47906-4238
PH: (765)496-3021
Phillips, Rhonda, President

National Council of Field Labor
  Locals **[23434]**
8 N 3rd St., Rm. 207
Lafayette, IN 47901
PH: (765)423-2152
Fax: (765)423-2194
DeMay, Denny, President

National Federation of Professional
  Trainers **[23336]**
PO Box 4579
Lafayette, IN 47903-4579
Toll free: 800-729-6378
Fax: (765)471-7369
Clark, Ron, CEO, Founder

American Harlequin Rabbit Club
  [4589]
c/o Pamela Granderson, Secretary/
  Treasurer
14991 Opera Rd.
Leopold, IN 47551
Byerley, Patti, President

International Carnival Glass Associa-
  tion **[21671]**
17186 Old State Road 37
Leopold, IN 47551
PH: (812)843-4611
Pitman, Brian, President

American Bonsai Society **[22066]**
PO Box 6
Lynnville, IN 47619
PH: (812)922-5451
Buehler, George, Treasurer

The Quilters Hall of Fame **[21781]**
926 S Washington St.
Marion, IN 46953
PH: (765)664-9333
Divine, Deborah, President

World Gospel Mission **[20477]**
3783 E State Road 18
Marion, IN 46952-0948
PH: (765)664-7731
Fax: (765)671-7230
Harriman, Dr. Hubert, President

American Camp Association **[22718]**
5000 State Road 67 N
Martinsville, IN 46151-7902

PH: (765)342-8456
Toll free: 800-428-2267
Fax: (765)342-2065
Bolger, Tisha, President

Association of Software Profession-
  als **[6272]**
PO Box 1522
Martinsville, IN 46151
PH: (765)349-4740
Fax: (815)301-3756
Holler, Mr. Richard, Exec. Dir.

American Oxford Sheep Association
  [4658]
9305 Zollman Rd.
Marysville, IN 47141
PH: (812)256-3478
Fax: (812)256-3478
Franzen, Jay, VP

Popular Rotorcraft Association
  [21244]
12296 West 600 South
Mentone, IN 46539
PH: (574)353-7227
Fax: (574)353-7021
Rountree, John

World Clown Association **[21603]**
PO Box 12215
Merrillville, IN 46411-2215
PH: (219)487-5317
Toll free: 800-336-7922
Fax: (765)807-8649
Christensen, Randy, President

HitchHikers of America International
  [22426]
58800 Executive Dr.
Mishawaka, IN 46544-6808
PH: (574)258-0571
Fax: (574)259-7105

Jayco Travel Club **[22428]**
58800 Executive Dr.
Mishawaka, IN 46544
PH: (574)258-0571
Toll free: 800-262-5178
Fax: (574)259-7105

Missionary Church Historical Society
  [20027]
Bethel College
1001 Bethel Cir.
Mishawaka, IN 46545
PH: (574)807-7000
Toll free: 800-422-4101
Cramer, Dr. Steven R., President

SunnyTravelers **[22433]**
58800 Executive Dr.
Mishawaka, IN 46544
PH: (574)258-0571
Toll free: 800-262-5178
Fax: (574)259-7105
Johnson, Patty, Founder

USS Nitro AE-2/AE-23 Association
  [4976]
PO BOX 1254
PO Box 1254
Mishawaka, IN 46546-1254
Timmons, James, President

Academy of Model Aeronautics
  [21210]
5161 E Memorial Dr.
Muncie, IN 47302
Toll free: 800-435-9262
Fax: (765)289-4248
Mathewson, Dave, Exec. Dir.

Cracker Jack Collectors Association
  [21644]
c/o Linda Farris, Membership
  Chairperson
4908 N Holborn Dr.

Muncie, IN 47304
Jaramillo, Alex, Jr., President

Lambda Alpha **[23676]**
Dept. of Anthropology
Ball State University
Burkhardt Bldg., Rm. 315
2000 W University Ave.
Muncie, IN 47306
PH: (765)285-1575
Fax: (765)285-2163
Groover, Dr. Mark, Exec. Sec.

Lambda Iota Tau **[23808]**
Ball State University
Dept. of English
2000 W University Ave.
Muncie, IN 47306-0460
PH: (765)285-8370
Fax: (765)285-3765
Clark-Flynn, Mary, Contact

American Board of Hair Restoration
  Surgery **[14898]**
8840 Calumet Ave., Ste 205
Munster, IN 46321
PH: (219)836-5858
Fax: (219)836-5525
Canalia, Peter B., JD, Exec. Dir.

Nikon Historical Society **[10143]**
RJR Publishing Inc.
PO Box 3213
Munster, IN 46321
Rotoloni, Robert J., Editor, Publisher

Norrie Disease Association **[14609]**
PO Box 3244
Munster, IN 46321-0244
Maguire, Bruce, President

Lifespan Resources **[10515]**
33 State St., 3rd Fl.
New Albany, IN 47151-0995
PH: (812)948-8330
Toll free: 888-948-8330
Fax: (812)948-0147
Stormes, Keith E., Exec. Dir.

Doll Costumer's Guild **[22001]**
PO Box 247
New Harmony, IN 47631
PH: (812)319-5300
Fax: (812)682-3815

American Maltese Association
  [21813]
c/o LaDonna Mosley, President
10029 N River Rd.
New Haven, IN 46774-9450
PH: (260)493-3413
Mosley, LaDonna, President

Natural Colored Wool Growers As-
  sociation **[4676]**
PO Box 406
New Palestine, IN 46163
PH: (317)861-4795
Merlau, John, President

Association of Life Insurance
  Counsel **[5312]**
14350 Mundy Dr., Ste. 800, No. 258
Noblesville, IN 46060
PH: (317)774-7500
Fax: (317)614-7147
Rasmussen, Teresa J., President

Destiny Rescue **[10954]**
PO Box 752
North Webster, IN 46555
PH: (574)457-2470
Kirwan, Tony, President, Founder

Association of Architecture School
  Librarians **[9682]**
c/o Jennifer Parker, Teasurer
117 Bond Hall

School of Architecture
University of Notre Dame
Notre Dame, IN 46556
PH: (574)631-9401
Palacios, Mar González, President

Center for Civil and Human Rights
[12026]
2150 Eck Hall of Law
Notre Dame Law School
Notre Dame, IN 46556
PH: (574)631-8555
Fax: (574)631-8702
McAward, Jennifer Mason, Dir.
(Actg.)

Fischoff National Chamber Music
Association **[9908]**
303 Brownson Hall
Notre Dame, IN 46556
PH: (574)631-0984
Divine, Ann, Exec. Dir.

History of Science Society **[9487]**
University of Notre Dame
440 Geddes Hall
Notre Dame, IN 46556
PH: (574)631-1194
Fax: (574)631-1533
Malone, Robert Jay, Exec. Dir.

Holy Cross Mission Center **[19841]**
PO Box 543
Notre Dame, IN 46556
PH: (574)631-5477
Olobo, Rev. Leonard, CSC, Director

Joan B. Kroc Institute for
International Peace Studies
[18801]
100 Hesburgh Center for
International Studies
University of Notre Dame
Notre Dame, IN 46556-5677
PH: (574)631-6970
Fax: (574)631-6973
Culbertson, Hal, Exec. Dir.

Northern Nut Growers Association
[4512]
c/o Jeanne Romero-Severson,
Treasurer
PO Box 489
Notre Dame, IN 46556
Fax: (203)974-8502
Miller, Greg, Director

Society for Hindu-Christian Studies
[20578]
232 Malloy Hall
University of Notre Dame
Notre Dame, IN 46556
PH: (574)631-7128
Bauman, Chad, President

Nigerian Dairy Goat Association
[4280]
1927 E 500 N
Ossian, IN 46777
PH: (260)307-1984
Craft, James, President

United States Flag Football for the
Deaf **[22802]**
Pendelton, IN
PH: (317)288-3590
Hamlow, Eric, Commissioner

Horizon International **[11040]**
350 JH Walker Dr.
Pendleton, IN 46064-0180
PH: (765)778-1016
Toll free: 866-778-7020
Fax: (765)778-9490
Pearson, Robert W., CEO, Founder

Chimney Safety Institute of America
[2126]
2155 Commercial Dr.
Plainfield, IN 46168

PH: (317)837-5362
Fax: (317)837-5365
Kelly, Frances, Exec. Dir.

Fiqh Council of North America
[20217]
PO Box 38
Plainfield, IN 46168
PH: (317)839-8157
Fax: (317)839-1840
Siddiqi, Dr. Muzammil, Chairman

Islamic Society of North America
[9606]
6555 S County Road 750 E
Plainfield, IN 46168
PH: (317)839-8157
Magid, Mohamed, President

National Chimney Sweep Guild
[2137]
2155 Commercial Dr.
Plainfield, IN 46168
PH: (317)837-1500
Fax: (317)837-5365
Biswell, Jeremy, President

Precision Aerobatics Model Pilots
Association **[21245]**
PO Box 320
Plainfield, IN 46168-0320
Adamisin, Dennis, President

Kustoms of America **[22399]**
5126 E ST RT 26
Portland, IN 47371
Auker, Jim, President

Friends United Meeting **[20171]**
101 Quaker Hill Dr.
Richmond, IN 47374-1926
PH: (765)962-7573
Muhanji, John, Director

Gene Stratton-Porter Memorial
Society **[9099]**
1205 Pleasant Pt.
Rome City, IN 46784
PH: (260)854-3790
Fax: (260)854-9102
Bry, John, President

Master Window Cleaners of America
[2135]
PO Box 193
Rushville, IN 46173
PH: (910)724-4442
(812)614-8329
Nelson, Jack, Founder

Continental Mi-Ki Association
[21861]
c/o Bonnie Campbell, President
6290 East 850 South
Saint Paul, IN 47272
PH: (317)512-7119
Rabb, Diana, Treasurer

UHL Collectors Society **[21729]**
398 S Star Dr.
Santa Claus, IN 47579
PH: (812)544-2987
Busler, Sam, Treasurer

Society for the Advancement of
Women's Imaging **[17062]**
PO Box 885
Schererville, IN 46375
PH: (219)588-2119
Bachman, Donald M., MD, President

Society for Airway Management
[15669]
5753 Tanager St.
Schererville, IN 46375
PH: (773)834-3171
Fax: (773)834-3166
Wali, Ashutosh, President

International Buckskin Horse As-
sociation **[4362]**
PO Box 268
Shelby, IN 46377
PH: (219)552-1013
Fax: (219)552-1013
Thompson, Fred, Exec. VP

Horatio Alger Society **[9033]**
1004 School St.
Shelbyville, IN 46176
Looney, Jeff, President

International Colored Appaloosa As-
sociation **[4363]**
PO Box 99
Shipshewana, IN 46565
PH: (574)238-4280
Higgins, David, Chairman

Montessori Educational Programs
International **[8353]**
PO Box 6
Smithville, IN 47458
PH: (812)824-6366
Toll free: 888-708-2470
Teien, Martha, President

Catholic Peace Fellowship **[18774]**
PO Box 4232
South Bend, IN 46634
PH: (574)232-2811
Storer, Shawn T., Director

Logan Community Resources
[11616]
2505 E Jefferson Blvd.
South Bend, IN 46615
PH: (574)289-4831
Fax: (574)234-2075
Bolser, Clint, President, CEO

Malawi Matters **[13552]**
PO Box 11694
South Bend, IN 46634
PH: (574)255-3570
Wezeman, Phyllis, President

National Citizens Police Academy
Association **[5498]**
PO Box 241
South Bend, IN 46624-0241
Vasquez, Tino, President

National One Design Racing Association **[22653]**
1225 E Bronson St.
South Bend, IN 46615
Donnatelli, Guy, Commodore

National Indy 500 Collectors Club
[21456]
PO Box 24105
Speedway, IN 46224
Darlington, John, President

United States Auto Club **[22530]**
4910 W 16th St.
Speedway, IN 46224-5703
PH: (317)247-5151
Fax: (317)248-5584
Miller, Kevin, CEO, President

African American Literature and
Culture Society **[9747]**
Indiana State University
English and Women's Studies
200 N 7th St.
Terre Haute, IN 47809
Byerman, Keith, President

Bibles for the Blind and Visually
Handicapped International **[19754]**
3228 E Rosehill Ave.
Terre Haute, IN 47805-1297
PH: (812)466-4899
Reedy, Keith, Director

Blair Society for Genealogical
Research **[20961]**
c/o Brenda Weeks, President
4430 Berrymore Ct.

Terre Haute, IN 47803-2085
Weeks, Brenda, President

Eugene V. Debs Foundation **[9387]**
451 N 8th St.
Terre Haute, IN 47807
PH: (812)232-2163
Beasley, Noel, President

Indiana State University Alumni As-
sociation **[19327]**
30 N 5th St.
Terre Haute, IN 47807
PH: (812)514-8400
Toll free: 800-258-6478
Fax: (812)237-8157
Kendall, Rex, Exec. Dir.

U.S. Scale Masters Association
[22206]
c/o Mitchell Baker
2878 Mariposa Dr.
Terre Haute, IN 47803
PH: (760)807-5519
(812)236-5351
Barbee, Mike, Officer

Lutheran Deaconess Association
[20305]
1304 LaPorte Ave.
Valparaiso, IN 46383
PH: (219)464-6925
Polito, Lisa, Exec. Dir.

Lutheran Deaconess Conference
[20306]
1304 LaPorte Ave.
Valparaiso, IN 46383
PH: (219)464-6925
Fax: (219)464-6928
Polito, Lisa, Exec. Dir.

Elgin Motorcar Owners Registry
[21376]
2226 E Apache Ln.
Vincennes, IN 47591
PH: (812)888-4172
Fax: (812)888-5471
Wolf, Mr. Jay, Contact

Belgian Draft Horse Corporation of
America **[4339]**
125 Southwood Dr.
Wabash, IN 46992
PH: (260)563-3205
Fax: (260)563-3205
Carey, Jim, VP

American Association of Nutritional
Consultants **[16200]**
220 Parker St.
Warsaw, IN 46580
PH: (574)269-6165
Toll free: 888-828-2262
Fax: (574)268-2120

National Consortium of Breast
Centers **[13851]**
PO Box 1334
Warsaw, IN 46581-1334
PH: (574)267-8058
Fax: (574)267-8268
Gass, Jennifer, MD, President

Antique Advertising Association of
America **[86]**
1002 SW 2nd St., No. 2
Washington, IN 47501

American Berkshire Association
[4705]
2637 Yeager Rd.
West Lafayette, IN 47906
PH: (765)497-3618
Fax: (765)497-2959
Smith, Amy, CEO

Conservation Technology Information
Center **[3841]**
3495 Kent Ave., Ste. L100
West Lafayette, IN 47906

PH: (765)494-9555
Fax: (765)463-4106
Scanlon, Karen A., Exec. Dir.

International Association for
Relationship Research [7094]
Purdue University
Dept. of Psychological Sciences
703 3rd St.
West Lafayette, IN 47907-2081
Simpson, Jeff, President

International Coalition for Genital
Integrity [11284]
1970 N River Rd.
West Lafayette, IN 47906
Bollinger, Dan, Exec. Dir.

International Federation of
Philosophical Societies [10093]
Purdue University
Dept. of Philosophy
100 N University St.
West Lafayette, IN 47907-2098
PH: (765)494-4285
Fax: (765)496-1616
Schrader, David, Chairman

Milton Society of America [9080]
c/o Angelica Duran, Treasurer
Purdue University, Heavilon Hall
500 Oval Dr.
West Lafayette, IN 47907
Mohamed, Feisal, Secretary

National Association of Multicultural
Engineering Program Advocates
[7861]
701 W Stadium Ave.
West Lafayette, IN 47907
PH: (765)400-0637
Womack, Virginia Booth, President,
Exec. Dir.

National Junior Swine Association
[4712]
2639 Yeager Rd.
West Lafayette, IN 47906
PH: (765)463-3594
Fax: (765)497-2959
Paul, Mike, CEO

National Rural Education Association
[8510]
100 N University St.
West Lafayette, IN 47907-2098
PH: (765)494-0086
Fax: (765)496-1228
Hill, Dr. John, Director

National Swine Registry [4716]
National Swine Registry
2639 Yeager Rd.
West Lafayette, IN 47906
PH: (765)463-3594
Fax: (765)497-2959
Anderson, Darrell D., CEO

North American Victorian Studies
Association [10299]
Dept. of English
Purdue University
500 Oval Dr.
West Lafayette, IN 47907
Fax: (765)494-3780
Tromp, Marlene, President

Purdue Alumni Association [19346]
Dick and Sandy Dauch Alumni Ctr.
403 W Wood St.
West Lafayette, IN 47907
PH: (765)494-5175
Toll free: 800-414-1541
Fax: (765)494-9179
Karl, Jim, Act. Pres.

Society of Early Americanists [8792]
c/o Kristina Bross, Advisory Officer
Dept. of English

Purdue University
500 Oval Dr.
West Lafayette, IN 47907
Stevens, Laura M., President

United Duroc Swine Registry [4718]
2639 Yeager Rd.
West Lafayette, IN 47996-2417
PH: (765)463-3594
Evans, Blaine

Walnut Council [4515]
Wright Forestry Ctr.
1007 N 725 W
West Lafayette, IN 47906-9431
PH: (765)583-3501
Fax: (765)583-3512
Van Sambeek, Jerry, President

World Federation of Athletic Training
& Therapy [17287]
c/o Larry J. Leverenz, President
Dept. of Health & Kinesiology
Purdue University
800 W Stadium Ave.
West Lafayette, IN 47907
PH: (765)494-3167
Leverenz, Larry J., President

Harness Horse Youth Foundation
[22915]
16575 Carey Rd.
Westfield, IN 46074-8925
PH: (317)867-5877
Fax: (317)867-1886
Gisser, Keith, Project Mgr.

Association of Grace Brethren
Ministers [20358]
PO Box 394
Winona Lake, IN 46590
PH: (209)872-4921
Olszewski, Bud, Treasurer

Spanish World Ministries [20466]
PO Box 542
Winona Lake, IN 46590-0542
PH: (574)267-8821
Sandoval, Daniel, Exec. Dir.

Water for Good [13360]
PO Box 247
Winona Lake, IN 46590
PH: (574)306-2810
Hocking, Jim, Founder, CEO

Securities and Insurance Licensing
Association [1925]
PO Box 498
Zionsville, IN 46077-0498
Toll free: 800-428-8329
Fax: (866)253-6026
Capes, Ms. Diana, Exec. VP

IOWA

Agricultural Drainage Management
Coalition [4767]
c/o Charlie Schafer, President
PO Box 458
Adair, IA 50002
Toll free: 800-232-4742
Fax: (800)282-3353
Schafer, Charlie, President

Barzona Breeders Association of
America [3718]
c/o Alecia Heinz, Executive
Secretary
604 Cedar St.
Adair, IA 50002
Fax: (641)743-6611
Boykin, Raymond, VP

Amana Heritage Society [9366]
PO Box 81
Amana, IA 52203

PH: (319)622-3567
Schaefer, Aaron, Treasurer

Communal Studies Association
[9382]
PO Box 122
Amana, IA 52203
PH: (319)622-6446

Council for Agricultural Science and
Technology [7474]
4420 W Lincoln Way
Ames, IA 50014-3447
PH: (515)292-2125
Fax: (515)292-4512
Gingerich, Dan, Treasurer

Distillers Grains Technology Council
[1518]
Iowa State University
3327 Elings Hall
Ames, IA 50011
PH: (515)294-4019
Toll free: 800-759-3448
Rosentrater, Kurt, Exec. Dir., CEO

Empower Tanzania, Inc. [12800]
5414 Cervantes Dr.
Ames, IA 50014
Latessa, Phil, Exec. Dir.

International Linear Algebra Society
[6821]
c/o Leslie Hogben, Secretary-
Treasurer
Carver Hall
Dept. of Mathematics
Iowa State University
Ames, IA 50011
Fax: (515)294-5454
Kirkland, Stephen, VP

National Farmers Organization
[4161]
528 Billy Sunday Rd., Ste. 100
Ames, IA 50010
Toll free: 800-247-2110
Riniker, Paul, VP

North American Mycological Association [6888]
2019 Ashmore Dr.
Ames, IA 50014
Yerich, Kathy, VP

Women, Food and Agriculture
Network [4704]
PO Box 611
Ames, IA 50010
PH: (515)460-2477
Adcock, Leigh, Exec. Dir.

National Traditional Country Music
Association [9980]
650 Main St.
Anita, IA 50020
PH: (712)762-4363
Everhart, Robert, CEO

Associated Construction Distributors
International [499]
1605 SE Delaware Ave., Ste. B
Ankeny, IA 50021
PH: (515)964-1335
Fax: (515)964-7668
Goetz, Tom, Exec. VP

Association of Boards of Certification
[5831]
2805 SW Snyder Blvd., Ste. 535
Ankeny, IA 50023
PH: (515)232-3623
Fax: (515)965-6827
Bishop, Paul D., CAE, CEO

Bicycle Tour Network [22746]
PO Box 1443
Ankeny, IA 50021

Federation of Exchange Accommo-
dators [3202]
1255 SW Prairie Trail Pky.
Ankeny, IA 50023
PH: (515)244-6515
Fax: (515)334-1174
Harkin, Lynn, Exec. Dir.

International Association of Lighting
Management Companies [2100]
1255 SW Prairie Trail Pky.
Ankeny, IA 50023-7068
PH: (515)243-2360
Fax: (515)334-1173
Frank, Chris, Treasurer

National Postsecondary Agricultural
Student Organization [7480]
1055 SW Prairie Trail Pky.
Ankeny, IA 50023
PH: (515)964-6866
McEnany, Craig A., Exec. Dir.

National Rural Economic Developers
Association [19076]
1255 SW Prairie Trail Pky.
Ankeny, IA 50023-7068
PH: (515)284-1421
Fax: (515)334-1167
Fisher, Rand, President

Plasticville Collectors Association
[21715]
601 SE 2nd St.
Ankeny, IA 50021-3207
PH: (515)964-0562
Ross, Frank, VP

Soil and Water Conservation Society
[3947]
945 SW Ankeny Rd.
Ankeny, IA 50023-9723
PH: (515)289-2331
Toll free: 800-843-7645
Fax: (515)289-1227
Gulliford, Jim, Exec. Dir.

Wings of Hope International [13097]
902 SE 5th St.
Ankeny, IA 50021
PH: (515)964-4164
Zama, Alec, President

Corben Club [21221]
PO Box 127
Blakesburg, IA 52536
PH: (515)938-2773
Fax: (515)938-2773
Taylor, Robert, President

International Pietenpol Association
[21233]
PO Box 127
Blakesburg, IA 52536-0127
PH: (515)938-2773
Fax: (515)938-2773

Interstate Club [21236]
c/o Brent Taylor
PO Box 127
Blakesburg, IA 52536-0127
Taylor, Brent, Contact

Mamie Doud Eisenhower Birthplace
Foundation [9408]
709 Carroll St.
Boone, IA 50036
PH: (515)432-1907
Fax: (515)432-1907

Winged Warriors/National B-Body
Owners Association [21522]
216 12th St.
Boone, IA 50036-2019

International Security Management
Association [3062]
PO Box 623
Buffalo, IA 52728-0623

PH: (563)381-4008
Fax: (563)381-4283
Howard, Mike, President

Country Music Showcase
  International **[9897]**
PO Box D
Carlisle, IA 50047-0368
PH: (515)989-3748
Luick, Barbara A., CEO

National Campus Ministry Associa-
  tion **[20086]**
2422 College St.
Cedar Falls, IA 50613
PH: (704)588-0183
Nielsen, Rev. Cody, President

National Program for Playground
  Safety **[19080]**
University of Northern Iowa
103 Human Performance Ctr.
Cedar Falls, IA 50614-0618
Toll free: 800-554-PLAY
Fax: (319)273-7308
Olsen, Heather, EdD, Exec. Dir.

Professional Farmers of America
  [4168]
6612 Chancellor Dr., Ste. 300
Cedar Falls, IA 50613
Toll free: 800-772-0023
Flory, Chip, Editor

American Association of Electrodiag-
  nostic Technologists **[15675]**
PO Box 2770
Cedar Rapids, IA 52406
Toll free: 877-333-2238
Lewis, Jim, Director

American Board of Certification
  [4984]
4403 1st Ave. SE, Ste. 113
Cedar Rapids, IA 52402-3221
PH: (319)365-2222
Toll free: 877-365-2221
Fax: (319)363-0127
Gilmore, Dian, Exec. Dir.

Association for Information Media
  and Equipment **[263]**
PO Box 9844
Cedar Rapids, IA 52409-9844
Gorsegner Ehlinger, Betty, Exec. Dir.

Journey to Solidarity **[14276]**
301 Cottage Grove Ave. SE
Cedar Rapids, IA 52403
Fax: (888)860-9263
Breitlow, Jay, Director, Founder

National Association of Media and
  Technology Centers **[2317]**
PO Box 9844
Cedar Rapids, IA 52409-9844
PH: (319)654-0608
Fax: (319)654-0609
Berger, Dan, President

National Systems Contractors As-
  sociation **[1056]**
3950 River Ridge Dr. NE
Cedar Rapids, IA 52402
PH: (319)366-6722
Toll free: 800-446-6722
Wilson, Chuck, Exec. Dir.

Western Fraternal Life Association
  [19420]
1900 1st Ave. NE
Cedar Rapids, IA 52402-5321
PH: (319)363-2653
Toll free: 877-935-2467
Fax: (319)363-8806
Van Dyke, Craig, President

Glenn Miller Birthplace Society
  [24043]
122 W Clark St.
Clarinda, IA 51632

PH: (712)542-2461
Fax: (712)542-2868
Negley, Marvin, President

National Association of Priest Pilots
  [19871]
c/o Rev. John Hemann, Treasurer
481 N Shore Dr., Apt. 301
Clear Lake, IA 50428
Hemann, Rev. Mel, Treasurer

Early American Pattern Glass
  Society **[21650]**
c/o Fred Phelps, Membership
  Coordinator
PO Box 266
Colesburg, IA 52035-0266
Yoder, Linda, Trustee, VP

American Pencil Collectors Society
  [21613]
c/o Aaron Bartholmey, Secretary-
  Treasurer
18 N Maple St., Apt 4
Colfax, IA 50054
Horsting, John, President

Midwest Free Community Papers
  [2801]
PO Box 5720
Coralville, IA 52241-5720
PH: (319)341-4352
Toll free: 800-248-4061
Fax: (319)343-1112
Shopper, Cresco, President

National Examining Board of Ocular-
  ists **[16396]**
David M. Bulgarelli, Executive Direc-
  tor
625 1st Ave., Ste. 220
Coralville, IA 52241-2101
PH: (319)339-1125
Fax: (319)354-3465
Bulgarelli, David M., Exec. Dir.

HIKE Fund **[15196]**
530 Elliott St.
Council Bluffs, IA 51503-0202
PH: (712)325-0812
Lux, Alexis, VP, Director

Rhinelander Rabbit Club of America
  [4611]
c/o Frank Gale, Vice President
802 N Division
Creston, IA 50801
PH: (515)782-2998
Ferchaud, Lorena, President

Hazardous Materials Training and
  Research Institute **[6704]**
ATEEC
201 N Harrison St., Ste. 101
Davenport, IA 52801-1918
PH: (563)441-4081
Toll free: 866-419-6761
Fax: (563)441-4080
Hanne, Gio, Contact

International Trumpet Guild **[9937]**
PO Box 2688
Davenport, IA 52809-2688
PH: (563)676-2435
Fax: (413)403-8899
Evans, Brian, President

National Ballroom and Entertainment
  Association **[1153]**
c/o John Matter, Executive Director
PO Box 274
Decorah, IA 52101-7600
PH: (563)382-3871
Matter, John, Exec. Dir.

Seed Savers Exchange **[22122]**
3094 N Winn Rd.
Decorah, IA 52101-7776

PH: (563)382-5990
Crotz, Keith, Chmn. of the Bd.

Society for Reformation Research
  [20204]
c/o Victoria and Robert Christman,
  Treasurer and Membership
  Secretary
Dept. of History
Luther College
700 College Dr.
Decorah, IA 52101-1045
Plummer, Beth, Rec. Sec.

Youth M.O.V.E. National **[13489]**
PO Box 215
Decorah, IA 52101
Toll free: 800-580-6199
Holt, Brittany, President

Cedar Tree Inc. **[8237]**
421 NW 52nd Ave.
Des Moines, IA 50313
PH: (515)243-1845
Fax: (515)282-3151
Morris, Paul, Contact

Child and Family Policy Center
  [10895]
505 5th Ave., Ste. 404
Des Moines, IA 50309
PH: (515)280-9027
Stover Wright, Michelle, Dir. of Res.

Council for Amusement and
  Recreational Equipment Safety
  [5746]
PO Box 8236
Des Moines, IA 50301
PH: (515)281-5387
McKernon, Dean, VP

Global Farmer Network **[6121]**
309 Court Ave., Ste. 214
Des Moines, IA 50309
PH: (515)274-0800
Fax: (240)201-8451
Boote, Mary, CEO

International Association for Food
  Protection **[5224]**
6200 Aurora Ave., Ste. 200W
Des Moines, IA 50322-2864
PH: (515)276-3344
Toll free: 800-369-6337
Fax: (515)276-8655
Tharp, Mr. David W., CAE, Exec. Dir.

La Sertoma International **[12895]**
PO Box 14521
Des Moines, IA 50306-4521
Toll free: 800-503-9227
Shomaker, Lynn, President

North American Saxophone Alliance
  [9988]
Dept. of Music
Drake University
2507 University Ave.
Des Moines, IA 50311-4505
PH: (515)271-3104
Romain, James, Dir. of Member
  Svcs.

PEO International **[8753]**
3700 Grand Ave.
Des Moines, IA 50312-2806
PH: (515)255-3153
Fax: (515)255-3820
Ledbetter, Beth, President

Sewing Educator Alliance **[8561]**
2724 2nd Ave.
Des Moines, IA 50313
PH: (515)282-9101
Toll free: 800-367-5651
Fax: (515)282-4483

Vacuum and Sewing Dealers Trade
  Association **[213]**
2724 2nd Ave.
Des Moines, IA 50313-4933

PH: (515)282-9101
Toll free: 800-367-5651
Fax: (515)282-4483
Patterson, Judy, President

United Catholic Music and Video
  Association **[19914]**
PO Box 230
Donnellson, IA 52625
PH: (319)835-9114
Fax: (319)835-3903

Stovall Family Association **[20931]**
c/o Tom Stovall, Treasurer
3345 Tibey Ct.
Dubuque, IA 52002-2849
PH: (563)581-7220
Stovall, Tom, Treasurer

Association for Glycogen Storage
  Disease **[15818]**
PO Box 896
Durant, IA 52747
PH: (563)514-4022
Peters, Matt, VP

National Science Education Leader-
  ship Association **[8554]**
55466 Forrester Valley Ln.
Glenwood, IA 51534
PH: (919)561-3612
Fax: (801)659-3351
Kaufmann, Janey, President

English Shepherd Club **[21873]**
2146 380th St.
Grafton, IA 50440
Partlow, Darlene, President

Society for Linguistic Anthropology
  [5924]
c/o Prof. Brigittine M. French, Editor
Dept. of Anthropology
Grinnell College
306 Goodnow Hall
1118 Park St.
Grinnell, IA 50112
Jaffe, Alexandra, Ed.-in-Chief

Two-Cylinder Club **[22458]**
506 2nd St.
Grundy Center, IA 50638
PH: (319)824-6060
Toll free: 888-782-2582
Fax: (319)824-2662

American School Band Directors As-
  sociation **[8360]**
227 N 1st St.
Guttenberg, IA 52052-9010
PH: (563)252-2500
Barrett, Susann, Secretary

A Promise of Health **[15060]**
PO Box 247
Hiawatha, IA 52233
PH: (719)547-1995
  (719)873-5450
Grannell, Barbara, Exec. Dir.,
  Founder

Balloon Federation of America
  [21529]
PO Box 400
Indianola, IA 50125-1484
Bradley, Troy, Director

Montadale Sheep Breeders Associa-
  tion **[4672]**
47 North 12th
Indianola, IA 50125
PH: (701)541-1120
Moenter, Kent, President

United States Ombudsman Associa-
  tion **[4969]**
200 W 2nd Ave.
Indianola, IA 50125
Toll free: 866-442-6751
Matsunaga, Robin, President

CARTHA [913]
85 Leamer Ct.
Iowa City, IA 52246
Balakrishnan, Usha R., Chairman,
CEO, President

Center for the Study of Group
Processes [7164]
c/o Alison Bianchi, Director
W28D Seashore Hall
Dept. of Sociology
University of Iowa
Iowa City, IA 52242-1401
PH: (319)335-2495
Bianchi, Alison, Director

Equipment Marketing and Distribu-
tion Association [2204]
PO Box 1347
Iowa City, IA 52244
PH: (319)354-5156
Fax: (319)354-5157
Wolters, Kevin, President

Historical Keyboard Society of North
America [22248]
c/o David C. Kelzenberg, Secretary
2801 Highway 6 E, Ste. 344
Iowa City, IA 52240
Funaro, Elaine, President

Infectious Diseases Society of
America Emerging Infections
Network [15403]
Carver College of Medicine
University of Iowa
200 Hawkins Dr., SW-34JGH
Iowa City, IA 52242
PH: (319)384-8622
Fax: (319)384-8860
Beekmann, Susan, RN, Program
Mgr.

International Society for
Interpersonal Psychotherapy
[16981]
University of Iowa
Department of Psychiatry
1-293 Medical Education Bldg.
Iowa City, IA 52242
PH: (319)353-4230
Fax: (319)353-3003
Stuart, Scott, Exec. Ofc.

National Association of State
Archaeologists [5943]
University of Iowa
Office of the State Archaeologist
700 S Clinton St.
Iowa City, IA 52242-1030
PH: (319)384-0732
Fax: (319)384-0768
De La Garza, Mary, Officer

National Co+op Grocers [908]
14 S Linn St.
Iowa City, IA 52240
Toll free: 866-709-COOP
Maher, Chris, VP

Perfusion Program Directors' Council
[14138]
c/o Thomas Rath, Chairman
University of Iowa Hospitals and
Clinics
Perfusion Technology Education
Program
200 Hawkins Dr.
Iowa City, IA 52242
PH: (319)356-8496
Fax: (319)353-7174
Kallies, Kirsten, V. Chmn. of the Bd.

Ponseti International Association
[13834]
University of Iowa Healthcare
International Office 118 CMAB
Iowa City, IA 52242
Morcuende, Jose, MD, Contact

Quill and Scroll International Honor-
ary Society [23795]
University of Iowa
100 Adler Journalism Bldg.
Iowa City, IA 52242
PH: (319)335-3457
Fax: (319)335-3989
Shelton, Vanessa, Exec. Dir.

Society for the Advancement of
Economic Theory [6400]
108 John Pappajohn Business Bldg.,
W288
Dept. of Economics
University of Iowa
Iowa City, IA 52242
Townsend, Robert, VP

University of Iowa Alumni Associa-
tion [19357]
PO Box 1970
Iowa City, IA 52244-1970
PH: (319)335-3294
Toll free: 800-469-2586
Fax: (319)335-1079
Lewis, Jim, Bd. Member

University of Iowa Injury Prevention
Research Center [7109]
2190 Westlawn
University of Iowa
Iowa City, IA 52242
PH: (319)467-4504
Roth, Lisa, Dep. Dir.

American Guinea Hog Association
[4706]
1830 P Ave.
Jefferson, IA 50129
PH: (515)370-1021
McDaniel, Jesse, President

The Gardeners of America [22095]
PO Box 241
Johnston, IA 50131-6245
PH: (515)278-0295
Fax: (515)278-6245
Forney, James, Treasurer

Aquatic Resources Education As-
sociation [4768]
c/o Barb Gigar, President
Iowa Dept. of Natural Resources
57744 Lewis Rd.
Lewis, IA 51544
PH: (641)747-2200
     (515)494-3891
Piper, Ti, Secretary

Affiliated Woodcarvers [8949]
1212 E Quarry St.
Maquoketa, IA 52060
PH: (563)505-2700
     (563)676-8264
Yudis, Carol, Chairperson

National Association of Rocketry
[22201]
PO Box 407
Marion, IA 52302-0407
Toll free: 800-262-4872
Fax: (319)373-8910
Barber, Arthur H., III, Liaison

United States Police Canine Association [5521]
c/o Melinda Ruopp, Secretary
1575 Wallace Ave.
Marshalltown, IA 50158
PH: (651)592-7874
     (540)226-4265
Ferland, David, Exec. Dir.

Allied Purchasing [967]
PO Box 1249
Mason City, IA 50402-1249
Toll free: 800-247-5956
Fax: (800)635-3775
Janssen, Brian, President

American Women's Self Defense
Association [12863]
PO Box 1533
Mason City, IA 50402
Toll free: 888-STOP RAPE
Fax: (641)424-3496
Tierney, Jessica Peterson, Exec. Dir.

Employers of America [3117]
310 Meadow Ln.
Mason City, IA 50401

Iowa Wesleyan College Alumni As-
sociation [19328]
601 N Main St.
Mount Pleasant, IA 52641
PH: (319)385-6215
Toll free: 800-582-2383
Phillips, James D., Bd. Member

Midwest Old Settlers and Threshers
Association [8903]
405 E Threshers Rd.
Mount Pleasant, IA 52641
PH: (319)385-8937
McWilliams, Terry, CEO

Concrete Foundations Association
[861]
113 W 1st St.
Mount Vernon, IA 52314
PH: (319)895-6940
Fax: (320)213-5556
Sauter, J. Edward, Exec. Dir.

Tilt-Up Concrete Association [902]
113 1st St. W
Mount Vernon, IA 52314
PH: (319)895-6911
Fax: (320)213-5555
Sauter, Ed, Exec. Dir.

American Art Pottery Association
[8829]
c/o Marie Latta, Trustee
2115 W Fulliam Ave.
Muscatine, IA 52761
Small, Arnie, President

Purple Flower Gang [24058]
1803 Lucas St.
Muscatine, IA 52761
Bryant, Cindy, Editor, President

Lutherans For Life [12780]
1101 5th St.
Nevada, IA 50201-1816
PH: (515)382-2077
Toll free: 888-364-LIFE
Fax: (515)382-3020
Auch, Lynette, President

American Quarter Pony Association
[4322]
PO Box 30
New Sharon, IA 50207
PH: (641)675-3669
Fax: (641)675-3969

Sigma Lambda Gamma National
Sorority [23977]
125 E Zeller St., Ste. D
North Liberty, IA 52317
PH: (319)774-5370
Jimenez, Vanessa, Exec. Dir.

Hobby Greenhouse Association
[22102]
922 Norwood Dr.
Norwalk, IA 50211-1329
PH: (724)744-7082
Karasek, Tom, President

William Penn University Alumni As-
sociation [19373]
201 Trueblood Ave.
Oskaloosa, IA 52577-1799
PH: (641)673-1046
Toll free: 800-779-7366
VanWyk, Jason, Officer

People Against Cancer [14044]
604 East St.
Otho, IA 50569
PH: (515)972-4444
Toll free: 800-662-2623
Fax: (515)972-4415
Wiewel, Frank D., Editor, Founder

Antique Airplane Association [21215]
22001 Bluegrass Rd.
Ottumwa, IA 52501
PH: (641)938-2773
Fax: (641)938-2093
Taylor, Robert L., President

Bluetick Breeders of America
[21843]
c/o Darren Batterson, President
17821 60th St.
Ottumwa, IA 52501
PH: (641)680-0117
Schulte, Travis, VP

452nd Bomb Group Association
[21182]
c/o Cally A. Boatwright, Secretary/
Editor
PO Box 72
Pacific Junction, IA 51561
Keating, J. Patrick, President

Many Hands for Haiti [13014]
PO Box 204
Pella, IA 50219
PH: (641)629-1243
Brand, Tim, Founder

American Association of Swine
Veterinarians [17601]
830 26th St.
Perry, IA 50220
PH: (515)465-5255
Fax: (515)465-3832
Burkgren, Dr. Tom, Exec. Dir.

Professional Animal Auditor Certifica-
tion Organization [3620]
PO Box 31
Redfield, IA 50233-0031
PH: (402)403-0104
Fax: (402)920-6396
Sjeklocha, Dave, Treasurer

APS Writers Unit No. 30 [22308]
c/o Kenneth Trettin, Secretary-
Treasurer
PO Box 56
Rockford, IA 50468-0056
Trettin, Kenneth, Secretary,
Treasurer

Massey Collectors Association
[22456]
c/o Bob Lynn, President
4273 280th St.
Shenandoah, IA 51601
Lynn, Bob, President

Indian Youth of America [12376]
PO Box 2786
Sioux City, IA 51106-0786
PH: (712)252-3230
Fax: (712)252-3712
Gordon, Patricia Trudell, Founder

Lyme Disease United Coalition
[15407]
PO Box 86
Story City, IA 50248
Toll free: 800-311-7518
Fax: (888)746-3810
Weeg, Judith, President

Police Car Owners of America
[21478]
1106 Lafayette Ave.
Story City, IA 50248-1434
PH: (515)778-5618
Spurlock, Norm, President

Christian Dental Society **[14423]**
PO Box 296
Sumner, IA 50674
PH: (563)578-8887
Yarbro, Dr. Jody, Treasurer

Outreach **[11123]**
301 Center St.
Union, IA 50258
PH: (641)486-2550
Toll free: 800-513-0935
Fax: (641)486-2570
Hammer, Floyd, President

Farm Safety For Just Kids **[12820]**
11304 Aurora Ave.
Urbandale, IA 50322
PH: (515)331-6506
Toll free: 800-423-5437
Schweitz, David T., Exec. Dir.

Forensic Accountants Society of
North America **[28]**
6200 Aurora Ave., Ste. 600W
Urbandale, IA 50322-2871
PH: (515)669-0415
Fax: (515)274-4807
Nearmyer, Roger, CPA, President,
Bd. Member

Medicine for Mali **[12290]**
4605 80th Pl.
Urbandale, IA 50322-7340
DeVore, Dr. Steven, Founder

National Deaf Women's Bowling Association **[22788]**
3314 64th St.
Urbandale, IA 50322
Willingham, Gayle, President

National Gymnastics Judges As-
sociation **[22902]**
c/o Dan Bachman, President
Guide Financial Group
2830 100th, No. 108
Urbandale, IA 50322
PH: (515)974-4561
Bachman, Dan, President

National Marriage Encounter **[12257]**
c/o Jeannette Babcock, Administrator
3922 77th St.
Urbandale, IA 50322
PH: (515)278-8458
Babcock, Jeannette, Administrator

International Motor Contest Associa-
tion **[22525]**
1800 W D St.
Vinton, IA 52349-2500
PH: (319)472-2201
Fax: (319)472-2218
Root, Kathy, President

American/Schleswig-Holstein
Heritage Society **[20955]**
PO Box 506
Walcott, IA 52773-0506
PH: (563)284-4184
Fax: (563)284-4184
Rehder, Jens, 1st VP

Champions of Autism and ADHD
[13760]
3025 Kimball Ave.
Waterloo, IA 50702
PH: (319)233-0380
Budke, Dr. Ken, CEO, President

International Association of Security
and Investigative Regulators
[2010]
PO Box 93
Waterloo, IA 50704
Toll free: 888-354-2747
Fax: (319)232-1488
McGee, Lisa D., President

RandomKid **[13477]**
PO Box 102
Waukee, IA 50263-0102
PH: (646)926-0778
Leman, Talia, CEO, Founder

Self-Help International **[12185]**
703 2nd Ave. NW
Waverly, IA 50677-2308
PH: (319)352-4040
Neal, Richard, President

Hoover Presidential Foundation
[10332]
302 Parkside Dr.
West Branch, IA 52358
PH: (319)643-5327
Fax: (319)643-2391
Fleagle, Jerry, Exec. Dir.

Association of Former Agents of the
U.S. Secret Service **[5356]**
6919 Vista Dr.
West Des Moines, IA 50266
PH: (515)282-8192
Fax: (515)282-9117
Rickenberger, Kathy, Exec. Dir.

National Pop Can Collectors **[21696]**
1082 S 46th St.
West Des Moines, IA 50265-5239
Wicker, Jim, President

Phi Beta Chi **[23959]**
PO Box 65426
West Des Moines, IA 50265
Johnson, Amy, Exec. Dir.

Phi Theta Pi **[23699]**
6552 Bradford Dr.
West Des Moines, IA 50266-2308
PH: (515)440-2045
    (515)271-1540
Pierce, Mr. David, Secretary,
Treasurer

Stadium Managers Association
[23268]
6919 Vista Dr.
West Des Moines, IA 50266
PH: (515)282-8192
Fax: (515)282-9117
Brown, Troy, Secretary, Treasurer

Sunbeam Rapier Registry **[21499]**
c/o James Mazour, Editor
3212 Orchard Cir.
West Des Moines, IA 50266-2140
PH: (515)226-9475
Mazour, James, Editor

Hudson-Essex-Terraplane Club
[21395]
7115 Franklin Ave.
Windsor Heights, IA 50324
Tuttle, Dave, TreasurerK

KANSAS

National Greyhound Association
[21922]
PO Box 543
Abilene, KS 67410-0543
PH: (785)263-7272
Guccione, Gary, Advisor

Tempered Steel **[13249]**
16039 274th Rd.
Atchison, KS 66002
PH: (913)370-0238
Fax: (866)377-3343
Schneider, Luana, Founder, Exec.
Dir.

Stickler Involved People **[14859]**
15 Angelina Dr.
Augusta, KS 67010-2207

PH: (316)259-5194
Houchin, Pat, Coord., Founder

Association for Informal Logic and
Critical Thinking **[10079]**
Center for Critical Thinking
Baker University
618 8th St.
Baldwin City, KS 66006
Hatcher, Donald, Treasurer

American Agriculture Movement
[17785]
c/o Larry Matlack, President
13118 E Stroud Rd.
Burton, KS 67020
PH: (620)463-3513
Matlack, Larry, President

Rubinstein-Taybi Parent Group
U.S.A. **[13835]**
24081 G Ln.
Cedar, KS 67628
Toll free: 888-447-2989
Baxter, Ms. Lorrie, Coord.

Manna House of Prayer **[11954]**
323 E 5th St.
Concordia, KS 66901
PH: (785)243-4428
Lander, Janet, CSJ, Facilitator

National Orphan Train Complex
[20986]
300 Washington St.
Concordia, KS 66901
PH: (785)243-4471
Sutton, Susan, President

Association for Honest Attorneys
[4996]
7145 Blueberry Ln.
Derby, KS 67037
PH: (316)788-0901
Heffington, Joan, CEO, Founder

Healthy Kids Challenge **[14194]**
2 W Road 210
Dighton, KS 67839
Toll free: 888-259-6287
Fax: (620)397-5979
James, Vickie L., Director

Bukovina Society of the Americas
[3724]
PO Box 81
Ellis, KS 67637
McClelland, Martha, President

National Smokejumper Association
[5213]
c/o John McDaniel, Membership
Coordinator
PO Box 105
Falun, KS 67442-0105
Cherry, James L., President

National Association of County Col-
lectors, Treasurers and Finance
Officers **[5707]**
c/o Cheryl Remington, President
PO Box 127
Gove, KS 67736
PH: (785)938-2275
Fax: (785)938-2222
Remington, Cheryl, President

Grant Professionals Association
[12479]
1333 Meadowlark Ln., Ste. 105
Kansas City, KS 66102-1200
PH: (913)788-3000
Fax: (913)788-3398
DiVirgilio, Debbie, President

International Brotherhood of
Boilermakers **[23457]**
753 State Ave., Ste. 570
Kansas City, KS 66101

PH: (913)371-2640
Fax: (913)281-8104
Jones, Newton B., President

International Brotherhood of
Boilermakers, Iron Ship Builders,
Blacksmiths, Forgers and Helpers -
Cement, Lime, Gypsum, and Allied
Workers Division **[23406]**
753 State Ave., Ste. 570
Kansas City, KS 66101
PH: (913)371-2640
Allen, Carey, Director

International Society for Fertility
Preservation **[14760]**
University of Kansas, School of
Medicine
Division of REI, Department of OB/
GYN
3901 Rainbow Blvd.
Kansas City, KS 66160
Kim, S. Samuel, President

Piano Technicians Guild **[2437]**
4444 Forest Ave.
Kansas City, KS 66106-3750
PH: (913)432-9975
Fax: (913)432-9986
Bruce, Shawn, Officer

Unbound **[13092]**
1 Elmwood Ave.
Kansas City, KS 66103-2118
PH: (913)384-6500
Toll free: 800-875-6564
Fax: (913)384-2211
Pearce, Paul, Director

Romagnola and RomAngus Cattle
Association **[3754]**
14305 W 379th St.
La Cygne, KS 66040
PH: (913)594-1080
Tanner, Maynard, Director

Accrediting Council on Education in
Journalism and Mass Communica-
tions **[8146]**
Stauffer-Flint Hall
1435 Jayhawk Blvd.
Lawrence, KS 66045-7575
PH: (785)864-3973
    (785)864-3986
Fax: (785)864-5225
Shaw, Susanne, Exec. Dir.

American Society of Ichthyologists
and Herpetologists **[6706]**
PO Box 1897
Lawrence, KS 66044-8897
PH: (785)843-1235
Toll free: 800-627-0326
Fax: (785)843-1274
Donnelly, Maureen A., Secretary

APA Division 54: Society of Pediatric
Psychology **[16896]**
PO Box 3968
Lawrence, KS 66046
PH: (785)856-0713
Fax: (785)856-0759
Wysocki, Tim, President

Association of Professional Piercers
[3198]
PO Box 1287
Lawrence, KS 66044
PH: (785)841-6060
Toll free: 888-888-1277
Fax: (267)482-5650
Skellie, Brian, President

Association of Reptilian and Amphib-
ian Veterinarians **[17636]**
810 E 10th St.
Lawrence, KS 66044
PH: (480)703-4941
Varble, Dana M., DVM, Exec. Dir.

Association of University Interior
Designers [1939]
c/o Lisa Kring, Treasurer
University of Kansas
1301 Jayhawk Blvd., Rm. 476
Lawrence, KS 66045
PH: (765)494-9603
Fax: (765)496-1579
Kring, Lisa, Treasurer

CREW Network [2858]
1201 Wakarusa Dr., Ste. D
Lawrence, KS 66049
PH: (785)832-1808
Fax: (785)832-1551
Ayers, Gail, PhD, CEO, President

CREW New York [2859]
1201 Wakarusa Dr., Ste. D
Lawrence, KS 66049
PH: (785)832-1808
Fax: (785)832-1551
Cole, Debra, Comm. Chm.

Foundation for Safer Athletic Field
Environments [22516]
805 New Hampshire St., Ste. E
Lawrence, KS 66044-2774
Toll free: 800-323-3875
Fax: (785)843-2977
Heck, Kim, Exec. Dir.

Golf Course Superintendents As-
sociation of America [3157]
1421 Research Park Dr.
Lawrence, KS 66049-3859
PH: (785)841-2240
Toll free: 800-472-7878
Fax: (785)832-3643
Evans, Rhett, CEO

International Association of Audio
Information Services [17714]
c/o Lori Kesinger
PO Box 847
Lawrence, KS 66044
Toll free: 800-280-5325
Fax: (785)864-5278
Pasquale, Andrea, Program Mgr.

International Bowling Pro Shop and
Instructors Association [22703]
c/o Russ Wilson, President
355 N Iowa St.
Lawrence, KS 66044
PH: (513)705-6497
Toll free: 800-255-6436
Supper, Bill, Exec. Dir.

International Society for Neuroethol-
ogy [5897]
PO Box 1897
Lawrence, KS 66044
PH: (785)865-9401
Toll free: 800-627-0629
Rankin, Catharine, President

Mycological Society of America
[6887]
PO Box 1897
Lawrence, KS 66044-8897
Toll free: 800-627-0326
Fax: (785)843-6153
Volk, Tom, VP

Phi Alpha Epsilon [23739]
c/o Civil, Environmental, and
Architectural Engineering Dept.
University of Kansas
2150 Learned Hall
1530 W 15th St.
Lawrence, KS 66045-7618
Rock, Brian, Fac. Adv.

Sisters in Crime [3519]
PO Box 442124
Lawrence, KS 66044
PH: (785)842-1325
Fax: (785)856-6314
Pullen, Karen, Contact

Society for Molecular Biology and
Evolution [6104]
810 E 10th St.
Lawrence, KS 66044
PH: (785)865-9405
Toll free: 800-627-0326
Fax: (785)843-6153
Zhang, George, President

Society for Quantitative Analyses of
Behavior [6049]
c/o Derek Reed, Executive Director
Department of Applied Behavioral
Science
University of Kansas
100 Sunnyside Ave.
Lawrence, KS 66045
Bizo, Lewis, Director, President

Society for Thermal Medicine
[17467]
c/o Allen Press
810 E 10th St.
Lawrence, KS 66044
PH: (785)865-9403
Toll free: 800-627-0326
Fax: (785)843-6153
McGough, Robert J., Counselor

Sociologists for Women in Society
[7191]
1415 Jayhawk Blvd.
University of Kansas
Department of Sociology, Rm. 716
Lawrence, KS 66045
PH: (785)864-9405
Jackson, Shirley A., PhD, Mem.

Sports Turf Managers Association
[2073]
805 New Hampshire St., Ste. E
Lawrence, KS 66044
PH: (785)843-2549
Toll free: 800-323-3875
Fax: (785)843-2977
Salmond, Jeff, President

Tire Society [3283]
810 E 10th St.
Lawrence, KS 66044
PH: (785)865-9403
Toll free: 800-627-0326
Fax: (785)843-6153
Fatt, Michell Hoo, Secretary

University of Kansas Alumni As-
sociation [19358]
1266 Oread Ave.
Lawrence, KS 66045
PH: (785)864-4760
Toll free: 800-584-2957
Fax: (785)864-5397
Corbett, Kevin, President

Weed Science Society of America
[3556]
810 E 10th St.
Lawrence, KS 66044
PH: (785)865-9520
Toll free: 800-627-0326
Lancaster, Joyce, Exec. Sec.

William Allen White Foundation
[9110]
c/o William Allen White School of
Journalism
Stauffer-Flint Hall
University of Kansas
1435 Jayhawk Blvd.
Lawrence, KS 66045-7515
PH: (785)864-4755
Anstaett, Doug, Trustee

Wildlife Disease Association [4912]
PO Box 7065
Lawrence, KS 66044-7065
PH: (785)865-9403
Toll free: 800-627-0326
Fax: (785)843-6153
Miller, Debra, VP

Xtal Set Society [6441]
PO Box 3636
Lawrence, KS 66046-0636
PH: (405)517-7347

American Academy of Family Physi-
cians [14746]
11400 Tomahawk Creek Pkwy.
Leawood, KS 66211-2680
PH: (913)906-6000
Toll free: 800-274-2237
Fax: (913)906-6075
Henley, Douglas E., MD, CEO,
Exec. VP

American Medical Society for Sports
Medicine [17275]
4000 W 114th St., Ste. 100
Leawood, KS 66211-2622
PH: (913)327-1415
    (626)445-1983
Fax: (913)327-1491
DiFiori, John, MD, Bd. Member

Association of Family Medicine
Residency Directors [15578]
11400 Tomahawk Creek Pky., Ste.
670
Leawood, KS 66211
PH: (913)906-6000
Toll free: 800-274-2237
Fax: (913)906-6105
Mazzone, Michael, MD, President

Association of Family Practice
Administrators [15579]
11400 Tomahawk Creek Pkwy.
Leawood, KS 66211-2672
Toll free: 800-274-2237
Fax: (913)906-6084

International Society of Laparoscopic
Colorectal Surgery [17391]
5019 W 147th St.
Leawood, KS 66224
PH: (913)402-7102
Fax: (913)273-9940
Marks, John H., MD, President

National Rural Health Association
[17013]
4501 College Blvd., No. 225
Leawood, KS 66211-1921
PH: (816)756-3140
Fax: (816)756-3144
Morgan, Alan, CEO

North American Primary Care
Research Group [13678]
11400 Tomahawk Creek Pky., Ste.
240
Leawood, KS 66211
PH: (913)906-6000
Toll free: 888-371-6397
Vansagi, Tom, PhD, Exec. Dir.

Society of Teachers of Family
Medicine [14751]
11400 Tomahawk Creek Pky., Ste.
240
Leawood, KS 66211
PH: (913)906-6000
Toll free: 800-274-7928
Fax: (913)906-6096
Brungardt, Stacy, CAE, Exec. Dir.

American Board of Genetic Counsel-
ing [14872]
PO Box 14216
Lenexa, KS 66285
PH: (913)895-4617
Fax: (913)895-4652
Hughey, Katherine, Assoc. Mgr.

American College of Clinical
Pharmacy [16637]
13000 W 87th Street Pky.
Lenexa, KS 66215-4530

PH: (913)492-3311
Fax: (913)492-0088
Maddux, Michael, Exec. Dir.

Association of Genetic Technologists
[6075]
PO Box 19193
Lenexa, KS 66285
PH: (913)895-4605
Fax: (913)895-4652
Sbeiti, Adam, Director

Heart to Heart International [12670]
13250 W 98th St.
Lenexa, KS 66215
PH: (913)764-5200
Fax: (913)764-0809
Aubrey, Curtis, CFO

International Assembly for Collegiate
Business Education [7551]
11374 Strang Line Rd.
Lenexa, KS 66215
PH: (913)631-3009
Fax: (913)631-9154
Gash, Dennis N., President

International Association of Opera-
tive Millers [2377]
12351 W 96th Ter., Ste. 100
Lenexa, KS 66215
PH: (913)338-3377
Fax: (913)338-3553
Farris, Melinda, CAE, Exec. VP

International Certified Floorcovering
Installers Association [870]
12201 W 88th St.
Lenexa, KS 66215
PH: (816)231-4646
Fax: (816)231-4343
Walker, Jim, CEO

National Association of Women Law
Enforcement Executives [5494]
12500 W 87th Street Pky.
Lenexa, KS 66215
PH: (847)404-8189
Fax: (913)477-7249
Layman, Dawn, President

National Cable Television Cooperative, Inc. [692]
11200 Corporate Ave.
Lenexa, KS 66219-1392
Holleran, Edward, Chairman

Nazarene Compassionate Ministries
[20000]
17001 Prairie Star Pky.
Lenexa, KS 66220
Toll free: 800-310-6362

Nazarene Missions International
[20444]
17001 Prairie Star Pkwy.
Lenexa, KS 66220
PH: (913)577-2970
Fax: (913)577-0861
Ketchum, Dr. Daniel D., Director

Transportation Lawyers Association
[5820]
PO Box 15122
Lenexa, KS 66285-5122
PH: (913)895-4615
Fax: (913)895-4652
Booth, Hillary Arrow, VP

International Yak Association [4457]
c/o Stephanie David, Secretary
-Treasurer
1676 Y Rd.
Lenora, KS 67645
Sprouse, Jandy, President

Singles in Agriculture [21741]
PO Box 51
Lincoln, KS 67455-0051

PH: (815)947-3559
Fritts, David, VP, Chairman

AIB International [365]
1213 Bakers Way
Manhattan, KS 66505-3999
PH: (785)537-4750
Toll free: 800-633-5137
Fax: (785)537-1493
Olewnik, Dr. Maureen C., VP of
Tech. Svcs.

Baking Industry Sanitation Standards
Committee [370]
PO Box 3999
Manhattan, KS 66505-3999
PH: (785)537-4750
Toll free: 866-342-4772
Fax: (785)537-1493
Biane, Andre, President, CEO

Global Alliance for Rabies Control
[14578]
529 Humboldt St., Ste. 1
Manhattan, KS 66502
Briggs, Dr. Deborah, Bd. Member

Journalism Education Association
[8156]
105 Kedzie Hall
828 Mid-Campus Dr. S
Manhattan, KS 66506-0008
PH: (785)532-5532
Toll free: 866-532-5532
Fax: (785)532-5563
Furnas, Kelly, Exec. Dir.

National Academic Advising Associa-
tion [7689]
Kansas State University
2323 Anderson Ave., Ste. 225
Manhattan, KS 66502-2912
PH: (785)532-5717
Fax: (785)532-7732
Nutt, Charlie, Exec. Dir.

Novelists Inc. [3517]
PO Box 2037
Manhattan, KS 66505
Fax: (785)537-1877
Leto, Julie, President

World Association of Veterinary
Anatomists [17677]
Dept. of Anatomy and Physiology
College of Veterinary Medicine
Kansas State University
Manhattan, KS 66506-5601
PH: (785)532-4530
Fax: (785)532-4557
Sotonyi, Dr. Peter, VP

World Organization for Early Child-
hood Education - U.S. National
Committee [7597]
c/o Bronwyn Fees, Ph.D., Member-
ship Chairperson
Family Studies & Human Services
College of Human Ecology
Kansas State University
303 Justin Hall
Manhattan, KS 66506
Wagner, Judith

99th Infantry Division Association
[20715]
PO Box 99
Marion, KS 66861-0099
Benefiel, Phil, President

Antique Telephone Collectors As-
sociation [22443]
PO Box 1252
McPherson, KS 67460
PH: (620)245-9555
Goldsmith, Cindy, Office Mgr.

Fibromyalgia Coalition International
[14766]
5201 Johnson Dr., Ste. 210
Mission, KS 66205-2920

PH: (913)384-4673
Fax: (913)384-8998
Keeny, Yvonne, Exec. Dir., Founder

Heavy Movable Structures, Inc.
[6163]
6701 W 64th St., Ste. 320
Mission, KS 66202
PH: (913)213-5110
Fax: (913)213-5149
Appelbaum, Daniel, Treasurer

Mennonite Women U.S.A. [20333]
718 N Main St.
Newton, KS 67114-1819
PH: (316)281-4396
Toll free: 866-866-2872
Fax: (316)283-0454
Roth, Carol, Bd. Member

Mennonite Central Committee
Overseas Peace Office [18804]
121 E 30th St.
North Newton, KS 67117
PH: (717)859-1151
Toll free: 888-563-4676
Hershberger, Ann Graber, Chmn. of
the Bd.

Alpha Rho Chi [23677]
PO Box 4671
Olathe, KS 66062
Buckberg, Phil, President

American College of Healthcare
Architects [14976]
18000 W 105th St.
Olathe, KS 66061-7543
PH: (913)895-4604
Fax: (913)895-4652
VanMeerhaeghe, Ms. Dana, Exec.
Dir.

American Society for Pain Manage-
ment Nursing [16113]
18000 W 105th St.
Olathe, KS 66061
PH: (913)895-4606
Toll free: 888-34-ASPMN
Fax: (913)895-4652
Schreiner, Ellyn T., MPH, President

American Whippet Club [21827]
c/o Kathy Rasmussen, Membership
Chairperson
11714 Harmony Ln.
Olathe, KS 66062
PH: (913)526-5702
Hopfenbeck, Jill, Dr., Director

Association of College and
University Auditors [7422]
18000 W 105th St.
Olathe, KS 66061
PH: (913)895-4620
Fax: (913)895-4652
Patel, Vijay, President

Cure CMD [15920]
PO Box 701
Olathe, KS 66051
Toll free: 866-400-3626
Rutkowski, Anne, Chairwoman

De Re Militari: The Society for
Medieval Military History [9801]
PO Box 2211
Olathe, KS 66051
Gillmor, Carroll, Secretary, Treasurer

Deaf Bilingual Coalition [11934]
c/o Chriz Dally, Treasurer
11541 S Penrose St.
Olathe, KS 66061
Kerr, David, Chairman

Deaf International [11936]
PO Box 3838
Olathe, KS 66063-3838

PH: (913)390-9010
Fax: (913)390-9011
Buchholz, Noah D., Founder

National Association of EMS Physi-
cians [14684]
18000 W 105th St.
Olathe, KS 66061
PH: (913)895-4611
Toll free: 800-228-3677
Fax: (913)895-4652
Kind, Jerrie Lynn, Exec. Dir.

National Association of Graduate
Admissions Professionals [7450]
18000 W 105th St.
Olathe, KS 66061-7543
PH: (913)895-4616
Fax: (913)895-4652
Evans-Lombe, Monica, Exec. Dir.

National Association for Healthcare
Recruitment [15586]
18000 W 105th St.
Olathe, KS 66061-7543
PH: (913)895-4627
Fax: (913)895-4652
Cunningham, Derek, President

National Board for Respiratory Care
[17455]
18000 W 105th St.
Olathe, KS 66061-7543
PH: (913)895-4900
Toll free: 888-341-4811
Fax: (913)895-4650
Smith, Gary A., Exec. Dir.

Pediatric Endocrinology Nursing
Society [16614]
18000 W 105th St.
Olathe, KS 66061
PH: (913)895-4628
Toll free: 877-936-7367
Fax: (913)895-4652
Johnson, Maryann, BSN, RN,
President

Railroadiana Collectors Association
Inc. [22411]
c/o Mary Ann James, Secretary
17675 W 113th St.
Olathe, KS 66061
James, Mary Ann, Mem.

USA Athletes International [22514]
13095 S Brentwood St.
Olathe, KS 66061
PH: (913)397-9024
Toll free: 800-413-6418
Fax: (913)782-5556
Edington, William, Founder, Exec.
Dir.

Academy of Veterinary Consultants
[17586]
PO Box 24305
Overland Park, KS 66283
PH: (913)766-4373
Fax: (913)766-0474
Portillo, Tom, President

Accordionists and Teachers Guild,
International [8355]
10349 Century Ln.
Overland Park, KS 66215
PH: (913)888-4706
Finch, Liz, VP

Accreditation Council for Business
Schools and Programs [7618]
11520 W 119th St.
Overland Park, KS 66213-2002
PH: (913)339-9356
Fax: (913)339-6226
Viehland, Mr. Douglas, CAE, Mem.

African Environmental Research and
Consulting Group [4034]
14912 Walmer St.
Overland Park, KS 66223

PH: (913)897-6132
Fax: (913)891-6132
Sam, Dr. Peter A., Chairman

American Association of School
Personnel Administrators [7417]
11863 W 112th St., Ste. 100
Overland Park, KS 66210-1375
PH: (913)327-1222
Fax: (913)327-1223
Reznicek, Larry, President

American Business Women's As-
sociation [607]
9820 Metcalf Ave., Ste. 110
Overland Park, KS 66212
Toll free: 800-228-0007
Fax: (913)660-0101
Montross, Lisa, President

Angel Capital Association [2017]
10977 Granada Ln., Ste. 103
Overland Park, KS 66211
PH: (913)894-4700
Hudson, Marianne, Exec. Dir.

ARMA International [1792]
11880 College Blvd., Ste. 450
Overland Park, KS 66210
Toll free: 800-422-2762
Fax: (913)341-3742
Bier, Marilyn, Director, Exec. Dir.

Aviation Insurance Association
[1841]
7200 W 75th St.
Overland Park, KS 66204
PH: (913)627-9632
Fax: (913)381-2515
Bannwarth, Amanda, Exec. Dir.

BEMA [371]
10740 Nall Ave., Ste. 230
Overland Park, KS 66211
PH: (913)338-1300
Fax: (913)338-1327
Brown, Kerwin, President, CEO

Cold War Veterans Association
[21119]
PO Box 13042
Overland Park, KS 66282-3042
Milum, Vince,, Chairman

Copper and Brass Servicenter As-
sociation [2346]
6734 W 121st St.
Overland Park, KS 66209
PH: (913)396-0697
Fax: (913)345-1006
Avery, Susan, CAE, CEO

Council for Learning Disabilities
[12233]
11184 Antioch Rd.
Overland Park, KS 66210
PH: (913)491-1011
Fax: (913)491-1011
Nease, Linda, Exec. Dir.

Epidermoid Brain Tumor Society
[16343]
c/o Kenneth D. Frevert
12573 Wedd St.
Overland Park, KS 66213-1845
Frevert, Kenneth D., Contact

Institute of Singles Dynamics
[20368]
PO Box 27222
Overland Park, KS 66225
Davidson, Don, Director, Founder

International Association of Crime
Analysts [5155]
9218 Metcalf Ave., No. 364
Overland Park, KS 66212
Toll free: 800-609-3419
Fritz, Dr. Noah, President

International Association of Plastics
Distribution [2624]
6734 W 121st St.
Overland Park, KS 66209
PH: (913)345-1005
Fax: (913)345-1006
Nelson, Whitney, Dir. of Mtgs.

International Essential Tremor
Foundation [15945]
11111 W 95th St., Ste. 260
Overland Park, KS 66214-1846
PH: (913)341-3880
Toll free: 888-387-3667
Fax: (913)341-1296
Rice, Catherine S., Exec. Dir.

International Wheat Gluten Associa-
tion [1348]
9393 W 110th St., Ste. 200
Overland Park, KS 66212-6319
PH: (913)381-8180
Fax: (913)381-8836
Bunn, G. Peter, III, Gen. Counsel

M&M's Collectors Club [21682]
c/o Carolyn McAlarney, Treasurer
13208 W 105th Terr.
Overland Park, KS 66215

National Agri-Marketing Association
[105]
11020 King St., Ste. 205
Overland Park, KS 66210
PH: (913)491-6500
Fax: (913)491-6502
Hunyor, Susan, Comm. Chm.

National Auctioneers Association
[261]
8880 Ballentine St.
Overland Park, KS 66214
PH: (913)541-8084
Fax: (913)894-5281
Combest, Hannes, CEO

National Crop Insurance Services
[1907]
8900 Indian Creek Pky., Ste. 600
Overland Park, KS 66210-1567
PH: (913)685-2767
Fax: (913)685-3080
Kovelan, Linda, Exec. Dir.

National Operating Committee on
Standards for Athletic Equipment
[3004]
c/o Mike Oliver, Executive Director
11020 King St., Ste. 215
Overland Park, KS 66210-1201
Oliver, Mike, Exec. Dir.

U.S.A. Federation of Pankration Ath-
lima [22518]
11301 W 88th St.
Overland Park, KS 66214-1701
PH: (816)728-7360
Fax: (816)222-0447
Sixel, Dave, President

Utilities Service Alliance [3425]
9200 Indian Creek Pky., Ste. 201
Overland Park, KS 66210
PH: (913)451-5641
Christensen, John, VP of Operations

We Care of India Association
[11183]
13816 Parkhill
Overland Park, KS 66221
Martin, Julie, Director

West Highland White Terrier Club of
America [21990]
c/o Vonda Kuechler, Membership
Chairperson
PO Box 25264
Overland Park, KS 66225-5264

PH: (913)963-3806
Trudeau, Lee, President

Western Surgical Association
[17418]
14005 Nicklaus Dr.
Overland Park, KS 66204
PH: (913)402-7102
Fax: (913)273-1116
Valentine, R. James, MD, President

World Waterpark Association [1163]
8826 Santa Fe Dr., Ste. 310
Overland Park, KS 66212
PH: (913)599-0300
Fax: (913)599-0520
Root, Rick, President

International Organization of Lace
Inc. [21763]
PO Box 132
Paola, KS 66071
Zeiss, Judy, President

Irish Setter Club of America [21901]
c/o Mary Goeke, Membership Chairman
31557 Lookout Rd.
Paola, KS 66071-4900
PH: (913)271-7554
Laabs, Mrs. Heidi, President

Gamewardens Association, Vietnam
to Present [21166]
PO Box 83
Parsons, KS 67357
Toll free: 866-220-7477
Larsen, David, President

COME International Baptist
Ministries [20136]
c/o Mark Gervais, Web Administrator
937 9th St.
Phillipsburg, KS 67661
PH: (651)470-2454
Beach, Rev. Bruce, Chairman

North American Gamebird Association [3608]
c/o Brian Beavers, Treasurer
01406 E Highway 50
Pierceville, KS 67868
PH: (620)335-5405
Stock, Fuzzy, VP

Association of Residency Coordina-
tors in Orthopaedic Surgery
[16471]
3965 W 83rd St.
Box 157
Prairie Village, KS 66208
PH: (816)404-5406
Kinowski, Anne, President

Mothers & More [11768]
PO Box 8091
Prairie Village, KS 66208-0091
Toll free: 855-373-MORE
Fax: (845)463-0537
Salamone, Liz, Secretary

Vintage Volkswagen Club of America
[21518]
PO Box 8559
Prairie Village, KS 66208
PH: (641)421-0965
Epstein, Michael, President

Burton Island Association [21051]
c/o Ralf Mauthe, Treasurer
13190 Cedarwood Dr.
Saint George, KS 66535
PH: (785)494-2502
Cox, Jim, Secretary

The Land Institute [4157]
2440 E Water Well Rd.
Salina, KS 67401

PH: (785)823-5376
Fax: (785)823-8728
Wright, Angus, Chairman

Alliance of Professional Tattooists,
Inc. [3197]
22052 W 66th St., Ste. 225
Shawnee, KS 66226
PH: (816)979-1300
Martin, Mike, President

National Association of Part-Time
and Temporary Employees [1096]
5800 Barton, Ste. 201
Shawnee, KS 66203
PH: (913)962-7740
Fax: (913)631-0489
Conner, Preston L., President

National Derby Rallies [23182]
c/o Terry Henry, Executive Director
6644 Switzer Ln.
Shawnee, KS 66203
PH: (913)962-6360
Shuff, Ruthie, President

Trucking Management, Inc. [3359]
PO Box 860725
Shawnee, KS 66286-0725
McMillan, Mike, President, CEO

American Reusable Textile Associa-
tion [3254]
PO Box 1142
Shawnee Mission, KS 66202
PH: (863)660-5350
    (913)709-0229
Jenkins, Nancy, Exec. Dir., Editor,
Secretary

Grassland Heritage Foundation
[3878]
PO Box 394
Shawnee Mission, KS 66201
PH: (785)691-9748
Babbitt, Angie, VP

International College of Applied Ki-
nesiology U.S.A. [15266]
6405 Metcalf Ave., Ste. 503
Shawnee Mission, KS 66202
PH: (913)384-5336
Fax: (913)384-5112
Domby, Gary, D.C., DIBAK, Chair-
man

Metal Building Contractors and Erec-
tors Association [2199]
PO Box 499
Shawnee Mission, KS 66201
PH: (913)432-3800
Toll free: 800-866-6722
Fax: (913)432-3803
Smith, Gary, President

North American Natural Bodybuilding
Federation [22698]
PO Box 25097
Shawnee Mission, KS 66225
PH: (913)963-5091

Professional Association of Small
Business Accountants [57]
6405 Metcalf Ave., Ste. 503
Shawnee Mission, KS 66202
Toll free: 866-296-0001
Fax: (913)384-5112
Woodman, Nick, CEO, Founder

Unity Coalition for Israel [8134]
3965 W 83rd St., No. 292
Shawnee Mission, KS 66208-5308
PH: (913)648-0022
Fax: (913)648-7997
Levens, Esther, CEO, Founder

Ankole Watusi International Registry
[3716]
22484 W 239 St.
Spring Hill, KS 66083-9306

PH: (913)592-4050
Lundgren, Dr. Elizabeth, Exec. Sec.

American Organ Transplant Associa-
tion [17502]
PO Box 418
Stilwell, KS 66085
PH: (713)344-2402
Fax: (281)617-4274
Terry, Pamela H., President

35th Infantry Division Association
[20701]
PO Box 5004
Topeka, KS 66605
Windham, Robert E., President

American Holistic Nurses Associa-
tion [15264]
2900 SW Plass Ct.
Topeka, KS 66612-1213
PH: (785)234-1712
Toll free: 800-278-2462
Fax: (785)234-1713
Roberts, Terri, Exec. Dir.

American Society of Mammalogists
[6790]
c/o Christy Classi, CAE
PO Box 4973
Topeka, KS 66604
PH: (785)550-6904
Lacey, Eileen, President

American Society of Victimology
[13257]
c/o Thomas Underwood, Treasurer
Washburn University
1700 SW College Ave.
Topeka, KS 66621
PH: (785)670-1242
Stanley, Debra, President

Bath Enclosure Manufacturers As-
sociation [2635]
PO Box 4730
Topeka, KS 66604
PH: (785)273-0393

Callerlab - International Association
of Square Dance Callers [9245]
200 SW 30th St., Ste. 104
Topeka, KS 66611
PH: (785)783-3665
Toll free: 800-331-2577
Fax: (785)783-3696
Clasper, Barry, Mem.

Clinical Legal Education Association
[8212]
c/o Janet T. Jackson, Co-President
1700 SW College Ave.
Topeka, KS 66621
PH: (785)670-1637
Jackson, Janet T., Co-Pres.

Foil and Specialty Effects Associa-
tion [2347]
2150 SW Westport Dr., Ste. 101
Topeka, KS 66614
PH: (785)271-5816
Fax: (785)271-6404
Peterson, Jeff, Exec. Dir.

Glass Association of North America
[1503]
800 SW Jackson St., Ste. 1500
Topeka, KS 66612-1200
PH: (785)271-0208
Sowell, Urmilla, Tech. Dir.

Glazing Industry Code Committee
[531]
800 SW Jackson St., Ste. 1500
Topeka, KS 66612-1200
PH: (785)271-0208
Fax: (785)271-0166
Block, Valerie, Chairperson

Home Baking Association [1336]
2931 SW Gainsboro Rd.
Topeka, KS 66614
PH: (785)478-3283
Fax: (785)478-3024

Casey Jones Railroad Unit [22337]
PO Box 5511
Topeka, KS 66605

National Association of Trailer
 Manufacturers [327]
2420 SW 17th St.
Topeka, KS 66604-2627
PH: (785)272-4433
Fax: (785)272-4455
Trusdale, Pam, Exec. Dir.

National Gulf War Resource Center
 [21133]
1725 SW Gage Blvd.
Topeka, KS 66604
PH: (785)221-0162
Toll free: 866-531-7183
Fax: (785)235-6531
Bunker, James A., Exec. Dir.

Protective Glazing Council [1508]
800 SW Jackson St., Ste. 1500
Topeka, KS 66612-1200
PH: (785)271-0208
Fax: (785)271-0166
Yanek, Bill, Exec. VP

Sports Car Club of America [21493]
PO Box 19400
Topeka, KS 66619-0400
PH: (785)357-7222
Toll free: 800-770-2055
Fax: (785)232-7228
Lemon, Joel, Mgr.

Transportation Safety Equipment
 Institute [3007]
4021 SW 10th Ave., No. 323
Topeka, KS 66604-1916
PH: (785)220-4062
Fax: (866)286-3641
Brown, Michelle, Exec. Dir.

Washburn Alumni Association
 [19370]
1700 SW College Ave.
Topeka, KS 66621
PH: (785)670-1641
    (785)670-1643
Hoffmann, Susie, Director

American Cheviot Sheep Society
 [4648]
PO Box 231
Wamego, KS 66547
PH: (785)456-8500
Fax: (785)456-8599
Ebert, Jeff, Exec. Sec.

American Delaine and Merino
 Record Association [4652]
305 Lincoln St.
Wamego, KS 66547
PH: (785)456-8500
Fax: (785)456-8599
Schroeder, Amy, Exec. Sec.

American Hampshire Sheep As-
 sociation [4654]
305 Lincoln St.
Wamego, KS 66547
PH: (785)456-8500
Fax: (785)456-8599
Lytle, David, Director

American Polypay Sheep Associa-
 tion [4659]
305 Lincoln St.
Wamego, KS 66547
PH: (785)456-8500
Fax: (785)456-8599
Jones, Glen, Treasurer

National Lincoln Sheep Breeders
 Association [4674]
305 Lincoln St.
Wamego, KS 66547
PH: (269)623-2549
    (585)494-1069
Meek, Robin, President

National Tunis Sheep Registry, Inc.
 [4675]
305 Lincoln St.
Wamego, KS 66547
PH: (785)456-8500
Fax: (785)456-8599
Murry, Lynn, President

North American Babydoll Southdown
 Sheep Association and Registry
 [4678]
305 Lincoln St.
Wamego, KS 66547-1629
PH: (785)456-8500
Fax: (785)456-8599
Spisak, Diane, Bd. Member

North American Shetland Sheep-
 breeders Association [4679]
305 Lincoln
Wamego, KS 66547
PH: (260)672-9623
Ludlum, Mike, President

American Academy of Environmental
 Medicine [14711]
6505 E Central Ave., No. 296
Wichita, KS 67206
PH: (316)684-5500
Fax: (316)684-5709
Rodgers-Fox, De, Exec. Dir.

American Bonanza Society [21213]
PO Box 12888
Wichita, KS 67277
PH: (316)945-1700
Fax: (316)945-1710
Kohout, Keith, President

American Overseas Schools Histori-
 cal Society [9373]
704 W Douglas Ave.
Wichita, KS 67203-6401
PH: (316)265-6837
Vaughn-Wiles, Gayle, President

Association of SIDS and Infant
 Mortality Programs [17332]
c/o The KIDS Network, Inc.
1148 S Hillside St., Ste. 10
Wichita, KS 67211
Toll free: 800-930-7437
Harvieux, Anne, LCSW, President

Clan Arthur Association USA [20797]
10821 E Glengate Cir.
Wichita, KS 67206-8902
Cochener, Nancy McArthur,
 President, Exec. Sec.

Congress of Chiropractic State As-
 sociations [14262]
12531 E Meadow Dr.
Wichita, KS 67206
PH: (316)613-3386
Fax: (316)633-4455
LaMonica, John, President

Crigler-Najjar Association [15254]
c/o Cory Mauck
3134 Bayberry St.
Wichita, KS 67226
Martin, Katie, President

Hospitals of Hope [15475]
3545 N Santa Fe St.
Wichita, KS 67219
PH: (316)262-0964
Fax: (316)262-0953
Wawrzewski, Michael J., CEO,
 Founder

Humane Water [4769]
PO Box 782916
wichita, KS 67278
PH: (316)788-1150
Leftwich, Sarah, CEO, President

MRFAC [467]
c/o BAC and Associates LLC
616 E 34th St. N
Wichita, KS 67219
PH: (316)832-9213
Elersich, Rich, Treasurer

National Association of Educational
 Office Professionals [7433]
1841 S Eisenhower Ct.
Wichita, KS 67209
PH: (316)942-4822
Fax: (316)942-7100
Tribble, Linda, Advisor

National Association of Victim
 Service Professionals in Correc-
 tions [13262]
212 S Market St.
Wichita, KS 67202
PH: (316)613-7263
Chambers, Monica, Chmn. of the
 Bd.

National Baseball Congress [22558]
110 S Main, Ste. 600
Wichita, KS 67202
PH: (316)977-9400
Fax: (316)462-4506
Sevier, Greg, Treasurer

National Championship Racing As-
 sociation [23083]
7700 N Broadway St.
Wichita, KS 67219
PH: (316)755-1781
Fax: (316)755-0665
Hall, C-Ray, President

National Depression Glass Associa-
 tion [22138]
PO Box 8264
Wichita, KS 67208
Cornelius, Danny, President

Orthodox Christian School Association [7613]
c/o Ro Kallail, Business Manager
13213 E Bridlewood Ct.
Wichita, KS 67230
PH: (316)734-6286
Bearer, Robert, Treasurer

Overseas Brats [19661]
PO Box 47112
Wichita, KS 67201
PH: (316)269-9610
Fax: (316)269-9610
Condrill, Joe, President

Running USA [23120]
3450 N Ridgewood St., No. 311
Wichita, KS 67220
PH: (313)408-3655
Harshbarger, Rich, CEO

Sigma Gamma Tau [23743]
c/o Dr. Shawn Keshmiri, Officer
Aerospace Engineering Dept.
University of Kansas
1530 W 15th St., 2120 Learned Hall
Wichita, KS 67260-0044
PH: (316)978-6328
    (785)864-4267
Fax: (316)978-3307
Myose, Roy, VP

Society of Decorative Painters
 [21784]
1220 E 1st st.
Wichita, KS 67203-5968
PH: (316)269-9300
Fax: (316)269-9191
Marler, Pat, President

Sport and Recreation Law Association [5768]
c/o Mary Myers
1621 N Melrose Dr.
Wichita, KS 67212
Seidler, Dr. Todd, Exec. Dir.

Trees for Life [12118]
3006 W St. Louis St.
Wichita, KS 67203
PH: (316)945-6929
Fax: (316)945-0909
Mathur, Balbir S., Founder

United States Deputy Sheriffs' As-
 sociation [5520]
319 S Hydraulic St., Ste. B
Wichita, KS 67211-1908
PH: (316)263-2583
Willis, Mike, Exec. Dir.

Vintage Thunderbird Club
 International [21516]
c/o Rod Wake, President
PO Box 75308
Wichita, KS 67275
PH: (316)722-2028
McNeill, Terri, Editor, Web Adm.

Pi Gamma Mu [23863]
1001 Millington St., Ste. B
Winfield, KS 67156
PH: (620)221-3128
Fax: (620)221-7124
Kinsella, Susan, Chancellor

KENTUCKY

National Conference of Firemen and
 Oilers [23417]
1212 Bath Ave., Fl. F and O
Ashland, KY 41101
PH: (606)324-3445
Fax: (606)326-7039
Thacker, John R., President

Jesse Stuart Foundation [9100]
4440 13th St.
Ashland, KY 41102-5432
PH: (606)326-1667
Toll free: 855-407-6243
Fax: (606)325-2519
Gifford, Dr. James M., CEO

United States Faceters Guild [6361]
c/o Sue Lichtenberger, Secretary-
 Treasurer
6625 Skyline Dr.
Ashland, KY 41102
Maxwell, Tom, President

National Saanen Breeders Association [3607]
c/o Amy Keach, President
4701 Lebanon Rd.
Bagdad, KY 40003
PH: (502)227-1044
Grossman, Marilyn, President

Substance Abuse Program
 Administrators Association [17329]
1014 Whispering Oak Dr.
Bardstown, KY 40004
Toll free: 800-672-7229
Fax: (281)664-3152
Morrison, Jeff, Exec. Dir.

American Forage and Grassland
 Council [4619]
PO Box 867
Berea, KY 40403
Toll free: 800-944-2342
Agee, Chris, President

American Society for Legal History
 [9457]
c/o Patricia Minter, Membership
 Committee

Western Kentucky University
1906 College Heights Blvd., No.
21086
Bowling Green, KY 42101-1000
Fax: (270)793-0040
Scott, Rebecca J., President

Miniature Motorsports Racing Association **[22519]**
PO Box 50906
Bowling Green, KY 42102-4206
PH: (270)784-8231
Neimeier, Pete, President

Phi Upsilon Omicron, Inc. **[23772]**
PO Box 50970
Bowling Green, KY 42102-4270
PH: (270)904-1340
Martin, Melissa, Exec. Dir.

Society for Values in Higher Education **[20090]**
c/o Western Kentucky University
1906 College Heights Blvd., No.
8020
Bowling Green, KY 42101-1041
PH: (270)745-2907
Fax: (270)745-5374
Bean, Cathy Bao, Chairperson

SunPower Afrique **[7213]**
188 Moorman Ln.
Bowling Green, KY 42101
PH: (610)489-1105
Costanza, Kira, Founder, Exec. Dir.

Aladdin Knights of the Mystic Light **[21605]**
c/o Bill Courter
550 Pioneer Ln.
Calvert City, KY 42029-9123
PH: (270)559-7900

Disabled American Veterans **[20766]**
3725 Alexandria Pke.
Cold Spring, KY 41076
Toll free: 877-426-2838

Disabled American Veterans
Auxiliary **[20767]**
3725 Alexandria Pke.
Cold Spring, KY 41076-1712
Toll free: 877-426-2838

Browning Collectors Association **[22018]**
c/o Charles P. Wagner, President
711 Scott St.
Covington, KY 41011
PH: (859)431-1712
Wagner, Charles P., President

International Order of E.A.R.S. **[10222]**
7712 Briarwood Dr.
Crestwood, KY 40014-9094
PH: (502)553-3406
Dotson, Heather, Secretary

Animal Welfare Council **[3621]**
PO Box 85
Eastwood, KY 40018-0085
PH: (719)440-7255
Schonholtz, Cindy, Mem.

American Academy of Physician Assistants in Occupational Medicine **[16310]**
174 Monticello Pl.
Elizabethtown, KY 42701
White, Regina Lee, President

International Youth Conditioning Association **[23377]**
PO Box 1539
Elizabethtown, KY 42702-1539
Toll free: 888-366-4922
Berry, Nick, CEO

American Shagya Arabian Verband **[4326]**
PO Box 169
Finchville, KY 40022
Boles, Steve, President

Association of Camp Nurses **[16117]**
19006 Hunt County Ln.
Fisherville, KY 40023-7704
PH: (502)232-2945
Erceg, Linda Ebner, RN, Author

American Bashkir Curly Registry **[4298]**
71 Cavalier Blvd., No. 124
Florence, KY 41042
PH: (859)485-9700
Toll free: 877-324-0956
Fax: (859)485-9777
Martino, Melinda, Treasurer

National Association for Family and Community Education **[7992]**
73 Cavalier Blvd., Ste. 106
Florence, KY 41042
Toll free: 877-712-4477
Fax: (859)525-6496
Teeples, Bonnie, Chairperson

National Association for PET
Container Resources **[3451]**
7310 Turfway Rd., Ste. 550
Florence, KY 41042
PH: (859)372-6635
Moore, Rick, Exec. Dir.

National Lieutenant Governors Association **[5785]**
71 Cavalier Blvd., Ste. 223
Florence, KY 41042
PH: (859)283-1400
   (859)244-8111
Toll free: 800-800-1910
Michels, Matt, Treasurer

101st Airborne Division Association **[5580]**
PO Box 929
Fort Campbell, KY 42223-0929
PH: (931)431-0199
Fax: (931)431-0195
Underhill, Randall, Exec. Sec.

Christian Universalist Association **[19967]**
14 Fairfield Pl.
Fort Thomas, KY 41075
PH: (269)352-4457
Koster, Rich, Coord.

USS Coral Sea CVA-43 Association **[21066]**
52 Woodland Pl.
Fort Thomas, KY 41075-1605
Phillips, Mil, President

Conference of Radiation Control
Program Directors **[5739]**
1030 Burlington Ln., Ste. 4B
Frankfort, KY 40601
PH: (502)227-4543
Fax: (502)227-7862
Meyer, Charles, Tech. Ofc.

International Association of
Workforce Professionals **[5165]**
1801 Louisville Rd.
Frankfort, KY 40601
PH: (502)223-4459
Toll free: 888-898-9960
Thomas, James, President

National Conference of State Social
Security Administrators **[5760]**
501 High St., 4th Fl.
Frankfort, KY 40601
PH: (502)564-3952
Fax: (502)564-2124
Bryan, J.W., Director

National Water Safety Congress **[12837]**
PO Box 4132
Frankfort, KY 40604-4132
PH: (502)352-8771
Brown, Mark, President

American Academy of Equine Art **[8828]**
160 E Main St.
Georgetown, KY 40324
PH: (502)570-8567
Conner, Frances Clay, Exec. Dir.

Purebred Morab Horse Association **[4404]**
PO Box 802
Georgetown, KY 40324
PH: (502)535-4803
Lassanske, Donna, President

Young Jumper Futurity **[22953]**
PO Box 1445
Georgetown, KY 40324-6445
PH: (502)535-6787
Fax: (502)535-4412

Clan Pollock International **[20837]**
PO Box 404
Greenville, KY 42345
PH: (615)456-1699
Fax: (208)362-5460
Pollock, A.D., Jr., President

National Cooperative of Health
Networks Association **[15046]**
400 S Main St.
Hardinsburg, KY 40143
PH: (970)712-0732
Fax: (970)417-4186
Czarnik-Laurin, Darcy, President

Friends-4-Cures **[13975]**
PO Box 324
Henderson, KY 42419-0324
Toll free: 866-469-2873

American Cave Conservation Association **[3798]**
119 E Main St.
Horse Cave, KY 42749
PH: (270)786-1466

Frontier Nursing Service **[16133]**
Frontier Nursing University
195 School St.
Hyden, KY 41749
PH: (606)672-2312
Lee, Nathan, CEO, President

National Adult Education Honor
Society **[7454]**
4953 Madison Pke.
Independence, KY 41051
PH: (859)685-8559
Bentti, Robert, Director

Chemical Coaters Association
International **[712]**
5040 Old Taylor Mill Rd., PMB 13
Latonia, KY 41015
PH: (859)356-1030

Industrial Heating Equipment Association **[1622]**
5040 Old Taylor Mill Rd.
Latonia, KY 41015
PH: (859)356-1575
Fax: (859)356-0908
Goyer, Anne, Exec. VP

Academy of Doctors of Audiology **[15164]**
446 E High St., Ste. 10
Lexington, KY 40517
Toll free: 866-493-5544
Czuhajewski, Stephanie, Exec. Dir.

Accounting and Financial Women's
Alliance **[2]**
2365 Harrodsburg Rd., Ste. A325
Lexington, KY 40504

PH: (859)219-3532
Toll free: 800-326-2163
Fax: (859)219-3577
Miles, Mrs. Monika P., CPA, Contact

All Star Association **[966]**
1050 Monarch St., Ste. 101
Lexington, KY 40513
Toll free: 800-930-3644
Fax: (859)255-3647
Sterne, Jeff, Exec. Dir.

Alpha Epsilon **[23735]**
University of Kentucky
Biosystems and Agricultural
Engineering
202 CE Barnhart Bldg.
Lexington, KY 40546
PH: (859)257-3000
Fax: (859)257-5671
Whysong, Christan, President

Alpha Tau Alpha **[7470]**
c/o Rebekah Barnes Epps
The University of Kentucky
College of Agriculture, Food, and
Environment
708 Garrigus Bldg.
Lexington, KY 40546
Graham, Dr. James, President

American Academy on Communication in Healthcare **[16732]**
201 E Main St., Ste. 1405
Lexington, KY 40507-2004
PH: (859)514-9211
Fax: (859)514-9207
Singler, Laura, CAE, Exec. Dir.

American Association of Equine
Practitioners **[17593]**
4033 Iron Works Pky.
Lexington, KY 40511
PH: (859)233-0147
Toll free: 800-443-0177
Fax: (859)233-1968
Baker, Sally J., Dir. of Public Rel.

American Board of Family Medicine **[14747]**
1648 McGrathiana Pky., Ste. 550
Lexington, KY 40511-1247
PH: (859)269-5626
Fax: (859)335-7501
Puffer, James C., MD, President,
CEO

American Carbon Society **[6180]**
2540 Research Park Dr.
Lexington, KY 40511
PH: (859)257-0322
Fax: (859)257-0220
Norley, Julian, VP

American Casting Association **[22838]**
c/o Patrick McFadden, Secretary
1719 Versailles Rd.
Lexington, KY 40504
Roberts, David, President

American Farrier's Association **[433]**
4059 Iron Works Pkwy., Ste. No. 1
Lexington, KY 40511
PH: (859)233-7411
Toll free: 877-268-4505
Fax: (859)231-7862
Heighton, Rachel, Office Mgr.

American Hackney Horse Society **[4307]**
4059 Iron Works Pky., A-3
Lexington, KY 40511-8462
PH: (859)255-8694
Fax: (859)255-0177
Campbell, Rich, President

American Hanoverian Society **[4310]**
4067 Iron Works Pkwy., Ste. 1
Lexington, KY 40511

PH: (859)255-4141
Fax: (859)255-8467
Schutte, Edgar, President

American Probation and Parole Association [5672]
1776 Ave. of the States, Bldg. B
Lexington, KY 40511
PH: (859)244-8203
Fax: (859)244-8001
Kincaid, Diane, Dep. Dir.

American Saddlebred Horse Association [4324]
4083 Iron Works Pky.
Lexington, KY 40511
PH: (859)259-2742
Fax: (859)259-1628
Patrick, Tandy, Director

American Tarot Association [22441]
1020 Liberty Rd.
Lexington, KY 40505-4035
Toll free: 888-211-1572
Fax: (859)514-9799
Hite, Tracy, Treasurer

American Volleyball Coaches Association [23349]
2365 Harrodsburg Rd., Ste. A325
Lexington, KY 40504
Toll free: 866-544-2822
DeBoer, Kathy, Exec. Dir.

Asphalt Institute [493]
2696 Research Park Dr.
Lexington, KY 40511-8480
PH: (859)288-4960
Fax: (859)288-4999
Grass, Peter T., President

Association for College and University Technology Advancement [8022]
152 W Zandale Dr., Ste. 200
Lexington, KY 40503
PH: (859)278-3338
Fax: (859)278-3268
Campbell, Tom, CFO

Association of Local Government Auditors [5268]
449 Lewis Hargett Cir., Ste. 290
Lexington, KY 40503-3669
PH: (859)276-0686
Fax: (859)278-0507
Waltmunson, Kymber, President

Association of Medical Illustrators [15632]
201 E Main St., Ste. 1405
Lexington, KY 40507
Toll free: 866-393-4264
Sandone, Cory, President

Association of Professional Dog Trainers [3984]
2365 Harrodsburg Rd., A325
Lexington, KY 40504
Toll free: 800-738-3647
Fax: (864)331-0767
Feldner, David, Exec. Dir.

Association of Racing Commissioners International [5738]
1510 Newtown Pke., Ste. 210
Lexington, KY 40511
PH: (859)224-7070
Martin, Edward, President

Association of State Dam Safety Officials [5745]
239 S Limestone
Lexington, KY 40508-2501
PH: (859)550-2788
Pawloski, Jim, President

Burley Tobacco Growers Cooperative Association [4720]
620 S Broadway
Lexington, KY 40508

PH: (859)252-3561
Warren, Eddie, VP

Carriage Association of America [21633]
4075 Iron Works Pky.
Lexington, KY 40511
PH: (859)231-0971
Fax: (859)231-0973
Swendson, Ted, Officer

CHA - Certified Horsemanship Association [22942]
1795 Alysheba Way, Ste. 7102
Lexington, KY 40509
PH: (859)259-3399
Fax: (859)255-0726
Stutz, Ward, Director

Chief Officers of State Library Agencies [9698]
201 E Main St., Ste. 1405
Lexington, KY 40507
PH: (859)514-9151
Fax: (859)514-9166
Wiggin, Kendall, President

Children of the Americas [10914]
PO Box 25046
Lexington, KY 40524
PH: (859)422-4278
Cottrill, Carol, MD, Bd. Member

Children's Healthcare is a Legal Duty [15530]
136 Blue Heron Pl.
Lexington, KY 40511
PH: (859)255-2200
    (208)985-0414
Swan, Rita, PhD, Founder, President

Christian Appalachian Project [12641]
PO Box 55911
Lexington, KY 40555-5911
Toll free: 866-270-4227
Fax: (859)269-0617
Adams, Guy, President, CEO

College Savings Plans Network [7925]
2760 Research Park Dr.
Lexington, KY 40511
Lochner, Betty, Chairperson

Concerned Philosophers for Peace [10084]
c/o Arnold Farr
1415 Patterson Office Twr.
Department of Philosophy
University of Kentucky
Lexington, KY 40506-0027
Gan, Barry, Exec. Dir.

Cookie Cutter Collectors Club [21641]
PO Box 22518
Lexington, KY 40522-2518
Birdsell, Chris, President

Council on Licensure, Enforcement and Regulation [5773]
403 Marquis Ave., Ste. 200
Lexington, KY 40502
PH: (859)269-1289
Fax: (859)231-1943
McKown, Kelly, Coord.

Emily Dickinson International Society [10150]
133 Lackawanna Rd.
Lexington, KY 40503
Smith, Martha Nell, President

Energy and Mineral Law Foundation [5651]
340 S Broadway, Ste. 101
Lexington, KY 40508

PH: (859)231-0271
Fax: (859)226-0485
Wells, G. Brian, President

Equine Land Conservation Resource [3859]
4037 Iron Works Pky., Ste. 120
Lexington, KY 40511-8508
PH: (859)455-8383
Fax: (859)455-8381
Gibson, Anna, CEO

Friesian Horse Association of North America [4351]
4037 Iron Works Pky., Ste. 160
Lexington, KY 40511-8483
PH: (859)455-7430
Fax: (859)455-7457
Steenbeek, Gerben, Director

Grayson-Jockey Club Research Foundation [4355]
821 Corporate Dr.
Lexington, KY 40503
PH: (859)224-2850
Fax: (859)224-2853
Hancock, Dell, Chairman

Half Saddlebred Registry of America [4358]
c/o American Saddlebred Horse Association
4083 Iron Works Pky.
Lexington, KY 40511
PH: (859)259-2742
Fax: (859)259-1628
Patrick, Tandy, President

Henry Clay Memorial Foundation [10331]
120 Sycamore Rd.
Lexington, KY 40502
PH: (859)266-8581
Fax: (859)268-7266

International Book Project [8079]
Van Meter Bldg.
1440 Delaware Ave.
Lexington, KY 40505
PH: (859)254-6771
Sprague, Daniel, President

International Coach Federation [22730]
2365 Harrodsburg Rd., Ste. A325
Lexington, KY 40504
PH: (859)219-3580
Toll free: 888-423-3131
Fax: (859)226-4411
Mook, Magdalena, Exec. Dir., CEO

International Spa Association [2910]
2365 Harrodsburg Rd., Ste. A325
Lexington, KY 40504
PH: (859)226-4326
Toll free: 888-651-4772
Fax: (859)226-4445
McNees, Ms. Lynne Walker, President

The Jockey Club [22920]
821 Corporate Dr.
Lexington, KY 40503
PH: (859)224-2700
    (859)514-6616
Fax: (859)224-2710
Gagliano, James L., President, COO

Jockeys' Guild [22921]
448 Lewis Hargett Cir., Ste. 220
Lexington, KY 40503
PH: (859)523-5625
Toll free: 866-465-6257
Fax: (859)219-9892
Velasquez, John, Chairman

KWPN of North America, Inc. [4375]
4037 Iron Works Pky., Ste. 160
Lexington, KY 40511

PH: (859)225-5331
Fax: (859)455-7457
Arts, Willy, Chairperson

Muslim Alliance in North America [10030]
PO Box 910375
Lexington, KY 40591
PH: (859)296-0206
Fax: (859)257-3743
Bagby, Ihsan, Gen. Sec.

National Academies of Practice [15037]
201 E Main St., Ste. 1405
Lexington, KY 40507
PH: (859)514-9184
Fax: (859)514-9188
Bowzer, Melanie, Exec. Dir.

National Association of Agricultural Educators [7476]
300 Garrigus Bldg.
University of Kentucky
Lexington, KY 40546-0215
PH: (859)257-2224
Toll free: 800-509-0204
Jackman, Dr. Jay, CAE, Exec. Dir.

National Association of Government Defined Contribution Administrators, Inc. [2030]
201 E Main St., Ste. 1405
Lexington, KY 40507
PH: (859)514-9161
Scott, Polly, President

National Association for Regulatory Administration [15042]
403 Marquis Ave., Ste. 200
Lexington, KY 40502
PH: (859)687-0262
Williams, Marcus, Exec. Dir.

National Association of State Administrators and Supervisor of Private Schools [8463]
403 Marquis Ave., Ste. 200
Lexington, KY 40502
Rosa-Casanova, Sylvia, President

National Association of State Auditors, Comptrollers, and Treasurers [5708]
449 Lewis Hargett Cir., Ste. 290
Lexington, KY 40503-3669
PH: (859)276-1147
Fax: (859)278-0507
Poynter, R. Kinney, Exec. Dir.

National Association of State Boating Law Administrators [5065]
1648 McGrathiana Pky., Ste. 360
Lexington, KY 40511-1385
PH: (859)225-9487
Graybeal, James, Liaison

National Association of State Chief Administrators [5778]
PO Box 708
Lexington, KY 40588
PH: (859)514-9156
Fax: (859)514-9166
Nelson, Doug, President

National Association of State Chief Information Officers [5306]
c/o AMR Management Services
201 E Main St., Ste. 1405
Lexington, KY 40507
PH: (859)514-9217
Fax: (859)514-9166
Given, Gale, Director

National Association of State Facilities Administrators [5697]
1776 Avenue of the States
Lexington, KY 40511

PH: (859)244-8181
Fax: (859)244-8001
Johnson, Marlene, Exec. Dir., CEO

National Association of State
Personnel Executives [5780]
2760 Research Park Dr.
Lexington, KY 40511
PH: (859)244-8182
Fax: (859)244-8001
Templet, Shannon, Officer

National Association of State
Procurement Officials [5736]
201 E Main St., Ste. 1405
Lexington, KY 40507
PH: (859)514-9159
Fax: (859)514-9166
Mash, Paul, President

National Association of State Retire-
ment Administrators [5078]
449 Lewis Hargett Cir., Ste. 290
Lexington, KY 40503-3669
PH: (202)624-1418
Hiatte, Mary, Coord.

National Association of State School
Nurse Consultants [16155]
1181 Wyndham Hills Dr.
Lexington, KY 40514
PH: (502)564-5279
Gerdes, Jessica, President

National Association of State
Technology Directors [3233]
2760 Research Park Dr.
Lexington, KY 40511
McCord, Mark, Exec. Dir.

National Association of State
Treasurers [5710]
2760 Research Park Dr.
Lexington, KY 40511-8482
Miller, Ken, VP

National Association of Supervisor of
Agricultural Education [7477]
c/o Jay Jackman, NASAE Executive
Treasurer
300 Garrigus Bldg.
Lexington, KY 40546-0215
PH: (859)257-2224
Toll free: 800-509-0204
Fax: (859)323-3919
Jackman, Dr. Jay, CAE, Treasurer

National Association of Unclaimed
Property Administrators [5688]
c/o National Association of State
Treasurers
The Council of State Governments
2760 Research Park Dr.
Lexington, KY 40578-1910
PH: (859)244-8150
Fax: (859)244-8053
Gabriel, John, Comm. Chm.

National Emergency Management
Association [14667]
1776 Avenue of the States
Lexington, KY 40511
PH: (859)244-8000
Fax: (859)244-8239
Richy, Brad, Treasurer

National Gerontological Nursing As-
sociation [14897]
446 E High St., Ste. 10
Lexington, KY 40507
PH: (859)977-7453
Toll free: 800-723-0560
Fax: (859)271-0607
Tanner, Elizabeth, Ph.D, Secretary

National Horsemen's Benevolent
and Protective Association [22923]
870 Corporate Dr., Ste. 300
Lexington, KY 40503-5419

PH: (859)259-0451
Toll free: 866-245-1711
Fax: (859)259-0452
Gessmann, Leroy, President, Chmn.
of the Bd.

National Hunter Jumper Association,
Inc. [22945]
PO Box 11635
Lexington, KY 40576
PH: (610)644-3283
(772)201-9340
Torano, Jimmy, VP

National Thoroughbred Racing As-
sociation [22926]
2525 Harrodsburg Rd., Ste. 510
Lexington, KY 40504
PH: (859)245-6872
Fax: (859)422-1230
Waldrop, Alex, CEO, President

National Tour Association [3387]
101 Prosperous Pl., Ste. 350
Lexington, KY 40509
PH: (859)264-6540
Toll free: 800-682-8886
Fax: (859)264-6570
Inman, Pam, President

National Walking Horse Association
[4390]
4059 Iron Works Pky., Ste. 4
Lexington, KY 40511
PH: (859)252-6942
Fax: (859)252-0640
Richwine, Linda, President

The Nursing Organizations Alliance
[16172]
201 E Main St., Ste. 1405
Lexington, KY 40507
PH: (859)514-9157
Fax: (859)514-9166
Hoying, Cheryl, RN, Treasurer

Paso Fino Horse Association [4400]
4047 Iron Works Pky., Ste. 1
Lexington, KY 40511
PH: (859)825-6000
Fax: (859)258-2125
Miller, Gregory, President

Phi Delta Gamma [23852]
1201 Red Mile Rd.
Lexington, KY 40504-2648
PH: (859)255-1848
Fax: (859)253-0779
Martin, Bill, Exec. Dir., Editor

Phi Gamma Delta [23911]
1201 Red Mile Rd.
Lexington, KY 40544-4599
PH: (859)255-1848
Martin, Bill, Exec. Dir.

Quest International Users Group
[6365]
2365 Harrodsburg Rd., Ste. A325
Lexington, KY 40504-3366
PH: (859)425-5081
Toll free: 800-225-0517
Lyle, David, Chmn. of the Bd.

Race Track Chaplaincy of America
[19938]
2365 Harrodsburg Rd., Ste. A120
Lexington, KY 40504
PH: (859)410-7822
Fax: (859)219-1424
Wiley, Chap. Craig, Exec. Dir.

Receptive Services Association of
America [3391]
2365 Harrodsburg Rd., Ste. A325
Lexington, KY 40504
PH: (859)219-3545
Toll free: 866-939-0934
Fax: (859)226-4404

Society of Behavioral Sleep
Medicine [17222]
1522 Player Dr.
Lexington, KY 40511
PH: (859)312-8880
Fax: (859)303-6055
Schmitz, Michael, PsyD, President

Society of Trauma Nurses [16186]
446 E High St., Ste. 10
Lexington, KY 40507
PH: (859)271-0607
Fax: (859)977-7456
Nash, Julie, Director

State Debt Management Network
[5788]
National Association of State
Treasurers
201 E Main St., Ste. 540
Lexington, KY 40507
PH: (859)721-2190
Pascarella, Mark, Chairman

Sustainable Agriculture Education
Association [7482]
c/o Krista Jacobsen, Treasurer
College of Agriculture, Food and
Environment
University of Kentucky
Lexington, KY 40506
Cotton, Julie, Chairman

Thoroughbred Club of America
[22929]
3555 Rice Rd.
Lexington, KY 40510-9643
PH: (859)254-4282
Fax: (859)231-6131
Broadbent, Happy, President

Thoroughbred Owners and Breeders
Association [22930]
3101 Beaumont Centre Cir., Ste. 110
Lexington, KY 40513
PH: (859)276-2291
Toll free: 888-606-TOBA
Fax: (859)276-2462
Metzger, Dan, President

United Professional Horsemen's As-
sociation [4416]
4059 Iron Works Pky., Ste. 2
Lexington, KY 40511
PH: (859)231-5070
Fax: (859)255-2774
Smith, Barbie, Secretary

United States Dressage Federation
[22948]
4051 Iron Works Pky.
Lexington, KY 40511
PH: (859)971-2277
Fax: (859)971-7722
Hienzsch, Stephan, Exec. Dir.

United States Equestrian Federation
[22949]
4047 Iron Works Pky.
Lexington, KY 40511
PH: (859)258-2472
Fax: (859)231-6662
Keating, Sonja, Sr. VP

United States Hunter Jumper As-
sociation [22951]
3870 Cigar Ln.
Lexington, KY 40511-8931
PH: (859)225-6700
Fax: (859)258-9033
Price, Kevin, Exec. Dir.

United States Pony Clubs [22952]
4041 Iron Works Pky.
Lexington, KY 40511
PH: (859)254-7669
Fax: (859)233-4652
Clark, Karen, Dir. of Fin. & Admin.

U.S.A. Deaf Sports Federation
[22803]
PO Box 22011
Lexington, KY 40591-0338
Lamberton, Jack C., President

World Association of Veterinary
Laboratory Diagnosticians [17678]
College of Agriculture
University of Kentucky
Livestock Disease Diagnostic Ctr.
1490 Bull Lea Rd.
Lexington, KY 40512-4125
PH: (859)253-0571
Fax: (859)255-1624
Carter, Dr. Craig N., Exec. Dir.

School Social Work Association of
America [8574]
PO Box 3068
London, KY 40743
Toll free: 800-588-4149
Oliver, Rebecca, Exec. Dir.

American Association of Preferred
Provider Organizations [15094]
974 Breckenridge Ln., No. 162
Louisville, KY 40207
PH: (502)403-1122
Fax: (502)403-1129
Greenrose, Karen, CEO, President

American Catholic Union [19791]
1207 Potomac Pl.
Louisville, KY 40214
PH: (502)368-0871
Fax: (502)361-9782
Facione, Francis P., Exec. Dir.

American Council of Blind Lions
[17682]
148 Vernon Ave.
Louisville, KY 40206
PH: (502)897-1472
Ruschival, Adam, Treasurer

American Craft Spirits Association
[176]
PO Box 701414
Louisville, KY 40270
PH: (502)299-0238
Lehrman, Margie A. S., Exec. Dir.

American Crappie Association
[22038]
220 Mohawk Ave.
Louisville, KY 40209
PH: (502)384-5924
(270)748-5703
Fax: (502)384-4232
VanVactor, Darrell, Operations Mgr.

American Institute of Wine and Food
[22145]
PO Box 4961
Louisville, KY 40204
Toll free: 800-274-2493
Fax: (502)456-1821
Giaimo, Frank, Chairman

American Printing House for the
Blind, Inc. [17686]
1839 Frankfort Ave.
Louisville, KY 40206-3148
PH: (502)895-2405
Toll free: 800-223-1839
Fax: (502)899-2284
Formenti, Inge, Librarian

American Turners [23213]
1127 E Kentucky St.
Louisville, KY 40204
PH: (502)636-2395
Fax: (502)636-1935
Luckhardt, Shirley, Secretary

Associated Cooperage Industries of
America [827]
10001 Taylorsville Rd., Ste. 201
Louisville, KY 40299-3116

PH: (502)261-2242
Fax: (502)261-9425
Roshkowski, Greg, Exec. VP

Association of Christian Therapists [19944]
PO Box 4961
Louisville, KY 40204
PH: (502)632-3036
Tipton, David, Treasurer

Association of Halfway House Alcoholism Programs of North America, Inc. [13125]
963 S 2nd St.
Louisville, KY 40203-2211
PH: (502)581-0765
Fax: (502)581-1748
Brown, Mac, President

Association for Healthcare Administrative Professionals [67]
328 E Main St.
Louisville, KY 40202
PH: (502)574-9040
Toll free: 888-320-0808
Fax: (502)589-3602
Featherston, Lisa, President

Association for Healthcare Foodservice [15313]
328 E Main St.
Louisville, KY 40202
PH: (502)574-9930
   (502)574-9934
Toll free: 888-528-9552
Fax: (502)589-3602

Blessings in a Backpack [10868]
4121 Shelbyville Rd.
Louisville, KY 40207
Toll free: 800-872-4366
Wiseman, Brooke, CEO

Bridge Kids International [13434]
501 W Kenwood Dr.
Louisville, KY 40214
PH: (502)457-1910
Bailey-Ndiaye, Stacy, Founder, Exec. Dir.

The Child Connection [12355]
2210 Meadow Dr., Ste. 28
Louisville, KY 40218-1335
PH: (502)459-6888
Fax: (502)459-8899
Herron, Keith, Sr., Coord.

Christians for Peace in El Salvador [20403]
808 Brookhill Rd.
Louisville, KY 40223
PH: (502)592-5295
Valiente, Ernesto O., Chmn. of the Bd.

Churches Uniting in Christ [20058]
PO Box 6496
Louisville, KY 40206
Winbush, Rev. Robina M., President

Cum Laude Society [23778]
4100 Springdale Rd.
Louisville, KY 40214
PH: (502)216-3814
Fax: (502)423-0445
McConnell, Robbie, Office Mgr.

Descendants of American Slaves [17890]
2100 W Muhammad Ali Blvd.
Louisville, KY 40212
PH: (502)939-6688
Shelton, Norris, Founder, President

Digital Screenmedia Association [3072]
13100 Eastpoint Park Blvd.
Louisville, KY 40223

PH: (502)489-3915
Toll free: 877-441-7545
Fax: (502)241-2795
Lynch, Bill, President

Dream Factory [11225]
410 W Chestnut St., Ste. 530
Louisville, KY 40202
PH: (502)561-3001
Toll free: 800-456-7556
Fax: (502)561-3004
Avery, Virginia, VP

Embroiderers' Guild of America [21755]
1355 Bardstown Rd., Ste. 157
Louisville, KY 40204-1353
PH: (502)589-6956
Fax: (502)584-7900
Nelson, Gwen T., President

Evangelical Theological Society [20120]
2825 Lexington Rd.
Louisville, KY 40280-0001
PH: (502)897-4388
Fax: (502)897-4386
House, Paul R., Mem.

The Fellowship Community [20521]
8134 New LaGrange Rd., Ste. 227
Louisville, KY 40222
PH: (502)425-4630
Detterman, Paul, Director

Foodservice Consultants Society International [820]
PO Box 4961
Louisville, KY 40204-0961
PH: (502)379-4122
Vaccaro, Nick, Administrator

Friend for Life Cancer Support Network [13974]
4003 Kresge Way, Ste. 100
Louisville, KY 40207
PH: (502)893-0643
Toll free: 866-374-3634
Fax: (502)896-3010
Houlette, Judy Kasey, Exec. Dir.

Hearts for Kenya [10723]
1514 Norris Pl.
Louisville, KY 40205
PH: (502)459-4582
Willingham, John, President

Independent Pilots Association [23387]
3607 Fern Valley Rd.
Louisville, KY 40219
PH: (502)968-0341
Fax: (502)753-3252
Kalfas, Tom, Secretary

International Amusement and Leisure Defense Association [2908]
PO Box 4563
Louisville, KY 40204
PH: (502)473-0956
Fax: (502)473-7352
Amaro, Michael L., President

International Barrel Racing Association [22918]
PO Box 91205
Louisville, KY 40291
PH: (502)239-4000
Fax: (502)239-4100

International Society of Heterocyclic Chemistry [6204]
c/o Dr. Frederick Luzzio, Treasurer
Dept. of Chemistry
University of Louisville
2320 S Brook St.
Louisville, KY 40208

PH: (502)852-7323
   (502)295-3469
Comins, Prof. Daniel, President

International Thomas Merton Society [9060]
2001 Newburg Rd.
Louisville, KY 40205
PH: (502)272-8177
Fax: (502)272-8452
Belcastro, David, President

Islamic Research Foundation International [8125]
7102 W Shefford Ln.
Louisville, KY 40242-6462
PH: (502)287-6262
   (502)423-1988
Ahmed, Dr. Tajuddin, Chairman

Les Dames d'Escoffier International [963]
PO Box 4961
Louisville, KY 40204-0961
PH: (502)456-1851
Fax: (502)456-1821
Jewell, Mr. Greg, Exec. Dir.

Life in Abundance International [10480]
211 Townepark Cir., Ste. 201
Louisville, KY 40243
PH: (502)749-7691
Toll free: 877-439-5566
Muindi, Dr. Florence, CEO, Founder, President

Mystery Shopping Providers Association North America [2294]
328 E Main St.
Louisville, KY 40202-1216
PH: (502)574-9033
Bradley, Richard, V. Chmn. of the Bd.

National Association for Community Mediation [4967]
PO Box 5246
Louisville, KY 40255
PH: (602)633-4213
Croucher, LaDessa, Secretary

National Association of Pizzeria Operators [1669]
c/o Pizza Today
908 S 8th St., Ste. 200
Louisville, KY 40203
PH: (502)736-9500
Lachapelle, Pete, Publisher

National Association of Specialty Health Organizations [15043]
222 S 1st St., Ste. 303
Louisville, KY 40202
PH: (502)403-1122
Fax: (502)403-1129
Roberts, Julian, Exec. Dir.

National Association of Vision Care Plans [15104]
974 Breckenridge Ln. No. 162
Louisville, KY 40202
PH: (502)403-1122
Fax: (502)403-1129
Roberts, Julian, Exec. Dir.

National Center for Families Learning [8248]
325 W Main St., Ste. 300
Louisville, KY 40202
PH: (502)584-1133
Darling, Sharon, Founder, President

National Crime Prevention Institute [11512]
University of Louisville
2301 S 3rd St.
Louisville, KY 40208-1838

PH: (800)334-8635
Edwards, Terry, Fac. Memb.

National Fastpitch Coaches Association [23243]
2641 Grinstead Dr.
Louisville, KY 40206-2840
PH: (502)409-4600
Fax: (502)409-4622
Revelle, Rhonda, President

National Safe Place Network [12834]
2429 Crittenden Dr.
Louisville, KY 40217
PH: (502)635-3660
Toll free: 888-290-7233
Fax: (502)635-3678
Jackson, Laurie, President, CEO

National Society, Sons of the American Revolution [20695]
809 W Main St.
Louisville, KY 40202
PH: (502)589-1776
Fax: (502)589-1671
Shaw, Donald, Exec. Dir.

North American Equine Ranching Information Council [4392]
PO Box 43968
Louisville, KY 40253-0968
PH: (502)245-0425
Fax: (502)245-0438
Allen, Carrie J., Coord.

North American One-Armed Golfer Association [22793]
8406 Cloverport Dr.
Louisville, KY 40228
PH: (502)964-7734
Dawley, Jeff, Secretary

North American Thermal Analysis Society [7330]
c/o Greg Jewell, Executive Director
PO Box 4961
Louisville, KY 40204
PH: (502)456-1851
Fax: (502)456-1821
Grady, Brian, Exec.

Presbyterian Association of Musicians [20495]
100 Witherspoon St.
Louisville, KY 40202-1396
PH: (502)569-5288
Toll free: 888-728-7228
Fax: (502)569-8465
Asbury, Jason, President

Presbyterian Health Education and Welfare Association [13082]
100 Witherspoon St.
Louisville, KY 40202-1396
Toll free: 800-728-7228
Valentine, Linda, President

Presbyterian Hunger Program [12108]
100 Witherspoon St.
Louisville, KY 40202-1396
PH: (502)569-8080
Toll free: 800-728-7228
Johnson, Harold

Presbyterian Men [20527]
100 Witherspoon St.
Louisville, KY 40202-1396
Toll free: 800-728-7228
James, Robert, President

Presbyterian Women [20529]
100 Witherspoon St.
Louisville, KY 40202-1396
Toll free: 888-728-7228
Fax: (502)569-8600
Paris, Debbie, Officer

Sharp WoundCare **[17529]**
10821 Plantside Dr., Ste. 104
Louisville, KY 40299
PH: (502)412-2995
Toll free: 866-540-9495

Society for Hospitality and Foodser-
vice Management **[1397]**
328 E Main St.
Louisville, KY 40202-2554
PH: (502)574-9931
Fax: (502)589-3602
Ventura, Bernadette, President

Society for Psychotherapy Research
[16952]
University of Louisville
401 E Chestnut St., Unit 610
Louisville, KY 40202-5711
Eells, Tracy D., PhD, Exec. Ofc.

Spalding University Alumni Associa-
tion **[19349]**
845 S 3rd St.
Louisville, KY 40203
PH: (502)585-7111
     (502)585-9911
Toll free: 800-896-8941
Boone, Deborah, President

Traditional Tae Kwon Do Chung Do
Association **[23016]**
1209 Gilmore Ln.
Louisville, KY 40213
PH: (502)964-3800
LaVanchy, Master Charlie, Exec. Dir.

University of Louisville Alumni As-
sociation **[19359]**
University Club and Alumni Ctr.
200 E Brandeis Ave.
Louisville, KY 40208
PH: (502)852-6186
Toll free: 800-813-8635
Fax: (502)852-6920
Dietzler, Deborah, Exec. Dir.

WaterStep **[13364]**
625 Myrtle St.
Louisville, KY 40208
PH: (502)568-6342
Hogg, Mark, Founder, CEO

Water With Blessings **[13362]**
11714 Main St., Ste. B
Middletown, KY 40243
PH: (502)356-9281
Lauter, Sr. Larraine, Founder

Guild of Professional Farriers **[1180]**
PO Box 4541
Midway, KY 40347
PH: (630)707-7877
Vanderlei, Russ, RJF, President

Organizational Systems Research
Association **[8664]**
Morehead State University
150 University Blvd.
Morehead, KY 40351-1689
PH: (606)783-2718
Fax: (606)783-5025
Regan, Elizabeth, President

United Beagle Gundog Federation
[21973]
1150 Millshed Rd.
Morgantown, KY 42261
PH: (931)629-6117
Mcdonald, Rick, President

American Ranch Horse Association
[4323]
PO Box 186
Nancy, KY 42544
PH: (606)636-4112
     (606)271-2963
Fax: (606)636-6197

Catholics United for Life **[12766]**
PO Box 10
New Hope, KY 40052-0010
Toll free: 800-764-8444
Musk, Dennis, Contact

National Softball Association **[23203]**
PO Box 7
Nicholasville, KY 40340
PH: (859)887-4114
Fax: (859)887-4874
Cantrell, Hugh, CEO

Primate Rescue Center **[10685]**
2515 Bethel Rd.
Nicholasville, KY 40356-8199
PH: (859)858-4866
Fax: (859)858-0044
Truitt, April D., Founder

National Scrip Collectors Association
[22275]
c/o Garrett Salyers, Secretary
86 McKenzie Ln.
Olive Hill, KY 41164
PH: (606)337-6622
Cawood, Steve, President

American Society of Interventional
Pain Physicians **[16553]**
81 Lakeview Dr.
Paducah, KY 42001
PH: (270)554-9412
Fax: (270)554-5394
Manchikanti, Laxmaiah, MD, Medical
Dir.

Society of Interventional Pain
Management Surgery Centers
[17402]
81 Lakeview Dr.
Paducah, KY 42001
PH: (270)554-9412
Fax: (270)554-5394
Martin, Melinda, Dir. of Operations

Order of Americans of Armorial
Ancestry **[20759]**
c/o David Carline Smith, Registrar/
Genealogist General
PO Box 339
Pembroke, KY 42266
PH: (270)475-4572
Phelps, Michael, Treasurer

American Academy of
Developmental Medicine and
Dentistry **[15894]**
PO Box 681
Prospect, KY 40059
Keller, Seth M., MD, President

National Turf Writers and Broadcast-
ers **[2708]**
PO Box 541
Prospect, KY 40059
PH: (646)337-6955
Pedulla, Tom, President

Association for Linen Management
[2075]
138 N Keeneland Dr., Ste. D
Richmond, KY 40475
PH: (859)624-0177
Toll free: 800-669-0863
Fax: (859)624-3580
Larson, Janice, Director

Arthrogryposis Multiplex Congenita
Support Inc. **[15903]**
PO Box 1883
Salyersville, KY 41465
Samargian, Ani, Founder

American Murray Grey Association
[3705]
PO Box 1222
Shelbyville, KY 40066

PH: (502)384-2335
Toll free: 866-571-2554
Gerow, John E., Exec. Dir.

Irish Draught Horse Society of North
America **[4373]**
1279 Bates Ln.
Smithfield, KY 40068
PH: (502)649-2037
Bryan, Fleur, President

Health Watch USA **[15014]**
3396 Woodhaven Dr.
Somerset, KY 42503
Kavanagh, Dr. Kevin T., Chmn. of
the Bd.

National Association of Scale Aero-
modelers **[22202]**
c/o Tina Patton, Secretary-Treasurer
572 Cedar Pointe Dr.
Somerset, KY 42501
Barbee, Mike, President

American English Spot Rabbit Club
[4587]
c/o Michael Wiley Sr., Secretary-
Treasurer
5772 Owenton Rd.
Stamping Ground, KY 40379
PH: (502)535-7051
     (651)674-7614
Wiley, Michael, Sr., Secretary,
Treasurer

National Association of the 6th
Infantry Div. **[20721]**
9733 Still Meadow Ct.
Union, KY 41091-6914
Kessen, Clifford, President

Japanese Chin Club of America, Inc.
[21907]
PO Box 74
Versailles, KY 40383-0074
Schnarrenberger, William, President

Mountain Pleasure Horse Associa-
tion **[4379]**
PO Box 33
Wellington, KY 40387
PH: (606)768-3847
Beal, Becky, Treasurer

Francis Asbury Society **[19757]**
1580 Lexington Rd.
Wilmore, KY 40390
PH: (859)858-4222
Fax: (859)858-4155
Key, Stan, President

Rocky Mountain Horse Association
[4406]
71 S Main St.
Winchester, KY 40391
PH: (859)644-5244
Fax: (859)644-5245
Beamer, Barbara, PresidentL

LOUISIANA

National Organization of Remedia-
tors and Mold Inspectors **[1166]**
22174 Prats Rd.
Abita Springs, LA 70420-2250
Toll free: 877-251-2296
Fax: (866)211-4324
Hoffman, D. Douglas, CEO

National Association of Veterans'
Affairs Chaplains **[19934]**
c/o Stephen Brandow, President
PO Box 69004
Alexandria, LA 71306
PH: (318)473-0010
Brandow, Chap. Stephen, President

National Black Home Educators
[7996]
13434 Plank Rd.
Baker, LA 70714

PH: (225)778-0169
Burges, Eric, Founder

Christian Methodist Episcopal
Church Women's Missionary
Council **[20341]**
c/o Dr. Princess Pegues, President
2309 Bonnie Ave.
Bastrop, LA 71220-4171
PH: (318)281-3044
Pegues, Mrs. Princess A., President

American Academy of Orthopaedic
Manual Physical Therapists
[17430]
8550 United Plaza Blvd., Ste. 1001
Baton Rouge, LA 70809
PH: (225)360-3124
Fax: (225)408-4422
Rivard, James, President

American Society of Sugar Cane
Technologists **[4692]**
c/o Freddie Martin, General
Secretary
LSU AgCenter
Sturgis Hall, No. 128
Baton Rouge, LA 70803
PH: (225)578-6930
Fax: (225)578-1403
Martin, Freddie, PhD, Gen. Sec.,
Treasurer

Association of Independent Informa-
tion Professionals **[1793]**
8550 United Plaza Blvd., Ste. 1001
Baton Rouge, LA 70809
PH: (225)408-4400
Langeman, Jane, President

Beta Kappa Chi **[23859]**
244 William James Hall
Baton Rouge, LA 70813
PH: (225)771-4854
James Mackie, Mrs. Deadra, Exec.
Sec.

Hope for Hemophilia **[15234]**
PO Box 77728
Baton Rouge, LA 70879
Toll free: 888-529-8023
James, Jonathan, President, Exec.
Dir.

International Society for Theoretical
Chemical Physics **[7026]**
c/o Dr. K. Rupnik
Dept. of Chemistry
Louisiana State University
Baton Rouge, LA 70803
Brandas, E., President

International Society of Trace Ele-
ment Biogeochemistry **[6058]**
c/o Magdi Selim, Committee Chairman
Sturgis Hall
Louisiana State University
Baton Rouge, LA 70803

Jump Start Your Heart **[14155]**
17732 Highland Rd., Ste. G150
Baton Rouge, LA 70810
PH: (225)751-8684
Fax: (225)751-9664
Kelley, Mrs. Danielle, Founder, Exec.
Dir.

Manuscript Society **[21684]**
14003 Rampart Ct.
Baton Rouge, LA 70810-8101
Dabrishus, Michael, President

National Association of the Holy
Name Society **[19870]**
6939 Sevenoaks Ave.
Baton Rouge, LA 70806
PH: (225)925-8921
     (225)266-8654
Bradley, John, Legal Counsel

National Committee for Latin and
Greek **[9165]**
Hodges 316
Dept. of Foreign Languages and
Literatures
Louisiana State University
Baton Rouge, LA 70803
PH: (225)578-6616
Pendergraft, Mary, Chairperson

National Senior Games Association
[23065]
PO Box 82059
Baton Rouge, LA 70884-2059
PH: (225)766-6800
Fax: (225)766-9115
White, John, Director

Phi Kappa Phi **[23791]**
7576 Goodwood Blvd.
Baton Rouge, LA 70806
PH: (225)388-4917
Toll free: 800-804-9880
Fax: (225)388-4900
Hulsey, Timothy L., President

Society for Mathematics and
Computation in Music **[6827]**
c/o Robert Peck, Founder
281 M&DA Bldg.
School of Music
Louisiana State University
Baton Rouge, LA 70803-2504
PH: (225)578-6830
Fax: (225)578-2562
Mazzola, Guerino, President

State Instructional Materials Review
Association **[8695]**
PO Box 94064
Baton Rouge, LA 70804-9064
PH: (225)342-1848
Fax: (225)342-0178
Buckle, Marcie, Treasurer

World Aquaculture Society **[3650]**
Louisiana State University
143 J.M Parker Coliseum
Baton Rouge, LA 70803
Fax: (225)578-3137
Mendoza, Carol, Director

Love Token Society **[22273]**
c/o Sid Gale, Secretary & Treasurer
PO Box 2351
Denham Springs, LA 70727
PH: (225)664-0718
Gale, Sid, Secretary, Treasurer

ECD Global Alliance **[14573]**
PO Box 775
Deridder, LA 70634
PH: (337)515-6987
Brewer, Kathy, President

National Association of Dramatic and
Speech Arts, Inc. **[10261]**
c/o Dr. King Godwin, President
Grambling State University
PO Box 4276
Grambling, LA 71245
PH: (318)274-3225
Skinner, Alexis, Exec. Sec.

After Death Communication
Research Foundation **[15340]**
PO Box 20238
Houma, LA 70360
Long, Dr. Jeff, Bd. Member

National Criminal Enforcement As-
sociation **[5500]**
PO Box 807
Jackson, LA 70748-0807
PH: (700)314-4543
Toll free: 877-468-2392
Fax: (770)679-8671
Cook, James, Chmn. of the Bd.

Chimp Haven, Inc **[10599]**
13600 Chimpanzee Pl.
Keithville, LA 71047
PH: (318)925-9575
Toll free: 888-982-4467
Fax: (318)925-9576
Brent, Dr. Linda, PhD, Trustee

American Guild of Hypnotherapists
[15358]
2200 Veterans Blvd., Ste. 108
Kenner, LA 70062-4005

National Federation of Tourist Guide
Associations USA **[23663]**
c/o Gene Reyes, President
3 Boimare Ave.
Kenner, LA 70065-3103
Reyes, Gene F, III, DTM, President

North American YMCA Development
Organization **[13419]**
21 Chateau Trianon Dr.
Kenner, LA 70065
PH: (504)464-7845
Washburn, Scott, CFRE, Treasurer

American Communication Associa-
tion **[7257]**
104 E University Cir.
Lafayette, LA 70503
PH: (337)482-1000
Auter, Phil, Exec. Dir.

American Professional Wound Care
Association **[17525]**
3639 Ambassador Caffery Pky., Ste.
605
Lafayette, LA 70503
PH: (215)942-6095
    (337)541-2223
Fax: (215)993-7922
Zinszer, Kathya, DPM, MAPWCA,
Secretary

Helicopter Safety Advisory Conference **[139]**
c/o Pat Attaway, Acting Chairman
PHI, Inc.
2001 SE Evangeline Thruway
Lafayette, LA 70508
Attaway, Pat, Act. Chm.

International Clinical Phonetics and
Linguistics Association **[9741]**
Dept. of Communicative Disorders
University of Louisiana at Lafayette
Lafayette, LA 70504-3170
Howard, Sara, President

International Radio Club of America
[21269]
PO Box 60241
Lafayette, LA 70596-0241

International Society of Endovascular Specialists **[17575]**
3639 Ambassador Caffery Pky., Ste.
605
Lafayette, LA 70503
PH: (337)993-7920
Diethrich, Edward B., MD, Chairman

National Association of Housing
Counselors and Agencies **[1691]**
PO Box 91873
Lafayette, LA 70509-1873
PH: (337)962-6600
Fax: (337)232-8834
Moore, Sandra L., President

United States Neapolitan Mastiff
Club **[21984]**
c/o Mike McDonald, Treasurer
40 Sam Carroll Rd.
Lecompte, LA 71364
Hosking, Rachel, VP

International Association for Truancy
and Dropout Prevention **[7822]**
c/o Ronnie Land, Executive Director
409 Mockingbird Ln.

Logansport, LA 71049
PH: (318)697-5003
Land, Ronnie, Exec. Dir.

Knowles/Knoles/Noles Family Association **[20982]**
c/o Robert B. Noles, Director
133 Acadian Ln.
Mandeville, LA 70471
PH: (985)845-4688
Noles, Robert B., Director

Mi Esperanza **[13383]**
PO Box 1575
Mandeville, LA 70470
PH: (205)533-8725
Connell, Lori, Founder

Randolph-Sheppard Vendors of
America **[3433]**
940 Parc Helene Dr.
Marrero, LA 70072-2421
PH: (504)328-6373
Toll free: 800-467-5299
Fax: (504)328-6372
Sippl, Dan, President

Fire Mark Circle of the Americas
[21654]
c/o Elaine Schlesinger, Secretary
PO Box 6738
Metairie, LA 70009-6738
Schlesinger, Elaine, Secretary

Keep Dentistry Alive **[14454]**
4825 Sanford St.
Metairie, LA 70006
David, Lauren K., Founder

Society for Costa Rica Collectors
[22365]
c/o Raul Hernandez, President
4204 Haring Rd.
Metairie, LA 70006
Hernandez, Mr. Raul, President

Southern Pine Council **[3511]**
c/o Southern Forest Product As-
sociation
6660 Riverside Dr., Ste. 212
Metairie, LA 70003-3200
PH: (504)443-4464
Fax: (504)443-6612
Wallace, Richard, VP, Comm.

Anglican Association of Biblical
Scholars **[19699]**
c/o Rev. Frank Hughes, Treasurer
1107 Broadway St.
Minden, LA 71055
PH: (318)377-1259
Davids, Peter H., Bd. Member

Live Oak Society **[4207]**
17832 River Rd.
Montz, LA 70068
Landry, Coleen Perilloux,
Chairperson

Society for Louisiana Irises **[22124]**
c/o Ron Killingsworth, Treasurer
10329 Caddo Lake Rd.
Mooringsport, LA 71060-9057
Wolford, Harry, Mem.

National Center for Preservation
Technology and Training **[9415]**
645 University Pky.
Natchitoches, LA 71457
PH: (318)356-7444
Fax: (318)356-9119
Cordell, Kirk A., Exec. Dir.

Southern Mutual Help Association,
Inc. **[11443]**
3602 Old Jeanerette Rd.
New Iberia, LA 70563
PH: (337)367-3277
Fax: (337)367-3279
Bourg, Lorna, President, CEO

AAAneurysm Outreach **[14920]**
1441 Canal St.
New Orleans, LA 70112
Arrington, Sheila G., Founder

Adjutants General Association of the
United States **[5581]**
6400 St. Claude Ave.
New Orleans, LA 70117
PH: (504)278-8357
Curtis, Maj. Gen. Glenn H.,
President

American Celiac Society Dietary
Support Coalition **[16202]**
New Orleans, LA 70123
PH: (504)305-2968
Bentley, Annette, BA, President

George H. Buck Jr. Jazz Foundation
[22246]
61 French Market Pl.
New Orleans, LA 70116
PH: (504)525-5000
Fax: (504)525-1776
Etegran, Lars, Contact

Knights of Peter Claver **[19405]**
1825 Orleans Ave.
New Orleans, LA 70116-2825
PH: (504)821-4225
Fax: (504)821-4253
Blackmon, Fredron Dekarlos, Chmn.
of the Bd., CEO

Historians Against Slavery **[12039]**
c/o Laura Murphy, Board Member
Dept. of English
Loyola University New Orleans
6363 St. Charles Ave.
New Orleans, LA 70116
PH: (504)865-2479
Murphy, Laura, Bd. Member

International Association of
Employee Assistance Profession-
als in Education **[11750]**
c/o Scott Embley, Treasurer
Clinical Education Bldg.
1542 Tulane Ave., 8th Fl., Office 866
New Orleans, LA 70112
PH: (504)568-8888
Fax: (504)568-3892
Kendall, Jim, President

International Association for
Research on Service-Learning and
Community Engagement **[7647]**
Tulane University Ctr. for Public
Service
Alcee Fortier Hall
6823 St. Charles Ave.
New Orleans, LA 70118
PH: (504)862-3366
Bargerstock, Burton, Chmn. of the
Exec. Committee

Junior Knights of Peter Claver
[19408]
1825 Orleans Ave.
New Orleans, LA 70116-2825
PH: (504)821-4425
Fax: (504)821-4253
Blackmon, Fredron Dekarlos, CEO,
Chmn. of the Bd.

Medical Mycological Society of the
Americas **[15850]**
c/o Mairi Noverr, Vice President
1100 Florida Ave.
New Orleans, LA 70119
Noverr, Mairi, VP

National MedPeds Residents' Association **[15430]**
School of Medicine
Tulane University
1430 Tulane Ave., SL-37

New Orleans, LA 70112
PH: (504)988-1332
Fax: (504)988-3971
Weber, Danielle, President

National Performance Network
[10264]
1024 Elysian Fields Ave.
New Orleans, LA 70117
PH: (504)595-8008
Fax: (504)595-8006
Wegmann, M.K., CEO, President

Offshore Marine Service Association
[2255]
935 Graver St., Ste. 2040
New Orleans, LA 70112-1657
PH: (504)528-9411
Fax: (504)528-9415
Wells, Richard, VP

People's Institute for Survival and
Beyond **[19115]**
601 N Carrollton Ave.
New Orleans, LA 70119
PH: (504)301-9292
Fax: (504)301-9291
Chisom, Ronald, Exec. Dir., Founder

Public Health Leadership Society
[17018]
1515 Poydras St., Ste. 1200
New Orleans, LA 70112-4536
PH: (504)301-9821
Fax: (504)301-9820
Stefanak, Matthew, Chairman

Society for the Philosophical Study
of Genocide and the Holocaust
[10125]
c/o Prof. James R. Watson,
President
Dept. of Philosophy
Loyola University
6363 St. Charles Ave.
New Orleans, LA 70118
PH: (501)922-3382
Watson, Prof. James R., President

Southern United States Trade As-
sociation **[3531]**
701 Poydras St., Ste. 3845
New Orleans, LA 70139
PH: (504)568-5986
Fax: (504)568-6010
Wiltz, Bernadette, Exec. Dir.

United States Track and Field and
Cross Country Coaches Associa-
tion **[23122]**
1100 Poydras St., Ste. 1750
New Orleans, LA 70163
PH: (504)599-8900
Fax: (504)599-8909
Seemes, Sam, CEO

Vespa Club of America **[22235]**
PO Box 23806
New Orleans, LA 70183
PH: (719)473-4692
Carolan, John J., President

Violent Death Bereavement Society
[10777]
Lavin-Bernick Ctr.
31 McAlister Dr.
New Orleans, LA 70118
PH: (206)223-6398
Rynearson, Edward K., MD, Director

World Society of Mixed Jurisdiction
Jurists **[5450]**
c/o Vernon Valentine Palmer,
President
Tulane Law School
6329 Freret St.
New Orleans, LA 70118
PH: (504)865-5978
 (504)862-8859
Palmer, Prof. Vernon, President

World Trade Center of New Orleans
[1973]
1 Canal Pl.
365 Canal St., Ste. 1120
New Orleans, LA 70130-1195
PH: (504)529-1601
Fax: (504)529-1691
Knoll, Dominik, CEO, President

Akashleena Literary and Cultural
Organization **[7529]**
c/o Quamrun Zinia, Editor
18055 Ira Babin Rd.
Prairieville, LA 70769
PH: (225)673-3277
Fax: (225)673-3277
Zinia, Quamrun, Editor

Children's Cup **[12637]**
PO Box 400
Prairieville, LA 70769
PH: (225)673-4505
Ohlerking, Jean, VP, Founder

National Pediatric Blood Pressure
Awareness Foundation **[15349]**
38261 Brown Rd.
Prairieville, LA 70769
PH: (225)955-2770
Fax: (225)677-8702
Goodwin, Celeste, President

Academy of Marketing Science
[8267]
PO Box 3072
Ruston, LA 71272
PH: (318)257-2612
Fax: (318)257-4253
Berkman, Harold W., Director, Exec.
VP

American Rose Society **[22084]**
8877 Jefferson Paige Rd.
Shreveport, LA 71119-8817
PH: (318)938-5402
Toll free: 800-637-6534
Fax: (318)938-5405
Ware, Jeff, Exec. Dir.

Centenary College of Louisiana
Alumni Association **[19314]**
PO Box 41188
Shreveport, LA 71134
PH: (318)869-5115
Toll free: 800-259-6447
Fax: (318)841-7266
Solomon, Saige W., Director

Elvis' Angels Fan Club **[24012]**
621 Dodd Dr.
Shreveport, LA 71107
PH: (318)424-5000
Harmon, Dianne, President

National Constables and Marshals
Association **[5499]**
1244 Texas Ave.
Shreveport, LA 71101
PH: (318)673-6800
McCloskey, Lennie, President

Society for Ultrastructural Pathology
[16595]
c/o Guillermo A. Herrera MD.,
Treasurer
1501 Kings Hwy.
Shreveport, LA 71103
PH: (318)675-4557
Fax: (318)675-4541
Miller, Sara E., President

American Sugar Cane League of the
U.S.A. **[4693]**
206 E Bayou Rd.
Thibodaux, LA 70301
PH: (985)448-3707
Fax: (985)448-3722
Simon, James H., Gen. Mgr.

European-American Unity and
Rights Organization **[17894]**
PO Box 5941
Thibodaux, LA 70302-5941
PH: (985)209-9937
Duke, David, PhD, President

Serama Council of North America
[3671]
PO Box 159
Vacherie, LA 70090
PH: (225)265-2238
Schexnayder, Jerry, Treasurer

Association of Resort and Leisure
Ministers **[20359]**
c/o Mary Gore
3840 Carter's Ferry Rd.
Zwolle, LA 71486
Gore, Mary, VP of Admin.M

MAINE

Disability Rights Maine **[11589]**
24 Stone St., Ste. 204
Augusta, ME 04330
PH: (207)626-2774
Toll free: 800-452-1948
Fax: (207)621-1419
Moody, Kim, Exec. Dir.

International Association of Milk
Control Agencies **[5225]**
c/o Charles Huff, Contact
28 SHS
Augusta, ME 04333
PH: (518)457-5731
Huff, Charles, Contact

Legal Services for the Elderly **[5542]**
5 Wabon St.
Augusta, ME 04330
PH: (207)621-0087
Toll free: 800-750-5353
Fax: (207)621-0742
Martin, Jaye, Exec. Dir.

Blue Knights International Law
Enforcement Motorcycle Club
[22214]
38 Alden St.
Bangor, ME 04401-3421

Professional Climbing Instructors
Association **[22728]**
PO Box 200
Bangor, ME 04402
PH: (541)704-7242
Fields, Dr. Andy, VP

Cetos Research Organization **[3995]**
11 Des Isle Ave.
Bar Harbor, ME 04609
PH: (207)266-6252
Zoidis, Ann, Exec. Dir.

Lipizzan Association of North
America **[4376]**
c/o Andrea Iannuzzi, Associate
Registrar
133 Seabury Dr.
Bar Harbor, ME 04609
Toth, Delphi, Director

Natural History Network **[6898]**
PO Box 533
Bar Harbor, ME 04609
Wheeler, Terry, President

Society for Human Ecology **[14725]**
c/o Barbara Carter, Secretary
105 Eden St.
Bar Harbor, ME 04609
PH: (207)801-5632
Carter, Ms. Barbara, Secretary,
Exec. Asst.

USS Intrepid Association of Former
Crew Members **[21067]**
c/o Robert Dunne, President
PO Box 654

Bingham, ME 04920-0654
PH: (207)672-3455
Giambalvo, Pete, Rep.

Association of Midwifery Educators
[14221]
24 S High St.
Bridgton, ME 04009
PH: (207)615-2566
Clegg, Justine, Chairperson

Expanding Opportunities **[10967]**
84 Payson Rd.
Brooks, ME 04921-3701
PH: (207)722-3708
Fax: (207)930-8012
Stone, Beverly G., Exec. Dir.,
President

American Musicological Society
[9863]
6010 College Sta.
Brunswick, ME 04011-8451
PH: (207)798-4243
Toll free: 877-679-7648
Fax: (207)798-4254
Judd, Robert, Exec. Dir.

Global Network Against Weapons
and Nuclear Power in Space
[18746]
PO Box 652
Brunswick, ME 04011
PH: (207)443-9502
Gagnon, Bruce K., Coord., Secretary

Goethe Society of North America
[9052]
c/o Professor Birgit Tautz, Executive
Secretary
Bowdoin College
Dept. of German
7700 College Sta.
Brunswick, ME 04011-8477
MacLeod, Prof. Catriona, VP

Gift From Within **[12523]**
16 Cobb Hill Rd.
Camden, ME 04843-4341
PH: (207)236-8858
Fax: (207)236-2818
Boaz, Joyce, Exec. Dir., Founder

Golden Rule Foundation **[9548]**
PO Box 658
Camden, ME 04843-0658
PH: (207)338-1866
Frye, Laurel, Administrator

Qajaq U.S.A. **[23363]**
88 Mason Cove Ln.
Cushing, ME 04563
Fuller, Ben, Treasurer

International Association of Clan MacInnes **[20886]**
c/o Eric MacGinnis Perry, Membership Director
14 Jakes Ln.
Dexter, ME 04930-2194
McInnis, Mr. John, President

Sustainable Harvest International
[3577]
104 Main St.
Ellsworth, ME 04605
PH: (207)669-8254
Fax: (207)591-4742
Reed, Florence, Founder, President

Homosexuals Anonymous Fellow-
ship Services **[11892]**
PO Box 176
Hancock, ME 04640
PH: (207)669-4264
McIntyre, Doug, Exec. Dir.

Domestic Abuse Helpline for Men
and Women **[11699]**
PO Box 252
Harmony, ME 04942

PH: (207)683-5758
Toll free: 888-743-5754

Morgan 3/4 Group [21441]
388 High Head Rd.
Harpswell, ME 04079
PH: (207)721-3206
Jacobsen, David, President

American RSDHope [16552]
PO Box 875
Harrison, ME 04040
PH: (207)583-4589
Orsini, Lynne, Exec. Dir.

American Society of Architectural
Illustrators [231]
c/o Tina Bryant, Executive Director
294 Merrill Hill Rd.
Hebron, ME 04238
PH: (207)966-2062
Dollus, John, Exec.

Email Sender and Provider Coalition
[6444]
PO Box 478
Kennebunk, ME 04043
PH: (207)351-5770
Formidoni, Kathleen Bagley, Dir. of
Public Rel.

North American Falconers Association [22829]
c/o Scott McNeff, President
64 High St.
Kennebunk, ME 04043
PH: (207)604-6283
Clarke, Ron, Director

United Ostomy Associations of
America, Inc. [16528]
PO Box 525
Kennebunk, ME 04043-0525
Toll free: 800-826-0826
Murray, Jim, 1st VP

Original Paper Doll Artists Guild
[22008]
PO Box 14
Kingfield, ME 04947
PH: (207)265-2500
Toll free: 800-290-2928
Johnson, Judy M., Editor

Military Toxics Project [4551]
PO Box 558
Lewiston, ME 04243
Thornton, Tara, Contact

Hospice Education Institute [15294]
3 Unity Sq.
Machiasport, ME 04655-0098
PH: (207)255-8800
Toll free: 800-331-1620
Fax: (207)255-8008

Alström Syndrome International
[14807]
14 Whitney Farm Rd.
Mount Desert, ME 04660
Toll free: 800-371-3628
Marshall, Robert P., Exec. Dir.

Friends of the Shakers [10213]
707 Shaker Rd.
New Gloucester, ME 04260

U.S. Biathlon Association [23168]
49 Pineland Dr., Ste. 301A
New Gloucester, ME 04260-5132
PH: (207)688-6500
Fax: (207)688-6505
Cobb, Max, President, CEO

Single Global Currency Association
[417]
PO Box 390
Newcastle, ME 04553

PH: (207)586-6078
Bonpasse, Morrison, Director

Antique Glass Salt and Sugar
Shaker Club [21622]
29 Autumn River Ln.
Ogunquit, ME 03907
Beverage, Jim, Membership Chp.

Littlefield Family Newsletter [20894]
PO Box 912
Ogunquit, ME 03907-0912

Cast Bullet Association [23127]
1317 Bennoch Rd.
1317 Bennoch Rd.
Old Town, ME 04468
Alexander, John, President

Wild Blueberry Association of North
America [4261]
PO Box 100
Old Town, ME 04468
PH: (207)570-3535
Fax: (207)581-3499

Homeworkers Organized for More
Employment [11765]
90 School House Rd.
Orland, ME 04472
PH: (207)469-7961
Fax: (207)469-1023
Poulin, Lucy, Exec. Dir.

Maine Folklife Center [9328]
University of Maine
5773 S Stevens Ste. 112 B
Orono, ME 04469-5773
PH: (207)581-1891
Fax: (207)581-1823
MacDougall, PhD, Pauleena, Direc-
tor

Potato Association of America [4248]
c/o Lori Wing, Administrator
5719 Crossland Hall, Rm. 220
University of Maine
Orono, ME 04469-5719
PH: (207)581-3042
Fax: (207)581-3015
Mikitzel, Loretta, President

Biomass Power Association [7052]
100 Middle St.
Portland, ME 04104-9729
PH: (207)228-7376
Cleaves, Bob, CEO, President

Breaking Ground [11320]
104 Neal St.
Portland, ME 04102
Fax: (207)772-7487
Clarke, Lindsay, Chmn. of the Bd.

Coalition of Essential Schools [7695]
482 Congress St., Ste. 500A
Portland, ME 04101
PH: (401)426-9638
Wood, George, Chairman

Common Dreams [12957]
PO Box 443
Portland, ME 04112-0443
PH: (207)775-0488
Fax: (207)775-0489
Brown, Craig, Founder, Editor

Council on International Educational
Exchange USA [8064]
300 Fore St.
Portland, ME 04101
PH: (207)553-4000
Fax: (207)553-4299
Fallon, Robert E., Chairman

Eastern Apicultural Society of North
America [3636]
c/o Erin M. Forbes, Chairman
188 Capisic St.

Portland, ME 04102
PH: (207)772-3380
Cottrill, Carol, MD, Secretary

Ecuador Children's Hope Organiza-
tion [10958]
94 Beckett St., No. 3
Portland, ME 04101-4473
PH: (207)615-7788
Guerette, Sarah, President

Great Schools Partnership [8537]
482 Congress St., Ste. 500
Portland, ME 04101
PH: (207)773-0505
Fax: (877)849-7052
Abbott, Stephen, Exec. Dir.

National Academy for State Health
Policy [15038]
10 Free St., 2nd Fl.
Portland, ME 04101
PH: (207)874-6524
Fax: (207)874-6527
Reinhardt, Susan, Chairman

National MIS User Group [6751]
c/o Nicci Bishop, Secretary
899 Riverside St.
Portland, ME 04103
PH: (207)871-1200
Fax: (207)797-6457
Bishop, Nicci, Secretary

Reverb [3932]
386 Fore St., No. 202
Portland, ME 04101
PH: (207)221-6553
Sullivan, Lauren, Director, Founder

Wine and Spirits Shippers Associa-
tion [193]
111 Commercial St., Ste. 202
Portland, ME 04101
PH: (207)805-1664
Toll free: 800-368-3167
Andretta, James V., Jr., Chmn. of
the Bd.

United States Cross Country
Snowmobile Racing Association
[23179]
782 Poland Range Rd.
Pownal, ME 04069

International Association for the
Study of Cooperation in Education
[7679]
11 South Rd.
Readfield, ME 04355
PH: (207)685-3171
Baloche, Lynda, Co-Pres.

Kitchen Gardeners International
[4237]
3 Powderhorn Dr.
Scarborough, ME 04074
PH: (207)956-0606
Doiron, Roger, Founder

National Association of African
American Studies [7467]
PO Box 6670
Scarborough, ME 04070
PH: (207)839-8004
Fax: (207)839-3776
Berry, Dr. Lemuel, Jr., Exec. Dir.,
Founder

American Polar Society [7038]
PO Box 300
Searsport, ME 04974
McLaren, Capt. Alfred S., President

Penobscot Marine Museum [9777]
5 Church St.
Searsport, ME 04974
PH: (207)548-2529
Toll free: 800-268-8030
Fax: (207)548-2520
Lodge, Liz, Exec. Dir.

Erskine Alumni Association [19323]
309 Windsor Rd.
South China, ME 04358-5118
PH: (207)445-4026
  (207)445-5945
McQuarrie, Michael, Officer

National Environmental, Safety and
Health Training Association [4553]
584 Main St.
South Portland, ME 04106
PH: (602)956-6099
Fax: (602)956-6399
Turner-Harris, Myrtle I., President

Partners for World Health [15487]
2112 Broadway
South Portland, ME 04106
PH: (207)774-5555
Fax: (207)772-9963
McLellan, Elizabeth, Founder,
President

Society for Slovene Studies [19655]
c/o Raymond Miller, President
381 Cathance Rd.
Topsham, ME 04086
Pogacar, Timothy, Treasurer

North American Society of
Homeopaths [15291]
PO Box 115
Troy, ME 04987
PH: (206)720-7000
Fax: (208)248-1942
Kell, Tanya, President

Organic Seed Growers and Trade
Association [4645]
PO Box 362
Washington, ME 04574
PH: (207)809-7530
Gerritsen, Jim, President

Baronial Order of Magna Charta
[9465]
c/o Robert Pond Vivian, Marshall
1285 Branch Rd.
Wells, ME 04090-6057
Vivian, Mr. Robert Pond, Contact

National Association of
Superintendents of U.S. Naval
Shore Establishments [5605]
89 Pine Legde Dr.
Wells, ME 04090

Parker Gun Collectors Association
[22022]
477 Ocean Ave.
Wells, ME 04090
Mullins, Bill, President

Harbour Lights Collectors Society
[21659]
PO Box 625
West Kennebunk, ME 04094
Toll free: 800-365-1219

International Association of Asian
Studies [7523]
850 Main St.
Westbrook, ME 04092
PH: (207)839-8004
Fax: (207)839-3776
Berry, Dr. Lemuel, Jr., Exec. Dir.,
Founder

National Association of Hispanic and
Latino Studies [9292]
850 Main St.
Westbrook, ME 04092
PH: (207)839-8004
Fax: (207)856-2800
Berry, Dr. Lemuel, Jr., Exec. Dir.,
Founder

National Association of Native
American Studies [8396]
850 Main St.
Westbrook, ME 04092

PH: (207)839-8004
Fax: (207)839-3776
Berry, Dr. Lemuel, Jr., Founder

Association of State Wetland Managers [3816]
32 Tandberg Trl., Ste. 2A
Windham, ME 04062
PH: (207)892-3399
Fax: (518)892-3089
Christie, Jeanne, Exec. Dir.

John Reich Collectors Society [22284]
c/o Stephen A. Crain, Secretary
PO Box 1680
Windham, ME 04062
Crain, Stephen A., Officer

Tugboat Enthusiasts Society of the Americas [22677]
PO Box 710
Winterport, ME 04496

Americans for Customary Weight and Measure [19152]
PO Box 248
Wiscasset, ME 04578
PH: (207)882-5554
Leslie, Seaver, President

Safe Passage [11145]
81 Bridge St., Ste. 104
Yarmouth, ME 04096
PH: (207)846-1188
Fax: (207)846-1688
Healy, Mariah, Assoc. Dir.

MARYLAND

American Holistic Veterinary Medical Association [17624]
33 Kensington Pky.
Abingdon, MD 21009
PH: (410)569-0795
Fax: (410)569-2346
Swartz, Ann, DVM, Secretary

American Veterinary Distributors Association [2541]
3465 Box Hill Corporate Center Dr., Ste. H
Abingdon, MD 21009
PH: (443)640-1040
Fax: (443)640-1086
King, Jackie, Exec. Dir.

Council for Textile Recycling [3449]
3465 Box Hill Corporate Center Dr., Ste. H
Abingdon, MD 21009
PH: (443)640-1050
Fax: (443)640-1086
King, Jackie, Exec. Dir.

Pet Care Trust [10679]
3465 Box Hill Corporate Center Dr., Ste. H
Abingdon, MD 21009
PH: (443)921-2825
Fax: (443)640-1086
Kollman, Rand, VP

Pet Industry Distributors Association [2548]
3465 Box Hill Corporate Center Dr., Ste. H
Abingdon, MD 21009
PH: (443)640-1060
Fax: (443)640-1086
Hickey, Marcia, Dir. of Mtgs., Dir. of Member Svcs.

Secondary Materials and Recycled Textiles [1766]
3465 Box Hill Corporate Center Dr., Ste. H

Abingdon, MD 21009
PH: (443)640-1050
Fax: (443)640-1086
King, Jackie, Exec. Dir.

Shippers of Recycled Textiles [3101]
3465 Box Hill Corporate Center Dr., Ste. H
Abingdon, MD 21009
PH: (443)640-1050
Fax: (443)640-1086

Stroke Network [17300]
PO Box 492
Abingdon, MD 21009
Mallory, Steve, CEO, President

Accokeek Foundation | National Colonial Farm [9362]
3400 Bryan Point Rd.
Accokeek, MD 20607
PH: (301)283-2113
Hayes, Lisa, President, CEO

Men Against Breast Cancer [14013]
PO Box 150
Adamstown, MD 21710-0150
Toll free: 866-547-MABC
Fax: (301)874-8657
Heyison, Marc, Founder, President

Airlines Electronic Engineering Committee [6525]
ARINC Inc.
2551 Riva Rd.
Annapolis, MD 21401-7435
PH: (240)334-2579
Swanson, Robert, Chairman

American Academy of Environmental Engineers and Scientists [6526]
147 Old Solomons Rd., Ste. 303
Annapolis, MD 21401
PH: (410)266-3311
Fax: (410)266-7653
Lafever, Howard B., President

American Boat & Yacht Council [2234]
613 3rd St., Ste. 10
Annapolis, MD 21403
PH: (410)990-4460
Fax: (410)990-4466
Sherman, Ed, Director

Asphalt Emulsion Manufacturers Association [492]
3 Church Cir., PMB 250
Annapolis, MD 21401
PH: (410)267-0023
Fax: (410)267-7546
Krissoff, Mike, Exec. Dir.

Asphalt Recycling and Reclaiming Association [3444]
3 Church Cir.
Annapolis, MD 21401-1933
PH: (410)267-0023
Fax: (410)267-7546
Krissoff, Mike, Exec. Dir.

Association of Transportation Law Professionals [5811]
c/o Lauren Michalski, Executive Director
PO Box 5407
Annapolis, MD 21403
PH: (410)268-1311
Fax: (410)268-1322
Charron, Kenneth G., President

Avionics Maintenance Conference [131]
Aeronautical Radio, Inc.
2551 Riva Rd.
Annapolis, MD 21401
PH: (240)334-2576
Buckwalter, Samuel, Exec. Sec.

BOMI International Independent Institute for Property and Facility Management Education [2851]
1 Park Pl., Ste. 475
Annapolis, MD 21401-3479
PH: (410)974-1410
Toll free: 800-235-2664
Fax: (410)974-0544
Horn, Jeffrey A., CEO, President

CATalyst Council [10598]
PO Box 3064
Annapolis, MD 21403
Brunt, Jane, DVM, Exec. Dir.

CharityHelp International [10891]
PO Box 1904
Annapolis, MD 21404
PH: (443)283-0677
Stevers, Paul H., Founder, Chmn. of the Bd., President

Disciples Justice Action Network [19972]
1040 Harbor Dr.
Annapolis, MD 21403-4251
PH: (410)212-7964
Langston, Ken Brooker, Director

Entomological Society of America [6612]
3 Park Pl., Ste. 307
Annapolis, MD 21401-3722
PH: (301)731-4535
Fax: (301)731-4538
Gammel, C. David, CAE, Exec. Dir.

Flexible Packaging Association [2476]
185 Admiral Cochrane Dr., Ste. 105
Annapolis, MD 21401
PH: (410)694-0800
Fax: (410)694-0900
Donahue, Marla, President

FPDA Motion and Control Network [1730]
105 Eastern Ave., Ste. 104
Annapolis, MD 21403-3300
PH: (410)940-6347
Fax: (410)263-1659
Gillig, Tim, President

Historic Naval Ships Association [9773]
626-C Admiral Dr.
Annapolis, MD 21401
PH: (443)949-8341
Hofwolt, Capt. Jerry, President

Industry Council for Tangible Assets [3196]
PO Box 3253
Annapolis, MD 21403
PH: (410)626-7005
Greenstein, Bob, Director

International Sealing Distributors Association [3472]
105 Eastern Ave., Ste. 104
Annapolis, MD 21403-3366
PH: (410)940-6344
Fax: (410)263-1659
Mitchell, Deborah B., Exec. Dir.

International Slurry Surfacing Association [538]
3 Church Cir., PMB 250
Annapolis, MD 21401
PH: (410)267-0023
Fax: (410)267-7546
Price, Rusty, President

International Star Class Yacht Racing Association [22639]
914 Bay Ridge Rd., Ste. 220
Annapolis, MD 21403
PH: (443)458-5733
Fax: (443)458-5735
Reynolds, Mark, Secretary

NAHAD - Association for Hose and Accessories Distribution [1752]
105 Eastern Ave., Ste. 104
Annapolis, MD 21403
PH: (410)940-6350
Toll free: 800-624-2227
Fax: (410)263-1659
Gordon, Dean, Bd. Member

National Association of Presort Mailers [2119]
c/o Bob Galaher, Executive Director
PO Box 3552
Annapolis, MD 21403-3552
Toll free: 877-620-6276
Galaher, Bob, Exec. Dir., CEO

National Boating Federation [22648]
PO Box 4111
Annapolis, MD 21403-4111
Toll free: 866-239-2070
Belmore, Carolyn, President

National Federation of Advanced Information Services [6749]
801 Compass Way, Ste. 201
Annapolis, MD 21401
PH: (410)221-2980
Bailey-Hainer, Brenda, Treasurer

National Marine Lenders Association [414]
1 Melvin Ave.
Annapolis, MD 21401
PH: (410)980-1401
Fax: (410)268-3755
Bryant, Michael D., President

Partnership for Quality Medical Donations [12298]
326 1st St., Ste. 32
Annapolis, MD 21403
PH: (410)848-7036
Fax: (410)871-9031
Weiss, Randy, Chairperson

Plasma Protein Therapeutics Association [13842]
147 Old Solomons Island Rd., Ste. 100
Annapolis, MD 21401
PH: (202)789-3100
Fax: (410)263-2298
Bell, David, Chairman

Preventing Colorectal Cancer [14049]
326 1st St., Ste. 29
Annapolis, MD 21403
PH: (410)777-5310
Fax: (410)777-8490
Madry, Randy, Exec. Dir.

Retail Packaging Association [2483]
105 Eastern Ave., Ste. 104
Annapolis, MD 21403-3366
PH: (410)940-6459
Fax: (410)263-1659
Van Belkom, Tony, President

Security Hardware Distributors Association [1576]
105 Eastern Ave., Ste. 104
Annapolis, MD 21403
PH: (410)940-6346
Fax: (410)263-1659
Steinmann, Sean, President

Social Integration and Community Development Association [11440]
3 Church Cir., Ste. 294
Annapolis, MD 21401
PH: (443)569-3578
Kittrie, Prof. Nicholas, Chairperson

South African Education and Environment Project U.S.A. [12188]
2116 Chesapeake Harbour Dr. E, Unit 102

Annapolis, MD 21403
PH: (410)295-5544
 (410)626-1747
Keen, Jane, Director

TRACE International [5111]
151 West St., Ste. 300
Annapolis, MD 21401
PH: (410)990-0076
Fax: (410)990-0707
Wrage, Alexandra, President

UniForum Association [6305]
PO Box 3177
Annapolis, MD 21403-0177
PH: (410)715-9500
Toll free: 800-333-8649
Fax: (240)465-0207
Fedder, Alan, President

United Association of Journeymen
 and Apprentices of the Plumbing
 and Pipe Fitting Industry of the
 United States, Canada [23503]
3 Park Pl.
Annapolis, MD 21401
PH: (410)269-2000
Fax: (410)267-0262
Hite, William P., President

United States Naval Academy
 Alumni Association [19590]
247 King George St.
Annapolis, MD 21402-1306
PH: (410)295-4000
Ryan, John R., Chairman

United States Naval Institute [5630]
291 Wood Rd.
Annapolis, MD 21402
PH: (410)268-6110
Toll free: 800-223-8764
Fax: (410)571-1703
Daly, V. Adm. (Ret.) Peter H., CEO

U.S. Naval Sailing Association
 [21063]
PO Box 4702
Annapolis, MD 21403
PH: (443)510-1421
Katz, Douglas J., Chairman

Wholesale Florist and Florist Sup-
 plier Association [1311]
Horn Point Harbor Marina
105 Eastern Ave., Ste. 104
Annapolis, MD 21403-3300
PH: (410)940-6580
Toll free: 888-289-3372
Fax: (410)263-1659
Lilly, Patricia A., Exec. VP

Yacht Brokers Association of
 America [2261]
105 Eastern Ave., Ste. 104
Annapolis, MD 21403
PH: (410)940-6345
Fax: (410)263-1659
Petrella, Vincent J., Exec. Dir.

National Association for the Self-
 Employed [3121]
PO Box 241
Annapolis Junction, MD 20701-
 0241
Toll free: 800-232-6273

American Board of Psychological
 Hypnosis [15356]
1509 Richie Hwy., Ste. F
Spectrum Behavioral Health
1509 Ritchie Hwy., Ste. F
Arnold, MD 21012
PH: (410)757-2077
Baker, Elgan, PhD, President

World Artists Experiences [9009]
PO Box 9753
Arnold, MD 21012

PH: (410)647-4482
McGinnis, Betty, Founder, President

4K for Cancer [13867]
1215 E Fort Ave., Ste. 104
Baltimore, MD 21230
PH: (410)964-0202
Ulman, Douglas, Founder

ABET [6522]
415 N Charles St.
Baltimore, MD 21201
PH: (410)347-7700
Fax: (410)625-2238
Daucher, Rachelle, Mgr.

ADHD Coaches Organization
 [15891]
701 Hunting Pl.
Baltimore, MD 21229
Toll free: 888-638-3999
Fax: (410)630-6991
Garrett, Robb, President

Advanced Laboratory Physics As-
 sociation [8436]
c/o Dr. Steven K. Wonnell, Treasurer
Bloomberg Ctr., Rm. 366
Physics and Astronomy Dept.
Johns Hopkins University
3400 N Charles St.
Baltimore, MD 21218
Peterson, Randy, Act. Pres., VP

Alpha Nu Omega [23708]
PO Box 39033
Baltimore, MD 21212
Toll free: 866-337-1988
Brown, Curtis M., President

Alpha Phi Alpha Fraternity [23864]
2313 St. Paul St.
Baltimore, MD 21218-5211
Toll free: 800-373-3089
Fax: (301)206-9789
Tillman, Mark S., President

Alternative Press Center [2645]
PO Box 13127
Baltimore, MD 21203-3127
PH: (312)451-8133
D'Adamo, Charles, Sen. Ed.

American Action Fund for Blind
 Children and Adults [17681]
1800 Johnson St.
Baltimore, MD 21230
PH: (410)659-9315
Loos, Barbara, President

American Board of Medicolegal
 Death Investigators [15628]
900 W Baltimore St.
Baltimore, MD 21223
PH: (410)807-3007
Fax: (410)807-3006
Zulauf, Dawn, President

American Hungarian Federation
 [19466]
c/o Tamas Teglassy, Treasurer
1805 Snow Meadow Ln., No. 103
Baltimore, MD 21209
Koszorus, Frank, Jr., President

American Institute of Floral Design-
 ers [1305]
720 Light St.
Baltimore, MD 21230
PH: (410)752-3318
Mason-Monheim, Joyce, President

American Restroom Association
 [7110]
PO Box 65111
Baltimore, MD 21209
PH: (571)354-6907
Toll free: 800-247-3864
Fax: (410)367-1254
Anthony, Kathryn, Bd. Member

American Society of Comparative
 Law [5348]
1420 N Charles St.
Baltimore, MD 21201
PH: (410)837-4689
Fax: (410)837-4560
Gerber, David J., President

American Society of Nepalese
 Engineers [6537]
PO Box 39524
Baltimore, MD 21212
Shrestha, Rajendra, PhD, President

Association for Asian American Stud-
 ies [7521]
PO Box 19966
Baltimore, MD 21211-0966
PH: (800)548-1784
Fax: (410)516-3866
Hsu, Madeline Y, Rep.

Association of Jewish Family and
 Children's Agencies [12219]
5750 Park Heights Ave.
Baltimore, MD 21215
Toll free: 800-634-7346
Fax: (410)664-0551
Sherman, Lee, President, CEO

Babe Ruth Birthplace and Museum
 [22547]
216 Emory St.
Baltimore, MD 21230
PH: (410)727-1539
Fax: (410)727-1652
Gibbons, Michael, Exec. Dir.

Baltimore and Ohio Railroad Histori-
 cal Society [10179]
5620 Southwestern Blvd.
Baltimore, MD 21227-0725
PH: (410)247-8165
Smith, Gregory, PhD, President

Believe In Tomorrow National
 Children's Foundation [11214]
6601 Frederick Rd.
Baltimore, MD 21228
Toll free: 800-933-5470
Fax: (410)744-1984
Morrison, Mr. Brian R., CEO,
 Founder, President

Black Mental Health Alliance [15764]
200 E Lexington St., Ste. 803
Baltimore, MD 21202
PH: (410)338-2642
Bryant, Tracee, Mem.

Black Women of Essence, Inc.
 [10494]
Baltimore, MD 21201
Ellis, Renee G., President

Braille Authority of North America
 [17693]
c/o National Federation of the Blind
200 E Wells St., Jernigan Pl.
Baltimore, MD 21230
PH: (612)767-5658
Dunnam, Jennifer, Chairperson

Burmese Medical Association of
 North America [15720]
PO Box 20052
Baltimore, MD 21284
Hsu, Dr. James, Div. Dir.

Business Solutions Association
 [3169]
3601 E Joppa Rd.
Baltimore, MD 21234
PH: (410)931-8100
Fax: (410)931-8111
Kreuzburg, Paula, Exec. VP

Catholic Relief Services [12586]
228 W Lexington St.
Baltimore, MD 21201-3443
Toll free: 888-277-7575
Woo, Carolyn, President, CEO

Center for Communication Programs
 [12509]
111 Market Pl., Ste. 310
Baltimore, MD 21202
PH: (410)659-6300
Krenn, Ms. Susan, Exec. Dir.

Center for Jewish Community Stud-
 ies [18590]
7 Church Ln., Ste. 9
Baltimore, MD 21208
PH: (410)653-7779
Fax: (410)653-8889
Eidelman, Prof. Arthur I, Chmn. of
 the Bd.

Child Literacy [10901]
201 N Charles St., Ste. 2406
Baltimore, MD 21201
PH: (212)531-1111
Cader, Naushard, Exec. Dir.

Coalition to End Childhood Lead
 Poisoning [4044]
Green & Healthy Homes Initiative
2714 Hudson St.
Baltimore, MD 21224
PH: (410)534-6447
Toll free: 800-370-5323
Fax: (410)534-6475
Norton, Ruth Ann, Exec. Dir.

College English Association [7866]
Johns Hopkins University Press
Journal Publishing Division
PO Box 19966
Baltimore, MD 21211-0966
Pestino, Joe, Hist.

Continental Divide Trail Society
 [23323]
3704 N Charles St., No. 601
Baltimore, MD 21218
PH: (410)235-9610
Wolf, James R., Director

Council of Colleges of Acupuncture
 and Oriental Medicine [16454]
PO Box 65120
Baltimore, MD 21209
PH: (410)464-6040
Fax: (410)464-6042
Sale, David M., JD, Exec. Dir.

Council for Exceptional Children
 Division on Career Development
 and Transition [8580]
PO Box 79026
Baltimore, MD 21279-0026
Toll free: 888-232-7733
Fax: (703)264-9494
Martin, Jim, President

Disability History Association [7715]
c/o Sara Scalenghe, Treasurer
Humanities Bldg., Rm. 322A
4501 N Charles St.
Loyola University Maryland
Baltimore, MD 21210
Brian, Kathleen, Treasurer

Faith Alliance Against Slavery and
 Trafficking [17895]
7 E Baltimore St.
Baltimore, MD 21202
Toll free: 855-333-2278

Fertilizer Industry Round Table
 [1181]
1701 S Highland Ave.
Baltimore, MD 21224
PH: (410)276-4466
Fax: (410)276-0241
McNaughton, Bob, Chmn. of the Bd.

Fire Suppression Systems Association [2995]
3601 E Joppa Rd.
Baltimore, MD 21234

PH: (410)931-8100
Fax: (410)931-8111
Aldridge, Ray, President

Ghana Relief Organization [10994]
PO Box 1722
Baltimore, MD 21203-1722
Iliasu, Iddrisu, Director

Healthy Teen Network [11842]
1501 St. Paul St., Ste. 124
Baltimore, MD 21202
PH: (410)685-0410
Fax: (410)685-0481
Paluzzi, Pat, President, CEO

Historic Ships in Baltimore [9774]
301 E Pratt St.
Baltimore, MD 21202
PH: (410)539-1797
Fax: (410)539-6238
Rowsom, Christopher, Exec. Dir.

Humanity First USA [11670]
300 E Lombard St., Ste. 840
Baltimore, MD 21202
Toll free: 877-994-3872
Naeem, Munum, Exec. Dir.

Immanuel Orphans [11043]
PO Box 43716
Baltimore, MD 21236
Mureithi, Robinson, President

International 505 Yacht Racing Association, American Section [22625]
519 Old Orchard Rd.
Baltimore, MD 21229
Nelson, G. Macy, Secretary, Treasurer

International Association of Ice Cream Distributors and Vendors [3430]
3601 E Joppa Rd.
Baltimore, MD 21234
PH: (410)931-8100
Fax: (410)931-8111
Rafaty, Hoss, President

International Association for Information and Data Quality [6743]
6920 Brookmill Rd.
Baltimore, MD 21215
PH: (410)484-0304
   (813)343-2163
Walenta, Christian, Advisor

International Book Bank [8078]
4000 Buena Vista Ave.
Baltimore, MD 21211
PH: (410)685-2665
Fax: (410)362-0336
Korenman, Victor, VP

International Chinese Snuff Bottle Society [21556]
2601 N Charles St.
Baltimore, MD 21218-4514
PH: (410)467-9400
Fax: (410)243-3451
Bozzo, Marion, Director

International Courtly Literature Society - North American Branch [9761]
c/o Leslie Zarker Morgan, President
Maryland Hall 461
Loyola University Maryland
4501 N Charles St.
Baltimore, MD 21210
Callahan, Christopher, Secretary, Treasurer

International Dyslexia Association [14630]
40 York Rd., 4th Fl.
Baltimore, MD 21204-5243

PH: (410)296-0232
Fax: (410)321-5069
Smith, Rick, Exec. Dir.

International Fortean Organization [7014]
PO Box 50088
Baltimore, MD 21211
Singer, Dave, VP

International Order of Alhambra [19407]
4200 Leeds Ave.
Baltimore, MD 21229-5421
PH: (410)242-0660
Toll free: 800-478-2946
Fax: (410)536-5729
Bass, Rev. Monsignor Ricardo E., Chap.

International Orthodox Christian Charities [19992]
110 West Rd., Ste. 360
Baltimore, MD 21204
PH: (410)243-9820
Toll free: 877-803-4622
Fax: (410)243-9824
Triantafilou, Constantine M., CEO, Exec. Dir.

International Police Mountain Bike Association [5475]
583 Frederick Rd., Ste. 5B
Baltimore, MD 21228
PH: (410)744-2400
Fax: (410)744-5504
Becker, Maureen, Exec. Dir.

International Social Service - United States of America Branch, Inc. [13110]
22 Light St., Ste. 200
Baltimore, MD 21202
PH: (443)451-1200
Fax: (443)451-1220
Miles, Robert G., Director

International Society for the Study and Prevention of Perinatal and Infant Death [16621]
1314 Bedford Ave., Ste. 210
Baltimore, MD 21208
Raven, Leanne, Chairperson

International Society for Third-Sector Research [12402]
Hampton House, No. 356
624 N Broadway
Baltimore, MD 21205-1900
PH: (410)614-4678
Fax: (410)502-0397
Daniels, Margery Berg, Exec. Dir.

International Union Against Sexually Transmitted Infections North America [17199]
c/o Charlotte A Gaydos, Regional Director
Division of Infectious Diseases
Johns Hopkins University
530 Rangos Bldg.
855 N Wolfe St.
Baltimore, MD 21205-1503
PH: (410)614-0932
Fax: (410)614-9775
Gaydos, Dr. Charlotte, Reg. Dir.

International Youth Foundation [13453]
32 South St.
Baltimore, MD 21202-3214
PH: (410)951-1500
Fax: (410)347-1188
Reese, William S., CEO, President

Iota Phi Theta Fraternity [23670]
1600 N Calvert St.
Baltimore, MD 21202

PH: (443)438-5691
Fax: (443)438-5692

John Hopkins Cleft and Craniofacial Center [14339]
4940 Eastern Ave.
Baltimore, MD 21224
PH: (410)955-7337
Jabs, Ethylin Wang, MD, Director

Johns Hopkins Center for Alternatives to Animal Testing [10654]
615 N Wolfe St., W7032
Baltimore, MD 21205
PH: (410)614-4990
Fax: (410)614-2871
Hartung, Thomas, MD, Director

KIDS COUNT [11057]
c/o Annie E. Casey Foundation
701 Saint Paul St.
Baltimore, MD 21202
PH: (410)547-6600
Fax: (410)547-6624

Kids Fund [11244]
416 Benninghaus Rd.
Baltimore, MD 21212
PH: (410)532-9330
Toll free: 877-532-9330
Cooper, George, Contact

Latin American Paper Money Society [22271]
c/o Arthur C. Matz, President, Secretary & Treasurer
1500 Bedford Ave., Apt. 209
Baltimore, MD 21206
Matz, Art C., President, Secretary, Treasurer

Leadership Council on Child Abuse & Interpersonal Violence [11705]
c/o Joyanna Silberg, Acting President
6501 N Charles St.
Baltimore, MD 21285-6815
Silberg, Joyanna, PhD, Act. Pres.

Let's Talk Pain [16561]
201 N Charles St., Ste. 710
Baltimore, MD 21201-4111
Toll free: 888-615-7246

Lutheran Immigration and Refugee Service [12593]
700 Light St.
Baltimore, MD 21230
PH: (410)230-2700
Fax: (410)230-2890
Grumm, Christine, Chmn. of the Bd.

Lutheran World Relief [20315]
700 Light St.
Baltimore, MD 21230
PH: (410)230-2800
Toll free: 800-597-5972
Fax: (410)230-2882
Speckhard, Daniel, CEO, President

Melville Society [9078]
c/o Johns Hopkins University Press
PO Box 19966
Baltimore, MD 21211-0966
Otter, Samuel, Editor

Mencken Society [9079]
PO Box 16218
Baltimore, MD 21210

Modernist Studies Association [8048]
Journals Publishing Div.
The Johns Hopkins University Press
PO Box 19966
Baltimore, MD 21211-0966
Toll free: 800-548-1784
Fax: (410)516-3866
Ross, Stephen, President

Museum Trustee Association [9837]
211 E Lombard St., Ste. 179
Baltimore, MD 21202-6102
PH: (410)402-0954
King, Maureen Pecht, Chairperson

Music Critics Association of North America, Inc. [9959]
722 Dulaney Valley Rd., Ste. 259
Baltimore, MD 21204
PH: (410)435-3881
Leininger, Robert, Managing Dir.

National Association for the Advancement of Colored People [17915]
4805 Mt. Hope Dr.
Baltimore, MD 21215
PH: (410)580-5777
Toll free: 877-NAACP-98
Brooks, Cornell William, President, CEO

National Association of Black Storytellers [10224]
PO Box 67722
Baltimore, MD 21215
PH: (410)947-1117
Fax: (410)947-1117
Abdul-Malik, Karen, President

National Association for Civil War Brass Music, Inc. [9966]
124 Maiden Choice Ln.
Baltimore, MD 21228
PH: (410)744-7708
Johnson, Don, President

National Association of Home Based Businesses [1645]
5432 Price Ave.
Baltimore, MD 21215
PH: (410)367-5308
   (410)367-5309

National Association for State Relay Administration [3232]
c/o Brenda Kelly-Frey, Chair
Telecommunications Access of Maryland
301 W Preston St., Ste. 1008A
Baltimore, MD 21201
PH: (443)453-5970
Toll free: 800-552-7724
Kelly-Frey, Brenda, Chairperson

National Black Catholic Congress [19874]
320 Cathedral St., 3rd Fl.
Baltimore, MD 21201
PH: (410)547-8496
Fax: (410)752-3958
Ricard, Rev. John, President

National Center on Institutions and Alternatives, Inc. [11537]
7205 Rutherford Rd.
Baltimore, MD 21244
PH: (443)780-1300
Fax: (410)597-9656
Miller, Dr. Jerome G., Founder

National Coalition for Sexual Freedom [12948]
Box 127
822 Guilford Ave.
Baltimore, MD 21202-3707
PH: (410)539-4824
Carlson, Kevin, Chairperson

National Correctional Industries Association [11539]
800 N Charles St., Ste. 550B
Baltimore, MD 21201-5343
PH: (410)230-3972
Fax: (410)230-3981
Honeycutt, Gina, Exec. Dir.

The National Council of Investigation and Security Services, Inc. [3064]
7501 Sparrows Point Blvd.
Baltimore, MD 21219-1927
Toll free: 800-445-8408
Beers, Dean A., President

National Federation of the Blind [17733]
200 E Wells St.
Baltimore, MD 21230-4850
PH: (410)659-9314
Fax: (410)685-5653
Maurer, Dr. Marc, President

National Information Standards Organization [6750]
3600 Clipper Mill Rd., Ste. 302
Baltimore, MD 21211
PH: (301)654-2512
Fax: (410)685-5278
Carpenter, Todd, Exec. Dir., Managing Dir.

National Office Products Alliance [3176]
3601 E Joppa Rd.
Baltimore, MD 21234-3314
PH: (410)931-8100
Manson, Rod, Chairman

National Organization for Continuing Education of Roman Catholic Clergy [20088]
110 E West St.
Baltimore, MD 21230
PH: (410)978-3676
Fax: (410)752-2703
Hartmayer, Bishop Gregory, Mem.

National Organization of Parents of Blind Children [17735]
1800 Johnson St.
Baltimore, MD 21230
PH: (410)659-9314
Cheadle, Barbara, Officer

National Summer Learning Association [8633]
575 S Charles St., Ste. 310
Baltimore, MD 21201
PH: (410)856-1370
Fax: (410)856-1146
Quinn, Jim, V. Ch.

National Women's Studies Association [8752]
11 E Mount Royal Ave., Ste. 100
Baltimore, MD 21202-5504
PH: (410)528-0355
Fax: (410)528-0357
Kimmich, Allison, Exec. Dir.

Newspaper Target Marketing Coalition [2297]
351 W Camden St., 6th Fl.
Baltimore, MD 21201-2473
PH: (202)386-6357
Coffelt, Doug, VP

North American Patristics Society [20515]
Johns Hopkins University
Press Journals Division
2715 N Charles St.
Baltimore, MD 21218
Toll free: 800-548-1784
Elm, Susanna, President

Old Old Timers Club [21272]
7634 Carla Rd.
Baltimore, MD 21208

Philosophy of Science Association [10114]
c/o Jessica Pfeifer, Executive Director
Dept. of Philosophy

University of Maryland, Baltimore County
1000 Hilltop Cir.
Baltimore, MD 21250
PH: (410)455-2014
Pfeifer, Jessica, Exec. Dir.

Physicians' Association for Anthroposophic Medicine [13648]
4801 Yellowwood Ave.
Baltimore, MD 21209
PH: (734)930-9462
Fax: (410)367-1961
Hinderberger, Peter, MD, Mem.

Polish/American/Jewish Alliance for Youth Action, Inc. [13474]
c/o Jay Pollack, Treasurer
13 Pipe Hill Ct., Unit B
Baltimore, MD 21209-1655
PH: (410)486-0698
Misler, Dennis, President

Polish Nobility Association Foundation [19612]
Villa Anneslie
529 Dunkirk Rd.
Baltimore, MD 21212-2014
Chylinski-Polubinski, Roger, Chairman

Professional Grounds Management Society [4289]
720 Light St.
Baltimore, MD 21230
PH: (410)223-2861
Fax: (410)752-8295
Doiron, John, President

Project Genesis [8144]
2833 Smith Ave., Ste. 225
Baltimore, MD 21209
PH: (410)602-1350
Toll free: 888-WWW-TORA
Fax: (410)602-1351
Menken, Rabbi Yaakov, Director

Regeneration [20044]
PO Box 9830
Baltimore, MD 21284-9830
PH: (410)661-0284
Fax: (443)275-7918
Glaser, Josh, Exec. Dir.

Register of Professional Archaeologists [5946]
3601 E Joppa Rd.
Baltimore, MD 21234
PH: (410)931-8100
Fax: (410)931-8111
Klein, Terry, President

Renal Pathology Society [16591]
c/o Lois J. Arend, Treasurer
Pathology 709
600 N Wolfe
Baltimore, MD 21287
Nickeleit, Volker, MD, Advisor

Representatives of Equal Access to Community Health-care in Ghana [11931]
1713 E Fairmount Ave., Ste. 9
Baltimore, MD 21231
Ama Manu, Aida Nana, MS, Founder, Bd. Member

Research Society for Victorian Periodicals [10300]
PO Box 19966
Baltimore, MD 21211-0966
Toll free: 800-548-1784
Fax: (410)516-3866
Shattock, Joanne, President

Reuse Development Organization, Inc. [4746]
The Loading Dock
2 N Kresson St.

Baltimore, MD 21224
PH: (410)558-3625
Fax: (410)558-1888
Kacandes, Tom, Bd. Member

Rushlight Club [9433]
4508 Elsrode Ave.
Baltimore, MD 21214-3107
PH: (443)433-6071
Mercer, Gerald, President

Sickle Cell Disease Association of America [15244]
3700 Koppers St., Ste. 570
Baltimore, MD 21227-1019
PH: (410)528-1555
Toll free: 800-421-8453
Fax: (410)528-1495
Banks, Sonja L., COO, President

Small Museum Association [9841]
Historic Ships
301 E Pratt St.
Baltimore, MD 21202
Illari, Jason, President

Society for the History of Authorship, Reading and Publishing [9135]
PO Box 19966
Baltimore, MD 21211-0966
PH: (410)516-6987
Toll free: 800-548-1784
Fax: (410)516-3866
Gadd, Ian, President

Society for the Study of Christian Spirituality [20007]
The Johns Hopkins University Press
PO Box 19966
Baltimore, MD 21211-0966
Toll free: 800-548-1784
Fax: (410)516-3866
Houck, Anita, Secretary, Treasurer

Society for Textual Scholarship [9769]
c/o Gabrielle Dean, Treasurer
The Sheridan Libraries
Johns Hopkins University
3400 N Charles St.
Baltimore, MD 21218
Young, Prof. John, Exec. Dir.

Star-Spangled Banner Flag House Association [20949]
844 E Pratt St.
Baltimore, MD 21202-4403
PH: (410)837-1793
Udoff, Amanda B., Coord.

Tissue Banks International [17519]
815 Park Ave.
Baltimore, MD 21201
PH: (410)752-3800
Toll free: 800-756-4824
Fax: (410)783-0183
Furlong, Douglas J., CEO

Trucking Industry Defense Association [3358]
3601 E Joppa Rd.
Baltimore, MD 21234
PH: (410)931-8100
Fax: (410)931-8111
Theragood, Renée, Exec. Dir.

United States of America Wushu-Kungfu Federation [23017]
7710 Harford Rd.
Baltimore, MD 21234
PH: (443)808-0048
Goh, Anthony, President

U.S. Lacrosse [22976]
113 W University Pkwy.
Baltimore, MD 21210
PH: (410)235-6882
Fax: (410)366-6735
Stenersen, Steve, CEO, President

United States Lacrosse Association-Women's Div. [22977]
113 W University Pky.
Baltimore, MD 21210
PH: (410)235-6882
Fax: (410)366-6735
Stenersen, Steve, CEO, President

Vegetarian Resource Group [10295]
PO Box 1463
Baltimore, MD 21203
PH: (410)366-8343

White Lung Association [17489]
PO Box 1483
Baltimore, MD 21203-1483
PH: (410)243-5864
Fite, James F., Librarian

World Association of Detectives [2014]
7501 Sparrows Point Blvd.
Baltimore, MD 21219
PH: (443)982-4586
Fax: (410)388-9746
Vinson, Christine, Chmn. of the Bd.

World Relief [20123]
7 E Baltimore St.
Baltimore, MD 21202-1602
PH: (443)451-1900
Toll free: 800-535-5433
Bauman, Stephan, President

Youth Action Network [18508]
32 South St.
Baltimore, MD 21202
PH: (410)951-1500
Fax: (410)347-1188
Regmi, Ashok, Mem.

Boardgame Players Association [22047]
1541 Redfield Rd.
Bel Air, MD 21015
Guttermuth, Ken, Chairman, Treasurer

National Weighing and Sampling Association [3466]
c/o David Hansel, Treasurer
1013 Shaffner Dr.
Bel Air, MD 21014
PH: (484)645-1464
Fax: (610)765-7753
Hansel, David, Treasurer

Shoe Service Institute of America [1403]
305 Huntsman Ct.
Bel Air, MD 21015
PH: (410)569-3425
Fax: (410)569-8333
Verbruggen, Sandra, President

Adoptions Together [10440]
4061 Powder Mill Rd., Ste. 320
Beltsville, MD 20705
PH: (301)439-2900
Fax: (301)937-2147
Goldwater, Janice, Founder, Exec. Dir.

Lewis Carroll Society of North America [9074]
11935 Beltsville Dr.
Beltsville, MD 20705
Burstein, Mark, Chairman

National Liquor Law Enforcement Association [5503]
11720 Beltsville Dr., Ste. 900
Beltsville, MD 20705-3102
PH: (301)755-2795
Fax: (301)755-2799
Cannon, Joseph, President

Operative Plasterers and Cement Masons International [23401]
11720 Beltsville Dr., Ste. 700
Beltsville, MD 20705

PH: (301)623-1000
Fax: (301)623-1032
Finley, Patrick D., President

Subud USA [20621]
4216 Howard Rd.
Beltsville, MD 20705
PH: (301)595-0626
Norton, Oswald, Exec. Dir.

Subud Youth Association [13481]
4216 Howard Rd.
Beltsville, MD 20705-2644
PH: (301)595-0626

Travelers Aid International [13091]
5000 Sunnyside Ave., Ste. 103
Beltsville, MD 20705-2327
PH: (202)546-1127
Davis, Floyd, Treasurer

Chrysler 300 Club International
[21353]
PO Box 40
Benson, MD 21018
Krausmann, Jim, President

Survivors of Incest Anonymous
[12939]
PO Box 190
Benson, MD 21018-9998
PH: (410)893-3322

Academy of Psychosomatic
Medicine [16953]
5272 River Rd., Ste. 630
Bethesda, MD 20816-1453
PH: (301)718-6520
Fax: (301)656-0989
Vrac, James, Exec. Dir.

Accuracy in Academia [7838]
4350 EW Hwy., Ste. 555
Bethesda, MD 20814
PH: (202)364-4403
Fax: (202)364-4098
Kline, Malcolm A., Exec. Dir.

Accuracy in Media [17935]
4350 E West Hwy., Ste. 555
Bethesda, MD 20814
PH: (202)364-4401
Fax: (202)364-4098
Irvine, Don, Chairman

The Adhesion Society [6176]
7101 Wisconsin Ave., Ste. 9901
Bethesda, MD 20814
PH: (301)986-9700
Fax: (301)986-9795
Barrios, Carlos, Editor

Adhesive and Sealant Council [60]
7101 Wisconsin Ave., Ste. 990
Bethesda, MD 20814
PH: (301)986-9700
Fax: (301)986-9795
Croson, Matt, President

African American Federal Executive
Association [5266]
6701 Democracy Blvd., Ste. 300
Bethesda, MD 20817
Toll free: 866-600-4894
Fax: (413)778-2563
Fraser, Leslye M., President

Alley Cat Allies [10563]
7920 Norfolk Ave., Ste. 600
Bethesda, MD 20814-2525
PH: (240)482-1980
Fax: (240)482-1990
Wilcox, Donna, VP, Chmn. of the Bd.

American Alliance for Theatre and
Education [10235]
4908 Auburn Ave.
Bethesda, MD 20814

PH: (301)200-1944
Fax: (301)280-1682
Minyard, Gary, President

American Association of Anatomists
[13687]
9650 Rockville Pke.
Bethesda, MD 20814-3999
PH: (301)634-7910
Fax: (301)634-7965
Mills, Ta'ice, Coord.

American Association of Blood
Banks [13836]
8101 Glenbrook Rd.
Bethesda, MD 20814-2749
PH: (301)907-6977
Fax: (301)907-6895
Marlow, Lisa, Exec. Asst.

American Association of Immunolo-
gists [15369]
1451 Rockville Pke., Ste. 650
Bethesda, MD 20814
PH: (301)634-7178
Fax: (301)634-7887
Berg, Leslie J., PhD, Chairman

American Beverage Licensees [175]
5101 River Rd., Ste. 108
Bethesda, MD 20816-1560
PH: (301)656-1494
Fax: (301)656-7539
Bodnovich, John D., Exec. Dir.

American Board of Medical Genetics
and Genomics [14873]
9650 Rockville Pke.
Bethesda, MD 20814-3998
PH: (301)634-7315
Fax: (301)634-7320
Robinson DelBusso, Ms. Sharon,
Administrator

The American College of Foot and
Ankle Orthopedics and Medicine
[16781]
5272 River Rd., Ste. 630
Bethesda, MD 20816
PH: (301)718-6505
Toll free: 800-265-8263
Fax: (301)656-0989
Wallis, Norman, PhD, Exec. Dir.

American College of Gastroenterol-
ogy [14776]
6400 Goldsboro Rd., Ste. 200
Bethesda, MD 20817
PH: (301)263-9000
Fax: (301)263-9025
Sarles, Harry E., Jr., MD, FACG,
Trustee

American College of Medical Genet-
ics and Genomics [14874]
7220 Wisconsin Ave., Ste. 300
Bethesda, MD 20814-4854
PH: (301)718-9603
Fax: (301)718-9604
Watson, Michael S., PhD, Exec. Dir.

American College of Medical Quality
[17027]
5272 River Rd., Ste. 630
Bethesda, MD 20816
PH: (301)718-6516
Fax: (301)656-0989
Casey, Donald E., Jr., VP

American College of Radiation
Oncology [17032]
5272 River Rd., Ste. 630
Bethesda, MD 20816
PH: (301)718-6515
Fax: (301)656-0989
Wallis, Norman, PhD, Exec. Dir.

American Employment Law Council
[4989]
4800 Hampden Ln., 7th Fl.
Bethesda, MD 20814

PH: (301)951-9326
Fax: (301)654-7354
Eastman, Hope B., Esq.,
Chairperson

American Fisheries Society [6713]
425 Barlow Pl., Ste. 110
Bethesda, MD 20814
PH: (301)897-8616
Fax: (301)897-8096
Hughes, Robert, President

American Gastroenterological As-
sociation [14777]
4930 Del Ray Ave.
Bethesda, MD 20814
PH: (301)654-2055
Fax: (301)654-5920
DeVault, Kenneth R., President

American Gastroenterological Association Research Foundation
[14778]
c/o American Gastroenterological
Association
4930 Del Ray Ave.
Bethesda, MD 20814
PH: (301)222-4002
Brotman, Martin, MD, Chairman

American Institute of Fishery
Research Biologists [6714]
7909 Sleaford Pl.
Bethesda, MD 20814-4625
Keegan, Tom, President

American International Recruitment
Council [7444]
4710 Rosedale Ave.
Bethesda, MD 20814
PH: (240)547-6400
Fax: (240)547-6400
Jennings, Ross, President

American Jewish Society for Service
[12218]
10319 Westlake Dr., Ste. 193
Bethesda, MD 20817
PH: (301)664-6400
Convissor, Rena, Exec. Dir.

American Medical Athletic Associa-
tion [23059]
4405 E West Hwy., Ste. 405
Bethesda, MD 20814-4535
PH: (301)913-9517
Toll free: 800-776-2732
Fax: (301)913-9520

American Medical Informatics As-
sociation [14361]
4720 Montgomery Ln., Ste. 500
Bethesda, MD 20814
PH: (301)657-1291
Fax: (301)657-1296
Greenwood, Karen, Exec. VP, COO

The American Occupational Therapy
Association, Inc. [17434]
4720 Montgomery Ln., Ste. 200
Bethesda, MD 20814-3449
PH: (301)652-6611
Toll free: 800-729-2682
Fax: (301)652-7711
Somers, Frederick P., Exec. Dir.

American Occupational Therapy
Foundation [16315]
4720 Montgomery Ln., Ste. 202
Bethesda, MD 20814-3449
PH: (240)292-1079
Fax: (240)396-6188
Campbell, Scott, CEO

American Physiological Society
[7033]
9650 Rockville Pke.
Bethesda, MD 20814-3991

PH: (301)634-7164
Fax: (301)634-7241
Frank, Martin, PhD, Exec. Dir.

American Podiatric Medical Associa-
tion [16783]
9312 Old Georgetown Rd.
Bethesda, MD 20814-1621
PH: (301)581-9200
Davis, R. Daniel, President

American Podiatric Medical
Students' Association [16784]
9312 Old Georgetown Rd.
Bethesda, MD 20814
PH: (301)581-9263
Toll free: 800-275-2762
McDonald, Dorothy Cahill, Exec. Dir.

American Pyrotechnics Association
[2821]
7910 Woodmont Ave., Ste. 1220
Bethesda, MD 20814
PH: (301)907-8181
Fax: (301)907-9148
Heckman, Ms. Julie L., Exec. Dir.

American Running Association
[23060]
4405 E West Hwy., Ste. 405
Bethesda, MD 20814-4535
Toll free: 800-776-2732
Fax: (301)913-9520
Watt, David, Bd. Member

American Society for Cell Biology
[6069]
8120 Woodmont Ave., Ste. 750
Bethesda, MD 20814
PH: (301)347-9300
Fax: (301)347-9310
Gorbsky, Gary J., Treasurer

American Society of Health-System
Pharmacists [16645]
7272 Wisconsin Ave.
Bethesda, MD 20814
PH: (301)664-8700
    (301)657-3000
Toll free: 866-279-0681
Fax: (301)657-1251
Abramowitz, Paul W., CEO

American Society of Human Genet-
ics [6666]
9650 Rockville Pke.
Bethesda, MD 20814
PH: (301)634-7300
Toll free: 866-HUM-GENE
Fax: (301)634-7079
Dietz, Harry C., MD, President

American Society for Investigative
Pathology [16575]
9650 Rockville Pke., Ste. E133
Bethesda, MD 20814
PH: (301)634-7130
Fax: (301)634-7990
Sobel, Mark E., PhD, Exec. Ofc.

American Society for Matrix Biology
[6070]
c/o Kendra LaDuca, Executive Director
9650 Rockville Pke.
Bethesda, MD 20814
PH: (301)634-7456
Fax: (301)634-7455
Pozzi, Ambra, Secretary, Treasurer

American Society of Nuclear Cardiol-
ogy [14094]
4340 East-West Hwy., Ste. 1120
Bethesda, MD 20814-4578
PH: (301)215-7575
Fax: (301)215-7113
Flood, Kathleen, CEO

American Society for Pharmacology and Experimental Therapeutics [16647]
9650 Rockville Pke.
Bethesda, MD 20814-3995
PH: (301)634-7060
Fax: (301)634-7061
Siuciak, Judith A., Exec. Ofc.

American Society of Podiatric Surgeons [16786]
9312 Old Georgetown Rd.
Bethesda, MD 20814
PH: (301)581-9214
Toll free: 877-277-7616
Palmer, Dr. Stephen, Chmn. of the Bd.

AMSUS - The Society of the Federal Health Professionals [15837]
9320 Old Georgetown Rd.
Bethesda, MD 20814-1653
PH: (301)897-8800
Toll free: 800-761-9320
Fax: (301)530-5446
Condrick, Diane, Exec. Asst.

ASHP Foundation [16651]
7272 Wisconsin Ave.
Bethesda, MD 20814
PH: (301)664-8612
Fax: (301)634-5712
Allen, Stephen J., MS, CEO

ASPRS, The Imaging and Geospatial Information Society [7018]
5410 Grosvenor Ln., Ste. 210
Bethesda, MD 20814-2160
PH: (301)493-0290
Fax: (301)493-0208
DeGloria, Stephen D., President

Associated Specialty Contractors [855]
3 Bethesda Metro Ctr., Ste. 1100
Bethesda, MD 20814
Smith, D. L., Chairman

Association of Biomolecular Resource Facilities [6776]
9650 Rockville Pke.
Bethesda, MD 20814-3999
PH: (301)634-7306
Fax: (301)634-7455
Friedman, David, Mem.

Association of Chiropractic Colleges [14256]
4424 Montgomery Ave., Ste. 202
Bethesda, MD 20814
Toll free: 800-284-1062
O'Bryon, David S., CAE, President

Association for Financial Professionals [1223]
4520 E West Hwy., Ste. 750
Bethesda, MD 20814
PH: (301)907-2862
Fax: (301)907-2864
Scaglione, Mr. Anthony, Chairman

Association for Molecular Pathology [16578]
9650 Rockville Pke., Ste. E133
Bethesda, MD 20814-3993
PH: (301)634-7939
Fax: (301)634-7995
Hill, Charles E., MD, PhD, President

Association of Pathology Chairs [16579]
9650 Rockville Pke., Ste. 4111
Bethesda, MD 20814-3993
PH: (301)634-7880
Fax: (301)576-5156
Markwood, Priscilla S., Exec. Dir.

Association of Program Directors in Surgery [17378]
6400 Goldsboro Rd., Ste. 200
Bethesda, MD 20817-5846

PH: (301)320-1200
Fax: (301)263-9025
Morris, Jon B., Mem.

Association for the Study of the Cuban Economy [7727]
5931 Beech Ave.
Bethesda, MD 20817
Henken, Ted, VP

Autism Society [13756]
4340 East-West Hwy., Ste. 350
Bethesda, MD 20814
Toll free: 800-328-8476
Badesch, Scott, COO, President, CEO

Auto Care Association [281]
7101 Wisconsin Ave., Ste. 1300
Bethesda, MD 20814-3415
PH: (301)654-6664
Fax: (301)654-3299
Klein, Michael, Chairman

Automotive Content Professionals Network [309]
7101 Wisconsin Ave., Ste. 1300
Bethesda, MD 20814-3415
PH: (301)654-6664
Slayter, Doreen, President

Automotive Warehouse Distributors Association [314]
7101 Wisconsin Ave., Ste. 1300
Bethesda, MD 20814-3415
PH: (301)654-6664
Fax: (301)654-3299
Fairbanks, Dick, Contact

Bladder Cancer Advocacy Network [13904]
4915 St. Elmo Ave., Ste. 202
Bethesda, MD 20814
PH: (301)215-9099
Toll free: 888-901-BCAN
Smith, Monica, Exec. Dir.

Brain Attack Coalition [17295]
Bldg. 31, Rm. 8A-16
31 Center Dr., MSC 2540
Bethesda, MD 20892
PH: (301)496-5751
Walker, Dr. Michael D., Chairman

Car Care Council [289]
7101 Wisconsin Ave., Ste. 1300
Bethesda, MD 20814
PH: (301)333-1088
White, Rich, Exec. Dir.

Rachel Carson Council [13221]
8600 Irvington Ave.
Bethesda, MD 20817
PH: (301)214-2400
Musil, Robert K., PhD, MPH, President, CEO

Center for Human Services [12966]
7200 Wisconsin Ave., Ste. 600
Bethesda, MD 20814
PH: (301)654-8338
Fax: (301)941-8427
Marshall, Ruth, Director

Child Trends [11219]
7315 Wisconsin Ave., Ste. 1200W
Bethesda, MD 20814
PH: (240)223-9200
Fax: (240)200-1238
Emig, Carol, President

Childhood Influenza Immunization Coalition [15376]
7201 Wisconsin Ave., Ste. 750
Bethesda, MD 20814-4850
PH: (301)656-0003
Fax: (301)907-0878
Baker, Carol J., MD, Chairperson

Chinese Biological Investigators Society [6079]
c/o Yingzi Yang, PhD, Treasurer
8102 Woodhaven Blvd.
Bethesda, MD 20817
Li, Guo-Min, Secretary

Circadian Sleep Disorders Network [17215]
4619 Woodfield Rd.
Bethesda, MD 20814
Mansbach, Peter, PhD, President

Circle of Rights [14154]
5802 Augusta Ln.
Bethesda, MD 20816
PH: (301)229-1355
    (301)948-5818
Emery, Susan, Exec. Dir.

Citizens for Effective Schools [8474]
c/o Gary Ratner, Executive Director
8209 Hamilton Spring Ct.
Bethesda, MD 20817
PH: (301)469-8000
Ratner, Gary, Exec. Dir., Founder

Clean Fuels Development Coalition [4541]
c/o Douglas Durante, Executive Director
4641 Montgomery Ave., Ste. 350
Bethesda, MD 20814
PH: (301)718-0077
Fax: (301)718-0606
Durante, Douglas A., Exec. Dir.

Coalition for the Life Sciences [7126]
8120 Woodmont Ave., Ste. 750
Bethesda, MD 20814-2762
PH: (301)347-9309
Fax: (301)347-9310
Yamamoto, Keith R., Chmn. of the Bd.

Coalition to Protect America's Health Care [15320]
PO Box 30211
Bethesda, MD 20824-0211
Toll free: 877-422-2349
Borgstrom, Marna P., Chairman

Compliance and Ethics Forum for Life Insurers [1849]
PO Box 30940
Bethesda, MD 20824
PH: (240)744-3030
Apostle, John G., II, Chairman

Council on Podiatric Medical Education [16787]
9312 Old Georgetown Rd.
Bethesda, MD 20814-1621
PH: (301)581-9200
Fax: (301)571-4903
Tinkleman, Alan R., MPA, Director

CureSearch for Children's Cancer [13956]
4600 EW Hwy., Ste. 600
Bethesda, MD 20814
Toll free: 800-458-6223
Fax: (301)718-0047
Thrall, Laura, President, CEO

Cystic Fibrosis Foundation [17138]
6931 Arlington Rd., Ste. B
Bethesda, MD 20814
PH: (301)657-8444
Toll free: 877-657-8444
Fax: (301)652-9571
Brownlee, Denise, Exec. Dir.

Czechoslovak Society of Arts and Sciences [9016]
PO Box 34617
Bethesda, MD 20827

PH: (301)881-7222
Hausner, Petr, MD, President

Decorative Plumbing and Hardware Association [2636]
7508 Wisconsin Ave., 4th Fl.
Bethesda, MD 20814-3561
PH: (301)657-3642
Toll free: 888-871-6520
Fax: (301)907-9326
Babbitt, Jim, Exec. Dir.

Democracy International [18866]
7600 Wisconsin Ave., Ste. 1010
Bethesda, MD 20814
PH: (301)961-1660
Fax: (301)961-6605
Bjornlund, Eric, Founder, Principal, President

Diabetes Action Research and Education Foundation [14522]
6701 Democracy Blvd., Ste. 300
Bethesda, MD 20817
PH: (202)333-4520
Fax: (202)558-5240
Faulkner, Patricia A., Chairperson

EarthShare [7888]
7735 Old Georgetown Rd., Ste. 900
Bethesda, MD 20814
PH: (240)333-0300
Toll free: 800-875-3863
Fax: (240)333-0301
Beard, Heather, Exec. Dir.

Editorial Projects in Education [7760]
6935 Arlington Rd., Ste. 100
Bethesda, MD 20814
PH: (301)280-3100
Toll free: 800-346-1834
Fax: (301)280-3200
Edwards, Virginia B., President, Editor

Education Network to Advance Cancer Clinical Trials [13962]
7625 Wisconsin Ave., 3rd Fl.
Bethesda, MD 20814
PH: (240)541-0366

ELECTRI International - The Foundation for Electrical Construction Inc. [1016]
3 Bethesda Metro Ctr., Ste. 1100
Bethesda, MD 20814-6302
PH: (301)215-4538
Fax: (301)215-4536
Alessi, Russell J., President

Farm Animal Rights Movement [10621]
10101 Ashburton Ln.
Bethesda, MD 20817
Toll free: 888-327-6872
Webermann, Michael A., Exec. Dir.

Federation of American Societies for Experimental Biology [6081]
9650 Rockville Pke.
Bethesda, MD 20814
PH: (301)634-7000
Fax: (301)634-7001
Fogleman, Guy C., Exec. Dir.

Foundation on Economic Trends [19108]
4520 East West Hwy., Ste. 600
Bethesda, MD 20814
PH: (301)656-6272
Fax: (301)654-0208
Rifkin, Jeremy R., President

Genetics Society of America [6667]
9650 Rockville Pke.
Bethesda, MD 20814-3998
PH: (301)634-7300
Toll free: 866-486-GENE
Fax: (301)634-7079
Fagen, Adam, PhD, Exec. Dir.

German Wine Society [3479]
5607 Huntington Pky.
Bethesda, MD 20814
Marling, George, Chmn. of the Bd.

Give an Hour [10742]
PO Box 5918
Bethesda, MD 20824-5918
Van Dahlen, Barbara, PhD,
President, Founder

Global Health Informatics Partner-
ship [15457]
American Medical Informatics As-
sociation
4720 Montgomery Ln., Ste. 500
Bethesda, MD 20814-3683
PH: (301)657-1291
Fax: (301)657-1296
Greenwood, Karen, Exec. VP, COO

Hearing Loss Association of America
[15195]
7910 Woodmont Ave., Ste. 1200
Bethesda, MD 20814
PH: (301)657-2248
Canniff, Teri, Mgr.

Heart Failure Society of America
[14113]
6707 Democracy Blvd., Ste. 925
Bethesda, MD 20817
PH: (301)312-8635
Toll free: 888-213-4417
Blair, Michele, CEO

Heavy Duty Distribution Association
[320]
Auto Care Association
7101 Wisconsin Ave., Ste. 1300
Bethesda, MD 20814-3415
PH: (301)654-6664
Fax: (301)654-3299
Scheer, David W., Mem.

Histochemical Society [6201]
9650 Rockville Pke.
Bethesda, MD 20814
PH: (301)634-7026
Fax: (301)634-7099
Stahl, William L., Exec. Dir.

Hope for Children-United States
[11036]
5801 Searl Terr.
Bethesda, MD 20816
Rhees, Carol A., President

Human Heredity and Health in Africa
[13514]
National Human Genome Research
Institute
National Institutes of Health
5635 Fishers Ln., Ste. 4076
Bethesda, MD 20892-9305
PH: (301)496-7531
Fax: (301)480-2770
Collins, Francis, Contact

Hydrocephalus Association [15943]
4340 East-West Hwy., Ste. 905
Bethesda, MD 20814-4447
PH: (301)202-3811
Toll free: 888-598-3789
Fax: (301)202-3913
Brown, Craig, V. Chmn. of the Bd.

IDB Family Association [19692]
1 Democracy Ctr., Ste. 110
6901 Rockledge Dr.
Bethesda, MD 20817
PH: (301)493-6576
Fax: (301)493-6456
Albarracin, Alejandra, President

Import Vehicle Community [321]
7101 Wisconsin Ave., Ste. 1300
Bethesda, MD 20814

PH: (301)654-6664
Fax: (301)654-3299
Bearden, Stephen, Mem.

Interdisciplinary Council on Development and Learning, Inc. [8585]
4938 Hampden Ln., Ste. 800
Bethesda, MD 20814
PH: (301)656-2667

International Association for Chronic
Fatigue Syndrome/Myalgic
Encephalomyelitis [14584]
9650 Rockville Pke.
Bethesda, MD 20814
PH: (301)634-7701
Fax: (301)634-7099
Friedberg, Fred, PhD, President

International Association for Vegeta-
tion Science [6144]
9650 Rockville Pke.
Bethesda, MD 20814
PH: (301)634-7255
    (301)634-7453
Bradham, Stefan R., Administrator

International Commission on Radia-
tion Units and Measurements
[7082]
7910 Woodmont Ave., Ste. 400
Bethesda, MD 20814-3076
PH: (301)657-2652
Fax: (301)907-8768
Schauer, David A., Exec. Sec.

International Cytokine and Interferon
Society [15648]
c/o Federation of American Societies
for Experimental Biology
9650 Rockville Pke.
Bethesda, MD 20814
PH: (301)634-7250
Fax: (301)634-7455
Taniguchi, Tadatsugu, President

International Lyme and Associated
Diseases Society [14587]
PO Box 341461
Bethesda, MD 20827-1461
PH: (301)263-1080
Fax: (301)263-0776
DeMio, Phillip C., MD, Director

International Municipal Lawyers As-
sociation [5012]
7910 Woodmont Ave., Ste. 1440
Bethesda, MD 20814
PH: (202)466-5424
Fax: (202)785-0152
Thompson, Chuck, Exec. Dir., Gen.
Counsel

International Neuroethics Society
[16052]
PO Box 34252
Bethesda, MD 20827
PH: (301)229-1660
Graham, Karen, Exec. Dir.

International Social Marketing Association [2287]
6414 Hollins Dr.
Bethesda, MD 20817-2343
Morgan, Winthrop, President

International Society for Advance-
ment of Cytometry [6085]
9650 Rockville Pke.
Bethesda, MD 20814
PH: (301)634-7435
Fax: (301)634-7429
Smith, Paul J., Mem.

International Society for Pharma-
coepidemiology [16668]
5272 River Rd., Ste. 630
Bethesda, MD 20816

PH: (301)718-6500
Fax: (301)656-0989
Epstein, Mark H., ScD, Exec. Sec.

International Society of Tropical
Foresters [4206]
5400 Grosvenor Ln.
Bethesda, MD 20814
PH: (301)530-4514
Fax: (301)897-3690

International Ultraviolet Association
[6494]
7720 Wisconsin Ave., Ste. 208
Bethesda, MD 20814
PH: (240)437-4615
Fax: (240)209-2340
Hunter, Gary, Secretary

Intersociety Council for Pathology
Information, Inc. [16588]
9650 Rockville Pke., Rm. E123
Bethesda, MD 20814-3993
PH: (301)634-7200
Fax: (301)634-7990
Stivers, Donna, Administrator,
Managing Ed.

Iran Freedom Foundation [18575]
PO Box 34422
Bethesda, MD 20827
PH: (301)215-6677
    (301)335-7717
Fax: (301)907-8877
Tabatabai, Mr. M.R., President

Japanese American Veterans As-
sociation [21127]
PO Box 341398
Bethesda, MD 20827
PH: (703)503-3431
Shima, Terry, Chairman

Mid-Atlantic Equity Consortium
[7780]
5272 River Rd., Ste. 340
Bethesda, MD 20816
PH: (301)657-7741
Toll free: 877-637-2736
Fax: (301)657-8782
Shaffer, Susan, President, Exec. Dir.

National Alliance for Caregiving
[11824]
4720 Montgomery Ln., Ste. 205
Bethesda, MD 20814
PH: (301)718-8444
Fax: (301)951-9067
Hunt, Gail Gibson, CEO, President

National Association of Community
Health Centers [14948]
7501 Wisconsin Ave., Ste. 1100W
Bethesda, MD 20814
PH: (301)347-0400
Van Coverden, Tom, CEO, President

National Association of School
Psychologists [16928]
4340 E West Hwy., Ste. 402
Bethesda, MD 20814
PH: (301)657-0270
Toll free: 866-331-NASP
Fax: (301)657-0275
Paige, Leslie, Secretary

National Association of Therapeutic
Schools and Programs [13800]
5272 River Rd., Ste. 600
Bethesda, MD 20816
PH: (301)986-8770
Fax: (301)986-8772
Brownstein, Clifford, Exec. Dir.

National Blood Foundation [13841]
8101 Glenbrook Rd.
Bethesda, MD 20814-2749
PH: (301)215-6552
Fax: (301)215-5751
Quiggins, Amy, Mgr.

National Collegiate Cancer Founda-
tion [14025]
4858 Battery Ln., No. 216
Bethesda, MD 20814
PH: (240)515-6262
Waeger, Daniel, Founder

National Council on Radiation
Protection and Measurements
[5740]
7910 Woodmont Ave., Ste. 400
Bethesda, MD 20814-3095
PH: (301)657-2652
Fax: (301)907-8768
Boice, John D., Jr., President

National Diabetes Information
Clearinghouse [14541]
1 Information Way
Bethesda, MD 20892-3560
Toll free: 800-860-8747
Fax: (301)634-0716
Rodgers, Griffin P., Director

National Electrical Contractors As-
sociation [888]
3 Bethesda Metro Ctr., Ste. 1100
Bethesda, MD 20814
PH: (301)657-3110
Fax: (301)215-4500
Grau, John, CEO

National Foundation for Cancer
Research [16351]
4600 E West Hwy., Ste. 525
Bethesda, MD 20814
PH: (301)654-1250
Toll free: 800-321-2873
Fax: (301)654-5824
Salisbury, Franklin C., Jr., CEO

National Foundation for Infectious
Diseases [15411]
7201 Wisconsin Ave., Ste. 750
Bethesda, MD 20814-5278
PH: (301)656-0003
Fax: (301)907-0878
Joseph, Patrick, President

National Institute on Deafness and
Other Communication Disorders
Information Clearinghouse [15206]
1 Communication Ave.
Bethesda, MD 20892-3456
Toll free: 800-241-1044
Battey, James F., Jr., MD, Director

National Institute of Health | National
Institute of Dental and Craniofacial
Reaserch | National Oral Health
Information Clearinghouse [14465]
1 NOHIC Way
Bethesda, MD 20892-3500
Somerman, Martha J., PhD, Director

National Institutes of Health |
National Institute of Dental and
Craniofacial Research [14466]
Bldg. 31, Rm. 5B55
31 Center Dr., MSC 2190
Bethesda, MD 20892-2190
PH: (301)496-4261
    (301)496-3571
Fax: (301)496-9988
Somerman, Martha J., PhD, Director

National Institutes of Health |
National Institute on Drug Abuse
[17323]
6001 Executive Blvd., Rm. 5213,
MSC 9561
Bethesda, MD 20892-9561
PH: (301)443-1124
Volkow, Dr. Nora D., Director

National Kidney and Urologic
Diseases Information
Clearinghouse [17554]
3 Information Way
Bethesda, MD 20892-3580
Toll free: 800-891-5390
Fax: (703)738-4929

National Latina Health Network
[14957]
7720 Wisconsin Ave., Ste. 212
Bethesda, MD 20814
PH: (301)664-9466
Fax: (301)527-1476
Alvarado, Elena M., CEO, President

Ornithological Council **[6964]**
c/o Ellen Paul, Executive Director
6512 E Halbert Rd.
Bethesda, MD 20817
PH: (301)986-8568
Fax: (301)986-5205
Elbin, Susan B., Chairperson

Parenteral Drug Association **[2565]**
Bethesda Towers, Ste. 150
4350 E West Hwy.
Bethesda, MD 20814-4485
PH: (301)656-5900
Fax: (301)986-0296
Johnson, Richard, President, CEO

Pediatric & Congenital Electrophysiology Society **[16768]**
9650 Rockville Pke.
Bethesda, MD 20814
PH: (301)634-7401
Fax: (301)634-7099
Collins, Kathryn K., MD, President

Property Management Association
[2887]
7508 Wisconsin Ave., 4th Fl.
Bethesda, MD 20814
PH: (301)657-9200
Fax: (301)907-9326
Block, Carolyn, Dir. of Fin.

Purine Research Society **[15834]**
5424 Beech Ave.
Bethesda, MD 20814-1730
PH: (301)530-0354
Fax: (301)564-1180

RadTech International North America
[7084]
7720 Wisconsin Ave., Ste. 208
Bethesda, MD 20814
PH: (240)497-1242
Weissman, Peter, President

James Renwick Alliance **[8885]**
4405 East West Hwy., Ste. 510
Bethesda, MD 20814
PH: (301)907-3888
Savage, Brigitte, VP of Dev.

RNA Society **[6061]**
9650 Rockville Pke.
Bethesda, MD 20814-3998
PH: (301)634-7166
Woodson, Sarah, President

Science Communication Network
[17020]
4833 West Ln.
Bethesda, MD 20814
PH: (301)654-6665
Kostant, Amy, Exec. Dir.

Sjogren's Syndrome Foundation
[17166]
6707 Democracy Blvd., Ste. 325
Bethesda, MD 20817
PH: (301)530-4420
Toll free: 800-475-6473
Fax: (301)530-4415
Taylor, Steven, CEO

Small Business Legislative Council
[3128]
4800 Hampden Ln., 6th Fl.
Bethesda, MD 20814
PH: (301)652-8302
Heppes, Jerry, Chairman

Smiles on Wings **[15161]**
6501 Democracy Blvd.
Bethesda, MD 20817

PH: (301)896-0064
Fax: (301)758-7401
Bunnag, Usa, DDS, Founder, President

Society of American Foresters
[4216]
5400 Grosvenor Ln.
Bethesda, MD 20814-2198
Toll free: 866-897-8720
Fax: (301)897-3691
Esguerra, Jorge, CFO

Society of Biological Inorganic Chemistry **[6214]**
9650 Rockville Pke.
Bethesda, MD 20814-3998
PH: (301)634-7194
Fax: (301)634-7099
Que, Lawrence, Ed.-in-Chief

Society for Developmental Biology
[6098]
9650 Rockville Pke.
Bethesda, MD 20814-3998
PH: (301)634-7815
Fax: (301)634-7825
Prince, Vicky, Secretary

Society for Leukocyte Biology
[17150]
9650 Rockville Pke.
Bethesda, MD 20814
PH: (301)634-7814
Fax: (301)634-7455
Richmond, Ann, Officer

Society of Medical Consultants to the Armed Forces **[15840]**
c/o Kevin G. Berry, MD, Secretary-Treasurer
5009 Overlea Ct.
Bethesda, MD 20816
PH: (301)320-0847
Alexander, A. Herbert, MD, President

Society for Radiation Oncology Administrators **[17071]**
5272 River Rd., Ste. 630
Bethesda, MD 20816
PH: (301)718-6510
Fax: (301)656-0989
Epstein, Mark H., Exec. Dir.

Society of Vertebrate Paleontology
[6975]
9650 Rockville Pke.
Bethesda, MD 20814
PH: (301)634-7024
Fax: (301)634-7455
Weisman, Serena, Exec. Dir.

Touch of Relief Inc. **[15271]**
Bethesda, MD
PH: (301)680-8867

U.S. Composting Council **[5847]**
5400 Grosvenor Ln.
Bethesda, MD 20814-2122
PH: (301)897-2715
Fax: (301)530-5072
King, Wayne, Sr., VP

U.S. Department of Health and Human Services I National Institutes of Health I National Cancer Institute I Alliance for Nanotechnology in Cancer **[15659]**
Bldg. 31, Rm. 10A52
31 Center Dr.
Bethesda, MD 20892-2580
PH: (301)451-8983
Grodzinski, Piotr, PhD, Director

U.S. Department of Health and Human Services I National Institutes of Health I National Center for Complementary and Intergrative Health **[13663]**
9000 Rockville Pke.
Bethesda, MD 20892
Toll free: 888-644-6226
Briggs, Josephine P., MD, Director

U.S. Department of Health and Human Services I National Institutes of Health I National Institute of Arthritis and Musculoskeletal and Skin Diseases Information Clearinghouse **[17171]**
1 AMS Cir.
Bethesda, MD 20892
PH: (301)495-4484
Toll free: 877-226-4267
Fax: (301)718-6366
Katz, Dr. Stephen I., Director

U.S. Department of Health and Human Services I National Institutes of Health I National Institute of Neurological Disorders and Stroke
[15999]
Bldg. 31, Rm 8A52
31 Center Dr.
Bethesda, MD 20892
PH: (301)496-5751
Toll free: 800-352-9424
Koroshetz, M.D., Walter J., Dir. (Actg.)

U.S. Department of Health and Human Services I National Institutes of Health I Eunice Kennedy Shriver National Institute of Child Health and Human Development **[14216]**
Bldg. 31, Rm. 2A32
31 Center Dr.
Bethesda, MD 20892-2425
Toll free: 800-370-2943
Spong, Catherine Y., MD, Dir. (Actg.)

Weight-Control Information Network
[16265]
1 WIN Way
Bethesda, MD 20892-3665

The Wildlife Society **[4917]**
5410 Grosvenor Ln., Ste. 200
Bethesda, MD 20814-2144
PH: (301)897-9770
Fax: (301)530-2471
Hutchins, Michael, Exec. Dir., CEO

Women's Learning Partnership
[13411]
4343 Montgomery Ave., Ste. 201
Bethesda, MD 20814
PH: (301)654-2774
Fax: (301)654-2775
Afkhami, Mahnaz, CEO, President

World Jurist Association **[5353]**
7910 Woodmont Ave., Ste. 1440
Bethesda, MD 20814
PH: (202)466-5428
Fax: (202)452-8540
Jones, Iris, Gen. Counsel

Wound Healing Society **[15074]**
9650 Rockville Pke.
Bethesda, MD 20814-3998
PH: (301)634-7600
Baird, Andrew, President

Zumunta Association USA **[19598]**
10411 Motor City Dr., Ste. 750
Bethesda, MD 20817
Salau, Dr. Ibrahim, President

Haitian Art Education and Appraisal Society **[8975]**
11 S Main St., Ste. 1
Boonsboro, MD 21713

PH: (301)637-4934
Fax: (240)715-6416
Wah, Marcel, Exec. Dir., Founder

Africa Environmental Watch **[3789]**
4207 Plummers Promise Dr., Ste. 100
Bowie, MD 20720
PH: (240)417-2545
(215)828-2010
Fax: (301)464-1664

Grantmakers for Children, Youth, and Families **[12481]**
12138 Central Ave., Ste. 422
Bowie, MD 20721
PH: (301)589-4293
Fax: (301)589-4289
Badio, Bernadette, Dir. of Operations

International Association of Women Police **[5137]**
12600 Kavanaugh Ln.
Bowie, MD 20715
PH: (301)464-1402
Fax: (301)560-8836
Humphrys, Andrea, Exec. Dir.

International Masonry Institute **[871]**
17101 Science Dr.
Bowie, MD 20715
PH: (301)291-2124
Toll free: 800-803-0295
Calambokidis, Joan Baggett, President

National Amateur Baseball Federation **[22555]**
PO Box 705
Bowie, MD 20718
PH: (410)721-4727
Fax: (410)721-4940
DiLauro, Vin, President

National Humanities Institute **[8007]**
PO Box 1387
Bowie, MD 20718-1387
PH: (301)464-4277
Baldacchino, Joseph, President

Tire Industry Association **[3280]**
1532 Pointer Ridge Pl., Ste. G
Bowie, MD 20716-1883
PH: (301)430-7280
Toll free: 800-876-8372
Fax: (301)430-7283
Nicholson, Glen, President

DateAble, Inc. **[11584]**
15520 Bald Eagle School Rd.
Brandywine, MD 20613-8545
PH: (301)888-1177
(301)657-3283
Watson, Robert, Exec. Dir.

TransWorld Development Initiatives
[12073]
PO Box 105
Brentwood, MD 20722
PH: (301)793-7551
Fax: (301)779-8892
Azuine, Dr. Magnus A., President

Capital PC User Group **[6296]**
19209 Mt. Airey Rd.
Brookeville, MD 20833
PH: (301)560-6442
Fax: (301)760-3303
Courtney, Dennis, President

National Health and Exercise Science Association **[16708]**
3701 Flintridge Ct.
Brookeville, MD 20833
PH: (301)576-0611
Toll free: 866-481-5957
Fax: (301)685-1819

Sidran Institute for Traumatic Stress Education and Advocacy **[12313]**
PO Box 436
Brooklandville, MD 21022-0436

PH: (410)825-8888
Fax: (410)560-0134
Giller, Esther, Director, President

Masonic Service Association of
North America [19563]
3905 National Dr., Ste. 280
Burtonsville, MD 20866
PH: (301)476-7330
(301)588-4010
Toll free: 855-476-4010
Fax: (301)476-9440
Braatz, George O., Exec. Sec.

Federal Law Enforcement Officers
Association [5359]
7945 MacArthur Blvd., Ste. 201
Cabin John, MD 20818
PH: (202)870-5503
Toll free: 866-553-5362
Catura, Nate, President

St. Gabriel Possenti Society, Inc.
[18254]
PO Box 183
Cabin John, MD 20818
PH: (202)239-8005
Snyder, John M., Founder, Chairman

Intermodal Association of North
America [3332]
11785 Beltsville Dr., Ste. 1100
Calverton, MD 20705
PH: (301)982-3400
Casey, Joanne F., CEO, President

Seafarers International Union
[23478]
5201 Auth Way
Camp Springs, MD 20746
PH: (301)899-0675
Fax: (301)899-7355
Sacco, Michael, President

Transportation Institute [3107]
5201 Auth Way
Camp Springs, MD 20746-4211
PH: (301)423-3335
Henry, James L., Chairman,
President

African American Holiday Associa-
tion [22437]
Positive Energy Ctr.
Capitol Heights, MD 20743
PH: (202)667-2577
Kendi, Ayo Handy, Director, Founder

African-American Life Alliance
[10493]
PO Box 3722
Capitol Heights, MD 20791
Roseboro, Paulette, Exec. Dir.

Association of African American
Financial Advisors [1273]
PO Box 4853
Capitol Heights, MD 20791
PH: (240)396-2530
Toll free: 888-392-5702
Davis, LeCount R., Chairman,
Founder

Institute for Operations Research
and the Management Sciences
[2174]
5521 Research Park Dr., Ste. 200
Catonsville, MD 21228
PH: (443)757-3500
Toll free: 800-446-3676
Fax: (443)757-3515
Jacobson, Sheldon H., Treasurer

Motor Maids [23039]
PO Box 9418
Catonsville, MD 21228
Gibson, Susan, President

National Opossum Society [10673]
PO Box 21197
Catonsville, MD 21228
Hughlett, Janice, President

American Rare Breed Association
[21818]
9921 Frank Tippett Rd.
Cheltenham, MD 20623
PH: (301)868-5718
Toll free: 800-693-2772

National Surf Schools and Instruc-
tors Association [23278]
PO Box 550
Chesapeake Beach, MD 20732
Gabrielson, Dr. Bruce, Founder

Distributed Computing Industry As-
sociation [6313]
2838 Cox Neck Rd., Ste. 200
Chester, MD 21619
PH: (410)476-7965
Fax: (410)643-3585
Lafferty, Marty, CEO

Mothers Supporting Daughters with
Breast Cancer [14015]
25235 Fox Chase Dr.
Chestertown, MD 21620-3409
PH: (410)778-1982
Fax: (410)778-1411
Dierker, Charmayne, Bd. Member

Gypsy Lore Society [9589]
5607 Greenleaf Rd.
Cheverly, MD 20785
PH: (301)341-1261
(212)229-5308
Fax: (810)592-1768
Salo, Sheila, Treasurer

Aid for Africa [12609]
6909 Ridgewood Ave.
Chevy Chase, MD 20815
PH: (202)531-2000
Fax: (301)986-7902
Rose, Barbara Alison, Exec. Dir.

American Association of Colleges of
Osteopathic Medicine [16502]
5550 Friendship Blvd., Ste. 310
Chevy Chase, MD 20815-7231
PH: (301)968-4100
Fax: (301)968-4101
Tillipman, Harvey, COO

American Board of Forensic
Psychology [16857]
c/o Lisa Drago Piechowski,
President
5425 Wisconsin Ave., Ste. 600
Chevy Chase, MD 20815-3588
PH: (870)740-4452
Piechowski, Lisa Drago, President

American Hungarian Educators Association [19465]
4515 Willard Ave., Apt. 2210
Chevy Chase, MD 20815
Basa, Eniko, Exec. Dir.

American Society of Addiction
Medicine [17307]
Upper Arcade, Ste. 101
4601 N Park Ave.
Chevy Chase, MD 20815-4520
PH: (301)656-3920
Fax: (301)656-3815
Mills, Penny S., MBA, CEO, Exec.
VP

Environmental Information Associa-
tion [525]
6935 Wisconsin Ave., Ste. 306
Chevy Chase, MD 20815-6112
PH: (301)961-4999
Toll free: 888-343-4342
Fax: (301)961-3094
Cannan, Kevin, President

Howard Hughes Medical Institute
[15644]
4000 Jones Bridge Rd.
Chevy Chase, MD 20815-6720

PH: (301)215-8500
Tjian, Robert, PhD, President

International Federation of Rabbis
[20252]
5600 Wisconsin Ave., No. 1107
Chevy Chase, MD 20815
Fax: (561)499-6316
Carter, Rabbi Suzanne H., President

International Society for ECT and
Neurostimulation [15777]
5454 Wisconsin Ave., Ste. 1220
Chevy Chase, MD 20815
PH: (301)951-7220
Fax: (301)299-4918
Moscarillo, Dr. Frank, MD, Exec. Dir.

National 4-H Council [13460]
7100 Connecticut Ave.
Chevy Chase, MD 20815
PH: (301)961-2800
Sirangelo, Jennifer, President, CEO

National Association of Veterans'
Research and Education Founda-
tions [5840]
5480 Wisconsin Ave., Ste. 214
Chevy Chase, MD 20815-3529
PH: (301)656-5005
Fax: (301)656-5008
Watterson-Diorio, Nancy, Exec. Dir.

Romanian-American Chamber of
Commerce [23654]
2 Wisconsin Cir., Ste. 700
Chevy Chase, MD 20815-7007
PH: (240)235-6060
Fax: (240)235-6061
McCrensky, Jay, Exec. Dir.

Setting Priorities for Retirement
Years [12758]
3916 Rosemary St.
Chevy Chase, MD 20815
PH: (301)656-3405
Fax: (301)656-6221
Markwood, Sandy, V. Ch., Secretary,
Treasurer

Sister to Sister: The Women's Heart
Health Foundation [14156]
4701 Willard Ave., Ste. 221
Chevy Chase, MD 20815
PH: (301)718-8033
Toll free: 888-718-8033
Pollin, Irene, PhD, Chairperson

Society of Professional Benefit
Administrators [1077]
2 Wisconsin Cir., Ste. 670
Chevy Chase, MD 20815
PH: (301)718-7722
Fax: (301)718-9440
Doney, Tom, Chairman

BrightFocus Foundation [15641]
22512 Gateway Center Dr.
Clarksburg, MD 20871
Toll free: 800-437-2423
Fax: (301)258-9454
Haller, Stacy Pagos, CEO, President

American Society of Peritoneal
Surface Malignancies [13887]
11806 Wollingford Ct.
Clarksville, MD 21029
PH: (410)368-2743
Fax: (410)951-4007
Esquivel, Jesus, MD, Bd. Member

American Horse Trials Foundation
[22938]
7913 Colonial Ln.
Clinton, MD 20735-1908
PH: (301)856-3064
Fax: (301)856-3065
Field, Donna L., Contact

Power of Pink! Foundation [14047]
6368 Coventry Way, No. 347
Clinton, MD 20735
PH: (240)389-4767
Crawford, DaChea, CEO

Surratt Society [9439]
Surratt House Museum
9118 Brandywine Rd.
Clinton, MD 20735
PH: (301)868-1121
Fax: (301)868-8177
Verge, Laurie, Director

World Mudo Federation [23032]
7137 Old Alexandria Ferry Rd.
Clinton, MD 20735
PH: (301)868-8880
Fax: (301)868-0805
Lee, Yong Sung, CEO, President,
Founder

No More Stolen Childhoods [10797]
PO Box 1553
Cockeysville, MD 21030
Toll free: 877-666-6735
Coffey, D. Wayne, Founder,
President

National Capital Trolley Museum
[9497]
1313 Bonifant Rd.
Colesville, MD 20905-5955
PH: (301)384-6088
Rucker, Kenneth, Dir. of Admin.,
President

Aerospace Department Chair's As-
sociation [7457]
University of Maryland
Dept. of Aerospace Engineering
Martin Hall, Rm. 3179F
College Park, MD 20742
PH: (315)443-2341
Fax: (315)443-9099
Messac, Prof. Achille, Exec. Chmn.
of the Bd.

Air Transport Research Society
[6023]
c/o Prof. Yanan Wang, Coordinator
3433 Van Munching Hall
Robert H. Smith School of Business
University of Maryland
College Park, MD 20742
PH: (301)405-2204
Fax: (301)314-1023
Wang, Yanan, Prof., Coord.

American Association of Physics
Teachers [7020]
1 Physics Ellipse
College Park, MD 20740-3841
PH: (301)209-3311
Fax: (301)209-0845
Cunningham, Beth A., Exec. Ofc.

American Center for Physics [7021]
1 Physics Ellipse
College Park, MD 20740
PH: (301)209-3000
Toll free: 866-773-2274
Cunningham, Beth, President

American Institute of Physics [7022]
1 Physics Ellipse
College Park, MD 20740
PH: (516)576-2200
(301)209-3100
Toll free: 888-491-8833
Fax: (516)349-7669
Brown, Robert G. W., CEO

American Physical Society [7023]
1 Physics Ellipse
College Park, MD 20740-3844
PH: (301)209-3200
Fax: (301)209-0865
Taylor, James, Exec. Ofc., COO

ARISE International Mission [20382]
PO Box 1014
College Park, MD 20741-1014
PH: (301)395-2385
Kim, Rev. Daniel, President

Association for India's Development
[12141]
5011 Tecumseh St.
College Park, MD 20740
PH: (304)825-5243
Bhagat, Mohan, President

Atmospheric Science Librarians
International [8230]
NOAA Center for Weather Prediction
Betty Peterson Memorial Library
5830 University Research Ct.
College Park, MD 20740
PH: (301)683-1307
    (310)825-3983
Fax: (301)683-1308
Kilbourn, Aldean, Secretary

Commission on Accreditation of
Medical Physics Education
Programs [8317]
1 Physics Ellipse
College Park, MD 20740
PH: (301)209-3346
Fax: (301)209-0862
Beckham, Wayne, President, Chair-
man

Food Recovery Network [11853]
4321 Hartwick Rd., Ste. 320
College Park, MD 20740
Minor, Ernie, President

Lotus Ltd. [21422]
PO Box L
College Park, MD 20741
PH: (301)982-4054
Fax: (301)982-4054
Vaccaro, Tony, Act. Pres.

National Association of Black
Journalists [2693]
1100 Knight Hall, Ste. 3100
College Park, MD 20742
PH: (301)405-0248
Fax: (301)314-1714
Berry, Scott, Program Mgr.

National Foreign Language Center
[8191]
Severn Bldg. 810
5245 Greenbelt Rd.
College Park, MD 20742
PH: (301)405-9828
Fax: (301)405-9829
Ellis, Dr. David, Exec. Dir.

National History Day [7989]
4511 Knox Rd., Ste. 205
College Park, MD 20740
PH: (301)314-9739
Gorn, Dr. Cathy, Exec. Dir.

National Marine Educators Associa-
tion [8263]
4321 Hartwick Rd., Ste. 300
College Park, MD 20740
PH: (844)687-6632
Rocha, Robert, President

Physics Teacher Education Coalition
[8656]
1 Physics Ellipse
College Park, MD 20740-3843
PH: (301)209-3263
    (301)209-3273
Hodapp, Theodore, Director

Quest for Peace [18440]
c/o Quixote Center
7307 Baltimore Ave., Ste. 214
College Park, MD 20740

PH: (301)699-0042
Hochhalter, Andrew, Exec. Dir.

Quixote Center [19898]
7307 Baltimore Ave.
College Park, MD 20740
PH: (301)699-0042
Dassow, Kelly, Operations Mgr.

Sigma Pi Sigma [23850]
1 Physics Ellipse
College Park, MD 20740
PH: (301)209-3007
Fax: (301)209-0839
Bentley, Dr. Sean, Director

Society of Directors of Academic
Medical Physics Programs [16766]
1 Physics Ellipse
College Park, MD 20740
PH: (301)209-3377
Fax: (301)209-0862
Bayouth, John, President

Society of Physics Students [7031]
1 Physics Ellipse
College Park, MD 20740
PH: (301)209-3007
White, Dr. Gary, Director

Alpha-1 Kids [14805]
PO Box 132
Coltons Point, MD 20626
PH: (410)243-4499
Toll free: 877-346-3212
Horsak, Cathy, Director

AMDA - The Society for Post-Acute
and Long-Term Care Medicine
[16195]
11000 Broken Land Pky., Ste. 400
Columbia, MD 21044
PH: (410)740-9743
Toll free: 800-876-2632
Fax: (410)740-4572
Pandya, MD, FACP, CMD, Naushira,
President

American Dance Therapy Associa-
tion [16959]
10632 Little Patuxent Pky., Ste. 108
Columbia, MD 21044
PH: (410)997-4040
Fax: (410)997-4048
Wager, Jody, President

American Small Business Coalition
[3112]
PO Box 2786
Columbia, MD 21045
PH: (410)381-7378
Timberlake, Margaret H., President

American Society of Breast
Surgeons [17371]
10330 Old Columbia Rd., Ste. 100
Columbia, MD 21046
PH: (410)381-9500
Toll free: 877-992-5470
Fax: (410)381-9512
Schuster, Jane, Exec. Dir.

Biscuit & Cracker Manufacturers As-
sociation [372]
6325 Woodside Ct., Ste. 125
Columbia, MD 21046
PH: (443)545-1645
Fax: (410)290-8585
Vial, Vanessa, Mgr.

Chain Link Fence Manufacturers
Institute [512]
10015 Old Columbia Rd., Ste. B-215
Columbia, MD 21046
PH: (301)596-2583
Fax: (301)596-2594
Finn, Don

Coalition Halting Obesity in Children
Everywhere [16255]
8630-M Guilford Rd., No. 168
Columbia, MD 21046

PH: (410)868-9286
Kan, Athena, Founder

COLA [15722]
9881 Broken Land Pky., Ste. 200
Columbia, MD 21046-3016
Toll free: 800-981-9883
Fax: (410)381-8611
Fedderly, Bradley J., Chairman

Enterprise Community Partners, Inc.
[11968]
11000 Broken Land Pky., Ste. 700
Columbia, MD 21044
Toll free: 800-624-4298
Ludwig, Terri, President, CEO

FCIB [1966]
8840 Columbia 100 Pky.
Columbia, MD 21045-2158
PH: (410)423-1840
Toll free: 888-256-3242
Fax: (410)740-5574
Shepherd, Ron, Dir. of Member
Svcs.

Foundation Fighting Blindness
[17700]
7168 Columbia Gateway Dr., Ste.
100
Columbia, MD 21046-3256
PH: (410)423-0600
Toll free: 800-683-5555
Petrou, Karen, Director

Global Health Linkages, Inc. [15458]
10810 Hickory Ridge Rd.
Columbia, MD 21044
Fax: (410)992-7553

International Society of Regulatory
Toxicology and Pharmacology
[14944]
6546 Belleview Dr.
Columbia, MD 21046-1054
PH: (410)992-9083
Fax: (410)740-9181
Ferenc, Sue, DVM, PhD, President

International Union of Elevator
Constructors [23447]
7154 Columbia Gateway Dr.
Columbia, MD 21046
PH: (410)953-6150
Fax: (410)953-6169
Bender, James K., II, Asst. Pres.

National Association of Catering and
Events [1668]
10440 Little Patuxent Pky., Ste. 300
Columbia, MD 21044
PH: (410)290-5410
Fax: (410)630-5768
Schultz, Allison, Comm. Chm.

National Association of Credit
Management [1253]
8840 Columbia 100 Pky.
Columbia, MD 21045
PH: (410)740-5560
Fax: (410)740-5574
Gaudette, Gary, Chairperson

National Association of Educational
Procurement [7434]
8840 Stanford Blvd., Ste. 2000
Columbia, MD 21045
PH: (443)543-5540
Fax: (443)219-9687
Murner, Doreen, CEO

National Society for HistoTechnology
[15697]
8850 Stanford Blvd., Ste. 2900
Columbia, MD 21045
PH: (443)535-4060
Fax: (443)535-4055
Sheppard, Beth, President

North American Jules Verne Society,
Inc. [10390]
c/o Mark Eckell
7106 Talisman Ln.
Columbia, MD 21045-4805
Margot, Jean-Michel, VP

Porsche Club of America [21480]
9689 Gerwig Ln., Unit 4C/D
Columbia, MD 21046
PH: (410)381-0911
Fax: (410)381-0924
Nguyen, Vu T.H., Exec. Dir.

Universities Space Research As-
sociation [5878]
7178 Columbia Gateway Dr.
Columbia, MD 21046
PH: (410)730-2656
Isaacson, Jeff, President, CEO

Zero Balancing Health Association
[15273]
8640 Guilford Rd., Ste. 241
Columbia, MD 21046-2667
PH: (410)381-8956
Fax: (410)381-9634
Pridgen, Cindi, Exec. Dir.

Annapolis Naval Sailing Association
[22597]
6807 Crofton Colony Ct.
Crofton, MD 21114-3276
Chappell, Dave, Commodore

Association of Professors of
Gynecology and Obstetrics
[16277]
2130 Priest Bridge Dr., Ste. 7
Crofton, MD 21114-2457
PH: (410)451-9560
Fax: (410)451-9568
Wachter, Donna, Exec. Dir.

Children's Medical Ministries [14182]
PO Box 3382
Crofton, MD 21114
PH: (301)536-3173
Fax: (410)721-6261
Collins, Bill, Founder

Compassion Care for Disabled
Children [16473]
PO Box 4712
Crofton, MD 21114
PH: (301)261-3211
Fax: (410)721-4647
Collins, Erma, Founder

Elvish Linguistic Fellowship [9740]
2509 Ambling Cir.
Crofton, MD 21114
Hostetter, Carl F., Editor

EPS Industry Alliance [4741]
1298 Cronson Blvd., Ste. 201
Crofton, MD 21114-2035
Toll free: 800-607-3772
Fax: (410)451-8343
Steiner, Betsy, Exec. Dir.

Insulating Concrete Form Associa-
tion [787]
1298 Cronson Blvd., Ste. 201
Crofton, MD 21114-2035
Toll free: 800-607-3772
Fax: (410)451-8343

International Association of Arson
Investigators [5205]
2111 Baldwin Ave., Ste. 203
Crofton, MD 21114
PH: (410)451-3473
Toll free: 800-468-4224
Fax: (410)451-9049
Marshall, Bill, Director

Plastic Loose Fill Council [4534]
1298 Cronson Blvd., Ste. 201
Crofton, MD 21114
Toll free: 800-828-2214
Mellott, John D., President

Bill Raskob Foundation [18171]
PO Box 507
Crownsville, MD 21032-0507
PH: (410)923-9123
Fax: (410)923-9124
Robinson, Edward H., Exec. Dir.,
Secretary

Brewster Kaleidoscope Society
[21629]
PO Box 95
Damascus, MD 20872
Karadimos, Charles, Director

Society of Atherosclerosis Imaging
and Prevention [17579]
26804 Ridge Rd.
Damascus, MD 20872
PH: (301)253-4155
Fax: (301)414-7535
Leong, Lawrence H., Exec. Dir.

Kurdish American Medical Associa-
tion [15734]
6117 Marlboro Pke.
District Heights, MD 20747
Kelli, Heval Mohammad, MD,
President

Aguayuda, Inc. [13314]
PO Box 2056
Easton, MD 21601
PH: (410)989-2134
Zimmermann, Sabrina, Sr. VP of
Operations, Founder

Global Vision 2020 [17704]
102 E Dover St.
Easton, MD 21601-3332
PH: (410)253-1543
White, Kevin, Founder, Exec. Dir.

American Healing Arts Alliance, Inc.
[15262]
3157 Rolling Rd.
Edgewater, MD 21037
PH: (410)956-0055
Yeager, Alice, President, Founder

Society of Mareen Duvall
Descendants [20858]
c/o Barrett L. McKown, President
3580 S River Terr.
Edgewater, MD 21037
McKown, Barrett L., President

Lawyer-Pilots Bar Association [5059]
PO Box 1510
Edgewater, MD 21037
PH: (410)571-1750
Fax: (410)571-1780
Griggs, Karen, Exec. Dir.

National Aircraft Finance Association
[2091]
PO Box 1570
Edgewater, MD 21037
PH: (410)571-1740
Jarvis, David, President

Water Design-Build Council [599]
PO Box 1924
Edgewater, MD 21037
PH: (410)798-0842
Fax: (410)798-5741
Bonner, Dr. Linda Hanifin, Opera-
tions Mgr.

National Emergency Medicine As-
sociation [14687]
PO Box 1039
Edgewood, MD 21040
PH: (443)922-7533
Toll free: 888-682-7947
Herzog, Kelly A., Director

National Heart Council [14136]
National Emergency Medicine Association

PO Box 1039
Edgewood, MD 21040
PH: (443)922-7533
Toll free: 888-682-7947

International Association of Forensic
Nurses [16136]
6755 Business Pky., Ste. 303
Elkridge, MD 21075-6740
PH: (410)626-7805
Fax: (410)626-7804
Krebs, Dee, President

Phi Sigma Sigma [23961]
8178 Lark Brown Rd., Ste. 202
Elkridge, MD 21075
PH: (410)799-1224
Fax: (410)799-9186
Ardern, Michelle, Exec. Dir.

Planet Aid [13016]
6730 Santa Barbara Ct.
Elkridge, MD 21075-6814
PH: (410)796-1510
Neltrup, Ester, President

National Steeplechase Association
[22925]
400 Fair Hill Dr.
Elkton, MD 21921
PH: (410)392-0700
Fax: (410)392-0706
Torsilieri, Guy J., President

Thoroughbred Racing Associations
[22931]
420 Fair Hill Dr., Ste. 1
Elkton, MD 21921-2573
PH: (410)392-9200
Fax: (410)398-1366
Pollard, Margie, Exec. Asst.

Thoroughbred Racing Protective
Bureau [22932]
420 Fair Hill Dr., Ste. 2
Elkton, MD 21921
PH: (410)398-2261
Mooney, John E., Chairman

United Fascist Union [18882]
PO Box 2209
Elkton, MD 21922

Association of Catholic Publishers
[2769]
4725 Dorsey Hall Dr., Ste. A
Ellicott City, MD 21042
PH: (410)988-2926
Fax: (410)571-4946
Brown, Therese, Exec. Dir.

Chinese American Doctors Associa-
tion [16747]
PO Box 6627
Ellicott City, MD 21042-0627
PH: (713)201-7928
Zhang, Dou Alvin, MD, President

Coalition Against Genocide [18303]
8480 Baltimore National Pke., No.
286
Ellicott City, MD 21043-3369
PH: (443)927-9039
Fax: (443)927-9039

Energy Kinesiology Association
[13620]
7862 Mayfair Cir.
Ellicott City, MD 21043
Toll free: 866-365-4336
Wayman, Ronald, President

IAC Vascular Testing [17573]
6021 University Blvd., Ste. 500
Ellicott City, MD 21043
PH: (443)973-3239
Toll free: 800-838-2110
Fax: (888)927-2637
Katanick, Sandra, CAE, CEO

International Critical Incident Stress
Foundation [17291]
3290 Pine Orchard Ln., Ste. 106
Ellicott City, MD 21042
PH: (410)750-9600
Fax: (410)750-9601
Stoll, Becky, LCSW, Officer

Investment Program Association
[2026]
PO Box 480
Ellicott City, MD 21041-0480
PH: (212)812-9799
Chereso, Tony, President, CEO

Joint Review Committee on Educa-
tion in Diagnostic Medical Sonog-
raphy [8297]
6021 University Blvd., Ste. 500
Ellicott City, MD 21043
PH: (443)973-3251
Toll free: 866-738-3444
Weiland, Cindy, Exec. Dir.

Medal Collectors of America [22274]
c/o Barry D. Tayman, Treasurer
3115 Nestling Pine Ct.
Ellicott City, MD 21042
Liechty, Skyler, President

National Alliance for Breastfeeding
Advocacy [13857]
c/o Barbara Heiser, Executive Director
9684 Oak Hill Dr.
Ellicott City, MD 21042-6321
Heiser, Barbara, RN, Exec. Dir.

National Episcopal Health Ministries
[14954]
9120 Fredrick Rd.
Ellicott City, MD 21042
PH: (203)451-9134
Ellis, Matthew, CEO

North American Sikh Medical and
Dental Association [15742]
4310 English Morning Ln.
Ellicott City, MD 21043
Narula, Amarjot, President

DECA The Decathlon Association
[23312]
c/o Frank Zarnowski, Founder
58 2nd Ave.
Emmitsburg, MD 21727
PH: (301)447-6122
Zarnowski, Dr. Frank, Founder

Marlowe Society of America [9077]
c/o Prof. Sarah K. Scott
Dept. of English
Mount St. Mary's University
16300 Old Emmitsburg Rd.
Emmitsburg, MD 21727-7700
Menzer, Prof. Paul, President

National Shrine of St. Elizabeth Ann
Seton [19891]
339 S Seton Ave.
Emmitsburg, MD 21727-9297
PH: (301)447-6606
Fax: (301)447-6061
Judge, Rob, Exec. Dir.

General Society of the War of 1812
[21175]
c/o Christos Christou, Registrar
General
303 Nicholson Rd.
Essex, MD 21221-6609
PH: (410)574-5467

International Double Reed Society
[9927]
2423 Lawndale Rd.
Finksburg, MD 21048-1401
PH: (410)871-0658
Fax: (410)871-0659
Stomberg, Eric, 1st VP

American Sports Builders Associa-
tion [851]
9 Newport Dr., Ste. 200
Forest Hill, MD 21050
PH: (410)730-9595
Toll free: 866-501-2722
Fax: (410)730-8833
Smith, Pete, Chairman

Association for Accounting Marketing
[2265]
9 Newport Dr., Ste. 200
Forest Hill, MD 21050
PH: (443)640-1061
Robertson, Sara, Treasurer

First Candle [17333]
9 Newport Dr., Ste. 200
Forest Hill, MD 21050
PH: (443)640-1049
Toll free: 800-221-7437
Schaffer, Michael J., Chairman

International Aviation Womens As-
sociation [362]
c/o Jennifer Miller, Executive Direc-
tor
9 Newport Dr., Ste. 200
Forest Hill, MD 21050
PH: (443)640-1056
Fax: (443)640-1031
Field, Ann Thornton, Treasurer,
Secretary

League of Historic American
Theatres [10257]
9 Newport Dr., Ste. 200
Forest Hill, MD 21050
PH: (443)640-1058
Fax: (443)640-1031
Stein, Ken, Exec. Dir.

National States Geographic Informa-
tion Council [6326]
9 Newport Dr., Ste. 200
Forest Hill, MD 21050
PH: (443)640-1075
Fax: (443)640-1031
Diller, Chris, President

Web Sling and Tie Down Association
[1778]
9 Newport Dr., Ste. 200
Forest Hill, MD 21050
PH: (443)640-1070
Fax: (443)640-1031
Iden, Jeff, President

Wood Machinery Manufacturers of
America [1779]
9 Newport Dr., Ste. 200
Forest Hill, MD 21050
PH: (443)640-1052
Fax: (443)640-1031
Hacker, Chris, President

The Fiber Society [6631]
c/o Janice R. Gerde, Secretary
PO Box 564
Fort Meade, MD 20755-0564
Schacher, Laurence, VP

Association of Black Psychologists
[16901]
7119 Allentown Rd., Ste. 203
Fort Washington, MD 20744
PH: (301)449-3082
Fax: (301)449-3084

29th Infantry Division Association
[20709]
PO Box 1546
Frederick, MD 21702-1546
PH: (410)242-1820
Wilcox, John E., Jr., Exec. Dir.

Advanced Biofuels USA [5880]
507 N Bentz St.
Frederick, MD 21701

PH: (301)644-1395
Ivancic, Joanne M., Exec. Dir.,
President

Airborne Law Enforcement Associa-
tion [5451]
50 Carroll Creek Way, Ste. 260
Frederick, MD 21701
PH: (301)631-2406
Fax: (301)631-2466
Schwarzbach, Daniel B., Exec. Dir.,
CEO

Aircraft Owners and Pilots Associa-
tion [124]
421 Aviation Way
Frederick, MD 21701
PH: (301)695-2000
Toll free: 800-872-2672
Fax: (301)695-2375
Baker, Mark, President, CEO

Aircrafts Owners and Pilots Associa-
tion [6024]
421 Aviation Way
Frederick, MD 21701
PH: (301)695-2000
Toll free: 800-872-2672
Trimble, William, Chairman

American Association for Laboratory
Accreditation [6773]
5202 President's Ct., Ste. 220
Frederick, MD 21703
PH: (301)644-3248
Fax: (240)454-9449
Whitehead, Robert, Chairman

American Ferret Association [21279]
PO Box 554
Frederick, MD 21705-0554
Toll free: 888-FERRET-1
Fax: (240)358-0673
Woodland, Paula, VP

American Society for Colposcopy
and Cervical Pathology [16275]
1530 Tilco Dr., Ste. C
Frederick, MD 21704-6726
PH: (301)733-3640
Toll free: 800-787-7227
Fax: (240)575-9880
Curtis, Kerry, Exec. Dir.

Association for Assessment and Ac-
creditation of Laboratory Animal
Care International [5896]
5283 Corporate Dr., Ste. 203
Frederick, MD 21703-2879
PH: (301)696-9626
Fax: (301)696-9627
Newcomer, Dr. Christian E., Exec.
Dir.

Association of Online Appraiser
[222]
PO Box 1292
Frederick, MD 21702-0292
PH: (301)228-2279
Katz-Schwartz, Judith, President

Care Wear Volunteers, Inc. [14171]
c/o Bonnie Hagerman, Founder
102 Mercer Ct., Ste. 23-5
Frederick, MD 21701
PH: (301)620-2858
Hagerman, Bonnie, Founder

Inter-Society Color Council [755]
7820B Wormans Mill Rd., Ste. 115
Frederick, MD 21701
Toll free: 866-876-4816
Conant, John, President

International Council of Aircraft
Owner and Pilot Associations [142]
421 Aviation Way
Frederick, MD 21701

PH: (301)695-2220
Fax: (301)695-2375
Baker, Mark, President

Mounted Games Across America
[23235]
c/o Matthew Brown, Membership
Chairman
120 Long Acre Ct.
Frederick, MD 21702
PH: (240)500-4906
Muldoon, Krista Wilson, President

National Auto Auction Association
[262]
5320 Spectrum Dr., Ste. D
Frederick, MD 21703
PH: (301)696-0400
Fax: (301)631-1359
Wallace, Don, Comm. Chm.

National Society of Professional
Surveyors [7252]
5119 Pegasus Ct., Ste. Q
Frederick, MD 21704
PH: (240)439-4615
Fax: (240)439-4952
Miller, Robert, Treasurer

Zambia Hope International [11195]
Hope Mountain Foundation
5235 Westview Dr., Ste. 100
Frederick, MD 21703
PH: (301)624-0061
Musonda, Anne, Exec. Dir.

Friend Family Association of America
[20866]
261 Maple St.
Friendsville, MD 21531-2131
PH: (301)746-4690
Friend, Donna M., Treasurer

Coalition of Higher Education As-
sociations for Substance Abuse
Prevention [13131]
c/o Spencer Deakin
Frostburg State University
101 Braddock Rd.
111 Sandspring Hall
Frostburg, MD 21532-1099
PH: (301)687-4234
Deakin, Spencer, Contact

National Association for Self-Esteem
[15790]
PO Box 597
Fulton, MD 20759-0597
Fountain, Sharon, President

American Academy of Forensic Sciences [5231]
c/o Susan Ballou, Secretary
100 Bureau Dr.
Gaithersburg, MD 20899-8102
PH: (301)975-8750
Warren, Anne, Exec. Dir.

American Association for Women in
Community Colleges [8744]
PO Box 3098
Gaithersburg, MD 20885
PH: (301)442-3374
DeWolf, Dawn, VP

American College of Dentists
[14401]
839J Quince Orchard Blvd.
Gaithersburg, MD 20878-1614
PH: (301)977-3223
Fax: (301)977-3330
Ralls, Dr. Stephen A., Exec. Dir.

Association of Collecting Clubs
[21626]
18222 Flower Hill Way, No. 299
Gaithersburg, MD 20879
PH: (301)926-8663
Krug, Larry L., President

Children of Fallen Soldiers Relief
Fund [10916]
PO Box 3968
Gaithersburg, MD 20885-3968
PH: (301)685-3421
Toll free: 866-96C-FSRF
Campbell, Rebecca, Founder

Clan MacIntyre Association [20821]
c/o Patty McIntire Hayes, President
306 Kent Oaks Way
Gaithersburg, MD 20878
Hayes, Patty McIntire, President

Corvette Club of America [21363]
Gaithersburg, MD 20885
Taylor, Rich, VP

Eduwatch [8070]
8817 Swallow Ct.
Gaithersburg, MD 20879
PH: (301)869-4720
Doherty-Mason, Enitan, Exec. Dir.,
Founder

Fusion Power Associates [6486]
2 Professional Dr., Ste. 249
Gaithersburg, MD 20879
PH: (301)258-0545
Fax: (301)975-9869
Dean, Stephen O., President

Historic Vehicle Association [9117]
7960 Cessna Ave.
Gaithersburg, MD 20879
PH: (301)407-1911
Gessler, Mark D., President

Humane Society Veterinary Medical
Association [10644]
700 Professional Dr.
Gaithersburg, MD 20879
PH: (202)452-1100
(301)258-1478
Kislak, Paula, Bd. Member

National Board for Certification in
Occupational Therapy, Inc. [17454]
12 S Summit Ave., Ste. 100
Gaithersburg, MD 20877
PH: (301)990-7979
Fax: (301)869-8492
Ammondson, Debra, V. Ch.

National Christian Choir [20493]
17B Firstfield Rd., Ste. 108
Gaithersburg, MD 20878
PH: (301)670-6331
Toll free: 800-599-4710
Tierney, Terry, Chairman, Exec. Dir.

National Environmental Balancing
Bureau [1633]
8575 Grovemont Cir.
Gaithersburg, MD 20877
PH: (301)977-3698
Toll free: 866-497-4447
Fax: (301)977-9589
Noel, Elana, Pub. Dir.

National Federation of Indian
American Associations [19476]
319 Summit Hall Rd.
Gaithersburg, MD 20877
PH: (301)926-3013
(301)935-5321
Fax: (301)926-3378
Nair, Satheesan, Secretary

Osteogenesis Imperfecta Foundation
[16490]
804 W Diamond Ave., Ste. 210
Gaithersburg, MD 20878
PH: (301)947-0083
Toll free: 844-889-7579
Fax: (301)947-0456
Carter, Erika Ruebensaal, Dir. of
Comm., Dir. of Dev.

Pretrial Justice Institute [5550]
305 Main St., Ste. 200
Gaithersburg, MD 20878
PH: (240)477-7152
Campbell, Robin, Dir. of Comm.

Society of Fire Protection Engineers
[6634]
9711 Washingtonian Blvd., Ste. 380
Gaithersburg, MD 20878
PH: (301)718-2910
Fax: (240)328-6225
Puchovsky, Milosh, PE, President

Society for Oncology Massage
[15564]
18679 Cross Country Ln.
Gaithersburg, MD 20879

Izaak Walton League of America
[3962]
707 Conservation Ln.
Gaithersburg, MD 20878
PH: (301)548-0150
Deschamps, Jeff, VP

World Folk Music Association
[10025]
PO Box 83583
Gaithersburg, MD 20883
Morse, Chuck, President

American College of Veterinary
Surgeons [17622]
19785 Crystal Rock Dr., Ste. 305
Germantown, MD 20874
PH: (301)916-0200
Toll free: 877-217-2287
Fax: (301)916-2287
Loew, Ann T., EdM, CEO

American Lumber Standard Commit-
tee, Incorporated [1426]
PO Box 210
Germantown, MD 20875-0210
PH: (301)972-1700
Fax: (301)540-8004
Parrish, R.B., Chairman

American Society of Psychoanalytic
Physicians [16842]
13528 Wisteria Dr.
Germantown, MD 20874
PH: (301)540-3197
Fax: (301)540-3511
Cotter, Christine, Exec. Dir.

Association of Liberian Engineers
USA, Inc. [6546]
PO Box 2960
Germantown, MD 20874
PH: (240)343-5971
ZayZay, Edman, President

Catholic Alumni Clubs International
[19313]
13517 Teakwood Ln.
Germantown, MD 20874-1034
Walczyk, Teresa, VP

Childhood Brain Tumor Foundation
[14569]
20312 Watkins Meadow Dr.
Germantown, MD 20876
PH: (301)515-2900
Toll free: 877-217-4166
Young, Jeanne P., President, Bd.
Member

Coalition of Handwriting Analysts
International [6702]
c/o Jerry Fishow
19025 Jamieson Dr.
Germantown, MD 20874
Weinberg, Karen Fisher, QDE,
President

Council for American Private Education [8462]
13017 Wisteria Dr., No. 457
Germantown, MD 20874-2621

PH: (301)916-8460
Fax: (301)916-8485
Heischman, Rev. Daniel R.,
President

Federation of Podiatric Medical
Boards [16788]
12116 Flag Harbor Dr.
Germantown, MD 20874-1979
PH: (202)810-3762
Fax: (202)318-0091
Levine, Robert, DPM, President

International Society of Weighing
and Measurement [3465]
13017 Wisteria Dr., No. 341
Germantown, MD 20874
PH: (240)753-4397
Toll free: 866-285-3512
Finnegan, Jerry, President

Microcirculatory Society [17576]
18501 Kingshill Rd.
Germantown, MD 20874
PH: (301)760-7745
Chilian, William M., President

National Fatherhood Initiative
[18198]
12410 Milestone Center Dr., Ste.600
Germantown, MD 20876
PH: (301)948-0599
(301)948-4325
Fax: (301)948-6776
Schoka, Andy, Chairman

North American Vascular Biology
Organization [17578]
18501 Kingshill Rd.
Germantown, MD 20874-2211
PH: (301)760-7745
Fax: (301)540-6903
Kitajewski, Jan, President

Society for Historical Archaeology
[5949]
13017 Wisteria Dr., No. 395
Germantown, MD 20874
PH: (301)972-9684
Fax: (866)285-3512
Joseph, J.W., President

World Chamberlain Genealogical
Society [21001]
c/o Patricia Sugg, Corresponding
Secretary
13305 Cloverdale Pl.
Germantown, MD 20874
Chamberlin, Donald L., VP

American Association for Long Term
Care Nursing [16090]
11104 Glen Arm
Glen Arm, MD 21057
Toll free: 888-458-2687
Fax: (888)741-0942
Eliopoulos, Charlotte, Exec. Dir.

Protection Sports Association
[23251]
7719 Leigh Rd.
Glen Burnie, MD 21060-8505
PH: (240)475-3637
Kardiasmenos, Katrina, Secretary

State Educational Technology Direc-
tors Association [8677]
PO Box 10
Glen Burnie, MD 21060
PH: (202)715-6636
Neugent, Lan, Exec. Dir.

Jagannath Organization for Global
Awareness [20576]
PO Box 152
Glenelg, MD 21737-0152
Biswal, Mr. Hemant, Chairman

People for Equality and Relief in
Lanka [18434]
PO Box 292
Glenn Dale, MD 70769

PH: (301)805-2465
Jeyalingam, Brintha, Bd. Member

Stop the Silence [10800]
PO Box 127
Glenn Dale, MD 20769
PH: (301)464-4791
Pine, Pamela, PhD, Founder

American Federation of Mineralogi-
cal Societies [6871]
c/o Steve Weinberger
PO Box 302
Glyndon, MD 21071-0302
PH: (410)833-7926
Weinberger, Steve, Administrator

Society of Government Travel
Professionals [3393]
PO Box 158
Glyndon, MD 21071-0158
PH: (202)241-7487
Fax: (202)379-1775
Stec, Marc, President

Chesapeake Bay Environmental
Center [4803]
600 Discovery Ln.
Grasonville, MD 21638
PH: (410)827-6694
Fax: (410)827-6713
Wink, Judy, Exec. Dir.

Academy of Criminal Justice Sci-
ences [11514]
7339 Hanover Pky., Ste. A
Greenbelt, MD 20770
PH: (301)446-6300
Toll free: 800-757-2257
Fax: (301)446-2819
Barth, Cathy L., Mgr.

Commercial Vehicle Safety Alliance
[291]
6303 Ivy Ln., Ste. 310
Greenbelt, MD 20770-6319
PH: (301)830-6143
Fax: (301)830-6144
Gildea, Adrienne L., Dep. Dir.

Dangerous Goods Advisory Council
[3084]
7501 Greenway Center Dr., Ste. 760
Greenbelt, MD 20770
PH: (202)289-4550
Fax: (202)289-4074
Arthur, Vaughn, President

Federation of Galaxy Explorers
[7459]
6404 Ivy Ln., Ste. 810
Greenbelt, MD 20770-1420
Fax: (610)981-8511
Eftimiades, Mr. Nicholas, Chairman,
Founder

Friends of Freddy [24016]
PO Box 912
Greenbelt, MD 20768-0912

IEEE - Oceanic Engineering Society
[6940]
c/o Stephen Holt, Web Administrator
National Aeronautics and Space
Administration
Code 444 Bldg. 3, Rm. 144
8800 Greenbelt Rd.
Greenbelt, MD 20771
Garello, Rene, President

National Association of Black Ac-
countants, Inc. [44]
7474 Greenway Center Dr., Ste.
1120
Greenbelt, MD 20770
PH: (301)474-6222
Toll free: 888-571-2939
Fax: (301)474-3114
Etienne, Jina, President, CEO

National Fenestration Rating Council
[557]
6305 Ivy Ln., Ste. 140
Greenbelt, MD 20770
PH: (301)589-1776
Fax: (301)589-3884
Benney, James C., CAE, CEO

National Volunteer Fire Council
[5214]
7852 Walker Dr., Ste. 375
Greenbelt, MD 20770
PH: (202)887-5700
Toll free: 888-275-6832
Fax: (202)887-5291
Schafer, Heather, CEO

Newah Organization of America
[11413]
7425 Morrison Dr.
Greenbelt, MD 20770
PH: (240)581-0078
Fax: (301)769-6264
Shrestha, Mr. Season, Advisor

American Jail Association [11519]
1135 Professional Ct.
Hagerstown, MD 21740-5853
PH: (301)790-3930
Fax: (301)790-2941
Kasabian, Robert J., MBA, Exec. Dir.

Association for Non-Traditional
Students in Higher Education
[7453]
19134 Olde Waterford Rd.
Hagerstown, MD 21742
PH: (301)992-2901
Fax: (301)766-9162
Powell, R.Todd, VP

Association of State Correctional
Administrators [11521]
1110 Opal Ct., Ste. 5
Hagerstown, MD 21740
PH: (301)791-2722
Fax: (301)393-9494
Bertsch, Leann, President

Miniature Piano Enthusiast Club
[21688]
633 Pennsylvania Ave.
Hagerstown, MD 21740
PH: (301)797-7675
Fax: (301)827-7029
Kelsh, Janice E., Founder

National Association for the
Advancement of Preborn Children
[12781]
21 Summit Ave.
Hagerstown, MD 21740
PH: (301)790-0640
Palmer, Martin, Founder

American College Health Association
[15132]
1362 Mellon Rd., Ste. 180
Hanover, MD 21076-3198
PH: (410)859-1500
Fax: (410)859-1510
Leino, Victor E., Dir. of Res.

International Federation of
Operational Research Societies
[6946]
7240 Pky. Dr., Ste. 310
Hanover, MD 21076
PH: (443)757-3534
Fax: (443)757-3535
Trick, Michael, President

International Union of Painters and
Allied Trades [23489]
7234 Parkway Dr.
Hanover, MD 21076
PH: (410)564-5900
Toll free: 800-554-2479
Rigmaiden, Kenneth E., President

National Automotive Finance As-
sociation [348]
7037 Ridge Rd., Ste. 300
Hanover, MD 21076-1343
PH: (410)712-4036
Toll free: 800-463-8955
Fax: (410)712-4038
Tracey, Jack, CAE, Exec. Dir.

All Kids Can Learn International
[11211]
224 N Washington St.
Havre de Grace, MD 21078
Toll free: 800-785-1015
Schwartz, Benedict, Founder

Doctors for United Medical Missions
[15446]
313 Tidewater Dr.
Havre de Grace, MD 21078-4144
PH: (410)688-0691
Fax: (240)331-2417
Sampson, John B., MD, Founder,
President

Early American Industries Associa-
tion [8901]
PO Box 524
Hebron, MD 21830-0524
PH: (508)993-9578
Verrill, Mr. John H., Exec. Dir.

Trail Riders of Today [22947]
PO Box 506
Highland, MD 20777
PH: (301)906-6089
MacNab, Ron, Coord.

American Society of Trial
Consultants [6028]
10534 York Rd., Ste. 102
Hunt Valley, MD 21030
PH: (410)560-7949
Fax: (410)560-2563
Batzer, Mary, Exec. Dir.

Gypsum Association [2379]
6525 Belcrest Rd., Ste. 480
Hyattsville, MD 20782
PH: (301)277-8686
Fax: (301)277-8747
Hines, Susan, Director

Minority Access, Inc. [8348]
5214 Baltimore Ave.
Hyattsville, MD 20781
PH: (301)779-7100
Fax: (301)779-9812
Mickle, Andrea, CEO, President

US-Southern Cameroons Foundation
[9220]
6475 New Hampshire Ave., Ste.
504-F
Hyattsville, MD 20783
PH: (301)891-2700
Asongu, Dr. Januarius J., Exec. Dir.

Air Force Historical Foundation
[9798]
1602 California Ave., Ste. F-162
JB Andrews, MD 20762
PH: (301)736-1959
Meyerrose, Maj. Gen. Dale, USAF,
President, Chmn. of the Bd.

American Childhood Cancer
Organization [13884]
10920 Connecticut Ave., Ste. A
Kensington, MD 20895
PH: (301)962-3520
Toll free: 855-858-2226
Fax: (301)962-3521
Phillips, Ken, Treasurer

Bakery, Confectionery, Tobacco
Workers and Grain Millers
International Union [23454]
10401 Connecticut Ave.
Kensington, MD 20895

PH: (301)933-8600
Durkee, David B., President

Dandy-Walker Alliance [15922]
10325 Kensington Pkwy., Ste. 384
Kensington, MD 20895
Toll free: 877-326-3992
Cole, Eric, Exec. Dir.

International Eye Foundation [16388]
10801 Connecticut Ave.
Kensington, MD 20895
PH: (240)290-0263
Fax: (240)290-0269
Sheffield, Victoria M., CEO, President

National Association for Children of Alcoholics [13162]
10920 Connecticut Ave., Ste. 100
Kensington, MD 20895
PH: (301)468-0985
Toll free: 888-554-COAS
Fax: (301)468-0987
Carpenter-Palumbo, Karen, Treasurer

Psoriasis Cure Now [14511]
PO Box 2544
Kensington, MD 20891
PH: (301)571-2393
Fax: (703)997-6528
Paranzino, Michael, President

Radio Amateur Satellite Corporation [7319]
10605 Concord St., No. 304
Kensington, MD 20895-2526
PH: (301)822-4376
Toll free: 888-322-6728
Fax: (301)822-4371
Saragovitz, Ms. Martha, Asst.

Society of Eye Surgeons [16408]
International Eye Foundation
10801 Connecticut Ave.
Kensington, MD 20895
PH: (240)290-0263
Fax: (240)290-0269
Sheffield, Victoria M., President, CEO

Asthma and Allergy Foundation of America [13574]
8201 Corporate Dr., Ste. 1000
Landover, MD 20785-2266
Toll free: 800-727-8462
Wilson, Kelli, Chairman

Biomedical Engineering Society [6110]
8201 Corporate Dr., Ste. 1125
Landover, MD 20785-2224
PH: (301)459-1999
Toll free: 877-871-2637
Fax: (301)459-2444
Hart, Richard T., President

Epilepsy Foundation [14740]
8301 Professional Pl. E, Ste. 200
Landover, MD 20785-2353
Toll free: 866-332-1000
Fax: (301)459-1569
Schneider, John, VP

National Academy of Opticianry [16414]
8401 Corporate Dr., Ste. 605
Landover, MD 20785
Toll free: 800-229-4828
Fax: (301)577-3880
Drake, Diane, President

National Phlebotomy Association [15242]
1901 Brightseat Rd.
Landover, MD 20785

PH: (301)386-4200
Fax: (301)386-4203
Crawford, Diane, CEO, President

United States Public Health Service I Commissioned Officers Association [5719]
8201 Corporate Dr., Ste. 200
Landover, MD 20785
PH: (301)731-9080
Fax: (301)731-9084
McElligott, John, Dep. Dir.

American Railway Engineering and Maintenance-of-Way Association [2833]
4501 Forbes Blvd., Ste. 130
Lanham, MD 20706
PH: (301)459-3200
Fax: (301)459-8077
Fisher, Vickie, Dir. of Fin. & Admin.

AMVETS [21109]
4647 Forbes Blvd.
Lanham, MD 20706-4380
PH: (301)459-9600
Toll free: 877-726-8387
Fax: (301)459-7924
King, Jim, Exec. Dir.

Asphalt Pavement Alliance [495]
5100 Forbes Blvd.
Lanham, MD 20706
PH: (301)918-8391
Toll free: 877-APA-0077
Fax: (301)731-4621
Staebell, Dan, Director

Children and Adults With Attention Deficit/Hyperactivity Disorder [15915]
4601 Presidents Dr., Ste. 300
Lanham, MD 20706
PH: (301)306-7070
Fax: (301)306-7090
MacKay, Michael, President

Children's Rights Council [11682]
9470 Annapolis Rd., Ste. 310
Lanham, MD 20706
PH: (301)459-1220
Fax: (301)459-1227
Morgan, Rev. E.F. Michael, Ph.D., President

Disaster Aid USA [11656]
9817 Lanham Severn Rd.
Lanham, MD 20706
PH: (240)487-6359
Fax: (410)956-3833
Agee, Kenneth, Exec. Dir.

International Association of Heat and Frost Insulators and Allied Workers [1624]
9602 Martin Luther King Jr. Hwy.
Lanham, MD 20706-1839
PH: (301)731-9101
Fax: (301)731-5058
McCourt, James P., President

National Asphalt Pavement Association [551]
5100 Forbes Blvd.
Lanham, MD 20706
PH: (301)731-4748
Toll free: 888-468-6499
Fax: (301)731-4621
Acott, Mike, President

National Association of Real Estate Brokers [2874]
9831 Greenbelt Rd.
Lanham, MD 20706
PH: (301)552-9340
Fax: (301)552-9216
Hughes, Robert, Chairperson

Society for Vascular Ultrasound [17582]
4601 Presidents Dr., Ste. 260
Lanham, MD 20706-4831

PH: (301)459-7550
Toll free: 800-788-8346
Fax: (301)459-5651
Stefaniak, Thomas L., MBA, Exec. Dir.

United Association for Labor Education [8166]
PO Box 598
Lanham, MD 20703
PH: (202)585-4393
McBride, Elissa, President

BioCommunications Association [13818]
c/o Connie Johansen, President
1394 Redwood Cir.
Laplata, MD 20646
PH: (571)557-1971
Johansen, Connie, President

American Tennis Association [23298]
9701 Apollo Dr., Ste. 301
Largo, MD 20774
PH: (240)487-5953
Scott, Dr. Franklyn, Jr., President

Black Data Processing Associates [68]
9500 Arena Dr., Ste. 106
Largo, MD 20774
PH: (301)584-3135
Fax: (301)560-8300

Council on Legal Education Opportunity [8213]
1101 Mercantile Ln., Ste. 294
Largo, MD 20774
PH: (240)582-8600
Fax: (240)582-8605
Ogden, Cassandra Sneed, CEO, Exec. Dir.

Educators Serving the Community [7808]
9701 Apollo Dr., Ste. 301
Largo, MD 20774-4783
PH: (301)498-2899
(301)584-3179
Smith, Brian K., Founder

National Association of Minority Automobile Dealers [2394]
9745 Lottsford Rd., Ste. 150
Largo, MD 20774
PH: (301)306-1614
Fax: (301)306-1493
Lester, Damon, President

National Council on Student Development [8607]
301 Largo Rd.
Largo, MD 20774
Toll free: 866-972-0717
Fax: (303)755-7363
Lee, Tyjaun, President

American Institute of Ultrasound in Medicine [17230]
14750 Sweitzer Ln., Ste. 100
Laurel, MD 20707-5906
PH: (301)498-4100
Toll free: 800-638-5352
Fax: (301)498-4450
Valente, Carmine M., PhD, CEO

American Spelean History Association [9458]
6304 Kaybro St.
Laurel, MD 20707
PH: (301)725-5877
Hoke, Robert, Secretary, Treasurer

Cave Research Foundation [7227]
c/o Bob Hoke, Treasurer
6304 Kaybro St.
Laurel, MD 20707
PH: (301)725-5877
House, Scott, Operating Ofc.

Correctional Education Association [11523]
PO Box 3430
Laurel, MD 20709
PH: (443)459-3080
Fax: (443)459-3088
Dews, Morris, President

Drycleaning and Laundry Institute International [2077]
14700 Sweitzer Ln.
Laurel, MD 20707
PH: (301)622-1900
Toll free: 800-638-2627
Johnson, Allan, III, Chairman

International Association for Chinese Management Research [2175]
c/o Xiaomeng Zhang, Executive Secretary
8636 Waterside Ct.
Laurel, MD 20723
PH: (316)978-6788
Fax: (316)978-3349
Yao, Zhijun, Exec. Dir.

International Hobie Class Association [22631]
c/o Rich McVeigh, President
15800 Bond Mill Rd.
Laurel, MD 20707-3257
PH: (301)435-7795
McVeigh, Rich, President

SOLE - The International Society of Logistics [6725]
14625 Baltimore Ave., Ste. 303
Laurel, MD 20707-4902
PH: (301)459-8446
Fax: (301)459-1522

Adoption Exchange Association [10438]
605 Global Way, Ste. 100
Linthicum, MD 21090
PH: (410)636-7030
Toll free: 888-200-4005
Fax: (410)636-7039
Bunn, Kamilah, CEO

American Midwifery Certification Board [14220]
849 International Dr., Ste. 120
Linthicum, MD 21090
PH: (410)694-9424
Toll free: 866-366-9632
Fax: (410)694-9425

American Urological Association [17549]
1000 Corporate Blvd.
Linthicum, MD 21090
PH: (410)689-3700
Toll free: 866-746-4282
Fax: (410)689-3800
Sheppard, Mr. Michael T., CPA, Exec. Dir.

International Organization of Masters, Mates and Pilots [23475]
700 Maritime Blvd., Ste. B
Linthicum, MD 21090-1953
PH: (410)850-8700
Toll free: 877-667-5522
Werse, Steven, Secretary, Treasurer

National Duckpin Bowling Congress [22706]
4991 Fairview Ave.
Linthicum, MD 21090
PH: (410)636-2695
Fax: (410)636-3256
Kellum, Stan, Exec. Dir.

Society for Basic Urologic Research [17558]
1000 Corporate Blvd.
Linthicum, MD 21090

PH: (410)689-3950
Fax: (410)689-3825
Shifflet, Drew, Exec. Dir.

Society for Fetal Urology [17559]
1000 Corporate Blvd.
Linthicum, MD 21090
PH: (410)689-3950
Fax: (410)689-3825
Gatti, John, President

Society of Genitourinary Reconstructive Surgeons [17560]
c/o Urology Management Services
1000 Corporate Blvd.
Linthicum, MD 21090
PH: (410)689-3950
Fax: (410)689-3824
Andrich, Daniela E., MD, President

Urology Care Foundation [17568]
1000 Corporate Blvd.
Linthicum, MD 21090
PH: (410)689-3700
Toll free: 800-828-7866
Fax: (410)689-3998
Memo, Richard A., MD, Chmn. of the Bd.

Family of the Americas Foundation [11840]
5929 Talbot Rd.
Lothian, MD 20711
PH: (301)627-3346
Toll free: 800-443-3395
Wilson, Mercedes Arzú, Founder, President

Foodservice Sales and Marketing Association [1387]
1810-J York Rd., No. 384
Lutherville, MD 21093
Toll free: 800-617-1170
Fax: (888)668-7496
Abraham, Rick, CEO, President

Jack Russell Terrier Club of America [21906]
PO Box 4527
Lutherville, MD 21094-4527
PH: (410)561-3655
Fax: (410)560-2563
Brown, Catherine, Chairperson

National Association of Drug Diversion Investigators [5490]
1810 York Rd., No. 435
Lutherville, MD 21093
PH: (410)321-4600
Cichon, Charlie, Exec. Dir.

United States Hydrofoil Association [23356]
320 Starlight Pl.
Lutherville, MD 21093
Toll free: 800-533-2972
Scott, Brad, President

Cotswold Breeders Association [3599]
PO Box 441
Manchester, MD 21102
PH: (410)374-4383
Fax: (410)374-2294
Updegrove, Lynne, VP

NASSCO [3419]
2470 Longstone Ln., Ste. M
Marriottsville, MD 21104
PH: (410)442-7473
Fax: (410)442-7788
Doheny, Kay, President

Scottish Harp Society of America [10001]
PO Box 681
Mechanicsville, MD 20659
Narkevicius, Jen, Coord.

United Drive-In Theatre Owners Association [1207]
PO Box 24771
Middle River, MD 21220
PH: (443)490-1250
Vincent, John, President

ReefGuardian International [4472]
PO Box 1316
Middletown, MD 21769-4668

Geriatric Oncology Consortium [16344]
672 E Old Mill Rd., No. 187
Millersville, MD 21108
PH: (410)941-9744
Toll free: 888-437-4662
Fax: (410)467-4100
Balducci, Lodovico, MD, Director

Military Order of the Carabao [20705]
PO Box 987
Millersville, MD 21108
PH: (703)946-7777
Ham, Gen. Carter F., Leader

The Swedenborg Project [20613]
c/o Washington New Church
11914 Chantilly Ln.
Mitchellville, MD 20721
Simons, Kurt, Director

HHT Foundation International, Inc. [14827]
PO Box 329
Monkton, MD 21111
PH: (410)357-9932
Fax: (410)357-0655
Clancy, Ms. Marianne, Exec. Dir.

Children of Persia [10922]
PO Box 2602
Montgomery Village, MD 20886
PH: (301)315-0750
Davoodpour, Shiva, VP

A is for Africa [11052]
14344 Harrisville Rd.
Mount Airy, MD 21771
Smith, Molly, Director

American Deafness and Rehabilitation Association [15170]
PO Box 480
Myersville, MD 21773-0480
Fax: (301)293-8969
Crump, Charlene, President

CTAM: Cable and Telecommunications Association for Marketing [460]
120 Waterfront St., Ste. 200
National Harbor, MD 20745
PH: (301)485-8900
Fax: (301)560-4964
Allen, Antoinette, Dir. of Mtgs.

American Boating Association [22593]
PO Box 690
New Market, MD 21774
PH: (614)497-4088
Toll free: 800-768-2121
Anderson, Mike, Director

Society for Applied Spectroscopy [7225]
168 W Main St., No. 300
New Market, MD 21774
PH: (301)694-8122
Fax: (301)694-6860
Saylor, Bonnie, Exec. Dir.

American Airborne Association [20717]
10301 McKinstry Mill Rd.
New Windsor, MD 21776-7903

PH: (410)775-7733
Toll free: 888-567-2927
Fax: (410)775-7760

Sales Exchange for Refugee Rehabilitation and Vocation [3305]
500 Main St.
New Windsor, MD 21776-0365
Toll free: 800-422-5915
Fax: (888)294-6376
Chase, Robert, CEO, President

National Institute of Electromedical Information [15696]
PO Box 43058
Nottingham, MD 21236
PH: (410)808-9700
Young, Dr. Mark A., President

Eastern Surfing Association [23275]
PO Box 4736
Ocean City, MD 21843
PH: (302)988-1953
Fax: (302)258-0735
Hodges, Debbie, Exec. Dir.

Lesley Gore International Fan Club [24053]
PO Box 1548
Ocean Pines, MD 21811
Natoli, Jack, President

Parents-Coaches Association [22707]
PO Box 224
Odenton, MD 21113
PH: (410)207-1570
Fax: (301)912-1039
Brady, Carole, President

American Society of Podiatric Dermatology [14488]
c/o Ken Silverstein, Executive Director
Ken Silverstein and Associates
17825 Sandcastle Ct.
Olney, MD 20832
PH: (301)570-6664
Silverstein, Ken, Exec. Dir.

Clan Shaw Society [20842]
c/o Meredith L. Shaw, President
3031 Appomattox Ave., No. 102
Olney, MD 20832-1498
Shaw, Mr. Meredith L., President

Professional Handlers' Association [21948]
17017 Norbrook Dr.
Olney, MD 20832
PH: (301)924-0089
Fetter, Nina, President

America's Survival [17873]
PO Box 146
Owings, MD 20736-0146
PH: (443)964-8208
Kincaid, Cliff, President

Association of Academic Physiatrists [17084]
10461 Mill Run Cir., Ste. 730
Owings Mills, MD 21117
PH: (410)654-1000
Fax: (410)654-1001
Knowlton, Tiffany, MBA, Exec. Dir.

Board for Orthotist/Prosthetist Certification [16495]
10451 Mill Run Cir., Ste. 200
Owings Mills, MD 21117-5575
PH: (410)581-6222
Toll free: 877-776-2200
Fax: (410)581-6228
Zacharias, Claudia, MBA, CAE, President, CEO

Parcel Shippers Association [2121]
PO Box 450
Oxon Hill, MD 20750

PH: (571)257-7617
Fax: (301)749-8684
Zwieg, Steve, Chairman

School Nutrition Association [8609]
120 Waterfront St., Ste. 300
National Harbor
Oxon Hill, MD 20745-1142
PH: (301)686-3100
Toll free: 800-877-8822
Fax: (301)686-3115
Phillips, Helen, SNS, Officer

Clean Islands International [4042]
8219 Elvaton Dr.
Pasadena, MD 21122-3903
PH: (410)647-2500
Brown, Randy, Exec. Dir.

Kunzang Palyul Choling [19780]
18400 River Rd.
Poolesville, MD 20837
PH: (301)710-6259
Lhamo, Jetsunma Ahkon, Director

Concrete Corrosion Inhibitors Association [784]
11836 Goya Dr.
Potomac, MD 20854
PH: (301)340-7368

Determined2heal Foundation [17254]
8112 River Falls Dr.
Potomac, MD 20854
PH: (703)795-5711
Basile, Josh, Founder

Food for Life Global [12662]
10310 Oaklyn Dr.
Potomac, MD 20854
PH: (202)407-9090
Turner, Paul Rodney, President

Heart Healers International [14114]
9601 Hall Rd.
Potomac, MD 20854
Sable, Dr. Craig, President

International Association for Women's Mental Health [15774]
c/o Debra Tucker Associates LLC
8213 Lakenheath Way
Potomac, MD 20854
PH: (301)983-6282
Fax: (301)983-6288
Tucker, Debra, CMP, Exec. Dir.

Set America Free [18194]
7811 Montrose Rd., Ste. 505
Potomac, MD 20854-3368
Toll free: 866-713-7527
Korin, Anne, Chairperson

South Asian Public Health Association [17023]
9408 Holbrook Ln.
Potomac, MD 20854
Dawood, Nazeera, President

Association of Research Directors [7087]
c/o Moses Kairo, Chairman
University of Maryland Eastern Shore
30665 Student Services Center
Princess Anne, MD 21853
PH: (410)651-6072
Brooks, Carolyn B., Exec. Dir.

Worldwide Friendship International [21743]
3607 Briarstone Rd.
Randallstown, MD 21133-4232
PH: (410)922-2795
Smith, Elton, President

International Beverage Dispensing Equipment Association [424]
PO Box 248
Reisterstown, MD 21136

PH: (410)602-0616
Toll free: 877-404-2332
Fax: (410)486-6799
Kint, Brian, President

United States Kuo Shu Federation
[23020]
PO Box 927
Reisterstown, MD 21136-0927
PH: (443)394-9200
Fax: (443)394-9202
Buckley, John, VP

The World Kuo Shu Federation
[23029]
PO Box 927
Reisterstown, MD 21136
PH: (443)394-9222
Fax: (443)394-9202
Huang, Chien Liang, Chairman

National Flag Foundation [10297]
PO Box 435
Riderwood, MD 21139
Toll free: 800-615-1776
Streufert, Duane, Jr., Contact

Orienteering USA [23051]
c/o Glen Schorr, Executive Director
PO Box 505
Riderwood, MD 21139
PH: (410)802-1125
Goodwin, Peter, President

Society of the Ark and the Dove
[20761]
PO Box 401
Riderwood, MD 21139-0401
Roberts, Eugene Bowie, Jr., Gov.

All Services Postal Chess Club
[21588]
c/o Robert A. MacDonald, Director
38 Louise Ct.
Rising Sun, MD 21911
PH: (410)378-5859
MacDonald, Robert A., Director

HomeFree - U.S.A. [1689]
6200 Baltimore Ave.
Riverdale, MD 20737-1054
PH: (301)891-8400
Toll free: 855-493-4002
Griffin, Marcia, Founder, President

Ogwashi-Uku Association USA
[19597]
PO Box 836
Riverdale, MD 20737
Okafor, Mary, President

Aeras [14726]
1405 Research Blvd.
Rockville, MD 20850
PH: (301)547-2900
Fax: (301)547-2901
Connolly, Jim, President, CEO

AHEAD-INC. [14922]
PO Box 2049
Rockville, MD 20847-2049
PH: (301)530-3697
Fax: (301)530-3697
Burgess, Ruby, Ed.D, President

Air Carrier Association of America
[121]
421 Watts Branch Pky.
Rockville, MD 20854
PH: (202)236-1018
Faberman, Edward P., Exec. Dir.

Alliance of Hazardous Materials
Professionals [4290]
9707 Key W Ave., Ste. 100
Rockville, MD 20850
PH: (301)329-6850
Fax: (301)990-9771
Graham, Ms. Zehra Schneider,
CHMM, Advisor, Director

Alpha Omega International Dental
Fraternity [23717]
50 W Edmonston Dr., No. 206
Rockville, MD 20852
PH: (301)738-6400
Toll free: 877-368-6326
Fax: (301)738-6403
Weber, Heidi, Exec. Dir.

American Academy of Appellate
Lawyers [4979]
9707 Key W Ave., Ste. 100
Rockville, MD 20850
PH: (240)404-6498
Fax: (301)990-9771
Winkelman, Nancy, President

American Association of Colleges of
Podiatric Medicine [16775]
15850 Crabbs Branch Way, Ste. 320
Rockville, MD 20855
PH: (301)948-9760
Fax: (301)948-1928
Parsley, Nancy L., DPM, MHPE,
Chairman

American Association on Health and
Disability [14544]
110 N Washington St., Ste. 328-J
Rockville, MD 20850
PH: (301)545-6140
Fax: (301)545-6144
Carlin, Roberta, MS, Exec. Dir.

American Association for Russian
Language, Culture and Education
[19628]
451 Hungerford Dr., Ste. 300
Rockville, MD 20850
PH: (240)372-3343
Fax: (405)625-5349
Foxman, Boris, Chmn. of the Bd.

American Chinese Pharmaceutical
Association [16634]
PO Box 10193
Rockville, MD 20849-0193
Yu, Lawrence, PhD, Chmn. of the
Bd.

American Citizens Abroad [19376]
11140 Rockville Pke., Ste. 100-162
Rockville, MD 20852
PH: (540)628-2426
Serrato, Marylouise, Exec. Dir.

American College Dance Association
[9240]
326 N Stonestreet Ave., Ste. 204
Rockville, MD 20850
PH: (240)428-1736
DeFries, Diane, Exec. Dir.

American College of Osteopathic
Internists [16505]
11400 Rockville Pke., No. 801
Rockville, MD 20852
PH: (301)231-8877
Toll free: 800-327-5183
Fax: (301)231-6099
Donadio, Brian J., Exec. Dir.

American College of Real Estate
Lawyers [4987]
11300 Rockville Pke., Ste. 903
Rockville, MD 20852-3034
PH: (301)816-9811
Fax: (301)816-9786
Jacobson, Kenneth M., President

American Kidney Fund [15870]
11921 Rockville Pke., Ste. 300
Rockville, MD 20852
PH: (301)984-5055
Toll free: 800-638-8299
Burton, LaVarne A., CEO, President

American Latvian Association
[19533]
400 Hurley Ave.
Rockville, MD 20850-3121

PH: (301)340-1914
Bataraga, Anita, President

American Lunar Society [5998]
c/o Andrew Martin
722 Mapleton Rd.
Rockville, MD 20850
Martin, Andrew, Contact

American Medical Writers Associa-
tion [2651]
30 W Gude Dr., Ste. 525
Rockville, MD 20850-4347
PH: (240)238-0940
Fax: (301)294-9006
Krug, Susan, CAE, Exec. Dir.

American Registry for Diagnostic
Medical Sonography [17231]
1401 Rockville Pke., Ste. 600
Rockville, MD 20852-1402
PH: (301)738-8401
Toll free: 800-541-9754
Fax: (301)738-0312
Wagner, Paul, Chairman

American Society for Biochemistry
and Molecular Biology [6050]
11200 Rockville Pke., Ste. 302
Rockville, MD 20852-3110
PH: (240)283-6600
Fax: (301)881-2080
Miller, Stephen, Deputy

American Society of Consulting Ar-
borists [4726]
9707 Key W Ave., Ste. 100
Rockville, MD 20850
PH: (301)947-0483
Fax: (301)990-9771
Neal, Barbara, President

American Society for Nutrition
[16206]
9211 Corporate Blvd., Ste. 300
Rockville, MD 20850
PH: (301)634-7050
   (240)428-3650
Fax: (301)634-7894
Courtney, John E., PhD, Exec. Ofc.

American Society of Plant Biologists
[6135]
15501 Monona Dr.
Rockville, MD 20855-2768
PH: (301)251-0560
Fax: (301)279-2996
Taylor, Dr. Crispin, Exec. Dir.

American Speech-Language-Hearing
Association [17237]
2200 Research Blvd.
Rockville, MD 20850-3289
PH: (301)296-5700
   (301)296-5650
Toll free: 800-638-8255
Fax: (301)296-8580
Pietranton, Arlene A., CEO

AOAC International [6187]
2275 Research Blvd., Ste. 300
Rockville, MD 20850-3250
PH: (301)924-7077
Toll free: 800-379-2622
Fax: (301)924-7089
Chelf, Lauren, Dir. of Mtgs.

Aplastic Anemia and MDS
International Foundation [15223]
100 Park Ave., Ste. 108
Rockville, MD 20850
PH: (301)279-7202
Toll free: 800-747-2820
Fax: (301)279-7205
Huber, John, Exec. Dir.

APSE: The Network on Employment
[11572]
416 Hungerford Dr., Ste. 418
Rockville, MD 20850

PH: (301)279-0060
Fax: (301)279-0075
Pavlak, Jeannine, Secretary

Asian American Music Society
[9873]
39 Eton Overlook
Rockville, MD 20850
PH: (301)424-3379
Yang, Mira, Director

Association of Adult Musicians with
Hearing Loss, Inc. [15175]
PO Box 522
Rockville, MD 20848
Cheng, Wendy, President

Association on American Indian Af-
fairs [18707]
966 Hungerford Dr., Ste. 12-B
Rockville, MD 20850
PH: (240)314-7155
Fax: (240)314-7159
DeRoin, DeeAnn, Chairman

Association of Community Cancer
Centers [13893]
11600 Nebel St., Ste. 201
Rockville, MD 20852-2557
PH: (301)984-9496
Fax: (301)770-1949
Marino, Monique, Managing Ed.

Association of Immunization Manag-
ers [15374]
620 Hungerford Dr., Ste. 29
Rockville, MD 20850
PH: (301)424-6080
Fax: (301)424-6081
Yett, Gerri, Chairman

Association of Language Companies
[3312]
9707 Key West Ave., Ste. 100
Rockville, MD 20850
PH: (240)404-6511
Palys, Beth W., CAE, Exec. Dir.

Association of Practicing Certified
Public Accountants [16]
932 Hungerford Dr., No. 17A
Rockville, MD 20850
PH: (301)340-3340
Ramos, Eileen, President

Association for Research in Vision
and Ophthalmology [16374]
1801 Rockville Pke., Ste. 400
Rockville, MD 20852-5622
PH: (240)221-2900
Fax: (240)221-0370
Rush, Iris M., Exec. Dir.

Association for Safe International
Road Travel [13230]
12320 Parklawn Dr.
Rockville, MD 20852-1726
PH: (240)249-0100
Fax: (301)230-0411
Sobel, Rochelle, Founder, President

Association of Schools and Colleges
of Optometry [16427]
6110 Executive Blvd., Ste. 420
Rockville, MD 20852
PH: (301)231-5944
Fax: (301)770-1828
Mancuso, Dawn M., CAE, Exec. Dir.

Association of Water Technologies
[3458]
9707 Key West Ave., Ste. 100
Rockville, MD 20850
PH: (301)740-1421
Fax: (301)990-9771
Zimmerman, Ms. Heidi, Exec. Dir.

Biophysical Society [6117]
11400 Rockville Pke., Ste. 800
Rockville, MD 20852

PH: (240)290-5600
Fax: (240)290-5555
Scarlata, Suzanne, President

Board of Nephrology Examiners
Nursing and Technology [15876]
100 S Washington St.
Rockville, MD 20850
PH: (202)462-1252
Fax: (202)463-1257
Anas, Mr. Peter, Exec. Dir.

Call For Action [11475]
11820 Parklawn Dr., Ste. 340
Rockville, MD 20852
PH: (240)747-0229
Wilcox, William E., Chmn. of the Bd.

Cancer Information Service [13924]
9609 Medical Center Dr.
Rockville, MD 20850
Toll free: 800-422-6237
Lowy, Dr. Douglas R., Dir. (Actg.)

Centers for Disease Control and
Prevention I National Prevention
Information Network [13535]
PO Box 6003
Rockville, MD 20849-6003
Toll free: 800-232-4636

Chinese Biopharmaceutical Association, U.S.A. [16656]
111 Rockville Pke., Ste. 800
Rockville, MD 20850
Jin, Feiyan, Treasurer

Council of State Administrators of
Vocational Rehabilitation [17087]
1 Research Ct., Ste. 450
Rockville, MD 20850
PH: (301)519-8023
Wooderson, Stephen A., CEO

Council of Teaching Hospitals
[15323]
15850 Crabbs Branch Way, Ste. 320
Rockville, MD 20855
PH: (301)948-9764
Dei, Randall I., Chairman

Disabled Sports USA [22780]
451 Hungerford Dr., Ste. 100
Rockville, MD 20850
PH: (301)217-0960
    (301)217-9838
Fax: (301)217-0968
Meserve, Robert, President

Employee Morale and Recreation
Association [12576]
PO Box 10517
Rockville, MD 20849
Schools, Randy, Chairman

Friends of the National Institute of
Dental and Craniofacial Research
[14436]
100 S Washington St.
Rockville, MD 20850
PH: (240)778-6117
Fax: (240)778-6112
Anas, Peter, Exec. Dir.

Funders Network on Population,
Reproductive Health and Rights
[17106]
PO Box 750
Rockville, MD 20851
PH: (301)294-4157
Shannon, Denise, Exec. Dir.

Gem and Lapidary Dealers Associa-
tion [2046]
120 Derwood Cir.
Rockville, MD 20850
PH: (301)294-1640
Duke, Arnold, President

Geoprofessional Business Associa-
tion [6221]
1300 Piccard Dr., No. LL14
Rockville, MD 20850-4303
PH: (301)565-2733
Fax: (301)589-2017
Carson, Joel G., Exec. Dir.

Goodwill Industries International
[11600]
15810 Indianola Dr.
Rockville, MD 20855
Toll free: 800-741-0186
Gibbons, Jim, CEO, President

Health and Development
International [14937]
318 Seth Pl.
Rockville, MD 20850
PH: (858)245-2410
Fax: (858)764-0604
Kirckpatrick, Amb. Barbro Owens,
Chairman

Indonesia Relief - USA [11671]
20 Bluehosta Way
Rockville, MD 20850-2871
Zaky, Mrs. Dwitra, President

Indoor Environmental Standards
Organization [4142]
12339 Carroll Ave.
Rockville, MD 20852
PH: (301)230-9636
Toll free: 800-406-0256
Fax: (301)230-9648
Fellman, Glenn, Exec. Dir.

Institute of Hazardous Materials
Management [4292]
11900 Parklawn Dr., Ste. 450
Rockville, MD 20852-2624
PH: (301)984-8969
Fax: (301)984-1516
Greenwald, Jeffrey H., CAE, Liaison

International Federation of Technical
Analysts [1246]
9707 Key West Ave., Ste. 100
Rockville, MD 20850
PH: (240)404-6508
Fax: (301)990-9771

Joint Baltic American National Com-
mittee [17823]
400 Hurley Ave.
Rockville, MD 20850-3121
PH: (301)340-1954
Fax: (301)309-1405
Rink-Abel, Marju, Treasurer

Mechanical Contractors Association
of America [876]
1385 Piccard Dr.
Rockville, MD 20850
PH: (301)869-5800
Fax: (301)990-9690

National Alliance for Eye and Vision
Research [17728]
1801 Rockville Pike, Ste. 400
Rockville, MD 20852
PH: (240)221-2905
Fax: (240)221-0370
Jorkasky, James, Exec. Dir.

National Association of Professional
Asian American Women [650]
304 Oak Knoll Ter.
Rockville, MD 20850
PH: (301)785-8585
Kim, Vivian C., MA, Chairperson

National Certified Pipe Welding
Bureau [2608]
1385 Piccard Dr.
Rockville, MD 20850-4329
PH: (301)869-5800
Toll free: 800-556-3653
Fax: (301)990-9690
Nikpourfard, Nick, Exec. Dir.

National Christ Child Society [19881]
6110 Executive Blvd., Ste. 504
Rockville, MD 20852
PH: (301)881-2490
Toll free: 800-814-2149
Fax: (301)881-2493
Rowe, Kaye, Treasurer

National Coalition of Oncology Nurse
Navigators [16159]
PO Box 1688
Rockville, MD 20849-1688
Toll free: 800-581-0175
Francz, Sharon, RN, Exec. Dir.,
President

National Coalition to Save Our Mall
[9416]
PO Box 4709
Rockville, MD 20849
PH: (301)340-3938
Feldman, Judy Scott, PhD,
Chairperson

National Council on Patient Informa-
tion and Education [16677]
200-A Monroe St., Ste. 212
Rockville, MD 20850-4448
PH: (301)340-3940
Fax: (301)340-3944
Keyes, Elizabeth K., Chairman

National Federation of Families for
Children's Mental Health [12309]
15883 Crabbs Branch Way
Rockville, MD 20855-2635
PH: (240)403-1901
Fax: (240)403-1909
Gargan, Lynda, Exec. Dir.

National Institute of Mental Health
[15797]
6001 Executive Blvd.
Rockville, MD 20852
PH: (301)443-4536
Toll free: 866-615-6464
Fax: (301)443-4279
Insel, Thomas, MD, Director

National Park Trust [4521]
401 E Jefferson St., Ste. 203
Rockville, MD 20850-2617
PH: (301)279-7275
Fax: (301)279-7211
Gualtieri, Ann, V. Chmn. of the Bd.

National School Public Relations As-
sociation [8472]
15948 Derwood Rd.
Rockville, MD 20855-2123
PH: (301)519-0496
Fax: (301)519-0494
Bagin, Richard D., APR, Exec. Dir.

National Student Speech Language
Hearing Association [17246]
2200 Research Blvd., No. 322
Rockville, MD 20850-3289
PH: (301)296-5700
Toll free: 800-498-2071
Fax: (301)296-8580
Boyer, Valerie, Editor

National Youth Rights Association
[19276]
PO Box 516
Rockville, MD 20848-0516
PH: (301)738-6769
Bystricky, Bill, Exec. Dir.

The Oceanography Society [6943]
PO Box 1931
Rockville, MD 20849-1931
PH: (301)251-7708
Fax: (301)251-7709
Ramarui, Jennifer, Exec. Dir.

Overseas Young Chinese Forum
[7603]
11423 Potomac Oaks Dr.
Rockville, MD 20850-3576
Zheng, Lu, President

Pediatric Nursing Certification Board
[16178]
9605 Medical Center Dr., Ste. 250
Rockville, MD 20850
PH: (301)330-2921
Toll free: 888-641-2767
Fax: (301)330-1504
Harrison, Peg, CEO

Physician Insurers Association of
America [15423]
2275 Research Blvd., Ste. 250
Rockville, MD 20850
PH: (301)947-9000
Fax: (301)947-9090
Anderson, Eric, VP of Mktg., VP,
Comm.

Prevent Alzheimer's Disease 2020
[13673]
451 Hungerford Dr.
PMB 119-355
Rockville, MD 20850
PH: (301)294-7201
Fax: (301)294-7203
Khachaturian, Zaven, President

Regulatory Affairs Professionals
Society [14963]
5635 Fishers Ln., Ste. 550
Rockville, MD 20852
PH: (301)770-2920
Fax: (301)841-7956
Brumfield, Martha A., Chmn. of the
Bd.

Renal Physicians Association
[15886]
1700 Rockville Pke., Ste. 220
Rockville, MD 20852-1631
PH: (301)468-3515
Fax: (301)468-3511
Singer, Dale, Exec. Dir.

Renewable Natural Resources
Foundation [3931]
3010 Executive Blvd., 5th Fl.
Rockville, MD 20852-3827
PH: (301)493-9101
Fax: (301)770-9104
Day, Robert D., Exec. Dir.

Reusable Industrial Packaging As-
sociation [843]
51 Monroe St., Ste. 812
Rockville, MD 20850
PH: (301)577-3786
Fax: (301)577-6476
Bernath, Eric, Bd. Member

Stop Abusive and Violent Environ-
ments [11714]
PO Box 1221
Rockville, MD 20849
PH: (301)801-0608
Stoddard, Teri, Prog. Dir.

Taxicab, Limousine & Paratransit
Association [3357]
3200 Tower Oaks Blvd., Ste. 220
Rockville, MD 20852
PH: (301)984-5700
Fax: (301)984-5703
LaGasse, Alfred, CEO

Transportation Communications
International Union [23516]
3 Research Pl.
Rockville, MD 20850
PH: (301)948-4910
Scardelletti, Robert A., President

Transportation Communications
Union - Brotherhood Railway Car-
men Division [23517]
3 Research Pl.
Rockville, MD 20850
PH: (301)840-8730
Scardelletti, Robert A., President

U.S. Department of Health and Human Services | Office of Disease Prevention and Health Promotion | National Health Information Center [14967]
1101 Wootton Pky., Ste. LL100
Rockville, MD 20852
PH: (301)565-4167
Toll free: 800-336-4797
Fax: (301)984-4256
Royall, Penelope, Director

United States Pharmacopeial Convention [16689]
12601 Twinbrook Pky.
Rockville, MD 20852-1790
PH: (301)881-0666
Toll free: 800-227-8772
Piervincenzi, Ronald T., PhD, CEO

U.S. Travel Insurance Association [3406]
9707 Key West Ave., Ste. 100
Rockville, MD 20850
PH: (240)342-3816
Evans, Peter, President

Universal Proutist Farmers Federation [4170]
6810 Tilden Ln.
Rockville, MD 20852
PH: (301)231-0110

Witness Justice [19232]
PO Box 2516
Rockville, MD 20847-2516
PH: (301)846-9110
Toll free: 800-394-2255
Luest, Helga, MA, CEO, Founder, President

World Federation of Free Latvians [18299]
400 Hurley Ave.
Rockville, MD 20850
PH: (301)340-7646
Garoza, Ilze, Secretary

International Consortium on Governmental Financial Management [1243]
PO Box 1077
Saint Michaels, MD 21663
PH: (410)745-8570
Fax: (410)745-8569
Anderson, Phyllis, Secretary

American Society for Ethnohistory [9289]
c/o James Joseph Buss, Secretary
1101 Camden Ave.
Salisbury, MD 21801
PH: (410)546-6902
Buss, James Joseph, Secretary

Czechoslovak Studies Association [9474]
c/o Gregory Ference, Secretary-Treasurer
Department of History
Salisbury University
Salisbury, MD 21801
Feinberg, Melissa, President

Horse Lovers United [18355]
PO Box 2744
Salisbury, MD 21802-2744
PH: (410)749-3599

Lone Ranger Fan Club [24086]
PO Box 1253
Salisbury, MD 21802-1253
Holland, Tex, Mgr.

Point of Care Communication Council [15058]
PO Box 4342
Salisbury, MD 21803

PH: (410)344-7580
McGuinness, Tom, Co-Chmn. of the Bd.

Better BedRest [16278]
PO Box 212
Savage, MD 20763
PH: (410)740-7662
Reisfeld, Joanie, Founder

Triumph Wedge Owners Association [21505]
c/o Gary Klein, Treasurer
8153 Quarterfield Farms Dr.
Severn, MD 21144
Elsberry, David, President

American Board of Periodontology [14399]
877 Baltimore Annapolis Blvd., Ste. 111
Severna Park, MD 21146
PH: (410)647-1324
Fax: (410)647-1260
Palcanis, Kent G., Assoc. Exec., Director

American Medical Association Alliance [15709]
550 M Ritchie Highway 271
Severna Park, MD 21146
Toll free: 800-549-4619
Borders, Emma, Comm. Chm.

Binge Eating Disorder Association [14634]
637 Emerson Pl.
Severna Park, MD 21146-3409
Toll free: 855-855-2332
Fax: (410)741-3037
Turner, Chevese, CEO, Founder

Industrial Steel Drum Institute [835]
120 Hatton Dr.
Severna Park, MD 21146-4400
PH: (410)544-0385
Stavig, Kyle R., Chairman

International Catalina 27/270 Association [22627]
c/o Peter Zahn, Commodore
106 Riggs Ave.
Severna Park, MD 21146
Zahn, Peter, Commodore, Assoc. Ed., Web Adm.

International Society for Ecological Modelling [4006]
550 M Ritchie Hwy.
Severna Park, MD 21146
Jorgensen, Sven E., President

National Marine Electronics Association [2253]
692 Ritchie Hwy., Ste. 104
Severna Park, MD 21146-3919
PH: (410)975-9425
Fax: (410)975-9450
Reedenauer, Mark, President, Exec. Dir.

Accreditation Commission for Midwifery Education [14219]
c/o Heather Maurer, Executive Director
American College of Nurse-Midwives
8403 Colesville Rd., Ste. 1550
Silver Spring, MD 20910
PH: (240)485-1803

Adventist Community Services [20600]
12501 Old Columbia Pke.
Silver Spring, MD 20904
PH: (301)680-6438
Toll free: 877-ACS-2702
Fax: (301)680-6125
Kwon, Sung, Exec. Dir.

Adventist Development and Relief Agency International [12606]
12501 Old Columbia Pke.
Silver Spring, MD 20904
Toll free: 800-424-2372
Duffy, Jonathan, President

African Women's Cancer Awareness Association [13873]
8701 Georgia Ave., Ste. 600
Silver Spring, MD 20910
PH: (301)565-0420
Nwabukwu, Ify Anne, Founder, Exec. Dir.

Alliance for a Stronger FDA [18260]
PO Box 7508
Silver Spring, MD 20907-7508
PH: (202)887-4211
   (301)539-9660
Fax: (301)576-5416
Wiley, Ladd, JD, Exec. Dir.

Amalgamated Transit Union [23525]
1000 New Hampshire Ave.
Silver Spring, MD 20903
PH: (301)431-7100
Toll free: 888-240-1196
Fax: (301)431-7117
Hanley, Lawrence J., President

American Board of Physician Nutrition Specialists [16201]
National Board of Physician Nutrition Specialists
8630 Fenton St., Ste. 412
Silver Spring, MD 20910
PH: (301)587-6315
Toll free: 800-727-4567
Fax: (301)587-2365
Kahana, Doron, MD, Secretary, Treasurer

American College of Nurse-Midwives [16104]
8403 Colesville Rd., Ste. 1550
Silver Spring, MD 20910
PH: (240)485-1800
Fax: (240)485-1818
Kinzelman, Cara, Assoc. Dir.

American Herbal Products Association [1639]
8630 Fenton St., Ste. 918
Silver Spring, MD 20910
PH: (301)588-1171
Fax: (301)588-1174
McGuffin, Michael, President

American Hiking Society [23320]
1422 Fenwick Ln.
Silver Spring, MD 20910
PH: (301)565-6704
Toll free: 800-972-8608
Fax: (301)565-6714
Miller, Gregory A., President

American Music Therapy Association [16961]
8455 Colesville Rd., Ste. 1000
Silver Spring, MD 20910
PH: (301)589-3300
Fax: (301)589-5175
Farbman, Dr. Andrea, Exec. Dir.

American Nurses Association [16106]
8515 Georgia Ave., Ste. 400
Silver Spring, MD 20910-3492
PH: (301)628-5000
Toll free: 800-284-2378
Fax: (301)628-5001
Drenkard, Karen, PhD, RN, NEA-BC, FAAN, Exec. Dir.

American Nurses Foundation [16107]
8515 Georgia Ave., Ste. 400
Silver Spring, MD 20910-3492

PH: (301)628-5227
Fax: (301)628-5354
Judge, Kate, Exec. Dir.

American Society for Information Science and Technology [6735]
8555 16th St., Ste. 850
Silver Spring, MD 20910
PH: (301)495-0900
Fax: (301)495-0810
Foss, Vanessa, Dir. of Mtgs., Dir. of Member Svcs.

American Society for Parenteral and Enteral Nutrition [16207]
8630 Fenton St., Ste. 412
Silver Spring, MD 20910-3805
PH: (301)587-6315
Fax: (301)587-2365
BenAvram, Ms. Debra, CEO

Americans for Religious Liberty [17872]
PO Box 6656
Silver Spring, MD 20916-6656
PH: (301)460-1111
Menendez, Albert J., Dir. of Res.

Amman Imman: Water is Life [13315]
914 Robin Rd.
Silver Spring, MD 20901-1871
PH: (240)418-1143
Alzhara Kirtley, Ariane, Exec. Dir., Founder

Anxiety and Depression Association of America [12503]
8701 Georgia Ave., Ste. 412
Silver Spring, MD 20910
PH: (240)485-1001
   (240)485-1030
Fax: (240)485-1035
Richards, Jennifer, Dir. of Mtgs.

Assassination Archives and Research Center [19228]
962 Wayne Ave., Ste. 910
Silver Spring, MD 20910
PH: (301)565-0249
Wrone, David, PhD, Secretary

Associates of Vietnam Veterans of America [21165]
8719 Colesville Rd., Ste. 100
Silver Spring, MD 20910
PH: (301)585-4000
Toll free: 800-882-1316
Fax: (301)585-0519
Mackey, Elayne

Association of Americans for Civic Responsibility [17858]
13316 Foxhall Dr.
Silver Spring, MD 20906-5308
PH: (301)933-1494
Cherian, Dr. Joy, PhD, Founder, President

Association of Indian Muslims of America [19470]
PO Box 10654
Silver Spring, MD 20914
Munshi, Dr. Anwar, President

Association for Information and Image Management International [1794]
1100 Wayne Ave., Ste. 1100
Silver Spring, MD 20910
PH: (301)587-8202
Toll free: 800-477-2446
Fax: (301)587-2711
Fraas, Lynn, V. Chmn. of the Bd., Chairman, Chairperson

Association for Public Health Laboratories [16996]
8515 Georgia Ave., Ste. 700
Silver Spring, MD 20910

PH: (240)485-2745
Fax: (240)485-2700

Association of Public Health
Laboratories **[16997]**
8515 Georgia Ave., Ste. 700
Silver Spring, MD 20910
PH: (240)485-2745
Fax: (240)485-2700
Atchison, Christopher G., MPA,
Secretary, Treasurer

Association for the Study of Classi-
cal African Civilizations **[8778]**
PO Box 2128
Silver Spring, MD 20915
Carr, Greg Kimathi, VP

Association of University Centers on
Disabilities **[12317]**
1100 Wayne Ave., Ste. 1000
Silver Spring, MD 20910
PH: (301)588-8252
Fax: (301)588-2842
Imparato, Andrew J., Exec. Dir.

Association of Zoos and Aquariums
[7399]
8403 Colesville Rd., Ste. 710
Silver Spring, MD 20910-3314
PH: (301)562-0777
Fax: (301)562-0888
Vehrs, Kris, JD, Exec. Dir.

Auxiliary to the National Medical As-
sociation **[15717]**
8403 Colesville Rd., Ste. 820
Silver Spring, MD 20910
PH: (301)495-3779
Fax: (301)495-0037
Clark, Velva, Chairperson

Bionomics International [7124]
3023 Kramer St.
Silver Spring, MD 20902
Krichevsky, Micah I., Director

Burma-America Buddhist Association
[19773]
1708 Powder Mill Rd.
Silver Spring, MD 20903
PH: (301)439-4035
Hurley, Wilson, Secretary

Cambodian Buddhist Society
[19774]
13800 New Hampshire Ave.
Silver Spring, MD 20904
PH: (301)622-6544
(301)602-6612
Tun, Dr. Sovan, President

Cameroon Center for Democracy
and Human Rights **[18380]**
8504 16th St., No. 715
Silver Spring, MD 20910
PH: (301)938-5221
Fax: (240)260-0766
Njungwe, Eric Ngonji, President

Catholic Legal Immigration Network
Inc. **[5290]**
8757 Georgia Ave., Ste. 850
Silver Spring, MD 20910-3742
PH: (301)565-4800
Fax: (301)565-4824
Vann, Rev. Kevin W., Chairman

Center for Construction Research
and Training **[23455]**
8484 Georgia Ave., Ste. 1000
Silver Spring, MD 20910
PH: (301)578-8500
Fax: (301)578-8572
Stafford, Pete, Exec. Dir.

Center for Ethics and Human Rights
[14745]
c/o American Nurses Association
8515 Georgia Ave., Ste. 400

Silver Spring, MD 20910-3492
PH: (301)628-5000
Toll free: 800-274-4262
Fax: (301)628-5001
Badzek, Laurie, Director

ChildAlive [15443]
14505 Gilpin Rd.
Silver Spring, MD 20906
PH: (301)598-1163
Macdonald, Donald Ian, MD, Chair-
man, Founder

Children's Health International
[14180]
110 W University Blvd., No. 3505
Silver Spring, MD 20918
PH: (301)681-8307
Aaron, Mrs. Grace Kumi, Founder

Citizens Network for Sustainable
Development **[11332]**
c/o ISF
PO Box 7458
Silver Spring, MD 20907
PH: (301)588-5550

Coalition for Patients' Rights [14988]
c/o Adam Sachs, Public Relations
Writer
American Nurses Association
8515 Georgia Ave., Ste. 400
Silver Spring, MD 20910-3492
PH: (301)628-5034
Fax: (301)628-5340
Sachs, Adam, Contact

Conference of Major Superiors of
Men **[19825]**
8808 Cameron St.
Silver Spring, MD 20910
PH: (301)588-4030
Fax: (301)587-4575
Pavlick, Rev. John A., Exec. Dir.

Consistent Life [18779]
PO Box 9295
Silver Spring, MD 20916-9295
Toll free: 866-444-7245
Fax: (413)485-2881
Samuel, Mr. Bill, President

Council on Education for Public
Health **[17002]**
1010 Wayne Ave., Ste. 220
Silver Spring, MD 20910
PH: (202)789-1050
Fax: (202)789-1895
King, Laura Rasar, MPH, Exec. Dir.

Council for Resource Development
[7834]
8720 Georgia Ave., Ste. 700
Silver Spring, MD 20910
PH: (202)822-0750
Murphy, John, Treasurer

Criminal Justice Policy Foundation
[18597]
8730 Georgia Ave., Ste. 400
Silver Spring, MD 20910
PH: (301)589-6020
Fax: (301)589-5056
Sterling, Mr. Eric E., President

Education Market Association [3021]
8380 Colesville Rd., Ste. 250
Silver Spring, MD 20910
Toll free: 800-395-5550
Fax: (301)495-3330
McGarry, Jim, CEO, President

Estonian American Fund [7729]
PO Box 7369
Silver Spring, MD 20907-7369
Ambre, Mr. Ago, COO

Global Communities [11969]
8601 Georgia Ave., Ste. 300
Silver Spring, MD 20910

PH: (301)587-4700
Fax: (301)587-7315
Weiss, David A., CEO, President

Groove Phi Groove Social Fellow-
ship, Inc. **[23900]**
PO Box 8337
Silver Spring, MD 20907
Thomas, Dennis, President

Handicap International-U.S. [11601]
8757 Georgia Ave., Ste. 420
Silver Spring, MD 20910
PH: (301)891-2138
Fax: (301)891-9193

HavServe Volunteer Service Network
[10722]
PO Box 4173
Silver Spring, MD 20914-4173
PH: (301)490-2368
Brice, Carline, Founder

Health & Environmental Funders
Network **[14716]**
817 Silver Spring Ave.
Silver Spring, MD 20910
PH: (301)565-0500
Sessions, Kathy, Director

Hepatitis Foundation International
[15256]
8121 Georgia Ave., Ste. 350
Silver Spring, MD 20910
PH: (301)565-9410
Toll free: 800-891-0707
Fuller, Ivonne Perlaza, MPA, NRPP,
CEO, President

Hostelling International-American
Youth Hostels **[12577]**
8401 Colesville Rd., Ste. 600
Silver Spring, MD 20910
PH: (240)650-2100
Fax: (240)650-2094
Azuma, Glenn, Chairperson

Interagency Council on Information
Resources in Nursing **[9707]**
c/o Richard Barry
American Nurses Association Library
8515 Georgia Ave., Ste. 400
Silver Spring, MD 20910-3492
Hutchinson, Gertrude B., President

International Aloe Science Council
[1604]
8630 Fenton St., Ste. 918
Silver Spring, MD 20910
PH: (301)476-9690
Fax: (301)588-1174
Dentali, Steven, Chairperson

International Coalition for Sustain-
able Production and Consumption
[17982]
c/o Integrative Strategies Forum
PO Box 7458
Silver Spring, MD 20907-7458
PH: (301)588-5550

International Leadership Association
[18631]
1110 Bonifant St., Ste. 510
Silver Spring, MD 20910
PH: (202)470-4818
Fax: (202)470-2724

International Montessori Accredita-
tion Council **[8351]**
International Montessori Society
9525 Georgia Ave., No. 200
Silver Spring, MD 20910
PH: (301)589-1127
Fax: (301)920-0764
Havis, Lee, Director

International Montessori Society
[8352]
9525 Georgia Ave., No. 200
Silver Spring, MD 20910

PH: (301)589-1127
Fax: (301)920-0764
Havis, Lee, Exec. Dir.

International NGO Safety and
Security Association **[12685]**
PO Box 7236
Silver Spring, MD 20907
PH: (202)643-6435
Crowley, Dominic, Chmn. of the Bd.

International Partners [12168]
15437 Tindlay St.
Silver Spring, MD 20905
PH: (301)318-2545
Fax: (301)587-3299
Stern, Andrew, Treasurer

International Partnership for Microbi-
cides **[13550]**
8401 Colesville Rd., Ste. 200
Silver Spring, MD 20910
PH: (301)608-2221
Fax: (301)608-2241
Rosenberg, Zeda F., CEO, Founder

International Possibilities Unlimited
[19127]
Metro Plz. II
8403 Colesville Rd., Ste. 865
Silver Spring, MD 20910
PH: (301)562-0883
Fax: (301)562-8084
Robinson, Deborah, Exec. Dir.,
Founder

International Religious Liberty As-
sociation **[19029]**
12501 Old Columbia Pke.
Silver Spring, MD 20904
PH: (301)680-6683
Fax: (301)680-6695
Graz, Dr. John, Sec. Gen.

International Society for
Performance Improvement **[8687]**
PO Box 13035
Silver Spring, MD 20910
PH: (301)587-8570
Fax: (301)587-8573
Wittkuhn, Klaus, President

The Jewish Peace Lobby [18270]
PO Box 7778
Silver Spring, MD 20907
PH: (301)589-8764
Fax: (301)589-2722
Segal, Dr. Jerome M., President

Leadership Conference of Women
Religious **[19854]**
8808 Cameron St.
Silver Spring, MD 20910-4152
PH: (301)588-4955
Fax: (301)587-4575
Mock, Janet, Mem.

Medical Care Development
International **[15483]**
8401 Colesville Rd., Ste. 425
Silver Spring, MD 20910-3391
PH: (301)562-1920
Fax: (301)562-1921
Battista, Mark, CEO, President

National Association of the Deaf
[15200]
8630 Fenton St., Ste. 820
Silver Spring, MD 20910
PH: (301)587-1788
Fax: (301)587-1791
Rosenblum, Howard A., CEO

National Association of Passport and
Visa Services **[3386]**
1417 Highland Dr.
Silver Spring, MD 20910
PH: (301)650-2321

National Association of Pastoral
Musicians **[8381]**
962 Wayne Ave., Ste. 210
Silver Spring, MD 20910-4461
PH: (240)247-3000
Fax: (240)247-3001
Hilgartner, Richard, President

National Association for Public
Health Information Technology
[6748]
962 Wayne Ave., Ste. 701
Silver Spring, MD 20910
PH: (301)563-6001

National Association for Public
Health Statistics and Information
Systems **[5718]**
962 Wayne Ave., Ste. 701
Silver Spring, MD 20910
PH: (301)563-6001
Fax: (301)563-6012
Potrzebowski, Patricia, PhD, Exec.
Dir.

National Association of School
Nurses **[16154]**
1100 Wayne Ave., Ste. 925
Silver Spring, MD 20910
PH: (240)821-1130
Toll free: 866-627-6767
Fax: (301)585-1791
Mazyck, Donna, MS, RN, NCSN,
Exec. Dir.

National Association of State Direc-
tors of Career Technical Education
Consortium **[8739]**
8484 Georgia Ave., Ste. 320
Silver Spring, MD 20910
PH: (301)588-9630
(301)588-9635
Fax: (301)588-9631
Green, Kimberly A., Exec. Dir.

National Association of State Utility
Consumer Advocates **[5834]**
8380 Colesville Rd., Ste. 101
Silver Spring, MD 20910
PH: (301)589-6313
Fax: (301)589-6380
Nelson, Robert, President

National Black Nurses Association
[16156]
8630 Fenton St., Ste. 330
Silver Spring, MD 20910-3803
PH: (301)589-3200
Fax: (301)589-3223
Gorham, Millicent, Exec. Dir.

National Board for Certified Clinical
Hypnotherapists **[15365]**
1110 Fidler Ln., Ste. 1218
Silver Spring, MD 20910
PH: (301)608-0123
Toll free: 800-449-8144
Fax: (301)588-9535
Klein, Ron, CACC, Exec. Dir.

National Catholic Office for the Deaf
[19879]
c/o Arrow Bookkeeping
8737 Colesville Rd., Ste. 501
Silver Spring, MD 20910
PH: (301)577-1684
Rhoades, Rev. Kevin C., Rep.

National Clearinghouse for English
Language Acquisition **[7789]**
8757 Georgia Ave., Ste. 460
Silver Spring, MD 20910-3750
Toll free: 866-347-6864

National Coalition Building Institute
[17988]
Metro Plaza Bldg.
8403 Colesville Rd., Ste. 1100

Silver Spring, MD 20910
PH: (202)785-9400
Fax: (202)785-3385
Brown, Cherie R., Exec. Dir.

National Coalition for Cancer Survi-
vorship **[14024]**
1010 Wayne Ave., Ste. 315
Silver Spring, MD 20910
Toll free: 877-622-7937
Kappel, Michael L., CEO, Act. Pres.

National Council for the Social Stud-
ies **[8566]**
8555 16th St., Ste. 500
Silver Spring, MD 20910
PH: (301)588-1800
Toll free: 800-683-0812
Fax: (301)588-2049
Daly, Timothy, Dir. of Admin.

National Council for the Traditional
Arts **[9330]**
8757 Georgia Ave., Ste. 450
Silver Spring, MD 20910
PH: (301)565-0654
Fax: (301)565-0472
Olin, Julia, Exec. Dir.

National Dance Education Organiza-
tion **[22762]**
8609 2nd Ave., Ste. 203-B
Silver Spring, MD 20910
PH: (301)585-2880
Fax: (301)585-2888
McGreevy-Nichols, Susan, Exec. Dir.

National Drug Strategy Network
[17920]
Criminal Justice Policy Foundation
8730 Georgia Ave., Ste. 400
Silver Spring, MD 20910
PH: (301)589-6020
Fax: (301)589-5056
Sterling, Eric E., Coord.

National Medical Association **[15741]**
8403 Colesville Rd., Ste. 920
Silver Spring, MD 20910
PH: (202)347-1895
Lenoir, Michael A., MD, Contact

National Ready Mixed Concrete As-
sociation **[793]**
900 Spring St.
Silver Spring, MD 20910
PH: (301)587-1400
Garbini, Robert A., PE, President

National Vulvodynia Association
[17762]
PO Box 4491
Silver Spring, MD 20914-4491
PH: (301)299-0775
Fax: (301)299-3999
Veasley, Ms. Christin, Mem.

NTL Institute **[7914]**
8380 Colesville Rd., Ste. 560
Silver Spring, MD 20910
PH: (301)565-3200
Osborne, David, Chmn. of the Bd.

The Obesity Society **[16263]**
8757 Georgia Ave., Ste. 1320
Silver Spring, MD 20910-3757
PH: (301)563-6526
Toll free: 800-974-3084
Fax: (301)563-6595
Dhurandhar, Nikhil V., PhD,
President

Peace Action **[18757]**
8630 Fenton St., Ste. 524
Silver Spring, MD 20910-3800
PH: (301)565-4050
Fax: (301)565-0850
Martin, Kevin, Exec. Dir.

Peace Action Education Fund
[18758]
Montgomery Ctr., Ste. 524
8630 Fenton St.
Silver Spring, MD 20910
PH: (301)565-4050
Fax: (301)565-0850
Martin, Kevin, Exec. Dir.

Population Association of America
[6368]
8630 Fenton St., Ste. 722
Silver Spring, MD 20910
PH: (301)565-6710
Fax: (301)565-7850
Staudt, Danielle, Exec. Dir.

Proutist Universal **[19116]**
2005 Wheaton Haven Ct.
Silver Spring, MD 20902
PH: (202)239-1171
Fax: (202)207-3525

Pulmonary Hypertension Association
[15350]
801 Roeder Rd., Ste. 1000
Silver Spring, MD 20910
PH: (301)565-3004
Toll free: 800-748-7274
Fax: (301)565-3994
White, Stephen L., Chairman

Salute Military Golf Association
[22894]
Argyle Country Club
14600 Argyle Club Rd.
Silver Spring, MD 20906-1999
PH: (301)500-7449
(301)525-1639
Estes, Jim, Founder

Seafood Choices Alliance **[3037]**
8401 Colesville Rd., Ste. 500
Silver Spring, MD 20910
PH: (301)495-9570
Fax: (301)495-4846
Martin, Dawn M., President

SeaWeb **[4473]**
8401 Colesville Rd., Ste. 1100
Silver Spring, MD 20910
PH: (301)495-9570
Toll free: 888-473-2932
Fax: (301)495-4846
Martin, Dawn M., President

Security Industry Association **[3069]**
8405 Colesville Rd., Ste. 500
Silver Spring, MD 20910
PH: (301)804-4700
Fax: (301)804-4701
Stroia, John, V. Chmn. of the Exec.
Committee

Sikh Council on Religion and Education **[20603]**
2621 University Blvd. W
Silver Spring, MD 20902
PH: (202)460-0630
(301)946-2800
Singh, Dr. Rajwant, Chairman

Soccer Industry Council of America
[3146]
c/o Sports & Fitness Industry Association
8505 Fenton St., Ste. 211
Silver Spring, MD 20910
PH: (301)495-6321
Fax: (301)495-6322
Cove, Tom, CEO, President

Solid Waste Association of North
America **[5846]**
1100 Wayne Ave., Ste. 650
Silver Spring, MD 20910
Toll free: 800-467-9262
Fax: (301)589-7068
Skinner, John H., PhD, Officer

Sports and Fitness Industry Associa-
tion **[3147]**
8505 Fenton St., Ste. 211
Silver Spring, MD 20910
PH: (301)495-6321
Fax: (301)495-6322
Cove, Tom, CEO, President

Street Law **[5553]**
1010 Wayne Ave., Ste. 870
Silver Spring, MD 20910
PH: (301)589-1130
Fax: (301)589-1131
Arbetman, Lee, Exec. Dir.

Telecommunications for the Deaf &
Hard of Hearing, Inc. **[15211]**
8630 Fenton St., Ste. 121
Silver Spring, MD 20910-3803
Stout, Claude, Exec. Dir.

Trees for the Future **[4736]**
1400 Spring St., Ste. 150
Silver Spring, MD 20910-2750
PH: (301)565-0630
Toll free: 800-643-0001
Moore, Dr. John R., Chairman

Truck Mixer Manufacturers Bureau
[333]
900 Spring St.
Silver Spring, MD 20910
PH: (301)587-1400
Garbini, Robert, Exec. Sec.

Tuberous Sclerosis Alliance **[15997]**
801 Roeder Rd., Ste. 750
Silver Spring, MD 20910
PH: (301)562-9890
Toll free: 800-225-6872
Fax: (301)562-9870
Rosbeck, Kari Luther, President,
CEO

United Burundian-American Com-
munity Association **[18531]**
14339 Rosetree Ct.
Silver Spring, MD 20906
PH: (240)669-6305
Fax: (240)669-6305
Niyiragira, Oscar, President

United States Association for Body
Psychotherapy **[16947]**
8639 B 16th St., Ste. 119
Silver Spring, MD 20910
PH: (202)466-1619
Swafford, Katy, PhD, Mem.

Uplift a Child International **[11280]**
8705 Kodiak Dr.
Silver Spring, MD 20903-3500
PH: (301)768-3020
(240)832-9234
Vonumu, Rena, Founder

Vietnam Veterans of America
[19227]
8719 Colesville Rd., Ste. 100
Silver Spring, MD 20910
PH: (301)585-4000
Toll free: 800-882-1316
Fax: (301)585-0519
Rowan, Mr. John, President

Wildlife Habitat Council **[3967]**
8737 Colesville Rd., Ste. 800
Silver Spring, MD 20910
PH: (301)588-8994
Bonneau, Josiane, Director

Women Proutists **[19123]**
2005 Wheaton Haven Ct.
Silver Spring, MD 20902
PH: (202)239-1171
Fax: (202)207-3525

Women's Alliance for Theology, Ethics and Ritual **[20648]**
8121 Georgia Ave., Ste. 310
Silver Spring, MD 20910

PH: (301)589-2509
Fax: (301)589-3150
Hunt, Ms. Mary E., PhD, Founder, Director

Women's Aquatic Network [6808]
c/o Daniel Basta, Advisor
NOAA National Marine Sanctuary
1305 E West Hwy., 11th Fl.
Silver Spring, MD 20910
Basta, Daniel, Advisor

Air Force Sergeants Association [5586]
5211 Auth Rd.
Suitland, MD 20746
PH: (301)899-3500
Toll free: 800-638-0594
Fax: (301)899-8136
Stevenson, Mark, COO

Alliance for Green Heat [6447]
6930 Carroll Ave., No. 407
Takoma Park, MD 20912
PH: (301)841-7755
(301)204-9562
Fax: (301)270-4000
Ackerly, John, President, Founder

Beyond Nuclear [18742]
6930 Carroll Ave., Ste. 400
Takoma Park, MD 20912
PH: (301)270-2209
Fax: (301)270-4000
Caldicott, Helen, President, Founder

Catholic Volunteer Network [19818]
6930 Carroll Ave., Ste. 820
Takoma Park, MD 20912
PH: (301)270-0900
Toll free: 800-543-5046
Fax: (301)270-0901
Lindsay, James, Exec. Dir.

Ecumenical Program on Central America and the Caribbean [18619]
102 Park Ave.
Takoma Park, MD 20912
PH: (240)770-8405
Hutchison, Whit, Director

FairVote [18909]
6930 Carroll Ave., Ste. 240
Takoma Park, MD 20912
PH: (301)270-4616
Richie, Robert, Exec. Dir.

Institute for Conservation Leadership [4069]
6930 Carroll Ave., Ste. 1050
Takoma Park, MD 20912
PH: (301)270-2900
Fax: (301)270-0610
Russell, Dianne J., President

Institute for Energy and Environmental Research [6489]
6935 Laurel Ave., Ste. 201
Takoma Park, MD 20912
PH: (301)270-5500
Fax: (301)270-3029
Makhijani, Arjun, PhD, President

Nuclear Information and Resource Service [18734]
6930 Carroll Ave., Ste. 340
Takoma Park, MD 20912
PH: (301)270-6477
Fax: (301)270-4291
Mariotte, Michael, President

Promicrofinance International [11849]
7777 Maple Ave., Apt. 208
Takoma Park, MD 20912
PH: (301)379-6127
Amani, Lwanzo, CEO

River Management Society [3934]
PO Box 5750
Takoma Park, MD 20913-5750
PH: (301)585-4677
Shimoda, Risa, Exec. Dir.

SMA Lay Missionaries [20463]
256 Manor Cir.
Takoma Park, MD 20912
PH: (301)891-2037
Fax: (301)270-6370
Hicks, Theresa, Coord.

South Asian Americans Leading Together [19131]
6930 Carroll Ave., Ste. 506
Takoma Park, MD 20912-4480
PH: (301)270-1855
Fax: (301)270-1882
Iyer, Deepa, Advisor

The TLT Group [7299]
PO Box 5643
Takoma Park, MD 20913-5643
PH: (301)270-8312
Gilbert, Sally, Dir. of Admin., Director

International Nippon Collectors Club [21582]
8 Geoley Ct.
Thurmont, MD 21788
Bittner, Dick, Membership Chp.

Child Health Foundation [14173]
110 E Ridgely Rd.
Timonium, MD 21093
PH: (410)992-5512
Black, Maureen, PhD, Chairperson

Foundation for PSP/CBD and Related Brain Diseases [14577]
30 E Padonia Rd., Ste. 201
Timonium, MD 21093-2308
PH: (410)785-7004
Toll free: 800-457-4777
Fax: (410)785-7009
Zyne, Richard G., Mem.

International Metal Decorators Association [1538]
9574 Deereco Rd.
Timonium, MD 21093
PH: (410)252-5205
Fax: (410)628-8079
Hurley, Art, President

Optometric Extension Program Foundation [16435]
2300 York Rd., Ste. 113
Timonium, MD 21093
PH: (410)561-3791
Fax: (410)252-1719
Lewis, Robin D., President

Parents' Choice Foundation [12422]
201 W Padonia Rd., Ste. 303
Timonium, MD 21093
PH: (410)308-3858
Fax: (410)308-3877
Green, Claire S., President

Coalition of Urban and Metropolitan Universities [7630]
8000 York Rd.
Towson, MD 21252
PH: (410)704-3700
Guarasci, Richard, President

Council of Parent Attorneys and Advocates [8582]
PO Box 6767
Towson, MD 21285
Toll free: 844-426-7224
Fax: (410)372-0209
Marshall, Denise, MS, Exec. Dir.

Council on Quality and Leadership [12321]
100 West Rd., Ste. 300
Towson, MD 21204

PH: (410)583-0060
(410)961-8124
Beattie, William, Chmn. of the Bd.

Immune Deficiency Foundation [15379]
110 West Rd., Ste. 300
Towson, MD 21204
Toll free: 800-296-4433
Fax: (410)321-9165
Boyle, Marcia, Founder, President

International Organization for Mycoplasmology [6084]
c/o Gail Gasparich, Treasurer
Towson University
8000 York Rd.
Towson, MD 21252
Gasparich, Gail, Treasurer

Phi Alpha Delta [23804]
606 Baltimore Ave., Ste. 303
Towson, MD 21204
PH: (410)347-3118
Sagan, Andrew, II, Exec. Dir.

Edgar Allan Poe Society of Baltimore [9091]
c/o Jeffrey A. Savoye, Secretary/Treasurer
1610 Dogwood Hill Rd.
Towson, MD 21286-1506
PH: (410)821-1285

The Society of Military Orthopaedic Surgeons [15841]
110 West Rd., Ste. 227
Towson, MD 21204
Toll free: 866-494-1778
Fax: (410)494-0515
Gerlinger, Col. Tad, MD, Rep.

Skinner Leadership Institute [20162]
PO Box 190
Tracys Landing, MD 20779
PH: (301)261-9800
Fax: (443)498-4935
Williams Skinner, Dr. Barbara, Founder, President

Space Transportation Association [5876]
4305 Underwood St.
University Park, MD 20782
PH: (703)855-3917
Coleman, Richard, President

Aaron Burr Association [10317]
c/o Stuart Johnson, President
1004 Butterworth Ln.
Upper Marlboro, MD 20774-2205
Fax: (301)350-5700
Johnson, Stuart F., President

International Association of Machinists and Aerospace Workers [23388]
9000 Machinists Pl.
Upper Marlboro, MD 20772-2687
PH: (301)967-4500
Martinez, Jr., Robert, President

Machinists Non-Partisan Political League [23448]
c/o International Association of Machinists and Aerospace Workers
9000 Machinists Pl.
Upper Marlboro, MD 20772-2687
PH: (301)967-4500
Buffenbarger, R. Thomas, President

Mocha Moms, Inc. [13384]
PO Box 1995
Upper Marlboro, MD 20773
Toll free: 877-456-7667
Mattox, Kuae Kelch, President

Shout Global Health [15496]
103 Azalea Ct.
Upper Marlboro, MD 20774-1668

PH: (240)293-3652
Akiyode, Olufunke, Exec. Dir.

Tamika and Friends, Inc. [14072]
PO Box 2942
Upper Marlboro, MD 20773-2942
Toll free: 866-595-2448
Felder, Tamika L., Founder

Dysautonomia Youth Network of America [15927]
1301 Greengate Ct.
Waldorf, MD 20601
PH: (301)705-6995
Dominelli, Debra L., Founder

North American Conference of Separated and Divorced Catholics [11686]
PO Box 568
Waldorf, MD 20604-0568
Toll free: 855-727-2269
Fax: (855)729-8751
Exman, Delphine, VP

International Society for Ethical Psychology and Psychiatry [16830]
5884 Joshua Pl.
Welcome, MD 20693
Galves, Albert, Ph.D., Director

Association of Independent Research Institutes [7086]
c/o David A. Issing, Executive Director
PO Box 844
Westminster, MD 21157
Issing, David, Exec. Dir.

Credit Research Foundation [1230]
1812 Baltimore Blvd., Ste. H
Westminster, MD 21157
PH: (443)821-3000
Fax: (443)821-3627
Balduino, William, President

Hope for Haiti [11377]
PO Box 496
Westminster, MD 21158-0496
PH: (410)635-4348
House, Brian, Founder

Libertarians for Life [18643]
13424 Hathaway Dr.
Wheaton, MD 20906
PH: (301)460-4141
Gordon, Doris, Founder, Coord.

National Association for Bilingual Education [7534]
c/o Ana G. Mendez University System
1106 Veirs Mills Rd., No. L-1
Wheaton, MD 20902
PH: (240)450-3700
Fax: (240)450-3799
Gomez, Leo, PhD, Rep.

The Public Lands Alliance [4580]
2401 Blueridge Ave., Ste. 303
Wheaton, MD 20902
PH: (301)946-9475
Fax: (301)946-9478
Cole, Jerryne, President

Farmers and Hunters Feeding the Hungry [12084]
PO Box 323
Williamsport, MD 21795
PH: (301)739-3000
Toll free: 866-438-3434
Fax: (301)745-6337
Wilson, Josh, Exec. Dir.

AMD Alliance International [17680]
10519 Old Court Rd.
Woodstock, MD 21163
Sharma, Mr. Narinder, President, CEO

MASSACHUSETTS

Ahern Association [20775]
298 Central St.
Acton, MA 01720-2444
Ahern, Dennis J., Secretary

Chinese Entrepreneur Association
[622]
PO Box 2752
Acton, MA 01720
PH: (978)266-1254
Ren, Justin, Mem.

Cliff Richard Fan Club of America
[24030]
c/o Heidi Schmelzer
3 Kelley Rd.
Acton, MA 01720-3614
Schmelzer, Heidi, Director

Jhamtse International [13011]
25 Duggan Rd.
Acton, MA 01720
PH: (978)502-6452
Foley, Mark, President, Secretary

Clan Chisholm Society - United
States [20802]
19 Green Meadow Dr.
Acushnet, MA 02743-1603
Chisholm, Kenneth, Secretary

Alliance for Renewable Energy
[6448]
PO Box 63
Amherst, MA 01004
PH: (413)549-8118
Barber, Lois, Exec. Dir.

The Association for Environmental
Health and Sciences [4684]
150 Fearing St.
Amherst, MA 01002-1941
PH: (413)549-5170
Fax: (413)549-0579
Kostecki, Paul, PhD, Editor, Exec.
Dir.

Association of Nutrition Departments
and Programs [16208]
c/o Dr. Nancy Cohen, Chairperson
University of Massachusetts-
Amherst, Chenoweth Lab
100 Holdsworth Way
Amherst, MA 01003
Cohen, Dr. Nancy, Chairperson

Center for Popular Economics
[6385]
PO Box 785
Amherst, MA 01004-0785
PH: (413)545-0743
Kawano, Emily, PhD, Exec. Dir.

Chartered Alternative Investment
Analyst Association [2022]
100 University Dr.
Amherst, MA 01002-2357
PH: (413)253-7373
Fax: (413)253-4494
Kelly, William J., CEO

EarthAction International [4054]
44 N Prospect St.
Amherst, MA 01002
PH: (413)427-8827
Fax: (413)256-8871
Barber, Lois, Exec. Dir., President

International Society of
Environmental Forensics [4073]
150 Fearing St., Ste. 21
Amherst, MA 01002
PH: (413)549-5170
Fax: (413)549-0579

Massachusetts Center for
Interdisciplinary Renaissance Studies [10195]
650 E Pleasant St.
Amherst, MA 01002

PH: (413)577-3600
Kinney, Arthur F., Director

Pan-American Aerobiology Associa-
tion [6095]
University of Massachusetts-Amherst
N239B Morril-I
639 N Pleasant St.
Amherst, MA 01003-9298
PH: (413)545-3052
Fax: (413)545-0964
Muilenberg, Michael L., Secretary,
Treasurer

Safe Haven Project [10552]
6 University Dr., Ste. 206-181
Amherst, MA 01002-3820
PH: (252)295-9073
Butler, David P., Treasurer, Director

Scandinavian Seminar [8090]
24 Dickinson St.
Amherst, MA 01002-2310
PH: (413)253-9737
Kaufmann, William J., Chairman

Society of Experimental Social
Psychology [7072]
c/o Nilanjana Dasgupta, Membership
Chair
Tobin Hall
Dept. of Psychology
University of Massachusetts at Am-
herst
135 Hicks Way
Amherst, MA 01003
PH: (413)545-0049
    (413)545-0996
Silver, Roxane Cohen, President

Union for Radical Political Econom-
ics [6404]
c/o Frances Boyes
University of Massachusetts
418 N Pleasant St.
Amherst, MA 01002-1735
PH: (413)577-0806
Fax: (413)577-0261
Moseley, Fred, Coord.

Verité [11787]
44 Belchertown Rd.
Amherst, MA 01002-2992
PH: (413)253-9227
Fax: (413)256-8960
Musuraca, Michael, Chairman

Veterans Education Project [13251]
PO Box 416
Amherst, MA 01004-0416
PH: (413)253-4947

Yiddish Book Center [9644]
Harry and Jeanette Weinberg Bldg.
1021 West St.
Amherst, MA 01002
PH: (413)256-4900
Fax: (413)256-4700
Lansky, Aaron, Founder, President

Massachusetts Bay Railroad
Enthusiasts [10183]
PO Box 4245
Andover, MA 01810-0814
PH: (617)489-5277
    (978)470-2066
Brown, David W., President

National Glaucoma Society [16397]
PO Box 4092
Andover, MA 01810
PH: (978)470-2555
Toll free: 800-661-6471
Fax: (978)470-4520
Thimons, J. James, Chairman

OneWorld Classrooms [8673]
180 Main St.
Andover, MA 01810

PH: (518)618-0571
Hurteau, Paul, Exec. Dir.

Election Defense Alliance [18180]
82 Hutchinson Rd.
Arlington, MA 02474-1920
PH: (617)538-6012
Simon, Jonathan, Director, Founder

GREY2K USA [4287]
7 Central St.
Arlington, MA 02476
PH: (781)488-3526
Fax: (617)666-3568
Theil, Carey M., Exec. Dir.

International Museum Theatre Alliance [9833]
c/o New England Museum Association
22 Mill St., Ste. 409
Arlington, MA 02476
Pickard, Elizabeth, President

Ugandan North American Associa-
tion [19291]
1337 Massachusetts Ave., No. 213
Arlington, MA 02476
Toll free: 855-873-8622
Atigo, Monday S., President, CEO

WAND Education Fund [18763]
691 Massachusetts Ave.
Arlington, MA 02476
PH: (781)643-6740
Fax: (781)643-6744
Shaer, Susan, Exec. Dir.

Women's Action for New Directions
[18764]
691 Massachusetts Ave.
Arlington, MA 02476
PH: (781)643-6740
Fax: (781)643-6744
Shaer, Susan, Exec. Dir.

Global Health through Education,
Training and Service [15456]
8 N Main St., Ste. 404
Attleboro, MA 02703
Mikhail, Mary, MPH, Exec. Dir.

Manufacturing Jewelers and Suppli-
ers of America [2058]
8 Hayward St.
Attleboro, MA 02703
PH: (508)316-2132
Fax: (508)316-1429
Arnold, Ann, Chairman

The Irish Ancestral Research Association [20976]
2120 Commonwealth Ave.
Auburndale, MA 02466-1909
Atkinson, Greg, Co-Pres.

Shakespeare Oxford Fellowship
[9096]
PO Box 66083
Auburndale, MA 02466
Joyrich, Richard, 1st VP

Association of Loudspeaker
Manufacturing and Acoustics
International [2420]
55 Littleton Rd., 13B
Ayer, MA 01432
Andrews, Peter, President

Lippitt Morgan Breeders Association
[4377]
c/o Grace Yaglou, President
728 Walnut Hill Rd.
Barre, MA 01005
PH: (978)355-2539
    (802)558-8144
Ayers, Wendy, Secretary, Treasurer

Association of Gastrointestinal Motility Disorders, Inc. [14782]
12 Roberts Dr.
Bedford, MA 01730

PH: (781)275-1300
Fax: (781)275-1304
DeGrazia-DiTucci, Mary-Angela,
Founder, President

Day Before Birth [14228]
101 Great Rd., Ste. 201
Bedford, MA 01730
Toll free: 866-213-1140
Fax: (781)313-8188
Ruthen, Russell, President

We Are AWARE [13403]
PO Box 242
Bedford, MA 01730
Bates, Lyn, Bd. Member, Inst.

The Wodehouse Society [9113]
236 Davis Rd.
Bedford, MA 01730-1500
Fowler, Ms. Kris, Treasurer

National Association for Armenian
Studies and Research [8826]
395 Concord Ave.
Belmont, MA 02478
PH: (617)489-1610
Fax: (617)484-1759
Yeghiayan, Raffi P., Chairman

American Shropshire Registry Association [4664]
c/o Becky Peterson, Secretary
41 Bell Rd.
Bernardston, MA 01337
PH: (413)624-9652
Dockter, Darrell, Bd. Member

American Association for Hand
Surgery [14905]
500 Cummings Ctr., Ste. 4550
Beverly, MA 01915
PH: (978)927-8330
Fax: (978)524-8890
McCabe, Steven, MD, Contact

American Association of Pediatric
Plastic Surgeons [16772]
500 Cummings Ctr., Ste. 4550
Beverly, MA 01915
PH: (978)927-8330
Fax: (978)524-0498
Mount, Delora L., MD, Chairperson

American Association of Plastic
Surgeons [14304]
500 Cummings Ctr., Ste. 4550
Beverly, MA 01915
PH: (978)927-8330
Fax: (978)524-0498
Bentz, Michael L., President

American Association for Thoracic
Surgery [17469]
500 Cummings Ctr., Ste. 4550
Beverly, MA 01915-6183
PH: (978)927-8330
Fax: (978)524-0498
Sugarbaker, David J., MD,
Counselor

American Council of Academic
Plastic Surgeons [14306]
500 Cummings Ctr., Ste. 4550
Beverly, MA 01915
PH: (978)927-8330
Fax: (978)524-0498
Kitzmiller, W. John, M.D., President

American Federation for Medical
Research [14287]
500 Cummings Ctr., Ste. 4550
Beverly, MA 01915-6534
PH: (978)927-8330
Fax: (978)524-8890
Ning, MingMing, M.D., President

American Society of Maxillofacial
Surgeons [16444]
500 Cummings Ctr., Ste. 4550
Beverly, MA 01915

PH: (978)927-8330
Fax: (978)524-0498
Lin, Kant Y., Contact

American Society of Plastic Surgical Nurses [16115]
500 Cummings Ctr., Ste. 4550
Beverly, MA 01915
Toll free: 877-337-9315
Fax: (978)524-0498
Spear, DNP, ACNP-BC, CWS, CPSN, Marcia, President

American Surgical Association [17376]
500 Cummings Ctr., Ste. 4550
Beverly, MA 01915
PH: (978)927-8330
Fax: (978)524-0498
Ledgerwood, Anna M., Counselor

Association of Physician Assistants in Cardiovascular Surgery [14100]
500 Cummings Ctr., Ste. 4550
Beverly, MA 01915
PH: (978)927-8330
Fax: (978)927-8330
Lizotte, David, Jr., President

Congenital Heart Surgeons' Society [17386]
500 Cummings Ctr., Ste. 4550
Beverly, MA 01915
PH: (978)927-8330
Fax: (978)524-0498
Backer, Carl L., President

Heart Valve Society [15217]
500 Cummings Ctr., Ste. 4550
Beverly, MA 01915-6534
PH: (978)927-8330
Fax: (978)524-8890
Sarano, Maurice, MD, Officer

International Society for Minimally Invasive Cardiothoracic Surgery [14129]
500 Cummings Ctr., Ste. 4550
Beverly, MA 01915
PH: (978)927-8330
Fax: (978)524-0498
Nifong, Wiley, Comm. Chm.

Pediatric Urology Nurse Specialists [16179]
500 Cummings Ctr., Ste. 4550
Beverly, MA 01915
PH: (978)927-8330
Fax: (978)524-0498
Plachter, Natalie, RN, Chairperson

Phi Sigma [23684]
Dept. of Arts and Sciences
Endicott College
376 Hale St.
Beverly, MA 01915-2096
Wong, Catherine, Exec. Dir.

Plastic Surgery Research Council [14321]
500 Cummings Ctr., Ste. 4550
Beverly, MA 01915
PH: (978)927-8330
Fax: (978)524-8890
Mehrara, Babak, Chairman

Society for Clinical Vascular Surgery [14144]
500 Cummings Ctr., Ste. 4550
Beverly, MA 01915
PH: (978)927-8330
Fax: (978)524-0498
Alger, Mr. Stan, Exec. Dir.

The Society for Pediatric Urology [17562]
500 Cummings Ctr., Ste. 4550
Beverly, MA 01915

PH: (978)927-8330
Fax: (978)524-0498
O'Grady, Lorraine, Exec. Dir.

Society for Surgery of the Alimentary Tract [17406]
500 Cummings Ctr., Ste. 4550
Beverly, MA 01915
PH: (978)927-8330
Fax: (978)524-8890
Matthews, Jeffrey B., President

Vascular and Endovascular Surgery Society [17414]
c/o Administrare, Inc.
100 Cummings Ctr., Ste. 124A
Beverly, MA 01915
PH: (978)927-7800
Fax: (978)927-7872
Maldonado, Thomas S., MD, President

North American Family Campers Association [22721]
PO Box 345
Billerica, MA 01821
PH: (781)584-6443
Richardson, Dennis, President

Basset Hound Club of America, Inc. [21836]
c/o Anne Testoni, Corresponding Secretary
8 Mount Wachusett Ln.
Bolton, MA 01740-2014
Wiginton, Norm, President

Access Project [14970]
89 South St., 7th Fl.
Boston, MA 02111
Dunham, Cathy, President

AfriHope International, Inc. [10471]
PO Box 190796
Boston, MA 02119
PH: (617)957-1613
Osemwenkhae, Steve, Contact

Agua Ecuador [13313]
183 Marlborough St., Apt. 2
Boston, MA 02116
PH: (443)858-5869
Harding, Alex, Founder

Aid to Incarcerated Mothers [11515]
434 Massachusetts Ave. 5th Fl., Ste. 503
Boston, MA 02118
PH: (617)536-0058
Fox, Jean, CEO, Founder

Albanian American Medical Society [15702]
58 E Springfield St., Ste. 2
Boston, MA 02118
PH: (617)236-0113
Fax: (617)236-0113
Coku, Lindita, MD, Mem.

Alliance for the Prudent Use of Antibiotics [16631]
M & V, Ste. 811
136 Harrison Ave.
Boston, MA 02111
PH: (617)636-0966
Young, Ms. Kathleen T., CEO

American Autonomic Society [16043]
c/o Christopher Gibbons, MD, President
Beth Israel Deaconess Medical Ctr.
1 Deaconess Rd., Palmer 111
Boston, MA 02215
PH: (952)469-5837
Gibbons, Christopher, MD, President

American Congregational Association [20034]
14 Beacon St., 2nd Fl.
Boston, MA 02108-3704

PH: (617)523-0470
Fax: (617)523-0491
Bendroth, Ms. Margaret, Exec. Dir.

American Council for International Studies [8053]
343 Congress St., Ste. 3100
Boston, MA 02210
PH: (617)236-2051
Toll free: 800-888-ACIS
Fax: (617)450-5601
Jones, Peter, President, Founder

American Institute for Afghanistan Studies [19285]
Boston University
232 Bay State Rd., Rm. 426
Boston, MA 02215
PH: (617)358-4649
Fax: (617)358-4650
Barfield, Thomas, President

American Ireland Fund [18578]
c/o Steve Greeley, Director
211 Congress St.
Boston, MA 02110
PH: (617)574-0720
Fax: (617)574-0730
McLoughlin, Kieran, President, CEO

American Meteorological Society [6854]
45 Beacon St.
Boston, MA 02108-3693
PH: (617)227-2425
Fax: (617)742-8718
Seitter, Keith L., Exec. Dir.

American Physicians and Friends for Medicine in Israel [12207]
2001 Beacon St., Ste. 210
Boston, MA 02135
PH: (617)232-5382
Frogel, Michael, M.D., Contact

American Schools of Oriental Research [9022]
Boston University
656 Beacon St., 5th Fl.
Boston, MA 02215
PH: (617)353-6570
Fax: (617)353-6575
Ackerman, Susan, President

American Society of Law, Medicine and Ethics [15528]
765 Commonwealth Ave., Ste. 1634
Boston, MA 02215-1401
PH: (617)262-4990
Fax: (617)437-7596
Hutchinson, Ted, Exec. Dir., Pub. Dir.

Archaeological Institute of America [5931]
656 Beacon St., 6th Fl.
Boston, MA 02215-2006
PH: (617)353-9361
Fax: (617)353-6550
Antonaccio, Carla, VP

Architectural Heritage Foundation [9374]
Old City Hall
45 School St.
Boston, MA 02108-3204
PH: (617)523-7210
Fax: (617)523-3782
McDonnell, Sean, President

Association of Commercial Finance Attorneys [4995]
c/o Paul Ricotta, Treasurer
1 Financial Ctr.
Boston, MA 02111
PH: (617)542-6000
Manzer, Alison, President

Association for Computers and the Humanities [8003]
c/o Vika Zafrin, Executive Secretary
Boston University Libraries

771 Commonwealth Ave.
Boston, MA 02215
PH: (617)358-6370
Guiliano, Jennifer, President

Association for Textual Scholarship in Art History [8847]
Beacon Hill
112 Charles St.
Boston, MA 02114-3201
PH: (617)367-1670
Fax: (617)557-2962
Cheney, Dr. Liana De Girolami, President, Treasurer

The Autism Research Foundation [13751]
School of Medicine
Boston University
72 E Concord St., R-1014
Boston, MA 02118
PH: (617)414-7012
Fax: (617)414-7207
LaPorte, Courtney, Exec. Dir.

Bostonian Society [9467]
Old State House Museum
206 Washington St.
Boston, MA 02109
PH: (617)720-1713
Fax: (617)720-3289
LeMay, Brian J., Exec. Dir., President

Campaign for a Commercial-Free Childhood [10881]
89 South St., Ste. 403
Boston, MA 02111-2651
PH: (617)896-9368
Fax: (617)896-9397
Linn, Susan, Director

Campus Compact [7749]
45 Temple Pl.
Boston, MA 02111
PH: (617)357-1881
Fax: (617)357-1889
Curley, Maureen F.

Cashmere and Camel Hair Manufacturers Institute [3256]
3 Post Office Sq., 8th Fl.
Boston, MA 02109-3905
PH: (617)542-7481
Spilhaus, Karl H., President

Catholic Democrats [18108]
PO Box 6262
Boston, MA 02114-0016
PH: (617)817-8617
Krueger, Steven, President

Ceres [4038]
99 Chauncy St., 6th Fl.
Boston, MA 02111
PH: (617)247-0700
Fax: (617)267-5400
Lubber, Mindy S., President

Chandler-Grant Society [17697]
Massachusetts Eye and Ear Infirmary
Glaucoma Service, Rm. 829
243 Charles St.
Boston, MA 02114
PH: (617)573-6487
Fax: (617)573-4300
Anderson, John, Contact

The Child is Innocent [10899]
139 E Berkeley St., Ste. 501
Boston, MA 02118
PH: (603)781-8346
Schwartz, Kevin, Director

ChildObesity180 [16253]
Tufts University
150 Harrison Ave.

Boston, MA 02111
Dolan, Peter R., MBA, Chairman

Christian Science Publishing Society
[2776]
210 Massachusetts Ave.
Boston, MA 02115
PH: (617)450-2000
Gerber, Russ, Mgr.

Clean Air Task Force [4539]
18 Tremont St., Ste. 530
Boston, MA 02108
PH: (617)624-0234
Fax: (617)624-0230
Cohen, Armond, Exec. Dir.

Clinton Health Access Initiative
[13536]
383 Dorchester Ave., Ste. 400
Boston, MA 02127
PH: (617)774-0110
Magaziner, Ira C., CEO, V. Ch.

Coalition of Jamaican Organizations
[12213]
351 Massachusetts Ave.
Boston, MA 02115
PH: (617)266-8604
Fax: (617)266-0185
Smith, Dennis, President

Committee for Accuracy in Middle
East Reporting in America [18679]
PO Box 35040
Boston, MA 02135-0001
PH: (617)789-3672
Fax: (617)787-7853
Levin, Andrea, President, Exec. Dir.

Community Catalyst [14991]
1 Federal St.
Boston, MA 02110
PH: (617)338-6035
Fax: (617)451-5838
Restuccia, Robert, Exec. Dir.

Concussion Legacy Foundation
[17282]
PO Box 181225
Boston, MA 02118
PH: (781)790-8922
(781)790-1921
Nowinski, Christopher, Founder

The Conservation Campaign [18017]
10 Milk St., Ste. 810
Boston, MA 02108
PH: (617)371-0526
Cook, Ernest, President

Consortium for Energy Efficiency,
Inc. [1109]
98 N Washington St., Ste. 101
Boston, MA 02114-1918
PH: (617)589-3949
Stockord, Michael, Chairman

Corporate Accountability
International [18745]
10 Milk St., Ste. 610
Boston, MA 02108
PH: (617)695-2525
Louaillier, Kelle, President

Dana-Farber Cancer Institute
[13958]
450 Brookline Ave.
Boston, MA 02215-5450
PH: (617)632-3000
Toll free: 866-408-3324
Benz, Dr. Edward J., Jr., CEO,
President

Design Management Institute [1555]
38 Chauncy St., Ste. 800
Boston, MA 02111
PH: (617)338-6380
Lyon, Anne, Dir. of Comm.

Dollars and Sense [6388]
95 Berkeley St., Ste. 305
Boston, MA 02116
PH: (617)447-2177
Fax: (617)447-2179
Piwko, Paul, Bus. Mgr.

Earthwatch Institute [7090]
114 Western Ave.
Boston, MA 02134
PH: (978)461-0081
Toll free: 800-776-0188
Fax: (978)461-2332
Wilson, Edward

Emerson College Alumni Association
[19322]
99 Summer St., 9th Fl.
Boston, MA 02110
PH: (617)824-8535
(617)824-8275
Rooney, Patrick, Bd. Member

Empower Peace [18782]
240 Commercial St., 2nd Fl.
Boston, MA 02109
PH: (617)912-3800
Raynard, Tricia, Exec. Dir.

Environment America [4057]
294 Washington St., Ste. 500
Boston, MA 02108
PH: (617)747-4449
Alt, Margie, Exec. Dir.

Esophageal Cancer Awareness As-
sociation [13965]
PO Box 55071
Boston, MA 02205-5071
Toll free: 800-601-0613
Small, Rhonda, President

European Club for Paediatric Burns
[16605]
c/o Matthias B. Donelan, MD,
Membership Chairperson
Shriners Hospitals for Children -
Boston
51 Blossom St.
Boston, MA 02114
Rode, Prof. Heinz, Gen. Sec.

Executives Without Borders [631]
281 Summer St., 5th Fl.
Boston, MA 02210
Toll free: 800-790-6134
Goodwin, Robert, Founder

Family Equality Council [11880]
225 Franklin St., Ste.2660
Boston, MA 02110
PH: (617)502-8700
Fax: (617)502-8701
Bernstein, Alan, Bd. Member

Family Firm Institute [3118]
200 Lincoln St., No. 201
Boston, MA 02111-2418
PH: (617)482-3045
Fax: (617)482-3049
Green, Judy L., PhD, President

Federation for Children with Special
Needs [12323]
529 Main St., Ste. 1M3
Boston, MA 02129
PH: (617)236-7210
Toll free: 800-331-0688
Fax: (617)241-0330
Robison, Richard J., Exec. Dir.

Federation of Pediatric Organiza-
tions [16606]
c/o Theodore C. Sectish, MD,
Executive Director
Boston's Children Hospital
300 Longwood Ave.
Boston, MA 02115
Sectish, Theodore C., MD, Exec. Dir.

Flying Kites [10978]
51 Melcher St.
Boston, MA 02210
PH: (401)575-0009
De Bruyne, Leila, Founder, Exec.
Dir.

Foundation for the Advancement of
Midwifery [14230]
PO Box 320667
Boston, MA 02132

Free Software Foundation [6275]
51 Franklin St., 5th Fl.
Boston, MA 02110-1301
PH: (617)542-5942
Fax: (617)542-2652
Stallman, Richard M., President,
Founder

Friends of Ethiopian Jews [17977]
PO Box 960059
Boston, MA 02196
PH: (202)262-5390
Pollack, Susan, Exec. Dir.

Gay and Lesbian Advocates and
Defenders [17898]
30 Winter St., Ste. 800
Boston, MA 02108
PH: (617)426-1350
Toll free: 800-455-GLAD
Fax: (617)426-3594
Bonauto, Mary L., Director

Global Lawyers and Physicians
[14935]
Talbot Bldg.
Boston University School of Public
Health
715 Albany St.
Boston, MA 02118
PH: (617)638-4626
Fax: (617)414-1464
Annas, George J., JD, Founder

Grassroots International [12158]
179 Boylston St., 4th Fl.
Boston, MA 02130
PH: (617)524-1400
Fax: (617)524-5525
Aziz, Nikhil, Exec. Dir.

Green Restaurant Association [2939]
89 South St., Ste. 802
Boston, MA 02111
PH: (617)737-3344
(617)737-4422
Oshman, Michael, CEO, Founder

Haitian Studies Association [11925]
University of Massachusetts Boston
McCormack Hall, Rm. 2-211
100 Morrissey Blvd.
Boston, MA 02125-3393
Michel, Claudine, Advisor

Helping Hands: Monkey Helpers for
the Disabled Inc. [11603]
541 Cambridge St.
Boston, MA 02134
PH: (617)787-4419
Talbert, Megan, Exec. Dir.

Historic New England [9398]
141 Cambridge St.
Boston, MA 02114
PH: (617)227-3956
Fax: (617)227-9204
Nold, Carl R., CEO, President

Informed Medical Decisions Founda-
tion [15686]
40 Court St., Ste. 300
Boston, MA 02108
PH: (617)367-2000
Barry, Michael J., MD, President

InterFuture [8120]
PO Box 51294
Boston, MA 02205
Robbins, David L., Coord.

International Association for Biological and Medical Research [15646]
140 Fenway
Boston, MA 02115
Chen, Tsute, President

International Catacomb Society
[9402]
71 Prince St.
Boston, MA 02113-1827
Hirschfeld, Amy, Exec. Dir.

International Health, Racquet and
Sportsclub Association [2600]
70 Fargo St.
Boston, MA 02210
PH: (617)951-0055
Toll free: 800-228-4772
Fax: (617)951-0056
Moore, Joe, CEO, President

International OCD Foundation
[15776]
18 Tremont St., Ste. 903
Boston, MA 02108
PH: (617)973-5801
Fax: (617)973-5803
Stack, Michael J., Treasurer

International Society of Gynecologi-
cal Pathologists [16290]
c/o Esther Oliva, Secretary
55 Fruit St.
Boston, MA 02114
Fax: (617)724-6564
McCluggage, Wilson Glenn,
President

International Society of Hotel As-
sociation Executives [2106]
374 Marlborough St.
Boston, MA 02115
PH: (617)536-0590
Pappas, Christina, Exec. Dir.

International Society for Low Vision
Research and Rehabilitation
[16391]
243 Charles St.
Boston, MA 02114
PH: (617)573-4177
Fax: (617)573-4178
van Rens, Ger, Mem.

International Sustainable Campus
Network [7634]
c/o Sustainserv
31 State St., 10th Fl.
Boston, MA 02109
PH: (617)330-5001
Schneider, André, President

InterPride [11895]
Boston, MA 02118
Doster, Sue, Co-Pres.

Irish American Partnership [9600]
15 Broad St., Ste. 501
Boston, MA 02109
PH: (617)723-2707
Toll free: 800-722-3893
Fax: (617)723-5478
McAleer, Mary Sugrue, Exec. Dir.

Jaw Joints and Allied Musculo-
Skeletal Disorders Foundation, Inc.
[16483]
790 Boylston St., Ste. 17-G
Boston, MA 02199
PH: (617)266-2550
Glass, Renee, Founder, President

Joslin Diabetes Center [14537]
1 Joslin Pl.
Boston, MA 02215
PH: (617)732-2400
(617)226-5815
Ketner, Saundra, Librarian

John F. Kennedy Library Foundation [9711]
Columbia Point
Boston, MA 02125
PH: (617)514-1550
Toll free: 866-JFK-1960
McNaught, Tom, Exec. Dir.

Kidney Transplant/Dialysis Association, Inc. [17513]
PO Box 51362
Boston, MA 02205-1362
PH: (781)641-4000
Wingren, Ann

Legal Sales and Services Organization [5540]
c/o Beth Marie Cuzzone, Founder
Goulston & Storrs
400 Atlantic Ave.
Boston, MA 02110
PH: (617)574-6525
MacDonagh, Catherine Alman, Esq., Founder, CEO

Les Clefs d'Or U.S.A. [1666]
68 Laurie Ave.
Boston, MA 02132
PH: (617)469-5397
Fax: (617)469-4397
Fermin, Marci, Dir. of Dev.

Media Access Group [11941]
1 Guest St.
Boston, MA 02135
PH: (617)300-3600
Fax: (617)300-1020
McDonald, Ian, Bus. Dev. Mgr.

Mil Milagros [11078]
400 Atlantic Ave.
Boston, MA 02110
PH: (617)330-7382
Blood, Margaret, Founder, Exec. Dir.

Millennium Campus Network [17806]
101 Huntington Ave., Ste. 2205
Boston, MA 02199-7603
PH: (617)492-9099
Vaghar, Sam, Exec. Dir.

MitoAction [15828]
PO Box 51474
Boston, MA 02205
Toll free: 888-648-6228
Balcells, Cristy, RN, Exec. Dir.

Moroccan American Business Council, Ltd. [1969]
1085 Commonwealth Ave., Ste. 194
Boston, MA 02215
PH: (508)230-5985
Fax: (508)230-9943
Alaoui, Moulay M., President

Murder Victims' Families for Human Rights [18428]
89 South St., Ste. 601
Boston, MA 02111
PH: (617)443-1102
Cushing, Renny, Exec. Dir.

Museum of African American History [8785]
14 Beacon St., Ste. 401
Boston, MA 02108
PH: (617)725-0022
Fax: (617)720-5225
Fields, Carmen, Chairman

National Alliance of HUD Tenants [18358]
42 Seaverns Ave.
Boston, MA 02130
PH: (617)522-4523
    (617)233-1885
Fax: (617)522-4857
Lucas, Ed, President

National Consumer Law Center [5106]
7 Winthrop Sq.
Boston, MA 02110-1245
PH: (617)542-8010
Fax: (617)542-8028
Ferry, Michael, President

National Immigration Project [5294]
14 Beacon St., Ste. 602
Boston, MA 02108
PH: (617)227-9727
Fax: (617)227-5495
Kesselbrenner, Dan, Exec. Dir.

National Initiative for Children's Healthcare Quality [14206]
30 Winter St., 6th Fl.
Boston, MA 02108
PH: (617)391-2700
Fax: (617)391-2701
Homer, Charles J., MD, Founder

National Jewish Coalition for Literacy [8251]
134 Beach St., No. 2A
Boston, MA 02111
PH: (617)423-0063
Fein, Leonard, Founder

National Network of Abortion Funds [10432]
PO Box 170280
Boston, MA 02117
Gupta-Brietzke, Shailey, Treasurer

National Partnership for Educational Access [7966]
155 Federal St., Ste. 800
Boston, MA 02110
PH: (617)423-6300
Fax: (617)423-6303
Elliott, Karin, Exec. Dir.

National Patient Safety Foundation [15049]
268 Summer St., 6th Fl.
Boston, MA 02210
PH: (617)391-9900
Fax: (617)391-9999
Anderson, Richard E., MD, Bd. Member

National Student Campaign Against Hunger and Homelessness [12104]
294 Washington St., Ste. 500
Boston, MA 02108
PH: (919)833-2070

National Tay-Sachs and Allied Diseases Association [15973]
2001 Beacon St., Ste. 204
Boston, MA 02135
PH: (617)277-4463
Toll free: 800-906-8723
Fax: (617)277-0134
Manning, Brian, President

New Ecology, Inc. [11412]
15 Court Sq., Ste. 420
Boston, MA 02108
PH: (617)557-1700
Fax: (617)557-1770
Connelly, Edward F., President

New Economy Coalition [17809]
89 S St., Ste. 406
Boston, MA 02111
PH: (617)946-3200
Tanaka, Aaron, Co-Chmn. of the Bd.

New Fuels Alliance [6501]
101 Tremont St., Ste. 700
Boston, MA 02108
PH: (617)275-8215
Coleman, R. Brooke, Exec. Dir.

New Generation Energy [6502]
98 N Washington St., No. 305
Boston, MA 02114-1913

PH: (617)624-3688

NIDCAP Federation International [14246]
c/o Sandra M. Kosta
Neurobehavioral Infant and Child Studies
Enders Pediatric Research Bldg. EN107
320 Longwood Ave.
Boston, MA 02115
PH: (617)355-8249
Fax: (617)730-0224
Als, Heidelise, PhD, Founder

NIDCD: National Temporal Bone, Hearing and Balance Pathology Resource Registry [15665]
243 Charles St.
Boston, MA 02114-3096
PH: (617)573-3711
Toll free: 800-822-1327
Fax: (617)573-3838
Nadol, Dr. Joseph B., Jr., Director

North American Alliance for Fair Employment [1099]
33 Harrison Ave., 5th Fl.
Boston, MA 02111
PH: (617)482-6300
Fax: (617)482-7300
Costello, Tim, Coord., Founder

North American Kant Society [10105]
c/o Pablo Muchnik, President
120 Boylston St.
Boston, MA 02116-4624
Muchnik, Pablo, President

North American Vexillological Association [10298]
PO Box 55701
Boston, MA 02205-5071
Hartvigsen, John M., President

Omega Theatre and the Omega Arts Network [8993]
41 Greenough Ave.
Boston, MA 02130
PH: (617)522-8300
Linden, Saphira, Director

Only a Child [11109]
PO Box 990885
Boston, MA 02199-0885
PH: (781)642-9317
Leger, George, Founder, Exec. Dir.

Organ Clearing House [9991]
PO Box 231127
Boston, MA 02123-1127
PH: (617)688-9290
Bishop, John, Exec. Dir.

Organizers' Collaborative [17997]
33 Harrison Ave., Fl. 5
Boston, MA 02111
PH: (617)720-6190
Fax: (617)848-9513
Cowan, Rich, Founder, Project Mgr.

Oxfam America [12557]
226 Causeway St., 5th Fl.
Boston, MA 02114
PH: (617)482-1211
Toll free: 800-776-9326
Fax: (617)728-2594
Offenheiser, Raymond C., President

Oxfam International Advocacy Office [12177]
226 Causeway St., 5th Fl.
Boston, MA 02114-2206
PH: (617)482-1211
Toll free: 800-776-9326
Fax: (617)728-2594
Offenheiser, Raymond C., President

Partners in Health [12297]
888 Commonwealth Ave., 3rd Fl.
Boston, MA 02215
PH: (617)998-8922
Fax: (617)998-8973
Dahl, Ophelia, Founder, Chairman, Trustee

Peace of Art, Inc. [8994]
PO Box 52416
Boston, MA 02205
PH: (617)435-7608
Hejinian, Daniel Varoujan, Founder, President

Peace First [12440]
25 Kingston St., 6th Fl.
Boston, MA 02111
PH: (617)261-3833
Dawson, Eric, President

Peace in Focus [18817]
281 Summer St.
Boston, MA 02210
Dietrich, Kyle, Exec. Dir., Founder

Private Equity CFO Association [1262]
c/o Citizens Financial Group
28 State St., 15th Fl.
Boston, MA 02109
McLaughlin, Jeff, Exec. Dir.

Public Responsibility in Medicine and Research [19085]
PO Box 845203
Boston, MA 02284-5203
PH: (617)423-4112
Fax: (617)423-1185
Norsigian, Judy, Director

RainforestMaker [4617]
1 Beacon St., Ste. 3333
Boston, MA 02108
Toll free: 877-763-6778
Glassman, Jeffrey, Founder

Reach Out and Read [8489]
89 South St., Ste. 201
Boston, MA 02111
PH: (617)455-0600
Fax: (617)455-0601
Gallagher, Brian, Exec. Dir.

Retirement Income Industry Association [2983]
101 Federal St., Ste. 1900
Boston, MA 02110
PH: (617)342-7390
Fax: (617)342-7080
Gadenne, Francois, Chairman, Exec. Dir.

Road Scholar [7673]
11 Ave. de Lafayette
Boston, MA 02111-1746
PH: (978)323-4141
Toll free: 800-454-5768
Fax: (877)426-2166
Moses, James A., CEO, President

Root Cause [19117]
11 Ave. de Lafayette
Boston, MA 02111
PH: (617)492-2300
Wolk, Andrew, CEO, Founder

Albert Schweitzer Fellowship [10351]
330 Brookline Ave.
Boston, MA 02215
PH: (617)667-5111
Fax: (617)667-7989
Auerbach, Bruce, Chmn. of the Bd.

Second Nature [7971]
18 Tremont St., Ste. 930
Boston, MA 02108

PH: (617)722-0036
Fax: (320)451-1612
White, Timothy P., Chairman

Society of Arts and Crafts [9000]
100 Pier 4 Blvd., Ste. 200
Boston, MA 02210
PH: (617)266-1810
Fax: (617)266-5654
Fernandez, Fabio, Exec. Dir.

Society of Directors of Research in
Medical Education [8337]
136 Harrison Ave., Sackler 321
Office of Educational Affairs
Tufts University School of Medicine
136 Harrison Ave., Sackler 321
Boston, MA 02111
PH: (617)636-6588
Fax: (617)636-0894
Blanco, Maria Alejandra, EdD,
President

Society for Music Teacher Education
[8389]
c/o Susan Conkling, Chairperson
Boston University
233 Bay State Rd.
Boston, MA 02215
Conkling, Susan, Chairperson

Society for Psychological Anthropol-
ogy [7076]
Dept. of Global Health and Social
Medicine
Harvard Medical School
641 Huntington Ave.
Boston, MA 02115
PH: (617)432-2612
Good, Byron, President

Society of University Otolaryngolo-
gists - Head and Neck Surgeons
[16542]
c/o Anand Devaiah, MD, Secretary/
Treasurer
Dept. of Otolaryngology – Head and
Neck Surgery
Boston University School of
Medicine/Boston Medical Ctr.
FGH Bldg., 4th Fl.
820 Harrison Ave.
Boston, MA 02118
PH: (312)202-5674
Fax: (312)268-6280
Bradford, Carol, President

Society for Vocational Psychology
[7077]
Kimberly Howard, PhD, Associate
Professor
Dept. of Educational Foundations,
Leadership, & Counseling
School of Education
Boston University
2 Silber Way
Boston, MA 02215
PH: (617)353-3378
Hammond, Marie, Treasurer

Gin Soon Tai Chi Chuan Federation
[23014]
33 Harrison Ave., Ground Fl.
Boston, MA 02111
PH: (617)542-4442
Chu, Vincent, Contact

South Africa Partners [18500]
89 South St., Ste. 701
Boston, MA 02111
PH: (617)443-1072
Fax: (617)443-1076
Tiseo, Mary, Exec. Dir.

Special Interest Group on Programming Languages of ACM [7060]
c/o Jan Vitek, Chairman
Northeastern University

College of Computer & Information
Science
440 Huntington Ave.
Boston, MA 02115
Fax: (765)494-0739
Vitek, Jan, Chairman

Story Shares [8493]
1313 Boylston St.
Boston, MA 02215
Baigelman, Louise, Founder, Exec.
Dir.

Strong Women, Strong Girls [13400]
262 Washington St., Ste. 602
Boston, MA 02108
PH: (617)338-4833
Hyde, Lindsay, Founder

Supreme Council of the Royal Arca-
num [19495]
61 Batterymarch St.
Boston, MA 02110-3208
Toll free: 888-272-2686
Ferrara, Peter D., Mem.

Tailored for Education [11738]
PO Box 171236
Boston, MA 02117
Kelly, Megan, President, Founder

Teach Plus [11739]
27-43 Wormwood St.
Tower Point, Ste. 410
Boston, MA 02210
PH: (617)533-9900
Coggins, Celine, Founder, CEO

Tear Film and Ocular Surface
Society [16439]
PO Box 130146
Boston, MA 02113
Sullivan, Rose, Operations Mgr.

Technical Assistance Collaborative
[13019]
31 St. James Ave., Ste. 950
Boston, MA 02116
PH: (617)266-5657
Crowley, Sheila, Chairperson

Theta Delta Chi [23937]
214 Lewis Wharf
Boston, MA 02110
Toll free: 800-999-1847
Wood, Richard E., Exec. Dir.

Unitarian Universalist Association
[20556]
24 Farnsworth St.
Boston, MA 02210-1262
PH: (617)742-2100
Fax: (617)367-3237
Morales, Rev. Peter, President

Unitarian Universalist Ministers As-
sociation [20629]
24 Farnsworth St.
Boston, MA 02210-1409
PH: (617)848-0498
Fax: (617)848-0973
Lallier, Janette M., Dir. of Admin.

United for a Fair Economy [18169]
62 Summer St.
Boston, MA 02110
PH: (617)423-2148
Huezo, Jeannette, Exec. Dir.

United States Distance Learning As-
sociation [8000]
76 Canal St., Ste. 400
Boston, MA 02114
PH: (617)399-1770
Fax: (617)399-1771
Collins, George R., President

U.S. ICE Hispanic Agents Association [5295]
10 Causeway St.
Boston, MA 02114
Garcia, Vicente M., President

U.S. National Oral Health Alliance
[14473]
465 Medford St.
Boston, MA 02129
Bush, Douglas M., Bd. Member

VHL Alliance [14865]
2001 Beacon St., Ste. 208
Boston, MA 02135-7787
PH: (617)277-5667
Toll free: 800-767-4845
Fax: (858)712-8712
Ramsey, Karen, Chairperson

VietHope [13270]
133 Clarendon St., No. 170649
Boston, MA 02217-4128
Duong, Quang, Exec. Ofc.

Whole Grains Council [16243]
266 Beacon St.
Boston, MA 02116
PH: (617)421-5500
Fax: (617)421-5511
Baer-Sinnott, Sara, President

Women in Solar Energy [7216]
225 Franklin St., 26th Fl.
Boston, MA 02110
Nicole, Kristen, Founder

Women's International League for
Peace and Freedom [18842]
11 Arlington St.
Boston, MA 02116
PH: (617)266-0999
Fax: (617)266-1688
Harrison, Mary, President

Women's International League for
Peace and Freedom U.S. Section
[18843]
11 Arlington St.
Boston, MA 02116
PH: (617)266-0999
Fax: (617)266-1688
Perry, Candace, Secretary

World Education [7456]
44 Farnsworth St.
Boston, MA 02210
PH: (617)482-9485
Fax: (617)482-0617
Lamstein, Joel H., President

World History Association [9528]
Northeastern University
Meserve Hall
360 Huntington Ave.
Boston, MA 02130
PH: (617)373-6818
Fax: (617)373-2661
Warner, Rick, President

Nuttall Ornithological Club [6963]
c/o David Larson, Vice President
736 Salem St.
Bradford, MA 01835
Larson, David, VP

Catholic Association of Foresters
[19400]
220 Forbes Rd., Ste. 404
Braintree, MA 02184
PH: (781)848-8221
Toll free: 800-282-2263
Anderson, John F., Jr., Secretary,
Treasurer

Child Rights and You America
[10904]
PO Box 850948
Braintree, MA 02185-0948
PH: (339)235-0792
(617)959-1273
Sunderlal, Shefali, President

MIB Group, Inc. [15420]
50 Braintree Hill Pk., Ste. 400
Braintree, MA 02184-8734

PH: (781)751-6000
O'Connor, Chris M., VP, CIO

Human Development and Capability
Association [12002]
PO Box 1051
Brewster, MA 02631
Richardson, Henry, President

National Children's Book and
Literacy Alliance [8249]
PO Box 1479
Brewster, MA 02631
PH: (508)533-5851
Barrett, Mary Brigid, President,
Exec. Dir.

Association of African Studies
Programs [7465]
c/o African Studies Program
Anthropology Dept.
Bridgewater State University
Hart Hall, Rm. 237
Bridgewater, MA 02325-0001
PH: (508)531-2166
Lelei, Macrina, Chairman

Justice Studies Association [12962]
c/o Jo-Ann Della Giustina, President
Dept. of Criminal Justice
Bridgewater State University
Maxwell Library, Rm. 311E
Bridgewater, MA 02325
Della Giustina, Jo-Ann, Ph.D., J.D.,
President

Assumption Guild [19801]
330 Market St.
Brighton, MA 02135
PH: (617)783-0495
Fax: (617)783-8030

International Society for Disease
Surveillance [14589]
26 Lincoln St., Ste. 3
Brighton, MA 02135
PH: (617)779-0880
Streichert, Laura, PhD, Exec. Dir.

Plastic Optical Fiber Trade Organiza-
tion [2459]
c/o Hui Pan, Secretary General
PO Box 35880
Brighton, MA 02135
PH: (617)782-5033
Pan, Dr. Hui, Sec. Gen.

American Medical Resource
Foundation [15437]
PO Box 3609
Brockton, MA 02304
PH: (508)946-0026

American Academy of the History of
Dentistry [14379]
c/o Marc B. Ehrlich, Secretary
1371 Beacon St.
Brookline, MA 02446
Ehrlich, Marc B., Secretary,
Treasurer

Asian Pacific American Medical
Student Association [8306]
c/o Calvin Sheng, Chief Financial
Officer
5 Winchester St., Apt. 202
Brookline, MA 02446
Riutzel, Kevin, President

Cross Cultural Collaborative [9207]
45 Auburn St.
Brookline, MA 02446
PH: (857)261-0474
Schimelman, Ellie, Clerk, President

Cure Alveolar Soft Part Sarcoma
International [13953]
260 Tappan St.
Brookline, MA 02445

PH: (617)731-1143
Landesman, Yosef, PhD, Dir. of Res., President

Facing History and Ourselves National Foundation [9476]
16 Hurd Rd.
Brookline, MA 02445
PH: (617)232-1595
Toll free: 800-856-9039
Fax: (617)232-0281
Strom, Margot Stern, Exec. Dir.

Hellenic Bioscientific Association in the USA [7132]
PO Box 1998
Brookline, MA 02446
Zervantonakis, Ioannis, Treasurer

ICA Group [1081]
1330 Beacon St., Ste. 355
Brookline, MA 02446
PH: (617)232-8765
Ward, Jonathan, Consultant

International Society for Infectious Diseases [15406]
9 Babcock St., 3rd Fl.
Brookline, MA 02446
PH: (617)277-0551
Fax: (617)278-9113
Klugman, Keith, Officer

Orthodox Christian Association of Medicine, Psychology and Religion [16931]
50 Goddard Ave.
Brookline, MA 02445-7415
Christakis, Michael, Bd. Member

SHARED Inc. [15494]
1018 Beacon St., Ste. 201
Brookline, MA 02446-4058
PH: (617)277-7800
Fax: (617)739-5929
Ziemba, Elizabeth A., President

Unitarian Universalist Women's Federation [20631]
258 Harvard St., No. 322
Brookline, MA 02446-2904
PH: (414)750-4404
Thomas, Lynn, VP of Fin. Admin.

American Chinese Medical Exchange Society [15434]
15 New England Executive Pk.
Burlington, MA 01803-5202
PH: (781)791-5066
Fax: (781)402-0284
Kong, Dr. June, President

Generation Excel [15081]
87 Cambridge St.
Burlington, MA 01803
PH: (617)448-8517
Marino, Gary, Founder

International Association for Human Resource Information Management [73]
PO Box 1086
Burlington, MA 01803
PH: (781)791-9488
Toll free: 800-804-3983
Murphy, Kevin, Bd. Member

Organization for the Advancement of Structured Information Standards [7289]
35 Corporate Dr., Ste. 150
Burlington, MA 01803-4238
PH: (781)425-5073
Fax: (781)425-5072
McGrath, Scott, COO

Society of the Companions of the Holy Cross [20115]
Adelynrood Retreat & Conference Ctr.

46 Elm St.
Byfield, MA 01922-2812
Butler, Susan, Contact

ACCION International [17964]
10 Fawcett St., Ste. 204
Cambridge, MA 02138
PH: (617)625-7080
Toll free: 800-931-9951
Fax: (617)625-7020
Taylor, Diana, Chairman

Addgene [6863]
75 Sidney St., Ste. 550A
Cambridge, MA 02139
PH: (617)225-9000
Fax: (617)300-8688
Kamens, Joanne, PhD, Exec. Dir.

African and Diasporic Religious Studies Association [20574]
12 Quincy St.
Barker Ctr.
Department of African and African American Studies
Harvard University
Cambridge, MA 02138
Wood, Funlayo E., Director

Alexander Technique International [13583]
1692 Massachusetts Ave., 3rd Fl.
Cambridge, MA 02138
PH: (617)497-5151
Toll free: 888-668-8996
Fax: (617)497-2615
Behrstock, David, Director

American Academy of Arts and Sciences [9013]
136 Irving St.
Cambridge, MA 02138
Randel, Don M., Chmn. of the Bd.

American Association for Ukrainian Studies [8107]
34 Kirkland St.
Cambridge, MA 02138
Chernetsky, Vitaly, President

American Association of Variable Star Observers [5996]
49 Bay State Rd.
Cambridge, MA 02138
PH: (617)354-0484
Fax: (617)354-0665
Larsen, Kristine, President

American Committee of Slavists [10214]
Dept. of Slavic Languages and Literatures, Barker Ctr., 3rd Fl.
Harvard University
12 Quincy St.
Cambridge, MA 02138
PH: (617)495-4065
Fax: (617)496-4466
Flier, Prof. Michael S., Chairman

Association of Population Centers [6366]
c/o Lisa Berkman, President
Massachusetts Hall
Harvard University
Cambridge, MA 02138
Reither, Eric, Secretary

BioBricks Foundation [6119]
955 Massachusetts Ave., Ste. 330
Cambridge, MA 02139
Million, Holly, Exec. Dir.

Boston Theological Institute [8705]
675 MAssachusetts Ave., 8th Fl.
Cambridge, MA 02139
PH: (617)527-4880
Fax: (617)527-1073
McClenahan, Ann, Exec. Dir.

Central Bureau for Astronomical Telegrams [6003]
Harvard University, Dept. of Earth and Planetary Sciences
Hoffman Lab 209
20 Oxford St.
Cambridge, MA 02138
Green, Dr. Daniel W.E., VP

Cervical Barrier Advancement Society [17195]
17 Dunster St., Ste. 201
Cambridge, MA 02138
Fax: (617)349-0041
Grindlay, Kate, Exec. Dir.

Circle of Women: Reach and Teach Across Borders [8534]
PO Box 381365
Cambridge, MA 02238-1365
Iqbal, Meher, Chmn. of the Bd.

Harry Connick, Jr. Fan Club [24031]
323 Broadway
Cambridge, MA 02139

Consortium on Financing Higher Education [8497]
c/o Dr. Kristine Dillon, President
238 Main St., Ste. 402
Cambridge, MA 02142
PH: (617)253-5030
Fax: (617)258-8280
Dillon, Kristine, President

Council for Responsible Genetics [19084]
5 Upland Rd., Ste. 3
Cambridge, MA 02140-2717
PH: (617)868-0870
Fax: (617)491-5344
Gruber, Mr. Jeremy, Exec. Dir., President

Cultural Survival [9533]
2067 Massachusetts Ave.
Cambridge, MA 02140
PH: (617)441-5400
Fax: (617)441-5417
Fuller, Sarah, President, Chmn. of the Bd.

Diagnostics for All [14996]
840 Memorial Dr.
Cambridge, MA 02139
PH: (617)494-0700
Smith, Marcus Lovell, CEO

Dialogue Foundation [20298]
PO Box 381209
Cambridge, MA 02238-1209
PH: (857)600-1620
Haglund, Kristine, Editor

EcoLogic Development Fund [3999]
186 Alewife Brook Pky., Ste. 214
Cambridge, MA 02138
PH: (617)441-6300
Vallarino, Barbara, Exec. Dir.

EF Foundation for Foreign Study [8071]
1 Education St.
Cambridge, MA 02141
Toll free: 800-447-4273
Fax: (617)619-1401

Electronic Literature Organization [2783]
Massachusetts Institute of Technology
77 Massachusetts Ave., 14N-234
Cambridge, MA 02139-4307
PH: (617)324-4845
Flores, Leonardo, Treasurer

Emerge: Counseling and Education to Stop Domestic Violence [11700]
2464 Massachusetts Ave., Ste. 101
Cambridge, MA 02140

PH: (617)547-9879
Fax: (617)547-0904
Adams, David, Director, Founder

Engaging Schools [18539]
23 Garden St.
Cambridge, MA 02138
PH: (617)492-1764
Toll free: 800-370-2515
Fax: (617)864-5164
Dieringer, Larry, Exec. Dir.

Farm Aid [17788]
501 Cambridge St., 3rd Fl.
Cambridge, MA 02141
PH: (617)354-2922
Toll free: 800-327-6243
Fax: (617)354-6992
Mugar, Carolyn, Exec. Dir.

Gardens for Health International [13538]
9 Waterhouse St.
Cambridge, MA 02138
PH: (845)204-5263
Cronan, Jessie, Exec. Dir.

Generation Rwanda [13446]
16 Highland St.
Cambridge, MA 02138

Global Action on Widowhood [13365]
3 Newport Rd., Ste. 1
Cambridge, MA 02140

Global Coral Reef Alliance [3876]
37 Pleasant St.
Cambridge, MA 02139
PH: (617)864-4226
(617)864-0433
Goreau, Dr. Thomas J., President

Green Pro Bono [5531]
727 Massachusetts Ave.
Cambridge, MA 02139
PH: (617)603-3537
Reiner, Nancy, Founder

Stanislav & Christina Grof Foundation [13626]
PO Box 400267
Cambridge, MA 02140
PH: (617)674-2474
Fax: (617)674-2474
Sloan, Kenneth Edwin, Exec. Dir.

Harvard Environmental Law Society [5182]
Wasserstein Hall
Harvard Law School
1563 Massachusetts Ave.
Cambridge, MA 02138
Ruby, Byron, President

Harvard University I Weatherhead Center for International Affairs [18523]
1737 Cambridge St.
Cambridge, MA 02138
PH: (617)495-4420
Fax: (617)495-8292
Bloomfield, Steven B., Exec. Dir.

Ibis Reproductive Health [17107]
17 Dunster St., Ste. 201
Cambridge, MA 02138
PH: (617)349-0040
Fax: (617)349-0041
Blanchard, Kelly, President

Institute for Defense and Disarmament Studies [18128]
675 Massachusetts Ave.
Cambridge, MA 02139
PH: (617)354-4337
Fax: (617)354-1450
Dean, Amb. (Ret.) Jonathan, President

Institute for Economic Analysis
[6389]
360 Mt. Auburn St., Ste. 001
Cambridge, MA 02138-5596
Atlee, John S., PhD, President,
Director

Institute for Foreign Policy Analysis
[18269]
Central Plz. Bldg.
675 Massachusetts Ave., 10th Fl.
Cambridge, MA 02139-3309
PH: (617)492-2116
Fax: (617)492-8242
Pfaltzgraff, Dr. Robert L., Jr.,
President

Institute for Healthcare Improvement
[15020]
20 University Rd., 7th Fl.
Cambridge, MA 02138
PH: (617)301-4800
Toll free: 866-787-0831
Fax: (617)301-4848
Feeley, Derek, CEO, President

Institute of Near Eastern and African
Studies [7773]
PO Box 425125
Cambridge, MA 02142-0004
Al-Natheema, Wafaa, Director,
Founder

Institute for Resource and Security
Studies [18987]
27 Ellsworth Ave.
Cambridge, MA 02139
PH: (617)491-5177
Fax: (617)491-6904
Smith, John, Accountant

Integrity USA [20182]
770 Massachusetts Ave., No.
390170
Cambridge, MA 02139
Toll free: 800-462-9498
Haines, Matt, President

International Academy of Periodon-
tology [14445]
c/o Alecha Pantaleon
The Forsyth Institute
245 First St.
Cambridge, MA 02142
PH: (617)892-8536
Fax: (617)262-4021
Bartold, Prof. P. Mark, Officer

International Association for
Comparative Mythology [10031]
c/o Dept. of South Asian Studies
Harvard University
1 Bow St., 3rd Fl.
Cambridge, MA 02138
PH: (617)496-2990
Witzel, Michael, President

International Economic Alliance
[1014]
1 Mifflin Pl., Ste. 400
Harvard Sq.
Cambridge, MA 02138-4946
PH: (617)418-1981
Fax: (617)812-0499
McCormick, Van, Director, Founder

Kurdistan Justice and Peace
Academy [19526]
955 Massachusetts Ave., Ste. 252
Cambridge, MA 02139
PH: (617)209-4331
Rahmani, M. Kajal, President,
Founder

LASPAU: Academic and Professional Programs for the Americas
[7635]
25 Mt. Auburn St., Ste. 300
Cambridge, MA 02138-6095

PH: (617)495-5255
Fax: (617)495-8990
DeShazo, Peter, Exec. Dir.

Lincoln Institute of Land Policy
[5402]
113 Brattle St.
Cambridge, MA 02138-3407
PH: (617)661-3016
Toll free: 800-526-3873
Fax: (617)661-7235
Flint, Anthony, Dir. Pub. Aff.

Marketing Science Institute [2292]
1000 Massachusetts Ave.
Cambridge, MA 02138-5396
PH: (617)491-2060
Fax: (617)491-2065
Clippinger, Marni Zea, COO

Medieval Academy of America
[9787]
17 Dunster St., Ste. 202
Cambridge, MA 02138
PH: (617)491-1622
Fax: (617)492-3303
Lyman, Eugene W., Treasurer

The Medieval Academy of America
Committee on Centers and
Regional Associations [9788]
17 Dunster St., Ste. 202
Cambridge, MA 02138
PH: (617)491-1622
Fax: (617)492-3303
Lester, Anne, Chairman

National Bureau of Economic
Research [6397]
1050 Massachusetts Ave.
Cambridge, MA 02138-5398
PH: (617)868-3900
Fax: (617)868-2742
Poterba, James, CEO, President

National Scientific Council on the
Developing Child [14161]
Harvard University
50 Church St., 4th Fl.
Cambridge, MA 02138
PH: (617)496-0578
Shonkoff, Jack, MD, Chairperson

Nieman Foundation for Journalism at
Harvard [8158]
Harvard University
Walter Lippmann House
1 Francis Ave.
Cambridge, MA 02138
PH: (617)495-2237
Lipinski, Ann Marie, Curator

Nonprofit VOTE [12393]
2464 Massachusetts Ave., Ste. 210
Cambridge, MA 02140
PH: (617)357-8683
Miller, Brian, Exec. Dir.

NRN National Coordination Council
of U.S. [19593]
48 Garden St.
Cambridge, MA 02138
PH: (617)640-1390
Fax: (617)267-1617
Prahlad, Mr. K.C., President

One Earth Designs [4092]
PO Box 382559
Cambridge, MA 02238
PH: (617)671-0727
Fax: (617)849-5661
Frank, Scot, CEO, Founder

Our Bodies, Ourselves [17765]
PO Box 400135
Cambridge, MA 02140-0002
PH: (617)245-0200
Rachlin, Joan, JD, Chairperson

Peace Educators Allied for Children
Everywhere [18759]
c/o Lucy Stroock
55 Frost St.
Cambridge, MA 02140
Stroock, Lucy, Contact

Provide [10434]
PO Box 410164
Cambridge, MA 02141
PH: (617)661-1161
Fax: (617)252-6878
Zurek, Melanie, Director

Public Conversations Project
[17953]
186 Alewife Brook Pky., Ste. 212
Cambridge, MA 02138
PH: (617)923-1216
Fax: (617)923-2757
Chasin, Laura, Bd. Member

Rebuild Africa [11424]
38 Porter Rd.
Cambridge, MA 02140
PH: (617)491-3539
Massaquoi, Bill, Founder, Exec. Dir.

Reform Sex Offender Laws [12934]
PO Box 400838
Cambridge, MA 02140
Toll free: 888-997-RSOL
Cordeiro, Jon R., Director

RefugePoint [12717]
689 Massachusetts Ave., 2nd Fl.
Cambridge, MA 02139
PH: (617)864-7800
Fax: (617)864-7802
Chanoff, Sasha, Exec. Dir., Founder

Relief Labs International [12720]
109 Windsor St., Ste. 4
Cambridge, MA 02139
Dixon, William, Founder, President

Right Question Institute [13085]
2464 Massachusetts Ave., Ste. 314
Cambridge, MA 02140
PH: (617)492-1900
Santana, Luz, Director

Root Capital [1264]
130 Bishop Allen Dr., 2nd Fl.
Cambridge, MA 02139
PH: (617)661-5792
Foote, William F., CEO, Founder

Samuel Rubin Foundation [13086]
50 Church St., 5th Fl.
Cambridge, MA 02138
PH: (617)547-0444
Longmire, Kaitlin, Administrator

Sino-American Bridge for Education
and Health [9585]
c/o Anne Watt, Development Committee Director
15R Sargent St.
Cambridge, MA 02140
PH: (617)497-1357
Thanas, Susan C., Chairperson

Soccer Without Borders [23191]
9 Waterhouse St.
Cambridge, MA 02138
PH: (857)264-0097
Gucciardi, Ben, Director, Founder

Society for Institutional &
Organizational Economics [2465]
1575 Massachusetts Ave.
Hauser 320
Harvard Law School
Cambridge, MA 02138

Society for Organizational Learning
[2466]
PO Box 425005
Cambridge, MA 02142

PH: (617)300-9500
Schneider, Frank, President

STG International [7212]
PO Box 426152
Cambridge, MA 02142
Orosz, Matt, Director, President

Teachers Resisting Unhealthy
Children's Entertainment [11165]
160 Lakeview Ave.
Cambridge, MA 02138-3367
Bartolini, Vicki, Contact

Together Against Malaria [15416]
220 Broadway
Cambridge, MA 02139-1904
Coons, Marnie, Contact

Union of Concerned Scientists
[18737]
2 Brattle Sq.
Cambridge, MA 02138-3780
PH: (617)547-5552
Fax: (617)864-9405
McCarthy, James J., Chairman

Unitarian Universalist Service Com-
mittee [20630]
689 Massachusetts Ave.
Cambridge, MA 02139-3302
PH: (617)868-6600
Toll free: 800-388-3920
Fax: (617)868-7102
Schulz, Rev. William F., CEO,
President, Act. Pres.

United States Offshore Wind Col-
laborative [7390]
1 Broadway, 14th Fl.
Cambridge, MA 02142
PH: (617)401-3145
Courtney, Fara, Exec. Dir.

Voices Beyond Walls [13487]
20 Ames St., E15-223
Cambridge, MA 02139
PH: (617)324-0031
Fax: (617)253-3977
Sawhney, Nitin, PhD, Contact

Women Entrepreneurs in Science
and Technology [3505]
1 Broadway, 14th Fl.
Cambridge, MA 02142-1187
PH: (617)682-3703
Fax: (617)588-1765
Glucksmann, Alexandra,
Chairperson

Women in Informal Employment:
Globalizing and Organizing
[13406]
Harvard University
79 John F. Kennedy St.
Cambridge, MA 02138
PH: (617)496-7037
Vanek, Joann, Director

World Science Fiction Society
[10207]
PO Box 426159, Kendall Square
Sta.
Cambridge, MA 02142
McMurray, Pat, Secretary

World Wide Web Consortium [6268]
Massachusetts Institute of Technol-
ogy
32 Vassar St., Rm. 32-G515
Cambridge, MA 02139
PH: (617)253-2613
Fax: (617)258-5999
Westhaver, Susan, Admin. Ofc.,
Memb. Ofc.

WorldTeach [7806]
1 Brattle Sq., Ste. 550
Cambridge, MA 02138-3723

PH: (857)259-6646
Fax: (857)259-6638
Grossman, Karen Doyle, Exec. Dir.

Association of Strategic Alliance
Professionals [2157]
960 Turnpike St., Ste. 3A
Canton, MA 02021-2818
PH: (781)562-1630
Carberry, Christine, Chairperson

International Association for Media
and History [268]
c/o Cynthia Miller, Treasurer
484 Bolivar St.
Canton, MA 02021
Engelen, Leen, Sec. Gen.

Journey Forward [17258]
755 Dedham St.
Canton, MA 02021
PH: (781)828-3233
Toll free: 866-680-5636
Fax: (781)828-4777
Walters, John, VP, Prog. Dir.

MatchingDonors [14623]
766 Turnpike St.
Canton, MA 02021
PH: (781)821-2204
Fax: (800)385-0422
Dooley, Mr. Paul, Founder, CEO

Cranberry Institute [4233]
PO Box 497
Carver, MA 02330
PH: (508)866-1118
Fax: (508)866-1199
Wilson, Bob, Chairman

Citroen Quarterly Car Club [21355]
PO Box 611
Centerville, MA 02632-0611

Families of Adults Affected by
Asperger's Syndrome [17337]
PO Box 514
Centerville, MA 02632-0514
PH: (508)790-1930
Rodman, Karen E., Founder,
President

Intercollegiate Rowing Association
[23110]
1311 Craigville Beach Rd.
Centerville, MA 02632-4129
PH: (857)257-3728
Fax: (508)771-9481
Chapman, Clayton, Director

National Wind Watch [7389]
63 W Hill Rd.
Charlemont, MA 01339
Rosenbloom, Eric, President

MissionSAFE [13459]
PO Box 290799
Charlestown, MA 02129
Flionis, Nikki, Exec. Dir.

International Motor Press Associa-
tion [2687]
783 Old Queen Anne Rd.
Chatham, MA 02633
PH: (508)945-2400
Frisch, Marianne Brunson, Secretary

American Physician Scientists Association [8304]
6 Boston Rd., Ste. 202
Chelmsford, MA 01824
Levi, Moshe, Chairman, Director

Association of Divorce Financial
Planners [1274]
6 Boston Rd., Ste. 202
Chelmsford, MA 01824
PH: (978)364-5035
Glazer, Cheryl, President

International Society for Computer-
ized Electrocardiology [14127]
6 Boston Rd., Ste. 202
Chelmsford, MA 01824
PH: (978)250-9847
Fax: (978)250-1117
Wagner, Susan, Exec. Dir.

National Association of College and
University Mail Services [2644]
6 Boston Rd., Ste. 202
Chelmsford, MA 01824-3075
Toll free: 877-NAC-UMS1
Dobson, Barbara, Treasurer

Society of Depreciation Profession-
als [58]
6 Boston Rd., Ste. 202
Chelmsford, MA 01824
PH: (978)364-5195
Fax: (978)250-1117
Fisher, Rick, President

Society for Clinical and Experimental
Hypnosis [15367]
Commoncove, Ste. 100
305 Commandants Way
Chelsea, MA 02150-4057
PH: (617)744-9857
Fax: (413)451-0668
Johnson, Anne Doherty, Exec. Dir.

Alliance for Nonprofit Management
[252]
12 Middlesex Rd., No. 67061
Chestnut Hill, MA 02467
Toll free: 888-776-2434
Alnes, Judy, Exec. Dir.

Citizens to End Animal Suffering and
Exploitation [10600]
PO Box 67278
Chestnut Hill, MA 02467
PH: (617)379-0535
Kimber, Evelyn, Bd. Member

Forum on European Expansion and
Global Interaction [9478]
c/o Owen Stanwood, Secretary
Stokes Hall, Rm. S347
140 Commonwealth Ave.
Department of History
Boston College
Chestnut Hill, MA 02467-3859
PH: (617)552-6342

Medically Induced Trauma Support
Services [17527]
830 Boylston St., Ste. 206
Chestnut Hill, MA 02467
PH: (617)232-0090
Toll free: 888-366-4877
Fax: (617)232-7181
Kenney, Linda, Exec. Dir., President,
Founder

National Association of Power
Engineers [7054]
1 Springfield St.
Chicopee, MA 01013
PH: (413)592-6273
Fax: (413)592-1998
Morin, Michael, President

Companion Animal Protection
Society [12454]
759 CJC Highway No. 332
Cohasset, MA 02025
PH: (339)309-0272
Howard, Deborah, President, Chmn.
of the Bd.

Workflow Management Coalition
[2197]
759 CJC Hwy., Ste. 363
Cohasset, MA 02025-2115
PH: (781)719-9209
Palmer, Nathaniel, Exec. Dir.

Louisa May Alcott Memorial Associa-
tion [9032]
399 Lexington Rd.
Concord, MA 01742-0343
PH: (978)369-4118
Turnquist, Jan, Exec. Dir.

Earth Drum Council [9231]
PO Box 1284
Concord, MA 01742
PH: (978)985-7421
Two Feathers, Morwen, Contact

Esperanza - Hope for the Children
[10963]
27 Captain Miles Ln.
Concord, MA 01742
PH: (978)808-8967
Collins, Emily, Founder

John Libby Family Association
[20893]
c/o Pat Libbey Davis, President
195 Deacon Haynes Rd.
Concord, MA 01742
PH: (978)369-6250
Davis, Patricia Libbey, President

The Nature Connection [10675]
PO Box 155
Concord, MA 01742
PH: (978)369-2585
Wadsworth, Sophie, Exec. Dir.

Thoreau Society [9104]
341 Virginia Rd.
Concord, MA 01742
PH: (978)369-5310
Fax: (978)369-5382
Frederick, Mr. Michael, Exec. Dir.

World Wide Essence Society
[15272]
PO Box 285
Concord, MA 01742
PH: (978)369-8454
Bier, Deborah, PhD, Founder

American Family Rights Association
[18196]
PO Box 1560
Cotuit, MA 02635

The International Educator [8103]
PO Box 513
Cummaquid, MA 02637
PH: (508)790-1990
Toll free: 877-375-6668
Fax: (508)790-1922
Thrasher, Julianne, Contact

United States Collegiate Ski and
Snowboard Association [23169]
320 Stage Rd.
Cummington, MA 01026-9646
PH: (413)634-0110
Fax: (413)634-0110
Sullivan, Laura, Exec. Dir., Secretary

American Bladder Cancer Society
[13878]
399 Main St., Ste. 2B
Dalton, MA 01226
PH: (413)684-2344
Toll free: 888-413-2344
Kinsella, Cynthia, President, CEO

Adam Hawkes Family Association
[20773]
c/o Cynthia Hawkes Meehan,
President
65 Center St.
Danvers, MA 01923
Meehan, Cynthia Hawkes, President

Epigraphic Society [5936]
97 Village Post Rd.
Danvers, MA 01923

PH: (978)774-1275
Totten, Norman, President

Scleroderma Foundation [17181]
300 Rosewood Dr., Ste. 105
Danvers, MA 01923
PH: (978)463-5843
Toll free: 800-722-4673
Fax: (978)463-5809
Riggs, Robert, CEO

Association of Family Practice Physi-
cian Assistants [15112]
77 Wollcott Ave.
Dartmouth, MA 02747
PH: (774)206-6774
Fax: (508)998-6001
Hughes, Tom, Treasurer

Dedham Pottery Collectors Society
[21648]
248 Highland St.
Dedham, MA 02026-5833
Toll free: 800-283-8070
Kaufman, Jim, Contact

Unitarian Universalist History and
Heritage Society [20628]
70 High St.
Dedham, MA 02026
Holt, Rev. Earl, President

Historic Deerfield [9396]
84B Old Main St.
Deerfield, MA 01342
PH: (413)774-5581
    (413)775-7125
Zea, Philip, President

Association to Preserve Cape Cod
[3814]
482 Main St.
Dennis, MA 02638
PH: (508)362-4226
DeWitt, Ed, Exec. Dir.

Association of Independents in
Radio [454]
1452 Dorchester Ave., 2nd Fl.
Dorchester, MA 02122
PH: (617)825-4400
Fax: (617)825-4422
Schardt, Sue, Mem.

Building Educated Leaders for Life
[8235]
60 Clayton St.
Dorchester, MA 02122
PH: (617)282-1567
Fax: (617)282-2698
Gueye, Dr. Tiffany Cooper, CEO

National Black Women's Society
[13388]
PO Box 240907
Dorchester, MA 02124
Smith, Janeen, President

Operation Paperback [10753]
PO Box 347
Dunstable, MA 01827
PH: (641)715-3900
Honeywell, Chrissy, Contact

United Fly Tyers [22853]
PO Box 148
Dunstable, MA 01827

Alden Kindred of America [20776]
105 Alden St.
Duxbury, MA 02332
PH: (781)934-9092
Osborne, Linda, Mem.

Cystic Fibrosis Worldwide [17139]
474 Howe St.
East Brookfield, MA 01515
PH: (774)230-1629
Messer, Mitch, Treasurer

Official Red Dwarf Fan Club [24088]
c/o Jupiter Mining Co.
PO Box 3152
East Falmouth, MA 02536
Bull, James, Chairman

Association of Reporters of Judicial
  Decisions [5378]
c/o Kevin J. Loftus, Treasurer
157 Pease Rd.
East Longmeadow, MA 01028-3113
Walker, Leah A., Chairperson

National Retail Tenants Association
  [2930]
60 Shaker Rd.
East Longmeadow, MA 01028-2760
PH: (413)525-4565
Fax: (413)525-4590
Kinney, Paul T., Exec. Dir.

Thornton W. Burgess Society [4036]
6 Discovery Hill Rd.
East Sandwich, MA 02537
PH: (508)888-6870
Fax: (508)888-1919
Maggio, Wendy, President

U.S. Life-Saving Service Heritage
  Association [9442]
PO Box 1031
Eastham, MA 02642
Toll free: 844-875-7742
Carlson, Michael S., Secretary

Country Dance and Song Society
  [9247]
116 Pleasant St., Ste. 345
Easthampton, MA 01027-2759
PH: (413)203-5467
Fax: (413)203-5471
Millstone, David, President

Independent Online Booksellers As-
  sociation [2790]
c/o Chris Korczak, Vice-President
PO Box 311
Easthampton, MA 01027
Volk, Christine, VP

Rosenberg Fund for Children
  [11266]
116 Pleasant St., Ste. 348
Easthampton, MA 01027-2759
PH: (413)529-0063
Fax: (413)529-0802
Black, Amber, Dir. of Comm.

SMART [13202]
PO Box 1295
Easthampton, MA 01027

Caledonian Foundation USA, Inc.
  [9883]
PO Box 1242
Edgartown, MA 02539-1242
Munro, Robert J., President

National Women's Sailing Association [22655]
c/o Scottie Robinson
4 Turtle Back Rd.
Essex, MA 01929
PH: (401)682-2064
Robinson, Scottie, Treasurer

Newspaper Association Managers
  [2711]
PO Box 458
Essex, MA 01929-0008
PH: (978)338-2555
Hills, Lisa, President

International Pedicure Association
  [921]
36 Washburn Ave.
Fairhaven, MA 02719
Toll free: 866-326-7573
Bourque, Debra, Exec. Dir.

National Enthronement Center
  [19884]
Box 111
Fairhaven, MA 02719
PH: (508)999-2680
Fax: (508)993-8233
Crotty, Columban, Contact

Stafford Canary Club of America
  [21551]
c/o John Ferreira
207 Rodman St.
Fall River, MA 02721
PH: (508)493-3311
Biers, Carl, VP

Bullseye Cancel Collectors' Club
  [22313]
c/o Stanley Alsis, Treasurer
PO Box 102
Feeding Hills, MA 01030

National Organization for Manyu
  Advancement [19288]
186 Olin Ave.
Fitchburg, MA 01420
PH: (617)388-8992
Egbe, Daniel, Officer

Folk Education Association of
  America [7768]
73 Willow St.
Florence, MA 01062
PH: (413)489-1012
Cattani, Mary, Co-Chmn. of the Bd.,
  Co-Ch.

SavetheInternet.com Coalition
  [18572]
40 Main St., Ste. 301
Florence, MA 01062
PH: (413)585-1533
Toll free: 877-888-1533
Fax: (413)585-8904

Options for Children in Zambia
  [11113]
20 Dassance Dr.
Foxboro, MA 02035
Morgan, John, Officer

Alumni Association - Framingham
  State College [19300]
100 State St.
Framingham, MA 01701-9101
PH: (508)626-4012
Fax: (508)626-4036
Gustafson, Eric, Exec. Dir.

Animal Law Coalition [10577]
c/o Jonathan Stone Rankin
Animal Law Offices of Jonathan
  Stone Rankin
PO Box 3311
Framingham, MA 01705-3311
Allen, Laura, Exec. Dir., Founder

Ovations for the Cure [14040]
79 Main St., Ste. 202
Framingham, MA 01702-2945
PH: (508)655-5412
Toll free: 866-920-6382
Fax: (508)655-5414
Flaherty, Paul, President

The Travel Institute [3400]
945 Concord St.
Framingham, MA 01701
PH: (781)237-0280
Toll free: 800-542-4282
Fax: (781)237-3860
Robb, Brian D., Chairman

Forward in Health [15002]
192 Lawrence St.
Gardner, MA 01440
PH: (978)808-5234
Mulqueen, John, MD, President,
  Founder

Brides Across America [10783]
28 W Main St.
Georgetown, MA 01833
Janson, Heidi, Founder

Save One Life, Inc. [15243]
65 Central St., Ste. 204
Georgetown, MA 01833
PH: (978)352-7652
Fax: (978)225-3492
Kelly, Laureen A., Founder

American Hockey Coaches Association [22906]
7 Concord St.
Gloucester, MA 01930
Bertagna, Joe, Exec. Dir.

National Basketry Organization
  [21772]
PO Box 1524
Gloucester, MA 01930-1524
PH: (617)863-0366
Saint-Pierre, Pamela, Treasurer

NeedyMeds [15609]
PO Box 219
Gloucester, MA 01931
PH: (978)221-6666
Toll free: 800-503-6897
Fax: (206)260-8850
Sagall, Rich, MD, President

Tag and Label Manufacturers
  Institute [3178]
1 Blackburn Ctr.
Gloucester, MA 01930
PH: (978)282-1400
Fax: (978)282-3238
Tibbetts, Mark, President

American Institute for Economic
  Research [6378]
250 Division St.
Great Barrington, MA 01230-1000
Toll free: 888-528-1216
Fax: (413)528-0103
Adams, Stephen, President

Council on Naturopathic Medical
  Education [15859]
PO Box 178
Great Barrington, MA 01230
PH: (413)528-8877
Blackshaw, G. Lansing, President

Association for Gravestone Studies
  [9376]
101 Munson St., Ste. 108
Greenfield, MA 01301
PH: (413)772-0836
Santore, Beth, Trustee

Northeast Sustainable Energy As-
  sociation [6504]
50 Miles St.
Greenfield, MA 01301
PH: (413)774-6051
Fax: (413)774-6053
Marrapese, Jennifer, Comm. Chm.,
  Exec. Dir.

Traprock Center for Peace and
  Justice [18831]
PO Box 1201
Greenfield, MA 01302
PH: (413)522-8892
Sweet, Sher, Bd. Member

VentureWell [6760]
100 Venture Way, 3rd Fl.
Hadley, MA 01035
PH: (413)587-2172
Fax: (413)587-2175
Weilerstein, Philip J., President

American Amputee Hockey Association [23210]
41 Buena Vista Way
Hanover, MA 02339
Crandell, David, MD, President

American Family Therapy Academy
  [11483]
150 Summer St.
Haverhill, MA 01830
PH: (978)914-6374
Fax: (978)914-7033
Arora, Kiran Shahreen Kaur, PhD,
  President

International Polymer Clay Association [22152]
162 Lake St.
Haverhill, MA 01832
Gallant, Alison, President

Art and Creative Materials Institute
  [1527]
99 Derby St., Ste. 200
Hingham, MA 02043
PH: (781)556-1044
Fax: (781)207-5550
Lilly, Joan, President

Children's Melanoma Prevention
  Foundation [13942]
PO Box 254
Hingham, MA 02043
PH: (781)875-1773
Eisen, Maryellen Maguire, RN,
  Founder, Exec. Dir.

College Diabetes Network [14520]
350 Lincoln St., Ste. 2400
Hingham, MA 02043
Roth, Christina, President, Founder

International 210 Association
  [22624]
59 Water St.
Hingham, MA 02043
PH: (781)985-5460
Lemaire, Tom, President

International Naval Research
  Organization [9803]
PO Box 48
Holden, MA 01520-0048
PH: (508)799-9229
Sullivan, David, Office Mgr.

Li-Fraumeni Syndrome Association
  [14836]
PO Box 6458
Holliston, MA 01746
Toll free: 855-239-5372
Perry, Jennifer, President, Founder

Greyhound Friends, Inc. [10631]
167 Saddle Hill Rd.
Hopkinton, MA 01748
PH: (508)435-5969
Coleman, Louise, Exec. Dir.

Alliance for Democracy [18935]
21 Main St.
Hudson, MA 01749
PH: (978)333-7971
Fax: (978)333-7972
Dugger, Ronnie, Founder

Mir Pace International [12700]
137 Hampton Cir.
Hull, MA 02045
PH: (781)925-0950
Weisslinger, Eileen M., Founder,
  Chairman

National Association for Moisture
  Management [1164]
76 D St.
Hull, MA 02045
PH: (781)925-0354
Fax: (781)925-0650
LaPierre, Mr. Rick, President,
  Founder

World Computer Exchange [7660]
936 Nantasket Ave.
Hull, MA 02045-1453
Alam, Muhammad Mukhtar, Bd.
  Member

Mystic Valley Railway Society
[10185]
PO Box 365486
Hyde Park, MA 02136-0009
PH: (617)361-4445
Fax: (617)361-4451
Rylko, Theresa E., President

Titanic Historical Society, Inc. [9778]
PO Box 51053
Indian Orchard, MA 01151-0053
PH: (413)543-4770
Fax: (413)583-3633
Kamuda, Edward S., President

Horn and Whistle Enthusiasts Group
[21662]
c/o Eric C. Larson, Publisher
2 Abell Ave.
Ipswich, MA 01938
Larson, Eric C., Publisher

Quebec-Labrador Foundation [4097]
55 S Main St.
Ipswich, MA 01938
PH: (978)356-0038
Fax: (978)356-7322
Bryan, Robert A., Chairman

Armenian Women's Welfare Association, Inc. [19388]
435 Pond St.
Jamaica Plain, MA 02130
Youssoufian, Annie, Secretary

Bikes Not Bombs [18772]
284 Amory St.
Jamaica Plain, MA 02130
PH: (617)522-0222
Fax: (617)522-0922
Sugerman-Brozan, Jodi, Exec. Dir.

Chlotrudis Society for Independent
Film [9302]
PO Box 301237
Jamaica Plain, MA 02130
PH: (781)526-5384
Colford, Michael, President

Clothes for the World [12646]
294 Chestnut Ave., No. 2
Jamaica Plain, MA 02130
PH: (857)492-3494
Rosenbaum, Erin, President, Direc-
tor

HandReach [13058]
28 Robinwood Ave.
Jamaica Plain, MA 02130
PH: (202)213-9267
Swartz, Brecken Chinn, PhD, Exec.
Dir.

National Center for Fair and Open
Testing [8689]
PO Box 300204
Jamaica Plain, MA 02130
PH: (617)477-9792
Neill, Dr. Monty, Exec. Dir.

The National Spiritual Alliance
[20509]
2 Montague Ave.
Lake Pleasant, MA 01347
PH: (413)367-0138
Midura, Rev. John E., President

History of Earth Sciences Society
[9484]
c/o David Spanagel, Treasurer
PO Box 70
Lancaster, MA 01523
Carneiro, Ana, President

Ancient Accepted Scottish Rite of
Free-Masonry, Northern Masonic
Jurisdiction Supreme Council
[19549]
33 Marrett Rd.
Lexington, MA 02421

PH: (781)862-4410
Toll free: 800-814-1432
Fax: (781)863-1833
McNaughton, John Wm., III, CEO

BasicNeeds US [15763]
9 Meriam St., Ste. 4
Lexington, MA 02420
PH: (781)869-6990
Dougherty, Richard H., President,
Founder

FSH Society [15934]
450 Bedford St.
Lexington, MA 02420
PH: (781)301-6060
   (781)301-6650
Fax: (781)862-1116
Perez, Daniel Paul, President, CEO

Global Warming Education Network
[4064]
8 Northbrook Park
Lexington, MA 02420
PH: (781)863-1400
Fax: (781)863-1441
Shamel, Roger, Founder

Information Technology Services
Marketing Association [2284]
91 Hartwell Ave.
Lexington, MA 02421-3137
PH: (781)862-8500
Fax: (781)674-1366
Munn, David C., CEO, President

International Medical Interpreters
Association [3314]
c/o William Colangeli
33 Bedford St., Ste. 9
Lexington, MA 02420
PH: (617)636-1798
Fax: (866)406-4642
Horton, Juana, President

Organization for Medical and
Psychological Assistance for
Children Overseas [14209]
14 Curve St.
Lexington, MA 02420
Collins, Martha, MD, Director,
President

Vision-Aid [17748]
8 Vine Brook Rd.
Lexington, MA 02421
PH: (781)333-5252
Ramakrishna, Revathy, VP

Women's International Network
[18239]
187 Grant St.
Lexington, MA 02420-2126
PH: (781)862-9431
Hosken, Fran P., Editor

Walden Woods Project [9444]
44 Baker Farm Rd.
Lincoln, MA 01773-3004
PH: (781)259-4700
Fax: (781)259-4710
Henley, Don, Chairman, Founder

Religious Witness for the Earth
[4144]
PO Box 642
Littleton, MA 01460
Bullitt-Jonas, Margaret, Co-Chmn. of
the Bd.

Pomegranate Guild of Judaic
Needlework [21777]
PO Box 60953
Longmeadow, MA 01116-5953
Big, Susan, VP

The Coblentz Society [7224]
c/o Mark Druy, President
41 Wellman St.

Lowell, MA 01851
Carrabba, Mary W., PhD, Treasurer

Light of Cambodian Children [11069]
Mogan Cultural Ctr., 3rd Fl.
40 French St.
Lowell, MA 01852
PH: (978)275-1822
Fax: (978)275-1824
Ye, Pov, President

Plastics Institute of America [7037]
Ball Hall
Plastics Engineering Department
University of Massachusetts Lowell
1 University Ave., Rm. 204
Lowell, MA 01854
PH: (978)934-2575
Fax: (978)934-3089
Crugnola, Dr. Aldo, Exec. Dir.

Society for Analytical Feminism
[10119]
c/o Carol Hay, Secretary/Treasurer
Dept. of Philosophy
University of Massachusetts Lowell
883 Broadway Ave.
Lowell, MA 01854
Norlock, Kate, President

Sustainable Hospitals Project
[15338]
Lowell Center for Sustainable
Production
1 University Ave.
Lowell, MA 01854
PH: (978)934-3386
Fax: (978)452-5711
Galligan, Catherine, MS, Mgr.

World Association for Cooperative
Education [7680]
Wannalancit Business Ctr., Ste. 125
600 Suffolk St.
Lowell, MA 01854
PH: (978)934-1867
Fax: (978)934-4084
van Rooijen, Dr. Maurits, Co-Chmn.
of the Bd.

Daughters of the Nile, Supreme
Temple [19554]
c/o Eleanor Green, Recorder
112 Skyridge St.
Ludlow, MA 01056
Sowers, Marsha D., Chairman

Clan Brown Society [20799]
38 High Rock St.
38 High Rock St.
Lynn, MA 01902-3815

CrossRef [2780]
50 Salem St.
Lynnfield, MA 01940
PH: (781)295-0072
Fax: (781)295-0077
Pentz, Ed, Exec. Dir.

Fire and Emergency Manufacturers
and Services Association [14694]
PO Box 147
Lynnfield, MA 01940-0147
PH: (781)334-2771
Fax: (781)334-2771
Cafaro, Kit, President

International Association for
Religious Freedom, U.S. Chapter
[19027]
c/o Nyla McCulloch
100 Woodland Rd.
Malden, MA 02148

National Association of Trade
Exchanges [3303]
926 Eastern Ave.
Malden, MA 02148

PH: (781)388-9200
Fax: (781)321-4443
Oshry, Gary, Treasurer

Promote Congo [18438]
87 Madison St., Unit 2L
Malden, MA 02148
PH: (781)321-3060
Liwanga, Roger-Claude, Exec. Dir.,
Founder

Green Schools [7893]
PO Box 323
Mansfield, MA 02048
PH: (508)272-9653
   (425)663-1757
Organ, Robin, Exec. Dir., Prog. Dir.

National Green Schools Society
[7897]
PO Box 323
Mansfield, MA 02048
Traggis, Hannah, Director

American Board of Examiners in
Clinical Social Work [13101]
214 Humphrey St.
Marblehead, MA 01945
PH: (781)639-5270
Toll free: 800-694-5285
Fax: (781)639-5278
Booth, Robert, Exec. Dir.

Jews for Animal Rights [10653]
Micah Publications, Inc.
255 Humphrey St.
Marblehead, MA 01945
PH: (781)631-7601
Kalechofsky, Roberta, Contact

Rhodes 19 Class Association
[22662]
c/o Jeff Shoreman, Secretary
34 Ticehurst Ln.
Marblehead, MA 01945-2837
Uhl, Steve, President

Clan Sutherland Society of North
America, Inc. [20844]
c/o Robert F. Sutherland, President
188 Simpson Rd.
Marlboro, MA 01752
Sutherland, George W., Commissioner

Association of Game and Puzzle
Collectors [22046]
197M Boston Post Rd. W
Marlborough, MA 01752
PH: (207)783-8732

National School Development
Council [7792]
28 Lord Rd.
Marlborough, MA 01752
PH: (508)481-9444
Fax: (508)481-5655
Schuhle, Betsey, President

Research Down Syndrome Founda-
tion [14628]
225 Cedar Hill St.
Marlborough, MA 01752
PH: (508)630-2177
Fax: (508)630-2101
Cronin, Carolyn, Exec. Dir.

Students Against Destructive Deci-
sions [12845]
255 Main St.
Marlborough, MA 01752-5505
Toll free: 877-SADD-INC
Fax: (508)481-5759
Scarola, Susan, Chairman

Historic Winslow House Association
[9400]
634 Careswell St.
Marshfield, MA 02050

PH: (781)837-5753
Dougherty, Aaron, Exec. Dir.

Illustrators' Partnership of America
[9349]
845 Moraine St.
Marshfield, MA 02050
PH: (781)837-9152

International Association of Pastel
Societies [8863]
PO Box 512
Marshfield Hills, MA 02051
Haywood-Sullivan, Liz, President

Follow A Dream [11596]
381 Old Falmouth Rd.
Marstons Mills, MA 02648
PH: (508)420-8319
Blake, Jay, Founder, President

All Hands Volunteers [11651]
6 County Rd., Ste. 6
Mattapoisett, MA 02739
PH: (508)758-8211
Campbell, David, Founder, Chairman

Usher Syndrome Coalition [14864]
2 Mill and Main Place, Ste. 418
Maynard, MA 01754
PH: (978)637-2625
Fax: (978)637-2618
Dunning, Mark, Chmn. of the Bd.

Society of the Descendants of the
Colonial Clergy [20763]
17 Lowell Mason Rd.
Medfield, MA 02052-1709

Dignity U.S.A. [20178]
PO Box 376
Medford, MA 02155-0004
PH: (202)861-0017
Toll free: 800-877-8797
Fax: (781)397-0584
Knowles, Alice, VP

International Institute of Forecasters
[6657]
53 Tesla Ave.
Medford, MA 02155
PH: (781)234-4077
Stroud, Ms. Pamela, Dir. of Bus.
Dev.

Charles Ives Society [9940]
c/o Donald Berman, Vice President
and Treasurer
Granoff Music Ctr.
Tufts University
20 Talbot Ave.
Medford, MA 02155
Magee, Gayle Sherwood, President

Law Enforcement Against Prohibition
[5477]
121 Mystic Ave., Ste. 9
Medford, MA 02155
PH: (781)393-6985
Fax: (781)393-2964
Franklin, Neill, Exec. Dir.

Tufts University Alumni Association
[19352]
Office Of Alumni Relations
80 George St., Ste. 100-3
Medford, MA 02155
PH: (617)627-3532
Toll free: 800-843-2586
Fax: (617)627-3938
Kaplan, Kate, President

Hope Through Health [12202]
PO Box 605
Medway, MA 02053
PH: (631)721-5917
Schechter, Jennifer, Exec. Dir.,
Founder

American Board of Abdominal
Surgery [17362]
824 Main St., 2nd Fl., Ste. 1
Melrose, MA 02176
PH: (781)665-6102
Fax: (781)665-4127

American Society of Abdominal
Surgeons [17370]
824 Main St., 2nd Fl., Ste. 1
Melrose, MA 02176
PH: (781)665-6102
Fax: (781)665-4127
Pothier, Diane, Editor, Dir. Ed.

North American Ring Association
[21931]
c/o Brian Branon, President
PO Box 760967
Melrose, MA 02176-0006
PH: (781)307-6540
Branon, Brian, President

First Signs [14160]
PO Box 358
Merrimac, MA 01860
PH: (978)346-4380
Fax: (978)346-4638
Wiseman, Nancy D., Founder,
President

Clan Drummond Society of North
America [20808]
c/o Charles McRobbie, President
6 Bernard Ln.
Methuen, MA 01844
PH: (978)682-0130
McRobbie, Charles E., Jr., President

Children Across America [10913]
23 Pine St.
Milford, MA 01757
PH: (508)381-8107
Fellows, Raymond, Founder, Exec.
Dir.

Merck Family Fund [4081]
PO Box 870245
Milton Village, MA 02187
PH: (617)696-3580
Fax: (617)696-7262
Chamberlin, Nat, President

Taft Family Association [20937]
c/o Patricia Allen, Secretary/
Treasurer
77 Greenfield Rd.
Montague, MA 01351
Allen, Patricia, Secretary, Treasurer

Maria Mitchell Association [6008]
4 Vestal St.
Nantucket, MA 02554
PH: (508)228-9198
     (508)228-2896
Sullivan, Brian, Director

Nurse Practitioner Associates for
Continuing Education [16167]
209 W Central St., Ste. 228
Natick, MA 01760
PH: (508)907-6424
Fax: (508)907-6425
Windle, Karen, Chmn. of the Bd.

Ovations for the Cure of Ovarian
Cancer [14041]
251 W Central St., Ste. 35
Natick, MA 01760
PH: (508)655-5412
Toll free: 866-920-6382
Fax: (508)655-5414
Flaherty, Paul, President, Director

ALS Therapy Alliance [13680]
16 Oakland Ave.
Needham, MA 02492
PH: (603)664-5005
Brown, Robert H., Jr., President

Business Modeling and Integration
Domain Task Force [617]
Object Management Group
109 Highland Ave.
Needham, MA 02494
PH: (781)444-0404
Fax: (781)444-0320
Cummins, Mr. Fred A., Co-Ch.

Catboat Association, Inc. [22605]
262 Forest St.
Needham, MA 02492-1326
Fallon, Tim, Treasurer

Debtors Anonymous [12871]
PO Box 920888
Needham, MA 02492-0009
PH: (781)453-2743
Toll free: 800-421-2383
Fax: (781)453-2745

Global Spatial Data Infrastructure
Association [7269]
PMB 194
946 Great Plain Ave.
Needham, MA 02492-3030
Longhorn, Roger, Sec. Gen.

National CFIDS Foundation [15964]
103 Aletha Rd.
Needham, MA 02492
PH: (781)449-3535
Fax: (781)449-8606
Kansky, Gail R., President

One Hen, Inc. [10821]
PO Box 920048
Needham, MA 02492-0001
PH: (650)400-0987
Bassey, Offiong, Secretary

Reel Recovery [10792]
160 Brookside Rd.
Needham, MA 02492
Toll free: 800-699-4490
Fax: (781)449-9031
Golub, Stan, Exec. Dir.

World Association for Case Method
Research and Application [7099]
23 Mackintosh Ave.
Needham, MA 02492-1218
PH: (781)444-8982
Fax: (781)444-1548
Klein, Dr. Hans E., President, Exec.
Dir.

Veterans of Safety [12847]
22 Logan St.
New Bedford, MA 02740-7324
Brown, Warren K., President

Amazon Promise [12263]
PO Box 1304
Newburyport, MA 01950
Webster, Patty, President

Association of Problem Gambling
Service Administrators [11865]
PO Box 135
PO Box 135
Newburyport, MA 01950-6619
PH: (617)548-8057
Linden, Mark Vander, VP

FRAXA Research Foundation
[17341]
10 Prince Pl., Ste. 203
Newburyport, MA 01950
PH: (978)462-1866
Clapp, Katherine, Founder, President

Online Learning Consortium [7795]
PO Box 1238
Newburyport, MA 01950-8238
PH: (617)716-1414
Fax: (888)898-6209
Cini, Marie, President

Society for Participatory Medicine
[15064]
PO Box 1183
Newburyport, MA 01950-1183
Sands, Danny, Chmn. of the Bd.

American Consumer Credit Counsel-
ing [940]
130 Rumford Ave., Ste. 202
Newton, MA 02466
PH: (617)559-5700
Toll free: 800-769-3571
Fax: (617)244-1116
Trumble, Steven R., CEO, President

Blind Sailing International [22600]
Carroll Center for the Blind
770 Centre St.
Newton, MA 02458

Carroll Center for the Blind [17695]
770 Centre St.
Newton, MA 02458-2597
PH: (617)969-6200
Abely, Joseph, President

Communities Without Borders
[10947]
PO Box 111
Newton, MA 02468
PH: (617)965-4713
Bail, Dr. Richard, Founder, President

Courageous Parents Network
[12411]
21 Rochester Rd.
Newton, MA 02458
Lord, Blyth, Founder

Friends of LADDERS [12235]
193 Oak St., Ste. 1
Newton, MA 02464-1453
PH: (781)860-1700
Bauman, Margaret L., Director

Gambling Portal Webmasters As-
sociation [5256]
95 Wells Ave.
Newton, MA 02459
PH: (617)332-2850
Fax: (617)964-2280

Minga [11079]
PO Box 610004
Newton, MA 02461
PH: (617)584-1305

National Brain Tumor Society
[14598]
55 Chapel St., Ste. 200
Newton, MA 02458
PH: (617)924-9997
Toll free: 800-770-8287
Fax: (617)924-9998
Corkin, Michael

National Pediculosis Association,
Inc. [17012]
1005 Boylston St., Ste. 343
Newton, MA 02461
PH: (617)905-0176
Fax: (800)235-1305
Altschuler, Deborah Z., President

Society for Terrorism Research
[13213]
PO Box 590094
Newton, MA 02459-0001
Walters, Tali K., PhD, Mem.

Fertility Within Reach [14758]
1005 Boylston St., No. 332
Newton Highlands, MA 02461
PH: (857)636-8674
Fankhauser, Davina, President,
Founder

Dante Society of America [9049]
PO Box 600616
Newtonville, MA 02460

PH: (617)831-9288
Vickers, Nancy, Treasurer

Model A Ford Foundation [21436]
PO Box 95151
Nonantum, MA 02495-0151
Smith, Loukie, President

Bichon Frise Club of America
[21841]
c/o Karen Chesbro, Membership
Administrator
140 Pine Ave.
North Adams, MA 01247
PH: (413)663-7109
Hansen, Keith, Contact

Chinese American Heart Association
[14109]
120 Liberty St.
North Andover, MA 01845
Li, Jianming, President

Global Occupational Therapy for
Orphans [16323]
820 Turnpike St., Ste. 104
North Andover, MA 01845
PH: (978)681-6605
McCormick, Dr. Tara, Founder

International Medical Equipment Col-
laborative [14943]
1620 Osgood St.
North Andover, MA 01845
PH: (978)557-5510
Fax: (978)557-5525
Keefe, Tom, Founder

Mobile Enhancement Retailers As-
sociation [2961]
85 Flagship Dr., Ste. F
North Andover, MA 01845
Toll free: 800-949-6372
Anderson, Mike, Chairman

Plumbing and Drainage Institute
[2638]
800 Turnpike St., Ste. 300
North Andover, MA 01845-6156
PH: (978)557-0720
Toll free: 800-589-8956

Bailey's Team for Autism [13759]
164 Westside Ave.
North Attleboro, MA 02760
PH: (508)699-4483
Robertson, Sammi, President

Navy & Marine Living History Association Inc. [9805]
41 Kelley Blvd.
North Attleboro, MA 02760-4734
Veit, Chuck, President

Photo Chemical Machining Institute
[2366]
11 Robert Toner Blvd., No. 234
North Attleboro, MA 02763
PH: (508)385-0085
Fax: (508)232-6005
Fox, William, President

Bionutrient Food Association [4189]
24 Hillsville Rd.
North Brookfield, MA 01535
PH: (978)257-2627
Fax: (978)277-6400
Kittredge, Dan, Exec. Dir.

Mediterranean Studies Association
[9794]
PO Box 79351
North Dartmouth, MA 02747-0984
PH: (508)979-8687
Taggie, Benjamin F., Exec. Dir.

Family Rosary [19832]
518 Washington St.
North Easton, MA 02356-1200

PH: (508)238-4095
Toll free: 800-299-7729
Phalen, Rev. John, CSC, President

CORPUS [19829]
2 Adamian Dr.
North Falmouth, MA 02556
PH: (508)523-4032
Moore, Allen, Co-Pres.

American College of Veterinary
Emergency and Critical Care
[17617]
Tufts Cummings School of
Veterinary Medicine
200 Westboro Rd.
North Grafton, MA 01536
PH: (508)839-5395
Fax: (508)887-4634
de Laforcade, Dr. Armelle, DVM,
Exec. Sec.

Phi Zeta [23983]
c/o Cheryl A. Blaze, Secretary-
Treasurer
Tufts Cummings School of
Veterinary Medicine
200 Westboro Rd.
North Grafton, MA 01536
PH: (508)887-4249
Fax: (508)839-7922
Williams, Susan Michelle, President

Tufts University | Cummings School
of Veterinary Medicine | Center for
Animals and Public Policy [10705]
200 Westboro Rd.
North Grafton, MA 01536
PH: (508)839-7991
Fax: (508)839-3337
Kochevar, Deborah, DVM, PhD,
Dean

Cruise Club of America [3375]
PO Box 318
North Pembroke, MA 02358
Toll free: 800-982-2276
Fax: (781)826-6156
Kraus, Bill, Founder

Hospitality Asset Managers Associa-
tion [1657]
c/o Stephanie Roy, Executive Direc-
tor
PO Box 381
North Scituate, MA 02060-0381
PH: (781)544-7330
Roy, Stephanie, Exec. Dir.

International Association of Asian
Crime Investigators and Specialists
[5153]
PO Box 612
North Scituate, MA 02060-0612
Leong, Benjamin, President

International Organization of Asian
Crime Investigators and Specialists
[5126]
PO Box 612
North Scituate, MA 02060-0612
Leong, Benjamin, Exec. Dir.,
President

Empower Dalit Women of Nepal
[13413]
PO Box 550076
North Waltham, MA 02455
PH: (617)864-1224
Pariyar, Bishnu Maya, Founder

Alumnae Association of Smith Col-
lege [19298]
33 Elm St.
Northampton, MA 01060
PH: (413)585-2040
Toll free: 800-526-2023
Chrisler, Jennifer, VP

Bill of Rights Defense Committee
[17879]
8 Bridge St., Ste. A
Northampton, MA 01060
PH: (413)582-0110
Fax: (413)582-0116
Graves, Lisa, President

Healing Across the Divides [15465]
72 Laurel Pk.
Northampton, MA 01060
Goldfield, Norbert, MD, Exec. Dir.

National Priorities Project [18313]
243 King St., Ste. 246
Northampton, MA 01060
PH: (413)584-9556
Bidwell, Dennis, Chairman

Remineralize the Earth [4687]
152 South St.
Northampton, MA 01060
Campe, Joanna, Exec. Dir., Founder

Stop it Now! [11160]
351 Pleasant St., Ste. B-319
Northampton, MA 01060
PH: (413)587-3500
Toll free: 888-PREVENT
Henry, Fran, Founder

SweatFree Communities [23462]
c/o Liana Foxvog
2 Conz St., Ste. 2B
Northampton, MA 01060
PH: (413)586-0974
Fax: (413)584-8987
Chakraborty, Rini, Co-Ch.

Women Outdoors [23053]
PO Box 158
Northampton, MA 01061

Women in Philanthropy [18854]
PO Box 224
Northampton, MA 01061
Perlmutter, Stacey, President

Golf Fights Cancer [13978]
300 Arnold Palmer Blvd.
Norton, MA 02766
PH: (774)430-9060
Fax: (774)430-9031
Oates, Brian, Founder, Chairman

International Berkeley Society
[10091]
26 E Main St.
Dept. of Philosophy
Wheaton College
Norton, MA 02766
Daniel, Stephen, Mem.

Naval Airship Association [5867]
c/o Frederick R. Morin, President
PO Box 136
Norwell, MA 02061-0136
Morin, Frederick R., President

AlKoura League [12612]
PO Box 95
Norwood, MA 02062
PH: (617)435-8687
Al-Dayaa, Dr. Hani, President

Infusion Nurses Society [17445]
315 Norwood Park S
Norwood, MA 02062
PH: (781)440-9408
Fax: (781)440-9409
Alexander, Mary, MA, CEO

American Society of Test Engineers
[7322]
PO Box 389
Nutting Lake, MA 01865-0389
Keller, Michael E., Ed.-in-Chief,
Exec. Dir., Treasurer

Dunkin' Donuts Independent
Franchise Owners [1459]
2 1st Ave., Ste. 127 - 3
Peabody, MA 01960
PH: (978)587-2581
Connelly, Dan, Chairman

Italian Genealogical Society of
America [9616]
PO Box 3572
Peabody, MA 01961-3572
Melnyk, Marcia Iannizzi D.,
President

Progeria Research Foundation
[17348]
PO Box 3453
Peabody, MA 01961-3453
PH: (978)535-2594
Fax: (978)535-5849
Gordon, Audrey, Esq., President,
Exec. Dir.

John Clough Genealogical Society
[20847]
21 Lowell Rd.
Pembroke, MA 02359
Clough, John W., President

Sacred Earth Network [4100]
93A Glasheen Rd.
Petersham, MA 01366
PH: (978)724-0120
Pfeiffer, Bill, Director, President,
Facilitator

Cushing's Support and Research
Foundation [14702]
60 Robbins Rd., No. 12
Plymouth, MA 02360
PH: (617)723-3674
Pace, Louise, Founder, President

General Society of Mayflower
Descendants [21082]
PO Box 3297
Plymouth, MA 02361-3297
PH: (508)746-3188

Pilgrim Society [21083]
Pilgrim Hall Museum
75 Court St.
Plymouth, MA 02360-3823
PH: (508)746-1620
Nutter, Robin, Dir. of Dev.

Plymouth Rock Foundation [7797]
1120 Long Pond Rd.
Plymouth, MA 02360
Toll free: 800-210-1620
Wolfe, Dr. Charles, President

World Bamboo Organization [4500]
9 Bloody Pond Rd.
Plymouth, MA 02360
Lucas, Susanne, CEO

American Cotswold Record Associa-
tion [4651]
18 Elm St.
Plympton, MA 02367
PH: (781)585-2026
Fax: (781)585-2026
Rigel, Vicki, Secretary, Treasurer

Triumph International Owners Club
[22232]
PO Box 158
Plympton, MA 02367-0158
PH: (508)946-1939
Fax: (508)946-1145

National Education for Assistance
Dog Services [15203]
305 Redemption Rock Trl. S
Princeton, MA 01541
PH: (978)422-9064
Deroche, Gerry, CEO

Coalition for Fire-Safe Cigarettes
[5202]
National Fire Protection Association
1 Batterymarch Pk.
Quincy, MA 02169-7471
PH: (617)770-3000
Fax: (617)770-0700
Shannon, James M., President, CEO

International Association of EMTs
and Paramedics [14681]
159 Thomas Burgin Pky.
Quincy, MA 02169
PH: (617)376-0220
Toll free: 866-412-7762
Holway, David J., President

International Brotherhood of Police
Officers [23470]
159 Burgin Pky.
Quincy, MA 02169
PH: (617)376-0220
Toll free: 866-412-7762
Fax: (617)984-5695
Holway, David J., President

International Fire Marshals Associa-
tion [5209]
1 Batterymarch Pk.
Quincy, MA 02169-7471
PH: (617)770-3000
Toll free: 800-344-3555
Fax: (617)770-0700
Tucker, Randolph W., Chairman

National Association of Government
Employees [23432]
159 Burgin Pky.
Quincy, MA 02169
PH: (617)376-0220
Fax: (617)984-5695
Holway, David J., President

National Association of State
Controlled Substances Authorities
[5158]
72 Brook St.
Quincy, MA 02170-1616
PH: (617)472-0520
Fax: (617)472-0521
Clifford, Peg, Comm. Chm.

National Fire Protection Association
[12832]
1 Batterymarch Pk.
Quincy, MA 02169-7471
PH: (617)770-3000
Fax: (617)770-0700
Bollon, Vincent J., Contact

Overseas Chinese - American
Entrepreneurs Association [3304]
219 Quincy Ave.
Quincy, MA 02169
Wu, Wanchu, Chairperson

Prostate Health Education Network
[14052]
500 Victory Rd., Ste. 4
Quincy, MA 02171
PH: (617)481-4020
Fax: (617)481-4021
Farrington, Thomas A., Founder,
President

Restoring Sight International [17740]
PO Box 692457
Quincy, MA 02269
PH: (617)327-6002
Tolentino, Felipe L., MD, President

World Organization of Building Officials [603]
c/o National Fire Protection Association
1 Batterymarch Pk.
Quincy, MA 02169-7471
PH: (617)984-7464
Fax: (617)984-7110
Eldurubi, Imad Y., President

Randolph for Haiti [12714]
41 S Main St.
Randolph, MA 02368
PH: (781)961-9779
    (781)308-0458
Fontaine, Pierre, President

The Barbara Pym Society [9093]
c/o Judy Horn
4 Summit Dr., Apt. 005
Reading, MA 01867-4050
Horn, Judy, Contact

United Brachial Plexus Network, Inc.
[16039]
32 William Rd.,
Reading, MA 01867
PH: (718)315-6161
Looby, Richard, President

Medicines for Humanity [14203]
800 Hingham St., Ste. 200N
Rockland, MA 02370-1067
PH: (781)982-0274
Bilodeau, Timothy W., Exec. Dir.

Bullseye Class Association [22602]
37 High St.
Rockport, MA 01966
Lee, Kym, President

Common Hope for Health [14990]
212 Highland St., Unit A
Roxbury, MA 02119
Lee, Scott, PhD, President

National Center of Afro-American
Artists [8786]
300 Walnut Ave.
Roxbury, MA 02119
PH: (617)442-8614
Burnham, Margaret, Co-Chmn. of
the Bd.

Nubian United Benevolent
International Association [12594]
149 Roxbury St.
Roxbury, MA 02119
PH: (617)669-2642
Stewart, Ronia, President

Company of Military Historians
[22182]
PO Box 910
Rutland, MA 01543-0910
PH: (508)799-9229
Bell, Craig, President

Child Aid International [10893]
125 Washington St., Ste. 201
Salem, MA 01970
PH: (978)338-4240
Fax: (978)236-7272
Hamilton, Jared, Founder, President

Harriet Beecher Stowe Society
[10374]
c/o Nancy Lusignan Schultz,
Treasurer
Dept. of English
Salem State University
352 Lafayette St.
Salem, MA 01970-5333
Lueck, Beth L., President

Human and Civil Rights Organiza-
tions of America [17900]
125 Washington St., Ste. 201
Salem, MA 01970
PH: (978)744-2608
Fax: (978)236-7272
Strauss, Marshall, President

Vascular Access Society of the
Americas [15888]
19 North St.
Salem, MA 01970
PH: (978)745-8331
    (978)745-8334
Henry, Mitchell L., MD, President

American Handel Society [9178]
c/o Marjorie Pomeroy, Secretary/
Treasurer
49 Christopher Hollow Rd.
Sandwich, MA 02563-2227
PH: (909)607-3568
Beeks, Graydon, President

International Clubmakers Guild
[3139]
38 Walden Pond Ave.
Saugus, MA 01906-1146
Newton, Steve, Mem.

Creative Education Foundation
[7758]
46 Watch Hill Dr.
Scituate, MA 02066
PH: (508)960-0000
Gonyeau, Thom, Chairman

American Working Dog Federation
[21830]
c/o Michelle Testa, Secretary
31 Mohawk St.
Sharon, MA 02067
Camper, Anne, President

Association for Commuter
Transportation [13229]
1 Chestnut Sq., 2nd Fl.
Sharon, MA 02067
PH: (202)792-8501
Straus, David, Exec. Dir.

Interweave Continental: Unitarian
Universalists for Lesbian, Gay,
Bisexual and Transgender
Concerns [20183]
156 Massapoag Ave.
Sharon, MA 02067-2749
Dwinell-Yardley, Dana, Dir. of
Comm.

Women in Health Care Management
[15071]
PO Box 150
Sharon, MA 02067-0150
Green, Linda, Treasurer

Global Emergency Care Collabora-
tive [15451]
PO Box 4404
Shrewsbury, MA 01545
Bisanzo, Mark, President, Exec. Dir.,
Founder

International Animal Rescue-US
[3626]
PO Box 137
Shrewsbury, MA 01545
PH: (508)826-1083

International Disaster Recovery As-
sociation [7312]
PO Box 4515
Shrewsbury, MA 01545
PH: (508)845-6000
Fax: (508)842-9003
Tartaglia, Benjamin W., Exec. Dir.

Hathaway Family Association
[20879]
2231 Riverside Ave.
Somerset, MA 02726-4104
PH: (508)889-6584
Hathaway, William S., Jr., President

Tin Can Sailors-The National As-
sociation of Destroyer Veterans
[21062]
PO Box 100
Somerset, MA 02726-0100
PH: (508)677-0515
Toll free: 800-223-5535
Fax: (508)676-9740
Miller, Terry, Exec. Dir.

Action for Clean Energy [4020]
21 Aldersey Rd., Apt. No. 5
Somerville, MA 02143

PH: (510)673-2440

Clean Production Action [4136]
1310 Broadway, Ste. 101
Somerville, MA 02144-1837
PH: (781)391-6743
Fax: (781)285-3091
Rossi, Mark, Exec. Dir.

Historians Against the War [19235]
PO Box 442154
Somerville, MA 02144
O'Brien, Jim, Contact

International Physicians for the
Prevention of Nuclear War [18750]
66-70 Union Sq., No. 204
Somerville, MA 02143
PH: (617)440-1733
Fax: (617)440-1734
Christ, Michael, Exec. Dir.

National History Club [7988]
PO Box 441812
Somerville, MA 02144
PH: (781)248-7921
Nasson, Robert, Exec. Dir.

Political Research Associates
[18919]
1310 Broadway, Ste. 201
Somerville, MA 02144-1837
PH: (617)666-5300
Fax: (617)666-6622
Rallapalli, Emelia, Secretary

Resist [18873]
PO Box 441155
Somerville, MA 02144
PH: (617)623-5110
O'Brien, Jim, Treasurer

World Peace Foundation [18567]
Tufts University
169 Holland St., Ste. 209
Somerville, MA 02144
PH: (617)627-2255
Fax: (617)627-3712
de Waal, Alex, Exec. Dir.

World Socialist Party of the United
States [18900]
PO Box 440247
Somerville, MA 02144

YouthBuild USA [13492]
58 Day St.
Somerville, MA 02144-2827
PH: (617)623-9900
Fax: (617)623-4331
Stoneman, Dorothy, Founder, CEO

Alliance for Animals [10564]
232 Silver St.
South Boston, MA 02127-2206
PH: (617)268-7800
Bishop, Donna, President, Founder

The Romanian Studies Association
of America [9590]
Mount Holyoke College
50 College St.
South Hadley, MA 01075
PH: (662)915-7716
Petrescu, Dr. Corina L., Secretary,
Treasurer

Evangelical Homiletics Society
[20206]
130 Essex St.
South Hamilton, MA 01982-2325
Gatzke, Nick, VP

Climate Crisis Coalition [3831]
c/o Tom Strokes, Project Director
PO Box 125
South Lee, MA 01260
PH: (413)243-5665
Stokes, Tom, Prog. Dir.

North American Farmers' Direct
  Marketing Association [4482]
62 White Loaf Rd.
Southampton, MA 01073
Fax: (413)233-4285
Touchette, Charlie, Exec. Dir.

American Hockey League [22907]
1 Monarch Pl., Ste. 2400
Springfield, MA 01144-4004
PH: (413)781-2030
Fax: (413)733-4767
Andrews, David, President, CEO

Ancient Coins for Education [22261]
PO Box 90193
Springfield, MA 01139-0193
Lehman, Mark, Director

Association of YMCA Professionals
  [13418]
Springfield College
Stitzer YMCA, 2nd Fl.
263 Alden St.
Springfield, MA 01109
PH: (413)748-3884
Fax: (413)748-3872
Norton, Natalie, President, CEO

Naismith Memorial Basketball Hall of
  Fame [22572]
1000 Hall of Fame Ave.
Springfield, MA 01105
Toll free: 877-4HO-OPLA
Doleva, John, President

National Association for Community
  College Entrepreneurship [7558]
Bldg. 101, 1 Federal St.
Springfield, MA 01105
PH: (413)306-3131
Fax: (413)372-4992
Massey, Edwin, Director

Paperboard Packaging Council
  [2480]
1350 Main St., Ste. 1508
Springfield, MA 01103-1628
PH: (413)686-9191
Fax: (413)747-7777
Markens, Ben, President

Association of Marian Helpers
  [19797]
Marians of the Immaculate Concep-
tion
Eden Hill
Stockbridge, MA 01263
PH: (413)298-3931
Toll free: 800-462-7426
Aguero, Dante, Priest

Dramatic Order Knights of Khoras-
  san [19522]
c/o Supreme Lodge Knights of Pythias
458 Pearl St.
Stoughton, MA 02072
PH: (781)436-5966
Fax: (781)341-0496

Junior Order, Knights of Pythias
  [19523]
Supreme Lodge Knights of Pythias
458 Pearl St.
Stoughton, MA 02072-1655
PH: (781)436-5966
Fax: (781)341-0496
Brown, Bruce, Chairman

National Scoliosis Foundation
  [17184]
5 Cabot Pl.
Stoughton, MA 02072-4624
PH: (781)341-6333
Toll free: 800-673-6922
Fax: (781)341-8333
O'Brien, Joseph P., CEO, President

Tanzania School Foundation [11451]
2 Canton St., Ste. 222
Stoughton, MA 02072-2878
PH: (781)718-4307
Lott, Christine, Founder, Director

AHRA: The Association for Medical
  Imaging Management [17037]
490B Boston Post Rd., Ste. 200
Sudbury, MA 01776
PH: (978)443-7591
Toll free: 800-334-2472
Fox, David, Officer

Goodenow Family Association
  [20872]
163 Landham Rd.
Sudbury, MA 01776-3156
Fox, Christine Banvard, President

Kate's Voice [16982]
PO Box 365
Sudbury, MA 01776-0365
PH: (978)440-9913
Rutherford, Laura Boyajian, Director,
President

Professional Lacrosse Players Association [23524]
52 Haynes Rd.
Sudbury, MA 01776
Schmitz, Peter E., President

Ecova Mali [3561]
69 Cherry St.
Swampscott, MA 01907
PH: (978)818-0751
Flatt, Gregory, Director

World Organization of Renal
  Therapies [15889]
21 Bradlee Ave.
Swampscott, MA 01907
PH: (781)586-8830
Trebbin, Wayne, MD, President

Homes for Our Troops [21124]
6 Main St.
Taunton, MA 02780
Toll free: 866-787-6677
Preston, Kenneth O., Director

American Scientific Affiliation
  [20594]
218 Boston St., Ste. 208
Topsfield, MA 01983-2210
PH: (978)887-8833
Fax: (978)887-8755
Herdrich, Marty, Exec. Asst.

American Society of Alternative
  Therapists [13602]
PO Box 303
Topsfield, MA 01983
PH: (978)561-1639
Hartl, Martin, President

International Desalination Associa-
  tion [7367]
94 Central St., Ste. 200
Topsfield, MA 01983-1838
PH: (978)887-0410
Fax: (978)887-0411
Sommariva, Dr. Corrado, President

Antibody Society [15373]
PO Box 162
Waban, MA 02468
Reichert, Janice M., PhD, President

Customer Experience Professionals
  Association [767]
401 Edgewater Pl., Ste. 600
Wakefield, MA 01880
PH: (781)876-8838
Fax: (781)623-0538
Magers, Diane M., Chairperson

Digital Analytics Association [6766]
401 Edgewater Pl., Ste. 600
Wakefield, MA 01880-6200

PH: (781)876-8933
Fax: (781)224-1239
Sterne, Jim, Chmn. of the Bd.

Feldenkrais Guild of North America
  [9545]
401 Edgewater Pl., Ste. 600
Wakefield, MA 01880
Feinstein, Carla, Mgr., Comm.

NFC Forum [6230]
401 Edgewater Pl., Ste. 600
Wakefield, MA 01880
PH: (781)876-8955
Fax: (781)610-9864
Tagawa, Koichi, Chairman

Search Engine Marketing Profes-
  sional Organization [2301]
401 Edgewater Pl., Ste. 600
Wakefield, MA 01880-6200
PH: (781)876-8866
Grehan, Mike, Chairperson

Air Barrier Association of America
  [487]
1600 Boston-Providence Hwy.
Walpole, MA 02081
Toll free: 866-956-5888
Fax: (866)956-5819
Schauffele, Roy, Chairman

Center for Independent
  Documentary [9300]
1600 Providence Hwy.
Walpole, MA 02081
PH: (888)220-0918
Walsh, Susi, Exec. Dir.

Accelerated Cure Project for Multiple
  Sclerosis [15890]
460 Totten Pond Rd., Ste. 140
Waltham, MA 02451
PH: (781)487-0008
McBurney, Robert, CEO, President

Action for Post-Soviet Jewry [18138]
24 Crescent St., Ste. 306
Waltham, MA 02453-4089
PH: (781)893-2331

Association for the Social Scientific
  Study of Jewry [8136]
c/o Prof. Leonard Saxe, Treasurer
Cohen Center for Modern Jewish
Studies
Brandeis University
415 South St.
Waltham, MA 02453
Benor, Sarah, VP

Brandeis University Alumni Associa-
  tion [19309]
415 South St.
Waltham, MA 02453-2728
PH: (781)736-4100
Toll free: 800-333-1948
Fax: (781)736-4101
Rifkin, Adam J., President

Children's Safety Network [10935]
Education Development Center, Inc.
43 Foundry Ave.
Waltham, MA 02453-8313
PH: (617)618-2918
Fogerty, Sally, MEd, Director

Rebecca Clarke Society, Inc. [9181]
Brandeis University
Women's Studies Research Ctr.
Mailstop 079
Waltham, MA 02454-9110
PH: (617)776-1809
Fax: (781)736-8117
Curtis, Liane, President

Education Development Center
  [7764]
43 Foundry Ave.
Waltham, MA 02453-8313

PH: (617)969-7100
Fax: (617)969-5979
Suomi, Marvin J., Chmn. of the Bd.

Families for Depression Awareness
  [15769]
391 Totten Pond Rd., Ste. 101
Waltham, MA 02451
PH: (781)890-0220
Fax: (781)890-2411
Totten, Julie, Founder, President

Federation of State Physician Health
  Programs, Inc. [16750]
860 Winter St.
Waltham, MA 02451-1414
PH: (781)434-7343
Fax: (781)464-4802
Bresnahan, Linda R., Exec. Dir.

Graduation Pledge Alliance [19111]
Bentley University
175 Forest St.
Waltham, MA 02452
PH: (781)891-2529
Fax: (781)891-2896
Buono, Anthony F., Treasurer

Guild for Human Services [17711]
411 Waverley Oaks Rd., Ste.104
Waltham, MA 02452-8468
PH: (781)893-6000
Fax: (781)893-1171
Belski, Thomas, CEO

International Foundation for Gender
  Education [12944]
272 Carroll St. NW
Waltham, MA 02454
PH: (202)207-8364
Leclair, Ms. Denise, Exec. Dir.

International Society of Psychoneu-
  roendocrinology [15649]
c/o Nicolas Rohleder, PhD,
  Secretary General
Dept. of Psychology
Brandeis University
415 South St.
Waltham, MA 02453
Yehuda, Rachel, PhD, Officer

Missionary Sisters of the Society of
  Mary [20441]
349 Grove St.
Waltham, MA 02453
PH: (781)893-0149
Fax: (781)899-6838
Rheaume, Sr. Claire, Contact

National Center for Jewish Film
  [9308]
Brandeis University
Lown 102 MS053
Waltham, MA 02454
PH: (781)736-8600
Fax: (781)736-2070
Rivo, Sharon Pucker, Exec. Dir.

Society for Craniofacial Morphometry
  [14347]
Shriver Center
Harvard Medical School
200 Trapelo Rd.
Waltham, MA 02452-6332
PH: (781)642-0163
Fax: (781)642-0196
Deutsch, Dr. Curtis K., Contact

SPRI [812]
465 Waverley Oaks Rd., Ste. 421
Waltham, MA 02452
PH: (781)647-7026
Fax: (781)647-7222
King, Linda, Managing Dir.

Two Ten Footwear Foundation
[1404]
1466 Main St.
Waltham, MA 02451
Toll free: 800-346-3210
Fax: (781)736-1554
Sullivan, Diane, Chairperson

World Connect [14247]
681 Main St., Ste. 3-37
Waltham, MA 02451
PH: (347)563-7452
Fax: (781)894-8050
Haney, Bill, Founder

Shields National Class Association
[22668]
PO Box 152
Wareham, MA 02571-0152
PH: (508)295-3550
Fax: (508)295-3551
Crocker, Collamore, President

Antiques Council [196]
PO Box 1508
Warren, MA 01083
PH: (413)436-7064
Fax: (413)436-7066
Shapiro, Marty, President

Armenian International Women's As-
sociation [13369]
65 Main St., No. 3A
Watertown, MA 02472
PH: (617)926-0171
Moranian, Suzanne, President

Armenian Relief Society of Eastern
U.S.A. [12622]
80 Bigelow Ave., Ste. 200
Watertown, MA 02472
PH: (617)926-3801
Fax: (617)924-7238
Attar, Ani, Mem.

Armenian Revolutionary Federation
[18703]
c/o Armenian Youth Federation
80 Bigelow Ave.
Watertown, MA 02472
PH: (617)923-1933
Fax: (617)924-1933

Armenian Youth Federation [18704]
80 Bigelow Ave.
Watertown, MA 02472
PH: (617)923-1933
Fax: (617)924-1933

Beverage Network [423]
44 Pleasant St., Ste. 110
Watertown, MA 02472
PH: (617)231-8800
Craven, John, CEO, Founder, Ed.
Dir.

Hairenik Association [19389]
80 Bigelow Ave.
Watertown, MA 02472
PH: (617)926-3974
  (617)926-3976
Fax: (617)926-1750

Pathfinder International [17115]
9 Galen St., Ste. 217
Watertown, MA 02472
PH: (617)924-7200
Fax: (617)924-3833
Mane, Purnima, President, CEO

SATELLIFE Global Health Informa-
tion Network [15062]
30 California St.
Watertown, MA 02472-2539
PH: (617)926-9400
Fax: (617)926-1212
Ladd, Holly, JD, Exec. Dir.

Open Geospatial Consortium [6329]
35 Main St., Ste. 5
Wayland, MA 01778-5037

PH: (508)655-5858
Fax: (508)655-2237
Reichardt, Mark, CEO, President

Eating for Life Alliance [14638]
396 Washington St., Ste. 392
Wellesley, MA 02481
Post, Whitney, Treasurer

Wellesley College Alumnae Associa-
tion [19371]
Green Hall, Rm. 246
106 Central St.
Wellesley, MA 02481-8203.
PH: (781)283-2331
Toll free: 800-358-3543
Fax: (781)283-3638
Lohin, Susan, Director

Rich Family Association [20920]
PO Box 142
Wellfleet, MA 02667
Rich, Craig R., President

Association for Moral Education
[7744]
c/o Kaye Cook PhD., President
Dept. of Psychology
Gordon College
255 Grapevine Rd.
Wenham, MA 01984-1813
Cook, Kaye, PhD, President

Christian College Consortium [7609]
255 Grapevine Rd.
Wenham, MA 01984-1813
PH: (978)468-1716
Fax: (978)867-4650
Gaede, Dr. Stan D., President

Compassionate Care ALS [13683]
PO Box 1052
West Falmouth, MA 02574
PH: (508)444-6775
Hoffman, Ron, Founder, Exec. Dir.

Bulgarian Studies Association [9148]
51 Davis Ave.
West Newton, MA 02465-1925
Warner, Vessela, President

Ambassadors for Sustained Health
[14974]
3 Petrel St.
West Roxbury, MA 02132-4110
PH: (646)481-0844
Nyatika, Zachary, Managing Dir.

Association of Veterans Affairs
Anesthesiologists [13699]
c/o Dr. Kay B. Leissner, Secretary
VA Boston Healthcare System
1400 VFW Pkwy.
West Roxbury, MA 02132

The Association of Travel Marketing
Executives [3373]
c/o Kristin Zern, Executive Director
PO Box 3176
West Tisbury, MA 02575
Zern, Kristin, Exec. Dir.

Great Dane Club of America, Inc.
[21889]
c/o Dianne Powers, President
PO Box 216
West Tisbury, MA 02575
Moriarty, Lynda, Director

Association for Episcopal Deacons
[20094]
PO Box 1516
Westborough, MA 01581-6516
PH: (508)873-1881
Campbell, Ernestina R., President

International District Energy Association [1626]
24 Lyman St., Ste. 230
Westborough, MA 01581-2841

PH: (508)366-9339
Fax: (508)366-0019
Thornton, Robert P., President, CEO

American Registry of Medical Assistants [15616]
61 Union St., Ste. 5
Westfield, MA 01085
PH: (413)562-7336

Churg Strauss Syndrome Associa-
tion [13786]
82 Pine Ridge Rd.
Westfield, MA 01085
PH: (413)862-3636
Dion, Jane, Director

Bikes for the Philippines, Inc.
[10779]
PO Box 43
Westminster, MA 01473
PH: (978)621-2599
Grant, Jo, President

Wood Products Manufacturers As-
sociation [1448]
PO Box 761
Westminster, MA 01473-0761
PH: (978)874-5445
Fax: (978)874-9946
Bibeau, Philip A., Exec. Dir.

Ocular Immunology and Uveitis
Foundation [16399]
348 Glen Rd.
Weston, MA 02493
PH: (617)494-1431
Fax: (617)621-2953
Foster, C. Stephen, MD, Founder,
President

Philippine Nurses Association of
America [16180]
656 Canton St.
Westwood, MA 02090
Doliente, Dino, III, President

No More Guantanamos [17923]
PO Box 618
Whately, MA 01093
PH: (413)665-1150
Talanian, Nancy, Director

Earthspirit Community [20504]
PO Box 723
Williamsburg, MA 01096
PH: (413)238-4240
Fax: (413)238-7785
Arthen, Deirdre Pulgram, Director

Institute for International Cooperation
and Development [12164]
1117 Hancock Rd.
Williamstown, MA 01267
PH: (413)441-5126
  (413)458-9466
Fax: (413)458-3323
Martinussen, Jytte, Exec. Dir.

iPods for Wounded Veterans
[13066]
4 Heather Dr.
Wilmington, MA 01887
PH: (603)770-5765
Cardello, Paul, Chairman

Afghanistan Samsortya [12022]
200 Swanton St., Ste. 418
Winchester, MA 01890
PH: (617)319-3717
Raqib, Mariam, Founder, Director

DuraSpace [6362]
28 Church St., Unit 2
Winchester, MA 01890
PH: (607)216-4548
Kimpton, Michele, CEO

International Galapagos Tour Opera-
tors Association [23667]
PO Box 1043
Winchester, MA 01890-8443

PH: (781)729-6262
Fax: (781)729-6262
Kareus, Matt, Exec. Dir.

House Rabbit Network [10639]
PO Box 2602
Woburn, MA 01888-1102
PH: (781)431-1211
Scafati, Laura, Treasurer

Lift Up Africa [11398]
PO Box 3112
Woburn, MA 01888
Toll free: 888-854-3887
Levy, Richard M., Founder, CEO

Medical Missions for Children
[14202]
600 W Cummings Pk., Ste. 2850
Woburn, MA 01801
PH: (508)697-5821
Fax: (781)501-5225
ODonnell, Frank, Exec. Dir.

International Society of Protistolo-
gists [6864]
c/o Virginia Edgcomb, President
Woods Hole Oceanographic Institu-
tion
Geology and Geophysics Dept.
220 McLean Laboratory, MS 8
Woods Hole, MA 02543
PH: (508)274-0963
Archibald, John M., VP

Sea Education Association [8264]
PO Box 6
Woods Hole, MA 02543-0006
PH: (508)540-3954
Toll free: 800-552-3633
Fax: (800)977-8516
Humphris, Susan, Chairperson

International Medical Volunteers As-
sociation [15602]
PO Box 205
Woodville, MA 01784
PH: (508)435-7377
Fax: (508)497-9568

American Antiquarian Society [9368]
185 Salisbury St.
Worcester, MA 01609-1634
PH: (508)755-5221
Fax: (508)753-3311
Dunlap, Ellen S., President

Associate Missionaries of the As-
sumption [20383]
16 Vineyard St.
Worcester, MA 01603
PH: (508)767-1356
Sherman, Michelle B., Director

Canines for Disabled Kids [11578]
255 Park Ave., Ste. 601
Worcester, MA 01609
PH: (978)422-5299
Fax: (978)422-7380
Law, Kristin Hartness, Contact

The Exodus Guild, Inc. [10488]
9 Sherer Trl.
Worcester, MA 01603
PH: (617)777-9338
Akinbuli, Funke Adenodi, Exec. Dir.,
Founder

Interdisciplinary Environmental As-
sociation [4117]
Assumption College
Dept. of Economics & Global Stud-
ies
500 Salisbury St.
Worcester, MA 01609
PH: (508)767-7296
Fax: (508)767-7382
Reiter, Dr. Kimberly, Chairperson

Light Path 4 Haiti [11399]
210 Park Ave., Ste. 261
Worcester, MA 01609
PH: (774)262-0603
Ignace, Fredo, Rep.

Small Business Service Bureau
[3129]
554 Main St.
Worcester, MA 01615-0014
Toll free: 800-343-0939
Carroll, Francis R., Chairman,
Founder

UHAI for Health, Inc. [15501]
PO Box 3603
Worcester, MA 01613
Kimani-Chomba, Jane, Bd. Member

Wake Up Narcolepsy [13791]
PO Box 60293
Worcester, MA 01606
PH: (978)751-3693
Gow, Monica, Exec. Dir., Founder

Worcester Polytechnic Institute
Alumni Association [19375]
100 Institute Rd.
Worcester, MA 01609-2280
PH: (508)831-5600
Fax: (508)831-5791
Delisle, Rachel, President

Graves Family Association [20873]
20 Binney Cir.
Wrentham, MA 02093
PH: (508)384-8084
Graves, Kenneth V., President

His Majesty's 10th Regiment of Foot
in America [8794]
40 Spring St.
Wrentham, MA 02093
PH: (781)862-2586
O'Shaughnessy, Lt. Col. Paul, Cmdr.

National Board of Trial Advocacy
[5827]
200 Stonewall Blvd., Ste. 1
Wrentham, MA 02093
PH: (508)384-6565
Fax: (508)384-8223
Sternbach, Melissa, Exec. Dir.

International Fund for Animal
Welfare [10648]
290 Summer St.
Yarmouth Port, MA 02675-0193
PH: (508)744-2000
Toll free: 800-932-4329
Fax: (508)744-2009
Savesky, Kathleen, Chairperson

MICHIGAN

Gleaner Life Insurance Society
[19484]
5200 W US Highway 223
Adrian, MI 49221-9461
Toll free: 800-992-1894
Fax: (517)265-7745
Warner, Bill, Mem.

World Association of International
Studies [9591]
Goldsmith Hall
Dept. of Modern Languages and
Cultures
Adrian College
Adrian, MI 49221
Hilton, Ronald, Founder

Intercollegiate Men's Choruses, Inc.
[9921]
c/o Clayton Parr, Executive
Secretary
Music Department

Albion College
611 E Porter St.
Albion, MI 49224
PH: (517)629-0251
Fax: (517)629-0784
Albinder, Frank, President

Fighting AIDS with Nutrition [10538]
PO Box 394
Allen Park, MI 48101
PH: (313)977-0259
Julian, Rev. Frank, RN, Founder

National Federation of Opticianry
Schools [16415]
c/o Randall L. Smith, Executive
Manager
4500 Enterprise Dr.
Allen Park, MI 48101
PH: (313)425-3815
Russo, Robert, President

Academia Ophthalmologica Interna-
tionalis [16360]
WK Kellog Eye Ctr.
1000 Wall St.
University of Michigan
Ann Arbor, MI 48105
PH: (734)764-6468
Fax: (734)647-0247

Aikido Yoshokai Association of North
America [22496]
Genyokan Dojo
3796 Plaza Dr., Ste. 3
Ann Arbor, MI 48108
PH: (734)662-4686

Alliance of Air National Guard Flight
Surgeons [17357]
3653 Larchmont Dr.
Ann Arbor, MI 48105
Howard, Cassandra, Col., VP

Alumni Association of the University
of Michigan [19302]
200 Fletcher St.
Ann Arbor, MI 48109-1007
PH: (734)764-0384
Toll free: 800-847-4764
Grafton, Steve, CEO, President

Amara Conservation [4780]
1531 Packard St., No. 12
Ann Arbor, MI 48104
PH: (734)761-5357
Bergemann, Lori, Exec. Dir.,
Founder

American Academy of Clinical Neu-
ropsychology [16001]
Dept. of Psychiatry
University of Michigan Health
System
1500 E Medical Center Dr.
Ann Arbor, MI 48109-5295
PH: (734)936-8269
Fax: (734)936-9761
Bieliauskas, Linas A., PhD, Exec.
Dir.

American Academy for Jewish
Research [9630]
202 S Thayer St., Ste. 211
Ann Arbor, MI 48104-1608
Hundert, Prof. Gershon, President

American Men's Studies Association
[11995]
1080 S University Ave.
Ann Arbor, MI 48109-1106
PH: (470)333-AMSA
Deeds, Dr. Jan, Dir. of Comm.

American Oriental Society [9021]
Hatcher Graduate Library
University of Michigan
Ann Arbor, MI 48109-1190

PH: (734)764-7555
Fax: (734)647-4760
Rodgers, Jonathan H., Secretary,
Treasurer

American Satin Rabbit Breeders'
Association [4593]
c/o Sue Moessner, President
3500 S Wagner Rd.
Ann Arbor, MI 48103
PH: (734)668-6709
Moessner, Sue, President

American Society for Clinical
Investigation [14288]
2015 Manchester Rd.
Ann Arbor, MI 48104
PH: (734)222-6050
Fax: (734)222-6058
Jain, Mukesh K., Chairman

Animals & Society Institute [10585]
2512 Carpenter Rd., Ste. 202-A
Ann Arbor, MI 48108-1188
PH: (734)677-9240
Fax: (734)677-9242
DeMello, Margo, Exec., Prog. Dir.

Anthroposophical Society in America
[19704]
1923 Geddes Ave.
Ann Arbor, MI 48104
PH: (734)662-9355
(718)644-7913
Fax: (734)662-1727
Finser, Torin, Gen. Sec.

APLIC [9678]
c/o Yan Fu, Vice President
University of Michigan
426 Thompson St.
Ann Arbor, MI 48104-2321
PH: (734)763-2152
Rosman, Lori, Rec. Sec.

Association for Advancing Automa-
tion [6016]
900 Victors Way, Ste. 140
Ann Arbor, MI 48108
PH: (734)994-6088
Fax: (734)994-3338
Ponce De Leon, Rusty, Chairman

Association for Asian Studies [7522]
825 Victors Way, Ste. 310
Ann Arbor, MI 48108
PH: (734)665-2490
Fax: (734)665-3801
Paschal, Michael, Exec. Dir.

Association for Executives in Health-
care Information Security [14982]
710 Avis Dr., Ste. 200
Ann Arbor, MI 48108
PH: (734)665-0000
Fax: (734)665-4922
Branzell, Russ, CEO

Association for Gender Equity
Leadership in Education [7900]
317 S Division St. Pmb 54
Ann Arbor, MI 48104
PH: (734)769-2456
Larson, Marta, Mgr.

Association of Outdoor Recreation
and Education [8399]
1100 N Main St., Ste. 101
Ann Arbor, MI 48104
PH: (810)299-2782
Fax: (810)299-3436
Watts, Russ, President

Automated Imaging Association
[7102]
900 Victors Way, Ste. 140
Ann Arbor, MI 48108
PH: (734)994-6088
Marini, Marc, Chairman

The Center for Social Gerontology,
Inc. [10503]
2307 Shelby Ave.
Ann Arbor, MI 48103
PH: (734)665-1126
Fax: (734)665-2071
Douglas, Clifford, President

Childhood Gynecologic Cancer As-
sociation [14175]
PO Box 3130
Ann Arbor, MI 48106
PH: (734)663-7251
Haefner, Hope, MD, Exec. Dir.

Chinese Economists Society [6386]
330 Packard St.
Ann Arbor, MI 48104-2910
PH: (734)647-9610
Fax: (734)763-0335
Bao, Dr. Shuming, Exec. Dir.

College of Healthcare Information
Management Executives [1796]
710 Avis Dr., Ste. 200
Ann Arbor, MI 48108
PH: (734)665-0000
Fax: (734)665-4922
Hadley, Jessica, Director

Community Systems Foundation
[16214]
219 S Main St., Ste. 206
Ann Arbor, MI 48104-2105
PH: (734)761-1357
Fax: (734)761-1356
Nystuen, John D., Chairman

Delta Kappa Epsilon [23894]
The Shant
611 1/2 E William St.
Ann Arbor, MI 48104
PH: (734)302-4210
McMillan, Stanford, Bd. Member,
Reg. Dir.

Delta Tau Lambda Sorority, Inc.
[23971]
PO Box 7714
Ann Arbor, MI 48107-7714
Madrigal, Damaris, President

Enterprise for a Sustainable World
[1004]
1609 Shadford Rd.
Ann Arbor, MI 48104-4464
PH: (734)369-8060
Hart, Stuart L., Founder, President

Extracorporeal Life Support
Organization [14351]
Bldg. 300, Rm. 303
2800 Plymouth Rd.
Ann Arbor, MI 48109-2800
PH: (734)998-6600
Fax: (734)998-6602
Fortenberry, James, Chairman

Fair Food Network [4190]
205 E Washington St., Ste. B
Ann Arbor, MI 48104
PH: (734)213-3999
Hesterman, Oran B., PhD,
President, CEO

Global Automotive Management
Council [293]
5340 Plymouth Rd., Ste. 205
Ann Arbor, MI 48105
PH: (734)997-9249
Fax: (734)786-2242
Uddin, M. Nasim, PhD, President

Great Lakes Commission [5652]
2805 S Industrial Hwy., Ste. 100
Ann Arbor, MI 48104-6791
PH: (734)665-9135
Fax: (734)665-9150
Crane, Thomas R., Dep. Dir.

Health Level Seven International **[15012]**
3300 Washtenaw Ave., Ste. 227
Ann Arbor, MI 48104-4261
PH: (734)677-7777
Fax: (734)677-6622
McDougall, Mark, Exec. Dir.

Homefront Hugs U.S.A. **[13241]**
1881 W Liberty St.
Ann Arbor, MI 48103
PH: (734)330-8203
Kellermann, Ms. Alessandra,
Founder, President

IEEE - Geoscience and Remote
Sensing Society **[6691]**
c/o Dr. Kamal Sarabandi, President
Dept. of Electrical Eng. and
Computer Science
Ann Arbor, MI 48109-2122
PH: (734)936-1575
Fax: (734)647-2106
Sarabandi, Prof. Kamal, President

Indo-American Eyecare Organization
[16386]
2975 Leslie Park Cir.
Ann Arbor, MI 48105
PH: (734)996-2866
Fax: (734)996-1638
Reddy, Vanita, President

Institute for Social Research **[7166]**
426 Thompson St.
Ann Arbor, MI 48104-2321
PH: (734)764-8354
(734)647-8043
Fax: (734)647-4575
Jackson, Prof. James S., PhD,
Director

Institute for Social Research
Program for Research on Black
Americans **[7183]**
5062 Institute for Social Research
Ann Arbor, MI 48106-1248
PH: (734)763-0045
Fax: (734)763-0044
Abelson, Jamie, Researcher

International Association for Great
Lakes Research **[6779]**
4840 S State Rd.
Ann Arbor, MI 48108
PH: (734)665-5303
(734)498-2007
Fax: (734)741-2055

International Association of Law
Libraries **[5563]**
c/o Barbara Garavaglia, Secretary
University of Michigan Law Library
801 Monroe St.
Ann Arbor, MI 48109
PH: (734)764-9338
Fax: (734)764-5863
Vervliet, Jeroen, President

International Council for Quality
Function Deployment **[2735]**
1140 Morehead Ct.
Ann Arbor, MI 48103-6181
PH: (206)203-3575

International Partnership for Critical
Markers of Disease **[14123]**
24 Frank Lloyd Wright Dr., Ste.
H1200
Ann Arbor, MI 48106
PH: (734)930-4400
Fax: (734)930-4414
Heinonen, Therese, DVM, Founder

International Society for Improvised
Music **[9934]**
PO Box 1603
Ann Arbor, MI 48106
Sarath, Ed, President

Islamic Assembly of North America
[20219]
3588 Plymouth Rd.
Ann Arbor, MI 48105
PH: (734)528-0006
Fax: (734)528-0066

Jewel Heart **[19779]**
1129 Oak Valley Dr.
Ann Arbor, MI 48108
PH: (734)994-3387
Rimpoche, Gelek, President,
Founder

Midwifery Education Accreditation
Council **[14236]**
850 Mt. Pleasant Ave.
Ann Arbor, MI 48103
PH: (360)466-2080
Young, Kristi Ridd, VP

Motor Control and Motion Associa-
tion **[1027]**
900 Victors Way, Ste. 140
Ann Arbor, MI 48108
PH: (734)994-6088
Payne, John, Chairperson

National Center for Manufacturing
Sciences **[2228]**
3025 Boardwalk St.
Ann Arbor, MI 48108
Toll free: 800-222-6267
Fax: (734)995-0380
Steinman, A., Chmn. of the Bd.

National Network of Depression
Centers **[15799]**
2350 Green Rd., Ste. 191
Ann Arbor, MI 48105
PH: (734)332-3914
Fax: (734)332-3939
Rinvelt, Patricia, MBA, Exec. Dir.

NSF International **[17015]**
789 N Dixboro Rd.
Ann Arbor, MI 48113
PH: (734)769-8010
Toll free: 800-673-6275
Fax: (734)769-0109
Bruursema, Tom, Director

Open DeviceNet Vendor Association
[6281]
4220 Varsity Dr., Ste. A
Ann Arbor, MI 48108-5006
PH: (734)975-8840
Fax: (734)922-0027
Voss, Katherine, President, Exec.
Dir.

Relief for Africa **[12718]**
3914 Trade Center Dr.
Ann Arbor, MI 48104
PH: (734)975-7200
Kannenje, Ramadhan, President

Robotic Industries Association
[7105]
900 Victors Way, Ste. 140
Ann Arbor, MI 48108
PH: (734)994-6088
Fax: (734)994-3338
Jacobs, Michael, Chairman

Sarcoma Alliance for Research
through Collaboration **[14060]**
24 Frank Lloyd Wright Dr., Lobby A,
Ste. 3100
Ann Arbor, MI 48105
PH: (734)930-7600
Fax: (734)930-7557
Reinke, Denise, President, CEO

Shudokan Martial Arts Association
[23013]
PO Box 6022
Ann Arbor, MI 48106-6022

PH: (734)645-6441
Suino, Mr. Nicklaus, Director

Society for College and University
Planning **[8442]**
1330 Eisenhower Pl.
Ann Arbor, MI 48108
PH: (734)669-3270
Santilli, Nicholas, Chairman

Society for Research on
Adolescence **[13479]**
2950 S State St., Ste. 401
Ann Arbor, MI 48104
PH: (734)926-0700
Fax: (734)926-0701
Crockett, Lisa, President

Society for Research in Child
Development **[10823]**
2950 S State St., Ste. 401
Ann Arbor, MI 48104
PH: (734)926-0600
Fax: (734)926-0601
Sherrod, Lonnie, PhD, Exec. Dir.

Thai Physicians Association of
America **[16762]**
c/o Chintana Paramagul, MD,
President
4972 Starak Ln.
Ann Arbor, MI 48105
PH: (734)604-6211
Kulwatdanaporn, Somchai, MD,
Comm. Chm.

Traumatic Incident Reduction As-
sociation **[17533]**
5145 Pontiac Trl.
Ann Arbor, MI 48105
PH: (734)761-6268
Toll free: 800-499-2751
Fax: (734)663-6861
Volkman, Marian, President

Universal Martial Arts Brotherhood
[23024]
2427 Buckingham Rd.
Ann Arbor, MI 48104-4913
PH: (734)971-7040
Humesky, Gr. Mast. Eugene A.,
PhD, Chairman, CEO, Founder

University of Michigan | Center for
the Education of Women **[8757]**
330 E Liberty St.
Ann Arbor, MI 48104-2274
PH: (734)764-6005
(734)764-6360
Fax: (734)998-6203
Miller, Jeanne E., Dir. of Info. Svcs.,
Pub. Dir.

Wood Engravers Network **[21788]**
3999 Waters Rd.
Ann Arbor, MI 48103
PH: (734)665-6044
Myers, Bill, Treasurer

IdeasAmerica **[1091]**
PO Box 210863
Auburn Hills, MI 48321
PH: (248)961-2674
Fax: (248)253-9252
Davis, Paula, Exec. Dir.

Independent Organization of Little
Caesar Franchisees **[1460]**
2685 Lapeer Rd., Ste. 101
Auburn Hills, MI 48326
PH: (248)377-1900
Fax: (248)377-1913
Messer, Todd, Exec. Dir.

International Show Car Association
[21405]
1092 Centre Rd.
Auburn Hills, MI 48326

PH: (248)371-1600
(586)703-2381
Millard, Bob, Gen. Mgr.

Science Fiction Research Associa-
tion **[10206]**
c/o Steven Berman, Treasurer
PO Box 214441
Auburn Hills, MI 48321
Berman, Steven, Treasurer

International Shipmasters Associa-
tion **[2247]**
c/o Robert Schallip, President
17592 Simonsen Rd.
Neebish Island
Barbeau, MI 49710-9416
PH: (906)635-0941
Schallip, Robert, President

W.K. Kellogg Foundation **[18946]**
1 Michigan Ave. E
Battle Creek, MI 49017
PH: (269)968-1611
Fax: (269)968-0413
Langenburg, Dianna, VP of HR

American Neurogastroenterology
and Motility Society **[14779]**
45685 Harmony Ln.
Belleville, MI 48111
PH: (734)699-1130
Fax: (734)699-1136
Ennis, Lori, Exec. Dir.

National Toy Fox Terrier Association
[21925]
c/o Julie Slauterbeck, Treasurer
22481 Bohn Rd.
Belleville, MI 48111
PH: (734)652-5184
Slauterbeck, Julie, Treasurer

DirectConnect Humanitarian Aid
[12656]
PO Box 37
Bellevue, MI 49021
PH: (269)763-3687
Toll free: 800-708-0296
Fax: (269)763-3689
Doty, Steven, Founder, President

Agoraphobics in Motion **[12502]**
PO Box 725363
Berkley, MI 48072
PH: (248)547-0400
Fortune, James, President

Association of Seventh-Day
Adventist Librarians **[9690]**
c/o Sarah Kimakwa, Treasurer
James White Library, Rm. 271
4910 Administration Dr.
Berrien Springs, MI 49104
Robertson, Terry, President

Lop Rabbit Club of America **[4600]**
c/o Russ Scott, President
7013 Fairland Rd.
Berrien Springs, MI 49103
PH: (269)687-8431
Parker, Tony, VP

Near East Archaeological Society
[5944]
Andrews University
Horn Archaeological Museum
9047 Old US 31
Berrien Springs, MI 49104-0990
PH: (269)471-3273
Lattimer, Suzanne, Treasurer

Albanian American National
Organization **[19296]**
c/o Gayle Orlow
31057 Rivers Edge Ct.
Beverly Hills, MI 48025
PH: (248)761-1184
Orlow, Gayle, Contact

Society of Medicolegal Death
Investigators [5370]
124 Elm St.
Big Rapids, MI 49307
Hargrave, Kathleen, President

American Supplier Institute [7259]
30200 Telegraph Rd., Ste. 100
Bingham Farms, MI 48025-4503
PH: (612)293-7337
Taguchi, Mr. Shin, President

AVKO Educational Research
Foundation [8577]
3084 Willard Rd.
Birch Run, MI 48415-9404
PH: (810)686-9283
Fax: (810)686-1101
McCabe, Don, President, Dir. of
Res.

Society of Automotive Analysts [302]
1729 Southfield Rd.
Birmingham, MI 48009
PH: (248)804-6433
Pratt, Anthony, Officer

UniteWomen.org [13417]
1221 Bowers St., No. 2225
Birmingham, MI 48012
Teegarden, Karen, President, CEO

Women's Automotive Association
International [304]
PO Box 2535
Birmingham, MI 48012
PH: (248)390-4952
Schultz, Lorraine H., CEO, Founder

National Association of Sales Profes-
sionals [3017]
555 Friendly St.
Bloomfield, MI 48302
Hairston, Rod, CEO, Chmn. of the
Bd.

Congregation Shema Yisrael [20244]
3600 Telegraph Rd.
Bloomfield Hills, MI 48302-2817
PH: (248)593-5150

Ethiopian North American Health
Professionals Association [15000]
Box 150
6632 Telegraph Rd.
Bloomfield Hills, MI 48301
PH: (313)872-2000
Fax: (313)871-1338
Asfaw, Dr. Ingida, MD, Founder,
President

Grandparents Rights Organization
[11918]
1760 S Telegraph Rd.
Bloomfield Hills, MI 48302
Victor, Richard S., Exec. Dir.,
Founder

Italian American Alliance for Busi-
ness and Technology [646]
41000 Woodward Ave., Office 231
Bloomfield Hills, MI 48304
PH: (248)258-1428
Denipoti, Massimo, President

National Aircraft Appraisers Associa-
tion [148]
7 W Square Lake Rd.
Bloomfield Hills, MI 48302
PH: (248)758-2333
Fax: (248)769-6084
Jacobson, Brian M., Contact

Organization for Bat Conservation
[4861]
Cranbrook Institute of Science
39221 Woodward Ave.
Bloomfield Hills, MI 48303

PH: (248)645-3232
Mies, Robert, Exec. Dir., Founder

Automotive Safety Council [313]
c/o Douglas Campbell, President
5572 Arbor Bay Ct.
Brighton, MI 48116
PH: (586)201-8653
Fax: (810)225-8567
Campbell, Douglas P., President

National Trailer Dealers Association
[3347]
9864 E Grand River Ave., Ste. 110-
290
Brighton, MI 48116
Toll free: 800-800-4552
Fax: (810)229-5961
Brown, Gwendolyn, Exec. Dir.,
President

Dysautonomia Information Network
[15926]
PO Box 55
Brooklyn, MI 49230
Lundy, Rachel, President

International Furniture Transportation
and Logistics Council [3089]
282 N Ridge Rd.
Brooklyn, MI 49230
PH: (517)467-9355
Matthews, Russ, Managing Dir.

Little Dresses for Africa [11070]
24614 Curtis Dr.
Brownstown, MI 48134
PH: (734)637-9064
O'Neill, Rachel, Contact

Life Action Revival Ministries [20150]
2727 Niles-Buchanan Rd.
Buchanan, MI 49107
PH: (269)697-8600
Fax: (269)695-2474
Paulus, Byron, Exec. Dir.

Morse Telegraph Club, Inc. [22442]
PO Box 192
Buchanan, MI 49107
PH: (269)548-8219
Galyen, Cindy, Director

Clan Moffat Society [20832]
c/o Roger Moffat, Membership
Chairperson
3020 76th St. SE
Caledonia, MI 49316-8398
Moffett, John, President

American Veterinary Society of
Animal Behavior [17631]
c/o Kari Krause, Treasurer
45298 Indian Creek Dr.
Canton, MI 48187
PH: (734)454-7470
Foote, Dr. Sally, President

Lithuanian-American Bar Association
[5021]
PO Box 871578
Canton, MI 48187
PH: (734)222-0088
Fax: (734)667-3357
Streeter, Patricia A., President

United Suffolk Sheep Association
[4682]
PO Box 872000
Canton, MI 48187
PH: (641)684-5291
Fax: (734)335-7646
Zelinsky, Rob, Director

American Shire Horse Association
[4328]
PO Box 336
Cedar Springs, MI 49319
Toll free: 888-302-6643
Naef, Heinz, Treasurer

National Organization for Raw
Materials [17791]
680 E 5 Point Hwy.
Charlotte, MI 48813
PH: (517)543-0111
Griepentrog, Paul, VP

Doberman Pinscher Club of America
[21869]
c/o Lesley Reeves-Hunt, Membership Secretary
6400 Tripp Rd.
China, MI 48054-2518
Santana, Michelle, President

America's Corvette Club of Michigan
[21325]
PO Box 986
Clarkston, MI 48347
PH: (248)884-3812

Amyloidosis Foundation [14559]
7151 N Main St., Ste. 2
Clarkston, MI 48346-1584
Toll free: 877-269-5643
Fax: (248)922-9620
O'Donnell, Mary, President

United Street Machine Association
[21511]
430 N Batchewana St.
Clawson, MI 48017
PH: (248)435-3091
Haney, Ralph A., Founder

Association for Interdisciplinary Stud-
ies [9580]
44575 Garfield Rd.
Clinton Township, MI 48038
PH: (513)529-2213
Fax: (513)529-5849
Newell, Prof. William H., Exec. Dir.

Charity Music [12368]
40736 Hayes Rd.
Clinton Township, MI 48038-2545
PH: (586)247-7444
Fax: (586)247-7443
Cavanaugh, Greg, CEO, President

Cryonics Institute [14356]
24355 Sorrentino Ct.
Clinton Township, MI 48035
PH: (586)791-5961
Toll free: 866-288-2796
Fax: (586)792-7062
Kowalski, Dennis, President, CEO

Immortalist Society [6356]
24355 Sorrentino Ct.
Clinton Township, MI 48035-3229
PH: (586)791-5961
Porter, York, President

Fairchild Club [21226]
c/o Mike Kelly, President
92 N Circle Dr.
Coldwater, MI 49036
Kelly, Mike, President

Triumph Register of America [21504]
c/o Jeff Kelley, President
443 Edgewater Ct.
Coldwater, MI 49036
PH: (269)251-1996
Kelley, Jeff, President

National Association of Mold Professionals [1165]
3130 Old Farm Ln., Ste. 1
Commerce Township, MI 48390
PH: (248)669-5673

The American Association of Riding
Schools, Inc. [22936]
8375 Coldwater Rd.
Davison, MI 48423-8966
PH: (810)496-0360
Pace, Colleen, President

American Arab Chamber of Com-
merce [23551]
12740 W Warren Ave.
Dearborn, MI 48126
PH: (313)945-1700
Fax: (313)945-6697
Dagher, Ali, Mem., Founder

Arab American Business Women's
Council [3485]
22952 Outer Dr.
Dearborn, MI 48124-4279
PH: (313)277-1986
Judeh, Jumana, President

Arab Community Center for
Economic and Social Services
[8813]
2651 Saulino Ct.
Dearborn, MI 48120
PH: (313)842-7010
Fax: (313)842-5150
Jaber, Hassan, Exec. Dir.

Association for Finishing Processes
[6225]
1 SME Dr.
Dearborn, MI 48128
PH: (313)425-3000
Toll free: 800-733-4763
Fax: (313)425-3400

Automotive Hall of Fame [283]
21400 Oakwood Blvd.
Dearborn, MI 48124
PH: (313)240-4000
Martini, Michael E., Chmn. of the Bd.

Imam Mahdi Association of Marjaeya
[20497]
22000 Garrison St.
Dearborn, MI 48124-2306
PH: (313)562-4626
Toll free: 888-SISTANI
Kashmiri, Sayyid Mohammad Baqir,
Chairman

International Association for Organ
Donation [17510]
PO Box 545
Dearborn, MI 48121
PH: (313)745-2379
Fax: (313)745-4509
Beydoun, Fouad, PhD, CEO,
President

International Feminist Approaches to
Bioethics [11801]
PO Box 1712
Dearborn, MI 48121-1712
Donchin, Anne, Advisor

International Society of Iraqi
Scientists [7138]
PO Box 4445
Dearborn, MI 48126
Fax: (248)538-6034
Jamil, Prof. Hikmet, MD, President

Islamic Center of America [20220]
19500 Ford Rd.
Dearborn, MI 48128
PH: (313)593-0000
Amen, Ron, Chairman

National Network for Arab American
Communities [10734]
c/o ACCESS
2651 Saulino Ct.
Dearborn, MI 48120
PH: (313)842-1933
Fax: (313)554-2801
Tonova, Nadia, Director

North American Manufacturing
Research Institution of SME [6797]
1 SME Dr.
Dearborn, MI 48128

PH: (313)425-3000
Toll free: 800-733-4763
Fax: (313)425-3400
Bartles, Dean L., PhD, President

Society of Manufacturing Engineers
[6798]
1 SME Dr.
Dearborn, MI 48128-2408
PH: (313)425-3000
Toll free: 800-733-4763
Fax: (313)425-3400
Krause, Jeffrey M., CEO

Society of Manufacturing Engineers -
Composites Manufacturing Tech
Group [2231]
1 SME Dr.
Dearborn, MI 48128
PH: (313)425-3000
Toll free: 800-733-4763
Fax: (313)425-3400
Smyth, Susan M., PhD, FSME,
Secretary

Society of Manufacturing Engineers
Education Foundation [7863]
1 SME Dr.
Dearborn, MI 48128-2408
Ruestow, Brian, President

Society of Manufacturing Engineers-
Machining and Material Removal
Community [7295]
1 SME Dr.
Dearborn, MI 48128
PH: (313)425-3000
Toll free: 800-733-4763

Society of Manufacturing Engineers -
Rapid Technologies and Additive
Manufacturing Community [6799]
1 SME Dr.
Dearborn, MI 48128-2408
PH: (313)425-3000
Toll free: 800-733-4763
Fax: (313)425-3400
Molnar, Michael F., President

International Catholic Stewardship
Council [19846]
26300 Ford Rd., No. 317
Dearborn Heights, MI 48127
Toll free: 800-352-3452
Fax: (313)446-8316
Murphy, Michael, Exec. Dir.

Mariannhill Mission Society [19858]
23715 Ann Arbor Trl.
Dearborn Heights, MI 48127
PH: (313)561-7140
Fax: (313)561-9486

41pounds.org [4031]
2000 Brush St., Ste. 262
Detroit, MI 48226
Fax: (248)738-2761

Alpha Iota Delta [23686]
c/o Gregory Ulferts, Executive Direc-
tor
University of Detroit Mercy
4001 W McNichols Rd.
Detroit, MI 48221
PH: (313)993-1219
Fax: (313)993-1052
Ulferts, Dr. Gregory W., Exec. Dir.

American Blind Bowling Association
[22771]
c/o Thomas Lester, President
19146 Ardmore St.
Detroit, MI 48235-1701
PH: (313)864-0448
Lester, Thomas, President

American Board of Dermatology
[14479]
Henry Ford Health System
1 Ford Pl.

Detroit, MI 48202-3450
PH: (313)874-1088
Fax: (313)872-3221

Black Mothers' Breastfeeding As-
sociation [13854]
9641 Harper Ave.
Detroit, MI 48213
Toll free: 800-313-6141
Green, Kidada, MAT, Founder, Exec.
Dir.

A Bone Marrow Wish [13847]
PO Box 21554
Detroit, MI 48221
Frierson, John, Founder

College for Creative Studies Alumni
Association [19316]
201 E Kirby St.
Detroit, MI 48202-4034
PH: (313)664-7400
Toll free: 800-952-2787
Guzman, Jessica, Mem.

Eta Phi Beta Sorority, Inc. [23693]
19983 Livernois Ave.
Detroit, MI 48221-1299
PH: (313)862-0600
Fax: (313)862-6245
Doublet, Barbara Ann H., 1st VP

Gospel Music Workshop of America
[9911]
3908 W Warren Ave.
Detroit, MI 48208
PH: (313)898-6900
Jamison, Dr. Albert L., Sr., Chairman

Helping Hand for Relief and
Development [11668]
12541 McDougall St., Ste. 100
Detroit, MI 48212
PH: (313)279-5378
Toll free: 877-521-6291
Fax: (313)366-0200
Farrukh, Raza, President, CEO

Instrumentation Testing Association
[6726]
PO Box 2611
Detroit, MI 48202
PH: (702)568-1445
Toll free: 877-236-1256
Fax: (702)568-1446
Assef, Saeed, President

International Association of Jesuit
Business Schools [7552]
4001 W McNichols Rd.
Detroit, MI 48221
PH: (313)993-1219
Fax: (313)993-1052
Ulferts, Dr. Gregory W., Exec. Dir.,
Secretary

International Association for
Language Learning Technology
[8184]
c/o Sangeetha Gopalakrishnan,
President
Wayne State University
385 Manoogian Hall
906 W Warren
Detroit, MI 48202
Gopalak, Sangeetha, President

International Proteolysis Society
[6055]
6105 Scott Hall
School of Medicine
Wayne State University
Detroit, MI 48201
PH: (313)577-0514
    (313)577-4451
Fax: (313)577-6739
Kini, Manjunatha, VP

Labor Notes [23468]
7435 Michigan Ave.
Detroit, MI 48210

PH: (313)842-6262
Fax: (313)842-0227
Brenner, Mark, Director

National American Arab Nurses As-
sociation [16144]
615 Griswold St., Ste. 925
Detroit, MI 48226
PH: (313)680-5049
Khalifa, Rose, RN, President

National Federation for Just Com-
munities [11289]
525 New Ctr. One
3031 W Grand Blvd.
Detroit, MI 48202-3025
PH: (804)515-7950
Fax: (804)515-7177
Zur, Jonathan, V. Chmn. of Admin.

National Socialist Movement [19240]
PO Box 13768
Detroit, MI 48213
PH: (651)659-6307
Schoep, Comdr. Jeff, Director

National Tots and Teens [13468]
16555 Wyoming Ave.
Detroit, MI 48221

Proving Innocence [11545]
535 Griswold St., Ste. 111-254
Detroit, MI 48226
PH: (313)718-2890
Proctor, Bill, Founder

Slovak Studies Association [19650]
c/o Kevin Deegan-Krause, President
Dept. of Political Science
Wayne Station University
2040 F/AB
Detroit, MI 48220
PH: (313)577-2630
Fax: (313)993-3435
Deegan-Krause, Dr. Kevin, President

Sphinx Organization [10015]
400 Renaissance Ctr., Ste. 2550
Detroit, MI 48243
PH: (313)877-9100
Fax: (313)887-0164
Dworkin, Aaron P., Founder,
President

Teamsters for a Democratic Union
[23526]
PO Box 10128
Detroit, MI 48210
PH: (313)842-2600
Fax: (313)842-0227

UAW Community Action Program
[18876]
Solidarity House
8000 E Jefferson Ave.
Detroit, MI 48214
PH: (313)926-5000
Williams, Dennis, President

United Auto Workers [23380]
Solidarity House
8000 E Jefferson Ave.
Detroit, MI 48214
PH: (313)926-5000
Toll free: 800-243-8829
Williams, Dennis, President

Vedic Friends Association [20618]
PO Box 15082
Detroit, MI 48215
Knapp, Stephen, President,
Treasurer

VIP Mentoring [11550]
7700 2nd Ave., Ste. 617
Detroit, MI 48202-2411
PH: (313)964-1110
Comer, Jim, Trustee

Woman Within International Ltd.
[13404]
269 Walker St., Ste. 204
Detroit, MI 48207-4258
Toll free: 800-732-0890
Fax: (519)732-0890
Renaud, Margaret, Administrator

Cherry Marketing Institute [4231]
12800 Escanaba Dr., Ste. A
Dewitt, MI 48820
Smith, George, Contact

Society of Physician Assistants in
Rheumatology [17167]
PO Box 492
Dimondale, MI 48821
PH: (517)646-9337
Giannelli, Antonio, President

Academy of International Business
[7539]
Eppley Ctr.
Michigan State University
645 N Shaw Ln., Rm. 7
East Lansing, MI 48824
PH: (517)432-1452
Fax: (517)432-1009
Kiyak, Dr. Tunga, Managing Dir.

Agriculture, Food & Human Values
Society [3542]
480 Wilson Rd., Rm 316
East Lansing, MI 48824
Howard, Phil, President

Allies for Change [19101]
PO Box 4353
East Lansing, MI 48826
Morrison, Melanie S., Founder,
Exec. Dir.

American Board of Emergency
Medicine [14672]
3000 Coolidge Rd.
East Lansing, MI 48823-6319
PH: (517)332-4800
Fax: (517)332-2234
Reisdorff, Earl J., MD, Exec. Dir.

American Council of Snowmobile
Associations [23175]
c/o Christine Jourdain, Executive
Director
271 Woodland Pass, Ste. 216
East Lansing, MI 48823-2060
PH: (517)351-4362
Fax: (517)351-1363
Jourdain, Christine, Exec. Dir.

American Society of Irrigation
Consultants [7363]
4700 S Hagadorn Rd., Ste. 195D
East Lansing, MI 48823-6808
PH: (508)763-8140
Munion, Ivy, President

Institute of Public Utilities [3418]
Michigan State University
Owen Graduate Hall
735 E Shaw Ln., Rm. W157
East Lansing, MI 48825-1109
PH: (517)355-1876
Fax: (517)355-1854
Beecher, Janice A., PhD, Director

International Rural Sociology As-
sociation [7184]
c/o Ray Jussaume, Jr., Secretary-
Treasurer
Michigan State University
317B Berkey Hall
East Lansing, MI 48824
PH: (517)353-6790
Lawrence, Geoffrey, AON, President

International Safe Transit Association
[3091]
1400 Abbott Rd., Ste. 160
East Lansing, MI 48823-1900

PH: (517)333-3437
Fax: (517)333-3813
Daum, Matt, Chairman

International Society for Concrete
Pavements [539]
c/o Neeraj Buch, President
3556 Engineering Bldg.
Department of Civil and
Environmental Engineering
Michigan State University
East Lansing, MI 48824
PH: (517)432-0012
Fax: (517)432-1827
Perrie, Brian, VP

Metropolitan Tree Improvement Alli-
ance [4732]
c/o Bert Cregg, Secretary/Treasurer
Michigan State University
Dept. of Horticulture
East Lansing, MI 48824-1325
St. Hilaire, Dr. Rolston, Exec. Dir.

Online Audiovisual Catalogers
[9720]
c/o Autumn Faulkner, Treasurer
366 W Circle Dr.
East Lansing, MI 48824
Traill, Stacie, President

Pan-American Association for
Biochemistry and Molecular Biol-
ogy [6059]
Michigan State University
Dept. of Biochemistry and Molecular
East Lansing, MI 48824-1319
Maccioni, Dr. Hugo J. F., Chairman

Save Yemen's Flora and Fauna
[3942]
1523 River Terrace Dr.
East Lansing, MI 48823
Almajrabi, Ibrahim, President

Slavic, East European, and Eurasian
Folklore Association [9331]
c/o Shannon Spasova
Dept. of Linguistics and Germanic,
Slavic, Asian and African
Languages, Michigan State
University
B-331 Wells Hall
619 Red Cedar Rd.
East Lansing, MI 48824-3402
Harris, Adrienne, VP

Society for the Study of Midwestern
Literature [9767]
c/o Mr. Roger J. Bresnahan, PhD,
Secretary/Treasurer
Michigan State University
Bessey Hall, Rm. 235
434 Farm Ln.
East Lansing, MI 48824
Comer, Dawn, President

Weave a Real Peace [10766]
6182 Pollard Ave.
East Lansing, MI 48823
PH: (517)333-8145
Allen, Judy, Coord., Admin.

World War Two Studies Association
[9529]
141h Old Horticulture
Michigan State University
506 E Circle Dr.
East Lansing, MI 48824
PH: (517)432-5134
Fax: (517)884-6994
Parillo, Mark P., Secretary, Editor

American Autoimmune Related
Diseases Association, Inc. [15370]
22100 Gratiot Ave.
Eastpointe, MI 48021
PH: (586)776-3900
Toll free: 800-598-4668
Fax: (586)776-3903
Ladd, Virginia, RT, Exec. Dir.,
President

American Power Boat Association
[22594]
17640 E 9 Mile Rd.
Eastpointe, MI 48021-2563
PH: (586)773-9700
Fax: (586)773-6490
Wheeler, Mark, President

American Association of Pro Life
Obstetricians and Gynecologists
[19054]
PO Box 395
Eau Claire, MI 49111-0395
PH: (202)230-0997
DeCook, Joseph, Mem.

American Coal Ash Association
[3443]
38800 Country Club Dr.
Farmington Hills, MI 48331
PH: (720)870-7897
Fax: (720)870-7889
Ward, John, Coord.

American College of Osteopathic
Neurologists and Psychiatrists
[16003]
28595 Orchard Lake Rd., Ste. 200
Farmington Hills, MI 48334
PH: (248)553-6207
Fax: (248)553-6222
Lage, Susan, President

American Concrete Institute [6344]
38800 Country Club Dr.
Farmington Hills, MI 48331-3439
PH: (248)848-3700
Fax: (248)848-3701
Burg, Ronald G., Exec. VP

American Institute for Preventive
Medicine [16799]
30445 Northwestern Hwy., Ste. 350
Farmington Hills, MI 48334
PH: (248)539-1800
Toll free: 800-345-2476
Fax: (248)539-1808
Powell, Don R., PhD, CEO,
President

American Shotcrete Association
[781]
38800 Country Club Dr.
Farmington Hills, MI 48331
PH: (248)848-3780
Fax: (248)848-3740
Hanskat, Charles S., P.E., Exec. Dir.

Council of Engineering and Scientific
Society Executives [6551]
38800 Country Club Dr.
Farmington Hills, MI 48331
PH: (734)972-3930
    (248)848-3191
Marlowe, Walter, Chmn. of the Bd.

Equipment and Tool Institute [318]
37899 W 12 Mile Rd., Ste. 220
Farmington Hills, MI 48331-3050
PH: (248)656-5080
Morgan, Tim, President

Fire Department Safety Officers As-
sociation [5747]
33365 Raphael Rd.
Farmington Hills, MI 48336
PH: (248)880-1864
Fax: (248)479-0491
Maddox, Richard, Chairman

Independent Professional
Representatives Organization
[266]
c/o Ray Wright, Executive Director
34157 W 9 Mile Rd.
Farmington Hills, MI 48335
PH: (248)474-0522
Toll free: 800-420-4268
Wright, Raymond, Exec. Dir.

JARC [12324]
30301 Northwestern Hwy., Ste. 100
Farmington Hills, MI 48334
PH: (248)538-6611
Friedberg, Rena, Officer

National Truck Equipment Associa-
tion [328]
37400 Hills Tech Dr.
Farmington Hills, MI 48331-3414
PH: (248)489-7090
Fax: (248)489-8590
Kastner, Michael, Managing Dir.

One World Medical Mission [12295]
PO Box 2784
Farmington Hills, MI 48333
Garmo, Nidhal, Founder

Post-Tensioning Institute [572]
38800 Country Club Dr.
Farmington Hills, MI 48331
PH: (248)848-3180
Fax: (248)848-3181
Sward, Robert, President

Slag Cement Association [797]
38800 Country Club
Farmington Hills, MI 48331
PH: (847)977-6920
Melander, John, Exec. Dir.

Society for Humanistic Judaism
[20282]
28611 W 12 Mile Rd.
Farmington Hills, MI 48334
PH: (248)478-7610
Fax: (248)478-3159
Logan, Richard, President

Tooling, Manufacturing and
Technologies Association [1774]
28237 Orchard Lake Rd., Ste. 101
Farmington Hills, MI 48334
PH: (248)488-0300
Toll free: 800-969-9682
Fax: (248)488-0500
Dumont, Robert J., President, CEO

Trinity Health International [15162]
34605 12 Mile Rd.
Farmington Hills, MI 48331-3221
PH: (248)489-6100
Williams, Patricia, Director

Cecchetti Council of America [7699]
23393 Meadows Ave.
Flat Rock, MI 48134
PH: (734)379-6710
Fax: (734)379-3886
Plansker, Stephanie, Rec. Sec.

International Association of Pipe
Smokers Clubs [22387]
647 S Saginaw St.
Flint, MI 48502
Spaniola, Dan, Chairman

International College of Dentists
[14450]
G3535 Beecher Rd., Ste. G
Flint, MI 48532-2700
PH: (810)820-3087
Fax: (810)265-7047
Hinterman, Dr. John V., Registrar

International Physical Fitness As-
sociation [3159]
3407 Southgate Dr.
Flint, MI 48507
Toll free: 877-520-4732
Fax: (810)239-3320
Sherrer, Ron, President

Charles Stewart Mott Foundation
[12982]
Mott Foundation Bldg.
503 S Saginaw St., Ste. 1200

Flint, MI 48502-1851
PH: (810)238-5651
White, William S., Chairman, CEO

Muslim Students Association of the
United States and Canada [8620]
4400 S Saginaw St., Ste. 1250
Flint, MI 48507
PH: (810)893-6011
Fiaz, Ali, President

American Dog Show Judges [21808]
c/o Carl Liepmann, Secretary
9144 W Mt. Morris Rd.
Flushing, MI 48433
PH: (480)991-0216
Fax: (480)991-0217
Penta, Dr. Gerard C., President

Tamburitza Association of America
[10017]
c/o Joseph R. Novosel, Esq.,
President
3894 Spartan Dr.
Fort Gratiot, MI 48059
PH: (810)385-9667
Novosel, Joseph R., Esq., President

National Association of Wheat
Weavers [21771]
c/o Kate Farris, Treasurer
9360 Warnick Rd.
Frankenmuth, MI 48734
PH: (989)928-0477
Ruff, Dianne, Comm. Chm.

Indo-American Chamber of Com-
merce USA [696]
PO Box 250125
Franklin, MI 48025
PH: (248)506-7555
Bhattiprolu, Nandita, Exec. Dir.

American Decency Association
[18031]
203 E Main St.
Fremont, MI 49412
PH: (231)924-4050
Johnson, Bill, Founder, President

Etruscan Foundation [5937]
PO Box 26
Fremont, MI 49412-0026
PH: (231)519-0675
Fax: (231)924-0777
String, Richard F., Exec. Dir.

National Association of Rural Health
Clinics [17009]
2 E Main St.
Fremont, MI 49412
Toll free: 866-306-1961
Fax: (866)311-9606

PRIDE Youth Programs [13175]
707 W Main St.
Fremont, MI 49412-1414
PH: (231)924-1662
Toll free: 800-668-9277
Dewispelaere, Jay, CEO, President

Model A Restorers Club [21437]
6721 Merriman Rd.
Garden City, MI 48135-1956
PH: (734)427-9050
Fax: (734)427-9054
Johnson, Gary, VP

National Association of
Environmental Law Societies
[5184]
6408 Western Ave.
Glen Arbor, MI 49636
PH: (617)610-7399
Worth, Dan, Exec. Dir.

American Yangjia Michuan Taijiquan
Association [22985]
PO Box 173
Grand Haven, MI 49417-0173

Blind Children's Fund **[17690]**
PO Box 187
Grand Ledge, MI 48837
PH: (989)779-9966
Fax: (269)756-3133
Kwast, Karla B., CEO, Exec. Dir.

Action Institute for the Study of
Religion and Liberty **[20531]**
98 E Fulton St.
Grand Rapids, MI 49503
PH: (616)454-3080
Toll free: 800-345-2286
Fax: (616)454-9454
Mauren, Kris Alan, Exec. Dir.

American Manual Medicine Association **[13596]**
2040 Raybrook SE, Ste. 103
Grand Rapids, MI 49546
Toll free: 888-375-7245
Fax: (616)575-9066
Hegstrand, Linda, PhD, Bd. Member

American Medical Massage Association **[15552]**
2040 Raybrook St. SE, Ste. 103
Grand Rapids, MI 49546
Toll free: 888-375-7245
Fax: (616)575-9066

American Reflexology Certification
Board **[13599]**
2586 Knightsbridge Rd. SE
Grand Rapids, MI 49546
PH: (303)933-6921
Fax: (303)904-0460
Rainone, Michael, President

Association for a More Just Society
[17877]
PO Box 888631
Grand Rapids, MI 49588
Toll free: 800-897-1135
Bandstra, Richard, Exec. Dir.

Bethany Christian Services
International **[10865]**
901 Eastern Ave. NE
Grand Rapids, MI 49501-0294
PH: (616)224-7550
Toll free: 800-238-4269
Blacquiere, William J., CEO,
President

Business and Institutional Furniture
Manufacturer's Association **[1476]**
678 Front Ave. NW, Ste. 150
Grand Rapids, MI 49504-5368
PH: (616)285-3963
Fax: (616)285-3765
Askren, Stan, Bd. Member

Christian Reformed Church-Spanish
and World Literature Committee
[19964]
1700 28th St. SE
Grand Rapids, MI 49508
PH: (616)241-1691
Toll free: 877-279-9994
Fax: (616)224-0834
Timmermans, Steven, Exec. Dir.

Copier Dealers Association **[2443]**
c/o John Lowery, President
5282 E Paris Ave. SE
Grand Rapids, MI 49512-9634
Weiss, Larry, Director

Council for Interior Design Accreditation **[8049]**
206 Grandville Ave. SW, Ste. 350
Grand Rapids, MI 49503-4079
PH: (616)458-0400
Fax: (616)458-0460
Mattson, Holly, Exec. Dir.

Dynamic Youth Ministries **[19973]**
Calvinist Cadet Corps
1333 Alger St. SE

Grand Rapids, MI 49507
PH: (616)241-5616
Fax: (616)241-5558
Broene, Mr. G. Richard, Exec. Dir.

Fellowship of Missions **[20417]**
1608 Aberdeen St. NE
Grand Rapids, MI 49505-3910
PH: (616)361-2396
Belt, Maynard H., President

Highway Melodies Inc. **[20367]**
PO Box 8451
Grand Rapids, MI 49518-8451
PH: (616)455-5760
Toll free: 800-452-0951
Tilburt, Bryan, Exec. Dir.

Historians of British Art **[8897]**
c/o Craig Ashley Hanson, President
Calvin College
3201 Burton St., SE
Grand Rapids, MI 49546
Hanson, Craig Ashley, President

International Association for Human
Caring **[15024]**
PO Box 6703
Grand Rapids, MI 49516-6703
France, Nancey E.M., President

International Society of Primerus
Law Firms **[5015]**
171 Monroe Ave. NW, Ste. 750
Grand Rapids, MI 49503
PH: (616)454-9939
Toll free: 800-968-2211
Fax: (616)458-7099
Buchanan, John C., Esq., Founder,
President

Joint Labor Management Committee
of the Retail Food Industry **[23418]**
2153 Wealthy St. SE
Grand Rapids, MI 49506
Toll free: 800-304-5540
Fax: (248)274-1036
Potter, Bob, Chairman

Life Matters Worldwide **[12779]**
5075 Clay Ave. SW, Ste. C
Grand Rapids, MI 49548
PH: (616)257-6800
Toll free: 800-968-6086
Lothamer, M. Thomas, President

National Association of School
Safety and Law Enforcement Officials **[8524]**
c/o Larry D. Johnson, President
1331 Franklin St.
Grand Rapids, MI 49504
PH: (616)819-2100
Fax: (616)819-2017
Johnson, Larry D., President

National Necrotizing Fasciitis
Foundation **[17346]**
2731 Porter SW
Grand Rapids, MI 49519-2140
PH: (862)213-5213
Batdorff, Donna, Founder, Exec. Dir.

NPAworldwide **[1100]**
1680 Viewpond Dr. SE
Grand Rapids, MI 49508
PH: (616)455-6555
Fax: (616)455-8255

Partners Worldwide **[20004]**
6139 Tahoe Dr.
Grand Rapids, MI 49546
PH: (616)818-4900
Toll free: 800-919-7307
Seebeck, Doug, President

Phoenix Society for Burn Survivors
[13865]
1835 RW Berends Dr. SW
Grand Rapids, MI 49519-4955

PH: (616)458-2773
Toll free: 800-888-2876
Fax: (616)458-2831
Acton, Amy, RN, Exec. Dir.

Progressive Democrats of America
[18117]
PO Box 150064
Grand Rapids, MI 49515-0064
Toll free: 877-239-2093
Buchan, Kimberly, Coord., Admin.

Society of Christian Philosophers
[10122]
Dept. of Philosophy
Calvin College
1845 Knollcrest Cir. SE
Grand Rapids, MI 49546-4402
Van Dyke, Christina, Exec. Dir.

Tasters Guild International **[191]**
1515 Michigan NE
Grand Rapids, MI 49503
PH: (616)454-7815
Fax: (616)459-9969
Borrello, Joe, CEO, President

Van Andel Education Institute **[7805]**
333 Bostwick Ave. NE
Grand Rapids, MI 49503
PH: (616)234-5000
Fax: (616)234-5001
Van Andel, David L., Chairman, CEO

World Renew **[12200]**
1700 28th St. SE
Grand Rapids, MI 49508
PH: (616)241-1691
(616)224-0740
Toll free: 800-552-7972
Zuidema, Roy, President

American and Foreign Christian
Union **[19942]**
2885 Sanford Ave. SW, No. 29934
Grandville, MI 49418-1342
Rislov, Ken, President

Association of Sewing and Design
Professionals **[200]**
2885 Sanford Ave. SW, No. 19588
Grandville, MI 49418
Toll free: 877-755-0303
Utberg, Debra, President

The Haunted Attraction Association
[1137]
2885 Stanford Ave. SW, No. 28015
Grandville, MI 49418
PH: (616)439-4220
Toll free: 866-490-9603
Bertolino, Brett, VP

IFCA International **[20025]**
3520 Fairlane Ave. SW
Grandville, MI 49418
PH: (616)531-1840
Fax: (616)531-1814
Lofquist, Dr. Les, Exec. Dir.

National Society of Pershing Angels
[23822]
2885 Sanford Ave. SW, Ste. 21820
Grandville, MI 49418

O'Dochartaigh Clann Association
[20989]
c/o Cameron Dougherty, Interim
Executive Committee
4078 Bruce Ct. SW
Grandville, MI 49418
PH: (616)534-8032
Daugherty, Steve, Exec. Ofc.

Organization for Computational
Neurosciences **[6919]**
2885 Sanford Ave. SW, No. 15359
Grandville, MI 49418
De Schutter, Dr. Erik, President

Students for Concealed Carry
[18257]
2885 Sanford Ave. SW, No. 24704
Grandville, MI 49418
Smith, Reid K., MD, Dir. of Dev.

Visitor Studies Association **[8719]**
2885 Sanford Ave. SW, No. 18100
Grandville, MI 49418
PH: (740)872-0566
Fax: (301)637-3312
Kiehl, Kimberlee, President

National Relief Network **[12703]**
PO Box 125
Greenville, MI 48838-0125
PH: (616)225-2525
Harding, R. Scott, CEO, Founder

American Revenue Association
[22304]
PO Box 74
Grosse Ile, MI 48138-0074
PH: (734)676-2649
Fax: (734)676-2959
Ivester, Hermann, VP

Association for Comprehensive NeuroTherapy **[16010]**
c/o Sheila Rogers DeMare, Director
PO Box 159
Grosse Ile, MI 48138-0159
DeMare, Sheila Rogers, MS, Director, Founder

Carriers and Locals Society, Inc.
[21634]
PO Box 74
Grosse Ile, MI 48138
PH: (734)676-2649
Fax: (734)676-2959
Morris, Vernon, President

Friends of Kenyan Orphans **[10986]**
920 Berkshire Rd.
Grosse Pointe, MI 48230-1822
PH: (313)815-9900
Fax: (313)822-9380
Ozar, Sue Horrigan, President,
Founder

Royal College of Physicians &
Surgeons of the United States of
America **[17535]**
485 Allard Rd.
Grosse Pointe, MI 48236
PH: (313)882-0641
Fax: (313)882-0979
Alli, Dr. Benjamin, Chancellor

Grosse Pointe War Memorial Association **[21122]**
32 Lake Shore Dr.
Grosse Pointe Farms, MI 48236-3726
PH: (313)881-7511
Fax: (313)884-6638
Everingham, J. Theodore, Chairman

Finnish American Historical Archives
[9321]
c/o Joanna Chopp
435 Quincy St.
Hancock, MI 49930
PH: (906)487-7347
Fax: (906)487-7557
Chopp, Joanna, Arch.

George Wright Society **[4110]**
PO Box 65
Hancock, MI 49930-0065
PH: (906)487-9722
Harmon, David, Exec. Dir.

Webb Deep-Sky Society **[6013]**
c/o John Isles, Secretary/Treasurer
10575 Darrel Dr.
Hanover, MI 49241
Isles, John, Secretary, Treasurer

Environmental Management Association **[2129]**
c/o Lauren Marosi, Executive Director
38575 Mallast St.
Harrison Township, MI 48045
Toll free: 866-999-4EMA
Fax: (586)463-8075
Kapral, Nancy K., Bookkeeper

Thompson Collectors Association **[22025]**
PO Box 66
Hartland, MI 48353
Troy, Bill, President

International Snowmobile Manufacturers Association **[2917]**
1640 Haslett Rd., Ste. 170
Haslett, MI 48840
PH: (517)339-7788
Fax: (517)339-7798

Iraqi Artists Association **[8926]**
c/o Amer Hanna Fatuhi, Founder
PO Box 171
Hazel Park, MI 48030
Namou-Yatooma, Weam, Founder, Director

Loyal Escorts of the Green Garter **[21011]**
c/o Michael Pearce, President
1645 E Madge Ave.
Hazel Park, MI 48030
Pearce, Michael, President

National Organization of Iraqi Christians **[12438]**
PO Box 833
Hazel Park, MI 48030
PH: (586)939-2554
Kalasho, Tahrir S., CEO, Founder

American Tolkien Society **[9037]**
PO Box 97
Highland, MI 48357
Helms, Amalie A., Exec. Dir.

Ridgeback Rescue of the United States **[10690]**
c/o Kitty Morgan
1790 Valley Dr.
Highland, MI 48356
PH: (786)309-7787
Marvin, Shellie, Director

American Guild of Town Criers **[10172]**
121 S Division Ave.
Holland, MI 49424
PH: (616)396-1043
Austin, Dennis, VP

Aqua Clara International **[13316]**
88 Sun Ridge Dr.
Holland, MI 49424
Knopke, Harry, President

Association for the Advancement of Dutch-American Studies **[9280]**
c/o Joint Archives of Holland
Hope College
PO Box 9000
Holland, MI 49422-9000
Reynolds, Geoffrey D., Secretary

Holland Historical Trust **[9281]**
16 W 9th St.
Holland, MI 49423-3508
PH: (616)796-3320

Trans Youth Family Allies **[18728]**
PO Box 1471
Holland, MI 49422-1471
Toll free: 888-462-8932
Pearson, Kim, Director

Helping Hearts Helping Hands **[12544]**
6250 Chinn Ct.
Holly, MI 48442

PH: (248)980-5090
(248)830-6871
Cale, Erica, Founder

43rd Bomb Group Association **[20675]**
c/o Louise V. Terrell, Secretary
207 Huron St.
Houghton, MI 49931
Lanson, Susan Clark, President

International Committee for the Conservation of the Industrial Heritage **[9490]**
c/o Prof. Patrick Martin, President
Michigan Technological University
1400 Townsend Dr.
Houghton, MI 49931-1200
PH: (906)487-2070
Martin, Prof. Patrick, President

Society for Industrial Archeology **[5950]**
Social Sciences Dept.
Michigan Technological University
1400 Townsend Dr.
Houghton, MI 49931-1295
PH: (906)487-1889
Tannenbaum, Saul, Director

Mustang II Network **[21445]**
115 McDonald Dr.
Houghton Lake, MI 48629
PH: (313)653-1516
Grahl, Timothy M., Founder

Vintage Triumph Register **[21517]**
PO Box 655
Howell, MI 48844
Discher, Blake J., President

Blackburn Family Association **[20784]**
25474 Wareham Dr.
Huntington Woods, MI 48070
PH: (248)677-7411
Myers, Linda, President

Interlochen Center for the Arts **[8977]**
9900 Diamond Park Rd.
Interlochen, MI 49643
PH: (231)276-7200
(231)276-7230
Toll free: 800-681-5912
Kimpton, Jeffrey S., President

107th Engineer Association **[4971]**
900 Palms Ave.
Ishpeming, MI 49849-1064
Perry, Thomas, Secretary

National Association of Photo Equipment Technicians **[2586]**
3000 Picture Pl.
Jackson, MI 49201
PH: (517)788-8100
Heinbokel, Raymond J., Jr., President

Photo Imaging Education Association **[8425]**
3000 Picture Pl.
Jackson, MI 49201
PH: (517)788-8100
Fax: (517)788-8371

Professional School Photographers Association International **[2592]**
3000 Picture Pl.
Jackson, MI 49201
PH: (517)788-8100
Toll free: 800-762-9287
Fax: (517)788-8371
Esp, Jim, Exec. Dir., Secretary

Association for Contextual Behavioral Science **[6033]**
1880 Pinegrove Dr.
Jenison, MI 49428
Rodrigues, Emily Neilan, Exec. Dir.

National Puzzlers' League **[22055]**
2507 Almar St.
Jenison, MI 49428
Hamilton, Craig, Editor

Philadelphia Society **[18998]**
11620 Rutan Cir.
Jerome, MI 49249
PH: (517)688-5111
Fax: (517)688-5113
Hales, Daniel B., Asst. Sec.

Association for Rehabilitation Programs in Computer Technology **[11575]**
Sangren Hall
Educational Leadership, Research and Technology Dept.
Western Michigan University
Kalamazoo, MI 49008-5275
PH: (269)387-2053
Fax: (269)387-3696
Kret, Dot, President

Clean Water for the World **[13318]**
PO Box 20416
Kalamazoo, MI 49019-1416
PH: (269)342-1354
Bohl, Anne, Founder

Crayons4Kids **[13042]**
601 John St., Ste. M-351
Kalamazoo, MI 49007
PH: (269)377-1860
Leinwand, Janis, Contact

International Association of Torch Clubs **[2741]**
2917 Duchess Dr.
Kalamazoo, MI 49008
PH: (269)312-8026
Toll free: 888-622-4101
Fax: (866)873-3690
Coppinger, Jim, Exec. Sec.

International Child Care U.S.A. **[11238]**
240 W Michigan
Kalamazoo, MI 49007
PH: (269)382-9960
Toll free: 800-722-4453
Mumma, Mr. Keith, Director

United Kennel Club **[21975]**
100 E Kilgore Rd.
Kalamazoo, MI 49002-5584
PH: (269)343-9020
Fax: (269)343-7037
Raab, Tanya, President

W.E. Upjohn Institute for Employment Research **[11786]**
300 S Westnedge Ave.
Kalamazoo, MI 49007-4686
PH: (269)343-5541
Fax: (269)343-3308
Parfet, Donald R., Chairman

WPC Club **[21524]**
Box 3504
Kalamazoo, MI 49003-3504
Fax: (269)694-2818
Bowman, Richard, President

Hunt for a Cure **[15645]**
2687 44th St. SE
Kentwood, MI 49512
PH: (616)455-9405
Fax: (616)897-0345
Odland, Peter, Founder

Citizens for Alternatives to Chemical Contamination **[4538]**
8735 Maple Grove Rd.
Lake, MI 48632-9511
PH: (989)544-3318
McManemy, Victor, Chairman

American Romanian Orthodox Youth **[20590]**
c/o Stephen Maxim, President
832 Indian Lake Rd.

Lake Orion, MI 48362
PH: (586)260-3342
Precop, Jessica, Officer

German Professional Women's Association **[3490]**
PO Box 476
Lake Orion, MI 48361-0476
PH: (248)693-9341
Fax: (248)693-9341
Griesser, Christina, President

National Catholic Council on Addictions **[13167]**
1601 Joslyn Rd.
Lake Orion, MI 48360
Toll free: 800-626-6910

National World War II Glider Pilots Association **[20671]**
c/o Charles L. Day
PO Box 439
Lambertville, MI 48144-0439
Theis, George I., Treasurer

Finnish North American Literature Association **[9323]**
c/o Beth L. Virtanen, President
PO Box 212
L'Anse, MI 49946
Virtanen, Beth L., PhD, President

American Academy of Podiatric Practice Management **[16774]**
1000 W St. Joseph Hwy., Ste. 200
Lansing, MI 48915
PH: (517)484-1930
Fax: (517)485-9408
Weaver, Benjamin W., DPM, President

American Board of Industrial Hygiene **[16311]**
6015 W St. Joseph, Ste. 102
Lansing, MI 48917
PH: (517)321-2638
Fax: (517)321-4624
Chung, Ulric K., CEO

American Society of Podiatric Medical Assistants **[16785]**
1000 W St. Joseph Hwy., Ste. 200
Lansing, MI 48915
Toll free: 888-882-7762
Fax: (517)485-9408
Keathley, Karen, PMAC, Exec. Dir.

Association of American Plant Food Control Officials **[4943]**
c/o April Hunt, President
PO Box 30017
Lansing, MI 48909
PH: (517)284-5644
Fax: (517)335-4540
Slater, Joe, Secretary

Clarity **[5529]**
c/o Joseph Kimble
Box 13038
Lansing, MI 48901-3038
PH: (517)371-5140
Fax: (517)334-5748
Kimble, Prof. Joseph, Treasurer

Hurst/Olds Club of America **[21397]**
304 S Clippert St.
Lansing, MI 48912
Worsham, Tara, Coord.

National Association of Legal Investigators **[5365]**
235 N Pine St.
Lansing, MI 48933
PH: (517)702-9835
Toll free: 866-520-6254
Fax: (517)372-1501
Johnson, Don C., Director

National Organization for Career Credentialing **[7571]**
c/o Barbara Bolin, President
1133 May St.

Lansing, MI 48906
PH: (804)310-2552
Bolin, Barbara, PhD, President

National Organization of State Associations for Children **[11095]**
c/o Michigan Federation for Children and Families
320 N Washington Sq., Suite 100
Lansing, MI 48933
Fischer, Megann Anderson, President

Oldsmobile Club of America **[21466]**
PO Box 80318
Lansing, MI 48908-0318
PH: (314)878-5651
Wilson, Jerry, President

United States Association of Consecrated Virgins **[19915]**
300 W Ottawa St.
Lansing, MI 48933-1577
Fax: (253)270-5507
Stegman, Judith M., President

Young Entomologists' Society **[6619]**
Minibeast Zooseum & Educational Ctr.
6907 W Grand River Ave.
Lansing, MI 48906
PH: (517)886-0630

American Voyager Association **[22211]**
c/o Bronson Barth, Membership Director
1418 Clark Rd.
Lapeer, MI 48446
McGee, Robin, Treasurer

Foundation for Aquatic Injury Prevention **[12821]**
631 Warner Dr.
Linden, MI 48451-9659
Toll free: 800-342-0330
Gilbert, Ronald R., Chairman

American Society of Employers **[1084]**
19575 Victor Pky., Ste. 100
Livonia, MI 48152
PH: (248)353-4500
Fax: (734)402-0462
Corrado, Mary, President, CEO

Incorporated Society of Irish American Lawyers **[5426]**
c/o Joseph P. McGill, President
Foley, Baron, Metzger & Juip, PLLC
38777 6 Mile Rd., Ste. 300
Livonia, MI 48152
McGill, Joseph P., President

International Hearing Society **[15198]**
16880 Middlebelt Rd., Ste. 4
Livonia, MI 48154
PH: (734)522-7200
Fax: (734)522-0200
Mennillo, Kathleen, MBA, Exec. Dir.

National Committee for Amish Religious Freedom **[19698]**
15343 Susanna Cir.
Livonia, MI 48154
PH: (734)464-3908
Lindholm, Rev. William C., Chairman

Seedlings Braille Books for Children **[13278]**
14151 Farmington Rd.
Livonia, MI 48154-5422
PH: (734)427-8552
Toll free: 800-777-8552
Fax: (734)427-8552
Bonde, Debra, Director, Founder

Society for Nonprofit Organizations **[258]**
PO Box 510354
Livonia, MI 48151

PH: (734)451-3582
Fax: (734)451-5935
Chmura, Jason, Dir. of Member Svcs.

Transcultural Nursing Society **[16189]**
Madonna University
36600 Schoolcraft Rd.
Livonia, MI 48150
Toll free: 888-432-5470
Fax: (734)793-2457
Lauderdale, Jana, PhD, Trustee

Unicycling Society of America **[22756]**
35011 Munger
Livonia, MI 48154-2412
Grzych, Wendy, Director

Worldwide Pollution Control Association **[4558]**
12190 Hubbard St.
Livonia, MI 48150
PH: (734)525-0300
Fax: (734)525-0303
Reinhold, Susan D., Chmn. of the Bd.

Cookware Manufacturers Association **[1681]**
PO Box 176
Lowell, MI 49331
PH: (205)592-0389
(616)987-3520
Fax: (205)599-5598

Benefit4Kids **[10864]**
21660 23 Mile Rd.
Macomb, MI 48044-1307
Toll free: 877-245-5430
Hearing, Steve, President

Bishop Baraga Association **[19804]**
347 Rock St.
Marquette, MI 49855-4725
PH: (906)227-9117
Paris, Benedetto, Director

National Association of State Veterans Homes **[13245]**
D.J. Jacobetti Home For Veterans
425 Fisher St.
Marquette, MI 49855-4521
PH: (906)226-3576
Sganga, Fred, Officer

Northern Michigan University Alumni Association **[19338]**
1401 Presque Isle Ave.
Marquette, MI 49855
PH: (906)227-2610
(906)227-1000
Toll free: 877-GRA-DNMU
Pickens, Jeremy, President

Distinguished Restaurants of North America **[2937]**
105 W Michigan Ave.
Marshall, MI 49068
PH: (269)789-9316
Fax: (269)789-0731

American Board of Veterinary Toxicology **[17611]**
c/o Jay Albretsen, Coordinator
54943 N Main St.
Mattawan, MI 49071
PH: (269)532-0169
Albretsen, Jay, Coord.

Whisky Pitcher Collectors Association of America **[21732]**
22862 Bluejay Ave.
Mattawan, MI 49071
PH: (269)668-4169

Token and Medal Society, Inc. **[22288]**
c/o Kathy Freeland, Secretary
PO Box 195

Mayville, MI 48744-0195
PH: (989)843-5247
Irion, Peter, Librarian

LandChoices **[3893]**
PO Box 181
Milford, MI 48381
PH: (248)685-0483
Manecke, Kirt, President

International D.N. Ice Yacht Racing Association **[22628]**
c/o Richard Potcova, Commodore
13790 Alton Dr.
Monroe, MI 48161

Biological Anthropology Section **[5911]**
c/o Rachel Caspari, Chairperson
Centeal Michigan University
Anspach Hall 142
Mount Pleasant, MI 48859
PH: (574)631-0299
Caspari, Rachel, Chairperson

Council for Elementary Science International **[8544]**
c/o James T. McDonald, President
EHS 134C
Department of Teacher Education
Central Michigan University
Mount Pleasant, MI 48859
Day, Jeanelle, Treasurer

International Association for Computer and Information Science **[6250]**
735 Meadowbrook Dr.
Mount Pleasant, MI 48858
PH: (989)774-3811
Lee, Roger Y., CEO, Treasurer

Steam Automobile Club of America **[21495]**
c/o David Lewis, Membership Secretary
602 S Fancher St.
Mount Pleasant, MI 48858-2619
PH: (586)214-4795
Helmick, Ken, President

World Leisure Organization **[22415]**
Central Michigan University
Warriner Hall 210
Mount Pleasant, MI 48859-0001
PH: (989)774-6099
Coles, Roger, Chairman

Aldea Development **[12797]**
1485 S Getty St.
Muskegon, MI 49442
Hughes, Patrick, President

Kuvasz Club of America **[21910]**
c/o Doreen MacPherson Hardt, Treasurer
3132 Snoblin Rd.
North Branch, MI 48461-8244
Brady, Lynn, President

Association for Constructivist Teaching **[8642]**
23900 Greening Dr.
Novi, MI 48375
Pelech, Jim, President

Brotherhood of Maintenance of Way Employees Division of the International Brotherhood of Teamsters **[23512]**
41475 Gardenbrook Rd.
Novi, MI 48375-1328
PH: (248)662-2660
Fax: (248)662-2659
Simpson, Freddie N., President

Chain Drug Marketing Association **[2555]**
43157 W 9 Mile Rd.
Novi, MI 48376

PH: (248)449-9300
Fax: (248)449-9396
Walker, Jack, VP

Vision Research ROPARD Foundation **[16409]**
39650 Orchard Hill Pl.
Novi, MI 48375
PH: (248)319-0161
Toll free: 800-788-2020

Kaiser-Darrin Owners Roster **[21412]**
c/o Terry Trasatti
3500 Collins Rd.
Oakland, MI 48363
PH: (248)656-1882
Trasatti, Terry, President

Association of College Honor Societies **[23776]**
1749 Hamilton Rd., Ste. 106
Okemos, MI 48864
PH: (517)351-8335
Fax: (517)351-8336
Yarbrough, Trisha, Secretary

Esperanza en Accion **[13047]**
PO Box 1011
Okemos, MI 48805
Perez, Yamileth, Director

Fatty Oxidation Disorders Family Support Group **[17338]**
1745 Hamilton Rd., Ste. 330
Okemos, MI 48864
PH: (517)381-1940
Fax: (866)290-5206
Gould, Deb Lee, Director

FOD Family Support Group **[15823]**
1745 Hamilton Rd., Ste. 330
Okemos, MI 48864
PH: (517)381-1940
Fax: (866)290-5206
Gould, Deb Lee, Director, President

Friends for Lesbian, Gay, Bisexual, Transgender, and Queer Concerns **[20180]**
2206 Iroquois Rd.
Okemos, MI 48864
Penn, Su, Treasurer

Islamic Schools League of America **[8126]**
PO Box 795
Okemos, MI 48805-0795
PH: (517)303-3905
Amri, Judi, Founder

Kappa Omicron Nu **[23771]**
1749 Hamilton Rd., Ste. 106
Okemos, MI 48864
PH: (517)351-8335
Mitstifer, Dr. Dorothy I., Exec. Dir.

National Association of College and University Food Services **[1393]**
2525 Jolly Rd., Ste. 280
Okemos, MI 48864-3681
PH: (517)332-2494
Fax: (517)332-8144
Couraud, Gretchen, Exec. Dir., CEO

National Consortium for Health Science Education **[15085]**
2123 University Park Dr., Ste.100
Okemos, MI 48864
PH: (517)253-8044
(517)331-8668
Stacy, Carole, Exec. Dir.

American Dutch Rabbit Club **[4586]**
c/o Janet Bowers, Secretary/ Treasurer
3520 Baker Hwy.
Olivet, MI 49076

PH: (517)449-8341
Graybeal, John, President

Miles Merwin Association [20900]
c/o Mimi M. McDonald
8416 Power Dr.
Oscoda, MI 48750-2016
PH: (989)739-9394
McDonald, Ms. Mimi M., Contact

United States Yngling Association
[22689]
c/o Mark Upham, President
7171 US Highway 23 S
Ossineke, MI 49766
PH: (989)471-3545
Upham, Mark, President

Syndromes Without a Name USA
[14614]
1745 Lorna Ln.
Otsego, MI 49078
PH: (269)692-2090
Toll free: 888-880-7926
Clugston, Amy, President, Treasurer

International Society of Antique
Scale Collectors [21679]
c/o Shirley Schmidt, Membership
Chairman
5790 N Lakeshore Rd.
Palms, MI 48465-9626
PH: (612)925-1386
Schmidt, Shirley, Mgr., Member
Svcs.

Dreamcatchers for Abused Children
[10794]
c/o Sandra Potter, Chief Executive
Officer/Founder
PO Box 142
Peck, MI 48466
PH: (810)275-0755
Potter, Sandra, CEO, Founder

Authors Coalition of America [9040]
PO Box 929
Pentwater, MI 49449
PH: (231)869-2011
Kelly, Dorien, Administrator

Social Contract Press [12406]
445 E Mitchell St.
Petoskey, MI 49770
PH: (231)347-1171
Toll free: 800-352-4843
Fax: (231)347-1185
Lutton, Wayne, PhD, Editor

Phi Delta Chi [23846]
PO Box 320
Pinckney, MI 48169
Toll free: 800-732-1883
Fax: (248)446-6065
Walkup, Kenny, Exec. Dir.

AppleWorks Users Group [6270]
PO Box 701010
Plymouth, MI 48170-0957

Lamborghini Club America [21417]
PO Box 701963
Plymouth, MI 48170
PH: (734)216-4455
Romanowski, Andrew, President

Mercy - U.S.A. for Aid and Develop-
ment [12699]
44450 Pinetree Dr., Ste. 201
Plymouth, MI 48170-3869
PH: (734)454-0011
Toll free: 800-556-3729
Fax: (734)454-0303
al-Qadi, Mr. Umar, CEO, President,
Secretary

Save a Family Plan [11829]
PO Box 610157
Port Huron, MI 48061

PH: (519)672-1115
Fax: (519)672-6379

Woman's Life Insurance Society
[19500]
1338 Military St.
Port Huron, MI 48060-5423
PH: (810)985-5191
Toll free: 800-521-9292
Fax: (810)985-6970
Martin, Christopher J., President

Association for Behavior Analysis
[6029]
550 W Centre Ave.
Portage, MI 49024
PH: (269)492-9310
Perone, Michael, Officer

Association for Behavior Analysis
International [6030]
550 W Centre Ave.
Portage, MI 49024
PH: (269)492-9310
Fax: (269)492-9316
Malott, Maria E., CEO, Secretary,
Treasurer, President

International Electrical Testing As-
sociation [1024]
3050 Old Centre Ave., Ste. 102
Portage, MI 49024
PH: (269)488-6382
Fax: (269)488-6383
Tanz, Jayne M., Exec. Dir.

National Association of Flight
Instructors [150]
3101 E Milham Ave.
Portage, MI 49002
Toll free: 866-806-6156
Poynor, Phil, VP of Government
Rel., VP of Indl. Rel.

National Paddleball Association
[22534]
7642 Kingston Dr.
Portage, MI 49002-4370
PH: (269)779-6615
Fax: (269)279-6275
Brigham, Lorri, Exec. VP, Treasurer

Society for the Advancement of
Behavior Analysis [6045]
550 W Centre Ave.
Portage, MI 49024
PH: (269)492-9310
Fax: (269)492-9316
Hayes, Linda J., President

American Behcet's Disease Associa-
tion [13812]
PO Box 80576
Rochester, MI 48308
PH: (631)656-0537
Toll free: 800-723-4238
Fax: (480)247-5377
Wise, Marcia, Secretary

Council of Supplier Diversity Profes-
sionals [681]
PO Box 70226
Rochester, MI 48307-0005
Gardner, Kenneth, Director

North American Chapter of the
International Group for the
Psychology of Mathematics Educa-
tion [6824]
c/o Ji-Eun Lee, Treasurer
470A Pawley Hall
Oakland University
2200 N Squirrel Rd.
Rochester, MI 48309
Hollebrands, Karen, Chairperson

RHEMA International [12723]
PO Box 82085
Rochester, MI 48308

PH: (248)652-2450
Fax: (248)652-9894
Beall Gruits, Rev. Patricia, DD, CEO,
Founder

Athletes with Disabilities Network
[22776]
2845 Crooks Rd.
Rochester Hills, MI 48309-3661
PH: (248)829-8353
Geno, Beth, Exec. Dir.

Leader Dogs for the Blind [17721]
1039 S Rochester Rd.
Rochester Hills, MI 48307
PH: (248)651-9011
Toll free: 888-777-5332
Daniels, Susan, CEO, President

Continental Baptist Missions [19728]
11650 Northland Dr. NE
Rockford, MI 49341
PH: (616)863-2226
Jenkin, Rev. Bill, III, President

Genealogical Society of Flemish
Americans [20969]
18740 13 Mile Rd.
Roseville, MI 48066
PH: (586)777-2770
Roets, Margaret, Corr. Sec.

International Union, Security, Police
and Fire Professionals of America
[23521]
25510 Kelly Rd.
Roseville, MI 48066
PH: (586)772-7250
Fax: (586)772-9644
Hickey, David L., President

Red Wing For'em Club [24079]
PO Box 66456
Roseville, MI 48066
Lefever, Sue, Liaison

Animals Deserve Absolute Protection
Today and Tomorrow [10584]
PO Box 725
Royal Oak, MI 48068-0725
Yourofsky, Gary, Founder

United States Quad Rugby Associa-
tion [23114]
302 S Main St., Ste. 201
Royal Oak, MI 48067
PH: (248)850-8973
Pate, Gary, Mem.

Volunteer Committees of Art
Museums of Canada and the
United States [9842]
5139 Thorncroft Ct.
Royal Oak, MI 48073
Milne, Peter, President

Lloyd Shaw Foundation [7703]
2124 Passolt St.
Saginaw, MI 48603
Fuller, Bob, President

Blue Star Mothers of America
[21039]
c/o Carla Brodacki, Financial
Secretary
PO Box 443
Saint Clair, MI 48079
Dorsey, Judy, President

International Society of Travel and
Tourism Educators [3382]
23220 Edgewater St.
Saint Clair Shores, MI 48082
PH: (586)294-0208
Fax: (586)294-0208
Dillane, Dominic, Chmn. of the Bd.

NARTS - The Association of Resale
Professionals [2964]
PO Box 190
Saint Clair Shores, MI 48080

PH: (586)294-6700
Toll free: 800-544-0751
Fax: (586)588-7018
Meyer, Adele, Exec. Dir.

American Society of Agricultural and
Biological Engineers [6533]
2950 Niles Rd.
Saint Joseph, MI 49085-8607
PH: (269)429-0300
Toll free: 800-371-2723
Fax: (269)429-3852
Drollinger, Darrin, Exec. Dir.

National Alliance of Wound Care and
Ostomy [15039]
717 St. Joseph Dr., Ste. 297
Saint Joseph, MI 49085
PH: (877)922-6292
Toll free: 888-352-4575
Fax: (800)352-8339
Hecker, Debbie, Exec. Dir.

United States Wayfarer Association
[22687]
c/o Gary Hirsch, Treasurer
1014 State St.
Saint Joseph, MI 49085-1466
PH: (919)942-6862
    (919)942-6862

Tillers International [12191]
10515 E OP Ave.
Scotts, MI 49088
PH: (269)626-0223
Toll free: 800-498-2700
Roosenberg, Dick, Exec. Dir.

Ladies Auxiliary of the Military Order
of the Purple Heart United States
of America [20735]
c/o Jan Knapp, President
PO Box 150
Six Lakes, MI 48886
PH: (231)881-0735
Knapp, Jan, President

Children With Hair Loss [14900]
12776 Dixie Hwy.
South Rockwood, MI 48179-1001
PH: (734)379-4400

Automotive Industry Action Group
[284]
26200 Lahser Rd., Ste. 200
Southfield, MI 48033-7100
PH: (248)358-3570
    (248)358-3003
Toll free: 877-275-2424
Fax: (248)358-3253
Batchik, John, V. Chmn. of the Bd.

Canada-United States Business Association [1981]
c/o Clayton & McKervey, P.C.
2000 Town Ctr., Ste. 1800
Southfield, MI 48075
High, Mark R., President

Chaldean Federation of America
[8816]
29850 Northwestern Hwy., Ste. 250
Southfield, MI 48034
PH: (248)996-8384
Fax: (248)996-8342
Kassab, Joseph T., Exec. Dir.

Ford Minority Dealers Association
[342]
c/o Dee Suber, Executive Assistant
PO Box 760386
Southfield, MI 48076
PH: (248)557-2500
Toll free: 800-247-0293
Fleming, Dr. A.V., Exec. Dir.

Global Accounting Aid Society [31]
19785 W 12 Mile Rd., Ste. 394
Southfield, MI 48076

PH: (765)206-6654
Fax: (765)662-3216
Taylor-Hopkins, Linda W., CPA, Contact

International Center for Reiki Training **[17101]**
21421 Hilltop St., Unit No. 28
Southfield, MI 48033
PH: (248)948-8112
Toll free: 800-332-8112
Fax: (248)948-9534
Rand, William Lee, Founder, President

Lawrence Technological University Alumni Association **[19332]**
21000 W 10 Mile Rd.
Southfield, MI 48075-1058
PH: (248)204-2309
Muccioli, Ron, Director

Life for Relief and Development **[12695]**
17300 W 10 Mile Rd.
Southfield, MI 48075-2930
PH: (248)424-7493
Toll free: 800-827-3543
Fax: (248)424-8325
Asamarai, Dr. Abdulwahab, Chairman

National Bone Marrow Transplant Link **[17516]**
20411 W 12 Mile Rd., Ste. 108
Southfield, MI 48076
PH: (248)358-1886
Toll free: 800-546-5268
Fax: (248)358-1889
Jacobs, Myra, MA, Founder

Original Equipment Suppliers Association **[661]**
25925 Telegraph Rd., Ste. 350
Southfield, MI 48033-2553
PH: (248)952-6401
Fax: (248)952-6404
Fream, Julie A., President, CEO

Phi Delta Psi Fraternity **[23671]**
PO Box 3088
Southfield, MI 48037-2105
Johnson, Q. Richards, President

Phi Kappa Upsilon Fraternity **[23740]**
21000 W 9 Mile Rd.
Southfield, MI 48075
Hui, James, President

United States Council for Automotive Research **[6022]**
1000 Town Center Dr., Ste. 300
Southfield, MI 48075-1219
PH: (248)223-9000
Zimmer, Steve, Exec. Dir.

Urban Farming **[4171]**
19785 W 12 Mile Rd., No. 537
Southfield, MI 48076
PH: (313)664-0615
Toll free: 877-679-8300
Fax: (313)664-0625
Sevelle, Taja, Exec. Dir., Founder

World Medical Relief **[12304]**
21725 Melrose Ave.
Southfield, MI 48075
PH: (313)866-5333
Fax: (313)866-5588
Samson, George V., CEO, President

Pilots for Christ International **[20159]**
9130 Vinto St.
Sparta, MI 49345
PH: (616)884-6241
Fax: (616)884-6079
Layne, Tim, President

Prostate Advocates Aiding Choices in Treatments **[14051]**
11555 Jadon Ct. NE
Sparta, MI 49345
PH: (616)453-1477
Fax: (616)453-1846
Profit, Richard H., Jr., CEO, President

International Aid **[12681]**
17011 Hickory St.
Spring Lake, MI 49456-9712
PH: (616)846-7490
Toll free: 800-968-7490
Fax: (616)846-3842
Anderson, Brian, CEO, President

International Association of Assistance Dog Partners **[14550]**
PO Box 638
Sterling Heights, MI 48311
PH: (586)826-3938
Toll free: 888-544-2237
Fax: (248)357-6209
Eames, Toni, President

National Organization of State Offices of Rural Health **[17011]**
44648 Mound Rd., No. 114
Sterling Heights, MI 48314-1322
PH: (586)739-9940
    (586)336-4627
Fax: (586)739-9941
Daniels, R. Scott, President

ConservAmerica **[3835]**
971 S Centerville Rd., PMB 139
Sturgis, MI 49091-2502
PH: (269)651-1808
Sisson, Rob, President

Inland Seas Education Association **[2243]**
100 Dame St.
Suttons Bay, MI 49682
PH: (231)271-3077
Fax: (231)271-3088
Chaney, Bill, Director

Antique Auto Racing Association **[21326]**
5295 S Linden Rd.
Swartz Creek, MI 48473-8200
PH: (810)655-2219
Brookshire, Lance, President

United Four Wheel Drive Associations **[21510]**
PO Box 316
Swartz Creek, MI 48473-0316
Toll free: 800-448-3932
Egbert, Steve, VP

American Board of Colon and Rectal Surgery **[16803]**
20600 Eureka Rd., Ste. 600
Taylor, MI 48180
PH: (734)282-9400
Fax: (734)282-9402
Schoetz, David J., Jr., Exec. Dir.

International Police and Fire Chaplain's Association **[19930]**
9393 Pardee Rd.
Taylor, MI 48180
PH: (313)291-2571
Tackett, Chief Daniel G., Director

National Association of Professional Canine Handlers **[5493]**
24800 Hayes St.
Taylor, MI 48180
PH: (313)291-2902
Fax: (313)291-2783
Foley, Terry, President

Association of Alternative Newsmedia **[2658]**
116 Cass St.
Traverse City, MI 49684

PH: (231)487-2261
Barna, Blair, President

Association of Directory Publishers **[2770]**
116 Cass St.
Traverse City, MI 49684
Toll free: 800-267-9002
Fax: (231)486-2182
Bills, Danny, Bd. Member

Flat-Coated Retriever Society of America **[21879]**
c/o Mary Ann Abbott, Membership Secreatary
19275 Whispering Trl.
Traverse City, MI 49686-9771
PH: (231)223-4473
Runyan, Nikki, President

Local Media Association **[2797]**
116 Cass St.
Traverse City, MI 49684
Toll free: 888-486-2466
Lane, Nancy, President

Seeking Ecology Education and Design Solutions **[4011]**
PO Box 2454
Traverse City, MI 49685
PH: (231)947-0312
Salzman, Sarna, Exec. Dir.

Youth Action International **[11193]**
125 Park St., Ste. 450
Traverse City, MI 49684
PH: (231)946-6283
Fax: (880)866-5437
Weeks, Kimmie, Exec. Dir., Founder

Asian Pacific American Chamber of Commerce **[23559]**
3155 W Big Beaver Rd., Ste. 106A
Troy, MI 48084
PH: (248)430-5855
Shahani, Ravinder, Chairman

Automotive Women's Alliance Foundation **[288]**
PO Box 4305
Troy, MI 48099
Toll free: 877-393-2923
Fax: (248)239-0291
Ziomek, Kim, Secretary

The Kresge Foundation **[12979]**
3215 W Big Beaver Rd.
Troy, MI 48084
PH: (248)643-9630
Rapson, Rip, CEO, President

Local Search Association **[2798]**
820 Kirts Blvd., Ste. 100
Troy, MI 48084-4836
PH: (248)244-6200
Fax: (248)244-0700
Norton, Neg, President

National Arab American Medical Association **[15126]**
2265 Livernois Rd., Ste. 720
Troy, MI 48083
PH: (248)646-3661
Fax: (248)646-0617
Dubaybo, Dr. Basim, President

One Child at a Time **[11105]**
AIAA/Corporate Office
2151 Livernois Rd., Ste. 200
Troy, MI 48083
PH: (248)362-1207
Fax: (248)362-8222
Fox, Nancy M., Contact

Professional Law Enforcement Association **[5517]**
PO Box 1197
Troy, MI 48099-1197
Toll free: 800-367-4321
Fax: (248)641-1197
Mcmahon, Leslie, Exec. Dir.

Rural Health International Non-Profit Organization **[15493]**
4447 Clarke Dr.
Troy, MI 48085
PH: (248)238-0636

Williams Syndrome Association **[14866]**
570 Kirts Blvd., Ste. 223
Troy, MI 48084-4156
PH: (248)244-2229
Toll free: 800-806-1871
Fax: (248)244-2230
Monkaba, Terry, Exec. Dir.

American Beefalo Association **[3588]**
9824 E YZ Ave.
Vicksburg, MI 49097
PH: (660)347-5448
Toll free: 800-BEEFALO
Skidmore, Kyle, Director

Hamilton National Genealogical Society **[20876]**
116 W Vine St.
Vicksburg, MI 49097
Hamilton, Larry, Jr., President

American Association of Teachers of Spanish and Portuguese **[8175]**
900 Ladd Rd.
Walled Lake, MI 48390
PH: (248)960-2180
Fax: (248)960-9570
Spinelli, Emily, Exec. Dir., Director

Associated Wire Rope Fabricators **[1712]**
PO Box 748
Walled Lake, MI 48390-0748
PH: (248)994-7753
Toll free: 800-666-2973
Fax: (248)994-7754

Sociedad Honoraria Hispánica **[7976]**
900 Ladd Rd.
Walled Lake, MI 48390
PH: (248)960-2180
Fax: (248)960-9570
Spinelli, Emily, Exec. Dir.

American Guild of Music **[9858]**
PO Box 599
Warren, MI 48090-0599
PH: (248)686-1975
Chizmadia, Richard, President

American MGC Register **[21322]**
c/o Fran Lewis, Treasury Director
1053 Forest Bay Dr.
Waterford, MI 48328
Sanders, Keith, Contact

Paws With a Cause **[11630]**
4646 S Division
Wayland, MI 49348
Toll free: 800-253-7297
Fax: (616)877-0248
Hendrickson, Portasue, Dir. of Admin.

Floor Covering Installation Contractors Association **[865]**
7439 Millwood Dr.
West Bloomfield, MI 48322
PH: (248)661-5015
Fax: (248)661-5018
Swift, Gerry, Bd. Member

American Federation of Ramallah, Palestine **[8812]**
27484 Ann Arbor Trl.
Westland, MI 48185
PH: (734)425-1600
Fax: (734)425-3985
Faris, Hanna, Contact

Vietnam Combat Veterans **[21170]**
PO Box 715
White Pine, MI 49971

PH: (906)885-5599
Devitt, John, Chairman, Founder

Travel and Tourism Research Association [3402]
5300 Lakewood Rd.
Whitehall, MI 49461-9626
PH: (248)708-8872
Fax: (248)814-7150
Mishell, Dan, Chairman

National Association of Agriculture Employees [4947]
9080 Torrey Rd.
Willis, MI 48191
Fax: (734)229-1654
Rehberg, Sarah, President

Association for People with Dogs Named Marty [21831]
22201 King Rd.
Woodhaven, MI 48183
Sheets, Marty, Exec. Dir.

Data Management Association International [6740]
c/o Dama Education & Research Foundation
PO Box 9937
Wyoming, MI 49508
PH: (813)778-5495
Fax: (813)464-7864
Edwards, Lee, VP of Mktg., VP, Comm.

Spiritual Unity of Nations [20612]
PO Box 9553
Wyoming, MI 49509
PH: (616)531-1339
Toll free: 800-704-2324
Fax: (616)531-2294

Women At Risk, International [12848]
2790 44th St. SW
Wyoming, MI 49519
PH: (616)855-0796
Toll free: 877-363-7528
McDonald, Rebecca, Founder, President

North American Kai Association [21929]
3410 Galbraith Line Rd.
Yale, MI 48097
Short, Marsha, President

Association for Applied and Clinical Sociology [7179]
c/o Fonda Martin, Executive Officer
Eastern Michigan University
Dept. of Sociology, Anthropology, and Criminology
926 E Forest Ave.
Ypsilanti, MI 48198
PH: (734)845-1206
Martin, Fonda, Exec. Ofc.

Association for Feminist Ethics and Social Theory [10078]
c/o Margaret A. Crouch, Treasurer
Dept. of History and Philosophy
Eastern Michigan University
701 Pray Harold
Ypsilanti, MI 48197
Rivera, Lisa, Chairperson

Association of Psychology Training Clinics [16908]
c/o Karen Saules, Secretary
Eastern Michigan University
611 W Cross St.
Ypsilanti, MI 48197
Saules, Karen, Secretary

Davis Registry [21368]
6487 Munger Rd.
Ypsilanti, MI 48197

PH: (734)434-5581
Wilson, Tom, Director

HighScope Educational Research Foundation [7696]
600 N River St.
Ypsilanti, MI 48198-2821
Toll free: 800-587-5639
Fax: (734)485-0704
Emdin, Ben, Exec. Dir.

Hotot Rabbit Breeders International [4599]
5988 S Mohawk Ave.
Ypsilanti, MI 48197
Wilkinson, Bob, President

International Society for the Study of Personality Disorders [15780]
c/o Ashley Stauffer
341 Science Complex
Eastern Michigan University
Psychology Dept.
Ypsilanti, MI 48197-6229
PH: (734)487-0047
Fax: (734)487-6553
Chanen, Andrew, President

MHP Salud [12341]
2111 Golfside Dr., Ste. 2B
Ypsilanti, MI 48197
Toll free: 800-461-8394
Ketterlinus, Jack, CPA, Treasurer

North American Society for the Sociology of Sport [7187]
c/o Brenda Riemer, Treasurer
School of HPHP
319 N Porter Bldg.
Eastern Michigan University
Ypsilanti, MI 48197
Riemer, Brenda, Treasurer

Twinless Twins Support Group International [12366]
PO Box 980481
Ypsilanti, MI 48198-0481
Toll free: 888-205-8962
Getchell, Michelle, Exec. Dir.

Christian Labor Association [19959]
405 Centerstone Ct.
Zeeland, MI 49464
Toll free: 877-CLA-1018
Fax: (616)772-9830
Merrill, Clarence, President

GM Futurliner [21387]
4521 Majestic Vue
Zeeland, MI 49464
PH: (616)875-3058
Mayton, Don M., Project Mgr.

MINNESOTA

National Association of Veterinary Technicians in America [17655]
PO Box 1227
Albert Lea, MN 56007
Toll free: 888-996-2882
Fax: (507)489-4518
Rose, Rebecca, President

Affirmation/Gay and Lesbian Mormons [20173]
PO Box 898
Anoka, MN 55303
PH: (661)367-2421
Thacker, Randall, President

American Water Spaniel Club [21826]
c/o Sue Liemohn, President
18515 Lake George Blvd. NW
Anoka, MN 55303-8439
PH: (651)748-2830
   (920)435-3558
Walker-Daniels, Kim, Secretary

Conservation Breeding Specialist Group [3836]
12101 Johnny Cake Ridge Rd.
Apple Valley, MN 55124-8151
PH: (952)997-9800
Fax: (952)997-9803
Byers, Onnie, Dr., Chairman

International Association of Facilitators [2740]
15050 Cedar Ave. S, No. 116-353
Apple Valley, MN 55124
PH: (952)891-3541
Toll free: 800-281-9948
Tan, Noel EK, Chairman

International Experimental Aerospace Society [5863]
14870 Granada Ave., No. 316
Apple Valley, MN 55124
PH: (952)583-2145

International Positive Psychology Association [16918]
14607 Felton Ct., Ste. 116
Apple Valley, MN 55124
Toll free: 888-389-9687
Fax: (888)389-9687
Fredrickson, Barbara, President

International Listening Association [7776]
Dr. Nan Johnson-Curiskis, Executive Director
943 Park Dr.
Belle Plaine, MN 56011
PH: (952)594-5697
Beall, Melissa, Comm. Chm.

Indigenous Environmental Network [4116]
PO Box 485
Bemidji, MN 56619
PH: (218)751-4967
Goldtooth, Tom, Exec. Dir.

Bethany International Missions [20387]
6820 Auto Club Rd., Ste. M
Bloomington, MN 55438
Brokke, Daniel, President

Disaster Response Communications [11659]
10719 Kell Ave. S
Bloomington, MN 55437
PH: (952)224-2045
Morgan, Dale R., Founder

PACER Center [14557]
8161 Normandale Blvd.
Bloomington, MN 55437
PH: (952)838-9000
Toll free: 800-537-2237
Fax: (952)838-0199
Reynolds, Karen, Treasurer

Partnership for Education of Children in Afghanistan [11260]
7121 W 113th St.
Bloomington, MN 55438
PH: (612)821-8759
Dasgupta, Santwana, Exec. Dir.

Portable Sanitation Association International [4744]
2626 E 82nd St., Ste. 175
Bloomington, MN 55425
PH: (952)854-8300
Toll free: 800-822-3020
Fax: (952)854-7560
Kos, Karleen, Exec. Dir.

Society for Siberian Irises [22126]
c/o Barbara Sautner
106th St., No. 2100
Bloomington, MN 55431
Sautner, Barbara, President

Stratis Health [14965]
2901 Metro Dr., Ste. 400
Bloomington, MN 55425-1525
PH: (952)854-3306
Toll free: 877-787-2847
Fax: (952)853-8503
Lundblad, Jennifer, PhD, CEO, President

United States Broomball Association [23258]
PO Box 20201
Bloomington, MN 55420
Toll free: 888-222-6731
Fax: (763)241-1736

U.S.A. Broomball [22537]
PO Box 20201
Bloomington, MN 55420-0201

International Peat Society - United States National Committee [6996]
10105 White City Rd.
Britt, MN 55710
PH: (218)741-2813
Fax: (218)741-2813
Grubich, Mr. Donald N., Chairman

Wildlife Forever [4913]
2700 Freeway Blvd., No. 1000
Brooklyn Center, MN 55430-1779
PH: (763)253-0222
Grann, Douglas H., CEO, President

Angel Eyes Foundation [13427]
7710 Brooklyn Blvd., Ste. 206F
Brooklyn Park, MN 55443
PH: (763)208-8339
Fax: (763)208-8526
Oni, Dr. Richard, Bd. Member

National Wheelchair Softball Association [22792]
c/o Brian Chavez, President
10004 Fallgold
Brooklyn Park, MN 55443
PH: (402)305-5020
Chavez, Brian, President

Autism Allies [13742]
2400 Prairie View Ln.
Buffalo, MN 55313-2450
PH: (612)384-4265
Strege, Roger, President, Treasurer

Sew Much Comfort [10759]
c/o Michele Cuppy, President/Chief Financial Officer/Co-Founder
13805 Frontier Ln.
Burnsville, MN 55337
PH: (952)431-6233
   (952)236-7300
Cuppy, Ms. Michele, CFO, President, Founder

Tee it up for the Troops [13248]
515 W Travelers Trl.
Burnsville, MN 55337
PH: (952)646-2490
Benson, Chuck, Chairman

Honor the Earth [19579]
607 Main Ave.
Callaway, MN 56521
PH: (218)375-3200
Fax: (218)375-2603
LaDuke, Winona, Exec. Dir.

Hazelden Betty Ford Foundation [13142]
PO Box 11
Center City, MN 55012-0011
PH: (651)213-4200
Toll free: 800-257-7810
Driscoll, John, Officer

ECKANKAR [20538]
PO Box 2000
Chanhassen, MN 55317-2000

PH: (952)380-2222
      (952)380-2200
Fax: (952)380-2295
Klemp, Harold, Leader

Carver-Scott Humane Society
  [10597]
210 N Chesnut St.
Chaska, MN 55318-0215
PH: (952)368-3553
Fasching, Larry, President

Educate Tanzania [7761]
858 Oriole Ln.
Chaska, MN 55318
PH: (952)250-9740
Hahn, Barbara, Director

International Association for Learning
  Alternatives [7487]
112103 Haering Cir.
Chaska, MN 55318-1378
PH: (612)716-5620
Jennings, Wayne, Chairman

International Lilac Society [22106]
c/o Karen McCauley, Treasurer
325 W 82nd St.
Chaska, MN 55318
Jordan, Nicole, President

North American Bowhunting Coali-
  tion [22167]
PO Box 493
Chatfield, MN 55923-0493
Brust, Mike, Chairman

Pope and Young Club [22506]
PO Box 548
Chatfield, MN 55923-0548
PH: (507)867-4144
Atwood, Roger, President

VoiceCare Network [8602]
Dept. of Music
St. John's University
Collegeville, MN 56321
PH: (320)363-3374
Fax: (320)363-2504

Feed My Starving Children [12085]
401 93rd Ave. NW
Coon Rapids, MN 55433
PH: (763)504-2919
Crea, Mark, Exec. Dir., CEO

University of Minnesota Crookston
  Alumni Association [19362]
Office of Development & Alumni
  Relations, Kiehle 115
2900 University Ave.
Crookston, MN 56716-5001
PH: (218)281-8439
Toll free: 800-862-6466
Fax: (218)281-8440
Kemmer, Mr. Corby, Dir. of Dev.

American Society of Plastic Surgery
  Administrators [14313]
6324 Fairview Ave. N
Crystal, MN 55428
PH: (717)249-2424
Fax: (717)249-4534
Fodor, Peter, MD, Liaison

North American Gladiolus Council
  [22115]
c/o Karen Otto, Secretary
302 Sandpiper Ct.
Delano, MN 55328-9783
Scripture, Burt, VP

Peruvian Partners [13081]
PO Box 735
Delano, MN 55328
Stavros, Gina, Founder

American Osler Society [15710]
c/o Renee Ziemer, Administrator
141 County Road 132 SE

Dover, MN 55929
PH: (507)259-5125
Swick, Herbert M., President

Academy of Integrative Health and
  Medicine [15260]
5313 Colorado St.
Duluth, MN 55804
PH: (218)525-5651
Fax: (218)525-5651
Cadwell, Steve, Exec. Dir.

American Academy of Health Care
  Providers in the Addictive
  Disorders [15895]
314 W Superior St., Ste. 508
Duluth, MN 55802
PH: (218)727-3940
Toll free: 888-429-3701
Fax: (218)722-0346
Hursh, Shannon, Prog. Dir.

The Antique Stove Association
  [21286]
2321 E Pioneer Rd.
Duluth, MN 55804

Association for Consumer Research
  [18040]
11 E Superior St., Ste. 210
Duluth, MN 55802
PH: (218)726-7853
Fax: (218)726-8016
Vaidyanathan, Rajiv, Exec. Dir.

College of St. Scholastica Alumni
  Association [19317]
Tower Hall 1410
1200 Kenwood Ave.
Duluth, MN 55811-4199
PH: (218)723-6071
      (218)723-6016
Toll free: 866-935-3731
Roseth, Lisa, Exec. Dir.

International Brain Barriers Society
  [16017]
c/o Lester R. Drewes, President
University of Minnesota - Medical
  School Duluth
1035 University Dr., 251 SMed
Duluth, MN 55812
Drewes, Lester R., President

Touching Hearts [10484]
314 W Superior St.
Duluth, MN 55802-1805
PH: (218)724-4743

Anti-Child Pornography Organization
  [18926]
PO Box 22338
Eagan, MN 55122-0388
Grigori, Natasha, Chairperson

Hearing Instrument Manufacturers'
  Software Association [15194]
2600 Eagan Woods Dr., Ste. 460
Eagan, MN 55121
PH: (651)644-2921
Toll free: 800-435-9246
Fax: (651)644-3046
Peterson, Scott, Contact

Houses for Haiti [11953]
1411 Deerwood Ct.
Eagan, MN 55122
Albright, Diane, President, Founder

The Abolitionist Vegan Society
  [10290]
PO Box 44875
Eden Prairie, MN 55344
Woodcock, Sarah K., Founder

Accreditation Commission for
  Acupuncture and Oriental Medicine
  [16451]
8941 Aztec Dr.
Eden Prairie, MN 55347

PH: (952)212-2434
Fax: (952)657-7068
McKenzie, Mark S., Exec. Dir.

Global Eye Mission [17703]
16526 W 78th St., No. 316
Eden Prairie, MN 55346
PH: (952)484-9710
Anderson, Dr. Steven, Founder

National Association of Women's
  Gymnastics Judges [22901]
c/o Barbara Tebben, Secretary
6913 Rosemary Rd.
Eden Prairie, MN 55346
Chandler, Evelyn, President

Peace House Africa [11129]
6581 City West Pky.
Eden Prairie, MN 55344-3248
PH: (952)465-0050
Fax: (952)465-0051

Star Legacy Foundation [15389]
11305 Hawk High Ct.
Eden Prairie, MN 55347
PH: (952)715-7731
Wimmer, Lindsay, Exec. Dir.

Starkey Hearing Foundation [15210]
6700 Washington Ave. S
Eden Prairie, MN 55344
Toll free: 866-354-3254
Fax: (952)828-6900
Austin, William F., Founder

Surface Mount Technology Associa-
  tion [1773]
6600 City W Pky., Ste. 300
Eden Prairie, MN 55344
PH: (952)920-7682
Fax: (952)926-1819
Barthel, Bill, President

Utility Management and Conservation Association [3427]
7607 Equitable Dr.
Eden Prairie, MN 55344
Blankenship, Arthur, Director

Colon Cancer Coalition [13947]
5666 Lincoln Dr., Ste. 270
Edina, MN 55436
PH: (952)426-6521
Fax: (952)674-1179
Tabor, Kristin, Founder, President

International Scleroderma Network
  [17179]
7455 France Ave. S, No. 266
Edina, MN 55435-4702
PH: (952)831-3091
Toll free: 800-564-7099
Ensz, Shelley, Founder, President

National Association for Proficiency
  Testing [7327]
4445 W 77th St., Ste. 212
Edina, MN 55435
PH: (952)303-6126
Fax: (305)425-5728
Brynteson, Richard, Managing Dir.

Outreach Asia [11124]
5608 Benton Ave.
Edina, MN 55436
PH: (952)922-8536
Fax: (952)920-2377
Peck, Mike, Founder, President

North American Bear Center [4854]
1926 Highway 169
Ely, MN 55731
PH: (218)365-7879
Toll free: 877-365-7879
Rogers, Lynn, Chairperson

Qigong Alliance International [13649]
PO Box 750
Ely, MN 55731
Toll free: 800-341-8895

Westar Institute [20558]
PO Box 346
Farmington, MN 55024
PH: (651)200-2372
Kea, Perry, Chairman

Communicating for America [3524]
112 E Lincoln Ave.
Fergus Falls, MN 56537
PH: (218)739-3241
Toll free: 800-432-3276
Fax: (218)739-3832
Strickland, Patty, President, COO

Spinal Cord Society [17262]
19051 County Highway 1
Fergus Falls, MN 56537-7609
PH: (218)739-5252
Fax: (218)739-5262

ChiroMission, Inc. [14259]
255 Highway 97, Ste. 2A
Forest Lake, MN 55025
Gerard, Dr. Jason, President, CEO

Utility Arborist Association [4737]
2009 W Broadway Ave., Ste. 400,
  PMB 315
Forest Lake, MN 55025
PH: (651)464-0380
Fax: (651)409-3819
Osborne, Joe, President

6th Bomb Group Association [20674]
29277 Garrard Ave.
Frontenac, MN 55026
Creek, John R., Jr., President

American Crossbow Federation
  [22959]
PO Box 251
Glenwood, MN 56334
Hendricks, Daniel, Contact

CAS Collectors [21578]
2000 Wisconsin Ave. N
Golden Valley, MN 55427-3363
Kuhlmann, Hank, President

Center of the American Experiment
  [18021]
8441 Wayzata Blvd., Ste. 350
Golden Valley, MN 55426
PH: (612)338-3605
Fax: (612)338-3621
Crockett, Kim, Exec. VP, COO, Gen.
  Counsel

Forius Business Credit Resources
  [1237]
8441 Wayzata Blvd., Ste. 270
Golden Valley, MN 55426
PH: (763)253-4300
Toll free: 800-279-6226
Corn, William, CCE, Chairman

Grain Elevator and Processing
  Society [1519]
4800 Olson Memorial Hwy.
Golden Valley, MN 55422
PH: (763)999-4300
Fax: (763)710-5328
Krejci, David, Exec. VP, Secretary

Headwaters Relief Organization
  [11666]
9400 Golden Valley Rd.
Golden Valley, MN 55427
PH: (612)251-2853
Thomley, Dr. Rebecca Hage, CEO

Organic Acidemia Association
  [14849]
c/o Kathy Stagni, Executive Director
9040 Duluth St.
Golden Valley, MN 55427
PH: (763)559-1797
Toll free: 866-539-4060
Fax: (866)539-4060
Pitre, Menta, Director

Haiti Outreach [10721]
50 9th Ave. S, Ste. 203
Hopkins, MN 55343
PH: (612)929-1122
Fax: (612)216-3777
Snyder, Dale, Exec. Dir.

Kids at Risk Action [13067]
PO Box 4091
Hopkins, MN 55343
PH: (612)508-7272
Fax: (952)400-8457
Tikkanen, Mike, Founder, President

Melanoma Awareness [14008]
PO Box 5512
Hopkins, MN 55343-7502
Buechele, Paul, President

National Council for Agricultural
Education [7478]
236 Maple Hill Rd.
Hopkins, MN 55343
PH: (317)709-0298
Fax: (317)802-5300
Allen, Ken, President

North American Elk Breeders As-
sociation [4857]
9086 Keats Ave. SW
Howard Lake, MN 55349-5500
PH: (320)543-3665
Fax: (320)543-2983
Seale, Charly, President

Wood Duck Society [4918]
c/o Lloyd Knudson, Secretary-
Treasurer
5581 129th Dr. N
Hugo, MN 55038
Molkenbur, John, President

American Association of Inside Sales
Professionals [3009]
1593 112th Ct. W
Inver Grove Heights, MN 55077
Toll free: 800-604-7085
Perkins, Bob, Chairman, Founder

White Plate Flat Trackers Association [23042]
18101 Johnson Memorial Dr.
Jordan, MN 55352
Parker, Lee, Exec. Dir.

FARMS International [12153]
PO Box 270
Knife River, MN 55609-0270
PH: (218)834-2676
Richter, Joseph E., Exec. Dir.

Columbia Sheep Breeders Associa-
tion of America [4668]
PO Box 722
Lakefield, MN 56150
PH: (507)360-2160
Fax: (507)662-6294
Crago, Mark, Director

Action for Children - Zambia [10831]
20855 Kensington Blvd.
Lakeville, MN 55044
McBrady, Carol, Director, Founder

Airedale Terrier Club of America
[21792]
c/o Richard Schlicht, Coordinator
9762 230th St. E
Lakeville, MN 55044-8292
PH: (952)461-5597
Clyde, April, President

International Society for the Study of
Women's Sexual Health [17198]
PO Box 1233
Lakeville, MN 55044
PH: (218)461-5115
Fax: (612)808-0491
Goldstein, Irwin, MD, President

Sexual Medicine Society of North
America, Inc. [17202]
c/o Status Plus
PO Box 1233
Lakeville, MN 55044
PH: (218)428-7072
Fax: (910)778-2586
Bivalacqua, Trinity J., Comm. Chm.

Wood Component Manufacturers
Association [1446]
PO Box 662
Lindstrom, MN 55045
PH: (651)332-6332
Fax: (651)400-3502
Anderson, Sid, III, President

Association of Asphalt Paving
Technologists [6347]
6776 Lake Dr., Ste. 215
Lino Lakes, MN 55014
PH: (651)293-9188
Fax: (651)293-9193
Anderson, Michael, Exec. Dir.

United States Women of Today
[12911]
c/o Jane Hanson, Secretary
31078 790th Ave.
Madelia, MN 56062
Harpster, Joyce, President

International Vocational Education
and Training Association [8738]
186 Wedgewood Dr.
Mahtomedi, MN 55115-2702
PH: (651)770-6719
Gardner, Christine, Exec. Sec.,
Treasurer

Betsy-Tacy Society [9043]
PO Box 94
Mankato, MN 56002-0094
PH: (507)345-9777
Schrader, Julie A., Director

Wordcraft Circle of Native Writers'
and Storytellers [10051]
230 Armstrong Hall
English Dept.
Minnesota State University
Mankato, MN 56001
PH: (505)948-4517
Roppolo, Dr. Kimberly G., Act. Pres.

Academy of Surgical Research
[15638]
15490 101st Ave. N, Ste. 100
Maple Grove, MN 55369
PH: (763)235-6464
Fax: (763)235-6461
Hachtman, Steve, Comm. Chm.

American Brain Coalition [15898]
6257 Quantico Ln. N
Maple Grove, MN 55311-3281
PH: (763)557-2913
Fax: (860)586-7550
Hieshetter, Janet, Certified Public
Accountant

American Conifer Society [4725]
PO Box 1583
Maple Grove, MN 55311
PH: (763)657-7251
Johnson, Ethan, President

Antique Motorcycle Club of America
[22212]
Cornerstone Registration Ltd.
PO Box 1715
Maple Grove, MN 55311-6715
PH: (763)420-7829
Toll free: 866-427-7583
Fax: (763)420-7849
Spagnolli, Richard, President

Antique Studebaker Club [21328]
PO Box 1715
Maple Grove, MN 55311-6715

PH: (763)420-7829
Wenzel, Frank, President

Avanti Owners Association
International [21336]
P.O. Box 1715
Maple Grove, MN 55311-6743
PH: (763)420-7829
Fax: (763)420-7849
Sexton, Dale, President

Early Ford V-8 Club of America
[21372]
PO Box 1715
Maple Grove, MN 55311
PH: (763)420-7829
Toll free: 866-427-7583
Bounds, Ken, Director

Elimu Africa [11201]
6480 Balsam Ln. N
Maple Grove, MN 55369
Blick, Kristy, Chairman

Laboratory Animal Management As-
sociation [13718]
15490 101st Ave. N, Ste. 100
Maple Grove, MN 55369
PH: (763)235-6483
Fax: (763)235-6461
Manke, Mr. Jim, CAE, Exec. Dir.

Lincoln and Continental Owners
Club [21419]
PO Box 1715
Maple Grove, MN 55311-6715
PH: (763)420-7829
Fax: (763)420-7849
Kramer, Glenn, Director

Lincoln Zephyr Owner's Club
[21420]
c/o Cornerstone Registration, Ltd.
PO Box 1715
Maple Grove, MN 55311-6715
PH: (763)420-7829
Toll free: 866-427-7583
Fax: (763)420-7849
Brunner, Thomas, Director

Packard Club [21472]
c/o Cornerstone Registration
PO Box 1715
Maple Grove, MN 55311-6715
PH: (763)420-7829
Toll free: 866-427-7583
Fax: (763)420-7849
Pyrtek-Blond, Stella, Secretary

Scottsdale Institute [15131]
7767 Elm Creek Blvd. N, Ste. 208
Maple Grove, MN 55369
PH: (763)710-7089
Fax: (763)432-5635
Williamson, Shelli, Exec. Dir.

Society of Automotive Historians
[21491]
PO Box 1715
Maple Grove, MN 55311-6715
Heitmann, John, President

Wiring Harness Manufacturer's As-
sociation [1034]
15490 101st Ave. N, Ste. 100
Maple Grove, MN 55369
PH: (763)235-6467
Fax: (763)235-6461
Bromm, Rick, Chairman

Sola Publishing/WordAlone [20319]
PO Box 521
Maple Lake, MN 55358
PH: (612)216-2055
Nestingen, Carolyn, Attorney

Pontiac-Oakland Club International
[21479]
PO Box 68
Maple Plain, MN 55359

PH: (763)479-2111
Toll free: 877-368-3454
Fax: (763)479-3571
Greene, Merle R., Jr., President

Vintage Base Ball Association
[22559]
2445 Londin Ln. E, Unit 410
Maplewood, MN 55119
PH: (651)739-6986
Show, Brad, President

Watchable Wildlife, Inc. [4898]
c/o James Mallman, President
PO Box 319
Marine on Saint Croix, MN 55047-
0319
PH: (651)433-4100
Fax: (651)433-4101
Mallman, James, President

International Sled Dog Racing As-
sociation [22826]
22702 Rebel Rd.
Merrifield, MN 56465
PH: (218)765-4297
Steele, Dave, Exec. Dir.

Abortion Care Network [10426]
PO Box 16323
Minneapolis, MN 55416
PH: (202)419-1444
Madsen, Nikki, Exec. Dir.

ACA International [981]
4040 W 70th St.
Minneapolis, MN 55435
PH: (952)926-6547
Fax: (952)926-1624
Bender, Leslie

African American Breast Cancer Alli-
ance [13872]
PO Box 8981
Minneapolis, MN 55408-0981
PH: (612)825-3675
Fax: (612)827-2977
Williams, Melanie, Bd. Member

Alliance for Community Media
[17936]
4248 Park Glen Rd.
Minneapolis, MN 55416
PH: (952)928-4643
Van Sickle, Mary, Chairman

Alliance for Sustainability [4148]
2801 21st Ave. S, Ste. 100
Minneapolis, MN 55407
PH: (612)250-0389
Gosiewski, Sean, Exec. Dir.

American Academy of Neurology
[16002]
201 Chicago Ave.
Minneapolis, MN 55415-1126
PH: (612)928-6000
Toll free: 800-879-1960
Fax: (612)454-2746
Cascino, Terrence L., President

American Chesterton Society [9035]
4117 Pebblebrook Cir.
Minneapolis, MN 55437
PH: (952)831-3096
Toll free: 800-343-2425
Fax: (952)831-0387
Ahlquist, Dale, President

American Council on Immersion
Education [8641]
University of Minnesota
Center for Advanced Research on
Language Acquisition
140 University International Ctr.
331 17th Ave. SE
Minneapolis, MN 55414
Miller, Kimerly, Editor

American Craft Council [21746]
1224 Marshall St. NE, Ste. 200
Minneapolis, MN 55413-1089
PH: (612)206-3100
Toll free: 800-836-3470
Fax: (612)355-2330
Amundsen, Chris, Exec. Dir.

American Indian Movement [18705]
PO Box 13521
Minneapolis, MN 55414

American Refugee Committee
[12584]
615 1st Ave. NE, Ste. 500
Minneapolis, MN 55413-2681
PH: (612)872-7060
Toll free: 800-875-7060
Fax: (612)607-6499
Boyum, Ben, V. Chmn. of the Bd.

American Relief Agency for the Horn
of Africa [12619]
PO Box 141117
Minneapolis, MN 55414
PH: (612)781-7646
Toll free: 866-992-7242
Fax: (612)781-7653
Idris, Mohamed, Exec. Dir.

American Society of Neuroimaging
[17047]
5841 Cedar Lake Rd., Ste. 204
Minneapolis, MN 55416
PH: (952)545-6291
Fax: (952)545-6073
Orvedahl, Leslie, Exec. Dir.

American Society of Neurorehabilita-
tion [16008]
5841 Cedar Lake Rd., Ste. 204
Minneapolis, MN 55416
PH: (952)545-6324
Fax: (952)545-6073
Winstein, Carolee, PhD, PT, FAPTA,
VP

American Society of Ophthalmic
Plastic and Reconstructive Surgery
[14311]
5841 Cedar Lake Rd. Ste. 204
Minneapolis, MN 55416-5657
PH: (952)646-2038
Fax: (952)545-6073
Karesh, James W., MD, Advisor

American Swedish Institute [10230]
2600 Park Ave.
Minneapolis, MN 55407-1090
PH: (612)871-4907
Karstadt, Bruce, CEO, President

American Technical Education As-
sociation [8660]
Dunwoody College of Technology
818 Dunwoody Blvd.
Minneapolis, MN 55403
PH: (612)381-3315
     (701)671-2301
Fax: (701)671-2260
Krebsbach, Sandra, Exec. Dir.

Animal Rights Coalition [10580]
317 W 48th St.
Minneapolis, MN 55419
PH: (612)822-6161
Cozzetto, Charlotte, President

Associated Collegiate Press [8148]
National Scholastic Press Associa-
tion
2221 University Ave. SE, Ste. 121
Minneapolis, MN 55414
PH: (612)625-8335
Fax: (612)605-0720
Mitsu Klos, Diana, Exec. Dir.

Association of Art Editors [2766]
3912 Natchez Ave. S
Minneapolis, MN 55416

PH: (952)922-1374
Fax: (952)922-1374
Freshman, Phil, President

Association for Chemoreception Sci-
ences [6188]
5841 Cedar Lake Rd.
Minneapolis, MN 55416
PH: (952)646-2035
Fax: (952)545-6073
Travers, Susan, President

Association of Himalayan Yoga
Meditation Societies International
[10419]
631 University Ave. NE
Minneapolis, MN 55413
PH: (612)379-2386
Dabral, Hari Shankar, Director

Association for Lesbian, Gay,
Bisexual and Transgender Issues
in Counseling [11872]
c/o Joy Whitman, Representative
Walden University
100 Washington Ave. S, Ste. 900
Minneapolis, MN 55401-2455
PH: (773)230-1789
Goodrich, Kristopher, President

Association of Missing and Exploited
Children's Organizations [12354]
416 E Hennepin Ave., Ste. 217
Minneapolis, MN 55414
PH: (703)399-0691
Toll free: 877-263-2620
Fax: (877)839-8279

Association of Personal Historians
[9462]
3208 E 25th St.
Minneapolis, MN 55406-1411
Coffin, Linda, Exec. Dir.

Association for Treatment and Train-
ing in the Attachment of Children
[15762]
310 E 38th St., Ste. 215
Minneapolis, MN 55409
PH: (612)861-4222
Fax: (612)866-5499
Blugerman, Michael, President

Association of University Professors
of Neurology [16011]
5841 Cedar Lake Rd., Ste. 204
Minneapolis, MN 55416
PH: (952)545-6724
Fax: (952)545-6073
Fink, David J., MD, President

Atheists For Human Rights [18376]
5146 Newton Ave. N
Minneapolis, MN 55430-3459
PH: (612)529-1200
     (612)326-6925
Toll free: 866-ATH-EIST
Castle, Marie Alena, Dir. of Comm.

Autism Recovery Foundation
[13750]
401 Groveland Ave.
Minneapolis, MN 55403
PH: (612)879-1817
Bachman, Randall, Chmn. of the Bd.

Be The Match Registry [13845]
National Marrow Donor Program
3001 Broadway St. NE, Ste. 100
Minneapolis, MN 55413-2196
PH: (612)627-5800
Toll free: 800-627-7692
Chell, Jeffrey W., MD, CEO

Blind LGBT Pride International
[11874]
PO Box 19561
Minneapolis, MN 55419

PH: (612)695-6991
Brown, Don, President

BlueGreen Alliance [4135]
1300 Godward St. NE, Ste. 2625
Minneapolis, MN 55413
Glas, Kim, Exec. Dir.

Brethren/Mennonite Council for
Lesbian, Gay, Bisexual and Trans-
gender Interest [20175]
PO Box 6300
Minneapolis, MN 55406
PH: (612)343-2060
Wise, Carol, Exec. Dir.

Building Bridges Coalition [13288]
129 N Second St., Ste. 102
Minneapolis, MN 55401
Clausen, Matthew, Chairman

Captive Insurance Companies As-
sociation [1843]
4248 Park Glen Rd.
Minneapolis, MN 55416
PH: (952)928-4655
Fax: (952)929-1318
Harwick, Dennis P., President

Category Management Association
[2158]
7900 Xerxes Ave. S, Ste. 980
Minneapolis, MN 55431
PH: (210)587-7203
Fritz, Wendy, CEO

Center for Global Education and
Experience [8118]
Augsburg College
2211 Riverside Ave.
Minneapolis, MN 55454
Anderson, Margaret, Program Mgr.

Charles Babbage Institute for the
History of Information Technology
[9471]
211 Andersen Library
222 21st Ave. S
Minneapolis, MN 55455
PH: (612)624-5050
Fax: (612)625-8054
Misa, Thomas J., PhD, Director

Child Neurology Foundation [15914]
201 Chicago Ave., No. 200
Minneapolis, MN 55415
PH: (877)263-5430
Shields, Donald, MD, President

Child Protection International
[10902]
267 19th Ave. S
Minneapolis, MN 55455-0499
PH: (612)624-8384
Skrebes, Robyn, Founder

Children and Nature Network [4039]
808 14th Ave. SE
Minneapolis, MN 55414
Charles, Cheryl, PhD, Consultant

Children's HeartLink [14108]
5075 Arcadia Ave.
Minneapolis, MN 55436
PH: (952)928-4860
Toll free: 888-928-6678
Fax: (952)928-4859
Kiser, Joseph, Founder

Children's Surgery International
[17384]
Medical Arts Bldg.
825 Nicollet Mall, Ste. 706
Minneapolis, MN 55402
PH: (612)746-4082
Fax: (612)746-4083
Koppel, Lora Stege, RN, Chair-
woman

College Gymnastics Association
[22900]
306 Cooke Hall
1900 University Ave. SE
Minneapolis, MN 55455
PH: (612)625-9567
Fax: (612)626-9922
Burns, Mike, President

Cooperative Grocer Network [906]
2600 E Franklin Ave., Ste. 3
Minneapolis, MN 55406-1172
PH: (612)436-9177
     (612)436-9166
Fax: (612)692-8563
Whitman, Martha, Treasurer

Cougar Network [4804]
c/o Michelle LaRue, Executive Direc-
tor
Dept. of Earth Sciences
University of Minnesota
310 Pillsbury Dr. SE
Minneapolis, MN 55455-0231
PH: (612)625-6358
Wilson, Bob, Director

Defence for Children International-
USA [10953]
2215 Pillsbury Ave. S
Minneapolis, MN 55404
PH: (612)626-9305
Goodwin, Dr. Michele Bratcher,
President

Diverse Emerging Music Organiza-
tion [9900]
PO Box 50252
Minneapolis, MN 55405
Martin, Ted, Chmn. of the Bd.

Diversity Information Resources
[2392]
2300 Kennedy St. NE, Ste. 230
Minneapolis, MN 55413
PH: (612)781-6819
Fax: (612)781-0109
Bonds, Leslie, Exec. Dir.

Ethiopia Reads [8240]
PO Box 581302
Minneapolis, MN 55458
PH: (612)354-2184
Roskey, Dana, Exec. Dir.

Evangelical Free Church of America
[20412]
901 E 78th St.
Minneapolis, MN 55420
PH: (952)854-1300
Toll free: 800-745-2202
Kompelien, Kevin, President

Faces of Loss, Faces of Hope
[12352]
PO Box 26131
Minneapolis, MN 55426
Cook, Kristin, Founder, Director

Fibre Channel Industry Association
[3227]
5353 Wayzata Blvd., Ste. 350
Minneapolis, MN 55416
PH: (415)561-6270
     (425)359-3326
Lyon, Chris, Exec. Dir.

Forest Stewardship Council - United
States [4202]
212 3rd Ave. N, Ste. 445
Minneapolis, MN 55401-1446
PH: (612)353-4511
Brinkema, Corey, President

Global Deaf Connection [15190]
1301 E American Blvd., Ste. 109
Minneapolis, MN 55425
PH: (612)724-8565
Fax: (612)729-3839
Runnels, Joel, Exec. Dir.

Global Health Ministries **[15005]**
7831 Hickory St. NE
Minneapolis, MN 55432-2500
PH: (763)586-9590
Fax: (763)586-9591
Gronert, Gary, President

Global Mamas **[13378]**
PO Box 18323
Minneapolis, MN 55418
PH: (612)781-0455
Toll free: 800-338-3032
Fax: (612)781-0450
Adam, Renae, Founder

Greater Public **[461]**
401 N 3rd St., Ste. 370
Minneapolis, MN 55401
Toll free: 888-454-2314
Jacobs, Paul, Chairman

Haiti Teen Challenge **[11745]**
1619 Portland Ave. S
Minneapolis, MN 55404
PH: (651)592-8774
Volcy, Dr. Julio, Exec. Dir.

Hardanger Fiddle Association of
America **[9916]**
PO Box 23046
Minneapolis, MN 55423-0046
PH: (612)568-7448
Kelley, Loretta, President

Health Care Administrators Associa-
tion **[15584]**
5353 Wayzata Blvd., Ste. 350
Minneapolis, MN 55416
Toll free: 888-637-1605
Fax: (952)252-8096
Wohlstein, Julie, CSFS, President

Health Care Compliance Association
[15008]
6500 Barrie Rd., Ste. 250
Minneapolis, MN 55435-2358
PH: (952)405-7900
(952)988-0141
Toll free: 888-580-8373
Fax: (952)988-0146
Wheeler, Sarah Kay, President

Human Biology Association **[6082]**
c/o Ellen W. Demerath, Ph.D.
Division of Epidemiology and Com-
munity Health, School of Public
Health
University of Minnesota
1300 S 2nd St., Ste. 300
Minneapolis, MN 55454
Worthman, Carol, President

Human Rights Resource Center
[18406]
University of Minnesota Law School
229 19th Ave. S, Ste. N-120
Minneapolis, MN 55455
PH: (612)626-0041
Toll free: 888-HRE-DUC8
Fax: (612)625-2011
Rudelius-Palmer, Ms. Kristi, Director

Incentive Gift Card Council **[1499]**
4248 Park Glen Rd.
Minneapolis, MN 55416
PH: (952)928-4649
Bowman, Betsi, President

Incentive Manufacturers and
Representatives Alliance **[2205]**
4248 Park Glen Rd.
Minneapolis, MN 55416
PH: (952)928-4661
Wesloh, Karen, Exec. Dir.

Incentive Marketing Association
[2283]
4248 Park Glen Rd.
Minneapolis, MN 55416

PH: (952)928-4649
Wesloh, Karen, Exec. Dir.

Institute for Agriculture and Trade
Policy **[17789]**
2105 1st Ave. S
Minneapolis, MN 55404
PH: (612)870-0453
Fax: (612)870-4846
Hoff, Kate, VP

Insurance Marketing & Communica-
tions Association **[1869]**
4248 Park Glen Rd.
Minneapolis, MN 55416-4758
PH: (952)928-4644
Fax: (952)929-1318
Grove, Gloria, Exec. Dir.

International Academy of Trial
Lawyers **[5009]**
5841 Cedar Lake Rd., Ste. 204
Minneapolis, MN 55416
PH: (952)546-2364
Fax: (952)545-6073
Burbidge, Richard, President

International Alliance of Law Firms
[5010]
527 Marquette Ave. S, Ste. 1925
Minneapolis, MN 55402
PH: (612)454-5242
Herbst, Michael, President

International Association of Com-
mercial Collectors, Inc. **[984]**
4040 W 70th St.
Minneapolis, MN 55435
PH: (952)925-0760
Toll free: 800-859-9526
Fax: (952)926-1624
Hamilton, Thomas J., Director

International Rescue and Emergency
Care Association **[14664]**
PO Box 431000
Minneapolis, MN 55443
Tanner, Randy, Contact

International Section of the National
Council on Family Relations
[11822]
1201 W River Pky., Ste. 200
Minneapolis, MN 55454
Toll free: 888-781-9331
Fax: (763)781-9348
Wiley, Angela R., Chairperson

International Society for Behavioral
Nutrition and Physical Activity
[13797]
University of Texas
313 E 12th St., Ste. 220
Minneapolis, MN 55455
Salmon, Jo, President

International Society of Bible Collec-
tors **[19760]**
PO Box 26654
Minneapolis, MN 55426
Johnson, Carl V., President

International Society of Coating Sci-
ence and Technology **[6226]**
Dept. of Chemical Engineering and
Materials Science
University of Minnesota
151 Amundson Hall
421 Washington Ave. SE
Minneapolis, MN 55455-0132
Kumar, Dr. Satish, President

International Women's Rights Action
Watch **[18420]**
University of Minnesota Human
Rights Ctr.
229 19th Ave. S
Minneapolis, MN 55455

PH: (612)625-4985
Fax: (612)625-2011
Freeman, Dr. Marsha A., Director

Irish Water Spaniel Club of America
[21903]
c/o Gregory L Johnson, Membership
Director
2316 NE 5th St.
Minneapolis, MN 55418-3504
PH: (612)205-0075
Louttit, Dana, President

Jean Piaget Society: Society for the
Study of Knowledge and Develop-
ment **[16923]**
c/o Phil Zelazo, President
University of Minnesota
Institute of Child Development
170 ChDev 51 E River Pky.
Minneapolis, MN 55455
PH: (612)625-5957
Zelazo, Phil, President

Jenny's Light **[17759]**
5021 Vernon Ave., Ste. 107
Minneapolis, MN 55436
Gibbs, Randy, Founder, Exec. Dir.

Lawyers Associated Worldwide
[5019]
Minneapolis, MN
PH: (952)404-1546
Fax: (952)404-1796
Mann, Hallie J., Exec. Dir.

Managed Care Risk Association
[1607]
333 Washington Ave. N, Ste. 5000
Minneapolis, MN 55401-1331
PH: (612)455-8324
Munger, Kelly, FSA, Coord.

Marine Retailers Association of
Americas **[2249]**
8401 73rd Ave. N, Ste. 71
Minneapolis, MN 55428
PH: (763)315-8043
Wattenbarger, Randy, Chairman

Men Against Destruction - Defending
Against Drugs and Social Disorder
[13152]
3026 4th Ave. S
Minneapolis, MN 55408
PH: (612)822-0802
Fax: (612)253-0663
Ferguson, Dwayne, VP, Dep. Dir.

Minneapolis Grain Exchange **[3779]**
400 S 4th St.
Minneapolis, MN 55415
PH: (612)321-7101
Toll free: 800-827-4746
Miller, John, Chief Executive Officer

Mother Bear Project **[11080]**
PO Box 62188
Minneapolis, MN 55426
Berman, Amy, Founder

National Alliance for Secondary
Education and Transition **[8559]**
6 Pattee Hall
150 Pillsbury Dr. SE
Minneapolis, MN 55455
PH: (612)624-2097
Johnson, David R., Director

National Association for the Educa-
tion of Homeless Children and
Youth **[7812]**
PO Box 26274
Minneapolis, MN 55426
Toll free: 866-862-2562
Fax: (763)545-9499
Scott, Dana, President

National Association of Tobacco
Outlets **[3285]**
15560 Boulder Pointe Rd.
Minneapolis, MN 55437
Toll free: 866-869-8888
Fax: (952)934-7442
Briant, Thomas A., Exec. Dir.

National Ataxia Foundation **[15963]**
2600 Fernbrook Ln., No. 119
Minneapolis, MN 55447
PH: (763)553-0020
Fax: (763)553-0167
Parent, Michael, Exec. Dir.

National Black Alcoholism and Ad-
diction Council **[13166]**
1500 Golden Valley Rd.
Minneapolis, MN 55411
Toll free: 877-622-2674
Fax: (407)532-2815
Hayden, Vincent, PhD, Chairman

National Concierge Association
[1670]
2920 Idaho Ave. N
Minneapolis, MN 55427
PH: (612)317-2932
Kasner, Sara-ann G., Founder, CEO

National Council on Family Relations
[14749]
1201 W River Pky., Ste. 200
Minneapolis, MN 55454-1115
PH: (763)781-9331
Toll free: 888-781-9331
Fax: (763)781-9348
Cushman, Diane L., Exec. Dir.

National Council on Family Relations
Education and Enrichment Section
[11825]
1201 W River Pky., Ste. 200
Minneapolis, MN 55454
PH: (763)781-9331
Toll free: 888-781-9331
Fax: (763)781-9348
Cushman, Diane L., Exec. Dir.

National Council on Family Relations
Family and Health Section **[14750]**
1201 W River Pky., Ste. 200
Minneapolis, MN 55454
PH: (763)781-9331
Toll free: 888-781-9331
Fax: (763)781-9348
Shreffler, Karina M., Chairperson

National Council on Family Relations
Feminism and Family Studies Sec-
tion **[11826]**
1201 W River Pky., Ste. 200
Minneapolis, MN 55454-1115
PH: (763)781-9331
Toll free: 888-781-9331
Fax: (763)781-9348
Cushman, Diane L., Exec. Dir.

National Council on Family Relations
- Religion and Family Life Section
[11827]
1201 W River Pky., Ste. 200
Minneapolis, MN 55454
Payne, Pamela, Secretary, Treasurer

National Council of the United
States, International Organization
of Good Templars **[19449]**
PO Box 202238
Minneapolis, MN 55420-7238
PH: (952)210-0382
Bakken, Ms. Vickie, Treasurer

National Exercise Trainers Associa-
tion **[22485]**
5955 Golden Valley Rd., Ste. 240
Minneapolis, MN 55422
PH: (763)545-2505
Toll free: 800-AEROBIC
Fax: (763)545-2524
Kelly, Tiffani, Contact

National Mail Order Association
[2295]
2807 Polk St. NE
Minneapolis, MN 55418-2954
PH: (612)788-1673
Schulte, John D., Mgr.

National Marrow Donor Program
[14624]
500 N 5th St.
Minneapolis, MN 55401-1206
PH: (612)627-5800
Toll free: 800-627-7692
Boo, Michael, Chief Strat. Ofc.

National Model United Nations
[8116]
2945 44th Ave. S, Ste. 600
Minneapolis, MN 55406
PH: (612)353-5649
Fax: (651)305-0093
Eaton, Michael, Exec. Dir.

National Orientation Directors Association **[7439]**
2829 University Ave., Ste. 415
Minneapolis, MN 55414
PH: (612)301-6632
Toll free: 866-521-6632
Fax: (612)624-2628
Holl, Joyce, Exec. Dir.

National Scholastic Press Association **[8456]**
2221 University Ave. SE, Ste. 121
Minneapolis, MN 55414-3074
PH: (612)625-8335
Klos, Diana Mitsu, Exec. Dir.

National Upper Cervical Chiropractic Association **[14279]**
5353 Wayzata Blvd., Ste. 350
Minneapolis, MN 55416-1300
PH: (952)564-3056
Toll free: 800-541-5799
Fax: (877)558-0410
Yardley, Dr. Lee, VP, Co-Ch.

Native Americans in Philanthropy
[12491]
2801 21st Ave. S, Ste. 132 D
Minneapolis, MN 55407
PH: (612)724-8798
Fax: (612)879-0613
Hare, Carly, Exec. Dir.

Neurocritical Care Society **[14352]**
5841 Cedar Lake Rd., Ste. 204
Minneapolis, MN 55416
PH: (952)646-2031
Fax: (952)545-6073
Manno, Edward, President

North American Neuro-Ophthalmology Society **[16398]**
5841 Cedar Lake Rd., Ste. 204
Minneapolis, MN 55416
PH: (952)646-2037
Fax: (952)545-6073
Subramanian, Prem S., Secretary

North American Voyageur Council
[9426]
4449 Xerxes Ave. S
Minneapolis, MN 55410
PH: (612)929-1087
Tomes, Charles, President

Northwestern Lumber Association
[1414]
5905 Golden Valley Rd., No. 110
Minneapolis, MN 55422
PH: (763)544-6822
Toll free: 888-544-6822
Fax: (763)595-4060
Miller, John, V. Chmn. of the Bd.

Organization for Human Brain Mapping **[6920]**
5841 Cedar Lake Rd., Ste. 204
Minneapolis, MN 55416

PH: (952)646-2029
Fax: (952)545-6073
Taie, JoAnn, Exec. Dir.

Pandora's Project **[12932]**
3109 W 50th St., Ste. 320
Minneapolis, MN 55410-2102
PH: (612)234-4204
L., Shannon, Founder, President

Peace and Hope International
[12996]
3400 Park Ave. S
Minneapolis, MN 55407
PH: (612)825-6864

Power-Motion Technology Representatives Association **[1759]**
5353 Wayzata Blvd., Ste. 350
Minneapolis, MN 55416-1300
Toll free: 888-817-7872
Fax: (949)252-8096
Crolla, Susan, Exec. Dir.

Professional Liability Underwriting Society **[1918]**
5353 Wayzata Blvd., Ste. 600
Minneapolis, MN 55416-1335
PH: (952)746-2580
Toll free: 800-845-0778
Fax: (952)746-2599
Cossu, Catherine, Secretary, Treasurer

Read Horn of Africa USA **[12181]**
2955 Chicago Ave. S
Minneapolis, MN 55407
Sugulle, Bile, Chmn. of the Bd.

Recycle Across America **[4634]**
Minneapolis, MN
Toll free: 855-424-5266
Hedlund, Mitch, Founder, Exec. Dir.

The Rita Hayworth Fan Club **[23998]**
c/o Caren Roberts-Frenzel
3943 York Ave. S
Minneapolis, MN 55410
Roberts-Frenzel, Caren, Contact

Scholarship America **[8520]**
7900 International Dr., Ste. 500
Minneapolis, MN 55425
PH: (952)830-7300
Toll free: 800-279-2083
Greene, Richard, CFO

Ski for Light **[22796]**
1455 W Lake St.
Minneapolis, MN 55408-2648
PH: (612)827-3232
Elmquist, Marion, President

Smile Network International **[14345]**
PO Box 3986
Minneapolis, MN 55403
PH: (612)377-1800
Cahill, Maureen, Exec. Dir.

Society of Corporate Compliance and Ethics **[1169]**
6500 Barrie Rd., Ste. 250
Minneapolis, MN 55435
PH: (952)933-4977
Toll free: 888-277-4977
Fax: (952)988-0146
Roach, Daniel R., Gen. Counsel

Society of Insurance Research
[1930]
4248 Park Glen Rd.
Minneapolis, MN 55416
PH: (952)928-4641
Markovsky, Sharon, President

Sons of Norway **[10053]**
1455 W Lake St.
Minneapolis, MN 55408-2666

PH: (612)827-3611
Toll free: 800-945-8851
Fax: (612)827-0658
Kristiansen, Marit, Mem.

Swedish Council of America **[19664]**
3030 W River Pky.
Minneapolis, MN 55406
PH: (612)871-0593
Baker, David, V. Chmn. of the Exec. Committee

The Trumpeter Swan Society **[4896]**
c/o Rivers Pk. District - French Regional Pk.
12615 Rockford Rd.
Minneapolis, MN 55441-1248
PH: (715)441-1994
Fax: (763)557-4943
Cornely, John, Advisor

Unclaimed Property Professionals Organization **[5689]**
8441 Wayzata Blvd., Ste. 270
Minneapolis, MN 55426
PH: (763)253-4340
Popal, Heela, President

United Council for Neurologic Subspecialties **[16040]**
201 Chicago Ave.
Minneapolis, MN 55415
Kohring, John, Exec. Dir.

United Council for Neurological Subspecialties **[16041]**
201 Chicago Ave.
Minneapolis, MN 55415
PH: (612)928-6106
Fax: (612)454-2750
Kohring, John, Exec. Dir.

United States Law Firm Group
[5052]
c/o Philip S. Garon, Executive Director
2200 Wells Fargo Ctr.
90 S 7th St.
Minneapolis, MN 55402
PH: (612)766-8101
Garon, Philip S., Exec. Dir.

University of Minnesota Alumni Association **[19361]**
McNamara Alumni Ctr.
200 Oak St. SE, Ste. 200
Minneapolis, MN 55455-2040
PH: (612)624-2323
Toll free: 800-862-5867
Fax: (612)626-8167
Lewis, Lisa, President, CEO

University of Minnesota Center for Bioethics **[6065]**
N504 Boynton Health Ctr.
410 Church St. SE
Minneapolis, MN 55455
PH: (612)624-9440
Fax: (612)624-9108
DeBruin, Debra, PhD, Director

US Cuba Artist Exchange **[9219]**
3359 36th Ave. S
Minneapolis, MN 55406
PH: (612)267-8363
Sun-Saenz, Mariesa, Director, Founder

Vida Volunteer **[11455]**
PO Box 856499
Minneapolis, MN 55485
Toll free: 888-365-VIDA
Elizondo, Sondra, Director

Viola da Gamba Society of America
[10020]
PO Box 582628
Minneapolis, MN 55458-2628
Toll free: 855-846-5415
Terry, Lisa, President

Jacob Wetterling Resource Center
[11186]
2021 E Hennepin Ave., Ste.360
Minneapolis, MN 55413
PH: (651)714-4673
Toll free: 800-325-HOPE
Fax: (612)767-8585
Vieth, Mr. Victor, Director

Wilderness Inquiry **[22722]**
808 14th Ave. SE
Minneapolis, MN 55414-1516
PH: (612)676-9400
Fax: (612)676-9401
Lais, Greg, Exec. Dir.

Windustry **[7392]**
201 Ridgewood Ave.
Minneapolis, MN 55403
PH: (612)200-0331
Toll free: 800-818-0936
Daniels, Lisa, Exec. Dir., Founder

Women Against Military Madness
[18699]
4200 Cedar Ave. S, Ste. 3
Minneapolis, MN 55407
PH: (612)827-5364
Fax: (612)827-6433
Beaudoin, Mary, Editor

World Mission Prayer League
[20322]
232 Clifton Ave.
Minneapolis, MN 55403-3466
PH: (612)871-6843

Diabetes Research Association of America **[14528]**
10560 Wayzata Blvd., Ste. 19
Minnetonka, MN 55305
PH: (612)730-2789
Hastings, Christopher Devin, Founder

More Light Presbyterians **[20186]**
4737 County Rd. 101
Minnetonka, MN 55345-2634
PH: (952)941-6494
McNeill, Alex Patchin, Exec. Dir.

National Association for Ambulatory Care **[13676]**
5396 Ashcroft Rd.
Minnetonka, MN 55345
PH: (952)544-6199
Toll free: 866-793-1396
Fax: (952)544-0979
Wenmark, William H., President

National Association of Purchasing Card Professionals **[2818]**
12701 Whitewater Dr., Ste. 110
Minnetonka, MN 55343
PH: (952)546-1880
Fax: (952)546-1857
McGuire, Diane, Managing Dir.

North American Fishing Club
[22851]
12301 Whitewater Dr.
Minnetonka, MN 55343
Toll free: 800-843-6232
Pennaz, Steve, Exec. Dir.

Shelter for Life International **[12727]**
10201 Wayzata Blvd., Ste. 230
Minnetonka, MN 55305-1505
PH: (763)253-4082
Fax: (763)253-4085
Patrick, Brint, Chmn. of the Bd.

International Association for the Study of Irish Literatures **[9759]**
c/o Dawn Duncan, Secretary
Dept. of English
Concordia College
901 8th St. S

Moorhead, MN 56562
Kelleher, Margaret, Chairperson

International Association of
Hydrological Sciences **[7366]**
c/o Chuck Onstad, Treasurer
18241 County Rd. 1
Morris, MN 56267
Savenije, Hubert H.G., President

American Society of
Temporomandibular Joint
Surgeons **[16445]**
4407 Wilshire Blvd., No. 302
Mound, MN 55364
PH: (952)472-4762
Fax: (952)472-1638
Sheridan, M. Kathleen, CAE, Exec.
Sec.

Society for the Arts in Religious and
Theological Studies **[8711]**
c/o United Theological Seminary of
the Twin Cities, 3000 5th St NW
3000 5th St. NW
New Brighton, MN 55112

Agricultural Relations Council **[2751]**
605 Columbus Ave. S
New Prague, MN 56071
PH: (952)758-5811
Fax: (952)758-5813
Gardner, Mr. Den, Exec. Dir.

American Agricultural Editors' As-
sociation **[2646]**
PO Box 156
New Prague, MN 56071
PH: (952)758-6502
Fax: (952)758-5813
Gardner, Den, Exec. Dir.

American Society of Agricultural
Consultants **[3523]**
605 Columbus Ave. S
New Prague, MN 56071
PH: (952)758-5811
Fax: (952)758-5813
Gilligan, Paige, Sr. VP, Director

Turf and Ornamental Communica-
tors Association **[2074]**
605 Columbus Ave. S
New Prague, MN 56071-1935
PH: (952)758-6340
Fax: (952)758-5813
Code, Cindy, Director

Archery Trade Association **[3134]**
PO Box 70
New Ulm, MN 56073-0070
PH: (507)233-8130
Toll free: 866-266-2776
Fax: (507)233-8140
McAninch, Jay, CEO, President

Lung Cancer Foundation of America
[15539]
15 S Franklin St.
New Ulm, MN 56073
PH: (507)354-1361
Norris, Kim, Founder, President

Kids for Saving Earth **[7879]**
37955 Bridge Rd.
North Branch, MN 55056-5398
PH: (763)559-1234
Fax: (651)674-5005
Hill, Tessa, President

International Ostomy Association
[16527]
PO Box 512
Northfield, MN 55057
Toll free: 800-826-0826
Fax: (507)645-5168
Buch, Dr. Harikesh, Officer

National Association of Geoscience
Teachers **[7936]**
c/o Carleton College W-SERC
1 N College St.

Northfield, MN 55057
PH: (507)222-7096
   (507)222-4545
Fax: (507)222-5175
Manduca, Dr. Cathryn, Exec. Dir.

Norwegian-American Historical As-
sociation **[10052]**
1510 St. Olaf Ave.
Northfield, MN 55057-1097
PH: (507)786-3221
   (507)786-3229
Fax: (507)786-3734
Hedberg, Blaine, Treasurer

Professional Risk Managers'
International Association **[1919]**
400 Washington St.
Northfield, MN 55057
PH: (612)605-5370
Fax: (212)898-9076
McCarthy, Oscar, Secretary

Student Pledge Against Gun
Violence **[18256]**
112 Nevada St.
Northfield, MN 55057
PH: (507)664-9494
Fax: (507)573-1775
Grow, Mary Lewis, Coord., Founder

Brothers and Sisters of Penance of
St. Francis **[19805]**
65774 County Road 31
Northome, MN 56661
PH: (218)897-5974
Fahey, Bruce, Administrator

Angel of Mercy **[10534]**
PO Box 28086
Oakdale, MN 55128
PH: (651)283-3546
Oyebog, Relindis A., President,
Founder, CEO

Automation Association **[2214]**
c/o Allan Hammel, President
7300 Hudson Blvd. N, Ste. 285
Oakdale, MN 55128
PH: (651)264-9841
Hammel, Allan, President

American Society of Exercise
Physiologists **[16695]**
503 8th Ave. W
Osakis, MN 56360
Boone, Prof. Tommy, PhD, Founder

Community Solutions for Africa's
Development **[11342]**
7111 Merrimac Ln. N
Osseo, MN 55311-3829
PH: (612)644-9905
Baitani, Smart P., Exec. Dir.,
Founder

North American Horsemen's As-
sociation **[4393]**
310 Washburne Ave.
Paynesville, MN 56362-1645
PH: (320)243-7250
Toll free: 800-328-8894
Fax: (320)243-7224
Liestman, Linda L., President,
Founder

British White Cattle Association of
America **[3598]**
6656 45th Ave. SW
Pequot Lakes, MN 56472
PH: (218)568-7003
Seep, Sue, Exec. Sec.

Rural Renewable Energy Alliance
[6511]
2330 Dancing Wind Rd. SW, Ste. 2
Pine River, MN 56474
PH: (218)947-3779
Edens, Jason, Director, Founder

Energy and Environmental Building
Alliance **[524]**
9900 13th Ave. N, Ste. 200
Plymouth, MN 55441
PH: (952)881-1098
Fax: (952)881-3048
Edwards, John, Bd. Member

International Orthopedic Rehabilita-
tion Organization **[16479]**
14254 43rd Ave. N, Unit C
Plymouth, MN 55446
PH: (763)291-7088
Fax: (763)432-3059
Thomas, Alvin B., Founder,
President

League of World War I Aviation
Historians **[21237]**
c/o Daniel Polglaze, Membership
Secretary
16820 25th Ave. N
Plymouth, MN 55447-2228
O'Neal, Mike, President

Algae Biomass Organization **[6446]**
125 St. Paul St.
Preston, MN 55965-1092
Toll free: 877-531-5512
Carr, Matt, Exec. Dir.

Humanitarian Services for Children
of Vietnam **[11042]**
2965 Spring Lake Rd. SW
Prior Lake, MN 55372
PH: (952)447-3502
Fax: (952)447-3573
De Vet, Chuck, President

Ride to Work **[22231]**
PO Box 1072
Proctor, MN 55810
PH: (218)722-9806
Fax: (218)720-3610

National Dysautonomia Research
Foundation **[14602]**
PO Box 301
Red Wing, MN 55066
PH: (651)327-0367
Fax: (651)323-5097

Red Wing Collectors Society **[21719]**
240 Harrison St., Unit No. 3
Red Wing, MN 55066-0050
PH: (651)388-4004
Toll free: 800-977-7927
Fax: (651)388-4042
Wichert, Paul, President

Pogo Fan Club and Walt Kelly
Society **[24006]**
Spring Hollow Books
6908 Wentworth Ave.
Richfield, MN 55423
Thompson, Steve, Editor

Presbyterian Frontier Fellowship
[20454]
7132 Portland Ave., Ste. 136
Richfield, MN 55423-3264
PH: (612)869-0062
Lewis, Bonnie Sue, Dr., V. Ch.

American Association of Neuromus-
cular and Electrodiagnostic
Medicine **[15897]**
2621 Superior Dr. NW
Rochester, MN 55901
PH: (507)288-0100
Fax: (507)288-1225
Aldrich, Patrick, Dir. of Fin.

American Board of Physical
Medicine and Rehabilitation
[17078]
3015 Allegro Park Ln. SW
Rochester, MN 55902-4139

PH: (507)282-1776
Fax: (507)282-9242
Kowalske, Karen J., MD, Chairman

Clinicians of the World **[15445]**
PO Box 116
Rochester, MN 55903
PH: (507)208-4202
Melduni, Rowlens M., MD, CEO,
President

Frisbie - Frisbee Family Association
of America **[20867]**
c/o Margaret Zimny, Secretary
5417 61st Ave. SE
Rochester, MN 55904
Frisbie, Fred, President

General Thoracic Surgical Club
[17475]
c/o Bonnie Lemmerman, Mayo
Clinic, 1241W, 200 First St. SW
Mayo Clinic, 1241W
200 1st St. SW
Rochester, MN 55905
PH: (507)538-4969
Fax: (507)284-0058

Global Bridges **[17313]**
200 1st St. SW
Rochester, MN 55905
Hurt, Richard D., MD, Chairman

International Genetic Epidemiology
Society **[14732]**
c/o Mariza de Andrade, PhD,
Treasurer
Mayo Clinic
200 1st St. SW
Rochester, MN 55905-0002
Dupuis, Josée, President

International Myeloma Society
[13991]
Mayo Clinic
200 1st St. SW
Rochester, MN 55905
PH: (507)284-3725
Fax: (507)284-1249
Anderson, Kenneth C., President

MusculoSkeletal Infection Society
[15409]
PO Box 422
Rochester, MN 55903-0422
Springer, Bryan, MD, President

National Beep Baseball Association
[22787]
1501 41st St. NW, Apt. G1
Rochester, MN 55901
PH: (507)208-8383
Toll free: 866-400-4551
Guerra, Stephen, Secretary

National Farm and Ranch Business
Management Education Associa-
tion, Inc. **[4160]**
6540 65th St. NE
Rochester, MN 55906-1911
PH: (507)951-3610
Toll free: 888-255-9735
Walter, Will, President

Professional Skaters Association
[23151]
3006 Allegro Park SW
Rochester, MN 55902
PH: (507)281-5122
Santee, Jimmie, Exec. Dir.

Society for Research into
Hydrocephalus and Spina Bifida
[17261]
c/o Dr. David Nash, Membership
Secretary
Pediatric Rehab Clinic Mayo
200 1st St. SW

Rochester, MN 55905
McAllister, James, President

Society of Thoracic Radiology
[**17074**]
c/o Matrix Meetings, Inc.
1202 1/2 7th St. NW, Ste. 209
Rochester, MN 55901
PH: (507)288-5620
Fax: (507)288-0014
McLeod, Barbara, Administrator

World Association of Sleep Medicine
[**17223**]
3270 19th St. NW, Ste. 109
Rochester, MN 55901-2950
PH: (507)316-0084
Toll free: 877-659-0760
Ferini-Strambi, Luigi, President

American Academy of Acupuncture
and Oriental Medicine [**13586**]
1925 County Road B2 W
Roseville, MN 55113-2703
PH: (651)631-0204
Fax: (651)631-0361
Gong, Changzhen, PhD, President

Geosynthetics Materials Association
[**6222**]
1801 County Road B W
Roseville, MN 55113-4061
PH: (651)225-6920
Gardner, Keith, Chairman

Narrow Fabrics Institute [**3263**]
1801 County Rd. B W
Roseville, MN 55113
PH: (651)222-6920
Hyland, Sarah, Mgr.

Professional Awning Manufacturers
Association [**3267**]
1801 County Road B W
Roseville, MN 55113
PH: (651)225-6944
Brienzo, Frank, Director

TARP Association [**303**]
1801 County Road B W
Roseville, MN 55113
PH: (651)225-6926
Aho, Andrew, VP of Operations

United States Industrial Fabrics
Institute [**3276**]
1801 County Road B W
Roseville, MN 55113-4061
PH: (651)225-6956
Kelley, Bret, Chmn. of the Bd.

Cardigan Welsh Corgi Club of
America [**21851**]
c/o Barbara Peterson, Membership
Chairperson
6263 Seville Rd.
Saginaw, MN 55779-9510
PH: (218)729-4527
Gladstone, Steve, President

Face It Foundation [**12308**]
2500 Hwy. 88, Ste. 114
Saint Anthony, MN 55418
PH: (612)789-9897
Meier, Mark, Founder, Exec. Dir.

American Monument Association
[**9372**]
c/o Mike Zniewski, Executive Director
414 Lincoln Ave. NE
Saint Cloud, MN 56304-0244
PH: (614)248-5866
Zniewski, Mike, Exec. Dir.

Associated Male Choruses of
America [**9874**]
5143 S 40th St.
Saint Cloud, MN 56301

PH: (320)260-1081
Wilson, Weldon, Chairman

Billings Ovulation Method Associa-
tion - USA [**11837**]
PO Box 2135
Saint Cloud, MN 56302
PH: (651)699-8139
Fax: (320)227-2532

National Wildlife Rehabilitators As-
sociation [**4849**]
2625 Clearwater Rd.
Saint Cloud, MN 56301
PH: (320)230-9920
Dohrmann, Deb, Office Mgr.

Society of Christian Ethics [**11804**]
PO Box 5126
Saint Cloud, MN 56302-5126
PH: (320)253-5407
Fax: (320)252-6984
Kaveny, M. Cathleen, Mem.

Society for the Study of Muslim Eth-
ics [**7906**]
PO Box 5126
Saint Cloud, MN 56302
PH: (320)253-5407
Hashmi, Sohail, President

American Benedictine Academy
[**19790**]
Monastery of St. Benedict
104 Chapel Ln.
Saint Joseph, MN 56374
Carrillo, Sr. Elizabeth, OSB, Exec.
Sec.

Society for Text and Discourse
[**8232**]
c/o Catherine Bohn-Gettler,
Treasurer, 125 HAB, 37 S College
Ave.
College of Saint Benedict
Education Department, 125 HAB
37 S College Ave.
Saint Joseph, MN 56374
Wolfe, Michael, Secretary

ImpactLives [**9173**]
6985 Oxford St.
Saint Louis Park, MN 55426
PH: (612)817-0791
Pastrano, Ramon A., President,
CEO

AACC International [**6175**]
3340 Pilot Knob Rd.
Saint Paul, MN 55121-2055
PH: (651)454-7250
Fax: (651)454-0766
Midness, Lydia Tooker, President

Advocating Change Together
[**11567**]
1821 University Ave. W, Ste. 306-S
Saint Paul, MN 55104
PH: (651)641-0297
Toll free: 800-641-0059
Fax: (651)641-4053
Cardenas, Rick, Contact

American Association for Medical
Chronobiology and Chronothera-
peutics [**13820**]
c/o Erhard Haus, President
Dept. of Pathology
University of Minnesota
640 Jackson St.
Saint Paul, MN 55101
PH: (651)254-9630
Fax: (651)254-2741
Haus, Erhard, PhD, President

American Association of Medical
Society Executives [**15704**]
1000 Westgate Dr., Ste. 252
Saint Paul, MN 55114

PH: (651)288-3432
Fax: (651)290-2266
Hubbard, Darrin, Exec. Dir.

American Association of Patholo-
gists' Assistants [**16570**]
2345 Rice St., Ste. 220
Saint Paul, MN 55113
PH: (651)697-9264
Toll free: 800-532-AAPA
Fax: (651)317-8048
Mitchell, John E., PA

American Association of Woodturn-
ers [**21744**]
222 Landmark Ctr.
75 5th St. W
Saint Paul, MN 55102-7704
PH: (651)484-9094
Toll free: 877-595-9094
Cook, Nick, Officer

American Composers Forum [**9177**]
75 W 5th St., Ste. 522
Saint Paul, MN 55102-1439
PH: (651)228-1407
Fax: (651)291-7978
Childs, Mary Ellen, Chmn. of the Bd.

American Phytopathological Society
[**6133**]
3340 Pilot Knob Rd.
Saint Paul, MN 55121
PH: (651)454-7250
Fax: (651)454-0766
Miller, Sally A., President

American Registry of Radiologic
Technologists [**15677**]
1255 Northland Dr.
Saint Paul, MN 55120
PH: (651)687-0048

American Society of Brewing Chem-
ists [**6186**]
3340 Pilot Knob Rd.
Saint Paul, MN 55121-2097
PH: (651)454-7250
Fax: (651)454-0766
Grider, Jody, Dir. of Operations

American Society for Theatre
Research [**10239**]
1000 Westgate Dr., Ste. 252
Saint Paul, MN 55114
PH: (651)288-3429
Fax: (651)290-2266
Ewald, Eric, Exec. Dir.

Anabaptist Sociology and Anthropol-
ogy Association [**7178**]
Bethel University
Dept. of Anthropology and Sociology
3900 Bethel Dr.
Saint Paul, MN 55112
PH: (651)638-6104
(651)635-8611
Schreck, Harley, Co-Ch.

APA Division 48: Society for the
Study of Peace, Conflict and
Violence [**16891**]
c/o Caitlin Mahoney, Secretary
Dept. of Psychology
Metropolitan State University
1450 Energy Park Dr.
Saint Paul, MN 55108
PH: (651)999-5823
Farley, Frank, Officer

Association of Child Neurology
Nurses [**16118**]
Child Neurology Society
1000 W County Road E, Ste. 290
Saint Paul, MN 55126
PH: (651)486-9447
Fax: (651)486-9436
Sheehan, Maureen, President

Association of College and
University Religious Affairs [**8605**]
Macalester College
Center for Religious and Spiritual
Life
1600 Grand Ave.
Saint Paul, MN 55105
PH: (651)696-6293
Fax: (651)696-6580
Forster-Smith, Rev. Lucy, Contact

Association for Continuing Legal
Education [**8211**]
1000 Westgate Dr., Ste. 252
Saint Paul, MN 55114
PH: (651)366-6082
Fax: (651)290-2266
Flynn, Jennifer, President

Association of Healthcare Value
Analysis Professionals [**14983**]
1000 Westgate Dr., Ste. 252
Saint Paul, MN 55114
PH: (651)290-6288
Fax: (651)290-2266
Graham, Gloria, President

Association of Image Consultants
International [**817**]
1000 Westgate Dr., Ste. 252
Saint Paul, MN 55114
PH: (615)290-7468
Fax: (615)290-2266
Seaman, Jane, President

Association of Professors of Mission
[**20385**]
University of Northwestern
3003 Snelling Ave. N
Saint Paul, MN 55113
PH: (651)631-5229
Fax: (651)628-3258
Caldwell, Larry, President

Association of Staff Physician
Recruiters [**16745**]
1000 Westgate Dr., Ste. 252
Saint Paul, MN 55114
Toll free: 800-830-2777
Gleason, Deborah, Bd. Member

Association of Technical Personnel
in Ophthalmology [**16375**]
2025 Woodlane Dr.
Saint Paul, MN 55125-2998
Toll free: 800-482-4858
Fax: (651)731-0410

Association for Theatre in Higher
Education [**8696**]
1000 Westgate Dr., Ste. 252
Saint Paul, MN 55114
PH: (651)288-3430
Toll free: 800-918-9216
Fax: (800)809-6374
Ewald, Eric, Exec. Dir.

Avian Welfare Coalition [**10592**]
PO Box 40212
Saint Paul, MN 55104
Kelly, Denise, Director

International Society for Hildegard
Von Bingen Studies [**10314**]
787 Iowa Ave. W
Saint Paul, MN 55117
PH: (651)487-6357
McGuire, K. Christian, Treasurer

Bird Strike Committee U.S.A. [**4796**]
Metropolitan Airports Commn.
Minneapolis-St. Paul International
Airport
4300 Glumack Dr.
Saint Paul, MN 55111
PH: (612)726-5780
Fax: (612)726-5074
Ostrom, John, Contact

Books For Africa **[9123]**
26 E Exchange St., Ste. 411
Saint Paul, MN 55101
PH: (651)602-9844
Fax: (651)602-9848
Plonski, Patrick, Exec. Dir.

Calix Society **[13128]**
PO Box 9085
Saint Paul, MN 55109
PH: (651)773-3117
Toll free: 800-398-0524
Montroy, William J., Founder

Catholic Rural Life **[19815]**
2115 Summit Ave.
Saint Paul, MN 55105-1078
PH: (651)962-5955
Fax: (651)962-5957
Ennis, James F., Exec. Dir.

Catholic United Financial **[19404]**
3499 Lexington Ave. N
Saint Paul, MN 55126
PH: (651)490-0170
Borrmann, Harald, President, Chairman

Center for School Change **[7751]**
Higher Ground Academy
1381 Marshall Ave.
Saint Paul, MN 55104
PH: (612)309-6571
Nathan, Joe, Director

Center for Victims of Torture **[13258]**
St. Paul Healing Ctr.
649 Dayton Ave.
Saint Paul, MN 55104-6631
PH: (612)436-4840
  (612)436-4800
Toll free: 877-265-8775
Goering, Curt, Exec. Dir.

Child Neurology Society **[16013]**
1000 W County Road E, Ste. 290
Saint Paul, MN 55126
PH: (651)486-9447
Fax: (651)486-9436
Schor, Nina F., MD, PhD, President

Citizens' Council for Health Freedom
  [18332]
161 St. Anthony Ave., Ste. 923
Saint Paul, MN 55103
PH: (651)646-8935
Fax: (651)646-0100
Brase, Twila J., RN, President

College Possible **[7753]**
450 N Syndicate St., Ste. 325
Saint Paul, MN 55104
PH: (651)917-3525
McCorkell, Jim, Founder, CEO

Commission on Accreditation of
  Ophthalmic Medical Programs
  [8294]
2025 Woodlane Dr.
Saint Paul, MN 55125
PH: (651)731-0410
Fax: (651)731-2944
Fey, Kristine, COMT, Bd. Member

Compatible Technology International
  [3536]
800 Transfer Rd., Ste. 6
Saint Paul, MN 55114-1414
PH: (651)632-3912
Fax: (651)204-9033
Healey, Paul, Chairman

Contact Lens Association of
  Ophthalmologists **[16382]**
2025 Woodlane Dr.
Saint Paul, MN 55125
Toll free: 855-264-8818
Fax: (703)434-3003
Massare, John S., PhD, Exec. Dir.

Contact Lens Society of America
  [1599]
2025 Woodlane Dr.
Saint Paul, MN 55125-2998
PH: (703)437-5100
Toll free: 800-296-9776
Fax: (703)437-0727
Grout, Trudy, Director

Controlled Release Society **[6196]**
3340 Pilot Knob Rd.
Saint Paul, MN 55121
PH: (651)454-7250
Fax: (651)454-0766
Bingham, Debra, President

Czechoslovak Genealogical Society
  International **[20964]**
PO Box 16225
Saint Paul, MN 55116-0225
PH: (651)964-2322
Blume, Nancy, Rec. Sec.

Degree of Honor Protective Associa-
  tion **[19483]**
287 W Lafayette Frontage Rd., Ste.
  200
Saint Paul, MN 55107-3464
PH: (651)228-7600
Toll free: 800-947-5812
Fax: (651)224-7446
Flanary, Lisa, CEO

Emotions Anonymous International
  Service Center **[12307]**
PO Box 4245
Saint Paul, MN 55104-0245
PH: (651)647-9712
Fax: (651)647-1593
Mead, Karen, Exec. Dir.

Farmers' Legal Action Group **[5530]**
6 W 5th St., Ste. 650
Saint Paul, MN 55102
PH: (651)223-5400
Carpenter, Stephen, Dep. Dir.

Flexible Intermediate Bulk Container
  Association **[833]**
PO Box 241894
Saint Paul, MN 55124-7019
PH: (952)412-8867
Fax: (661)339-0023
Anderson, Lewis, Exec. Dir.

Freshwater Society **[4547]**
2424 Territorial Rd., Ste. B
Saint Paul, MN 55114
PH: (651)313-5800
Fax: (651)666-2569
Bateson, Rick, Chmn. of the Bd.

Geospatial Information and Technol-
  ogy Association **[6314]**
1360 University Ave. W, Ste. 455
Saint Paul, MN 55104-4086
PH: (303)337-0513
Toll free: 844-447-4482
Fax: (303)337-1001
Rosales, Henry, Dir. of Operations

Give Us Wings **[11363]**
450 N Syndicate St., Ste. 290
Saint Paul, MN 55104
PH: (651)789-5606
Anderson, Therese Dosch, Exec.
  Dir. (Actg.)

Global Volunteers **[18546]**
375 E Little Canada Rd.
Saint Paul, MN 55117-1628
Toll free: 800-487-1074
Fax: (651)482-0915
Philbrook, Bud, Founder, Chairman,
  Trustee

Help the Helpless **[12126]**
PO Box 270308
Saint Paul, MN 55127

PH: (651)762-8857
Toll free: 877-762-8857
Altier, Fr. Robert, President

Higher Education Consortium for
  Urban Affairs **[8724]**
2233 University Ave. W, Ste. 210
Saint Paul, MN 55114
PH: (651)287-3300
Fax: (651)659-9421
Keyser, Jenny, PhD, Exec. Dir.

Hospitality Institute of Technology
  and Management **[1658]**
PO Box 13734
Saint Paul, MN 55113-0734
PH: (651)646-7077
Snyder, Dr. O. Peter, Jr., Founder,
  President

Immunization Action Coalition
  [15380]
2550 University Ave. W, Ste. 415 N
Saint Paul, MN 55114
PH: (651)647-9009
Fax: (651)647-9131
Wexler, Deborah L., MD, Exec. Dir.

Insurance Regulatory Examiners
  Society **[1870]**
1821 University Ave. W, Ste. S256
Saint Paul, MN 55104
PH: (651)917-6250
Fax: (651)917-1835
Sherman, Tanya, President

International Concrete Repair
  Institute **[789]**
1000 Westgate Dr., Ste. 252
Saint Paul, MN 55114
PH: (651)366-6095
Fax: (651)290-2266
Levin, Mike, Exec. Dir.

International Humic Substances
  Society **[7136]**
1991 Upper Buford Cir., Rm. 439
Saint Paul, MN 55108
PH: (612)626-1204
Olk, Dr. Dan, Coord.

International Magnesium Association
  [2351]
1000 Westgate Dr., Ste. 252
Saint Paul, MN 55114
PH: (847)526-2010
  (651)379-7305
Fax: (847)526-3993
Guy, Jan, President

International Society for Molecular
  Plant-Microbe Interactions **[6148]**
3340 Pilot Knob Rd.
Saint Paul, MN 55121
PH: (651)454-7250
Fax: (651)454-0766
He, Sheng Yang, President

Joint Commission on Allied Health
  Personnel in Ophthalmology
  [16393]
2025 Woodlane Dr.
Saint Paul, MN 55125-2998
PH: (651)731-2944
Toll free: 800-284-3937
Fax: (651)731-0410
Astle, Dr. William F., Officer

Joy Project **[14643]**
PO Box 16488
Saint Paul, MN 55116
Nollenberg, Joy, Exec. Dir.,
  Secretary

Lexington Group in Transportation
  History **[10182]**
c/o Byron Olsen, Vice President/
  Secretary

1543 Grantham St.
Saint Paul, MN 55108-1449
Hofsommer, Don L., Treasurer, Edi-
  tor

Master Brewers Association of the
  Americas **[428]**
3340 Pilot Knob Rd.
Saint Paul, MN 55121
PH: (651)454-7250
Fax: (651)454-0766
Hope, Amy, Exec. VP

Melpomene Institute **[17760]**
550 Rice St., Ste. 104
Saint Paul, MN 55103
Monahan, Shawne, Exec. Dir.

NACEL Open Door **[8085]**
380 Jackson St., Ste. 200
Saint Paul, MN 55101-4810
PH: (651)686-0080
Toll free: 800-622-3553
Fax: (651)686-9601
Tarsitano, Dr. Frank, CEO, President

National Alfalfa and Forage Alliance
  [4176]
4630 Churchill St., Ste. 1
Saint Paul, MN 55126
PH: (651)484-3888
Fax: (651)638-0756
Nelson, Beth, President

National Association of
  Governmental Labor Officials
  [5399]
c/o Ken Peterson, President
443 Lafayette Rd. N
Saint Paul, MN 55155
PH: (651)284-5010
Fax: (651)284-5721
Peterson, Ken, President

National Chevy Association **[21449]**
947 Arcade St.
Saint Paul, MN 55106
PH: (651)778-9522
Fax: (651)778-9686

National Evangelization Teams
  [19885]
110 Crusader Ave. W
Saint Paul, MN 55118
PH: (651)450-6833
Fax: (651)450-9984
Cozzens, Bishop Andrew, Chmn. of
  the Bd.

National Health Freedom Coalition
  [15047]
2136 Ford Pky.
Saint Paul, MN 55116-1863
PH: (507)663-9018

National Qigong Association **[13642]**
PO Box 270065
Saint Paul, MN 55127
Toll free: 888-815-1893
Furbush, Lori, Chairperson

National Qigong Chi Kung Associa-
  tion **[13643]**
PO Box 270065
Saint Paul, MN 55127
Toll free: 888-815-1893
Fax: (888)359-9526
Roberts, Annie, Chmn. of the Bd.

National Youth Leadership Council
  [8200]
1667 Snelling Ave. N, Ste. D300
Saint Paul, MN 55108
PH: (651)631-3672
Fax: (651)631-2955
Bak, Kelita Svoboda, CEO

Nonviolent Peaceforce **[18810]**
2610 University Ave. W, Ste. 550
Saint Paul, MN 55114

PH: (612)871-0005
Fax: (612)871-0006
Mariani, Doris, CEO

North American Association of Inventory Services [660]
PO Box 120145
Saint Paul, MN 55112
PH: (651)402-9032
Paul, Randy, President

North American Burn Society [13864]
c/o Holly Schnetzler, Treasurer
1290 Hammond Rd.
Saint Paul, MN 55110-5959
Wibbenmeyer, Lucy, MD, President

North American Council on Adoptable Children [10461]
970 Raymond Ave., Ste. 106
Saint Paul, MN 55114
PH: (651)644-3036
Fax: (651)644-9848
Badeau, Sue, President

North American Gaming Regulators Association [5258]
1000 Westgate Dr., Ste. 252
Saint Paul, MN 55114
PH: (651)203-7244
Fax: (651)290-2266
Christiansen, Lisa M., President

Pheasants Forever [4870]
1783 Buerkle Cir.
Saint Paul, MN 55110
PH: (651)773-2000
Toll free: 877-773-2070
Fax: (651)773-5500
Vincent, Howard K., CEO, President

Power Washers of North America [2139]
PO Box 270634
Saint Paul, MN 55127
PH: (651)213-0060
Toll free: 800-393-7962
Fax: (651)213-0369
Nearon, John, President

Progressive Librarians Guild [9722]
St. Catherine University
2004 Randolph Ave., No. 4125
Saint Paul, MN 55105
Hudson, Mark, Coord.

Quail Forever [4874]
1783 Buerkle Cir.
Saint Paul, MN 55110
PH: (651)773-2000
Toll free: 877-773-2070
Gottschalk, John, Director

Qualitative Research Consultants Association [7096]
1000 Westgate Dr., Ste. 252
Saint Paul, MN 55114
PH: (651)290-7491
Toll free: 888-674-7722
Fax: (651)290-2266
Thompson, Shannon Pfarr, Exec. Dir.

Recognition Professionals International [11782]
1000 Westgate Dr., Ste. 252
Saint Paul, MN 55114
PH: (651)290-7490
Fax: (651)290-2266
Stark, Kathy, CRP, President

ReconcilingWorks [20188]
1669 Arcade St., Ste. 2
Saint Paul, MN 55106-1054
PH: (651)665-0861
Fax: (651)665-0863

Scandinavian Collectors Club [22361]
PO Box 16213
Saint Paul, MN 55116-0213
Quinby, Roger, President

Sigma Delta Epsilon, Graduate Women in Science [23860]
PO Box 240607
Saint Paul, MN 55124-0607
PH: (952)236-9112
McManus, Ms. Dee, Exec. Dir.

Society of Insurance Trainers and Educators [8039]
1821 University Ave. W, Ste. S256
Saint Paul, MN 55104
PH: (651)999-5354
Fax: (651)917-1835
Davenport, Deborah, President

Society of Sensory Professionals [7147]
3340 Pilot Knob Rd.
Saint Paul, MN 55121
PH: (651)454-7250
Fax: (651)454-0766
Newton, Jason, PhD, Chairperson

Society for Veterinary Medical Ethics [17663]
University of Minnesota College of Veterinary Medicine
Dept. Veterinary Clinical Sciences
1352 Boyd Ave.
Saint Paul, MN 55108

Surfaces in Biomaterials Foundation [6124]
1000 Westgate Dr., Ste. 252
Saint Paul, MN 55114
PH: (651)290-6267
Wilkerson, Katie, Exec. Dir.

WINGS [17121]
1043 Grand Ave., No. 299
Saint Paul, MN 55105
PH: (415)230-0441
Patterson, Sue, Founder

WINGS Guatemala [17122]
1043 Grand Ave., No. 299
Saint Paul, MN 55105
PH: (415)230-0441
Simon, Janeen, Exec. Dir.

World Press Institute [17963]
3415 University Ave.
Saint Paul, MN 55114
Gahlon, Dan E., Chairman

World Wide Village [11463]
616 Sims Ave.
Saint Paul, MN 55130
PH: (651)777-6908
Mortensen, Randy, President

Zeta Phi Eta, Inc. [23713]
c/o Tyler Wilson, Executive Director
85 Victoria St. N, Apt. 2
Saint Paul, MN 55104
Shiff, Blair, President

Gluckstal Colonies Research Association [9480]
4544 N River Run
Savage, MN 55378
PH: (958)447-8654

Western Saddle Clubs Association [4428]
c/o Leslie Mason, Secretary
15128 240th St.
Scandia, MN 55073
PH: (651)724-3421
Sparks, Ben, VP

Music EdVentures [8375]
c/o Leah Steffen, President
26276 Redwing Ave.

Shafer, MN 55074
PH: (651)257-1698
Steffen, Leah, President

Christian Deer Hunters Association [19955]
PO Box 432
Silver Lake, MN 55381
PH: (320)327-2266
(320)587-7127
Rakow, Dr. Tom C., Founder, President

Irish Genealogical Society International [20979]
1185 Concord St. N, Ste. 218
South Saint Paul, MN 55075-1150

Antique Snowmobile Club of America [22417]
c/o Valdi Stefanson, President
8660 Fawn Lake Dr. NE
Stacy, MN 55079-9306
PH: (651)462-4497
Stefanson, Valdi, President

Fifty Lanterns International [7199]
47399 Anchor Ave.
Stanchfield, MN 55080
PH: (612)747-9516
Cullen, Linda, Exec. Dir.

A.C. Gilbert Heritage Society [22449]
c/o Robert Asleson
39330 Jay St. NW
Stanchfield, MN 55080-8807
Asleson, Robert, Contact

Down Syndrome Diagnosis Network [14625]
PO Box 140
Stillwater, MN 55082
PH: (612)460-0765
Bradley, Heather, President

ReSpectacle [16406]
c/o Jeffrey Lynch, MD, Chief Executive Officer and Founder
1719 Tower Dr.
Stillwater, MN 55082
Lynch, Jeffrey, MD, CEO, Founder

Association of Cooperative Educators [7676]
1057 Parkview Ln.
Victoria, MN 55386-3709
PH: (763)432-2032
Gracie, Tanya, President

Day Spa Association [15140]
1551 Sandbar Cir.
Waconia, MN 55387
PH: (952)767-2202
Toll free: 877-851-8998
Fax: (844)344-8990
Share, Allan, President

International Medical Spa Association [15149]
1551 Sandbar Cir.
Waconia, MN 55387
PH: (952)283-1252
Toll free: 877-851-8998
Fax: (952)767-0742
Leavy, Hannelore R., Exec. Dir., Founder

International Association for Bear Research and Management [4827]
15542 County Road 72
Warba, MN 55793
PH: (218)259-6686
(830)324-6550
Fax: (865)974-3555
Doan-Crider, Dr. Diana, Mem.

Advertising and Marketing International Network [80]
3587 Northshore Dr.
Wayzata, MN 55391

PH: (952)471-7752
Barton, Doug, President

National Association for Ambulatory Urgent Care [13677]
18870 Rutledge Rd.
Wayzata, MN 55391-3157

Pulmonary Fibrosis Advocates [17146]
c/o Paul A. Fogelberg, Director
700 Twelve Oaks Center Dr., Ste. 716
Wayzata, MN 55391-4450
PH: (952)933-9990
Toll free: 800-229-2531
Fogelberg, Paul A., Director

Commission for the Accreditation of Birth Centers [14227]
c/o Rosemary Senjem, Executive Director
2269 5th St.
White Bear Lake, MN 55110
PH: (305)420-5198
Toll free: 877-241-0262
Senjem, Rosemary, Exec. Dir.

H2O for Life [13326]
1310 Highway 96 E, No. 235
White Bear Lake, MN 55110
PH: (651)756-7577
Toll free: 866-427-7183
Schoonover, Jim, Chairman

Lutheran Braille Evangelism Association [17723]
1740 Eugene St.
White Bear Lake, MN 55110-3312
PH: (651)426-0469
Olson, Gary, VP

Parents of Infants and Children with Kernicterus [15981]
PO Box 10744
White Bear Lake, MN 55110-0744
Dornbos, Vicki, President

Association of Faith Churches and Ministers [20356]
PO Box 1918
Willmar, MN 56201
PH: (320)235-3838
Fax: (320)235-1802
Kaseman, Dr. Julius, Founder

E-quip Africa [11348]
PO Box 3178
Willmar, MN 56201-8178
Wilkowske, Doug, Founder

International Society for Computers and their Applications [6319]
64 White Oak Ct.
Winona, MN 55987
PH: (507)458-4517
Debnath, Dr. Narayan, Contact

International Society for Philosophical Enquiry [9343]
Dr. Patrick M. O'Shea, Acting Comptroller
700 Terrace Heights, No. 60
Winona, MN 55987
O'Shea, Dr. Patrick, DSPE, Officer

Hope for the Child [11035]
8315 Emerald Ln.
Woodbury, MN 55125
PH: (651)246-0552
Williams, Akinyi, Founder, Exec. Dir.

Plastic Lumber Trade Association [2628]
PO Box 211
Worthington, MN 56187
PH: (507)372-5558
Fax: (507)372-5726
Larsen, Brian, PE, President

Efficient Windows Collaborative
[3476]
c/o Kerry Haglund
21629 Zodiac St. NE
Wyoming, MN 55092
PH: (202)530-2254
Fax: (202)331-9588
Petermann, Mr. Nils, Project Mgr.

National Association of Competitive
Mounted Orienteering [23050]
c/o Jim Klein, Treasurer/National
Pointskeeper
24305 98th St. NW
Zimmerman, MN 55398
PH: (763)856-6735
Hall, Doug, VP

MISSISSIPPI

National Juneteenth Observance
Foundation [17783]
PO Box 269
Belzoni, MS 39038
PH: (662)392-2016
Fax: (662)247-1471
Myers, Rev. Ronald V., MD, Chair-
man, Founder

International Internet Leather Craft-
ers' Guild [2083]
c/o Pat Hay, Treasurer
PO Box 98
Cary, MS 39054
Talbott, Joel, President

Kappa Pi International Art Honor
Society [23679]
307 S 5th Ave.
Cleveland, MS 38732
PH: (662)846-4729
Stanley, Michael, President

American Society of Diagnostic and
Interventional Nephrology [15872]
134 Fairmont St., Ste. B
Clinton, MS 39056
PH: (601)924-2220
Fax: (601)924-6249
Yevzlin, Alexander S., MD, Officer

National Association of Emergency
Medical Technicians [14683]
132-A E Northside Dr.
Clinton, MS 39056
PH: (601)924-7744
Toll free: 800-34-NAEMT
Fax: (601)924-7325
Lane, Pamela, Exec. Dir.

National Association of Women
Highway Safety Leaders, Inc.
[12830]
c/o KAy Brodbeck, President
PO Box 1379
Clinton, MS 39060
PH: (601)924-7815
Fax: (601)924-7747
Brodbeck, Kay, President

Fell Pony Society of North America,
Inc. [4350]
c/o Kim Owens, General Secretary
1041 Scott Rd.
Coldwater, MS 38618-3070
PH: (662)622-0267
Fax: (901)212-2034
Gould-Earley, Mary Jean, Rep.

National Association of Junior
Auxiliaries, Inc. [12899]
845 S Main St.
Greenville, MS 38701-5871
PH: (662)332-3000
Fax: (662)332-3076
Knauer, Amanda, President

International Dodge Ball Federation
[23229]
3451A Washington Ave.
Gulfport, MS 39507

PH: (228)863-9000
Walker, Rusty, President

American Board of Cardiovascular
Perfusion [14088]
2903 Arlington Loop
Hattiesburg, MS 39401
PH: (601)268-2221
Fax: (601)268-2229
Palmer, David A., CCP, Officer

American Kinesiotherapy Association
[17080]
118 College Dr., No. 5142
Hattiesburg, MS 39406
Toll free: 800-296-2582
Ziegler, Mrs. Melissa, Exec. Dir.

American Therapeutic Recreation
Association [17083]
629 N Main St.
Hattiesburg, MS 39401
PH: (601)450-2872
Fax: (601)582-3354
Devries, Dawn, DHA, MPA, CTRS,
President

Business Retention and Expansion
International [1003]
PO Box 15011
Hattiesburg, MS 39404
Toll free: 800-677-9930
Scott, Ida, President

International Society for Comparative
Psychology [16919]
University of Southern Mississippi
Dept. of Psychology
118 College Dr., No. 5025
Hattiesburg, MS 39406
Gutiérrez, Germán, President

National Association of Call Centers
[772]
100 S 22nd Ave.
Hattiesburg, MS 39401
PH: (480)922-5949
(601)447-8300
Butler, David L., PhD, Exec. Dir.

National Verbatim Reporters As-
sociation [3515]
629 N Main St.
Hattiesburg, MS 39401
PH: (601)582-4345
Schmelz, Brenda, CCR, CVR-M,
President

University of Southern Mississippi
Alumni Association [19366]
118 College Dr., No. 5013
Hattiesburg, MS 39406-0001
PH: (601)266-5013
Fax: (601)266-4214
DeFatta, Jerry, Exec. Dir.

Box Project [12629]
315 Losher St., Ste. 100
Hernando, MS 38632-2124
PH: (662)449-5002
Toll free: 800-268-9928
Fax: (662)449-5006
Tyner, Rob, Chairman

Society of Stukely Westcott
Descendants of America [20930]
c/o Lyle Wescott, Editor
180 Pleasant Valley Dr.
Holly Springs, MS 38635
PH: (847)304-1755
Hulkow, Lynn, VP

American Contract Bridge League
[21559]
6575 Windchase Blvd.
Horn Lake, MS 38637-1523
PH: (662)253-3100
Fax: (662)253-3187
Hartman, Robert, CEO

National Association of Charterboat
Operators [2250]
PO Box 1070
Hurley, MS 39555
Toll free: 866-981-5136
Blackburn, Capt. Percy, Director

Catfish Farmers of America [3638]
1100 Highway 82 E, Ste. 202
Indianola, MS 38751

National Conference of Black Politi-
cal Scientists [7048]
14000 Highway 82 W, MVSU 5098
Itta Bena, MS 38941-1400
PH: (601)750-7318
Fax: (662)254-3130
Shaw, Todd, PhD, President

Association for the Treatment of
Tobacco Use and Dependence
[17308]
c/o Thomas Payne, President
University of Mississippi Medical Ctr.
Jackson Medical Mall, Ste. 61
350 W Woodrow Wilson Dr.
Jackson, MS 39213
Payne, Thomas, President

The Catfish Institute [3639]
6311 Ridgewood Rd., Ste. W404
Jackson, MS 39211
PH: (601)977-9559
Barlow, Roger, President

Christian Fellowship of Art Music
Composers [9180]
c/o Andrew Sauerwein, President
Belhaven University
1500 Peachtree St., No. 286
Jackson, MS 39202
PH: (585)567-9424
Sauerwein, Andrew, President

Council of American Jewish
Museums [9827]
PO Box 12025
Jackson, MS 39236-2025
Sievers, Leah, Secretary

Energy Farm [6479]
PO Box 1834
Jackson, MS 39215-1834
Dortch, Richard, Project Mgr.

Jackson State University National
Alumni Association, Inc. [19329]
PO Box 17820
Jackson, MS 39217
PH: (601)979-2281
Toll free: 800-578-6622
Fax: (601)979-3701
Terrell-Brooks, Tabatha, Exec. Dir.

Mothers Against Munchausen
Syndrome by Proxy Allegations
[14205]
210 E Capitol St., Ste. 800
Jackson, MS 39201
PH: (601)359-1406
Fax: (601)576-2532

National Tile Contractors Association
[892]
626 Lakeland East Dr.
Jackson, MS 39232
PH: (601)939-2071
Fax: (601)932-6117
Bettiga, Bart, Exec. Dir.

Parents for Public Schools [11734]
125 S Congress St., Ste. 1218
Jackson, MS 39201
PH: (601)969-6936
Toll free: 800-880-1222
Fax: (601)397-6132
Cushinberry, Dr. Catherine, Exec.
Dir.

Phi Theta Kappa, International
Honor Society [23733]
1625 Eastover Dr.
Jackson, MS 39211
PH: (601)984-3518
(601)984-3504
Toll free: 800-946-9995
Fax: (601)984-3544
Risley, Dr. Rod A., Exec. Dir.

US Oil & Gas Association - Missis-
sipi/Alabama Divison [2539]
513 N State St., Ste. 202
Jackson, MS 39201
PH: (601)948-8903
Fax: (601)948-8919
Thompson, Ben, President

United States Freshwater Prawn and
Shrimp Growers Association
[3038]
c/o Dolores Fratesis, Secretary-
Treasurer
655 Napanee Rd.
Leland, MS 38756
PH: (662)686-2894
(662)390-3528
Jacobs, Charlene, President

National Society of Physical Activity
Practitioners in Public Health
[16710]
102 Parkdale Pl.
Madison, MS 39110
Newkirk, Jimmy, Exec. Dir.

Preemie Parent Alliance [12426]
201 Cotton Wood Dr.
Madison, MS 39110
PH: (601)345-1772
Sorrells, Keira, President

USS Wisconsin Association [21073]
PO Box 227
Marion, MS 39342
Fox, John, Treasurer

Amateur Field Trial Clubs of America
[21795]
c/o Piper Huffman, Secretary
2873 Whippoorwill Rd.
Michigan City, MS 38647
PH: (662)223-0126
Fax: (662)223-0126
Trimble, Preston, Rep.

Agricultural History Society [9448]
PO Box H
Mississippi State, MS 39762
PH: (662)268-2247
Giesen, James C., PhD, Exec. Sec.

William Faulkner Society [10370]
c/o Ted Atkinson, President
PO Box 5272
Mississippi State, MS 39762
Hagood, Taylor, VP

Ulysses S. Grant Association
[10328]
395 Hardy Rd.
Mississippi State, MS 39762-5408
PH: (662)325-4552
Williams, Frank J., President

Sea Grant Association [6807]
703 E Beach Dr.
Ocean Springs, MS 39564
PH: (228)818-8842
De Guise, Sylvain, President

Show Mercy International [11270]
PO Box 1003
Port Gibson, MS 39150
PH: (541)981-1469
Salley, Mike, Founder, Exec. Dir.,
Dir. of Operations

Beef Improvement Federation [6642]
10223 Highway 382
Prairie, MS 39756

PH: (662)369-4426
Fax: (662)369-9547
Parish, Jane, Exec. Dir.

Evidenced-Based Veterinary
   Medicine Association [17646]
c/o Northwest Registered Agent
270 Trace Colony Pk., Ste. B
Ridgeland, MS 39157
Moberly, Heather, Secretary

American KuneKune Pig Society
   [4707]
c/o Matt Burton, Webmaster
321 Hurricane Creek Rd.
Sandy Hook, MS 39478
Petersen, Kathy, President

National Cotton Batting Institute
   [936]
4322 Bloombury St.
Southaven, MS 38672
PH: (901)218-2393
Arnall, Weston, President

Network of International Christian
   Schools [7612]
3790 Goodman Rd. E
Southaven, MS 38672
PH: (662)892-4300
Toll free: 800-887-6427
Fax: (662)892-4310
Phillips, Harry, V. Ch.

Women in Corporate Aviation [6026]
4450 Nicholas Ln.
Southaven, MS 38672
PH: (901)277-7078
Kotrla, Stacey, President

Care Ministries [17694]
PO Box 1830
Starkville, MS 39760-1830
PH: (662)323-4999
Toll free: 800-336-2232
LeJeune, B.J., Director

Southern Pressure Treaters' As-
   sociation [1421]
PO Box 1784
Starkville, MS 39760
PH: (601)405-1116
Fax: (662)205-8589

U.S. Naval Research Laboratory |
   Marine Geosciences Division |
   Seafloor Sciences Branch [6944]
Bldg. 1005, Code 7430
Stennis Space Center, MS 39529
PH: (228)688-4657

American Family Association
   [17937]
PO Box 2440
Tupelo, MS 38803
PH: (662)844-5036
Wildmon, Donald E., Chairman,
   Founder

United Methodist Association of
   Health and Welfare Ministries
   [14966]
218 S Thomas St., Ste. 212
Tupelo, MS 38801-3027
PH: (662)269-2955
Fax: (662)269-2956
Vinson, Mr. Stephen L., CEO,
   President

Society for the Study of Southern
   Literature [9768]
PO Box 1848
University, MS 38677-1848
Hutchison, Coleman, President

University of Mississippi Alumni Association [19363]
651 Grove Loop
651 Groove Loop

University, MS 38677
PH: (662)915-7375
Fax: (662)915-7756
Maloney, Mr. Eddie, President

University of Mississippi School of
   Applied Sciences | Institute of
   Child Nutrition [1398]
6 Jeanette Phillips Dr.
University, MS 38677
PH: (662)915-7658
Toll free: 800-321-3054
Fax: (800)321-3061
Wilson, Dr. Katie, Exec. Dir.

Sacred Heart League [19902]
6050 Highway 161
Walls, MS 38680
Toll free: 800-232-9079
Kurps, Rev. Jack, Director

Easterling Family Genealogical
   Society [20859]
1124 Pearl Valley Rd.
Wesson, MS 39191-9361
Easterling, Letson E., Sr., President

MISSOURI

Mid-America Buddhist Association
   [19781]
299 Heger Ln.
Augusta, MO 63332-1445
PH: (636)482-4037
Fax: (636)482-4078
Ru, Ji, Chairman

American Mini Pig Association
   [4708]
PO Box 735
Aurora, MO 65605
Hubert, Jaimee, President

Missouri Fox Trotting Horse Breed
   Association [4378]
1 Mile N Highway 5
Ava, MO 65608
PH: (417)683-2468
Fax: (417)683-6144
Graening, Joyce, President

Council of Chiropractic Acupuncture
   [14263]
c/o A. Rand Olso, President
1360 Big Bend Sq.
Ballwin, MO 63021
PH: (636)225-2121
Fax: (636)225-8122
Myerowitz, Dr. Zev J., D.C., Officer

Median Iris Society [22109]
c/o Jean Morris, President
682 Huntley Heights Dr.
Ballwin, MO 63021-5878
Morris, Jean, President

Parents for Window Blind Safety
   [11127]
PO Box 205
Barnhart, MO 63012
PH: (314)494-7890
Kaiser, Linda, Founder

National Autumn Leaf Collectors
   Club [21692]
8426 Clint Dr.
Belton, MO 64012
Didriksen, Judie, President

International Society for the Study of
   Subtle Energies and Energy
   Medicine [7661]
PO Box 297
Bolivar, MO 65613
Toll free: 888-272-6109
Fax: (417)777-7711
Gaither, James, ThD, President

American Karakul Sheep Registry
   [4655]
11500 Hwy. 5
Boonville, MO 65233
PH: (660)838-6340

International Rose O'Neill Club
   Foundation [22003]
PO Box 668
Branson, MO 65615
Trim, Donna, President

United States Pilots Association
   [160]
1652 Indian Point Rd.
Branson, MO 65616
PH: (417)338-2225
Hoynacki, Jan, Exec. Dir.

Boys Hope Girls Hope [13432]
12120 Bridgeton Square Dr.
Bridgeton, MO 63044
PH: (314)298-1250
Toll free: 877-878-HOPE
Fax: (314)298-1251
Minorini, Paul A., President, CEO

North American Association of Utility
   Distributors [3422]
c/o Mary Jane Reinhardt, Director
3105 Corporate Exchange Ct.
Bridgeton, MO 63044
PH: (314)506-0724
Fax: (314)506-0790
Reinhardt, Mary Jane, Director

Concerns of Police Survivors [5461]
846 Old South 5
Camdenton, MO 65020-3199
PH: (573)346-4911
Fax: (573)346-1414
Bernhard, Dianne, Exec. Dir.

National Federation of Pachyderm
   Clubs [18915]
PO Box 1295
Cape Girardeau, MO 63702-1295
Toll free: 888-467-2249
Shults, Bob, President

Out of Poverty thru Education
   [10730]
2128 William St., No. 107
Cape Girardeau, MO 63703-5847
PH: (573)334-0930

Kustom Kemps of America [21416]
26 Main St.
Cassville, MO 65625-9400
PH: (417)847-2940
Fax: (417)847-3647

Reach International Healthcare and
   Training [15491]
PO Box 152
Caulfield, MO 65626
Evans, Samuel C., MD, Director

Alpha Zeta [23673]
16020 Swingley Ridge Rd., Ste. 300
Chesterfield, MO 63017
PH: (636)449-5090
Fax: (636)449-5051
Lee, Teresa, CEO

Consortium for Graduate Study in
   Management [8261]
229 Chesterfield Business Pky.
Chesterfield, MO 63005
PH: (636)681-5460
   (636)681-5553
Fax: (636)681-5499
Aranda, Peter J., III, CEO, Exec. Dir.

Germany Philatelic Society [22330]
PO Box 6547
Chesterfield, MO 63006-6547
Peter, Mike, Secretary, Treasurer

Incentive Federation [2282]
c/o Melissa Van Dyke, Co-Chair
The Incentive Research Foundation
100 Chesterfield Business Pky., Ste.
   200
Chesterfield, MO 63005-1271
PH: (636)549-3193
Bellantone, Paul, CAE, V. Ch.

International Fruit Tree Association
   [4729]
16020 Swingley Ridge Rd., Ste. 300
Chesterfield, MO 63017
PH: (636)449-5083
Fax: (636)449-5051
Schwallier, Phil, President

Junior Chamber International, Inc.
   [12891]
15645 Olive Blvd., Ste. A
Chesterfield, MO 63017-1722
PH: (636)778-3010
Fax: (636)449-3107
Kwemain, Roland, President

National Broadcasting Society -
   Alpha Epsilon Rho [23685]
PO Box 4206
Chesterfield, MO 63006
PH: (636)536-1943
Fax: (636)898-6920
Wilson, Mr. Jim, Exec. Dir.

National Christmas Tree Association
   [4733]
16020 Swingley Ridge Rd., Ste. 300
Chesterfield, MO 63017
PH: (636)449-5070
Fax: (636)449-5051
Rafeld, Blake, President

National Corn Growers Association
   [3766]
632 Cepi Dr.
Chesterfield, MO 63005
PH: (636)733-9004
Fax: (636)733-9005
Claiborne, Susan, Receptionist

National Wood Flooring Association
   [564]
111 Chesterfield Industrial Blvd., Ste.
   B
Chesterfield, MO 63005
PH: (636)519-9663
Toll free: 800-422-4556
Fax: (636)519-9664
Martin, Michael, CEO, President

Shop America Alliance LLC [2977]
1308 Westhampton Woods Ct.
Chesterfield, MO 63005-6324
PH: (707)224-3795
McCormick, Rosemary, Founder,
   President

United Soybean Board [4254]
16305 Swingley Ridge Rd., Ste. 150
Chesterfield, MO 63017
Toll free: 800-989-USB1
Fax: (636)530-1560
Becherer, John, CEO

United States Junior Chamber
   [23632]
15645 Olive Blvd., Ste. A
Chesterfield, MO 63017
PH: (636)778-3010
Fax: (636)449-3107
Harper, Joel, Exec. Dir.

Wings of Hope [12735]
18370 Wings of Hope Blvd.
Chesterfield, MO 63005
PH: (636)537-1302
Toll free: 800-448-9487
Akre, Steven H., Chmn. of the Bd.

CHAN Healthcare Auditors [7752]
231 S Bemiston Ave., Ste. 300
Clayton, MO 63105-1914

PH: (314)802-2000
Fax: (314)802-2020
Cole, Sarah, CEO

**International Arthurian Society -
North American Branch [9758]**
c/o Evelyn Meyer, Secretary/
Treasurer
6637A San Bonita Ave.
Clayton, MO 63105-3121
Whetter, Kevin, VP

**Silver Star Families of America
[12350]**
525 Cave Hollow Rd.
Clever, MO 65631-6313
PH: (417)743-2508
Newton, Steven, Founder, CEO

**American Society of News Editors
[2655]**
209 Reynolds Journalism Institute
Missouri School of Journalism
Columbia, MO 65211
PH: (573)882-2430
Fax: (573)884-3824
Stewart, Mizell, President

**Association for Education Finance
and Policy [7830]**
226 Middlebush Hall
Columbia, MO 65211
PH: (573)814-9878
Fax: (573)884-4872
Goldhaber, Dan, President

**Association of Health Care Journal-
ists [2663]**
10 Neff Hall
Missouri School of Journalism
Columbia, MO 65211
PH: (573)884-5606
Fax: (573)884-5609
Bruzzese, Len, Exec. Dir.

**Association for International
Agriculture and Rural Development
[7473]**
c/o Christy Copeland, Treasurer
213D Mumford Hall
Columbia, MO 65211
Copeland, Christy, Treasurer

**Association for Temperate Agrofor-
estry [4195]**
University of Missouri
Center for Agroforestry
203 ABNR Bldg.
Columbia, MO 65211
PH: (573)882-3234
Fax: (573)882-1977
Zamora, Diomy, President

A Call to Serve International [11329]
610 West Blvd.
Columbia, MO 65203
James, Elizabeth, MD, Officer

**Historians of German and Central
European Art [8859]**
c/o James A. Van Dyke, Treasurer
365 McReynolds Hall
Dept. of Art History and Archaeology
University of Missouri
Columbia, MO 65211-2015
Morton, Dr. Marsha, President

Humanity for Children [16608]
2101 W Broadway, No. 103-131
Columbia, MO 65203-7632
Toll free: 866-406-2006
Fax: (206)420-5353
Berg, Bradley R., MD, Founder

**International Association of Human-
Animal Interaction Organizations
[17447]**
2005 W Broadway, Ste 100
Columbia, MO 65203
Johnson, Rebecca, President

**International Association for Obsid-
ian Studies [5941]**
Archaeometry Laboratory
University of Missouri Research
Reactor
1513 Research Park Dr.
Columbia, MO 65211
PH: (573)882-5241
Fax: (573)882-6360
Ferguson, Jeffrey, President

**Investigative Reporters and Editors,
Inc. [2691]**
Missouri School of Journalism
141 Neff Annex
Columbia, MO 65211
PH: (573)882-2042
Dowdell, Jamie, Director

Kappa Tau Alpha [23794]
University of Missouri
School of Journalism
76 Gannett Hall
Columbia, MO 65211-1200
PH: (573)882-7685
Fax: (573)884-1720
Sanders, Dr. Keith P., Exec. Dir.

MarineParents.com [12251]
3208 LeMone Industrial Blvd.
Columbia, MO 65205
PH: (573)449-2003
Fax: (573)303-5502
Vecchia, Tracy Della, Exec. Dir.

**National Association of Animal
Breeders [4459]**
PO Box 1033
Columbia, MO 65205
PH: (573)445-4406
Fax: (573)446-2279
Doak, Dr. Gordon A., Secretary,
Treasurer, President

**National Freedom of Information
Coalition [18958]**
University of Missouri-Columbia
Journalism Institute
101 Reynolds
Columbia, MO 65211
PH: (573)882-4856
Leary, Mal, President

**Orthopedic Foundation for Animals
[17659]**
2300 E Nifong Blvd.
Columbia, MO 65201-3806
PH: (573)442-0418
Fax: (573)875-5073

**Religion Newswriters Association
[2718]**
30 Neff Annex
Columbia, MO 65211-2600
PH: (573)882-9257
Mason, Dr. Debra L., Exec. Dir.

Veterinary Cancer Society [17668]
PO Box 30855
Columbia, MO 65205
PH: (573)823-8497
Fax: (573)445-0353
Strother, Ms. Sandi, Exec. Dir.

**Fabry Support and Information
Group [14576]**
108 NE 2nd St., Ste. C
Concordia, MO 64020-8324
PH: (660)463-1355
Fax: (660)463-1356
Johnson, J., Founder

Lutheran Bible Translators [19761]
PO Box 789
Concordia, MO 64020
PH: (660)255-0810
Toll free: 800-532-4253
Fax: (660)225-0810
Rodewald, Dr. Mike, Exec. Dir.

**Automotive Communications Council
[282]**
28203 Woodhaven Rd.
Edwards, MO 65326
PH: (240)333-1089
Savine, Steffanie, President

Endangered Wolf Center [4814]
PO Box 760
Eureka, MO 63025
PH: (636)938-5900
Fax: (636)938-6490
Busch, Virginia, Exec. Dir.

**Brewery Collectibles Club of America
[21628]**
747 Merus Ct.
Fenton, MO 63026-2092
PH: (636)343-6486
Smith, Charlie, VP, Treasurer

**Concordia Deaconess Conference
[20302]**
c/o Kim Schave, Webmaster
5000 Romaine Spring Dr.
Fenton, MO 63026
Naumann, Cheryl D.

**North American Equipment Dealers
Association [171]**
1195 Smizer Mill Rd.
Fenton, MO 63026-3480
PH: (636)349-5000
Fax: (636)349-5443
Williams, Michael, VP of Operations

Precancel Stamp Society [22357]
c/o T.G. Rehkop, Secretary
PO Box 1013
Fenton, MO 63026-1013
Rehkop, T.G., Secretary

Jon-Erik Hexum Fan Club [23994]
32 Lee Ave.
Ferguson, MO 63135
Carell, Mr. Alan J., Secretary

**National Mossberg Collectors As-
sociation [22021]**
PO Box 487
Festus, MO 63028
PH: (636)937-6401
Havlin, Victor, President

Friends of Old St. Ferdinand [19837]
1 rue St. Francois
Florissant, MO 63031
PH: (314)837-2110
Keller, Thomas, VP

**Military Police Regimental Associa-
tion [21049]**
Bldg. 1607
495 S Dakota Ave.
Fort Leonard Wood, MO 65473
PH: (573)329-6772
Fax: (573)596-0603
Harne, Rick, Exec. Dir.

**Ancient Coin Collectors Guild
[22260]**
PO Box 911
Gainesville, MO 65655
PH: (417)499-9831
Sayles, Wayne G., Exec. Dir.

**Wabash, Frisco and Pacific Associa-
tion [10194]**
101 Grand Ave.
Glencoe, MO 63038
PH: (636)587-3538
Lorance, Michael, Treasurer

Spuria Iris Society [22128]
c/o Jim Hedgecock, President
12421 SE State Route 116
Gower, MO 64454-8613
Hedgecock, Jim, President

**Owner-Operator Independent Drivers
Association [3353]**
1 NW OOIDA Dr.
Grain Valley, MO 64029-7903
PH: (816)229-5791
Toll free: 800-444-5791
Fax: (816)229-0518
Johnston, Jim, President

**American Bridge Teachers' Associa-
tion [21558]**
PO Box 232
Greenwood, MO 64034-0232
PH: (816)237-0519
Tucker, Patty, President

**American Dorper Sheep Breeders'
Society [4653]**
PO Box 259
Hallsville, MO 65255-0259
PH: (573)696-2550
Fax: (573)696-2030
Sparks, Ronda, Registrar

**Mark Twain Boyhood Home Associ-
ates [9075]**
120 N Main St.
Hannibal, MO 63401-3537
PH: (573)221-9010
Fax: (573)221-7975
Sweets, Henry, Exec. Dir.

**Mark Twain Home Foundation
[9106]**
120 N Main St.
Hannibal, MO 63401
PH: (573)221-9010
Fax: (573)221-7975
Sweets, Henry, Exec. Dir.

**Aiding Mothers and Fathers
Experiencing Neonatal Death
[11554]**
c/o Martha Eise
1559 Ville Rosa
Hazelwood, MO 63042
PH: (314)291-0892
  (314)487-7582
Eise, Martha, Contact

**Daniel Boone and Frontier Families
Research Association [9466]**
c/o Ken Kamper
1770 Hickory Hill Dr.
Hermann, MO 65041
Kamper, Ken, Hist.

**International Machine Quilters As-
sociation, Inc. [21762]**
PO Box 419
Higginsville, MO 64037-0419
PH: (660)584-8171
Fax: (660)584-3841
Hibbs, Mary, President

**American College of Counselors
[11811]**
273 Glossip Ave.
Highlandville, MO 65669-8133
PH: (417)885-7632
Fax: (417)443-3002
Croskey, Raymond Bazemore,
President

**Coalition for Animal Rescue and
Education [10601]**
PO Box 2203
Hillsboro, MO 63050
PH: (636)535-3253
  (314)280-5428
Pitzer, Carole, President

**National Human Resources Associa-
tion [2500]**
PO Box 36
House Springs, MO 63051
Toll free: 866-523-4417
Perry, Lynne, Contact

Guide Dog Users, Inc. **[17707]**
3603 Morgan Way
Imperial, MO 63052-4106
PH: (636)942-5956
Toll free: 866-799-8436
Mehta, Laurie, Officer

Alpha Phi Omega National Service
Fraternity **[23865]**
14901 E 42nd St.
Independence, MO 64055-7347
PH: (816)373-8667
Fax: (816)373-5975
London, Bob, Exec. Dir.

Military Vehicle Preservation Association **[22183]**
3305 Blue Ridge Cutoff
Independence, MO 64055
PH: (816)833-6872
Toll free: 800-365-5798
Fax: (816)833-5115
Cadorette, David, President

National Association of Parliamentarians **[5671]**
213 S Main St.
Independence, MO 64050-3808
PH: (816)833-3892
Toll free: 888-627-2929
Fax: (816)833-3893
Jones, James, VP

National Dog Registry **[10668]**
9018 E Wilson Rd.
Independence, MO 64053-1022
Toll free: 800-637-3647

Reed Organ Society, Inc. **[9999]**
c/o Charlie Robison, Treasurer/
Membership Secretary
PO Box 47
Independence, MO 64051-0047
PH: (816)461-7300
Hendron, Michael, President

Truman Library Institute **[10353]**
500 W US Highway 24
Independence, MO 64050
PH: (816)268-8200
Toll free: 800-833-1225
Sherman, John J., Chairman

American Walnut Manufacturers Association **[1427]**
c/o Brian Brookshire, Executive
Director
505 E State St.
Jefferson City, MO 65101
PH: (573)635-7877
Fax: (573)636-2591
Brookshire, Brian, Exec. Dir.

Association of Conservation
Engineers **[3810]**
c/o Howard David Thomas,
Treasurer
PO Box 180
Jefferson City, MO 65102-0180
PH: (573)522-4115
Fax: (573)522-2324
Gunter, Dale, President

International Association of School
Librarianship **[9709]**
PO Box 684
Jefferson City, MO 65102
PH: (573)635-6044
Fax: (573)635-2858
Manck, Katy, President

Lincoln University Alumni Association
[19333]
820 Chestnut St.
Jefferson City, MO 65101
PH: (573)681-5573
(573)681-5572
Fax: (573)681-5892
Harris, Alfred L., Sr., President

National Association of Public Pension Attorneys **[5030]**
2410 Hyde Park Rd., Ste. B
Jefferson City, MO 65109
PH: (573)616-1895
Fax: (573)616-1897
Dahl, Susie, Exec. Dir.

National Biodiesel Board **[1466]**
605 Clark Ave.
Jefferson City, MO 65101
PH: (573)635-3893
Toll free: 800-929-3437
Fax: (573)635-7913
Anderson, Greg, Treasurer

National Conference of State Fleet
Administrators **[5817]**
301 W High St., Rm. 760
Jefferson City, MO 65101
Edwards, Scott, VP

National Rural Recruitment and
Retention Network **[15128]**
228 Little Creek Ln.
Jefferson City, MO 65109
Toll free: 800-787-2512
Shimmens, Mike, Exec. Dir.

Show Me Solar **[7205]**
303 Norris Dr.
Jefferson City, MO 65109
PH: (573)556-8653
Allemann, Kevin, Director, Secretary

Vintage Sailplane Association
[22493]
31757 Honey Locust Rd.
Jonesburg, MO 63351-3195
Short, James, President

International Society of Weekly
Newspaper Editors **[2690]**
Missouri Southern State University
3950 E Newman Rd.
Joplin, MO 64801-1595
Stebbins, Chad, Exec. Dir.

National Association of Health Care
Assistants **[14895]**
501 E 15th St.
Joplin, MO 64804
PH: (417)623-6049
(417)623-2230
Sweet, Lisa, Chief Clin. Ofc.,
Founder

Agriculture Future of America **[3540]**
PO Box 414838
Kansas City, MO 64141-4838
PH: (816)472-4232
Toll free: 888-472-4232
Fax: (816)472-4239
Weathers, K. Russell, Chairman,
CEO

Alpha Delta Gamma **[23880]**
1100 Rockhurst Rd.
Kansas City, MO 64110
Bal, Kevin, President

Alpha Delta Kappa **[23727]**
1615 W 92nd St.
Kansas City, MO 64114
PH: (816)363-5525
Toll free: 800-247-2311
Fax: (816)363-4010
Griggs, Ruth Ann, President

Alpha Gamma Rho **[23672]**
10101 NW Ambassador Dr.
Kansas City, MO 64153-1395
PH: (816)891-9200
Fax: (816)891-9401
Josephson, Philip, Bus. Mgr.

American Association of Grain
Inspection and Weighing Agencies
[1516]
PO Box 26426
Kansas City, MO 64196

PH: (816)912-2993
(816)912-2084
Petersen, Bob, Officer

American Association of Veterinary
State Boards **[17606]**
380 W 22nd St., Ste. 101
Kansas City, MO 64108
PH: (816)931-1504
Toll free: 877-698-8482
Fax: (816)931-1604
Roeder, Jennifer, Exec. Asst., Office
Mgr.

American Hereford Association
[3694]
PO Box 014059
Kansas City, MO 64101
PH: (816)842-3757
Fax: (816)842-6931
Shaw, Sam, President

American Institute of Musical Studies
[8358]
28 E 69th St.
Kansas City, MO 64113-2512
PH: (816)268-3657
Rouse, James, Chairman

American-International Charolais Association **[3696]**
11700 NW Plaza Cir.
Kansas City, MO 64153
PH: (816)464-5977
Fax: (816)464-5759
Ludeke, Larry, VP

American Junior Brahman Association **[3698]**
PO Box 14100
Kansas City, MO 64101-4100
PH: (816)595-2442
Fax: (816)842-6931
Spies, Rhaelee, Secretary

American Junior Shorthorn Association **[3700]**
7607 NW Prairie View Rd.
Kansas City, MO 64151
PH: (816)599-7777
Fax: (816)599-7782
Smith, Mitchell, VP

American Peony Society **[22081]**
713 White Oak Ln.
Kansas City, MO 64116-4607
Tretheway, Dana, President

American Royal Association **[4452]**
1701 American Royal Ct.
Kansas City, MO 64102
PH: (816)221-9800
Fax: (816)221-8189
Parman, Lynn, President, CEO

American Shorthorn Association
[3712]
7607 NW Prairie View Rd.
Kansas City, MO 64151
PH: (816)599-7777
Fax: (816)599-7782
Soules, Montie D., CEO, Exec. Sec.

American Society of Baking **[369]**
7809 N Chestnut Ave.
Kansas City, MO 64119
Toll free: 800-713-0462
Fax: (888)315-2612
Rivera, Ramon, Chairman

American Society of Electroneurodiagnostic Technologists **[14656]**
402 E Bannister Rd., Ste. A
Kansas City, MO 64131-3019
PH: (816)931-1120
Fax: (816)931-1145
Reimnitz, Arlen, Exec. Dir.

American Truck Historical Society
[22472]
PO Box 901611
Kansas City, MO 64190-1611

PH: (816)891-9900
(816)891-9903
Fax: (816)891-9903
Johnson, Bill, Exec. Dir.

Americas Hepato-Pancreato-Biliary
Association **[15250]**
PO Box 410454
Kansas City, MO 64141
PH: (913)402-7102
Fax: (913)273-1140
Lendoire, Javier C., MD, President

Association of Diesel Specialists
[1125]
400 Admiral Blvd.
Kansas City, MO 64106
PH: (816)285-0810
Fax: (847)770-4952
Reed, Lea Ann, Dir. of Operations

Association of Mailing, Shipping and
Office Automation Specialists
[2116]
11310 Wornall Rd.
Kansas City, MO 64114
Toll free: 888-750-6245
Fax: (888)836-9561
Chambers, Rick, Exec. Dir.

Astronomical League **[6001]**
9201 Ward Pky., Ste. 100
Kansas City, MO 64114
PH: (816)333-7759
Glaze, Mitch, Office Mgr.

Avant Ministries **[20386]**
10000 N Oak Trafficway
Kansas City, MO 64155
PH: (816)734-8500
Toll free: 800-468-1892
Fax: (816)734-4601
Holbrook, Scott, CEO, President

Beta Sigma Phi **[23870]**
1800 W 91st Pl.
Kansas City, MO 64114
PH: (816)444-6800
Toll free: 888-238-2221
Fax: (816)333-6206
Wingfield, Laura Ross, Div. Dir.

Black Archives of Mid-America
[8820]
1722 E 17th Ter.
Kansas City, MO 64108
PH: (816)221-1600
Fields, Taylor, Chairperson

Business Technology Association
[2442]
12411 Wornall Rd., Ste. 200
Kansas City, MO 64145
PH: (816)941-3100
Toll free: 800-325-7219
Fax: (816)941-4843
Hoskins, Brent, Exec. Dir.

Camp Fire **[13436]**
1801 Main, Ste. 200
Kansas City, MO 64108
PH: (816)285-2010
Tisdale, Cathy, President, CEO

Cardiovascular Outcomes **[14153]**
18 W 52nd St.
Kansas City, MO 64112
PH: (816)932-8270
Fax: (816)932-5613
Spertus, John, Director

Children International **[20393]**
2000 E Red Bridge Rd.
Kansas City, MO 64121
PH: (816)942-2000
Toll free: 800-888-3089
Fax: (816)942-3714
Cook, James

China Stamp Society [22316]
c/o H. James Maxwell, President
1050 West Blue Ridge Blvd.
Kansas City, MO 64145-1216
PH: (816)210-1234
Gault, Paul H., Secretary

Compasio Relief and Development
[12648]
9111 N Oregon Ave.
Kansas City, MO 64154
PH: (612)216-5565
Brown, Allan, Exec. Dir.

Council on Chiropractic Orthopedics
[16474]
4409 Sterling Ave.
Kansas City, MO 64133-1854
PH: (816)358-5100
Fax: (816)358-6565
Swank, Larry, Secretary

CrossWorld [20407]
10000 N Oak Trafficway
Kansas City, MO 64155
PH: (816)479-7300
Toll free: 888-785-0087
Fax: (816)734-4601
Losch, Dale, President

A Cup of Water International, Inc.
[4755]
PO Box 9809
Kansas City, MO 64134
PH: (267)242-1798
Kwon, Daniel J., Contact

Electric Utility Industry Sustainable
Supply Chain Alliance [3415]
638 W 39th St.
Kansas City, MO 64111
PH: (816)561-5323
Fax: (816)561-1991
Male, Ms. Jane, Exec. Dir.

Electrical Equipment Representa-
tives Association [1018]
638 W 39th St.
Kansas City, MO 64111
PH: (816)561-5323
Fax: (816)561-1991
Cooper, Kier, President

Emphysema Foundation for Our
Right to Survive [17140]
PO Box 20241
Kansas City, MO 64195
Toll free: 866-END-COPD
Watson, Linda, President

Express Delivery and Logistics As-
sociation [3085]
400 Admiral Blvd.
Kansas City, MO 64106
PH: (816)221-0254
Toll free: 888-838-0761
Fax: (816)472-7765
Conway, Jim, Exec. Dir.

FarmHouse Fraternity, Inc. [23899]
7306 NW Tiffany Spring Pky., Ste.
210
Kansas City, MO 64153
PH: (816)891-9445
Fax: (816)891-0838
Harris, Chad, Exec. Dir.

Fellowship of Christian Athletes
[20141]
8701 Leeds Rd.
Kansas City, MO 64129
PH: (816)921-0909
Toll free: 800-289-0909
Fax: (816)921-8755
Steckel, Les, President, CEO

Gabriel Marcel Society [10087]
c/o Brendan Sweetman, PhD,
President

Rockhurst University
Dept. of Philosophy
1100 Rockhurst Rd.
Kansas City, MO 64110-2561
PH: (816)501-4681
Sweetman, Prof. Brendan, PhD,
President

Gifted Learning Project [12236]
10E 125th St., No. 481551
Kansas City, MO 64148-1551
PH: (816)200-0457

Hotel Brokers International [2862]
1420 NW Vivion Rd., Ste. 111
Kansas City, MO 64118
PH: (816)505-4315
Fax: (816)505-4319
Niehaus, H. Brandt, CHB, President

International Association of
Administrative Professionals [72]
10502 N Ambassador Dr., Ste. 100
Kansas City, MO 64153
PH: (816)891-6600
Fax: (816)891-9118
Donohue, Jay, President, CEO

International Association of Assess-
ing Officers [5795]
314 W 10th St.
Kansas City, MO 64105
PH: (816)701-8100
Toll free: 800-616-4226
Fax: (816)701-8149
Jacks, Dorthy, VP

International Association of Attune-
ment Practitioners [13631]
PO Box 28574
Kansas City, MO 64188-8574
PH: (816)221-7123
Jorgensen, Chris, Founder,
President

International Association for Group
Psychotherapy and Group
Processes [16975]
c/o Bonnie Buchele, PhD, President-
Elect
411 Nichols Rd., Ste. 194
Kansas City, MO 64112
PH: (816)531-2600
Gutmann, David, PhD, President

International Association of Insur-
ance Fraud Agencies [5314]
PO Box 10018
Kansas City, MO 64171
PH: (816)756-5285
Fax: (816)756-5287
Moody, Maximiliane, Exec. Dir.

International Midas Dealers Associa-
tion [346]
400 Admiral Blvd.
Kansas City, MO 64106
PH: (816)285-0811
Toll free: 877-543-6203
Fax: (816)472-7765
DeJong, Tina, President

Investment Recovery Association
[3191]
638 W 39th St.
Kansas City, MO 64111
PH: (816)561-5323
Toll free: 800-728-2272
Fax: (816)561-1991
Male, Jane, Exec. Dir.

Irish Genealogical Foundation
[20978]
PO Box 7575
Kansas City, MO 64116
PH: (816)399-0905
O'Laughlin, Michael C., President,
Founder

Kansas City Barbeque Society
[22149]
11514 Hickman Mills Dr.
Kansas City, MO 64134
PH: (816)765-5891
Toll free: 800-963-5227
Wells, Carolyn, Exec. Dir.

Ewing Marion Kauffman Foundation
[647]
4801 Rockhill Rd.
Kansas City, MO 64110
PH: (816)932-1000
Guillies, Wendy, President, CEO

KidsAndCars.org [19079]
7532 Wyoming St.
Kansas City, MO 64114
PH: (816)216-7085
   (913)732-2792
Fennell, Janette E., Founder,
President

Ladies of Charity of the United
States of America [13068]
National Service Ctr.
850 Main St.
Kansas City, MO 64105
PH: (816)260-3853

Livestock Marketing Association
[4477]
10510 NW Ambassador Dr.
Kansas City, MO 64153
Toll free: 800-821-2048
Harris, Dan, President

Mutual Fund Education Alliance
[3046]
2345 Grand Blvd., Ste. 1750
Kansas City, MO 64108
PH: (816)454-9344

National Association of Basketball
Coaches [22573]
1111 Main St., Ste. 1000
Kansas City, MO 64105-2136
PH: (816)878-6222
Fax: (816)878-6223
Haney, Jim, Exec. Dir.

National Association of Collegiate
Women Athletics Administrators
[8430]
2024 Main St., No. 1W
Kansas City, MO 64108
PH: (816)389-8200
Phillips, Patti, CEO

National Association of Construction
Contractors Cooperation [553]
6301 Rockhill Rd., Ste 316
Kansas City, MO 64130
PH: (816)923-5399
Fax: (816)444-3226
James, John, Secretary

National Association of Insurance
Commissioners [5316]
1100 Walnut St., Ste. 1500
Kansas City, MO 64106-2277
PH: (816)842-3600
Fax: (816)783-8175
Huff, John M., President

National Association of Intercol-
legiate Athletics [23239]
1200 Grand Blvd.
Kansas City, MO 64106
PH: (816)595-8000
Fax: (816)595-8200
Carr, Jim, CEO, President

National Association of Professional
Surplus Lines Offices [1901]
4131 N Mulberry Dr., Ste. 200
Kansas City, MO 64116
PH: (816)741-3910
Kelley, Brady, Exec. Dir.

National Chronic Fatigue Syndrome
and Fibromyalgia Association
[14600]
PO Box 18426
Kansas City, MO 64133-8426
PH: (816)737-1343
Fax: (816)524-6782
Prewitt, Orvalene, President

National Fireworks Association
[6629]
8224 NW Bradford Ct.
Kansas City, MO 64151
PH: (816)741-1826
Blake, Bob, VP

National Junior Hereford Association
[3741]
PO Box 014059
Kansas City, MO 64101
PH: (816)842-3757
Fax: (816)842-6931
Stotz, Keysto, Chairman

National Soccer Coaches Associa-
tion of America [23189]
30 W Pershing Rd., Ste. 350
Kansas City, MO 64108-2463
PH: (816)471-1941
Fax: (816)474-7408
Cummings, Joe, CEO

Negro Leagues Baseball Museum
[22564]
1616 E 18th St.
Kansas City, MO 64108-1610
PH: (816)221-1920
Toll free: 888-221-NLBM
Fax: (816)221-8424
Kendrick, Bob, President

Nonprofit Leadership Alliance [8202]
1801 Main St., Ste. 200
Kansas City, MO 64108
PH: (816)561-6415
Fax: (816)531-3527
Tisdale, Cathy, Secretary

North American Bangladeshi As-
sociation for Bangladesh [7531]
PO Box 55103
Kansas City, MO 64138
Kaikobad, Mahmudul H., Exec. Sec.

PE4life [8434]
127 W 10th St., Ste. 208
Kansas City, MO 64105
PH: (816)472-7345
Stevens, John, Bd. Member

People to People International
[18554]
2405 Grand Blvd., Ste. 500
Kansas City, MO 64105-5305
PH: (816)531-4701
Toll free: 800-676-7874
Fax: (816)561-7502
Kubic, Micah, Chairman

Public Works Historical Society
[9507]
2345 Grand Blvd., Ste. 700
Kansas City, MO 64108-2625
PH: (816)472-6100
Toll free: 800-848-APWA
Fax: (816)472-1610
Smith, Lois, Mgr.

Scaffold and Access Industry As-
sociation [578]
400 Admiral Blvd.
Kansas City, MO 64106
PH: (816)595-4860
Fax: (816)472-7765
Loar, Granville, Exec. Dir.

Scaffolding, Shoring & Forming
Institute [579]
400 Admiral Blvd.
Kansas City, MO 64106

PH: (816)471-4922
Fax: (816)472-7765

Sealant, Waterproofing and Restoration Institute [62]
400 Admiral Blvd.
Kansas City, MO 64106
PH: (816)472-7974
Fax: (816)472-7765
Raffio, Cindy, President

Sertoma Inc. [12908]
1912 E Meyer Blvd.
Kansas City, MO 64132
PH: (816)333-8300
Fax: (816)333-4320
Murphy, Mr. Steven, Secretary

Species Iris Group of North America [22127]
8871 NW Brostrom Rd.
Kansas City, MO 64152-2711
Waddick, Jim, Chairman

Tile Contractors Association of America [901]
10434 Indiana Ave.
Kansas City, MO 64137
Toll free: 800-655-8453
Fax: (816)767-0194
Schwartz, Ron, President, Chmn. of the Bd.

Transportation, Elevator and Grain Merchants Association [1522]
PO Box 26426
Kansas City, MO 64196
PH: (816)569-4020
    (816)912-2084
Fax: (816)221-8189
Petersen, Robert R., President

United Federation of Doll Clubs [22009]
10900 N Pomona Ave.
Kansas City, MO 64153-1256
PH: (816)891-7040
Gula, Janet, President

Vasculitis Foundation [17352]
PO Box 28660
Kansas City, MO 64188-8660
PH: (816)436-8211
Toll free: 800-277-9474
Fax: (816)656-3838
Kullman, Joyce A., Exec. Dir.

Vetarans Voices Writing Project [17100]
406 W 34th St., Ste. 103
Kansas City, MO 64111
PH: (816)701-6844
Mitchell, Deann, President

Veterans of Foreign Wars of the United States [21149]
406 W 34th St.
Kansas City, MO 64111
.PH: (816)756-3390
Fax: (816)968-1169
Thien, William A., Cmdr.

Veterans of Foreign Wars of the United States, Ladies Auxiliary [21150]
406 W 34th St., 10th Fl.
Kansas City, MO 64111
PH: (816)561-8655
Fax: (816)931-4753
Guilford, Francisca, President

Water.org [13349]
920 Main St., Ste. 1800
Kansas City, MO 64105
PH: (816)877-8400
White, Mr. Gary, CEO, Founder

World Atlatl Association [22173]
c/o Justin Garnett, Executive Treasurer

905 E 76th Ter.
Kansas City, MO 64131
Garnett, Justin, Treasurer

In-Plant Printing and Mailing Association [2787]
455 S Sam Barr Dr., Ste. 203
Kearney, MO 64060
PH: (816)919-1691
Fax: (816)902-4766
Golden, Tammy, Secretary, Treasurer

North American Alliance for the Advancement of Native Peoples [18712]
29780 Highway UU
Keytesville, MO 65261-2455
Randall, Harriet L., CEO, President

Piedmontese Association of the United States [3750]
6134 NW Theil Dr.
Kidder, MO 64649
PH: (816)786-3155
Morris, Chris, President

American Osteopathic College of Dermatology [14483]
2902 N Baltimore St.
Kirksville, MO 63501
PH: (660)665-2184
Toll free: 800-449-2623
Fax: (660)627-2623
Wise, Marsha A., Exec. Dir.

National Osteopathic Women Physician's Association [23841]
ATSU - Kirksville College of Osteophatic Medicine
800 W Jefferson St.
Kirksville, MO 63501
Sigler, Rachel, President

Beyond the Rainbow [23986]
956 Briar Green Ct.
Kirkwood, MO 63122-5149
PH: (314)799-1724
Fax: (314)596-4549
Willingham, Elaine, Founder

Canadian Poolplayers Association [22585]
1000 Lake St. Louis Blvd., Ste. 325
Lake Saint Louis, MO 63367
PH: (636)625-8611
Fax: (636)625-2975
Hubbart, Larry, Founder

For the Love of Horses [18354]
605 Oak St.
Lathrop, MO 64465
PH: (814)474-5382
Toll free: 866-537-7336
Leaman, Crystal, Gen. Mgr.

Two Hearts for Hope [11174]
PO Box 1928
Lebanon, MO 65536-1928
Prud'homme, Kimberly, Exec. Dir., Founder

Aircraft Electronics Association [123]
3570 NE Ralph Powell Rd.
Lees Summit, MO 64064
PH: (816)347-8400
Fax: (816)347-8405
Derks, Paula, President

International Feng Shui Guild [9278]
705 B SE Melody Ln., Ste. 166
Lees Summit, MO 64063
PH: (816)246-1898
Calamia, Maureen, Secretary

National Association of Division Order Analysts [2528]
PO Box 2300
Lees Summit, MO 64063-7300
Hinton, Jean, Secretary

National Lubricating Grease Institute [2531]
249 SW Noel St., Ste. 249
Lees Summit, MO 64063-2241
PH: (816)524-2500
Fax: (816)524-2504
Hartley, Kimberly, Exec. Dir.

Unity Worldwide Ministries [20029]
PO Box 610
Lees Summit, MO 64063
PH: (816)524-7414
Fax: (816)525-4020
Johnson, Donna, President, CEO

International Air Filtration Certifiers Association [1623]
c/o Michael Alleman, 129 S Gallatin
129 S Gallatin St.
Liberty, MO 64068
Toll free: 888-679-1904
Fax: (816)792-8105
Alleman, Michael, Contact

National Perinatal Association [16623]
PO Box 392
Lonedell, MO 63060
Toll free: 888-971-3295

Hope Imaging [17232]
14248 F Manchester Rd., No. 187
Manchester, MO 63011
PH: (206)588-9931
Fax: (636)527-7700
Gregory, Kama, Director, Consultant

National Federation of Professional Bullriders [23098]
2222 Highway F
Mansfield, MO 65704
PH: (417)924-3591
    (417)259-3361
Jackson, Clint, President

National Association of Medical Examiners [15630]
c/o Denise D. McNally, Executive Director
National Association of Medical Examiners
362 Bristol Rd.
Marceline, MO 64658
PH: (660)734-1891
McNally, Denise D., Exec. Dir.

Beta Gamma Sigma [23688]
125 Weldon Pky.
Maryland Heights, MO 63043
PH: (314)432-5650
Toll free: 800-337-4677
Fax: (314)432-7083
Hunter, William C., President

National Council of the United States Society of St. Vincent de Paul [13074]
58 Progress Pky.
Maryland Heights, MO 63043-3706
PH: (314)576-3993
Fax: (314)576-6755
Gilbert, Sheila, President

North American Strongman [22699]
PO Box 1973
Maryland Heights, MO 63043
PH: (314)565-5970
Wessels, Dione, President, CEO

Painting and Decorating Contractors of America [896]
2316 Millpark Dr.
Maryland Heights, MO 63043
PH: (314)514-7322
Toll free: 800-332-7322
Fax: (314)890-2068
French, Rod, Chmn. of the Bd.

Lightning Protection Institute [2999]
25475 Magnolia Dr.
Maryville, MO 64468
Toll free: 800-488-6864
Fax: (660)582-0430
Loehr, Kim, Dir. of Comm.

Sigma Gamma Epsilon [23768]
c/o Aaron Johnson, President
Dept. of Natural Sciences
Northwest Missouri State University
1335 Garret-Strong
800 College Park Dr.
Maryville, MO 64468
PH: (660)562-1569
Fax: (660)562-1055
Walters, James, Secretary, Treasurer

American Osteopathic College of Radiology [17042]
119 E 2nd St.
Milan, MO 63556-1331
PH: (660)265-4011
Fax: (660)265-3494
Houston, Carol, Exec. Dir.

American Gerbil Society [21280]
18893 Lawrence 2100
Mount Vernon, MO 65712
Hanna, Libby, President

Palomino Horse Association [4399]
c/o Patricia Rebuck
10171 Nectar Ave.
Nelson, MO 65347
PH: (660)859-2064
    (660)859-2058
Rebuck, Patricia, Contact

American Cat Fanciers Association [21565]
PO Box 1949
Nixa, MO 65714-1949
PH: (417)725-1530
Fax: (417)725-1533
Blackmore, Doug, President

Ophthalmic Photographers' Society [16401]
1887 W Ranch Rd.
Nixa, MO 65714-8262
PH: (417)725-0181
Toll free: 800-403-1677
Fax: (417)724-8450
McCalley, Barbara S., Exec. Dir.

International Spotted Horse Registry Association [4372]
2120 Scotch Hollow Rd.
Noel, MO 64854
PH: (417)475-6273
Toll free: 866-201-3098
Rogers, Rebecca, Founder, President

Business Products Credit Association [1225]
607 Westridge Dr.
O Fallon, MO 63366
PH: (360)612-9507
    (636)754-0567
Toll free: 888-514-2722

Children's Relief Mission [10933]
PO Box 597
Owensville, MO 65066-0597
PH: (818)502-1989
Fax: (818)502-9040
Sholer, Michael, Asst. Sec.

Teen Challenge International [20663]
5250 N Towne Centre Dr.
Ozark, MO 65721
PH: (417)581-2181
Batluck, Rev. Joseph S., Sr., President, CEO

Animal Health Foundation [17632]
3615 Bassett Rd.
Pacific, MO 63069
Walsh, Dr. Donald, President, Founder

The Hardware Companies Kollectors Klub [21660]
c/o Barbara Keener, Secretary-Treasurer
PO Box 325
Pacific, MO 63069-0325
PH: (636)257-2926
Hester, Mike, President

Association of the Miraculous Medal [19798]
1811 W St. Joseph St.
Perryville, MO 63775
Toll free: 800-264-6279

American Chianina Association [3690]
1708 N Prairie View Rd.
Platte City, MO 64079
PH: (816)431-2808
Fax: (816)431-5381
Miller, Ed, Cmte. Mgmt. Ofc.

American Junior Chianina Association [3699]
1708 N Prairie View Rd.
Platte City, MO 64079
PH: (816)431-2808
Fax: (816)431-5381
Upperman, Jaclyn, Director, Editor

American Maine-Anjou Association [3701]
204 Marshall Rd.
Platte City, MO 64079-1100
PH: (816)431-9950
Fax: (816)431-9951
Vliet, Marty Van, President

National Association of Farm Broadcasters [471]
1100 Platte Falls Rd.
Platte City, MO 64079
PH: (816)431-4032
Fax: (816)431-4087
Winnekins, Brian, President

National EMS Management Association [14688]
2901 Williamsburg Terr., Ste. G
Platte City, MO 64079
Toll free: 888-424-9850
Touchstone, Mike, President

Simian Society of America, Inc. [10696]
c/o Brenda Keller, Membership Chairman
16322 S Graham Rd.
Pleasant Hill, MO 64080
Newman, Ann, President

General Association of General Baptists [19730]
100 Stinson Dr.
Poplar Bluff, MO 63901
PH: (573)785-7746
Fax: (573)785-0564
Cook, Clint, Exec. Dir.

Purebred Dexter Cattle Association of North America [3751]
25979 Highway EE
Prairie Home, MO 65068
PH: (660)841-9502

Stained Glass Association of America [1511]
9313 E 63rd St.
Raytown, MO 64133
PH: (816)737-2090
Toll free: 800-438-9581
Fax: (816)737-2801
Gross, Richard, Editor

American Appaloosa Association [4296]
PO Box 429
Republic, MO 65738-0429

PH: (417)466-3633
Green-Carpenter, Heidi, Contact

DeSoto Club of America [21370]
403 S Thorton St.
Richmond, MO 64085
PH: (816)470-3048
    (816)421-6006
O'Kelly, Walter, Contact

National Utility Locating Contractors Association [894]
1501 Shirkey Ave.
Richmond, MO 64085
Toll free: 888-685-2246
Fax: (504)889-9898
Tarosky, Dennis, VP

Allison Family Association [20778]
10095 County Road 5120
Rolla, MO 65401
PH: (573)341-3549

Omega Chi Epsilon [23738]
c/o Dr. Douglas K. Ludlow, President
Chemical & Biological Engineering Dept.
Missouri University of Science and Technology
132 Schrenk Hall
Rolla, MO 65409-1230
PH: (573)341-6477
Fax: (573)341-4377
Davis, Dr. Richard A., Exec. Sec.

Scottish-American Military Society [9807]
c/o Mike Gibbens, National Adjutant
37 McFarland Dr.
Rolla, MO 65401
PH: (573)578-9194
Anderson, Robert, Comptroller

Society for Natural Philosophy [6828]
c/o Professor Gearoid P. MacSithigh, Treasurer
Toomey Hall
Dept. of Mechanical and Aerospace Engineering
Missouri University of Science and Technology
400 W 13th St.
Rolla, MO 65409-0500
MacSithigh, Prof. Gearoid P., Treasurer

Fellowship for Intentional Community [9171]
PO Box 156
Rutledge, MO 63563-9720
Toll free: 800-462-8240
Schaub, Laird, Exec. Sec., Coord.

Fellowship for Intentional Community [17975]
PO Box 156
Rutledge, MO 63563-9720
Toll free: 800-462-8240
Schaub, Laird, Exec. Sec., Coord.

Council of State Science Supervisors [8545]
c/o C. J. Evans, Treasurer
614 Indian Hills Dr.
Saint Charles, MO 63301-0561
PH: (314)614-7701
Jordan, Linda K., Exec. Sec.

I.B.M. Youth [22177]
The International Brotherhood of Magicians
13 Point W Blvd.
Saint Charles, MO 63301-4431
PH: (636)724-2400
Fax: (636)724-8566

International Brotherhood of Magicians [22178]
13 Point West Blvd.
Saint Charles, MO 63301-4431

PH: (636)724-2400
Fax: (636)724-8566
Munoz, Oscar, President

Monocoupe Club [21239]
1218 Kingstowne Pl.
Saint Charles, MO 63304

National Association of Peer Program Professionals [11495]
58 Portwest Ct.
Saint Charles, MO 63303
Toll free: 888-691-1088
Fax: (888)691-1088

Powder Actuated Tool Manufacturers' Institute [1758]
136 S Main St., Ste. 2E
Saint Charles, MO 63301
PH: (636)578-5510
Fax: (314)884-4414

SHARE: Pregnancy and Infant Loss Support [12427]
c/o Patti Budnik, RN
National Share Office
402 Jackson St.
Saint Charles, MO 63301-3468
PH: (636)947-6164
Margherio, Michael, President

Travelers Protective Association of America [19496]
2041 Exchange Dr.
Saint Charles, MO 63303
Toll free: 877-872-2638
Fax: (636)724-2457
McGrew, George S., President

American Angus Association [3682]
3201 Frederick Ave.
Saint Joseph, MO 64506
PH: (816)383-5100
Fax: (816)233-9703
Schumann, Bryce, CEO

American Board of Funeral Service Education [2397]
3414 Ashland Ave., Ste. G
Saint Joseph, MO 64506-1333
PH: (816)233-3747
Fax: (816)233-3793
Kann, Karl, VP

National Junior Angus Association [3740]
3201 Frederick Ave.
Saint Joseph, MO 64506
PH: (816)383-5100
Fax: (816)233-9703
Rogen, Alex, Chairman

Pony Express Historical Association [9506]
1202 Penn St.
Saint Joseph, MO 64503
PH: (816)232-8206

United States Animal Health Association [17666]
4221 Mitchell Ave.
Saint Joseph, MO 64507
PH: (816)671-1144
Fax: (816)671-1201
King, Bruce, President

1904 World's Fair Society [22482]
2605 Causeway Dr.
Saint Louis, MO 63125
King, Linda, Exhibits Dir.

Accreditation Council on Optometric Education [16418]
American Optometric Association
243 N Lindbergh Blvd., 1st Fl.
Saint Louis, MO 63141-7881
Toll free: 800-365-2219
Campbell, J. Bart, OD, Chairman

African Great Lakes Initiative [13023]
1001 Park Ave.
Saint Louis, MO 63104
PH: (314)647-1287
Bucura, David, Coord.

Alpha Eta Rho [23682]
4579 Laclede Ave., Ste. 1929
Saint Louis, MO 63108

American Academy of Fertility Care Professionals [11835]
11700 Studt Ave., Ste. C
Saint Louis, MO 63141
PH: (314)489-3733
Fax: (402)488-6525
Danis, Peter, President

American Association of Bioanalysts [15513]
906 Olive St., Ste. 1200
Saint Louis, MO 63101-1448
PH: (314)241-1445
Fax: (314)241-1449
Birenbaum, Mark S., Administrator

American Association of Orthodontists [14392]
401 N Lindbergh Blvd.
Saint Louis, MO 63141-7816
PH: (314)993-1700
Toll free: 800-424-2841
Fax: (314)997-1745
Vranas, Chris, Exec. Dir.

American Board of Bioanalysis [6774]
906 Olive St., Ste. 1200
Saint Louis, MO 63101
PH: (314)241-1445
Fax: (314)241-1449

The American Board of Nuclear Medicine [16073]
4555 Forest Park Blvd., Ste. 119
Saint Louis, MO 63108-2173
PH: (314)367-2225

American Board of Optometry [16421]
243 N Lindbergh Blvd., Ste. 312
Saint Louis, MO 63141
PH: (314)983-4244
Ajamian, Paul C., OD, Chairman

American Board of Orthodontics [14398]
401 N Lindbergh Blvd., Ste. 300
Saint Louis, MO 63141-7839
PH: (314)432-6130
Fax: (314)432-8170
Dugoni, Dr. Steven A., Secretary, Treasurer

American Clan Gregor Society [20779]
c/o Jeanne Lehr, Registrar
11 Ballas Ct.
Saint Louis, MO 63131-3038
PH: (801)899-6157
    (314)432-2842
Garlitz, Lois Ann, Dep. Chief

American Independent Cockpit Alliance [23384]
PO Box 220670
Saint Louis, MO 63122-0670
PH: (603)528-2552
Long, Chuck, President

American Optometric Association [16422]
243 N Lindbergh Blvd., 1st Fl.
Saint Louis, MO 63141-7881
PH: (314)991-4100
    (314)983-4136
Toll free: 800-365-2219
Fax: (314)991-4101
Hopping, Ronald L., O.D., President

American Optometric Student Association [16425]
243 N Lindbergh, Ste. 311
Saint Louis, MO 63141
PH: (314)983-4231
Foster, Robert, Exec. Dir.

American Society of Concrete Contractors [850]
2025 S Brentwood Blvd., Ste. 105
Saint Louis, MO 63144
PH: (314)962-0210
Toll free: 866-788-2722
Fax: (314)968-4367
Garnant, Beverly, Exec. Dir.

American Soybean Association [4691]
12125 Woodcrest Executive Dr., Ste. 100
Saint Louis, MO 63141-5009
PH: (314)576-1770
Toll free: 800-688-7692
Fax: (314)576-2786
Wilkins, Richard, President

American Youth Foundation [20657]
6357 Clayton Rd.
Saint Louis, MO 63117
PH: (314)719-4343
Wittkamp, Nancy, Dir. of Fin.

America's Future [18279]
7800 Bonhomme Ave.
Saint Louis, MO 63105
PH: (314)725-6003
Fax: (314)721-3373
Duplantier, F.R., Ed. Dir.

Association of Hebrew Catholics [19796]
4120 W Pine Blvd.
Saint Louis, MO 63108-2802
Friedman, Elias, OCD, Founder

Basket of Hope [10784]
PO Box 510860
Saint Louis, MO 63151
PH: (314)268-1515
Furrey, Mike, President

Black Radical Congress [19293]
PO Box 24795
Saint Louis, MO 63115

Botanical Society of America [6138]
4475 Castleman Ave.
Saint Louis, MO 63110-3201
PH: (314)577-9566
Fax: (314)577-9515
Dahl, Bill, Exec. Dir.

Cardinal Mindszenty Foundation [17801]
7800 Bonhomme Ave.
Saint Louis, MO 63105
PH: (314)727-6279
Fax: (314)727-5897
Schlafly, Eleanor, President

Catholic Health Association of the United States [15317]
4455 Woodson Rd.
Saint Louis, MO 63134-3701
PH: (314)427-2500
Fax: (314)427-0029
Keehan, Sr. Carol, DC, CEO, President

Chinese American Chromatography Association [6195]
c/o Tao Jiang, President
Covidien/Mallinckrodt
3600 N 2nd St.
Saint Louis, MO 63147
PH: (314)654-1744
Jiang, Tao, President

Christian Fencers Association [22831]
c/o Bruce Sikes
912 S Rock Hill

Saint Louis, MO 63119
Sikes, Rev. Robert Bruce, Contact

Christian Life Community of the United States of America [19822]
3601 Lindell Blvd.
Saint Louis, MO 63108-3301
PH: (202)425-2572
Nguyen, Sophie, Treasurer

Coast Guard Auxiliary Association [20748]
9449 Watson Industrial Pk.
Saint Louis, MO 63126
Toll free: 877-875-6296
Mallison, Thomas, VP

College of Diplomates of the American Board of Orthodontics [14424]
401 N Lindbergh Blvd.
Saint Louis, MO 63141
Toll free: 888-217-2988
Fax: (314)997-1745
Guess, Dr. Michael, Officer

Concordia Historical Institute [20303]
804 Seminary Pl.
Saint Louis, MO 63105-3014
PH: (314)505-7900
     (314)505-7911
Fax: (314)505-7901
Meyer, Mr. Scott, President

Council of Conservative Citizens [19155]
PO Box 221683
Saint Louis, MO 63122
PH: (636)940-8474
Baum, Gordon, CEO

Credit Professionals International [1229]
10726 Manchester Rd., Ste. 210
Saint Louis, MO 63122
PH: (314)821-9393
Fax: (314)821-7171
Westenhofer, Cindy, President

Disability Rights Advocates for Technology [11587]
500 Fox Ridge Rd.
Saint Louis, MO 63131
Toll free: 800-401-7940
Fax: (314)965-4956
Kerr, Jerry, Founder, President

The Discussion Club [17891]
c/o Racquet Club Ladue
1600 Log Cabin Ln.
Saint Louis, MO 63124
PH: (314)416-7722
Fax: (314)416-7760
Jozwiak, Mrs. Mary Ann, Bd. Member

Dozenal Society of America [7230]
5106 Hampton Ave., Ste. 205
Saint Louis, MO 63109-3115
De Vlieger, Michael, Director

Electrical Apparatus Service Association [1017]
1331 Baur Blvd.
Saint Louis, MO 63132
PH: (314)993-2220
Fax: (314)993-1269
Raynes, Linda J., CEO, President

Energy Storage Council [6482]
3963 Flora Pl., 2nd Fl.
Saint Louis, MO 63110
PH: (314)495-4545

Farm Equipment Manufacturers Association [167]
1000 Executive Pky., Ste. 100
Saint Louis, MO 63141-6369

PH: (314)878-2304
Fax: (314)732-1480
Irish, Michael, Secretary

Global Aquaculture Alliance [3640]
4111 Telegraph Rd., Ste. 302
Saint Louis, MO 63129
PH: (314)293-5500
Stevens, Wally, Exec. Dir.

Walter Burley Griffin Society of America [5969]
1152 Center Dr.
Saint Louis, MO 63117
PH: (314)644-4546
Griffin, Peter Burley, President

Idoma Association USA [19596]
12031 Lackland Rd.
Saint Louis, MO 63146
PH: (314)878-1400
Ogwuche, Grace Dama, Secretary

INROADS [8195]
10 S Broadway, Ste. 300
Saint Louis, MO 63102
PH: (314)241-7488
Fax: (314)241-9325
Harper, Mr. Forest T., CEO, President

Institute for Challenging Disorganization [9538]
1693 S Hanley Rd.
Saint Louis, MO 63144
PH: (314)416-2236
Quick-Andrews, Beth, CAE, Exec. Dir.

Institute for Peace and Justice [18793]
475 E Lockwood Ave.
Saint Louis, MO 63119
PH: (314)918-2630
     (314)533-4445
Fax: (314)918-2643
McGinnis, Kathleen, Exec. Dir.

Institute for Theological Encounter with Science and Technology [12006]
20 Archbishop May Dr., Ste. 3400A
Saint Louis, MO 63119
PH: (314)792-7220
Fax: (314)977-7211
Sheahen, Dr. Thomas P., Director

International Crisis Aid [12683]
PO Box 510167
Saint Louis, MO 63151
PH: (314)487-1400
Toll free: 888-740-7779
Fax: (314)487-1409
Bradley, Patrick, Chairman, President

International Lutheran Laymen's League [20304]
660 Mason Ridge Center Dr.
Saint Louis, MO 63141
PH: (314)317-4100
Toll free: 800-876-9880
Krauss, Philip, II, Chairman

International Psoriasis Council [14497]
1034 S Brentwood Blvd., Ste. 600
Saint Louis, MO 63117-1206
PH: (972)861-0503
Fax: (214)242-3391
Griffiths, Christopher, President

International Steel Guitar Convention [9935]
9535 Midland Blvd.
Saint Louis, MO 63114-3314
PH: (314)427-7794
Fax: (314)427-0516
DeWitt, Scott, Founder

Jewish Federation of St. Louis [19519]
12 Millstone Campus Dr.
Saint Louis, MO 63146-5776
PH: (314)432-0020
Fax: (314)432-6150

Junior Optimist Octagon International [12892]
4494 Lindell Blvd.
Saint Louis, MO 63108
PH: (314)371-6000
Toll free: 800-500-8130
Fax: (314)371-6006
Bourgeois, Marie-Claude, President

Kinship Circle [10655]
7380 Kingsbury Blvd.
Saint Louis, MO 63130
PH: (314)795-2646
Shoss, Brenda, President, Founder

Latin Liturgy Association [19851]
c/o Regina Morris, President
3526 Oxford Blvd.
Saint Louis, MO 63143-4209
Mooney, James, VP

Lentz Peace Research Association [18802]
366 Social Sciences Bldg.
University of Missouri
1 University Blvd.
Saint Louis, MO 63121-4400

Lutheran Deaf Mission Society [20307]
9907 Sappington Rd.
Saint Louis, MO 63128
Konkel, Rev. Dennis, Director

Lutheran Women's Missionary League [20314]
3558 S Jefferson Ave.
Saint Louis, MO 63118
Toll free: 800-252-5965
Fax: (314)268-1532
Ross, Patti, President

Lymphology Association of North America [15545]
PO Box 16183
Saint Louis, MO 63105
PH: (773)756-8971
Feldman, Joseph L., MD, President

Materials Technology Institute [721]
1215 Fern Ridge Pky., Ste. 206
Saint Louis, MO 63141-4405
PH: (314)576-7712
Fax: (314)576-6078
Whitcraft, Paul, Chmn. of the Bd.

Meds & Food for Kids [11076]
4488 Forest Park Ave., Ste. 230
Saint Louis, MO 63108-2215
PH: (314)420-1634
Wolff, Patricia B., MD, Exec. Dir., Founder

Melanoma Hope Network [14009]
101 W Argonne Dr., No. 220
Saint Louis, MO 63122
Thornberry, Jeannie, Founder

Metal Roofing Alliance [2357]
12430 Tesson Ferry Rd., No. 112
Saint Louis, MO 63128
PH: (314)495-5906
Hippard, William, Exec. Dir.

Mission Continues [13243]
1141 S 7th St.
Saint Louis, MO 63104
PH: (314)588-8805
Fax: (314)571-6227
Greitens, Eric, CEO

Mobile Health Clinics Association [15036]
2275 Schuetz Rd.
Saint Louis, MO 63146

PH: (314)764-2288
Fax: (314)569-0721
Wallace, Elizabeth, Exec. Dir.

Museum of Transportation [10184]
2967 Barrett Station Rd.
Saint Louis, MO 63122
PH: (314)965-6885
McEachern, Terri O., Exec. Dir.

NAED Education and Research
Foundation [2182]
1181 Corporate Lake Dr.
Saint Louis, MO 63132-1716
PH: (314)991-9000
Toll free: 888-791-2512
Fax: (314)991-3060
McNamara, Michelle, Exec. Dir., Sr.
VP

National Association of Academies of
Science [7140]
c/o Academy of Science of St. Louis
5050 Oakland Ave.
Saint Louis, MO 63110-1404
PH: (314)533-8083
Fax: (314)533-8885
Brogie, Ed M., Exec. Dir.

National Association of Electrical
Distributors [1028]
1181 Corporate Lake Dr.
Saint Louis, MO 63132-1716
PH: (314)991-9000
Toll free: 888-791-2512
Fax: (314)991-3060
Naber, Tom, President, CEO

National Association of Portable
X-ray Providers [15694]
1065 Executive Pkwy., No. 220
Saint Louis, MO 63141
PH: (314)227-2700
Fax: (800)533-9729
Schwartz, Tamara, Treasurer

National Association for Pseudox-
anthoma Elasticum [14504]
8760 Manchester Rd.
Saint Louis, MO 63144-2724
PH: (314)301-7345
Fax: (314)301-7345
Benham, Frances, PhD, Chairman,
President

National Association of the Van Valk-
enburg Family [20905]
PO Box 411010
Saint Louis, MO 63141

National Automatic Pistol Collectors
Association [21297]
PO Box 15738
Saint Louis, MO 63163-0738
Knox, Tom, President

National Catholic Conference for
Total Stewardship [19877]
4579 Laclede Ave., No. 483
Saint Louis, MO 63108
PH: (314)552-1679

National Children's Cancer Society
[14023]
500 N Broadway, Ste. 800
Saint Louis, MO 63102
PH: (314)241-1600
Fax: (314)241-1996
Slocomb, Mark, Chairman

National Garden Clubs [22111]
4401 Magnolia Ave.
Saint Louis, MO 63110-3406
PH: (314)776-7574
Fax: (314)776-5108
Robinson, Sandra, President

National Hockey League Booster
Clubs [24076]
PO Box 805
Saint Louis, MO 63188
Sharp, Chris, President

New Chaucer Society [9763]
Adorjan Hall, Rm. 127
St. Louis University
3800 Lindell Blvd.
Saint Louis, MO 63108
PH: (314)520-7067
Fax: (314)977-1514
Evans, Ruth, Exec. Dir.

Optimist International [12903]
4494 Lindell Blvd.
Saint Louis, MO 63108-2404
PH: (314)371-6000
Toll free: 800-500-8130
Fax: (314)735-4100
Garner, Ken, President

Optometric Historical Society
[16436]
Optometry Cares
243 N Lindbergh Blvd.
Saint Louis, MO 63141-7881
PH: (314)983-4200
Amos, John F., President

Partners in Sustainable Develop-
ment International [12558]
PO Box 16505
Saint Louis, MO 63105-1005
PH: (314)993-5599
Klein, Virginia, Exec. Dir.

Personal Freedom Outreach [20049]
PO Box 26062
Saint Louis, MO 63136-0062
PH: (314)921-9800
Goedelman, M. Kurt, Exec. Dir.,
Founder

The Pesticide Stewardship Alliance
[14721]
11327 Gravois Rd., No. 201
Saint Louis, MO 63126-3657
PH: (314)849-9137
Fax: (314)849-0988
Rogers, Jeff, President

Post-Polio Health International
[11632]
4207 Lindell Blvd., No. 110
Saint Louis, MO 63108-2930
PH: (314)534-0475
Fax: (314)534-5070
Stothers, William G., Chairperson,
President

Project Appleseed: The National
Campaign for Public School
Improvement [7824]
520 Melville Ave.
Saint Louis, MO 63130-4506
PH: (314)292-9760
Fax: (314)725-2319
Walker, Kevin S., Director, President,
Founder

Sociedad Internacional Brecht
[9098]
c/o Paula Hanssen, Secretary-
Treasurer
Webster University
470 E Lockwood Ave.
Saint Louis, MO 63119-3141
PH: (314)968-6900
Fax: (314)963-6926
Heeg, Günther, VP

Society for Economic Botany [6155]
PO Box 299
Saint Louis, MO 63166-0299
Fax: (314)577-9515
Brosi, Sunshine, Secretary

Society for Medieval and Renaissance Philosophy [9790]
c/o Jon McGinnis, Secretary-
Treasurer
599 Lucas Hall, MC 73

Department of Philosophy
University of Missouri, St. Louis
1 University Blvd.
Saint Louis, MO 63121-4400
PH: (314)516-5439
McGinnis, Jon, Secretary, Treasurer

Society of the Sacred Heart, United
States-Canada [19911]
4120 Forest Park Ave.
Saint Louis, MO 63108
PH: (314)652-1500
Fax: (314)534-6800
Miller, Shirley, RSCJ, Director

Society of Saint Peter Apostle
[19913]
20 Archbishop May Dr.
Saint Louis, MO 63119
PH: (314)792-7655
Henrion, Connie, Coord.

Society for the Study of Evolution
[6623]
4475 Castleman Ave.
Saint Louis, MO 63110-3201
PH: (314)577-9554
Weinig, Cynthia, Secretary

A Soldier's Wish List [10760]
11143 Larimore Rd.
Saint Louis, MO 63138
Najar, Julieann, Founder

Sponge and Chamois Institute
[2087]
10024 Office Center Ave., Ste. 203
Saint Louis, MO 63128
PH: (314)842-2230
Fax: (314)842-3999
Waters, Susan, Contact

Support Dogs, Inc. [11641]
10995 Linpage Pl.
Saint Louis, MO 63132
PH: (314)997-2325
Fax: (314)997-7202
Klein, Anne, President, CEO

Terminal Railroad Association of St.
Louis Historical and Technical
Society, Inc. [10193]
PO Box 1688
Saint Louis, MO 63188-1688
PH: (314)535-3101
(636)326-3026
Thomas, Larry, Editor, Secretary,
Treasurer

Theta Xi [23938]
745 Craig Rd., Ste.222
Saint Louis, MO 63141
Toll free: 800-783-6294
Fax: (314)993-8760
Baker, Stephen, Chairman

United Schutzhund Clubs of America
[21977]
4407 Meramec Bottom Rd., Ste. J
Saint Louis, MO 63129
PH: (314)638-9686
Fax: (314)638-0609
Phillips, Frank, VP

U.S. Basketball Writers Association
[22577]
1818 Chouteau Ave.
Saint Louis, MO 63103
PH: (314)444-4325
Mitch, Joe, Exec. Dir.

United States Bocce Federation
[22695]
c/o Julie Belfi, Treasurer
10013 Shapfield Ln.
Saint Louis, MO 63123
PH: (630)257-2854
San Rafael, Jerry South, President

Veteran Feminists of America
[18236]
18 Aberdeen Pl.
Saint Louis, MO 63105
Ceballos, Jacqui, Founder

Veterans for Peace [18837]
1404 N Broadway
Saint Louis, MO 63102
PH: (314)725-6005
Fax: (314)227-1981
McPhearson, Michael, Exec. Dir.

Vision USA [16440]
243 N Lindbergh Blvd., Fl. 1
Saint Louis, MO 63141
PH: (314)983-4200
Toll free: 800-365-2219
Fax: (314)991-4101
Bennett, Irving, Treasurer, Secretary

Walter E. Dandy Neurosurgical
Society [16071]
3635 Vista Ave., 5th Fl., FDT
Saint Louis, MO 63110
PH: (314)577-8716
Fax: (314)577-8720
Abdulrauf, Saleem I., MD, President

WaterJet Technology Association
and Industrial and Municipal
Cleaning Association [6637]
906 Olive St., Ste. 1200
Saint Louis, MO 63101-1448
PH: (314)241-1445
Fax: (314)241-1449
Savanick, George, PhD, Treasurer

Women for Faith and Family [19921]
PO Box 300411
Saint Louis, MO 63130
PH: (314)863-8385
Fax: (314)863-5858
Hitchcock, Mrs. Helen Hull,
President

World Federation of Orthodontists
[14476]
401 N Lindbergh Blvd.
Saint Louis, MO 63141-7816
Fax: (314)985-1036
Maplethorp, F. Amanda, BSc, VP

World Initiative for Soy in Human
Health [3777]
12125 Woodcrest Executive Dr., Ste.
100
Saint Louis, MO 63141
PH: (314)576-1770
Fax: (314)576-2786
Hershey, Jim, Exec. Dir.

World Internet Numismatic Society
[22291]
PO Box 220401
Saint Louis, MO 63122
Noble, Dave, President

Writing Academy [10408]
c/o Nancy Remmert, Treasurer
312 St. Louis Ave.
Saint Louis, MO 63135-3718
PH: (314)522-7718

Bereaved Parents of the USA
[10771]
PO Box 622
Saint Peters, MO 63376
PH: (636)947-9403
Francisco, Mike, President

International Coalition for Autism and
All Abilities [13770]
PO Box 781
Saint Peters, MO 63376-0014
Malabey, Emily, Founder, VP

National 4th Infantry Ivy Division As-
sociation [20720]
PO Box 1914
Saint Peters, MO 63376-0035

PH: (678)480-4422

National Collegiate Table Tennis Association [23293]
154 Mill Run Ln.
Saint Peters, MO 63376-7106
Toll free: 800-581-6770
Leparulo, Willy, President

Paint and Decorating Retailers Association [1958]
1401 Triad Center Dr.
Saint Peters, MO 63376-7353
PH: (636)326-2636
Bond, Craig, President

Association of North American Missions [20384]
PO Box 610
Salem, MO 65560
PH: (573)261-0057
Clark, Rev. Douglas, Exec. Dir.

Scott Joplin International Ragtime Foundation [10000]
111 W 5th St.
Sedalia, MO 65301
PH: (660)826-2271
Toll free: 866-218-6258
Ballard, Terri, Exec. Dir.

Dream Pursuit [11226]
205 Holmes Dr.
Sikeston, MO 63801
PH: (573)421-5580
Davis, Rick, Founder, President

National Angora Rabbit Breeders Club [4602]
c/o Margaret Bartold, Secretary
909 Highway E
Silex, MO 63377
PH: (573)384-5866
Hastings, Joan, President

P.O.W. Network [21092]
PO Box 68
Skidmore, MO 64487-0068
PH: (660)928-3304
Schantag, Mary, Chairperson

Ambassadors for Children [11212]
500 W Battlefield St., Ste. B
Springfield, MO 65807-4294
PH: (417)708-0565
Fax: (417)708-0566
Cron, Amber, Coord.

American Association of Integrative Medicine [15703]
2750 E Sunshine St.
Springfield, MO 65804-2047
PH: (417)881-9995
Toll free: 877-718-3053
Fax: (417)823-9959
O'Block, Dr. Robert, Founder, Publisher

American College of Forensic Examiners International [5235]
2750 E Sunshine St.
Springfield, MO 65804
PH: (417)881-3818
Toll free: 800-423-9737
Fax: (417)881-4702
O'Block, Robert L., PhD, CEO, Founder

American Dexter Cattle Association [3691]
1325 W Sunshine No. 519
Springfield, MO 65807
PH: (970)858-1931
   (605)745-4755
Malcuit, Pam, President

American Integrative Medical Association [15706]
2750 E Sunshine
Springfield, MO 65804

PH: (417)823-9959
Toll free: 877-718-3053

American Psychotherapy Association [16962]
2750 E Sunshine St.
Springfield, MO 65804
PH: (417)823-0173
Toll free: 800-205-9165
Tasker, Wayne E., Chairman

Baptist Bible Fellowship International [19720]
720 E Kearney St.
Springfield, MO 65803
PH: (417)862-5001
Fax: (417)865-0794
Lyons, Eddie, President

Convoy of Hope [12652]
330 S Patterson Ave.
Springfield, MO 65802
PH: (417)823-8998
Fax: (417)823-8244
Donaldson, Hal, Founder, President

Enactus [18283]
1959 E Kerr St.
Springfield, MO 65803-4775
PH: (417)831-9505
Rohrs, Alvin, President, CEO

HealthCare Ministries [20365]
521 W Lynn St.
Springfield, MO 65802-1829
PH: (417)866-6311
Fax: (417)866-4711
Highfill, Dr. Deborah M., PhD, Director

International Association of Fairs and Expositions [2331]
3043 E Cairo St.
Springfield, MO 65802-6204
PH: (417)862-5771
Toll free: 800-516-0313
Calico, Marla, President, CEO

Miracle Wings Foundation [10775]
PO Box 9841
Springfield, MO 65801
PH: (417)576-5471
Kyger, Alliena, President

Musical Box Society International [22251]
PO Box 10196
Springfield, MO 65808-0196
PH: (417)886-8839
Fax: (417)886-8839
Harris, Rosanna, Editor

National Association for Poetry Therapy [16983]
c/o Dottie Joslyn
1403 E Dunkirk St.
Springfield, MO 65804
Rolfs, Alma, President

One Missing Link [12363]
PO Box 10581
Springfield, MO 65808
PH: (417)886-5836
Toll free: 800-555-7037

Retail Confectioners International [1371]
2053 S Waverly, Ste. C
Springfield, MO 65804
Toll free: 800-545-5381
Burlison, Angie, Exec. Dir., Secretary, Treasurer

Short Wing Piper Club [21246]
PO Box 10822
Springfield, MO 65808-0822
PH: (417)883-1457
Toll free: 855-797-2411
Stevens, Constance, MBA, President

Society for Pentecostal Studies [20519]
1435 N Glenstone Ave.
Springfield, MO 65802
PH: (417)268-1084
Grey, Jacqui, President

North American Truck Stop Network [2973]
PO Box 337
Sullivan, MO 63080
PH: (573)468-6288
Toll free: 800-771-6016
Fax: (573)468-5885
Bird, Marsha, CEO

Collie Club of America [21859]
c/o Susan Houser
12736 W Watson
Sunset Hills, MO 63127-1325
PH: (314)842-4832
Myers, Robert, Mem.

Pi Beta Phi [23919]
1154 Town and Country Commons Dr.
Town and Country, MO 63017
PH: (636)256-0680
Fax: (636)256-8095
Willeman, Juli, Exec. Dir.

Electrical Rebuilder's Association [317]
PO Box 906
Union, MO 63084
PH: (636)584-7400
Fax: (636)584-7401
Henke, Henry, Contact

Monster Truck Racing Association [23082]
c/o Brenda Noelke, Secretary, 947 Crider Ln.
947 Crider Ln.
Union, MO 63084
PH: (636)234-6162
Fax: (636)583-1660
Hall, Tim, President

Quaker Parakeet Society [3670]
PO Box 343
Valley Park, MO 63088
Gildhouse, Vern, President

World Bird Sanctuary [4919]
125 Bald Eagle Ridge Rd.
Valley Park, MO 63088
PH: (636)225-4390
Fax: (636)861-3240
Crawford, Walter, Exec. Dir.

American Gulf War Veterans Association [21106]
PO Box 85
Versailles, MO 65084
PH: (573)378-6049
Toll free: 877-817-9829
Riley, Joyce, RN, Spokesperson

Kindness in a Box [11063]
5955 Grayling View Ct.
Villa Ridge, MO 63089
Burgman, Lynda, Founder, Exec. Dir.

Kappa Mu Epsilon [23812]
c/o Dr. Rhonda McKee, President
Dept. of Mathematics and Computer Science
University of Central Missouri
Warrensburg, MO 64093
PH: (660)543-8929
Fax: (417)865-9599
Hollenbeck, Brian, VP

Sigma Tau Gamma Fraternity, Inc. [23933]
101 Ming St.
Warrensburg, MO 64093

PH: (660)747-2222
Fax: (660)747-9599
Johnston, Jim, Treasurer

World Safety Organization [12849]
PO Box 518
Warrensburg, MO 64093
PH: (660)747-3132
Fax: (660)747-2647
Senkovich, Dr. Vlado Z., President

Child Evangelism Fellowship [20132]
17482 Hwy. M
Warrenton, MO 63383-3414
PH: (636)456-4321
Toll free: 800-748-7710
Fax: (636)456-9935
Kauffman, Reese R., President

Primero Agua [13333]
2675 Stonecrest Dr.
Washington, MO 63090
PH: (636)239-1573
Quattlebaum, Jay L., Exec. Dir., Founder

Weatherby Collectors Association [22026]
PO Box 1217
Washington, MO 63090-8217
PH: (636)239-0348
Hart, Guy, Exec. Dir.

Society of Army Physician Assistants [16725]
PO Box 4068
Waynesville, MO 65583-4068
PH: (573)528-2307
Fax: (888)711-8543
Miller, Jim, Treasurer

American Darters Association [22765]
PO Box 627
Wentzville, MO 63385-0627
PH: (636)614-4380
Fax: (636)673-1092
Remick, Gloria, CEO

Interfaith Church of Metaphysics [20607]
163 Moon Valley Rd.
Windyville, MO 65783
PH: (417)345-8411
Spretnjak, Christine, President

MONTANA

Sustainable Smiles [3952]
Box 148
Alberton, MT 59820
PH: (406)370-0226
Franklin, Kelly, CEO, President

Irish Black Cattle Association [3734]
PO Box 7
Arlee, MT 59821
PH: (406)696-5977
Boney, Maurice W., Founder

National Council of Exchangors [2882]
11 W Main St., Ste. 223
Belgrade, MT 59714
PH: (858)222-1608
Jones, William, Treasurer

Association of Administrative Law Judges [5377]
c/o Jessica H. Pugrud, Secretary
3024 Mactavish Cir.
Billings, MT 59101-9451
Fax: (406)247-7555
Pugrud, Jessica H., Secretary

National Alliance of Families for the Return of America's Missing Servicemen [21091]
2528 Poly Dr.
Billings, MT 59102-1442

PH: (406)652-3528
Holland, Ann, Dir. of Operations

Sharps Collector Association [22023]
PO Box 81566
Billings, MT 59108
Sears, Matt, President

Mothers Against Sexual Predators At Large [12928]
PO Box 606
Bonner, MT 59823
Ogle, Jan, President

Adventurers and Scientists for Conservation [3788]
PO Box 1834
Bozeman, MT 59771
PH: (406)624-3320
Treinish, Gregg, Founder, Exec. Dir.

Aid to Orphans of Madagascar [10842]
13670 Lone Bear Rd.
Bozeman, MT 59715
De Meij, Annie, Founder

American College for Advancement in Medicine [16797]
380 Ice Center Ln., Ste. C
Bozeman, MT 59718
Toll free: 800-532-3688
Fax: (406)587-2451
Green, MD, Allen, President

American Fly Fishing Trade Association [3133]
321 E Main St., Ste. 300
Bozeman, MT 59715
PH: (406)522-1556
Fax: (406)522-1557
Klug, Jim, Dir. of Operations

American Independent Business Alliance [3111]
222 S Black Ave.
Bozeman, MT 59715-4716
PH: (406)582-1255
Rockne, Jennifer, Chmn. of the Bd., Founder

American Simmental Association [3713]
1 Genetics Way
Bozeman, MT 59718
PH: (406)587-4531
Fax: (406)587-9301
Shafer, Wade, PhD, Exec. VP

Antahkarana Society International [12621]
PO Box 1543
Bozeman, MT 59771-1543
PH: (406)581-5963
Campbell, Deanna, Exec. Dir.

Global Wildlife Resources [4822]
PO Box 10248
Bozeman, MT 59719
PH: (406)586-4624
Johnson, Mark R., DVM, Exec. Dir.

Greater Yellowstone Coalition [3880]
215 S Wallace Ave.
Bozeman, MT 59715
PH: (406)586-1593
Toll free: 800-775-1834
Barrett, Heidi, Mgr.

Keystone Conservation [4838]
104 E Main St., Ste. 307
Bozeman, MT 59715
PH: (406)587-3389
Fax: (406)587-3178
Upson, Lisa, Exec. Dir.

North American Sturgeon and Paddlefish Society [3918]
c/o Dr. Molly Webb, President

USFWS, Bozeman Fish Technology Center
4050 Bridger Canyon Rd.
Bozeman, MT 59715
PH: (406)994-9907
Fax: (406)586-5942
Webb, Dr. Molly, President

Polar Bears International [4871]
PO Box 3008
Bozeman, MT 59772
Wright, Krista, Exec. Dir.

Property and Environment Research Center [4095]
2048 Analysis Dr., Ste. A
Bozeman, MT 59718
PH: (406)587-9591
Anderson, Terry L., President

Radiation Research Society [7083]
380 Ice Center Ln., Ste. C
Bozeman, MT 59718
Toll free: 877-216-1919
Haynes, Veronica, Exec. Dir.

Reclaim Democracy! [18106]
222 S Black Ave.
Bozeman, MT 59715
PH: (406)582-1224
Milchen, Jeff, Founder

Red Feather Development Group [11992]
PO Box 907
Bozeman, MT 59771-0907
PH: (406)585-7188
(928)440-5119
Echohawk, Sarah, President

Wildlife Conservation Society - North America [4911]
212 S Wallace Ave., Ste. 101
Bozeman, MT 59715
PH: (406)522-9333
Fax: (406)522-9377

Winchester Arms Collectors Association [21299]
PO Box 10427
Bozeman, MT 59719
PH: (541)526-5929
Fax: (971)285-9046
Hill, Rick, Treasurer

American Cormo Sheep Association [4649]
c/o Charlotte Carlat, Treasurer/ Registrar
100 E River Rd.
Broadus, MT 59317
PH: (406)427-5449
Carlat, Charlotte, Secretary

International Organic Inspectors Association [4517]
PO Box 6
Broadus, MT 59317
PH: (406)436-2031
Mcmillan, Stuart, Chairman

Mai Wah Society [9028]
7 W Mercury St.
Butte, MT 59703-0404
PH: (406)723-3231

Maternal Life International [17109]
326A S Jackson St.
Butte, MT 59701
PH: (406)782-1719
Mulcaire-Jones, Dr. George, Founder, President

National Affordable Housing Network [11975]
PO Box 632
Butte, MT 59703-0632
PH: (406)782-8579
Fax: (406)782-5539
Knox, Meg, Chmn. of the Bd.

National Center for Appropriate Technology [17808]
PO Box 3838
Butte, MT 59702
PH: (406)494-4572
Toll free: 800-275-6228
Fax: (406)494-2905
Brady, Gene, Chairman

Shape Up America [16713]
PO Box 149
Clyde Park, MT 59018-0149
PH: (406)686-4844
Fax: (406)686-4424
Moore, Barbara J., PhD, CEO, President

World Hypertension League [15351]
415 Bass Ln.
Corvallis, MT 59828
Niebylski, Dr. Mark L., CEO

Big Wild Advocates [4793]
222 Tom Miner Creek Rd.
Emigrant, MT 59027-6010
PH: (406)848-7000
Wolke, Howie, President, Founder

Foundation for Research on Economics and the Environment [3868]
16380 Cottonwood Rd.
Gallatin Gateway, MT 59730
PH: (406)585-1776
Baden, John A., PhD, Chairman

Church Universal and Triumphant [20535]
63 Summit Way
Gardiner, MT 59030-9314
PH: (406)848-9500
Toll free: 800-245-5445
Fax: (406)848-9555
Prophet, Elizabeth Claire, Founder

International Truck Parts Association [323]
1720 10th Ave. S, Ste. 4
Great Falls, MT 59405
Toll free: 866-346-5692
Fax: (800)895-4654
Zentner, Gerard, Chairman

Lewis and Clark Trail Heritage Foundation [9492]
4201 Giant Springs Rd.
Great Falls, MT 59405
PH: (406)454-1234
Toll free: 888-701-3434
Lee, Steve, President

Custer Battlefield Historical and Museum Association [9473]
PO Box 902
Hardin, MT 59034-0902
O'Keefe, Mike, Bd. Member

Alternative Energy Resources Organization [6450]
PO Box 1558
Helena, MT 59624
PH: (406)443-7272
Fax: (406)442-9120
Williamson, Corrie, Officer

American Council on Criminal Justice Training [5128]
PO Box 7053
Helena, MT 59604
PH: (406)241-6150
Webb, Howard, Exec. Dir.

Association for the Rights of Catholics in the Church [19799]
PO Box 6512
Helena, MT 59604-6512
PH: (870)235-5209
Edgar, Patrick B., President

Feathered Pipe Foundation [11998]
2409 Bear Creek Rd.
Helena, MT 59601
PH: (406)442-8196
Fax: (406)442-8110
Supera, India, Founder

Fully Informed Jury Association [18598]
PO Box 5570
Helena, MT 59604-5570
PH: (406)442-7800
Toll free: 800-TEL-JURY
Lewis, Lisa, Media Spec.

Indian Law Resource Center [18708]
602 N Ewing St.
Helena, MT 59601-3603
PH: (406)449-2006
Fax: (406)449-2031
Coulter, Robert T., Exec. Dir., President

International Chinese Boxing Association Worldwide [22713]
3465 Blackhawk St.
Helena, MT 59602
PH: (214)796-4039
Grago, David M., Sr., Chairman

International Livestock Identification Association [4455]
c/o Tammy Bridges, Secretary/ Treasurer
6335 Mt. Vista
Helena, MT 59602
PH: (406)457-0087
Reister, Christian, President

National Association of Medicare Supplement Advisors [15041]
PO Box 4459
Helena, MT 59604
PH: (406)442-4016
Iverson, Ron, Contact

National Parliamentary Debate Association [8599]
Carroll College
1601 N Benton Ave.
Helena, MT 59625-0001
PH: (503)768-7729
Fax: (503)768-7620
Northup, Prof. Brent, Treasurer

Professional Knifemakers Association, Inc. [21779]
2905 N Montana Ave., Ste. 30027
Helena, MT 59601
PH: (618)753-2147
Waites, Dick, Secretary

Sustainable Obtainable Solutions [4583]
PO Box 1424
Helena, MT 59624
PH: (406)495-0738
Fax: (406)495-9703
Flora, Gloria, Director

American Miniature Llama Association [3595]
PO Box 8
Kalispell, MT 59903-0008
PH: (406)755-3438
Chapman, Julie, President

Christian Jujitsu Association [22989]
PO Box 7174
Kalispell, MT 59904-0174
PH: (406)257-3245
Edwards, Prof. Gene, CEO

International Lama Registry [3601]
11 1/2 Meridian Rd.
Kalispell, MT 59901
PH: (406)755-3438
Fax: (406)755-3439
Baum, Karen, Secretary

Orphan's Lifeline of Hope
International [11121]
135 Kelly Rd.
Kalispell, MT 59901
PH: (406)257-0868
Murphy, Tim, Coord.

United States Association of Profes-
sional Investigators [5372]
175 Hutton Ranch Rd., Ste. 103-165
Kalispell, MT 59901
PH: (406)545-2177
Toll free: 877-894-0615
Torgerson, Randy, President

Federation of Fly Fishers [22843]
5237 US Highway 89 S, Ste. 11
Livingston, MT 59047
PH: (406)222-9369
Snyder, Judy, Admin. Asst.

Operation Never Forgotten [10752]
PO Box 1229
Manhattan, MT 59741
Kelly, Linda, President

International Bridge Press Association [21560]
611 Pleasant
Miles City, MT 59301
Jourdain, Patrick, President

Adventure Cycling Association
[22743]
150 E Pine St.
Missoula, MT 59807
PH: (406)721-1776
Toll free: 800-755-2453
Fax: (406)721-8754
Garst, Jennifer, Director

American Indian Business Leaders
[608]
Gallagher Business Bldg., Ste. 366
Missoula, MT 59812
Fax: (406)243-2298
Bighorn, Prairie, Exec. Dir.

Association for Technology in Music
Instruction [8362]
312 E Pine St.
Missoula, MT 59802
Phillips, Scott, President

Bear Trust International [4792]
PO Box 4006
Missoula, MT 59806-4006
PH: (406)523-7779
Reynolds-Hogland, Melissa, PhD,
Exec. Dir.

Boone and Crockett Club [4799]
250 Station Dr.
Missoula, MT 59801
PH: (406)542-1888
Toll free: 888-840-4868
Fax: (406)542-0784
Schoonen, Tony, Chief of Staff

John Clare Society [7981]
c/o James McKusick, Dean
The Davidson Honors College
University of Montana
Missoula, MT 59812
Curry, Linda, Chairperson

College Music Society [8364]
312 E Pine St.
Missoula, MT 59802
PH: (406)721-9616
Fax: (406)721-9419
Barry, Nancy, Secretary

Ecology Project International [7875]
315 S 4th St. E
Missoula, MT 59801
PH: (406)721-8784
Fax: (406)721-7060
Pankratz, Scott, Exec. Dir., Founder

Great Bear Foundation [4823]
PO Box 9383
Missoula, MT 59807-9383
PH: (406)829-9378
Fax: (406)829-9379
Jonkel, Chuck, Founder, Act. Pres.

International Association of Wildland
Fire [4205]
1418 Washburn St.
Missoula, MT 59801
PH: (406)531-8264
Toll free: 888-440-4293
Robinson, Mikel, Exec. Dir.

International Society of Folk Harpers
and Craftsmen [9933]
Alice Williams, Secretary
1614 Pittman Dr.
Missoula, MT 59803
PH: (406)542-1976
Kolacny, Dave, President

Kamut Association of North America
[3764]
PO Box 4903
Missoula, MT 59806
PH: (406)251-4903
Blyth, Trevor, CEO

National Forest Foundation [3904]
Bldg. 27, Ste. 3
Fort Missoula Rd.
Missoula, MT 59804-7212
PH: (406)542-2805
Fax: (406)542-2810
Possiel, Bill, President

Native Forest Network [3911]
PO Box 8251
Missoula, MT 59807
PH: (406)542-7343
Fax: (406)542-7347
Koehler, Matthew, Exec. Dir.

Natural Trails and Waters Coalition
[4579]
PO Box 7516
Missoula, MT 59807-7516
PH: (406)543-9551
Kiely, Jason, Contact

Outdoor Writers Association of
America [2714]
615 Oak St., Ste. 201
Missoula, MT 59801
PH: (406)728-7434
Freeman, Mark, President

Rural Institute: Center for Excellence
in Disability Education, Research
and Service [11636]
52 Corbin Hall
University of Montana
Missoula, MT 59812
PH: (406)243-5467
Toll free: 800-732-0323
Fax: (406)243-4730
Blair, Martin, Exec. Dir.

Society for Wilderness Stewardship
[3946]
3225 Fort Missoula Rd., B30
Missoula, MT 59804
PH: (435)962-9453
MacSlarrow, Heather, Exec. Dir.

Women's Voices for the Earth [4109]
114 W Pine St.
Missoula, MT 59807
PH: (406)543-3747
Fax: (406)543-2557
Switalski, Erin, Exec. Dir.

United Native American Housing Association [1693]
56423 Highway 93
Pablo, MT 59855

PH: (406)675-4491
Adams, Jason, Chairman

English Setter Association of
America [21872]
c/o Dr. Rhonda Dillman
62 Dillman Rd.
Roundup, MT 59072
PH: (256)435-9652
Gray, Janet, President

Women Involved in Farm Economics
[17793]
c/o Linda Newman, President
442 4 Rd.
Roundup, MT 59072-6404
PH: (406)323-8299
   (406)462-5597
Cammack, Mary Ellen, VP

Chemical Injury Information Network
[17487]
PO Box 301
White Sulphur Springs, MT 59645
PH: (406)547-2255
Wilson, Cynthia, Exec. Dir., Founder

North American Ski Joring Associa-
tion [23248]
PO Box 1602
Whitefish, MT 59937
PH: (406)261-7464
Smith, Geoffrey, VPN

NEBRASKA

Hearts United for Animals [10635]
Box 286
Auburn, NE 68305
PH: (402)274-3679
Fax: (402)274-3689

Foundation for Veterinary Dentistry
[14435]
3905 Twin Creek Dr., No. 103
Bellevue, NE 68123
PH: (402)505-9033
Rachwitz, Dr. Erich, Treasurer

Pyrotechnics Guild International
[2822]
c/o Dan Creagan, President
1501 Cobblestone Lane Cir.
Bellevue, NE 68005
PH: (402)212-9200
Toll free: 877-223-3552
Creagan, Dan, President

Tripoli Rocketry Association [8557]
PO Box 87
Bellevue, NE 68005
PH: (402)884-9530
Fax: (402)884-9531
Barrett, Stu, President

Danish America Heritage Society
[9475]
1717 Grant St.
Blair, NE 68008
PH: (402)426-9610
Jensen, Timothy, President

Danish American Heritage Society
[9275]
1717 Grant St.
Blair, NE 68008
PH: (402)426-9610
Nielsen, John Mark, Secretary

Society of the Third Infantry Division,
United States Army [20726]
510 W York St.
Blue Hill, NE 68930
Ball, Joe, President

Boys Town [12791]
14100 Crawford St.
Boys Town, NE 68010-7520

PH: (402)498-1300
Toll free: 800-488-3000
Fax: (402)498-1348
Rasmussen, Judy, Exec. VP, CFO

Museum of the Fur Trade [9496]
6321 Highway 20
Chadron, NE 69337
PH: (308)432-3843
Fax: (308)432-5963
Leas, Alyson, Director

American Association of Philatelic
Exhibitors [21606]
c/o Mike Ley, Secretary
330 Sonja Dr.
Doniphan, NE 68832-9795
PH: (248)540-0948
Fax: (248)540-0905
Walker, Patricia, President

American Tarentaise Association
[3714]
9150 N 216th St.
Elkhorn, NE 68022
PH: (402)639-9808
Kullman, Maureen Mack, President

Indoor Football League [22858]
3123 W Stolley Park Rd.
Grand Island, NE 68801
PH: (804)643-7277
Fax: (804)643-7278
Loving, Robert, CFO

The Mastocytosis Society [14593]
PO Box 129
Hastings, NE 68902-0129
PH: (508)842-3080
Fax: (508)842-2051
Slee, Valerie, RN, Chairperson

Alpaca Owners Association, Inc.
[3585]
8300 Cody Dr., Ste. A
Lincoln, NE 68512
PH: (402)437-8484
Fax: (402)437-8488

Alumni Association of the University
of Nebraska [19303]
1520 R St.
Lincoln, NE 68508
PH: (402)472-2841
Toll free: 888-353-1874
Zaborowski, Shelley, Exec. Dir.

American Distance Education
Consortium [7740]
PO Box 830952
Lincoln, NE 68583-0952
PH: (402)472-7000
Fax: (402)472-9060
Tebbett, Ian, President

American Historical Society of
Germans From Russia [19443]
631 D St.
Lincoln, NE 68502-1199
PH: (402)474-3363
Fax: (402)474-7229
Wilson, Diane, Librarian

American Quilt Study Group [21748]
1610 L St.
Lincoln, NE 68508-2509
PH: (402)477-1181
Fax: (402)477-1181
Brott Buss, Judy J., PhD, Exec. Dir.

Antique Fan Collectors Association
[21621]
c/o Dick Boswell, Treasurer
2245 Harrison Ave.
Lincoln, NE 68502
Hill, Rick, President

The Association of American
Cultures [8964]
1635 S 15th St.
Lincoln, NE 68502

PH: (402)472-0208
Kewl-Durfey, Grace, Chairperson

Christian Record Services for the
Blind [13275]
4444 S 52nd St.
Lincoln, NE 68516-1302
PH: (402)488-0981
Fax: (402)488-7582
Pitcher, Larry, Secretary, President

College of Psychiatric and
Neurologic Pharmacists [16658]
8055 O St., Ste. S113
Lincoln, NE 68510
PH: (402)476-1677
Fax: (888)551-7617
Burghart, Steven, PhD, President

Contact Lens Manufacturers As-
sociation, Inc. [1598]
PO Box 29398
Lincoln, NE 68529-0398
PH: (402)465-4122
Toll free: 800-344-9060
Fax: (402)465-4187
Svochak, Jan, President

Golf Course Builders Association of
America [3156]
6040 S 58th St., Ste. D
Lincoln, NE 68516
PH: (402)476-4444
Fax: (402)476-4489
Apel, Justin, Exec. Dir.

The Groundwater Foundation [4758]
3201 Pioneers Blvd., Ste. 105
Lincoln, NE 68502-5963
PH: (402)434-2740
Toll free: 800-858-4844
Fax: (402)434-2742
Griffin, Jane, President

International Association for Feminist
Economics [6391]
371 CBA
Dept. of Economics
College of Business Administration
University of Nebraska-Lincoln
Lincoln, NE 68588-0479
PH: (402)472-3372
Fax: (866)257-8304
Conrad, Cecilia, VP, Chmn. of the
Bd.

International Association for the
Plant Protection Sciences [3567]
6517 S 19th St.
Lincoln, NE 68512
PH: (402)805-4748
Fax: (402)472-4687
Heinrichs, Dr. E. A., Sec. Gen.

National Collegiate Honors Council
[7791]
University of Nebraska-Lincoln
1100 Neihardt Residence Ctr.
540 N 16th St.
Lincoln, NE 68588-0627
PH: (402)472-9150
Fax: (402)472-9152
Savage, Hallie, Exec. Dir.

National Conference on Weights and
Measures [5771]
1135 M St., Ste. 110
Lincoln, NE 68508
PH: (402)434-4880
Fax: (402)434-4878
Benjamin, Stephen, Comm. Chm.

National Hair Society [1586]
1672 Van Dorn St.
Lincoln, NE 68502
PH: (402)302-0822
Garner, Christina, President

Organic Crop Improvement Association [4167]
1340 N Cotner Blvd.
Lincoln, NE 68505-1838

PH: (402)477-2323
Fax: (402)477-4325
Laberge, Guy, Chairman

Organization for Competitive
Markets [3530]
PO Box 6486
Lincoln, NE 68506
PH: (402)817-4443
Heffernan, Judy, Secretary

Society for Applied Research in
Memory and Cognition [7069]
University of Alaska
223 Burnett Hall
Lincoln, NE 68588-0308
Mori, Kaz, Exec. Dir.

Tiny Hands International [11166]
PO Box 67195
Lincoln, NE 68506
PH: (402)601-4816
Orduna, KC, Admin. Asst.

United States Consortium of Soil
Science Associations [4690]
c/o Mr. Jim Culver, Coordinator
611 Jeffrey Dr.
Lincoln, NE 68505
PH: (402)483-0604
Culver, Mr. Jim, Coord.

U.S.A. Roller Sports [23159]
4730 South St.
Lincoln, NE 68506
PH: (402)483-7551
Fax: (402)483-1465
Hawkins, Richard J., Exec. Dir.

Women on Wheels Motorcycle As-
sociation [23043]
PO Box 83076
Lincoln, NE 68501-3076
PH: (402)477-1280
Baldwin, Cris, President

World Association for Public Opinion
Research [18925]
201 N 13th St.
Lincoln, NE 68588-0242
PH: (402)472-7720
Fax: (402)472-7727
Moy, Patricia, President

Center for Rural Affairs [17787]
145 Main St.
Lyons, NE 68038
PH: (402)687-2100
Depew, Brian, Exec. Dir.

National Association of Hepatitis
Task Forces [15257]
Miller Depot
Miller, NE 68858
PH: (308)457-2641
Fax: (308)457-2641
Remak, Bill, BSc, Chairman

Arbor Day Foundation [19148]
100 Arbor Ave.
Nebraska City, NE 68410
PH: (402)474-5655
Toll free: 888-448-7337
Fax: (402)474-0820
Empson, Ray, Chmn. of the Bd.

American Penstemon Society
[22080]
c/o Dale Lindgren, Membership
Secretary
9202 Maloney Dr.
North Platte, NE 69101
Tatroe, Randy, President

Homer Laughlin China Collectors
Association [21661]
PO Box 721
North Platte, NE 69103-0721
Fax: (308)534-7015
Bond, Sandra, President

American Academy of Maxillofacial
Prosthetics [14381]
c/o Dr. Jeffery C. Markt, Vice
President
Dept. of Otolaryngology - Head &
Neck Surgery
University of Nebraska Medical Ctr.
981225 Nebraska Medical Ctr.
Omaha, NE 68198-1225
Grant, Dr. Gerald T., President

American Impressionist Society
[8909]
PO Box 27818
Omaha, NE 68127
PH: (402)592-3399
Dickinson, Charlotte, Founder

American Laryngological, Rhinologi-
cal and Otological Society [16535]
13930 Gold Cir., Ste. 103
Omaha, NE 68144
PH: (402)346-5500
Fax: (402)346-5300
Brackmann, Derald E., MD,
President

Association of Leadership Educators, Inc. [8192]
c/o Jennifer Moss Breen, President
2500 California Plz.
Omaha, NE 68178
PH: (402)280-3952
Breen, Jennifer Moss, President

Christ for the City International
[20361]
5332 S 138th St., Ste. 200
Omaha, NE 68137-2946
PH: (402)592-8332
Toll free: 888-526-7551
Fax: (402)592-8312
Anderson, Duane, President

Christian Family Movement [11815]
PO Box 540550
Omaha, NE 68154
Toll free: 800-581-9824
Fax: (888)354-1094
Poprac, John, President

CityMatch [14185]
982170 Nebraska Medical Ctr.
University of Nebraska Medical
Center
Omaha, NE 68198-2170
PH: (402)552-9500
Fax: (402)552-9593
Peck, Magda G., ScD, Advisor,
Founder

Drug Watch International [18137]
PO Box 45218
Omaha, NE 68145-0218
PH: (402)384-9212
Coleman, John J., PhD, President

Guild of Carillonneurs in North
America [9913]
2255 S 133rd Ave.
Omaha, NE 68144-2506
vanden Wyngaard, Julianne, VP

Health and Science Communications
Association [14295]
PO Box 31323
Omaha, NE 68132
PH: (402)915-5373
Huff, Jim, President

International Association of Reserva-
tion Executives [3291]
c/o Denise Pullen
9805 Q St.
Omaha, NE 68127
PH: (402)915-1905
Trog, Ronda, Dir. of Member Svcs.

International Society for Sports
Psychiatry [16831]
c/o Todd Stull, MD, Treasurer
Inside Performance Mindroom

16262 L St.
Omaha, NE 68135
PH: (402)917-7132
Fax: (402)595-1874
Stull, Todd, MD, Treasurer

Kids Against Hunger [12099]
13702 B St.
Omaha, NE 68144
PH: (952)542-5600
Toll free: 866-654-0202
Proudfit, Richard, CEO, Founder

Military Impacted Schools Associa-
tion [8345]
6327 S 196th St.
Omaha, NE 68135
PH: (402)305-6468
Toll free: 800-291-6472
Proctor, Ray, Reg. Dir.

National Association of Economic
Educators [7732]
c/o Dr. Kim Sosin, Executive
Secretary
PO Box 27925
Omaha, NE 68127
Ferrarini, Tawni, President

Project Harmony [8089]
11949 Q St.
Omaha, NE 68137
PH: (402)595-1326
Jensen, Patty, Chairman

Society on Neuroimmune
Pharmacology [16055]
University of Nebraska Medical
Center
Department of Pharmacology and
Experimental Neuroscience
985880 Nebraska Medical Ctr., DRC
8011
Omaha, NE 68198-5880
PH: (402)559-3165
Fax: (402)559-3744
Buch, Shilpa, PhD, Secretary

VOSH International [12303]
12660 Q St.
Omaha, NE 68137
Weiss, Ellen, President

Wellness Council of America [15163]
17002 Marcy St., Ste. 140
Omaha, NE 68118-2933
PH: (402)827-3590
Fax: (402)827-3594
LaCagnin, Stephen Michael, Chair-
man

Woodmen of the World/Omaha
Woodmen Life Insurance Society
[19694]
1700 Farnam St.
Omaha, NE 68102-2025
Toll free: 800-225-3108
King, Larry R., President, CEO

Job's Daughters International
[19562]
233 W 6th St.
Papillion, NE 68046-2210
PH: (402)592-7987
Fax: (402)592-2177
Goolsby, Susan M., Mgr.

The Willa Cather Foundation [9047]
413 N Webster St.
Red Cloud, NE 68970-2466
PH: (402)746-2653
Toll free: 866-731-7304
Fax: (402)746-2652
Krieger, Lynette, President

Missionary Society of St. Columban
[19865]
PO Box 10
Saint Columbans, NE 68056

PH: (402)291-1920
Toll free: 877-299-1920
Fax: (402)291-4984
Mulroy, Fr. Timothy, Reg. Dir.

Celiac Support Association United
 States of America [14785]
413 Ash St.
Seward, NE 68434
PH: (402)643-4101
Toll free: 877-272-4272
Fax: (402)643-4108
Schluckebier, Mary A., Exec. Dir.

North American Grouse Partnership
 [4858]
10630 North 135th St.
Waverly, NE 68462-1256
Fax: (402)786-5547
Belinda, Steve, Exec. Dir.

NEVADA

National Association of Home and
 Workshop Writers [2695]
PO Box 12
Baker, NV 89311
Toll free: 866-457-2582
Burch, Monte, President

Internet Infidels [10098]
711 S Carson St., Ste. 4
Carson City, NV 89701
Toll free: 877-501-5113
Augustine, Keith, Exec. Dir., Editor

United States Mondioring Associa-
 tion [22822]
PO Box 4432
Carson City, NV 89702
PH: (775)848-0041
Lee, Don, President

American Welara Pony Society
 [4333]
471 4th St., Nevelco Unit 1
Crescent Valley, NV 89821

Miracle Flights for Kids [14666]
2764 N Green Valley Pky., No. 115
Green Valley, NV 89014-2120
PH: (702)261-0494
Toll free: 800-359-1711
Fax: (702)261-0497
McGee, Ann, Founder, President

Society for Animal Homeopathy
 [15292]
272 Lucille Dr.
Hawthorne, NV 89415
PH: (775)945-2395
 (775)313-5884
McKay, Pat, Founder, Secretary,
 Treasurer

American Board of Hypnotherapy
 [15355]
PO Box 531605
Henderson, NV 89053
PH: (702)456-3267
Toll free: 888-823-4823
Fax: (702)436-3267

American Society for Management
 [2147]
2505 Anthem Village Dr., Ste. E-222
Henderson, NV 89052
PH: (702)293-7389
 (818)974-4004
Fax: (702)293-5260
Tapanian, Aza, Principal

Association of Gaming Equipment
 Manufacturers [22060]
c/o Marcus Prater, Executive Director
PO Box 50049

Henderson, NV 89016-0049
PH: (702)812-6932
Prater, Marcus, Exec. Dir.

Independent Photo Imagers [2580]
2518 Anthem Village Dr., Ste. 104
Henderson, NV 89052-5554
PH: (702)617-1141
Fax: (702)617-1181
DiVincenzo, Brenda, Director

International Female Boxers As-
 sociation [22714]
PO Box 91957
Henderson, NV 89009
PH: (702)900-7464
Fax: (310)541-9708

International Virtual Assistants As-
 sociation [74]
2360 Corporate Cir., Ste. 400
Henderson, NV 89074-7739
PH: (702)583-4970
Toll free: 877-440-2750
Weld, Yvonne, President

Julian Jaynes Society [16922]
PO Box 778153
Henderson, NV 89077-8153
Kuijsten, Marcel, Exec. Dir.

Macular Degeneration Foundation
 [17726]
PO Box 531313
Henderson, NV 89053
PH: (702)450-2908
Toll free: 888-633-3937
Fax: (702)450-3396
Trauernicht, Ms. Liz, President, Dir.
 of Comm.

National Conference of Personal
 Managers, Inc. [163]
PO Box 50008
Henderson, NV 89016-0008
Toll free: 866-916-2676
Billups, Mr. Clinton Ford, Jr.,
 President

Saigon Mission Association [19224]
1762 Clear River Falls Ln.
Henderson, NV 89012
PH: (702)435-4055
 (731)967-1595
Mohler, Lee, President

Association for Support of Graduate
 Students [7956]
PO Box 4698
Incline Village, NV 89450-4698
PH: (775)831-1399
Fax: (775)831-1221
Dave, Ronda, Contact

International Production Planning
 and Scheduling Association [2222]
PO Box 5031
Incline Village, NV 89450-5031
PH: (775)833-3922

American Academy of Somnology
 [17209]
PO Box 27077
Las Vegas, NV 89126-1077
PH: (702)371-0947
Hopper, Dr. David, Director

American Association of Clinical
 Coders and Auditors [15108]
1350 E Flamingo Rd., No. 517
Las Vegas, NV 89119
PH: (909)579-0507
Toll free: 877-810-9464
Fax: (909)680-3157

American Credit Union Mortgage
 Association [945]
PO Box 400955
Las Vegas, NV 89140-0955
Toll free: 877-442-2862
Fax: (702)823-3950
Dorsa, Robert, President

American Gem Society [2039]
8881 W Sahara Ave.
Las Vegas, NV 89117
Batson, Ruth, RJ, CEO

American Naturopathic Medical As-
 sociation [15856]
P O Box 96273
Las Vegas, NV 89193
PH: (702)450-3477
Morgan, Julie, Contact

American Sanctuary Association
 [10570]
9632 Christine View Ct.
Las Vegas, NV 89129
PH: (702)804-8562
Fax: (702)804-8561
Hedren, Tippi, President

AmeriFace [14329]
PO Box 751112
Las Vegas, NV 89136
PH: (702)769-9264
Toll free: 888-486-1209
Fax: (702)341-5351
Oliver, Debbie, Exec. Dir.

Arabian Horse Breeders Alliance
 [4337]
9777 S Las Vegas Blvd.
Las Vegas, NV 89101
Bailey, Scott, Director

Asian American/Pacific Islander
 Nurses Association, Inc. [16116]
c/o Jennifer Kawi, PhD, MSN,
 Treasurer
School of Nursing
University of Nevada, Las Vegas
4505 Maryland Pky.
Las Vegas, NV 89154-9900
Alpert, Patricia T., President

Association for the Study of Higher
 Education [7955]
4505 S Maryland Pky.
Las Vegas, NV 89154-9900
PH: (702)895-2737
Fax: (702)895-4269
Nehls, Kim, PhD, Exec. Dir.

Association of Women Martial Arts
 Instructors [22987]
PO Box 28166
Las Vegas, NV 89126
Grate, Shifu/Sensei Koré, Exec. Dir.

Atomic Age Alliance [9378]
2620 S Maryland Pky., No. 345
Las Vegas, NV 89109

Cottage Industry Miniaturists Trade
 Association, Inc. [21643]
848 N Rainbow Blvd., No. 3459
Las Vegas, NV 89107
PH: (702)997-2077
McClain, Marcia, VP

Do Right Foundation [20537]
2540 S Maryland Pky., No. 178
Las Vegas, NV 89109

Earth Ecology Foundation [3996]
4175 S Decatur 205
Las Vegas, NV 89103
PH: (702)778-9930
Wunstell, Erik, Director, Founder

Ex-Masons for Jesus [19975]
PO Box 28702
Las Vegas, NV 89126
Washum, Duane, Director

Exotic Dancers League of America
 [9255]
Burlesque Hall of Fame
520 Fremont St., No. 120

Las Vegas, NV 89101
Toll free: 888-661-6465
Roth, Debra, Chmn. of the Bd.

Fine Chocolate Industry Association
 [1324]
2265 Georgia Pine Ct.
Las Vegas, NV 89134
PH: (206)577-9983
Williams, Pam, President

Government Investment Officers As-
 sociation [5373]
10655 Park Run Dr., Ste. 120
Las Vegas, NV 89144
PH: (702)489-8993
Fax: (702)575-6670
Day, Maurine, Exec. Dir.

Health For All Missions [12281]
9101 W Sahara Ave., Ste. 105-F11
Las Vegas, NV 89117
PH: (702)795-6776
Fax: (702)838-8436
Joseph, Angelina M., MA, Founder

Institute of Inspection, Cleaning and
 Restoration Certification [1945]
4043 S Eastern Ave.
Las Vegas, NV 89119
PH: (775)553-5458
Fax: (775)553-5458
Duncanson, Pete, Chairman, Act.
 Pres.

International Association of Certified
 Surveillance Professionals [3057]
8438 Langhorne Creek St.
Las Vegas, NV 89139
PH: (270)724-4368
Boss, Derk, CSP, President

International Association of Coroners
 and Medical Examiners [15629]
c/o Nicole Coleman, Executive
 Administrator
1704 Pinto Ln.
Las Vegas, NV 89106
PH: (702)455-1937
Fax: (702)380-9669
Fudenberg, Mr. John, Chairman

International Association for Physicians in Aesthetic Medicine
 [14315]
848 N Rainbow Blvd., No. 713
Las Vegas, NV 89107
Toll free: 800-485-5759
Russell, Jeff, Exec. Dir.

International Cellular Medicine
 Society [14879]
PO Box 371034
Las Vegas, NV 89137
PH: (702)664-0017
Toll free: 866-878-7717
Vitelli, Francesca, Secretary

International Hospitality Information
 Technology Association [7279]
c/o Mehmet Erdem, PhD, President
Box 456021
Harrah College of Hotel Administra-
 tion
University of Nevada
4505 Maryland Pky.
Las Vegas, NV 89154-6021
PH: (702)895-5811
Fax: (702)895-4872
Erdem, Mehmet, PhD, President

International Masters of Gaming Law
 [5259]
PO Box 27106
Las Vegas, NV 89126
PH: (702)375-5812
Ellinger, Marc H., Treasurer

International Ozone Association
 [6661]
c/o Southern Nevada Water Authority

PO Box 97075
Las Vegas, NV 89193-7075
PH: (480)529-3787
Fax: (480)533-3080

International Society of Women
Airline Pilots **[144]**
723 S Casino Center Blvd., 2nd Fl.
Las Vegas, NV 89101-6716
Novaes, Nancy, Contact

International Soundex Reunion
Registry, Inc. **[10454]**
PO Box 371179
Las Vegas, NV 89137
Toll free: 888-886-4777
Rillera, Marri J., Registrar

International Star Riders Association
[22227]
848 N Rainbow Blvd., No. 793
Las Vegas, NV 89107
Herbert, Barry, President

Media Guilds International **[2316]**
9651 Trailwood Dr.
Las Vegas, NV 89164
PH: (702)255-1179
Lougaris, Betty I., Exec. Dir.,
Treasurer

Medical Association of Billers
[15635]
2620 Regatta Dr., Ste. 102
Las Vegas, NV 89128
PH: (702)240-8519
Fax: (702)243-0359
Watson, Sharon D., Contact

National Association of Supervisor of
Business Education **[7559]**
c/o Melissa Scott, Treasurer
9890 S Maryland Pky., Ste. 221
Las Vegas, NV 89183
PH: (702)486-6625
Morrison, Dawn, President

National Association of Supervisors
of Business Education **[7560]**
c/o Melissa Scott, Treasurer
Nevada Department of Education
9890 S Maryland Pky., Ste. 221
Las Vegas, NV 89183
PH: (702)486-6625
Morrison, Dawn, President

National Construction Investigators
Association Inc. **[5367]**
4328 Murillo St.
Las Vegas, NV 89121
Nuby, Glenn, President

National Latino Cosmetology As-
sociation **[927]**
7925 W Russell Rd., Unit 401285
Las Vegas, NV 89140
PH: (702)448-5020
Toll free: 877-658-3801
Fax: (702)448-8993
Zepeda, Julie, President, CEO

National Procurement Institute
[2819]
PO Box 370192
Las Vegas, NV 89137
PH: (702)989-8095
Toll free: 866-877-7641
Fax: (702)967-0744
Rowley, Craig, Exec. Dir.

North American Boxing Federation
[22715]
c/o Duane B. Ford, President
5255 S Decatur Blvd., Ste. 110
Las Vegas, NV 89118
PH: (702)382-8360
Ford, Duane B., President

Peanut Pals **[21710]**
c/o Ruth Augustine, Treasurer
6052 Canter Glen Ave.

Las Vegas, NV 89122
PH: (301)604-5858
Augustine, Ruth, Treasurer

Donald W. Reynolds Foundation
[14140]
1701 Village Center Cir.
Las Vegas, NV 89134
PH: (702)804-6000
Fax: (702)804-6099
Anderson, Steven L., President

Robinson Jeffers Association
[10395]
c/o Charles Rodewald, Treasurer
5140 Cutty Way
Las Vegas, NV 89130
Gano, Geneva, President

Sex Workers Anonymous **[12879]**
3395 S Jones Blvd., No. 217
Las Vegas, NV 89146-4660
PH: (702)649-5587

Society of American Fight Directors
[8701]
1350 E Flamingo Rd., No. 25
Las Vegas, NV 89119
Brimmer, J. David, President

Society of Building Science Educa-
tors **[7856]**
c/o Alfredo Fernandez-Gonzalez,
President
Paul B. Sogg Architecture Bldg.
4505 Maryland Pky.
Las Vegas, NV 89154-4018
Fernandez-Gonzalez, Alfredo,
President

Society for Scientific Exploration
[7017]
c/o Stephen E. Braude, Ph.D.
University of Maryland - Baltimore
County
8022 S Rainbow Blvd., Ste. 236
Las Vegas, NV 89139
Bengston, Prof. William, President

United States Lipizzan Federation
[4420]
8414 W Farm Rd., Ste. 180
Las Vegas, NV 89143-1235
PH: (503)589-3172
Isgreen, Cheri

Vietnam Dog Handler Association
[21160]
c/o Robert Palochik, Treasurer
8203 Parting Clouds Ct.
Las Vegas, NV 89117-7614
PH: (702)255-6265
Palochik, Robert, Treasurer

Western Veterinary Conference
[17675]
2425 E Oquendo Rd.
Las Vegas, NV 89120
PH: (702)739-6698
Toll free: 866-800-7326
Fax: (702)739-6420
Howell, Joe M., DVM, President

World Relief Organization for
Children **[11191]**
3157 N Rainbow Blvd., No. 234
Las Vegas, NV 89108-4578
PH: (916)242-8970

Pierre Fauchard Academy **[14432]**
PO Box 3718
Mesquite, NV 89024-3718
PH: (702)345-2950
Toll free: 800-232-0099
Fax: (702)345-5031
Castagna, Dr. Daniel M., Officer

Lifeboat Foundation **[19184]**
1638 Esmeralda Ave.
Minden, NV 89423

PH: (775)853-5212
Fax: (775)853-5214
Klien, Eric, Chairman, President,
Founder

Native American Water Association
[3461]
1662 Highway 395, Ste. 212
Minden, NV 89423
PH: (775)782-6636
Toll free: 866-632-9992
Fax: (775)782-1021
Crawford, Tom, President

Indigenous Peoples Council on Bio-
colonialism **[12129]**
PO Box 72
Nixon, NV 89424
PH: (775)574-0248
Fax: (775)574-0345
Harry, Debra, Exec. Dir.

Another Joy Foundation **[13002]**
2629 E Craig Rd., Ste. F
North Las Vegas, NV 89030
PH: (702)808-3967
Crowley, Nadia, President, Founder

National Association of Reunion
Managers **[2743]**
PO Box 335428
North Las Vegas, NV 89033-5428
Toll free: 800-654-2776
McEvoy, Carol, VP

American Mammoth Jackstock
Registry **[3594]**
PO Box 9062
Pahrump, NV 89060
PH: (830)330-0499
Coffman, Linda, Owner

Beach Boys Fan Club **[24026]**
50 S Emery St., No. 4E
Pahrump, NV 89048
Wilson, Brian, Bd. Member

Bounders United **[22463]**
c/o Pat Hoffman,Treasurer
1970 N Leslie St.
Pahrump, NV 89060-3678
Nicholson, Harold, President

American Mule Association **[3596]**
260 Neilson Rd.
Reno, NV 89521
PH: (775)849-9437
    (916)390-1861
Fairbanks, Casie, President

American Radio Association **[23395]**
1755 E Plumb Ln., Ste. 111
Reno, NV 89502-3545
PH: (510)281-0706
Young, Carl, Secretary, Treasurer,
Coord.

Association of International Product
Marketing and Management **[2266]**
9120 Double Diamond Pky., Ste.
1996
Reno, NV 89521
PH: (202)449-8658
Toll free: 877-275-5500
Fax: (866)731-8421

Association of State and Territorial
Dental Directors **[14421]**
3858 Cashill Blvd.
Reno, NV 89509
PH: (775)626-5008
Fax: (775)626-9268
Yineman, Kimberlie, President

Association TransCommunication
[7008]
PO Box 13111
Reno, NV 89507
Estep, Sarah, Founder

Davidson Institute for Talent
Development **[11914]**
9665 Gateway Dr., Ste. B
Reno, NV 89521
PH: (775)852-3483
Davidson, Bob, Founder

International Development Missions
[12166]
PO Box 5600
Reno, NV 89513-5600
Mutua, Muthoka, Chairman,
President

Les Amis de Panhard and Deutsch-
Bonnet USA **[21418]**
c/o John A. Peterson, Editor
7992 Oak Creek Dr.
Reno, NV 89511-1065
PH: (775)853-8452
Peterson, John A., Editor

Martial Arts International Federation
[23002]
3816 Bellingham Dr.
Reno, NV 89511
PH: (775)851-8875
Bethers, Bruce R., President

National Association of State Judicial
Educators **[8219]**
c/o Kelly Tait, Committee Chairman
KT Consulting
362 Hillcrest Dr.
Reno, NV 89509
Tait, Kelly, Comm. Chm.

National Council of Juvenile and
Family Court Judges **[5396]**
PO Box 8970
Reno, NV 89507
PH: (775)507-4777
Fax: (775)507-4855
Dailey, Cheryl, CFO

National Judicial College **[5398]**
Judicial College Bldg., MS 358
Reno, NV 89557
PH: (775)784-6747
Toll free: 800-255-8343
Fax: (775)784-1253
Sweeney, Matt, Chairman

National Wilderness Stewardship
Alliance **[3907]**
PO Box 5293
Reno, NV 89513
Hodge, Bill, Chairperson

Saluki Club of America **[21955]**
c/o Sharon Walls
100 Wrangler Rd.
Reno, NV 89510-9303
Roush, Gary, President

Statue of Liberty Club **[21723]**
c/o Lebo Newman, Treasurer
3705 Barron Way
Reno, NV 89511
Swift, Mr. Vince, President

American Miniature Cheviot Sheep
Breeders Association **[4656]**
403 Cheryl Way
Silver Springs, NV 89429
PH: (775)629-1211

Sporting Goods Shippers Associa-
tion **[3104]**
3250 Spanish Springs Ct.
Sparks, NV 89434
PH: (775)356-9931
Fax: (775)356-9932
Munson, Angela, Managing Dir.

NEW HAMPSHIRE

70th Infantry Division Association
[21177]
c/o Diane Kessler, Secretary
73 Providence Hill Rd.

Atkinson, NH 03811
Dixon, Steve, Web Adm.

Society of Parrot Breeders and
Exhibitors **[21550]**
c/o Ray Schwartz, Membership
Director
19 Olde Common Dr.
Atkinson, NH 03811-2177
Tucker, Pat, Chairman

Student Conservation Association
[3950]
689 River Rd.
Charlestown, NH 03603-4171
PH: (603)543-1700
Toll free: 888-722-9675

American College of Laboratory
Animal Medicine **[17613]**
96 Chester St.
Chester, NH 03036
PH: (603)887-2467
Fax: (603)887-0096
Balk, Dr. Melvin W., Exec. Dir.

GeoVisions **[8074]**
PO Box 167
Chesterfield, NH 03443
PH: (603)363-4187
Toll free: 888-830-9455
LeGrant, Randy, Exec. Dir.

Academy of Applied Science **[7113]**
24 Warren St.
Concord, NH 03301
PH: (603)228-4530
Fax: (603)228-4730
Cousens, Doris, Officer

American Ground Water Trust
[3456]
50 Pleasant St., Ste. 2
Concord, NH 03301
PH: (603)228-5444
Toll free: 800-423-7748
Fax: (603)228-6557
McGinnis, Kevin, Chairman

Association of Forensic Quality Assurance Managers **[5243]**
c/o Lise A. Swacha, Secretary
NH State Police Forensic Laboratory
33 Hazen Dr.
Concord, NH 03305
Bond, Jason, President

Examination Board of Professional
Home Inspectors **[1815]**
53 Regional Dr., Ste. 1
Concord, NH 03301-8500
PH: (847)298-7750
Harper, George, Director

Marlin Auto Club **[21423]**
5 Howards Grove
Derry, NH 03038
Zeno, Mark, Act. Pres.

New England Trail Rider Association
[23328]
PO Box 1235
Derry, NH 03038
PH: (508)306-1410
Burton, Chris, President

New England Trails Conference
[23329]
c/o Bob Spoerl
242 Island Pond Rd.
Derry, NH 03038
PH: (603)473-0541
Spoerl, Bob, Contact

Egg Clearinghouse, Inc. **[4566]**
PO Box 817
Dover, NH 03821
Toll free: 800-736-7286
Niewedde, Bob, Chairman

American Brahms Society **[9176]**
Music Dept.
University of New Hampshire
30 Academic Way
Durham, NH 03824
PH: (206)543-0400
Fax: (206)284-0111
Bozarth, George S., Bd. Member

Association for Communication
Excellence in Agriculture, Natural
Resources, and Life and Human
Sciences **[3546]**
Taylor Hall
59 College Rd.
Durham, NH 03824
PH: (603)862-1564
Toll free: 855-657-9544
Fax: (603)862-1585
Young, Holly, Exec. Dir.

Climate Counts **[3830]**
131 Main St., No. 107
Durham, NH 03824
PH: (603)862-0121
Martin, Michael, V. Chmn. of the Bd.

Interhostel **[8077]**
UNH CIS Training Ctr.
1 Leavitt Ln.
Durham, NH 03824
PH: (603)862-4242

Education-A-Must, Inc. **[11594]**
PO Box 216
East Derry, NH 03041
PH: (603)437-6286
Fax: (603)434-0371
French, Dorothy, Exec. Dir., Founder

National Organization for Albinism
and Hypopigmentation **[15832]**
PO Box 959
East Hampstead, NH 03826-0959
PH: (603)887-2310
Toll free: 800-648-2310
Fax: (800)648-2310
McGowan, Michael, Exec. Dir.

Fan Association of North America
[21653]
2 Sterling Hill Ln., No. 228
Exeter, NH 03833
Lukas, Katherine, President

National Association of Professional
Accident Reconstruction Special-
ists **[5749]**
PO Box 866
Farmington, NH 03835
PH: (603)332-3267
Veppert, Chuck, President

International Association of Law
Enforcement Firearms Instructors
[5470]
25 Country Club Rd., Ste. 707
Gilford, NH 03249
PH: (603)524-8787
Fax: (603)524-8856
Johnson, R. Steven, President

Pius X Secular Institute **[19896]**
c/o Fr. Marcel Caron
27 Cove St.
Goffstown, NH 03045
PH: (418)626-5882
Caron, Fr. Marcel, Dir. Gen.

Cleveland Bay Horse Society of
North America **[4343]**
PO Box 483
Goshen, NH 03752
PH: (703)401-4054
    (817)431-8775
Gordon, Gabrielle, VP

Kupenda for the Children **[11065]**
PO Box 473
Hampton, NH 03843

PH: (978)626-1625
Bauer, Cynthia, Exec. Dir., Founder

Quimper Club International **[21304]**
c/o Sherry Lohnes, Secretary
561 Ocean Blvd., Unit 10
Hampton, NH 03842

Association of Nepal and Himalayan
Studies **[9588]**
Dept. of Anthropology
Dartmouth College
6047 Silsby Hall
Hanover, NH 03755
PH: (603)646-9356
Fax: (603)646-1140
Hindman, Heather, President, Web
Adm.

International Society of Aesthetic
Plastic Surgery **[14316]**
45 Lyme Rd., Ste. 304
Hanover, NH 03755
PH: (603)643-2325
Fax: (603)643-1444
Takayanagi, Susumu, MD, President

International Society for Terrain-
Vehicle Systems **[6727]**
72 Lyme Rd.
Hanover, NH 03755
PH: (603)646-4405
Fax: (603)646-4280
Shoop, Dr. Sally, Deputy

Medical Outcomes Trust **[15033]**
c/o Dr. Michael Zubkoff, President
Dept. of Community and Family
Medicine
Darmouth Medical School, HB 7250
Hanover, NH 03755
Zubkoff, Dr. Michael, President

Society for the Study of Early China
[9156]
Dartmouth College
HB 6191
Hanover, NH 03755
Toll free: 800-872-7423
Allan, Sarah, Chairperson, Editor

Visual Resources Association **[269]**
c/o Jen Green, President
6025 Baker, Office 180
Dartmounth Library
Darmounth College
Hanover, NH 03755
PH: (603)646-2132
Green, Jen, President

World Phenomenology Institute
[10134]
1 Ivy Pointe Way
Hanover, NH 03755
PH: (802)295-3487
Fax: (802)295-5963
Smith, William S., Exec. Ofc.

Homeopaths Without Borders
[15289]
20 Brookside Ln.
Hebron, NH 03241
Stemm, Laurie Defrain, VP

Global Routes **[9209]**
1 World Way
Hillsborough, NH 03244
PH: (413)585-8895
Fax: (413)585-8810
Hahn, Kenneth, Founder

National Society for the Preservation
of Covered Bridges **[9421]**
c/o Jennifer Caswell, Membership
Chair
535 2nd NH Tpke.
Hillsborough, NH 03244-4601
Smedley, Gloria, Treasurer,
Secretary

Centennial Legion of Historic Military
Commands **[21079]**
46 Highland Ave.
Jaffrey, NH 03452
Moore, Neal, Cmdr.

Association for the Study of
Literature and Environment **[9752]**
PO Box 502
Keene, NH 03431-0502
PH: (603)357-7411
Fax: (603)357-7411
McIntyre, Amy, Mgr. Dir.

Cross Country Ski Areas Association
[3153]
88 S Lincoln St., No. 1
Keene, NH 03431
PH: (603)239-4341
Frado, Chris, Exec. Dir., President

Elm Research Institute **[4199]**
c/o Liberty Tree Society
11 Kit St.
Keene, NH 03431
PH: (603)358-6198
Fax: (603)358-6305
Hansel, John P., Officer

National Association of Certified
Professional Midwives **[16295]**
PO Box 340
Keene, NH 03431
PH: (603)358-3322
Lawlor, Mary, CPM, Exec. Dir.

United States Canoe Association
[23364]
581 W St.
581 West St.
Keene, NH 03431
PH: (603)209-2299
Heed, Peter, President

Lakes Region Sled Dog Club
[22827]
PO Box 341
Laconia, NH 03247
PH: (603)524-4314
Lyman, James, President

Post-Landfill Action Network **[4745]**
1 Depot Ln.
Lee, NH 03861
PH: (603)608-9859
Freid, Alex, Founder, Director

Tree Care Industry Association
[4735]
136 Harvey Rd., Ste. 101
Londonderry, NH 03053
PH: (603)314-5380
Toll free: 800-733-2622
Fax: (603)314-5386
Garvin, Mark, President

Z Car Club Association **[21525]**
6 Jason Dr.
Londonderry, NH 03053
PH: (603)425-2270
Fax: (603)218-6149
Karl, Chris, Exec. Dir.

Preservation Trades Network **[573]**
75 Holt Rd.
Lyndeborough, NH 03082-5815
Toll free: 866-853-9336
Jackson, Sarah, Secretary

American-Canadian Genealogical
Society **[20951]**
PO Box 6478
Manchester, NH 03108-6478
PH: (603)622-1554
Cusson, Pauline, Editor

For Inspiration and Recognition of
Science and Technology **[7810]**
200 Bedford St.
Manchester, NH 03101

PH: (603)666-3906
Toll free: 800-871-8326
Fax: (603)666-3907
Havenstein, Walter P., Director

International Design Guild [1949]
670 N Commercial St.
Manchester, NH 03101
Toll free: 800-450-7595
Fax: (603)626-3444
Eliason, Krista, President

International Rebecca West Society [10380]
100 St. Anselm Dr.
Manchester, NH 03102-1308
PH: (718)488-1098
Schweizer, Bernard, Secretary, Treasurer

Kappa Delta Phi [23904]
373 S Willow St., Ste. 111
Manchester, NH 03103
Kadel, Jon, Exec. Dir.

National Association of Melkite Youth [19997]
c/o Fr. Thomas P. Steinmetz, Director
140 Mitchell St.
Manchester, NH 03103
PH: (603)623-8944
Steinmetz, Fr. Thomas P., Director

National Guild of Hypnotists [15366]
PO Box 308
Merrimack, NH 03054-0308
PH: (603)429-9438
Fax: (603)424-8066
Damon, Dr. Dwight F., President

International Association of Reiki Professionals [13632]
PO Box 6182
Nashua, NH 03063-6182
PH: (603)881-8838
Fax: (603)882-9088

ChildVoice International [10938]
202 Kent Pl.
Newmarket, NH 03857
PH: (603)842-0132
Bryon, Bill, Chmn. of the Bd.

Antiques Dealers Association of America [21624]
PO Box 218
Northwood, NH 03261
PH: (603)942-6498
Fax: (603)942-5035
Loto, Judith Livingston, Exec. Dir.

Hawk Migration Association of North America [6960]
PO Box 721
Plymouth, NH 03264
Randell, Gil, Secretary

Association of Medical Laboratory Immunologists [15375]
40 Prospect St.
Portsmouth, NH 03801
PH: (603)610-7766
Fax: (603)610-7288
Fogel, Maggie, Administrator

Global Grassroots [13415]
Box 1
1950 Lafayette Rd., Ste. 200
Portsmouth, NH 03801
PH: (603)643-0400
Fax: (603)619-0076
Sullivan, Michael, Treasurer

International Association of Privacy Professionals [1800]
75 Rochester Ave., Ste. 4
Portsmouth, NH 03801

PH: (603)427-9200
(209)351-1500
Toll free: 800-266-6501
Fax: (603)427-9249
Hughes, J. Trevor, CIPP, CEO, President

National Electrical Manufacturers Representatives Association [1030]
28 Deer St., Ste. 302
Portsmouth, NH 03801
PH: (914)524-8650
Toll free: 800-446-3672
Fax: (914)524-8655
Hooper, Kenneth W., President

Rain for the Sahel and Sahara [12180]
56 Middle St.
Portsmouth, NH 03801
PH: (603)371-0676
Fax: (603)397-0681
Palmisciano, Bess, Exec. Dir., Founder

The Society of Standards Professionals [7237]
1950 Lafayette Rd., Ste. 200
Portsmouth, NH 03801
PH: (603)926-0750
Fax: (603)610-7101
Mikoski, Edward F., Jr., VP

Gamma Sigma Sigma [23874]
PO Box 248
Rindge, NH 03461
PH: (603)674-4931
Fax: (603)899-3225
Connor, Keli, Chairman

Association for Conservation Information [3811]
c/o Judy Stokes Weber, Treasurer
854 Quincy Rd.
Rumney, NH 03266
Weber, Judy Stokes, Treasurer

The Fuller Foundation, Inc. [12973]
PO Box 479
Rye Beach, NH 03871
PH: (603)964-6998
Bottomley, John T., Exec. Dir.

Air Charter Association of North America [172]
2 Main St.
Salem, NH 03079
Toll free: 888-359-2226
Zaher, Richard, Chairman

Kelsey Kindred of America [20890]
c/o Jarman Kelsey, President
37 Ackerman St.
Salem, NH 03079
PH: (603)893-6814
Kelsey, Jarman J., President

Ecological Landscape Alliance [4445]
PO Box 3
Sandown, NH 03873
PH: (617)436-5838
Smith, Trevor, President

Ecological Landscaping Association [4446]
PO Box 3
Sandown, NH 03873
PH: (617)436-5838
Smith, Trevor, President

AdoptaPlatoon [10735]
PO Box 1457
Seabrook, NH 03874
PH: (956)748-4206
Hagg, Ida, Exec. Dir.

Fisher-Price Collector's Club [22447]
60 Spring St.
Spofford, NH 03462

Unfinished Furniture Association [1490]
PO Box 520
Spofford, NH 03462
Toll free: 800-487-8321
Moriarty, Fred, Exec. Dir.

Wooden Canoe Heritage Association [22693]
PO Box 117
Tamworth, NH 03886
PH: (603)323-8992
Kelly, Ken, President

Metanoia Ministries [20043]
PO Box 448
Washington, NH 03280
PH: (603)495-0035
Van Yperen, Jim, Founder, President

Personal Submersibles Organization [6905]
PO Box 53
Weare, NH 03281
PH: (603)232-9157
Wallace, Jon, Founder

Wenzi kwa Afya [15089]
24 Wildwood Dr.
West Lebanon, NH 03784
Greenstein, Susan, President

United States Classic Racing Association [22234]
441 Athol Rd.
Winchester, NH 03470
PH: (413)341-6780
Coy, Bob, Exec. Dir.

London Vintage Taxi Association - American Section [21421]
PO Box 445
Windham, NH 03087
PH: (603)893-8919
Freeston, John, V. Ch.

Felton Family Association [20865]
PO Box 215
Wolfeboro, NH 03894
Anderson, Cora Felton, Hist., Co-Pres.

NEW JERSEY

Touch the World [20163]
1 Maple St.
Allendale, NJ 07401
PH: (201)760-9925
Fax: (201)760-9926
Kroeze, Andrea, Contact

Clean Water Construction Coalition [4751]
PO Box 728
Allenwood, NJ 08720
PH: (732)292-4300
Fax: (732)292-4310

Species Alliance [4891]
PO Box 54
Annandale, NJ 08801
PH: (973)207-5457
Landig, Rhea, Exec. Dir.

World Apostolate of Fatima - USA [19923]
674 Mountain View Rd. E
Asbury, NJ 08802-1400
PH: (908)689-1700
(908)689-3590
Ellis, Deacon Robert F., Coord.

Middle East Peace Dialogue Network, Inc. [12437]
PO Box 943
Atco, NJ 08004
PH: (856)768-0938
Fax: (856)768-1444
Goodwin, Richard C., Chairman

Miss America Organization [21735]
PO Box 1919
Atlantic City, NJ 08404-1919
PH: (609)344-1800
Randle, Josh, COO

National Impala Association [21455]
PO Box 111
Atlantic Highlands, NJ 07716-0111
PH: (732)291-7668
Naasz, Byrdi, Mem.

American Bantam Association [4560]
PO Box 127
Augusta, NJ 07822
PH: (419)234-4427
(716)592-0766
Halbach, Jeff, Comm. Chm.

Fields of Growth International [11358]
PO Box 2
Avon by the Sea, NJ 07717-0002
Toll free: 888-318-8541
Dugan, Kevin, Director, Founder

International Society of Cosmetogynecology [14317]
350 Kennedy Blvd.
Bayonne, NJ 07002
PH: (201)436-8025
Fax: (201)339-5030
Pelosi, Dr. Marco A., II, Founder, President

Amazigh Cultural Association in America [8777]
75 Washington Rd., CN753 PMB163
Bedminster, NJ 07921
Benslimane, Mr. Aomar, PhD, President

Breast Health and Healing Foundation [13850]
36 Newark Ave., Ste. 130
Belleville, NJ 07109
PH: (973)450-9955
Fax: (973)450-2552
Ruddy, Kathleen T., Founder

Council for Healing [13618]
c/o Daniel J. Benor, MD, Founder
PO Box 76
Bellmawr, NJ 08099
PH: (609)714-1885
Benor, Daniel J., M.D., Founder

Friends of Israel Gospel Ministry [20143]
PO Box 908
Bellmawr, NJ 08099
PH: (856)853-5590
Toll free: 800-257-7843
Fax: (856)384-8522
Showers, Jim, Exec. Dir.

Marketing Agencies Association Worldwide [2289]
60 Peachcroft Dr.
Bernardsville, NJ 07924
PH: (908)428-4300
Fax: (908)766-1277
Mahoney, Simon, President

American Society for the Advancement of Anesthesia and Sedation in Dentistry [13693]
6 E Union Ave.
Bound Brook, NJ 08805
PH: (732)469-9050
Crystal, Dr. David, Exec. Sec.

Crowncap Collectors Society International [21645]
c/o Kevin Kirk, Treasurer
1990 Holland Brook Rd.
Branchburg, NJ 08876
Oremland, Barry, President

International Side Saddle Organization **[22944]**
75 Lamington Rd.
Branchburg, NJ 08876-3314
PH: (706)871-4776
Liggett, Shelly, President

Association of Professional Insurance Women **[1840]**
c/o Susan Barros
The Beaumont Group, Inc.
990 Cedar Bridge Ave., Ste. B, PMB 210
Brick, NJ 08723-4157
PH: (973)941-6024
Vollweiler, Cheryl, President

Audubon Artists **[8848]**
c/o Vincent J. Nardone, President/Admissions Chair
3 Lamb Rd.
Brick, NJ 08724
PH: (732)903-7468
Nardone, Vincent J., Chairperson, President

Parents Of Autistic Children **[13776]**
1989 Route 88
Brick, NJ 08724
PH: (732)785-1099
Fax: (732)785-1003
Weitzen, Gary, Exec. Dir.

Golden Glow of Christmas Past **[22438]**
c/o Lillie Ghidiu
7 Turnbridge Dr.
Bridgeton, NJ 08302

Marine Mammal Stranding Center **[4842]**
3625 Brigantine Blvd.
Brigantine, NJ 08203
PH: (609)266-0538
Schoelkopf, Robert C., Director, Founder

Common Sense for Animals **[10605]**
2420 Route 57
Broadway, NJ 08808
PH: (908)859-3060
Fax: (908)859-3738
Blease, Robert R., DVM, President

United States War Dogs Association **[21035]**
1313 Mt. Holly Rd.
Burlington, NJ 08016
PH: (609)747-9340
Aiello, Ronald L., President

Holistic Moms Network **[12415]**
PO Box 408
Caldwell, NJ 07006
Toll free: 877-465-6667
Massotto, Nancy, Chairperson, Exec. Dir., Founder

Society of Insurance Financial Management **[1266]**
61 Mountain Ave.
Caldwell, NJ 07006
PH: (973)303-6297
Nivia, Adriana, Exec. VP

Society for the History of Children and Youth **[9517]**
c/o Kriste Lindenmeyer, Secretary-Treasurer
Armitage Hall, Rm. 379
311 N 5th St.
Rutgers University
Camden, NJ 08102-1405
Lindenmeyer, Kriste, Secretary, Treasurer

National Intercollegiate Soccer Officials Association **[23188]**
c/o NISOA Foundation Fund
1030 Ohio Ave.

Cape May, NJ 08204
Wescott, George, President

American Society of Certified Engineering Technicians **[6534]**
PO Box 95
Cape May Court House, NJ 08210
PH: (609)600-2097
Fax: (609)600-2097
Freier, Russel E., CET, Chmn. of the Bd.

Association of the Sons of Poland **[19602]**
333 Hackensack St.
Carlstadt, NJ 07072
PH: (201)935-2807
Fax: (201)935-2752
Knurowski, Frank, President

Circulo de Cultura Panamericano **[9659]**
PO Box 469
Cedar Grove, NJ 07009-0469
Alba-Buffill, Dr. Elio, PhD, Exec. Sec.

Discover Worlds **[12969]**
908 B2 Pompton Ave.
Cedar Grove, NJ 07009
Bhatia, Anjali, CEO, President

Women's Overseas Service League **[21156]**
PO Box 124
Cedar Knolls, NJ 07927-0124
Kuhns, Martha, President

American Bureau of Metal Statistics Inc. **[6839]**
PO Box 805
Chatham, NJ 07928-0805
PH: (973)701-2299
Fax: (973)701-2152

Global Learning **[8114]**
PO Box 1011
Chatham, NJ 07928
PH: (201)317-8796
Coleman, Shay, Exec. Dir.

American Association of Teachers of German **[8171]**
112 Haddontowne Ct., Ste. 104
Cherry Hill, NJ 08034-3662
PH: (856)795-5553
Fax: (856)795-9398
Boland, Hal, President

American Society of PeriAnesthesia Nurses **[16114]**
90 Frontage Rd.
Cherry Hill, NJ 08034-1424
Toll free: 877-737-9696
Fax: (856)616-9601
Godfrey, Kimberly, Reg. Dir.

Destination ImagiNation **[8410]**
1111 S Union Ave.
Cherry Hill, NJ 08002
Toll free: 888-321-1503
Fax: (856)881-3596
Cadle, Chuck, CEO

International Association of Jewish Genealogical Societies **[20974]**
PO Box 3624
Cherry Hill, NJ 08034-0556
Bravo, Ken, VP

International Fluid Power Society **[6635]**
PO Box 1420
Cherry Hill, NJ 08034-0054
PH: (856)489-8983
Toll free: 800-308-6005
Fax: (856)424-9248

Kingdom Chamber of Commerce **[23600]**
383 N Kings Hwy., Ste. 201
Cherry Hill, NJ 08034

PH: (856)414-0818
Fax: (856)414-6140

Multiple Sclerosis Association of America **[15955]**
375 Kings Hwy. N
Cherry Hill, NJ 08034
PH: (856)488-4500
Toll free: 800-532-7667
Fax: (856)661-9797
Franklin, Douglas G., CEO, President

Multiple Sclerosis Coalition **[15956]**
706 Haddonfield Rd.
Cherry Hill, NJ 08002
Toll free: 800-532-7667
Fax: (856)661-9797
Skutnik, Lisa, President

National Association for Media Literacy Education **[8290]**
10 Lauren Hill Dr.
Cherry Hill, NJ 08003
Toll free: 888-775-2652
Brown, David W., President

Cancer Hope Network **[13923]**
2 North Rd., Ste. A
Chester, NJ 07930
PH: (908)879-4039
Toll free: 800-552-4366
Fax: (908)879-6518
Diak, Wanda, Exec. Dir., COO

International 22q11.2 Deletion Syndrome Foundation **[14829]**
PO Box 2269
Cinnaminson, NJ 08077
Toll free: 877-739-1849
Kambin, Sheila, MD, Chairperson

Women in Toys **[3295]**
300 Winston Dr., Ste. 1509
Cliffside Park, NJ 07010
PH: (201)224-2190
Mady, Ashley, President

Drums and Disabilities **[12234]**
1360 Clifton Ave., Unit No. 231
Clifton, NJ 07012-1453
PH: (973)725-5150
Gesualdo, Pat, Founder

IEEE - Instrumentation and Measurement Society **[6761]**
c/o Robert M. Goldberg
1360 Clifton Ave., PMB 336
Clifton, NJ 07012
PH: (785)532-6224
Yan, Ruqiang, VP

International Alumni Association of Shri Mahavir Jain Vidyalaya **[19634]**
24 River Rd., Unit 1
Clifton, NJ 07014
PH: (919)661-3904
Shah, Ketan M., President

National Council on Public Polls **[18924]**
1425 Broad St., Ste. 7
Clifton, NJ 07013
PH: (202)293-4710
Fax: (202)293-4757
Taylor, Humphrey, Chairman

United in Group Harmony Association **[10019]**
PO Box 185
Clifton, NJ 07011
PH: (973)365-0049
Italiano, Ronnie, President, Founder

MG Drivers Club of North America **[21431]**
18 George's Pl.
Clinton, NJ 08809-1334

PH: (908)713-6251
Fax: (908)713-6251
Miller, Richard F., Director

Hold the Door for Others **[10774]**
PO Box 755
Closter, NJ 07624
PH: (732)851-3667
Fazio, Lauren, Founder, President

National Association of Environmental Professionals **[4083]**
PO Box 460
Collingswood, NJ 08108
PH: (856)283-7816
Fax: (856)210-1619
Bower, Tim, CAE, Managing Dir.

Small Steps in Speech **[14296]**
PO Box 134
Collingswood, NJ 08108
Toll free: 888-577-3256
Fax: (856)632-7741
Charney, Amanda, Exec. Dir.

American Atheists **[19708]**
225 Cristiani St.
Cranford, NJ 07016
PH: (908)276-7300
Cary, Neal, Chmn. of the Bd.

Veterinary Laboratory Association **[17672]**
PO Box 433
Cream Ridge, NJ 08514
PH: (732)492-8019
Jenkins-Perez, Jenni, LVT, President

National Seasoning Manufacturers Association **[1304]**
228 Phelps Ave.
Cresskill, NJ 07626
PH: (201)657-1989
Sonntag, Tim, President

American Ivy Society **[22079]**
PO Box 163
Deerfield Street, NJ 08313
Dapp, Veronica, Contact

Knights of Saint John International **[19849]**
c/o Bruce Stowers, Membership Chairman
29 Cranberry Ln.
Delran, NJ 08075
PH: (856)764-3147
Gossiaux, Gen. Dale, President

ALMA Society, Inc. **[10441]**
PO Box 85
Denville, NJ 07834
PH: (973)586-1358
Anderson, Marie, Coord.

Hypertrophic Cardiomyopathy Association **[14118]**
18 E Main St., Ste. 202
Denville, NJ 07834
PH: (973)983-7429
Fax: (973)983-7870
Salberg, Lisa, CEO, Founder

Society of American Bayonet Collectors **[21298]**
PO Box 5866
Deptford, NJ 08096
Morrison, Dan, Founder

American Self-Help Group Clearinghouse **[12867]**
375 E McFarlan St.
Dover, NJ 07801-3638
PH: (973)989-1122
Toll free: 800-367-6274
Fax: (973)989-1159

Chinese-American Golf Association **[22876]**
2 Doloree Dr.
East Brunswick, NJ 08816

PH: (732)422-9558
Fax: (732)422-9558
Lin, Peter K.R., President

Black Cops Against Police Brutality
[5457]
PO Box 4256
East Orange, NJ 07019
PH: (973)926-5717

SOKOL U.S.A. [19651]
276 Prospect St.
East Orange, NJ 07017-2889
PH: (973)676-0281
Fax: (973)676-3348
Bielecki, Joseph, President

Canadian Corkscrew Collectors Club
[21631]
1 Madison St., Ste. 5B
East Rutherford, NJ 07073-1605
PH: (973)773-9224
Becker, Milt, Coord., Member Svcs.

Dawn Bible Students Association
[19756]
199 Railroad Ave.
East Rutherford, NJ 07073-1915
Toll free: 888-440-3296
Gorecki, Robert, Chairman

The Society of Marine Port
Engineers of New York [3102]
111 Broad St.
Eatontown, NJ 07724
PH: (732)389-2009
Fax: (732)389-2264
Walla, Joseph, Chmn. of the Bd.

Cosmopolitan Soccer League
[23186]
115 River Rd., Ste. 1029
Edgewater, NJ 07020
PH: (201)943-3390
Fax: (201)943-3394
Strumpf, Peter, Treasurer

Craft and Hobby Association [1641]
319 E 54th St.
Elmwood Park, NJ 07407
PH: (201)835-1200
Murray, David, Chairman

Guang Ping Yang T'ai Chi Association [23295]
268 Kinderkamack Rd.
Emerson, NJ 07630
Riddle, Lawrence, President

NOVA Hope for Haiti, Inc. [12294]
176 Palisade Ave.
Emerson, NJ 07630
PH: (201)675-9413
Nuzzi, Joseph F., President

Fellowship of St. John the Divine
[20054]
PO Box 5238
Englewood, NJ 07631
PH: (201)871-1355
Fax: (201)871-7954
Zain, Thomas, Officer

International Academy of Olympic
Chiropractic Officers [14272]
546 Broad Ave.
Englewood, NJ 07631
PH: (201)569-1444
Press, Dr. Stephen J., DC, Chairman

Association of Ship Brokers and
Agents, Inc. [2239]
510 Sylvan Ave., Ste. 201
Englewood Cliffs, NJ 07632
PH: (201)569-2882
Cardona, Jeanne L., Exec. Dir.,
Secretary

Korean American Medical Association [15733]
200 Sylvan Ave., Ste. 22
Englewood Cliffs, NJ 07632

PH: (201)567-1434
Fax: (201)567-1753
Kim, Dr. Stanley Y., VP, Treasurer

National Organization of Social
Security Claimants' Representa-
tives [19139]
560 Sylvan Ave., Ste. 2200
Englewood Cliffs, NJ 07632
PH: (201)567-4228
Fax: (201)567-1542
Shifrin, Debra, Mem.

Educational Testing Service [8684]
225 Phillips Blvd.
Ewing, NJ 08628
PH: (609)921-9000
Fax: (609)734-5410
MacDonald, Walt, President, CEO

Graduate Record Examinations
Board [8685]
225 Phillips Blvd.
Ewing, NJ 08618-1426
PH: (609)771-7670
Toll free: 866-473-4373
Fax: (610)290-8975
Huntoon, Jacqueline, Chairperson

Thornton Wilder Society [10405]
c/o College of New Jersey
PO Box 7718
Ewing, NJ 08628-0718
PH: (609)771-2346
Konkle, Dr. Lincoln, Exec. Dir.

American Catholic Lawyers Associa-
tion [5411]
420 US Highway Route 46, Ste. 7
Fairfield, NJ 07004
PH: (973)244-9895
Fax: (973)244-9897
Ferrara, Christopher A., Counsel,
President

Association of Dental Implant
Auxiliaries [14419]
55 Lane Rd., Ste. 305
Fairfield, NJ 07004
PH: (973)783-6300
Fax: (973)783-1175
Mortilla, Lynn, Exec. Dir.

Healthcare Businesswomen's As-
sociation [15015]
Bldg. E, Ste. 215
373 Route 46 West
Fairfield, NJ 07004
PH: (973)575-0606
Fax: (973)575-1445
Cooke, Laurie, CEO

International Congress of Oral Im-
plantologists [14452]
55 Lane Rd., Ste. 305
Fairfield, NJ 07004
PH: (973)783-6300
Toll free: 800-442-0525
Fax: (973)783-1175
Judy, Dr. Kenneth W.M., Co-Chmn.
of the Bd.

Textile Care Allied Trades Associa-
tion [2080]
271 Route 46 W, Ste. C205
Fairfield, NJ 07004
PH: (973)244-1790
Fax: (973)244-4455
Cotter, David, CEO

Unico National [19509]
271 US Highway 46, Ste. F-103
Fairfield, NJ 07004-2447
PH: (973)808-0035
Toll free: 800-877-1492
Fax: (973)808-0043
D'Arminio, Richard, President

Schiffli Lace and Embroidery
Manufacturers Association [3268]
22 Industrial Ave.
Fairview, NJ 07022

PH: (201)941-0766
Fax: (201)941-1507

United States Golf Association
[22895]
PO Box 708
Far Hills, NJ 07931
PH: (908)234-2300
Fax: (908)234-1883
Stulack, Nancy, Librarian

USGA Green Section [22898]
77 Liberty Cor. Rd.
Far Hills, NJ 07931-2570
PH: (908)234-2300
Fax: (908)781-1736
Erusha, Kimberly S., PhD, Managing
Dir.

American Beveren Rabbit Club
[22396]
c/o Meg Whitehouse, Secretary-
Treasurer
480 Colts Neck Rd.
Farmingdale, NJ 07727
PH: (732)919-0909
Calloway, Kim, President

Pine Creek Railroad [22410]
New Jersey Museum of Transporta-
tion, Inc.
PO Box 622
Farmingdale, NJ 07727-0622
PH: (732)938-5524
Smith, David, V. Chmn. of the Bd.

Therapy Dogs International [17466]
88 Bartley Rd.
Flanders, NJ 07836
PH: (973)252-9800
Fax: (973)252-7171
Kempe, Ursula A., CEO, President

Dachshund Club of America [21864]
c/o Neal Hamilton, Membership
Administrator
59 Cloverhill Rd.
Flemington, NJ 08822-9801
PH: (908)782-4724
Holder, Carl, President

International Disease Management
Alliance [14586]
32 Sutton Farm Rd.
Flemington, NJ 08822
PH: (908)806-3961
Fax: (908)806-8267

Starve Poverty International [10733]
6 Norwick Dr.
Forked River, NJ 08731
PH: (609)249-5392
Fax: (609)971-6827
Fraser, Ron, Founder, CEO

Association of Intellectual Property
Firms [5674]
2125 Center Ave., Ste. 406
Fort Lee, NJ 07024-5874
PH: (201)403-0927
Fax: (201)461-6635
Crenshaw, Diallo, Treasurer

National Valentine Collectors' As-
sociation [21701]
c/o Nancy Rosin, President
PO Box 647
Franklin Lakes, NJ 07417
PH: (201)337-5834
Fax: (201)337-3356
Rosin, Nancy, President

Kidney & Urology Foundation of
America [15880]
63 W Main St., Ste. G
Freehold, NJ 07728
PH: (732)866-4444
Toll free: 800-633-6628
Giarrusso, Sam, President

Professional Picture Framers As-
sociation [8883]
83 South St., Ste. 303
Freehold, NJ 07728
PH: (732)536-5160
Fax: (732)536-5161
Ausili, Gene, Mem.

Society for the Prevention of Teen
Suicide [13198]
110 W Main St.
Freehold, NJ 07728
Fritz, Scott, President

Well Spouse Association [17353]
63 W Main St., Ste. H
Freehold, NJ 07728
Toll free: 800-838-0879
Fax: (732)577-8644
Saunders, Dorothy, Co-Pres.

Association of Caribbean Historians
[9460]
c/o Michelle Craig McDonald,
Secretary/Treasurer
Dept. of History
Richard Stockton College
101 Vera King Farris Dr.
Galloway, NJ 08205-9441
Dumont, Jacques, President

Christian Overcomers [11581]
PO Box 2007
Garfield, NJ 07026
PH: (973)253-2343
White, Debbie, Director

Amateur Astronomers, Inc. [21305]
PO Box 111
Garwood, NJ 07027-0111
Ducca, Mary, President

Cosmetic Industry Buyers and Suppliers [1584]
c/o Jenifer Brady, Recording
Secretary
124 South Ave.
Garwood, NJ 07027
Carey, Laura, Director

Congenital Hyperinsulinism
International [16567]
PO Box 135
Glen Ridge, NJ 07028
PH: (973)544-8372
Hopkins, Matthew M., President

Women in Flavor and Fragrance
Commerce, Inc. [3507]
55 Harristown Rd., Ste. 106
Glen Rock, NJ 07452
PH: (732)922-0500
    (201)857-8955
Fax: (732)922-0560
Roche, Celine, Account Exec.

Foster Family-based Treatment As-
sociation [10982]
294 Union St.
Hackensack, NJ 07601-4303
PH: (201)343-2246
Toll free: 800-414-3382
Fax: (201)489-6719
Cole, Ms. Melissa, Administrator

International Organization of Multiple
Sclerosis Nurses [16139]
359 Main St., Ste. A
Hackensack, NJ 07601-5806
PH: (201)487-1050
Fax: (201)678-2291
Halper, June, MSN, Exec. Dir.

Parent Project Muscular Dystrophy
[15980]
401 Hackensack Avenue, 9th Floor
Hackensack, NJ 07601
PH: (201)250-8440
Toll free: 800-714-5437
Fax: (201)250-8435
Furlong, Pat, President

517th Parachute Regimental Combat Team Association [21186]
c/o K. Allan Johnson, President
215 Mission Rd.
Hackettstown, NJ 07840
Johnson, Allan, President

Antique Doorknob Collectors of America [21620]
PO Box 803
Hackettstown, NJ 07840
PH: (908)684-5253
Kennedy, Rich, Secretary

National Kitchen and Bath Association [1955]
687 Willow Grove St.
Hackettstown, NJ 07840
Toll free: 800-843-6522
Fax: (908)852-1695
Darcy, Bill, CEO

Phi Mu Delta [23915]
216 Haddon Ave., Ste. 602
Haddon Township, NJ 08108
PH: (609)220-4975
Murphy, Thomas A., Exec. Dir.

Sedgwick Society [10398]
c/o Deborah Gussman
619 Wayne Ave.
Haddonfield, NJ 08033
Damon-Bach, Lucinda, Founder, President

Tau Epsilon Rho Law Society [23805]
133 Paisley Pl.
133 Paisley Pl.
Hainesport, NJ 08036
PH: (609)864-1838
(609)284-4584
Tepper, Alan M., Exec. Dir., Treasurer

Iranian American Medical Association [15732]
PO Box 8218
Haledon, NJ 07538
PH: (973)595-8888
Fax: (973)790-7755
Sharifzadeh, Khalil, DVM, President

National Birman Fanciers [21572]
c/o Joann Lamb, Secretary
7 Cornwall Ct.
Hamburg, NJ 07419-1359
Lamb, Joann, Secretary

International Sculpture Center [10209]
14 Fairgrounds Rd., Ste. B
Hamilton, NJ 08619-3447
PH: (609)689-1051
Fax: (609)689-1061
Kaneko, Ree, Chairman

Deep Foundations Institute [863]
326 Lafayette Ave.
Hawthorne, NJ 07506
PH: (973)423-4030
Fax: (973)423-4031
Engler, Theresa, Exec. Dir.

International Association of Dinnerware Matchers [1682]
67 Beverly Rd.
Hawthorne, NJ 07506

Affiliated Warehouse Companies [3435]
PO Box 295
Hazlet, NJ 07730-0295
PH: (732)739-2323
Ritter, Wayne, CFO

Securities Transfer Association [3051]
PO Box 5220
Hazlet, NJ 07730

PH: (732)888-6040
Fax: (732)888-2121
May, Todd J., President

Harley Hummer Club [22222]
13 Sylvan Rd.
High Bridge, NJ 08829
Hennessey, David, President

Pedals for Progress [12710]
PO Box 312
High Bridge, NJ 08829
PH: (908)638-4811
Schweidenback, Dave, Founder, CEO

American Littoral Society [3800]
18 Hartshorne Dr., Ste. 1
Highlands, NJ 07732
PH: (732)291-0055
Fax: (732)291-3551
Dillingham, Tim, Exec. Dir.

American Littoral Society - Northeast Region [6800]
18 Hartshorne Dr., Ste. 1
Highlands, NJ 07732
PH: (732)291-0055
Riepe, Don, Director

Citizens Against Greyhound Racing [18324]
PO Box 944
Hightstown, NJ 08520

American Association of Feline Practitioners [17595]
390 Amwell Rd., Ste. 402
Hillsborough, NJ 08844-1247
Toll free: 800-874-0498
Fax: (908)292-1188
Smith, Dr. Roy, Treasurer

Hark [13684]
PO Box 6627
Hillsborough, NJ 08844
PH: (908)285-9202
York, Donna, President

International Association of Pet Cemeteries and Crematories [2542]
390 Amwell Rd., Ste. 402
Hillsborough, NJ 08844
Toll free: 800-952-5541
Fax: (908)450-1398
Bjorling, Debra, Treasurer

Society for Medical Decision Making [15746]
390 Amwell Rd., Ste. 402
Hillsborough, NJ 08844
PH: (908)359-1184
Fax: (908)450-1119
Helfand, Mark, President

American Indian Law Alliance [18372]
PO Box 3036
Hoboken, NJ 07030
Lyons, Betty, President, Exec. Dir.

American Musical Instrument Society [9862]
c/o Joanne Kopp, Treasurer
1106 Garden St.
Hoboken, NJ 07030
PH: (201)656-0107
Kopp, Joanne, Treasurer

National Society of Leadership and Success [8626]
50 Harrison St., Ste. 308
Hoboken, NJ 07030
PH: (201)222-6544
Toll free: 800-601-6248
Fax: (201)839-4604
Tuerack, Gary, Founder

Containerization and Intermodal Institute [831]
960 Holmdel Rd., Bldg. 2, Ste. 201
Holmdel, NJ 07733
PH: (732)817-9131
Fax: (732)817-9133
Clifford, Allen, V. Chmn. of the Bd.

Seeds to Sew International, Inc. [11429]
PO Box 22
Hopewell, NJ 08525
PH: (609)564-0441
Ito, Ellyn M., Exec. Dir., Trustee

Greek American Chamber of Commerce, Inc. [23588]
111 Wood Ave. S
Iselin, NJ 08830-2700
PH: (609)431-8000
(215)909-6000
Antonakakis, Stavros, Contact

Pediatric Hydrocephalus Foundation [15986]
2004 Green Hollow Dr.
Iselin, NJ 08830
PH: (732)634-1283
Fax: (847)589-1250
Illions, Kim, President

ChangeALife Uganda [10890]
46 Oakmont Ln.
Jackson, NJ 08527
Semler, Jean, Founder, President

Empower the Children [10961]
PO Box 1412
Jackson, NJ 08527
Giffoniello, Rosalie, Founder

Lyme Disease Association [14591]
PO Box 1438
Jackson, NJ 08527
Toll free: 888-366-6611
Fax: (732)938-7215
Smith, Patricia V., BA, President

Afro-American Historical Society Museum [8782]
1841 Kennedy Blvd.
Jersey City, NJ 07305
PH: (201)547-5262
Fax: (201)547-5392
Brunson, Neal E., Esq., Director

Doors of Hope [18579]
PO Box 5291
Jersey City, NJ 07305

Global Association of Risk Professionals [1238]
111 Town Square Pl., 14th Fl.
Jersey City, NJ 07310
PH: (201)719-7210
Fax: (201)222-5022
Apostolik, Richard, CEO, President

Insurance Data Management Association [1865]
545 Washington Blvd., 17th Fl.
Jersey City, NJ 07310
PH: (201)469-3069
Fax: (201)748-1690
Yassine, Farouk N., Exec. Dir.

Psi Sigma Phi Multicultural Fraternity Inc. [23868]
PO Box 3613
Jersey City, NJ 07303-3062
Castro, Ceasar, Contact

Rainforest Relief [4616]
PO Box 8451
Jersey City, NJ 07308
PH: (917)543-4064
Keating, Tim, Exec. Dir.

Rising Tide Capital [1008]
334 Martin Luther King Dr.
Jersey City, NJ 07305

PH: (201)432-4316
Fax: (201)432-3504
Demmellash, Alfa, CEO, Founder

United Seamen's Service [12862]
104 Broadway, Ground Fl.
Jersey City, NJ 07306
PH: (201)369-1100
Fax: (201)369-1105
Korner, Roger T., Exec. Dir.

Wheel Wishers [13095]
Jersey City, NJ
Mellegers, Marije, Founder

Waves of Health [15506]
206 Bergen Ave., Ste. 203
Kearny, NJ 07032
Boni, Chris, VP

The Parkinson Alliance [15982]
PO Box 308
Kingston, NJ 08528-0308
PH: (609)688-0870
Toll free: 800-579-8440
Fax: (609)688-0875
Walton, Carol J., CEO

Professor Chen Wen-Chen Memorial Foundation [9221]
PO Box 136
Kingston, NJ 08528
PH: (609)936-1352

National Association for Developmental Education [7713]
170 Kinnelon Rd., Ste. 33
Kinnelon, NJ 07405
Toll free: 877-233-9455
Fax: (973)838-7124
Ozz, Robin, President

Radio Club of America [22404]
170 Kinnelon Rd., No. 33
Kinnelon, NJ 07405
PH: (973)283-0626
Fax: (973)838-7124
McIntyre, Bruce, President

Professional Car Society [21481]
64 Mudcut Rd.
Lafayette, NJ 07848-4607
Skivolocke, Daniel, VP

JOY for Our Youth [11053]
1805 Swarthmore Ave.
Lakewood, NJ 08701
Toll free: 866-GIV-EJOY
Mintz, Eliyohu, Director

Lung Cancer Circle of Hope [14005]
7 Carnation Dr., Ste. A
Lakewood, NJ 08701
PH: (732)363-4426
Fax: (732)370-9180
Levin, Susan, President, Founder

National Intercollegiate Women's Fencing Association [22833]
c/o Denise C. O'Connor, Secretary/Treasurer
224C Buckingham Ct.
Lakewood, NJ 08701-7802
Everson, Sharon, President

Runkle Family Association [20922]
1281 Route 179
Lambertville, NJ 08530-3502
Masterson, Patricia, Editor, President

Advanced Practitioner Society for Hematology and Oncology [16328]
Bldg. 1, Ste. 205
3131 Princeton Pke.
Lawrenceville, NJ 08648
PH: (609)832-3000
Viale, Pamela Hallquist, RN, President

GS1 US [273]
Princeton Pike Corporate Ctr.
1009 Lenox Dr., Ste. 202
Lawrenceville, NJ 08648
PH: (609)620-0200
Carpenter, Bob, President, CEO

International Society for Pharmaco-
economics and Outcomes
Research [16667]
505 Lawrence Square Blvd. S
Lawrenceville, NJ 08648-2675
PH: (609)586-4981
Toll free: 800-992-0643
Fax: (609)586-4982
Dix Smith, Marilyn, RPh, Exec. Dir.

Certification Board for Sterile
Processing and Distribution
[15663]
148 Main St., Ste. C-1
Lebanon, NJ 08833
PH: (908)236-0530
Toll free: 800-555-9765
Fax: (908)236-0820
Chobin, Nancy, RN, Bd. Member

ColombiaCare [10944]
PO Box 254
Lincroft, NJ 07738-0254
Perez, Victoria, Bd. Member

State Revenue Society [22372]
27 Pine St.
Lincroft, NJ 07738-1827
Bowman, John, Gov.

SETI League [6011]
433 Liberty St.
Little Ferry, NJ 07643
PH: (201)641-1770
Toll free: 800-TAU-SETI
Fax: (201)641-1771
Factor, Richard, President

C.H.A.S.E. for Life [14661]
PO Box 443
Little Silver, NJ 07739
Toll free: 888-547-4460
Boyle, Farley, Exec. Dir., Founder,
President

Chinese Language Association of
Secondary-Elementary Schools
[7600]
PO Box 2348
Livingston, NJ 07039
Lin, Dr. Yu-Lan, Exec. Dir.

Correspondence Chess League of
America [21591]
PO Box 142
Livingston, NJ 07039-0142
Lines, Daniel, President

United States Maritime Alliance
[2258]
125 Chubb Ave., Ste. 350NC
Lyndhurst, NJ 07071
PH: (732)404-2960
Adam, David F., Chairman, CEO

Confrerie de la Chaîne des Rotis-
seurs, Bailliage des U.S.A. [22146]
285 Madison Ave.
Madison, NJ 07940
PH: (973)360-9200
Fax: (973)360-9330
Braunstein, Clyde, Exec. Dir.

General Commission on Archives
and History of the United Method-
ist Church [20343]
36 Madison Ave.
Madison, NJ 07940
PH: (973)408-3189
Fax: (973)408-3909
Day, Alfred T., III, Gen. Sec.

World Methodist Historical Society
[20352]
PO Box 127
Madison, NJ 07940
PH: (973)408-3189
Fax: (973)408-3909
Williams, Robert, PhD, Editor

American Vegan Society [10291]
56 Dinshah Ln.
Malaga, NJ 08328
PH: (856)694-2887
Fax: (856)694-2288
Dinshah, Freya, President

Dinshah Health Society [13619]
PO Box 707
Malaga, NJ 08328-0707
PH: (856)692-4686
Dinshah, Darius, President

National Conference of Insurance
Legislators [5318]
2317 Route 34, Ste. 2B
Manasquan, NJ 08736
PH: (732)201-4133
Fax: (609)989-7491
Holdman, Travis, President

L.C. Smith Collectors Association
[22024]
c/o Frank Finch, Executive Director
1322 Bay Ave.
Mantoloking, NJ 08738
Finch, Frank, Corr. Sec., Exec. Dir.

Dark Shadows Official Fan Club
[24085]
PO Box 92
Maplewood, NJ 07040

Ethiopia's Tomorrow [10966]
28 Hoffman St.
Maplewood, NJ 07040
PH: (973)951-8035
    (763)350-1115
Mischel, Emmebeth, Founder,
Treasurer

Cultural Association of Bengal
[9229]
35 Windfall Ln.
Marlboro, NJ 07746
Sarkar, Kajal, Chairman

New Hope Foundation [13171]
80 Conover Rd.
Marlboro, NJ 07746
PH: (732)946-3030
Toll free: 800-705-4673
Fax: (732)946-3541
Comerford, Tony, PhD, CEO,
President

Patidar Cultural Association of USA
[9570]
32 Stevenson Dr.
Marlboro, NJ 07746
PH: (732)761-9829
Ghodasara, Kiran, President

ChemoClothes [13938]
Five Greentree Center
525 Lincoln Dr., Ste. 104, Rte. 73
Marlton, NJ 08053
PH: (609)706-3896
Toll free: 888-852-5858
Levy, Jared R., President

Music Business Association [2902]
1 Eves Dr., Ste. 138
Marlton, NJ 08053
PH: (856)596-2221
Fax: (856)596-7299
Wilson, Bill, VP of Bus. Dev.

National Limousine Association
[3344]
49 S Maple Ave.
Marlton, NJ 08053

PH: (856)596-3344
Toll free: 800-652-7007
Fax: (856)596-2145
Gazi, Sarah, Exec. Dir.

Organization for International
Cooperation [18552]
Bldg. C, Ste. 196
100 Conestoga Dr.
Marlton, NJ 08053
PH: (856)596-6679
Fax: (856)282-1184
Keiser, Arnold, President, Project
Mgr.

Adler Aphasia Center [13725]
60 W Hunter Ave.
Maywood, NJ 07607
PH: (201)368-8585
Fax: (201)587-1909
Tucker, Karen, Exec. Dir.

Eliminate Poverty Now [10720]
PO Box 67
Mendham, NJ 07945
Craig, Judy, Founder

Pediatric Angel Network [11261]
PO Box 213
Mendham, NJ 07945
Toll free: 800-620-3620
Fax: (866)546-7493
Ratynski, Deborah, RN, Founder,
President, CEO

Power Sources Manufacturers As-
sociation [1119]
PO Box 418
Mendham, NJ 07945-0418
PH: (973)543-9660
Fax: (973)543-6207
Oliver, Stephen, President

Shenpen America [13089]
PO Box 12
Mendham, NJ 07945
Wangpo, Jigme Losel, Contact

Stamps on Stamps Collectors Club
[22371]
c/o Michael Merritt
73 Mountainside Rd.
Mendham, NJ 07945-2014
Guadagno, Lou, President

United States Running Streak Association, Inc. [23121]
c/o Mark Washburne, President
31 Galway Dr.
Mendham, NJ 07945
Washburne, Mark, President

Amateur Radio Lighthouse Society
[9367]
114 Woodbine Ave.
Merchantville, NJ 08109
PH: (856)486-1755
Weidner, Jim, Founder

Asian Indian Chamber of Commerce
[23558]
402 Main St., Ste. 214
Metuchen, NJ 08840
PH: (732)777-4666
Pandya Patel, Priti, President

U.S.-China Exchange Association
[18533]
52 Bridge St.
Metuchen, NJ 08840
PH: (732)771-5083
Fax: (732)494-5802
Wang, Dr. George, President

American Microchemical Society
[6184]
c/o Herk Felder, Treasurer
2 June Way

Middlesex, NJ 08846
Ferrari, Hal, Chairman

Focus Fusion Society [6485]
128 Lincoln Blvd.
Middlesex, NJ 08846
PH: (732)356-5900
Fax: (732)377-0381
Razani, Rezwan, Exec. Dir.

Titanic International Society [9779]
c/o Robert Bracken, Treasurer
47 Van Blarcom Ave.
Midland Park, NJ 07432
Haas, Charles A., President

Les Amis d'Escoffier Society of New
York [1351]
787 Ridgewood Rd.
Millburn, NJ 07041
PH: (212)414-5820
    (973)564-7575
Fax: (973)379-3117
Keller, Kurt, Exec. Dir., Treasurer

Centered Riding, Inc. [22941]
PO Box 429
Millstone Township, NJ 08510
PH: (609)208-1100
Fax: (609)208-1101
Swift, Sally, Founder

Order of the Noble Companions of
the Swan [9336]
PO Box 404
Milltown, NJ 08850
de Alabona-Ostrogojsk, William,
Master

Holly Society of America [4728]
309 Buck St.
Millville, NJ 08332-0803
PH: (856)825-4300
Fax: (856)825-5283
Swintosky, John A., President

Plymouth Rock Fanciers Club of
America [4570]
2724 Cedarville Rd.
2724 Cedarville Rd.
Millville, NJ 08332
PH: (856)265-7278
Beauchamp, John, President

National Ski Council Federation
[23165]
c/o Joe Harvis, President
4 Green Rd.
Mine Hill, NJ 07803-2908
Harvis, Joe, President

Dow Jones News Fund, Inc. [8154]
Bldg. 5
4300 Route 1 N
Monmouth Junction, NJ 08852
PH: (609)452-2820
Fax: (609)520-5804
Shockley, Linda, Managing Dir.

American Engineering Association
[6530]
c/o Harold Ruchelman
533 Waterside Blvd.
Monroe Township, NJ 08831
Tax, Richard F., President

Association for Value-Based Cancer
Care [13895]
241 Forsgate Dr., Ste. 205B
Monroe Township, NJ 08831
PH: (732)992-1538
Owens, Gary, MD, Co-Chmn. of the
Bd.

American Acne and Rosacea
Society [14478]
201 Claremont Ave.
Montclair, NJ 07042

PH: (973)783-4575
Toll free: 888-744-3376
Fax: (973)783-4576
Thiboutot, Diane, MD, President

American Psychopathological Association [16950]
39 Marion Rd.
Montclair, NJ 07043
Shrout, Patrick E., PhD, Treasurer

American Society of Pain Educators [16554]
6 Erie St.
Montclair, NJ 07042
PH: (973)233-5570
Fax: (973)453-8246
McPherson, Mary Lynn, Chairperson

Montclair State University | Institute for the Advancement of Philosophy for Children [10103]
1 Normal Ave.
College of Education & Human Services
1 Normal Ave.
Montclair, NJ 07043
PH: (973)655-4000
Gregory, Maughn, Director

National Housing Institute [11981]
60 S Fullerton Ave., Ste. 202
Montclair, NJ 07042
PH: (973)509-1600
Atlas, John, President

National Music Council [9974]
c/o Dr. David Sanders, Director
425 Park St.
Montclair, NJ 07043
PH: (973)655-7974
Sanders, Dr. David, Director

Presbyterian Youth Workers' Association [20662]
c/o Nick Wallwork
Grace Presbyterian Church
153 Grove St.
Montclair, NJ 07042

Rwanda Gift for Life [12935]
PO Box 840
Montclair, NJ 07042
PH: (973)783-4057
Urdang, Stephanie, Coord.

Institute of Management Accountants, Cost Management Group [2172]
10 Paragon Dr., Ste. 1
Montvale, NJ 07645-1760
PH: (201)573-9000
Toll free: 800-638-4427
Fax: (201)474-1600
Thomson, Jeffrey C., President, CEO

Institute of Management Accountants, Inc. [33]
10 Paragon Dr., Ste. 1
Montvale, NJ 07645-1774
PH: (201)573-9000
Toll free: 800-638-4427
Knese, Bill, Bd. Member

Investment Casting Institute [1740]
136 Summit Ave.
Montvale, NJ 07645
PH: (201)573-9770
Fax: (201)573-9771
D'Ambra, Nora, Coord., Member Svcs.

Midwives Alliance of North America [16294]
PO Box 373
Montvale, NJ 07645
Toll free: 844-626-2674
Farrell, LM, CPM, Marinah Valenzuela, President

Sky Help, Inc. [17530]
218 Evergreen Dr.
Moorestown, NJ 08057
Toll free: 877-SKY-HELP
Howland, Susan, Founder

Africa Surgery [17356]
70 Macculloch Ave.
Morristown, NJ 07960
PH: (973)292-3320
Johnson, Tom, Jr., Founder

Cardiovascular and Metabolic Health Foundation [14152]
Educational Concepts in Medicine
163 Madison Ave., Ste. 401
Morristown, NJ 07960
Toll free: 800-732-2161
Fax: (973)525-1891
Brinton, Eliot A., MD, Bd. Member

Geraldine R. Dodge Foundation [12970]
14 Maple Ave., Ste. 400
Morristown, NJ 07960
PH: (973)540-8442
Fax: (973)540-1211
Daggett, Christopher, CEO, President

Financial Executives International [1233]
West Twr., 7th Fl.
1250 Headquarters Plz.
Morristown, NJ 07960
PH: (973)765-1000
Toll free: 877-359-1070
Fax: (973)765-1018
Chase, Paul, VP, CFO

Financial Executives Research Foundation [2166]
Financial Executives International
West Twr., 7th Fl.
1250 Headquarters Plz.
Morristown, NJ 07960
PH: (973)765-1000
    (973)765-1004
Fax: (973)765-1018
Sinnett, William, Director

International Society for Performance Improvement - Europe [7325]
ISPI Europe/EMEA
66 Fanok Rd.
Morristown, NJ 07960-6551
PH: (973)455-0420
Panza, Carol M., CPT, President

Irish American Cultural Institute [9599]
PO Box 1716
Morristown, NJ 07962
PH: (973)605-1991
Halas, Dr. F. Peter, Chairman

North American Butterfly Association [6783]
4 Delaware Rd.
Morristown, NJ 07960-5725
PH: (973)285-0907
Glassberg, Jeffrey, President

Seeing Eye [17744]
10 Washington Valley Rd.
Morristown, NJ 07960-3412
PH: (973)539-4425
Fax: (973)539-0922
Kutsch, Dr. James A., Jr., CEO, President

American Association of Heart Failure Nurses [16089]
1120 Route 73, Ste. 200
Mount Laurel, NJ 08054
Toll free: 888-452-2436
Fax: (856)439-0525
Prasun, Marilyn A., President

American Mosquito Control Association [4522]
1120 Route 73, Ste. 200
Mount Laurel, NJ 08054
PH: (856)439-9222
Fax: (856)439-0525
Smith, Larry, Dir. of Indl. Rel.

American Neurological Association [16004]
1120 Route 73, Ste. 200
Mount Laurel, NJ 08054
PH: (856)380-6892
Fax: (856)439-0525
Elliott, Victoria, RPh, MBA, CAE, Exec. Dir.

American Society of Hand Therapists [14907]
1120 Route 73, Ste. 200
Mount Laurel, NJ 08054-2212
PH: (856)380-6856
Fax: (856)439-0525
Hardy, Maureen, Bd. Member

American Society for Histocompatibility and Immunogenetics [15372]
1120 Route 73, Ste. 200
Mount Laurel, NJ 08054
Fax: (856)439-0500
Miranda, Kathy, Exec. Dir.

American Society of Transplantation [17505]
1120 Route 73, Ste. 200
Mount Laurel, NJ 08054
PH: (856)439-9986
Fax: (856)581-9604
Allan, James S., MD, MBA, President

Association of Information Technology Professionals [7652]
1120 Route 73, Ste. 200
Mount Laurel, NJ 08054-5113
PH: (856)380-6910
Toll free: 800-224-9371
Fax: (856)439-0525
Wade, Julian, President

Association of Medical Media Inc. [2313]
1120 Route 73, Ste. 200
Mount Laurel, NJ 08054
PH: (856)380-6814
Fax: (856)439-0525

Church Benefits Association [20516]
1120 Rte., Ste. 200
Mount Laurel, NJ 08054
PH: (856)439-0500
Fax: (856)439-0525
Hamlett, James, Chairman

Commission for Case Manager Certification [15117]
1120 Route 73, Ste. 200
Mount Laurel, NJ 08054
PH: (856)380-6836
Fax: (856)439-0525
Sminkey, Patrice V., CEO

Council for Chemical Research [6197]
1120 Route 73, Ste. 200
Mount Laurel, NJ 08054
PH: (856)439-0500
Fax: (856)439-0525
Lin, Eric, Officer

International Energy Credit Association [1244]
1120 Route 73, Ste. 200
Mount Laurel, NJ 08054
PH: (856)380-6854
Fax: (856)439-0525
Biordi, Michele, Exec. Dir.

International Hard Anodizing Association [2350]
PO Box 5
Mount Laurel, NJ 08054-0005

PH: (856)234-0330
Downing, Denise, Exec. Dir., Secretary

International Liver Transplantation Society [17511]
1120 Route 73, Ste. 200
Mount Laurel, NJ 08054-5113
Fax: (856)439-0525
Stern, Diann, Exec. Dir.

Juvenile Products Manufacturers Association [2064]
1120 Route 73, Ste. 200
Mount Laurel, NJ 08054
PH: (856)638-0420
Fax: (856)439-0525
Dwyer, Michael, President

National Air Duct Cleaners Association [2136]
1120 Route 73, Ste. 200
Mount Laurel, NJ 08054
PH: (856)380-6810
Fax: (856)439-0525
Lantz, Richard, 1st VP

National Association of Professional Organizers [6711]
1120 Route 17, Ste. 200
Mount Laurel, NJ 08054
PH: (856)380-6828
Fax: (856)439-0525
Mark, Lisa, Treasurer

National Association of Professional Pet Sitters [2545]
1120 Route 73, Ste. 200
Mount Laurel, NJ 08054
PH: (856)439-0324
Fax: (856)439-0525
Gonzales, Yvette, President

National Football League Alumni [22862]
8000 Midlantic Dr., Ste. 130 S
Mount Laurel, NJ 08054-1526
Toll free: 877-258-6635
Fax: (862)772-0277

OsteoArthritis Research Society International [17163]
1120 Route 73, Ste. 200
Mount Laurel, NJ 08054
PH: (856)642-4215
    (856)439-1385
Fax: (856)439-0525
Stern, Diann, MS, Exec. Dir.

QiGong Research Society [13650]
3802 Church Rd.
Mount Laurel, NJ 08054-1106
PH: (856)234-3056
Hou, Master FaXiang, Founder, Director

Society for Biomaterials [6114]
1120 Route 73, Ste. 200
Mount Laurel, NJ 08054
PH: (856)439-0826

Society for Information Management [2193]
1120 Route 73, Ste. 200
Mount Laurel, NJ 08054-5113
PH: (856)380-6807
Toll free: 800-387-9746
More, Kevin, Chairman

Wolfensberger Family Association [20944]
c/o Barbara Snavely, Treasurer
218 Belaire Dr.
Mount Laurel, NJ 08054-2702
Wolfersberger, Jon Rhan, President

Wound, Ostomy and Continence
Nurses Society [16192]
1120 Route 73, Ste. 200
Mount Laurel, NJ 08054
Toll free: 888-224-9626
Fax: (856)439-0525
Kupsick, Phyllis, President

American Headache and Migraine
Association [14915]
19 Mantua Rd.
Mount Royal, NJ 08061
PH: (856)423-0043
Fax: (856)423-0082
Dehlin, Jill, Chairperson

American Headache Society [14916]
19 Mantua Rd.
Mount Royal, NJ 08061
PH: (856)423-0043
Fax: (856)423-0082
McGillicuddy, Dr. Linda, CEO

Association for Governmental Leas-
ing and Finance [5704]
19 Mantua Rd.
Mount Royal, NJ 08061
PH: (856)423-3259
Fax: (856)423-3420
Jones, Chris, President

Association for Research in
Otolaryngology [16539]
19 Mantua Rd.
Mount Royal, NJ 08061-1006
PH: (856)423-0041
Fax: (856)423-3420
Kelley, Matthew W., PhD, President

Association of Women in the Metal
Industries [3487]
19 Mantua Rd.
Mount Royal, NJ 08061
PH: (856)423-3201
Fax: (856)423-3420
Brust, Haley J., Exec. Dir.

Comparative and International
Education Society [8112]
19 Mantua Rd.
Mount Royal, NJ 08061-1006
PH: (856)423-3629
Baker, David P., Chairperson

International Game Developers Association [6253]
19 Mantua Rd.
Mount Royal, NJ 08061
Hightower, Tristin, Dir. of Operations

National Society for Experiential
Education [7913]
c/o Talley Management Group, Inc.
19 Mantua Rd.
Mount Royal, NJ 08061-1006
PH: (856)423-3427
Fax: (856)423-3420
Lorenz, Greg, VP

North American Society for Pediatric
and Adolescent Gynecology
[16301]
19 Mantua Rd.
Mount Royal, NJ 08061
PH: (856)423-3064
Fax: (856)423-3420
Rome, Ellen, MD, President

SAVE International [6724]
19 Mantua Rd.
Mount Royal, NJ 08061
PH: (856)423-3215
Fax: (856)423-3420
Baldwin, Melissa, Program Mgr.

Society for Cardiovascular Magnetic
Resonance [15699]
19 Mantua Rd.
Mount Royal, NJ 08061

PH: (856)423-8955
Fax: (856)423-3420
Schulz-Menger, Jeanette, President

Eire Philatelic Association [22326]
1559 Grouse Ln.
1559 Grouse Ln.
Mountainside, NJ 07092-1340
Kelly, Richard, President

Foundation for Innovation in
Medicine [15725]
PO Box 1220
Mountainside, NJ 07092
PH: (908)233-2448
DeFelice, Stephen L., MD, Chair-
man, Founder

Smile Bangladesh [14344]
PO Box 1403
Mountainside, NJ 07092
PH: (908)400-1226
Fax: (866)558-4311
Aziz, Shahid R., MD, President,
Founder

United States Stamp Society
[22378]
c/o Nicholas Lombardi, President
PO Box 1005
Mountainside, NJ 07092-0005
Ballantyne, Larry, Secretary

International Center for Assault
Prevention [11704]
107 Gilbreth Pky., Ste. 200
Mullica Hill, NJ 08062
PH: (856)582-7000
Toll free: 800-258-3189
Fax: (856)582-3588
Collins, Jeannette, Dir. of Operations

National Council of Corvette Clubs
[21452]
c/o Stephen Johnson, Vice President
of Membership
10 Earlington Ave.
Mullica Hill, NJ 08062-9417
PH: (817)561-9314
Fax: (817)483-6758

Alpha Chi Rho [23879]
109 Oxford Way
Neptune, NJ 07753
PH: (732)869-1895
Fax: (732)988-5357
Carlson, Mr. Scott A., CPA, CEO,
Secretary

Association of Food Industries
[1318]
3301 Route 66, Ste. 205, Bldg. C
Neptune, NJ 07753
PH: (732)922-3008
Fax: (732)922-3590
Mortati, Fred, Chairman

Chemical Sources Association
[1450]
Bldg. C, Ste. 205
3301 Route 66
Neptune, NJ 07753
PH: (732)922-3008
Fax: (732)922-3590
Roman, Alpa, President

Move For Hunger [12103]
Bldg. 1, Ste. 1
1930 Heck Ave.
Neptune, NJ 07753
PH: (732)774-0521
Fax: (732)774-6683
Lowy, Stephan, Exec. Dir., Founder

National Association of Flavors and
Food-Ingredient Systems [1352]
3301 Route 66, Bldg. C, Ste. 205
Neptune, NJ 07753

PH: (732)922-3218
Fax: (732)922-3590
Henzi, Pia, President

National Honey Packers and Dealers
Association [1360]
Bldg. C, Ste. 205
3301 Route 66
Neptune, NJ 07753
PH: (732)922-3008
Fax: (732)922-3590

North American Olive Oil Association
[2456]
Bldg. C
3301 Route 66, Ste. 205
Neptune, NJ 07753
PH: (732)922-3008
Fax: (732)922-3590

Society of Flavor Chemists [6216]
Bldg. C, Ste. 205
3301 Route 66
Neptune, NJ 07753
PH: (732)922-3393
Fax: (732)922-3590
Lipka, Cyndie, President

Rolling Thunder [21093]
PO Box 216
Neshanic Station, NJ 08853
PH: (908)369-5439
Fax: (908)369-2072
Muller, Artie, Exec. Dir.

American Hungarian Foundation
[19467]
300 Somerset St.
New Brunswick, NJ 08901-2248
PH: (732)846-5777
Fax: (732)249-7033
Hajdu-Nemeth, Gergely, Exec. Dir.

Environmental Research Foundation
[13575]
PO Box 160
New Brunswick, NJ 08903
PH: (732)828-9995
Toll free: 888-272-2435
Fax: (732)791-4603
Montague, Peter, Exec. Dir.

Friends' Health Connection [21736]
PO Box 114
New Brunswick, NJ 08903
PH: (732)418-1811
Toll free: 800-483-7436
Fax: (732)249-9897
Black-Weisheit, Roxanne, Founder,
Exec. Dir.

Global Literacy Project [8242]
PO Box 1859
New Brunswick, NJ 08903-1859
Olubayi, Dr. Olubayi, Trustee

Society for Cultural Anthropology
[5921]
c/o Yarimar Bonilla, Secretary
Rutgers University
Dept. of Anthropology
131 George St.
New Brunswick, NJ 08901-1414
Hetherington, Kregg, Secretary

Recreational Fishing Alliance [4186]
PO Box 3080
New Gretna, NJ 08224
Toll free: 888-564-6732
Fax: (609)294-3812
Donofrio, Jim, Exec. Dir.

Association of Consulting Chemists
and Chemical Engineers [6189]
PO Box 902
New Providence, NJ 07974
PH: (908)464-3182
Fax: (908)464-3182
Borne, Tom, VP

Ireland Chamber of Commerce
U.S.A. [23595]
219 South St., Ste. 203
New Providence, NJ 07974
PH: (908)286-1300
Fax: (908)286-1200
Buckley, Maurice A., CEO, Founder,
President

National Council of Self-Insurers
[1906]
1253 Springfield Ave.
PMB 345
New Providence, NJ 07974
PH: (908)665-2152
Fax: (908)665-4020

AIDS Resource Foundation for
Children [13525]
77 Academy St.
Newark, NJ 07102
PH: (973)643-0400
Fax: (973)242-3583
Anderson, Ms. Avis, Bd. Member

Associated Humane Societies
[10590]
124 Evergreen Ave.
Newark, NJ 07114-2133
PH: (973)824-7080
Fax: (973)824-2720
Trezza, Roseann, Exec. Dir.

Association of African Biomedical
Scientists [7121]
c/o Rutgers School of Dental
Medicine
185 S Orange Ave., MSB C-636
Newark, NJ 07103
Tsiagbe, Vincent K., PhD, President

Bikers Against Breast Cancer
[13900]
PO Box 3183
Newark, NJ 07103
PH: (973)819-3519
Green-Barnhill, Shelia, Founder,
CEO

Center for Seafarers' Rights [5574]
118 Export St.
Newark, NJ 07114
PH: (973)589-5828
Fax: (973)817-8565
Stevenson, Douglas B., Director

Community College Humanities As-
sociation [8004]
Essex County College
303 University Ave.
Newark, NJ 07102
PH: (973)877-3577
Fax: (973)877-3578
Berry, Prof. David, Exec. Dir.

Devils Fan Club [24073]
Prudential Ctr.
25 Lafayette St.
Newark, NJ 07102-3611
PH: (201)768-9680
Stetter, Trudy, President

Eighteenth-Century Scottish Studies
Society [7983]
New Jersey Institute of Technology
University Heights
Newark, NJ 07102-1982
Sher, Prof. Richard B., Exec. Sec.

Expansionist Party of the United
States [18889]
295 Smith St.
Newark, NJ 07106-2517
PH: (973)416-6151
Schoonmaker, L. Craig, Chairman

HEART 9/11: Healing Emergency
Aid Response Team 9/11 [11667]
614 Frelinghuysen Ave.
Newark, NJ 07114
Keegan, Bill, Founder, President

International Institute for Scientific
and Academic Collaboration
[12167]
15 Honiss Pl., Ste. 1
Newark, NJ 07104
PH: (973)699-2550
Huang, Dr. Ngan, Chairperson

National Association of Black Law
Enforcement Officers [5487]
PO Box 1182
Newark, NJ 07102
PH: (401)465-9152
Wilson, Charles P., Chairman

National Black United Fund [12404]
17 Academy St.
Newark, NJ 07102
PH: (973)643-5122
Toll free: 800-223-0866
Williams, J. Robert, Chairman

One Heart for Haiti [11730]
54 Barbara St.
Newark, NJ 07105
PH: (973)589-6611
Fax: (973)817-8011
Parlapiano, Joe, Founder, CEO

Worldwide Dragonfly Association
[6618]
c/o Jessica Ware, Secretary
206 Boyden Hall
Dept. of Biological Sciences
Rutgers University
195 University Ave.
Newark, NJ 07102
Fincke, Ola, President

Unexpected Wildlife Refuge [10706]
PO Box 765
Newfield, NJ 08344-0765
PH: (856)697-3541
Summerville, Sarah, Director

Hungarian Scouts Association
[12853]
c/o Gabor Szorad
2850 Route 23 N
Newfoundland, NJ 07435-1443
PH: (973)874-0384
Szorad, Gabor, Gen. Sec.

International Longshoremen's As-
sociation [23474]
5000 W Side Ave.
North Bergen, NJ 07047
PH: (212)425-1200
Fax: (212)425-2928
Knott, Stephen, Secretary, Treasurer

Association of Commercial Profes-
sionals - Life Sciences [1597]
1691 Holly Rd.
North Brunswick, NJ 08902
PH: (908)824-0318
Drucker, Chuck, President

Educate These Children [11228]
5 Meadow Ct.
Norwood, NJ 07648
PH: (201)767-5806

Triple Negative Breast Cancer
Foundation [13853]
PO Box 204
Norwood, NJ 07648
PH: (646)942-0242
Dinerman, Hayley, Exec. Dir. (Actg.)

Association for Pet Loss and
Bereavement [12453]
PO Box 55
Nutley, NJ 07110
PH: (718)382-0690
Dwyer, Joe, President

Sri Lanka Wildlife Conservation
Society [4892]
127 Kingsland St.
Nutley, NJ 07110

PH: (973)667-0576
Corea, Ravi, CEO, President

National Association of Health and
Educational Facilities Finance
Authorities [1590]
PO Box 906
Oakhurst, NJ 07755
Toll free: 888-414-5713
Murr, Donna, President, Director

Railroad Station Historical Society
[10189]
c/o Jim Dent, Business Manager
26 Thackeray Rd.
Oakland, NJ 07436-3312
PH: (212)818-8085
Dent, Jim, Bus. Mgr.

Radiation and Public Health Project
[17036]
PO Box 1260
Ocean City, NJ 08226
Mangano, Joseph, Exec. Dir.

American Academy of Orofacial Pain
[14385]
174 S New York Ave.
Oceanville, NJ 08231
PH: (609)504-1311
Fax: (609)573-5064
Cleveland, Kenneth, Exec. Dir.

Egg Cup Collectors' Corner [21651]
c/o Joan George
67 Stevens Ave.
Old Bridge, NJ 08857
George, Joan, Contact

National Senior Golf Association
[22889]
200 Perrine Rd., Ste. 201
Old Bridge, NJ 08857-2842
Toll free: 800-282-6772
Fax: (732)525-9590
Gartenfeld, Mr. Mark, Operations
Mgr.

British American Educational
Foundation [8061]
c/o Laurel Zimmermann, Executive
Director
520 Summit Ave.
Oradell, NJ 07649
PH: (201)261-4438
Zimmermann, Laurel, Exec. Dir.

Armenian Missionary Association of
America [19706]
31 W Century Rd.
Paramus, NJ 07652
PH: (201)265-2607
Fax: (201)265-6015
Filian, Mr. Levon, Exec. Dir.

Motor Bus Society [21444]
PO Box 261
Paramus, NJ 07653-0261
Mandros, Dino, President

National Council of Young Israel
[20271]
50 Eisenhower Dr., Ste. 102
Paramus, NJ 07652
PH: (212)929-1525
Toll free: 800-617-NCYI
Fax: (212)727-9526
Weiss, Farley, President

Neshama: Association of Jewish
Chaplains [19936]
50 Eisenhower Dr.
Paramus, NJ 07652
PH: (973)929-3168
Kaprow, Moe, President

Hydraulic Institute [1734]
6 Campus Dr., 1st Fl. N
Parsippany, NJ 07054-4405

PH: (973)267-9700
Fax: (973)267-9055
Harris, George, Chairman

Lambda Theta Phi Latin Fraternity
[23759]
181 New Rd., Ste. 304
Parsippany, NJ 07054-5625
Toll free: 866-4-A-LAMBDA
Grajales, José, President

Ukrainian National Association
[19680]
2200 Route 10
Parsippany, NJ 07054
Toll free: 800-253-9862
Fax: (973)292-0900
Kaczaraj, Stefan, President

Vishwam [12581]
3 Eastmans Rd.
Parsippany, NJ 07054-3702
PH: (973)886-8170
Swami, Nishwant, Founder

Slovak Catholic Sokol [19649]
205 Madison St.
Passaic, NJ 07055
Toll free: 800-886-7656
Fax: (973)779-8245
Horvath, Michael J, President

Electrochemical Society [6198]
Bldg. D
65 S Main St.
Pennington, NJ 08534-2827
PH: (609)737-1902
Fax: (609)737-2743
Calvo, Roque J., Exec. Dir.

Fund for an OPEN Society [17978]
3403 Palace Ct., Ste. C
Pennsauken, NJ 08109
PH: (856)910-9210
Klein, Mrs. Arlene, Chairwoman

American Auditory Society [15168]
PO Box 779
Pennsville, NJ 08070
Toll free: 877-746-8315
Fax: (650)763-9185
Abrams, Harvey, President, Comm.
Chm.

Association of Military Osteopathic
Physicians and Surgeons [16519]
PO Box 4
Phillipsburg, NJ 08865-0004
PH: (908)387-1750
Fax: (866)925-8568
Wilson, Stephanie, Exec. Dir.

African Studies Association [8776]
Rutgers University Livingston
Campus
54 Joyce Kilmer Ave.
Piscataway, NJ 08854
PH: (848)445-8173
Fax: (732)445-1366
DeLancey, Renee, Mgr.

American Society of Perfumers
[1449]
PO Box 1256
Piscataway, NJ 08855-1256
PH: (201)500-6101
Fax: (877)732-0090
Krivda, James, Secretary

BAPS Charities, Inc. [13033]
81 Suttons Ln., Ste. 103
Piscataway, NJ 08854-5723
Toll free: 888-227-3881
Patel, Mr. Nilkanth, President

IEEE - Aerospace and Electronics
Systems Society [6422]
445 Hoes Ln.
Piscataway, NJ 08854-4141

PH: (571)220-9257
Pace, Teresa, President

IEEE - Broadcast Technology
Society [7306]
445 Hoes Ln.
Piscataway, NJ 08854
PH: (732)562-6061
Fax: (732)981-1769
Hayes, William T., President

IEEE - Components, Packaging, and
Manufacturing Technology Society
[6424]
445 Hoes Ln.
Piscataway, NJ 08854
PH: (732)562-5529
Fax: (732)465-6435
Tickman, Marsha, Exec. Dir.

IEEE Computational Intelligence
Society [6555]
c/o Jo-Ellen B. Snyder, Senior
Administrator
445 Hoes Ln.
Piscataway, NJ 08855
PH: (732)465-5892
Fax: (732)465-6435
Estevez, pablo, President

IEEE - Electromagnetic Compatibility
Society [6426]
445 Hoes Ln.
Piscataway, NJ 08855-6802
PH: (732)562-5539
Fax: (732)981-0225
Sabath, F, President

IEEE - Electron Devices Society
[6427]
IEEE Operations Ctr.
445 Hoes Ln.
Piscataway, NJ 08854
PH: (732)562-3926
Fax: (732)235-1626
Gilbert, Kellie, Administrator

IEEE - Engineering in Medicine and
Biology Society [6112]
445 Hoes Ln.
Piscataway, NJ 08854
PH: (732)981-3433
Fax: (732)465-6435
Wolf, Laura J., Exec. Dir.

IEEE-Eta Kappa Nu [23737]
445 Hoes Ln.
Piscataway, NJ 08854
PH: (732)465-5846
Toll free: 800-406-2590
Fax: (732)465-5808
Ramesh, S.K., President

IEEE - Industry Applications Society
[6722]
445 Hoes Ln.
Piscataway, NJ 08854
PH: (732)465-5804
McCarren, Patrick, Exec. Dir.

IEEE - Magnetics Society [6429]
445 Hoes Ln.
Piscataway, NJ 08855-0459
PH: (908)981-0060
Fax: (908)981-0225
Terris, Bruce, President

IEEE - Photonics Society [6430]
445 Hoes Ln.
Piscataway, NJ 08854-1331
PH: (732)562-3926
Fax: (732)562-8434
Choquette, Kent, President

IEEE - Power Electronics Society
[6431]
445 Hoes Ln.
Piscataway, NJ 08855-1331
Florek, Ms. Donna, Specialist

IEEE - Power Engineering Society
[6410]
445 Hoes Ln.
Piscataway, NJ 08854-1331
PH: (732)562-3883
Fax: (732)562-3881
Ryan, Patrick P., Exec. Dir.

IEEE - Professional Communication
Society [6432]
445 Hoes Ln.
Piscataway, NJ 08854-6804
PH: (732)981-0060
Toll free: 800-678-4333
Fax: (732)981-0225
Labun, Carolyn, Secretary

IEEE - Robotics and Automation
Society [7104]
445 Hoes Ln.
Piscataway, NJ 08854
PH: (732)562-3906
    (732)562-6585
Colabaugh, Kathy, Specialist

IEEE - Signal Processing Society
[5853]
445 Hoes Ln.
Piscataway, NJ 08854-4141
PH: (732)562-3888
Fax: (732)235-1627
Baseil, Rich, Exec. Dir.

IEEE - Solid-State Circuits Society
[6411]
445 Hoes Ln.
Piscataway, NJ 08854
PH: (732)981-3400
    (732)981-3410
Fax: (732)981-3401
Kelly, Mike

NALGAP: The Association of
Lesbian, Gay, Bisexual, and Trans-
gender Addiction Professionals and
Their Allies [13155]
c/o Phil McCabe
Rutgers School of Public Health/
OPHP
683 Hoes Ln.
Piscataway, NJ 08854
PH: (937)972-9537
McCabe, Philip T., President

Academy of Medical-Surgical Nurses
[16079]
PO Box 56
Pitman, NJ 08071
Toll free: 866-877-2676
Fax: (856)589-7463
Nowicki Hnatiuk, Cynthia, CEO

American Academy of Ambulatory
Care Nursing [16083]
E Holly Ave.
Pitman, NJ 08071-0056
Toll free: 800-262-6877
Cox, Debra L., President

American Nephrology Nurses' As-
sociation [15871]
E Holly Ave.
Pitman, NJ 08071-0056
PH: (856)256-2320
Fax: (856)589-7463
Cunningham, Mike, Exec. Dir.

Certification Board for Urologic
Nurses and Associates [17550]
E Holly Ave.
Pitman, NJ 08071-0056
PH: (856)256-2351
Borch, Marianne, President

Gerontological Advanced Practice
Nurses Association [14891]
Box 56 E Holly Ave.
Pitman, NJ 08071-0056

PH: (866)355-1392

Histiocytosis Association [15233]
332 N Broadway
Pitman, NJ 08071
PH: (856)589-6606
Fax: (856)589-6614
Toughhill, Jeffrey M., CEO, President

JEM Cure for CLL [15535]
140 S Broadway
Pitman, NJ 08071
PH: (856)256-1490
Cesare, Dennis, Contact

Society of Urologic Nurses and As-
sociates [16187]
Box 56
E Holly Ave.
Pitman, NJ 08071-0056
PH: (856)256-2335
Toll free: 888-827-7862
Fax: (856)589-7463
Spears, Vanessa, President

United Sportsman's Association of
North America [22508]
224 Sand Bridge Rd.
Pittsgrove, NJ 08318-3613
PH: (856)358-4891

National Black Bridal Association
[446]
68 Abbond Ct.
Plainfield, NJ 07063
Toll free: 888-299-2250
Magee, Dion, President

Drinking Water for India, Inc.
[13321]
PO Box 244
Plainsboro, NJ 08536-0244
PH: (609)843-0176

Independent Association of Publish-
ers' Employees [23511]
5 Schalks Crossing Rd., Ste. 220
Plainsboro, NJ 08536
PH: (609)275-6020
Toll free: 800-325-4273
Fax: (609)275-6023
Johnson, Robert, Treasurer

Descendants of Founders of New
Jersey [20750]
c/o Evelyn Ogden, Registrar
816 Grove St.
Point Pleasant Beach, NJ 08742
Hahn, Gail Bennett, Gov., Rec. Sec.

Knights of Life Motorcycle Club
[12826]
53 Jefferson Ave.
Pompton Lakes, NJ 07442
Festa, John P., President

Aging with Autism [13738]
704 Marten Rd.
Princeton, NJ 08540
PH: (908)904-9319
Hayes, Dr. Cyndy, President,
Founder

Alumni Association of Princeton
University [19301]
PO Box 291
Princeton, NJ 08542-0291
PH: (609)258-1900
Wieser, Jeffrey N., President

American College of Orgonomy
[16450]
PO Box 490
Princeton, NJ 08542
PH: (732)821-1144
Fax: (732)821-0174
Baker, Dr. Elsworth F., Founder

American Ethnological Society
[5902]
c/o Carol Greenhouse, President
125 Aaron Burr Hall

Princeton, NJ 08544
PH: (609)258-7369
Gusterson, Hugh, Asst. Pres.

American Iranian Council [18574]
PO Box 707
Princeton, NJ 08542-0707
PH: (609)252-9099
Fax: (609)252-9698
Johnston, J. Bennett, Jr., Chairman

American Literature Association
[9750]
Dept. of English
Princeton University
Princeton, NJ 08544
Bendixen, Prof. Alfred, Exec. Dir.

American Parliamentary Debate As-
sociation [8593]
1 Whig Hall
Princeton University
Princeton, NJ 08544
Demsas, Jerusalem

American Society of Group
Psychotherapy and Psychodrama
[16964]
301 N Harrison St., No. 508
Princeton, NJ 08540
PH: (609)737-8500
Fax: (609)737-8510
Condon, Linda, President

APMI International [6840]
105 College Rd. E
Princeton, NJ 08540-6992
PH: (609)452-7700
Fax: (609)987-8523
Trombino, C. James, Exec. Dir.,
CEO

Business Today [7548]
48 University Pl.
Princeton, NJ 08544
PH: (609)258-1111
Hastings, Jonathan, President

The Charlotte W. Newcombe
Foundation [11580]
35 Park Pl.
Princeton, NJ 08542-6918
PH: (609)924-7022
Wilfrid, Thomas N., Exec. Dir.

Community Options, Inc. [11563]
16 Farber Rd.
Princeton, NJ 08540
PH: (609)951-9900
Fax: (609)951-9112
Stack, Robert, Founder, President,
CEO

Construction Financial Management
Association [862]
100 Village Blvd., Ste. 200
Princeton, NJ 08540
PH: (609)452-8000
Toll free: 888-421-9996
Fax: (609)452-0474
Binstock, Stuart, President, CEO

Council of Ivy League Presidents
[23224]
228 Alexander St., 2nd Fl.
Princeton, NJ 08540-7121
PH: (609)258-6426
Fax: (609)258-1690
Harris, Ms. Robin, Exec. Dir.

Diabetes Advocacy Alliance [14523]
Novo Nordisk Inc.
100 College Rd. W
Princeton, NJ 08540
Geigle, Ron, Contact

Fellowship in Prayer [20061]
291 Witherspoon St.
Princeton, NJ 08542-3227

PH: (609)924-6863
Newton, David, President

IEEE - Society on Social Implica-
tions of Technology [7271]
c/o Terri Bookman, Managing Editor
PO Box 7465
Princeton, NJ 08543
Bookman, Terri, Editor

International Panel on Fissile Materi-
als [18749]
Princeton University
221 Nassau St., 2nd Fl.
Princeton, NJ 08542
PH: (609)258-4677
Fax: (609)258-3661
Burnett, Nancy A., Program Mgr.

International Schools Services
[8105]
15 Roszel Rd.
Princeton, NJ 08543-5910
PH: (609)452-0990
Fax: (609)452-2690
Stitt, Malcolm, Dir. of Info. Technol-
ogy

ITAP International Alliance [683]
353 Nassau St., 1st Fl.
Princeton, NJ 08540
Bing, Catherine Mercer, CEO

Metal Injection Molding Association
[2354]
105 College Rd. E
Princeton, NJ 08540-6992
PH: (609)452-7700
Fax: (609)987-8523
Trombino, C. James, Exec. Dir.

Metal Powder Industries Federation
[2355]
105 College Rd. E
Princeton, NJ 08540
PH: (609)452-7700
Abbott, Turner T., Mgr.

Metal Powder Producers Association
[2356]
Metal Powder Institute Federation
105 College Rd. E
Princeton, NJ 08540-6992
PH: (609)452-7700
Fax: (609)987-8523
Howard, Dean, President

NAFA Fleet Management Associa-
tion [297]
125 Village Blvd., Ste. 200
Princeton, NJ 08540
PH: (609)720-0882
Fax: (609)452-8004
Alfson, Ruth A., President

Naturopathic Medicine for Global
Health [15863]
PO Box 483
Princeton, NJ 08540
PH: (609)310-1340
Cunningham, Carlos, ND, CEO,
Founder

Play Soccer Nonprofit International
[10492]
PO Box 106
Princeton, NJ 08542-0106
PH: (609)683-4941
    (609)651-0854
McPherson, Ms. Judy, Exec. Dir.,
Chmn. of the Bd.

Shark Research Institute [6811]
PO Box 40
Princeton, NJ 08540
PH: (609)921-3522
Fax: (609)921-1505
Levine, Marie, Exec. Dir.

Tobacco Merchants Association
[3287]
PO Box 8019
Princeton, NJ 08543-8019
PH: (609)275-4900
Fax: (609)275-8379
Delman, Farrell, President

Travel Goods Association [3399]
301 N Harrison St., No. 412
Princeton, NJ 08540-3512
Toll free: 877-842-1938
Fax: (877)842-1938
Pittenger, Michele Marini, President,
CEO

TRI Princeton [3274]
601 Prospect Ave.
Princeton, NJ 08542
PH: (609)430-4820
Graham, David E., Chairperson

USRowing [23113]
2 Wall St.
Princeton, NJ 08540
PH: (609)751-0700
Toll free: 800-314-4769
Fax: (609)924-1578
Cipollone, Peter, Rep.

Woodrow Wilson National Fellowship
Foundation [7930]
5 Vaughn Dr., Ste. 300
Princeton, NJ 08540-6313
PH: (609)452-7007
Fax: (609)452-0066
Sanford, Ms. Beverly, Secretary, VP,
Comm.

Acoustic Emission Working Group
[5851]
c/o Mark Carlos, Secretary-
Treasurer
MISTRAS Group Inc.
195 Clarksville Rd.
Princeton Junction, NJ 08550
PH: (609)716-4030
Kosnik, Dr. David, Chairman

American Dystonia Society [15899]
17 Suffolk Ln.
Princeton Junction, NJ 08550
PH: (310)237-5478
Fax: (609)275-5663
Valero, Noel, Founder, President

Event Service Professionals As-
sociation [2327]
191 Clarksville Rd.
Princeton Junction, NJ 08550
PH: (609)799-3712
Fax: (609)799-7032
McCullough, Lynn, Exec. Dir.

Hands to Clinical Labs of Third
World Countries [15519]
5 Compton Ln.
Princeton Junction, NJ 08550
PH: (609)468-5673
Fax: (609)301-8737
Goel, Mahesh, Founder

Healthcare Manufacturers Manage-
ment Council [15077]
191 Clarksville Rd.
Princeton Junction, NJ 08550
PH: (609)297-2211
Fax: (609)799-7032
LoDuca, Gerry, President

International Card Manufacturers
Association [2626]
191 Clarksville Rd.
Princeton Junction, NJ 08550-5391
PH: (609)799-4900
Fax: (609)799-7032
Barnhart, Jeffrey E., Exec. Dir.,
Founder

International Function Point Users
Group [642]
191 Clarksville Rd.
Princeton Junction, NJ 08550
PH: (609)799-4900
Fax: (609)799-7032
Lawrence, Kriste, Officer

MediaGlobal [12170]
7 Whitney Pl.
Princeton Junction, NJ 08550
PH: (609)716-1296
Fax: (609)716-1297
Nalavala, Nosh, Exec. Dir.

National Association of Independent
Lighting Distributors [2102]
191 Clarksville Rd.
Princeton Junction, NJ 08550
PH: (609)297-2216
Fax: (609)799-7032
Watt, Robin, Secretary, Treasurer

North American Association of Com-
mencement Officers [7968]
191 Clarksville Rd.
Princeton Junction, NJ 08550
PH: (254)710-8534
Toll free: 877-622-2606
Walker, Lisa, President

Smart Card Alliance [7293]
191 Clarksville Rd.
Princeton Junction, NJ 08550
Toll free: 800-556-6828
Fax: (609)799-7032
Vanderhoof, Randy, Exec. Dir.

Technology Channel Association
[7658]
191 Clarksville Rd.
Princeton Junction, NJ 08550-5391
PH: (609)799-4900
Fax: (609)799-7032
Ponts, Jeff, President

United Front Against Riverblindness
[17536]
PO Box 218
Princeton Junction, NJ 08550
PH: (609)771-3674
Shungu, Dr. Daniel L., Exec. Dir.,
Chairman

International Isotope Society [6054]
c/o David Hesk, Executive Secretary
Merck Research Laboratories
126 E Lincoln Ave.
Rahway, NJ 07065
ElMasri, Marwan, President

North American Shippers Association
[3099]
1600 St. Georges Ave., Ste. 301
Rahway, NJ 07065
PH: (732)850-7610
Fax: (732)340-9133
Ballas, Stephen, President

American Association of Professional
Technical Analysts [3206]
c/o Larry McMillan, Treasurer
39 Meadowbrook Rd.
Randolph, NJ 07869
Young, Jeanette, President

Sturge-Weber Foundation [15993]
1240 Sussex Tpke., Ste. 1
Randolph, NJ 07869
PH: (973)895-4445
Toll free: 800-627-5482
Fax: (973)895-4846
Ball, Karen L., President, CEO

American Association of Dental Office Managers [15568]
125 Half Mile Rd., Ste. 200
Red Bank, NJ 07701

PH: (732)842-9977
Colicchio, Heather, Founder,
President

HealthyWomen [17757]
PO Box 430
Red Bank, NJ 07701
PH: (732)530-3425
Toll free: 877-986-9472
Fax: (732)865-7225
Battaglino, Beth, Founder

Collectors of Religion on Stamps
[22322]
c/o Matthew C. Brogan, President
308 Stevens Ave.
Ridgewood, NJ 07450-5204

National Coalition of Estheticians,
Manufacturers/Distributors and As-
sociations [925]
484 Spring Ave.
Ridgewood, NJ 07450-4624
PH: (201)670-4100
Fax: (201)670-4265
Warfield, Susanne S., Exec. Dir.

Pharma & Biopharma Outsourcing
Association [2566]
10 Alta Vista Dr.
Ringwood, NJ 07456
PH: (201)788-7994
Roth, Gil, President

International Match Safe Association
[21674]
PO Box 227
Riverdale, NJ 07457
PH: (973)835-2803

American Lead Poisoning Help As-
sociation [17494]
PO Box 403
Riverside, NJ 08075
Howell, Leann, Exec. Dir., President

Drug, Chemical & Associated
Technologies Association [2557]
1 Union St., Ste. 208
Robbinsville, NJ 08691
PH: (609)208-1888
Toll free: 800-640-3228
Fax: (609)208-0599
Timony, Margaret M., Exec. Dir.

Organization for Entrepreneurial
Development [7566]
21 Pine St., Ste. 109
Rockaway, NJ 07866
Toll free: 800-767-0999
Fax: (973)784-1099

Communications Fraud Control As-
sociation [1786]
4 Becker Farm Rd., 4th Fl.
Roseland, NJ 07068
PH: (973)871-4032
Fax: (973)871-4075
Aronoff, Roberta, Exec. Dir.

Help Darfur Now [18307]
51 Schweinberg Dr.
Roseland, NJ 07068
Wisotsky, Arielle, Founder, VP

Telecommunications Risk Manage-
ment Association [3242]
4 Becker Farm Rd.
Roseland, NJ 07068
PH: (973)871-4080
Fax: (973)871-4075
Roberts, Tom, Partner

Angelwish [10856]
PO Box 186
Rutherford, NJ 07070
PH: (201)672-0722
Mehta, Shimmy, Founder, CEO

CPA Associates International [23]
Meadows Office Complex
301 Route 17
Rutherford, NJ 07070
PH: (201)804-8686
Fax: (201)804-9222
Burnett, Michael J., Secretary

North American Celtic Trade As-
sociation [9149]
27 Addison Ave.
Rutherford, NJ 07070-2303
PH: (201)842-9922
Fax: (201)804-9143
Hughes, Cheryl, VP

Moore Stephens North America, Inc.
[42]
Plaza II, Ste. 200
250 Pehle Ave., Park 80 W
Saddle Brook, NJ 07663
PH: (201)291-2660
Fax: (201)368-1944
Sacks, Steven E., CPA, Exec. Dir.

Hepatitis C Association, Inc. [15255]
1351 Cooper Rd.
Scotch Plains, NJ 07076-2844
PH: (908)769-8479
Simon, Sue, President

Tesla Memorial Society [10352]
21 Maddaket
Scotch Plains, NJ 07076-3136
Terbo, William H., Exec. Sec.

Association for Historical Fencing
[22830]
PO Box 2013
Secaucus, NJ 07096-2013
Peterson, Mr. Ivan, President

Office Furniture Distribution Associa-
tion [3475]
PO Box 2548
Secaucus, NJ 07096
Russo, Domenico, Chairman

The Prostate Net [14053]
PO Box 2192
Secaucus, NJ 07096-2192
Toll free: 888-477-6763
Fax: (270)294-1565
Simons, Virgil, Founder, President

American Nursing Informatics As-
sociation [16108]
200 E Holly Ave.
Sewell, NJ 08080
Toll free: 866-552-6404
Sengstack, Patricia, Bd. Member

Mariner Class Association [22646]
PO Box 273
Ship Bottom, NJ 08008
Toll free: 866-457-2582
Schuss, Russell E., President

New Eyes for the Needy [12293]
549 Millburn Ave.
Short Hills, NJ 07078-3330
PH: (973)376-4903
Gajano, Jean, Exec. Dir.

One in Four, Inc. [12931]
10 Shirlawn Dr.
Short Hills, NJ 07078
PH: (405)338-8046
Heinrichs, Kris, Bd. Member

Professional Autograph Dealers Association [21716]
c/o Stuart Lutz, Membership Chairman
784 Morris Tpke.
Short Hills, NJ 07078-2698
Toll free: 877-428-9362
Kaller, Seth, VP

Christopher and Dana Reeve
Foundation [17260]
636 Morris Tpke., Ste. 3A
Short Hills, NJ 07078
PH: (973)379-2690
    (973)467-8270
Toll free: 800-225-0292
Wilderotter, Peter T., President, CEO

InterCollegiate Tennis Association
[23300]
174 Tamarack Cir.
Skillman, NJ 08558-2021
PH: (609)497-6920
Fax: (609)497-9586
Benjamin, David A., Exec. Dir.

Secondary School Admission Test
Board [8691]
862 Route 518
Skillman, NJ 08558
PH: (609)683-5558
Fax: (609)683-4507
Hoerle, Heather, Exec. Dir.

Muslim Women's Coalition [20501]
1283 Highway 27
Somerset, NJ 08873
PH: (732)545-8833
    (732)745-4844
Fax: (732)545-3423
Shamim, Tasneem, MD, Exec. Dir.

American Romney Breeders Association [4662]
c/o Chris Posbergh, President
381 Burnt Mill Rd.
Somerville, NJ 08876
PH: (908)310-8548
Mast, JoAnn, Secretary, Treasurer

Equipment Managers Council of
America [806]
PO Box 794
South Amboy, NJ 08879-0794
PH: (732)354-7264
Eder, Mike

Aphra Behn Society [10363]
Seton Hall University
Dept. of English
400 S Orange Ave.
South Orange, NJ 07079
Gevirtz, Dr. Karen, President

International Association of
Genocide Scholars [18308]
c/o Borislava Manojlovic, Secretary-
Treasurer
Seton Hall University
400 S Orange Ave.
South Orange, NJ 07079
Feierstein, Prof. Daniel, President

International Federation of Stamp
Dealers' Associations [22335]
c/o Sam Malamud, Vice President
161 Helen St.
South Plainfield, NJ 07080
PH: (908)548-8088
Fax: (908)822-7379
Johnson, Richard, President

National Police Officers Association
of America [5510]
150 Maple Ave., No. 224
South Plainfield, NJ 07080-0663
Fax: (908)226-8715

Society of Polish-American Travel
Agents [3396]
36 Main St.
South River, NJ 08882
PH: (732)390-1750

National Council of Certified
Dementia Practitioners [15965]
1 A Main St., Ste. 8
Sparta, NJ 07871-1909

PH: (973)729-6601
Toll free: 877-729-5191
Fax: (973)860-2244
Stimson, Sandra, CALA, CEO

Christian Missions in Many Lands
[20401]
PO Box 13
Spring Lake, NJ 07762-0013
PH: (732)449-8880
Fax: (732)974-0888
Dadd, Robert F., President

International Boxing Federation
[22711]
899 Mountain Ave., Ste. 2C
Springfield, NJ 07081
PH: (973)564-8046
Fax: (973)564-8751
Peoples, Daryl J., President

Russian Nobility Association in
America [20994]
c/o Roberta Maged
DRG International, Inc.
841 Mountain Ave.
Springfield, NJ 07081
Geacintov, Dr. Cyril E., President

Association of Lifecasters
International [10208]
18 Bank St.
Summit, NJ 07901
PH: (908)273-5600
Fax: (908)273-9256
McCormick, Edmund, Director

Clan Currie Society [20805]
PO Box 541
Summit, NJ 07902-0541
Currie, Robert, President

Family Promise, Inc. [11950]
71 Summit Ave.
Summit, NJ 07901
PH: (908)273-1100
Fax: (908)273-0030
Hardy, Cary, Chairman

Programmers Guild [7290]
PO Box 1250
Summit, NJ 07902-1250
Berry, Mr. Kim, President

International Miniature Aircraft Association [22413]
1 Campbell Dr.
Sussex, NJ 07461
PH: (973)875-9584

Beyond Tears Worldwide [12628]
123 Saratoga Ln.
Swedesboro, NJ 08085
PH: (570)309-0324
Kjellson, Emily, Contact

Official Gumby Fan Club [24005]
5 Hanley Ct.
Tabernacle, NJ 08088
PH: (609)268-6680
Toll free: 877-988-6900

Association of Avian Veterinarians
[17634]
PO Box 9
Teaneck, NJ 07666
PH: (720)458-4111
Fax: (720)398-3496
Welle, Kenneth, President

Association of Jewish Libraries
[9685]
PO Box 1118
Teaneck, NJ 07666
PH: (201)371-3255
Warshenbrot, Amalia

International Association of Medical
Equipment Remarketers and Ser-
vicers [15687]
85 Edgemont Pl.
Teaneck, NJ 07666-4605

PH: (201)357-5400
Fax: (201)833-2021
Fall, Jeff, VP

Retail Marketing Society [2300]
PO Box 3376
Teaneck, NJ 07666
PH: (201)692-8087
Fax: (201)692-1291
DeParis, Lawrence C., President

Risk Strategies Company [1924]
1086 Teaneck Rd., Ste. 5B
Teaneck, NJ 07666
PH: (201)837-1100
    (212)826-9744
Fax: (201)837-5050
Boak, Brian P., Contact

Sharsheret [14061]
1086 Teaneck Rd., Ste. 2G
Teaneck, NJ 07666
PH: (201)833-2341
Toll free: 866-474-2774
Fax: (201)837-5025
Shoretz, Rochelle, Exec. Dir.,
Founder

Association of Laboratory Managers
[6777]
c/o Dominion Administrators, LLC
PO Box 652
Tenafly, NJ 07670-0652

Children's Cardiomyopathy Founda-
tion [14107]
PO Box 547
Tenafly, NJ 07670
Toll free: 866-808-2873
Fax: (201)227-7016
Yue, Lisa, President, Exec. Dir.

Direct Marketing Fundraisers As-
sociation [1468]
PO Box 51
Tenafly, NJ 07670
PH: (646)675-7314
Fax: (201)266-4006
Froehlich, Steve, Director

Friends of Falun Gong [17848]
24 W Railroad Ave., No. 124
Tenafly, NJ 07670
Toll free: 866-343-7436
Adler, Alan, Exec. Dir.

Loss Executives Association [1884]
PO Box 37
Tenafly, NJ 07670
PH: (201)569-3346
Owens, Dean M., Contact

Oriental Rug Importers Association
[1956]
400 Tenafly Rd., No. 699
Tenafly, NJ 07670
PH: (201)866-5054
Fax: (201)866-6169
Momeni, Reza, President

SAFE-BioPharma Association [2571]
82 N Summit St., Ste. 2
Tenafly, NJ 07670-1018
PH: (201)925-2173
Celik, Emre, CEO, President

Society of African Missions [19906]
23 Bliss Ave.
Tenafly, NJ 07670-3001
PH: (201)567-0450
    (201)567-9085
Toll free: 800-670-8328
Fax: (201)541-1280
Paladino, Ms. Martha, Mgr.

Jewish Coaches Association [22732]
PO Box 167
Tennent, NJ 07763

PH: (732)322-5145
Belzer, Jason, Exec. Dir.

BioPharma Research Council [6111]
1 Sheila Dr.
Tinton Falls, NJ 07724
PH: (732)403-3137
Gere, Joanne, Exec. Dir.

The Fuller Society [20868]
42 Sugar Maple Ln.
Tinton Falls, NJ 07724
Yingst, Deb, Deputy, Gov.

Holiday Express [13297]
968 Shrewsbury Ave.
Tinton Falls, NJ 07724
PH: (732)544-8010
Fax: (732)544-8020
McLoone, Tim, Founder

The Inter-American Conductive
Education Association, Inc. [8584]
PO Box 3169
Toms River, NJ 08756-3169
PH: (732)797-2566
Toll free: 800-824-2232
Fax: (732)797-2599
Riley, Patrick F., President

North American Quilling Guild
[21302]
2422 Torrington Dr.
Toms River, NJ 08755-2556
Anderson, Ms. Rita, Dir. of Member
Svcs.

World Healthcare Educational
Resources, Etc. [15510]
17 Sun Ray Dr.
Toms River, NJ 08753
PH: (732)255-4738
Konn, Dr. Terry, Founder, Chairman

Babe Ruth Baseball/Softball [22546]
1770 Brunswick Ave.
Trenton, NJ 08648-4632
PH: (609)695-1434
Toll free: 800-880-3142
Fax: (609)695-2505
Tellefsen, Mr. Steven, CEO,
President

International Healthcare Volunteers
[15025]
PO Box 8231
Trenton, NJ 08650
PH: (609)259-8807
Ayers, Charletta, Chairperson

The League of Professional System
Administrators [6323]
PO Box 5161
Trenton, NJ 08638-0161
PH: (202)567-7201
Fax: (609)219-6787
Moore, Warner, Comm. Chm.

National Association of State
Aquaculture Coordinators [3645]
c/o Joe Myers, Secretary-Treasurer
PO Box 330
Trenton, NJ 08625
PH: (609)984-2502
Fax: (609)633-7229
Sloan, Debra, President

One Simple Wish [11107]
1977 N Olden Ave., No. 292
Trenton, NJ 08618
PH: (609)883-8484
Gletow, Danielle, Founder, Exec. Dir.

Bunker Family Association [20790]
c/o Gil Bunker, President
9 Sommerset Rd.
Turnersville, NJ 08012-2122
PH: (856)589-6140
    (520)940-7225
Bunker, Mr. Gil, President

Computer Measurement Group
[6244]
3501 Route 42, Ste. 130, No. 121
Turnersville, NJ 08012-1734
PH: (856)401-1700
   (303)773-7985
Drake, Bryan, Chairman

Holocaust Resource Center [18348]
Kean University
1000 Morris Ave.
Union, NJ 07083
PH: (908)737-5326
Morell, Ada, Chmn. of the Bd.

Food Institute [1327]
10 Mountainview Rd., Ste. S125
Upper Saddle River, NJ 07458
PH: (201)791-5570
Fax: (201)791-5222
Todd, Brian, President, CEO

Little Kids Rock [8373]
Bldg. E2
271 Grove Ave.
Verona, NJ 07044
PH: (973)746-8248
Fax: (973)746-8240
Wish, David, CEO, Founder

Beta Sigma Kappa [23840]
PO Box 1765
Voorhees, NJ 08043
Silbert Aumiller, Mira, Exec. Dir.

National Center for Environmental
   Health Strategies [14718]
c/o Mary Lamielle, Executive Direc-
   tor
1100 Rural Ave.
Voorhees, NJ 08043-2234
PH: (856)429-5358
Lamielle, Mary, Exec. Dir.

Tau Epsilon Phi Fraternity, Inc.
   [23934]
1000 White Horse Rd., Ste. 512
Voorhees, NJ 08043-4411
Koplon, Lane, Consul Gen.

United States Marine Safety As-
   sociation [5567]
5050 Industrial Rd., Ste. 2
Wall Township, NJ 07727
PH: (732)751-0102
Fax: (732)751-0508
Thompson, Tom, Exec. Dir.

Chinese American Society of
   Anesthesiology [13700]
4 Hickory Ln.
Warren, NJ 07059
Zhou, Henry Haifeng, President

Certified Audit of Circulations [116]
155 Willowbrook Blvd.
Wayne, NJ 07470
PH: (973)785-3000
Barrett, Stephen, Director

Childhood Cancer Society [13939]
189 Berdan Ave., No. 221
Wayne, NJ 07470
Head, Thomas M., Founder

Life Raft Group [14002]
155 Route 46 W, Ste. 202
Wayne, NJ 07470
PH: (973)837-9092
Fax: (973)837-9095
Scherzer, Norman, Exec. Dir.

Metropolitan Air Post Society
   [22344]
c/o Ernest Wheeler, President
7 Evelyn Ter.
Wayne, NJ 07470-3446
Wheeler, Ernest, President

Xaverian Missionaries of the United
   States [20483]
12 Helene Ct.
Wayne, NJ 07470
PH: (973)942-2975
Fax: (973)492-5012
Conforti, St. Guido, Founder

American Swan Boat Association
   Inc. [23079]
312 Duff Ave.
Wenonah, NJ 08090
PH: (856)468-4646
Fax: (856)468-4646

American Organization for Bodywork
   Therapies of Asia [15553]
PO Box 343
West Berlin, NJ 08091
PH: (856)809-2953
Fax: (856)809-2958
Mylin, Wayne, Mgr. Dir.

Ancient Order of Hibernians in
   America [19504]
PO Box 539
West Caldwell, NJ 07007
PH: (315)252-3895
Fax: (315)252-6996
McKay, James, VP

World for Christ Crusade [20476]
1005 Union Valley Rd.
West Milford, NJ 07480-1220
PH: (973)728-3267
Stelpstra, Rev. William, Founder,
   Director

Greenlaw Family Association
   [20874]
c/o Barbara Britton, Treasurer
104 W Upper Ferry Rd.
West Trenton, NJ 08628
Hernan, Richard A., Jr., President

Council of Hotel and Restaurant
   Trainers [1654]
PO Box 2835
Westfield, NJ 07091
PH: (908)389-9277
Toll free: 800-463-5918
Davey, Tara, Exec. Dir.

Poe Studies Association [9092]
c/o Carole Shaffer-Koros, Secretary-
   Treasurer
58 Normandy Dr.
Westfield, NJ 07090-3432
Phillips, Philip Edward, President

Rabbinic Center for Research and
   Counseling [16989]
PO Box 897
Westfield, NJ 07091-0897
PH: (908)233-0419
Fishbein, Rabbi Irwin H., Director

American Accordion Musicological
   Society [9849]
322 Haddon Ave.
Westmont, NJ 08108
PH: (856)854-6628
Darrow, Joanna, Officer

Concerned Persons for Adoption
   [10449]
PO Box 179
Whippany, NJ 07981
PH: (973)293-2621
Bennett, Pat, Comm. Chm.

National Exchange Carrier Association [3420]
c/o Kathy McNary, Director
80 S Jefferson Rd.
Whippany, NJ 07981-1009
Toll free: 800-228-8563
Hegmann, Bill, CEO, President

Accord Alliance [17189]
531 Route 22 E, No. 244
Whitehouse Station, NJ 08889
PH: (908)349-0534
Fax: (801)349-0534
Green, Janet, Exec. Dir.

National Life Center [12783]
686 N Broad St.
Woodbury, NJ 08096-1607
PH: (856)848-1819
   (856)848-5683
Toll free: 800-848-5683
Cocciolone, Denise F., Founder,
   President

The Moles [19659]
577 Chestnut Ridge Rd.
Woodcliff Lake, NJ 07677
PH: (201)930-1923
Fax: (201)930-8501
Junco, Kirk, Comm. Chm.

Research Institute for Fragrance
   Materials [1453]
50 Tice Blvd.
Woodcliff Lake, NJ 07677
PH: (201)689-8089
Mirzayantz, Nicolas, V. Chmn. of the
   Exec. Committee

North American Guild of Change
   Ringers [9987]
c/o A. Thomas Miller, Membership
   Secretary
229 Howard Ave.
Woodstown, NJ 08098-1249
Martin, Ann, Officer

Northeastern Weed Science Society
   [4447]
PO Box 25
Woodstown, NJ 08098
PH: (315)209-7580
Lingenfelter, Dwight, Comm. Chm.

American Chesapeake Club [21805]
c/o Joanne Silver, Membership
   Chairperson
412 Woodbury Dr.
Wyckoff, NJ 07481-1514
Colvin, JoAnn, Chairperson

NEW MEXICO

Arab World and Islamic Resources
   and School Services [8814]
PO Box 174
Abiquiu, NM 87510
PH: (505)685-4533
   (510)704-0517
Fax: (505)685-4533
Shabbas, Audrey, Exec. Dir.,
   President

F-4 Phantom II Society [21225]
PO Box 2680
Alamogordo, NM 88310
Thompson, Helen, Secretary

ACMHA: The College for Behavioral
   Health Leadership [15753]
7804 Loma del Norte Rd. NE
Albuquerque, NM 87109-5419
PH: (505)822-5038
Ericson, Dr. Kris, Exec. Dir.

Acupuncturists Without Borders
   [13501]
3538 Anderson SE
Albuquerque, NM 87106
PH: (505)266-3878

Alliance for Student Activities [8610]
1129 Ortega Rd. NW
Albuquerque, NM 87114
Fax: (505)212-0468

American Association of Public
   Health Veterinarians [17598]
PO Box 66419
Albuquerque, NM 87193
Baravik, Jeff, President

American Indian Council of
   Architects and Engineers [5952]
c/o Beverly Diddy, President
Beverly Diddy Designs, LLC
PO Box 36647
Albuquerque, NM 87176
PH: (505)884-4815
Fax: (505)884-4914
Begay, Jefferson, Bd. Member

American Indian Graduate Center
   [7922]
3701 San Mateo Blvd. NE, No. 200
Albuquerque, NM 87110
PH: (505)881-4584
Toll free: 800-628-1920
Fax: (505)884-0427
Bird, Michael, President

American Indian Science and
   Engineering Society [6531]
2305 Renard Pl. SE, Ste. 200
Albuquerque, NM 87106
PH: (505)765-1052
Fax: (505)765-5608
Echohawk, Sarah, CEO

American Portuguese Studies As-
   sociation [10169]
University of New Mexico
Dept. of Spanish and Portuguese
MSC03-2100
Albuquerque, NM 87131-0001
Lehnen, Leila, Secretary

American Ski-Bike Association
   [23212]
PO Box 65220
Albuquerque, NM 87193
PH: (505)350-9835
   (505)350-3844
Kimball, Randy, President, Chmn. of
   the Bd., Owner

American Society of Radiologic
   Technologists [15680]
15000 Central Ave. SE
Albuquerque, NM 87123-3909
PH: (505)298-4500
Toll free: 800-444-2778
Fax: (505)298-5063
Brennan, William J., Jr., Chmn. of
   the Bd.

American Theatre Critics Association
   [10240]
12809 Northern Sky NE
Albuquerque, NM 87111-8089
PH: (505)856-2101
Gaines, Barry, Administrator

Americans for Indian Opportunity
   [12374]
1001 Marquette Ave. NW
Albuquerque, NM 87102-1937
PH: (505)842-8677
Fax: (505)842-8658
Harris, Laura, Exec. Dir.

Archaeological Conservancy [5930]
1717 Girard Blvd. NE
Albuquerque, NM 87106
PH: (505)266-1540
Michel, Mark, CEO, President

Aril Society International [22085]
c/o Reita Jordan, Secretary
3500 Avenida Charada NW
Albuquerque, NM 87107-2604
Jordan, Reita, Secretary

Association of Educators in Imaging
   and Radiologic Sciences [17052]
PO Box 90204
Albuquerque, NM 87199-0204

PH: (505)823-4740
Christensen, Ms. Valerie, Exec. Sec.

Association of Firearm and Tool
Mark Examiners [5215]
5350 2nd St. NW
Albuquerque, NM 87107
PH: (505)823-4260

Catching the Dream [7923]
8200 Mountain Rd. NE, Ste. 203
Albuquerque, NM 87110-7856
PH: (505)262-2351
Fax: (505)262-0534
Lujan, James, President

Center for Nonviolent Communica-
tion [18716]
9301 Indian School Rd. NE, Ste.
204
Albuquerque, NM 87112-2861
PH: (505)244-4041
Toll free: 800-255-7696
Fax: (505)547-0414
Wisbauer, Stefan, Bd. Member

Citizens' Alliance for Responsible
Energy [6467]
PO Box 52103
Albuquerque, NM 87181
PH: (505)239-8998
Noon, Marita, Exec. Dir.

Clean Energy Alliance [1108]
c/o Suzanne Roberts, Director
1155 University Blvd. SE
Albuquerque, NM 87106
PH: (505)843-4091
Groelinger, James F., Exec. Dir.

Directed Energy Professional
Society [6472]
7770 Jefferson St. NE, Ste. 440
Albuquerque, NM 87109
PH: (505)998-4910
Fax: (505)998-4917
Maloney, Jeff, President

EC-Council [997]
101C Sun Ave. NE
Albuquerque, NM 87109
PH: (505)341-3228
Fax: (505)341-0050
Bavisi, Sanjay, President

Faith Encouragement Ministries
[20106]
PO Box 51776
Albuquerque, NM 87181-1776
PH: (505)255-3233
    (505)472-1992

Family Voices [14189]
3701 San Mateo Blvd. NE, Ste. 103
Albuquerque, NM 87110
PH: (505)872-4774
Toll free: 888-835-5669
Fax: (505)872-4780
Autin, Diana, Coord.

Federation of Indian Service
Employees [8395]
1218 Lomas Blvd. NW
Albuquerque, NM 87102-1856
PH: (505)243-4088
Toll free: 888-433-2382
Fax: (505)243-4098
Parton, Sue, President

Futures for Children [11232]
9600 Tennyson St. NE
Albuquerque, NM 87122
Toll free: 800-545-6843
Gomez, Teresa C., President, CEO

Gathering of Nations [10040]
3301 Coors Blvd. NW, Ste. R300
Albuquerque, NM 87120

PH: (505)836-2810

Global Health Partnerships [15459]
PO Box 4385
Albuquerque, NM 87196
Tomedi, Angelo, MD, President

Holistic Management International
[3882]
5941 Jefferson St. NE, Ste. B
Albuquerque, NM 87109
PH: (505)842-5252
Fax: (505)843-7900
Nuckols, Dan, Director, Chairman

Indian Arts and Crafts Association
[10041]
4010 Carlisle Blvd. NE, Ste. C
Albuquerque, NM 87107
PH: (505)265-9149
Fax: (505)265-8251
Ouellet, Kathi, President

International Biometals Society
[6838]
c/o Prof. Larry L. Barton, Secretary
Dept. of Biology, MSC03 2020
University of New Mexico
Albuquerque, NM 87131
PH: (505)277-2537
Fax: (505)277-0304
Barton, Prof. Larry L., Secretary

La Raza Unida Party [18891]
PO Box 40376
Albuquerque, NM 87196-0376

Mission Society of the Mother of
God of Boronyavo [20547]
1838 Palomas Dr. NE
Albuquerque, NM 87110
Fax: (505)256-1278
Zugger, Fr. Christopher L., Chap.,
Editor

National Council for Marketing and
Public Relations [8471]
5901 Wyoming Blvd. NE, No. J-254
Albuquerque, NM 87109
PH: (505)349-0500
Boehmer, Jennifer, President

National Indian Council on Aging,
Inc. [10524]
10501 Montgomery Blvd. NE, Ste.
210
Albuquerque, NM 87111
PH: (505)292-2001
Fax: (505)292-1922
DeLaCruz, James T., Sr., V. Chmn.
of the Bd.

National Indian Youth Council
[10044]
318 Elm St. SE
Albuquerque, NM 87102
PH: (505)247-2251
Fax: (505)247-4251

National Information Center for
Educational Media [8035]
c/o Access Innovations, Inc.
4725 Indian School Rd. NE, Ste.100
Albuquerque, NM 87110
Toll free: 800-926-8328
Fax: (505)256-1080
Pannell, Alan, Web Adm.

National Native American Law
Students Association [8221]
1001 Marquette Ave. NW
Albuquerque, NM 87102
PH: (505)289-0810
Mojado, Alexandra, Secretary

Operation Identity [10462]
1818 Somervell St. NE
Albuquerque, NM 87112

PH: (505)350-1344
Free, Barbara, VP

Phylaxis Society [19567]
PO Box 5675
Albuquerque, NM 87185-5675
Campbell, Robert, President

Prall Family Association [20916]
14104 Piedras Rd. NE
14104 Piedras Rd. NE
Albuquerque, NM 87123
Prall, Richard D., Editor

Radix Institute [13652]
3212 Monte Vista Blvd. NE
Albuquerque, NM 87106-2120
PH: (310)570-2439
    (808)256-3347
Lindsay, Melissa, Chairman

Restaurant Marketing and Delivery
Association [1396]
3636 Menaul Blvd. NE, Ste. 323
Albuquerque, NM 87110
Farmer, David, VP

Society of Vacuum Coaters [749]
71 Pinon Hill Pl. NE
Albuquerque, NM 87122
PH: (505)856-7188
Fax: (505)856-6716
Martinu, Ludvik, Officer

Southwest Research and Information
Center [18060]
105 Stanford SE
Albuquerque, NM 87196
PH: (505)262-1862
Fax: (505)262-1864
Pino, Manuel, President

Tamarind Institute [7948]
2500 Central Ave. SE
Albuquerque, NM 87106-3562
PH: (505)277-3901
Fax: (505)277-3920
Gaston, Diana, Director

Vietnam Security Police Association
[21162]
c/o Paul Shave, Membership
Chairperson
2909 Sol De Vida NW
Albuquerque, NM 87120
PH: (501)831-9401
Smith, Edwin, VP

American Toy Fox Terrier Club
[21825]
c/o Cindy Enroughty, President
143 County Road 2400
Aztec, NM 87410-9309
PH: (505)334-0380
    (585)729-1711

American Rottweiler Club [21819]
c/o Nancy Griego, President
PO Box 1004
Belen, NM 87002-1004
PH: (505)681-8020
Shaver, Jeff, Liaison

American Society of Picture Profes-
sionals [2574]
12126 Hwy. 14 N, No. A-4
Cedar Crest, NM 87008
PH: (505)281-3177
    (213)760-1176
Masterson, Michael, President

National Latino Behavioral Health
Association [15798]
6555 Robin St.
Cochiti Lake, NM 87083
PH: (505)980-5156
Mancini, Pierluigi, President

Center for Advancement of Public
Policy [18965]
323 Morning Sun Trl.
Corrales, NM 87048-9645

Natural Dyes International [7726]
HCR74, Box 21912
El Prado, NM 87529
Toll free: 800-665-9786
Collier, Robin, President

National Latino Alliance for the
Elimination of Domestic Violence
[11709]
PO Box 2787
Espanola, NM 87532
PH: (505)753-3334
Medina, Adelita Michelle, Exec. Dir.

American Amateur Baseball
Congress [22540]
100 W Broadway
Farmington, NM 87401
PH: (505)327-3120
Fax: (507)327-3132
Neely, Richard, President

Thai Burma Border Health Initiative
[17024]
1127 Boggio Dr.
Gallup, NM 87301
Crook, Larry, MD, President

Builders Without Borders [11965]
119 Main St.
Hillsboro, NM 88042
PH: (510)525-0525
Roff, Derek, Director

National Soaring Foundation [22490]
PO Box 684
Hobbs, NM 88240

One Love Worldwide [12708]
1223 El Caminito Dr.
Hobbs, NM 88240-0961
McMurray, Karli Sue, Founder, CEO

Soaring Society of America [22491]
PO Box 2100
Hobbs, NM 88241-2100
PH: (575)392-1177
Layton, Denise, COO

Animal Kind International [10576]
PO Box 300
Jemez Springs, NM 87025
Menczer, Karen, Founder, Exec. Dir.

American Society of Theatre
Consultants [816]
PO Box 22
La Luz, NM 88337
Toll free: 855-800-2782
Wilson, Duane, Secretary, CFO

Committee to Abolish Sport Hunting
[10604]
PO Box 13815
Las Cruces, NM 88013
PH: (575)640-7372
Miele, Joe, President

North American Invasive Species
Management Association [3553]
Bldg. 4, Ste. 5
205 W Boutz Rd.
Las Cruces, NM 88005
PH: (575)649-7157
Schultz, Rob, President

American Computer Scientists As-
sociation [6233]
General Delivery Box ACSA
Los Alamos, NM 87544-9999
Toll free: 888-532-5540
Vanoceur, Andrew, Chairman

Diabetic Supply Rescue [14533]
3060 Los Lentes Rd. SE
Los Lunas, NM 87031
PH: (505)565-8526
Koch, Jay, Founder

American Youth Horse Council
[4334]
1 Gainer Rd.
McDonald, NM 88262
PH: (817)320-2005
Fax: (575)356-3721
Nadeau, Jenifer, President

Spanish Barb Horse Association
[4410]
PO Box 30
Mule Creek, NM 88051-0030
Engler, Maggie, Treasurer

American Society of Parasitologists
[6993]
c/o Lee Couch, Secretary/Treasurer
76 Homesteads Rd.
Placitas, NM 87043
PH: (505)867-9480
Esch, Gerald W., President

Antique Tribal Art Dealers Association [236]
c/o Larry Cornelius, Treasurer
PO Box 45628
Rio Rancho, NM 87174
PH: (505)823-4560
    (415)863-3173
Fax: (415)431-1939
Begner, Steve, Treasurer

Antique Tribal Art Dealers Association [8837]
c/o Larry Cornelius, Treasurer
PO Box 45628
Rio Rancho, NM 87174
PH: (505)823-4560
    (415)863-3173
Fax: (415)431-1939
Begner, Steve, Treasurer

Overeaters Anonymous World
Service Office [12398]
6075 Zenith Ct. NE
Rio Rancho, NM 87144-6424
PH: (505)891-2664
Fax: (505)891-4320
Lippel, Naomi, Managing Dir.

Cowboy Mounted Shooting Association [23128]
PO Box 157
Roswell, NM 88202
PH: (719)426-2774
Toll free: 888-960-0003
Plaster, Dan, President

Lama Foundation [9540]
PO Box 240
San Cristobal, NM 87564-0240
PH: (575)586-1269
Fax: (206)984-0916
White, Megan, Coord.

3HO Foundation [20651]
PO Box 1560
Santa Cruz, NM 87567
Toll free: 888-346-2420
Fax: (424)731-8348
Bhajan, Yogi, Founder

Alliance for Nuclear Accountability
[18740]
c/o Nuclear Watch of New Mexico
903 W Alameda St., No. 505
Santa Fe, NM 87505-1681
PH: (505)989-7342
Sinha, Ashish, Prog. Dir.

American Society for Mass
Spectrometry [7223]
Bldg. I-1
2019 Galisteo St.
Santa Fe, NM 87505
PH: (505)989-4517
Fax: (505)989-1073
Brodbelt, Jennifer S., President

Architecture 2030 [4133]
607 Cerrillos Rd.
Santa Fe, NM 87505
PH: (505)988-5309
Mazria, Edward, CEO, Founder

Association of Food Journalists
[2662]
7 Avenida Vista Grande, Ste. B7,
No. 467
Santa Fe, NM 87508-9198
Moose, Debbie, President

Biographers International Organization [10364]
PO Box 33020
Santa Fe, NM 87594
Jones, Brian Jay, President

Bread for the Journey International
[12463]
101 Coronado Ln., Ste. 732
Santa Fe, NM 87505
Cacciatore, Marianna, Exec. Dir.

Concerned Citizens for Nuclear
Safety [18744]
107 Cienega St.
Santa Fe, NM 87501
PH: (505)986-1973
Fax: (505)986-0997
Arends, Joni, Exec. Dir.

Earth Care [7887]
Bldg. A
6600 Valentine Way
Santa Fe, NM 87507
PH: (505)983-6896
Gonzales, Jorge, President

Federation of Analytical Chemistry
and Spectroscopy Societies [6200]
Bldg. I
2019 Gallisteo St.
Santa Fe, NM 87505-2143
PH: (505)820-1648
Fax: (505)989-1073
Pettit, Cindi, Exec. Asst.

Forest Guild [3865]
2019 Galisteo St., Ste. N7
Santa Fe, NM 87505
PH: (505)983-8992
Fax: (505)986-0798
Evans, Zander, Dir. of Res.

Hanuman Foundation [11999]
Box 269
223 N Guadalupe St.
Santa Fe, NM 87501

Institute of American Indian Arts
[10042]
83 Avan Nu Po Rd.
Santa Fe, NM 87508-1300
PH: (505)424-2300
Fax: (505)424-0050
James, Jennifer, Librarian

International Institute for Building-
Biology and Ecology [4005]
PO Box 8520
Santa Fe, NM 87504
Toll free: 866-960-0333
Conn, Michael, Exec. Dir.

National New Deal Preservation Association [10068]
PO Box 602
Santa Fe, NM 87504-0602
PH: (505)473-3985
Flynn, Kathryn A., Exec. Dir.

Project Tibet [19191]
403 Canyon Rd.
Santa Fe, NM 87501
PH: (505)982-3002
Fax: (505)988-4142
Thundup, Paljor, Administrator

Saq' Be': Organization for Mayan
and Indigenous Spiritual Bodies
[9578]
PO Box 31111
Santa Fe, NM 87594
Rubel, Adam, Founder, Director

Society of Tempera Painters [8944]
c/o Michael Bergt, Tutor
PO Box 30766
Santa Fe, NM 87592-0766
PH: (505)473-9654
Bergt, Michael, Contact

Spanish Colonial Arts Society [9361]
750 Camino Lejo
Santa Fe, NM 87505
PH: (505)982-2226
Fax: (505)982-4585
Setford, David, Exec. Dir.

ThinkTwice Global Vaccine Institute
[15387]
PO Box 9638
Santa Fe, NM 87504
PH: (505)983-1856
Fax: (505)983-1856
Wright, Nathan, Contact

United States Human Proteome
Organization [6106]
Bldg. I-1
2019 Galisteo St.
Santa Fe, NM 87505
PH: (505)989-4876
Fax: (505)989-1073
Ahn, Natalie, Bd. Member

Water Engineers for the Americas
[13359]
1201 Parkway Dr.
Santa Fe, NM 87507
PH: (505)473-9211
Toll free: 800-460-5366
Fax: (505)471-6675
Fant, Peter, President

World Wide Martial Arts Association
[23034]
1000 Cordoval Pl., Ste. 505
Santa Fe, NM 87505
PH: (402)250-4618

African Wild Dog Conservancy
[4778]
208 N California Ave.
Silver City, NM 88061
Robbins, Dr. Robert, Founder

Western New Mexico University
Alumni Association [19372]
PO Box 680
Silver City, NM 88062
PH: (575)538-6675
Toll free: 800-872-9668
Moffett, Ms. Danielle, Director

Taos Watercolor Society [8893]
PO Box 282
Taos, NM 87571
PH: (575)224-3166
Blair, Karen McCurtain, President

Home Study Exchange [7995]
c/o Santa Fe Community School
PO Box 289
Torreon, NM 87061-0289
PH: (505)847-2909
Toll free: 866-703-9375

International Curly Horse Organization [4364]
322 Tulie Gate Rd.
Tularosa, NM 88352
PH: (575)740-4159
Richardson, Jackie, Registrar

NEW YORK

Indoor Gardening Society of America
[22103]
, NY
Fuchs, Tibor, VP

International Neuro-Linguistic
Programming Association [16979]
, NY
Faraone, Barbara, Exec. Dir.

Advancing the Gospel in Angola
[12605]
25 Maple St.
Addison, NY 14801-1009
Bloise, John R., President

Volvo Club of America [21520]
Box 16
Afton, NY 13730-0016
Fax: (607)639-2280

Academy of Certified Archivists
[8819]
1450 Western Ave., Ste. 101
Albany, NY 12203-3539
PH: (518)463-8644
Fax: (518)463-8656
Linn, Mott, President

Academy of Rehabilitative Audiology
[15165]
PO Box 2323
Albany, NY 12220-0323
Fax: (866)547-3073
Olsen, Anne D., PhD, President

American Academy of
Psychotherapists [16955]
1450 Western Ave., Ste. 101
Albany, NY 12203
PH: (518)694-5360
    (202)328-2035
Fax: (518)463-8656
Shaffer, Diane Christie, Secretary

Association of Financial Guaranty
Insurers [1837]
c/o Teresa M. Casey, Executive
Director
Mackin & Casey, LLC
139 Lancaster St.
Albany, NY 12210-1903
PH: (518)449-4698
Casey, Teresa M., Exec. Dir.

Association of Philanthropic Counsel
[818]
136 Everett Rd.
Albany, NY 12205-1418
PH: (518)694-5525
Fax: (518)677-1668
Carter, Julie, Secretary

Association for Psychological Type
International [16907]
1450 Western Ave., Ste. 101
Albany, NY 12203
PH: (518)320-7416

Civil Service Employees Association
[23429]
143 Washington Ave.
Albany, NY 12210
PH: (518)257-1000
Toll free: 800-342-4146
Donohue, Danny, President

Cleaning Management Institute
[2128]
125 Wolf Rd., Ste. 112
Albany, NY 12205
Toll free: 800-225-4772
Fax: (847)982-1012

Council of State Archivists [8821]
Cultural Education Ctr., Rm. 9B70
222 Madison Ave.

Albany, NY 12230
PH: (608)264-6480
(518)473-9098
Fax: (518)473-7058
Blessing, Matt, President

Excelsior College Alumni Association **[19324]**
7 Columbia Cir.
Albany, NY 12203-5159
PH: (518)464-8500
Toll free: 888-647-2388
Fax: (518)464-8777
Senn, William, President

Healthy Schools Network **[4141]**
773 Madison Ave.
Albany, NY 12208
PH: (518)462-0632
(202)543-7555
Fax: (518)462-0433
Anderko, Laura, VP

Helping Honduras Kids **[11024]**
1525 Western Ave., Maildrop 8
Albany, NY 12203
Ashby, David, Chairman, President

Holocaust Survivors and Friends Education Center **[18349]**
184 Washington Ave.
Albany, NY 12203-5347
PH: (518)694-9984
(518)694-9965
Fax: (518)783-1557
Shapiro, Shelly Zima, Director

Institute of Certified Records Managers **[1799]**
1450 Western Ave., Ste. 101
Albany, NY 12203
PH: (518)694-5362
Toll free: 877-244-3128
Fax: (518)463-8656
Haliday, Rae Lynn, CRM, Chairman

International Lexical Functional Grammar Association **[8185]**
University at Albany, State University of New York
Arts and Sciences Bldg., Rm. 239
1400 Washington Ave.
Albany, NY 12222
Broadwell, George Aaron, Secretary, Treasurer

International Narcotic Enforcement Officers Association **[5226]**
112 State St., Ste. 1200
Albany, NY 12207-2023
PH: (518)463-6232
Fax: (518)463-6232

International Society of the Arts, Mathematics, and Architecture **[8047]**
University at Albany
1400 Washington Ave.
Albany, NY 12222
Friedman, Nat, Editor, Founder

National Alliance for Direct Support Professionals **[1701]**
240 Washington Avenue Ext., Ste. 501
Albany, NY 12203
PH: (518)449-7551
Laws, Carol Britton, PhD, MSW, President

National Association for Health and Fitness **[16706]**
10 Kings Mill Ct.
Albany, NY 12205-3632
PH: (518)456-1058
Haberstro, Philip, Exec. Dir.

National Association for Pupil Transportation **[5815]**
1840 Western Ave.
Albany, NY 12203-4624

PH: (518)452-3611
Toll free: 800-989-6278
Fax: (518)218-0867
Martin, Michael J., Exec. Dir.

National Client Protection Organization **[5439]**
c/o Michael J. Knight, President
New York Lawyers' Fund for Client Protection
119 Washington Ave.
Albany, NY 12210
PH: (518)434-1935
Toll free: 800-442-3863
Fax: (518)434-5614
Peifer, Kathryn J., Co-Pres.

North American Drama Therapy Association **[16986]**
1450 Western Ave., Ste. 101
Albany, NY 12203
PH: (518)463-8656
Toll free: 888-416-7167

North American Geosynthetics Society **[6224]**
c/o L. Davis Suits, Executive Director
PO Box 12063
Albany, NY 12212-2063
PH: (518)869-2917
Fax: (518)869-2917
Henderson, John, President

Oley Foundation for Home Parenteral and Enteral Nutrition **[15281]**
c/o Albany Medical Center
43 New Scotland Ave., MC-28
Albany, NY 12208-3478
PH: (518)262-5079
Toll free: 800-776-6539
Fax: (518)262-5528
Bishop, Joan, Exec. Dir.

Renew the Earth **[7204]**
428 Sand Creek Rd.
Albany, NY 12205
PH: (518)797-3377
Beller, Jeff, Treasurer

Society for Integrative Oncology **[16357]**
136 Everett Rd.
Albany, NY 12205
PH: (347)676-1746
Mao, Jun, MD, MSCE, President

Society of Quantitative Analysts **[1267]**
1450 Western Ave., Ste. 101
Albany, NY 12203
Toll free: 800-918-7930
Okounkova, Inna, President

Welfare Research, Inc. **[13094]**
14 Columbia Cir., Ste. 104
Albany, NY 12203
PH: (518)713-4726
Fax: (518)608-5435
Lounsbury, Lee, Exec. Dir.

Women in Cognitive Science **[7078]**
c/o Laurie B. Feldman, Officer
University at Albany - State University of New York
Department of Psychology
1400 Washington Ave.
Albany, NY 12222
PH: (518)442-4820
Fax: (518)442-4867
Feldman, Laurie B., Officer

Women in Insurance and Financial Services **[1935]**
136 Everett Rd.
Albany, NY 12205
PH: (518)694-5506
Toll free: 866-264-9437
Fax: (518)935-9232
Duffy, Deb, Exec. Dir.

World's Window **[11742]**
40 Van Schoick Ave.
Albany, NY 12208
Casey, Chris, Exec. Dir.

National Business and Disability Council **[11771]**
201 I.U. Willets Rd.
Albertson, NY 11507
PH: (516)465-1400
Kemp, John D., President, CEO

The Viscardi Center **[11644]**
201 I.U. Willets Rd.
Albertson, NY 11507-1516
PH: (516)465-1400
(516)465-1450
Kemp, John D., Esq., CEO, President

Center for Inquiry **[18294]**
PO Box 741
Amherst, NY 14226
PH: (716)636-4869
Fax: (716)636-1733
Goddard, Debbie, Director

Committee for Skeptical Inquiry **[6985]**
Box 703
Amherst, NY 14226
PH: (716)636-1425
Toll free: 800-634-1610
Kurtz, Paul, Founder

Council for Secular Humanism **[20210]**
PO Box 664
Amherst, NY 14226-0664
PH: (716)636-7571
Toll free: 800-458-1366
Fax: (716)636-1733
Lindsay, Mr. Ronald, PhD, CEO, President

Food Service Enablers **[3013]**
4256 Ridge Lea Rd., Ste. 100
Amherst, NY 14226
PH: (716)819-6600
Toll free: 866-377-8833
Hobart, Tom, Contact

Hope for Two.. The Pregnant With Cancer Network **[13983]**
PO Box 253
Amherst, NY 14226
Toll free: 800-743-4471
Murray, Patty, JD, Chairman

Students for the Exploration and Development of Space **[7461]**
3840 E Robinson Rd.
PMB 176
Amherst, NY 14228
Zaslow, Molly, Mgr.

Hypospadias and Epispadias Association **[13829]**
PO Box 607
Amsterdam, NY 12010
PH: (917)861-8339
Arnold, Chris, President

Economists for Peace and Security **[18127]**
PO Box 5000
Annandale on Hudson, NY 12504-5000
PH: (845)758-0917
Fax: (845)758-1149
Galbraith, James K., Chairman

Catholic Kolping Society of America **[19812]**
c/o Bernhard Preisser, President
19 Revere Rd.
Ardsley, NY 10502-1219
PH: (914)693-5537
(516)364-0800
Fax: (516)364-0802
Preisser, Bernhard, President

Choose Responsibility **[13129]**
PO Box 284
Ardsley on Hudson, NY 10503-0284
PH: (202)543-8760
Seaman, Barrett, President

Alliance for Southern African Progress **[12137]**
1424 31st Ave., Ste. 3R
Astoria, NY 11106
Toll free: 877-375-5778
Fax: (877)375-5778
DeWitt, Sean, Exec. Dir.

American MidEast Leadership Network **[18513]**
PO Box 2156
Astoria, NY 11102
PH: (347)924-9674
Fax: (917)591-2177
Nuseir, Rami, Director, Founder

Chian Federation **[19451]**
44-01 Broadway
Astoria, NY 11103
PH: (718)204-2550
Fax: (718)278-6199

Good Shepherd Volunteers **[13295]**
25-30 21st Ave.
Astoria, NY 11105
PH: (718)943-7488
(718)943-7489
Fax: (718)408-2332
Fedeli, Sean, Chairman

The Optimists **[11112]**
25-78 31st St.
Astoria, NY 11102
PH: (718)278-4953
(718)577-1048
Salam, Sarwar B., CPA, Chairman

TDF Costume Collection **[9190]**
34-12 36th St., Ste. 1
Astoria, NY 11106
PH: (212)989-5855
Fax: (212)206-0922

Federation of Metal Detector and Archaeological Clubs **[22151]**
c/o Mark Schuessler, President
1464 Graft Rd.
Attica, NY 14011
PH: (585)591-0010
Burke, Ed, VP

American Correctional Chaplains Association **[19924]**
ACCA Chaplains Office
Auburn Correctional Facility
135 State St.
Auburn, NY 13021
PH: (347)783-7684
Fax: (315)253-8401
Deshaies, Richard, 1st VP

American Political Items Collectors **[21614]**
PO Box 55
Avon, NY 14414-0055
PH: (585)226-8620
Puechner, Ron, President

Shwachman-Diamond Syndrome Foundation **[17351]**
2334 Rolling Ridge Dr.
Avon, NY 14414-9642
Toll free: 888-825-7373
James, Christine, President

Bible Believers Fellowship **[19752]**
PO Box 0065
Baldwin, NY 11510-0065
PH: (516)739-7746
Kaestner, Mr. Eric, CEO, President

Richardson Boat Owners Association **[22663]**
c/o Bill Beall, 2nd Vice-President
3623 Melvin Rd. S

Baldwinsville, NY 13027-9229
PH: (315)635-1356
Shatrau, Mike, Director

The Meader Family Association, Inc.
  [20899]
158 Ashdown Rd.
Ballston Lake, NY 12019
PH: (518)399-5013
Nye, Jane Meader, Secretary

Newfoundland Club of America
  [21926]
1155 Raymond Rd.
Ballston Spa, NY 12020-3719
Toll free: 866-622-6393
Saunders, Pam, President

Borgward Owners' Club **[21340]**
77 New Hampshire Ave.
Bay Shore, NY 11706-2520
PH: (516)273-0458
Fax: (516)666-5446

Baseball Writers Association of
  America **[2667]**
PO Box 610611
Bayside, NY 11361-0611
PH: (718)767-2582
Fax: (718)767-2583
O'Connell, Jack, Secretary,
  Treasurer

Children in Need Haitian Project
  [10919]
PO Box 604846
Bayside, NY 11360
Felix, Jeanette, Founder, VP

Dance Masters of America **[7702]**
PO Box 610533
Bayside, NY 11361-0533
PH: (718)225-4013
Fax: (718)225-4293
Mann, Robert, Exec. Sec.

Tourette Association of America
  [15994]
42-40 Bell Blvd., Ste. 205
Bayside, NY 11361
PH: (718)224-2999
Fax: (718)279-9596
Miller, John, President, CEO

Damien-Dutton Society for Leprosy
  Aid **[15532]**
616 Bedford Ave.
Bellmore, NY 11710
PH: (516)221-5829
  (516)221-9588
Fax: (516)221-5909

Society of Professional Investigators
  [5371]
PO Box 1087
Bellmore, NY 11710
PH: (718)490-7288
Sackman, Bruce, President

Nesbitt/Nisbet Society of North
  America **[20907]**
c/o Nick Nesbitt, Treasurer
4573 Colburn Rd.
Bemus Point, NY 14712
Nesbitt, Nick, Treasurer

Italian Genealogical Group **[20980]**
PO Box 626
Bethpage, NY 11714-0626
DiBartolo, Anthony, Director

American Civic Association **[12122]**
131 Front St.
Binghamton, NY 13905-3101
PH: (607)723-9419
Fax: (607)723-0023
Baranoski, Andrew, Exec. Dir.

American Name Society **[10058]**
c/o Dr. Michael F. McGoff, Senior
  Vice Provost

Binghamton University
State University of New York
Office of the Provost
Binghamton, NY 13902-6000
PH: (607)777-2143
Toll free: 866-297-5154
Fax: (607)777-4831
McGoff, Dr. Michael F., Provost,
  Treasurer

Fluoride Action Network **[14433]**
104 Walnut St.
Binghamton, NY 13905
PH: (802)338-5577
Connett, Michael, Exec. Dir.

Link Foundation **[7304]**
c/o Binghamton University Founda-
  tion
PO Box 6005
Binghamton, NY 13902-6005
Kelly, Thomas F., PhD, Chairman

Society for Ancient Greek
  Philosophy **[10120]**
Binghamton University
Binghamton, NY 13902-6000
PH: (607)777-2886
  (607)777-2646
Fax: (607)777-6255
Preus, Anthony, Secretary

State University of New York at
  Binghamton I Center for Medieval
  and Renaissance Studies **[9791]**
PO Box 6000
Binghamton, NY 13902-6000
PH: (607)777-2130
Fax: (607)777-2408
Desmond, Marilyn, Director

Antique Wireless Association
  [22401]
PO Box 421
Bloomfield, NY 14469-0421

Adirondack Historical Association
  [9363]
c/o Adirondack Museum
Route 28N & 30
Blue Mountain Lake, NY 12812
PH: (518)352-7311
Fax: (518)352-7653
Kahn, David, Exec. Dir.

Flexographic Technical Association
  [1533]
3920 Veterans Memorial Hwy., Ste.
  9
Bohemia, NY 11716-1074
PH: (631)737-6020
Fax: (631)737-6813
Cisternino, Mark, President

National Association of Puerto Rican
  Hispanic Social Workers **[13112]**
PO Box 651
Brentwood, NY 11717
PH: (631)864-1536
Fax: (631)864-1536
Velazquez, Pauline, MSW, Founder

Crystal Ball Cruise Association
  [13441]
PO Box 390
Brewerton, NY 13029
PH: (315)668-2277
Fax: (315)676-5782
McGill, Matt, Founder

Academy of Management **[8260]**
PO Box 3020
Briarcliff Manor, NY 10510-8020
PH: (914)923-2607
Fax: (914)923-2615
Urbanowicz, Nancy, Exec. Dir.

KISS Rocks Fan Club **[24052]**
c/o Jon Rubin, Founder
15 Maple Rd.

Briarcliff Manor, NY 10510
Rubin, Jon, Founder, President

American Association for Technology
  in Psychiatry **[16816]**
PO Box 11
Bronx, NY 10464-0011
PH: (718)502-9469
Kennedy, Robert, Exec. Dir., Exec.
  VP

American Catholic Historical As-
  sociation **[9452]**
Dealy Hall, Rm. 637
441 E Fordham Rd.
Bronx, NY 10458
PH: (718)817-3830
Fax: (718)817-5690
Brockey, Liam Matthew, President

American Pan-African Relief Agen-
  cies **[12617]**
PO Box 723
Bronx, NY 10467
PH: (646)558-6363
  (646)558-6364
Toll free: 877-368-8241
Fax: (646)853-3393
Omokha, Emmanuel M.I., Sr., Exec.
  Dir.

American Society of Botanical Artists
  [8911]
The New York Botanical Garden
2900 Southern Blvd.
Bronx, NY 10458-5126
PH: (718)817-8814
Toll free: 866-691-9080
Williams, Jody, President

The Center for Family Support
  [12320]
2811 Zulette Ave.
Bronx, NY 10461
PH: (718)518-1500
Fax: (718)518-8200
Vernikoff, Steven, Exec. Dir.

Christopher Columbus Philatelic
  Society **[22318]**
c/o Leslie Seff, Secretary
3750 Hudson Manor Ter. E
Bronx, NY 10463-1126
Nye, Mr. David E., President

Coalition of Irish Immigration
  Centers **[12125]**
PO Box 210
Bronx, NY 10470
PH: (914)837-2007
Collins, Michael, Secretary

Council on Botanical and
  Horticultural Libraries **[9701]**
c/o Esther Jackson, Secretary
LuEsther T. Mertz Library
New York Botanical Garden
2900 Southern Blvd.
Bronx, NY 10458-5126
Teghtmeyer, Suzi, Mgr., Member
  Svcs.

Gaia Institute **[4002]**
440 City Island Ave.
Bronx, NY 10464
Mankiewicz, Paul, PhD, Exec. Dir.

Grassroots Artists MovEment, Inc.
  [8924]
2427 Morris Ave., 1st Fl.
Bronx, NY 10468
PH: (718)690-3393
Fax: (646)792-3323
Adewale, Omowale, Exec. Dir.

Hall of Fame for Great Americans
  [10329]
Bronx Community College
2155 University Ave.

Bronx, NY 10453
PH: (718)289-5160
LeMelle, Therese, Contact

Independent Media Arts Preservation
  [9784]
c/o Lehman College
Lief Library 201
250 Bedford Park Blvd. W
Bronx, NY 10468
Schlesinger, Kenneth, President

Institute for Mediation and Conflict
  Resolution **[4959]**
384 E 149th St., Ste. 330
Bronx, NY 10455-3908
PH: (718)585-1190
Slate, Stephen, Exec. Dir.

Joseph Conrad Society of America
  [9065]
c/o Christopher GoGwilt, President
Fordham University
Dealy 512W
Bronx, NY 10458-9993
PH: (718)817-4020
Larabee, Mark, Treasurer, Exec. Ed.

National Amateur Body Builders As-
  sociation U.S.A. **[22697]**
PO Box 531
Bronx, NY 10469
PH: (718)882-6413
Gruskin, Bob, President

National Double Dutch League
  [23106]
888 Grand Concourse, Ste. 6i
Bronx, NY 10451
PH: (212)865-9606
Walker, David A., Founder, President

Nietzsche Society **[10104]**
Fordham University
Graduate School of Arts and Sci-
  ences
441 E Fordham Rd.
Bronx, NY 10458
PH: (212)636-6297
Babich, Babette E., Exec. Dir.

North American Society for the
  Study of Personality Disorders
  [15801]
c/o Marianne Goodman, Treasurer
Icahn School of Medicine at Mount
  Sinai
130 W Kingsbridge Rd.
Bronx, NY 10468
Hopwood, Chris, PhD, VP

Organization for Flora Neotropica
  [6151]
c/o Dr. Wm. Wayt Thomas, Execu-
  tive Director
Institute of Systematic Botany
New York Botanical Garden
Bronx, NY 10458-5126
PH: (718)817-8625
Fax: (718)817-8648
Thomas, Dr. Wayt, Exec. Dir.

Osborne Association **[11542]**
809 Westchester Ave.
Bronx, NY 10455
PH: (718)707-2600
Fax: (718)707-3102
Osborne, Frederik R-L., V. Chmn. of
  the Bd.

Per Scholas **[7796]**
804 E 138th St., 2nd Fl.
Bronx, NY 10454
PH: (718)991-8400
Fax: (718)991-0362
Ayala, Dr. Plinio, CEO, President

PHI **[1594]**
400 E Fordham Rd., 11th Fl.
Bronx, NY 10458

PH: (718)402-7766
Fax: (718)585-6852
Sturgeon, Jodi, President

Rebuild A Nation [10731]
866 E 175th St., Ste. 1
Bronx, NY 10460
PH: (718)207-7142
Davies, Moses, President

Save Humanity Initiative [12725]
PO Box 647
Bronx, NY 10469
PH: (914)219-3355
    (914)219-3344
Toll free: 877-657-3121
Fax: (914)412-7676
Rhodes, Allen, Chairman

Sisters of Life [20589]
St. Frances de Chantal Convent
198 Hollywood Ave.
Bronx, NY 10465-3350
PH: (718)863-2264
Fax: (718)409-2033

Society for the Study of Process
  Philosophies [10131]
c/o Jude Jones
Collins Hall
Dept. of Philosophy
Fordham University
441 E Fordham Rd.
Bronx, NY 10458
PH: (718)817-4721
Jones, Dr. Jude, Director

Wildlife Conservation Society [4910]
2300 Southern Blvd.
Bronx, NY 10460
PH: (718)220-5100
Samper, Cristian, PhD, President,
  CEO

Alpha Beta Gamma International
  [23700]
1160 Midland Ave., Ste. 4C
Bronxville, NY 10708
PH: (914)771-9987
Christesen, Dr. John D., CEO

Rene Dubos Center for Human
  Environments [4047]
The Rene Dubos Center, Ste. 387
Bronxville, NY 10708-3818
PH: (914)337-1636
Fax: (914)771-5206
Eblen, Ruth A., Founder, President

350.org [3783]
20 Jay St., Ste. 1010
Brooklyn, NY 11201
PH: (518)635-0350
McKibben, Bill, President, Founder

Aid to the Church in Need [19788]
725 Leonard St.
Brooklyn, NY 11222-2350
PH: (718)609-0939
Toll free: 800-628-6333
Barbour, Fr. Hugh, Director

Alliance For Relief Mission in Haiti
  [12613]
PO Box 250028
Brooklyn, NY 11225
PH: (516)499-7452
Damour, Yvon, MD, President

Alliance of Guardian Angels [11499]
982 E 89th St.
Brooklyn, NY 11236
PH: (718)649-2607
Sliwa, Curtis, President, Founder

Amateur Astronomers Association
  [5995]
PO Box 150253
Brooklyn, NY 11215

PH: (212)535-2922
Cabrera, Marcelo, President

Asian American Arts Alliance [8962]
20 Jay St., Ste. 740
Brooklyn, NY 11201
PH: (212)941-9208
Fax: (212)366-1778
Louie, Andrea, Exec. Dir.

Asian CineVision [9297]
30 John St.
Brooklyn, NY 11201
PH: (212)989-1422
Fax: (212)727-3584
Woo, John C., Exec. Dir.

Association for Birth Psychology
  [16900]
9115 Ridge Blvd.
Brooklyn, NY 11209-5748
PH: (347)517-4607
Feher, Leslie, PhD, Exec. Dir.

Association of Concerned Africa
  Scholars [17774]
c/o Michael Walker, Treasurer
538 Pacific St., Apt. 5-6
Brooklyn, NY 11217-2280
Barnes, Teresa, Co-Ch.

Association of Haitian Physicians
  Abroad [15714]
1166 Eastern Pky.
Brooklyn, NY 11213
PH: (718)245-1015
Fax: (718)735-8015
Cadet, Dr. Joseph Pierre-Paul,
  Contact

Association of Professional Art Advi-
  sors [240]
433 3rd St., Ste. 3
Brooklyn, NY 11215
PH: (718)788-1425
Isenberg, Michelle, Principal

Association for Union Democracy
  [23466]
104 Montgomery St.
Brooklyn, NY 11225
PH: (718)564-1114
Kornblum, William, Director

Bangladeshi-American Pharmacists'
  Association [16654]
1108 Liberty Ave.
Brooklyn, NY 11208
PH: (718)304-6261
Fax: (718)277-0193
Ahmed, Shahab, Exec.

Batey Relief Alliance [12627]
PO Box 300565
Brooklyn, NY 11230-5656
PH: (917)627-5026
Gaillard, Ulrick, JD, CEO, Founder

Beta Gamma Sigma Alumni [23689]
PO Box 297-006
Brooklyn, NY 11229-7006
PH: (585)542-9181
Mendels, David B., President

Black Veterans for Social Justice
  [21112]
665 Willoughby Ave.
Brooklyn, NY 11206
PH: (718)852-6004
Fax: (718)852-4805
Sweat, Herbert, Director

Blacks in Law Enforcement [5458]
591 Vanderbilt Ave., Ste. 133
Brooklyn, NY 11238
PH: (718)455-9059
Daniels, Ron, Exec. Dir.

Brighter Green [3822]
165 Court St., No. 171
Brooklyn, NY 11201

PH: (212)414-2339
MacDonald, Mia, Exec. Dir.

Brooklyn College Alumni Association
  [19310]
2900 Bedford Ave.
Brooklyn, NY 11210
PH: (718)951-5065
Schweiger, Ron, President

Buckminster Fuller Institute [10315]
181 N 11th St., Ste. 402
Brooklyn, NY 11211
PH: (718)290-9280
    (718)290-9283
Fax: (718)290-9281
Thompson, Elizabeth, Exec. Dir.

Canine Cancer Awareness, Inc.
  [17642]
44 Devoe St.
Brooklyn, NY 11211
Storto, Pamela, President

Canteens for the Children of Haiti
  [10882]
1468 Flatbush Ave., Ste. 3
Brooklyn, NY 11210
PH: (718)434-1799
Fax: (718)434-0805

Caribbean American Chamber of
  Commerce and Industry, Inc.
  [23570]
Bldg. No. 5, Unit 239
Brooklyn Navy Yard
63 Flushing Ave.
Brooklyn, NY 11205
PH: (718)834-4544
Fax: (718)834-9774
Hastick, Roy A., Sr., Founder,
  President, CEO

Caribbean-American Netball As-
  sociation Inc. [23046]
Empire Blvd., Lefferts Sta.
Brooklyn, NY 11225
Beaumont, Devon, VP

Caribbean People International Col-
  lective [19395]
4710 Church Ave., 3rd Fl.
Brooklyn, NY 11203
PH: (718)576-1839
Stewart, Dawn C., MPA, Founder,
  CEO

Catalogue Raisonne Scholars Association [7503]
c/o Suzi Villiger, Director
294 E 7th St.
Brooklyn, NY 11218
Cooke, Susan, Dir. of Programs

Center for Communication [7536]
195 Plymouth St., Ste. 320
Brooklyn, NY 11201
PH: (212)686-5005
Barrett, David J., Chairman

Chabad Lubavitch [20240]
Lubavich World Headquarters
770 Eastern Pky.
Brooklyn, NY 11213
PH: (718)774-4000
Fax: (718)774-2718
Levine, Shalom, Dir. of Lib. Svcs.

Conservative Party [18888]
486 78th St.
Brooklyn, NY 11209-3404
PH: (718)921-2158
Fax: (718)921-5268
Long, Michael R., Chairman

Dance Films Association [7701]
252 Java St., Ste. 333
Brooklyn, NY 11222

PH: (347)505-8649
Vander Veer, Greg, VP

Delta Sigma Chi Multicultural Soror-
  ity, Inc. [23970]
New York City Technical College
300 Jay St.
Brooklyn, NY 11201-1909
Crowder, Chaquita, VP

Dictionary Society of North America
  [9126]
c/o Rebecca Shapiro, Executive
  Secretary
Dept. of English
New York City College of Technology
300 Jay St.
Brooklyn, NY 11201
Shapiro, Rebecca, PhD, Exec. Sec.

Dorcas Medical Mission, Inc.
  [15447]
907 Utica Ave.
Brooklyn, NY 11203
PH: (718)342-2928
Fax: (718)342-5721
Mullings, Lorna, RN, President

East Timor and Indonesia Action
  Network/US [18395]
PO Box 21873
Brooklyn, NY 11202-1873
PH: (718)596-7668
    (917)690-4391

Equal Justice USA [18072]
81 Prospect St.
Brooklyn, NY 11201
PH: (718)801-8940
Fax: (718)801-8947
Silberstein, Shari, Exec. Dir.

Federation of International Trade
  Associations [1967]
172 5th Ave., No. 118
Brooklyn, NY 11217
PH: (703)634-3482
Toll free: 888-491-8833
Park, Kimberly, President, CEO

The Edward E. Ford Foundation
  [12972]
26 Court St., Ste. 2200
Brooklyn, NY 11242-1122
PH: (718)596-1950
Fax: (718)596-1988
Gulla, John C., Exec. Dir.

France and Colonies Philatelic
  Society [22329]
PO Box 102
Brooklyn, NY 11209
Nilsestuen, Ken, President

Franklin Furnace Archive [8855]
c/o Pratt Institute
ISC Bldg., Rm. 209-211
200 Willoughby Ave.
Brooklyn, NY 11205
PH: (718)687-5800
Fax: (718)687-5830
Wilson, Martha, Director

Freelancers Union [23421]
20 Jay St., Ste. 1102
Brooklyn, NY 11201
Toll free: 800-856-9981
Horowitz, Sara, Founder, Exec. Dir.

Gift Sales Manager Association
  [3015]
c/o Ari D. Lowenstein
105 Atlantic Ave.
Brooklyn, NY 11201
PH: (718)243-9492
Lowenstein, Prof. Ariela, PhD,
  Contact

Global Autism Project [13767]
252 3rd Ave.
Brooklyn, NY 11215

PH: (718)764-8225
Pinney, Molly Ola, CEO, Founder

Global Jewish Assistance and Relief
Network [12037]
1485 Union St.
Brooklyn, NY 11213
PH: (212)868-3636
(718)774-6497
Avtzon, Eliezer, Exec. Dir.

Global Workers Justice Alliance
[12338]
789 Washington Ave.
Brooklyn, NY 11238
PH: (646)351-1160
Caron, Cathleen, Exec. Dir., Founder

Global Youth Action Network [19273]
540 President St., 3rd Fl.
Brooklyn, NY 11215-1493
PH: (212)661-6111
Ahluwalia, Dr. Poonam, Exec. Dir.

Global Youth Coalition on HIV/AIDS
[10541]
155 Water St.
Brooklyn, NY 11201-1040
PH: (917)677-9927
Dolce, Gillian, Program Mgr.

Goods for Good [11007]
45 Main St., Ste. 518
Brooklyn, NY 11201
PH: (646)963-6076
Kushner, Melissa, Exec. Dir.,
Founder

Guardians of Hydrocephalus
Research Foundation [15937]
2618 Avenue Z
Brooklyn, NY 11235
PH: (718)743-4473
Fax: (718)743-1171
Fischetti, Mrs. Marie, Founder

Habonim Dror North America
[20247]
1000 Dean St., No. 353
Brooklyn, NY 11238
PH: (718)789-1796
Fax: (718)789-1799
Silverman, Kali, Director

Haiti Cultural Exchange [9211]
c/o FiveMyles Gallery
558 St. John Pl.
Brooklyn, NY 11238
PH: (347)565-4429
Roumain, Regine M., Exec. Dir.

Health and Education Relief for
Guyana [15467]
883 Flatbush Ave.
Brooklyn, NY 11226
PH: (718)282-2262
Fax: (718)282-2263
Mitchell, John, MD, Mem.

Health and Educational Relief
Organization [15144]
883 Flatbush Ave.
Brooklyn, NY 11226
PH: (718)282-2262
Fax: (718)282-2263
Mitchell, John, MD, President

Health Global Access Project
[10544]
540 President St., 3rd Fl.
Brooklyn, NY 11215
PH: (347)263-8438
Fax: (347)263-8439
Baker, Brook, Analyst

Heart's Home USA [20366]
108 St. Edwards St.
Brooklyn, NY 11205

PH: (718)522-2121
de Roucy, Fr. Thierry, Founder

Helpers of God's Precious Infants
[19059]
Monastery of the Precious Blood
5300 Fort Hamilton Pky.
Brooklyn, NY 11219
Fax: (718)853-0599
Reilly, Mgr. Phillip, Founder

Heritage Foods USA [6647]
790 Washington Ave., PMB 303
Brooklyn, NY 11238
PH: (718)389-0985
Fax: (718)389-0547
Martins, Patrick, Founder, President

Historical Society of Jews from
Egypt [9638]
PO Box 230445
Brooklyn, NY 11223
Fax: (718)998-2497
Fteha, Elie F., MD, President

Hitchcock Institute for Studies in
American Music [8371]
Brooklyn College, CUNY
2900 Bedford Ave.
Brooklyn, NY 11210-2889
PH: (718)951-5655
(718)951-5000
Taylor, Jeffrey, PhD, Director

Housing Works [13546]
57 Willoughby St., 2nd Fl.
Brooklyn, NY 11201
PH: (347)473-7400
Ward, Earl, Chairman

Ijaw National Alliance of the
Americas [11381]
PO Box 24435
Brooklyn, NY 11202-4435
Whyte, Dr. Tonye, Gen. Sec.

Independent Filmmaker Project
[1193]
30 John St.
Brooklyn, NY 11201
PH: (212)465-8200
Fax: (212)465-8525
Vicente, Joana, Exec. Dir.

INFORM Inc. [19133]
PO Box 320403
Brooklyn, NY 11232
PH: (212)361-2400
Fax: (212)361-2412
Ramsey, Virginia, Exec. Producer

Inter-Governmental Philatelic
Corporation [22334]
172 Empire Blvd., 3rd Fl.
Brooklyn, NY 11225
PH: (212)629-7979
Fax: (212)629-3350

International Association of Former
Soviet Political Prisoners and
Victims of the Communist Regime
[18412]
1310 Avenue R, Ste. 6-F
Brooklyn, NY 11229
PH: (718)339-4563
Bolonkin, Alexander, PhD, President

International MultiCultural Institute
[11492]
595 6th St.
Brooklyn, NY 11215
PH: (718)832-8625
Regan, Margaret, President, CEO

JazzReach, Inc. [9942]
45 Main St., Ste. 728
Brooklyn, NY 11201
PH: (718)625-5188
Fax: (718)625-4979
Schuman, Hans, Exec. Dir.

Jewish Stuttering Association
[17302]
PO Box 301072
Brooklyn, NY 11230
PH: (347)855-7520

Keepers of the Waters [4760]
191 22nd St.
Brooklyn, NY 11232
PH: (917)977-1411
Damon, Betsy, Director, Founder

Kolel Chibas Jerusalem [20262]
4802-A 12th Ave.
Brooklyn, NY 11219
PH: (718)633-7112
Toll free: 866-787-4520
Fax: (718)633-5783
Haness, Rabbi Mayer Baal, Contact

Konbit pou Rebati Bele [11206]
2804 Church Ave.
Brooklyn, NY 11226
Denis, Jean Claude, Founder

Laban/Bartenieff Institute of Move-
ment Studies [9266]
138 S Oxford St., Ste. 2D
Brooklyn, NY 11217
PH: (212)643-8888
Fax: (347)422-0948
Bradley, Karen, Exec. Dir., Dir. of
Res.

Latin America Parents Association
[10458]
PO Box 339-340
Brooklyn, NY 11234
PH: (718)236-8689
Quatrale, Andrea, President

The League of Young Voters [18912]
540 President St., 3rd Fl.
Brooklyn, NY 11215
PH: (347)464-8683
Baker, Rob, Exec. Dir.

Lesbian Herstory Archives [10306]
484 14th St.
Brooklyn, NY 11215
PH: (718)768-3953
Fax: (718)768-4663
Wolfe, Maxine, Coord.

Linguistic Association of Canada and
the United States [9744]
2900 Bedford Ave.
Brooklyn, NY 11210
PH: (713)348-2820
Fax: (713)348-5846
Embleton, Sheila, Chairman

Lubavitch Youth Organization
[20264]
770 Eastern Pky.
Brooklyn, NY 11213-3409
PH: (718)953-1000
Fax: (718)771-6315
Butman, Rabbi Shmuel M., Director

Machne Israel Development Fund
[12227]
770 Eastern Pky.
Brooklyn, NY 11213
PH: (718)774-4000
Fax: (718)774-2718
Krinsky, Rabbi Yehuda, Chairman

May First/People Link [18570]
237 Flatbush Ave., No. 278
Brooklyn, NY 11217
Fax: (815)642-9756
McClelland, Jamie, Founder, Director

Mercado Global [3495]
33 Nassau Ave., Ste. 54
Brooklyn, NY 11222
PH: (718)838-9908
Fax: (203)772-4493
DeGolia, Ruth, Exec. Dir.

Ms. Foundation for Women [18219]
12 MetroTech Ctr., 26th Fl.
Brooklyn, NY 11201
PH: (212)742-2300
Fax: (212)742-1653
Barbara, Rosina, VP of Fin. &
Admin.

Muslim Ummah of North America
[9607]
1033 Glenmore Ave.
Brooklyn, NY 11208
PH: (646)683-2174
Fax: (718)277-7901
Chowdhury, Sayedur Rahman, Dir.
Ed.

National Committee for Furtherance
of Jewish Education [8142]
824 Eastern Pky.
Brooklyn, NY 11213
PH: (718)735-0200
Fax: (718)735-4455
Hecht, Rabbi Sholem Ber, Director

National Conference of Black
Lawyers [5035]
PO Box 25162
Brooklyn, NY 11202
Toll free: 866-266-5091
Jackson, Deborah A., Ph.D, Editor

National Conference of Law Enforcement Emerald Societies [19537]
2121 New York Ave.
Brooklyn, NY 11210-5423
Tinker, William, Exec. Dir.

National Student Nurses' Association
[8335]
45 Main St., Ste. 606
Brooklyn, NY 11201
PH: (718)210-0705
Fax: (718)797-1186
Hunt, Kelly, President

National War Tax Resistance
Coordinating Committee [19174]
PO Box 150553
Brooklyn, NY 11215
PH: (718)768-3420
Toll free: 800-269-7464
Benn, Ruth, Coord.

North American Humanitarian Aid
and Relief [12707]
23 Doscher St.
Brooklyn, NY 11208
PH: (516)864-5078

Nurses Educational Funds, Inc.
[16168]
137 Montague St.
Brooklyn, NY 11201
PH: (212)590-2443
(917)524-8051
Fax: (212)590-2446
Bowar-Ferres, Susan, PhD,
President

NURTUREart Non-Profit, Inc. [8935]
56 Bogart St.
Brooklyn, NY 11206
PH: (718)782-7755
Fax: (718)569-2086
Marston, Karen, President

Nutrition and Metabolism Society
[16233]
60 Terrace Pl.
Brooklyn, NY 11218
PH: (646)685-8892

Ocular Surface Society of Optometry
[16433]
1 Prospect Park SW, Ste. 4B
Brooklyn, NY 11215
Schaeffer, Jack, President

OK Kosher Certification [20273]
391 Troy Ave.
Brooklyn, NY 11213
PH: (718)756-7500
Fax: (718)756-7503
Levy, Rabbi Don Yoel, President

Organizing for Haiti [12055]
879 E 93rd St.
Brooklyn, NY 11236
PH: (718)496-5103
Foreste, Suze, President, Chmn. of
the Bd.

Patience T'ai Chi Association
[23011]
845 65th St., 2nd Fl.
Brooklyn, NY 11220
PH: (718)332-3477
Phillips, William C., Founder

Jozef Pilsudski Institute of America
for Research in the Modern History
of Poland [10165]
138 Greenpoint Ave.
Brooklyn, NY 11222
PH: (212)505-9077
Fax: (347)763-9469
Korga, Dr. Iwona, Exec. Dir.,
Treasurer

Polish American Golf Association
[22890]
616 Manhattan Ave.
Brooklyn, NY 11222
PH: (718)389-8536
Gasior, Pawel, President

Progressive Labor Party [18894]
PO Box 808
Brooklyn, NY 11202
PH: (212)629-0002

Responsible Endowments Coalition
[8771]
33 Flatbush Ave., 5th Fl.
Brooklyn, NY 11217
PH: (718)989-3949
Smith, Marcie, Exec. Dir.

Scenarios U.S.A. [19277]
80 Hanson Pl., Ste. 305
Brooklyn, NY 11217
PH: (718)230-5125
Toll free: 866-414-1044
Fax: (718)230-4381
Minsky, Maura, Founder, Exec. Dir.

Sculptors Guild [10211]
55 Washington St., Ste. 256
Brooklyn, NY 11201
PH: (718)422-0555
Smith, Robert Michael, Comm. Chm.

Slow Food USA [3576]
1000 Dean St., Ste. 222
Brooklyn, NY 11238
PH: (718)260-8000
Toll free: 877-SLOWFOOD
Fax: (718)260-8068
Krauss, Kate, Managing Dir.

Social Psychiatry Research Institute
[16835]
3044 Coney Island Ave., Ste. 201
Brooklyn, NY 11235
Toll free: 888-345-7774
Kiev, Ari, MD, Founder, President

Social Science Research Council
[7173]
300 Cadman Plz. W, 15th Fl.
Brooklyn, NY 11201-2701
PH: (212)377-2700
Fax: (212)377-2727
Katznelson, Ira, President

Society for the Advancement of the
Caribbean Diaspora [19398]
PO Box 24556
Brooklyn, NY 11202

PH: (917)771-7935
Hamilton-LaFortune, Minna,
President, Secretary

Solidarity and Action Against the HIV
Infection in India [10553]
c/o Rachel Yaasky, Treasurer
20 Plaza St. E, Apt. C11
Brooklyn, NY 11238
Yaasky, Rachel, Treasurer

START Treatment and Recovery
Centers [13184]
22 Chapel St.
Brooklyn, NY 11201
PH: (718)260-2900
Fax: (718)875-2817
Lopez, Sonia, Medical Dir.

Stoked [13480]
10 Jay St., Ste. 908
Brooklyn, NY 11201
PH: (646)710-3600
Fax: (212)859-7357
Larosiliere, Steven, President

Student Global AIDS Campaign
[13562]
540 President Street, 3rd Floor
540 President St., 3rd Fl.
Brooklyn, NY 11215
Sanderson, Emily, Contact

Tamizdat [9216]
20 Jay St., Ste. 308
Brooklyn, NY 11201-8322
PH: (718)254-0022
Fax: (413)513-1157
Covey, Matthew, Director

Torah Umesorah - The National
Society for Hebrew Day Schools
[20197]
620 Foster Ave.
Brooklyn, NY 11230-1399
PH: (212)227-1000
Fax: (212)406-6934
Fruchter, Y., Mgr.

Tzivos Hashem [9643]
792 Eastern Pkwy.
Brooklyn, NY 11213
PH: (718)907-8855
    (718)467-6630
Benjaminson, Rabbi Yerachmiel,
Exec. Dir.

Unified for Global Healing [15502]
106 Waverly Ave.
Brooklyn, NY 11205
PH: (212)555-0123
Bruce, Zola Z., Contact

Watch Tower Bible and Tract Society
of Pennsylvania [20222]
25 Columbia Hts.
Brooklyn, NY 11201-2483
PH: (718)560-5000
Sinclair, David G., Director

Water Collective [13358]
209 Quincy St. Ste., 2R
Brooklyn, NY 11216
Sunwoo, Sophia, CEO, Founder

WCFO, Inc. [22823]
4547 Bedford Ave.
Brooklyn, NY 11235-2525
PH: (718)332-8336
Schloff, Anna, COO, President

The Well Project [13564]
PO Box 220410
Brooklyn, NY 11222
Bridge, Dawn Averitt, Founder, Bd.
Member

WITNESS [18452]
80 Hanson Pl., Ste. 5
Brooklyn, NY 11217

PH: (718)783-2000
Fax: (718)783-1593
Alberdingk Thijm, Yvette, Exec. Dir.

Women of Wind Energy [7393]
155 Water St.
Brooklyn, NY 11201
PH: (718)210-3666
Graf, Kristen, Exec. Dir.

Working Families Party [18899]
1 Metrotech Ctr. N, 11th Fl.
Brooklyn, NY 11217
PH: (718)222-3796
Clements, Holly, Dir. of HR

World Martial Arts Association
[23030]
Our Savior Church
414 80th St.
Brooklyn, NY 11209-3903
PH: (917)796-5254

Wyckoff House and Association
[9843]
5816 Clarendon Rd.
Brooklyn, NY 11203
PH: (718)629-5400
Wikoff, Naj, President, Chairman

American Geographical Society
[6671]
32 Court St., Ste. 201
Brooklyn Heights, NY 11201
PH: (917)745-8354
Black, Jason, Mem.

Aid and Care [11311]
338 Auburn Ave.
Buffalo, NY 14213
Diing, Dominic, Founder

American Crystallographic Associa-
tion [6359]
PO Box 96
Buffalo, NY 14205-0096
PH: (716)898-8690
Fax: (716)898-8695
Koetzle, Thomas, Editor

Association for Research of Child-
hood Cancer [13894]
PO Box 251
Buffalo, NY 14225-0251
PH: (716)681-4433
O'Donnell, Anne, President

Coated Abrasives Fabricators Association [2217]
c/o Jim Schnorr, Director, Communications
259 Chicago St.
Buffalo, NY 14204
PH: (636)272-7432
    (716)972-0333
Fax: (716)972-0334
Schnorr, Jim, Dir. of Comm.

Computers for Children Inc. [8666]
701 Seneca St., Ste. 601
Buffalo, NY 14210
PH: (716)823-7248
Carr, Christine, Exec. Dir.

D'Youville College Alumni Associa-
tion [19321]
631 Niagara St.
Buffalo, NY 14201
PH: (716)829-7805
Fax: (716)829-7821
Vrana Cunningham, Jodene,
President

Elephants Without Borders [4812]
500 Linwood Ave.
Buffalo, NY 14209
PH: (716)884-1548
Chase, Mike, Director, Founder

Every Person Influences Children
[10817]
1000 Main St.
Buffalo, NY 14202
PH: (716)332-4100
Fax: (716)332-4101
Murphy, Dennis P., Chairman

Gilda Radner Familial Ovarian
Cancer Registry [13967]
Roswell Park Cancer Institute
Elm and Carlton St.
Buffalo, NY 14263
PH: (716)845-4503
Toll free: 800-682-7426
Odunsi, Kunle, MD, Investigator,
Director

Global Outreach Mission [12277]
PO Box 2010
Buffalo, NY 14231-2010
PH: (716)688-5048
Fax: (716)688-5049
Albrecht, Dr. Brian M., President

International Society for Transgenic
Technologies [6113]
Roswell Park Cancer Institute
Elm and Carlton St.
Buffalo, NY 14263
PH: (716)845-5843
Fax: (716)845-5908
Parker-Thornburg, Jan, President

National Chemical Credit Association
[1257]
500 Seneca St., Ste. 400
Buffalo, NY 14204-1963
PH: (716)885-4444
Toll free: 844-937-3268
Liflieri, Glenn, Exec. Chmn. of the
Bd.

National Council of State Sociologi-
cal Associations [7186]
Medaille College
Buffalo, NY 14214-2695
Fuller, Paul, Secretary

Pediatric Digestion and Motility
Disorders Society, Inc. [16613]
701 Washington St.
Buffalo, NY 14205
LoFaso, Marcella A., President

Print Alliance Credit Exchange
[1261]
1100 Main St.
Buffalo, NY 14209-2356
Fax: (716)878-2807
Meyers, Michael, Dir. of Member
Svcs.

Radical Philosophy Association
[10115]
c/o Brandon Absher
320 Porter Ave.
Buffalo, NY 14201
Absher, Brandon, Coord.

Skating Association for the Blind and
Handicapped [23156]
2607 Niagara St.
Buffalo, NY 14207-1029
PH: (716)362-9600
Fax: (716)362-9601
O'Brien, Sheila, Exec. Dir.

Society for Disability Studies [11638]
University at Buffalo
538 Park Hall
Buffalo, NY 14260
PH: (716)645-0276
Fax: (716)645-5954
Hamlin-Smith, Stephan J.

Adirondack Forty-Sixers [23317]
PO Box 180
Cadyville, NY 12918-0180

PH: (518)293-6401
Corell, Phil, Treasurer

International Boxing Hall of Fame
    Museum [22712]
1 Hall of Fame Dr.
Canastota, NY 13032
PH: (315)697-7095
Fax: (315)697-5356
Brophy, Edward P., Exec. Dir.

Streeter Family Association [20932]
3273 State Route 248
Canisteo, NY 14823
Streeter, Perry, President

Commission on Opticianry Accredita-
    tion [16413]
c/o Debra White, Director of Ac-
    creditation
PO Box 592
Canton, NY 13617
PH: (703)468-0566
White, Debra, Dir. of Accred.

Ephemera Society of America
    [22012]
PO Box 95
Cazenovia, NY 13035-0095
PH: (315)655-9139
Fax: (315)655-9139
Freund, David, Director

H.H. Franklin Club, Inc. [21385]
Cazenovia College
Cazenovia, NY 13035
PH: (201)384-1530
    (518)883-5765
Fax: (518)773-7742
Eby, Bill, President

Jewish Educators Assembly [8139]
Broadway & Locust Ave.
Cedarhurst, NY 11516
PH: (516)569-2537
Fax: (516)295-9039
Edelstein, Edward, Exec. Dir.

Disability Resources, Inc. [11586]
4 Glatter Ln.
Centereach, NY 11720-1032
PH: (631)585-0290
Fax: (631)585-0290
Klauber, Avery, Exec. Dir., Founder

Holy Face Association [19842]
PO Box 821
Champlain, NY 12919-0821
PH: (518)320-8570
Deery, Gordon, Director

Camp Fire Club of America [3823]
230 Campfire Rd.
Chappaqua, NY 10514
PH: (914)941-0199

Equine Advocates [10617]
PO Box 354
Chatham, NY 12037-0354
PH: (518)245-1599
Wagner, Susan, Founder, President

International Order of the King's
    Daughters and Sons [19991]
34 Vincent Ave.
Chautauqua, NY 14722
PH: (716)357-4951
Fax: (716)357-3762
Cote, Joyce S., President

Buffalo Sabres Booster Club [24072]
PO Box 1065
Cheektowaga, NY 14225

Building Stone Institute [3182]
Bldg. 2
5 Riverside Dr.
Chestertown, NY 12817

PH: (518)803-4336
Toll free: 866-786-6313
Fax: (518)803-4338
Bennett, Jane, Exec. VP

Antique and Classic Boat Society
    [22598]
422 James St.
Clayton, NY 13624
PH: (315)686-2628
Fax: (315)686-2680
Howard, John, President

Gar Wood Society [22615]
c/o The Antique Boat Museum
750 Mary St.
Clayton, NY 13624
PH: (315)686-4104

International Water Levels Coalition
    [4770]
PO Box 316
Clayton, NY 13624
Schebaum, Bill, Bd. Member

International Waterless Printing As-
    sociation [1539]
5 Southside Dr., Unit 11-328
Clifton Park, NY 12065-3870
PH: (518)387-9321
O'Rourke, John, VP

Medical Image Computing and
    Computer Assisted Intervention
    Society [15690]
c/o Stephen Aylward, Treasurer
Kitware, Inc.
28 Corporate Dr.
Clifton Park, NY 12065
Niessen, Wiro, Chmn. of the Bd.,
    President

National Association of Independent
    Insurance Auditors and Engineers
    [1895]
PO Box 794
Clifton Park, NY 12065
Toll free: 800-232-2342
Lowry, Fred, Jr., VP

North American Board of Certified
    Energy Practitioners [6503]
56 Clifton Country Rd., Ste. 202
Clifton Park, NY 12065
Toll free: 800-654-0021
Fax: (518)899-1092
Spies, Jeff, Secretary

North American Sankethi Association
    [9174]
34 Longwood Dr.
Clifton Park, NY 12065
Rudrapatna, Ashok, President

Society for Melanoma Research
    [14065]
c/o Site Solution Worldwide
PO Box 113
Clifton Park, NY 12065
Toll free: 866-374-6338
Fisher, David, President

To Love a Child, Inc. [11167]
PO Box 165
Clifton Park, NY 12065-0165
PH: (518)859-4424
Pierre, Colleen, President

Zebrafish Disease Models Society
    [5895]
1023 Route 146
Clifton Park, NY 12065
PH: (518)399-7181
Amatruda, James F., MD, President

International Association Auto Theft
    Investigators [5466]
PO Box 223
Clinton, NY 13323-0223

PH: (315)853-1913
Fax: (315)883-1310
Abounader, John V., Exec. Dir.

Intimate Apparel Square Club
    [11859]
326 Field Rd.
Clinton Corners, NY 12514
PH: (845)758-5752
Fax: (845)758-2546
Costello, Walter, Secretary

Underfashion Club, Inc. [113]
326 Field Rd.
Clinton Corners, NY 12514
PH: (845)758-6405
Fax: (845)758-2546
Costello, Walter A., Director

Lifetime Benefit Solutions [3120]
2457 State Route 7, Ste. 1
Cobleskill, NY 12043
Toll free: 800-322-3920
Fax: (518)234-3026

National Caves Association [1154]
PO Box 625
Cobleskill, NY 12043
PH: (270)749-2228
Toll free: 866-552-2837
Fax: (270)749-2428
Beckler, Greg, VP

North American Association for
    Laser Therapy [15524]
142 Whitbeck Rd.
Coeymans Hollow, NY 12046
Choy, Daniel S.J., MD, Exec. Dir.

National Coalition for Electronics
    Education [6438]
71 Columbia St.
Cohoes, NY 12047-2939
Toll free: 888-777-8851
Sawyer, Ron, Administrator

Professional Service Association
    [3077]
71 Columbia St.
Cohoes, NY 12047
Toll free: 888-777-8851
Fax: (518)237-0418
Campbell, Jim, Director

The Whaling Museum & Education
    Center [9781]
279 Main St.
Cold Spring Harbor, NY 11724
PH: (631)367-3418
Aitken, Patricia, President

Association for the Advancement of
    Blind and Retarded [17688]
1508 College Point Blvd.
College Point, NY 11356
PH: (718)321-3800
McAlvanah, Tom, Exec. Dir.

Chess Collectors International
    [21589]
PO Box 166
Commack, NY 11725
PH: (631)543-1330
Fax: (516)543-7901
Flowers, Brian, Gen. Mgr.

National Coalition of Mental Health
    Professionals and Consumers
    [15793]
PO Box 438
Commack, NY 11725
PH: (631)979-5307
Toll free: 866-826-2548
Fax: (631)979-5293
Saccardi, Kathleen, Office Mgr.

Sportsmen's Association for
    Firearms Education, Inc. [18255]
PO Box 343
Commack, NY 11725S

PH: (631)475-8125
Cushman, John L., President

Historical Society of Early American
    Decoration [8902]
PO Box 30
Cooperstown, NY 13326-0030
PH: (607)547-5667
Toll free: 866-304-7323
Stewart, Ann, Admin. Asst.

National Baseball Hall of Fame and
    Museum [22559]
25 Main St.
Cooperstown, NY 13326
PH: (607)547-7200
Toll free: 888-425-5633
Fax: (607)547-2044
Clark, Jane Forbes, Chairperson,
    Director

Ladies Kennel Association of
    America [21911]
c/o Patricia Cruz, Secreatary
15 Shiloh Ct.
Coram, NY 11727
PH: (631)928-1517
Rechler, Evelyn, President

Love and Hope Ministries
    International [12215]
1 East Ave.
Coram, NY 11727
PH: (631)828-4062
    (718)658-1920

The National Center For Men
    [18667]
117 Pauls Path, No. 531
Coram, NY 11727
PH: (613)476-2115
Feit, Mel, Exec. Dir.

Omnilogy, Inc. [12175]
22 Camp Fire Ln.
Coram, NY 11727
Dequito, April, CEO, Founder

United States Snowshoe Association
    [23180]
678 County Route 25
Corinth, NY 12822
PH: (518)654-7648
    (518)420-6961
Elmore, Mark, Sports Dir.

American Overseas Dietetic Associa-
    tion [16205]
PO Box 1346
Corning, NY 14830

Corning Cinderella Softball League,
    Inc. [23200]
Baker St.
Corning, NY 14830
PH: (607)346-5838
Robertson, John

Education Credit Union Council
    [951]
PO Box 426
Corning, NY 14830
Toll free: 855-888-5851
Fax: (866)861-8132
Conway, Chris, President

Ananda Marga [20653]
9738 42nd Ave.
Corona, NY 11368
PH: (718)898-1603

Automotive Lift Institute [312]
80 Wheeler Ave.
Cortland, NY 13045
PH: (607)756-7775
Fax: (607)756-0888
Schanze, Stet, Chairman

National Academy of Arbitrators
    [4966]
NAA Operations Ctr.
1 N Main St., Ste. 412

Cortland, NY 13045
PH: (607)756-8363
Toll free: 888-317-1729
Ponak, Allen, President

Bellanca-Champion Club [21216]
PO Box 100
Coxsackie, NY 12051
Szego, Robert, President

Xeroderma Pigmentosum Society
[14868]
437 Snydertown Rd.
Craryville, NY 12521-5224
PH: (518)851-3466
Mahar, Caren, Exec. Dir.

CEDAM International [3825]
2 Fox Rd.
Croton on Hudson, NY 10520
PH: (914)271-5365

Physicians Against World Hunger
[12107]
19 Old Post Rd. S
Croton on Hudson, NY 10520
PH: (914)737-8570
Altamura, Michael, M.D., Contact

Scottish Deerhound Club of America
[21958]
c/o Wendy Fast, Membership
Secretary
8406 Green Rd.
Dansville, NY 14437
Smith, Kris, President

LittleLight International [12550]
2061 Deer Park Ave.
Deer Park, NY 11729
PH: (631)940-9966
Fax: (631)940-9960
Felton, David, Director

Professional Women Singers As-
sociation [9998]
PO Box 29
Deer Park, NY 11729
Kerns, Madeline Abel, Mem.

American Lutheran Publicity Bureau
[20301]
PO Box 327
Delhi, NY 13753-0327
PH: (607)746-7511
Sauer, Paul R., Exec. Dir.

Therapeutic Touch International As-
sociation [15270]
PO Box 130
Delmar, NY 12054
PH: (518)325-1185
Fax: (509)693-3537
Conlin, Sue, President

Family Campers and RVers [22720]
Bldg. 2
4804 Transit Rd.
Depew, NY 14043
PH: (716)668-6242
Toll free: 800-245-9755
Ludwig, Dave, President

American Fox Terrier Club [21810]
6838 Lake Shore Rd.
Derby, NY 14047-9749
Smith, J. W., Director

North American Vegetarian Society
[10293]
PO Box 72
Dolgeville, NY 13329
PH: (518)568-7970
Lehmkuhl, Vance, Mgr.

Project HEAL [14650]
38-18 W Dr.
Douglaston, NY 11363
Fax: (718)709-7787
Lenz, Ashley, COO

National Coalition for Assistive and
Rehab Technology [15695]
54 Towhee Ct.
East Amherst, NY 14051
PH: (716)839-9728
Fax: (716)839-9624
Clayback, Don, Exec. Dir.

Dunlop - Dunlap Family Society
[20857]
PO Box 652
East Aurora, NY 14052
PH: (716)655-2521
Dunlop, Mr. Peter, President

Foundation for the Study of the Arts
and Crafts Movement at Roycroft
[21289]
46 Walnut St.
East Aurora, NY 14052-2330
PH: (716)653-4477
Turgeon, Kitty, Exec. Dir.

Roycrofters-at-Large Association
[21782]
1054 Olean Rd.
East Aurora, NY 14052
PH: (716)655-7252
Peters, Christine, Exec. Dir.

Alliance for International Women's
Rights [19253]
PO Box 165
East Chatham, NY 12060
PH: (518)632-4797
Herb, Lisa, Exec. Dir.

National Latino Officers Association
[5443]
27-14 Kearney St.
East Elmhurst, NY 11369
Toll free: 866-579-5806
Fax: (347)426-2188
Gonzalez, Manny, President

Accreditation Commission for
Homeopathic Education in North
America [15285]
105 State Route 151
East Greenbush, NY 12061
PH: (518)477-1416
Cotroneo, Rick, President

Afghan Hands [10464]
220 Treescape Dr.
East Hampton, NY 11937
PH: (312)786-3309
Maulawizada, Matin, Founder

United States Billiard Association
[22587]
58 Hawthorne Ave.
East Islip, NY 11730-1926
PH: (516)238-6193
Shovak, Jim, President

Mothers' Home Business Network
[1644]
PO Box 423
East Meadow, NY 11554
PH: (516)997-7394
Fax: (516)997-0839
Fiumara, Georganne, Founder

National Infertility Network Exchange
[12419]
PO Box 204
East Meadow, NY 11554
PH: (516)794-5772
Fax: (516)794-0008
Stargot, Ilene, President

Performance Poets Association
[10155]
c/o Cliff Bleidner
2176 3rd St.
East Meadow, NY 11554-1810
PH: (516)582-8910

The Magic Penny, Inc. [12803]
c/o Lucy Sumner,President and
International Director
24 Eldorado Dr.
East Northport, NY 11731
PH: (631)486-3822
Sumner, Lucy, President, Director

Surgical Infection Society [17411]
PO Box 1278
East Northport, NY 11731
PH: (631)368-1880
Fax: (631)368-4466
Namias, Nicholas, President

Van Voorhees Association [20939]
c/o Albert T. Van
9 Purdy Ave.
East Northport, NY 11731-4501
Van, Albert T., Contact

National Community Oncology
Dispensing Association, Inc.
[16350]
PO Box 308
East Syracuse, NY 13057
PH: (315)256-4935
Reff, Michael J., RPh, Founder,
President

Adirondack Council [3786]
103 Hand Ave., No. 3
Elizabethtown, NY 12932
PH: (518)873-2240
Toll free: 877-873-2240
Fax: (518)873-6675
Kafin, Robert J., Chairman

Dharma Drum Mountain Buddhist
Association [19775]
90-56 Corona Ave.
Elmhurst, NY 11373
PH: (718)592-6593
Yen, Master Sheng, President

National Association of Nigerian
Nurses in North America [16150]
2195 Hoffman Ave.
Elmont, NY 11003
PH: (516)528-1644
Ugorji, Julia, RN, President

Reach the Children [11137]
14 Chesham Way
Fairport, NY 14450
PH: (585)223-3344
Clawson, Kevin, President

American Historical Print Collectors
Society [21285]
94 Marine St.
Farmingdale, NY 11735-5605

American Solar Action Plan [7196]
52 Columbia St.
Farmingdale, NY 11735-2606
PH: (516)694-0759
Mason, James, Director, Founder

Association of Average Adjusters of
the United States and Canada
[1835]
126 Midwood Ave.
Farmingdale, NY 11735
Sales, Brian, Chairman

Coma/Traumatic Brain Injury
Recovery Association [15919]
8300 Republic Airport, Ste. 106
Farmingdale, NY 11735
PH: (631)756-1826

Craniosynostosis and Positional Pla-
giocephaly Support [14333]
208 NY-190 No. 205
Farmingdale, NY 11735
Toll free: 888-572-5526
Galm, Amy, President, Exec. Dir.

Workmen's Benefit Fund of the
U.S.A. [19501]
399 Conklin St., Ste. 310
Farmingdale, NY 11735-2614
PH: (516)938-6060
Fax: (516)706-9020

Honest Ballot Association [18182]
27246 Grand Central Pky.
Floral Park, NY 11005
Toll free: 800-541-1851
Gibbs, Linda Chiarelli, President

Indian Dental Association (USA)
[14441]
140 Tulip Ave.
Floral Park, NY 11001
PH: (516)345-8261
Gehani, Dr. Chad P., Exec. Dir.

Italic Institute of America [9618]
PO Box 818
Floral Park, NY 11001
PH: (516)488-7400
Fax: (516)488-4889
Mancini, John, Exec. Dir.

Pedal Steel Guitar Association
[9994]
PO Box 20248
Floral Park, NY 11002-0248
PH: (516)616-9214
Fax: (516)616-9214
Maickel, Bob, President

Association of Chinese American
Physicians [16741]
33-70 Prince St., Ste. 703
Flushing, NY 11354
PH: (718)321-8798
Fax: (718)321-8836
He, Zili, Dr., CEO

International Cell Death Society
[14359]
c/o Dr. Zahra Zakeri, President
Dept. of Biology
Queens College and Graduate
Center of CUNY
65-30 Kissena Blvd.
Flushing, NY 11367-1575
PH: (718)997-3450
Fax: (718)997-3429
Zakeri, Dr. Zahra, President

International Counter-Terrorism Of-
ficers Association [19182]
PO Box 580009
Flushing, NY 11358-0009
PH: (212)564-5048

Joint Industry Board of the Electrical
Industry [873]
158-11 Harry Van Arsdale Jr. Ave.
Flushing, NY 11365
PH: (718)591-2000
Fax: (718)380-7741
Finkel, Dr. Gerald, Chairman

Korean American Civic Empower-
ment [18602]
35-20 147th St., No. 2D
Flushing, NY 11354
PH: (718)961-4117
Fax: (718)961-4603
Kim, Dongchan, President

Pictorial Photographers of America
[10145]
147-10 41st Ave.
Flushing, NY 11355-1266
PH: (212)243-0273
Buck, Kathryn, President

China American Psychoanalytic Alliance [16911]
76-26 113th St., 5G
Forest Hills, NY 11375
Snyder, Dr. Elise, President

Institute of General Semantics
[10212]
72-11 Austin St., No. 233
Forest Hills, NY 11375
PH: (212)729-7973
Fax: (718)793-2527
Levinson, Martin H., President

We, The World [12964]
PO Box 750651
Forest Hills, NY 11375-0651
PH: (212)867-0846
Ulfik, Rick, Chmn. of the Bd.,
Founder

Global Associates for Health
Development, Inc. [15450]
PO Box 790
Freeport, NY 11520
PH: (516)771-1200
Fax: (516)771-1210
Smith, Mignon, RN, Founder,
President

Athletic Equipment Managers As-
sociation [23215]
460 Hunt Hill Rd.
Freeville, NY 13068-9643
PH: (607)539-6300
Fax: (607)539-6340
Cutting, Dorothy, Office Mgr.

Association of Orthodox Jewish
Scientists [7122]
69-09 172nd St.
Fresh Meadows, NY 11365
PH: (718)969-3669
Fax: (718)969-1947

Pi Delta Psi Fraternity, Inc. [9334]
176-25 Union Tpke.
Fresh Meadows, NY 11366
Kayserian, Andrew, President

Women for Afghan Women [12064]
158-24 73rd Ave.
Fresh Meadows, NY 11366-1024
PH: (718)591-2434
Fax: (718)591-2430
Naderi, Manizha, Exec. Dir.

Children's Leukemia Research As-
sociation [13941]
585 Stewart Ave., Ste. 18
Garden City, NY 11530
PH: (516)222-1944
Fax: (516)222-0457
Weinberg, Allan D., Exec. Dir.

National Association of Professional
Women [3497]
1325 Franklin Ave., Ste. 160
Garden City, NY 11530
PH: (516)877-5500
Toll free: 866-540-6279
Ishak, Sherry, Mem.

Scientific Equipment and Furniture
Association [3031]
65 Hilton Ave.
Garden City, NY 11530
PH: (516)294-5424
Toll free: 877-294-5424
Fax: (516)294-2758
Sutton, David J., CAE, Exec. Dir.,
Gen. Counsel

Garden Conservancy [3875]
20 Nazareth Way
Garrison, NY 10524
PH: (845)424-6500
Fax: (845)424-6501
Young du Pont, Jenny, President

The Hastings Center [11800]
21 Malcolm Gordon Rd.
Garrison, NY 10524
PH: (845)424-4040
Fax: (845)424-4545
Adelson, Andrew S.

Pi Delta Phi [23765]
c/o Dr. Beverly J. Evans, Executive
Director
State University of New York at
Geneseo
Dept. of Languages and Literatures
Welles 211
1 College Cir.
Geneseo, NY 14454
PH: (585)245-5247
Fax: (585)245-5399
Evans, Dr. Beverly J., PhD, Exec.
Dir.

International Association of Liberal
Religious Women [20641]
c/o Susan Caravello, Treasurer
50 Harwood Dr. E
Glen Cove, NY 11542

Veterans Rebuilding Life [13253]
PO Box 327
Glen Cove, NY 11542
PH: (212)560-2235
Popow, Dre, Exec. Ofc.

National Association of Stationary
Operating Engineers [6728]
212 Elmwood Ave. Ext., Ste. 500
Gloversville, NY 12078
PH: (518)620-3683
OBrien, John, Exec. Asst.

Harness Racing Museum and Hall of
Fame [22916]
240 Main St.
Goshen, NY 10924
PH: (845)294-6330
Fax: (845)294-3463
DeVan, Lawrence S., President

American Society of Professional
Graphologists [6701]
23 South Dr.
Great Neck, NY 11021
PH: (516)487-5287
Siegel, Patricia, President

American Society for the Protection
of Nature in Israel [3806]
c/o Robin Gordon, Director
28 Arrandale Ave.
Great Neck, NY 11024
Toll free: 800-411-0966
Gordon, Robin, Director

Brain and Body Alternatives [15597]
290 Community Dr.
Great Neck, NY 11021
PH: (631)807-6819
(631)873-6366
Fax: (516)686-0641
DiPeri, Frances, Founder

International Seven-Star Mantis
Style Lee Kam Wing Martial Art
Association USA [22994]
Ortiz Chinese Boxing Academy
148-B Middle Neck Rd.
Great Neck, NY 11021
PH: (516)972-1670
Ortiz, Raul, Contact

National Adrenal Diseases Founda-
tion [14708]
505 Northern Blvd.
Great Neck, NY 11021
PH: (516)487-4992
Wong, Ms. Melanie G., Exec. Dir.

National InterScholastic Swimming
Coaches Association of America
[23286]
29 Fairview Ave.
Great Neck, NY 11023-1206
PH: (843)637-4663
McElroy, Arvel

National Money Transmitters Association [1258]
12 Welwyn Rd., Ste. C
Great Neck, NY 11021

PH: (516)829-2742
Landsman, David, Exec. Dir.

Interhelp [19112]
PO Box 111
Greenwich, NY 12834-0111
PH: (518)475-1929
Harley, Carol, President

Project Children [11263]
PO Box 933
Greenwood Lake, NY 10925
Mulcahy, Denis, Chairman, Founder

Nurses House, Inc. [16170]
2113 Western Ave., Ste. 2
Guilderland, NY 12084-9559
PH: (518)456-7858
Mahoney, Elizabeth, President

Professional Football Researchers
Association [22866]
257 Joslyn Rd.
Guilford, NY 13780-3138
Ford, Mark L., President, Exec. Dir.

CSB Ministries [20659]
PO Box 1010
Hamburg, NY 14075
PH: (716)526-0026
(716)951-5515
Toll free: 800-815-5573
Haima, Scott, Director

Association of Professional Model
Makers [6548]
PO Box 165
Hamilton, NY 13346-0165
PH: (315)750-0803
Toll free: 877-765-6950
Martinez, Samanthi, Exec. Dir.

Association for Research in
Personality [7062]
c/o Rebecca Shiner, Executive Of-
ficer
Dept. of Psychology
13 Oak Dr.
Hamilton, NY 13346
PH: (217)333-3486
Fax: (217)244-5876
Funder, David, President

D.H. Lawrence Society of North
America [9072]
c/o Matthew Leone, Treasurer
45 Broad St.
Hamilton, NY 13346
Laird, Holly

EPIE Institute [8030]
PO Box 590
Hampton Bays, NY 11946-0509
PH: (631)728-9100
Komoski, P. Kenneth, Exec. Dir.,
President

James Joyce Society [9066]
80 E Hartsdale Ave., No. 414
Hartsdale, NY 10530-2805
PH: (516)764-3119
Fargnoli, A. Nicholas, President

Stroke Help Association [17299]
65 Circle Dr.
Hastings on Hudson, NY 10706
PH: (914)478-3687
Schor, Robert H., President, Chair-
man

National Junior Baseball League
[22562]
4 White Spruce Ln.
Hauppauge, NY 11788
PH: (631)582-5191
Sullivan, Frank, Commissioner

International Watch Collectors
Society [22445]
257 Adams Ln.
Hewlett, NY 11557

PH: (516)295-2516
Fax: (516)374-5060
Destino, Ralph, Chairman

Optometrists Network [16438]
58 Mohonk Rd.
High Falls, NY 12440
PH: (212)923-0496
Cooper, Rachel, Founder

International Psychohistorical Association [9491]
c/o Denis O'Keefe, Treasurer
142A Main St.
Highland Falls, NY 10928
O'Keefe, Denis J., Treasurer

World T.E.A.M. Sports [22806]
4250 Veterans Memorial Hwy., Ste.
420 E
Holbrook, NY 11741-4020
Toll free: 855-987-8326
Fax: (855)288-3377
Bell, Sarah, Director

Association of Holocaust Organiza-
tions [18345]
PO Box 230317
Hollis, NY 11423
PH: (516)582-4571
Shulman, Dr. William L., President

Protect Allergic Kids [13581]
PO Box 227
Holtsville, NY 11742
PH: (631)207-1681
Stainkamp, Cristina, President

All Roads Ministry [19789]
55 Palen Rd., No. 3
Hopewell Junction, NY 12533
PH: (845)226-4172
Lewis, Vincent P., Founder,
President

Rose Hybridizers Association
[22121]
c/o Mr. Larry Peterson, Treasurer
21 S Wheaton Rd.
Horseheads, NY 14845-1077
Peterson, Mr. Larry, Treasurer

Arthur Miller Society [10360]
c/o Steve Manio
100-14 160 Ave.
Howard Beach, NY 11414
PH: (212)556-5600
Abbotson, Sue, Web Adm.

Bee Native [3635]
Mantis Farm
68 Fingar Rd.
Hudson, NY 12534-7208
PH: (917)679-0567
Young, Helen Faraday, Founder

National Young Farmers Coalition
[4165]
PO Box 1074
Hudson, NY 12534
PH: (518)643-3564
Bryan, Alex, President

Transportation and Logistics Council,
Inc. [3109]
120 Main St.
Huntington, NY 11743-8001
PH: (631)549-8988
Fax: (631)549-8962
Pezold, George Carl, Exec. Dir.

H2 Empower [11371]
PO Box 493
Huntington Station, NY 11746
PH: (631)549-9346
Boxwill, Helen, Exec. Dir.

Walt Whitman Birthplace Association
[9111]
246 Old Walt Whitman Rd.

Huntington Station, NY 11746-4148
PH: (631)427-5240
Fax: (631)427-5247
Shor, Cynthia, Exec. Dir.

Frederick A. Cook Society **[10320]**
PO Box 247
Hurleyville, NY 12747
PH: (845)434-8044
Fax: (845)434-8056
Gibbons, Russell W., Editor, Exec. Dir.

International Foodservice Editorial Council **[2686]**
7 Point Pl.
Hyde Park, NY 12538
PH: (845)229-6973
(845)527-5679
Fax: (845)229-6973
Oches, Sam, Co-Ch.

American Youth Circus Organization **[9160]**
PO Box 482
Ithaca, NY 14851
PH: (914)441-8834
AlFord, Jesse, President

Association of Field Ornithologists **[3657]**
c/o Paul Rodewald, President
Cornell Lab of Ornithology
159 Sapsucker Woods Rd.
Ithaca, NY 14850
PH: (607)254-6276
Rodewald, Paul, President

Committee for Crescent Observation International **[9603]**
1069 Ellis Hollow Rd.
Ithaca, NY 14850
PH: (607)277-6706
Fax: (607)277-6706
Afzal, Dr. Omar, Chairman

Committee on US/Latin American Relations **[19529]**
316 Anabel Taylor Hall
Cornell University
Ithaca, NY 14853
PH: (607)255-7293
Fax: (607)255-9550
Wessels, Sally, Chmn. of the Bd.

Cornell Feline Health Center **[17645]**
235 Hungerford Hill Rd.
Ithaca, NY 14853
PH: (607)253-3414
(607)253-3000
Toll free: 800-548-8937
Fax: (607)253-3419
Kornreich, Dr. Bruce, DVM, Assoc. Dir.

Cornell Lab of Ornithology **[6957]**
159 Sapsucker Woods Rd.
Ithaca, NY 14850
PH: (607)254-2165
Toll free: 800-843-2473
Fax: (607)254-2415
Fitzpatrick, Dr. John W., Exec. Dir.

Cross World Africa **[13043]**
14 Redwood Ln., B-101
Ithaca, NY 14850
PH: (607)227-1594
Thompson, Mr. Kevin, Exec. Dir.

Educate the Children International **[11227]**
PO Box 414
Ithaca, NY 14851-0414
PH: (607)272-1176
Prentice, Elisabeth, President

Global Applied Disability Research and Information Network on Employment and Training **[14549]**
201 Dolgen Hall
Yang-Tan Institute

Cornell University
Ithaca, NY 14853
Kamp, Michael, Chairperson

Group of Universities for the Advancement of Vietnamese in America **[10302]**
Rockefeller Hall
Department of Asia Studies
Cornell University
Ithaca, NY 14853
Tran, VietThuy, President

Historians of Eighteenth-Century Art and Architecture **[8898]**
Ithaca College, 953 Danby Rd.
113 Gannett Ctr.
Ithaca, NY 14850
Yonan, Michael, President

International Association of Law Schools **[8215]**
c/o Barbara Holden-Smith, Secretary-Treasurer
Cornell Law School
124 Myron Taylor Hall
Ithaca, NY 14853
Fax: (607)255-7033
Wang, Francis S.L., President

International Service for the Acquisition of Agri-biotech Applications **[3570]**
105 Leland Lab
Cornell University
Ithaca, NY 14853
PH: (607)255-1724
Fax: (607)255-1215
Meenen, Ms. Patricia, Administrator

Omega Tau Sigma **[23982]**
PO Box 876
Ithaca, NY 14851-0876
Vredenburg, Seth, President

Paleontological Research Institution **[6972]**
1259 Trumansburg Rd.
Ithaca, NY 14850
PH: (607)273-6623
Fax: (607)273-6620
Allmon, Warren D., Director

Phi Gamma Nu **[23698]**
213 E King Rd.
Ithaca, NY 14850
PH: (630)412-1746
Hagiwara, Tuesday, Exec. Dir.

Planners Network **[18999]**
106 W Sibley Hall
Cornell University
Ithaca, NY 14853
Hartman, Chester, Founder

Social Science History Association **[7172]**
391 Pine Tree Rd.
905 W Main St., Ste. 18-B
Ithaca, NY 14850
Block, William C., Exec. Dir.

Society for the Humanities **[9558]**
Cornell University
Andrew D. White House
27 East Ave.
Ithaca, NY 14853
PH: (607)255-4086
Fax: (607)255-1422
Ahl, Mary, Mgr. of Admin.

Society for the Psychological Study of Lesbian, Gay, Bisexual and Transgender Issues **[16941]**
c/o Brenda J. Marston, Curator
Cornell University
Human Sexuality Collection and Library Women's Studies Selector

2B Carl A Kroch Library
Ithaca, NY 14853
Balsam, Kimberly, President

Telluride Association **[7803]**
217 West Ave.
Ithaca, NY 14850-3911
PH: (607)273-5011
Fax: (607)272-2667
Baer, Ellen, Dir. of Admin.

InterCollegiate Outing Club Association **[23324]**
35-41 72 St.
35-41 72 St.
Jackson Heights, NY 11372
Nowak, Jonathan, Exec. Sec.

Leschetizky Association **[9948]**
37-21 90th St., Apt. 2R
Jackson Heights, NY 11372-7838
Drago, Ms. Young, Registrar, Treasurer

Bangladesh Medical Association of North America **[15718]**
87-46 168 St.
Jamaica, NY 11432
Fax: (718)526-6661
Ahmed, Rafique, MD, PhD, President

Hip-Hop Summit Youth Council, Inc. **[9256]**
PO Box 300925
Jamaica, NY 11430
PH: (212)316-7639
Fax: (805)800-1459
Fisher, Randy, Exec. Dir.

National Organization of Industrial Trade Unions **[23449]**
148-06 Hillside Ave.
Jamaica, NY 11435
PH: (718)291-3434
Jones, Gerard A., President

Dog Writers Association of America **[2677]**
c/o Susan Ewing, Secretary
66 Adams St.
Jamestown, NY 14701
Santi, Pat, Secretary

Magnolia Society International **[6150]**
3000 Henneberry Rd.
Jamesville, NY 13078-9640
Edward, Beth, Secretary

rock CAN roll **[12110]**
PO Box 700
Jericho, NY 11753
PH: (516)822-3457
Holtzman, Aimee, Founder, President

Iroquois Studies Association **[10043]**
28 Zevan Rd.
Johnson City, NY 13790
PH: (607)729-0016

OPP Concerned Sheep Breeders Society **[17657]**
228 Main St.
Jordanville, NY 13361
PH: (315)858-6042
(952)955-2596
Walsh, Jean T., Treasurer

Adirondack Trail Improvement Society **[23318]**
PO Box 565
Keene Valley, NY 12943
PH: (518)576-9157

Keuka College Alumni Association **[19331]**
Office of Alumni and Family Relations

141 Central Ave., Ball 122
Keuka Park, NY 14478
PH: (315)279-5238
(315)279-5338
Hourihan, Jeremy, President

Dominicans on Wall Street **[1231]**
41 Kew Gardens Rd, Apt. 6A
Kew Gardens, NY 11415
Gutierrez, Frank, President, Bd. Member

Intermed International **[15479]**
125-28 Queens Blvd., Ste. 538
Kew Gardens, NY 11415
PH: (646)820-7360
Chaney, Dr. Verne E., Jr., Founder

Friends of Lindenwald **[9391]**
PO Box 64
Kinderhook, NY 12106

Ohashi Institute **[16458]**
PO Box 505
Kinderhook, NY 12106
PH: (518)758-6879
Toll free: 800-810-4190
Fax: (518)758-6609
Ohashi, Wataru, Director

National Association for the Dually Diagnosed **[14555]**
132 Fair St.
Kingston, NY 12401
PH: (845)331-4336
Toll free: 800-331-5362
Fax: (845)331-4569
Fletcher, Dr. Robert J., CEO

American Austin/Bantam Club **[21316]**
c/o Marilyn Sanson, Treasurer
PO Box 63
Kirkville, NY 13082-0063
PH: (315)656-7568
Sanson, Marilyn, Treasurer

World Class Ghana **[12065]**
PO Box 325
Lagrangeville, NY 12540
Willsey, Judy, Founder

Cover Collectors Circuit Club **[22324]**
PO Box 266
Lake Clear, NY 12945-0266
Thompson, Renate, Managing Dir.

Creativity Coaching Association **[22729]**
PO Box 328
Lake George, NY 12845
PH: (518)798-6933
Down, Beverly, CEO, President

U.S. Bobsled and Skeleton Federation **[23178]**
196 Old Military Rd.
Lake Placid, NY 12946
PH: (518)523-1842
Fax: (518)523-9491
Steele, Darrin, CEO

United States Luge Association **[22978]**
57 Church St.
Lake Placid, NY 12946-1805
PH: (518)523-2071
Fax: (518)523-4106
Bell, Dwight, President

Kappa Alpha Society **[23903]**
3109 N Triphammer Rd.
Lansing, NY 14882
Toll free: 877-895-1825
Enteman, John, President

Atlantic Legal Foundation **[5419]**
2039 Palmer Ave., Ste. 104
Larchmont, NY 10538

PH: (914)834-3322
Fax: (914)833-1022
Fisk, Hayward D., Chairman, Act. Pres.

Angela Thirkell Society [9102]
c/o Lynne Crowley, Treasurer
PO Box 203
Larchmont, NY 10538
Fritzer, Dr. Penelope, Secretary, President

Association of Governmental Risk Pools [5311]
9 Cornell Rd.
Latham, NY 12110
PH: (518)389-2782
Gergen, Ann, Exec. Dir.

Interstate Renewable Energy Council [6495]
PO Box 1156
Latham, NY 12110-1156
PH: (518)621-7379
Weissman, Jane, President, CEO

Women's Motorcyclist Foundation [22239]
7 Lent Ave.
Le Roy, NY 14482-1009
PH: (585)768-6054
    (585)415-8230
Fax: (585)502-0418
Shear, Gin, Exec. Dir.

Canadian/American Border Trade Alliance [3299]
PO Box 929
Lewiston, NY 14092
PH: (716)754-8824
Fax: (716)754-8824
Phillips, Jim, President

National Spiritualist Association of Churches [20510]
13 Cottage Row
Lily Dale, NY 14752
PH: (716)595-2000
Fax: (716)595-2020
Gosselin, Rev. Bradley, President

Coalition of Landlords, Homeowners, & Merchants [18931]
656C N Wellwood Ave.
Lindenhurst, NY 11757
PH: (631)376-2110
    (631)661-7015
Fax: (631)376-2148
Akujuo, Uzo, Contact

Merrill's Marauders Association [21197]
c/o Robert Passanisi, Chairman
111 Kramer Dr.
Lindenhurst, NY 11757-5407
Passanisi, Robert, Chairman

Association of Free Community Papers [2771]
7445 Morgan Rd., Ste. 203
Liverpool, NY 13090
Toll free: 877-203-2327
Fax: (781)459-7770
Colburn, Loren, Exec. Dir.

Support for People with Oral and Head and Neck Cancer [14071]
PO Box 53
Locust Valley, NY 11560-0053
Toll free: 800-377-0928
Fax: (516)671-8794
Leupold, Nancy E., Founder, President

Cure Mommy's Breast Cancer [13954]
PO Box 434
Long Beach, NY 11561

PH: (516)967-1148
Toll free: 888-519-9185
Siddiqui, Ellen, Contact

Green Zionist Alliance, Inc. [4067]
PO Box 1176
Long Beach, NY 11561
PH: (347)559-4492
Cohen, Rabbi Michael, Dir. of Operations, Founder

Multicultural Golf Association of America [22886]
Long Island, NY
PH: (631)288-8255
David, Paul G., Exec. VP, Founder

Afghanistan Blind Women and Children Foundation [17679]
40-10 12th St., Apt 1C
Long Island City, NY 11101
PH: (718)784-4541
Nodrat, Nooria, President

American Sambo Association [22983]
PO Box 5773
Long Island City, NY 11105
PH: (718)728-8054
Koepfer, Stephen R., President

American Wu Shu Society [22984]
PO Box 5898
Long Island City, NY 11105-5898
PH: (718)504-2981
Aguirre, Edward, President

Building Bridges Worldwide, Inc. [11323]
509 48th Ave., Apt. 8E
Long Island City, NY 11101-5622
Basile, Matthew, Founder, Director

Central Yiddish Culture Organization [9634]
CYCO Publishing
51-02 21st St., 7th Fl. A-2
Long Island City, NY 11101-5357
PH: (718)392-0002
Wolfe, Hy, Director

The Floating Hospital [15326]
41-43 Crescent St.
Long Island City, NY 11101
PH: (718)784-2240
Granahan, Sean T., Esq, Gen. Counsel, President

Fortune Society [11526]
29-76 Northern Blvd.
Long Island City, NY 11101
PH: (212)691-7554
Rothenberg, David, Founder

Greek Food and Wine Institute [1333]
34-80 48th St.
Long Island City, NY 11101
PH: (718)729-5277

Healing Arts Initiative, Inc. [10253]
33-02 Skillman Ave. 1st Fl.
Long Island City, NY 11101
PH: (212)575-7676
Fax: (212)575-7669
Dyer, D.Alexandra, Exec. Dir.

Larger Than Life [11067]
54-15 35th St.
Long Island City, NY 11101
PH: (201)567-8990
Toll free: 888-644-4040
Fax: (201)567-8991
Nathaniel, Netta, Exec. Dir.

MoMA PS1 [8985]
22-25 Jackson Ave.
Long Island City, NY 11101

PH: (718)784-2084
Biesenbach, Klaus, Director

Pact Training [11497]
c/o Steven R. Hitt, Team Leader
LaGuardia Community College
31-10 Thomson Ave., Ste. E-241
Long Island City, NY 11101
PH: (718)482-5154
St. George, Joyce, Director

Urban Design Forum [5980]
45-50 30th St., Ste. 10
Long Island City, NY 11101
PH: (718)663-8478
Fax: (718)663-8390
Rose, Daniel, Chairman

American Car Rental Association [2924]
PO Box 584
Long Lake, NY 12847
Toll free: 888-200-2795
Faulkner, Sharon, Exec. Dir.

National Jobs for All Coalition [18188]
PO Box 96
Lynbrook, NY 11563
PH: (203)856-3877
Bell, Charles, V. Ch.

The American Scientific Glassblowers Society [3024]
PO Box 453
Machias, NY 14101-0453
PH: (716)353-8062
Toll free: 866-880-3216
Cornell, Jim, Officer

National Amputation Foundation [11621]
c/o Paul Bernacchio, President
40 Church St.
Malverne, NY 11565
PH: (516)887-3600
Fax: (516)887-3667
Bernacchio, Paul, President

Animal Welfare Advocacy [10582]
141 Halstead Ave., Ste. 301
Mamaroneck, NY 10543
PH: (914)381-6177
Fax: (914)381-6176
Goldberg, Brad, Director, President

New York Turtle and Tortoise Society [4851]
1214 W Boston Post Rd.
Mamaroneck, NY 10543
Toll free: 800-847-7332
Cramer, Lorri, Director

African American Women in Cinema [9293]
Manhattan, NY
PH: (212)769-7949
Fax: (212)871-2074
Renee, Terra, President

Production Equipment Rental Association [1204]
101 W 31st St.
Manhattan, NY 10001-3507
PH: (646)839-0430
Johnston, John, Exec. Dir.

Cingulum NeuroSciences Institute [16044]
4435 Stephanie Dr.
Manlius, NY 13104
Vogt, Dr. Brent A., Founder

Church Periodical Club [20097]
PO Box 1206
Manorville, NY 11949
PH: (631)447-3996
Markert, Rebecca, Treasurer

Norwegian Elkhound Association of America [21934]
c/o Karen V. Freudendorf, Corresponding Secretary
4 Jerusalem Hollow Rd.
Manorville, NY 11949
Viken, Pat, President

CitiHope International [12644]
629 Main St., Ste. 2
Margaretville, NY 12455
PH: (845)586-6202
Moore, Rev. Paul S., Sr., Chmn. of the Bd.

Maryknoll Lay Missioners [20432]
PO Box 307
Maryknoll, NY 10545-0307
PH: (914)762-6364
Toll free: 800-867-2980
Stanton, Sam, Exec. Dir.

Maryknoll Sisters of Saint Dominic [20433]
PO Box 311
Maryknoll, NY 10545-0311
PH: (914)941-7575
Toll free: 866-662-9900
Fax: (914)923-0733
Reddy, Karra, Mgr.

Lithuanian Catholic Religious Aid [19857]
64-25 Perry Ave.
Maspeth, NY 11378-2441
PH: (718)326-5202
Fax: (718)326-5206
Kungys, Salvijus, Administrator

Space Topic Study Unit [22369]
PO Box 780241
Maspeth, NY 11378-0241
Steiner, Tom, President

Gam-Anon International Service Office, Inc. [11866]
PO Box 307
Massapequa Park, NY 11762-0307
PH: (718)352-1671

Mom-mentum [12416]
4940 Merrick Rd., No. 300
Massapequa Park, NY 11762
PH: (516)750-5365
Toll free: 877-939-MOMS
Fierstein, Sharon Sabba, Chairperson

Acoustical Society of America [5852]
c/o Elaine Moran, Office Manager
1305 Walt Whitman Rd., Ste. 300
Melville, NY 11747-4300
PH: (516)576-2360
Fax: (516)576-2377
Holland, Christy K., President

Alliance for Oral Health Across Borders [14371]
135 Duryea Rd., No. E-310
Melville, NY 11747
PH: (631)777-5275
Ismail, Amid, Chairman

Docs for Tots [14187]
128 Breeley Blvd.
Melville, NY 11747
PH: (856)362-4868
Lieser, Dina, MD, Director

International Society of Gastrointestinal Oncology [14794]
200 Broadhollow Rd., Ste. 207
Melville, NY 11747
PH: (631)390-8390
Fax: (631)393-5026
Moore, Malcolm, MD, Contact

National Association of Shareholder and Consumer Attorneys [5088]
c/o Samuel H. Rudman, President
58 S Service Rd., Ste. 200

Melville, NY 11747
PH: (631)367-7100
Fax: (631)367-1173
Riebel, Karen Hanson, Treasurer

National Association for Shoplifting
Prevention [12877]
225 Broadhollow Rd., Ste. 400E
Melville, NY 11747
PH: (631)923-2737
Toll free: 800-848-9595
Fax: (631)923-2743
Kochman, Caroline, Exec. Dir.

Society of Rheology [7100]
c/o American Institute of Physics
Publishing
1305 Walt Whitman Rd., Ste. 300
Melville, NY 11747-4300
PH: (516)576-2397
Fax: (516)349-9704

United States Judo Association
[22966]
2005 Merrick Rd., No. 313
Merrick, NY 11566
Toll free: 877-411-3409
Fax: (888)276-3432
Cohen, Marc, President

Copywriter's Council of America
[764]
CCA Bldg.
7 Putter Ln.
Middle Island, NY 11953-0102
PH: (631)924-8555
Fax: (631)924-3890

Council on National Literatures
[9757]
68-02 Metropolitan Ave.
Middle Village, NY 11379
PH: (718)821-3916

Ontario and Western Railway
Historical Society [10187]
22 Cottage St.
Middletown, NY 10940
PH: (845)283-2637
Barberio, Doug, Chairman

Dyson Foundation [12471]
25 Halcyon Rd.
Millbrook, NY 12545-9611
PH: (845)677-0644
Fax: (845)677-0650
Dyson, Robert R., Chairman

American Air Mail Society [22297]
PO Box 110
Mineola, NY 11501-0110
Graue, Jim, President

Arba Sicula [19643]
c/o Prof. Gaetano Cipolla, President
PO Box 149
Mineola, NY 11501
Cipolla, Prof. Gaetano, President

Music & Memory Inc. [12370]
160 1st St.
Mineola, NY 11501
Cohen, Dan, Exec. Dir.

National Conference of CPA
Practitioners [49]
22 Jericho Tpke., Ste. 110
Mineola, NY 11501
PH: (516)333-8282
Toll free: 888-488-5400
Fax: (516)333-4099
Coscetta, Holly, Exec. Dir.

International Castor Oil Association,
Inc. [2450]
PO Box 595
Mohegan Lake, NY 10547
Knight, Deirdre, Admin. Asst.

American Philosophical Practitioners
Association [8418]
PO Box 166
Monroe, NY 10949-0166
Marinoff, Prof. Lou, PhD, Director,
Editor

The Fight Against Hunger Organiza-
tion [12089]
PO Box 2250
Monroe, NY 10949
PH: (845)232-1420
Forestieri, Christina, Exec. Dir.,
President, Treasurer

American Communities Helping
Israel [12206]
PO Box 556
Monsey, NY 10952-0550
Fax: (845)426-5392
Weilgus, Suzanne, Founder

Hovawart Club of North America
[21893]
PO Box 455
Montgomery, NY 12549-0455
Rutkowski, John, President

Better School Food [8531]
487 E Main St.
Mount Kisco, NY 10549
PH: (914)671-1373

International Thymic Malignancy
Interest Group [13995]
6 Cold Spring Ct.
Mount Kisco, NY 10549
Bruce, Pamela, Project Mgr.

Zeiss Historical Society of America
[21733]
PO Box 556
Mount Kisco, NY 10549

Council on Size and Weight
Discrimination [12395]
PO Box 305
Mount Marion, NY 12456
PH: (845)679-1209
Fax: (845)679-1206
Berg, Ms. Miriam, President

American Association for the
Improvement of Boxing [22710]
86 Fletcher Ave.
Mount Vernon, NY 10552-3319
PH: (914)664-4571
Fax: (914)664-3164

International Association for Insur-
ance Law in the United States
[5315]
PO Box 9001
Mount Vernon, NY 10552
PH: (914)966-3180
Fax: (914)966-3264
Acunto, Steve, Managing Dir.

National Association of Blessed Bil-
lionaires [7556]
199 N Columbus Ave.
Mount Vernon, NY 10553
PH: (914)559-8765
Smart, Audrey D.F., Exec. Dir.,
Founder

Veterans Bedside Network [11797]
10 Fiske Pl., Rm. 328
Mount Vernon, NY 10550
PH: (914)699-6069

Worldwide Kennel Club [21997]
PO Box 62
Mount Vernon, NY 10552
PH: (914)654-8574
Fax: (914)654-0364

Sino-American Pharmaceutical
Professionals Association [16686]
PO Box 282
Nanuet, NY 10954
Tang, Lei, Officer

Falun Dafa Information Center
[18397]
PO Box 577
New City, NY 10956-9998
PH: (845)418-4870
Browde, Levi, Exec. Dir.

National Council for Therapeutic
Recreation Certification [17456]
7 Elmwood Dr.
New City, NY 10956
PH: (845)639-1439
Fax: (845)639-1471
Hilton, Jennifer, Chairperson

National Jewish Committee on Girl
Scouting [12858]
5 McLeod Ter.
New City, NY 10956

Breathe Easy Play Hard Foundation
[16696]
3003 New Hyde Park Rd., Ste. 204
New Hyde Park, NY 11042
PH: (516)355-2374
Schaeffer, Janis I., MD, Founder

Caribbean American Medical and
Scientific Association [15114]
410 Lakeville Rd., Ste. 202
New Hyde Park, NY 11042
Toll free: 866-648-2620
Haynes, Milton O., Chmn. of the Bd.

Obsessive-Compulsive Anonymous
[12312]
PO Box 215
New Hyde Park, NY 11040
PH: (516)739-0662

Child Find of America [10896]
PO Box 277
New Paltz, NY 12561-0277
PH: (845)883-6060
Fax: (845)883-6614
Linder, Donna, Exec. Dir.

Hasbrouck Family Association
[20878]
PO Box 176
New Paltz, NY 12561
PH: (845)255-3223
Fax: (845)255-0624
Hasbrouck, Robert W., Jr., President

Huguenot Historical Society [21002]
88 Huguenot St.
New Paltz, NY 12561-1403
PH: (845)255-1660
   (845)255-0180
Fax: (845)255-0376
Stessin-Cohn, Susan, Dir. Ed.

United States Society for Education
Through the Arts [7520]
SUNY New Paltz, Department of Art,
Art Education
SUNY New Paltz
Dept. of Art
New Paltz, NY 12561
PH: (845)257-3850
   (845)257-3837
Willis, Steve, Exec. Sec.

Wild Earth [3964]
29 S Chestnut St., Ste. 201
New Paltz, NY 12561
PH: (845)256-9830
Brownstein, David, Exec. Dir.

American Import Shippers Associa-
tion [3080]
662 Main St.
New Rochelle, NY 10801
PH: (914)633-3770
Fax: (914)633-4041
Wiesenmaier, Hubert, Exec. Dir.

American Society of Jewelry
Historians [9629]
1333A North Ave., No. 103
New Rochelle, NY 10804

PH: (914)235-0983
Fax: (914)235-0983
Singer, Diana, President

Cross-Cultural Solutions [9228]
2 Clinton Pl.
New Rochelle, NY 10801
PH: (914)632-0022
Toll free: 800-380-4777
Fax: (914)632-8494
Rosenthal, Steven C., Exec. Dir.

Esther's Aid for Needy and
Abandoned Children [10964]
271 N Ave.
New Rochelle, NY 10801
PH: (914)365-1544
   (914)365-1545
Effiong, Clare, Founder

Israel Service Organization [12210]
151 Oxford Rd.
New Rochelle, NY 10804
Weiss, Rabbi Avi, Chairman

The Medical Letter, Inc. [16670]
145 Huguenot St., Ste. 312
New Rochelle, NY 10801-7537
PH: (914)235-0500
Toll free: 800-211-2769
Fax: (914)632-1733
Valentino, Joanne, Dir. of Comm.,
Dir. of Mktg.

Thomas Paine National Historical
Association [10343]
983 North Ave.
New Rochelle, NY 10804-3609
PH: (914)434-7270
Fax: (914)632-5376
Jacobs, Matthew, President

Philosophy of Education Society
[8422]
c/o James Stillwaggon, Executive
Director
Iona College
715 North Ave.
New Rochelle, NY 10801
Stillwaggon, James, Exec. Dir.

Salesian Missions [20459]
2 Lefevre Ln.
New Rochelle, NY 10801-5710
PH: (914)633-8344
Fax: (914)633-7404
Hyde, Mark, SDB, Director

Society for Adolescent and Young
Adult Oncology [16354]
140 Huguenot St., 3rd Fl.
New Rochelle, NY 10801
PH: (914)740-2242
Sender, Leonard S., MD, President

Intercollegiate Broadcasting System
Inc. [7537]
367 Windsor Hwy.
New Windsor, NY 12553-7900
PH: (845)565-0003
Fax: (845)565-7446
Kass, Fritz, CEO

4 Real Women International [13366]
299 Broadway, Ste. 1508
New York, NY 10007-2061
Toll free: 866-494-4794
Fletcher, Angela, CFO

4Ekselans [10825]
PO Box 1407
New York, NY 10150
Najt, Beverly A., Exec. Dir., Founder

100 Women in Hedge Funds [1214]
888C 8th Ave., No. 453
New York, NY 10019
Pullinger, Amanda, CEO

369th Veterans' Association Inc.
[21100]
369th Armory 2366 5th Ave., - 1
369th Plz.
2366 5th Ave.
New York, NY 10037
PH: (516)378-5328
James, Nathaniel, President

Academy of American Poets **[10148]**
75 Maiden Ln., Ste. 901
New York, NY 10038
PH: (212)274-0343
Fax: (212)274-9427
Houghton, Helen, Secretary

Academy of Political Science **[7040]**
475 Riverside Dr., Ste. 1274
New York, NY 10115-1274
PH: (212)870-2500
Fax: (212)870-2202
Corrales, Carmen A., Gen. Counsel

ACCESS Health International, Inc.
[14969]
1016 5th Ave., Ste. 11A
New York, NY 10028
Haseltine, William A., PhD, Founder,
President, Chairman

Access Now **[17861]**
PO Box 115
New York, NY 10113
Toll free: 888-414-0100
Solomon, Brett, Exec. Dir.

Accessories Council **[197]**
224 W 30th St., Ste. 201
New York, NY 10001
PH: (212)947-1135
Fax: (646)674-0205
Giberson, Karen, President

Achilles International **[22768]**
42 W 38th St., 4th Fl.
New York, NY 10018-6242
PH: (212)354-0300
Fax: (212)354-3978
Traum, Richard, PhD, Founder,
President

Ackerman Institute for the Family
[11808]
936 Broadway, 2nd Fl.
New York, NY 10010
PH: (212)879-4900
Fax: (212)744-0206
Rogers, Gregory T., V. Chmn. of the
Bd.

ACLU Foundation **[17862]**
125 Broad St., 18th Fl.
New York, NY 10004
PH: (212)549-2500
Romero, Anthony D., Exec. Dir.

ACM SIGGRAPH **[6232]**
2 Penn Plz., Ste. 701
New York, NY 10121
PH: (212)626-0500
Fax: (212)944-1318
Jortner, Jeff, President

ACMP - The Chamber Music
Network **[9846]**
1133 Broadway, Rm. 810
New York, NY 10010
PH: (212)645-7424
Fax: (212)741-2678
Turner, Ivy A., V. Chmn. of the Bd.

ACT Alliance-New York **[12603]**
Ecumenical UN Office
Church Centre for the United Na-
tions
777 United Nations Plaza, Ste. D
New York, NY 10017
PH: (212)867-5890
Nduna, John, Gen. Sec.

Action Against Hunger **[12075]**
1 Whitehall St., 2nd Fl.
New York, NY 10004
PH: (212)967-7800
Toll free: 877-777-1420
Fax: (212)967-5480
Garcia, Luis Manuel, Dir. of Fin.

Action to Cure Kidney Cancer
[13869]
150 W 75th St., Ste. 4
New York, NY 10023
PH: (212)714-5341
Bitkower, Jay, President

Action Without Borders/Idealist.org
[18291]
302 5th Ave., 11th Fl.
New York, NY 10001-3604
PH: (646)786-6886
Fax: (212)695-7243
Dar, Ami, Exec. Dir.

Actors' Equity Association **[23491]**
165 W 46th St.
New York, NY 10036
PH: (212)869-8530

Actors' Fund **[11793]**
729 7th Ave., 10th Fl.
New York, NY 10019
PH: (212)221-7300
Toll free: 800-825-0911
Benincasa, Joseph P., CEO,
President

Ad Council **[18934]**
815 2nd Ave., 9th Fl.
New York, NY 10017
PH: (212)922-1500
Fax: (212)922-1676
Hill, Nancy, Scientist

American Friends of Magen David
Adom **[12604]**
352 7th Ave., Ste. 400
New York, NY 10001-5012
PH: (212)757-1627
Toll free: 866-632-2763
Fax: (212)757-4662
Lebow, Mark D., Chairman

Advancement for Rural Kids **[10832]**
10 E 85th St.
New York, NY 10028-0412
Vera-Yu, Ayesha, CEO, Founder

Advancing Human Rights **[18364]**
PO Box 85
New York, NY 10008
PH: (646)678-5626
Fax: (212)207-5047
Keyes, David, Exec. Dir.

Advancing Women Professionals
and the Jewish Community
[13368]
520 8th Ave., 4th Fl.
New York, NY 10018
PH: (212)542-4280
Bronznick, Shifra, Founder,
President

Advertising Council **[79]**
815 2nd Ave., 9th Fl.
New York, NY 10017
PH: (212)922-1500
Sherman, Lisa, President, CEO

Advertising Research Foundation
[81]
432 Park Ave. S, 6th Fl.
New York, NY 10016-8013
PH: (212)751-5656
Fax: (212)319-5265
Poltrack, David, Chairman

Advertising Women of New York **[82]**
25 W 43rd St., Ste. 912
New York, NY 10036

PH: (212)221-7969
Fax: (212)221-8296
Walker, Kiera, Associate

Aesthetic Realism Foundation
[10074]
141 Greene St.
New York, NY 10012
PH: (212)777-4490
Reiss, Ellen, Chairperson, Chmn. of
the Bd.

Afghan Hindu Association, Inc.
[20198]
45-32 Bowne St.
New York, NY 11355
PH: (718)961-8838
Lund, Sena P., Secretary

The Africa-America Institute **[17770]**
420 Lexington Ave., Ste. 1706
New York, NY 10170-0002
PH: (212)949-5666
Fax: (212)682-6174
Kajunju, Amini, CEO, President

African Action on AIDS **[13517]**
511 Ave. of the Americas, No. 302
New York, NY 10011
Engo, Ruth Bamela, President

African-American Institute **[17772]**
420 Lexington Ave., Ste. 1706
New York, NY 10170-0002
PH: (212)949-5666
Fax: (212)682-6174
Appenteng, Kofi, Chairperson

African Development Institute
[17773]
PO Box 1644
New York, NY 10185
Toll free: 888-619-7535
Fax: (908)850-3016
Akonor, Kwame, Chairman

African Federation, Inc. **[12135]**
PO Box 2186
New York, NY 10163
PH: (646)863-5880
Fax: (646)863-5000
Addow-Langlais, Grace, Consultant

African Health Now **[15433]**
PO Box 3243
New York, NY 10163
PH: (347)389-2461
Eyeson-Akiwowo, Nana, Founder,
President

AFS Intercultural Programs **[9198]**
71 W 23rd St., 6th Fl.
New York, NY 10010-4102
PH: (212)807-8686
Fax: (212)807-1001
Morlini, Dr. Vincenzo, CEO,
President

Agni Yoga Society **[20652]**
319 W 107th St.
New York, NY 10025-2799
PH: (212)864-7752
Fax: (212)864-7704
Roerich, Helena, Director

Agricultural Missions, Inc. **[20380]**
475 Riverside Dr., Ste. 700
New York, NY 10115
PH: (212)870-2553
Rivera, Doris, Admin. Asst.

Aid for AIDS **[13519]**
515 Greenwich St., Ste. 506
New York, NY 10013
PH: (212)337-8043
Fax: (212)337-8045
Aguais, Jesus, Exec. Dir.

Elton John AIDS Foundation **[10532]**
584 Broadway, Ste. 906
New York, NY 10012

PH: (212)219-0670
Campbell, Scott, Exec. Dir.

AIESEC United States **[7540]**
11 Hanover Sq., Ste. 1700
New York, NY 10005
PH: (212)757-3774
Smith, Domenic, President

Airline Passenger Experience As-
sociation **[358]**
355 Lexington Ave., 15th Fl.
New York, NY 10017
PH: (212)297-2177
Fax: (212)370-9047
Celestino, Linda, Bd. Member

Alcoholics Anonymous World
Services, Inc. **[13120]**
475 Riverside Dr., 11th Fl.
W 120th St.
New York, NY 10115
PH: (212)870-3400
Giannone, Garry, VP

Alfred Adler Institute of New York
[16854]
372 Central Pk. W
New York, NY 10025
PH: (212)254-1048
Hotaling, Brock, BSc, Exec. Dir.

Algerian American Scientists As-
sociation **[7115]**
1825 Madison Ave., Apt. 6H
New York, NY 10035
PH: (646)641-7615
Merghoub, Tara, President

All for Africa **[10472]**
277 Park Ave., 40th Fl.
New York, NY 10172
PH: (212)351-0055
Fax: (212)351-0001
Wrobel, Bruce, Chairman, Exec. Dir.

All Healers Mental Health Alliance
[15755]
c/o United Social Services, Inc.
2 W 64th St., Ste. 505
New York, NY 10023
PH: (212)874-5210
Fax: (212)721-4407
Harrison-Ross, Dr. Phyllis, President

Alliance for the Arts **[8950]**
330 W 42nd St.
New York, NY 10036
PH: (212)947-6340
Robb, Lisa, Exec. Dir.

Alliance for Childhood **[10814]**
Park W PO
New York, NY 10025
PH: (202)643-8242
Rhoads, Linda, Exec. Dir.

Alliance for Human Research
Protection **[18368]**
142 W End Ave., Ste. 28P
New York, NY 10023
Sharav, Vera, President

Alliance for Inclusion in the Arts
[10234]
1560 Broadway, Ste. 709
New York, NY 10036
PH: (212)730-4750
Jensen, Sharon, Exec. Dir.

Alliance for Preventive Health
[15106]
817 Broadway, 5th Fl.
New York, NY 10003
PH: (212)257-6105
Fax: (212)631-3619
Kaur, Ravneet, Chairperson

Allied Artists of America **[8906]**
15 Gramercy Pk. S
New York, NY 10003
Valenti, Thomas, President

Alumni Association of City College of
New York [19299]
Shepard Hall, Rm. 162
160 Convent Ave.
138th St.
New York, NY 10027
PH: (212)234-3000
Fax: (212)368-6576
Jordan, Donald K., Exec. VP

Alzheimer's Foundation of America
[13670]
322 8th Ave., 7th Fl.
New York, NY 10001
PH: (646)638-1542
Toll free: 866-232-8484
Fax: (646)638-1546
Fuschillo, Charles J., Jr., CEO,
President

Amandla Development [7807]
42 Water St., 4th Fl.
New York, NY 10004
Clarke, Scott, Founder, Exec. Dir.

Ameinu [19514]
424 W 33rd St., Ste. 150
New York, NY 10001
PH: (212)366-1194
Fax: (212)675-7685
Bob, Kenneth, President

America-Israel Cultural Foundation,
Inc. [9199]
1140 Broadway, Ste. No. 304
New York, NY 10001
PH: (212)557-1600
Fax: (212)557-1611
Homan, David, Exec. Dir.

America-Israel Friendship League
[9609]
1430 Broadway, Ste. 1804
New York, NY 10018
PH: (212)213-8630
(646)892-9142
Bialkin, Kenneth J., Chairman,
President

America Needs You [11744]
589 8th Ave., 5th Fl.
New York, NY 10018
PH: (212)571-0202
Harris, Kimberly, CEO

America Scores [23183]
2nd Fl., Ste. 201C
520 8th Ave.
New York, NY 10018
PH: (212)868-9510
Fax: (212)868-9533
Twombly, A.J., V. Chmn. of the Bd.

American Abstract Artists [8907]
PO Box 1076
New York, NY 10013
Voisine, Don, Asst. Sec.

American Academy of Arts and Let-
ters [9551]
633 W 155 St.
New York, NY 10032
PH: (212)368-5900
Fax: (212)491-4615
McClatchy, J. D., Mem.

American Academy in Rome [9611]
7 E 60 St.
New York, NY 10022-1001
PH: (212)751-7200
Fax: (212)751-7220
Robbins, Mark, President, CEO

American Academy of Teachers of
Singing [8356]
c/o Jeannette LoVetri, Secretary/
Director
317 W 93rd St., Apt. 3B

New York, NY 10025
PH: (301)649-5260
Randall, Martha L., Chairperson

American Arbitration Association
[4955]
1633 Broadway, 10th Fl.
New York, NY 10019
PH: (212)716-5800
Toll free: 800-778-7879
Slate, William K., II, CEO, President

American Artists Professional
League [8908]
47 5th Ave.
New York, NY 10003
PH: (212)645-1345
Faust, Kate, VP

American Assembly [18959]
475 Riverside Dr., Ste. 456
New York, NY 10115-0084
PH: (212)870-3500
Stamas, Stephen, Chairman

American Associates Ben-Gurion
University of the Negev [8128]
1001 Avenue of the Americas, 19th
Fl.
New York, NY 10018-5460
PH: (212)687-7721
Toll free: 800-962-2248
Fax: (212)302-6443
Krakow, Doron, Exec. VP

American Association of Advertising
Agencies [85]
1065 Avenue of Americas, 16th Fl.
New York, NY 10018
PH: (212)682-2500
Hill, Nancy, President, CEO

American Association for Chinese
Studies [7598]
The City College of New York -
CUNY
NAC R4/116
Convent Ave. & 138th St.
New York, NY 10031
PH: (212)650-6206
(212)650-8268
Fax: (212)650-8287
Chow, Prof. Peter C.Y., Exec. Dir.

American Association of
Independent Music [2900]
132 Delancey St.
New York, NY 10002
PH: (646)692-4877
Bengloff, Rich, Mem.

American Association for the
International Commission of Jurists
[18370]
280 Madison Ave., Ste. 1102
New York, NY 10016
PH: (212)972-0883
Fax: (212)972-0888
Fox, Donald T., Chmn. of the Bd.

American Association for the Treat-
ment of Opioid Dependence
[17305]
225 Varick St., Ste. 402
New York, NY 10014-4304
PH: (212)566-5555
Fax: (212)566-4647
Parrino, Mark W., MPA, President

American Association of Wine
Economists [3478]
Economics Dept.
New York University
19 W 4th St., 6th Fl.
New York, NY 10012
PH: (212)992-8083
Fax: (212)995-4186
Ashenfelter, Orley C., President

American Australian Association
[9200]
50 Broadway, Ste. 2003
New York, NY 10004
PH: (212)338-6860
Fax: (212)338-6864
Cassidy, Frances M., President

American Board of Multiple Special-
ties in Podiatry [16778]
555 8th Ave., Ste. 1902
New York, NY 10018
PH: (646)779-8438
Toll free: 888-852-1442
Fax: (646)786-4488
Horowitz, Earl R., DPM, President

American Board of Perianesthesia
Nursing Certification [16103]
475 Riverside Dr., 6th Fl.
New York, NY 10115-0089
Toll free: 800-6-ABPANC
Fax: (212)367-4256
Brancati, Annette, Secretary,
Treasurer

American Board of Rabbis [20223]
276 5th Ave., Ste. 704
New York, NY 10001-4527
PH: (212)714-3598
(646)996-4040
Toll free: 800-539-4743
Friedman, Rabbi Mordechai Yitz-
chok, President

American Board of Spine Surgery
[17364]
1350 Broadway, 17th Fl., Ste. 1705
New York, NY 10018
PH: (212)356-0682
Fax: (212)356-0678
Eckert, Mimi, Exec. Dir.

American Book Producers Associa-
tion [2761]
31 W 8th St., 2nd Fl.
New York, NY 10011-4116
PH: (212)944-6600
Rothschild, Richard, President

American Buddhist Study Center
[19770]
331 Riverside Dr.
New York, NY 10025
PH: (212)864-7424
Seki, Hoshin, Coord., President

American Center for the Alexander
Technique Inc. [13591]
39 W 14th St., Ste. 507
New York, NY 10011
PH: (212)633-2229
Kent, Barbara, Fac. Memb.

American Civil Liberties Union
[17867]
125 Broad St., 18th Fl.
New York, NY 10004
PH: (212)549-2500
Romero, Anthony D., Exec. Dir.

American Committee for Shaare
Zedek Medical Center in
Jerusalem [12205]
55 W 39th St., 4th Fl.
New York, NY 10018
PH: (212)354-8801
Fax: (212)391-2674
Wolf, Rachel, CEO

American Committee for Shenkar
College [8129]
307 7th Ave., No.1805
New York, NY 10001
PH: (212)947-1597
Helfand, Ivan, Exec. Dir.

American Committee for the Weiz-
mann Institute of Science [7117]
633 3rd Ave.
New York, NY 10017

PH: (212)895-7900
Toll free: 800-242-2947
Merlo, Ellen, Chairperson

American Composers Alliance
[9855]
PO Box 1108
New York, NY 10040
PH: (212)568-0036
Genova, Gina, Exec. Dir., Gen. Mgr.

American Council for Drug Educa-
tion [13124]
164 W 74th St.
New York, NY 10023
PH: (646)505-2061
(212)595-5810
Toll free: 800-488-3784
Fax: (212)595-2553
Lozada, Herman, Contact

American Council on Germany
[19441]
14 E 60th St., Ste. 1000
New York, NY 10022
PH: (212)826-3636
Fax: (212)758-3445
Kimmitt, Robert M., Chairman

American Council of Learned Societ-
ies [9552]
633 3rd Ave., 8th Fl.
New York, NY 10017-6795
PH: (212)697-1505
Fax: (212)949-8058
Yu, Pauline, President

American Council on Science and
Health [14923]
1995 Broadway, Ste. 202
New York, NY 10023-5882
Toll free: 866-905-2694
Fax: (212)362-4919
Whelan, Elizabeth M., Founder

American Dance Guild [9242]
240 W 14th St.
New York, NY 10011
McLean, Gloria, President

American Ditchley Foundation
[18510]
275 Madison Ave., 6th Fl.
New York, NY 10016
PH: (212)878-8854
Talbott, Strobe, Chairman

American Egyptian Cooperation
Foundation [18511]
235 E 40th St.
New York, NY 10016
PH: (212)867-2323
(347)470-4622
Fax: (212)697-0465
Zaki, Abdel Fattah, CEO, President

American Engineering Alliance
[6529]
Bowling Green Sta.
New York, NY 10004-1415
PH: (212)606-4053
Galletta, Salvatore, PE, Chairperson

American Ethical Union [20207]
2 W 64th St.
New York, NY 10023-7183
PH: (212)873-6500
Fax: (212)624-0203
Koral, Richard, President

American Federation for Aging
Research [14887]
55 W 39th St., 16th Fl.
New York, NY 10018-0541
PH: (212)703-9977
Toll free: 888-582-2327
Fax: (212)997-0330
Lederman, Stephanie, EdM, Exec.
Dir.

American Federation of Arts [8952]
305 E 47th St., 10th Fl.
New York, NY 10017
PH: (212)988-7700
Toll free: 800-232-0270
Fax: (212)861-2487
Loewy, Jeffrey M., Chairman

American Federation of Musicians
[23492]
1501 Broadway, Ste. 600
New York, NY 10036
Hair, Ray, President

American Festival of Microtonal
Music [9857]
c/o Johnny Reinhard, Director
318 E 70th St., Ste. 5FW
New York, NY 10021
Reinhard, Johnny, Director, Founder

American Foreign Law Association
[5347]
c/o Paul Downs, President
222 E 41st St.
New York, NY 10017
Downs, Paul, President

American Forum for Global Educa-
tion [8054]
120 Wall St., Ste. 2600
New York, NY 10005
PH: (212)624-1300
Fax: (212)624-1412

American Foundation for the Blind
[17684]
2 Penn Plz., Ste. 1102
New York, NY 10121-1100
PH: (212)502-7600
Selsdon, Helen, Arch.

American Foundation for Suicide
Prevention [13192]
120 Wall St., 29th Fl.
New York, NY 10005
PH: (212)363-3500
    (212)826-3577
Toll free: 888-333-AFSP
Fax: (212)363-6237
Gebbia, Robert T., CEO

American Friends of ALYN Hospital
[10850]
122 E 42nd St., No. 1519
New York, NY 10168
PH: (212)869-8085
Toll free: 877-568-3259
Fax: (212)768-0979
Lanyard, Cathy M., Exec. Dir.

American Friends of Bucerius
[19442]
10 Rockefeller Plz., 16th Fl.
New York, NY 10020
PH: (212)713-7651
Smidt, Nina, President

American Friends of the Hebrew
University [8130]
1 Battery Park Plz., 25th Fl.
New York, NY 10004
PH: (212)607-8500
Toll free: 800-567-AFHU
Fax: (212)809-4430
Schlessinger, Daniel, President

American Friends of the Israel
Museum [9817]
545 5th Ave., Ste. 920
New York, NY 10017
PH: (212)997-5611
Fax: (212)997-5536
Gregory, Alexis, Officer

American Friends Musee d'Orsay
[8832]
c/o PJSC
1345 Ave. of the Americas, 31st Fl.

New York, NY 10105
PH: (212)508-1614
Thornton, Verena, Exec. Dir.

American Friends of the National
Gallery of Australia [9818]
50 Broadway, Ste. 2003
New York, NY 10004
PH: (212)338-6860
Fax: (212)338-6864
Cobran, Philip L., Chmn. of the Bd.

American Friends of Neot Kedumim
[19747]
42 E 69th St.
New York, NY 10021
PH: (212)737-1337
Aberbach, Susan, President

American Friends of the Paris Opera
and Ballet [8953]
972 5th Ave.
New York, NY 10075
PH: (212)439-1426
Fax: (212)439-1455
Witt, Hal J., VP

American Friends of Tel Aviv
University [8131]
39 Broadway, Ste. 1510
New York, NY 10006
PH: (212)742-9070
Toll free: 800-989-1198
Fax: (212)742-9071
Reiss, Gail, CEO, President

American Fund for Czech and
Slovak Leadership Studies [12582]
Bohemian National Hall
321 E 73rd St.
New York, NY 10021-3705
Kallan, Henry, President

American Gathering of Jewish
Holocaust Survivors and Their
Descendants [18343]
c/o The American Gathering
122 W 30th St., Ste. 304A
New York, NY 10001
PH: (212)239-4230
Levine, Joyce, Secretary

American Geriatrics Society [14888]
40 Fulton St., 18th Fl.
New York, NY 10038-5082
PH: (212)308-1414
Fax: (212)832-8646
Hansen, Jennie Chin, CEO

American Go Association [22045]
PO Box 4668
New York, NY 10163
Okun, Andy, President

American Group Psychotherapy As-
sociation [16960]
25 E 21st St., 6th Fl.
New York, NY 10010
PH: (212)477-2677
Fax: (212)979-6627
Block, Marsha S., CAE, CEO

American Guild of Musical Artists
[23493]
1430 Broadway, 14th Fl.
New York, NY 10018
PH: (212)265-3687
Toll free: 800-543-2462
Fax: (212)262-9088
Odom, James, President

American Guild of Organists [9859]
475 Riverside Dr., Ste. 1260
New York, NY 10115
PH: (212)870-2310
Fax: (212)870-2163
Thomashower, James E., Exec. Dir.

American Hungarian Library and
Historical Society [19468]
215 E 82nd St.
New York, NY 10028

PH: (212)744-5298
Hámos, László, President

American Indian Ritual Object
Repatriation Foundation [18706]
463 E 57th St.
New York, NY 10022-3003
PH: (212)980-9441
Fax: (212)421-2746
Sackler, Elizabeth A., PhD, Founder,
President

American Indonesian Chamber of
Commerce [23552]
521 5th Ave., Ste. 1700
New York, NY 10175
PH: (212)687-4505
Fax: (212)867-5844
Forrest, Wayne, President, Secretary

American Institute of Certified Public
Accountants [10]
1211 Avenue of the Americas
New York, NY 10036-8775
PH: (212)596-6200
Fax: (212)596-6213
Christen, Tim, Chairman

American Institute of Graphic Arts
[1526]
223 Broadway, 17th Fl.
New York, NY 10279
PH: (212)807-1990
Cox, Kathleen, Controller

American Institute of Iranian Studies
[9201]
c/o Dr. Erica Ehrenberg, Executive
Director
118 Riverside Dr.
New York, NY 10024
Ehrenberg, Dr. Erica, Exec. Dir.

American Institute of Marine
Underwriters [1830]
14 Wall St., Ste. 820
New York, NY 10005-2101
PH: (212)233-0550
Fax: (212)227-5102
Miklus, John A., President

American Institute for Stuttering
[17235]
27 W 20th St., Ste. 1203
New York, NY 10011
PH: (212)633-6400
Toll free: 877-378-8883
Fax: (212)220-3922
Russo, Nolan, Jr., Chairman

American Institute for Verdi Studies
[9861]
Music Dept., Rm. 268
New York University
24 Waverly Pl.
New York, NY 10003-6757
PH: (212)998-2587
Fax: (212)995-4147
Fairtile, Linda B., Director

American Irish Historical Society
[9598]
991 5th Ave.
New York, NY 10028
PH: (212)288-2263
Fax: (212)628-7927
Kelleher, Dennis P., Chairman

American Jewish Committee [20226]
165 E 56th St.
New York, NY 10022
PH: (212)891-1314
    (212)751-4000
Fax: (212)891-1460
Schonfeld, Victoria, COO

American Jewish Congress [20227]
260 Madison Ave., 2nd Fl.
New York, NY 10016

PH: (212)879-4500
Fax: (212)758-1633
Rosen, Jack, President

American Jewish Historical Society
[9632]
15 W 16th St.
New York, NY 10011-6301
PH: (212)294-6160
Fax: (212)294-6161
Lapidus, Sidney, Chmn. of the Bd.

American Jewish Joint Distribution
Committee [12217]
New York, NY
PH: (212)687-6200
Fax: (212)370-5467
Blumenstein, Penny, Chmn. of the
Bd.

American Jewish World Service
[12615]
45 W 36th St.
New York, NY 10018-7641
PH: (212)792-2900
Toll free: 800-889-7146
Fax: (212)792-2930
Messinger, Ruth W., President

American Liver Foundation [15249]
39 Broadway, Ste. 2700
New York, NY 10006
PH: (212)668-1000
Toll free: 800-465-4837
Fax: (212)483-8179
Nealon, Thomas F., III, Chmn. of the
Bd.

American Management Association
[2146]
1601 Broadway
New York, NY 10019
PH: (212)586-8100
Toll free: 877-566-9441
Fax: (212)903-8168
Craig, Charles R., Chairman

American Montessori Society [8349]
116 E 16th St.
New York, NY 10003-2163
PH: (212)358-1250
Fax: (212)358-1256
Ungerer, Richard A., Exec. Dir.

American Non-Governmental
Organizations Coalition for the
International Criminal Court
[18069]
Columbia University Institute for the
Study of Human Rights
MC 3365
New York, NY 10027
PH: (212)851-2106
Washburn, John L., Facilitator

American Numismatic Society
[22257]
75 Varick St., 11th Fl.
New York, NY 10013
PH: (212)571-4470
Fax: (212)571-4479
Kagan, Ute W., Exec. Dir.

American Printing History Associa-
tion [9347]
PO Box 4519
Grand Central Sta.
New York, NY 10163
Schreiner, Erin, Secretary

American Psychoanalytic Association
[16841]
309 E 49th St.
New York, NY 10017-1601
PH: (212)752-0450
Stein, Dean K., Exec. Dir.

American Renaissance for the
Twenty-First Century [8955]
PO Box 8379
New York, NY 10150

PH: (212)759-7765
Fax: (212)759-1922

The American-Scandinavian Foundation [10199]
58 Park Ave. 38th St.
New York, NY 10016
PH: (212)779-3587
    (212)847-9716
Gallagher, Edward P., CEO, President

American-Scottish Foundation [19635]
575 Madison Ave., 10th Fl.
New York, NY 10022-2511
PH: (212)605-0338
Fax: (212)605-0222
Bain, Heather L., Chairman

American Sephardi Federation [20229]
15 W 16th St.
New York, NY 10011-6301
PH: (212)548-4486
Dangoor, David E. R., President

American Skin Association [14484]
6 E 43rd St., 28th Fl.
New York, NY 10017-4605
PH: (212)889-4858
Toll free: 800-499-SKIN
Fax: (212)889-4959
Milstein, Howard P., Chairman

American Society of Composers, Authors and Publishers [5322]
1900 Broadway
New York, NY 10023
PH: (212)621-6000
Fax: (212)621-8453
Williams, Paul, President, Chmn. of the Bd.

American Society of Contemporary Artists [8912]
150 W 96th St., No. 14G
New York, NY 10025
Karp, Erin, Chairperson

American Society for Dental Aesthetics [14414]
635 Madison Ave.
New York, NY 10022-1009
PH: (212)371-4575
Toll free: 888-988-ASDA
Fax: (212)308-5182
Smigel, Irwin, DDS, President, Founder

American Society of Geolinguistics [9737]
c/o Prof. Wayne H. Finke, Faculty Member
Department of Modern Languages
Baruch College, B6-280
17 Lexington Ave.
New York, NY 10010-5585
PH: (646)312-1000

American Society of Hypertension [15346]
244 Madison Ave., Ste. 136
New York, NY 10016
PH: (212)696-9099
Fax: (347)916-0267
Sansone, Torry Mark, Exec. Dir.

American Society of Illustrators Partnership [910]
536 Broadway, 5th Fl.
New York, NY 10012
PH: (212)420-9160
Holland, Brad, Co-Chmn. of the Bd.

American Society for Jewish Music [9868]
Center for Jewish History
15 W 16th St.

New York, NY 10011
PH: (212)874-3990
Fax: (212)874-8605
Leavitt, Michael, President

American Society of Journalists and Authors [10359]
355 Lexington Ave. 15th Fl.
New York, NY 10017
PH: (212)997-0947
Owens, Alexandra, Exec. Dir.

American Society of Magazine Editors [2654]
757 3rd Ave., 11th Fl.
New York, NY 10017-2194
PH: (212)872-3700
Fax: (212)906-0128
Holt, Sid, CEO

American Society of Mechanical Engineers Auxiliary [6830]
2 Park Ave.
New York, NY 10016-5990
PH: (973)882-1170
Toll free: 800-843-2763
Sims, J. Robert, President

American Society for Muslim Advancement [9602]
475 Riverside Dr., Ste. 248
New York, NY 10115
Khan, Daisy, Exec. Dir., Founder

American Society for the Prevention of Cruelty to Animals [10571]
424 E 92nd St.
New York, NY 10128-6804
PH: (212)876-7700
Toll free: 800-582-5979
Tanne, Frederick, Chairman

American Society for Psychical Research [6983]
5 W 73rd St.
New York, NY 10023
PH: (212)799-5050
Fax: (212)496-2497
Keane, Patrice, Exec. Dir., Director

American Sommelier Association [178]
580 Broadway, Ste. 714
New York, NY 10012
PH: (212)226-6805
Fax: (212)226-6407
Bell, Andrew F., President, CEO

American Sportscasters Association [453]
225 Broadway, Ste. 2030
New York, NY 10007
PH: (212)227-8080
Fax: (212)571-0556
Enberg, Dick, Chmn. of the Bd.

American Swiss Foundation [19666]
271 Madison Ave., Ste. 1403
New York, NY 10016
PH: (212)754-0130
Fax: (212)754-4512
Hoch, Steven G., Chairman

American Synesthesia Association, Inc. [16009]
75 E 4th St., Ste. 573
New York, NY 10003
Steen, Carol, Founder

American Technion Society [8132]
55 E 59th St.
New York, NY 10022-1112
PH: (212)407-6300
Fax: (212)753-2925
Leemaster, Scott, President

American Textbook Council [8693]
1150 Park Ave., 12th Fl.
New York, NY 10128

PH: (212)289-5177
Sewall, Gilbert T., Director

American Thoracic Society [17471]
25 Broadway
New York, NY 10004
PH: (212)315-8600
Fax: (212)315-6498
Crane, Stephen C., PhD, Exec. Dir.

American Turkish Society [19672]
1460 Broadway Ste. 10023
New York, NY 10036
PH: (646)434-4409
Fax: (646)434-4405
Koprulu, Mr. Murat, Chairman

American Veterans of Israel [21005]
136 E 39th St.
New York, NY 10016
PH: (212)685-8548

American Watercolor Society [8836]
47 5th Ave.
New York, NY 10003-4679
PH: (212)206-8986
Fax: (212)206-1960
McFarlane, James, President

American Zionist Movement [20230]
40 Wall St.
New York, NY 10005
PH: (212)318-6100
Fax: (212)935-3578
Bob, Kenneth, Chairman

Americans for Middle East Understanding [18674]
475 Riverside Dr., Rm. 245
New York, NY 10115-0245
PH: (212)870-2053
Fax: (212)870-2050
Norberg, Robert L., President

Americans for a Safe Israel [18675]
1751 2nd Ave., 91st St.
New York, NY 10128-5363
PH: (212)828-2424
Toll free: 800-235-3658
Fax: (212)828-4538
Freedman, Helen, Exec. Dir.

America's Foundation [20729]
30 Vesey St., Ste. 506
New York, NY 10007
PH: (212)732-4333
Fax: (212)732-0660

Americas Society/Council of the Americas [17795]
680 Park Ave.
New York, NY 10065-5072
PH: (212)249-8950
Fax: (212)249-5868
Negroponte, John D., Chairman

amfAR, The Foundation for AIDS Research [13528]
120 Wall St., 13th Fl.
New York, NY 10005-3908
PH: (212)806-1600
Fax: (212)806-1601
Cole, Kenneth, Chmn. of the Bd.

AMIT [20231]
817 Broadway, 3rd Fl.
New York, NY 10003
PH: (212)477-4720
Toll free: 800-989-2648
Fax: (212)353-2312
Isaac, Debbie, President

Amnesty International of the USA [18373]
5 Penn Plz.
New York, NY 10001
PH: (212)807-8400
Fax: (212)627-1451
Huang, Margaret, Exec. Dir.

Amref Health Africa, USA [16994]
4 W 43rd St., 2nd Fl.
New York, NY 10036
PH: (212)768-2440
Fax: (212)768-4230
Wilson, Timothy, Chairman

Anglican Society [20091]
c/o Linda Bridges, 215 Lexington Ave., 11th Fl.
215 Lexington Ave., 11th Fl.
New York, NY 10016
Wright, Rev. J. Robert, President

Animal Medical Center [10579]
510 E 62nd St.
New York, NY 10065
PH: (212)838-8100
    (212)838-7053
Fax: (212)752-2592
Coyne, Kathryn, CEO

Anne Frank Center U.S.A. [18344]
44 Park Pl.
New York, NY 10007-2500
PH: (212)431-7993
Fax: (212)431-8375
Rapaport, Peter, Chairman

Anthology Film Archives [9295]
32 2nd Ave., 2nd St.
New York, NY 10003-8631
PH: (212)505-5181
Fax: (212)477-2714
Mekas, Jonas, President

Anti-Defamation League [17874]
605 3rd Ave., Fl. 9
New York, NY 10158
PH: (212)885-7700
    (212)885-7800
Fax: (212)867-0779
Nathan, Marvin, Chairman

Antiquarian Booksellers Association of America [9119]
20 W 44th St., Ste. 507
New York, NY 10036-6604
PH: (212)944-8291
Fax: (212)944-8293
Thomson, John, Trustee

Appeal of Conscience Foundation [19024]
119 W 57th St.
New York, NY 10019-2401
PH: (212)535-5800
Fax: (212)628-2513
Schneier, Rabbi Arthur, Founder, President

Appraisers Association of America [219]
212 W 35th St., 11th Fl. S
New York, NY 10001
PH: (212)889-5404
Fax: (212)889-5503
Moore, Anne, Director

Arab Bankers Association of North America [380]
150 W 28th St., Ste. 801
New York, NY 10001
PH: (212)599-3030
Fax: (212)599-3131
Peters, Ms. Susan, President, COO

Architecture for Health in Vulnerable Environments [11962]
894 6th Ave., 5th Fl.
New York, NY 10001
PH: (917)793-5901
Williams, Peter, Founder, Exec. Dir.

Arcus Foundation [18851]
44 W 28th St., 17th Fl.
New York, NY 10001
PH: (212)488-3000
Fax: (212)488-3010
Stryker, Jon, Founder, President

Argentine-American Chamber of
Commerce **[23556]**
150 E 58th St.
New York, NY 10155
PH: (212)698-2238
Fax: (212)698-1144
Alfaro, Carlos, President

Armenian American Society for Studies on Stress and Genocide
[15760]
185 E 85th St., Mezzanine No. 4
New York, NY 10028
PH: (201)723-9578
Kalayjian, Ani, Dr., Founder

Armenian Church Youth Organiza-
tion of America **[19705]**
630 2nd Ave.
New York, NY 10016-4806
PH: (212)686-0710
Maslar, Mallory, Treasurer

Armenian General Benevolent Union
[19385]
55 E 59th St.
New York, NY 10022-1112
PH: (212)319-6383
Setrakian, Berge, President

Aromatherapy Registration Council
[13604]
1350 Broadway, 17th Fl.
New York, NY 10018-0903
PH: (503)244-0726
Petersen, Dorene, Chairperson

Art and Antique Dealers League of
America, Inc. **[237]**
Lennox Hill Sta.
New York, NY 10021
PH: (212)879-7558
Fax: (212)772-7197
Simon, Robert, VP

Art in a Box **[10764]**
463 W St., Ste. G-122
New York, NY 10014
PH: (212)691-2543
DuBasky, Valentina, Director,
Founder

Art Dealers Association of America
[238]
205 Lexington Ave., Rm. 901
New York, NY 10016
PH: (212)488-5550
Fax: (646)688-6809
Waxter, Dorsey, Officer

Art Directors Club **[8840]**
106 W 29th St.
New York, NY 10001
PH: (212)643-1440
Fax: (212)643-4266
Oreamuno, Ignacio, Exec. Dir.

Art for Refugees in Transition
[12585]
100 Bank St., 5G
New York, NY 10014
PH: (917)757-6191
Green, Sara M., Exec. Dir., Founder

Art and Science Collaborations Inc.
[9015]
130 E End Ave. 1A
New York, NY 10028
PH: (505)990-0781
Pannucci, Cynthia, Exec. Dir.

Art Students League of New York
[8915]
215 W 57th St.
New York, NY 10019
PH: (212)247-4510
Fax: (212)541-7024
Goldberg, Ira, Exec. Dir.

Art21 **[8842]**
133 W 25th St., No. 3E
New York, NY 10001
PH: (212)741-7133
Fax: (212)741-5709
Sollins, Susan, Founder

Artfully AWARE **[8959]**
201 E 17th St., 27D
New York, NY 10003
Wallis, Hilary, Exec. Dir., Founder

Artists' Fellowship, Inc. **[19573]**
47 5th Ave.
New York, NY 10003-4679
PH: (212)255-7740
Caporale, Wende, President

Artists for Israel International **[8844]**
PO Box 2056
New York, NY 10163-2056
PH: (212)245-4188
Fax: (646)607-0667
Goble, Dr. Phillip, President

Artists for Peace and Justice
[12994]
87 Walker St., No. 6B
New York, NY 10013
PH: (646)398-7804
Fax: (646)398-8343
Haggis, Paul, Founder

Artists Rights Society **[239]**
536 Broadway, 5th Fl.
New York, NY 10012
PH: (212)420-9160
Fax: (212)420-9286
Feder, Dr. Theodore H., President

Artists Striving to End Poverty
[12526]
165 W 46th St., Ste. 1303
New York, NY 10036
PH: (212)921-1227
Fax: (212)840-0551
Campbell, Mary-Mitchell, Exec. Dir.,
Founder

A.R.T.S. Anonymous **[12868]**
PO Box 230175
New York, NY 10023
PH: (718)251-3828
B., Abigail, Founder

Arts Resources in Collaboration
[9243]
70 E 10th St., Rm. 19D
New York, NY 10003
PH: (212)206-6492
Ipiotis, Ms. Celia, Director

ArtTable **[8916]**
1 E 53rd St., 5th Fl.
New York, NY 10022
PH: (212)343-1735
Fax: (866)363-4188
Harris, Deborah, Bd. Member

ArtWatch International Inc. **[8961]**
Ruth Osborne
47 5th Ave.
New York, NY 10003-4396
Daley, Mike, Director

Ascend **[12]**
120 Wall St., 9th Fl.
New York, NY 10005
PH: (212)248-4888
Nam, Gina, Secretary

Asia Catalyst **[12389]**
1270 Broadway, Suite 1109
New York, NY 10001
PH: (212)967-2123
Davis, Sara L.M., PhD, Founder, Bd.
Member

Asia Society **[9023]**
725 Park Ave.
New York, NY 10021

PH: (212)288-6400
Fax: (212)517-8315
Sheeran, Josette, President

Asian American Arts Centre **[8963]**
111 Norfolk St.
New York, NY 10002
PH: (212)233-2154
Fax: (360)283-2154
Lee, Robert, Exec. Dir., Curator

Asian American Federation **[19390]**
120 Wall St., 9th Fl.
New York, NY 10005-3904
PH: (212)344-5878
Fax: (212)344-5636
Yoo, Jo-Ann, Exec. Dir.

Asian American Legal Defense and
Education Fund **[17876]**
99 Hudson St., 12th Fl.
New York, NY 10013
PH: (212)966-5932
Fax: (212)966-4303
Shi, Tommy, President

Asian American Writers' Workshop
[3513]
110-112 W 27th St., Ste. 600
New York, NY 10001
PH: (212)494-0061
Chen, Ken, Exec. Dir.

Asian Financial Society **[1220]**
PO Box 357, Church St. Sta.
New York, NY 10008
PH: (646)580-5066
Wan, Tracy, Bd. Member

Asian Women in Business **[611]**
42 Broadway, Ste. 1748
New York, NY 10004-3876
PH: (212)868-1368
Toll free: 877-686-6870
Azuma, Julie, Chairperson

ASME International **[6831]**
2 Park Ave.
New York, NY 10016-5990
PH: (973)882-1170
Toll free: 800-843-2763
Fax: (973)882-1717
Loughlin, Thomas G., Exec. Dir.

Asset Managers Forum **[1221]**
c/o SIFMA
120 Broadway, 35th Fl.
New York, NY 10017
PH: (212)313-1389
Cameron, Tim, Managing Dir.

Associated Press Media Editors
[2657]
450 W 33rd St.
New York, NY 10001
PH: (212)621-7007
Sellers-Earl, Laura, President

Associated Press Photo Managers
[2576]
450 W 33rd St.
New York, NY 10001-2603
Sell, Rebecca, President

Association for Advancement of
Psychoanalysis **[16843]**
80 8th Ave., Ste. 1501
New York, NY 10011
PH: (212)741-0515
Fax: (212)366-4347

Association of American Publishers
[2765]
71 5th Ave., 2nd Fl.
New York, NY 10003-3004
PH: (212)255-0200
Fax: (212)255-7007
Allen, Tom, CEO, President

Association of American University
Presses **[8021]**
28 W 36th St., Ste. 602
New York, NY 10018
PH: (212)989-1010
Fax: (212)989-0275
McLaughlin, Brenna, Dir. of Mktg.

Association of Art Museum Curators
[9821]
174 E 80th St.
New York, NY 10075
PH: (646)405-8057
Fax: (212)537-5571
Pineiro, Judith, Exec. Dir.

Association of Art Museum Directors
[9822]
120 E 56th St., Ste. 520
New York, NY 10022-3673
PH: (212)754-8084
Fax: (212)754-8087
Cole, Johnnetta Betsch, PhD,
President

Association of Authors' Representatives, Inc. **[161]**
302A W 12th St., No. 122
New York, NY 10014
Kahn, Jody, Admin. Sec.

Association for Behavioral and
Cognitive Therapies **[13794]**
305 7th Ave., 16th Fl.
New York, NY 10001-6008
PH: (212)647-1890
Fax: (212)647-1865
Eimer, Mary Jane, CAE, Exec. Dir.

Association of Biomedical Com-
munications Directors **[14294]**
c/o Susan Weil-Kazzaz, President
Memorial Sloan-Kettering Cancer
Ctr.
1275 York Ave.
New York, NY 10065
PH: (646)888-2040
Fax: (646)422-0161
Weil-Kazzaz, Susan, President

Association of Black Cardiologists
[14097]
122 East 42nd St., 18th Fl.
New York, NY 10168-1898
Toll free: 800-753-9222
McCullough, Cassandra A., MBA,
CEO, Exec. Dir.

Association of Black Women At-
torneys **[4994]**
1001 Avenue of the Americas, 11th
Fl.
New York, NY 10017
Wittingham, Kaylin L., President

Association of Business Information
& Media Companies **[2768]**
675 3rd Ave., 7th Fl.
New York, NY 10017-5704
PH: (212)661-6360
Fax: (212)370-0736
Pettit, Clark, CEO, President

Association of Cancer Online
Resources **[13892]**
173 Duane St., Ste. 3A
New York, NY 10013-3334
PH: (212)226-5525

Association of Chartered Ac-
countants in the United States **[13]**
347 5th Ave., Ste. 1406
New York, NY 10016
PH: (212)481-7950
Holbeck, Natasha, VP

Association of Commercial Stock
Image Licensors **[1187]**
630 9th Ave.
New York, NY 10036

PH: (301)920-4054

Association for Computing
Machinery **[6292]**
2 Penn Plz., Ste. 701
New York, NY 10121-0701
PH: (212)869-7440
Toll free: 800-342-6626
Stephenson, Chris, Exec. Dir.

Association for Computing
Machinery - Special Interest Group
on Accessible Computing **[6293]**
2 Penn Plz., Ste. 701
New York, NY 10121-0701
PH: (212)626-0500
Toll free: 800-342-6626
Fax: (212)944-1318
Trewin, Shari, Chairman

Association for Computing
Machinery-Special Interest Group
on Array Programming Languages
[7057]
1515 Broadway
New York, NY 10036
PH: (212)626-0500
Toll free: 800-342-6626
Fax: (212)944-1318

Association for Computing
Machinery Special Interest Group
on Artificial Intelligence **[5984]**
2 Penn Plz., Ste. 701
New York, NY 10121-0701
PH: (212)626-0605
　(212)302-5826
Frawley, Irene, Prog. Dir.

Association for Computing
Machinery - Special Interest Group
on Computer and Human Interac-
tion **[6032]**
1515 Broadway
New York, NY 10036
PH: (212)626-0500
Toll free: 800-342-6626
Fax: (212)944-1318
van der Veer, Gerrit, President

Association for Computing
Machinery - Special Interest Group
on Computer Science Education
[7651]
2 Penn Plz., Rm. 701
New York, NY 10121-0799
Rodger, Susan H., Chairperson

Association for Computing
Machinery - Special Interest Group
for Design Automation **[6237]**
c/o Debra Venedam, Program Direc-
tor
Office of SIG Services
2 Penn Plz., Ste. 701
New York, NY 10121
PH: (212)626-0614
Fax: (212)302-5826
Narayanan, Vijaykrishnan, Chairman

Association for Computing
Machinery - Special Interest Group
on Design of Communication
[6308]
2 Penn Plz., Ste. 701
New York, NY 10121-0701
PH: (212)626-0500
Toll free: 800-342-6626
Fax: (212)944-1318
Potts, Liza, Chairperson

Association for Computing
Machinery - Special Interest Group
on Measurement and Evaluation
[6239]
PO Box 30777
New York, NY 10087
PH: (212)869-7440
Toll free: 800-342-6626
Misra, Vishal, President

Association for Computing
Machinery - Special Interest Group
on Mobility Systems Users, Data
and Computing **[6310]**
2 Penn Plz., Ste. 701
New York, NY 10121-0701
PH: (212)626-0603
Fax: (212)302-5826
Spinola, Fran, Coord.

Association for Computing
Machinery - Special Interest Group
on MultiMedia **[6311]**
2 Penn Plz., Ste. 701
New York, NY 10121-0701
PH: (212)869-7440
Toll free: 800-342-6626
Fax: (212)944-1318
Spinola, Fran, Program Mgr.

Association for Computing
Machinery - Special Interest Group
on Simulation and Modelling
[6241]
2 Penn Plz., Ste. 701
New York, NY 10121-0701
PH: (212)626-0605
Fishwick, Paul, Chairman

Association for Computing
Machinery - Special Interest Group
on University and College Comput-
ing Services **[7423]**
c/o ACM
PO Box 3077
New York, NY 10087-0777
PH: (814)863-0421
Fax: (814)863-7049
Vaught, Russel S., Director

Association of Departments of
English **[7865]**
c/o David Laurence, Director
26 Broadway, 3rd Fl.
New York, NY 10004-1789
PH: (646)576-5137
　(646)576-5130
Fax: (646)835-4056
Laurence, David, Director

Association of Departments of
Foreign Languages **[8178]**
85 Broad St., Ste. 500
New York, NY 10004-2434
PH: (646)576-5140
Goldberg, David, Assoc. Dir.

Association of Directors of Geriatric
Academic Programs **[14889]**
American Geriatrics Society
40 Fulton St., 18th Fl.
New York, NY 10038
PH: (212)308-1414
Fax: (212)832-8646
Busby-Whitehead, Jan, MD, Chair-
man

Association of Episcopal Colleges
[7625]
Colleges and Universities of the
Anglican Communion
815 2nd Ave.
New York, NY 10017-4559
PH: (212)716-6149
Fax: (212)986-5039
Thompson, Rev. Donald

Association of Executive Search and
Leadership Consultants **[1086]**
425 5th Ave., 4th Fl.
New York, NY 10016
PH: (212)398-9556
Rooney, Patrick, Managing Dir.

Association of Former International
Civil Servants - New York **[5077]**
1 United Nations Plz., Rm. DC1-580
New York, NY 10017

PH: (212)963-2943
Fax: (212)963-5702
Saputelli, Ms. Linda, President

Association for the Help of Retarded
Children **[15813]**
83 Maiden Ln.
New York, NY 10038
PH: (212)780-2500
　(212)780-4491
VanReepinghen, Sharyn, VP

Association of Hispanic Healthcare
Executives **[15113]**
153 W 78th St., Ste. 1
New York, NY 10024
PH: (212)877-1615
Fax: (212)877-2406
Zeppenfeldt-Cestero, George A.,
President

Association of Independent Com-
mercial Producers **[89]**
3 W 18th St., 5th Fl.
New York, NY 10011
PH: (212)929-3000
Fax: (212)929-3359
Miller, Matt, CEO, President

Association of Independent Creative
Editors **[2664]**
3 W 18th St., 5th Fl.
New York, NY 10011
PH: (212)665-2679
Madden, Rachelle, Exec. Dir.

Association of Inspectors General
[5265]
524 W 59th St., 3400 N
New York, NY 10019
PH: (212)237-8001
Fax: (718)732-2480
Miguel, Melinda M., Director

Association for Interactive Marketing
[3217]
1430 Broadway, 8th Fl.
New York, NY 10018
PH: (212)790-1408
Fax: (212)391-9233
Nooman, Kevin M., Exec. Dir.

Association of Jewish Reform
Educators **[20233]**
633 3rd Ave.
New York, NY 10017
PH: (212)452-6510
Fax: (212)452-6512
Novak Winer, Rabbi Laura, RJE,
President

Association for Jewish Studies
[8135]
15 W 16th St.
New York, NY 10011-6301
PH: (917)606-8249
Fax: (917)606-8222
Sheramy, Rona, PhD, Exec. Dir.

Association of Junior Leagues
International **[13284]**
80 Maiden Ln., Ste. 305
New York, NY 10038
PH: (212)951-8300
Toll free: 800-955-3248
Fax: (212)481-7196
Danish, Susan, Exec. Dir.

Association for Macular Diseases
[16372]
210 E 64th St.
New York, NY 10065
PH: (212)605-3719
Fax: (212)605-3795
Landou, Bernard, President

Association of Management Consulting Firms **[2154]**
370 Lexington Ave., Ste. 2209
New York, NY 10017

PH: (212)262-3055
Fax: (212)262-3054
Caputo, Sally, President, COO

Association of Minor League
Umpires **[22544]**
80 8th Ave., Ste. 205
New York, NY 10011
Francis, Shaun, Exec. Dir.

Association of Music Producers
[2421]
3 W 18th St., 5th Fl.
New York, NY 10011
PH: (212)924-4100
Fax: (212)675-0102
Menkes, Jason, President

Association of Muslim American
Lawyers **[4997]**
233 Broadway, Ste. 801
New York, NY 10279
PH: (212)608-7776
Mohammedi, Omar, Esq., President

Association of National Advertisers
[90]
708 3rd Ave., 33rd Fl.
New York, NY 10017
PH: (212)697-5950
Fax: (212)687-7310
Liodice, Robert D., CEO, President

Association of Productivity Specialists **[2155]**
521 5th Ave., Ste. 1700
New York, NY 10175
Quinn, James, Treasurer

Association for Psychohistory **[9463]**
140 Riverside Dr., Ste. 14H
New York, NY 10024-2605
PH: (212)799-2294
Fax: (212)799-2294
Hein, Susan, Publisher, Administra-
tor

Association for Religion and Intel-
lectual Life **[20074]**
475 Riverside Dr., Ste. 1945
New York, NY 10115
PH: (212)870-2544
Fax: (212)870-2539
Henderson, Charles P., Jr., Exec.
Ed.

Association for the Study of Food
and Society **[6641]**
c/o Amy Bentley, Editor
NYU Steinhardt
Dept. of Nutrition, Food Studies, and
Public Health
411 Lafayette St., 5th Fl.
New York, NY 10003
Ray, Krishnendu, President

Association for the Study of
Nationalities **[9290]**
420 W 118th St., 12th Fl.
The Harriman Institute
Columbia University
New York, NY 10027
Kreider, Ryan, Exec. Dir.

Association for the Study of Persian-
ate Societies **[9593]**
Stony Brook-Manhattan
387 Park Ave. S, 3rd Fl.
New York, NY 10016
PH: (631)632-7746
Fax: (631)632-8203
Gross, Jo-Ann, Director

Association of Theatrical Press
Agents and Managers **[23494]**
14 Penn Plz., Ste. 1703
225 W 34th St.
New York, NY 10122

PH: (212)719-3666
Fax: (212)302-1585
Calhoun, David R., President

**Association of Women Industrial
Designers [6720]**
Old Chelsea St.
New York, NY 10008-0461
Doering, Erika, Founder

Aston Martin Owners Club [21329]
120 E 75th St.
New York, NY 10021
PH: (212)628-7448
Wright, Anne, Events Coord.

**Audience Development Committee
[10242]**
Manhattanville Sta.
New York, NY 10027
PH: (212)368-6906
Jones, Grace L., President

Audio Engineering Society [6417]
551 5th Ave., Ste. 1225
New York, NY 10165-2520
PH: (212)661-8528
Moses, Bob, Exec. Dir.

**Australian Trade and Investment
Commission [3297]**
150 E 42nd St., 34th Fl.
New York, NY 10017-5612
PH: (646)344-8111
Fax: (212)867-7710
Gosper, Bruce, CEO

Austrian Cultural Forum [9197]
11 E 52nd St.
New York, NY 10022
PH: (212)319-5300
Fax: (212)644-8660
Moser, Christine, Director

Austrian Tourist Office [23543]
PO Box 1142
New York, NY 10108-1142
PH: (212)575-7723
    (212)944-6885
Fax: (212)730-4568
Gigl, Michael, Director

Authors Guild [10362]
31 E 32nd St., 7th Fl.
New York, NY 10016
PH: (212)563-5904
Fax: (212)564-5363
Russo, Richard, VP

Autism Link [13748]
900 John St.
New York, NY 10038
PH: (412)364-1886
Carosso, Dr. John, Exec. Dir.

Autism Science Foundation [13753]
10 W 32nd St., Ste. 182
New York, NY 10001
PH: (914)810-9100
Singer, Alison Tepper, Founder,
President

Autism Speaks [13757]
1 E 33rd St., 4th Fl.
New York, NY 10016
PH: (212)252-8584
Fax: (212)252-8676
Geiger, Angela, President, CEO

**AVS Science and Technology
Society [7359]**
125 Maiden Ln., 15th Fl.
New York, NY 10038
PH: (212)248-0200
Fax: (212)248-0245
Wolden, Colin, Editor

**AZRA/World Union for Progressive
Judaism North America [20234]**
633 3rd Ave., 7th Fl.
New York, NY 10017-6778

PH: (212)650-4280
Fax: (212)650-4289
Miller, Rabbi Bennett, Chairman

Leo Baeck Institute [9633]
15 W 16th St.
New York, NY 10011-6301
PH: (212)744-6400
    (212)294-8340
Sobel, Ronald, President

Ballet Theatre Foundation [9244]
890 Broadway, 3rd Fl.
New York, NY 10003
PH: (212)477-3030
Fax: (212)254-5938
Moore, Rachel S., CEO

**Barbados Cancer Association USA
[13897]**
PO Box 3094
Grand Central Sta.
New York, NY 10163-3094
Toll free: 866-729-1011
Parris, O'Neall E., Chairman

**Barbados Tourism Marketing, Inc.
[23657]**
820 2nd Ave., 5th Fl.
New York, NY 10017
PH: (212)986-6516
Toll free: 800-221-9831
Fax: (212)573-9850

Basic Health International [17752]
25 Broadway, 5th Fl.
New York, NY 10004
PH: (646)593-8694
Cremer, Dr. Miriam, Founder

BCA Global [960]
244 Madison Ave., Ste. 305
New York, NY 10016
PH: (212)643-6570
Askew, Alex, President, CEO

James Beard Foundation [10313]
167 W 12th St.
New York, NY 10011
PH: (212)675-4984
Ungaro, Susan, President

Beaux Arts Alliance [8967]
119 E 74th St.
New York, NY 10021
PH: (212)639-9120

**Belgian American Chamber of Com-
merce [23564]**
1177 Avenue of the Americas, 7th Fl.
New York, NY 10036
PH: (212)541-0771
Burggraeve, Chris, President

Belgian Tourist Office [23658]
300 E 42nd St., 14th Fl.
New York, NY 10017
PH: (212)758-8130

Bend the Arc [12528]
330 7th Ave., 19th Fl.
New York, NY 10001
PH: (212)213-2113
Rohde, Stephen, Chairman

**Bermuda Department of Tourism
[23659]**
675 3rd Ave., 20th Fl.
New York, NY 10017
Toll free: 800-223-6106
Darrell, Karin, Director

Bernard Shaw Society [9042]
PO Box 1159
Madison Square Sta.
New York, NY 10159-1159
Nathan, Rhoda, President

Beth Din of America [20236]
305 7th Ave., 12th Fl.
New York, NY 10001-6008

PH: (212)807-9042
    (212)807-9072
Fax: (212)807-9183
Weissmann, Rabbi Shlomo, Director

A Better Chance [7816]
253 W 35th St., 6th Fl.
New York, NY 10001-1907
PH: (646)346-1310
Toll free: 800-562-7865
Fax: (646)346-1311
Timmons, Ms. Sandra E., President

Better Future International [10866]
PO Box 20196
New York, NY 10014
Johnson, Starlene, Exec. Dir.

Better World Chorus [12367]
PO Box 20934
New York, NY 10025

**Bibliographical Society of America
[9120]**
PO Box 1537, Lenox Hill Sta.
New York, NY 10021
PH: (212)452-2710
Fax: (212)452-2710
Antonetti, Martin, President

Bideawee [10594]
410 E 38th St.
New York, NY 10016
Toll free: 866-262-8133
Lawrence, Guy B.

Bioethics International [13815]
733 3rd Ave., 15th Fl.
New York, NY 10017
PH: (646)549-0233
Miller, Jennifer, PhD, President,
CEO, Founder

BKR International [18]
19 Fulton St., Rm. 401
New York, NY 10038
PH: (212)964-2115
Toll free: 800-BKR-INTL
Fax: (212)964-2133
Schwartz, Maureen, Exec. Dir.

Black Culinarian Alliance [961]
244 Madison Ave., Ste. 305
New York, NY 10016-2817
PH: (212)643-6570
Fax: (212)967-4184
Stanford, Howard, Chairman

**Black Entertainment and Sports
Lawyers Association [5174]**
PO Box 230794
New York, NY 10023-0014
Suber, Elke, Chairman

Black Filmmaker Foundation [9299]
131 Varick St., Ste. 937
New York, NY 10013
PH: (212)253-1690
Hudlin, Warrington, Founder

Black Retail Action Group [2948]
68 E 131st St., Ste. 704
New York, NY 10037
PH: (212)234-3050
Fax: (212)234-3053
Cokley-Dunlap, Nicole, Co-Pres.

Black Rock Coalition [9285]
PO Box 1054
New York, NY 10276
Davis, LaRonda, President

**Jacob Blaustein Institute for the
Advancement of Human Rights
[18378]**
165 E 56th St.
New York, NY 10022
PH: (212)891-1315
Fax: (212)891-1460
Sideman, Richard, President

The Blue Card, Inc. [12220]
171 Madison Ave., Ste. 1405
New York, NY 10016
PH: (212)239-2251
Fax: (212)594-6881
Machlin, Gia, Chmn. of the Bd.

Bnai Zion Foundation [19515]
1430 Broadway, Ste. 1804
New York, NY 10018
PH: (212)725-1211
Fax: (212)684-6327
Kesten, Robert, Consultant

**Bnei Akiva of the United States and
Canada [20238]**
520 W 8th Ave., 15th Fl.
New York, NY 10018
PH: (212)465-9536
Fax: (212)216-9578
Feldman, Shaul, Director

Bond Club of New York [389]
c/o Peter F. Ricciardi
Dresver Securities
75 Wall St.
New York, NY 10005
PH: (212)363-5191
Ricciardi, Peter F., Secretary

Bone Marrow Foundation [13846]
515 Madison Ave., Ste. 1130
New York, NY 10022
PH: (212)838-3029
Toll free: 800-365-1336
Fax: (212)223-0081
Merrill, Christina, Exec. Dir.

Book Industry Study Group [2774]
145 W 45th St., Ste. 601
New York, NY 10036
PH: (646)336-7141
Fax: (646)336-6214
Michaels, Ken, Director

**Boston Terrier Club of America
[21846]**
c/o Margaret Noble, Corresponding
Secretary
233 E 69th St., Unit 7D
New York, NY 10021-5447
PH: (212)452-2324
Lajoye, Dane, President

**Boys' and Girls' Towns of Italy
[13431]**
250 E 63rd St., Ste. 204
New York, NY 10065
PH: (212)980-8770
Fax: (212)409-8740
Romita, Mauro C., Chmn. of the Bd.

**Boys Town Jerusalem Foundation of
America [13433]**
1 Penn Plz., Ste. 6250
New York, NY 10119
Toll free: 800-469-2697
Fax: (866)730-2697
Kaswell, Robert, Chmn. of the Bd.

Brand Activation Association [2269]
708 3rd Ave., 33rd Fl.
New York, NY 10017
PH: (212)697-5950
Mavreshko, Lana, CFO

Braun Holocaust Institute [18346]
Anti-Defamation League
605 3rd Ave.
New York, NY 10158
PH: (212)885-7700
Toll free: 866-386-3235
Foxman, Abraham H., Director

**Brazilian-American Chamber of
Commerce [23567]**
509 Madison Ave., Ste. 304
New York, NY 10022

PH: (212)751-4691
Fax: (212)751-7692
Vieira, Carlos Alberto, President,
Chmn. of the Bd.

**Brazilian Government Trade Bureau
of the Consulate General of Brazil
in New York [23544]**
220 E 42nd St.
New York, NY 10017-5806
PH: (917)777-7777
Fax: (212)827-0225

Breakthrough [18379]
4 W 43rd St., Ste. 715
New York, NY 10036
PH: (212)868-6500
Fax: (212)868-6501
Dutt, Mallika, CEO, President,
Founder

A Bridge for Children [10872]
PO Box 1054
New York, NY 10268
Hwang, Steve, Exec. Dir.

**Bridge Engineering Association
[6549]**
11 Broadway, 21st Fl.
New York, NY 10004
PH: (212)286-8014
Fax: (435)203-1166
Mahmoud, Khaled M., PhD, Chair-
man

Bridges of Understanding [18516]
PO Box 2232
New York, NY 10101-2232
PH: (917)755-2179
Al-Juburi, Faisal, Exec. Dir.

**British-American Business Council
[616]**
52 Vanderbilt Ave., 20th Fl.
New York, NY 10017
PH: (212)661-4060
Fax: (212)661-4074
Allen, Steve, President

**British Schools and Universities Club
of New York [7628]**
PO Box 4116
New York, NY 10163
PH: (212)465-3270
Bradley, Orton, Founder

**British Schools and Universities
Foundation [7629]**
575 Madison Ave., Ste. 1006
New York, NY 10022-8511
PH: (212)662-5576
Lipson, Mr. David, Chairman

**BritishAmerican Business Inc. of
New York and London [23568]**
52 Vanderbilt Ave., 20th Fl.
New York, NY 10017
PH: (212)661-4060
Fax: (212)661-4074
Mendenhall, Wendy, Managing Dir.

**Broadcasters' Foundation of America
[457]**
125 W 55th St., 4th Fl.
New York, NY 10019-5366
PH: (212)373-8250
Fax: (212)373-8254
Thompson, Jim, President

**Broadway Cares/Equity Fights AIDS
[10535]**
165 W 46th St., Ste. 1300
New York, NY 10036
PH: (212)840-0770
Fax: (212)840-0551
Viola, Tom, Exec. Dir.

Broadway League [10245]
729 7th Ave., 5th Fl.
New York, NY 10019

PH: (212)764-1122
Fax: (212)944-2136
St. Martin, Charlotte, President

**Builders Hardware Manufacturers
Association [1566]**
355 Lexington Ave., 15th Fl.
New York, NY 10017
PH: (212)297-2122
Fax: (212)370-9047
Picard, Dan, President

**Building Community Bridges, Inc.
[11324]**
244 5th Ave., Ste. E283
New York, NY 10001-7604
Toll free: 888-834-8611
Fax: (888)397-3717
Nanevie, Enyonam, CEO, Founder,
Co-Ch., Exec. Dir.

**Building Trades Employers' Associa-
tion [509]**
1430 Broadway, Ste. 1106
New York, NY 10018
PH: (212)704-9745
Fax: (212)704-4367
Coletti, Louis J., CEO, President

**Business Council for International
Understanding [18518]**
1501 Broadway, Ste. 2300
New York, NY 10018
PH: (212)490-0460
Fax: (212)697-8526
Tichansky, Peter J., CEO, President

Business Council for Peace [13372]
2576 Broadway, No. 317
New York, NY 10025
PH: (212)696-9696
Maloney, Toni, Bd. Member

**Business Marketing Association
[2270]**
708 3rd Ave.
New York, NY 10017
PH: (212)697-5950
Goodman, Meg, Mem.

Cambridge in America [9138]
1120 Avenue of the Americas, 17th
Fl.
New York, NY 10036
PH: (212)984-0960
Fax: (212)984-0970
Yun Won, Cho, Exec. Dir.

Cancer Care [13917]
275 7th Ave., 22nd Fl.
New York, NY 10001-6708
PH: (212)712-8400
Toll free: 800-813-4673
Fax: (212)712-8495
Perez, Hector, Dir. of Info. Technol-
ogy

Cancer101 [13932]
304 Park Ave. S, 11th Fl.
New York, NY 10010
PH: (646)638-2202
Fax: (646)349-3035
Knoll, Monica, Founder

Career Gear [8409]
40 Fulton St., Ste. 701
New York, NY 10038
PH: (212)577-6190
Fields, Gary, Exec. Dir., Founder

**Caribbean Cultural Center African
Diaspora Institute [9226]**
1825 Park Ave., Ste. 602
New York, NY 10035
PH: (212)307-7420
Capote, Melody, Dep. Dir.

**Caribbean Tourism Organization,
American Branch [23548]**
80 Broad St., Ste. 3302
New York, NY 10004

PH: (212)635-9530
Fax: (212)635-9511
Bramble, Sylma Brown, Director

**Carnegie Corporation of New York
[7750]**
437 Madison Ave.
New York, NY 10022
PH: (212)371-3200
Fax: (212)754-4073
Gregorian, Vartan, President

**Carnegie Council for Ethics in
International Affairs [18476]**
Merrill House
170 E 64th St.
New York, NY 10065-7478
PH: (212)838-4120
Fax: (212)752-2432
Rosenthal, Joel H., President

**Catalog and Multichannel Marketing
Council [1532]**
1333 Broadway, Ste. 301
New York, NY 10018
PH: (212)768-7277
Woolley, Linda A., President, CEO

Catalyst, Inc. [10303]
120 Wall St., 15th Fl.
New York, NY 10005-3904
PH: (212)514-7600
Fax: (212)514-8470
Fong, Serena, VP

**Catholic Daughters of the Americas
[19401]**
10 W 71st St.
New York, NY 10023-4201
PH: (212)877-3041
Impellizeri, Mary, Exec. Dir.

Catholic Guardian Services [10887]
1011 1st Ave. 10th Fl.
New York, NY 10022
PH: (212)371-1011
Fax: (212)758-5892
Kelleher, Rory, Chairman

**Catholic League for Religious and
Civil Rights [19813]**
450 7th Ave.
New York, NY 10123
PH: (212)371-3191
Fax: (212)371-3394
Eichner, Rev. Philip, Chairman

**Catholic Medical Mission Board
[12267]**
100 Wall St., 9th Fl.
New York, NY 10005
PH: (212)242-7757
Toll free: 800-678-5659
Wilkinson, Bruce, President, CEO

**Catholic Near East Welfare Associa-
tion [18678]**
1011 1st Ave.
New York, NY 10022-4195
PH: (212)826-1480
Fax: (212)838-1344
Kozar, John E., President, Secretary

Catholic Worker Movement [18715]
36 E 1st St.
New York, NY 10003
PH: (212)777-9617
Allaire, Jim, Web Adm.

**Cayman Islands Department of Tour-
ism [23660]**
Empire State Bldg., Ste. 2720
350 5th Ave.
New York, NY 10118
PH: (212)889-9009

CEC ArtsLink [18077]
291 Broadway, 12th Fl.
New York, NY 10007 -

PH: (212)643-1985
Fax: (212)643-1996
Brown, Fritzie, Exec. Dir.

**Center to Advance Palliative Care
[15318]**
55 W 125th St., 13th Fl.
New York, NY 10027
PH: (212)201-2670
Sieger, Carol E., JD, COO

Center for Book Arts [9124]
28 W 27th St., 3rd Fl.
New York, NY 10001
PH: (212)481-0295
Campos, Alexander, Exec. Dir.,
Curator

**Center for Chemical Process Safety
[6193]**
120 Wall St., 23rd Fl.
New York, NY 10005-4020
PH: (203)702-7660
Toll free: 800-242-4363
Fax: (203)775-5177
Berger, Scott, Exec. Dir.

Center for Christian Studies [19949]
7 W 55th St.
New York, NY 10019
PH: (212)247-0490
Johnston, Rev. Scott Black, Pastor

**Center for Constitutional Rights
[17881]**
666 Broadway, 7th Fl.
New York, NY 10012
PH: (212)614-6464
Fax: (212)614-6499
Warren, Vincent, Exec. Dir.

**Center for Contemporary Opera
[9885]**
236 E 31st St.
New York, NY 10016
PH: (646)481-8110
Schaeffer, Jim, Dir. Gen.

Center for Cuban Studies [9194]
231 W 29th St., 4th Fl.
New York, NY 10001
PH: (212)242-0559
Fax: (212)242-1937
Levinson, Sandra, Exec. Dir.

**Center for Hearing and Communica-
tion [15179]**
50 Broadway, 6th Fl.
New York, NY 10004
PH: (917)305-7766
Hanin, Laurie, PhD, Exec. Dir.

Center for Jewish History [19516]
15 W 16th St.
New York, NY 10011
PH: (212)294-8301
Lapidus, Sidney, Treasurer

Center for LGBTQ Studies [11877]
365 5th Ave., Rm. 7115
New York, NY 10016
PH: (212)817-1955
Fax: (212)817-1567
Blint, Rich, Director

**Center for Medical Consumers
[14931]**
239 Thompson St.
New York, NY 10012
PH: (212)674-7105
Napoli, Maryann, Assoc. Dir.

Center for Migration Studies [9796]
37 E 60th St., 4th Fl.
New York, NY 10022
PH: (212)337-3080
Kerwin, Donald M., Jr., Exec. Dir.

**Center for Reproductive Rights
[19032]**
199 Water St.
New York, NY 10038

PH: (917)637-3600
Fax: (917)637-3666
McQuade, Laura, COO, Exec. VP

Center for Sports and Osteopathic
  Medicine [16801]
317 Madison Ave., Ste. 400
New York, NY 10017
PH: (212)685-8113
Fax: (212)697-4541
Bachrach, Dr. Richard M., DO,
  President

Center for U.N. Reform Education
  [19208]
PO Box 3195
New York, NY 10163-3195
PH: (646)465-8520
Pace, William R., President

Center for United States-China Arts
  Exchange [9151]
423 W 118th St., No. 1E
New York, NY 10025
PH: (212)280-4648
Fax: (212)662-6346
Bollinger, Lee C., Chmn. of the Bd.

Center for War/Peace Studies
  [18520]
866 United Nations Plz., Rm. 4050
New York, NY 10017
PH: (646)553-3464
Kean, Hamilton, Chairman

The Century Foundation [18969]
1 Whitehall St., 15 Fl.
New York, NY 10004
PH: (212)452-7700
Fax: (212)535-7534
Abelow, Bradley, Chairman

CFDA Foundation [201]
65 Bleecker St., 11th Fl.
New York, NY 10012
PH: (212)302-1821
Fax: (212)768-0515
Kolb, Steven, President, CEO

Chamber Music America [9886]
12 W 32nd St., 7th Fl.
New York, NY 10001-0802
PH: (212)242-2022
Fax: (212)967-9747
Lioi, Margaret M., CEO

Change for Change [12467]
PO Box 230426
New York, NY 10023
PH: (212)918-9303
Fax: (212)918-9220
Hork, Dana, President, Founder

charity: water [13317]
40 Worth St., Ste. 330
New York, NY 10013
PH: (646)688-2323
Fax: (646)883-3456
Harrison, Scott, Founder, President

Chefs for Humanity [12081]
c/o Jaime Wolf, Esq.
The Woolworth Bldg.
233 Broadway, Ste. 2208
New York, NY 10279
Cora, Cat, Founder, President

Chemists' Club [19656]
30 W 44th St.
New York, NY 10036
PH: (212)626-9300
Stefandel, Roland, President

Chemo Comfort [10785]
154 Christopher St., Ste 3C
New York, NY 10014
PH: (212)675-3744
Fax: (212)675-3786
Paolucci, Anne Marie, Founder

Chemotherapy Foundation [16340]
183 Madison Ave., Ste. 403
New York, NY 10016
PH: (212)213-9292
Fax: (212)213-3831
Cox, Shirley, Exec. Dir.

Cherished Feet [13004]
115 E 34th St., No. 1870
New York, NY 10156
PH: (646)770-6892
Koeningsberg, Karen, Founder,
  President

Chess in the Schools [21590]
520 8th Ave., 2nd Fl.
New York, NY 10018
PH: (212)643-0225
Fax: (212)564-3524
Walsh, Mike, Chairman

Children of Nowhere [10921]
601 W 26th St., Rm. 1105
New York, NY 10001-1133
Jonas, Richard, Contact

Children's Advertising Review Unit
  [92]
112 Madison Ave., 3rd Fl.
New York, NY 10016
PH: (212)705-0100
Fax: (212)705-0134
Keeley, Wayne J., Director

Children's Book Council [9125]
54 W 39th St., 14th Fl.
New York, NY 10018-7480
PH: (212)966-1990
Feresten, Nancy, Director

Children's Brain Tumor Foundation
  [14177]
1460 Broadway
New York, NY 10016-0715
Toll free: 866-228-4673
Edmiaston, Mark, President

Children's Cancer and Blood
  Foundation [15226]
333 E 38th St., Ste. 830
New York, NY 10016-2772
PH: (212)297-4336
Fax: (212)297-4340
Zaleski, Jennifer, Exec. Dir.

Children's Health Fund [14179]
215 W 125th St., Ste. 301
New York, NY 10027
PH: (212)535-9400
Redlener, Irwin, MD, Founder,
  President

The Children's Tumor Foundation
  [15916]
120 Wall St., 16th Fl.
New York, NY 10005-3904
PH: (212)344-6633
Toll free: 800-323-7938
Fax: (212)747-0004
Tiven, Rachel B., V. Ch.

China General Chamber of
  Commerce-U.S.A. [23573]
19 E 48th St., 5th Fl.
New York, NY 10017
PH: (646)918-7804
Fax: (917)639-3124
Niu, Candice, Exec. Dir.

China Institute in America [9152]
100 Wasington St.
New York, NY 10006
PH: (212)744-8181
Fax: (212)628-4159
Mei, Ingrid, Office Mgr.

Chinese-American Arts Council
  [8970]
456 Broadway, 3rd Fl.
New York, NY 10013

PH: (212)431-9740
Fax: (212)431-9789
Chow, Alan, Founder, Director

Chinese American Medical Society
  [15721]
265 Canal St., Ste. 515
New York, NY 10013
PH: (212)334-4760
Fax: (646)304-6373
Fong, Danny, MD, VP

Chinese Consolidated Benevolent
  Association [19414]
62 Mott St.
New York, NY 10013
PH: (212)226-6280
Fax: (212)431-5883
Shiao, Jerry, President

The Chinese Finance Association
  [1226]
PO Box 4058, Grand Central Sta.
New York, NY 10163
Xing, Fan, President

Choices in Childbirth [14225]
441 Lexington Ave., 19th Fl.
New York, NY 10017
PH: (212)983-4122
Fax: (212)983-0281
McAllister, Elan, Exec. Dir.

Christian Herald Association [19957]
432 Park Ave. S
New York, NY 10016
PH: (212)684-2800
Toll free: 800-269-3791
Fax: (212)684-3740
Morgan, Edward H., CEO, President

The Christophers [19823]
5 Hanover Sq., 22nd Fl.
New York, NY 10004
PH: (212)759-4050
Toll free: 888-298-4050
Fax: (212)838-5073
Okulski, Robert V., President,
  Treasurer

Church Women United [20640]
475 Riverside Dr., Ste. 243
New York, NY 10115
PH: (212)870-2347
Toll free: 800-298-5551
Fax: (212)870-2338
Samad, Djamillah, Exec. Dir.

Church World Service - Immigration
  and Refugee Program [19017]
475 Riverside Dr., Ste. 700
New York, NY 10115
PH: (212)870-2061
   (212)870-3300
Fax: (212)870-3194
McCullough, Rev. John L., CEO,
  President

Winston Churchill Foundation of the
  United States [7924]
600 Madison Ave., Ste. 1601
New York, NY 10022-1737
PH: (212)752-3200
Fax: (212)246-8330
Patrikis, Peter C., Exec. Dir.

Cinema Advertising Council [623]
122 E 42nd St., Ste. 511
New York, NY 10168
PH: (212)931-8106
Marks, Cliff, Chairman, President

Cinema Tropical [9303]
611 Broadway, Ste. 836
New York, NY 10012
PH: (212)254-5474
Gutierrez, Carlos A., Founder, Exec.
  Dir.

Circulation Council of DMA [2273]
1120 Avenue of the Americas
New York, NY 10036-6700
PH: (212)768-7277
Fax: (212)302-6714

Circumnavigators Club [6624]
50 Vanderbilt Ave.
New York, NY 10017
PH: (201)612-9100
Fax: (201)786-9133
Parke, Margaret Ellen, President

CityKids Foundation [13437]
601 W 26th St., Ste. 325
New York, NY 10001
PH: (212)925-3320
Finn, Brian, V. Ch.

CIVICUS: World Alliance for Citizen
  Participation [18901]
355 Lexington Ave.
New York, NY 10017
Gumbonzvanda, Nyaradzayi, Chmn.
  of the Bd., Chmn. of the Exec.
  Committee

CLAL - The National Jewish Center
  for Learning and Leadership
  [20241]
440 Park Ave. S, 4th Fl.
New York, NY 10016-8012
PH: (212)779-3300
Fax: (212)779-1009
Hirschfield, Rabbi Brad, President

Robert Sterling Clark Foundation
  [9227]
135 E 64th St.
New York, NY 10065
PH: (212)288-8900
Fax: (212)288-1033
Smith, James Allen, Chairman

The Climate Group [3832]
145 W 58th St., Ste. 2A
New York, NY 10019
PH: (646)233-0550
Davidsen, Amy, Exec. Dir.

Clinical Directors Network [15139]
5 W 37th St., 10th Fl.
New York, NY 10018
PH: (212)382-0699
Tobin, Jonathan N., PhD, CEO,
  President

Coalition Against Trafficking in
  Women [18384]
PO Box 7160, JAF Sta.
New York, NY 10116
Fax: (212)643-9895
Bien-Aime, Taina, Exec. Dir.

Coalition for Healthcare Communica-
  tion [14987]
405 Lexington Ave.
New York, NY 10174-1801
PH: (212)850-0708
Kamp, John, Exec. Dir.

The Coalition for Hemophilia B
  [15228]
835 3rd Ave., Ste. 226
New York, NY 10022
PH: (212)520-8272
Fax: (212)520-8501
Taylor, John, Founder

Coalition for Innovative Media
  Measurement [2315]
1115 Broadway, 12th Fl.
New York, NY 10010
PH: (212)590-2431
Clarke, Jane, CEO, Managing Dir.

Coalition for the International
  Criminal Court [5131]
c/o WFM
708 3rd Ave., Ste. 1715

New York, NY 10017
PH: (212)687-2863
Fax: (212)599-1332
Pace, William R., Facilitator

Coalition for Rainforest Nations
[4613]
52 Vanderbilt Ave., 14th Fl.
New York, NY 10017-3808
PH: (646)448-6870
Fax: (646)448-6889
Conrad, Amb. Kevin M., Exec. Dir.

Cocoa Merchants' Association of
America **[1321]**
55 E 52nd St., 40th Fl.
New York, NY 10055
PH: (212)748-4193
Diez, Daniel V., Chairman

Coffee Kids **[11333]**
1 Penn Plz., Ste. 2225
New York, NY 10119
Singer, Rebecca, Exec. Dir.

The Collectors Club **[22321]**
22 E 35th St.
New York, NY 10016-3806
PH: (212)683-0559
Marsden, R. Bruce, President

College Art Association **[7509]**
50 Broadway, 21st Fl.
New York, NY 10004
PH: (212)691-1051
Fax: (212)627-2381
Downs, Linda, Exec. Dir.

The College Board **[8682]**
45 Columbus Ave.
New York, NY 10023-6917
PH: (212)713-8000
Caperton, Gaston, President

College Media Association **[8151]**
355 Lexington Ave., 15th Fl.
New York, NY 10017-6603
PH: (212)297-2195
Lash, Kelley, President

Colleges and Universities of the
Anglican Communion **[19700]**
Association of Episcopal Colleges
815 2nd Ave.
New York, NY 10017
PH: (212)716-6149
Fax: (212)986-5039
Callaway, Rev. Canon James G.,
Gen. Sec.

Colombian American Association
[23545]
641 Lexington Ave., Ste. 1430
New York, NY 10022
PH: (212)233-7776
Fax: (212)233-7779
Murrle, Christian, President

Color Association of the United
States **[752]**
33 Whitehall St., Ste. M3
New York, NY 10004
PH: (212)947-7774
Donghia, Sherri, Officer

Columbia Scholastic Press Advisers
Association **[8453]**
Columbia Scholastic Press Associa-
tion
Columbia University
90 Morningside Dr., Ste. B01, MC
5711
New York, NY 10027-6902
PH: (212)854-9400
Westbrook, Ray, Chairperson

Columbia Scholastic Press Association **[8454]**
Columbia University
90 Morningside Dr., Ste. B01

New York, NY 10027
PH: (212)854-9400
Sullivan, Edmund J., Exec. Dir.

Columbia University | Institute for
Learning Technologies **[7841]**
Teachers College
525 W 120th St.
New York, NY 10027-6605
PH: (212)678-3000
Lowes, Susan, Assoc. Dir.

Columbia University | Institute for the
Study of Human Rights **[18385]**
Riverside Church Twr., 7th Fl.
91 Claremont Ave.
New York, NY 10027
PH: (212)854-2479
Barkan, Elazar, Director

Comedy Fights Cancer **[13949]**
c/o Nuforms Media
116 W 23rd St., Ste. 500
New York, NY 10011
PH: (212)396-2015
Fax: (267)540-6597

Commercial Finance Association
[2090]
370 7th Ave., Ste. 1801
New York, NY 10001
PH: (212)792-9390
Fax: (212)564-6053
Trojan, Robert, CEO

Committee Against Anti-Asian
Violence **[17813]**
55 Hester St., Storefront
New York, NY 10002
PH: (212)473-6485
Dang, Cathy, Exec. Dir.

Committee of Concerned Scientists
[18386]
222 W 135th St., Ste. 3A
New York, NY 10030
Lebowitz, Joel L., Co-Ch.

Committee Encouraging Corporate
Philanthropy **[12469]**
5 Hanover Sq., Ste. 2102
New York, NY 10004
PH: (212)825-1000
Short, Barb, Managing Dir.

Committee of French Speaking
Societies **[19437]**
c/o Gerard Epelbaum, President
30 E 40th St., Ste. 906
New York, NY 10016
Epelbaum, Dr. Gerard, President

Committee for Humanitarian As-
sistance to Iranian Refugees
[12587]
17 Battery Pl., Rm. 605N
New York, NY 10004
PH: (212)747-1046
Fax: (212)425-7240
Namazie, Maryam, Contact

Committee of Interns and Residents
[23443]
520 8th Ave., Ste. 1200
New York, NY 10018
PH: (212)356-8100
      (212)356-8180
Toll free: 800-247-8877
Fax: (212)356-8111
Eshak, David, MD, President

Committee to Protect Journalists
[17942]
330 7th Ave., 11th Fl.
New York, NY 10001
PH: (212)465-1004
Fax: (212)465-9568
Rowe, Sandra Mims, Chairman

Committee for Truth in Psychiatry
[15765]
c/o Linda Andre, Director
PO Box 1214
New York, NY 10003
PH: (212)665-6587
Andre, Linda, Director

Committee for a Unified Independent
Party **[18886]**
225 Broadway, Ste. 2010
New York, NY 10007
PH: (212)609-2800
Salit, Jacqueline, President

The Commonwealth Fund **[17001]**
1 E 75th St.
New York, NY 10021
PH: (212)606-3800
Fax: (212)606-3500
Blumenthal, David, M.D., President

Communications Coordination Committee for the United Nations
[19209]
1140 Avenue of the Americas, 9th Fl.
New York, NY 10036
Carll, Dr. Elizabeth, President

Communist Party USA **[18887]**
235 W 23rd St., 7th Fl.
New York, NY 10011-2302
PH: (212)989-4994
Fax: (212)229-1713
Webb, Sam, Chairman

Community Alliance for the Ethical
Treatment of Youth **[10948]**
450 Lexington Ave., No. 1319
New York, NY 10163
PH: (202)681-8499
Whitehead, Kathryn, Founder, Exec.
Dir.

Community Development
International **[11338]**
PO Box 3417
New York, NY 10163
Jamison, Kevin, Founder, Director

Community Development Venture
Capital Alliance **[11339]**
424 W 33rd St., Ste. 320
New York, NY 10001-2618
PH: (212)594-6747
Fax: (212)594-6717
Moncrief, L. Raymond, Chairman

Community Information and
Epidemiological Technologies
[14728]
511 Avenue of the Americas, No.
132
New York, NY 10011
PH: (212)242-3428
Fax: (212)504-0848
Sioui, Georges, Investigator

Computer Science Teachers As-
sociation **[7654]**
PO Box 30778
New York, NY 10117-3509
PH: (212)626-0530
Toll free: 800-342-6626
Fax: (212)944-1318
Nelson, Mark R., Exec. Dir.

Concern Worldwide **[12651]**
355 Lexington Ave., 16th Fl.
New York, NY 10017
PH: (212)557-8000
Fax: (212)557-8004
Moran, Thomas J., Chairman

The Conference Board **[6387]**
845 3rd Ave.
New York, NY 10022-6600
PH: (212)759-0900
Ferguson, Roger W., Jr., Chairman

Conference on Jewish Material
Claims Against Germany **[12221]**
1359 Broadway, Rm. 2000
New York, NY 10018
PH: (646)536-9100
Fax: (212)685-5299
Bloch, Sam E., Bd. Member

Conference of Presidents of Major
American Jewish Organizations
[20243]
633 3rd Ave.
New York, NY 10017
PH: (212)318-6111
Fax: (212)644-4135
Greenberg, Stephen M., Chairman

Confluence Philanthropy **[12470]**
475 Riverside Dr., Ste. 900
New York, NY 10115
PH: (212)812-4367
Lanza, Dana, CEO, Founder

Congress for Jewish Culture **[9635]**
PO Box 1590
New York, NY 10159
PH: (212)505-8040

Congress of Racial Equality **[17780]**
817 Broadway, 3rd Fl.
New York, NY 10003
PH: (212)598-4000
Toll free: 800-439-2673
Fax: (212)982-0184
Holmes, George, Secretary,
Treasurer

Consolidated Tape Association
[3040]
c/o Kerry Baker Relf, Representative
Thompson Reuters
195 Broadway
New York, NY 10007

Consortium on Science, Technology
and Innovation for the South
[7129]
United Nations Headquarters
New York, NY 10017
PH: (212)963-4777
Fax: (212)963-3515

The Content Council **[2779]**
355 Lexington Ave., 15th Fl.
New York, NY 10017
PH: (212)297-2191
Fax: (212)297-2149
Seibert, Andrew, Chairman

Cooley's Anemia Foundation Inc.
[15229]
330 7th Ave., No. 200
New York, NY 10001
PH: (212)279-8090
Butler, Craig D., Exec. Dir.

Copper Development Association
Inc. **[6879]**
260 Madison Ave.
New York, NY 10016-2401
PH: (212)251-7200
Fax: (212)251-7234
Isayama, Maki, Info. Technology
Mgr.

Copyright Society of the U.S.A.
[5328]
1 E 53rd St., 8th Fl.
New York, NY 10022
PH: (212)354-6401
Wolff, Nancy E., VP

Cordell Hull Foundation for
International Education **[8113]**
1745 Broadway, 17th Fl.
New York, NY 10019
PH: (646)289-8620
Fax: (646)349-3455
Mason, Marianne, Exec. Dir.

Corporate Counsel Women of Color
[5000]
Radio City Sta.
New York, NY 10101-2095
PH: (646)483-8041
Robinson Haden, Laurie, CEO,
Founder

Cosmetic Executive Women **[1583]**
159 W 25th St., 8th Fl.
New York, NY 10001
PH: (212)685-5955
     (646)929-8000
Fax: (212)685-3334
Jacobson, Carlotta, President

Council on Accreditation **[13039]**
45 Broadway, 29th Fl.
New York, NY 10006
PH: (212)797-3000
Fax: (212)797-1428
Noelker, Timothy F., Director

Council for Aid to Education **[7833]**
215 Lexington Ave., 16th Fl.
New York, NY 10016-6056
PH: (212)661-5800
Fax: (212)661-9766
Benjamin, Roger, PhD, President,
CEO

Council for American Students in
International Negotiations **[8098]**
PO Box 2243
New York, NY 10101-2240
Zia, Maimoona, Chairperson

Council of the Americas **[23649]**
680 Park Ave.
New York, NY 10065
PH: (212)249-8950
Fax: (212)249-5868
Segal, Susan L., CEO, President

Council for Economic Education
[7728]
122 E 42nd St., Ste. 2600
New York, NY 10168
PH: (212)730-7007
Fax: (212)730-1793
Morrison, Nan J., CEO, President

Council for European Studies **[7907]**
Columbia University
420 W 118 St., MC 3307
New York, NY 10027
PH: (212)854-4172
Fax: (212)854-8808
Medrano, Juan Diez, Chairperson

Council on Foreign Relations
[18265]
The Harold Pratt House
58 E 68th St.
New York, NY 10065
PH: (212)434-9400
Fax: (212)434-9800
Hills, Carla A., Chairwoman

Council of Literary Magazines and
Presses **[2674]**
154 Christopher St., Ste. 3C
New York, NY 10014-9110
PH: (212)741-9110
Fax: (212)741-9112
Lependorf, Jeffrey, Exec. Dir.

Council of Overseas Chinese
Services, Inc. **[19415]**
430 E 6th St., Apt. 13A
New York, NY 10009-6432
PH: (415)860-6932
Li, Ge, President

Council of PR Firms **[2752]**
32 E 31st St., 9th Fl.
New York, NY 10016
PH: (646)588-0139
Toll free: 877-773-4767
Graves, Chris, Chmn. of the Exec.
Committee

Council of Protocol Executives
[2324]
101 W 12th St., Ste. PH-H
New York, NY 10011
PH: (212)633-6934
Cronin, Jim, President

Council of State Governments
Justice Center **[5133]**
100 Wall St., 20th Fl.
New York, NY 10005
PH: (212)482-2320
Thompson, Michael, Director

The Cousteau Society **[7874]**
Greeley Square Sta.
4 E 27th St.
New York, NY 10001
PH: (212)532-2588
Cousteau, Francine, President

Covenant House **[13439]**
461 8th Ave.
New York, NY 10001
Toll free: 800-388-3888
Ryan, Mr. Kevin, President, CEO

The Creative Coalition **[18864]**
360 Park Ave. S, 11th Fl.
New York, NY 10010-1717
PH: (646)717-9908
Bronk, Robin, CEO

Creative Time **[8972]**
59 E 4th St., 6th Fl.
New York, NY 10003
PH: (212)206-6674
Fax: (212)255-8467
Pasternak, Anne, Art Dir., President

Crohn's and Colitis Foundation of
America **[14786]**
733 3rd Ave., Ste. 510
New York, NY 10017
PH: (212)685-3440
Toll free: 800-932-2423
Fax: (212)779-4098
Granieri, Marie, Chief of Staff

Crossdressers International **[12943]**
404 W 40th St., Apt. 2
New York, NY 10018
PH: (212)564-4847
Lamar, Nancy, Treasurer, Secretary

Crutches 4 Kids, Inc. **[10951]**
459 Columbus Ave., Ste. 381
New York, NY 10024
PH: (646)535-4629
Stein, Ken Shubin, Founder, Chair-
man

Cultural Vistas **[8067]**
440 Park Ave. S, 2nd Fl.
New York, NY 10016-8012
PH: (212)497-3500
Fenstermacher, Rob, President,
CEO

Nathan Cummings Foundation
[12968]
475 10th Ave., 14th Fl.
New York, NY 10018-9715
PH: (212)787-7300
Fax: (212)787-7377
Alpert, Sharon, President, CEO

Cyprus Embassy Trade Center
[23578]
13 E 40th St.
New York, NY 10016
PH: (212)213-9100
Fax: (212)213-2918

Cyprus-US Chamber of Commerce
[23579]
805 3rd Ave., 10th Fl.
New York, NY 10017

PH: (201)444-5609
Fax: (201)444-0445
Nicolaou, Nicolas, President

Damon Runyon Cancer Research
Foundation **[13957]**
1 Exchange Plz.
55 Broadway, Ste. 302
New York, NY 10006-3720
PH: (212)455-0500
Egan, Lorraine W., CEO, President

Dana Alliance for Brain Initiatives
[16014]
505 5th Ave., 6th Fl.
New York, NY 10017
PH: (212)223-4040
Fax: (212)593-7623
Gill, Barbara E., Exec. Dir.

Dance Critics Association **[9250]**
Old Chelsea Sta.
New York, NY 10113-1881
Abrams, Robert, President

Dance Notation Bureau **[9253]**
111 John St., Ste. 704
New York, NY 10038
PH: (212)571-7011
Fax: (212)571-7012
Weber, Lynne, Exec. Dir.

Danish American Chamber of Commerce **[23580]**
1 Dag Hammarskjold Plz.
885 2nd Ave., 18th Fl.
New York, NY 10017-2201
PH: (646)790-7169
Frederiksen, Peter, Chairman

Darwin Animal Doctors **[3623]**
222 E 89th St., No. 8
New York, NY 10128-4309
Emko, Tod, President, Founder

Daughters of the Cincinnati **[20690]**
20 W 44th St., Rm. 508
New York, NY 10036
PH: (212)991-9945

Deadline Club **[2676]**
c/o The Salmagundi Club
47 5th Ave.
New York, NY 10003
PH: (646)481-7584
Gin, Catherine, Asst. Sec.

Delta Gamma Pi Multicultural Soror-
ity **[23968]**
PO Box 1414
New York, NY 10113-1414
Campbell, Rishona, Contact

Democratic Socialists of America
[19140]
75 Maiden Ln., Ste. 702
New York, NY 10038
PH: (212)727-8610
Fax: (212)608-6955
Svart, Maria, Director

Demos **[18095]**
220 5th Ave., 2nd Fl.
New York, NY 10001
PH: (212)633-1405
Tyagi, Amelia Warren, Chairman

Design Industries Foundation Fight-
ing AIDS **[10537]**
16 W 32nd St., Ste. 402
New York, NY 10001
PH: (212)727-3100
Fax: (212)727-2574
Osburn, Johanna, Exec. Dir.

Deutsch-Amerikanische Handel-
skammern **[23581]**
80 Pine St., 24th Fl.
New York, NY 10005

PH: (212)974-8830
Fax: (212)974-8867
Rieg, Dietmar, President, CEO

Deutscher Akademischer Austausch
Dienst **[8068]**
871 United Nations Plz.
New York, NY 10017
PH: (212)758-3223
Fax: (212)755-5780
Kerrigan, Peter, Dep. Dir., Dir. of
Mktg.

Diamond Dealers Club **[2043]**
580 5th Ave., 10th Fl.
New York, NY 10036
PH: (212)790-3600
Fax: (212)869-5164
Kaufman, Reuven, President

Diamond Manufacturers & Importers
Association of America **[2044]**
580 5th Ave. No.2000
New York, NY 10036
PH: (212)382-2200
     (212)944-2066
Fax: (212)202-7525
Shah, Parag, Treasurer

Digital Content Next **[2781]**
1350 Broadway, Rm. 606
New York, NY 10018-7205
PH: (646)473-1000
Fax: (646)473-0200
Kosner, John, Advisor

Digital Divide Data **[7263]**
115 W 30th St., Ste. 400
New York, NY 10001
PH: (212)461-3700
Fax: (212)813-3209
Hockenstein, Jeremy, CEO, Founder

Digital Place Based Advertising As-
sociation **[93]**
205 E 42nd St., 20th Fl.
New York, NY 10017
PH: (212)371-8961
Frey, Barry, President

Direct Care Alliance **[15118]**
4 W 43rd St., Unit 610
New York, NY 10036
PH: (212)730-0741
Fax: (212)302-4345
Washington, Carla D., Exec. Dir.

Direct Marketing Association **[2279]**
1333 Broadway, Ste. No. 301
New York, NY 10018
PH: (212)768-7277
Woolley, Linda A., President, CEO

Disabled and Alone/Life Services for
the Handicapped **[11590]**
1440 Broadway, 23rd Fl.
New York, NY 10018-2326
PH: (212)532-6740
Toll free: 800-995-0066
Fax: (212)532-6740
Ackerman, Lee, Exec. Dir.

Disarm Education Fund **[18126]**
113 University Pl., 8th Fl.
New York, NY 10003
PH: (212)353-9800
Fax: (212)353-9676
Schwartz, Bob, Exec. Dir.

Disaster Relief for Kids **[11658]**
800 B 5th Ave.
New York, NY 10065
Ahmad, Samoon, MD, Founder,
President

Do Something **[17974]**
19 W 21st St., 8th Fl.
New York, NY 10010

PH: (212)254-2390
Radford, Katie, Office Mgr.

DOCOMOMO US [9388]
PO Box 230977
New York, NY 10023-0017
Prudon, Theo, President

Doctors Without Borders USA
[12657]
333 7th Ave., 2nd Fl.
New York, NY 10001-5004
PH: (212)679-6800
Toll free: 888-392-0392
Fax: (212)679-7016
Lawrence, John, VP

The Domestic/Foreign Missionary
Society of the Episcopal Church
[20408]
Episcopal Church Ctr.
815 2nd Ave.
New York, NY 10017-4594
PH: (212)716-6000
Toll free: 800-334-7626
Arias, Ana, Exec. Asst., Mgr.

Drama Desk [10246]
New York, NY
Karam, Ed, Treasurer

The Drama League [10247]
32 Avenue of the Americas, 1st Fl.
New York, NY 10013
PH: (212)244-9494
Fax: (212)244-9191
Shanks, Gabriel J., Exec. Dir.

Dramatists Guild of America [10248]
1501 Broadway, Ste. 701
New York, NY 10036
PH: (212)398-9366
Fax: (212)944-0420
Sevush, Ralph, Exec. Dir.

The Drawing Center [8853]
35 Wooster St.
New York, NY 10013
PH: (212)219-2166
Fax: (888)380-3362
Littman, Brett, Exec. Dir.

Dress for Success Worldwide
[13375]
32 E 31st St., 7th Fl.
New York, NY 10016
PH: (212)532-1922
Fax: (212)684-9563
Gordon, Joi, CEO

Camille and Henry Dreyfus Founda-
tion, Inc. [7759]
555 Madison Ave., 20th Fl.
New York, NY 10022-3301
PH: (212)753-1760
Fax: (212)593-2256
Cardillo, Dr. Mark, Exec. Dir.

DRI International [5075]
1115 Broadway, 12th Fl.
New York, NY 10010
Toll free: 866-542-3744
Berman, Al, CEO, President

Doris Duke Charitable Foundation
[12971]
650 5th Ave., 19th Fl.
New York, NY 10019
PH: (212)974-7000
Fax: (212)974-7590
Henry, Edward P., President

The Duke Ellington Society [9902]
Church Street Sta.
New York, NY 10008-0031
Carman, Ray, President

Dysautonomia Foundation, Inc.
[15925]
315 W 39th St., Ste. 701
New York, NY 10018

PH: (212)279-1066
Fax: (212)279-2066
Brenner, David, Exec. Dir.

Dystrophic Epidermolysis Bullosa
Research Association of America
[14493]
75 Broad St., Ste. 300
New York, NY 10004
PH: (212)868-1573
Toll free: 855-287-3432
Fax: (212)868-9296
Kopelan, Brett, Exec. Dir., Bd.
Member

Earth Child Institute [4048]
777 United Nations Plz.
New York, NY 10017
Goodman, Donna L., Founder

Earth Society Foundation [4053]
238 E 58th St., Ste. 2400
New York, NY 10022
PH: (212)832-3659
Dowd, Thomas C., President

EastWest Institute [18477]
11 E 26th St., 20th Fl.
New York, NY 10010
PH: (212)824-4100
Mroz, John Edwin, Founder

EcoHealth Alliance [4810]
460 W 34th St., 17th Fl.
New York, NY 10001-2320
PH: (212)380-4460
Fax: (212)380-4465
Epstein, Dr. Jonathan H., Assoc. VP

Econometric Society [7241]
Dept. of Economics
19 W 4th St., 6th Fl.
New York, NY 10012
PH: (212)998-3820
Fax: (212)995-4487
Sashi, Claire, Gen. Mgr.

EcoVitality [3852]
224 Centre St., 2nd Fl.
New York, NY 10013
PH: (212)966-8803
Fax: (212)966-8803
Latin, Prof. Howard A., President

Ecuadorean American Association
[19424]
641 Lexington Ave., Ste. 1430
New York, NY 10022
PH: (212)233-7776
Caicedo-Selinger, Juana, President

Editorial Freelancers Association
[2678]
71 W 23rd St., 4th Fl.
New York, NY 10010-4102
PH: (212)929-5400
Toll free: 866-929-5425
Fax: (212)929-5439

Education Through Music [8367]
122 E 42nd St., Ste. 1501
New York, NY 10168
PH: (212)972-4788
Fax: (212)972-4864
Schaefer, Michael R., Officer

Educational Broadcasting Corp.
[9143]
c/o THIRTEEN
825 8th Ave.
New York, NY 10019
PH: (212)560-1313
Fax: (212)560-1314
Croen, Caroline C., VP, CFO,
Treasurer

Educational Equity Center [7901]
71 5th Ave., 6th Fl.
New York, NY 10003

PH: (212)243-1110
Fax: (212)627-0407
Martin, Antonia Cottrell, Founder,
President

Educational Records Bureau [8683]
470 Park Ave. S, 2nd Fl., South
Tower
New York, NY 10016
Toll free: 800-989-3721
Clune, Dr. David, President, CEO

Elder Craftsmen [10505]
307 7th Ave., Ste. 1401
New York, NY 10001
Manzione, Patricia, Exec. Dir.,
Secretary

Electric Railroaders' Association
[10181]
PO Box 3323
New York, NY 10163-3323
Colorafi, Robert, VP, Secretary

Albert Ellis Institute [16969]
145 E 32nd St., 9 Fl.
New York, NY 10016
PH: (212)535-0822
Toll free: 800-323-4738
Fax: (212)249-3582
Stuart, Jay, Treasurer

Ellis Island Medal of Honor Society
[19428]
National Ethnic Coalition of
Organizations
12 East 33rd St., 12th Fl.
New York, NY 10016
PH: (212)755-1492
Fax: (212)755-3762
Taglione, Rosemarie, Exec. Dir.

Emerging Practitioners in
Philanthropy [12473]
601 W 26th St., No. 325-7
New York, NY 10001
PH: (212)584-8249
Novotny, Tamir, Exec. Dir.

EMTA [3042]
360 Madison Ave., 17th Fl.
New York, NY 10017
PH: (646)289-5410
Fax: (646)289-5429
Ortiz, Suzette, Office Mgr.

Emunah of America [12208]
363 7th Ave., 2nd Fl.
New York, NY 10001
PH: (212)564-9045
Fax: (212)643-9731
Hirmes, Fran, Chmn. of the Bd.

Emunah Women of America [20245]
7 Penn Plz.
New York, NY 10001
PH: (212)564-9045
Toll free: 800-368-6440
Fax: (212)643-9731
Hirmes, Fran, Chmn. of the Bd.

Energy Vision [6484]
138 E 13th St.
New York, NY 10003
PH: (212)228-0225
Underwood, Joanna D.,
Chairperson, Founder

Engenderhealth [11839]
440 9th Ave.
New York, NY 10001
PH: (212)561-8000
Toll free: 800-564-2872
Fax: (212)561-8067
Müller, Ulla E., President, CEO

English-Speaking Union of the
United States [9651]
144 E 39th St.
New York, NY 10016

PH: (212)818-1200
Fax: (212)867-4177
Broadwell, Christopher, Exec. Dir.

Environmental Defense Fund [4058]
257 Park Ave. S
New York, NY 10010
Toll free: 800-684-3322
Hamburg, Steven, Scientist

Environmental Grantmakers Associa-
tion [4533]
475 Riverside Dr., Ste. 960
New York, NY 10115
PH: (212)812-4310
Fax: (212)812-4311
Leon, Rachel, Exec. Dir.

The Episcopal Actors' Guild of
America, Inc. [10249]
1 E 29th St.
New York, NY 10016-7405
PH: (212)685-2927
Lehman, Karen A., Exec. Dir.

Episcopal Partnership for Global
Mission [20102]
815 2nd Ave.
New York, NY 10017-4503
PH: (212)716-6000
Toll free: 800-334-7626
Wilson, Constance, Administrator

Episcopal Relief and Development
[12659]
815 2nd Ave.
New York, NY 10017
Toll free: 855-312-4325
Fax: (212)687-5302
Radtke, Robert W., President

Equality Now Americas Office
[13414]
PO Box 20646
Columbus Circle Sta.
New York, NY 10023
PH: (212)586-0906
Fax: (212)586-1611

Equator Initiative [11355]
Bureau for Policy and Programme
Support
304 E 45th St., Rm. 614
New York, NY 10017
PH: (646)781-4023
Virnig, Annie, Consultant

John Ericsson Society [10325]
5 E 48th St.
New York, NY 10017
PH: (845)704-2080

Estonian American Chamber of
Commerce & Industry [23583]
111 John St., Ste. 1910
New York, NY 10038
PH: (917)744-2765
Tassa, Krista Altok, Founder,
President

Estonian Relief Committee [12660]
243 E 34th St.
New York, NY 10016-4852
Kilm, Toomas, Chairman, President

European-American Chamber of
Commerce [23584]
The New York Times Bldg.
620 8th Ave., 37th Fl.
New York, NY 10018
PH: (212)808-2730
(212)808-2707
Rosener, James, President

European American Musical Alliance
[9906]
1160 5th Ave., Ste. 201
New York, NY 10029

PH: (212)831-7424
Shea, Brian, Chairman

Evangelicals Concerned [20179]
311 E 72nd St., Ste. 1G
New York, NY 10021
Blair, Dr. Ralph, Founder

Events of the Heart [15215]
350 Central Park W, Ste. 12G
New York, NY 10025
PH: (212)662-7887
Serure, Pamela, Exec. Dir.

Executive Protection Institute [8560]
16 Penn Plz., Ste. 1130
New York, NY 10001
PH: (212)268-4555
Toll free: 800-947-5827
Fax: (212)563-4783
Kobetz, Dr. Richard W., CST,
   Founder

The Explorers Club [6625]
46 E 70th St.
New York, NY 10021
PH: (212)628-8383
Fax: (212)288-4449
Roseman, Will, Exec. Dir.

Eye-Bank for Sight Restoration
   [14619]
120 Wall St.
New York, NY 10005-3902
PH: (212)742-9000
Fax: (212)269-3139
D'Ambrosio, Joseph J., President,
   Founder

FACE Foundation [8031]
972 5th Ave.
New York, NY 10075
PH: (212)439-1439
Dibie-Violante, Maia, Treasurer

FACES [14741]
223 E 34th St.
New York, NY 10016
PH: (646)558-0900
Fax: (646)385-7163
Mohr, Pamela, Exec. Dir.

Fairness and Accuracy in Reporting
   [17945]
124 W 30th St., Ste. 201
New York, NY 10001
PH: (212)633-6700
Jackson, Janine, Prog. Dir.

Families with Children from China
   [10451]
Ansonia Sta.
New York, NY 10023
PH: (212)579-0115

Families of September 11 [19179]
1560 Broadway, Ste. 305
New York, NY 10036
PH: (212)575-1878
Fax: (212)575-1877
Holmes, Anastasia, MPA, Exec. Dir.

Families and Work Institute [11817]
245 5th Ave., Ste. 1002
New York, NY 10016
PH: (212)465-2044
Fax: (212)465-8637
Galinsky, Ellen, Founder, President

Family Care International [17196]
45 Broadway, Ste. 320
New York, NY 10006
PH: (212)941-5300
Fax: (212)941-5563
Sligar, James S., Secretary

Family Justice Program [11525]
233 Broadway, 12th Fl.
New York, NY 10279-1299

PH: (212)334-1300
Fax: (212)941-9407
Turner, Nicholas, President, Director

Fashion Group International, Inc.
   [203]
8 W 40th St., 7th Fl.
New York, NY 10018
PH: (212)302-5511
Fax: (212)302-5533
Evins, Louise, Treasurer

Federation of Jewish Men's Clubs
   [20246]
475 Riverside Dr., Ste. 832
New York, NY 10115-0022
PH: (212)749-8100
Simon, Rabbi Charles E., Exec. Dir.

Federation of Modern Painters and
   Sculptors [8917]
c/o Anneli Arms, President
113 Greene St.
New York, NY 10012
PH: (212)966-4864
Arms, Anneli, President

Federation of Protestant Welfare
   Agencies [20530]
40 Broad St.
New York, NY 10004
PH: (212)777-4800
Fax: (212)533-8792
Storen, Stephen J., Chairman

Federation of Turkish American As-
   sociations [19674]
821 United Nations Plz.
New York, NY 10017
PH: (212)682-7688
Toll free: 888-352-9886
Fax: (646)290-6171
Cinar, Ali, President

Fertility Research Foundation
   [14757]
877 Park Ave.
New York, NY 10021
PH: (212)744-5500
Toll free: 888-439-2999
Fax: (212)744-6536
Khatamee, Dr. Masood, Exec. Dir.

FilmAid International [12590]
234 5th Ave., Ste. 206
New York, NY 10001
PH: (212)920-3663
Baron, Caroline, Founder

Financial Services Volunteer Corps
   [18489]
10 E 53rd St., 36th Fl.
New York, NY 10022
PH: (212)771-1429
Fax: (212)771-1462
Donaldson, William H., Chairman

Fine Press Book Association [2680]
c/o Russell Maret, Vice-Chair
140 E 71st St., Apt. 5B
New York, NY 10021
McCamant, Robert, Editor, Treasurer

Louis Finkelstein Institute for
   Religious and Social Studies
   [20080]
c/o Jewish Theological Seminary
3080 Broadway
New York, NY 10027-4650
PH: (212)678-8989
Visotzky, Rabbi Burton L., PhD,
   Director

Finnish American Chamber of Com-
   merce [23586]
54 W 40th St.
New York, NY 10018
PH: (917)414-1603
Student, Michael, Director

Finnish and American Women's
   Network [13377]
PO Box 3623
New York, NY 10163-3623
Nordin, Kerstin, Chairperson

FireFlag/EMS [14695]
208 W 13th St.
New York, NY 10011
PH: (917)885-0127
Vissichelli, Mike, Officer

First Hungarian Literary Society
   [19469]
323 E 79th St.
New York, NY 10021
PH: (212)288-5002
Fax: (212)772-3175
Allen, Louis, President

First Zen Institute of America
   [19777]
113 E 30th St.
New York, NY 10016
PH: (212)686-2520
Hotz, Michael, President

Fixed Income Analysts Society, Inc.
   [1279]
c/o Executive Director
244 5th Ave., Ste. L230
New York, NY 10001
PH: (212)726-8100
Fax: (212)591-6534
Nauser, Ms. Lauren, Exec. Dir.

The Flaherty [9306]
6 E 39th St., 12th Fl.
New York, NY 10016
PH: (212)448-0457
Fax: (212)448-0458
Yang, Chi-Hui, President

Food & Environment Reporting
   Network [2062]
576 5th Ave., Ste. 903
New York, NY 10036
Laskawy, Tom, Founder, Exec. Dir.

FoodCorps [16221]
281 Park Ave. S
New York, NY 10010
PH: (212)596-7045
Fax: (347)244-7213
Ellis, Curt, Exec. Dir.

Ford Foundation [18943]
320 E 43rd St.
New York, NY 10017-4801
PH: (212)573-5000
Fax: (212)351-3677
Dawson, Victoria A., Librarian

Foreign Policy Association [18266]
470 Park Ave. S
New York, NY 10016-6819
PH: (212)481-8100
Toll free: 800-477-5836
Fax: (212)481-9275
King, MacDara, Dir. of Comm.

Foreign Press Association [2681]
333 E 46th St., Ste. 1-K
New York, NY 10017
PH: (212)370-1054
Fax: (212)370-1058
Fields, Cindy, Treasurer

Forward Face [14335]
317 E 34th St., Ste. 901A
New York, NY 10016
PH: (212)684-5860

Foundation for Advancement in
   Cancer Therapy [13971]
Old Chelsea Sta.
New York, NY 10113

Foundation for the Advancement of
   Monetary Education [7919]
909 3rd Ave., No. 625
New York, NY 10150

PH: (212)818-1206
Parks, Dr. Lawrence M., Exec. Dir.

Foundation for the Advancement of
   Sephardic Studies and Culture
   [19517]
34 W 15th St., 3rd Fl.
New York, NY 10011
Bedford, Robert, Exec. VP

Foundation for Child Development
   [10818]
295 Madison Ave., 40th Fl.
New York, NY 10017
PH: (212)867-5777
Fax: (212)867-5844
Jones, Jacqueline, President, CEO

Foundation for the Study of
   Independent Social Ideas [18637]
120 Wall St., 31st Fl.
New York, NY 10005
Phillips, Maxine, Editor

Fractured Atlas [8918]
248 W 35th St., 10th Fl.
New York, NY 10001
Toll free: 888-692-7878
Fax: (212)277-8025
Huttler, Adam, Exec. Dir.

Fragrance Foundation [1451]
621 2nd Ave., 2nd Fl.
New York, NY 10016
PH: (212)725-2755
Fax: (646)786-3260
Policastro, Cosimo, Director

Free Expression Policy Project
   [17897]
170 W 76th St., No. 301
New York, NY 10023
Heins, Marjorie, Director, Founder

French-American Aid for Children
   [19438]
150 E 58th St., 27th Fl.
New York, NY 10155
PH: (212)486-9593
Fax: (212)486-9594
Klebe, Mrs. Joerg, Mem.

French-American Chamber of Com-
   merce [23587]
1375 Broadway, Ste. 504
New York, NY 10018
PH: (212)867-0123
Fax: (212)867-9050
Gallagher, Christopher, Exec. Dir.,
   Director

French-American Foundation
   [18540]
28 W 44th St., Ste. 1420
New York, NY 10036
PH: (212)829-8800
Arifi, Dana, VP, COO

French Heritage Society [9390]
14 E 60th St., No. 605
New York, NY 10022-7131
PH: (212)759-6846
Fax: (212)759-9632
Stribling, Elizabeth F., Chmn. of the
   Bd.

French Institute Alliance Francaise
   [9335]
22 E 60th St.
New York, NY 10022
PH: (212)355-6100
Steckel, Marie-Monique, President

Frére Independent [8919]
149 W 24th St., No. 3A
New York, NY 10011-1960
PH: (347)284-0040

Friars Club [10252]
57 E 55th St.
New York, NY 10022

PH: (212)751-7272
Fax: (212)355-0217
Gyure, Michael, Exec. Dir.

Friends of Africa International
[18401]
619 W 140th St., Ste. 2H
New York, NY 10031
PH: (917)261-4472
Fax: (212)590-6164
Obasi, Onyeka, President

Friends of the American Museum in
Britain/Halcyon Foundation [8791]
555 5th Ave., 17th Fl.
New York, NY 10017
PH: (212)370-0198
Wendorf, Richard, Director

Friends of the Australian Koala
Foundation [4819]
c/o The Nolan Lehr Group, Inc.
214 W 29th St., Ste. 1002
New York, NY 10001
PH: (212)967-8200
Fax: (212)967-7292
Tabart, Deborah, CEO

Friends of Bezalel Academy of Arts
[9610]
370 Lexington Ave., Ste. 1612
New York, NY 10017
PH: (212)687-0542
Fax: (212)687-1140
Rifkin, Bathsheva, President

Friends of Israel Disabled Veterans
[21006]
1133 Broadway, Ste. 232
New York, NY 10010
PH: (212)689-3220
Leichtling, Michael, Chairman

Friends of Terra Cotta [9392]
771 W End Ave., No. 10E
New York, NY 10025
Tunick, Susan, President

Friends of the United Nations
[19211]
866 UN Plz., Ste. 544
New York, NY 10017
PH: (212)355-4192
Brown, Dr. Noel J., President, CEO

Fuel for Truth [19110]
42 E 69th St., 5th Fl.
New York, NY 10021

The Fund for Animals [10625]
200 W 57th St.
New York, NY 10019
Toll free: 866-482-3708
Markarian, Michael, President

Fund for Modern Courts [5384]
205 E 42nd St., 6th Fl.
New York, NY 10017
PH: (212)541-6741
Fax: (212)541-7301
Starr, Amelia, V. Chmn. of the Bd.

Funders' Collaborative on Youth
Organizing [12475]
330 7th Ave., Ste. 1902
New York, NY 10001
PH: (212)725-3386
James, Taj, Exec. Dir.

Games for Change [22052]
205 E 42nd St., 20th Fl.
New York, NY 10017
PH: (212)242-4922
Burak, Asi, Director

Garden Club of America [22094]
14 E 60th St., 3rd Fl.
New York, NY 10022

PH: (212)753-8287
Fax: (212)753-0134
Butler, Anne, Receptionist

Gay and Lesbian Dominican
Empowerment Organization
[11884]
24 W 25th St., 9th Fl.
New York, NY 10010
PH: (718)596-0342
    (212)463-0342
Fax: (718)596-1328

Gay, Lesbian, and Straight Educa-
tion Network [11885]
110 William St., 30th Fl.
New York, NY 10003
PH: (212)727-0135
Byard, Eliza, PhD, Exec. Dir.

Gay Men's Health Crisis [13539]
446 W 33rd St.
New York, NY 10001-2601
PH: (212)367-1000
    (212)807-6655
Bimblick, Warren N., Treasurer

Gay Officers' Action League [11886]
PO Box 1774, Old Chelsea Sta.
New York, NY 10113
PH: (212)691-4625

GBCHealth [10539]
1 Rockefeller Plz., 28th Fl.
New York, NY 10020
PH: (212)584-1600
Fax: (212)584-1699
Cohen, Gary, Acting CEO

General Society of Mechanics and
Tradesmen of the City of New York
[8661]
20 W 44th St.
New York, NY 10036
PH: (212)840-1840
Dengel, Victoria A., Exec. Dir.

Henry George Institute [19170]
90 John St., Ste. 501
New York, NY 10038
PH: (212)889-8020
Achenbaum, Wyn, Bd. Member

German Convention Bureau [23546]
122 E 42nd St., Ste. 2000
New York, NY 10168
PH: (212)661-4582
Fax: (212)661-6192
d'Elsa, Laura, Reg. Dir.

German National Tourist Office
[3377]
122 E 42nd St., Ste. 2000
New York, NY 10168-0072
PH: (212)661-4796
Fax: (212)661-7174
Laepple, Klaus, Chmn. of the Bd.

GesherCity [19518]
c/o JCC Association
15 E 26th St.
New York, NY 10018
PH: (212)786-5130
Fax: (212)481-4174

Gilbert & Sullivan Society of New
York [9182]
c/o Samuel Silvers, Membership
Secretary
117 Broadway, Apt. 28
New York, NY 10027
Kravetz, Dan, President, Editor

Girl Scouts of the U.S.A. [12852]
420 5th Ave.
New York, NY 10018-2798
PH: (212)852-8000
Toll free: 800-478-7248
Chavez, Anna Maria, CEO

Girls Educational and Mentoring
Services [12923]
298B W 149th St.
New York, NY 10039
PH: (212)926-8089
Fax: (212)491-2696
Lloyd, Rachel, CEO, Founder

Girls Inc. [13447]
120 Wall St.
New York, NY 10005-3902
PH: (212)509-2000
Vredenburgh, Judy, CEO, President

Girls Who Code [11479]
28 W 23rd St., 4th Fl.
New York, NY 10010
PH: (646)629-9735
Saujani, Reshma, Founder, CEO

Givat Haviva Educational Foundation
[18682]
424 W 33rd St., Ste. 150
New York, NY 10001
PH: (212)989-9272
Pickering, Thomas, Chmn. of the Bd.

The Glaucoma Foundation [16383]
80 Maiden Ln., Ste. 700
New York, NY 10038-4965
PH: (212)285-0080
Christensen, Scott R., CEO,
President

Global Action to Prevent War
[18720]
866 UN Plz., Ste. 4050
New York, NY 10017
PH: (212)818-1815
Fax: (212)818-1857
Frydland, Michael, Exec.

Global Action Project [19271]
130 W 25th St., Fl. 2C
New York, NY 10001-7406
PH: (212)594-9577
Winn, Robert, Chairman

Global Advertising Lawyers Alliance
[5425]
c/o Stacy D. Bess, Executive Director
488 Madison Ave., 10th Fl.
New York, NY 10022
PH: (212)705-4895
Fax: (347)438-2185
Bess, Stacy D., Exec. Dir.

Global Alliance for Community
Development [11364]
PO Box 20511
New York, NY 10017
McCoy, David L., Exec. Dir.

Global Alliance for Women's Health
[17756]
777 United Nation Plz., 7th Fl.
New York, NY 10017
PH: (212)286-0424
Fax: (212)286-9561
Wolfson, Elaine M., PhD, Founder,
President

Global Business and Technology
Association [633]
PO Box 8021
New York, NY 10116
PH: (631)662-1336
Fax: (215)628-2436
Delener, Dr. Nejdet, Founder,
President

Global Children [11001]
37 W 28th St., 3rd Fl.
New York, NY 10001
PH: (917)359-7085
Pollard, Eli, Chairman

Global China Connection [8099]
116 E 55th St.
New York, NY 10022
Tedesco, Daniel, Chairman

Global Education Associates [18544]
475 Riverside Dr., Ste. 1848
New York, NY 10115-0033
PH: (212)870-3290
Fax: (212)870-2729
Mische, Gerald F., President

Global Emergency Relief [14696]
107 Suffolk St.
New York, NY 10002-3300
PH: (212)213-0213
Lobel-Weiss, Nick, Exec. Dir.,
Founder

Global Goods Partners [12155]
115 W 30th St., Ste. 400
New York, NY 10001
PH: (212)461-3647
Toll free: 800-463-3802
Shifrin, Joan, Founder, Co-Pres.

Global Health Corps [15454]
5 Penn Plz., 3rd Fl.
New York, NY 10001
Bush, Barbara, Founder, CEO

Global Health Partners [15006]
113 University Pl., 8th Fl.
New York, NY 10003
PH: (212)353-9800
Fax: (212)353-9676
Schwartz, Bob, Exec. Dir., Founder

Global HIV Vaccine Enterprise
[13542]
64 Beaver St., No. 352
New York, NY 10004
PH: (212)461-3692
Fax: (866)966-4483
Snow, William, Director

Global Kids [7811]
137 E 25th St., 2nd Fl.
New York, NY 10010
PH: (212)226-0130
Fax: (212)226-0137
Roberts, Richard, Chairman

Global Medic Force [15461]
101 W 23rd St., Ste. 179
New York, NY 10011
Toll free: 866-232-4954
Charles, Dr. Marie, MD,
Chairperson, CEO

Global Nomads Group [8768]
132 Nassau St., Ste. 822
New York, NY 10038
PH: (212)529-0377
Plutte, Chris, Exec. Dir.

Global Organization of People of
Indian Origin [19474]
PO Box 560117
New York, NY 11356
PH: (818)708-3885
Singh, Inder, Chairman

Global Partnership for Afghanistan
[10469]
PO Box 1237
New York, NY 10276-1237
PH: (212)735-2080
Freyer, Dana H., Chairman, Founder

Global Peace Initiative of Women
[18789]
301 E 57th St., 4th Fl.
New York, NY 10022
Marstrand, Marianne, Exec. Dir.

Global Policy Forum [18490]
866 UN Plz., Ste. 4050
New York, NY 10017
PH: (646)553-3460
Adams, Barbara, Chmn. of the Bd.

The Global Poverty Project [12543]
594 Broadway, Ste. 207
New York, NY 10012
Evans, Hugh, CEO

Global and Regional Asperger
  Syndrome Partnership [15936]
419 Lafayette St.
New York, NY 10003
Toll free: 888-474-7277
Palmer, Kate, MA, CCP, CAS,
  President, CEO

Global Security Institute [18747]
866 United Nations Plz., Ste. 4050
New York, NY 10017
PH: (646)289-5170
Fax: (646)289-5171
Cranston, Kim, Chmn. of the Bd.

Global Sourcing Council [2471]
750 3rd Ave., 11th Fl.
New York, NY 10017
PH: (914)645-0605
Judex, Angeline, Exec. Dir.

Global Youth Connect [19274]
PO Box 1342
New York, NY 10159-1342
PH: (845)657-3273
Hawkes, Jesse, Exec. Dir., Prog. Dir.

God's Love We Deliver [10542]
166 Avenue of the Americas
New York, NY 10013
PH: (212)294-8100
   (212)294-8102
Toll free: 800-747-2023
Fax: (212)294-8101
Bruckner, Scott, Chmn. of the Bd.

Goethe-Institut [9339]
30 Irving Pl.
New York, NY 10003
PH: (212)439-8700
Fax: (212)439-8705
Lindner, Ulrich, Regional Mgr.

Adolph and Esther Gottlieb Founda-
  tion [8922]
380 W Broadway
New York, NY 10012
PH: (212)226-0581
Fax: (212)274-1476
Hirsch, Sanford, Exec. Dir.

William T. Grant Foundation [10819]
570 Lexington Ave., 18th Fl.
New York, NY 10022-6837
PH: (212)752-0071
Fax: (212)752-1398
Pennoyer, Russell, Chairman

Graphic Artists Guild [8923]
31 W 34th St., 8th Fl.
New York, NY 10001
PH: (212)791-3400
Fax: (212)791-0333
McKiernan, Ms. Patricia, Exec. Dir.

Graymoor Ecumenical and Inter-
  religious Institute [20062]
c/o Elizabeth Matos, Secretary
475 Riverside Dr., Rm. 1960
New York, NY 10115
PH: (212)870-2330
Fax: (212)870-2001
Sullivan, Ms. Veronica, Bus. Mgr.

Greek National Tourist Organization
  [3330]
305 E 47th St., 2nd Fl.
New York, NY 10017
PH: (212)421-5777
Fax: (212)826-6940
Pallis, Dr. Christos, President

Greek Orthodox Ladies Philoptochos
  Society [20193]
126 E 37th St.
New York, NY 10016
PH: (212)977-7770
Fax: (212)977-7784
Logus, Maria, Esq., President

Greek Orthodox Young Adult League
  [20194]
8 E, 79 th St.
New York, NY 10024
PH: (646)519-6780
Fax: (646)478-9358
Roll, Fr. Jason, Director

Grolier Club [9128]
47 E 60th St.
New York, NY 10022
PH: (212)838-6690
Fax: (212)838-2445
Holzenberg, Eric, Director

Grow and Know [11202]
35 W 64th St., Ste. 6B
New York, NY 10023
Sommer, Marni, Exec. Dir.

Gruppo Esponenti Italiani [19505]
60 E 42nd St., Ste. 2214
New York, NY 10165
PH: (212)867-2772
Fax: (212)867-4114

Guild of Book Workers [9129]
521 5th Ave.
New York, NY 10175
PH: (212)292-4444
Haller, Cindy, Editor

Guild of Italian American Actors
  [23495]
PO Box 123
New York, NY 10013-0123
PH: (201)344-3411
Fiorletta, Carlo, President

Guinea Development Foundation,
  Inc. [17777]
140 W End Ave., Ste. 17G
New York, NY 10023
PH: (212)874-2911
Sylla, Dr. Sekou M., President

Guitar and Accessories Marketing
  Association [2424]
875 W 181st St., No. 2D
New York, NY 10033
PH: (212)795-3630
Olsen, Tim, Officer

Guttmacher Institute [11841]
125 Maiden Ln., 7th Fl.
New York, NY 10038
PH: (212)248-1111
Toll free: 800-355-0244
Fax: (212)248-1951
Coles, Matthew, Chairman

GWA: The Association for Garden
  Communicators [22098]
355 Lexington Ave., 5th Fl.
New York, NY 10017
PH: (212)297-2198
Fax: (212)297-2149
Ungaro, Maria, Exec. Dir.

Hadassah, The Women's Zionist
  Organization of America [20248]
40 Wall St.
New York, NY 10005
PH: (212)355-7900
Toll free: 888-303-3640
Fax: (212)303-8282
Weinman, Janice, CEO

Haiti Support Network [11923]
International Action Ctr.
39 W 14th St., Ste. 206
New York, NY 10011
PH: (212)633-6646
Ives, Kim, Director

HaitiCorps International [11665]
4 Washington Square Village, Apt.
  2-ORT

New York, NY 10012
PH: (347)674-4241
Gibson, Brent, President, Founder

Harlem Children's Zone Inc. [11374]
35 E 125th St.
New York, NY 10035
PH: (212)534-0700
Canada, Geoffrey, President

Harm Reduction Coalition [13141]
22 W 27th St., 5th Fl.
New York, NY 10001
PH: (212)213-6376
Clear, Allan, Exec. Dir.

The John A. Hartford Foundation
  [10509]
55 E 59th St., 16th Fl.
New York, NY 10022-1713
PH: (212)832-7788
Fax: (212)593-4913
Fulmer, Terry, PhD, President

Harvey Society [15726]
c/o M. Elizabeth Ross, PhD,
  Treasurer
Weill Cornell Medical College
1300 York Ave.
New York, NY 10065
PH: (718)270-1370
   (212)746-5550
Singer, Robert H., Contact

Hashomer Hatzair Zionist Youth
  Movement [20249]
424 W 33rd St., Ste. 150
New York, NY 10001
PH: (212)627-2830
Angel, Shaked, Director

HeadCount [18181]
104 W 29th St., 11th Fl.
New York, NY 10001
Bernstein, Andy, Exec. Dir.

Health Jam [15083]
221 E 122nd St., 5th Fl.
New York, NY 10035
PH: (212)722-7987
Fax: (212)722-7252

HealthCare Chaplaincy Network
  [20561]
65 Broadway, 12th Fl.
New York, NY 10006
PH: (212)644-1111
Fax: (212)486-1440
Weldon, James R., Secretary

HealthRight International [12283]
240 Greene St., 2nd Fl.
New York, NY 10003
PH: (212)226-9890
Fax: (212)226-7026
Sharp, Victoria L., MD, President

Hearing Health Foundation [15193]
363 7th Ave., 10th Fl.
New York, NY 10001-3904
PH: (212)257-6140
Toll free: 866-454-3924
Eberts, Shari, Chairman

Heart Valve Society of America
  [14116]
PO Box 1365
New York, NY 10021
Borer, Jeffrey S., MD, President

Hearts and Minds Network [19180]
165 W 105th St.
New York, NY 10025
PH: (212)280-0333
Fax: (212)280-0336
Blackman, Bill, Founder, President

Hebrew Free Burial Association
  [20250]
224 W 35th St., Rm. 300
New York, NY 10001

PH: (212)239-1662
Fax: (212)239-1981
Koplow, Amy, Exec. Dir.

Hebrew Immigrant Aid Society
  [12222]
333 7th Ave., 16th Fl.
New York, NY 10001
PH: (212)967-4100
Toll free: 800-HIAS-714
Fax: (212)967-4442

Hedge Fund Association [2023]
415 Madison Ave., 14th Fl.
New York, NY 10017
PH: (646)762-9668
Ackles, Mitch, President

Hedge Funds Care [10795]
330 7th Ave., Ste. 2B
New York, NY 10001
PH: (212)991-9600
Fax: (646)214-1079
Davis, Rob, Founder

Helen Keller International [17712]
352 Park Ave. S, 12th Fl.
New York, NY 10010-1723
PH: (212)532-0544
Quinn, Victoria, Sr. VP

Hellenic American Bankers Associa-
  tion [399]
PO Box 7244
New York, NY 10150
PH: (212)421-1057
Kellas, Costas, Director

Hellenic-American Chamber of Com-
  merce [23589]
370 Lexington Ave., 27th Fl.
New York, NY 10017
PH: (212)629-6380
Fax: (212)564-9281
Stratakis, John C., Advisor

HELP USA [11952]
5 Hanover Sq., 17th Fl.
New York, NY 10004
PH: (212)400-7000
Toll free: 800-311-7999
Fax: (212)400-7005
Hameline, Thomas, PhD, President,
  CEO

Hereditary Disease Foundation
  [15939]
3960 Broadway, 6th Fl.
New York, NY 10032
PH: (212)928-2121
Fax: (212)928-2172
Wexler, Nancy S., PhD, President

Heritage of Pride [11889]
154 Christopher St., Ste. 1D
New York, NY 10014-2840
PH: (212)807-7433
Fax: (212)807-7436
Williams, Craig, Contact

Hermandad, Inc. [17840]
PO Box 286269
New York, NY 10128
PH: (347)709-0190
Reyes, Zoila, Exec. Dir.

Hetrick-Martin Institute [11890]
2 Astor Pl.
New York, NY 10003
PH: (212)674-2400
Krever, Thomas, CEO

Hineni [9637]
232 W End Ave.
New York, NY 10023-3604
PH: (212)496-1660
Janov, Barbara, Exec. Dir.

Hispanic Neuropsychological Society **[16015]**
151 E 31st St., No. 22C
New York, NY 10016
Cagigas, Xavier E., Ph.D., President

Hispanic Organization of Latin Actors **[9357]**
107 Suffolk St., Ste. 302
New York, NY 10002
PH: (212)253-1015
Fax: (212)256-9651
Oliva, Manolo Garcia, President

Hispanic Society of America **[9358]**
613 W 155th St.
New York, NY 10032
PH: (212)926-2234
Fax: (212)690-0743
Anderson, Ruth Matilda, Publisher

Historic Brass Society **[9918]**
148 W 23rd St., No. 5F
New York, NY 10011
PH: (212)627-3820
Fax: (212)627-3820
Nussbaum, Jeffrey, President, Founder

Home Fashion Products Association **[1944]**
355 Lexington Ave.
New York, NY 10017
PH: (212)297-2122
Kaufmann, Jeff, President

Hong Kong Trade Development Council **[23547]**
219 E 46th St.
New York, NY 10017
PH: (212)838-8688
Fax: (212)838-8941
Mak, Anthony, Director

Karen Horney Clinic **[16845]**
329 E 62nd St.
New York, NY 10011
PH: (212)838-4333
Fax: (212)838-7158

Horror Writers Association **[10376]**
244 5th Ave., Ste. 2767
New York, NY 10001-7604
PH: (818)220-3965
McKinney, Joe, Secretary

Hospitality Committee for United Nations Delegations **[18547]**
United Nations General Assembly Bldg. Rm. GA-0142
New York, NY 10017
PH: (212)963-8753
Fax: (212)963-1320
Soon-taek, Mrs. Ban, Chairwoman

HPV and Anal Cancer Foundation **[13985]**
PO Box 232
New York, NY 10028
PH: (646)593-7739
Almada, Justine, Contact

Huguenot Society of America **[20972]**
20 W 44th St., Ste. 510
New York, NY 10036-6603
PH: (212)755-0592
Fax: (212)317-0676
Bertschmann, Mary, Exec. Dir.

Human Life Foundation **[12772]**
The Human Life Review
353 Lexington Ave., Ste. 802
New York, NY 10016
PH: (212)685-5210
Angelopoulos, Christina, Production Mgr., Dir. of Info. Technology

Human Right First **[18404]**
75 Broad St., 31st Fl.
New York, NY 10001-5108

PH: (212)845-5200
Fax: (212)845-5299
Massimino, Elisa, CEO, President

Human Rights in China **[12041]**
450 7th Ave., Ste. 1301
New York, NY 10123
PH: (212)239-4495
Fax: (212)239-2561
Hom, Sharon, Exec. Dir.

Human Rights First **[18405]**
75 Broad St., 31st Fl.
New York, NY 10004
PH: (212)845-5200
Fax: (212)845-5299
Massimino, Elisa, President, CEO

Human Rights Watch **[18407]**
350 5th Ave., 34th Fl.
New York, NY 10118-3299
PH: (212)290-4700
Fax: (212)736-1300
Roth, Kenneth, Exec. Dir.

Human Rights Watch - Asia **[18408]**
350 5th Ave., 34th Fl.
New York, NY 10118-3299
PH: (212)290-4700
Roth, Kenneth, Exec. Dir.

Human Rights Watch - Children's Rights **[18409]**
350 5th Ave., 34th Fl.
New York, NY 10118-3299
PH: (212)290-4700
Fax: (212)736-1300
Roth, Kenneth, Exec. Dir.

Humanity in Action **[12042]**
601 W 26th St., Rm. 325
New York, NY 10001
PH: (212)828-6874
Fax: (212)704-4130
Goldstein, Dr. Judith S., Founder, Exec. Dir.

The Hunger Project **[18456]**
5 Union Sq. W, 7th Fl.
New York, NY 10003-3306
PH: (212)251-9100
Fax: (212)532-9785
Ariola, Lena, CFO

Huntington's Disease Society of America **[15942]**
505 8th Ave., Ste. 902
New York, NY 10018
PH: (212)242-1968
Toll free: 800-345-4372
Vetter, Louise, CEO, President

I Have a Dream Foundation **[13450]**
330 7th Ave., 20th Fl.
New York, NY 10001
PH: (212)293-5480
Fax: (212)293-5478
Lawrence, Donna, President, CEO

IEEE - Communications Society **[7307]**
3 Park Ave., 17th Fl.
New York, NY 10016
PH: (212)705-8900
Fax: (212)705-8999
Brooks, Susan, Exec. Dir.

IEEE Information Theory Society **[7308]**
3 Park Ave., 17th Fl.
New York, NY 10016-5997
El Gamal, Abbas, President

IEEE - Nuclear and Plasma Sciences Society **[6927]**
3 Park Ave.
New York, NY 10016-5902
Ritt, Stefan, VP

IEEE - Reliability Society **[6433]**
3 Park Ave., 17th Fl.
New York, NY 10016-5997
PH: (212)419-7900
Fax: (212)752-4929
Hansen, Christian, President

IEEE - Systems, Man, and Cybernetics Society **[6247]**
3 Park Ave., 17th Fl.
New York, NY 10016-5997
PH: (212)419-7900
Fax: (212)752-4929
Nuernberger, Andreas, VP

IEEE - Vehicular Technology Society **[6434]**
3 Park Ave., 17th Fl.
New York, NY 10016-5997
PH: (212)419-7900
Fax: (212)752-4929
Labeau, Fabrice, VP

Illuminating Engineering Society of North America **[6784]**
120 Wall St., 17th Fl.
New York, NY 10005
PH: (212)248-5000
Fax: (212)248-5018
Roush, Mark, President

Imaging and Perimetry Society **[16385]**
c/o Mitchell Dul, Treasurer
33 W 42nd St.
Department of Clinical Sciences
SUNY State College of Optometry
New York, NY 10036
PH: (212)938-5816

Immigration Equality **[11894]**
40 Exchange Pl., Ste. 1300
New York, NY 10005
PH: (212)714-2904
Fax: (212)714-2973
Morris, Aaron, Exec. Dir.

Incontinentia Pigmenti International Foundation **[14828]**
30 E 72nd St., Ste. No. 16
New York, NY 10021-4265
PH: (212)452-1231
Fax: (212)452-1231
Emmerich, Susanne Bross, Founder, Exec. Dir.

Indego Africa **[10479]**
51 W 52nd St., Ste. 2300
New York, NY 10019
PH: (212)506-3697
Mitro, Matthew T., Chairman, Founder

Independent Curators International **[8861]**
401 Broadway, Ste. 1620
New York, NY 10013
PH: (212)254-8200
Fax: (212)477-4781
Fowle, Kate, Director

Independent Diplomat **[18479]**
45 E 20th St., 6th Fl.
New York, NY 10003
PH: (212)594-8295
Fax: (212)594-8430
Ogur, Scott, Treasurer

Indian Diamond and Colorstone Association **[2049]**
56 W 45th St., Ste. 705
New York, NY 10036
PH: (212)921-4488
Fax: (212)769-7935
Sancheti, Ashok, President

Indo-American Arts Council, Inc. **[8976]**
351 E 74th St., 3rd Fl.
New York, NY 10021

PH: (212)594-3685
Fax: (212)594-8476
Shivdasani, Aroon, Exec. Dir., President

Inland Marine Underwriters Association **[1861]**
14 Wall St., 8th Fl.
New York, NY 10005
PH: (212)233-0550
Fax: (212)227-5102
O'Brien, Kevin, President

Innocence Project **[5135]**
40 Worth St., Ste. 701
New York, NY 10013
PH: (212)364-5340
Scheck, Barry C., Director, Founder

Innovation: Africa **[5884]**
520 8th Ave., 15th Fl.
New York, NY 10018-6507
PH: (646)472-5380
Borowich, Sivan, Founder, CEO

Innovation Norway - United States **[23592]**
655 3rd Ave., Ste. 1810
New York, NY 10017-9111
PH: (212)885-9700
Fax: (212)885-9710

Institute for American Values **[11821]**
1841 Broadway, Ste. 211
New York, NY 10023
PH: (212)246-3942
Blankenhorn, David, Founder, President

Institute for Children, Poverty and Homelessness **[11044]**
44 Cooper Sq.
New York, NY 10003
PH: (212)358-8086
Fax: (212)358-8090
Bazerjian, Linda, Director

Institute of Electrical and Electronics Engineers **[6435]**
3 Park Ave., 17th Fl.
New York, NY 10016-5997
PH: (212)419-7900
Fax: (212)752-4929

Institute for Expressive Analysis **[16974]**
303 5th Ave., Ste. 1103
New York, NY 10016
PH: (646)494-4324
Sullivan, Janet, Membership Chp.

Institute of International Bankers **[401]**
299 Park Ave., 17th Fl.
New York, NY 10171
PH: (212)421-1611
Fax: (212)421-1119
Blissett, Roger, Chairman

Institute of International Education **[8075]**
IIE New York City
809 United Nations Plz.
New York, NY 10017-3503
PH: (212)883-8200
Fax: (212)984-5452
Goodman, Dr. Allan E., CEO, President

Institute of Judicial Administration **[5385]**
Wilf Hall, Rm. 116
New York University School of Law
139 MacDougal St.
New York, NY 10012
PH: (212)998-6149
Fax: (212)995-4769
Whitman, Torrey L., Exec. Dir.

Institute for Retired Professionals
[12756]
6 E 16th St., Rm. 905
New York, NY 10011
PH: (212)229-5682
Markowitz, Michael, Director

Institute for the Study of Genocide
[18410]
c/o Joyce Apsel, President
New York University
726 Broadway, 6th Fl.
New York, NY 10003
Fein, Helen, Chmn. of the Bd.

Institute for Transportation and
Development Policy [18491]
9 E 19th St., 7th Fl.
New York, NY 10003
PH: (212)629-8001
Fax: (646)380-2360
Lane, Clayton, CEO

Insurance Information Institute
[1866]
110 William St.
New York, NY 10038
PH: (212)346-5500
Fax: (212)267-9591
Hartwig, Dr. Robert P., President

Inter-American Commercial Arbitration Commission [4960]
c/o American Arbitration Association,
140 West 51st St.
140 W 51st St.
New York, NY 10020-1203
PH: (212)484-4000
Fax: (212)765-4874
Slate, William K., III, Director

Interactive Advertising Bureau [97]
116 E 27th St., 7th Fl.
New York, NY 10016
PH: (212)380-4700
Rothenberg, Randall, CEO,
President

Interchurch Center [20063]
475 Riverside Dr.
New York, NY 10115
PH: (212)870-2200
    (212)870-3804
Mayo, Paula M., President, Exec.
Dir.

Intercollegiate Taiwanese American
Students Association [19668]
PO Box 654
New York, NY 10163
Ko, Austin, President

Intercultural Alliance of Artists and
Scholars, Inc. [8925]
PO Box 4378, Grand Central Sta.
New York, NY 10163-4378
PH: (646)801-4227
Fax: (646)998-1314
David, Gabrielle, Exec. Dir., Chmn.
of the Bd.

InterExchange [8076]
100 Wall St., Ste. 301
New York, NY 10005
PH: (212)924-0446
Fax: (212)924-0575
Christianson, Uta, Founder

Interfaith Center on Corporate
Responsibility [18067]
475 Riverside Dr., Ste. 1842
New York, NY 10115
PH: (212)870-2295
    (212)870-2318
Fax: (212)870-2023
McCloskey, Kathryn, Secretary

Intergovernmental Renewable
Energy Organization [6490]
Dag Hammarskjold UN Ctr.
884 2nd Ave., No. 20050

New York, NY 10017
PH: (917)862-6444
Hill, John, Sec. Gen.

International Academy of Television
Arts and Sciences [463]
25 W 52nd St.
New York, NY 10019
PH: (212)489-6969
    (212)489-1946
Fax: (212)489-6557
Paisner, Bruce, CEO, President

International Action Center [18695]
147 W 24th St., 2nd Fl.
New York, NY 10011
PH: (212)633-6646
Fax: (212)633-2889
Clark, Ramsey, Founder

International Advertising Association
[98]
747 3rd Ave., 2nd Fl.
New York, NY 10017
PH: (646)722-2612
Fax: (646)722-2501
Lee, Michael, Managing Dir.

International AIDS Vaccine Initiative
[13548]
125 Broad St., 9th Fl.
New York, NY 10004
PH: (212)847-1111
Fax: (212)847-1112
Schwartz, Louis, CFO

International Alliance of Theatrical
Stage Employees, Moving Picture
Technicians, Artists and Allied
Crafts of the United States, Its Ter-
ritories and Canada [23496]
207 W 25th St., 4th Fl.
New York, NY 10001
PH: (212)730-1770
Fax: (212)730-7809
Loeb, Matthew D., President

International Association of Art Crit-
ics - United States Section [8979]
PO Box 20533, London Terrace Sta.
New York, NY 10011
Mac Adam, Barbara, Bd. Member

International Association of Credit
Portfolio Managers [943]
360 Madison Ave., 17th Fl.
New York, NY 10017-7111
PH: (646)289-5430
Fax: (646)289-5429
Leung, Som-lok, Exec. Dir.

International Association of Crime
Writers - North American Branch
[10377]
243 5th Ave., No. 537
New York, NY 10016
Davis, J. Madison, President

International Association of Culinary
Professionals [1388]
45 Rockefeller Plz., Ste. 2000
New York, NY 10111
PH: (646)358-4957
Toll free: 866-358-4951
Fax: (866)358-2524
Duda, Doug, Dir. of Strat. Plan.

International Association for Ecology
and Health [4004]
c/o Ecohealth Alliance
460 W 34th St., 17th Fl.
New York, NY 10001
PH: (212)380-4460
Zinsstag, Jakob, President

International Association for the
Exchange of Students for Technology Experience [8617]
440 Park Ave. S, 2nd Fl.
New York, NY 10016

PH: (212)497-3538
    (212)497-3500
Fax: (212)497-3534

International Association of
Independent Private Sector Inspec-
tors General [5308]
PO Box 5017
New York, NY 10185-5017
Toll free: 888-70I-PSIG
Getnick, Neil V., Chairman,
President

International Association for
Quantitative Finance [1241]
555 8th Ave., Rm. 1902
New York, NY 10018-4349
PH: (646)736-0705
Jaffe, David, Exec. Dir.

International Association for
Relational Psychoanalysis and
Psychotherapy [16846]
799 Broadway, Ste. 305
New York, NY 10003-6811
Ullman, Chana, President

International Association for the
Study of Maritime Mission [9782]
c/o Rev. Clint Padgitt
123 E 15th St.
New York, NY 10003
Friend, Stephen, Secretary

International Association of Tour
Managers-North American Region
[3380]
345 W 58th St.
New York, NY 10019
Seidelman, Carole-Anne, Chairman

International Brain Education As-
sociation [16050]
866 United Nations Plz., Ste. 479
New York, NY 10017
PH: (212)319-0848
Fax: (212)319-8671
Lee, Ilchi, Founder, President

International Bridal Manufacturers
Association [445]
118 W 20th St., 3rd Fl.
New York, NY 10011-3627
Warshaw, Larry, President

International Cargo Gear Bureau
[5566]
321 W 44th St.
New York, NY 10036
PH: (212)757-2011
Fax: (212)757-2650
Visconti, Charles G., Chairman,
President

International Center for Fabry
Disease [17343]
c/o Dana Doheny
One Gustave L. Levy Pl.
Mt. Sinai School of Medicine
New York, NY 10029-6574
PH: (212)241-6500
    (212)241-6696
Davis, Kenneth, President, CEO

International Center of Medieval Art
[9786]
The Cloisters, Fort Tryon Pk.
99 Margaret Corbin Dr.
New York, NY 10040
PH: (212)928-1146
Fax: (212)928-9946
Sevcenko, Nancy Patterson,
President

International Center of Photography
[8424]
1114 Avenue of the Americas
New York, NY 10036

PH: (212)857-0000
    (212)857-0004
Rosen, Jeffrey A., President

International Center for Transitional
Justice [18413]
5 Hanover Sq., 24th Fl.
New York, NY 10004
PH: (917)637-3800
Fax: (917)637-3900
Tolbert, David, President

International Chamber of Commerce
- USA [23593]
US Council for International Busi-
ness
1212 Avenue of the Americas
New York, NY 10036-1689
PH: (212)354-4480
Fax: (212)575-0327
Robinson, Peter M., CEO, President

International Cinema Technology
Association [1196]
c/o Robert H. Sunshine, Executive
Director
825 8th Ave. 29th Fl.
New York, NY 10019
PH: (212)493-4097
    (212)493-4058
Fax: (212)257-6428
Sunshine, Robert H., Exec. Dir.

International Civil Service Commis-
sion [23486]
2 United Nations Plz., 10th Fl.
New York, NY 10017
PH: (212)963-5465
Fax: (212)963-0159
Rhodes, Mr. Kingston, Chairman

International Coalition for the
Responsibility to Protect [19013]
c/o World Federalist Movement
Institute for Global Policy
708 3rd Ave., Ste. 1715
New York, NY 10017
PH: (212)599-1320
Fax: (212)599-1332
Schmidt, Megan, Officer

International Coalition of Sites of
Conscience [9403]
10 W 37th St., 6th Fl.
New York, NY 10018
PH: (646)397-4272
Silkes, Elizabeth, Exec. Dir.

International Colored Gemstone As-
sociation [3185]
30 W 47th St., Ste. 201
New York, NY 10036
PH: (212)620-0900
Fax: (212)352-9054
Goyal, Sushil, Director

International Consortium for
Emergency Contraception [11843]
Family Care International
45 Broadway, Ste. 320
New York, NY 10006
PH: (212)941-5300
Westley, Elizabeth, Coord.

International Council for Archaeozo-
ology [5942]
c/o Pam J. Crabtree, Treasurer
25 Waverly Pl.
New York, NY 10003
Lefevre, Christine, Secretary

International Council for Caring
Communities [5096]
24 Central Park S
New York, NY 10019
PH: (212)688-4321
Fax: (212)759-5893

International Council of the Museum
of Modern Art [8865]
11 W 53rd St.
New York, NY 10019

PH: (212)708-9400
Toll free: 888-999-8861
Lowry, Glenn D., Director

International Council of Psychologists [16917]
c/o Janet Sigel, President
Pace University 888, 8th Ave., Apt 1p
New York, NY 10019
Sigal, Janet, President

International Council of Shopping Centers [2956]
1221 Avenue of the Americas, 41st Fl.
New York, NY 10020-1099
PH: (646)728-3800
Fax: (732)694-1755
Kelly, Terri, Bus. Dev. Mgr.

International Council of Toy Industries [3293]
c/o Toy Industry Association
1115 Broadway, Ste. 400
New York, NY 10010-3466
PH: (212)675-1141
(202)459-0355
Carroll, Molly, Contact

International Counselor Exchange Program [8080]
38 W 88th St.
New York, NY 10024
PH: (212)787-7706
Paul, Suresh, Exec. Dir.

International Debate Education Association [8594]
222 Broadway, 19th Fl.
New York, NY 10038
PH: (212)300-6076
Moreau, Sandra, Exec. Dir.

International E-Learning Association [7488]
Kaleidoscope Learning
304 Park Ave. S, 11th Fl.
New York, NY 10010
PH: (646)397-3710
Guralnick, David, President, Treasurer

International Federation of Accountants [37]
529 5th Ave., 6th Fl.
New York, NY 10017
PH: (212)286-9344
Fax: (212)286-9570
Kirtley, Olivia, President

International Federation of Family Associations of Missing Persons from Armed Conflicts [12362]
750 3rd Ave., 9th Fl.
New York, NY 10017
PH: (212)335-0220
Fax: (646)476-9657

International Fine Print Dealers Association [250]
250 W 26th St., Ste. 405
New York, NY 10001-6737
PH: (212)674-6095
Fax: (212)674-6783
Senecal, Michele, Exec. Dir.

International Foundation for Art Research [8866]
500 5th Ave., Ste. 935
New York, NY 10110
PH: (212)391-6234
Fax: (212)391-8794
Flescher, Dr. Sharon, Exec. Dir.

International Healthcare Leadership [15122]
Columbia University Medical Ctr.
3959 Broadway, 8 N

New York, NY 10032
Roye, Dr. David P., Jr., CEO, President

International Institute for Conflict Prevention and Resolution [4962]
30 E 33rd St., 6th Fl.
New York, NY 10016
PH: (212)949-6490
Fax: (212)949-8859
Hanft, Noah J., President, CEO

International Institute of Rural Reconstruction U.S. Chapter [12802]
601 W 26th St., Ste. 325-1
New York, NY 10001
PH: (908)347-5585
Bekalo, Isaac B., President

International Insurance Society [1879]
101 Astor Pl., Ste. 202
New York, NY 10003-7132
PH: (212)277-5171
Fax: (212)277-5172

International League for Human Rights [18415]
352 7th Ave., Ste. 1234
New York, NY 10001
PH: (212)661-0480
Fax: (212)661-0416

International Legal Defense Counsel [5352]
405 Lexington Ave., 26th Fl.
New York, NY 10174
Toll free: 888-534-9106
Griffith, Michael J., Esq., Contact

International Legal Foundation [5534]
111 John St., Ste. 1040
New York, NY 10038
PH: (212)608-1188
Smith, Jennifer, Exec. Dir.

International Licensing Industry Merchandisers' Association [5332]
350 5th Ave., Ste. 6410
New York, NY 10118
PH: (212)244-1944
Riotto, Charles M., President

International Molded Fiber Association [2492]
355 Lexington Ave., 15 Fl.
New York, NY 10017
PH: (630)544-5056
Fax: (630)544-5055
Grygny, Joseph, Exec. Dir.

International Multiracial Shared Cultural Organization [18548]
4 Park Ave.
New York, NY 10016-5339
PH: (212)532-5449
Weston, Frank, Chairman, President

International Peace Institute [18361]
777 United Nations Plz.
New York, NY 10017-3521
PH: (212)687-4300
Fax: (212)983-8246
Hauser, Dr. Rita E., Chairwoman

International Planned Parenthood Federation - Western Hemisphere Region [11844]
125 Maiden Ln., 9th Fl.
New York, NY 10038-4730
PH: (212)248-6400
Fax: (212)248-4221
Cohen, Andrea, Chairperson

International PNH Interest Group [15236]
521 5th Ave., 6th Fl.
New York, NY 10175
Hillmen, Peter, PhD, Chairman

International Psycho-Oncology Society [13993]
244 5th Ave., Ste. L296
New York, NY 10001
PH: (416)968-0260
Fax: (416)968-6818
Jacobsen, Paul, VP

International Radio and Television Society Foundation [464]
1697 Broadway, 10th Fl.
New York, NY 10019
PH: (212)867-6650
Tudryn, Joyce M., President, CEO

International Refugee Rights Initiative [18416]
1483 York Ave., No. 20463
New York, NY 10021
PH: (646)867-1991
Akello, Sandrah, Administrator, Mgr. of Fin.

International Rescue Committee USA [12687]
122 E 42nd St.
New York, NY 10168-1289
PH: (212)551-3000
Toll free: 855-9RE-SCUE
Fax: (212)551-3179
Johnson, David, CFO

International RFID Business Association, Inc. [275]
5 W 37th St. & 5th Ave., 9th Fl.
New York, NY 10018
PH: (610)357-0990
Pappas, Harry P., CEO, Founder, President

International Senior Lawyers Project [5014]
96 Morton St., 7th Fl.
New York, NY 10014
PH: (646)798-3289
Berman, Ms. Jean C., Esq., Advisor

International Service for Human Rights-New York Office [18418]
777 UN Plz., 8th Fl.
New York, NY 10017
PH: (212)490-2199

International Society for the Comparative Study of Civilizations [7168]
c/o David Hahn, Treasurer
School for Management
Metropolitan College of New York
431 Canal St.
New York, NY 10013
PH: (212)343-1234
Fax: (212)343-8476
Rosner, David, President

International Society for Contemporary Music USA [9932]
24 Waverly Pl., Rm. 268
New York, NY 10003
PH: (347)559-5376
Fax: (516)694-1340
Kern, Friedrich Heinrich, Officer

International Society for Forensic Genetics [14774]
c/o Mechthild Prinz, President
Dept. of Sciences
John Jay College of Criminal Justice
524 W 59th St.
New York, NY 10019
Prinz, Mechthild, VP

International Society for Hyaluronan Sciences [6056]
c/o Mary K. Cowman, President
433 1st Ave., Rm. 910
New York, NY 10010
PH: (212)992-5971
Fax: (405)271-3092
Hascall, Vincent, Trustee

International Society on Metabolic Eye Disease [16392]
1125 Park Ave.
New York, NY 10128
PH: (212)427-1246
Fax: (212)360-7009
Haddad, Prof. Heskel M., MD, Chairman

International Society of Orthopaedic Centers [16481]
c/o Hospital for Special Surgery
535 E 70th St.
New York, NY 10021
PH: (212)774-2315
Fax: (212)734-3833
Sculco, Thomas P., MD, Exec. Dir.

International Society for the Performing Arts Foundation [8982]
630 9th Ave., Ste. 213
New York, NY 10036-4752
PH: (212)206-8490
Fax: (212)206-8603
Baile, David, CEO

The International Society for the Study of Ghosts and Apparitions [6987]
29 Washington Sq. W
Penthouse N
New York, NY 10011-9180
Youngson, Dr. Jeanne Keyes, Founder, President

International Society for Urban Health [15150]
New York Academy of Medicine
1216 5th Ave.
New York, NY 10029
O'Campo, Patricia, Treasurer

International Swaps and Derivatives Association [2024]
360 Madison Ave., 16th Fl.
New York, NY 10017-7111
PH: (212)901-6000
Fax: (212)901-6001
O'Malia, Scott, CEO

International Thyroid Eye Disease Society [13787]
Columbia University
635 W 165th St.
New York, NY 10032
PH: (212)305-5477
Kazim, Michael, President

International Trademark Association [5333]
655 3rd Ave., 10th Fl.
New York, NY 10017
PH: (212)642-1700
Fax: (212)768-7796
Deutsch, Ayala, Treasurer

International Vintage Poster Dealers Association [99]
PO Box 501
New York, NY 10113-0501

International Women's Health Coalition [17758]
333 7th Ave., 6th Fl.
New York, NY 10001
PH: (212)979-8500
Hess, Marlene, Chairman

Interreligious Foundation for Community Organization [11472]
418 W 145th St.
New York, NY 10031
PH: (212)926-5757
Fax: (212)926-5842
Walker, Gail, Exec. Dir.

Investorside Research Association
[2027]
61 Broadway, Ste. 1910
New York, NY 10006-2701
Toll free: 877-834-4777
Fax: (877)834-4777
Eade, John, President

Iranian Alliances Across Borders
[9595]
154 Grand St.
New York, NY 10013
Kharrazi, Mana, Exec. Dir.

Iranian Refugees' Alliance [12591]
Cooper Sta.
New York, NY 10276-0316
PH: (212)260-7460
Fax: (267)295-7391
Abadi, Deljou, Founder, Exec. Dir.

Iraq and Afghanistan Veterans of
America [21126]
114 W 41st St., 19th Fl.
New York, NY 10036
PH: (212)982-9699
Fax: (917)591-0387
Rieckhoff, Paul, CEO, Founder

Iraq Veterans Against the War
[19236]
PO Box 3565
New York, NY 10008-3565
PH: (646)723-0989
Fax: (646)723-0996
Howard, Matt, Dir. of Comm.

Irish Arts Center [9601]
553 W 51st St.
New York, NY 10019
PH: (212)757-3318
Toll free: 866-811-4111
Fax: (212)247-0930
Connolly, Aidan, Exec. Dir.

Israel Aliyah Center [20253]
633 3rd Ave.
New York, NY 10017-6706
PH: (212)339-6000
Ratner, Charles Horowitz, Chmn. of
the Bd.

Israel Humanitarian Foundation -
New York [12209]
2 W 46th St., Ste. 1500
New York, NY 10036
Hoter-Ishay, Arnon, President

Israeli Committee Against House
Demolitions - USA [18797]
PO Box 8118
New York, NY 10150-8101
PH: (646)308-1322
Efrati, Eran, Exec. Dir.

Israeli Dance Institute [9264]
225 W 34th St., Ste. 1607
New York, NY 10122
PH: (212)983-4806
Fax: (212)983-4084
Goodman, Ruth, Mgr.

Istituto Italiano di Cultura [9613]
686 Park Ave.
New York, NY 10065-5009
PH: (212)879-4242
Fax: (212)861-4018
Barlera, Paolo, Officer

Italian American Studies Association
[9614]
The Calandra Institute
25 W 43rd St., 17th Fl.
New York, NY 10036
Pardini, Samuele F.S., VP

Italian Historical Society of America
[9617]
410 Park Ave., Ste. 1530
New York, NY 10022
LaCorte, John N., PhD, Exec. Dir.

Italian Wine and Food Institute
[1350]
1 Grand Central Pl.
60 E 42nd St., Ste. 2214
New York, NY 10165
PH: (212)867-4111
Fax: (212)867-4114
Caputo, Dr. Lucio, President,
Founder

Italy-America Chamber of Com-
merce [23597]
730 5th Ave., Ste. 502
New York, NY 10019
PH: (212)459-0044
Fax: (212)459-0090
Viola, Giulio, Rep.

Ittleson Foundation [12978]
c/o Anthony C. Wood, Executive
Director
15 E 67th St.
New York, NY 10065
PH: (212)794-2008
Wood, Anthony C., Exec. Dir.,
Secretary

Jackie Robinson Foundation [13454]
1 Hudson Sq., 2nd Fl.
75 Varick St.
New York, NY 10013-1917
PH: (212)290-8600
Fax: (212)290-8081
Baeza, Della Britton, CEO, President

Jamaica Impact, Inc. [12214]
PO Box 3794
New York, NY 10163
PH: (212)459-4390
Todd, Dale, President

Jane Addams Peace Association
[18798]
777 United Nations Plz., 6th Fl.
New York, NY 10017
PH: (212)682-8830
Belle, Linda B., Exec. Dir.

Japan Center for International
Exchange USA [18549]
135 W 29th St., Rm. 303
New York, NY 10001
PH: (212)679-4130
Gannon, James, Exec. Dir.,
Secretary, Treasurer

Japan Convention Bureau [23643]
1 Grand Central Pl.
60 E 42nd St., Ste. 448
New York, NY 10165
PH: (212)757-5640
Fax: (212)307-6754
Galbreath, Dana, Convention Mgr.

Japan Foundation [9623]
152 W 57th St., 17th Fl.
New York, NY 10019
PH: (212)489-0299
Fax: (212)489-0409
Wada, Yoshihiro, Dep. Dir.

Japan International Christian
University Foundation [20084]
475 Riverside Dr., Ste. 439
New York, NY 10115-0090
PH: (212)870-3386
Vikner, David W., President

Japan National Tourist Organization
[23644]
1 Grand Central Pl.
60 E 42nd St., Ste. 448
New York, NY 10165
PH: (212)757-5640
Fax: (212)307-6754
Mamiya, Tadatoshi, President

Japan Society [9624]
333 E 47th St.
New York, NY 10017

PH: (212)832-1155
(212)715-1270
Sakurai, Motoatsu, President

Jazzmobile Inc. [9941]
91 Claremont Ave.
New York, NY 10027
PH: (212)866-4900
(212)866-3616

JBI International [17718]
110 E 30th St.
New York, NY 10016
PH: (212)889-2525
Toll free: 800-433-1531
Fax: (212)689-3692
Isler, Dr. Ellen, CEO, President

JCC Association [12223]
520 8th Ave.
New York, NY 10018
PH: (212)532-4949
Fax: (212)481-4174
Seiden, Stephen, Chairman

JCC Association of North America
[20254]
520 8th Ave.
New York, NY 10018
PH: (212)532-4949
Fax: (212)481-4174
Arnoff, Stephen Hazan, President

JETRO New York [23645]
565 5th Ave., 4th Fl.
New York, NY 10017
PH: (212)997-0400
Fax: (212)997-0464

Jewelers of America [2050]
120 Broadway, Ste. 2820
New York, NY 10271
PH: (646)658-5806
Toll free: 800-223-0673
Bonaparte, David J., President, CEO

Jewelers' Security Alliance [2052]
6 E 45th St.
New York, NY 10017
Toll free: 800-537-0067
Fax: (212)808-9168
Kennedy, John J., President

Jewelers Vigilance Committee
[2054]
801 2nd Ave., Ste. 303
New York, NY 10017
PH: (212)997-2002
Fax: (212)997-9148
Gardner, Cecilia L., Esq., CEO, Gen.
Counsel, President

Jewelry Information Center [2056]
120 Broadway, Ste. 2820
New York, NY 10271
PH: (646)658-0246
Toll free: 800-223-0673
Fax: (646)658-0256
Gizzi, Amanda, Contact

Jewish Alcoholics, Chemically
Dependent Persons and Significant
Others [13149]
135 W 50th St.
New York, NY 10020
PH: (212)632-4600
Fax: (212)399-3525
Darack, Ms. Sharon, Dir. of
Programs

Jewish Book Council [9130]
520 8th Ave., 4th Fl.
New York, NY 10018
PH: (212)201-2920
Fax: (212)532-4952
Krule, Lawrence J., President

Jewish Council for Public Affairs
[12224]
116 E 27th St.
New York, NY 10016-8942

PH: (212)684-6950
Bernstein, David, President

Jewish Education Service of North
America [8138]
247 W 37th St., 5th Fl.
New York, NY 10018
PH: (212)284-6877
Fax: (212)532-7518
Gottlieb, Cass, Chairman

The Jewish Federations of North
America [12225]
25 Broadway, 17th Fl.
New York, NY 10004
PH: (212)284-6500
(212)284-6903
Toll free: 866-844-0070
Silverman, Jerry, CEO, President

Jewish Foundation for the Righteous
[18350]
305 7th Ave., 19th Fl.
New York, NY 10001-6008
PH: (212)727-9955
Fax: (212)727-9956
Stahl, Ms. Stanlee Joyce, Exec. VP

Jewish Genealogical Society [20981]
PO Box 631
New York, NY 10113-0631
PH: (212)294-8318
Berenbeim, Jane Rosen, President

Jewish Guild for the Blind [17719]
15 W 65th St.
New York, NY 10023-6601
PH: (212)769-6200
(212)769-6331
Toll free: 800-284-4422
Fax: (212)769-6266
Morse, Alan R., CEO, President

Jewish Labor Committee [18591]
140 W 31st St., 3rd Fl.
New York, NY 10001-3411
PH: (212)477-0707
Fax: (212)477-1918
Appelbaum, Stuart, President

Jewish Lawyers Guild [20256]
c/o Shoshana T. Bookson, President
570 Lexington Ave., Ste. 1600
New York, NY 10022
PH: (646)300-8100
Bookson, Shoshana T., President

Jewish National Fund [20257]
42 E 69th St.
New York, NY 10021
Toll free: 800-542-8733
Fax: (212)409-8548
Lauder, Ronald, Chairman

Jewish Orthodox Feminist Alliance
[20258]
520 8th Ave., 4th Fl.
New York, NY 10018
PH: (212)679-8500
Alperovich, Allie, Treasurer

Jewish Student Press Service [8140]
125 Maiden Ln., 8th Fl.
New York, NY 10038
Sobel, Chloe, Exec. Dir.

Jewish Telegraphic Agency [18592]
24 W 30th St., 4th Fl.
New York, NY 10001
PH: (212)643-1890
Fax: (212)643-8499
Eden, Ami, CEO, Exec. Ed.

JPRO Network [12226]
25 Broadway, Ste. 1700
New York, NY 10004
PH: (212)284-6945
Fax: (212)284-6566
Terrill, Marc B., Bd. Member

C.G. Jung Foundation for Analytical Psychology **[16924]**
28 E 39th St.
New York, NY 10016-2587
PH: (212)697-6430
Fax: (212)953-3989

Juvenile Diabetes Cure Alliance **[14538]**
14 E 60th St., Ste. 208
New York, NY 10022
Kelly, Brian G., Founder

Juvenile Diabetes Research Foundation International **[14539]**
26 Broadway
New York, NY 10004
Toll free: 800-533-CURE
Fax: (212)785-9595
Brewer, Jeffrey, President, CEO

JWB Jewish Chaplains Council **[19931]**
520 8th Ave.
New York, NY 10018-6507
PH: (212)532-4949
Fax: (212)481-4174
Robinson, Rabbi Harold, Director

Kafka Society of America **[9067]**
c/o Marie Luise Caputo-Mayr, Director
160 E 65th St., No. 2C
New York, NY 10065
PH: (212)744-0821
Fax: (212)744-0821
Rajec, Elizabeth, President

Kageno Worldwide **[11392]**
261 Broadway
New York, NY 10007
PH: (212)227-0509
Andolino, Frank C., Founder, Exec. Dir.

Keats-Shelley Association of America **[9068]**
New York Public Library, Rm. 226
476 5th Ave.
New York, NY 10018-2788
Curran, Stuart, President

Keep a Child Alive **[13551]**
11 Hanover Sq., 14th Fl.
New York, NY 10005
PH: (646)762-8200
Fax: (646)762-8201
Keys, Alicia, Founder

Keren Or **[17720]**
350 7th Ave., Ste. 701
New York, NY 10001-1942
PH: (212)279-4070
Fax: (212)279-4043
Steinberg, Edward L., MSc, Chairman

Kibbutz Program Center **[18586]**
424 W 33rd St., Ste. 150
New York, NY 10001
PH: (212)462-2764
Fax: (212)675-7685

Esther A. and Joseph Klingenstein Fund, Inc **[15651]**
125 Park Ave., Ste. 1700
New York, NY 10017-5529
PH: (212)492-6195
Klingenstein, Mr. Andrew D., President

Klingenstein Third Generation Foundation **[14198]**
125 Park Ave., Ste. 1700
New York, NY 10017-5529
PH: (212)492-6179
Klingenstein Martell, Sally, Exec. Dir.

The Korea Society **[23648]**
950 3rd Ave., 8th Fl.
New York, NY 10022

PH: (212)759-7525
Fax: (212)759-7530
Byrne, Thomas J., President

Korean American League for Civic Action **[18604]**
149 W 24th St., 6th Fl.
New York, NY 10011
PH: (212)633-2000
Kim, Judy H., V. Chmn. of the Bd.

Kosciuszko Foundation **[10164]**
15 E 65th St.
New York, NY 10065
PH: (212)734-2130
Fax: (212)628-4552
Storozynski, Alex, Chmn. of the Bd.

Samuel H. Kress Foundation **[12980]**
174 E 80th St.
New York, NY 10075
PH: (212)861-4993
Fax: (212)628-3146
Marmor, Max, President

La Unidad Latina, Lambda Upsilon Lambda Fraternity **[23800]**
511 6th Ave., PMB 39
New York, NY 10011
Acosta-Thompson, Hermano Ignacio U., President

Lambda Legal **[11896]**
120 Wall St., 19th Fl.
New York, NY 10005-3919
PH: (212)809-8585
Fax: (212)809-0055
Cathcart, Kevin M., Exec. Dir.

The Lambs, Inc. **[10256]**
3 W 51st St.
New York, NY 10019
PH: (212)586-0306
Baron, Marc, President

Langston Hughes Society **[9070]**
English Dept.
City College of New York/CUNY
160 Convent Ave.
New York, NY 10031
Thompson, Gordon, PhD, Treasurer

Latin American Venture Capital Association **[1248]**
589 8th Ave., 18th Fl.
New York, NY 10018
PH: (646)315-6735
Fax: (646)349-1047
Ambrose, Cate, CEO, President

Latinas Promoviendo Comunidad/ Lambda Pi Chi Sorority **[23801]**
PO Box 1522
New York, NY 10028
Banuelos, Cristina, President

Latino America Unida, Lambda Alpha Upsilon Fraternity **[23802]**
244 5th Ave., Ste. C-140
New York, NY 10001
PH: (203)392-5792
Rosario, Tristian, COO

Latino Center on Aging **[10512]**
576 5th Ave., Ste. 903
New York, NY 10036
PH: (212)330-8120
Tapia, Mario E., CEO, President

LatinoJustice PRLDEF **[17905]**
99 Hudson St., 14th Fl.
New York, NY 10013-2815
PH: (212)219-3360
Toll free: 800-328-2322
Fax: (212)431-4276
Cartagena, Juan, President, Gen. Counsel

Lawyers Committee on Nuclear Policy **[18751]**
866 UN Plz., Ste. 4050
New York, NY 10017-1830
PH: (212)818-1861
Fax: (212)818-1857
Burroughs, John, Exec. Dir.

Leadership Enterprise for a Diverse America **[8619]**
501 7th Ave., 7th Fl.
New York, NY 10018
PH: (212)672-9750
Fax: (212)986-1857
Roberts, John C., President

Leading Jewelers of the World **[2057]**
500 7th Ave., Ste. 12B
New York, NY 10018-4502
PH: (212)398-6401
Fax: (212)398-6406
Barlerin, Michael, Exec. Dir.

League of American Orchestras **[9946]**
33 W 60th St.
New York, NY 10023
PH: (212)262-5161
Fax: (212)262-5198
Rosen, Jesse, CEO, President

League of Resident Theatres **[10258]**
1501 Broadway, Ste. 2401
New York, NY 10036
PH: (212)944-1501
Fax: (212)768-0785
Shields, Tim, President

League for the Revolutionary Party **[19142]**
PO Box 1936, Murray Hill Sta.
New York, NY 10156
PH: (212)330-9017

League for Yiddish, Inc. **[20263]**
64 Fulton St., Ste. 1101
New York, NY 10038
PH: (212)889-0380
Fax: (212)889-0380
Zucker, Dr. Sheva, Exec. Dir.

A Leg To Stand On **[11614]**
401 Park Ave. S, 10th Fl.
New York, NY 10016
PH: (212)683-8805
Fax: (212)683-8813
Mueller, Gabriella, Exec. Dir.

Legal Momentum **[18217]**
5 Hanover Sq., Ste. 1502
New York, NY 10004
PH: (212)925-6635
Knowles, Ralph I., Director

Lennox-Gastaut Syndrome Foundation **[14742]**
192 Lexington Ave., Ste. 216
New York, NY 10016
PH: (718)374-3800
SanInocencio, Christina, President, Founder

Leslie-Lohman Museum of Gay and Lesbian Art **[8870]**
26 Wooster St.
New York, NY 10013
PH: (212)431-2609
Fax: (212)431-2666
Katz, Jonathan David, PhD, President

Liberian Shipowners' Council **[2248]**
99 Park Ave., Ste. 1700
New York, NY 10016
PH: (212)973-3896
Fax: (212)217-3869

Liederkranz Foundation, Inc. **[9949]**
6 E 87th St.
New York, NY 10128
PH: (212)534-0880
Fax: (212)828-5372
Pfeifer, Joseph, President

Lifebeat Inc. **[10545]**
302A W 12th St., Ste. 186
New York, NY 10014
PH: (212)459-2590

Lifespire **[12326]**
1 Whitehall St., 9th Fl.
New York, NY 10004-2141
PH: (212)741-0100
Fax: (212)463-9814
van Voorst, Mark, CEO, President

Lighthouse International **[17722]**
15 W 65th St.
New York, NY 10023-6601
Toll free: 800-284-4422
Morse, Alan R., President, CEO

Gerda Lissner Foundation **[9950]**
15 E 65th St., 4th Fl.
New York, NY 10065-6501
PH: (212)826-6100
Fax: (212)826-0366
De Maio, Stephen, President

Literacy Design Collaborative **[8245]**
48 Wall St., 11th Fl.
New York, NY 10005
Vignola, Chad, Exec. Dir.

Literary Managers and Dramaturgs of the Americas **[10259]**
PO Box 36
New York, NY 10129
Toll free: 800-680-2148
Quirt, Brian, Chmn. of the Bd.

Lithuanian Alliance of America **[19540]**
307 W 30th St.
New York, NY 10001-2703
PH: (212)563-2210
Fax: (212)331-0001

Lithuanian National Foundation **[18423]**
307 W 30th St.
New York, NY 10001-2703
PH: (212)868-5860
Fax: (212)868-5815
Kumpikas, Giedre M., PhD, Bd. Member

Litigation Counsel of America **[5022]**
641 Lexington Ave., 15th Fl.
New York, NY 10022
PH: (212)724-4128
Fax: (212)918-9144
Henry, G. Steven, Founder, Exec. Dir., Gen. Counsel

Loan Syndications and Trading Association **[404]**
366 Madison Ave., 15th Fl.
New York, NY 10017
PH: (212)880-3000
Fax: (212)880-3040
Smith, Bram, Exec. Dir.

Local Initiatives Support Corporation **[17984]**
501 7th Ave.
New York, NY 10018
PH: (212)455-9800
Fax: (212)682-5929
Rubinger, Michael, President, CEO

Love Our Children USA **[11071]**
220 E 57th St.
New York, NY 10022
PH: (212)629-2099
Toll free: 888-347-KIDS
Ellis, Ross, CEO, Founder

Henry Luce Foundation **[11728]**
51 Madison Ave., 30th Fl.
New York, NY 10010
PH: (212)489-7700
Fax: (212)581-9541
Gilligan, Michael, President

Lucis Trust **[18362]**
120 Wall St., 24th Fl.
New York, NY 10005
PH: (212)292-0707
Fax: (212)292-0808
Morgan, Christine, Chairman,
President

Lupus Clinical Trials Consortium
[15540]
221 E 48th St., 2nd Fl.
New York, NY 10017
PH: (212)593-7227
Snider, Katherine, President

Luxembourg-American Chamber of
Commerce **[23601]**
17 Beekman Pl.
New York, NY 10022
PH: (212)888-6701
Fax: (212)935-5896
Lamesch, Fernand, Chairman

Lymphatic Education and Research
Network **[15544]**
261 Madison Ave., 9th Fl.
New York, NY 10016
PH: (516)625-9675
Fax: (516)625-9410
Braginsky, Philip, Esq., Secretary

Lymphoma Research Foundation
[14006]
115 Broadway, Ste. 1301
New York, NY 10006-1623
PH: (212)349-2910
Toll free: 800-500-9976
Fax: (212)349-2886
Werner, Michael, Exec. VP

Macedonian Arts Council **[8984]**
380 Rector Pl., Apt. 21E
New York, NY 10280-1449
PH: (212)799-0009
Fax: (815)301-3893
Proevska, Pavlina, Exec. Dir.,
Founder

Josiah Macy Jr. Foundation **[14945]**
44 E 64th St.
New York, NY 10065-7306
PH: (212)486-2424
Fax: (212)644-0765
Goodwin, Peter, Treasurer, COO

MADRE **[12287]**
121 W 27th St., No. 301
New York, NY 10001
PH: (212)627-0444
Fax: (212)675-3704
Susskind, Yifat, Exec. Dir.

Major League Baseball **[22552]**
75 9th Ave., 5th Fl.
New York, NY 10167-3000
Fax: (212)949-5654
Robinson, Frank, Exec. VP of Dev.

Major League Baseball Players As-
sociation **[23392]**
12 E 49th St., 24th Fl.
New York, NY 10017
PH: (212)826-0808
Fax: (212)752-4378
Clark, Tony, Exec. Dir.

Major League Eating **[23234]**
18 E 41st St., 15th Fl.
New York, NY 10017
PH: (212)352-8651
Fax: (212)627-5430
Shea, George, Contact

Malaria No More **[14592]**
432 Park Ave. S, 4th Fl.
New York, NY 10016
Edlund, Martin, CEO

Malecare **[14007]**
419 Lafayette St., 2nd Fl.
New York, NY 10003
PH: (212)673-4920
Mitteldorf, Darryl, LCSW, Founder

MaleSurvivor: The National
Organization Against Male Sexual
Victimization **[12926]**
4768 Broadway, No. 527
New York, NY 10034
Followell, Ken, President

Manhattan Institute for Policy
Research **[18956]**
52 Vanderbilt Ave.
New York, NY 10017
PH: (212)599-7000
Fax: (212)599-3494
Singer, Paul E., Chairman

Mano A Mano: Mexican Culture
Without Borders **[9795]**
550 W 155th St.
New York, NY 10032
PH: (212)587-3070
Fax: (212)587-3071
Aguirre, Juan Carlos, Exec. Dir.

MARHO: The Radical Historians'
Organization **[9493]**
New York University
Tamiment Library, 10th Fl.
70 Washington Sq. S
New York, NY 10012
Chazkel, Amy, Chairman

Market Technicians Association
[1249]
61 Broadway, Ste. 514
New York, NY 10006
PH: (646)652-3300
Fax: (646)652-3322
Licitra, Tim, Exec. Dir.

Marketing EDGE **[8271]**
1333 Broadway, Rm. 301
New York, NY 10018
PH: (212)768-7277
Fax: (212)790-1561
Bartlett, Terri L., President

Markle Foundation **[6229]**
10 Rockefeller Plz., 16th Fl.
New York, NY 10020-1903
PH: (212)713-7600
Fax: (212)765-9690
Kaden, Lewis B., Chmn. of the Bd.

Marriage Equality USA, Inc. **[12255]**
PO Box 121, Old Chelsea Sta.
New York, NY 10113
PH: (347)913-6369
Fax: (347)479-1700
Silva, Brian, Exec. Dir.

Master Drawings Association **[8871]**
225 Madison Ave.
New York, NY 10016
PH: (212)590-0369
Fax: (212)685-4740
Turner, Jane, Editor

Math for America **[8281]**
915 Broadway, 16th Fl.
New York, NY 10010
PH: (646)437-0904
Fax: (646)437-0935
Ewing, John, President

Maudsley Parents **[14644]**
c/o National Eating Disorder Association

165 W 46th St., No. 402
New York, NY 10036
Brown, Harriet, Bd. Member

Media Coalition **[17910]**
19 Fulton St., Ste. 407
New York, NY 10038
PH: (212)587-4025
Finan, Chris, Chmn. of the Bd.

Media & Content Marketing Associa-
tion **[2800]**
225 W 34th St., Ste. 946
New York, NY 10122
PH: (818)487-2090
Fax: (818)487-4501
Knowles, Brian, Chairperson

Media Law Resource Center **[5433]**
266 W 37th St., 20th Fl.
New York, NY 10018
PH: (212)337-0200
Fax: (212)337-9893
Oberlander, Lynn, Chairman

Media Rating Council **[466]**
420 Lexington Ave., Ste. 343
New York, NY 10170
PH: (212)972-0300
Fax: (212)972-2786
Ivie, George, CEO, Exec. Dir.

MediaChannel.org **[18659]**
PO Box 677
New York, NY 10035
Schechter, Danny, Editor

Medical Relief Alliance **[12696]**
244 5th Ave., Ste. B293
New York, NY 10001
PH: (917)292-4866
Walters, Ms. Davie, Founder

Medicare Rights Center **[18328]**
266 W 37th St., 3rd Fl.
New York, NY 10018
PH: (212)869-3850
Toll free: 800-333-4114
Fax: (212)869-3532
Vladeck, Bruce C., Chairperson

The Andrew W. Mellon Foundation
[12487]
140 E 62nd St.
New York, NY 10065-8124
PH: (212)838-8400
Fax: (212)888-4172
Tirfe, Abyssinia, Asst.

Melodious Accord **[9953]**
Park West Sta.
New York, NY 10025-01516
PH: (413)339-8508
    (212)665-4405
Parker, Alice, Art Dir.

Melorheostosis Association **[14842]**
410 E 50th St.
New York, NY 10022
Gordy, Jennifer, President

Memorial Foundation for Jewish
Culture **[9640]**
50 Broadway, 34th Fl.
New York, NY 10004
PH: (212)425-6606
Fax: (212)425-6602
Schorsch, Prof. Ismar, President

Men of Reform Judaism **[20265]**
633 3rd Ave.
New York, NY 10017
PH: (212)650-4100
Portnoy, Steven, President

Menopause Alliance **[16293]**
350 Broadway, Ste. 307
New York, NY 10013

PH: (212)625-3311
Fax: (917)591-5606
Woodin, Mary Beth, President

MERCAZ USA **[20266]**
475 Riverside Dr., Ste. 820
New York, NY 10115
PH: (212)533-2061
Fax: (212)870-3897
Tobin, Janet, President

Metastatic Breast Cancer Network
[14014]
PO Box 1449
New York, NY 10159
Toll free: 888-500-0370
Przypyszny, Michele, President

Metropolitan Opera Association
[9954]
Lincoln Center for the Performing
Arts
30 Lincoln Center Plz.
New York, NY 10023
PH: (212)870-7457
    (212)362-6000
Fisher, John, Dir. of Admin.

Metropolitan Opera Guild **[9955]**
70 Lincoln Center Plz., 6th Fl.
New York, NY 10023-6593
PH: (212)769-7000
Rutherfurd, Winthrop, Jr., Chmn. of
the Bd.

Mexico Tourism Board **[23651]**
152 Madison Ave., Ste. 1800
New York, NY 10016
PH: (212)308-2110
Fax: (212)308-9060
Vega, Ivan Martinez, Director

Middle Powers Initiative **[18129]**
866 United Nations Plz., Ste. 4050
New York, NY 10017
PH: (646)289-5170
Fax: (646)289-5171
Roche, Douglas, Advisor

Midori & Friends **[7514]**
352 7th Ave., Ste. 301
New York, NY 10001
PH: (212)767-1300
Fox, Nancy, Officer

Millennium Promise Alliance Inc.
[10727]
475 Riverside Dr., Ste. 1040
New York, NY 10115
PH: (212)870-2490
McArthur, John, CEO, Exec. Dir.

Minority Peace Corps Association
[18847]
Village Sta.
PO Box 244
New York, NY 10044
PH: (770)498-3353
Fax: (770)498-7350

Miracle Corners of the World
[13458]
152 Madison Ave., Ste. 1702
New York, NY 10016
PH: (212)453-5811
Fax: (212)213-4890
Bergman, Edward, President,
Founder

Missionary Childhood Association
[19863]
70 W 36th St., 8th Fl.
New York, NY 10018
PH: (212)563-8700
Fax: (212)563-8725
Small, Rev. Andrew, OMI, Director

Missionary Society of Saint Paul the
Apostle **[19866]**
415 W 59th St.
New York, NY 10019

PH: (202)269-2500
Andrews, Rev. Eric, CSP, President

Mobile Marketing Association [102]
41 E 11 St., 11th Fl.
New York, NY 10003
PH: (646)257-4515
Stuart, Greg Stuart, CEO

Jeffrey Modell Foundation [15383]
780 3rd Ave.
New York, NY 10017
Fax: (212)764-4180
Modell, Vicki, Founder

Modern Language Association of America [8187]
85 Broad St., Ste. 500
New York, NY 10004-1789
PH: (646)576-5000
Fax: (646)458-0030
Feal, Rosemary G., Exec. Dir.

Modern Language Association of America Committee on Scholarly Editions [10386]
85 Broad St., Ste. 500
New York, NY 10004-2434
PH: (646)576-5000
Fax: (646)458-0030
Fitzpatrick, Kathleen, Liaison

Morris-Jumel Mansion [10340]
65 Jumel Ter.
New York, NY 10032
PH: (212)923-8008
Gruchow, Emilie, Dir., Archives

Mozart Society of America [9183]
c/o Suzanne Forsberg
865 W End Ave., Apt. 8C
New York, NY 10025-8405
Hettrick, Jane Schatkin, Secretary

MPA - The Association of Magazine Media [2802]
757 3rd Ave., 11th Fl.
New York, NY 10017
PH: (212)872-3700
Jimenez, Sandy, Dir. of Info. Svcs.

Museum of American Finance [9834]
48 Wall St.
New York, NY 10005
PH: (212)908-4110
Fax: (212)908-4601
Meyers, Chris, Dir. Ed.

Music Performance Trust Fund [9960]
1501 Broadway, Ste. 600
New York, NY 10036
PH: (212)391-3950
Fax: (212)221-2604
Beck, Dan, Trustee

Music Publishers' Association of the United States [2429]
243 5th Ave., Ste. 236
New York, NY 10016
Keiser, Lauren, VP

Musicians' Assistance Program [12371]
322 W 48th St., 6th Fl.
New York, NY 10036
PH: (212)397-4802
Shundi, Siena, Coord.

Musicians Foundation, Inc. [9961]
875 6th Ave., Ste. 2303
New York, NY 10001
PH: (212)239-9137
Fax: (212)239-9138
Vermeersch, B.C., Exec. Dir.

Musicians for Harmony [18807]
345 E 93rd St., Ste. 12B
New York, NY 10128

PH: (212)996-8010
Fax: (212)996-8010

Muslim Urban Professionals [10171]
244 Fifth Ave., Ste. N-270
New York, NY 10001
Iqbal, Naiel, President

A. J. Muste Memorial Institute [18808]
339 Lafayette St.
New York, NY 10012
PH: (212)533-4335
Fax: (212)228-6193
Boghosian, Heidi, Exec. Dir.

Myasthenia Gravis Foundation of America, Inc. [15960]
355 Lexington Ave., 15th Fl.
New York, NY 10017
Toll free: 800-541-5454
Fax: (212)370-9047
Schulhof, Sam, Chairperson

myFace [14342]
Lobby Office
333 E 30th St.
New York, NY 10016
PH: (212)263-6656
Fax: (212)263-7534
Gordon, John R., Chairman

Mystery Writers of America [10387]
1140 Broadway, Ste. 1507
New York, NY 10001
PH: (212)888-8171
Fax: (212)888-8107
Andrews, Donna, Exec. VP

NAACP Legal Defense and Educational Fund [17912]
40 Rector St., 5th Fl.
New York, NY 10006
PH: (212)965-2200
Mills, David W., Chairman

Nation Institute [18989]
116 E 16th St., 8th Fl.
New York, NY 10003
PH: (212)822-0250
Fax: (212)253-5356
Jones, David R., Chmn. of the Bd.

National Academy of Popular Music [9964]
330 W 58th St., Ste. 411
New York, NY 10019-1827
David, Hal, Chairman

National Academy of Television Arts and Sciences [468]
1697 Broadway, Ste. 404
New York, NY 10019
PH: (212)586-8424
Fax: (212)246-8129
Pillitteri, Paul, Sr. VP of Comm. & Planning

National Action Network [17913]
106 W 145th St.
New York, NY 10039-4138
PH: (212)690-3070
Toll free: 877-626-4651
Sharpton, Rev. Al, Founder, President

National Advertising Division [103]
112 Madison Ave., 3rd Fl.
New York, NY 10016
Harris, Sheryl, Mgr. of Admin.

National Advertising Review Board [104]
c/o Camille Sasena, Coordinator
112 Madison Ave., 3rd Fl.
New York, NY 10016
PH: (212)705-0115
Fax: (212)705-0134
Sasena, Camille, Coord.

National Advocates for Pregnant Women [18429]
875 6th Ave., Ste. 1807
New York, NY 10001
PH: (212)255-9252
Fax: (212)255-9253
Paltrow, Lynn M., JD, Exec. Dir.

National AIDS Treatment Advocacy Project [13555]
580 Broadway, Ste. 1010
New York, NY 10012
PH: (212)219-0106
Toll free: 888-26N-ATAP
Fax: (212)219-8473
Levin, Jules, Exec. Dir.

National Alliance for Medication Assisted Recovery [17320]
435 2nd Ave.
New York, NY 10010-3101
PH: (212)595-6262
Fax: (212)595-6262
Davis, Brenda, Treasurer

National Alliance for Musical Theatre [9965]
520 8th Ave., Ste. 301
New York, NY 10018
PH: (212)714-6668
Fax: (212)714-0469
Militello, Betsy King, Exec. Dir.

National Antique & Art Dealers Association of America, Inc. [247]
220 E 57th St.
New York, NY 10022
PH: (212)826-9707
McConnaughy, James, President

National Association for the Advancement of Psychoanalysis [16848]
80 8th Ave., Ste. 1501
New York, NY 10011-7158
PH: (212)741-0515
Fax: (212)366-4347
Quackenbush, Margery, Exec. Dir.

National Association of Commissions for Women [18220]
1732 1st Ave., No. 27315
New York, NY 10128-5177
PH: (415)492-4420
(317)232-6720
Toll free: 855-703-6229
Zamora, Cecilia, President

National Association on Drug Abuse Problems [13163]
355 Lexington Ave., 2nd Fl.
New York, NY 10017
PH: (212)986-1170
Fax: (212)697-2939
Darin, John A., CEO, President

National Association of Episcopal Schools [20112]
815 2nd Ave., 3rd Fl.
New York, NY 10017-4509
PH: (212)716-6134
Toll free: 800-334-7626
Fax: (212)286-9366
Heischman, Rev. Daniel R., Exec. Dir.

National Association for Female Executives [649]
2 Park Ave.
New York, NY 10016
Spence, Dr. Betty, President

National Association of Independent Publishers Representatives [2804]
111 E 14th St.
New York, NY 10003-4103
PH: (267)546-6561
Toll free: 888-624-7779
Rooney, Robert, Exec. Dir.

National Association for Multi-Ethnicity in Communications [773]
50 Broad St., Ste. 1801
New York, NY 10004
PH: (212)594-5985
Fax: (212)594-8391
Rice, Michelle L., Chairman

National Association for Parents of Children With Visual Impairments [17729]
c/o Susan LaVenture, Executive Director
15 W 65th St.
New York, NY 10023
Toll free: 800-562-6265
LaVenture, Susan, Exec. Dir.

National Association of Pediatric Nurse Practitioners [16153]
5 Hanover Sq., Ste. 1401
New York, NY 10004
PH: (917)746-8300
(856)857-9700
Toll free: 877-662-7627
Fax: (212)785-1713
Martin, Jean, PhD, President

National Association of Professional Women in Construction, Inc. [881]
1001 Avenue of the Americas, Ste. 405
New York, NY 10018
PH: (212)486-7745
Fax: (212)486-0228
LeMar, Chelsea, Exec. Dir.

National Association of Scholars [7964]
8 W 38th St., Ste. 503
New York, NY 10018
PH: (917)551-6770
Ricketts, Glenn, Dir. Pub. Aff.

National Association of Travel Healthcare Organizations [15156]
558 8th Ave., Ste. 1902
New York, NY 10018
PH: (646)350-4083
Kinnas, Cynthia, President

National Association of Women Artists [8930]
80 5th Ave., Ste. 1405
New York, NY 10011
PH: (212)675-1616
Stark, Sonia, Director

National Audubon Society [3903]
225 Varick St.
New York, NY 10014
Toll free: 800-274-4201
Yarnold, David, President, COO

National Basketball Association [22574]
Olympic Tower
645 5th Ave.
New York, NY 10022
PH: (212)407-8000
Fax: (212)832-3861
Stern, David J., Commissioner

National Basketball Players Association [23523]
1133 Avenue of Americas
New York, NY 10036
PH: (212)655-0880
Toll free: 800-955-6272
Fax: (212)655-0881
Roberts, Michele, Exec. Dir.

National Basketball Wives Association [12488]
555 Madison Ave., 5th Fl.
New York, NY 10022
PH: (917)472-0539
Fax: (917)472-0501
Wright, Mia, President

National Bible Association [20296]
488 Madison Ave., 24th Fl.
New York, NY 10022
PH: (212)658-0365
Fax: (212)898-1147
Fieler, Sean, Chairman

National Black Programming
  Consortium [9144]
68 E 131st St., 7th Fl.
New York, NY 10037
PH: (212)234-8200
Fields-Cruz, Leslie, Exec. Dir. (Actg.)

National Board of Review of Motion
  Pictures [9307]
40 W 37th St., Ste. 501
New York, NY 10018
PH: (212)465-9166
Fax: (212)465-9168
Schulhof, Annie, President

National Book Critics Circle [9133]
160 Varick St., 11th Fl.
New York, NY 10013
Ciabattari, Jane, VP

National Book Foundation [9134]
90 Broad St., Ste. 604
New York, NY 10004
PH: (212)685-0261
Fax: (212)213-6570
Lucas, Lisa, Exec. Dir.

National Cargo Bureau [3094]
17 Battery Pl., Ste. 1232
New York, NY 10004-1110
PH: (212)785-8300
Fax: (212)785-8333
Lennard, Mr. Ian J., President

National Center for Children in
  Poverty [11255]
215 W 125th St., 3rd Fl.
New York, NY 10027
PH: (646)284-9600
Fax: (646)284-9623
O Connell, Wanda, Coord.

The National Center for Jewish
  Healing [9641]
135 W 50th St., 6th Fl.
New York, NY 10020-1201
PH: (212)632-4500
Fax: (212)399-2475

National Center for Law and
  Economic Justice [19014]
275 7th Ave., Ste. 1506
New York, NY 10001-6660
PH: (212)633-6967
Fax: (212)633-6371
Selendy, Jennifer, Chairwoman

National Center for Learning Disabilities [12239]
32 Laight St., 2nd Fl.
New York, NY 10013-2152
Kalikow, Mary, V. Chmn. of the Bd.

National Center for the Study of Collective Bargaining in Higher Education and the Professions [5082]
425 E 25th St., No. 615
New York, NY 10010-2547
PH: (212)481-7550
Hicks, Steve, President

National Child Labor Committee
  [13465]
1501 Broadway, Ste. 1908
New York, NY 10036-5600
PH: (212)840-1801
Fax: (212)768-0963
Butler, Erik, Chmn. of the Bd.

National Coalition Against Censorship [17837]
19 Fulton St., Ste. 407
New York, NY 10038

PH: (212)807-6222
Fax: (212)807-6245
Mintcheva, Svetlana, Dir. of
  Programs

National Coalition of Anti-Violence
  Programs [19230]
116 Nassau St., 3rd Fl.
New York, NY 10038
PH: (212)714-1184
    (212)714-1141
Grasinger, Todd, Chmn. of the Bd.

National Coalition for Haitian Rights
  [19018]
275 7th Ave.
New York, NY 10001
McCalla, Jocelyn, Exec. Dir.

National Coffee Association of U.S.
  A., Inc. [429]
45 Broadway, Ste. 1140
New York, NY 10006
PH: (212)766-4007
Fax: (212)766-5815
Murray, William, CEO, President

National Committee on American
  Foreign Policy [18271]
320 Park Ave., 3rd Fl.
New York, NY 10022-6815
PH: (212)224-1120
Fax: (212)224-2524
DiCarlo, Rosemary A., President,
  CEO

National Committee on United
  States-China Relations [17849]
6 E 43rd St., 24th Fl.
New York, NY 10017-4650
PH: (212)645-9677
Fax: (212)645-1695
Hills, Carla A., Chairwoman

National Conference of Shomrim
  Societies [12228]
PO Box 598
Knickerbocker Sta.
New York, NY 10002
Wein, Lawrence, President

National Conference of Synagogue
  Youth [20269]
11 Broadway
New York, NY 10004
PH: (212)613-8233
Fax: (212)613-0793
Greenland, Micah, Director

National Council on Alcoholism and
  Drug Dependence, Inc. [13168]
217 Broadway, Ste. 712
New York, NY 10007
PH: (212)269-7797
Bensinger, Roger, Secretary

National Council of Churches U.S.A.
  - Communication Commission
  [19768]
475 Riverside Dr., Rm. 852
New York, NY 10115

National Council of Jewish Women
  [20270]
475 Riverside Dr., Ste. 1901
New York, NY 10115
PH: (212)645-4048
Fax: (212)645-7466
Frank, Robin, Mgr.

National Council of Women of the
  United States [19256]
777 United Nations Plz.
New York, NY 10017
PH: (212)697-1278
Browne, Saideh, President, CEO

National Council on Women's Health
  [17761]
1300 York Ave.
New York, NY 10021
Devi, Gayatri, MD, President

National Dance Institute [7706]
217 W 147th St.
New York, NY 10039-3427
PH: (212)226-0083
Fax: (212)226-0761
Landau, Kathy, Exec. Dir.

National Development Council
  [18155]
24 Whitehall St., Ste. 710
New York, NY 10004
PH: (212)682-1106
    (859)578-4850
Fax: (212)573-6118
Davenport, Robert W., President

National Down Syndrome Society
  [15816]
666 Broadway, 8th Fl.
New York, NY 10012
Toll free: 800-221-4602
Gerhardt, Charles H., III, Bd.
  Member

National Eating Disorders Associa-
  tion [14648]
165 W 46th St., Ste. 402
New York, NY 10036
PH: (212)575-6200
Toll free: 800-931-2237
Fax: (212)575-1650
Renner, Judy, Dir. of HR

National Economic and Social Rights
  Initiative [18431]
90 John St., Ste. 308
New York, NY 10038
PH: (212)253-1710
Fax: (212)385-6124
Albisa, Catherine, Exec. Dir.

National Emphysema/COPD As-
  sociation [17144]
850 Amsterdam Ave., Ste. 9A
New York, NY 10025
PH: (212)666-2210
Fax: (212)666-0642
Rogers, Barbara, President, CEO

National Employment Law Project
  [11774]
75 Maiden Ln., Ste. 601
New York, NY 10038
PH: (212)285-3025
Fax: (212)285-3044
Owens, Christine L., Exec. Dir.

National Ethnic Coalition of
  Organizations [19430]
16 W 36th St., Ste. 801
New York, NY 10018
PH: (212)755-1492
Fax: (212)755-3762
Kazeminy, Nasser J., Chairman,
  CEO

National Father's Day/Mother's Day
  Council [19149]
37 W 39th St., Ste. 1102
New York, NY 10018-0580
PH: (212)594-5977
    (212)594-6421
Fax: (212)594-9349
Rivers, Mr. C. Joseph, Bd. Member

National Federation of Community
  Development Credit Unions [958]
39 Broadway, Ste. 2140
New York, NY 10006-3063
PH: (212)809-1850
Toll free: 800-437-8711
Fax: (212)809-3274
Chan, Michael A., Director

National Football League [22861]
345 Park Ave.
New York, NY 10017
PH: (212)450-2000
Goodell, Roger, Commissioner

National Guild for Community Arts
  Education [7518]
520 8th Ave., Ste. 302
New York, NY 10018
PH: (212)268-3337
Fax: (212)268-3995
Herman, Jonathan, Exec. Dir.

National Hemophilia Foundation
  [15241]
116 W 32nd St., 11th Fl.
New York, NY 10001
PH: (212)328-3700
Fax: (212)328-3777
Bias, Val, CEO

National Hispanic Business Group
  [654]
45 W 21st St., Ste. 6D
New York, NY 10010
PH: (212)265-2664
Fax: (212)265-2675
Linares, Jesus, Chairman

National Kidney Foundation [15882]
30 E 33rd St.
New York, NY 10016-5337
Toll free: 800-622-9010
Fax: (212)689-9261
Bernstein, Jeffrey, President

National Latina Institute for
  Reproductive Health [17111]
50 Broad St., Ste. 1937
New York, NY 10004
PH: (212)422-2553
Fax: (212)422-2556
González-Rojas, Jessica, Exec. Dir.

National Lawyers Guild [5042]
132 Nassau St., Rm. 922
New York, NY 10038
PH: (212)679-5100
Fax: (212)679-2811
White, Claire, VP

National LGBT Cancer Network
  [14029]
136 W 16th St., No. 1E
New York, NY 10011
PH: (212)675-2633
Margolies, Liz, Founder, Exec. Dir.

National Mah Jongg League [22054]
250 W 57th St.
New York, NY 10107-0001
PH: (212)246-3052
Fax: (212)246-4117

National Medical Fellowships [8333]
347 5th Ave., Rm. 510
New York, NY 10016-5007
PH: (212)483-8880
Fax: (212)483-8897
Dyer, Dr. Esther R., CEO, President

National Minority Business Council
  [2395]
100 Church St., Ste. 800
New York, NY 10007
PH: (347)289-7620
    (212)245-2652
Robinson, John F., CEO, President,
  Publisher

National Minority Supplier Develop-
  ment Council [2396]
1359 Broadway, 10th Fl., Ste. 1000
New York, NY 10018
PH: (212)944-2430
Seaberry, Nettie, Director

National Mobilization Against
  Sweatshops [18612]
Lower E Side Ctr.
345 Grand St.
New York, NY 10003
PH: (212)358-0295
Fax: (212)358-0297

National Multicultural Greek Council,
Inc. **[23760]**
PO Box 250430
New York, NY 10025
Rencher, Jen, President

National Multiple Sclerosis Society
[15968]
733 3rd Ave., 3rd Fl.
New York, NY 10017
PH: (212)463-7787
Toll free: 800-344-4867
Fax: (212)986-7981
Zagieboylo, Cyndi, President, CEO

National Music Theater Network
[10262]
36 W 44th St.
New York, NY 10019
PH: (212)664-0979
Fax: (212)664-0978
Markley, Dan, President, Exec. Dir.

National Orchestral Association
[9977]
PO Box 7016
New York, NY 10150-7016
PH: (212)208-4691
Fax: (212)208-4691
Trachtenberg, Matthew J., Chair-
man, CEO, President

National Organization on Disability
[11629]
77 Water St., Ste. 204
New York, NY 10005
PH: (646)505-1191
Fax: (646)505-1184
Glazer, Carol, President

National Organization of Italian-
American Women **[19507]**
25 W 43rd St. Ste. 1005
New York, NY 10036-7406
PH: (212)642-2003
Fax: (212)642-2006
Sirey, Aileen Riotto, PhD,
Chairperson, Founder

National Organization of Legal
Services Workers **[23436]**
256 W 38th St., Ste. 705
New York, NY 10018
PH: (212)228-0992
Fax: (212)228-0097
Deane, Gordon, President

National Police Accountability Project
[5507]
499 7th Avenue 12N
New York, NY 10018-7058
PH: (212)630-9939
Fax: (212)659-0695
Keller, Brigitt, Esq., Exec. Dir.

National Psychological Association
for Psychoanalysis **[16849]**
40 W 13th St.
New York, NY 10011
PH: (212)924-7440
Fax: (212)989-7543
Werden, Jeffrey, President

National Queer Asian Pacific
Islander Alliance **[12954]**
233 5th Ave., Ste. 4A
New York, NY 10016
PH: (917)439-3158
Magpantay, Glenn D., Exec. Dir.

National Ramah Commission **[8143]**
3080 Broadway
New York, NY 10027
PH: (212)678-8881
Fax: (845)358-6284
Cohen, Rabbi Mitchell, Director

National Schools Committee for
Economic Education **[7733]**
250 E 73rd St., Apt. 12G
New York, NY 10021-4310

PH: (212)535-9534
Fax: (212)535-4167
Donnelly, John E., Exec. Dir.

National Sculpture Society **[10210]**
75 Varick St., 11th Fl.
New York, NY 10013
PH: (212)764-5645
Fax: (212)764-5651
Pier, Gwen, Exec. Dir.

National Society of Mural Painters
[8933]
450 W 31st St., 7th Fl.
New York, NY 10001
PH: (212)244-2800
Greene, Jeff, President

National Stigma Clearinghouse
[15800]
245 8th Ave., No. 213
New York, NY 10011
PH: (212)255-4411
Arnold, Jean, Contact

National Stuttering Association
[17247]
119 W 40th St., 14th Fl.
New York, NY 10018
PH: (212)944-4050
Toll free: 800-937-8888
Fax: (212)944-8244
Maguire, Gerald, MD, Chmn. of the
Bd.

National Traditionalist Caucus
[18028]
PO Box 971
New York, NY 10116
PH: (212)685-4689
Rosenberg, Donald P., Founder

National Urban Fellows **[19218]**
1120 Avenue of the Americas, 4th Fl.
New York, NY 10036
PH: (212)730-1700
Fax: (212)730-1823
Garcia, Miguel A., Jr., President,
CEO

National Urban League **[17922]**
120 Wall St.
New York, NY 10005
PH: (212)558-5300
Fax: (212)344-5332
Morial, Marc H., President, CEO

National Urban Squash and Educa-
tion Association **[23273]**
555 8th Ave., Ste. 1102
New York, NY 10018-4311
PH: (646)218-0456
Wyant, Tim, Exec. Dir.

National Urban Technology Center
[7287]
80 Maiden Ln., Ste. 606
New York, NY 10038
PH: (212)528-7350
Bransford, Patricia, Founder,
President

National Writers Union **[23541]**
256 W 38th St., Ste. 703
New York, NY 10018
PH: (212)254-0279
Fax: (212)254-0673
Goldbetter, Larry, President

Native American Art Studies Association **[7504]**
c/o Kathleen Ash-Milby, President
NMAI-George Gustav Heye Ctr.
1 Bowling Green
New York, NY 10004
Morris, Kate, President

Natural Color Diamond Association
[2060]
22 W 48th St., 4th Fl.
New York, NY 10036

PH: (212)644-9747
Fax: (212)840-0607
Fine, Jordan, President

Natural Resources Defense Council
[4496]
40 W 20th St.
New York, NY 10011
PH: (212)727-2700
Fax: (212)727-1773
Tishman, Daniel R., Chairman

Neighborhood Cats **[3630]**
2576 Broadway, No. 555
New York, NY 10025
PH: (212)662-5761
Richmond, Susan, Exec. Dir.

Netherlands Board of Tourism and
Conventions **[23653]**
Netherlands Board of Tourism and
Conventions
215 Park Ave. S
New York, NY 10003
Van Tiggelen, Conrad, Dir. of Mktg.

Netherlands Chamber of Commerce
in the United States **[23606]**
267 5th Ave., Ste. 910
New York, NY 10016-7503
PH: (212)265-6460

Nets for Life Africa **[13077]**
Episcopal Relief and Development
815 2nd Ave.
New York, NY 10017
Toll free: 855-312-4325
Walsh, Shaun, Director

Network 20/20, Inc. **[18632]**
850 7th Ave., Ste. 1101
New York, NY 10019
PH: (212)582-1870
Fax: (212)586-3291
Kunstadter, Geraldine S., Chairman

Network Against Coercive Psychiatry
[12311]
172 W 79th St., No. 2E
New York, NY 10024
PH: (212)560-7288

Network of Conservation Educators
and Practitioners **[3917]**
Ctr. for Biodiversity and Conserva-
tion
American Museum of Natural History
79th St., Central Pk. W
New York, NY 10024
PH: (212)769-5742
Fax: (212)769-5292

Network for Teaching Entrepreneurship **[7565]**
120 Wall St., 18th Fl.
New York, NY 10005
Mariotti, Steve, Founder

The Neuropathy Association, Inc.
[16031]
60 E 42nd St., Ste. 942
New York, NY 10165
PH: (212)692-0662
Fax: (212)692-0668
Gardner, James R., PhD, Chairman

New Art Dealers Alliance **[8877]**
55-59 Chrystie St., Ste. 410
New York, NY 10002
PH: (212)594-0883
Fax: (212)594-0884
Hubbs, Heather, Director

New Democratic Dimensions
[18116]
152 Madison Ave., Ste. 804
New York, NY 10016-5424
PH: (212)481-7251
Fax: (212)481-9015
Acosta, Thomas, Chairman

New Dramatists **[10266]**
424 W 44th St.
New York, NY 10036
PH: (212)757-6960
Fax: (646)390-8705
Ruark, Joel K., Exec. Dir.

New Israel Fund **[18587]**
6 E 39th St., Ste. 301
New York, NY 10016-0112
PH: (212)613-4400
Fax: (212)714-2153
Chazan, Naomi, Director

New Leaders **[8201]**
30 W 26th St.
New York, NY 10010-2011
PH: (646)792-1070
Schnur, Jonathan, Founder

New Music USA **[9982]**
90 Broad St. Ste. 1902
New York, NY 10004
PH: (212)645-6949
Fax: (646)490-0998
Harsh, Ed, CEO, President

New Wilderness Foundation **[9984]**
307 7th Ave., Ste. 1402
New York, NY 10001
PH: (646)912-7990
Chadabe, Joel, President

New York Center for Independent
Publishing **[2806]**
20 W 44th St.
New York, NY 10036
PH: (212)764-7021

New York Live Arts **[8992]**
219 W 19th St.
New York, NY 10011
PH: (212)691-6500
Fax: (212)633-1974
Davidson, Jean, CEO

New York Stock Exchange Inc.
[3048]
11 Wall St.
New York, NY 10005-1905
PH: (212)656-3000
Davis, Bruce, Assistant Vice
President

New York University School of Law I
Brennan Center for Justice **[5680]**
161 Avenue of the Americas, 12th
Fl.
New York, NY 10013
PH: (646)292-8310
Fax: (212)463-7308
Waldman, Michael, President

New York Women in Communica-
tions Foundation **[774]**
355 Lexington Ave., 15th Fl.
New York, NY 10017-6603
PH: (212)297-2133
Fax: (212)370-9047
Ungaro, Maria, Exec. Dir.

NEXCO **[1990]**
PO Box 3949
New York, NY 10163
Toll free: 877-291-4901
Fax: (646)349-9628

Next Generation Nepal **[11098]**
527 3rd Ave., Ste. 196
New York, NY 10016
PH: (646)820-0696
Howe, Anne, Exec. Dir.

NGO Committee on Disarmament,
Peace and Security **[18130]**
The Church Ctr., 7th Fl.
777 United Nations Pl.
New York, NY 10017

PH: (212)986-5165
Kamiya, Masamichi, Treasurer

Nigerian Lawyers Association [5046]
305 Broadway, 14th Fl.
New York, NY 10007-1134
PH: (212)323-7408
Fax: (212)323-7409
Sea, Nexus U., President

Nine Lives Associates [3065]
c/o Executive Protection Institute
16 Penn Pl., Ste. 1570
New York, NY 10001
Heying, Dr. Jerry, Exec. Dir.

Nippon Club [19512]
145 W 57th St.
New York, NY 10019-2220
PH: (212)581-2223
Fax: (212)581-3332
Takahashi, Motomu, President, CEO

No Peace Without Justice [18809]
866 Union Plz., No. 408
New York, NY 10017
PH: (212)980-2558
Fax: (212)980-1072
Bonino, Emma, Founder

Nocturnal Adoration Society [19892]
184 E 76th St.
New York, NY 10021
PH: (212)266-5679
Reynell, John, Contact

Norcross Wildlife Foundation [4853]
PO Box 611
New York, NY 10024
PH: (212)362-4831
Fax: (212)362-4783
Outlaw, Karen, Exec. Dir.

NORMAL In Schools [14649]
339 E 19th St., Ste. 2B
New York, NY 10003
PH: (917)771-4977
Farrell, Robyn Hussa, MFA,
Founder, CEO

Norman Foundation, Inc. [12985]
147 E 48th St.
New York, NY 10017
PH: (212)230-9830
Fax: (212)230-9849
Lassalle, Honor, President

North American Association of
Synagogue Executives [20565]
Rapaport House
120 Broadway, No. 1540
New York, NY 10271
PH: (631)732-9461
Fax: (631)732-9461
Rothenberg, David, Secretary

North American-Chilean Chamber of
Commerce [23609]
866 United Nations Plz., Rm. 4019
New York, NY 10017
PH: (212)317-1959
Fax: (212)758-8598
Stephens, Oscar, VP

North American Conference on
Ethiopian Jewry [18593]
255 W 36th St., Rm. 701
New York, NY 10018
PH: (212)233-5200
Gordon, Barbara Ribakove, Exec.
Dir., Founder

North American Congress on Latin
America [17797]
c/o NYU CLACS
53 Washington Sq. S, Fl. 4W
New York, NY 10012
PH: (646)535-9085
    (646)613-1440
Rockefeller, Stuart, Director

North American Federation of
Temple Youth [19521]
c/o Union for Reform Judaism
633 3rd Ave., 7th Fl.
New York, NY 10017
PH: (212)650-4070
Fax: (212)650-4064
Cronig, Jeremy, President

North American Natural Casing As-
sociation [1365]
494 8th Ave., Ste. 805
New York, NY 10001
PH: (212)695-4980
Fax: (212)695-7153
Negron, Barbara, President

North American Performing Arts
Managers and Agents [164]
459 Columbus Ave., No. 133
New York, NY 10024
PH: (212)769-1000
Ross, Jerry, VP

North American Sartre Society
[10108]
150 Broadway, Ste. 812
New York, NY 10038

North Star Fund [12405]
520 8th Ave., Ste. 1800
New York, NY 10018-6656
PH: (212)620-9110
Fax: (212)620-8178
Atre, Nisha, Chairwoman

Norwegian-American Chamber of
Commerce [23610]
655 3rd Ave., Ste. 1810
New York, NY 10017
PH: (212)885-9737
Landi, Giacomo, Exec. VP

Not On Our Watch [18433]
162 5th Ave., 8th Fl.
New York, NY 10010
Cheadle, Don, Founder

NYPD Shomrim Society [12229]
c/o Murray Ellman, Financial
Secretary
PO Box 598
New York, NY 10002
Podber, Michael, President

Office and Professional Employees
International Union [77]
80 8th Ave., 20th Fl.
New York, NY 10011
PH: (212)367-0902
Toll free: 800-346-7348
Mahoney, Mary, Secretary, Treasurer

Ohr Torah Institutions of Israel
[8133]
49 W 45th St., Ste. 701
New York, NY 10036
PH: (212)935-8672
Fax: (212)935-8683
Riskin, Rabbi Shlomo, Chancellor

OnBehalf.org [13247]
223 E 88th St., No. 3A
New York, NY 10128
Gifford, Mike, Founder, Exec. Dir.

One to World [8087]
285 W Broadway, Ste. 450
New York, NY 10013
PH: (212)431-1195
Fax: (212)941-6291
Clifford, Deborah L., Exec. Dir.

Open Society Foundations [18526]
224 W 57th St.
New York, NY 10019-3212
PH: (212)548-0600
Fax: (212)548-4600
Grabbe, Heather, Director

Open Space Institute [4093]
1350 Broadway, Ste. 201
New York, NY 10018-7799
PH: (212)290-8200
Adams, John H., Chairman

OpenPlans [6283]
148 Lafayette St., 12th Fl.
New York, NY 10013
PH: (917)388-9033
Fax: (646)390-2624
Gorton, Mark, President, Founder

OPERA America [9989]
330 7th Ave.
New York, NY 10001-5010
PH: (212)796-8620
Fax: (212)796-8621
Scorca, Marc A., CEO, President

Opera Foundation [9990]
712 5th Ave., 32nd Fl.
New York, NY 10019
PH: (212)664-8843
Koepp, Bernhard, President

Operation Crossroads Africa [17778]
PO Box 5570
New York, NY 10027
PH: (212)289-1949
Fax: (212)289-2526
Logan, Willis, Coord.

Operation Respect [7905]
199 New Rd., Ste. 61, No. 397
New York, NY 10121
PH: (866)546-9291
Weiss, Mark, Dir. Ed.

ORBIS International [16403]
520 8th Ave., 11th Fl.
New York, NY 10018
Toll free: 800-ORBIS-US
Fax: (646)674-5599
McAllister, Kevin G., Chairman

Order of Lafayette [21208]
243 W 70th St., Apt. 6f
New York, NY 10023
PH: (212)873-9162
Laue, Bruce A., President

Order of Saint Andrew the Apostle
[20195]
8 E 79th St.
New York, NY 10075-0192
PH: (212)570-3550
Fax: (212)774-0214
Limberakis, Anthony J., MD, Cmdr.

Organization for Advancement of
Afghan Women [10470]
PO Box 946
New York, NY 10024
PH: (212)998-8994
Homayun, Dr. Tahira, President

Origami USA [22292]
15 W 77th St.
New York, NY 10024-5192
PH: (212)769-5635
Fax: (212)769-5668
Zeichner, Wendy, President, CEO

Orphans' Futures Alliance [11731]
244 5th Ave., Ste. 2247
New York, NY 10001
PH: (212)726-2247
Hoang, Chau, Founder, CEO, Direc-
tor

Orphans International Worldwide,
Inc. [11258]
55 Exchange Pl., 4th Fl.
New York, NY 10005
Luce, Jim, President, Founder

ORT America [12230]
75 Maiden Ln., 10th Fl.
New York, NY 10038

PH: (212)505-7700
Toll free: 800-519-2678
Fax: (212)674-3057
Dreifuss, Shelly, VP

Orthodox Union [20274]
11 Broadway
New York, NY 10004
PH: (212)563-4000
Tzvi Friedman, Howard, Chairman

Our Time [17303]
330 W 42nd St., 12th Fl.
New York, NY 10036
PH: (212)414-9696
Alexander, Taro, Founder

OutRight Action International [11904]
80 Maiden Ln., Ste. 1505
New York, NY 10038
PH: (212)430-6054
Fax: (212)430-6060
Gómez, María Mercedes, Coord.

Overseas Press Club of America
[2715]
40 W 45th St.
New York, NY 10036
Kranz, Patrica, Exec. Dir.

Overseas Press Club Foundation
[8159]
40 W 45 St.
New York, NY 10036
PH: (201)493-9087
Fax: (201)612-9915
Reilly, Jane, Exec. Dir.

Oxalosis and Hyperoxaluria Founda-
tion [15885]
201 E 19th St., Ste. 12E
New York, NY 10003
PH: (212)777-0470
Toll free: 800-OHF-8699
Hollander, Kim, Exec. Dir.

PanAmerican Society for Pigment
Cell Research [15654]
c/o Prashiela Manga, PhD,
Secretary and Treasurer
Ronald O. Perelman Department of
Dermatology
NYU Langone Medical Ctr., Smilow
401
522 First Ave.
New York, NY 10016
PH: (212)263-9086
Fax: (212)263-5819
Le Poole, Caroline, President

Panthera [4868]
8 W 40th St., 18th Fl.
New York, NY 10018-2218
PH: (646)786-0400
Fax: (646)786-0401
Kaplan, Thomas S., PhD, Chairman,
Founder

Parapsychology Foundation [6990]
PO Box 1562
New York, NY 10021-0043
PH: (212)628-1550
Fax: (212)628-1559
Coly, Lisette, VP, Exec. Dir.

Parkinson's Disease Foundation
[15984]
1359 Broadway, Ste. 1509
New York, NY 10018
PH: (212)923-4700
Fax: (212)923-4778
Holt, Valerie, Exec. Asst.

Parliamentarians for Global Action
[18131]
132 Nassau St., Ste. 1419
New York, NY 10038
PH: (212)687-7755
Fax: (212)687-8409
Robertson, Mr. H. V. Ross, President

Partners for Progressive Israel **[18813]**
424 W 33rd St., Ste. 150
New York, NY 10001
PH: (212)242-4500
Fax: (212)242-5718
Shapiro, Harold M., President

Partnership for Drug-Free Kids **[13172]**
352 Park Ave. S, 9th Fl.
New York, NY 10010
PH: (212)922-1560
Toll free: 855-378-4373
Fax: (212)922-1570
Castiello, Andrea, Coord.

Passionists International **[19894]**
246 East 46th St. No. 1F
New York, NY 10017

Pastel Society of America **[8880]**
15 Gramercy Pk. S
New York, NY 10003
PH: (212)533-6931
Fax: (212)353-8140
Wright, Jimmy, President

Path2Parenthood **[14762]**
315 Madison Ave., Ste. 901
New York, NY 10017
Toll free: 888-917-3777
Hribek, Donald, Chmn. of the Bd.

PCI-Media Impact **[12511]**
777 United Nations Plz., 5th Fl.
New York, NY 10017
PH: (212)687-3366
Fax: (212)661-4188
Southey, Sean, CEO

Peace Boat US **[8407]**
777 United Nations Plz., Ste. 3E
New York, NY 10017
PH: (212)687-7214
Armstrong-Yoshioka, Rachel,
President

PEF Israel Endowment Funds Inc.
[12211]
630 3rd Ave., 15th Fl.
New York, NY 10017
PH: (212)599-1260
Fax: (212)599-5981
Stern, Geoffrey, President

PEN American **[10391]**
588 Broadway, Rm. 303
New York, NY 10012-5258
PH: (212)334-1660
Fax: (212)334-2181
Aiello, Antonio, Director

Pen and Brush **[8937]**
29 E 22nd St.
New York, NY 10010
PH: (212)475-3669
Sands, Janice, Exec. Dir.

People's Movement for Human
Rights Learning **[18435]**
526 W 111th St., Ste. 4E
New York, NY 10025
PH: (212)749-3156
Fax: (212)666-6325
Kesten, Robert, Exec. Dir.

People's Rights Fund **[17925]**
147 W 24th St., 2nd Fl.
New York, NY 10011
PH: (212)633-6646

Perhaps Kids Meeting Kids Can
Make a Difference **[18555]**
380 Riverside Dr.
New York, NY 10025-1858
PH: (212)662-2327
Sochet, Mary, Chairperson

Periodic Paralysis Association
[15666]
c/o Jacob Levitt, MD, FAAD,
President/Medical Director
Periodic Paralysis Association
155 W 68th St., Ste. 1732
New York, NY 10023
PH: (407)339-9499
Levitt, Jacob, MD, President, Medi-
cal Dir., Bd. Member

Periodical and Book Association of
America **[2809]**
481 8th Ave., Ste. 526
New York, NY 10001
PH: (212)563-6502
Fax: (212)563-4098
Michalopoulos, William, Chmn. of
the Bd.

PET Resin Association **[2627]**
355 Lexington Ave., Ste. 1500
New York, NY 10017
PH: (212)297-2108
Fax: (212)370-9047
Vasami, Ralph, Esq., Exec. Dir.

Philatelic Foundation **[22353]**
341 W 38th St., 5th Fl.
New York, NY 10018-9692
PH: (212)221-6555
Fax: (212)221-6208
Walske, Steven C., Author

Philolexian Society **[9764]**
Columbia University
116th St. & Broadway
New York, NY 10027

Phoenix House **[13173]**
164 W 74th St., 4th Fl.
New York, NY 10023-2301
PH: (646)505-2080
Toll free: 888-671-9392
Fax: (212)595-6365
Bray, Ann, President, CEO

Physicians for Human Rights
[18436]
256 W 38th St., 9th Fl.
New York, NY 10018
PH: (646)564-3720
Fax: (646)564-3750
McKay, Donna, Exec. Dir.

Physicians for Reproductive Health
[17116]
55 W 39th St., Ste. 1001
New York, NY 10018-3889
PH: (646)366-1890
Fax: (646)366-1897
Magee, Jodi, President, CEO

Physicians' Research Network
[16761]
39 W 19th St., Ste. 605
New York, NY 10011
PH: (212)924-0857
Fax: (212)924-0759
Vladich, Edward, Office Mgr.

Picture the Homeless **[11959]**
104 E 126th St.
New York, NY 10468
PH: (646)314-6423
Lewis, Lynn, Exec. Dir.

Pipe Fabrication Institute **[2611]**
511 Avenue of the Americas, No.
601
New York, NY 10011-8436
PH: (514)634-3434
Fax: (514)634-9736
Cottington, Robert B.

Pirandello Society of America **[9089]**
c/o Casa Italiana Zerilli-Marimo
24 W 12th St.

New York, NY 10011
D'Aponte, Mimi Gisolfi, President

Planned Parenthood Federation of
America **[11847]**
New York, NY
PH: (212)541-7800
Fax: (212)245-1845
Richards, Cecile, President

The Players **[10269]**
16 Gramercy Park S
New York, NY 10003
PH: (212)475-6116
Collins, Michael, Secretary

Poetry Project **[10157]**
St. Marks Church
131 E 10th St.
New York, NY 10003
PH: (212)674-0910
Szymaszek, Stacy, Director

Poetry Society of America **[10158]**
15 Gramercy Park
New York, NY 10003
PH: (212)254-9628
Fax: (212)673-2352
Hahn, Kimiko, President

Poets and Writers **[10159]**
90 Broad St., Ste. 2100
New York, NY 10004
PH: (212)226-3586
Fax: (212)226-3963
Figman, Elliot, Exec. Dir.

Polish Assistance **[19607]**
15 E 65th St.
New York, NY 10065
PH: (212)570-5560
Fax: (212)570-5561
Palade, Jadwiga, Exec. Ofc.

Polish Institute of Arts and Sciences
of America **[10167]**
208 E 30th St.
New York, NY 10016
PH: (212)686-4164
Fax: (212)545-1130
Baron, Krystyna, Librarian

Pollock-Krasner Foundation **[8938]**
863 Park Ave.
New York, NY 10075-0342
PH: (212)517-5400
Fax: (212)288-2836
Sachs, Samuel, II, President

Pontifical Mission for Palestine
[12596]
c/o Catholic Church of the Holy Land
1011 1st Ave.
New York, NY 10022-4195
PH: (212)826-1480
Fax: (212)838-1344
Kozar, John E., President

Pontifical Mission Societies in the
United States **[19897]**
70 W 36th St., 8th Fl.
New York, NY 10018
PH: (212)563-8700
Fax: (212)563-8725
Small, Rev. Andrew, OMI, Director

Population Council **[12515]**
1 Dag Hammarskjold Plz.
New York, NY 10017
PH: (212)339-0500
Toll free: 877-339-0500
Fax: (212)755-6052
Walker, Mark A., Chmn. of the Bd.

Possible **[15488]**
30 Broad St., 9th Fl.
New York, NY 10004
Arnoldy, Mark, CEO

Postgraduate Center for Mental
Health **[16987]**
Westside Rehabilitation Ctr.
344 W 36th St.
New York, NY 10018-1843
PH: (212)889-5500
Barak, Dr. Jacob, MBA, CEO,
President

PowerMyLearning **[7659]**
520 8th Ave., 10th Fl.
New York, NY 10018
PH: (212)563-7300
Fax: (212)563-1215
Stock, Elisabeth, CEO, Founder

PR Council **[2756]**
32 E 31st St., 9th Fl.
New York, NY 10016
PH: (646)588-0139
Fax: (646)651-4770
Cripps, Kathy, President

Practising Law Institute **[8224]**
1177 Avenue of the Americas, 2nd
Fl.
New York, NY 10036
PH: (212)824-5700
Toll free: 800-260-4754
Geller, Sandra R., Exec. VP

Pregones Theater Puerto Rican
Traveling Theater **[10270]**
304 W 47th St.
New York, NY 10036
PH: (212)354-1293
Colon Valle, Miriam, Director

Preservation Volunteers **[9429]**
1995 Broadway, Ste. 605
New York, NY 10023
PH: (212)769-2900
Guerrieri, Dexter, President, Founder

Private Art Dealers Association **[248]**
Lenox Hill Sta.
New York, NY 10021
PH: (917)302-3087
Simon, Robert, President

Private Label Manufacturers As-
sociation **[2298]**
630 3rd Ave.
New York, NY 10017
PH: (212)972-3131
Fax: (212)983-1382

Pro-Choice Public Education Project
[10433]
PO Box 3952
New York, NY 10163
PH: (212)977-4266
Wagoner, James, Director

Pro Mujer **[13394]**
253 W 35th St., 11th Fl.
New York, NY 10001
PH: (646)626-7000
Fax: (212)904-1038
Landis, Gail, Chairman

Professional Association of Social
Workers in HIV and AIDS **[13558]**
1000 10th Ave., Ste. 2T
New York, NY 10019
PH: (212)523-6683
Rice, Alan, President

Professional Organization for
Women in the Arts **[8998]**
New York, NY
Kay, Sara, Founder

Professional Women Photographers
[2593]
119 W 72nd St., No. 223
New York, NY 10023
Shaw, Beth Portnoi, President

Project for Public Spaces **[17993]**
419 Lafayette, 7th Fl.
New York, NY 10003
PH: (212)620-5660
Fax: (212)620-3821
Johnson, Minnie Fells, Chairwoman

Project Renewal **[13177]**
200 Varick St. 9th Fl.
New York, NY 10014
PH: (212)620-0340
Netburn, Mitchell, President, CEO

Project Sunshine **[11135]**
211 E 43rd St., Ste. 401
New York, NY 10017
PH: (212)354-8035
Fax: (212)354-8052
Kernan, Beatrice, Exec. Dir.

Prospect Hill Foundation **[10822]**
99 Park Ave., Ste. 2220
New York, NY 10016-1601
PH: (212)370-1165
Fax: (212)599-6282
Fujiko Willgerodt, Penny, Exec. Dir.

Public Agenda **[19002]**
6 E 39th St., 9th Fl.
New York, NY 10016-0112
PH: (212)686-6610
Fax: (212)889-3461
Yankelovich, Daniel, Chairman,
Founder

Public Art Fund **[17994]**
1 E 53rd St.
New York, NY 10022
PH: (212)223-7800
Fax: (212)223-7801
Kraus, Jill, Chairman

Public Patent Foundation **[5676]**
55 5th Ave.
New York, NY 10003
PH: (212)545-5337
Fax: (212)591-6038
Ravicher, Daniel B., President, Exec.
Dir.

Public Relations Society of America
[2757]
33 Maiden Ln., 11th Fl.
New York, NY 10038-5150
PH: (212)460-1400
Dvorak, Jane, APR, Officer

Public Relations Student Society of
America **[8473]**
33 Maiden Ln., 11th Fl.
New York, NY 10038-5150
PH: (212)460-1474
Fax: (212)995-0757
Daronatsy, Laura, President

Publishers Information Bureau **[117]**
c/o John Ciotoli, Director
Kantar Media
11 Madison Ave., 12th Fl.
New York, NY 10010
Telliho, Nancy, President

Puerto Rican Family Institute, Inc.
[11946]
145 W 15th St.
New York, NY 10011
PH: (212)924-6320
Fax: (212)691-5635
O'Toole, Milagros Baez, Contact

Puerto Rican Studies Association
[19621]
Dept. of Africana, Puerto Rican/
Latino Studies
Hunter College, City University of
New York
695 Park Ave., HW 1711
New York, NY 10065

PH: (860)486-9052
Fax: (860)486-3794
Venator-Santiago, Charles, Mem.

Queen Sofia Spanish Institute
[10220]
684 Park Ave.
New York, NY 10065
PH: (212)628-0420
Fax: (212)734-4177
de Habsburgo-Lorena, Immaculada,
President, CEO

Rabbinical Assembly **[20275]**
3080 Broadway
New York, NY 10027
PH: (212)280-6000
Fax: (212)749-9166
Schonfeld, Rabbi Julie, Exec. VP

Rabbinical Council of America
[20276]
305 7th Ave., 12th Fl.
New York, NY 10001
PH: (212)807-9000
(212)741-7522
Fax: (212)727-8452
Baum, Rabbi Shalom, President

Racial Justice 911 **[17927]**
c/o CAAAV: Organizing Asian Communities
55 Hester St.
New York, NY 10002
PH: (718)473-6485
Dang, Cathy, Exec. Dir.

Rainforest Alliance **[4497]**
233 Broadway, 28th Fl.
New York, NY 10279
PH: (212)677-1900
Fax: (212)677-2187
Katz, Daniel R., Chmn. of the Bd.

Ramakrishna - Vivekananda Center
of New York **[20634]**
17 E 94th St.
New York, NY 10128-0611
PH: (212)534-9445
Fax: (212)828-1618
Yuktatmananda, Swami, Min.,
Founder

Re:Gender **[18234]**
11 Hanover Sq.
New York, NY 10005-2843
PH: (212)785-7335
Thomas, Gloria, Secretary

Reach Grenada **[11138]**
575 Madison Ave., 10th Fl.
New York, NY 10022
PH: (212)605-0281
Lawson, Karen, PhD, Founder

Reach the World **[7915]**
222 Broadway, 21st Fl.
New York, NY 10007
PH: (212)288-6987
Toll free: 866-411-5090
Halstead, Heather, Exec. Dir.

Reaching Critical Will **[18134]**
c/o Women's International League
for Peace and Freedom
777 UN Plz., 6th Fl.
New York, NY 10017
PH: (212)682-1265
Acheson, Ray, Director

Reading Hamlets **[12248]**
PO Box 575
New York, NY 10116
PH: (347)856-8357
Ude, Christina, Founder

Ready Hands International **[11140]**
PO Box 925
New York, NY 10274
Toll free: 877-732-3942
Osei-Boateng, Marian, MPA, Exec.
Dir.

RedLight Children **[10798]**
75 Rockefeller Plz., 17th Fl.
New York, NY 10019-6927
Jacobson, Guy, Exec. Dir., Founder

Reform Jewish Appeal **[20278]**
Union for Reform Judaism
633 3rd Ave.
New York, NY 10017-6778
PH: (212)650-4000

Rehabilitation International **[17098]**
866 United Nations Plz., Office 422
New York, NY 10017
PH: (212)420-1500
Fax: (212)505-0871
Ilagan, Ms. Venus, Sec. Gen.

Religion Communicators Council
[20032]
475 Riverside Dr., Rm. 1505
New York, NY 10115
PH: (212)870-2402
Rollins, James, President

Religions for Peace International
[18825]
777 United Nations Plz., 9th Fl.
New York, NY 10017
PH: (212)687-2163
Vendley, Dr. William F., Sec. Gen.

Renaissance Society of America
[10196]
CUNY Graduate Ctr.
365 5th Ave., Rm. 5400
New York, NY 10016-4309
PH: (212)817-2130
Fax: (212)817-1544
Terpstra, Nicholas, Editor

Reprieve-U.S. **[12058]**
PO Box 3627
New York, NY 10163
PH: (917)885-8064

Reproductive Health Access Project
[17117]
PO Box 21191
New York, NY 10025
PH: (212)206-5247
Fax: (314)584-3260
Katzman, Harlene, JD, VP

Research to Prevent Blindness
[17739]
360 Lexington Ave., 22nd Fl.
New York, NY 10017
PH: (212)752-4333
Toll free: 800-621-0026
Fax: (212)688-6231
Swift, Diane S., Chmn. of the Bd.

Resolution Project **[12999]**
1120 Avenue of the Americas, 4th Fl.
New York, NY 10036
PH: (212)626-6504
Tsiatis, George M., Exec. Dir.

Resource Generation **[12997]**
18 W 27th St., 2nd Fl.
New York, NY 10001
PH: (646)634-7727
Fax: (646)417-7950
Spier, Zeke, President

Retail, Wholesale and Department
Store Union **[23519]**
370 7th Ave., Ste. 501
New York, NY 10001
PH: (212)684-5300
Appelbaum, Stuart, President

Riders for Health **[15061]**
88 Pine St., 26th Fl.
New York, NY 10005
Coleman, Barry, Exec. Dir.

Rigoberta Menchu Tum Foundation
[17929]
c/o Ali El-Issa, Representative
11 Broadway, 2nd Fl.

New York, NY 10004-1300
PH: (212)982-5358
Fax: (212)982-5346
El-Issa, Ali, Rep.

Risk and Insurance Management
Society **[1923]**
5 Bryant Park, 13th Fl.
New York, NY 10018
PH: (212)286-9292
Fleming, Terry, Director

Sylvia Rivera Law Project **[13228]**
147 W 24th St., 5th Fl.
New York, NY 10011
PH: (212)337-8550
Fax: (212)337-1972
Spade, Dean, Founder

Road Recovery Foundation **[17327]**
PO Box 1680
New York, NY 10101-1680
PH: (212)489-2425
Bowen, Gene, Founder

Rockefeller Brothers Fund **[12494]**
475 Riverside Dr., Ste. 900
New York, NY 10115
PH: (212)812-4200
Fax: (212)812-4299
Heintz, Stephen B., President

Rockefeller Family Fund **[12495]**
475 Riverside Dr., Ste. 900
New York, NY 10115
PH: (212)812-4252
Fax: (212)812-4299
Wasserman, Lee, Secretary

Romanian National Tourist Office
[3392]
355 Lexington Ave., 8th Fl.
New York, NY 10017-6603
PH: (212)545-8484

Romanian-U.S. Business Council
[23655]
620 8th Ave.
New York, NY 10018
PH: (646)678-2905

Roosevelt Institute **[10350]**
570 Lexington Ave., 5th Fl.
New York, NY 10022
PH: (212)444-9130
Wong, Felicia, President, CEO

Royal Oak Foundation **[9432]**
20 W 44th St., Ste. 606
New York, NY 10036-6603
PH: (212)480-2889
Toll free: 800-913-6565
Fax: (212)785-7234
Sawyer, Mr. Sean E., PhD, Exec.
Dir.

Russian-American Chamber of Com-
merce **[23615]**
30 Wall St., 8th Fl.
New York, NY 10005-3817
PH: (212)844-9455
Fax: (678)559-0418
Shperling, Andrey, Exec. VP

Russian Children's Welfare Society
[11143]
16 W 32nd St., No. 405
New York, NY 10001
PH: (212)473-6263
Fax: (212)473-6301
Fekula, Vladimir P., Mem.

Safe Water Network **[13335]**
122 E 42nd St., Ste. 2600
New York, NY 10168
PH: (212)355-7233
Soderlund, Kurt, CEO

Russell Sage Foundation **[7171]**
112 E 64th St.
New York, NY 10065

PH: (212)750-6000
Lee, John, Director

St. Anthony's Guild [20458]
144 W 32nd St.
New York, NY 10001-3202
PH: (212)564-8799
Toll free: 800-848-4538
Convertino, Fr. David I., OFM, Exec.
Dir.

Saint Lucia Tourist Board [23549]
800 2nd Ave., Rm. 910
New York, NY 10017
PH: (212)867-2950
Toll free: 800-456-3984
Devaux, Odile, Mgr.

Salmagundi Club [8999]
47 5th Ave.
New York, NY 10003-4679
PH: (212)255-7740
Fax: (212)229-0172
Clancy, Eileen, Officer

Saving Antiquities for Everyone
[21292]
PO Box 231172, Ansonia Sta.
New York, NY 10023-0020
Ho, Cindy, Founder

Scandinavian Tourist Boards [23664]
655 3rd Ave., Ste. 1810
New York, NY 10017
PH: (212)885-9700
Muri, Ina, Contact

Schechter Day School Network
[8145]
85 Broad St., 18th Fl.
New York, NY 10004
PH: (646)655-7730
Wyner, Susan, Consultant

The Scherman Foundation [13088]
16 E 52nd St., Ste. 601
New York, NY 10022
PH: (212)832-3086
Fax: (212)838-0154
Pratt, Mike, President

Scholars at Risk Network [7407]
c/o New York University
194 Mercer St., Rm. 410
New York, NY 10012
PH: (212)998-2179
Fax: (212)995-4402
Stimpson, Catharine R., Chairman

School Food FOCUS [12113]
40 Worth St., 5th Fl.
New York, NY 10013
PH: (616)619-6449
Fax: (646)619-6777
Liquori, Toni, Exec. Dir.

Sculpture in the Environment
[17995]
25 Maiden Ln.
New York, NY 10038
PH: (212)285-0120
Wines, James, Creative Dir.,
Founder, President

Seafarers and International House
[20318]
123 E 15th St.
New York, NY 10003
PH: (212)677-4800
Drege, Pastor Marsh Luther, Exec.
Dir., Pastor

Seamen's Church Institute of New
York and New Jersey [20114]
50 Broadway, Fl. 26
New York, NY 10004-3802
PH: (212)349-9090
Rider, Rev. David M., Exec. Dir.,
President

Securities Industry and Financial
Markets Association [3050]
120 Broadway, 35th Fl.
New York, NY 10271
PH: (212)313-1200
Fax: (212)313-1301
Crispen, Cheryl, Exec. VP

Security Traders Association [3052]
1115 Broadway, Ste. 1110
New York, NY 10010
PH: (646)699-5995
Clark, Doug, Treasurer

Seeds of Peace [18828]
370 Lexington Ave., Ste. 1201
New York, NY 10017
PH: (212)573-8040
Fax: (212)573-8047
Lewin, Leslie Adelson

Sense of Smell Institute [1454]
c/o The Fragrance Foundation
621 2nd Ave., 2nd Fl.
New York, NY 10016
PH: (212)725-2755
Fax: (212)786-3260
Belasco, Jill, Chairman

September 11th Families' Association [11678]
22 Cortlandt St., Rm. 801
New York, NY 10007-3128
Ielpi, Lee, President

September Eleventh Families for
Peaceful Tomorrows [12442]
Park West Finance Sta.
New York, NY 10025
PH: (212)598-0970
Greene, Terry, Director

September's Mission [13212]
548 Broadway, 3rd Fl.
New York, NY 10012-3950
PH: (212)312-8800
Toll free: 888-424-4685
Iken, Monika, Chairperson, Founder

Services and Advocacy for GLBT
Elders [11908]
305 7th Ave., 15th Fl.
New York, NY 10001
PH: (212)741-2247
Fax: (212)366-1947
Adams, Michael, CEO

Sesame Workshop [11269]
1 Lincoln Plz.
New York, NY 10023
PH: (212)595-3456
    (212)595-3457
Dunn, Jeffrey D., President, CEO

Shakespeare Society [9097]
191 7th Ave., Ste. 2S
New York, NY 10011
Fax: (267)381-5283
Davidson, Betsy, Exec. Dir.

Shevchenko Scientific Society
[19678]
63 4th Ave.
New York, NY 10003
PH: (212)254-5130
Fax: (212)254-5239
Grabowicz, George, President

Shining Hope for Communities
[11435]
175 Varick St., 6th Fl.
New York, NY 10014
PH: (860)218-9854
Odede, Kennedy, CEO, President

Shipowners Claims Bureau, Inc.
[1927]
1 Battery Park Plz., 31st Fl.
New York, NY 10004

PH: (212)847-4500
Fax: (212)847-4599
Hughes, Joseph E.M., Chairman,
CEO

Sigma Beta Rho Fraternity, Inc.
[23926]
PO Box 4668
New York, NY 10163-4668
Malik, Hersh, President

Sikh Coalition [19099]
50 Broad St., Ste. 1537
New York, NY 10004
PH: (212)655-3095
Kaur, Sapreet, Exec. Dir.

William E. Simon Foundation
[18168]
140 E 45th St., Ste. 14D
New York, NY 10017
PH: (212)661-8366
Fax: (212)661-9450
Piereson, James, President

Single Mothers By Choice [12428]
PO Box 1642
New York, NY 10008-1642
PH: (212)988-0993
Mattes, Jane, Director, Founder

The Single Parent Resource Center,
Inc. [12429]
228 E 45th St., 5th Fl.
New York, NY 10017
PH: (212)951-7030
Fax: (212)951-7037
Dackerman, Rosemarie E., Exec.
Dir.

SingleStop USA [12565]
123 William St., Ste. 901
New York, NY 10038
PH: (212)480-2870
Reeves, Christy, CEO

Skin Cancer Foundation [14063]
149 Madison Ave., Ste. 901
New York, NY 10016
PH: (212)725-5176
Robins, Perry, MD, President,
Founder

Slavic Heritage Coalition [10219]
51 W 14th St., Ste. 4R
New York, NY 10011
PH: (212)366-5406
Toll free: 888-699-7531

Alfred P. Sloan Foundation [18950]
630 5th Ave., Ste. 2200
New York, NY 10111
PH: (212)649-1649
Fax: (212)757-5117
Joskow, Paul L., President

Slovak-American Cultural Center
[19647]
PO Box 5395
New York, NY 10185
Krcmar, Zuzana, President

Small Luxury Hotels of the World
[1679]
12 E 49th St., Ste. 1211
New York, NY 10017
PH: (212)953-2064
Toll free: 877-234-7033
Kerr, Paul, CEO

Smile Train USA [14346]
41 Madison Ave., 28th Fl.
New York, NY 10010
Toll free: 800-932-9541
Schaefer, Susannah, CEO

Social Accountability International
[18443]
15 W 44th St., 6th Fl.
New York, NY 10036

PH: (212)684-1414
Fax: (212)684-1515
Cook, Richard, CFO

Social Welfare Action Alliance
[13090]
PO Box 20563
New York, NY 10023

Socialist Party U.S.A. [18897]
339 Lafayette St., Ste. 303
New York, NY 10012
PH: (212)537-4728

Societe Culinaire Philanthropique
[19494]
305 E 47th St., Ste. 11B
New York, NY 10017-2323
PH: (212)308-0628
Fax: (212)308-0588
Santamaria, Thomas, Rec. Sec.

Society for Accessible Travel and
Hospitality [11637]
347 5th Ave., Ste. 605
New York, NY 10016-5010
PH: (212)447-7284
Fax: (212)447-1928
Nayar, Jani, Coord.

Society for the Advancement of
Judaism [20281]
15 W 86th St.
New York, NY 10024
PH: (212)724-7000
Clott, Abe, Chairman

Society of American Graphic Artists
[9350]
32 Union Sq. E, Rm. 1214
New York, NY 10003-3225
Di Cerbo, Michael, President

Society of American Registered
Architects [5977]
14 E 38th St.
New York, NY 10016
PH: (920)395-2330
Fax: (866)668-9858
Moscato, Cathie, Administrator

Society of Asian Federal Officers
[5519]
PO Box 1021
New York, NY 10002
Tang, Sheldon, President

Society of Australasian Specialists/
Oceania [22364]
c/o Steven Zirinsky, President
PO Box 49
New York, NY 10008
PH: (925)934-3847
McNamee, David, Secretary,
Treasurer

Society for Classical Studies [9657]
New York University
20 Cooper Sq., 2nd Fl.
New York, NY 10003
PH: (215)992-7828
Cullyer, Helen, Exec. Dir.

Society of Corporate Secretaries and
Governance Professionals [78]
240 W 35th St., Ste. 400
New York, NY 10001
PH: (212)681-2000
Fax: (212)681-2005
Chia, Douglas K., Chmn. of the Bd.

Society of Cosmetic Chemists
[6215]
120 Wall St., Ste. 2400
New York, NY 10005-4088
PH: (212)668-1500
Fax: (212)668-1504

Society for Emotional Well-Being
Worldwide **[15807]**
PO Box 41
New York, NY 10024
Collins, Pamela Y., MD, Founder

Society for Folk Arts Preservation
Inc. **[9332]**
308 E 79th St.
New York, NY 10075-0906
PH: (845)436-7314
Stern, Kalika, Exec. Dir.

Society of General Physiologists
[7035]
555 8th Ave., Ste. 1902
New York, NY 10018
PH: (646)595-1800
Fax: (646)417-6378
Shapiro, Mark, President

Society for the History of
Czechoslovak Jews, Inc. **[9642]**
PO Box 230255, Ansonia Sta.
New York, NY 10023

Society of Illustrators **[8943]**
128 E 63rd St.
New York, NY 10065-7303
PH: (212)838-2560
Fax: (212)838-2561
Green, Karen, VP

Society of Jewish Science **[20284]**
109 E 39th St.
New York, NY 10016
PH: (212)682-2626
Katz, Terry, Exec. Dir.

Society of Maritime Arbitrators
[4968]
1 Penn Plz., 36th Fl.
New York, NY 10119
PH: (212)786-7404
Fax: (212)786-7317
Shaw, Robert G., VP

Society for New Communications
Research **[6231]**
845 3rd Ave.
New York, NY 10022-6600
PH: (212)759-0900
Hoffman, David, VP, Managing Dir.

Society for Pediatric Pathology
[16593]
355 Lexington Ave., 15th Fl.
New York, NY 10017
PH: (706)364-3375
(212)297-2196
Fax: (706)733-8033
Kapur, Raj, Director

Society for the Preservation of
Natural History Collections **[9436]**
PO Box 526
New York, NY 10044-0526
Bentley, Andy, President

Society for Prevention of Human
Infertility **[17127]**
877 Park Ave.
New York, NY 10075-0341
PH: (212)744-5500
Toll free: 888-439-2999
Fax: (212)744-6536
Khatamee, Dr. Masood A., Exec. Dir.

Society of Professional Audio
Recording Services **[2905]**
c/o Kirk Imammura, President
Avatar Studios
441 W 53rd St.
New York, NY 10019
Toll free: 800-771-7727
Fax: (214)722-1442

Society for the Propagation of the
Faith **[19910]**
70 W 36th St., 8th Fl.
New York, NY 10018-8007

PH: (212)563-8700
Fax: (212)563-8725
Small, Rev. Andrew, OMI, Director

Society of Publication Designers
[1558]
27 Union Sq. W, Ste. 207
New York, NY 10003
PH: (212)223-3332
Fax: (212)223-5880
Leong, Tim, President

Society of Satellite Professionals
International **[3239]**
The New York Information Technol-
ogy Ctr.
250 Park Ave., 7th Fl.
New York, NY 10177-0799
PH: (212)809-5199
Fax: (212)825-0075
Stott, Chris, Director

Society of Scribes **[10416]**
PO Box 933
New York, NY 10150
PH: (212)452-0139
Nguyen, Chi, President

Society of the Silurians **[2724]**
PO Box 1195, Madison Square Sta.
New York, NY 10159
Frank, Allan Dodds, Chairperson

Society for the Study of Myth and
Tradition **[10032]**
Parabola
20 W 20th St., 2nd Fl.
New York, NY 10011
PH: (212)822-8806
Toll free: 877-593-2521
Zaleski, Jeff, Ed.-in-Chief

Society of Trust and Estate
Practitioners USA **[1168]**
40 E 84th St., Ste. 5D
New York, NY 10028
PH: (212)737-3690
Fax: (917)206-4306
Pine, Jeryl, Dir. of Member Svcs.

Society of Turkish American
Architects, Engineers and
Scientists **[6600]**
821 United Nations Plz.
Turkish Ctr., 2nd Fl.
New York, NY 10017
PH: (646)312-3366
Alpoge, Oguz, Bd. Member

Software and Technology Vendors'
Association **[6288]**
555 8th Ave., Ste. 1902
New York, NY 10019
PH: (646)233-0167
Jaffe, David, Exec. Dir.

Soliya **[19278]**
261 Madison Ave., 9th Fl.
New York, NY 10016
PH: (718)701-5855
Fax: (718)701-5856
Chambers, Liza, Founder

Sommelier Society of America **[190]**
West Village Sta.
New York, NY 10014
PH: (212)679-4190
Moody, Robert R., Chairman

South African Tourism **[23665]**
500 5th Ave., 20th Fl., Ste. 2040
New York, NY 10110
PH: (212)730-2929
Toll free: 800-593-1318
Fax: (212)764-1980

South Asian Journalists Association
[2725]
Columbia University Graduate
School of Journalism

New York, NY 10020
PH: (212)854-5979
Shrivastava, Anusha, Contact

Spain-United States Chamber of
Commerce **[23618]**
80 Broad St., Ste. 2103
New York, NY 10004
PH: (212)967-2170
Ruiz, Xavier, Director

Spartacist League **[19145]**
PO Box 1377
New York, NY 10116
PH: (212)732-7860

SPCA International **[10697]**
PO Box 8682
New York, NY 10001
PH: (212)244-7722
Toll free: 888-690-7722
Barnoti, Pierre, Founder, President

Special Interest Group on Applied
Computing **[6336]**
c/o Irene Frawley, Program
Coordinator
Association for Computing
Machinery
2 Penn Plaza, Ste. 701
New York, NY 10121-0701
Frawley, Irene, Coord.

Special Spectators **[13209]**
333 E 79th St., No. 1W
New York, NY 10075
Rockwell, Blake, Exec. Dir.

Specialty Food Association, Inc.
[1373]
136 Madison Ave., 12th Fl.
New York, NY 10016
PH: (212)482-6440
(212)921-1690
Fax: (212)921-1898

Spinal Muscular Atrophy Foundation
[17271]
888 7th Ave., Ste. 400
New York, NY 10019
PH: (646)253-7100
Toll free: 877-386-3762
Fax: (212)247-3079
Eng, Loren A., President

Spirituality & Practice **[7674]**
15 W 24th St., 10th Fl.
New York, NY 10010
Brussat, Mary Ann, Director,
Founder

Spoons Across America **[16240]**
630 9th Ave., Ste. 418
New York, NY 10036-4750
PH: (212)245-1145
Magaram, Kate, VP

Stage Directors and Choreographers
Foundation **[10273]**
321 W 44th St.
New York, NY 10036-5653
PH: (646)524-2226
Fax: (212)302-6195
Penn, Laura, Exec. Dir.

Stage Directors and Choreographers
Society **[23500]**
321 W 44th St., Ste. 804
New York, NY 10036
PH: (212)391-1070
Toll free: 800-541-5204
Fax: (212)302-6195
Rando, John, Exec. VP

Stage Managers' Association
[10233]
PO Box 275
New York, NY 10108-0275
Nathan, Melissa A., Secretary

Stand Up 4 Haiti **[12732]**
PO Box 3314
New York, NY 10008
Maceno, Witlet, President

Standing Commission on Ecumeni-
cal Relations of the Episcopal
Church **[20116]**
815 2nd Ave.
New York, NY 10017-4594
PH: (212)716-6000
Toll free: 800-334-7626
Alvero, Demetrio, Dep. Dir.

Statue of Liberty - Ellis Island
Foundation **[9438]**
History Ctr.
17 Battery Pl., No. 210
New York, NY 10004-3507
PH: (212)561-4588
O'Bannon, Michael J., President

Stepfamily Foundation, Inc. **[11831]**
310 W 85th St.
New York, NY 10024
PH: (212)877-3244
(631)725-0911
Lofas, Jeannette, PhD, Founder,
President

Structured Employment Economic
Development Corporation **[18160]**
22 Cortlandt St., 33rd Fl.
New York, NY 10007-3107
PH: (212)473-0255
Dwyer Gunn, Barbara, CEO,
President

Students Active For Ending Rape
[12573]
222 Broadway, 19th Fl.
New York, NY 10004
PH: (347)465-7233
Glowa-Kollisch, Anya, Coord.

Stupid Cancer **[14068]**
40 Worth St., Ste. 808
New York, NY 10013
Toll free: 877-735-4673
Zachary, Matthew, Founder

Suicide Prevention Initiatives
[13200]
1045 Park Ave., Ste. 3C
New York, NY 10028
Hendin, Herbert, CEO

Surdna Foundation **[12497]**
330 Madison Ave., 30th Fl.
New York, NY 10017
PH: (212)557-0010
Henderson, Phillip, President

Surgeons of Hope **[17409]**
1675 Broadway, 8th Fl.
New York, NY 10019
PH: (212)474-5994
Fax: (212)474-5996
da Cruz, Eduardo, MD, President

Sustainable Travel International
[3398]
222 Broadway
New York, NY 10010
Mullis, Brian Thomas, CEO, Founder

Swedish-American Chamber of
Commerce Inc. **[23619]**
570 Lexington Ave., 20th Fl.
New York, NY 10022
PH: (212)838-5530
Fax: (212)755-7953
Lundholm, Renee, President

Swiss Benevolent Society of New
York **[19667]**
500 5th Ave., Rm. 1800
New York, NY 10110

PH: (212)246-0655
Fax: (212)246-1366
Hubacher, Christine, Exec. Dir.

Synergos [12566]
3 E 54th St., 14th Fl.
New York, NY 10022
PH: (646)963-2100
Fax: (646)201-5220
Dunn, Robert H., Advisor

Systems Building Research Alliance [1692]
1776 Broadway, Ste. 2205
New York, NY 10019-2016
PH: (212)496-0900
Fax: (212)496-5389
Levy, Emanuel, Exec. Dir.

Taipei Economic and Cultural Office in New York [9157]
1 E 42nd St., 4th Fl.
New York, NY 10017
PH: (212)486-0088
Fax: (212)421-7866
Chang, Paul Wen-liang, Amb.

Tea Association of the U.S.A. [431]
362 5th Ave., Ste. 801
New York, NY 10001
PH: (212)986-9415
Fax: (212)697-8658
Simrany, Joseph P., President

Tea Council of the United States of America [432]
362 5th Ave., Ste. 801
New York, NY 10001
PH: (212)986-9415
Fax: (212)697-8658
Simrany, Joseph P., President

Teach For America [7802]
25 Broadway, 12th Fl.
New York, NY 10004-1056
Toll free: 800-832-1230
Beard, Elisa Villanueva, CEO

Teachers and Writers Collaborative [8766]
520 8th Ave., Ste. 2020
New York, NY 10018
PH: (212)691-6590
Fax: (212)675-0171
Schrader, Steven, Treasurer

TeleTruth: The Alliance for Customers' Telecommunications Rights [18061]
568 Broadway, Ste. 404
New York, NY 10012
Toll free: 800-780-1939
Kushnick, Bruce, Chairman

Television Bureau of Advertising [111]
120 Wall St., 15th Fl.
New York, NY 10005-3908
PH: (212)486-1111
Fax: (212)935-5631
Lanzano, Steve, CEO, President

Temple of Understanding [20614]
777 United Nations Plz., Office 3E
New York, NY 10017
PH: (914)610-5146
Van Dyk, Alison, Chairperson

Thanks to Scandinavia [7927]
366 Amsterdam Ave., Ste. 205
New York, NY 10024
PH: (347)855-4109
Larson, Kim, VP

Theatre Communications Group [10274]
520 8th Ave., 24th Fl.
New York, NY 10018-4156

PH: (212)609-5900
Fax: (212)609-5901
Eyring, Teresa, Exec. Dir.

Theatre Development Fund [10275]
520 8th Ave., Ste. 801
New York, NY 10018-6507
PH: (212)912-9770
Bailey, Victoria, Exec. Dir.

Theatre Forward [10276]
505 8th Ave., Ste. 2303
New York, NY 10018
PH: (212)750-6895
Fax: (212)750-6977
Whitacre, Bruce E., Exec. Dir.

Theatre Library Association [9730]
The New York Public Library for the Performing Arts
40 Lincoln Center Plz.
New York, NY 10023
Friedland, Nancy, President

Thyroid Cancer Survivors' Association [17482]
PO Box 1545
New York, NY 10159-1545
Toll free: 877-588-7904
Fax: (630)604-6078
Bloom, Gary, Exec. Dir.

Thyroid, Head and Neck Cancer Foundation [14075]
10 Union Sq. E, Ste. 5B
New York, NY 10003
PH: (212)844-6832
Fax: (212)844-8465
Markowitz, Erika, Exec. Dir.

TIAA [8507]
730 3rd Ave.
New York, NY 10017-3206
PH: (212)490-9000
    (212)913-2803
Toll free: 866-842-2442
Ferguson, Roger W., Jr., CEO, President

The Tibet Fund [10281]
241 E 32 St.
New York, NY 10016
PH: (212)213-5011
Fax: (212)213-1219
Lemle, Mr. Michael, Chairman

Tinker Foundation [9664]
55 E 59th St.
New York, NY 10022-1112
PH: (212)421-6858
Rennie, Ms. Renate, President

Toy Industry Association, Inc. [3294]
1115 Broadway, Ste. 400
New York, NY 10010
PH: (212)675-1141
Hargreaves, David, Chairman

Traditional Chinese Medicine Association and Alumni [13661]
108-A E 38th St.
New York, NY 10016
PH: (212)889-4802
Fax: (646)309-7633
Peng, Dr. Ding Lun, President

Traffic Audit Bureau for Media Measurement, Inc. [112]
561 7th Ave., 12th Fl.
New York, NY 10018
PH: (212)972-8075
Fax: (212)972-8928
Allman, Donald R., President, CEO

Trans-Atlantic American Flag Liner Operators/Trans-Pacific American Flag Berth Operators [3105]
80 Wall St., Ste. 1117
New York, NY 10005-3688

PH: (802)383-1689

The Transition Network [13401]
505 8th Ave., Ste. 1212
New York, NY 10128
PH: (347)735-6035
Bartoldus, Ellen, Bd. Member

Transportation Alternatives [7351]
111 John St., Ste. 260
New York, NY 10038
PH: (212)629-8080
    (648)873-6008
Fax: (212)629-8334
Miller, Richard B., Secretary

Treatment Action Group [13563]
261 5th Ave., Ste. 2110
New York, NY 10016-7701
PH: (212)253-7922
Fax: (212)253-7923
Morgan, Scott, Dep. Dir.

Treatment and Research Advancements Association for Personality Disorder [15810]
23 Greene St.
New York, NY 10013
PH: (212)966-6514
Porr, Valerie, MA, Founder, President

Trickle Up Program [12192]
104 W 27th St., 12th Fl.
New York, NY 10001-6210
PH: (212)255-9980
Toll free: 866-246-9980
Fax: (212)255-9974
Barry, Thomas C., Founder, CEO

T'ruah: The Rabbinic Call for Human Rights [18446]
333 7th Ave., 13th Fl.
New York, NY 10001
PH: (212)845-5201
Jacobs, Jill, Exec. Dir.

The True Nature Network, Inc. [10704]
PO Box 20672
Columbus Cir. Sta.
New York, NY 10023-1487
Bullington, Allan, Founder

Trust for Mutual Understanding [12193]
1 Rockefeller Pl., Rm. 2500
New York, NY 10020
PH: (212)649-5776
Fax: (212)649-5777
Chasin, Laura, Advisor

Tuesday's Children [11680]
10 Rockefeller Plz., Ste. 1007
New York, NY 11020
PH: (516)562-9000
    (516)332-2980
Weild, David, IV, Chairman

Turkish American Business Improvement and Development Council [686]
535 5th Ave., 6th Fl.
New York, NY 10017
PH: (917)601-8685
Fax: (212)696-2660

Turkish American Chamber of Commerce & Industry [23623]
2 W 45th St., Ste. 1709
New York, NY 10036
PH: (212)354-5470
Fax: (212)354-8050
Secilmis, Mr. Celal, VP

Twana Twitu [11172]
Mwinzi Kaluva Bldg.
350 5th Ave. 59th Fl.

New York, NY 10022
PH: (212)537-5927
Fax: (914)470-1320
Mwinzi-Edozie, Mwende, Exec. Dir.

Twenty-First Century Foundation [12499]
c/o Nathaniel Thompkins, Executive Director
55 Exchange Pl. No. 402
New York, NY 10005-3304
PH: (212)662-3700
Fax: (212)662-3700
Thompkins, Nathaniel, Exec. Dir.

Tyndale Society [20580]
c/o Mary Clow, Chairman
3 E 85th St., Apt. 7a
New York, NY 10028
Clow, Mrs. Mary, Chairperson

Type Directors Club [6700]
347 W 36th St., Ste. 603
New York, NY 10018
PH: (212)633-8943
Fax: (212)633-8944
Clouse, Doug, President

The Typophiles [9351]
PO Box 36-20594
New York, NY 10129
Toll free: 800-996-2556
Beletsky, Misha, Exec. VP

Ukrainian Academy of Arts and Sciences in the U.S. [10287]
206 W 100th St.
New York, NY 10025
PH: (212)222-1866
Fax: (212)864-3977
Kipa, Albert, President

Ukrainian Congress Committee of America [19206]
203 2nd Ave.
New York, NY 10003
PH: (212)228-6840
Fax: (212)254-4721
Olexy, Tamara Gallo, President

Ukrainian Educational Council [10288]
Cooper Sta.
New York, NY 10276-0391
PH: (212)477-1200
Fax: (212)777-7201
Fedorenko, Eugene, President

Ukrainian Engineers' Society of America [6602]
PO Box 1592
New York, NY 10276

Ukrainian Institute of America [10289]
2 E 79th St.
New York, NY 10075
PH: (212)288-8660
Fax: (212)288-2918
Swistel, Daniel, President

Ukrainian National Women's League of America Inc. [19681]
203 2nd Ave.
New York, NY 10003-5706
PH: (212)533-4646
Fax: (212)533-5237
Zajac, Marianna, President

UN Women for Peace Association [12444]
410 Park Ave., Ste. 1500
New York, NY 10022
Winston, Barbara, President

UNANIMA International [19132]
845 3rd Ave., Rm. 671
New York, NY 10017

PH: (917)426-8285
Fax: (646)290-5001
Morek, Michele, OSU, Coord.

UNICEF [12733]
125 Maiden Ln., 11th Fl.
New York, NY 10038
PH: (212)686-5522
Fax: (212)779-1679
Lake, Anthony, Exec. Dir.

Union for Reform Judaism [20285]
633 3rd Ave.
New York, NY 10017-6778
PH: (212)650-4000
Toll free: 855-URJ-1800
Jacobs, Rabbi Rick, President

Union Settlement Association [12567]
237 E 104th St.
New York, NY 10029-5404
PH: (212)828-6000
Fax: (212)828-6022
Rockoff, Maxine L., PhD, Officer

Union for Traditional Judaism [20286]
82 Nassau St., No. 313
New York, NY 10038
PH: (201)801-0707
Fax: (201)801-0449
Pilavin, Rabbi Robert, Chairman

Unite Here [23463]
275 7th Ave., 16th Fl.
New York, NY 10001-6708
PH: (212)265-7000
Ward, Peter, Rec. Sec.

United Action for Animals [10707]
PO Box 635
New York, NY 10021
PH: (212)249-9178
Panton, Jennifer, President

United Against Nuclear Iran [18762]
PO Box 1028
New York, NY 10185-1028
PH: (212)554-3296
Fax: (212)682-1238
Wallace, Mark, CEO

United Board for Christian Higher Education in Asia [8106]
475 Riverside Dr., Ste. 1221
New York, NY 10115
PH: (212)870-2600
Fax: (212)870-2322
Chapman, Nancy E., President

United Confederation of Taino People [19399]
PO Box 4515
New York, NY 10163
PH: (123)456-7890
Borrero, Roberto, President, Chairman

United Methodist Committee on Relief [20349]
475 Riverside Dr., Rm. 1520
New York, NY 10115
PH: (212)870-3951
Toll free: 800-554-8583
Rollins, James, Dir. of Mktg., Dir. of Comm.

United Nations Alliance of Civilizations [18560]
730 3rd Ave., 20th Fl.
New York, NY 10017
PH: (929)274-6217
Fax: (929)274-6233
Al-Nasser, Nassir Abdulaziz, Rep.

United Nations Association of the United States of America [19212]
801 2nd Ave.
New York, NY 10017

PH: (212)697-3315
Fax: (212)697-3316
Ki-Moon, Ban, Sec. Gen.

United Nations Association of the United States of America - Council of Organizations [19213]
801 2nd Ave., 9th Fl.
New York, NY 10017
PH: (212)697-3315
Fax: (212)697-3316
Johnson, Monika, Mgr.

United Nations Commission on the Status of Women [19214]
405 East 42 St.
New York, NY 10017
PH: (646)781-4400
Fax: (646)781-4444
Mlambo-Ngcuka, Phumzile, Exec. Dir.

United Nations Correspondents Association [2727]
United Nations Secretariat Bldg., Rm. S-308
405 E 42nd St.
New York, NY 10017
PH: (212)963-7137
Pioli, Giampaolo, President

United Nations Development Programme [18503]
1 United Nations Plz.
New York, NY 10017
PH: (212)963-1234
     (212)906-5382
Fax: (212)906-5364
Clark, Helen, Administrator

United Nations Development Programme in Asia and the Pacific [18504]
Regional Bureau for Asia and the Pacific
1 United Nations Plz.
New York, NY 10017
PH: (212)906-5000
Fax: (212)906-5898
Xu, Haoliang, Director

United Nations Economic and Social Council [18161]
Office for ECOSOC Support and Coordination
1 United Nations Plz.
New York, NY 10017
PH: (212)963-8415
Fax: (212)963-1712
Joon, Oh, President

United Nations Population Fund [17120]
605 3rd Ave.
New York, NY 10158-0180
PH: (212)297-5000
Fax: (212)370-0201
Mnatsakanyan, Zohrab, President

United Nations Population Fund - Cuba [12521]
1 United Nations Plz.
New York, NY 10017
PH: (537)204-2491

United Nations Staff Union [23488]
866 United Nations Plz., 2nd Fl., Rm. A-0248
48th St.
New York, NY 10017
PH: (212)963-7075
Fax: (212)963-3367
Tavora-Jainchill, Barbara, President

United Nations Women [18235]
405 E 42nd St.
New York, NY 10017
PH: (646)781-4400
Fax: (646)781-4444
Mlambo-Ngcuka, Phumzile, Exec. Dir.

United Nations Women's Guild [12910]
DC-1, Rm. 0775
1 United Nations Plz.
New York, NY 10017
PH: (212)963-4149
Chang, Ms. Tsu-Wei, Director

United for Peace and Justice [18832]
244 5th Ave., Ste. D55
New York, NY 10001
PH: (212)868-5545

United Scenic Artists Local USA 829 [23501]
29 W 38th St., 15th Fl.
New York, NY 10018
PH: (212)581-0300
Toll free: 877-728-5635
Fax: (212)977-2011
Miller, Beverly, President

UNITED SIKHS [12019]
PO Box 7203
New York, NY 10116
PH: (646)688-3525
Toll free: 888-243-1690
Fax: (810)885-4264

United States Aikido Federation [22498]
c/o Yoshimitsu Yamada
142 W 18th St.
New York, NY 10011-5403
PH: (212)242-6246
Fax: (212)242-9749
McGinnis, Charles, Chairman

United States Air Consolidator Association [3403]
C and H International
4751 Wilshire Blvd., Ste. 201
New York, NY 10036
Toll free: 800-833-8888
White, Donald, President

United States of America Netball Association [23047]
PO Box 1105
New York, NY 10274-1105

United States Association of Independent Gymnastic Clubs [3165]
450 N End Ave., Apt. 20F
New York, NY 10282
Spadaro, Paul, President, Comm. Chm.

U.S. Austrian Chamber of Commerce [23626]
165 W 46th St., Ste. 1113
New York, NY 10036
PH: (212)819-0117
Eder, Stefen, Exec. VP

U.S. Branch of the World Association for Psychosocial Rehabilitation [17099]
c/o The Bridge
248 W 108th St.
New York, NY 10025
PH: (212)663-3000
Fax: (212)663-3181
Gutierrez, Denise, Administrator

United States Committee for a Free Lebanon [18635]
445 Park Ave., 9th Fl.
New York, NY 10022-8632
Abdelnour, Ziad K., President

United States Council for International Business [672]
1212 Avenue of the Americas
New York, NY 10036
PH: (212)354-4480
Fax: (212)575-0327
McGraw, Harold, III, Chairman

U.S. Federation for Middle East Peace [18834]
777 United Nations Plz.
44th St. & 1st Ave., Ste. 7H
New York, NY 10017-3521
PH: (973)568-8384
     (917)331-4699
Fax: (646)688-5582
Kader, Ralph, CEO

United States-Japan Foundation [9218]
145 E 32nd St., 12th Fl.
New York, NY 10016
PH: (212)481-8753
Fax: (212)481-8762
Packard, Dr. George R., President

United States Othello Association [22057]
c/o Othello Quarterly
7 Peter Cooper Rd., No. 10G
New York, NY 10010
Yiu, Edmund, President

U.S. Tibet Committee [19193]
241 E 32nd St.
New York, NY 10016
PH: (212)481-3569
     (212)481-3569
Wangdu, Sonam, Chairman

United States Tour Operators Association [3404]
345 7th Ave., Ste. 1801
New York, NY 10001
PH: (212)599-6599
Fax: (212)599-6744
Dale, Terry, President, CEO

United Synagogue of Conservative Judaism [20287]
120 Broadway, Ste. 1540
New York, NY 10271-0016
PH: (212)533-7800
Fax: (212)353-9439
Wernick, Rabbi Steven C., CEO

United Synagogue Youth [20288]
120 Broadway, Ste. 1540
New York, NY 10271
PH: (212)533-7800
Fax: (212)353-9439
Feuer, Ethan, President

Universal Torah Registry [20289]
225 W 34th St., Ste. 1607
New York, NY 10122-1693
PH: (212)983-4800

University Resident Theatre Association [8702]
1560 Broadway, Ste. 1103
New York, NY 10036
PH: (212)221-1130
Fax: (212)869-2752
Steele, Scott L., Exec. Dir.

Unreserved American Indian Fashion and Art Alliance [9006]
55 Bethune St., 13th Fl.
New York, NY 10014
PH: (212)206-6580
Bruce, Gail, Founder

Up2Us [13486]
520 8th Ave., 2nd Fl.
New York, NY 10018
PH: (212)563-3031
     (212)563-4046
Caccamo, Paul, Founder, CEO

Urasenke Tea Ceremony Society [9628]
153 E 69th St.
New York, NY 10021
PH: (212)988-6161
Fax: (646)370-6452

Urban Homesteading Assistance
Board [11994]
120 Wall St., 20th Fl.
New York, NY 10005
PH: (212)479-3300
Laven, Charles, President

Uruguayan-American Chamber of
Commerce in the USA [23637]
401 E 88th St., Ste. 12-A
New York, NY 10128
PH: (212)722-3306
Fax: (212)996-2580
O'Keefe, Thomas Andrew, President

US-Cuba Reconciliation Initiative
[18322]
355 W 39th St.
New York, NY 10118
PH: (212)760-9903
Fax: (212)760-9906
McAuliff, John, Exec. Dir.

US Squash [23274]
555 8th Ave., Ste. 1102
New York, NY 10018-4311
PH: (212)268-4090
Fax: (212)268-4091
Heinrich, Dan, Director

Van Alen Institute: Projects in Public
Architecture [7501]
30 W 22nd St.
New York, NY 10010
PH: (212)924-7000
van der Leer, David, Exec. Dir.

Venceremos Brigade [18562]
PO Box 230527, Ansonia Sta.
New York, NY 10023

Venezuelan American Association of
the United States [23668]
641 Lexington Ave., Ste. 1430
New York, NY 10022
PH: (212)233-7776
Baquerizo, Maria Rosa, CEO

Vera Institute of Justice [11549]
233 Broadway, 12th Fl.
New York, NY 10279
PH: (212)334-1300
Fax: (212)941-9407
Savarese, John F., Chairman

Veteran Wireless Operators Associa-
tion [3246]
Peck Slip
New York, NY 10272-1003
Ehrlich, Alan, President

Veterans Association of America,
Inc. [21146]
Audubon Sta.
New York, NY 10032
Toll free: 800-590-2173
Fax: (888)859-8131
Works, Raphael K., PhD, Chairman,
CEO

G. Unger Vetlesen Foundation
[12500]
1 Rockefeller Plz., Ste. 301
New York, NY 10020-2002
PH: (212)586-0700
Fax: (212)245-1863
Monell, Ambrose K., President,
Treasurer, Director

VisitSweden [3408]
PO Box 4649, Grand Central Sta.
New York, NY 10163-4649
PH: (212)885-9700
Fax: (212)885-9710
Thiringer, Lotta, Mem.

Visual Artists and Galleries Association [5343]
111 Broadway, Ste. 1006
New York, NY 10006

PH: (212)736-6666
Fax: (212)736-6767

Viva! USA [10713]
1123 Broadway, Ste. 912
New York, NY 10010
PH: (212)989-8482
Fax: (212)627-6037
Gellatley, Juliet, Founder, President

Voices of African Mothers, Inc.
[12445]
777 United Nations Plz., Ste. 6G
New York, NY 10017
PH: (212)661-5860
Fax: (212)661-5861
Randall, Nana-Fosu, Founder,
President

Volunteer Lawyers for the Arts
[5554]
1 E 53rd St., 6th Fl.
New York, NY 10022-4200
PH: (212)319-2787
Paul, Elena M., Esq., Exec. Dir.

Volunteers for Israel [18589]
330 W 42nd St., Ste. 1618
New York, NY 10036
PH: (212)643-4848
Toll free: 866-514-1948
Feldman, Larry, President

Voter Rights March [18187]
PO Box 3275
New York, NY 10163
Posner, Louis, Esq., Director,
Founder

Wallace Foundation [11740]
5 Penn Plz., 7th Fl.
New York, NY 10001
PH: (212)251-9700
Fax: (212)679-6990
Miller, Will, President

Raoul Wallenberg Committee of the
United States [18143]
37 W 26th St., Ste. 403
New York, NY 10010
PH: (646)678-3711
Blake, Diane, President

War and Peace Foundation [18839]
20 E 9th St., No. 23E
New York, NY 10003
PH: (212)228-5836
Fax: (212)228-5791

War Resisters League [18729]
339 Lafayette St.
New York, NY 10012
PH: (212)228-0450
Fax: (212)228-6193
Heinz, Kimber, Contact

Waste-to-Energy Research and
Technology Council [4747]
Mudd Bldg., Rm. 926
Earth Engineering Ctr.
Columbia University
500 W 120th St.
New York, NY 10027
PH: (212)854-9136
Fax: (212)854-5213
Langenohl, Marc William,
Administrator

Watchlist on Children and Armed
Conflict [11182]
122 E 42nd St., 16th Fl., Ste. 1620
New York, NY 10168-1289
PH: (212)972-0695
Fax: (212)972-0701
Smets, Eva, Exec. Dir.

WaterAid America, Inc. [13348]
315 Madison Ave., Rm. 2301
New York, NY 10017

PH: (212)683-0430
(202)833-1341
Fax: (212)683-0293
Prabasi, Sarina, CEO

Webgrrls International, Inc. [3501]
119 W 72nd St., No. 314
New York, NY 10023
Toll free: 888-932-4775
Fax: (866)935-1188

Wedding and Portrait Photographers
International [2596]
Emerald Expositions
85 Broad St., 11th Fl.
New York, NY 10004
Groupp, Jason, Dir. Ed.

Kurt Weill Foundation for Music
[10022]
7 E 20th St., 3rd Fl.
New York, NY 10003
PH: (212)505-5240
Fax: (212)353-9663
Kowalke, Kim H., President

Westminster Kennel Club [21991]
149 Madison Ave., Ste. 402
New York, NY 10016-6722
PH: (212)213-3165
Fax: (212)213-3270
McCarthy, Sean, President

Why Hunger [18459]
505 8th Ave., Ste. 2100
New York, NY 10018
PH: (202)629-8850
Toll free: 800-548-6479
Ayres, Bill, Founder, Amb.

Wildcat Service Corporation [11789]
2 Washington St. 3rd Fl.
New York, NY 10004-3415
PH: (212)209-6000
Samuels, Peter, Chairman

The Willi Hennig Society [6108]
c/o Mark E. Siddall, Treasurer
Division of Invertebrate Zoology
American Museum of Natural History
Central Park W at 79th St.
New York, NY 10024
PH: (212)769-5638
Fax: (212)769-5277
Giribet, Prof. Dr. Gonzalo, President

Window Covering Manufacturers Association [1962]
355 Lexington Ave., 15th Fl.
New York, NY 10017
PH: (212)297-2122

Window Covering Safety Council
[3477]
355 Lexington Ave., Ste. 1500
New York, NY 10017
PH: (212)297-2100
Fax: (212)370-9047
Rush, Peter, Exec. Dir.

Wolfe Pack [9114]
PO Box 230822, Ansonia Sta.
New York, NY 10023

Women in Black [18841]
PO Box 20554
New York, NY 10021
PH: (212)560-0905
Kajosevic, Indira, Contact

Women Deliver [17123]
584 Broadway, Ste. 306
New York, NY 10012
PH: (646)695-9100
Fax: (646)695-9145
Sheffield, Jill, President

Women Make Movies [10311]
115 W 29th St., Ste. 1200
New York, NY 10001

PH: (212)925-0606
Fax: (212)925-2052
Zimmerman, Debra, Exec. Dir.

Women of Reform Judaism [20290]
633 3rd Ave.
New York, NY 10017-6778
PH: (212)650-4050
Feldman, Rabbi Marla J., Exec. Dir.

Women's Caucus for Art [8947]
PO Box 1498, Canal Street Sta.
New York, NY 10013
PH: (212)634-0007
Takata, Yuriko, Contact

Women's Economic Round Table
[19010]
The Journalism School, Columbia
University
Knight-Bagehot Fellowship Program
2950 Broadway, MC 3850
New York, NY 10027
PH: (914)922-1747
Fax: (914)922-1747
Augustus, Dr. Amelia, Director,
Founder

Women's Environment and Develop-
ment Organization [18238]
355 Lexington Ave., 3rd Fl.
New York, NY 10017
PH: (212)973-0325
Fax: (212)973-0335
Restrepo, Marcela Tovar,
Chairperson

Women's Federation for World
Peace International [12446]
4 W 43rd St.
New York, NY 10036-7408
PH: (203)661-5820
Fax: (203)360-5895
Moon, Dr. Hak Ja Han, Founder

Women's League for Conservative
Judaism [20291]
475 Riverside Dr., Ste. 820
New York, NY 10115
PH: (212)870-1260
Toll free: 800-628-5083
Fax: (212)870-1261
Kogen, Lisa, Dir. Ed.

Women's National Basketball Play-
ers Association [22579]
310 Lenox Ave.
New York, NY 10027
PH: (212)655-0880
Toll free: 800-955-6272
Fax: (212)655-0881
Appel, Jayne, Secretary, Treasurer

Women's National Book Association
[2733]
PO Box 237
New York, NY 10150
PH: (212)208-4629
Fax: (212)208-4629
Tomaselli, Valerie, Bd. Member

Women's National Republican Club
[19052]
3 W 51st St.
New York, NY 10019
PH: (212)582-5454
Fax: (212)265-5633
Weaver, Robin, President

Women's Prison Association [11552]
110 2nd Ave.
New York, NY 10003
PH: (646)292-7740
Fax: (646)292-7763
Lerner, Georgia, Exec. Dir.

Women's Project Theater [19124]
55 W End Ave.
New York, NY 10023

PH: (212)765-1706
Fax: (212)765-2024
Leeming, Jann, Bd. Member

Women's Sports Foundation [23265]
424 W 33rd St., Ste. 150
New York, NY 10001
PH: (646)845-0273
Fax: (212)967-2757
Olson, Kathryn, CEO

**Women's World Banking - USA
[13412]**
122 E 42nd St., 42nd Fl.
New York, NY 10168
PH: (212)768-8513
Fax: (212)768-8519
Iskenderian, Ms. Mary Ellen, CEO,
President

WonderWork [17419]
420 5th Ave., 27th Fl.
New York, NY 10018
PH: (212)729-1855
Fax: (212)729-4541
Mullaney, Brian, Founder, CEO

Workers World Party [19146]
147 W 24th St., 2nd Fl.
New York, NY 10011
PH: (212)627-2994
Fax: (212)675-7869
Flounders, Sara, Contact

Workmen's Circle [19502]
247 W 37th St., 5th Fl.
New York, NY 10018
PH: (212)889-6800
Toll free: 800-922-2558
Fax: (212)532-7518
Goldstein, David, Secretary

**World Animal Protection - North
America [10717]**
Nelson Tower Bldg., 31st Fl.
450 7th Ave.
New York, NY 10123
PH: (646)783-2200
Fax: (212)564-4250

World Bible Project, Inc. [19766]
PO Box 1606, FDR Sta.
New York, NY 10150
Toll free: 888-576-2210
Jackson, Miguel M., Founder,
President

World Corrosion Organization [3978]
PO Box 2544
New York, NY 10116-2544
Hays, George, Dir. Gen.

**World Council of Conservative/
Masorti Synagogues [20292]**
3080 Broadway
New York, NY 10027
PH: (212)280-6039
Fax: (212)678-5321
Graetz, Rabbi Tzvi, Exec. Dir.

**World Council of Religious Leaders
[20568]**
Empire State Bldg.
350 5th Ave., 59th Fl.
New York, NY 10118-5999
PH: (212)967-2891
Fax: (212)967-2898
Jain, Bawa, Sec. Gen.

**World Day of Prayer International
Committee [20650]**
475 Riverside Dr., Rm. 729
New York, NY 10115
PH: (212)870-3049
Oliveira, Rosângela, Exec. Dir.

**A World of Difference Institute
[17933]**
605 3rd Ave.
New York, NY 10158

PH: (212)885-7700

World Evangelical Alliance [20122]
PO Box 3402
Church St. Sta.
New York, NY 10008-3402
PH: (212)233-3046
Fax: (646)957-9218
Artz, Kenneth, Treasurer

World Federalist Movement [19215]
708 3rd Ave., Ste. 1715
New York, NY 10017
PH: (212)599-1320
Fax: (212)599-1332
Pace, William R., Exec. Dir.

**World Federation of Therapeutic
Communities [13667]**
54 W 40th St.
New York, NY 10018
Gelormino, Anthony, President,
Comm. Chm.

**World Glaucoma Patient Association
[16410]**
The Glaucoma Foundation
80 Maiden Ln., Ste. 1206
New York, NY 10038
PH: (212)651-1900
Fax: (212)651-1888
Christensen, Scott, President

World Gold Council [2384]
444 Madison Ave.
New York, NY 10022
PH: (212)317-3800
Fax: (212)688-0410
Telfer, Ian, Chairman

World Goodwill [18363]
120 Wall St., 24th Fl.
New York, NY 10005
PH: (212)292-0707
Fax: (212)292-0808

World of Hope International [12199]
Dag Hammarskjold Ctre., No. 20149
884 2nd Ave., UN Plz.
New York, NY 10017
PH: (347)323-9333
Fax: (347)323-9333
Westin, Monica, Founder, President

World Investigators Network [2015]
875 6th Ave., Ste. 206
New York, NY 10001
PH: (212)779-2000
Toll free: 888-946-6389
Fax: (212)779-2545
Fruedenthaler, Tatianna, Exec. Dir.

**World Jewish Congress, American
Section [18595]**
501 Madison Ave.
New York, NY 10022
PH: (212)755-5770
Lauder, Ronald S., President

**World Organization and Public
Education Corp. of the National
Association for the Advancement
of Psychoanalysis [16853]**
80 8th Ave., Ste. 1501
New York, NY 10011
PH: (212)741-0515
Fax: (212)366-4347
Quackenbush, Margery, Exec. Dir.

World Parkinson Coalition [16000]
1359 Broadway, Ste. 1509
New York, NY 10018
PH: (212)923-4700
Fax: (212)923-4778
Pollard, Elizabeth, Exec. Dir.

World Policy Institute [18277]
108 W 39th St., Ste. 1000
New York, NY 10018

PH: (212)481-5005
Fax: (212)481-5009
Watts, John, Chairman

World Rehabilitation Fund [11649]
16 E 40th St., Ste. 704
New York, NY 10016
PH: (212)532-6000
Fax: (212)532-6012
Karam, Dr. Nadim, Exec. Dir.

**World Student Christian Federation-
North America [11462]**
475 Riverside Dr., Ste. 700
New York, NY 10115
PH: (212)870-2470
Fax: (212)870-3220
Kovacs, Luciano, Secretary

World Teleport Association [3249]
250 Park Ave., 7th Fl.
New York, NY 10177
PH: (212)825-0218
Fax: (212)825-0075
Bell, Robert, Exec. Dir.

**World Trade Center Survivors'
Network [13214]**
511 Avenue of the Americas, Ste.
302 G
New York, NY 10011-8436
Zimbler, Richard, Act. Pres.

**World Trade Centers Association
[3308]**
120 Broadway, Ste. 3350
New York, NY 10271
PH: (212)432-2626
Dahl, Eric, CEO

World Water Organization [13351]
866 United Nations Plz.
New York, NY 10017
PH: (212)759-1639
Fax: (646)666-4349
HyunSuk Oh, Dr. Harold, Chairman .

World Youth Alliance [19280]
228 E 71st St.
New York, NY 10021
PH: (212)585-0757
Fax: (917)463-1040
Ndaba, Obadias, President

**Wyman Worldwide Health Partners
[15512]**
c/o Oliver Wyman
1166 Avenue of the Americas
New York, NY 10036-2708
PH: (212)345-8000
McDonald, Scott, CEO

Xavier Society for the Blind [17750]
2 Penn Plz., Ste. 1102
New York, NY 10121
PH: (212)473-7800
Toll free: 800-637-9193
Fax: (212)473-7801
Sheehan, Fr. John R., Chairman,
CEO

YAI Network [12334]
460 W 34th St., 11th Fl.
New York, NY 10001-2382
PH: (212)273-6100
(212)273-6199
Toll free: 877-924-4438
Contos, George, CEO

**YIVO Institute for Jewish Research
[9645]**
15 W 16th St.
New York, NY 10011-6301
PH: (212)246-6080
(212)294-6139
Fax: (212)292-1892
Brent, Jonathan, Exec. Dir.

**YMA Fashion Scholarship Fund
[210]**
1501 Broadway, Ste. 1810
New York, NY 10036

PH: (212)278-0008
Rosengard, Paul, Co-Ch.

YMCA International Branch [13420]
5 W 63rd St., 2nd Fl.
New York, NY 10023
PH: (212)727-8800

**Young Audiences Arts for Learning
[9010]**
171 Madison Ave., Ste. 200
New York, NY 10016-5110
PH: (212)831-8110
Fax: (212)289-1202
Dik, David A., Exec. Dir.

Young Concert Artists [10027]
250 W 57th St., Ste. 1222
New York, NY 10107
PH: (212)307-6655
Fax: (212)581-8894
Wadsworth, Susan, Director,
Founder

Young Democratic Socialists [19147]
75 Maiden Ln., Ste. 702
New York, NY 10038
PH: (212)727-8610
Fax: (212)608-6955
Porter, Matt, Contact

Young Judaea [20293]
575 8th Ave., 11th Fl.
New York, NY 10018
PH: (917)595-2100
Klarfeld, Simon, Exec. Dir.

Young Survival Coalition [14083]
80 Broad St., Ste. 1700
New York, NY 10004
Toll free: 877-972-1011
Fax: (646)257-3030

Yugntruf - Youth for Yiddish [9646]
419 Lafayette St., 2nd Fl.
New York, NY 10003
PH: (212)796-5782
Kutzik, Jordan, Chairman

Yum-O Organization [12121]
132 E 43rd St., No. 223
New York, NY 10017
Ray, Rachael, Founder

Zen Studies Society [19785]
223 E 67th St.
New York, NY 10065
PH: (212)861-3333
Fax: (212)628-6968

Ziegfeld Club [10280]
593 Park Ave.
New York, NY 10065
PH: (212)751-6688
Lansbury, Emily Bickford, Chairman

**Zionist Organization of America
[20294]**
4 E 34th St.
New York, NY 10016
PH: (212)481-1500
Fax: (212)481-1515
Klein, Morton A., President

**American Rhododendron Society
[22083]**
c/o Laura Grant, Exectuive Director
PO Box 525
Niagara Falls, NY 14302
Grant, Laura, Exec. Dir.

**Emergency Committee to Defend
Constitutional Welfare Rights USA
[18974]**
c/o Mr. Martin J. Sawma, Executive
Director
3501 Westwood Dr., Rm. 4
Niagara Falls, NY 14305-3416

PH: (716)297-7273
Fax: (630)929-3839
Sawma, Mr. Martin J., Exec. Dir.

Foundation for the Support of
International Medical Training
[15449]
c/o International Association for
Medical Assistance to Travellers
1623 Military Rd., No. 279
Niagara Falls, NY 14304-1745
PH: (716)754-4883
Uffer-Marcolongo, M. Assunta,
President

International Association for Medical
Assistance to Travellers [13238]
1623 Military Rd., No. 279
Niagara Falls, NY 14304-1745
PH: (716)754-4883
Forgey, William W., Director

Union for Democratic Communica-
tions [17959]
c/o Doug Tewksbury, Treasurer
Niagara University
PO Box 1922
Niagara University, NY 14109-1922

Neuroendocrine Cancer Awareness
Network [14033]
2480 Hull Ave.
North Bellmore, NY 11710
PH: (516)781-7814
Toll free: 866-850-9555
Wahmann, Robert, President

Friends of Karen [11231]
118 Titicus Rd.
North Salem, NY 10560
PH: (914)277-4547
Toll free: 800-637-2774
Fax: (914)277-4967
Factor, Ms. Judith, Exec. Dir.

National Institute for Jewish Hospice
[15298]
732 University St.
North Woodmere, NY 11581
PH: (516)791-9888
Toll free: 800-446-4448
Lamm, Dr. Maurice, Founder,
President

A Midwinter Night's Dream [13685]
155 Main St., Ste. 4
Northport, NY 11768
PH: (631)262-7428
(516)680-6658
Strasser, Don, CEO, Exec. Dir.

World Ocean and Cruise Liner
Society [22471]
PO Box 329
Northport, NY 11768-0329
Toll free: 866-631-0611
Cassidy, Thomas E., President, Edi-
tor

American Willow Growers Network
[4727]
412 County Rd. 31
Norwich, NY 13815-3149
PH: (607)336-9031
Fax: (607)336-9031
Gale, Bonnie, Founder

Wagner and Griswold Society
[22158]
c/o Diana Hickling
5409 State Highway 23
Norwich, NY 13815
PH: (512)282-3924
Hickling, Diana, Secretary

National American Legion Press Association [20689]
3 Morton St.
Norwood, NY 13668-1100
Buskirk, George A., Treasurer

Children's Creative Response to
Conflict [11222]
521 N Broadway
Nyack, NY 10960
PH: (845)353-1796
Fax: (845)358-4924
Prutzman, Priscilla, Officer

Fellowship of Reconciliation - USA
[18783]
PO Box 271
Nyack, NY 10960
PH: (845)358-4601
Fax: (845)358-4924
Kelly, Linda, Dir. of Comm.

Jewish Peace Fellowship [18799]
PO Box 271
Nyack, NY 10960-0271
PH: (845)358-4601
Fax: (845)358-4924
Merken, Stefan, Chairman

Society of U.S. Pattern Collectors
[22287]
PO Box 806
Nyack, NY 10960
Lustig, Andy, Contact

Pediatric Neurotransmitter Disease
Association [15987]
28 Prescott Pl.
Old Bethpage, NY 11804
Kannusamy, Priya, Director

Center for Energy, Environment and
Economics [6464]
New York Institute of Technology
Northern Blvd.
Old Westbury, NY 11568-8000
PH: (516)686-1000
Fox, Dr. Herbert, Director

International Association of Educa-
tors [7851]
320 Fitzelle Hall
Ravine Pky.
Oneonta, NY 13820
Kahveci, Nihat Gurel, PhD, Gen.
Sec.

American Association of Philosophy
Teachers [8416]
Cominican College
470 Westen Hwy.
Orangeburg, NY 10962
PH: (434)220-3300
Toll free: 800-444-2419
Fax: (434)220-3301
Esch, Dr. Emily, Exec. Dir.

AIDSfreeAFRICA [13526]
125 S Highland Ave., No. 3-B1
Ossining, NY 10562
PH: (914)236-0658
Hodel, Rolande R., PhD, Founder,
President

Albanian American Civic League
[19295]
PO Box 70
Ossining, NY 10562
PH: (914)762-5530
Fax: (914)762-5102
DioGuardi, Joseph J., Founder,
President

Bridges to Community [13287]
95 Croton Ave.
Ossining, NY 10562
PH: (914)923-2200
Fax: (914)923-8396
Hannan, John, Exec. Dir.

Maryknoll Fathers and Brothers
[19861]
55 Ryder Rd.
Ossining, NY 10562

PH: (914)941-7590
Toll free: 888-627-9566
Dougherty, Rev. Edward, Gen.

National Milk Glass Collectors
Society [22143]
c/o Helen Engel
32 Brown Dr.
Oswego, NY 13126
PH: (315)343-9678
Truby, Cindy, Director

John More Association [20902]
c/o Mike Williams, Treasurer
295 Williams Rd.
Oxford, NY 13830
Yewcic, Patricia Hile, Officer

Association of Indians in America
[19471]
26 Pleasant Ln.
Oyster Bay, NY 11771
PH: (516)624-2460
Goenka, Animesh, Mem.

Hermansky-Pudlak Syndrome
Network Inc [14826]
1 South Rd.
Oyster Bay, NY 11771-1905
Toll free: 800-789-9HPS
Fax: (516)624-0640
Appell, Donna Jean, Founder,
President

Theodore Roosevelt Association
[10349]
PO Box 719
Oyster Bay, NY 11771
PH: (516)921-6319
Fax: (516)921-6481
Pels, Laurence, Exec. Dir.

Wales North America Business
Chamber [23640]
69 Closter Rd.
Palisades, NY 10964
PH: (845)398-0619
Jones, Chris, President

Arabian F.O.A.L. Association [10589]
PO Box 198
Parksville, NY 12768-0198
PH: (845)392-7797
(845)292-7797
Fax: (845)292-7797
Lohnes, Robin C., Secretary

Steuben Society of America [19448]
1 S Ocean Ave.
Patchogue, NY 11772-3738
PH: (631)730-5111
Ratje, Randall J., Chairman

National Fire Sprinkler Association
[3002]
40 Jon Barrett Rd.
Patterson, NY 12563-2164
PH: (845)878-4200
Fax: (845)878-4215
Thau, Larry, Chairperson

Aiding Children Together [10843]
1055 W Dover Rd.
Pawling, NY 12564
PH: (845)832-7594
Fax: (845)832-7594
Kohomban, Lisa, President, Exec.
Dir.

Crew's Voice [13762]
14 Maple Ln.
Pawling, NY 12564
PH: (914)804-4740
Reinhardt, Christy, Chmn. of the Bd.

International Boys' Schools Coalition
[7774]
700 Route 22
Pawling, NY 12564

PH: (207)841-7441
Armstrong, David, Exec. Dir.

ACORD [1820]
1 Blue Hill Plz., 15th Fl.
Pearl River, NY 10965-3104
PH: (845)620-1700
Fax: (845)620-3600
Maciag, Gregory A., CEO, President

American Society of Polar
Philatelists [22305]
c/o John Young, President
146 N Lincoln St.
Pearl River, NY 10965
Warren, Alan, Secretary

Irish Northern Aid [18582]
38 S Main St.
Pearl River, NY 10965
Toll free: 800-473-5263

Medical Mission Group [15485]
134 Grove St.
Pearl River, NY 10965
PH: (845)920-9001
Upton, Devin, President

Zeta Psi Fraternity, Inc. [23940]
15 S Henry St.
Pearl River, NY 10965
PH: (845)735-1847
Toll free: 800-477-1847
Fax: (845)735-1989
Hunter, Dave, Exec. Dir.

Get Your Guts in Gear, Inc. [14792]
1000 N Division St., Ste. 10-8
Peekskill, NY 10566-1830
PH: (718)875-2123
Toll free: 866-944-6848

National Maritime Historical Society
[9783]
5 John Walsh Blvd.
Peekskill, NY 10566
PH: (914)737-7878
Toll free: 800-221-6647
Fax: (914)737-7816
Slotnick, Howard, Treasurer

United States Intercollegiate
Lacrosse Association [22975]
3738 W Lake Rd.
Perry, NY 14530
PH: (585)237-5886
Fax: (585)237-5886
Mitrano, Chuck, President

Building Minds in South Sudan
[13034]
5880 Pittsford Palmyra Rd.
Pittsford, NY 14534
PH: (585)350-4035
Maroundit, Sebastian, President,
Founder

University Athletic Association
[23263]
115 Sully's Trl., Ste. 14
Pittsford, NY 14534-4571
PH: (585)419-0575
Fax: (585)218-0951
Rasmussen, Dick, Exec. Sec.

Association for Children with Down
Syndrome [12316]
4 Fern Pl.
Plainview, NY 11803
PH: (516)933-4700
Fax: (516)933-9524
Smith, Michael M., Exec. Dir.

Association of Pediatric Hematology
Oncology Educational Specialists
[15224]
c/o Karen DeMairo, Treasurer
5 Eileen Ave.

Plainview, NY 11803
PH: (631)370-7532
Fax: (631)370-7560
Irwin, Mary Kay, EdD, Chairperson

Irish Family History Forum [20977]
PO Box 67
Plainview, NY 11803-0067
Carragher, Michael, President

National Cancer Center [16348]
88 Sunnyside Blvd., Ste. 307
Plainview, NY 11803-1518
PH: (516)349-0610
Fax: (516)349-1755
Sherman, Jack, MD, President

Seeds For Hope [11677]
PO Box 145
Plainview, NY 11803
Kist, Nadia, Chmn. of the Bd.,
    Founder

American Military Retirees Associa-
    tion [21107]
5436 Peru St., No. 1
Plattsburgh, NY 12901
PH: (518)563-9479
Toll free: 800-424-2969
Fax: (518)324-5204
Bergeron, Margaret, Exec. Dir.

Water Without Borders [13363]
10 Cole Rd., Ste. A
Pleasant Valley, NY 12569
Evert, Frank, President

Program of Academic Exchange
    [8088]
14 Willett Ave.
Port Chester, NY 10573
Toll free: 800-555-6211
Fax: (914)690-0350
Stewart, Walter, Chmn. of the Bd.

Saab Club of North America [21487]
30 Puritan Dr.
Port Chester, NY 10573-2504
Powers, Daryle, President

Accredited Certifiers Association,
    Inc. [4516]
PO Box 472
Port Crane, NY 13833
PH: (607)648-3259
Fax: (607)648-3259
Cox, Duncan, Director

Council of American Survey
    Research Organizations [18923]
170 N Country Road, Ste. 4
Port Jefferson, NY 11777
PH: (631)928-6954
Fax: (631)928-6041
Collins, Meg, Mktg. Mgr.

Content Delivery and Storage As-
    sociation [1189]
39 N Bayles Ave.
Port Washington, NY 11050
PH: (516)767-6720
Fax: (516)883-5793
Porter, Martin, Exec. Dir.

Grassroots Environmental Education
    [7892]
52 Main St.
Port Washington, NY 11050
PH: (516)883-0887
Wood, Patricia J., Exec. Dir.

International Federation of Marfan
    Syndrome Organizations [14830]
c/o National Marfan Foundation
22 Manhasset Ave.
Port Washington, NY 11050
Ciccariello, Priscilla, President

Marfan Foundation [17484]
22 Manhasset Ave.
Port Washington, NY 11050

PH: (516)883-8712
Toll free: 800-8 MARFAN
Fax: (516)883-8040
Murray, Karen, Chairman

Pet Savers Foundation [10681]
750 Port Washington Blvd.
Port Washington, NY 11050
PH: (516)883-1461
Fax: (516)883-1595

APA Division 23: Society for
    Consumer Psychology [16875]
c/o Larry D. Compeau, Executive
    Officer
Clarkson University School of Busi-
    ness
Snell Hall
Potsdam, NY 13699
Compeau, Prof. Larry D., PhD,
    Exec. Ofc.

National Association of Crisis
    Organization Directors [11553]
c/o Karen Butler Easter, President
PO Box 5051
Potsdam, NY 13676
PH: (315)265-2422
Easter, Karen Butler, President

Alumnae and Alumni of Vassar Col-
    lege [7491]
Alumnae House
161 College Ave.
Poughkeepsie, NY 12603
PH: (845)437-5400
Toll free: 800-443-8196
Fax: (845)437-7425

American Topical Association,
    Americana Unit [22307]
17 Peckham Rd.
Poughkeepsie, NY 12603
PH: (845)452-2126
Fax: (817)274-1184
Dengel, Dennis M., Treasurer

Association for Symbolic Logic
    [6817]
Vassar College
124 Raymond Ave.
Poughkeepsie, NY 12604
PH: (845)437-7080
Fax: (845)437-7830
Kohlenbach, Ulrich, VP

International Association of
    Outsourcing Professionals [2472]
2600 S Rd., Ste. 44-240
Poughkeepsie, NY 12601
PH: (845)452-0600
Fax: (845)452-6988
Corbett, Michael F., Chairman,
    Founder

Women's Jewelry Association [2061]
82 Washington St., Ste. 203A
Poughkeepsie, NY 12601
PH: (212)687-2722
Fax: (646)355-0219
Mack, Bernadette, Exec. Dir.

Aging in America [10496]
2975 Westchester Ave., Ste. 301
Purchase, NY 10577
PH: (914)205-5030
Smith, Dr. William T., CEO,
    President

Soft Power Health [15498]
2887 Purchase St.
Purchase, NY 10577-2214
PH: (914)282-7354
Stone, Dr. Jessie, Director, Founder

Hungarian Studies Association
    [9488]
c/o Susan Glanz, St. John's
    University, College of Professional
    Studies, 8000 Utopia Pky.

8000 Utopia Pky.
Dept. of Administration and Econom-
    ics
College of Professional Studies
St. John's University
Queens, NY 11439

Islamic Circle of North America
    [20499]
166-26 89th Ave.
Queens, NY 11432
PH: (718)658-1199
Fax: (718)658-1255
Bukhari, Dr. Zahid, President

Sumi-e Society of America [8892]
c/o Veronica Lowe, Membership
    Secretary
94-72 220th St.
Queens Village, NY 11428
PH: (718)468-4061
Nolan, Betty, Bd. Member

American Women Artists [8914]
PO Box 4125
Queensbury, NY 12804
Swanson, Diane, Exec. Dir.

Council on Safe Transportation of
    Hazardous Articles, Inc. [3082]
10 Hunter Brook Ln.
Queensbury, NY 12804
PH: (518)761-0389
Fax: (518)792-7781
Currie, John V., Administrator, Chief
    Tech. Ofc.

International Relief Friendship
    Foundation [13065]
39 N Jefferson Rd.
Red Hook, NY 12571
PH: (917)319-6202
Fax: (845)835-8214
Han Moon, Dr. Hak Ja, President

World War 1 Aeroplanes [21258]
PO Box 730
Red Hook, NY 12571-0730
Polapink, Tom, Secretary, Treasurer

Citizens Aviation Watch Association
    [361]
97-37 63rd Rd. 15 E
Rego Park, NY 11374-1600
PH: (718)275-3932
Fax: (718)275-3932
Verhagen, Dr. Frans C., President

The Myanmar American Medical
    Education Society, Inc. [8327]
PO Box 740576
Rego Park, NY 11374-0576
San, Dr. Myat, Chairman

National Association of Jewelry Ap-
    praisers [2059]
c/o Gail Brett Levine, GG, Executive
    Director
PO Box 18
Rego Park, NY 11374-0018
PH: (718)896-1536
Fax: (718)997-9057
Levine, Gail Brett, Exec. Dir.

Toy Train Collectors Society [22191]
c/o Robert D Richter, President
2015 Bay Rd.
Remsen, NY 13438-4286
PH: (315)831-8302
Richter, Robert D., President

STRIDE [7719]
476 N Greenbush Rd., Ste. 9
Rensselaer, NY 12144
PH: (518)598-1279
Fax: (518)391-2563
Earing, Amy, Treasurer

WAVES for Development [23279]
166 Thornberry Ln.
Rensselaer, NY 12144
Aabo, David, Exec. Dir.

American Spoon Collectors [21616]
PO Box 243
Rhinecliff, NY 12574
PH: (845)876-0303
Fax: (845)876-0303
Wilhelm, Robert M., Editor

Light Millennium [17909]
87-82 115th St.
Richmond Hill, NY 11418
PH: (718)846-5776
Unver, Bircan, Founder, President

United States Muay Thai Association
    [23021]
6535 Broadway, Ste. 1K
Riverdale, NY 10471
Fax: (718)549-6122
Heyliger, Arjarn Clint, President,
    Founder

American College of Tax Counsel
    [5412]
2604 Elmwood Ave., No. 350
Rochester, NY 14618
Toll free: 888-549-4177
Arnold, Joan C., President

American Precision Optics
    Manufacturers Association [3023]
PO Box 20001
Rochester, NY 14602
Mahanna, Justin J., President

Association of NROTC Colleges and
    Universities [8343]
c/o Lauren Heary
University of Rochester, 208 Latti-
    more Hall
Rochester, NY 14627
PH: (585)273-2425
Fax: (585)275-8531
Nordahl, Regina T., President

The Association for the Study of
    Play [10147]
1 Manhattan Sq.
Rochester, NY 14607
PH: (585)263-2700
Nwokah, Eva, President

Biological Stain Commission [6077]
c/o Chad Fagan
University of Rochester Medical Ctr.
601 Elmwood Ave.
Rochester, NY 14642-0001
PH: (585)275-2751
Fax: (585)442-8993
Dapson, Richard, Trustee

Center for Environmental Information
    [4037]
700 W Metro Pk.
Rochester, NY 14623
PH: (585)233-6086
    (585)262-2870
Fax: (585)262-4156
Thomas, George, Exec. Dir.

Center for Governmental Research
    [18966]
1 S Washington St., Ste. 400
Rochester, NY 14614
PH: (585)325-6360
Toll free: 888-388-8521
Barnes, Susan, Treasurer

Children Awaiting Parents [10448]
274 N Goodman St., Ste. D103
Rochester, NY 14607
PH: (585)232-5110
Toll free: 888-835-8802
Fax: (585)232-2634
Reaves, Charles, Exec. Dir.

Collaborative Family Healthcare As-
    sociation [14989]
PO Box 23980
Rochester, NY 14692-3980

PH: (585)482-8210
Fax: (585)482-2901
Kurtz, Polly, Exec. Dir.

Custom Tailors and Designers Association [202]
229 Forest Hills Rd.
Rochester, NY 14625
Toll free: 888-248-2832
Fax: (866)661-1240
Gambert, Mitch, President

Discovering Deaf Worlds [11940]
PO Box 10063
Rochester, NY 14610
PH: (585)234-8144
Mowl, Harold, President

Emerald Society of the Federal Law Enforcement Agencies [19534]
PO Box 16413
Rochester, NY 14616-0413
Smart, Tom, President

Feminists For Nonviolent Choices [18208]
1255 University Ave., Ste. 146
Rochester, NY 14607
PH: (585)319-4565
Vincent-Brunacini, Kelly, Exec. Dir.

Governmental Research Association [18981]
c/o Center for Governmental Research
1 S Washington St., Ste. 400
Rochester, NY 14614
PH: (205)870-2482
(205)726-2482
Fax: (205)726-2900
Gardner, Kent, Secretary

Gravure Education Foundation [7947]
PO Box 25617
Rochester, NY 14625-0617
PH: (201)523-6042
Fax: (201)523-6048
Vail, Walter, President

International Association of Therapeutic Drug Monitoring and Clinical Toxicology [17496]
2604 Elmwood Ave., No. 350
Rochester, NY 14618
PH: (613)531-8166
Fax: (866)303-0626
Langman, Loralie, President

National Braille Association [17730]
95 Allens Creek Rd., Bldg. 1, Ste. 202
Rochester, NY 14618
PH: (585)427-8260
Fax: (585)427-0263
Venneri, Joanna E., Director

Nitric Oxide Society [6209]
2604 Elmwood Ave., No. 350
Rochester, NY 14618
Gow, Andrew, President

NTID's Center on Employment [11778]
Rochester Institute of Technology
Lyndon Baines Johnson Bldg.
52 Lomb Memorial Dr.
Rochester, NY 14623-5604
PH: (585)475-6219
Fax: (585)475-7570
Macko, John, Director

Organization of Bricklin Owners [21470]
PO Box 24775
Rochester, NY 14624-0775
PH: (585)247-1575
DeLorenzo, Joseph F., Founder, President

Parenthood for Me [11846]
PO Box 67750
Rochester, NY 14617
Schlaefer, Erica Walther, President, Founder

PeaceArt International [8995]
PO Box 40028
Rochester, NY 14604-0028
PH: (585)482-0778
Fax: (585)288-2572
Warfield, Thomas, Founder, Art Dir.

The Photographic Historical Society [10144]
PO Box 10342
Rochester, NY 14610
PH: (585)475-2411
Calandra, Frank, Secretary

Polio Children [16793]
155 Dunrovin Ln.
Rochester, NY 14618
PH: (585)442-2505
Patel, Shirish, Director

Society for Pastoral Theology [20623]
c/o Dr. Roslyn Karaban
St. Bernard's School of Theology and Ministry
120 French Rd.
Rochester, NY 14618
PH: (585)750-6693
Fax: (585)271-2045
Lee, Insook, PhD, President

Society for the Study of Early Modern Women [8756]
c/o Deborah Uman, Treasurer
3690 E Ave.
Rochester, NY 14618
PH: (585)385-5258
Ray, Meredith K., President

Sportsplex Operators and Developers Association [23257]
PO Box 24617
Rochester, NY 14624-0617
PH: (585)426-2215
Toll free: 800-878-4308
Fax: (585)247-3112
Aselin, Don, Exec. Dir.

Support Organization for Trisomy 18, 13, and Related Disorders [14861]
2982 S Union St.
Rochester, NY 14624
Toll free: 800-716-7638
VanHerreweghe, Barb, President

Tall Clubs International [13207]
c/o Walter J. Narog Jr., President
Tall Club of Rochester
PO Box 20197
Rochester, NY 14602
Narog, Walt, President

United States Deaf Ski and Snowboard Association [22801]
76 Kings Gate N
Rochester, NY 14617-5409
Di Giovanni, Anthony, Treasurer

Visual Studies Workshop [9318]
31 Prince St.
Rochester, NY 14607
PH: (585)442-8676
Fax: (585)442-1992
Shaw, Tate, Director

Water for South Sudan [13345]
PO Box 25551
Rochester, NY 14625-0551
PH: (585)383-0410
Dut, Salva, Founder

Complementary and Alternative Medicine Initiative [13616]
75 Winchell Dr.
Rock Tavern, NY 12575

PH: (718)877-0292
Egwuonwu, Dr. Uchenna, Founder, President

A Call To Men [12305]
250 Merrick Rd., Ste. 813
Rockville Centre, NY 11570
PH: (917)922-6738
Bunch, Ted, Founder, Director

International Organization for Women and Development Inc. [17108]
PO Box 616
Rockville Centre, NY 11571-0616

National Coalition on Auditory Processing Disorders [15202]
PO Box 494
Rockville Centre, NY 11571-0494
Lucker, Jay R., President

Electrical Overstress/Electrostatic Discharge Association [6418]
Bldg. 3
7900 Turin Rd.
Rome, NY 13440-2069
PH: (315)339-6937
Fax: (315)339-6793
Welsher, Terry, President

National Miniature Donkey Association [4461]
6450 Dewey Rd.
Rome, NY 13440-8006
PH: (315)336-0154
Fax: (315)339-4414
Gattari, Lynn, Director

American Academy of Experts in Traumatic Stress [17522]
203 Deer Rd.
Ronkonkoma, NY 11779
PH: (631)543-2217
Fax: (631)543-6977
Lindell, Brad, PhD, President

Christopher Morley Knothole Association [9081]
c/o The Bryant Library
2 Paper Mill Rd.
Roslyn, NY 11576-2133
Cohn, Peter, President

Alternative Education Resource Organization [7735]
417 Roslyn Rd.
Roslyn Heights, NY 11577
PH: (516)621-2195
Toll free: 800-769-4171
Fax: (516)625-3257
Mintz, Jerry, Director, Founder

Communication Institute for Online Scholarship [7484]
PO Box 57
Rotterdam Junction, NY 12150-0057
PH: (518)887-2443
Fax: (518)887-5186
Stephen, Timothy, President

Archivists and Librarians in the History of the Health Sciences [9679]
c/o Barbara Niss, Treasurer
14 Elmwood Ave.
Rye, NY 10580
PH: (310)825-6940
Letocha, Phoebe Evans, Secretary

Wainwright House [20619]
260 Stuyvesant Ave.
Rye, NY 10580-3115
PH: (914)967-6080
Kelly, Laura, Dir. of Operations

Leukemia and Lymphoma Society [14001]
3 International Dr., Ste. 200
Rye Brook, NY 10573

PH: (914)949-5213
Fax: (914)949-6691
Degennaro, Louis J., PhD, CEO, President

Insulating Glass Certification Council [1506]
PO Box 730
Sackets Harbor, NY 13685
PH: (315)646-2234
Fax: (315)646-2297
Ackley, Erin M., Admin. Asst.

Safety Glazing Certification Council [577]
205 W Main St.
Sackets Harbor, NY 13685
PH: (315)646-2234
Fax: (315)646-2297
Weismantle, Peter, President

Cancer Simplified [13930]
No. 34 Bay St., Ste. 202
Sag Harbor, NY 11963
PH: (631)725-4646
Darrow, Duncan N., Founder

Embrace It Africa [11350]
PO Box 25
Saint Bonaventure, NY 14778
Pohlman, Lindsay, President

International Bank Note Society [22270]
c/o Roger Urce, General Secretary
PO Box 289
Saint James, NY 11780-0289
Lutz, Dennis, President

International Maple Syrup Institute [1346]
647 Bunker Hill Rd.
Salem, NY 12865
PH: (518)854-7669
Campbell, David, Treasurer

National Elevator Industry [1753]
1677 County Route 64
Salem, NY 12865-0838
PH: (518)854-3100
Fax: (518)854-3257
Lloyd, Sterrett, Director

Helen Keller National Center for Deaf-Blind Youths and Adults [15199]
141 Middle Neck Rd.
Sands Point, NY 11050
PH: (516)944-8900
Fax: (516)944-7302
Bruno, Joseph F., President, CEO

National Family Association for Deaf-Blind [15204]
141 Middle Neck Rd.
Sands Point, NY 11050
Toll free: 800-255-0411
Fax: (516)883-9060
Green, Susan, Bd. Member

American Copper Council [2341]
475 Broadway
Saratoga Springs, NY 12866-6735
PH: (518)871-1062
Boland, Betsy, Exec. Dir.

Angel Names Association [12131]
PO Box 423
Saratoga Springs, NY 12866
PH: (518)654-2411
Mosca, Michelle, President

Godolphin Society [23081]
National Museum of Racing and Hall of Fame
191 Union Ave.
Saratoga Springs, NY 12866
PH: (518)584-0400
Toll free: 800-562-5394
Fax: (518)584-4574
Dragone, Mr. Christopher, Director

Handcrafted Soap and Cosmetic Guild **[21759]**
178 Elm St.
Saratoga Springs, NY 12866-4009
PH: (518)306-6934
Toll free: 866-900-7627
O'Donnell, Leigh, Exec. Dir.

HUMOR Project **[9561]**
10 Madison Ave.
Saratoga Springs, NY 12866
PH: (518)587-8770
Goodman, Dr. Joel, Director, Founder

National Museum of Racing and Hall of Fame **[22924]**
191 Union Ave.
Saratoga Springs, NY 12866-3566
PH: (518)584-0400
Toll free: 800-562-5394
Fax: (518)584-4574
Dragone, Christopher, Director

Thoroughbred Retirement Foundation **[10702]**
10 Lake Ave.
Saratoga Springs, NY 12866
PH: (518)226-0028
Fax: (518)226-0699
Moore, John C., Chairman

New York Triathlon Club **[23338]**
PO Box 50
Saugerties, NY 12477-0050
PH: (845)247-0271

World Pen Pals **[8094]**
PO Box 337
Saugerties, NY 12477
PH: (845)246-7828
       (914)246-7828
Fax: (914)246-7828

Chinese American Hematologist and Oncologist Network **[15227]**
PO Box 1308
Scarsdale, NY 10583
Sun, Weijing, President

National Aphasia Association **[13726]**
PO Box 87
Scarsdale, NY 10583
Toll free: 800-922-4622
Williamson, Darlene S., President

The Bridge Line Historical Society **[22407]**
2476 Whitehall Ct.
Schenectady, NY 12309
Milczarek, John, President, Treasurer

Remove Intoxicated Drivers - USA **[12841]**
PO Box 520
Schenectady, NY 12301
PH: (518)372-0034
Toll free: 888-283-5144
Fax: (518)370-4917
Aiken, Doris, Founder, President

Peter Warlock Society **[9188]**
c/o Richard Valentine, Representative
1109 2nd Ave.
Schenectady, NY 12303-1643
PH: (518)209-8052
Mitchell, John R., Treasurer

Word of Life Fellowship **[20165]**
PO Box 600
Schroon Lake, NY 12870
PH: (518)494-6000
Lough, Donald H., Jr., Exec. Dir.

National Women's Hall of Fame **[20738]**
76 Fall St.
Seneca Falls, NY 13148

PH: (315)568-8060
Ryder, Beverly P., Bd. Member

National Academy of Building Inspection Engineers **[550]**
PO Box 860
Shelter Island, NY 11964
Binder, Alexandra M., Exec. Dir.

Malignant Hyperthermia Association of the United States **[14841]**
PO Box 1069
Sherburne, NY 13460
PH: (607)674-7901
Fax: (607)674-7910
Daugherty, Dianne M., Exec. Dir.

Neuroleptic Malignant Syndrome Information Service **[15975]**
Box 1069
Sherburne, NY 13460-1069
PH: (607)674-7920
Toll free: 888-667-8367
Fax: (607)674-7910
Daugherty, Dianne, Exec. Dir.

Sustainable Organic Integrated Livelihoods **[11448]**
124 Church Rd.
Sherburne, NY 13460
Kramer, Sasha, Exec. Dir., Founder

Guide Dog Foundation for the Blind **[17706]**
371 E Jericho Tpke.
Smithtown, NY 11787-2976
PH: (631)930-9000
Fax: (631)930-9009
Jones, Wells B., CAE, CEO

American Association for Women Podiatrists **[16776]**
c/o Karen A. Langone, DMP, Treasurer
365 Country Road 39A, Ste. 9
Benton Plz.
Southampton, NY 11968
Spector, Jennifer, Secretary

International Surgical Mission Support **[17393]**
365 County Rd. 39A, Ste. 11
Southampton, NY 11968
PH: (631)287-6202
Fax: (631)287-6213
Allam, Medhat E., MD, Chairman

North American Association for the Study of Religion **[20550]**
c/o Craig Martin, Executive Secretary/Treasurer
St. Thomas Aquinas College
125 Route 340
Sparkill, NY 10976
McCutcheon, Russell T., President

IOCALUM **[23326]**
c/o Roland Vinyard, Executive Secretary, 597 State Highway 162
597 State Highway 162
Sprakers, NY 12166
PH: (518)673-3212
Fax: (518)673-3219
Vinyard, Roland, Exec. Sec.

Waldorf Early Childhood Association of North America **[8451]**
285 Hungry Hollow Rd.
Spring Valley, NY 10977
PH: (845)352-1690
       (413)549-5930
Fax: (845)352-1695
Howard, Susan, Chairperson, Coord.

All4Israel **[12204]**
53 Dewhurst St.
Staten Island, NY 10314
Toll free: 877-812-7162
Indig, Zalman, Director

American Parkinson Disease Association **[15900]**
135 Parkinson Ave.
Staten Island, NY 10305
PH: (718)981-8001
Toll free: 800-223-2732
Fax: (718)981-4399
Greene, Fred, Chairman

Border Terrier Club of America **[21844]**
c/o Susan Friedenberg, Membership Chairperson
55 Marble St.
Staten Island, NY 10314-2131
PH: (718)761-2439
Steinbacher, Ann, Director

Earth's Physical Features Study Unit **[22325]**
c/o Jeffrey Hayward, President
163 Baden Pl.
Staten Island, NY 10306-6048
Hayward, Jeffrey, President

Egbe Omo Yoruba, North America **[19594]**
173 Hagaman Pl.
Staten Island, NY 10302
PH: (646)209-5158
Bolu Omodele, Agba-Akin, President

Forum for Religious Freedom **[20572]**
PO Box 60425
Staten Island, NY 10306-0425
PH: (240)506-0396
Shivaram, Indu, Contact

Freedom From Fear **[15770]**
308 Seaview Ave.
Staten Island, NY 10305-2246
PH: (718)351-1717
Guardino, Mary, Exec. Dir., Founder, President

Haiti Verte Foundation **[11372]**
169 Arlington Ave.
Staten Island, NY 10303
Brutus, Emmanuel, Founder

International Customer Service Association **[3075]**
1110 South Ave., Ste. 50
Staten Island, NY 10314
Toll free: 888-900-8503
Gessert, Bill, President

National Pro-Life Religious Council **[19064]**
PO Box 61838
Staten Island, NY 10306
PH: (718)980-4400
Fax: (718)980-6515
Van der Swaagh, Rev. Kirk, VP

Priests for Life **[19068]**
PO Box 141172
Staten Island, NY 10314
PH: (718)980-4400
Toll free: 888-735-3448
Fax: (718)980-6515
Morana, Janet A., Exec. Dir.

World Traditional Karate Organization **[23033]**
c/o John Mullin, Executive Chairman
521 Jewett Ave.
Staten Island, NY 10314
PH: (347)609-3608
Mullin, Mr. John J., Exec. Chmn. of the Bd.

World Trichology Society **[14904]**
2550 Victory Blvd., Ste. 305
Staten Island, NY 10314
PH: (718)698-4700
Kingsley, Dr. David, Chairman

International Association for Philosophy and Literature **[10090]**
310 Administration Bldg.
Philosophy Dept.
Stony Brook University
Stony Brook, NY 11794
PH: (631)331-4598
Silverman, Prof. Hugh J., Exec. Dir.

Ride for Life **[13686]**
Stony Brook University
Health Sciences Center, Level 2, Rm. 106
Stony Brook, NY 11794-8231
PH: (631)444-1292
Pendergast, Christopher, Founder, President

Sri Lanka Medical Association of North America **[15066]**
2500 Nesconset Hwy., Bldg. 16A
Stony Brook, NY 11790-2563
PH: (631)246-5454
Fax: (631)246-5902
Denepitiya, Lakshman, DDS, President

Presbyterian Peace Fellowship **[18823]**
17 Cricketown Rd.
Stony Point, NY 10980
PH: (845)786-6743
Ufford-Chase, Rick, Director

Coalition to Protect Animals in Parks and Refuges **[10602]**
PO Box 26
Swain, NY 14884-0026

Friends: The National Association of Young People Who Stutter **[17240]**
38 S Oyster Bay Rd.
Syosset, NY 11791
Toll free: 866-866-8335
Caggiano, Lee, Exec. Dir., Founder

Interactive Multimedia and Collaborative Communications Alliance **[769]**
PO Box 756
Syosset, NY 11791
PH: (516)818-8184
Zelkin, Carol, Exec. Dir.

National Urban Alliance for Effective Education **[8729]**
33 Queens St., Ste. 100
Syosset, NY 11791
PH: (516)802-4192
Toll free: 800-682-4556
Fax: (516)921-0298
Jackson, Dr. Yvette, CEO

Outsourcing Institute **[662]**
6800 Jericho Tpke., Ste. 120W
Syosset, NY 11791
PH: (516)279-6850

Alpha Kappa Delta **[7175]**
2507 James St., Ste. 210
Syracuse, NY 13206
PH: (315)883-0528
Fax: (315)410-5408
Titus, Bethany, Exec. Dir.

Association for Rehabilitation Marketing **[2268]**
118 Julian Pl.
Syracuse, NY 13210
Brown, Bill, Treasurer

Autism Network International **[13749]**
PO Box 35448
Syracuse, NY 13235-5448
PH: (315)476-2462
Sinclair, Jim, Contact

Ernst Bacon Society **[9905]**
8 Drovers Ln.
Syracuse, NY 13214-1805
Bacon, Ellen, President

International Betta Congress **[22033]**
c/o Steve Van Camp, Secretary
923 Wadsworth St.
Syracuse, NY 13208
Griffin, Gerald, President

International Society for Dialogical
Science **[7063]**
Psychology Dept.
Le Moyne College
1419 Salt Springs Rd.
Syracuse, NY 13214
Hermans, Hubert, President

National Board for Certification of
Orthopaedic Technologists, Inc.
[16484]
4736 Onondaga Blvd., No. 166
Syracuse, NY 13219
Toll free: 866-466-2268
Fax: (866)466-7067
Virgo, Mr. Jeffery J., OTC, Chairman

Near East Foundation **[18692]**
230 Euclid Ave.
Syracuse, NY 13210
PH: (315)428-8670
Ashby, John, Sr. VP, CFO

New Environment Association **[4091]**
c/o Charlotte Haas Quirk
1200 Euclid Ave.
Syracuse, NY 13210-2610
Schwarzlander, Pat, Contact

ProLiteracy **[8253]**
104 Marcellus St.
Syracuse, NY 13204
PH: (315)422-9121
Toll free: 888-528-2224
Fax: (315)422-6369
Morgan, Kevin, CEO, President

Kate Smith Commemorative Society
[24063]
PO Box 242
Syracuse, NY 13214-0242
Wood, Rev. Raymond B., President

United States Institute for Theatre
Technology **[10279]**
315 S Crouse Ave., Ste. 200
Syracuse, NY 13210-1844
PH: (315)463-6463
Toll free: 800-938-7488
Fax: (315)463-6525
Shanda, Mark, President

United States Society for Ecological
Economics **[4018]**
c/o Valerie Luzadis, President
106 Marshall Hall
1 Forestry Dr.
Syracuse, NY 13210-2712
PH: (315)470-6636
    (315)470-6695
Richardson, Robert, Secretary,
Treasurer

Association of Retired Hispanic
Police, Inc. **[5456]**
PO Box 722
Tallman, NY 10982-0722
PH: (845)521-4716
Cabo, Ralph, Treasurer

American Wire Cloth Institute **[1709]**
25 N Broadway
Tarrytown, NY 10591
PH: (914)332-0040
Fax: (914)332-1541

The William H. Donner Foundation,
Inc. **[13961]**
520 White Plains Rd., Ste. 500
Tarrytown, NY 10591
PH: (914)524-0404
Fax: (914)524-0407
Winsor, Rebecca D., President

Expansion Joint Manufacturers Association Inc. **[2605]**
25 N Broadway
Tarrytown, NY 10591
Fax: (914)332-1541

Hand Tools Institute **[1568]**
25 N Broadway
Tarrytown, NY 10591
PH: (914)332-0040
Fax: (914)332-1541

Intact America **[11283]**
PO Box 8516
Tarrytown, NY 10591
Bollinger, Daniel H., Officer

International Society for Medical
Publication Professionals **[2795]**
520 White Plains Rd., Ste. 500
Tarrytown, NY 10591
Toll free: 888-252-7904
Fax: (914)618-4453
Goldin, Kimberly, Gen. Mgr.

Network of Trial Law Firms **[5045]**
303 S Broadway, Ste. 222
Tarrytown, NY 10591
PH: (914)332-4400
Fax: (914)332-1671
Schultz, David, V. Chmn. of the Bd.

Tubular Exchanger Manufacturers
Association **[1638]**
25 N Broadway
Tarrytown, NY 10591
PH: (914)332-0040
Fax: (914)332-1541

Universal Peace Federation **[18836]**
200 White Plains Rd., 1st Fl.
Tarrytown, NY 10591
PH: (914)631-1331
Fax: (914)332-1582
Walsh, Dr. Thomas G., President

World Association of Non-
Governmental Organizations
[10767]
200 White Plains Rd., 1st Fl.
Tarrytown, NY 10591
Hwang, Dr. Sun Jo, Chairman

Intermediaries & Reinsurance
Underwriters Association, Inc.
[1872]
c/o The Beaumont Group, Inc.
3626 E Tremont Ave., Ste. 203
Throggs Neck, NY 10465
PH: (718)892-0228
Brost, James A., Mem.

Chromosome 9p- Network **[14812]**
PO Box 71
Tillson, NY 12486
PH: (920)931-2644
Constantino, Kris, Treasurer

Elizabeth Madox Roberts Society
[10369]
16 Montgomery St.
Tivoli, NY 12583
Nickel, Matthew, VP

American Automatic Control Council
[270]
Department of Chemical and Biologi-
cal Engineering
Rensselaer Polytechnic Institute
110 8th St.
Troy, NY 12180-3590
PH: (512)471-3061
Judd, Robert P., Div. Dir.

Audubon International **[3817]**
120 Defreest Dr.
Troy, NY 12180
PH: (518)767-9051
Toll free: 844-767-9051
Fax: (518)767-9076
Aylesworth, Ryan, President, CEO

Clan MacCarthy Society **[20819]**
c/o Robert P. McCarthy, 5 Fox Hollow Rd.
5 Fox Hollow Rd.
Troy, NY 12180-7224
McCarty, William M., MD, Secretary,
Treasurer

Electronic Music Foundation **[9904]**
176 3rd St.
Troy, NY 12180
PH: (518)434-4110
    (212)206-1505
Toll free: 888-749-9998
Fax: (518)434-0308
Chadabe, Benjamin, Exec. Dir.

Coalition Against Unsolicited Com-
mercial Email **[6442]**
PO Box 727
Trumansburg, NY 14886
PH: (303)800-6345
Schwartzman, Neil, Exec. Dir.

Welsh North American Association
[19689]
PO Box 1054
Trumansburg, NY 14886
PH: (607)279-7402
Fax: (877)448-6633
Williams, Dr. Megan, Exec. Sec.

AIDS-Free World **[13521]**
501 Northern Pky.
Uniondale, NY 11553
PH: (212)729-5084
Donovan, Paula, Director

Foundation for Accounting Education
[30]
PO Box 10490
Uniondale, NY 11555-0490
Toll free: 866-495-1354
Barry, Joanne S., Exec. Dir.

Haitian Orphans Wish **[11010]**
PO Box 138
Uniondale, NY 11553
Toussaint, Marcel, President

International Association for Protein
Structure Analysis and Proteomics
[6053]
c/o Carl W. Anderson, Secretary
Biology Dept.
Bookhaven National Laboratory
50 Bell Ave.
Upton, NY 11973-5000
Anderson, Dr. Carl W., Secretary

Gift of Life International **[12276]**
22 Clovebrook Rd.
Valhalla, NY 10595
PH: (845)546-2104
Toll free: 855-734-3278
Raylman, Rob, Exec. Dir., CEO

Kate Chopin International Society
[10385]
c/o Heather Ostman, President
English Dept.
Westchester Community College
75 Grasslands Rd.
Valhalla, NY 10595
Ostman, Heather, President

NAVAH **[13211]**
616 Corporate Way, Ste. 2 - 4560
Valley Cottage, NY 10989-2050
PH: (718)689-1493

Tolstoy Foundation Inc. **[19632]**
104 Lake Rd.
Valley Cottage, NY 10989
PH: (845)268-6722
Fax: (845)268-6937
Wohlsen, Victoria, Exec. Dir.

Building Homes for Heroes **[10738]**
65 Roosevelt Ave., Ste. 105
Valley Stream, NY 11581-1106

PH: (516)684-9220
Fax: (516)206-0181
Pujol, Andrew, Chairman, President,
Founder

International Federation of American
Homing Pigeon Fanciers **[22386]**
c/o Richard Smith, President
289 W Valley Stream Blvd.
Valley Stream, NY 11580-5340
PH: (516)794-3612
Smith, Richard, President

Tibetan Spaniel Club of America
[21969]
c/o William Chaffee, President
469 Langford Creek Rd.
Van Etten, NY 14889-9752
PH: (607)589-6868
    (419)352-1176
Briggs, Jean, VP

Cardio-Facio-Cutaneous
International **[14811]**
183 Brown Rd.
Vestal, NY 13850
PH: (607)772-9666
Fax: (607)748-0409
Conger, Brenda, Exec. Dir.,
President

Persons United Limiting Substan-
dards and Errors in Health Care
[15056]
PO Box 353
Wantagh, NY 11793-0353
PH: (516)579-4711
Toll free: 800-96P-ULSE
Fax: (516)520-8105
Corina, Ilene, Rep.

Student Letter Exchange **[21742]**
3280 Sunrise Hwy., PMB 62
Wantagh, NY 11793
PH: (631)393-0216
Fax: (631)759-3866

American Rhinologic Society **[16537]**
PO Box 495
Warwick, NY 10990
PH: (845)988-1631
Fax: (845)986-1527
Perez, Wendi, Administrator

Association for Computers and Taxa-
tion **[3201]**
PO Box 1093
Warwick, NY 10990
PH: (845)987-9690
Mattiola, Paul, Treasurer

World Peace Prayer Society **[18845]**
26 Benton Rd.
Wassaic, NY 12592
PH: (845)877-6093
Fax: (845)877-6862
Nobel, Mr. Claes, Chairman

Leafy Greens Council **[4238]**
PO Box 143
Waterport, NY 14571-0143
PH: (716)517-0248

Farm Sanctuary **[10623]**
3100 Aikens Rd.
Watkins Glen, NY 14891
PH: (607)583-2225
Fax: (607)583-2041
Lynch, Harry, CEO, Exec. Dir.

Society for the Advancement of
Education **[7799]**
766 Bermuda Rd., Ste. 2
West Babylon, NY 11704
PH: (516)729-4618
Rashid, Abbas, Exec. Dir.

Finnsheep Breeders Association
[4670]
c/o Mary Tucker, Secretary
PO Box 85

West Clarksville, NY 14786
PH: (585)928-1721
Tucker, Mary, Secretary

International Grooving & Grinding
Association **[790]**
12573 Route 9W
West Coxsackie, NY 12192
PH: (518)731-7450
Fax: (518)731-7490
Roberts, John, Exec. Dir.

John Burroughs Association **[6895]**
261 Floyd Ackert Rd.
West Park, NY 12493
PH: (845)384-6320
Breslof, Lisa, Secretary

National Collegiate Emergency
Medical Services Foundation
[14686]
PO Box 93
West Sand Lake, NY 12196
Toll free: 877-623-6731
Fax: (877)623-6731
Koenig, Dr. George J., DO,
President

North American Serials Interest
Group **[9719]**
1902 Ridge Rd., PMB 305
West Seneca, NY 14224-3312
Getz, Kelli, Secretary

Polish Union of America **[19614]**
745 Center Rd.
West Seneca, NY 14224-2108
PH: (716)677-0220
Fax: (716)677-0246

World Modern Arnis Alliance **[23031]**
PO Box 5
West Seneca, NY 14224
PH: (716)247-5254
Hartman, Timothy J., President,
Tech. Dir.

Catholic Traditionalist Movement
[19817]
210 Maple Ave.
Westbury, NY 11590-3117
PH: (516)333-6470
Fax: (516)333-7535
Cuneo, Richard A., President

Doc2Doc **[15599]**
1299 Corporate Dr., Ste. 703
Westbury, NY 11590
Charash, Bruce, MD, Founder

International EECP Therapists As-
sociation **[17449]**
PO Box 315
Westbury, NY 11590
PH: (513)777-0964
Tempich, Louanne, VP

National Circus Project **[9164]**
56 Lion Ln.
Westbury, NY 11590
PH: (516)334-2123
Fax: (516)334-2249
Milstein, Greg, Exec. Dir.

Society for Strings **[10012]**
Meadowmount School of Music
1424 County Route 10
Westport, NY 12993
PH: (518)962-2400
McGowan, Mary, Director

American Booksellers Association
[2944]
333 Westchester Ave., Ste. S202
White Plains, NY 10604
PH: (914)406-7500
Toll free: 800-637-0037
Fax: (914)417-4013
Teicher, Oren, CEO

American Booksellers Foundation for
Free Expression **[18292]**
c/o American Book Seller Associa-
tion
333 Westchester Ave., Ste. S202
White Plains, NY 10604
PH: (914)406-7576
(917)509-0340
Toll free: 800-727-4203
Fax: (212)587-2436
Finan, Chris, Director

American Maritime Safety **[2235]**
445 Hamilton Ave., Ste. 1204
White Plains, NY 10601-1833
PH: (914)997-2916
Fax: (914)997-6959
Middlebrook, Lucas, VP

Anguilla Tourist Board **[23656]**
246 Central Ave.
White Plains, NY 10606
PH: (914)287-2400
Toll free: 877-4AN-GUILLA
Fax: (914)287-2404
Walker, Marie, Contact

APA Division 24: Society for
Theoretical and Philosophical
Psychology **[16876]**
c/o Mary Beth Morrissey, Treasurer
7 Ellis Dr.
White Plains, NY 10605
Teo, Thomas, President

Ardent Lion Society **[11474]**
PO Box 356
White Plains, NY 10605
PH: (914)874-4480
Amoako-Agyeman, Romeo, CEO,
Founder

Carcinoid Cancer Foundation
[13935]
333 Mamaroneck Ave., No. 492
White Plains, NY 10605
PH: (914)683-1001
Toll free: 888-722-3132
Fax: (914)683-0183
Warner, Keith R.P., CEO

Center for Judicial Accountability,
Inc. **[18596]**
PO Box 8101
White Plains, NY 10602-8101
PH: (914)421-1200
Fax: (914)684-6554
Sassower, Doris L., JD, Administra-
tor, Founder

Corporate Angel Network **[13951]**
Westchester County Airport
1 Loop Rd.
White Plains, NY 10604-1215
PH: (914)328-1313
Fax: (914)328-3938
Fleiss, Mr. Peter H., Exec. Dir.

Encephalitis Global **[14574]**
1 Franklin Ave., Apt. 4C
White Plains, NY 10601
Guerci, Ingrid, Treasurer

International Academy of Matrimonial
Lawyers **[5577]**
1 N Lexington Ave.
White Plains, NY 10601
Longrigg, William, President

International Percy Grainger Society
[9539]
c/o Susan Edwards Colson
6 Benedict Ave.
White Plains, NY 10603
Hess, Lucinda, Contact

March of Dimes Foundation **[13831]**
1275 Mamaroneck Ave.
White Plains, NY 10605

PH: (914)997-4488
Howse, Dr. Jennifer L., President

National Action Council for Minorities
in Engineering **[7860]**
1 N Broadway, Ste. 601
White Plains, NY 10601-2318
PH: (914)539-4010
Fax: (914)539-4032
McPhail, Irving Pressley, President,
CEO

National Junior Tennis and Learning
[23302]
c/o United States Tennis Association
70 W Red Oak Ln.
White Plains, NY 10604-3602
Pasarell, Charlie, Founder

New York State Turf and Landscape
Association **[2072]**
1 Prospect Ave.
White Plains, NY 10607
PH: (914)993-9455
Fax: (914)993-9051
Wager, Joe, VP

NSX Club of America **[21464]**
333 Mamaroneck Ave., PMB No.
399
White Plains, NY 10605
Toll free: 877-679-2582
Fax: (844)329-6790
Urlage, Brian, President

Society of Motion Picture and Televi-
sion Engineers **[6594]**
3 Barker Ave., 5th Fl.
White Plains, NY 10601
PH: (914)761-1100
Fax: (914)761-3115
Lange, Barbara, Exec. Dir.

United States Tennis Association
[23309]
70 W Red Oak Ln., 4th Fl.
White Plains, NY 10604
PH: (914)697-2300
Fax: (914)694-2402
Smith, Gordon, Exec. Dir., COO

American Society of Master Dental
Technologists **[14417]**
146-21 13th Ave.
Whitestone, NY 11357-2420
Fax: (718)746-8355
Heppenheimer, Sue, Exec. Dir.

Angiosarcoma Awareness **[14562]**
PO Box 570442
Whitestone, NY 11357
Ryan, Lauren, Founder

Aviation Development Council **[129]**
14107 20th Ave., Ste. 404
Whitestone, NY 11357
PH: (718)746-0212
Fax: (718)746-1006
Huisman, Bill, Exec. Dir.

Society of Kastorians Omonoia
[19457]
150-28 14th Ave.
Whitestone, NY 11357
PH: (718)746-4505
(718)747-3246
Fax: (718)746-4506
Jimas, George, Bd. Member

American Banjo Fraternity **[9852]**
c/o Paul Heilman, Executive
Secretary
6929 Tuckahoe Rd.
Williamson, NY 14589
Heilman, Paul, Exec. Sec.

American Society of Tax Problem
Solvers **[5789]**
2250 Wehrle Dr., Ste. 3
Williamsville, NY 14221

PH: (716)630-1650
Fax: (716)630-1651
Lawler, Lawrence M., CPA, Director

Association for Scientific Advance-
ment in Psychological Injury and
Law **[13809]**
University at Buffalo
School of Medicine, Ste. 203
5820 Main St.
Williamsville, NY 14221
PH: (716)866-8517
Fax: (716)565-1511
Young, Gerald, PhD, President

Polish Singers Alliance of America
[9996]
208 Caesar Blvd.
Williamsville, NY 14221
Krenglicki, Mrs. Teresa, President

International Association of Master
Penmen, Engrossers, and Teachers of Handwriting **[10412]**
c/o Kathleen Markham, Treasurer
609 Marcellus Rd., 2nd Fl.
Williston Park, NY 11596
Gray, Linda, Rec. Sec.

Colon Club **[13948]**
17 Peach Tree Ln.
Wilton, NY 12831
Morgoslepov, Molly McMaster,
President, Founder

Haiti Air Ambulance **[12279]**
1 Media Crossways
Woodbury, NY 11797
Dolan, Patrick, Founder

International Mystery Shopping Alli-
ance **[2958]**
210 Crossways Park Dr.
Woodbury, NY 11797
PH: (516)576-1188
Tarica, Marcelo, Chairman

Photoimaging Manufacturers and
Distributors Association **[2589]**
7600 Jericho Tpke., Ste. 301
Woodbury, NY 11797
PH: (516)802-0895
Fax: (516)364-0140
Grossman, Jerry, Exec. Dir.

Emerald Isle Immigration Center
[18463]
59-26 Woodside Ave.
Woodside, NY 11377
PH: (718)478-5502
Fax: (718)446-3727
Dennehy, Siobhan, Exec. Dir.

Federation of French War Veterans
[21206]
39-45 51st St., Ste. 6F
Woodside, NY 11377-3165
PH: (718)426-1474
Dupuis, Alain H., President

MAAWS for Global Welfare **[12169]**
64-17 Broadway, 2nd Fl.
Woodside, NY 11377
PH: (718)478-1045
Fax: (718)565-6941
Yusuf, Dr. Nurun N., M.D, President

Topaz Arts **[9004]**
55-03 39th Ave.
Woodside, NY 11377
PH: (718)505-0440
Richmond, Mr. Todd, Director,
President

Creative Music Foundation **[9898]**
PO Box 671
Woodstock, NY 12498
PH: (845)679-8847
(845)679-5616
Berger, Dr. Karl Hans, Director,
Founder

Afya Foundation [15596]
140 Saw Mill River Rd.
Yonkers, NY 10701
PH: (914)920-5081
Fax: (914)920-5082
Butin, Danielle, MPH, Exec. Dir.

Groundwork USA [11370]
22 Main St., 2nd Fl.
Yonkers, NY 10701
PH: (914)375-2151
Fax: (914)375-2153
Magder, Rick, Exec. Dir.

International Imagery Association
[9546]
18 Edgecliff Ter.
Yonkers, NY 10705
PH: (914)476-0781
Fax: (914)476-5796
Ahsen, Akhter, PhD, Chairman,
Founder

Orthodox Christians for Life [20587]
c/o Hierodeacon Herman
575 Scarsdale Rd.
Yonkers, NY 10707
PH: (914)961-8313
Protopapas, Deacon John, Director,
Founder

Reserve Police Officers Association
[5518]
c/o Brooke Webster, President
89 Rockland Ave.
Yonkers, NY 10705
Toll free: 800-326-9416
Webster, Brooke, President

Standardbred Owners Association of
New York [22928]
733 Yonkers Ave., Ste. 102
Yonkers, NY 10704-2659
PH: (914)968-3599
Fax: (914)968-3943
Faraldo, Joe, President

Alpha Zeta Omega [23843]
c/o Lou Flacks, Director
2485 Pine Grove Ct.
Yorktown Heights, NY 10598
Ortega, Leonardo, Contact

Guiding Eyes for the Blind [17710]
611 Granite Springs Rd.
Yorktown Heights, NY 10598-3411
PH: (914)245-4024
Toll free: 800-942-0149
Fax: (914)245-1609
Panek, Thomas, CEO, President

Support Connection [14070]
40 Triangle Ctr., Ste. 100
Yorktown Heights, NY 10598
PH: (914)962-6402
Toll free: 800-532-4290
Fax: (914)962-1926
Quinn, Katherine, MBA, Exec. Dir.

NORTH CAROLINA

Art in the Public Interest [8958]
, NC
Burnham, Linda Frye, Director, Editor

Association of Shelter Veterinarians
[17637]
3225 Alphawood Dr.
Apex, NC 27539
PH: (919)803-6113
DiGangi, Brian A., DVM, MS,
DABVP, President

CR3 Diabetes Association, Inc.
[14521]
PO Box 792
Apex, NC 27502-0792

PH: (919)303-6949
Fax: (919)267-9629
Ray, Charles, III, CEO, Founder,
President

Food Aid International [12090]
PO Box 853
Apex, NC 27502
Toll free: 888-407-5125
Swartz, John, Founder, Chairman

The American Chestnut Foundation
[6129]
50 N Merrimon Ave., Ste. 115
Asheville, NC 28804
PH: (828)281-0047
Fax: (828)253-5373
Rea, Glen, Director

American Helvetia Philatelic Society
[22299]
c/o Richard T. Hall, Secretary
PO Box 15053
Asheville, NC 28813-0053
Heath, Roger, President

American Herbalists Guild [13595]
PO Box 3076
Asheville, NC 28802-3076
PH: (617)520-4372
Hernandez, Mimi, Exec. Dir.

The Association of Boarding Schools
[8460]
1 N Pack Sq., Ste. 301
Asheville, NC 28801
PH: (828)258-5354
Fax: (828)258-6428
Upham, Peter, Exec. Dir.

Center for Craft, Creativity and
Design [9012]
67 Broadway St.
Asheville, NC 28801
PH: (828)785-1357
Fax: (828)785-1372
Moore, Stephanie, Exec. Dir.

Environmental Paper Network [3858]
13 1/2 W Walnut St.
Asheville, NC 28801
PH: (828)251-8558

Foundation for P.E.A.C.E. [18785]
PO Box 9151
Asheville, NC 28815-0151
PH: (828)296-0194
Roush, James L., Editor

Helps International Ministries
[20423]
1340-J Patton Ave.
Asheville, NC 28806
PH: (828)277-3812
Fax: (828)274-7770
Harris, Bo, Exec. Dir.

International Disabled Self-Defense
Association [12864]
22-C New Leicester Hwy., No. 259
Asheville, NC 28806
Schmidt, Master Jurgen R.,
President

Jargon Society [9327]
56 Broadway St.
Asheville, NC 28801
PH: (828)350-8484
Arnal, Jeff, Exec. Dir.

National Paideia Center [7845]
29 1/2 Page Ave.
Asheville, NC 28801
PH: (828)575-5592
Roberts, Dr. Terry, Director

Pediatric Brain Tumor Foundation
[14043]
302 Ridgefield Ct.
Asheville, NC 28806

PH: (828)665-6891
Toll free: 800-253-6530
Fax: (828)665-6894
Eckert, Emilie, Exec. Asst., Office
Mgr.

Public Radio Program Directors Association [2826]
150 Hilliard Ave.
Asheville, NC 28801
PH: (828)424-7510
Goldstein, Abby, Secretary

Quilt Alliance [21780]
67 Broadway St., Ste. 200
Asheville, NC 28801
PH: (828)251-7073
Fax: (828)251-7073
Milne, Amy, Exec. Dir.

Sigma Alpha Iota International Music
Fraternity [23833]
1 Tunnel Rd.
Asheville, NC 28805
PH: (828)251-0606
Fax: (828)251-0644
Johnson, Ruth Sieber, Exec. Dir.

Small World Foundation, Inc.
[17399]
PO Box 25004
Asheville, NC 28813
Arnold, Laurence I., MD, CEO,
President

Swiss American Historical Society
[9440]
c/o Ernest Thurston, Membership
Secretary
65 Town Mountain Rd.
Asheville, NC 28804
Gillespie, Fred, President

Council of American Maritime
Museums [9828]
c/o Paul Fontenoy, Treasurer
North Carolina Maritime Museum
315 Front St.
Beaufort, NC 28516
Gorga, Greg, President

Christian Cheerleaders of America
[22725]
PO Box 49
Bethania, NC 27010-0049
Toll free: 877-243-3722
Fax: (866)222-1093
Clevenger, Rose, President

Presbyterian-Reformed Ministries
International [20528]
3227 N Fork Left Fork Rd.
Black Mountain, NC 28711-0429
PH: (828)669-7373
Fax: (828)669-4880
Long, Rev. Brad, Exec. Dir.

Natural Fibers Group [21301]
c/o Lynn Hoyt, President
549 Bluebird Trl.
Blounts Creek, NC 27814
Hoyt, Lynn, President

Access Health Africa [10828]
PO Box 57
Boone, NC 28607
PH: (828)263-6877
Pipes, Jesse, Exec. Dir.

Hannah's Promise International Aid
[12669]
120 Juniper Dr.
Boone, NC 28607
Kivette, Rad, CEO, Founder, Director

International Virginia Woolf Society
[9061]
c/o Jeanne Dubino, Secretary-
Treasurer

Appalachian State University
131 Living Learning Ctr.
Boone, NC 28608
PH: (828)262-7598
Fax: (828)262-6400
Hankins, Leslie Kathleen

Samaritan's Purse [12301]
PO Box 3000
Boone, NC 28607
PH: (828)262-1980
Fax: (828)266-1056
Graham, Franklin, Chmn. of the Bd.,
President

Wine to Water [13350]
747 W King St., Ste. 200, 2nd Fl.
Boone, NC 28607
PH: (828)355-9655
Hendley, Doc, Founder, President

World Medical Mission [15751]
c/o Samaritan's Purse
PO Box 3000
Boone, NC 28607
PH: (828)262-1980
Fax: (828)266-1056
Graham, W. Franklin, III, President,
Chairman

National Center for Homeless
Education [11956]
5900 Summit Ave., No. 201
Browns Summit, NC 27214
Toll free: 800-308-2145
Fax: (336)315-7457
Hancock, George, Director

Delta Chi Xi Honorary Dance
Fraternity [23716]
3218 Hiddenwood Ln.
Burlington, NC 27215
PH: (336)437-4479
Wade, Kara Jenelle, Founder

Second Marine Division Association
[21020]
PO Box 8180
Camp Lejeune, NC 28547
PH: (910)451-3176
Deitle, John O., 1st VP

Save A Generation [12724]
PO Box 370
Carolina Beach, NC 28428
Coffer, Rony, President, Founder

International Society on Thrombosis
and Haemostasis [15239]
610 Jones Ferry Rd., Ste. 205
Carrboro, NC 27510-6113
PH: (919)929-3807
Fax: (919)929-3935
Reiser, Thomas, Exec. Dir.

Business Golf Association of
America [22875]
c/o David Pitkin, Executive Director
PO Box 157
Cary, NC 27512-0157
PH: (919)906-2076
Thenstedt, Paul, Director

Clothed in Hope [13036]
314 Bonniewood Dr.
Cary, NC 27518
Bardi, Amy, Founder

Cotton Inc. [934]
6399 Weston Pky.
Cary, NC 27513
PH: (919)678-2220
Fax: (919)678-2230
Hake, Kater D., PhD, VP

Gastric Cancer Foundation [13977]
c/o The V Foundation for Cancer
Research

106 Towerview Ct.
Cary, NC 27513
Feinstein, Wayne, Chmn. of the Bd.

Global Warming Initiatives [4549]
108 Piperwood Dr.
Cary, NC 27518
PH: (919)829-7052

INDA, Association of the Nonwoven
Fabrics Industry [3259]
1100 Crescent Green, Ste. 115
Cary, NC 27518
PH: (919)459-3700
(919)233-1210
Fax: (919)459-3701
Ogle, Steve, Tech. Dir.

National Agritourism Professionals
Association [3573]
c/o Martha Glass, Executive Director
108 Forest Holls Ct.
Cary, NC 27511
PH: (919)467-5809
Glass, Martha, Exec. Dir.

National Council for Air and Stream
Improvement [4210]
1513 Walnut St., Ste. 200
Cary, NC 27511
PH: (919)941-6400
Fax: (919)941-6401
Joseph, Tommy, Chairman

National Pharmaceutical Association
[16679]
107 Kilmayne Dr., Ste. C
Cary, NC 27511
Toll free: 877-215-2091
Fax: (919)469-5858
Maxwell, Dr. Carleton B., President

Sigma Gamma Rho Sorority, Inc.
[23876]
1000 Southill Dr., Ste. 200
Cary, NC 27513
PH: (919)678-9720
Toll free: 888-747-1922
Fax: (919)678-9721
Morris, Rachel, Exec. Dir.

Trans World Radio [20469]
PO Box 8700
Cary, NC 27512
PH: (919)460-3700
Toll free: 800-456-7897
Fax: (919)460-3702
Libby, Lauren, President, CEO

Two Cents of Hope [11173]
423 Westfalen Dr.
Cary, NC 27519-9751
Swaroop, Prem, President

Vietnamese Nom Preservation
Foundation [9770]
229 Beachers Brook Ln.
Cary, NC 27511
Collins, Lee, President

Ladyslipper Music [10305]
PO Box 14
Cedar Grove, NC 27231
PH: (919)245-3737

Able Flight [11565]
91 Oak Leaf Ln.
Chapel Hill, NC 27516
PH: (919)942-4699
Stites, Charles H., Exec. Dir.

The American Board of Orthopaedic
Surgery [16464]
400 Silver Cedar Ct.
Chapel Hill, NC 27514
PH: (919)929-7103
Fax: (919)942-8988
Martin, David F., M.D., Exec. Dir.

American Board of Pediatrics
[16599]
111 Silver Cedar Ct.
Chapel Hill, NC 27514
PH: (919)929-0461
Fax: (919)929-9255
Nichols, David G., MD., President,
CEO

American Board of Professional
Psychology [16859]
600 Market St., Ste. 201
Chapel Hill, NC 27516
PH: (919)537-8031
Fax: (919)537-8034
Otto, Randy K., PhD, President

American Cleft Palate-Craniofacial
Association [14328]
1504 E Franklin St., Ste. 102
Chapel Hill, NC 27514-2820
PH: (919)933-9044
Toll free: 800-242-5338
Fax: (919)933-9604
Cohen, Marilyn A., President

Center for Urban and Regional Stud-
ies [8723]
University of North Carolina at
Chapel Hill
108 Battle Ln.
Chapel Hill, NC 27599-3410
PH: (919)962-3074
Fax: (919)962-2518
Rohe, Dr. William M., Director

Coalition for Peace with Justice
[18777]
PO Box 2081
Chapel Hill, NC 27515
PH: (919)914-9881

Empowerment Project [17943]
8218 Farrington Mill Rd.
Chapel Hill, NC 27517
PH: (919)225-5449

Group B Strep Association [14192]
PO Box 16515
Chapel Hill, NC 27516
Burns, Gina, President

Historians of Islamic Art Association
[8899]
c/o Glaire D. Anderson, Treasurer
UNC-Chapel Hill
115 S Columbia St., CB 3405
Chapel Hill, NC 27514
Fax: (919)962-0722
Canby, Sheila, President

International Brotherhood of Bioler-
makers - Stove, Furnace, Energy
and Allied Appliance Workers Division [23456]
1504 E Franklin St., Ste. 101
Chapel Hill, NC 27514

International Mammalian Genome
Society [6668]
c/o Darla Miller
Dept. of Genetics
University of North Carolina at
Chapel Hill
5047 Genetic Medicine Bldg.
Chapel Hill, NC 27599
Gunn, Teresa, President

IntraHealth International [15123]
6340 Quadrangle Dr., Ste. 200
Chapel Hill, NC 27517-7891
PH: (919)313-9100
(919)433-5720
Fax: (919)313-9108
Gaye, Pape Amadou, President,
CEO

National Alliance of Concurrent
Enrollment Partnerships [7636]
PO Box 578
Chapel Hill, NC 27514

PH: (919)593-5205
Toll free: 877-572-8693
Stetter, Tim, Officer

National Council Against Health
Fraud [18329]
11312 US 15-501 N, Ste. 107/108
Chapel Hill, NC 27517
PH: (919)533-6009
Barrett, Stephen, Bd. Member, Editor

Noise Free America [6924]
PO Box 2754
Chapel Hill, NC 27515
Toll free: 877-664-7366
Rueter, Mr. Ted, Contact

Nourish International [10728]
723 Mt. Carmel Church Rd.
Chapel Hill, NC 27517
PH: (919)338-2599
Phoenix, Kelly Leonhardt, Exec. Dir.

The Order of the Coif [23789]
University of North Carolina
CB No. 3385
Chapel Hill, NC 27599-3385
Gasaway, Laura N., Secretary,
Treasurer

OrganicAthlete [22513]
19 S Circle Dr.
Chapel Hill, NC 27516-3104
PH: (707)861-0004
Saul, Bradley, Founder, President

Phi Sigma Nu Native American
Fraternity, Inc. [23918]
Jackson Hall
University of Carolina at Chapel Hill
Chapel Hill, NC 27599

The Rho Chi Society [23847]
c/o UNC Eshelman School of
Pharmacy
University of North Carolina
3210 Kerr Hall, CB 7569
Chapel Hill, NC 27514
PH: (919)843-9001
Fax: (919)962-0644
Boucher, Bradley A., President

Society of Civil War Historians
[9512]
c/o UNC Press Journals Dept.
116 S Boundary St.
Chapel Hill, NC 27514
PH: (814)863-0151
(919)962-4201
Janney, Caroline E., President

Southeast Institute for Group and
Family Therapy [19119]
659 Edwards Ridge Rd.
Chapel Hill, NC 27517-9201
PH: (919)929-1171
Fax: (919)929-1174
Joines, Vann, PhD, Director,
President

Tanzer 16 Class Association [22674]
7111 Crescent Ridge Dr.
Chapel Hill, NC 27516
PH: (919)933-8208
Thorn, Pete, Contact

University of North Carolina General
Alumni Association [19364]
CB No 9180, Stadium Dr.
Chapel Hill, NC 27514
PH: (919)962-1208
Fax: (919)962-0010
Myers, Dan A., Chairman

WiderNet Project [8679]
104 S Estes Dr., Ste. 301A
Chapel Hill, NC 27514
PH: (919)240-4622
Missen, Cliff, MA, Director

325th Glider Infantry Association
[21181]
c/o Jesse Oxendine, Chairman
1812 Woodberry Rd.
Charlotte, NC 28212
PH: (704)537-4912
Oxendine, Jesse, Chairman

Action for Child Protection [10830]
2101 Sardis Rd. N, Ste. 204
Charlotte, NC 28227
PH: (704)845-2121

Advent Christian General Confer-
ence [19695]
14601 Albemarle Rd.
Charlotte, NC 28227
PH: (704)545-6161
Toll free: 800-676-0694
Fax: (704)573-0712
Lawson, Steve, Exec. Dir.

All We Want Is LOVE [18366]
300 Rampart St.
Charlotte, NC 28203
PH: (704)625-6263
Mourning, Jillian, Founder

American Kempo-Karate Association
[22981]
5760 Oak Dr.
Charlotte, NC 28216
PH: (704)393-1077
Toll free: 800-320-2552
Farrell, Soke Ray, President

American Recorder Society [9866]
PO Box 480054
Charlotte, NC 28269-5300
PH: (704)509-1422
Toll free: 844-509-1422
Podeschi, David, President

Association of Pediatric
Gastroenterology and Nutrition
Nurses [16121]
c/o Emmala Ryan Shonce, RN,
President
Levine Children's Hospital
1001 Blythe Blvd., MCP Ste. 200F
Charlotte, NC 28203
PH: (704)381-8898
Fax: (704)381-6851
Shonce, Emmala Ryan, RN,
President

Association of Professional Material
Handling Consultants [819]
8720 Red Oak Blvd., Ste. 201
Charlotte, NC 28217-3992
PH: (704)676-1190
Fax: (704)676-1199

Association of Regulatory Boards of
Optometry [16426]
200 S College St., Ste. 2030
Charlotte, NC 28202
PH: (704)970-2710
Toll free: 866-869-6852
Fax: (704)970-2720
Ritch, Jerry, OD

Austin-Healey Club of America
[21332]
c/o Fred Dabney, 2327 Christensens
Ct.
2327 Christensens Ct.
Charlotte, NC 28270
PH: (704)366-9808
Brierton, Gary, Chairman

Automatic Guided Vehicle Systems
[1717]
c/o MHI
8720 Red Oak Blvd., Ste. 201
Charlotte, NC 28217
PH: (704)676-1190
Fax: (704)676-1199
Kelly, Stacy, Chairman

Baptist Peace Fellowship of North America [18771]
300 Hawthorne Ln., Ste. 205
Charlotte, NC 28204-2434
PH: (704)521-6051
Fax: (704)521-6053
Paksoy, Allison, Mgr., Comm.

Billy Graham Evangelistic Association [20130]
1 Billy Graham Pkwy.
Charlotte, NC 28201-0001
PH: (704)401-2432
Toll free: 877-247-2426
Graham, Billy, Chairman

Campus Pride [11875]
PO Box 240473
Charlotte, NC 28224
PH: (704)277-6710
Self, Desi, Admin. Asst.

Christian Friends of Israel USA [19956]
c/o Hannele Pardain, Executive Director
PO Box 470258
Charlotte, NC 28247-0258
PH: (704)544-9110
Pardain, Hannele, Exec. Dir.

Christian Research Institute [19965]
PO Box 8500
Charlotte, NC 28271
Toll free: 888-700-0274
Hanegraaff, Hank, Chairman, President

Christian Small Publishers Association [2777]
PO Box 481022
Charlotte, NC 28269
PH: (704)277-7194
Fax: (704)717-2928
Bolme, Sarah, Director, Founder

Conference on Latin American History [9660]
Dept. of History
University of North Carolina at Charlotte
9201 University City Blvd.
Charlotte, NC 28223
PH: (704)687-5129
Fax: (704)687-3218

Craft Retailers Association for Tomorrow [21753]
11238 Home Place Ln.
Charlotte, NC 28227
PH: (980)938-4574
Milstein, Donna, VP

Crane Manufacturers Association of America [1725]
c/o MHI
8720 Red Oak Blvd., Ste. 201
Charlotte, NC 28217-3996
PH: (704)676-1190
Fax: (704)676-1199
Becker, Chris, President

Electrification and Controls Manufacturers Association [1726]
c/o MHI
8720 Red Oak Blvd., Ste. 201
Charlotte, NC 28217-3996
PH: (704)676-1190
Fax: (704)676-1199
Sparks, Mike, Chairman

The Employers Association [1068]
3020 W Arrowood Rd.
Charlotte, NC 28273
PH: (704)522-8011
Fax: (704)522-8105
Colbert, Kenny L., SPHR, President, CEO

Evrytanian Association of America [19453]
121 Greenwich Rd., Ste. 212
Charlotte, NC 28211
PH: (704)366-6571
Fax: (704)366-6678
Kazakos, Sophia, Secretary

Flags Across the Nation [20946]
PO Box 78995
Charlotte, NC 28271-7045
PH: (704)962-1868
Schwartz, Eileen A., Founder, President

FreeThoughtAction [10086]
PO Box 12238
Charlotte, NC 28220

Friends of Feral Felines [21569]
PO Box 473385
Charlotte, NC 28247-3385
PH: (704)348-1578

From Hunger to Harvest [12096]
Charlotte, NC
Nyei, Mr. Abraham Habib, Founder, President

Girls on the Run International [23117]
801 E Morehead St., Ste. 201
Charlotte, NC 28202
PH: (704)376-9817
Toll free: 800-901-9965
Fax: (704)376-1039
Kunz, Elizabeth, CEO

Hagar USA [12038]
1609 E 5th St., Ste. 2
Charlotte, NC 28204
PH: (803)322-2221
   (980)272-0114
Casey, Ray, CEO

Hoist Manufacturers Institute [1733]
c/o MHI
8720 Red Oak Blvd., Ste. 201
Charlotte, NC 28217-3996
PH: (704)676-1190
Fax: (704)676-1199
Burkey, Bob, President

International Marking and Identification Association [3174]
PO Box 49649
Charlotte, NC 28277
Hewitt, Steve, Exec. Dir., Director

International Nanny Association [10808]
PO Box 18126
Charlotte, NC 28218
Toll free: 888-878-1477
Fax: (508)638-6462
Gibson, Cortney, President

International Tinnitus Awareness Association [17241]
8408 Markethouse Ln.
Charlotte, NC 28227
PH: (704)567-6860
Hunt, William Randolph, Founder, President

Latin America Mission [20430]
United World Mission
205 Regency Executive Park Dr., Ste. 430
Charlotte, NC 28217
PH: (704)357-3355
Toll free: 800-825-5896
Bernard, John, President

Latin American Women's Association [13381]
3440 Toringdon Way, Ste. 205
Charlotte, NC 28277

PH: (704)552-1003
Rey, Ana Silva, President

Loading Dock Equipment Manufacturers [1742]
c/o MHI
8720 Red Oak Blvd., Ste. 201
Charlotte, NC 28217-3996
PH: (704)676-1190
Fax: (704)676-1199
Pilgrim, Mike, Chairman

Material Handling Industry [1748]
8720 Red Oak Blvd., Ste. 201
Charlotte, NC 28217-3996
PH: (704)676-1190
Toll free: 800-345-1815
Fax: (704)676-1199
Paxton, John, Chmn. of the Bd.

Material Handling Industry of America - Order Fulfillment Solutions [3439]
8720 Red Oak Blvd., Ste. 201
Charlotte, NC 28217-3996
PH: (704)676-1190
Fax: (704)676-1199
Paxton, John, Chairman

Material Handling Institute of American - Lift Manufacturers Product Section [1749]
8720 Red Oak Blvd., Ste. 201
Charlotte, NC 28217-3996
PH: (704)676-1190
Fax: (704)676-1199
Carbott, Tom, VP

Materials Handling Institute [6814]
8720 Red Oak Blvd., Ste. 201
Charlotte, NC 28217
PH: (704)676-1190
Fax: (704)676-1199
Paxton, John, Chairman

The Mommies Network [13385]
8116 S Tryon St., Ste. B-3, No. 202
Charlotte, NC 28273
PH: (980)429-4666
Meininger, Heather, Founder, President

Monorail Manufacturers Association [1751]
c/o MHI
8720 Red Oak Blvd., Ste. 201
Charlotte, NC 28217
PH: (704)676-1190
Fax: (704)676-1199
Beightol, Rob, President

Mothering Across Continents [11081]
310 Arlington Ave., Ste. 303
Charlotte, NC 28203
PH: (704)607-1333
Shafer, Patricia, Contact

Multiple System Atrophy Coalition [15958]
9935-D Rea Rd., Ste. 212
Charlotte, NC 28277
Toll free: 866-737-5999
Crouse, Don, VP

National African-American RV'ers Association [22430]
614 Chipley Ave.
Charlotte, NC 28205
PH: (704)333-3070
Fax: (704)333-3071
Horton, Lemeul, President

National Board of Examiners in Optometry [16430]
200 S College St., No. 2010
Charlotte, NC 28202
PH: (704)332-9565
Toll free: 800-969-EXAM
Fax: (704)332-9568
Terry, Jack, PhD, CEO

National Optometric Association [16432]
1801 N Tryon St., Ste. 315
Charlotte, NC 28206
PH: (704)918-1809
Toll free: 877-394-2020
Johnson-Brown, Stephanie, Officer

Neurosurgery Executives' Resource Value and Education Society [16066]
1300 Baxter St., Ste. 360
Charlotte, NC 28204
PH: (704)940-7386
Fax: (704)365-3678
Butler, Scott, President

North American Young Generation in Nuclear [6931]
PO Box 32642
Charlotte, NC 28232-2642
Ashworth, Bobby, President

Patient Access Network Foundation [11930]
PO Box 221858
Charlotte, NC 28222
PH: (202)347-9271
Toll free: 866-316-7263
McKercher, Patrick, PhD, President

Pi Kappa Phi [23921]
2015 Ayrsley Town Blvd., Ste. 200
Charlotte, NC 28273
PH: (704)504-0888
Fax: (980)318-5295
Timmes, Mr. Mark E., CEO

Professional Construction Estimators Association of America, Inc. [899]
PO Box 680336
Charlotte, NC 28216
PH: (704)489-1494
Toll free: 877-521-7232
Barton, Bill, President

Rack Manufacturers Institute [1764]
8720 Red Oak Blvd., Ste. 201
Charlotte, NC 28217-3996
PH: (704)676-1190
Fax: (704)676-1199
Schwebel, David, Exec.

Reiki Education and Research Institute [17102]
725 Providence Rd., Ste. 200
Charlotte, NC 28207
PH: (704)644-3644
Coryer, Bill, Founder

Retail Solutions Providers Association [6332]
9920 Couloak Dr., Unit 120
Charlotte, NC 28216
Toll free: 800-782-2693
Fax: (704)357-3127
Seymour, Mike, Chmn. of the Bd.

Ryukyu Philatelic Specialist Society [22360]
PO Box 240177
Charlotte, NC 28224-0177
Weiss, Dr. Gary B., VP

Samaritan's Feet [11146]
1836 Center Park Dr.
Charlotte, NC 28217
PH: (980)939-8150
Toll free: 866-833-7463
Fax: (704)341-1687
Ohonme, Emmanuel, Founder, President

Section for Women in Public Administration [5701]
c/o Phin Xaypangna, Treasurer
2828 Mt. Isle Harbor Dr.
Charlotte, NC 28214
Nichol, Heather, Secretary

Storage Manufacturers Association
[1771]
c/o Material Handling Institute
8720 Red Oak Blvd., Ste. 201
Charlotte, NC 28217
PH: (704)676-1190
Fax: (704)676-1199
Schwebel, David, Exec.

Unitarian Universalist Musicians'
Network [20496]
c/o Donna Fisher, Executive
Administrator
2208 Henery Tuckers Ct.
Charlotte, NC 28270
Toll free: 800-969-8866
Fisher, Donna, Administrator

United Israel World Union [20009]
2124 Crown Centre Dr., Ste. 300
Charlotte, NC 28227

United World Mission [20472]
205 Regency Executive Park Dr.,
Ste. 430
Charlotte, NC 28217
PH: (704)357-3355
Toll free: 800-825-5896
Fax: (704)357-6389
Bernard, Rev. John, President

American Flock Association [3253]
PO Box 1090
Cherryville, NC 28021
PH: (617)303-6288
Fax: (617)671-2366
Shah, Raj, Chmn. of the Exec. Com-
mittee

TVR Car Club North America
[21507]
c/o Terry Telke, Membership
Chairperson
267 Ocean Dr.
Clayton, NC 27520
Hess, Tony, President

Ekissa [12031]
PO Box 370
Clemmons, NC 27012
PH: (336)971-4855
Hales, Sarah, Founder, Treasurer

International Association of Applied
Control Theory [6039]
643 Barrocliff Rd.
Clemmons, NC 27012-8543
PH: (336)813-8484
Smith, Glenn, Fac. Memb.

Emergency Response Massage
International [15555]
227 S Peak St.
Columbus, NC 28722-9493
PH: (704)763-6099
Yandle, Abbie G., President

International Society of Political
Psychology [16921]
126 Ward St., Ste. 1213
Columbus, NC 28722
PH: (828)894-5422
Fax: (828)894-5422
Bennett, Severine, CGMP, PMP,
Exec. Dir.

Challenge Coin Association [22263]
1375 Mistletoe Ridge Pl. NW
Concord, NC 28027
PH: (704)723-1170
(704)918-6992
Fax: (704)723-9202
Medford, Jesse L., President

International Society for the History
of the Neurosciences [6916]
c/o Sherry R. Ginn, Secretary
Rowan-Cabarrus Community College

1531 Trinity Church Rd.
Concord, NC 28027
PH: (704)216-3799
Fax: (704)216-0992
Ginn, Sherry R., Secretary,
Treasurer

Lionel Railroader Club [22187]
6301 Performance Dr.
Concord, NC 28027-3426
PH: (586)949-4100
Toll free: 800-454-6635
Cowen, Joshua Lionel, Founder

The Safer Racer Tour [12843]
4537 Orphanage Rd.
Concord, NC 28027
PH: (704)795-7474
LaJoie, Randy, Founder

Mobile Riverine Force Association
[21167]
c/o Albert B. Moore, President
106 Belleview Dr. NE
Conover, NC 28613
PH: (828)464-7228
Moore, Albert B., President

National Country Ham Association
[1356]
PO Box 948
Conover, NC 28613
PH: (828)466-2760
Toll free: 800-820-4426
Fax: (828)466-2770
Goonight, Bill, President

Addi's Cure [15538]
c/o Bo Johnson, Founder
19520 W Catawba Ave., Ste. 200
Cornelius, NC 28031
Johnson, Bo, Founder

International Art Materials Associa-
tion [245]
20200 Zion Ave.
Cornelius, NC 28031
PH: (704)892-6244
Fax: (704)892-6247
Hall, Reggie, Exec. Dir.

National Art Materials Trade Associa-
tion [1541]
20200 Zion Ave.
Cornelius, NC 28031
PH: (704)892-6244
Hall, Reggie, Exec. Dir.

Public Choice Society [7049]
224C Forsyth Hall
College of Business
Western Carolina University
1 University Way
Cullowhee, NC 28723
PH: (608)363-2775
Herzberg, Roberta Q., President

Antiques and Collectibles National
Association [195]
PO Box 4389
Davidson, NC 28036
Toll free: 800-287-7127
Fax: (704)895-0230
Becker, Ms. Angie, President

International Vladimir Nabokov
Society [9083]
Davidson College
English Dept.
Davidson, NC 28036
Kuzmanovich, Zoran, Editor, VP

Gravure Association of the Americas,
Inc. [1536]
8281 Pine Lake Rd.
Denver, NC 28037
PH: (201)523-6042
Fax: (201)523-6048
Schenk, Pamela W., Dir. of Admin.

ACLU Capital Punishment Project
[17827]
201 W Main St., Ste. 402
Durham, NC 27701-3228
PH: (919)682-5659
Fax: (919)682-5961
Herman, Susan N., President

American Association for Gifted
Children [7941]
Erwin Mill Bldg.
2024 W Main St.
Durham, NC 27705
PH: (919)684-8459
Evans Gayle, Margaret, Exec. Dir.

American Dance Festival [9241]
715 Broad St.
Durham, NC 27705
PH: (919)684-6402
Fax: (919)684-5459
Nimerichter, Jodee, Director

American Dialect Society [9736]
PO Box 90660
Durham, NC 27708-0660
PH: (919)688-5134
Toll free: 888-651-0122
Metcalf, Allan A., Exec. Sec.

American Sexually Transmitted
Diseases Association [17193]
1005 Slater Rd., Ste. 330
Durham, NC 27703
PH: (919)861-9399
Fax: (919)361-8425
Rietmeijer, Cornelis A., MD,
President

American Society of Papyrologists
[10063]
233 Allen Bldg.
Dept. of Classical Studies
Duke University
Durham, NC 27708-0103
Fax: (919)681-4262
Johnson, William A., Secretary,
Treasurer

Ashraya Initiative for Children
[10857]
5804 Renee Dr.
Durham, NC 27705
PH: (607)301-1242
Sholtys, Elizabeth, Founder

Associated Parishes for Liturgy and
Mission [20093]
3405 Alman Dr.
Durham, NC 27705
Koyle, Jay, President

Association of Graduate Liberal
Studies Programs [8227]
Duke University
2114 Campus Dr.
Durham, NC 27708-9940
PH: (919)684-1987
Fax: (919)681-8905
Finkel, Deborah, President

Association of International Educa-
tion Administrators [7425]
2204 Erwin Rd., Rm. 030
Durham, NC 27708-0404
PH: (919)668-1928
Fax: (919)684-8749
Latz, Dr. Gil, President

Association of Nigerian Physicians in
the Americas [16742]
506 Summer Storm Dr.
Durham, NC 27704
PH: (919)230-1488
(913)402-7102
Fax: (928)496-7006
Chukwumerije, Nkem, President

Autoimmune Encephalitis Alliance
[15394]
920 Urban Ave.
Durham, NC 27701
McDow, Will, Chairman

Beta Alpha Psi [23669]
220 Leigh Farm Rd.
Durham, NC 27707
PH: (919)402-4044
Fax: (919)402-4040
Baum, Hadassah, CPA

Center for Professional Well-Being
[15115]
21 W Colony Pl., Ste. 150
Durham, NC 27705
PH: (919)489-9167
Fax: (919)419-0011
Pfifferling, John-Henry, PhD, Direc-
tor, Founder

Childhood Arthritis and Rheumatol-
ogy Research Alliance [17156]
2608 Erwin Rd., Ste. 148-191
Durham, NC 27705
PH: (919)668-7531
Toll free: 800-377-5731
Wallace, Carol, Chairman

Chordoma Foundation [13943]
PO Box 2127
Durham, NC 27702
PH: (919)809-6779
Fax: (866)367-3910
Sommer, Josh, Exec. Dir.

Committee on the Status of Women
in the Economics Profession
[5159]
Duke University
Durham, NC 27708-0097
PH: (850)562-1211
Fax: (919)684-8974
McElroy, Marjorie, Chairperson

Consortium of Humanities Centers
and Institutes [9553]
Box 90403
Duke University
114 S Buchanan Blvd.
Durham, NC 27708-0403
Aravamudan, Srinivas, President

DiabetesSisters [14532]
2530 Meridian Pkwy., Ste. 2123
Durham, NC 27713
PH: (919)361-2012
Toll free: 855-361-2012
Barnes, Brandy, CEO, Founder

Divers Alert Network [22810]
6 W Colony Pl.
Durham, NC 27705
PH: (919)684-2948
Toll free: 800-446-2671
Fax: (919)490-6630
Ziefle, William, President, CEO

Engineering World Health [15448]
The Prizery, Ste. 200
302 E Pettigrew St.
Durham, NC 27701
PH: (919)682-7788
Peck, Catherine, Bd. Member

Federation of Schools of Ac-
countancy [7408]
c/o Megan Tarasi, Administrator
Pailadian I
220 Leigh Farm Rd.
Durham, NC 27707-8110
PH: (919)402-4825
Tarasi, Megan, Administrator

FHI 360 [8469]
359 Blackwell St., Ste. 200
Durham, NC 27701

PH: (919)544-7040
  (212)367-4573
Fax: (919)544-7261
Temeemi, Sean, CFE, CICA, Comp.
  Ofc.

Fitness Forward [16700]
202 Remington Cir.
Durham, NC 27705
PH: (919)309-4446
Langheier, Jason, Chairman,
  Founder, Exec. Dir.

Forest History Society [9477]
701 William Vickers Ave.
Durham, NC 27701
PH: (919)682-9319
Fax: (919)682-2349
Kelly, L. Michael, Chairman

Furniture Society [1479]
4711 Hope Valley Rd., Ste. 4F, No.
  512
Durham, NC 27707-5651
PH: (828)581-9663
Dickey, Forest, VP

Green Home Council [534]
PO Box 51008
Durham, NC 27717-1008
PH: (919)624-7903
Fax: (919)493-1240
Beasley, Bill, Exec. Dir., Founder

Institute for Southern Studies [8798]
PO Box 531
Durham, NC 27702
PH: (919)419-8311
Fax: (919)419-8315
Kromm, Chris, Exec. Dir., Publisher

Insurance Accounting and Systems
  Association [1862]
3511 Shannon Rd., Ste. 160
Durham, NC 27707
PH: (919)489-0991
Fax: (919)489-1994
Pomilia, Joe, Exec. Dir.

International Association for Account-
  ing Education & Research [35]
c/o Katherine Schipper, President
Duke University
The Fuqua School of Business
100 Fuqua Dr.
Durham, NC 27708
Schipper, Katherine, President

International Association for Near-
  Death Studies [7013]
Bldg. 500
2741 Campus Walk Ave.
Durham, NC 27705-8878
PH: (919)383-7940
Fax: (919)383-7940
Amsden, Susan, Bus. Mgr.

International Lead Zinc Research
  Organization [6845]
1822 NC Hwy. 54 E, Ste. 120
Durham, NC 27713-3210
PH: (919)361-4647
Fax: (919)361-1957
Reid, Eustace

International Neurotoxicology As-
  sociation [7342]
c/o Edward D. Levin, PhD, President
Psychiatry and Behavioral Sciences
School of Medicine
Duke Institute for Brain Sciences
Durham, NC 27708
PH: (919)681-6273
Levin, Edward D., PhD, President

International Organization of
  Chinese Physicist and
  Astronomers [7025]
c/o Albert M. Chang, President-elect
PO Box 90305

Durham, NC 27708
PH: (919)660-2569
Fax: (919)660-2525
Xu, Nu, VP

International Society of Barristers
  [5825]
210 Science Dr.
Durham, NC 27708-0360
PH: (919)613-7085
Barrasso, Judy, VP

International Society for Bayesian
  Analysis [6822]
Box 90251
Duke University
Durham, NC 27708-0251
MacEachern, Steven, President

International Society for Heart
  Research [14128]
c/o Dr. Leslie Anderson Lobaugh,
  Executive Secretary
PO Box 52643
Durham, NC 27717-2643
Fax: (919)493-4418
Avkiran, Dr. Metin, President

International Zinc Association United
  States [2353]
2530 Meridian Pky., Ste. 115
Durham, NC 27713
PH: (919)361-4647

Junior Shag Association [9265]
c/o Gene Pope, President
3753 E Geer St.
Durham, NC 27704
PH: (919)682-4266
Pope, Gene, President

Just for Openers [21681]
c/o John Stanley
PO Box 51008
Durham, NC 27717
Stanley, John, Contact

Labor and Working Class History
  Association [8165]
Duke University
226 Carr Bldg.
Durham, NC 27708
PH: (919)688-5134
Toll free: 888-651-0122
Gregory, James, President

National Association of Blacks in
  Criminal Justice [11536]
Whiting Criminal Justice Bldg.
1801 Fayetteville St.
Durham, NC 27707
PH: (919)683-1801
Toll free: 866-846-2225
Fax: (919)683-1903
Holder, Carlyle I., President

National Association of Negro Musi-
  cians [9968]
PO Box 51669
Durham, NC 27717
PH: (919)489-4139
Lawton, Dr. Orville, Asst. Treas.

National MPS Society [15830]
PO Box 14686
Durham, NC 27713
PH: (919)806-0101
Toll free: 877-MPS-1001
Bozarth, Stephanie, President

North American Taiwan Studies As-
  sociation [9214]
c/o Hong, Gou-Juin, Advisor
Campus Box 90414
2204 Erwin Rd., Rm. 220
Durham, NC 27708
PH: (919)660-4396
Fax: (919)981-7871
Cheng, Eric Siu-kei, Secretary

Organization for Tropical Studies -
  North American Office [7353]
410 Swift Ave.
Durham, NC 27705-4831
PH: (919)684-5774
Fax: (919)684-5661
Losos, Elizabeth, CEO, President

OurEarth.org [3927]
PO Box 62133
Durham, NC 27715
PH: (410)878-6485
Ullman, John, President

People of Faith Against the Death
  Penalty [17832]
PO Box 61943
Durham, NC 27701
PH: (919)933-7567
Dear, Stephen, Exec. Dir.

Rhine Research Center [6991]
Bldg. 500
2741 Campus Walk Ave.
Durham, NC 27705
PH: (919)309-4600
Bennett, Lisa, Office Mgr.

Rock Against Cancer [14057]
4711 Hope Valley Rd.
Durham, NC 27707
Toll free: 877-246-0976
White, Lisa L., PhD, Founder, Exec.
  Dir.

Sequoia Helping Hands [11148]
PO Box 13015
Durham, NC 27709-3015
PH: (919)469-3095
Asiyo, Juni, Chairman, Founder

Society for French Historical Studies
  [9514]
905 W Main St., Ste. 18B
Durham, NC 27701
Zdatny, Steven, Exec. Dir.

Society of Systematic Biologists
  [7404]
c/o Anne Yoder, President
Dept. of Biology
Duke University
315 Science Dr.
Durham, NC 27708
Yoder, Anne, President

Society for Translational Oncology
  [16359]
318 Blackwell St., Ste. 270
Durham, NC 27701
PH: (919)433-0489
Goldberg, Richard M., MD, Co-Ch.

Stop Soldier Suicide [13199]
318 Blackwell St., Ste. 130
Durham, NC 27701
Kinsella, Brian, Founder, CEO

Turnbull Clan Association [20938]
c/o Wally Turnbull, President
5216 Tahoe Dr.
Durham, NC 27713
PH: (919)361-5041
Fax: (866)585-4635
Turnbull, Brian P., Treasurer, VP

U.S.A. Baseball [22568]
1030 Swabria Crt., Ste. 201
Durham, NC 27701
PH: (919)474-8721
Fax: (919)474-8822
Seiler, Paul, Exec. Dir., CEO

Sustainable Furnishings Council
  [1489]
100 E King St., Ste. 1
Edenton, NC 27932
PH: (252)368-1098
Smith, Amy, Secretary

United States Equine Rescue
  League, Inc. [4418]
1851 W Erhinghaus St., Ste. 146
Elizabeth City, NC 27909
Toll free: 800-650-8549
Woodard, Amy, Chairperson

Society for Indian Philosophy and
  Religion [9572]
PO Box 79
Elon, NC 27244
Chakrabarti, Dr. Chandana, VP

Champagne Horse Breeders' and
  Owners' Association [4342]
619 Raiford Rd.
Erwin, NC 28339
PH: (910)891-5022
Hamilton, Vonda, President

82nd Airborne Division Association
  [21097]
PO Box 87482
Fayetteville, NC 28304-7482
PH: (910)223-1182
Toll free: 844-272-0047
Shoppe, Allen E., President

Civil Affairs Association [5596]
6689 Kodiak Dr.
Fayetteville, NC 28304
PH: (910)835-1314
Kirlin, Joseph P., III, President

International Association for the
  Study of Popular Romance [9760]
887 Flintwood Rd.
Fayetteville, NC 28314
Frantz, Sarah S.G., President

Saleeby-Saliba Association of
  Families [20923]
PO Box 87094
Fayetteville, NC 28304
Saleeby, Eli Leonard, President

Special Forces Association [21032]
4990 Doc Bennett Rd.
Fayetteville, NC 28306
PH: (910)485-5433
Fax: (910)485-1041
Tobin, Jack, President

Spirit of the Sage Council [3948]
439 Westwood SC, No. 144
Fayetteville, NC 28314-1532
Vera Rocha, Ya'anna, Founder

National Technical Honor Society
  [23985]
PO Box 1336
Flat Rock, NC 28731
PH: (828)698-8011
Fax: (828)698-8564
Powell, Allen C., Exec. Dir.

American Association of Radon
  Scientists and Technologists
  [6659]
4989 Hendersonville Rd.
Fletcher, NC 28732
Fax: (828)214-6299
Hendrick, Peter, Exec. Dir.

Chromosome 22 Central [14814]
c/o Murney Rinholm, President
7108 Partinwood Dr.
Fuquay Varina, NC 27526
PH: (919)567-8167
Rinholm, Murney, President

Coin Operated Collectors Association [21638]
4804 Clubview Ct.
Fuquay Varina, NC 27526-8681
PH: (330)837-2265
  (419)350-0477
Cain, Doug, President

National Adult Day Services Association **[10516]**
1421 E Broad St., Ste. 425
Fuquay Varina, NC 27526-1968
Toll free: 877-745-1440
Fax: (919)825-3945
Anderson, Keith, Secretary

4 the World **[11300]**
404 Butler Dr.
Garner, NC 27529
Froom, Robert Keith, Founder

504th Parachute Infantry Regiment Association **[21183]**
c/o Ronald H. Rath, Treasurer
22 Club Hill Dr.
Garner, NC 27529-6528
PH: (919)803-4554
Fax: (919)803-2400
Briseno, Michael A., President

American Society of Crime Laboratory Directors **[5238]**
139A Technology Dr.
Garner, NC 27529
PH: (919)773-2044
Fax: (919)861-9930
Stover, Jean, Exec. Dir.

Association of Health Facility Survey Agencies **[5712]**
5105 Solemn Grove Rd.
Garner, NC 27529
Linneman, Dean, President

Feral Cat Friends, Inc. **[21568]**
8255 White Oak Rd.
Garner, NC 27529-8816
PH: (919)662-3989

National Association of Produce Market Managers **[4478]**
PO Box 1617
Garner, NC 27529
PH: (919)779-5258
Kane, Dan, President

Association of American Seed Control Officials **[4944]**
c/o Fawad Shah, Director
801 Summit Crossing Pl., Ste. C
Gastonia, NC 28054-2194
PH: (704)810-8884
Malone, Steve, President

Southern Textile Association, Inc. **[3269]**
PO Box 66
Gastonia, NC 28053-0066
PH: (704)215-4543
Fax: (704)215-4160
Boehmer, Judson L., Chairman

American Collectors of Infant Feeders **[21608]**
c/o Charna Sansbury, Treasurer
30 White Birch Ct.
Gibsonville, NC 27249
Thomason, Metty, President

International Cesarean Awareness Network **[16287]**
PO Box 573
Glen Alpine, NC 28628
Toll free: 800-686-4226
Seger, Lindsey, President

American Academy of Micropigmentation **[14302]**
c/o Charles S. Zwerling, Chairman of the Board
2709 Medical Office Pl.
Goldsboro, NC 27534
PH: (919)736-3937
Toll free: 888-302-3482
Fax: (919)735-3701
Zwerling, Charles S., MD, Chmn. of the Bd.

National Association of Human Rights Workers **[12051]**
c/o LaTerrie Ward, Treasurer
PO Box 283
Goldsboro, NC 27533
PH: (919)580-4359
Ward, LaTerrie, Treasurer

American Board of Science in Nuclear Medicine **[16074]**
c/o Gregory Beavers, PhD
3098 Creek Point Rd.
Graham, NC 27253
PH: (336)508-5148
DiFilippo, Frank, Ph.D, VP

International Fibrinogen Research Society **[15235]**
c/o Frances Woodlief
1513 Stonegate Dr.
Graham, NC 27253
Ariens, Robert, PhD, President

International Society of Limnology **[6780]**
c/o Denise Johnson, Business Manager
5020 Swepsonville-Saxapahaw Rd.
Graham, NC 27253
Johnson, Denise, Bus. Mgr.

Vulvar Pain Foundation **[16308]**
Graham Office Bldg., Ste. 203
203 1/2 N Main St.
Graham, NC 27253-2836
PH: (336)226-0704
Fax: (336)226-8518
Yount, Joanne, Exec. Dir.

Alliance for Global Good **[12458]**
445 Dolley Madison Rd., Ste. 208
Greensboro, NC 27410
PH: (336)376-7710
Brand, David, CEO

Alpha Psi Omega **[23723]**
1601 E Market St.
North Carolina A&T University
1601 E Market St.
Greensboro, NC 27411-0002
Day, Frankie, President

AMBUCS **[12883]**
4285 Regency Dr.
Greensboro, NC 27410-8101
Toll free: 800-838-1845
Fax: (336)852-6830
Graham, Bob, Chairperson

American Association of Pharmacy Technicians **[16633]**
PO Box 1447
Greensboro, NC 27402
PH: (336)333-9356
Toll free: 877-368-4771
Fax: (336)333-9068
Knorr, Marci, CPht, President

American Baseball Coaches Association **[22541]**
4101 Piedmont Pky., Ste. C
Greensboro, NC 27410
PH: (336)821-3140
Schaly, John, Director

American Boccaccio Association **[9034]**
c/o Timothy Kircher, President
5800 W Friendly Ave.
Greensboro, NC 27410-4108
Olson, Kristina, Treasurer

American Polarity Therapy Association **[13597]**
122 N Elm St., Ste. 504
Greensboro, NC 27401-2818
PH: (336)574-1121
Fax: (336)574-1151
Henderson, Johny, VP

Association of Chinese Professors of Social Sciences in the United States **[7162]**
c/o Yunqiu Zhang, Treasurer
210 Heritage Creek Way
Greensboro, NC 27405
Huang, Yonggang, VP

Association of Legal Writing Directors **[5527]**
c/o Catherine Wasson, Treasurer
Elon University School of Law
201 N Greene St.
Greensboro, NC 27401
Tiscione, Kristen, Secretary

Association for Research in Business Education **[23701]**
c/o Lisa Gueldenzoph Synder, President
North Carolina A&T State University
1601 E Market St.
Greensboro, NC 27411
PH: (501)219-1866
Mitchell, Robert, Dir. of Comm.

Atlantic Coast Conference **[23216]**
4512 Weybridge Ln.
Greensboro, NC 27407
PH: (336)854-8787
Fax: (336)854-8797
Swofford, John D., Commissioner

Center for Creative Leadership **[2159]**
1 Leadership Pl.
Greensboro, NC 27410-9427
PH: (336)288-7210
   (336)545-2810
Fax: (336)282-3284
Deal, Jennifer J., Scientist

Children of Vietnam **[10924]**
4361 Federal Dr., Ste. 160
Greensboro, NC 27410-8147
PH: (336)235-0981
Fax: (336)294-9566
Wilson, Mr. Benjamin C., Founder, President

FISA **[1382]**
1207 Sunset Dr.
Greensboro, NC 27408
PH: (336)274-6311
Fax: (336)691-1839
Morava, Bob, President

International Alliance of Furnishing Publications **[1483]**
7025 Albert Pick Rd.
Greensboro, NC 27409
PH: (336)605-1033
do Lago, Carlos Bessa, Sec. Gen.

National AMBUCS **[11620]**
4285 Regency Dr.
Greensboro, NC 27410
PH: (336)852-0052
Toll free: 800-838-1845
Fax: (336)852-6830
Copeland, J. Joseph, Exec. Dir.

National Board for Certified Counselors, Inc. and Affiliates **[11496]**
3 Terrace Way
Greensboro, NC 27403-3660
PH: (336)547-0607
Fax: (336)547-0017
Allen, Sherry, Exec. Dir.

National Fair Access Coalition on Testing **[7328]**
3 Terrace Way
Greensboro, NC 27403-3660
PH: (336)547-0607
Fax: (336)547-0017

National Organization of Vascular Anomalies **[17577]**
PO Box 38216
Greensboro, NC 27438-8216
Clemens, Roy, President

North American Society for the Psychology of Sport and Physical Activity **[23076]**
c/o Jennifer Etnier, President
University of North Carolina at Greensboro
Dept. of Kinesiology
PO Box 26170
Greensboro, NC 27402-6170
Fax: (336)334-3037

Society for Romanian Studies **[21094]**
c/o William Crowther, Treasurer
Dept. of Political Science
University of North Carolina-Greensboro
Greensboro, NC 27402-6170
PH: (480)965-4658
Livezeanu, Irina, President

United States Border Collie Club **[21979]**
1712 Hertford St.
Greensboro, NC 27403
Carson, Laura, Treasurer

Worlds Apart One Heart **[11466]**
402 Country Club Dr.
Greensboro, NC 27408
Hankins, Rose, Founder

Institute of Outdoor Theatre **[10254]**
East Carolina University
201 Erwin Bldg., MS 528
Greenville, NC 27858-4353
PH: (252)328-5363
Fax: (252)328-0968
Hardy, Michael C., Director

National Association of Bariatric Nurses Inc. **[16259]**
110 E Arlington Blvd.
East Carolina University, Mail Stop 162
Greenville, NC 27858
PH: (252)744-6440
Sarvey, Sharon Isenhour, PhD

Pi Omega Pi **[23702]**
BITE Dept., Bate 2318A
East Carolina University
Greenville, NC 27858
PH: (252)328-6983
Faulk, Emma, President

United States Society for Education Through Art **[7519]**
c/o Nanyoung Kim, Treasurer
East Carolina University
Jenkins Fine Arts Ctr.
Greenville, NC 27858-4353
PH: (252)328-1298
Kim, Dr. Nanyoung, Treasurer

Chevrolet Nomad Association **[21351]**
1720 Laurie Dr.
Haw River, NC 27258
Darcy, Gina, President

United Poodle Breeds Association **[21976]**
c/o Andrea Hungerford, Treasurer
1175 Peckerwood Rd.
Hayesville, NC 28904
Tayeb, Lorraine, President

Welsh Springer Spaniel Club of America **[21989]**
c/o Carla Vooris, Secretary
284 Welshie Way Ln.

Henderson, NC 27537
Ford, Cindy, President

Scouts on Stamps Society
   International **[22362]**
c/o Jay Rogers
15 Hickory Court Ln.
Hendersonville, NC 28792-1229
PH: (803)466-4783
Clay, Mr. Lawrence E., President

ADED, Inc. **[7722]**
200 1st Ave. NW, Ste. 505
Hickory, NC 28601-6113
Toll free: 866-672-9466
Fax: (828)855-1672
Benoit, Dana, President

Clan Mackintosh of North America
   [20825]
c/o Randy Holbrook, Treasurer
1037 35th Avenue Ln. NE
Hickory, NC 28601-9601
McIntosh, Rob, Treasurer

American Home Furnishings Alliance
   [1473]
1912 Eastchester Dr., Ste. 100
High Point, NC 27265
PH: (336)884-5000
Fax: (336)884-5303
O'Connor, Kevin, Chmn. of the Bd.

American Society of Furniture
   Designers **[1474]**
4136 Coachmans Ct.
High Point, NC 27262-5445
PH: (336)307-0999
Fax: (336)885-3291
Phillips, Jason, President

Appalachian Hardwood Manufactur-
   ers **[1430]**
816 Eastchester Dr.
High Point, NC 27262
PH: (336)885-8315
Fax: (336)886-8865
Inman, Tom, President

Beauty 4 Ashes International
   [13370]
3713 Lexham Dr.
High Point, NC 27265
PH: (336)209-7405
Fax: (336)574-0277
Johnson, Jacquelyn Clark, PHR,
   Exec. Dir.

Collegiate Women's Lacrosse Of-
   ficiating Association **[22972]**
2310 N Centennial St., Ste. 102
High Point, NC 27265
Williams, Nikki, Exec. Dir.

Council for Qualification of
   Residential Interior Designers
   [1943]
Interior Design Society
164 S Main St., Ste. 404
High Point, NC 27260
PH: (336)884-4437
Toll free: 888-884-4469
Fax: (336)885-3291
Knott, Bruce, President

High Point Market Authority **[1481]**
164 S Main St., Ste. 700
High Point, NC 27260
PH: (336)869-1000
Toll free: 800-874-6492
Conley, Tom, President, CEO

Interior Design Society **[1946]**
164 S Main St., Ste. 404
High Point, NC 27260
PH: (336)884-4437
Fax: (336)885-3291
Cregier, Jan, President

International Casual Furnishings Association **[1484]**
1912 Eastchester Dr., Ste. 100
High Point, NC 27265

PH: (336)881-1016
Fax: (336)884-5303
Sanicola, Doug, V. Chmn. of the
   Exec. Committee

International Home Furnishings
   Representatives Association **[1486]**
209 S Main St.
High Point, NC 27260
PH: (336)889-3920
Weed, Geoff, President

International Textile Market Associa-
   tion **[3262]**
305 W High Ave.
High Point, NC 27260
PH: (336)885-6842
Nifong, Todd, President

Upholstered Furniture Action Council
   [1492]
Box 2436
High Point, NC 27261
PH: (336)885-5065
Fax: (336)885-5072

Addington Association **[20774]**
100 Oak Beech Ct.
Holly Springs, NC 27540
Bowersox, Jerry Sue, Secretary,
   Treasurer

Giant Screen Cinema Association
   [3277]
624 Holly Springs Rd., Ste. 243
Holly Springs, NC 27540
PH: (919)346-1123
Fax: (919)573-9100
Barker, Jonathan, Secretary

Model T Ford Club International
   [21439]
PO Box 355
Hudson, NC 28638-0355
PH: (828)728-5758
Lilleker, Ross, President

Association on Higher Education and
   Disability **[7714]**
107 Commerce Centre Dr., Ste. 204
Huntersville, NC 28078
PH: (704)947-7779
Fax: (704)948-7779
Smith, Stephan J., Exec. Dir.

A Place of Hope **[11735]**
PO Box 3341
Huntersville, NC 28070
PH: (980)230-6511
Tiandem-Adamou, Yvonne, Founder

Lightning Strike and Electric Shock
   Survivors International Inc. **[14653]**
PO Box 1156
Jacksonville, NC 28541-1156
PH: (910)346-4708
Fax: (910)346-4708
Marshburn, Mr. Steve, Sr., Founder,
   President

United States Marine Corps Motor
   Transport Association, Inc. **[5628]**
PO Box 1372
Jacksonville, NC 28541-1372
PH: (910)450-1841
Davidson, Dwight, President

Food Distribution Research Society
   [6646]
c/o Jonathan Baros, Vice President
   for Membership
600 Laureate Way
Kannapolis, NC 28081
PH: (704)250-5458
Fax: (704)250-5427
Baros, Jonathan, VP

Y's Men International **[13422]**
101 YMCA Dr.
Kannapolis, NC 28081
Crosby, Brett, President

Shwachman Diamond America
   [14857]
931-B S Main St., No. 332
Kernersville, NC 27284
PH: (336)423-8158
Curran, Pattie, Director

American Hosta Society **[22076]**
PO Box 7539
Kill Devil Hills, NC 27948-7539
Dean, Don, President

Vacation Rental Housekeeping
   Professionals **[992]**
PO Box 1883
Kill Devil Hills, NC 27948
PH: (252)455-4121

Pet Sitters International **[2550]**
201 E King St.
King, NC 27021
PH: (336)983-9222
Fax: (336)983-5266
Moran, Patti J., President, CEO

First Flight Society **[21227]**
PO Box 1903
Kitty Hawk, NC 27949
PH: (252)441-1903
Woodruff, Phil, President

World Methodist Council **[20351]**
545 N Lakeshore Dr.
Lake Junaluska, NC 28745
PH: (828)456-9432
Lockmann, Paulo, President

Moms Against Mercury **[13223]**
55 Carson's Trl.
Leicester, NC 28748
PH: (828)776-0082
Fax: (828)683-6866
Carson, Amy, President, Founder

The Amarun Organization **[3795]**
9505 Seany Dr. NE
Leland, NC 28451
PH: (910)508-3630
Crawford, Rachel, Prog. Dir.

National Association of Left-Handed
   Golfers **[22887]**
c/o jim Bradley, Treasurer
PO Box 640
Leland, NC 28451
PH: (910)383-0339
Flowers, Jon, President

Books For Soldiers **[10737]**
116 Lowes Food Dr., No. 123
Lewisville, NC 27023
Williams, Storm, Founder

Working Riesenschnauzer Federation **[21995]**
c/o Tim Nyx, President
2303 Pete Smith Rd.
Louisburg, NC 27549
Nyx, Tim, President

Fell Pony Society and Conservancy
   of the Americas **[4349]**
775 Flippin Rd.
Lowgap, NC 27024
PH: (336)352-5520
Tollman, Victoria, Secretary,
   Treasurer

Chronic Syndrome Support Association **[14571]**
801 Riverside Dr.
Lumberton, NC 28358-4625
Solo, Nancy, Founder

International Compressor Remanufacturers Association **[1625]**
1505 Carthage Rd.
Lumberton, NC 28358

PH: (910)301-7060
Fax: (910)738-6994
Walker, Sandra, Officer

Protect All Children's Environment
   [14723]
396 Sugar Cove Rd.
Marion, NC 28752
PH: (828)724-4221
O'nan, E.M.T., Director

Squire SS-100 Registry **[21494]**
c/o Chuck Blethen
PO Box 4
Marshall, NC 28753
PH: (828)606-3130
Blethen, Chuck, Contact

Parrotlet Alliance **[3668]**
3405 Camden Rd.
Marshville, NC 28103
Rogers, Ruth, Contact

Always Believe, Inc. **[11743]**
PO Box 1884
Matthews, NC 28106
PH: (704)430-6149
Bogues, Tyrone, Founder

American Singles Golf Association
   [22874]
1122 Industrial Dr., Ste. 170
Matthews, NC 28105
PH: (980)833-6450
Toll free: 888-465-3628
Fax: (704)889-4607
Price, Jane, President

American Station Wagon Owners
   Association **[21324]**
PO Box 914
Matthews, NC 28106
PH: (704)847-7510
Cleary, Tim, President

Give Children a Choice **[8448]**
PO Box 2298
Matthews, NC 28106
Shimoda, Dori, Founder, President

Legacy Creators **[19113]**
13663 Providence Rd., No. 305
Matthews, NC 28104
PH: (704)661-5702
Toll free: 800-224-0579
Allen, Horace D., CEO, Founder

Professional Association for Investment Communications Resources
   [2036]
10020 Monroe Rd., Ste. 170
Matthews, NC 28105
PH: (704)724-5753
Farro, Anne, VP

Silent Images **[12991]**
100 W John St., Ste. H
Matthews, NC 28105
PH: (704)999-5010
Johnson, David, Founder, Director

Financial & Security Products As-
   sociation **[397]**
1024 Mebane Oaks Rd., No. 273
Mebane, NC 27302
PH: (919)648-0664
Toll free: 800-843-6082
Fax: (919)648-0670
Abell, Linda, Chairman

National Organization of Single
   Mothers **[12956]**
PO Box 68
Midland, NC 28107
Engber, Andrea, Director, Founder

Montreat College Alumni Association
   [19335]
310 Gaither Cir.
Montreat, NC 28757

PH: (828)669-8012
Toll free: 800-849-3347
Clark, Caroline, Officer

Samaritans International [20460]
c/o Stephen Ferguson, Secretary
370 E Cedar St.
Mooresville, NC 28115-2806
PH: (704)663-7951
Ferguson, Stephen, Secretary

Trauma Center Association of
America [17531]
108 Gateway Blvd., Ste. 103
Mooresville, NC 28117
PH: (704)360-4665
Fax: (704)677-7052
Ward, Jennifer, President

Crisis Response International
[11655]
PO Box 1122
Moravian Falls, NC 28654
Malone, Sean, Director

Home Ventilating Institute [1621]
4915 Arendell St., Ste. J
Morehead City, NC 28557
Toll free: 855-484-8368
Fax: (480)559-9722
Donner, Jacki, Exec. Dir., CEO

American Dairy Products Association
[970]
2501 Aerial Center Pky.
Morrisville, NC 27560-7655
PH: (919)459-2076
Fax: (919)459-2075
Yates, Tom, President

American Society of Echocardiogra-
phy [14093]
2100 Gateway Centre Blvd., Ste.
310
Morrisville, NC 27560
PH: (919)861-5574
Wiegerink, Robin L., MNPL, CEO

The International Childbirth Educa-
tion Association [16288]
2501 Aerial Center Pky., Ste. 103
Morrisville, NC 27560
PH: (919)863-9487
    (919)674-4183
Toll free: 800-624-4934
Fax: (919)787-4916
Lytle, Jessica, Exec. Dir.

International Lactation Consultant
Association [11240]
2501 Aerial Center Pky., Ste. 103
Morrisville, NC 27560
PH: (919)861-5577
Toll free: 888-452-2478
Fax: (919)459-2075
Lytle, Jessica, Dir. of Operations

International Nursing Association for
Clinical Simulation and Learning
[16138]
2501 Aerial Center Pky., Ste. 103
Morrisville, NC 27560
PH: (919)674-4182
Fax: (919)459-2075
Owens, Linda, President

National Association of County
Recorders, Election Officials, and
Clerks [5115]
2501 Aerial Center Pky., Ste. 103
Morrisville, NC 27560
PH: (919)459-2080
Fax: (919)459-2075
Johnsrud, Ann, President

National Association of Professional
Background Screeners [1697]
2501 Aerial Center Pky., Ste. 130
Morrisville, NC 27560-7655

PH: (919)459-2082
Fax: (919)459-2075
Sorenson, Melissa, Exec. Dir.

National Public Records Research
Association [1804]
2501 Aerial Center Pky., Ste. 103
Morrisville, NC 27560
PH: (919)459-2078
Fax: (919)459-2075
Hopton, Melissa, VP

Property Records Industry Associa-
tion [2750]
2501 Aerial Center Pky., Ste. 103
Morrisville, NC 27560
PH: (919)459-2081
Fax: (919)459-2075
Kernick, Stevie Hughes, Chief of
Staff

Professional Air Sports Association
[23250]
PO Box 1839
Nags Head, NC 27959
Harris, John, President, Founder

SATS/EAF Association [21019]
2514 Hickory St.
New Bern, NC 28562
Goodwin, Frank, President

Trollope Society [9105]
c/o Midge Fitzgerald
6 Pier Pointe
New Bern, NC 28562
PH: (212)683-4023
Hall, John, Bd. Member

Calorie Restriction Society [16211]
187 Ocean Dr.
Newport, NC 28570
PH: (252)241-3079
Toll free: 877-511-2702
Cavanaugh, Bob, Managing Dir.

Rainbow Division Veterans Memorial
Foundation [21209]
1400 Knolls Dr.
Newton, NC 28658
PH: (828)464-1466
Remple, Melanie, Secretary

Clan Davidson Society [20806]
235 Fairmont Dr.
North Wilkesboro, NC 28659-9050
Dawson, John D., President

Single Booklovers [21740]
2205 Oak Ridge Rd.
Oak Ridge, NC 27310
PH: (336)298-1767
Leach, Ruth, Founder

Association for Pet Obesity Preven-
tion [16248]
51 Newport St.
Ocean Isle Beach, NC 28469
PH: (910)579-5550
Ward, Ernie, DVM, Founder

AASP - The Palynological Society
[6976]
University of N Carolina at Pem-
broke
Geology, Old Main 213
Pembroke, NC 28372
PH: (910)521-6478
Norton, Norman J., Chairman

Phi Sigma Nu American Indian
Fraternity [23917]
PO Box 2040
Pembroke, NC 28372
Lowery, John, VP

Newborns in Need [11197]
3323 Transou Rd.
Pfafftown, NC 27040

PH: (336)469-8953
Edwards, Connie, President

Council of Scottish Clans and As-
sociations [19639]
Bldg. 2, Ste. 10
315 N Page Rd.
Pinehurst, NC 28370
PH: (980)333-4686
Belassai, John King, President

Medical Fitness Association [16705]
90 Cherokee Rd., Ste. 3A
Pinehurst, NC 28374
PH: (910)420-8610
Toll free: 844-312-3541
Fax: (910)420-8733
Nordan, Rebecca, VP of Operations

Scottish Heritage U.S.A. [19641]
Bldg. 2, Ste. 10
315 N Page Rd.
Pinehurst, NC 28374-8751
PH: (910)295-4448
Kelly, Rev. Douglas F., President

American Academy of Advertising
[83]
c/o Pat Rose, Executive Director
831 Fearrington Post
Pittsboro, NC 27312
Morton, Cynthia, Treasurer

Families Affected by Fetal Alcohol
Spectrum Disorder [17310]
PO Box 427
Pittsboro, NC 27312
PH: (919)360-7073
Schanzenbach, Janet, VP

Livestock Conservancy [4458]
33 Hillsborough St.
Pittsboro, NC 27312
PH: (919)542-5704
Hallman, Eric, Exec. Dir.

Rural Advancement Foundation
International-USA [3555]
274 Pittsboro Elementary School Rd.
Pittsboro, NC 27312
PH: (919)542-1396
Hart, Archie, Director

United White Shepherd Club [21986]
128 Cavalier Dr.
Raeford, NC 28376
PH: (253)468-6673
Lee, Missy, President

Actively Moving Forward [10769]
3344 Hillsborough St., Ste. 260
Raleigh, NC 27607
PH: (919)803-6728
Toll free: 877-830-7442
Fajgenbaum, David, MSc, Founder,
Chmn. of the Bd.

AKC Reunite [10561]
8051 Arco Corporate Dr., Ste. 200
Raleigh, NC 27617-3900
Toll free: 800-252-7894
Fax: (919)233-1290
Kalter, Alan, Chairman

Alliance of Professionals and
Consultants, Inc. [814]
8200 Brownleigh Dr.
Raleigh, NC 27617-7411
PH: (919)510-9696
Roberts, Roy, CEO

American Board of Anesthesiology
[13691]
4208 Six Forks Rd., Ste. 1500
Raleigh, NC 27609-5765
Toll free: 866-999-7501
Fax: (866)999-7503
Post, Mary E., MBA, Exec. Dir.

American Board of Toxicology [7334]
PO Box 97786
Raleigh, NC 27624
PH: (919)841-5022
Fax: (919)841-5042

American College of Epidemiology
[14727]
1500 Sunday Dr., Ste. 102
Raleigh, NC 27607
PH: (919)861-5573
Fax: (919)787-4916
Kralka, Peter, Exec. Dir.

American Kennel Club [21811]
8051 Arco Corporate Dr., Ste. 100
Raleigh, NC 27617-3390
PH: (919)233-9767
Sprung, Dennis B., CEO, President

American Society for Cytotechnology
[14358]
1500 Sunday Dr., Ste. 102
Raleigh, NC 27607-5151
PH: (919)861-5571
Toll free: 800-948-3947
Fax: (919)787-4916
Denny, Beth, Exec. Dir.

American Society for Precision
Engineering [6539]
PO Box 10826
Raleigh, NC 27605-0826
PH: (919)839-8444
Fax: (919)839-8039
Leach, Richard K., Director

Association of Appraiser Regulatory
Officials [220]
13200 Strickland Rd., Ste. 114-264
Raleigh, NC 27613
PH: (919)235-4544
Fax: (919)870-5392
Petit, Anne, President

Association of Forensic Document
Examiners [5242]
c/o Emily J. Will, President
PO Box 58552
Raleigh, NC 27658
PH: (919)556-7414
Will, Emily J., President

Australian Labradoodle Association
of America [3985]
c/o Butch Charlton, Treasurer and
Registrar
10729 Grassy Creek Pl.
Raleigh, NC 27614
Fax: (309)418-9916
Hale, Heather, President

Avery's Angels Gastroschisis
Foundation [13824]
PO Box 58312
Raleigh, NC 27658
Toll free: 855-692-8379
Fax: (919)400-4595
Hall, Meghan, Founder, CEO

Cardiovascular Credentialing
International [14106]
1500 Sunday Dr., Ste. 102
Raleigh, NC 27607
Toll free: 800-326-0268
Fax: (919)787-4916
Horton, RCS, RCIS, FASE, Ken,
President

Chosen Children International
[10939]
PO Box 97112
Raleigh, NC 27624
PH: (719)634-5437
Cohn, Marilyn, Director

Clan Gillean U.S.A. [20812]
PO Box 61066
Raleigh, NC 27661-1066

PH: (919)334-8977
Fax: (919)881-5228
MacLean, Reverend Canon Patrick,
President

Coalition for Improving Maternity
Services [16281]
PO Box 33590
Raleigh, NC 27636-3590
Toll free: 866-424-3635
Hotelling, Barbara, Co-Ch.

Collegiate Association of Table Top
Gamers [22049]
Campus Box 7306
North Carolina State University
Raleigh, NC 27695
PH: (919)809-9456
Roselli, Mike, Exec. Dir.

Community-Campus Partnerships
For Health [11336]
PO Box 12124
Raleigh, NC 27605
PH: (206)666-3406
Fax: (206)666-3406
Seifer, Sarena, Founder, Exec. Dir.

Controlled Environment Testing As-
sociation [7324]
1500 Sunday Dr., Ste. 102
Raleigh, NC 27607-5151
PH: (919)861-5576
Fax: (919)787-4916
Caughron, Tony, President

Culture and Animals Foundation
[10609]
3509 Eden Croft Dr.
Raleigh, NC 27612
PH: (919)782-3739
Regan, Tom, Founder, President

Delta Theta Phi Law Fraternity
International [23803]
Campbell University
Wiggins School of Law
225 Hillsborough St., Ste. 432
Raleigh, NC 27603
PH: (919)866-4667
    (919)865-4667
Toll free: 800-783-2600
Evola, Vito M., Exec. Dir.

Environmental Research and Educa-
tion Foundation [4139]
3301 Benson Dr., Ste. 101
Raleigh, NC 27609
PH: (919)861-6876
Fax: (919)861-6878
Staley, Bryan F., PhD, CEO,
President

Federation of Earth Science Informa-
tion Partners [6374]
6300 Creedmoor Rd., Ste. 170-315
Raleigh, NC 27612
PH: (314)369-9954
Robinson, Erin, Exec. Dir.

The Fishermen [10977]
PO Box 17171
Raleigh, NC 27619
PH: (919)452-2405
Gowen, Alex, Founder, Director

Grey Muzzle Organization [10629]
14460 Falls of Neuse Rd., Ste. 149-
269
Raleigh, NC 27614
PH: (919)529-0309
Dudley, Julie, Founder, Advisor

International Association of
Structural Integrators [13633]
PO Box 31381
Raleigh, NC 27622
Toll free: 855-253-4274
Fax: (919)787-8081
Foster-Scott, Denise, President

International Association for
Structural Mechanics in Reactor
Technology [7276]
Campus Box 7908
North Carolina State University
Raleigh, NC 27695-7908
PH: (919)515-5277
Shepherd, Dave, President

International Epidemiological As-
sociation [14731]
1500 Sunday Dr., Ste. 102
Raleigh, NC 27607
PH: (919)861-5586
Fax: (919)787-4916
Beral, Valerie, President

International Society for Adult
Congenital Heart Disease [14124]
1500 Sunday Dr., Ste. 102
Raleigh, NC 27607
PH: (919)861-5578
Fax: (919)787-4916
Oechslin, Erwin N., MD, FRCPC,
President

Libertarian Nation Foundation
[18642]
335 Mulberry St.
Raleigh, NC 27604
Emory, Bobby Yates, President

Military Order of the Stars and Bars
[20744]
PO Box 18901
Raleigh, NC 27619-8901

Multi-Housing Laundry Association
[2079]
1500 Sunday Dr., Ste. 102
Raleigh, NC 27607
PH: (919)861-5579
Fax: (919)787-4916
Marsden, Mike, President

Murder Victims' Families for
Reconciliation [17830]
PO Box 27764
Raleigh, NC 27611-7764
Toll free: 877-896-4702
Lytle, Rosemary, Chmn. of the Bd.

Nanodermatology Society [14502]
4414 Lake Boone Trl., Ste. 408
Raleigh, NC 27607
PH: (919)781-4375
Fax: (919)781-3909
Nasir, Dr. Adnan, President

National Association of County
Information Officers [5114]
c/o Rita McGee, Membership
Coordinator
102 Minden Ln.
Raleigh, NC 27607-4989
PH: (919)715-7336
Beyer, Jessica, President

National Association of Disability
Examiners [14298]
PO Box 243
9404 N Manor Dr.
Raleigh, NC 27602
PH: (919)212-3222
Toll free: 800-443-9359
Fax: (919)212-3155
Nottingham, Jennifer, Officer

National Association of Extension
4-H Agents [13461]
3801 Lake Boone Trl., Ste. 190
Raleigh, NC 27607
PH: (919)232-0112
Fax: (919)779-5642
Mallory, Lene, President

National Association for Holistic
Aromatherapy [15269]
PO Box 27871
Raleigh, NC 27611-7871

PH: (919)894-0298
Fax: (919)894-0271
Davis, Annette, President

National Association of Medical
Minority Educators [8331]
1500 Sunday Dr., Ste. 102
Raleigh, NC 27607
PH: (919)573-1309
Toll free: 855-201-6247
Fax: (919)573-1310
Cannon, Aise, Secretary

National Association of Public Auto
Auctions [260]
PO Box 41368
Raleigh, NC 27629
PH: (919)876-0687
Martin, W. David, Director

National Association of State Ap-
proving Agencies [5838]
120 Penmarc Dr., Ste. 103
Raleigh, NC 27603-2434
PH: (919)733-7535
Fax: (919)733-1284
Kelly, Elizabeth, Specialist

National Association of State
Comprehensive Health Insurance
Plans [15103]
3739 National Dr., Ste. 228
Raleigh, NC 27612
PH: (919)783-5766
Fax: (919)783-5767

National Association of State Park
Directors [5664]
PO Box 91567
Raleigh, NC 27675
Ledford, Lewis, Exec. Dir.

National Farm Worker Ministry
[12343]
112 Cox Ave., Ste. 208
Raleigh, NC 27605-1817
PH: (919)807-8707
Fax: (919)807-8708
Taylor, Julie, Exec. Dir.

National Federation of Licensed
Practical Nurses [16161]
3801 Lake Boone Trl., Ste. 190
Raleigh, NC 27607
PH: (919)779-0046
Toll free: 800-948-2511
Fax: (919)779-5642
Morgan, Beverly, President

The National Organization for
Diversity in Sales and Marketing,
Inc. [2296]
PO Box 99640
Raleigh, NC 27624-9640
Toll free: 800-691-6380
Fax: (888)260-0836
Willingham-Hinton, Shelley, CEO,
Founder

North American Pet Health Insur-
ance Association [15105]
PO Box 37940
Raleigh, NC 27627
Toll free: 877-962-7442
Horan, Bill, VP

North American Rock Garden
Society [4271]
c/o Bobby J. Ward, Membership
Director
PO Box 18604
Raleigh, NC 27619-8604
PH: (919)781-3291
    (914)762-2948
George, Peter, Comm. Chm.

North American Rock Garden
Society [22118]
c/o Bobby J. Ward, Membership
Director

PO Box 18604
Raleigh, NC 27619-8604
PH: (919)781-3291
    (914)762-2948
George, Peter, Comm. Chm.

Postpartum Education and Support
[16625]
PO Box 33751
Raleigh, NC 27636
PH: (919)889-3221
Pence, Caroline, Exec. Dir.

Public Media Foundation [18665]
Campus Box 7016
Office of Development
College of humanities and Social
Sciences
Raleigh, NC 27695-7016
PH: (919)515-5973
Hooker, Deborah, Director

RCI, Inc. [900]
1500 Sunday Dr., Ste. 204
Raleigh, NC 27607
PH: (919)859-0742
Toll free: 800-828-1902
Fax: (919)859-1328
Birdsong, James R., CEO, Exec. VP

Sewn Products Equipment and Sup-
pliers of the Americas [1767]
9650 Strickland Rd., Ste. 103-324
Raleigh, NC 27615-1902
PH: (919)872-8909
Fax: (919)872-1915
Gardner, Benton, President

Society for In Vitro Biology [6101]
514 Daniels St., Ste. 411
Raleigh, NC 27605
PH: (919)562-0600
Fax: (919)562-0608
Elmore, Eugene, President

Society of Invasive Cardiovascular
Professionals [14147]
1500 Sunday Dr., Ste. 102
Raleigh, NC 27607-5151
PH: (919)861-4546
Fax: (919)787-4916
Shore, Nicole, Exec. Dir.

Stop Hunger Now [12116]
615 Hillsborough St., Ste. 200
Raleigh, NC 27603
PH: (919)839-0689
Toll free: 888-501-8440
Fax: (919)839-8971
Brooks, Rod, President, CEO

Striving for More [14067]
PO Box 97443
Raleigh, NC 27624
PH: (919)339-1214
Moore, Diane, Founder, President,
Exec. Dir.

Students Against Violence
Everywhere [18727]
322 Chapanoke Rd., No. 110
Raleigh, NC 27603
PH: (919)661-7800
Toll free: 866-343-SAVE
Fax: (919)661-7777
Wray, Ms. Carleen, Exec. Dir.

Sweet Sorghum Association [5891]
8912 Brandon Station Rd.
Raleigh, NC 27613
PH: (919)870-0782
Eggleston, Gillian, President

Touch for Health Kinesiology As-
sociation [13660]
4917 Waters Edge Dr., Ste. 125
Raleigh, NC 27606
PH: (919)637-4938
Lewis, Darcy, Contact

UCA International Users Group
[7357]
10604 Candler Falls Ct.
Raleigh, NC 27614
PH: (919)847-2944
Fax: (919)869-2700
Clinard, Kay N., President

United States Power Squadrons
[22683]
1504 Blue Ridge Rd.
Raleigh, NC 27607
PH: (919)821-0281
Toll free: 888-367-8777
Hoffee, James, Mem.

U.S. Tobacco Cooperative, Inc.
[4722]
1304 Annapolis Dr.
Raleigh, NC 27608
PH: (919)821-4560
Fax: (919)821-4564
Lynch, Mike, Sr. VP of Sales & Mktg.

U.S. Trout Farmers Association
[3649]
PO Box 61342
Raleigh, NC 27661
PH: (919)909-1943
Conklin, Charlie, President

AASA Technology Council [63]
10 Laboratory Dr.
Research Triangle Park, NC 27709
PH: (919)406-8830
Gardner, Chris, Exec. Dir.

American Association of Medical
Review Officers [15109]
PO Box 12873
Research Triangle Park, NC 27709
Toll free: 800-489-1839
Fax: (919)490-1010

American Sexual Health Association
[17192]
PO Box 13827
Research Triangle Park, NC
27709-3827
PH: (919)361-8400
Wysocki, Susan, Treasurer

Association of Textile, Apparel and
Materials Professionals [6191]
1 Davis Dr.
Research Triangle Park, NC
27709-2215
PH: (919)549-8141
Fax: (919)549-8933
Daniels, John Y., Exec. VP

Automation Federation [6017]
67 Alexander Dr.
Research Triangle Park, NC
27709-0185
PH: (919)314-3920
Fax: (919)314-3921
Roop, Rick, Chairman

Automotive Aftermarket Suppliers
Association | Filter Manufacturers
Council [308]
10 Laboratory Dr.
Research Triangle Park, NC
27709-3966
PH: (919)406-8825
Fax: (919)549-4824
Messier, Krysta, Contact

The Hamner Institutes for Health
Sciences [7338]
6 Davis Dr.
Research Triangle Park, NC 27709
PH: (919)558-1200
Fax: (919)558-1400
Hamner, Charles E., V. Chmn. of the
Bd.

Heavy-Duty Business Forum [294]
c/o Heavy Duty Manufacturers Association

10 Laboratoty Dr.
Research Triangle Park, NC
27709-3966
Hjalmquist, Jennifer, Contact

Heavy Duty Manufacturers Associa-
tion [2221]
10 Laboratory Dr.
Research Triangle Park, NC
27709-3966
PH: (919)549-4800
    (919)549-4824
Fax: (919)506-1465
Kraus, Timothy R., COO, President

International Society of Automation
[6762]
67 TW Alexander Dr.
Research Triangle Park, NC 27709
PH: (919)549-8411
Fax: (919)549-8288
Eby, Debbie, Mgr.

International Union of Pure and Ap-
plied Chemistry [6205]
Bldg. 4201, Ste. 260
79 TW Alexander Dr.
Research Triangle Park, NC 27709
PH: (919)485-8700
Fax: (919)485-8706
Soby, Dr. Lynn, Exec. Dir.

Motor and Equipment Manufacturers
Association [326]
10 Laboratory Dr.
Research Triangle Park, NC 27709
PH: (919)549-4800
Fax: (919)406-1465
Handschuh, Steve, President, CEO

National Cervical Cancer Coalition
[14022]
PO Box 13827
Research Triangle Park, NC 27709
Toll free: 800-685-5531
Fax: (919)361-8425
Wysocki, Susan, Treasurer

National Humanities Center [9556]
7 TW Alexander Dr.
Research Triangle Park, NC 27709
PH: (919)549-0661
Fax: (919)990-8535
Harpham, Geoffrey, Director,
President

National Institute of Statistical Sci-
ences [7244]
19 TW Alexander Dr.
Research Triangle Park, NC 27709
PH: (919)685-9300
Fax: (919)685-9310
Sedransk, Nell, Director

Overseas Automotive Council [301]
c/o Automotive Aftermarket Suppliers
Association
10 Laboratory Dr.
Research Triangle Park, NC 27709
PH: (919)406-1464
Jordan, Mick, Chairman

Sigma Xi, The Scientific Research
Society [23861]
3106 E NC Highway 54, Ste. 300
Research Triangle Park, NC 27709
PH: (919)549-4691
Toll free: 800-243-6534
Fax: (919)549-0090
Peeples, Mark, President

U.S. National Committee for the
International Union of Pure and
Applied Chemistry [6218]
Bldg. 4201, Ste. 260
79 TW Alexander Dr.
Research Triangle Park, NC 27709
PH: (202)334-2807
Fax: (202)334-2231
Hughes, Kathryn, Program Mgr.

American Belgian Malinois Club
[21796]
c/o Sara Andersen
308 Scott Rd.
Rocky Point, NC 28457
PH: (717)487-3323
Bradie, Alice, President

Mastiff Club of America [21913]
c/o Jodi LaBombard, Recording
Secretary
189 Miranda Ln.
Roxboro, NC 27574-6602
LaBombard, Jodi, Secretary

Association for Evolutionary
Economics [6380]
c/o Eric R. Hake, Secretary-
Treasurer
Catawba College
2300 W Innes St.
Salisbury, NC 28144-2488
PH: (704)637-4293
Fax: (704)637-4491
Figart, Deborah M., President

National Sports Media Association
[2707]
307 Summit Ave.
Salisbury, NC 28144
PH: (704)633-4275
Goren, Dave, Exec. Dir.

Sole Hope [13018]
605 E Innes St., Ste. 3263
Salisbury, NC 28145
Toll free: 855-516-4673
Collie, Asher, Founder, Exec. Dir.

Equipment Service Association
[3073]
c/o Curt Williams, President
5225 Womack Rd.
Sanford, NC 27330
PH: (443)640-1053
Toll free: 866-372-3155
Fax: (443)640-1031
Tombrello, Pat, Secretary, Treasurer

Jaguar Clubs of North America
[21409]
500 Westover Dr., No. 8354
Sanford, NC 27330
Toll free: 888-258-2524
Matejek, Bob, Secretary

United States Powered Paragliding
Association [23052]
500 Westover Dr., No. 2384
Sanford, NC 27330
Toll free: 866-378-7772
Goin, Jeff, President

International Wild Waterfowl As-
sociation [4832]
500 Sylvan Heights Pkwy.
Scotland Neck, NC 27874
PH: (252)826-3186
Schouton, Arnold, President

National Association of Safety
Professionals [7108]
1531 S Post Rd.
Shelby, NC 28152
Toll free: 800-922-2219
Fax: (704)487-1579
Abbey, Charlie, Advisor

Stolen Horse International [10698]
PO Box 1341
Shelby, NC 28151
PH: (704)484-2165
Kirby, Angela, Coord.

Dermatology Nurses' Association
[16130]
435 N Bennett St.
Southern Pines, NC 28387
Toll free: 800-454-4362
Fax: (856)439-0525
Onoday, Heather, BSN, MN, FNP-C,
President

American Association of Retirement
Communities [12754]
PO Box 10981
Southport, NC 28461
Toll free: 866-531-5567
Nabors, Andre, Exec. Dir.

Force 5 Class Association [22614]
3438 Scupper Run SE
Southport, NC 28461
Barrere, John, President

Sacro Occipital Technique Organiza-
tion U.S.A. [14282]
PO Box 1357
Sparta, NC 28675
PH: (336)793-6524
Fax: (336)372-1541
Benner, Christine, VP

American Dairy Goat Association
[3591]
161 W Main St.
Spindale, NC 28160
PH: (828)286-3801
Fax: (828)287-0476
Cassette, Philip M., VP

Support Our Arthritic Kids [17169]
PO Box 624
Spring Lake, NC 28390
PH: (919)842-3484
Cavalier, Crystal, President, Founder

International Association of Clerks,
Recorders, Election Officials and
Treasurers [5262]
c/o Brenda Bell, Chief Administrator
156 Old Pond Ln.
Statesville, NC 28625
Toll free: 800-890-7368
Nanney, Timothy, President

Food Industry Association Executives [2953]
c/o Bev Lynch, President
664 Sandipiper Bay Dr. SW
Sunset Beach, NC 28468
PH: (910)575-3423
Taylor, Ellie, Chairman

American Whitewater [23092]
629 W Main St.
Sylva, NC 28779
PH: (828)586-1930
Toll free: 866-262-8429
Fax: (828)586-2840
Singleton, Mark, Exec. Dir.

Professional Bowhunters Society
[22507]
PO Box 246
Terrell, NC 28682-0246
PH: (704)664-2534
Fax: (704)664-7471
Akenson, Jim, President

Chi Sigma Iota [14326]
PO Box 1829
Thomasville, NC 27360
PH: (336)841-8180
Fax: (336)844-4323
Hartwig Moorhead, Holly J., CEO

Black Farmers and Agriculturists As-
sociation [3559]
PO Box 61
Tillery, NC 27887-0061
PH: (252)826-3017
Fax: (252)826-3244
Grant, Gary R., President

Land Loss Fund [12231]
PO Box 61
Tillery, NC 27887-0061
PH: (252)826-3017
Fax: (252)826-3244

Bobby Labonte Fan Club [24075]
PO Box 358
Trinity, NC 27370

Proposition One Campaign [18133]
PO Box 26
Tryon, NC 28782
PH: (202)210-3886

American Waldensian Society
[20637]
208 Rodoret St. S
Valdese, NC 28690-0398
PH: (828)874-3500
Toll free: 866-825-3373
Fax: (828)874-0880
Lewis, Dr. Brad, President

CHERUBS - Association of
Congenital Diaphragmatic Hernia
Research, Awareness and Support
[13827]
152 S White St., Upstairs Ste.
Wake Forest, NC 27587
PH: (919)610-0129
Toll free: 855-CDH-BABY
Fax: (815)425-9155
Williamson, Dawn, Founder,
President

Clan Bell North America [20798]
1513 Anterra Dr.
Wake Forest, NC 27587
PH: (919)528-7959
Bell, David E., President

Embrace Uganda [11351]
PO Box 742
Wake Forest, NC 27588
Bowman, Dorothy, Vol., Exec. Dir.

Start Thinking About Romanian
Children Relief [11158]
100 Traylee Dr.
Wake Forest, NC 27587
PH: (919)521-5851
Henderson, Adriana, Founder,
President, Bd. Member

Window Coverings Association of
America [1963]
PO Box 731
Wake Forest, NC 27588
PH: (919)263-9850
Fax: (919)426-2047
Hoag, Mary, Asst.

International Association of Mission-
ary Aviation [20425]
6922 Davis Rd.
Waxhaw, NC 28173
PH: (704)562-2481
Egeler, Jon, President

International Society for the Study of
Vulvovaginal Disease [16291]
PO Box 586
Waxhaw, NC 28173
PH: (704)814-9493
Marchitelli, Claudia, MD, President

Libros for Learning [11068]
7614 Sims Rd.
Waxhaw, NC 28173
PH: (704)562-4596
Baron, Glenn, Contact

Association for the Advancement of
Computing in Education [8665]
PO Box 719
Waynesville, NC 28786
Fax: (828)246-9557

Society for Information Technology
and Teacher Education [8675]
PO Box 719
Waynesville, NC 28786
Fax: (828)246-9557
Searson, Michael, Officer

Wild Bird Feeding Institute [4181]
PO Box 502
West End, NC 27376

PH: (855)233-6362
Toll free: 888-839-1237
Hays, Sue, Contact

Feministas Unidas [9356]
c/o Mayte De Lama, Professor
919 Creek Crossing Trl.
Whitsett, NC 27377
Chacón, Hilda, Vice Cmdr.

American Netherland Dwarf Rabbit
Club [4591]
c/o Susan Smith, Secretary and
Treasurer
864 Barkers Creek Rd.
Whittier, NC 28789
Smith, Susan, Secretary, Treasurer

National Council on Bible Curriculum
in Public Schools [20577]
1504 Mall Sq.
Wilkesboro, NC 28697
PH: (336)272-3799
Toll free: 877-662-4253
Fax: (336)272-7199
Ammerman, Jim, VP

Critical Messaging Association [766]
441 N Crestwood Dr.
Wilmington, NC 28405-2609
Toll free: 866-301-2272
Fax: (910)792-9733
Jackson, Tom, Secretary, Treasurer

Global Economic Outreach [20419]
PO Box 12778
Wilmington, NC 28405-0138

National Association for Weight Loss
Surgery [16260]
609A Piner Rd., No. 319
Wilmington, NC 28409
Toll free: 877-746-5759
Jay, Katie, Founder, Director

National Organization of Rheumatol-
ogy Managers [17161]
1121 Military Cutoff Rd., No. 337
Wilmington, NC 28405
PH: (910)520-0515
Fax: (910)254-1091
Owen, Ethel, President

Oracle Development Tools User
Group [6285]
2601 Iron Gate Dr., Ste. 101
Wilmington, NC 28412
PH: (910)452-7444
Toll free: 855-853-0491
Fax: (910)523-5504
Delemar, Natalie, President

Roger Sessions Society [9184]
Dept. of Music
University of North Carolina Wilming-
ton
601 S College Rd.
Wilmington, NC 28403-3201
PH: (910)962-3890
Fax: (910)962-7106
Salwen, Dr. Barry D., Exec. Dir.

Senepol Cattle Breeders Association
[3756]
2321 Chestnut St.
Wilmington, NC 28405
PH: (910)444-0234
Toll free: 800-SEN-EPOL
Fax: (704)919-5871
Lawaetz, Mr. Hans, VP

USS North Carolina Battleship As-
sociation [21203]
1 Battleship Rd.
Wilmington, NC 28401
PH: (910)251-5797
Fax: (910)251-5807
Bragg, Capt. Terry A., Exec. Dir.

Working Films [9319]
624 1/2 S 7th St
Wilmington, NC 28401
PH: (910)342-9000
Fax: (910)342-9003
West, Robert, Exec. Dir., Founder

381st Bomb Group Memorial Association [20678]
145 Kimel Park Dr., Ste. 370
Winston Salem, NC 27103-6972
Klein, Virgil A., President

American Belarussian Relief
Organization [12614]
PO Box 25303
Winston Salem, NC 27114-5303
PH: (336)407-6062
Hinchman, Kristen, Director

American Society for Eighteenth-
Century Studies [9456]
PO Box 7867
Winston Salem, NC 27109-6253
PH: (336)727-4694
Fax: (336)727-4697
Aravamudan, Srinivas, President

APA Division 39: Psychoanalysis
[16885]
c/o Ruth Helein, Administrator
2615 Amesbury Rd.
Winston Salem, NC 27103
PH: (336)768-1113
    (336)448-4198
Fax: (336)464-2974
Helen, Ruth, Administrator

Better Marriages [12254]
PO Box 21374
Winston Salem, NC 27120
Toll free: 800-634-8325
Hunt, Priscilla, Exec. Dir.

Cancer Biology Training Consortium
[13916]
834 Madison Ave.
Winston Salem, NC 27103
PH: (520)222-8722
Fax: (480)393-4589
Der, Channing J., PhD, President

Cataract Pack Organization [17696]
331 Hanover Arms Ct.
Winston Salem, NC 27104
PH: (813)476-2704
Kesty, Katarina, Bd. Member

Conchologists of America [21640]
c/o Karlynn Morgan, Membership
Director
3098 Shannon Dr.
Winston Salem, NC 27106-3647
Morgan, Karlynn, Dir. of Member
Svcs.

Independent Order of Odd Fellows
[19599]
422 Trade St.
Winston Salem, NC 27101
PH: (336)725-5955
Toll free: 800-235-8358
Fax: (336)722-7317
Barrett, Terry L., Secretary

International Alliance for Women in
Music [9923]
c/o Susan Borwick, President
Dept. of Music
Wake Forest University
PO Box 7345
Winston Salem, NC 27109-7345
Borwick, Susan, President

International Association of Rebekah
Assemblies, IOOF [19600]
422 Trade St.
Winston Salem, NC 27101

PH: (336)725-5955
Toll free: 800-235-8358
Fax: (336)722-7317
Barrett, Terry L., Secretary

Moravian Music Foundation [9957]
457 S Church St.
Winston Salem, NC 27101-5314
PH: (336)725-0651
Fax: (336)725-4514
Knouse, Dr. Nola Reed, Director

Society for Acupuncture Research
[13505]
130 Cloverhurst Ct.
Winston Salem, NC 27103-9503
Napadow, Vitaly, PhD, LAc, Co-Pres.

Steel Erectors Association of
America [6351]
401 E 4th St., No. 204
Winston Salem, NC 27101-4171
PH: (336)294-8880
Fax: (413)208-6936
Johnson, Charlie, Mem.

Board Retailers Association [2949]
PO Box 1170
Wrightsville Beach, NC 28480
PH: (910)509-0109
Duncan, Mike, President

Biodynamic Craniosacral Therapy
Association of North America
[14349]
115 Williamston Ridge Dr.
Youngsville, NC 27596
PH: (708)837-8090
Harader, Joyce, RCST, President

National Utility Training and Safety
Education Association [3421]
PO Box 1163
Youngsville, NC 27596
PH: (919)671-4496
Williams, Michael, Director

NORTH DAKOTA

Delta Waterfowl [4806]
PO Box 3128
Bismarck, ND 58502
Toll free: 888-987-3695
Petrie, Scott, CEO

Germans From Russia Heritage
Society [19446]
1125 W Turnpike Ave.
Bismarck, ND 58501-8115
PH: (701)223-6167
Fax: (701)223-4421
Hopkins, Wanda, Director

God's Child Project [11005]
721 Memorial Hwy.
Bismarck, ND 58504-5398
PH: (701)255-7956
    (612)351-8020
Atkinson, Patrick, Founder, Exec.
Dir.

Lignite Energy Council [738]
1016 E Owens Ave.
Bismarck, ND 58502
PH: (701)258-7117
Toll free: 800-932-7117
Fax: (701)258-2755
Bohrer, Jason, President, CEO

National Horseshoe Pitchers Association of America [22957]
c/o Stuart Sipma, President
2826 Domino Dr.
Bismarck, ND 58503-0831
PH: (701)258-5686
Sipma, Stuart, President

STEER, Inc. [20467]
1025 N 3rd St.
Bismarck, ND 58502

PH: (701)258-4911
Fax: (701)258-7684
Kost, Mr. Keith, CEO, Exec. Dir.

United States Durum Growers Association [3773]
1605 E Capitol Ave.
Bismarck, ND 58501
PH: (701)214-3203
Fax: (701)223-4645
Martinson, Mark, VP

University of Mary Alumni Association [19360]
7500 University Dr.
Bismarck, ND 58504
PH: (701)355-8030
Toll free: 800-408-6279
Fax: (701)255-7687
Borlaug, Nicolette, President

Plymouth Owners Club [21477]
PO Box 416
Cavalier, ND 58220-0416
Desimone, Nick, Director

African Soul, American Heart [10839]
300 NP Ave., Ste. 308
Fargo, ND 58102
PH: (701)478-7800
Dawson, Deb, President

American Oil Chemists' Society Agricultural Microscopy Division [4175]
c/o Kim Koch, Chairperson
National Crops Institute
PO Box 6050
Fargo, ND 58108
PH: (701)235-3662
Koch, Kim, Chairperson

International Association for Impact Assessment [7273]
1330 23rd St. S, Ste. C
Fargo, ND 58103-3705
PH: (701)297-7908
Fax: (701)297-7917
Hamm, Rita R., CEO

National Alliance of General Agents [1887]
Concorde General Agency, Inc.
720 28th St. SW
Fargo, ND 58103
Fax: (701)239-9941
Rainley, Paul, President

National Association of Teacher Educators for Family and Consumer Sciences [7993]
c/o Mari Borr, Treasurer/Membership Chairperson
PO Box 6050
Fargo, ND 58108-6050
PH: (701)231-7968
Browne, Lorna, Editor

National High School Athletic Coaches Association [22734]
c/o Dave Dougherty, Executive Director
PO Box 10277
Fargo, ND 58106
PH: (701)570-1008
Dougherty, Dave, Exec. Dir.

North Dakota State University Foundation and Alumni Association [19337]
1241 University Dr. N
Fargo, ND 58102-2524
PH: (701)231-6800
(701)231-6834
Toll free: 800-279-8971
Fax: (701)231-6801
Wald, Sara, Mem.

Transportation Research Forum [7352]
PO Box 6050
Fargo, ND 58108-6050
PH: (701)231-7766
McCarthy, Pat, Exec. VP

World Vets [10718]
802 1st Ave. N
Fargo, ND 58102-4906
Toll free: 877-688-8387
Fax: (701)282-9324
King, Cathy, DVM, CEO, Founder

Indians Into Medicine [8325]
c/o School of Medicine and Health Sciences
501 N Columbia Rd., Stop 9037
Grand Forks, ND 58202-9037
PH: (701)777-3037
Fax: (701)777-3277
DeLorme, Eugene, JD, Director

Christian Alliance for Indian Child Welfare [10940]
PO Box 253
Hillsboro, ND 58045-0253
Morris, Elizabeth, Dir. of Admin.

Farm Rescue [4155]
PO Box 28
Horace, ND 58047
PH: (701)252-2017
Fax: (708)221-6488
Gross, Bill, Founder, President

National Sunflower Association [3768]
2401 46th Ave. SE, Ste. 206
Mandan, ND 58554-4829
PH: (701)328-5100
Toll free: 888-718-7033
Sandbakken, John, Exec. Dir.

Retailers of Art Glass and Supplies [1509]
c/o Margie Bolton, Treasurer
109 Main St. S
Minot, ND 58701-3913
PH: (701)837-8555
Berry, Jim, PresidentO

OHIO

All-American Soap Box Derby [23181]
789 Derby Downs Dr.
Akron, OH 44306
PH: (330)733-8723
Fax: (330)733-1370
Mazur, Joseph, President, CEO

American Chemical Society - Rubber Division [2984]
411 Wolf Ledges, Ste. 201
Akron, OH 44311
PH: (330)595-5531
Fax: (330)972-5269
Berkheimer, Beth, Mgr. of Mtgs. & Exhibits

APA Division 26: Society for the History of Psychology [16878]
c/o Cathy Faye, Council Representative
University of Akron
73 College St.
Akron, OH 44325-4302
PH: (202)336-6121
Lamiell, James, President

Association of Nurses in AIDS Care [13529]
3538 Ridgewood Rd.
Akron, OH 44333
PH: (330)670-0101
Toll free: 800-260-6780
Fax: (330)670-0109
Farley, Jason, President

Dogue de Bordeaux Society of America [21870]
679 W Market St.
Akron, OH 44303-1407
Smith, Victor, VP

International Society for Applied Cardiovascular Biology [14125]
c/o Steven P. Schmidt, PhD
1023 Rambling Way
Akron, OH 44333
PH: (330)730-3331
Vorp, David A., PhD, President

Radiology Mammography International [13852]
1037 Robinwood Hills Dr.
Akron, OH 44333-1553
PH: (330)666-1967
Hirsh, Dr. Richard N., Founder

The Tire and Rim Association, Inc. [3282]
175 Montrose West Ave., Ste. 150
Akron, OH 44321
PH: (330)666-8121
Fax: (330)666-8340

Transgender American Veterans Association [21141]
574 E Cuyahoga Falls Ave., Unit 4513
Akron, OH 44310
PH: (516)828-2911
(616)427-5724
Ewing, Jamie, Secretary

Wire and Cable Industry Suppliers Association [1063]
1741 Akron Peninsula Rd.
Akron, OH 44313
PH: (330)864-2122
Fax: (330)864-5298
McNulty, Michael J., Exec. Dir.

Cat Fanciers' Association [21566]
260 E Main St.
Alliance, OH 44601-2423
PH: (330)680-4070
Fax: (330)680-4633
Kallmeyer, Dick, VP

Sport Marketing Association [3164]
1972 Clark Ave.
Alliance, OH 44601
PH: (330)829-8207
Mcevoy, Chad, President

National Residential Appraisers Institute [2885]
2001 Cooper Foster Park Rd.
Amherst, OH 44001
PH: (440)935-1698
Fax: (888)254-5314
Schreiber, Brian, President

Registered Financial Planners Institute [1286]
2001 Cooper Foster Park Rd.
Amherst, OH 44001
PH: (440)282-7176
Fax: (888)254-5314

Committee on Research Materials on Southeast Asia [9700]
c/o Jeffrey R. Shane, Chairperson
Ohio University
Alden Library
Athens, OH 45701-2978
PH: (740)593-2657
Fax: (740)597-1879
Shane, Jeffrey R., Chairman

International Society for Landscape, Place, & Material Culture [9405]
c/o Timothy G. Anderson, Treasurer
Dept. of Geography
Ohio University

122 Clippinger Laboratories
Athens, OH 45701
Brew, Wayne, Exec. Dir.

Last Chance Corral [10657]
5350 US-33 S
Athens, OH 45701
PH: (740)594-4336
Goss, Victoria, President

National Network of Forest Practitioners [4211]
8 N Court St., Ste. 411
Athens, OH 45701
PH: (740)593-8733
Donohue, Colin, Exec. Dir.

Old Lesbians Organizing for Change [10527]
PO Box 5853
Athens, OH 45701
Toll free: 888-706-7506
Griesinger, Jan, Officer

The Pawpaw Foundation [4247]
PO Box 2609
Athens, OH 45701

American Board of Nursing Specialties [16101]
610 Thornhill Ln.
Aurora, OH 44202
PH: (330)995-9172
Fax: (330)995-9743
Niebuhr, Bonnie, RN, MS, CAE, CEO

College of Optometrists in Vision Development [16428]
215 W Garfield Rd., Ste. 200
Aurora, OH 44202
PH: (330)995-0718
Fax: (330)995-0719
Happ, Ms. Pamela R., CAE, Exec. Dir.

National Ice Carving Association [8874]
PO Box 109
Aurora, OH 44202
PH: (630)871-8431
Diederich, Ken, Exec. Dir.

Association of Modified Asphalt Producers [500]
PO Box 305
Avon, OH 44011
PH: (330)714-4117
(440)249-0144
Murphy, John, VP

American Haflinger Registry [4308]
1064 Northview Ave.
Barberton, OH 44203
PH: (330)784-0000
Fax: (330)784-9843
Schwab, Ruth, Managing Dir.

Advertising Media Credit Executives Association [1215]
24600 Detroit Rd., Ste. 100
Bay Village, OH 44140-0036
PH: (410)992-7609
Fax: (410)740-5574
Bolinger, Vickie, President

Bonsai Clubs International [22087]
PO Box 40463
Bay Village, OH 44140-0463
Degroot, David, Secretary

Theta Phi Alpha [23966]
27025 Knickerbocker Rd.
Bay Village, OH 44140-2300
PH: (440)899-9282
Foley, Laura, President

Dwarf Iris Society of America [22092]
c/o Dorothy Willott, President
26231 Shaker Blvd.

Beachwood, OH 44122
Willott, Dorothy, President

First Catholic Slovak Ladies Association **[19644]**
24950 Chagrin Blvd.
Beachwood, OH 44122-5634
PH: (216)464-8015
Toll free: 800-464-4642
Fax: (216)464-9260
Maleski, Cynthia M., President

Institute of Mathematical Statistics **[7242]**
PO Box 22718
Beachwood, OH 44122
PH: (216)295-2340
Toll free: 877-557-4674
Fax: (216)295-5661
Davis, Richard, President

Milestones Autism Resources **[13772]**
23880 Commerce Pk., Ste. 2
Beachwood, OH 44122
PH: (216)464-7600
Fax: (216)464-7602
Skoff, Ilana Hoffer, MA, Exec. Dir.

B-52 Stratofortress Association **[5861]**
498 Carthage Dr.
Beavercreek, OH 45434-5865
Fax: (937)426-1289
Hooppaw, James, President

Catholic Academy of Communication Professionals **[9141]**
1645 Brook Lynn Dr., Ste. 2
Beavercreek, OH 45432-1944
PH: (937)458-0265
Fax: (937)458-0263
Morock, Frank, Director

Society of Air Force Physician Assistants **[20686]**
2833 Gramercy Pl.
Beavercreek, OH 45431
Mathews, Terry, Mem.

Society of Israel Philatelists **[22367]**
25250 Rockside Rd.
Bedford Heights, OH 44146
Rotterdam, Howard, Comm. Chm.

National Imperial Glass Collectors Society **[22142]**
PO Box 534
Bellaire, OH 43906
Wilson, Mike, Officer

Federal Government Distance Learning Association **[7767]**
166 Bledsoe Dr.
Bellbrook, OH 45305
PH: (937)904-5480
Autry, Alex, President

Nu Rho Psi **[23836]**
Baldwin Wallace University
275 Eastland Rd.
Berea, OH 44017-2088
PH: (440)826-8526
Becker, Lora, PhD, President

Christian Aid Ministries **[20397]**
PO Box 360
Berlin, OH 44610
PH: (330)893-2428
Fax: (330)893-2305

American Sighthound Field Association **[21823]**
c/o Jeff Lipps, Chief Financial Officer
3052 Mann Rd.
Blacklick, OH 43004
PH: (614)855-5067
(724)586-6158
Lipps, Jeff, CFO

Scrollsaw Association of the World **[22481]**
116 E Lynn St.
Botkins, OH 45306
PH: (937)693-3309
Bengtson, Carol, President

Epsilon Pi Tau **[23692]**
Bowling Green State University
Technology Bldg.
Bowling Green, OH 43403
PH: (419)372-2425
Fax: (419)372-9502
Olson, Jerry C., Consultant

Historical Construction Equipment Association **[9579]**
16623 Liberty Hi Rd.
Bowling Green, OH 43402
PH: (419)352-5616
Fax: (419)352-6086
Berry, Thomas, Arch.

International Society for Research on Aggression **[6043]**
c/o Eric F. Dubow, PhD, Treasurer
Dept. of Psychology
Bowling Green State University
Bowling Green, OH 43403-0232
Fax: (419)372-6013
Potegal, Mike, President

National Band Association **[9970]**
c/o Bruce Moss, Music Education Committee Chair
537 Monroe Ct.
Bowling Green, OH 43402-1541
Good, Richard, President

National Threshers Association **[8904]**
c/o Steve Lashaway, President
20550 Carter Rd.
Bowling Green, OH 43402
Lashaway, Steve, President

Society For Industrial Organizational Psychology **[16936]**
440 E Poe Rd., Ste. 101
Bowling Green, OH 43402-2756
PH: (419)353-0032
Fax: (419)352-2645
Below, Stephany, Mgr., Comm.

Society for Industrial and Organizational Psychology **[16937]**
440 E Poe Rd., Ste. 101
Bowling Green, OH 43402-1355
PH: (419)353-0032
Fax: (419)352-2645
Nershi, Mr. David, Exec. Dir.

Precision Machined Products Association **[2111]**
6880 W Snowville Rd., Ste. 200
Brecksville, OH 44141
PH: (440)526-0300
Fax: (440)526-5803
Nagle, Bernard, Exec. Dir.

National Drilling Association **[887]**
4036 Center Rd., Ste. B
Brunswick, OH 44212
Toll free: 877-632-4748
Fax: (216)803-9900
Gibel, Larry, Secretary, Treasurer

Crown Victoria Association **[21365]**
PO Box 6
Bryan, OH 43506-0006
PH: (419)636-2475
Fax: (419)636-8449
Gorny, Toby, Founder, President

National Reye's Syndrome Foundation **[17151]**
426 N Lewis St.
Bryan, OH 43506
Toll free: 800-233-7393
Freudenberger, Mr. John, President

Hubbell Family Historical Society **[20883]**
c/o Jan Fulton, Treasurer
4933 Stetzer Rd.
Bucyrus, OH 44820
Hlava, Margie, President

Basal Cell Carcinoma Nevus Syndrome Life Support Network **[14809]**
14525 N Cheshire St.
Burton, OH 44021
PH: (440)834-0011
Toll free: 866-834-1895
Fax: (440)834-0132
Ginn, William D., President

North American Montessori Teachers' Association **[8354]**
13693 Butternut Rd.
Burton, OH 44021-9571
PH: (440)834-4011
Fax: (440)834-4016

United States Trager Association **[13664]**
13801 W Center St., Ste. C
Burton, OH 44021
PH: (440)834-0308
Fax: (440)834-0365

Dodge Brothers Club **[21371]**
PO Box 1648
Cambridge, OH 43725
PH: (740)439-5102
Cogan, Barry, President

National Cambridge Collectors, Inc. **[22137]**
136 S 9th St.
Cambridge, OH 43725-2453
PH: (740)432-4245
Ray, David, President

USS St. Louis CL-49 Association **[9780]**
1112 N 18th St.
Cambridge, OH 43725
PH: (740)432-5305
Jones, Jack R., Editor

Center for Effective Discipline **[7720]**
327 Groveport Pke.
Canal Winchester, OH 43110
PH: (614)834-7946
Fax: (614)321-6308
Block, Nadine, Co-Ch., Co-Chmn. of the Bd.

Feng Shui Institute of America **[9277]**
7547 Bruns Ct.
Canal Winchester, OH 43110
PH: (614)837-8370
Wydra, Nancilee, Founder

National Association of Flour Distributors **[1353]**
c/o G. Timothy Dove
5350 Woodland Pl.
Canfield, OH 44406
PH: (330)718-6563
Fax: (877)573-1230
Valente, Dominic S., Bd. Member

American Institute of Organbuilders **[2417]**
PO Box 35306
Canton, OH 44735
PH: (330)806-9011
Sullivan, Robert, Exec. Dir.

Association of Church Sports and Recreation Ministries **[20017]**
5350 Broadmoor Cir. NW
Canton, OH 44709
PH: (330)493-4824
Linville, Dr. Greg, Exec. Dir.

Catholic Migrant Farmworker Network **[12336]**
701 Walnut Ave. NE
Canton, OH 44702
PH: (330)454-6754
Lopez, Jose, President

International Association of Information Technology Asset Managers Inc. **[1790]**
4848 Munson St. NW
Canton, OH 44718
PH: (330)628-3012
Toll free: 877-942-4826
Fax: (330)628-3289
Rembiesa, Barbara, Founder, President, CEO

North American Deer Farmers Association **[4166]**
4501 Hills and Dales Rd. NW, Ste. C
Canton, OH 44708-1572
PH: (330)454-3944
Fax: (330)454-3950
Schafer, Shawn, Exec. Dir.

Brain Injury Recovery Network **[14910]**
840 Central Ave.
Carlisle, OH 45005

Association of Christian Librarians **[9683]**
PO Box 4
Cedarville, OH 45314-0004
PH: (937)766-2255
Fax: (937)766-5499
Gray, Anita, Secretary

Midstates Jeepster Association **[21432]**
7721 Howick Rd.
7721 Howick Rd.
Celina, OH 45822
Barnikow, Al, President

Children of Promise International **[10923]**
6844 Loop Rd.
Centerville, OH 45459-2159
PH: (937)436-5397
Toll free: 888-667-7426
Fax: (937)438-4972
Haitz, Linn, Founder

National Association of Catholic Family Life Ministers **[20374]**
5818 Wilmington Pke., No. 230
Centerville, OH 45459
PH: (937)431-5443
Fax: (937)431-5443

American Orff-Schulwerk Association **[9865]**
147 Bell St., Ste. 300
Chagrin Falls, OH 44022
PH: (440)600-7329
Fax: (440)600-7332
Barnette, Carrie, Exec. Dir.

Council of International Programs USA **[13108]**
100 N Main St., Ste. 309
Chagrin Falls, OH 44022
PH: (440)247-1088
Fax: (440)247-1490
Purdy, Lisa L., CEO, President

Inter-Lake Yachting Association **[22622]**
18705 Mt. Pleasant Dr.
Chagrin Falls, OH 44023-6061
PH: (440)543-5008
Pribe, Bill, President

Synthetic Amorphous Silica and Silicates Industry Association **[731]**
c/o David A. Pavlich, Association Manager

116 Countryside Dr.
Chagrin Falls, OH 44022
PH: (440)897-8780
Bramante, Christina, Chairperson

The Caucasian Ovcharka Club of
America, Inc. **[21852]**
PO Box 227
Chardon, OH 44024
PH: (440)286-2374

International Borzoi Council **[21897]**
c/o Roger Katona, Treasurer
7617 Pelham Dr.
Chesterland, OH 44026-2011
Katona, Roger, Treasurer

Organization Development Institute
[2463]
11234 Walnut Ridge Rd.
Chesterland, OH 44026
PH: (440)729-7419
Fax: (440)729-9319
Cole, Dr. Donald W., President

Maverick/Comet Club International
[21427]
c/o Don Comfort, Treasurer
4952 Black Run Rd.
Chillicothe, OH 45601
Simpson, Shawn, President

African Society for Toxicological Sci-
ences **[7333]**
c/o Michael Dourson, Advisor
2300 Montana Ave., Ste. 409
Cincinnati, OH 45211
PH: (513)542-7475
Fax: (513)542-7587
Afeseh, Hilary, PhD, Gen. Mgr. of
Sales & Mktg.

American Association for Community
Dental Programs **[14388]**
635 W 7th St., Ste. 309
Cincinnati, OH 45203
PH: (513)621-0248
Fax: (513)621-0288
Hill, Larry, Exec. Dir.

American Conference of
Governmental Industrial Hygienists
[16313]
1330 Kemper Meadow Dr.
Cincinnati, OH 45240-4147
PH: (513)742-2020
    (513)742-6163
Fax: (513)742-3355
Arnold, Susan, Chairman

American Council of the Blind Radio
Amateurs **[21264]**
c/o Robert R Rogers
1121 Morado Dr.
Cincinnati, OH 45238
Duke, Mike, Treasurer

American Jewish Archives **[9631]**
3101 Clifton Ave.
Cincinnati, OH 45220-2404
PH: (513)221-1875
Fax: (513)221-7812
Zola, Gary P., PhD, Exec. Dir.

Annapolis Coalition on the
Behavioral Health Workforce
[15759]
3665 Erie Ave.
Cincinnati, OH 45208-1982
PH: (203)494-7491
    (513)404-3232
Stuart, Gail W., Ph.D., President

Association for the Education of
Children with Medical Needs
[7582]
c/o Scott Menner, Treasurer
580 Chapelacres Ct.

Cincinnati, OH 45233
Rose, Tifanie, President

Association of Luxury Suite Directors
[3151]
10017 McKelvey Rd.
Cincinnati, OH 45231
PH: (513)674-0555
Fax: (513)674-0577
Dorsey, Bill, Chairman, Founder

Association for Women in Aviation
Maintenance **[3486]**
2330 Kenlee Dr.
Cincinnati, OH 45230
PH: (386)416-0248
Ashland, Lynette, President

Catholic Campus Ministry Associa-
tion **[19809]**
330 W Vine St.
Cincinnati, OH 45215
PH: (513)842-0167
Toll free: 888-714-6631
Fax: (513)842-0171
Moran, Rev. Martin O., III, Exec. Dir.

Catholic Social Workers National
Association **[13106]**
PO Box 498531
Cincinnati, OH 45249-8531
PH: (317)416-8285
Neher, Kathleen, Founder, President

A Child's Hope International **[10937]**
2430 E Kemper Rd.
Cincinnati, OH 45241
PH: (513)771-2244
Bergeron, Larry, Exec. Dir., Founder

Chinese Overseas Transportation
Association **[3325]**
c/o Dr. Heng Wei
University of Cincinnati
792 Rhodes Hall
2850 Campus Way
Cincinnati, OH 45221-0071
Heng, Wei, PhD, Bd. Member

Cooperative Education and Intern-
ship Association **[7677]**
PO Box 42506
Cincinnati, OH 45242
PH: (513)793-2342
Fax: (513)793-0463
Cayse, Dan, VP of Fin., VP of Dev.

Couple to Couple League **[11838]**
4290 Delhi Ave.
Cincinnati, OH 45238-5829
PH: (513)471-2000
Toll free: 800-745-8252
Fax: (513)557-2449
Turrentine, Deacon Bill, Chairman

Educational Theatre Association
[8698]
2343 Auburn Ave.
Cincinnati, OH 45219-2815
PH: (513)421-3900
Fax: (513)421-7077
Woffington, Julie, Exec. Dir.

Electrocoat Association **[7264]**
PO Box 541083
Cincinnati, OH 45254-1083
Fax: (513)527-8801
McGlothlin, Ms. Karen, Exec. Dir.

Environmental Policy Center **[5181]**
PO Box 670056
Cincinnati, OH 45267-0056
PH: (513)558-5439
    (513)558-0105
Fax: (513)558-4397
Martin, Joyce, Director

Family Motor Coach Association
[22423]
8291 Clough Pke.
Cincinnati, OH 45244

PH: (513)474-3622
Toll free: 800-543-3622
Fax: (513)474-2332
Adcock, Charlie, President

Food Ingredient Distributors Associa-
tion **[1326]**
3206 Columbia Pky.
Cincinnati, OH 45226
PH: (513)235-6786
Johannigman, Roger, Exec. Dir.

FootPrints for Peace **[18784]**
1225 N Bend Rd.
Cincinnati, OH 45224
PH: (513)843-1205
Toren, Jim, Contact

Foundation of Compassionate
American Samaritans **[20418]**
64 E McMicken Ave.
Cincinnati, OH 45202-8510
PH: (513)621-5300
Taylor, Mr. Dick, Founder

Free Store Food Bank **[12540]**
112 E Liberty St.
Cincinnati, OH 45202-6510
PH: (513)241-1064
Dressman, Jim, Chmn. of the Bd.

Handbell Musicians of America
[9915]
201 E 5th St., Ste. 1900-1025
Cincinnati, OH 45202
PH: (937)438-0085
Fax: (937)438-0085
Cauhorn, Jennifer A., Exec. Dir.

Hope for Haiti's Children **[11039]**
12020 Southwick Ln.
Cincinnati, OH 45241
Toll free: 866-314-9330
Fax: (888)316-9646
Bever, Ken, President, Founder

Interlake Sailing Class Association
[22623]
c/o Thomas Humprey, Secretary-
Treasurer
8 Little Creek Ln.
Cincinnati, OH 45246-4724
PH: (513)772-6441
Aspery, Steve, Director

International Association of Peer
Supporters **[15772]**
PO Box 19265
Cincinnati, OH 45219
PH: (585)797-4641
Christian, Gladys DeVonne,
President

International Enneagram Association
[8411]
4010 Executive Park Dr., Ste. 100
Cincinnati, OH 45241
PH: (513)232-5054
Fax: (513)563-9743
Gore, Belinda, VP

International Fantasy Gaming
Society **[22053]**
PO Box 36555
Cincinnati, OH 45236
Jones, John, President

International Pediatric Hypertension
Association **[15347]**
c/o Melinda Andrews, Assistant
Cincinnati Children's Hospital Medi-
cal Ctr.
3333 Burnet Ave.
MLC 7002
Cincinnati, OH 45229
PH: (513)636-8265
Fax: (513)636-0162
Faulkner, Bonita, Chairman

International Rett Syndrome Founda-
tion. **[15946]**
4600 Devitt Dr.
Cincinnati, OH 45246
PH: (513)874-3020
Toll free: 800-818-7388
Fax: (513)874-2520
Gordon, Rich, COO

International Society of Airbreathing
Engines **[6605]**
c/o Prof. Awatef Hamed, Executive
Secretary
745 Baldwin Hall
Dept. of Aerospace Engineering and
Engineering Mechanics
University of Cincinnati
Cincinnati, OH 45221-0070
Hamed, Prof. Awatef, Exec. Sec.

The International Society of Motor
Control **[6917]**
c/o Michael A. Riley, Secretary/
Treasurer
Psychology Dept., ML 0376
University of Cincinnati
Cincinnati, OH 45221-0376
Riley, Michael, Secretary, Treasurer

Joubert Syndrome and Related
Disorders Foundation **[14834]**
1415 W Ave.
Cincinnati, OH 45215
PH: (614)864-1362
Mack, Stephen, President

Kappa Gamma Pi **[23782]**
7250 Overcliff Rd.
Cincinnati, OH 45233-1038
PH: (305)525-3744
Fax: (305)718-9362
Haden, Kelly, President

Harry Stephen Keeler Society **[9069]**
4745 Winton Rd.
Cincinnati, OH 45232-1522
PH: (513)591-1226
Polt, Richard, Editor

Kundalini Research Network **[15267]**
c/o Lawrence Edwards, Ph.D.
PO Box 541166
Cincinnati, OH 45254
Edwards, Lawrence, PhD, Contact

LAM Foundation **[14590]**
4520 Cooper Rd., Ste. 300
Cincinnati, OH 45242
PH: (513)777-6889
Toll free: 877-287-3526
Pearson, Maria, Mgr.

Lionel Operating Train Society
[22186]
6376 W Fork Rd.
Cincinnati, OH 45247-5704
PH: (513)598-8240
Fax: (866)286-6416
Howe, Phil, President

Melanoma Know More **[14010]**
PO Box 9155
Cincinnati, OH 45209
PH: (513)364-6653
Kindel, Susan, MD, President

Music Teachers National Association
[8378]
1 W 4th St., Ste. 1550
Cincinnati, OH 45202
PH: (513)421-1420
Toll free: 888-512-5278
Johnson, Rebecca Grooms,
President

Nathaniel Hawthorne Society **[9084]**
University of Cincinnati
2600 Clifton Ave.

Cincinnati, OH 45220
PH: (513)556-6000
Mitchell, Mr. Thomas R., President

National Association of Directors of
Nursing Administration in Long
Term Care **[16147]**
1329 E Kemper Rd., Ste. 4100A
Cincinnati, OH 45246
PH: (513)791-3679
Toll free: 800-222-0539
Arnicar, Robin, RN, CDONA, FAC-
DONA, President

National Association of Sports Com-
missions **[23269]**
9916 Carver Rd., Ste. 100
Cincinnati, OH 45242
PH: (513)281-3888
Fax: (513)281-1765
Schumacher, Don, Exec. Dir.

The National Bowling Association
[22705]
9944 Reading Rd.
Cincinnati, OH 45241
PH: (513)769-1985
Fax: (513)769-3596
Davis, Pauline, Div. Mgr.

National Corvette Restorers Society
[21451]
6291 Day Rd.
Cincinnati, OH 45252-1334
PH: (513)385-8526
    (513)385-6367
Fax: (513)385-8554
Burnett, Joan, Chairman

National Real Estate Investors As-
sociation **[2034]**
7265 Kenwood Rd., Ste. 368
Cincinnati, OH 45236-4412
PH: (513)827-9563
Toll free: 888-762-7342
Fax: (859)422-4916
McLean, Rebecca, Exec. Dir.

National Vitiligo Foundation Inc.
[14508]
11250 Cornell Park Dr., Ste. 207
Cincinnati, OH 45242
PH: (513)793-6834
Fax: (513)793-6887

National Wood Carvers Association
[21776]
PO Box 43218
Cincinnati, OH 45243

Nigerian Association of Pharmacists
and Pharmaceutical Scientists in
the Americas **[2564]**
483 Northland Blvd.
Cincinnati, OH 45240
PH: (513)641-3300
Fax: (513)861-3629
Onyewuenyi, Nonye, Ph.D,
Secretary

North American Railcar Operators
Association **[3350]**
PO Box 9035
Cincinnati, OH 45209
Knight, Bob, President

Parents of Murdered Children, Inc.
[12423]
4960 Ridge Ave., Ste. 2
Cincinnati, OH 45209-1075
PH: (513)721-5683
Toll free: 888-818-7662
Fax: (513)345-4489
Levey, Dan, Exec. Dir.

Patrol Craft Sailors Association
[21060]
c/o Jim Heywood, Membership Officer

7005 Bridge Rd.
Cincinnati, OH 45230
PH: (513)233-2775
Brenner, August K., President

Phi Sigma Rho **[23741]**
PO Box 58304
Cincinnati, OH 45258
Bush, Colleen, Exec. Dir.

pureHOPE **[18928]**
110 Boggs Ln., Ste. 302
Cincinnati, OH 45246
PH: (513)521-6227
Matthews, Gary, Treasurer

Retail Design Institute **[2975]**
126A W 4th St., 2nd Fl.
Cincinnati, OH 45202
PH: (513)751-5815
Fax: (513)961-1192
McQuilkin, Andrew, Chairman

Save Babies Through Screening
Foundation **[14213]**
PO Box 42197
Cincinnati, OH 45242
Toll free: 888-454-3383
Levy-Fisch, Jill, President

Scripps Howard Foundation **[8160]**
PO Box 5380
Cincinnati, OH 45201
PH: (513)977-3035
Toll free: 800-888-3000
Fax: (513)977-3800
Rose, Lee, Director

Soccer Association for Youth **[23190]**
Enterprise Business Park
2812 E Kemper Rd.
Cincinnati, OH 45241
PH: (513)769-3800
Toll free: 800-233-7291
Fax: (513)769-0500
Wood, Doug, Exec. Dir.

Society for Design Administration
[5978]
8190-A Beechmont Ave., No. 276
Cincinnati, OH 45255
PH: (513)268-5302
Toll free: 800-711-8199
Fax: (513)448-1921
Kirschner, Stephanie L., Exec. Dir.

Society for Philosophy and Psychol-
ogy **[10127]**
206 McMicken Hall
Dept. of Philosophy
University of Cincinnati
Cincinnati, OH 45221
PH: (513)556-6324
Fax: (513)556-2939
Gendler, Tamar Szabo, President

SOTENI International **[10554]**
1662 Blue Rock St., Ste. 3
Cincinnati, OH 45223
PH: (513)729-9932
Fax: (513)961-2101
Marsh, Randie, Exec. Dir.

Testicular Cancer Society **[14074]**
792 Woodlyn Dr. S
Cincinnati, OH 45230
PH: (513)696-9827
Craycraft, Michael, RPh, President

Toxicology Excellence for Risk As-
sessment **[7344]**
2300 Montana Ave., Ste. 409
Cincinnati, OH 45211
PH: (513)542-7475
Fax: (513)542-7487
Dourson, Michael L., PhD, President

VOICES in Action **[12940]**
8041 Hosbrook Rd., Ste. 236
Cincinnati, OH 45236
Toll free: 800-786-4238
Fax: (773)327-4590
Sowels-Jenkins, Holly, President

World Piano Competition **[10026]**
1241 Elm St.
Cincinnati, OH 45202-7531
PH: (513)744-3501
Fax: (513)744-3504
Smith, Gary, Treasurer

Vintage BMW Motorcycle Owners
[22236]
PO Box 341
Clarksville, OH 45113-0341
PH: (414)333-6987
Fax: (414)456-9790
Rosenstein, Hans, President

Academy of Accounting Historians
[9447]
Case Western Reserve University
Weatherhead School of Manage-
ment
10900 Euclid Ave.
Cleveland, OH 44106-7235
PH: (216)368-2058
Colson, Robert, President

African American Museum of
Cleveland **[9814]**
1765 Crawford Rd.
Cleveland, OH 44106
PH: (216)721-6555

American Association of Automatic
Door Manufacturers **[993]**
1300 Sumner Ave.
Cleveland, OH 44115-2851
PH: (216)241-7333
Fax: (216)241-0105
Addington, John H., Exec. Dir.

American Mutual Life Association
[19652]
19424 S Waterloo Rd.
Cleveland, OH 44119
PH: (216)531-1900
Fax: (216)531-8123

American Sickle Cell Anemia As-
sociation **[17206]**
DD Bldg.
10900 Carnegie Ave., Ste. DD1-201
Cleveland, OH 44106
PH: (216)229-8600
Fax: (216)229-4500
Bragg-Grant, Ira, Exec. Dir.

American Society of Greek and Latin
Epigraphy **[10411]**
1201 Euclid Ave.
11201 Euclid Ave.
Cleveland, OH 44106-7111
PH: (261)368-2348
Fax: (261)368-4681
Iversen, Prof. Paul, VP

American Train Dispatchers Associa-
tion **[23513]**
4239 W 150th St.
Cleveland, OH 44135
PH: (216)251-7984
Fax: (216)251-8190
Dowell, Ed, Secretary, Treasurer

Aquarium and Zoo Facilities Association **[7397]**
3900 Wildlife Way
Cleveland, OH 44109
Castañeda, Rudy, President

Association of Ingersoll-Rand
Distributors **[1714]**
1300 Sumner Ave.
Cleveland, OH 44115-2851

PH: (216)241-7333
Fax: (216)241-0105
Michel, Jonathan, VP

Association of Marshall Scholars
[8514]
1120 Chester Ave., Ste. 470
Cleveland, OH 44114
Toll free: 866-276-0741
Fax: (216)696-2582
Klaber, Andrew, President

Association for Patient Experience
[14930]
PO Box 21875
Cleveland, OH 44121
PH: (216)316-5787
Merlino, James, MD, Chmn. of the
Bd., President

BVU: The Center for Nonprofit
Excellence **[13289]**
1300 E 9th St., Ste. 1805
Cleveland, OH 44114-1509
PH: (216)736-7711
Fax: (216)736-7710
Clark, Julie, Director

Center on Urban Poverty and Com-
munity Development **[12533]**
Jack, Joseph and Morton Mandel
School of Applied Social Sciences
Case Western Reserve University
10900 Euclid Ave.
Cleveland, OH 44106-7167
PH: (216)368-6946
Fax: (216)368-8592
Coulton, Claudia, Director

CEOs for Cities **[19216]**
1717 Euclid Ave., UR 130
Cleveland, OH 44115
PH: (216)687-4704
Fisher, Lee, CEO, President

Chemical Fabrics and Film Associa-
tion Inc. **[2622]**
1300 Sumner Ave.
Cleveland, OH 44115-2851
PH: (216)241-7333
Fax: (216)241-0105

Christian Vegetarian Association
[20635]
PO Box 201791
Cleveland, OH 44120
PH: (216)283-6702
Toll free: 866-202-9170
Fax: (216)283-6702
Kaufman, Stephen R., MD, Chair-
man

Compressed Air and Gas Institute
[1720]
1300 Sumner Ave.
Cleveland, OH 44115
PH: (216)241-7333
Fax: (216)241-0105

Concrete and Masonry Anchor
Manufacturers Association **[785]**
1300 Sumner Ave.
Cleveland, OH 44115
PH: (216)241-7333
Fax: (216)241-0105

Congregation of the Blessed Sacra-
ment **[19827]**
5384 Wilson Mills Rd.
Cleveland, OH 44143-3023
PH: (440)442-6311
Stark, Robert, Treasurer

Congress of Secular Jewish
Organizations **[9636]**
320 Claymore Blvd.
Cleveland, OH 44143
PH: (216)481-0850
Toll free: 866-874-8608
Feinstein, Ms. Roberta E., Exec. Dir.

Council for Health and Human Service Ministries of the United Church of Christ **[13040]**
700 Prospect Ave.
Cleveland, OH 44115
PH: (216)736-2260
Toll free: 866-822-8224
Sickbert, Bryan W., Consultant

Czech Catholic Union **[19419]**
5349 Dolloff Rd.
Cleveland, OH 44127
PH: (216)341-0444
Fax: (216)341-0711
Malec, Elsie T., Officer

Door and Access Systems Manufacturers Association International **[2220]**
1300 Sumner Ave.
Cleveland, OH 44115-2851
PH: (216)241-7333
Fax: (216)241-0105
Addington, John H., Exec. Dir.

Education Law Association **[5525]**
2121 Euclid Ave. LL 212
Cleveland, OH 44115-2214
PH: (216)523-7377
 (937)229-3589
Fax: (216)687-5284
Smith, Cate K., Exec. Dir.

Federation Internationale de Gynecologie Infantile et Juvenile **[16284]**
9500 Euclid Ave., No. A120
Cleveland, OH 44195-0001
PH: (216)444-3566
Fax: (216)445-3523
Rome, Dr. Ellen S., President

Fire Equipment Manufacturers' Association **[2994]**
1300 Sumner Ave.
Cleveland, OH 44115
PH: (216)241-7333

Flashes of Hope **[10787]**
6009 Landerhaven Dr., Ste. I
Cleveland, OH 44124
PH: (440)442-9700
DiFiore, Kristine, CFO

Fluid Controls Institute **[1728]**
1300 Sumner Ave.
Cleveland, OH 44115
PH: (216)241-7333
Fax: (216)241-0105

Forging Industry Association **[2348]**
1111 Superior Ave., Ste. 615
Cleveland, OH 44114
PH: (216)781-6260
Fax: (216)781-0102
DiLorenzo, Michael J., Mgr.

Forging Industry Educational and Research Foundation **[6844]**
1111 Superior Ave., Ste. 615
Cleveland, OH 44114-2568
PH: (216)781-5040
Fax: (216)781-0102
Lewis, Karen S., Exec. Dir.

Health Action Council **[15143]**
6133 Rockside Rd., Ste. 210
Cleveland, OH 44131
PH: (216)328-2200
Gough, Karen, Coord.

Heat Exchange Institute **[1619]**
1300 Sumner Ave.
Cleveland, OH 44115-2815
PH: (216)241-7333
Fax: (216)241-0105

Intermuseum Conservation Association **[9830]**
2915 Detroit Ave.
Cleveland, OH 44113

PH: (216)658-8700
Fax: (216)658-8709
Beckenbach, William C., President

International Association for Energy Economics **[6491]**
28790 Chagrin Blvd., Ste. 350
Cleveland, OH 44122
PH: (216)464-5365

International Endotoxin and Innate Immunity Society **[7341]**
c/o Amy Hise, Treasurer
Dept. of Pathology
Case Western Reserve University
2109 Adelbert Rd.
Cleveland, OH 44106
Schromm, Andra, Secretary

International Maillard Reaction Society **[6203]**
c/o David R. Sell, Secretary-Treasurer
Dept. of Patholoy
Case Western Reserve University
10900 Euclid Ave.
Cleveland, OH 44106
Miyazawa, Teruo, President

International Society of Explosives Engineers **[6564]**
30325 Bainbridge Rd.
Cleveland, OH 44139
PH: (440)349-4400
Fax: (440)349-3788
Forde, J. Winston, Exec. Dir.

International Society for Genetic Eye Diseases and Retinoblastoma **[16390]**
9500 Euclid Ave., I32
Cleveland, OH 44195
Lorenz, Birgit, President

International Special Tooling and Machining Association **[1739]**
c/o Dave Tilstone, President
1357 Rockside Rd.
Cleveland, OH 44134
PH: (301)248-6862
Tilstone, Mr. Dave, President

International Union of Physiological Sciences **[7034]**
c/o Steven Webster, Manager
Dept. of Physiology and Biophysics
Case Western Reserve University
10900 Euclid Ave.
Cleveland, OH 44106-4970
PH: (216)368-5520
Fax: (216)368-5586
Boron, Walter, Sec. Gen.

Iota Sigma Pi **[23704]**
c/o QuynhGiao Nguyen, President
21000 Brookpark Rd.
MS 49-3
Cleveland, OH 44135
PH: (216)433-6073
Nguyen, QuynhGiao N., PhD, President

Ishmael and Isaac **[18685]**
1 Bratenahl Pl., Ste. 1302
Cleveland, OH 44108-1156
PH: (216)233-7333
 (216)751-6446
Gray, Anita, President

LifeBanc **[14621]**
4775 Richmond Rd.
Cleveland, OH 44128-5919
PH: (216)752-5433
Toll free: 888-558-5433
Fax: (216)292-8191
Bowen, Gordon, CEO

Lyman Boat Owners Association **[22645]**
PO Box 40052
Cleveland, OH 44140

PH: (440)241-4290
Gundlach, Tina, Secretary

The Macula Society **[16394]**
3401 Enterprise Pky., Ste. 310
Cleveland, OH 44122
PH: (216)839-4949
Fax: (216)831-8221

Medical Dermatology Society **[14501]**
526 Superior Ave. E, Ste. 540
Cleveland, OH 44114-1900
PH: (216)579-9300
Fax: (216)579-9333
Kroshinsky, Daniela, President

Metal Building Manufacturers Association **[544]**
1300 Sumner Ave.
Cleveland, OH 44115-2851
PH: (216)241-7333
Fax: (216)241-0105
Curtis, Brad, Chairman

MHE Coalition **[14843]**
c/o Chele Zelina, President
6783 York Rd., No. 104
Cleveland, OH 44130-4596
PH: (440)842-8817
Zelina, Chele, President

NASBITE International **[7555]**
c/o Donna Davisson, Executive Director
Monte Ahuja College of Business
1860 E 18th St., BU327
Cleveland, OH 44115
PH: (216)802-3381
Davisson, Donna, Exec. Dir.

National Association of Estate Planners & Councils **[1282]**
1120 Chester Ave., Ste. 470
Cleveland, OH 44114
Toll free: 866-226-2224
Fax: (216)696-2582
Lehmann, Lawrence M., President

National Association of Graphic and Product Identification Manufacturers, Inc. **[2361]**
1300 Sumner Ave.
Cleveland, OH 44115-2851
PH: (216)241-7333
Fax: (216)241-0105
Anderson, Dean, VP

National Association for Justice Information Systems **[5141]**
c/o Thomas Welch, President
984 Keynote Cr.
Cleveland, OH 44131
PH: (216)739-6254
Fax: (216)739-3520
Radke, Laura, Director

National Coalition of Advanced Technology Centers **[8671]**
33607 Seneca Dr.
Cleveland, OH 44139-5578
PH: (440)318-1558
McAtee, J. Craig, Exec. Dir.

National Coil Coating Association **[746]**
1300 Sumner Ave.
Cleveland, OH 44115
PH: (216)241-7333
Fax: (216)241-0105
Small, Aaron, President

National Confectionery Sales Association **[2968]**
Spitfire House
3135 Berea Rd.
Cleveland, OH 44111
PH: (216)631-8200
Fax: (216)631-8210
Leipold, John A., Jr., Director, President

National Juvenile Court Services Association **[5192]**
c/o George S. Tsagaris, President
Cleveland State University
2121 Euclid Ohio
Cleveland, OH 44115
PH: (216)523-7474
Tsagaris, George S., President

National Sunroom Association **[562]**
1300 Sumner Ave.
Cleveland, OH 44115-2851
PH: (216)241-7333
Fax: (216)241-0105
Goss, Martin, VP

National Tooling and Machining Association **[2109]**
1357 Rockside Rd.
Cleveland, OH 44134
Toll free: 800-248-6862
Fax: (216)264-2840
Tilstone, Mr. Dave, President

New Avenues to Independence **[12331]**
17608 Euclid Ave.
Cleveland, OH 44112
PH: (216)481-1907
Fax: (216)481-2050
Lewins, Thomas, Exec. Dir.

Nonprofit Academic Centers Council **[12392]**
1717 Euclid Ave.
Cleveland, OH 44115-2214
PH: (216)687-5233
Palmer, Paul, VP

North American Society for Trenchless Technology **[7356]**
14500 Lorain Ave., No. 110063
Cleveland, OH 44111
PH: (216)570-8711
Staheli, Kimberlie, Chairperson

PediaWorks **[16617]**
10000 Cedar Ave., Ste. 16
Cleveland, OH 44106
PH: (216)223-8877
Moran, Tim, Founder

Percussion Marketing Council **[2435]**
PO Box 33252
Cleveland, OH 44133
PH: (440)582-7006
Fax: (440)230-1346
Smith, Brad, Exec. Dir.

Platelet Disorder Support Association **[13789]**
8751 Brecksville Rd., Ste. 150
Cleveland, OH 44141
PH: (440)746-9003
Toll free: 877-528-3538
Fax: (844)270-1277
Kruse, Caroline, Exec. Dir.

Power Tool Institute, Inc. **[1574]**
1300 Sumner Ave.
Cleveland, OH 44115-2851
PH: (216)241-7333
Fax: (216)241-0105

Pressure Washer Manufacturers Association **[1762]**
1300 Sumner Ave.
Cleveland, OH 44115-2851
PH: (216)241-7333
Fax: (216)241-0105

The Refractories Institute **[6174]**
1300 Sumner Ave.
Cleveland, OH 44115
PH: (216)241-7333
Fax: (216)241-0105

Scleral Lens Education Society **[14299]**
c/o Mindy Toabe, Secretary
MetroHealth Medical Ctr.

2500 MetroHealth Dr.
Cleveland, OH 44109
Barnett, Melissa, President

Society of Ethical and Religious
Vegetarians **[20636]**
c/o Stephen Kaufman, Coordinator
PO Box 201791
Cleveland, OH 44120
PH: (216)283-6702
Fax: (216)283-6702

Society for Heart and Vascular
Metabolism **[14146]**
10900 Euclid Ave.
Case Western Reserve University
School of Medicine E521
10900 Euclid Ave.
Cleveland, OH 44106-4970
Abel, E. Dale, MD, President

Society for Investigative Dermatol-
ogy **[14513]**
526 Superior Ave. E, Ste. 540
Cleveland, OH 44114-1999
PH: (216)579-9300
Fax: (216)579-9333
Rumsey, Jim, Exec. Dir., COO

Society for Photographic Education
[8426]
2530 Superior Ave., Ste. 403
Cleveland, OH 44114
PH: (216)622-2733
Fax: (216)622-2712
Cutshaw, Stacey McCarroll, Editor

Steel Window Institute **[584]**
1300 Sumner Ave.
Cleveland, OH 44115-2851
PH: (216)241-7333
Fax: (216)241-0105

The Transformer Association **[1578]**
1300 Sumner Ave.
Cleveland, OH 44115
PH: (216)241-7333
Fax: (216)241-0105
Graham, Susan, VP

Twentieth Century Society USA
[8895]
PO Box 110148
Cleveland, OH 44111
PH: (828)778-6425
Beyer, Mick, President

Unified Abrasives Manufacturers'
Association - Grain Committee
[1775]
30200 Detroit Rd.
Cleveland, OH 44145-1967
PH: (440)899-0010
Fax: (440)892-1404

Union and League of Romanian
Societies **[19624]**
Cleveland, OH
Istrate, Daniela, President

United Abrasives Manufacturers' As-
sociation **[2307]**
30200 Detroit Rd.
Cleveland, OH 44145-1967
PH: (440)899-0010
Fax: (440)892-1404
Gaylord, Rick, President

United Church of Christ Coalition for
Lesbian, Gay, Bisexual and Trans-
gender Concerns **[20190]**
700 Prospect Ave.
Cleveland, OH 44115
PH: (216)736-3228
Lang, Andy, Exec. Dir.

United States Association for Energy
Economics **[6514]**
28790 Chagrin Blvd., Ste. 350
Cleveland, OH 44122-4642

PH: (216)464-2785
Fax: (216)464-2768
Smith, James, President

United States Book Exchange
[9732]
2969 W 25th St.
Cleveland, OH 44113
PH: (216)241-6960
Fax: (216)241-6966

United States Cutting Tool Institute
[1776]
1300 Sumner Ave.
Cleveland, OH 44115-2851
PH: (216)241-7333
Fax: (216)241-0105
Stokey, Steve, President

Universal Health Care Action
Network **[15067]**
2800 Euclid Ave., No. 520
Cleveland, OH 44115-2418
PH: (216)241-8422
Toll free: 800-634-4442
Fax: (216)241-8423
DeGolia, Rachel, Exec. Dir.

Preventive Oncology International
[16352]
2762 Fairmount Blvd.
Cleveland Heights, OH 44118
PH: (216)312-3663
Belinson, Jerome L., President

Vasa Order of America **[19498]**
c/o Bruce Elfvin, Membership Chairman
2924 E Overlook Rd.
Cleveland Heights, OH 44118-2434
Kellgren, Tore, Master

Roofing Industry Committee on
Weather Issues, Inc. **[575]**
6314 Kungle Rd.
Clinton, OH 44216
PH: (330)671-4569
Fax: (330)825-7172
Cook, Joan, Exec. Dir.

Gale Storm Appreciation Society
[23993]
PO Box 212
Coalton, OH 45621-0212
Baker, Ron, Co-Pres.

America in Bloom **[3780]**
2130 Stella Ct.
Columbus, OH 43215
PH: (614)453-0744
Fax: (614)487-1216
Hall, Charlie, PhD, Contact

American Academy of Fixed Prost-
hodontics **[14376]**
Office of the Secretary
6661 Merwin Rd.
Columbus, OH 43235
PH: (614)761-1927
Fax: (614)292-0941
Rosenstiel, Stephen F., Secretary

American Association for Agricultural
Education **[7471]**
Columbus, OH
Trefz, Marilyn, Exec. Dir.

American Association for Italian
Studies **[9612]**
c/o Dana Renga, Executive
Secretary
200 Hagerty Hall
Dept. of French and Italian
Ohio State University
1775 College Rd.
Columbus, OH 43210-1340
PH: (573)882-2030
Past, Elena, Treasurer

American Guernsey Association
[3693]
1224 Alton Darby Creek Rd., Ste. G
Columbus, OH 43228
PH: (614)864-2409
Fax: (614)864-5614
Trotter, David, President

American Professional Society on
the Abuse of Children **[10851]**
1706 E Broad St.
Columbus, OH 43203
PH: (614)827-1321
Toll free: 877-402-7722
Fax: (614)251-6005
Haney, Michael L., PhD, Exec. Dir.

American Society of Criminology
[5152]
1314 Kinnear Rd., Ste. 212
Columbus, OH 43212-1156
PH: (614)292-9207
Fax: (614)292-6767
Peterson, Ruth, President

American Society for Nondestructive
Testing **[7321]**
1711 Arlingate Ln.
Columbus, OH 43228
PH: (614)274-6003
Toll free: 800-222-2768
Fax: (614)274-6899
Morgan, Ricky, President

Association of Anesthesia Clinical
Directors **[16739]**
c/o Kimberly R. Corey
3757 Indianola Ave.
Columbus, OH 43214-3753
PH: (614)784-9772
Fax: (614)784-9771
Judge, Lisa M., M.D., Treasurer

Association of Capitol Reporters and
Editors **[2660]**
c/o Alan Johnson, Treasurer
34 S 3rd St.
Columbus, OH 43215-4201
Leslie, Laura, President

Association of College and
University Housing Officers
International **[8604]**
1445 Summit St.
Columbus, OH 43201-2105
PH: (614)292-0099
Fax: (614)292-3205
Glenn, Emily, Librarian

Association for Financial Technology
[66]
c/o Jeannine Windbigler, Managing
Director
96 Northwoods Blvd., Ste. B2
Columbus, OH 43235
PH: (614)895-1208
Fax: (614)436-6181
Bannister, James R., Exec. Dir.

Association of Public Pension Fund
Auditors **[23490]**
PO Box 16064
Columbus, OH 43216-6064
Priestas, Matt, President

Association of Residential Cleaning
Services International **[2124]**
7870 Olentangy River Rd., Ste. 301
Columbus, OH 43235
PH: (614)547-0887
Fax: (614)505-7136
Hartong, Ernie, Exec. Dir.

Association for the Study of the
Worldwide African Diaspora **[7466]**
c/o Dr. Leslie Alexander
486N University Hall
230 N Oval Mall

Columbus, OH 43210
Alexander, Leslie, President

Australian Football Association of
North America **[22856]**
PO Box 27623
Columbus, OH 43227-0623
PH: (614)571-8986
Fax: (866)334-9884
de Santos, Rob, Chairman

Ayrshire Breeders' Association
[3717]
1224 Alton Darby Creek Rd., Ste. B
Columbus, OH 43228
PH: (614)335-0020
Fax: (614)335-0023
Fenton, Tom, VP

Battelle for Kids **[7584]**
1160 Dublin Rd., Ste. 500
Columbus, OH 43215-1085
PH: (614)481-3141
Toll free: 866-543-7555
Mahoney, Jim, PhD, Exec. Dir.

Batten Disease Support and
Research Association **[15909]**
1175 Dublin Rd.
Columbus, OH 43215
Toll free: 800-448-4570
Fax: (800)648-8718
Collins, Mike, Secretary

Better Healthcare for Africa **[15080]**
PO Box 361132
Columbus, OH 43236
PH: (614)475-6038
Ward, Darrell, Bd. Member

Buick Club of America **[21344]**
PO Box 360775
Columbus, OH 43236-0775
PH: (614)472-3939
Fax: (614)472-3222
DePouli, Brian, President

Business Professionals of America
[8736]
5454 Cleveland Ave.
Columbus, OH 43231-4021
PH: (614)895-7277
Toll free: 800-334-2007
Fax: (614)895-1165
Lawson, Kirk, Exec. Dir.

Cadillac-LaSalle Club **[21346]**
PO Box 360835
Columbus, OH 43236-0835
PH: (614)478-4622
Fax: (614)472-3222
Kneller, Lars, Director

Center for African Studies **[19242]**
318 Oxley Hall
1712 Neil Ave.
Columbus, OH 43210-1219
PH: (614)292-8169
Fax: (614)292-4273
Agunga, Dr. Robert, Director

Center for Humane Options in
Childbirth Experiences **[16279]**
2584 Oakstone Dr.
Columbus, OH 43231
PH: (614)263-2229
Fax: (614)263-2228

Central Eurasian Studies Society
[8111]
2873 W Broad St.
Columbus, OH 43204-2673
Koch, Natalie, Secretary

Community Development Society
[17973]
17 S High St., Ste. 200
Columbus, OH 43215

PH: (614)221-1900
Fax: (614)221-1989
Lamie, David, President

Council of Development Finance
  Agencies [18149]
100 E Broad St., Ste. 1200
Columbus, OH 43215
PH: (614)705-1300
  (614)705-1317
Rittner, Toby, CEO, President

Council for Ethical Leadership [626]
1 College and Main
Columbus, OH 43209
PH: (614)236-7222
Abrams, Jim, Chairman

Delta Gamma [23951]
3250 Riverside Dr.
Columbus, OH 43221
PH: (614)481-8169
Toll free: 800-644-5414
McGuire, Colleen, Exec. Dir.

Edison Welding Institute [7383]
1250 Arthur E Adams Dr.
Columbus, OH 43221-3585
PH: (614)688-5000
Fax: (614)688-5001
Cialone, Dr. Henry J., CEO,
  President

The Entrepreneurship Institute [629]
3700 Corporate Dr., Ste. 145
Columbus, OH 43231
PH: (614)895-1153

Farm Show Council [3563]
c/o Chuck Gamble, Secretary-
  Treasurer
232 Ag Engineering Bldg.
590 Woody Hayes Dr.
Columbus, OH 43210
PH: (614)292-4278
Fax: (614)292-9448
Gamble, Chuck, Secretary,
  Treasurer

For Mother Earth [18471]
1101 Bryden Rd.
Columbus, OH 43205
PH: (614)252-9255
Brown, Pat, Contact

Free to Smile Foundation [14336]
75 E Gay St., Ste. 300
Columbus, OH 43215
PH: (614)778-5344
Henry, Dr. Byron, Founder

Game Manufacturers Association
  [1136]
240 N 5th St., Ste. 340
Columbus, OH 43215
PH: (614)255-4500
Fax: (614)255-4499
Ward, John, Exec. Dir.

Greek Olympic Society [23048]
555 N High St.
Columbus, OH 43215
PH: (614)224-9020
Mardas, Denny, President

Heartbeat International [12769]
5000 Arlington Center Blvd., Ste.
  2277
Columbus, OH 43220-2913
Toll free: 888-550-7577
Fax: (614)885-8746
Hartshorn, Peggy, PhD, Chmn. of
  the Bd.

Heating Airconditioning and
  Refrigeration Distributors
  International [1620]
445 Hutchinson Ave., Ste. 550
Columbus, OH 43235

PH: (614)345-4328
Toll free: 888-253-2128
Fax: (614)345-9161
Bergaminiinc, William, President, VP

Industrial Diamond Association
  [1735]
PO Box 29460
Columbus, OH 43229
PH: (614)797-2265
Fax: (614)797-2264
Kane, Terry M., Exec. Dir.

International Association for
  Comparative Research on
  Leukemia and Related Diseases
  [15534]
c/o Clara D. Bloomfield, MD,
  Secretary-General
1216 James Cancer Hospital
300 W 10th Ave.
Columbus, OH 43210
PH: (614)293-7518
Fax: (614)366-1637
Bloomfield, Dr. Clara D., Sec. Gen.

International Association of
  Geochemistry [7938]
c/o Chris Gardner, Office Manager
275 Mendenhall Laboratory
125 S Oval Mall
Columbus, OH 43210-1308
PH: (614)688-7400
Fax: (614)292-7688
Negrel, Philippe, VP

International Clarinet Association
  [9925]
829 Bethel Rd., No. 216
Columbus, OH 43214
Lynch, Evan, Exec. Dir. (Actg.)

International Community Corrections
  Association [11532]
2100 Stella Ct.
Columbus, OH 43215
PH: (614)252-8417
Fax: (614)252-7987
Connell-Freund, Anne, President

International Society of Glass Bead-
  makers [8981]
118 Graceland Blvd., Ste. 316
Columbus, OH 43214
PH: (614)222-2243
Fax: (614)983-0389
Ramey, Angie, President

Iron Casting Research Institute, Inc.
  [1741]
2802 Fisher Rd.
Columbus, OH 43204
PH: (614)275-4201
Fax: (614)275-4203
Blatzer, Bruce T., Exec. Dir.

Kappa Kappa Gamma [23958]
530 E Town St.
Columbus, OH 43215
PH: (614)228-6515
Toll free: 866-KKG-1870
Fax: (614)228-7809
Kittrell, Kari, Exec. Dir.

Mon American Association [17825]
1357 Worthington Centre Dr.
Columbus, OH 43085
PH: (614)456-9136
Nai, Janoi Marn, Chairman

Mortar Board, Inc. [23783]
c/o Motor Board National College
  Senior Honor Society
1200 Chambers Rd., Ste. 201
Columbus, OH 43212
PH: (614)488-4094
Toll free: 800-989-6266
Fax: (614)488-4095
Hamblin, Ms. Jane, JD, Exec. Dir.

National Agricultural Communicators
  of Tomorrow [8157]
c/o Dr. Emily Buck, Adviser
208 Agricultural Administration Bldg.
Department of Agricultural Communication, Education, and
  Leadership
The Ohio State University
2120 Fyffe Rd.
Columbus, OH 43210
Kennedy, Taylor, President

National Amateur Press Association
  [22391]
184 Reinhard Ave.
Columbus, OH 43206-2635
Klosterman, Michelle, President

National Association of Attorneys
  with Disabilities [5026]
1491 Polaris Pky., PMB 295
Columbus, OH 43240
PH: (347)455-1521
Pixley, Stuart, President

National Association of Barber
  Boards of America [923]
2886 Airport Dr.
Columbus, OH 43219
PH: (614)523-0203
Kirkpatrick, Charles, Exec. Dir.
  (Actg.)

National Association of Bionutrition-
  ists [16227]
c/o Sarah Rusnak
Ohio State University
376 W 10th Ave., Ste. 260
Columbus, OH 43210
Hanson, Michelle, President

National Association of Consumer
  Credit Administrators [5105]
PO Box 20871
Columbus, OH 43220-0871
PH: (614)326-1165
Fax: (614)326-1162
Mulberry, Joe, President

National Association of Diaconate
  Directors [19868]
7625 N High St.
Columbus, OH 43235
PH: (614)985-2276
Dubois, Deacon Thomas R., MPS,
  Exec. Dir.

National Association for the Educa-
  tion of African American Children
  with Learning Differences [12238]
PO Box 09521
Columbus, OH 43209
PH: (614)237-6021
Fax: (614)238-0929
Myers, Linda James, PhD, Chairman

National Association of Unemployment Insurance Appeals Professionals [5317]
c/o Kathryn Todd, President
4020 E 5th Ave.
Columbus, OH 43219-1811
Fax: (405)208-4552
Todd, Kathryn, President

National Board of Boiler and Pres-
  sure Vessel Inspectors [5309]
1055 Crupper Ave.
Columbus, OH 43229-1183
PH: (614)888-8320
Fax: (614)888-0750
Douin, David A., Exec. Dir.

National Council for Continuing
  Education and Training [7672]
PO Box 2916
Columbus, OH 43216
Toll free: 888-771-0179
Fax: (877)835-5798
Starkey, Jennifer, Exec. Dir.

National Council of State Supervi-
  sors for Languages [8190]
25 S Front St.
Ohio Dept. of Education
25 S Front St.
Mail Stop No. 509
Columbus, OH 43215-4183
PH: (614)728-4630
Wertz, Ryan, President

National InterCollegiate Flying As-
  sociation [21242]
2160 W Case Rd.
Columbus, OH 43235
PH: (614)247-5444
Smith, Richard G., III, Exec. Dir.

National Quilting Association [21775]
PO Box 12190
Columbus, OH 43212-0190
PH: (614)488-8520
Fax: (614)488-8521
Miller, Marcel, President

National Registry of Emergency
  Medical Technicians [14689]
6610 Busch Blvd.
Columbus, OH 43229
PH: (614)888-4484
Fax: (614)888-8920
Persse, David, MD, Chairman

National Society of Insurance
  Premium Auditors [1910]
PO Box 936
Columbus, OH 43216-0936
Toll free: 888-846-7472
Fax: (877)835-5798
Lang, Kurt, President

National Starwind/Spindrift Class
  Association [22654]
PO Box 21262
Columbus, OH 43221
Hull, S., Contact

National Tractor Pullers Association
  [23316]
6155-B Huntley Rd.
Columbus, OH 43229
PH: (614)436-1761
Fax: (614)436-0964
Schreier, David P., President

North American Society of Pipe Col-
  lectors [21702]
PO Box 9642
Columbus, OH 43209
Tolle, John, President

Nursery and Landscape Association
  Executives of North America
  [4504]
2130 Stella Ct.
Columbus, OH 43215
PH: (614)487-1117
Fax: (614)487-1216
McGuire-Schoeff, Margaret, Exec.
  Dir.

Order of United Commercial Travel-
  ers of America [19491]
1801 Watermark Dr., Ste. 100
Columbus, OH 43215
PH: (614)487-9680
Toll free: 800-848-0123
Fax: (614)487-9675
Hoffmann, Tom, President

Orphan World Relief [11117]
700 Morse Rd., Ste. 100
Columbus, OH 43214
Toll free: 855-677-4265
Riggle, Doug, Founder

Palatines to America German
  Genealogy Society [20991]
4601 N High St., Ste. C
Columbus, OH 43214

PH: (614)267-4700
Lieby, Joseph, Ed.D, President

Parapsychological Association
[6989]
c/o Annalisa Ventola, Executive
Director
PO Box 24173
Columbus, OH 43224
PH: (202)318-2364
Fax: (202)318-2364

Pilot Dogs [17737]
625 W Town St.
Columbus, OH 43215-4444
PH: (614)221-6367
Fax: (614)221-1577
Straub, Ed, President

Polar Libraries Colloquy [9721]
c/o Laura Kissel, Secretary
Byrd Polar Research Center Archival
Program
134 University Archives
2700 Kenny Rd.
Columbus, OH 43210
PH: (614)688-8173
Kissel, Laura, Secretary

Ride for World Health [22753]
PO Box 8234
Columbus, OH 43201
Suchocki, Andrew, Founder

Rosedale Mennonite Missions
[20334]
2120 E 5th Ave.
Columbus, OH 43219
PH: (614)429-3211
Toll free: 866-883-1367
Showalter, Joe, President

Scale Manufacturers Association
[3467]
PO Box 26972
Columbus, OH 43226-0972
Toll free: 866-372-4627
Upright, Rob, President

Second Wind Lung Transplant Association, Inc. [17147]
c/o Cheryl Keeler, President
2781 Chateau Cir.
Columbus, OH 43221
PH: (614)488-1149
(815)723-3622
Toll free: 888-855-9463
Martin, Julie, Director

Secular Student Alliance [20212]
1550 Old Henderson Rd., Ste. W200
Columbus, OH 43220
PH: (614)441-9588
Toll free: 877-842-9474
Brunsman, August E., IV, Exec. Dir.

Society for Natural Immunity [15386]
c/o Dr. Michael A. Caligiuri,
President
Ohio State University
460 W 10th Ave.
Columbus, OH 43210
Caligiuri, Dr. Michael A., President

Society of Pi Kappa Lambda [23834]
Capital University, 1 College & Main
Conservatory of Music
1 College and Main
Columbus, OH 43209
PH: (614)236-7211
Fax: (614)236-6935
Lochstampfor, Dr. Mark, Exec. Dir.

Special Wish Foundation [11273]
1250 Memory Ln. N, Ste. B
Columbus, OH 43209
PH: (614)258-3186
Toll free: 800-486-WISH
Fax: (614)258-3518
Fickle, Ramona, Founder

TECH CORPS [13308]
6600 Busch Blvd., Ste. 210
Columbus, OH 43229-8259
PH: (614)583-9211
Fax: (614)340-9840
Beach, Gary, Founder, V. Ch.

United Ford Owners [21509]
PO Box 32419
Columbus, OH 43232
Tippett, Terry, President

United Producers, Inc. [3578]
8351 N High St., Ste. 250
Columbus, OH 43235
Toll free: 800-456-3276
Rayburn, Mr. Eric, Info. Technology
Mgr.

U.S. Sportsmen's Alliance [22964]
801 Kingsmill Pky.
Columbus, OH 43229
PH: (614)888-4868
Fax: (614)888-0326
Pinizzotto, Nick, President

Youth to Youth International [13491]
1420 Fields Ave.
Columbus, OH 43211
PH: (614)224-4506
Fax: (614)675-3318
Smock, Jill, Director

Research for Health [15492]
4321 Northampton Rd.
Cuyahoga Falls, OH 44223
Hess, Rosanna F., Founder,
President

Teachers Saving Children Inc.
[19073]
PO Box 125
Damascus, OH 44619-0125
PH: (330)821-2747
Bancroft, Ms. Connie, Exec. Dir.

71 429 Mustang Registry [21308]
c/o Marvin Scothorn, Dir.
6250 Germantown Pke.
Dayton, OH 45439-6634
Scothorn, Mr. Marvin, Director

Adventures in Movement for the
Handicapped [17428]
945 Danbury Rd.
Dayton, OH 45420
PH: (937)294-4611
Toll free: 800-332-8210
Fax: (937)294-3783
Geiger, Dr. Jo A., Exec. Dir.,
Founder

American Academy of Research
Historians of Medieval Spain
[9449]
c/o Miguel Gomez, Treasurer
Dept. of History
University of Dayton
300 College Pk.
Dayton, OH 45469
Kosto, Adam J., Officer

American Society for the Alexander
Technique [13601]
11 W Monument Ave., Ste. 510
Dayton, OH 45402-1233
PH: (937)586-3732
Toll free: 800-473-0620
Carbaugh, Rick, Chairman

American Society for Composites
[6161]
University of Dayton
Dept. of Civil and Environmental
Engineering
422 Kettering Laboratory
300 College Park Ave.
Dayton, OH 45469-0243

PH: (937)229-3847
Fax: (937)229-3491
Donaldson, Prof. Steven L.,
Treasurer

Association of Destination Management Executives International
[3371]
11 W Monument Ave., Ste 510
Dayton, OH 45402
PH: (937)586-3727
Ferrell, Brian, Officer

Association for Institutional Thought
[6381]
Dept. of Economics
Raj Soin College of Business
Wright State University
3640 Colonel Glenn Hwy.
Dayton, OH 45435-0001
Warnecké, Tonia, President

Cash Registers Collectors Club
[21635]
PO Box 20534
Dayton, OH 45429-0534
Kloda, Harry, President

Cellulose Insulation Manufacturers
Association [510]
S Keowee St.
Dayton, OH 45402
PH: (937)222-2462
Toll free: 888-881-2462
Fax: (937)222-5794
Leuthold, Doug, President,
Treasurer, Director

Center for the Evangelical United
Brethren Heritage [20117]
4501 Denlinger Rd.
Dayton, OH 45426
PH: (937)529-2201
Deichmann, Dr. Wendy J., President

CPA Firm Management Association
[24]
136 S Keowee St.
Dayton, OH 45402
PH: (937)222-0030
Fax: (937)222-5794
Fantaci, Kim, President

The Educational Foundation for
Women in Accounting [8747]
136 S Keowee St.
Dayton, OH 45402
PH: (937)424-3391
Fax: (937)222-5794
Weiss, Susan, President

Health Ministries Association [20540]
c/o Michelle Randall, Office Manager
PO Box 60042
Dayton, OH 45406
Toll free: 800-723-4291
Fax: (937)558-0453
Feagan, Marlene, President

IUE-CWA [23414]
2701 Dryden Rd.
Dayton, OH 45439
PH: (937)298-9984
Fax: (937)298-2636
Clark, James D., President

Mariological Society of America
[19859]
The Marian Library
University of Dayton
300 College Pk.
Dayton, OH 45469-1390
PH: (937)229-4294
(313)883-8515
Fax: (937)229-4258
Phalan, Fr. James H., Officer

Monument Builders of North America
[2410]
136 S Keowee St.
Dayton, OH 45402
Toll free: 800-233-4472
Fax: (937)222-5794
Johns, Michael N., VP

National Association of Nephrology
Technicians/Technologists [15881]
11 W Monument Ave., Ste. 510
Dayton, OH 45402
PH: (937)586-3705
Toll free: 877-607-NANT
Fax: (937)586-3699
Rickenbach, Fran, CAE, Exec. Dir.

National Concrete Burial Vault As-
sociation [2411]
136 S Keowee St.
Dayton, OH 45402
Toll free: 888-88N-CBVA
Fax: (937)222-5794
Russell, Jerry, President

National Issues Forums Institute
[18993]
100 Commons Rd.
Dayton, OH 45459-2777
Toll free: 800-433-7834
Mathews, David, Chairman

National Management Association
[2187]
2210 Arbor Blvd.
Dayton, OH 45439
PH: (937)294-0421
Bailey, Steve, CM, Exec. Dir.

National Shellfisheries Association
[6788]
c/o Karolyn Mueller Hansen,
President
300 College Park Ave.
Dayton, OH 45469-0001
PH: (937)229-2141
Fax: (937)229-2021
Davis, Christopher, Comm. Chm.

National Society of Accountants for
Cooperatives [53]
136 S Keowee St.
Dayton, OH 45402
PH: (937)222-6707
Fax: (937)222-5794
Strain, Gary, Officer

North American Association for the
Catechumenate [19893]
c/o Elise Eslinger
1843 Ruskin Rd.
Dayton, OH 45406
PH: (623)444-6963
Piro, Bev, President

North American Power Sweeping
Association [2138]
136 S Keowee St.
Dayton, OH 45402
PH: (937)424-3344
Toll free: 888-757-0130
Fax: (937)222-5794
Phillips, Peter, VP

One More Soul [19066]
1846 N Main St.
Dayton, OH 45405-3832
PH: (937)279-5433
Toll free: 800-307-7685
Fax: (937)275-3902
Koob, Steve, Exec. Dir., Founder

Pro Vita Advisors [20588]
PO Box 292813
Dayton, OH 45429
PH: (937)306-1504
Toll free: 888-438-0800

School and Office Products Network
[2446]
PO Box 751705
Dayton, OH 45475-1705

PH: (937)610-3333
Brous, David, VP of Sales

Technology First [1810]
714 E Monument Ave., Ste. 106
Dayton, OH 45402
PH: (937)229-0054
Gallaher, Ann, COO

Ultrasonic Industry Association
[3032]
11 W Monument Ave., Ste. 510
Dayton, OH 45402
PH: (937)586-3725
Fax: (937)586-3699
DeAngelis, Dominick, Chairperson

Wallcovering Installers Association
[1960]
136 S Keowee St.
Dayton, OH 45402
PH: (937)222-6477
Toll free: 800-254-6477
Fax: (937)222-5794
Mead, Heidi Wright, Treasurer

National Society of Professional
Insurance Investigators [1911]
PO Box 88
Delaware, OH 43015
Toll free: 888-677-4498
Fax: (740)369-7155
Brown, Scott, Officer

Society for Medieval Feminist
Scholarship [8755]
Ohio Wesleyan University
Sturges 208
61 S Sandusky St.
Department of Comparative
Literature
Ohio Wesleyan University
Delaware, OH 43015
Mitchell, Linda, VP

Ladies of the Grand Army of the
Republic [20742]
c/o Madeline Rock, Editor
68 W Marion St.
Doylestown, OH 44230
Rock, Elizabeth, Treasurer

Wilderness Education Association
[8402]
PO Box 601
Dresden, OH 43821
PH: (740)607-9759
Toll free: 888-365-4639
McMahan, Kelli, PhD, President

International League of Professional
Baseball Clubs [22549]
55 S High St., Ste. 202
Dublin, OH 43017
PH: (614)791-9300
Fax: (614)791-9009
Mobley, Randy, President, Treasurer

Machine Cancel Society [22339]
c/o Gary Carlson
3097 Frobisher Ave.
Dublin, OH 43017-1652
Liebson, Matthew E., President

North American Association of
Wardens and Superintendents
[11541]
PO Box 3573
Dublin, OH 43016
Lindamood, Cherry, President

Society of Cardiovascular Patient
Care [16564]
6161 Riverside Dr.
Dublin, OH 43017
PH: (614)442-5950
Toll free: 877-271-4176
Fax: (614)442-5953
Kontos, Michael C., MD, President

Stutz Club [21497]
PO Box 2031
Dublin, OH 43017
PH: (330)730-9498
Barry, Michael P., VP of Corp. &
Member Svcs.

Surveyors Historical Society [9523]
6465 Reflections Dr., Ste. 100
Dublin, OH 43017-2353
PH: (614)798-5257
Fax: (614)761-2317
Gilpin, Melinda, Exec. Dir.

Sacred Cat of Burma Fanciers
[21573]
c/o Kent Thompson, Secretary
5395 Ridge Ave. SW
East Sparta, OH 44626-2332
PH: (330)484-4739
Garner, Margaret, President

Association of American Military
Uniform Collectors [22181]
PO Box 1876
Elyria, OH 44036
PH: (440)365-5321
Sanow, Gil, II, Editor

Hard Hatted Women [3491]
41957 N Ridge, Unit 2
Elyria, OH 44035
PH: (216)861-6500
Sandu, Terri Burgess, President

Senior Roller Skaters of America
[23154]
Elyria, OH 44035
PH: (440)365-6843
Toll free: 800-605-0067
Alten, Kenneth H., President

American Wine Society [4926]
PO Box 279
Englewood, OH 45322
Toll free: 888-297-9070
Hames, John, Exec. Dir.

American-Slovenian Polka Founda-
tion [9867]
605 E 222nd St.
Euclid, OH 44123
PH: (216)261-3263
Fax: (216)261-4134
Valencic, Joe, President

The Society of United States Air
Force Flight Surgeons [13511]
PO Box 1776
Fairborn, OH 45324-7776
Wood, Michael, Secretary

Glenmary Research Center [19839]
Glenmary Home Missioners
4119 Glenmary Trace
Fairfield, OH 45014-5549
PH: (513)874-8900
Fax: (513)874-1690
Artysiewicz, Fr. Chet, President

SonLight Power Inc. [11442]
7100 Dixie Hwy.
Fairfield, OH 45014
PH: (513)285-9960
Rainey, Allen, Founder, Dir. of
Programs

Cantors Assembly [20239]
55 S Miller Rd., Ste. 201
Fairlawn, OH 44333-4168
PH: (330)864-8533
Fax: (330)864-8343
Mizrahi, Alberto, President

American Harp Society [9860]
624 Crystal Ave.
Findlay, OH 45840
PH: (805)410-4277
Fax: (508)803-8383
McManus, Kathryn, Exec. Dir.

Rutherford B. Hayes Presidential
Center [10330]
Spiegel Grove
1337 Hayes Ave.
Fremont, OH 43420-2796
PH: (419)332-2081
Toll free: 800-998-PRES
Fax: (419)332-4952
Hayes, Stephen A., President

McDonald's Collectors Club [21686]
c/o Jim Gegorski, Treasurer
424 White Rd.
Fremont, OH 43420-1539
Williams, Dale, VP

Automatic Fire Alarm Association
[2991]
81 Mill St., Ste. 300
Gahanna, OH 43230
PH: (614)416-8076
Toll free: 844-438-2322
Fax: (614)453-8744
Hammerberg, Thomas P., Director

Christians Overcoming Cancer
[13945]
PO Box 307133
Gahanna, OH 43230
PH: (614)985-3750
Jenkins, Mary, President, CEO

FORE Cancer Research [13970]
PO Box 30827
Gahanna, OH 43230
PH: (614)975-8319
Thomas, Mark, Founder

Grottoes of North America [19559]
430 Beecher Rd.
Gahanna, OH 43230
PH: (614)933-9193
Fax: (614)933-9098
Phillips, Pat, Admin. Asst.

Kya's Krusade [14553]
947 E Johnstown Rd., Ste. 143
Gahanna, OH 43230
PH: (614)750-2198
Fax: (614)478-3223
Miles, Kylie, Founder, CEO

63rd Infantry Division Association
[20711]
c/o Judith Schaefer, Secretary
6152 George Fox Dr.
Galloway, OH 43119
PH: (614)818-6440
Fowle, Edward, President

North American Trap Collector Association [21704]
c/o Tom Parr, Director
6106 Bausch Rd.
Galloway, OH 43119
PH: (614)878-6011
Parr, Tom, Director

Union of Poles in America [19617]
9999 Granger Rd.
Garfield Heights, OH 44125
PH: (216)478-0120
Fax: (216)478-0122
Milcinovic, David, VP

Christmas Philatelic Club [22317]
PO Box 744
Geneva, OH 44041-0744
Sanders, Christine, President

North American Association of State
and Provincial Lotteries [5565]
1 S Broadway
Geneva, OH 44041
PH: (440)466-5630
(440)361-7962
Grief, Gary, Director

American Bladesmith Society
[21745]
c/o Cindy Sheely, Office Manager
PO Box 160

Grand Rapids, OH 43522-0160
PH: (419)832-0400
Keeslar, Joe, Chairman

Africa Network [18365]
c/o Jim Pletcher, Chairman
Denison University
100 W College St.
Granville, OH 43023
Ejikeme, Anene, PhD, Exec. Dir.

International Association for
Environmental Philosophy [10089]
c/o Steven Vogel, Co-Director
Dept. of Philosophy
Denison University
100 W College St.
Granville, OH 43023-1100
McWhorter, Ladelle, Secretary

Cat Fanciers' Federation [21567]
PO Box 661
Gratis, OH 45330
PH: (937)787-9009
Merrill, Vicky, President

Grand Aerie, Fraternal Order of
Eagles [19423]
1623 Gateway Cir. S
Grove City, OH 43123-9309
PH: (614)883-2200
(614)883-2177
Fax: (614)883-2201
Tice, David, President

National Council on Laser Certifica-
tion [15565]
Professional Medical Education As-
sociation
3136 Broadway, Ste. 101
Grove City, OH 43123
PH: (614)883-1739
Toll free: 800-435-3131
Fax: (305)946-0232
Absten, Gregory T., Chairman

Women's International Network of
Utility Professionals [1035]
PO Box 64
Grove City, OH 43123-0064
Powell, Claudia, Exec. Dir.

American Classical League [8176]
860 NW Washington Blvd., Ste. A
Hamilton, OH 45013
PH: (513)529-7741
Toll free: 800-670-8346
Fax: (513)529-7742
Elifrits, Kathy, President

Deaf Friends International [11935]
PO Box 13192
Hamilton, OH 45013-0192
PH: (513)658-4879
Griffin, Jeanne, Director

National Junior Classical League
[9166]
860 NW Washington Blvd., Ste. A
Hamilton, OH 45013
PH: (513)529-7741
Clough, Brier, President

American Watchmakers-
Clockmakers Institute [2041]
701 Enterprise Dr.
Harrison, OH 45030
PH: (513)367-9800
Toll free: 866-367-2924
Fax: (513)367-1414
Ficklin, Jordan, Exec. Dir.

Dog Scouts of America [11689]
PO Box 158
Harrison, OH 45030
PH: (989)389-2000
Puls, Chris, President

American Trakehner Association
[4330]
663 Hopewell Dr.
Heath, OH 43056

PH: (740)344-1111
Fax: (740)344-3225
Cottongnim, Anissa, Secretary

Academy of Dentistry International
[14364]
3813 Gordon Creek Dr.
Hicksville, OH 43526
PH: (419)542-0101
Fax: (419)542-6883
Ramus, Dr. Robert L., DDS, Exec.
Dir.

Numismatic Bibliomania Society
[22278]
c/o Terry White, Treasurer
PO Box 39
Hilliard, OH 43026
Ricard, Marc, President

Perennial Plant Association [4441]
3383 Schirtzinger Rd.
Hilliard, OH 43026
PH: (614)771-8431
Fax: (614)876-5238
Brennan, Jennifer, President

All-American Indian Motorcycle Club
[22208]
c/o Teri Clement
140 N Centennial Rd.
Holland, OH 43528
Clement, Paul, Treasurer

National Child Abuse Defense and
Resource Center [13264]
PO Box 638
Holland, OH 43528
PH: (419)865-0513
Fax: (419)865-0526
Hart, Kimberly A., Exec. Dir.

American Osteopathic Colleges of
Ophthalmology and Otolaryngology
- Head and Neck Surgery [16517]
4764 Fishburg Rd., Ste. F
Huber Heights, OH 45424
Toll free: 800-455-9404
Fax: (937)233-5673
Sibia, Sirtaz Singh, DO, President

Angel Harps [16965]
c/o Carolyn Weislogel
6813 Windsor Rd.
Hudson, OH 44236-3253
PH: (330)655-2185
Weislogel, Carolyn, Contact

Association of Concert Bands [9875]
6613 Cheryl Ann Dr.
Independence, OH 44131-3718
Toll free: 800-726-8720
Montgomery, Mike, CIO

Brotherhood of Locomotive
Engineers and Trainmen [23514]
7061 E Pleasnt Valley Rd.
Independence, OH 44131
PH: (216)241-2630
Fax: (216)241-6516
Pierce, Dennis R., President

First Catholic Slovak Union of the
U.S.A. and Canada [19645]
6611 Rockside Rd., Ste. 300
Independence, OH 44131
PH: (216)642-9406
Toll free: 800-533-6682
Fax: (216)642-4310
Rajec, Andrew M., President

Industrial Fasteners Institute [1569]
6363 Oak Tree Blvd.
Independence, OH 44131
PH: (216)241-1482

International Business Brokers Association, Inc. [2865]
7100 E Pleasant Valley Rd., Ste.
160

Independence, OH 44131
Toll free: 888-686-4222
Fax: (800)630-2380
Bushkie, Scott, Chmn. of the Bd.

Precision Metalforming Association
[2368]
6363 Oak Tree Blvd.
Independence, OH 44131
PH: (216)901-8800
Fax: (216)901-9190
Flando, Andrew, VP

Precision Metalforming Association -
Custom Roll Forming Division
[2369]
6363 Oak Tree Blvd.
Independence, OH 44131-2500
PH: (216)901-8800
Fax: (216)901-9190
Adler, William, Chairman

Wally Byam Caravan Club
International [22420]
PO Box 612
Jackson Center, OH 45334
PH: (937)596-5211
Fax: (937)596-5542
Reed, Ms. Cindy, Mgr.

Capri Club North America [21348]
PO Box 701
Johnstown, OH 43031
Robertson, Mike, Membership Chp.

Institute for Vietnamese Music
[9920]
2005 Willow Ridge Cir.
Kent, OH 44240
Fax: (330)673-4434
Nguyen, Phong, PhD, Exec. Dir.

International Liquid Crystal Society
[6360]
c/o Hiroshi Yokoyama, President
Liquid Crystal Institute
Kent State University
1425 Lefton Esplanade
Kent, OH 44242
Yokoyama, Hiroshi, PhD, President

International Palestinian Cardiac
Relief Organization [14122]
PO Box 1926
Kent, OH 44240
PH: (330)678-2645
Fax: (330)678-2661
Nasir, Dr. Musa, Chmn. of the Bd.

Kent State University Alumni As-
sociation [19330]
PO Box 5190
Kent, OH 44242-0001
PH: (330)672-5368
Toll free: 888-320-5368
Fax: (330)672-4723
Bartz, Elizabeth, Bd. Member

National Network of Embroidery
Professionals [2440]
4693 Kent Rd.
Kent, OH 44240
Toll free: 800-866-7396
Cox, Jennifer, Founder

Large Black Hog Association [4710]
c/o Felicia Krock, Secretary
16383 County Road 75
Kenton, OH 43326
Toll free: 800-687-1942
Fax: (800)687-2089
Bradford, Alec, President

Driving School Association of the
Americas [7724]
Communications Office
3125 Wilmington Pke.
Kettering, OH 45429-4003
Toll free: 800-270-3722
Fax: (937)290-0696
Chauncy, Charles Bud, Coord.

Herb Society of America [6142]
9019 Kirtland Chardon Rd.
Kirtland, OH 44094
PH: (440)256-0514
Fax: (440)256-0541

The International Amphicar Owners
Club [21400]
c/o Pat DePasquale, Treasurer
9938 Forest St.
Lakeview, OH 43331
Clark, Mike, President

FutureChurch [19838]
17307 Madison Ave.
Lakewood, OH 44107
PH: (216)228-0869
Fax: (216)228-4872
Graf, Marie, Chairman

International J/22 Class Association
[22633]
12900 Lake Ave., No. 2001
Lakewood, OH 44107
PH: (216)226-4411
Princing, Chris, Comm. Chm.

United States J/24 Class Association
[22681]
12900 Lake Ave., No. 2001
Lakewood, OH 44107
PH: (617)285-9455
Lai, Lambert, Exec.

American Concrete Pumping As-
sociation [780]
606 Enterprise Dr.
Lewis Center, OH 43035
PH: (614)431-5618
Langhauser, Beth, President

American Daffodil Society [22070]
3670 E Powell Rd.
Lewis Center, OH 43035-9530
PH: (614)882-5720
Matthews, Becky, Chairperson

National Show Horse Registry
[4387]
PO Box 862
Lewisburg, OH 45338
PH: (937)962-4336
Fax: (937)962-4332
Mikosz, David, Chairman

Show Horse Alliance [4408]
PO Box 862
Lewisburg, OH 45338
PH: (937)962-4336
Fax: (937)962-4332

Combat Martial Art Practitioners Association [22990]
2277 E Elm St.
Lima, OH 45804
Brado, John Frank, Director

Organized Flying Adjusters [1916]
1380 W Hume Rd.
Lima, OH 45806-1860
PH: (567)712-2097
Fax: (800)207-9324
Popper, Eric, President

Circus Fans Association of America
[9161]
3660 Morningside Way, No. 105
Lorain, OH 44053
Payne, Gary C., President

National Circus Preservation Society
[9163]
2704 Marshall Ave.
Lorain, OH 44052

National Eosinophilia-Myalgia
Syndrome Network [17498]
767 Tower Blvd.
Lorain, OH 44052-5213
Heston, Jann, President

United Yorkie Rescue [10710]
c/o Carl Sullenberger, Treasurer
3924 Miami Ave.
Lorain, OH 44053
Rand, Ilene, Asst. Treas.

Society of Nematologists [6910]
c/o Rosewood Business Solutions
108 W Burwell Ave.
Loudonville, OH 44842
PH: (419)994-3419
Adams, Byron, President

CancerFree KIDS [13934]
PO Box 575
Loveland, OH 45140
PH: (513)575-5437
Flannery, Ellen M., Founder, Exec.
Dir.

Grailville [19840]
932 O Bannonville Rd.
Loveland, OH 45140-9705
PH: (513)683-2340
Barr, Elizabeth, Mem.

Thistle Class Association [22675]
PO Box 741
Loveland, OH 45140
PH: (513)461-3845
Finefrock, Kyle, President

American Self-Protection Association
[23123]
7792 Capital Blvd., No. 4
Macedonia, OH 44056
PH: (330)467-7110

96th Infantry Division Association
[20714]
c/o Don Klimkowicz, President
2817 Townline Rd.
Madison, OH 44057
PH: (440)259-4212
O'Brien, Dennis, Treasurer

American Board of Clinical Metal
Toxicology [17492]
c/o James Smith, Treasurer
367 Hennepin Dr.
Maineville, OH 45039
PH: (513)942-3226
Fax: (513)942-3934
Smith, James, DO, Treasurer

Vintage Garden Tractor Club of
America [22459]
c/o Doug Tallman, President
804 N Trimble Rd.
Mansfield, OH 44906
PH: (419)545-2609
Franklin, Joe, Rep.

International King Midget Car Club,
Inc. [21402]
c/o Brenda Arnold, Secretary
20280 State Route 676
Marietta, OH 45750-6552
Seats, Lee, President

International Planetarium Society
[6007]
c/o Ann Bragg, Treasurer
Marietta College
215 5th St.
Marietta, OH 45750
PH: (407)376-4589
Laatsch, Shawn, President

National Fenton Glass Society
[22140]
PO Box 4008
Marietta, OH 45750
PH: (740)374-3345
Fax: (740)374-3345
Davison, Susan Jean, Treasurer

Sons and Daughters of Pioneer Riv-
ermen [21089]
PO Box 352
Marietta, OH 45750
Spear, Jeffrey W., President

Christian Law Association [19960]
PO Box 8600
Mason, OH 45040
Toll free: 888-252-1969
Fax: (888)600-9899
Gibbs, Dr. David C., Jr., Founder, President

Christian Restoration Association [19966]
7133 Central Parke Blvd.
Mason, OH 45040
PH: (513)229-8000
Fax: (513)229-8003
Nichols, Jim, Director

American Lock Collectors Association [21612]
c/o David Rankl
13115 Millersburg Rd. SW
Massillon, OH 44647-9773
Rankl, David, Contact

League of St. Dymphna [19855]
206 Cherry Rd. NE
Massillon, OH 44646
PH: (330)833-8478
Fax: (330)833-5193
Gretchko, Fr. Ed, Contact

National Russell Collectors Association [21697]
561 29th St. NW
Massillon, OH 44647
PH: (330)875-6022
(330)833-6493

ASM International [6841]
9639 Kinsman Rd.
Materials Park, OH 44073
PH: (440)338-5151
Tirpak, Jon D., PE, FASM, President

Japanese Sword Society of the United States [21295]
427 W Dussel, No. 128
Maumee, OH 43537-4208
Hennick, Barry, Omb.

North American Menopause Society [16299]
5900 Landerbrook Dr., Ste. 390
Mayfield Heights, OH 44124
PH: (440)442-7550
Fax: (440)442-2660
Utian, Wulf H., PhD, Medical Dir.

National Grigsby Family Society [20906]
c/o Phyllis J. Bryant, Administrator
69 Plymouth St.
Medina, OH 44256-2418
Braden, Mrs. Sharon, President

Out of Love Sugar Glider Rescue [10676]
PO Box 183
Medina, OH 44258
PH: (330)722-1627
Schira, Dottie, Founder

Super Coupe Club of America [21500]
4322 Hamilton Rd.
Medina, OH 44256
PH: (330)242-1122
Davenport, George, Contact

National Quarter Pony Association [4385]
PO Box 171
Melrose, OH 45861
PH: (419)594-2968
Stephey, Wendy, Secretary, Treasurer

Alcohol and Drug Abuse Self-Help Network [17304]
7304 Mentor Ave., Ste. F
Mentor, OH 44060

PH: (440)951-5357
Toll free: 866-951-5357
Fax: (440)951-5358
Horvath, Thomas, PhD, President

American Measuring Tool Manufacturers Association [7229]
8562 East Ave.
Mentor, OH 44060
PH: (440)974-6829
Fax: (440)974-6828
Hollis, Thomas, Jr., President

Project EverGreen [4448]
8500 Station St., Ste. 230
Mentor, OH 44060
Toll free: 877-758-4835
Code, Cindy, Exec. Dir.

U.S. Flag & Touch Football League [22869]
6946 Spinach Dr.
Mentor, OH 44060
PH: (440)974-8735
Fax: (440)974-8441
Cihon, Michael, Exec. Dir.

Association of Medical Professionals with Hearing Losses [15177]
10708 Nestling Dr.
Miamisburg, OH 45342
McKee, Michael, President

International Society for Fall Protection [16324]
2500 Newmark Dr.
Miamisburg, OH 45342-5407
PH: (937)259-6350
Toll free: 877-472-8483
Fax: (937)259-5100
Kramer, Thomas, President

North American Brass Band Association [9985]
PO Box 113
Miamiville, OH 45147
Bulla, Randi, President

Baptist Mid-Missions [19724]
7749 Webster Rd.
Middleburg Heights, OH 44130-8011
PH: (440)826-3930
Fax: (440)826-4457
Anderson, Dr. Gary L., President

Society to Advance Opticianry [16417]
14901 N State Ave.
Middlefield, OH 44062
Pierce, Laurie, President

International Association of Registered Financial Consultants [1242]
2507 N Verity Pky.
Middletown, OH 45042-0506
Toll free: 800-532-9060
Fax: (513)424-5752
Morrow, Edwin P., CEO

Edison Birthplace Association [10324]
c/o Edison Birthplace Museum
9 N Edison Dr.
Milan, OH 44846
PH: (419)499-2135
Wolf, Lois, Director

American Checkered Giant Rabbit Club [4585]
c/o David Freeman, Secretary
1119 Klondyke Rd.
Milford, OH 45150-9659
PH: (513)576-0804
Long, Danny, President

Families with Autism Spectrum Disorders [13764]
PO Box 269
Milford, OH 45150

PH: (513)444-4979
Smith, Mrs. Julia Ann, Founder

Jerusalem Institute of Justice - USA [12995]
PO Box 610
Milford, OH 45150
Myers, Shimon, Dir. of Dev.

Klippel-Trenaunay Support Group [13830]
1471 Greystone Ln.
Milford, OH 45150
PH: (513)722-7724
Vessey, Mrs. Judy, Exec. Dir.

Blue Key Honor Society [23777]
7501 Whitehill Ln.
Whitehill Farm
Millersburg, OH 44654-9270
PH: (330)674-2570
Sieverdes, Dr. Christopher M., Exec. Dir.

African Sky [11308]
PO Box 203
Munroe Falls, OH 44262
Lacy, Scott M., PhD, Exec. Dir.

National Catholic College Admission Association [19876]
PO Box 267
New Albany, OH 43054
PH: (614)633-5444
Fax: (614)839-9232
Masek, Joyce A., Exec. Dir.

National Aeronca Association [21240]
10563 Milton Carlisle Rd.
New Carlisle, OH 45344
Thompson, Jim, President

The Way International [20475]
PO Box 328
New Knoxville, OH 45871-0328
PH: (419)753-2523
Rivenbark, Rev. Rosalie F., Chairperson

Heisey Collectors of America [22135]
169 W Church St.
Newark, OH 43055
PH: (740)345-2932
Fax: (740)345-9638
Heisey, Emie, VP

National Heisey Glass Museum [22141]
169 W Church St.
Newark, OH 43055-4945
PH: (740)345-2932
Fax: (740)345-9638
Eggert, Roy, President

Allied Stone Industries [3180]
c/o Brundene Van Ness, President
10500 Kinsman Rd.
Newbury, OH 44065
Van Ness, Brundene, President

Hebron USA [20422]
12375 Kinsman Rd., Ste. H11
Newbury, OH 44065
PH: (440)804-5733
Toll free: 888-598-8276
Fax: (440)564-1273
DuVall, Randy, President

Army & Navy Union U.S.A. [21110]
PO Box 686
Niles, OH 44446
Goode, Carl, Jr., Cmdr.

Bridge Grid Flooring Manufacturers Association [504]
300 E Cherry St.
North Baltimore, OH 45872-1227
Toll free: 877-257-5499
Kaczinski, Mark, Exec. Dir.

Association for Living History, Farm and Agricultural Museums [9824]
8774 Route 45 NW
North Bloomfield, OH 44450
PH: (440)685-4410
Fax: (440)685-4410
Baker, Edward, Secretary, Treasurer

Hoover Historical Center [21293]
1875 E Maple St.
North Canton, OH 44720-3331
PH: (330)499-0287
(330)490-7435
Fax: (330)494-4725
Haines, Mrs. Ann, Coord.

Military Aviation Preservation Society [20670]
2260 International Pky.
North Canton, OH 44720
PH: (330)896-6332
Kovesci, Kim, Exec. Dir.

Jet 14 Class Association [22643]
6176 Winding Creek Ln.
North Olmsted, OH 44070
PH: (440)716-1859
Hennon, Paula, Mem.

United Transportation Union [23518]
SMART Transportation Division
24950 Country Club Blvd., Ste. 340
North Olmsted, OH 44070-5333
PH: (216)228-9400

Bricklin International Owners Club [21343]
George Malaska, VP Membership
Bl, 38083 Princeton Dr.
38083 Princeton Dr.
North Ridgeville, OH 44039
Stratton, Steve, President

Infant Massage USA [15557]
34760 Center Ridge Rd., No. 39006
North Ridgeville, OH 44039
Toll free: 800-497-5996
Fax: (440)385-0197
Del Castillo, Mercedes, Exec. Dir.

National Network of Career Nursing Assistants [16163]
3577 Easton Rd.
Norton, OH 44203-5661
PH: (330)825-9342
Fax: (330)825-9378
Gipson, Genevieve, RN, Director

International Hot Rod Association [22524]
300 Cleveland Rd.
Norwalk, OH 44857
PH: (419)663-6666
Fax: (419)663-4472
Gardner, Scott, President

International Organization on Shape Memory and Superelastic Technologies [6846]
9639 Kinsman Rd.
Novelty, OH 44073-0001
PH: (440)338-5151
Fax: (440)338-4634
Stebner, Dr. Aaron, President

American Single Shot Rifle Association [23126]
c/o Keith Foster, Membership Administrator
15770 Road 1037
Oakwood, OH 45873
PH: (630)898-4229
Glen, Bob, President

Association of Specialty Cut Flower Growers [1306]
MPO Box 268
Oberlin, OH 44074

PH: (440)774-2887
Laushman, Judy, Exec. Dir.

Double Harvest [3537]
55 S Main St.
Oberlin, OH 44074
PH: (440)714-1694
Giesbrecht, Rev. Vernon, Coord.

Marble Institute of America [3186]
380 E Lorain St.
Oberlin, OH 44074
PH: (440)250-9222
Fax: (440)250-9223
Hieb, James A., CEO

National Association of College
Stores [2967]
500 E Lorain St.
Oberlin, OH 44074
PH: (440)775-7777
Toll free: 800-622-7498
Ellis, Tony, VP

Central States Association [21217]
9283 Lindbergh Blvd.
Olmsted Falls, OH 44138-2407

Iota Lambda Sigma [23984]
c/o Anna Skinner, Executive
Secretary-Treasurer
607 Park Way W
Oregon, OH 43616
PH: (419)693-6860
Fax: (419)693-6859
Skinner, Anna, Exec. Sec., Treasurer

American Council of Christian
Churches [19941]
PO Box 628
Orwell, OH 44076
PH: (440)579-2416
McKnight, Dr. John, President

Anxiety Disorders Special Interest
Group [12504]
c/o Laurel Sarfan, Treasurer
90 N Patterson Ave.
Oxford, OH 45056
Cathy, Angela, President

Beta Theta Pi [23891]
5134 Bonham Rd.
Oxford, OH 45056
Toll free: 800-800-2382
Fax: (513)523-2381
Horras, Judson A., CAE, Admin.
Sec.

Chris Craft Antique Boat Club
[22607]
PO Box 787
Oxford, OH 45056
Riggs, Andy, Director

Delta Sigma Pi [23897]
330 S Campus Ave.
Oxford, OH 45056-2405
PH: (513)523-1907
Fax: (513)523-7292
Shaver, Joe, Coord.

Delta Zeta [23954]
202 E Church St.
Oxford, OH 45056
PH: (513)523-7597
Fax: (513)523-1921
Menges, Cynthia Winslow, Exec. Dir.

Learning Forward [7430]
504 S Locust St.
Oxford, OH 45056
Toll free: 800-727-7288
Fax: (513)523-0638
Hirsh, Stephanie, Exec. Dir.

National Senior Classical League
[9167]
422 Wells Mills Dr.
Oxford, OH 45056

PH: (701)799-1210
Kraft, Ethan, President

Phi Delta Theta International
Fraternity [23910]
2 S Campus Ave.
Oxford, OH 45056-1801
PH: (513)523-6345
Toll free: 877-563-1848
Fax: (513)523-9200
Biggs, Robert A., CAE, Exec. VP

Phi Kappa Tau [23913]
5221 Morning Sun Rd.
Oxford, OH 45056
PH: (513)523-4193
Toll free: 800-PKT-1906
Fax: (513)523-9325
Hudson, Tim, CEO

Josiah Royce Society [10117]
150 Charleston Dr.
Oxford, OH 45056
Brodrick, Michael, PhD, Treasurer

Gyro International [12890]
1096 Mentor Ave.
Painesville, OH 44077-0489
PH: (440)352-2501
Bernard, Harold, Contact

American Lawyers Alliance [4990]
2756 Patterson Rd. SW
Pataskala, OH 43062-7704
Bennett, Sue, President

International Thunderbird Club
[21407]
PO Box 24041
Pepper Pike, OH 44124-9998
PH: (216)375-2808
   (205)938-7494
Bartasavich, Gerard, President

North American Police Work Dog
Association [5513]
4222 Manchester Rd.
Perry, OH 44081
PH: (502)523-4452
Toll free: 888-4-CANINE
Fax: (866)236-0753
Watson, Jim, Secretary

Alliance for Paired Donation [15867]
PO Box 965
Perrysburg, OH 43552
PH: (419)866-5505
Toll free: 877-273-4255
Fax: (419)383-5579
Rees, Michael, CEO, Medical Dir.

The Needmor Fund [12984]
539 E Front St.
Perrysburg, OH 43551
PH: (419)872-1490
Sanchez, Frank, Exec. Dir.

A.L.E.R.T. International [14691]
PO Box 74
Pickerington, OH 43147
Toll free: 866-402-5378
Liebno, Albert, President

American Motorcycle Heritage
Foundation [23035]
13515 Yarmouth Dr.
Pickerington, OH 43147
PH: (614)856-1924
   (614)856-1900
Heininger, Jeffrey V., Chairman

American Motorcyclist Association
[23036]
13515 Yarmouth Dr.
Pickerington, OH 43147
PH: (614)856-1900
Toll free: 800-262-5646
Fax: (614)856-1924
Simpson, Stan, Chairman

Thimble Collectors International
[21727]
1209 Hill Rd. N, No. 253
Pickerington, OH 43147
Walbrun, Dan, President

Roy Rogers - Dale Evans Collectors
Association [24061]
PO Box 1166
Portsmouth, OH 45662
PH: (740)259-1195
   (740)727-4444
Lilly, Jane, President

Airport Ground Transportation As-
sociation [3319]
1538 Powell Rd.
Powell, OH 43065
PH: (314)753-3432
Fax: (314)667-3850
Mundy, Ray, Exec. Dir.

American Association of Service
Coordinators [1700]
499 Village Park Dr.
Powell, OH 43065-1178
PH: (614)848-5958
Fax: (614)848-5954
Monks, Janice C., LSW, President,
CEO

Human-Wildlife Conflict Collaboration [4826]
c/o The Columbus Zoo
9990 Riverside Dr.
Powell, OH 43065-0400
PH: (202)746-4421
Madden, Francine, Exec. Dir.

Maple Syrup Urine Disease Family
Support Group [15827]
9517 Big Bear Ave.
Powell, OH 43065
Bulcher, Sandy, Director

Pharmacists for Life International
[12787]
PO Box 1281
Powell, OH 43065-1281
PH: (740)881-5520
Toll free: 800-227-8359
Fax: (740)206-1260
Kuhar, Bogomir M., Bd. Member,
Exec. Dir.

Transverse Myelitis Association
[15995]
1787 Sutter Pky.
Powell, OH 43065-8806
PH: (614)317-4884
Toll free: 855-380-3330
Siegel, Sanford J., Officer

American Jersey Cattle Association
[3697]
6486 E Main St.
Reynoldsburg, OH 43068-2362
PH: (614)861-3636
Fax: (614)861-8040
Smith, Neal, CEO

A Future Without Poverty, Inc.
[12542]
PO Box 73
Ripley, OH 45167-9715
Flores, Syl, President

Fibromuscular Dysplasia Society of
America, Inc. [15931]
20325 Center Ridge Rd., Ste. 360
Rocky River, OH 44116
PH: (216)834-2410
Toll free: 888-709-7089
Mace, Pamela, Exec. Dir.

National Advisory Group [2965]
19111 Detroit Rd., Ste. 201
Rocky River, OH 44116

PH: (440)250-1583
Fax: (440)333-1892
Harris, Tony, Chmn. of the Bd.

Polonus Philatelic Society [22354]
PO Box 60438
Rossford, OH 43460-0438
Mikucki, Chester, Founder

United Plant Savers [13662]
PO Box 147
Rutland, OH 45775
PH: (740)742-3455
Bancroft, Betzy, Bd. Member

American Medical Autism Board
[13739]
320 Orchardview Ave., Ste. 2
Seven Hills, OH 44131
PH: (216)901-0441
DeMio, Phillip C., MD, Chairman,
Exec. Dir.

Materials Properties Council [6848]
c/o Welding Research Council
PO Box 201547
Shaker Heights, OH 44120-8109
PH: (216)658-3847
Fax: (216)658-3854
Prager, Dr. Martin, President

Medical Research Modernization
Committee [15652]
3200 Morley Rd.
Shaker Heights, OH 44122
PH: (216)283-6702
Fax: (216)283-6702
Kaufman, Stephen R., MD, Co-Ch.

National Association of Test Directors [8688]
c/o Dr. Dale Whittington, Director -
Research, Evaluation and Assessment
15600 Parkland Dr.
Shaker Heights, OH 44120
PH: (216)295-4363
Swan, Bonnie, President

Pontius Family Association [20915]
21810 Fairmount Blvd.
Shaker Heights, OH 44118-4816
Johnson, Ginger, President

Pressure Vessel Research Council
[2615]
c/o Welding Research Council
PO Box 201547
Shaker Heights, OH 44122
PH: (216)658-3847
Fax: (216)658-3854
Prager, Dr. Martin, Contact

Welding Research Council [7385]
PO Box 201547
Shaker Heights, OH 44122
PH: (216)658-3847
Fax: (216)658-3854

Association of Ohio Longrifle Collectors [22017]
6778 Columbus Rd.
Shreve, OH 44676

Crosscurrents International Institute
[18537]
7122 Hardin-Wapak Rd.
Sidney, OH 45365
PH: (937)492-0407
Eisenhower, Dwight D., President

United States Twirling Association
[22581]
c/o Julie Jenkins, Business Manager
244 Overland Dr.
Sidney, OH 45365
Chamberlain, John, President

Leadership to Keep Children Alcohol
Free [13150]
2933 Lower Bellbrook Rd.
Spring Valley, OH 45370

PH: (937)848-2993
Baldacci, Karen, Chairperson

Honor Flight Network [21125]
300 E Auburn Ave.
Springfield, OH 45505-4703
PH: (937)521-2400
    (614)558-6220
McLaughlin, Jim, Chmn. of the Bd.

**National Association for Practical
    Nurse Education and Service
    [8332]**
2071 N Bechtle Ave., No. 307
Springfield, OH 45504-1583
PH: (703)933-1003
Fax: (703)940-4089
Bauer, Ann, LPN, President

**Catholics United for the Faith
    [19820]**
827 N 4th St.
Steubenville, OH 43952
PH: (740)283-2484
Toll free: 800-398-5470
Fax: (740)283-4011
Mohr, Michael, Chmn. of the Bd.

Patients Rights Council [11807]
PO Box 760
Steubenville, OH 43952
PH: (740)282-3810
Toll free: 800-958-5678
Marker, Rita L., Exec. Dir.

**Forum for Education and Democracy
    [7821]**
PO Box 15
Stewart, OH 45778
PH: (740)590-1579
Wood, George, Exec. Dir.

United Peafowl Association [3673]
c/o Loretta Smith, Vice President/
    Membership
5156A US Highway 52
Stout, OH 45684
PH: (740)935-6556
Potente, Daniel, President

U.S.A. Karate Federation [23023]
1550 Ritchie Rd.
Stow, OH 44224
PH: (330)388-3115
Hickey, Patrick M., President

Ductile Iron Society [6843]
15400 Pearl Rd., Ste. 238
Strongsville, OH 44136
PH: (440)665-3686
Fax: (440)878-0070
Galvin, Mike, President

**International Watch Fob Association
    [3279]**
c/o Louise Harting, Secretary and
    Treasurer
18458 Boston Rd.
Strongsville, OH 44136-8642
Toth, Dimitrie, President

**Assistance Dogs of America, Inc.
    [11573]**
5605 Monroe St.
Sylvania, OH 43560
PH: (419)885-5733
Fax: (419)882-4813
Tedhams, Gale, Bd. Member

**Association of U.S. Catholic Priests
    [19800]**
200 St. Francis Ave.
Tiffin, OH 44883-3458
PH: (872)205-5862
Doepker, Jacquelyn, Secretary

Tiffin Glass Collectors Club [22144]
25 S Washington St.
Tiffin, OH 44883

PH: (419)448-0200

**Studebaker Family National Associa-
    tion [20934]**
6555 S State Rte. 202
Tipp City, OH 45371
PH: (937)405-6539
Studebaker, Charles, Trustee

Adopt America Network [10435]
3100 W Central Ave., Ste. 225
Toledo, OH 43606
PH: (419)726-5100
Toll free: 800-246-1731
Fax: (419)726-5089
Spoerl, Wendy, President

American Society for Virology [6051]
c/o Dr. Dorothea L. Sawicki,
    Secretary-Treasurer
3000 Arlington Ave., Mail Stop 1021
Department of Medical Microbiology
    and Immunology
University of Toledo College of
    Medicine
Toledo, OH 43614-2598
PH: (419)383-5173
Fax: (419)383-2881
Sawicki, Dr. Dorothea L., Secretary,
    Treasurer

**Automobile Racing Club of America
    [22523]**
PO Box 5217
Toledo, OH 43611
PH: (734)847-6726
Drager, Ron, CEO, President

**Farm Labor Organizing Committee
    [23378]**
1221 Broadway St.
Toledo, OH 43609
PH: (419)243-3456
Fax: (419)243-5655
Velasquez, Baldemar, President

Good Bears of the World [12889]
PO Box 13097
Toledo, OH 43613
PH: (419)531-5365
Toll free: 877-429-2327
Taylor, Elizabeth, V. Ch.

**International Association of Animal
    Massage and Bodywork [15558]**
c/o Beth Farkas, Coordinator
2950 Douglas Rd.
Toledo, OH 43606
Toll free: 800-903-9350
Farkas, Beth, Coord.

**International Model Power Boat As-
    sociation [22198]**
c/o Chris Rupley, President
4630 Stengel Ave.
Toledo, OH 43614
PH: (419)360-3230
    (517)321-6230
Sheren, Kevin, VP

**International Society for Plastination
    [16587]**
Dept. of Neurosciences
College of Medicine and Life Sci-
    ences
University of Toledo
3000 Arlington Ave.
Toledo, OH 43614-2598
PH: (419)383-4283
Fax: (419)383-3008
Baptista, Prof. Carlos A.C., PhD,
    President

National Exchange Club [12901]
3050 Central Ave.
Toledo, OH 43606-1700
PH: (419)535-3232
Toll free: 800-924-2643
Fax: (419)535-1989
Edwards, Tracey, Exec. VP

**National Exchange Club Foundation
    [11093]**
3050 Central Ave.
Toledo, OH 43606-1700
PH: (419)535-3232
Fax: (419)535-1989
Edwards, Tracey, Exec. VP

**Student African American Brother-
    hood [19697]**
PO Box 350842
Toledo, OH 43635
PH: (419)530-3221
Fax: (419)530-3223
Bledsoe, Dr. Tyrone, CEO, Founder

Women in the Wind [22238]
PO Box 8392
Toledo, OH 43605
Brown, Becky, Founder

**American Society of Healthcare
    Publication Editors [14978]**
8870 Darrow Rd., Ste. F106-155
Twinsburg, OH 44087
PH: (330)487-0344
Fax: (330)487-0530

**Sports Philatelists International
    [22370]**
1320 Bridget Ln.
Twinsburg, OH 44087-2729
Maestrone, Mark C., President

**Catholic Theological Society of
    America [19816]**
John Carroll University
1 John Carroll Blvd.
University Heights, OH 44118
PH: (216)397-4980
Fax: (216)397-1804
Hollenbach, David, President

**Middle East Librarians Association
    [9717]**
c/o Jaleh Fazelian, President
Grasselli Library and Breen Learning
    Center
John Carroll University
1 John Carroll Blvd.
University Heights, OH 44118
PH: (216)397-1509
Fazelian, Jaleh, President

**National Council for History Educa-
    tion [7987]**
13940 Cedar Rd., No. 393
University Heights, OH 44118
PH: (240)696-6600
Fax: (240)523-0245
Steiner, Dale, Chairman

T-Ten Class Association [22672]
2655 S Belvoir Blvd.
University Heights, OH 44118
PH: (330)592-5243
Barker, John, President

**National Society Sons of the
    American Colonists [20757]**
c/o Robert Darrell Pollock, Registrar
    General
PO Box 86
Urbana, OH 43078-0086
Lucas, Col. Charles Clement, M.D.,
    Gov.

**Rathkamp Matchcover Society
    [21718]**
1509 S Dugan Rd.
1509 S Dugan Rd.
Urbana, OH 43078-9209
PH: (937)653-3947

**Accredited Snow Contractors As-
    sociation [848]**
5811 Canal Rd.
Valley View, OH 44125

PH: (216)393-0303
Toll free: 800-456-0707
Gilbride, Kevin, Exec. Dir.

Alive Alone [10770]
PO Box 182
Van Wert, OH 45891
Bevington, Kay, Founder

**U.S.A. Ploughing Organization
    [4169]**
c/o Roger Neate, Secretary/
    Treasurer
14837 Greenville Rd.
Van Wert, OH 45891
Postlethwait, David, President

Vintage Motor Bike Club [22237]
c/o Kaitlyn Edelbrock, Secretary
419 W Ervin Rd.
Van Wert, OH 45891-3403
PH: (419)605-5336
Chafin, Darren, President

**American Kerry Bog Pony Society
    [4314]**
13010 W Darrow Rd.
Vermilion, OH 44089
PH: (440)967-2680
Ashar, Linda C., President

**International Bowhunting Organiza-
    tion [22960]**
PO Box 398
Vermilion, OH 44089-0398
PH: (440)967-2137
Fax: (440)967-2052

**Darkride and Funhouse Enthusiasts
    [21276]**
PO Box 484
Vienna, OH 44473-0484
Davis, Rick, Director

**Veterinary Neurosurgical Society
    [17673]**
5671 Crooked Stick Dr.
Wadsworth, OH 44281
Axlund, Todd, President

**National Association of Land Title
    Examiners and Abstractors [2872]**
7490 Eagle Rd.
Waite Hill, OH 44094
Fax: (440)256-2404
Gunther, Ed, Director

Construction Innovation Forum [804]
6494 Latcha Rd.
Walbridge, OH 43465
PH: (419)725-3108
Fax: (419)725-3079
Alter, Mr. Timothy A., Chmn. of the
    Bd.

**Cast Iron Seat Collectors Associa-
    tion [22169]**
c/o Olan Bentley, President
1168 Jamison Rd.
Washington Court House, OH
    43160-8479
PH: (740)335-0964
Stead, Mark, VP

**Teacup Dogs Agility Association
    [21968]**
14543 State Route 676
Waterford, OH 45786
PH: (740)749-3597
Houston, Marsha, Contact

**Sanitary Supply Wholesaling As-
    sociation [2141]**
1432 Riverwalk Ct.
Waterville, OH 43566
PH: (419)878-2787
Fax: (614)340-7938
Eanes, Gordon, Treasurer

Animal House Rescue **[10575]**
PO Box 264
Wauseon, OH 43567
PH: (419)374-0310

Gypsy Vanner Horse Society **[4357]**
PO Box 65
Waynesfield, OH 45896
Toll free: 888-520-9777
Litz, Michael, Bd. Member

Women in Aviation International
[3502]
Morningstar Airport
3647 State Route 503 S
West Alexandria, OH 45381-9354
PH: (937)839-4647
Fax: (937)839-4645
Chabrian, Dr. Peggy, President

AFCOM **[6291]**
9100 W Chester Towne Centre Rd.
West Chester, OH 45069
PH: (513)322-1550
Roberts, Tom, President

Care2Share **[13268]**
PO Box 911
West Chester, OH 45071-0911
PH: (513)319-0548

International Door Association **[537]**
PO Box 246
West Milton, OH 45383
PH: (937)698-8042
Toll free: 800-355-4432
Fax: (937)698-6153
Gibson, Bill, Officer

National Professional Anglers Association **[22850]**
PO Box 117
West Milton, OH 45383
PH: (937)698-4188
Fax: (937)698-6153
Neu, Mr. Pat, Exec. Dir.

United States Agricultural Information Network **[3579]**
c/o Chris Long & Associates
PO Box 117
West Milton, OH 45383
PH: (937)698-4188
Fax: (937)698-6153
Williams, Sarah, President

Nevus Network **[17347]**
c/o Congenital Nevus Support Group
PO Box 305
West Salem, OH 44287-0305
PH: (419)853-4525
(405)377-3403
Bett, BJ, Founder

American Ceramic Society **[6169]**
600 N Cleveland Ave., Ste. 210
Westerville, OH 43082
PH: (240)646-7054
Toll free: 866-721-3322
Fax: (204)396-5637
Spahr, Charles, Exec. Dir.

Association of American Ceramic
Component Manufacturers **[6170]**
600 N Cleveland Ave., Ste 210
Westerville, OH 43082
PH: (614)794-5894
Fax: (614)794-5892

Association for Middle Level Education **[8341]**
4151 Executive Pky., Ste. 300
Westerville, OH 43081-3871
PH: (614)895-4730
Toll free: 800-528-6672
Fax: (614)895-4750
Waidelich, William D., EdD, Exec. Dir.

Ceramic Educational Council **[6171]**
600 N Cleveland Ave., Ste. 210
Westerville, OH 43082
PH: (240)646-7054
(866)721-3322
Fax: (240)396-5637
Gorzkowski, Ed, Secretary

Cooperative Business International
Inc. **[905]**
507 Executive Campus Dr., Ste. 120
Westerville, OH 43082
PH: (614)839-2700
Fax: (614)839-2709
Clark, Robert W., CEO, President

Glass Manufacturing Industry
Council **[1504]**
600 N Cleveland Ave., Ste. 210
Westerville, OH 43082
PH: (614)818-9423
Fax: (614)818-9485
Lipetz, Robert Weisenburger, Exec. Dir.

International Biochar Initiative **[5885]**
640 Brook Run Dr.
Westerville, OH 43081
PH: (802)257-5359
Reed, Debbie, Exec. Dir.

International Executive Housekeepers Association **[2130]**
1001 Eastwind Dr., Ste. 301
Westerville, OH 43081-3361
PH: (614)895-7166
Toll free: 800-200-6342
Fax: (614)895-1248
Patterson, Michael, President

My Very Own Blanket **[11085]**
PO Box 2691
Westerville, OH 43086
PH: (614)530-3327
Hollins, Jessica, Founder, CEO

National Ground Water Association **[3460]**
601 Dempsey Rd.
Westerville, OH 43081
PH: (614)898-7791
Toll free: 800-551-7379
Fax: (614)898-7786
McCray, Kevin B., CEO

National Institute of Ceramic
Engineers **[6172]**
American Ceramic Society
600 N Cleveland Ave., Ste. 210
Westerville, OH 43082-6921
PH: (614)794-5821
Fax: (614)794-5881
Castro, Ricardo, President

Potters Council **[6173]**
Ceramic Publications Co.
600 N Cleveland Ave., Ste. 210
Westerville, OH 43082
Toll free: 800-424-8698
Fax: (818)487-2054
Branfman, Steven, Officer

Rhetoric Society of America **[10198]**
c/o Kathie Cesa, Member Services Officer
1143 Tidewater Ct.
Westerville, OH 43082
PH: (702)895-4825
Clark, Gregory, Officer

Sigmund Freud Archives, Inc. **[16852]**
c/o Louis Rose, Executive Director
Dept. of History
Otterbein University
Westerville, OH 43081
Stuart, Jennifer, President

Technology for the Poor **[4703]**
877 Pelham Ct.
Westerville, OH 43081
Ebenezer, Job S., PhD, President

United States Trotting Association
[22935]
6130 S Sunbury Rd.
Westerville, OH 43081
PH: (614)224-2291
(614)224-3281
Toll free: 877-800-8782
Langley, F. Phillip, President

1953-54 Buick Skylark Club **[21309]**
c/o Gary Di Lillo, Newsletter Editor
27315 Hemlock Dr.
Westlake, OH 44145
Fax: (440)871-5484
De Peppo, Vin, Membership Chp.

American Knife Manufacturers Association **[2065]**
30200 Detroit Rd.
Westlake, OH 44145
PH: (440)899-0010
Fax: (440)892-1404
Peppel, Alan, President

Christian Educators Association
International **[20077]**
PO Box 45610
Westlake, OH 44145
Toll free: 888-798-1124
Laursen, Finn, Exec. Dir.

National Association of Academic
Advisors for Athletics **[7690]**
24651 Detroit Rd.
Westlake, OH 44145
PH: (440)892-4000
Fax: (440)892-4007
Boyd, Jean, President

National Association of Athletic
Development Directors **[23236]**
24651 Detroit Rd.
Westlake, OH 44145-2524
PH: (440)892-4000
Fax: (440)892-4007
Schneider, Scarlett, VP

National Association of Collegiate
Directors of Athletics **[23237]**
c/o Brian Horning, Director
24651 Detroit Rd.
Westlake, OH 44145-2524
PH: (847)491-8880
(401)456-8007
Alden, Mike, Director

National Association of Collegiate
Marketing Administrators **[23238]**
24651 Detroit Rd.
Westlake, OH 44145
PH: (440)892-4000
Fax: (440)892-4007
Parke, Becky, President

Steel Door Institute **[582]**
30200 Detroit Rd.
Westlake, OH 44145
PH: (440)899-0010
Fax: (440)892-1404
Berhinig, Robert, Chairman

COAR Peace Mission **[18174]**
28700 Euclid Ave.
Wickliffe, OH 44092-2585
PH: (440)943-7615
Fax: (440)943-7618
Stevenson, Mary, Exec. Dir.

S.U.C.C.E.S.S. for Autism **[13779]**
28700 Euclid Ave., No. 120
Wickliffe, OH 44092
PH: (440)943-7607
Scotese-Wojtila, Lynette, Founder

American Checker Federation **[22044]**
34490 Ridge Rd., Apt. 115
Willoughby, OH 44094
Millhone, Alan, President

Russian American Medical Association **[15745]**
36100 Euclid Ave., Ste. 330-B
Willoughby, OH 44094
PH: (440)953-8055
Fax: (440)953-0242
Osipoff, Olga, Exec. Dir.

Kids in Flight **[14197]**
PO Box 5234
Willowick, OH 44095-0234
Knausz, Maria, Founder

Caricature Carvers of America
[21751]
c/o Donald K. Mertz, Secretary
729 Prairie Rd.
Wilmington, OH 45177-9683
Rhadigan, Floyd, Mem.

Anneke Jans and Everardus Bogardus Descendants Association
[20888]
c/o Mr. William Bogardus
1121 Linhof Rd.
Wilmington, OH 45177-2917
Bogardus, Mr. William, Founder

Rural Electricity Resource Council **[6510]**
2333 Rombach Ave.
Wilmington, OH 45177
PH: (937)383-0001
Fax: (937)383-0003
Hiatt, Richard S., PE, Exec. Dir., President

Conference of Research Workers in
Animal Diseases **[17644]**
Ohio State University
Research Services Bldg., Rm. 209e
Wooster, OH 44691
PH: (330)263-3703
Fax: (330)263-3688
Gershwin, Dr. Laurel J., President

William James Society **[10354]**
Philosophy Dept.
The College of Wooster
1189 Beall Ave.
Wooster, OH 44691
PH: (330)263-2548
Hester, D. Micah, Contact

International Medical Health
Organization **[15026]**
400 W Wilson Bridge Rd., Ste. 230
Worthington, OH 43085-2259
PH: (614)659-9922
Fax: (614)659-9933
Theventhiran, Rajam, MD, VP

Reading Recovery Council of North
America **[8491]**
500 W Wilson Bridge Rd., Ste. 250
Worthington, OH 43085-2238
PH: (614)310-7323
Toll free: 877-883-READ
Fax: (614)310-7345
Johnson, Jady, Exec. Dir.

Athletes in Action **[20127]**
651 Taylor Dr.
Xenia, OH 45385-7246
PH: (937)352-1000
Fax: (937)352-1001
Hannah, Dave, Founder

Highlander Class International Association **[22620]**
2280 US 68 S
Xenia, OH 45385
PH: (937)271-8658
Fisher, Doug, President

Hispanic Organization of Toxicologists **[7339]**
c/o Ranulfo Lemus-Olalde, Treasurer
2131 Annandale Pl.

Xenia, OH 45385
PH: (804)852-4439
DePass, Linval, President

Mission2Guatemala [13071]
301 Sutton Rd.
Xenia, OH 45385
PH: (937)830-1478
Batres, Manuel, President

Dental Anthropology Association
[14428]
c/o Dr. Loren R. Lease, Secretary
and Treasurer
Dept. of Sociology and Anthropology
Youngstown State University
1 University Plz.
Youngstown, OH 44555
Lease, Dr. Loren, Secretary,
Treasurer

International Association of Hygienic
Physicians [15852]
c/o Mark A. Huberman, Secretary/
Treasurer
4620 Euclid Blvd.
Youngstown, OH 44512
PH: (330)788-5711
Fax: (330)788-0093
Huberman, Mark A., Secretary,
Treasurer

National Health Association [15853]
PO Box 477
Youngstown, OH 44501-0477
PH: (330)953-1002
Fax: (330)953-1030
Epstein, Mark Alan, Treasurer

Pi Mu Epsilon [23814]
c/o Angela Spalsbury, President
Dept. of Mathematics and Statistics
Youngstown State University
Youngstown, OH 44555
PH: (330)941-1803
Edwards, Stephanie, Secretary,
Treasurer

A Way With Words Foundation
[10793]
PO Box 2334
Youngstown, OH 44509
PH: (330)538-7000
    (330)360-3300
Rider, Brenda M., President

Art Glass Association [1501]
PO Box 2537
Zanesville, OH 43702-2537
PH: (740)450-6547
Toll free: 866-301-2421
Fax: (740)454-1194
Shupper, Steve, Chmn. of the Bd.

Association of Environmental &
Engineering Geologists [6679]
1100-H Brandywine Blvd.
Zanesville, OH 43701
Toll free: 844-331-7867
Fax: (740)452-2552
Troost, Dr. Kathy, Treasurer

Crochet Guild of America [22254]
1100-H Brandywine Blvd.
Zanesville, OH 43701-7303
PH: (740)452-4541
Fax: (740)452-2552
Smith, Marcy, Bd. Member

International Window Cleaning As-
sociation [2134]
1100-H Brandywine Blvd.
Zanesville, OH 43701-7303
Toll free: 800-875-4922
Fax: (740)452-2552
Pedersen, Noa, President

The Knitting Guild Association
[21768]
1100-H Brandywine Blvd.
Zanesville, OH 43701-7303

PH: (740)452-4541
Sitler, Ms. Penny, Exec. Dir.

The National Needle Arts Associa-
tion [3266]
1100-H Brandywine Blvd.
Zanesville, OH 43701-7303
PH: (740)455-6773
Toll free: 800-889-8662
VanStralen, Dave, President

Parents Without Partners, Inc.
[12424]
1100-H Brandywine Blvd.
Zanesville, OH 43701-7303
Toll free: 800-637-7974
Fax: (740)452-2552
Gallinati, Janet, President

Professional Lighting and Sign
Management Companies of
America [2105]
1100-H Brandywine Blvd.
Zanesville, OH 43701-7303
PH: (740)452-4541
Bailey, Jarad, Director

Society of Glass and Ceramic
Decorated Products [1510]
PO Box 2489
Zanesville, OH 43702
PH: (740)588-9882
Fax: (740)588-0245
Warne, Myra, Exec. Dir.

Spinning and Weaving Group [3270]
c/o The National NeedleArts As-
sociation
1100-H Brandywine Blvd.
Zanesville, OH 43701-7303
Toll free: 800-889-8662
Fax: (740)452-2552
Nachtrieb, Cheryl, Chairperson

OKLAHOMA

Association of Trust Companies
[1276]
2313 N Broadway
Ada, OK 74820
PH: (405)680-7869
Fax: (580)332-4714
Nunn, Douglas, Officer

The Samuel Roberts Noble Founda-
tion [3529]
2510 Sam Noble Pky.
Ardmore, OK 73401
PH: (580)223-5810
Buckner, Bill, President, CEO

Carp Anglers Group [22039]
PO Box 1502
Bartlesville, OK 74005-1502
Shanmuga, Santosh, President

Nevus Outreach, Inc [14608]
600 SE Delaware Ave., Ste. 200
Bartlesville, OK 74003
PH: (918)331-0595
Toll free: 877-426-3887
Fax: (281)417-4020
Beckwith, Mark, Exec. Dir.

Voice of the Martyrs [20474]
PO Box 443
Bartlesville, OK 74005-0443
PH: (918)337-8015
Toll free: 877-337-0302
Fax: (918)338-0189
Little, Mr. Harvey, Chairman

Pinto Horse Association of America
Inc. [4401]
7330 NW 23rd St.
Bethany, OK 73008
PH: (405)491-0111
Fax: (405)787-0773
Davidson, Wendy, President

American Veterinary Chiropractic
Association [17627]
442154 E 140 Rd.
Bluejacket, OK 74333
PH: (918)784-2231
Fax: (918)784-2675

Aerostar Owners Association
[21211]
2608 W Kenosha St., No. 704
Broken Arrow, OK 74012
PH: (918)258-2346
Fax: (918)258-2346
Bliss, Bob, President

American Association of State
Counseling Boards [14325]
305 N Beech Cir.
Broken Arrow, OK 74012
PH: (918)994-4413
Fax: (918)663-7058
Enegess, Karen, President

Blessings International [12266]
1650 N Indianwood Ave.
Broken Arrow, OK 74012-1284
PH: (918)250-8101
Fax: (918)250-1281
Harder, Harold C., PhD, Mem.

International Council for Machinery
Lubrication [2108]
2208 W Detroit St., Ste. 101
Broken Arrow, OK 74012-3630
PH: (918)259-2950
Fax: (918)259-0177
Johnson, Bryan, Chairman

National Career Development As-
sociation [11772]
305 N Beech Cir.
Broken Arrow, OK 74012
PH: (918)663-7060
Toll free: 866-367-6232
Fax: (918)663-7058
Pennington, Deneen, Exec. Dir.

National Environmental Coalition of
Native Americans [4086]
PO Box 988
Claremore, OK 74018
PH: (405)567-4297
Fax: (405)567-4297
Thorpe, Grace, President

American Mookee Association
[3656]
c/o Steve Bieberich, President
22523 E 1020 Rd.
Clinton, OK 73601
PH: (580)323-6259
Nowak, Ed, VP

American Medical Billing Association
[15575]
2465 E Main St.
Davis, OK 73030
PH: (580)369-2700
Fax: (580)369-2703
Housberg, Steven, Bd. Member

Androgen Insensitivity Syndrome-
Disorders of Sex Development
Support Group [14808]
PO Box 2148
Duncan, OK 73534-2148
Saviano, Kimberly, President

National Rural Water Association
[12805]
2915 S 13th St.
Duncan, OK 73533
PH: (580)252-0629
Fax: (580)255-4476
Wade, Sam, CEO

Southwest Case Research Association [7570]
c/o Robert Stevens, President
John Massey School of Business

Southern Oklahoma State University
1405 N 4th Ave.
Durant, OK 74701
PH: (580)745-3181
    (580)745-3190
Stevens, Robert, President

ALL FRETS [9847]
2501 Saddleback Dr.
Edmond, OK 73034
PH: (405)819-3883
Baier, Johnny, Editor

American Weather and Climate
Industry Association [6855]
c/o Steven Root, 1015 Waterwood
Pky., Ste. J
Weatherbank Inc.
1015 Waterwood Pky., Ste. J
Edmond, OK 73034
Root, Steven, CCM, President, CEO

Law Enforcement Thermographers'
Association [5482]
PO Box 6485
Edmond, OK 73083
PH: (405)330-6988
Carignan, Joe, President

National Church Conference of the
Blind [13277]
PO Box 276
Edmond, OK 73083-0276
PH: (405)330-1331
Ohadi, Pauline, Membership Chp.

United States Fencing Coaches Association [22835]
514 NW 164th St.
Edmond, OK 73013-2001
Burchard, Peter, President

U.S. Cavalry Association and Memo-
rial Research Library [9810]
7107 W Cheyenne St.
El Reno, OK 73036
PH: (405)422-6330
Bolte, Brig. Gen. (Ret.) Philip L.,
Chairman

Comanche Language and Cultural
Preservation Committee [10037]
1375 NE Cline Rd.
Elgin, OK 73538-3086
PH: (580)492-4988
Toll free: 877-492-4988
Fax: (580)492-5119
Goodin, Barbara, Secretary,
Treasurer

Air Force Navigators Observer Association [20681]
c/o James Faulkner, Director
4109 Timberlane
Enid, OK 73703-2825
PH: (580)242-0526
Barrett, Ron, President

Southwest Spanish Mustang As-
sociation [4409]
PO Box 329
Hugo, OK 74743
PH: (580)579-3467
Rickman, Bryant, Chairman

Ballew Family Association of
America [20782]
c/o Paul Ballew
PO Box 2808
Lawton, OK 73502
PH: (580)595-1007
Murphy, Allen, President

Institute of the Great Plains [9352]
601 NW Ferris Ave.
Lawton, OK 73507
PH: (580)581-3460
Fisher, Paul, President

Allied Trades of the Baking Industry
[366]
PO Box 688
Maysville, OK 73057
PH: (405)664-8762
Hellman, John, VP

Sears Family Association [20925]
821 SW 42nd St.
Moore, OK 73160-7658
PH: (405)703-0779

Road Race Lincoln Register [21485]
5847 E 201st St. S
5847 E 201st St. S
Mounds, OK 74047
Denney, Mike, Editor

Softball Players Association [23206]
PO Box 1307
Mustang, OK 73064
PH: (405)376-7034
Fax: (405)376-7035

American Indian Institute [10034]
1639 Cross Center Dr.
Norman, OK 73019
PH: (405)325-4127
    (405)325-0473
Neely, Norma, Ph.D., Director

Association for Continuing Higher
Education [7668]
OCCE Admin Bldg.
1700 Asp Ave., Rm. 129C
Norman, OK 73072-6407
Toll free: 800-807-2243
Fax: (405)325-4888
Pappas, James, Exec. VP

Citizens United for the Rehabilitation ·
of Errants-Sex Offenders Restored
through Treatment [12920]
c/o Wayne Bowers, Executive Director
PO Box 1022
Norman, OK 73070-1022
PH: (405)639-7262
Bowers, Wayne, Exec. Dir.

Gamma Delta Pi [23973]
900 Asp Ave., Rm. 370
Norman, OK 73019
Metzner, Traci, President

Golf Coaches Association of America
[22880]
1225 W Main St., Ste. 110
Norman, OK 73069
PH: (405)329-4222
Fax: (405)573-7888
Grost, Gregg, CEO

HIS Nets [13513]
PO Box 721701
Norman, OK 73070-8301
PH: (405)443-4014
    (828)782-0705
Lewis, Dr. Jimmy, Bd. Member

Mu Alpha Theta [23813]
c/o Kay Weiss, Executive Director
University of Oklahoma
3200 Marshall Ave., Ste. 190
Norman, OK 73019
PH: (405)325-4489
Fax: (405)325-7184
Weiss, Kay, Exec. Dir.

National Weather Association [6857]
3100 Monitor Ave., Ste. 123
Norman, OK 73072
PH: (405)701-5167
Fax: (405)701-5227
Murray, William, VP

Native American Journalists Association [2710]
395 W Lindsey St.
Norman, OK 73019

PH: (405)325-1649
Fax: (405)325-6945
Navajo, Jason Begay, President

Northamerican Association of
Masters In Psychology [8468]
PO Box 721270
Norman, OK 73070 ·
PH: (405)329-3030
Toll free: 800-919-9330
Doan, Lesia Foerster, President

Oklahoma University Alumni As-
sociation [19342]
900 Asp Ave., Rm. 427
Norman, OK 73019-5142
PH: (405)325-1710
Audas, JP, Assoc. VP

OURMedia Network [18663]
610 Elm Ave.
Norman, OK 73019
PH: (405)325-1570

Public Investors Arbitration Bar As-
sociation [5374]
2415 A Wilcox Dr.
Norman, OK 73069
PH: (405)360-8776
Toll free: 888-621-7484
Fax: (405)360-2063
Ringo, Robin S., Exec. Dir.

Society for Cinema and Media Stud-
ies [9312]
Wallace Old Science Hall, Rm. 300
640 Parrington Oval
Norman, OK 73019
PH: (405)325-8075
Fax: (405)325-7135
Cohan, Steven, President

International Coleman Collectors
Club [21672]
c/o Leonard Johnson, Treasurer
PO Box 122
Okemah, OK 74859
Smith, James, President

Association of Ignition Interlock
Program Administrators [280]
5030 N May Ave., Ste. 212
Oklahoma, OK 73112
Bailey, Laura, President

95th Infantry Division Association
[20713]
PO Box 1113
Oklahoma City, OK 73101
Archer, Jim, President

Amateur Softball Association of
America [23199]
ASA Hall of Fa,e Studio Complex
2801 NE 50th St.
Oklahoma City, OK 73111
PH: (405)424-5266
Fax: (405)424-3855
Dooley, Andy, VP

American Association of Pediatric
Urologists [17545]
c/o Dominic Frimberger, MD,
Secretary and Treasurer
The Children's Hospital of Oklahoma
1200 Children's Ave.
Oklahoma City, OK 73104
PH: (405)271-6900
Fax: (405)271-3118
Ewalt, David, MD, President

American Choral Directors Associa-
tion [9854]
545 Couch Dr.
Oklahoma City, OK 73102-2207
PH: (405)232-8161
Fax: (405)232-8162
Sharp, Dr. Tim, Exec. Dir.

American Racing Pigeon Union
[22385]
PO Box 18465
Oklahoma City, OK 73154
PH: (405)848-5801
Fax: (405)848-5888
Rivera, Freddie, President

Association of Alternate Postal
Systems [2115]
1725 Oaks Way
Oklahoma City, OK 73131
PH: (405)478-0006
Somers, Keith, President

Association of American Indian
Physicians [16737]
1225 Sovereign Row, Ste. 103
Oklahoma City, OK 73108-1854
PH: (405)946-7072
Fax: (405)946-7651
Hill, Gerald, President

Association of Native American
Medical Students [15621]
1225 Sovereign Row, Ste. 103
Oklahoma City, OK 73108-1854
PH: (405)946-7072
Fax: (405)946-7651
Wilson, Ryan, MS III, Mem.

Black Caucus of the American
Library Association [9695]
c/o Denyvetta Davis, President
PO Box 13367
Oklahoma City, OK 73113
Davis, Denyvetta, President

Domestic Energy Producers Alliance
[1110]
PO Box 18359
Oklahoma City, OK 73154-0359
PH: (405)424-1699
Hamm, Harold, Chairman

Downed Bikers Association [22220]
PO Box 21713
Oklahoma City, OK 73156
PH: (405)789-5565
Holley, Cary, President

Feed the Children [12661]
333 N Meridian
Oklahoma City, OK 73107
Toll free: 800-627-4556
Watts, J.C, Jr., President, CEO

Golden Retriever Club of America
[21887]
c/o Jolene Carey, Administrative Assistant
PO Box 20434
Oklahoma City, OK 73156
Chase, Jonathan, President

Ground Water Protection Council
[3450]
13308 N MacArthur Blvd.
Oklahoma City, OK 73142
PH: (405)516-4972
Paque, Mike, Exec. Dir.

Hugs Project [10748]
720 W Wilshire Blvd., Ste. 105
Oklahoma City, OK 73116-7737
PH: (405)651-8359
Corbeil, Susan, President

International Professional Rodeo As-
sociation [23096]
1412 S Agnew
Oklahoma City, OK 73108
PH: (405)235-6540
Fax: (405)235-6577
Schick, Tom, Chairman

Interstate Oil and Gas Compact
Commission [5170]
900 NE 23rd St.
Oklahoma City, OK 73105

PH: (405)525-3556
Fax: (405)525-3592
Smith, Mike, Exec. Dir.

Limbs for Life Foundation [14554]
218 E Main St.
Oklahoma City, OK 73104
PH: (405)605-5462
Toll free: 888-235-5462
Fax: (405)823-5123
Fraser, Lucy, Exec. Dir.

Medical Missions Response [20325]
PO Box 57011
Oklahoma City, OK 73157-7011
Toll free: 866-667-8996

National Association of Perinatal
Social Workers [17228]
3319 N Youngs Blvd.
Oklahoma City, OK 73112-7835
Cross, JaNeen, DSW, President

National Collegiate Choral Organiza-
tion [9159]
c/o Randi Von Ellefson, President
Wanda L. Bass School of Music
Oklahoma City University
2501 N Blackwelder Ave.
Oklahoma City, OK 73106
Von Ellefson, Randi, President

National Cowboy and Western
Heritage Museum [8801]
1700 NE 63rd St.
Oklahoma City, OK 73111
PH: (405)478-2250
Fax: (405)478-4714
Muno, Ed, Mgr.

National Reining Horse Association
[4386]
3000 NW 10th St.
Oklahoma City, OK 73107-5302
PH: (405)946-7400
Fax: (405)946-8425
Clark, Rick, President

National Women in Agriculture As-
sociation [3574]
1701 N Martin Luther King Ave.
Oklahoma City, OK 73111
PH: (405)424-4623
Fax: (405)424-4624
Steele, Tammy, Exec. Dir.

Ninety Nines, Inc. International
Organization of Women Pilots
[153]
4300 Amelia Earhart Dr., Ste. A
Oklahoma City, OK 73159
PH: (405)685-7969
Toll free: 800-994-1929
Fax: (405)685-7985
Ohrenberg, Laura, Comm. Chm.

Oklahoma City University Alumni
Office [19341]
2501 N Blackwelder Ave.
Oklahoma City, OK 73106-1493
PH: (405)208-5463
    (405)208-5077
Pirrong, Cary, Director

PAMBE Ghana [11732]
PO Box 18813
Oklahoma City, OK 73154-0813
Iddi-Gubbels, Alice Azumi, Founder,
Exec. Dir.

Photographic Society of America
[22384]
8421 S Walker Ave., Ste. 104
Oklahoma City, OK 73139
PH: (405)843-1437
Toll free: 855-772-4636
Key, John R., Asst.

Red Earth [19588]
6 Santa Fe Plz.
Oklahoma City, OK 73102

PH: (405)427-5228
Fax: (405)427-8079
Norick, Vickie L., Chairman

Rodeo Historical Society **[8803]**
National Cowboy and Western
Heritage Museum
1700 NE 63rd St.
Oklahoma City, OK 73111
PH: (405)478-2250
Fax: (405)478-4714

Society for Applied Anthropology
[5920]
PO Box 2436
Oklahoma City, OK 73101-2436
PH: (405)843-5113
Fax: (405)843-8553
Musante, Kathleen, President

Society for the Study of Occupation:
U.S.A. **[7532]**
University of Oklahoma Health Sci-
ences Ctr.
1200 N Stonewall Ave.
Oklahoma City, OK 73117
PH: (734)487-2280
Gupta, Jyothi, Chairman

VITA **[6339]**
9100 Paseo del Vita
Oklahoma City, OK 73131
Gipper, Jerry, Exec. Dir.

Westerners International **[8807]**
c/o National Cowboy & Western
Heritage Museum
1700 NE 63rd St.
Oklahoma City, OK 73111-7906
PH: (405)478-8408
Toll free: 800-541-4650
McInnis, Kent, Exec., Chairman, Bd.
Member

World Neighbors **[18566]**
PO Box 270058
Oklahoma City, OK 73137-0058
PH: (405)752-9700
Toll free: 800-242-6387
Schecter, Kate, President, CEO

World Organization of China Paint-
ers **[21789]**
2700 N Portland
Oklahoma City, OK 73107-5400
PH: (405)521-1234
Fax: (405)521-1265
Pine, Dee, Exec. Dir.

Future Fisherman Foundation
[22845]
5998 N Pleasant View Rd.
Ponca City, OK 74601
PH: (580)716-4251
Gintert, Mark, Exec. Dir.

National Bass Anglers Association
[22849]
5998 N Pleasant View Rd.
Ponca City, OK 74601
PH: (580)765-2319
Fax: (580)765-2890

National Association of Publicly
Funded Truck Driving Schools
[3339]
1324 S 220 W Ave.
Sand Springs, OK 74063
PH: (918)770-6446
Behnke, Robert, Bd. Member

PODS Association **[7234]**
PO Box 1726
Sand Springs, OK 74063
PH: (918)246-9343
Mayo, Kathy, Exec. Dir.

Marine Corps Counterintelligence
Association **[19546]**
PO Box 1948
Seminole, OK 74818-1948
Dubrule, Mike, Chairman

Conference on Faith and History
[20203]
c/o Glenn Sanders
Dept. of History
Oklahoma Baptist University
PO Box 61232
Shawnee, OK 74804
PH: (405)585-4157
Wigger, John H., President

Oklahoma Baptist University Alumni
Association **[19340]**
500 W University
500 W University St.
Shawnee, OK 74804
PH: (405)275-2850
     (405)585-5413
Toll free: 800-654-3285
Hagans, Lori Renegar, Exec. Dir.

American Association of Veterinary
Immunologists **[17603]**
c/o Dr. Glenn Zhang, Secretary-
Treasurer
212 Animal Science
Animal Molecular Biology
Oklahoma State University
Stillwater, OK 74074
Sylte, Matt, Secretary, Treasurer

International Fire Service Training
Association **[8662]**
930 N Willis
Stillwater, OK 74078
PH: (405)744-5723
Toll free: 800-654-4055
Fax: (405)744-8204
Moore-Merrell, Lori, Asst. Pres.

International Ground Source Heat
Pump Association **[1627]**
1201 S Innovation Way Dr., Ste. 400
Stillwater, OK 74074-1583
PH: (405)744-5175
Toll free: 800-626-4747
Fax: (405)744-5283
Smith, Cary, Treasurer

Kappa Kappa Psi **[23827]**
401 E 9th Ave.
Stillwater, OK 74074-4704
PH: (405)372-2333
Fax: (405)372-2363
Chestnutt, Rod, Chairman

National Association of Government
Guaranteed Lenders **[2093]**
215 E 9th Ave.
Stillwater, OK 74074
PH: (405)377-4022
Wilkinson, Anthony R., CEO,
President

National Association of University
Fisheries and Wildlife Programs
[7880]
c/o Dr. Keith Owens, President-Elect
Dept. of Natural Resource Ecology
and Management
Oklahoma State University
008C Agricultural Hall
Stillwater, OK 74078
PH: (405)744-5438
Hallerman, Dr. Eric, President

Overseas Chinese Entomologists
Association **[6617]**
136 Ag Hall
Stillwater, OK 74078-6015
PH: (405)744-5395
Jiang, Haobo, Ph.D., Secretary

Society for Tropical Veterinary
Medicine **[17661]**
250 McElroy Hall
Center for Veterinary Health Sciences
Department of Veterinary Pathobiology

Oklahoma State University
Stillwater, OK 74078
PH: (405)744-6726
     (405)744-7271
Blouin, Edmour, Secretary, Treasurer

Tau Beta Sigma **[23835]**
PO Box 849
Stillwater, OK 74076-0849
PH: (405)372-2333
Toll free: 800-543-6505
Fax: (405)372-2363
Kelly, Kathryn, President

Cherokee National Historical Society
[10036]
PO Box 515
Tahlequah, OK 74465-0515
PH: (918)456-6007
Toll free: 888-999-6007
Plumb, Susan, President

National Indian Child Care Associa-
tion **[12379]**
c/o Eloise Locust, Treasurer
PO Box 2146
Tahlequah, OK 74465
PH: (918)453-5051
Locust, Eloise, Treasurer

National Tribal Child Support As-
sociation **[11256]**
PO Box 557
Tahlequah, OK 74465
PH: (918)458-7660
     (918)453-5444

American Association of Petroleum
Geologists **[6675]**
1444 S Boulder Ave.
Tulsa, OK 74119
PH: (918)584-2555
Toll free: 800-364-2274
Fax: (918)560-2665
Smith, Tom, Manager

American Buckskin Registry As-
sociation **[4300]**
320 S Boston Ave., Ste. 808
Tulsa, OK 74103
PH: (918)936-4707
Cain, Amy, VP

American Guild of Court Videogra-
phers **[5526]**
1437 S Border Ave., Ste. 170
Tulsa, OK 74119
Toll free: 800-678-1990
Marquette, Dr. Gayle, Founder

American Osteopathic College of
Occupational and Preventive
Medicine **[16514]**
PO Box 3043
Tulsa, OK 74101
PH: (253)968-3423
Toll free: 800-558-8686
LeBoeuf, Mr. Jeffrey J., CAE, Exec.
Dir.

Association of Desk and Derrick
Clubs **[2513]**
5321 S Sheridan Rd., Ste. 24
Tulsa, OK 74145
PH: (918)622-1749
Fax: (918)622-1675
Harrison, Connie, President

Blessings of Joy **[10869]**
PO Box 701143
Tulsa, OK 74170
PH: (918)282-3623
Mutebi, Solomon, President

Engineers in Action **[11353]**
10759 E Admiral Pl.
Tulsa, OK 74116
PH: (918)770-9840
     (918)481-9009
Stephenson, David, Exec. Dir.

Gas Processors Association **[2521]**
6060 American Plz., Ste. 700
Tulsa, OK 74135
PH: (918)493-3872
Sutton, Mark, President, CEO

Gas Processors Suppliers Associa-
tion **[2522]**
6060 American Plz., Ste. 700
Tulsa, OK 74135
PH: (918)493-3872
Fax: (918)493-3875
Tzap, Steve, 1st VP

Global Organization for Organ Dona-
tion **[14620]**
PO Box 52757
Tulsa, OK 74105
PH: (918)605-1994
Fax: (918)745-6637
Koontz, Shelly Brady, Founder

International Christian Accrediting
Association **[20083]**
2448 E 81st St., Ste. 600
Tulsa, OK 74137
PH: (918)493-8880
Fax: (918)493-8041
Pratt, Michael, Chairman

International FireStop Council **[6633]**
2660 S Utica Ave.
Tulsa, OK 74114
PH: (918)200-3757
Stahl, Jim, Jr., President

Jana Jae Fan Club **[24048]**
PO Box 35726
Tulsa, OK 74153
PH: (918)786-8896
Deal, Evelyn, President

Knowledge & Information Profes-
sional Association **[1801]**
PO Box 4107
Tulsa, OK 74159-4107
Colannino, Joseph, President

Lawn and Garden Dealers Associa-
tion **[4270]**
5616 S 122nd East Ave., Ste. N
Tulsa, OK 74146
Toll free: 800-752-5296
Fax: (918)254-0713

Literacy and Evangelism
International **[8246]**
1800 S Jackson Ave.
Tulsa, OK 74107-1857
PH: (918)585-3826
Fax: (918)585-3224
Rice, Dr. Robert F., Owner

NALS **[5545]**
8159 E 41st St.
Tulsa, OK 74145-3313
PH: (918)582-5188
Fax: (918)582-5907
Hailey, Tammy, CAE, Exec. Dir.

NALS The Association for Legal
Professionals **[76]**
8159 E 41st St.
Tulsa, OK 74145-3313
PH: (918)582-5188
Fax: (918)582-5907
McElroy, Karen S., PP, PL-SC,
President

National Association of Legal As-
sistants **[5659]**
7666 E 61st St., Ste. 315
Tulsa, OK 74133
PH: (918)587-6828
Fax: (918)582-6772
Zeimetz, Greta P., Exec. Dir.

National Association of Royalty Owners **[2529]**
15 W 6th St., Ste. 2626
Tulsa, OK 74119

PH: (918)794-1660
Toll free: 800-558-0557
Fax: (918)794-1662
Wagner, Emily, Secretary

National Biplane Association [21241]
7215 E 46th St.
Tulsa, OK 74145
PH: (918)665-0755
Harris, Charles W., Chairman

National Kappa Kappa Iota [23731]
1875 E 15th St.
Tulsa, OK 74104-4610
PH: (918)744-0389
Toll free: 800-678-0389
Fax: (918)744-0578
Huhn, Wanda, President

National Resource Center for Youth
Services [11096]
Bldg. 4W
Schusterman Ctr.
4502 E 41st St.
Tulsa, OK 74135-2512
PH: (918)660-3700
Fax: (918)660-3737
Charles, Kristi, Assoc. Dir.

Palomino Horse Breeders of
America [3611]
15253 E Skelly Dr.
Tulsa, OK 74116-2637
PH: (918)438-1234
Fax: (918)438-1232
Goble, Terry L., Sr., Liaison

Petroleum Equipment Institute
[2533]
PO Box 2380
Tulsa, OK 74101
PH: (918)494-9696
Fax: (918)491-9595
Trabilsy, Steve, President

Reach Now International [12715]
PO Box 35133
Tulsa, OK 74153
PH: (918)361-0452
Meyer, Bill, Founder

Society of Exploration Geophysicists
[6695]
8801 S Yale, Ste. 500
Tulsa, OK 74137-3575
PH: (918)497-5500
    (918)497-5581
Fax: (918)497-5557
Koster, Dr. Klaas, President

Society for Sedimentary Geology
[6974]
4111 S Darlington Ave., Ste. 100
Tulsa, OK 74135-6373
PH: (918)610-3361
Toll free: 800-865-9765
Fax: (918)621-1685
Harper, Dr. Howard, Exec. Dir.

Sweet Adelines International [10016]
9110 S Toledo Ave.
Tulsa, OK 74137
PH: (918)622-1444
Toll free: 800-992-7464
Fax: (918)665-0894
Talbot, Tammy, COO

Union Youth Football Association
[22868]
10026-A S Mingo Rd., No. 124
Tulsa, OK 74133
PH: (918)289-8916
Farquhar, Mark, President

Unitarian Universalist Christian Fel-
lowship [20627]
PO Box 6702
Tulsa, OK 74156

PH: (918)794-4637
Robinson, Rev. Ron, Exec. Dir.

Voice of China and Asia Missionary
Society [20473]
PO Box 702015
Tulsa, OK 74170-2015
PH: (918)392-0560
Toll free: 877-392-0560
Brooks, Jonathan, President

World Jeet Kune Do Federation
[23028]
8086 S Yale Ave., No. 133
Tulsa, OK 74136
Hargrave, Prof. Carter, President,
Founder

Zarrow Families Foundation [13099]
401 S Boston, Ste. 900
Tulsa, OK 74103-4012
PH: (918)295-8004
Major, Bill, Exec. Dir.

Clan Leslie Society International
[20817]
302 SW 3rd St.
Tuttle, OK 73089-8927
PH: (405)381-3577
Flowers, Linda, Contact

Barrel Futurities of America [22914]
c/o Cindy Arnold, Secretary
Box 120 K, Route 2
Vian, OK 74962
Roper, Jimmy, President

American Kiko Goat Association
[4273]
8222 Kay Rd.
Wakita, OK 73771
PH: (254)423-5914
Guffey, Jean, President

Table Shuffleboard Association, Inc.
[23148]
c/o Lynda French, Chief Finanacial
Officer/Treasurer
8155 Meadow Lark Dr.
Wynnewood, OK 73098-8949
PH: (512)619-6030
Fax: (512)597-0609
French, Lynda P., CFO, Treasurer

Energy Training Council [6483]
PO Box 850359
Yukon, OK 73085
Murphy, David, Contact

OREGON

Refrigerating Engineers and Techni-
cians Association [6583]
1035 2nd Ave. SE
Albany, OR 97321
PH: (541)497-2955
Fax: (541)497-2966
Barron, Jim, Exec. Dir.

American Alliance for Medical Can-
nabis [15550]
44500 Tide Ave.
Arch Cape, OR 97102
PH: (503)436-1882
Livermore, Arthur, Director

Gifted Homeschoolers Forum
[11915]
1467 Siskiyou Blvd., No. 174
Ashland, OR 97520
Goodwin, Corin Barsily, President,
Exec. Dir.

Life Resources Institute [15268]
c/o Kristin Abbott, Financial Director
61 Morse Ave.
Ashland, OR 97520

PH: (541)482-1289
Rawson, Cheryl, Contact

Long Way Home [10725]
c/o Mike Smith
227 W Hersey St.
Ashland, OR 97520
Paz, Daniel, President

Tube Collectors Association [21728]
PO Box 636
Ashland, OR 97520
PH: (541)855-5207
Sibley, Ludwell, President, Editor

American Society of Forensic
Podiatry [14773]
PO Box 549
Bandon, OR 97411
Dimaggio, John A., DPM, President

AirFuel Alliance [7051]
3855 SW 153rd Dr.
Beaverton, OR 97003
PH: (503)619-0666
Fax: (503)644-6708
Butler, Edward, Chmn. of the Bd.

American Association of Professional
Hypnotherapists [15354]
16055 SW Walker Rd., No. 406
Beaverton, OR 97006
PH: (503)533-7106

Association for the Treatment of
Sexual Abusers [6036]
4900 SW Griffith Dr., Ste. 274
Beaverton, OR 97005
PH: (503)643-1023
Fax: (503)643-5084
Christopher, Maia, Exec. Dir.

Building Commissioning Association
[505]
1600 NW Compton Dr., Ste. 200
Beaverton, OR 97006
PH: (503)747-2903
Toll free: 877-666-2292
Miller, Mark F., Mem.

Compassion First [12649]
16055 SW Walker Rd., PMB 239
Beaverton, OR 97006
PH: (503)207-1320
Fax: (503)614-1599
Mercer, Mike, President

Digital Watermarking Alliance [6697]
9405 SW Gemini Dr.
Beaverton, OR 97008-7192
PH: (818)444-4777
    (503)469-4771
Fax: (503)469-4686
Oakes, Graham, Chairman

Ethernet Alliance [7266]
3855 SW 153rd Dr.
Beaverton, OR 97003-5105
PH: (503)619-0564
Fax: (503)644-6708
D'Ambrosia, John, Chmn. of the Bd.

Ethiopian Orphan Relief, Inc.
[10965]
3020 SW Christy Ave.
Beaverton, OR 97005
Pasion, Kimberley, President

The Green Grid [3211]
3855 SW 153rd Dr.
Beaverton, OR 97006
PH: (503)619-0653
Fax: (503)644-6708
Tipley, Roger, President, Chmn. of
the Bd.

InfiniBand Trade Association [6249]
3855 SW 153rd Dr.
Beaverton, OR 97006-5105

PH: (503)619-0565

LCD TV Association [3251]
16055 SW Walker Rd., Ste. 264
Beaverton, OR 97006
PH: (215)206-6506
Berkoff, Mr. Bruce, Chairman

National Association of Medics and
Corpsmen [4974]
c/o Lloyd Beemer, Treaduer
13915 SW Azalea Ct.
Beaverton, OR 97008
Pardue, Kerry, Exec. Sec.

National Women's Martial Arts
Federation [23008]
9450 SW Gemini Dr.
Beaverton, OR 97005-2343
PH: (206)339-5251
Fax: (206)339-5251
Stevenson, Jennifer, Treasurer

Open Gaming Alliance [6328]
9450 SW Gemini Dr., No. 67608
Beaverton, OR 97008
Ployhar, Matt, Bd. Member

Luis Palau Association [20158]
1500 NW 167th Pl.
Beaverton, OR 97006
PH: (503)614-1500
Fax: (503)614-1599
Palau, Kevin, President

Personal Connected Health Alliance
[15055]
3855 SW 153rd Dr.
Beaverton, OR 97003
PH: (503)619-0867
Fax: (503)644-6708
Merkle, Horst, President, Chairman

RF Energy Alliance [6509]
3855 SW 153rd Dr.
Beaverton, OR 97003
PH: (503)619-0692
Fax: (503)644-6708
Scaburri, Adriano, Chairman

Serial ATA International Organization
[6335]
3855 SW 153rd Dr.
Beaverton, OR 97006
PH: (503)619-0572
Fax: (503)644-6708
Grimsrud, Knut, President

USB Implementers Forum [6338]
3855 SW 153rd Dr.
Beaverton, OR 97006
PH: (503)619-0426
Fax: (503)644-6708
Ravencraft, Jeff, President, COO

American Cross Country Skiers
[23161]
PO Box 604
Bend, OR 97709
PH: (541)317-0217
Downing, J. D., Director

Cancer Adventures [13915]
PO Box 7353
Bend, OR 97708-7353
PH: (541)610-7278
Johnson, Gary, Contact

Education for Chinese Orphans
[7762]
PO Box 8630
Bend, OR 97708
PH: (541)610-6967
Tadjiki, Brian, President

Exhibit and Event Marketers Association [1172]
2214 NW 5th St.
Bend, OR 97701

PH: (541)317-8768
Fax: (541)317-8749
Wurm, Jim, Exec. Dir.

Kite Trade Association International
[3140]
PO Box 6898
Bend, OR 97708
PH: (541)994-9647
Toll free: 800-243-8548
Fax: (503)419-4369
Leitner, Elaine, President

Natural Areas Association [3913]
PO Box 1504
Bend, OR 97709
PH: (541)317-0199
Heidorn, Randy R., President

North American Dog Agility Council
[22819]
24605 Dodds Rd.
Bend, OR 97701

Scientists Center for Animal Welfare
[10695]
2660 NE Highway 20, Ste. 610-115
Bend, OR 97701
PH: (301)345-3500
Fax: (541)383-4655
Braunschweiger, Paul, PhD, VP

Sparrow Clubs U.S.A. [11272]
906 NE Greenwood Ave., Ste. 2
Bend, OR 97701
PH: (541)312-8630
Wilson, Dr. Nancy, Contact

Thirst Relief International [13339]
PO Box 2266
Bend, OR 97709
Toll free: 866-584-4778
Hicks, Jim Davis, Founder, President

Toy Car Collectors Association
[22450]
c/o Dana Johnson
PO Box 1824
Bend, OR 97709-1824
PH: (541)318-7176
Johnson, Mr. Dana, Contact

World Masters Cross-Country Ski
Association [23174]
c/o John Downing, Director
PO Box 604
Bend, OR 97709
PH: (541)317-0217
Fax: (541)317-0217
Downing, John, Director

National Men's Resource Center
[18670]
PO Box 12
Brookings, OR 97415
Clay, Gordon, President, Editor

American North Country Cheviot
Sheep Association [4657]
PO Box 9275
Brooks, OR 97305
PH: (503)792-3448
Fax: (503)792-4416
Kessler, Brett, President

Wilderness International [3965]
PO Box 491
Canby, OR 97013-0491
PH: (503)593-0199
Hall, Russ, Consultant

International College of Cranio-
Mandibular Orthopedics [16477]
PO Box 1491
Cannon Beach, OR 97110
PH: (503)436-0703
Toll free: 866-379-3656
Fax: (503)436-0612
Thomas, Norman R., Chancellor

National Rex Rabbit Club [4607]
c/o Arlyse DeLoyola, Secretary-
Treasurer
PO Box 1465
Cave Junction, OR 97523
PH: (541)592-4865
DeLoyola, Arlyse, Secretary,
Treasurer

Dogs for the Deaf [15188]
10175 Wheeler Rd.
Central Point, OR 97502
PH: (541)826-9220
Toll free: 800-990-DOGS
Dickson, Mrs. Robin, Bd. Member

Cambodia America Mobile Clinic
[14245]
PO Box 1913
Clackamas, OR 97015
PH: (725)333-2262
Iv, Mr. Tin, Founder, President

American Ornithologists' Union
[6953]
c/o Scott Lanyon, President
University of Minnesota
1987 Upper Buford Cir.
Corvallis, OR 97331
PH: (612)624-6291
Lanyon, Scott M., President

FG Syndrome Family Alliance
[17339]
922 NW Circle Blvd., Ste. 160
Corvallis, OR 97330
Morford, Jackie, President

Charlotte Perkins Gilman Society
[10373]
c/o Peter Betjemann, President
Dept. of English
Oregon State University
Moreland Hall
Corvallis, OR 97331
So, Brandi, Exec. Dir.

Global Nutrition Empowerment
[16222]
3205 NW Elmwood Dr.
Corvallis, OR 97330
Long, Marie, MD, Founder, Chairman

Integrated Plant Protection Center
[3566]
2040 Cordley Hall
Dept. of Environmental and
Molecular Toxicology
Oregon State University
Corvallis, OR 97331-2915
PH: (541)737-3541
Fax: (541)737-3080
Jepson, Paul, Director

International Institute of Fisheries
Economics and Trade [1299]
Dept. of Agricultural and Resource
Economics
Oregon State University
Corvallis, OR 97331-3601
PH: (541)737-1439
    (541)737-1416
Fax: (541)737-2563
Shriver, Ann L., Exec. Dir.

National Pesticide Information
Center [13225]
c/o Oregon State University
310 Weniger Hall
Corvallis, OR 97331-6502
Toll free: 800-858-7378
Miller, Terry L., Director

NIRSA [23246]
4185 SW Research Way
Corvallis, OR 97333-1067
PH: (541)766-8211
Fax: (541)766-8284
Braden, Laurie, President

North American Association of
Fisheries Economists [1302]
213 Ballard Hall
Oregon State University
Corvallis, OR 97330-3601
PH: (541)737-1439
Fax: (541)737-2563
Sylvia, Dr. Gilbert, President

North American Truffling Society
[6889]
3200 Jefferson Way
Corvallis, OR 97339-0296
Kenneke, Jon, Editor

Abundant Life Seeds [3784]
c/o Territorial Seed Company
PO Box 158
Cottage Grove, OR 97424
Toll free: 800-626-0866
Fax: (888)657-3131

International Sport Horses of Color
[4370]
PO Box 1567
Cottage Grove, OR 97424
Toll free: 877-266-9757

Jew's Harp Guild [9943]
69954 Hidden Valley Ln.
Cove, OR 97824
Morgan, Deirdre, Exec. Dir.

SAFE Association [5872]
300 N Mill St., Unit B
Creswell, OR 97426
PH: (541)895-3012
Fax: (541)895-3014
Loving, Allen, Advisor

North American Fastpitch Associa-
tion [23205]
c/o Benjie Hedgecock, Executive
Director
PO Box 566
Dayton, OR 97114
PH: (503)864-3939
Fax: (503)864-3939
Kopp, Ronn, President

Soil Carbon Coalition [4688]
501 South St.
Enterprise, OR 97828-1345
PH: (541)263-1888

AHA International [8051]
1585 E 13th Ave., No. 333
Eugene, OR 97403
PH: (541)346-5888
Toll free: 800-654-2051
Fax: (541)346-9100
Poole, Kathy, Exec. Dir.

Association for Fire Ecology [3990]
PO Box 50412
Eugene, OR 97405
PH: (541)852-7903
Oswald, Dr. Brian, Comm. Chm.

Association for Fire Ecology of the
Tropics [3991]
PO Box 50412
Eugene, OR 97405-0412
PH: (541)852-7903
Kobziar, Dr. Leda, President

Association for Professional Observ-
ers [4183]
PO Box 933
Eugene, OR 97440
PH: (541)344-5503
Mitchell, Liz, Bd. Member

Association for Recorded Sound
Collections [9688]
c/o Nathan Georgitis, Executive
Director
Knight Library

1299 University of Oregon
Eugene, OR 97403-1299
Georgitis, Nathan, Exec. Dir.

Association of University Architects
[5964]
1277 University of Oregon
Eugene, OR 97403-1277
PH: (541)346-3537
Toll free: 800-280-6218
Fax: (541)346-3545
Fenwick, Jack, Contact

Binders' Guild [9122]
2925 Powell St.
Eugene, OR 97405-1992
PH: (541)485-6527

blueEnergy [6463]
1595 Walnut St.
Eugene, OR 97403
PH: (415)509-0155
Craig, Mathias, Exec. Dir.

Country Coach International [22465]
1574 Coburg Rd., No. 530
Eugene, OR 97401-4802
PH: (515)708-3391
Toalson, Tammy, Coord.

Early Slavic Studies Association
[10217]
Eugene, OR
Ostrowski, Don

Edurelief [12658]
85334 Lorane Hwy.
Eugene, OR 97405
PH: (541)554-2992
Fax: (541)343-0568
Renich, Jonathan, CEO, Founder

Electrathon America [23080]
2495 Cleveland St.
Eugene, OR 97405
PH: (541)915-9834
Hodgert, Mike, President

Environmental Law Alliance
Worldwide [5179]
1412 Pearl St.
Eugene, OR 97401
PH: (541)687-8454
Fax: (541)687-0535
Johnson, Mr. Bern, Exec. Dir.

Fanconi Anemia Research Fund
[14822]
1801 Willamette St., Ste. 200
Eugene, OR 97401
PH: (541)687-4658
Toll free: 888-326-2664
Hays, Laura, Exec. Dir.

Firefighters United for Safety, Ethics
and Ecology [5204]
2852 Willamette St., No. 125
Eugene, OR 97405-8200
PH: (541)338-7671
Ingalsbee, Timothy, PhD, Exec. Dir.

Forest Industries Telecommunica-
tions [1408]
1565 Oak St.
Eugene, OR 97401
PH: (541)485-8441
Fax: (541)485-7556
McCarthy, Kevin, President

Forest Service Employees for
Environmental Ethics [4578]
PO Box 11615
Eugene, OR 97440
PH: (541)484-2692
Fax: (541)484-3004
Stahl, Andy, Exec. Dir.

Holt International Children's Services
[11236]
250 Country Club Rd.
Eugene, OR 97401

PH: (541)687-2202
Toll free: 888-355-4658
Fax: (541)683-6175
Littleton, Phillip A., CEO, President

HOPE Animal-Assisted Crisis
   Response [12742]
1292 High St., No. 182
Eugene, OR 97401
Toll free: 877-467-3597
Dunbar, Melanie, President

Imagery International [15341]
1574 Coburg Rd., No. 555
Eugene, OR 97401-4802
PH: (541)632-4197
   (514)938-6131
Toll free: 866-494-9985
Garrison, Jenny, RN, President

India Partners [12679]
PO Box 5470
Eugene, OR 97405-0470
PH: (541)683-0696
Toll free: 877-874-6342
Cannon, Susan, Chairperson

International Association for Dance
   Medicine and Science [15728]
Dept. of Dance
1214 University of Oregon
Eugene, OR 97403-1214
PH: (541)465-1763
Fax: (541)465-1763
Chatfield, Steven J., PhD, CFO, Dir.
   of Member Svcs.

International Wildlife Rehabilitation
   Council [4834]
PO Box 3197
Eugene, OR 97403
Toll free: 866-871-1869
Fax: (408)876-6153
Miller, Lynn, President

MindFreedom International [18426]
454 Willamette, Ste. 216
Eugene, OR 97401-2643
PH: (541)345-9106
Toll free: 877-623-7743
Fax: (480)287-8833
Brown, Celia, President

Mobility International USA [11618]
132 E Broadway, Ste. 343
Eugene, OR 97401-3155
PH: (541)343-1284
Fax: (541)343-6812
Sygall, Susan, CEO, Founder

National Association of Tax
   Consultants [5799]
321 W 13th Ave.
Eugene, OR 97401
Millerchip, EA, CFP, Jean, President

Native Forest Council [3910]
PO Box 2190
Eugene, OR 97402
PH: (541)688-2600
Fax: (541)461-2156
Hermach, Timothy G., Director

Santana 20 Class Association
   [22666]
c/o Zoe Gilstrap, 1266 Napa Creek
   Dr.
1266 Napa Creek Dr.
Eugene, OR 97404
Mayer, Lyle, President

Society of North American
   Goldsmiths [21785]
PO Box 1355
Eugene, OR 97440
PH: (541)345-5689
   (813)977-5326
Fax: (541)345-1123
McDonah, Becky, Secretary

Steamboaters [3949]
PO Box 41266
Eugene, OR 97404
Volland, Len, Assoc. Dir.

Students Helping Street Kids
   International [11275]
PO Box 2069
Eugene, OR 97402
PH: (541)505-9738
Toll free: 877-543-7697

Tariro: Hope and Health for
   Zimbabwe's Orphans [11164]
PO Box 50273
Eugene, OR 97405
PH: (541)729-2972
Bandera, Memory, Founder

Golf Collectors Society [21657]
c/o Karen Bednarski, Executive
   Director
PO Box 2386
Florence, OR 97439
PH: (541)991-7313
Fax: (541)997-3871
Bednarski, Karen, Exec. Dir.

International Sports Heritage As-
   sociation [23232]
PO Box 2384
Florence, OR 97439
PH: (541)991-7315
Fax: (541)997-3871
Walls, Rick, Officer

National Judges Association [5397]
222 Gilbert Ave.
Glendale, OR 97442
Fax: (541)832-2647
Hissong, Hon. Candace, Exec. Dir.,
   Treasurer

Foundation of Human Understanding
   [9792]
PO Box 1000
Grants Pass, OR 97528
PH: (541)956-6700
Toll free: 800-877-3227
Fax: (541)956-6705
Masters, Roy, President

Organization for the Advancement of
   Knowledge [3770]
1212 SW 5th St.
Grants Pass, OR 97526-6104
PH: (541)476-5588
Fax: (541)476-1823
Miller, Richard Alan, Consultant

American Association of Naturopathic Midwives [15854]
c/o Jill Edwards
Vibrant Family Medicine & Midwifery
22400 SE Stark St.
Gresham, OR 97030
Ohgushi, Sara, ND, President

Edsel Owner's Club [21375]
c/o Lois Roth
1740 NW 3rd St.
Gresham, OR 97030
PH: (503)492-0878
Fakely, Carolyn, Officer

Healthcare Hospitality Network
   [15328]
PO Box 1439
Gresham, OR 97030
Toll free: 800-542-9730
Glawe, Amber, Treasurer

United States Adult Cystic Fibrosis
   Association [17149]
PO Box 1618
Gresham, OR 97030-0519
PH: (248)349-4553
Honaker, Meranda, VP

Supportive Care Coalition [15283]
18530 NW Cornell Rd., Ste. 101
Hillsboro, OR 97124
PH: (503)216-5376
Picchi, Tina, MA, Exec. Dir.

Athletes for Cancer [13896]
216 Cascade Ave., No. 227
Hood River, OR 97031
Farman, Tonia, Founder

National Cherry Growers and
   Industries Foundation [4241]
2667 Reed Rd.
Hood River, OR 97031
PH: (541)386-5761
Fax: (541)386-3191
Kroupa, Cheryl, Dir. of Mktg.

Wireless Technology Association
   [6267]
PO Box 680
Hood River, OR 97031-0021
PH: (541)490-5140
Fax: (413)410-8447
Kowalski, Gloria, Director

Helping Assist Nepal's Disabled
   [11602]
315 Laurelwood Dr.
Jacksonville, OR 97530
Smith, Brian, Founder, President

Perfins Club [22352]
6500 Upper Applegate Rd.
Jacksonville, OR 97530-9314
Endicott, Steve, President

Euthanasia Research and Guidance
   Organization [11806]
24829 Norris Ln.
Junction City, OR 97448-9559
PH: (541)998-1873
Fax: (541)998-1873
Humphry, Derek, President, Founder

Friends of Kenya Schools and
   Wildlife [11359]
95363 Grimes Rd.
Junction City, OR 97448
PH: (541)998-3724
Meyer, Gwen, Director

Association for Communal Harmony
   in Asia [12433]
4410 Verda Ln. NE
Keizer, OR 97303
Rohila, Pritam, PhD, Exec. Dir.

Sacred Circle [10047]
c/o Teresa Norris, Executive Director
PO Box 21451
Keizer, OR 97303
PH: (971)239-5697
Norris, Teresa, Exec. Dir.

American Institute for Full Employ-
   ment [11754]
2636 Biehn St.
Klamath Falls, OR 97601
PH: (541)273-6731
Toll free: 800-562-7752
Fax: (541)273-6496
Abram, Ted, Exec. Dir.

Academy of Dental Materials
   [14363]
21 Grouse Ter.
Lake Oswego, OR 97035
PH: (503)636-0861
Fax: (503)675-2738
Breschi, Dr. Lorenzo, Secretary

Teens Fighting Hunger [12117]
PMB 410
3 Monroe Pky., Ste. P
Lake Oswego, OR 97035
PH: (971)285-5588
Carlton, J. Steven, Director

National Association of Atomic
   Veterans, Inc. [13244]
130 Cleveland St.
Lebanon, OR 97355-4505
PH: (541)258-7453
Schafer, Fred, Cmdr.

National Wildfire Suppression As-
   sociation [4212]
PO Box 330
Lyons, OR 97358
PH: (541)389-3526
Toll free: 877-676-6972
Fax: (866)854-8186
Dice, Rick, President

Pilgrim Edward Doty Society [20751]
c/o Judy Wilson
PO Box 247
Manzanita, OR 97130
Reiman, Rose, Gov.

Africa Bridge [10835]
PO Box 115
Marylhurst, OR 97036-0115
PH: (503)699-6162
Childs, Barry, Founder

Association of Insolvency and
   Restructuring Advisors [14]
221 W Stewart Ave., Ste. 207
Medford, OR 97501
PH: (541)858-1665
Fax: (541)858-9187
Schwartz, Matthew, Chairman

Elliot Clan Society USA [20862]
c/o Patricia Tennyson Bell, Treasurer
2984 Siskiyou Blvd.
Medford, OR 97504-8161
Elliott, Bill, VP

Fur Commission USA [10626]
PO Box 1532
Medford, OR 97501
PH: (541)595-8568
Fax: (541)566-7489
Platt, Teresa, Exec. Dir.

International Association of Marine
   Investigators [2245]
711 Medford Ctr., No. 419
Medford, OR 97504
PH: (573)691-9569
Skrdla, Lt. Wayne, Mem.

International Post Polio Support
   Organization [16792]
2252 Table Rock Rd., SPC 40
Medford, OR 97501-1426
PH: (541)772-1102
Fax: (541)772-1102
Fiksdal, Shari, Founder, President

Association of Northwest Steelhead-
   ers [22840]
6641 SE Lake Rd.
Milwaukie, OR 97222
PH: (503)653-4176
Domenico, Joe, VP

Jesuit Volunteer Corps Northwest
   [19848]
2780 SE Harrison St.
Milwaukie, OR 97222
PH: (503)335-8202
Fax: (503)249-1118
Haster, Jeanne, Exec. Dir.

Society for Old Ivory and Ohme
   Porcelains [22389]
1650 SE River Ridge Dr.
Milwaukie, OR 97222
Hillman, Alma, Contact

Home Orchard Society [4234]
PO Box 12
Molalla, OR 97038

PH: (503)338-8479

Sarcoid Networking Association
[14612]
12619 S Wilderness Way
Molalla, OR 97038
PH: (503)905-2092
Anderson, Kristi, Exec. Dir.

National Center on Deaf-Blindness
[17731]
345 N Monmouth Ave.
Monmouth, OR 97361
PH: (503)838-8754
Fax: (503)838-8150
Baroncelli, Brenda, Admin. Asst.

International Organization for Victim
Assistance [13260]
32465 NE Old Parrett Mountain Rd.
Newberg, OR 97132
PH: (503)554-1552
Fax: (503)554-1532
Waller, Irvin, President

MamaBaby Haiti [14235]
PO Box 3061
Newberg, OR 97132
Gallardo, Jennifer, President

American Genetic Association [6664]
c/o Anjanette Baker, Manager
2030 SE Marine Science Dr.
Newport, OR 97365
PH: (541)264-5612
Baker, Anjanette, Mgr.

United States Judo Federation
[22967]
PO Box 338
Ontario, OR 97914
PH: (541)889-8753
Fax: (541)889-5836
Asano, Kevin, President

American Part-Blooded Horse
Registry [4319]
PO Box 986
Oregon City, OR 97045
PH: (503)702-6410
Abbett, John, Founder

Caring Ambassadors Hepatitis C
Program [15252]
PO Box 1748
Oregon City, OR 97045
PH: (503)632-9032
Fax: (503)632-9038
Sandt, Lorren, Exec. Dir., Founder

Native Fish Society [4850]
813 7th St., Ste 200A
Oregon City, OR 97045
PH: (503)344-4218
Fortino, Paul, Chmn. of the Bd.

Patton Society [10344]
17010 S Potter Rd.
Oregon City, OR 97045
Province, Charles M., Founder,
President

Demeter Association, Inc. [4151]
PO Box 1390
Philomath, OR 97370
PH: (541)929-7148
Fullmer, Jim, Exec. Dir.

New Horizons International Music
Association [9981]
c/o William Gates, Treasurer
PO Box 127
Philomath, OR 97370
Summers, Nancy, President

North American Heather Society
[22116]
c/o Ella May Wulff, Membership
Chairperson

2299 Wooded Knolls Dr.
Philomath, OR 97370
Wulff, Ella May, Membership Chp.

Affiliated Tribes of Northwest Indians
[19575]
6636 NE Sandy Blvd.
Portland, OR 97213
PH: (503)249-5770
Fax: (503)249-5773
Sharp, Fawn, President

African American Alliance for Home-
ownership [1687]
825 NE 20th Ave.
Portland, OR 97232
PH: (503)595-3517
Fax: (503)595-3519
Roberts, Cheryl L., Exec. Dir.

Alfa Romeo Owners Club [21314]
c/o Barbara Clark, Administrator
PO Box 92155
Portland, OR 97292
PH: (816)459-7462
Banzer, Cindy, President

Alliance for Coffee Excellence [420]
2250 NW 22nd Ave., Ste. 612
Portland, OR 97210
PH: (503)208-2872
Watts, Geoff, Chairman

Alliance for Contraception in Cats
and Dogs [12452]
11145 NW Old Cornelius Pass Rd.
Portland, OR 97231
PH: (503)358-1438
Briggs, Joyce, President

Alliance for a Healthier Generation
[14165]
606 SE 9th Ave.
Portland, OR 97214
Toll free: 888-KID-HLTH
Wechsler, Dr. Howell, CEO

America Walks [17751]
PO Box 10581
Portland, OR 97296
PH: (503)757-8342
    (414)241-3805
Bricker, Scott, Exec. Dir.

American Amateur Press Association
[22390]
1327 NE 73rd Ave.
1327 NE 73rd Ave.
Portland, OR 97213-6112
Snyder, Ivan D., Secretary,
Treasurer

American Iranian Friendship Council
[18512]
PO Box 1235
Portland, OR 97207-1235
PH: (503)523-7368

American Kitefliers Association
[22971]
PO Box 22365
Portland, OR 97269
PH: (609)755-5483
Lutter, John, President

American Mental Health Alliance
[15757]
c/o Michaele P. Dunlap, PsyD,
President
Mentor Professional Corporation
818 NW 17th Ave., No. 11
Portland, OR 97209
PH: (503)227-2027
Dunlap, Michaele, President

American Philatelic Congress
[22300]
c/o Dr. Michael D. Dixon, Second
Vice President

7321 SE Taylor St.
Portland, OR 97215-2262
PH: (415)861-0515
Banchik, Dr. Mark E., President

American Society for Political and
Legal Philosophy [10077]
c/o Andrew Valls, Secretary-
Treasurer, 7749 SE 17th Ave.
7749 SE 17th Ave.
Portland, OR 97202
Satz, Debra, President

American Tinnitus Association
[17238]
522 SW 5th Ave., Ste. 825
Portland, OR 97204
PH: (503)248-9985
Toll free: 800-634-8978
Fax: (503)248-0024
West, Melanie F., CEO, Exec. Dir.

L'Arche USA [11561]
1130 SW Morrison St., Ste. 230
Portland, OR 97205
PH: (503)282-6231
Fax: (503)249-9264
Smith, Luther E., Jr., PhD, VP

Arts and Crafts Society [8845]
5015 SE Hawthorne Blvd., Ste. C
Portland, OR 97215
PH: (503)459-4422

ASHA International [15761]
PO Box 91232
Portland, OR 97291-0004
PH: (971)340-7190
Ramprasad, Gayathri, MBA,
Founder, President

Association for the Advancement of
Gestalt Therapy [16899]
PO Box 42221
Portland, OR 97242
PH: (971)238-2248
Fax: (212)202-3974
Gilligan, Toni, VP

Austin Healey Club USA [21333]
c/o Mark Schneider, President
12465 NW McDaniel Rd.
Portland, OR 97229
PH: (503)643-7208
Schneider, Mark, President

Building Material Dealers Association
[507]
1006 SE Grand Ave., Ste. 301
Portland, OR 97214-2323
PH: (503)208-3763
Toll free: 888-960-6329
Fax: (971)255-0790
Matras, Gwyneth, Exec. Dir.

Child Aid [15180]
917 SW Oak St., Ste. 208
Portland, OR 97205
PH: (503)223-3008
Fax: (503)223-4017
Carroll, Richard, Treasurer

Church and Synagogue Library As-
sociation [9699]
10157 SW Barbur Blvd., No. 102C
Portland, OR 97219
PH: (503)244-6919
Toll free: 800-542-2752
Fax: (503)977-3734
Janzen, Judith, Administrator

Climate Trust [4543]
65 SW Yamhill St., Ste. 400
Portland, OR 97204
PH: (503)238-1915
Beane, Laura, Chairman

Coalition of Communities of Color
[12030]
5135 NE Columbia Blvd.
Portland, OR 97218

PH: (503)288-8177
Meier, Julia, Director

Community Acupuncture Network
[13503]
Working Class Acupuncture
3526 NE 57th Ave.
Portland, OR 97213
PH: (503)335-9440

The Culinary Trust [7692]
PO Box 5485
Portland, OR 97228-5485
Flinn, Kathleen, Chairperson

Death with Dignity National Center
[17889]
520 SW 6th Ave., Ste. 1220
Portland, OR 97204-1510
PH: (503)228-4415
Sandeen, Peg, Exec. Dir.

Digital Living Network Alliance
[1041]
PO Box 8637
Portland, OR 97286
Parikh, Nidhish, Director

Economics for Equity and the
Environment Network [4114]
Ecotrust
721 NW 9th Ave., Ste. 200
Portland, OR 97209
PH: (503)467-0811
Sheeran, Kristen A., PhD, Exec. Dir.,
Founder

The Education Conservancy [7447]
c/o Lloyd Thacker, Executive Direc-
tor
805 SW Broadway, Ste. 1600
Portland, OR 97205
PH: (503)290-0083
Fax: (503)973-5252
Thacker, Lloyd, Exec. Dir.

Educational Research Associates
[7765]
PO Box 8795
Portland, OR 97207-8795
PH: (503)228-6345
Fax: (810)885-5811

Equality Federation [18301]
818 SW 3rd Ave., No. 141
Portland, OR 97204-2405
PH: (415)252-0510
Isaacs, Rebecca, Exec. Dir.

Exotic Bird Rescue [10620]
PO Box 14863
Portland, OR 97293
PH: (541)461-4333
Shaw, Jarrine, Chmn. of the Bd.

Farm Forward [10622]
PO Box 4120
Portland, OR 97208
Toll free: 877-313-3276
Fax: (877)313-3276
Mackey, John, Chairman

Federation of Naturopathic Medicine
Regulatory Authorities [15860]
9220 SW Barbur Blvd., Ste.119, No.
321
Portland, OR 97219
PH: (503)244-7189
Walsh, Anne, President

Fetal Alcohol Syndrome Consulta-
tion, Education and Training
Services [17311]
PO Box 69242
Portland, OR 97239
PH: (503)621-1271
Fax: (503)621-1271
Temko, Wendy, Admin. Ofc.

Finnish-American Historical Society
of the West **[9322]**
PO Box 5522
Portland, OR 97228-5522
Tolonen, Andrea, President

Focus the Nation **[18191]**
240 N Broadway, Ste. 212
Portland, OR 97227-1881
PH: (503)224-9440
Brennan, Garett, Bd. Member

Food Alliance **[6645]**
PO Box 86457
Portland, OR 97286
PH: (503)267-4667
Buck, Matthew, Director

Foundation for the Preservation of
the Mahayana Tradition **[19778]**
1632 SE 11th Ave.
Portland, OR 97214-4702
PH: (503)808-1588
Toll free: 866-241-9886
Fax: (503)232-0557
Williams, George, Dir. of Operations

Free Geek **[12580]**
1731 SE 10th Ave.
Portland, OR 97214
PH: (503)232-9350
Lloyd, Larry, Treasurer

Friends of the Children **[10983]**
44 NE Morris
Portland, OR 97212
PH: (503)281-6633
Campbell, Duncan, Founder

Friends of Malawi **[9208]**
c/o Lance Cole, Treasurer
7940 SW 11th Ave.
Portland, OR 97219
Cole, Lance, Treasurer

Friends of Sabeel - North America
[18787]
PO Box 9186
Portland, OR 97207
PH: (503)653-6625
Toll, Rev. Richard K., Trustee,
Secretary

Global ADE **[11469]**
8094 N Burlington Ave.
Portland, OR 97203
PH: (425)346-0921
King, Kenny, CEO

Global Envision **[18284]**
c/o Mercy Corps
45 SW Ankeny St.
Portland, OR 97204
Keny-Guyer, Neal, CEO

Global Service Corps **[13293]**
1306 NW Hoyt St., Ste. 310
Portland, OR 97209
PH: (503)954-1659
Lathrop, Rick, Exec. Dir., Founder

GLOBIO **[7890]**
5544 N Burrage Ave.
Portland, OR 97217
PH: (503)367-2874
Crisco, J. Keith, Chmn. of the Bd.

Green Building Initiative **[533]**
PO Box 80010
Portland, OR 97280
PH: (503)274-0448
Toll free: 877-424-4241
Thomas, Jay, Chmn. of the Bd.

Green Electronics Council **[6421]**
227 SW Pine St., Ste. 300
Portland, OR 97204
PH: (503)279-9383
Fax: (503)279-9381
Keith, Alan, Chairman

Green Empowerment **[3781]**
140 SW Yamhill St.
Portland, OR 97204
PH: (503)284-5774
Fax: (503)460-0450
Royce, Michael, Founder

Health Bridges International **[15466]**
PO Box 8813
Portland, OR 97207
PH: (608)354-7567
Centrone, Dr. Wayne, President

HomePlug Powerline Alliance, Inc.
[1049]
10260 SW Greenburg Rd., Ste. 400
Portland, OR 97223
PH: (503)766-2516
Fax: (503)766-2516
Ranck, Rob, President

A Hope for Autism Foundation
[13769]
2900 SW Peaceful Ln.
Portland, OR 97239
PH: (503)516-9085
Sobotka-Soles, Robbin, President,
Exec. Dir.

Information Systems Security As-
sociation **[1788]**
9220 SW Barbur Blvd., Ste. 119-333
Portland, OR 97219
PH: (206)388-4584
Toll free: 866-349-5818
Fax: (206)299-3366
Richard, Kevin, President

Institute for Traditional Medicine and
Preventive Health Care **[13630]**
2017 SE Hawthorne Blvd.
Portland, OR 97214
PH: (503)233-4907
Fax: (503)233-1017
Dharmananda, Subhuti, PhD, Direc-
tor

International Center for Traditional
Childbearing **[14233]**
5257 NE Martin Luther King Jr.
Blvd., Ste. 202-D
Portland, OR 97211
PH: (503)460-9324
Fax: (503)972-0365

International Federation of Psoriasis
Associations **[14496]**
6600 SW 92nd, Ste. 300
Portland, OR 97223
PH: (503)244-7404
Toll free: 800-723-9166
Fax: (503)245-0626
Ettarp, Lars, President

International Steamboat Society
[21553]
10325 NE Hoyt St.
Portland, OR 97220-4016

Jamii Moja **[11390]**
10110 NW Ash St.
Portland, OR 97229
Andersen, Anne, Bd. Member

Kasese Wildlife Conservation Aware-
ness Organization **[4836]**
PO Box 10664
Portland, OR 97296
Mukobi, Asaba, President

Kids Need Both Parents **[18197]**
PO Box 6481
Portland, OR 97228-6481
PH: (503)727-3686
(516)942-2020
Whinston, James P., Contact

Kiger Mesteno Association **[4374]**
11124 NE Halsey St., Ste. 591
Portland, OR 97220
Sink, Kevin, President

Men's Resource Center **[12010]**
12 SE 14th Ave.
Portland, OR 97214-1404
PH: (503)235-3433
Fax: (503)235-4762
Lee, Paul, Counselor

Mercy Corps **[18494]**
45 SW Ankeny St.
Portland, OR 97204
PH: (503)896-5000
Toll free: 800-292-3355
Keny-Guyer, Neal, CEO

Mothers Against Misuse and Abuse
[17316]
5217 SE 28th Ave.
Portland, OR 97202
PH: (503)233-4202
Toll free: 866-559-3369
Burbank, Sandee, Exec. Dir.

National Animal Interest Alliance
[10663]
PO Box 66579
Portland, OR 97290
PH: (503)761-8962
(503)227-8450
Greer, Dr. Marty, DVM, JD, Chmn. of
the Bd.

National Association of Consumer
Shows **[1177]**
147 SE 102nd Ave.
Portland, OR 97216-2703
PH: (503)253-0832
Toll free: 800-728-6227
Fax: (503)253-9172
Adams, Mark, President

National Association of Professional
Process Servers **[5685]**
PO Box 4547
Portland, OR 97208-4547
PH: (503)222-4180
Toll free: 800-477-8211
Fax: (503)222-3950
Yellon, Lawrence, VP

National Conference of Women's
Bar Associations **[5036]**
PO Box 82366
Portland, OR 97282
PH: (503)775-4396
(816)360-4116
Rynerson, Diane, Exec. Dir.

National Indian Child Welfare As-
sociation **[19583]**
5100 SW Macadam Ave., Ste. 300
Portland, OR 97239
PH: (503)222-4044
Fax: (503)222-4007
Cross, Mr. Terry, Advisor

National Psoriasis Foundation USA
[14506]
6600 SW 92nd Ave., Ste. 300
Portland, OR 97223-7195
PH: (503)244-7404
Toll free: 800-723-9166
Fax: (503)245-0626
Beranek, Randy, President, CEO

National Stereoscopic Association
[10142]
PO Box 86708
Portland, OR 97286
PH: (503)771-4440
Kaufman, Mr. Lawrence, Chairman

Naturopathic Medical Student As-
sociation **[15862]**
049 SW Porter St.
Portland, OR 97201
PH: (503)334-4153
Mehrmann, Craig S., President

NETWORK **[7794]**
23 NE Morgan St.
Portland, OR 97211
Toll free: 800-877-5400
Fax: (503)336-1014
Crandall, Dr. David, President

New Buildings Institute **[5070]**
623 SW Oak St.
Portland, OR 97205
PH: (503)761-7339
Fax: (503)968-6160
Goldstein, David B., PhD, President

North American Snowsports Journal-
ists Association **[2712]**
11728 SE Madison St.
Portland, OR 97216
PH: (503)255-3771
Fax: (503)255-3771
Griff, Martin, President

Northwest Energy Efficiency Alliance
[4028]
421 SW 6th Ave., Ste. 600
Portland, OR 97204
PH: (503)688-5400
Toll free: 800-411-0834
Fax: (503)688-5447
Stolarski, Bob, Chmn. of the Bd.

Oncology Youth Connection **[14036]**
205 SE Spokane St., Ste. 300-64
Portland, OR 97202
PH: (503)869-7632
Roesler, Grant, Founder, Prog. Dir.

Open Arms International **[12709]**
PO Box 343
Portland, OR 97207
PH: (503)296-9989
Fax: (503)297-0193
Havens, Scott, Exec. Dir.

Oregon Horsemen's Benevolent and
Protective Association **[22927]**
10350 N Vancouver Way, No. 351
Portland, OR 97217
PH: (503)285-4941
Fax: (503)285-4942
Funk, Debbie, VP

Pacific Lumber Exporters Associa-
tion **[1416]**
720 NE Flanders St., Ste. 207
Portland, OR 97232
PH: (503)701-6510
Fax: (503)238-2653
Setzer, Chip, VP

Pacific Printing Industries Associa-
tion **[1545]**
6825 SW Sandburg St.
Portland, OR 97223
PH: (503)221-3944
Toll free: 877-762-7742
Fax: (503)221-5691
Van Sant, Ms. Jules, Exec. Dir.

Pan African Sanctuary Alliance
[4866]
1405 NE 52nd Ave.
Portland, OR 97213
PH: (971)712-8360
Sherman, Julie, Exec. Dir.

Pan American Taekwondo Union
[23010]
c/o Rick W. Shin, Secretary General
8001 SE Powell Blvd., Ste. O
Portland, OR 97206
PH: (503)970-8928
Choi, Mr. Ji Ho, President

Peace Corps Iran Association
[18849]
4101 SW Hillsdale Ave.
Portland, OR 97239
Yale, Carolyn, President

Postpartum Support International
[12425]
6706 SW 54th Ave.
Portland, OR 97219
PH: (503)894-9453
Toll free: 800-944-4773
Fax: (503)894-9452
Davis, Wendy, PhD, Exec. Dir.

Society of Bead Researchers [5948]
PO Box 13719
Portland, OR 97213
PH: (503)655-3078
Scherer, Alice, Secretary, Treasurer

The Society for German Idealism
[9341]
c/o J.M. Fritzman
Dept. of Philosophy
Lewis and Clark College
615 SW Palatine Hill Rd.
Portland, OR 97219-7879
PH: (503)768-7477
Fritzman, J. M., Contact

Softwood Export Council [1419]
720 NE Flanders, Ste. 207
Portland, OR 97232
PH: (503)620-5946
Foster, Dacia, Acct. Mgr.

Sons and Daughters of Oregon
Pioneers [21088]
PO Box 6685
Portland, OR 97228
Miller, Merle, Contact

Thanhouser Company Film
Preservation Inc. [9315]
2335 NE 41st Ave.
Portland, OR 97212
Thanhouser, Ned, President

United States PostgreSQL Associa-
tion [6289]
9220 SW Barbur Blvd., Ste. 119-230
Portland, OR 97219
PH: (503)778-5428
Fax: (503)276-5813
Brewer, Michael, Director

Vestibular Disorders Association
[16543]
5018 NE 15th Ave.
Portland, OR 97211
Toll free: 800-837-8428
Fax: (503)229-8064
Ryan, Cynthia, MBA, Exec. Dir.

Veterinary Ventures [10712]
c/o Amber Holland, Treasurer
PO Box 10553
Portland, OR 97296
Sutton, Dr. Joi, Founder

Western Forestry and Conservation
Association [4223]
4033 SW Canyon Rd.
Portland, OR 97221
PH: (503)226-4562
Zabel, Richard A., Exec. Dir.

Women in Balance Institute [17767]
049 SW Porter St.
Portland, OR 97201-4848
PH: (503)552-1527
Murray, Jane, MD, Chairperson

World Food Travel Association [704]
4110 SE Hawthorne Blvd., Ste. 440
Portland, OR 97214
PH: (503)213-3700
Wolf, Erik, Founder, Exec. Dir.

World Forest Institute [4224]
World Forestry Ctr.
4033 SW Canyon Rd.
Portland, OR 97221

PH: (503)228-1367
    (503)488-2130
Vines, Eric, Exec. Dir.

World Forestry Center [4225]
4033 SW Canyon Rd.
Portland, OR 97221
PH: (503)228-1367
    (503)488-2111
Fax: (503)228-4608
Hampton, David, Chairman

World Spark [11192]
PO Box 83479
Portland, OR 97206-2378
PH: (503)245-7899
Fax: (503)245-4639
Maslowsky, Michael, President,
   Founder

Xerces Society [4922]
628 NE Broadway, Ste. 200
Portland, OR 97232
PH: (503)232-6639
Toll free: 855-232-6639
Fax: (503)233-6794
Black, Scott Hoffman, Exec. Dir.

Zero Waste International Alliance
[4748]
227 SW Pine St., No. 220
Portland, OR 97204
PH: (503)279-9383

National Silver Rabbit Club [4609]
c/o Patty Beamer, Secretary/
   Treasurer
1239 NW Dogwood Ave.
Redmond, OR 97756
PH: (541)815-8160
Hall, Jann, President

Wood I-Joist Manufacturers Associa-
tion [1447]
c/o Dave Anderson, Member
Roseburg Forest Products
PO Box 1088
Roseburg, OR 97470
Stefani, Jeff, Secretary, Treasurer

Companion Animal Parasite Council
[17643]
6331 Walina Ct. SE
Salem, OR 97317
Carpenter, Christopher, DVM, MBA,
   Exec. Dir.

Cork Forest Conservation Alliance
[3843]
565 Oxford St. SE
Salem, OR 97302-3001
PH: (503)931-9690
Spencer, Patrick, Exec. Dir.

Hollow Earth Research Society
[12001]
c/o Danny Weiss
1529 Kenard St. NW
Salem, OR 97304
PH: (503)990-6969
Weiss, Danny L., Director, CEO

International Professional Groomers
[2544]
6475 Wallace Rd. NW
Salem, OR 97304
PH: (503)551-2397
Easton, Linda, Exec. Dir.

Mold Help Organization [14947]
1255 Broadway St. NE, Ste. 410
Salem, OR 97301
PH: (503)763-0808
Lillard, Susan, Contact

National Association of the Sixth
Infantry Division [20722]
c/o Thomas E. Price
317 Court St. NE, Ste. 203

Salem, OR 97301
PH: (503)363-7334
Fax: (503)581-2260
Kessen, Clifford, President

National Fibromyalgia Research As-
sociation [15967]
PO Box 500
Salem, OR 97308
PH: (503)315-7257
Fax: (503)315-7205
Scott, Jack, Founder

National Home Education Research
Institute [7999]
PO Box 13939
Salem, OR 97309
PH: (503)364-1490
Fax: (503)364-2827
Ray, Brian D., PhD, Founder

National Lamb Feeders Association
[4673]
1270 Chemeketa St. NE
Salem, OR 97301-4145
PH: (503)370-7024
Fax: (503)585-1921
Harlan, Bob, President

Natural Doctors International [15861]
9240 Alaska St. SE
Salem, OR 97317
Parker, Dr. Tabatha, Exec. Dir.,
   Founder

North American Association of
Educational Negotiators [23412]
PO Box 1068
Salem, OR 97308
PH: (519)503-0098
Petrarca, Justin, President

Pacific Northwest Christmas Tree
Association [4734]
PO Box 3366
Salem, OR 97302
PH: (503)364-2942
Fax: (503)581-6819
Ramsby, Mike, Researcher

Tall Bearded Iris Society [22129]
4728 Jade St., NE
Salem, OR 97305-3138
PH: (806)792-1878
Stout, Hugh, President

United Sidecar Association [22233]
c/o Steve Woodward
PO Box 4301
Salem, OR 97302-8301
PH: (612)759-4666
Olme, Al, President

Association of Support Professionals
[3070]
38954 Proctor Blvd., Ste. 396
Sandy, OR 97055
PH: (503)668-9004
Hahn, Al, Exec. Dir.

Parents Via Egg Donation Organiza-
tion [14761]
PO Box 597
Scappoose, OR
PH: (503)987-1433
Gatlin, Marna, Founder, CEO

National Retriever Club [22818]
c/o Gary Zellner, President
39300 Montgomery Dr.
Scio, OR 97374
PH: (503)394-2139
Zellner, Gary, President

FosterClub [13443]
753 1st Ave.
Seaside, OR 97138
PH: (503)717-1552
Fax: (503)717-1702
Bodner, Celeste, CEO, Founder

Sea Turtles Forever [4886]
PO Box 845
Seaside, OR 97138
PH: (503)739-1446
Ward, Marc W., President

International Desert Lynx Cat As-
sociation [3680]
PO Box 511
Selma, OR 97538
Magrino, Arlene, President

Swedish Warmblood Association of
North America [4414]
24875 SW Middleton Rd.
Sherwood, OR 97140
PH: (575)835-1318
Fax: (575)835-1321
Wadeborn, Ulf, President

Ninos del Lago [11100]
PO Box 1005
Silverton, OR 97381
Cervantes, Arlaine, Founder, Exec.
   Dir.

A Family for Every Child [10968]
880 Beltline Rd.
Springfield, OR 97477
PH: (541)343-2856
Toll free: 877-343-2856
Fax: (541)343-2866
Obie-Barrett, Christy, Exec. Dir.

Mooncircles [20609]
c/o Dana Gerhardt, MA
397 Arnos St.
Talent, OR 97540
Gerhardt, Dana, M.A., Contact

Breast Friends [13910]
14050 SW Pacific Hwy., Ste. 201
Tigard, OR 97224
Toll free: 888-386-8048
Fax: (866)734-3762
Olson, Becky, Founder, CEO

Alagille Syndrome Alliance [14803]
10500 SW Starr Dr.
Tualatin, OR 97062-8411
PH: (503)885-0455
Hahn, Cindy L., Exec. Dir.

Autism Service Dogs of America
[13754]
20340 SW Boones Ferry Rd.
Tualatin, OR 97062
PH: (503)488-5983
Taylor, Priscilla, Founder

HumaniNet [12676]
4068 Ridge Ct.
West Linn, OR 97068-8285
PH: (503)957-2960
Swanson, Gregg, Exec. Dir., Chmn.
   of the Bd.

Society for Inherited Metabolic
Disorders [15835]
c/o Leslie Lublink, Administrator
18265 Lower Midhill Dr.
West Linn, OR 97068
PH: (503)636-9228
Fax: (503)210-1511
Lublink, Leslie, Administrator

Transload Distribution Association of
North America [3106]
1980 Willamette Falls Dr., No. 120-
   282
West Linn, OR 97068
PH: (503)656-4282
Fax: (888)347-9933
Braithwaite, Steve, President

American Holsteiner Horse Association [4311]
25195 SW Parkway Ave., Ste. 201
Wilsonville, OR 97070

PH: (503)570-7779
Fax: (503)570-7781
McElvain, Guy, VPP

PENNSYLVANIA

Associates for Biblical Research
[19749]
PO Box 144
Akron, PA 17501
PH: (717)859-3443
Toll free: 800-430-0008
Fax: (717)859-3393
Livingston, Dr. David, Founder

Mennonite Central Committee
[20327]
21 S 12th St.
Akron, PA 17501-0500
PH: (717)859-1151
Toll free: 888-563-4676
Byler, J. Ron, Exec. Dir.

Church Army USA [20096]
380 Franklin Ave.
Aliquippa, PA 15001
PH: (724)375-5659
Carlile, Rev. Wilson, Founder

Community of Celebration [19969]
809 Franklin Ave.
Aliquippa, PA 15001-3302
PH: (724)375-1510
Fax: (724)375-1138

Fellowship International Mission
[20416]
555 S 24th St.
Allentown, PA 18104-6666
PH: (610)435-9099
Toll free: 888-346-9099
Fax: (610)435-2641
Wilt, Mr. Steve, Dir. Gen.

National Tattoo Association, Inc.
[3199]
485 Business Park Ln.
Allentown, PA 18109-9120
PH: (610)433-7261
Makofske, Florence, Treasurer

Quality Bakers of America Coopera-
tive [375]
1275 Glenlivet Dr., Ste. 100
Allentown, PA 18106-3107
PH: (203)531-7100
Fax: (203)531-1406
Trapp, Norm, Contact

Ukrainian American Veterans
[21142]
3535 Fox Run Dr.
Allentown, PA 18103
Hron, Ihor, Cmdr.

Youth Education in the Arts [9011]
601 W Hamilton St.
Allentown, PA 18101
PH: (610)821-0345
Fax: (610)821-1451
Hopkins, George, CEO, Exec. Dir.

Association for the Rhetoric of Science and Technology [10197]
c/o William J. White, Treasurer
3000 Ivyside Pk.
Altoona, PA 16601
White, Bill, Treasurer

International Committee for the
Defense of the Breton Language,
US Branch [9653]
c/o Lois Kuter, Secretary
605 Montgomery Rd.
Ambler, PA 19002
PH: (215)886-6361
Kuter, Lois, Editor, Secretary,
Treasurer

Society of the First Infantry Division
[20725]
c/o Jen Sanford
PO Box 607
Ambler, PA 19002
PH: (215)654-1969
Fax: (215)654-0392
Wallace, Darrell, Exec. Dir.,
Secretary, Treasurer

Three Stooges Fan Club [24011]
904 Sheble Ln.
Ambler, PA 19002
PH: (267)468-0810
Lassin, Gary, Curator

Brotherhood of Saint Andrew
[20095]
PO Box 632
Ambridge, PA 15003
PH: (724)266-5810
Hanstein, Jack, Sr. VP

New Wineskins Missionary Network
[20447]
PO Box 278
Ambridge, PA 15003
PH: (724)266-2810
Steinmiller, Sharon, Director

Society of Anglican Missionaries and
Senders [20464]
PO Box 399
Ambridge, PA 15003
PH: (724)266-0669
Fax: (724)266-5681
Wicker, Stewart, Director, President

International Digital Media and Arts
Association [6836]
c/o Digital Communications
101 N College Ave.
Annville, PA 17003
PH: (423)794-9996
Olin, Joseph, Exec. Dir.

Association for Comprehensive
Energy Psychology [16902]
233 E Lancaster Ave., Ste. 104
Ardmore, PA 19003
PH: (619)861-2237
Fax: (484)418-1019
Gallo, Fred P., PhD, DCEP,
President

Global Exploration for Educators
Organization [8636]
2945 Morris Rd.
Ardmore, PA 19003
Toll free: 877-600-0105
Weisz, Jesse, Exec. Dir.

American Board of Wound Medicine
and Surgery [15705]
PO Box 133
Aspers, PA 17304
PH: (717)677-0165
Fax: (717)398-0396
Simman, Richard, MD, President,
Chairman

Delta Epsilon Sigma [23779]
c/o Dr. Claudia Marie Kovach,
Secretary-Treasurer
1 Neumann Dr.
Aston, PA 19014-1298
Lorentz, Dr. Christopher, President

American Mushroom Institute [4226]
1284 Gap Newport Pke.
Avondale, PA 19311
PH: (610)268-7483
Fax: (610)268-8015
Carroll, David, Contact

Gravely Tractor Club of America
[22454]
PO Box 194
Avondale, PA 19311
Howland, Jim, Director

American Board of Ophthalmology
[16365]
111 Presidential Blvd., Ste. 241
Bala Cynwyd, PA 19004-1075
PH: (610)664-1175
Fax: (610)664-6503
Clarkson, John G., MD, Exec. Dir.,
CEO

Catholic Medical Association [16746]
29 Bala Ave., Ste. 205
Bala Cynwyd, PA 19004-3206
PH: (484)270-8002
Fax: (866)666-2319
Brehany, John, PhD, Contact

Hysterectomy Educational
Resources and Services Founda-
tion [16286]
422 Bryn Mawr Ave.
Bala Cynwyd, PA 19004
PH: (610)667-7757
Toll free: 888-750-4377
Fax: (610)667-8096
Coffey, Nora W., President

Scholars for Peace in the Middle
East [18693]
PO Box 2241
Bala Cynwyd, PA 19004
Schumann, Ralf R., VP

Greek Catholic Union of the U.S.A.
[19454]
5400 Tuscarawas Rd.
Beaver, PA 15009
PH: (800)722-4428
Fax: (724)495-3421
Juba, George N., CEO, President

American Association of Daily
Money Managers [1272]
174 Crestview Dr.
Bellefonte, PA 16823-8516
Toll free: 877-326-5991
Fax: (814)355-2452
Conklin, Pete, Director

American Philatelic Research Library
[22301]
100 Match Factory Pl.
Bellefonte, PA 16823-1367
PH: (814)933-3803
Fax: (814)933-6128
Brody, Roger, President

American Philatelic Society [22302]
100 Match Factory Pl.
Bellefonte, PA 16823
PH: (814)933-3803
Fax: (814)933-6128
Walker, W. Danforth, Officer

American Society for Plasticulture
[3545]
174 Crestview Dr.
Bellefonte, PA 16823
PH: (814)357-9198
Fax: (814)355-2452

Cooperative Communicators As-
sociation [763]
174 Crestview Dr.
Bellefonte, PA 16823-8516
Toll free: 877-326-5994
Fax: (814)355-2452
Simmons, Tammy, President

Independent Turf and Ornamental
Distributors Association [2069]
174 Crestview Dr.
Bellefonte, PA 16823-8516
PH: (814)357-9197
Fax: (814)355-2452
Hart, William T., President

International Plant Propagators
Society [4435]
174 Crestview Dr.
Bellefonte, PA 16823
Fax: (814)355-2467
Jones, Alan, Chmn. of the Bd.

National Board of Podiatric Medical
Examiners [16790]
PO Box 510
Bellefonte, PA 16823
PH: (814)357-0487
Park, Philip I., Exec. Dir.

National Guardianship Association,
Inc. [1560]
174 Crestview Dr.
Bellefonte, PA 16823
Toll free: 877-326-5992
Fax: (814)355-2452
Ott, Denise, Bus. Mgr.

Young Stamp Collectors of America
[22382]
100 Match Factory Pl.
Bellefonte, PA 16823-1367
PH: (814)933-3803
Fax: (814)933-6128
Reinhard, Stephen, President

Another Chance 4 Horses [10587]
166 Station Rd.
Bernville, PA 19506
PH: (610)488-5647
Fax: (610)488-5648
Sheidy, Ricky, Founder, President

Dual Laminate Fabrication Associa-
tion [2623]
PO Box 582
Berwyn, PA 19312-0582
PH: (609)636-0826
Fax: (610)695-8446
Blazejewski, Arek, President

International Society of Hypnosis
[15364]
PO Box 602
Berwyn, PA 19312
Toll free: 800-550-4741
Linden, Julie H., PhD, Bd. Member

Scriabin Society of America [10002]
353 Lindsey Dr.
Berwyn, PA 19312
Rieber, Edith Finton, Director,
President

American Federation of New
Zealand Rabbit Breeders [4588]
c/o Bruce Himmelberger, Director,
Box 173
PO Box 173
Bethel, PA 19507
PH: (717)865-5803
Cardinal, David, President

Archconfraternity of the Holy Ghost
[19794]
6230 Brush Run Rd.
Bethel Park, PA 15102-2214
PH: (412)831-0302
Promis, Fr. Christopher P., Director

Beyond Labels and Limitations
[14810]
3391 Church Rd.
Bethlehem, PA 18015

Eastern Amputee Golf Association
[22878]
2015 Amherst Dr.
Bethlehem, PA 18015-5606
PH: (610)867-9295
Fax: (610)867-9295
Buck, Bob, Exec. Dir.

Electronic Commerce Code Manage-
ment Association [998]
2980 Linden St., Ste. E2
Bethlehem, PA 18017-3283
PH: (610)861-5990
Fax: (610)625-4657
Benson, Peter, Chief Tech. Ofc.,
Exec. Dir.

Emulsion Polymers Institute **[6199]**
Lehigh University
111 Research Dr.
Bethlehem, PA 18015
PH: (610)758-3602
Fax: (610)758-5880
Daniels, Dr. Eric S., Exec. Dir.

International Association for Bridge
Maintenance and Safety **[6157]**
c/o Professor Dan M. Frangopol,
President
Lehigh University
ATLSS Research Ctr.
117 ATLSS Dr.
Bethlehem, PA 18015-4729
PH: (610)758-6103
Fax: (610)758-5902
Frangopol, Prof. Dan M., President

Metal Buildings Institute **[545]**
PO Box 4308
Bethlehem, PA 18018
PH: (484)239-3337
Smith, Gary, President

National Association of Colleges and
Employers **[8438]**
62 Highland Ave.
Bethlehem, PA 18017-9481
PH: (610)868-1421
Mackes, Marilyn, Exec. Dir.

Professional Manufacturing
Confectioners Association **[1369]**
2980 Linden St., Ste. E3
Bethlehem, PA 18017
PH: (610)625-4655
Fax: (610)625-4657
Marcanello, Steve, Director

U.S. Albacore Association **[22679]**
c/o Kay Marsh, Membership
Secretary
1031 Graham St.
Bethlehem, PA 18015-2520
Heinsdorf, Michael, President

International Veterinary Ultrasound
Society **[17653]**
PO Box 524
Birdsboro, PA 19508
Lindquist, Eric, President

Crosley Automobile Club **[21364]**
307 Schaeffer Rd.
Blandon, PA 19510
Anspach, Dave, President

Association for Positive Behavior
Support **[6035]**
PO Box 328
Bloomsburg, PA 17815
PH: (570)441-5418
Knoster, Tim, Exec. Dir.

American Society for Automation in
Pharmacy **[2552]**
492 Norristown Rd., Ste. 160
Blue Bell, PA 19422
PH: (610)825-7783
Fax: (610)825-7641
Lockwood, Bill, Exec. Dir.

Independent Board for Presbyterian
Foreign Missions **[20522]**
PO Box 1346
Blue Bell, PA 19422-0435
PH: (610)279-0952
Fax: (610)279-0954
Gsell, Brad, President

National Organization for the Profes-
sional Advancement of Black
Chemists and Chemical Engineers
[6207]
PO Box 255
Blue Bell, PA 19422
Toll free: 866-599-0253
Hampton, Talitha, President

National Coalition for Dialogue and
Deliberation **[8482]**
PO Box 150
Boiling Springs, PA 17007
PH: (717)243-5144
Heierbacher, Sandy, Director,
Founder

Antique Truck Club of America
[22473]
85 S Walnut St.
Boyertown, PA 19512
PH: (610)367-2567
Fax: (610)367-9712
Chase, Fred, President

United Nations Philatelists Inc.
[22374]
c/o Blanton Clement, Jr., Secretary
PO Box 146
Boyertown, PA 19512-0146
Fillion, Larry, President

Case Collectors Club **[22174]**
c/o WR Case & Sons Cutlery
50 Owens Way
Bradford, PA 16701-3749
Toll free: 800-523-6350
Fax: (814)368-1736

Alternative Aquaculture Association
[3637]
630 Independent Rd.
Breinigsville, PA 18031
PH: (610)398-1062
    (610)393-5918
Fax: (610)395-8202

Collegiate Water Polo Association
[23351]
129 W 4th St.
Bridgeport, PA 19405
PH: (610)277-6787
Fax: (610)277-7382
Sharadin, Daniel, Commissioner

United States Sign Council **[114]**
211 Radcliffe St.
Bristol, PA 19007-5017
PH: (215)785-1922
Fax: (215)788-8395
Charles, Earl, President

International Glove Association
[1738]
PO Box 146
Brookville, PA 15825
PH: (814)328-5208
Fax: (814)328-2308
O'Leary, Kim, President

Contemporary Record Society
[9894]
724 Winchester Rd.
Broomall, PA 19008
PH: (610)205-9897
Fax: (707)549-5920
Shusterman, Jack, Contact

International Association of Golf
Administrators **[22883]**
1974 Sproul Rd., Ste. 400
Broomall, PA 19008-9998
PH: (610)687-2340
Fax: (610)687-2082
Heaney, Kevin, President

North American Araucanian Royalist
Society **[9425]**
PO Box 211
Bryn Athyn, PA 19009-0211
Morrison, Daniel, Gen. Sec.

Missionary Sisters of the Holy
Rosary **[19864]**
Holy Rosary Convent
741 Polo Rd.
Bryn Mawr, PA 19010

PH: (610)520-1974
Shanahan, Bishop Joseph, Founder

National Association for Adults with
Special Learning Needs **[7718]**
PO Box 716
Bryn Mawr, PA 19010
Cooper, Richard, Co-Pres.

United for Libraries **[9731]**
859 W Lancaster Ave., Unit 2-1
Bryn Mawr, PA 19010
PH: (312)280-2161
Toll free: 800-545-2433
Fax: (484)383-3407
Nawalinski, Beth, Dep. Dir.

American Poultry Association **[4563]**
PO Box 306
Burgettstown, PA 15021-0306
PH: (724)729-3459
Fax: (724)729-1003
Brush, Sam, Director

Society of the Fifth Division **[21031]**
c/o Wayne Cumer, President
150 Cumer Ln.
Burgettstown, PA 15021
PH: (724)947-3859
Robertson, Robb, President

Abrasive Engineering Society **[6523]**
144 Moore Rd.
Butler, PA 16001
PH: (724)282-6210
Fax: (724)234-2376

Abrasives Engineering Society
[6524]
144 Moore Rd.
Butler, PA 16001
PH: (724)282-6210
Fax: (724)234-2376

Jewelry Industry Distributors As-
sociation **[2055]**
c/o Diehl Accounting and Financial
Services, P.C.
703 Old Route 422 W
Butler, PA 16001
PH: (203)254-4492
Livesay, Richard, Treasurer

North American Society for Sport
Management **[8433]**
135 Winterwood Dr.
Butler, PA 16001
PH: (724)482-6277
Ammon, Dr. Robin, Jr., Office Mgr.

International Association for
Computer Information Systems
[6251]
c/o Gary DeLorenzo, Vice President
California University of Pennsylvania
250 University Ave.
California, PA 15419-1341
Behling, Susan Haugen, Treasurer

Birth Without Boundaries **[14222]**
8 Riddle Rd.
Camp Hill, PA 17011
PH: (717)654-9810
Gaby, Elizabeth, ND, V. Ch.

International Lawyers in Alcoholics
Anonymous **[13148]**
c/o Laurie Besden, Treasurer
55 Central Blvd.
Camp Hill, PA 17011
Toll free: 800-335-2572
Heiting, James O., Chairman

Citizens Coal Council **[4023]**
125 W Pike St., Ste. B
Canonsburg, PA 15317
PH: (724)338-4629
Erickson, Aimee, Exec. Dir.

Association of Reformed Baptist
Churches of America **[19717]**
401 E Louther St., Ste. 303
Carlisle, PA 17013-2652
PH: (717)249-7473
Giarrizzo, Pastor John, Coord.

International Association of Approved
Basketball Officials **[22571]**
PO Box 355
Carlisle, PA 17013-0344
PH: (717)713-8129
Fax: (717)718-6164
Lopes, Tommy, Exec. Dir.

Daguerreian Society **[10138]**
PO Box 306
Cecil, PA 15321-0306
PH: (412)221-0306
Isenburg, Matthew, Founder

American Hearing Aid Associates
[15171]
225 Wilmington W Chester Pike,
Ste. 300
Chadds Ford, PA 19317-9011
Toll free: 800-984-3272
Russomagno, Vince, CEO, Founder

Marine Corps Mustang Association,
Inc. **[21016]**
PO Box 12
Chalfont, PA 18914-0012
Toll free: 866-937-6262
Cook, Tim, Secretary

Society of Clinical Research Associ-
ates **[15657]**
530 W Butler Ave., Ste. 109
Chalfont, PA 18914-3209
PH: (215)822-8644
Toll free: 800-762-7292
Green, Jody L., PhD, President

Royal Order of Scotland **[19569]**
400 Fallowfield Ave.
Charleroi, PA 15022
PH: (724)489-0670
Fax: (724)489-0688
Fowler, Sir Edward H., Jr., Secretary

Physical Therapy Pro Bono National
Honor Society **[23849]**
c/o Widener University, One
University Pl.
Institute for Physical Therapy Educa-
tion
One University Pl.
Chester, PA 19013
Pierce, Sam, PT, Contact

American Saddlebred Sport Horse
[4325]
520 Byers Rd.
Chester Springs, PA 19425

Laymen's Home Missionary Movement **[20149]**
1156 St. Matthews Rd.
Chester Springs, PA 19425-2700
Herzig, Ralph M., Director

Phi Kappa Sigma **[23912]**
2 Timber Dr.
Chester Springs, PA 19425
PH: (610)469-3282
Fax: (610)469-3286
Smith, Dave, Secretary

National Dog Groomers Association
of America, Inc. **[2546]**
PO Box 101
Clark, PA 16113-0101
PH: (724)962-2711
Fax: (724)962-1919

Genetic Toxicology Association
[7337]
c/o Leon Stankowski, Treasurer
1712 DaVinci Ln.

Clarks Summit, PA 18411
Dobo, Krista, Officer

International Society for Animal
Rights **[10651]**
PO Box F
Clarks Summit, PA 18411
PH: (570)586-2200
Fax: (570)586-9580
Dapsis, Susan, President

Episcopal Peace Fellowship **[19106]**
c/o Allison Liles, Executive Director
PO Box 15
Claysburg, PA 16625
PH: (312)922-8628
Liles, Allison, Exec. Dir.

Equipment Appraisers Association of
North America **[223]**
1270 State Route 30
Clinton, PA 15026
Toll free: 800-790-1053
Fax: (724)899-2001
Miceli, Carl, President

Borzoi Club of America **[21845]**
c/o Joy Windle, Recording Secretary
2255 Strasburg Rd.
Coatesville, PA 19320-4437
PH: (610)380-0850
  (678)957-9544
Peters-Campbell, Rebecca,
  President

International Society for Mushroom
Science **[4236]**
c/o Christine Smith, Secretary
1507 Valley Rd.
Coatesville, PA 19320
PH: (610)384-5031
Fax: (610)384-0390
Van Greuning, Martmari

Bright Futures Farm **[4340]**
238 Old Franklin Pke.
Cochranton, PA 16314
PH: (724)496-4960
Dee, Beverlee, Exec. Dir.

American Counsel Association
[4988]
3770 Ridge Pike
Collegeville, PA 19426
PH: (610)489-3300
Bertschy, Timothy, President

Foundation for Ichthyosis and
Related Skin Types **[14494]**
2616 N Broad St.
Colmar, PA 18915
PH: (215)997-9400
Toll free: 800-545-3286
Fax: (215)997-9403
Hoerle, Jeff, President

National Association of Watch and
Clock Collectors **[22446]**
514 Poplar St.
Columbia, PA 17512-2124
PH: (717)684-8261
Fax: (717)684-0878
Humphrey, J. Steven, Exec. Dir.

OutreachPARAGUAY **[11290]**
761 Chickies Dr.
Columbia, PA 17512
PH: (717)684-6062
Sosa, Eileen, Founder, Director

Life Counseling Ministries **[20184]**
250 Meadow Ln.
Conestoga, PA 17516
PH: (717)871-0540
Fax: (717)871-0547
Martin, Titus R., Chairman

Center for Assessment and Policy
Development **[12965]**
268 Barren Hill Rd.
Conshohocken, PA 19428

PH: (610)828-1063
Leiderman, Sally H., President

Association of Ayurvedic Profession-
als of North America **[13606]**
567 Thomas St., Ste. 400
Coopersburg, PA 18036
PH: (484)550-7725
  (484)347-6110
Annambhotla, Dr. Shekhar,
  President, Founder

Paper Shipping Sack Manufacturers'
Association, Inc. **[840]**
5050 Blue Church Rd.
Coopersburg, PA 18036
PH: (610)282-6845
Fax: (610)282-1577
Belmont, Donald P., Chmn. of the
  Bd.

Ruffed Grouse Society **[4878]**
451 McCormick Rd.
Coraopolis, PA 15108
PH: (412)262-4044
Toll free: 888-564-6747
Oliver, James H., Chairman

Environmental Education and
Conservation Global **[7889]**
204 E Locust St.
Coudersport, PA 16915
PH: (814)260-9138
McCrea, Edward J., CEO, President

AIM **[271]**
20399 Route 19, Ste. 203
Cranberry Township, PA 16066
PH: (724)742-4470
Fax: (724)742-4476
Bosco, Mary Lou, COO

Association for Automatic Identification and Mobility North America
[272]
1 Landmark N
20399 Route 19, Ste. 203
Cranberry Township, PA 16066
PH: (724)742-4473
Fax: (724)742-4476
Hall, Doug, Officer

International Association of Animal
Behavior Consultants **[7402]**
565 Callery Rd.
Cranberry Township, PA 16066
Basciano, Danielle, VP

Military Writers Society of America
[22484]
PO Box 1768
Cranberry Township, PA 16066
Doerr, Bob, VP

Air Forces Escape and Evasion
Society **[20682]**
c/o Richard Shandor, Membership
and Corresponding Secretary
PO Box 254
Cresson, PA 16630-2129
PH: (814)886-2735
  (978)869-3035
White, John, Treasurer

American Livebearer Association
[22029]
5 Zerbe St.
Cressona, PA 17929-1513
PH: (570)385-0573
Brady, Timothy J., Membership Chp.

American Romeldale/CVM Associa-
tion, Inc. **[4661]**
c/o John Savage, Register
1039 State Route 168
Darlington, PA 16115
PH: (724)843-2084
Fax: (724)891-1440
Savage, John, Registrar

International Fainting Goat Associa-
tion **[4276]**
c/o John Savage, Registrar
1039 State Rte. 168
Darlington, PA 16115
PH: (724)843-2084
Fax: (724)891-1440
Lenoci, Terri, President

Attention Deficit Disorder Association
[15907]
PO Box 103
Denver, PA 17517-0103
Toll free: 800-939-1019
Fax: (800)939-1019
Gordon, Duane, President

Griswold and Cast Iron Cookware
Association **[22157]**
210 Kralltown Rd.
Dillsburg, PA 17019-9683
PH: (315)376-6328
  (717)432-3370
Schwarting, Brad, President

National Peach Council **[4243]**
22 Triplett Ct.
Dillsburg, PA 17019-9490
PH: (717)329-8421
Fax: (717)432-2200

International Al Jolson Society
[24045]
c/o Sandra K. Gerloff
419 Glenwood Dr.
Douglassville, PA 19518-1125
Hernstat, Jan, President

Taijiquan Enthusiasts Organization
[17424]
PO Box 564
Douglassville, PA 19518
PH: (484)332-3331
Rhoads, CJ, Managing Dir.

94th Infantry Division Association
[20712]
c/o Harry Helms, Secretary
609 Dogwood Dr.
Downingtown, PA 19335-3907
PH: (484)288-2778
Helms, Mr. Harry, Secretary

Certification Board for Music
Therapists **[16968]**
506 E Lancaster Ave., Ste. 102
Downingtown, PA 19335
PH: (610)269-8900
Toll free: 800-765-2268
Fax: (610)269-9232
Schneck, Joy S., Exec. Dir.

Friedreich's Ataxia Research Alliance
[14775]
533 W Uwchlan Ave.
Downingtown, PA 19335-1763
PH: (484)879-6160
Fax: (484)872-1402
Bartek, Mr. Ronald J., Director,
  Founder, President

Integrated Business Communica-
tions Alliance **[274]**
81 Cottage St.
Doylestown, PA 18901
PH: (215)489-1722
Bushnell, Rick, Contact

International Academy of Myodontics
[14443]
777 Ferry Rd., P-6
Doylestown, PA 18901
PH: (215)345-1149
Cooperman, Dr. Harry N., DDS,
  President

National Tactical Officers Association
[5512]
PO Box 797
Doylestown, PA 18901
Toll free: 800-279-9127
Fax: (215)230-7552
Lomax, Mark, Exec. Dir.

Industrial Auctioneers Association
[259]
3213 Ayr Ln.
Dresher, PA 19025
PH: (215)366-5450
Toll free: 800-805-8359
Fax: (215)657-1964
Jacobs, Terrance, Director

Association of Coupon Professionals
[2946]
1051 Pontiac Rd.
Drexel Hill, PA 19026
PH: (610)789-1478
Fax: (610)789-5309
Morgan, John, Exec. Dir.

National Team Cheng Martial Arts
Association **[23007]**
2269 Garrett Rd.
Drexel Hill, PA 19026
PH: (610)622-5260
Cheng, Paul, Mgr.

Nature Abounds **[4090]**
PO Box 506
Dubois, PA 15801-0506
PH: (814)765-1453
Fax: (855)629-7329
Hughes-Wert, Melinda, Founder,
  President

World Freestyle Watercraft Alliance
[23367]
c/o Eric Malone Enterprises LLC
16432 Dunnings Hwy.
Duncansville, PA 16635
PH: (814)207-9709
Malone, Eric, Founder

Carpet Cushion Council **[1940]**
5103 Brandywine Dr.
Eagleville, PA 19403
PH: (484)687-5170
Fax: (610)885-5131
Ambrose, Bob, Secretary

Coast Guard Combat Veterans As-
sociation **[21118]**
c/o Gary Sherman, Secretary/
  Treasurer
3245 Ridge Pke.
Eagleville, PA 19403
PH: (610)539-1000
Swifth, Ed, LM, Chairman

Jim Smith Society **[19658]**
c/o Jim Smith, Membership Chairman
256 Lake Meade Dr.
East Berlin, PA 17316-9374
Smith, James Wayne, President

Alliance of National Heritage Areas
[9224]
c/o C. Allen Sachse, President
2750 Hugh Moore Park Rd.
Easton, PA 18042-7120
PH: (610)923-3548
Fax: (610)923-0537
McCollum, Michelle, Director

American Friends of Lafayette
[10312]
PO Box 9463
Easton, PA 18042-1798
Hoffman, Alan, President

Associate Degree Early Childhood
Teacher Educators **[7580]**
14 Freedom Ter.
14 Freedom Terr.

Easton, PA 18045
PH: (610)861-4162
Bulat, Cheryl, President

American Association of Meat
   Processors [2308]
1 Meating Pl.
Elizabethtown, PA 17022
PH: (717)367-1168
Fax: (717)367-9096
Hankes, Doug, President

Southern Public Administration
   Education Foundation [5702]
122 W High St.
Elizabethtown, PA 17022
PH: (717)689-6126

National American Glass Club
   [22136]
PO Box 24
Elkland, PA 16920
Taylor, Gay LeCleire, President

National Sexual Violence Resource
   Center [12930]
123 N Enola Dr.
Enola, PA 17025
PH: (717)909-0710
Toll free: 877-739-3895
Fax: (717)909-0714
Brown, Peggy, Exec. Dir.

Orphan Resources International
   [11116]
550 W Trout Run Rd.
Ephrata, PA 17522-9604
PH: (717)733-7444
Martin, Rod, Director, President

Pennsylvania German Society
   [10065]
PO Box 118
Ephrata, PA 17522
PH: (717)597-7940
Gerhart, Mr. Thomas J., President,
   Bd. Member

Associated Pipe Organ Builders of
   America [2418]
PO Box 8268
Erie, PA 16505
Toll free: 800-473-5270
Rusczyk, Bob, Exec., Administrator

Chosen International Medical As-
   sistance [12270]
3638 W 26th St.
Erie, PA 16506-2037
PH: (814)833-3023
Fax: (814)833-4091
King, Mr. Richard, Exec. Dir.

Christian Bowhunters of America
   [22500]
2423 Oak Orchard River Rd.
Erie, PA 16504
PH: (716)402-5650
Toll free: 877-912-5724
Roose, David, Founder

Cody's Wheels of Hope [10942]
PO Box 8735
Erie, PA 16505
PH: (814)460-8228
Filson, Cindy, President

Hearts for the Hungry [12098]
PO Box 10701
Erie, PA 16514-0701
PH: (814)873-1397
Hess, Robert, Bd. Member

International Association for Intel-
   ligence Education [8041]
PO Box 10508
Erie, PA 16514-0508
PH: (814)824-2131
Fax: (814)824-2008
Gordon, Dr. Joseph, Chairman

Loyal Christian Benefit Association
   [19488]
8811 Peach St.
Erie, PA 16509-4738
PH: (888)382-2716
Toll free: 800-234-5222
Tuttle, Doug, CEO, President

Ophelia Project [13472]
718 Nevada Dr.
Erie, PA 16505
PH: (814)456-5437
Fax: (814)455-2090
Wellman, Susan, Founder

People for Life [12786]
1625 W 26th St.
Erie, PA 16508-1262
PH: (814)459-1333
   (814)882-1333
Broderick, Tim, Director, Editor

Purple Martin Conservation Associa-
   tion [4873]
301 Peninsula Dr., Ste. 6
Erie, PA 16505
PH: (814)833-7656
Fax: (814)833-2451
Chambers, Louise, Dir. of Comm.

Truck-Frame and Axle Repair Association [356]
c/o Ken Dias, Consultant
364 W 12th St.
Erie, PA 16501
Jones, Paul, Officer

Gastroparesis Patient Association for
   Cures and Treatments, Inc.
   [14791]
185-132 Newberry Commons
Etters, PA 17319
Toll free: 888-874-7228
Haston, Carissa, President

InFaith [20424]
145 John Robert Thomas Dr.
Exton, PA 19341
PH: (610)527-4439
Wisneski, Gerald D., Chairman

National Association for Choice in
   Education [8478]
64 E Uwchlan Ave., No. 259
Exton, PA 19341-1203
PH: (610)296-2821
Fax: (610)993-3139
Sax, Dr. Leonard, Founder

Society of Cable Telecommunica-
   tions Engineers [6590]
14 Philips Rd.
Exton, PA 19341-1318
PH: (610)363-6888
Toll free: 800-542-5040
Fax: (610)363-5898
Williams, Steve, Secretary

Paperweight Collectors' Association
   [21709]
PO Box 334
Fairless Hills, PA 19030
Edelman, Phil, President

National Shaving Mug Collectors
   Association [21698]
c/o Carl Mitchell, Treasurer
7058 Ballybunion Ct.
Fayetteville, PA 17222-9443
Mitchell, Carl, Treasurer

American Society of Inventors
   [6769]
PO Box 354
Feasterville, PA 19053
PH: (215)546-6601

Sunshine Foundation [11276]
1041 Mill Creek Dr.
Feasterville, PA 19053

PH: (215)396-4770
Fax: (215)396-4774
Sample, Kate, President

American White Shepherd Association [21828]
c/o Shelley Caldwell, Chair
48 Aber Rd.
Finleyville, PA 15332
PH: (412)384-5537
Vest, Terri, President

25th Infantry Division Association
   [20708]
PO Box 340
Flourtown, PA 19031-0340
PH: (215)248-2572
Fax: (215)248-5250

North American Society for Pediatric
   Gastroenterology, Hepatology and
   Nutrition [14795]
PO Box 6
Flourtown, PA 19031
PH: (215)233-0808
Fax: (215)233-3918
Stallings, Margaret K., Exec. Dir.

Prana International [12562]
PO Box 362
Flourtown, PA 19031-9998
PH: (267)270-5551
Sinha, Amit, Founder, Bd. Member,
   President

Aerie Africa, Inc. [10834]
1249 Hazelwood Dr.
Fort Washington, PA 19034
Kelemu, Mekdes, Founder

Life Laboratory [15030]
1244 Fort Washington Ave., Ste. N1
Fort Washington, PA 19034
PH: (215)646-6504
Lezzi, S. Nicholas, Chmn. of the Bd.

National Comprehensive Cancer
   Network [14027]
275 Commerce Dr., Ste. 300
Fort Washington, PA 19034
PH: (215)690-0300
Fax: (215)690-0280
Weyhmuller, Gary J., MBA, Exec.
   VP, COO

Vietnam Women's Memorial
   Foundation [21174]
c/o Eastern National
470 Maryland Dr., Ste. 1
Fort Washington, PA 19034
Toll free: 877-463-3647
Evans, Diane Carlson, RN, Founder,
   President

WEC International [20164]
PO Box 1707
Fort Washington, PA 19034
PH: (215)646-2322
Toll free: 888-646-6202
Hall, David, Director

Kids with Food Allergies [13579]
5049 Swamp Rd., Ste. 303
Fountainville, PA 18923-9660
PH: (215)230-5394
Fax: (215)340-7674
Mitchell, Lynda, President

A Hero's Welcome [20703]
PO Box 14
Frederick, PA 19435-0014
PH: (484)679-1717
Keyser, Sharon Hyland, Founder

American Canal Society [9369]
117 Main St.
Freemansburg, PA 18017-7231
PH: (610)691-0956
Barber, David G., President

Equine Protection Network [4815]
c/o Horse Cruelty Fund
PO Box 232
Friedensburg, PA 17933
Lohnes, Robin C., Exec. Dir.

Wildlife Management Institute [4914]
1440 Upper Bermudian Rd.
Gardners, PA 17324
PH: (802)563-2087
   (717)677-4480
Dunfee, Matt, Program Mgr.

English Toy Spaniel Club of America
   [21875]
c/o Susan Plance, Secretary
505 Whitehill Rd.
Georgetown, PA 15043-9634
PH: (714)893-0053
Fax: (714)893-5085
Van Deman, Bruce, President

Forestry Conservation Communica-
   tions Association [3867]
122 Baltimore St.
Gettysburg, PA 17325
PH: (717)398-0815
Toll free: 844-458-0298
Fax: (717)778-4237
Mitchell, Lloyd M., President

Gettysburg Foundation [9394]
1195 Baltimore Pke.
Gettysburg, PA 17325-7034
PH: (717)338-1243
Toll free: 866-889-1243
Fax: (717)338-1244
Eisenhower, Susan, Director

Timber Frame Business Council
   [593]
46 Chambersburg St.
Gettysburg, PA 17325
PH: (717)334-5234
Toll free: 888-560-9251
Fax: (717)334-5571

International Surface Fabricators As-
   sociation [2223]
2400 Wildwood Rd.
Gibsonia, PA 15044
PH: (412)487-3207
Fax: (412)487-3269
Langenderfer, Mike, Exec. Dir.

International Intelligence Network
   [3060]
PO Box 350
Gladwyne, PA 19035-0350
PH: (610)520-9222
Toll free: 800-784-2020
Psarouthakis, Peter, Exec. Dir.

Tibetan Terrier Club of America
   [21970]
c/o Ron Pankiewicz, President
1645 Seaks Run Rd.
Glen Rock, PA 17327-8484
Pankiewicz, Ron, President

The American Bouvier des Flandres
   Club [21798]
c/o Karen Florentine, Secretary
79 W Indian Springs Dr.
Glenmoore, PA 19343-3989
PH: (610)458-7179
Costanzo, Susan, President, Chmn.
   of the Bd.

Charcot-Marie-Tooth Association
   [15913]
PO Box 105
Glenolden, PA 19036
PH: (610)499-9264
Toll free: 800-606-2682
Fax: (610)499-9267
Livney, Patrick A., CEO

Academy of Behavioral Medicine
Research [13793]
810 Scott Ave.
Glenshaw, PA 15116
McCubbin, David, President

Presbyterians Pro-Life [12788]
PO Box 461
Glenshaw, PA 15116
PH: (412)487-1990
Fax: (412)487-1994
Bowen, Mrs. Marie, Exec. Dir.

Steel Deck Institute [581]
PO Box 426
Glenshaw, PA 15116
PH: (412)487-3325
Fax: (412)487-3326
Roehrig, Steven A., Managing Dir.

Responsible Policies for Animals,
Inc. [10688]
PO Box 891
Glenside, PA 19038
PH: (215)886-7721
Cantor, David, Exec. Dir., Founder,
President

Kappa Delta Rho [23905]
331 S Main St.
Greensburg, PA 15601
PH: (724)838-7100
Toll free: 800-536-5371
Fax: (724)838-7101
Spencer, Gene L., President

National Brittany Rescue and Adop-
tion Network [10665]
PO Box 5046
Greensburg, PA 15601-5058
Spaid, Susan, President

National Monte Carlo Owners Association [21457]
204 Shelby Dr.
Greensburg, PA 15601-4974
Harvey, Mr. John W., Director

Seton Hill University's E-magnify
[7567]
Seton Hill University
1 Seton Hill Dr.
Greensburg, PA 15601
Toll free: 800-826-6234
Huston, Ms. Jayne H., Director

Deep Springs International [4756]
PO Box 694
Grove City, PA 16127
Ritter, Mr. Michael, CEO

Slate Roofing Contractors Associa-
tion of North America [580]
143 Forest Ln.
Grove City, PA 16127
PH: (814)786-7015
Fax: (814)786-8209
Jenkins, Mr. Joe, Exec. Dir.

Enders Family Association [20863]
c/o David G. Enders, President
56 Marie Dr.
Halifax, PA 17032
PH: (717)877-9214
Enders, David G., President

American Society for the Defense of
Tradition, Family and Property
[18032]
PO Box 341
Hanover, PA 17331
PH: (717)225-7147
Toll free: 888-317-5571
Fax: (717)225-7382
Drake, Raymond E., President

Hebrew Christian Fellowship [20145]
PO Box 245
Harleysville, PA 19438

PH: (215)256-4500
Wambold, Rev. Roger L., Director

National Duck Stamp Collectors
Society [22349]
PO Box 43
Harleysville, PA 19438-0043
Cotton, Dr. Ira, President

American College of Veterinary
Radiology [17621]
777 E Park Dr.
Harrisburg, PA 17105
PH: (717)558-7865
Fax: (717)558-7841
Drost, Tod, Exec. Dir.

American Equestrian Trade Associa-
tion [4306]
2207 Forest Hills Dr.
Harrisburg, PA 17112
PH: (717)724-0204
Fax: (717)238-9985
Birsh, Hope, Contact

Association of Outdoor Lighting
Professionals [2099]
2207 Forest Hills Dr.
Harrisburg, PA 17112
PH: (717)238-2504
Fax: (717)238-9985
Frye, Lisa, Exec. Dir.

Association of Professional
Landscape Designers [2067]
2207 Forest Hills Dr.
Harrisburg, PA 17112
PH: (717)238-9780
Fax: (717)238-9985
Calabrese, Denise, Exec. Dir.

Association of Science Fiction and
Fantasy Artists [241]
PO Box 60933
Harrisburg, PA 17106-0933
Dashoff, Joni Brill, VP

International Play Equipment
Manufacturers Association [2909]
2207 Forest Hills Dr.
Harrisburg, PA 17112
PH: (717)238-1744
Toll free: 888-944-7362
Fax: (717)238-9985

International Playground Contractors
Association [872]
2207 Forest Hills Dr.
Harrisburg, PA 17112
PH: (717)724-0594
Fax: (717)238-9985
Fry, Jack, Comm. Chm.

International RadioSurgery Associa-
tion [17035]
PO Box 5186
Harrisburg, PA 17110-0186
PH: (717)260-9808

National Frozen and Refrigerated
Foods Association [1358]
4755 Linglestown Rd., Ste. 300
Harrisburg, PA 17112
PH: (717)657-8601
Fax: (717)657-9862
Troutman, Tracy, Asst.

National Greenhouse Manufacturers
Association [170]
2207 Forest Hill Dr.
Harrisburg, PA 17112
PH: (717)238-4530
Toll free: 800-792-6462
Fax: (717)238-9985
Scantland, Leah, President

Perlite Institute [2388]
2207 Forest Hills Dr.
Harrisburg, PA 17112

PH: (717)238-9723
Calabrese, Denise, Exec. Dir.

Platt Family Association [20914]
4081 Greystone Dr.
Harrisburg, PA 17112
Bretz, Joan, Contact

Retail Energy Supply Association
[1122]
PO Box 6089
Harrisburg, PA 17112
PH: (717)566-5405
(301)717-2988
McCormick, Tracy, Exec. Dir.

Sons of Union Veterans of the Civil
War [20746]
National Civil War Museum
1 Lincoln Circle at Reservoir Park,
Ste. 240
Harrisburg, PA 17103-2411
PH: (717)232-7000
Fax: (717)412-7492
Demmy, David W., Sr., Exec. Dir.

Tall Cedars of Lebanon of North
America [19571]
4309 Linglestown Rd.Ste 116
Harrisburg, PA 17112
PH: (717)232-5991
Fax: (717)232-5997
Ward, William W., Sr., Chairman

Three Mile Island Alert [18736]
315 Peffer St.
Harrisburg, PA 17102-1834
PH: (717)233-7897
Epstein, Eric, Chmn. of the Bd.,
Chairman

Tigers East/Alpines East [21502]
c/o Joe McConlogue
820 Fishing Creek Valley Rd.
Harrisburg, PA 17112-9227
PH: (717)474-8311
McConlogue, Joe, Officer

The Vermiculite Association [2389]
2207 Forest Hills Dr.
Harrisburg, PA 17112
PH: (717)238-9902
Fax: (717)238-9985
McDermott, Damien, President

Association for the Behavioral Sci-
ences and Medical Education
[6031]
PO Box 368
Harrison City, PA 15636
PH: (724)590-9187
Fax: (724)744-0146
Humbert, Laurel, Exec. Dir.

Remembering ADAM, Inc. [13180]
PO Box 665
Hastings, PA 16646
PH: (814)954-1556

Nurses Service Organization [1915]
159 E County Line Rd.
Hatboro, PA 19040-1218
Toll free: 800-247-1500
Fax: (800)758-3635

Interdisciplinary Biblical Research
Institute [20082]
PO Box 423
Hatfield, PA 19440-0423
PH: (215)368-7002
Bossard, Steve, Mgr.

Committee to Support the Antitrust
Laws [18282]
c/o Joe Sauder, Treasurer
1 Haverford Centre
361 W Lancaster Ave.
Haverford, PA 19041

PH: (202)789-3960
(610)645-4717
Cuneo, Jonathan W., Gen. Counsel

Friends Historical Association
[20170]
Haverford College
370 Lancaster Ave.
Haverford, PA 19041-1336
PH: (610)896-1161
Fax: (610)896-1102
Cherry, Charles L., Editor

Historical Harp Society [9919]
PO Box 662
Havertown, PA 19083-0662
Johnston, Gordon, VP

International Alliance of Messianic
Congregations and Synagogues
[20335]
PO Box 1570
Havertown, PA 19083
PH: (215)452-5900
Toll free: 866-426-2766
Lowinger, Rabbi, Chairman

Slovak Catholic Federation [19648]
173 Berner Ave.
Hazleton, PA 18201
PH: (570)454-5547
Evanko, Dolores M., Secretary,
Treasurer

Eastern Bird Banding Association
[6958]
c/o Donald Mease, Treasurer
2366 Springtown Hill Rd.
Hellertown, PA 18055
PH: (610)346-7754
Mease, Donald, Treasurer

International Federation of
Chiropractors and Organizations
[14275]
2276 Wassergass Rd.
Hellertown, PA 18055
Toll free: 800-521-9856
Walker, Shane, Director

Antique Automobile Club of America
[21327]
501 W Governor Rd.
Hershey, PA 17033
PH: (717)534-1910
(717)534-2082
Fax: (717)534-9101
Ritter, Chris, Librarian

High Hopes for Haiti - Mortel
Foundation [11470]
PO Box 405
Hershey, PA 17033
Toll free: 888-355-6065
Mortel, Dr. Rodrigue, President

Information Resources Management
Association [1798]
701 E Chocolate Ave., Ste. 200
Hershey, PA 17033-1240
PH: (717)533-8845
Fax: (717)533-8661
Khosrow-Pour, Dr. Mehdi, Exec. Dir.

International Association of
Trampoline Parks [3309]
PO Box 594
Hershey, PA 17033
PH: (717)910-4534
Evans, Bethany, Exec. VP

National Junior Horticultural Association [22113]
c/o Carole Carney, Executive
Secretary
15 Railroad Ave.
Homer City, PA 15748-1378
Carney, Carole, Exec. Sec.

Himalayan Institute [12000]
952 Bethany Tpke.
Honesdale, PA 18431-4194
PH: (570)253-5551
Toll free: 800-822-4547
Tigunait, Pandit Rajmani, Chairman

Institute for Safe Medication
Practices [15021]
200 Lakeside Dr., Ste. 200
Horsham, PA 19044-2321
PH: (215)947-7797
Fax: (215)914-1492
Cohen, Michael R., RPh, President

International Medication Safety
Network [16666]
c/o Institute for Safe Medication
Practices
200 Lakeside Dr., Ste. 200
Horsham, PA 19044
PH: (215)947-7797
Fax: (215)914-1492
Cohen, Michael R., RPh,
Chairperson

Medication Safety Officers Society
[15124]
200 Lakeside Dr., Ste. 200
Horsham, PA 19044
PH: (215)947-7797
Fax: (215)914-1492
Hartman, Christian, Founder

American Pastured Poultry Produc-
ers Association [4562]
PO Box 85
Hughesville, PA 17737-0085
PH: (570)584-2309
Toll free: 888-662-7772
Mattocks, Jeff, Treasurer

Child Aid Africa [10892]
551 Roslaire Dr.
Hummelstown, PA 17036-9165
PH: (877)288-9666
(205)967-0441
Mbito, Dr. Michael Njoroge, Founder,
President, Chairman, Exec. Dir.

College Broadcasters, Inc. [458]
UPS - Hershey Square Ctr.
1152 Mae St.
Hummelstown, PA 17036
Toll free: 855-275-4224
Weston, Greg, President

International Management Develop-
ment Association [643]
PO Box 216
Hummelstown, PA 17036-0216
PH: (717)566-3054
Kaynak, Erdener, PhD, Ed.-in-Chief

Parke Society [20913]
c/o Ronald Neal Parks, Registrar
722 Warm Springs Ave.
Huntingdon, PA 16652-2424
PH: (814)643-2576
Parks, Fr. Michael, Exec. Dir.

Bringing Hope to Nigeria [11321]
3301 Creek Rd.
Huntingdon Valley, PA 19006
PH: (215)947-6345
Agber, Rev. Philip, Contact

National Mine Rescue Association
[6882]
c/o Chris Melvin, President
132 Forest Glen Dr.
Imperial, PA 15126
Stanchek, Jeffrey, VP

Slovene National Benefit Society
[19653]
247 W Allegheny Rd.
Imperial, PA 15126-9774

PH: (724)695-1100
Toll free: 800-843-7675
Fax: (724)695-1555
Pintar, Karen A, Secretary

American Driver and Traffic Safety
Education Association [7723]
Highway Safety Services, LLC
1434 Trim Tree Rd.
Indiana, PA 15701
PH: (724)801-8246
Toll free: 877-485-7172
Fax: (724)349-5042
Brody, Barbara, Liaison

American Society for Competitiveness [7541]
304 Eberly, IUP
664 Pratt Dr.
Indiana, PA 15705
PH: (724)357-5928
(724)357-5759
Fax: (724)357-7768
Ali, Abbas J., Exec. Dir.

Anglican Fellowship of Prayer
[19702]
1106 Mansfield Ave.
Indiana, PA 15701
PH: (724)463-6436
(814)725-4484
Williams, Dr. William C., President

National Association of State
Motorcycle Safety Administrators
[5750]
1434 Trim Tree Rd.
Indiana, PA 15701
PH: (724)801-8075
Fax: (724)349-5042
Krajewski, Andrew, Contact

Our Hearts to your Soles [13015]
PO Box 243
Ingomar, PA 15127
Conti, Matt, Founder

Association for Hospital Medical
Education [15316]
109 Brush Creek Rd.
Irwin, PA 15642
PH: (724)864-7321
Mohn, Kimball, MD, Exec. Dir.

Coast to Coast Dachshund Rescue
[10603]
PO Box 147
Jacobus, PA 17407
McCornick, Joni, President

International Fetal Medicine and
Surgery Society [16620]
c/o Dr. Frank Craparo, Secretary-
Treasurer
2406 April Dr.
Jamison, PA 18929
Deprest, Jan, President

American Anti-Vivisection Society
[10565]
801 Old York Rd., Ste. 204
Jenkintown, PA 19046
Toll free: 800-729-2287
Letterman, Tracie, Exec. Dir.

A Chance to Heal [14635]
PO Box 2342
Jenkintown, PA 19046
PH: (215)885-2420
Osterman, Kate, Contact

Society of Environmental Journalists
[8161]
PO Box 2492
Jenkintown, PA 19046-8492
PH: (215)884-8174
Fax: (215)884-8175
Parke, Beth, Exec. Dir.

Dreams Blossom [13046]
PO Box 5293
Johnstown, PA 15904-5293
PH: (814)659-7595
Ateya, Theresa, Founder, Exec. Dir.

Napoléonic Age Philatelists [22348]
c/o Don Smith, President
PO Box 576
Johnstown, PA 15907-0576
Berry, Ken, Editor

Professional Outdoor Media Associa-
tion [2318]
PO Box 1569
Johnstown, PA 15907
PH: (814)254-4719
Fax: (206)350-1047
Opre, Tom, President

School of Living [9542]
215 Julian Woods Ln.
Julian, PA 16844-8617
PH: (814)353-0130
Stupski, Karen, Exec. Dir.

Hawk Mountain Sanctuary [4825]
1700 Hawk Mountain Rd.
Kempton, PA 19529
PH: (610)756-6961
Fax: (610)756-4468
Regan, Jerry, President

American Public Gardens Associa-
tion [4429]
351 Longwood Rd.
Kennett Square, PA 19348
PH: (610)708-3010
Fax: (610)444-3594
Sclar, Dr. Casey, Exec. Dir.

North American Clivia Society [4438]
PO Box 1098
Kennett Square, PA 19348
Petravich, Alan, Director, President

Farmers Market Coalition [3538]
PO Box 499
Kimberton, PA 19442
Yeago, Sharon, Treasurer

American Association of Managing
General Agents [1827]
610 Freedom Business Ctr., Ste. 110
King of Prussia, PA 19406
PH: (610)992-0022
Fax: (610)992-0021
Heinze, Bernd G., Esq., Exec. Dir.

American Baptist Churches USA
[19711]
588 N Gulph Rd.
King of Prussia, PA 19406
PH: (610)768-2000
Toll free: 800-222-3872
Fax: (610)768-2309
Gillies, Susan, Officer

American Horticultural Therapy Association [17433]
610 Freedom Business Ctr., No. 110
King of Prussia, PA 19406
PH: (610)992-0020

International Association of Insur-
ance Receivers [1875]
610 Freedom Business Ctr., Ste. 110
King of Prussia, PA 19406
PH: (610)992-0017
Fax: (610)992-0021
Wilson, Donna, President

International Furnishings and Design
Association [1950]
610 Freedom Business Ctr., Ste. 110
King of Prussia, PA 19406
PH: (610)992-0011
Fax: (610)992-0021
Jones, Jennifer, Exec. Dir.

Rough and Tumble Engineers'
Historical Association [22439]
PO Box 9
Kinzers, PA 17535-0009
PH: (717)442-4249
Bashore, Harvey, Director

ARPKD/CHF Alliance [15875]
PO Box 70
Kirkwood, PA 17536
PH: (717)529-5555
Toll free: 800-708-8892
Fax: (800)807-9110
Zak, Colleen B., President, Founder

International Alliance of Professional
Hypnotists [15361]
8852 SR 3001
Laceyville, PA 18623
PH: (570)869-1021
Fax: (570)869-1249
Otto, Robert, CEO

International Association of
Counselors and Therapists [15362]
8852 SR 3001
Laceyville, PA 18623
PH: (570)869-1021
Toll free: 800-553-6886
Fax: (570)869-1249
Otto, Linda, Exec. Dir.

International Medical and Dental
Hypnotherapy Association [15363]
8852 SR 3001
Laceyville, PA 18623
PH: (570)869-1021
Toll free: 800-553-6886
Fax: (570)869-1249
Otto, Linda, Exec. Dir.

American Carnival Glass Association
[22130]
PO Box 10022
Lancaster, PA 17605-0022
Yung, Larry A., Jr., President

American Home Life International
[8055]
2137 Embassy Dr., Ste. 202
Lancaster, PA 17603
PH: (717)560-2840
Fax: (717)560-2845
Mayer, Keith, CEO

BCM International [19750]
201 Granite Run Dr., Ste. 260
Lancaster, PA 17601
PH: (717)560-9601
Toll free: 888-226-4685
Fax: (717)560-9607
Windle, Rev. Martin, President

Central American Relief Efforts
[12268]
2117 Saddleridge Rd.
Lancaster, PA 17601
PH: (717)299-4942
Mentzer, Steven C., President

CHAP International [12636]
1390 Columbia Ave., No. 251
Lancaster, PA 17603
PH: (717)553-2427
Weaver, Stan, Founder

Common Sense for Drug Policy
[18970]
1377-C Spencer Ave.
Lancaster, PA 17603
Zeese, Kevin B., President

Cork Institute of America [1435]
c/o Don Scantling, 715 Fountain
Ave.
Ecore International
715 Fountain Ave.
Lancaster, PA 17601

PH: (717)295-3400
Fax: (717)295-3414

Cosmopolitan International [12888]
PO Box 7351
Lancaster, PA 17604
PH: (717)295-7142
Toll free: 800-648-4331
Fax: (717)295-7143
Gordon, Richard, President

Distribution Business Management
Association [3469]
2938 Columbia Ave., Ste. 1102
Lancaster, PA 17603
PH: (717)295-0033
Fax: (717)299-2154
Thorn, Amy Z., Ed. Dir.

Epicor Users Group [6300]
PO Box 10368
Lancaster, PA 17605
PH: (717)209-7177
Fax: (717)209-7189
Wolfe, Bill, II, VP

Evangelical and Reformed Historical
Society [20632]
555 W James St.
Lancaster, PA 17603
PH: (717)290-8734
Gruber, Rev. Linda, President

First Response Team of America
[11660]
1060 N Charlotte St., Ste. 102
Lancaster, PA 17603
Agoglia, Tad, Founder

HOPE International [13379]
227 Granite Run Dr., Ste. 250
Lancaster, PA 17601-6826
PH: (717)464-3220
Fax: (717)255-0306
Greer, Peter, President, CEO

Lancaster Mennonite Historical
Society [20983]
2215 Millstream Rd.
Lancaster, PA 17602-1499
PH: (717)393-9745
Fax: (717)393-8751
Santiago, Rolando, Exec. Dir.

Mennonite Economic Development
Associates - Lancaster Chapter
[20329]
1891 Santa Barbara Dr., Ste. 201
Lancaster, PA 17601-4106
PH: (717)560-6546
Toll free: 800-665-7026
Fax: (717)560-6549
Hershey, Lyle, Chairman

Navy Club of the United States of
America Auxiliary [5617]
c/o Andrew Murphy, Liason Officer
194 Lepore Dr.
Lancaster, PA 17602-2646
PH: (717)392-4479
Gainey, Judy, Officer

Phi Sigma Pi National Honor
Fraternity [23807]
2119 Ambassador Cir.
Lancaster, PA 17603
PH: (717)299-4710
Fax: (717)390-3054
Schaffer, Suzanne, Editor, Exec. Dir.

Spanish American Civic Association
[11288]
545 Pershing Ave.
Lancaster, PA 17602
PH: (717)397-6267

International Norton Owners' Association [22226]
c/o Tari Norum, 276 Butterworth Ln.
276 Butterworth Ln.

Langhorne, PA 19047-2616
PH: (215)741-0110
Greenway, Suzi, President

Pop Warner Little Scholars, Inc.
[22864]
586 Middletown Blvd., Ste. C-100
Langhorne, PA 19047-1867
PH: (215)752-2691
Fax: (215)752-2879
Butler, Jon, Exec. Dir.

Anthracite Railroads Historical
Society [10178]
PO Box 519
Lansdale, PA 19446

Hemophilia Alliance [15230]
1758 Allentown Rd., Ste. 183
Lansdale, PA 19446
PH: (215)279-9236
Fax: (215)279-8679
Pugliese, Joe

Mobile Air Conditioning Society
[1631]
225 S Broad St.
Lansdale, PA 19446
PH: (215)631-7020
Fax: (215)631-7017
Fiffick, Andrew, Chairman

Pharmaceutical Business Intel-
ligence and Research Group
[2567]
114 Madison Way
Lansdale, PA 19446
PH: (215)855-5255
Fax: (215)855-5622
Reilly, Carol, Exec. Dir.

African-American Female
Entrepreneurs Alliance [3484]
45 Scottdale Ave.
Lansdowne, PA 19050
PH: (215)747-9282
Fax: (610)394-0264
Edwards, Dr. Germaine, Chmn. of
the Bd.

American Association for Social
Psychiatry [16815]
c/o Carol Coffman, Office
Administrator
250 Crawford Ave.
Lansdowne, PA 19050
PH: (610)626-5133
Pumariega, Andres, President

Support Our Shelters [10700]
100 Walsh Rd.
Lansdowne, PA 19050-2117
PH: (610)626-6647
White, Judith, Contact

American Association of Chairs of
Departments of Psychiatry [16809]
c/o Lucille F. Meinsler, Executive
Director
20 Woodland Est
Lebanon, PA 17042
PH: (717)270-1673
    (717)228-7687
Fax: (717)270-1673
Meinsler, Lucille F., Exec. Dir.

Boss 302 Registry [21341]
1817 Janet Ave.
Lebanon, PA 17046-1845

Cast Stone Institute [783]
c/o Jan Boyer, Executive Director
813 Chesnut St.
Lebanon, PA 17042-0068
PH: (717)272-3744
Fax: (717)272-5147
Boyer, Jan, Exec. Dir.

Sons of Spanish American War
Veterans [21096]
c/o James McAteer, President
145 Tiverton Ct.

Lebanon, PA 17042
PH: (803)345-2025
O'Bryan, Bernard, III, Trustee

American Stamp Dealers Association
[1640]
PO Box 692
Leesport, PA 19533
Toll free: 800-369-8207
Reasoner, Mark, President

Patriotic Order Sons of America
[21081]
240 S Centre Ave., Rte. 61
Leesport, PA 19533
PH: (610)926-3324
Fax: (610)926-3340
Shultz, Scott M., President

United States of America Coton de
Tulear Club [21978]
c/o Eileen Narieka, Membership
Secretary
1103 Snyder Dr.
Leesport, PA 19533
PH: (610)926-1681
Narieka, Eileen, Secretary

United States Blind Golf Association
[22799]
125 Gilberts Hill Rd.
Lehighton, PA 18235
Pomo, Dick, President

CURE International [14186]
701 Bosler Ave.
Lemoyne, PA 17043
PH: (717)730-6706
Fax: (717)730-6747
Harrison, Dr. C. Scott, MD, Founder

Longwave Club of America [21270]
45 Wildflower Rd.
Levittown, PA 19057-3209
Oliver, Bill, Publisher

North American Shortwave Association [21271]
45 Wildflower Rd.
Levittown, PA 19057-3209
D'Angelo, Richard A., Counsel

International Confederation of As-
sociations for Pluralism in Econom-
ics [6394]
Dept. of Economics
Bucknell University
1 Dent Dr.
Lewisburg, PA 17837
PH: (570)577-1666
Starr, Prof. Martha A., Contact

Society of American Mosaic Artists
[8941]
PO Box 624
Ligonier, PA 15658-0624
PH: (724)238-3087
Fax: (724)238-3973
Zimmerman, Ms. Dawnmarie, Exec.
Dir.

Mennonite Disaster Service [12698]
583 Airport Rd.
Lititz, PA 17543-9339
PH: (717)735-3536
Toll free: 800-241-8111
Fax: (717)735-0809
King, Kevin, Exec. Dir.

The Pocket Testament League
[19762]
PO Box 800
Lititz, PA 17543-7026
Toll free: 844-376-2538
Brickley, Michael, President

International Cops for Christ [19988]
c/o John McTernan
PO Box 444

Liverpool, PA 17045
PH: (717)329-0470
McTernan, John, Chap.

American Medical Fly Fishing As-
sociation [3801]
PO Box 768
Lock Haven, PA 17745
PH: (570)769-7375
Frye, Dr. Veryl F., Secretary,
Treasurer

International Benchrest Shooters
[23130]
c/o Jeff Stover, President
84 Susquehanna Ave.
Lock Haven, PA 17745
PH: (570)660-6102
Borden, Joan, Rec. Sec.

National Federation of Flemish Giant
Rabbit Breeders [4603]
c/o Wayne Bechdel, Secretary/
Treasurer
117 Hollow Rd.
Lock Haven, PA 17745
Bomia, Robert, President

Alliance of Families Fighting
Pancreatic Cancer [16566]
PO Box 2023
Lower Burrell, PA 15068
Toll free: 800-704-9080
Dukovich, Theresa, Exec. Dir.

Candy Container Collectors of
America [21632]
c/o Jim Olean, Membership
Chairperson
115 Mac Beth Dr.
Lower Burrell, PA 15068-2628
Olean, Jim, Membership Chp.

American Risk and Insurance As-
sociation [8038]
716 Providence Rd.
Malvern, PA 19355-3402
PH: (610)640-1997
Fax: (610)725-1007
Biacchi, Mr. Anthony, Exec. Dir.

Association for the Advancement of
Wound Care [14929]
70 E Swedesford Rd., Ste. 100
Malvern, PA 19355
PH: (610)560-0484
Toll free: 866-AAWC-999
Fax: (610)560-0502
Thomas, Tina, Exec. Dir.

CPCU Society [1853]
720 Providence Rd.
Malvern, PA 19355
PH: (610)251-2716
    (610)644-2100
Toll free: 800-932-2728
Fax: (610)725-5969
Brown, Kevin H., Exec. Dir., Sr. VP

Insurance Research Council [1871]
718 Providence Rd.
Malvern, PA 19355
Kilgore, Victoria, Dir. of Res.

National Wrestling Coaches Associa-
tion [23371]
330 Hostetter St.
Manheim, PA 17545
PH: (717)653-8009
Fax: (717)653-8270
Moyer, Mike, Exec. Dir.

Society of Outdoor Recreation
Professionals [5669]
PO Box 221
Marienville, PA 16239
PH: (814)927-8212
Fax: (814)927-6659
Baas, John, President

Transport for Christ, International **[20470]**
1525 River Rd.
Marietta, PA 17547-9403
PH: (717)426-9977
Toll free: 877-797-7729
Fax: (717)426-9980
Weidner, Mr. Scott A., CEO,
President

Association of Emergency Physicians **[14676]**
911 Whitewater Dr.
Mars, PA 16046-4221
Toll free: 866-772-1818
Fax: (866)422-7794
Hayes, Jim, President

AE/AOE Sailors Association **[5582]**
603 S Market St.
Martinsburg, PA 16662
PH: (772)340-2709
Gohde, William, President

Society for the Arts, Religion and
Contemporary Culture **[9001]**
15811 Kutztown Rd., Box 15
Maxatawny, PA 19538
PH: (610)683-7581
Fax: (610)683-7581
Vos, Nelvin, Exec. Dir.

Society of Carbide & Tool Engineers
[6851]
PO Box 77
McKeesport, PA 15135

National Slovak Society of the
United States of America **[19646]**
351 Valley Brook Rd.
McMurray, PA 15317-3337
PH: (724)731-0094
Toll free: 800-488-1890
Fax: (724)731-0145
Blazek, David G., FIC, President,
CEO

Phi Sigma Iota **[23798]**
Allegheny College, Box 30
520 N Main St.
Meadville, PA 16335-3902
PH: (814)332-4886
Fax: (814)337-4445
Marx, Joann, President

Brethren in Christ World Missions
[20389]
431 Grantham Rd.
Mechanicsburg, PA 17055-5812
PH: (717)697-2634
Fax: (717)691-6053
Lloyd, Jonathan, Exec. Dir.

Children's Medical Mission of Haiti
[10930]
925 Hertzler Rd.
Mechanicsburg, PA 17055-6128
PH: (717)796-1852
Squire, Rev. Bill, President

Modern Car Society **[21440]**
Rolls-Royce Owners Club
191 Hempt Rd.
Mechanicsburg, PA 17050
Facinelli, James, Chairman

MOMSTELL **[13153]**
PO Box 450
Mechanicsburg, PA 17055
PH: (717)384-6066
Smith-LeGore, Sharon, President

Rolls-Royce Owners' Club **[21486]**
191 Hempt Rd.
Mechanicsburg, PA 17050-2605
PH: (717)697-4671
Fax: (717)697-7820
Austin, Bob, Exec. Dir.

United States Harness Writers' Association **[2729]**
PO Box 1314
Mechanicsburg, PA 17055
PH: (717)651-5889
Wolf, Steve, Chmn. of the Bd.

American Coon Hunters Association
[22958]
PO Box 2015
Media, PA 19063-9015
PH: (484)234-0582
Toll free: 855-WIN-ACHA
Monroe, John J., President

The Decorative Arts Trust **[8973]**
20 S Olive St., Ste. 304
Media, PA 19063
PH: (610)627-4970
Fairbanks, Jonathan, Chairman

Elwyn **[12069]**
111 Elwyn Rd.
Media, PA 19063-4622
PH: (610)891-2000
Andrade, Raul, Director

Glass Molders, Pottery, Plastics, and
Allied Workers International Union
[23422]
608 E Baltimore Pke.
Media, PA 19063-0607
PH: (610)565-5051
Fax: (610)565-0983
Smith, Bruce, President

Holistic Pediatric Alliance **[13628]**
327 N Middletown Rd.
Media, PA 19063
PH: (610)565-2360

International Chiropractic Pediatric
Association **[14273]**
327 N Middletown Rd.
Media, PA 19063
PH: (610)565-2360
Fax: (610)656-3567
Ohm, Dr. Jeanne, Exec. Dir.

Scotch-Irish Foundation **[20996]**
PO Box 53
Media, PA 19063

Scotch-Irish Society of the United
States of America **[20997]**
PO Box 53
Media, PA 19063
Smith, Carole, Editor

UNITE **[12430]**
c/o Riddle Hospital
1068 W Baltimore Pke.
Media, PA 19063
PH: (610)296-2411
Toll free: 888-488-6483
Flanagan, John, Treasurer

VALUEUSA **[8255]**
1 W 2nd St.
Media, PA 19063
PH: (484)443-8457
Fax: (484)443-8458
Finsterbusch, Marty, Exec. Dir.

Association for X and Y Chromosome Variations **[17336]**
PO Box 861
Mendenhall, PA 19357
Toll free: 888-999-9428
Miller, Robert, Dir. (Actg.)

White German Shepherd Dog Club
of America **[21992]**
c/o Barb Hively, President, 8837 N
Mountain Dr.
8837 N Mountain Dr.
Mercersburg, PA 17236
Hively, Barb, President

Syrian Studies Association **[8340]**
c/o Geoffrey D. Schad, Treasurer
and Secretary
312 Maplewood Rd.
Merion Station, PA 19066-10331
Kalmbach, Hilary, President

Secular Institute of Saint Francis de
Sales **[19904]**
c/o DeSales Secular Institute
104 W Main St.
Middletown, PA 17057-1215
Reisinger, Rev. Franz, Founder

American Bandstand Fan Club
[24083]
c/o David Frees, President
52 Stauffer Park Ln.
Mohnton, PA 19540-7751
Frees, David, President

Rhodesian Ridgeback Club of the
United States **[21953]**
1185 Alleghenyville Rd.
Mohnton, PA 19540
Jones, Ross, President

National Veteran-Owned Business
Association **[5842]**
420 Rouser Rd., Ste. 101
Moon Township, PA 15108
PH: (412)269-1663
Hale, Chris, President

International Association for Pain
and Chemical Dependency
[16557]
101 Washington St.
Morrisville, PA 19067-7111
Fax: (215)337-0959
Buttfield, Dr. Ian, Chairman

International Modern Hapkido
Federation **[22992]**
210 Homestead Dr.
Moscow, PA 18444
PH: (570)842-1558
Fax: (570)842-3741
Cushing, Victor, Founder, CEO

Society of Phantom Friends **[9136]**
40 S Vine St.
Mount Carmel, PA 17851
Emburg, Kate, President

National Association of Forensic
Economics **[5561]**
PO Box 394
Mount Union, PA 17066
PH: (814)542-3253
Toll free: 866-370-6233
Fax: (814)542-3253
Weinstein, Marc A., Exec. Dir.

Colonial Coin Collectors Club
[22265]
c/o Charlie Rohrer, Treasurer
PO Box 25
Mountville, PA 17554
Rosen, Jim, President

Carpatho-Rusyn Society **[19629]**
915 Dickson St.
Munhall, PA 15120-1929
PH: (412)567-3077
Sivak, Maryann, President

American Malacological Society
[6787]
c/o Charles Sturm, Jr., Treasurer
5024 Beech Rd.
Murrysville, PA 15668-9613

American British White Park Association **[3689]**
PO Box 409
Myerstown, PA 17067
Toll free: 877-900-BEEF
Fax: (208)979-2008
Bledsoe, Doug, President

National Antique Oldsmobile Club
[21448]
121 N Railroad St.
Myerstown, PA 17067
Schultz, Jim E., President

Numismatic Literary Guild **[22279]**
c/o Ed Reiter, Executive Director
1517 Stewart Dr.
Nanticoke, PA 18634
PH: (570)740-2181
Fax: (570)740-2723
Reiter, Ed, Exec. Dir.

American Color Print Society **[8830]**
c/o Elizabeth MacDonald
205 Woodside Ave.
Narberth, PA 19072-2430
Meyers, Carole J., President

American Osteopathic College of
Physical Medicine and Rehabilitation **[16516]**
210 Lantwyn Ln.
Narberth, PA 19072
PH: (908)387-1750
(610)664-4466
Fax: (866)925-8568
Wilson, Stephanie, Exec. Dir.

Guillain-Barre Syndrome/Chronic
Inflammatory Demyelinating Polyneuropathy Foundation
International **[15938]**
The Holly Bldg.
104 1/2 Forrest Ave.
Narberth, PA 19072
PH: (610)667-0131
Toll free: 866-224-3301
Fax: (610)667-7036
Butler, Lisa, Exec. Dir.

International Society for Psychological and Social Approaches to
Psychosis - United States Chapter
[15779]
PO Box 491
Narberth, PA 19072
Koehler, Dr. Brian, Exec. Ofc.

Moravian Historical Society **[20485]**
214 E Center St.
Nazareth, PA 18064
PH: (610)759-5070
Fax: (610)759-2461

Open Air Campaigners U.S.A.
[20157]
PO Box D
Nazareth, PA 18064
PH: (610)746-0508
Toll free: 888-886-5661
Briscoe, Eric, Director

Vintage Sports Car Club of America
[21515]
39 Woodland Dr.
New Britain, PA 18901
Leith, Sandy, President

Pepsi-Cola Collectors Club **[21712]**
c/o Diane Gabriel, Secretary
335 Mathews Way
New Castle, PA 16101
PH: (724)658-6310
(804)748-5769
Stoddard, Bob, Founder

Association of Baptists for World
Evangelism **[19716]**
522 Lewisberry Rd.
New Cumberland, PA 17070
PH: (717)774-7000
Fax: (717)774-1919
Cockrell, Al, Act. Pres.

Marx Brotherhood **[24010]**
335 Fieldstone Dr.
New Hope, PA 18938-1012

PH: (215)862-9734
Wesolowski, Paul G., Director

Medical Care International **[15484]**
PO Box 69
New Hope, PA 18938-0069
Kasirsky, Gilbert, PhD, President

USMC Vietnam Tankers Association
[21159]
5537 Lower Mountain Rd.
New Hope, PA 18938
Wear, John, President

International Graphoanalysis Society
[10413]
842 5th Ave.
New Kensington, PA 15068
PH: (724)472-9701
Fax: (509)271-1149
Greco, Greg, President

Arabian Professional & Amateur
  Horseman's Association **[4338]**
c/o Johnny Ryan, President
216 Irish Dr.
New Oxford, PA 17350
PH: (609)558-4616
    (507)867-2981
Harvey, Katie G., VP

Ngwa National Association USA
[9577]
56 Scheller Rd.
New Providence, PA 17560
PH: (717)786-6620
Anosike-Byron, C., VP

Clumber Spaniel Club of America
[21858]
c/o Jack Poole
874 Orchard Terrace Dr.
New Wilmington, PA 16142-4222
Cole, Milford, President

Law School Admission Council
[8216]
662 Penn St.
Newtown, PA 18940
PH: (215)968-1001
Margolis, Wendy, Dir. of Comm.

Project Management Institute **[2191]**
14 Campus Blvd.
Newtown Square, PA 19073-3299
PH: (610)356-4600
Toll free: 855-746-4849
Fax: (610)482-9971
Nieto-Rodriguez, Antonio, Chairman

Society of Financial Service Profes-
  sionals **[1929]**
3803 W Chester Pke., Ste. 225
Newtown Square, PA 19073
PH: (610)526-2500
Toll free: 800-392-6900
Fax: (610)359-8115
Rigney, Anne M., Gen. Counsel

World Arnold Chiari Malformation
  Association **[17355]**
31 Newtown Woods Rd.
Newtown Square, PA 19073
PH: (610)353-4737
Justin, Sandi, Contact

Independent Laboratory Distributors
  Association **[3026]**
827 Maple Ave.
North Versailles, PA 15137
PH: (412)829-5190
Toll free: 888-878-4532
Fax: (412)829-5191
DeMeis, Jonathan, Chairman

Six of One Club: The Prisoner Appreciation Society **[24089]**
871 Clover Dr.
North Wales, PA 19454-2749
Clark, Bruce A., Coord.

International Susan Glaspell Society
[10381]
c/o Dr. Doug Powers
555 Jefferson St.
Northumberland, PA 17857-9634
Carpentier, Martha C., President,
  Web Adm.

Women Marines Association **[21022]**
PO Box 377
Oaks, PA 19456-0377
Toll free: 888-525-1943
Cook, Betty, VP

Catholic Golden Age **[19811]**
PO Box 249
Olyphant, PA 18447-0249
Toll free: 855-586-1091
Dino, Rev. Gerald N., President

Council on Brain Injury **[14911]**
16 Industrial Blvd., Ste. 203
Paoli, PA 19301-1609
Finegan, Joanne, President

Society of the Descendants of the
  Schwenkfeldian Exiles **[10066]**
105 Seminary St.
Pennsburg, PA 18073
PH: (215)679-3103
Fax: (215)679-8175
Luz, Rev. David W., President

Tan Son Nhut Association **[21158]**
PO Box 236
Penryn, PA 17564-0236
PH: (803)463-7555
    (870)932-8085
Brown, Randall, President

Pearl S. Buck International **[10877]**
520 Dublin Rd.
Perkasie, PA 18944
PH: (215)249-0100
Fax: (215)249-9657
Mintzer, Janet L., CEO, President

Chess Journalists of America **[2671]**
c/o Stan Booz, Secretary-Treasurer
511 Solliday Ct.
Perkasie, PA 18944
Capron, Mark, VP

American Association of Birth
  Centers **[16267]**
3123 Gottschall Rd.
Perkiomenville, PA 18074
PH: (215)234-8068
Toll free: 866-542-4784
Fax: (215)234-8829
Bauer, Kate E., MBA, Exec. Dir.

Academy of Natural Sciences of
  Drexel University **[6891]**
1900 Benjamin Franklin Pky.
Philadelphia, PA 19103
PH: (215)299-1000
Gephart, George W., Jr., CEO,
  President

Adult Congenital Heart Association
[14085]
3300 Henry Ave., Ste. 112
Philadelphia, PA 19129
PH: (215)849-1260
Toll free: 888-921-2242
Fax: (215)849-1261
Tringali, Glenn R., Exec. Dir.

African American Collaborative
  Obesity Research Network **[16244]**
University of Pennsylvania
Perelman School of Medicine
415 Curie Blvd.
Philadelphia, PA 19104
Kumanyika, Shiriki K., PhD,
  Founder, Chairperson

African Cultural Alliance of North
  America **[10485]**
5530 Chester Ave.
Philadelphia, PA 19143-5328

PH: (215)729-8225
Jabateh, Voffee, Exec. Dir.

AGLP: The Association of LGBTQ
  Psychiatrists **[11870]**
4514 Chester Ave.
Philadelphia, PA 19143-3707
PH: (215)222-2800
Fax: (215)222-3881
Harker, Roy, Exec. Dir.

Aid for the Children of Liberia
[10841]
3320 Fairdale Rd.
Philadelphia, PA 19154
PH: (484)202-4082
Fax: (267)338-1016
Morris-Fello, M. Yassah, Founder,
  President

Aikido Association of North America
[22495]
5836 Henry Ave., No. 38
Philadelphia, PA 19128-1703
PH: (215)483-3000
Utada, Yukio, President

Al-Bustan Seeds of Culture **[8811]**
526 S 46th St.
Philadelphia, PA 19143
PH: (267)303-0070
    (267)809-3668
Saah, Andrea Imredy, Treasurer

Al-Rafidain Humanitarian Aid for
  Women and Children **[12611]**
PO Box 45906
Philadelphia, PA 19149
Jasim, Azhar, CEO

ALEPH: Alliance for Jewish Renewal
[18739]
7000 Lincoln Dr., No. B2
Philadelphia, PA 19119-3046
PH: (215)247-9700
Fax: (215)247-9703
Schechter-Shaffin, Shoshanna,
  Exec. Dir.

American Academy of Political and
  Social Science **[7041]**
Annenberg Public Policy Ctr.
202 S 36th St.
Philadelphia, PA 19104-3806
PH: (215)746-6500
Fax: (215)573-2667
Kecskemethy, Tom, Exec. Dir.

American Aging Association **[14886]**
Dept. of Pathology, College of
  Medicine
Drexel University
New College Bldg.
245 N 15th St.
Philadelphia, PA 19102
Nikolich-Zugich, Janko, MD,
  Chairperson

American Assembly for Men in Nurs-
  ing **[16086]**
c/o Karen Mota, Account Executive
PO Box 7867
Philadelphia, PA 19101-7867
PH: (215)243-5813
Fax: (215)387-7497
Patterson, Bob, President

American Association for Cancer
  Research **[16329]**
615 Chestnut St., 17th Fl.
Philadelphia, PA 19106-4406
PH: (215)440-9300
Toll free: 866-423-3965
Fax: (215)440-9313
Foti, Margaret, PhD, CEO

American Association of Teachers of
  Turkic Languages **[10283]**
c/o Dr. Feride Hatiboglu, Treasurer

Dept. of Near Eastern languages
  and Civilizations
Williams Hall, Rm. 847
255 S 36th St.
Philadelphia, PA 19104-6305
Schamiloglu, Dr. Uli, President

American Bible Society **[19746]**
101 N Independence Mall E, 8th Fl.
Philadelphia, PA 19106-2155
PH: (215)309-0900
Fax: (215)689-4308
Curtin, Sr. Joan, Advisor

American Board of Allergy and Im-
  munology **[13571]**
1835 Market St., Ste. 1210
Philadelphia, PA 19106-2512
Toll free: 866-264-5568
Fax: (215)592-9411
Wasserman, Stephen I., MD,
  President

American Board of Internal Medicine
[15425]
510 Walnut St., Ste. 1700
Philadelphia, PA 19106-3699
Toll free: 800-441-ABIM
Fax: (215)446-3590
Baron, Richard J., President, CEO

The American Board of Plastic
  Surgery, Inc. **[14305]**
7 Penn Ctr., Ste. 400
1635 Market St.
Philadelphia, PA 19103-2204
PH: (215)587-9322
Fax: (215)587-9622
Noone, Dr. R. Barrett, Officer

American Board of Surgery **[17365]**
1617 John F. Kennedy Blvd., Ste.
  860
Philadelphia, PA 19103
PH: (215)568-4000
Fax: (215)563-5718
Evans, Stephen R. T., Chairman

American Catholic Historical Society
[9453]
263 S 4th St.
Philadelphia, PA 19106
PH: (717)632-3535
Finnegan, Michael H., President

American College of Physicians
[15426]
190 N Independance Mall W
Philadelphia, PA 19106-1572
PH: (215)351-2400
    (215)351-2600
Toll free: 800-523-1546
Hood, Virginia L., Specialist

American College of Physicians -
  Ethics, Professionalism and Hu-
  man Rights Committee **[14744]**
190 N Independence Mall W
Philadelphia, PA 19106-1572
PH: (215)351-2400
    (215)351-2835
Toll free: 800-523-1546
Sulmasy, Lois Snyder, Director

American Creativity Association
[9530]
School of Education
Drexel University
3141 Chestnut St.
Philadelphia, PA 19104
PH: (215)895-6771
O'Boyle, Mr. Jamie, Treasurer

American Friends Service Commit-
  tee **[13027]**
1501 Cherry St.
Philadelphia, PA 19102
PH: (215)241-7000
    (215)241-7104
Cretin, Shan, Gen. Sec.

American Institute of Chemists
[6182]
315 Chestnut St.
Philadelphia, PA 19106-2702
PH: (215)873-8224
Fax: (215)629-5224
Jasinski, Jerry, Chairman

American Latvian Artists Association
[8834]
639 Kerper St.
Philadelphia, PA 19111
PH: (215)904-7265
Treija, Linda, President

American Law Institute [5414]
4025 Chestnut St.
Philadelphia, PA 19104
PH: (215)243-1600
Fax: (215)243-1636
Cooper Ramo, Roberta, President

American Law Institute Continuing
Legal Education [8208]
4025 Chestnut St.
Philadelphia, PA 19104
Toll free: 800-CLE-NEWS
Fax: (215)243-1664
Scribner, Julie, CFO, Director

American Philosophical Society
[7118]
104 S 5th St.
Philadelphia, PA 19106-3387
PH: (215)440-3400
Fax: (215)440-3423
Thomson, Keith Stewart, Exec. Ofc.

American Research Institute in
Turkey [10284]
3260 S St.
Philadelphia, PA 19104-6324
PH: (215)898-3474
Leinwand, Dr. Nancy, Exec. Dir.

American Society of Media
Photographers [2573]
150 N 2nd St.
Philadelphia, PA 19106-1912
PH: (215)451-2767
Fax: (215)451-0880
Kennedy, Tom, Exec. Dir.

American Swedish Historical
Museum [10229]
1900 Pattison Ave.
Philadelphia, PA 19145-5901
PH: (215)389-1776
Beck, Ms. Tracey R., Exec. Dir.

Artisans Order of Mutual Protection
[19482]
8100 Roosevelt Blvd.
Philadelphia, PA 19152
PH: (215)708-1000
Toll free: 800-551-1873
Bornmann, Carl F., Jr., Managing
Ed.

Associated Services for the Blind
[17687]
919 Walnut St.
Philadelphia, PA 19107
PH: (215)627-0600
Toll free: 800-732-0999
Fax: (215)922-0692
Bryant, Cedric, Director

Association for the Advancement of
Philosophy and Psychiatry [8419]
c/o Claire Pouncey, President
Eudaimonia Associates, LLC
210 W Rittenhouse Sq., Ste. 404
Philadelphia, PA 19103
PH: (215)545-9700
Potter, Nancy Nyquist, PhD, Exec.

Association for the Advancement of
Sustainability in Higher Education
[7952]
2401 Walnut St., Ste. 102
Philadelphia, PA 19103

PH: (303)395-1331
Toll free: 888-552-0329
Ahmed, Fahmida, Chairperson

Association of Black Women in
Higher Education [8746]
University of Pennsylvania
3537 Locust Walk, Ste. 200
Philadelphia, PA 19104-6225
Ray, Michelle, VP

Association of Educational Publish-
ers [8452]
325 Chestnut St., Ste. 1110
Philadelphia, PA 19106
PH: (267)351-4310
Fax: (267)351-4317
Gaynor, Charlene F., CEO

Association of Islamic Charitable
Projects [20216]
4431 Walnut St.
Philadelphia, PA 19104-2924
PH: (215)387-8888

Athenaeum of Philadelphia [9693]
219 S 6th St.
Philadelphia, PA 19106-3794
PH: (215)925-2688
Fax: (215)925-3755
Davison, William M., Treasurer

Audio Publishers Association [2901]
100 N 20th St., Ste. 400
Philadelphia, PA 19103
PH: (215)564-2729
Lee, Linda, President

Aviation Distributors and Manufactur-
ers Association [130]
100 N 20th St., Ste. 400
Philadelphia, PA 19103-1462
PH: (215)320-3872
Fax: (215)564-2175
Diggs, Tia, Exec. Dir.

Beta Phi Mu [9694]
PO Box 42139
Philadelphia, PA 19101
PH: (267)361-5018
Abels, Eileen G., PhD, President

Big Picture Alliance [17280]
Stenton Artists Guild
4732 Stenton Ave.
Philadelphia, PA 19144
PH: (215)381-2588
Fax: (215)381-2593
Rosard, Steve, President

Bike & Build [10778]
6153 Ridge Ave.
Philadelphia, PA 19128
PH: (267)331-8488
Fax: (661)752-9806
Anderson, Kristin, Chairperson

Bockus International Society of
Gastroenterology [14783]
220 W Rittenhouse Sq., No. 18C
Philadelphia, PA 19103
PH: (215)732-5468
Fax: (215)732-4989
Bernstein, David E., MD, VP

Brazil Philatelic Association [22312]
c/o William V. Kriebel, Secretary-
Treasurer, 1923 Manning St.
1923 Manning St.
Philadelphia, PA 19103-5728
Hawkins, John, President

Peggy Browning Fund [5524]
100 S Broad St., Ste. 1208
Philadelphia, PA 19110
PH: (267)273-7990
Fax: (267)273-7688
Lurie, Joseph, President, Founder

Carpenters' Company of the City
and County of Philadelphia [9380]
320 Chestnut St., Carpenters Hall
Philadelphia, PA 19106
PH: (215)925-0167
Thompson, Christy, Administrator

Carriage Operators of North America
[693]
1648 N Hancock St.
Philadelphia, PA 19122-3120
PH: (215)923-8516
Kramer, Linda, Liaison

Center for Advocacy for the Rights
and Interests of the Elderly
[10502]
2 Penn Ctr.
1500 JFK Blvd., Ste. 1500
Philadelphia, PA 19102-1718
PH: (215)545-5728
Toll free: 800-356-3606
Fax: (215)545-5372
Menio, Diane, Exec. Dir.

Center for the Study of Economics
[19166]
1501 Cherry St.
Philadelphia, PA 19102
PH: (267)519-5312
Mastalski, Frank, Mem.

Central Association of the
Miraculous Medal [19821]
475 E Chelten Ave.
Philadelphia, PA 19144
PH: (215)848-1010
Toll free: 800-523-3674
Fax: (215)848-1014
Pieber, Rev. Carl L., PhD, Exec. Dir.

CGFNS International [16127]
3600 Market St., Ste. 400
Philadelphia, PA 19104-2651
PH: (215)222-8454
Shaffer, Franklin A., EdD, CEO

Challah for Hunger [12080]
201 S Camac St., 2nd Fl.
Philadelphia, PA 19107
Winkelman, Ms. Eli, Founder

Chemical Heritage Foundation
[9472]
315 Chestnut St.
Philadelphia, PA 19106
PH: (215)925-2222
Tritton, Tom, CEO, President

Children's Literacy Initiative [8238]
2314 Market St., 3rd Fl.
Philadelphia, PA 19103
PH: (215)561-4676
Toll free: 888-408-3388
Fax: (215)561-4677
Bloom, David J, V. Chmn. of the Bd.

Citizens for Responsible Care and
Research, Inc. [6063]
1024 N 5th St.
Philadelphia, PA 19123-1404
PH: (215)627-5335
Fax: (267)639-4950
Woeckner, Elizabeth, President

Coalition of Cancer Cooperative
Groups [13946]
1818 Market St., Ste. 1100
Philadelphia, PA 19103
PH: (215)789-3600
Fax: (215)789-3655
Comis, Robert L., MD, Chairman,
President

Conservation Center for Art and
Historic Artifacts [8852]
264 S 23rd St.
Philadelphia, PA 19103

PH: (215)545-0613
Fax: (215)735-9313
Cades, Stewart R., Treasurer

Corporate Responsibility Association
[915]
123 S Broad St., Ste. 1930
Philadelphia, PA 19109
PH: (215)606-9520
Fax: (267)800-2701
Murren, James J., Chairman

Dance Affiliates [9249]
Bldg. 46B
4701 Bath St.
Philadelphia, PA 19137-2235
PH: (215)636-9000
Fax: (267)672-2912
Swartz, F. Randolph, Art Dir., Bd.
Member

Darfur Human Rights Organization
[18393]
8171 Castor Ave.
Philadelphia, PA 19152
PH: (267)784-7073
Adam, Dr. Abdel Gabar, Founder

Delta Phi Epsilon Sorority [23952]
251 S Camac St.
Philadelphia, PA 19107
PH: (215)732-5901
Fax: (215)732-5906
DeFeo, Nicole L., Exec. Dir.

Educational Commission for Foreign
Medical Graduates [16748]
3624 Market St.
Philadelphia, PA 19104-2685
PH: (215)386-5900
Fax: (215)386-9196
Cassimatis, N. Emmanuel G., MD,
CEO, President

EducationWorks [7645]
3149 Germantown Ave.
Philadelphia, PA 19133
PH: (215)221-6900
Fax: (215)221-6901
Friedman, Mr. Martin, Exec. Dir.,
Founder

Estonian American National Council
[19427]
c/o Linda Rink, Executive Director
1420 Locust St., Ste. 31N
Philadelphia, PA 19102
PH: (215)546-5863
Rink-Abel, Marju, President

False Memory Syndrome Foundation
[16914]
PO Box 30044
Philadelphia, PA 19103-8044
PH: (215)940-1040
Fax: (215)940-1042
Freyd, Pamela, PhD, Exec. Dir.

Federation of Malayalee Associa-
tions of Americas [19473]
1922 Cottman Ave.
Philadelphia, PA 19111
PH: (267)549-1196
Fax: (267)742-4142
Niravel, Anandan, President

Foreign Policy Research Institute
[18268]
1528 Walnut St., Ste. 610
Philadelphia, PA 19102
PH: (215)732-3774
Fax: (215)732-4401
McDougall, Walter A., Chairman

Foundation for Advancement of
International Medical Education
and Research [8321]
3624 Market St.
Philadelphia, PA 19104
Fax: (215)966-3121
Cassimatis, Emmanuel G., MD,
Chmn. of the Bd.

Friends Association for Higher
Education **[7961]**
1501 Cherry St.
Philadelphia, PA 19102
PH: (215)241-7116
Fax: (215)241-7078
Weinholtz, Donn, Clerk

Friends Council on Education **[8483]**
1507 Cherry St.
Philadelphia, PA 19102
PH: (215)241-7245
     (215)241-7289
Fax: (215)241-7299
Smith, Drew, Exec. Dir.

Friends General Conference **[20169]**
1216 Arch St., Ste. 2B
Philadelphia, PA 19107
PH: (215)561-1700
Toll free: 800-966-4556
Crossno, Barry, Gen. Sec.

Friends World Committee for
Consultation **[18788]**
1506 Race St.
Philadelphia, PA 19102-1406
PH: (215)241-7250
Fax: (215)241-7285
Mohr, Robin, Exec. Sec.

Frontiers International, Inc. **[11360]**
6301 Crittenden St.
Philadelphia, PA 19138-1031
PH: (215)549-4550
Fax: (215)549-4209
Evans, Wilma J., Chairperson

General Building Contractors As-
sociation **[530]**
36 S 18th St.
Philadelphia, PA 19103
PH: (215)568-7015
Fax: (215)568-3115
Bittenbender, Emily L., Chmn. of the
Bd.

Global Interdependence Center
[19261]
Federal Reserve Bank of
Philadelphia
100 N 6th St., 5th Fl. SE
Philadelphia, PA 19106
PH: (215)238-0990
Fax: (215)238-0966
Fornito, Jill, Dir. of Operations

Gynecologic Oncology Group
[16345]
4 Penn Ctr., Ste. 1020
1600 John F. Kennedy Blvd.
Philadelphia, PA 19103
PH: (215)854-0770
Toll free: 800-225-3053
DiSaia, Dr. Philip J., Chairman

History of Dermatology Society
[9483]
c/o Lawrence Charles Parish, MD,
President
1760 Market St., Ste. 301
Philadelphia, PA 19103
PH: (215)563-8333
Fax: (215)563-3044
Parish, Lawrence C., MD, President

Hobby Manufacturers Association
[1642]
1410 E Erie Ave.
Philadelphia, PA 19124
PH: (267)341-1604
Fax: (215)744-4699
Hill, Fred, Treasurer

HRO Today Services and Technology Association **[1695]**
SharedXpertise Media, LLC
123 S Broad St., Ste. 1930

Philadelphia, PA 19109
PH: (215)606-9520
Reim, Jason, Mgr.

Independence Seaport Museum
[21095]
211 S Columbus Blvd.
Philadelphia, PA 19106
PH: (215)413-8655
Fax: (215)925-6713
Good, Megan, Director

International Academy of Cosmetic
Dermatology **[14495]**
c/o Ms. Anna Gjeci, Executive
Secretary
1508 Creswood Rd.
Philadelphia, PA 19115
PH: (215)677-3060
Fax: (215)695-2254
Parish, Lawrence Charles, President

International Association of Hand
Papermakers and Paper Artists
[10062]
c/o Nicole Donnelly, President
2120 E Westmoreland St.
Philadelphia, PA 19133
Larrea, Ma. Carolina J., VP,
Secretary

International Association of Jewish
Vocational Services **[8737]**
1845 Walnut St., Ste. 640
Philadelphia, PA 19103
PH: (215)854-0233
Fax: (215)854-0212
Cohen, Genie, CEO

International Association of Word
and Image Studies **[8501]**
c/o Prof. Catriona MacLeod,
Secretary
745 Williams Hall
University of Pennsylvania
Philadelphia, PA 19104-6305
PH: (215)898-7332
Fax: (215)573-7794
MacLeod, Prof. Catriona, Secretary

International Children's Anophthal-
mia & Microphthalmia Network
[17715]
c/o Center for Developmental
Medicine and Genetics
Genetics, Levy 2 W
5501 Old York Rd.
Philadelphia, PA 19141
PH: (215)456-8722
Toll free: 800-580-4226
McGrady, Ryan, President

International Clinical Epidemiology
Network **[14730]**
1735 Market St., Ste. A427
Philadelphia, PA 19103
PH: (215)898-2368
Fax: (215)573-5315
Arora, Dr. Narendra, Prog. Dir.

International Complement Society
[15381]
c/o Dr. Wenchao Song, Treasurer
1254 BRBII/III
University of Pennsylvania
421 Curie Blvd.
Philadelphia, PA 19104
PH: (215)573-6641
Fax: (215)746-8941
Tenner, Andrea Joan, President

International Hustle Dance Associa-
tion **[9262]**
PO Box 11655
Philadelphia, PA 19116
McGee, Daniel, Treasurer

International Kitchen Exhaust Cleaning Association **[1290]**
100 N 20th St., Ste. 400
Philadelphia, PA 19103-1462

PH: (215)320-3876
Fax: (215)564-2175
Hagy, Sarah, Exec. Dir.

International Organization for
Septuagint and Cognate Studies
[19759]
c/o Jay C. Treat, Editor
University of Pennsylvania
255 S 36th St.
Philadelphia, PA 19104-6305
Joosten, Jan, President

International People's Democratic
Uhuru Movement **[18101]**
PO Box 22370
Philadelphia, PA 19110-2370
PH: (973)826-0702

International Performing Arts for
Youth **[10067]**
c/o CultureWorks
The Philadelphia Bldg.
1315 Walnut St., Ste. 320
Philadelphia, PA 19107
PH: (267)690-1325
Fax: (267)519-3343
Gargano, Ray, President

International Society of Bone and
Soft Tissue Pathology **[16585]**
800 Spruce St.
Philadelphia, PA 19107
PH: (215)829-3541
Fax: (215)829-7564
Bridge, Dr. Julia, President

International Society of NeuroVirol-
ogy **[16026]**
Dept. of Neuroscience, Rm. 740
Temple University School of
Medicine
3500 N Broad St.
Philadelphia, PA 19140
PH: (215)707-9788
Fax: (215)707-9838
Pulliam, Lynn, Bd. Member

International Society of Ocular
Oncology **[16346]**
Wills Eye Hospital
Ocular Oncology Service
840 Walnut St.
Philadelphia, PA 19107
Fax: (215)928-1140
Pe'er, Jacob, MD, President

International Society for Presence
Research **[7095]**
Media Interface and Network Design
Lab.
Dept. of Broadcasting, Telecom-
munications, and Mass Media
Temple University
Philadelphia, PA 19122
PH: (215)204-7182
Fax: (215)204-5402
Lombard, Matthew, President

International Society for Research
on Emotion **[7065]**
La Salle University
1900 W Olney Ave., Wister 219
Philadelphia, PA 19141
Kappas, Arvid, President

International Society for the Study of
Time **[10282]**
c/o Jo Alyson Parker
St. Joseph's University
English Dept.
5600 City Ave.
Philadelphia, PA 19131-1395
Steineck, Raji, President

International Visual Literacy Association **[7777]**
c/o Dr. Carolyn Berenato, Treasurer
Merion Hall 212

St. Joseph's University
5600 City Ave.
Philadelphia, PA 19131
Tardrew, Karen, President

Jewish Publication Society **[9639]**
2100 Arch St., 2nd Fl.
Philadelphia, PA 19103
PH: (215)832-0600
Toll free: 800-234-3151
Fax: (215)568-2017
Schwartz, Rabbi Barry L., CEO

Kappa Alpha Psi Fraternity **[23902]**
2322-24 N Broad St.
Philadelphia, PA 19132-4590
PH: (215)228-7184
Fax: (215)228-7181
Brown, Ernest H., Exec. Dir.

Kappa Psi Kappa Fraternity, Inc.
[23757]
PO Box 733
Philadelphia, PA 19105
PH: (516)841-5865
Raby, Dedrick J., President

Lamp for Haiti **[11928]**
PO Box 39703
Philadelphia, PA 19106
PH: (267)295-2822
Reimer, Henry, Chairman

The Life After Trauma Organization
[13235]
PO Box 56243
Philadelphia, PA 19130
Perkins, Clara Whaley, PhD, Chair-
man

Linguistic Data Consortium **[9745]**
3600 Market St., Ste. 810
Philadelphia, PA 19104-2653
PH: (215)898-0464
Fax: (215)573-2175
Cieri, Dr. Christopher, Exec. Dir.

Maccabi USA/Sports for Israel
[23233]
1511 Walnut St., Ste. 401
Philadelphia, PA 19102
PH: (215)561-6900
Fax: (215)561-5470
Carner, Ron, President

Medical Mission Sisters **[20434]**
8400 Pine Rd.
Philadelphia, PA 19111-1385
PH: (215)742-6100
Lanfermann, Sr. Agnes, MMS,
Coord.

Medical Students for Choice **[17110]**
PO Box 40188
Philadelphia, PA 19106
PH: (215)625-0800
Fax: (215)625-4848
Henderson, Miquia, Contact

Military Order of the Loyal Legion of
the United States **[20743]**
121 S Broad St., Ste. 1910
Philadelphia, PA 19107
Burden, Jeffry C., Cmdr.

National Adoption Center **[10459]**
1500 Walnut St., Ste. 701
Philadelphia, PA 19102
PH: (215)735-9988
Toll free: 800-TO-ADOPT
Fax: (215)735-9410
Mullner, Ken, Exec. Dir.

National Association of African
Americans for Positive Imagery
[17781]
1231 N Broad St.
Philadelphia, PA 19122

PH: (215)235-6488
Fax: (215)235-6491
Brown, Rev. Jesse W., Jr., Exec. Dir.

**National Association of Catholic
School Teachers [7576]**
1700 Sansom St., Ste. 903
Philadelphia, PA 19103
Toll free: 800-99N-ACST
Schwartz, Rita C., President

**National Association of Clinical
Nurse Specialists [16146]**
100 N 20th St., 4th Fl.
Philadelphia, PA 19103-1462
PH: (215)320-3881
Fax: (215)564-2175
Ray, Melinda Mercer, Exec. Dir.

**National Association of Early Child-
hood Teacher Educators [8652]**
3017 Tilton St.
Philadelphia, PA 19134
Davis, Sara McCormick, President

**National Association of Equipment
Leasing Brokers [2928]**
100 N 20th St., Ste. 400
Philadelphia, PA 19103
Toll free: 800-996-2352
Fax: (215)564-2175
Casey, Joe, Exec. Dir.

**National Association of Prudential
Retirees and Vested Terminators,
Inc. [12757]**
2018 Bergen St.
Philadelphia, PA 19152
Toll free: 888-730-6090
Fax: (215)722-1017
Ciocca, Joseph R., CLU, President

**National Black Leadership Initiative
on Cancer [14019]**
8500 Lindbergh Blvd., Ste. 2216
1415 N Broad St., Ste. 221B
Philadelphia, PA 19153
PH: (267)639-3057

**National Board of Medical Examin-
ers [15631]**
3750 Market St.
Philadelphia, PA 19104-3102
PH: (215)590-9500

**National Council of Chain
Restaurants [1671]**
c/o National Retail Federation
PO Box 781081
Philadelphia, PA 19178-1081
PH: (202)626-8183
Green, Rob, Exec. Dir.

**National Council on Measurement in
Education [8690]**
100 N 20th St., Ste. 400
Philadelphia, PA 19103
PH: (215)461-6263
Fax: (215)564-2175
Casey, Joe, Exec. Dir.

**National Dental Hygienists' Associa-
tion [14462]**
c/o LaVerna Wilson, Treasurer
366 E Gorgas Ln.
Philadelphia, PA 19119
Newbern, T. Carla, RDH, Trustee

**National Greyhound Adoption
Program [10670]**
10901 Dutton Rd.
Philadelphia, PA 19154-3203
PH: (215)331-7918
Fax: (215)331-1947
Wolf, David G., Director

**National Havurah Committee
[20272]**
7135 Germantown Ave., 2nd Fl.
Philadelphia, PA 19119

PH: (215)248-1335
Fax: (215)248-9760
Goldfield, Matthew, Chairman

National Liberty Museum [18351]
321 Chestnut St.
Philadelphia, PA 19106
PH: (215)925-2800
Fax: (215)925-3800
Caramanico, Thomas, President

**National Medical and Dental As-
sociation [19604]**
Philadelphia, PA
PH: (484)431-0111
Fax: (610)566-6888
Czarnecki, Dr. Barbara, President

**National Mental Health Consumers'
Self-Help Clearinghouse [12310]**
1211 Chestnut St., Ste. 1100
Philadelphia, PA 19107
PH: (215)751-1810
Toll free: 800-553-4539
Fax: (215)636-6312
Rogers, Joseph, Exec. Dir.

National News Bureau [2702]
PO Box 43039
Philadelphia, PA 19129
PH: (215)849-9016
Fax: (215)754-4488
Cruz, Debra Renee, Editor

**National Railway Historical Society
[10186]**
100 N 20th St., Ste. 400
Philadelphia, PA 19103-1462
PH: (215)557-6606
Fax: (215)963-9785
Ernst, Robert, Asst. Sec.

**National Renal Administrators As-
sociation [15591]**
100 N 20th St., Ste. 400
Philadelphia, PA 19103-1462
PH: (215)320-4655

**North American Horticultural Supply
Association [4439]**
100 N 20th St., 4th Fl.
Philadelphia, PA 19103-1443
PH: (215)564-3484
Fax: (215)963-9784
Smith, Richard, President

**OBTS Teaching Society for Manage-
ment Educators [6044]**
c/o Joe Seltzer, President
900 W Olney Ave.
Philadelphia, PA 19141
PH: (215)951-1037
Allen, Scott, Secretary

OIC of America [11779]
Leon H. Sullivan Human Services
Ctr.
1415 N Broad St., Ste. 227
Philadelphia, PA 19122-3323
PH: (215)236-4500
Fax: (215)236-7480
Taylor, H. Art, Chairman

**Opportunity Finance Network
[17991]**
Public Ledger Bldg., Ste. 572
620 Chestnut St.
Philadelphia, PA 19106
PH: (215)923-4754
Fax: (215)923-4755
Pinsky, Mark, President, CEO

Partners for Sacred Places [20552]
1700 Sansom St., 10th Fl.
Philadelphia, PA 19103
PH: (215)567-3234
Fax: (215)567-3235
Jaeger, A. Robert, President

**Partnership for Global Security
[19096]**
1911 Pine St.
Philadelphia, PA 19103
PH: (202)332-1412
Fax: (202)332-1413
Luongo, Kenneth N., President,
Founder

Penn Center for Bioethics [6064]
3420 Walnut St.
Philadelphia, PA 19104-3318
PH: (215)898-7555
Wipperman, Sarah, Mgr.

Pension Research Council [12450]
The Wharton School of the
University of Pennsylvania
3620 Locust Walk
3000 Steinberg Hall - Dietrich Hall
Philadelphia, PA 19104-6302
PH: (215)898-7620
Fax: (215)573-3418
Mitchell, Dr. Olivia S., Exec. Dir.

Pew Charitable Trusts [12986]
1 Commerce Sq., Ste. 2800
2005 Market St.
Philadelphia, PA 19103-7077
PH: (215)575-9050
Fax: (215)575-4939
Rimel, Rebecca W., CEO, President

Phi Alpha Sigma [23817]
313 S 10th St.
Philadelphia, PA 19107

**Philadelphia Flyers Fan Club
[24077]**
3601 S Broad St.
Philadelphia, PA 19148
Fisher, Joe, III, President

**Philomathean Society of the
University of Pennsylvania [9765]**
3450 Woodland Walk
Philadelphia, PA 19104
Marchi, Ben, Mem.

Polish Beneficial Association [19608]
2595 Orthodox St.
Philadelphia, PA 19137
PH: (215)535-2626
Fax: (215)535-0169
Zekanis, Loretta, President

Power Up Gambia [7203]
4724 Kingsessing Ave.
Philadelphia, PA 19143
Cunningham Hall, Kathryn, Founder

**Presbyterian Historical Society
[20525]**
425 Lombard St.
Philadelphia, PA 19147
PH: (215)627-1852
Fax: (215)627-0115
Taylor, Nancy, Dir. of Programs

The Print Center [8939]
1614 Latimer St.
Philadelphia, PA 19103-6308
PH: (215)735-6090
Fax: (215)735-5511
Spungen, Elizabeth F., Exec. Dir.

**Printing Brokerage/Buyers Associa-
tion International [1546]**
1530 Locust St., Mezzanine 124
Philadelphia, PA 19102
PH: (215)821-6581
Mallardi, Vincent, Chairman

Prometheus Radio Project [18664]
PO Box 42158
Philadelphia, PA 19101
PH: (215)727-9620
Gomez, Allan, Prog. Dir.

**Providence Association of Ukrainian
Catholics in America [19676]**
817 N Franklin St.
Philadelphia, PA 19123-2004
Toll free: 877-857-2284
Fax: (215)238-1933
Iwaskiw, Leo, Editor

**Prune Belly Syndrome Network
[14854]**
PO Box 16071
Philadelphia, PA 19154
Toll free: 855-275-7276
Hall, Maryann, President

The Questers [21291]
210 S Quince St.
Philadelphia, PA 19107-5534
PH: (215)923-5183
Stokebrand, Jeanne, President

**Radiation Therapy Oncology Group
[16353]**
1818 Market St., Ste. 1720
Philadelphia, PA 19103-3609
PH: (215)574-3189
Toll free: 800-227-5463
Machtay, Dr. Mitchell, Deputy Chmn.

Risk Management Association [416]
1801 Market St., Ste. 300
Philadelphia, PA 19103-1613
PH: (215)446-4000
Toll free: 800-677-7621
Fax: (215)446-4101
Blakey, Kevin M., President, CEO

Sight For Souls [17745]
3300 Tyson Ave.
Philadelphia, PA 19149
PH: (215)222-1933
Tadesse, Demissie, MD, Contact

Society for Clinical Trials [14293]
100 N 20th St., 4th Fl.
Philadelphia, PA 19103
PH: (215)320-3878
Fax: (215)564-2175
Kim, KyungMann, President

Society of Family Planning [11848]
255 S 17th St., Ste. 2709
Philadelphia, PA 19103
Toll free: 866-584-6758
Higginbotham, Susan, Exec. Dir.

Society of Family Planning [14752]
255 S 17th St., Ste. 2709
Philadelphia, PA 19103
Toll free: 866-584-6758
Higginbotham, Susan, Exec. Dir.

**Society for Historians of the Early
American Republic [9516]**
3355 Woodland Walk
Philadelphia, PA 19104-4531
PH: (215)746-5393
Smith, Gene A., Treasurer

Society of Hospital Medicine [15336]
1500 Spring Garden St., Ste. 501
Philadelphia, PA 19130
PH: (267)702-2601
Toll free: 800-843-3360
Fax: (267)702-2690
Wellikson, Laurence, MD, CEO

**Society for Industrial and Applied
Mathematics [6826]**
3600 Market St., 6th Fl.
Philadelphia, PA 19104-2688
PH: (215)382-9800
Toll free: 800-447-7426
Fax: (215)386-7999
Gubins, Samuel, Treasurer

**Society for Social Work Leadership
in Health Care [13116]**
100 N 20th St., Ste. 400
Philadelphia, PA 19103-1462
Toll free: 866-237-9542
Thompson, Pam, Officer

Society of Spanish and Spanish-
American Studies **[10221]**
Anderson Hall, 4th Fl.
Dept. of Spanish and Portuguese
Temple University
1114 W Berks St.
Philadelphia, PA 19122
PH: (215)204-8285
    (215)204-1706
Gonzalez-del-Valle, Luis T., Fac.
Memb.

Soroptimist International of the
Americas **[12909]**
1709 Spruce St.
Philadelphia, PA 19103-6103
PH: (215)893-9000
Fax: (215)893-5200
Standiford, Cathy, Contact

Swedish Colonial Society **[10232]**
916 S Swanson St.
Philadelphia, PA 19147-4332
Berich, Ms. Peg, Registrar

Technology for Liberia **[11746]**
PO Box 40882
Philadelphia, PA 19107
Saye, Matu, President, Founder

Training for Change **[12993]**
PO Box 30914
Philadelphia, PA 19104
PH: (267)289-2288
Amador, Nico, Inst.

United Engineering Foundation
[6603]
1650 Market St., Ste. 1200
Philadelphia, PA 19103
Natale, Patrick J., PE, Exec. Dir.

United States Lakeland Terrier Club
[21983]
c/o Mark Brandsema
PO Box 7292
Philadelphia, PA 19101
PH: (215)266-6059
Peterka, Sara, President

United Ukrainian American Relief
Committee Inc. **[19682]**
1206 Cottman Ave.
Philadelphia, PA 19111
PH: (215)728-1630
Fax: (215)728-1631
Kyj, Larissa, President

Veterans of the Battle of the Bulge
[21204]
PO Box 27430
Philadelphia, PA 19118
PH: (703)528-4058
Bruno, Duane R., Treasurer

Victorian Society in America **[10301]**
1636 Sansom St.
Philadelphia, PA 19103
PH: (215)636-9872
    (202)265-6669
Fax: (215)636-9873
Robertson, Charles, Comm. Chm.

Voice Foundation **[17249]**
219 N Broad St., 10th Fl.
Philadelphia, PA 19107
PH: (215)735-7999
Fax: (215)762-5572
Sataloff, Robert Thayer, Chmn. of
the Bd.

Water and Sewer Distributors of
America **[3429]**
100 N 20th St., Ste. 400
Philadelphia, PA 19103-1462
PH: (215)320-3882
Fax: (215)564-2175
King, Kevin, Director

Wider Quaker Fellowship **[20172]**
1506 Race St.
Philadelphia, PA 19102-1406
PH: (215)241-7250
Fax: (215)241-7285
Mohr, Robin, Exec. Sec.

Women's Law Project **[18240]**
125 S 9th St., Ste. 300
Philadelphia, PA 19107
PH: (215)928-9801
Miller, Dabney, Assoc. Dir.

Workers Compensation Insurance
Organizations **[1936]**
30 S 17th St., Ste. 1500
Philadelphia, PA 19103-4007
PH: (215)320-4456
Piacentino, Bonnie, Comm. Chm.

Lyre Association of North America
[22250]
13 Morgan St.
Phoenixville, PA 19460
PH: (610)608-9281
Seidenberg, Channa A., VP

Nuclear Information Technology
Strategic Leadership **[6933]**
c/o Mary Lou Furtek
30 Thayer Way
Phoenixville, PA 19460
Gordon, Bruce, Chairperson

369th Fighter Squadron Association
[20677]
511 Crest Haven Dr.
Pittsburgh, PA 15239
PH: (412)793-7619
Chardella, Anthony, Chairman

Air & Waste Management Associa-
tion **[4535]**
1 Gateway Ctr., 3rd Fl.
420 Fort Duquesne Blvd.
Pittsburgh, PA 15222-1435
PH: (412)232-3444
Toll free: 800-270-3444
Fax: (412)232-3450
Brown, Ron, Mgr. of Fin.

American Cable Association **[690]**
7 Parkway Ctr., Ste. 755
Pittsburgh, PA 15220
PH: (412)922-8300
Fax: (412)922-2110
Polka, Matthew M., Treasurer

American Platform Tennis Associa-
tion **[23297]**
109 Wesport Dr.
Pittsburgh, PA 15238
Toll free: 888-744-9490
Coster, Rob, President

American Society of Professional
Communicators **[760]**
4885 McKnight Rd., Ste. 325
Pittsburgh, PA 15237-3400
PH: (412)695-4009
Fax: (412)625-4094

American Society of Regional
Anesthesia and Pain Medicine
[13695]
4 Penn Center W, Ste. 401
Pittsburgh, PA 15222
PH: (412)471-2718
Toll free: 855-795-ASRA
Neal, Joseph M., MD, President

Amizade Global Service-Learning
[13282]
305 34th St.
Pittsburgh, PA 15201
PH: (412)586-4986
Fax: (757)257-8358
Blache-Cohen, Brandon, Exec. Dir.

Association of American Cancer
Institutes **[13890]**
Medical Arts Bldg., Ste. 503
3708 5th Ave.
Pittsburgh, PA 15213
PH: (412)647-6111
Duffy Stewart, Barbara, MPH, Exec.
Dir.

Association for Bridge Construction
and Design **[5963]**
c/o Todd Carroll, Secretary
117 Industry Dr.
Pittsburgh, PA 15275
PH: (412)788-0472
Fax: (412)787-3588
Ferko, Bill, President

Association of Earth Science Editors
[2661]
c/o Mary Ann Schmidt
554 Chess St.
Pittsburgh, PA 15205-3212
Farguharson, Phil, Treasurer

Association of Otolaryngology
Administrators **[15582]**
2400 Ardmore Blvd., Ste. 302
Pittsburgh, PA 15221
PH: (412)243-5156
Fax: (412)243-5160
White, Camille, Contact

Association for Pathology Informatics
[16580]
c/o Nova Smith, Executive Director
Dept. of Biomedical Informatics
University of Pittsburgh
5607 Baum Blvd., Rm. 518A
Pittsburgh, PA 15206
PH: (412)648-9552
Fax: (412)624-5100
Riben, Mike, President

Association for Slavic, East
European, and Eurasian Studies
[10215]
University of Pittsburgh
203C Bellefield Hall
Pittsburgh, PA 15260-6424
PH: (412)648-9911
Fax: (412)648-9815
Walker, Wendy, Coord.

Association of Theological Schools
[8704]
10 Summit Park Dr.
Pittsburgh, PA 15275-1110
PH: (412)788-6505
Fax: (412)788-6510
Hudnut-Beumler, James, VP

Ayn Rand Society **[10082]**
Dept. of History and Philosophy of
Science
University of Pittsburgh
4200 5th Ave.
Pittsburgh, PA 15260
Lennox, James G., Co-Ch.

Brother's Brother Foundation
[12630]
1200 Galveston Ave.
Pittsburgh, PA 15233-1604
PH: (412)321-3160
Fax: (412)321-3325
Hingson, Luke L., President

Canned Food Alliance **[1320]**
Foster Plaza Plz. 10
680 Andersen Dr.
Pittsburgh, PA 15220
PH: (412)922-2772
Tavoletti, Rich, Exec. Dir.

Carnegie Hero Fund Commission
[12885]
436 7th Ave., Ste. 1101
Pittsburgh, PA 15219-1841

PH: (412)281-1302
Toll free: 800-447-8900
Fax: (412)281-5751
Laskow, Mark, Chairman

Center for Organ Recovery and
Education **[17509]**
RIDC Pk.
204 Sigma Dr.
Pittsburgh, PA 15238
PH: (412)963-3550
Toll free: 800-366-6777
Stuart, Susan A., CEO, President

Chemistry and Physics on Stamps
Study Unit **[22315]**
960 Lakemont Dr.
Pittsburgh, PA 15243
Morgan, Michael A., President

Childhood Apraxia of Speech As-
sociation **[17239]**
416 Lincoln Ave., 2nd Fl.
Pittsburgh, PA 15209
PH: (412)343-7102
Gretz, Sharon, Exec. Dir.

Christian Literacy Associates **[8239]**
541 Perry Hwy.
Pittsburgh, PA 15229-1857
PH: (412)364-3777
Kofmehl, Dr. William E., Jr., Founder,
President

CHWMEG, Inc. **[3447]**
470 William Pitt Way
Pittsburgh, PA 15238-1330
PH: (412)826-3055
Fax: (586)461-1856
Hill, Becky, Administrator

Combustion Institute **[7024]**
5001 Baum Blvd., Ste. 664
Pittsburgh, PA 15213-1851
PH: (412)687-1366
Fax: (412)687-0340
Kohse-Hoinghaus, Katharina,
President

Communications Workers of America
- Printing, Publishing and Media
Workers Sector **[23439]**
219 Fort Pitt Blvd., 3rd Fl.
Pittsburgh, PA 15222
PH: (412)281-7268
Fax: (412)281-7815
Wasser, Dan, President

Cool Metal Roofing Coalition **[517]**
680 Andersen Dr.
Pittsburgh, PA 15220
PH: (412)922-2772
Fax: (412)922-3213
Crawford, Gregory L., Exec. Dir.

Croatian Fraternal Union of America
[9192]
100 Delaney Dr.
Pittsburgh, PA 15235
PH: (412)843-0380
Fax: (412)823-1594
Pazo, Edward W, President

Developmental Delay Resources
[14159]
5801 Beacon St.
Pittsburgh, PA 15217
Toll free: 800-497-0944
Fax: (412)422-1374
Lerner, Patricia S., Exec. Dir.,
Founder

Early Music America **[8366]**
801 Vinial St., Ste. 300
Pittsburgh, PA 15212
PH: (412)642-2778
Fax: (412)642-2779
Rosenberg, Donald, Editor

Educational Audiology Association
[15189]
700 McKnight Park Dr., Ste. 708
Pittsburgh, PA 15237
Toll free: 800-460-7322
Fax: (888)729-3489
Pillow, Gary, President

Engineers for a Sustainable World
[11354]
3715 Beechwood Blvd.
Pittsburgh, PA 15217
Dale, Alexander, Exec. Dir.

GALA Choruses [9909]
PO Box 99998
Pittsburgh, PA 15233
PH: (412)418-7709
Godfrey, Robin, Exec. Dir.

Grinnell Family Association of
America [20875]
c/o David R. Grinnell, President
2924 Marshall Rd.
Pittsburgh, PA 15214
PH: (412)321-4963
   (561)439-8519
Asbury, Mrs. Kathleen L.G., Officer

Haitian Families First [11924]
PO Box 99834
Pittsburgh, PA 15233
McMutrie, Jamie, Founder, President

Hardwood Manufacturers Associa-
tion [1440]
665 Rodi Rd., Ste. 305
Pittsburgh, PA 15235
PH: (412)244-0440
Fax: (412)244-9090
Jovanovich, Linda, Exec. VP

Hospice and Palliative Nurses As-
sociation [16135]
1 Penn Ctr. W, Ste. 425
Pittsburgh, PA 15276
PH: (412)787-9301
Buck, Joy, PhD, President

Institute for Global Labour and Hu-
man Rights [17841]
5 Gateway Ctr., 6th Fl.
Pittsburgh, PA 15222
PH: (412)562-2406
Fax: (412)562-2411
Kernaghan, Charles, Director

Institute of Professional
Environmental Practice [4070]
339 Fisher Hall
600 Forbes Ave.
Pittsburgh, PA 15282
PH: (412)396-1703
Fax: (412)396-1704
Kobus, Diana, Exec. Dir.

International Council of Employers of
Bricklayers and Allied Craftworkers
[23177]
1306 Lancaster Ave.
Pittsburgh, PA 15218
PH: (202)210-6069
Aquiline, Matthew S., Exec. Dir.

International Society for Bipolar
Disorders [13722]
PO Box 7168
Pittsburgh, PA 15213
PH: (412)624-4407
Fax: (412)624-4484
Daversa, Chad, Exec. Dir.

International Society of Nurses in
Genetics [14880]
461 Cochran Rd.
Pittsburgh, PA 15228
PH: (412)344-1414
Fax: (412)344-0599
Kassalen, Ms. Beth, MBA, Exec. Dir.

International Visual Sociology Association [7185]
c/o Doug Harper, President
504 College Hall
Duquesne University
1100 Locust St.
Pittsburgh, PA 15219
PH: (412)396-6490
Harper, Doug, President

ISDA - Association of Storage and
Retrieval Professionals [2444]
750 Holiday Dr., Bldg. 9, Ste. 500
Pittsburgh, PA 15220
Toll free: 877-921-3501
Fax: (412)921-3525

Jewish Vegetarians of North America
[10292]
9 Hawthorne Rd.
Pittsburgh, PA 15221
PH: (412)965-9210
Schwartz, Richard, President

Junior Tamburitzans [9193]
100 Delaney Dr.
Pittsburgh, PA 15235-5416
PH: (412)843-0380
Fax: (412)823-1594
Luketich, Bernard M., President

Latin American Studies Association
[9662]
315 S Bellefield Ave.
Pittsburgh, PA 15260
PH: (412)648-7929
Fax: (412)624-7145
Rappaport, Joanne, President

Learning Disabilities Association of
America [12237]
4156 Library Rd.
Pittsburgh, PA 15234-1349
PH: (412)341-1515
Toll free: 888-300-6710
Fax: (412)344-0224
Reynolds, Mary- Clare, Exec. Dir.

Marketing and Advertising Global
Network [101]
c/o Cheri D. Gmiter, Executive Direc-
tor
MAGNET Global
226 Rostrevor Pl.
Pittsburgh, PA 15202
Gmiter, Cheri D., Exec. Dir.

Mechanical Bank Collectors of
America [21687]
PO Box 13323
Pittsburgh, PA 15243-0323

Nash Car Club of America [21447]
c/o Tom Ritter, 27 Sunny Dr.
27 Sunny Dr.
Pittsburgh, PA 15236-2652

National Association of EMS Educa-
tors [8329]
250 Mt. Lebanon Blvd., Ste. 209
Pittsburgh, PA 15234-1248
PH: (412)343-4775
Fax: (412)343-4770
Todaro, John, President

National Association of Myofascial
Trigger Point Therapists [17453]
88 Union Ave.
Pittsburgh, PA 15205-2724
Brown, Heather, Secretary

National Association of Subrogation
Professionals [2744]
3 Robinson Plz., Ste. 130
6600 Steubenville Pke.
Pittsburgh, PA 15205
Toll free: 800-574-9961
Fax: (412)706-7164
Foster, John, Consultant

National Black Association for
Speech-Language and Hearing
[17243]
700 McKnight Park Dr., Ste. 708
Pittsburgh, PA 15237
Toll free: 855-727-2836
Williams, Rachel M., PhD,
Chairperson

National Center for Juvenile Justice
[11538]
3700 S Water St., Ste. 200
Pittsburgh, PA 15203
PH: (412)227-6950
Fax: (412)227-6955
Sickmund, Melissa, PhD, Director

National Club Baseball Association
[22560]
850 Ridge Ave., Ste. 301
Pittsburgh, PA 15212
PH: (412)321-8440
Fax: (412)321-4088
Sanderson, Sandy, President,
Treasurer

National Cyber-Forensics & Training
Alliance [6653]
2000 Technology Dr., Ste. 450
Pittsburgh, PA 15219
PH: (412)802-8000
Fax: (412)802-8510

National Federation of Municipal
Analysts [51]
PO Box 14893
Pittsburgh, PA 15234
Southwell, Gil, Comm. Chm.

North American Computational
Social and Organization Sciences
[6259]
Carnegie Mellon University
Wean Hall 1325
5000 Forbes Ave.
Pittsburgh, PA 15213
PH: (412)268-3163
Cioffi-Revilla, Claudio, President

Oncology Nursing Certification
Corporation [16173]
125 Enterprise Dr.
Pittsburgh, PA 15275
PH: (412)859-6104
Toll free: 877-769-ONCC
Fax: (412)859-6168
Murphy, Cynthia Miller, Exec. Dir.

Oncology Nursing Society [16174]
125 Enterprise Dr.
Pittsburgh, PA 15275
PH: (412)859-6100
Toll free: 877-369-5497
Fax: (412)859-6162
Burke, Margaret Barton, PhD, RN,
FAAN, President

Oncology Nursing Society Founda-
tion [16175]
125 Enterprise Dr.
Pittsburgh, PA 15275-1214
PH: (412)859-6228
Toll free: 866-257-4667
Fax: (412)859-6163
Worrall, Linda, RN, Exec. Dir.

Pittsburgh Penguins Booster Club
[24078]
PO Box 903
Pittsburgh, PA 15230
Harty, Melinda, President

Polish Falcons of America [19609]
381 Mansfield Ave.
Pittsburgh, PA 15220
PH: (412)922-2244
Toll free: 800-535-2071
Fax: (412)922-5029
Kuzma, Timothy L., CEO, President

Religious Communication Associa-
tion [20033]
c/o Janie Harden Fritz, Executive
Secretary
340 College Hall
Dept. of Communication & Rhetori-
cal Studies
Duquesne University
600 Forbes Ave.
Pittsburgh, PA 15282
Fritz, Janie Harden, Exec. Sec.,
Exec. Dir.

Sarah Scaife Foundation [19004]
1 Oxford Ctre.
301 Grant St., Ste. 3900
Pittsburgh, PA 15219-6402
PH: (412)392-2900
Gleba, Michael W., Chairman,
Treasurer

Serb National Federation [19642]
615 Iron City Drive Ste. 302
Pittsburgh, PA 15205
PH: (412)458-5227
Fax: (412)875-5924
Marjanovic, Michael Miroslav, Mem.

Service Specialists Association [353]
c/o Sean Ryan, President
7307 Grand Ave.
Pittsburgh, PA 15225
PH: (847)760-0067
Ryan, Sean, President

Social Democrats USA [18874]
PO Box 16161
Pittsburgh, PA 15242-0161
PH: (412)894-1799
D'Loss, Rick, Secretary, Treasurer

Societas Liturgica [20072]
c/o Peter C. Bower, Editor
587 Moorhead Pl.
Pittsburgh, PA 15232-1426
Lathrop, Prof. Dr. Gordon, Mem.

Society for American Music [10003]
PO Box 99534
Pittsburgh, PA 15233
PH: (412)624-3031
Whitmer, Mariana, Exec. Dir.

Society for Economic Measurement
[6402]
c/o Stephen Spear, Secretary-
Treasurer
Posner Hall, Rm. 251
5000 Forbes Ave.
Tepper School of Business
Carnegie Mellon University
Pittsburgh, PA 15213
PH: (412)468-8831

Society for Middle Ear Disease
[16541]
c/o Charles D. Bluestone, MD,
Founder
Children's Hospital of Pittsburgh
Faculty Pavilion, 7th Fl.
One Children's Hospital Dr.
4401 Penn Ave.
Pittsburgh, PA 15224
PH: (412)924-1026
Auld, Ruth Gabig, EdD, Chairperson

SSPC: The Society for Protective
Coatings [2489]
800 Trumbull Dr.
Pittsburgh, PA 15222
PH: (412)281-2331
Toll free: 877-281-7772
Fax: (412)281-9992
Worms, William M., Exec. Dir.

Steel Recycling Institute [3455]
680 Andersen Dr.
Pittsburgh, PA 15220-2700

PH: (412)922-2772
Woods, James, Dir. of Public Rel.

Theatre Historical Society of America [10277]
461 Cochran Rd.
Pittsburgh, PA 15228-1253
PH: (412)528-1801
   (630)782-1800
Masher, Joe, Treasurer

United Electrical, Radio and Machine Workers of America [23415]
1 Gateway Ctr., Ste. 1400
Pittsburgh, PA 15222
PH: (412)471-8919
Knowlton, Peter, President

United Mitochondrial Disease Foundation [17148]
8085 Saltsburg Rd., Ste. 201
Pittsburgh, PA 15239-1977
PH: (412)793-8077
Toll free: 888-317-8633
Fax: (412)793-6477
Mohan, Charles A., CEO, Exec. Dir.

United Steelworkers [23482]
60 Boulevard of the Allies
Pittsburgh, PA 15222-1214
PH: (412)562-2400
Fax: (412)562-2445
Gerard, Leo W., President

University Economic Development Association [8740]
PO Box 97930
Pittsburgh, PA 15227
PH: (216)200-8332
Toll free: 877-583-8332
Hindes, Tim, Exec. Dir.

William Penn Association [19499]
709 Brighton Rd.
Pittsburgh, PA 15233
PH: (412)231-2979
Toll free: 800-848-7366
Fax: (412)231-8535
Charles, George S., Jr., President

World Association for Chinese Biomedical Engineers [6116]
210 Lothrop St., E1641 BST
Pittsburgh, PA 15213-2536
PH: (412)648-1494
Fax: (412)648-8548
Woo, Savio L-Y., PhD, Founder, Chairperson

World Peace One [12020]
5135 Dearborn St.
Pittsburgh, PA 15224

Veteran's Coalition [21147]
805 S Township Blvd.
Pittston, PA 18640-3327
PH: (570)603-9740
Toll free: 800-843-8626
Fax: (570)603-9741

Veterans of the Vietnam War [21169]
805 S Township Blvd.
Pittston, PA 18640-3327
PH: (570)603-9740
Toll free: 800-843-8626
Fax: (570)603-9741
Verespy, Nancy, Exec. Dir.

National Entomology Scent Detection Canine Association [2503]
PO Box 121
Pleasant Mount, PA 18453
Skinner, Jim, Bd. Member

ECRI Institute [15685]
5200 Butler Pke.
Plymouth Meeting, PA 19462-1298

PH: (610)825-6000
Fax: (610)834-1275
Lerner, Jeffrey C., PhD, President, CEO

Unite for HER [14077]
PO Box 351
Pocopson, PA 19366
PH: (610)322-9552
   (484)431-6776
Weldon, Susan, Founder, President

Institute for Briquetting and Agglomeration [2498]
PO Box 205
Portersville, PA 16051
PH: (724)368-4004
Fax: (715)368-4014
Hinkle, Bob, Exec. Dir.

Austin-Healey Sports and Touring Club [21334]
309 E Broad St.
Quakertown, PA 18951-1703
PH: (215)536-6912
Brodeur, Rick, Membership Chp.

Rosicrucian Fraternity [19627]
PO Box 220
Quakertown, PA 18951
Clymer, George, Mem.

Women for Sobriety, Inc. [13189]
PO Box 618
Quakertown, PA 18951
PH: (215)536-8026
Fax: (215)538-9026
Kirkpatrick, Jean, Mgr.

Association for Frontotemporal Degeneration [15905]
Radnor Station Bldg. 2, Ste. 320
290 King of Prussia Rd.
Radnor, PA 19087
PH: (267)514-7221
Toll free: 866-507-7222
Dickinson, Susan, Exec. Dir.

Business Travel Coalition [23666]
214 Grouse Ln.
Radnor, PA 19087
PH: (610)999-9247
Mitchell, Kevin P., Chairman, Founder

Cabrini Mission Corps [20390]
610 King of Prussia Rd.
Radnor, PA 19087
PH: (610)971-0821
Fax: (610)971-0396

Inflammation Research Association [14582]
c/o Joel E. Tocker, President
145 King of Prussia Rd.
Radnor, PA 19087
PH: (610)651-6107
Tocker, Joel E., President

Society for Orphaned Armenian Relief [12730]
c/o George Yacoubian Jr., Chairman
150 N Radnor Chester Rd., Ste. F-200
Radnor, PA 19087
PH: (267)515-1944
Fax: (610)229-5168
Yacoubian, George S., Chairman

American Camaro Association [21318]
1116 Laurelee Ave.
Reading, PA 19605
Scheffy, Karl, Contact

Water for Waslala [13347]
c/o Justin Knabb
2000 Friedensburg Rd.

Reading, PA 19606
Nespoli, Matt, Founder, President

North American Teckel Club [21932]
536 Orchard Rd.
Reinholds, PA 17569-9632
PH: (610)285-2469
Hamilton, Carrie, President

United Chainsaw Carvers Guild [21786]
PO Box 255
Ridgway, PA 15853-0255
Schieffer, Jerry, President

Patients Against Lymphoma [15548]
3774 Buckwampum Rd.
Riegelsville, PA 18077
PH: (610)346-8419
Fax: (801)409-5736
Schwartz, Karl, Founder, President

Association of Asthma Educators [17135]
70 Buckwalter Rd., Ste. 900
Royersford, PA 19468
Toll free: 888-988-7747
Metz, Gregory, VP

USS LSM-LSMR Association [21070]
c/o David K. Miller, President
21850 Vista Dr.
Saegertown, PA 16433
PH: (814)763-3090
   (727)360-5718
Miller, David K., President

International Guild of Lamp Researchers [21290]
Lamplighters Farm
10111 Lincoln Way W
Saint Thomas, PA 17252-9513
Vantiger, D., Secretary

REO Club of America [21483]
203 Crestwood Dr
203 Crestwood Dr.
Sarver, PA 16055
Zingaro, Susan, Membership Chp.

KidsPeace [11062]
4085 Independence Dr.
Schnecksville, PA 18078-2574
Toll free: 800-257-3223
Fax: (610)799-8001
Isemann, Dr. William, CEO, President

American Alliance of Ethical Movers [824]
118A Gerloff Rd.
Schwenksville, PA 19473
Toll free: 888-764-2936
Presson, Greg, CEO, President

Moringa Community [11403]
242 N Limerick Rd.
Schwenksville, PA 19473
PH: (610)287-7802
Lohr, Jeffry, Founder, President, Treasurer

Johannes Schwalm Historical Association [20995]
PO Box 127
Scotland, PA 17254
Schwalm, Hal, Contact

Aimee's Army [13874]
PO Box 37
Scranton, PA 18504
McKeon, Annette, Founder

Polish National Union of America [19611]
1002 Pittston Ave.
Scranton, PA 18505

PH: (570)344-1513
Toll free: 800-724-6352

Society for Italian Historical Studies [9620]
c/o Prof. Roy Domenico, Executive Secretary/Treasurer
University of Scranton
800 Linden St.
Scranton, PA 18510
Domenico, Prof. Roy, Exec. Sec., Treasurer

Ukrainian Fraternal Association [19679]
371 N 9th Ave.
Scranton, PA 18504-2005
PH: (570)342-0937
Fax: (570)347-5649

National Black Deaf Advocates [11623]
PO Box 564
Secane, PA 19018
Ogunyipe, Benro, MPA, Comm. Chm.

Anglicans for Life [12763]
405 Frederick Ave.
Sewickley, PA 15143
Toll free: 800-707-6635
Forney, Mrs. Georgette, President

Commission on Religious Counseling and Healing [13615]
456 Nimick St.
Sharon, PA 16146
PH: (724)308-6218
Lawrence, Rev. Stephen, Officer

National Montford Point Marine Association, Inc. [5611]
PO Box 1070
Sharon Hill, PA 19079
Averhart, Mr. James, President

National Welsh-American Foundation [19688]
c/o Jack Pritchard, NWAF
24 Carverton Rd.
Shavertown, PA 18708-1711
PH: (717)696-1525
Fax: (717)696-1808
Pritchard, Jack, Contact

American Hair Loss Council [14482]
30 S Main St.
Shenandoah, PA 17976
PH: (615)721-8085
Budgen, Betty, Dir. of Member Svcs., Treasurer

Challenger T/A Registry [21349]
c/o Barry Washington
4511 Spring Rd.
Shermans Dale, PA 17090-9403
Washington, Barry, Contact

Estrela Mountain Dog Association of America [21876]
c/o Tracey Conner, President
102 Cherokee Dr.
Shickshinny, PA 18655
PH: (570)592-8784
Conner, Tracey, President

Herb Growing and Marketing Network [4293]
PO Box 245
Silver Spring, PA 17575-0245
PH: (717)393-3295
Fax: (717)393-9261
Rogers, Maureen, Director

American Association for Employment in Education [8437]
PO Box 173
Slippery Rock, PA 16057

PH: (614)485-1111
Fax: (360)244-7802
Kennedy, Jason, President

Coalition for Student and Academic
Rights **[7406]**
PO Box 491
Solebury, PA 18963-0491
PH: (215)862-9096
Fax: (215)862-9557
Lindsay, C.L., III, Exec. Dir., Founder

National Paralegal Association
[5661]
Box 406
Solebury, PA 18963
PH: (215)297-8333
Fax: (215)297-8358

Recovered Alcoholic Clergy Associa-
tion **[13178]**
PO Box 377
Solebury, PA 18963-0377
PH: (215)297-5135
Vinson, Rev. Richard, Director,
President

Guild of American Papercutters
[21758]
214 S Harrison Ave.
Somerset, PA 15501
PH: (456)867-2365
Reed, Kathy Trexel, VP

National Fellowship of Child Care
Executives **[13466]**
c/o Robert Miller, Executive
Secretary
PO Box 1195
Somerset, PA 15501
Fahner, Thomas, President

International Foundation for Terror
Act Victims **[19183]**
1300 Industrial Blvd., Ste. 204
Southampton, PA 18966
PH: (321)213-0198
Fax: (206)333-0505
Mogilyansky, Andrew, Chairman,
Founder

Homeopathic Pharmacopoeia of the
United States **[15288]**
PO Box 2221
Southeastern, PA 19399-2221
PH: (513)813-2940
Fax: (484)970-9835

Landscape Artists International
[8928]
c/o Karl Eric Leitzel, Founder
155 Murray School Ln.
Spring Mills, PA 16875
PH: (814)422-8461
Leitzel, Karl Eric, Director, Founder

Rachel Carson Homestead Associa-
tion **[10318]**
613 Marion Ave.
Springdale, PA 15144
PH: (724)274-5459
Carlisle, David, President

Adults with Autism: Living with
Independence, Value and Esteem
[13737]
PO Box 431
Springfield, PA 19064
PH: (610)544-5914

Messianic Jewish Alliance of
America **[20338]**
PO Box 274
Springfield, PA 19064
Toll free: 800-225-6522
Fax: (610)338-0471
Feldman, Larry, President

Historic Building Inspectors Associa-
tion **[9395]**
PO Box 201
Springtown, PA 18081

Ghana Medical Relief **[15600]**
114 Jules Dr.
State College, PA 16801
Owusu, Dr. Samuel Kwapong,
Founder

Professional Football Players Moth-
ers' Association **[22865]**
c/o Chris Johnson, Treasurer
340 Glengarry Ln.
State College, PA 16801
PH: (504)392-7781
Fax: (740)879-4454
Wayne, Euwayne Denise, President

Train Collectors Association **[22193]**
PO Box 248
Strasburg, PA 17579-0248
PH: (717)687-8623
Fax: (717)687-0742
Sheriff, Wayne S., President

Association for Computational
Linguistics **[9738]**
209 N 8th St.
Stroudsburg, PA 18360
PH: (570)476-8006
Fax: (570)476-0860
Bhattacharyya, Pushpak, President

Association for Machine Translation
in the Americas **[3313]**
c/o Priscilla Rasmussen, Business
Manager
209 N 8th St.
Stroudsburg, PA 18360
PH: (570)476-8006
Fax: (570)476-0860

International Association of Women
Ministers **[20642]**
579 Main St.
Stroudsburg, PA 18360
PH: (412)734-2263
Shearer, Rev. Marian P., President

Quiet Valley Living Historical Farm
[9508]
347 Quiet Valley Rd.
Stroudsburg, PA 18360
PH: (570)992-6161
Fax: (570)992-9587
Durham, David, President

North American Sports Federation
[22512]
311 Race St.
Sunbury, PA 17801
PH: (717)278-2474
Greiner, Scott, CEO

Waksman Foundation for Microbiol-
ogy **[6107]**
Swarthmore College
Dept. of Biology
500 College Ave.
Swarthmore, PA 19081-1390
PH: (610)328-8044
Fax: (610)328-8663
Vollmer, Amy Cheng, President

Floating Harbor Syndrome Support
Group **[14823]**
PO Box 774
Terre Hill, PA 17581
PH: (254)721-8184

NiUG International **[6752]**
300 Community Dr., Ste. B2
Tobyhanna, PA 18466
PH: (570)243-8700
Toll free: 866-301-6484
Fax: (775)257-1661
Serrano, Lisa, Specialist

United States Mine Rescue Associa-
tion **[6885]**
PO Box 1010
Uniontown, PA 15401

PH: (724)366-5272
McGee, Robert, Secretary, Treasurer

Academy of Legal Studies in Busi-
ness **[8205]**
c/o Dan Cahoy, President
Dept. of Risk Management
Smeal College of Business
Penn State University
310 Business Bldg.
University Park, PA 16802
PH: (814)865-6205
Thomas, Robert, Sec. (Actg.),
Treasurer

American Pomological Society
[4227]
102 Tyson Bldg.
University Park, PA 16802
PH: (814)863-6163
Fax: (814)863-6139
Pritts, Marvin, VP

Association for Computing
Machinery - Special Interest Group
on Security, Audit and Control
[6240]
c/o Trent Jaeger, Chairman
Pennsylvania State University
Dept. of Computer Science and
Engineering
346A IST Bldg.
University Park, PA 16802
PH: (814)865-1042
Fax: (814)865-3176
Jaeger, Trent, Chairman

The Association of Religion Data
Archives **[20533]**
211 Oswald Twr.
Dept. of Sociology
Pennsylvania State University
University Park, PA 16802-6207
PH: (814)865-6258
Fax: (814)863-7216
Finke, Roger, Director

Charles Johnson Society **[10383]**
c/o Dr. Linda Selzer, Treasurer
Penn State University
116 Burrowes Bldg.
University Park, PA 16802
Nash, Dr. Will, President

North American Case Research As-
sociation **[3516]**
c/o Deborah Ettington, Editor
Smeal College of Business
Pennsylvania State University
University Park, PA 16802
PH: (306)585-5647
Harris, Randall, President

North American Society for Sport
History **[9500]**
c/o Jaime Schultz, Secretary
Pennsylvania State University
268M Recreation Bldg.
University Park, PA 16802
Wamsley, Kevin, President

Peace Science Society
(International) **[18819]**
c/o Glenn Palmer, Executive Director
The Pennsylvania State University
Dept. of Political Science
208 Pond Bldg.
University Park, PA 16802
Palmer, Glenn, Exec. Dir.

Society for Phenomenology and
Existential Philosophy **[10124]**
c/o Christopher P. Long, Webmaster
119 Sparks Bldg.
Pennsylvania State University
University Park, PA 16802
Schroeder, Brian, Exec. Dir.

InterServe U.S.A. **[20427]**
PO Box 418
Upper Darby, PA 19082-0418
Toll free: 800-809-4440
Fax: (610)352-4394
Mulholland-Wozniak, Ken, PhD.,
Secretary

Black Indians and Intertribal Native
American Association **[19576]**
PO Box 143
Upperstrasburg, PA 17265
PH: (717)491-1065
Fax: (775)418-6031

American Baptist International
Ministries **[19714]**
PO Box 851
Valley Forge, PA 19482
Toll free: 800-222-3872
Trulson, Reid, Exec. Dir.

American Baptist Women's
Ministries **[19715]**
PO Box 851
Valley Forge, PA 19482-0851
PH: (610)768-2288
Fax: (610)768-2286
Sullivan, Rev. Angel L, President

Freedoms Foundation at Valley
Forge **[18296]**
1601 Valley Forge Rd.
Valley Forge, PA 19481
PH: (610)933-8825
Fax: (610)935-0522
Di Yeso, Michael E., CEO, President

Scripture Union-USA **[19764]**
PO Box 215
Valley Forge, PA 19481
PH: (610)935-2807
Toll free: 800-621-5267
Fax: (610)935-2809
Ross, Steven, Dir. of Corp. Comm.

Humility of Mary Volunteer Service
[19844]
PO Box 534
Villa Maria, PA 16155
PH: (724)964-8920
Stanco, Sr. Mary, Prog. Dir.

Association for Computing
Machinery - Special Interest Group
on Management Information
Systems **[6309]**
c/o Janice C. Sipior, Chairperson
800 Lancaster Ave.
Villanova, PA 19085
PH: (610)519-4347
Sipior, Janice C., Chairperson

Comparative Cognition Society
[5893]
c/o Michael Brown, Treasurer
Dept. of Psychology
Villanova University
800 Lancaster Ave.
Villanova, PA 19085
Kelly, Debbie, President

Devereux National **[13795]**
444 Devereux Dr.
Villanova, PA 19085
Toll free: 800-345-1292
Kreider, Robert Q., CEO, President

Heirs, Inc. **[18051]**
PO Box 292
Villanova, PA 19085
PH: (610)527-6260
Smith, Standish, Founder

Lonergan Philosophical Society
[10100]
c/o Prof. Mark Doorley, Secretary-
Treasurer

St. Augustine Ctr., Rm. 481
Dept. of Philosophy
Villanova University
800 Lancaster Ave.
Villanova, PA 19085
Murray, Dr. Elizabeth A., Founder,
President

National Catholic Band Association
[9971]
Villanova University
800 E Lancaster Ave.
Villanova, PA 19085
Desrosiers, Philip, President

American Association of University
Administrators **[7418]**
10 Church Rd.
Wallingford, PA 19086
PH: (814)460-6498
Fax: (610)565-8089
King, Dan L., CEO, President

The Erythromelalgia Association
[14575]
200 Old Castle Ln.
Wallingford, PA 19086-6027
PH: (610)566-0797
Coimbra, Beth, President, Treasurer

Colorado Ranger Horse Association
[4345]
1510 Greenhouse Rd.
Wampum, PA 16157
PH: (724)535-4841

Independent Time & Labor Manage-
ment Association **[3278]**
2049 Stout Dr., Ste. A-1
Warminster, PA 18974
PH: (215)443-8720
Fax: (215)443-8709
Rubin, Barry, President

NGA - Needlework Guild of America
[12902]
822 Veterans Way
Warminster, PA 18974-3500
PH: (215)682-9183
Toll free: 866-295-9974
Fax: (215)682-9185
Rich-Bonn, Michelle, Exec. Dir.

Society of Saint Gianna Beretta
Molla **[11830]**
PO Box 2946
Warminster, PA 18974-0095
PH: (215)657-3101
White, Robert, President

American Academy of Attorney-
CPAs **[8]**
PO Box 706
Warrendale, PA 15095
PH: (703)352-8064
Toll free: 888-272-2889
Fax: (703)352-8073
Driegert, Robert S., Director

Association for Iron and Steel
Technology **[6842]**
186 Thorn Hill Rd.
Warrendale, PA 15086-7528
PH: (724)814-3000
Fax: (724)814-3001
Carter, Wendell L., President

Association of Occupational Health
Professionals in Healthcare
[16317]
125 Warrendale Bayne Rd., Ste. 375
Warrendale, PA 15086
Toll free: 800-362-4347
Fax: (724)935-1560
Bliss, Mary, President

Binding Industries Association **[1529]**
301 Brush Creek Rd.
Warrendale, PA 15086

PH: (412)259-1736
     (317)347-2665
Fax: (412)749-9890
Eckhart, Chris, Chairman

Label Printing Industries of America
[3175]
301 Brush Creek Rd.
Warrendale, PA 15086
PH: (412)741-6860
Toll free: 800-910-4283
Fax: (412)741-2311
Olberding, David A., Chmn. of the
Bd.

Materials Research Society **[6815]**
506 Keystone Dr.
Warrendale, PA 15086-7573
PH: (724)779-3003
Fax: (724)779-8313
Osman, Todd, Exec. Dir.

The Minerals, Metals, and Materials
Society **[6849]**
184 Thorn Hill Rd.
Warrendale, PA 15086
PH: (724)776-9000
Toll free: 800-759-4867
Fax: (724)776-3770
Bazzy, Michael, Mktg. Mgr.

Printing Industries of America's
Center for Technology and
Research **[1547]**
301 Brush Creek Rd.
Warrendale, PA 15086
PH: (412)741-6860
Toll free: 800-910-4283
Fax: (412)741-2311

SAE International **[6584]**
400 Commonwealth Dr.
Warrendale, PA 15096-0001
PH: (724)776-4841
Toll free: 877-606-7323
Fax: (724)776-0790
Greaves, Richard W., President

Technical Association of the Graphic
Arts **[6699]**
301 Brush Creek Rd.
Warrendale, PA 15086
PH: (412)259-1706
Fax: (412)741-2311
Workman, Jim, Managing Dir.

Web Offset Association **[1551]**
Printing Industries of America
301 Brush Creek Rd.
Warrendale, PA 15086
PH: (412)741-6860
Toll free: 800-910-4283
Fax: (412)741-2311
Goldstein, Justin, Administrator

Ice Screamers **[21664]**
PO Box 465
Warrington, PA 18976
PH: (215)343-2676
Fussel, Larry, Officer

World Team **[20480]**
1431 Stuckert Rd.
Warrington, PA 18976
PH: (215)491-4900
Toll free: 800-967-7109
Oessenich, Kevin, Exec. Dir.

Delta Phi Alpha **[23769]**
c/o Michael Shaughnessy,
Secretary-Treasurer
Washington & Jefferson College
60 S Lincoln St.
Washington, PA 15301
PH: (724)223-6170
Davidheiser, Dr. James, President

National Duncan Glass Society
[22139]
PO Box 965
Washington, PA 15301

PH: (724)225-9950
Fax: (724)225-1620

Pony Baseball and Softball **[22565]**
1951 Pony Pl.
Washington, PA 15301-5889
PH: (724)225-1060
Fax: (724)225-9852
Key, Abraham, CEO, President

Aircraft Locknut Manufacturers As-
sociation **[1561]**
c/o Robert H. Ecker, Executive
Director
994 Old Eagle School Rd., Ste.
1019
Wayne, PA 19087
PH: (610)971-4850
Fax: (610)971-4859
Ecker, Robert H., Exec. Dir.

Clery Center for Security on Campus
[11502]
110 Gallagher Rd.
Wayne, PA 19087-2959
PH: (484)580-8754
Fax: (484)580-8759
Swanson, Mary, Chairman

Clinical and Laboratory Standards
Institute **[15518]**
950 W Valley Rd., Ste. 2500
Wayne, PA 19087
PH: (610)688-0100
Toll free: 877-447-1888
Fax: (610)688-0700
Gantzer, Mary Lou, PhD, Contact

Cordage Institute **[911]**
994 Old Eagle School Rd., Ste.
1019
Wayne, PA 19087
PH: (610)971-4854
Fax: (610)971-4859
Padilla, Luis, VP

Evangelicals for Social Action
[19107]
PO Box 367
Wayne, PA 19087
PH: (484)384-2988
Alexander, Paul, President

Flag Manufacturers Association of
America **[20945]**
994 Old Eagle School Rd., Ste.
1019
Wayne, PA 19087
PH: (610)971-4850
Fax: (610)971-4859
Tannahill, Mrs. Sharon K., Exec. Dir.

Fluid Sealing Association **[1729]**
994 Old Eagle School Rd., No. 1019
Wayne, PA 19087-1866
PH: (610)971-4850

Gasket Fabricators Association
[1732]
994 Old Eagle School Rd., Ste.
1019
Wayne, PA 19087-1866
PH: (610)971-4850
Lance, Peter M., Exec. Dir.

NCMS Inc. - The Society of
Industrial Security Professionals
[1789]
994 Old Eagle School Rd., Ste.
1019
Wayne, PA 19087-1802
PH: (610)971-4856
Fax: (610)971-4859
Tannahill, Sharon K., Exec. Dir.

Renaissance Transgender Association **[12951]**
987 Old Eagle School Rd., Ste. 719
Wayne, PA 19087

PH: (610)636-1990
Wannabe, Ms. Katie, Chairperson

Society of the Hawley Family
[20929]
c/o Linda D. Hawley, Interim
President
63 Shelbourne Ct.
Wayne, PA 19087-5723
Hawley, Paul, Secretary

Society of Professional Rope Access
Technicians **[1768]**
994 Old Eagle School Rd., Ste.
1019
Wayne, PA 19087-1866
PH: (610)971-4850
Fax: (610)971-4859
Gault, Iain, President

Vibration Isolation and Seismic
Control Manufacturers Association
[7159]
994 Old Eagle School Rd., Ste.
1019
Wayne, PA 19087-1866
PH: (610)971-4850
Ecker, Robert H., Exec. Dir.

American Academy of Veterinary
Nutrition **[17588]**
721 Inverness Dr.
West Chester, PA 19380-6880
Amand, Dr. Wilbur B., VMD, Exec.
Dir.

Brinton Association of America
[20963]
William Brinton 1704 House and
Historic Site
21 Oakland Rd.
West Chester, PA 19382
PH: (610)399-0913
Jacobs, Mr. Francis Brinton, II,
President

e-Learning for Kids **[7586]**
c/o Marlene Zimmerman
953 Cloud Ln.
West Chester, PA 19382
Williams, Michael, Director

HomeAID for Africa **[10477]**
1191 Shady Grove Way
West Chester, PA 19382
PH: (610)399-0823
Phreaner, Linda, Treasurer

Leif Ericson Viking Ship **[10335]**
PO Box 779
West Chester, PA 19381-0779
PH: (410)275-8516
Segermark, Mr. David O., President

National Association of Traffic Ac-
cident Reconstructionists and
Investigators **[5366]**
PO Box 2588
West Chester, PA 19382
PH: (610)696-1919
Camlin, William C., President

National Cristina Foundation **[11625]**
339 Lea Dr.
West Chester, PA 19382
PH: (203)863-9100
Marrin, Yvette, PhD, Founder,
President, Bd. Member

Swedenborg Foundation **[9101]**
320 N Church St.
West Chester, PA 19380
PH: (610)430-3222
Fax: (610)430-7982
McLaughlin, Valerie, Bus. Mgr.

White Ironstone China Association
[21587]
c/o Mary Ann and Chuck Ulmann
1320 Ashbridge Rd.

West Chester, PA 19380
Riley, Dorothy, President

Women's Caucus for Political Science [7050]
c/o Michelle Wade, Treasurer
West Chester University Graduate Ctr., Ste. 101
Dept. of Public Policy and Administration
1160 McDermott Dr.
West Chester, PA 19383
Walsh, Denise, President

ASTM International [7323]
100 Barr Harbor Dr.
West Conshohocken, PA 19428-2959
PH: (610)832-9585
(610)832-9598
Toll free: 877-909-2786
Thomas, James, Asst. VP of Mktg. & Sales

John Templeton Foundation [20555]
300 Conshohocken State Rd., Ste. 500
West Conshohocken, PA 19428
PH: (610)941-2828
Fax: (610)825-1730
Templeton Dill, Heather, President

National Registry of Certified Chemists [6208]
c/o Russ Phifer, Executive Director
125 Rose Ann Ln.
West Grove, PA 19390-8946
PH: (610)322-0657
Fax: (800)858-6273
Phifer, Russ, Exec. Dir.

National Hyperbaric Association [15345]
PO Box 438
Westtown, PA 19395
PH: (484)886-4272
Hoffecker, Paul S., CEO

National Automotive Radiator Service Association [349]
3000 Village Run Rd., Ste. 103, No. 221
Wexford, PA 15090-6315
PH: (724)799-8415
Fax: (724)799-8416
Juchno, Wayne, Exec. Dir.

Eastern Winter Sports Reps Association [3154]
PO Box 88
White Haven, PA 18661
PH: (570)443-7180
Fax: (570)443-0388
Kleeschulte, Dave, VP

National Commission for Health Education Credentialing [15084]
1541 Alta Dr., Ste. 303
Whitehall, PA 18052-5642
PH: (484)223-0770
Toll free: 888-624-3248
Fax: (800)813-0727
Lysoby, Linda, Exec. Dir.

National Society of Painters in Casein and Acrylic [8934]
c/o Douglas Wiltraut, Membership Chairperson
969 Catasauqua Rd.
Whitehall, PA 18052
Wiltraut, Douglas, Membership Chp.

Society for the Scientific Study of Sexuality [17204]
881 3rd St., Ste. B5
Whitehall, PA 18052
PH: (610)443-3100
Fax: (610)443-3105
Koken, Juline, PhD, Mem.

American Freedom Union [18885]
PO Box 218
Wildwood, PA 15091
Wassall, Donald B., Exec. Dir.

Fellowship of Orthodox Christians in America [20591]
892 Scott St.
Wilkes-Barre, PA 18705-3630
PH: (570)824-0562
Fax: (516)922-0954
Kovach, Marge, President

Polish Union of the United States of North America [19615]
53-59 N Main St.
Wilkes-Barre, PA 18701
PH: (570)823-1611
Fax: (570)829-7849
Kolodziej, Bernard, President

American Rescue Workers Inc. [13030]
25 Ross St.
Williamsport, PA 17701-5149
PH: (570)323-8693
Fax: (570)323-8694
Astin, Gen. Claude S., Jr., Cmdr.

Little League Baseball and Softball [22550]
539 US Route 15 Hwy.
Williamsport, PA 17701-0485
PH: (570)326-1921
Fax: (570)326-1074
Keener, Stephen D., President, CEO

Little League Foundation [22551]
539 US Route 15 Hwy.
Williamsport, PA 17701-0485
PH: (570)326-1921
Fax: (570)326-1074
Paster, Howard, President

National Association of Pupil Services Administrators [7436]
PO Box 113
Williamsport, PA 17701
PH: (570)323-2050
Fax: (570)323-2051
Fausnaught, Wayne D., Exec. Dir.

International Association of Forensic Toxicologists [7340]
3701 Welsh Rd.
Willow Grove, PA 19090
Chung, Ms. Hee-Sun, President

National Association of Mobile Entertainers [1150]
PO Box 144
Willow Grove, PA 19090
Toll free: 800-434-8274
Keslar, carol, President

Christian History Institute [19958]
PO Box 540
Worcester, PA 19490
Toll free: 800-468-0458
Fax: (610)584-6643

Jewish Reconstructionist Movement [20260]
1299 Church Rd.
Wyncote, PA 19095-1824
PH: (215)576-0800
Fax: (215)576-6143
Roberts, David, Chairperson

Reconstructionist Rabbinical Association [20277]
1299 Church Rd.
Wyncote, PA 19095
PH: (215)576-5210
Fax: (215)576-8051
Klein, Jason, Exec.

Institutes for the Achievement of Human Potential [11237]
8801 Stenton Ave.
Wyndmoor, PA 19038

PH: (215)233-2050
Fax: (215)233-9312
Dimencescu, Dr. Mihai, Contact

International Academy for Child Brain Development [16016]
c/o Institutes for the Achievement of Human Potential
8801 Stenton Ave.
Wyndmoor, PA 19038
PH: (215)233-2050
Fax: (215)233-9312
Doman, Janet, Director

National Association of Town Watch [11509]
308 E Lancaster Ave., Ste. 115
Wynnewood, PA 19096
Toll free: 800-648-3688
Fax: (610)649-5456

Tabitha USA [11449]
PO Box 449
Wynnewood, PA 19096
Broach, Mary, President

Women and Mathematics Education [8287]
c/o Lorraine Howard, Treasurer
PO Box 88
Wynnewood, PA 19096
Hosten, Melissa, President

Children's Alopecia Project [13785]
PO Box 6036
Wyomissing, PA 19610
PH: (610)468-1011
Woytovich, Betsy, Exec. Dir.

Ukrainian Philatelic and Numismatic Society [22373]
157 Lucinda Ln.
Wyomissing, PA 19610
Martyniuk, Andrew O., President

Council of International Neonatal Nurses [16129]
c/o Carole Kenner, Chief Executive Officer
2110 Yardley Rd.
Yardley, PA 19067
PH: (405)684-1476
Fax: (267)392-5637
Pointer, Mary, CFO

Empower Orphans [10962]
1415 Hidden Pond Dr.
Yardley, PA 19067
PH: (610)909-1778
Gupta, Neha, Founder

Gamma Iota Sigma [23695]
PO Box 356
Yardley, PA 19067
PH: (484)991-4471
Codispoti, Noelle, Exec. Dir.

Russian Brotherhood Organization of the U.S.A. [19631]
301 Oxford Valley Rd., Ste. 1602B
Yardley, PA 19067
PH: (215)563-2537
Fax: (215)563-8106
Wanko, John, President

Association of Food and Drug Officials [5221]
2550 Kingston Rd., Ste. 311
York, PA 17402
PH: (717)757-2888
Fax: (717)650-3650
Read, David, Bd. Member

Crickett's Answer for Cancer [13952]
1110 Skyview Dr.
York, PA 17406
PH: (717)843-7903
Julius, Bonnie, President

League of Chiropractic Women [14277]
PO Box 21772
York, PA 17402
PH: (413)353-4636
Fax: (678)669-2786
Giuliano, Patti, Co-Pres.

National Nostalgic Nova [21458]
PO Box 29177
York, PA 17402-0109
PH: (717)252-4192
(717)252-2383
Fax: (717)252-1666
Bushey, Wayne, Founder

Pi Nu Epsilon [23832]
2159 White St., Ste. 3, No. 104
York, PA 17404
Jenkins, Chanel, President

Pro-Life Alliance of Gays and Lesbians [12789]
PO Box 3005
York, PA 17402
PH: (202)223-6697
Brown, Cecilia, President

Eastern Museum of Motor Racing [21373]
100 Baltimore Rd.
York Springs, PA 17372
PH: (717)528-8279
Miller, Nancy, President

American Association for Lost Children [12360]
PO Box 386
Youngstown, PA 15696
PH: (724)537-6970
Toll free: 800-375-5683
Fax: (724)537-6971
Miller, Mark, Founder

Christian Sports International [23221]
PO Box 254
Zelienople, PA 16063
PH: (724)453-1400
Fax: (724)240-1617
Grinder, N. Scott, PresidentR

RHODE ISLAND

Seventh Day Baptist Missionary Society [19739]
19 Hillside Ave.
Ashaway, RI 02804
PH: (401)596-4326
Fax: (401)348-9494
Brown, Clinton, Exec. Dir.

Society for the Anthropology of Lowland South America [5918]
c/o Jeremy Campbell, Secretary-Treasurer
Roger Williams University
1 Old Ferry Rd.
Bristol, RI 02809
Hill, Jonathan, President

United States A-Class Catamaran Association [22678]
33 Broadcommon Rd.
Bristol, RI 02809-2721
White, Bailey, President

eMarketing Association [999]
40 Blue Ridge Dr.
Charlestown, RI 02813
Toll free: 800-496-2950
Fax: (408)884-2461
Fleming, Robert, CEO

American Border Leicester Association [4647]
c/o Polly Hopkins, President
Maybe Tomorrow Farm

494 Evans Rd.
Chepachet, RI 02814
PH: (401)949-4619
Hopkins, Polly, President

Association for Medical Education
and Research in Substance Abuse
[8309]
135 Lyndon Rd.
Cranston, RI 02905
PH: (401)243-8460
Toll free: 877-418-8769
MacLane-Baeder, Doreen, Exec. Dir.

Jewelers Shipping Association
[2053]
125 Carlsbad St.
Cranston, RI 02920
PH: (401)943-6020
Toll free: 800-688-4572
Roche, David, Managing Dir.

Survivor Connections **[12938]**
52 Lyndon Rd.
Cranston, RI 02905-1121
PH: (401)941-2548
Fax: (401)941-2335
Fitzpatrick, Mr. Francis L., Founder

43rd Infantry Division Veterans As-
sociation **[20710]**
c/o Howard F. Brown, Assistant
Secretary-Treasurer
150 Lakedell Dr.
East Greenwich, RI 02818-4716
Brown, Howard F., Secretary,
Treasurer

Plymouth Barracuda/Cuda Owners
Club **[21476]**
c/o Ann M. Curfman, Secretary, 36
Woodland Rd.
36 Woodland Rd.
East Greenwich, RI 02818-3430
Fisher, Jay M., Director, Founder

American Academy of Addiction
Psychiatry **[16806]**
400 Massasoit Ave., 2nd Fl., Ste.
307
East Providence, RI 02914-2012
PH: (401)524-3076
Fax: (401)272-0922
Cates-Wessel, Ms. Kathryn, Exec.
Dir.

Swan Owners Association of
America **[22671]**
PO Box 347
Jamestown, RI 02835
PH: (401)423-0600
Beltrano, Bob, President

International Flying Dutchman Class
Association of the U.S. **[22630]**
c/o Chris Liberti, Secretary-
Treasurer, 60 Spring Hill Rd.
60 Spring Hill Rd.
Kingston, RI 02881-1806
PH: (401)487-3062
Ballenger, Buzz, President

Merleau-Ponty Circle **[10101]**
University of Rhode Island
Kingston, RI 02881
PH: (401)874-1000
Weiss, Prof. Gail, Gen. Sec.

National Association of Geriatric
Education Centers **[14894]**
c/o Phil Clark, ScD, President
University of Rhode Island
55 Lower College Rd.
Kingston, RI 02881
Clark, Phil, ScD, President

National Disability Sports Alliance
[22789]
25 W Independence Way
Kingston, RI 02881

PH: (401)792-7130
Fax: (401)792-7132
McCole, Jerry, Exec. Dir.

Steiff Club **[21724]**
24 Albion Rd., Ste. 220
Lincoln, RI 02865
PH: (401)312-0080
Toll free: 888-978-3433
Fax: (401)475-2147

1000 Jobs **[12524]**
316 W Main Rd.
Little Compton, RI 02837
Fax: (401)635-1838
Close, Leroy S., Founder, President

Historical Writers of America **[10375]**
PO Box 4238
Middletown, RI 02842
PH: (401)847-6832
Fax: (401)537-9159
Davis, Paul, Treasurer

International Association of
Antarctica Tour Operators **[3379]**
c/o Janeen Haase, Administrative
Officer
320 Thames St., Ste. 264
Newport, RI 02840
PH: (401)841-9700
Fax: (401)841-9704
Crosbie, Dr. Kim, Exec. Dir.

International Tennis Hall of Fame
[23301]
194 Bellevue Ave.
Newport, RI 02840
PH: (401)849-3990
Toll free: 800-457-1144
Martin, Todd, CEO

Navy Nurse Corps Association
[16166]
PO Box 3289
Newport, RI 02840
PH: (401)619-4432
Bibb, Sandra, President

Newport Restoration Foundation
[9423]
51 Touro St.
Newport, RI 02840
PH: (401)849-7300
Fax: (401)849-0125
Roos, Pieter N., Exec. Dir.

Prayers for Life **[20071]**
c/o Dr. James F. Nugent, President
Salve Regina University
100 Ochre Point Ave.
Newport, RI 02840-4149
PH: (401)849-5421
Nugent, Dr. James F., President

Sailors for the Sea **[3937]**
449 Thames St., 300D
Newport, RI 02840
PH: (401)846-8900
Fax: (401)846-7200
Rockefeller, David, Jr., Chairman

Tall Ships America **[22673]**
Bldg. 2, Ste. 101
221 3rd St.
Newport, RI 02840-1088
PH: (401)846-1775
Fax: (401)849-5400
Rogers, Bert, President

Touro Synagogue Foundation **[9441]**
85 Touro St.
Newport, RI 02840
PH: (401)847-4794
Hurley, Diane, Chairman

Urban History Association **[9526]**
100 Ochre Point Ave.
Department of History

Salve Regina University
Newport, RI 02840-4149
PH: (401)341-3292

Association of Migraine Disorders
[14917]
PO Box 870
North Kingstown, RI 02852
Godley, Frederick, MD, President

Fashion Jewelry & Accessories
Trade Association **[2045]**
25 Sea Grass Way
North Kingstown, RI 02852
PH: (401)667-0520
Fax: (401)267-9096
Cleaveland, Brent, Exec. Dir.

Narcolepsy Network **[17219]**
46 Union Dr., No. A212
North Kingstown, RI 02852
PH: (401)667-2523
Toll free: 888-292-6522
Fax: (401)633-6567
Kowalczyk, Sara, Bd. Member

CartoPhilatelic Society **[22314]**
c/o Marybeth Sulkowski, Secretary
1117 Douglas Ave., Unit 209
North Providence, RI 02904-5374

Continental Dorset Club **[4669]**
c/o Debra Hopkins, Executive
Secretary/Treasurer
PO Box 506
North Scituate, RI 02857-0506
PH: (401)647-4676
Fax: (401)647-4679
Sidwell, Casey, Director

Liberty Seated Collectors Club
[22272]
c/o Dennis Fortier
PO Box 1841
Pawtucket, RI 02862
Fortin, Gerry, President

Volunteers in Health Care **[15069]**
111 Brewster St.
Pawtucket, RI 02860
Toll free: 877-844-8442
Geller, Stephanie, Ed.M,
Researcher, Director

National Autism Association **[13773]**
1 Park Ave., Ste. 1
Portsmouth, RI 02871
PH: (401)293-5551
Toll free: 877-622-2884
Fax: (401)293-5342
Fournier, Wendy, President

United States Sailing Association
[22684]
15 Maritime Dr.
Portsmouth, RI 02871-0907
PH: (401)683-0800
Toll free: 800-877-2451
Fax: (401)683-0840

United States Sailing Foundation
[22685]
15 Maritime Dr.
Portsmouth, RI 02871-0907
PH: (401)683-0800
Toll free: 800-877-2451
Fax: (401)683-0840
Larkin, Amy, Dir. of Mktg.

Adopt a Doctor **[16730]**
101 Dyer St.
Providence, RI 02903
PH: (401)421-0606
Rickman, Ray, President, Founder

American Friends of the Hakluyt
Society **[9749]**
c/o The John Carter Brown Library
PO Box 1894

Providence, RI 02912
O'Donnell, Maureen, Secretary

American Mathematical Society
[6816]
201 Charles St.
Providence, RI 02904-2294
PH: (401)455-4000
Toll free: 800-321-4267
Fax: (401)331-3842
Lebron, Maria L., Mem.

Association of Independent Colleges
of Art and Design **[7626]**
236 Hope St.
Providence, RI 02906
PH: (401)270-5991
Fax: (401)270-5993
Obalil, Deborah, Exec. Dir.

Big Picture Learning **[7839]**
325 Public St.
Providence, RI 02905
PH: (401)752-3442
Fax: (919)573-0787
Littky, Dennis, Director, Founder

Brazilian Studies Association **[8060]**
Watson Institute for International and
Public Affairs
Brown University
111 Thayer St.
Providence, RI 02912-1970
Fax: (401)863-2928
McCann, Bryan, President

Council of Women's and Infants'
Specialty Hospitals **[15324]**
National Perinatal Information Ctr.
225 Chapman St., Ste. 200
Providence, RI 02905-4533
PH: (401)274-0650
McLaughlin, Maribeth, RN, BSN,
President

Cure Alliance for Mental Illness
[15767]
470 Lloyd Ave.
Providence, RI 02906
Cunningham, Robin, Founder

International Association of Teachers
of Czech **[9652]**
Dept. of Slavic Languages
Brown University
20 Manning Walk, Box E
Providence, RI 02912
Kresin, Susan, Editor

Kazakh Aul of the United States
[9584]
PO Box 6185
Providence, RI 02940
PH: (401)486-4023
Saxon, Susan, Founder, Exec. Dir.

Khadarlis for Sierra Leone **[11393]**
105 Dodge St.
Providence, RI 02907
PH: (401)454-6916

Multicultural Foodservice and
Hospitality Alliance **[1392]**
1144 Narragansett Blvd.
Providence, RI 02905
PH: (401)461-6342
Fax: (401)461-9004
Howell, Andrew, VP of Operations

National Perinatal Information Center
[16624]
225 Chapman St., Ste. 200
Providence, RI 02905-3633
PH: (401)274-0650
Fax: (401)455-0377
Muri, Janet H., MPA, President

North American Society of Obstetric
Medicine **[16300]**
146 W River St.
Providence, RI 02904

PH: (401)793-7410
Fax: (401)793-7801

Rites and Reason Theatre [10271]
Dept. of Africana Studies
Brown University
155 Angell St.
Providence, RI 02912
PH: (401)863-3137
Fax: (401)863-3559
Morgan, Elmo Terry, Director

Scleroderma Support Group [17183]
Roger Williams Meeical Ctr., 1st Fl.,
    825 Chalkstone Ave.
825 Chalkstone Ave.
Providence, RI 02908
PH: (401)781-5013
Cowell, Carole, Leader

What Kids Can Do [19279]
PO Box 603252
Providence, RI 02906
PH: (401)247-7665
Fax: (401)245-6428
Cervone, Barbara, Founder,
    President

Automotive Body Parts Association
    [336]
400 Putnam Pke., Ste. J, No. 503
Smithfield, RI 02917-2442
PH: (401)949-0912
Toll free: 800-323-5832
Fax: (401)262-0193
Morrissey, Dan, Chairman

Weimaraner Club of America
    [21988]
c/o Ellen Dodge, Executive
    Secretary
PO Box 489
Wakefield, RI 02880-0489
PH: (401)782-3725
Fax: (401)789-8279
Bonner, John, President

International Marina Institute [2246]
50 Water St.
Warren, RI 02885
Toll free: 866-367-6622
Fax: (401)247-0074
Rose, Jeff, Officer

Sail America [438]
50 Water St.
Warren, RI 02885-3034
PH: (401)289-2540
Fax: (401)247-0074
West, Scot, President

Armenian Students' Association of
    America Inc. [19387]
333 Atlantic Ave.
Warwick, RI 02888
PH: (401)461-6114
Assadourian, Brian, Chairman

Cleaning for Heroes [13005]
221B Hallene Rd.
Warwick, RI 02886
PH: (401)732-6243
Fax: (866)389-3445
Aldridge-Baligian, Anne, Founder

International Sprout Growers As-
    sociation [3539]
685 Bald Hill Rd., Box No. 8
Warwick, RI 02886
PH: (508)657-4742
Wolfe, Richard, Treasurer, Exec.
    Sec.

Jewelers Board of Trade [2051]
95 Jefferson Blvd.
Warwick, RI 02888
PH: (401)467-0055
Fax: (401)467-6070

Plan International U.S.A. [11262]
155 Plan Way
Warwick, RI 02886
PH: (401)562-8400
Toll free: 800-556-7918
San Martin, Tessie, CEO

Project Sweet Peas [12132]
45 Boylston St.
Warwick, RI 02889
PH: (724)268-0465
King, Sarah, President, CEO

Steamship Historical Society of
    America [22440]
2500 Post Rd.
Warwick, RI 02886
PH: (401)463-3570
Fax: (401)463-3572
Ryan, Erik, President

Association of Certified Marine
    Surveyors [2237]
19 Nooseneck Hill Rd.
West Greenwich, RI 02817
PH: (401)397-1888
Toll free: 800-714-5040
Cross, Jim, Memb. Ofc.

American Computer Science League
    [7650]
10 Brisas Dr.
West Warwick, RI 02893

Association of College and
    University Clubs [7623]
185 Providence St., Unit A315
West Warwick, RI 02893
PH: (239)687-8819
Lindgren, Rob, President

Society of American Silversmiths
    [3195]
PO Box 786
West Warwick, RI 02893
PH: (401)461-6840
Toll free: 800-339-0417
Fax: (401)828-0162
Herman, Jeffrey, Founder, Exec. Dir.

Crandall Family Association [20850]
PO Box 1472
Westerly, RI 02891-0907
Potter, Donna, President, Genealo-
    gist, Editor

International Ski Dancing Association
    [23162]
22 Fountain Dr.
Westerly, RI 02891
PH: (401)596-8009
Malfetti, Cheryl, Exec. Dir., Founder

Nuclear Suppliers Association [6934]
PO Box 1354
Westerly, RI 02891
PH: (401)637-4224
Fax: (401)637-4822
McCormick, Rick, President

American-French Genealogical
    Society [20953]
78 Earle St.
Woonsocket, RI 02895
PH: (401)765-6141
Fax: (401)597-6290
Burkhart, Janice, Librarian, Presi-
    dentS

SOUTH CAROLINA

Society for the Preservation and Ap-
    preciation of Antique Motor Fire
    Apparatus in America [22015]
c/o Candy Bennett, Membership
    Secretary
8035 Bird Pond Rd.

Adams Run, SC 29426-5545
Dundas, William, President

Ameraucana Breeders Club [3654]
c/o Susan Mouw, Secretary-
    Treasurer
156 Titanic Rd.
Aiken, SC 29805
Redden, Clif, President

American Bicycle Polo Association
    [23068]
305 Magnolia Lake Ct.
Aiken, SC 29803-2654
PH: (803)648-4993
Baker, Carl P., President

Association of Ecosystem Research
    Centers [3989]
c/o Olin E. Rhodes, Jr.,Past
    President
PO Drawer E
Aiken, SC 29802
PH: (803)725-8191
Arnone, John A., III, Contact

SEAMS Association [2230]
1908 Richland Ave. E
Aiken, SC 29801
PH: (803)772-5861
    (803)642-1111
Fax: (803)731-7709
Friedman, Sarah, Exec. Dir.

Commission on Accreditation of
    Medical Transport Systems
    [14692]
117 Chestnut Ln.
Anderson, SC 29625
PH: (864)287-4177
Fax: (864)287-4251
Rogers, Ralph, MD, Chairman

Tile Council of North America [591]
100 Clemson Research Blvd.
Anderson, SC 29625
PH: (864)646-8453
Fax: (864)646-2821
Astrachan, Eric, Exec. Dir.

United States Isshinryu Karate As-
    sociation [23019]
2202 Surfside Dr.
Anderson, SC 29625
PH: (864)225-8610
Little, Gr. Mast. Phil E., President

International Cornish Breeders As-
    sociation [3665]
c/o Mark Beasley, President
1264 Old Allendale Hwy.
Barnwell, SC 29812
PH: (803)259-3752
Beasley, Mark, President

Fourth Marine Division Association
    [21195]
3 Black Skimmer Ct.
Beaufort, SC 29907
Baker, Norman L., Asst. Treas.

American Game Fowl Society [3655]
PO Box 800
Belton, SC 29627-0800
PH: (864)237-5280
Saville, Anthony, President

Ashburn Institute [18878]
198 Okatie Village Dr., Ste. 103
PMB No. 301
Bluffton, SC 29909
PH: (703)728-6482
Fax: (843)705-7643
Carter, McCall, Director

American Polocrosse Association
    [22774]
PO Box 158
Bonneau, SC 29431-0158

PH: (843)825-2686
Caldwell, Rob, President

Alliance for Full Acceptance [11871]
29 Leinbach Dr.
Charleston, SC 29407
PH: (843)883-0343
Fax: (843)723-3859
Redman-Gress, Warren, Exec. Dir.

ASCEND Foundation [13889]
PO Box 80925
Charleston, SC 29416
PH: (843)225-4055
Pritchard, J. Russ, Jr., President

Darkness to Light [10952]
1064 Gardner Rd., Ste. 210
Charleston, SC 29407
PH: (843)965-5444
Toll free: 866-FOR-LIGHT
Fax: (843)965-5449
Haviland, Lyndon, CEO

Dictionary Project [12245]
PO Box 1845
Charleston, SC 29402-1845
PH: (843)388-8375
    (843)856-2706
French, Mary, Director

Gulf Yachting Association [22617]
c/o Sarah Ashton, Regional
    Administrative Judge
79 Pitt St.
Charleston, SC 29403
Johnson, David, Comm. Chm.

International Hyperhidrosis Society
    [14707]
1260 Smythe St.
Charleston, SC 29492
Pieretti, Lisa J., Exec. Dir., Founder

International Order of St. Vincent
    [20110]
126 Coming St.
Charleston, SC 29403
PH: (843)722-7345
Fax: (843)722-2105
Dixon, Philip G., Director, Gen.

Louie's Kids [16258]
PO Box 21291
Charleston, SC 29413
PH: (843)883-5026
Fax: (800)457-7497
Yuhasz, Louis H., Founder

Metabolomics Society [15653]
331 Ft. Johnson Rd.
Charleston, SC 29412
Bearden, Dan, Treasurer

National Golf Course Owners As-
    sociation [3161]
291 Seven Farms Dr.
Charleston, SC 29492
PH: (843)881-9956
Toll free: 800-933-4262
Fax: (843)881-9958
Karen, Jay, CEO

North American Chinese Clinical
    Chemists Association [6210]
c/o Yusheng Zhu, PhD, Advisor
Medical University of South Carolina
165 Ashley Ave., Ste. 309
Charleston, SC 29425-8905
Zhang, Dr. Yan, President

North American Society of Head and
    Neck Pathology [16589]
Medical University of South Carolina
Dept. of Pathology and Laboratory
    Medicine
Division of Anatomic Pathology
PO Box 250908

Section 1: Geographic Index

SOUTH CAROLINA

Geographic Index

Charleston, SC 29425-0686
PH: (843)792-1994
Fax: (843)792-8974
Richardson, Mary S., MD, President

People Against Rape [12933]
PO Box 1723
Charleston, SC 29402
PH: (843)745-0144
     (843)577-9882
Lauve, Janie Ward, Exec. Dir.

Psi Omega Fraternity [23720]
1040 Savannah Hwy.
Charleston, SC 29407-7804
PH: (843)556-0573
Fax: (843)556-6311
Steinberg, Arthur, President

Select Registry [1678]
295 Seven Farms Dr., Ste. C-279
Charleston, SC 29492
PH: (269)789-0393
Toll free: 800-344-5244
Fax: (269)789-0970

Sigma Delta Pi [23979]
c/o Mark P. Del Mastro, Executive
  Director
College of Charleston
66 George St.
Charleston, SC 29424-0001
PH: (843)953-6748
Toll free: 866-920-7011
Del Mastro, Mark P., Exec. Dir.

Society of School Librarians
International [9727]
c/o Jeanne Schwartz, Executive
  Director
19 Savage St.
Charleston, SC 29401
PH: (843)577-5351
Schwartz, Jeanne, Exec. Dir.

U.S. Club Soccer [23193]
192 E Bay St., Ste. 301
Charleston, SC 29401
PH: (843)614-4140
Fax: (843)614-4146
Payne, Kevin, Exec. Dir., CEO

We Are Family [11912]
29 Leinbach Dr., Ste. D-3
Charleston, SC 29407
PH: (843)637-3697
Moore, Ms. Melissa, Exec. Dir.

American Real Estate Society [2846]
300 Sirrine Hall
Clemson University
Clemson, SC 29634
PH: (864)656-1373
Fax: (864)656-4982
Harrison, David, President

International Society for Human
Ethology [6040]
c/o Thomas Alley, President
312J Brackett Hall
Clemson, SC 29634
PH: (864)656-4974
Schiefenhovel, Wulf, Trustee

International Town & Gown Associa-
tion [11387]
1250 Tiger Blvd.
Clemson, SC 29631
PH: (864)624-1148
Fax: (864)653-2032
Bagwell, Beth, MPA, Exec. Dir.

National Council of Examiners for
Engineering and Surveying [6574]
PO Box 1686
Clemson, SC 29633
PH: (864)654-6824
Toll free: 800-250-3196
Fax: (864)654-6033
Carter, Jerry T., CEO

National Dropout Prevention Center/
Network [7823]
Clemson University
209 Martin St.
Clemson, SC 29631-1555
PH: (864)656-2599
Fax: (864)656-0136
Collins, Bob, Chairman

World's Poultry Science Association,
U.S.A. Branch [4576]
PO Box 1705
Clemson, SC 29633-7105
PH: (864)633-8633
     (864)654-0809
Taylor, Dr. R.L., President

American Agricultural Law Associa-
tion [4941]
c/o Kristy Thomason Ellenberg,
  Executive Director
PO Box 5861
Columbia, SC 29250
PH: (803)728-3200
Ellenberg, Kristy Thomson, Exec.
  Dir.

American Association of State
Climatologists [6853]
c/o Hope Mizzell, PhD, President
South Carolina State Climatologist
South Carolina State Climatology
  Office
SC Department of Natural
  Resources
PO Box 167
Columbia, SC 29202
PH: (803)734-9568
Kerr, Glenn D., Exec. Dir.

American Comparative Literature
Association [9748]
University of South Carolina
Dept. of Languages, Literatures &
  Cultures
1620 College St., Rm. 813A
Columbia, SC 29208
Beecroft, Alexander, Secretary,
  Treasurer

American Fats and Oils Association
[2447]
PO Box 11035
Columbia, SC 29211
PH: (803)252-7128
Fax: (803)252-7799
Jackson, Eric, President

Angels With Special Needs [11571]
PO Box 25555
Columbia, SC 29224-5555
PH: (803)419-5136
Fax: (803)788-3236
Duckett, Helen, Founder

Apert International [13823]
PO Box 2571
Columbia, SC 29202
PH: (803)732-2372
Sears, Donald A., President

Association for Documentary Editing
[9461]
c/o Constance B. Schulz, Secretary
Department of History
University of South Carolina
Columbia, SC 29208
Stertzer, Jennifer E., President

Association for Education in Journal-
ism and Mass Communication
[8149]
234 Outlet Pointe Blvd., Ste. A
Columbia, SC 29210-5667
PH: (803)798-0271
Fax: (803)772-3509
McGill, Jennifer H., Exec. Dir.

Association of Programs for Female
Offenders [11520]
c/o Judy Anderson, Treasurer
PO Box 5293

Columbia, SC 29250-5293
Smith, Gregory V., President

Association of Schools of Journalism
and Mass Communication [7428]
234 Outlet Pointe Blvd.
Columbia, SC 29210-5667
PH: (803)798-0271
Fax: (803)772-3509
McGill, Jennifer H., Exec. Dir.

Audiology Awareness Campaign
[13733]
1 Windsor Cove, Ste. 305
Columbia, SC 29223
Toll free: 800-445-8629
Fax: (803)765-0860
Goodman, Kathy Landau, AuD,
  Chairperson

Benedict College National Alumni
Association [19307]
1600 Harden St.
Columbia, SC 29204
PH: (803)705-4600
Toll free: 800-868-6598
Fax: (803)705-6654
Hill, Willie J., Dr., President

Kay Boyle Society [10365]
Dept. of English
Columbia College
1301 Columbia College Dr.
Columbia, SC 29203
Reynes-Delobel, Anne, President

Clan Montgomery Society
International [20834]
9 Poplar Springs Ct.
Columbia, SC 29223
Waugh, Don, VP

Flying Scot Sailing Association
[22613]
1 Windsor Cove, Ste. 305
Columbia, SC 29223
PH: (803)252-5646
Gerry, Frank, President

Habele [7590]
701 Gervais St., Ste. 150-244
Columbia, SC 29201
Mellen, Neil, President

National Alliance of Highway
Beautification Agencies [5734]
PO Box 191
Columbia, SC 29202
Knox, Wendy, Chairman

National Association of Bankruptcy
Trustees [5087]
1 Windsor Cove, Ste. 305
Columbia, SC 29223
PH: (803)252-5646
Toll free: 800-445-8629
Fax: (803)765-0860
Nelson, Richard D., President

National Association for Campus
Activities [8606]
13 Harbison Way
Columbia, SC 29212-3401
PH: (803)732-6222
Cummings, Toby, Exec. Dir.

National Association of Decorative
Fabric Distributors [3264]
1 Windsor Cove, Ste. 305
Columbia, SC 29223
PH: (803)765-0860
Toll free: 800-445-8629
Gowdy, Kathy, Secretary, Treasurer

National Board of Diving &
Hyperbaric Medical Technology
[15344]
9 Medical Pk., Ste. 330
Columbia, SC 29203

PH: (803)434-7802
Toll free: 866-451-7231
Clarke, Dick, President

National College of District Attorneys
[5033]
University of South Carolina Law
  School
1600 Hampton St., Ste. 414
Columbia, SC 29208
PH: (803)705-5005
Fax: (803)705-5301

National Educational Telecom-
munications Association [7827]
939 S Stadium Rd.
Columbia, SC 29201
PH: (803)799-5517
     (803)978-1581
Fax: (803)771-4831
Hinton, Skip, President

Ocean Wishes [4131]
PO Box 291030
Columbia, SC 29229
PH: (803)419-2838
Fax: (843)353-2537
Peyton, Margo, Founder

Serendib [11430]
PO Box 11081
Columbia, SC 29211
Fax: (877)799-3383
McCravy, Tucker, Founder, President

William Gilmore Simms Society
[10399]
c/o Dr. Todd Hagstette, Secretary-
  Treasurer
South Caroliniana Library
University of South Carolina
910 Sumter St.
Columbia, SC 29208-1760
Lackey, Sam, Secretary, Treasurer

Society of Ultrasound in Medical
Education [17541]
PO Box 212334
Columbia, SC 29221-2334
PH: (803)216-3360
Fax: (803)216-3362
Abuhamad, Alfred, President

United States Sweet Potato Council
[4258]
12 Nicklaus Ln., Ste. 101
Columbia, SC 29229-3363
Earp, Jamie, President

U.S.S. LCI National Association
[21144]
101 Rice Bent Way, No. 6
Columbia, SC 29229
PH: (803)865-5665
Cummer, John, Chmn. of the Bd.

Coastal Carolina University Alumni
Association [19315]
PO Box 261954
Conway, SC 29528
PH: (843)349-2846
     (843)349-2586
Forbus, Brian, President

YoungStroke, Inc. [17301]
PO Box 692
Conway, SC 29528
PH: (843)655-2835
Edmunds, Amy, Founder, CEO

National Wild Turkey Federation
[4846]
770 Augusta Rd.
Edgefield, SC 29824-0530
PH: (803)637-3106
Toll free: 800-843-6983
Hinkle, Jim, Bd. Member

Waterfowl U.S.A. [3963]
Waterfowl Bldg.
Edgefield, SC 29824

Encyclopedia of Associations, 56th Edition: Geographic and Executive Indexes

3553

PH: (803)637-5767
Wentz, Darrin, Sales Mgr.

Association of American Schools in Central America, Colombia, Caribbean and Mexico [8528]
c/o Sonia Keller, Executive Director
2812 Cypress Bend Rd.
Florence, SC 29506-8353
PH: (843)799-5754
Sims, Robert, President

International Sungja-Do Association [22996]
2009 Butterfly Lake Dr.
Florence, SC 29505-3343
PH: (843)676-5280
Petrotta, George I., Director, Founder

Pulp & Paperworkers' Resource Council [23420]
USW Local 9-1877
Florence, SC 29505
Wise, David, Chmn. of the Bd.

Steel Joist Institute [583]
234 W Cheves St.
Florence, SC 29501
PH: (843)407-4091
Charles, J. Kenneth, III, Managing Dir.

Association of International Mettalizers, Coaters and Laminators [744]
201 Springs St.
Fort Mill, SC 29715
PH: (803)948-9470
Fax: (803)948-9471
Sheppard, Craig, Exec. Dir.

Church Planting International [20405]
5186 Cressingham Dr.
Fort Mill, SC 29707
Navarette, Brian, Chairman

Commercial Food Equipment Service Association [1381]
3605 Centre Cir.
Fort Mill, SC 29715
PH: (336)346-4700
Fax: (336)346-4745
Potvin, Gary, President

Converting Equipment Manufacturers Association [1722]
201 Springs St.
Fort Mill, SC 29715
PH: (803)802-7820
Fax: (803)802-7821
Sheppard, Mr. Craig, Exec. Dir.

Instrument Contracting and Engineering Association [867]
c/o Nick Theisen, Executive Director
4312 Rochard Ln.
Fort Mill, SC 29707-5851
PH: (704)905-0319
Fax: (803)547-7697
Theisen, Nick, Exec. Dir.

South America Mission [20465]
1021 Maxwell Mill Rd., Ste. B
Fort Mill, SC 29708
PH: (803)802-8580
Fax: (803)548-7955
Ogden, Kirk, Exec. Dir.

McCoy Pottery Collectors' Society [21584]
420 Quail Run Cir.
Fountain Inn, SC 29644
Harrington, Tony, President

Silver Ghost Association [21490]
c/o Jim Bannon, Membership Chairman

306 Cross Hill Rd.
Fountain Inn, SC 29644-9239
PH: (864)862-5494
Fax: (864)862-5494
Newman, Maggie, President

Boykin Spaniel Club and Breeders Association of America [21847]
PO Box 42
Gilbert, SC 29054
PH: (713)501-1661
Copeland, Greg, Contact

Clan Carmichael U.S.A. [20801]
c/o Benjamin DeRosia, Membership Chairman
333 Clarine Dr.
Goose Creek, SC 29445
Gambill, Kathy, Mem.

North American Meteor Network [6859]
101 Margate Cir.
Goose Creek, SC 29445
Davis, Mark, Coord.

The Voluntaryists [18644]
PO Box 275-D
Gramling, SC 29348
Watner, Carl, Editor

American Academy of Thermology [15674]
500 Duvall Dr.
Greenville, SC 29607
PH: (864)236-1073
Fax: (864)236-5918
Uricchio, Joesph, Jr., MD, Treasurer

American Leprosy Missions [15531]
1 Alm Way
Greenville, SC 29601
Toll free: 800-543-3135
Fax: (866)881-9769
Genheimer, Stephen R., Ph.D, Chairman

American Mock Trial Association [5824]
c/o Paige Blankenship, Department of Political Science3300 Poinsett Hwy.
Dept. of Political Science
3300 Poinsett Hwy.
Greenville, SC 29613
PH: (515)259-6625
Fax: (864)294-3513
Pavely, Melissa, Chairperson

Association of Traumatic Stress Specialists [11486]
5000 Old Buncombe Rd., Ste. 27-11
Greenville, SC 29617
PH: (864)294-4337
Hood, Linda, President

BMW Car Club of America [21338]
640 S Main St., Ste. 201
Greenville, SC 29601-2564
PH: (864)250-0022
Toll free: 800-878-9292
Fax: (864)250-0038
Hazard, Bruce, President

BMW Motorcycle Owners of America [22215]
640 S Main St., Ste. 201
Greenville, SC 29601
PH: (864)438-0962
Feeler, Greg, Director

CBM U.S. [14547]
228 Adley Way
Greenville, SC 29607
Toll free: 800-937-2264
Coborn, J.Michael, Dir. of Dev.

Clan Sinclair USA [20843]
c/o Mel Sinclair, President Emeritus
224 Bransfield Rd.

Greenville, SC 29615
PH: (919)542-2795
Sinclair, Mel, President

Dining for Women [13374]
PO Box 25633
Greenville, SC 29616-0633
PH: (864)335-8401
Wallace, Marsha, Founder

National Anger Management Association [15786]
100 Orchard Park Dr., No. 26629
Greenville, SC 29616-9998
PH: (646)485-5116
Fax: (646)390-1571
Pfeiffer, Richard, PhD, President

National Christian College Athletic Association [23240]
302 W Washington St.
Greenville, SC 29601-1919
PH: (864)250-1199
Fax: (864)250-1141
Wood, Dan, Exec. Dir.

Surgeons for Sight [17746]
113 Doctors Dr.
Greenville, SC 29605
McNair, Wallace, Chairman

Veterans Healing Initiative [13252]
108 Veronese Dr.
Greenville, SC 29609
PH: (917)509-7873
Toll free: 855-247-8500
Stone, Margaret, Chairman, President

World Witness, The Board of Foreign Missions of the Associate Reformed Presbyterian Church [20482]
1 Cleveland St., Ste. 220
Greenville, SC 29601
PH: (864)233-5226
Fax: (864)233-5326
Pettett, Alex, Exec. Dir.

Alpha Kappa Mu [23774]
101 Longwood Ln.
Greenwood, SC 29646-9262
Morris, Dr. Ann W., Exec. Sec., Treasurer

National Academy of Needlearts [21770]
c/o Debbie Stiehler
1 Riverbanks Ct.
Greer, SC 29651
Stiehler, Debbie, Contact

Atrial Fibrillation Association - USA [14102]
PO Box 5507
Hilton Head Island, SC 29938
PH: (843)785-4101
Lobban, Trudie C.A., Founder, CEO

International Association for the Scientific Study of Intellectual Disabilities [15647]
School of Medicine and Dentistry
University of Rochester
10 Ellis Ct.
Hilton Head Island, SC 29926-2701
Timmons, Vianne, President

Professional Tennis Registry [23305]
4 Office Way, Ste. 200
Hilton Head Island, SC 29928
PH: (843)785-7244
Toll free: 800-421-6289
Fax: (843)686-2033
Barth, Roy, President

Tennis Industry Association [3148]
117 Executive Ctr.
1 Corpus Christie Pl.

Hilton Head Island, SC 29928
PH: (843)686-3036
Toll free: 866-686-3036
Fax: (843)686-3078
Mason, Greg, President

Affordable Housing Investors Council [485]
PO Box 986
Irmo, SC 29063
PH: (347)392-9983
Toll free: 800-246-7277
Fax: (803)732-0135
Pelletier, William, President

Manpower Education Institute [8034]
1835 Charles Ave.
Lancaster, SC 29720-1512
PH: (718)548-4200
McFadden, Elizabeth, President

Oriental Rug Retailers of America [1957]
PO Box 53
Landrum, SC 29356-0053
PH: (864)895-6544
Joseph, Michael, President

Pure Puerto Rican Paso Fino Federation of America, Inc. [4403]
PO Box 2027
Leesville, SC 29070
Fax: (803)657-7780
Brown, Gail, President

Council on Chiropractic Guidelines and Practice Parameters [14265]
PO Box 2542
Lexington, SC 29071-2542
PH: (803)356-6809
Fax: (803)356-6826
Augat, Thomas J., Mem.

Maritime Postmark Society [22341]
c/o Fred McGary, Secretary and Treasurer
955 E Main St., Ste. E
Lexington, SC 29072

Reach Across [20456]
PO Box 2047
Lexington, SC 29071-2047
PH: (803)358-2330

Wirehaired Vizsla Club of America [21993]
100 Gill Field Ct.
Lexington, SC 29072
Goodwein, Mark, Director

National Hispanic Landscape Alliance [2071]
c/o Jose Arroyo, Secretary
PO Box 309
Lyman, SC 29365
Toll free: 877-260-7995
Torres, Juan, President

Operation Quiet Comfort [10754]
c/o Jan Hogg, President
307 Palmer Ln.
McCormick, SC 29835
PH: (864)614-1894
Schafnitz-Hogg, Jan, President

Association of Corporate Contributions Professionals [912]
1150 Hungryneck Blvd., Ste. C344
Mount Pleasant, SC 29464
PH: (734)655-3221
(843)216-3442
Shamley, Mark, CEO, President

Congressional Medal of Honor Society [20731]
40 Patriots Point Rd.
Mount Pleasant, SC 29464-4377
PH: (843)884-8862
Fax: (843)884-1471
Fritz, Harold A., President

National Association for Continence [17553]
1415 Stuart Engals Blvd.
Mount Pleasant, SC 29464
PH: (843)377-0900
Toll free: 800-252-3337
Jeter, Katherine F., EdD, Founder

Marines Helping Marines [12252]
512 Thorton Ct.
Myrtle Beach, SC 29579
PH: (443)465-1406
Short, Ron, Chairman

National Silver Fox Rabbit Club [4608]
c/o Kimberly R. Esquilla, Secretary
648 Forestbrook Rd.
Myrtle Beach, SC 29579
PH: (843)450-9019
Williams, Gordon, President

Vets With a Mission [17817]
1307 Caldwell St., 3rd Fl.
Newberry, SC 29108-2799
PH: (803)405-9926
Fax: (803)405-9926
Ward, Mr. Charles, Exec. Dir.

Lineolated Parakeet Society [3666]
c/o June DiCiocco, Treasurer
606 Cherokee Dr.
North Augusta, SC 29841
Whittaker, Jamie, President

Water Missions International [13344]
PO Box 71489
North Charleston, SC 29415
PH: (843)769-7395
Toll free: 866-280-7107
Fax: (843)763-6082
Greene, George C., III, CEO, Founder

Personal Injury Lawyers Marketing and Management Association [5047]
802 41st Ave. S
North Myrtle Beach, SC 29582
PH: (843)361-1700
Toll free: 800-497-1890
Fax: (866)859-8126
Hardison, Kenneth L., Founder, President

US ProMiniGolf Association [22897]
3210 Highway 17 S
North Myrtle Beach, SC 29582
PH: (843)458-2585
(843)272-7812
Fax: (843)361-7922
Detwiler, Bob, Contact

Orangeburgh German Swiss Genealogical Society [20990]
PO Box 974
Orangeburg, SC 29116-0974
Johnson, Pam, Editor

Let Me Live [12775]
130 Amberwood Rd.
Pickens, SC 29671
Wilson, Wesley, President

Homeless Children International [11034]
PO Box 416
Reidville, SC 29375-0416
High, David M., President

Fight Staph Infections [15397]
624 Station West Ln.
Roebuck, SC 29376
PH: (864)431-1411
Getz, Bonnie, Founder

Self-Insurance Institute of America [1926]
PO Box 1237
Simpsonville, SC 29681
Toll free: 800-851-7789
Fax: (864)962-2483
Link, Steven J., Chmn. of the Bd.

Navy Nuclear Weapons Association [21058]
c/o Frank Kelly, Treasurer
1087 Frank Kelly Rd.
Society Hill, SC 29593
PH: (843)378-4026
Salisbury, Tom, President

Catholic Radio Association [19814]
PO Box 172051
Spartanburg, SC 29301
PH: (864)438-4801
Fax: (509)479-1186
Gajdosik, Stephen, President

Impact Sports International [23227]
PO Box 5765
Spartanburg, SC 29304
PH: (864)278-8006

National Beta Club [23866]
151 Beta Club Way
Spartanburg, SC 29306
Toll free: 800-845-8281
Fax: (864)542-9300
Bright, Bob, CEO

Rice Bowls [12109]
951 S Pine St., Ste. 252
Spartanburg, SC 29302
Toll free: 866-312-5791
Caldwell, Dodd, President

Wofford College National Alumni Association [19374]
429 N Church St.
Spartanburg, SC 29303
PH: (864)597-4208
(864)597-4192
Gray, Charlie, Mem.

America's Great Loop Cruisers' Association [21552]
500 Oakbrook Ln.
Summerville, SC 29485
Toll free: 877-478-5667
Russo, Kimberly, Director

Chase After a Cure [13937]
89B Old Trolley Rd., Ste. 201
Summerville, SC 29483
Ringler, Whitney, Contact

International Primate Protection League [10650]
PO Box 766
Summerville, SC 29484-0766
PH: (843)871-2280
Fax: (843)871-7988
McGreal, Dr. Shirley, Founder, Exec. Dir.

USAF Medical Service Corps Association [15844]
4008 Plantation House Rd.
Summerville, SC 29485-6239
PH: (404)500-6722
Law, Col. Denise, Chairman

Christian Golfers' Association [22877]
1285 Clara Louise Kellogg Dr.
Sumter, SC 29153
Toll free: 800-784-2171
Winstead, Mr. Tom, Sr., President

Confederate Stamp Alliance [22323]
c/o Col. Larry Baum
316 W Calhoun St.
Sumter, SC 29150-4512

McAdams Historical Society [20898]
711 17th Ave. N
Surfside Beach, SC 29575-4354
PH: (818)789-1086
McAdams, R. Michael, Director

Iron Disorders Institute [15825]
PO Box 675
Taylors, SC 29687
Koenig, Gerry, Chmn. of the Bd.

National Association of Christian Ministers [20375]
2801 Wade Hampton Blvd., Ste. 115-227
Taylors, SC 29687
Mooney, Michael, President

First Foundations Inc. [13050]
PO Box 991
Travelers Rest, SC 29690
PH: (864)834-2300
Jensen, Dick, President

Mothers Against Sexual Abuse [12927]
404 Wilson St.
Union, SC 29379
Reeves, Claire R., CCDC, Founder

SOUTH DAKOTA

Abundant Wildlife Society of North America [4777]
PO Box 2
Beresford, SD 57004
PH: (605)751-0979

Carriage Travel Club [22464]
514 Americans Way, No. 3384
Box Elder, SD 57719-7600
PH: (931)707-0299
Winstel, Thomas, President

The Coleopterists Society [6609]
c/o Insect Biodiversity Lab
South Dakota State University
Box 2207A, SAG 361
Brookings, SD 57007
PH: (605)688-4438
Fax: (605)688-4602
Carlton, Christopher E., President

The Creativity Movement [19238]
c/o Rev. Chappel
PO Box 8044
Brookings, SD 57006
Klassen, Ben, Founder

National Association of College Wind and Percussion Instructors [8379]
c/o Michael Walsh, President
Box 2212
Lincoln Music Hall, SLM 205
Department of Music
South Dakota State University
Brookings, SD 57007
Ardovino, Lori, VP

Crazy Horse Memorial Foundation [10038]
12151 Avenue of the Chiefs
Crazy Horse, SD 57730-8900
PH: (605)673-4681
Brown, Jerry, V. Chmn. of the Bd.

Miniature Australian Shepherd Club of America, Inc. [21914]
PO Box 712
Custer, SD 57730
McCormick, Marla, President

Laura Ingalls Wilder Memorial Society [9071]
105 Olivet Ave.
De Smet, SD 57231-2445
PH: (605)854-3383
Toll free: 800-880-3383

American Red Cross Overseas Association [12618]
c/o Dorris Heaston, Treasurer
27118 Eagle Ridge Pl.
Harrisburg, SD 57032
MacSwain, Debby Griffith, President

International Association for Property and Evidence, Inc. [5471]
PO Box 652
Hot Springs, SD 57747
PH: (818)846-2926
Toll free: 800-449-4273
Fax: (818)846-4543
Campbell, Steve, Secretary

Lakota Student Alliance [19581]
PO Box 225
Kyle, SD 57752
PH: (605)867-1507
Quiver, Robert, Contact

Native American Community Board [12383]
PO Box 572
Lake Andes, SD 57356-0572
PH: (605)487-7072
Fax: (605)487-7964
Asteoyer, Charon, Exec. Dir., CEO

Native American Women's Health Education Resource Center [17764]
PO Box 572
Lake Andes, SD 57356-0572
PH: (605)487-7072
(605)487-7097
Fax: (605)487-7964
Asteoyer, Charon, Exec. Dir., CEO

International Society for the Protection of Mustangs and Burros [4831]
PO Box 55
Lantry, SD 57636-0055
PH: (605)964-6866
(605)430-2088
Sussman, Karen A., President

Association for Distance Education and Independent Learning [7483]
c/o Susan Eykamp, 820 N Washington Ave.
Dakota State University
Madison, SD 57042
PH: (605)256-5798
Eykamp, Susan, President

Association of Community Tribal Schools [8394]
220 Omaha St.
Mission, SD 57555
PH: (605)838-0424
Fax: (605)838-0424
Bordeaux, Dr. Roger, Exec. Dir.

National Council of State Agricultural Finance Programs [4182]
c/o Terri LaBrie
South Dakota Department of Agriculture
523 E Capitol Ave.
Pierre, SD 57501
PH: (605)773-4026
Fax: (605)773-3481
LaBrie, Terri, President

International Guild of Glass Artists [251]
27829 365th Ave.
Platte, SD 57369
PH: (313)886-0099
Baxter, Ann, Chairperson

Intermountain Forest Association [1411]
2218 Jackson Blvd., No. 10
Rapid City, SD 57702-3452

PH: (605)341-0875
Fax: (605)341-8651
Troxel, Tom, Exec. Dir.

Intertribal Buffalo Council [3627]
2497 W Chicago St.
Rapid City, SD 57702
PH: (605)394-9730
Fax: (605)394-7742
Stone, Jim, Exec. Dir.

Mount Rushmore Society [9411]
711 N Creek Dr.
Rapid City, SD 57703
PH: (605)341-8883
Fax: (605)341-0433
Allen, Judy, President

National Bowhunter Education
Foundation [22503]
PO Box 2934
Rapid City, SD 57709-2934
PH: (605)716-0596
Fax: (309)401-6096
Clayton, Doug, President

Native American Coalition for
Healthy Alternatives [12382]
1038 E Tallent St.
Rapid City, SD 57701
PH: (605)891-9413
Fax: (605)791-5225
Pourier, Cholena, Exec. Dir.

Native Financial Education Coalition
[7932]
1010 9th St., Ste. 3
Rapid City, SD 57701
PH: (605)342-3770
Meeks, Elsie, Chairperson

Vinegar Connoisseurs International
[22150]
The Vinegar Man
PO Box 41
Roslyn, SD 57261
Diggs, Lawrence, Contact

Abstinence Clearinghouse [17188]
801 E 41st St.
Sioux Falls, SD 57105
PH: (605)335-3643
Toll free: 888-577-2966
Unruh, Leslee J., Founder, President

American Coalition for Ethanol
[4021]
5000 S Broadband Ln., Ste. 224
Sioux Falls, SD 57108
PH: (605)334-3381
Alverson, Ron, President

ATM Industry Association [384]
PO Box 88433
Sioux Falls, SD 57109-8433
PH: (605)271-7371
    (605)271-7371
Lee, Mike, CEO

Beaver Ambassador Club [22419]
c/o Iris Schmidt, Membership Director
3916 N Potsdam Ave.
Sioux Falls, SD 57104-7048
PH: (541)953-3595
Humble, Mike, President

Evangelical Lutheran Good
Samaritan Society [13048]
4800 W 57th St.
Sioux Falls, SD 57108
PH: (605)362-3100
Toll free: 866-928-1635
Fax: (605)362-3240
Horazdovsky, Mr. David J., CEO,
President

Lutheran Educational Conference of
North America [8259]
2601 S Minnesota Ave., Ste. 105
Sioux Falls, SD 57105

PH: (605)271-9894
Brill, Laurie, Exec. Dir. (Actg.)

Teton Club International [22434]
c/o TCI Secretary-Treasurer
3916 N Potsdam Ave., No. 2590
Sioux Falls, SD 57104-7048
Inman, Dennis, President

American Azteca Horse International
Association [4297]
PO Box 460
Sturgis, SD 57785
PH: (605)342-2322

Public Radio News Directors
Incorporated [480]
PO Box 838
Sturgis, SD 57785
Bodarky, George, President

Czech Heritage Preservation Society
[9385]
PO Box 3
Tabor, SD 57063-0003
PH: (605)463-2571
Novak, Alex, President

Institute for American Indian Studies
[5939]
Slagle Hall, Rm. 102
414 E Clark St.
Vermillion, SD 57069
PH: (605)677-6497
Fax: (605)677-6651

International Coalition for Addiction
Studies Education [13146]
PO Box 224
Vermillion, SD 57069-0224
PH: (605)677-5520
Korkow, John, Chairman

University of South Dakota Alumni
Association [19365]
414 E Clark St.
Vermillion, SD 57069-2390
PH: (605)677-6734
Toll free: 800-655-2586
Johnson, Kersten, Exec. Dir.

National Association of Tower Erec-
tors [6165]
8 2nd St. SE
Watertown, SD 57201-3624
PH: (605)882-5865
Toll free: 888-882-5865
Cipov, Pat, Chairperson

Mt. Marty College Alumni Associa-
tion [19336]
1105 W 8th St.
Yankton, SD 57078-3725
PH: (605)668-1545
Toll free: 855-686-2789
Fax: (605)668-1508
Heimes, Amy, Admin. Asst.

National Field Archery Association
[22505]
800 Archery Ln.
Yankton, SD 57078-4119
PH: (605)260-9279
Cull, Bruce, PresidentT

TENNESSEE

International Automotive Remarket-
ers Alliance [295]
257 N Calderwood St., No. 316
Alcoa, TN 37701
PH: (865)805-5954
Toll free: 866-277-6996
Graham, Bob, Chmn. of the Bd.

National Safe Skies Alliance, Inc.
[19198]
110 McGhee Tyson Blvd., Ste. 201
Alcoa, TN 37701

PH: (865)970-0515
Toll free: 888-609-4957
Roberts, Jennifer, CFO, Sr. VP

Master's Men of the National As-
sociation of Free Will Baptists
[19732]
5233 Mount View Rd.
Antioch, TN 37013-2306
PH: (615)731-6812
Toll free: 877-767-7659
Fax: (615)731-0771
Hodges, Eddie, Chmn. of the Bd.

National Association of Free Will
Baptists [19734]
5233 Mount View Rd.
Antioch, TN 37013-2306
PH: (615)731-6812
Toll free: 877-767-7659
Fax: (615)731-0771
Burden, Keith, Exec. Sec.

Women Nationally Active for Christ
[19744]
PO Box 5002
Antioch, TN 37011-5002
PH: (615)731-6812
Toll free: 877-767-7662
Fax: (615)727-1157
Hodges, Elizabeth, Exec. Dir.

Swift Museum Foundation [21251]
223 County Road 552
Athens, TN 37303
PH: (423)745-9547
Fax: (423)745-9869
Roberson, Will, Jr., Chmn. of the Bd.

American College of Apothecaries
[16635]
2830 Summer Oaks Dr.
Bartlett, TN 38134
PH: (901)383-8119
Fax: (901)473-8187
Hesterlee, Edward J., Exec. VP

Restoration Path [20045]
PO Box 343418
Bartlett, TN 38184
PH: (901)751-2468
Toll free: 877-320-5217
Jones, David, Exec. Dir., Counselor

Alpha Omicron Pi [23944]
5390 Virginia Way
Brentwood, TN 37027
PH: (615)370-0920
Toll free: 855-230-1183
Fax: (615)371-9736
Whipple, Krista, VP

American College of Neuropsychop-
harmacology [16638]
5034-A Thoroughbred Ln.
Brentwood, TN 37027
PH: (615)324-2360
Fax: (615)523-1715
Wilkins, Ronnie D., EdD, Exec. Dir.

American Society of Clinical Psy-
chopharmacology [16643]
5034 Thoroughbred Ln., Ste. A
Brentwood, TN 37027-4231
PH: (615)649-3085
Fax: (888)417-3311
Rapaport, Mark, MD, President

Artists in Christian Testimony
[20126]
7003 Chadwick Dr., Ste. 354
Brentwood, TN 37027
PH: (615)376-7861
Toll free: 888-376-7861
Fax: (615)376-7863
Spradlin, Rev. Byron, CEO,
President

Hope Force International [11669]
7065 Moores Ln., Ste. 200
Brentwood, TN 37027

PH: (615)371-1271
Fax: (615)371-1261
Minton, Jack, CEO, Founder

International Society of Psychiatric
Genetics [14881]
5034 Thoroughbred Ln., Ste. A
Brentwood, TN 37027-4231
PH: (615)649-3086
Toll free: 888-417-3311
Rice, John, Treasurer

Alan Jackson Fan Club [24047]
PO Box 1955
Brentwood, TN 37024

Leuva Patidar Samaj of USA [9567]
9005 Overlook Blvd.
Brentwood, TN 37027
Toll free: 866-201-2353
Fax: (866)201-5183
Patel, Harshad, President

Marce Society [15782]
5034-A Thoroughbred Ln.
Brentwood, TN 37027
PH: (615)324-2362
Glover, Vivette, Treasurer

North Central Wholesalers Associa-
tion [2637]
7107 Crossroads Blvd., Ste. 106
Brentwood, TN 37027-7972
PH: (615)371-5004
Fax: (615)371-5444
Shafer, Terry, Exec. VP

Organization of Teratology Informa-
tion Specialists [13833]
5034A Thoroughbred Ln.
Brentwood, TN 37027
PH: (615)649-3082
Toll free: 866-626-6847
Fax: (615)523-1715
Felix, Robert, President

Schizophrenia International
Research Society [15804]
5034-A Thoroughbred Ln.
Brentwood, TN 37027
PH: (615)324-2370
Kahn, René, M.D., President

Sexaholics Anonymous [12916]
PO Box 3565
Brentwood, TN 37024-3565
PH: (615)370-6062
Toll free: 866-424-8777
Fax: (615)370-0882

Songwriters Guild of America [5342]
5120 Virginia Way, Ste. C22
Brentwood, TN 37027-7594
PH: (615)742-9945
Toll free: 800-524-6742
Fax: (615)630-7501
Carnes, Rick, President

American Academy of Medical Eth-
ics [14743]
PO Box 7500
Bristol, TN 37621
PH: (423)844-1095
Stevens, Dr. David, Exec. Dir.

Christian Medical and Dental As-
sociations [20323]
2604 Highway 421
Bristol, TN 37620
PH: (423)844-1000
Toll free: 888-231-2637
Fax: (423)844-1005
Stevens, Dr. David, CEO

Christian Pharmacists Fellowship
International [16657]
PO Box 1154
Bristol, TN 37621-1154

PH: (423)844-1043
Eckel, Fred, President

Presbyterian Evangelistic Fellowship
[20524]
100 5th St., Ste. 330
Bristol, TN 37620
PH: (423)573-5308
Toll free: 800-225-5733
Fax: (423)573-5309
Light, Rev. Rick J., Exec. Dir.

WTCARES [21998]
c/o Lyn Hollis
164 N Forrest Ave.
Camden, TN 38320-1217
Hollis, Lyn, Comm. Chm.

Airlift/Tanker Association [5056]
655 Julian Rd.
Chattanooga, TN 37421
PH: (423)902-2297
Reynolds, Michael C., President

American Polygraph Association
[5237]
PO Box 8037
Chattanooga, TN 37414-0037
PH: (423)892-3992
Toll free: 800-272-8037
Fax: (423)894-5435
Slupski, Charles, Chairman

AMG International [20381]
6815 Shallowford Rd.
Chattanooga, TN 37421
PH: (423)894-6060
Toll free: 800-251-7206
Fax: (423)894-6863
Hardin, William S., Chairman

Association of Private Enterprise
Education [8461]
c/o Probasco Chair of Free
Enterprise
University of Tennessee at Chat-
tanooga
313 Fletcher Hall, Dept. 6106
615 McCallie Ave.
Chattanooga, TN 37403-2598
Clark, Dr. J.R., Secretary, Treasurer

Christian Business Men's Connec-
tion [19952]
Osborne Ctr., Ste. 602
5746 Marlin Rd.
Chattanooga, TN 37411
PH: (423)698-4444
Toll free: 800-566-2262
Fax: (423)629-4434
Truax, Lee, President

Craniofacial Foundation of America
[14332]
975 E 3rd St.
Chattanooga, TN 37403
PH: (423)778-9176
Toll free: 800-418-3223
Fax: (423)778-8172
Butler, Cindy, VP

FACES: The National Craniofacial
Association [14334]
PO Box 11082
Chattanooga, TN 37401
PH: (423)266-1632
Toll free: 800-322-2373
Teems, Kim, Prog. Dir., Dir. of
Comm.

Fellowship of Christian Peace Of-
ficers U.S.A. [19978]
105 Lee Parkway Dr., Ste. C
Chattanooga, TN 37421
PH: (423)553-8806
Fax: (423)553-8846
Lee, Paul, Exec. Dir.

Maclellan Foundation, Inc. [20546]
820 Broad St., Ste. 300
Chattanooga, TN 37402

PH: (423)755-1366

National Alternative Education As-
sociation [7489]
PO Box 22185
Chattanooga, TN 37422
Lamb, Lori L., Mem.

National Inhalant Prevention Coali-
tion [17322]
318 Lindsay St.
Chattanooga, TN 37403
PH: (423)265-4662
Toll free: 855-704-4400
Fax: (423)265-4889
Weiss, Harvey, Exec. Dir.

National Knife Collectors Association
[22176]
PO Box 21070
Chattanooga, TN 37424-0070
PH: (423)667-8199
Sebenick, Lisa, President

Partners and Peers for Diabetes
Care [14542]
PO Box 5128
Chattanooga, TN 37406
PH: (423)505-0558
Nunnally, Philip, Chairman

Psi Chi, The International Honor
Society in Psychology [23855]
825 Vine St.
Chattanooga, TN 37403
PH: (423)756-2044
Toll free: 877-774-2443
Zlokovich, Dr. Martha S., Exec. Dir.

Southern Economic Association
[6403]
313 Fletcher Hall, Dept. 6106
615 McCallie Ave.
Chattanooga, TN 37403-2598
PH: (423)425-4118
Fax: (423)425-5218
Clark, J.R., Secretary, Treasurer

International French Brittany Club of
America [21898]
870 Barren Valley Rd.
Chuckey, TN 37641-5808

Fairlane Club of America [21378]
340 Clicktown Rd.
Church Hill, TN 37642-6622
PH: (423)245-6678
Fax: (423)245-2456
Bender, Doug, President

State Guard Association of the
United States [5623]
PO Box 2441
Clarksville, TN 37042
PH: (931)624-0588
Martinez, Carlos, President

Church of God World Missions
[20404]
2490 Keith St. NW
Cleveland, TN 37311
Toll free: 800-345-7492
Hill, Tim, Director

American Association of Moderate
Sedation Nurses [16092]
322 Commerce St.
Clinton, TN 37716
PH: (865)230-9995
Fax: (865)269-4613
Eslinger, Ron, MA, President,
Treasurer

National Alliance of Independent
Crop Consultants [3525]
349 E Nolley Dr.
Collierville, TN 38017
PH: (901)861-0511
Fax: (901)861-0512
Keenan, Debra, President

Independent Free Papers of America
[2789]
104 Westland Dr.
Columbia, TN 38401
PH: (931)224-8151
Fry, Douglas, Exec. Dir.

James K. Polk Memorial Association
[10334]
301-305 W 7th St.
Columbia, TN 38401
PH: (931)388-2354
Price, Tom, Curator

Sons of Confederate Veterans
[20745]
PO Box 59
Columbia, TN 38402-0059
Toll free: 800-380-1896
Fax: (931)381-6712

National Sweet Sorghum Producers
and Processors Association [3769]
c/o James Baier, Executive
Secretary
PO Box 1356
Cookeville, TN 38503-1356
PH: (931)644-7764
Baier, James, Exec. Sec.

The Cotton Foundation [933]
PO Box 783
Cordova, TN 38088
PH: (901)274-9030
Fax: (901)725-0510
Norman, Dr. Bill, Exec. Dir.,
Secretary

National Cotton Council of America
[937]
7193 Goodlett Farms Pky.
Cordova, TN 38016-4909
PH: (901)274-9030
Fax: (901)725-0510
Johnson, Fred, VP of Admin.

National Cotton Ginners' Association
[938]
7193 Goodlett Farms Pky.
Cordova, TN 38016-4909
PH: (901)274-9030
Fax: (901)725-0510
Craft, Ron, President

National Cottonseed Products As-
sociation [2452]
866 Willow Tree Cir.
Cordova, TN 38018
PH: (901)682-0800
Morgan, Ben, Exec. VP, Secretary

U.S. Chess Federation [21593]
137 O'Brien Dr.
Crossville, TN 38555
PH: (931)787-1234
Fax: (931)787-1200
DuBois, Joan, Dir. of Public Rel.

American Association of Christian
Schools [7605]
602 Belvoir Ave.
East Ridge, TN 37412-2602
PH: (423)629-4280
Fax: (423)622-7461
Wiebe, Dr. Keith, President

Roger Wyburn-Mason and Jack M.
Blount Foundation for the Eradica-
tion of Rheumatoid Disease
[17165]
7376 Walker Rd.
Fairview, TN 37062-8141
PH: (615)799-1002
Fax: (615)799-1002

Technology Institute for Music
Educators [8391]
7503 Kingwood Ct.
Fairview, TN 37062

PH: (615)870-9333
Lawson, Mike, Exec. Dir.

American Bunka Embroidery Association [22252]
c/o Cathy Dean, Treasurer
222 Double Springs Rd.
Fall Branch, TN 37656
PH: (317)882-2851
(423)863-1023
Palmer, Anita, President

American Veterinary Dental Society
[17628]
PO Box 803
Fayetteville, TN 37334
PH: (931)438-0238
Toll free: 800-332-2837
Fax: (931)433-6289
Bannon, Dr. Kris, President

Americana Music Association [9872]
PO Box 628
Franklin, TN 37065
PH: (615)386-6936
Fax: (615)386-6937
Hilly, Jed, Exec. Dir.

Doctors at War Against Trafficking
Worldwide [12921]
PO Box 681364
Franklin, TN 37068
Toll free: 888-552-8927
Bercu, Dr. Daniel, Founder,
President

Multiples of America [12365]
2000 Mallory Ln., Ste. 130-600
Franklin, TN 37067-8231
PH: (248)231-4480
Krell, Pam, President

Open Schools Worldwide [11110]
PO Box 972
Franklin, TN 37065
PH: (615)599-2059
McIlhenny, Dr. Alan, CEO

Presbyterian Lay Committee [20526]
PO Box 682247
Franklin, TN 37068-2247
PH: (615)591-4388
Toll free: 800-368-0110
Fowler LaBerge, Rev. Carmen S.,
Editor, President

Association of Procurement Technical Assistance Centers [1512]
360 Sunset Island Trl.
Gallatin, TN 37066
PH: (615)268-6644

American Society of Military Insignia
Collectors [22180]
c/o Garth Thompson, Secretary
7350 Green Clover Cove
Germantown, TN 38138
McDuff, James M, President

Automotive Distribution Network
[310]
3085 Fountainside Dr., No. 210
Germantown, TN 38138
Toll free: 800-727-8112
Fax: (901)682-9098
Barstow, Bob, Contact

Orthopedic Surgical Manufacturers
Association [1605]
c/o Valerie Frank
7302 Texas Heights Ave.
Germantown, TN 38183-0805
PH: (901)758-0806
Starowicz, Sharon, President

P.T. Boats Inc. [21200]
PO Box 38070
Germantown, TN 38183-0070

PH: (901)755-8440
Fax: (901)751-0522
Shannon, Don, Coord.

Society of Gynecologic Surgeons
[16305]
7800 Wolf Trail Cove
Germantown, TN 38138
PH: (901)682-2079
Fax: (901)682-9505
Sung, Vivian, MD, President

American Credit Card Collectors
Society [21609]
c/o Scott Nimmo
3563 B Long Hollow Pk.
Goodlettsville, TN 37072
Tylenda, Ed, Chairman

American Historic Racing Motorcycle
Association [22210]
c/o David Lamberth, Executive
Director
309 Buffalo Run
Goodlettsville, TN 37072
PH: (615)420-6435
Fax: (615)420-6438
Lamberth, David, Exec. Dir.

Independent Medical Specialty Deal-
ers Association [1603]
113 Space Pk. N
Goodlettsville, TN 37072
Toll free: 866-463-2937
Fax: (614)467-2071
Sizemore, Don, President

Society for Excellence in Eyecare,
Inc. [16407]
PO Box 2153
Goodlettsville, TN 37070-2153
PH: (615)892-0863
Fax: (615)859-3941

Burley Stabilization Corporation
[4719]
1427 W Main St.
Greeneville, TN 37743
PH: (615)212-0508
Toll free: 866-828-6501

The Maserati Club [21425]
325 Walden Ave.
Harriman, TN 37748-2738
PH: (865)882-9230
Demyanovich, Michael A., President

George Strait Fan Club [24042]
PO Box 2119
Hendersonville, TN 37077

National Association of Timetable
Collectors [22462]
PO Box 1266
Hendersonville, TN 37077-1266
Hannah, Kent, Jr., President

New Hope Construction Inc. [11989]
PO Box 1186
Hendersonville, TN 37077
PH: (615)822-0111
Toll free: 866-396-4673

Eddy Raven Fan Club [24059]
PO Box 2476
Hendersonville, TN 37077-2476
PH: (615)368-7433

American Chevelle Enthusiasts
Society [21319]
4636 Lebanon Pike, Ste. 195
Hermitage, TN 37076-1316
PH: (615)773-2237
Hanson, Chuck, Contact

Andrew Jackson Foundation [10333]
4580 Rachel's Ln.
Hermitage, TN 37076-1331

PH: (615)889-2941
Fax: (615)889-9909
Kittell, Howard J., President, CEO

International Board of Jewish Mis-
sions [20146]
5106 Genesis Ln.
Hixson, TN 37343
PH: (423)876-8150
Fax: (423)876-8156
Frampton, Ed, President

Elephant Care International [4811]
166 Limo View Ln.
Hohenwald, TN 38462
PH: (931)796-7102
Hammatt, Hank, Exec. Dir., Founder

Elephant Sanctuary in Tennessee
[10615]
27 E Main St.
Hohenwald, TN 38462
PH: (931)796-6500
Fax: (931)796-1360
Spivey, Angela, Exec. Asst.

El Ayudante Nicaragua [13006]
PO Box 10805
Jackson, TN 38308
Coley, Liz, Director

The Pig Preserve Association
[10682]
PO Box 555
Jamestown, TN 38556
Austin, Gail, President, Treasurer

Delta Omicron International Music
Fraternity [23826]
910 Church St.
Jefferson City, TN 37760
PH: (865)471-6155
Fax: (865)475-9716
Beckner, Debbie, Exec. Sec.

National Association of Rhythm and
Blues Dee Jay's [9969]
c/o Sue Kestner, Secretary
5375 Ridge Rd.
Joelton, TN 37080
PH: (615)876-2343
Hall, Mike, President

Develop Africa [10487]
1906 Knob Creek Rd., Ste. 3
Johnson City, TN 37604
PH: (423)282-0006
Renner, Sylvester, Founder,
President

EEG and Clinical Neuroscience
Society [16046]
East Tennessee State University
Department of Psychology
807 University Pkwy.
Johnson City, TN 37614
Toll free: 888-531-5335
Fax: (888)531-5335
Galderisi, Silvana, MD, President

International Society of Biomechan-
ics in Sports [6087]
c/o East Tennessee State University
PO Box 70300
Johnson City, TN 37614
PH: (423)439-1000
Hamill, Joseph, Contact

Artist-Blacksmith's Association of
North America [434]
259 Muddy Fork Rd.
Jonesborough, TN 37659
PH: (423)913-1022
Fax: (423)913-1023
Rainey, Eddie, President

National Storytelling Network
[10225]
PO Box 795
Jonesborough, TN 37659

PH: (423)913-8201
Toll free: 800-525-4514
Fax: (423)753-9331
Rogers, Kit, Office Mgr.

National Chaplains Association
[20028]
c/o Dr. Doyle E. Varvel, National
Commander
PO Box 6418
Kingsport, TN 37663-1437
PH: (276)466-0599
Varvel, Dr. Doyle E., Cmdr.

North American Vodder Association
of Lymphatic Therapy [15547]
317 Cherokee St., Ste. 101
Kingsport, TN 37660-4335

America Outdoors Association
[23091]
PO Box 10847
Knoxville, TN 37939
PH: (865)558-3595
Toll free: 800-524-4814
Fax: (865)558-3598
Brown, David L., Exec. Dir.

American Association of Blind
Teachers [8638]
c/o John Buckley
1025 Ree Way
Knoxville, TN 37909
PH: (865)692-4888
Buckley, John, Contact

American Association of Physician
Offices and Laboratories [15514]
c/o Doctors Management
10401 Kingston Pke.
Knoxville, TN 37922
Toll free: 800-635-4040
Fax: (865)531-0722
Bachman, Ms. Ann, Director

Chet Atkins Appreciation Society
[24025]
c/o Mark Pritcher, President
3716 Timberlake Rd.
Knoxville, TN 37920
PH: (865)577-2828
Pritcher, Mark, President

Autism 4 Parents [13740]
209 Lawton Blvd.
Knoxville, TN 37934
Toll free: 855-273-5437
Stein, Terry L., President, CEO

Cavalier King Charles Spaniel Club
of America [21853]
2301 E Emory Rd.
Knoxville, TN 37938-4518
PH: (865)688-2484
Fax: (865)219-0363
Henry, Bruce B., President

College and University Professional
Association for Human Resources
[8414]
1811 Commons Point Dr.
Knoxville, TN 37932-1989
PH: (865)637-7673
Toll free: 877-287-2474
Fax: (865)637-7674
Brantley, Andy, CEO, President

Intercoiffure America/Canada [920]
1645 Downtown W Blvd.
Knoxville, TN 37919
Toll free: 800-442-3007
Gambuzza, Frank, President

International Alliance of Composers
[9922]
9701 Clearwater Dr.
Knoxville, TN 37923-2021
PH: (323)306-3057
(347)767-2952
Merritt, Chris, Exec. Dir.

International Textile and Apparel As-
sociation [3261]
PO Box 70687
Knoxville, TN 37938-0687
PH: (865)992-1535
Rutherford, Nancy, Exec. Dir.

Mission Services Association
[20438]
2004 E Magnolia Ave.
Knoxville, TN 37917
PH: (865)525-7010
Fax: (865)525-7012
Hundley, Reggie, Exec. Dir.

National Association of Blind
Merchants [2966]
7450 Chapman Hwy., Ste. 319
Knoxville, TN 37920
PH: (719)527-0488
Toll free: 866-543-6808
Gacos, Nicky, President

National Association of Ordnance
Contractors [880]
c/o Kyra Donell, Membership
Chairperson
2095 Lakeside Center Way, Ste. 200
Knoxville, TN 37922
PH: (865)560-2883
Fax: (865)560-2802
Donnell, Kyra, VP

National Association to Protect
Children [11086]
PO Box 2187
Knoxville, TN 37901
PH: (865)525-0901
Weeks, Grier, Exec. Dir.

National Information Officers As-
sociation [2755]
PO Box 10125
Knoxville, TN 37939-0125
PH: (865)389-8736
Fronimos, Mike, Officer

National Swine Improvement
Federation [4715]
102 McCord Hall
Dept. of Animal Science
University of Tennessee
2640 Morgan Cir.
Knoxville, TN 37996-4588
PH: (865)974-7238
Fax: (865)974-9043
Conatser, Glenn, Officer

One Vision International [11419]
2915 Alcoa Hwy.
Knoxville, TN 37920
PH: (865)579-3353
Miller, John, Exec. Dir., Founder

Professional Paddlesports Associa-
tion [3145]
PO Box 10847
Knoxville, TN 37939
PH: (865)558-3595
Roberts, Don, Chairman

Random Acts of Flowers [11850]
3500 Workman Rd., Ste. 101A
Knoxville, TN 37921
PH: (865)248-3045
Fax: (865)240-2933
Jay, Larsen, Founder, CEO

Saving Little Hearts [14141]
PO Box 52285
Knoxville, TN 37950
PH: (865)748-4605
Coulter, Karin, Exec. Dir., Founder,
President

Society for the Study of Social
Problems [12992]
University of Tennessee
901 McClung Twr.

Knoxville, TN 37996-0490
PH: (865)689-1531
Fax: (865)689-1534
Delgado, Dr. Hector L., Exec. Ofc.

Special Interest Group on Information Retrieval **[6758]**
c/o Diane Kelly, Chairperson
School of Information Sciences
University of Tennessee
1345 Circle Park Dr., Ste. 451
Knoxville, TN 37996-0341
Kelly, Diane, Chairperson

Tau Beta Pi Association, Inc. **[23745]**
508 Dougherty Engineering Bldg.
1512 Middle Dr.
Knoxville, TN 37996
PH: (865)546-4578
Fax: (865)546-4579
Gomulinski, Curtis D., Exec. Dir., Editor

Opticians Association of America **[16416]**
3740 Canada Rd.
Lakeland, TN 38002
PH: (901)388-2423
Fax: (901)388-2348
Allen, Christopher M., Exec. Dir.

TECH, Technical Exchange for Christian Healthcare **[20326]**
PO Box 912
Lawrenceburg, TN 38464
PH: (989)600-6536
Fax: (989)600-6536
Wood, Jennie, Exec. Dir.

Harden - Hardin - Harding Family Association **[20877]**
c/o Colleen Taylor, Membership Coordinator
380 Powell Grove Rd.
Lebanon, TN 37090-8275
PH: (615)449-4806
Hardin, William, Director

Sigma Pi Fraternity, International **[23932]**
106 N Castle Heights Ave.
Lebanon, TN 37087
PH: (615)921-2300
Toll free: 800-332-1897
Fax: (615)373-8949
Walker, Jason, Exec. Dir.

Tennessee Walking Horse Breeders' and Exhibitors' Association **[4415]**
250 N Ellington Pky.
Lewisburg, TN 37091
PH: (931)359-1574
Fax: (931)359-7530
Smith, Stephen, President

The Doe Network **[12361]**
420 Airport Rd.
Livingston, TN 38570-1268
PH: (931)397-3893
Wells, Rocky, Gen. Mgr.

Polyurethane Foam Association, Inc. **[2630]**
334 Lakeside Plz.
Loudon, TN 37774-4165
PH: (865)657-9840
Fax: (865)381-1292
Luedeka, Robert J., Exec. Dir.

International Quarter Pony Association **[4369]**
PO Box 230
Lyles, TN 37098
PH: (931)996-3987
    (931)996-8242
Whitling, Laurie, President

Kitty Wells-Johnny Wright-Bobby Wright International Fan Club **[24068]**
619 Due West Ave.
Madison, TN 37115

PH: (615)868-2600

God's Planet for Haiti **[13055]**
PO Box 4462
Maryville, TN 37802
PH: (865)257-7680
Maignan, Jemps, Exec. Dir., Founder

American Association of Cheerleading Coaches and Administrators **[22724]**
6745 Lenox Center Ct., Ste. 318
Memphis, TN 38115
Toll free: 800-533-6583
Lord, Jim, Exec. Dir.

American Association for Laboratory Animal Science **[13715]**
9190 Crestwyn Hills Dr.
Memphis, TN 38125-8538
PH: (901)754-8620
Fax: (901)753-0046
Turner, Ann Tourigny, Exec. Dir.

American Cancer Assistance **[13881]**
5865 Ridgeway Center Pkwy., Ste. 300
Memphis, TN 38120-4014
Toll free: 877-767-9948
Miller, David E., Chairman, CEO

American Cotton Shippers Association **[931]**
88 Union Ave., Ste. 1204
Memphis, TN 38103
PH: (901)525-5352
Fax: (901)527-8303
Walton, Bobby, Chairman

American Mathematical Association of Two-Year Colleges **[8275]**
Southwest Tennessee Community College
5983 Macon Cove
Memphis, TN 38134
PH: (901)333-5643
Garner, Wanda L., Exec. Dir.

American Society of Geriatric Otolaryngology **[16538]**
c/o Dr. Brian J. McKinnon, Treasurer
Shea Ear Clinic
6133 Poplar Pke.
Memphis, TN 38119
Eibling, David, MD, President

Ancient Arabic Order of the Nobles of the Mystic Shrine for North America **[19551]**
2239 Democrat Rd.
Memphis, TN 38132
PH: (901)395-0150
Fax: (901)395-0115

Ancient Egyptian Arabic Order Nobles of the Mystic Shrine **[19552]**
2239 Democrat Rd.
Memphis, TN 38132-1802
PH: (901)395-0150
Fax: (901)395-0115
Buchanan, Homer L., Leader

Animal World USA **[3622]**
PO Box 11126
Memphis, TN 38111
PH: (901)791-2455
    (703)625-1392
Fax: (901)249-3253
Buckalew, Michelle, Founder, President

Association for Veterinary Family Practice **[17638]**
c/o Jen Clay, Secretary-Treasurer
1157 Madison Ave.

Memphis, TN 38104-2202
Clay, Jennifer, Secretary, Treasurer

The Blues Foundation **[9881]**
421 S Main St.
Memphis, TN 38103-4464
PH: (901)527-2583
Fax: (901)529-4030
Newman, Barbara, President, CEO

Brilliant Scientists of Tomorrow **[7748]**
5100 Poplar Ave., Ste. 2700
Memphis, TN 38137
Toll free: 800-984-0379

Center for Southern Folklore **[8797]**
119 S Main St.
Memphis, TN 38101
PH: (901)525-3655
Peiser, Judy, Exec. Producer, Director

Chi Omega **[23949]**
3395 Players Club Pky.
Memphis, TN 38125
PH: (901)748-8600
Fax: (901)748-8686
Potter, Shelley Eubanks, President

Commission on Missing and Exploited Children **[10945]**
616 Adams Ave., Ste. 102
Memphis, TN 38105
PH: (901)405-8441
Waddell, Kristen Myers, President

Cooperative Association of Tractor Dealers, Inc. **[904]**
6075 Poplar Ave., Ste. 125
Memphis, TN 38119
PH: (901)333-8600
Fax: (901)333-8640
McCain, Shellie G., President

Developmental Neurotoxicology Society **[15924]**
c/o Helen J. K. Salbe, PhD
Department of Psychology
University of Memphis
400 Innovation Dr.
Memphis, TN 38152
Makris, Sue, Liaison

Ducks Unlimited **[4808]**
1 Waterfowl Way
Memphis, TN 38120
PH: (901)758-3825
Toll free: 800-453-8257
Bonderson, Paul, Jr., President

Eta Sigma Phi, National Classics Honorary Society **[23711]**
c/o David H. Sick, Executive Secretary
Greek and Roman Studies
Rhodes College
2000 N Pkwy.
Memphis, TN 38112
PH: (901)843-3907
Fax: (901)843-3363
Sienkewicz, Thomas J., Exec. Sec.

International Neuroendocrine Federation **[16051]**
c/o William Armstrong, Treasurer
University of Tennessee Health Science Ctr.
855 Monroe Ave.
Memphis, TN 38117
PH: (901)448-5966
Fax: (901)448-4685
Millar, Robert, President

Kappa Delta **[23957]**
3205 Players Ln.
Memphis, TN 38125
Toll free: 888-668-4293
Stockton, Susan, VP

Lessing Society **[9073]**
c/o Dr. Monika Nenon, President
University of Memphis
Dept. of Foreign Languages and Literatures
Memphis, TN 38152
PH: (901)678-4094
Fax: (901)678-5338
Dupree, Dr. Mary Helen, Secretary, Treasurer

Memphis Cotton Exchange **[3778]**
65 Union Ave.
Memphis, TN 38103
PH: (901)531-7826
Fax: (901)531-7827
Webster, Ross, President

National Association of Black Female Executives in Music and Entertainment **[1148]**
111 S Highland, Ste. 388
Memphis, TN 38111
PH: (901)236-8439
Walker, Johnnie, Chairperson, Founder

National Coalition of Pastors' Spouses **[13073]**
950 Mt. Moriah Rd., Ste. 100
Memphis, TN 38117
PH: (901)517-6537
Toll free: 866-901-5044
Berryhill, Vivian, Founder, President

National Foundation for Transplants **[17517]**
5350 Poplar Ave., Ste. 430
Memphis, TN 38119
PH: (901)684-1697
Toll free: 800-489-3863
Fax: (901)684-1128
Gonitzke, Connie, President, CEO

National Hardwood Lumber Association **[1443]**
6830 Raleigh LaGrange Rd.
Memphis, TN 38134
PH: (901)377-1818
Toll free: 800-933-0318
Barford, Mark, CEO

National Street Rod Association **[21459]**
4030 Park Ave.
Memphis, TN 38111-7406
PH: (901)452-4030
Reynolds, Bob, Dir. of Advertising

Pediatric Pharmacy Advocacy Group **[16615]**
5865 Ridgeway Center Pky., Ste. 300
Memphis, TN 38120
PH: (901)820-4434
Fax: (901)767-0704
Helms, Matthew R., CAE, Exec. Dir.

Pi Kappa Alpha **[23920]**
8347 W Range Cove
Memphis, TN 38125
PH: (901)748-1868
Fax: (901)748-3100
Bobango, John A., President

Promotional Glass Collectors Association **[21717]**
4595 Limestone Ln.
Memphis, TN 38141
PH: (901)794-8723
Sehnert, Carl, Contact

St. Jude Children's Research Hospital **[14212]**
262 Danny Thomas Pl.
Memphis, TN 38105-3678
PH: (901)595-2305
    (901)535-3300
Toll free: 800-822-6344
Sarrouf, Camille, Jr., V. Chmn. of the Bd.

Southern Cotton Ginners Association
[939]
874 Cotton Gin Pl.
Memphis, TN 38106
PH: (901)947-3104
Fax: (901)947-3103
Shoaf, Holt, Chmn. of the Bd.

Stuttering Foundation of America
[17248]
1805 Moriah Woods Blvd., Ste. 3
Memphis, TN 38117-0749
Fax: (901)761-0484
Fraser, Ms. Jane, President

Marine Corps Air Transport Associa-
tion [21012]
PO Box 1134
Millington, TN 38083
Driscoll, Rich, President

United States Navy Retired Activities
Branch [5631]
OPNAV N170C
5720 Integrity Dr.
Millington, TN 38055-6220
Toll free: 866-827-5672

American Armsport Association
[22509]
176 Dean Rd.
Mooresburg, TN 37811
PH: (423)272-6162
Fax: (423)272-6162
Bean, Frank, Exec. Dir.

National Counter Intelligence Corps
Association [21029]
1185 Bastion Cir.
Mount Juliet, TN 37122-6148
PH: (615)758-6092
Washbush, Charles E., Chairman

American Budgerigar Society
[21533]
c/o Luemma McWilliams, Secretary
1407 Southport Rd.
Mount Pleasant, TN 38474-1987
PH: (931)626-2230
Hyatt, David, President

Neurotoxicity Society [17499]
PO Box 370
Mountain Home, TN 37684
Segura-Aguilar, Juan, Secretary

Australian Cattle Dog Club of
America [21832]
c/o Lib Nichols, Membership
Secretary
1861 Central Valley Rd.
Murfreesboro, TN 37129-7618
Maclennan, Sherry, President

Baptist Association of Christian
Educators [19719]
3151 Winfield Ct.
Murfreesboro, TN 37129
PH: (615)274-1567
McClendon, John, Contact

National Spotted Saddle Horse As-
sociation [4389]
PO Box 898
Murfreesboro, TN 37133-0898
PH: (615)890-2864
Manis, Justin, Chmn. of the Bd.

Operation Troop Aid [10758]
2441-Q Old Fort Pky., No. 317
Murfreesboro, TN 37128
PH: (921)355-8844
Toll free: 877-435-7682
Woods, Mark H., CEO, Founder

Society for Historians of American
Foreign Relations [9515]
Dept. of History
Middle Tennessee State University

1301 E Main St.
Murfreesboro, TN 37132
PH: (617)458-6156
Fax: (615)898-5881
Hahn, Peter L., Exec. Dir.

Walking Horse Owners' Association
[4424]
PO Box 4007
Murfreesboro, TN 37129
PH: (615)494-8822
Beech, Jill, Director

William Dean Howells Society [9112]
English Dept.
Middle Tennessee State University
1301 E Main St.
Murfreesboro, TN 37132
Rubin, Lance, President

Accessibility Equipment Manufactur-
ers Association [11566]
PO Box 92255
Nashville, TN 37209
Toll free: 800-514-1100
Fax: (949)270-7710
Page, Bill, Secretary

African American Cultural Alliance
[8781]
1215 9th Ave., Ste. 210
Nashville, TN 37208
PH: (615)942-0706

Agricultural Development Initiatives,
Inc. [3534]
PO Box 50006
Nashville, TN 37205
PH: (540)278-4596
Schnipke, Rita J., Bd. Member

Alliance of Veterinarians for the
Environment [4122]
c/o Gwen Griffith, Board Member,
836 W Hillwood Dr.
836 W Hillwood Dr.
Nashville, TN 37205
PH: (615)353-0272
Fax: (615)353-8904
Griffith, Gwen, D.V.M., Bd. Member

American Association of Human-
Animal Bond Veterinarians [10566]
618 Church St., Ste. 220
Nashville, TN 37219
PH: (766)621-0830
Takashima, Dr. Gregg, President

American Association for State and
Local History [9451]
1717 Church St.
Nashville, TN 37203-2991
PH: (615)320-3203
Fax: (615)327-9013
Davis, Terry, CEO, President

American Board of Disability
Analysts [17077]
Belle Mead Office Pk.
4525 Harding Rd., 2nd Fl.
Nashville, TN 37205
Horwitz, Alexander E., MD, Exec.
Ofc.

American Economic Association
[6377]
2014 Broadway, Ste. 305
Nashville, TN 37203
PH: (615)322-2595
Fax: (615)343-7590
Shiller, Robert J., President

American Filtration and Separations
Society [7258]
618 Church St., Ste. 220
Nashville, TN 37219
Fax: (615)254-7047
DeWaal, Klaas, Chairman

American Institute of Parliamentar-
ians [5670]
618 Church St., Ste. 220
Nashville, TN 37219
PH: (615)522-5269
Toll free: 888-664-0428
Fax: (615)248-9253
Crews, Kay Allison, President

American Judicature Society [5376]
Center Bldg.
2014 Broadway, Ste. 100
Nashville, TN 37203-2425
PH: (615)873-4675
Toll free: 800-626-4089
Fax: (615)873-4671
Jamison, Martha Hill, President

American Laryngological Association
[16534]
Nashville, TN 37212-8186
Fax: (615)739-6459

American Society of Professional
Estimators [7663]
2525 Perimeter Place Dr., Ste. 103
Nashville, TN 37214
PH: (615)316-9200
Fax: (615)316-9800
Phillips, Doyle T., President

Amusement Industry Manufacturers
and Suppliers International [1132]
PO Box 92366
Nashville, TN 37209
PH: (714)425-5747
Fax: (714)276-9666

The Andy Griffith Show Rerun
Watchers Club [24084]
118 16th Ave. S
Nashville, TN 37203-3100
Clark, Jim, Founder

Annie Sims International Fan Club
[24022]
PO Box 218478
Nashville, TN 37221-8478
Foster, Jan, President

Association of Academic Museums
and Galleries [9819]
c/o Joseph S. Mella, Director
Vanderbilt University Fine Arts Gallery
230 Appleton Pl.
Nashville, TN 37203
PH: (765)658-6556
      (402)882-2264
Hartz, Jill, President

Association of Exotic Mammal
Veterinarians [17635]
618 Church St., Ste. 220
Nashville, TN 37219
Kohles, Micah, DVM, President

Association for Gerontology Educa-
tion in Social Work [7939]
PO Box 198136
Nashville, TN 37219-8136
Cummings, Sherry, PhD, Bd.
Member

Association of Presbyterian Church
Educators [20018]
404 BNA Dr., Ste. 650
Nashville, TN 37217
PH: (615)953-4648
Toll free: 855-566-5657
Lamberson, Zeta, President

Auto Dealers CPAs [17]
1801 West End Ave., Ste. 800
Nashville, TN 37203
PH: (615)373-9880
Toll free: 800-231-2524
Fax: (615)377-7092
Pruett, Patrick, Exec. Dir.

W.T. Bandy Center for Baudelaire
and Modern French Studies [9041]
419 21st Ave. S
Nashville, TN 37203-2405
PH: (615)343-0372
Barsky, Robert, Director

Baptist Global Response [12626]
402 BNA Dr., Ste. 411
Nashville, TN 37217-2546
PH: (615)367-3678
Toll free: 866-974-5623
Fax: (615)290-5045
Palmer, Jeff, Exec. Dir.

Barbershop Harmony Society [9880]
110 7th Ave. N
Nashville, TN 37203-3704
PH: (615)823-3993
Toll free: 800-876-7464
Monson, Marty, Exec. Dir., CEO

Blake Shelton Fan Club [24027]
c/o Warner Music Nashville
20 Music Sq. E
Nashville, TN 37203

Blood: Water [10474]
PO Box 60381
Nashville, TN 37206
PH: (615)550-4296
Nardella, Jena Lee, Founder, Chief
Strat. Ofc.

Cardiac Muscle Society [14104]
c/o Bjorn Knollmann
2215B Garland Ave.
Nashville, TN 37232-0575
PH: (615)343-6493
Fax: (615)343-4522
Knollmann, Bjorn C., President

Chi Psi [23893]
Jeffrey Hall
45 Rutledge St.
Nashville, TN 37210
PH: (615)736-2520
Fax: (615)736-2366
Bessey, Samuel C., Exec. Dir.

Church Music Publishers Association
[20489]
PO Box 158992
Nashville, TN 37215-8992
PH: (615)791-0273
Fax: (615)790-8847
Shorney, John, President

College Band Directors National As-
sociation [8363]
c/o Thomas Verrier, Executive
Secretary
Blair School of Music
Vanderbilt University
2400 Blakemore Ave.
Nashville, TN 37212
PH: (615)322-7651
Fax: (615)343-0324
Verrier, Thomas, Exec. Sec.

Country Music Association [9895]
1 Music Cir. S
Nashville, TN 37203-4312
PH: (615)244-2840
Simmons, Bill, Officer

Country Music Foundation [9896]
222 5th Ave. S
Nashville, TN 37203
PH: (615)416-2001
Toll free: 800-852-6437
Young, Kyle, Director

Country Radio Broadcasters Inc.
[459]
1009 16th Ave. S
Nashville, TN 37212
PH: (615)327-4487
Fax: (615)329-4492
Mayne, Bill, Exec. Dir.

Diamond Council of America **[2042]**
3212 W End Ave., Ste. 400
Nashville, TN 37203
PH: (615)385-5301
Toll free: 877-283-5669
Fax: (615)385-4955
Chandler, Terry, President, CEO

Disciples of Christ Historical Society
[20022]
1101 19th Ave. S
Nashville, TN 37212-
PH: (615)327-1444
Carson, Glenn Thomas, PhD, Mem.

Donna Fargo International Fan Club
[24034]
PO Box 210877
Nashville, TN 37221
Cottingham, Linda, Coord.

Ethics and Religious Liberty Com-
mission of the Southern Baptist
Convention **[19729]**
901 Commerce St., Ste. 550
Nashville, TN 37203-3600
PH: (615)244-2495
Fax: (615)242-0065
Moore, Russell D., President

Fellowship of United Methodists in
Music and Worship Arts **[20342]**
PO Box 24787
Nashville, TN 37202-4787
Toll free: 800-952-8977
Fax: (615)749-6874
Bone, David, Exec. Dir.

Fraternal Order of Police **[19535]**
701 Marriott Dr.
Nashville, TN 37214
PH: (614)224-1856
Canterbury, Chuck, President

The Gideons International **[20144]**
PO Box 140800
Nashville, TN 37214-0800
PH: (615)564-5000
Hill, Samuel E., President

Gospel Music Association **[9910]**
4012 Granny White Pke.
Nashville, TN 37204-3924
PH: (615)242-0303
Fax: (615)254-9755
Fratt, Justin, Dir. of Operations

Harmony Foundation International
[9917]
110 7th Ave. N, Ste. 200
Nashville, TN 37203
PH: (615)823-5611
Toll free: 866-706-8021
Fax: (615)823-5612
Caldwell, Clarke A., CEO, President

The Heads Network **[8457]**
c/o Dr. Margaret Wade, Executive
Director
2140 Chickering Ln.
Nashville, TN 37215
PH: (615)533-6022
Fax: (615)523-1952
Curtis, Alex, VP

Healing Hands International **[13009]**
455 McNally Dr.
Nashville, TN 37211-3311
PH: (615)832-2000
Fax: (615)832-2002
Merry, Bill, Jr., Chairman

Hope Beyond Hope **[15472]**
4230 Harding Rd., Ste. 307
Nashville, TN 37205
PH: (615)292-8299
Wolf, Dr. Bruce, Founder

Hope Through Healing Hands
[15473]
2908 Poston Ave.
Nashville, TN 37203

PH: (615)320-7888
(615)818-5579
Dyer, Jenny Eaton, PhD, Exec. Dir.

Intellectbase International
Consortium **[8500]**
1615 7th Ave. N
Nashville, TN 37208

International Bluegrass Music As-
sociation **[9924]**
608 W Iris Dr.
Nashville, TN 37204
PH: (615)256-3222
Toll free: 888-438-4262
Fax: (615)256-0450
Schiminger, Paul, Exec. Dir.

International Conference of
Symphony and Opera Musicians
[9926]
1609 Tammany Dr.
Nashville, TN 37206
PH: (615)227-2379
Moore, Michael, Treasurer

International Entertainment Buyers
Association **[1140]**
412 E Iris Dr.
Nashville, TN 37204
PH: (615)679-9601
Matthews, Pam, Exec. Dir.

Japan Studies Association **[9625]**
c/o John Paine, Editor
Belmont University
1900 Belmont Blvd.
Nashville, TN 37212
PH: (615)460-6244
Overton, Joe, President

Sammy Kershaw Fan Club **[24051]**
833 Todd Preis Dr.
Nashville, TN 37221
PH: (615)564-2580
Fax: (615)646-4721
Holland, Billy, Contact

Kids for a Clean Environment **[4079]**
PO Box 158254
Nashville, TN 37215
PH: (615)331-7381
Poe, Melissa, Founder

Lamia Afghan Foundation **[12694]**
4014 Skyline Dr.
Nashville, TN 37215
PH: (615)783-2899
Bradley, John, Founder

LiveBeyond **[12286]**
1508 Delmar Ave., Ste. 122
Nashville, TN 37212
PH: (615)460-8296
Vanderpool, David, MD, Founder,
CEO

Manufacturing CPAs **[40]**
1801 West End Ave., Ste. 800
Nashville, TN 37203
PH: (615)373-9880
Toll free: 800-231-2524
Fax: (615)377-7092
Coakley, Michael, President

Martina McBride Fan Club **[24054]**
PO Box 291627
Nashville, TN
PH: (512)371-6924
Weaver, Tracy, Director

Music and Entertainment Industry
Educators Association **[8376]**
1900 Belmont Blvd.
Nashville, TN 37212-3758
PH: (615)460-6946
Elton, Serona, Bd. Member

Nashville Songwriters Association
International **[9963]**
1710 Roy Acuff Pl.
Nashville, TN 37203

PH: (615)256-3354
Toll free: 800-321-6008
Fax: (615)256-0034
Herbison, Barton, Exec. Dir.

National Association of Federal
Defenders **[5139]**
PO Box 22223
Nashville, TN 37202

National Association of Nonprofit Ac-
countants and Consultants **[48]**
1801 West End Ave., Ste. 800
Nashville, TN 37203
PH: (615)373-9880
Toll free: 800-231-2524
Hoskins, Harvey, President

National Association of State Boards
of Accountancy **[4940]**
150 4th Ave. N, Ste. 700
Nashville, TN 37219-2417
PH: (615)880-4200
Fax: (615)880-4290
Bishop, Ken L., President, CEO

National Association of State Charity
Officials **[5254]**
c/o Janet M. Kleinfelter, Deputy At-
torney General
PO Box 20207
Nashville, TN 37202
PH: (615)741-7403
Kleinfelter, Janet, Dep. Atty. Gen.

National Baptist Convention U.S.A.
Inc. **[19735]**
1700 Baptist World Center Dr.
Nashville, TN 37207
PH: (615)228-6292
Toll free: 866-531-3054
Fax: (615)262-3917
Scruggs, Dr. Julius R., Mem.

National CPA Health Care Advisors
Association **[50]**
1801 W End Ave., Ste. 800
Nashville, TN 37203
PH: (615)373-9880
Toll free: 800-231-2524
Fax: (615)377-7092
White, James, President

National Federation of Independent
Business **[3123]**
53 Century Blvd., Ste. 250
Nashville, TN 37214
PH: (615)872-5800
Toll free: 800-634-2669
McDevitt, Caitlin, Program Mgr.

National Health Care for the Home-
less Council **[15158]**
PO Box 60427
Nashville, TN 37206-0427
PH: (615)226-2292
Fax: (615)226-1656
Lozier, Mr. John, Exec. Dir.

National Latina/Latino Law Student
Association **[18622]**
900 19th Ave. S, Apt. 509
Nashville, TN 37212-2172
Pena, Alex, Chmn. of the Bd.

North-American Association of
Uniform Manufacturers and
Distributors **[208]**
4400 Belmont Park Ter., No. 195
Nashville, TN 37215
PH: (516)393-5838
(615)480-8420
Donahue, Dan, Comm. Chm.

North American Society for Dialysis
and Transplantation **[15884]**
c/o Phyllis Helderman
1113 Chickering Park Dr.

Nashville, TN 37215-4507
PH: (615)665-0566
Fax: (615)665-2951
Helderman, Phyllis, Contact

Official Fan Club of the Grand Ole
Opry **[24056]**
2804 Opryland Dr.
Nashville, TN 37214
PH: (615)871-6779
(615)871-5043
Toll free: 800-SEE-OPRY

Parents' Action For Children **[12421]**
4117 Hillsboro Pike, Ste. 103-130
Nashville, TN 37215
Toll free: 888-447-3400
Fax: (954)745-1133
Reiner, Rob, Founder

Jeannie Seely's Circle of Friends
[24062]
c/o Ron Harman
101 Cottage Pl.
Nashville, TN 37214
Harman, Ron, Contact

Social Enterprise Alliance **[19118]**
41 Peabody St.
Nashville, TN 37210
PH: (202)758-0194
(615)727-8551
Schorr, Jim, President, CEO

Society for Evolutionary Analysis in
Law **[6046]**
Vanderbilt University Law School
Attn: SEAL Administrative Assistant
131 21st Ave. S
Nashville, TN 37203-1181
PH: (615)322-1435

Society for Workforce Planning
Professionals **[1699]**
6508 Grayson Ct.
Nashville, TN 37205
PH: (615)352-4292
Fax: (615)352-4204
Herrell, Vicki, Exec. Dir.

Southern Baptist Foundation **[19741]**
901 Commerce St., Ste. 600
Nashville, TN 37203
PH: (615)254-8823
Toll free: 800-245-8183
Fax: (615)255-1832
Peek, Warren, President

Southern Baptist Historical Library
and Archives **[19742]**
901 Commerce St., Ste. 400
Nashville, TN 37203-3630
PH: (615)244-0344
Fax: (615)782-4821
Sumners, Mr. Bill, Director

Stars for Stripes **[21034]**
109 Rivers Edge Ct.
Nashville, TN 37214
PH: (615)872-2122
Seale, Judy G., CEO, President

Sumner Family Association **[20935]**
c/o Charles H. Sumner, Director
7540 Rolling River Pky.
Nashville, TN 37221-3322
PH: (615)646-9946
Sumner, Mr. Charles Hanson, Director

Sweet Sleep **[11163]**
PO Box 40486
Nashville, TN 37204-9998
PH: (615)730-7671
Gash, Jen, Founder

Tennessee Regulatory Authority
[5836]
502 Deaderick St.
Nashville, TN 37243

PH: (615)741-2904
Toll free: 800-342-8359
Hilliard, Herbert H., Chairman

Pam Tillis Fan Club [24066]
c/o Johanna Michell
PO Box 128575
Nashville, TN 37212

Transitions Global [12060]
PO Box 50165
Nashville, TN 37205
PH: (615)356-0946

United Furniture Workers Insurance
Fund [1491]
1910 Air Lane Dr.
Nashville, TN 37210
PH: (615)889-8860
Fax: (615)391-0865
Walker, Dee Anne, Secretary,
Treasurer

United South and Eastern Tribes,
Inc. [12385]
711 Stewarts Ferry Pke.
Nashville, TN 37214
PH: (615)872-7900
Fax: (615)872-7417
Patterson, Brian, President

Visiting Orphans [11181]
449 Metroplex Dr.
Nashville, TN 37211
Toll free: 866-683-7554
Fax: (866)683-5087
Kerr, Autumn, Exec. Dir.

Hank Williams Jr. Fan Club [24070]
c/o Ken Levitan
Vector Management
PO Box 120479
Nashville, TN 37212
Levitan, Ken, Contact

World Convention of Churches of
Christ [20031]
Vine Street Christian Church
4101 Harding Pke.
Nashville, TN 37205
PH: (615)298-1824
Holloway, Mr. Gary, Exec. Dir.

You Have the Power [18731]
2814 12th Ave. S
Nashville, TN 37204-2513
PH: (615)292-7027
Fax: (615)292-4088
Gurley, Cathy, Exec. Dir.

American Design Drafting Associa-
tion [6696]
105 E Main St.
Newbern, TN 38059
PH: (731)627-0802
Fax: (731)627-9321
Whitus, Tony, Dep. Dir.

Gamma Beta Phi Society [23780]
99 E Midway Ln.
Oak Ridge, TN 37830
PH: (865)483-6212
McCauley, Margaret C., Exec. Dir.

Integrated Manufacturing Technology
Initiative [6795]
PO Box 5296
Oak Ridge, TN 37831
PH: (865)385-7002
Neal, Richard, Contact

International Guards Union of
America [23520]
c/o Scott Sanders, Treasurer
PO Box 4098
Oak Ridge, TN 37831
PH: (865)456-9110
Sanders, Scott, Treasurer

Korea Stamp Society [22338]
PO Box 6889
Oak Ridge, TN 37831-3588
Beck, Peter M., President

National Organization of Test,
Research, and Training Reactors
[6930]
Oak Ridge National Laboratory
1 Bethel Valley Rd.
Oak Ridge, TN 37831-6249
PH: (765)496-3573
Miller, Stephen, Treasurer

SpeakingOut Against Child Sexual
Abuse [12937]
PO Box 5826
Oak Ridge, TN 37831
PH: (865)230-8600
Suafoa-Dinino, Susan, Founder,
President

Australian Terrier Club of America
[21834]
c/o Marilyn Harban, Corresponding
Secretary
6675 Sawtooth Dr.
Ooltewah, TN 37363-5865
Samarotto, Alexa, President

International Radio Controlled
Helicopter Association [22200]
6104 Hunter Valley Rd.
Ooltewah, TN 37363
PH: (765)287-1256
Toll free: 800-435-9262
Millner, Dave, President

Owsley Family Historical Society
[20911]
6185 Oilskin Dr.
Ooltewah, TN 37363
PH: (423)910-0058
Bodine, Ronny O., President

Friends of Paul Overstreet [24038]
PO Box 320
Pegram, TN 37143
PH: (615)557-2183
Toll free: 888-739-8086

American Indian Heritage Founda-
tion [10033]
PO Box 750
Pigeon Forge, TN 37868
PH: (703)354-2270
Moon, Princess Pale, Chairman,
President

Dollywood Foundation [24033]
Dolly Parton's Imagination Library
1020 Dollywood Ln.
Pigeon Forge, TN 37863
PH: (865)428-9606
Fax: (865)428-9612
Dotson, David, President

Children's Art Foundation [11221]
PO Box 567
Selmer, TN 38375
Toll free: 800-447-4569
Mandel, Ms. Gerry, Founder

American Black Hereford Association
[3683]
1704 S Cannon Blvd.
Shelbyville, TN 37160
PH: (913)677-1111
Smith, Marc, VP

Spotted Saddle Horse Breeders' and
Exhibitors Association [4413]
PO Box 1046
Shelbyville, TN 37162
PH: (931)684-7496
Fax: (931)684-7215
Prince, Janice, Operations Mgr.

Walking Horse Trainers Association
[4425]
PO Box 61
Shelbyville, TN 37162

PH: (931)684-5866
Fax: (931)684-5895
Hankins, Jamie, VP

Sam Davis Memorial Association
[10323]
1399 Sam Davis Rd.
Smyrna, TN 37167
PH: (615)459-2341
Patterson, James G., President

National Amputee Golf Association
[22786]
701 Orkney Ct.
Smyrna, TN 37167-6395
PH: (615)967-4555
Wilson, Mr. Bob, Consultant

University and College Designers
Association [8037]
199 Enon Springs Rd. W, Ste. 400
Smyrna, TN 37167
PH: (615)459-4559
Fax: (615)459-5229
Bussey, Tadson, Exec. Dir.

National Model Railroad Association
[22189]
PO Box 1328
Soddy Daisy, TN 37384-1328
PH: (423)892-2846
Fax: (423)899-4869
Getz, Charles W., President

Chandler Family Association [20792]
c/o Helen Chandler, Secretary-
Treasurer, 5020 Monk House Rd.
5020 Monk House Rd.
Somerville, TN 38068
PH: (901)355-5614
Chandler, B. Glenn, VP

International Narcotics Interdiction
Association [5227]
PO Box 1757
Spring Hill, TN 37174
Toll free: 866-780-4642
Goodman, Benny, Exec. Dir.

Bamboo of the Americas [3818]
c/o Sue Turtle, Treasurer
30 Myers Rd.
Summertown, TN 38483-7323
Ruiz-Sanchez, Eduardo, Exec. Dir.

Global Village Institute [5732]
184 Schoolhouse Ridge Rd.
Summertown, TN 38483-0090
PH: (931)964-4474
Fax: (931)964-2200
Bates, Albert K., Chairman

Plenty International [12713]
PO Box 394
Summertown, TN 38483-0394
PH: (931)964-4323
Schweitzer, Peter, Exec. Dir.

Children's Bible Ministries [20133]
160 Bear Lodge Dr.
Townsend, TN 37882
PH: (865)448-1200
Fax: (865)448-1233
Kain, Rev. Greg, President

Twin Bonanza Association [21252]
Beechcraft Heritage Museum
570 Old Shelbyville Hwy.
Tullahoma, TN 37388
PH: (931)455-1974
Fax: (931)455-1994

Hugs for Our Soldiers [10747]
PO Box 532
Vonore, TN 37885
Orcutt, Kathy, Founder, President

Lorrie Morgan International Fan Club
[24055]
PO Box 213
White Creek, TN 37189

PH: (615)724-1818
Conway, Tony, Contact

TEXAS

Bowen USA [13612]
710 Butternut St., Ste. B
Abilene, TX 79602
Hall, Neil, President

Society of Cleaning and Restoration
Technicians [2142]
142 Handsome Jack Rd.
Abilene, TX 79602
Toll free: 800-949-4728
Fax: (325)692-1823
Glenn, Gary, President

Soulforce [11909]
PO Box 2499
Abilene, TX 79604
Toll free: 800-810-9143
Herrin, Haven, Exec. Dir.

Concentra Occupational Health
Research Institute [16322]
5080 Spectrum Dr., Ste. 1200
Addison, TX 75001
Fogarty, W. Tom, President,
Treasurer

International and American Associa-
tions of Clinical Nutritionists
[16224]
15280 Addison Rd., Ste. 130
Addison, TX 75001
PH: (972)407-9089
Fax: (972)250-0233
Henry, Kevin P., Web Adm.

International Society for Heart &
Lung Transplantation [17512]
14673 Midway Rd., Ste. 200
Addison, TX 75001
PH: (972)490-9495
Fax: (972)490-9499
Rowe, Amanda, Exec. Dir.

Moon Society [7219]
5015 Addison Cir., No. 420
Addison, TX 75001
PH: (214)507-7911
Murphy, Ken, President

International Society for Burn Injuries
[13863]
584 Arbor View
Adkins, TX 78101
Gamelli, Richard L., Contact

National Kindergarten Alliance
[8450]
c/o Penny Pillack, President
PO Box 309
Agua Dulce, TX 78330
Fax: (361)998-2333
Pillack, Penny, President

International Federation of Postcard
Dealers [21673]
PO Box 749
Alamo, TX 78516
PH: (956)787-1717
Taylor, Dr. Jim, President

Christian Mission for the Deaf
[20399]
PO Box 1651
Aledo, TX 76008
Foster, Prof. Andrew D., PhD,
Founder

Madison Project [19039]
PO Box 655
Aledo, TX 76008
Ryun, Jim, Chairman

Asian American Real Estate As-
sociation [2849]
PO Box 1762
Alief, TX 77411

PH: (281)799-4939
Chen, David, Treasurer

Amazing Little Hearts CHD Support
Group [15212]
1314 W McDermott Dr., Ste. 106,
No. 818
Allen, TX 75013
Cooper, Jennifer, Bd. Member

Angels for Premature Babies
[16794]
1112 Scotts Bluff Dr.
Allen, TX 75002
PH: (469)441-2387
Fax: (214)291-5242
Ogbuta, Chidi, RN, Founder,
President

American Miniature Horse Associa-
tion [4315]
5601 S Interstate 35 W
Alvarado, TX 76009
PH: (817)783-5600
Fax: (817)783-6403
Kahre, Joe, President

Clan MacDuff Society of America
[20820]
8105 Rainfall Rd.
Alvarado, TX 76009-4505
PH: (817)783-2942
Bradshaw, Sean, Membership Chp.

National Association of Catastrophe
Adjusters [1889]
PO Box 499
Alvord, TX 76225
PH: (817)498-3466
Hatcher, Chris, President

American Quarter Horse Association
[4320]
1600 Quarter Horse Dr.
Amarillo, TX 79104
PH: (806)376-4811
Huffhines, Craig, Exec. VP

American Quarter Horse Youth As-
sociation [4321]
1600 Quarter Horse Dr.
Amarillo, TX 79104
PH: (806)376-4811
Fax: (806)349-6411
Huffhines, Craig, Exec. VP

Ulster-Scots Society of America
[20999]
PO Box 3969
Amarillo, TX 79116

Working Ranch Cowboys Associa-
tion [4621]
408 SW 7th Ave.
Amarillo, TX 79101
PH: (806)374-9722
Whipple, Randy, Treasurer

National Toothpick Holder Collectors'
Society [21700]
PO Box 852
Archer City, TX 76351-0852
Knauer, Judy, Founder

American Ex-Prisoners of War
[21090]
c/o Clydie J. Morgan, Executive
Director
3201 E Pioneer Pky., No. 40
Arlington, TX 76010
PH: (817)649-2979
Fax: (817)649-0109
Morgan, Clydie J., COO

American Journalism Historians As-
sociation [7978]
Arlington, TX
PH: (662)325-0983
(405)585-4158
Humphrey, Carol Sue, Admin. Sec.

American Mensa [9342]
1229 Corporate Dr. W
Arlington, TX 76006-6103
PH: (817)607-0060
Fax: (817)649-5232
Donahoo, Pamela L., CAE, Exec.
Dir.

Billiard and Bowling Institute of
America [3137]
PO Box 6573
Arlington, TX 76005-6573
PH: (817)649-5105
Fax: (817)385-8268
Supper, Bill, Exec. Dir.

Bowling Proprietors' Association of
America [3152]
621 Six Flags Dr.
Arlington, TX 76011
Toll free: 800-343-1329
Martino, Tom, President

Children's Hemiplegia and Stroke
Association [17296]
4101 W Green Oaks Blvd., Ste. 305,
No. 149
Arlington, TX 76016
Atwood, Nancy, Exec. Dir., Founder

Delta Delta Delta [23950]
2331 Brookhollow Plaza Dr.
Arlington, TX 76006
PH: (817)633-8001
Fax: (817)652-0212
Hughes White, Karen, Exec. Dir.

International Convention of Faith
Ministries [19987]
5500 Woodland Park Blvd.
Arlington, TX 76013
PH: (817)451-9620
Toll free: 877-348-4236
Fax: (817)451-9621
Willoughby, Dr. Jim, Trustee

National Association of Church
Design Builders [552]
1000 Ballpark Way, Ste. 306
Arlington, TX 76011
PH: (817)200-2622
Toll free: 866-416-2232
Fax: (817)275-4519
McFerren, Amanda, Exec. Dir.

National Independent Automobile
Dealers Association [350]
2521 Brown Blvd.
Arlington, TX 76006-5203
PH: (817)640-3838
Toll free: 800-682-3837
Fax: (817)649-5866
Linn, Michael, CPP, CEO

National One Coat Stucco Association [559]
1615 W Abram St. Ste. U
Arlington, TX 76012-1325
Griffin, Mike, President

Pan-American Association of
Ophthalmology [16405]
1301 S Bowen Rd., No. 450
Arlington, TX 76013
PH: (817)275-7553
Fax: (817)275-3961
Bradshaw, Teresa J., Exec. Dir.

Schipperke Club of America [21957]
c/o Deb Decker, Membership
Chairperson
5100 Andalusia Trl.
Arlington, TX 76017
Morrison, Kristin, VP

Sixth Marine Division Association
[21201]
704 Cooper Ct.
Arlington, TX 76011-5550
Houseweart, Connie, President

Theta Chi Omega National
Multicultural Sorority [23978]
University of Texas at Arlington
701 S Nedderman Dr.
Arlington, TX 76019
Trevino, Amy, President

United States Bowling Congress
[22709]
621 Six Flags Dr.
Arlington, TX 76011
Toll free: 800-514-2695
Cain, Andrew, President

United States Marine Raider As-
sociation [5629]
704 Cooper Ct.
Arlington, TX 76011-5550
PH: (817)275-1552
(940)580-0298
Dornan, Hon. Florence R.,
Secretary, Director

Vietnamese Medical Association of
the U.S.A. [15749]
1926 SW Green Oaks Blvd.
Arlington, TX 76017
PH: (687)667-1016
Lam, Jonathan Hoang, MD,
President

Watchman Fellowship [20051]
PO Box 13340
Arlington, TX 76094-0340
PH: (817)277-0023
Fax: (817)277-8098
Walker, James K., President

Alliance of Claims Assistance
Professionals [1821]
c/o Rebecca Stephenson, Co-
President
9600 Escarpment, Ste. 745-65
Austin, TX 78749-1982
Toll free: 888-394-5163
Stephenson, Rebecca, ACAP, Co-
Pres.

American Academy of Mechanics
[6829]
University of Texas at Austin
Dept. of Aerospace Engineering and
Engineering Mechanics
210 E 24th St.
Austin, TX 78712-1221
PH: (512)471-4273
Fax: (512)471-5500
Aref, Hassan, Bd. Member

American Association of Bariatric
Counselors [16245]
9901 Brodie Ln., Ste. 160-278
Austin, TX 78748
Toll free: 866-284-3682
Indelicato, Dr. Joseph, Dir. of Res.

American Association of Nurse
Practitioners [16096]
Bldg. II, Ste. 450
911 S MoPac Expy.
Austin, TX 78711-2846
PH: (512)442-4262
(703)740-2529
Fax: (512)442-6469
Hebert, David E., CEO

American Botanical Council [6127]
6200 Manor Rd.
Austin, TX 78723
PH: (512)926-4900
Toll free: 800-373-7105
Fax: (512)926-2345
Blumenthal, Mark, Exec. Dir.,
Founder

American College of Construction
Lawyers [4986]
PO Box 4646
Austin, TX 78765-4646

PH: (512)343-1808
Smith, Robert J., Secretary

American College of Musicians
[8357]
PO Box 1807
Austin, TX 78767
PH: (512)478-5775

American Federation of Aviculture
[21537]
PO Box 91717
Austin, TX 78709-1717
PH: (512)585-9800
Fax: (512)858-7029
Whittaker, Jamie, President

American Fern Society [6130]
c/o Dr. Blanca Leon, Membership
Secretary
1 University Sta.
Austin, TX 78712-0471
Yatskievych, Dr. George, Curator

Asleep at the Wheel Fan Club
[24024]
PO Box 463
Austin, TX 78767
PH: (512)444-9885
Fax: (512)444-4699
Benson, Ray, President, Chairman

Association of Certified Background
Investigators [5354]
c/o Donald Johnson, Secretary
6873 Auckland Dr.
Austin, TX 78749
Gould, Earl, Founder

Association of Certified Fraud
Examiners [1783]
The Gregor Bldg.
716 West Ave.
Austin, TX 78701-2727
PH: (512)478-9000
Toll free: 800-245-3321
Fax: (512)478-9297
Ratley, James D., President

Association for Child Psychoanalysis
[16844]
900 Ranch Rd. 620 S, Ste. C101
Austin, TX 78734
PH: (512)261-3422
Fax: (866)534-7555
Blomquist, Janet, Administrator

Association of Donor Recruitment
Professionals [13838]
PO Box 150790
Austin, TX 78715
PH: (512)658-9414
Fax: (866)219-7008
Peterson, Carla, President

Association for Early Learning Lead-
ers [10803]
8000 Center Park Dr., Ste. 170
Austin, TX 78754
Toll free: 800-537-1118
Hornbeck, Mary, President

Association of Historians of
Nineteenth-Century Art [8846]
PO Box 5730
Austin, TX 78763-5730
Trippi, Peter, President

Association for Mexican Cave Stud-
ies [7226]
PO Box 7672
Austin, TX 78713
Mixon, Bill, Editor

Association for Neurologically
Impaired Children [15906]
2109 Eva St.
Austin, TX 78704

PH: (972)264-7983
Powers, D. J., President

Association of Progressive Rental Organizations [2926]
1504 Robin Hood Trl.
Austin, TX 78703
Toll free: 800-204-2776
Fax: (512)794-0097
Keese, Bill, Exec. Dir.

Association for Refugee Service Professionals [12123]
PO Box 80692
Austin, TX 78708
Palm, Bob, President

Atticus Circle [18300]
Bldg. 6, Ste. 450
2901 Via Fortuna
Austin, TX 78746
PH: (512)275-7880
(512)450-5188
Wynne, Anne S., Founder

Bat Conservation International [4791]
PO Box 162603
Austin, TX 78716
PH: (512)327-9721
Toll free: 800-538-BATS
Geiselman, Cullen, Chairman

Best Answer for Cancer Foundation [13899]
8127 Mesa, B-206, No. 243
Austin, TX 78759
PH: (512)342-8181
Fax: (512)276-6678
Brandt, Annie, Exec. Dir.

Bromeliad Society International [22088]
c/o Annette Dominguez, Membership Chairpersom
8117 Shenandoah Dr.
Austin, TX 78753
PH: (512)619-2750
Wegner, Lyn, President

Caring for Cambodia [7585]
900 RR 620 S, No. C101-304
Austin, TX 78734
Amelio, Jamie, CEO

Circle of Health International [15598]
c/o Sera Bonds
1905 Paramount Ave.
Austin, TX 78704
PH: (347)712-1721
(512)210-7710
Johnson, Leilani, Exec. Dir.

Clan Scott Society [20841]
PO Box 13021
Austin, TX 78711-3021
Scott, Mr. David, Secretary

Clean Technology and Sustainable Industries Organization [3675]
3925 W Braker Ln.
Austin, TX 78759
PH: (925)886-8461
Laudon, Matthew, Chairman, President

Connect Worldwide [6299]
PO Box 204086
Austin, TX 78720-4086
Lesan, Rob, President

Consortium for Advanced Management International [2218]
6836 Bee Cave Rd., Ste. 256
Austin, TX 78746
PH: (512)296-6872
Vadgama, Ashok, President

Council on Contemporary Families [11816]
305 E 23rd St., G1800
Austin, TX 78712

PH: (512)471-8339
Risman, Barbara, President

Credit Union Information Security Professionals Association [6757]
1717 W 6th St., Ste. 112
Austin, TX 78703
PH: (512)465-9711
Toll free: 888-475-4440
Dowell, Kelly, Exec. Dir.

Culligan Dealers Association of North America [1458]
Bldg. 1600-B
14101 Highway 290 W
Austin, TX 78737
PH: (512)894-4106
Fax: (512)858-0486
Gibson, Susan, Account Exec.

Dart Music International [9899]
2704 E 2nd St.
Austin, TX 78702
PH: (707)836-3278
Dart, Dave, Founder, Exec. Dir.

Daughters of the Republic of Texas [20965]
510 E Anderson Ln.
Austin, TX 78752
PH: (512)339-1997
Fax: (512)339-1998
Edwards, Dr. Betty J., President

Deaf Women United [11938]
PO Box 91563
Austin, TX 78709-1563
Hermatz, Lisa, Officer

The Delta Kappa Gamma Society International [19432]
PO Box 1589
Austin, TX 78767
PH: (512)478-5748
Toll free: 888-762-4685
Fax: (512)478-3961

DogsBite.org [12819]
PO Box 12443
Austin, TX 78711
Lynn, Colleen, Founder

Ecumenical and Interreligious Leaders Network [20060]
Bldg. D, Ste. 3
2921 E 17th St.
Austin, TX 78702
PH: (512)386-9145
Fax: (512)385-1430
Flowers, Simon Talma, Secretary

EMDR International Association [16970]
5806 Mesa Dr., Ste. 360
Austin, TX 78731-3785
Toll free: 866-451-5200
Fax: (512)451-5256
Doherty, Mark G., Exec. Dir.

Federation of Genealogical Societies [20967]
PO Box 200940
Austin, TX 78720-0940
Toll free: 888-347-1350
Taylor, Joshua, President

Fertile Hope [14756]
c/o Livestrong Foundation
2201 E 6th St.
Austin, TX 78702
Toll free: 877-236-8820
Beck, Lindsay Nohr, Exec. Dir., Founder

FP2 Inc. [808]
8100 West Ct.
Austin, TX 78759
PH: (512)977-1854
Moulthrop, Jim, Exec. Dir.

German-Texan Heritage Society [19445]
PO Box 684171
Austin, TX 78768-4171
PH: (512)467-4569
Toll free: 855-892-6691
Fax: (512)467-4574
Boehm, Teddy, Advisor

Girlstart [7946]
1400 W Anderson Ln.
Austin, TX 78757
PH: (512)916-4775
Toll free: 888-852-6481
Hudgins, Tamara, Exec. Dir.

Global Animal Partnership [3625]
7421 Burnet Rd., No. 237
Austin, TX 78757
Toll free: 877-427-5783
Siemon, George, Chairman

Global Wildlife Conservation [4821]
PO Box 129
Austin, TX 78767
PH: (512)593-1883
Sechrest, Wes, PhD, CEO

Government Management Information Sciences [5303]
PO Box 27923
Austin, TX 78755
Toll free: 877-963-4647
Fax: (512)857-7711

Hand to Hold [14232]
13492 Research Blvd., Ste. 120
Austin, TX 78750
PH: (512)293-0165
Toll free: 855-424-6428
Kelley, Kelli D., Founder, Exec. Dir.

Helping Autism through Learning and Outreach [13768]
PO Box 303399
Austin, TX 78703-0057
PH: (512)465-9595
Toll free: 866-465-9595
Fax: (512)465-9598
Jackson, Brian, President

Hispanic Dental Association [14439]
3910 South IH 35., Ste. 245
Austin, TX 78704-7441
PH: (512)904-0252
Pena, David, Jr., CEO, Exec. Dir.

Hood's Texas Brigade Association [20741]
605 Pecan Grove Rd.
Austin, TX 78704-2507
Hartzog, Martha, President

Hospitality Financial and Technology Professionals [1239]
11709 Boulder Ln., Ste. 110
Austin, TX 78726
PH: (512)249-5333
Toll free: 800-646-4387
Fax: (512)249-1533
Trieber, Jerry, Contact

International Aeronauts League [21530]
PO Box 200931
Austin, TX 78720-0931
PH: (512)740-2506
Craparo, John S., Contact

International Association of Software Architects [6277]
12325 Hymeadow Dr., Ste. 2-200
Austin, TX 78750-1847
PH: (512)637-4272
Toll free: 866-399-4272
Fax: (512)382-5327
Preiss, Paul, CEO, Founder

International Biopharmaceutical Association [16665]
PMB 143
11521 N FM 620, No. 250

Austin, TX 78726
PH: (713)366-8062
Fax: (713)366-8062
Hudasek, Ms. Kristin, Coord.

International Order of the Golden Rule [2408]
3520 Executive Center Dr., Ste. 300
Austin, TX 78731
PH: (512)334-5504
Toll free: 800-637-8030
Fax: (512)334-5514
Brock Jr., William, President

International Palm Society [6147]
9300 Sandstone St.
Austin, TX 78737-1135
PH: (512)301-2744
Fax: (512)870-9366
Jackson, Tom, Treasurer

International Society of Six Sigma Professionals [2742]
7301 RR 620 N, Ste. 155 O362
Austin, TX 78726-4537
PH: (512)233-2721
Toll free: 844-477-7746
O'Brasky-Britland, Roxanne, Founder, Chairperson

International Tap Association [9263]
PO Box 150574
Austin, TX 78715
PH: (303)443-7989
Gray, Acia, President

Knowbility [11613]
1033 La Posada Dr., Ste. 372
Austin, TX 78752
PH: (512)527-3138
Toll free: 800-735-2989
Rush, Sharron, Exec. Dir.

Lady Bird Johnson Wildflower Center [6149]
4801 La Crosse Ave.
Austin, TX 78739
PH: (512)232-0100
Fax: (512)232-0156
Newman, Patrick, Exec. Dir.

Lights. Camera. Help. [6014]
PO Box 270069
Austin, TX 78727
PH: (512)524-7227
Bramley, Aaron, Exec. Dir.

LIVESTRONG Foundation [14003]
2201 E 6th St.
Austin, TX 78702
Toll free: 877-236-8820
Ulman, Doug, President, CEO

Marine Corps Engineer Association [5571]
10018 Estancia Ln.
Austin, TX 78739
PH: (512)394-9333

Mission of Hope [12701]
PO Box 171500
Austin, TX 78717
PH: (239)791-8125
Fax: (239)791-8133
Lubin, Marc Jean, Exec. Dir.

National Alliance for Insurance Education and Research [1888]
3630 N Hills Dr.
Austin, TX 78731
Toll free: 800-633-2165
Fax: (512)349-6194
Hold, William T., PhD, CEO, President

National Association of Investigative Specialists [2012]
PO Box 82148
Austin, TX 78708-2148

PH: (512)719-3595
Fax: (512)719-3594
Thomas, Ralph D., President, Director

National Council of Lawyer Disciplinary Boards [5037]
1414 Colorado St., Ste. 610
Austin, TX 78701
Hayashi, Leslie A., President

National Council on Qualifications for the Lighting Professions [2103]
PO Box 142729
Austin, TX 78714-2729
PH: (512)973-0042
Fax: (512)973-0043
Kolar, Mary Jane, CAE, Exec. Dir.

National Domestic Violence Hotline [11708]
PO Box 161810
Austin, TX 78716
PH: (512)794-1133
Toll free: 800-799-7233
Purcell, Dyanne, CEO

National Flood Determination Association [4488]
PO Box 82642
Austin, TX 78708
PH: (512)977-3007
Hanson, Mike, President

National Fraternity of Student Musicians [8385]
American College of Musicians
Austin, TX 78767
PH: (512)478-5775

National Hispanic Professional Organization [7975]
PO Box 41780
Austin, TX 78704
PH: (512)662-0249
Gonzales, J.R., President

National Organization of Hispanics in Criminal Justice [5145]
PO Box 19748
Austin, TX 78760
PH: (512)708-0647
Aguirre, Ana, President

National Student Employment Association [8439]
9600 Escarpment Blvd., Ste. 745, PMB 11
Austin, TX 78749
PH: (512)423-1417
Fax: (972)767-5131
Wessman, Ann, President

Patient Privacy Rights [15636]
1006 Mopac Cir., Ste. 102
Austin, TX 78746
PH: (512)732-0033
Fax: (512)732-0036
Gropper, Adrian, MD, Chief Tech. Ofc.

Pro-Moskitia Foundation of Nicaragua [12130]
2435 Oak Crest
Austin, TX 78704
PH: (512)444-8640
Fax: (512)443-1212
Espinoza, Rev. Melesio Peter, President

Progressive Technology Project [7291]
PO Box 303190
Austin, TX 78703
PH: (612)724-2600
Toll free: 866-298-6463
Aguilar, Alice, Exec. Dir.

Psychology Beyond Borders [11676]
1000 Rio Grande St.
Austin, TX 78701

PH: (512)900-8898
Ryan, Dr. Pamela, Bd. Member, Founder

Rainforest Partnership [4615]
800 W 34th St., Ste. 105
Austin, TX 78705
PH: (512)420-0101
Spelman, Niyanta, Exec. Dir.

RapidIO Trade Association [6260]
8650 Spicewood Springs, No. 145-515
Austin, TX 78759
PH: (512)401-2900
    (512)827-7680
O'Connor, Rick, Exec. Dir.

Research Society on Alcoholism [17326]
7801 N Lamar Blvd., Ste. D-89
Austin, TX 78752-1038
PH: (512)454-0022
Fax: (512)454-0812
Sher, Dr. Kenneth, VP

Restless Legs Syndrome Foundation [17349]
3006 Bee Caves Rd., Ste. D206
Austin, TX 78746
PH: (512)366-9109
Fax: (512)366-9189
Dzienkowski, Karla, Exec. Dir.

RGK Foundation [15656]
1301 W 25th St., Ste. 300
Austin, TX 78705-4248
PH: (512)474-9298
Fax: (512)474-7281
Kozmetsky, Gregory A., Chairman, President, Treasurer

Society for Asian Music [10004]
PO Box 7819
Austin, TX 78713-7819
PH: (512)232-7621
Fax: (512)232-7178
Lau, Frederick, President

Society for Features Journalism [2721]
c/o Lisa Glowinski, Preident
More Content Now
9001 IH-35 N, Ste. 102
Austin, TX 78753
PH: (217)816-3343
Guzior, Betsey, Chairperson

Society of Folk Dance Historians [9333]
2100 Rio Grande St.
Austin, TX 78705-5578

Society of Infectious Diseases Pharmacists [16688]
823 Congress Ave., Ste. 230
Austin, TX 78701-2435
PH: (512)328-8632
Fax: (512)495-9031
Neuhauser, Melinda, Pharm.D., President

SpineHope [16070]
PO Box 684261
Austin, TX 78768
PH: (512)750-0788
Felker, Beth, Exec. Dir.

Subud International Cultural Association U.S.A. [9003]
9509 Ketona Cove
Austin, TX 78759
PH: (512)560-3397
Taormina, Latifah, Director

SunGard Public Sector Users' Group Association [6304]
PO Box 171028
Austin, TX 78717

PH: (309)781-8810
Anderson, Nanette, President

Technology Transfer Society [7297]
2005 Arthur Ln.
Austin, TX 78704
Paleari, Stefano, President

Texas Search and Rescue [12749]
PO Box 171258
Austin, TX 78717
PH: (512)956-6727
Hohnstreiter, Shawn, Chairman

Theta Tau [23746]
1011 San Jacinto, Ste. 205
Austin, TX 78701
PH: (512)472-1904
Toll free: 800-264-1904
Fax: (512)472-4820
Abraham, Michael T., Exec. Dir.

U.S. Association for Computational Mechanics [6832]
PO Box 8137
Austin, TX 78713
PH: (512)743-3273
Ghosh, Somnath, President

U.S. Business Council for Sustainable Development [1009]
411 W Monroe St.
Austin, TX 78704-3025
PH: (512)981-5417
Fax: (512)309-5456
Mangan, Andrew, Exec. Dir., Founder

Water to Thrive [13346]
PO Box 26747
Austin, TX 78755
PH: (512)206-4495
Wilson, Susanne, Exec. Dir.

Wi-Fi Alliance [6341]
10900-B Stonelake Blvd., Ste. 126
Austin, TX 78759-5748
PH: (512)498-9434
Fax: (512)498-9435
Figueroa, Edgar, CEO, President

Women's Flat Track Derby Association [23160]
PO Box 14100
Austin, TX 78761
PH: (512)587-1859
Sane, Alassin, President

International Behavioral Neuroscience Society [16048]
1123 Comanche Path
Bandera, TX 78003-4212
PH: (830)796-9393
Toll free: 866-377-4416
Fax: (830)796-9394
Van Wagner, Marianne, Coord.

International Behavioural and Neural Genetics Society [16049]
1123 Comache Path
Bandera, TX 78003-4212
PH: (919)843-7292
Tarantino, Lisa M., President

International Neural Network Society [16020]
1123 Comanche Path
Bandera, TX 78003-4212
PH: (830)796-9393
Fax: (830)796-9394
Sun, Prof. Ron, Bd. Member

International Society for Developmental Psychobiology [16920]
1123 Comanche Path
Bandera, TX 78003-4212
PH: (830)796-9393
Toll free: 866-377-4416
Fax: (830)796-9394
Van Wagner, Marianne, Web Adm.

International Primatological Society [5914]
c/o Steve Schapiro, Treasurer
650 Cool Water Dr.
Bastrop, TX 78602
PH: (512)321-3991
Fax: (512)332-5208
Caine, Nancy, Sec. Gen.

Federation of Employers and Workers of America [1090]
2901 Bucks Bayou Rd.
Bay City, TX 77414
PH: (979)245-7577
Toll free: 877-422-3392
Fax: (979)245-8969
Evans, Scott, President

International Public Debate Association [8481]
c/o Joe Ganakos, Chairman of the Board
Lee College
200 Lee Dr.
Baytown, TX 77520
Milstead, Keith, President

African Violet Society of America [22064]
2375 N St.
Beaumont, TX 77702-1722
PH: (409)839-4725
Toll free: 844-400-2872
Goretsk, Winston J., President

Benign Essential Blepharospasm Research Foundation [15910]
637 N 7th St., Ste. 102
Beaumont, TX 77702
PH: (409)832-0788
Fax: (409)832-0890
Smith, Mary, Secretary

Association of Biblical Counselors [20038]
209 N Industrial Blvd., Ste. 237
Bedford, TX 76021-6128
Toll free: 877-222-4551
Lelek, Jeremy, President

Committee on Accreditation for Respiratory Care [17440]
1248 Harwood Rd.
Bedford, TX 76021-4244
PH: (817)283-2835
Fax: (817)354-8519
Smalling, Tom, PhD, Exec. Dir.

Council of American Instructors of the Deaf [15184]
PO Box 377
Bedford, TX 76095-0377
PH: (817)354-8414
Mousley, Keith, President

Forward in Faith North America [20107]
PO Box 210248
Bedford, TX 76095-7248
Toll free: 800-225-3661
Ackerman, Rev. Keith L., President

Grand Encampment of Knights Templar [19558]
5909 West Loop South, Ste. 495
Bellaire, TX 77401-2402
PH: (713)349-8700
Fax: (713)349-8710
Vaught, Sir Knight Duane L, Officer

Society for Color and Appearance in Dentistry [14470]
5116 Bissonnet St., No. 394
Bellaire, TX 77401
PH: (281)687-8752
Fax: (877)255-6075
Chu, Stephen J., President

Wimbum Cultural and Development
Association in the United States of
America **[8780]**
PO Box 3108
Bellaire, TX 77402-3108
Ndimbie, Oliver, Chairperson

American Drum Horse Association
[4304]
6700 Kuykendall Rd.
Bellville, TX 77418
PH: (832)558-1630
McKeever, Rebecca, President

National Association of Baptist
Professors of Religion **[8710]**
900 College St.
UMHB Box 8374
Belton, TX 76513
Turner, Helen Lee, Secretary

Big Bend Natural History Association
[6894]
Big Bend National Park, TX

Industrial Foundation of America
[1092]
179 Enterprise Pky., Ste. 102
Boerne, TX 78006
PH: (830)249-7899
Toll free: 800-592-1433
Fax: (800)628-2397
Smith, Bill, Exec. Dir.

Quartus Foundation for Spiritual
Research **[12014]**
PO Box 1768
Boerne, TX 78006
PH: (830)249-3985

Committee for the Advancement of
Role-Playing Games **[22050]**
1127 Cedar St.
Bonham, TX 75418-2913
Thomas, Alan M., II, Chairman

Society of Philippine Surgeons in
America, Inc. **[17404]**
c/o Edward E. Quiros, MD, Website
Editor
PO Box 5284
Borger, TX 79008
Calica, Carl, MD, President

North American Saddle Mule As-
sociation **[21283]**
PO Box 1108
Boyd, TX 76023
Hamilton, Peggy, President

Sanctuary Workers and Volunteers
Association **[10691]**
PO Box 637
Boyd, TX 76023
PH: (940)433-5091
Fax: (940)433-5092
Hicks, Bandy, Keeper

Heart of Texas Country Music As-
sociation **[24044]**
1701 S Bridge St.
Brady, TX 76825-7031
PH: (325)597-1895
Fax: (325)597-0515

American Cutting Horse Association
[22937]
PO Box 2443
Brenham, TX 77834
PH: (979)836-3370
Fax: (979)251-9971
Wilson, David, VP

American Junior Rodeo Association
[23094]
c/o Mary McMullan, Secretary and
Manager
PO Box 398

Bronte, TX 76933-0298
PH: (325)277-5824
(530)662-8246
Ingham, Stella, President

Professional Aerial Photographers
Association International **[2591]**
12069 Cessna Pl.
Brookshire, TX 77423
PH: (713)721-6523
(713)721-6593
Toll free: 800-373-2135
Fax: (713)721-6586
Belanger, Julie, Exec. Dir.

American Backflow Prevention As-
sociation **[7354]**
3016 Maloney Ave.
Bryan, TX 77801-3121
PH: (979)846-7606
Toll free: 877-227-2127
Fax: (979)846-7607
Graham, John, President

Australian Shepherd Club of America
[21833]
6091 E State Highway 21
Bryan, TX 77808
PH: (979)778-1082
Fax: (979)778-1898
Dolan, Pete, Treasurer

National Center for Farmworker
Health **[15045]**
1770 FM 967
Buda, TX 78610
PH: (512)312-2700
Toll free: 800-531-5120
Fax: (512)312-2600
Ryder, E. Roberta, President, CEO

German Shorthaired Pointer Club of
America **[21884]**
c/o Cynthia McCracken, Membership
Chairperson
3026 Tidwell Rd.
Burke, TX 75941-6173
PH: (814)421-2946
Chandler, Terry, President

Farm and Ranch Freedom Alliance
[4154]
PO Box 809
Cameron, TX 76520-0809
PH: (254)697-2661
McGeary, Judith, Exec. Dir.

National Bucking Bull Association
[23097]
PO Box 867
Canton, TX 75103
PH: (903)848-4150
Toll free: 800-878-1454
Foutch, Marty, President

National Opera Association **[9976]**
PO Box 60869
Canyon, TX 79016-0869
PH: (806)651-2843
Fax: (806)651-2958
Hansen, Robert, Exec. Dir.

Association of Premier Nanny Agen-
cies **[10804]**
2125 N Josey Ln., No. 100
Carrollton, TX 75006
PH: (301)654-1242
Swift, Ginger, President

Craft Yarn Council of America
[21754]
3740 N Josey Ln., Ste. 102
Carrollton, TX 75007
PH: (972)325-7232
Fax: (972)215-7333
Colucci, Mary, Exec. Dir.

Force Recon Association **[21054]**
PO Box 111000
Carrollton, TX 75011-1000
Bierlein, Allan, President

Furniture Bank Association of North
America **[13052]**
c/o Dallas Furniture Bank
1417 Upfield Dr., Ste. 104
Carrollton, TX 75006
Dohm, Paul, Exec. Dir.

Joint Commission on Sports
Medicine & Science **[17284]**
1620 Valwood Pky., No. 115
Carrollton, TX 75006
PH: (972)532-8854
Whitehead, James, Exec. Ofc.

National Athletic Trainers' Associa-
tion **[23334]**
1620 Valwood Pkwy., Ste. 115
Carrollton, TX 75006
PH: (214)637-6282
Fax: (214)637-2206
Thornton, Jim, MS, President

Phi Chi Theta **[23697]**
1508 E Belt Line Rd., Ste. 104
Carrollton, TX 75006
PH: (972)245-7202
Finley, Saundra, Exec. Dir.

Society of Paper Money Collectors
[22286]
c/o Frank Clark, Membership Director
PO Box 117060
Carrollton, TX 75011-7060
Anderson, Mark B., Gov.

National Narcotic Detector Dog As-
sociation **[5504]**
379 County Road 105
Carthage, TX 75633
Toll free: 888-289-0070
Bounds, Alan, President

Afghan Hound Club of America, Inc.
[21791]
PO Box 1838
Cedar Park, TX 78630
Saia, Tony, VP

Boone Society **[20787]**
1303 Hunter Ace Way
Cedar Park, TX 78613
Compton, Sam, President

International Barbeque Cookers As-
sociation **[22147]**
202 Walton Way, Ste. 192-200
Cedar Park, TX 78613
PH: (682)232-7972
Sharry, Craig, Exec. Dir.

Sigma Sigma Phi **[23842]**
c/o Deborah Ann Brimelow, Execu-
tive Director/Secretary-Treasurer
PO Box 4096
Cedar Park, TX 78613
PH: (512)553-1705
Brimelow, Deborah Ann, Exec. Dir.,
Secretary, Treasurer

Original Doll Artists Council of
America **[22007]**
c/o Donna Sims, Treasurer
105 Cedar Ln.
Channelview, TX 77530
Vasina, Ute, VP

Fullblood Simmental Fleckvieh
Federation **[3726]**
PO Box 321
Cisco, TX 76437
Toll free: 855-353-2584
Fax: (855)638-2582
Davis, Mikell, President

Field Spaniel Society of America
[21877]
c/o Barbara Cox, Secretary - Corresponding

404 Santa Anna Ave
Coleman, TX 76834
Neumeyer, Tom

American Academy of Counseling
Psychology **[16855]**
c/o James Deegear, PhD, President
Texas A&M University
1263 TAMU
College Station, TX 77843
PH: (979)845-4427
Fax: (979)862-4383
Wright, Esther, Secretary

American Association of Professional
Apiculturists **[3631]**
c/o Dr. Juliana Rangel-Posada,
President
Texas A&M University
401 Joe Routt Blvd.
College Station, TX 77843-2475
PH: (979)845-3211
(517)353-8136
Fax: (517)353-4354
Rangel-Posada, Juliana, President

American Peanut Research and
Education Society **[4507]**
PO Box 15825
College Station, TX 77841
PH: (979)845-8278
(229)329-2949
Gallo, Maria, President

American Taxation Association
[5790]
c/o John Robinson, President
Dept. of Accounting
College of Business Administration
Texas A&M University
College Station, TX 77843-4353
PH: (979)845-3457
Robinson, John, President

Committee on South Asian Women
[18204]
Texas A&M University
Dept. of Psychology
College Station, TX 77843-4235
PH: (979)845-2576
Fax: (979)845-4727
Vaid, Dr. Jyotsna, Editor

Gamma Sigma Delta **[23674]**
c/o Edward Rister, President
Texas A & M University
College Station, TX 77843-2124
PH: (979)845-3801
Brugger, Michael, Secretary

Ignitus Worldwide **[13451]**
1199 Haywood Dr.
College Station, TX 77845
PH: (800)316-4311
Edwards, Dr. Steve, CEO, Bd.
Member

Institute of Nautical Archaeology
[5940]
PO Box HG
College Station, TX 77841-5137
PH: (979)845-6694
Fax: (979)847-9260
Carlson, Deborah, PhD, President

International Association for China
Planning **[18855]**
Texas A&M University
Dept. of Landscape Architecture and
Urban Planning
MS 3137
College Station, TX 77843-3137
Pan, Qisheng, Chairperson

International HACCP Alliance **[4567]**
120 Rosethal Ctr., 2471 TAMU
College Station, TX 77843-2471
PH: (979)862-3643
Fax: (979)862-3075
Mucklow, Rosemary, V. Chmn. of the
Bd.

Society of Herbarium Curators
[6156]
3380 University Dr. E
College Station, TX 77845
PH: (979)845-4328
Fax: (979)889-9898
Feist, Mary Ann, Secretary

11th Armored Cavalry's Veterans of
Vietnam and Cambodia [21163]
PO Box 956
Colleyville, TX 76034-0956
Hathaway, Allen, President

Association of Finance and Insur-
ance Professionals [1836]
4104 Felps Dr., Ste. H
Colleyville, TX 76034
PH: (817)428-2434
Fax: (817)428-2534
Robertson, David N., Exec. Dir.

International Association of Currency
Affairs [403]
PO Box 821
Colleyville, TX 76034
PH: (613)985-5723
Fax: (972)692-8186
Baxter, Mrs. Sybil, Secretary,
Administrator

Philip Roth Society [10393]
c/o Christopher Gonzalez, Treasurer
Dept. of Literature and Languages
Texas A&M University-Commerce
PO Box 3011
Commerce, TX 75429
Shipe, Matthew, President

Texas A&M University - Commerce
Alumni Association [19351]
1706 Stonewall
Commerce, TX 75429
PH: (903)886-5765
Toll free: 866-268-4844
Fax: (903)886-5768
Peace, Derryle, Director

Model A Ford Cabriolet Club [21434]
PO Box 1487
Conroe, TX 77305
PH: (936)441-8209
Machacek, Larry, Coord.

Society of Military Otolaryngologists
- Head and Neck Surgeons
[15842]
PO Box 923
Converse, TX 78109-0923
PH: (210)945-9006
Fax: (210)867-5495
Pearce, Sue, Administrator

American Carp Society [22037]
106 N Denton Tap Rd., Ste. 210-178
Coppell, TX 75019
PH: (818)240-4842

Bradley O'Martin Melanoma Founda-
tion [13907]
655 Duncan Dr.
Coppell, TX 75019
PH: (972)462-7326
O'Martin, Yvonne, Exec. Dir.

International Association of Venue
Managers [2321]
635 Fritz Dr., Ste. 100
Coppell, TX 75019-4442
PH: (972)906-7441
Toll free: 800-935-4226
Fax: (972)906-7418
Mayne, Brad, Chairman

Secret Society of Happy People
[9563]
240 N Denton Tap Rd., PMB 112
Coppell, TX 75019

PH: (972)459-7031
Johnson, Pamela Gail, Founder

Western Music Association [10023]
PO Box 648
Coppell, TX 75019
PH: (505)563-0673
Taylor, Steve, President

Utility Supply Management Alliance
[3428]
c/o Alan Morris, Treasurer
2800 Quail Run Dr., Ste. 100
Corinth, TX 76208
Gorman, Pat, President

Society for Advancement of Manage-
ment [2192]
6300 Ocean Dr.
Corpus Christi, TX 78412-5808
PH: (361)825-3045
Toll free: 888-827-6077
Fax: (361)825-5609
Abdelsamad, Dr. Moustafa H., CEO,
President

Society of Our Lady of the Most
Holy Trinity [19909]
1200 Lantana St.
Corpus Christi, TX 78407
Fax: (361)387-8800
Flanagan, Fr. James, Founder

Theta Rho Girls' Club [13484]
3440 W 2nd Ave.
Corsicana, TX 75110
PH: (903)872-7438
Fax: (903)872-7277
Barrett, Mr. Terry, Secretary

Cleaning Equipment Trade Associa-
tion [2127]
11450 US Highway 380, Ste. 130
Crossroads, TX 76227-8322
PH: (704)635-7362
Toll free: 800-441-0111
Fax: (704)635-7363
Braber, Curtis, President

Alpaca Llama Show Association
[21278]
17102 Mueschke Rd.
Cypress, TX 77433
PH: (281)516-1442
Fax: (281)516-1449
Doyle, Jim, VP

National Energy Services Associa-
tion [6498]
17515 Spring-Cypress Rd., Ste.
C-327
Cypress, TX 77429
PH: (713)856-6525
Fax: (713)856-6199
Plentl, Selena, Bd. Member

Pharmacy Technician Educators
Council [16683]
c/o Lisa McCartney
7366 FM 672
Dale, TX 78616-2526
Broke Stokely, Hannah, President

106th Infantry Division Association
[21179]
PO Box 140535
PO Box 140535
Dallas, TX 75214
PH: (214)823-3004
Coy, Jacquelyn, Membership Chp.

508th Parachute Infantry Regiment
Association [21184]
3630 Townsend Dr.
Dallas, TX 75229
PH: (214)632-1360
Peters, Ellen, Treasurer

Academic Language Therapy Association [12232]
14070 Proton Rd., Ste. 100, LB 9
Dallas, TX 75244-3601

PH: (972)233-9107
Fax: (972)490-4219
Mathis, Marilyn, President

Academy of Psychic Arts and Sci-
ences [6981]
PO Box 191129
Dallas, TX 75219-8129
PH: (214)219-2020
Latus, Timothy D., DPMP, Founder

Accounting Group International [3]
10830 N Central Expy., Ste. 300
Dallas, TX 75231
PH: (214)378-8111
Fax: (214)378-8118
Lasky, George, Chairman

African Love Bird Society [21531]
3831 Whitehall
Dallas, TX 75229-2757
Miller, Mike, Chairman

Aim For Success [8562]
PO Box 550336
Dallas, TX 75355
PH: (972)422-2322
Morris, Marilyn, Founder, President

ALOA Security Professionals As-
sociation, Inc. [1562]
3500 Easy St.
Dallas, TX 75247
PH: (214)819-9733
Toll free: 800-532-2562

American Association of Community
Psychiatrists [16810]
c/o Francis Roton Bell, Administra-
tive Director
PO Box 570218
Dallas, TX 75357-0218
PH: (972)613-0985
      (972)613-3997
Fax: (972)613-5532
Roton, Francis M., Dir. of Admin.

American Association of Psychiatric
Administrators [15303]
c/o Frances M. Bell, Executive
Director
PO Box 570218
Dallas, TX 75357-0218
PH: (972)613-0985
Fax: (972)613-5532
Bell, Frances M., Exec. Dir.

American Board of Obstetrics and
Gynecology, Inc. [16269]
2915 Vine St.
Dallas, TX 75204
PH: (214)871-1619
      (214)721-7520
Fax: (214)871-1943
Gilstrap, Dr. Larry C., III, Exec. Dir.

American Board of Trial Advocates
[5822]
2001 Bryan St., Ste. 3000
Dallas, TX 75201
PH: (214)871-7523
Toll free: 800-932-2682
Fax: (214)871-6025
Tyson, Brian, Exec. Dir.

American Board of Trial Advocates
Foundation [4985]
2001 Bryan St., Ste. 3000
Dallas, TX 75201
PH: (214)871-7523
Toll free: 800-932-2682
Fax: (214)871-6025
Tyson, Brian, Exec. Dir.

American Environmental Health
Foundation [14712]
8345 Walnut Hill Ln., Ste. 225
Dallas, TX 75231

PH: (214)361-9515
Toll free: 800-428-2343
Fax: (214)361-2534
Rea, William J., MD, Founder

American Fire Sprinkler Association
[2988]
12750 Merit Dr., Ste. 350
Dallas, TX 75251-1273
PH: (214)349-5965
Fax: (214)343-8898
Montalvo, D'Arcy, Mgr. of Public Rel.

American Gem Trade Association
[2040]
3030 LBJ Fwy., Ste. 840
Dallas, TX 75234
PH: (214)742-4367
Toll free: 800-972-1162
Fax: (214)742-7334
Hucker, Douglas, CEO

American Heart Association-Council
on Arteriosclerosis, Thrombosis
and Vascular Biology [14091]
American Heart Association
7272 Greenville Ave.
Dallas, TX 75231
Toll free: 800-242-8721
Moore, Kathryn J., PhD, Chairman

American Heart Association - Dallas
[14092]
7272 Greenville Ave.
Dallas, TX 75231
PH: (214)441-4200
Fax: (214)441-4201
Michel, Marchelle, Comm. Spec.

American Lighting Association
[2098]
2050 N Stemmons Fwy., Unit 100
Dallas, TX 75207-3206
PH: (214)698-9898
Toll free: 800-605-4448
Rollins, Wendy E., Dir. of Fin.

American Orthodontic Society
[14412]
11884 Greenville Ave., Ste. 112
Dallas, TX 75243
Toll free: 800-448-1601
Newman, Michael J., Officer

American Society for Adolescent
Psychiatry [16823]
PO Box 570218
Dallas, TX 75357-0218
PH: (972)613-0985
      (866)672-9060
Fax: (972)613-5532
Barclay, Gregory P., Contact

American Society of Genealogists
[20956]
Joseph C. Anderson II
5337 Del Roy Dr.
Dallas, TX 75229-3016

American Stroke Association [17294]
7272 Greenville Ave.
Dallas, TX 75231
Toll free: 888-478-7653
Royse, Alvin J., JD, Chairman

American Viola Society [9871]
14070 Proton Rd., Ste. 100, LB 9
Dallas, TX 75244
PH: (972)233-9107
Crouch, Madeleine, Gen. Mgr.

Art Alliance for Contemporary Glass
[8839]
11700 Preston Rd., Ste. 660, No.
327
Dallas, TX 75230
PH: (214)890-0029
Fax: (214)890-0029
Fischer, Harlan J., President

Associated Locksmiths of America
[1565]
3500 Easy St.
Dallas, TX 75247
PH: (214)819-9733
Toll free: 800-532-2562
Schofield, Lee, President

Association of Attorney-Mediators
[4993]
PO Box 741955
Dallas, TX 75374-1955
PH: (972)669-8101
Toll free: 800-280-1368
Fax: (972)669-8180
Rachuig, Brenda, Exec. Dir.

Association of Marketing and Communication Professionals [2267]
127 Pittsburgh St.
Dallas, TX 75207
PH: (214)377-3524

Association of Women Psychiatrists
[16828]
PO Box 570218
Dallas, TX 75357-0218
PH: (972)613-0985
Fax: (972)613-5532
Barber, Mary E., MD, President

Camino Global [20391]
8625 La Prada Dr.
Dallas, TX 75228
PH: (214)327-8206
Toll free: 800-366-2264
Fax: (214)327-8201
Raymer, Dr. Roger, Chairman

CAS Forum of the Violin Society of
America [9884]
14070 Proton Rd., Ste. 100, LB 9
Dallas, TX 75244-3601
PH: (972)233-9107
VandeKopple, Julius J., Chairman

Center for Exhibition Industry
Research [1170]
12700 Park Central Dr., Ste. 308
Dallas, TX 75251
PH: (972)687-9242
Fax: (972)692-6020
Bludworth, Aaron, Chmn. of the Bd.

Charley Pride Fan Club [24028]
3198 Royal Ln.
Dallas, TX 75229
PH: (214)350-8477
Fax: (214)350-0534
Daines, John, Contact

Children's Craniofacial Association
[14330]
13140 Coit Rd., Ste. 517
Dallas, TX 75240
PH: (214)570-9099
Toll free: 800-535-3643
Fax: (214)570-8811
Mecklenburg, Bill, Chairman

Choristers Guild [20487]
12404 Park Central Dr., Ste. 100
Dallas, TX 75251-1802
PH: (469)398-3606
Toll free: 800-246-7478
Fax: (469)398-3611
Rindelaub, Jim, Exec. Dir.

Christ for the Nations [20395]
3404 Conway St.
Dallas, TX 75224
PH: (214)376-1711
Toll free: 800-933-2364
Lindsay, Dennis, CEO, President

Christian Women in Media Associa-
tion [2314]
PO Box 571566
Dallas, TX 75357
Roberts, Suellen, President, Founder

Commemorative Air Force [21219]
PO Box 764769
Dallas, TX 75376-4769
PH: (214)330-1700
Toll free: 877-767-7175
Fax: (214)623-0014
Brown, Mr. Stephan C., President

Cooper Institute [16697]
12330 Preston Rd.
Dallas, TX 75230
PH: (972)341-3200
Toll free: 800-635-7050
Fax: (972)341-3227
Cooper, Kenneth H., MD, Founder

Council of International Restaurant
Real Estate Brokers [2935]
8350 N Central Expy., Ste. 1300
Dallas, TX 75206-1620
Toll free: 866-247-2123
Fax: (866)247-2329
Evans, John T., II, President

Cyberspace Bar Association [5422]
8828 Greenville Ave.
Dallas, TX 75243
PH: (214)343-7400
Martin, E.X., III, President

The Elisa Project [14639]
10300 N Central Expy., Ste. 330
Dallas, TX 75231
PH: (972)369-5222
Toll free: 866-837-1999
Fax: (214)987-4518
Wade, Alvin, Treasurer

Empower African Children [10960]
3333 Lee Pkwy., Ste. 110
Dallas, TX 75219
PH: (214)828-9323
Hefley, Alexis, Founder, President

Esperanza International [11356]
PO Box 140807
Dallas, TX 75214
PH: (425)451-4359
Fax: (425)451-4360
Valle, David, CEO

Football Writers Association of
America [22857]
18652 Vista Del Sol Dr.
Dallas, TX 75287-4021
PH: (972)713-6198
Richardson, Steve, Exec. Dir.

Global Semiconductor Alliance
[1048]
12400 Coit Rd., Ste. 650
Dallas, TX 75251
PH: (972)866-7579
Toll free: 888-322-5195
Fax: (972)239-2292
Shelton, Jodi, President

Globe Aware [13294]
6500 E Mockingbird Ln., Ste. 104
Dallas, TX 75214-2497
PH: (214)824-4562
Toll free: 877-588-4562
Fax: (214)824-4563
Shahani, Shanti, Dir. of Comm.

Golden Crown Literary Society
[9337]
PO Box 720154
Dallas, TX 75372
Gibson, Liz, Exec. Dir., President

Group for the Advancement of
Psychiatry [16829]
PO Box 570218
Dallas, TX 75357-0218
PH: (972)613-0985
Fax: (972)613-5532
Sharfstein, Steven, President

Holiday and Decorative Association
[1308]
2050 N Stemmons Fwy., Ste. 1F312
Dallas, TX 75207
PH: (214)742-2747
Fax: (214)742-2648
Malcom, Cathy, Chmn. of the Bd.

Institute for Creation Research
[20585]
1806 Royal Ln.
Dallas, TX 75229
Toll free: 800-337-0375
Ford, Mr. Lawrence, Dir. of Comm.

InterAmerican Heart Foundation
[14119]
7272 Greenville Ave.
Dallas, TX 75231-4596
Richaud, PT, Yvonne Garcia,
President

International Adhesions Society
[16556]
Synechion, Inc.
18208 Preston Rd., Ste. D9
Dallas, TX 75252-6011
PH: (972)931-5596
Fax: (972)931-5476
Wiseman, Dr. David, PhD, Founder

International Aikido Association
[22497]
726 W Jefferson Blvd.
Dallas, TX 75208
PH: (214)331-6696
Sensei, Bill Sosa, Founder

International Airline Passengers As-
sociation [22468]
PO Box 700188
Dallas, TX 75370
PH: (972)404-9980
Toll free: 800-821-4272
Fax: (972)233-5348

International Association of Exhibi-
tions and Events [1175]
12700 Park Central Dr., Ste. 308
Dallas, TX 75251
PH: (972)458-8002
Fax: (972)458-8119
Dubois, David, President, CEO

International Banking, Economics
and Finance Association [6393]
c/o John V. Duca, Vice President
Federal Reserve Bank of Dallas
2200 N Pearl St.
Dallas, TX 75201
PH: (214)922-5154
Duca, John V., VP, Assoc. Dir.

International Network of Prison
Ministries [20371]
Box 227475
Dallas, TX 75222
Mitchel, Beth, Contact

International News Media Associa-
tion [18654]
PO Box 740186
Dallas, TX 75374
PH: (214)373-9111
Fax: (214)373-9112
Challinor, Mark, President

International Newsmedia Marketing
Association [2793]
PO Box 740186
Dallas, TX 75374
PH: (214)373-9111
Fax: (214)373-9112
Loubier, Andrea, Operations Mgr.

International Society of Bassists
[9931]
14070 Proton Rd., Ste. 100
Dallas, TX 75244

PH: (972)233-9107
Fax: (972)490-4219
Villaflor, Marcel, Treasurer

International Society of Beverage
Technologists [426]
14070 Proton Rd., Ste. 100, LB 9
Dallas, TX 75244-3601
PH: (972)233-9107
Fax: (972)490-4219
Ringo, Stefanie, Treasurer

KinderUSA [11247]
PO Box 224846
Dallas, TX 75222-9785
Toll free: 888-451-8908
Al-Marayati, Laila, MD, Chairperson

Susan G. Komen for the Cure
[13999]
5005 LBJ Freeway, Ste. 250
Dallas, TX 75244
Toll free: 877-465-6636
Salerno, Judith A., President, CEO

Korean War Project [5837]
PO Box 180190
Dallas, TX 75218-0190
PH: (214)320-0342
Barker, Hal, Founder

Leadership America [8198]
c/o Selection Committee
25 Highland Park Village, Ste. 100-
371
Dallas, TX 75205
PH: (214)421-5566
Farmer, Martha P., Founder, Exec.
Dir.

Leadership Women [8749]
25 Highland Park Village, No. 100-
371
Dallas, TX 75205
PH: (214)421-5566
Porter, Lana G., President

Lighthouse Station, Inc. [12549]
2215 Canton St., Unit 121
Dallas, TX 75201
PH: (214)676-9999
Mathews, Mark, President

Major Orchestra Librarians' Association, Inc. [9715]
c/o Karen Schnackenberg
Dallas Symphony Orchestra
2301 Flora St., Ste. 300
Dallas, TX 75201
Fredrickson, Ella M., Coord.

MediSend International [12291]
9244 Markville Dr.
Dallas, TX 75243
PH: (214)575-5006
Fax: (214)570-9284
Hallack, Nick, President, CEO

Meeting Professionals International
[2334]
3030 Lyndon B. Johnson Fwy., Ste.
600
Dallas, TX 75234-7349
PH: (972)702-3000
Fax: (972)702-3070
Pelham, Fiona, Chairman

Mended Hearts, Inc. [14133]
8150 N Central Expy., M2248
Dallas, TX 75206
PH: (214)206-9259
Toll free: 888-432-7899
Fax: (214)295-9552
Elsner, Tim

Mozambique Conservation
Organization [3900]
PO Box 610623
Dallas, TX 75261
Fax: (888)810-3161
Muns, William R., Founder

Music Distributors Association **[2428]**
14070 Proton Rd., Ste. 100, LB 9
Dallas, TX 75244
PH: (972)233-9107
Fax: (972)490-4219

National Asian Pacific American Law
Student Association **[5435]**
c/o Lianne Baldridge, Treasurer
8910 Southwestern Blvd., No. 1226
Dallas, TX 75214
Shimada, Alexis, President

National Association of Dental Plans
[15421]
12700 Park Central Dr., Ste. 400
Dallas, TX 75251
PH: (972)458-6998
Fax: (972)458-2258
Ireland, Evelyn F., CAE, Exec. Dir.

National Association of Hispanic
Firefighters **[5211]**
PO Box 225037
Dallas, TX 75222-5037
PH: (972)814-6766
Garcia, Joe, Secretary

National Association of School Music
Dealers, Inc. **[2433]**
14070 Proton Rd., Ste. 100
Dallas, TX 75244
PH: (972)233-9107
Fax: (972)490-4219
Crouch, Madeleine, Officer

National Association of State Farm
Agents **[1903]**
14070 Proton Rd., Ste. 100
Dallas, TX 75244
PH: (972)233-9107
Fax: (972)490-4219
Kaminsky, Joan, Secretary,
Treasurer

National Black Police Association
[5495]
3100 Main St., No. 256
Dallas, TX 75226
PH: (214)942-2022
Toll free: 855-879-6272
Fax: (855)879-6272
Aziz, Malik, Chairman

National Business Association
[3122]
5151 Beltline Rd., No. 1150
Dallas, TX 75254
Toll free: 800-456-0440
Fax: (972)960-9149

National Center for Policy Analysis
[18990]
14180 Dallas Pky., Ste. 350
Dallas, TX 75254
PH: (972)386-6272
Stevens, Rachel, Director

National Corrugated Steel Pipe As-
sociation **[2610]**
14070 Proton Rd., Ste. 100, LB 9
Dallas, TX 75244
PH: (972)850-1907
Fax: (972)490-4219
Johnson, Wallace, Officer

National Ovarian Cancer Coalition
[14030]
2501 Oak Lawn Ave., Ste. 435
Dallas, TX 75219
PH: (214)273-4200
Toll free: 888-682-7426
Fax: (214)273-4201
Barley, David D., CEO

National Piano Foundation **[8387]**
14070 Proton Rd., Ste. 100
Dallas, TX 75244

PH: (972)233-9107
Fax: (972)490-4219

National Truckers Association **[3348]**
3131 Turtle Creek Blvd., Ste. 1120
Dallas, TX 75219
Toll free: 800-823-8454

Nicotine Anonymous World Services
[12878]
6333 E Mockingbird Ln., No. 147-
817
Dallas, TX 75214
PH: (469)737-9304
Toll free: 877-879-6422

North America Wu (Hao) Taiji
Federation **[23009]**
PO Box 742703
Dallas, TX 75374
PH: (214)878-4598
Wong, Master Jimmy K., Founder,
President

North American Strategy for
Competitiveness **[3351]**
4347 W Northwest Hwy., Ste. 130-
250
Dallas, TX 75220
PH: (214)744-1042
Melvin, Tiffany, JD, President

Numismatics International **[22280]**
PO Box 570842
Dallas, TX 75357-0842
Young, Carl, Pres. of Indl. Cos.

Operation Save America **[19067]**
PO Box 740066
Dallas, TX 75374
PH: (254)304-0016
Thomas, Rusty, Director

Optical Women's Association **[6950]**
14070 Proton Rd., Ste. 100, LB9
Dallas, TX 75244
PH: (972)233-9107
Smith, Heather, President

Photomedicine Society **[15668]**
c/o Jo Urquhart, Administrative
Coordinator
Dept. of Dermatology
UT Southwestern Medical Center
5323 Harry Hines Blvd.
Dallas, TX 75390-9069
Fax: (214)648-5556
Kang, Sewon, MD, President

Piano Manufacturers Association
International **[2436]**
14070 Proton Rd., Ste. 100
Dallas, TX 75244
PH: (972)233-9107
Fax: (972)490-4219

Pipe Line Contractors Association
[2536]
1700 Pacific Ave., Ste. 4100
Dallas, TX 75201-4675
PH: (214)969-2700
Tielborg, J. Patrick, Gen. Counsel,
Managing Dir.

Retail Print Music Dealers Associa-
tion **[2438]**
14070 Proton Rd., Ste. 100
Dallas, TX 75244-3601
PH: (972)233-9107
Fax: (972)490-4219
Smith, Christie, President

Safe and Vault Technicians Associa-
tion **[3067]**
3500 Easy St.
Dallas, TX 75247
PH: (214)819-9733
Toll free: 800-532-2562
Cortie, Mr. Joseph, President

Siempre Salud **[11436]**
9839 Crest Meadow Dr.
Dallas, TX 75230
PH: (214)363-0362
Deaver, John, MD, President, Direc-
tor

Society for Design and Process Sci-
ence **[6372]**
3824 Cedar Springs Rd., Ste. 368
Dallas, TX 75219
PH: (214)253-9025
Fax: (214)520-0227
Juric, Radmilla, VP

Society of Independent Professional
Earth Scientists **[6683]**
4925 Greenville Ave., Ste. 1106
Dallas, TX 75206
PH: (214)363-1780
Fax: (214)363-8195

Society for the Preservation and
Advancement of the Harmonica
[10010]
PO Box 551381
Dallas, TX 75355-1381
D'Eath, Michael, President

Southwest Celtic Music Association
[9150]
2528 Elm St., Ste. B
Dallas, TX 75226-1472
PH: (214)821-4173
Bush, Shery, President

Thanks-Giving Foundation **[19150]**
1627 Pacific Ave.
Dallas, TX 75201-3601
PH: (214)969-1977
Altabef, Jennifer, Chairperson

Thanks-Giving Square **[20615]**
1627 Pacific Ave.
Dallas, TX 75201
PH: (214)969-1977
Slaughter, Chris, President, CEO

Ugandan American Partnership
Organization **[12194]**
3311 Elm St.
Dallas, TX 75226
PH: (214)310-0964
Merrill, Brittany, Founder, President

Uni-Bell PVC Pipe Association
[2617]
2711 LBJ Fwy., Ste. 1000
Dallas, TX 75234
PH: (972)243-3902
Fax: (972)243-3907

United States Christian Chamber of
Commerce **[23629]**
2201 Main St., Ste. 501
Dallas, TX 75201
PH: (214)801-5419
Bills, Lisa E., Exec. Dir.

United States National Tennis
Academy **[23307]**
3839 McKinney Ave., Ste. 155-208
Dallas, TX 75204
Toll free: 800-452-8519

U.S.A. Film Festival **[9316]**
6116 N Central Expy., Ste. 105
Dallas, TX 75206
PH: (214)821-6300
Fax: (214)821-6364

Violin Society of America **[10021]**
14070 Proton Rd., Ste. 100
Dallas, TX 75244
PH: (972)233-9107
Kirr, Lori, President

Women's Foodservice Forum **[1399]**
6730 LBJ Fwy., Bldg. B
Dallas, TX 75240

PH: (972)770-9100
Fax: (972)770-9150
Davidson, Wendy, President

World Craniofacial Foundation
[14348]
7777 Forest Ln., Ste. C-616
Dallas, TX 75230
PH: (972)566-6669
Toll free: 800-533-3315
Fax: (972)566-3850
Salyer, Kenneth E., MD, Chairman,
Founder

Worldwide Employee Benefits
Network **[1079]**
11520 N Central Expy., Ste. 201
Dallas, TX 75243-6608
Toll free: 888-795-6862
Fax: (214)382-3038
Corpora, Corine R., President

Young Professionals in Energy
[6521]
1601 Elm St., Ste. 3130
Dallas, TX 75201
PH: (214)550-8991
Cravens, Stephen, Founder, Exec.
Dir.

The Association for the Gifted **[7942]**
PO Box 316
De Leon, TX 76444
PH: (270)745-5991
Boswell, Cecelia, President

North American Model Horse Shows
Association **[22156]**
PO Box 1271
Decatur, TX 76234
McClelland, Carra, Mem.

Aquatic Gardeners Association
[4269]
PO Box 51536
Denton, TX 76206
Rogers, Cheryl, President

Association for Modern and
Contemporary Art of the Arab
World, Iran, and Turkey **[8966]**
PO Box 305100
Denton, TX 76203
Shabout, Nada, PhD, President

Developmental Disabilities Nurses
Association **[16131]**
1501 S Loop 288, Ste. 104 - 381
Denton, TX 76205
Toll free: 800-888-6733
Fax: (844)336-2329
Herbers, Wendy, RN, VP

International Council on Materials
Education **[7775]**
3940 N Elm St.
Denton, TX 76207
PH: (940)565-3262
(940)565-4337
Brostow, Prof. Witold, President

Majolica International Society
[21583]
c/o Amy C. Griffin
8912 Crestview Dr.
Denton, TX 76207
Matthes, Wanda Rawson, President

Red Angus Association of America
[3752]
4201 N Interstate 35
Denton, TX 76207-3415
PH: (940)387-3502
Toll free: 888-829-6069
Mccuistion, Jeanene, Director

Sigma Lambda Alpha Sorority Inc.
[23976]
PO Box 424613
Denton, TX 76204-4296
Castro, Karina, Assoc. Dir.

Society for the Study of Indigenous
Languages of the Americas **[9658]**
PO Box 1295
Denton, TX 76202-1295
Rice, Keren, VP

World Dance Alliance Americas
[9273]
c/o Scott Martin, Vice President
816 N Bell Ave., No. 14
Denton, TX 76209
PH: (214)460-6844
Warner, Mary Jane, President

Society of Air Force Physicians
[15839]
c/o JoAnn Honn, Administrative As-
sistant
PO Box 64
Devine, TX 78016
PH: (830)665-4048
May, Kimberly, Gov.

National Society of Artists **[8932]**
PO Box 1885
Dickinson, TX 77539
Lee, Brenda, President

American Red Brangus Association
[3708]
3995 E Highway 290
Dripping Springs, TX 78620
PH: (512)858-7285

Arte Sana **[10765]**
PO Box 1334
Dripping Springs, TX 78620
Toll free: 800-656-4673
Zarate, Laura, Exec. Dir., Founder

Groundwater Management Districts
Association **[4759]**
PO Box 356
Dumas, TX 79029
PH: (806)935-6401
    (402)443-4675
Fax: (806)935-6633
Angle, Larry, President

Bill Glass Champions for Life
[20129]
1101 S Cedar Ridge Dr.
Duncanville, TX 75137
PH: (972)298-1101
Fax: (972)298-1104
Glass, Bill, Founder

Cloud Family Association **[20846]**
508 Crestwood Dr.
Eastland, TX 76448
Jones, James, President

Pan-American Alumni Association
[19344]
1201 W University Dr., UC108
Edinburg, TX 78541
PH: (956)381-2500
    (956)665-2005
Fax: (956)381-2385
Lara, Carmen, President

Association of Professional Flight
Attendants **[23386]**
1004 W Euless Blvd.
Euless, TX 76040
PH: (817)540-0108
Fax: (817)540-2077
Glading, Laura, President

Federation of State Medical Boards
[15724]
400 Fuller Wiser Rd.
Euless, TX 76039
PH: (817)868-4000
    (817)868-4041
Toll free: 888-ASK-FCVS
Fax: (817)868-4099
Chaudhry, Humayon J., FACP, CEO,
President

International Association of Medical
Regulatory Authorities **[15730]**
400 Fuller Wiser Rd., Ste. 300
Euless, TX 76039
PH: (817)868-4006
Fax: (817)868-4097
Chaudhry, Humayun, Dr., Chairman,
Secretary

Parrots & People, Inc. **[3669]**
521 Essex Pl.
Euless, TX 76039
PH: (817)267-3366

American Small Business Travelers
Alliance **[3368]**
3112 Bent Oak Cir.
Flower Mound, TX 75022
PH: (972)836-8064
Sharp, Chuck, President

CCNG International **[2272]**
2201 Long Prairie Rd., Ste. 107-365
Flower Mound, TX 75022
Toll free: 855-599-2264
Fax: (972)539-9661
Hendrickson, Lon, Exec. Dir.

International Association of Audio
Visual Communicators **[1195]**
The CINDYS
PO Box 270779
Flower Mound, TX 75027-0779
PH: (469)464-4180
Fax: (469)464-4170

Mozambique Development in Motion
[11405]
3634 Long Prairie Rd., Ste. 108-128
Flower Mound, TX 75022
Whitehead-Stotland, Tara, President

Pug Dog Club of America **[21949]**
c/o Joella Collier-Flory, Membership
Chairperson
3920 Raintree Dr.
Flower Mound, TX 75022-6323
Huff, Jason, President

National Association of Farm Service
Agency County Office Employees
[5269]
PO Box 598
Floydada, TX 79235
PH: (724)853-5555
Daniels, Wes, President

Chihuahuan Desert Research
Institute **[3828]**
43869 State Hwy. 19
Fort Davis, TX 79734
PH: (432)364-2499
Fax: (432)364-2686
Powell, Shirley, President

80th Fighter Squadron Headhunters'
Association **[20676]**
2830 S Hulen, PMB 174
Fort Worth, TX 76109
Riedel, Col. Jay E., President

Allied Pilots Association **[23383]**
14600 Trinity Blvd., Ste. 500
Fort Worth, TX 76155-2512
PH: (817)302-2272

Alpha Epsilon Delta **[23815]**
Texas Christian University, Box
298810
Fort Worth, TX 76129
PH: (817)257-4550
Fax: (817)257-0201
Stanfield, Cindy, PhD, President

American Association of Community
Theatre **[10236]**
1300 Gendy St.
Fort Worth, TX 76107

PH: (817)732-3177
Toll free: 866-687-2228
Fax: (817)732-3178
McCullough, Rod, Chairman

American Association of Professional
Landmen **[2507]**
800 Fournier St.
Fort Worth, TX 76102
PH: (817)847-7700
Fax: (817)847-7704
Bell, Melanie, Exec. VP

American College of Osteopathic
Obstetricians and Gynecologists
[16271]
8851 Camp Bowie W, Ste. 275
Fort Worth, TX 76116
PH: (817)377-0421
Toll free: 800-875-6360
Fax: (817)377-0439
Alderson, Thomas, President

American Institute of Stress **[17289]**
6387B Camp Bowie Blvd., No. 334
Fort Worth, TX 76116
PH: (682)239-6823
Fax: (817)394-0593
Rosch, Dr. Paul J., Chairman

American Paint Horse Association
[4318]
2800 Meacham Blvd.
Fort Worth, TX 76137
PH: (817)834-2742
Fax: (817)834-3152
McCulley, Kaitlyn, Treasurer

Association for Contract Textiles
[3255]
PO Box 101981
Fort Worth, TX 76185
PH: (817)924-8048
Fax: (817)924-8050
Rabiah, Janan, Exec. Dir.

Association for Ocular Pharmacology
and Therapeutics **[16373]**
c/o Thomas Yorio, President
University of North Texas Health Science Ctr.
3500 Camp Bowie Blvd.
Fort Worth, TX 76107
PH: (817)765-0268
Yorio, Dr. Thomas, President

Beta Upsilon Chi **[23709]**
12650 N Beach St., Ste. 114, No.
305
Fort Worth, TX 76244
Toll free: 877-250-4512
Hoyt, Jason, President, COO

Cowboys for Christ **[19971]**
PO Box 7557
Fort Worth, TX 76111
PH: (817)236-0023
Harvey, Dave, President, Exec. Dir.

EarthWave Society **[4055]**
16151 S Highway 377
Fort Worth, TX 76126
PH: (817)443-3780
Toll free: 800-668-WAVE
Fax: (817)443-3858
Wills, Betty, Founder, Exec. Dir.

Genetic Metabolic Dietitians
International **[15824]**
c/o Carol Williams, Program
Coordinator
PO Box 33985
Fort Worth, TX 76162
Williams, Carol, Program Mgr.

GI Joe Collectors' Club **[22448]**
225 Cattle Baron Parc
Fort Worth, TX 76108

PH: (817)448-9863
Savage, Brian, President

Hardwood Distributor's Association
[1438]
PO Box 1921
Fort Worth, TX 76101
Landwehr, Kurt, President

Human Milk Banking Association of
North America **[14195]**
4455 Camp Bowie Blvd., Ste. 114-88
Fort Worth, TX 76107
PH: (817)810-9984
Fax: (817)810-0087
Sakamoto, Pauline, MS, President

International Coalition of Apostolic
Leaders **[20370]**
PO Box 164217
Fort Worth, TX 76161
PH: (817)232-5815
Fax: (817)232-1290
Pfeifer, Mark, Director

International Society of Certified
Electronics Technicians **[1051]**
3000-A Landers St.
Fort Worth, TX 76107-5642
PH: (817)921-9101
Toll free: 800-946-0201
Fax: (817)921-3741
Blakely, Mack, Exec. Dir.

Life Outreach International **[20152]**
PO Box 982000
Fort Worth, TX 76182-8000
Toll free: 800-947-5433
Robison, James, Founder, President,
Chairman

Livestock Publications Council
[2796]
200 W Exchange Ave.
Fort Worth, TX 76164
PH: (817)247-1200
Brown, Carey, Secretary, Treasurer

Manufacturers Representatives of
America **[2478]**
4604 Ringold Dr.
Fort Worth, TX 76133
PH: (817)690-4308
Battle, Pamela L., Exec. Dir.

National Association of Hearing Of-
ficials **[5389]**
PO Box 330865
Fort Worth, TX 76163-0865
Deshais, Janice B., President

National Association of Presbyterian
Scouters **[12854]**
c/o Steve Baker, Treasurer
5620 Charlott St.
Fort Worth, TX 76112
PH: (301)948-7121
    (512)458-9889
Baker, Steve, Treasurer

National Association of Women in
Construction **[885]**
327 S Adams St.
Fort Worth, TX 76104
PH: (817)877-5551
Toll free: 800-552-3506
Fax: (817)877-0324
Lovejoy, Riki F., President

National Cutting Horse Association
[4381]
260 Bailey Ave.
Fort Worth, TX 76107
PH: (817)244-6188
Fax: (817)244-2015
Smith, Chuck, President

National Electronics Service Dealers
Association **[1055]**
3000-A Landers St.
Fort Worth, TX 76107-5642

PH: (817)921-9061
Fax: (817)921-3741
Blakely, Mack, Exec. Dir.

Native Workplace [12384]
PO Box 136757
Fort Worth, TX 76136
Mussato-Allen, Cristala, Exec. Dir.,
Founder

North American Society for Oceanic
History [9776]
Dept. of History
Texas Christian University
Box 297260
Fort Worth, TX 76129
Smith, Gene, President

Outside Sales Support Network
[3390]
320 Hemphill St.
Fort Worth, TX 76104
PH: (941)322-9700
Fax: (941)981-1902
Marxen, Dic, President, CEO

OV-10 Bronco Association [5869]
3300 Ross Ave.
Fort Worth, TX 76106-3646
Toll free: 800-575-0535
Kemp, Tom, Treasurer

Sharing of Ministries Abroad U.S.A.
[20461]
2501 Ridgmar Plz., No. 99
Fort Worth, TX 76116
PH: (817)737-7662
Speare, Ed, Chairman

Shine Therapy [15563]
1450 8th Ave.
Fort Worth, TX 76104
PH: (817)372-8998
Bashore, Lisa, President

Soles for Kidz [11151]
5821 Imes Ln.
Fort Worth, TX 76179
Toll free: 866-905-5439
Savage, Kelly, Founder

Stop Calling It Autism! [13777]
PO Box 155728
Fort Worth, TX 76155
Toll free: 888-724-2123
Rodriguez, Juan, Founder

Texas Longhorn Breeders Associa-
tion of America [3757]
2315 N Main St., Ste. 402
Fort Worth, TX 76164
PH: (817)625-6241
Fax: (817)625-1388
Mcknight, Todd, Chmn. of the Bd.

Turtle Survival Alliance [4897]
1989 Colonial Pky.
Fort Worth, TX 76110
PH: (817)759-7262
Fax: (817)759-7501
Hudson, Rick, President

Water Harvest International [13361]
3131 W 7th St., Ste. 400
Fort Worth, TX 76107
PH: (817)632-5200
Huber, Stephen, Project Mgr.

A Wish With Wings [11281]
3751 West Fwy.
Fort Worth, TX 76107
PH: (817)469-9474
Kalina, Greg, President

International Nubian Breeders Association [3602]
c/o Caroline Lawson, Secretary/
Treasurer

5124 FM 1940
Franklin, TX 77856
PH: (979)828-4158
Losey, Marshall, President

International Bird Dog Association
[21229]
c/o Suzanne Cobb, Membership
Director
2829 Aviation Loop
Fredericksburg, TX 78624
Cobb, Suzanne, Dir. of Member
Svcs.

American Southdown Breeders' As-
sociation [4665]
100 Cornerstone Rd.
Fredonia, TX 76842
PH: (325)429-6226
Fax: (325)429-6225
Scramlin, L.C., Comm. Chm.

Pink Isn't Always Pretty [14046]
PO Box 697
Fresno, TX 77545-0697
Toll free: 877-495-7427
Porterfield, Naomi, Chmn. of the Bd.,
Founder

Association of Energy Service
Companies [1106]
121 E Magnolia St., Ste. 103
Friendswood, TX 77546
PH: (713)781-0758
Fax: (713)781-7542
Jordan, Kenny, Exec. Dir.

American College Counseling As-
sociation [7682]
c/o Amy M. Lenhart, President
Collin College - PRC Campus
9700 Wade Blvd.
Frisco, TX 75035
PH: (972)377-1008
Lenhart, Amy M., President

American Society of Breast Disease
[13849]
2591 Dallas Pky., Ste. 300
Frisco, TX 75034-8563
PH: (214)368-6836
Pruthi, Sandhya, President

Bluefaced Leicester Union of North
America [4667]
PO Box 2304
Frisco, TX 75034
PH: (610)905-1136
Barndt, Kristen, Contact

Hand in Hand in Africa [13544]
7653 Bridge Water Cir.
Frisco, TX 75034
Toll free: 866-908-3518
Wilkinson, Bert Andrew, Chairman,
President

Human Touch International [13515]
12392 Hawk Creek Dr.
Frisco, TX 75033
PH: (513)593-1850
Aguwa, Alozie, Chmn. of the Bd.

National Breast Cancer Foundation
[14021]
2600 Network Blvd., Ste. 300
Frisco, TX 75034
Hail, Janelle, CEO, Chmn. of the
Bd., Founder

Para Sa Bata [11125]
11331 Cedar Springs Dr.
Frisco, TX 75035
PH: (469)579-4544
Alvarez, Ariel, Founder

United States Youth Soccer Associa-
tion [23197]
9220 World Cup Way
Frisco, TX 75033
Toll free: 800-4SOCCER
Fax: (972)334-9960
Moore, Christopher, CEO

American Alternative Medical As-
sociation [13587]
2200 Market St., Ste. 803
Galveston, TX 77550-1530
PH: (409)621-2600
Toll free: 888-764-2237
Fax: (775)703-5334
Rosenthal, Donald A., MD, Exec. Dir.

American Association of Drugless
Practitioners [13589]
2200 Market St., Ste. 803
Galveston, TX 77550-1530
PH: (409)621-2600
Toll free: 888-764-2237
Fax: (775)703-5334

American Society for Rickettsiology
[13792]
c/o Jere McBride, PhD, President
University of Texas Medical Branch
301 University Blvd., Keiller 1.136
Galveston, TX 77555-0609
McBride, Jere W., PhD, President

Artist Boat [3809]
2627 Ave. O
Galveston, TX 77550
PH: (409)770-0722
Klay, Karla, Exec. Dir.

International Oleander Society
[22107]
PO Box 3431
Galveston, TX 77552
Miller, Lydia, President

National Network for Immunization
Information [15384]
301 University Blvd.
Galveston, TX 77555-0350
PH: (702)200-0201
Fax: (409)772-5208
Myers, Dr. Martin G., MD, Ed.-in-
Chief, Exec. Dir.

Mercy Ships International Operations
Center [15606]
PO Box 2020
Garden Valley, TX 75771-2020
PH: (903)939-7000
Toll free: 800-772-7447
Ullman, Myron E., III, Chairman

Aesthetics International Association
[917]
310 E Interstate 30, Ste. B107
Garland, TX 75043
Toll free: 877-968-7539
Lawrence, Melissa, Officer

Alveolar Capillary Dysplasia Association [13821]
c/o Donna Hanson, Treasurer
5902 Marcie Ct.
Garland, TX 75044-4958
Hanson, Steve, President

Christian Adult Higher Education As-
sociation [7608]
c/o Renee Hyatt, Coordinator
2100 Westway Ave.
Garland, TX 75042
PH: (972)864-2010
Fax: (972)278-8486
Pauls, Toni, Contact

Descendants of Mexican War
Veterans [21023]
PO Box 461941
Garland, TX 75046-1941
Heath, Rebecca, Editor

Gene Summers International Fan
Club [24041]
222 Tulane St.
Garland, TX 75043-2239

Helping Hands, Inc. [11023]
2918 Churchill Way
Garland, TX 75044-4626
PH: (972)635-3903
Toll free: 877-623-5200
Fax: (214)703-3283
Siriwardana, Mrs. Kaushalya,
Founder

Last Harvest - The Outreach [12774]
1813 Eldorado Dr.
Garland, TX 75042
PH: (214)703-0505
   (908)926-2607
Freeman, Ken, President

American Stewards of Liberty
[18929]
624 S Austin Ave., Ste. 101
Georgetown, TX 78626
PH: (512)591-7843
Fax: (512)365-7931
Byfield, Margaret H., Exec. Dir.

National Institute for Technology in
Liberal Education [8228]
1001 E University Ave.
McCook-Crain Bldg.
Georgetown, TX 78626
PH: (512)863-1603
Fax: (512)819-7684
Nanfito, Michael, Exec. Dir.

Organization for Research on
Women and Communication
[10309]
Box 7381
Dept. of Communication Studies
Southwestern University
1001 E University Ave.
Georgetown, TX 78626
Goins, Marnel Niles, VP

United States Calf Ropers Associa-
tion [23104]
PO Box 690
Giddings, TX 78942
PH: (979)542-1239

International Texas Longhorn As-
sociation [3733]
1600 Texas Dr.
Glen Rose, TX 76043
PH: (254)898-0157
Fax: (254)898-0165
Lonero, Larry, President

American Coaster Enthusiasts
[21275]
PO Box 540261
Grand Prairie, TX 75054-0261
PH: (469)278-6223
Altman, Dave, President

MannaRelief [12100]
PO Box 540669
Grand Prairie, TX 75054-0669
PH: (817)557-8700
Fax: (817)557-8750
Caster, Sam, Founder

National Institute of Packaging,
Handling and Logistics Engineers
[6969]
5903 Ridgeway Dr.
Grand Prairie, TX 75052
PH: (817)466-7490
Werneke, Mike, Contact

Veteran Motor Car Club of America
[21512]
c/o Don Knight, Acting President
1610 Knight Circle

Grand Prairie, TX 75050-2848
PH: (972)641-4517
Knight, Don, Act. Pres.

Vietnam Helicopter Pilots Association **[21172]**
2100 N Highway 360, Ste. 907
Grand Prairie, TX 75050-1030
Toll free: 800-505-8472
Fax: (817)200-7309
Roush, Gary, Officer

American Association of Certified Wedding Planners **[441]**
210 W College St., Ste. 400
Grapevine, TX 76051
Toll free: 844-202-2297
Baade, Trudy, President

American Council of Spotted Asses **[3590]**
2933 Silvercrest Ln.
Grapevine, TX 76051
Brown, June, Registrar

Brothers and Sisters in Christ **[19947]**
PO Box 633
Grapevine, TX 76099
PH: (228)255-9251
Pulsifer, Henry, Founder

Children's Eye Foundation **[16379]**
1631 Lancaster Dr., Ste. 200
Grapevine, TX 76051-2116
PH: (817)310-2641
Fax: (817)423-6672
Gibson, William E., PhD, President

Kids Making a Difference **[3628]**
1527 W State Highway 114; Ste. 500, No. 106
Grapevine, TX 76051-8647
Cohen, Stephanie, Founder, President

Production Engine Remanufacturers Association **[1129]**
3931 Kelsey Ct.
Grapevine, TX 76051-6414
PH: (817)243-2646

Snowball Express **[12351]**
611 S Main St., Ste. 400
Grapevine, TX 76051
PH: (817)410-4673
Kern, Francis, Exec. Dir.

International German Coolie Society and Registry **[21899]**
c/o Ida Parmer
1139 LCR 454
Groesbeck, TX 76642
PH: (903)390-0300
Parmer, Ida, Contact

Military Child Education Coalition **[8344]**
909 Mountain Lion Cir.
Harker Heights, TX 76548-5709
PH: (254)953-1923
Fax: (254)953-1925
Keller, Dr. Mary M., CEO, President

The International Cat Association **[21570]**
306 E Jackson
Harlingen, TX 78550-6892
PH: (956)428-8046
Fax: (956)428-8047
Mays, Fate, President

International Pet and Animal Transportation Association **[2543]**
2129 S FM 2869, Ste. 4
Hawkins, TX 75765
PH: (903)769-2267
Fax: (903)769-2867
Huntington, Derek, President

American Rambouillet Sheep Breeders' Association **[4660]**
c/o Robbie G. Eckhoff, Executive Secretary
PO Box 214
Hawley, TX 79525
PH: (409)256-3687
Crawford, Scott, President

Collins Collectors Association **[21267]**
c/o Scott Kerr, President
2500 Chantilly Ct.
Heath, TX 75032
PH: (972)772-9750
Kerr, Scott, President

American Loggers Council **[1407]**
c/o Daniel J. Dructor, Executive Vice President
PO Box 966
Hemphill, TX 75948
PH: (409)625-0206
Fax: (409)625-0207
Schwab, Richard, President

Americal Division Veterans Association **[21188]**
4493 Highway 64 W
Henderson, TX 75652
PH: (830)377-8115
Ellis, Ronald, Finance Ofc.

Preemptive Love Coalition **[14139]**
1300 Darbyton Dr.
Hewitt, TX 76643
PH: (254)400-2033
Courtney, Jeremy, President, Founder

Habitat for Horses **[10632]**
PO Box 213
Hitchcock, TX 77563
PH: (409)935-0277
Toll free: 866-434-5737
Fax: (409)515-0657
Finch, Jerry, President

Barbados Blackbelly Sheep Association International **[4666]**
801 County Road 243
Hondo, TX 78861
PH: (301)440-4808
Kahn, Patrick, Treasurer

Haiti Share **[11922]**
PO Box 9208
Horseshoe Bay, TX 78657
PH: (830)598-2172
Harmsen, Dr. Betty Jean, Exec. Dir.

Abriendo Mentes **[12795]**
Guanacaste Literacy Inc.
3310 Crosspark Ln.
Houston, TX 77007
PH: (832)548-4493
Leebrick, Meradith, Founder

Accounting and Finance Benchmarking Consortium **[604]**
4606 FM 1960 Rd. W, Ste. 250
Houston, TX 77069-9949
PH: (281)440-5044

Africa Cancer Care Inc. **[13871]**
6011 Telephone Rd.
Houston, TX 77087
PH: (713)995-8000
Fax: (713)645-5588
Iwuanyanwu, Eucharia, President

Amanda Jimeno Foundation **[13876]**
1155 Dairy Ashford, Ste. 610
Houston, TX 77079
PH: (281)920-2668
Jimeno-Nieto, July, Founder

American Association of Breast Care Professionals **[13848]**
3375 Westpark Dr., No. 573
Houston, TX 77005
Fax: (888)892-1684
Turner, Rhonda F., PhD, Founder, President

American Association of Drilling Engineers **[6997]**
PO Box 107
Houston, TX 77001
PH: (281)293-9800
Fax: (281)293-9800
Day, Jeffrey D., Chairperson

American Board of Forensic Document Examiners **[5234]**
7887 San Felipe St., Ste. 122
Houston, TX 77063
PH: (713)784-9537
Fax: (713)784-3985
Burkes, Ted, Secretary

American Board of Otolaryngology **[16532]**
5615 Kirby Dr., Ste. 600
Houston, TX 77005
PH: (713)850-0399
Fax: (713)850-1104
Miller, Robert H., Exec. Dir.

American Brahman Breeders Association **[3686]**
3003 S Loop W, Ste. 520
Houston, TX 77054
PH: (713)349-0854
Fax: (713)349-9795
Kempfer, George, VP

American Breeds Coalition **[3688]**
3003 S Loop W, Ste. 520
Houston, TX 77054
Graham, Dr. Charles, President

American Catholic Philosophical Association **[8417]**
Ctr. for Thomistic Studies
University of St. Thomas
3800 Montrose Blvd.
Houston, TX 77006-4626
PH: (713)942-3483
Toll free: 800-444-2419
Fax: (713)525-6964
Flannery, Kevin, President

American Friends of Guinea **[15436]**
PO Box 940505
Houston, TX 77079
PH: (832)456-8100
Fax: (832)300-2516
Watts, Kenn, Chmn. of the Bd.

American Neuropsychiatric Association **[16820]**
The Menninger Clinic
12301 Main St.
Houston, TX 77035
PH: (713)275-5777
Schmahmann, Jeremy, MD, FANPA, President

American Porphyria Foundation **[15817]**
4900 Woodway, Ste. 780
Houston, TX 77056-1837
PH: (713)266-9617
Toll free: 866-273-3635
Fax: (713)840-9552
Lyon, Desiree H., Exec. Dir.

American Sewing Guild **[21749]**
9660 Hillcroft, Ste. 510
Houston, TX 77096-3866
PH: (713)729-3000
Fax: (713)721-9230
Martin, Margo, Exec. Dir.

American Society of Emergency Radiology **[17044]**
4550 Post Oak Pl., Ste. 342
Houston, TX 77027

PH: (713)965-0566
Fax: (713)960-0488
John, Susan D., MD, FACR, Exec.

American Woman's Society of Certified Public Accountants **[11]**
701 N Post Oak Rd., Ste. 635
Houston, TX 77024
PH: (937)222-1872
    (713)893-5685
Toll free: 800-297-2721
Fax: (937)222-5794
Cox, Cynthia, President

Amigos de las Americas **[13281]**
5618 Star Ln.
Houston, TX 77057
PH: (713)782-5290
Toll free: 800-231-7796
Howick, Andrew, Chairman

Anesthesia History Association **[13696]**
c/o Martin Giesecke, M.D., Treasurer
5010 Crawford St.
Houston, TX 77004-5735
Kopp, Sandra, MD, President

APQC **[2148]**
123 N Post Oak Ln., 3rd Fl.
Houston, TX 77024
Toll free: 800-776-9676
Fax: (713)681-8578
O'Dell, Carla, PhD, CEO

Asian/Pacific American Heritage Association **[9025]**
6220 Westpark, Ste. 245BC
Houston, TX 77057
PH: (713)784-1112
Gee, Betty, Officer

Association for Adult Development and Aging **[10499]**
c/o Andrew Daire, President-Elect
214 Farish Hall, Rm. 466G
College of Education
University of Houston
Houston, TX 77204-5023
PH: (713)743-5443
Killam, Wendy, Ph.D., President

Association for the Advancement of Mexican Americans **[11316]**
Bldg. E
6001 Gulf Fwy.
Houston, TX 77023-5423
PH: (713)967-6700
Fax: (713)926-8035
Garza, Beatrice G., President, CEO

Association for Benchmarking Health Care **[1589]**
4606 FM 1960 Rd. W, Ste. 250
Houston, TX 77069-9949
PH: (281)440-5044
Fax: (281)440-6677

Association of Chinese-American Professionals **[19412]**
10303 Westoffice Dr.
Houston, TX 77042-5306
Lin, Hsin-Hui, President

Association for Continuing Dental Education **[7709]**
c/o Yvette Haas, President
The University of Texas
School of Dentistry at Houston
7500 Cambridge St., Ste. 6130
Houston, TX 77054
PH: (713)486-4028
Fax: (713)486-4037
Haas, Yvette, President

Association of Diving Contractors International **[856]**
5206 FM 1960 W, Ste. 202
Houston, TX 77069

PH: (281)893-8388
Fax: (281)893-5118
Newsum, Phil, Exec. Dir.

Association of Nigerian Petroleum
Professionals Abroad [6998]
PO Box 218865
Houston, TX 77218
Inikori, Solomon, PhD, President

Association of Psychology
Postdoctoral and Internship
Centers [8312]
Onyx One, Ste. 170
17225 El Camino Real
Houston, TX 77058-2748
PH: (832)284-4080
Fax: (832)284-4079
Baker, Jeff, PhD, Exec. Dir.

Association of Starwood Franchisees
and Owners North America [1652]
c/o John Shingler, President
420A Lovett Blvd.
Houston, TX 77006
PH: (713)523-1352
Fax: (713)524-3319
Shingler, John, CEO, President

Auto Suppliers Benchmarking As-
sociation [615]
4606 FM 1960 Rd. W, Ste. 250
Houston, TX 77069-9949
PH: (281)440-5044
Fax: (281)440-6677

The Benchmarking Network, Inc.
[2441]
4606 FM 1960 W, Ste. 300
Houston, TX 77069-9949
PH: (281)440-5044
Toll free: 888-323-6246
Fax: (281)440-6677
Czarnecki, Mark T., Owner,
President

Bilateral US-Arab Chamber of Com-
merce [23565]
PO Box 571870
Houston, TX 77257-1870
PH: (713)880-8168
Phillips, David L., Chmn. of the Bd.

Breast Cancer Initiative East Africa
[13909]
8903 Emerald Heights Ln.
Houston, TX 77083
PH: (281)564-0974
Kibugu-Decuir, Philippa, Founder

Breathe the Cure [13613]
Houston, TX
Buergermeister, Jennifer, Founder

Casino Chip and Gaming Token Col-
lectors Club [21636]
PO Box 691085
Houston, TX 77269-1085

Chapman Family Association
[20793]
c/o Robert L. Sonfield, Executive
Director
770 S Post Oak Ln., Ste 435
Houston, TX 77056-1913
PH: (713)877-8333
Gustafson, Dian, Bd. Member

Chinese Historians in the United
States [7980]
c/o Xiaoping Cong, President
University of Houston
Dept. of History
524 Agnes Arnold Hall
Houston, TX 77204
PH: (713)743-3096
Xiaoping, Cong, PhD, President

Chinese School Association in the
United States [8533]
5925 Sovereign Dr., Ste. 115
Houston, TX 77036

Christian Communications, Inc. of
USA [19954]
9600 Bellaire Blvd., No. 111
Houston, TX 77036
PH: (713)778-1155
(713)778-1144
Chen, Lillien, Exec. Dir.

Citizens for Affordable Energy [6466]
1302 Waugh Dr., No. 940
Houston, TX 77019-3908
PH: (713)523-7333
Fax: (888)318-7878
Hofmeister, Dr. Karen, Bd. Member

Coastal Conservation Association
[3834]
6919 Portwest Dr., Ste. 100
Houston, TX 77024-8049
PH: (713)626-4234
Fax: (713)626-5852

Community Colleges for International
Development [8063]
c/o Lone Star College
Bldg. 11, Rm. 11296
20515 State Highway 249
Houston, TX 77070
PH: (281)401-5389
Rafn, Jeffrey, President, Chmn. of
the Bd.

Consumer Energy Alliance [6471]
2211 Norfolk St., Ste. 410
Houston, TX 77098
PH: (713)337-8800
Holt, David, President

Cooling Technology Institute [519]
3845 Cypress Creek Pky., Ste. 420
Houston, TX 77068
PH: (281)583-4087
Fax: (281)537-1721
Michell, Frank, President

COSA [12914]
9219 Katy Fwy., Ste. 212
Houston, TX 77024-1514
Toll free: 866-899-2672

Council for Environmental Education
[7873]
5555 Morningside Dr., Ste. 212
Houston, TX 77005
PH: (713)520-1936
Fax: (713)520-8008
Hawthorne, Josetta, Exec. Dir.

Council of Societies for the Study of
Religion [8708]
Rice University
PO Box 1892
Houston, TX 77251-1892
PH: (713)348-5721
Fax: (713)348-5725
Elliott, Scott, Editor

Customer Satisfaction Measurement
Benchmarking Association [627]
4606 FM 1960 Rd. W, Ste. 250
Houston, TX 77069-9949
PH: (281)440-5044
Fax: (281)440-6677

Michael E. DeBakey International
Surgical Society [14111]
c/o Kenneth L. Mattox, MD,
Secretary-Treasurer
1 Baylor Plz.
Houston, TX 77030
PH: (713)798-4557
Soltero, Ernesto, MD, President

Decision Sciences Institute [7550]
C.T. Bauer College of Business
334 Melchor Hall
4750 Calhoun Rd., Ste. 325
Houston, TX 77204-6021

PH: (713)743-4815
Fax: (713)743-8984
Sahin, Funda, President

Delta Phi Omega Sorority, Inc.
[23969]
2020 Bailey St.
Houston, TX 77006
Morisetty, Harini, President

Delta Phi Upsilon Fraternity, Inc.
[23705]
PO Box 573013
Houston, TX 77257
Wilson, Darryl L., Jr., Exec. Dir.

Drilling Engineering Association
[2519]
International Association of Drilling
Contractors
10370 Richmond Ave., Ste. 760
Houston, TX 77042
PH: (713)292-1945
Fax: (713)292-1946
Bloys, Ben, Chairman

Dysphagia Research Society
[14572]
International Meeting Managers, Inc.
4550 Post Oak Place Dr., Ste. 342
Houston, TX 77027-3167
PH: (713)965-0566
Fax: (713)960-0488
Belafsky, Peter C., MD, Officer

Electric Utility Benchmarking As-
sociation [6408]
Houston, TX
PH: (281)440-5044

Elephant Managers Association
[10614]
1513 Cambridge St.
Houston, TX 77030
PH: (407)938-1988
Hoffman, Daryl, Exec. Dir.

Empowering Leadership Alliance
[7960]
6100 Main St., MS 134
Houston, TX 77005-1827
PH: (713)348-6122
Fax: (713)348-3679
Stipeche, Juliet, Program Mgr.

Energy Security Council [1787]
9720 Cypresswood Dr., Ste. 206
Houston, TX 77070
PH: (281)587-2700
Fax: (281)807-6000
Ream, Rob, Chairman

Eta Sigma Alpha National Home
School Honor Society [7485]
11665 Fuqua St., Ste. A-100
Houston, TX 77034
PH: (281)922-0478
Juren, Joanne E., BA, Director,
Founder

Fathers for Equal Rights [11684]
1314 Texas St., Ste. 609
Houston, TX 77002-3521
PH: (512)588-7900
Clark, Doug, Exec. Dir.

Federation of Historical Bottle Col-
lectors [21555]
c/o Elizabeth Meyer, Business
Manager
101 Crawford St., Studio 1A
Houston, TX 77002
PH: (713)222-7979
Meyer V, Ferdinand, President

Federation Internationale des associations vexillologiques [10296]
c/o Charles A. Spain, Secretary
General

504 Branard St.
Houston, TX 77006-5018
PH: (713)249-0416
Fax: (713)752-2304
Lupant, Michel R., President

Fiberglass Tank and Pipe Institute
[832]
14323 Heatherfield Dr.
Houston, TX 77079-7407
Curran, Sullivan D., PE, Exec. Dir.

Financial Services and Banking
Benchmarking Association [632]
4606 FM 1960 Rd. W, Ste. 250
Houston, TX 77069-9949
PH: (281)440-5044
Fax: (281)440-6677

Golf Writers Association of America
[22882]
10210 Greentree Rd.
Houston, TX 77042
PH: (713)782-6664
Fax: (713)781-2575
Hauser, Melanie, Secretary,
Treasurer

Green Hotels Association [1656]
1611 Mossy Stone Dr.
Houston, TX 77077-4109
PH: (713)789-8889
Fax: (713)789-9786
Griffin, Patricia, Founder, President

HALTER, Inc. [17443]
17410 Clay Rd.
Houston, TX 77084
PH: (281)861-9138
(281)508-6501
Pigozzi, Maria, President

Health Empowering Humanity
[15011]
PO Box 300618
Houston, TX 77230
Preidis, Geoff, Founder, President

Hispanic Genealogical Society
[20971]
PO Box 231271
Houston, TX 77223-1271
Fax: (281)449-4020
Guerra, Jose O., Web Adm.

Historical Society for Twentieth-
Century China [9481]
c/o Xiaoping Cong, Secretary-
Treasurer
Department of History
University of Houston
Houston, TX 77204
Wang, Dong, President

Hope Through Grace [13982]
4660 Beechnut St., Ste. 102
Houston, TX 77096
PH: (713)668-4673
Fax: (713)668-6040
Butler, Grace L., PhD, Founder,
Chmn. of the Bd.

Human Resources Benchmarking
Association [635]
4606 FM 1960 Rd. W, Ste. 250
Houston, TX 77069-9949
PH: (281)440-5044
Fax: (281)440-6677

The Hydrographic Society of
America [7251]
PO Box 841361
Houston, TX 77284
PH: (774)773-8470
Cooper, Paul, President

Igbere Progressive Association
International [11380]
c/o Chuck Oko, Board Secretary
PO Box 540814

Houston, TX 77254
PH: (713)773-4887
Fax: (713)779-0233
Onyeuku, Saul, President

Indian American Cancer Network
[10789]
PO Box 741886
Houston, TX 77274
PH: (713)370-3489
Kabad, Kanchan, MBA, President

Indicorps [12127]
3418 Highway 6 S, Ste. B, No. 309
Houston, TX 77082

Information Systems Management
Benchmarking Consortium [636]
4606 FM 1960 Rd. W, Ste. 250
Houston, TX 77069-9949
PH: (281)440-5044
Fax: (281)440-6677

Institute of Chinese Culture [9155]
10550 Westoffice Dr.
Houston, TX 77042
PH: (713)781-2888
   (713)339-1992
Shih, Francoise, VP

Intercultural Cancer Council [13988]
1 Baylor Plz., MS 620
Houston, TX 77030-3411
PH: (713)798-4614
Fax: (713)798-3990
Jackson, Pamela M., Exec. Dir.

International Association of Butterfly
Exhibitors and Suppliers [1174]
Houston Museum of Natural Science
Cockerell Butterfly Ctr.
5555 Hermann Park Dr.
Houston, TX 77030
PH: (713)639-4750
Fax: (713)639-4788
Buckman, Michael, President

International Association of
Directional Drilling [7001]
525 North Sam Houston Pky. E, No.
525
Houston, TX 77060
PH: (281)931-8811
Oberkircher, Jim, Exec. Dir.

International Association of Drilling
Contractors [2525]
10370 Richmond Ave., Ste. 760
Houston, TX 77042
PH: (713)292-1945
Fax: (713)292-1946
Burke, Thomas, Chairman

International Association of Elevator
Consultants [1737]
448 W 19th St., No. 484
Houston, TX 77008
PH: (713)426-1662
Fax: (713)690-0004
Fenili, Leo, VP

International Association of Gay/
Lesbian Country Western Dance
Clubs [9258]
5380 W 34th St., No. 207
Houston, TX 77092-6626
Monroe, Charlie, Chairperson

International Association of
Geophysical Contractors [2526]
1225 North Loop W, Ste. 220
Houston, TX 77008-1761
PH: (713)957-8080
Toll free: 866-558-1756
Fax: (713)957-0008
Rosenbursch, Walt, COO, Exec. VP

International Association for Hospice
and Palliative Care [15279]
5535 Memorial Dr., Ste. F, PMB 509
Houston, TX 77007

PH: (936)321-9846
Toll free: 866-374-2472
Fax: (713)589-3657
De Lima, Liliana, MHA, Exec. Dir.

International Association for
Mathematical Geosciences [6692]
5868 Westheimer Rd., No. 537
Houston, TX 77057
PH: (832)380-8833
Cheng, Qiuming, President

International Atherosclerosis Society
[14120]
6535 Fannin St.
Houston, TX 77030-2703
PH: (713)797-0401
Fax: (713)796-8853
Jackson, Ann, Exec. Dir.

International Contact Center
Benchmarking Consortium [639]
4606 FM 1960 Rd. W, Ste. 250
Houston, TX 77069-9949
PH: (281)440-5044
Fax: (281)440-6677

International Facility Management
Association [2747]
800 Gessner Rd., Ste. 900
Houston, TX 77024-4257
PH: (713)623-4362
Fax: (713)623-6124
Feldman, Michael D., FMP, CM,
Chairperson

International Institute of Synthetic
Rubber Producers, Inc. [2985]
207 S Gessner Rd., Ste. 133
Houston, TX 77063
PH: (713)783-7511
Fax: (713)783-7253
O'Connor, Mary, Secretary

International Maintenance Institute
[2132]
c/o Joyce Rhoden, Executive
Secretary
PO Box 751896
Houston, TX 77275
PH: (281)481-0869
Toll free: 888-207-1773
Fax: (281)481-8337
Fortier, Kenneth J., Secretary

International Oil Scouts Association
[2527]
PO Box 940310
Houston, TX 77094-7310
Sarrat, Christi, Exec. VP

International Quilt Association
[21764]
7660 Woodway, Ste. 550
Houston, TX 77063-1528
PH: (713)781-6882
Fax: (713)781-8182
Pumphrey, Linda, President

International Society for Brachial
Plexus and Peripheral Nerve Injury
[16023]
2201 W Holcombe Blvd., Ste. 225
Houston, TX 77030
PH: (713)592-9900
Melcher, Sonya, Gen. Mgr.

International Society for Rotary
Blood Pumps [14130]
Baylor College of Medicine
1 Baylor Plz., BMC M390
Houston, TX 77030
PH: (713)798-6309
Fax: (713)798-8439
Slepian, Prof. Marvin, President

International Transportation Manage-
ment Association [5814]
PO Box 670228
Houston, TX 77267-0228

PH: (832)399-1032
Brightwell, David, Secretary

IT Service Management Forum USA
[6746]
20333 State Highway 249, Ste. 200
Houston, TX 77070-2613
PH: (626)963-1900
Toll free: 888-959-0673
Erskine, Pamela, President

It's My Heart [14131]
1304 Langham Creek, No. 235
Houston, TX 77084
PH: (713)334-4244
   (713)334-4243
Toll free: 888-HEART-07
Fax: (866)222-0334
Stassen, Ms. Corrie, Exec. Dir.

Lex Mundi [5020]
2100 W Loop S, Ste. 1000
Houston, TX 77027-3537
PH: (713)626-9393
Fax: (713)626-9933
Anduri, Carl E., Jr., President

The Living Bank [14622]
4545 Post Oak Pl., Ste. 340
Houston, TX 77027
PH: (713)961-9431
Toll free: 800-528-2971
Biscone, Mark J., V. Chmn. of the
Bd.

MAES: Latinos in Science and
Engineering [6569]
2437 Bay Area Blvd., No. 100
Houston, TX 77058
PH: (281)557-3677
Fax: (281)715-5100
Davis, Will, President

The Maritime Law Association of the
United States [5576]
c/o Robert Clyne, President
16855 Northchase Dr.
Houston, TX 77060
PH: (281)877-5989
Fax: (281)877-6646
Parrish, Robert B., Director

Materials & Methods Standards Association [543]
4000 Pinemont Dr.
Houston, TX 77018
Whitfield, Jim, VP

Maybee Society [20897]
718 Pachester Dr.
Houston, TX 77079
Mabie, Steve, VP

Medical Bridges [15604]
2706 Magnet St.
Houston, TX 77054
PH: (713)748-8131
Fax: (713)748-0118
Weill, Michael A., Chmn. of the Bd.

MentorCONNECT [14645]
1302 Waugh Dr., No. 660
Houston, TX 77019
Cutts, Shannon, Founder, Exec. Dir.,
Chmn. of the Bd.

Mission K9 Rescue [10660]
14027 Memorial Dr., No. 185
Houston, TX 77079
PH: (713)589-9362
Maurer, Kristen, President, Founder

NACE International [6571]
15835 Park Ten Pl.
Houston, TX 77084
PH: (281)228-6200
Fax: (281)228-6300
Chalker, Bob, CEO

National Association of Black
Geoscientists [6694]
4212 San Felipe St., Ste. 420
Houston, TX 77027
Carroll, Michael, President

National Association of Dog Obedi-
ence Instructors [21919]
7910 Picador Dr.
Houston, TX 77083-4918
PH: (972)296-1196
Kincaid, Marti, VP

National Association of Healthcare
Transport Management [14952]
c/o Pamela Douglas-Ntagha, DNP,
   1400 Holcombe Blvd. Ste. 0422
1400 Holcombe Blvd., Unit 0422
Houston, TX 77030-4009
PH: (713)563-7700
Douglas-Ntagha, Pamela, DNP,
President

National Association of Pipe Coating
Applicators [745]
500 Dallas St., Ste. 3000
Houston, TX 77002
PH: (713)655-5761
Fax: (713)655-0020
Chastain, Merritt B., III, Managing
Dir.

National Birth Defects Prevention
Network [13832]
1321 Upland Dr., Ste. 1561
Houston, TX 77043
PH: (404)498-3918
Anderka, Marlene, President

National Pan-American Junior Golf
Association [22888]
1700 Seaspray, Ste. 1213
1700 Seaspray, No. 1213
Houston, TX 77008
PH: (713)862-1911
Garcia, Alex, Secretary

National Pharmacy Technician As-
sociation [16680]
PO Box 683148
Houston, TX 77268-3148
Toll free: 888-247-8700
Fax: (888)247-8706
Johnston, Mike, CPhT, Chairman

National Search Dog Alliance
[12747]
1302 Waugh Dr., Ste. 121
Houston, TX 77019
PH: (360)808-0894
Fleming, Susan, President

National Senior Women's Tennis Association [23304]
c/o Sue Bramlette
96 Sugarberry Cir.
Houston, TX 77024
Langer, Kathy, President

Nature Healing Nature [11410]
514 Byrne St.
Houston, TX 77009
PH: (832)423-8425
Illian, Mark, President

North American Carbon Capture &
Storage Association [6580]
c/o Michael Moore, Executive Direc-
tor
FearnOil, Inc.
12012 Wickchester Ln., Ste. 350
Houston, TX 77079
PH: (281)759-0245
Moore, Michael, Exec. Dir.

Pakistan Chamber of Commerce
USA [23611]
11110 Bellaire Blvd., Ste. 202
Houston, TX 77072-2610

PH: (832)448-0520
Toll free: 888-712-5111
Faraz, Ahmed, Gen. Sec.

Petroleum Equipment Suppliers Association [2534]
2500 Citywest Blvd., Ste. 1110
Houston, TX 77055
PH: (713)932-0168
Rahimian, Saeid, Chairman

Pink Door Nonprofit Organization [14045]
PO Box 6990
Houston, TX 77265-6990
PH: (832)727-3121
Cole, Ms. Cortney A., Founder, President

Plumeria Society of America [22119]
PO Box 22791
Houston, TX 77227
Arend, Bob, President

Pratham U.S.A. [12128]
9703 Richmond Ave., Ste. 102
Houston, TX 77042
PH: (713)774-9599
Ahuja, Avinash, Director

Procurement and Supply Chain Benchmarking Association [665]
4606 FM 1960 Rd. W, Ste. 250
Houston, TX 77069-9949
PH: (281)440-5044
Fax: (281)440-6677

Professional Sporting Clays Association [23142]
9219 Katy Fwy., Ste. 291
Houston, TX 77024
PH: (614)660-6174
Robertson, Scott, President

Reasoning Mind [8285]
2000 Bering Dr., Ste. 300
Houston, TX 77057-3774
PH: (281)579-1110
Toll free: 800-994-1306
Khachatryan, Alexander R., PhD, CEO, President, Founder

Rice Design Alliance [5976]
M.D. Anderson Hall, Rm. 149
Rice University
6100 Main St.
Houston, TX 77005-1827
PH: (713)348-4876
Fax: (713)348-5924
Sylvan, Ms. Linda L., Exec. Dir.

Romance Writers of America [10396]
14615 Benfer Rd.
Houston, TX 77069
PH: (832)717-5200
Kelley, Allison, CAE, Exec. Dir.

Schizophrenia and Related Disorders Alliance of America [15805]
PO Box 941222
Houston, TX 77094-8222
PH: (240)423-9432
Toll free: 866-800-5199
Stalters, Linda, Founder

Sewa International U.S.A. [12187]
PO Box 820867
Houston, TX 77082-0867
PH: (708)872-7392
Bhutada, Ramesh, Director

Sex Addicts Anonymous [12915]
PO Box 70949
Houston, TX 77270-0949
PH: (713)869-4902
Toll free: 800-477-8191
H., Joe, Exec. Dir.

Sisters Network, Inc. [14062]
2922 Rosedale St.
Houston, TX 77004
PH: (713)781-0255
Toll free: 866-781-1808
Fax: (713)780-8998
Jackson, Karen E., CEO, Founder

Society of Abdominal Radiology [17557]
4550 Post Oak Pl., Ste. 342
Houston, TX 77027
PH: (713)965-0566
Fax: (713)960-0488
Mayo-Smith, William W., MD, President

Society of Engineering Science [6591]
c/o Pradeep Sharma, Vice-President
Dept. of Mechanical Engineering
Cullen College of Engineering
University of Houston
Houston, TX 77204-4006
Saif, Taher, President

Society for Heart Attack Prevention and Eradication [14145]
2500 W Loop S, Ste. 360-A
Houston, TX 77027
Toll free: 877-SHA-PE11
Naghavi, Morteza, Exec. Chmn. of the Bd., Founder

Society of Iranian-American Women for Education [8123]
PO Box 572371
Houston, TX 77257
PH: (713)532-6666
Barazandeh, Vajeh, Contact

Society of Mexican American Engineers and Scientists [6593]
2437 Bay Area Blvd., No. 100
Houston, TX 77058
PH: (281)557-3677
Fax: (281)715-5100
Davis, Will, President

Society for Neuro-Oncology [16054]
PO Box 273296
Houston, TX 77277
PH: (281)554-6589
Fax: (713)583-1345
Haynes, J. Charles, JD, Exec. Dir.

Society of Petroleum Evaluation Engineers [7003]
c/o Debbie Suter, Executive Secretary
20333 State Highway 249, Ste. 200
Houston, TX 77070
PH: (832)972-7733
Suter, Debbie, Exec. Dir.

Society of Petrophysicists and Well Log Analysts [7004]
8866 Gulf Fwy., Ste. 320
Houston, TX 77017
PH: (713)947-8727
Fax: (713)947-7181
Liu, Shujie, VP

Society of Piping Engineers and Designers [6596]
9668 Westheimer Rd., Ste. 200-242
Houston, TX 77063
PH: (832)286-3404
Noakes, Kevin, Consultant

Society for the Second Self [12952]
PO Box 20785
Houston, TX 77225
PH: (832)431-7104
Fairfax, Jane Ellen, Chmn. of the Bd., Treasurer

Together in Hope [11169]
1250 Wood Branch Park Dr., Ste. 625

Houston, TX 77079
PH: (832)758-2971
McGehee, Diane, Founder, Exec. Dir.

Turner Syndrome Society of the U.S. [14862]
11250 West Rd., Ste. G
Houston, TX 77065
PH: (832)912-6006
Toll free: 800-365-9944
Fax: (832)912-6446
Scurlock, Cindy, Exec. Dir.

U.S. Cancellation Club [22376]
1715 Valley Vista Dr.
Houston, TX 77077-4938
Donnes, John, President

U.S. National Committee for International Union of Radio Science [7150]
c/o David Jackson, Chairman
Dept. of Electrical and Computer Engineering
University of Houston
4800 Calhoun Rd.
Houston, TX 77004
PH: (713)743-4426
Fax: (713)743-4444
Brown, Gary S., Acct. Mgr.

United States Professional Tennis Association [23308]
3535 Briarpark Dr., Ste. 202
Houston, TX 77042-5233
PH: (713)978-7782
Fax: (713)978-7780
Gill, Chuck, President

US Rice Producers Association [1524]
2825 Wilcrest Dr., Ste. 218
Houston, TX 77042-6041
PH: (713)974-7423
Fax: (713)974-7696
Roberts, Dwight, CEO, President

Vietnamese-American Nurses Association [16190]
PO Box 691994
Houston, TX 77269-1994
Ho, Vi, PhD, Founder, Chairman

Voices Breaking Boundaries [10070]
PO Box 541247
Houston, TX 77254-1247
PH: (713)524-7821
Alvarado, Yolanda, President

We Improve Tomorrow [11184]
1054 Lehman St.
Houston, TX 77018
Crompton, Joanne, Founder

Wireless Industry Association [3248]
9746 Tappenbeck Dr.
Houston, TX 77055
PH: (713)467-0077
Hutchinson, Robert, Founder, President

Women Contractors Association [3503]
PO Box 70966
Houston, TX 77270
PH: (713)807-9977
Fax: (713)807-9917
Scheffer, Sherri, CPA, Treasurer

Women in the Visual and Literary Arts [9008]
PO Box 130406
Houston, TX 77219-0406
Mulholland, Jane, President

World Energy Cities Partnership [1124]
c/o Matthew Shailer, Executive Director

901 Bagby St., 4th Fl.
Houston, TX 77002
Shailer, Matthew, Exec. Dir.

World Federation for Coral Reef Conservation [3972]
PO Box 311117
Houston, TX 77231
PH: (281)309-1201
Ferguson, Vic, Exec. Dir., Founder

Canary and Finch Society [3659]
c/o Helen Jones, Treasurer
348 Magnolia Dr.
Huffman, TX 77336
PH: (281)259-7951
Peters, Don, Director

American APS Association [13783]
6942 FM 1960 E, No. 363
Humble, TX 77346
PH: (281)812-3384
Crowson, Seresa, Founder, President

American Collegiate Horsemen's Association [4301]
PO Box 2088
Huntsville, TX 77341-2088
PH: (936)294-1214
Martin, Kamry, President

Association of Doctoral Programs in Criminology & Criminal Justice [7691]
c/o Amanda L. Burris, Secretariat Administrator
College of Criminal Justice
Sam Houston State University
Box 2296
Huntsville, TX 77341-2296
PH: (936)294-3799
(936)294-1658
Brennan, Dr. Pauline, President

Association of Paroling Authorities International [5673]
Sam Houston State University
George J. Beto Criminal Justice Ctr.
Huntsville, TX 77341-2296
PH: (936)294-1706
Toll free: 877-318-2724
Fax: (936)294-1671
Morris, Monica, Chief Adm. Ofc.

International Association for Society and Natural Resources [4493]
c/o Sam Houston State University Sociology Dept.
1901 Avenue I, Ste. 270
Huntsville, TX 77341
PH: (936)294-4446
(936)294-4143
Carroll, Matthew, Exec. Dir.

National Association of Probation Executives [5142]
c/o Christie Davidson, Executive Director
National Association of Probation Executives
Correctional Management Institute
George J. Beto Criminal Justice Center
Sam Houston State University
Huntsville, TX 77341-2296
PH: (936)294-3757
Fax: (936)294-1671
Davidson, Ms. Christie, Exec. Dir.

USA Jump Rope [23107]
2431 Crosstimbers Dr.
Huntsville, TX 77320
PH: (936)295-3332
Fax: (936)295-3309
Fletcher, Marian, Exec. Dir.

Covenant of Unitarian Universalist Pagans [20513]
479 W Harwood Rd.
Hurst, TX 76054-2943

PH: (330)892-8877

Electronic Document Systems Foundation [1797]
1845 Precinct Line Rd., Ste. 212
Hurst, TX 76054
PH: (817)849-1145
Fax: (817)849-1185
Kai, Brenda, Exec. Dir.

Exotic Wildlife Association [4816]
105 Henderson Branch Rd. W
Ingram, TX 78025-5078
PH: (830)367-7761
Fax: (830)367-7762
Seale, Charly, Exec. Dir.

ADSC: The International Association of Foundation Drilling [849]
8445 Freeport Pky., Ste. 325
Irving, TX 75063
PH: (469)359-6000
Fax: (469)359-6007
Kitchens, Lance, President

American Association for Respiratory Care [17431]
9425 N MacArthur Blvd., Ste. 100
Irving, TX 75063-4706
PH: (972)243-2272
Fax: (972)484-2720
Kallstrom, Tom, Exec. Dir., CEO

American Association of Women Emergency Physicians [14671]
c/o American College of Emergency Physicians
1125 Executive Cir.
Irving, TX 75038-2522
PH: (972)550-0911
Toll free: 800-798-1822
Fax: (972)580-2816
Santistevan, Jamie, Contact

American College of Emergency Physicians [14673]
1125 Executive Cir.
Irving, TX 75038-2522
PH: (972)550-0911
Toll free: 800-798-1822
Fax: (972)580-2816
Wilkerson, Dean, Exec. Dir.

American Concrete Pipe Association [2601]
8445 Freeport Pky., Ste. 350
Irving, TX 75063-2595
PH: (972)506-7216
Fax: (972)506-7682
Gossett, A. C., III, Chmn. of the Bd.

American Pregnancy Association [16274]
1425 Greenway Dr., Ste. 440
Irving, TX 75038
PH: (972)550-0140
Toll free: 800-672-2296
Rydfors, Jan, Chief Med. Ofc.

American Recovery Association [982]
5525 N MacArthur Blvd., No. 135
Irving, TX 75038
PH: (972)755-4755
Wilson, Jerry, President

Association of Baptists for Scouting [12850]
PO Box 152079
Irving, TX 75015-2079
PH: (706)366-4998
Spangenberg, Ted, Jr., President

Baitulmaal, Inc. [12625]
PO Box 166911
Irving, TX 75016-6911
PH: (972)257-2564
Toll free: 800-220-9554
Fax: (972)258-1396
Jillaow, Ugas, Chairman

Boy Scouts of America [12851]
1325 W Walnut Hill Ln.
Irving, TX 75038-3008
PH: (972)580-2000
Ashline, Michael, CFO

Caregivers4Cancer [13936]
PO Box 153448
Irving, TX 75015
PH: (972)513-0668
Garrett, Betty, Contact

Electronic Security Association [3054]
6333 N State Highway 161, Ste. 350
Irving, TX 75038
PH: (972)807-6800
Toll free: 888-447-1689
Fax: (972)807-6883
Guilbeau, Merlin, Exec. Dir.

Emergency Medicine Foundation [14678]
1125 Executive Cir.
Irving, TX 75038-2522
Toll free: 800-798-1822
Heard, Robert, CAE, Exec. Dir.

Emergency Medicine Residents' Association [14679]
1125 Executive Cir.
Irving, TX 75038
PH: (972)550-0920
Toll free: 866-566-2492
Fax: (972)692-5995
Celeste, Jordan, MD, Bd. Member

Energy Telecommunications and Electrical Association [1022]
5005 W Royal Ln., Ste. 291
Irving, TX 75063
Toll free: 888-503-8700
Nation, Richard, Secretary, Treasurer

Hearts Across Romania [11019]
2544 Brookside Dr.
Irving, TX 75063-3172
PH: (972)849-4359
Achiriloaie, Mariana, Founder, Bd. Member

International Association of Microsoft Channel Partners [6276]
c/o The TransSynergy Group
909 Lake Carolyn Pky., Ste. 320
Irving, TX 75039
PH: (425)746-1572
Mackay, Gail Mercer, President

International Black Aerospace Council [140]
7120 Sugar Maple Dr.
Irving, TX 75063-5522
PH: (972)373-9551
Fax: (972)373-9551
Eddins, Lt. Col. Tim, Treasurer

Mothers Against Drunk Driving [12827]
511 E John Carpenter Fwy., Ste. 700
Irving, TX 75062-3983
Toll free: 877-275-6233
Fax: (972)869-2206
Strickland, David, Chmn. of the Bd.

National Catholic Committee on Scouting [12855]
1325 W Walnut Hill Ln.
Irving, TX 75038-3008
PH: (972)580-2114
Fax: (972)580-2535
Sparks, George, Chairman

National Collegiate Baseball Writers Association [2699]
c/o Russell Anderson, Associate Executive Director

Conference USA
5201 N O'Connor Blvd., Ste. 300
Irving, TX 75039-3765
PH: (214)418-6132
Anderson, Russell, Assoc. Dir.

National Colorbred Association [21543]
c/o Henry Vela, Treasurer
620 Arawe Cir. E
Irving, TX 75060
Vela, Henry, Treasurer

National Eagle Scout Association [12856]
Boy Scouts of America
1325 W Walnut Hill Ln.
Irving, TX 75038-3008
PH: (972)580-2000
Adams, Glenn, President

National Football Foundation and College Hall of Fame [22860]
433 E Las Colinas Blvd., Ste. 1130
Irving, TX 75039
PH: (972)556-1000
Fax: (972)556-9032
Manning, Archie, Chairman

The National Jewish Committee on Scouting [12859]
Boy Scouts of America
PO Box 152079
Irving, TX 75015-2091
PH: (972)580-2000
Hyman, Peter, Chap.

National Society of Hispanic MBAs [659]
450 E John Carpenter Fwy., Ste. 200
Irving, TX 75062
PH: (214)596-9338
Toll free: 877-467-4622
Fax: (214)596-9325
Lopez, Anthony, Chairman

Plastics Pipe Institute [2614]
105 Decker Ct., Ste. 825
Irving, TX 75062
PH: (469)499-1044
Fax: (469)499-1063
Radoszewski, Tony, President

Promotional Products Association International [107]
3125 Skyway Cir. N
Irving, TX 75038-3526
PH: (972)252-0404
Toll free: 888-426-7724
Fax: (972)258-3004
Bellantone, Paul, CAE, CEO, President

Radio Advertising Bureau [108]
1320 Greenway Dr., Ste. 500
Irving, TX 75038-2587
Toll free: 800-232-3131
Farber, Erica, President, CEO

SER National [11783]
100 E Royal Ln., Ste. 130
Irving, TX 75039
PH: (469)549-3600
Fax: (469)549-3684
Moran, Margaret, V. Chmn. of the Bd.

Society of Emergency Medicine Physician Assistants [16727]
4950 W Royal Ln.
Irving, TX 75063
Toll free: 877-297-7594
Parker, Michelle, Exec. Dir.

United States Helice Association [23143]
7750 N MacArthur Blvd., Ste. 120-324

Irving, TX 75063
PH: (817)296-3104
Crum, Dr. Glen, President

VHA [15339]
290 E John Carpenter Fwy.
Irving, TX 75062
Toll free: 800-750-4972
Nonomaque, Curt, CEO, President

Vintage Radio and Phonograph Society [22406]
PO Box 165345
Irving, TX 75016-5345
PH: (972)742-8085
Sargent, Jim, President

World Presidents Organization [675]
600 E Las Colinas Blvd., Ste. 1000
Irving, TX 75039
PH: (972)587-1500
(972)587-1618
Toll free: 800-773-7976
Fax: (972)587-1611

Young Presidents' Organization [676]
600 E Las Colinas Blvd., Ste. 1000
Irving, TX 75039
PH: (972)587-1500
Toll free: 800-773-7976
Fax: (972)587-1611
Auyang, Bernie, Chairman

National Gardening Association [22112]
5452 County Road 1405
Jacksonville, TX 75766
Metallo, Michael, Contact

National Cursillo Movement [19883]
PO Box 799
Jarrell, TX 76537
PH: (512)746-2020
Fax: (512)746-2030
Tran, Hoang, Administrator

United We Serve [21046]
5645 US Highway 59 S
Jefferson, TX 75657
PH: (903)665-2647

Southwestern Donkey and Mule Society [21284]
PO Box 1633
Johnson City, TX 78636
PH: (830)868-4645
Tippie, Jim, President

SPARK Worldwide [11155]
PO Box 1349
Joshua, TX 76058
PH: (817)645-6200
Fax: (817)645-2208
Brewer, Leanna, Founder, CEO

American Meat Goat Association [2309]
PO Box 333
Junction, TX 76849-0333
PH: (915)446-3921
Laning, Bill, President

Clan Young Society [20845]
5414 Tim Donald Rd.
Justin, TX 76247

National Association of State Election Directors [18184]
21946 Royal Montreal Dr., Ste. 100
Katy, TX 77450
PH: (281)396-4314
Fax: (281)396-4315
Giles, Bob, Treasurer

National Firearms Act Trade and Collectors Association [1293]
20603 Big Wells Dr.
Katy, TX 77449-6269

PH: (281)492-8288
Toll free: 866-897-0182
Brown, John, President

Vegan Society of People for the
Earth, Animals, Compassion and
Enlightenment [17585]
PO Box 6128
Katy, TX 77491-6128
PH: (832)303-0834
Ohanyan, Kristen Lee, President,
Founder

Guinea Fowl International Association [3662]
2812 FM 987
Kaufman, TX 75142
Gibson, Cindy, President

World Health Services [15509]
PO Box 186
Keene, TX 76059
PH: (817)933-2088
Simons, Barbie, President

Council of Educators in Landscape
Architecture [4444]
PO Box 1915
Keller, TX 76244
PH: (817)741-9730
Fax: (817)741-9731
Taylor, Mr. Pat D., Exec. Dir.

Glocal Ventures, Inc. [12156]
1870 Rufe Snow Dr.
Keller, TX 76248-5629
PH: (817)656-5136
Fax: (817)656-4671
Roberts, Bob, Jr., Founder, Chair-
man

Hobby Distiller's Association [21262]
5970 Park Vista Cir., Ste. 190
Keller, TX 76244
PH: (817)750-2739

International Wheelchair Aviators
[21235]
82 Corral Dr.
Keller, TX 76244
PH: (817)229-4634

National Pawnbrokers Association
[2095]
PO Box 508
Keller, TX 76248
PH: (817)337-8830
Fax: (817)337-8875
Meinecke, Dana, Exec. Dir.

Bread for Life International [12078]
PO Box 291307
Kerrville, TX 78029
PH: (830)896-8326
Fax: (830)866-5262
Ehabe, Ernest, President

Standard Schnauzer Club of
America [21967]
c/o Lynne Schuneman, Membership
Chairperson
2903 Dry Hollow Dr.
Kerrville, TX 78028-8051
Mohrenweiser, Liz, President

New Hope for Cambodian Children
[11097]
PO Box 690597
Killeen, TX 76549
Tucker, John, Founder, Advisor

National Junior Santa Gertrudis As-
sociation [3743]
PO Box 1257
Kingsville, TX 78364
PH: (361)592-9357
Fax: (361)592-8572
Ford, John E., Exec. Dir.

Santa Gertrudis Breeders
International [3755]
PO Box 1257
Kingsville, TX 78364
PH: (361)592-9357
Fax: (361)592-8572
Ford, John E., Exec. Dir.

The Atlas Society [10080]
800 Rockmead Dr., Ste. 200
Kingwood, TX 77339-9958
PH: (202)296-7263
Fax: (202)296-0771
Grossman, Jennifer, CEO

Big Thicket Natural Heritage Trust
[3820]
Box 1049
Kountze, TX 77625
Ruppel, Jan, President

Communications Marketing Associa-
tion [3221]
PO Box 5680
Lago Vista, TX 78645
PH: (512)267-7747
Walsh, Elaine Baugh, Comm. Chm.

Foundation for Rational Economics
and Education [18036]
PO Box 1776
Lake Jackson, TX 77566
Paul, Congressman Ron, Founder,
Chairman

National Electric Drag Racing Association [22828]
264 Plum Cir.
Lake Jackson, TX 77566
Metric, John, President

National Military Fish and Wildlife
Association [4845]
103 W Highway 33
Lake Jackson, TX 77566
PH: (831)656-2850
(720)542-3085
Cobb, Coralie, President

Proclaim Justice [18074]
2303 RR 620 S
Lakeway, TX 78734
PH: (512)605-7525
Baldwin, Jason, Founder

Textile Exchange [4518]
511 S 1st St.
Lamesa, TX 79331
PH: (806)428-3411
Pepper, La Rhea, Managing Dir.

International Association of Canine
Professionals [3986]
PO Box 928
Lampasas, TX 76550
PH: (512)564-1011
Fax: (512)556-4220
Deeley, Martin, Exec. Dir.

American Society of Bookplate Collectors and Designers [21615]
5802 Bullock Loop, Ste. C1 No.
84404
Laredo, TX 78041-8807
Keenan, James P., Director

Country School Association of
America [9384]
210 N Kansas Ave.
League City, TX 77573
PH: (281)554-2994
Dewalt, Dr. Mark, VP

International Association of Hispanic
Meeting Professionals [2332]
2600 S Shore Blvd., Ste. 300
League City, TX 77573-2944
PH: (281)245-3330
Fax: (281)668-9199
Gonzalez, Margaret, Founder,
President

Legal Secretaries International [75]
2951 Marina Bay Dr., Ste. 130-641
League City, TX 77573-2735
PH: (713)651-2933
Fax: (713)651-2908
Harbolt, Elizabeth, President

Lisle Intercultural Project [8084]
PO Box 1932
Leander, TX 78646
PH: (512)259-4404
Toll free: 800-477-1538
Kinney, Bill, President

American Suffolk Horse Association
[4329]
c/o Mary Margaret Read, Secretary
4240 Goehring Rd.
Ledbetter, TX 78946-5004
PH: (979)249-5795
Jensen, Jerry F., VP

Alport Syndrome Hope for the Cure
Foundation [14806]
2560 King Arthur Blvd., Ste. 124-76
Lewisville, TX 75056
PH: (469)951-6533
De Serrano, Jodi, Founder,
President

American Donkey and Mule Society
[3592]
PO Box 1210
Lewisville, TX 75067
PH: (972)219-0781
Patton, Leah, Office Mgr.

Bhojpuri Association of North
America [9649]
801 Hebron Pky., No. 7210
Lewisville, TX 75057
Mishra, Mr. Sailesh, Chairman

Cleaning for a Reason [10786]
211 S Stemmons, Ste. G
Lewisville, TX 75067
Toll free: 877-337-3348
Frankenfield, Lynne, Exec. Dir.

American Deer and Wildlife Alliance
[4782]
PO Box 10
Liberty Hill, TX 78642
Perry, Mathew, Officer

Escapees [22422]
100 Rainbow Dr.
Livingston, TX 77351-9340
PH: (936)327-8873
Toll free: 888-757-2582
Fax: (936)327-4388
Carr, Cathie, President

American Indian Horse Registry
[4313]
9028 State Park Rd.
Lockhart, TX 78644-4310
PH: (512)398-6642
Falley, Nanci, President

American Syringomyelia & Chiari
Alliance Project [15901]
PO Box 1586
Longview, TX 75606-1586
PH: (903)236-7079
Toll free: 800-ASAP-282
Fax: (903)757-7456
Schaublin, Patrice, President

Educational Research Analysts
[8692]
PO Box 7518
Longview, TX 75607-7518
PH: (903)753-5993
Fax: (903)753-8424
Frey, Neal, President

Missionary TECH Team [20442]
25 FRJ Dr.
Longview, TX 75602-4703

PH: (903)757-4530
Toll free: 800-871-7795
Wiley, Birne D., Founder

American Cowboy Culture Associa-
tion [8800]
PO Box 6638
Lubbock, TX 79493
PH: (806)798-7825
Querner, Mike, Bd. Member

American Leather Chemists Associa-
tion [6183]
1314 50th St., Ste. 103
Lubbock, TX 79412-2940
PH: (806)744-1798
Fax: (806)744-1785
Adcock, Carol, Exec. Sec.

American Society of Forensic Odontology [14416]
4414 82nd St., Ste. 212
Lubbock, TX 79424
Schrader, Dr. Bruce, Exec. Dir.

Architectural Research Centers
Consortium [5959]
c/o Saif Haq, Treasurer
College of Architecture, Rm. 604B
Texas Tech University
1800 Flint Ave.
Lubbock, TX 79409-2091
PH: (806)834-6317
Rinehart, Michelle A., President

Asociación National de Sacerdotes
Hispanos en Estados Unidos
[19795]
1120 52nd St.
Lubbock, TX 79411
PH: (806)781-7832
Solorzano, Rev. Miguel, Secretary

Association for Politics and the Life
Sciences [7044]
c/o Gregg R. Murray, PhD, Execu-
tive Director
Texas Tech University
Political Science Dept.
Lubbock, TX 79409
PH: (806)834-4017
Murray, Gregg R., PhD, Exec. Dir.

Association for the Study of Free
Institutions [7954]
c/o Stephen H. Balch, Chairman
Institute for the Study of Western
Civilization
Box 41017
Lubbock, TX 79409-1017
PH: (806)834-8289
Holloway, Carson, Exec. Dir.

International Society for Aeolian
Research [6693]
c/o Dr. Jeff Lee, Secretary/Treasurer
Dept. of Geosciences
Texas Tech University
Lubbock, TX 79409-1053
Bullard, Dr. Joanna E., President

Kappa Delta Chi Sorority [23799]
PO Box 4317
Lubbock, TX 79409
Rodriguez, Melanie, President

Mathematical Study Unit [22342]
c/o Monty Strauss
4209 88th St.
Lubbock, TX 79423
Strauss, Monty J., Officer

National Sorghum Producers [3767]
4201 N Interstate 27
Lubbock, TX 79403-7507
PH: (806)749-3478
Toll free: 800-658-9808
Fax: (806)749-9002
Lust, Tim, CEO

National Storm Shelter Association
[3464]
c/o TTU Student Media Bldg.
1009 Canton Ave., Rm. 117
Lubbock, TX 79409
Toll free: 877-700-6772
Fax: (806)742-3446
Kiesling, Dr. Ernst W., Exec. Dir.

Physicians Aiding Physicians Abroad
[15057]
3004 50th St, Ste. D
Lubbock, TX 79413
PH: (806)729-9061
Sheets, Kyle, MD, Founder, Chairman

Ranching Heritage Association
[9509]
3121 4th St.
Lubbock, TX 79409
Spears, Tony, President

Society for Eighteenth-Century
Music [10005]
School of Music
Texas Tech University
Lubbock, TX 79409-2033
Fax: (806)742-2294
Eyerly, Sarah, President

Tau Sigma Delta [23678]
c/o Maria Jeffrey, Administrartive Assistant
College of Architecture, Box 42091
Texas Tech University
Lubbock, TX 79409
Fowler, Thomas, President

Teethsavers International [14472]
3306 34th St.
Lubbock, TX 79410
PH: (806)368-7513
Lee, Beth, President

National Puro Conjunto Music Association [9978]
9200 Lockwood Springs Rd.
Manor, TX 78653
PH: (512)853-0034
Balderrama, Arturo, Founder

International Federation of Leather
Guilds [2082]
c/o David Smith, Executive Director
10 Park Pl.
Mansfield, TX 76063
PH: (817)453-2386
Smith, Dave, Exec. Dir.

National Fishing Lure Collectors
Club [21694]
PO Box 509
Mansfield, TX 76063
PH: (817)473-6748
Hays, Steve, President

We Care Act [11681]
2722 Garden Falls Dr.
Manvel, TX 77578
PH: (832)298-5888
Li, Grace, Founder

National Hispanic Institute [9360]
PO Box 220
Maxwell, TX 78656
PH: (512)357-6137
Fax: (512)357-2206
Nieto, Ernesto, Founder, President

Association of Arts Administration
Educators [7507]
PO Box 721031
McAllen, TX 78504
PH: (312)469-0795
Laughlin, Sherburne, VP

Optometric Retina Society [16437]
4500 Knightsbridge Dr.
McKinney, TX 75070

PH: (214)548-6345

Reach Out Honduras [11139]
PO Box 2993
McKinney, TX 75070
Ginn, Clay, President, Chmn. of the
Bd.

Federation of Fire Chaplains [19926]
c/o Ed Stauffer, Executive Director
PO Box 437
Meridian, TX 76665
PH: (254)435-2256
Fax: (254)435-2256
Cook, Jim, Secretary

Alford American Family Association
[20777]
427 Wheatridge St.
Mesquite, TX 75150-5857
PH: (972)288-1175
Alford, Max Ray, President, Chmn.
of the Bd.

Art Greenhaw Official International
Fan Club [24023]
105 Broad St.
105 Broad St.
Mesquite, TX 75149-4201
PH: (214)739-2664
Carlson, Larry, Mgr.

China Aid Association [20569]
PO Box 8513
Midland, TX 79708
PH: (432)689-6985
Toll free: 888-889-7757
Fax: (432)686-8355
Xiqiu, Bob Fu, Founder, President

Electronic Components Certification
Corporation [1042]
1002 Shell Ave.
Midland, TX 79705
Baker, Don, Director

National Association of University-
Model Schools [7638]
103 N 1st St.
Midlothian, TX 76065
PH: (972)525-7005
Toll free: 888-485-8525
Fax: (888)506-6597
Freeman, Barbara Nicholson, MEd,
Exec. Dir.

Stampe Club International [21249]
2940 Falcon Way
Midlothian, TX 76065
PH: (214)723-1504
Peterson, Don, Contact

Society of Composers, Inc. [9185]
PO Box 687
Mineral Wells, TX 76068-0687
McFerron, Mike, Chmn. of the Exec.
Committee

Bihar Association of North America
[9565]
3618 Battle Creek Dr.
Missouri City, TX 77459
PH: (281)892-9187
Jha, Santosh, President

Coalition for Justice in the
Maquiladoras [19103]
3611 Golden Tee Ln.
Missouri City, TX 77459
PH: (210)732-8957
      (210)210-1084
Ojeda, Martha A., Exec. Dir.

International Academy of
Compounding Pharmacists [16664]
4638 Riverstone Blvd.
Missouri City, TX 77459-6157
PH: (281)933-8400
Toll free: 800-927-4227
Fax: (281)495-0602
Stephens, Pat, Chmn. of the Bd.

National Medical Malpractice
Advocacy Association [12052]
9119 Hwy. 6, Ste. 230
Missouri City, TX 77459
Toll free: 800-379-1054
Dickson-Gilbert, Deirdre, Director,
Founder

Phi Beta Mu [23830]
c/o David Lambert, Executive
Secretary
3323 Meadowcreek Dr.
Missouri City, TX 77459
Lambert, David, Exec. Sec.

Scottish Terrier Club of America
[21959]
c/o Kelli Edell, Membership Chairman
2727 Cheryl Ct.
Missouri City, TX 77459-2930
PH: (281)261-6031
Kelly, Lori, President

Toyota Territory Off-Roaders Association [22435]
1715 Earl Porter Dr.
Mont Belvieu, TX 77580
PH: (281)414-1645
Fax: (281)576-5413
Brookshire, Shannon, Founder

Flying Physicians Association
[16751]
11626 Twain Dr.
Montgomery, TX 77356
PH: (936)588-6505
Fax: (832)415-0287
Johnson, Douglas W., President

Intervention & Coiled Tubing Association [7036]
PO Box 1082. 8
Montgomery, TX 77356
PH: (936)520-1549
Fax: (832)201-9977
Babin, Allison, Administrator,
Secretary

Powder Coating Institute [747]
PO Box 2112
Montgomery, TX 77356
PH: (936)597-5060
Toll free: 800-988-2628
Fax: (936)597-5059
Sudges, John, President

Reynolds Family Association [20919]
c/o Larry Reynolds, President
1007 Stone Shore St.
Mount Pleasant, TX 75455
PH: (903)717-8608
Jones, Debbie, Registrar

Colored Angora Goat Breeder's Association [4275]
c/o Polly Holmes, Treasurer
2JP Ranch
150 Scenic Dr.
Mountain Home, TX 78058-2152
PH: (817)675-9352
Meyer, Cheryl, President

OSU Tour [11796]
120 E FM 544, Ste. 72, No. 108
Murphy, TX 75094
Spinks, Jonathan, CEO, President

American Blue Cattle Association,
Inc. [3685]
PO Box 633404
Nacogdoches, TX 75963
PH: (936)652-2550
Brooks, Connie, Bd. Member

Mosquito Association, Inc. [20684]
2202 County Road 331
Nacogdoches, TX 75961
Parther, Hal, Secretary

Special Interest Group on Ada
[7059]
c/o David Cook, Chairperson
PO Box 13063
Nacogdoches, TX 75962
PH: (936)468-2508
Fax: (936)468-7086
Cook, David, Chairperson

Painted Desert Sheep Society
[4681]
11819 Puska Rd.
Needville, TX 77461
PH: (979)793-4207
Garza, Anita, Founder

The Crustacean Society [7400]
1320 Winding Way
New Braunfels, TX 78132
PH: (210)842-9152
Belk, Mary, Exec. Dir.

American Rosie the Riveter Association [21191]
c/o Stephanie Davis
8336 Valley Oak Dr.
North Richland Hills, TX 76182
PH: (205)822-4106
Toll free: 888-557-6743
Carter, Dr. Frances Tunnell, Exec.
Dir., Founder

Automotive Service Association
[341]
8209 Mid Cities Blvd.
North Richland Hills, TX 76182-
4712
PH: (817)514-2900
      (817)514-2900
Fax: (817)514-0770
Seyfer, Donny, Chairman

Rotarian Action Group for the Alleviation of Hunger and Malnutrition [12111]
4015 Boulder Ave.
Odessa, TX 79762
Fax: (432)550-0538
Bobanick, David, President

One-Arm Dove Hunt Association
[22794]
PO Box 582
Olney, TX 76374
Northrup, Jack, Founder

Trull Foundation [12498]
404 4th St.
Palacios, TX 77465
PH: (361)972-5241
Fax: (361)972-1109
Trull, R. Scott, Chmn. of the Bd.

STARFLEET [24081]
c/o Wayne Killough, President
1053 E Palestine Ave., Apt. 204
Palestine, TX 75801
Toll free: 888-734-8735
Blaser, Dave, Cmdr.

Council on Diagnostic Imaging
[17056]
c/o Doctor Brian Batenchuk,
President
PO Box 5092
Pasadena, TX 77508
PH: (281)881-4578
Fax: (281)954-6800
Strehlow, Ammon, VP

Christian Alliance For Humanitarian
Aid, Inc. [12640]
1525 Mmain St., L-3
Pearland, TX 77581
PH: (281)412-2285
      (713)644-2010
Stokely, Fran, President, Treasurer

PBCers Organization [15258]
1426 Garden Rd.
Pearland, TX 77581

PH: (346)302-1620
Moore, Linda A., Founder, President

Primary Biliary Cirrhosis Organization **[14611]**
1426 Garden Rd.
Pearland, TX 77581
PH: (346)302-1620
Moore, Linie A., CEO, Founder

ATAYAL **[9574]**
900 E Pecan St., Ste. 300
Pflugerville, TX 78660
PH: (407)459-7766
Coolidge, Tony, Exec. Dir.

National Foster Parent Association **[12418]**
1102 Prairie Ridge Trl.
Pflugerville, TX 78660
Toll free: 800-557-5238
Fax: (888)925-5634
Clements, Irene, Exec. Dir.

Railway and Locomotive Historical Society **[10190]**
PO Box 2913
Pflugerville, TX 78691-2913
PH: (512)989-2480
Holzweiss, Robert, President

National Reined Cow Horse Association **[22155]**
1017 N Highway 377
Pilot Point, TX 76258
PH: (940)488-1500
Fax: (940)488-1499
Crawford, Todd, Chairperson

American Goat Society **[3593]**
PO Box 63748
Pipe Creek, TX 78063
PH: (830)535-4247
Fax: (830)535-4561
Kowalik, Amy, Registrar

Vawter - Vauter - Vaughter Family Association **[20940]**
c/o Patricia Vawter Renton
2372 Bear Creek Rd.
Pipe Creek, TX 78063
PH: (903)624-9632
Vawter, Bruce, President

American Fence Association **[799]**
6404 International Pky., Ste. 2048-A
Plano, TX 75093
Toll free: 800-822-4342
Fax: (314)480-7118
Gregg, David, President

American Muslim Women Physicians Association **[16736]**
6300 Stonewood Dr., Ste. 412
Plano, TX 75025
Ashfaq, Dr. Raheela, Bd. Member

Association of Indian Pathologists in North America **[16577]**
1812 Kings Isle Dr.
Plano, TX 75093-2422
Singh, Meenakshi, Dr., Liaison

Center for American and International Law **[5420]**
5201 Democracy Dr.
Plano, TX 75024
PH: (972)244-3400
Toll free: 800-409-1090
Fax: (972)244-3401
Miers, Harliet E., Chairman

Cheng Ming USA **[22988]**
3916 McDermott Dr., Ste. 160
Plano, TX 75025
PH: (972)740-8458
Hung, Eric, Inst.

East West Ministries International **[12472]**
2001 W Plano Pky., Ste. 3000
Plano, TX 75075-8644

PH: (972)941-4500
Fax: (469)440-7633
Whitehead, Bruce, Director

Exposition Services & Contractors Association **[2328]**
5068 W Plano Pky., Ste. 300
Plano, TX 75093
PH: (972)447-8212
Toll free: 877-792-3722
Fax: (972)447-8209
Arnaudet, Larry, Exec. Dir.

Hemochromatosis Information Society **[15247]**
3017 Princeton Dr.
Plano, TX 75075
PH: (214)702-2698
Edwards, Jason, Exec. Dir.

Ice Skating Institute **[23150]**
6000 Custer Rd., Bldg. 9
Plano, TX 75023
PH: (972)735-8800
Fax: (972)735-8815
Kibat, Elizabeth, Controller

International Oral Cancer Association **[13992]**
424 Maplelawn Dr.
Plano, TX 75075
PH: (972)612-7886
Fax: (972)612-7842
Fitzgerald, Armaiti, Founder

Lowe Syndrome Association **[14838]**
PO Box 864346
Plano, TX 75086-4346
PH: (972)733-1338
Jacobs, Debbie, President

National Association of Mortgage Brokers **[408]**
2701 W 15th St., Ste. 536
Plano, TX 75075
PH: (972)758-1151
Fax: (530)484-2906
Stevens, John, VP

National Tick-Borne Disease Advocates **[15412]**
PO Box 866096
Plano, TX 75086
PH: (972)832-6703
Torrey, Lisa, Contact

Probe Ministries International **[7614]**
2001 W Plano Pky., Ste. 2000
Plano, TX 75075
PH: (972)941-4565
Anderson, Kerby, President

Research Advocacy Network **[14055]**
6505 W Park Blvd., Ste. 305
Plano, TX 75093
Toll free: 877-276-2187
Smith, Mary Lou, President, Founder

Restaurant Facility Management Association **[2941]**
5600 Tennyson Pky., Ste. 265
Plano, TX 75024
PH: (972)805-0905
Fax: (972)805-0906
Tomson, Tracy, Exec. Dir.

Society of Diagnostic Medical Sonography **[17233]**
2745 Dallas Pky., Ste. 350
Plano, TX 75093-8730
PH: (214)473-8057
Toll free: 800-229-9506
Fax: (214)473-8563
Rodriguez, Mary, COO, Dep. Dir.

Apostleship of the Sea in the United States of America **[19793]**
1500 Jefferson Dr.
Port Arthur, TX 77642-0646

PH: (409)985-4545
Fax: (409)985-5945
Tordillo, Señor Myrna, MSCS, Director

Meningitis Angels **[14594]**
PO Box 448
Porter, TX 77365-0448
PH: (281)572-1998
Milley, Frankie, Exec. Dir., Founder

American Half Quarter Horse Registry **[4309]**
PO Box 693
Proctor, TX 76468
PH: (254)592-7827

On the Lighter Side, International Lighter Collectors **[21707]**
PO Box 1733
Quitman, TX 75783
Sanders, Judith, Secretary

African Blackwood Conservation Project **[3790]**
PO Box 26
Red Rock, TX 78662
Harris, James E., Founder

Alliance for Higher Education **[7951]**
2602 Rutford Ave.
Richardson, TX 75080
PH: (972)234-8373
Smith, Maria, Director

CHRISTAR **[20396]**
1500 International Pky., Ste. 300
Richardson, TX 75081
PH: (214)838-3800
Toll free: 800-755-7955
Fax: (214)237-7515
Coffey, Steve, President

Council on Ionizing Radiation Measurements and Standards **[7081]**
PO Box 851391
Richardson, TX 75085-1391
PH: (301)591-8776
Fax: (972)883-5725
Voit, Walter E., President

Distribution Contractors Association **[23502]**
101 W Renner Rd., Ste. 460
Richardson, TX 75082-2024
PH: (972)680-0261
Fax: (972)680-0461
Anderson, Dale, President

Heritage Rose Foundation **[22099]**
PO Box 831414
Richardson, TX 75083
Scanniello, Stephen, President

International Association of Electrical Inspectors **[1023]**
901 Waterfall Way, Ste. 602
Richardson, TX 75080
PH: (972)235-1455
Toll free: 800-786-4234
Clements, David, Exec. Dir., CEO

International Cessna 120/140 Association **[21230]**
PO Box 830092
Richardson, TX 75083
PH: (989)339-1009
Adkins, Gene, VP

John Gary International Fan Club **[24049]**
7 Briarwood Cir.
Richardson, TX 75080-4854

Kappa Psi Pharmaceutical Fraternity, Inc. **[23844]**
2060 N Collins Blvd., Ste. 128
Richardson, TX 75080-2657

PH: (972)479-1879
Fax: (972)231-5171
Porter, Johnny W., Exec. Dir.

Muslim American Society **[20500]**
1206 Apollo Rd., No. 851255
Richardson, TX 75085
PH: (913)888-5555
Siddiqi, Nadeem, Chairman

National Association of Church Business Administration **[20562]**
100 N Central Expy., Ste. 914
Richardson, TX 75080-5326
PH: (972)699-7555
Toll free: 800-898-8085
Fax: (972)699-7617
Mirau, Tammy, Admin. Asst.

National Association of Shooting Sports Athletes **[23134]**
2103 Wheaton Dr.
Richardson, TX 75081
Ordesch, Edward L., Act. Pres.

National Write Your Congressman **[18917]**
2435 N Central Expy., Ste. 300
Richardson, TX 75080
PH: (214)342-0299
Fax: (214)324-2455

Ogbaru National Association **[12054]**
PO Box 832701
Richardson, TX 75083
PH: (214)734-1343
Chukwuemeka, Odili P., President

Production and Operations Management Society **[2190]**
The University of Texas at Dallas
800 W Campbell Rd., SM 30
Richardson, TX 75080
PH: (972)883-4834
Fax: (972)883-5834
Gupta, Prof. Sushil, PhD, Exec. Dir.

Society for Mathematical Psychology **[7073]**
c/o Richard Golden, Secretary-Treasurer
University of Texas at Dallas
School of Behavioral and Brain Sciences, GR41
800 W Campbell Rd.
Richardson, TX 75080
Criss, Amy, President

Society of Petroleum Engineers **[6595]**
222 Palisades Creek Dr.
Richardson, TX 75080-2040
PH: (972)952-9393
Toll free: 800-456-6863
Fax: (972)952-9435
Fattahi, Behrooz, President

United States Dog Agility Association **[22821]**
PO Box 850955
Richardson, TX 75085
PH: (972)487-2200
Fax: (972)231-9700
Tatsch, Kenneth, President

Brahman Samaj of North America **[20200]**
c/o BSNA Treasurer
8418 Bishop Oaks Dr.
Richmond, TX 77406
Pandey, Sanjay, VP

Nouris International **[13078]**
4029 Dellman Dr.
Roanoke, TX 76262

American Angora Goat Breeder's Association **[3587]**
PO Box 195
Rocksprings, TX 78880

PH: (830)683-4483
Fax: (830)683-2559
Flach, Freddie, Director

Christian Wrestling Federation [23370]
331 County Line Rd.
Rockwall, TX 75032
PH: (214)460-0477
Vaughn, Rob, Founder

Souvenir Building Collectors Society [21722]
c/o Katherine Isbell, Treasurer
809 Jackson St.
Rockwall, TX 75087-6106
PH: (703)532-4532
    (703)477-4781
Misuriellio, Harry, Dir. of Member
Svcs.

CADASIL Together We Have Hope [14567]
3605 Monument Dr.
Round Rock, TX 78681-3707
PH: (512)255-0209
Toll free: 877-519-4673
Duncan-Smith, Billie, Founder

National Episcopal Scouters Association [12857]
PO Box 294
Round Top, TX 78954

Committee on Accreditation for Educational Programs for the Emergency Medical Services Professions [8295]
8301 Lakeview Pky., Ste. 111-312
Rowlett, TX 75088
PH: (214)703-8445
Fax: (214)703-8992
Hatch, George W., Jr., Exec. Dir.

Road Map Collectors Association [21720]
PO Box 478
Rowlett, TX 75030
Perucca, Kirk P., VP

Three Dog Night Fan Club [24065]
c/o Madonna Nuckolls, President
PO Box 1975
Rowlett, TX 75030
Nuckolls, Madonna, Editor, President

International Union of Industrial and Independent Workers [23534]
5250 Highway 78, Ste. 750-227
Sachse, TX 75048
Miller, Jim, Secretary, Treasurer

National Public Parks Tennis Association [23303]
c/o Ron Melvin, President
13925 FM 1346
Saint Hedwig, TX 78152
McAllister, Ken, President

Dance/Drill Team Directors of America [9251]
339 Van Bibber Rd.
Salado, TX 76571
PH: (254)947-0613
Toll free: 800-462-5719
Fax: (254)947-3040
Pennington, Joyce Eaton, Owner,
President, CEO

International Willow Collectors [21680]
c/o Brenda Nottingham, Membership
Chairperson
969 County Road 3357
Saltillo, TX 75478
Kowen, Ken, Treasurer

Angelo State University Alumni Association [19304]
ASU Station No. 11049
San Angelo, TX 76909
Tutle, Gene, President

Gilstrap Family Association [20870]
1921 N Harrison
San Angelo, TX 76901-1335
PH: (325)949-0792
Gilstrap, Marcus D., Contact

Mohair Council of America [3604]
233 W Twohig Ave.
San Angelo, TX 76903
PH: (325)655-3161
Toll free: 800-583-3161
Hartgrove, Mary, Exec. Dir.

Acid Maltase Deficiency Association [13499]
PO Box 700248
San Antonio, TX 78270-0248
PH: (210)494-6144
Fax: (210)490-7161
House, Tiffany, President

Air Weather Reconnaissance Association [21104]
c/o Bernie Barris, Membership
Chairman
11019 Oaktree Park
San Antonio, TX 78249-4440
PH: (760)793-4733
Faubus, Stoney, President

American Association of Anthropological Genetics [6663]
c/o Ellen Quillen, Secretary/
Treasurer
Texas Biomedical Research Institute
Dept. of Genetics
San Antonio, TX 78245
Quillen, Ellen, PhD, Secretary,
Treasurer

American Blind Golf [22872]
c/o Bruce Hooper, Co-Director
7410 Quail Run Dr.
San Antonio, TX 78209-3129
PH: (210)822-6366
Hooper, Bruce, Director

American Clinical and Climatological Association [14286]
c/o Richard A. Lange, MD,
Secretary-Treasurer
507 Blackjack Oak
San Antonio, TX 78230
PH: (210)567-4812
Fax: (210)567-4654
Lange, Richard A., MD, Secretary,
Treasurer

American Council for Construction Education [7662]
1717 N Loop 1604 E, Ste. 320
San Antonio, TX 78232-1570
PH: (210)495-6161
Fax: (210)495-6168
Carr, Jim, Treasurer

American Druze Society [20215]
PO Box 781628
San Antonio, TX 78278
Faraj, Dr. Walid, Director

American Payroll Association - San Antonio [1083]
660 N Main Ave., Ste. 100
San Antonio, TX 78205-1217
PH: (210)226-4600
    (210)224-6406
Fax: (210)226-4027
Maddux, Daniel J., Exec. Dir.

American Psychotherapy and Medical Hypnosis Association [16963]
11827 Button Willow Cove
San Antonio, TX 78213
PH: (956)203-0608
Mugford, J. Gerry, Dr., President

American Society of Primatologists [5903]
c/o Dr. Corinna Ross, Treasurer
Dept. of Arts and Sciences

Texas A&M University
1 University Way
San Antonio, TX 78224
PH: (210)784-2227
Fax: (210)784-2299
Phillips, Kimberley, PhD, President

American Sunrise [11961]
2007 W Commerce St.
San Antonio, TX 78207-3836
PH: (210)212-2227
Cisneros, Mary Alice P., Founder,
President

Army Nurse Corps Association [15838]
8000 IH-10
San Antonio, TX 78218-1235
PH: (210)650-3534
Fax: (210)650-3494
Bartz, Claudia C., President

Association of Christian Investigators [5355]
2553 Jackson Keller Rd., Ste. 200
San Antonio, TX 78230
PH: (210)342-0509
Fax: (210)342-0731
Riddle, Kelly, President

Association of Medical and Graduate Departments of Biochemistry [6052]
c/o Bruce J. Nicholson, President
University of Texas
7703 Floyd Curl Dr., MC 7760
San Antonio, TX 78229-3901
PH: (210)567-3770
Fax: (210)567-6595
Nicholson, Bruce J., President

Beefmaster Breeders United [3719]
6800 Park 10 Blvd., Ste. 290 W
San Antonio, TX 78213
PH: (210)732-3132
Fax: (210)732-7711
Pendergrass, Bill, Exec. VP

BISH Foundation [13902]
20770 US 281 N, No. 108-114
San Antonio, TX 78258
PH: (210)287-9881
Gonzalez, Darlene, President

Braunvieh Association of America [3721]
c/o Patti Teeler, Frances Miller
5750 Epsilon, Ste. 200
San Antonio, TX 78249-3407
PH: (210)561-2892
Fax: (210)696-5031
Jernigan, Jerry, VP

Burleson Family Association [20791]
14343 Markham Glen
San Antonio, TX 78247
Mills, Kaye P., VP

Care Highway International [12632]
PO Box 100986
San Antonio, TX 78201
Morrison, Christopher, Director,
Founder

Catholic Life Insurance [19402]
1635 NE Loop 410
San Antonio, TX 78209-1625
PH: (210)828-9921
    (210)828-5529
Toll free: 800-262-2548
Fax: (210)828-4629
Laskowski, Sixtus, Mem.

Chromosome 18 Registry and Research Society [14813]
7155 Oakridge Dr.
San Antonio, TX 78229-3640
PH: (210)657-4968
Traa, Claudia, Director

Clan Johnstone in America [20815]
c/o J. J. Johnston, President
4207 Leona River
San Antonio, TX 78253
PH: (210)560-2639
Johnston, J.J., President

Clan MacKinnon Society [20824]
c/o Sharon MacKinnon
518 Penstemon Trl.
San Antonio, TX 78256
PH: (231)861-6453
McKinnon, John G., Chairman

Constitution Society [5101]
11447 Woollcott St.
San Antonio, TX 78251
PH: (512)299-5001
Roland, Jon, Founder, President,
Web Adm.

CUE: An Organization for Positive Employee Relations [23533]
900 NE Loop 410, Ste. D-103
San Antonio, TX 78209
PH: (210)545-3499
Toll free: 866-409-4283
Fax: (210)545-4284
Vandervort, Michael, Exec. Dir.

DUSTOFF Association [20719]
PO Box 8091, Wainwright Sta.
San Antonio, TX 78208
Gower, Dan, Exec. Dir.

Episcopal Communicators [20100]
PO Box 6885
San Antonio, TX 78209
Slocumb, Bill, Treasurer

Grand Lodge Order of the Sons of Hermann in Texas [19485]
515 S Saint Mary St.
San Antonio, TX 78205
PH: (210)226-9261
Toll free: 800-234-4124
Fax: (210)892-0299
Prewitt, Stephen R., Mem.

The Heart Smiles [11017]
PO Box 592798
San Antonio, TX 78259
PH: (210)771-8157
Osei-Bonsu, Ama, Founder

Hispanic Association of Colleges and Universities [7633]
8415 Datapoint Dr., Ste. 400
San Antonio, TX 78229
PH: (210)692-3805
Fax: (210)692-0823
Flores, Dr. Antonio R., President,
CEO

Intercultural Development Research Association [7533]
5815 Callaghan Rd., Ste. 101
San Antonio, TX 78228-1102
PH: (210)444-1710
Fax: (210)444-1714
Robledo Montecel, Maria, PhD,
CEO, President

International Association of Christian Chaplains [19927]
5804 Babcock Rd.
San Antonio, TX 78240-2134
PH: (210)696-7313
Kraus, Rev. Paul D., President

International Association for Colon Hydrotherapy [14942]
11103 San Pedro, Ste. 117
San Antonio, TX 78216
PH: (210)366-2888
Fax: (210)366-2999
Kolbo, Russell, President

International Association of Colon Hydrotherapy [16805]
11103 San Pedro Ave., Ste. 117
San Antonio, TX 78216-3117

PH: (210)366-2888
Fax: (210)366-2999
Jablonski, Tiffany, VP

International Bond and Share
Society [21668]
116 Parklane Dr.
San Antonio, TX 78212-1748
Hensley, Mr. Max, President

International Brangus Breeders As-
sociation [3729]
5750 Epsilon
San Antonio, TX 78249
PH: (210)696-8231
Fax: (210)696-8718
Perkins, Tommy, PhD, Exec. VP

International Junior Brangus Breed-
ers Association [3730]
5750 Epsilon
San Antonio, TX 78249
PH: (405)867-1421
Wallace, Kacie, President

International Military Community
Executives Association [21026]
14080 Nacogdoches Rd.
San Antonio, TX 78247-1944
PH: (940)463-5145
Fax: (866)369-2435
Schaffner, Melissa A., Officer

International Order of Saint Luke the
Physician [20544]
PO Box 780909
San Antonio, TX 78278-0909
PH: (210)492-5222
Toll free: 877-992-5222
Rice, Rev. John, Chap.

Last Chance Forever [4839]
PO Box 460993
San Antonio, TX 78246-0993
PH: (210)499-4080
Fax: (210)499-4305

Liberia Now [11397]
Po Box 781767
San Antonio, TX 78278
Toll free: 877-582-7906
Anderson, Allyn, Exec. Dir.

Men of God Christian Fraternity
[23710]
5423 Oxbow
San Antonio, TX 78228
Toll free: 877-822-3706

Mexican American Catholic College
[20373]
3115 W Ashby Pl.
San Antonio, TX 78228-5104
PH: (210)732-2156
Toll free: 866-893-6222
Fax: (210)732-9072
Chavez, Arturo, PhD, President,
CEO

Mexican American Unity Council
[11945]
2300 W Commerce St., Ste. 200
San Antonio, TX 78207
PH: (210)978-0500
Godinez, Fernando S., CEO,
President

Mexicans and Americans Thinking
Together [1965]
329 Old Guilbeau St.
San Antonio, TX 78204
PH: (210)270-0300
Garcia Granados, Aracely, Exec. Dir.

Mind Science Foundation [6988]
117 W El Prado Dr.
San Antonio, TX 78212
PH: (210)821-6094
Fax: (210)821-6199
Good, Meriam, Exec. Dir.

National Association of Latino Arts
and Culture [8989]
1208 Buena Vista St.
San Antonio, TX 78207
PH: (210)432-3982
Fax: (210)432-3934
De Leon, Maria Lopez, Exec. Dir.

National Board for Colon
Hydrotherapy [13641]
11103 San Pedro Ave., Ste. 117
San Antonio, TX 78216
PH: (210)308-8288
Medsker, Bekki, President

National Chief Petty Officers' Association [21056]
c/o Richard A. Oubre, Treasurer
5730 Misty Glen
San Antonio, TX 78247-1373
PH: (210)637-6304
Sweeney, Jerry L., Officer

National Coalition of Independent
Scholars [7965]
PO Box 120182
San Antonio, TX 78212
Haste, Amanda, Act. Pres., VP

National Huguenot Society [21004]
7340 Blanco Rd., Ste. 104
San Antonio, TX 78216
PH: (210)366-9995
Gradeless, Rex L., Treasurer

National Native American Veterans
Association [21135]
3903 County Rd. 382
San Antonio, TX 78253
Cates, James, Chairman

National Organization for Mexican
American Rights, Inc. [18341]
c/o Dan J. Solis, President
PO Box 681205
San Antonio, TX 78268-1205
PH: (210)520-1831
Fax: (210)520-1831
Solis, Dan J., President

National Skeet Shooting Association
[23138]
5931 Roft Rd.
San Antonio, TX 78253
PH: (210)688-3371
Toll free: 800-877-5338
Fax: (210)688-3014
Hampton, Michael, Jr., Exec. Dir.

National Sporting Clays Association
[23139]
5931 Roft Rd.
San Antonio, TX 78253
PH: (210)688-3371
Toll free: 800-877-5338
Fax: (210)688-3014
Hampton, Michael, Exec. Dir.

NOAH Nature Alliance [4852]
PO Box 6768
San Antonio, TX 78209
PH: (210)826-0599
Fax: (210)824-3161
deJori, Charlene, Founder

Omega Delta Phi Fraternity [23908]
8111 Mainland, Ste. 104-417
San Antonio, TX 78240
PH: (206)234-6424
Pagliocco, Tony, President

Operation Homefront [12348]
1355 Central Pky. S, Ste. 100
San Antonio, TX 78232-5056
PH: (210)659-7756
Toll free: 800-722-6098
Fax: (210)566-7544
Blades, Catherine, Chmn. of the Bd.

Pan-American Allergy Society
[13580]
c/o Ann Brey, Executive Director
1317 Wooded Knoll
San Antonio, TX 78258
PH: (210)495-9853
Fax: (210)495-9852
Brey, Ann, Exec. Dir.

Primarily Primates, Inc. [10684]
26099 Dull Knife Trl.
San Antonio, TX 78255
PH: (830)755-4616
Fax: (830)755-4618
Feral, Priscilla, President,
Chairperson

Research and Development Associ-
ates for Military Food and Packag-
ing Systems [6649]
16607 Blanco Rd., Ste. 501
San Antonio, TX 78232
PH: (210)493-8024
Fax: (210)493-8036
Zimmerman, Tim, Chmn. of the Bd.

Sigma Zeta [23862]
Our Lady of the Lake University
411 SW 24th St.
San Antonio, TX 78207-4689
Hall, Dr. Jim, Exec. Dir.

Society of Ethical Attorneys at Law
[5049]
PO Box 5993
San Antonio, TX 78201-0993
PH: (210)785-0935
Fax: (210)785-9254
Wright, Wyatt, President

Society for Physician Assistants in
Pediatrics [16728]
PO Box 90434
San Antonio, TX 78209
PH: (614)824-2102
(210)722-7622
Fax: (614)824-2103
Wingrove, Brian, President

Soldiers' Angels [19383]
2700 NE Loop 410, Ste. 310
San Antonio, TX 78217
PH: (210)629-0020
Fax: (210)629-0024
Beauchamp, Curtis, Chairman

Strategic and Competitive Intel-
ligence Professionals [6754]
7550 IH 10 W, Ste. 400
San Antonio, TX 78229
PH: (703)739-0696
Fax: (703)739-2524
Bulger, Nan, Exec. Dir., CEO

Student National Pharmaceutical
Association [8415]
PO Box 761388
San Antonio, TX 78245
PH: (210)383-7381
Fax: (210)579-1059
Hwang, Jessie Nia, President

Student Veterinary Emergency and
Critical Care Society [17665]
6335 Camp Bullis Rd., Ste. 12
San Antonio, TX 78257-9721
PH: (210)698-5575
Masciana, Joe, President

Students for the Second Amendment
[18258]
9624 Braun Run
San Antonio, TX 78254
PH: (210)674-5559
Bragg, Ryan T., Chairman, Founder

William C. Velasquez Institute
[19532]
1426 El Paso St., Ste. A
San Antonio, TX 78207

PH: (210)223-2918
Fax: (210)922-7095
González, Antonio, President

Veterinary Emergency and Critical
Care Society [17669]
6335 Camp Bullis Rd., Ste. 12
San Antonio, TX 78257
PH: (210)698-5575
Fax: (210)698-7138
Johnson, Scott, PhD, President

Voice for Animals, Inc. [10714]
PO Box 120095
San Antonio, TX 78212
PH: (210)737-3138

Women's Global Connection [13409]
University of the Incarnate Word
4503 Broadway St.
San Antonio, TX 78209
PH: (210)828-2224
Buck, Alison, Assoc. Dir.

Women's Regional Publications of
America [3509]
c/o J.M. Gaffney
San Antonio Woman
8603 Botts Ln.
San Antonio, TX 78217
PH: (210)826-5375
Green, Karen, President

Computer Assisted Language
Instruction Consortium [8025]
Texas State University
214 Centennial Hall
San Marcos, TX 78666
PH: (512)245-1417
Fax: (512)245-9089
Horn, Ms. Esther, Mgr.

Instream Flow Council [3885]
c/o Kevin Mayes, President
Texas Parks and Wildlife Department
PO Box 1685
San Marcos, TX 78667
Mayes, Kevin, President

International Society of Applied Intel-
ligence [5986]
Dept. of Computer Science
Texas State University, San Marcos
601 University Dr.
San Marcos, TX 78666-4616
PH: (512)245-8050
Fax: (512)245-8750
Ali, Moonis, President

Big Thicket Association [3819]
PO Box 198
Saratoga, TX 77585
PH: (936)274-1181
Ruppel, Jan, President

American Ostrich Association [3597]
PO Box 218
Scurry, TX 75158
PH: (972)968-8546
Brust, Joel, President

International Association of Equine
Dentistry [14448]
PO Box 1141
Seguin, TX 78156
PH: (830)268-5005
Bass, Jessica, Exec. Sec.

Non Commissioned Officers As-
sociation of the United States of
America [5619]
9330 Corporate Dr., Ste. 701
Selma, TX 78154
PH: (210)653-6161
Toll free: 800-662-2620
Fax: (210)637-3337
Overstreet, Gene, CEO, President

Operation Appreciation [20771]
Non-Commissioned Officers Association of the USA

9330 Corporate Dr., Ste. 701
Selma, TX 78154
PH: (210)653-6161
Toll free: 800-662-2620
Fax: (210)637-3337
Schneider, Richard, Exec. Dir.

National Association of Chamber
Ambassadors **[23602]**
PO Box 1198
Seminole, TX 79360
Toll free: 800-411-6222
Fax: (432)758-6698
Concotelli, Ms. Shelby, Dir. of Admin.

Mulch and Soil Council **[1442]**
7809 FM 179
Shallowater, TX 79363
PH: (806)832-1810
Fax: (806)832-5244
Salmon, Scott, President

Progressive Gardening Trade As-
sociation **[4272]**
7809 FM 179
Shallowater, TX 79363-3637
PH: (806)832-5306
Fax: (806)832-5244
Edwards, Jeff, VP

Roving Volunteers in Christ's Service
[22469]
1800 SE 4th St.
Smithville, TX 78957-2906
Toll free: 800-727-8914
Swetland, Paul, President

American Airgun Field Target As-
sociation **[23125]**
c/o Scott York, Treasurer
PO Box 245
Somerville, TX 77879
PH: (979)255-8324
York, Scott, Treasurer

Health Occupations Students of
America **[8323]**
548 Silicon Dr., Ste. 101
Southlake, TX 76092
Toll free: 800-321-4672
Allen, Nancy, Assoc. Dir.

Kids Matter International **[11059]**
535 S Nolen Dr., Ste. 300
Southlake, TX 76092
PH: (817)488-7679
Fax: (817)488-7685
Conner, Coye, Jr., Chmn. of the Bd.

Missions International **[20155]**
PO Box 93235
Southlake, TX 76092-0112
Mason, Dr. Bob, Founder, President

National Aircraft Resale Association
[149]
PO Box 92013
Southlake, TX 76092
Toll free: 866-447-1777
Foster, Johnny, Chmn. of the Bd.

National Association of Christian
Women Entrepreneurs **[3496]**
2140 E Southlake Blvd., Ste. L-643
Southlake, TX 76092
PH: (940)247-0090
Cunningham, Diane, Founder,
President

National Floor Safety Institute **[3003]**
PO Box 92607
Southlake, TX 76092
PH: (817)749-1700
Fax: (817)749-1702
Kendzior, Russell J., Chairman,
President

Sove Lavi **[11444]**
401 N Carroll Ave., Ste. 124
Southlake, TX 76092

PH: (817)239-7298
Simeus, Kimberly, President

Sportscar Vintage Racing Associa-
tion **[22529]**
1598 Hart St., Ste. 100
Southlake, TX 76092
PH: (817)521-5158
Fax: (817)953-3550
Parella, Tony, President, CEO

United States Boer Goat Association
[4282]
PO Box 663
Spicewood, TX 78669
Toll free: 866-668-7242
Fax: (877)640-4060

Home-Based Working Moms **[634]**
PO Box 1628
Spring, TX 77383-1628
PH: (281)757-2207
Pyle, Lesley Spencer, Founder,
President

Interprofessional Fostering of
Ophthalmic Care for Underserved
Sectors **[17717]**
18555 Kuykendahl Rd.
Spring, TX 77379
PH: (281)547-7477
Toll free: 866-398-7525
Fax: (877)302-6385
Dollak, Joseph, OD, President, CEO

Railway Industrial Clearance As-
sociation **[3355]**
8900 Eastloch Dr., Ste. 215
Spring, TX 77379
PH: (281)826-0009
Toll free: 888-203-5580
Collins, Kelli, President

Water Assurance Technology Energy
Resources **[6517]**
40 Sun Valley Dr.
Spring Branch, TX 78070
Fax: (830)885-4827
Korth, Peggy G., President

Medical Benevolence Foundation
[15153]
10707 Corporate Dr., Ste. 220
Stafford, TX 77477-4001
PH: (281)201-2043
Toll free: 800-547-7627
Fax: (281)903-7627
Mayo, E. Andrew, CEO

Southwestern Association of Natural-
ists **[6900]**
c/o Philip D. Sudman, President
Box T-0620
Department of Biological Sciences
Tarleton State University
Stephenville, TX 76402
Sudman, Philip D., President

Asaba National Association, USA,
Inc. **[19286]**
PO Box 1627
Sugar Land, TX 77487-1627
PH: (678)860-9602
Kwentua, Victor, Secretary

Energy Traffic Association **[2520]**
935 Eldridge Rd., No. 604
Sugar Land, TX 77478-2809
Lopez, Ralph, President

International Association of Innova-
tion Professionals **[1811]**
4422 Castle Wood St., Ste. 200
Sugar Land, TX 77479
Toll free: 800-276-1180
Trusko, Brett, President, CEO

Mapping Your Future **[7962]**
PO Box 2578
Sugar Land, TX 77487
Mueller, Cathy, Exec. Dir.

Money Management International
[1280]
14141 Southwest Fwy., Ste. 1000
Sugar Land, TX 77478-3494
Toll free: 866-889-9347
Hand, Ivan L., Jr., CEO, President

Research Partnership to Secure
Energy for America **[6508]**
1650 Highway 6, Ste. 325
Sugar Land, TX 77478
PH: (281)313-9555
Fax: (281)313-9560
Warren, Dr. John, Director

South Asian Bar Association of North
America **[5446]**
c/o Faisal Charania
Prime Communications
3006 Arrowhead Dr.
Sugar Land, TX 77479
Gwal, Anne, President

Sparkles of Life **[14242]**
11569 Hwy. 6 S, Ste. 148
Sugar Land, TX 77498
PH: (281)397-3260
Lewis-Nwosu, Rhonda, Founder

World Malayalee Council **[19479]**
PO Box 823
Sugar Land, TX 77487-0823
Jose, A.S., President

Myotubular Myopathy Resource
Group **[17345]**
2602 Quaker Dr.
Texas City, TX 77590
PH: (409)945-8569
Fax: (409)945-2162
Scoggin, Gary, Contact

Africa's Promise Village **[12023]**
15 Monarch Oaks Ln.
The Hills, TX 78738
PH: (512)291-3593
Gunn, Dr. Donna, President

American Pediatric Society **[16600]**
3400 Research Forest Dr., Ste. B-7
The Woodlands, TX 77381
PH: (281)419-0052
Fax: (281)419-0082
Fenton, Eileen G., Exec. Dir.

American Society of Pediatric Neph-
rology **[15874]**
3400 Research Forest Dr., Ste. B7
The Woodlands, TX 77381-4259
PH: (346)980-9752
Fax: (346)980-9752
Norwood, Victoria F., President

Business for Orphans **[10878]**
8 Hickory Oak Dr.
The Woodlands, TX 77381
PH: (832)693-9185
Doherty, James

Good News, A Forum for Scriptural
Christianity **[20344]**
PO Box 132076
The Woodlands, TX 77393-2076
PH: (832)813-8327
Fax: (832)813-5327
Renfroe, Rev. Rob, President

Independent Armored Car Operators
Association, Inc. **[3086]**
8000 Research Forest Dr., Ste. 115
The Woodlands, TX 77382
PH: (281)292-8208
Fax: (281)292-9308
Margaritis, John, Secretary

National Algae Association **[5888]**
4747 Research Forest Dr., Ste. 180
The Woodlands, TX 77381

PH: (936)321-1125

Society for Pediatric Research
[16619]
3400 Research Forest Dr., Ste. B-7
The Woodlands, TX 77381
PH: (281)419-0052
Fax: (281)419-0082
Lee, Brendan H., President

Wind Energy Association Latin
America **[7391]**
9418 FM 2920 Rd.
Tomball, TX 77375
PH: (281)710-7456

American Association of Code
Enforcement **[5452]**
114 Lakeshore Loop
Tow, TX 78672-4900
PH: (830)613-4268
Benisch, Johnny, Mem.

American Cuemakers Association
[22582]
2231 Galloway Blvd.
Trophy Club, TX 76262
PH: (817)683-5652
Espiritu, Russ, Chmn. of the Bd.

American Collegiate Retailing As-
sociation **[8268]**
c/o Robert Jones, Secretary
University of Texas at Tyler
Business Bldg. 122
3900 University Blvd.
Tyler, TX 75799
Fiorito, Susan S., Treasurer

Christian Hunters and Anglers As-
sociation **[22165]**
PO Box 132379
Tyler, TX 75712-0072
PH: (903)312-7390
Brasher, Bobby, Officer

Early Day Gas Engine and Tractor
Association **[22011]**
c/o Carrie Jo Parmley, Secretary
15246 Seven League Rd.
Tyler, TX 75703
PH: (903)360-0396
Young, Don, VP, Director

International Council of Associations
for Science Education **[8548]**
c/o Prof. Teresa Kennedy, President
3900 University Blvd.
Tyler, TX 75799
Kennedy, Teresa, President

National Alliance of State Science
and Mathematics Coalitions **[8549]**
Ingenuity Ctr., The University of
Texas at Tyler
3900 University Blvd.
Tyler, TX 75799-6600
PH: (903)617-6813
Fax: (903)617-6814
Heydrick, Kenneth W., EdD, Exec.
Dir.

North American Council of Automo-
tive Teachers **[7525]**
1820 Shiloh Rd., Ste. 1403
Tyler, TX 75703
PH: (682)465-4662
Ward, Curt, President

Therapet Animal Assisted Therapy
Foundation **[17465]**
PO Box 130118
Tyler, TX 75713
PH: (903)535-2125
Sites, Carianne, Exec. Dir.

United Braford Breeders **[3758]**
Box 358
5380 Old Bullard Rd. Ste. 600

Tyler, TX 75703
PH: (904)563-1816
Smith, Jim, Director

American Volkssport Association
[23214]
1001 Pat Booker Rd., Ste. 101
Universal City, TX 78148-4147
PH: (210)659-2112
Fax: (210)659-1212
Purcell, Candace, Dir. of Fin., Dir. of
Operations

Daedalian Foundation **[20669]**
PO Box 249
Universal City, TX 78148-0249
PH: (210)945-2111
Fax: (210)945-2112

National Association of Steel Pipe
Distributors **[2607]**
1501 E Mockingbird Ln., Ste. 307
Victoria, TX 77904
PH: (361)574-7878
Fax: (832)201-9479
Porr, Susannah F., Exec. Dir.

Rotary on Stamps Fellowship
[22359]
c/o Gerald FitzSimmons, Secretary
105 Calle Ricardo
Victoria, TX 77904-1203
Peters, Gerhard, Chairman

American Football Coaches Associa-
tion **[22854]**
100 Legends Ln.
Waco, TX 76706
PH: (254)754-9900
Fax: (254)754-7373
Welch, Mike, President

Association for the Sciences of Lim-
nology and Oceanography **[6937]**
5400 Bosque Blvd., Ste. 680
Waco, TX 76710-4446
PH: (254)399-9635
Toll free: 800-929-2756
Fax: (254)776-3767
Elser, Jim, President

Center for Occupational Research
and Development **[7840]**
4901 Bosque Blvd., 2nd Fl.
Waco, TX 76710
PH: (254)772-8756
Toll free: 800-972-2766
Fax: (254)772-8972
Hinckley, Dr. Richard, CEO,
President

Christian Association of World
Languages **[8179]**
c/o Jennifer Good
Dept. of Modern Foreign Languages
1 Bear Pl., No. 97390
Waco, TX 76798-7390
Vaughan, Alex, Treasurer

Degree of Pocahontas, Improved
Order of Red Men **[19622]**
4521 Speight Ave.
Waco, TX 76711
PH: (254)756-1221
Fax: (254)756-4828
Washburn, Mary K., Officer

Great Council of U.S. Improved
Order of Red Men **[19623]**
4521 Speight Ave.
Waco, TX 76711
PH: (254)756-1221
Fax: (254)756-4828
Wilson, David, Officer

International Society for Reef Studies **[4076]**
c/o Schneider Group Meeting and
Marketing Services

5400 Bosque Blvd., Ste. 680
Waco, TX 76710-4446
PH: (254)776-3550
Golbuu, Yimnang, VP

Mental Health Grace Alliance
[15784]
105 Old Hewitt Dr., Ste. 100A
Waco, TX 76712
PH: (254)235-0616
Padilla, Joe, Founder, Exec. Dir.

National Association for Professional
Development Schools **[8539]**
1 Bear Pl., No. 97477
Waco, TX 76798-7477
Toll free: 855-936-2737
Stoicovy, Donnan, Officer

National Career Pathways Network
[7843]
PO Box 21689
Waco, TX 76702-1689
PH: (254)772-5095
Toll free: 800-518-1410
Fax: (254)776-2306
Warner, Teemus, Mktg. Coord.

North American Llewellin Breeders
Association, Inc. **[21930]**
3413 Forrester Ln.
Waco, TX 76708-1719
PH: (254)752-1526
Wilson, Chuck, President

Ornithological Societies of North
America **[6965]**
c/o Helen Schneider Lemay, Execu-
tive Director
USNA Business Office
5400 Bosque Blvd., Ste. 680
Waco, TX 76710
PH: (254)399-9636
Fax: (254)776-3767
Lemay, Helen Schneider, Exec. Dir.

Religious Research Association
[20586]
c/o Kevin D. Dougherty
1 Bear Pl., No. 97326
Waco, TX 76798
PH: (254)710-6232
Fax: (254)710-1175
Swatos, William H., Ph.D., Exec.
Ofc.

Society for Freshwater Science
[4015]
5400 Bosque Blvd., Ste. 680
Waco, TX 76710-4446
PH: (254)399-9636
Fax: (254)776-3767
Bernhardt, Emily, President

Society for Freshwater Science
[6375]
5400 Bosque Blvd., Ste. 680
Waco, TX 76710-4446
PH: (254)399-9636
Fax: (254)776-3767
Bernhardt, Emily, President

Wilson Ornithological Society **[6966]**
5400 Bosque Blvd., Ste. 680
Waco, TX 76710
PH: (254)399-9636
Fax: (254)776-3767
Deutschlander, Dr. Mark, VP

Workroom Resource Group **[1964]**
802 N Robinson Dr.
Waco, TX 76706
PH: (254)662-4021
Toll free: 888-395-1959
Plumlee, Mary Ann, Founder

Gulf Coast GTOs **[21391]**
429 Apache Run
Wallisville, TX 77597

PH: (281)452-0855
Toll free: 800-935-7663
Siracusa, Mimi, President

World Watusi Association **[3759]**
PO Box 201
Walnut Springs, TX 76690
PH: (254)797-3032
Burnett, Pat, Jr., President

United States Team Penning As-
sociation **[22934]**
PO Box 1359
Weatherford, TX 76086
PH: (817)599-4455
Fax: (817)599-4461
O'Dea, Joe, President

Association of Space Explorers
U.S.A. **[5860]**
141 Bay Area Blvd.
Webster, TX 77598
PH: (281)280-8172
Turnage, Andy, Secretary

United States Adventure Racing As-
sociation **[23085]**
PO Box 514
Wellborn, TX 77881-0514
PH: (979)703-5018
Farrar, Troy, President

Association of Forensic DNA
Analysts and Administrators **[5241]**
2525 N International Blvd.
Weslaco, TX 78599

American Brahmousin Council
[3687]
PO Box 88
Whitesboro, TX 76273
PH: (903)564-3995
Cummins, Bob, Dir. (Actg.)

Law Enforcement and Emergency
Services Video Association, Inc.
[5480]
84 Briar Creek Rd.
Whitesboro, TX 76273-4603
PH: (469)285-9435
Fax: (469)533-3659
Peloquin, Tracy, Chmn. of the Bd.

Association of Extremity Nerve
Surgeons **[16062]**
15577 Ranch Rd. 12, Ste. 103
Wimberley, TX 78676
Toll free: 888-708-9575
Fax: (888)394-1123
Bregman, Peter, DPM, President

North American Stone Skipping As-
sociation **[22414]**
PO Box 2986
Wimberley, TX 78676-7886
McGhee, Jerdone, FounderU

UTAH

United Precious Metals Association
[2374]
270 N Main St., Ste. B
Alpine, UT 84004
Toll free: 888-210-8488
Hilton, Lawrence D., Esq., Gen.
Counsel

Mothers Without Borders **[11083]**
125 E Main St., Ste. 402
American Fork, UT 84003
PH: (801)607-5641
Headlee-Miner, Kathy, Founder

American Canyoneering Academy
[21594]
Cedar City, UT
Toll free: 877-RAPPEL-8

American Sulphur Horse Association
[22154]
1245 South 6300 West
Cedar City, UT 84720-9206
Nield, Naylene, Contact

National Mustang Association **[4383]**
PO Box 1367
Cedar City, UT 84721
Toll free: 888-867-8662

Society for Epidemiologic Research
[14734]
PO Box 990
Clearfield, UT 84089
PH: (801)525-0231
Fax: (801)525-6549
Bevan, Sue, Director

Society for Pediatric and Perinatal
Epidemiologic Research **[14736]**
PO Box 160191
Clearfield, UT 84016
PH: (617)432-3942
Drews-Botsch, Carolyn, President

American Apitherapy Society
[13588]
14942 S Eagle Crest Dr.
Draper, UT 84020
PH: (631)470-9446
Fax: (631)693-2528
Keller, Frederique, President

The American Civil Defense Associa-
tion **[5074]**
12162 S Business Park Dr., No. 208
Draper, UT 84020
PH: (801)501-0077
Toll free: 800-425-5397
Fax: (888)425-5339
Packer, Sharon, Secretary, Treasurer

U.S. Autism and Asperger Associa-
tion **[13781]**
PO Box 532
Draper, UT 84020-0532
PH: (801)816-1234
Toll free: 888-928-8476
Kaplan, Lawrence P., PhD, Chair-
man, CEO

Mormon History Association **[20299]**
175 South 1850 East
Heber City, UT 84032
PH: (801)521-6565
Fax: (801)521-8686
Cannon, Brian Q., President

Association for Vascular Access
[17571]
5526 West 13400 South, Ste. 229
Herriman, UT 84096
PH: (801)792-9079
Toll free: 877-924-2821
Fax: (801)601-8012
Brazunas, Michael, RN, BSN,
President

International Sharps Injury Prevention Society **[17173]**
6898 Maria Way
Herriman, UT 84096-6500

American Pomeranian Club Inc.
[21817]
c/o Kelly D. Reimschiissel, 6214 W
10150 N
6214 West 10150 North
Highland, UT 84003
PH: (801)361-8619
Oelerich, Vikki, President

Best Friends Animal Society **[10593]**
5001 Angel Canyon Rd.
Kanab, UT 84741-5000
PH: (435)644-2001
Fax: (435)644-2078
Castle, Gregory, CEO

Affordable Housing Association of
   Certified Public Accountants **[1686]**
459 North 300 West, Ste. 11
Kaysville, UT 84037
PH: (801)547-0809
Toll free: 800-532-0809
Sparks, Les, President

The Bulldog Club of America Rescue
   Network, Inc. **[10596]**
c/o Shar Kynaston
PO Box 1049
Kaysville, UT 84037
PH: (801)546-0265
Kynaston, Shar, Treasurer

ManKind Project **[12874]**
PO Box 383
Kaysville, UT 84037
Toll free: 800-870-4611
Fax: (800)405-7840
Powell, Robert, Chairman

National Association of Arms Shows
   [22020]
PO Box 290
Kaysville, UT 84037-0290
PH: (801)544-9125
Templeton, Robert, President

National Association of Certified
   Public Bookkeepers **[45]**
238 North 300 West, Ste. 504
Kaysville, UT 84037
Toll free: 866-444-9989
Fax: (801)451-4688
Bybee, David B., CPA, CEO,
   President

U.S. Speedskating **[23158]**
5662 South Cougar Ln.
Kearns, UT 84118
PH: (801)417-5360
Fax: (801)417-5361
Plant, Mike, President

National Quarter Horse Registry
   [4384]
PO Box 513
La Verkin, UT 84745
PH: (435)915-6747
Fax: (734)917-6747
Holdaway, Tamara, Exec. Dir.

National EMS Pilots Association
   [14669]
PO Box 2128
Layton, UT 84041-9128
PH: (801)436-7505
Williams, Kurt, President

National Softball Association of the
   Deaf **[23204]**
c/o Rod Jex, Treasurer
1039 E Wyndom Way
Layton, UT 84040
Jex, Rod, Treasurer

Pro Energy Alliance **[1120]**
1665 N 1200 W
Lehi, UT 84043-3573
PH: (801)935-4360
Toll free: 888-316-8285
Beckman, Eric, Operations Mgr.

International Plutarch Society
   [10095]
Utah State University
Dept. of History
0710 Old Main Hill
Logan, UT 84322-0710
PH: (435)797-1290
Fax: (435)797-3899
Titchener, Dr. Frances B., Editor

International Union for the Study of
   Social Insects **[6614]**
c/o Karen Kapheim
Dept. of Biology

Utah State University
Logan, UT 84322-5305
PH: (630)915-1738
Breed, Michael, Ed.-in-Chief

National Fibromyalgia and Chronic
   Pain Association **[14769]**
31 Federal Ave.
Logan, UT 84321-4640
PH: (801)200-3627
Chambers, Janet Favero, President

National Resource Center for Para-
   educators **[8591]**
2865 Old Main Hill
Logan, UT 84322-2865
PH: (435)797-7272
Likins, Dr. Marilyn, Exec. Dir.

Western Literature Association
   [9771]
PO Box 6815
Logan, UT 84341
Witschi, Nicolas, Exec. Sec.

All One People **[10473]**
460 East 100 North
Manti, UT 84642
PH: (435)851-1548
Johnson, Fred, President

German Gun Collectors' Association
   [21656]
PO Box 429
Mayfield, UT 84643-0429
PH: (435)979-9723
Fax: (435)528-7966
Devers, Thomas, President

American Honey Producers Associa-
   tion **[3633]**
c/o Cassie Cox, Executive Secretary
PO Box 435
Mendon, UT 84325
PH: (281)900-9740
Cox, Darren, President

Advanced Conservation Strategies
   [3787]
c/o Josh Donlan, Founder and Director
PO Box 1201
Midway, UT 84049-1201
PH: (435)200-3031
   (607)227-9768
Donlan, Josh, Founder, Director

Canyonlands Field Institute **[3993]**
1320 S Highway 191
Moab, UT 84532
PH: (435)259-7750
Toll free: 800-860-5262
Fax: (435)259-2335
VanderZanden, Karla, Exec. Dir.

Threshold, Inc. **[4105]**
PO Box 152
Moab, UT 84532
PH: (435)259-0816
Milton, John P., Founder, President

Fifty Caliber Shooters Association
   [23129]
PO Box 111
Monroe, UT 84754-0111
PH: (435)527-9245
Fax: (435)527-0948

National Association for Research
   and Therapy of Homosexuality
   [14801]
301 West 5400 South, Ste. 203
Murray, UT 84107
Toll free: 888-364-4744

Association of Communication
   Engineers **[6544]**
c/o Mike Riley, Secretaty/Treasurer
1475 North 200 West

Nephi, UT 84648-0311
PH: (435)623-8601
Riley, Mike, Secretary, Treasurer

Association of Mormon Counselors
   and Psychotherapists **[16966]**
PO Box 540385
North Salt Lake, UT 84054
PH: (801)425-3490
Fax: (801)931-2010
Coombs, Ms. Emily, Exec. Sec.

Producers Livestock Marketing As-
   sociation **[4484]**
PO Box 540477
North Salt Lake, UT 84054-0477
PH: (801)936-2424
Lovell, Rick, Gen. Mgr.

Sabu Help International **[12809]**
743 N Wilton Dr.
North Salt Lake, UT 84054
PH: (801)834-4992
Ayeliya, Dr. Abio, Founder, Exec. Dir.

Hope and a Future **[15940]**
PO Box 13646
Ogden, UT 84412
PH: (801)395-1979
Fax: (801)627-1831
Kane, Linda M., Officer

Medical Equipment & Technology
   Association **[15689]**
c/o Dustin Telford, President
McKay-Dee Hospital
4401 Harrison Blvd.
Ogden, UT 84403-3195
PH: (801)879-5433
Telford, Dustin, President

Society for Skeptical Studies **[10129]**
c/o Dr. Richard Greene, Executive
   Director
Dept. of Political Science and
   Philosophy
Weber State University
1203 University Cir.
Ogden, UT 84408-1203
Greene, Dr. Richard, Exec. Dir.

World Championship Cutter and
   Chariot Racing Association **[22723]**
2632 S 4300 W
Ogden, UT 84401
PH: (801)731-8021
   (801)731-3820
Fax: (801)731-8021
Adams, J. Victor, Mgr., Secretary

Grow Learn Give **[15082]**
1495 N 450 E
Orem, UT 84097
Brown, Kristin, President, Founder

International Aid Serving Kids
   [11045]
1135 N 650 E
Orem, UT 84097
Dort, Illens, President, Founder

Thomas Minor Society **[20901]**
c/o Ray Howell, Secretary
38 West 1600 South
Orem, UT 84058
Burdick, Frederick, President

Unitus Labs **[12196]**
435 South 660 West
Orem, UT 84058-6078
PH: (206)926-3700
Grenny, Joseph, Chairman

National Ability Center **[22784]**
1000 Ability Way
Park City, UT 84060
PH: (435)649-3991
Fax: (435)658-3992
Loveland, Gail, Exec. Dir.

Seeley Genealogical Society **[20926]**
c/o Lynda Simmons,
125 Parkview Dr.
Park City, UT 84098
PH: (453)649-9878
Taylor, Paul, VP

Sundance Institute **[9314]**
1825 Three Kings Dr.
Park City, UT 84060
PH: (435)658-3456
Fax: (435)658-3457
Redford, Robert, President, Founder

United States Ski and Snowboard
   Association **[23171]**
1 Victory Ln.
Park City, UT 84060
PH: (435)649-9090
Fax: (435)649-3613
Shaw, Tiger, President, CEO

United States Ski Team Foundation
   [23172]
1 Victory Ln.
Park City, UT 84060
PH: (435)647-2075

Kathy Mattea Fan Club **[24050]**
866 N Sage Dr.
Pleasant Grove, UT 84062

National Slag Association **[561]**
PO Box 1197
Pleasant Grove, UT 84062
PH: (801)785-4535
Fax: (801)785-4539
Kiggins, Karen, President

Victorian Hairwork Society **[21787]**
c/o Marlys Fladeland, Founder
PO Box 806
Pleasant Grove, UT 84062
PH: (816)833-2955
Cohoon, Leila, Contact

National Insulator Association
   [21695]
c/o Don Briel, President
PO Box 188
Providence, UT 84332
Briel, Don, President

One Heart Bulgaria **[11106]**
165 N Main St.
Providence, UT 84332
PH: (435)764-3093
Gardner, Deborah Dushku, Founder,
   President

American Association of Presidents
   of Independent Colleges and
   Universities **[8008]**
c/o Steven M. Sandberg, Executive
   Director
PO Box 7070
Provo, UT 84602-7070
PH: (801)422-2235
Fax: (801)422-0265
Westmoreland, Andrew, President

American Student Association of
   Community Colleges **[8611]**
2250 N University Pky., No. 4865
Provo, UT 84604
PH: (801)785-9784
Toll free: 888-240-4993
Fax: (801)406-4385
Clegg, Philip, Exec. Dir.

American Translation and Interpret-
   ing Studies Association **[8714]**
Brigham Young University
3190 JFSB
Provo, UT 84602
PH: (801)422-2005
Fax: (801)422-0628
Angelelli, Claudia, President

Cantonese Language Association
[20297]
Brigham Young University
A-41 ASB
Provo, UT 84602
PH: (801)422-4636
   (801)422-1211
Bourgerie, Dana Scott, Dept. Chm.

Donny Osmond International
Network [24035]
223 W Bulldog Blvd., No. 520
Provo, UT 84604
Toll free: 800-732-2111

National Dance Council of America
[7705]
PO Box 22018
Provo, UT 84602-2018
PH: (801)422-8124
Fax: (801)422-0541
McDonald, Brian, President

Renew America [3782]
PO Box 50502
Provo, UT 84605-0502
Stone, Stephen, President

Society for the Advancement of
Scandinavian Study [10201]
Brigham Young University
3168 JFSB
Provo, UT 84602-6702
Wantland, Clydette L., Exec. Dir.

Weather Modification Association
[6861]
PO Box 845
Riverton, UT 84065
PH: (801)598-4392
Capece, Laurie, Exec. Sec.,
Treasurer

303rd Bomb Group (H) Association
[21180]
303rd Bomb Group
237 Oasis Dr.
Saint George, UT 84770-0901
Moncur, Gary L., Editor

Discovery Owners Association, Inc.
[22421]
PO Box 95
Saint George, UT 84771-0095
Toll free: 888-594-6818
Baker, John, Contact

Heart Walk Foundation [9172]
437 S Bluff St., Ste. 202
Saint George, UT 84770-3590
PH: (435)619-0797
Eicher, Penelope, Exec. Dir.

Academy of Clinical Laboratory
Physicians and Scientists [16729]
c/o Becky Lubbers, Administrative
Assistant
500 Chipeta Way
Salt Lake City, UT 84108
PH: (801)583-2787
Fax: (801)584-5207
Frank, Karen, President

Air Medical Physician Association
[16731]
951 E Montana Vista Ln.
Salt Lake City, UT 84124-2467
PH: (801)263-2672
Fax: (801)534-0434
Petersen, Patricia, Exec. Dir.

American Academy of Professional
Coders [15107]
2233 S Presidents Dr., Ste. F
Salt Lake City, UT 84120
PH: (801)236-2200
Toll free: 800-626-2633
Fax: (801)236-2258
Johnson Kipreos, Jaci, President

American Association of Nurse Life
Care Planners [16095]
3267 East 3300 South, No. 309
Salt Lake City, UT 84109
PH: (801)274-1184
Fax: (801)274-1535
Powell, Victoria, RN, President

American Dog Breeders Association
[21807]
PO Box 1771
Salt Lake City, UT 84110
PH: (801)936-7513
Fax: (801)936-4229
Greenwood, Hank, President, Chmn.
of the Bd.

American Finance Association
[1218]
c/o James Schallheim, Executive
Secretary/Treasurer
1655 E Campus Center Dr.
Salt Lake City, UT 84112
PH: (781)388-8599
Toll free: 800-835-6770
Schallheim, James, Exec. Sec.,
Treasurer

American Mustang and Burro As-
sociation, Inc. [4317]
PO Box 27703
Salt Lake City, UT 84127-0703

Assembly of Episcopal Healthcare
Chaplains [20092]
c/o Susan Roberts, Secretary
The University of Utah
50 N Medical Dr., Rm. 1C351
Salt Lake City, UT 84132
PH: (801)587-9064
Cobb, Dr. Matthew, President

Association for Configuration and
Data Management [6736]
PO Box 58888
Salt Lake City, UT 84158-0888
Hauer, Cynthia, President

Association of Medical School
Pharmacology Chairs [16653]
University of Utah
Department of Pharmacology and
Toxicology
30 S 2000 E, Rm. 201
Salt Lake City, UT 84112
PH: (801)581-6287
Fax: (801)585-5111
Haywood, J.R., PhD, Secretary

Center for Resource Management
[3827]
1861 E Beaumont Cir.
Salt Lake City, UT 84121-1204
PH: (801)509-5308
Parker, Paul, President

Community of Caring [10949]
1721 Campus Center Dr.
Salt Lake City, UT 84112
PH: (801)581-8221
Keith, Penny, Coord.

Crown Council [14427]
975 Woodoak Ln., Ste. 200
Salt Lake City, UT 84117-7275
PH: (801)293-8522
Toll free: 800-276-9658
Fax: (801)293-8524

Drilling, Observation and Sampling
of the Earth's Continental Crust
[6373]
2075 S Pioneer Rd., Ste. B
Salt Lake City, UT 84104-4231
PH: (801)583-2150
Fax: (801)583-2153
Nielson, Dennis, Bd. Member

Executive Women International [69]
3860 South 2300 East, Ste. 211
Salt Lake City, UT 84109

PH: (801)355-2800
Fax: (801)355-2852
Stokes, Lisa, Advisor

Family Support America [11819]
307 West 200 South, Ste. 2004
Salt Lake City, UT 84101-1261
PH: (312)338-0900
Toll free: 877-338-3722
Fax: (312)338-1522
Mason, Virginia L., Manager

Globus Relief [12278]
1775 West 1500 South
Salt Lake City, UT 84104
PH: (801)977-0444
Fax: (801)977-3999
Driggs, Daniel, Mem.

Guild for Structural Integration
[13627]
150 S State St.
Salt Lake City, UT 84111
PH: (800)447-0150
Toll free: 800-447-0150
Fax: (801)906-8157
Hutchins, Emmett, Fac. Memb., VP

Hawkwatch International [6961]
2240 South 900 East
Salt Lake City, UT 84106
PH: (801)484-6808
Fax: (801)484-6810
Nelson, Janet, Educator

HelpMercy International [15019]
Salt Lake City, UT
Williams, Lloyd B., Chairman

Institute of Business Appraisers
[226]
5217 S State St., Ste. 400
Salt Lake City, UT 84107
Toll free: 800-299-4130
Fax: (866)353-5406
Smith, Sharon, Chairperson

International Academies of
Emergency Dispatch [14697]
110 S Regent St., Ste. 800
Salt Lake City, UT 84111
PH: (801)359-6916
Toll free: 800-960-6236
Fax: (801)359-0996
Freitag, Scott, President

The International Neuropsychological
Society [16022]
2319 S Foothill Dr., Ste. 260
Salt Lake City, UT 84109
PH: (801)487-0475
Haaland, Kathleen Y., President

International Society Daughters of
Utah Pioneers [21084]
300 N Main St.
Salt Lake City, UT 84103-1699
PH: (801)532-6479
Fax: (801)532-4436
Smith, Maurine P., President

Kids with Cameras [10141]
122 S Main St.
Salt Lake City, UT 84101
PH: (801)746-7600
Briski, Zana, Founder

Kids Together, Inc. [11612]
60 W Burton Ave.
Salt Lake City, UT 84115-2609

Latin American Art Song Alliance
[9945]
3333 S 900 E, No. 110
Salt Lake City, UT 84106-3167
Weiss, Allison, President

Law and Society Association [5432]
383 S University St.
Salt Lake City, UT 84112

PH: (801)581-3219
Fax: (888)292-5515
Hans, Valerie, President

Make Early Diagnosis to Prevent
Early Death [14840]
School of Medicine, Rm. 1160
University of Utah
420 Chipeta Way
Salt Lake City, UT 84108
Toll free: 888-244-2465
Hopkins, Prof. Paul N., MD, Director,
Investigator

Movable Book Society [9132]
PO Box 9190
Salt Lake City, UT 84109-0190
PH: (801)277-6700
Montanaro, Ann, Director

National Association of Certified
Valuators and Analysts [46]
5217 S State St., Ste. 400
Salt Lake City, UT 84107-4812
PH: (801)486-0600
Toll free: 800-677-2009
Fax: (801)486-7500
Black, Parnell, CEO

National Association for Family Child
Care [5189]
1743 W Alexander St., Ste. 201
Salt Lake City, UT 84119-2000
PH: (801)886-2322
Toll free: 800-359-3817
Fax: (801)886-2325
Dischler, Patricia, President

National Association of Financial and
Estate Planning [1254]
515 E 4500 S, No. G-200
Salt Lake City, UT 84107
Toll free: 800-454-2649
Fax: (877)890-0929
Janko, Scott, President

National Association of Health Data
Organizations [14949]
124 S 400 E, Ste. 220
Salt Lake City, UT 84111-5312
PH: (801)532-2299
Fax: (801)532-2228
Love, Denise, Exec. Dir.

National Center for Voice and
Speech [17244]
136 S Main St., Ste. 320
Salt Lake City, UT 84101-1623
PH: (801)596-2012
Fax: (801)596-2013
Titze, Ingo R., PhD, Exec. Dir.

National Energy Foundation [7881]
4516 South 700 East, Ste. 100
Salt Lake City, UT 84107
PH: (801)327-9500
Toll free: 800-616-8326
Fax: (801)908-5400
Bonner, Wayne, VP of Fin. & Admin.

National Episcopal Historians and
Archivists [9418]
c/o Cathedral Church of St. Mark
231 East 100 South
Salt Lake City, UT 84111
PH: (920)543-6342
Stonesifer, Susan, President

National Society of the Sons of Utah
Pioneers [21085]
3301 E Louise Ave.
Salt Lake City, UT 84109
PH: (801)484-4441
Toll free: 866-724-1847
Fax: (801)484-2067
Davis, Heather, Office Mgr.,
Secretary

One Hour for Life [11929]
678 E 3rd Ave., Unit 5
Salt Lake City, UT 84103

PH: (435)565-1663
Kraft, Ira, Founder, Treasurer

Professionals in Nutrition for
Exercise and Sport [16238]
358 South 700 East (B-247)
Salt Lake City, UT 84102
Pearce, Jeni, President

Society for Ear, Nose, and Throat
Advances in Children [16540]
32 West 200 South, No. 105
Salt Lake City, UT 84101
PH: (407)650-7440
Fax: (407)650-7955
Barck, Patrick, Secretary

Society for Transplant Social Workers [17229]
c/o Patricia Voorhes, Treasurer
2273 E Tara Ln., No. 3
Salt Lake City, UT 84117
Hart, Jan, President

Stepping Stones International
[11159]
693 17th Ave.
Salt Lake City, UT
PH: (801)359-2746
    (801)651-1771
Jamu, Lisa, Founder, Exec. Dir.

Sudden Arrhythmia Death
Syndromes Foundation [14860]
4527 South 2300 East, Ste. 104
Salt Lake City, UT 84117-4448
PH: (801)272-3023
Lara, Alice, RN, CEO, President

Sudden Cardiac Arrest Coalition
[14149]
Sudden Arrhythmia Death Sydromes
Foundation
508 E South Temple, Ste. 202
Salt Lake City, UT 84102
PH: (801)531-0937
Lara, Alice A., Chairperson

Tread Lightly! [4622]
353 East 400 South, Ste. 100
Salt Lake City, UT 84111
PH: (801)627-0077
Toll free: 800-966-9900
McCullough, Lori, CEO

United Natural Products Alliance
[15079]
1075 E Hollywood Ave.
Salt Lake City, UT 84105-3446
PH: (801)474-2572
Fax: (801)474-2571
Israelsen, Loren D., President

Water Alliance for Africa [13341]
3267 East 3300 South, No. 535
Salt Lake City, UT 84109
Lloyd, Brian, Bd. Member

Wilderness Medical Society [15750]
2150 South 1300 East, Ste. 500
Salt Lake City, UT 84106-4375
PH: (801)990-2988
Fax: (801)990-4601
Bennett, Brad, President

Women's World Health Initiative
[17768]
PO Box 9635
Salt Lake City, UT 84109
Allison, Dana, Exec. Dir.

American Association of State
Compensation Insurance Funds
[1828]
c/o Donna Garfield
PO Box 2227
Sandy, UT 84091
PH: (385)351-8024
Toll free: 866-935-6773
Fax: (385)351-7845
Adams, Gerard, VP

American Home Business Associa-
tion [1643]
53 W 9000 S
Sandy, UT 84070
Toll free: 866-396-7773
Fax: (866)396-7773

Burma Humanitarian Mission
[11326]
3395 E Deer Hollow Cir.
Sandy, UT 84092
PH: (435)487-9244
Isherwood, Mike, Chairman

Wings and Dreams for Kids [14218]
3210 E Fur Hollow Dr.
Sandy, UT 84092

Equine Assisted Growth and Learn-
ing Association [16971]
PO Box 993
Santaquin, UT 84655
PH: (801)754-0400
Toll free: 877-858-4600
Fax: (801)754-0401
Thomas, Lynn, Exec. Dir.

Casual Games Association [22048]
861 Upper Canyon Rd.
Smithfield, UT 84335
PH: (435)770-5369

Afflicted War Heroes [20764]
PO Box 95794
South Jordan, UT 84095
Butterfield, Jason, President,
Founder

Southern Sudan Humanitarian
[12731]
9959 S 3200 W
South Jordan, UT 84095
PH: (801)323-2007
Jenkins, Scott R., Chmn. of the Bd.

Women Against Gun Control [18259]
PO Box 95357
South Jordan, UT 84095
PH: (801)328-9660
Tobias, Janalee, Founder, President

Foundation of East European Family
History Studies [20968]
PO Box 321
Springville, UT 84663
Edlund, Thomas, President

Bridge of Love [10873]
PO Box 1869
West Jordan, UT 84084-8869
Lundberg, Laurie, Founder,
President, Exec. Dir.

Clan Forsyth Society U.S.A. [20811]
4336 South 3150 West
West Valley City, UT 84119-5856
Sandusky, Dale, President

World Association of Benchers and
Dead Lifters [23369]
PO Box 515
Willard, UT 84340
PH: (503)901-1622
Fax: (435)723-0308
Rethwisch, Gus, Chairman, Presi-
dentV

VERMONT

World Sound Healing Organization
[12448]
PO Box 389
Ascutney, VT 05030-0389
PH: (802)674-9585
Fax: (802)674-9585
Blackburn, Zacciah, Director

American Cream Draft Horse Association [4303]
193 Crossover Rd.
Bennington, VT 05201
Tremel, Frank, President

Hormone Refractory Prostate
Cancer Association [13984]
PO Box 260
Bennington, VT 05201
PH: (802)879-1131
Laumeister, Bruce, President

Wuqu' Kawoq [15511]
PO Box 91
Bethel, VT 05032-0091
PH: (513)393-9878
Tummons, Emily, Founder

Safer Society Foundation [11546]
PO Box 340
Brandon, VT 05733-0340
PH: (802)247-3132
Fax: (802)247-4233
Burchard, Brenda, Exec. Dir.

Holstein Association U.S.A. [3728]
1 Holstein Pl.
Brattleboro, VT 05302-0808
PH: (802)254-4551
Toll free: 800-952-5200
Fax: (802)254-8251
Meyer, John, Secretary

National Junior Holstein Association
[3742]
1 Holstein Pl.
Brattleboro, VT 05302-0808
PH: (802)254-4551
Toll free: 800-952-5200
Fax: (802)254-8251
Dunklee, Kelli F., Liaison

Vote Hemp [18649]
PO Box 1571
Brattleboro, VT 05302-1571
PH: (202)318-8999
Fax: (202)318-8999
Steenstra, Eric, President

World Learning [8093]
1 Kipling Rd.
Brattleboro, VT 05301
Toll free: 800-257-7751
Fax: (802)258-3248
Hiatt, Thomas, Chairman

World Learning Visitor Exchange
Program [18565]
1 Kipling Rd.
Brattleboro, VT 05302-0676
PH: (800)257-7751
Hiatt, Thomas, Chmn. of the Bd.

International Society of Ethnobiology
[6091]
PO Box 303
Bristol, VT 05443
PH: (802)453-6996
Fax: (802)453-3420
Cuerrier, Alain, President

1-800 American Free Trade Associa-
tion [3410]
PO Box 1049
Burlington, VT 05402-1049
PH: (802)383-0816
Fax: (802)860-4821
Carpenter, Jay, President

Chinese Language Teachers As-
sociation [7601]
c/o Dept. of Asian Langauges &
Literatures
University of Vermont
479 Main St.
Burlington, VT 05405
PH: (802)656-5764
Fax: (802)656-8472
Jing-hua Yin, John, Exec. Dir.

Democracy for America [18865]
PO Box 1717
Burlington, VT 05402
PH: (802)651-3200
Fax: (802)651-3299
Dean, Jim, Chairman

Free Press Media [18652]
100 Bank St., Ste. 700
Burlington, VT 05401
PH: (802)660-1896
Getler, Al, President, Publicist

Lumunos [20067]
38 S Winooski Ave.
Burlington, VT 05401
PH: (802)860-1936
Wysockey-Johnson, Doug, Exec. Dir.

North American Conference on Brit-
ish Studies [9140]
c/o Paul Deslandes, Executive
Secretary
University of Vermont
133 S Prospect St.
Burlington, VT 05405
PH: (802)656-3535
Pennybacker, Susan, President

Toward Freedom [18298]
PO Box 468
Burlington, VT 05402
PH: (802)657-3733
Lloyd, Robin, Chairman, Publisher

Volunteers for Peace [18563]
7 Kilburn St., Ste. 316
Burlington, VT 05401
PH: (802)540-3060
Messier, Matt, President

Society for Menstrual Cycle
Research [16306]
c/o Ingrid Johnston-Robeldo,
President
Castleton State College
Castleton, VT 05735
Johnston-Robeldo, Ingrid, President

Imaging the World [15146]
PO Box 25
Charlotte, VT 05445
PH: (802)734-1440
DeStigter, Dr. Kristen, Founder

American Agri-Women [17784]
PO Box 743
Colchester, VT 05446
PH: (586)530-1771
Fax: (802)479-5414
Mold, Doris, President

North American British Music Studies Association [9986]
c/o Nathaniel Lew, Secretary
St. Michael's College
1 Winooski Pk.
Colchester, VT 05439-1000
Saylor, Eric, President

American Society of Dowsers [7007]
184 Brainerd St.
Danville, VT 05828
PH: (802)684-3417
Fax: (802)684-2565

Funeral Ethics Organization [11799]
87 Upper Access Rd.
Hinesburg, VT 05461
PH: (802)482-6021
Carlson, Lisa, Exec. Dir.

Keeping Track [4837]
2209 Main Rd.
Huntington, VT 05462
PH: (802)434-7000
Fax: (802)434-5383
Morse, Susan C., Director, Founder

International College of Angiology
[17574]
161 Morin Dr.
Jay, VT 05859-9283
PH: (802)988-4065
Fax: (802)988-4066
Prasad, Kailash, MD, Chmn. of the
Bd.

American Milking Devon Cattle Association [3702]
c/o Raymond Clark, Director
1429 Red Village Rd.
Lyndonville, VT 05851
Hall, John L., III, President,
Treasurer

International Skiing History Associa-
tion [23163]
PO Box 1064
Manchester Center, VT 05255
PH: (802)366-1158
Fry, John, Chairman

American Association of Teachers of
Korean [8163]
c/o Dr. Sahie Khang, The School of
Korean,Middlebury College
The School of Korean
Middlebury College
Middlebury, VT 05753
PH: (802)443-5215
Kang, Sahie, Dr., President

Bread Loaf Writers Conference
[10366]
204 College St.
Middlebury, VT 05753-1054
PH: (802)443-5286
Fax: (802)443-2087
Cargill, Noreen, Mgr. of Admin.

World Reuse, Repair and Recycling
Association [4637]
PO Box 1010
Middlebury, VT 05753
Ingenthron, Robin, President

Association for the Advancement of
Restorative Medicine [13605]
PO Box 874
Montpelier, VT 05601
Toll free: 866-962-2276
Friedman, Michael, ND, Founder,
Exec. Dir.

Clean Energy Group [6468]
50 State St., Ste. 1
Montpelier, VT 05602
PH: (802)223-2554
Fax: (802)223-4967
Milford, Lewis, Founder, President

Clean Energy States Alliance [6469]
50 State St., Ste. 1
Montpelier, VT 05602
PH: (802)223-2554
Fax: (802)223-4967
Milford, Lewis, Founder

Global Community Initiatives [11366]
12 Parkside Dr.
Montpelier, VT 05602
PH: (802)851-7697
Hallsmith, Gwendolyn, Exec. Dir.,
Founder

Institute for Sustainable Communi-
ties [11385]
535 Stone Cutters Way
Montpelier, VT 05602-3795
PH: (802)229-2900
Fax: (802)229-2919
Hamilton, George, President

International Association of Lemon
Law Administrators [5055]
c/o Pauline Liese, President
New Motor Vehicle Arbitration Board

14 Baldwin St., Rm. 103
Montpelier, VT 05602-2109
PH: (802)828-2943
Fax: (802)828-5809
Soletski, Rick, Exec. Dir.

Mercury Policy Project [17488]
1420 North St.
Montpelier, VT 05602-9592
PH: (802)223-9000
Williams, Jane, Exec. Dir.

Planting Hope [11422]
1 Granite St., 3rd Fl.
Montpelier, VT 05601
PH: (802)778-0344
Bloom, Darryl, Bd. Member

Regulatory Assistance Project [5835]
50 State St., Ste. 3
Montpelier, VT 05602
PH: (802)223-8199
Fax: (802)223-8172
Weinberg, Carl, V. Chmn. of the Bd.

Rwanda Knits [11425]
122 Ward Brook Rd.
Montpelier, VT 05602
PH: (518)791-0212
Clement, Cari, Director, Founder

The Global Child [11000]
5 Short Bluff Rd.
Newport, VT 05855
PH: (518)423-8780
Wheeler, Judy, Chmn. of the Bd.

Direct Aid International [12655]
PO Box 394
Northfield, VT 05663
Hoffman, Jonathan I., Director,
Founder

ACTS Honduras [11304]
PO Box 433
Norwich, VT 05055
Bisceglia, Lisa, Officer

DROKPA [11347]
95 Stowell Rd.
Norwich, VT 05055
Bauer, Ken, President

Grassroot Soccer [10543]
198 Church St.
Norwich, VT 05055
PH: (802)649-2900
Fax: (802)649-2910
Clark, Tommy, MD, CEO, Founder

Calvin Coolidge Presidential
Foundation, Inc. [10321]
PO Box 97
Plymouth, VT 05056
PH: (802)672-3389
Fax: (802)672-3289
Denhart, Matthew, Exec. Dir.

Friends in Adoption [10453]
212 Main St.
Poultney, VT 05764
Toll free: 800-982-3678
Smith-Pliner, Dawn, Director,
Founder

Welsh-American Genealogical
Society [21000]
60 Norton Ave.
Poultney, VT 05764-1029
Roberts, Dr. Arturo, President

United States Telemark Ski Associa-
tion [23173]
PO Box 844
Putney, VT 05346
PH: (406)862-3303
Long, Garrett, President

Jefferson Legacy Foundation [8445]
PO Box 76
Ripton, VT 05766

PH: (802)388-7676
Fax: (802)388-1776
Stokes, Sydney N., Jr., Chairman

Divine Science Federation
International [20052]
Bldg. 18, Unit 303
Howe Ctr., Ste. 51
1 Scale Ave.
Rutland, VT 05701
PH: (802)779-9019
Toll free: 800-644-9680
Mercer, William, Mem.

Pure Water for the World Inc.
[13334]
PO Box 55
Rutland, VT 05702
PH: (802)747-0778
Fax: (802)773-8575
Manganello, Rick, President

National Education Alliance for
Borderline Personality Disorder
[15796]
10 Quarry Ct.
Saint Albans, VT 05478
Hoffman, Perry D., PhD, President

Friends of Robert Frost [10151]
121 Historic Route 7A
Shaftsbury, VT 05262
Thompson, Carole J., President,
Treasurer

International Association of Service
Evaluators [2823]
c/o Matt Corrow, President
1988 E Rd.
Shaftsbury, VT 05262-9778
PH: (802)681-7940
San Roman, Tina, Treasurer

American Morgan Horse Association
[4316]
4066 Shelburne Rd., Ste. 5
Shelburne, VT 05482
PH: (802)985-4944
Fax: (802)985-8897
Broadway, Julie, Exec. Dir.

Farm-Based Education Network
[7475]
c/o Shelburne Farms
1611 Harbor Rd.
Shelburne, VT 05482
PH: (802)985-0382
Redmond, Brooke G., Dir. of Comm.,
Dir. of Dev.

Population Media Center [12518]
PO Box 547
Shelburne, VT 05482-0547
PH: (802)985-8156
Fax: (802)985-8119
Ryerson, William, President

Autism National Committee [18377]
3 Bedford Green
South Burlington, VT 05403
PH: (802)658-3374
Fax: (802)658-8061
Titon, Emily, President

Children of the Earth [12434]
26 Baycrest Dr.
South Burlington, VT 05403
PH: (802)862-1936
Meyerhof, Dr. Nina, President,
Founder

Funeral Consumers Alliance [2404]
33 Patchen Rd.
South Burlington, VT 05403
PH: (802)865-8300
Fax: (802)865-2626
Powsner, Laurie, President

National Truck Leasing System
[2931]
36 San Remo Dr.
South Burlington, VT 05403

Real Foundation [13395]
550 Hinesburg Rd.
South Burlington, VT 05403
PH: (802)846-7871
O'Brien, Kathy, Director, President

French Bull Dog Club of America
[21881]
c/o Adrienne Soler
206 Smedley Rd.
South Royalton, VT 05068
Rowland, Virginia, President

National Guild of Decoupeurs
[21774]
1017 Pucker St.
Stowe, VT 05672-4496
Fax: (802)253-9552
Peer, Marion D., Contact

Help Kids India [11021]
PO Box 12
Topsham, VT 05076
Dailey, Betsy, President

Action Coalition for Media Education
[18650]
PO Box 1121
Waitsfield, VT 05673
Williams, Rob, President

National Association of State Head
Injury Administrators [14913]
PO Box 878
Waitsfield, VT 05673
PH: (802)498-3349
Fax: (205)823-4544
Wargo, Lorraine, Exec. Dir.

National Association of Comics Art
Educators [7516]
94 South Main St.
The Center for Cartoon Studies
PO Box 125
White River Junction, VT 05001
PH: (802)295-3319
Fax: (802)295-3399
Sturm, James, Director

U.S. Department of Veterans Affairs
I National Center for Post-
Traumatic Stress Disorder [17293]
1234 VA Cut Off Rd.
White River Junction, VT 05009
PH: (802)296-6300
Hamblen, Jessica, Exec. Dir.

Grounds for Health [13979]
600 Blair Park, Ste. 330
Williston, VT 05495
PH: (802)876-7835
Fax: (802)876-7795
Stallworthy, Guy, President, CEO

American Nyckelharpa Association
[9864]
c/o Tim Newcomb
579 Hampshire Hill Rd.
Worcester, VT 05682
PH: (802)229-4604
Oines, Dough, President

VIRGINIA

Association for Multicultural Counsel-
ing and Development [11484]
, VA
Frazier, Kimberly N., Ph.D., LPC,
LMFT, NCC, President

BethanyKids [17382]
PO Box 1297
Abingdon, VA 24212-1297
Toll free: 800-469-1512
Davis, Donald, Dir. of Dev.

Reflexology Association of America
[13653]
PO Box 220
Achilles, VA 23001

PH: (980)234-0159
Earl, Mia, President

National Beagle Club of America
[21920]
22265 Oatlands Rd.
Aldie, VA 20105
Eichler, Caroline, Secretary

60 Plus Association [10495]
515 King St., Ste. 315
Alexandria, VA 22314
PH: (703)807-2070
Fax: (703)807-2073
Martin, James L., Chairman,
President

Academy of Managed Care
Pharmacy [16629]
100 N Pitt St., Ste. 400
Alexandria, VA 22314-3141
PH: (703)683-8416
Toll free: 800-827-2627
Fax: (703)683-8417
Cantrell, Susan, CEO

Accreditation Council for Ac-
countancy and Taxation [4]
1330 Braddock Pl., Ste. 540
Alexandria, VA 22314-1574
Toll free: 888-289-7763
Fax: (703)549-2984
Frick, Roy, Director

Adoptee-Birthparent Support
Network [10437]
6439 Woodridge Rd.
Alexandria, VA 22312-1336
PH: (301)442-9106
Ashford, Suzanne, Contact

Advocates International [5404]
2920 King St.
Alexandria, VA 22302-3512
PH: (571)319-0100
McBurney, Brent, CEO, President

Aeronautical Repair Station Associa-
tion [118]
121 N Henry St.
Alexandria, VA 22314-2903
PH: (703)739-9543
Fax: (703)299-0254
Hudnall, Gary, President

Aerospace Medical Association
[13506]
320 S Henry St.
Alexandria, VA 22314-3579
PH: (703)739-2240
Fax: (703)739-9652
Kildall, Sheryl, Mgr.

Aerospace Physiology Society
[7032]
c/o The Aerospace Medical Association
320 S Henry St.
Alexandria, VA 22314-3579
Thomas, Ashley, Mem.

AFBA [19377]
909 N Washington St.
Alexandria, VA 22314
PH: (703)549-4455
Toll free: 800-776-2322
Fax: (703)706-5961
Eberhart, Ralph E., Chairman,
President

AHOPE for Children [10840]
104 Hume Ave.
Alexandria, VA 22301-1015
PH: (703)683-7500
Fax: (703)683-4482
Wadler, Julie, President, Exec. Dir.

Air Traffic Control Association [122]
1101 King St., Ste. 300
Alexandria, VA 22314

PH: (703)299-2430
Fax: (703)299-2437
Belger, Monte, Contact

Airport Consultants Council [813]
908 King St., Ste. 100
Alexandria, VA 22314
PH: (703)683-5900
Fax: (703)683-2564
Schulz, T.J., President

Alliance for Academic Internal
Medicine [15424]
330 John Carlyle St., Ste. 610
Alexandria, VA 22314
PH: (703)341-4540
Fax: (703)519-1893
Cotroneo, Bergitta E., CEO, Exec.
VP

Alliance of Artists and Recording
Companies [2899]
700 N Fairfax St., Ste. 601
Alexandria, VA 22314
PH: (703)535-8101
Fax: (703)535-8105
Sherman, Cary, Chairman, CEO

Alliance for Childhood Cancer
[13875]
2318 Mill Rd., Ste. 800
Alexandria, VA 22314
Fax: (571)366-9595
Leach, Danielle, Chairperson

Alliance for Conflict Transformation
[17998]
PO Box 9117
Alexandria, VA 22304
PH: (703)879-7039
Carstarphen, Nike, Consultant,
Founder, Director

Alliance for National Defense [5848]
PO Box 184
Alexandria, VA 22313
PH: (703)445-4263
de Vries, Lt. Col. Sherry, USMCR,
President

Alliance for Regional Stewardship
[18625]
c/o American Chamber of Commerce Executives
1330 Braddock Pl., Ste. 300
Alexandria, VA 22314-6400
PH: (703)998-0072
Fax: (888)577-9883
Fleming, Mick, President

Ambulatory Surgery Center Associa-
tion [17358]
1012 Cameron St.
Alexandria, VA 22314-2427
PH: (703)836-8808
Fax: (703)549-0976
Bohlke, Terry, President

AMC Institute [253]
700 N Fairfax St., Ste. 510
Alexandria, VA 22314
PH: (571)527-3108
Fax: (571)527-3105
Payne, Michael, Treasurer

American Academy of Facial Plastic
and Reconstructive Surgery
[14301]
310 S Henry St.
Alexandria, VA 22314-3524
PH: (703)299-9291
Toll free: 800-332-FACE
Fax: (703)299-8898
Duffy, Stephen C., Exec. VP, CEO

American Academy of Forensic
Psychology [5230]
c/o Anita L. Boss, President
1200 Prince St.

Alexandria, VA 22314
PH: (703)299-2422
Otto, Randy K., PhD, Officer

American Academy of Otolaryngol-
ogy - Head and Neck Surgery
[16531]
1650 Diagonal Rd.
Alexandria, VA 22314-2857
PH: (703)836-4444
Fax: (703)683-5100
Edelstein, David R., Chairman

American Academy of Physician As-
sistants [16721]
2318 Mill Rd., Ste. 1300
Alexandria, VA 22314
PH: (703)836-2272
Fax: (703)684-1924
Gables, Lisa, Chief Dev. Ofc., Exec.
Dir.

American Art Therapy Association
[16956]
4875 Eisenhower Ave., Ste. 240
Alexandria, VA 22304
PH: (703)548-5860
Toll free: 888-290-0878
Fax: (703)783-8468
Woodruff, Cynthia, Exec. Dir.

American Association of Airport
Executives [127]
The Barclay Bldg. I
601 Madison St., Ste. 400
Alexandria, VA 22314
PH: (703)824-0500
(703)824-0504
Fax: (703)820-1395
Williams, Craig, Comm. Chm.

American Association of Colleges of
Pharmacy [16632]
1727 King St.
Alexandria, VA 22314
PH: (703)739-2330
Fax: (703)836-8982
Maine, Lucinda L., CEO, Exec. VP

American Association for Dental
Research [14390]
1619 Duke St.
Alexandria, VA 22314-3406
PH: (703)548-0066
Fax: (703)548-1883
Fox, Christopher H., Exec. Dir.

American Association of Family and
Consumer Sciences [11810]
400 N Columbus St., Ste. 202
Alexandria, VA 22314
PH: (703)706-4600
Toll free: 800-424-8080
Fax: (703)706-4663
Barnhart, Carolyn, President

American Association for Marriage
and Family Therapy [16957]
112 S Alfred St.
Alexandria, VA 22314-3061
PH: (703)838-9808
Fax: (703)838-9805
Todd, Tracy, PhD, Exec. Dir.

American Association of Physicists
in Medicine [16763]
1631 Prince St.
Alexandria, VA 22314
PH: (571)298-1300
Fax: (571)298-1301

American Association of Poison
Control Centers [17491]
515 King St., Ste. 510
Alexandria, VA 22314
PH: (703)894-1858
Toll free: 800-222-1222
Fax: (703)683-2812
Kaminski, Stephen T., CEO, Exec.
Dir.

American Association of Port
Authorities [23423]
1010 Duke St.
Alexandria, VA 22314-3589
PH: (703)684-5700
Fax: (703)684-6321
Monteverde, Susan, VP of Rel.

American Association of School
Administrators [7416]
1615 Duke St.
Alexandria, VA 22314
PH: (703)528-0700
Fax: (703)841-1543
Domenech, Daniel A., Exec. Dir.

American Association for the Study
of Liver Diseases [15248]
1001 N Fairfax St., Ste. 400
Alexandria, VA 22314-1587
PH: (703)299-9766
Cathcart, Sherrie, Exec. Dir.

American-Austrian Cultural Society
[9030]
c/o Ulli Wiesner, Managing Director
5618 Dover Ct.
Alexandria, VA 22312
Wiesner, Ms. Ulrike, Managing Dir.

American Automotive Leasing As-
sociation [2923]
675 N Washington St., Ste. 410
Alexandria, VA 22314
PH: (703)548-0777
Fax: (703)548-1925
Bloom, Steven, President

American Bankruptcy Institute [5083]
66 Canal Center Plz., Ste. 600
Alexandria, VA 22314
PH: (703)739-0800
Fax: (703)739-1060
Thorne, Deborah L., VP, Comm.

American Board for Certification in
Orthotics, Prosthetics and Pedorth-
ics [16493]
330 John Carlyle St., Ste. 210
Alexandria, VA 22314
PH: (703)836-7114
Fax: (703)836-0838
Carter, Catherine, Exec. Dir.

American Board of Facial Plastic
and Reconstructive Surgery
[17363]
115C S St. Asaph St.
Alexandria, VA 22314
PH: (703)549-3223
Fax: (703)549-3357
Wirth, Laurie, Exec. Dir.

American Board of Physical Therapy
Residency and Fellowship Educa-
tion [16716]
c/o American Physical Therapy As-
sociation
1111 N Fairfax St.
Alexandria, VA 22314-1488
PH: (703)706-3152
Fax: (703)706-8186
DeWitt, John, Chmn. of the Bd.

American Board of Physical Therapy
Specialties [16717]
c/o American Physical Therapy As-
sociation
1111 N Fairfax St.
Alexandria, VA 22314-1488
PH: (703)706-8520
Toll free: 800-999-2782
Fax: (703)706-8186
Irion, Jean, Chairperson

American Civil Rights Union [17869]
3213 Duke St., No. 625
Alexandria, VA 22314

PH: (703)217-2660
Toll free: 877-730-2278
Carleson, Susan A., Chairman, CEO

American College of International
  Physicians [15435]
9323 Old Mt. Vernon Rd.
Alexandria, VA 22309
PH: (703)221-1500
Yadao, Alex, MD, Chairman,
  President

American College of Osteopathic
  Surgeons [16507]
123 N Henry St.
Alexandria, VA 22314-2903
PH: (703)684-0416
Toll free: 800-888-1312
Fax: (703)684-3280
Ayers, Linda, CEO

American Correctional Association
  [11517]
206 N Washington St.
Alexandria, VA 22314
PH: (703)224-0000
Fax: (703)224-0179
Gondles, James A., Jr., Exec. Dir.

American Council on the Teaching of
  Foreign Languages [8177]
1001 N Fairfax St., Ste. 200
Alexandria, VA 22314
PH: (703)894-2900
Fax: (703)894-2905
Abbott, Marty, Exec. Dir.

American Counseling Association
  [11482]
6101 Stevenson Ave.
Alexandria, VA 22304
PH: (703)823-9800
Toll free: 800-347-6647
Fax: (703)823-0252
Yep, Richard, Exec. Dir.

American Defense Institute [18081]
1055 N Fairfax St., Ste. 200
Alexandria, VA 22314
PH: (703)519-7000
Fax: (703)519-8627
McDaniel, Eugene, President

American Diabetes Association
  [14518]
1701 N Beauregard St.
Alexandria, VA 22311
PH: (800)342-2383
    (202)331-8303
Toll free: 800-342-2383
Bennett, Vaneeda, CRO

American Foundation for
  Pharmaceutical Education [16639]
6076 Franconia Rd., Ste. C
Alexandria, VA 22310-1758
PH: (703)875-3095
Toll free: 855-624-9526
Fax: (703)875-3098
Kadlec, Gary, Chairman

American Friends of the
  Shakespeare Birthplace Trust
  [10357]
1423 Powhatan St., Ste.1
Alexandria, VA 22314
PH: (703)566-3805
Fax: (703)566-3806
Chwat, John, President

American Gear Manufacturers As-
  sociation [1706]
1001 N Fairfax St., Ste. 500
Alexandria, VA 22314-1587
PH: (703)684-0211
Fax: (703)684-0242
Croson, Matthew, President

American Geosciences Institute
  [6676]
4220 King St.
Alexandria, VA 22302

PH: (703)379-2480
Fax: (703)379-7563

American Horticultural Society
  [22075]
7931 E Boulevard Dr.
Alexandria, VA 22308-1300
PH: (703)768-5700
Fax: (703)768-8700
Underwood, Tom, Exec. Ofc.

American Indian Higher Education
  Consortium [8393]
121 Oronoco St.
Alexandria, VA 22314
PH: (703)838-0400
Fax: (703)838-0388
Billy, Carrie L., JD, CEO, President

American Indian Youth Running
  Strong, Inc. [12373]
8301 Richmond Hwy., Ste. 200
Alexandria, VA 22309-2324
PH: (703)317-9881
Toll free: 888-491-9859
Fax: (703)317-9690
Finkelstein, Lauren Haas, Exec. Dir.

American Institute of Constructors
  [6345]
700 N Fairfax St., Ste. 510
Alexandria, VA 22314
PH: (703)683-4999
Fax: (571)527-3105
Matthews, Tanya, FAIC, DBIA, Direc-
  tor

American International Automobile
  Dealers Association [335]
500 Montgomery St., Ste. 800
Alexandria, VA 22314
Toll free: 800-462-4232
Fax: (703)519-7810
Kaminsky, Greg, Chairman

American Lebanese Coalition
  [18633]
4900 Leesburg Pke., Ste. 203
Alexandria, VA 22302
PH: (703)578-4214
Fax: (703)578-4615
Gebeily, Joseph, MD, President

American Medical Group Association
  [15135]
1 Prince St.
Alexandria, VA 22314-3318
PH: (703)838-0033
Fax: (703)548-1890
Fisher, Dr. Donald W., CAE, CEO,
  President

American Mental Health Counselors
  Association [15758]
675 N Washington, Ste. 470
Alexandria, VA 22314
PH: (703)548-6002
Toll free: 800-326-2642
Miller, Joel E., CEO, Exec. Dir.

American Moving and Storage As-
  sociation [3081]
1611 Duke St.
Alexandria, VA 22314-3406
PH: (703)683-7410
Toll free: 888-849-2672
Fax: (703)683-7527
Becker, John, Director

American Network of Community
  Options and Resources [12314]
1101 King St., Ste. 380
Alexandria, VA 22314-2962
PH: (703)535-7850
Fax: (703)535-7860
Yu, Tony, Dir. of Info. Technology

American Orthotic and Prosthetic
  Association [1596]
330 John Carlyle St., Ste. 200
Alexandria, VA 22314

PH: (571)431-0876
Fax: (571)431-0899
Fise, Tom, Exec. Dir., Secretary

American Peanut Council [4506]
1500 King St., Ste. 301
Alexandria, VA 22314
PH: (703)838-9500
Archer, Patrick, President

American Physical Therapy Associa-
  tion [16718]
1111 N Fairfax St.
Alexandria, VA 22314-1488
PH: (703)684-2782
Toll free: 800-999-2782
Fax: (703)684-7343
Dunn, Sharon L., President

American Public Communications
  Council, Inc. [3216]
3213 Duke St., Ste. 806
Alexandria, VA 22314
PH: (703)739-1322
Fax: (703)739-1324
Nichols, Willard R., President

American Rock Mechanics Associa-
  tion [3181]
600 Woodland Ter.
Alexandria, VA 22302-3319
PH: (703)683-1808
Fax: (703)997-6112
Smeallie, Peter H., Exec. Dir.

American School Counselor Associa-
  tion [7683]
1101 King St., Ste. 310
Alexandria, VA 22314
PH: (703)683-2722
Toll free: 800-306-4722
Fax: (703)997-7572
Wong, Prof. Richard, Exec. Dir.

American Seed Research Founda-
  tion [4640]
1701 Duke St., Ste. 275
Alexandria, VA 22314
PH: (703)837-8140
Fax: (703)837-9365
Austin, Glenn D., President

American Seed Trade Association
  [4641]
1701 Duke St., Ste. 275
Alexandria, VA 22314-3415
PH: (703)837-8140
Toll free: 888-890-7333
Fax: (703)837-9365
LaVigne, Andrew W., President,
  CEO

American Society of Aerospace
  Medicine Specialists [13508]
c/o Aerospace Medical Association
320 S Henry St.
Alexandria, VA 22314
Shoor, Dr. Daniel, President

American Society of Clinical Oncol-
  ogy [16335]
2318 Mill Rd., Ste. 800
Alexandria, VA 22314
PH: (571)483-1300
Toll free: 888-282-2552
Hudis, Clifford, MD, President

American Society for Clinical
  Pharmacology and Therapeutics
  [16642]
528 N Washington St.
Alexandria, VA 22314-2314
PH: (703)836-6981
Fax: (703)836-5223
Swan, Sharon J., CAE, CEO

American Society of Consultant
  Pharmacists [16644]
1321 Duke St.
Alexandria, VA 22314-3563

PH: (703)739-1300
Toll free: 800-355-2727
Fax: (703)739-1321
Grosso, Frank, Exec. Dir., CEO

American Society for Horticultural
  Science [6134]
1018 Duke St.
Alexandria, VA 22314
PH: (703)836-4606
Fax: (703)836-2024
Neff, Michael W., Exec. Dir.

American Society of Military
  Comptrollers [5591]
415 N Alfred St.
Alexandria, VA 22314
PH: (703)549-0360
Toll free: 800-462-5637
Fax: (703)549-3181
Bennett, Craig, President

American Society of Naval
  Engineers [6904]
1452 Duke St.
Alexandria, VA 22314
PH: (703)836-6727
Fax: (703)836-7491
Huling, Mike, Officer

American Society of Travel Agents
  [3369]
675 N Washington St., Ste. 490
Alexandria, VA 22314
PH: (703)739-2782
Toll free: 800-275-2782
Kerby, Zane, President, CEO

American Sportfishing Association
  [22839]
1001 N Fairfax St., Ste. 501
Alexandria, VA 22314
PH: (703)519-9691
Fax: (703)519-1872
Nussman, Mike, CEO, President

American Staffing Association [1085]
277 S Washington St., Ste. 200
Alexandria, VA 22314
PH: (703)253-2020
Fax: (703)253-2053
Wahlquist, Mr. Richard, CEO,
  President

American Statistical Association
  [7240]
732 N Washington St.
Alexandria, VA 22314-1943
PH: (703)684-1221
Toll free: 888-231-3473
Fax: (703)684-2037
Wasserstein, Ronald, Exec. Dir.

American Subcontractors Associa-
  tion [852]
1004 Duke St.
Alexandria, VA 22314
PH: (703)684-3450
Fax: (703)836-3482
Nelson, Collette, Officer

American Translators Association
  [3311]
225 Reinekers Ln., Ste. 590
Alexandria, VA 22314
PH: (703)683-6100
Fax: (703)683-6122
Rumsey, David C., President

American Wire Producers Associa-
  tion [1710]
PO Box 151387
Alexandria, VA 22315-1387
PH: (703)299-4434
Fax: (703)299-4434
Korbel, KImberly A., Exec. Dir.

Americans for Better Care of the Dying [13215]
1700 Diagonal Rd., Ste. 635
Alexandria, VA 22314-2866

PH: (703)647-8505
Fax: (703)837-1233
Lily, Maureen, Exec. Dir.

Analytical, Life Science and
Diagnostics Association [7119]
500 Montgomery St., Ste. 400
Alexandria, VA 22314-1560
PH: (703)647-6214
Fax: (703)647-6368
Alpert, Briar, V. Chmn. of the Bd.

Argentum [11963]
1650 King St., Ste. 602
Alexandria, VA 22314
PH: (703)894-1805
Fax: (703)894-1831
Bacon, Brenda J., Chmn. of the Bd.

Army Emergency Relief [19380]
200 Stovall St., Rm. 5S33
Alexandria, VA 22332-4005
PH: (703)428-0000
Toll free: 866-878-6378
Fax: (703)325-7183
Reimer, Gen. Dennis J., President

Army Engineer Association [4972]
PO Box 30260
Alexandria, VA 22310-8260
PH: (703)428-7084
      (703)428-6049
Fax: (703)428-6043
O'Neill, Colonel (Retired) Jack,
Exec. Dir.

Art Services International [8841]
119 Duke St.
Alexandria, VA 22314
PH: (703)548-4554
Fax: (703)548-3305
McAllister, Michael F., Gen. Counsel

ASCD [7693]
1703 N Beauregard St.
Alexandria, VA 22311-1714
PH: (703)578-9600
Toll free: 800-933-2723
Fax: (703)575-5400
McClure, Matt, President

ASIS International [1782]
1625 Prince St.
Alexandria, VA 22314-2882
PH: (703)519-6200
Fax: (703)519-6299
O'Neil, Peter J., FASAE, CAE, Exec.
VP, CEO

Assisting Children in Need [10802]
c/o Frank O. Klein II, President
600 Cameron St.
Alexandria, VA 22314-2506
PH: (703)340-1677
Klein, Melissa, VP, Director

Association of Air Medical Services
[14660]
909 N Washington St., Ste. 410
Alexandria, VA 22314-3143
PH: (703)836-8732
Fax: (703)836-8920
Sherlock, Rick, Contact

Association for Assessment and
Research in Counseling [8681]
c/o American Counseling Association
6101 Stevenson Ave., Ste. 600
Alexandria, VA 22304-3540
Toll free: 800-347-6647
Fax: (800)473-2329
Sheperis, Carl, President

Association of Baccalaureate Social
Work Program Directors [8568]
1701 Duke St., Ste. 200
Alexandria, VA 22314
PH: (703)519-2045
Fax: (703)683-8493
Battle, DuWayne, President

Association for Career and Technical
Education [8733]
1410 King St.
Alexandria, VA 22314
Toll free: 800-826-9972
Fax: (703)683-7424
Comer, Jim, Comm. Chm.

Association of Chamber of Com-
merce Executives [23561]
1330 Braddock Pl., Ste. 300
Alexandria, VA 22314
PH: (703)998-0072
Toll free: 888-577-9883
Fleming, Mick, President

Association of Clinical Research
Professionals [16652]
99 Canal Center Plz., Ste. 200
Alexandria, VA 22314
PH: (703)254-8100
Fax: (703)254-8101
Lancaster, Giovanna, Administrator

Association for Computing
Machinery - Special Interest Group
on Ada [7055]
c/o Clyde Roby, Secretary-Treasurer
Institute for Defense Analyses
4850 Mark Center Dr.
Alexandria, VA 22311
PH: (703)845-6666
Fax: (703)845-6848
Cook, David, Chairman

Association of Consulting Foresters
of America [4194]
312 Montgomery St., Ste. 208
Alexandria, VA 22314
PH: (703)548-0990
Wilson, Lynn C., Exec. Dir.

Association of Corporate Travel
Executives [3370]
510 King St., Ste. 220
Alexandria, VA 22314
PH: (262)763-1902
Toll free: 800-375-2283
Knackstedt, Kurt, President

Association of Credit Union Internal
Auditors [946]
1727 King St., Ste. 300
Alexandria, VA 22314
PH: (703)688-2284
Fax: (703)348-7602
Swenson, Dean

Association for Education and
Rehabilitation of the Blind and
Visually Impaired [17689]
1703 N Beauregard St., Ste. 440
Alexandria, VA 22311
PH: (703)671-4500
Tutt, Lou, Contact

Association for Federal Information
Resources Management [5300]
400 N Washington St., Ste. 300
Alexandria, VA 22314
PH: (703)778-4646
Fax: (703)683-5480
Foster, Robert, President

Association for Financial Counseling
and Planning Education [1275]
1940 Duke St., Ste. 200
Alexandria, VA 22314-3452
PH: (703)684-4484
Fax: (703)684-4485
Wiggins, Rebecca, Exec. Dir.

Association of Government Ac-
countants [4938]
2208 Mt. Vernon Ave.
Alexandria, VA 22301-1314
PH: (703)684-6931
Toll free: 800-AGA-7211
Fax: (703)548-9367
Ebberts, Ann M., CEO

Association for Humanistic Counseling [8001]
5999 Stevenson Ave.
Alexandria, VA 22304
Lopez, Belinda, Secretary

Association of Independent Cor-
rugated Converters [828]
PO Box 25708
Alexandria, VA 22313
PH: (703)836-2422
Toll free: 877-836-2422
Fax: (703)836-2795
Williams, Mark, Chairman

Association of Machinery and Equip-
ment Appraisers [221]
315 S Patrick St.
Alexandria, VA 22314
PH: (703)836-7900
Toll free: 800-537-8629
Fax: (703)836-9303
Mendenhall, Jack, President

Association Montessori International
USA [8350]
206 N Washington St., Ste. 330
Alexandria, VA 22314
PH: (703)746-9919
Lewis, Adam, President

Association of Old Crows [6416]
1000 N Payne St., Ste. 200
Alexandria, VA 22314-1652
PH: (703)549-1600
Fax: (703)549-2589
Dolim, Mike, Exec. Dir.

Association of Pool and Spa Profes-
sionals [2906]
2111 Eisenhower Ave., Ste. 500
Alexandria, VA 22314
PH: (703)838-0083
Fax: (703)549-0493
Nielsen, April, Mem.

Association for Postal Commerce
[2117]
1100 Wyne St., Unit 1268
Alexandria, VA 22313
PH: (703)524-0096
Fax: (703)997-2414
Del Polito, Gene A., PhD, President

Association of Professors of
Medicine [8311]
330 John Carlyle St., Ste. 610
Alexandria, VA 22314
PH: (703)341-4540
Marsh, James, President

Association of Program Directors in
Internal Medicine [15427]
Alliance for Academic Internal
Medicine
330 John Carlyle St., Ste. 610
Alexandria, VA 22314-5946
PH: (703)341-4540
Fax: (703)519-1893
Bellini, Lisa M., MD, Comm. Chm.

Association of Residential Construc-
tion Workers [801]
3680 Wheeler Ave., Ste. 100
Alexandria, VA 22304
PH: (703)212-8294
Fax: (703)386-6444
Gonzalez, Rick, Contact

Association of Specialty Professors
[15428]
c/o Alliance for Academic Internal
Medicine
330 John Carlyle St., Ste. 610
Alexandria, VA 22314
PH: (703)341-4540
Fax: (703)519-1893
Bater, D. Craig, MD, President

Association for Spiritual, Ethical and
Religious Values in Counseling
[20039]
c/o American Counseling Association
6101 Stevenson Ave., Ste. 600
Alexandria, VA 22304-3580
Giordano, Amanda, Treasurer

Association for Talent Development
[7546]
1640 King St.
Alexandria, VA 22314-2746
PH: (703)683-8100
Toll free: 800-628-2783
Fax: (703)683-1523
Bingham, Tony, CEO, President

Association of the United States
Navy [5594]
1619 King St.
Alexandria, VA 22314
PH: (703)548-5800
Toll free: 877-628-9411
Fax: (703)683-3647
Totushek, John, Exec. Dir.

Association for Women in Com-
munications [761]
3337 Duke St.
Alexandria, VA 22314
PH: (703)370-7436
Fax: (703)342-4311
Valenzuela, Pamela, Exec. Dir.

Association for Women in Science
[7123]
1321 Duke St., Ste. 210
Alexandria, VA 22314
PH: (703)894-4490
Fax: (703)894-4489
Koster, Janet Bandows, Exec. Dir.,
CEO

Aviation Technician Education
Council [7458]
117 North Henry St.
Alexandria, VA 22314-2903
PH: (703)548-2030
Goertzen, Ryan, President

Better Sleep Council [17214]
501 Wythe St.
Alexandria, VA 22314-1917
PH: (703)683-8371

Boat Owners Association of the
United States [22601]
880 S Pickett St.
Alexandria, VA 22304-4606
Toll free: 800-395-2628
La, Kirk, Chairman

Bodomase Development Association
USA Inc. [11319]
4527 Arendale Sq.
Alexandria, VA 22309

CAF America [13003]
King Street Sta.
1800 Diagonal Rd., Ste. 150
Alexandria, VA 22314-2840
PH: (202)793-2232
Fax: (703)549-8934
Hart, Ted, AFCRE, CEO

Cancer Quality Alliance [13928]
2318 Mill Rd., Ste. 800
Alexandria, VA 22314
PH: (571)483-1300
Ganz, Patricia, Co-Ch.

Catholic Athletes for Christ [22510]
3703 Cameron Mills Rd.
Alexandria, VA 22305
PH: (703)239-3070
McKenna, Ray, Founder, President

Catholic Charities USA [13035]
2050 Ballenger Ave., Ste. 400
Alexandria, VA 22314

PH: (703)549-1390
Toll free: 800-919-9338
Fax: (703)549-1656
Markham, Donna, President, CEO

Catholic War Veterans of the U.S.A.
[21114]
441 N Lee St.
Alexandria, VA 22314
PH: (703)549-3622
Fax: (703)684-5196
Finkel, James C., Sr., Cmdr.

Center for Competitive Politics
[17880]
124 S West St., Ste. 201
Alexandria, VA 22314
PH: (703)894-6800
Fax: (703)894-6811
Smith, Bradley A., Founder, Chairman

Center for the Ministry of Teaching
[20076]
3737 Seminary Rd.
Alexandria, VA 22304
PH: (703)370-6600
Toll free: 800-941-0083
Linthicum, Dorothy, Coord.

Children's Hospice International
[15293]
500 Montgomery St., Ste. 400
Alexandria, VA 22314
PH: (703)684-0330
Armstrong-Dailey, Ann, Director, Founder

Christian Relief Services [12642]
8301 Richmond Hwy., Ste. 900
Alexandria, VA 22309
PH: (703)317-9086
    (703)317-9690
Toll free: 800-33-RELIEF
Krizek, Eugene L., Exec. Dir., Gen. Counsel

Clerkship Directors in Internal Medicine [15429]
330 John Carlyle St., Ste. 610
Alexandria, VA 22314-5946
PH: (703)341-4540
Fax: (703)519-1893
Fazio, Sara B., Chairman

Close Up Foundation [17855]
1330 Braddock Pl., Ste. 400
Alexandria, VA 22314
PH: (703)706-3300
Toll free: 800-CLOSE UP
Davis, Timothy S., President, CEO

Club Managers Association of America [732]
1733 King St.
Alexandria, VA 22314
PH: (703)739-9500
Fax: (703)739-0124
Morgan, Jeff, CEO

Coalition Against Bigger Trucks
[13231]
1001 N Fairfax St., Ste. 515
Alexandria, VA 22314
PH: (703)535-3131
Toll free: 888-CAB-T123

Coalition for Tactical Medicine
[16319]
3337 Duke St.
Alexandria, VA 22314
PH: (703)370-7436
Fax: (703)342-4311
Clinchy, Richard A., Chairman

Color Marketing Group [753]
1908 Mt. Vernon Ave.
Alexandria, VA 22301

PH: (703)329-8500
Fax: (703)329-0155
Woodman, Mark, President

Commission on Accreditation for Marriage and Family Therapy Education [8273]
112 S Alfred St.
Alexandria, VA 22314-3061
PH: (703)253-0473
Fax: (703)253-0508
Tamarkin, Tanya A., Dir. of Accred.

Commission for Certification in Geriatric Pharmacy [16659]
1321 Duke St., Ste. 400
Alexandria, VA 22314-3563
PH: (703)535-3036
Fax: (703)739-1500
Clark, Thomas R., RPh, Exec. Dir.

Community Anti-Drug Coalitions of America [13133]
625 Slaters Ln., Ste. 300
Alexandria, VA 22314
Toll free: 800-54-CADCA
Fax: (703)706-0565
Dean, Arthur T., Chairman, CEO

Community Financial Services Association of America [1227]
515 King St., Ste. 300
Alexandria, VA 22314
Toll free: 888-572-9329
Fax: (703)684-1219
DeVault, Lynn, Comm. Chm.

Community Health Charities [11858]
1240 N Pitt St., 3rd Fl.
Alexandria, VA 22314
PH: (703)528-1007
Toll free: 800-654-0845
Fax: (703)528-5975
Bognanno, Thomas G., President, CEO

Community Members Interested
[11340]
205 Yoakum Pky., Unit 807
Alexandria, VA 22304
PH: (301)273-5679
Hada, Jayjeev, Chairman, Exec. Dir., Founder

Composite Can and Tube Institute
[830]
50 S Pickett St., Ste. 110
Alexandria, VA 22304-7206
PH: (703)823-7234
Fax: (703)823-7237
Garland, Kristine, Exec. VP

Concern for Helping Animals in Israel [10608]
PO Box 3341
Alexandria, VA 22302
PH: (703)658-9650
Natelson, Nina, Exec. Dir.

Conexxus [2516]
1600 Duke St.
Alexandria, VA 22314
PH: (703)518-7960
Taylor, Gray, Exec. Dir.

Connective Tissue Oncology Society
[16342]
PO Box 320574
Alexandria, VA 22320
PH: (301)502-7371
Fax: (703)548-4882
Rapp, Barbara, Exec. Dir.

Construction Specifications Institute
[6349]
110 S Union St., Ste. 100
Alexandria, VA 22314
Toll free: 800-689-2900
Dorsey, Mark, Exec. Dir., CEO

Convention Industry Council [3290]
700 N Fairfax St., Ste. 510
Alexandria, VA 22314
PH: (571)527-3116
Fax: (571)527-3105
Hinton, Kevin, Bd. Member

Council for Accreditation of Counseling and Related Educational Programs [7687]
1001 N Fairfax St., Ste. 510
Alexandria, VA 22314
PH: (703)535-5990
Fax: (703)739-6209
Parsons, Jeffrey, Chairman

Council for Affordable and Rural Housing [11967]
1112 King St.
Alexandria, VA 22314
PH: (703)837-9001
Fax: (703)837-8467
Flynn, Kevin, Chmn. of the Bd.

Council of Citizens With Low Vision International [11583]
1703 N Beauregard St., Ste. 420
Alexandria, VA 22311-1764
Toll free: 800-733-2258
Smith, Dan, 1st VP

Council for Electronic Revenue Communication Advancement
[3224]
600 Cameron St., Ste. 309
Alexandria, VA 22314
PH: (703)340-1655
Fax: (703)340-1658
Cavanagh, Mike, Exec. Dir.

Council of Ethical Organizations
[11798]
214 S Payne St.
Alexandria, VA 22314
PH: (703)683-7916
Quinn, Howard, Advisor

Council for Global Immigration
[1088]
1800 Duke St.
Alexandria, VA 22314
PH: (703)535-6365
Toll free: 855-686-4777
Fragomen, Austin T., Jr., Chairman

Council on Sexual Orientation and Gender Identity and Expression
[8570]
Council on Social Work Education
1701 Duke St., Ste. 200
Alexandria, VA 22314-3457
PH: (703)683-8080
Fax: (703)683-8099
Balestrery, Jean E., Fac. Memb.

Council on Social Work Education
[8571]
1701 Duke St., Ste. 200
Alexandria, VA 22314
PH: (703)683-8080
Fax: (703)683-8099
Shank, Barbara W., Chmn. of the Bd.

Council for Standards in Human Service Education [13041]
3337 Duke St.
Alexandria, VA 22314
PH: (571)257-3959
Kaufmann, Jacquelyn, MS, HS-BCP, VP

Council on Standards for International Educational Travel
[8066]
212 S Henry St.
Alexandria, VA 22314
PH: (703)739-9050
Tackett, Julian, Chairman

Crude Accountability [4046]
PO Box 2345
Alexandria, VA 22301
PH: (703)299-0854
Fax: (703)299-0854
Watters, Ms. Kate, Exec. Dir.

Darfur Peace and Development Organization [12150]
PO Box 10384
Alexandria, VA 22310
Giddo, Suliman A., CEO, President

Defense Advisory Committee on Women in the Services [5597]
4000 Mark Center Dr., Ste. 04J25-01
Alexandria, VA 22350-9000
PH: (703)697-2122
Anderson, Kristy, Officer

Economics of National Security Association [5753]
c/o John Whitley, Secretary
4850 Mark Center Dr.
Alexandria, VA 22311
Feldstein, Martin, President

EcoVentures International [4115]
2016 Mt. Vernon Ave., Ste. 203
Alexandria, VA 22301
Brand, Margie, Founder

Electronic Industry Citizenship Coalition [1044]
1737 King St., Ste. 330
Alexandria, VA 22314
PH: (517)858-5720
Fax: (517)431-6317
Anderson, Kenneth, Dir. of Info. Technology

Employer Support of the Guard and Reserve [5598]
4800 Mark Center Dr., Ste. 3E25
Alexandria, VA 22350-1200
Toll free: 800-336-4590
Fax: (571)372-0705
Mock, Paul E., Chairman

Enlisted Association of National Guard of the United States [5599]
3133 Mount Vernon Ave.
Alexandria, VA 22305-2640
Toll free: 800-234-3264
Fax: (703)519-3849
Harris, John, President

Entrepreneurs' Organization [628]
500 Montgomery St., Ste. 700
Alexandria, VA 22314
PH: (703)519-6700
Fax: (703)519-1864
Crombé, Gilberto, Chairman

Envelope Manufacturers Association
[3171]
500 Montgomery St., Ste. 550
Alexandria, VA 22314
PH: (703)739-2200
Fax: (703)739-2209
Benjamin, Maynard H., CAE, CEO, President

Epicomm [94]
1800 Diagonal Rd., Ste. 320
Alexandria, VA 22314-2806
PH: (703)836-9200
Fax: (703)548-8204
Garner, Ken, COO, President

Ex-Partners of Servicemembers for Equality [11683]
PO Box 11191
Alexandria, VA 22312-0191
PH: (703)941-5844

The Executive Leadership Council
[2393]
1001 N Fairfax St., Ste. 300
Alexandria, VA 22314

PH: (703)706-5200
Fax: (703)535-6830
Parker, Ronald C., President, CEO

Fats and Proteins Research Foundation, Inc. [2448]
500 Montgomery St., Ste. 310
Alexandria, VA 22314
PH: (703)683-2914
Meisinger, Jessica, PhD, Dir. Ed.

Federal Bureau of Investigation Agents Association [5462]
PO Box 320215
Alexandria, VA 22320
PH: (703)247-2173
Fax: (703)247-2175
Tariche, Reynaldo, President

Federal Managers Association [5196]
1641 Prince St.
Alexandria, VA 22314-2818
PH: (703)683-8700
Fax: (703)683-8707
Johnson, Renee, President

Federation of State Boards of Physical Therapy [16719]
124 West St. S, 3rd Fl.
Alexandria, VA 22314
PH: (703)299-3100
Fax: (703)299-3110
Hatherill, William, CEO

Feminists for Life of America [19058]
PO Box 320667
Alexandria, VA 22320
PH: (703)836-3354
Foster, Serrin M., President

Fight Colorectal Cancer [13968]
1414 Prince St., Ste. 204
Alexandria, VA 22314
PH: (703)548-1225
Toll free: 877-427-2111
Roach, Nancy, Chairperson, Founder

FishAmerica Foundation [3863]
1001 N Fairfax St., Ste. 501
Alexandria, VA 22314
PH: (703)519-9691
Fax: (703)519-1872
Bulthuis, Dave, Certified Public Accountant

Fleet Reserve Association [21053]
125 N West St.
Alexandria, VA 22314-2709
PH: (703)683-1400
Toll free: 800-FRA-1924
Snee, Thomas J., Exec. Dir.

Flight Safety Foundation [135]
701 N Fairfax St., Ste. 250
Alexandria, VA 22314-1754
PH: (703)739-6700
Fax: (703)739-6708
Rosenkrans, Wayne, Editor

Forest Landowners Tax Council [5792]
1602 Belle View Blvd. No. 245
Alexandria, VA 22307-6531
PH: (703)549-0347
Stewart, Frank, Exec. Dir.

Foster Care Alumni of America [10981]
5810 Kingstowne Center Dr., Ste. 120-730
Alexandria, VA 22315
PH: (703)299-6767
Toll free: 888-ALU-MNI0
Herrick, Mary Anne, President, Chairman

Foundation for Physical Therapy [17441]
1111 N Fairfax St.
Alexandria, VA 22314
Toll free: 800-875-1378
Malm, Barbara, MBA, Exec. Dir.

Free Congress Foundation [18868]
901 N Washington, Ste. 206
Alexandria, VA 22314-1535
PH: (703)837-0030
Blackwell, Morton C., Director, Treasurer

Fund for UFO Research [7010]
PO Box 7501
Alexandria, VA 22307
Berliner, Don, Chairman

Global Business Travel Association [3378]
123 N Pitt St.
Alexandria, VA 22314
PH: (703)684-0836
Fax: (703)342-4324
Kelliher, Donna, CTC, GLP, President, CEO

Global Cold Chain Alliance [1616]
1500 King St., Ste. 201
Alexandria, VA 22314-2730
PH: (703)373-4300
Fax: (703)373-4301
Costello, Megan, VP

Global Envelope Alliance [3172]
700 S Washington St., Ste. 260
Alexandria, VA 22314
PH: (703)739-2200
Fax: (703)739-2209
Berkley, Bert, Chmn. of the Bd.

Global Health Council [15455]
1199 N Fairfax St., Ste. 300
Alexandria, VA 22314
PH: (703)717-5200
Fax: (703)717-5215
Sow, Dr. Christine, Exec. Dir., President

GlobalSecurity.org [18792]
300 N Washington St., Ste. B-100
Alexandria, VA 22314
PH: (703)548-2700
Fax: (703)548-2424
Pike, John E., Director

Good360 [12478]
675 N Washington St. Ste. 330
Alexandria, VA 22314
Schwartz, Bob, Co-Ch.

Haiti Philatelic Society [22332]
5709 Marble Archway
Alexandria, VA 22315-4013
Deltoro, Ubaldo, President, Secretary, Treasurer

Health Industry Distributors Association [1601]
310 Montgomery St.
Alexandria, VA 22314-1516
PH: (703)549-4432
    (703)838-6118
Fax: (703)549-6495
Rowan, Matthew, President, CEO

Heart4Kids Society, Inc. [11018]
2801 Park Center Dr.
Alexandria, VA 22302
PH: (404)957-9014
Denenga, Sandra, Exec. Dir., Founder

Helicopter Association International [137]
1920 Ballenger Ave.
Alexandria, VA 22314-2898

PH: (703)683-4646
Toll free: 800-435-4976
Fax: (703)683-4745
Dicampli, Edward F., COO, Secretary

Helicopter Foundation International [138]
1920 Ballenger Ave.
Alexandria, VA 22314-2898
PH: (703)683-4646
    (703)360-1521
Dicampli, Edward F., Secretary, COO

High Frontier Organization [18478]
500 N Washington St.
Alexandria, VA 22314
PH: (703)535-8774
Cooper, Amb. Henry F., Chairman

Horatio Alger Association of Distinguished Americans [20734]
99 Canal Center Plz., Ste. 320
Alexandria, VA 22314-1588
PH: (703)684-9444
Toll free: 844-422-4200
Sokol, David L., Chairman

HR Certification Institute [2499]
1725 Duke St., Ste. 700
Alexandria, VA 22314
PH: (571)551-6700
Toll free: 866-898-4724
Morgan, Kerry, Chief Mktg. Ofc.

HR People and Strategy [2169]
1800 Duke St.
Alexandria, VA 22314
Toll free: 888-602-3270
Fax: (703)535-6490
Vosburgh, Richard, Chairman

Human Resources Research Organization [6038]
66 Canal Center Plz., Ste. 700
Alexandria, VA 22314-1578
PH: (703)549-3611
Fax: (703)549-9025
Kracker, Thomas, VP, Director

Idealliance [1537]
1800 Diagonal Rd., Ste. 320
Alexandria, VA 22314
PH: (703)837-1070
    (703)837-1066
Fax: (703)837-1072
Bonoff, Steve, Sr. VP of Mktg.

Independent Electrical Contractors [866]
4401 Ford Ave., Ste. 1100
Alexandria, VA 22302
PH: (703)549-7351
Toll free: 800-456-4324
Fax: (703)549-7448
Long, Thayer, Exec. VP, CEO

Independent Insurance Agents and Brokers of America Inc. [1860]
127 S Peyton St.
Alexandria, VA 22314
Toll free: 800-221-7917
Fax: (703)683-7556

Independent Lubricant Manufacturers Association [2523]
400 N Columbus St., Ste. 201
Alexandria, VA 22314-2264
PH: (703)684-5574
Fax: (703)836-8503
Hamilton, Frank H., III, President

The Infrastructure Security Partnership [3056]
607 Prince St.
Alexandria, VA 22314
PH: (703)549-3800
    (703)373-7981
Edgar, C. Ernest, LTC, Chairperson

Institute for Alternative Futures [6656]
2331 Mill Rd., Ste. 100
Alexandria, VA 22314
PH: (703)684-5880
Bezold, Clement, PhD, Chairman

Institute for Defense Analyses [5755]
4850 Mark Center Dr.
Alexandria, VA 22311-1882
PH: (703)845-2000
Chu, David, President

Insulation Contractors Association of America [868]
1321 Duke St., Ste. 303
Alexandria, VA 22314
PH: (703)739-0356
Fax: (703)739-0412
Blanchard, Ted, President

International Association of Addictions and Offender Counselors [11490]
5999 Stevenson Ave.
Alexandria, VA 22304-3300
PH: (703)823-9800
Toll free: 800-347-6647
Fax: (703)461-9260
Gray, Geneva M., PhD, LPC, NCC, Treasurer

International Association of Amusement Parks and Attractions [1138]
1448 Duke St.
Alexandria, VA 22314
PH: (703)836-4800
Fax: (703)836-4801
Mosedale, Susan, Exec. VP

International Association of Chiefs of Police [5468]
44 Canal Center Plz., Ste. 200
Alexandria, VA 22314
PH: (703)836-6767
De Lucca, Donald W., VP

International Association of Chiefs of Police - Law Enforcement Information Management Section [5304]
44 Canal Center Plz., Ste. 200
Alexandria, VA 22314
PH: (800)843-4227
    (703)836-6767
Cunningham, Terrence M., President

International Association of Counseling Services [7688]
101 S Whiting St., Ste. 211
Alexandria, VA 22304-3416
PH: (703)823-9840
Fax: (703)823-9843
Beale, Charles L., President

International Association for Dental Research [14446]
1619 Duke St.
Alexandria, VA 22314-3406
PH: (703)548-0066
Fax: (703)548-1883
Fox, Christopher H., Exec. Dir.

International Association of Movers [3087]
5904 Richmond Hwy., Ste. 404
Alexandria, VA 22303
PH: (703)317-9950
Fax: (703)317-9960
Head, Terry R., President

International Bottled Water Association [425]
1700 Diagonal Rd., Ste. 650
Alexandria, VA 22314
PH: (703)683-5213
Fax: (703)683-4074
Caradec, Philippe, Bd. Member

International Brain Injury Association [14912]
c/o MCC Association Management
5909 Ashby Manor Pl.

Alexandria, VA 22310-2267
PH: (703)960-0027
Fax: (703)960-6603
Zasler, Nathan, V. Ch.

International Child Empowerment
Network **[11239]**
8605-B Engleside Office Park Dr.
Alexandria, VA 22309-4130
PH: (571)332-1179
Barwuah, Adwoa K., President, CEO

International Corrugated Packaging
Foundation **[12485]**
113 SW St., 3rd. Fl
Alexandria, VA 22314
PH: (703)549-8580
Fax: (703)549-8670
Flaherty, Richard M., President

International Institute of Ammonia
Refrigeration **[1628]**
1001 N Fairfax St., Ste. 503
Alexandria, VA 22314
PH: (703)312-4200
Fax: (703)312-0065
Stencel, Mark, Chairperson

International Parking Institute **[2496]**
1330 Braddock Pl., Ste. 350
Alexandria, VA 22314
PH: (571)699-3011
Fax: (703)566-2267
Campbell, Cindy, Specialist

International Public Management
Association for Human Resources
[1094]
1617 Duke St.
Alexandria, VA 22314
PH: (703)549-7100
Fax: (703)684-0948
Reichenberg, Neil, Exec. Dir.

International Refrigerated
Transportation Association **[3336]**
Global Cold Chain Alliance
1500 King St., Ste. 201
Alexandria, VA 22314-2730
PH: (703)373-4300
Fax: (703)373-4301
Luckas, Matt, Chairman

International Road Federation **[3337]**
Madison Pl., 5th Fl.
500 Montgomery St.
Alexandria, VA 22314
PH: (703)535-1001
Fax: (703)535-1007
Al-Mogbel, Abdullah A., Chairman

International Sign Association **[1026]**
1001 N Fairfax St., Ste. 301
Alexandria, VA 22314
PH: (703)836-4012
Fax: (703)836-8353
Anderson, Lori, CEO, President

International Sleep Products As-
sociation **[1685]**
501 Wythe St.
Alexandria, VA 22314-1917
PH: (703)683-8371
Fax: (703)683-4503

International Strategic Studies As-
sociation **[18084]**
PO Box 320608
Alexandria, VA 22320
PH: (703)548-1070
Fax: (703)684-7476
von Gruber, Pamela, Exec. Dir.,
Publisher

International Wood Products Association **[1412]**
4214 King St.
Alexandria, VA 22302

PH: (703)820-6696
Fax: (703)820-8550
Squires, Cindy L., Exec. Dir.

Islamic Relief U.S.A. **[12690]**
PO Box 22250
Alexandria, VA 22304
PH: (703)370-7202
Toll free: 855-447-1001
Fax: (866)917-0667
Attawia, Mohamed Amr, MD, Contact

Jobs for America's Graduates
[11766]
1729 King St., Ste. 100
Alexandria, VA 22314
PH: (703)684-9479
Fax: (703)684-9489
Bryant, Phil, Chairman

Johnny Adams Blues Organization
[9944]
PO Box 11205
Alexandria, VA 22312
Toll free: 888-316-5235
Fax: (703)722-0649
Adams, Judy A., Exec. Dir.

Joint Council on International
Children's Services **[10456]**
117 S St. Asaph St.
Alexandria, VA 22314
PH: (703)535-8045
Fax: (703)535-8049
DiFilipo, Thomas, CEO, President

Junior Engineering Technical Society
[7859]
1420 King St., Ste. 510
Alexandria, VA 22314
PH: (703)548-5387
Fax: (703)548-0769

Kerr Family Association of North
America **[20891]**
c/o Katharine R. Kerr, Treasurer
6540 Greyledge Ct.
Alexandria, VA 22310
Kerr, David, Director

Koinonia Foundation **[20065]**
6037 Franconia Rd.
Alexandria, VA 22310
PH: (703)971-1991
Miles, Mrs. Jack, Founder

Learning First Alliance **[7778]**
1615 Duke St.
Alexandria, VA 22314
PH: (703)518-6290
Fax: (703)548-6021
Williams, Cheryl, Exec. Dir.

Libertarian National Committee
[18892]
1444 Duke St.
Alexandria, VA 22314-3403
PH: (202)333-0008
Toll free: 800-ELECT-US
Fax: (202)333-0072
Benedict, Wes, Exec. Dir.

Liberty's Promise **[5293]**
2900-A Jefferson Davis Hwy.
Alexandria, VA 22305
PH: (703)549-9950
Fax: (703)549-9953
Hendry, Krista, Chairperson

Licensing Executives Society **[5336]**
1800 Diagonal Rd., Ste. 280
Alexandria, VA 22314-2840
PH: (703)836-0026
Fax: (703)836-3107
Sobieraj, Jim, President

Machinery Dealers National Association **[1743]**
315 S Patrick St.
Alexandria, VA 22314-3501

PH: (703)836-9300
Toll free: 800-872-7807
Fax: (703)836-9303
Khoury, Kim, President

Major County Sheriffs' Association
[5484]
1450 Duke St.
Alexandria, VA 22314
PH: (202)237-2001
Toll free: 855-625-2689
Hutchens, Sher. Sandra, President

Manufacturing Skill Standards
Council **[7232]**
901 N Washington St., Ste. 600
Alexandria, VA 22314
PH: (703)739-9000
(703)739-9000
Reddy, Leo, Chmn. of the Bd.,
President, CEO

Mental Health America **[15783]**
2000 N Beauregard St., 6th Fl.
Alexandria, VA 22311
PH: (703)684-7722
Toll free: 800-969-6642
Fax: (703)684-5968
Shern, David, PhD, CEO, President

Meso Foundation **[14595]**
1317 King St.
Alexandria, VA 22314
Toll free: 877-363-6376
Fax: (703)299-0399
Kotzian, Melinda, CEO

Methanol Institute **[6662]**
124 S West St., Ste. 203
Alexandria, VA 22314-2872
PH: (703)248-3636
Dolan, Gregory A., CEO

Migraine Awareness Group: A
National Understanding for Mi-
graineurs **[14918]**
100 N Union St., Ste. B
Alexandria, VA 22314
PH: (703)349-1929
Coleman, Michael John, Exec. Dir.,
Founder, President

Military and Government Counseling
Association **[11493]**
c/o American Counseling Association
5999 Stevenson Ave.
Alexandria, VA 22304-3300
PH: (703)823-9800
Toll free: 800-347-6647

Military Officers Association of
America **[21076]**
201 N Washington St.
Alexandria, VA 22314-2537
PH: (703)549-2311
Toll free: 800-234-6622
Ryan, V. Adm. (Ret.) Norbert R., Jr.,
President

Military Order of the World Wars
[21207]
435 N Lee St.
Alexandria, VA 22314
PH: (703)683-4911
Toll free: 877-320-3774
Fax: (703)683-4501
Morrill, Brig. Gen. Arthur B., III, Chief
of Staff

Missile Defense Advocacy Alliance
[18087]
515 King St., Ste. 320
Alexandria, VA 22314
PH: (703)299-0060
Ellison, Riki, Chmn. of the Bd.,
Founder

The Myositis Association **[15962]**
1737 King St., Ste. 600
Alexandria, VA 22314-2764

PH: (703)299-4850
Toll free: 800-821-7356
Fax: (703)535-6752
Goldberg, Bob, Exec. Dir.

NAADAC: The Association for Addic-
tion Professionals **[17317]**
1001 N Fairfax St., Ste. 201
Alexandria, VA 22314
Toll free: 800-548-0497
Fax: (703)377-1136
Bowden, Kirk, PhD, President

NACS: The Association for
Convenience and Fuel Retailing
[2963]
1600 Duke St., 7th Fl.
Alexandria, VA 22314
PH: (703)684-3600
Toll free: 800-966-6227
Fax: (703)836-4564
Armour, Henry, Liaison, CEO,
President

National Accrediting Commission of
Career Arts and Sciences **[7412]**
4401 Ford Ave., Ste. 1300
Alexandria, VA 22302-1432
PH: (703)600-7600
Fax: (703)379-2200
Mirando, Tony, MS, Exec. Dir.

National Active and Retired Federal
Employees Association **[5197]**
606 N Washington St.
Alexandria, VA 22314
PH: (703)838-7760
Fax: (703)838-7785
Thissen, Richard G., President

National Affordable Housing
Management Association **[1690]**
400 N Columbus St., Ste. 203
Alexandria, VA 22314
PH: (703)683-8630
Cook, Kris, CAE, Exec. Dir.

National Agricultural Aviation As-
sociation **[3652]**
1440 Duke St.
Alexandria, VA 22314
PH: (202)546-5722
Fax: (202)546-5726
Watts, Brenda, President

National Alcohol Beverage Control
Association **[4953]**
4401 Ford Ave., Ste. 700
Alexandria, VA 22302-1433
PH: (703)578-4200
Fax: (703)820-3551
Sgueo, James M., President, CEO

National Art Education Association
[7515]
901 Prince St.
Alexandria, VA 22314
PH: (703)860-8000
Toll free: 800-299-8321
Fax: (703)860-2960
Franklin, Patricia, President

National Association of Career
Travel Agents **[3384]**
675 N Washington St., Ste. 490
Alexandria, VA 22314
PH: (703)739-6826
Toll free: 877-22-NACTA
Fax: (703)739-6861
Kerby, Zane, Treasurer

National Association of Church
Personnel Administrators **[20564]**
2050 Ballenger Ave., Ste. 200
Alexandria, VA 22314
PH: (703)746-8315
Haney, Dr. Regina M., Exec. Dir.

National Association of Crime Victim
Compensation Boards **[13261]**
PO Box 16003
Alexandria, VA 22302

PH: (703)780-3200
Eddy, Dan, Exec. Dir.

National Association of Deans and
Directors of Schools of Social
Work [8572]
1701 Duke St., Ste. 200
Alexandria, VA 22314
PH: (703)683-8080
Fax: (703)683-8099
Mondros, Jacqueline B., President

National Association of Drug Court
Professionals [13164]
1029 N Royal St., Ste. 201
Alexandria, VA 22314
PH: (703)575-9400
Huddleston, West, CEO

National Association of Elementary
School Principals [8458]
1615 Duke St.
Alexandria, VA 22314
PH: (703)684-3345
Toll free: 800-386-2377
Fax: (703)549-5568
Connelly, Gail, Exec. Dir.

National Association of Farmers'
Market Nutrition Programs [4158]
PO Box 9080
Alexandria, VA 22304-0080
PH: (703)837-0451
Fax: (919)471-0137
Blalock, Phil, Exec. Dir.

National Association of Free and
Charitable Clinics [15155]
1800 Diagonal Rd., Ste. 600
Alexandria, VA 22314
PH: (703)647-7427
Toll free: 866-875-3827
Worel, Nann, President

National Association of Mental
Health Planning and Advisory
Councils [15788]
2000 N Beauregard St., 6th Fl.
Alexandria, VA 22311
PH: (703)797-2595
Fax: (703)684-5968
Stange, Judy, Ph.D., Exec. Dir.

National Association of Police
Organizations [5492]
317 S Patrick St.
Alexandria, VA 22314
PH: (703)549-0775
Fax: (703)684-0515
McHale, Mick, President

National Association of Postal
Supervisors [23507]
1727 King St., Ste. 400
Alexandria, VA 22314-2753
PH: (703)836-9660
Fax: (703)836-9665
Atkins, Louis M., President

National Association of Postmasters
of the United States [5681]
8 Herbert St.
Alexandria, VA 22305
PH: (703)683-9027
Fax: (703)683-0923
Leonardi, Anthony D., President

National Association of Professional
Employer Organizations [1098]
707 N St. Asaph St.
Alexandria, VA 22314
PH: (703)836-0466
Fax: (703)836-0976
Cleary, Pat, CEO, President

National Association of Professional
Insurance Agents [1900]
400 N Washington St.
Alexandria, VA 22314

PH: (703)836-9340
(703)518-1360
Fax: (703)836-1279
Clements, Richard A., President

National Association for Rehabilita-
tion Leadership [17090]
c/o National Rehabilitation Associa-
tion
PO Box 150235
Alexandria, VA 22315
PH: (703)836-0850
Fax: (703)836-0848
Jones, Evan, Web Adm.

National Association of Service
Providers in Private Rehabilitation
[17092]
c/o National Rehabilitation Associa-
tion
PO Box 150235
Alexandria, VA 22315
PH: (703)836-0850
Fax: (703)836-0848
Nortz, Kim, President

National Association of Sign Supply
Distributors [3473]
1001 N Fairfax St., Ste. 301
Alexandria, VA 22314-1587
PH: (703)836-4013
Fax: (703)836-8353
Clemons, Mr. Cal, CAE, Exec. Dir.

National Association of Specialty
Pharmacy [16675]
1800 Diagonal Rd., Ste. 600
Alexandria, VA 22314
PH: (703)842-0122
Zweigenhaft, Burt, President

National Association of State Boards
of Education [8521]
333 John Carlyle St., Ste. 530
Alexandria, VA 22314
PH: (703)684-4000
Johnson, Scott, Secretary, Treasurer

National Association of State Direc-
tors of Developmental Disabilities
Services [12329]
301 N Fairfax St., Ste. 101
Alexandria, VA 22314-2633
PH: (703)683-4202
Nuss, Laura L., President

National Association of State Direc-
tors of Special Education [8589]
225 Reinekers Ln., Ste. 420
Alexandria, VA 22314
PH: (703)519-3800
Fax: (703)519-3808
East, Bill, Exec. Dir.

National Association of State Direc-
tors of Veterans Affairs [5839]
107 S West St., Ste. 550
Alexandria, VA 22314
PH: (208)780-1300
Fax: (208)780-1301
Brasuell, David, President

National Association of State Mental
Health Program Directors [15791]
66 Canal Center Plz., Ste. 302
Alexandria, VA 22314
PH: (703)739-9333
Fax: (703)548-9517
Hepburn, Brian, Exec. Dir.

National Association of Telecom-
munications Officers and Advisors
[3234]
3213 Duke St., Ste. 695
Alexandria, VA 22314
PH: (703)519-8035
Fax: (703)997-7080
Hovis, Joanne, President

National Association of Triads
[12829]
1450 Duke St.
Alexandria, VA 22314
PH: (703)836-7827
Fax: (703)519-8567
Thompson, Jonathan, Exec. Dir.

National Beer Wholesalers Associa-
tion [188]
1101 King St., Ste. 600
Alexandria, VA 22314-2944
PH: (703)683-4300
Toll free: 800-300-6417
Fax: (703)683-8965
Purser, Craig A., Ph.D., President

National Biosolids Partnership
[4552]
601 Wythe St.
Alexandria, VA 22314-1994
PH: (800)666-0206
Fax: (703)684-2492
McFadden, Lisa, Mgr.

National Cancer Registrars Associa-
tion [16349]
1330 Braddock Pl., Ste. 520
Alexandria, VA 22314
PH: (703)299-6640
Fax: (703)299-6620
Corrigan, Kathy, Coord.

National Center for Missing and
Exploited Children [11088]
Charles B Wang International
Children's Bldg.
699 Prince St.
Alexandria, VA 22314-3175
PH: (703)224-2150
Toll free: 800-843-5678
Fax: (703)224-2122
Kolodziej, Richard R., Officer

National Coalition of Black Meeting
Planners [2335]
700 N Fairfax St., Ste. 510
Alexandria, VA 22314
PH: (571)527-3110
Robinson, Monica, Exec. Dir.

National Coalition for Child Protec-
tion Reform [11091]
53 Skyhill Rd., Ste. 202
Alexandria, VA 22314-4997
PH: (703)212-2006
Wexler, Richard, Exec. Dir.

National Coalition for Technology in
Education and Training [8672]
2724 Kenwood Ave.
Alexandria, VA 22302
PH: (202)263-2577
Bernstein, Jon

National Commission on Orthotic
and Prosthetic Education [16497]
Ste. 200
330 John Carlyle St.
Alexandria, VA 22314
PH: (703)836-7114
Fax: (703)836-0838
Gillis, Arlene, Chairperson

National Committee on Uniform Traf-
fic Laws and Ordinances [5805]
107 S West St., No. 110
Alexandria, VA 22314-2824
Toll free: 800-807-5290
Fax: (540)465-5383

National Community Pharmacists
Association [16676]
100 Daingerfield Rd.
Alexandria, VA 22314
PH: (703)683-8200
Toll free: 800-544-7447
Fax: (703)683-3619
Mullins, DeAnn, Chairman

National Council for Adoption
[10460]
225 N Washington St.
Alexandria, VA 22314-2561
PH: (703)299-6633
Fax: (703)299-6004
Johnson, Charles, President, CEO

National Council of Commercial
Plant Breeders [4643]
1701 Duke St., Ste. 275
Alexandria, VA 22314
PH: (703)837-8140
Fax: (703)837-9365
LaVigne, Andrew W., Exec. VP

National Defense Transportation As-
sociation [5608]
50 S Pickett St., Ste. 220
Alexandria, VA 22304-7296
PH: (703)751-5011
Fax: (703)823-8761
Buzby, Mark, President, COO

National District Attorneys Associa-
tion [5039]
99 Canal Center Plz., Ste. 330
Alexandria, VA 22314
PH: (703)549-9222
Hemphill, Jean, Contact

National Emergency Number As-
sociation [14668]
1700 Diagonal Rd., Ste. 500
Alexandria, VA 22314-2846
PH: (202)466-4911
Fax: (202)618-6370
Fontes, Brian, CEO

National Federation of Republican
Women [19041]
124 N Alfred St.
Alexandria, VA 22314
PH: (703)548-9688
Fax: (703)548-9836
Almond, Carrie, President

National Foundation for Women
Legislators [5849]
1727 King St., Ste. 300
Alexandria, VA 22314
PH: (703)518-7931
Frederick, Amy Noone, Treasurer

National GEM Consortium [7862]
1430 Duke St.
Alexandria, VA 22314-3403
PH: (703)562-3646
Fax: (202)207-3518
Lezama, Michele, Exec. Dir.

National Head Start Association
[8449]
1651 Prince St.
Alexandria, VA 22314
PH: (703)739-0875
Toll free: 866-677-8724
Rich, Vanessa, Chairperson

National Healthy Mothers, Healthy
Babies Coalition [16297]
PO Box 3360
Alexandria, VA 22302-3360
PH: (703)838-7552
Lewis, Janine, PhD, Chairperson

National Home Infusion Association
[15740]
100 Daingerfield Rd.
Alexandria, VA 22314
PH: (703)549-3740
Fax: (703)683-1484
Wilson, Tyler J., President, CEO

National Hospice and Palliative Care
Organization [15297]
1731 King St., Ste. 100
Alexandria, VA 22314

PH: (703)837-1500
Rock, Linda, Chairperson

National Industries for the Blind
[17734]
1310 Braddock Pl.
Alexandria, VA 22314-1691
PH: (703)310-0500
Lynch, Kevin A., CEO, President

National Institute for Certification in
Engineering Technologies [6576]
1420 King St.
Alexandria, VA 22314-2794
PH: (703)548-1518
Toll free: 888-476-4238
Clark, Michael A., CAE, COO

National Investor Relations Institute
[2033]
225 Reinekers Ln., Ste. 560
Alexandria, VA 22314
PH: (703)562-7700
Fax: (703)562-7701
Young, Kirsten, VP

National League of Postmasters of
the United States [23508]
1 Beltway Ctr.
5904 Richmond Hwy., Ste. 500
Alexandria, VA 22303-1864
PH: (703)329-4550
Fax: (703)329-0466
Strong, Mark W., Bd. Member

National Military Family Association
[21042]
3601 Eisenhower Ave., Ste. 425
Alexandria, VA 22304
PH: (703)931-6632
Fax: (703)931-4600
Raezer, Joyce Wessel, Exec. Dir.

National Mitigation Banking Associa-
tion [3905]
107 SW St., No. 573
Alexandria, VA 22314
PH: (202)457-8409
White, Wayne, President

National Motor Freight Traffic As-
sociation, Inc. [3095]
1001 N Fairfax St., Ste. 600
Alexandria, VA 22314-1798
PH: (703)838-1810
Toll free: 866-411-6632
Fax: (703)683-6296
Levine, Paul, Exec. Dir.

National Multifamily Resident
Information Council [2884]
3337 Duke St.
Alexandria, VA 22314
PH: (703)370-7436
Fax: (703)342-4311
Valenzuela, Pamela, Exec. Dir.

National Naval Officers Association
[5612]
PO Box 10871
Alexandria, VA 22310-0871
PH: (703)828-7308
Chestnut, Maj. Melissa, Secretary

National Oilheat Research Alliance
[1118]
600 Cameron St., Ste. 206
Alexandria, VA 22314
PH: (703)340-1660
Fax: (703)340-1642
Huber, John J., President

National Onsite Wastewater
Recycling Association [4743]
1199 N Fairfax St., Ste. 410
Alexandria, VA 22314
PH: (703)836-1950
Toll free: 800-966-2942
Moore, Curtis, Secretary, Treasurer

National Order of Women Legisla-
tors [5556]
National Foundation for Women
Legislators
1727 King St., Ste. 300
Alexandria, VA 22314
PH: (703)518-7931
Keeley, Rep. Helene, Chairperson

National Organization of Black Law
Enforcement Executives [5506]
4609-F Pinecrest Office Park Dr.
Alexandria, VA 22312-1442
PH: (703)658-1529
Fax: (703)658-9479
Nelson, Thomas Lee, Rec. Sec.

National Organization for Victim As-
sistance [13265]
510 King St., Ste. 424
Alexandria, VA 22314-3132
PH: (703)535-6682
Toll free: 800-879-6682
Fax: (703)535-5500
Jeffries, Hon. Tim, Contact

National Organizations for Youth
Safety [13467]
901 N Washington St., Ste. 703
Alexandria, VA 22314
PH: (571)367-7171
Toll free: 866-559-9398
Boles, Anita, CEO

National PACE Association [10526]
675 N Washington St., Ste. 300
Alexandria, VA 22314
PH: (703)535-1565
Fax: (703)535-1566
Greenwood, Robert, VP of Public
Affairs

National Preservation Institute
[9420]
PO Box 1702
Alexandria, VA 22313
PH: (703)765-0100
Gibber, Jere, Exec. Dir.

National PTA [8403]
1250 N Pitt St.
Alexandria, VA 22314
PH: (703)518-1200
Toll free: 800-307-4782
Fax: (703)836-0942
Monell, Nathan R., CAE, Exec. Dir.

National Rehabilitation Association
[17094]
PO Box 150235
Alexandria, VA 22315
PH: (703)836-0850
Toll free: 888-258-4295
Fax: (703)836-0848
Schroeder, Dr. Fredric K., Exec. Dir.

National Renderers Association
[2455]
500 Montgomery St., Ste. 310
Alexandria, VA 22314
PH: (703)683-0155
Fax: (571)970-2279
Foster, Nancy, President

National Rural Education Advocacy
Coalition [8509]
1615 Duke St.
Alexandria, VA 22314
PH: (703)528-0700
Fax: (703)841-1543
Patrick, Ray, Chairman

National Rural Letter Carriers' As-
sociation [23510]
1630 Duke St.
Alexandria, VA 22314-3465
PH: (703)684-5545
Dwyer, Jeanette P., President

National School Boards Association
[8522]
1680 Duke St., FL2
Alexandria, VA 22314-3493
PH: (703)838-6722
Fax: (703)683-7590
Tuttle, John D., President

National School Transportation As-
sociation [3346]
122 S Royal St.
Alexandria, VA 22314
PH: (703)684-3200
Huss, Alexandra, Mktg. Coord.

National Security Whistleblowers
Coalition [19093]
PO Box 320518
Alexandria, VA 22320
Edmonds, Sibel, Founder, President

National Sheriffs' Association [5511]
1450 Duke St.
Alexandria, VA 22314
Toll free: 800-424-7827
Fax: (703)838-5349
Hall, Daron, Treasurer

National Society of Accountants [52]
1330 Braddock Pl., Ste. 540
Alexandria, VA 22314
PH: (703)549-6400
Toll free: 800-966-6679
Fax: (703)549-2984
Hanson, Steven J., CPA, Officer

National Society of Black Engineers
[6577]
205 Daingerfield Rd.
Alexandria, VA 22314
PH: (703)549-2207
Fax: (703)683-5312
Green, Neville, Chairman

National Society of Professional
Engineers [6578]
1420 King St.
Alexandria, VA 22314
Toll free: 888-285-6773
Fax: (703)836-4875
Hnatiuk, Harve D., President

National Stone, Sand and Gravel
Association [3188]
1605 King St.
Alexandria, VA 22314
PH: (703)525-8788
Johnson, Mike W., President, CEO

National Voluntary Organizations
Active in Disaster [12704]
615 Slaters Ln.
Alexandria, VA 22314
PH: (703)778-5088
Fax: (703)778-5091
Wood, April, Chairman

National Wooden Pallet and
Container Association [839]
1421 Prince St., Ste. 340
Alexandria, VA 22314-2805
PH: (703)519-6104
Fax: (703)519-4720

NATSO [2971]
1330 Braddock Pl., No. 501
Alexandria, VA 22314
PH: (703)549-2100
Toll free: 800-527-1666
Mullings, Lisa J., CEO, President

Nature's Voice Our Choice [4761]
1940 Duke St., Ste. 200
Alexandria, VA 22314
PH: (202)341-9180
  (202)360-8373
Strassberg, Valerie, PE, Exec. Dir.

Negative Population Growth [12510]
2861 Duke St., Ste. 36
Alexandria, VA 22314

PH: (703)370-9510
Fax: (703)370-9514
Mann, Donald, President

North America-Mongolia Business
Council, Inc. [1991]
1015 Duke St.
Alexandria, VA 22314
PH: (703)549-8444
Fax: (703)549-6526
Saunders, Steve, President

North American Brain Injury Society
[14914]
PO Box 1804
Alexandria, VA 22313
PH: (703)960-6500
Fax: (703)960-6603
Savage, Ronald C., Chairman

North American Insulation
Manufacturers Association [568]
11 Canal Center Plz., Ste. 103
Alexandria, VA 22314
PH: (703)684-0084
Fax: (703)684-0427
Andrews, Mark, Chmn. of the Bd.

North American Manx Association
[19545]
1751 Olde Towne Rd.
Alexandria, VA 22307-1457
PH: (703)718-0172
  (410)531-6685
Prendergast, John, Treasurer

Operation Lifesaver [12839]
1420 King St., Ste. 201
Alexandria, VA 22314
PH: (703)739-0308
Toll free: 800-537-6224
Fax: (703)519-8267
Mercier, Anika, Officer

OPSEC Professionals Society
[19095]
PO Box 150515
Alexandria, VA 22315-0515
McCarthy, John, President

Outdoor Power Equipment
Aftermarket Association [1126]
341 S Patrick St.
Alexandria, VA 22314
PH: (703)549-7608
Fax: (703)549-7609
Harris, Scott, President

Outdoor Power Equipment Institute
[1128]
341 S Patrick St.
Alexandria, VA 22314
PH: (703)549-7600
Teske, Todd J., Chairman

Passenger Vessel Association
[2256]
103 Oronoco St., Ste. 200
Alexandria, VA 22314
PH: (703)518-5005
Toll free: 800-807-8360
Fax: (703)518-5151
Whitaker, Jeff, VP

Patent Office Professional Associa-
tion [5338]
PO Box 25287
Alexandria, VA 22313
PH: (571)272-7161
Reip, David O., Treasurer

PCIA - The Wireless Infrastructure
Association [3236]
500 Montgomery St., Ste. 500
Alexandria, VA 22314
PH: (703)535-7492
Fax: (703)836-1608
Ganzi, Marc, Chmn. of the Bd.

Peanut & Tree Nut Processors Association **[1366]**
PO Box 2660
Alexandria, VA 22301
PH: (301)365-2521
Ezell, Brian, Chairman

Pharmaceutical Industry Labor-Management Association **[2568]**
101 N Union St., No. 305
Alexandria, VA 22314
PH: (703)548-4721
Dean, Eric, Chairman

Plant Growth Regulation Society of America **[6153]**
1018 Duke St.
Alexandria, VA 22314
PH: (703)836-4606
Fax: (703)836-4607
Maki, Dr. Sonja L., Exec. Dir.

Power & Communication Contractors Association **[898]**
1908 Mt. Vernon Ave., 2nd Fl.
Alexandria, VA 22301
PH: (703)212-7734
Toll free: 800-542-7222
Fax: (703)548-3733
Myers, Todd, President

Prevent Cancer Foundation **[14048]**
1600 Duke St., Ste. 500
Alexandria, VA 22314-3421
PH: (703)836-4412
Toll free: 800-227-2732
Fax: (703)836-4413
McIntyre, Scott, Chairman

Private Practice Section of the American Physical Therapy Association **[17461]**
1055 N Fairfax St., Ste. 204
Alexandria, VA 22314
PH: (703)299-2410
Toll free: 800-517-1167
Fax: (703)299-2411
Brown, Terry, President

Professional Aviation Maintenance Association **[156]**
400 N Washington St., Ste. 300
Alexandria, VA 22314
Toll free: 866-610-5549
Fax: (817)769-2674
Sickler, Roger, Chairman

Professional Truck Driver Institute **[3354]**
555 E Braddock Rd.
Alexandria, VA 22314
PH: (703)647-7015
Fax: (703)836-6610
Burch, Kevin, V. Chmn. of the Bd.

Public Risk Management Association **[5320]**
700 S Washington St., Ste. 218
Alexandria, VA 22314
PH: (703)528-7701
Fax: (703)739-0200
Davies, Marshall, PhD, Exec. Dir.

Public Technology Institute **[5700]**
1420 Prince St., Ste. 200
Alexandria, VA 22314
PH: (202)626-2400
Cable, Susan, Program Mgr.

Reagan Alumni Association **[18921]**
122 S Royal St.
Alexandria, VA 22314-3328
PH: (703)461-7250
Fax: (703)461-7251

Registry of Interpreters for the Deaf, Inc. **[15208]**
333 Commerce St.
Alexandria, VA 22314

PH: (703)838-0030
Fax: (703)838-0454
Butts, Ryan, Officer

Republicans for Choice **[19036]**
3213 Duke St., No. 808
Alexandria, VA 22314
PH: (703)447-1404
Stone, Ann, Chairperson

Research! America **[15655]**
1101 King St., Ste. 520
Alexandria, VA 22314-2960
PH: (703)739-2577
Fax: (703)739-2372
Woolley, Mary, President

Salvation Army **[13087]**
615 Slaters Ln.
Alexandria, VA 22314-1112
Toll free: 800-728-7825
Gaither, Commissioner Israel L., Cmdr.

Self Storage Association **[3441]**
1901 N Beauregard St., Ste. 106
Alexandria, VA 22311
PH: (703)575-8000
Toll free: 888-735-3784
Fax: (703)575-8901
Dietz, Timothy J., President, CEO

SHRM Global Forum **[2501]**
1800 Duke St.
Alexandria, VA 22314
PH: (703)548-3440
Toll free: 800-283-7476
Fax: (703)535-6490

Sierra Leone Relief and Development Outreach, Inc. **[12728]**
4231-B Duke St.
Alexandria, VA 22304-2485
PH: (703)507-5576
Kamara-Bangura, Mrs. Bernadette, Founder

SOCAP International **[2758]**
625 N Washington St., Ste. 304
Alexandria, VA 22314
PH: (703)519-3700
Fax: (703)549-4886
Dumais, Céline, Chairperson

Society of American Florists **[1310]**
1001 N Fairfax St., Ste. 201
Alexandria, VA 22314
Toll free: 800-336-4743
Fax: (703)836-8700
Moran, Peter J., CEO, Exec. VP

Society of American Military Engineers **[6588]**
607 Prince St.
Alexandria, VA 22314-3117
PH: (703)549-3800
Fax: (703)684-0231
Schroedel, Brig. Gen. Joseph, PE, Exec. Dir.

Society for Financial Education and Professional Development **[7572]**
500 Montgomery St., Ste. 400
Alexandria, VA 22314
PH: (703)920-3807
Fax: (703)920-3809
Daniels, Theodore R., CEO, President

Society of General Internal Medicine **[15431]**
1500 King St., Ste. 303
Alexandria, VA 22314
PH: (202)887-5150
Toll free: 800-822-3060
Ovington, Kay, Exec. Dir.

Society of Government Meeting Professionals **[2338]**
PO Box 321025
Alexandria, VA 22320-5125

PH: (703)549-0892
Fax: (703)549-0708
Milligan, Michelle, President

Society for Human Resource Management **[2502]**
1800 Duke St.
Alexandria, VA 22314
PH: (703)548-3440
Toll free: 800-253-7476
Fax: (703)535-6490
Silva, Brian D., Chairperson

Society for Marketing Professional Services **[2303]**
123 N Pitt St., Ste. 400
Alexandria, VA 22314
PH: (703)549-6117
Toll free: 800-292-7677
Fax: (703)549-2498
Geary, Michael V., CEO

Society of Naval Architects and Marine Engineers **[6906]**
99 Canal Center Plz., Ste. 310
Alexandria, VA 22314
PH: (703)997-6701
Hall, Mike, Dir. of Member Svcs.

Spill Control Association of America **[2643]**
103 Oronoco St., Ste. 200
Alexandria, VA 22314
PH: (571)451-0433
Allen, John, Exec. Dir.

State Government Affairs Council **[18321]**
515 King St., Ste. 325
Alexandria, VA 22314
PH: (703)684-0967
Dehrmann, Gerard, President

Team HOPE: Help Offering Parents Empowerment **[12359]**
699 Prince St.
Charles B. Wang International Children's Bldg.
699 Prince St.
Alexandria, VA 22314
Toll free: 800-843-5678
Jezycki, Michelle, Project Mgr., Director

TechServe Alliance **[823]**
1420 King St., Ste. 610
Alexandria, VA 22314
PH: (703)838-2050
Fax: (703)838-3610
Laine, Steven, Chairman

TESOL International Association **[7871]**
1925 Ballenger Ave., Ste. 550
Alexandria, VA 22314-6822
PH: (703)836-0774
Fax: (703)836-7864
Aronson, Rosa, Exec. Dir.

Textile Rental Services Association of America **[2933]**
1800 Diagonal Rd., Ste. 200
Alexandria, VA 22314
PH: (703)519-0029
Toll free: 877-770-9274
Fax: (703)519-0026
Ricci, Joseph, President, CEO

Transportation Intermediaries Association **[3108]**
1625 Prince St., Ste. 200
Alexandria, VA 22314
PH: (703)299-5700
Fax: (703)836-0123
Voltmann, Robert A., President, CEO

Truck Renting and Leasing Association **[2934]**
675 N Washington St., Ste. 410
Alexandria, VA 22314

PH: (703)299-9120
Fax: (703)299-9115
Anderson, Scott, Director

Truckload Carriers Association **[3360]**
555 E Braddock Rd.
Alexandria, VA 22314
PH: (703)838-1950
Fax: (703)836-6610
Giroux, William, Exec. VP

Truss Plate Institute **[595]**
218 N Lee St., Ste. 312
Alexandria, VA 22314
PH: (703)683-1010
Fax: (866)501-4012

United Motorcoach Association **[3361]**
113 S W St., 4th Fl.
Alexandria, VA 22314-2824
Toll free: 800-424-8262
Fax: (703)838-2950
Parra, Victor, President, CEO

United Way Worldwide **[11863]**
701 N Fairfax St.
Alexandria, VA 22314-2045
PH: (703)836-7112
Baldwin, Phillip N., Chmn. of the Bd.

USS Pyro AE-1 and AE-24 Association **[21072]**
3808 Brighton Ct.
Alexandria, VA 22305-1571
Cameron, Jared S., President

The Vision Council **[1606]**
225 Reinekers Ln., Ste. 700
Alexandria, VA 22314
PH: (703)548-4560
Toll free: 866-826-0290
Fax: (703)548-4580
Daley, Mike, CEO

Vision Council Lab Division **[2460]**
225 Reinekers Ln., Ste. 700
Alexandria, VA 22314
PH: (703)548-4560
Toll free: 866-826-0290
Bassett, Martin, Chairman

Volunteers of America **[13093]**
1660 Duke St.
Alexandria, VA 22314
PH: (703)341-5000
Toll free: 800-899-0089
King, Michael, President, CEO

Water Environment Federation **[4557]**
601 Wythe St.
Alexandria, VA 22314-1994
Toll free: 800-666-0206
Fax: (703)684-2492
Mixon, Theresa, Officer

WateReuse Association **[4766]**
1199 N Fairfax St., Ste. 410
Alexandria, VA 22314
PH: (703)548-0880
Fax: (703)548-5085
Trejo, Gilbert, Secretary

WISH List **[5255]**
333 N Fairfax St., Ste. 302
Alexandria, VA 22314-2632

Women Chefs and Restaurateurs **[703]**
115 S Patrick St., Ste. 101
Alexandria, VA 22314
Toll free: 877-927-7787
Gresser, Ruth, President

Women Construction Owners and
Executives U.S.A. [903]
1004 Duke St.
Alexandria, VA 22314
Toll free: 800-788-3548
Fax: (202)330-5151
Boisen, Caryn, Director

Women in Housing and Finance
[1271]
400 N Washington St., Ste. 300
Alexandria, VA 22314
PH: (703)683-4742
Fax: (703)683-0018
Bellesi, Karen, President

Women of the National Agricultural
Aviation Association [3653]
c/o National Agricultural Aviation As-
sociation
1440 Duke St.
Alexandria, VA 22314
PH: (202)546-5722
Fax: (202)546-5726
Moore, Andrew D., Exec. Dir.

Women's Dermatologic Society
[14516]
700 N Fairfax St., Ste. 510
Alexandria, VA 22314
PH: (856)423-7222
Toll free: 877-937-7673
Fax: (856)423-3420
Bergfeld, Wilma F., MD, Founder

Woodworking Machinery Industry
Association [1780]
225 Reinekers Ln., Ste. 410
Alexandria, VA 22314
PH: (571)279-8340
Fax: (571)279-8343
Besonen, Jim, Treasurer, Secretary

World Hope International [20378]
1330 Braddock Pl., Ste. 301
Alexandria, VA 22314-6400
PH: (703)594-8527
Toll free: 888-466-4673
Lyon, John, President, CEO

ZERO-The Project to End Prostate
Cancer [14084]
515 King St., Ste. 420
Alexandria, VA 22314-3137
PH: (202)463-9455
Toll free: 888-245-9455
Fax: (571)257-8559
Bearse, Jamie, CEO, President

Association of Full Gospel Women
Clergy [20357]
PO Box 1504
Annandale, VA 22003
PH: (301)879-6958
Vance, Rev. Suzanne, Exec. Dir.

Connected International Meeting
Professionals Association [2323]
8803 Queen Elizabeth Blvd.
Annandale, VA 22003
PH: (512)684-0889
Fax: (267)390-5193
Peterson, Jeff, Mgr.

Hope for the Warriors [10746]
5101C Backlick Rd.
Annandale, VA 22003
Toll free: 877-246-7349
Kelleher, Robin, CEO, President

Korean American Sharing Movement
[12692]
7004 Little River Tpke., Ste. O
Annandale, VA 22003
PH: (703)867-0846
Fax: (703)354-0427
Cho, Man, V. Ch.

Military Order of the Purple Heart of
the United States of America
[20737]
PO Box 49
Annandale, VA 22003
PH: (703)354-2140
      (352)753-5535
Toll free: 800-273-8255
Fax: (703)642-2054

Naval Submarine League [18088]
5025D Backlick Rd.
Annandale, VA 22003-6044
PH: (703)256-0891
Toll free: 877-280-7827
Fax: (703)642-5815
Padgett, John B., III, President

Potomac Antique Tools and
Industries Association [22172]
c/o David Murphy
9121 Bramble Pl.
Annandale, VA 22003-4015
PH: (301)253-4892
Williams, John G., President

Society for Chemical Hazard Com-
munication [727]
PO Box 1392
Annandale, VA 22003-9392
PH: (703)658-9246
Fax: (703)658-9247
Mahoney, Jennifer, VP

World Health Ambassador [15073]
7611 Little River Tpke., Ste. 108W
Annandale, VA 22003
PH: (703)658-7060
Do, Thien, Founder, CEO, Director

Accrediting Commission of Career
Schools and Colleges [7410]
2101 Wilson Blvd., Ste. 302
Arlington, VA 22201
PH: (703)247-4212
      (703)247-4520
Fax: (703)247-4533
McComis, Michale S., Exec. Dir.

Action for Enterprise [11303]
4600 N Fairfax Dr., Ste. 304
Arlington, VA 22203-1553
PH: (703)243-9172
Fax: (703)243-9123
Lusby, Frank, Exec. Dir., Founder

Aerospace Industries Association of
America [119]
1000 Wilson Blvd., Ste. 1700
Arlington, VA 22209-3928
PH: (703)358-1000
Fax: (703)358-1011
Bodmer, Leonardo, Director

Agricultural and Food Transporters
Conference [3316]
c/o Jon Samson, Secretary
950 N Glebe Rd., Ste. 210
Arlington, VA 22203-4181
PH: (703)838-1700
Fax: (703)838-1781
Samson, Jon, Secretary

Air Conditioning Contractors of
America Association, Inc. [1610]
2800 S Shirlington Rd., Ste. 300
Arlington, VA 22206
PH: (703)575-4477
Toll free: 888-290-2220
Stalknecht, Paul T., CEO, President

Air-Conditioning, Heating, and
Refrigeration Institute [1611]
2111 Wilson Blvd., Ste. 500
Arlington, VA 22201
PH: (703)524-8800
Fax: (703)562-1942
Yurek, Stephen, President, CEO,
Contact

Air Force Aid Society [19378]
241 18th St. S, Ste. 202
Arlington, VA 22202
PH: (703)972-2650
Fax: (703)972-2646
McKeown, Dr. Mick, President

Air Force Association [5584]
1501 Lee Hwy.
Arlington, VA 22209-1198
PH: (703)247-5800
Toll free: 800-727-3337
Fax: (703)247-5853
Van Cleef, Scott, Chmn. of the Bd.

Airport Minority Advisory Council
[2391]
2001 Jefferson Davis Hwy., Ste. 500
Arlington, VA 22202
PH: (703)414-2622
Fax: (703)414-2686
Terry, Simeon, Secretary

Alliance for Global Conservation
[3792]
4245 Fairfax Dr., Ste. 100
Arlington, VA 22203
Adams, John S., Mem.

Alliance for Responsible
Atmospheric Policy [707]
2111 Wilson Blvd., 8th Fl.
Arlington, VA 22201
PH: (703)243-0344
Fax: (703)243-2874
Lapin, Phil, Bd. Member

Aluminum Association [2339]
1400 Crystal Dr., Ste. 430
Arlington, VA 22202
PH: (703)358-2960
Brock, Heidi Biggs, President

American Alliance of Museums
[9815]
2451 Crystal Dr., Ste. 1005
Arlington, VA 22202
PH: (202)289-1818
Toll free: 866-226-2150
Fax: (202)289-6578
Levine, Susan V., Creative Dir.

American Anthropological Associa-
tion - Evolutionary Anthropology
Society [5898]
2200 Wilson Blvd., Ste. 600
Arlington, VA 22201-3357
PH: (703)528-1902
Richerson, Peter, President

American Anthropological Associa-
tion Society for the Anthropology of
Europe [5900]
2300 Clarendon Blvd., Ste. 1301
Arlington, VA 22201
PH: (703)528-1902
Fax: (703)528-3546

American Association of Eye and
Ear Centers of Excellence [15302]
1655 Noth Fort Myer Dr., Ste. 700
Arlington, VA 22209
PH: (703)243-8848
Fax: (703)351-5298
Paterno, Mia, President

American Association of Motor
Vehicle Administrators [5054]
4401 Wilson Blvd., Ste. 700
Arlington, VA 22203
PH: (703)522-4200
Ferro, Anne, CEO, President

American Association of
Pharmaceutical Scientists [7005]
2107 Wilson Blvd., Ste. 700
Arlington, VA 22201-3042
PH: (703)243-2800
Benet, Dr. Les, Founder

American Butter Institute [968]
2101 Wilson Blvd., Ste. 400
Arlington, VA 22201
PH: (703)243-5630
Fax: (703)841-9328
Holmes, Irv, President

American Chiropractic Association
[14250]
1701 Clarendon Blvd., Ste. 200
Arlington, VA 22209
PH: (703)276-8800
Fax: (703)243-2593
Herd, David, President

American Composites Manufacturers
Association [489]
3033 Wilson Blvd., Ste. 420
Arlington, VA 22201-3843
PH: (703)525-0511
Fax: (703)525-0743
Garoufalis, Leon, V. Chmn. of the
Bd.

American Council of Blind Students
[17683]
American Council of the Blind
2200 Wilson Blvd., Ste. 650
Arlington, VA 22201-3354
PH: (202)467-5081
Toll free: 800-424-8666
Fax: (202)465-5085
Conrad, Sara, Director

American Court and Commercial
Newspapers, Inc. [2762]
PO Box 5337
Arlington, VA 22205-0437
PH: (703)237-9806
Fax: (703)237-9808
Morris, Greg, VP, Secretary

American Feed Industry Association
[4174]
2101 Wilson Blvd., Ste. 916
Arlington, VA 22201
PH: (703)524-0810
Fax: (703)524-1921
Newman, Joel, President, Treasurer,
CEO

American Feed Industry Association
- Equipment Manufacturers Council
[165]
2101 Wilson Blvd., Ste. 916
Arlington, VA 22201
PH: (703)524-0810
Fax: (703)524-1921
Newman, Joel G., President,
Treasurer

American Fiber Manufacturers As-
sociation [3252]
3033 Wilson Blvd., Ste. 700
Arlington, VA 22201
PH: (703)875-0432
Fax: (703)875-0907
O'Day, Paul T., President

American Homeowners Grassroots
Alliance [18357]
6776 Little Falls Rd.
Arlington, VA 22213-1213
Hahn, Mr. Bruce, CAE, President

American Intellectual Property Law
Association [5321]
241 18th St. S, Ste. 700
Arlington, VA 22202
PH: (703)415-0780
Fax: (703)415-0786
DeFranco, Denise W., President

American Legislative Exchange
Council [18961]
2900 Crystal Dr., 6th Fl.
Arlington, VA 22202
PH: (703)373-0933
Fax: (703)373-0927
Hyde, Montana, Exec. Asst.

American Press Institute **[8147]**
4401 Wilson Blvd., Ste. 900
Arlington, VA 22203-4195
PH: (571)366-1200
   (571)366-1035
Rosenstiel, Tom, Exec. Dir.

American Psychiatric Association
[16822]
1000 Wilson Blvd., Ste. 1825
Arlington, VA 22209-3901
PH: (703)907-7300
Toll free: 888-357-7924
Fax: (703)907-1097
Levin, Saul, MD, CEO

American Public Power Association
[5830]
2451 Crystal Dr., Ste. 1000
Arlington, VA 22202-4804
PH: (202)467-2900
Hunter, Douglas, Chairman

American Society of Pension Profes-
sionals and Actuaries **[1065]**
4245 N Fairfax Dr., Ste. 750
Arlington, VA 22203
PH: (703)516-9300
Fax: (703)516-9308
Nichols, Joseph A., President

American Society for Radiation
Oncology **[17050]**
251 18th St. S, 8th Fl.
Arlington, VA 22202
PH: (703)502-1550
Toll free: 800-962-7876
Fax: (703)502-7852
Minsky, Bruce D., Chairman

American Society of Transplant
Surgeons **[17504]**
2461 S Clark St., Ste. 640
Arlington, VA 22202
PH: (703)414-7870
Fax: (703)414-7874
Gifford, Kimberly A., MBA, Exec. Dir.

American Sugar Alliance **[1315]**
2111 Wilson Blvd., Ste. 600
Arlington, VA 22201
PH: (703)351-5055
Fax: (703)351-6698
Myers, Vickie Rideout, Exec. Dir.

American Trucking Associations
[3322]
950 N Glebe Rd., Ste. 210
Arlington, VA 22203-4181
PH: (703)838-1700
Thomas, Pat, Chairman

American Trucking Associations
Technology and Maintenance
Council **[3323]**
950 N Glebe Rd., Ste. 210
Arlington, VA 22203-4181
PH: (703)838-1763
Toll free: 800-333-1759
Fax: (703)838-1701
Graves, Bill, CEO, President

The American Waterways Operators
[2236]
801 N Quincy St., Ste. 200
Arlington, VA 22203
PH: (703)841-9300
Fax: (703)841-0389
Allegretti, Tom, President, CEO

American Youth Understanding
Diabetes Abroad **[14519]**
1700 N Moore St., Ste. 2000
Arlington, VA 22209
PH: (703)527-3860
Cuttriss, Nicolas, Founder, Chmn. of
the Bd.

Animal Agriculture Alliance **[1316]**
2101 Wilson Blvd., Ste. 916-B
Arlington, VA 22201

PH: (703)562-5160
Smith, Ms. Kay Johnson, CEO,
President

Armenian American Cultural As-
sociation, Inc **[8823]**
1300 Crystal Dr., Ste. 1504
Arlington, VA 22202
PH: (703)416-2555
Balian, Rita, CEO, President

Army Historical Foundation **[9799]**
2425 Wilson Blvd.
Arlington, VA 22201
Toll free: 800-506-2672
Fax: (703)522-7929
Abrams, Creighton W., Exec. Dir.

Arnold Air Society **[23821]**
1501 Lee Hwy., Ste. 400
Arlington, VA 22209
PH: (843)467-5855

Ashoka Innovators for the Public
[12139]
1700 N Moore St., Ste. 2000
Arlington, VA 22209
PH: (703)527-8300
Fax: (703)527-8383
Drayton, Bill, Founder, CEO, Chair-
man

Associated General Contractors of
America **[854]**
2300 Wilson Blvd., Ste. 300
Arlington, VA 22201
PH: (703)548-3118
Toll free: 800-242-1767
Fax: (703)548-3119
Sandherr, Stephen E., CEO

Associates of the American Foreign
Service Worldwide **[23427]**
4001 N 9th St., Ste. 214
Arlington, VA 22203
PH: (703)820-5420
Fax: (703)820-5421
Miller, Debbie, Bd. Member

Association for the Advancement of
Medical Instrumentation **[6109]**
4301 N Fairfax Dr., Ste. 301
Arlington, VA 22203-1633
PH: (703)525-4890
Fax: (703)276-0793
Bernat, Patrick, Director

Association for Africanist Anthropol-
ogy **[5905]**
American Anthropological Associa-
tion
2200 Wilson Blvd., Ste. 600
Arlington, VA 22201-3357
PH: (703)528-1902
Toll free: 800-545-4703
Fax: (703)528-3546
Coffman, Jennifer, Officer

Association of Black Anthropologists
[5906]
AAA Member Services
2300 Clarendon Blvd., Ste. 1301
Arlington, VA 22201
PH: (703)528-1902
Simmons, David, President

Association of Children's Museums
[9823]
2711 Jefferson Davis Hwy., Ste. 600
Arlington, VA 22202
PH: (703)224-3100
Fax: (703)224-3099
Farrington, Jennifer, VP

Association for Enterprise Information **[613]**
2111 Wilson Blvd., Ste. 400
Arlington, VA 22201

PH: (703)247-2597
Fax: (703)522-3192
Witter, Ray, Chairman

Association of Fundraising Profes-
sionals **[11856]**
4300 Wilson Blvd., Ste. 300
Arlington, VA 22203
PH: (703)684-0410
Toll free: 800-666-3863
Fax: (703)684-0540
Watt, Andrew, President, CEO

Association for Political and Legal
Anthropology **[5907]**
American Anthropological Associa-
tion
2300 Clarendon Blvd., Ste. 1301
Arlington, VA 22201
PH: (703)528-1902
Adelman, Madelaine, Officer

Association of Public Data Users
[6738]
PO Box 100155
Arlington, VA 22210
PH: (703)522-4980
Fax: (480)393-5098
Brown, Warren, President

Association of Public Television Sta-
tions **[455]**
2100 Crystal Dr., Ste. 700
Arlington, VA 22202
PH: (202)654-4200
Fax: (202)654-4236
Butler, Patrick, President, CEO

Association of Senior Anthropolo-
gists **[5909]**
2300 Clarendon Blvd., Ste. 1301
Arlington, VA 22201
PH: (703)528-1902
Fax: (703)528-3546
Lewis, Prof. Herbert S., President

Association of State Drinking Water
Administrators **[5713]**
1401 Wilson Blvd., Ste. 1225
Arlington, VA 22209
PH: (703)812-9505
Fax: (703)812-9506
Taft, Jim, Exec. Dir.

Association of State and Territorial
Health Officials **[5714]**
2231 Crystal Dr., Ste. 450
Arlington, VA 22202
PH: (202)371-9090
Fax: (571)527-3189
Mullen, Jewel, MD, MPH, MPA,
President

The Association of Union Construc-
tors **[857]**
1501 Lee Hwy., Ste. 202
Arlington, VA 22209-1109
PH: (703)524-3336
Fax: (703)524-3364
Acord, David, Exec. Dir.

Association of the United States
Army **[5593]**
2425 Wilson Blvd.
Arlington, VA 22201
PH: (703)841-4300
Toll free: 800-336-4570
Sullivan, Gordon R., President, CEO

Association for Unmanned Vehicle
Systems International **[7101]**
2700 S Quincy St., Ste. 400
Arlington, VA 22206
PH: (703)845-9671
Fax: (703)845-9679
Davidson, Daryl, Exec. Dir.

Beyond AIDS **[13532]**
2200 Wilson Blvd., No. 102-232
Arlington, VA 22201
Fax: (888)BEY-AIDS
Hattis, Ronald, MD, President

Bicycle Helmet Safety Institute
[12816]
4611 7th St. S
Arlington, VA 22204-1419
PH: (703)486-0100

Bikes for the World **[10780]**
1408 N Fillmore St., Ste. 11
Arlington, VA 22201
PH: (703)740-7856
Hendrixson, Karen, Chairperson

BiNet U.S.A. **[11873]**
4201 Wilson Blvd., No. 110-311
Arlington, VA 22203-1859
Toll free: 800-585-9368
Cheltenham, Faith, President

Castle Coalition **[18930]**
901 N Glebe Rd., Ste. 900
Arlington, VA 22203-1854
PH: (703)682-9320
Fax: (703)682-9321
Walsh, Christina, Director

Casualty Actuarial Society **[1844]**
4350 N Fairfax Dr., Ste. 250
Arlington, VA 22203
PH: (703)276-3100
Fax: (703)276-3108
Ziegler, Cynthia R., Exec. Dir.,
Secretary, Treasurer

Cement Kiln Recycling Coalition
[4627]
PO Box 7553
Arlington, VA 22207
PH: (703)624-4513
Benoit, Mike, Exec. Dir.

Center for Climate and Energy Solu-
tions **[4126]**
2101 Wilson Blvd., Ste. 550
Arlington, VA 22201
PH: (703)516-4146
Fax: (703)516-9551
Claussen, Hon. Eileen, President

Child Care Aware of America
[10805]
1515 N Courthouse Rd., 2nd Fl.
Arlington, VA 22201
Toll free: 800-424-2246
Fax: (703)341-4101
Rohde, Steve, President

Child Life Council **[14174]**
1820 N Fort Myer Dr., Ste. 520
Arlington, VA 22209
PH: (571)483-4500
Toll free: 800-252-4515
Fax: (571)483-4482
Gandorf, Jim, CAE, CEO, Exec. Dir.

Chlorine Institute **[714]**
1300 Wilson Blvd., Ste 525
Arlington, VA 22209
PH: (703)894-4140
Fax: (703)894-4130
Reiner, Frank, President

Climate, Community and Biodiversity
Alliance **[3829]**
c/o Joanna Durbin, Director
2011 Crystal Dr., Ste. 500
Arlington, VA 22202-3787
PH: (703)341-2461
Durbin, Joanna, Director

College Parents of America **[7957]**
2200 Wilson Blvd., Ste. 102-396
Arlington, VA 22201
Toll free: 888-761-6702

College Theology Society **[8707]**
c/o Brian Flanagan, Treasurer
Marymount University
Butler Hall

2807 N Glebe Rd.
Arlington, VA 22207
PH: (937)229-4435
   (703)284-6516
Portier, William, President

Committee for Economic Development **[18146]**
1530 Wilson Blvd., Ste. 400
Arlington, VA 22209
PH: (202)296-5860
Toll free: 800-676-7353
Fax: (202)223-0776
West, Todd, Dir. of Dev.

Common Ground Alliance **[12818]**
2300 Wilson Blvd., Ste. 310
Arlington, VA 22201
PH: (703)836-1709
Smith, Greg, V. Chmn. of the Bd.

Communities In Schools **[7818]**
2345 Crystal Dr., Ste. 700
Arlington, VA 22202
PH: (703)519-8999
Toll free: 800-247-4543
Milliken, William E., Founder, V. Ch.

Concord Coalition **[18147]**
1011 Arlington Blvd., Ste. 300
Arlington, VA 22209-2299
PH: (703)894-6222
Fax: (703)894-6231
Bixby, Robert, Exec. Dir.

The Conservation Fund **[3837]**
1655 N Fort Myer Dr., Ste. 1300
Arlington, VA 22209
PH: (703)525-6300
Fax: (703)525-4610
Leonard, Michael, Chmn. of the Bd.

Conservation International -
   Headquarters **[3838]**
2011 Crystal Dr., Ste. 500
Arlington, VA 22202
PH: (703)341-2400
Toll free: 800-429-5660
Seligmann, Peter A., Chairman,
   CEO

Consumer Electronics Association,
   TechHome Division **[1039]**
1919 S Eads St.
Arlington, VA 22202
PH: (703)907-7600
Toll free: 866-858-1555
Fax: (703)907-7675
Inns, David, V. Ch.

Consumer Technology Association
   [1040]
1919 S Eads St.
Arlington, VA 22202-3028
PH: (703)907-7600
   (703)907-7650
Fax: (703)907-7690
Shapiro, Gary, CEO, President

Council for Children with Behavior
   Disorders **[8579]**
Council for Exceptional Children
2900 Crystal Dr., Ste. 1000
Arlington, VA 22202-3557
Oakes, Wendy Peia, President

Council for Community and
   Economic Research **[23577]**
1700 N Moore St., Ste. 2225
Arlington, VA 22209
PH: (703)522-4980
Fax: (480)393-5098
Poole, Dr. Kenneth E., Exec. Dir.

Council of Defense and Space
   Industry Associations **[134]**
1000 Wilson Blvd., Ste. 1800
Arlington, VA 22209

PH: (703)243-2020
Fax: (703)243-8539

Council for Exceptional Children
   [8667]
2900 Crystal Dr., Ste. 1000
Arlington, VA 22202-3557
Toll free: 888-232-7733
Graham, Alexander T., Exec. Dir.

Council on Foundations **[12401]**
2121 Crystal Dr., Ste. 700
Arlington, VA 22202-3706
PH: (703)879-0600
Toll free: 800-673-9036
Spruill, Vikki N., President, CEO

Counterpart International **[12149]**
2345 Crystal Dr., Ste. 301
Arlington, VA 22202
PH: (571)447-5700
Fax: (703)412-5035
Nolan, Deborah, Chmn. of the Bd.

CRDF Global **[7131]**
1776 Wilson Blvd., Ste. 300
Arlington, VA 22209
PH: (703)526-9720
Fax: (703)526-9721
Hurley, John, President, CEO

Crude Oil Quality Association **[2518]**
2324 N Dickerson St.
Arlington, VA 22207-2641
PH: (703)282-2461
Sutton, Dennis L., Exec. Dir.

Cyber Conflict Studies Association
   [7698]
c/o Karl Grindal
4600 N Fairfax Dr., Ste. 906
Arlington, VA 22203
Healey, Jason, Secretary

Dental Trade Alliance **[1600]**
4350 N Fairfax Dr., Ste. 220
Arlington, VA 22203-1673
PH: (703)379-7755
Fax: (703)931-9429

Department of Boards and Councils
   of Catholic Education **[7575]**
National Catholic Educational As-
   sociation
1005 N Glebe Rd., Ste. 525
Arlington, VA 22201
PH: (202)337-6232
Toll free: 800-711-6232
Fax: (703)243-0025
Haney, Dr. Regina M., Exec. Dir.

Educators Rising **[7849]**
1525 Wilson Blvd., Ste. 705
Arlington, VA 22209
Toll free: 800-766-1156
Brown, Dan, Director

Employee Assistance Professionals
   Association **[13109]**
4350 N Fairfax Dr., Ste. 740
Arlington, VA 22203
PH: (703)387-1000
Fax: (703)522-4585
DeLapp, Greg, CEO

Energy Recovery Council **[4740]**
2200 Wilson Blvd., Ste. 310
Arlington, VA 22201
PH: (202)467-6240
Michaels, Ted, President

Ethics and Compliance Initiative
   [630]
2345 Crystal Dr., Ste. 201
Arlington, VA 22202
PH: (703)647-2185
Fax: (703)647-2180
Harned, Patricia J., Ph.D., CEO

Ethics Research Center **[17856]**
2345 Crystal Dr., Ste. 201
Arlington, VA 22202-4807
PH: (703)647-2185
Fax: (703)647-2180
Boswell, Nancy, Co-Chmn. of the
   Bd.

Ethiopian Community Development
   Council **[12589]**
901 S Highland St.
Arlington, VA 22204
PH: (703)685-0510
Fax: (703)685-0529
Teferra, Tsehaye, PhD, President

Evangelical Education Society of the
   Episcopal Church **[20105]**
PO Box 7297
Arlington, VA 22207
PH: (703)807-1862
Pritchartt, Day Smith, Exec. Dir.

Experience Works **[11764]**
4401 Wilson Blvd., Ste. 1100
Arlington, VA 22203
Toll free: 800-397-9757
Noonan, Roger, Chairman

Families Fighting Flu **[17141]**
4201 Wilson Blvd., No. 110-702
Arlington, VA 22203
Toll free: 888-236-3358
Kanowitz, Richard, President

Fashion Fights Poverty **[12537]**
1101 Wilson Blvd., Ste. 932
Arlington, VA 22209
PH: (571)969-3121
Luanghy, Sylvie, VP, Founder

Federal Bar Association **[5005]**
1220 N Fillmore St., Ste. 444
Arlington, VA 22201
PH: (571)481-9100
Fax: (571)481-9090
Vincent, Mark, President

Federation of State Humanities
   Councils **[9554]**
1600 Wilson Blvd., Ste. 902
Arlington, VA 22209
PH: (703)908-9700
Allen, Jeff, VP

Feminist Majority Foundation
   [18207]
1600 Wilson Blvd., Ste. 801
Arlington, VA 22209
PH: (703)522-2214
Fax: (703)522-2219
Smeal, Eleanor, President

Fiber Economics Bureau **[6630]**
3033 Wilson Blvd., Ste. 700
Arlington, VA 22201
PH: (703)875-0676
Fax: (703)875-0675
Snowman, Stanwood, Officer

Firefly, Inc. **[10975]**
1405 S Fern St., No. 552
Arlington, VA 22202
PH: (917)359-7207
Fax: (240)396-2107
Levine, Nicole, President

Food Marketing Institute **[2954]**
2345 Crystal Dr., Ste. 800
Arlington, VA 22202
PH: (202)452-8444
Fax: (202)429-4519
Garland, Jerry, Chairman

Foundation for Advancing Alcohol
   Responsibility **[17312]**
2345 Crystal Dr., Ste. 710
Arlington, VA 22202

PH: (202)637-0077
Fax: (202)637-0079
Seikaly, Fadi, Dir. of Programs

Foundation of the Federal Bar Association **[5424]**
1220 N Fillmore St., Ste. 444
Arlington, VA 22201
Méndez, Néstor M., President

Friends of Tent of Nations North
   America **[12436]**
c/o Kay Plitt, Finance Director
5621 N 9th Rd.
Arlington, VA 22205
PH: (703)524-5657
Plitt, Kay, Dir. of Fin.

Gasification and Syngas Technolo-
   gies Council **[1497]**
3030 Clarendon Blvd., Ste. 330
Arlington, VA 22201-6518
PH: (703)276-0110
Fax: (703)276-0141
Kerester, Alison, Exec. Dir.

George Mason University I Center
   for Media and Public Affairs
   [17947]
2338 S Queen St.
Arlington, VA 22202
PH: (202)302-5523
Rieck, Donald, Exec. Dir.

Glass Packaging Institute **[834]**
1220 N Fillmore St., Ste. 400
Arlington, VA 22201
PH: (703)684-6359
Fax: (703)546-0588
Bragg, Lynn M., President

Global Centurion **[10999]**
PO Box 17107
Arlington, VA 22216-7107
PH: (703)919-6828
Lederer, Laura J., President

Global Water **[13325]**
1901 N Fort Myer Dr., Ste. 405
Arlington, VA 22209
PH: (703)528-3863
Fax: (703)528-5776
Dickman, Karen, Exec. Dir.

Global Water Challenge **[4757]**
2900 S Quincy St., Ste. 375
Arlington, VA 22206
PH: (703)379-2713
Reilly, William K., Co-Ch.

Governors' Wind Energy Coalition
   [7388]
2200 Wilson Blvd., Ste. 102-22
Arlington, VA 22201
PH: (402)651-2948
Pearce, Larry, Exec. Dir.

Grantmakers In Aging **[12482]**
2001 Jefferson Davis Hwy., Ste. 504
Arlington, VA 22202
Feather, John, PhD, CEO

Halogenated Solvents Industry Alli-
   ance, Inc. **[719]**
3033 Wilson Blvd., Ste. 700
Arlington, VA 22201
PH: (703)875-0683
Fax: (703)875-0675

Healthcare Distribution Management
   Association **[16662]**
901 N Glebe Rd., Ste. 1000
Arlington, VA 22203
PH: (703)787-0000
Fax: (703)812-5282
Scherr, Ted, Chairman

Hearth, Patio and Barbecue Association **[1617]**
1901 N Moore St., Ste. 600
Arlington, VA 22209

PH: (703)522-0086
Fax: (703)522-0548
Goldman, Jack, President, CEO

Hearth, Patio and Barbecue Education Foundation [1618]
1901 N Moore St., Ste. 600
Arlington, VA 22209
PH: (703)522-0086
Fax: (703)522-0548
Goldman, Jack, President, CEO

High Performance Building Council [6164]
3101 Wilson Blvd., Ste. 900
Arlington, VA 22201
PH: (703)682-1630
Moy, Get W., Chairman

Highway Loss Data Institute [1859]
1005 N Glebe Rd., Ste. 700
Arlington, VA 22201
PH: (703)247-1600
Fax: (703)247-1595
O'Donnell, Brenda, VP

HIV Medicine Association [13545]
1300 Wilson Blvd., Ste. 300
Arlington, VA 22209
PH: (703)299-1215
Fax: (703)299-8766
Rio, Carlos del, MD, Chairman

Joseph A. Holmes Safety Association [23483]
PO Box 9375
Arlington, VA 22219
PH: (304)256-3223
Fax: (304)256-3319
Kravitz, Jeffrey, President

Industrial Research Institute [7091]
2300 Clarendon Blvd., Ste. 400
Arlington, VA 22201
PH: (703)647-2580
Fax: (703)647-2581
Bernstein, Edward, President

Infectious Diseases Society of America [15402]
1300 Wilson Blvd., Ste. 300
Arlington, VA 22209
PH: (703)299-0200
Fax: (703)299-0204
Murray, Barbara E., MD, Exec.

Institute of Clean Air Companies [2641]
3033 Wilson Blvd., Ste. 700
Arlington, VA 22201
PH: (571)858-3707
Fax: (703)243-8696
Stafford, Michael, Exec. Dir.

Institute for Humane Studies [12044]
George Mason University
3434 Washington Blvd., MS 1C5
Arlington, VA 22201
PH: (703)993-4880
Toll free: 800-697-8799
Fax: (703)993-4890
Zupan, Marty, President, CEO

Institute for Justice [5427]
901 N Glebe Rd., Ste. 900
Arlington, VA 22203
PH: (703)682-9320
Fax: (703)682-9321
Bullock, Scott, President, Gen. Counsel

Insurance Institute for Highway Safety [12822]
1005 N Glebe Rd., Ste. 800
Arlington, VA 22201
PH: (703)247-1500
Fax: (703)247-1588
Lund, Adrian, President

Intelligence and National Security Alliance [5344]
NRECA Bldg.
4301 Wilson Blvd., Ste. 910
Arlington, VA 22203
PH: (703)224-4672
Fax: (571)777-8481
Alsup, Chuck, President

International Association for College Admission Counseling [7448]
PO Box 41348
Arlington, VA 22204
PH: (678)827-1622
Fleischmann, Samuel, VP

International Association for Counterterrorism and Security Professionals [19181]
PO Box 100688
Arlington, VA 22210-3688
PH: (201)224-0588
Fax: (202)315-3459
Fustero, Steven J., Dir. of Operations

International Coordinating Council of Aerospace Industries Associations [141]
c/o Doug Farren, Executive Secretary
Aerospace Industries Association of America
1000 Wilson Blvd., Ste. 1700
Arlington, VA 22209-3928
PH: (703)358-1064
Melcher, David, Chairman

International Crosby Circle [24046]
c/o Wig Wiggins
5608 N 34th St.
Arlington, VA 22207
PH: (703)241-5608
Crosby, Kathryn, President

International Federation of Inspection Agencies - Americas Committee, Inc. [1818]
1600 N Oak St., No. 1710
Arlington, VA 22209
PH: (703)528-2737
Fax: (703)533-1612
Bush, Milton, Exec. Dir.

International Foundation for Election Systems [18183]
2011 Crystal Dr., 10th Fl.
Arlington, VA 22202
PH: (202)350-6700
Fax: (202)350-6701
Sweeney, Bill, President, CEO

International Fragrance Association North America [1452]
1655 Fort Myer Dr., Ste. 875
Arlington, VA 22209
PH: (571)317-1500
Fax: (571)312-8033
Ahmed, Farah, President

International Initiative on Exploitative Child Labor [11048]
1016 S Wayne St., Apt. 702
Arlington, VA 22204
PH: (703)920-0435
Fax: (703)328-3401
Mull, Ms. Lynda Diane, Exec. Dir., President

International Liquid Terminals Association [3437]
1005 N Glebe Rd., Ste. No. 600
Arlington, VA 22201
PH: (703)875-2011
Fax: (703)875-2018
Lidiak, Peter, VP of Government Rel.

International Pharmaceutical Excipients Council of the Americas [2560]
3138 N 10th St., Ste. 500
Arlington, VA 22201

PH: (571)814-3449
(571)814-3451
Beals, Kimberly, Exec. Dir.

International Relief & Development [11386]
1621 N Kent St., 4th Fl.
Arlington, VA 22209
PH: (703)248-0161
Fax: (703)248-0194
Ervin, Roger, President, CEO

International Safety Equipment Association [2998]
1901 N Moore St.
Arlington, VA 22209-1762
PH: (703)525-1695
Fax: (703)528-2148
Shipp, Daniel K, President

International Society on Hypertension in Blacks [15348]
2111 Wilson Blvd., Ste. 700
Arlington, VA 22201
PH: (703)351-5023
Fax: (703)351-9292
Kountz, David, M.D. Trustee

International Society for NeuroImmunoModulation [16025]
PO Box 41269
Arlington, VA 22204-8269
Fax: (703)521-3462
Majde-Cottrell, Jeannine A., PhD, Exec. Dir., Treasurer

International Society for Technology in Education [7657]
1530 Wilson Blvd., Ste. 730
Arlington, VA 22209
PH: (703)348-4784
Toll free: 800-336-5191
Fax: (703)348-6459
Lewis, Brian, CEO

International Training and Simulation Alliance [6254]
2111 Wilson Blvd., Ste. 400
Arlington, VA 22201-3061
PH: (703)247-9471

Interstate Council on Water Policy [5653]
505 N Ivy St.
Arlington, VA 22201-1707
PH: (573)303-6644
Mueller, Ryan, Exec. Dir.

JEDEC [1054]
3103 N 10th St., Ste. 240-S
Arlington, VA 22201-2107
PH: (703)907-7515
Kelly, John, President

Leadership Institute [8199]
Steven P.J. Wood Bldg.
1101 N Highland St.
Arlington, VA 22201-2807
PH: (703)247-2000
Fax: (703)247-2001
Blackwell, Morton C., President

Lighting Controls Association [2101]
c/o National Electrical Manufacturers Association
1300 N 17th St., Ste. 1752
Arlington, VA 22209
PH: (403)802-1809
DiLouie, Craig, Contact

Live Action [19060]
2200 Wilson Blvd., Ste. 102
Arlington, VA 22201-3324
PH: (323)454-3304
Rose, Lila, Founder, President

Logistics Officer Association [18696]
PO Box 2264
Arlington, VA 22202
Dabney, Dennis, President

Manufactured Housing Institute [2198]
1655 N Fort Myer Dr., Ste. 104
Arlington, VA 22209-3108
PH: (703)558-0400
Fax: (703)558-0401
Smith, Nathan, Chairman

Manufacturers Alliance for Productivity and Innovation [1745]
1600 Wilson Blvd., 11th Fl.
Arlington, VA 22209-2594
PH: (703)841-9000
Fax: (703)841-9514
Keating, Neal J., Chairman

Manufacturers of Emission Controls Association [2642]
2200 Wilson Blvd., Ste. 310
Arlington, VA 22201
PH: (202)296-4797
Santos, Antonio, Contact

Master Limited Partnership Association [2029]
4350 N Fairfax Dr., Ste. 815
Arlington, VA 22203
PH: (703)822-4995
Fax: (703)842-8333
Lyman, Ms. Mary, Exec. Dir.

Meals on Wheels America [12102]
1550 Crystal Dr., Ste. 1004
Arlington, VA 22202
Toll free: 888-998-6325
Fax: (703)548-5274
Seman, Liz, Chairman

The Media Institute [17950]
2300 Clarendon Blvd., Ste. 602
Arlington, VA 22201
PH: (703)243-5700
Fax: (703)243-8808
Coto, Susanna, Director

Mediators Beyond Borders International [4964]
1901 N Fort Myer Dr., Ste. 405
Arlington, VA 22209
PH: (703)528-6552
Fax: (703)528-5776
Pillsbury, Charlie, Exec. Dir.

Military Chaplains Association of the U.S.A. [19932]
PO Box 7056
Arlington, VA 22207-7056
PH: (703)533-5890
Fax: (770)649-1972
McCoy, Michael, President

Military Operations Research Society [5604]
2111 Wilson Blvd., Ste. 700
Arlington, VA 22201
PH: (703)933-9070
Fax: (703)933-9066
Reardon, Susan K., CEO

National Accounting and Finance Council [43]
c/o Joe Howard, Manager
950 N Glebe Rd., Ste. 210
Arlington, VA 22203-4181
PH: (703)838-1763
Fax: (703)838-1701
Howard, Joe, Mgr.

National Air Carrier Association [146]
1000 Wilson Blvd., Ste. 1700
Arlington, VA 22209
PH: (703)358-8060
Fax: (703)358-8070
Brooks, A. Oakley, President

National Alliance on Mental Illness [15785]
3803 N Fairfax Dr., Ste. 100
Arlington, VA 22203

PH: (703)524-7600
Toll free: 800-950-6264
Giliberti, Mary, J.D, Exec. Dir.

National Apartment Association
[2867]
4300 Wilson Blvd., Ste. 400
Arlington, VA 22203
PH: (703)518-6141
Fax: (703)248-9440
Ross, Marc, Chmn. of the Bd.

National Association of Chain Drug
Stores [16674]
1776 Wilson Blvd., Ste. 200
Arlington, VA 22209
PH: (703)549-3001
Fax: (703)836-4869
Otto, Martin, Chairman

National Association of Chemical
Distributors [723]
1560 Wilson Blvd., Ste. 1100
Arlington, VA 22209
PH: (703)527-6223
Fax: (703)527-7747
Brainerd, Mathew A., Chairman

National Association for College
Admission Counseling [7449]
1050 N Highland St., Ste. 400
Arlington, VA 22201-2197
PH: (703)836-2222
Toll free: 800-822-6285
Fax: (703)243-9375
Smith, Joyce E., CEO

National Association of Federal
Credit Unions [955]
3138 10th St. N
Arlington, VA 22201-2149
Toll free: 800-336-4644
Templeton, Ed, Chairman

National Association of Immigration
Judges [5390]
c/o Judge Lawrence Burman,
Secretary-Treasurer
Arlington Immigration Court
1901 S Bell St., Ste. 200
Arlington, VA 22202
PH: (703)603-1306
Marks, Hon. Dana Leigh, President

National Association of Parish Cat-
echetical Directors [20085]
c/o National Catholic Educational
Association
1005 N Glebe Rd., Ste. 525
Arlington, VA 22201
Toll free: 800-711-6232
Fax: (703)243-0025

National Association for the Practice
of Anthropology [5916]
c/o Kathleen Terry-Sharp
American Anthropological Association
2200 Wilson Blvd., Ste. 600
Arlington, VA 22201
PH: (703)528-1902
Hall-Clifford, Rachel, Secretary

National Association of State Credit
Union Supervisor [5124]
1655 N Ft. Myer Dr., Ste. 650
Arlington, VA 22209
PH: (703)528-8351
Fax: (703)528-3248
West, Terry, Secretary, Treasurer

National Association of State Depart-
ments of Agriculture [4949]
4350 N Fairfax Dr., No. 910
Arlington, VA 22203
PH: (202)296-9680
Fax: (703)880-0509
Ibach, Greg, President

National Association of State Energy
Officials [5172]
2107 Wilson Blvd., Ste. 850
Arlington, VA 22201
PH: (703)299-8800
Fax: (703)299-6208
Clark, Vaughn, Chairman

National Association of Veterans Af-
fairs Physicians and Dentists
[16758]
PO Box 15418
Arlington, VA 22215-0418
Toll free: 866-836-3520
Fax: (540)972-1728
Spagnolo, Samuel V., MD, President

National Board for Professional
Teaching Standards [8653]
1525 Wilson Blvd., Ste. 700
Arlington, VA 22209
PH: (703)465-2700
Brookins, Peggy, President, CEO

National Catholic Educational As-
sociation [7577]
1005 N Glebe Rd., Ste. 525
Arlington, VA 22201
PH: (571)257-0010
Toll free: 800-711-6232
Fax: (703)243-0025
Comeau, Stephen, Exec. Asst.

National Center for Advanced
Technologies [7285]
1000 Wilson Blvd., Ste. 1700
Arlington, VA 22209-3901
PH: (703)358-1000
Fax: (703)358-1012
Forest, Don, President

National Center for Prosecution of
Child Abuse [11089]
1400 Crystal Dr., Ste. 330
Arlington, VA 22202
PH: (703)549-9222
Fax: (703)836-3195
Phillips, Allie, Director

National Commission on Teaching
and America's Future [8654]
1525 Wilson Blvd., Ste. 705
Arlington, VA 22209
PH: (202)429-2570
George, Melinda, President

National Council on Aging [10522]
251 18th St. S, Ste. 500
Arlington, VA 22202
PH: (571)527-3900
Browdie, Richard, Chmn. of the Bd.,
Chairman

National Council of Catholic Women
[19882]
200 N Glebe Rd., Ste. 725
Arlington, VA 22203
PH: (703)224-0990
Toll free: 800-506-9407
Fax: (703)224-0991
Hopkins, Sheila, President

National Council of Social Security
Management Associations [5761]
3303 S Wakefield St.
Arlington, VA 22206
PH: (202)547-8530
Fax: (202)547-8532
Dirago, Joe, Exec. Ofc.

National Defense Industrial Associa-
tion [5607]
2111 Wilson Blvd., Ste. 400
Arlington, VA 22201
PH: (703)522-1820
McKinley, Gen. Creg R., President,
CEO

National Federation of Press Women
[2700]
PO Box 5556
Arlington, VA 22205

PH: (804)746-1033
Hoffman, Marsha, President

National Fusion Center Association
[5345]
1609 N Edgewood St.
Arlington, VA 22201
Sena, Mike, President

National Genealogical Society
[20985]
3108 Columbia Pke., Ste. 300
Arlington, VA 22204-4370
PH: (703)525-0050
Toll free: 800-473-0060
Fax: (703)525-0052
Jones, Jordan, President

National Grocers Association [2969]
1005 N Glebe Rd., Ste. 250
Arlington, VA 22201-5758
PH: (703)516-0700
Fax: (703)516-0115
Lynch, Brian P., VP

National Ice Cream Mix Association
[1703]
2101 Wilson Blvd., Ste. 400
Arlington, VA 22201
PH: (703)243-5630
Fax: (703)841-9328
Galloway, Pat, President

The National Industrial Transporta-
tion League [3343]
1700 N Moore St., Ste. 1900
Arlington, VA 22209
PH: (703)524-5011
Fax: (703)524-5017
Gilanshah, Ellie, VP of Fin., VP of
Admin.

National Institute of Senior Centers
[10525]
National Council on Aging
251 18th St. S, Ste. 500
Arlington, VA 22202
PH: (571)527-3900

National Lime Association [724]
200 N Glebe Rd., Ste. 800
Arlington, VA 22203
PH: (703)243-5463
Fax: (703)243-5489
Herz, William C., Exec. Dir.

National Milk Producers Federation
[3982]
2101 Wilson Blvd., Ste. 400
Arlington, VA 22201-3062
PH: (703)243-6111
Fax: (703)841-9328

National Osteoporosis Foundation
[16485]
251 18th St. S, Ste. 630
Arlington, VA 22202
PH: (703)647-3000
Toll free: 800-231-4222
Fax: (703)414-3742
Gagel, Robert F., M.D., President

National Private Truck Council
[3345]
950 N Glebe Rd., Ste. 2300
Arlington, VA 22203-4183
PH: (703)683-1300
Fax: (703)683-1217
Mundell, George, Exec. VP, COO

National Rural Electric Cooperative
Association [1031]
4301 Wilson Blvd.
Arlington, VA 22203
PH: (703)907-5500
(703)907-5732
Coleman, Mel, President

National Science Foundation [7142]
4201 Wilson Blvd.
Arlington, VA 22230

PH: (703)292-5111
Toll free: 800-877-8339
Cordova, France A., Director

National Science Teachers Associa-
tion [8555]
1840 Wilson Blvd.
Arlington, VA 22201-3000
PH: (703)243-7100
Fax: (703)243-7177
Simmons, Dr. Patricia, President

National Sleep Foundation [17220]
1010 N Glebe Rd., Ste. 310
Arlington, VA 22201
PH: (703)243-1697
Cloud, David, MBA, CEO

National Society of Black Physicists
[7028]
3303 Wilson Blvd., Ste. 700
Arlington, VA 22201
PH: (703)617-4176
Fax: (703)536-4203
Horton, Renee, President

National Tank Truck Carriers [3097]
950 N Glebe Rd., Ste. 520
Arlington, VA 22203
PH: (703)838-1960
Sumerford Jr., Harold, Chmn. of the
Bd.

National Training and Simulation As-
sociation [6257]
2111 Wilson Blvd., Ste. 400
Arlington, VA 22201-3061
PH: (703)247-9471
(703)247-2567
Fax: (703)243-1659
Robb, James A., President

National Waterways Conference
[3098]
1100 N Glebe Rd., Ste. 1010
Arlington, VA 22201
PH: (703)224-8007
Fax: (866)371-1390
Larson, Amy W., Esq., President

The Nature Conservancy [3914]
4245 N Fairfax Dr., Ste. 100
Arlington, VA 22203-1606
PH: (703)841-5300
Toll free: 800-628-6860
Fax: (703)841-1283
McCaw, Craig O., Chmn. of the Bd.

Naval Sea Cadet Corps [5615]
2300 Wilson Blvd., Ste. 200
Arlington, VA 22201-5435
PH: (703)243-6910
Fax: (703)243-3985
Monahan, Capt. James E., Exec.
Dir.

Navy League of the United States
[5618]
2300 Wilson Blvd., Ste. 200
Arlington, VA 22201
PH: (703)528-1775
Toll free: 800-356-5760
Fax: (703)528-2333
Offutt, James, Counsel

Navy-Marine Corps Relief Society
[19382]
875 N Randolph St., Ste. 225
Arlington, VA 22203-1767
Toll free: 800-654-8364
Amos, James, Bd. Member

New Forests Project [12173]
PO Box 41720
Arlington, VA 22204
PH: (202)285-4328
Foote, Virginia B., President

Newspaper Association of America
[2807]
4401 Wilson Blvd., Ste. 900
Arlington, VA 22203-1867

PH: (571)366-1000
Fax: (571)366-1195
Golden, Michael, Director

North American Technician Excellence [1634]
2111 Wilson Blvd., Ste. 510
Arlington, VA 22201-3051
PH: (703)276-7247
Toll free: 877-420-6283
Fax: (703)527-2316
Yurek, Stephen, Officer

NTCA, The Rural Broadband Association [3423]
4121 Wilson Blvd., Ste. 1000
Arlington, VA 22203
PH: (703)351-2000
Fax: (703)351-2001
Boone, Doug, President

NumbersUSA [18995]
1400 Crystal Dr., Ste. 240
Arlington, VA 22202
PH: (703)816-8820
Beck, Roy, Founder, CEO

Obscure Organization [7288]
300 S Jackson St.
Arlington, VA 22204
PH: (703)979-4380
Bullington-McGuire, Richard, President

Organization for Autism Research [13775]
2000 N 14th St., Ste. 240
Arlington, VA 22201
PH: (703)243-9710
Maloney, Michael V., Exec. Dir., Secretary

Our Task [4094]
1900 N Harvard St.
Arlington, VA 22201
Barney, Dr. Gerald O., Exec. Dir., Founder

Partnership for Food Safety Education [16234]
2345 Crystal Dr., Ste. 800
Arlington, VA 22202
PH: (202)220-0651
Feist, Shelley, Exec. Dir.

Patent and Trademark Office Society [5339]
PO Box 2089
Arlington, VA 22202
PH: (571)270-1805
Troutman, Matthew, Comm. Chm.

Pediatric Infectious Diseases Society [15414]
1300 Wilson Blvd., Ste. 300
Arlington, VA 22209
PH: (703)299-6764
Fax: (703)299-0473
Gilsdorf, Janet R., President

Professional Services Council [18289]
4401 Wilson Blvd., Ste. 1110
Arlington, VA 22203
PH: (703)875-8059
Fax: (703)875-8922
Goodman, John, Chairman

Public Broadcasting Service [9147]
2100 Crystal Dr.
Arlington, VA 22202
PH: (703)739-5000
Jones, Michael, Exec. VP

Public Lands Foundation [4582]
PO Box 7226
Arlington, VA 22207
PH: (703)935-0916
Toll free: 866-985-9636
Fax: (888)204-9814
Allen, Tom, Director

Radio Technical Commission for Maritime Services [3237]
1611 N Kent St., Ste. 605
Arlington, VA 22209-2128
PH: (703)527-2000
Fax: (703)351-9932
Markle, Robert, President

RARE [4498]
1310 N Courthouse Rd., Ste. 110
Arlington, VA 22201
PH: (703)522-5070
Fax: (703)522-5027
Galvin, Dale, Managing Dir.

Regional and Distribution Carriers Conference [3100]
c/o Robert Farrell
950 N Glebe Rd., Ste. 210
Arlington, VA 22203-4181
Farrell, Robert P., Contact

Rehabilitation Engineering and Assistive Technology Society of North America [11634]
1700 N Moore St., Ste. 1540
Arlington, VA 22209-1903
PH: (703)524-6686
Fax: (703)524-6630
Mihailidis, Alex, Officer

Restore America's Estuaries [4762]
2300 Clarendon Blvd., Ste. 603
Arlington, VA 22201-3392
PH: (703)524-0248
Benoit, Jeff, CEO, President

Retail Industry Leaders Association [2976]
1700 N Moore St., Ste. 2250
Arlington, VA 22209
PH: (703)841-2300
Fax: (703)841-1184
White, Deborah, Exec. VP

Road Runners Club of America [23119]
1501 Lee Hwy., Ste. 140
Arlington, VA 22209
PH: (703)525-3890
Garner, Mitchell, President

Sea Service Leadership Association [21077]
PO Box 40371
Arlington, VA 22204
Goscinski, Lt. Comdr. Rosie, President

Security Analysis and Risk Management Association [3068]
PO Box 100284
Arlington, VA 22210
PH: (703)635-7906
Fax: (703)635-7935
Ezell, Dr. Barry C., President

SNAC International [1372]
1600 Wilson Blvd., Ste. 650
Arlington, VA 22209
PH: (703)836-4500
Toll free: 800-628-1334
Wells, Elizabeth, VP

Society for Anthropology in Community Colleges [7495]
2200 Wilson Blvd., Ste. 600
Arlington, VA 22201-3357
PH: (703)528-1902
Paskey, Amanda, President

Society for the Anthropology of Consciousness [7496]
American Anthropological Association
2300 Clarendon Blvd., Ste. 1301
Arlington, VA 22201
PH: (703)528-1902
Fax: (703)528-3546
Rill, Bryan, President

Society for the Anthropology of North America [5919]
c/o American Anthropological Association
2300 Clarendon Blvd., Ste. 1301
Arlington, VA 22201-3386
PH: (703)528-1902
Fax: (703)528-3546
Falls, Susan, President

Society for Conservation GIS [3944]
c/o Healy Hamilton, President
NatureServe
4600 N Fairfax Dr., 7th Fl.
Arlington, VA 22203
PH: (703)908-1889
Beardsley, Karen, Officer

Society of Federal Labor and Employee Relations Professionals [5401]
PO Box 25112
Arlington, VA 22202
PH: (703)403-3039
Fax: (703)852-4461
Schwartz, Scott, President

Society for Healthcare Epidemiology of America [14735]
1300 Wilson Blvd., Ste. 300
Arlington, VA 22209
PH: (703)684-1006
Fax: (703)684-1009
Humphreys, Eve, MBA, CAE, Exec. Dir.

Society for International Affairs Inc. [1994]
PO Box 9466
Arlington, VA 22219
PH: (703)946-5683
Weinel, Jennifer, President

Society for Latin American and Caribbean Anthropology [5923]
c/o American Anthroplological Association
4350 N Fairfax Dr., Ste. 640
Arlington, VA 22203-1620
Little, Walter E., PhD, President

Society for Urban, National and Transnational/Global Anthropology [5926]
American Anthropological Association
2200 Wilson Blvd., Ste. 600
Arlington, VA 22201-3357
PH: (703)528-1902
Fax: (703)528-3546
Newman, Andrew, Secretary

Society for Visual Anthropology [5927]
c/o American Anthropological Associatoin
2300 Clarendon Blvd., Ste. 1301
Arlington, VA 22201
Takaragawa, Stephanie, President

Sons and Daughters In Touch [21045]
PO Box 1596
Arlington, VA 22210
Toll free: 800-984-9994
Cordero, Tony, Chairman

Space Enterprise Council [159]
1525 Wilson Blvd., Ste. 540
Arlington, VA 22209-2444
PH: (202)682-9110
Fax: (202)682-9111
Logsdon, David, Exec. Dir.

Spina Bifida Association of America [17250]
1600 Wilson Blvd., Ste. 800
Arlington, VA 22209

PH: (202)944-3285
Fax: (202)944-3295
Struwe, Sara, President

Synthetic Yarn and Fiber Association [3272]
c/o Diane Bayatafshar, Managing Director
3033 Wilson Blvd., Ste. 700
Arlington, VA 22201
Crossfield, Roger, President

Telecommunications Industry Association [3241]
1320 N Courthouse Rd., Ste. 200
Arlington, VA 22201
PH: (703)907-7700
Fax: (703)907-7727
Schramm, Susan, Director

TIPS Program [11513]
c/o Health Communications, Inc.
1400 Key Blvd., Ste. 700
Arlington, VA 22209
Toll free: 800-438-8477
Fax: (703)524-1487
Chafetz, Adam, CEO, President

Tortilla Industry Association [1376]
1600 Wilson Blvd., Ste. 650
Arlington, VA 22209
Toll free: 800-944-6099
Fax: (800)944-6177
Kabbani, Jim, CEO, Exec. Dir.

Tragedy Assistance Program for Survivors [10762]
3033 Wilson Blvd., Ste. 630
Arlington, VA 22201
PH: (202)588-8277
Toll free: 800-959-8277
Fax: (571)385-2524
Carroll, Bonnie, Founder, President

Travel Technology Association [3401]
c/o Stephen Shur, President
3033 Wilson Blvd., Ste. 700
Arlington, VA 22201
PH: (202)503-1422
(703)842-3745
Shur, Stephen, President

Trout Unlimited [4895]
1777 N Kent St., Ste. 100
Arlington, VA 22209
PH: (703)522-0200
Toll free: 800-834-2419
Fax: (703)284-9400
Coley, Hillary, CFO, Asst. VP of Admin.

Truck Safety Coalition [12846]
2020 14th St. N, Ste. 710
Arlington, VA 22201
PH: (703)294-6404
Fax: (703)294-6406
Lannen, John, Exec. Dir.

U.S.-Algeria Business Council [1996]
2001 Jefferson Davis Hwy., Ste. 208
Arlington, VA 22202
PH: (703)418-4150
Fax: (703)418-4151
Chikhoune, Dr. Ismael, CEO, President

United States Braille Chess Association [21592]
c/o Alan Schlank, Treasurer
1881 N Nash St., Unit 702
Arlington, VA 22209
PH: (516)223-8685
Pietrolungo, Al, President

United States Committee for Refugees and Immigrants [19022]
2231 Crystal Dr., Ste. 350
Arlington, VA 22202

PH: (703)310-1130
Toll free: 800-307-4712
Fax: (703)769-4241
Limon, Lavinia, CEO, President

U.S. Council of Better Business
Bureaus [671]
3033 Wilson Blvd., Ste. 600
Arlington, VA 22201
PH: (703)276-0100
Power, Mary E., CAE, President,
CEO

United States Dairy Export Council
[3983]
2101 Wilson Blvd., Ste. 400
Arlington, VA 22201-3061
PH: (703)528-3049
Fax: (703)528-3705
Suber, Tom, President

U.S.-Taiwan Business Council
[2005]
1700 N Moore St., Ste. 1703
Arlington, VA 22209
PH: (703)465-2930
Fax: (703)465-2937
Wolfowitz, Paul D., Chairman

U.S. Wheat Associates [3774]
3103 10th St. N, Ste. 300
Arlington, VA 22201
PH: (202)463-0999
Fax: (703)524-4399
Miller, Mike, Secretary, Treasurer

U.S.A. Rice Council [3775]
2101 Wilson Blvd., Ste. 610
Arlington, VA 22201
PH: (703)236-2300
Fax: (703)236-2301
Towery, Justin, Chairman

U.S.A. Rice Federation [1523]
2101 Wilson Blvd., Ste. 610
Arlington, VA 22201-3040
PH: (703)236-2300
Fax: (703)236-2301
Lucas, Frank, Chairman

US-Ireland Alliance [689]
2800 Clarendon Blvd., Ste. 502W
Arlington, VA 22201
Vargo, Trina, President, Founder

Vietnam Veterans Memorial Fund
[21173]
1235 S Clark St., Ste. 910
Arlington, VA 22202
PH: (202)393-0090
Knotts, Jim, President, CEO

VII Corps Desert Storm Veterans
Association [21155]
2425 Wilson Blvd.
Arlington, VA 22201
PH: (703)562-4163
Hotop, Arthur R., Comm. Chm.

Visiting Nurse Associations of
America [16191]
2121 Crystal Dr., Ste. 750
Arlington, VA 22202
PH: (571)527-1520
Toll free: 888-866-8773
Fax: (571)527-1521
Moorhead, Tracey, President, CEO

Women in Defense, a National
Security Organization [18090]
2111 Wilson Blvd., Ste. 400
Arlington, VA 22201-3061
PH: (703)522-1820
(703)247-2551
Fax: (703)522-1885
Courter, Maj Gen Amy S., President

Women in Federal Law Enforcement, Inc. [5522]
2200 Wilson Blvd., Ste. 102
PMB 204

Arlington, VA 22201-3324
PH: (301)805-2180
Fax: (301)560-8836
Moore, Margaret M., Chmn. of the
Bd.

Women Grocers of America [2980]
1005 N Glebe Rd., Ste. 250
Arlington, VA 22201-5758
PH: (703)516-0700
Fax: (703)516-0115
Mottese, Lorelei, President

Worldwide ERC [1104]
4401 Wilson Blvd., Ste. 510
Arlington, VA 22203
PH: (703)842-3400
Fax: (703)527-1552
Smith, Peggy, SCRP, CEO,
President

Worldwide Responsible Accredited
Production [209]
2200 Wilson Blvd., Ste. 601
Arlington, VA 22201-3357
PH: (703)243-0970
Fax: (703)243-8247
Jowell, Russell, Mgr., Comm.

Yoga Alliance [10425]
1560 Wilson Blvd., Ste. 700
Arlington, VA 22209
PH: (571)482-3355
Toll free: 888-921-9642
Hartsell, Brandon, Chmn. of the Bd.

Young Americans for Liberty [19281]
PO Box 2751
Arlington, VA 22202-0751
Frazee, Jeff, Exec. Dir.

Youth Venture [13490]
1700 N Moore St., Ste. 2000
Arlington, VA 22209
PH: (703)527-8300
Fax: (703)527-8383
Gamse, Roy, Act. Pres.

Advanced Transit Association [7346]
c/o Tony Newkirk, Treasurer
44027 Florence Terr.
Ashburn, VA 20147
Young, Stan, President

American College of Clinical
Pharmacology [16636]
21750 Red Rum Dr., Ste. 137
Ashburn, VA 20147
PH: (571)291-3493
Fax: (571)918-4167
Meibohm, PhD, FCP, Bernd,
President

American Watercraft Association
[23361]
PO Box 1993
Ashburn, VA 20146-1993
Toll free: 800-913-2921
Fax: (703)777-1566

Coalition for Responsible Waste
Incineration [3448]
44121 Harry Byrd Hwy., Ste. 225
Ashburn, VA 20147
PH: (703)431-7343

National Contract Management As-
sociation [1514]
21740 Beaumeade Cir., Ste. 125
Ashburn, VA 20147
PH: (571)382-0082
Toll free: 800-344-8096
Fax: (703)448-0939
White, Penny L., JD, President

National Recreation and Park Association [5667]
22377 Belmont Ridge Rd.
Ashburn, VA 20148-4501

PH: (703)858-0784
Toll free: 800-262-6772
Tulipane, Barbara, CEO, President

National Therapeutic Recreation
Society [17457]
22377 Belmont Ridge Rd.
Ashburn, VA 20148-4501
PH: (703)858-0784
Fax: (703)858-0794

APA Division 38: Health Psychology
[16884]
PO Box 1838
Ashland, VA 23005-2544
PH: (804)752-4987
Klonoff, Elizabeth, PhD, Rep.

National Alliance for Medicaid in
Education, Inc. [15101]
c/o Mary Hall
12055 Meriturn Pl.
Ashland, VA 23005
PH: (614)752-1493
Wright, Steven, Director

National Association of Independent
Writers and Editors [2696]
PO Box 549
Ashland, VA 23005-0549
PH: (804)767-5961
Campbell, Janice, Director

National Black Farmers Association
[4159]
68 Wind Rd.
Baskerville, VA 23915
PH: (804)691-8528
Boyd, Dr. John W., Jr., Founder,
President

Canine Freestyle Federation [22815]
14430 Overlook Ridge Ln.
Beaverdam, VA 23015-1787
PH: (804)883-1174
Tennille, Carl, Treasurer

Legacy International [8121]
1020 Legacy Dr.
Bedford, VA 24523
PH: (540)297-5982
Fax: (540)297-1860
Thompson, Shanti, Director, VP

Society of St. Andrew [12115]
3383 Sweet Hollow Rd.
Big Island, VA 24526
PH: (434)299-5956
Toll free: 800-333-4597
Fax: (434)299-5949
Jones, Debbie, Production Mgr.

Alpha Pi Mu [23736]
3005 Lancaster Dr.
Blacksburg, VA 24060
PH: (540)553-2043
Balachandran, S., Treasurer

American Association of Veterinary
Clinicians [17602]
125 N Main St., Ste. 500-403
Blacksburg, VA 24060
PH: (614)358-0417
Fax: (540)242-3385
Austin, Jonathan, Exec. Dir.

Association for Business Communication [7543]
355 Shanks Hall
181 Turner St. NW
Blacksburg, VA 24061
PH: (540)231-1939
(540)231-8460
Dubinsky, James, Exec. Dir.

International Commission on Il-
lumination - U.S. National Committee [6785]
Virginia Tech Transportation Institute
3500 Transportation Research Plz.

Blacksburg, VA 24061
PH: (540)231-1581
Fax: (540)231-1555
Leland, James, President

International Society for Educational
Planning [8441]
2903 Ashlawn Dr.
Blacksburg, VA 24060-8101
Chandler, Mary, President

Peacework Volunteer Organization
[18821]
620 N Main St., Ste. 306
Blacksburg, VA 24060
PH: (540)953-1376
Darr, Stephen, Exec. Dir.

Phycological Society of America
[6152]
PO Box 90001
Blacksburg, VA 24062-9001
PH: (540)231-6170
Gabrielson, Paul, President

Poverty Awareness Coalition for
Equality [12560]
210 Burrus Hall
Blacksburg, VA 24061
Stone, Kendall, Treasurer, Secretary

Society of Reliability Engineers
[6598]
c/o Joel A. Nachlas, PhD, Commit-
tee Chairman
Virginia Tech
250 Durham Hall
Blacksburg, VA 24061-0118
PH: (540)231-5357
Fax: (540)231-3322
Dalton, Robert K., President

HealthCare Compliance Packaging
Council [16661]
2711 Buford Rd., No. 268
Bon Air, VA 23235-2423
PH: (804)338-5778
Toll free: 888-812-4272
Berghahn, Mr. Walt, Exec. Dir.

American Spaniel Club [21824]
c/o Kevin Carter, Assistant Treasurer
6973 Davis-Bonne Rd.
Boones Mill, VA 24065
PH: (540)772-1272
Ward, Calvin, President

American Boxwood Society [22067]
PO Box 85
Boyce, VA 22620
Boyd, Mr. John, III, President

American Nigerian Dwarf Dairy Association [4274]
c/o Angel Cole, President
72 Highway 92
Boydton, VA 23917
PH: (434)738-8527
Cole, Angel, President

Fellowship of Christian Firefighters
International [5203]
249 Rochiri Dr.
Boydton, VA 23917
PH: (443)336-9859
Hall, Ken, Director

Humanity Road [13064]
230 Washington St.
Boydton, VA 23917
Thompson, Christine, President,
Chmn. of the Bd.

U.S. Complete Shooting Dog As-
sociation [21981]
3329 Redlawn Rd.
Boydton, VA 23917
PH: (434)738-9757
McKeag, Yvonne, Secretary,
Treasurer

Act for Africa International **[12796]**
9040 Falcon Glen Ct.
Bristow, VA 20136
PH: (804)994-4962
  (571)212-6167
Drame, Papa, President

American Association of Housecall
  and Mobile Veterinarians **[17597]**
c/o Around Town Mobile Veterinary
  Clinic
9030 Sainsbury Ct.
Bristow, VA 20136
PH: (703)753-7988
Price, Michele, VMD, Contact

American Association for
  Psychoanalysis in Clinical Social
  Work **[13100]**
10302 Bristow Center Dr.
Bristow, VA 20136
PH: (703)369-1268
Rosen, Penny, Comm. Chm.

American Rescue Dog Association
  [12741]
PO Box 613
Bristow, VA 20136-0613
Toll free: 888-775-8871
Massey, Jennifer, VP

American Society for Gravitational
  and Space Research **[7217]**
12209 Wheat Mill Loop
Bristow, VA 20136
PH: (703)392-0272
Ronca, April, President

America's Small Business Develop-
  ment Center **[3114]**
8990 Burke Lake Rd., 2nd Fl.
Burke, VA 22015
PH: (703)764-9850
Fax: (703)764-1234
Petrilli, Mark, Chairman

Association of Cable Communicators
  [5089]
9259 Old Keene Mill Rd., Ste. 202
Burke, VA 22015
PH: (703)372-2215
Toll free: 800-210-3396
Fax: (703)782-0153
Jones, Mr. Steven R., Exec. Dir.

Atlantic Seaboard Wine Association
  [4927]
PO Box 11332
Burke, VA 22009
PH: (703)323-6873
Fax: (703)323-1271
Brandhorst, Carl G., President

Defense Orientation Conference As-
  sociation **[19090]**
9245 Old Keene Mill Rd., Ste. 100
Burke, VA 22015
PH: (703)451-1200
Currie, Robert, Chairman

Egyptians Relief Association **[11349]**
6121 Winnepeg Dr.
Burke, VA 22015-3847
PH: (703)503-8816
Tadros, Nadia, President

International Council on Infertility
  Information Dissemination **[14759]**
5765 F Burke Center Pky.
Box 330
Burke, VA 22015
PH: (703)379-9178
Fax: (703)379-1593
Hemenway, Nancy, Exec. Dir.

Naval Intelligence Professionals
  [5614]
PO Box 11579
Burke, VA 22009-1579
Porterfield, Robert, President

Pakistan American Business Association **[663]**
9302 Old Keene Mill Rd., Ste. B
Burke, VA 22015-4278
Webster, Steve, Director

American Society of Marine Artists
  [8913]
PO Box 557
Carrollton, VA 23314
PH: (314)241-2339
Kramer, Russ, President

Pierce-Arrow Society **[21475]**
PO Box 402
Catharpin, VA 20143-0402
Wozney, John, Chairman

International Society for Fire Service
  Instructors **[5210]**
14001C St. Germain Dr., Ste. 128
Centreville, VA 20121
Toll free: 800-435-0005
Fax: (800)235-9153
Pegram, Steve, President

National Association for Search and
  Rescue **[12745]**
PO Box 232020
Centreville, VA 20120-2020
Toll free: 877-893-0702
Rice, George, Director

Specialized Carriers and Rigging
  Association **[3103]**
5870 Trinity Pky., Ste. 200
Centreville, VA 20120
PH: (703)698-0291
Fax: (703)698-0297
Dandrea, Joel, Exec. VP

America's Charities **[11855]**
14150 Newbrook Dr., Ste. 110
Chantilly, VA 20151-2274
Toll free: 800-458-9505
Fax: (703)222-3867
Young, Kimberly H., VP of Bus. Dev.

Clay Minerals Society **[6873]**
3635 Concorde Pky., Ste. 500
Chantilly, VA 20151-1110
PH: (703)652-9960
Fax: (703)652-9951
Srodon, Jan, VP

Club de l'Epagneul Breton of the
  United States **[21857]**
c/o Fatmi Anders, Secretary
25900 Poland Rd.
Chantilly, VA 20152
Hutwagner, Jackie, President

Compressed Gas Association **[1496]**
14501 George Carter Way, Ste. 103
Chantilly, VA 20151
PH: (703)788-2700
Fax: (703)961-1831
Tiller, Michael, President, CEO

DHI **[1567]**
14150 Newbrook Dr., Ste. 200
Chantilly, VA 20151
PH: (703)222-2010
Fax: (703)222-2410
Heppes, Jerry, CEO

Entertainment Industries Council Inc.
  [13138]
4206 Technology Ct., Ste. E
Chantilly, VA 20151
PH: (703)481-1414
Fax: (703)481-1418
Dyak, Brian L., Bd. Member,
  Secretary, Founder, Exec.
  Producer

Helping Children Worldwide **[11022]**
14101 Parke Long Ct., Ste. T
Chantilly, VA 20151

PH: (703)793-9521
Fax: (703)956-6866
Duston, Rob, Chairman

Interlocking Concrete Pavement
  Institute **[788]**
14801 Murdock St., Ste.230
Chantilly, VA 20151
PH: (703)657-6900
Fax: (703)657-6901
McGrath, Charles A., CAE, Exec.
  Dir.

Military Benefit Association **[19381]**
14605 Avion Pky.
Chantilly, VA 20151-1104
PH: (703)968-6200
Toll free: 800-336-0100
Fax: (703)968-6423
Reyna, Michael, President

Mineralogical Society of America
  [6875]
3635 Concorde Pky., Ste. 500
Chantilly, VA 20151-1110
PH: (703)652-9950
Fax: (703)652-9951
Speer, Dr. J. Alexander, Exec. Dir.

National Captioning Institute **[15201]**
3725 Concorde Pky., Ste. 100
Chantilly, VA 20151
PH: (703)917-7600
Fax: (703)917-9853
Chao, Gene, CEO, President, Chair-
  man

Professional Scripophily Trade As-
  sociation **[666]**
PO Box 223795
Chantilly, VA 20153
PH: (703)579-4209
Toll free: 888-786-2576
Fax: (703)995-4422
Kerstein, Bob, President

Sheet Metal and Air Conditioning
  Contractors' National Association
  [1637]
4201 Lafayette Center Dr.
Chantilly, VA 20151-1209
PH: (703)803-2980
Fax: (703)803-3732
Sandusky, Vincent R., CEO

Defense Intel Alumni Association
  [19320]
PO Box 354
Charlotte Court House, VA 23923
PH: (571)426-0098
Demulling, Judi, Secretary

National Military Intelligence As-
  sociation **[5369]**
PO Box 354
Charlotte Court House, VA 23923
Fax: (703)738-7487
Williams, James A., CEO

Advancing Native Missions **[19939]**
PO Box 5303
Charlottesville, VA 22905
PH: (540)456-7111
Fax: (540)456-7222
Zodhiates, Philip, Chairman

Air Weather Association **[21103]**
1697 Capri Way
Charlottesville, VA 22911-3534
Lavin, James Kevin, Chairman, Editor, Treasurer

Alliance for Transforming the Lives
  of Children **[10848]**
901 Preston Ave., Ste. 400
Charlottesville, VA 22903
PH: (206)666-4145
Callander, Meryn, President

American Association for Cancer
  Education **[13877]**
154 Hansen Rd., Ste. 201
Charlottesville, VA 22911-8839
PH: (434)284-4445
Fax: (434)977-1856
Alluisi, Jennifer, MA Ed, Dir. of
  Programs

American Board of Urology **[17546]**
c/o Gerald H. Jordan MD, Executive
  Secretary
600 Peter Jefferson Pky., Ste. 150
Charlottesville, VA 22911
PH: (434)979-0059
Fax: (434)979-0266
Thrasher, J. Brantley, MD, VP

American Psychosocial Oncology
  Society **[16333]**
154 Hansen Rd., Ste. 201
Charlottesville, VA 22911-8839
PH: (434)293-5350
Toll free: 866-276-7443
Fax: (434)977-1856
Schuermeyer, Isabel, President

American Renewal Foundation
  [18858]
PO Box 930
Charlottesville, VA 22904
PH: (703)758-4600

Aniridia Foundation International
  [13822]
c/o University of Virginia
  Ophthalmology
PO Box 800715
Charlottesville, VA 22908-0715
PH: (434)243-3357
Nerby, Jill, Founder, Exec. Dir.

Association of Theatre Movement
  Educators **[8697]**
977 Seminole Trl., No. 228
Charlottesville, VA 22901-2824
Saltzberg, Matt, Secretary

Bibliographical Society of the
  University of Virginia **[9121]**
PO Box 400152
Charlottesville, VA 22904-4152
PH: (434)924-7013
Fax: (434)924-1431
Ribble, Anne, Secretary, Treasurer

Breath of Hope, Inc. **[13826]**
PO Box 6627
Charlottesville, VA 22906-6627
Toll free: 888-264-2340
Doyle-Propst, Elizabeth, Contact

Byron Society of America **[9046]**
Univ. of English, Dept. of English
219 Bryan Hall
PO Box 400121
Charlottesville, VA 22904
Graham, Peter W., President

Center for a New American Dream
  [18016]
PO Box 797
Charlottesville, VA 22902
PH: (301)891-3683
Bowen, Tracy, Exec. Dir.

Center for Oceans Law and Policy
  [6938]
580 Massie Rd.
Charlottesville, VA 22903-1789
PH: (434)924-7441
Fax: (434)924-7362
Moore, Prof. John Norton, Director

CFA Institute **[2021]**
915 E High St.
Charlottesville, VA 22902
PH: (434)951-5499
Fax: (434)951-5262
Franklin, Margaret E., Bd. Member

Christian Aid Mission [20398]
1201 5th St.
Charlottesville, VA 22902
PH: (434)977-5650
Finley, Cynthia, President

Clowns Without Borders - U.S.A.
[12306]
705 Rockcreek Rd.
Charlottesville, VA 22903
PH: (707)363-5513
Cohen, Moshe, Founder

Community College Business Officers [7549]
3 Boar's Head Ln., Ste. B
Charlottesville, VA 22903-4604
PH: (434)293-2825
Fax: (434)245-8453
Dove, Tangila, PhD, President

Council of Alumni Marketing and
Membership Professionals [2276]
211 Emmet St. S
Charlottesville, VA 22903-2431
PH: (434)243-9020
Fansler, Greg, President

Council on America's Military Past
[9383]
PO Box 4209
Charlottesville, VA 22905
Gjernes, Marylou, President

Focused Ultrasound Foundation
[17537]
1230 Cedars Ct., Ste. F
Charlottesville, VA 22903
PH: (434)220-4993
Fax: (434)220-4978
Kassell, Neal F., MD, Chairman,
Founder

Focused Ultrasound Surgery
Foundation [17538]
1230 Cedars Ct., Ste. F
Charlottesville, VA 22903
PH: (434)220-4993
Fax: (434)220-4978
Kassell, Neal F., MD, Founder,
Chairman

Hagiography Society [20575]
302 Cabel Hall
Charlottesville, VA 22904
Ogden, Amy, Secretary, Treasurer

Hegel Society of America [9053]
PO Box 7147
Charlottesville, VA 22906-7147
PH: (804)220-3300
Toll free: 800-444-2419
Fax: (804)220-3301
Collins, Ardis, Treasurer

International Society for Prenatal
Diagnosis [17427]
154 Hansen Rd., Ste. 201
Charlottesville, VA 22911
PH: (434)979-4773
Fax: (434)977-1856
Otaño, Lucas, President

Kappa Sigma Fraternity [23906]
1610 Scottsville Rd.
Charlottesville, VA 22902
PH: (434)295-3193
Fax: (434)296-9557
Wilson, Mitchell B., Exec. Dir.

Modular Building Institute [2445]
944 Glenwood Station Ln., Ste. 204
Charlottesville, VA 22901
PH: (434)296-3288
Toll free: 888-811-3288
Fax: (434)296-3361
Hardiman, Tom, CAE, Exec. Dir.

Montessori Accreditation Council for
Teacher Education [7781]
420 Park St.
Charlottesville, VA 22902

PH: (434)202-7793
Toll free: 888-525-8838
Pelton, Rebecca, Exec. Dir.,
President

National Alliance for Model State
Drug Laws [5157]
420 Park St.
Charlottesville, VA 22902
PH: (703)836-6100
Fax: (662)892-8660
Kelsey, Sarah, CEO

National Association of College
Auxiliary Services [3022]
3 Boar's Head Ln., Ste B
Charlottesville, VA 22903
PH: (434)245-8425
Fax: (434)245-8453
Finn, Kelsey H., CEO

National Coalition of Girls' Schools
[7790]
Po Box 5729
Charlottesville, VA 22905-5729
PH: (434)205-4496
Murphy, Megan, Exec. Dir.

North American Society for Social
Philosophy [10109]
PO Box 7147
Charlottesville, VA 22906-7147
PH: (434)220-3300
Toll free: 800-444-2419
Fax: (434)220-3301
Scholz, Sally J., President

Philosophy Documentation Center
[10112]
701 Charlton Ave.
Charlottesville, VA 22903-5203
PH: (434)220-3300
Toll free: 800-444-2419
Fax: (434)220-3301
Leaman, George, Director

The Rutherford Institute [19030]
PO Box 7482
Charlottesville, VA 22906-7482
PH: (434)978-3888
Toll free: 800-225-1791
Fax: (434)978-1789
Whitehead, John W., Chairman

Scientific Committee on Frequency
Allocations for Radio Astronomy
and Space Science [6010]
c/o Harvey S. Liszt, Chairman
National Radio Astronomy Observatory
520 Edgemont Rd.
Charlottesville, VA 22903-2475
PH: (434)227-6356
Fax: (434)296-0278

Robert H. Smith International Center
for Jefferson Studies [8446]
PO Box 316
Charlottesville, VA 22902
PH: (434)984-9800
Toll free: 800-243-0743
O'Shaughnessy, Andrew Jackson,
Director

Society for Philosophy in the
Contemporary World [10126]
PO Box 7147
Charlottesville, VA 22906-7147
PH: (434)220-3300
Toll free: 800-444-2419
Fax: (434)220-3301
Matheis, Christian, Treasurer

Society of Quality Assurance [2824]
154 Hansen Rd., Ste. 201
Charlottesville, VA 22911
PH: (434)297-4772
Fax: (434)977-1856
Bens, Catherine M., President

Society for Social and Political
Philosophy [10130]
PO Box 7147
Charlottesville, VA 22906-7147
Toll free: 800-444-2419
Sharp, Hasana, Sec. Gen.

Sustainable Packaging Coalition
[2484]
600 E Water St., Ste. C
Charlottesville, VA 22902-5361
PH: (434)817-1424
Goodrich, Nina, Director

University Council for Educational
Administration [7442]
Ruffner Hall
Curry School of Education
University of Virginia
405 Emmet St., Rm. 141
Charlottesville, VA 22903
PH: (434)243-1041
Young, Michelle D., Exec. Dir.

American Optometric Society
[16424]
801 Volvo Pkwy., Ste. 133
Chesapeake, VA 23320
PH: (805)768-4267
Fax: (805)456-3005
Miller, Dr. Pamela J., President,
Chmn. of the Bd.

American Shetland Sheepdog Association [21821]
500 Millstone Rd.
Chesapeake, VA 23322-4367
PH: (757)436-4868
Bianchi, Liz, Corr. Sec.

Association of Physician Assistants
in Psychiatry [16827]
732 Eden Way N, No. 261, Ste. E
Chesapeake, VA 23320
PH: (678)666-0289
Toll free: 888-973-9477
Combs, Glen E., President

Association of Structural Pest
Control Regulatory Officials [4526]
663 Lacy Oak Dr.
Chesapeake, VA 23320
PH: (757)753-8162
Trossbach, Liza Fleeson, President

Foundation for American Christian
Education [7611]
4225 Portsmouth Blvd.
Chesapeake, VA 23321
Toll free: 800-352-3223
Fax: (757)488-5593
Adams, Dr. Carole G., President

German Shepherd Dog Club of
America [21882]
c/o Dania Karloff, Recording
Secretary
2136 Mt. Pleasant Rd.
Chesapeake, VA 23322-1215
PH: (757)482-3966
Battaglia, Dr. Carmen, President

Holland Lop Rabbit Specialty Club
[4598]
c/o Pandora Allen, Secretary
2633 Seven Eleven Rd.
Chesapeake, VA 23322
PH: (757)421-9607
Allen, Pandora, Secretary

International Mobjack Association
[22636]
1313 Cambridge Way
Chesapeake, VA 23320-8247
PH: (757)312-0768
Roberts, Tom, Secretary

Law Enforcement United Inc. [5483]
PO Box 2126
Chesapeake, VA 23327-2126
Chadwick, Wallace, Exec. Dir.

Miniature Pinscher Club of America
[21916]
c/o Joanne Wilds-Snell, Secretary
1800 Coral Ivy Ct.
Chesapeake, VA 23323-6370
Hofheins-Wackerfuss, Gretchen,
President

National Association of Marine
Surveyors [6806]
3105 American Legion Rd., Ste. E
Chesapeake, VA 23321-5654
PH: (757)638-9638
Toll free: 800-822-6267
Fax: (757)638-9639
Weiss, Steven P., President

National Association of Residential
Property Managers [2748]
638 Independence Pky., Ste. 100
Chesapeake, VA 23320
Toll free: 800-782-3452
Fax: (866)466-2776
Sturzl, Bart, President

National School Plant Management
Association [7440]
c/o Dr. John A. Bailey, President
1021 Great Bridge Blvd.
Chesapeake, VA 23320
PH: (757)547-0139
Fax: (757)547-2091
Mertens, Mike, President

Urban Superintendent's Association
of America [8726]
PO Box 1248
Chesapeake, VA 23327-1248
PH: (757)436-1032
Bateman, C. Fred, Exec. Dir.

National Association of State 911
Administrators [7316]
c/o Dorothy Spears-Dean, Secretary
11751 Meadowville Ln.
Chester, VA 23836-6315
PH: (804)416-6201
Fax: (804)416-6353
Branson, Daryl, Treasurer, VP

National Society of Minorities in
Hospitality [1675]
6933 Commons Plz., Ste. 537
Chesterfield, VA 23832
PH: (703)549-9899
Fax: (703)539-1049
Washington, Kadeem, Chairperson

American Pheasant and Waterfowl
Society [4783]
7153 Piney Island Rd.
Chincoteague Island, VA 23336
PH: (757)824-5828
Smith, Terry, Secretary

Project Underground [6883]
c/o Carol Zokaites, Coordinator
8 Radford St., Ste. 201
Christiansburg, VA 24073
PH: (540)381-7132
Zokaites, Carol, Coord.

Care for Children International
[10884]
Neuropsychological and Family
Therapy Associates
13310 Compton Rd.
Clifton, VA 20124-1512
PH: (703)830-6052
Federici, Dr. Ronald Steven, CEO,
President

Chesapeake and Ohio Historical
Society [10180]
312 E Ridgeway St.
Clifton Forge, VA 24422
PH: (540)862-2210
Toll free: 800-453-COHS
Fax: (540)863-9159

Power of Pain Foundation [16563]
213 Nottingham Dr.
Colonial Heights, VA 23834
PH: (804)657-7246
Taylor, Ken, Exec. Dir.

Gleaning for the World [12663]
7539 Stage Rd.
Concord, VA 24538-3590
PH: (434)993-3600
Toll free: 877-913-9212
Fax: (434)993-2300
Davidson, Rev. Ronald T., COO,
  Founder, President

Aquacultural Engineering Society
  [6541]
8969 Mountain View Dr.
Copper Hill, VA 24079
Guerdat, Dr. Todd C., President

SCI - International Voluntary Service
  [13307]
5505 Walnut Level Rd.
Crozet, VA 22932
PH: (206)350-6585
Fax: (206)350-6585
Axtell, Mr. David, Contact

Association of Social Work Boards
  [13104]
400 S Ridge Pky., Ste. B
Culpeper, VA 22701
PH: (540)829-6880
Toll free: 800-225-6880
Fax: (540)829-0562
Comer, Jenise M., President

Operation First Response [10750]
20037 Dove Hill Rd.
Culpeper, VA 22701
Toll free: 888-289-0280
Fax: (888)505-2795
Baker, Peggy, President

Republican Majority for Choice
  [19048]
RMC Finance Office
15191 Montanus Dr., PMB 206
Culpeper, VA 22701
PH: (516)316-6982
Fax: (516)338-6723

Instructional Systems Association
  [8032]
5868 Mapledale Plz., No. 120
Dale City, VA 22193
PH: (703)730-2838
Fax: (703)730-2857
Schmidt, Ms. Pamela J., Exec. Dir.

American Humor Studies Association
  [9560]
Averett University, 316 Frith Hall
Danville, VA 24541
PH: (434)791-7242
McIntire-Strasburg, Janice, PhD,
  Exec. Dir.

Heritage Preservation Association
  [17899]
975 Main St.
Danville, VA 24541-1822
PH: (434)822-8165

International Miniature Zebu As-
  sociation [3732]
17500 Hamilton Arms Ct.
Dewitt, VA 23840
PH: (407)717-0084
DeMoor, Steve, Director

Ruritan National, Inc. [12907]
5451 Lyons Rd.
Dublin, VA 24084
PH: (540)674-5431
Toll free: 877-787-8727
Fax: (540)674-2304
Chrisley, Michael, Exec. Dir.

Association of Albanian Girls and
  Women [12919]
6240 Mumbai Pl.
Dulles, VA 20189-6240
Sebes, Amy L., Director, Founder

Freedom Alliance [8790]
22570 Markey Ct., Ste. 240
Dulles, VA 20166
PH: (703)444-7940
Toll free: 800-475-6620
Fax: (703)444-9893
Kilgannon, Thomas P., President

Marine Corps Heritage Foundation
  [21014]
3800 Fettler Park Dr., Ste. 104
Dumfries, VA 22025
PH: (703)640-7965
Toll free: 800-397-7585
Fax: (703)640-9546
Aronson, Maj. (Ret.) Edgar D.,
  Director

Panamerican/Panafrican Association
  [18078]
3986 Melting Snow Pl.
Dumfries, VA 22025
PH: (202)487-4143
Fax: (703)373-2347
Pritchard, Dr. Robert Starling, II,
  Chairman, Founder

Society of Former Special Agents of
  the Federal Bureau of Investigation
  [19538]
3717 Fettler Park Dr.
Dumfries, VA 22025
PH: (703)445-0026
Fax: (703)445-0039
Scudieri, Alfred W., Comm. Chm.

Moroccan-American Society for Life
  Sciences [6896]
PO Box 324
Dunn Loring, VA 22027-0324
PH: (202)413-6025
  (860)944-7934
Benjelloun, Karim, Secretary

Civilian Conservation Corps Legacy
  [23430]
PO Box 341
Edinburg, VA 22824
PH: (540)984-8735
Sharpe, Joan, President

American Bloodhound Club [21797]
c/o Cindy Andrews, Membership
  Chairperson
129 Little Bear Trail
Elkton, VA 22827-3922
PH: (540)298-9899
  (386)788-0137
Fax: (386)788-0137
McArdle, Camille, President

The Monroe Institute [6918]
365 Roberts Mountain Rd.
Faber, VA 22938
PH: (434)361-1500
Toll free: 866-881-3440
Fax: (434)361-1237
McMoneagle, Nancy, Exec. Dir.,
  President

AFCEA International [5583]
4400 Fair Lakes Ct.
Fairfax, VA 22033-3899
PH: (703)631-6100
Toll free: 800-336-4583
Fax: (703)631-6169
Cofoni, Paul, Director

AHS International [120]
2701 Prosperity Ave., Ste. 210
Fairfax, VA 22031
PH: (703)684-6777
Toll free: 855-247-4685
Fax: (703)739-9279
Hirschberg, Mike, Exec. Dir.

Alliance of Information and Referral
  Systems [6734]
c/o Moayad Zahralddin, Membership
  Director
11240 Waples Mill Rd., Ste. 200
Fairfax, VA 22030
PH: (703)218-2477
Fax: (703)359-7562
Hipes, Charlene, COO

American Association of Healthcare
  Administrative Management
  [15569]
11240 Waples Mill Rd., Ste. 200
Fairfax, VA 22030
PH: (703)281-4043
Fax: (703)359-7562
Stottlemyer, Christine, Contact

American Association of Pastoral
  Counselors [20037]
9504A Lee Hwy.
Fairfax, VA 22031-2303
PH: (703)385-6967
Fax: (703)352-7725
Ronsheim, Douglas M., Exec. Dir.

American Council for Technology
  [5298]
3040 Williams Dr., Ste. 500
Fairfax, VA 22031
PH: (703)208-4800
Fax: (703)208-4805
Allen, Kenneth, Exec. Dir.

American Institute of Homeopathy
  [15286]
c/o Sandra M. Chase, MD, Trustee
10418 Whitehead St.
Fairfax, VA 22030
Toll free: 888-445-9988
Sebastian, Irene, Trustee

American Society of Cataract and
  Refractive Surgery [16369]
4000 Legato Rd., Ste. 700
Fairfax, VA 22033
PH: (703)591-2220
Cionni, Robert J., President

American Society for Cellular and
  Computational Toxicology [7336]
4094 Majestic Ln., Ste. 286
Fairfax, VA 22033
PH: (202)527-7335
Fax: (202)527-7435
Sullivan, Kristie, Secretary

American Society of Ophthalmic
  Administrators [15576]
4000 Legato Rd., Ste. 700
Fairfax, VA 22033
PH: (703)788-5777
Mueller, Shannon, Mgr.

American String Teachers Associa-
  tion [8361]
4155 Chain Bridge Rd.
Fairfax, VA 22030
PH: (703)279-2113
Fax: (703)279-2114
Schulz, Monika, Exec. Dir., CEO

Association for Directors of Radia-
  tion Oncology Programs [17033]
8280 Willow Oaks Corporate Dr.,
  Ste. 500
Fairfax, VA 22031
PH: (703)502-1550
Toll free: 800-962-7876
Fax: (703)502-7852
Vapiwala, Neha, MD, President

Association of Hispanic Advertising
  Agencies [88]
8280 Willow Oaks Corporate Dr.,
  Ste. 600
Fairfax, VA 22031

PH: (703)745-5531
Gavilan, Horacio, CMP, Exec. Dir.

Association of Independent
  Consumer Credit Counseling
  Agencies [941]
10332 Main St.
Fairfax, VA 22030
PH: (434)939-6006
Toll free: 866-703-8787
Fax: (434)939-6030
Bedker, Shari, Exec. Dir.

Association of Military Colleges and
  Schools of the United States
  [8342]
12332 Washington Brice Rd.
Fairfax, VA 22033-2428
PH: (703)272-8406
Rottman, Colonel (Retired) Ray,
  Exec. Dir.

Association of Nepalis in the
  Americas [19591]
10560 Main St., Ste. 209
Fairfax, VA 22030
PH: (347)355-8237
Adhikari, Roger, President

Association of Residents in Radia-
  tion Oncology [16339]
8280 Willow Oaks Corporate Dr.,
  Ste. 500
Fairfax, VA 22031
PH: (703)502-1550
Toll free: 800-962-7876
Fax: (703)502-7852
Burt, Lindsay, MD, Chairperson

Association of Teacher Educators
  [8644]
11350 Random Hills Rd., Ste. 800
PMB 6
Fairfax, VA 22030
PH: (703)659-1708
Fax: (703)595-4792
Lefever, Shirley, President

Association for Women in Mathemat-
  ics [6818]
11240 Waples Mill Rd., Ste. 200
Fairfax, VA 22030
PH: (703)934-0163
Fax: (703)359-7562
Beery, Janet, Officer

Association of Writers & Writing
  Programs [10361]
George Mason University
4400 University Dr.
MSN 1E3
Fairfax, VA 22030-4444
PH: (703)993-4301
Fax: (703)993-4302
Baumel, Judith, President

Bambi Uganda Orphans [10861]
4400 Oak Creek Ct., No. 205
Fairfax, VA 22033
McGarr, Conche, Founder

BiOptic Driving Network U.S.A.
  [16412]
5520 Ridgeton Hill Ct.
Fairfax, VA 22032

Bite Me Cancer [13903]
4094 Majestic Ln., Ste. 335
Fairfax, VA 22033
Ferraro, C. Michael, Chairman

Bowlers to Veterans Link [22701]
11350 Random Hills Rd., Ste. 800
Fairfax, VA 22030
PH: (703)934-6039
Fax: (703)591-3049
LaSpina, John, Chairman

Cause - Comfort for America's
  Uniformed Services [10739]
4114 Legato Rd., Ste. B
Fairfax, VA 22033-4002

PH: (703)591-4965
Caldwell, John S., Jr., President

Clean Water Council [4752]
c/o National Utility Contractors Association
3925 Chain Bridge Rd., Ste. 300
Fairfax, VA 22030
PH: (703)358-9300
Fax: (703)358-9307
Hillman, Bill, CEO

Democrats for Life of America
[19057]
10521 Judicial Dr., Unit 200
Fairfax, VA 22030
PH: (703)424-6663
Day, Kristen, Exec. Dir.

Electronic Funds Transfer Association [393]
4000 Legato Rd., Ste. 1100
Fairfax, VA 22033
PH: (571)318-5556
    (571)318-5555
Hanisch, Jim, Chairman

End Hunger Network [18454]
3819 Hunt Manor Dr.
Fairfax, VA 22033
PH: (703)731-6109
Bridges, Jeff, Founder

Frontiers of Freedom [18024]
4094 Majestic Blvd., No. 380
Fairfax, VA 22033-2104
PH: (703)246-0110
Fax: (703)246-0129
Landrith, George C., CEO, President

Future of Freedom Foundation
[18025]
11350 Random Hills Rd., Ste. 800
Fairfax, VA 22030
PH: (703)934-6101
Fax: (703)352-8678
Hornberger, Jacob G., President, Founder

Galapagos Conservancy [3874]
11150 Fairfax Blvd., Ste. 408
Fairfax, VA 22030
PH: (703)383-0077
Fax: (703)383-1177
Rayner, Wendy, President

Independent Educational
Consultants Association [7771]
3251 Old Lee Hwy., Ste. 510
Fairfax, VA 22030-1504
PH: (703)591-4850
Fax: (703)591-4860
Meyer, Gail, President

InfoComm International [267]
11242 Waples Mill Rd., Ste. 200
Fairfax, VA 22030
PH: (703)273-7200
Toll free: 800-659-7469
Fax: (703)991-8259
Jeffreys, Greg, President

Institute for Philosophy and Public
Policy [18984]
4400 University Dr., 3F1
Fairfax, VA 22030-4422
PH: (703)993-1290
Sagoff, Prof. Mark, PhD, Founder

International Association of Fire
Chiefs [5207]
4025 Fair Ridge Dr., Ste. 300
Fairfax, VA 22033-2868
PH: (703)273-0911
Fax: (703)273-9363
Light, Mark, Exec. Dir., CEO

International Association of Women
in Fire and Emergency Services
[5208]
4025 Fair Ridge Dr., Ste. 300
Fairfax, VA 22033

PH: (703)896-4858
Fax: (703)273-9363
Jones, Susan, Chairman

International Board of Lactation
Consultant Examiners [13855]
10301 Democracy Ln., Ste. 400
Fairfax, VA 22030
PH: (703)560-7330
Fax: (703)560-7332
Lake, Sara, Exec. Dir.

International Council on Korean
Studies [8164]
5508 Chestermill Dr.
Fairfax, VA 22030-7248
PH: (703)803-7088
Fax: (703)803-7088
Shin, Richard T., VP

International Insolvency Institute
[1812]
10332 Main St.
PMB 112
Fairfax, VA 22030-2410
PH: (703)591-6336
Fax: (703)802-0207
Peck, James M., President

International Propeller Club of the
United States [3090]
3927 Old Lee Hwy., Ste. 101A
Fairfax, VA 22030
PH: (703)691-2777
Schiappacasse, Rick, President

International Test and Evaluation
Association [7326]
4400 Fair Lakes Ct., Ste. 104
Fairfax, VA 22033-3801
PH: (703)631-6220
Fax: (703)631-6221
Surch, Randell, VP

Irrigation Association [169]
8280 Willow Oaks Corporate Dr.,
Ste. 400
Fairfax, VA 22031
PH: (703)536-7080
Fax: (703)536-7019
Hamlin, Deborah M., CAE, CEO

Laboratory Products Association
[3027]
PO Box 428
Fairfax, VA 22038
PH: (703)836-1360
Fax: (703)836-6644
Mulligan, Clark, CAE, President

Logical Language Group [9656]
2904 Beau Ln.
Fairfax, VA 22031
PH: (703)385-0273
LeChevalier, Robert, President

Marine Corps League [5572]
8626 Lee Hwy., Ste. 201
Fairfax, VA 22031
PH: (703)207-9588
Toll free: 800-625-1775
Fax: (703)207-0047
Gore, Richard D., Sr., CEO

Marine Corps League Auxiliary
[21015]
8626 Lee Hwy., Ste. 207
Fairfax, VA 22031-2135
PH: (703)207-0626
Fax: (703)207-0264
Hunter, Jackie, President

Marine Corps Reserve Association
[5573]
8626 Lee Hwy., Ste. 205
Fairfax, VA 22031-2135
PH: (703)289-1204
Green, Tom, Secretary, Dep. Dir.

National Association of Independent
Life Brokerage Agencies [1896]
11325 Random Hills Rd., Ste. 110
Fairfax, VA 22030
PH: (703)383-3081
Fax: (703)383-6942
Long, David, Secretary, Treasurer

National Association of Korean
Americans [17917]
3883 Plaza Dr.
Fairfax, VA 22030-2512
PH: (703)267-2388
Fax: (703)267-2396
Hong, Dukjin, Rev., Sec. Gen.

National Association of Reinforcing
Steel Contractors [882]
PO Box 280
Fairfax, VA 22038
PH: (703)591-1870
Fax: (703)591-1895

National Commission for the
Certification of Crane Operators
[810]
2750 Prosperity Ave., Ste. 505
Fairfax, VA 22031
PH: (703)560-2391
Fax: (703)560-2392
Bent, Graham, CEO

National Community Education Association [7648]
3929 Old Lee Hwy., No. 91-A
Fairfax, VA 22030-2401
PH: (703)359-8973
Fax: (703)359-0972
Simmons, Virginia, President

National Energy Management
Institute [6497]
8403 Arlington Blvd., Ste. 100
Fairfax, VA 22031
PH: (703)739-7100
Fax: (703)683-7615
Bernett, David, Administrator

National Institute for Metalworking
Skills [6850]
10565 Fairfax Blvd., Ste. 10
Fairfax, VA 22030
PH: (703)352-4971
Toll free: 844-839-6467
Fax: (703)352-4991
Chambers, Greg, Chairman

National Institute for Public Policy
[18992]
9302 Lee Hwy., Ste. 750
Fairfax, VA 22031-1214
PH: (703)293-9181
Fax: (703)293-9198
Payne, Dr. Keith B., CEO, President

National Pest Management Association [2504]
10460 N St.
Fairfax, VA 22030
PH: (703)352-6762
Toll free: 800-678-6722
Fax: (703)352-3031
Ives, H. Russell, President

National Postal Forum [5682]
3998 Fair Ridge Dr., Ste. 150
Fairfax, VA 22033-2907
PH: (703)218-5015
Fax: (703)218-5020
Genick, Michael J., Secretary

National Rifle Association of America
[23137]
11250 Waples Mill Rd.
Fairfax, VA 22030-7400
Toll free: 800-672-3888

National RV Dealers Association
[2918]
3930 University Dr.
Fairfax, VA 22030

PH: (703)591-7130
Ingrassia, Phil, CAE, President

National Utility Contractors Association [893]
3925 Chain Bridge Rd., Ste. 300
Fairfax, VA 22030
PH: (703)358-9300
Fax: (703)358-9307
Hillman, Bill, CEO

NetHope [12705]
10615 Judicial Dr., Ste. 402
Fairfax, VA 22030
PH: (703)388-2845
McMillan, Laura, COO

Network Branded Prepaid Card Association [1260]
10332 Main St., Ste. 312
Fairfax, VA 22030
PH: (202)548-7200
Fauss, Brad, President, CEO

North Korea Freedom Coalition
[18606]
c/o Jubilee Campaign USA
9689 Main St., Ste. C
Fairfax, VA 22031
Scholte, Dr. Suzanne, Chairman

Optical Imaging Association [6869]
PO Box 428
Fairfax, VA 22038
PH: (703)836-1360
Fax: (703)836-6644

Precious Metals Association of North
America [2367]
3930 Walnut St., Ste. 210
Fairfax, VA 22030
PH: (703)930-7790
Fax: (703)359-7562

Professional Audio Manufacturers
Alliance [1060]
11242 Waples Mill Rd., Ste. 200
Fairfax, VA 22030
PH: (703)279-9938
Wilbert, Duffy J., Exec. Dir.

Radiology Business Management
Association [15593]
9990 Fairfax Blvd.
Fairfax, VA 22030
PH: (703)621-3355
Toll free: 888-224-7262
Fax: (703)621-3356
Hamilton, Jim, President

Recreation Vehicle Rental Association [2921]
c/o RVDA
3930 University Dr.
Fairfax, VA 22030
PH: (703)591-7130
Fax: (703)359-0152

Screen Printing Technical Foundation [1548]
c/o Specialty Graphic Imaging Association
10015 Main St.
Fairfax, VA 22031
Toll free: 888-385-3588

September 11 Digital Archive
[19186]
Center for History and New Media
Dept. of History and Art History,
MSN 1E7
George Mason University
4400 University Dr.
Fairfax, VA 22030
PH: (703)993-9277
    (212)817-1970
Brennan, Ms. Sheila, Director

Sheet Metal Occupational Health
Institute Trust [12844]
8403 Arlington Blvd., Ste. 100
Fairfax, VA 22031

PH: (703)739-7130
Krocka, Randall A., Administrator

Society of American Federal Medical
  Laboratory Scientists [15521]
PO Box 2549
Fairfax, VA 22031-0549
More, Col. Lucia, President

Society of Independent Gasoline
  Marketers of America [2537]
3930 Pender Dr., Ste. 340
Fairfax, VA 22030
PH: (703)709-7000
Kelly, Kevin, CFO

Society for Industrial Microbiology
  and Biotechnology [6102]
3929 Old Lee Hwy., Ste. 92A
Fairfax, VA 22030
PH: (703)691-3357
Fax: (703)691-7991
Johnson, Jennifer, Director

Society of Interventional Radiology
  [17068]
3975 Fair Ridge Dr., Ste. 400 N
Fairfax, VA 22033
PH: (703)691-1805
Toll free: 800-488-7284
Fax: (703)691-1855
Sedory Holzer, Susan E., Exec. Dir.

Society of NeuroInterventional
  Surgery [17069]
3975 Fair Ridge Dr., Ste. 200 N
Fairfax, VA 22033
PH: (703)691-2272
Fax: (703)537-0650
Meyers, Philip M., MD, Bd. Member

Society for Prevention Research
  [17328]
11240 Waples Mill Rd., Ste. 200
Fairfax, VA 22030-6078
PH: (703)934-4850
Fax: (703)359-7562
Lewis, Jennifer, Exec. Dir.

Society for Social Work and
  Research [8575]
11240 Waples Mill Rd., Ste. 200
Fairfax, VA 22030-6078
PH: (703)352-7797
Fax: (703)359-7562
Williams, James Herbert, President

Society for Technical Communication
  [777]
9401 Lee Hwy., Ste. 300
Fairfax, VA 22031
PH: (703)522-4114
Aschwanden, Bernard, President

Specialty Graphic Imaging Associa-
  tion [1550]
10015 Main St.
Fairfax, VA 22031
Toll free: 888-385-3588
Peck, Hoddy, Chairman

Stop Alcohol Deaths [13185]
12103 Green Leaf Ct., Ste. 202
Fairfax, VA 22033
Fax: (202)670-1448
Polastre, Shevonne, President

Uttaranchal Association of North
  America [9573]
10560 Main St., Ste. L1-1
Fairfax, VA 22030
Pant, Dinesh, VP

Cartoonists Rights Network
  International [18381]
PO Box 7272
Fairfax Station, VA 22039
Russell, Dr. Robert, Exec. Dir.

Community Development Corporation of the Americas [11337]
8110 Haddington Ct.
Fairfax Station, VA 22039
Sheffel, Ashley, Contact

Great Dads [12414]
PO Box 7537
Fairfax Station, VA 22039
PH: (571)643-4526
Toll free: 888-478-3237
Hamrin, Dr. Robert, Founder, Chair-
  man

North American Thoroughbred
  Society [22956]
1390 Sterrett Rd.
Fairfield, VA 24435-2628
Adamski, Anita, Contact

Accrediting Bureau of Health Educa-
  tion Schools [15671]
7777 Leesburg Pke., Ste. 314 N
Falls Church, VA 22043
PH: (703)917-9503
Fax: (703)917-4109
Tate, Florence, Exec. Dir.

American Apparel and Footwear Association [198]
2200 Wilson Blvd.
Falls Church, VA 22040
Herman, Nate, VP

American Association for Budget and
  Program Analysis [5703]
PO Box 1157
Falls Church, VA 22041
PH: (703)941-4300
Stehle, Jon, Director

American Health Planning Associa-
  tion [14925]
7245 Arlington Blvd., Ste. 319
Falls Church, VA 22042
PH: (703)573-3101
Fax: (703)573-3101

American Industrial Hygiene As-
  sociation [16314]
3141 Fairview Park Dr., Ste. 777
Falls Church, VA 22042
PH: (703)849-8888
Fax: (703)207-3561
Keithline, Judy, Exec. Asst.

American Institute for International
  Steel [2342]
701 W Broad St., Ste. 301
Falls Church, VA 22046
PH: (703)245-8075
Fax: (703)610-0215
Chriss, Richard, Exec. Dir.

American Psychiatric Nurses As-
  sociation [16111]
3141 Fairview Park Dr., Ste. 625
Falls Church, VA 22042
PH: (571)533-1919
Toll free: 855-863-2762
Fax: (855)883-2762
Croce, Nicholas, Jr., Exec. Dir.

American Textile Machinery Associa-
  tion [1708]
201 Park Washington Ct.
Falls Church, VA 22046
PH: (703)538-1789
Moore, Allen, Treasurer

American Thyroid Association
  [17480]
6066 Leesburg Pke., Ste. 550
Falls Church, VA 22041
PH: (703)998-8890
Fax: (703)998-8893
Smith, Barbara R., CAE, Exec. Dir.

American Trauma Society [17526]
201 Park Washington Ct.
Falls Church, VA 22046

PH: (703)538-3544
Toll free: 800-556-7890
Fax: (703)241-5603
Weston, Ian, Exec. Dir.

Association of Executive and
  Administrative Professionals [65]
900 S Washington St., Ste. G-13
Falls Church, VA 22046
PH: (703)237-8616
Fax: (703)533-1153
Bowles, Cheryl, Contact

Association of Former Intelligence
  Officers [5357]
7700 Leesburg Pke., Ste. 324
Falls Church, VA 22043
PH: (703)790-0320
Fax: (703)991-1278
Bancroft, Elizabeth A., Exec. Dir.

Association for Healthcare
  Philanthropy [15314]
313 Park Ave., Ste. 400
Falls Church, VA 22046
PH: (703)532-6243
Fax: (703)532-7170
Pritchard-Kerr, Mrs. Jory, Exec. Dir.

Association of Vacuum Equipment
  Manufacturers [1716]
201 Park Washington Ct.
Falls Church, VA 22046
PH: (703)538-3543
    (703)538-3542
Fax: (703)241-5603
Shiley, Dawn M., Exec. Dir.

Association of the Wall and Ceiling
  Industries International [502]
513 W Broad St., Ste. 210
Falls Church, VA 22046
PH: (703)538-1600
Fax: (703)534-8307
Etkin, Steven A., Exec. VP, CEO

Baptist World Alliance [19726]
405 N Washington St.
Falls Church, VA 22046
PH: (703)790-8980
Fax: (703)893-5160
Msiza, Paul, President

Belgian Sheepdog Club of America
  [21838]
c/o Julie Fiechter, Corresponding
  Secretary
7805 Sherve Rd.
Falls Church, VA 22043-3313
Trethewey, Claire, Corr. Sec.

CCAL - Advancing Person-Centered
  Living [10501]
2342 Oak St.
Falls Church, VA 22046
PH: (732)212-9036
Pinkowitz, Jackie, MPH, Chairperson

Center for Equal Opportunity
  [12124]
7700 Leesburg Pike, Ste. 231
Falls Church, VA 22043
PH: (703)442-0066
Fax: (703)442-0449
Chavez, Linda, Chairman

Center For Health, Environment and
  Justice [4738]
105 Rowell Ct., 1st Fl.
Falls Church, VA 22046
PH: (703)237-2249
Gibbs, Lois Marie, Founder

Circle of Friends for American
  Veterans [21116]
210 E Broad St., Ste. 202
Falls Church, VA 22046
PH: (703)237-8980
Fax: (703)237-8976
Hampton, Brian, Founder

Community Association Managers
  International Certification Board
  [2162]
6402 Arlington Blvd., Ste. 510
Falls Church, VA 22042
PH: (703)970-9300
Toll free: 866-779-2622
Skiba, Tom, CEO

Community Associations Institute
  [17972]
6402 Arlington Blvd., Ste. 500
Falls Church, VA 22042
PH: (703)970-9220
Toll free: 888-224-4321
Fax: (703)970-9558
Skiba, Thomas M., CEO

Defense Forum Foundation [18083]
6312 Seven Corners Ctr., No. 167
Falls Church, VA 22044
PH: (703)534-4313
Scholte, Dr. Suzanne, President

EIFS Industry Members Association
  [521]
513 W Broad St., Ste. 210
Falls Church, VA 22046-3257
Toll free: 800-294-3462
Fax: (703)538-1736
Buchanan, Buck

Food for the Hungry International
  Federation [12092]
2937 Strathmeade St.
Falls Church, VA 22042
PH: (703)966-1901
Tuk Su, Koo, Rev., CEO, Gen. Sec.

Foodservice and Packaging Institute
  [2477]
7700 Leesburg Pke., Ste. 421
Falls Church, VA 22043
PH: (703)592-9889
Fax: (703)592-9864
Dyer, Lynn, President

Foundation of the Wall and Ceiling
  Industry [529]
513 W Broad St., Ste. 210
Falls Church, VA 22046
PH: (703)538-1600
Fax: (703)538-1728
Kimmel-Schary, Carol, President

Friends of the Children of Angola
  [10984]
6210 Homespun Ln.
Falls Church, VA 22044-1012
PH: (703)237-7468
Fax: (703)237-7467
Abrantes, Maria Luisa, Chairperson

GAMA International [1857]
2901 Telestar Ct., Ste. 140
Falls Church, VA 22042
Toll free: 800-345-2687
Fax: (571)499-4311
Godsman, Bonnie, CEO

International Association of
  Emergency Managers [1240]
201 Park Washington Ct.
Falls Church, VA 22046-4527
PH: (703)538-1795
Fax: (703)241-5603
Armstrong, Elizabeth B., CAE, CEO

International Association Emergency
  of Managers [5076]
201 Park Washington Ct.
Falls Church, VA 22046-4527
PH: (703)538-1795
Fax: (703)241-5603
Armstrong, Elizabeth B., CEO

International Chiropractors Association [14274]
6400 Arlington Blvd., Ste. 800
Falls Church, VA 22042

PH: (703)528-5000
Toll free: 800-423-4690
Fax: (703)528-5023
Walsemann, Gary, DC, Chmn. of the Bd.

International Hyperbaric Medical Association [15342]
6155 Beachway Dr.
Falls Church, VA 22041-1431
PH: (703)339-0900
Duncan, William A., President

Iran Rooyan [19255]
6402 Arlington Blvd., Ste. 300
Falls Church, VA 22042
PH: (571)282-6194
Milani, Leila, JD, Founder

Mustard Seed Foundation [20443]
7115 Leesburg Pke., Ste. 304
Falls Church, VA 22043
PH: (703)524-5620
Bakke, Dennis, Co-Ch., Treasurer

National Association of Dental Assistants [14456]
900 S Washington St., No. G13
Falls Church, VA 22046-4020
PH: (703)237-8616
Fax: (703)533-1153

National Association of Government Communicators [5092]
201 Park Washington Ct.
Falls Church, VA 22046-4527
PH: (703)538-1787
Fax: (703)241-5603
Armstrong, Elizabeth B., CAE, Exec. Dir., Secretary

National Association of Insurance and Financial Advisors [1897]
2901 Telestar Ct.
Falls Church, VA 22042-1205
Toll free: 877-866-2432
McNeely, Juli, CFP, CLU, LUTCF, President

National Association of State EMS Officials [14685]
201 Park Washington Ct.
Falls Church, VA 22046-4527
PH: (703)538-1799
Fax: (703)241-5603
Armstrong, Elizabeth B., Exec. VP

National Corvette Owners Association [21450]
900 S Washington St., Ste. G-13
Falls Church, VA 22046-4009
PH: (703)533-7222
Fax: (703)533-1153

National League of Families of American Prisoners and Missing in Southeast Asia [18697]
5673 Columbia Pke., Ste. 100
Falls Church, VA 22041
PH: (703)465-7432
Griffiths, Ann Mills, Chmn. of the Bd.

National Legal and Policy Center [18319]
107 Park Washington Ct.
Falls Church, VA 22046
PH: (703)237-1970
Fax: (703)237-2090
Boehm, Ken, Chairman

National Organization of Portuguese Americans [19618]
PO Box 2652
Falls Church, VA 22042
PH: (703)389-3512
Perry, George, PhD, Chairman

National Standard Plumbing Code Committee [5069]
180 S Washington St.
Falls Church, VA 22046

PH: (703)237-8100
Toll free: 800-533-7694
Fax: (703)237-7442
Wagner, J. Richard, Chairman

Naval Enlisted Reserve Association [5613]
6703 Farragut Ave.
Falls Church, VA 22042-2189
Toll free: 800-776-9020
Purtill, Yvette, Ed.-in-Chief

North American Tiddlywinks Association [22056]
5505 Seminary Rd., Ste. 1206 N
PO Box 1701
Falls Church, VA 22041
PH: (703)671-7098

Plumbing-Heating-Cooling Contractors Association [2639]
180 S Washington St., Ste. 100
Falls Church, VA 22046
PH: (703)237-8100
Toll free: 800-533-7694
Fax: (703)237-7442
Kennedy, Gerard J., Jr., Exec. VP

Process Equipment Manufacturers Association [1763]
201 Park Washington Ct.
Falls Church, VA 22046
PH: (703)538-1796
Schieber, Doug, President

Society for Personality Assessment [16938]
6109H Arlington Blvd.
Falls Church, VA 22044
PH: (703)534-4772

Society of Research Administrators [7097]
500 N Washington St., Ste. 300
Falls Church, VA 22046
PH: (703)741-0140
Fax: (703)741-0142
Kulakowski, Elliott, CEO

Spastic Paraplegia Foundation [15992]
7700 Leesburg Pike, Ste. 123
Falls Church, VA 22043
Toll free: 877-773-4483
Davis, Frank, President

Tax Analysts [19175]
400 S Maple Ave., Ste. 400
Falls Church, VA 22046
PH: (703)533-4400
Toll free: 800-955-2444
Fax: (703)533-4444
Lobel, Martin, Chmn. of the Bd.

Tire Retread & Repair Information Bureau [3281]
1013 Birch St.
Falls Church, VA 22046
PH: (703)533-7677
Fax: (703)533-7678
Hayes, Brian, President

U.S. Copts Association [12061]
5116 Arlington Blvd., Ste. 155
5116 Arlington Blvd., Ste. 155
Falls Church, VA 22042
Meunier, Michael, President

Voluntary Protection Programs Participants' Association [16327]
7600E Leesburg Pke., Ste. 100
Falls Church, VA 22043-2004
PH: (703)761-1146
Fax: (703)761-1148
Layne, R. Davis, Advisor

Worldwide Assurance for Employees of Public Agencies [5264]
433 Park Ave.
Falls Church, VA 22046

PH: (703)790-8011
Toll free: 800-368-3484

Josephine Porter Institute for Applied Bio-Dynamics [3554]
201 E Main St., Ste. 14
Floyd, VA 24091
PH: (540)745-7030
Fax: (540)745-7033
Frazier, Pat, President

American Association of Christian Counselors [20036]
PO Box 739
Forest, VA 24551
Toll free: 800-526-8673
Clinton, Timothy E., EdD, President

Christian Action Network [19951]
PO Box 606
Forest, VA 24551
Toll free: 888-499-4226
Mawyer, Martin J., Founder

Hindustan Bible Institute [20081]
PO Box 584
Forest, VA 24551
PH: (434)525-5847
Toll free: 877-424-4634
Gupta, Dr. Paul R., Director, President

Thomas Jefferson's Poplar Forest [9406]
PO Box 419
Forest, VA 24551-0419
PH: (434)525-1806
Fax: (434)525-7252
Nichols, Mr. Jeffrey L., President, CEO

American Armed Forces Mutual Aid Association [19379]
102 Sheridan Ave.
Fort Myer, VA 22211-1110
PH: (703)707-4600
Toll free: 800-522-5221
Fax: (888)210-4882
Lincoln, Maj. (Ret.) Walt, CFP, President, Treasurer

American Canoe Association [23360]
503 Sophia St., Ste. 100
Fredericksburg, VA 22401
PH: (540)907-4460
Toll free: 888-229-3792
Blackwood, Wade, Exec. Dir.

American Traffic Safety Services Association [2989]
15 Riverside Pkwy., Ste. 100
Fredericksburg, VA 22406-1077
PH: (540)368-1701
Toll free: 800-272-8772
Fax: (540)368-1717
Seeley, Scott, Chairman

Catholic Association of Diocesan Ecumenical and Interreligious Officers [20056]
1009 Stafford Ave.
Fredericksburg, VA 22401
PH: (540)373-6491
Fax: (540)371-0251
Rooney, Rev. Don, President

Christian Media Association [20363]
6310 Wendover Ct.
Fredericksburg, VA 22407
Shields, Tim, President

E3 Kids International [10957]
PO Box 8111
Fredericksburg, VA 22404
PH: (540)538-3437
Turner, Carol A., Exec. Dir.

Empowering the Poor [12152]
PO Box 42031
Fredericksburg, VA 22404

PH: (540)735-6806
Coulibaly, Darius, MA, CEO, Founder, President

First Peoples Worldwide [9575]
877 Leeland Rd.
Fredericksburg, VA 22405
PH: (540)899-6545
Fax: (540)899-6501
Adamson, Rebecca L., Founder, President

Health and Life International [15013]
PO Box 7822
Fredericksburg, VA 22404
PH: (540)295-2374
Uchefuna, Rev. Gloria Obioma, Exec. Dir.

International Association of Bomb Technicians and Investigators [6627]
1120 International Pky., Ste. 105
Fredericksburg, VA 22406
PH: (540)752-4533
Fax: (540)752-2796

Miniature Bull Terrier Club of America [21915]
c/o Kathleen Coffman
11200 Newman Ct.
Fredericksburg, VA 22407
PH: (540)219-3751
Lethin, Linda, President

National Association for Gun Rights [17916]
PO Box 7002
Fredericksburg, VA 22404
Toll free: 877-405-4570
Fax: (202)351-0528
Brown, Dudley, Exec. VP

National Petroleum Management Association [2532]
10908 Courthouse Rd., Ste. 102-301
Fredericksburg, VA 22408-2658
PH: (540)507-4371
Fax: (540)507-4372
Lavin, Jack, Director

National Wildlife Control Operators Association [4847]
PO Box 655
Fredericksburg, VA 22404
PH: (540)374-5600
Toll free: 855-GON-WCOA
Reger, Jason, President

Students Helping Honduras [11161]
1213 Dandridge St.
Fredericksburg, VA 22401
PH: (703)445-5497
Fujiyama, Shin, Exec. Dir.

United States Parachute Association [23057]
5401 Southpoint Centre Blvd.
Fredericksburg, VA 22407
PH: (540)604-9740
Fax: (540)604-9741
Butcher, Sherry, President

U.S.A. Canoe/Kayak [23366]
503 Sophia St., Ste. 100
Fredericksburg, VA 22401
PH: (540)907-4460
Blackwood, Wade, CEO

Brotherhood of Railroad Signalmen [23515]
917 Shenandoah Shores Rd.
Front Royal, VA 22630
PH: (540)622-6522
Fax: (540)622-6532
Boles, Jerry C., Secretary, Treasurer

Christian Freedom International
[20570]
986 John Marshall Hwy.
Front Royal, VA 22630-0011
Toll free: 800-323-2273
Jacobson, James B., President,
Founder

Human Life International [12773]
4 Family Life Ln.
Front Royal, VA 22630
Toll free: 800-549-5433
Fax: (540)622-6247
Boquet, Fr. Shenan J., President

Life Decisions International [12778]
PO Box 439
Front Royal, VA 22630-0009
PH: (540)631-0380
Scott, Douglas R., Founder,
President

Red River Valley Fighter Pilots As-
sociation [21138]
PO Box 1553
Front Royal, VA 22630-0033
PH: (540)636-9798
Fax: (540)636-9776
Preston, Jim, Gen. Sec.

Automotive Parts Remanufacturers
Association [340]
7250 Heritage Village Plz., Ste. 201
Gainesville, VA 20155
PH: (703)968-2772
Fax: (703)753-2445
Dunn, Tom, Secretary

Commission on Accreditation for
Law Enforcement Agencies [5460]
13575 Heathcote Blvd., Ste. 320
Gainesville, VA 20155
PH: (703)352-4225
Fax: (703)890-3126
Webre, Craig, VP

NORA, An Association of
Responsible Recyclers [4633]
7250 Heritage Village Plz., Ste. 201
Gainesville, VA 20155
PH: (703)753-4277
Fax: (703)753-2445
Parker, Scott D., Exec. Dir.

Transplant Recipients International
Organization [17520]
13705 Currant Loop
Gainesville, VA 20155-3031
PH: (202)293-0980
Toll free: 800-TRIO-386
Gleason, Jim, President

Truck Trailer Manufacturers Associa-
tion [334]
7001 Heritage Village Plz., Ste. 220
Gainesville, VA 20155
PH: (703)549-3010
Sims, Jeff, President

Clinical Social Work Association
[13107]
PO Box 10
Garrisonville, VA 22463
PH: (202)203-9350
Ward, Susanna, President

National Association of Shell Market-
ers [2530]
PO Box 658
Garrisonville, VA 22463-0658
PH: (703)582-8478
Fax: (540)356-0029
Richards, Jennifer, President

National Windshield Repair Associa-
tion [352]
PO Box 569
Garrisonville, VA 22463

PH: (540)720-7484
Fax: (540)720-5687
Reddell, Jeff, President

American Association of Integrated
Healthcare Delivery Systems
[15570]
4435 Waterfront Dr., Ste. 101
Glen Allen, VA 23060
PH: (804)747-5823
Fax: (804)747-5316

American Association of Managed
Care Nurses [16091]
4435 Waterfront Dr., Ste. 101
Glen Allen, VA 23060
PH: (804)747-9698
Fax: (804)747-5316
Smith, Jacquelyn, RN, President

American Association of Working
People [11752]
4435 Waterfront Dr., Ste. 101
Glen Allen, VA 23058
PH: (804)527-1905
Fax: (804)747-5316
Williams, Bill, MD, President,
Founder

American Board of Managed Care
Nursing [16099]
4435 Waterfront Dr., Ste. 101
Glen Allen, VA 23060
PH: (804)527-1905
Fax: (804)747-5316
Snyder, April, Contact

Environic Foundation International
[7877]
12035 Stonewick Pl.
Glen Allen, VA 23059-7152
PH: (804)360-9130
Sherman, Terry, Treasurer

International Society for Intelligence
Research [6763]
12340 Morning Creek Rd.
Glen Allen, VA 23059-7100
PH: (804)727-0209
Keith, Timothy, Secretary, Treasurer

National Association of Managed
Care Physicians [16756]
4435 Waterfront Dr., Ste. 101
Glen Allen, VA 23060
PH: (804)527-1905
Fax: (804)747-5316
Williams, Jeremy, Contact

Enough Is Enough [18568]
746 Walker Rd., Ste. 116
Great Falls, VA 22066
Toll free: 888-744-0004
Hughes, Donna Rice, CEO,
President

Organization of Chinese American
Women [18232]
PO Box 815
Great Falls, VA 22066
PH: (301)907-3898
Fax: (301)907-3899
Chang, Christina K., President

Serve a Village [11431]
11732 Thomas Ave.
Great Falls, VA 22066
PH: (571)213-1978
Cozzens, Alisa, Exec. Dir.

Society for the Preservation of Old
Mills [9437]
PO Box 422
Great Falls, VA 22066
PH: (860)423-2033
Yeske, Charles, President

International Waterlily and Water
Gardening Society [22108]
PO Box 546
Greenville, VA 24440

PH: (540)337-4507
Fax: (540)337-0738

Methacrylate Producers Association,
Inc. [722]
17260 Vannes Ct.
Hamilton, VA 20158
Hunt, Elizabeth K., Exec. Dir.

Society for the Development of
Austrian Economics [6401]
c/o Tony Carilli, Treasurer
Hampden-Sydney College
Hampden Sydney, VA 23943
Stringham, Edward, President

Automobile License Plate Collectors
Association [21335]
118 Quaker Rd.
Hampton, VA 23669-2024
McCabe, Cyndi, President

Central Intercollegiate Athletic As-
sociation [23220]
22 Enterprise Pky., Ste. 210
Hampton, VA 23666-6416
PH: (757)865-0071
Fax: (757)865-8436
McLean, Ed, President

The Judge GTO International
[21411]
c/o Robert J. McKenzie
114 Prince George Dr.
Hampton, VA 23669-3604
PH: (757)838-2059
McKenzie, Robert, Contact

National Association of Veterans Affairs Optometrists [16429]
c/o Dr. Makesha Sink, Treasurer
111 Harbor Dr.
Hampton, VA 23661
Wong, Nancy, OD, President

Patient Advocate Foundation
[15054]
421 Butler Farm Rd.
Hampton, VA 23666
Toll free: 800-532-5274
Fax: (757)873-8999
Davenport-Ennis, Nancy, CEO,
President

International Wildfowl Carvers As-
sociation [21766]
PO Box 115
Hanover, VA 23069-0115
PH: (804)537-5033
Sutton, Bob L., Chmn. of the Bd.

Institute of Certified Professional
Managers [2170]
c/o James Madison University
800 S Main St.
Harrisonburg, VA 22807
PH: (540)568-3247
Powell, Lynne, Exec. Dir.

Mid-West Tool Collectors Association
[22170]
c/o Vaughn Simmons, Treasurer
3315 Clement Dr.
Harrisonburg, VA 22801
Simmons, Vaughn, Treasurer

Society of Multivariate Experimental
Psychology [7074]
821 S Main Str.,
James Madison University
821 S Main Street
Harrisonburg, VA 22801
Nicewander, Alan, President

Society for Police and Criminal
Psychology [16939]
c/o JoAnne Brewster, PhD.,
Membership Chair

Department of Graduate Psychology,
MSC 7704, Miller 1151
James Madison University
Harrisonburg, VA 22807
PH: (540)568-6107
Aumiller, Gary S., PhD, Exec. Dir.

Universal Design Partners [990]
PO Box 570
Harrisonburg, VA 22803
PH: (540)908-3473
Pruett, Sarah, MOT, Contact

Nail Patella Syndrome Worldwide
[14844]
14980 Stream Valley Ct.
Haymarket, VA 20169
Mansour, Joanne, Director

World Partners for Development
[13098]
14658 Gap Way, Ste. 165
Haymarket, VA 20168
PH: (571)435-2657
Darko, Philip, Dir. of Programs

Good News Jail and Prison Ministry
[11528]
PO Box 9760
Henrico, VA 23228-0760
PH: (804)553-4090
Toll free: 800-220-2202
Fax: (804)553-4144
Patterson, Don, Chairman

Hymn Society in the United States
and Canada [20492]
8040 Villa Park Dr.
Henrico, VA 23228
Toll free: 800-843-4966
Carlton Loftis, Deborah, Exec. Dir.

International Trombone Association
[9936]
PO Box 3241
Henrico, VA 23228
Toll free: 888-236-6241
Fax: (206)600-5845
Nilsson, Magnus, Exec. Dir.

American Association of Medical Do-
simetrists [15660]
2201 Cooperative Way, Ste. 600
Herndon, VA 20171
PH: (703)677-8071
Fax: (703)677-8071
Mckenzie, Craig, Treasurer

American Society of Ocularists
[15662]
PO Box 5275
Herndon, VA 20172
PH: (661)633-1746
Toll free: 888-973-4066
Fax: (661)458-1660
Tannehill, Doss K., President

American Tai Chi and Qigong Association [17422]
2465 J-17 Centreville Rd., No. 150
Herndon, VA 20171
Jahnke, Roger, Officer

Association for Facilities Engineering
[6545]
8200 Greensboro Dr., Ste. 400
Herndon, VA 20170
PH: (571)203-7171
Fax: (571)766-2142
Saya, Wayne P., Sr., Exec. Dir.

Association of Major City Building
Officials [5066]
505 Huntmar Park Dr., Ste. 210
Herndon, VA 20170-5139
PH: (703)481-2038
Toll free: 800-DOC-CODE
Fax: (703)481-3596
Cooper, Claude, Chmn. of the Bd.

Association for Radiologic and Imaging Nursing [17054]
2201 Cooperative Way, Ste. 600
Herndon, VA 20171
PH: (703)884-2229
Toll free: 866-486-2762
Wempe, Evelyn P., President

Association of Vascular and Interventional Radiographers [17572]
2201 Cooperative Way, Ste. 600
Herndon, VA 20171-3005
PH: (571)252-7174
Ramaswamy, Izzy, Comm. Chm.

Checker Car Club of America [21350]
Herndon, VA
Garrison, James, President

Clan MacRae Society of North America [20828]
c/o Stuart Macrae
12623 Terrymill Dr.
Herndon, VA 20170-2874
MacRae-Hall, Capt. John M., VP

Enterprise Wireless Alliance [3226]
2121 Cooperative Way, Ste. 225
Herndon, VA 20171
Toll free: 800-482-8282
Fax: (703)524-1074
Leonard, Catherine, Chmn. of the Bd.

Humane Farm Animal Care [10641]
PO Box 727
Herndon, VA 20172
PH: (703)435-3883
Douglass, Adele, CEO

Industrial Designers Society of America [6721]
555 Grove St., Ste. 200
Herndon, VA 20170
PH: (703)707-6000
Fax: (703)787-8501
Barratt, John, Chairman

International Association of Muslim Scientists and Engineers [6560]
500 Grove St.
Herndon, VA 20170
Alam, Mohammad, PhD, President

International Electronics Manufacturing Initiative [6796]
2214 Rock Hill Rd., Ste. 110
Herndon, VA 20170-4214
PH: (703)834-0330
Fax: (703)834-2735
Bader, Bill, Mem.

International Institute of Islamic Thought [9605]
500 Grove St., Ste. 200
Herndon, VA 20170
PH: (703)471-1133
    (703)230-2850
Fax: (703)471-3922
Hadsell, Heidi, President

The International Lepidoptera Survey [6613]
PO Box 1124
Herndon, VA 20172
Pavulaan, Harry, Bd. Member

International Society for Environmental Epidemiology [14733]
c/o Infinity Conference Group, Inc.
1035 Sterling Rd., Ste. 202
Herndon, VA 20170
PH: (703)925-0178
Toll free: 844-369-4121
Fax: (703)925-9453
Kogevinas, Manolis, President

International Society of Exposure Science [6620]
c/o Infinity Conference Group Inc.
1035 Sterling Rd., Ste. 202
Herndon, VA 20170-3838
PH: (703)925-9620
Toll free: 800-869-1551
Fax: (703)925-9453
Riederer, Anne, Treasurer

Interstate Mining Compact Commission [5634]
445 Carlisle Dr.
Herndon, VA 20170
PH: (703)709-8654
Fax: (703)709-8655
Conrad, Gregory E., Exec. Dir.

Land Mobile Communications Council [3231]
c/o Mark Crosby, Secretary-Treasurer
2121 Cooperative Way, Ste. 225
Herndon, VA 20171
PH: (703)528-5115
Crosby, Mark E., Secretary, Treasurer

NACHA: The Electronic Payments Association [406]
2550 Wasser Ter., Ste. 400
Herndon, VA 20171
PH: (703)561-1100
Fax: (703)787-0996
Estep, Janet O., CEO, President

National Association of Industrial and Office Properties [2871]
2201 Cooperative Way, Ste. 300
Herndon, VA 20171-3034
PH: (703)904-7100
Fax: (703)904-7942
Hunt, William E.

National Association of Landscape Professionals [2070]
950 Herndon Pky., Ste. 450
Herndon, VA 20170-5528
PH: (703)736-9666
Toll free: 800-395-2522
Fax: (703)736-9668
Keener, Jackie, Events Coord.

National Concrete Masonry Association [791]
13750 Sunrise Valley Dr.
Herndon, VA 20171
PH: (703)713-1900
Fax: (703)713-1910
Thomas, Robert D., President

National Organization of Life and Health Insurance Guaranty Associations [1593]
13873 Park Center Rd., Ste. 329
Herndon, VA 20171-3247
PH: (703)481-5206
Fax: (703)481-5209
Gallanis, Peter G., President

NIGP: The Institute for Public Procurement [5737]
2411 Dulles Corner Pk., Ste. 350
Herndon, VA 20171
PH: (703)736-8900
Toll free: 800-367-6447
Fax: (703)736-9644
Grimm, Rick, CEO, Secretary

North American Association of Islamic and Muslim Studies [7170]
PO Box 5502
Herndon, VA 20172
Mandaville, Jon, President

Petroleum Technology Transfer Council [2535]
c/o Kathy Chapman, Operations Director

PO Box 710942
Herndon, VA 20171
PH: (703)928-5020
Fax: (571)485-8255
Carr, Mary, Exec. Dir.

Promised Land International [19397]
13509 Martha Jefferson Pl.
Herndon, VA 20171
PH: (703)723-0089
Toll free: 877-754-7137
Fax: (703)723-0089
Graves, Deborah C., Founder, President, Chairman, Sec. (Actg.)

SCORE [3125]
1175 Herndon Pky., Ste. 900
Herndon, VA 20170
Toll free: 800-634-0245
Yancey, Kenneth W., Jr., CEO

United States Army Warrant Officers Association [5625]
462 Herndon Pky., Ste. 207
Herndon, VA 20170-5235
PH: (703)742-7727
Toll free: 800-587-2962
Fax: (703)742-7728
Hill, Kenneth B. N., Secretary

Vesalius Trust [7949]
491 Carlisle Dr., Ste. A
Herndon, VA 20170
PH: (703)437-9555
Fax: (703)437-0727
Schott, Tina M., Exec. Dir.

International Society of Indoor Air Quality and Climate [4074]
c/o Infinity Conference Group, Inc.
1035 Sterling Rd., Ste. 202
Herndorn, VA 20170-3838
PH: (703)925-9455
Fax: (703)925-9453
Loomans, Marcel, President

National Association of Christian Child and Family Agencies [19996]
c/o Joy Ranch
PO Box 727
Hillsville, VA 24343
PH: (276)236-5578
Toll free: 888-862-2232

Antique Poison Bottle Collectors Association [21623]
312 Summer Ln.
Huddleston, VA 24104
Jones, Jerry, President

International Hydrofoil Society [22632]
PO Box 157
Hume, VA 22639
Bebar, Mark R., President

The Richard III Foundation, Inc. [10346]
PO Box 524
Irvington, VA 22480-0524

Horseplayers Association of North America [22153]
93 Campbell Rd.
Keswick, VA 22947
Platt, Jeff, President

Alberg 37 International Owners Association [22592]
PO Box 32
Kinsale, VA 22488
Assenmacher, Tom, Contact

Law Enforcement Alliance of America [5478]
12427 Hedges Run Dr., Ste. 113
Lake Ridge, VA 22192-1715
PH: (202)706-9218
Fotis, James J., Director, Exec. Dir.

Care Net [18033]
44180 Riverside Pky., Ste. 200
Lansdowne, VA 20176
PH: (703)554-8734
Toll free: 800-518-7909
Fax: (703)554-8735
Warren, Mr. Roland, President, CEO

Prison Fellowship Ministries [11544]
44180 Riverside Pky.
Lansdowne, VA 20176
Toll free: 877-478-0100
Liske, Jim, President, CEO

American Roentgen Ray Society [17043]
44211 Slatestone Ct.
Leesburg, VA 20176-5109
PH: (703)729-3353
Toll free: 866-940-2777
Fax: (703)729-4839
Castillo, Mauricio, MD, President

American Wood Council [3510]
222 Catoctin Cir. SE, Ste. 201
Leesburg, VA 20175
PH: (202)463-2766
Toll free: 800-890-7732
Glowinski, Robert W., President, CEO

Automotive Training Managers Council [287]
101 Blue Seal Dr. SE
Leesburg, VA 20175
PH: (703)669-6670
Zilke, Tim, Secretary

Coalition to Salute America's Heroes [21117]
552 Ft. Evans Rd., Ste. 300
Leesburg, VA 20176-3378
PH: (703)291-4605
Toll free: 888-447-2588
Walker, David W., President, CEO

Composite Panel Association [1434]
19465 Deerfield Ave., Ste. 306
Leesburg, VA 20176
PH: (703)724-1128
Fax: (703)724-1588
Morrill, Jackson, President

The Equine Rescue League, Inc. [10618]
PO Box 4366
Leesburg, VA 20177
PH: (540)822-4577
Rogers, Patricia, Founder

Food and Drug Administration Alumni Association [18261]
c/o Karen Carson, Membership Chair
540 N St. SW, No. S104
Leesburg, VA 20176
Levitt, Joseph, Director

Hyperemesis Education and Research Foundation [16285]
932 Edwards Ferry Rd., No. 23
Leesburg, VA 20176-3324
PH: (703)399-1272
King, Ann Marie, Founder

International Association of Computer Investigative Specialists [7656]
PO Box 2411
Leesburg, VA 20177
PH: (304)915-0555
Toll free: 888-884-2247
Elrick, Doug, Chmn. of the Bd.

International Council of Air Shows [21232]
748 Miller Dr. SE, Ste. G-3
Leesburg, VA 20175-8919

PH: (703)779-8510
Fax: (703)779-8511
Cudahy, John, President

Issue Management Council [2179]
207 Loudoun St. SE
Leesburg, VA 20175-3115
PH: (703)777-8450
Crane, Teresa Yancey, President,
Founder

**National Automotive Technicians
Education Foundation [7524]**
101 Blue Seal Dr. SE, Ste. 101
Leesburg, VA 20175
PH: (703)669-6650
Fax: (703)669-6125

**National Institute for Automotive
Service Excellence [351]**
101 Blue Seal Dr. SE, Ste. 101
Leesburg, VA 20175
PH: (703)669-6600
Toll free: 877-346-9327
Fax: (703)669-6127
Zilke, Tim, CEO, President

**Professional Housing Management
Association [5284]**
154 Ft. Evans Rd. NE
Leesburg, VA 20176
PH: (703)771-1888
Fax: (703)771-0299
Eulberg, Del, President

SkillsUSA Inc. [8018]
14001 Skills USA Way
Leesburg, VA 20176-5494
PH: (703)777-8810
Toll free: 800-321-8422
Fax: (703)777-8999
Kindred, Brent, President

**Society for Imaging Informatics in
Medicine [17067]**
19440 Golf Vista Plz., Ste. 330
Leesburg, VA 20176-8264
PH: (703)723-0432
Fax: (703)723-0415
Brown, David E., CIIP, Chairman

**United States Eventing Association
[22950]**
525 Old Waterford Rd. NW
Leesburg, VA 20176
PH: (703)779-0440
Fax: (703)779-0550
Whitehouse, Jo, CEO

**US Iran People Friendship Society
[9586]**
215 Depot Ct. SE, Ste. 201
Leesburg, VA 20175
Herischi, Ali, President

World Priorities [19011]
38664 Mt. Gilead Rd.
Leesburg, VA 20175
PH: (703)777-4352
Sivard, Jim, Contact

**Ag Container Recycling Council
[4623]**
223 S Main St.
Lexington, VA 24450
Toll free: 877-952-2272
Perkins, Ron, Exec. Dir.

Kappa Alpha Order [23901]
115 Liberty Hall Rd.
Lexington, VA 24450
PH: (540)463-1865
Fax: (540)463-2140
Wiese, Mr. Larry, Exec. Dir.

**George C. Marshall Foundation
[10338]**
1600 VMI Parade
Lexington, VA 24450-1600

PH: (540)463-7103
Fax: (540)464-5229
Barron, Paul B., Dir., Archives, Dir.
of Lib. Svcs.

**Omicron Delta Kappa Society
[23788]**
224 McLaughlin St.
Lexington, VA 24450-2002
PH: (540)458-5336
Toll free: 877-635-6437
Fax: (540)458-5342
Christakis, Michael, President,
Trustee

Sigma Nu Fraternity, Inc. [23928]
9 N Lewis St.
Lexington, VA 24450
PH: (540)463-1869
Fax: (540)463-1669
Beacham, R. Brad, Exec. Dir.

Society for Military History [9809]
George C. Marshall Library
Virginia Military Institute
Lexington, VA 24450-1600
PH: (540)464-7468
(928)237-1289
Fax: (540)464-7330
Berlin, Dr. Robert H., Exec. Dir.

**Home School Sports Network
[23226]**
153 Old Linden Rd.
Linden, VA 22642
PH: (540)631-5683
(540)636-3713
Davis, Chris, Exec. Dir., Founder

**National Fibromyalgia Partnership
Inc. [14770]**
140 Zinn Way
Linden, VA 22642-5609
Toll free: 866-725-4404
Rothenberg, Russell, MD, Chairman

**Air Force Public Affairs Alumni As-
sociation [5585]**
PO Box 447
Locust Grove, VA 22508-0447
Gaines, Clem, Chmn. of the Bd.

**Memorial Foundation of the Ger-
manna Colonies in Virginia [9410]**
PO Box 279
Locust Grove, VA 22508-0279
PH: (540)423-1700
Fax: (540)423-1747
Wheat, J. Marc, President

**National Service Committee/
Chariscenter USA [19890]**
PO Box 628
Locust Grove, VA 22508-0628
PH: (540)972-0225
Toll free: 800-338-2445
Matthews, Walter, Exec. Dir.

Abigail Alliance [13868]
8881 White Orchid Pl.
Lorton, VA 22079
PH: (703)646-5306
Burroughs, Frank, Founder

Vacations for Veterans [13250]
9435 Lorton Market St., No. 105
Lorton, VA 22079
PH: (202)731-0109
Carr, Peggy, CEO, Founder

**American Sealyham Terrier Club
[21820]**
c/o Sharon Yard, President
14111 Rehoboth Church Rd.
Lovettsville, VA 20180-3217
PH: (540)882-3492
Yard, Sharon, President

**Association of Coffee Mill
Enthusiasts [21625]**
c/o Shane Branchcomb, Treasurer
12031 George Farm Dr.

Lovettsville, VA 20180
Branchcomb, Shane, Treasurer

**Shenandoah National Park Associa-
tion [9434]**
3655 US Highway 211 E
Luray, VA 22835
PH: (540)999-3582
Fax: (540)999-3583

**Association of Collegiate Marketing
Educators Inc. [8269]**
c/o Silvia Lozano Martin, Secretary
School of Business and Economics
Lynchburg College
1501 Lakeside Dr.
Lynchburg, VA 24501
PH: (434)544-8177
Natarajan, Vivek S., President

Liberty Godparent Home [12776]
124 Liberty Mountain Dr.
Lynchburg, VA 24502
PH: (434)845-3466
Toll free: 800-542-4453
Fax: (434)845-1751
Basham, Janelle, Director

**North American Border Terrier
Welfare [11693]**
c/o Cindy Peebles, Treasurer
822 George St.
Lynchburg, VA 24502
PH: (434)239-4576
Moon, Camilla, President

**Professional Putters Association
[22893]**
8105 Timberlake Rd.
Lynchburg, VA 24502

Vitiligo Support International [14515]
PO Box 3565
Lynchburg, VA 24503-0565
PH: (434)326-5380
Gardner, Ms. Jackie, Exec. Dir.

United Poultry Concerns [10708]
PO Box 150
Machipongo, VA 23405
PH: (757)678-7875
Fax: (757)678-5070
Davis, Karen, PhD, President

**Air and Expedited Motor Carriers
Association [3318]**
9532 Liberia Ave., No. 705
Manassas, VA 20110
PH: (703)361-5208
Fax: (703)361-5274
Klever, Scott, President

**American Type Culture Collection
[6073]**
10801 University Blvd.
Manassas, VA 20110
PH: (703)365-2700
Toll free: 800-638-6597
Fax: (703)365-2750
Cypess, Raymond, PhD, Chairman,
CEO

**Amputee Coalition of America
[14545]**
9303 Center St., Ste. 100
Manassas, VA 20110
Toll free: 888-267-5669
Richmond, Jack, Chairman

**Automotive Recyclers Association
[3446]**
9113 Church St.
Manassas, VA 20110
PH: (571)208-0428
Toll free: 888-385-1005
Fax: (571)208-0430
Wilson, Michael E., CEO

Christ In Action [20134]
PO Box 4200
Manassas, VA 20108

PH: (703)368-6286
Fax: (703)368-6470
Nissley, Rev. Denny, President,
Founder

Institute of Navigation [6907]
8551 Rixlew Ln., Ste. 360
Manassas, VA 20109
PH: (703)366-2723
Fax: (703)366-2724
Beaty, Lisa, Exec. Dir.

**International Federation of
Pharmaceutical Wholesalers, Inc.
[2559]**
10569 Crestwood Dr.
Manassas, VA 20109-3406
PH: (703)331-3714
Fax: (703)331-3715
Zwisler, Eric V., Director

**International Senior Softball Associa-
tion [23201]**
9114 I-Beam Ln.
Manassas, VA 20110
PH: (571)436-9704
Fax: (703)361-0344
Thomas, R.B., Jr., Exec. Dir.

Marine Machinery Association [2262]
8665 Sudley Rd., Ste. 270
Manassas, VA 20110-4588
PH: (703)791-4800
Fax: (703)791-4808
Richard, Leslie, Exec. Dir.

Medical Missionaries [15605]
9590 Surveyor Ct.
Manassas, VA 20110
PH: (703)361-5116
Irwin, Gilbert, MD, President

**National Association for Public
Safety Infection Control Officers
[15410]**
9250 Mosby St., Ste. 100
Manassas, VA 20110
PH: (703)365-8388
Cross, James, Exec. Dir.

**National Energy Education Develop-
ment Project [18192]**
8408 Kao Cir.
Manassas, VA 20110
PH: (703)257-1117
Toll free: 800-875-5029
Fax: (703)257-0037
Luthi, Randall, Treasurer

**National Rehabilitation Counseling
Association [17095]**
PO Box 4480
Manassas, VA 20108
PH: (703)361-2077
Fax: (703)361-2489
Wilson, Thomas, President

**National Religious Broadcasters
[19769]**
9510 Technology Dr.
Manassas, VA 20110-4149
PH: (703)330-7000
Fax: (703)330-7100
Bott, Richard P., Director

**National Safe Boating Council
[12833]**
9500 Technology Dr., Ste. 104
Manassas, VA 20110
PH: (703)361-4294
Moore, Richard, Chairman

**National Teen Age Republicans
[19045]**
10610-A Crestwood Professional Ctr.
Manassas, VA 20108
PH: (703)368-4220
Wells, Barby, Director

Cardinal Newman Society [7578]
9720 Capital Ct., Ste. 201
Manassas, VA 20110
PH: (703)367-0333
Fax: (703)396-8668
Reilly, Patrick J., President

Portuguese American Leadership
Council of the United States
[19619]
9255 Center St., Ste. 404
Manassas, VA 20110
PH: (202)466-4664
Fax: (202)466-4661
Rosa, Mr. Fernando G., Chairman,
CEO

International Window Film Associa-
tion [540]
PO Box 3871
Martinsville, VA 24115
PH: (276)666-4932
Smith, Darrell L., Exec. Dir.

Melungeon Heritage Association
[8810]
PO Box 3604
Martinsville, VA 24115
Arthur, S.J., Act. Pres.

3-A Sanitary Standards, Inc. [965]
6888 Elm St., Ste. 2D
McLean, VA 22101
PH: (703)790-0295
Fax: (703)761-6284
Schmidt, Ronald, Director

Academic Pediatric Association
[16597]
6728 Old McLean Village Dr.
McLean, VA 22101
PH: (703)556-9222
Fax: (703)556-8729
Schuster, Mark, President

Afghan-American Chamber of Com-
merce [23550]
8201 Greensboro Dr., Ste. 103
McLean, VA 22102
PH: (703)442-5005
Fax: (703)442-5008
Ritter, Hon. Donald, CEO, President

Alliance for Potato Research and
Education [4559]
2000 Corporate Ridge, Ste. 1000
McLean, VA 22102
PH: (703)245-7694
Storey, Maureen, PhD, President,
CEO

America World Adoption Association
[10442]
6723 Whittier Ave.
McLean, VA 22101
PH: (703)356-8447
Toll free: 800-429-3369
Luwis, Brian Andrew, CEO

American Academy of Clinical
Toxicology [17490]
6728 Old McLean Village Dr.
McLean, VA 22101
PH: (703)556-9222
Fax: (703)556-8729
Simone, Karen, PharmD, President

American Academy of Health Phys-
ics [17429]
c/o Nancy Johnson
1313 Dolley Madison Blvd., Ste. 402
McLean, VA 22101
PH: (703)790-1745
Fax: (703)790-2672
Lambert, Kent, President

American Ambulance Association
[14659]
8400 Westpark Dr., 2nd Fl.
McLean, VA 22102

PH: (703)610-9018
Toll free: 800-523-4447
Fax: (703)610-0210
Hall, Mike, President

American Association for Geriatric
Psychiatry [16813]
6728 Old McLean Village Dr.
McLean, VA 22101
PH: (703)556-9222
Fax: (703)556-8729

American Association of Physical
Anthropologists [5901]
1313 Dolley Madison Blvd., Ste. 402
McLean, VA 22101
PH: (302)831-1855
Fax: (302)831-4002
Antón, Susan, President

American Association of Political
Consultants [18902]
8400 Westpark Dr.
McLean, VA 22102
PH: (703)245-8020
Hackney, Arthur, Chairman

American Association of Tissue
Banks [17501]
8200 Greensboro Dr., Ste. 320
McLean, VA 22102
PH: (703)827-9582
Fax: (703)356-2198
Crandall, Kathy

American Board of Health Physics
[16764]
c/o Nancy J. Johnson, Program
Director/Executive Secretary
1313 Dolley Madison Blvd., Ste. 402
McLean, VA 22101
PH: (703)790-1745
Fax: (703)790-2672
Johnson, Nancy J., Prog. Dir., Exec.
Sec.

American Cochlear Implant Alliance
[15169]
PO Box 103
McLean, VA 22101-0103
PH: (703)536-6146
Sorkin, Donna L., MA, Exec. Dir.

American Frozen Food Institute
[1313]
2000 Corporate Ridge, Ste. 1000
McLean, VA 22102
PH: (703)821-0770
Fax: (703)821-1350
Cope, Larry W., Chairman

American Health Quality Association
[17028]
7918 Jones Branch Dr., Ste. 300
McLean, VA 22102
PH: (202)331-5790
Arias, Anthony

American Institute of Biological Sci-
ences [6067]
1313 Dolley Madison Blvd., Ste. 402
McLean, VA 22101
PH: (703)790-1745
    (202)628-1500
Toll free: 800-992-2427
Fax: (703)790-2672
Skog, Judith, Secretary

American Psychosomatic Society
[16954]
6728 Old McLean Village Dr.
McLean, VA 22101-3906
PH: (703)556-9222
Fax: (703)556-8729
Herrmann-Lingen, Christoph,
President

American School Health Association
[15136]
7918 Jones Branch, Ste. 500
McLean, VA 22102

PH: (703)506-7675
Fax: (703)506-3266
Conley, Stephen, Director

American Society for Clinical
Laboratory Science [15516]
1861 International Dr., Ste. 200
McLean, VA 22102
PH: (571)748-3770

American Society for Photobiology
[6072]
1313 Dolley Madison Blvd., Ste. 402
McLean, VA 22101
PH: (703)790-1745
Wondrak, Georg, President

American Truck Dealers, a Division
of NADA [278]
8400 Westpark Dr.
McLean, VA 22102
PH: (703)821-7230
Toll free: 800-352-6232
Fax: (703)749-4700
Jorgensen, Eric, Contact

Archer Association [20780]
PO Box 6233
McLean, VA 22106
Archer, George W., President

Associated Owners and Developers
[800]
PO Box 4163
McLean, VA 22103-4163
PH: (703)405-5324
Kornbluh, Harvey L., Chairman,
CEO, Founder

Association of Clinicians for the Un-
derserved [14980]
1420 Spring Hill Rd., Ste. 600
McLean, VA 22102
Toll free: 844-442-5318
Fax: (703)562-8801
Kennedy, Craig, Exec. Dir.

Association for Manufacturing
Technology [6793]
7901 W Park Dr.
McLean, VA 22102-4206
PH: (703)893-2900
Toll free: 800-524-0475
Fax: (703)893-1151
Jones, Greg, VP

Association of Medical School
Pediatric Department Chairs
[16602]
6728 Old McLean Village Dr.
McLean, VA 22101
PH: (703)556-9222
Fax: (703)556-8729
Degnon, Laura, CAE, Exec. Dir.

Association of Pediatric Program
Directors [8310]
6728 Old McLean Village Dr.
McLean, VA 22101
PH: (703)556-9222
Fax: (703)556-8729
Degnon, Laura E., CAE, Exec. Dir.

Automotive Trade Association
Executives [286]
8400 Westpark Dr.
McLean, VA 22102
PH: (703)821-7072
Fax: (703)556-8581
Colman, Jennifer, Exec. Dir.

Board of Registered Polysomno-
graphic Technologists [15683]
8400 Westpark Dr., 2nd Fl.
McLean, VA 22102
PH: (703)610-9020
Fax: (703)610-0229
Magruder, Jim, Exec. Dir.

Catholic Academy of Sciences in the
United States of America [20075]
c/o Lee T. Grady, PhD, Secretary
1205 Carol Raye St.
McLean, VA 22101-2620
Carroll, Austin David, PhD, Bd.
Member

Christian Alliance for Orphans
[10941]
6723 Whittier Ave., Ste. 202
McLean, VA 22101
Medefind, Jedd, President

Construction Industry Round Table
[803]
8115 Old Dominion Dr., Ste. 210
McLean, VA 22102-2325
PH: (202)466-6777
Gilbane, Thomas F., Jr., Chairman

Construction Management Associa-
tion of America [2164]
7926 Jones Branch Dr., Ste. 800
McLean, VA 22102-3303
PH: (703)356-2622
Fax: (703)356-6388
D'Agostino, Bruce, CEO, President

Council for the National Interest
[18680]
1350 Beverly Rd., Ste. 115-100
McLean, VA 22101
PH: (202)863-2951
Findley, Paul, Founder

Council of Pediatric Subspecialties
[16604]
6728 Old McLean Village Dr.
McLean, VA 22101
PH: (703)556-9222
Fax: (703)556-8729
Spicer, Robert, Rep.

Data Interchange Standards As-
sociation [19153]
8300 Greensboro Dr., Ste. 800
McLean, VA 22102
PH: (703)970-4480
Fax: (703)970-4488
Leach, Jim, Treasurer

Ehlers Danlos National Foundation
[17483]
7918 Jones Branch Dr., Ste. 300
McLean, VA 22102
PH: (703)506-2892
Fax: (703)506-3266
Robinson, Shane, Exec. Dir.

Emergency Department Practice
Management Association [14677]
8400 Westpark Dr., 2nd Fl.
McLean, VA 22102
PH: (703)610-0314
Fax: (703)995-4678
Mundinger, Elizabeth, Esq., Exec.
Dir.

Food Allergy Research and Educa-
tion [13577]
7925 Jones Branch Dr., Ste. 1100
McLean, VA 22102
PH: (703)691-3179
Toll free: 800-929-4040
Fax: (703)691-2713
Atwater, Janet, Chmn. of the Bd.

Food Processing Suppliers Associa-
tion [974]
1451 Dolley Madison Blvd., Ste. 101
McLean, VA 22101
PH: (703)663-1200
Fax: (703)761-4334
Seckman, David, President, CEO

Health Physics Society [16765]
1313 Dolley Madison Blvd., Ste. 402
McLean, VA 22101

PH: (703)790-1745
Fax: (703)790-2672
Cherry, Robert, President

Healthcare Convention and Exhibitors Association [1173]
7918 Jones Branch Dr., Ste. 300
McLean, VA 22102
PH: (703)935-1961
Fax: (703)506-3266
Farmer, Christine, President

Hospitality Sales and Marketing Association International [1659]
7918 Jones Branch Dr., Ste. 300
McLean, VA 22102
PH: (703)506-3280
Fax: (703)506-3266

International Defense Equipment Exhibitors Association [1176]
6233 Nelway Dr.
McLean, VA 22101
PH: (703)760-0762
Fax: (703)760-0764

International Foodservice Distributors Association [1391]
1410 Spring Hill Rd., Ste. 210
McLean, VA 22102
PH: (703)532-9400
Fax: (703)538-4673
Caldwell, Chris, Dir. of Comm., Dir. of Mktg.

International Society for Neurofeedback and Research [6912]
c/o Cindy A. Yablonski, Executive Director
1350 Beverly Rd., Ste. 115, PMB 114
McLean, VA 22101-3633
PH: (415)485-1344
Fax: (703)738-7341
Yablonski, Cindy A., PhD, Exec. Dir.

International Society for Neurofeedback and Research [16024]
c/o Cindy A. Yablonski, Exeutive Director
1350 Beverly Rd., Ste. 115, PMB 114
McLean, VA 22101-3633
PH: (415)485-1344
Fax: (703)738-7341
Yablonski, Cindy A., PhD, Exec. Dir.

International Society for the Study of Trauma and Dissociation [15781]
8400 Westpark Dr., 2nd Fl.
McLean, VA 22102
PH: (703)610-9037
Fax: (703)610-0234
Danylchuk, Lynette S., PhD, Chairman

International Technology Law Association [5091]
7918 Jones Branch Dr., Ste. 300
McLean, VA 22102
PH: (703)506-2895
Fax: (703)579-4366
Weiss, Robert, Treasurer

Interstitial Cystitis Association [17551]
7918 Jones Branch Dr., Ste. 300
McLean, VA 22102
PH: (703)442-2070
Fax: (703)506-3266
Zarnikow, Barbara, Co-Ch.

Mobile Satellite Users Association [7112]
1350 Beverly Rd., Ste. 115, No. 341
McLean, VA 22101
PH: (650)839-0376
August, Frank, Secretary

National Association of Marine Laboratories [6805]
1313 Dolley Madison Blvd., Ste. 402
McLean, VA 22101
PH: (703)790-1745
Toll free: 800-955-1236
Fax: (703)790-2672
Rabalais, Nancy, President

National Association of State Aviation Officials [5060]
8400 Westpark Dr., 2nd Fl.
McLean, VA 22102
PH: (703)417-1880
Fax: (703)417-1885
Principato, Greg, President, CEO

National Capital Lyme Disease Association [14599]
PO Box 8211
McLean, VA 22106-8211
PH: (703)821-8833
Green, Susan, Counsel

National Center for Homeopathy [15290]
7918 Jones Branch Dr., Ste. 300
McLean, VA 22102
PH: (703)506-7667
Fax: (703)506-3266
Jerome, Ann, PhD, CCH, RSHom, President

National Child Support Enforcement Association [5191]
7918 Jones Branch Dr., Ste. 300
McLean, VA 22102
PH: (703)506-2880
Fax: (703)506-3266
Golightly, Steven, President

National Fisheries Institute [3033]
7918 Jones Branch Dr., Ste. 700
McLean, VA 22102-3319
PH: (703)752-8880
Fax: (703)752-7583
Connelly, John, President

National Frozen Pizza Institute [1357]
2000 Corporate Ridge, Ste. 1000
McLean, VA 22102
PH: (703)245-7696
Fax: (703)821-1350
Henry, Corey

National Hospice Regatta Alliance [22652]
PO Box 1054
McLean, VA 22101
Kluttz, Jean Swink, Bd. Member

National Investment Company Service Association [2032]
8400 Westpark Dr., 2nd Fl.
McLean, VA 22102
PH: (508)485-1500
Fax: (508)485-1560
Fitzpatrick, Jim, President

National Science and Technology Education Partnership [12983]
PO Box 9644
McLean, VA 22102
McCloskey, Peter F., Chairman

National Yogurt Association [977]
2000 Corporate Ridge, Ste. 1000
McLean, VA 22102
PH: (703)245-7698
   (703)821-0770
Clayton, Joseph, President

Natural Science Collections Alliance [6093]
1313 Dolley Madison Blvd., Ste. 402
McLean, VA 22101
PH: (202)628-1500
Page, Lawrence, Secretary

Our Military Kids [12349]
6861 Elm St., Ste. 2A
McLean, VA 22101
PH: (703)734-6654
Toll free: 866-691-6654
Fax: (703)734-6503
Davidson, Linda, Exec. Dir., Founder

Partner for Surgery [17397]
PO Box 388
McLean, VA 22101
PH: (703)893-4335
Peterson, Frank, Founder, President

PMA-The Worldwide Community of Imaging Associations [2590]
7918 Jones Branch Dr., Ste. 300
McLean, VA 22102
PH: (703)665-4416
Toll free: 800-762-9287
Fax: (703)506-3266
McCabe, Georgia, CEO

Psychiatric Rehabilitation Association [17097]
7918 Jones Branch Dr., Ste. 300
McLean, VA 22102
PH: (703)422-2078
Fax: (703)506-3266
Gibson, Tom, CEO

Public Media Business Association [479]
7918 Jones Branch Dr., Ste. 300
McLean, VA 22102
PH: (703)506-3292
Fax: (703)506-3266
Chen, John, Mgr. Dir.

RESOLVE: The National Infertility Association [14764]
7918 Jones Branch Dr., Ste. 300
McLean, VA 22102
PH: (703)556-7172
Fax: (703)506-3266
Collura, Barbara, President, CEO

Safety Equipment Institute [3005]
1307 Dolley Madison Blvd., Ste. 3A
McLean, VA 22101-3913
PH: (703)442-5732
Fax: (703)442-5756
Sant, Bradley M., Director

Semiconductor Environmental, Safety and Health Association [6439]
1313 Dolley Madison Blvd., Ste. 402
McLean, VA 22101-3926
PH: (703)790-1745
Fax: (703)790-2672
Burk, Brett, Exec. Dir.

Shrimp Council [4639]
7918 Jones Branch Dr., Ste. 700
McLean, VA 22102
PH: (703)752-8880

SnowSports Industries America [3163]
8377B Greensboro Dr.
McLean, VA 22102-3587
PH: (703)556-9020
Fax: (703)821-8276
Gundram, Bob, Chmn. of the Bd.

Society of Dermatology Physician Assistants [16726]
8400 Westpark Dr., 2nd Fl.
McLean, VA 22102
Toll free: 800-380-3992
Fax: (703)563-9263
Conner, Jennifer, President

Society for Developmental and Behavioral Pediatrics [16618]
6728 Old McLean Village Dr.
McLean, VA 22101

PH: (703)556-9222
Fax: (703)556-8729
Degnon, Laura, CAE, Exec. Dir.

Society for Integrative and Comparative Biology [7403]
1313 Dolley Madison Blvd., Ste. 402
McLean, VA 22101
PH: (703)790-1745
Toll free: 800-955-1236
Fax: (703)790-2672
Burk, Brett J., Exec. Dir.

Society for Risk Analysis [1932]
1313 Dolley Madison Blvd., Ste. 402
McLean, VA 22101
PH: (703)790-1745
Drupa, David A., Exec. Sec.

Special Libraries Association [9728]
7918 Jones Branch Dr., Ste. 300
McLean, VA 22102
PH: (703)647-4900
Fax: (703)506-3266
Burke, Amy Lestition

Student & Youth Travel Association [3397]
8400 Westpark Dr., 2nd Fl.
McLean, VA 22102-5116
PH: (703)610-1263
Fax: (703)610-0270
Assante, Carylann, Exec. Dir.

Sudan-American Foundation for Education [7595]
1700 Westwind Way
McLean, VA 22102
PH: (571)297-4099
Badri, Hala, President

Tobacco Associates [3286]
8452 Holly Leaf Dr.
McLean, VA 22102
PH: (703)821-1255
Fax: (703)821-1511
Wayne, Kirk, President

Tomorrow's Youth Organization [13485]
1356 Beverly Rd., Ste. 200
McLean, VA 22101-3640
PH: (703)893-1143
Fax: (703)893-1227
Masri, Hani, Founder, President

Women in Government Relations [18323]
8400 Westpark Dr., 2nd Fl.
McLean, VA 22102
PH: (703)610-9030
Fax: (703)995-0528
Bardach, Emily, Exec. Dir.

Caring Voice Coalition [12465]
8249 Meadowbridge Rd.
Mechanicsville, VA 23116
PH: (804)427-6468
Toll free: 888-267-1440
Harris, Ms. Pamela, Chairperson, President, Founder

International Association of Bedding and Furniture Law Officials [5307]
c/o Margaret Davis, Treasurer
6758 Crump Dr.
Mechanicsville, VA 23111-6517
PH: (804)864-8146

International Microwave Power Institute [6870]
PO Box 1140
Mechanicsville, VA 23111
PH: (804)559-6667
Poisant, Molly, Exec. Dir.

Alliance for Marriage [12253]
PO Box 2490
Merrifield, VA 22116-2490

PH: (703)934-1212
Fax: (703)934-1211
Rodriguez, Samuel, Contact

Campaign for Working Families
[18862]
PO Box 1222
Merrifield, VA 22116-1222
PH: (703)671-8800
Bauer, Gary, Founder

Coptic Orphans Support Association
[10950]
PO Box 2881
Merrifield, VA 22116
PH: (703)641-8910
Fax: (703)641-8787
Riad, Mrs. Nermien, Founder

Family and Home Network [12412]
PO Box 492
Merrifield, VA 22116
Myers, Cathy, Exec. Dir.

Glories Happy HATS, Inc. [13448]
PO Box 624
Merrifield, VA 22116-0624
PH: (703)506-1415
Carlson-Khorsand, Ms. Susan,
Founder

Postal History Society [22356]
c/o Joseph J. Geraci, President
PO Box 4129
Merrifield, VA 22116-4129
Geraci, Joseph J., President

Public Advocate of the U.S. [19156]
PO Box 1360
Merrifield, VA 22116
PH: (703)845-1808
Toll free: 800-293-8436
Delgaudio, Eugene A., Mem.

American Connemara Pony Society
[4302]
PO Box 100
Middlebrook, VA 24459
Eyles, Marynell, Secretary

American College of Veterinary
Anesthesia and Analgesia [17615]
c/o Dr. Lydia Donaldson, Executive
Secretary
22499 Polecat Hill Rd.
Middleburg, VA 20118
PH: (540)687-5270
Donaldson, Dr. Lydia, Exec. Sec.

American Water Resources Associa-
tion [7364]
PO Box 1626
Middleburg, VA 20118
PH: (540)687-8390
Fax: (540)687-8395
Reid, Kenneth D., CAE, Exec. VP

Norwich Terrier Club of America
[21936]
c/o Patty Warrender, Membership
Chairperson
PO Box 1431
Middleburg, VA 20118
PH: (540)364-4901
Schubart, Jane, President

Alliance of Cardiovascular Profes-
sionals [14086]
PO Box 2007
Midlothian, VA 23113
PH: (804)632-0078
Fax: (804)639-9212
Beveridge, Richard, President

Balm in Gilead [13531]
620 Moorefield Park Dr., Ste. 150
Midlothian, VA 23236
PH: (804)644-2256
Seele, Pernessa C., CEO, Founder

Health Professions Network [15119]
PO Box 2007
Midlothian, VA 23113
PH: (804)639-9211
Fax: (804)639-9212
Ellingson, Stephanie, Secretary

Huguenot Society of the Founders of
Manakin in the Colony of Virginia
[21003]
981 Huguenot Trail
Midlothian, VA 23113
Woodlief, Dr. Ann, Librarian

Jessie's Wish [14642]
742 Colony Forest Dr.
Midlothian, VA 23114
PH: (804)378-3032
Fax: (804)378-3032
Inlow, Brand, President

National Association of Lutheran
Interim Pastors [20316]
PO Box 5235
Midlothian, VA 23112
PH: (804)564-5389
Seng, Daniel, Chairman

Opel Association of North America
[21468]
630 Watch Hill Rd.
Midlothian, VA 23113
PH: (804)379-9737
Goin, Charles, Founder, President

Recruitment Process Outsourcing
Association [1698]
14621 Charter Walk Pl.
Midlothian, VA 23114
PH: (804)897-1310
Mayeux, Mike, President

Talking Page Literacy Organization
[8254]
1500 King William Woods Rd.
Midlothian, VA 23113
PH: (949)510-1804
Chekel, Martin J., President

Teaching-Family Association [11832]
PO Box 2007
Midlothian, VA 23113-9007
PH: (804)632-0155
Fax: (804)639-9212
Altom, Andy, President

Vietnam Era Seabees [21161]
PO Box 5177
Midlothian, VA 23112-0020
Koch, Bob, Memb. Ofc.

Masters of Foxhounds Association of
America [22962]
PO Box 363
Millwood, VA 22646
PH: (540)955-5680
Fax: (540)955-5682
Kelly, Edward W., MFH, Director

Project HOPE [14962]
255 Carter Hall Ln.
Millwood, VA 22646
PH: (540)837-2100
Toll free: 800-544-4673
Heitzman, Linda N., Exec. VP

American Immigration Control
Foundation [18461]
PO Box 525
Monterey, VA 24465
PH: (540)468-2023
Fax: (540)468-2026
Vinson, John, President

Higdon Family Association [20880]
c/o Janice M. Higdon, Treasurer
Box 315
Moon, VA 23119-0315
Higdon, Janice M., Treasurer

Mount Vernon Ladies' Association
[10341]
3600 Mt. Vernon Memorial Hwy.
Mount Vernon, VA 22121
PH: (703)780-2000
Viebranz, Curtis G., President, CEO

Sustainable Food Trade Association
[1375]
49 Race St.
New Castle, VA 24127-6397
PH: (413)624-6678
New, Hansel, President

The Coalition of Spirit-filled
Churches, Inc. [20020]
PO Box 6606
Newport News, VA 23606
Toll free: 877-208-8189
Fax: (425)977-1360
Plummer, David B., Chairperson

Inflammatory Skin Disease Institute
[14583]
PO Box 1074
Newport News, VA 23601
PH: (757)223-0795
Fax: (757)595-1842
Finch, LaDonna, Exec. Dir.

International Theodore Dreiser
Society [9059]
c/o Roark Mulligan, Secretary-
Treasurer
Christopher Newport University
Dept. of English
1 Avenue of the Arts
Newport News, VA 23606
Davies, Jude, President

National Association of Independent
Labor [23433]
One City Ctr., Ste. 300
11815 Fountain Way
Newport News, VA 23606
PH: (757)926-5216
Fax: (757)926-5204
Priest, Dannis, President

Morgan Car Club of Washington DC
[21442]
c/o Marline Riehle, Membership/
Registrar
PO Box 539
Nokesville, VA 20182
PH: (703)594-2054
Trabb, Bruce, President

American Society of Biomechanics
[6068]
c/o Stacie Ringleb, Secretary/
Membership Chairman
Old Dominion University
Norfolk, VA 23529
PH: (757)683-5934
Troy, Karen, Ph.D, Treasurer

Angioma Alliance [15902]
520 W 21st St., Ste. G2-411
Norfolk, VA 23517-1950
PH: (571)306-2873
Fax: (757)623-0616
Lee, Dr. Cornelia, President

Coal Trading Association [737]
PO Box 3146
Norfolk, VA 23514-3146
PH: (703)418-0392
Fax: (703)416-0014
McLean, Robert E., CAE, Exec. Dir.

College Swimming Coaches As-
sociation of America [23282]
1585 Wesleyan Dr., Unit A
Norfolk, VA 23502
PH: (540)460-6563
Wadley, Bill, President

Creative Global Relief [12654]
749 Boush St.
Norfolk, VA 23510

PH: (757)627-7672
Strickland, James, Jr., Founder

Employee Assistance Society of
North America [11489]
PO Box 3146
Norfolk, VA 23514-3146
PH: (703)416-0060
McLean, Bob, CAE, Exec. Dir.

Escort Carrier Sailors and Airmen
Association [21025]
c/o Anthony Looney, President
1215 N Military Hwy., No. 128
Norfolk, VA 23502
Toll free: 855-505-2469
Hathaway, Oscar, III, Secretary

Hampton One-Design Class Racing
Association [22618]
c/o Charlie McCoy, Treasurer
1721 Cloncurry Rd.
Norfolk, VA 23505
McCoy, Charles H., Jr., Treasurer

International Black Women's
Congress [18215]
645 Church St., Ste. 200
Norfolk, VA 23510-1772
PH: (757)625-0500
Fax: (757)625-1905
Rodgers-Rose, Dr. La Francis,
Founder

National Alliance of Preservation
Commissions [9412]
208 E Plume St., Ste. 327
Norfolk, VA 23510
PH: (757)802-4141
Pollard, Paige, Exec. Dir.

National Gay Pilot's Association
[152]
PO Box 11313
Norfolk, VA 23517
PH: (757)626-1848
Pettet, David J., Exec. Dir.

National Town Builders' Association
[563]
9655 24th Bay St.
Norfolk, VA 23518
PH: (914)715-5576
Freeman, Herbert L., VP

Nationwide Insurance Independent
Contractors Association [1913]
c/o Bob McLean, Executive Director
PO Box 3146
Norfolk, VA 23514-3146
PH: (703)416-4422
Fax: (703)416-0014
Gardner, David, President

People for the Ethical Treatment of
Animals [10677]
501 Front St.
Norfolk, VA 23510
PH: (757)622-7382
Fax: (757)622-0457
Newkirk, Ingrid E., President

Physicians for Peace [15612]
500 E Main St., Ste. 900
Norfolk, VA 23510-2204
PH: (757)625-7569
Arfaa, Lisa, President, CEO

Purcell Family of America [20917]
9101 Mace Arch
Norfolk, VA 23503-4503
PH: (334)687-9787
Purcell, Douglas Clare, President

Society of Black Academic Surgeons
[17401]
c/o Lovie Brown
825 Fairfax Ave., 6th Fl.

Norfolk, VA
Brown, Lovie, Contact

Society for the History of Navy
Medicine **[9520]**
Old Dominion University
Norfolk, VA 23529-0091
Finley-Croswhite, Annette, Exec. Dir.

United States Collegiate Athletic As-
sociation **[23259]**
150 Boush St., Ste. 603
Norfolk, VA 23510
PH: (757)706-3756
Fax: (757)706-3758
Casto, Mr. Bill, Commissioner, Exec.
Dir.

Children Inc. **[11220]**
PO Box 72848
North Chesterfield, VA 23235
PH: (804)359-4562
Toll free: 800-538-5381
Carter, Ronald, President, CEO

NATCO, The Organization for
Transplant Professionals **[17515]**
12820 Rose Grove Dr.
Oak Hill, VA 20171
PH: (703)483-9820
Fax: (703)879-7544

Biopesticide Industry Alliance **[4528]**
PO Box 313
Oakton, VA 22124
PH: (202)570-1411
Jones, Keith, Exec. Dir.

Craft Beverage Association **[182]**
2911 Hunter Mill Rd., Ste. 303
Oakton, VA 22124
PH: (202)449-3739
Fax: (202)478-5189

endPoverty.org **[12536]**
PO Box 3380
Oakton, VA 22124
PH: (240)396-1146
Fax: (240)235-3550
Roadman, Larry, Exec. Dir.

National AfterSchool Association
[10809]
2961A Hunter Mill Rd., No. 626
Oakton, VA 22124
PH: (703)610-9002
Tang, Carol, Exec. Dir.

Order of the Founders and Patriots
of America **[20760]**
12010 Vale Rd.
12010 Vale Rd.
Oakton, VA 22124
PH: (703)476-9705

World Federation for Mental Health
[15811]
PO Box 807
Occoquan, VA 22125
Fax: (703)490-6926
Geller, Jeffrey, Director

Measurement, Control, and Automa-
tion Association **[3028]**
200 City Hall Ave., Ste. D
Poquoson, VA 23662
PH: (757)258-3100
Esher, Cynthia A., President

Association for Ambulatory
Behavioral Healthcare **[16825]**
247 Douglas Ave.
Portsmouth, VA 23707
PH: (757)673-3741
Fax: (757)966-7734
Meikel, Larry, President

International Reciprocal Trade Association **[3302]**
524 Middle St.
Portsmouth, VA 23704

PH: (757)393-2292
Fax: (757)257-4014
Whitney, Ron D., Exec. Dir.

Urban Awareness USA **[20011]**
601 Dinwiddie St.
Portsmouth, VA 23704
Toll free: 866-975-8722
Brown, Mr. Tracy J., Founder

Architectural Woodwork Institute
[491]
46179 Westlake Dr., Ste. 120
Potomac Falls, VA 20165
PH: (571)323-3636
Fax: (571)323-3630
Duvic, Philip, Exec. VP

National Association of Public Insur-
ance Adjusters **[1902]**
21165 Whitfield Pl., No. 105
Potomac Falls, VA 20165
PH: (703)433-9217
Fax: (703)433-0369
Denison, Karl, President

LaPerm Society of America **[21571]**
4403 Old Buckingham Rd.,
4403 Old Buckingham Rd.
Powhatan, VA 23139
Anderson, Patsi, President

Together for Tanzania **[11452]**
PO Box 395
Powhatan, VA 23139
Brannan, Jeanette, Founder, Exec.
Dir.

Home School Legal Defense As-
sociation **[7828]**
PO Box 3000
Purcellville, VA 20134
PH: (540)338-5600
Fax: (540)338-2733
Smith, J. Michael, President

Intercessors for America **[19984]**
PO Box 915
Purcellville, VA 20134
Toll free: 800-872-7729
Beckett, John, Bd. Member

Romania Reborn **[11142]**
PO Box 2027
Purcellville, VA 20134-2027
PH: (540)751-9490
Metzgar, Jayme, Founder, President

Society of Amateur Radio
Astronomers **[21307]**
904 Towering Oak Court.,
904 Towering Oak Ct.
Purcellville, VA 20132

Marine Corps Association **[5568]**
PO Box 1775
Quantico, VA 22134
Toll free: 866-622-1775
Usher, Maj. Gen. Edward, CEO,
President

Marine Corps Aviation Association
[5569]
715 Broadway St.
Quantico, VA 22134
PH: (703)630-1903
Toll free: 800-280-3001
Fax: (703)630-2713
Gallinetti, Jon, Deputy

Marine Corps Intelligence Associa-
tion, Inc. **[19547]**
PO Box 1028
Quantico, VA 22134
Harrison, Kathleen, Secretary

United States Marine Corps Scout
Sniper Association **[21021]**
PO Box 762
Quantico, VA 22134
Mann, Jason, President

Professional Administrative Co-
Employers **[1102]**
c/o Ray O'Leary, Administrator
3535 S Woodland Cir.
Quinton, VA 23141
PH: (804)932-9159
Toll free: 888-436-6227
Fax: (804)932-9461
O'Leary, Ray, Administrator

Gordon Institute for Music Learning
[8368]
PO Box 3466
Radford, VA 24143
McDonel, Jennifer, Exec. Dir.

International Philosophers for Peace
and Prevention of Nuclear Omni-
cide **[18795]**
c/o Professor Glen T. Martin,
President
PO Box 6943
Radford, VA 24142
Murphy, Patricia Anne, Chairperson

Parents and Friends of Ex-Gays and
Gays **[11906]**
PO Box 510
Reedville, VA 22539
PH: (804)453-4737
Griggs, Regina, Exec. Dir.

Academy for Eating Disorders
[14631]
12100 Sunset Hills Rd., Ste. 130
Reston, VA 20190
PH: (703)234-4079
Fax: (703)435-4390
Becker, Carolyn, PhD, President

Alliance for Building Regulatory
Reform in the Digital Age **[6160]**
10702 Midsummer Dr.
Reston, VA 20191
PH: (703)568-2323
Fax: (703)620-0015
Wible, Robert C., Secretary

American Academy of Audiology
[17234]
11480 Commerce Park Dr., Ste. 220
Reston, VA 20191
PH: (703)790-8466
Toll free: 800-222-2336
Fax: (703)790-8631
Carlson, Deborah, PhD, Comm.
Chm.

American Academy of Craniofacial
Pain **[16459]**
12100 Sunset Hills Rd., Ste. 130
Reston, VA 20190
PH: (703)234-4142
Toll free: 800-322-8651
Fax: (703)435-4390
Light, Rick, Secretary

American Academy of Otolaryngic
Allergy **[13569]**
11130 Sunrise Valley Dr., Ste. 100
Reston, VA 20191
PH: (202)955-5010
(202)955-5016
Lucas, Jami, Exec. Dir., CEO

American Academy of Otolaryngic
Allergy and Foundation **[13570]**
11130 Sunrise Valley Dr., Ste. 100
Reston, VA 20191
PH: (202)955-5010
Fax: (202)955-5016
Lucas, Jami, CEO, Exec. Dir.

American Association for Aerosol
Research **[6177]**
12100 Sunset Hills Rd., Ste. 130
Reston, VA 20190
PH: (703)437-4377
Toll free: 800-485-3106
Smith, James, Secretary

American Association of Engineering
Societies **[6527]**
1801 Alexander Bell Dr.
Reston, VA 20191
PH: (202)296-2237
Toll free: 888-400-2237
Fax: (202)296-1151
Cowan, Wendy, Exec. Dir., Secretary

American Association for Women
Radiologists **[17038]**
1891 Preston White Dr.
Reston, VA 20191
PH: (703)476-7650
Ackerman, Susan Johnston, M.D.,
President

American Brachytherapy Society
[13879]
12100 Sunset Hills Rd., Ste. 130
Reston, VA 20190-5202
PH: (703)234-4078
Fax: (703)435-4390
Guggolz, Rick, Exec. Dir.

American College of Nuclear
Medicine **[16075]**
1850 Samuel Morse Dr.
Reston, VA 20190-5316
PH: (703)326-1190
(703)708-9000
Fax: (703)708-9015
Pappas, Virginia, CAE, CEO

American College of Radiology
[17041]
1891 Preston White Dr.
Reston, VA 20191
PH: (703)648-8900
Thorwarth, William T., CEO

American College of Toxicology
[7335]
1821 Michael Farady Dr., Ste. 300
Reston, VA 20190
PH: (703)547-0875
Fax: (703)438-3113
Ghantous, Hanan, PhD, President

American Congress of Rehabilitation
Medicine **[17079]**
11654 Plaza America Dr., Ste. 535
Reston, VA 20190-4700
PH: (703)435-5335
Fax: (866)692-1619
Bushnik, Tamara, PhD. FACRM,
Contact

American Hardwood Export Council
[1406]
1825 Michael Faraday Dr.
Reston, VA 20190
PH: (703)435-2900
Fax; (703)435-2537
Snow, Michael, Exec. Dir.

American Institute of Aeronautics
and Astronautics **[5857]**
12700 Sunrise Valley Dr., Ste. 200
Reston, VA 20191-5807
PH: (703)264-7500
Toll free: 800-639-2422
Fax: (703)264-7551
Marko, Tammy, Dir. of Info. Technol-
ogy

American Medical Women's Associa-
tion **[15110]**
12100 Sunset Hills Rd., Ste. 130
Reston, VA 20190
PH: (703)234-4069
Toll free: 866-564-2483
Fax: (703)435-4390
Templeton, Kimberly, MD, President

American Society of Appraisers
[215]
11107 Sunset Hills Rd., Ste. 310
Reston, VA 20190

PH: (703)478-2228
Toll free: 800-272-8258
Fax: (703)742-8471
Trugman, Linda B., President

American Society of Civil Engineers
[6219]
1801 Alexander Bell Dr.
Reston, VA 20191
PH: (703)295-6300
Toll free: 800-548-2723
Mattei, Norma Jean, President

American Women's Hospitals
Service Committee of AMWA
[15311]
12100 Sunset Hills Rd.
Reston, VA 20190
PH: (703)234-4069
Luu, Jennie, President

Animal Transportation Association
[10581]
12100 Sunset Hills Rd., Ste. 130
Reston, VA 20190-3221
PH: (703)437-4377
Fax: (703)435-4390
Wheeler, Kelly, President

Architectural Engineering Institute of
ASCE [5958]
c/o American Society of Civil
Engineers
1801 Alexander Bell Dr.
Reston, VA 20191-4400
PH: (703)295-6300
Toll free: 800-548-2723
Ling, Moses D.F., PE, RA, President

Association for Advanced Life
Underwriting [1834]
11921 Freedom Dr., Ste. 1100
Reston, VA 20190
PH: (703)641-9400
Toll free: 888-275-0092
Fax: (703)641-9885
Stertzer, David, FLMI, CEO

Association of Freestanding Radia-
tion Oncology Centers [17034]
12100 Sunset Hills Rd., Ste. 130
Reston, VA 20190
PH: (202)442-3762
Fax: (202)638-0604
Smith, Stacey, Exec. Dir.

Association of Investment Manage-
ment Sales Executives [2020]
12100 Sunset Hills Rd., Ste. 130
Reston, VA 20190
PH: (703)234-4098
Fax: (703)435-4390
Hoskins, Kathy, Exec. Dir.

Association of School Business Of-
ficials International [7427]
11401 N Shore Dr.
Reston, VA 20190-4232
Toll free: 866-682-2729
Fax: (703)478-0205
Musso, John D., CAE, Exec. Dir.

Brick Industry Association [503]
1850 Centennial Park Dr., Ste. 301
Reston, VA 20191
PH: (703)620-0010
Fax: (703)620-3928
Sears, Stephen, COO

Cemetery Consumer Service Council
[18041]
PO Box 2028
Reston, VA 20195-0028
PH: (703)391-8407
Toll free: 800-645-7700
Fax: (703)391-8416

The Children of War [18775]
11874 Sunrise Valley Dr., No. 200-B
Reston, VA 20191-3323

PH: (510)396-5084
(703)625-9147
Anthony, Mary, Bd. Member

Circum-Pacific Council for Energy
and Mineral Resources [6872]
c/o Michele Redner, Secretariat
12201 Sunrise Valley Dr.
MS-917
Reston, VA 20192
PH: (703)648-5042
Fax: (703)648-4227
Redner, Michele

Coalition on the Public Understand-
ing of Science [7127]
American Institute of Biological Sci-
ences
1900 Campus Commons Dr., Ste.
200
Reston, VA 20191
PH: (571)748-4415
Fax: (703)674-2509
Potter, Sheri, Project Mgr.

College of Performance Management [2161]
12100 Sunset Hills Rd., Ste. 130
Reston, VA 20190
Abba, Wayne, President

Convenience Distribution Association
[1322]
11311 Sunset Hills Rd.
Reston, VA 20190
PH: (703)208-3358
Toll free: 800-482-2962
Fax: (703)573-5738
Owen, Chad, Chairman

Council of Landscape Architectural
Registration Boards [5965]
1840 Michael Faraday Dr., Ste. 200
Reston, VA 20190
PH: (571)432-0332
Albizo, Joel, Exec. Dir.

DECA Inc. [8270]
1908 Association Dr.
Reston, VA 20191-1502
PH: (703)860-5000
Reisenauer, Kevin, Officer

Environmental Mutagenesis and
Genomics Society [6080]
1821 Michael Faraday Dr., Ste. 300
Reston, VA 20190
PH: (703)438-8220
Fax: (703)438-3113
Engelward, Bevin P., President

Family, Career and Community
Leaders of America [7916]
1910 Association Dr.
Reston, VA 20191-1584
PH: (703)476-4900
Fax: (703)439-2662
Spavone, Sandy, Exec. Dir.

Future Business Leaders of America
- Phi Beta Lambda [23694]
1912 Association Dr.
Reston, VA 20191-1591
Toll free: 800-325-2946
Harshbarger, Ted L., Chairman

Global Camps Africa [10540]
1606 Washington Plz.
Reston, VA 20190
PH: (703)437-0808
Lilienthal, Philip, Founder, President

Graduate Management Admission
Council [8262]
PO Box 2969
Reston, VA 20195
PH: (703)668-9600
Toll free: 866-505-6559
Fax: (703)668-9601
Alig, Bob, Exec. VP

Graphic Arts Education and
Research Foundation [1534]
1899 Preston White Dr.
Reston, VA 20191-4367
PH: (703)264-7200
Toll free: 866-381-9839
Fax: (703)620-3165
Nappi, Ralph J., President

Graphic Communications Council
[1535]
c/o Graphic Arts Education and
Research Foundation
1899 Preston White Dr.
Reston, VA 20191-4367
Toll free: 866-381-9839
Fax: (703)620-3165
Hurlburt, Carol, Administrator

Graphic Communications Education
Association [9348]
1899 Preston White Dr.
Reston, VA 20191-4367
PH: (417)690-2511
Loch, Tom, President

Hardwood Plywood and Veneer As-
sociation [1441]
1825 Michael Faraday Dr.
Reston, VA 20190
PH: (703)435-2900
Fax: (703)435-2537
Mentel, Eva, Office Mgr.

Health Care Without Harm [15009]
12355 Sunrise Valley Dr., Ste. 680
Reston, VA 20191
PH: (703)860-9790
Fax: (703)860-9795
Cohen, Gary, Founder, President

History of Education Society [9486]
c/o Ralph Kidder, Treasurer
2020 Chadds Ford Dr.
Reston, VA 20191
Nelson, Adam, President

Institute for a Drug-Free Workplace
[13144]
10701 Parkridge Blvd., Ste. 300
Reston, VA 20191
PH: (703)391-7222
Fax: (703)391-7223
de Bernardo, Mark A., Exec. Dir.

Institute of Noise Control Engineer-
ing [6923]
12100 Sunset Hills Rd., Ste. 130
Reston, VA 20190
PH: (703)234-4124
Fax: (703)435-4390
Cuschieri, Joseph M., Exec. Dir.

International Association for Continu-
ing Education and Training [7669]
12100 Sunset Hills Rd., Ste. 130
Reston, VA 20190
PH: (703)234-4065
Fax: (703)435-4390
Meier, Sara, MSEd, Exec. Dir.

International Association of
Environmental Mutagenesis and
Genomics Societies [6083]
1821 Michael Faraday Dr., Ste. 300
Reston, VA 20190
PH: (703)438-3103
Fax: (703)438-3113
Nohmi, Takehiko, President

International Color Consortium [757]
1899 Preston White Dr.
Reston, VA 20191
PH: (703)264-7200
Orf, Deborah, Secretary

International Council for Health,
Physical Education, Recreation,
Sport, and Dance [8428]
1900 Association Dr.
Reston, VA 20191-1502

PH: (703)476-3462
Fax: (703)476-9527
Elnashar, Dr. Adel M., President

International Institute for Energy
Conservation [6493]
1850 Centennial Park Dr., Ste. 105
Reston, VA 20191
PH: (443)934-2279
Pratt, Robert L., Chmn. of the Bd.

International Professional Partnerships for Sierra Leone [18493]
2042 Swans Neck Way
Reston, VA 20191-4030
O'Connell, Mr. Jamie, JD, President

International Society of Radiology
[17059]
1891 Preston White Dr.
Reston, VA 20191
PH: (703)648-8360
Fax: (703)648-8361
Borgstede, James P., President

International Technology and
Engineering Educators Association
[8669]
1914 Association Dr., Ste. 201
Reston, VA 20191-1539
PH: (703)860-2100
Fax: (703)860-0353
Barbato, Steven, Exec. Dir.

International Technology and
Engineering Educators Association
- Council for Supervision and
Leadership [8670]
c/o ITEEA
1914 Association Dr., Ste. 201
Reston, VA 20191-1539
PH: (703)860-2100
Fax: (703)860-0353
Moye, Johnny, Membership Chp.

Internet Society [6767]
1775 Wiehle Ave., Ste. 201
Reston, VA 20190-5108
PH: (703)439-2120
Fax: (703)326-9881
St. Amour, Lynn, Trustee

Kitchen Cabinet Manufacturers As-
sociation [1952]
1899 Preston White Dr.
Reston, VA 20191-5435
PH: (703)264-1690
Fax: (703)620-6530
Natz, Betsy, CEO

Mammography Saves Lives [15688]
American College of Radiology
1891 Preston White Dr.
Reston, VA 20191
Toll free: 800-227-5463
Fax: (703)295-6773
Farley, Shawn, Contact

Management Association for Private
Photogrammetric Surveyors [7019]
1856 Old Reston Ave., Ste. 205
Reston, VA 20190
PH: (703)787-6996
Fax: (703)787-7550
Byrd, John, Mgr.

Media Research Center [12262]
1900 Campus Commons Dr., Ste.
600
Reston, VA 20191
PH: (571)267-3500
Toll free: 800-672-1423
Fax: (571)375-0099
Bozell, L. Brent, III, Founder,
President

Microscopy Society of America
[6868]
12100 Sunset Hills Rd., Ste. 130
Reston, VA 20190

PH: (703)234-4115
Toll free: 800-538-3672
Fax: (703)435-4390
Crozier, Peter A., Treasurer

**National Armored Car Association
[3093]**
11911 Fawn Ridge Ln.
Reston, VA 20194
PH: (202)642-1970
Ulman, Josh, Exec. Dir.

**National Association for Business
Teacher Education [7557]**
1914 Association Dr.
Reston, VA 20191-1538
PH: (703)860-8300
Fax: (703)620-4483
Fisher, Diane J., Director

**National Association of Corporate
Treasurers [1252]**
12100 Sunset Hills Rd., Ste. 130
Reston, VA 20190-3221
PH: (703)437-4377
Fax: (703)435-4390
Deas, Thomas C., Sr., Chairman

**National Association for Music
Education [8380]**
1806 Robert Fulton Dr.
Reston, VA 20191
PH: (703)860-4000
Toll free: 800-336-3768
Butera, Michael A., CEO, Exec. Dir.

**National Association for Research in
Science Teaching [8550]**
12100 Sunset Hills Rd., Ste. 130
Reston, VA 20190-3221
PH: (703)234-4138
Fax: (703)435-4390
Atwater, Mary M., President

**National Association of Schools of
Art and Design [7517]**
11250 Roger Bacon Dr., Ste. 21
Reston, VA 20190-5248
PH: (703)437-0700
Fax: (703)437-6312
Mullen, Denise, President

**National Association of Schools of
Dance [7704]**
11250 Roger Bacon Dr., Ste. 21
Reston, VA 20190-5248
PH: (703)437-0700
Fax: (703)437-6312
Moynahan, Karen P., Exec. Dir.

**National Association of Schools of
Music [8382]**
11250 Roger Bacon Dr., Ste. 21
Reston, VA 20190-5248
PH: (703)437-0700
Fax: (703)437-6312
Moynahan, Karen P., Exec. Dir.

**National Association of Schools of
Theatre [8699]**
11250 Roger Bacon Dr., Ste. 21
Reston, VA 20190-5248
PH: (703)437-0700
Fax: (703)437-6312
Moynahan, Karen P., Exec. Dir.

**National Association of Secondary
School Principals [8459]**
1904 Association Dr.
Reston, VA 20191-1502
PH: (703)860-0200
Toll free: 800-253-7746
Allison, Michael, President

**National Association for Sport and
Physical Education [8431]**
1900 Association Dr.
Reston, VA 20191-1598

PH: (703)476-3410
Toll free: 800-213-7193
Fax: (703)476-8316
Jefferies, Steve, President

**National Association of Student
Councils [8623]**
1904 Association Dr.
Reston, VA 20191-1537
PH: (703)860-0200
Bartoletti, JoAnn D., Exec. Dir.

**National Business Education As-
sociation [7563]**
1914 Association Dr.
Reston, VA 20191-1596
PH: (703)860-8300
Fax: (703)620-4483
Blair, Robert B., President

**National Business Honor Society
[23785]**
1914 Association Dr.
1914 Association Dr.
Reston, VA 20191-1596
PH: (703)860-8300
Fax: (703)620-4483
Nelson, Lydia, Chairperson

**National Center for Housing
Management [11978]**
1801 Old Reston Ave., Ste. 203
Reston, VA 20190-3356
Toll free: 800-368-5625
Fax: (904)372-2324
Abrams-Bell, Martha, Fac. Memb.

**National Center on Nonprofit
Enterprise [12391]**
10717 Oldfield Dr.
Reston, VA 20195
PH: (757)214-5084
Brewster, Richard P., Exec. Dir.

**National Committee for Accreditation
of Coaching Education [7617]**
1900 Association Dr.
Reston, VA 20191
PH: (703)476-3487
Alexander, CaSandra, Program Mgr.

**National Council of Teachers of
Mathematics [8284]**
1906 Association Dr.
Reston, VA 20191-1502
PH: (703)620-9840
Toll free: 800-235-7566
Fax: (703)476-2970
Larson, Matt, President

**National Court Reporters Association
[5121]**
12030 Sunrise Valley Dr., Ste. 400
Reston, VA 20191
PH: (703)556-6272
Toll free: 800-272-6272
Fax: (703)391-0629
Zinone, Stephen, President

National Honor Society [23786]
1904 Association Dr.
Reston, VA 20191-1537
PH: (703)860-0200
Toll free: 866-647-7253
Fax: (703)476-5432
Cordts, David, Assoc. Dir.

National Insulation Association [890]
12100 Sunset Hills Rd., Ste. 330
Reston, VA 20190
PH: (703)464-6422
Fax: (703)464-5896
Freeman, Kenneth, President

National Journalism Center [18288]
11480 Commerce Park Dr., Ste. 600
Reston, VA 20191
Toll free: 800-USA-1776
Fax: (702)318-9122
Jensen, Jessica, Chief of Staff

**National Junior Honor Society
[23787]**
1904 Association Dr.
Reston, VA 20191-1537
PH: (703)860-0200
Fax: (703)476-5432
Cordts, David, Assoc. Dir.

**National Society of Certified Health-
care Business Consultants [15129]**
12100 Sunset Hills Rd., Ste. 130
Reston, VA 20190
PH: (703)234-4099
Fax: (703)435-4390
Wynne, Carol, Exec. Dir.

National Wildlife Federation [3908]
11100 Wildlife Center Dr.
Reston, VA 20190
PH: (703)438-6000
Toll free: 800-822-9919
O'Mara, Collin, President, CEO

**North American Society for
Cardiovascular Imaging [14137]**
1891 Preston White Dr.
Reston, VA 20191
PH: (703)476-1350
    (703)476-1121
Fax: (703)716-4487
Wittling, Michele, Exec. Dir.

**NPES: Association for Suppliers of
Printing, Publishing and Converting
Technologies [1544]**
1899 Preston White Dr.
Reston, VA 20191
PH: (703)264-7200
Fax: (703)620-0994
Long, Thayer, President

NRI Vasavi Association [9569]
PO Box 2492
Reston, VA 20195
Toll free: 855-936-7482
Gupta, V Nagendra, President

**Packaging Machinery Manufacturers
Institute [2479]**
1191 Freedom Dr., Ste. 600
Reston, VA 20190
PH: (571)612-3200
Fax: (703)243-8556
Egan, Tom, VP

**PMMI, the Association for Packaging
and Processing Technologies
[2110]**
11911 Freedom Dr., Ste. 600
Reston, VA 20190
PH: (571)612-3200
Toll free: 888-275-7664
Fax: (703)243-8556
Abromavage, Caroline, Dir. of
Operations

Practice Greenhealth [14722]
12355 Sunrise Valley Dr., Ste. 680
Reston, VA 20191
Toll free: 888-688-3332
Fax: (866)379-8705
Wenger, Laura, RN, Contact

**Recreation Vehicle Industry Associa-
tion [2920]**
1896 Preston White Dr.
Reston, VA 20191
PH: (703)620-6003
Fax: (703)620-5071
Reed, Lyle, Chairman, Exec. Dir.

**Safety Pharmacology Society
[16685]**
1821 Michael Faraday Dr., Ste. 300
Reston, VA 20190
PH: (703)547-0874
Fax: (703)438-3113
Correll, Krystle G., Exec. Dir.

Society of Breast Imaging [17063]
1891 Preston White Dr.
Reston, VA 20191
PH: (703)715-4390
Fax: (703)295-6776
Morris, Elizabeth A., MD, President

**Society of Computed Body
Tomography and Magnetic
Resonance [17066]**
1891 Preston White Dr.
Reston, VA 20191
PH: (703)476-1117
Fax: (703)716-4487
Paulson, Erik, President

**Society of Financial Examiners
[5711]**
12100 Sunset Hills Rd., Ste. 130
Reston, VA 20190
PH: (703)234-4140
Toll free: 800-787-7633
Fax: (703)435-4390
Knief, Annette, President

**Society of Health and Physical
Educators [16715]**
1900 Association Dr.
Reston, VA 20191-1598
Toll free: 800-213-7193
Fax: (703)476-9527
Roetert, E. Paul, CEO

**Society of Nuclear Medicine and
Molecular Imaging [16077]**
1850 Samuel Morse Dr.
Reston, VA 20190
PH: (703)708-9000
Fax: (703)708-9015
Milanchus, Robert, Dir. of Bus. Dev.

**Society of Nuclear Medicine and
Molecular Imaging Technologist
Section [16078]**
1850 Samuel Morse Dr.
Reston, VA 20190
PH: (703)708-9000
Fax: (703)708-9015
Johnson, Sara G., President

**The Society for Organic Petrology
[7002]**
US Geological Survey
956 National Ctr.
Reston, VA 20192
PH: (703)648-6458
Fax: (703)648-6419
Hackley, Paul, Membership Chp.

**The Society for Pediatric Radiology
[17070]**
1891 Preston White Dr.
Reston, VA 20191-4397
PH: (703)648-0680
Boylan, Jennifer K., Exec. Dir.

**Society of Radiologists in Ultrasound
[17072]**
1891 Preston White Dr.
Reston, VA 20191
PH: (703)858-9210
Fax: (703)880-0295
Tublin, Mitchell E.

**Society of Toxicologic Pathology
[16594]**
1821 Michael Faraday Dr., Ste. 300
Reston, VA 20190
PH: (703)438-7508
Fax: (703)438-3113

Society of Toxicology [7343]
1821 Michael Faraday Dr., Ste. 300
Reston, VA 20190
PH: (703)438-3115
Toll free: 800-826-6762
Fax: (703)438-3113
Goering, Peter, President

Sports Lawyers Association [5769]
12100 Sunset Hills Rd., Ste. 130
Reston, VA 20190
PH: (703)437-4377
Fax: (703)435-4390
Guggolz, Richard A., Exec. Dir.

Sudan Sunrise [12443]
11404 Summer House Ct.
Reston, VA 20194-2006
PH: (202)499-6984
Jane, Amanda, Chairman

Sun Safety Alliance [14069]
1856 Old Reston Ave., Ste. 215
Reston, VA 20190
PH: (703)481-1414
Dyak, Brian, Membership Chp., Advisor

Technology Student Association [8019]
1914 Association Dr.
Reston, VA 20191-1538
PH: (703)860-9000
Toll free: 888-860-9010
Fax: (703)758-4852
Schmidt, Rick, President

Teratology Society [6105]
1821 Michael Faraday Dr., Ste. 300
Reston, VA 20190
PH: (703)438-3104
Fax: (703)438-3113
White, Tacey, President

Toxicology Forum [7345]
1821 Michael Faraday Dr., Ste. 300
Reston, VA 20190
PH: (703)547-0876
Fax: (703)438-3113
Klaunig, James, President

TRI-M Music Honor Society [10018]
National Association for Music Education
1806 Robert Fulton Dr.
Reston, VA 20191
PH: (703)860-4000
Toll free: 800-336-3768
Fax: (703)860-1531

The Wheelmen [22760]
c/o Kenneth Gray, Membership Chairman
1552 Autumn Ridge Cir.
Reston, VA 20194-1563
Allen, James, Cmdr.

Wireless Innovation Forum [6290]
12100 Sunset Hills Rd., Ste. 130
Reston, VA 20190
PH: (602)843-1634
Fax: (604)608-9593
Pucker, Lee, CEO

Workgroup for Electronic Data Interchange [1595]
1984 Isaac Newton Sq., Ste. 304
Reston, VA 20190
PH: (202)618-8788
Narcisi, Jean, Chairman

World Press Freedom Committee [17962]
11690 Sunrise Valley Dr., Ste. C
Reston, VA 20191-1436
PH: (703)715-9811
Fax: (703)620-6790

Young Americans for Freedom [18029]
c/o Patrick X. Coyle, Executive Director
11480 Commerce Park Dr.
Reston, VA 20191
Toll free: 800-USA-1776
Fax: (703)318-9122
Coyle, Patrick X., Exec. Dir.

Young America's Foundation [18030]
11480 Commerce Park Dr., Ste. 600
Reston, VA 20191-1556
PH: (703)318-9608
Toll free: 800-USA-1776
Fax: (703)318-9122
Coyle, Patrick X., VP

American Association for the History of Medicine [15259]
c/o Jodi Koste, Secretary
509 N 12th St.
Richmond, VA 23298
PH: (804)828-9898
Fax: (804)828-6098
Humphreys, Margaret, MD, President

American College of Osteopathic Pediatricians [16506]
2209 Dickens Rd.
Richmond, VA 23230-2005
PH: (804)565-6333
Fax: (804)282-0090
Packer, Edward E., VP

American Insurance Marketing and Sales Society [1832]
PO Box 35718
Richmond, VA 23235
PH: (804)674-6466
Toll free: 877-674-2742
Fax: (703)579-8896
Gray, Donna M., Administrator

American Osteopathic Academy of Orthopedics [16467]
2209 Dickens Rd.
Richmond, VA 23230-2005
PH: (804)565-6370
Toll free: 800-741-2626
Fax: (804)282-0090
Lugt, Lee Vander, DO, Exec. Dir.

American Society of Trace Evidence Examiners [5240]
c/o Chad Schennum, Treasurer
Virginia Department of Forensic Science
700 N 5th St.
Richmond, VA 23219
PH: (804)588-4105
Fax: (804)786-6305
Olsson, Kristine, President

American Spinal Injury Association [17251]
2209 Dickens Rd.
Richmond, VA 23230
PH: (804)565-6396
Fax: (804)282-0090
Mulcahey, Mary Jane, President

Apiary Inspectors of America [3634]
Virginia Department of Agriculture and Consumer Services
PO Box 1163
Richmond, VA 23218
Dykes, Mark, President

Association of Management/
International Association of Management [6034]
PO Box 72894
Richmond, VA 23235
PH: (757)482-2273
Fax: (757)482-0325
Hamel, Dr. Willem Arthur, Founder, President

Association of Physician Assistants in Cardiology [14099]
2415 Westwood Ave., Ste. B
Richmond, VA 23230
Toll free: 800-863-1207
Fax: (804)288-3551
Zeb, Shazad, PA-C, MPAS, President

Atlantic Flyway Council [4789]
PO Box 11104
Richmond, VA 23230

Cancer Dancer [13921]
PO Box 7416
Richmond, VA 23221
Nicholas, Kyle, President, Founder

ChildFund International [10911]
2821 Emerywood Pky.
Richmond, VA 23294
Toll free: 800-776-6767
Hill, Nancy, Secretary

Church Music Association of America [20488]
12421 New Point Dr.
Richmond, VA 23233
Mahrt, William P., President

Citizens to Stop Nuclear Terrorism [19178]
612 S Laurel St.
Richmond, VA 23220
PH: (214)478-8314
Rennolds, Edmund, Exec. Dir., Founder

Clinical Orthopaedic Society [16472]
2209 Dickens Rd.
Richmond, VA 23230-2005
PH: (804)565-6366
Fax: (804)282-0090
Hinckley, Stewart, Exec. Dir.

Conductors Guild Inc. [9892]
719 Twinridge Ln.
Richmond, VA 23235-5270
PH: (804)553-1378
Fax: (804)553-1876
Winger, Amanda Burton, Exec. Dir.

Congenital Cardiac Anesthesia Society [13701]
2209 Dickens Rd.
Richmond, VA 23230-2005
PH: (804)282-9780
Fax: (804)282-0090
Mossad, Emad, President

Jefferson Davis Association [10322]
2545 Bellwood Rd.
Richmond, VA 23237
PH: (804)275-5190
Fax: (804)275-5192
McGee, Sterry, Treasurer

Descendants of the Signers of the Declaration of Independence [20691]
c/o Laurie Croft, President
21 W Glenbrooke Cir.
Richmond, VA 23229-8036
Alexander, Johnny D., Treasurer

Donate Life America [14617]
701 E Byrd St., 16th Fl.
Richmond, VA 23219-3921
PH: (804)377-3580
Orlowski, Jeff, Secretary

Episcopal Church Building Fund [20099]
563A Southlake Blvd.,
Richmond, VA 23236
PH: (804)893-3436
Fax: (804)893-3439
Rowe, Rev. Sean, Chmn. of the Bd.

Faces of HOPE [12396]
PO Box 35229
Richmond, VA 23235
PH: (804)592-4751
Fax: (804)592-4752
Cordor, Jeannette, Founder, CEO

FightSMA [17270]
8016 Staples Mill Rd.
Richmond, VA 23228-2713

PH: (703)299-1144
Slay, Joe, Chmn. of the Bd.

Folk Art Society of America [9326]
PO Box 17041
Richmond, VA 23226-7041
Toll free: 800-355-6709
Brumfield, Thomas, Jr., VP

Honduras Outreach Medical Brigada Relief Effort [15471]
c/o Dr. Steve Crossman
West Hospital, 14th Fl.
1200 E Broad St.
Richmond, VA 23298-0251
Crossman, Dr. Steve, Contact

IEEE - Industrial Electronics Society [6428]
c/o Milos Manic, Secretary
Virginia Commonwealth University
401 W Main St., Rm. E2254
Richmond, VA 23284
PH: (804)827-3999
Martin, Prof. Terry, Treasurer

Independent Research Libraries Association [9706]
c/o Charles Bryan, President
Virginia Historical Society
428 N Blvd.
Richmond, VA 23221-0311
PH: (804)358-4901
Bryan, Charles, President

Initiatives of Change [18360]
2201 W Broad St., Ste. 200
Richmond, VA 23220-2022
PH: (804)358-1764
Fax: (804)358-1769
Elliott, William S., Exec. Dir.

International Association of Law Enforcement Intelligence Analysts [5362]
PO Box 13857
Richmond, VA 23225
Fax: (804)565-2059
Dauzier, Jennifer, Treasurer

International Council on Hotel, Restaurant, and Institutional Education [1664]
2810 N Parham Rd., Ste. 230
Richmond, VA 23294
PH: (804)346-4800
Fax: (804)346-5009
McCarty, Kathy, CEO

International Mission Board [20426]
3806 Monument Ave.
Richmond, VA 23230-0767
Toll free: 800-999-3113
Elliff, Tom, President

Jamestowne Society [20753]
PO Box 6845
Richmond, VA 23230
PH: (804)353-1226
Hofmeyer, Bonnie, Exec. Dir.

Kidney End-of-Life Coalition [15296]
300 Arboretum Pl., Ste. 310
Richmond, VA 23236
PH: (804)320-0004
Toll free: 866-651-6272
Fax: (804)320-5918

John Marshall Foundation [9409]
1108 E Main St., Ste. 800
Richmond, VA 23219
PH: (804)775-0861
Fax: (804)775-0862
Parkinson, Rev. Caroline Smith, President

Midwives for Haiti [15125]
7130 Glen Forest Dr., Ste. 101
Richmond, VA 23226

PH: (804)662-6060
Brunk, Nadene S., CNM, Founder,
Exec. Dir.

James Monroe Memorial Foundation
[10339]
113 N Foushee St.
Richmond, VA 23220
PH: (804)231-1827
Thomas, G. William, Jr., President

Museum of the Confederacy [9495]
1201 E Clay St.
Richmond, VA 23219
PH: (804)649-1861
Toll free: 855-649-1861
Rawls, Mr. S. Waite, III, CEO

National Alliance of State Pharmacy
Associations [16672]
2530 Professional Rd., Ste. 202
Richmond, VA 23235
PH: (804)285-4431
Fax: (804)612-6555
Snead, Rebecca P., CEO, Exec. VP

National Anemia Action Council
[15240]
2209 Dickens Rd.
Richmond, VA 23230
PH: (804)565-6399
Fax: (804)282-0090

National Association of Appellate
Court Attorneys [5024]
c/o Mary Ellen Donaghy, Executive
Director
University of Richmond Law School
Richmond, VA 23173
PH: (804)289-8204
Fax: (804)289-8992
Tucker, John, Treasurer

National Association for Ethnic Stud-
ies [9291]
Founders Hall
Virginia Commonwealth University
827 W Franklin St., 3rd Fl.
Richmond, VA 23284
PH: (804)828-2706
    (804)828-8051
Perry, Ravi K., President, Comm.
Chm.

National Bridal Service [447]
2225 Grove Ave.
Richmond, VA 23220
PH: (804)342-0055
Fax: (804)342-6062
Wright, Gary, CEO

National Coalition for Aviation and
Space Education [7527]
c/o Virginia Dept. of Aviation
5702 Gulfstream Rd.
Richmond, VA 23250-2422
PH: (505)362-8232
Wilson, Betty P., Secretary

National Council of State Agencies
for the Blind, Inc. [17732]
397 Azalea Ave.
Richmond, VA 23227
PH: (804)371-3145
Fax: (804)371-3157
Hopkins, Raymond E., President

National Forum of Greek Orthodox
Church Musicians [20494]
9030 Kings Crown Rd.
Richmond, VA 23236-1302
PH: (804)745-8606
Fax: (804)745-9726
Keritsis, Maria, Chairman

Nims Family Association [20908]
c/o Jane D. Nimbs, Treasurer
1103 Peachtree Blvd.

Richmond, VA 23226-1137
Wiscombe, Allan, Director

Organ Historical Society [9992]
PO Box 26811
Richmond, VA 23261
PH: (804)353-9226
Fax: (804)353-9266
Marks, Christopher, Chmn. of the
Bd.

Pediatric Cardiac Intensive Care
Society [16612]
2209 Dickens Rd.
Richmond, VA 23230-2005
PH: (804)565-6398
Fax: (804)282-0090
Chang, Anthony C., Group VP, Intl.

Poe Foundation [9090]
c/o Poe Museum
1914-16 E Main St.
Richmond, VA 23223
PH: (804)648-5523
Inge, M. Thomas, VP

Preservation Virginia [9428]
204 W Franklin St.
Richmond, VA 23220-5012
PH: (804)648-1889
Fax: (804)775-0802
Kostelny, Elizabeth, Exec. Dir.

Resort Hotel Association [1677]
2100 E Cary St., Ste. 3
Richmond, VA 23223
PH: (804)525-2020
Fax: (804)525-2021
Riehle, Gregory, President, CEO

Rural Education and Community
Health for Ghana [11932]
PO Box 889
Richmond, VA 23218
PH: (804)925-8548
Powers, Jeremy, Founder

Sigma Phi Epsilon [23930]
310 S Blvd.
Richmond, VA 23220
PH: (804)353-1901
Toll free: 800-767-1901
Fax: (804)359-8160
Warren, Brian, Exec. Dir.

Society for the Advancement of
Blood Management [15245]
2209 Dickens Rd.
Richmond, VA 23230-2005
PH: (804)565-6399
Fax: (804)282-0090
Bracey, Arthur W., MD, President

Society for Animation Studies [7493]
c/o Pamela Turner, Chairperson
2615 Fendall Ave.
Richmond, VA 23222
PH: (804)937-2942
Turner, Pamela, Chairperson

Society for Neuroscience in
Anesthesiology and Critical Care
[16069]
2209 Dickens Rd.
Richmond, VA 23230-2005
PH: (804)565-6360
Fax: (804)282-0090
Avitsian, Rafi, MD, Secretary,
Treasurer

Society for Pediatric Anesthesia
[13712]
2209 Dickens Rd.
Richmond, VA 23230-2005
PH: (804)282-9780
Fax: (804)282-0090
Martin, Lynn D., MD, Comm. Chm.

Society for Pediatric Sedation
[13713]
2209 Dickens Rd.
Richmond, VA 23230-2005

PH: (804)565-6354
Fax: (804)282-0090
Connors, J. Michael, MD, President

Society of Veterinary Behavior
Technicians [17662]
c/o Donna Dyer
7400 Kirkwall Dr.
Richmond, VA 23235
Yuschak, Sherrie, RVT, Director

Uniformed Services Academy of
Family Physicians [15843]
1503 Santa Rosa Rd., Ste. 207
Richmond, VA 23229
PH: (804)968-4436
Fax: (804)968-4418
Flynn, Mark, Contact

United Daughters of the
Confederacy [20747]
328 N Blvd.
Richmond, VA 23220-4009
PH: (804)355-1636
Fax: (804)353-1396
Likins, Jamesene E., President

United Network for Organ Sharing
[17521]
700 N 4th St.
Richmond, VA 23219
PH: (804)782-4800
    (804)782-4862
Toll free: 888-894-6361
Fax: (804)782-4817
Shepard, Brian, CEO

Vegan Action [10294]
PO Box 7313
Richmond, VA 23221-0313
PH: (804)502-8341
Fax: (804)254-8346
Vandenberg, Kristine, Exec. Dir.

Weddings Beautiful Worldwide [449]
2225 Grove Ave.
Richmond, VA 23220
PH: (804)342-6061
Fax: (804)342-6062
Mahoney, Pat, Director

Zellweger Baby Support Network
[14870]
c/o Pam Freeth, Pres.
9310 Groundhog Dr.
Richmond, VA 23235
PH: (919)741-9778
Freeth, Pam, President

American Charities for Reasonable
Fundraising Regulation [11854]
333 Church Ave. SW
Roanoke, VA 24016
PH: (301)675-7741
Fax: (831)603-3462
Peters, Mr. Geoffrey, Esq., Gen.
Counsel, Secretary

American Hemerocallis Society
[22073]
c/o Julie Covington, President
4909 Labradore Dr.
Roanoke, VA 24012
PH: (540)977-1704
Covington, Julie, President

Association of United States Night
Vision Manufacturers [2376]
7040 Highfields Farm Dr.
Roanoke, VA 24018
PH: (540)774-1783
Fax: (540)774-1802
Toohig, Michael, President

Godparents for Tanzania [11004]
PO Box 20221
Roanoke, VA 24018
Westermann, Dwayne, President

Life Sciences Trainers & Educators
Network [3016]
4423 Pheasant Ridge Rd., Ste. 100
Roanoke, VA 24014-5274
PH: (540)725-3859
Fax: (540)989-7482
Lannone, Susan, VP

National Association of Air Medical
Communication Specialists [13510]
2311 Yellow Mountain Rd.
Roanoke, VA 24014
PH: (262)409-8884
Toll free: 877-396-2227
Fax: (866)827-2296
Ross, David, Bd. Member

National Chrysanthemum Society
[22110]
c/o Anette M. Lloyd, Secretary
PO Box 20456
Roanoke, VA 24018-0046
PH: (516)263-2717
Capobianco, John, President

National Healthcare Collectors As-
sociation [1609]
1502 Williamson Rd. NE, Ste. 100
Roanoke, VA 24012
Toll free: 888-698-8022
Fax: (540)344-1211

Respiratory Nursing Society [16182]
c/o Gina Martin
1018 Jamison Ave. SE
Roanoke, VA 24013
Fax: (540)981-8643
Moore, Wendy, President

National Electrical Manufacturers
Association [1029]
1300 N 17th St., Ste. 1752
Rosslyn, VA 22209
PH: (703)841-3200
    (703)841-3272
Gaddis, Evan R., President, CEO

Council of Professional Geropsychol-
ogy Training Programs [14890]
c/o Mary Lindsey Jacobs, Secretary
Salem VA Medical Ctr.
1970 Roanoke Blvd., Bldg. 9
Salem, VA 24153
Allen, Rebecca S., Chairman

US China Peoples Friendship As-
sociation [17850]
105 Treva Rd.
Sandston, VA 23150
PH: (804)737-2704
    (561)747-9487
Greer, Diana, President

Dogs Deserve Better [11691]
1915 Moonlight Rd.
Smithfield, VA 23430
PH: (757)357-9292
Thayne, Tamira Ci, Founder

1st Fighter Wing Association [21205]
c/o Steve Grass, Secretary/
Treasurer
11512 Henegan Pl.
Spotsylvania, VA 22551
Marty, Pete, President

North American Torquay Society
[21703]
13607 Maxson Ct.
Spotsylvania, VA 22553
O'Connor, Jen, VP

Rock For Life [19071]
9900 Courthouse Rd.
Spotsylvania, VA 22553
PH: (540)834-4600
Whittington, Erik, Exec. Dir.

Students for Life of America [12790]
9900 Courthouse Rd.
Spotsylvania, VA 22553

PH: (540)834-4600
Fax: (866)582-6420
Hawkins, Ms. Kristan, President

World Organization of Dredging Associations [2260]
c/o Thomas M. Verna, Executive Director
PO Box 2035
Spotsylvania, VA 22553
PH: (619)839-9474
Mohan, Ram, President, Chairman

American Astronautical Society [5856]
6352 Rolling Mill Pl., Ste. 102
Springfield, VA 22152-2370
PH: (703)866-0020
Fax: (703)866-3526
Slazer, Frank A., Director

American Board of Opticianry [16411]
6506 Loisdale Rd., Ste. 330
Springfield, VA 22150
PH: (703)719-5800
Toll free: 800-296-1379
Fax: (703)719-9144

Azalea Society of America [22086]
c/o Leslie Nanney, Secretary
8646 Tuttle Rd.
Springfield, VA 22152-2243
Beck, Paul, Treasurer

Center on National Labor Policy [18616]
5211 Port Royal Rd., Ste. 610
Springfield, VA 22151-2100
PH: (703)321-9180

Christian Legal Society [5073]
8001 Braddock Rd., Ste. 302
Springfield, VA 22151-2110
PH: (703)642-1070
     (312)853-8709
Fax: (703)642-1075
Nammo, David, Exec. Dir., CEO

Concerned Educators Against Forced Unionism [18608]
c/o Cathy Jones, Director
8001 Braddock Rd.
Springfield, VA 22160
PH: (703)321-8519
Toll free: 800-336-3600
Fax: (703)321-9319
Jones, Cathy, Director

English First [9282]
8001 Forbes Pl., Ste. 102
Springfield, VA 22151
McGlynn, Frank, Exec. Dir.

Gun Owners of America [5217]
8001 Forbes Pl., Ste. 102
Springfield, VA 22151
PH: (703)321-8585
Fax: (703)321-8408
Pratt, Larry, Exec. Dir.

Gun Owners Foundation [5218]
8001 Forbes Pl., Ste. 102
Springfield, VA 22151
PH: (703)321-8585
Fax: (703)321-8408
McGlynn, Frank, Chief Adm. Ofc.

Heroes of '76 [19560]
National Sojourners, Inc.
7942R Cluny Ct.
Springfield, VA 22153-2810
PH: (703)765-5000
Fax: (703)765-8390
Vanden Berghe, 1st Lt. Raymond J, Sr., Cmdr.

Mine Warfare Association [19092]
6551 Loisdale Ct., Ste. 222
Springfield, VA 22150-1808

PH: (703)960-6804
Fax: (703)960-6807
Holt, David, President

National Association for Uniformed Services [5606]
5535 Hempstead Way
Springfield, VA 22151
Toll free: 800-842-3451
Wilkerson, Thomas L., President, CEO

National Congress of Vietnamese Americans [19685]
6433 Northanna Dr.
Springfield, VA 22150
PH: (703)971-9178
Toll free: 877-592-4140
Fax: (703)719-5764

National Contact Lens Examiners [16431]
6506 Loisdale Rd., Ste. 330
Springfield, VA 22150
PH: (703)719-5800
Toll free: 800-296-1379
Fax: (703)719-9144

National Pro-Life Alliance [19063]
5211 Port Royal Rd., Ste. 500
Springfield, VA 22151
PH: (703)321-9200
Fox, Martin E., President

National Right to Work Committee [18617]
8001 Braddock Rd., Ste. 500
Springfield, VA 22160
Toll free: 800-325-7892
Fax: (703)321-7342

National Right to Work Legal Defense and Education Foundation [18618]
8001 Braddock Rd.
Springfield, VA 22160
PH: (703)321-8510
Toll free: 800-336-3600
Fax: (703)321-9613
Mix, Mark A., President

National Sojourners Inc. [19565]
7942R Cluny Ct.
Springfield, VA 22153-2810
PH: (703)765-5000
Fax: (703)765-8390
Higdon, Capt. James N, President

Naval Order of the United States [21057]
PO Box 2142
Springfield, VA 22152-0142
PH: (703)323-0929
Morrison, Capt. Vance H., Cmdr.

Pharmacy Quality Alliance [16682]
6213 Old Keene Mill Ct.
Springfield, VA 22152
PH: (703)690-1987
Fax: (703)842-8150
Cranston, Laura, Exec. Dir.

Protestant Church-Owned Publishers Association [2810]
6631 Westbury Oaks Ct.
Springfield, VA 22152
PH: (703)220-5989
Mulder, Gary, Director

Retired Military Police Officers Association [21050]
PO Box 5477
Springfield, VA 22150
Fax: (703)533-7207
Mullins, Mack H., Exec. Dir.

Scruggs Family Association [20924]
c/o Mary Beth Scruggs Rephlo, Secretary-Treasurer

6130 Sherborn Ln.
Springfield, VA 22152
PH: (703)451-9473
Kelly, Bill, President

Senior Conformation Judges Association [21960]
c/o Lt. Col. Wallace H. Pede, Chief Executive Officer
7200 Tanager St.
Springfield, VA 22150
PH: (703)451-5656
Fax: (703)451-5979
Pede, Lt. Col. Wallace H., CEO

Society for Imaging Science and Technology [7294]
7003 Kilworth Ln.
Springfield, VA 22151
PH: (703)642-9090
Fax: (703)642-9094
Smith, Donna, Exec. Asst.

Society of Military Widows [21043]
5535 Hempstead Way
Springfield, VA 22151-4010
Toll free: 800-842-3451
Walker, Patricia, President

United States Coast Guard Chief Petty Officers Association [20749]
5520 Hempstead Way, Ste. G
Springfield, VA 22151
Fax: (703)941-0397
Lorigan, Kim, President

Vietnamese American Armed Forces Association [4977]
6200 Rolling Rd.
Springfield, VA 22152
PH: (714)386-9896
Nguyen, Ross, Chairman, Exec. Dir.

Washington Capitals Fan Club [24080]
PO Box 2802
Springfield, VA 22152
Rogers, Nancy, President

American Life League [12760]
PO Box 1350
Stafford, VA 22555
PH: (540)659-4171
Fax: (540)659-2586
Brown, Judie, President

Auto Glass Safety Council [1502]
20 PGA Dr., Ste. 201
Stafford, VA 22554
PH: (540)720-7484
Fax: (540)720-5687
Levy, Debra, President

A Child For All, Inc. [10897]
21 Arbor Ln.
Stafford, VA 22554
PH: (540)659-6497
Sidibe, Kadiatou Fatima, CEO, Founder

Landstuhl Hospital Care Project [12284]
29 Greenleaf Ter.
Stafford, VA 22556
Grimord, Karen, Founder, President

STOPP International [19072]
c/o American Life League
PO Box 1350
Stafford, VA 22555-1350
PH: (540)659-4171
Fax: (540)659-2586
Diller, Rita, Director

American College of Bankruptcy [5084]
PO Box 249
Stanardsville, VA 22973

PH: (434)939-6004
Fax: (434)939-6030
Bedker, Shari, Exec. Dir.

Association of College Administration Professionals [7421]
PO Box 1389
Staunton, VA 24402
PH: (540)885-1873
Fax: (540)885-6133

Organization Chemen Lavi [8252]
PO Box 1952
Staunton, VA 24402
PH: (540)480-4852
     (540)607-1212
Eugene, Patrick, Founder

Willys-Overland-Knight Registry [21521]
c/o Duanne Perrin
4177 Spring Hill Rd.
Staunton, VA 24401-6320
Young, Mark, President

Woodrow Wilson Presidential Library and Museum [10355]
20 N Coalter St.
Staunton, VA 24401
PH: (540)885-0897
Shortt, Elizabeth, Arch.

Welsh Pony & Cob Society of America [4426]
720 Green St.
Stephens City, VA 22655
PH: (540)868-7669
Benedict, Dr. Mary I., Director

American Medical Student Association [8303]
45610 Woodland Rd., Ste. 300
Sterling, VA 20166
PH: (703)620-6600
Toll free: 800-767-2266
Fax: (703)620-6445
Caulfield, Joshua, Exec. Dir.

Christian Connections for International Health [14932]
1329 Shepard Dr., Ste. 6
Sterling, VA 20164
PH: (703)444-8250
Grigsby, Garrett, Exec. Dir.

Foster Care to Success [11230]
21351 Gentry Dr., Ste. 130
Sterling, VA 20166
PH: (571)203-0270
Fax: (571)203-0273
McCaffrey, Eileen, Exec. Dir.

Hockey North America [22909]
PO Box 78
Sterling, VA 20167-0078
PH: (703)430-8100
Fax: (703)421-9205

INMED Partnerships for Children [15478]
21630 Ridgetop Cir., Ste. 130
Sterling, VA 20166-6564
PH: (703)729-4951
Fax: (703)858-7253
Pfeiffer, Linda, PhD, CEO, President

International Cemetery, Cremation and Funeral Association [2406]
107 Carpenter Dr., Ste. 100
Sterling, VA 20164
PH: (703)391-8400
Toll free: 800-645-7700
Fax: (703)391-8416
Lohman, Nancy R.

International Society of Air Safety Investigators [12824]
c/o Ann Schull, International Office Manager

107 E Holly Ave., Ste. 11
Sterling, VA 20164
PH: (703)430-9668
Fax: (703)430-4970
Del Gandio, Frank S., President

Jewish Funeral Directors of America
[2409]
107 Carpenter Dr., Ste. 100
Sterling, VA 20164
Toll free: 800-645-7700
Fax: (703)391-8416
Botbol, Mindy Moline, President

National Association of Urban
Hospitals **[15334]**
21351 Gentry Dr., Ste. 210
Sterling, VA 20166
PH: (703)444-0989
Fax: (703)444-3029
Kugler, Ellen, Esq., Exec. Dir.

National Vaccine Information Center
[14207]
21525 Ridgetop Cir., Ste. 100
Sterling, VA 20166
PH: (703)938-0342
Fax: (571)313-1268
Wrangham, Theresa, Exec. Dir.

Nurses Organization of Veterans Af-
fairs **[16171]**
47595 Watkins Island Sq.
Sterling, VA 20165
PH: (703)444-5587
Fax: (703)444-5597
Dove, Susan H., Exec. Dir.

PRISMS: Parents and Researchers
Interested In Smith-Magenis
Syndrome **[14853]**
21800 Town Center Plz., Ste. No.
266A-633
Sterling, VA 20164
PH: (972)231-0035
Fax: (972)499-1832
Beall, Randy, Bd. Member

National Right to Read Foundation
[8487]
PO Box 560
Strasburg, VA 22657
PH: (913)788-6773
Sweet, Mr. Robert, Jr., President,
Founder

Robert E. Lee Memorial Association
[10348]
Stratford Hall Plantation
483 Great House Rd.
Stratford, VA 22558-0001
PH: (804)493-8038
Refo, Carter B., Exec. Dir.

North American Truffle Growers' Association **[4485]**
c/o Koru Farm/CMTGMT Farm
1541 Little Russell Creek Rd.
Stuart, VA 24171-2553
Cromer, Andy, President

World Flute Society **[10024]**
3351 Mintonville Point Dr.
Suffolk, VA 23435
PH: (757)651-8328
Fax: (757)538-2937
Joyce-Grendahl, Dr. Kathleen, Exec.
Producer

Association for Skilled and Technical
Sciences **[8015]**
c/o Ed Sullivan, Executive Director
176 Rappahannock Beach Dr.
Tappahannock, VA 22560
Shockney, Bethany, Secretary

American Bird Conservancy **[4781]**
4249 Loudoun Ave.
The Plains, VA 20198-2237

PH: (540)253-5780
Toll free: 888-247-3624
Fax: (540)253-5782
Morrison, Merrie, VP of Operations

Bird Conservation Alliance **[3658]**
PO Box 249
The Plains, VA 20198-0249
PH: (202)234-7181
Holmer, Steve, Director

International Society of Equine
Locomotor Pathology **[16586]**
2716 Landmark School Rd.
The Plains, VA 20198
Toll free: 800-363-2034
Denoix, Jean-Marie, President

Technology Without Borders **[7298]**
PO Box 445
The Plains, VA 20198-0445
PH: (703)220-7327

Marine Toys for Tots Foundation
[11251]
The Cooper Ctr.
18251 Quantico Gateway Dr.
Triangle, VA 22172
Fax: (703)649-2054
Shea, Robert M., Chmn. of the Bd.

United Mine Workers of America
[23484]
18354 Quantico Gateway Dr., Ste.
200
Triangle, VA 22172
PH: (703)291-2400
Roberts, Cecil E., President

National Automobile Dealers As-
sociation **[347]**
8400 Westpark Dr.
Tysons, VA 22102
PH: (703)821-7000
Toll free: 800-252-6232
Fax: (703)821-7234
Welch, Peter, President

System Safety Society **[3006]**
PO Box 70
Unionville, VA 22567-0070
PH: (540)854-8630
Schmedake, Robert, Exec. VP

Allergy and Asthma Network Moth-
ers of Asthmatics **[17132]**
8229 Boone Blvd., Ste. 260
Vienna, VA 22182
Toll free: 800-878-4403
Fax: (703)288-5271

The Alliance for Safe Children
[14166]
213 Adahi Rd.
Vienna, VA 22180-5937
PH: (703)652-3873
Peterson, Douglas B., Chairman,
Founder

American Boiler Manufacturers As-
sociation **[1705]**
8221 Old Courthouse Rd., Ste. 380
Vienna, VA 22182
PH: (703)356-7172
Giaier, Thomas, Secretary, Treasurer

The American Cause **[18293]**
PO Box 7
Vienna, VA 22183
PH: (703)255-9224
Fax: (703)255-2219
Buchanan, Patrick J., Chairman

American Eskimo Dog Club of
America **[21809]**
c/o Cathy Hammer, Membership
Chairman
423 Center St. N

Vienna, VA 22180
PH: (703)999-7300
Hammer, Cathy, Chairperson

Americans Against Union Control of
Government **[18615]**
Public Service Research Council
320D Maple Ave. E
Vienna, VA 22180-4742
PH: (703)242-3575
Fax: (703)242-3579
Denholm, David Y., President

Association of American Rhodes
Scholars **[19633]**
8229 Boone Blvd., Ste. 240
Vienna, VA 22182-2623
PH: (703)821-7377
Toll free: 866-746-0283
Fax: (703)821-2770
Crown, Steven A., President

Association of Organ Procurement
Organizations **[14616]**
8500 Leesburg Pke., Ste. 300
Vienna, VA 22182-2409
PH: (703)556-4242
Fax: (703)556-4852
Eidbo, Elling, CEO

The Bolling Family Association
[20785]
PO Box 591
Vienna, VA 22183-0591
Bentley, Woody, President

Brain Injury Association of America
[14909]
1608 Spring Hill Rd., Ste. 110
Vienna, VA 22182
PH: (703)761-0750
Toll free: 800-444-6443
Fax: (703)761-0755
Connors, Susan H., President, CEO

Central Station Alarm Association
[2993]
8150 Leesburg Pke., Ste. 700
Vienna, VA 22182-2721
PH: (703)242-4670
McMahon, Madeline Fullerton, Sr.
VP of Fin.

Chris4Life Colon Cancer Foundation
[13944]
8330 Boone Blvd., Ste. 450
Vienna, VA 22182
Toll free: 855-610-1733
Sapienza, Michael, Exec. Dir.

Community Coalition for Haiti
[11920]
PO Box 1222
Vienna, VA 22183
PH: (703)880-4160
Singleton, Knox, President

Doane Family Association of
America **[20854]**
c/o Jane MacDuff, Membeship Chair
2618 Occidental Dr.
Vienna, VA 22180
Doane, Kenneth M., President

Eco Energy Finance **[6473]**
129 Pleasant St., NW
Vienna, VA 22180-4419
PH: (202)262-0412
Khan, Ms. Shazia, Esq., Exec. Dir.

International Association for K-12
Online Learning **[7486]**
1934 Old Gallows Rd., Ste. 350
Vienna, VA 22182-4040
PH: (703)752-6216
Toll free: 888-956-2265
Fax: (703)752-6201
Patrick, Susan, President

International Council for the Life Sci-
ences **[7134]**
1713 Gosnell Rd., Ste. 203
Vienna, VA 22182
PH: (202)659-8058
Fax: (202)659-8074
Taylor, Terence, Chairman, President

International Neuro-Linguistic
Programming Trainers Association
[16980]
1201 Delta Glen Ct.
Vienna, VA 22182
Woodsmall, Wyatt L., PhD, Director,
Founder

Jane Goodall Institute **[4835]**
1595 Spring Hill Rd., Ste. 550
Vienna, VA 22182
PH: (703)682-9220
Fax: (703)682-9312
Goodall, Jane, Founder

Korean-American Scientists and
Engineers Association **[6568]**
1952 Gallows Rd., Ste. 300
Vienna, VA 22182
PH: (703)748-1221
Fax: (703)748-1331
Yoon, Euna, Mgr. of Admin.

La Vallee Alliance **[11207]**
PO Box 75
Vienna, VA 22183
Bazzarone, Anne, Founder

Manufacturers Standardization
Society **[1746]**
127 Park St. NE
Vienna, VA 22180-4602
PH: (703)281-6613
Fax: (703)281-6671
O'Neill, Robert, Exec. Dir.

Mother Health International **[15608]**
8004 Trevor Pl.
Vienna, VA 22182
Maurer, Heather L., Founder

National Academy of Elder Law At-
torneys **[5546]**
1577 Spring Hill Rd., Ste. 310
Vienna, VA 22182
PH: (703)942-5711
Fax: (703)563-9504
Wacht, Peter G., CAE, Exec. Dir.

National Association for Medical
Direction of Respiratory Care
[15587]
8618 Westwood Center Dr., Ste. 210
Vienna, VA 22182-2222
PH: (703)752-4359
Fax: (703)752-4360
Porte, Phillip, Exec. Dir.

National Blood Clot Alliance **[14134]**
8321 Old Courthouse Rd., Ste. 255
Vienna, VA 22182
PH: (703)935-8845
Toll free: 877-4NO-CLOT
Smith, Kathy, President

National Glass Association **[1507]**
1945 Old Gallows Rd., Ste. 750
Vienna, VA 22182
PH: (703)442-4890
Toll free: 866-342-5642
Fax: (703)442-0630
Albert, Michael, Chairman

National Woodland Owners Associa-
tion **[4213]**
374 Maple Ave. E, Ste. 310
Vienna, VA 22182
PH: (703)255-2700
Fax: (703)281-9200
Argow, Dr. Keith A., CEO, President

Network of Employers for Traffic
  Safety [19081]
344 Maple Ave. W, No. 357
Vienna, VA 22180
PH: (703)755-5350
Hanley, Jack, Exec. Dir.

Public Service Research Council
  [18613]
320-D Maple Ave. E
Vienna, VA 22180-4742
PH: (703)242-3575
Fax: (703)242-3579
Denholm, David Y., President

Small Business and Entrepreneur-
  ship Council [3126]
301 Maple Ave. W, Ste. 690
Vienna, VA 22180-4320
PH: (703)242-5840
Kerrigan, Karen, CEO, President

Society of Cardiovascular Computed
  Tomography [17064]
415 Church St. NE, Ste. 204
Vienna, VA 22180-4751
PH: (703)766-1706
Toll free: 800-876-4195
Fax: (888)849-1542
Min, James K., MD, President

SourceAmerica [11639]
8401 Old Courthouse Rd., Ste. 200
Vienna, VA 22182-3820
PH: (571)226-4660
Toll free: 800-411-8424
Fax: (703)849-8916
Beaman, Rick, Chairman

U.S. Apple Association [4255]
8233 Old Courthouse Rd., Ste. 200
Vienna, VA 22182
PH: (703)442-8850
Fax: (703)790-0845
Kurrle, Diane, Sr. VP

U.S.-Saudi Arabian Business Council
  [2004]
8081 Wolftrap Rd., Ste. 300
Vienna, VA 22182
PH: (703)962-9300
Toll free: 888-638-1212
Fax: (703)204-0332
Burton, Edward, CEO, President

Window & Door Dealers Alliance
  [600]
1945 Old Gallows Rd., Ste. 750
Vienna, VA 22182
Toll free: 866-342-5642
Fax: (703)442-0630
Albert, Michael, Chairman

Wolf Trap Foundation for the
  Performing Arts [9007]
1645 Trap Rd.
Vienna, VA 22182
PH: (703)255-1900
Toll free: 877-WOLFTRAP
Obama, Michelle, Chairman

Antique Outboard Motor Club, Inc.
  [22599]
PO Box 251
Vinton, VA 24179

Air Compassion for Veterans [21102]
4620 Haygood Rd., Ste. 1
Virginia Beach, VA 23455
Hoffmann, Rev. John W., Chairman

Al-Anon Family Group [13118]
1600 Corporate Landing Pky.
Virginia Beach, VA 23454-5617
PH: (757)563-1600
Fax: (757)563-1656

Alateen [13119]
1600 Corporate Landing Pky.
Virginia Beach, VA 23454-5617

PH: (757)563-1600
Fax: (757)563-1655

American Guild for Infant Survival
  [17330]
301 Eastwood Cir.
Virginia Beach, VA 23454
PH: (757)463-3845
Hessek, Scott, President

Association for Research and
  Enlightenment [6984]
215 67th St.
Virginia Beach, VA 23451
PH: (757)428-3588
Toll free: 800-333-4499
Hoff, Laura, Dir. of Lib. Svcs.

Dalit Freedom Network [18391]
PO Box 3459
Virginia Beach, VA 23454
PH: (202)233-9110
Fax: (202)280-1340
D'Souza, Dr. Joseph, President

Great War Association [9802]
c/o Chris Garcia, Treasurer
418 Chinaberry Ct.
Virginia Beach, VA 23454-3331
PH: (757)631-0661
Werner, Bret, VP

International 190SL Group [21399]
c/o Jim Villers, President
3133 Inlet Rd.
Virginia Beach, VA 23454
PH: (757)481-6398
Villers, Jim, President

Knowledge Management Profes-
  sional Society [1802]
PO Box 68549
Virginia Beach, VA 23471
PH: (206)395-2556
Kirsch, Dr. Dan, CKM, MKMP, CEO,
  President

Man Will Never Fly Memorial Society
  Internationale [22163]
103 Caribbean Ave.
Virginia Beach, VA 23451-4716

National Air Filtration Association
  [1632]
PO Box 68639
Virginia Beach, VA 23471
PH: (757)313-7400
Fax: (757)313-7401
Justice, Tom, Comm. Chm.

National Certification Council for
  Activity Professionals [1591]
PO Box 62589
Virginia Beach, VA 23466
PH: (757)552-0653
Fax: (757)552-0491
Bradshaw, Cindy, MS, ACC, Exec.
  Dir.

National Legal Foundation [5723]
PO Box 64427
Virginia Beach, VA 23467-4427
PH: (757)463-6133
Fax: (757)463-6055
Fitschen, Steven W., President

Operation Blessing International
  [20003]
977 Centerville Tpke.
Virginia Beach, VA 23463-1001
PH: (757)226-3401
    (757)226-3440
Toll free: 800-730-2537
Fax: (757)226-3657
Horan, Bill, COO, President

Operation Smile [15159]
3641 Faculty Blvd.
Virginia Beach, VA 23453

PH: (757)321-7645
Toll free: 888-677-6453
Magee, Kathleen S., M.S.W., M.Ed.,
  President, Founder

United States Indoor Sports Associa-
  tion [23194]
1340 N Great Neck Rd., Ste. 1272-
142
Virginia Beach, VA 23454-2268
Fax: (509)357-7096
Shapero, Donald L., Founder,
  President

Women of Hope Project [13405]
4876-118 Princess Anne Rd., No.
203
Virginia Beach, VA 23462
Beamon, Betsy, Founder

Air Serv International [12610]
410 Rosedale Ct., Ste. 190
Warrenton, VA 20186
PH: (540)428-2323
Fax: (540)428-2326
Abbott, Mark, Chairman

American Children of SCORE [9853]
PO Box 3423
Warrenton, VA 20188
PH: (540)428-2313
Krumich, Mr. John, Art Dir.

Americans for Constitutional Liberty
  [18020]
92 Main St., Ste. 202-8
Warrenton, VA 20186
PH: (540)219-4536
Phillips, Howard, Founder

Association of Military Banks of
  America [383]
PO Box 3335
Warrenton, VA 20188-1935
PH: (540)347-3305
Fax: (540)347-5995
Jacobs, Christiane, Exec. Asst.

Conservative Caucus Research
  Analysis and Education Foundation
  [18022]
92 Main St., Ste. 202-8
Warrenton, VA 20186
PH: (703)281-6782
Phillips, Howard, President

Council of Industrial Boiler Owners
  [1724]
6801 Kennedy Rd., Ste. 102
Warrenton, VA 20187
PH: (540)349-9043
Fax: (540)349-9850
Bessette, Robert D., President

Educational Book and Media As-
  sociation [2782]
37 Main St., Ste. 203
Warrenton, VA 20186
PH: (540)318-7770
Fax: (202)962-3939
Allen, Jennifer, Bd. Member

Families Empowered and Supporting
  Treatment of Eating Disorders
  [14640]
PO Box 331
Warrenton, VA 20188
PH: (540)227-8518
Krevans, Sarah, Chmn. of the Bd.

International Massage Association
  [15560]
PO Box 421
Warrenton, VA 20188-0421
Toll free: 800-776-6268
Fax: (540)351-0815

National Association of Biology
  Teachers [8650]
PO Box 3363
Warrenton, VA 20188

PH: (703)264-9696
Toll free: 888-501-NABT
Fax: (202)962-3939
Reeves-Pepin, Jaclyn, Exec. Dir.

Northern Haiti Hope Foundation
  [11414]
332 W Lee Hwy., Ste. 119
Warrenton, VA 20186
Lavin, James, Jr., Chairman

Rainforest Trust [4098]
7078 Airlie Rd.
Warrenton, VA 20187
Toll free: 800-456-4930
Swift, Byron, Founder

Society for Applied Learning
  Technology [8036]
50 Culpeper St.
Warrenton, VA 20186
PH: (540)347-0055
Fax: (540)349-3169
Morgan, Thomas, Systems Mgr.

Share and Care Cockayne
  Syndrome Network [14856]
PO Box 282
Waterford, VA 20197-0282
PH: (703)727-0404
Clark, Jackie, Exec. Dir., President

International Brotherhood of DuPont
  Workers [23404]
PO Box 10
Waynesboro, VA 22980
Fax: (540)337-5442
Flickinger, Jim, President

American Ceramic Circle [21576]
PO Box 224
Williamsburg, VA 23187
Forschler-Tarrasch, Anne, President

American Judges Association [5375]
300 Newport Ave.
Williamsburg, VA 23185-4147
PH: (757)259-1841
Fax: (757)259-1520
Burke, Kevin S., Treasurer

The Coastal Society [6939]
55 Winster Fax
Williamsburg, VA 23185
PH: (757)565-0999
Fax: (757)565-0922
Tucker, Judy, CAE, Exec. Dir.

Conference of Chief Justices [5379]
c/o Association and Conference
  Services
300 Newport Ave.
Williamsburg, VA 23185-4147
PH: (757)259-1841
Fax: (757)259-1520
Gilbertson, David, President

Council of Colleges of Arts and Sci-
  ences [7511]
c/o College of William & Mary
PO Box 8795
Williamsburg, VA 23187-8795
PH: (757)221-1784
Fax: (757)221-1776
McCartan, Dr. Anne-Marie, Exec. Dir.

General Society, Sons of the
  Revolution [20692]
412 W Francis St.
Williamsburg, VA 23185
PH: (757)345-0757
Toll free: 800-593-1776
Fax: (757)345-0780
Simpson, Laurence, DDS, Gen. Sec.

International Council of Academies
  of Engineering and Technological
  Sciences [8547]
3004 The Mall
Williamsburg, VA 23185

PH: (703)527-5782
Salmon, William C., PE, Secretary, Treasurer

Mid Atlantic Fiber Association [246]
c/o David Banks, Membership Chairman
215 Charter House Ln.
Williamsburg, VA 23188-7808
PH: (757)258-8632
Wall, Lori, Corr. Sec.

National Association for Court Management [5118]
National Center for State Courts
300 Newport Ave.
Williamsburg, VA 23185-4147
PH: (757)259-1841
Toll free: 800-616-6165
Fax: (757)259-1520
Burke, Kevin, Director

National Center for State Courts [5392]
300 Newport Ave.
Williamsburg, VA 23185
PH: (757)259-1525
Toll free: 800-616-6164
Clarke, Thomas M., VP of Res.

National Conference of Appellate Court Clerks [5120]
Association Services National Center for State Courts
300 Newport Ave.
Williamsburg, VA 23185
PH: (757)259-1841
May, Marilyn, Mem.

Native American Television [9286]
PO Box 1754
Williamsburg, VA 23187
PH: (703)554-2815

Omohundro Institute of Early American History and Culture [9501]
PO Box 8781
Williamsburg, VA 23187-8781
PH: (757)221-1114
Fax: (757)221-1047
Holl, Shawn A., Dir. of Dev.

American History Forum | Civil War Education Association [7977]
PO Box 78
Winchester, VA 22604
PH: (540)678-8598
Toll free: 800-298-1861
Fax: (540)667-2339
Maher, Robert, President, Founder

Evangelical Council for Financial Accountability [20138]
440 W Jubal Early Dr., Ste. 100
Winchester, VA 22601-6319
PH: (540)535-0103
Toll free: 800-323-9473
Fax: (540)535-0533
Busby, Mr. Dan, President

North-South Skirmish Association [23140]
480 Chalybeate Springs Rd.
Winchester, VA 22603-2364
PH: (540)888-4334
Spaugy, Phil, Cmdr.

Project Esperanza [11423]
1291 Valley Mill Rd.
Winchester, VA 22602
McHale, Caitlin, Director

Association of Civilian Technicians [23428]
12620 Lake Ridge Dr.
Woodbridge, VA 22192
PH: (703)494-4845
Fax: (703)494-0961
Garnett, Terry W., Officer

Federal Criminal Investigators Association [5148]
5868 Mapledale Plz., Ste. 104
Woodbridge, VA 22193
Toll free: 800-403-3374
Zehme, Richard, President

Federal Physicians Association [16749]
5868 Mapledale Plz., Ste. 104
Woodbridge, VA 22193
Toll free: 877-FED-PHYS
Ribeiro, Brian, President

National Association of Assistant United States Attorneys [5025]
5868 Mapledale Plz., Ste. 104
Woodbridge, VA 22193
Toll free: 800-455-5661
Cook, Steven H., President

Working Pit Bull Terrier Club of America [21994]
c/o Amanda Tsampas, Secretary
5406 Melvin Ct.
Woodbridge, VA 22193

Opening Door [3389]
8049 Ormesby Ln.
Woodford, VA 22580

Armed Forces Stamp Exchange Club [22309]
c/o Hal Stout, Executive Secretary
PO Box 342
Woodstock, VA 22664

Sigma Sigma Sigma [23965]
Mabel Lee Walton House
225 N Muhlenberg St.
Woodstock, VA 22664-1424
PH: (540)459-4212
Fax: (540)459-2361
Schendel, Kaye, President

American Cockatiel Society [21535]
c/o Julie Mitchell, Secretary
100 Bailey Dr.
Yorktown, VA 23692-3052
PH: (757)898-8397
Mitchell, Julie, President, Chmn. of the Bd.

Burroughs Bibliophiles [9045]
318 Patriot Way
Yorktown, VA 23693-4639
Bledig, Joan, Chairperson

Conrad Veidt Society [23990]
407 Kingston Ct.
Yorktown, VA 23693W

WASHINGTON

Grays Harbor Historical Seaport Authority [8265]
500 N Custer St.
Aberdeen, WA 98520
PH: (360)532-8611
Toll free: 800-200-5239
Fax: (360)533-9384
Howden, Tim, Treasurer

End Violence Against Women International [13272]
PO Box 33
Addy, WA 99101-0033
PH: (509)684-9800
Fax: (509)684-9801
Archambault, Joanne, Exec. Dir.

The Emergency Vehicle Owners & Operators Association [21377]
PO Box 1149
Airway Heights, WA 99001-1149
Bujosa, John, Founder, President

North American Bungee Association [23247]
32016 NE Healy Rd.
Amboy, WA 98601

PH: (503)520-0303
Dale, Casey, President, Founder

American Board of Operative Dentistry [14397]
c/o Dr. Jeanette Gorthy, Secretary
PO Box 1276
Anacortes, WA 98221
PH: (310)794-4387
Fax: (310)825-2536
Kolker, Justine L., President

Foundation for Nager and Miller Syndromes [14824]
13210 SE 342nd St.
Auburn, WA 98092
PH: (253)333-1483
Toll free: 800-507-3667
Fax: (253)288-7679
Van Quill, DeDe, Exec. Dir.

Gluten Intolerance Group [16223]
31214 124th Ave. SE
Auburn, WA 98092-3667
PH: (253)833-6655
Fax: (253)833-6675
Kupper, Cynthia, CEO

Maserati Information Exchange [21426]
1620 Industry Dr. SW, No. F
Auburn, WA 98001
PH: (253)833-2598
Fax: (253)735-0946
McMullen, Mr. Kerry, President

Cruising Club of America [22610]
298 Winslow Way W
Bainbridge Island, WA 98110
Hamilton, Paul, Capt.

Earthstewards Network [11996]
PO Box 10697
Bainbridge Island, WA 98110
PH: (206)842-7986
Fax: (206)842-8918
Brusseau, Jerilyn, Bd. Member

Extend the Day [13007]
710 John Nelson Ln. NE
Bainbridge Island, WA 98110
Lonseth, Andrew, Founder

International Molyneux Family Association [20887]
PO Box 10306
Bainbridge Island, WA 98110
Seddon, Brian, President

Positive Futures Network [19265]
284 Madrona Way NE, Ste. 116
Bainbridge Island, WA 98110
PH: (206)842-0216
Toll free: 800-937-4451
Fax: (206)842-5208
Arakaki, Rod, Director

American Land Rights Association [5690]
30218 NE 82nd Ave.
Battle Ground, WA 98604
PH: (360)687-3087
Fax: (360)687-2973
Cushman, Charles, Exec. Dir., Founder

Bible Sabbath Association [20592]
802 NW 21st Ave.
Battle Ground, WA 98604
PH: (253)447-7913
Toll free: 888-687-5191
Ryland, Kenneth, VP

American Canine Foundation [21803]
23969 NE State Rte. 3, Ste. G101
Belfair, WA 98528
PH: (703)451-5656
Fax: (703)451-5979
Tiechner, Renee, President

Center for the Defense of Free Enterprise [18280]
12500 NE 10th Pl.
Bellevue, WA 98005
PH: (425)455-5038
Noon, Marita, Advisor

Citizens Committee for the Right to Keep and Bear Arms [17886]
Liberty Park
12500 NE 10th Pl.
Bellevue, WA 98005
PH: (425)454-4911
Toll free: 800-486-6963
Fax: (425)451-3959
Gottlieb, Alan M., Chairman

CRU Institute [18000]
16301 NE 8th St., Ste. 231
Bellevue, WA 98008
PH: (425)869-4041
Toll free: 800-922-1988
Fax: (425)867-0491
Kaplan, Nancy, MSW, Exec. Dir.

International League of Electrical Associations [1025]
c/o Brook Walker
13563 SE 27th Pl.
Bellevue, WA 98005
Morris, Skip, Exec. Dir.

International.NET Association [6278]
PO Box 6713
Bellevue, WA 98008-0713
Guadagno, Joseph, VP

Jews for the Preservation of Firearms Ownership [17904]
12500 NE 10th Pl.
Bellevue, WA 98005
Toll free: 800-869-1884
Fax: (425)451-3959
Gottlieb, Alan, Director

Kids Without Borders [11061]
PO Box 24
Bellevue, WA 98009-0024
PH: (425)836-5354

National Association of Reversionary Property Owners [18932]
227 Bellevue Way NE, Ste. 719
Bellevue, WA 98004
PH: (425)646-8812
Welsh, Richard, Exec. Dir.

Online Trust Alliance [6327]
11011 NE 9th St., Ste. 420
Bellevue, WA 98004
PH: (425)455-7400
Spiezle, Craig, Exec. Dir., President

Pet Partners [17460]
875 124th Ave. NE, No. 101
Bellevue, WA 98005
PH: (425)679-5500
    (425)679-5530
Williams, David E., Chief Med. Ofc.

Project Kesho [11208]
PO Box 677
Bellevue, WA 98009
PH: (206)501-0758
Barnes, Ian, President

Second Amendment Foundation [17930]
12500 NE 10th Pl.
Bellevue, WA 98005
PH: (425)454-7012
Gottlieb, Alan, Founder

Spiritual Directors International [20554]
PO Box 3584
Bellevue, WA 98009
PH: (425)455-1565
Fax: (425)455-1566
McAlpin, Kathleen, RSM, DMin, Chairman

Stop Exploitation Now! [10799]
15100 SE 38th St., Ste. 101, No.
753
Bellevue, WA 98006
Jester, Molly, Founder, President

African Children's Choir [8774]
PO Box 29690
Bellingham, WA 98228-1690
Toll free: 877-532-8651
Fax: (360)752-2402
Barnett, Ray, Founder, President

Center for Pacific Northwest Studies
[7163]
Western Washington University
808 25th St.
Bellingham, WA 98225-9103
PH: (360)650-7534
Fax: (360)650-3323
Steele, Ruth, Arch.

Childcare Worldwide [10910]
1971 Midway Ln., Ste. N
Bellingham, WA 98226-7682
PH: (360)647-2283
Toll free: 800-553-2328
Fax: (360)647-2392
Lange, Dr. G. Max, Founder,
President, Chmn. of the Bd.

Council for Educational Travel
U.S.A. - Washington State Office
[8716]
110 Grand Ave.
Bellingham, WA 98225
PH: (949)940-1140
Toll free: 888-238-8725
Fax: (949)940-1141
Anaya, Rick, CEO, Founder

Facing the Future [7809]
516 High St., MS 9102
Bellingham, WA 98225
Toll free: 844-284-2151
Corrigan, Kimberly E., Exec. Dir.

Metal Boat Society [436]
721 Marine Dr.
Bellingham, WA 98225
PH: (425)485-2100
Palanca, Rod, President

Missing Pet Partnership [12455]
PO Box 31158
Bellingham, WA 98228
PH: (253)529-3999
Albrecht, Ms. Kathy, Founder

National Chincoteague Pony As-
sociation [4380]
2595 Jensen Rd.
Bellingham, WA 98226
PH: (360)671-8338
Fax: (360)671-7603
Frederick, Gale Park, Director

National Council for Workforce
Education [7854]
1050 Larrabee Ave., No. 104-308
Bellingham, WA 98225
PH: (603)714-1918
Albrecht, Christal M., President

North American Truck Camper Own-
ers Association [22475]
PO Box 30408
Bellingham, WA 98228
Quinn, Dan, Contact

SPIE [6951]
PO Box 10
Bellingham, WA 98227-0010
PH: (360)685-5580
    (360)676-3290
Toll free: 888-902-0894
Fax: (360)647-1445
Arthurs, Dr. Eugene G., CEO

Timber Framers Guild [1422]
1106 Harris Ave.
Bellingham, WA 98225
PH: (530)746-6571
Toll free: 855-598-1803
Arvin, Jeff, Exec. Dir.

Wildlife Media [4915]
1208 Bay St., Ste. 202
Bellingham, WA 98225
PH: (360)734-6060
Taylor, John, Chairman, Founder,
CEO

Workplace Bullying Institute [16948]
PO Box 29915
Bellingham, WA 98228
PH: (360)656-6630
Namie, Gary, PhD, Director

World Sweeping Association [2145]
PO Box 667
Bellingham, WA 98227
PH: (360)724-7355
Toll free: 866-635-2205
Fax: (866)890-0912
Kidwell-Ross, Ranger, Exec. Dir.,
Founder

United States Canada Peace An-
niversary Association [18833]
PO Box 2564
Blaine, WA 98231-2564
PH: (360)332-7165
Alexander, Christina, Founder,
President

Bicycle Stamps Club [22311]
c/o Bill Eubanks
21304 2nd Ave. SE
Bothell, WA 98021-7550
Eubanks, Bill, Contact

International Yang Family Tai Chi
Chuan Association [22998]
PO Box 786
Bothell, WA 98041
PH: (425)869-1185
Zhenduo, Yang, Chairman

Tex Ritter Fan Club [24064]
23914 Willow Cir.
23914 Willow Cir.
Bothell, WA 98021

Clean Technology Trade Alliance
[5882]
441 NE Silver Pine Dr.
Bremerton, WA 98311
PH: (360)824-5417
Frost, Mark D., Exec. Dir.

Inner Circle of Advocates [5560]
c/o Richard H. Friedman, Director
1126 Highland Ave.
Bremerton, WA 98337
PH: (360)782-4300
Davis, Mark S., Director

Twelve Lights League [5557]
PO Box 1415
Bremerton, WA 98337
PH: (360)373-9999
Struble, Robert, Jr., Founder

U.S. Boomerang Association [22700]
c/o Betsylew Miale-Gix, Treasurer
3351 236th St. SW
Brier, WA 98036-8421
PH: (425)485-1672
Hirsch, David, Bd. Member

American Council for Medicinally
Active Plants [13593]
18110 NE 189th St.
Brush Prairie, WA 98606
Fax: (360)882-2089
Stutte, Gary, Exec. Dir.

Western Snow Conference [7381]
PO Box 485
Brush Prairie, WA 98606
PH: (530)414-3267
Lea, Jon, Secretary, Treasurer, Mgr.

Association of Environmental Health
Academic Programs [4124]
PO Box 66057
Burien, WA 98166
PH: (206)522-5272
Fax: (206)985-9805
Murphy, Tim, Treasurer

Disabled Americans Have Rights
Too [11591]
616 SW 152nd St.
Burien, WA 98166
PH: (206)241-1697
Fax: (206)241-1697
Lawrence, Joanne, Founder,
Chairperson

Pedro Rescue Helicopter Association
[20672]
16610 14th Ave. SW
Burien, WA 98166
PH: (503)653-7727
Christianson, John, President

United States Practical Shooting As-
sociation [23144]
827 N Hill Blvd.
Burlington, WA 98233
PH: (360)855-2245
Fax: (360)855-0380
Foley, Mike, President

Our Family in Africa [10483]
PO Box 626
Camas, WA 98607
PH: (602)330-6337
MacDonald, Cami, Exec. Dir.

Akhal-Teke Association of America
[4295]
c/o Catrina Quantrell, President
Gods Cavalry Ranch
1010 Randall Rd.
Centerville, WA 98613
PH: (509)823-0877
Shearer-McMahon, Jas, VP

Komondor Club of America [21909]
c/o Anna Quigley, President
159 Beville Rd.
Chehalis, WA 98532-9115
PH: (360)245-3464
Quigley, Ann, President

Society of Photo-Technologists
[2594]
11112 S Spotted Rd.
Cheney, WA 99004
PH: (509)710-4464
Bertone, Charles, Exec. Dir.

Smile Alliance International [11271]
PO Box 240
Cle Elum, WA 98922-0240
PH: (509)674-2274

Rivers Without Borders [3936]
c/o Terry Portillo, Finance and
Outreach Director
PO Box 154
Clinton, WA 98236
PH: (360)341-1976
Patric, Will, Exec. Dir.

American Balint Society [16856]
912 E Burk Rd.
Colbert, WA 99005
Lichtenstein, Albert, Contact

November Coalition [17325]
282 W Astor
Colville, WA 99114

PH: (509)680-4679
Callahan, Nora, Exec. Dir.

International Miniature Cattle Breed-
ers Society and Registry [3731]
16000 SE 252nd Pl.
Covington, WA 98042
PH: (253)631-1911
Fax: (253)631-5774
Gradwohl, Prof. Richard, Director,
Founder

Wear Blue: Run to Remember
[13255]
PO Box 76
DuPont, WA 98327
Hallett, Lisa, President

North American ZY Qigong Associa-
tion [13646]
Duvall, WA
Mingtang, Xu, Contact

Aglow International [20639]
123 2nd Ave., Ste. 100
Edmonds, WA 98020-8457
PH: (425)775-7282
Fax: (425)778-9615
Hoyt, Jane Hansen, President, CEO

Breakthrough Partners [20360]
110 3rd Ave. N, Ste. 101
Edmonds, WA 98020
PH: (425)775-3362
Fax: (425)640-3671
Edmonds, Gary L., President

Institute of Tax Consultants [5794]
7500 - 212th St. SW, Ste. 205
Edmonds, WA 98026
PH: (425)774-3521
Kraemer, Carol, CCCE, Registrar

Scale Ship Modelers Association of
North America [22205]
7325, 176th St. SW
7325 176th St. SW
Edmonds, WA 98026
Speilberger, Don, Director

Viva Bolivia [11458]
PO Box 1505
Edmonds, WA
PH: (206)347-7054
Fax: (206)400-1586
Schoenhals, Jonathan, President

Family and Consumer Sciences
Education Association [7917]
Dept. of Family and Consumer Sci-
ences
Central Washington University
400 E University Way, MS 7565
Ellensburg, WA 98926-7565
PH: (509)963-2766
Bowers, Jan, Exec. Dir.

Children of the Dump [10915]
718 Griffin Ave.
Enumclaw, WA 98022
PH: (360)825-1099
    (322)299-3515
Toll free: 877-224-2792
Parker, Michael L., Sr., Officer

Global Helps Network [11293]
PO Box 1238
Enumclaw, WA 98022
McDaniel, Mic, President

U.S. Philatelic Classics Society
[22377]
2913 Fulton St.
Everett, WA 98201-3733
Barwis, John, President

Experience International [3861]
PO Box 680
Everson, WA 98247

PH: (360)966-3876
Fax: (360)966-4131
Walkinshaw, Charlie, Director

American Association of the Deaf-
Blind [15167]
PO Box 24493
Federal Way, WA 98093
PH: (770)492-8646
Drake, Adam, Treasurer

Geary 18 International Yacht Racing
Association [22616]
PO Box 4763
Federal Way, WA 98063-4763

Hardy Fern Foundation [4431]
PO Box 3797
Federal Way, WA 98063-3797
PH: (253)838-4646
Fax: (253)838-4686
Steffen, Richie, President

Institute for Functional Medicine
[13629]
505 S 336th St., Ste. 600
Federal Way, WA 98003
PH: (253)661-3010
Toll free: 800-228-0622
Fax: (253)661-8310
Hofmann, Laurie, MPH, CEO

Pacific Lumber Inspection Bureau
[1417]
909 S 336th St., Ste. 203
Federal Way, WA 98003
PH: (253)835-3344
Fax: (253)835-3371
Fantozzi, Jeff, President

Rhododendron Species Foundation
[6154]
PO Box 3798
Federal Way, WA 98063
PH: (253)838-4646
Fax: (253)838-4686
Hootman, Steve, Exec. Dir., Curator

Touch the Life of a Child Organiza-
tion [11171]
31811 Pacific Hwy. S, Ste. B-220
Federal Way, WA 98003
PH: (253)838-2038
Springman, Anthony, Founder

World Vision [12739]
PO Box 9716
Federal Way, WA 98063-9716
Toll free: 888-511-6548
Stearns, Richard, President

Community Empowerment Network
[12799]
1685 Grandview Pl.
Ferndale, WA 98248
PH: (206)329-6244
Fax: (617)344-7868
Bortner, Robert, Founder, President

Technocracy Inc. [19120]
2475 Harksell Rd.
Ferndale, WA 98248-9764
PH: (360)366-1012
Toll free: 855-277-3748
Fax: (360)547-7664
Scott, Howard, Founder, Chief
Engineer

Soft Coated Wheaten Terrier Club of
America, Inc. [21964]
c/o Mary Ann Curtis, Treasurer
6206 Sheffield Ln. E
Fife, WA 98424-2268
Skinner, Cecily, President

Heritage Institute [19578]
PO Box 1273
Freeland, WA 98249

PH: (360)341-3020
Toll free: 800-445-1305
Fax: (360)341-3070
Seymour, Mike, President, Director

Center for Whale Research [6791]
PO Box 1577
Friday Harbor, WA 98250
Toll free: 866-ORC-ANET
Giles, Dr. Deborah, Dir. of Res.

Interspecies [6768]
301 Hidden Meadows Ln.
Friday Harbor, WA 98250
Nollman, Jim, Director, Founder

Sea Shepherd Conservation Society
[4884]
PO Box 2616
Friday Harbor, WA 98250
PH: (360)370-5650
Fax: (360)370-5651
Watson, Capt. Paul, Founder

401st Bombardment Group Heavy
Association [20679]
PO Box 2718
Gig Harbor, WA 98335
Anderson, Dale, Chmn. of the Bd.

Association of Stained Glass Lamp
Artists [242]
5070 Cromwell Dr. NW
Gig Harbor, WA 98335
Kanick, Steve, VP, Secretary

Dutch Bantam Society [4565]
c/o Jerrod Alcaida, Secretary
10814 131st St. NW
Gig Harbor, WA 98329
PH: (310)991-5799
Howell, Stewart, President

International Association of
Architectural Photographers [2581]
2901 136th St. NW
Gig Harbor, WA 98332-9111
Toll free: 877-845-4783
Bliss, Thomas, Site Mgr.

International Association of Certified
Thermographers [7331]
38 Raft Island Dr. NW
Gig Harbor, WA 98335
PH: (253)509-3742
Wood, Scott, Treasurer

International Latino Gang Investiga-
tors Association [5364]
PO Box 1148
Gig Harbor, WA 98335
Arriaga, Nelson, President

Navajo-Churro Sheep Association
[4677]
1029 Zelinski Rd.
Goldendale, WA 98620
PH: (509)773-3671
Taylor, Connie, Registrar

Back Country Horsemen of America
[22940]
PO Box 1367
Graham, WA 98338-1367
PH: (360)832-2461
Toll free: 888-893-5161
Fax: (360)832-1564
Greiwe, Peg, Exec. Sec.

United States Lighthouse Society
[9443]
9005 Point No Point Rd. NE
Hansville, WA 98340-8759
PH: (415)362-7255
Fax: (415)362-7464
Gonzalez, Henry, VP

The Traditional Cat Association, Inc.
[21574]
PO Box 178
Heisson, WA 98622
Fineran, Diana, Founder

The Compassionate Listening
Project [11477]
PO Box 17
Indianola, WA 98342
Green, Leah, Exec. Dir., Founder

Coffin-Lowry Syndrome Foundation
[14817]
675 Kalmia Pl. NW
Issaquah, WA 98027
PH: (425)427-0939
Hoffman, Mary C., Founder

Environmental Outreach and
Stewardship Alliance [4059]
1445 NW Mall St., Ste. 4
Issaquah, WA 98027
PH: (425)270-3274
Workman, James, Exec. Dir.

National Association of Rural
Landowners [18933]
PO Box 1031
Issaquah, WA 98027
PH: (425)837-5365
Toll free: 800-662-7848
Fax: (425)837-5365
Ewart, Ron, President

Saints Alive in Jesus [20161]
PO Box 1347
Issaquah, WA 98027
Toll free: 800-861-9888
Decker, J. Edward, Founder

Take Root [12358]
PO Box 930
Kalama, WA 98625
PH: (360)673-3720
Toll free: 800-ROOT-ORG
Fax: (360)673-3732
Haviv, Melissa, Exec. Dir.

Media Fellowship International
[20154]
PO Box 82685
Kenmore, WA 98028
PH: (425)488-3965
Fax: (425)488-8531
Rieth, Pastor Bob, Exec. Dir.,
Founder, President

American Academy for Oral
Systemic Health [14384]
8911 W Grandridge Blvd., Ste. D
Kennewick, WA 99336
Toll free: 855-246-9133
Kammer, Chris, President

Children's Reading Foundation
[12244]
515 W Entiat Ave.
Kennewick, WA 99336
PH: (509)735-9405
Fax: (509)396-7730
Kerr, Nancy, President

National Booster Club Training
Council [3160]
100 N Morain St., No. 312
Kennewick, WA 99336
PH: (509)736-6877
Fax: (509)736-6895

International Occultation Timing As-
sociation [6006]
c/o Chad K. Ellington, Secretary/
Treasurer
PO Box 7152
Kent, WA 98042
Ellington, Chad, Secretary, Treasurer

Pacific Northwest Region of the
Lincoln and Continental Owners
Club [21471]
c/o Roger Clements
16630 SE 235th St.
Kent, WA 98042
Toll free: 866-427-7583
D'Ambrosia, Becky, Contact

Wells Family Research Association
[20942]
PO Box 5427
Kent, WA 98064-5427
PH: (253)630-5296
Fax: (253)639-2701
Wells, Orin R., President

Association for Innovative
Cardiovascular Advancements
[14098]
13661 62nd Ave. NE
Kirkland, WA 98034
PH: (858)204-4116
Fax: (425)823-0669
Rhyne, Rhonda F., President, CEO

Association for Women Soil
Scientists [7192]
c/o Kelly Counts
PO Box 8264
Kirkland, WA 98034
Greenberg, Wendy, Chairperson

Windward Foundation [13096]
55 Windward Ln.
Klickitat, WA 98628
PH: (509)369-2000

Maremma Sheepdog Club of
America [21912]
c/o, Kristi Zwicker, Secretary
31606 NE 40th Ave.
La Center, WA 98629
PH: (360)430-3430
Mills, Michael, Director

Western International Walking Horse
Association [4427]
c/o Kim Swingley, Secretary
9101 NE LaView St.
La Center, WA 98629
Brown, Stephen, President

Society for Japanese Irises [22123]
c/o Patrick Spence, President
PO Box 1062
Lake Stevens, WA 98258
Coble, John, VP

Vre Lavi Ayiti [11459]
10422 37th St. SE
Lake Stevens, WA 98258
Shelton, Allan, President, Exec. Dir.

Well Done Organization [11461]
10813 27th St. SE
Lake Stevens, WA 98258-5179
Finley, Daryl, Founder

Context Institute [19104]
PO Box 946
Langley, WA 98260
Gilman, Diane, Founder

Giraffe Heroes Project [9547]
PO Box 759
Langley, WA 98260
PH: (360)221-7989
Fax: (360)221-7817
Patterson, Bob, Co-Ch.

New Road Map Foundation [12013]
PO Box 1363
Langley, WA 98260
Dominguez, Joe, Founder

Rainbow Alliance of the Deaf
[11943]
c/o Barbara Hathaway, Treasurer
PO Box 1616
Langley, WA 98260
Puhlmann, Greg, President

Sister Island Project [11437]
PO Box 1413
Langley, WA 98260
PH: (360)321-4012
Santos, Victoria, Director

Orphan's Hope [11120]
10190 B Suncrest Dr.
Leavenworth, WA 98826
PH: (952)941-1546
Toll free: 888-251-2871
Cassidy, Steve, Founder, President

International Association of Round
Dance Teachers [9260]
2803 Louisiana St.
Longview, WA 98632-3536
PH: (360)423-7423
Toll free: 877-943-2623
Gotta, Roy, Chairman

Mothers of Military Support [12346]
1105 D 15th Ave., No. 111
Longview, WA 98632
PH: (360)430-3597
    (360)577-1351

Association of VA Hematology/
Oncology [15225]
PO Box 2459
Lynnwood, WA 98036
PH: (206)794-9124
Fax: (206)319-4601
Ascensao, Joao, MD, President

Association of VA Surgeons [17380]
2610 164th St. SW, No. A524
Lynnwood, WA 98087
PH: (206)794-9124
Fax: (206)319-4601
Spector, Seth, MD, President

African Promise Foundation [13001]
25545 SE 274th Pl.
Maple Valley, WA 98038
PH: (630)947-2805
Gillies, Suzy Benson, Founder,
President

Pacific Logging Congress [1415]
PO Box 1281
Maple Valley, WA 98038
PH: (425)413-2808
Wellman, Rikki, Exec. Dir.

33rd Infantry Division Association
[20700]
617 143rd St. NW
Marysville, WA 98271
Endicott, Bill, Editor

National Hot Rod Diesel Association
[23084]
14702 Smokey Point Blvd.
Marysville, WA 98271
PH: (360)658-4353
Fax: (360)322-3334
Cole, Randy, President

National Hay Association [4179]
24064 SW Rd. L
Mattawa, WA 99349
PH: (615)854-5574
Fax: (509)932-4514
Blackmer, Carl, Comm. Chm.

Maasai Association [10490]
PO Box 868
Medina, WA 98039
PH: (206)697-9826
Ole Maimai, Kakuta, Managing Dir.

International Thunderbird Class As-
sociation [22641]
PO Box 1033
Mercer Island, WA 98040
Burnell, Craig, Treasurer

MED25 International [15032]
PO Box 1459
Mercer Island, WA 98040
Okelo, Rebecca Conte, Exec. Dir.

North American Native Fishes As-
sociation [6717]
PO Box 1596
Milton, WA 98354-1596

PH: (256)824-6992
Rohde, Fritz, President

EyeCare WeCare Foundation
[17698]
304 N Talbot
Montesano, WA 98563
PH: (360)593-2353
Fax: (360)249-3024
Weyrich, Dr. James, CEO

Ghana Together [11468]
808 Addison Pl.
Mount Vernon, WA 98273
PH: (360)848-6568
    (360)708-5735
Ward, Maryanne, President,
Treasurer

Action International Ministries
[20124]
PO Box 398
Mountlake Terrace, WA 98043-0398
PH: (425)775-4800
Fax: (425)775-0634
Lee, Rex, Director

Hop Growers of America [3762]
301 W Prospect Pl.
Moxee, WA 98936
PH: (509)453-4749
Fax: (509)457-8561
Brophy, Jaki, Contact

1394 Trade Association [3204]
315 Lincoln, Ste. E
Mukilteo, WA 98275
PH: (425)870-6574
Fax: (425)320-3897
Bassler, Max, Chairman

Disability Advocates for Cystic
Fibrosis [11585]
C/O Julie Pereira 513 203rd PL SW
Mukilteo, WA 98275
PH: (425)280-7310
Fax: (425)672-5133
Raysbrook, Julie, Contact

Hugs for Ghana [11041]
PO Box 694
Mukilteo, WA 98275
Bervell, Rachel, Founder

Society for Hungarian Philately
[22366]
4889 76th St. SW, Unit A403
Mukilteo, WA 98275
PH: (770)840-8766
Toll free: 888-868-8293
Caswell, Lyman, Director

American Lumberjack Association
[23211]
c/o Chrissy Ramsey, Secretary
11800 US Highway 12
Naches, WA 98937
Hartley, James, President

Society for Pacific Coast Native Iris
[22125]
c/o Kathleen Sayce, Secretary
PO Box 91
Nahcotta, WA 98637-0091
Sussman, Bob, President

Icelandic Sheepdog Association of
America [21896]
24417 E Rosewood
Newman Lake, WA 99025
Williamson, Spike, VP

International MYOPAIN Society
[16559]
PO Box 268
Nine Mile Falls, WA 99026-0268
PH: (714)423-4863
Fricton, James, President

Hear See Hope Foundation [14825]
19655 1st Ave. S, Ste. 101
Normandy Park, WA 98148
PH: (206)429-3884
Fax: (206)299-9519
McKittrick, Todd, Founder, Director

Semiotic Society of America [7160]
204 Raven Ln.
Olga, WA 98279
PH: (206)268-4910
Seif, Prof. Farouk Y., Exec. Dir.

Center for World Indigenous Studies
[18470]
1001 Cooper Point Rd. SW, Ste. 140
Olympia, WA 98502-1107
PH: (360)529-4896
Korn, Leslie E., Ph.D., MPH, Dir. of
Res.

Cooper Ornithological Society [6956]
c/o Martin Raphael, President
3625 93rd Ave. SW
Olympia, WA 98512
PH: (360)753-7662
Powell, Abby, Secretary

Fourth World Documentation Project
[18472]
1001 Cooper Point Rd. SW, No.
104, PMB 214
Olympia, WA 98502-1107
PH: (360)529-4896
Ryser, Rudolph C., Chairman

Freedom Foundation [5729]
PO Box 552
Olympia, WA 98507
PH: (360)956-3482
Fax: (360)352-1874
Minnich, Brian, Exec. VP

Friendly Water for the World [13322]
1717 18th Ct. NE
Olympia, WA 98506
PH: (360)352-0506
Albert, David H., Chmn. of the Bd.,
Founder

Global Alliance for Community
Empowerment [10476]
8300 Steamboat Island Rd. NW
Olympia, WA 98502
PH: (360)866-8500

North American English and
European Ford Registry [21462]
PO Box 11415
Olympia, WA 98508
PH: (360)754-9585
MacSems, Michael, Director

Pacific Coast Shellfish Growers As-
sociation [3035]
120 State Ave. NE, No. 142
Olympia, WA 98501
PH: (360)754-2744
Fax: (360)754-2743
Barrette, Margaret Pilaro, Exec. Dir.

Pacific Shellfish Institute [3646]
120 State Ave. NE, No. 1056
Olympia, WA 98501
PH: (360)754-2741
Fax: (360)754-2246
Hudson, Bobbi, Exec. Dir.

Society for Northwestern Vertebrate
Biology [6899]
2103 Harrison Ave. NW, No. 2132
Olympia, WA 98502
Thurman, Lindsey, Secretary

World Whale Police [4921]
PO Box 814
Olympia, WA 98506
PH: (360)561-7492
Moss, Bill, President

Children's Welfare International
[10936]
223 Pacific Ave. S
Pacific, WA 98047-1214
PH: (206)317-3545
Jarbah, Joseph Fatinyan, President,
Founder

Ride and Tie Association [23252]
2709 Road 64
Pasco, WA 99301
PH: (509)521-6249
Volk, Ben, Bd. Member

Friends of the Trees Society [3872]
PO Box 1133
Port Hadlock, WA 98339
PH: (360)643-9178
Pilarski, Michael, Director, Founder

Horace Mann League of the U.S.A.
[8476]
c/o Jack McKay, Executive Director
560 Rainier Ln.
Port Ludlow, WA 98365
PH: (360)821-9877
McKay, Dr. Jack, Exec. Dir.

Clan Guthrie USA [20813]
c/o Carrie Guthrie-Whitlow,
Treasurer
PO Box 121
Port Orchard, WA 98366
Moore, William, President

Prison Mission Association [20455]
PO Box 2300
Port Orchard, WA 98366
PH: (360)876-0918
Anderson, Dwight, Exec. Dir.

Spokane, Portland and Seattle
Railway Historical Society [10192]
c/o Bill Baker, Treasurer
6345 Peppermill Pl. SE
Port Orchard, WA 98366
Hobbs, Paul, VP

Organic Seed Alliance [4644]
PO Box 772
Port Townsend, WA 98368
PH: (360)385-7192
Colley, Micaela, Exec. Dir.

Mobile Post Office Society [22347]
PO Box 1058
Poulsbo, WA 98370-0048
PH: (508)428-9132
Clark, Douglas N., President

National Denturist Association
[14463]
PO Box 2344
Poulsbo, WA 98370
PH: (360)232-4353
Fax: (360)779-6879
Anderson, Bruce, Bd. Member

Society of Collision Repair Special-
ists [354]
PO Box 909
Prosser, WA 99350
PH: (302)423-3537
Toll free: 877-841-0660
Fax: (877)851-0660
Reichen, Ron, Officer

American Ecological Engineering
Society [3987]
c/o Anand Jayakaran, Treasurer
2606 W Pioneer
Puyallup, WA 98371-4900
PH: (253)445-4523
Fax: (253)445-4571
Austin, Dave, President

Pentecostal Charismatic Churches of
North America [20518]
8408 131st St., Ct. E
Puyallup, WA 98373-5402

PH: (253)446-6475
Blake, Bishop Charles E., Co-Ch.

Professional Football Chiropractic
Society [14280]
PO Box 552
Puyallup, WA 98371
PH: (253)948-6039
Fax: (253)435-1053
Ellis, Brenda, Exec. Dir.

Society of Inkwell Collectors [21721]
c/o Jeffrey Pisetzner
2203 39th St. SE
Puyallup, WA 98372-5223
Wirth, Fritz, Exec. Dir.

Vietnam Dustoff Association [21171]
3103 31st Ave. SE
Puyallup, WA 98374
PH: (253)906-2938
Vermillion, Steve, Contact

North American Lionhead Rabbit
Club [4610]
c/o Theresa Mueller
PO Box 43
Ravensdale, WA 98051
PH: (425)413-5995
Schneegas-Nevills, Lea A., President

Blind Judo Foundation [22778]
24145 NE 122nd St.
Redmond, WA 98053
PH: (425)444-8256
Peck, Ronald C., MBA, Founder

Medical Relief International [12697]
12316 134th Ct. NE
Redmond, WA 98052
PH: (425)284-2630
Mays, William E., PhD, Exec. Dir.,
President

Microsoft Health Users Group
[15154]
1 Microsoft Way
Redmond, WA 98052-6399
PH: (425)870-4880
Soti, Praveen, Chairman

Organization of Regulatory and Clini-
cal Associates [6123]
PO Box 3490
Redmond, WA 98073
PH: (206)464-0825
Bhend, Dave, Mktg. Mgr.

Relief and Education for Afghan
Children [11265]
PO Box 304
Redmond, WA 98073
PH: (206)463-3839
   (425)844-8591
Fax: (206)463-2832
Hunziker, Jim, President

Black Box Voting [18179]
330 SW 43rd St., Ste. K
Renton, WA 98057
PH: (206)335-7747
Harris, Bev, Director

Food Shippers Association of North
America [1329]
4632 NE 5th Ct.
Renton, WA 98059-5702
Fax: (425)458-9054

World Association for Children and
Parents [11188]
315 S 2nd St.
Renton, WA 98057
PH: (206)575-4550
Toll free: 800-732-1887
Fax: (206)575-4148
Rosnik, Phil, Chmn. of the Bd.

Vietnam Veteran Wives [21154]
12 Trout Creek Rd.
Republic, WA 99166

PH: (509)775-8893
Hughes, Danna, Founder, President

GridWise Architecture Council [7053]
902 Battelle Blvd.
Richland, WA 99352
PH: (509)372-6410
   (509)372-6777
Melton, Ron, Administrator

National Air-Racing Group [22489]
1932 Mahan
Richland, WA 99352-2121
PH: (509)946-5690
Sherman, Betty, Treasurer

Radiochemistry Society [6212]
PO Box 3091
Richland, WA 99354
PH: (509)460-7474
Burchfield, Larry A., PhD, CEO,
President, Founder

SIGN Fracture Care International
[17398]
451 Hills St., Ste. B
Richland, WA 99354
PH: (509)371-1107
Fax: (509)371-1316
Zirkle, Lewis J., MD, Founder

American Federation of Violin and
Bow Makers [9856]
1035 S Josephine Ave.
Rosalia, WA 99170-9551
Bonsey, David, President

200 Orphanages Worldwide [10826]
704 228th Ave. NE, No. 236
Sammamish, WA 98074
Hanson, Jan M., Exec. Dir., Founder

Airflow Club of America [21312]
1651 209th Pl. NE
Sammamish, WA 98074-4212
PH: (425)868-7448
Daly, Frank, President

International Smile Power [14453]
704 228th Ave. NE, No. 204
Sammamish, WA 98074-7222
PH: (206)715-6322
Shinn, Jerri, Founder

Songea's Kids [11152]
3020 Issaquah Pine Lake Rd. SE,
No. 539
Sammamish, WA 98075
PH: (425)961-0623
Hines, Linda, President

International Association of Confer-
ence Center Administrators [1663]
PO Box 1012
Seabeck, WA 98380
Kraining, Chuck, President

Broad Universe [22483]
4725 S 172nd Pl.
Seatac, WA 98188
Rhoads, Loren, Contact

Action for Animals [10558]
PO Box 45843
Seattle, WA 98145-0843
PH: (206)227-5752

Adventure Travel Trade Association
[3365]
601 Union St., 42nd Fl.
Seattle, WA 98101
PH: (360)805-3131
   (206)290-4410
Fax: (360)805-0649
Stowell, Mr. Shannon, President

African American Advocates for
Victims of Clergy Sexual Abuse
[12918]
4020 E Madison St., Ste. 205
Seattle, WA 98112

PH: (425)232-0504
Harris, Ruby Dell, Exec. Dir.

African Communities Against Malaria
[15390]
3644 36th Ave. S, Unit A
Seattle, WA 98144
Casazza, Dr. Larry, Director

Agros International [11310]
2225 4th Ave., 2nd Fl.
Seattle, WA 98121
PH: (206)528-1066
Solano, Alberto, Exec. Dir.

American Academy of Oral Medicine
[14383]
2150 N 107th St., Ste. 205
Seattle, WA 98133
PH: (206)209-5277
Reeder, Michele M., Exec. Dir.

American Fighter Aces Association
[20666]
9404 E Marginal Way S
Seattle, WA 98108-4907
PH: (206)764-5700
Cleveland, Lt. Gen. Charles,
President

American Medical Tennis Association
[23296]
2414 43rd Ave. E, B-1
Seattle, WA 98112
Toll free: 800-326-2682
Kirkpatrick, John, Exec. Dir.

Art with Heart [13727]
316 Broadway, Ste. 316
Seattle, WA 98122-5325
PH: (206)362-4047
Nelson, Jeff, President

Arts Council of Mongolia-US [9812]
2025 23rd Ave. E
Seattle, WA 98112
Morrow, Peter, Chairman

Associates in Cultural Exchange
[9204]
200 W Mercer St., Ste. 108
Seattle, WA 98119-3958
PH: (206)217-9644
Fax: (206)217-9643
Woodward, David, President, CEO

Association for the Advancement of
Baltic Studies [9205]
University of Washington, Box
353420
Seattle, WA 98195-3420
PH: (301)977-8491
Fax: (301)977-8492
Blekys, Irena, Dir. of Admin.

Association for Computing
Machinery - Special Interest Group
on Algorithms and Computation
Theory [7056]
c/o Paul Beame, Chairman
University of Washington
PO Box 352350
Seattle, WA 98195
Beame, Paul, Chairman

Association for Computing
Machinery - Special Interest Group
on Management of Data [6238]
c/o Magdalena Balazinska,
Treasurer
Computer Science & Engineering
University of Washington, Box
352350
Seattle, WA 98195-2350
PH: (206)616-1069
Balazinska, Magdalena, Treasurer

Association for Crime Scene
Reconstruction [11500]
c/o Amy Jagmin, Membership Chairman

Forensic Analytical Sciences, Inc.
2203 Airport Way S, Ste. 250
Seattle, WA 98134
PH: (206)262-6067
DeFrance, Charles S., Editor

Association of Donor Relations
Professionals [12461]
2150 N 107th St., No. 205
Seattle, WA 98133-9009
Toll free: 800-341-0014
Fax: (206)367-8777
Bostian, Julie, President

Association for Library and Informa-
tion Science Education [8229]
2150 N 107th St., Ste. 205
Seattle, WA 98133
PH: (206)209-5267
Fax: (206)367-8777
Spiteri, Louise, President

Association of Workplace Investiga-
tors [5358]
2150 N 107th St., Ste. 205
Seattle, WA 98133
PH: (206)209-5278
Estep, Andrew, Exec. Dir.

Avenues, National Support Group for
Arthrogryposis Multiplex Congenita
[15908]
c/o Cathy Graubert
Seattle Children's Hospital
4800 Sand Point Way NE
Seattle, WA 98105
PH: (206)987-2113
Schmidt, Jim, Director

Ayni Education International [7583]
PO Box 17672
Seattle, WA 98127
PH: (206)331-3786
Brelsford, Ms. Ginna, Exec. Dir.

Basel Action Network [4291]
206 1st Ave. S, Ste. 410
Seattle, WA 98104
PH: (206)652-5555
Fax: (206)652-5750
Gilbert, Steven G., President

Bill and Melinda Gates Foundation
[12529]
500 5th Ave. N
Seattle, WA 98109
PH: (206)709-3400
   (206)709-3100
Desmond-Hellmann, Sue, CEO

BIO Ventures for Global Health
[15440]
401 Terry Ave. N
Seattle, WA 98109
Greenwood, James C., Chmn. of the
Bd.

Black World Foundation [8779]
c/o The Black Scholar
Dept. of English
University of Washington
Padelford A-101, Box 354330
Seattle, WA 98105-4412
Lewis, Shireen K., Sen. Ed.

Blue Earth Alliance [10137]
4557 51st Pl SW
Seattle, WA 98116
PH: (206)569-8754
Fobes, Natalie, President

Blue Nile Children's Organization
[10871]
PO Box 28658
Seattle, WA 98118-8658
PH: (206)633-1508
Kifle, Selamawit, Founder

Boreal Songbird Initiative [4800]
1904 3rd Ave., Ste. 305
Seattle, WA 98101

PH: (206)956-9040
Fax: (206)447-4824
Reid, Fritz, President

The Borgen Project [12530]
1416 NW 46th St., Ste. 105, PMB 145
Seattle, WA 98107
PH: (206)414-1032
Borgen, Clint, President

Brain Injury Resource Center [17085]
PO Box 84151
Seattle, WA 98124-5451
PH: (206)621-8558
Miller, Constance, MA, Founder, Author

Caffeine Awareness Association [17309]
93 S Jackson St.
Seattle, WA 98104
PH: (888)710-5870
Kushner, Marina, Founder

Cartoonists Northwest [8969]
PO Box 31122
Seattle, WA 98103
Fruchter, Jason, President

Center for Wooden Boats [22606]
1010 Valley St.
Seattle, WA 98109-4468
PH: (206)382-2628
Fax: (206)382-2699
Wagner, Dick, Founder, Curator

Child United [10905]
500 Yale Ave. N, 1st Fl.
Seattle, WA 98109
PH: (425)954-5288
Umayam, Christine, Founder

Childhood Obesity Prevention Coalition [16252]
419 3rd Ave. W
Seattle, WA 98119
PH: (206)859-2500
Colman, Victor, Director

Classic Yacht Association [22608]
5267 Shilshole Ave. NW
Seattle, WA 98107
PH: (206)937-6211
Meyer, Ken, President

Clear Path International [18122]
1700 N Northlake Way, Ste. 201
Seattle, WA 98103
PH: (754)444-8885
Creamer, Kellie, Officer

Coastal and Estuarine Research Federation [6801]
2150 N 107th St., Ste. 205
Seattle, WA 98133-9009
PH: (206)209-5262
Fax: (206)367-8777
Sutula, Martha, Secretary

CodeBlueNow! [17000]
705 2nd Ave., Ste. 901
Seattle, WA 98104
PH: (206)217-9430
Snider, Pamela, ND, Secretary

Code.org [7653]
1301 5th Ave., Ste. 1225
Seattle, WA 98101
Partovi, Hadi, Founder, CEO

COLAGE [11878]
3815 S Othello St., Ste. 100, No. 310
Seattle, WA 98118
PH: (504)313-0555
Toll free: 855-426-5243
Perry, Paul, Officer

Committee for Children [10946]
2815 2nd Ave., Ste. 400
Seattle, WA 98121-3207
PH: (206)343-1223
Toll free: 800-634-4449
Fax: (206)438-6765
Stanley, Sarah, Bd. Member

Comprehensive Health Education Foundation [8319]
419 3rd Ave. W
Seattle, WA 98119
PH: (206)824-2907
Toll free: 800-323-2433
Fax: (206)824-3072
Johnson, Whitney, Coord.

Contemporary Quilt Art Association [21752]
PO Box 95685
Seattle, WA 98145-2685

CorgiAid [21862]
2108 N 38th St.
Seattle, WA 98103
Fax: (208)693-8342
Neff, Vicki, President

Council of Engineers and Scientists Organizations [23532]
15205 52nd Ave. S
Seattle, WA 98188
PH: (205)433-0991
Shuler, Tonya, V. Chmn. of the Bd.

Council on Medical Student Education in Pediatrics [8320]
c/o Sherilyn Smith, President
4800 Sand Point Way NE
Seattle, WA 98105
PH: (206)987-2008
Fax: (206)987-2890
Degnon, Laura, CAE, Exec. Dir.

Council of Vedic Astrology [5991]
PO Box 84312
Seattle, WA 98124-5612
Flaherty, Dennis, President

Crooked Trails [8717]
PO Box 94034
Seattle, WA 98124
PH: (206)383-9828
Mackay, Christine Torrison, Founder, Exec. Dir.

Cross Cultural Health Care Program [14995]
1200 12th Ave. S, Ste. 1001
Seattle, WA 98144-2712
PH: (206)860-0329
SenGupta, Ira, MA, Exec. Dir.

DigitalEve [6835]
1902 NE 98th St.
Seattle, WA 98115
Cullom, Elaine, President

Doctors Opposing Circumcision [11282]
2442 NW Market St., S-42
Seattle, WA 98107-4137
PH: (415)647-2687
(225)383-8067
Denniston, George C., MD, CEO, President

Dream Jamaica [13442]
PO Box 14424
Seattle, WA 98114
Bailey, Arthur, President

Editorial Photographers [2578]
PO Box 51192
Seattle, WA 98115
Smith, Brian, President

FaithTrust Institute [11702]
2900 Eastlake Ave. E, Ste. 200
Seattle, WA 98102

PH: (206)634-1903
Toll free: 877-860-2255
Fax: (206)634-0115
Fredricksen, Jane, Exec. Dir.

Family for Every Orphan [10969]
PO Box 34628
Seattle, WA 98124
PH: (360)358-3293
Siler, Micala, Exec. Dir.

Feminist Karate Union [22991]
1426 S Jackson St., 3rd Fl.
Seattle, WA 98144
PH: (206)325-3878
Van Petten, Aleeta, Inst.

Filipino American National Historical Society [9389]
810 18th Ave., Rm. 100
Seattle, WA 98122
PH: (206)322-0204
(707)477-1159
Orpilla, Mel, President

Freedom Socialist Party [19141]
4710 University Way NE, No. 102
Seattle, WA 98105
PH: (206)985-4621
Fax: (206)985-8965
Barnes, Doug, Leader

Friends of the Jose Carreras International Leukemia Foundation [13976]
1100 Fairview Ave. N
Seattle, WA 98109-1024
PH: (206)667-7108
Fax: (206)667-6498
Carreras, Jose, President

GALA: Globalization and Localization Association [1005]
4000 NE 41st St., Ste. 201
Seattle, WA 98105
PH: (206)494-4686
Fax: (815)346-2361
Brandon, Laura, Exec. Dir.

Gesneriad Hybridizers Association [22096]
1122 E Pike St., PMB 637
Seattle, WA 98122-3916
Hudson, Julie, President

Gesneriad Society [22097]
1122 E Pike St.
Seattle, WA 98122-3916
Susi, Paul, President

Glass Art Society [22134]
6512 23rd Ave. NW, Ste. 329
Seattle, WA 98117
PH: (206)382-1305
Fax: (206)382-2630

Global Alliance to Prevent Prematurity and Stillbirth [14231]
1100 Olive Way, Ste. 1000
Seattle, WA 98101
PH: (206)884-2777
Fax: (206)884-1040
Rubens, Craig E., PhD, Exec. Dir.

Global Brigades [11365]
220 2nd Ave. S
Seattle, WA 98104
PH: (206)489-4798
Hay, Jeff, Chairman

Global Visionaries [12974]
2524 16th Ave. S, Rm. 206 and 305
Seattle, WA 98144
PH: (206)322-9448
Fax: (206)322-9719
Fontana, Chris, CEO

Grantmakers in the Arts [12480]
4055 21st Ave. W, Ste. 100
Seattle, WA 98199-1247

PH: (206)624-2312
Fax: (206)624-5568
Brown, Janet, President, CEO

GreaterGood.org [12975]
1 Union Sq., Ste. 1000
600 University St.
Seattle, WA 98101-4107
Toll free: 888-811-5271
Christophersen, Julia, President

Healing Minds [15771]
PO Box 45836
Seattle, WA 98145
PH: (206)718-2022
(253)632-1547
Turner, Raechelle, Exec. Dir.

Heart of America Northwest [18944]
444 NE Ravenna Blvd., Ste. 406
Seattle, WA 98115
PH: (206)382-1014
Pollet, Gerry, Exec. Dir.

Helping and Loving Orphans [11025]
2416 2nd Ave. N
Seattle, WA 98109
PH: (206)282-7337
Tisdale, Betty, Founder, President

Historical Society of the United Methodist Church [9482]
c/o Priscilla Pope-Levison, President
Seattle Pacific University
3307 3rd Ave. W
Seattle, WA 98119
Pope-Levison, Priscilla, President

Inlandboatmen's Union of the Pacific [2244]
1711 W Nickerson St., Ste. D
Seattle, WA 98119-1663
PH: (206)284-6001
Fax: (206)284-5043
Cote, Alan, President

InterConnection [11480]
3415 Stone Way N
Seattle, WA 98103
PH: (206)633-1517
Brennick, Charles, Director, Founder

International Association of Aquatic and Marine Science Libraries and Information Centers [9708]
c/o Brian Voss
U.S NOAA Seattle Library
7600 Sand Point Way NE, Bldg. 3
Seattle, WA 98115-6349
Anderson, Kristen, President

International Bicycle Fund [13232]
4887 Columbia Dr. S
Seattle, WA 98108-1919
PH: (206)767-0848
Mozer, David, Director

International Guild of Symphony, Opera and Ballet Musicians [23498]
c/o Nancy Griffin, President
PO Box 20013
Seattle, WA 98102
Agent, Betty, Treasurer

International Pacific Halibut Commission [1300]
2320 W Commodore Way, Ste. 300
Seattle, WA 98199
PH: (206)634-1838
Fax: (206)632-2983
Leaman, Dr. Bruce M., Exec. Dir.

International Society for Knowledge Organization [6745]
Mary Gates Hall, Ste. 370
The Information School
Seattle, WA 98195-2840
David, Amos, Secretary

International Society for the Study of
Human Ideas on Ultimate Reality
and Meaning **[10097]**
c/o David J. Leigh
English Dept.
Seattle University
901 12th Ave.
Seattle, WA 98122
PH: (206)296-5414
    (403)220-7124
Fax: (403)282-6716
Glasberg, Prof. Ronald, President

International Thermoelectric Society
[7332]
c/o Jihui Yang, President
Materials Science and Engineering
Dept.
University of Washington
302 Roberts Hall
Seattle, WA 98195
Yang, Jihui, President

Internet Business Alliance **[7303]**
PO Box 11518
Seattle, WA 98110-5518
Cook, Guy R., Director, President

Ivory Coast Medical Relief Team
[15603]
PO Box 55996
Seattle, WA 98155
PH: (206)622-0549
Adjorlolo, Alain, PhD, President

B.K.S. Iyengar Yoga National As-
sociation of the U.S. **[10422]**
PO Box 538
Seattle, WA 98111
PH: (206)623-3562
Beach, Chris, President

Henry M. Jackson Foundation
[18170]
1501 4th Ave., Ste. 1580
Seattle, WA 98101-1653
PH: (206)682-8565
Fax: (206)682-8961
Iglitzin, Lara, Exec. Dir.

Jewish Prisoner Services
International **[20259]**
PO Box 85840
Seattle, WA 98145-1840
PH: (206)985-0577
Fax: (206)526-7113
Friedman, Gary, Chairman

Literacy Bridge **[8244]**
1904 3rd Ave., Ste. 733
Seattle, WA 98101
PH: (425)780-5669
Fax: (425)780-5669
Schmidt, Cliff, Founder, President

Lutheran Peace Fellowship **[18803]**
1710 11th Ave.
Seattle, WA 98122-2420
PH: (206)349-2501

Marine Stewardship Council **[4638]**
2110 N Pacific St., Ste. 102
Seattle, WA 98103
PH: (206)691-0188
Fax: (206)691-0190
Howes, Rupert, CEO

Maternity Acupuncture Association
[13504]
c/o Patrice Hapke, President
340 15th Ave. E, No. 304
Seattle, WA 98122
PH: (206)851-0228
Hapke, Patrice, President

Merchant Risk Council **[1000]**
1809 7th Ave., Ste. 1403
Seattle, WA 98101-4405

PH: (206)364-2789
Fax: (206)367-1115
Murphy, Tim, Treasurer

Military Postal History Society
[22346]
PO Box 15927
Seattle, WA 98115-0927
Brooks, Tony, President

Mobility Builders **[11617]**
Washington Assistive Technology
Foundation
100 S King St., Ste. 280
Seattle, WA 98104
PH: (206)328-5116
Lefkowicz, Todd, Founder, Exec. Dir.

Mobility Outreach International
[17395]
192 Nickerson St., Ste. 201
Seattle, WA 98109
PH: (206)726-1636
Fax: (206)726-1637
Ignacio, Jose, Director

Mountaineers **[23327]**
7700 Sand Point Way NE
Seattle, WA 98115
PH: (206)521-6000
Toll free: 800-573-8484
Fax: (206)523-6763
Woody, Gavin, Director

Multiple Myeloma Opportunities for
Research & Education **[14016]**
117 E Louisa St., No. 554
Seattle, WA 98102
Toll free: 888-486-4240
Kaufmann, Nancy, President,
Founder

National Asian Pacific Center on Ag-
ing **[10517]**
1511 3rd Ave., Ste. 914
Seattle, WA 98101
PH: (206)624-1221
Toll free: 800-336-2722
Fax: (206)624-1023
Lum, Wesley, President, CEO

National Council for Private School
Accreditation **[7415]**
PO Box 13686
Seattle, WA 98198-1010
Fax: (253)874-3409
Petry, Dr. Don D., Exec. Dir.

National Court Appointed Special
Advocate Association **[11092]**
North Twr., Ste. 500
100 W Harrison St.
Seattle, WA 98119
Toll free: 800-628-3233
Collins, Bill, Chmn. of the Bd.

National Environmental Health Sci-
ence and Protection Accreditation
Council **[14720]**
PO Box 66057
Seattle, WA 98105
PH: (206)522-5272
Fax: (206)985-9805
Hatfield, Tom, PhD, Dir. of Programs

National Network for Educational
Renewal **[7844]**
2125 1st Ave., No. 2305
Seattle, WA 98121
PH: (206)850-2017
Fax: (206)441-5697
Foster, Ann, Exec. Dir.

National Urban Indian Family Coalition **[12381]**
2626 Eastlake Ave. E, Ste. D
Seattle, WA 98102
Comenote, Janeen, Director

Northwest Schooner Society **[22658]**
PO Box 75421
Seattle, WA 98175
PH: (206)577-7233

Omicron Kappa Upsilon **[23719]**
c/o Hai Zhang, President
Box 357456
School of Dentistry
University of Washington
1959 NE Pacific St.
Seattle, WA 98195-7456
PH: (206)543-5948
Fax: (206)543-7783
Suzuki, Brian J., JD, MPP, Exec. Dir.

One By One **[15087]**
2622 NW Market St., Ste. C
Seattle, WA 98107
PH: (206)297-1418
Fax: (206)374-3010
Breeze-Harris, Heidi, Founder, CEO

One Nurse At A Time **[16176]**
7747 38th Ave. NE
Seattle, WA 98115
Averill, Sue, RN, President, Founder

OneAmerica **[18105]**
1225 S Weller St., Ste. 430
Seattle, WA 98144
PH: (206)723-2203
Fax: (206)826-0423
Lopez, Fe, President

OneWorld Now! **[8629]**
220 2nd Ave. S, Ste. 102
Seattle, WA 98104
PH: (206)223-7703
Fax: (206)223-0371
Hayden, Kristin, Advisor, Founder

Orphans to Ambassadors **[11119]**
4742 42nd Ave. SW, No. 479
Seattle, WA 98116
Gentry, Jake, Founder, President

Pacific Seafood Processors Associa-
tion **[3036]**
1900 W Emerson Pl., Ste. 205
Seattle, WA 98119
PH: (206)281-1667
Reed, Glenn, President

Partners Task Force for Gay and
Lesbian Couples **[11907]**
c/o Demian, Director
PO Box 9685
Seattle, WA 98109-0685
PH: (206)935-1206
Demian, Director

Peace Winds America **[11675]**
2341 Eastlake Ave. E, Ste. 1
Seattle, WA 98102
PH: (206)432-3712
Aanenson, Dr. Charles, CEO

PeaceTrees Vietnam **[18132]**
509 Olive Way, Ste. 1226
Seattle, WA 98101
PH: (206)441-6136
Yunker, Claire, Exec. Dir.

Pellet Fuels Institute **[4267]**
2150 N 107th St., Ste. 205
Seattle, WA 98133
PH: (206)209-5277
Fax: (206)367-8777
Reid, Mike, Director

Pilgrim Africa **[12712]**
2200 6th Ave., No. 804
Seattle, WA 98121
PH: (206)706-0350
Echodu, Calvin, Founder, V. Chmn.
of the Bd.

Plumbers Without Borders **[13332]**
PO Box 16082
Seattle, WA 98116

PH: (206)390-5000
    (206)384-3222
DiGregorio, Domenico, Chmn. of the
Bd., President

Professional Women of Color
Network **[3499]**
PO Box 22367
Seattle, WA 98122
PH: (206)659-6356
Lawson, Meko L., Founder

Program for Appropriate Technology
in Health **[17811]**
2201 Westlake Ave., Ste. 200
Seattle, WA 98121
PH: (206)285-3500
Fax: (206)285-6619
Allen, Dean, Chairman

Pulmonary Pathology Society
[16590]
Virginia Mason Medical Center
Department of Pathology, C6-PTH
1100 9th Ave.
Seattle, WA 98101
Guinee, Dr. Donald G., Jr., President

Refugee Women's Alliance **[19020]**
4008 Martin Luther King, Jr. Way S
Seattle, WA 98108
PH: (206)721-0243
Fax: (206)721-0282
Eshetu, Mahnaz K., Exec. Dir.

Schedules Direct **[6333]**
8613 42nd Ave. S
Seattle, WA 98118
Petersen, Chris, Exec. Dir.

Snow Leopard Network **[4888]**
4649 Sunnyside Ave. N
Seattle, WA 98103
PH: (206)632-2421
Mishra, Charudutt, Exec. Dir.

Snow Leopard Trust **[4889]**
4649 Sunnyside Ave. N, Ste. 325
Seattle, WA 98103
PH: (206)632-2421
Fax: (206)632-3967
Mishra, Charudutt, Exec. Dir.

Social Work Hospice and Palliative
Care Network **[15299]**
1521 2nd Ave., Ste. 609
Seattle, WA 98101
PH: (412)701-1192
Christ, Grace, PhD, Chairperson

Socialist Alternative **[5767]**
PO Box 45343
Seattle, WA 98145-0343
PH: (206)526-7185

Society for Medical Anthropology
[5925]
American Anthropological Associa-
tion
Box 353100
Seattle, WA 98195
Rödlach, Alexander, Treasurer

Splash **[13337]**
1115 E Pike St.
Seattle, WA 98122
PH: (206)535-7375
Stowe, Eric, Director, Founder

Technology and Information for All
[8678]
333 18th Ave. E
Seattle, WA 98112
Le Du, Emma, President, Founder

Tile Roofing Institute **[592]**
2150 N 107th St., Ste. 205
Seattle, WA 98133

PH: (206)209-5300
Burlingame, Kevin, Chairman

True Compassion Advocates
[15300]
PO Box 27514
Seattle, WA 98165
PH: (206)366-2715
Geller, Eileen, President

United Indians of All Tribes Foundation [18714]
5011 Bernie Whitebear Way
Seattle, WA 98199
PH: (206)285-4425
Smith, Jeff, Chairman

United States Tchoukball Association
[22536]
4250 W Cramer St.
Seattle, WA 98199
PH: (240)505-5951

U.S. Women and Cuba Collaboration [18535]
6508 27th Ave. NW
Seattle, WA 98117
Domingo, Cindy, Director

Uplift International [15504]
PO Box 27696
Seattle, WA 98165-2696
PH: (206)455-0916
Schlansky, Mark, CEO, Founder

Vietnam Veterans Against the War
Anti-Imperialist [19226]
PO Box 21604
Seattle, WA 98111-3604
PH: (206)374-2215
Fax: (206)374-2215

Village Volunteers [12197]
5100 S Dawson St., Ste. 202
Seattle, WA 98118
PH: (206)577-0515
Greene, Shana, Exec. Dir., Founder

Water 1st International [13340]
1904 3rd Ave., Ste. 1012
Seattle, WA 98101
PH: (206)297-3024
Smith-Nilson, Marla, Exec. Dir.,
Founder

Wild Entrust International [4902]
5140 Ballard Ave. NW, Ste. A
Seattle, WA 98107
PH: (206)687-7956
Fulghum, Christian, President, Chairman

Wild Steelhead Coalition [4905]
117 E Louisa St., No. 329
Seattle, WA 98102
Kelly, Luke, V. Chmn. of the Bd.

Wildlands Network [4108]
1402 3rd Ave., Ste. 1019
Seattle, WA 98101
PH: (206)538-5363
Toll free: 877-554-5234
Olson, Steve, President

World Concern [12569]
19303 Fremont Ave. N
Seattle, WA 98133
PH: (206)546-7201
Toll free: 800-755-5022
Fax: (206)546-7269
Lonac, Robert, CEO

World Juggling Federation [22969]
7511 Greenwood Ave. N, No. 315
Seattle, WA 98103
Garfield, Jason, Founder, President

Youth Maritime Training Association
[8266]
PO Box 70425
Seattle, WA 98127-0425

PH: (206)300-5559
Stauffer, Gary, President

Zoological Registrars Association
[4937]
c/o Krista Adelhardt, President
Woodland Park Zoo
5500 Phinney Ave. N
Seattle, WA 98103
PH: (206)548-2513
Fax: (206)632-2556
Adelhardt, Krista, President

The Appliqué Society [21750]
PO Box 89
Sequim, WA 98382-0089
Toll free: 800-597-9827
Keane, Eileen, VP

International Association of Orofacial
Myology [16583]
PO Box 2352
Sequim, WA 98382
PH: (360)683-5794
Fax: (503)345-6858
Lee-White, Marsha, President

National Entlebucher Mountain Dog
Association [21921]
c/o Sue Tom, Membership
Chairperson
34 Wild Rose Ln.
Sequim, WA 98382

Hungarian Pumi Club of America
Inc. [21894]
c/o Tammy Hall, Vice President
211 SE Maplewood Ln.
Shelton, WA 98584
PH: (360)427-8918
Levy, Chris, President

Business Espionage Controls and
Countermeasures Association
[1785]
Box 55582
Shoreline, WA 98155-0582
Kanalis, John, Administrator

Coalition of Organic Landscape
Professionals [2068]
1125 NE 152nd St.
Shoreline, WA 98155
PH: (206)362-8947
Stoller, David, President

International Society of Veterinary
Dermatopathology [17650]
c/o Jennifer Ward, DVM
14810 15th Ave. NE
Shoreline, WA 98155
Fax: (206)453-3309
Shearer, David, President

RISE-UP From Poverty [12563]
15613 5th Ave. NE
Shoreline, WA 98155
Amin, Narima, Founder

Children of the Nations International
[10918]
11992 Clear Creek Rd. NW
Silverdale, WA 98383
PH: (360)698-7227
Clark, Chris, Founder

National Seafood Educators [3034]
PO Box 93
Skamokawa, WA 98647
Hansen, Evie, Director, Founder

American Dobermann Association
[21806]
PO Box 2231
Snohomish, WA 98291-2231
PH: (425)397-7630
Fax: (425)397-8747

Continental Luscombe Association
[21220]
1913 Vaughn Ct.
Snohomish, WA 98290

PH: (360)815-3314

Early Childhood Music and Movement Association [12369]
805 Mill Ave.
Snohomish, WA 98290
PH: (360)568-5635
Fax: (360)568-5635
Stratton, Torie, Office Mgr.

Healing the Culture [12768]
605 2nd St., Ste. 218
Snohomish, WA 98290
PH: (360)243-3811
Spitzer, Fr. Robert J., PhD, Chairman, Founder

International Academy of
Gnathology-American Section
[14442]
1322 Ave. D, Ste. A
Snohomish, WA 98290
PH: (210)567-3644
Fax: (210)493-7046
Hasegawa, Paul, Secretary,
Treasurer

National Pygmy Goat Association
[3606]
1932 149th Ave. SE
Snohomish, WA 98290
PH: (425)334-6506
Fax: (425)334-5447
Fraser, Denise, Director

American Baptist Homes and Caring
Ministries [19713]
PO Box 239
Southworth, WA 98386
Painter, Bill, President

All As One - USA [10844]
PO Box 4903
Spanaway, WA 98387
PH: (253)846-0815
Fax: (253)846-0815
Wallace, Deanna, Founder, Exec.
Dir.

American Association of Handwriting
Analysts [10409]
PO Box 4576
Spanaway, WA 98387
PH: (360)455-4551
Toll free: 800-826-7774
Fax: (253)846-6448
O'Brien, Jane, Treasurer

Academy of Ambulatory Foot and
Ankle Surgery [16773]
3707 S Grand Blvd., Ste. A
Spokane, WA 99203
PH: (509)624-1452
Toll free: 800-433-4892
Fax: (509)624-1128
Horsley, Victor, Dr., President

American Exploration & Mining Association [2385]
10 N Post St., Ste. 305
Spokane, WA 99201
PH: (509)624-1158
Heywood, Pat, Dir. of Operations

Association of Change Management
Professionals [2152]
3625 E 16th Ave.
Spokane, WA 99223
PH: (301)200-2362
Darby, Maria, President

Association for the Development of
Human Potential [9544]
406 S Coeur d'Alene St., Ste. T
Spokane, WA 99201
PH: (509)838-3575
Fax: (509)838-6652

Bastard Nation: The Adoptee Rights
Organization [10446]
PO Box 9959
Spokane, WA 99209-0959

PH: (415)704-3166
Fax: (415)704-3166
Greiner, Marley, Exec. Chmn. of the
Bd., Founder

Boss 429 Mustang World Registry
[21342]
PO Box 8035
Spokane, WA 99203
PH: (509)448-0252
Strange, Steve, Contact

Forensic CPA Society [29]
PO Box 31060
Spokane, WA 99223
PH: (509)448-9318
Toll free: 800-923-2797
Fax: (509)448-9302
Larsen, Donna, CEO

Genesis Institute [20596]
1220 N Howard St.
Spokane, WA 99201
PH: (509)467-7913
Fax: (509)467-0344
Hutchins, Dave, Exec. Dir., Founder

Healing the Children [11235]
c/o Carol Borneman
PO Box 9065
Spokane, WA 99209-9065
PH: (509)327-4281
Fax: (509)327-4284
Borneman, Carol, Contact

International Association of Medical
Intuitives [15729]
PO Box 30752
Spokane, WA 99223-3021
PH: (509)389-7290
Lightwalker, Mr. Charles, PhD,
Treasurer

International Doctors in Alcoholics
Anonymous [13147]
8514 E Maringo Dr.
Spokane, WA 99212
Metcalf, Michael, Exec. Dir.

Metaphysical Society of America
[10102]
c/o Brian G. Henning
Dept. of Philosophy
Gonzaga University
502 E Boone Ave.
Spokane, WA 99258-1774
PH: (509)313-5885
Frankenberry, Nancy K., President

National Barley Foods Council
[1520]
2702 W Sunset Blvd.
Spokane, WA 99224
PH: (509)456-2481
Ritter, Cindy, Rep., Media Spec.

Roots and Wings International
[12183]
5018 N Allen Pl.
Spokane, WA 99205
PH: (503)564-8831
Swanson, Mr. Erik, Founder, Exec.
Dir.

Ships on Stamps Unit [22363]
c/o Myron Molnau, Secretary
1616 E 32nd Ct.
Spokane, WA 99203-3918
Molnau, Myron P., Secretary

Sit and Be Fit [16714]
PO Box 8033
Spokane, WA 99203-0033
PH: (509)448-9438
Toll free: 888-678-9438
Fax: (509)448-5078
Wilson, Mary Ann, RN, Founder,
Exec. Dir.

Timber Products Manufacturers **[1423]**
951 E 3rd Ave.
Spokane, WA 99202
PH: (509)535-4646
Fax: (509)534-6106
Molenda, Adam, President

Cedar Shake and Shingle Bureau **[1432]**
PO Box 1178
Sumas, WA 98295-1178
Christensen, Lynne, Dir. of Operations

North America Indigenous Ministries **[20448]**
PO Box 499
Sumas, WA 98295
PH: (604)850-3052
Toll free: 888-942-5468
Fax: (604)504-0178
Hartwig, Ron, Exec. Dir.

Sales and Marketing Executives International **[3019]**
PO Box 1390
Sumas, WA 98295-1390
PH: (312)893-0751
Turner, Willis, President

Adenoid Cystic Carcinoma Organization International **[13870]**
PO Box 112186
Tacoma, WA 98411
Toll free: 888-223-7983
Curry, Tom, President

American Academy of Gold Foil Operators **[14378]**
c/o Marc D. Tollefson, Secretary
701 Regents Blvd.
Tacoma, WA 98466
PH: (253)565-5414
Tollefson, Marc D., Secretary

American Leadership Forum **[18627]**
738 Broadway, Ste. 301
Tacoma, WA 98402-3777
PH: (713)807-1253
Fax: (713)807-1064
Snyder, Kent, Treasurer

American Society for Environmental History **[7872]**
Interdisciplinary Arts & Sciences Program
University of Washington
1900 Commerce St.
Tacoma, WA 98402
Mighetto, Lisa, Exec. Dir.

APA: The Engineered Wood Association **[1429]**
7011 S 19th St.
Tacoma, WA 98466
PH: (253)565-6600
    (253)620-7400
Fax: (253)565-7265
Nyblad, Mary Jo, Trustee

Carpet Cleaners Institute of the Northwest **[711]**
2661 N Pearl St.
Tacoma, WA 98407
PH: (360)687-6156
Toll free: 877-692-2469
Joner, Dan, Officer

Children's International Health Relief **[14181]**
c/o Dr. Robin Jones, President
4218 S Steele St., Ste. 220
Tacoma, WA 98409
PH: (253)476-0556
Jones, Dr. Robin, President, Founder

Clan Phail Society in North America **[20836]**
Box 16
403 Garfield St. S

Tacoma, WA 98444
PH: (253)531-4112
Fax: (253)539-0921
MackFall, John, President

Del Shannon Appreciation Society **[24032]**
PO Box 44201
Tacoma, WA 98448
Young, Brian C., Contact

Engineered Wood Technology Association **[1437]**
7011 S 19th St.
Tacoma, WA 98466
PH: (253)620-7237
Kerwood, Terry, Managing Dir.

Euler Society **[8279]**
c/o Erik R. Tou, Secretary-Treasurer
School of Interdisciplinary Arts and Sciences
University of Washington - Tacoma
1900 Commerce St.
Tacoma, WA 98402
Bradley, Robert E., President

Guild of American Luthiers **[2423]**
8222 S Park Ave.
Tacoma, WA 98408-5226
PH: (253)472-7853
Olsen, Timothy L., President

Hearts for Zambia **[11020]**
PO Box 11161
Tacoma, WA 98411-0161
PH: (253)565-3114

Orphans Africa **[11421]**
2612 N 8th St.
Tacoma, WA 98406-7207
PH: (253)252-3544
Gann, Carl, Founder, President

Professional Loadmaster Association **[5621]**
PO Box 4351
Tacoma, WA 98438
Toll free: 800-239-4524
Disney, Kathy, President

Professionals in Workers' Compensation **[23540]**
PO Box 65893
Tacoma, WA 98464
PH: (206)249-7922
Fax: (206)888-4697
Thomas, Marilyn, Coord.

Society of Ethnobiology **[6099]**
Dept. of Sociology and Anthropology
University of Puget Sound
1500 N Warner St., CMB 1092
Tacoma, WA 98416
Parker, Karen, Secretary

Wolf Haven International **[3968]**
3111 Offut Lake Rd. SE
Tenino, WA 98589
PH: (360)264-4695
Toll free: 800-448-9653
Fax: (360)264-4639
Sleeter, John, President

Cogswell Family Association **[20848]**
c/o Edward R. Cogswell, Secretary
214 140th St. NW
Tulalip, WA 98271-8105
PH: (360)652-4615
Cogswell, Howard, President

Association of Green Property Owners and Managers **[2746]**
3400 Capitol Blvd. SE, Ste. 101
Tumwater, WA 98501
PH: (425)233-6481
Teegarden, Heather, CSEP, Exec. Dir.

Logistics and Transportation Association of North America **[3092]**
PO Box 426
Union, WA 98592
Toll free: 877-858-8627
Dejonge, Katie, Exec. Dir.

Acupuncture Relief Project **[13500]**
3712 NE 40th Ave.
Vancouver, WA 98661
PH: (360)695-9591
Schlabach, Andrew, Founder, President

American Navion Society **[5858]**
16420 SE McGillivray, Ste. 103
Vancouver, WA 98683-3461
PH: (360)833-9921
    (623)975-4052

Clean Water for Haiti **[4754]**
PO Box 871181
Vancouver, WA 98687
PH: (360)450-2929
Rolling, Chris, Exec. Dir.

The Fabric Shop Network, Inc. **[3257]**
PO Box 820128
Vancouver, WA 98682-0003
Harsh, Laurie, Founder

Great Pyrenees Club of America **[21890]**
c/o Ilene Agosto, Membership Committee Chairman
11604 NW 27th Ave.
Vancouver, WA 98685-4418
PH: (360)576-6857
Seeley, Valerie, President

Intracranial Hypertension Research Foundation **[15949]**
6517 Buena Vista Dr.
Vancouver, WA 98661
PH: (360)693-4473
Fax: (360)694-7062
Tanne, Emanuel, MD, Founder, Chairman

National Society of Tax Professionals **[54]**
11700 NE 95th St., Ste. No. 100
Vancouver, WA 98682
PH: (360)695-8309
Toll free: 800-367-8130
Fax: (360)695-7115
Huebel, Keith, President

North American NeuroEndocrine Tumor Society **[14709]**
800 NE Tenney Rd., Ste. 110-412
Vancouver, WA 98685
PH: (360)314-4112
Brendtro, Kari, Exec. Dir., Founder

Parents of Kids with Infectious Diseases **[15413]**
PO Box 5666
Vancouver, WA 98668
PH: (360)695-0293
Toll free: 877-55P-KIDS
Fax: (360)695-6941
Abramson, Jon, MD, Advisor

Shared Hope International **[13416]**
PO Box 65337
Vancouver, WA 98665
PH: (360)693-8100
    (703)351-8062
Toll free: 866-437-5433
Smith, Linda, Founder, President

Stein Collectors International **[21725]**
8002 NE Highway 99
Vancouver, WA 98665
PH: (708)323-9283
Estep, Ms. Carolyn, Treasurer

Western United States Agricultural Trade Association **[3582]**
4601 NE 77th Ave., Ste. 240
Vancouver, WA 98662-6860
PH: (360)693-3373
Fax: (360)693-3464
Anderson, Andy, Exec. Dir.

Alliance for Tompotika Conservation **[3794]**
c/o Marcy Summers, Director
21416 86th Ave. SW
Vashon, WA 98070
PH: (206)463-7720
Fax: (206)463-7720
Summers, Marcy, Director

Gaited Horse International Association **[4353]**
507 N Sullivan Rd., Ste. A-Z
Veradale, WA 99037-8531
PH: (509)928-8389
Fax: (509)927-2012

Conservation through Poverty Alleviation International **[3839]**
712 S Palouse St.
Walla Walla, WA 99362
Craig, Catherine L., PhD, President, Founder

Embracing Orphans **[10959]**
PO Box 2615
Walla Walla, WA 99362
PH: (509)540-9408
Robanske, Carl, Chairman

National InterCollegiate Rodeo Association **[23100]**
2033 Walla Walla Ave.
Walla Walla, WA 99362
PH: (509)529-4402
Fax: (509)525-1090
Walters, Roger, Commissioner

Society for Comparative Literature and the Arts **[9766]**
345 Boyer Avenue
Whitman College
345 Boyer Ave.
Walla Walla, WA 99362

Log Home Builders Association **[874]**
14241 NE Woodinville-Duvall Rd., No. 345
Woodinville, WA 98072
PH: (360)794-4469
Ellsworth, Skip, Founder

MX for Children **[11084]**
PO Box 141
Woodinville, WA 98072
PH: (425)301-0527
Gross, Paul, Founder

Portuguese Water Dog Club of America **[21947]**
20217 NE 163rd St.
Woodinville, WA 98077-9446
Smith, David, President

Stories of Autism **[13778]**
13110 NE 177th Pl., No. 237
Woodinville, WA 98072
PH: (425)501-9725
Cotugno, Charlie, President

Toy Australian Shepherd Association of America **[21971]**
c/o Kelli Reichert, Championship Secretary
495 Robinson Rd.
Woodland, WA 98674
Reichert, Kelli, Secretary

Academy of Organizational and Occupational Psychiatry **[16309]**
402 E Yakima Ave., No. 1080
Yakima, WA 98901-2760

PH: (509)457-4611
Fax: (509)454-3295
Hammer, Paul, VP

Alpine Coach Association **[22416]**
5808 A Summitview Ave., No. 337
Yakima, WA 98908-3042
PH: (509)457-4133
Cook, Tim, President

WEST VIRGINIA

Charles A. and Anne Morrow Lindbergh Foundation **[4080]**
PO Box 861
Berkeley Springs, WV 25411
PH: (703)623-1944
Welf, Kelley A., Dir. of Comm.

Association of Scottish Games and Festivals **[19637]**
c/o Deb Anderson, Treasurer
1836 Boothsville Rd.
Bridgeport, WV 26330
PH: (719)630-0923
Young, Peggy, President

Autism Community of Africa **[13747]**
PO Box 502
Charles Town, WV 25414-0504
PH: (443)718-1824
Kobenan, Mrs. Brigitte, Founder

The National Humane Education Society **[10671]**
PO Box 340
Charles Town, WV 25414-0340
PH: (304)725-0506
Fax: (304)725-1523
Taylor, James D., President

United States Kerry Blue Terrier Club **[21982]**
c/o Mary McGreevy, Membership Chairman
25 New Castle Dr.
Charles Town, WV 25414
PH: (681)252-0816
Feldges, Melanie, President

Center for Economic Options **[11759]**
910 Quarrier St., Ste. 206
Charleston, WV 25301
PH: (304)345-1298
Fax: (304)342-0641
Curry, Pam, Exec. Dir.

Flagon and Trencher Descendants of Colonial Tavern Keepers **[20752]**
1716 Bigley Ave.
Charleston, WV 25302-3938
PH: (304)340-0200
Bannerman, Alexander N., President

Hereditary Order of the Families of the Presidents and First Ladies of America **[21080]**
1716 Bigley Ave.
Charleston, WV 25302-3938
Power, Jane Routt, President

Treeing Walker Breeders and Fanciers Association **[21972]**
c/o Danielle Champ, Secretary
293 Paddy Rd.
Duck, WV 25063
PH: (304)651-9028
Starns, Gary, President

Institute for Earth Education **[7878]**
Cedar Cove
Greenville, WV 24945
PH: (304)832-6404
van Matre, Steve, Chmn. of the Bd.

Appalachian Trail Conservancy **[23322]**
799 Washington St.
Harpers Ferry, WV 25425

PH: (304)535-6331
Fax: (304)535-2667
Marshall, Stacey, Dir. of Fin. & Admin.

Diabetes Alert Dog Alliance **[14524]**
719 Mission Rd.
Harpers Ferry, WV 25425
Kay, Debby, Exec. Dir.

National Gaucher Foundation **[15829]**
61 General Early Dr.
Harpers Ferry, WV 25425
Toll free: 800-504-3189
Fax: (770)934-2911
Berman, Brian E., President

Council for the Advancement of Science Writing **[2673]**
PO Box 910
Hedgesville, WV 25427
PH: (304)754-6786
McGurgan, Diane, Administrator

Pearl S. Buck Birthplace Museum **[9044]**
PO Box 126
Hillsboro, WV 24946-0126
PH: (304)653-4430
Gudmundsson, BJ, President

American Board of Independent Medical Examiners **[15627]**
6470A Merritts Creek Rd.
Huntington, WV 25702-9739
PH: (304)733-0095
    (304)733-0096
Toll free: 877-523-1415
Fax: (304)733-5243
Ranavaya, Prof. Mohammed, MD, President, Director

Appalachian Studies Association, Inc. **[8809]**
1 John Marshall Dr.
Huntington, WV 25755-0002
PH: (304)696-2904
Fax: (304)696-6221
Thomas, Mary K., Exec. Dir.

Autism Services Center **[13755]**
929 4th Ave.
Huntington, WV 25710-0507
PH: (304)525-8014
Fax: (304)525-8026
Sullivan, Ruth C., PhD, Founder

International Association of Medical Science Educators **[15624]**
c/o JulNet Solutions, LLC
1404 1/2 Adams Ave.
Huntington, WV 25704
PH: (304)522-1270
Fax: (304)523-9701
Michaelsen, Veronica, MD, President

International Network for Social Network Analysis **[7167]**
c/o JulNet Solutions, LLC
1404 1/2 Adams Ave.
Huntington, WV 25704
PH: (304)208-8001
Fax: (304)523-9701
Skvoretz, John, President

Oberhasli Breeders of America **[3610]**
c/o Michelle Liga, Secretary/Treasurer
4140 Dogtown Rd.
Kingwood, WV 26537
McCorkle, Betty, VP

Federation for Accessible Nursing Education and Licensure **[16132]**
PO Box 1418
Lewisburg, WV 24901-4418

PH: (304)645-4357
Wallace, Twyla, President, Editor

American Glass Guild **[1500]**
c/o Carol Slovikosky, Treasurer
612 S Queen St.
Martinsburg, WV 25401
Leap, J. Kenneth, Comm. Chm.

AACE International **[6354]**
1265 Suncrest Towne Centre Dr.
Morgantown, WV 26505-1876
PH: (304)296-8444
Fax: (304)291-5728
Quick, Charity A., MBA, Exec. Dir.

American Council on Rural Special Education **[8576]**
West Virginia University
509 Allen Hall
Morgantown, WV 26506-6122
PH: (304)293-3450
Courtade, Ginevra, Chairman

Association of Pediatric Oncology Social Workers **[16603]**
c/o Anita Graham, MSW, LCSW, President
Dept. of Pediatrics, Section of Hematology/Oncology
WVU Healthcare Children's Hospital
Morgantown, WV 26506-9214
PH: (304)293-1205
Fax: (304)293-1216
Graham, Anita, President

Council on Forest Engineering **[4198]**
c/o Appalachian Hardwood Ctr.
PO Box 6125
Morgantown, WV 26505
PH: (240)382-2633

Freeman-Sheldon Research Group, Inc. **[14337]**
c/o Gregory Sabak, Treasurer
115 Birds Eye Dr.
Morgantown, WV 26501

Job Accommodation Network **[11609]**
PO Box 6080
Morgantown, WV 26506-6080
Toll free: 800-526-7234
Hirsh, Anne E., Director

North American Forensic Entomology Association **[6615]**
c/o Rachel Mohr, Treasurer
103 Open Ridge Rd.
Morgantown, WV 26508
Kimsey, Bob, President

United States Football Alliance **[22870]**
c/o Danial Marshall, League Commissioner
Morgantown, WV 26505
PH: (724)866-1714
Goodnight, Randy, Founder, President

Fostoria Glass Society of America **[22133]**
511 Tomlinson Ave.
Moundsville, WV 26041
PH: (304)845-9188
Davis, Jim, President

National Association of State Land Reclamationists **[5636]**
47 School St., Ste. 301
Philippi, WV 26416

The National Crossbowmen of the USA, Inc. **[22504]**
38 B Ave.
Richwood, WV 26261

PH: (304)846-6420
Pimm, William G., Jr., President

Conservation Leadership Network **[4491]**
National Conservation Training Ctr.
698 Conservation Way
Shepherdstown, WV 25443
PH: (304)876-7462
Fax: (304)876-7751
Allen, Katie, Director

National Lighting Bureau **[2104]**
180 Reachcliff Dr.
Shepherdstown, WV 25443
PH: (301)587-9572
    (304)870-4249
Yorgey, James M., Chairman

SkyTruth **[4145]**
PO Box 3283
Shepherdstown, WV 25443-3283
PH: (304)885-4581
Shearer, David, Chairman

Society for the Study of American Women Writers **[10401]**
c/o Heidi Hanrahan, Vice President
PO Box 5000
Dept. of English
Shepherd University
Shepherdstown, WV 25443-5000
Garcia, Magda, VP of Fin.

American Anthropological Association - General Anthropology Division **[5899]**
Marshall University Graduate College
100 Angus E Peyton Dr.
South Charleston, WV 25303
PH: (304)746-1923
Lassiter, Luke Eric, PhD, President

National Institute for Chemical Studies **[13224]**
3200 Kanawha Tpke.
South Charleston, WV 25303
Toll free: 800-611-2296
Fax: (800)611-2296
DiGregorio, Kevin, Exec. Dir.

Catholic Committee of Appalachia **[20392]**
885 Orchard Run Rd.
Spencer, WV 25276
PH: (304)927-5798
Rausch, Fr. John, Director

National Association of Cognitive-Behavioral Therapists **[16951]**
102 Gilson Ave.
Weirton, WV 26062-3912
PH: (304)224-2534
Toll free: 800-253-0167
Pucci, Aldo R., DCBT, President

American Defenders of Bataan and Corregidor **[21189]**
945 Main St.
Wellsburg, WV 26070
Wallace, Mr. J.W. George, Editor

509th Parachute Infantry Association **[21185]**
47 Washington Ave.
Wheeling, WV 26003
Persun, Hal, President

Brooks Bird Club **[4801]**
PO Box 4077
Wheeling, WV 26003
McCullough, Carol, President

Fenton Art Glass Collectors of America **[22132]**
702 W 5th St.
Williamstown, WV 26187-0384

PH: (304)375-6196
Boyle, Miriam, President

WISCONSIN

The Izaak Walton League of
America Endowment [3890]
George M. Guyant, 10598 Hotvedt
Rd.
10598 Hotvedt Rd.
Amherst Junction, WI 54407-9073
PH: (715)824-2405
Shepherd, Robert, President

Center for the Study of Film and History [9301]
Lawrence University
Memorial Hall B5
711 E Boldt Way
Appleton, WI 54911
PH: (920)832-6649
Baybrook, Loren, Editor

Historical Society of the Episcopal
Church [20109]
82 Cherry Ct.
Appleton, WI 54915
PH: (920)383-1910
Prichard, Rev. Robert W., President

The John Birch Society [18027]
770 N Westhill Blvd.
Appleton, WI 54914
PH: (920)749-3780
Toll free: 800-527-8721
Fax: (920)749-5062
Thompson, Arthur R., CEO

Littlest Tumor Foundation [14837]
PO Box 7051
Appleton, WI 54912
PH: (920)475-6599
Wirtanen, Tracy, Founder

National Association of Tax Professionals [5800]
PO Box 8002
Appleton, WI 54914-8002
Toll free: 800-558-3402
Fax: (800)747-0001
Artman, Scott, Exec. Dir.

Puli Club of America [21950]
1616 E Calumet St.
Appleton, WI 54915-4222
PH: (920)730-1885
Exum, Jane Slade, President

Thrivent Financial for Lutherans
[20320]
4321 N Ballard Rd.
Appleton, WI 54919-0001
Toll free: 800-847-4836
Hewitt, Brad, CEO, President

United Barrel Racing Association
[22933]
960 Bunyan Ave.
Balsam Lake, WI 54810
PH: (715)857-6343
Beauvais, Jessica, Mgr.

International Crane Foundation
[4829]
E-11376 Shady Lane Rd.
Baraboo, WI 53913-0447
PH: (608)356-9462
Fax: (608)356-9465
Healy, Hall, Director

North American Crane Working
Group [4856]
c/o Barry Hartup
E-11376 Shady Lane Rd.
Baraboo, WI 53913
Chavez-Ramirez, Felipe, President

Vergilian Society [9109]
c/o Keely Lake, Secretary
Wayland Academy

101 N University Ave.
Beaver Dam, WI 53916
O'Hara, Jim, Officer

American Milking Shorthorn Junior
Society [3703]
800 Pleasant St.
Beloit, WI 53511
PH: (608)365-3332
Fax: (608)365-6644
Cailteux, Scott, President

American Milking Shorthorn Society
[3704]
800 Pleasant St.
Beloit, WI 53511
PH: (608)365-3332
Fax: (608)365-6644
Marak, Steve, Director

Brown Swiss Association [3722]
800 Pleasant St.
Beloit, WI 53511-5456
PH: (608)365-4474
Fax: (608)365-5577
Wallace, David, Exec. Sec.

Dead Theologians Society [19831]
PO Box 368
Black Earth, WI 53515-0368
PH: (608)767-4063
Fax: (608)767-4064
Cotter, Edmond J., Jr., Founder,
Exec. Dir.

American Society of Golf Course
Architects [5955]
125 N Executive Dr., Ste. 302
Brookfield, WI 53005
PH: (262)786-5960
Fax: (262)786-5919
Ritterbusch, Chad, Exec. Dir.

International Foundation of
Employee Benefit Plans [1072]
18700 W Bluemound Rd.
Brookfield, WI 53045
PH: (262)786-6700
(262)786-6710
Toll free: 888-334-3327
Van Alstyne, Stacy, Mgr.

International Society of Certified
Employee Benefit Specialists
[1073]
18700 W Bluemound Rd.
Brookfield, WI 53008-0209
PH: (262)786-8771
Fax: (262)786-8670
Murphy, Wayne C.

National Funeral Directors Association [2412]
13625 Bishop's Dr.
Brookfield, WI 53005
PH: (262)789-1880
Toll free: 800-228-6332
Fax: (262)789-6977
Pepper, Christine, CEO

Society of Risk Management
Consultants [1933]
330 S Executive Dr., Ste. 301
Brookfield, WI 53005-4275
Toll free: 800-765-7762
Harder, Robert, ARM, President

United States Amateur Tug of War
Association [23340]
W504 State Road 92
Brooklyn, WI 53521
Toll free: 800-TUG-O-WAR
Heindel, Lisa

Burlington Liars Club [22160]
113 E Chestnut St., Ste. B
Burlington, WI 53105

Association of Pedestrian and
Bicycle Professionals [19196]
PO Box 93
Cedarburg, WI 53012-0093

PH: (262)228-7025
Fax: (866)720-3611
Hefferan, Jennifer, President

American Paintball Players Association [23054]
530 E South Ave.
Chippewa Falls, WI 54729
PH: (715)720-9131
Raehl, Chris, Coord.

National Collegiate Paintball Association [23055]
530 E South Ave.
Chippewa Falls, WI 54729
PH: (612)605-8323
Fax: (612)605-9255
Raehl, Chris, President

Havana Rabbit Breeders Association
[4597]
c/o Tanya Zimmerman, Secretary/
Treasurer
N-9487 Walnut Rd.
Clintonville, WI 54929
PH: (715)823-5020
Zimmerman, Tanya, Secretary,
Treasurer

American Driving Society, Inc.
[22955]
1837 Ludden Dr., Ste. 120
Cross Plains, WI 53528-9007
PH: (608)237-7382
Fax: (608)237-6468
Arnold, Mike, President

Miniature Arms Collectors/Makers
Society [21296]
c/o Alice McGinnis, Treasurer
2109 Spring St.
Cross Plains, WI 53528
Driskill, Wayne, President

Navy Club of the United States of
America [5616]
PO Box 6051
De Pere, WI 54115-6051
PH: (765)447-2766
(317)473-5087
Krick, Cecil, Cmdr.

Autism Alert [13741]
PO Box 282
Deerfield, WI 53531
PH: (608)628-7852
Lacey, Christine, Founder

National Dairy Shrine [3981]
PO Box 725
Denmark, WI 54208
PH: (920)863-6333
Fax: (920)863-6333
Hendricks, Fred, President

International Morab Breeders' Association [4367]
c/o Wendy Konichek, Chairperson/
Registrar
S101 W 34628 Hwy. LO
Eagle, WI 53119
PH: (262)594-3667
Licht, Jane, V. Chmn. of the Bd.

International Morab Registry [4368]
S 101 W 34628 Highway LO
Eagle, WI 53119
PH: (262)594-3667
Smith, Karen, Exec. Dir.

Trees for Tomorrow [4221]
519 Sheridan E St.
Eagle River, WI 54521
PH: (715)479-6456
Fax: (715)479-2318
Cloninger, Chuck, President

Adventist World Aviation [19696]
8023 County Road L (Hangar S-3)
East Troy, WI 53120

PH: (414)226-5196
Fax: (414)231-9430
Haase, Betty, CFO

American Latex Allergy Association
[13573]
63334 Lohmann LN
Eastman, WI 54626
PH: (608)874-4044
Toll free: 888-972-5378
Lockwood, Sue, CST, Exec. Dir.,
Founder

Association for Science Teacher
Education [8643]
c/o Dr. Bob Hollon, Executive Director
9324 27th Ave.
Eau Claire, WI 54703
PH: (715)838-0893
Fax: (715)838-0893
Butler, Malcolm, President

Association for Social Economics
[6383]
c/o Sanjukta Chaudhuri, Secretary
University of Wisconsin
Department of Economics
463 Schneider Hall
Eau Claire, WI 54701
PH: (715)836-6046
Fontana, Giuseppe, President

National Association of Show Trucks
[3340]
2425 Seymour Rd.
Eau Claire, WI 54703
PH: (715)832-6666
Kemner, Chuck, Exec. Dir.

University of Wisconsin - Eau Claire
Alumni Association [19368]
213 Schofield Hall
Eau Claire, WI 54702-4004
PH: (715)836-3266
Fax: (715)836-4375
Allaman, Lisa, Officer

National Clay Pipe Institute [2609]
N6369 US Highway 12, Ste. A
Elkhorn, WI 53121
PH: (262)742-2904
Fax: (360)242-9094
Boschert, Jeff, President

Global Partners Running Waters,
Inc. [11367]
13105 Watertown Plank Rd.
Elm Grove, WI 53122
PH: (262)787-1010
Gregorcich, Sr. Jan, SSND, Exec.
Dir.

Honorable Order of the Blue Goose,
International [19486]
12940 Walnut Rd.
Elm Grove, WI 53122
PH: (414)221-0341
Fax: (262)782-7608
Maloney, Terrence M., Officer

Specialty Tools and Fasteners
Distributors Association [1769]
500 Elm Grove Rd., Ste. 210
Elm Grove, WI 53122
PH: (262)784-4774
Toll free: 800-352-2981
Fax: (262)784-5059
Earley, Terry, President

American Pinzgauer Association
[3707]
W5702 Grouse Dr.
Endeavor, WI 53930
PH: (608)697-5968
(936)443-9205
Wamsley, Lisa, President

Otterhound Club of America [21938]
c/o Becky Van Houten, Secretary
3846 Juddville Rd.

Fish Creek, WI 54212
PH: (570)739-7074
Houten, Becky, Secretary

National Dairy Herd Improvement
Association **[3738]**
5940 Seminole Centre Ct., Ste. 200
Fitchburg, WI 53711
PH: (608)848-6455
Fax: (608)260-7772
Mattison, Jay, Administrator, CEO

Congregation of Sisters of Saint
Agnes **[19828]**
320 County Road K
Fond du Lac, WI 54937-8158
PH: (920)907-2300
Craig, Carol A., Exec. Asst.

Inland Lake Yachting Association
[22621]
PO Box 662
Fontana, WI 53125-0311
PH: (847)675-6434
Berg, Dave, Exec. Dir.

National Niemann Pick Disease
Foundation **[15831]**
401 Madison Ave., Ste. B
Fort Atkinson, WI 53538
PH: (920)563-0930
Toll free: 877-287-3672
Fax: (920)563-0931
Fey, Margo

Text and Academic Authors Associa-
tion **[10404]**
PO Box 367
Fountain City, WI 54629
PH: (727)563-0020
Pawlak, Kim, Dir..of Operations

English Cocker Spaniel Club of
America **[21871]**
c/o Shannon Loritz, Secretary
903 Lake St.
Fremont, WI 54940
PH: (920)216-2855
Nawrocki, Chereen, President

Association of Professional Reserve
Analysts **[2739]**
W175 N11117 Stonewood Dr., Ste.
204
Germantown, WI 53022
Toll free: 877-858-5047
Fax: (262)532-2430
Thompson, Richard, President

Berean Bible Society **[19751]**
PO Box 756
Germantown, WI 53022-0756
PH: (262)255-4750
Fax: (262)255-4195
Sadler, Pastor Paul M., President

Federation of Environmental
Technologists, Inc. **[4546]**
W175 N11081 Stonewood Dr., Ste.
203
Germantown, WI 53022
PH: (262)437-1700
Fax: (262)437-1702
Hurula, Barbara, Exec. Dir.

Columbia College of Nursing Alumni
Association **[19319]**
4425 N Port Washington Rd.
Glendale, WI 53212
PH: (414)326-2330
Fax: (414)326-2331
Blair, Tracy, President, Treasurer

Irish Terrier Club of America **[21902]**
c/o Susan Bednar, Secretary
7170 N Seneca Ave.
Glendale, WI 53217-3870
PH: (414)228-0268
Brouillette, Don, President

American CueSports Alliance
[22583]
101 S Military Ave., Ste. P, No. 131
Green Bay, WI 54303
PH: (920)662-1705
Fax: (920)662-1706
Lewis, John, Exec. Dir.

Global Association of Holistic
Psychotherapy **[16973]**
2221 S Webster Ave.
PMB 122
Green Bay, WI 54301
Toll free: 877-346-1167
Riutta, Shelley, MSE, Founder,
President

Kids With Heart National Association
for Children's Heart Disorders, Inc.
[14132]
1578 Careful Dr.
Green Bay, WI 54304-2941
Rintamaki, Michelle, BA, President,
Treasurer

MUMS National Parent-to-Parent
Network **[17344]**
150 Custer Ct.
Green Bay, WI 54301-1243
PH: (920)336-5333
Fax: (920)339-0995

PKS Kids **[14851]**
PO Box 12211
Green Bay, WI 54307
Zane, Mike, Chairperson

Save Your Future Association **[4101]**
2641 Trojan Dr., No. 309
Green Bay, WI 54304
PH: (920)857-9520
Nforba, Dieudonne Tantoh, Founder

Volunteer Missionary Movement -
U.S. Office **[19920]**
5980 W Loomis Rd.
Greendale, WI 53129-1824
PH: (414)423-8660
Fax: (414)423-8964
Muth, R.Timothy, President

Mu Kappa Tau **[23810]**
5217 S 51st St.
Greenfield, WI 53220
PH: (414)328-1952
Fax: (414)235-3425
Hartman, Dr. Katie, President

Pi Sigma Epsilon **[23811]**
5217 S 51st St.
Greenfield, WI 53220
PH: (414)328-1952
Fax: (414)235-3425
Salvani, Jon, President

Professional Fraternity Association
[23764]
5217 S 51st St.
Greenfield, WI 53220
PH: (512)789-9530
Schaffer, Suzane, President

Citizens Equal Rights Alliance
[12028]
PO Box 0379
Gresham, WI 54128
Bachman, Judy, Chairperson

Italian Folk Art Federation of
America **[9615]**
5275 Robinwood Ln.
Hales Corners, WI 53130
Gigliotti, Leslie, President, CEO

Kissel Kar Klub **[21415]**
Wisconsin Automotive Museum
147 N Rural St.
Hartford, WI 53027

PH: (262)673-7999

Fishing Has No Boundaries Inc.
[22844]
15453 County Highway B
Hayward, WI 54843
PH: (715)634-3185
Toll free: 800-243-3462
Fax: (715)634-1305
Koppa, Jim, President

International Log Rolling Association
[23231]
c/o Polly Pappadopoulos
3111 S Pleasant Dr.
Holmen, WI 54636
Pappadopoulos, Polly, Contact

National Alaska Native American
Indian Nurses Association **[16143]**
c/o Pelagie Snesrud, RN, Treasurer
418 Russell Dr. S
Holmen, WI 54636
Bishop, Jewel, RN, President

North American Squirrel Association
[22293]
PO Box 186
Holmen, WI 54636
PH: (608)234-5988
Johnson, Steve, Secretary

U.S. Log Rolling Association **[23365]**
c/o Polly Pappadopoulos, Secretary
3111 S Pleasant Dr.
Holmen, WI 54636
Hadley, Sam, VP

Bellarmine Forum **[19803]**
PO Box 542
Hudson, WI 54016-0542
PH: (651)276-1429
Rice, Charles E., Chairman,
President

Piper Owner Society **[21243]**
N7450 Aanstad Rd.
Iola, WI 54945
PH: (715)445-5000
Toll free: 800-331-0038
Fax: (715)445-4053
Jones, Joe, Publisher

National Baton Twirling Association
USA **[22580]**
PO Box 266
Janesville, WI 53547
PH: (608)754-2238
Fax: (608)754-1986

Seventh Day Baptist General
Conference **[19736]**
PO Box 1678
Janesville, WI 53547-1678
PH: (608)752-5055
Fax: (608)752-7711
Appel, Robert F., Exec. Dir.

Seventh Day Baptist General
Conference of the United States
and Canada **[19737]**
PO Box 1678
Janesville, WI 53547-1678
PH: (608)752-5055
Fax: (608)752-7711
Appel, Robert, Exec. Dir.

Seventh Day Baptist Historical
Society **[19738]**
PO Box 1678
Janesville, WI 53547-1678
PH: (608)752-5055
Fax: (608)752-7711
Kersten, Mr. Nicholas J., Hist.,
Librarian

American Motors Owners Association **[21323]**
892 N Jackson Ave.
Jefferson, WI 53549

PH: (920)674-4482
Salisbury, Darryl A., Chairman

O.J. Noer Research Foundation
[4284]
PO Box 94
Juneau, WI 53039-0094
Wiley, J.I., President

NANDA International **[16142]**
PO Box 157
Kaukauna, WI 54130
Herdman, Dr. T. Heather, Exec. Dir.,
CEO

Gene Pitney International Fan Club
[24040]
6201 39th Ave.
Kenosha, WI 53142-7015

International Law Enforcement
Educators and Trainers Association
[5474]
4742 79 St.
Kenosha, WI 53142
PH: (262)767-1406
Fax: (262)767-1813
Hedden, Harvey V., Exec. Dir.

Noah's Never Ending Rainbow
[14848]
7737 6th Ave.
Kenosha, WI 53143
PH: (262)605-3690
Tehako-Esser, Dana, President,
CEO

Brick by Brick for Tanzania! **[8447]**
539 Braatz Dr.
Kewaskum, WI 53040
PH: (262)573-9032
Kenworthy, John, Exec. Dir.,
Founder

Association of Physician Assistants
in Obstetrics and Gynecology
[16276]
563 Carter Ct., Ste. B
Kimberly, WI 54136-2201
PH: (920)560-5620
Toll free: 800-545-0636
Fax: (920)882-3655
Fosnight, Aleece, MSPAS, PA-C,
President

National Association of Local Boards
of Health **[17008]**
563 Carter Ct., Ste. B
Kimberly, WI 54136
PH: (920)560-5644
Fax: (920)882-3655
Hughes, Barbara Ann, President

National Defender Investigator As-
sociation **[5368]**
PO Box 169
Kohler, WI 53044
PH: (920)395-2330
Fax: (866)668-9858
Carlson, Larry, VP

Patterdale Terrier Club of America
[21941]
511 Lower Rd.
Kohler, WI 53044

ADOREMUS - Society for the
Renewal of the Sacred Liturgy
[19787]
PO Box 385
La Crosse, WI 54602-0385
PH: (608)521-0385
Hitchcock, Helen Hull, Editor

African American Mutual Assistance
Network **[11307]**
2709 South Ave., Ste. E
La Crosse, WI 54601
Toll free: 800-765-4050
Boone, Elverta, President

American Physical Therapy Association - Orthopaedic Section [17435]
2920 East Ave. S, Ste. 200
La Crosse, WI 54601
PH: (608)788-3982
Toll free: 800-444-3982
Fax: (608)788-3965
DeFlorian, Terri, Exec. Dir.

APS Foundation of America [13784]
PO Box 801
La Crosse, WI 54602-0801
PH: (608)782-2626
Fax: (608)782-6569
Pohlman, Tina, President, Founder, Exec. Dir.

Association of Recovering Motorcyclists [13126]
1503 Market St.
La Crosse, WI 54601

Bereavement Services [10772]
1900 South Ave., AVS-003
La Crosse, WI 54601
PH: (608)782-7300
Toll free: 800-362-9567
Sturm, Brad, Chmn. of the Bd.

Center for Grief & Death Education [13216]
University of Wisconsin - La Crosse
Center for Grief & Death Education
302G Graff Main Hall
La Crosse, WI 54601-3742
PH: (608)785-8440
Srinivasan, Dr. Erica, Director

Cliometric Society [18145]
c/o Michael Haupert, Executive Director
Dept. of Economics
University of Wisconsin - La Crosse
1725 State St.
La Crosse, WI 54601
PH: (608)785-6863
Fax: (608)785-8549
Haupert, Michael, Exec. Dir.

Lutheran Girl Pioneers [20309]
1611 Caledonia St.
La Crosse, WI 54603-2234
PH: (608)781-5232
Fax: (608)781-5233

Freshwater Mollusk Conservation Society [4818]
c/o Teresa Newton, President
Upper Midwest Environ. Science Ctr.
U.S. Geological Survey
2630 Fanta Reed Rd.
Lacrosse, WI 54603
PH: (608)781-6217
Morrison, Patricia, President

Global Orphan Outreach [11002]
PO Box 193
Ladysmith, WI 54848
PH: (715)415-4401
Barber, Donna, Exec. Dir., Founder

Contemporary Art Pottery Collectors Association [21579]
PO Box 175
Lake Geneva, WI 53147
Rowe, Carol, President

Nukewatch [18735]
740-A Round Lake Rd.
Luck, WI 54853
PH: (715)472-4185
Fax: (715)472-4184
Peterson, Arianne, Officer

International Silo Association [168]
E106 Church Rd.
Luxemburg, WI 54217
PH: (920)655-3301
Shefchik, Leroy, President

International Society for Aviation Photography, Inc. [2585]
c/o Bonnie Kratz, Treasurer
N4752 Valley Rd.
Luxemburg, WI 54217
Collins, Mike, Secretary

Advanced Media Workflow Association [3205]
436 N Westfield Rd.
Madison, WI 53717
PH: (608)513-5992
Main, Barbara, Operations Mgr.

Alliance for Life Ministries [19940]
PO Box 5102
Madison, WI 53705
Lagan, Paul, President

Alliance of State Pain Initiatives [16545]
University of Wisconsin
School of Medicine and Public Health
1300 University Ave., Ste. 3795
Madison, WI 53706
PH: (608)262-0978
Fax: (608)265-4014

ALS Worldwide [13681]
5808 Dawley Dr
Madison, WI 53711-7209
PH: (608)663-0920
Byer, Barbara, Exec. Dir.

American Academy of Cosmetic Dentistry [14372]
402 W Wilson St.
Madison, WI 53703
PH: (608)222-8583
Toll free: 800-543-9220
Fax: (608)222-9540
Gibson, Chiann, DMD, President

American Bryological and Lichenological Society [6128]
c/o Susan Wolf, Secretary
430 Lincoln Dr.
Madison, WI 53706-1381
PH: (608)262-2754
St. Clair, Larry, President

American College of Veterinary Pathologists [17620]
2424 American Ln.
Madison, WI 53704
PH: (608)443-2466
Fax: (608)443-2474
Coe, Wendy, Exec. Dir.

American Conference for Irish Studies [9597]
Theatre and Drama Dept.
University of Wisconsin-Madison
821 University Ave., 6192 Vilas Hall
Madison, WI 53706-1497
PH: (212)180-3590
Burke, Mary, Mgr.

American Electrophoresis Society [6407]
Kendrick Laboratories, Inc.
1202 Ann St.
Madison, WI 53713-2410
Hoelter, Matt, Exec. Dir.

American Institute of Bangladesh Studies [7530]
B488 Medical Science Ctr.
1300 University Ave.
Madison, WI 53706
PH: (608)261-1471
Mathbor, Dr. Golam, President

American Institute of the History of Pharmacy [16640]
777 Highland Ave.
Madison, WI 53705-2222

PH: (608)262-5378
Stroud, Dr. Elaine C., Asst. Dir.

American Institute of Pakistan Studies [10061]
B488 Medical Science Ctr.
University of Wisconsin - Madison
1300 University Ave.
Madison, WI 53706
PH: (608)265-1471
(608)261-1194
Ali, Kamran Asdar, President

American Needlepoint Guild, Inc. [21747]
2424 American Ln.
Madison, WI 53704-3102
PH: (608)443-2476
Fax: (608)443-2474
McEnerney, Cathe, President

American Orthoptic Council [16368]
3914 Nakoma Rd.
Madison, WI 53711
PH: (608)233-5383
Fax: (608)263-4247
France, Ms. Leslie, CO, Exec. Dir.

American Osteopathic Academy of Sports Medicine [17277]
2424 American Ln.
Madison, WI 53704
PH: (608)443-2477
Fax: (608)443-2474
Cook, R. Scott, President

American Society of Agronomy [3544]
5585 Guilford Rd.
Madison, WI 53711-5801
PH: (608)273-8080
Bergfeld, Ellen G.M., PhD, CEO

American Society of Preventive Oncology [16337]
330 WARF Bldg.
610 Walnut St.
Madison, WI 53726
PH: (608)263-9515
Fax: (608)263-4497
Newcomb, Polly, President

American Society for Veterinary Clinical Pathology [17626]
2424 American Ln.
Madison, WI 53704
PH: (608)443-2479
Fax: (608)443-2474
Johnson, Jennifer, Treasurer

Andean Health and Development [15439]
UW Dept. of Family Medicine
1100 Delaplaine Ct.
Madison, WI 53715
PH: (619)788-6833
Gaus, Dr. David, Exec. Dir., Founder

Association of Family and Conciliation Courts [5188]
6525 Grand Teton Plz.
Madison, WI 53719
PH: (608)664-3750
Fax: (608)664-3751
Boshier, Peter, President

Association for Korean Music Research [9877]
455 North Park St.,
University of Wisconsin-Madison
455 N Park St.
Madison, WI 53706
PH: (608)263-1900
Sutton, Prof. R. Anderson, President

Association of Ringside Physicians [16744]
2424 American Ln.
Madison, WI 53704
Estwanik, Joe, Bd. Member

Association of State Energy Research & Technology Transfer Institutions [6460]
455 Science Dr., Ste. 200
Madison, WI 53711
PH: (703)395-1076
Fay, Jake, Treasurer, Secretary

Association of State Floodplain Managers [3815]
575 D'Onofrio Dr., Ste. 200
Madison, WI 53719
PH: (608)828-3000
Fax: (608)828-6319
Larson, Mr. Larry A., CFM, Pol. Dir.

Balalaika and Domra Association of America [9879]
2801 Warner St.
Madison, WI 53713-2160
Rappaport, Charley, Founder

International Association of Jim Beam Bottle and Specialties Club [21554]
2965 Waubesa Ave.
Madison, WI 53711-5964
PH: (608)663-9661
Fax: (608)663-9664
Hellwig, Beth, President

Business Forms Management Association [3168]
1147 Fleetwood Ave.
Madison, WI 53716-1417
Toll free: 888-367-3078

Children of the Earth United [4113]
PO Box 258035
Madison, WI 53725
PH: (608)237-6577
Reinfeld, Jennifer, Exec. Dir., Founder

Christians in the Visual Arts [8971]
849 E Washington Ave., Ste. 212
Madison, WI 53703
PH: (608)433-9339
Anderson, Cameron, Exec. Dir.

Clinic at a Time [15444]
PO Box 14457
Madison, WI 53708-0457
PH: (608)239-3091
Yayehyirad, Mulusew, Exec. Dir., Founder

Collegians Activated to Liberate Life [12767]
PO Box 259806
Madison, WI 53725-9806
PH: (608)256-2255

Control Systems Integrators Association [3192]
22 N Carroll St., Ste. 300
Madison, WI 53703
PH: (608)310-7851
Toll free: 800-661-4914
Fax: (888)581-3666
Rivera, Jose, CEO

Council of Teachers of Southeast Asian Languages [8181]
c/o Sheila Zamar, Secretary
1240 Van Hise Hall
University of Wisconsin-Madison
1220 Linden Dr.
Madison, WI 53706
Pandin, Jolanda M., VP

Credit Union Executives Society [948]
5510 Research Park Dr.
Madison, WI 53711-5377
PH: (608)271-2664
Toll free: 800-252-2664
Fax: (608)271-2303
Pembroke, John, President, CEO

Credit Union National Association [949]
5710 Mineral Point Rd.
Madison, WI 53705
PH: (202)638-5777
Toll free: 800-356-9655
Fax: (202)638-7734
Staatz, Rod, Chairman

Crop Science Society of America [3547]
5585 Guilford Rd.
Madison, WI 53711-5801
PH: (608)273-8080
Grusak, Michael A., President

CUES Financial Suppliers Forum [2277]
5510 Research Park Dr.
Madison, WI 53711-5377
PH: (608)271-2664
Toll free: 800-252-2664
Fax: (608)271-2303
Ramirez, Robert D., CCE, Director

Environmental Design Research Association [5967]
22 N Caroll St., Ste. 300
Madison, WI 53703
PH: (608)310-7540
Fax: (608)251-5941
Lang, Marechiel Santos, Exec. Dir.

Family Farm Defenders [4153]
122 State St., No. 405A
Madison, WI 53703
PH: (608)260-0900
Fax: (608)260-0900
Greeno, Joel, President

Foster Care Children & Family Fund [12413]
PO Box 2534
Madison, WI 53701-2534
PH: (608)274-9111
Fax: (608)274-4838
White, Cora E., President, CEO

Free to Breathe [13973]
1 Point Pl., Ste. 200
Madison, WI 53719
PH: (608)833-7905
Fax: (608)833-7906
Vidaver, Regina, PhD, Exec. Dir.

Freedom From Religion Foundation [20014]
PO Box 750
Madison, WI 53701
PH: (608)256-8900
Fax: (608)204-0422
Harburg, Ernie, Bd. Member

Friends of Liberia [12961]
c/o Nimu Sidhu, Treasurer
648 E Johnson St., No. 3
Madison, WI 53703
Vickers, Stephanie, President

Green Schools National Network [7895]
PO Box 14744
Madison, WI 53708-0744
Seydel, Jennifer, PhD, Exec. Dir.

Health Care Education Association [7769]
2424 American Ln.
Madison, WI 53704-3102
PH: (608)441-1054
Fax: (608)443-2474
Cornett, Sandy, President

Institute for Chemical Education [6202]
Dept. of Chemistry
University of Wisconsin-Madison
1101 University Ave.

Madison, WI 53706-1322
PH: (608)262-3033
Toll free: 888-220-9822
Fax: (608)265-8094
Fanis, Linda, Mktg. & Sales Mgr.

Institute for Global Ethics [6621]
10 E Doty St., Ste. 825
Madison, WI 53703
PH: (608)204-5902
Toll free: 888-607-0883
Kidder, Dr. Rushworth M., Founder

International Association of Industrial Accident Boards and Commissions [5164]
5610 Medical Cir., Ste. 24
Madison, WI 53719
PH: (608)663-6355
Maynard, R.D., President

International Dairy-Deli-Bakery Association [1340]
636 Science Dr.
Madison, WI 53711-1073
PH: (608)310-5000
Fax: (608)238-6330

International Society of Psychiatric-Mental Health Nurses [16140]
2424 American Ln.
Madison, WI 53704-3102
PH: (608)443-2463
Fax: (608)443-2478
Horton-Deutsch, Sara, Mem.

Interstate Postgraduate Medical Association of North America [14748]
PO Box 5474
Madison, WI 53705
PH: (608)231-9045
Toll free: 877-292-4489
Lopez, Carolyn, Chairperson

InterVarsity Christian Fellowship [20428]
635 Science Dr.
Madison, WI 53707-7895
PH: (608)274-9001
Fax: (608)274-7882
Hill, Alec D., CEO, President

InterVarsity Link [8618]
635 Science Dr.
Madison, WI 53711
PH: (608)443-4558
Molitor, Renee, Coord.

Lumbar Spine Research Society [17259]
1685 Highland Ave.
Madison, WI 53705-2281
PH: (608)770-8992
Currier, Bradford, MD, President

Media Communications Association - International [1198]
2810 Crossroads Dr., Ste. 3800
Madison, WI 53705-0135
Toll free: 888-899-6224
Fax: (888)862-8150
Alberth, Brian

Microanalysis Society [6867]
c/o Thomas F. Kelly, President
5500 Nobel Dr., Ste. 100
Madison, WI 53711-4951
Lowers, Heather A., Secretary

Minority Student Achievement Network [7903]
Wisconsin Center for Education Research
467 Education Sciences Bldg.
1025 W Johnson St.
Madison, WI 53706
PH: (608)263-1565
Fax: (608)263-6448
Hafner, Madeline M., PhD, Exec. Dir.

National Association of Professional Allstate Agents [1899]
22 N Carroll St., Ste. 300
Madison, WI 53703
Toll free: 877-627-2248
Fax: (866)627-2232
Fish, Jim, President

National Association of Professors of Hebrew [8141]
907 Van Hise Hall
University of Wisconsin-Madison
1220 Linden Dr.
Madison, WI 53706-1525
Fax: (608)262-8570
Morahg, Prof. Gilead, Exec. VP

National Center for Student Leadership [8624]
2718 Dryden Dr.
Madison, WI 53704
Toll free: 800-433-0499
Fax: (608)246-3597
Kueppers, Mark, Asst. Dir.

National Class E Scow Association [22651]
337 Woodland Cir.
Madison, WI 53704
PH: (608)347-1480
Cole, Robert, Commodore

National Conference of Bar Examiners [5440]
302 S Bedford St.
Madison, WI 53703
PH: (608)280-8550
Fax: (608)280-8552
Moeser, Erica, CEO, President

National Resume Writers' Association [3514]
5113 Monona Dr.
Madison, WI 53716
Toll free: 877-843-6792
Bryce, Shauna C., President

National Telemedia Council [9146]
1922 University Ave.
Madison, WI 53726
PH: (608)218-1182
Fax: (608)218-1183
Rowe, Marieli, Editor

No Stomach for Cancer [14034]
PO Box 46070
Madison, WI 53711
PH: (608)692-5141
Toll free: 855-355-0241
Gauger, Meghan, Exec. Dir.

North American Lake Management Society [6781]
PO Box 5443
Madison, WI 53705-0443
PH: (608)233-2836
Fax: (608)233-3186
Forsberg, Philip, Dir. of Programs

Norwegian American Genealogical Center [20988]
415 W Main St.
Madison, WI 53703-3116
PH: (608)255-2224
Fax: (608)255-6842

Outside the Bean [18623]
PO Box 1565
Madison, WI 53701-1565
Earley, Matt, President

Pediatric Congenital Heart Association [15219]
14 Ellis Potter Ct., Ste. 100
Madison, WI 53711
PH: (608)370-3739
Kasnic, David M., Exec. Dir.

Preventive Cardiovascular Nurses Association [16181]
613 Williamson St., Ste. 200
Madison, WI 53703-3515

PH: (608)250-2440
Dennison Himmelfarb, Cheryl R., RN, ANP, President

Psychonomic Society [16933]
2424 American Ln.
Madison, WI 53704-3102
PH: (608)441-1070
Fax: (608)443-2474
Moore, Cathleen, Chairperson

Re-Formed Congregation of the Goddess - International [20646]
PO Box 6677
Madison, WI 53716-0677
PH: (608)226-9998

Sarvodaya U.S.A. [11427]
1127 University Ave.
Madison, WI 53715
PH: (608)567-4421
Fax: (608)310-5865
Warbington, Joseph, Chairperson

Sharing Resources Worldwide [15495]
2405 Industrial Dr.
Madison, WI 53713
PH: (608)445-8503
Thompson, Richard, President

Society for Clinical and Medical Hair Removal [14658]
2424 American Ln.
Madison, WI 53704-3102
PH: (608)443-2470
Fax: (608)443-2474
Moore, William A., President

Society for Psychophysiological Research [16943]
2424 American Ln.
Madison, WI 53704
PH: (608)443-2472
Fax: (608)443-2474
Rees, Susan, Director

Society for Research on Nicotine and Tobacco [4721]
2424 American Ln.
Madison, WI 53704
PH: (608)443-2462
Fax: (608)443-2474
McClure, Jennifer, Mem.

Society for the Study of Reproduction [17130]
1619 Monroe St., Ste. 3
Madison, WI 53711-2063
PH: (608)256-2777
Fax: (608)256-4610
Murphy, Bruce D., President

Society of Wetland Scientists [3945]
22 N Carroll St., Ste. 300
Madison, WI 53703-2798
PH: (608)310-7855
Fax: (608)251-5941
Battaglia, Loretta, Sec. Gen., Membership Chp.

Soil Science Society of America [7194]
5585 Guilford Rd.
Madison, WI 53711
PH: (608)273-8080
Fax: (608)273-2021
van Es, Harold M., President

Structural Building Components Association [585]
6300 Enterprise Ln.
Madison, WI 53719
PH: (608)274-4849
Fax: (608)274-3329
Grundahl, Kirk, PE, Officer

Working Capital for Community Needs [18564]
517 N Segoe Rd., Ste. 209
Madison, WI 53705-3172

PH: (608)257-7230
Harris, Will, President

World Council of Credit Unions [959]
5710 Mineral Point Rd.
Madison, WI 53705-4454
PH: (608)395-2000
Fax: (608)395-2001
Branch, Brian, President, CEO

World Sturgeon Conservation
Society U.S.A. [3974]
Wisconsin Dept. of Natural
Resources
PO Box 7921
Madison, WI 53707-7921
PH: (608)267-7591
Fax: (608)266-2244
Brunch, Dr. Ron, Officer

American Breweriana Association
[21259]
c/o Darrell Smith, Executive Director
PO Box 269
Manitowish Waters, WI 54545-0269
PH: (715)604-2774
Grier, John A., Editor

32nd Red Arrow Veteran Association
[20699]
c/o Theodor J. Welch, 1st Vice
President
1113 N 8th St.
Manitowoc, WI 54220-2817
PH: (608)271-3075
Welch, Theodor J., 1st VP

Society for German-American Studies [9340]
c/o Karyl Rommelfanger, Membership Chair
4824 Morgan Dr.
Manitowoc, WI 54220
Roba, William H., Officer

Soo Line Historical and Technical
Society [10191]
PO Box 603
Manitowoc, WI 54221-0603

Laurence-Moon-Bardet-Biedl
Syndrome Network [14835]
c/o Robert Haws, Committee Chair
Marshfield Clinic
1000 N Oak Dr.
Marshfield, WI 54449
PH: (715)387-5240
Ogden, Tim, President

Acres of Hope Liberia [11302]
29525 Four Corners Store Rd.
Mason, WI 54856-2054
PH: (715)765-4118
Fax: (715)765-4119
Anglin, Patty, Exec. Dir.

United States of America Deaf
Basketball [22576]
5313 Windwood Cir.
McFarland, WI 53558-9676
Costello, Christina, Commissioner

Automotive Fleet and Leasing As-
sociation [337]
N83 W13410 Leon Rd.
Menomonee Falls, WI 53051
PH: (414)386-0366
Fax: (414)359-1671
Mott, Gary, Comm. Chm.

Farm Financial Standards Council
[3562]
c/o Carroll Merry
N78 W14573 Appleton Ave., No. 287
Menomonee Falls, WI 53051
PH: (262)253-6902
Fax: (262)253-6903
Severe, Stephen, VP

Federation of Clinical Immunology
Societies [15378]
N83 W13410 Leon Rd.
Menomonee Falls, WI 53051
PH: (414)359-1670
Fax: (414)359-1671
Bast, Gail L., Director

International Association of Special
Investigation Units [1876]
N83 W13410 Leon Rd.
Menomonee Falls, WI 53051
PH: (414)375-2992
Fax: (414)359-1671
Wickre, Wade, President

National Vehicle Leasing Association
[2932]
N83 W13410 Leon Rd.
Menomonee Falls, WI 53051
PH: (414)533-3300
Fax: (414)359-1671
Mcmahon, PJ, President

Ophthalmic Anesthesia Society
[16400]
N83 W13410 Leon Rd.
Menomonee Falls, WI 53051
PH: (414)359-1628
Fax: (414)359-1671
Feldman, Marc, MD, President

Simple Hope [12729]
PO Box 4
Menomonee Falls, WI 53052-0004
Schwalbach, Pamela, Founder

Society for Mucosal Immunology
[15385]
N83 W13410 Leon Rd.
Menomonee Falls, WI 53051
PH: (414)359-1650
Fax: (414)359-1671
Mowat, Allan, MD, PhD, President

Society for Vascular Nursing [16188]
N83 W13410 Leon Rd.
Menomonee Falls, WI 53051
PH: (414)376-0001
Fax: (414)359-1671
Bast, Gail L., President

American Veterinary Exhibitors' Association [17629]
712 N Broadway
Menomonie, WI 54751-1511
Gadomski, Brent, President

Association of Lutheran Secondary
Schools [8257]
c/o Ross Stueber, Head Administra-
tor
12800 N Lake Shore Dr.
Mequon, WI 53097
PH: (262)243-4210
Stueber, Dr. Ross, Administrator

Professional Association of Innkeep-
ers International [1676]
108 South Cleveland St.
Merrill, WI 54452-2435
PH: (715)257-0128
Karen, Jay, CEO, President

American Hearing Impaired Hockey
Association [22773]
c/o Jeff Sauer, Head Coach
6623 Columbus Dr.
Middleton, WI 53562
Mikita, Stan, Founder

American Hindu Association [20199]
PO Box 628243
Middleton, WI 53562
PH: (608)234-8634
Reddy, Narend, President

Biology Fortified, Inc. [6078]
6907 University Ave., No. 354
Middleton, WI 53562

PH: (608)284-8842
von Mogel, Karl Haro, Chairman

Environmental Risk Resources As-
sociation [4060]
7780 Elmwood Ave, Ste 130
Middleton, WI 53562
Toll free: 877-735-0800
Fax: (608)836-9565

Jussi Bjorling Society U.S.A. [8927]
c/o Dan Shea, Director
3337 Conservancy Ln.
Middleton, WI 53562
PH: (608)836-6911
Rudolph, Walter, President

Kidlinks World [11056]
PO Box 628283
Middleton, WI 53562-8283
PH: (608)658-1171

Music Library Association [9718]
1600 Aspen Commons, Ste. 100
Middleton, WI 53562
PH: (608)836-5825
Fax: (608)831-8200
Rogan, Michael, President

9 to 5, National Association of Work-
ing Women [18199]
207 E Buffalo St., Ste. 211
Milwaukee, WI 53202
PH: (414)274-0925
    (404)222-0077
Toll free: 800-522-0925
Fax: (414)272-2870
Meric, Linda, Exec. Dir.

9 to 5 Working Women Education
Fund [18200]
207 E Buffalo St., Ste. 211
Milwaukee, WI 53202
PH: (414)274-0925
Fax: (414)272-2870
Barnard, Linda Garcia, Dir. of Opera-
tions

Agricultural and Applied Economics
Association [6376]
555 E Wells St., Ste. 100
Milwaukee, WI 53202
PH: (414)918-3190
    (919)515-4620
Goodwin, Barry, President

Alpha Sigma Nu [23775]
707 N 11th St., No. 330
Milwaukee, WI 53201
PH: (414)288-7542
Fax: (414)288-3259
Gaertner, Kate, Exec. Dir.

American Academy of Allergy
Asthma & Immunology [13568]
555 E Wells St., Ste. 100
Milwaukee, WI 53202-3823
PH: (414)272-6071
Fleisher, Dr. Thomas A., President

American Academy for Cerebral
Palsy and Developmental Medicine
[15893]
555 E Wells St., Ste. 100
Milwaukee, WI 53202-3800
PH: (414)918-3014
Fax: (414)276-2146
Stevenson, Richard, Officer

American Academy of Emergency
Medicine [14670]
555 E Wells St., Ste. 100
Milwaukee, WI 53202-3823
Toll free: 800-884-2236
Fax: (414)276-3349
Rodgers, Kevin, MD, FAAEM,
President

American Association of Children's
Residential Centers [13424]
11700 W Lake Park Dr.
Milwaukee, WI 53224
Toll free: 877-332-2272
Bellonci, Christopher, President

American Association of Dental Edi-
tors [2647]
750 N Lincoln Memorial Dr., Ste. No.
422
Milwaukee, WI 53202
PH: (414)272-2759
Fax: (414)272-2754
Moore, Detlef B., Exec. Dir.

American Clinical Neurophysiology
Society [14655]
555 E Wells St., Ste. 1100
Milwaukee, WI 53202-3800
PH: (414)918-9803
Fax: (414)276-3349
Herman, Susan T., MD, Mem.

American College of Mohs Surgery
[16330]
555 E Wells St., Ste. 1100
Milwaukee, WI 53202-3823
PH: (414)347-1103
Toll free: 800-500-7224
Fax: (414)276-2146
Brandt, Rebecca, Exec. Dir.

American Council for School Social
Work [8567]
5011 W Fairy Chasm Ct.
Milwaukee, WI 53223
Fax: (224)649-4408
Shine, Judith Kullas, President

American Malting Barley Association
[3761]
740 N Plankinton Ave., Ste. 830
Milwaukee, WI 53203
PH: (414)272-4640
Heisel, Scott E., VP

American Society of Gene and Cell
Therapy [14875]
555 E Wells St., Ste. 1100
Milwaukee, WI 53202-3800
PH: (414)278-1341
Fax: (414)276-3349
Sukup, Alicia, Assoc. Dir.

American Society for Mohs Histo-
technology [15679]
555 E Wells St., Ste. 1100
Milwaukee, WI 53202-3800
PH: (414)918-9813
Fax: (414)276-3349
Wade, Jeanie, HT, President

American Society of Photographers
[10135]
3120 N Argonne Dr.
Milwaukee, WI 53222
PH: (414)871-6600
Henderson, Kalen, Chmn. of the Bd.

American Society for Quality [7079]
600 N Plankinton Ave.
Milwaukee, WI 53201
PH: (414)272-8575
Toll free: 800-248-1946
Fax: (414)272-1734
Troy, Bill, CEO

Apostleship of Prayer [19792]
1501 S Layton Blvd.
Milwaukee, WI 53215-1924
PH: (414)486-1152
Fax: (414)486-1159
Kubicki, Rev. James M., SJ, Director

Association of Equipment
Manufacturers [166]
6737 W Washington St., Ste. 2400
Milwaukee, WI 53214-5647

PH: (414)272-0943
Toll free: 866-AEM-0442
Fax: (414)272-1170
Slater, Dennis, Secretary

Association of Manpower Franchise Owners [1087]
6737 W Washington St., Ste. 4210
Milwaukee, WI 53214
PH: (414)276-2651

Biodynamic Association [4150]
1661 N Water St., Ste. 307
Milwaukee, WI 53202
PH: (262)649-9212
Fax: (262)649-9213
Carlson, Thea Maria, Director

Black Holocaust Society [17779]
6622 N Bourbon St., Rm. 16
Milwaukee, WI 53224
PH: (414)446-4377
Brown, Dr. Gregory E., Director

British Biker Cooperative [22217]
PO Box 371021
Milwaukee, WI 53237-2121
Aretz, Doug, President

Center for Consumer Affairs [18042]
UWM School of Continuing Education
161 W Wisconsin Ave., Ste. 6000
Milwaukee, WI 53203-2602
PH: (414)227-3252
Longhini, Liza, Director

Center for Self-Sufficiency [11331]
728 N James Lovell St.
Milwaukee, WI 53233
PH: (414)270-4679
Fax: (414)449-4775

Center for Veterans Issues [21115]
315 W Court St.
Milwaukee, WI 53212
PH: (414)345-3917
    (414)345-4272
Fax: (414)342-1073
Cocroft, Robert A., CEO, President

Certification Board of Infection Control and Epidemiology [15116]
555 E Wells St., Ste. 1100
Milwaukee, WI 53202
PH: (414)918-9796
Fax: (414)276-3349
Krolikowski, Anne, Exec. Dir.

Chrysler Town and Country Owners Registry [21354]
3006 S 40th St.
Milwaukee, WI 53215
PH: (414)384-1843
Fax: (414)384-1843
Slusar, John, Editor, Contact

Clinical Immunology Society [15377]
555 E Wells St., Ste. 1100
Milwaukee, WI 53202-3823
PH: (414)224-8095
Fax: (414)272-6070
Krolikowski, Anne, Exec. Dir.

Council for Accreditation in Occupational Hearing Conservation [16320]
555 E Wells St., Ste. 1100
Milwaukee, WI 53202-3823
PH: (414)276-5338
Fax: (414)276-2146
Stanton, Kim, Exec. Dir.

Cyclic Vomiting Syndrome Association [14787]
PO Box 270341
Milwaukee, WI 53227
PH: (414)342-7880
Fax: (414)342-8980
Hill, Connie, Secretary

Endometriosis Association [16283]
8585 N 76th Pl.
Milwaukee, WI 53223
PH: (414)355-2200
Fax: (414)355-6065
Ballweg, Mary Lou, Exec. Dir., President

Growing Power Inc. [3564]
5500 W Silver Spring Dr.
Milwaukee, WI 53218-3261
PH: (414)527-1546
Fax: (414)527-1908
Allen, Will, Founder, CEO

Guitars For Vets [20769]
PO Box 617
Milwaukee, WI 53201-0617
Toll free: 855-448-4376
Nettesheim, Patrick, Founder

Harley Owners Group [22223]
PO Box 453
Milwaukee, WI 53201
Toll free: 800-258-2464
Fax: (414)343-4515

Hemostasis and Thrombosis Research Society [15232]
8733 Watertown Plank Rd.
Milwaukee, WI 53226-3548
PH: (414)937-6569
Jacobsen-Tews, Lorilyn, Exec. Dir.

Industrial Perforators Association [2349]
6737 W Washington St., Ste. 1300
Milwaukee, WI 53214
PH: (414)389-8618
Fax: (414)276-7704

International Academy for Quality [7080]
c/o American Society for Quality
600 N Plankinton Ave.
Milwaukee, WI 53203-2914
PH: (414)272-2241
Molnar, Dr. Pal, President

International Adam Smith Society [10088]
Dept. of Political Science
Marquette University
Milwaukee, WI 53201-1881
PH: (414)288-6842
Hanley, Prof. Ryan Patrick

International Association of Agricultural Economists [6390]
555 E Wells St., Ste. 1100
Milwaukee, WI 53202-3800
PH: (414)918-3199
Fax: (414)276-3349
Swinnen, Prof. Johan, President

International Association for Orthodontics [14449]
750 N Lincoln Memorial Dr., Ste. 422
Milwaukee, WI 53202
PH: (414)272-2757
Toll free: 800-447-8770
Fax: (414)272-2754
Moore, Detlef B., Exec. Dir.

International Association for Radio, Telecommunications and Electromagnetics [7311]
600 N Plankinton Ave.
Milwaukee, WI 53201
PH: (414)272-3937
Toll free: 888-722-2440
Fax: (414)765-8661
Holtmann, Peter, President, CEO

International Federation of Engineering Education Societies [7858]
College of Engineering
Marquette University
Milwaukee, WI 53201-1881

PH: (414)288-0736
Fax: (414)288-1516
Hoyer, Dr. Hans J., Sec. Gen.

International Foundation for Functional Gastrointestinal Disorders [14793]
700 W Virginia St., No. 201
Milwaukee, WI 53204
PH: (414)964-1799
Toll free: 888-964-2001
Fax: (414)964-7176
Norton, Nancy J., President

International Parkinson and Movement Disorder Society [15027]
555 E Wells St., Ste. 1100
Milwaukee, WI 53202-3823
PH: (414)276-2145
Fax: (414)276-3349
Gershanik, Oscar S., President

International Psychogeriatric Association [14893]
555 E Wells St., Ste. 1100
Milwaukee, WI 53202
PH: (414)918-9889
Fax: (414)276-3349
Wang, Huali, Secretary

International Society for Anaesthetic Pharmacology [13703]
6737 W Washington St., Ste. 4210
Milwaukee, WI 53214
PH: (414)755-6296
Fax: (414)276-7704
Svinicki, Jane, CAE, Exec. Dir.

International Society of Biometeorology [6088]
c/o Dr. Jonathan M. Hanes, Secretary
Dept. of Geography
University of Wisconsin-Milwaukee
Milwaukee, WI 53201
PH: (414)229-6611
Fax: (414)229-3981
Hanes, Dr. Jonathan M., Secretary

International Society for Quality of Life Research [6041]
555 E Wells St., Ste. 1100
Milwaukee, WI 53202
PH: (414)918-9797
Fax: (414)276-3349
Snyder, Claire, Ph.D., President

International Society for the Scholarship of Teaching and Learning [8515]
c/o Anthony Ciccone, President
University of Wisconsin-Milwaukee
Milwaukee, WI
Ciccone, Anthony, President

Iprex [2753]
735 N Water St., No. 200
Milwaukee, WI 53202
PH: (414)272-6898
Scheibel, Mary, Contact

Largely Positive [16257]
PO Box 170223
Milwaukee, WI 53217-8021
Johnson, Carol A., MA, Founder, President

Living Church Foundation [20111]
816 E Juneau Ave.
Milwaukee, WI 53202-2793
PH: (414)276-5420
    (414)292-1240
Toll free: 800-211-2771
Fax: (414)276-7483
Wells, Dr. Christopher, Exec. Dir., Editor

Marquette University Alumni Association [19334]
PO Box 1881
Milwaukee, WI 53201-1881

PH: (414)288-7448
Toll free: 800-344-7544
Dillow, Katharine, Officer

Morris Pratt Institute Association [20508]
11811 Watertown Plank Rd.
Milwaukee, WI 53226-3342
PH: (414)774-2994
Fax: (414)774-2964

National Association for Black Veterans [21129]
PO Box 11432
Milwaukee, WI 53211
Toll free: 877-622-8387
Fax: (414)562-6455
Allen, Charles, Chairman

National Association of Catholic Chaplains [19933]
4915 S Howell Ave., Ste. 501
Milwaukee, WI 53207
PH: (414)483-4898
Fax: (414)483-6712
Lichter, David A., D.Min, Exec. Dir.

National Association of Scientific Materials Managers [3030]
c/o Dave Ross, President
Wisconsin Lutheran College
8800 W Bluemound Rd.
Milwaukee, WI 53226

National Association of Service Managers [3076]
PO Box 250796
Milwaukee, WI 53225-6512
PH: (414)466-6060
Gasparovic, Walt, Officer

National Black State Troopers Coalition [5496]
PO Box 18192
Milwaukee, WI 53218
Burrell, Tony, President

National Conference on Fluid Power [6636]
6737 W Washington St., Ste. 2350
Milwaukee, WI 53214
PH: (414)778-3344
Fax: (414)778-3361
Lanke, Eric, CEO

National Fluid Power Association [1754]
6373 W Washington St., Ste. 2350
Milwaukee, WI 53214
PH: (414)778-3344
Fax: (414)778-3361
Chase, Sue, Dir. of Fin.

National Industrial Belting Association [1755]
6737 W Washington St., Ste. 1300
Milwaukee, WI 53214
PH: (414)389-8606
Fax: (414)276-7704
Rzepka, Jennifer, Exec. Dir.

National Registration Center for Study Abroad [8086]
PO Box 1393
Milwaukee, WI 53202-5712
PH: (414)278-0631
Fax: (414)271-8884

National United Church Ushers Association of America [20633]
c/o Geneva Clark-Cole, President
6231 W Spencer Pl.
Milwaukee, WI 53218
PH: (414)462-4997
Cole, Geneva Clark, President

New Order [19241]
Box 270486
Milwaukee, WI 53227

North American Cartographic Information Society [6168]
American Geographical Society Library

2311 E Hartford Ave.
Milwaukee, WI 53211
PH: (414)229-6282
Fax: (414)229-3624
Griffin, Amy, President

Polyurethane Manufacturers Association **[2631]**
6737 W Washington St., Ste. 1300
Milwaukee, WI 53214
PH: (414)431-3094
Fax: (414)276-7704
Katz, Linda, VP, Treasurer, Secretary

Royal Academy of Dance **[9270]**
3211 S Lake Dr., Ste. R317
Milwaukee, WI 53235
PH: (414)747-9060
Fax: (414)747-9062
Ashby, Patti, Director

Scoliosis Research Society **[17186]**
555 E Wells St., Ste. 1100
Milwaukee, WI 53202-3823
PH: (414)289-9107
Fax: (414)276-3349
Goulding, Tressa, CAE, Exec. Dir.

Snow & Ice Management Association, Inc. **[5819]**
7670 N Port Washington Rd., Ste. 105
Milwaukee, WI 53217-3174
PH: (414)375-1940
Fax: (414)375-1945
Tirado, Martin, CAE, CEO

Society of Anesthesia and Sleep Medicine **[13708]**
6737 W Washington St., Ste. 1300
Milwaukee, WI 53214
PH: (414)389-8608
Fax: (414)276-7704
Svinicki, Jane, CAE, Exec. Dir.

Society of Behavioral Medicine **[13803]**
555 E Wells St., Ste. 1100
Milwaukee, WI 53202-3800
PH: (414)918-3156
Fax: (414)276-3349
Wilson, Dawn K., PhD, Exec.

The Society for Education in Anesthesia **[13711]**
6737 W Washington St., Ste. 4210
Milwaukee, WI 53214
PH: (414)389-8614
Fax: (414)276-7704
Bronson, Andrew, CAE, Exec. Dir.

Society for Immunotherapy of Cancer **[14064]**
555 E Wells St., Ste. 1100
Milwaukee, WI 53202-3823
PH: (414)271-2456
Fax: (414)276-3349
Kaufman, Howard, President

Society for Obstetric Anesthesia and Perinatology **[16628]**
6737 W Washington St., Ste. 4210
Milwaukee, WI 53214
PH: (414)389-8611
Fax: (414)276-7704
Svinicki, Jane, CAE, Exec. Dir.

Society for Reproductive Investigation **[16307]**
555 E Wells St., Ste. 1100
Milwaukee, WI 53202-3823
PH: (414)918-9888
Fax: (414)276-3349
Sadovsky, Yoel, President

Society for Technology in Anesthesia **[13714]**
6737 W Washington St., Ste. 4210
Milwaukee, WI 53214-5636
PH: (414)389-8600
Fax: (414)275-7704
Rothman, Brian, President

Society of Vascular and Interventional Neurology **[16036]**
6737 W Washington St., Ste. 1300
Milwaukee, WI 53214
PH: (414)389-8613
Fax: (414)276-7704
Nogueira, Raul G., President

Tesla Engine Builders Association **[590]**
5464 N Port Washington Rd., No. 293
Milwaukee, WI 53217-4925

TMJ Association **[16565]**
PO Box 26770
Milwaukee, WI 53226-0770
PH: (262)432-0350
Cowley, Terrie, Founder, President

TOPS Club Inc. **[12399]**
4575 S Fifth St.
Milwaukee, WI 53207-0360
PH: (414)482-4620
Toll free: 800-932-8677
Fax: (414)482-1655
Cady, Barb, President

UNITY Journalists for Diversity **[2731]**
PO Box 511783
Milwaukee, WI 53203
PH: (414)335-1478
Altoro, Eloiza, Exec. Dir.

Urban Affairs Association **[8725]**
University of Wisconsin-Milwaukee
Urban Studies Program
3210 N Maryland Ave.
Bolton 702
Milwaukee, WI 53211
PH: (414)229-3025
Wilder, Margaret, Exec. Dir.

Welfare Warriors **[18766]**
2711 W Michigan Ave.
Milwaukee, WI 53208
PH: (414)342-6662
Gowens, Pat, Editor

Wilson Disease Association International **[14615]**
5572 N Diversey Blvd.
Milwaukee, WI 53217
PH: (414)961-0533
Toll free: 866-961-0533
Graper, Mary L., President

Wilson's Disease Association **[15836]**
5572 N Diversey Blvd.
Milwaukee, WI 53217
PH: (414)961-0533
Toll free: 866-961-0533
Graper, Mary L., President

World Allergy Organization **[13582]**
555 E Wells St., Ste. 1100
Milwaukee, WI 53202-3823
PH: (414)276-1791
Fax: (414)276-3349
Dodge, Justin, Exec. Dir.

World Gastroenterology Organisation **[14799]**
555 E Wells St., Ste. 1100
Milwaukee, WI 53202-3823
PH: (414)918-9798
Fax: (414)276-3349
Quigley, Prof. Eamonn, Comm. Chm.

Wound, Ostomy and Continence Nursing Certification Board **[16193]**
555 E Wells St., Ste. 1100
Milwaukee, WI 53202-3823
Toll free: 888-496-2622
Fax: (414)276-2146
Reimanis, Cathy, DNP, MS, CNS, ANP-BC, CWOCN, President

Nepali American Friendship Association **[19592]**
408 Midland Ln.
Monona, WI 53716
PH: (608)222-0646
Batajoo, Ayodhya, Treasurer

Society of Wood Science and Technology **[4218]**
PO Box 6155
Monona, WI 53716-6155
PH: (608)577-1342
Fax: (608)254-2769
Smith, Bob, VP

Association for Pelvic Organ Prolapse Support **[14984]**
8225 State Road 83
Mukwonago, WI 53149-8901
PH: (262)642-4338
Palm, Sherrie, Founder, CEO

BMW Riders Association International **[22216]**
PO Box 570
Mukwonago, WI 53149-0570
PH: (262)409-2899
Toll free: 866-924-7102
Fax: (262)409-2899
Nyktas, George, President

MC Sailing Association **[22647]**
W257 S10550 Horseshoe Ln.
Mukwonago, WI 53149
PH: (847)255-0210
Toll free: 866-457-2582
Cole, Robert H., Jr., Officer

Ehlers-Danlos Syndrome Network CARES **[14821]**
PO Box 66
Muskego, WI 53150
PH: (262)514-2851
Fax: (262)514-2851
Sanders, Lynn, Founder, President

Future Corvette Owners Association **[21386]**
c/o Pat Kelly, Director
S68W17323 Rossmar Ct.
Muskego, WI 53150-8575
PH: (262)971-5046
Kelly, Pat, Director

International Edsel Club **[21401]**
PO Box 312
Muskego, WI 53150
Whipple, Jack, Secretary

Lambda Kappa Sigma **[23845]**
PO Box 570
Muskego, WI 53150-0570
Toll free: 800-557-1913
Fax: (262)679-4558
Rogala, Joan E., CAE, Exec. Dir.

Sigma Alpha Sorority **[23875]**
Po Box 570
Muskego, WI 53150-0570
PH: (262)682-4690
Bujol, K. Angelle, Exec. Dir.

International Association of Structural Movers **[3088]**
PO Box 2104
Neenah, WI 54956-2104
PH: (803)951-9304
Fax: (920)486-1519
Blaney, Tammie DeVooght, Exec. Dir.

Pueblo a Pueblo **[17992]**
PO Box 303
Neenah, WI 54957-0303
PH: (920)209-0488
Cabrera, Ana, Officer

Songwriters of Wisconsin International **[9186]**
PO Box 1027
Neenah, WI 54957-1027

PH: (920)725-5129
Fax: (920)720-0195
Ansems, Tony, President

Wild Ones **[4449]**
2285 Butte des Morts Beach Rd.
Neenah, WI 54956
PH: (920)730-3986
Toll free: 877-394-9453
Lewis, Tim, President

World Umpires Association **[23393]**
PO Box 394
Neenah, WI 54957
PH: (920)969-1580
Janssen, Phil, Contact

Delta Sigma Delta **[23718]**
c/o Dr. John Prey, Supreme Scribe
296 15th Ave.
Nekoosa, WI 54457
PH: (715)325-6320
Toll free: 800-335-8744
Fax: (715)325-3057
Prey, Dr. John H., Secretary

Marklin Digital Special Interest Group **[22188]**
PO Box 510559
New Berlin, WI 53151-0559
Fax: (262)522-7288
Catherall, Dr. Tom, Consultant

Belted Galloway Society **[3720]**
c/o Victor Eggleston, DVM, Executive Director
N8603 Zentner Rd.
New Glarus, WI 53574
PH: (608)220-1091
Fax: (608)527-4811
Eggleston, Victor, Exec. Dir.

Mid-Continent Railway Historical Society **[22409]**
E8948 Diamond Hill Rd.
North Freedom, WI 53951
PH: (608)522-4261
Toll free: 800-930-1385
Fax: (608)522-4490
Meyer, Don, Mgr.

American Association of Medical Audit Specialists **[15571]**
7044 S 13th St.
Oak Creek, WI 53154
PH: (414)908-4941
Fax: (414)768-8001
Shane, Allen, President

American Society of Anesthesia Technologists and Technicians **[15617]**
7044 S 13th St.
Oak Creek, WI 53154-1429
PH: (414)908-4942
(808)547-9872
Fax: (414)768-8001
Wyatt, Jeremy, President

Art Libraries Society of North America **[9680]**
7044 S 13th St.
Oak Creek, WI 53154
PH: (734)764-3166
Toll free: 800-817-0621
Gendron, Heather, President

Association of Public Treasurers of the United States and Canada **[5705]**
7044 S 13th St.
Oak Creek, WI 53154
PH: (414)908-4947
Fax: (414)768-8001
Rucker, Tumiko, Advisor

College Reading and Learning Association **[8484]**
7044 S 13th St.
Oak Creek, WI 53154

PH: (414)908-4961
Briggs, Dorothy, President

Congress on Research in Dance
[9246]
7044 S 13th St.
Oak Creek, WI 53154
Amin, Takiyah Nur, PhD, Director

International Network of Somewhere
in Time Enthusiasts [24019]
8110 S Verdev Dr.
Oak Creek, WI 53154-3042
Addie, Jo, President

NaSPA [6303]
7044 S 13th St.
Oak Creek, WI 53154
PH: (414)908-4945
Fax: (414)768-8001
Wrobel, Leo A., President, Director

National Association of
Congregational Christian Churches
[20035]
8473 S Howell Ave.
Oak Creek, WI 53154
PH: (414)764-1620
Toll free: 800-262-1620
Fax: (414)764-0319
Miller, Linda, Coord.

National Auto Body Council [300]
7044 S 13th St.
Oak Creek, WI 53154-1429
PH: (414)908-4957
Fax: (414)768-8001
Sulkala, Chuck, Exec. Dir.

Anxiety Disorders Foundation
[13721]
PO Box 560
Oconomowoc, WI 53066
PH: (262)567-6600
Fax: (262)567-7600
Riemann, Bradley C., PhD,
President

United States Icelandic Horse
Congress [4419]
c/o Kari Pietsch-Wangard
300 S Sawyer Rd.
Oconomowoc, WI 53066
Toll free: 866-929-0009
Elwell, Anne, Bd. Member

Great Lakes Indian Fish and Wildlife
Commission [4824]
72682 Maple St.
Odanah, WI 54861
PH: (715)682-6619
Isham, Mic, Chairman

Midwest Treaty Network [19582]
PO Box 43
Oneida, WI 54155
PH: (920)496-5360
(715)295-0018
Manthe, Laura, Director

Archery Range and Retailers
Organization [3150]
156 N Main St., Ste. D
Oregon, WI 53575
PH: (608)835-9060
Toll free: 800-234-7499
Fax: (608)835-9360
Stubstad, Martin, President

North American Industrial Hemp
Council [6632]
PO Box 232
Oregon, WI 53575
Sholts, Erwin A., Chairman

American Quaternary Association
[6892]
c/o Colin Long, Secretary
800 Algoma Blvd.
Oshkosh, WI 54901-8642

PH: (920)424-2182
Smith, Alison, President

EAA Vintage Aircraft Association
[21222]
3000 Poberezny Rd.
Oshkosh, WI 54902
PH: (920)426-6110
Toll free: 800-843-3612
Fax: (920)426-6579
Robison, Geoff L., President

EAA Warbirds of America [21223]
PO Box 3086
Oshkosh, WI 54903-3086
PH: (920)426-4800
Fischer, Bill, Exec. Dir.

Experimental Aircraft Association
[5862]
EAA Aviation Ctr.
3000 Poberezny Rd.
Oshkosh, WI 54902-8939
PH: (920)426-4800
Toll free: 800-564-6322
Fax: (920)426-6865
Diana, Janine, VP

History of Economics Society [9485]
c/o Marianne Johnson, Secretary
Dept. of Economics
University of Wisconsin Oshkosh
800 Algoma Blvd.
Oshkosh, WI 54901
PH: (920)424-2230
Fax: (920)424-1441
Berdell, John, Mem.

Institute for Theatre Journalism and
Advocacy [10255]
c/o Jane Purse-Wiedenhoeft,
Coordinator
University of Wisconsin Oshkosh
Arts and Communication Theatre
Dept.
800 Algoma Blvd.
Oshkosh, WI 54901-8657
PH: (920)424-4425
Purse-Wiedenhoeft, Jane, Coord.

International Aerobatic Club [22488]
PO Box 3086
Oshkosh, WI 54903
PH: (920)426-4800
Bartlett, Doug, President

Man from U.N.C.L.E. Fan Club
[24087]
PO Box 1733
Oshkosh, WI 54903
Cole, Sue, President

The Naturist Society, LLC [10057]
627 Bay Shore Dr., Ste. 100
Oshkosh, WI 54901
PH: (920)426-5009
Toll free: 800-886-7230
Hoffman-Lee, Nicky, Mgr. Dir.

Friends for Health in Haiti [15003]
PO Box 122
Pewaukee, WI 53072
PH: (262)227-9581
Wolf, Dr. Catherine, Exec. Dir.

National C Scow Sailing Association
[22650]
N30 W29273A Hillcrest Dr.
Pewaukee, WI 53072
Porter, Christine, President

National Council for Print Industry
Certifications [1543]
W232 N2950 Roundy Cir. E, Ste.
200
Pewaukee, WI 53072
PH: (262)522-2215
Burton, Tim, President

Society for Chaos Theory in
Psychology and Life Sciences
[7070]
c/o Society for Chaos Theory in
Psychology & Life Sciences

PO Box 484
Pewaukee, WI 53072
Pincus, David, Comm. Chm.

Ferguson Enthusiasts of North
America [22452]
5604 Southwest Rd.
Platteville, WI 53818-8923
PH: (608)348-6344
Lory, David, Treasurer, Secretary

University of Wisconsin-Platteville
Alumni Association [19369]
1500 Ullsvik Hall
1 University Plz.
Platteville, WI 53818-3099
PH: (608)342-1181
Toll free: 800-897-2586
Fax: (608)342-1196
Schmelz, Kim, Director

Women in Trucking [3362]
PO Box 400
Plover, WI 54467-0400
Toll free: 888-464-9482
Voie, Ellen, CEO, President

Silver Marten Rabbit Club [4612]
c/o Katie Peltier, Secretary/Treasurer
9599 E Highway 2
Poplar, WI 54864
PH: (715)364-6801
Burant, Connie, President

American Association of Candy
Technologists [6638]
711 W Water St.
Princeton, WI 54968
PH: (920)295-6969
Fax: (920)295-6843
Wieland, Lynn, Secretary

Concrete Pump Manufacturers As-
sociation [6343]
2310 S Green Bay Rd., Ste. C
Racine, WI 53406
Fax: (262)284-7878
Schantz, John, President

Ford/Fordson Collectors Association
[22453]
2435 Hansen Ave.
Racine, WI 53405-2518
Ted, Foster, Exec. Dir., Secretary

National Association of Sports Of-
ficials [23270]
2017 Lathrop Ave.
Racine, WI 53405
PH: (262)632-5448
Fax: (262)632-5460
Mano, Barry, President

North American Normande Associa-
tion [3747]
748 Enloe Rd.
Rewey, WI 53580
PH: (608)943-6091
Toll free: 800-573-6254
Lange, Robert, President

Blue Mountain Project [12212]
PO Box 473
Ripon, WI 54971
PH: (985)212-2356

National Speech & Debate Associa-
tion [8600]
125 Watson St.
Ripon, WI 54971
PH: (920)748-6206
Fax: (920)748-9478
Wunn, J. Scott, Exec. Dir.

American Forensic Association
[8592]
PO Box 256
River Falls, WI 54022
PH: (715)425-3198
Toll free: 800-228-5424
Fax: (715)425-9533
Pratt, James W., Exec. Sec.

Learning Resources Network [7670]
PO Box 9
River Falls, WI 54022
PH: (715)426-9777
Toll free: 800-678-5376
Fax: (888)234-8633
Draves, William A., CAE, President

Society for Social Studies of Science
[7148]
Dept. of Sociology, Anthropology and
Criminal Justice
University of Wisconsin
River Falls, WI 54022
Shrum, Dr. Wesley, Officer

Arctic Cat Club of America [22418]
c/o Paul Wustrack
PO Box 528
Rosendale, WI 54974-0528
Wustrack, Paul, Mgr., Web Adm.

Carousel Organ Association of
America [22247]
c/o Marc Dannecker, Treasurer
1900 E Cora Ave.
Saint Francis, WI 53235
Rulli, Angelo, President

August Derleth Society [9038]
PO Box 481
Sauk City, WI 53583
Schweitzer, Mary, Treasurer

Cardiac Arrhythmias Research and
Education Foundation [14103]
PO Box 69
Seymour, WI 54165
PH: (920)833-7000
(425)785-5836
Toll free: 800-404-9500
Fax: (920)833-7005
Myerburg, Robert J., MD, President

Muskies Inc. [3643]
1509 Stahl Rd.
Sheboygan, WI 53081-8894
Toll free: 888-710-8286
Zahn, Mr. Jay, President

Kids First Fund [10796]
1916 E Kensington Blvd.
Shorewood, WI 53211
PH: (414)961-1939
Sorensen, Jay, President

Polycystic Ovarian Syndrome As-
sociation [16302]
4230 N Oakland Ave., Ste. 204
Shorewood, WI 53211
Dezarn, Ms. Christine G., CEO,
Founder

Delta Nu Alpha Transportation
Fraternity [23981]
1720 Manistique Ave.
South Milwaukee, WI 53172
PH: (414)764-3063
Fax: (630)499-8505
Plizka, Laura, Asst. Sec., Treasurer

International Council of Kinetography
Laban [9261]
c/o Susan Gingrasso, Treasurer
4308 Heffron St.
Stevens Point, WI 54481-5338
Lepczyk, Billie, Chairperson

National Wellness Institute [16802]
1300 College Ct.
Stevens Point, WI 54481-0827
PH: (715)342-2969
Fax: (715)342-2979
Howard, Linda, Treasurer

United States Curling Association
[22742]
5525 Clem's Way
Stevens Point, WI 54482-8841
PH: (715)344-1199
Toll free: 888-287-5377
Fax: (715)344-2279
Carlson, Dave, Chmn. of the Bd.

World Scientific and Engineering
  Academy and Society [6604]
c/o Charles A. Long, Chairman
University of Wisconsin
2100 Main St.
Stevens Point, WI 54481-3897
Long, Prof. Charles A., Chairman

Whitetails Unlimited [4899]
2100 Michigan St.
Sturgeon Bay, WI 54235
PH: (920)743-6777
Toll free: 800-274-5471
Fax: (920)743-4658
Gerl, Peter J., Exec. Dir.

National Butterfly Association
  [22649]
14341 Marina Dr.
Sturtevant, WI 53177
Fax: (262)925-6980

Heavenly Hats Foundation [13059]
1813 Coach Ln.
Suamico, WI 54173
PH: (920)362-2668
Leanna, DeeAnn, President, Chmn.
  of the Bd.

Metropolitan Owners Club of North
  America [21430]
2308 Co. Hwy. V
2308 County Hwy. V
Sun Prairie, WI 53590
PH: (608)825-1903
Swiggart, Brad, President

Cinnamon Rabbit Breeders Associa-
  tion [4596]
N59 W22476 Silver Spring Dr.
W248 N7411 Beverly Ln.
Sussex, WI 53089
PH: (765)463-4616
    (262)894-3647
Howard-Weigel, Maggie, Secretary,
  Treasurer

National PKU Alliance [16690]
PO Box 501
Tomahawk, WI 54487
PH: (715)437-0477
Brown, Christine, Exec. Dir.

Siberian Husky Club of America, Inc.
  [21961]
c/o Delbert Thacker, Membership
  Chairman
3413 67th Dr.
Union Grove, WI 53182-9405
Jessop, Sandy, President

National Dairy Herd Information As-
  sociation [3739]
421 S Nine Mound Rd.
Verona, WI 53593
PH: (608)848-6455
Fax: (608)848-7675

NMC [17656]
421 S Nine Mound Rd.
Verona, WI 53593
PH: (608)848-4615
Fax: (608)848-4671
Gardner, Den, Exec. Dir.

Inspiration Ministries [11604]
N2270 State Road 67
Walworth, WI 53184
PH: (262)275-6131
Knoll, Robin, Chap.

National Association of Fraternal
  Insurance Counselors [1892]
211 Canal Rd.
Waterloo, WI 53594
Toll free: 866-478-3880
Kolarik, Randall, FIC, President

Bethesda Lutheran Communities
  [12319]
600 Hoffmann Dr.
Watertown, WI 53094

PH: (920)261-3050
Toll free: 800-369-4636
Fax: (920)261-8441
Bauer, Dr. John E., CEO, President

National Flag Day Foundation
  [20947]
PO Box 55
Waubeka, WI 53021-0055
PH: (262)692-9111
    (262)692-2811
Janik, John J., President

Association for High Technology
  Distribution [1037]
N19 W24400 Riverwood Dr.
Waukesha, WI 53188
Schatzman, Leigha, Exec. Dir.

Cornish American Heritage Society
  [9139]
c/o Kathryn Herman, President
222 Park Pl., No. 476
Waukesha, WI 53186-4815
PH: (608)342-1719
Haines, Carolyn, VP

MRA - The Management Association
  [2181]
N19 W24400 Riverwood Dr.
Waukesha, WI 53188
PH: (262)523-9090
Toll free: 800-488-4845
Fronk, Susan, President

International Society of Lyophiliza-
  tion - Freeze Drying, Inc. [6122]
917 Lexington Way
Waunakee, WI 53597
PH: (608)577-6790
Tebrinke, Kevin, PE, President

National Motorists Association
  [13233]
402 W 2nd St.
Waunakee, WI 53597
Toll free: 800-882-2785
Fax: (888)787-0381
Biller, Mr. Gary, President

National Lilac Rabbit Club of
  America [4605]
c/o Bob Koch, Secretary-Treasurer
N3650 Oak Ridge Rd.
Waupaca, WI 54981
PH: (715)281-3106
Koch, Bob, Secretary, Treasurer

American Society for Laser Medicine
  and Surgery [15522]
2100 Stewart Ave., Ste. 240
Wausau, WI 54401-1709
PH: (715)845-9283
Toll free: 877-258-6028
Fax: (715)848-2493
Dalsky, Dianne, Exec. Dir.

Marine Embassy Guard Association
  [21018]
PO Box 6226
Wausau, WI 54402-6226
Hermening, Kevin, Treasurer

Performing Arts Foundation [8997]
401 N 4th St.
Wausau, WI 54403-5420
PH: (715)842-0988
Wright, Sean, Exec. Dir.

American College of Chiropractic
  Orthopedists [14254]
c/o Boyd M. Peterson, President
1155 N Mayfair Rd.
Wauwatosa, WI 53226
PH: (414)955-7999
Fax: (414)955-0110
Peterson, Boyd M., D.C., F.A.C.O.,
  President

Learn for Life Kenya [11395]
2477 N 91st St.
Wauwatosa, WI 53226
Lee, Bonnie, President, Founder

Professional Association of Volleyball
  Officials [23272]
c/o Julie Voeck, President
6905 Wellauer Dr.
Wauwatosa, WI 53213
PH: (414)607-9918
Toll free: 888-791-2074
Voeck, Julie, President

Association for the Bladder Exstro-
  phy Community [14564]
6737 W Washington St., Ste. 3265
West Allis, WI 53214
PH: (425)941-1475
Block, Pamela, President, Exec. Dir.

International Memorialization Supply
  Association [2407]
PO Box 425
West Bend, WI 53095-0425
Toll free: 800-375-0335
Kaniuk, Anthony R., President

United States Association for Small
  Business and Entrepreneurship
  [3130]
c/o Patrick Snyder, Executive Direc-
  tor
1214 Hyland Hall
University of Wisconsin, Whitewater
Whitewater, WI 53190
PH: (262)472-1449
Snyder, Patrick, Exec. Dir.

Firearms Engravers Guild of America
  [21757]
6120 David Dr.
Wisconsin Rapids, WI 54494
PH: (616)929-6146
Hands, Barry Lee, President

WYOMING

National Association of State Fire
  Marshals [5212]
315 S Main St., Ste. 1
Burns, WY 82053
PH: (202)737-1226
Fax: (307)547-2260
Browning, Butch, President

Clan MacKenzie Society in the
  United States [20823]
c/o Barbara Mackenzie, Treasurer
PO Box 20454
Cheyenne, WY 82003-7011
PH: (307)214-4817
Tobyne, Claire, Regional VP

Partners for Rural America [19077]
c/o Mary Randolph, Treasurer
214 W 15th St.
Cheyenne, WY 82002
PH: (307)777-6430
Fax: (307)777-2935
Randolph, Mary, Treasurer

Buffalo Bill Center of the West
  [10316]
720 Sheridan Ave.
Cody, WY 82414-3428
PH: (307)587-4771
    (307)578-4008
Eldredge, Bruce, CEO, Exec. Dir.

Dude Ranchers' Association [1655]
1122 12th St.
Cody, WY 82414
PH: (307)587-2339
Toll free: 866-399-2339
Hodson, Colleen, Exec. Dir.

International Brick Collectors' Association [21670]
c/o Donna Johnson, Treasurer
3141 S Fork Rd.
Cody, WY 82414-8009
PH: (307)587-5061
Johnson, Donna, Treasurer

The International Cessna 170 As-
  sociation [21231]
22 Vista View Ln.
Cody, WY 82414
PH: (307)587-6397
Fax: (307)587-8296
Billeb, Ms. Jan, Exec. Sec.

Wild Sheep Foundation [4683]
720 Allen Ave.
Cody, WY 82414
PH: (307)527-6261
Fax: (307)527-7117
Thornton, Gray, CEO, President

Organization for the Support of
  Albania's Abandoned Babies
  [11114]
PO Box 1672
Dubois, WY 82513
PH: (303)989-7260
Janiszewski, Claudia, Founder,
  President

Western Writers of America, Inc.
  [10406]
271 CR 219
Encampment, WY 82325
Monahan, Sherry, President

American Kenpo Karate International
  [22982]
PO Box 768
Evanston, WY 82931-0768
PH: (307)789-4124
Mills, Mr. Paul, Founder, President

Never Too Weak to Wander [15978]
PO Box 4424
Jackson, WY 83001
Mishev, Dina, Founder

United States Dry Bean Council
  [4256]
c/o Jeane Wharton, Executive Direc-
  tor
PO Box 9224
Jackson, WY 83002
PH: (307)201-1894
Bratter, Rebecca, Exec. Dir.

American Society of Plant
  Taxonomists [6136]
University of Wyoming
Laramie, WY 82071
PH: (307)766-2556
Brown, Linda, Bus. Mgr.

National Acupuncture Detoxification
  Association [17318]
PO Box 1066
Laramie, WY 82073
PH: (307)460-2771
Toll free: 888-765-6232
Fax: (573)777-9956
Stuyt, Elizabeth, MD, President

Spanish Mustang Registry [4411]
c/o Josie Brislawn, President
2740 D Rd.
Moorcroft, WY 82721
Brislawn, Josie, President

National Bench Rest Shooters As-
  sociation [23135]
PO Box 6770
Sheridan, WY 82801-6770
PH: (307)655-7415
Campbell, Wayne, Rep.

United States Ski Mountaineering
  Association [23170]
PO Box 495
Wilson, WY 83014

Cleft Lip and Palate Foundation of
  Smiles [14331]
1270 Blanchard SW
Wyoming, WY 49509
PH: (616)329-1335
Mancuso, Rachel, Founder, CEO

A

A., Larry, Chairman
Adult Children of Alcoholics World
Service Organization Inc. [12866]
PO Box 3216
Torrance, CA 90510
Ph: (310)534-1815

Aabo, David, Exec. Dir.
WAVES for Development [23279]
166 Thornberry Ln.
Rensselaer, NY 12144

Aanenson, Dr. Charles, CEO
Peace Winds America [11675]
2341 Eastlake Ave. E, Ste. 1
Seattle, WA 98102
Ph: (206)432-3712

Aaron, Dr. Debra K., President
American Society of Animal Science
[3615]
PO Box 7410
Champaign, IL 61826-7410
Ph: (217)356-9050
Fax: (217)568-6070

Aaron, Mrs. Grace Kumi, Founder
Children's Health International
[14180]
110 W University Blvd., No. 3505
Silver Spring, MD 20918
Ph: (301)681-8307

Aaronson, Mel, President
National Conference on Public
Employee Retirement Systems
[5079]
444 N Capitol St. NW, Ste. 630
Washington, DC 20001
Ph: (202)624-1456
Toll Free: 877-202-5706
Fax: (202)624-1439

Abadi, Deljou, Founder, Exec. Dir.
Iranian Refugees' Alliance [12591]
Cooper Sta.
New York, NY 10276-0316
Ph: (212)260-7460
Fax: (267)295-7391

Abadie, Jude, President
American Board of Clinical
Chemistry [6179]
900 17th St. NW, Ste. 400
Washington, DC 20006
Ph: (202)835-8717
Fax: (202)833-4576

Abba, Wayne, President
College of Performance Management [2161]
12100 Sunset Hills Rd., Ste. 130
Reston, VA 20190

Abbate, Jim, Director
National Amusement Park Historical
Association [21277]
PO Box 871
Lombard, IL 60148-0871

Abbett, John, Founder
American Part-Blooded Horse
Registry [4319]
PO Box 986
Oregon City, OR 97045
Ph: (503)702-6410

Abbey, Charlie, Advisor
National Association of Safety
Professionals [7108]
1531 S Post Rd.
Shelby, NC 28152
Toll Free: 800-922-2219
Fax: (704)487-1579

Abbotson, Sue, Web Adm.
Arthur Miller Society [10360]
c/o Steve Manio

100-14 160 Ave.
Howard Beach, NY 11414
Ph: (212)556-5600

Abbott, Bart, President
Emerging Humanity [12151]
2279 Makanani Dr.
Honolulu, HI 96817

Abbott, Corinne, Sr. VP
ULI Foundation [19219]
1025 Thomas Jefferson St. NW, Ste.
500 W
Washington, DC 20007
Ph: (202)624-7000
Fax: (855)442-6702

Abbott, Mark, Chairman
Air Serv International [12610]
410 Rosedale Ct., Ste. 190
Warrenton, VA 20186
Ph: (540)428-2323
Fax: (540)428-2326

Abbott, Marty, Exec. Dir.
American Council on the Teaching of
Foreign Languages [8177]
1001 N Fairfax St., Ste. 200
Alexandria, VA 22314
Ph: (703)894-2900
Fax: (703)894-2905

Abbott, Stephen, Exec. Dir.
Great Schools Partnership [8537]
482 Congress St., Ste. 500
Portland, ME 04101
Ph: (207)773-0505
Fax: (877)849-7052

Abbott, Turner T., Mgr.
Metal Powder Industries Federation
[2355]
105 College Rd. E
Princeton, NJ 08540
Ph: (609)452-7700

Abdallah, Bobbie, Contact
Veterinary Institute of Integrative
Medicine [17671]
PO Box 740053
Arvada, CO 80006
Ph: (303)277-8227

Abdelnour, Ziad K., President
United States Committee for a Free
Lebanon [18635]
445 Park Ave., 9th Fl.
New York, NY 10022-8632

Abdelsamad, Dr. Moustafa H., CEO,
President
Society for Advancement of Manage-
ment [2192]
6300 Ocean Dr.
Corpus Christi, TX 78412-5808
Ph: (361)825-3045
Toll Free: 888-827-6077
Fax: (361)825-5609

Abdinur, Ali Haji, President, CEO
Humanitarian African Relief
Organization [12677]
6161 El Cajon Blvd., No. 912
San Diego, CA 92115
Ph: (612)315-5691
      (619)741-9260
Fax: (612)315-5693

Abdou, Sherif, President
Egyptian Student Association in
North America [8615]

Abdoulaye, Kone, Founder,
President
International Agro Alliance [4697]
173 NW 89th St.
Miami, FL 33150
Ph: (844)422-7333
Toll Free: 877-292-3921
Fax: (844)422-7333

Abdul-Malik, Karen, President
National Association of Black
Storytellers [10224]
PO Box 67722
Baltimore, MD 21215
Ph: (410)947-1117
Fax: (410)947-1117

Abdulrauf, Saleem I., MD, President
Walter E. Dandy Neurosurgical
Society [16071]
3635 Vista Ave., 5th Fl., FDT
Saint Louis, MO 63110
Ph: (314)577-8716
Fax: (314)577-8720

Abe, Toshi, VP of Member & Public
Rel.
Japanese American Citizens League
[19510]
1765 Sutter St.
San Francisco, CA 94115
Ph: (415)921-5225
      (415)345-1077

Abel, E. Dale, MD, President
Society for Heart and Vascular
Metabolism [14146]
10900 Euclid Ave.
Case Western Reserve University
School of Medicine E521
10900 Euclid Ave.
Cleveland, OH 44106-4970

Abel, Mike Van, Exec. Dir., President
International Mountain Bicycling As-
sociation [22748]
4888 Pearl East Cir., Ste. 200E
Boulder, CO 80301
Ph: (303)545-9011
Toll Free: 888-442-4622
Fax: (303)545-9026

Abelin, Bob, Commodore
San Juan 21 Class Association
[22665]
6 Stately Oaks Ln.
Belleville, IL 62220

Abell, Linda, Chairman
Financial & Security Products As-
sociation [397]
1024 Mebane Oaks Rd., No. 273
Mebane, NC 27302
Ph: (919)648-0664
Toll Free: 800-843-6082
Fax: (919)648-0670

Abelow, Bradley, Chairman
The Century Foundation [18969]
1 Whitehall St., 15 Fl.
New York, NY 10004
Ph: (212)452-7700
Fax: (212)535-7534

Abels, Eileen G., PhD, President
Beta Phi Mu [9694]
PO Box 42139
Philadelphia, PA 19101
Ph: (267)361-5018

Abelson, Jamie, Researcher
Institute for Social Research
Program for Research on Black
Americans [7183]
5062 Institute for Social Research
Ann Arbor, MI 48106-1248
Ph: (734)763-0045
Fax: (734)763-0044

Abely, Joseph, President
Carroll Center for the Blind [17695]
770 Centre St.
Newton, MA 02458-2597
Ph: (617)969-6200

Aberbach, Susan, President
American Friends of Neot Kedumim
[19747]

42 E 69th St.
New York, NY 10021
Ph: (212)737-1337

Abercrombie, Karin Moen, Exec. Dir.
Swedish American Museum Associa-
tion of Chicago [20998]
5211 N Clark St.
Chicago, IL 60640
Ph: (773)728-8111

Abernathy, Paul, Exec. Dir.
Association of Lighting and Mercury
Recyclers [4624]
4139 Rhine Ct.
Napa, CA 94558
Ph: (707)927-3844
Fax: (707)927-3936

Abidi, Syed E., President
Universal Muslim Association of
America [20502]
1701 Pennsylvania Ave. NW
Washington, DC 20004
Ph: (202)559-9123

Abijaodi, Carlos Eduardo, Chmn. of
the Bd.
Brazil Industries Coalition [1979]
818 18th St. NW, Ste. 630
Washington, DC 20006
Ph: (202)471-4020
Fax: (202)471-4024

Abji, Minaz, Chairman
American Hotel & Lodging
Educational Foundation [1648]
1250 I St. NW, Ste. 1100
Washington, DC 20005-3931
Ph: (202)289-3180
Fax: (202)289-3199

Ablard, Linda Welch, CEO
Alpha Delta Pi [23882]
1386 Ponce de Leon Ave. NE
Atlanta, GA 30306
Ph: (404)378-3164

Ables, Scott, President
Association for Advanced Training in
the Behavioral Sciences [8467]
5126 Ralston St.
Ventura, CA 93003
Ph: (805)676-3030
Toll Free: 800-472-1931
Fax: (805)676-3033

Abosch, Aviva, President
American Society for Stereotactic
and Functional Neurosurgery
[16060]
c/o Aviva Abosch, President
Dept. of Neurosurgery
University Colorado
12631 E 17th Ave., C307
Aurora, CO 80045
Ph: (303)724-2204
Fax: (303)724-2300

Abounader, John V., Exec. Dir.
International Association Auto Theft
Investigators [5466]
PO Box 223
Clinton, NY 13323-0223
Ph: (315)853-1913
Fax: (315)883-1310

Abraham, Garry, President
Conveyor Equipment Manufacturers
Association [1723]
5672 Strand Ct., Ste. 2
Naples, FL 34110
Ph: (239)514-3441
Fax: (239)514-3470

Abraham, Michael T., Exec. Dir.
Theta Tau [23746]
1011 San Jacinto, Ste. 205

Executive Index

Austin, TX 78701
Ph: (512)472-1904
Toll Free: 800-264-1904
Fax: (512)472-4820

Abraham, Rick, CEO, President
Foodservice Sales and Marketing
Association [1387]
1810-J York Rd., No. 384
Lutherville, MD 21093
Toll Free: 800-617-1170
Fax: (888)668-7496

Abrahams, Edward, PhD, President
Personalized Medicine Coalition
[15743]
1710 Rhode Island Ave. NW, Ste.
700
Washington, DC 20036
Ph: (202)589-1770

Abram, Ted, Exec. Dir.
American Institute for Full Employ-
ment [11754]
2636 Biehn St.
Klamath Falls, OR 97601
Ph: (541)273-6731
Toll Free: 800-562-7752
Fax: (541)273-6496

Abramov, Frida, Contact
Gastroenterology Physician As-
sistants [14790]
PO Box 82511
Tampa, FL 33682
Ph: (813)766-8807
Fax: (813)856-3533

Abramowitz, Paul W., CEO
American Society of Health-System
Pharmacists [16645]
7272 Wisconsin Ave.
Bethesda, MD 20814
Ph: (301)664-8700
    (301)657-3000
Toll Free: 866-279-0681
Fax: (301)657-1251

Abrams, Creighton W., Exec. Dir.
Army Historical Foundation [9799]
2425 Wilson Blvd.
Arlington, VA 22201
Toll Free: 800-506-2672
Fax: (703)522-7929

Abrams, Harvey, President, Comm.
Chm.
American Auditory Society [15168]
PO Box 779
Pennsville, NJ 08070
Toll Free: 877-746-8315
Fax: (650)763-9185

Abrams, Jim, Chairman
Council for Ethical Leadership [626]
1 College and Main
Columbus, OH 43209
Ph: (614)236-7222

Abrams, Robert, President
Dance Critics Association [9250]
Old Chelsea Sta.
New York, NY 10113-1881

Abrams-Bell, Martha, Fac. Memb.
National Center for Housing
Management [11978]
1801 Old Reston Ave., Ste. 203
Reston, VA 20190-3356
Toll Free: 800-368-5625
Fax: (904)372-2324

Abramson, Jon, MD, Advisor
Parents of Kids with Infectious
Diseases [15413]
PO Box 5666
Vancouver, WA 98668
Ph: (360)695-0293
Toll Free: 877-55P-KIDS
Fax: (360)695-6941

Abrantes, Maria Luisa, Chairperson
Friends of the Children of Angola
[10984]
6210 Homespun Ln.
Falls Church, VA 22044-1012
Ph: (703)237-7468
Fax: (703)237-7467

Abrantes, Roger, PhD, President
Association of Companion Animal
Behavior Counselors [7398]
PO Box 104
Seville, FL 32190-0104
Toll Free: 866-224-2728

Abrate, Jayne, Exec. Dir.
American Association of Teachers of
French [8170]
302 N Granite St.
Marion, IL 62959
Ph: (815)310-0490
Fax: (815)310-5754

Abreu Paez, Victor Manuel, Exec.
Dir.
Interamerican Accounting Associa-
tion [34]
275 Fountainebleau Blvd., Ste. 245
Miami, FL 33172-4576
Ph: (305)225-1991
Fax: (305)225-2011

Abreu, Tanya, President
Spirit of Women [15337]
Spirit Health Group
2424 N Federal Hwy., Ste. 100
Boca Raton, FL 33431
Ph: (561)544-0755

Abromavage, Caroline, Dir. of
Operations
PMMI, the Association for Packaging
and Processing Technologies
[2110]
11911 Freedom Dr., Ste. 600
Reston, VA 20190
Ph: (571)612-3200
Toll Free: 888-275-7664
Fax: (703)243-8556

Abrusci, Richard, COO
LAM Health Project [17142]
1909 Capitol Ave., Ste. 203
Sacramento, CA 95811-4242
Ph: (617)460-7339
Fax: (617)864-0614

Absher, Brandon, Coord.
Radical Philosophy Association
[10115]
c/o Brandon Absher
320 Porter Ave.
Buffalo, NY 14201

Absten, Gregory T., Chairman
National Council on Laser Certifica-
tion [15565]
Professional Medical Education As-
sociation
3136 Broadway, Ste. 101
Grove City, OH 43123
Ph: (614)883-1739
Toll Free: 800-435-3131
Fax: (305)946-0232

Abuhamad, Alfred, President
Society of Ultrasound in Medical
Education [17541]
PO Box 212334
Columbia, SC 29221-2334
Ph: (803)216-3360
Fax: (803)216-3362

Abukhalaf, Nadira, President
House of Palestine [9212]
6161 El Cajon Blvd., No. 149
San Diego, CA 92115
Ph: (760)802-5255

Abukittah, Sam, Founder, Bd.
Member
Association of Natural Health
[13607]
108 Buchanan St. N
Bremen, GA 30110
Ph: (202)505-2664

Abu-Niber, Mohammed, Founder,
President
Salam Institute for Peace and
Justice [18010]
1628 16th St. NW
Washington, DC 20009
Ph: (202)360-4955

Aceves, Margaret, President
American Board of Criminalistics
[5233]
PO Box 1358
Palmetto, FL 34220
Ph: (941)729-9050

Achenbaum, Wyn, Bd. Member
Henry George Institute [19170]
90 John St., Ste. 501
New York, NY 10038
Ph: (212)889-8020

Acheson, Daniel E., CEO, Exec. Dir.
Drum Corps International, Inc.
[9901]
110 W Washington St., Ste. C
Indianapolis, IN 46204
Ph: (317)275-1212

Acheson, Ray, Director
Reaching Critical Will [18134]
c/o Women's International League
for Peace and Freedom
777 UN Plz., 6th Fl.
New York, NY 10017
Ph: (212)682-1265

Achiriloaie, Mariana, Founder, Bd.
Member
Hearts Across Romania [11019]
2544 Brookside Dr.
Irving, TX 75063-3172
Ph: (972)849-4359

Ackerly, John, President, Founder
Alliance for Green Heat [6447]
6930 Carroll Ave., No. 407
Takoma Park, MD 20912
Ph: (301)841-7755
    (301)204-9562
Fax: (301)270-4000

Ackerman, Andy, President
North American Trailer Dealers As-
sociation [3352]
111 2nd Ave. NE, Unit 1405
Saint Petersburg, FL 33701
Ph: (727)360-0304
Fax: (727)231-8356

Ackerman, Glenn W., President,
Founder
Talk About Curing Autism [13780]
2222 Martin St., Ste. 140
Irvine, CA 92612
Ph: (949)640-4401
Toll Free: 855-726-7810
Fax: (949)640-4424

Ackerman, Rev. Keith L., President
Forward in Faith North America
[20107]
PO Box 210248
Bedford, TX 76095-7248
Toll Free: 800-225-3661

Ackerman, Lee, Exec. Dir.
Disabled and Alone/Life Services for
the Handicapped [11590]
1440 Broadway, 23rd Fl.
New York, NY 10018-2326
Ph: (212)532-6740
Toll Free: 800-995-0066
Fax: (212)532-6740

Ackerman, Susan, President
American Schools of Oriental
Research [9022]
Boston University
656 Beacon St., 5th Fl.
Boston, MA 02215
Ph: (617)353-6570
Fax: (617)353-6575

Ackerman, Susan Johnston, M.D.,
President
American Association for Women
Radiologists [17038]
1891 Preston White Dr.
Reston, VA 20191
Ph: (703)476-7650

Ackles, Mitch, President
Hedge Fund Association [2023]
415 Madison Ave., 14th Fl.
New York, NY 10017
Ph: (646)762-9668

Ackley, Erin M., Admin. Asst.
Insulating Glass Certification Council
[1506]
PO Box 730
Sackets Harbor, NY 13685
Ph: (315)646-2234
Fax: (315)646-2297

Ackley, Terry, Exec. Dir.
Diabetes Education and Camping
Association [14525]
PO Box 385
Huntsville, AL 35804
Ph: (256)757-8114
Fax: (256)230-3171

Acord, David, Exec. Dir.
The Association of Union Construc-
tors [857]
1501 Lee Hwy., Ste. 202
Arlington, VA 22209-1109
Ph: (703)524-3336
Fax: (703)524-3364

Acosta, Jody, VP
Bowfishing Association of America
[22842]
c/o MemberPlanet Inc.
23224 Crenshaw Blvd.
Torrance, CA 90505
Ph: (501)730-3169

Acosta, Jose, President
Cuban American Association of Civil
Engineers [6220]
2191 NW 97th Ave.
Miami, FL 33172

Acosta, Thomas, Chairman
New Democratic Dimensions
[18116]
152 Madison Ave., Ste. 804
New York, NY 10016-5424
Ph: (212)481-7251
Fax: (212)481-9015

Acosta-Thompson, Hermano Ignacio
U., President
La Unidad Latina, Lambda Upsilon
Lambda Fraternity [23800]
511 6th Ave., PMB 39
New York, NY 10011

Acott, Mike, President
National Asphalt Pavement Associa-
tion [551]
5100 Forbes Blvd.
Lanham, MD 20706
Ph: (301)731-4748
Toll Free: 888-468-6499
Fax: (301)731-4621

Acquard, Charles, VP of Gvt. Affairs
Electricity Consumers Resource
Council [1021]

1101 K St. NW, Ste. 700
Washington, DC 20005
Ph: (202)682-1390
Fax: (202)289-6370

Acton, Amy, RN, Exec. Dir.
Phoenix Society for Burn Survivors
 [13865]
1835 RW Berends Dr. SW
Grand Rapids, MI 49519-4955
Ph: (616)458-2773
Toll Free: 800-888-2876
Fax: (616)458-2831

Acunto, Steve, Managing Dir.
International Association for Insur-
 ance Law in the United States
 [5315]
PO Box 9001
Mount Vernon, NY 10552
Ph: (914)966-3180
Fax: (914)966-3264

Adam, Dr. Abdel Gabar, Founder
Darfur Human Rights Organization
 [18393]
8171 Castor Ave.
Philadelphia, PA 19152
Ph: (267)784-7073

Adam, David F., Chairman, CEO
United States Maritime Alliance
 [2258]
125 Chubb Ave., Ste. 350NC
Lyndhurst, NJ 07071
Ph: (732)404-2960

Adam, Renae, Founder
Global Mamas [13378]
PO Box 18323
Minneapolis, MN 55418
Ph: (612)781-0455
Toll Free: 800-338-3032
Fax: (612)781-0450

Adamsin, Dennis, President
Precision Aerobatics Model Pilots
 Association [21245]
PO Box 320
Plainfield, IN 46168-0320

Adamowicz, W.L., President
Association of Environmental and
 Resource Economists [3812]
c/o Dr. Alan J. Krupnick, President
1616 P St. NW, Ste. 600
Washington, DC 20036
Ph: (202)328-5125
Fax: (202)939-3460

Adams, Aaron, PhD, Science Dir.
Bonefish & Tarpon Trust [4184]
24 Dockside Ln.
Key Largo, FL 33037
Ph: (321)674-7758

Adams, Barbara, Chmn. of the Bd.
Global Policy Forum [18490]
866 UN Plz., Ste. 4050
New York, NY 10017
Ph: (646)553-3460

Adams, Byron, President
Society of Nematologists [6910]
c/o Rosewood Business Solutions
108 W Burwell Ave.
Loudonville, OH 44842
Ph: (419)994-3419

Adams, Dr. Carole G., President
Foundation for American Christian
 Education [7611]
4225 Portsmouth Blvd.
Chesapeake, VA 23321
Toll Free: 800-352-3223
Fax: (757)488-5593

Adams, Chris, Director
National Association of Criminal
 Defense Lawyers [5150]

1660 L St. NW, 12th Fl.
Washington, DC 20036
Ph: (202)872-8600
Fax: (202)872-8690

Adams, Chris, Director
National Press Foundation [2705]
1211 Connecticut Ave. NW, Ste. 310
Washington, DC 20036
Ph: (202)663-7280

Adams, David, Director, Founder
Emerge: Counseling and Education
 to Stop Domestic Violence [11700]
2464 Massachusetts Ave., Ste. 101
Cambridge, MA 02140
Ph: (617)547-9879
Fax: (617)547-0904

Adams, Deborah, President
National Association of Early Childhood Specialists in State Departments of Education [7591]
c/o Amy Corriveau, Treasurer
Arizona Department of Education
1535 W Jefferson St., Bin 15
Phoenix, AZ 85007
Ph: (602)364-1530

Adams, Douglas Q., Editor
Institute for the Study of Man [5913]
1133 13th St. NW, Ste. C2
Washington, DC 20005
Ph: (202)371-2700
Fax: (202)371-1523

Adams, Gerard, VP
American Association of State
 Compensation Insurance Funds
 [1828]
c/o Donna Garfield
PO Box 2227
Sandy, UT 84091
Ph: (385)351-8024
Toll Free: 866-935-6773
Fax: (385)351-7845

Adams, Glenn, President
National Eagle Scout Association
 [12856]
Boy Scouts of America
1325 W Walnut Hill Ln.
Irving, TX 75038-3008
Ph: (972)580-2000

Adams, Guy, President, CEO
Christian Appalachian Project
 [12641]
PO Box 55911
Lexington, KY 40555-5911
Toll Free: 866-270-4227
Fax: (859)269-0617

Adams, J. Victor, Mgr., Secretary
World Championship Cutter and
 Chariot Racing Association [22723]
2632 S 4300 W
Ogden, UT 84401
Ph: (801)731-8021
 (801)731-3820
Fax: (801)731-8021

Adams, James, VP
States Organization for Boating Ac-
 cess [439]
231 S LaSalle St., Ste. 2050
Chicago, IL 60604
Ph: (312)946-6283
Fax: (312)946-0388

Adams, Jason, Chairman
United Native American Housing As-
 sociation [1693]
56423 Highway 93
Pablo, MT 59855
Ph: (406)675-4491

Adams, Jay, Exec. Dir.
Marine Corps Cryptologic Association [21013]

4486 Sandlewood St.
Napa, CA 94558-1766
Toll Free: 877-856-9562

Adams, John H., Chairman
Open Space Institute [4093]
1350 Broadway, Ste. 201
New York, NY 10018-7799
Ph: (212)290-8200

Adams, John S., Mem.
Alliance for Global Conservation
 [3792]
4245 Fairfax Dr., Ste. 100
Arlington, VA 22203

Adams, Joseph L., Chairperson
National Association of Boards of
 Pharmacy [16673]
1600 Feehanville Dr.
Mount Prospect, IL 60056
Ph: (847)391-4406
Fax: (847)391-4502

Adams, Judy A., Exec. Dir.
Johnny Adams Blues Organization
 [9944]
PO Box 11205
Alexandria, VA 22312
Toll Free: 888-316-5235
Fax: (703)722-0649

Adams, Kerry, Exec. Dir.
American Institute for Maghrib Stud-
 ies [7464]
Marshall Bldg., Rm. 470
Center for Middle Eastern Studies
845 N Park Ave.
Tucson, AZ 85719-4871
Ph: (520)626-6498
Fax: (520)621-9257

Adams, Marc, Exec. Dir.
HeartStrong [11888]
478 E Altamonte Dr., Ste. 108, No.
 714
Altamonte Springs, FL 32701
Ph: (206)388-3894

Adams, Mark, President
National Association of Consumer
 Shows [1177]
147 SE 102nd Ave.
Portland, OR 97216-2703
Ph: (503)253-0832
Toll Free: 800-728-6227
Fax: (503)253-9172

Adams, Michael, CEO
Services and Advocacy for GLBT
 Elders [11908]
305 7th Ave., 15th Fl.
New York, NY 10001
Ph: (212)741-2247
Fax: (212)366-1947

Adams, Mike, Gen. Counsel, Dep.
 Dir.
Republican Governors Association
 [5786]
1747 Pennsylvania Ave. NW, Ste.
 250
Washington, DC 20006-4643
Ph: (202)662-4140

Adams, Nevin E., Director
American Savings Education Council
 [7931]
1100 13th St. NW, Ste. 878
Washington, DC 20005-4204
Ph: (202)659-0670
Fax: (202)775-6312

Adams, Noland, President, Founder
Solid Axle Corvette Club [21492]
c/o Noland Adams, Founding
 President
PO Box 1134

El Dorado, CA 95623
Ph: (916)991-7040
Fax: (916)991-7044

Adams, Richard, Chmn. of the Bd.,
 Treasurer
Ferrari Owners Club [21381]
PO Box 3671
Granada Hills, CA 91394-0671
Ph: (714)213-4775
Fax: (714)960-4262

Adams, Stephen, President
American Institute for Economic
 Research [6378]
250 Division St.
Great Barrington, MA 01230-1000
Toll Free: 888-528-1216
Fax: (413)528-0103

Adams, Vikki A., Contact
Beyond Hunger [14633]
PO Box 151148
San Rafael, CA 94915
Ph: (415)459-2270

Adamski, Anita, Contact
North American Thoroughbred
 Society [22956]
1390 Sterrett Rd.
Fairfield, VA 24435-2628

Adamson, Jason, President
Olson 30 National Class Association
 [22659]
3695 Via Pacifica Walk
Oxnard, CA 93035

Adamson, Jo, President
WAVES National [21075]
c/o Monica O'Hara, Treasurer
6383 Kimmy Ct.
San Diego, CA 92114-5631

Adamson, Rebecca L., Founder,
 President
First Peoples Worldwide [9575]
877 Leeland Rd.
Fredericksburg, VA 22405
Ph: (540)899-6545
Fax: (540)899-6501

Adcock, Carol, Exec. Sec.
American Leather Chemists Associa-
 tion [6183]
1314 50th St., Ste. 103
Lubbock, TX 79412-2940
Ph: (806)744-1798
Fax: (806)744-1785

Adcock, Charlie, President
Family Motor Coach Association
 [22423]
8291 Clough Pke.
Cincinnati, OH 45244
Ph: (513)474-3622
Toll Free: 800-543-3622
Fax: (513)474-2332

Adcock, Mr. Gene, Director
Empress Chinchilla Breeders
 Cooperative [3600]
5525 Heidi St.
La Mesa, CA 91942-2411
Ph: (619)825-6204

Adcock, Leigh, Exec. Dir.
Women, Food and Agriculture
 Network [4704]
PO Box 611
Ames, IA 50010
Ph: (515)460-2477

Addie, Jo, President
International Network of Somewhere
 in Time Enthusiasts [24019]
8110 S Verdev Dr.
Oak Creek, WI 53154-3042

Addington, John H., Exec. Dir.
American Association of Automatic
Door Manufacturers [993]
1300 Sumner Ave.
Cleveland, OH 44115-2851
Ph: (216)241-7333
Fax: (216)241-0105

Addington, John H., Exec. Dir.
Door and Access Systems
Manufacturers Association
International [2220]
1300 Sumner Ave.
Cleveland, OH 44115-2851
Ph: (216)241-7333
Fax: (216)241-0105

Addiss, David, MD, Director
Children Without Worms [14176]
c/o The Task Force for Global Health
325 Swanton Way
Decatur, GA 30030
Ph: (404)371-0466

Addiss, Susan S., MPH, MUrS, Bd.
Member
Environment and Human Health, Inc.
[14715]
1191 Ridge Rd.
North Haven, CT 06473-4437
Ph: (203)248-6582
Fax: (203)288-7571

Addonizio, Lane, Assoc. VP
National Association for Olmsted
Parks [5098]
1200 18th St. NW, Ste. 330
Washington, DC 20036
Ph: (202)223-9113
Fax: (202)223-9112

Addow-Langlais, Grace, Consultant
African Federation, Inc. [12135]
PO Box 2186
New York, NY 10163
Ph: (646)863-5880
Fax: (646)863-5000

Adelhardt, Krista, President
Zoological Registrars Association
[4937]
c/o Krista Adelhardt, President
Woodland Park Zoo
5500 Phinney Ave. N
Seattle, WA 98103
Ph: (206)548-2513
Fax: (206)632-2556

Adelman, Madelaine, Officer
Association for Political and Legal
Anthropology [5907]
American Anthropological Associa-
tion
2300 Clarendon Blvd., Ste. 1301
Arlington, VA 22201
Ph: (703)528-1902

Adelson, Andrew S.
The Hastings Center [11800]
21 Malcolm Gordon Rd.
Garrison, NY 10524
Ph: (845)424-4040
Fax: (845)424-4545

Adelson, Sheldon G., Chairman
Republican Jewish Coalition [19046]
50 F St. NW, Ste. 100
Washington, DC 20001
Ph: (202)638-6688
Fax: (202)638-6694

Adem, Jenet, Dir. of Fin. & Admin.
American Association of State
Highway and Transportation Of-
ficials [5808]
444 N Capitol St. NW, Ste. 249
Washington, DC 20001
Ph: (202)624-5800
Fax: (202)624-5806

Aderton, Alex, Dir. of Mktg.
Investment Adviser Association
[3044]
1050 17th St. NW, Ste. 725
Washington, DC 20036-5514
Ph: (202)293-4222
Fax: (202)293-4223

Adewale, Omowale, Exec. Dir.
Grassroots Artists MovEment, Inc.
[8924]
2427 Morris Ave., 1st Fl.
Bronx, NY 10468
Ph: (718)690-3393
Fax: (646)792-3323

Adhikari, Roger, President
Association of Nepalis in the
Americas [19591]
10560 Main St., Ste. 209
Fairfax, VA 22030
Ph: (347)355-8237

Adjorlolo, Alain, PhD, President
Ivory Coast Medical Relief Team
[15603]
PO Box 55996
Seattle, WA 98155
Ph: (206)622-0549

Adkins, Gene, VP
International Cessna 120/140 As-
sociation [21230]
PO Box 830092
Richardson, TX 75083
Ph: (989)339-1009

Adkins, Lowell, Exec. Dir.
National Association of Campus
Card Users [3194]
2226 W Northern Ave., Ste C-120
Phoenix, AZ 85021
Ph: (602)395-8989
Fax: (602)395-9090

Adler, Alan, Exec. Dir.
Friends of Falun Gong [17848]
24 W Railroad Ave., No. 124
Tenafly, NJ 07670
Toll Free: 866-343-7436

Adler, Gary R., CEO, Founder,
President
Pro Players Association [13306]
PO Box 396
Peyton, CO 80831
Ph: (720)327-9207

Adler, William, Chairman
Precision Metalforming Association -
Custom Roll Forming Division
[2369]
6363 Oak Tree Blvd.
Independence, OH 44131-2500
Ph: (216)901-8800
Fax: (216)901-9190

Adolphson, Rev. Dan, Officer
GLAD Alliance [20181]
PO Box 44400
Indianapolis, IN 46244-0400
Ph: (317)721-5230

Adorno, Wilfredo Estrada, Secretary
Asociacion para la Educacion Teo-
logica Hispana [8703]
PO Box 677848
Orlando, FL 32867-7848
Ph: (407)482-7598
(407)482-7599
Fax: (407)641-9198

Adsay, N. Volkan, MD, President
United States and Canadian
Academy of Pathology [16596]
404 Town Park Blvd., Ste. 201
Evans, GA 30809
Ph: (706)733-7550
Fax: (706)733-8033

Adu-Gyamfi, Yaw, Founder, Exec.
Dir.
Shea Yeleen International [1588]
733 Euclid St. NW, 2nd Fl.
Washington, DC 20001
Ph: (202)285-3435

Advincula, Arnold P., President
Society of Robotic Surgery [17405]
WJ Weiser and Associates, Inc.
Two Woodfield Lake
1100 E Woodfield Rd., Ste. 520
Schaumburg, IL 60173
Ph: (847)517-7225
Fax: (847)517-7229

Afeseh, Hilary, PhD, Gen. Mgr. of
Sales & Mktg.
African Society for Toxicological Sci-
ences [7333]
c/o Michael Dourson, Advisor
2300 Montana Ave., Ste. 409
Cincinnati, OH 45211
Ph: (513)542-7475
Fax: (513)542-7587

Affolter, James, President
Botanic Gardens Conservation
International U.S. [3674]
c/o Kate Sackman, Executive Direc-
tor
Chicago Botanic Garden
1000 Lake Cook Rd.
Glencoe, IL 60022
Ph: (847)835-6928

Afkhami, Mahnaz, CEO, President
Women's Learning Partnership
[13411]
4343 Montgomery Ave., Ste. 201
Bethesda, MD 20814
Ph: (301)654-2774
Fax: (301)654-2775

Afzal, Dr. Omar, Chairman
Committee for Crescent Observation
International [9603]
1069 Ellis Hollow Rd.
Ithaca, NY 14850
Ph: (607)277-6706
Fax: (607)277-6706

Agamah, Dr. Edem, President
International Health and Develop-
ment Network [15480]
3950 Mill Stone Dr.
Springfield, IL 62711
Ph: (217)787-6530

Agber, Rev. Philip, Contact
Bringing Hope to Nigeria [11321]
3301 Creek Rd.
Huntingdon Valley, PA 19006
Ph: (215)947-6345

Agbor-Baiyee, Baiyee-Mbi, PhD,
CEO, President
African University Foundation [7463]
545 Edgemere Dr.
Indianapolis, IN 46260
Ph: (317)252-0123
Toll Free: 855-252-0432
Fax: (317)252-0124

Age, Zina, CEO, Founder
Aniz, Inc. [12068]
236 Forsyth St., Ste. 300
Atlanta, GA 30303
Ph: (404)521-2410
Toll Free: 866-521-2410
Fax: (404)521-2499

Agee, Chris, President
American Forage and Grassland
Council [4619]
PO Box 867
Berea, KY 40403
Toll Free: 800-944-2342

Agee, Kenneth, Exec. Dir.
Disaster Aid USA [11656]
9817 Lanham Severn Rd.
Lanham, MD 20706
Ph: (240)487-6359
Fax: (410)956-3833

Agee, Mary Cunningham, Founder,
President
Nurturing Network [13391]
1241 Adam St., Ste. 1142
Saint Helena, CA 94574
Ph: (509)493-4026
Fax: (509)493-4027

Agent, Betty, Treasurer
International Guild of Symphony,
Opera and Ballet Musicians
[23498]
c/o Nancy Griffin, President
PO Box 20013
Seattle, WA 98102

Agliata, Tony, President
National Association for County
Community and Economic
Development [17986]
2025 M St. NW, Ste. 800
Washington, DC 20036-3309
Ph: (202)367-1149
Fax: (202)367-2149

Agoglia, Tad, Founder
First Response Team of America
[11660]
1060 N Charlotte St., Ste. 102
Lancaster, PA 17603

Agostini, Augusto, Founder, CEO
Coalition to Defeat Childhood
Obesity [16254]
600 Northern Way, Ste. 1803
Winter Springs, FL 32708
Ph: (407)542-3150

Aguais, Jesus, Exec. Dir.
Aid for AIDS [13519]
515 Greenwich St., Ste. 506
New York, NY 10013
Ph: (212)337-8043
Fax: (212)337-8045

Aguero, Dante, Priest
Association of Marian Helpers
[19797]
Marians of the Immaculate Concep-
tion
Eden Hill
Stockbridge, MA 01263
Ph: (413)298-3931
Toll Free: 800-462-7426

Aguerre, Fernando, President
International Surfing Association
[23276]
5580 La Jolla Blvd., No. 145
La Jolla, CA 92037-7651
Ph: (858)551-8580
Fax: (858)551-8563

Aguilar, Alice, Exec. Dir.
Progressive Technology Project
[7291]
PO Box 303190
Austin, TX 78703
Ph: (612)724-2600
Toll Free: 866-298-6463

Aguirre, Ana, President
National Organization of Hispanics in
Criminal Justice [5145]
PO Box 19748
Austin, TX 78760
Ph: (512)708-0647

Aguirre, Edward, President
American Wu Shu Society [22984]
PO Box 5898

Long Island City, NY 11105-5898
Ph: (718)504-2981

Aguirre, Juan Carlos, Exec. Dir.
Mano A Mano: Mexican Culture
Without Borders [9795]
550 W 155th St.
New York, NY 10032
Ph: (212)587-3070
Fax: (212)587-3071

Aguirre, Stephen, President
American Civil War Association
[9454]
298 Warren Dr.
Ukiah, CA 95482

Aguirre, Tobias, Exec. Dir.
Sustainable Fishery Advocates
[4188]
PO Box 233
Santa Cruz, CA 95061-0233
Ph: (831)427-1707
Fax: (309)213-4688

Agunga, Dr. Robert, Director
Center for African Studies [19242]
318 Oxley Hall
1712 Neil Ave.
Columbus, OH 43210-1219
Ph: (614)292-8169
Fax: (614)292-4273

Aguwa, Alozie, Chmn. of the Bd.
Human Touch International [13515]
12392 Hawk Creek Dr.
Frisco, TX 75033
Ph: (513)593-1850

Ahearn, John, Chairman
Bankers Association for Finance and
Trade [388]
1120 Connecticut Ave. NW
Washington, DC 20036
Ph: (202)663-7575
Fax: (202)663-5538

Ahearn, Mary, V. Ch.
The Council on Food, Agricultural
and Resource Economics [3560]
c/o Caron Gala, Executive Director
502 C St. NE
Washington, DC 20002
Ph: (202)408-8522
Fax: (202)408-5385

Ahern, Dennis J., Secretary
Ahern Association [20775]
298 Central St.
Acton, MA 01720-2444

Ahern, Maureen, President
Our Journey [11122]
15617 US Hwy. 17
Townsend, GA 31331
Ph: (912)832-2809

Ahl, Mary, Mgr. of Admin.
Society for the Humanities [9558]
Cornell University
Andrew D. White House
27 East Ave.
Ithaca, NY 14853
Ph: (607)255-4086
Fax: (607)255-1422

Ahlquist, Dale, President
American Chesterton Society [9035]
4117 Pebblebrook Cir.
Minneapolis, MN 55437
Ph: (952)831-3096
Toll Free: 800-343-2425
Fax: (952)831-0387

Ahlquist, Margaret Sikkens, Officer
Swedish Women's Educational As-
sociation International, Inc. [19665]
PO Box 4128

Fort Lauderdale, FL 33338

Ahlquist, Roberta, President
Our Developing World [18553]
13004 Paseo Presada
Saratoga, CA 95070-4125
Ph: (408)379-4431

Ahluwalia, Dr. Poonam, Exec. Dir.
Global Youth Action Network [19273]
540 President St., 3rd Fl.
Brooklyn, NY 11215-1493
Ph: (212)661-6111

Ahmad, Samoon, MD, Founder,
President
Disaster Relief for Kids [11658]
800 B 5th Ave.
New York, NY 10065

Ahmed, Basheer, Secretary
Indian Muslim Relief and Charities
[12680]
849 Independence Ave., Ste. A
Mountain View, CA 94043
Ph: (650)856-0440
Fax: (650)856-0444

Ahmed, Fahmida, Chairperson
Association for the Advancement of
Sustainability in Higher Education
[7952]
2401 Walnut St., Ste. 102
Philadelphia, PA 19103
Ph: (303)395-1331
Toll Free: 888-552-0329

Ahmed, Farah, President
International Fragrance Association
North America [1452]
1655 Fort Myer Dr., Ste. 875
Arlington, VA 22209
Ph: (571)317-1500
Fax: (571)312-8033

Ahmed, Rafique, MD, PhD,
President
Bangladesh Medical Association of
North America [15718]
87-46 168 St.
Jamaica, NY 11432
Fax: (718)526-6661

Ahmed, Shahab, Exec.
Bangladeshi-American Pharmacists'
Association [16654]
1108 Liberty Ave.
Brooklyn, NY 11208
Ph: (718)304-6261
Fax: (718)277-0193

Ahmed, Dr. Tajuddin, Chairman
Islamic Research Foundation
International [8125]
7102 W Shefford Ln.
Louisville, KY 40242-6462
Ph: (502)287-6262
(502)423-1988

Ahn, Natalie, Bd. Member
United States Human Proteome
Organization [6106]
Bldg. I-1
2019 Galisteo St.
Santa Fe, NM 87505
Ph: (505)989-4876
Fax: (505)989-1073

Aho, Andrew, VP of Operations
TARP Association [303]
1801 County Road B W
Roseville, MN 55113
Ph: (651)225-6926

Ahsen, Akhter, PhD, Chairman,
Founder
International Imagery Association
[9546]

18 Edgecliff Ter.
Yonkers, NY 10705
Ph: (914)476-0781
Fax: (914)476-5796

Ahuja, Avinash, Director
Pratham U.S.A. [12128]
9703 Richmond Ave., Ste. 102
Houston, TX 77042
Ph: (713)774-9599

Ahuja, Sarita, Director
Neighborhood Funders Group
[12492]
436 14th St., Ste. 425
Oakland, CA 94612
Ph: (510)444-6063

Aiello, Antonio, Director
PEN American [10391]
588 Broadway, Rm. 303
New York, NY 10012-5258
Ph: (212)334-1660
Fax: (212)334-2181

Aiello, Ronald L., President
United States War Dogs Association
[21035]
1313 Mt. Holly Rd.
Burlington, NJ 08016
Ph: (609)747-9340

Aiken, Doris, Founder, President
Remove Intoxicated Drivers - USA
[12841]
PO Box 520
Schenectady, NY 12301
Ph: (518)372-0034
Toll Free: 888-283-5144
Fax: (518)370-4917

Ainley, Marshall, Chmn. of the Bd.
American Maritime Congress [5578]
444 N Capitol St. NW, Ste. 800
Washington, DC 20001
Ph: (202)347-8020
Fax: (202)347-1550

Ainley, Marshall, President
Marine Engineers' Beneficial As-
sociation [6803]
444 N Capitol St. NW, Ste. 800
Washington, DC 20001-1570
Ph: (202)257-2825
Fax: (202)638-5369

Aitken, Patricia, President
The Whaling Museum & Education
Center [9781]
279 Main St.
Cold Spring Harbor, NY 11724
Ph: (631)367-3418

Ajamian, Paul C., OD, Chairman
American Board of Optometry
[16421]
243 N Lindbergh Blvd., Ste. 312
Saint Louis, MO 63141
Ph: (314)983-4244

Akello, Sandrah, Administrator, Mgr.
of Fin.
International Refugee Rights Initiative [18416]
1483 York Ave., No. 20463
New York, NY 10021
Ph: (646)867-1991

Akenson, Jim, President
Professional Bowhunters Society
[22507]
PO Box 246
Terrell, NC 28682-0246
Ph: (704)664-2534
Fax: (704)664-7471

Akerman, Debby, President
Woman's Missionary Union [19743]
100 Missionary Ridge

Birmingham, AL 35283-0010
Ph: (205)991-8100
Toll Free: 800-968-7301
Fax: (888)422-7032

Akhwand, Mustafa, Founder, Exec.
Dir.
Shia Rights Watch [18442]
1050 17th St. NW, Ste. 800
Washington, DC 20036
Ph: (202)350-4302

Akinbuli, Funke Adenodi, Exec. Dir.,
Founder
The Exodus Guild, Inc. [10488]
9 Sherer Trl.
Worcester, MA 01603
Ph: (617)777-9338

Akins, Nick, Chairman
Edison Electric Institute [3414]
701 Pennsylvania Ave. NW
Washington, DC 20004-2696
Ph: (202)508-5000
Toll Free: 800-334-5453

Akiyode, Olufunke, Exec. Dir.
Shout Global Health [15496]
103 Azalea Ct.
Upper Marlboro, MD 20774-1668
Ph: (240)293-3652

Akonor, Kwame, Chairman
African Development Institute
[17773]
PO Box 1644
New York, NY 10185
Toll Free: 888-619-7535
Fax: (908)850-3016

Akre, Steven H., Chmn. of the Bd.
Wings of Hope [12735]
18370 Wings of Hope Blvd.
Chesterfield, MO 63005
Ph: (636)537-1302
Toll Free: 800-448-9487

Aksikas, Jaafar, President
Cultural Studies Association [9230]
3333 York Ln.
Island Lake, IL 60042
Ph: (630)999-1711
Toll Free: 800-519-6057

Akujuo, Uzo, Contact
Coalition of Landlords, Homeowners,
& Merchants [18931]
656C N Wellwood Ave.
Lindenhurst, NY 11757
Ph: (631)376-2110
(631)661-7015
Fax: (631)376-2148

Akutagawa, Linda, President, CEO
Leadership Education for Asian Pa-
cifics, Inc. [9027]
327 E 2nd St., Ste. 226
Los Angeles, CA 90012
Ph: (213)485-1422

Alam, Mohammad, PhD, President
International Association of Muslim
Scientists and Engineers [6560]
500 Grove St.
Herndon, VA 20170

Alam, Muhammad Mukhtar, Bd.
Member
World Computer Exchange [7660]
936 Nantasket Ave.
Hull, MA 02045-1453

Alaoui, Moulay M., President
Moroccan American Business
Council, Ltd. [1969]
1085 Commonwealth Ave., Ste. 194
Boston, MA 02215
Ph: (508)230-5985
Fax: (508)230-9943

Alba-Buffill, Dr. Elio, PhD, Exec. Sec.
Circulo de Cultura Panamericano [9659]
PO Box 469
Cedar Grove, NJ 07009-0469

Albarracin, Alejandra, President
IDB Family Association [19692]
1 Democracy Ctr., Ste. 110
6901 Rockledge Dr.
Bethesda, MD 20817
Ph: (301)493-6576
Fax: (301)493-6456

Alberdingk Thijm, Yvette, Exec. Dir.
WITNESS [18452]
80 Hanson Pl., Ste. 5
Brooklyn, NY 11217
Ph: (718)783-2000
Fax: (718)783-1593

Albert, Christine, Chairperson
National Academy of Recording Arts and Sciences [2903]
3030 Olympic Blvd.
Santa Monica, CA 90404
Ph: (310)392-3777
Fax: (310)392-2188

Albert, David H., Chmn. of the Bd., Founder
Friendly Water for the World [13322]
1717 18th Ct. NE
Olympia, WA 98506
Ph: (360)352-0506

Albert, Michael, Chairman
National Glass Association [1507]
1945 Old Gallows Rd., Ste. 750
Vienna, VA 22182
Ph: (703)442-4890
Toll Free: 866-342-5642
Fax: (703)442-0630

Albert, Michael, Chairman
Window & Door Dealers Alliance [600]
1945 Old Gallows Rd., Ste. 750
Vienna, VA 22182
Toll Free: 866-342-5642
Fax: (703)442-0630

Alberth, Brian
Media Communications Association - International [1198]
2810 Crossroads Dr., Ste. 3800
Madison, WI 53705-0135
Toll Free: 888-899-6224
Fax: (888)862-8150

Albert-Konecky, Lisa, VP
National Association of Youth Courts [19275]
PO Box 48927
Sarasota, FL 34230
Ph: (410)528-0143
Fax: (410)528-0170

Albinder, Frank, President
Intercollegiate Men's Choruses, Inc. [9921]
c/o Clayton Parr, Executive Secretary
Music Department
Albion College
611 E Porter St.
Albion, MI 49224
Ph: (517)629-0251
Fax: (517)629-0784

Albisa, Catherine, Exec. Dir.
National Economic and Social Rights Initiative [18431]
90 John St., Ste. 308
New York, NY 10038
Ph: (212)253-1710
Fax: (212)385-6124

Albizo, Joel, Exec. Dir.
Council of Landscape Architectural Registration Boards [5965]
1840 Michael Faraday Dr., Ste. 200
Reston, VA 20190
Ph: (571)432-0332

Albrecht, Dr. Brian M., President
Global Outreach Mission [12277]
PO Box 2010
Buffalo, NY 14231-2010
Ph: (716)688-5048
Fax: (716)688-5049

Albrecht, Christal M., President
National Council for Workforce Education [7854]
1050 Larrabee Ave., No. 104-308
Bellingham, WA 98225
Ph: (603)714-1918

Albrecht, Ms. Kathy, Founder
Missing Pet Partnership [12455]
PO Box 31158
Bellingham, WA 98228
Ph: (253)529-3999

Albretsen, Jay, Coord.
American Board of Veterinary Toxicology [17611]
c/o Jay Albretsen, Coordinator
54943 N Main St.
Mattawan, MI 49071
Ph: (269)532-0169

Albright, Bruce, Director
Lutheran Volunteer Corps [20313]
1226 Vermont Ave. NW
Washington, DC 20005
Ph: (202)387-3222
Fax: (202)667-0037

Albright, Craig, VP
Business Software Alliance [5324]
20 F St. NW, Ste. 800
Washington, DC 20001
Ph: (202)872-5500
Fax: (202)872-5501

Albright, David, Founder, President, Chairman
Institute for Science and International Security [7133]
440 1st St. NW, Ste. 800
Washington, DC 20001
Ph: (202)547-3633
Fax: (202)547-3634

Albright, Diane, President, Founder
Houses for Haiti [11953]
1411 Deerwood Ct.
Eagan, MN 55122

Albright, Madeleine K., Chairman
America Abroad Media [18651]
1701 Pennsylvania Ave. NW, Ste. 300
Washington, DC 20006
Ph: (202)249-7380

Albright, Madeleine K., Chairman
National Democratic Institute for International Affairs [18525]
455 Massachusetts Ave. NW, 8th Fl.
Washington, DC 20001-2783
Ph: (202)728-5500
Toll Free: 888-875-2887

Albright, Tom, PhD, President
Academy of Neuroscience for Architecture [6913]
1249 F St.
San Diego, CA 92101
Ph: (619)235-0221

Albuelouf, Alma, BSN, RN, FCN, Bd. Member
National Association of Catholic Nurses-U.S.A. [16145]

c/o Diocese of Joliet
Blanchette Catholic Center
16555 Weber Rd.
Crest Hill, IL 60403
Ph: (774)413-5084

Alcairo, Pet, Director
Tremor Action Network [15996]
PO Box 5013
Pleasanton, CA 94566-0513
Ph: (510)681-6565
Fax: (925)369-0485

Al-Dayaa, Dr. Hani, President
AlKoura League [12612]
PO Box 95
Norwood, MA 02062
Ph: (617)435-8687

Alden, Mike, Director
National Association of Collegiate Directors of Athletics [23237]
c/o Brian Horning, Director
24651 Detroit Rd.
Westlake, OH 44145-2524
Ph: (847)491-8880
(401)456-8007

Alderman, E. Joseph, DDS, Exec. Dir.
American Board of Dental Public Health [14395]
827 Brookridge Dr. NE
Atlanta, GA 30306-3618
Ph: (404)876-3530

Alderson, Thomas, President
American College of Osteopathic Obstetricians and Gynecologists [16271]
8851 Camp Bowie W, Ste. 275
Fort Worth, TX 76116
Ph: (817)377-0421
Toll Free: 800-875-6360
Fax: (817)377-0439

Aldrich, Patrick, Dir. of Fin.
American Association of Neuromuscular and Electrodiagnostic Medicine [15897]
2621 Superior Dr. NW
Rochester, MN 55901
Ph: (507)288-0100
Fax: (507)288-1225

Aldridge, Ray, President
Fire Suppression Systems Association [2995]
3601 E Joppa Rd.
Baltimore, MD 21234
Ph: (410)931-8100
Fax: (410)931-8111

Aldridge-Baligian, Anne, Founder
Cleaning for Heroes [13005]
221B Hallene Rd.
Warwick, RI 02886
Ph: (401)732-6243
Fax: (866)389-3445

Alegria, Mr. Eric, President
International Sonoran Desert Alliance [4077]
38 W Plz.
Ajo, AZ 85321
Ph: (520)387-6823
Fax: (520)387-3005

Alemayhu, Ted M., Chairman, Founder
US Doctors for Africa [15505]
14945 Ventura Blvd., Ste. 224
Sherman Oaks, CA 91403
Ph: (818)728-6629

Aleong, Aki, President
Media Action Network for Asian Americans [18658]

PO Box 6188
Burbank, CA 91510-6188
Ph: (213)486-4433

Alessandri, Gina, Mem.
Association of American Pesticide Control Officials [4523]
PO Box 466
Milford, DE 19963
Ph: (302)422-8152

Alessi, Dr. David, Founder
Face Forward [11701]
9735 Wilshire Blvd., Ste. 300
Beverly Hills, CA 90210
Ph: (310)657-2253

Alessi, Russell J., President
ELECTRI International - The Foundation for Electrical Construction Inc. [1016]
3 Bethesda Metro Ctr., Ste. 1100
Bethesda, MD 20814-6302
Ph: (301)215-4538
Fax: (301)215-4536

Alexander, A. Herbert, MD, President
Society of Medical Consultants to the Armed Forces [15840]
c/o Kevin G. Berry, MD, Secretary-Treasurer
5009 Overlea Ct.
Bethesda, MD 20816
Ph: (301)320-0847

Alexander, CaSandra, Program Mgr.
National Committee for Accreditation of Coaching Education [7617]
1900 Association Dr.
Reston, VA 20191
Ph: (703)476-3487

Alexander, Christina, Founder, President
United States Canada Peace Anniversary Association [18833]
PO Box 2564
Blaine, WA 98231-2564
Ph: (360)332-7165

Alexander, Dan, Chmn. of the Bd.
National Antique Tractor Pullers Association [22457]
c/o Brad Begeman, President
1863 E 1000th St.
Mendon, IL 62351-2213
Ph: (217)242-4634

Alexander, John, President
Cast Bullet Association [23127]
1317 Bennoch Rd.
1317 Bennoch Rd.
Old Town, ME 04468

Alexander, Johnny D., Treasurer
Descendants of the Signers of the Declaration of Independence [20691]
c/o Laurie Croft, President
21 W Glenbrooke Cir.
Richmond, VA 23229-8036

Alexander, Leslie, President
Association for the Study of the Worldwide African Diaspora [7466]
c/o Dr. Leslie Alexander
486N University Hall
230 N Oval Mall
Columbus, OH 43210

Alexander, Lisa, President
American Contract Compliance Association [11753]
17 E Monroe St., No. 150
Chicago, IL 60603
Toll Free: 866-222-2298
Fax: (510)287-2158

Alexander, Mary, MA, CEO
Infusion Nurses Society [17445]
315 Norwood Park S

Norwood, MA 02062
Ph: (781)440-9408
Fax: (781)440-9409

Alexander, Paul, President
Evangelicals for Social Action
[19107]
PO Box 367
Wayne, PA 19087
Ph: (484)384-2988

Alexander, Sarah Stokes, VP
Keystone Policy Center [6731]
1628 St. John Rd.
Keystone, CO 80435
Ph: (970)513-5800
Fax: (970)262-0152

Alexander, Steve, Exec. Dir.
Association of Postconsumer Plastic
Recyclers [2619]
1001 G St. NW, Ste. 500 W
Washington, DC 20001
Ph: (202)316-3046

Alexander, Taro, Founder
Our Time [17303]
330 W 42nd St., 12th Fl.
New York, NY 10036
Ph: (212)414-9696

Alfaro, Carlos, President
Argentine-American Chamber of
Commerce [23556]
150 E 58th St.
New York, NY 10155
Ph: (212)698-2238
Fax: (212)698-1144

Alford, Diane, Exec. Dir.
Miracle League Association [22783]
1506 Klondike Rd., Ste. 105
Conyers, GA 30094
Ph: (770)760-1933
Fax: (770)483-1223

Alford, Harry C., CEO, President
National Black Chamber of Com-
merce [23603]
4400 Jenifer St. NW, Ste. 331
Washington, DC 20015-2133
Ph: (202)466-6888
Fax: (202)466-4918

AlFord, Jesse, President
American Youth Circus Organization
[9160]
PO Box 482
Ithaca, NY 14851
Ph: (914)441-8834

Alford, Max Ray, President, Chmn.
of the Bd.
Alford American Family Association
[20777]
427 Wheatridge St.
Mesquite, TX 75150-5857
Ph: (972)288-1175

Alford-Jones, Ms. Kelsey, Exec. Dir.
Guatemala Human Rights Commis-
sion USA [18403]
3321 12th St. NE
Washington, DC 20017-4008
Ph: (202)529-6599
Fax: (202)526-4611

Alfson, Ruth A., President
NAFA Fleet Management Associa-
tion [297]
125 Village Blvd., Ste. 200
Princeton, NJ 08540
Ph: (609)720-0882
Fax: (609)452-8004

Alger, George, President
Artists for a Better World
International [8960]

PO Box 1872
Ventura, CA 93002

Alger, Mr. Stan, Exec. Dir.
Society for Clinical Vascular Surgery
[14144]
500 Cummings Ctr., Ste. 4550
Beverly, MA 01915
Ph: (978)927-8330
Fax: (978)524-0498

Al-Hardan, Yousif, Exec. VP
Iraqi American Chamber of Com-
merce and Industry [23594]
15265 Maturin Dr., No. 184
San Diego, CA 92127-2323
Ph: (858)613-9215
Toll Free: 877-684-5162
Fax: (858)408-2624

Ali, Abbas J., Exec. Dir.
American Society for Competitiveness [7541]
304 Eberly, IUP
664 Pratt Dr.
Indiana, PA 15705
Ph: (724)357-5928
   (724)357-5759
Fax: (724)357-7768

Ali, Kamran Asdar, President
American Institute of Pakistan Stud-
ies [10061]
B488 Medical Science Ctr.
University of Wisconsin - Madison
1300 University Ave.
Madison, WI 53706
Ph: (608)265-1471
   (608)261-1194

Ali, Moonis, President
International Society of Applied Intel-
ligence [5986]
Dept. of Computer Science
Texas State University, San Marcos
601 University Dr.
San Marcos, TX 78666-4616
Ph: (512)245-8050
Fax: (512)245-8750

Ali, Somy, Founder, President
No More Tears [11711]
10097 Clearly Blvd., Ste. 150
Plantation, FL 33324
Ph: (954)324-7669

Ali, Subhi D., MD, Chairman
The Jerusalem Fund | Palestine
Center [8083]
2425 Virginia Ave. NW
Washington, DC 20037
Ph: (202)338-1958
Fax: (202)333-7742

Alig, Bob, Exec. VP
Graduate Management Admission
Council [8262]
PO Box 2969
Reston, VA 20195
Ph: (703)668-9600
Toll Free: 866-505-6559
Fax: (703)668-9601

Alikakos, Dr. Maria, CEO, Founder
Global Physicians Corps [15462]
PO Box 25118
Los Angeles, CA 90025-0118

Aliniece, Pamala Gail, Founder,
CEO
Laughing at Leukemia [15536]
260 Peachtree St., Ste. 2200
Atlanta, GA 30303
Ph: (404)784-1839

Al-Juburi, Faisal, Exec. Dir.
Bridges of Understanding [18516]
PO Box 2232

New York, NY 10101-2232
Ph: (917)755-2179

Allaire, Jim, Web Adm.
Catholic Worker Movement [18715]
36 E 1st St.
New York, NY 10003
Ph: (212)777-9617

Allam, Medhat E., MD, Chairman
International Surgical Mission Sup-
port [17393]
365 County Rd. 39A, Ste. 11
Southampton, NY 11968
Ph: (631)287-6202
Fax: (631)287-6213

Allaman, Lisa, Officer
University of Wisconsin - Eau Claire
Alumni Association [19368]
213 Schofield Hall
Eau Claire, WI 54702-4004
Ph: (715)836-3266
Fax: (715)836-4375

Allan, James S., MD, MBA,
President
American Society of Transplantation
[17505]
1120 Route 73, Ste. 200
Mount Laurel, NJ 08054
Ph: (856)439-9986
Fax: (856)581-9604

Allan, Sarah, Chairperson, Editor
Society for the Study of Early China
[9156]
Dartmouth College
HB 6191
Hanover, NH 03755
Toll Free: 800-872-7423

Allaster, Stacey, Chairman
WTA Tour Players Association
[23311]
100 2nd Ave. S, Ste. 1100S
Saint Petersburg, FL 33701
Ph: (727)895-5000
Fax: (727)894-1982

Allbright, Amy, Director
American Bar Association - Commis-
sion on Disability Rights [5271]
1050 Connecticut Ave. NW, Ste. 400
Washington, DC 20036
Ph: (202)662-1570
Fax: (202)442-3439

Allbright, Jay, Founder
Recovery Ministries [13179]
22015 N 64th Ave.
Glendale, AZ 85310
Ph: (623)433-9643

Allegretti, Tom, President, CEO
The American Waterways Operators
[2236]
801 N Quincy St., Ste. 200
Arlington, VA 22203
Ph: (703)841-9300
Fax: (703)841-0389

Alleman, Michael, Contact
International Air Filtration Certifiers
Association [1623]
c/o Michael Alleman, 129 S Gallatin
129 S Gallatin St.
Liberty, MO 64068
Toll Free: 888-679-1904
Fax: (816)792-8105

Allemann, Kevin, Director, Secretary
Show Me Solar [7205]
303 Norris Dr.
Jefferson City, MO 65109
Ph: (573)556-8653

Allen, Antoinette, Dir. of Mtgs.
CTAM: Cable and Telecommunications Association for Marketing
[460]

120 Waterfront St., Ste. 200
National Harbor, MD 20745
Ph: (301)485-8900
Fax: (301)560-4964

Allen, Barbara, VP
Compassionate Friends [12410]
1000 Jorie Blvd., Ste. 140
Oak Brook, IL 60523-4494
Ph: (630)990-0010
Toll Free: 877-969-0010
Fax: (630)990-0246

Allen, Brent, Exec. Dir.
American Equestrian Alliance [4305]
PO Box 6230
Scottsdale, AZ 85261
Toll Free: 800-874-9191
Fax: (602)992-8327

Allen, Carey, Director
International Brotherhood of
Boilermakers, Iron Ship Builders,
Blacksmiths, Forgers and Helpers -
Cement, Lime, Gypsum, and Allied
Workers Division [23406]
753 State Ave., Ste. 570
Kansas City, KS 66101
Ph: (913)371-2640

Allen, Carrie J., Coord.
North American Equine Ranching
Information Council [4392]
PO Box 43968
Louisville, KY 40253-0968
Ph: (502)245-0425
Fax: (502)245-0438

Allen, Charles, Chairman
National Association for Black
Veterans [21129]
PO Box 11432
Milwaukee, WI 53211
Toll Free: 877-622-8387
Fax: (414)562-6455

Allen, Charles, Director
National Association of Home
Inspectors [1819]
4426 5th St. W
Bradenton, FL 34207
Ph: (941)462-4265
Toll Free: 800-448-3942
Fax: (941)896-3187

Allen, Christopher M., Exec. Dir.
Opticians Association of America
[16416]
3740 Canada Rd.
Lakeland, TN 38002
Ph: (901)388-2423
Fax: (901)388-2348

Allen, Dean, Chairman
Program for Appropriate Technology
in Health [17811]
2201 Westlake Ave., Ste. 200
Seattle, WA 98121
Ph: (206)285-3500
Fax: (206)285-6619

Allen, Eleanor, CEO, Secretary
Water for People [12198]
100 E Tennessee Ave.
Denver, CO 80209
Ph: (720)488-4590

Allen, Horace D., CEO, Founder
Legacy Creators [19113]
13663 Providence Rd., No. 305
Matthews, NC 28104
Ph: (704)661-5702
Toll Free: 800-224-0579

Allen, Ines, President
IMAHelps [15477]
PO Box 2727
Rancho Mirage, CA 92270

Allen, James, Cmdr.
The Wheelmen [22760]
c/o Kenneth Gray, Membership
Chairman
1552 Autumn Ridge Cir.
Reston, VA 20194-1563

Allen, Jeff, VP
Federation of State Humanities
Councils [9554]
1600 Wilson Blvd., Ste. 902
Arlington, VA 22209
Ph: (703)908-9700

Allen, Jeff, CFO
Tournament of Roses Association
[9287]
391 S Orange Grove Blvd.
Pasadena, CA 91184
Ph: (626)449-4100

Allen, Jeff, CFO
United States Futsal Federation
[23260]
PO Box 40077
Berkeley, CA 94704-4077
Ph: (510)836-8733
Fax: (650)242-1036

Allen, Jennifer, Bd. Member
Educational Book and Media As-
sociation [2782]
37 Main St., Ste. 203
Warrenton, VA 20186
Ph: (540)318-7770
Fax: (202)962-3939

Allen, John, Exec. Dir.
Spill Control Association of America
[2643]
103 Oronoco St., Ste. 200
Alexandria, VA 22314
Ph: (571)451-0433

Allen, Josh, RN, Director
American Assisted Living Nurses
Association [16087]
PO Box 10469
Napa, CA 94581
Ph: (707)622-5628

Allen, Judy, President
Mount Rushmore Society [9411]
711 N Creek Dr.
Rapid City, SD 57703
Ph: (605)341-8883
Fax: (605)341-0433

Allen, Judy, Coord., Admin.
Weave a Real Peace [10766]
6182 Pollard Ave.
East Lansing, MI 48823
Ph: (517)333-8145

Allen, Katie, Director
Conservation Leadership Network
[4491]
National Conservation Training Ctr.
698 Conservation Way
Shepherdstown, WV 25443
Ph: (304)876-7462
Fax: (304)876-7751

Allen, Ken, President
National Council for Agricultural
Education [7478]
236 Maple Hill Rd.
Hopkins, MN 55343
Ph: (317)709-0298
Fax: (317)802-5300

Allen, Kenneth, Exec. Dir.
American Council for Technology
[5298]
3040 Williams Dr., Ste. 500
Fairfax, VA 22031
Ph: (703)208-4800
Fax: (703)208-4805

Allen, Kimberly, VP
Organization of Black Screenwriters
[1157]
3010 Wilshire Blvd., No. 269
Los Angeles, CA 90010
Ph: (323)735-2050

Allen, Laura, Exec. Dir., Founder
Animal Law Coalition [10577]
c/o Jonathan Stone Rankin
Animal Law Offices of Jonathan
Stone Rankin
PO Box 3311
Framingham, MA 01705-3311

Allen, Louis, President
First Hungarian Literary Society
[19469]
323 E 79th St.
New York, NY 10021
Ph: (212)288-5002
Fax: (212)772-3175

Allen, Mark, Director
International Monetary Fund [18153]
700 19th St. NW
Washington, DC 20431
Ph: (202)623-7000
Fax: (202)623-4661

Allen, Martha Leslie, PhD, Director
Women's Institute for Freedom of
the Press [17961]
1940 Calvert St. NW
Washington, DC 20009-1502
Ph: (202)656-0893

Allen, Nancy, Assoc. Dir.
Health Occupations Students of
America [8323]
548 Silicon Dr., Ste. 101
Southlake, TX 76092
Toll Free: 800-321-4672

Allen, Pandora, Secretary
Holland Lop Rabbit Specialty Club
[4598]
c/o Pandora Allen, Secretary
2633 Seven Eleven Rd.
Chesapeake, VA 23322
Ph: (757)421-9607

Allen, Patricia, Secretary, Treasurer
Taft Family Association [20937]
c/o Patricia Allen, Secretary/
Treasurer
77 Greenfield Rd.
Montague, MA 01351

Allen, Rebecca S., Chairman
Council of Professional Geropsychol-
ogy Training Programs [14890]
c/o Mary Lindsey Jacobs, Secretary
Salem VA Medical Ctr.
1970 Roanoke Blvd., Bldg. 9
Salem, VA 24153

Allen, Roger, VP
Traditional Small Craft Association
[22676]
PO Box 350
Mystic, CT 06355-0350

Allen, Ms. Sally, President
U.S.A. Defenders of Greyhounds
[10709]
PO Box 1256
Carmel, IN 46082
Ph: (317)244-0113

Allen, Samuel R., Chairman
Council on Competitiveness [3300]
900 17th St. NW, Ste. 700
Washington, DC 20006
Ph: (202)682-4292
Fax: (202)682-5150

Allen, Scott, President
Disciple Nations Alliance [20021]
1110 E Missouri Ave., No. 393

Phoenix, AZ 85014
Ph: (602)386-4560
Fax: (602)386-4564

Allen, Scott, Secretary
OBTS Teaching Society for Management Educators [6044]
c/o Joe Seltzer, President
900 W Olney Ave.
Philadelphia, PA 19141
Ph: (215)951-1037

Allen, Sharon L., Chmn. of the Bd.
YMCA of the U.S.A. [13421]
101 N Wacker Dr.
Chicago, IL 60606
Ph: (312)977-0031
Toll Free: 800-872-9622

Allen, Sherry, Exec. Dir.
National Board for Certified
Counselors, Inc. and Affiliates
[11496]
3 Terrace Way
Greensboro, NC 27403-3660
Ph: (336)547-0607
Fax: (336)547-0017

Allen, Stacy, Bd. Member
Association of National Park Rang-
ers [5662]
PO Box 984
Davis, CA 95617

Allen, Stephen J., MS, CEO
ASHP Foundation [16651]
7272 Wisconsin Ave.
Bethesda, MD 20814
Ph: (301)664-8612
Fax: (301)634-5712

Allen, Steve, President
British-American Business Council
[616]
52 Vanderbilt Ave., 20th Fl.
New York, NY 10017
Ph: (212)661-4060
Fax: (212)661-4074

Allen, Steven H., Exec. Dir.
Green Mechanical Council [6554]
PO Box 521
Mount Prospect, IL 60056
Ph: (847)342-0049
Toll Free: 800-726-9696

Allen, Teresa, DO, President
International Association of Medical
Thermographers [17468]
5120 S Florida Ave., Ste. 301
Lakeland, FL 33813
Ph: (863)646-1599

Allen, Tom, CEO, President
Association of American Publishers
[2765]
71 5th Ave., 2nd Fl.
New York, NY 10003-3004
Ph: (212)255-0200
Fax: (212)255-7007

Allen, Tom, Director
Public Lands Foundation [4582]
PO Box 7226
Arlington, VA 22207
Ph: (703)935-0916
Toll Free: 866-985-9636
Fax: (888)204-9814

Allen, Tracy, President
Specialty Coffee Association of
America [430]
117 W 4th St., Ste. 300
Santa Ana, CA 92701

Allen, Vinit, Founder, Exec. Dir.
Sustainable World Coalition [3954]
c/o Earth Island Institute

2150 Allston Way, Ste. 460
Berkeley, CA 94704-1375
Ph: (415)717-0422

Allen, Will, Founder, CEO
Growing Power Inc. [3564]
5500 W Silver Spring Dr.
Milwaukee, WI 53218-3261
Ph: (414)527-1546
Fax: (414)527-1908

Alli, Dr. Benjamin, Chancellor
Royal College of Physicians &
Surgeons of the United States of
America [17535]
485 Allard Rd.
Grosse Pointe, MI 48236
Ph: (313)882-0641
Fax: (313)882-0979

Allinson, Marc, President
International Society of Transport
Aircraft Trading [143]
330 N Wabash Ave., Ste. 2000
Chicago, IL 60611
Ph: (312)321-5169
Fax: (312)673-6579

Allison, Allen, PhD, Chmn. of the Bd.
Indo-Pacific Conservation Alliance
[3884]
1525 Bernice St.
Honolulu, HI 96817
Ph: (808)848-4124
Fax: (808)847-8252

Allison, Dana, Exec. Dir.
Women's World Health Initiative
[17768]
PO Box 9635
Salt Lake City, UT 84109

Allison, James, CEO, President
Flair Bartenders' Association [185]
104 E Fairview Ave., No. 283
Meridian, ID 83642-1733
Ph: (208)888-3146
Toll Free: 877-794-9446
Fax: (208)887-1505

Allison, Michael, President
National Association of Secondary
School Principals [8459]
1904 Association Dr.
Reston, VA 20191-1502
Ph: (703)860-0200
Toll Free: 800-253-7746

Allman, Donald R., President, CEO
Traffic Audit Bureau for Media
Measurement, Inc. [112]
561 7th Ave., 12th Fl.
New York, NY 10018
Ph: (212)972-8075
Fax: (212)972-8928

Allmon, Warren D., Director
Paleontological Research Institution
[6972]
1259 Trumansburg Rd.
Ithaca, NY 14850
Ph: (607)273-6623
Fax: (607)273-6620

Alluisi, Jennifer, MA Ed, Dir. of
Programs
American Association for Cancer
Education [13877]
154 Hansen Rd., Ste. 201
Charlottesville, VA 22911-8839
Ph: (434)284-4445
Fax: (434)977-1856

Allvin, Rhian Evans, Exec. Dir.
National Association for the Educa-
tion of Young Children [7592]
1313 L St. NW, Ste. 500
Washington, DC 20005
Ph: (202)232-8777
Toll Free: 800-424-2460
Fax: (202)328-1846

Alm, Kathy, CEO
Professional Association of
  Therapeutic Horsemanship
  International [22795]
PO Box 33150
Denver, CO 80221-6920
Ph: (303)452-1212
Toll Free: 800-369-7433
Fax: (303)252-4610

Almada, Justine, Contact
HPV and Anal Cancer Foundation
  [13985]
PO Box 232
New York, NY 10028
Ph: (646)593-7739

Almajrabi, Ibrahim, President
Save Yemen's Flora and Fauna
  [3942]
1523 River Terrace Dr.
East Lansing, MI 48823

Al-Marayati, Laila, MD, Chairperson
KinderUSA [11247]
PO Box 224846
Dallas, TX 75222-9785
Toll Free: 888-451-8908

Al-Marayati, Salam, President
Muslim Public Affairs Council
  [18702]
3010 Wilshire Blvd., No. 217
Los Angeles, CA 90010
Ph: (323)258-6722
Fax: (323)258-5879

Almasi, Janice, President
Literacy Research Association
  [8486]
222 S Westmonte Dr., Ste. 101
Altamonte Springs, FL 32714
Ph: (407)774-7880
Fax: (407)774-6440

Almeida, Paul E., President
AFL-CIO- Department Professional
  Employees [23452]
815 16th St. NW, 7th Fl.
Washington, DC 20006
Ph: (202)638-0320

Almodovar, Norma Jean,
  Chairperson, President
International Sex Worker Foundation
  for Art, Culture and Education
  [12945]
8801 Cedros Ave., No. 7
Panorama City, CA 91402
Ph: (818)924-2776

Al-Mogbel, Abdullah A., Chairman
International Road Federation [3337]
Madison Pl., 5th Fl.
500 Montgomery St.
Alexandria, VA 22314
Ph: (703)535-1001
Fax: (703)535-1007

Almond, Carrie, President
National Federation of Republican
  Women [19041]
124 N Alfred St.
Alexandria, VA 22314
Ph: (703)548-9688
Fax: (703)548-9836

Al-Nasser, Nassir Abdulaziz, Rep.
United Nations Alliance of Civiliza-
  tions [18560]
730 3rd Ave., 20th Fl.
New York, NY 10017
Ph: (929)274-6217
Fax: (929)274-6233

Al-Natheema, Wafaa, Director,
  Founder
Institute of Near Eastern and African
  Studies [7773]

PO Box 425125
Cambridge, MA 02142-0004

Alnes, Judy, Exec. Dir.
Alliance for Nonprofit Management
  [252]
12 Middlesex Rd., No. 67061
Chestnut Hill, MA 02467
Toll Free: 888-776-2434

Aloma, Angel, Exec. Dir.
Food for the Poor [12538]
6401 Lyons Rd.
Coconut Creek, FL 33073
Ph: (954)427-2222
Toll Free: 800-427-9104

Alonso, Gabriel, Director
American Wind Energy Association
  [7386]
1501 M St. NW, Ste. 1000
Washington, DC 20005
Ph: (202)383-2500
Fax: (202)383-2505

Alonso, Shantha Ready, Exec. Dir.
Eco-Justice Working Group [19105]
110 Maryland Ave. NE, Ste. 203
Washington, DC 20002
Ph: (202)827-3975

Alperovich, Allie, Treasurer
Jewish Orthodox Feminist Alliance
  [20258]
520 8th Ave., 4th Fl.
New York, NY 10018
Ph: (212)679-8500

Alpert, Briar, V. Chmn. of the Bd.
Analytical, Life Science and
  Diagnostics Association [7119]
500 Montgomery St., Ste. 400
Alexandria, VA 22314-1560
Ph: (703)647-6214
Fax: (703)647-6368

Alpert, Patricia T., President
Asian American/Pacific Islander
  Nurses Association, Inc. [16116]
c/o Jennifer Kawi, PhD, MSN,
  Treasurer
School of Nursing
University of Nevada, Las Vegas
4505 Maryland Pky.
Las Vegas, NV 89154-9900

Alpert, Sharon, President, CEO
Nathan Cummings Foundation
  [12968]
475 10th Ave., 14th Fl.
New York, NY 10018-9715
Ph: (212)787-7300
Fax: (212)787-7377

Alpoge, Oguz, Bd. Member
Society of Turkish American
  Architects, Engineers and
  Scientists [6600]
821 United Nations Plz.
Turkish Ctr., 2nd Fl.
New York, NY 10017
Ph: (646)312-3366

Alps, Diane, President
American Cetacean Society [6789]
PO Box 1391
San Pedro, CA 90733-1391
Ph: (310)548-6279
Fax: (310)548-6950

al-Qadi, Mr. Umar, CEO, President,
  Secretary
Mercy - U.S.A. for Aid and Develop-
  ment [12699]
44450 Pinetree Dr., Ste. 201
Plymouth, MI 48170-3869
Ph: (734)454-0011
Toll Free: 800-556-3729
Fax: (734)454-0303

Al-Rahim, Rend, President
Iraq Foundation [12048]
1012 14th St. NW, Ste. 1110
Washington, DC 20005
Ph: (202)347-4662
Fax: (202)347-7897

Als, Heidelise, PhD, Founder
NIDCAP Federation International
  [14246]
c/o Sandra M. Kosta
Neurobehavioral Infant and Child
  Studies
Enders Pediatric Research Bldg.
  EN107
320 Longwood Ave.
Boston, MA 02115
Ph: (617)355-8249
Fax: (617)730-0224

Alsup, Chuck, President
Intelligence and National Security
  Alliance [5344]
NRECA Bldg.
4301 Wilson Blvd., Ste. 910
Arlington, VA 22203
Ph: (703)224-4672
Fax: (571)777-8481

Al-Suwaij, Zainab, Exec. Dir.
Hands Across the Mideast Support
  Alliance [18683]
American Islamic Congress
1718 M St. NW, No. 243
Washington, DC 20036
Ph: (202)595-3160
Fax: (202)621-6005

Alt, Margie, Exec. Dir.
Environment America [4057]
294 Washington St., Ste. 500
Boston, MA 02108
Ph: (617)747-4449

Altabef, Jennifer, Chairperson
Thanks-Giving Foundation [19150]
1627 Pacific Ave.
Dallas, TX 75201-3601
Ph: (214)969-1977

Altamura, Michael, M.D., Contact
Physicians Against World Hunger
  [12107]
19 Old Post Rd. S
Croton on Hudson, NY 10520
Ph: (914)737-8570

Altay, Ayse Nil, Secretary
International Association of Dental
  Traumatology [14447]
4425 Cass St., Ste. A
El Cajon, CA 92019
Ph: (858)272-1018
Fax: (858)272-7687

Alten, Kenneth H., President
Senior Roller Skaters of America
  [23154]
Elyria, OH 44035
Ph: (440)365-6843
Toll Free: 800-605-0067

Alter, Mr. Timothy A., Chmn. of the
  Bd.
Construction Innovation Forum [804]
6494 Latcha Rd.
Walbridge, OH 43465
Ph: (419)725-3108
Fax: (419)725-3079

Alterman, Stephen A., President
Cargo Airline Association [132]
1620 L St. NW, Ste. 610
Washington, DC 20036
Ph: (202)293-1030

Altier, Fr. Robert, President
Help the Helpless [12126]
PO Box 270308

Saint Paul, MN 55127
Ph: (651)762-8857
Toll Free: 877-762-8857

Altman, Dave, President
American Coaster Enthusiasts
  [21275]
PO Box 540261
Grand Prairie, TX 75054-0261
Ph: (469)278-6223

Altman, Drew, PhD, CEO, President
Kaiser Family Foundation [15028]
2400 Sand Hill Rd.
Menlo Park, CA 94025
Ph: (650)854-9400
Fax: (650)854-4800

Altman, Isaac, CEO
World Salsa Federation [9274]
8080 SW 81 Dr.
Miami, FL 33143
Ph: (305)746-1282

Altom, Andy, President
Teaching-Family Association [11832]
PO Box 2007
Midlothian, VA 23113-9007
Ph: (804)632-0155
Fax: (804)639-9212

Altoro, Eloiza, Exec. Dir.
UNITY Journalists for Diversity
  [2731]
PO Box 511783
Milwaukee, WI 53203
Ph: (414)335-1478

Altschuler, Deborah Z., President
National Pediculosis Association,
  Inc. [17012]
1005 Boylston St., Ste. 343
Newton, MA 02461
Ph: (617)905-0176
Fax: (800)235-1305

Alvarado, Elena M., CEO, President
National Latina Health Network
  [14957]
7720 Wisconsin Ave., Ste. 212
Bethesda, MD 20814
Ph: (301)664-9466
Fax: (301)527-1476

Alvarado, Nelson, President
Peruvian American Chamber of
  Commerce [23612]
1948 NW 82nd Ave.
Doral, FL 33126
Ph: (305)599-1057

Alvarado, Yolanda, President
Voices Breaking Boundaries [10070]
PO Box 541247
Houston, TX 77254-1247
Ph: (713)524-7821

Alvarez, Ariel, Founder
Para Sa Bata [11125]
11331 Cedar Springs Dr.
Frisco, TX 75035
Ph: (469)579-4544

Alvarez, Frank, III, President
United States Professional Poolplayers Association [22588]
4340 E Indian School Rd., Ste. 21-
  115
Phoenix, AZ 85018

Alvarez, Jeffrey J., MD, CCHP,
  Director
National Commission on Cor-
  rectional Health Care [15157]
1145 W Diversey Pky.
Chicago, IL 60614
Ph: (773)880-1460
Fax: (773)880-2424

Alvarez, Julia, Exec. Dir.
Elephant Energy [6476]
1031 33rd St., Ste. 174
Denver, CO 80205
Ph: (720)446-8609

Alvero, Demetrio, Dep. Dir.
Standing Commission on Ecumeni-
cal Relations of the Episcopal
Church [20116]
815 2nd Ave.
New York, NY 10017-4594
Ph: (212)716-6000
Toll Free: 800-334-7626

Alverson, Ron, President
American Coalition for Ethanol
[4021]
5000 S Broadband Ln., Ste. 224
Sioux Falls, SD 57108
Ph: (605)334-3381

Alzhara Kirtley, Ariane, Exec. Dir.,
Founder
Amman Imman: Water is Life
[13315]
914 Robin Rd.
Silver Spring, MD 20901-1871
Ph: (240)418-1143

Al-Zu'bi, Dr. Raed, President
Society of Plastics Engineers [6597]
6 Berkshire Blvd., Ste. 306
Bethel, CT 06801
Ph: (203)775-0471
Fax: (203)775-8490

Ama Manu, Aida Nana, MS,
Founder, Bd. Member
Representatives of Equal Access to
Community Health-care in Ghana
[11931]
1713 E Fairmount Ave., Ste. 9
Baltimore, MD 21231

Amador, Nico, Inst.
Training for Change [12993]
PO Box 30914
Philadelphia, PA 19104
Ph: (267)289-2288

Aman, Reinhold A., PhD, Editor,
Publisher
International Maledicta Society
[9742]
PO Box 14123
Santa Rosa, CA 95402-6123
Ph: (707)795-8178

Amand, Dr. Wilbur B., VMD, Exec.
Dir.
American Academy of Veterinary
Nutrition [17588]
721 Inverness Dr.
West Chester, PA 19380-6880

Amani, Lwanzo, CEO
Promicrofinance International
[11849]
7777 Maple Ave., Apt. 208
Takoma Park, MD 20912
Ph: (301)379-6127

Amaro, Michael L., President
International Amusement and
Leisure Defense Association
[2908]
PO Box 4563
Louisville, KY 40204
Ph: (502)473-0956
Fax: (502)473-7352

Amatruda, James F., MD, President
Zebrafish Disease Models Society
[5895]
1023 Route 146
Clifton Park, NY 12065
Ph: (518)399-7181

Ambegaonkar, Dr. Prakash, CEO,
Founder
Bridging Nations Foundation [18517]
1779 Massachusetts Ave. NW, Ste.
715
Washington, DC 20036
Ph: (202)518-1247

Ambos, Elizabeth, Exec. Ofc.
Council on Undergraduate Research
[8499]
734 15th St. NW, Ste. 550
Washington, DC 20005-1013
Ph: (202)783-4810
Fax: (202)783-4811

Ambre, Mr. Ago, COO
Estonian American Fund [7729]
PO Box 7369
Silver Spring, MD 20907-7369

Ambriz, Robert, Contact
Leathercraft Guild [2085]
c/o Robert Ambriz
PO Box 4603
Ontario, CA 91761-4603
Ph: (909)983-9544

Ambrogio, Frank, Contact
1956 Studebaker Golden Hawk
Owners Register [21310]
31654 Wekiva River Rd.
Sorrento, FL 32776-9233

Ambrose, Bob, Secretary
Carpet Cushion Council [1940]
5103 Brandywine Dr.
Eagleville, PA 19403
Ph: (484)687-5170
Fax: (610)885-5131

Ambrose, Cate, CEO, President
Latin American Venture Capital As-
sociation [1248]
589 8th Ave., 18th Fl.
New York, NY 10018
Ph: (646)315-6735
Fax: (646)349-1047

Ambrose, Laurie Fenton, CEO,
President
Lung Cancer Alliance [14004]
1700 K St. NW, Ste. 660
Washington, DC 20006
Ph: (202)463-2080
Toll Free: 800-298-2436

Ambrosio, Kathy, Treasurer
Food Addicts Anonymous [11852]
529 NW Prima Vista Blvd., Ste.
301A
Port Saint Lucie, FL 34983
Ph: (772)878-9657

Amelio, Jamie, CEO
Caring for Cambodia [7585]
900 RR 620 S, No. C101-304
Austin, TX 78734

Amen, Ron, Chairman
Islamic Center of America [20220]
19500 Ford Rd.
Dearborn, MI 48128
Ph: (313)593-0000

Ames, Dr. Steve, Exec. Sec.,
Treasurer
Community College Journalism As-
sociation [8153]
163 E Loop Dr.
Camarillo, CA 93010
Ph: (805)389-3744
Fax: (520)438-4886

Amin, Narima, Founder
RISE-UP From Poverty [12563]
15613 5th Ave. NE
Shoreline, WA 98155

Amin, Shahira, Officer
International Women's Forum
[13380]
2120 L St. NW, Ste. 460
Washington, DC 20037
Ph: (202)387-1010
Fax: (202)387-1009

Amin, Takiyah Nur, PhD, Director
Congress on Research in Dance
[9246]
7044 S 13th St.
Oak Creek, WI 53154

Amirkhanian, Charles, Exec. Dir.
Other Minds [9993]
55 Taylor St.
San Francisco, CA 94102-3916
Ph: (415)934-8134
Fax: (415)934-8136

Ammerman, Jim, VP
National Council on Bible Curriculum
in Public Schools [20577]
1504 Mall Sq.
Wilkesboro, NC 28697
Ph: (336)272-3799
Toll Free: 877-662-4253
Fax: (336)272-7199

Ammon, Dr. Robin, Jr., Office Mgr.
North American Society for Sport
Management [8433]
135 Winterwood Dr.
Butler, PA 16001
Ph: (724)482-6277

Ammondson, Debra, V. Ch.
National Board for Certification in
Occupational Therapy, Inc. [17454]
12 S Summit Ave., Ste. 100
Gaithersburg, MD 20877
Ph: (301)990-7979
Fax: (301)869-8492

Amoako-Agyeman, Romeo, CEO,
Founder
Ardent Lion Society [11474]
PO Box 356
White Plains, NY 10605
Ph: (914)874-4480

Amos, James, Bd. Member
Navy-Marine Corps Relief Society
[19382]
875 N Randolph St., Ste. 225
Arlington, VA 22203-1767
Toll Free: 800-654-8364

Amos, John F., President
Optometric Historical Society
[16436]
Optometry Cares
243 N Lindbergh Blvd.
Saint Louis, MO 63141-7881
Ph: (314)983-4200

Amri, Judi, Founder
Islamic Schools League of America
[8126]
PO Box 795
Okemos, MI 48805-0795
Ph: (517)303-3905

Amsden, Susan, Bus. Mgr.
International Association for Near-
Death Studies [7013]
Bldg. 500
2741 Campus Walk Ave.
Durham, NC 27705-8878
Ph: (919)383-7940
Fax: (919)383-7940

Amselle, Jorge, Dir. of Comm.
Salt Institute [2382]
405 5th Ave. S, Ste. 7G
Naples, FL 34102
Ph: (703)549-4648
Fax: (703)548-2194

Amster, Randall, Exec. Dir.
Peace and Justice Studies Association [18818]
1421 37th St. NW, Ste. 130
Washington, DC 20057

Amuedo-Dorantes, Catalina,
President
American Society of Hispanic
Economists [1011]
c/o Catalina Amuedo-Dorantes,
President
Dept. of Economics
San Diego State University
5500 Campanile Dr.
San Diego, CA 92182
Ph: (619)594-1663

Amundsen, Chris, Exec. Dir.
American Craft Council [21746]
1224 Marshall St. NE, Ste. 200
Minneapolis, MN 55413-1089
Ph: (612)206-3100
Toll Free: 800-836-3470
Fax: (612)355-2330

Amutah, Dr. Ndidi, President
Society for the Analysis of African-
American Public Health Issues
[17021]
PO Box 360350
Decatur, GA 30036

Anas, Mr. Peter, Exec. Dir.
Board of Nephrology Examiners
Nursing and Technology [15876]
100 S Washington St.
Rockville, MD 20850
Ph: (202)462-1252
Fax: (202)463-1257

Anas, Peter, Exec. Dir.
Friends of the National Institute of
Dental and Craniofacial Research
[14436]
100 S Washington St.
Rockville, MD 20850
Ph: (240)778-6117
Fax: (240)778-6112

Anastasia, Marsha L., President
National Association of Women
Lawyers [5031]
American Bar Ctr., MS 19.1
321 N Clark St.
Chicago, IL 60654
Ph: (312)988-6186
Fax: (312)932-6450

Anaya, Bill, Exec. Dir.
International Furniture Rental As-
sociation [1485]
c/o Alston & Bird LLP
950 F St. NW, 10th Fl.
Washington, DC 20004
Ph: (202)239-3818
Fax: (202)654-4818

Anaya, Rick, CEO, Founder
Council for Educational Travel
U.S.A. - Washington State Office
[8716]
110 Grand Ave.
Bellingham, WA 98225
Ph: (949)940-1140
Toll Free: 888-238-8725
Fax: (949)940-1141

Andere, Amanda, President, CEO
Wider Opportunities for Women
[11788]
1001 Connecticut Ave. NW, Ste. 930
Washington, DC 20036-5565
Ph: (202)464-1596
Fax: (202)354-4638

Anderka, Marlene, President
National Birth Defects Prevention
Network [13832]

1321 Upland Dr., Ste. 1561
Houston, TX 77043
Ph: (404)498-3918

Anderko, Laura, VP
Healthy Schools Network [4141]
773 Madison Ave.
Albany, NY 12208
Ph: (518)462-0632
    (202)543-7555
Fax: (518)462-0433

Andersen, Anne, President
International Doll Makers Association
    [22002]
515 Harrison Ave.
Panama City Beach, FL 32401

Andersen, Anne, Bd. Member
Jamii Moja [11390]
10110 NW Ash St.
Portland, OR 97229

Andersen, Crossan, President, CEO
Entertainment Merchants Association
    [265]
16530 Ventura Blvd., Ste. 400
Encino, CA 91436-4551
Ph: (818)385-1500
Fax: (818)933-0911

Anderson, Allyn, Exec. Dir.
Liberia Now [11397]
Po Box 781767
San Antonio, TX 78278
Toll Free: 877-582-7906

Anderson, Andy, Exec. Dir.
Western United States Agricultural
    Trade Association [3582]
4601 NE 77th Ave., Ste. 240
Vancouver, WA 98662-6860
Ph: (360)693-3373
Fax: (360)693-3464

Anderson, Anne, Director
National Association of Locum
    Tenens Organizations [16755]
222 S Westmonte Dr., Ste. 101
Altamonte Springs, FL 32714
Ph: (407)774-7880
Fax: (407)774-6440

Anderson, Ms. Avis, Bd. Member
AIDS Resource Foundation for
    Children [13525]
77 Academy St.
Newark, NJ 07102
Ph: (973)643-0400
Fax: (973)242-3583

Anderson, B.A., CEO
USA BMX [22758]
1645 W Sunrise Blvd.
Gilbert, AZ 85233
Ph: (480)961-1903
Fax: (480)961-1842

Anderson, Bernadine, Exec. Dir.
Bridge2Peace [7747]
1574 Asylum Ave.
West Hartford, CT 06117

Anderson, Bobby, VP
The Holiday Project [13298]
c/o Melinda Sedlacek, Treasurer
2632 Tartan Dr.
Santa Clara, CA 95051
Ph: (408)984-6555

Anderson, Brian, CEO, President
International Aid [12681]
17011 Hickory St.
Spring Lake, MI 49456-9712
Ph: (616)846-7490
Toll Free: 800-968-7490
Fax: (616)846-3842

Anderson, Bruce, President
National Bison Association [4479]
8690 Wolff Ct., No. 200

Westminster, CO 80031
Ph: (303)292-2833
Fax: (303)845-9081

Anderson, Bruce, Bd. Member
National Denturist Association
    [14463]
PO Box 2344
Poulsbo, WA 98370
Ph: (360)232-4353
Fax: (360)779-6879

Anderson, Cameron, Exec. Dir.
Christians in the Visual Arts [8971]
849 E Washington Ave., Ste. 212
Madison, WI 53703
Ph: (608)433-9339

Anderson, Dr. Carl W., Secretary
International Association for Protein
    Structure Analysis and Proteomics
    [6053]
c/o Carl W. Anderson, Secretary
Biology Dept.
Bookhaven National Laboratory
50 Bell Ave.
Upton, NY 11973-5000

Anderson, Carolyn, Director,
    Founder
Global Family [13008]
17756 Minnow Way
Penn Valley, CA 95946
Ph: (530)277-2804

Anderson, Cora Felton, Hist., Co-
    Pres.
Felton Family Association [20865]
PO Box 215
Wolfeboro, NH 03894

Anderson, D. Greg, MD, President
Society for Minimally Invasive Spine
    Surgery [16067]
8880 Rio San Diego Dr., Ste. 260
San Diego, CA 92108
Ph: (619)265-5222
Fax: (619)265-5858

Anderson, Dale, Chmn. of the Bd.
401st Bombardment Group Heavy
    Association [20679]
PO Box 2718
Gig Harbor, WA 98335

Anderson, Dale, President
Distribution Contractors Association
    [23502]
101 W Renner Rd., Ste. 460
Richardson, TX 75082-2024
Ph: (972)680-0261
Fax: (972)680-0461

Anderson, Danyle, Exec. Dir.
Global Equity Organization [1071]
1442 E Lincoln Ave., No. 487
Orange, CA 92865
Ph: (714)630-2908
Fax: (714)421-4900

Anderson, Darrell D., CEO
National Swine Registry [4716]
National Swine Registry
2639 Yeager Rd.
West Lafayette, IN 47906
Ph: (765)463-3594
Fax: (765)497-2959

Anderson, Daryl, Exec. Dir.
Phi Beta Sigma Fraternity [23867]
145 Kennedy St. NW
Washington, DC 20011-5294
Ph: (202)726-5434
Fax: (202)882-1681

Anderson, Dean, VP
National Association of Graphic and
    Product Identification Manufactur-
    ers, Inc. [2361]

1300 Sumner Ave.
Cleveland, OH 44115-2851
Ph: (216)241-7333
Fax: (216)241-0105

Anderson, Dixie, V. Ch.
World Affairs Councils of America
    [19267]
1200 18th St. NW, Ste. 902
Washington, DC 20036
Ph: (202)833-4557
Fax: (202)833-4555

Anderson, Duane, President
Christ for the City International
    [20361]
5332 S 138th St., Ste. 200
Omaha, NE 68137-2946
Ph: (402)592-8332
Toll Free: 888-526-7551
Fax: (402)592-8312

Anderson, Dwight, Exec. Dir.
Prison Mission Association [20455]
PO Box 2300
Port Orchard, WA 98366
Ph: (360)876-0918

Anderson, E. Byron, Bd. Member
Liturgical Conference [20066]
c/o First Congregational Church
    UCC
1125 Wilmette Ave.
Wilmette, IL 60091
Toll Free: 800-354-1420

Anderson, Ed, CEO
Healing Waters International [13327]
15000 W 6th Ave., Ste. 404
Golden, CO 80401
Ph: (303)526-7278
Toll Free: 866-913-8522

Anderson, Edna, Exec. Ofc.
American Medical Technologists
    [15676]
10700 W Higgins Rd., Ste. 150
Rosemont, IL 60018
Ph: (847)823-5169
Toll Free: 800-275-1268
Fax: (847)823-0458

Anderson, Elizabeth, Exec. Dir.
Pilates Method Alliance [16712]
1666 Kennedy Cswy., Ste. 402
North Bay Village, FL 33141
Ph: (305)573-4946
Toll Free: 866-573-4945
Fax: (305)573-4461

Anderson, Eric, Exec. Dir.
Cartography and Geographic
    Information Society [6166]
c/o Michael P. Finn, President
Box 25046, MS 510
Denver, CO 80225-0046

Anderson, Eric, VP of Mktg., VP,
    Comm.
Physician Insurers Association of
    America [15423]
2275 Research Blvd., Ste. 250
Rockville, MD 20850
Ph: (301)947-9000
Fax: (301)947-9090

Anderson, Gail, Mem.
Citizens' Stamp Advisory Committee
    [22319]
475 L'Enfant Plz. SW, Rm. 3300
Washington, DC 20260

Anderson, Gary, Secretary
American Association of Teachers of
    Esperanto [8169]
c/o Dorothy Holland, Corresponding
    Secretary
5140 San Lorenzo Dr.

Santa Barbara, CA 93111-2521

Anderson, Gary, President
Jacob Sheep Breeders Association
    [4671]
c/o Mickey Ramirez, Liaison
2540 W Mulberry
Fort Collins, CO 80521
Ph: (970)491-9750

Anderson, Dr. Gary L., President
Baptist Mid-Missions [19724]
7749 Webster Rd.
Middleburg Heights, OH 44130-8011
Ph: (440)826-3930
Fax: (440)826-4457

Anderson, Geoffrey, CEO, President
Smart Growth America [11438]
1707 L St. NW, Ste. 250
Washington, DC 20036
Ph: (202)207-3355

Anderson, George, Exec. Dir.
American Association of Anger
    Management Providers [15756]
2300 Westridge Rd.
Los Angeles, CA 90049
Ph: (310)476-0908
Fax: (310)476-6789

Anderson, Greg, Treasurer
National Biodiesel Board [1466]
605 Clark Ave.
Jefferson City, MO 65101
Ph: (573)635-3893
Toll Free: 800-929-3437
Fax: (573)635-7913

Anderson, James A., Jr., VP
National Association of Wholesaler-
    Distributors [3474]
1325 G St. NW, Ste. 1000
Washington, DC 20005
Ph: (202)872-0885
Fax: (202)785-0586

Anderson, Jamie, Administrator
NewTithing Group [18853]
c/o Webster Systems, LLC dba
    Data360
1 Maritime Plz., Ste. 1545
San Francisco, CA 94111
Ph: (415)733-9740

Anderson, Janet, President
Desert Protective Council [3846]
PO Box 3635
San Diego, CA 92163-1635
Ph: (619)342-5524
    (619)228-6316

Anderson, Jennifer, Mgr.
Museum Store Association [2962]
789 Sherman St., Ste. 600
Denver, CO 80203
Ph: (303)504-9223

Anderson, Jeremy, President
Education Commission of the States
    [7763]
700 N Broadway, Ste. 810
Denver, CO 80203-3442
Ph: (303)299-3600

Anderson, Jim, Treasurer
Clan Anderson Society [20796]
360 Silver Creek Run
Lawrenceville, GA 30044-4800

Anderson, John, Contact
Chandler-Grant Society [17697]
Massachusetts Eye and Ear
    Infirmary
Glaucoma Service, Rm. 829
243 Charles St.
Boston, MA 02114
Ph: (617)573-6487
Fax: (617)573-4300

Anderson, John F., Jr., Secretary,
Treasurer
Catholic Association of Foresters
[19400]
220 Forbes Rd., Ste. 404
Braintree, MA 02184
Ph: (781)848-8221
Toll Free: 800-282-2263

Anderson, Kathi, Exec. Dir.,
President
Survivors of Torture International
[18444]
PO Box 151240
San Diego, CA 92175-1240
Ph: (619)278-2400
Fax: (619)294-9405

Anderson, Keith, Secretary
National Adult Day Services Associa-
tion **[10516]**
1421 E Broad St., Ste. 425
Fuquay Varina, NC 27526-1968
Toll Free: 877-745-1440
Fax: (919)825-3945

Anderson, Kenneth C., President
International Myeloma Society
[13991]
Mayo Clinic
200 1st St. SW
Rochester, MN 55905
Ph: (507)284-3725
Fax: (507)284-1249

Anderson, Kenneth, Dir. of Info.
Technology
Electronic Industry Citizenship Coali-
tion **[1044]**
1737 King St., Ste. 330
Alexandria, VA 22314
Ph: (517)858-5720
Fax: (517)431-6317

Anderson, Kerby, President
Probe Ministries International **[7614]**
2001 W Plano Pky., Ste. 2000
Plano, TX 75075
Ph: (972)941-4565

Anderson, Kristen, President
International Association of Aquatic
and Marine Science Libraries and
Information Centers **[9708]**
c/o Brian Voss
U.S NOAA Seattle Library
7600 Sand Point Way NE, Bldg. 3
Seattle, WA 98115-6349

Anderson, Kristi, Exec. Dir.
Sarcoid Networking Association
[14612]
12619 S Wilderness Way
Molalla, OR 97038
Ph: (541)905-2092

Anderson, Kristin, Chairperson
Bike & Build **[10778]**
6153 Ridge Ave.
Philadelphia, PA 19128
Ph: (267)331-8488
Fax: (661)752-9806

Anderson, Kristy, Officer
Defense Advisory Committee on
Women in the Services **[5597]**
4000 Mark Center Dr., Ste. 04J25-01
Alexandria, VA 22350-9000
Ph: (703)697-2122

Anderson, Lewis, Exec. Dir.
Flexible Intermediate Bulk Container
Association **[833]**
PO Box 241894
Saint Paul, MN 55124-7019
Ph: (952)412-8867
Fax: (661)339-0023

Anderson, Lisa, Mem.
Pen Collectors of America **[21711]**
PO Box 705

Parrish, FL 34219
Ph: (920)809-5182

Anderson, Lori, CEO, President
International Sign Association **[1026]**
1001 N Fairfax St., Ste. 301
Alexandria, VA 22314
Ph: (703)836-4012
Fax: (703)836-8353

Anderson, Margaret, Program Mgr.
Center for Global Education and
Experience **[8118]**
Augsburg College
2211 Riverside Ave.
Minneapolis, MN 55454

Anderson, Maria, President
International Oracle Users Group
[6302]
330 N Wabash Ave., Ste. 2000
Chicago, IL 60611
Ph: (312)245-1579

Anderson, Marie, Coord.
ALMA Society, Inc. **[10441]**
PO Box 85
Denville, NJ 07834
Ph: (973)586-1358

Anderson, Mark B., Gov.
Society of Paper Money Collectors
[22286]
c/o Frank Clark, Membership Director
PO Box 117060
Carrollton, TX 75011-7060

Anderson, Mark C., CAE, CEO,
Exec. VP
American Foundation for Surgery of
the Hand **[14906]**
822 W Washington Blvd.
Chicago, IL 60607
Ph: (312)880-1900
Fax: (847)384-1435

Anderson, Mark C., CAE, CEO,
Exec. VP
American Society for Surgery of the
Hand **[14908]**
822 W Washington Blvd.
Chicago, IL 60607
Ph: (312)880-1900
Fax: (847)384-1435

Anderson, Dr. Megory, Founder,
Exec. Dir.
Sacred Dying Foundation **[11558]**
PO Box 210328
San Francisco, CA 94121
Ph: (415)585-9455

Anderson, Michael, Exec. Dir.
Association of Asphalt Paving
Technologists **[6347]**
6776 Lake Dr., Ste. 215
Lino Lakes, MN 55014
Ph: (651)293-9188
Fax: (651)293-9193

Anderson, Michael G., Exec. Dir.
Native American Contractors As-
sociation **[895]**
750 1st St. NE, Ste. 950
Washington, DC 20002
Ph: (202)758-2676
Fax: (202)758-2699

Anderson, Mike, Director
American Boating Association
[22593]
PO Box 690
New Market, MD 21774
Ph: (614)497-4088
Toll Free: 800-768-2121

Anderson, Mike, Chairman
Mobile Enhancement Retailers Association **[2961]**

85 Flagship Dr., Ste. F
North Andover, MA 01845
Toll Free: 800-949-6372

Anderson, Nanette, President
SunGard Public Sector Users' Group
Association **[6304]**
PO Box 171028
Austin, TX 78717
Ph: (309)781-8810

Anderson, Patsi, President
LaPerm Society of America **[21571]**
4403 Old Buckingham Rd.,
4403 Old Buckingham Rd.
Powhatan, VA 23139

Anderson, Paul, President
International Association of Natural
Resource Pilots **[3651]**
222 7 Oaks Rd.
Glenwood Springs, CO 81601
Ph: (701)220-7248
     (970)618-9483

Anderson, Paul, Chairman
National Business Aviation Associa-
tion **[151]**
1200 G St. NW, Ste. 1100
Washington, DC 20005
Ph: (202)783-9000
Fax: (202)331-8364

Anderson, Phyllis, Secretary
International Consortium on
Governmental Financial Manage-
ment **[1243]**
PO Box 1077
Saint Michaels, MD 21663
Ph: (410)745-8570
Fax: (410)745-8569

Anderson, Richard E., MD, Bd.
Member
National Patient Safety Foundation
[15049]
268 Summer St., 6th Fl.
Boston, MA 02210
Ph: (617)391-9900
Fax: (617)391-9999

Anderson, Richard, President
Renewable Energy Markets Associa-
tion **[1121]**
1211 Connecticut Ave. NW, Ste. 600
Washington, DC 20036-2701
Ph: (202)640-6597
Fax: (202)223-5537

Anderson, Ms. Rita, Dir. of Member
Svcs.
North American Quilling Guild
[21302]
2422 Torrington Dr.
Toms River, NJ 08755-2556

Anderson, Robert, Comptroller
Scottish-American Military Society
[9807]
c/o Mike Gibbens, National Adjutant
37 McFarland Dr.
Rolla, MO 65401
Ph: (573)578-9194

Anderson, Russell, Assoc. Dir.
National Collegiate Baseball Writers
Association **[2699]**
c/o Russell Anderson, Associate
Executive Director
Conference USA
5201 N O'Connor Blvd., Ste. 300
Irving, TX 75039-3765
Ph: (214)418-6132

Anderson, Ruth Matilda, Publisher
Hispanic Society of America **[9358]**
613 W 155th St.
New York, NY 10032
Ph: (212)926-2234
Fax: (212)690-0743

Anderson, Sarah, Secretary
Institute for Policy Studies **[18985]**
1301 Connecticut Ave. NW, Ste. 600
Washington, DC 20036
Ph: (202)234-9382

Anderson, Scott, President
College Athletic Trainers' Society
[23333]
c/o Robert Murphy, Treasurer/
Secretary
PO Box 250325
Atlanta, GA 30325

Anderson, Scott, Director
Truck Renting and Leasing Associa-
tion **[2934]**
675 N Washington St., Ste. 410
Alexandria, VA 22314
Ph: (703)299-9120
Fax: (703)299-9115

Anderson, Sid, III, President
Wood Component Manufacturers
Association **[1446]**
PO Box 662
Lindstrom, MN 55045
Ph: (651)332-6332
Fax: (651)400-3502

Anderson, Steve, President
Land Improvement Contractors of
America **[3891]**
3080 Ogden Ave., Ste. 300
Lisle, IL 60532
Ph: (630)548-1984
Fax: (630)548-9189

Anderson, Dr. Steven, Founder
Global Eye Mission **[17703]**
16526 W 78th St., No. 316
Eden Prairie, MN 55346
Ph: (952)484-9710

Anderson, Steven L., President
Donald W. Reynolds Foundation
[14140]
1701 Village Center Cir.
Las Vegas, NV 89134
Ph: (702)804-6000
Fax: (702)804-6099

Anderson, Terry L., President
Property and Environment Research
Center **[4095]**
2048 Analysis Dr., Ste. A
Bozeman, MT 59718
Ph: (406)587-9591

Anderson, Terry, President
National Police Canine Association
[5509]
PO Box 538
Waddell, AZ 85355
Toll Free: 877-362-1219

Anderson, Theresa, Admin. Asst.
Society for Creative Anachronism,
Inc. **[9789]**
PO Box 360789
Milpitas, CA 95036-0789
Ph: (408)263-9305
Toll Free: 800-789-7486
Fax: (408)263-0641

Anderson, Therese Dosch, Exec.
Dir. (Actg.)
Give Us Wings **[11363]**
450 N Syndicate St., Ste. 290
Saint Paul, MN 55104
Ph: (651)789-5606

Andolino, Frank C., Founder, Exec.
Dir.
Kageno Worldwide **[11392]**
261 Broadway
New York, NY 10007
Ph: (212)227-0509

Andrade, Raul, Director
Elwyn [12069]
111 Elwyn Rd.
Media, PA 19063-4622
Ph: (610)891-2000

Andre, Kristine, Admin. Asst.
Council on Rehabilitation Education
[17086]
1699 E Woodfield Rd., Ste. 300
Schaumburg, IL 60173
Ph: (847)944-1345
Fax: (847)944-1346

Andre, Linda, Director
Committee for Truth in Psychiatry
[15765]
c/o Linda Andre, Director
PO Box 1214
New York, NY 10003
Ph: (212)665-6587

Andrejeski, Mark, Secretary
International League of Associations
for Rheumatology [17159]
c/o Mark Andrejeski, Secretary
2200 Lake Blvd. NE
Atlanta, GA 30319

Andreolli-Comstock, Rev. Lindsay,
Exec. Dir.
The Beatitudes Society [19946]
2345 Channing Way
Berkeley, CA 94704

Andres, Charles, President
Fur Takers of America [4723]
PO Box 3
Buckley, IL 60918
Ph: (217)394-2577

Andretta, James V., Jr., Chmn. of
the Bd.
Wine and Spirits Shippers Associa-
tion [193]
111 Commercial St., Ste. 202
Portland, ME 04101
Ph: (207)805-1664
Toll Free: 800-368-3167

Andreucci, Patricia, Mgr., Coord.
Human Relations Area Files, Inc.
[9549]
755 Prospect St.
New Haven, CT 06511-1225
Ph: (203)764-9401
Toll Free: 800-520-4723
Fax: (203)764-9404

Andrews, David, President, CEO
American Hockey League [22907]
1 Monarch Pl., Ste. 2400
Springfield, MA 01144-4004
Ph: (413)781-2030
Fax: (413)733-4767

Andrews, Donna, Exec. VP
Mystery Writers of America [10387]
1140 Broadway, Ste. 1507
New York, NY 10001
Ph: (212)888-8171
Fax: (212)888-8107

Andrews, Rev. Eric, CSP, President
Missionary Society of Saint Paul the
Apostle [19866]
415 W 59th St.
New York, NY 10019
Ph: (202)269-2500

Andrews, Mark, Chmn. of the Bd.
North American Insulation
Manufacturers Association [568]
11 Canal Center Plz., Ste. 103
Alexandria, VA 22314
Ph: (703)684-0084
Fax: (703)684-0427

Andrews, Mary, CEO
MAGIC Foundation [14201]
6645 W North Ave.

Oak Park, IL 60302
Ph: (708)383-0808
Toll Free: 800-362-4423

Andrews, Peter, President
Association of Loudspeaker
Manufacturing and Acoustics
International [2420]
55 Littleton Rd., 13B
Ayer, MA 01432

Andrews, Tom, President, CEO
United to End Genocide [18310]
1010 Vermont Ave. NW, Ste. 1100
Washington, DC 20005
Ph: (202)556-2100

Andrich, Daniela E., MD, President
Society of Genitourinary Reconstruc-
tive Surgeons [17560]
c/o Urology Management Services
1000 Corporate Blvd.
Linthicum, MD 21090
Ph: (410)689-3950
Fax: (410)689-3824

Andringa, Mary Vermeer, Exec. Ofc.
National Association of Manufactur-
ers [2227]
733 10th St. NW, Ste. 700
Washington, DC 20001
Ph: (202)637-3000
Toll Free: 800-814-8468
Fax: (202)637-3182

Andrus, Sabrina, Exec. Dir.
Law Students for Reproductive
Justice [19033]
1730 Franklin St., Ste. 212
Oakland, CA 94612-3417
Ph: (510)622-8134
Fax: (510)622-8138

Andruscavage, Willam, President
American Association of Cat
Enthusiasts [21564]
PO Box 321
Ledyard, CT 06339-0321
Ph: (973)658-5198
Fax: (866)890-2223

Anduri, Carl E., Jr., President
Lex Mundi [5020]
2100 W Loop S, Ste. 1000
Houston, TX 77027-3537
Ph: (713)626-9393
Fax: (713)626-9933

Anduri, Carl E., Jr., President
Lex Mundi Pro Bono Foundation
[5543]
2001 K St. NW, Ste. 400
Washington, DC 20006-1040
Ph: (202)429-1630
(925)962-0115

Angel, Bradley, Exec. Dir.
Greenaction for Health and
Environmental Justice [5274]
559 Ellis St.
San Francisco, CA 94109
Ph: (415)447-3904
Fax: (415)447-3905

Angel, Dr. Ken, President
National Association of Federal
Veterinarians [17654]
1910 Sunderland Pl. NW
Washington, DC 20036-1608
Ph: (202)223-4878

Angel, Shaked, Director
Hashomer Hatzair Zionist Youth
Movement [20249]
424 W 33rd St., Ste. 150
New York, NY 10001
Ph: (212)627-2830

Angelelli, Claudia, President
American Translation and Interpreting Studies Association [8714]

Brigham Young University
3190 JFSB
Provo, UT 84602
Ph: (801)422-2005
Fax: (801)422-0628

Angelides, Phil, Chairperson
Apollo Alliance Project [6456]
155 Montgomery St., Ste. 1001
San Francisco, CA 94104

Angelopoulos, Christina, Production
Mgr., Dir. of Info. Technology
Human Life Foundation [12772]
The Human Life Review
353 Lexington Ave., Ste. 802
New York, NY 10016
Ph: (212)685-5210

Angha, Dr. Nahid, Founder
International Association of Sufism
[20218]
14 Commercial Blvd., Ste. 101
Novato, CA 94949
Ph: (415)472-6959
(415)382-7834

Angle, Larry, President
Groundwater Management Districts
Association [4759]
PO Box 356
Dumas, TX 79029
Ph: (806)935-6401
(402)443-4675
Fax: (806)935-6633

Anglin, Patty, Exec. Dir.
Acres of Hope Liberia [11302]
29525 Four Corners Store Rd.
Mason, WI 54856-2054
Ph: (715)765-4118
Fax: (715)765-4119

Angood, Peter, CEO
American Association for Physician
Leadership [15572]
400 N Ashley Dr., Ste. 400
Tampa, FL 33602
Toll Free: 800-562-8088
Fax: (813)287-8993

Angus, Walt, Treasurer, Secretary
Society of Antique Modelers [21248]
c/o Walt Angus, Secretary
PO Box 73215
Phoenix, AZ 85050
Ph: (707)255-3547

Anis, Wagdy, Bd. Member
Building Enclosure Technology and
Environment Council [506]
c/o National Institute of Building Sci-
ences
1090 Vermont Ave. NW, Ste. 700
Washington, DC 20005
Ph: (202)289-7800
Fax: (202)289-1092

Annambhotla, Dr. Shekhar,
President, Founder
Association of Ayurvedic Profession-
als of North America [13606]
567 Thomas St., Ste. 400
Coopersburg, PA 18036
Ph: (484)550-7725
(484)347-6110

Annas, George J., JD, Founder
Global Lawyers and Physicians
[14935]
Talbot Bldg.
Boston University School of Public
Health
715 Albany St.
Boston, MA 02118
Ph: (617)638-4626
Fax: (617)414-1464

Annotti, Mr. Joseph J., CEO,
President
American Fraternal Alliance [19481]
1301 W 22nd St., Ste. 700

Oak Brook, IL 60523
Ph: (630)522-6322
Fax: (630)522-6326

Anosike-Byron, C., VP
Ngwa National Association USA
[9577]
56 Scheller Rd.
New Providence, PA 17560
Ph: (717)786-6620

Anselme, Lisa, Exec. Dir.
Healing Beyond Borders [15007]
445 Union Blvd., Ste. 105
Lakewood, CO 80228
Ph: (303)989-7982

Anselmo, Mary Sendra, President
Legion of Young Polish Women
[19603]
PO Box 56-110
Chicago, IL 60656

Ansems, Tony, President
Songwriters of Wisconsin
International [9186]
PO Box 1027
Neenah, WI 54957-1027
Ph: (920)725-5129
Fax: (920)720-0195

Anson, Cynthia, Chairman
Native Seeds/SEARCH [3912]
3584 E River Rd.
Tucson, AZ 85718
Ph: (520)622-0830
(520)622-5561
Fax: (520)622-0829

Anspach, Dave, President
Crosley Automobile Club [21364]
307 Schaeffer Rd.
Blandon, PA 19510

Anstaett, Doug, Trustee
William Allen White Foundation
[9110]
c/o William Allen White School of
Journalism
Stauffer-Flint Hall
University of Kansas
1435 Jayhawk Blvd.
Lawrence, KS 66045-7515
Ph: (785)864-4755

Anthony, Clarence E., Exec. Dir.
National League of Cities [5644]
1301 Pennsylvania Ave. NW, Ste.
550
Washington, DC 20004
Toll Free: 877-827-2385

Anthony, Donald K., Jr., President
United States Fencing Association
[22834]
4065 Sinton Rd., Ste. 140
Colorado Springs, CO 80907
Ph: (719)866-4511
Fax: (719)632-5737

Anthony, Dr. John Duke, CEO,
Founder, President
National Council on U.S.-Arab Rela-
tions [18691]
1730 M St. NW, Ste. 503
Washington, DC 20036
Ph: (202)293-6466
Fax: (202)293-7770

Anthony, Kathryn, Bd. Member
American Restroom Association
[7110]
PO Box 65111
Baltimore, MD 21209
Ph: (571)354-6907
Toll Free: 800-247-3864
Fax: (410)367-1254

Anthony, Mary, Bd. Member
The Children of War [18775]
11874 Sunrise Valley Dr., No. 200-B

Reston, VA 20191-3323
Ph: (510)396-5084
   (703)625-9147

Anthony, Wayne, President
House of Heroes [13242]
4709 Milgen Rd.
Columbus, GA 31907
Ph: (706)562-1032

Antón, Susan, President
American Association of Physical
  Anthropologists [5901]
1313 Dolley Madison Blvd., Ste. 402
McLean, VA 22101
Ph: (302)831-1855
Fax: (302)831-4002

Antolick, Steven, Exec. Dir.
Check Payment Systems Associa-
  tion [3170]
2025 M St. NW, Ste. 800
Washington, DC 20036-3309
Ph: (202)367-1144
Fax: (202)367-2144

Antolick, Steven, Assoc. Dir.
International Association of Airport
  Duty Free Stores [2955]
2025 M St. NW, Ste. 800
Washington, DC 20036-3309
Ph: (202)367-1184
Fax: (202)429-5154

Antonaccio, Carla, VP
Archaeological Institute of America
  [5931]
656 Beacon St., 6th Fl.
Boston, MA 02215-2006
Ph: (617)353-9361
Fax: (617)353-6550

Antonakakis, Stavros, Contact
Greek American Chamber of Commerce, Inc. [23588]
111 Wood Ave. S
Iselin, NJ 08830-2700
Ph: (609)431-8000
   (215)909-6000

Antonakakis, Stavros, Officer
Hellenic American National Council
  [9353]
1220 16th St. NW
Washington, DC 20036
Ph: (610)446-1463
Fax: (610)446-3189

Antonetti, Martin, President
Bibliographical Society of America
  [9120]
PO Box 1537, Lenox Hill Sta.
New York, NY 10021
Ph: (212)452-2710
Fax: (212)452-2710

Antonini, Jack M., CEO, President
National Association of Credit Union
  Services Organizations [953]
3419 Via Lido, PMB No. 135
Newport Beach, CA 92663
Ph: (949)645-5296
Toll Free: 888-462-2870
Fax: (949)645-5297

Antonio, Dr. Jose, PhD, CEO,
  Founder
International Society of Sports Nutri-
  tion [16226]
c/o Jose Antonio, Founder
4511 NW 7th St.
Deerfield Beach, FL 33442
Fax: (561)239-1754

Antonishak, John, Exec. Dir.
National Council on Skin Cancer
  Prevention [14028]
c/o John Antonishak, Executive
  Director

1875 I St. NW, Ste. 500
Washington, DC 20006
Ph: (301)801-4422
Fax: (301)831-5062

Antonvich, Pete, President
American Track Racing Association
  [22744]
PO Box 93245
Atlanta, GA 30377

Aossey, Nancy A., CEO, President,
  Treasurer
International Medical Corps [12684]
12400 Wilshire Blvd., Ste. 1500
Los Angeles, CA 90025
Ph: (310)826-7800
Fax: (310)442-6622

Aoyagi, Fay, President
Haiku Society of America [10152]
c/o Fay Aoyagi, President
930 Pine St., No. 105
San Francisco, CA 94108

Apel, Justin, Exec. Dir.
Golf Course Builders Association of
  America [3156]
6040 S 58th St., Ste. D
Lincoln, NE 68516
Ph: (402)476-4444
Fax: (402)476-4489

Apostle, John G., II, Chairman
Compliance and Ethics Forum for
  Life Insurers [1849]
PO Box 30940
Bethesda, MD 20824
Ph: (240)744-3030

Apostolik, Richard, CEO, President
Global Association of Risk Profes-
  sionals [1238]
111 Town Square Pl., 14th Fl.
Jersey City, NJ 07310
Ph: (201)719-7210
Fax: (201)222-5022

Appel, Jayne, Secretary, Treasurer
Women's National Basketball Play-
  ers Association [22579]
310 Lenox Ave.
New York, NY 10027
Ph: (212)655-0880
Toll Free: 800-955-6272
Fax: (212)655-0881

Appel, Robert F., Exec. Dir.
Seventh Day Baptist General
  Conference [19736]
PO Box 1678
Janesville, WI 53547-1678
Ph: (608)752-5055
Fax: (608)752-7711

Appel, Robert, Exec. Dir.
Seventh Day Baptist General
  Conference of the United States
  and Canada [19737]
PO Box 1678
Janesville, WI 53547-1678
Ph: (608)752-5055
Fax: (608)752-7711

Appelbaum, Daniel, Treasurer
Heavy Movable Structures, Inc.
  [6163]
6701 W 64th St., Ste. 320
Mission, KS 66202
Ph: (913)213-5110
Fax: (913)213-5149

Appelbaum, Stuart, President
Jewish Labor Committee [18591]
140 W 31st St., 3rd Fl.
New York, NY 10001-3411
Ph: (212)477-0707
Fax: (212)477-1918

Appelbaum, Stuart, President
Retail, Wholesale and Department
  Store Union [23519]
370 7th Ave., Ste. 501
New York, NY 10001
Ph: (212)684-5300

Appell, Donna Jean, Founder,
  President
Hermansky-Pudlak Syndrome
  Network Inc [14826]
1 South Rd.
Oyster Bay, NY 11771-1905
Toll Free: 800-789-9HPS
Fax: (516)624-0640

Appenteng, Kofi, Chairperson
African-American Institute [17772]
420 Lexington Ave., Ste. 1706
New York, NY 10170-0002
Ph: (212)949-5666
Fax: (212)682-6174

Appleby, James, Exec. Dir., CEO
Gerontological Society of America
  [14892]
1220 L St. NW, Ste. 901
Washington, DC 20005-4001
Ph: (202)842-1275

Appleman, Marc, Exec. Dir.
Society for American Baseball
  Research [22567]
4455 E Camelback Rd., Ste. D140
Phoenix, AZ 85018-2847
Ph: (602)343-6455
Toll Free: 800-969-7227
Fax: (602)595-5690

Aquiline, Matthew S., Exec. Dir.
International Council of Employers of
  Bricklayers and Allied Craftworkers
  [23477]
1306 Lancaster Ave.
Pittsburgh, PA 15218
Ph: (202)210-6069

Aquines, Justin G., Exec. Dir.
National Spasmodic Torticollis As-
  sociation [15972]
9920 Talbert Ave.
Fountain Valley, CA 92708
Ph: (714)378-9837
Toll Free: 800-487-8385

Arago, Marie, Exec. Dir.
Fotokonbit [13051]
12555 Biscayne Blvd., No. 926
Miami, FL 33181
Ph: (305)962-8568

Aragon, Janice, Exec. Dir.
National Scholastic Surfing Associa-
  tion [23277]
17381 Nichols Ln., Ste. L
Huntington Beach, CA 92647
Ph: (714)906-7423

Arakaki, Rod, Director
Positive Futures Network [19265]
284 Madrona Way NE, Ste. 116
Bainbridge Island, WA 98110
Ph: (206)842-0216
Toll Free: 800-937-4451
Fax: (206)842-5208

Aranda, Peter J., III, CEO, Exec. Dir.
Consortium for Graduate Study in
  Management [8261]
229 Chesterfield Business Pky.
Chesterfield, MO 63005
Ph: (636)681-5460
   (636)681-5553
Fax: (636)681-5499

Aravamudan, Srinivas, President
American Society for Eighteenth-
  Century Studies [9456]

PO Box 7867
Winston Salem, NC 27109-6253
Ph: (336)727-4694
Fax: (336)727-4697

Aravamudan, Srinivas, President
Consortium of Humanities Centers
  and Institutes [9553]
Box 90403
Duke University
114 S Buchanan Blvd.
Durham, NC 27708-0403

Arbetman, Lee, Exec. Dir.
Street Law [5553]
1010 Wayne Ave., Ste. 870
Silver Spring, MD 20910
Ph: (301)589-1130
Fax: (301)589-1131

Archambault, Joanne, Exec. Dir.
End Violence Against Women
  International [13272]
PO Box 33
Addy, WA 99101-0033
Ph: (509)684-9800
Fax: (509)684-9801

Archer, Anne, Founder, Director
Artists for Human Rights [18374]
23679 Calabasas Rd., Ste. 636
Calabasas, CA 91302
Toll Free: 800-334-2802

Archer, George W., President
Archer Association [20780]
PO Box 6233
McLean, VA 22106

Archer, Jim, President
95th Infantry Division Association
  [20713]
PO Box 1113
Oklahoma City, OK 73101

Archer, Patrick, President
American Peanut Council [4506]
1500 King St., Ste. 301
Alexandria, VA 22314
Ph: (703)838-9500

Archibald, John M., VP
International Society of Protistolo-
  gists [6864]
c/o Virginia Edgcomb, President
Woods Hole Oceanographic Institu-
  tion
Geology and Geophysics Dept.
220 McLean Laboratory, MS 8
Woods Hole, MA 02543
Ph: (508)274-0963

Archibald, LaRita, Director, Founder
HEARTBEAT Grief Support Follow-
  ing Suicide [13193]
PO Box 16985
Colorado Springs, CO 80935-6985
Ph: (719)596-2575

Ardemagni, Enrica, PhD, President
National Council on Interpreting in
  Health Care [1592]
5614 Connecticut Ave. NW, Ste. 119
Washington, DC 20015-2604

Ardern, Michelle, Exec. Dir.
Phi Sigma Sigma [23961]
8178 Lark Brown Rd., Ste. 202
Elkridge, MD 21075
Ph: (410)799-1224
Fax: (410)799-9186

Ardouny, Bryan, Exec. Dir.
Armenian Assembly of America
  [8824]
734 15th St. NW, Ste. 500
Washington, DC 20005
Ph: (202)393-3434
Fax: (202)638-4904

Ardovino, Lori, VP
National Association of College Wind
    and Percussion Instructors [8379]
c/o Michael Walsh, President
Box 2212
Lincoln Music Hall, SLM 205
Department of Music
South Dakota State University
Brookings, SD 57007

Aref, Hassan, Bd. Member
American Academy of Mechanics
    [6829]
University of Texas at Austin
Dept. of Aerospace Engineering and
    Engineering Mechanics
210 E 24th St.
Austin, TX 78712-1221
Ph: (512)471-4273
Fax: (512)471-5500

Arend, Bob, President
Plumeria Society of America [22119]
PO Box 22791
Houston, TX 77227

Arends, Joni, Exec. Dir.
Concerned Citizens for Nuclear
    Safety [18744]
107 Cienega St.
Santa Fe, NM 87501
Ph: (505)986-1973
Fax: (505)986-0997

Arens, Christine, Director
American Federation of Astrologers
    [5987]
6535 S Rural Rd.
Tempe, AZ 85283-3746
Ph: (480)838-1751
Toll Free: 888-301-7630
Fax: (480)838-8293

Arens, Christine, President
Friends of Astrology Inc. [5992]
5122 S May St.
Chicago, IL 60609-5009
Ph: (630)654-4742

Arensberg, Walter, Founder
Francis Bacon Foundation [9051]
100 Corson St.
Pasadena, CA 91103

Aretz, Doug, President
British Biker Cooperative [22217]
PO Box 371021
Milwaukee, WI 53237-2121

Arfaa, Lisa, President, CEO
Physicians for Peace [15612]
500 E Main St., Ste. 900
Norfolk, VA 23510-2204
Ph: (757)625-7569

Argarwal, Sam, CFO
Pacifica Foundation [10060]
1925 Martin Luther King Jr. Way
Berkeley, CA 94704-1037
Ph: (510)849-2590

Argow, Dr. Keith A., CEO, President
National Woodland Owners Associa-
    tion [4213]
374 Maple Ave. E, Ste. 310
Vienna, VA 22180
Ph: (703)255-2700
Fax: (703)281-9200

Arias, Ana, Exec. Asst., Mgr.
The Domestic/Foreign Missionary
    Society of the Episcopal Church
    [20408]
Episcopal Church Ctr.
815 2nd Ave.
New York, NY 10017-4594
Ph: (212)716-6000
Toll Free: 800-334-7626

Arias, Anthony
American Health Quality Association
    [17028]
7918 Jones Branch Dr., Ste. 300
McLean, VA 22102
Ph: (202)331-5790

Arias, Patricia, Managing Dir.
Latin Chamber of Commerce of
    U.S.A. [23650]
1401 W Flagler St.
Miami, FL 33135
Ph: (305)642-3870
Fax: (305)642-3961

Arias, Yanira, President
Salvadoran American National
    Network [18177]
2845 W 7th St.
Los Angeles, CA 90005

Ariens, Robert, PhD, President
International Fibrinogen Research
    Society [15235]
c/o Frances Woodlief
1513 Stonegate Dr.
Graham, NC 27253

Arifi, Dana, VP, COO
French-American Foundation
    [18540]
28 W 44th St., Ste. 1420
New York, NY 10036
Ph: (212)829-8800

Ariola, Lena, CFO
The Hunger Project [18456]
5 Union Sq. W, 7th Fl.
New York, NY 10003-3306
Ph: (212)251-9100
Fax: (212)532-9785

Ariturk, Selim, Officer
Gays and Lesbians in Foreign Affairs
    Agencies USA [23431]
PO Box 18774
Washington, DC 20036-8774

Arizumi, Koji, Exec. Dir.
National Association of Self-
    Instructional Language Programs
    [8188]
University of Arizona
1717 E Speedway Blvd., Ste. 3312
Tucson, AZ 85719-4514
Ph: (520)621-3387
Fax: (520)626-8205

Arkills, Bobby, Exec. Dir.
Youth for Christ/U.S.A. [20665]
7670 S Vaughn Ct.
Englewood, CO 80112
Ph: (303)843-9000

Armanaviciute, Vaida, Managing Ed.
Lituanus Foundation, Inc. [19544]
47 W Polk St., Ste. 100-300
Chicago, IL 60605
Ph: (312)341-9396

Armijo, Oscar Raziel, President,
    Exec. Dir.
Adelante Bolivia [10782]
41-990 Cook St., Ste. 501
Palm Desert, CA 92211

Armour, Henry, Liaison, CEO,
    President
NACS: The Association for
    Convenience and Fuel Retailing
    [2963]
1600 Duke St., 7th Fl.
Alexandria, VA 22314
Ph: (703)684-3600
Toll Free: 800-966-6227
Fax: (703)836-4564

Arms, Anneli, President
Federation of Modern Painters and
    Sculptors [8917]

c/o Anneli Arms, President
113 Greene St.
New York, NY 10012
Ph: (212)966-4864

Arms, Suzanne, Founder, Director
Birthing the Future [14223]
PO Box 1040
Bayfield, CO 81122
Ph: (970)884-4005

Armstrong, Angela, Mem.
Maids of Athena [19455]
1909 Q St. NW, Ste. 500
Washington, DC 20009
Ph: (202)232-6300
Fax: (202)232-2145

Armstrong, David, Exec. Dir.
International Boys' Schools Coalition
    [7774]
700 Route 22
Pawling, NY 12564
Ph: (207)841-7441

Armstrong, Elizabeth B., CAE, CEO
International Association of
    Emergency Managers [1240]
201 Park Washington Ct.
Falls Church, VA 22046-4527
Ph: (703)538-1795
Fax: (703)241-5603

Armstrong, Elizabeth B., CEO
International Association Emergency
    of Managers [5076]
201 Park Washington Ct.
Falls Church, VA 22046-4527
Ph: (703)538-1795
Fax: (703)241-5603

Armstrong, Elizabeth B., CAE, Exec.
    Dir., Secretary
National Association of Government
    Communicators [5092]
201 Park Washington Ct.
Falls Church, VA 22046-4527
Ph: (703)538-1787
Fax: (703)241-5603

Armstrong, Elizabeth B., Exec. VP
National Association of State EMS
    Officials [14685]
201 Park Washington Ct.
Falls Church, VA 22046-4527
Ph: (703)538-1799
Fax: (703)241-5603

Armstrong, James, Consultant
Business Sweden [3298]
150 N Michigan Ave., Ste. 1950
Chicago, IL 60601-7550
Ph: (312)781-6222
Fax: (312)276-8606

Armstrong, Larry, Director
World Wide Association of Treasure
    Seekers [22393]
361 S Camino Del Rio, Ste. 241
Durango, CO 81303-7997

Armstrong, Lawrence E., President
American College of Sports
    Medicine [17274]
401 W Michigan St.
Indianapolis, IN 46202-3233
Ph: (317)637-9200
Toll Free: 800-486-5643
Fax: (317)634-7817

Armstrong, Michael J., CEO
National Council of Architectural
    Registration Boards [5973]
1801 K St. NW, Ste. 700K
Washington, DC 20006-1301
Ph: (202)879-0520
Fax: (202)783-0290

Armstrong, Peter, President, Director
Armstrong Clan Society [19636]
2101 Mc Dowling Dr.

Huntsville, AL 35803-1225

Armstrong, Robert, President
American Academy of Estate Plan-
    ning Attorneys [4980]
9444 Balboa Ave., Ste. 300
San Diego, CA 92123-1696
Ph: (858)453-2128
Toll Free: 877-679-6411
Fax: (858)874-5804

Armstrong-Dailey, Ann, Director,
    Founder
Children's Hospice International
    [15293]
500 Montgomery St., Ste. 400
Alexandria, VA 22314
Ph: (703)684-0330

Armstrong-Yoshioka, Rachel,
    President
Peace Boat US [8407]
777 United Nations Plz., Ste. 3E
New York, NY 10017
Ph: (212)687-7214

Arn, Dr. Charles, EdD, President
Church Growth Inc. [20584]
2530 Vista Way, Ste. F78
Oceanside, CA 92054

Arnal, Jeff, Exec. Dir.
Jargon Society [9327]
56 Broadway St.
Asheville, NC 28801
Ph: (828)350-8484

Arnall, Gail, PhD, President
Coalition Against Landmines [18123]
1516 Crittenden St. NW
Washington, DC 20011
Ph: (202)465-5213
Fax: (270)747-0935

Arnall, Weston, President
National Cotton Batting Institute
    [936]
4322 Bloombury St.
Southaven, MS 38672
Ph: (901)218-2393

Arnaudet, Larry, Exec. Dir.
Exposition Services & Contractors
    Association [2328]
5068 W Plano Pky., Ste. 300
Plano, TX 75093
Ph: (972)447-8212
Toll Free: 877-792-3722
Fax: (972)447-8209

Arney, Jan, Director
Partners in Parenting Haiti [11128]
3970 Newport Ln.
Boulder, CO 80304

Arnicar, Robin, RN, CDONA, FAC-
    DONA, President
National Association of Directors of
    Nursing Administration in Long
    Term Care [16147]
1329 E Kemper Rd., Ste. 4100A
Cincinnati, OH 45246
Ph: (513)791-3679
Toll Free: 800-222-0539

Arnoff, Stephen Hazan, President
JCC Association of North America
    [20254]
520 8th Ave.
New York, NY 10018
Ph: (212)532-4949
Fax: (212)481-4174

Arnold, Ann, Chairman
Manufacturing Jewelers and Suppli-
    ers of America [2058]
8 Hayward St.
Attleboro, MA 02703
Ph: (508)316-2132
Fax: (508)316-1429

Arnold, Bud, President
Veitch Historical Society [20941]
909 W Oak Hill Rd.
Crawfordsville, IN 47933
Ph: (765)362-2503

Arnold, Chris, President
Hypospadias and Epispadias Association [13829]
PO Box 607
Amsterdam, NY 12010
Ph: (917)861-8339

Arnold, Christina, Founder, Exec. Dir.
Prevent Human Trafficking [12056]
4410 Massachusetts Ave. NW, No. 210
Washington, DC 20016
Ph: (202)330-2800

Arnold, Jean, Contact
National Stigma Clearinghouse [15800]
245 8th Ave., No. 213
New York, NY 10011
Ph: (212)255-4411

Arnold, Jeffrey, Exec. Dir.
Association of Presbyterian Colleges and Universities [20520]
Agnes Scott College
141 E College Ave.
Decatur, GA 30030
Ph: (470)443-1948

Arnold, Jeffrey, Exec. Dir.
Delta Mu Delta Honor Society [23691]
9217 Broadway Ave.
Brookfield, IL 60513-1251
Ph: (708)485-8494
Toll Free: 866-789-7067
Fax: (708)221-6183

Arnold, Joan C., President
American College of Tax Counsel [5412]
2604 Elmwood Ave., No. 350
Rochester, NY 14618
Toll Free: 888-549-4177

Arnold, Katie, Exec. Dir.
Sibling Leadership Network [11564]
332 S Michigan Ave., Ste. 1032-S240
Chicago, IL 60604-4434

Arnold, Laurence I., MD, CEO, President
Small World Foundation, Inc. [17399]
PO Box 25004
Asheville, NC 28813

Arnold, Mike, President
American Driving Society, Inc. [22955]
1837 Ludden Dr., Ste. 120
Cross Plains, WI 53528-9007
Ph: (608)237-7382
Fax: (608)237-6468

Arnold, Susan, Chairman
American Conference of Governmental Industrial Hygienists [16313]
1330 Kemper Meadow Dr.
Cincinnati, OH 45240-4147
Ph: (513)742-2020
   (513)742-6163
Fax: (513)742-3355

Arnoldy, Mark, CEO
Possible [15488]
30 Broad St., 9th Fl.
New York, NY 10004

Arnone, John A., III, Contact
Association of Ecosystem Research Centers [3989]

c/o Olin E. Rhodes, Jr.,Past President
PO Drawer E
Aiken, SC 29802
Ph: (803)725-8191

Arnone, William J., Chmn. of the Bd.
National Academy of Social Insurance [19136]
1200 New Hampshire Ave. NW, Ste. 830
Washington, DC 20036
Ph: (202)452-8097
Fax: (202)452-8111

Arnwine, Barbara, President
Capital Press Club [2669]
PO Box 75114
Washington, DC 20013-5114

Aron, Cathy, Exec. Dir.
Digital Media Licensing Association [2577]
3165 S Alma School Rd., Ste. 18
Chandler, AZ 85248-3760
Ph: (714)815-8427
Fax: (866)427-1464

Aron, Nan, President
Alliance for Justice [5720]
11 Dupont Cir. NW, 2nd Fl.
Washington, DC 20036
Ph: (202)822-6070
Fax: (202)822-6068

Aronoff, Roberta, Exec. Dir.
Communications Fraud Control Association [1786]
4 Becker Farm Rd., 4th Fl.
Roseland, NJ 07068
Ph: (973)871-4032
Fax: (973)871-4075

Aronson, Maj. (Ret.) Edgar D., Director
Marine Corps Heritage Foundation [21014]
3800 Fettler Park Dr., Ste. 104
Dumfries, VA 22025
Ph: (703)640-7965
Toll Free: 800-397-7585
Fax: (703)640-9546

Aronson, Rosa, Exec. Dir.
TESOL International Association [7871]
1925 Ballenger Ave., Ste. 550
Alexandria, VA 22314-6822
Ph: (703)836-0774
Fax: (703)836-7864

Arora, Kiran Shahreen Kaur, PhD, President
American Family Therapy Academy [11483]
150 Summer St.
Haverhill, MA 01830
Ph: (978)914-6374
Fax: (978)914-7033

Arora, Dr. Narendra, Prog. Dir.
International Clinical Epidemiology Network [14730]
1735 Market St., Ste. A427
Philadelphia, PA 19103
Ph: (215)898-2368
Fax: (215)573-5315

Arora, Parul, RN, BSN, Director
National Organization of Nurses with Disabilities [16165]
1640 W Roosevelt Rd., Rm. 736
Chicago, IL 60608

Arounnarath, Meiling, President
Laotian American Society [19528]
PO Box 1558
Suwanee, GA 30024

Arredondo, Crystal, Chairperson
National Association of Women Business Owners [651]
South Bldg., Ste. 900
601 Pennsylvania Ave. NW
Washington, DC 20004
Toll Free: 800-556-2926
Fax: (202)403-3788

Arria, Dr. Sal, President
National Board of Fitness Examiners [16707]
1650 Margaret St., Ste. 302-342
Jacksonville, FL 32204-3869

Arriaga, Kristina, Exec. Dir.
Becket Fund for Religious Liberty [19025]
1200 New Hampshire Ave. NW, Ste. 700
Washington, DC 20036
Ph: (202)955-0095
   (202)349-7220
Fax: (202)955-0090

Arriaga, Nelson, President
International Latino Gang Investigators Association [5364]
PO Box 1148
Gig Harbor, WA 98335

Arrington, Sheila G., Founder
AAAneurysm Outreach [14920]
1441 Canal St.
New Orleans, LA 70112

Arsht, Leslye A., Founder
StandardsWork [8542]
Ph: (202)835-2000

Arteaga, Roland A., Officer
Defense Credit Union Council [950]
South Bldg., Ste. 600
601 Pennsylvania Ave. NW
Washington, DC 20004
Ph: (202)638-3950
Fax: (202)638-3410

Arthen, Deirdre Pulgram, Director
Earthspirit Community [20504]
PO Box 723
Williamsburg, MA 01096
Ph: (413)238-4240
Fax: (413)238-7785

Arthur, S.J., Act. Pres.
Melungeon Heritage Association [8810]
PO Box 3604
Martinsville, VA 24115

Arthur, Vaughn, President
Dangerous Goods Advisory Council [3084]
7501 Greenway Center Dr., Ste. 760
Greenbelt, MD 20770
Ph: (202)289-4550
Fax: (202)289-4074

Arthurs, Dr. Eugene G., CEO
SPIE [6951]
PO Box 10
Bellingham, WA 98227-0010
Ph: (360)685-5580
   (360)676-3290
Toll Free: 888-902-0894
Fax: (360)647-1445

Artiga, Jose, Exec. Dir.
SHARE El Salvador [18178]
2425 College Ave.
Berkeley, CA 94704
Ph: (510)848-8487

Artis, Claude, Treasurer
National Technical Association [7286]
2705 Bladensburg Rd. NE

Washington, DC 20018

Artis, Edward A., PhD, Chairman, Founder
Knightsbridge International [12691]
PO Box 4394
West Hills, CA 91308-4394
Ph: (818)372-6902
Fax: (818)716-9494

Artman, Scott, Exec. Dir.
National Association of Tax Professionals [5800]
PO Box 8002
Appleton, WI 54914-8002
Toll Free: 800-558-3402
Fax: (800)747-0001

Arts, Willy, Chairperson
KWPN of North America, Inc. [4375]
4037 Iron Works Pky., Ste. 160
Lexington, KY 40511
Ph: (859)225-5331
Fax: (859)455-7457

Artysiewicz, Fr. Chet, President
Glenmary Research Center [19839]
Glenmary Home Missioners
4119 Glenmary Trace
Fairfield, OH 45014-5549
Ph: (513)874-8900
Fax: (513)874-1690

Artz, Kenneth, Treasurer
World Evangelical Alliance [20122]
PO Box 3402
Church St. Sta.
New York, NY 10008-3402
Ph: (212)233-3046
Fax: (646)957-9218

Arvin, Jeff, Exec. Dir.
Timber Framers Guild [1422]
1106 Harris Ave.
Bellingham, WA 98225
Ph: (360)746-6571
Toll Free: 855-598-1803

Arwood, Jim, Exec. Dir.
Energy Services Coalition [6481]
5590 Crestbrook Dr.
Morrison, CO 80465

Arzt, Leonard, Mem.
National Association for Proton Therapy [16347]
1155 15th Street NW, Ste. 500
Washington, DC 20005
Ph: (202)495-3133
Fax: (202)530-0659

Asali, Ziad J., President
American Task Force on Palestine [18514]
1634 Eye St. NW, Ste. 725
Washington, DC 20006
Ph: (202)887-0177
Fax: (202)887-1920

Asamarai, Dr. Abdulwahab, Chairman
Life for Relief and Development [12695]
17300 W 10 Mile Rd.
Southfield, MI 48075-2930
Ph: (248)424-7493
Toll Free: 800-827-3543
Fax: (248)424-8325

Asano, Kevin, President
United States Judo Federation [22967]
PO Box 338
Ontario, OR 97914
Ph: (541)889-8753
Fax: (541)889-5836

Asbury, Jason, President
Presbyterian Association of Musicians [20495]

100 Witherspoon St.
Louisville, KY 40202-1396
Ph: (502)569-5288
Toll Free: 888-728-7228
Fax: (502)569-8465

Asbury, Mrs. Kathleen L.G., Officer
Grinnell Family Association of
   America [20875]
c/o David R. Grinnell, President
2924 Marshall Rd.
Pittsburgh, PA 15214
Ph: (412)321-4963
   (561)439-8519

Ascensao, Joao, MD, President
Association of VA Hematology/
   Oncology [15225]
PO Box 2459
Lynnwood, WA 98036
Ph: (206)794-9124
Fax: (206)319-4601

Ascher, Yvonne, Advisor
Freedom Fields USA [11292]
PO Box 221820
Carmel, CA 93922

Aschwanden, Bernard, President
Society for Technical Communication
   [777]
9401 Lee Hwy., Ste. 300
Fairfax, VA 22031
Ph: (703)522-4114

Aselin, Don, Exec. Dir.
Sportsplex Operators and Develop-
   ers Association [23257]
PO Box 24617
Rochester, NY 14624-0617
Ph: (585)426-2215
Toll Free: 800-878-4308
Fax: (585)247-3112

Asfaw, Dr. Ingida, MD, Founder,
   President
Ethiopian North American Health
   Professionals Association [15000]
Box 150
6632 Telegraph Rd.
Bloomfield Hills, MI 48301
Ph: (313)872-2000
Fax: (313)871-1338

Ashar, Linda C., President
American Kerry Bog Pony Society
   [4314]
13010 W Darrow Rd.
Vermilion, OH 44089
Ph: (440)967-2680

Ashby, David, Chairman, President
Helping Honduras Kids [11024]
1525 Western Ave., Maildrop 8
Albany, NY 12203

Ashby, Golden, President
Social Media Club [2319]
PO Box 14881
San Francisco, CA 94114-0881

Ashby, John, Sr. VP, CFO
Near East Foundation [18692]
230 Euclid Ave.
Syracuse, NY 13210
Ph: (315)428-8670

Ashby, Patti, Director
Royal Academy of Dance [9270]
3211 S Lake Dr., Ste. R317
Milwaukee, WI 53235
Ph: (414)747-9060
Fax: (414)747-9062

Ashenfelter, Orley C., President
American Association of Wine
   Economists [3478]
Economics Dept.

New York University
19 W 4th St., 6th Fl.
New York, NY 10012
Ph: (212)992-8083
Fax: (212)995-4186

Ashenfelter, Orley, VP
Western Economic Association
   International [6405]
18837 Brookhurst St., Ste. 304
Fountain Valley, CA 92708-7302
Ph: (714)965-8800
Fax: (714)965-8829

Ashenhurst, Maj. Gen. Deborah A.,
   Chairman
National Guard Association of the
   United States [5609]
1 Massachusetts Ave. NW
Washington, DC 20001
Ph: (202)789-0031
Fax: (202)682-9358

Ashfaq, Dr. Raheela, Bd. Member
American Muslim Women Physicians
   Association [16736]
6300 Stonewood Dr., Ste. 412
Plano, TX 75025

Ashford, Suzanne, Contact
Adoptee-Birthparent Support
   Network [10437]
6439 Woodridge Rd.
Alexandria, VA 22312-1336
Ph: (301)442-9106

Ashland, Lynette, President
Association for Women in Aviation
   Maintenance [3486]
2330 Kenlee Dr.
Cincinnati, OH 45230
Ph: (386)416-0248

Ashline, Michael, CFO
Boy Scouts of America [12851]
1325 W Walnut Hill Ln.
Irving, TX 75038-3008
Ph: (972)580-2000

Ashlock, Joy Austin, Founder,
   President
Green Parent Association, Inc.
   [3881]
2601 Westhall Ln.
Maitland, FL 32751
Ph: (407)493-1372
   (321)331-7456

Ashmen, John, President, CEO
Association of Gospel Rescue Mis-
   sions [13032]
7222 Commerce Center Dr., Ste.
   120
Colorado Springs, CO 80919
Ph: (719)266-8300
Toll Free: 800-473-7283
Fax: (719)266-8600

Ashwill, Barbi, President
National Square Dance Convention
   National Executive Committee
   [9269]
Montgomery, AL 36117

Ashworth, Bobby, President
North American Young Generation in
   Nuclear [6931]
PO Box 32642
Charlotte, NC 28232-2642

Asis, Moises, Contact
Bees for Life [13610]
PO Box 65-0707
Miami, FL 33265-0707

Asiyo, Juni, Chairman, Founder
Sequoia Helping Hands [11148]
PO Box 13015

Durham, NC 27709-3015
Ph: (919)469-3095

Askew, Alex, President, CEO
BCA Global [960]
244 Madison Ave., Ste. 305
New York, NY 10016
Ph: (212)643-6570

Askren, Stan, Bd. Member
Business and Institutional Furniture
   Manufacturer's Association [1476]
678 Front Ave. NW, Ste. 150
Grand Rapids, MI 49504-5368
Ph: (616)285-3963
Fax: (616)285-3765

Asleson, Robert, Contact
A.C. Gilbert Heritage Society
   [22449]
c/o Robert Asleson
39330 Jay St. NW
Stanchfield, MN 55080-8807

Asongu, Dr. Januarius J., Exec. Dir.
US-Southern Cameroons Foundation
   [9220]
6475 New Hampshire Ave., Ste.
   504-F
Hyattsville, MD 20783
Ph: (301)891-2700

Aspery, Steve, Director
Interlake Sailing Class Association
   [22623]
c/o Thomas Humprey, Secretary-
   Treasurer
8 Little Creek Ln.
Cincinnati, OH 45246-4724
Ph: (513)772-6441

Aspromonte, Kenneth J, Exec. VP
National Italian American Foundation
   [9619]
1860 19th St. NW
Washington, DC 20009
Ph: (202)387-0600
Fax: (202)387-0800

Aspros, Douglas G., DVM, President
Pet Nutrition Alliance [16235]
5003 SW 41st Blvd.
Gainesville, FL 32608

Assadourian, Brian, Chairman
Armenian Students' Association of
   America Inc. [19387]
333 Atlantic Ave.
Warwick, RI 02888
Ph: (401)461-6114

Assante, Carylann, Exec. Dir.
Student & Youth Travel Association
   [3397]
8400 Westpark Dr., 2nd Fl.
McLean, VA 22102-5116
Ph: (703)610-1263
Fax: (703)610-0270

Assassa, Dr. Sam B., President
American Association of Aesthetic
   Medicine and Surgery [14303]
9478 W Olympic Blvd., Ste. 301
Beverly Hills, CA 90212
Ph: (310)274-9955

Assef, Saeed, President
Instrumentation Testing Association
   [6726]
PO Box 2611
Detroit, MI 48202
Ph: (702)568-1445
Toll Free: 877-236-1256
Fax: (702)568-1446

Assenmacher, Tom, Contact
Alberg 37 International Owners Association [22592]

PO Box 32
Kinsale, VA 22488

Asteoyer, Charon, Exec. Dir., CEO
Native American Community Board
   [12383]
PO Box 572
Lake Andes, SD 57356-0572
Ph: (605)487-7072
Fax: (605)487-7964

Asteoyer, Charon, Exec. Dir., CEO
Native American Women's Health
   Education Resource Center
   [17764]
PO Box 572
Lake Andes, SD 57356-0572
Ph: (605)487-7072
   (605)487-7097
Fax: (605)487-7964

Astin, Gen. Claude S., Jr., Cmdr.
American Rescue Workers Inc.
   [13030]
25 Ross St.
Williamsport, PA 17701-5149
Ph: (570)323-8693
Fax: (570)323-8694

Astle, Dr. William F., Officer
Joint Commission on Allied Health
   Personnel in Ophthalmology
   [16393]
2025 Woodlane Dr.
Saint Paul, MN 55125-2998
Ph: (651)731-2944
Toll Free: 800-284-3937
Fax: (651)731-0410

Aston, Kane, Chairman, Secretary
Fighting Robots Association [7103]

Astrachan, Eric, Exec. Dir.
Tile Council of North America [591]
100 Clemson Research Blvd.
Anderson, SC 29625
Ph: (864)646-8453
Fax: (864)646-2821

Astrene, Tom, Exec. Dir.
Society of Tribologists and Lubrica-
   tion Engineers [6599]
840 Busse Hwy.
Park Ridge, IL 60068-2302
Ph: (847)825-5536

Atchison, Christopher G., MPA,
   Secretary, Treasurer
Association of Public Health
   Laboratories [16997]
8515 Georgia Ave., Ste. 700
Silver Spring, MD 20910
Ph: (240)485-2745
Fax: (240)485-2700

Ateya, Theresa, Founder, Exec. Dir.
Dreams Blossom [13046]
PO Box 5293
Johnstown, PA 15904-5293
Ph: (814)659-7595

Atigo, Monday S., President, CEO
Ugandan North American Associa-
   tion [19291]
1337 Massachusetts Ave., No. 213
Arlington, MA 02476
Toll Free: 855-873-8622

Atkins, Charles, President
Military Intelligence Corps Associa-
   tion [4973]
PO Box 13020
Fort Huachuca, AZ 85670-3020

Atkins, Jody Rosen, Exec. Dir.
National Extension Association of
   Family and Consumer Sciences
   [5107]

140 Island Way, Ste. 316
Clearwater Beach, FL 33767
Ph: (561)477-8100
Fax: (561)910-0896

Atkins, Louis M., President
National Association of Postal
Supervisors [23507]
1727 King St., Ste. 400
Alexandria, VA 22314-2753
Ph: (703)836-9660
Fax: (703)836-9665

Atkinson, Carol, Coord.
Insulin for Life USA [14535]
5745 SW 75th St., No. 116
Gainesville, FL 32608
Ph: (352)327-8649

Atkinson, Dale J., Exec. Dir.
Federation of Associations of
Regulatory Boards [14933]
1466 Techny Rd.
Northbrook, IL 60062
Ph: (847)559-3272
Fax: (847)714-9796

Atkinson, Greg, Co-Pres.
The Irish Ancestral Research Association [20976]
2120 Commonwealth Ave.
Auburndale, MA 02466-1909

Atkinson, John, President
Fellowship of Christian Released
Time Ministries [20079]
5722 Lime Ave.
Long Beach, CA 90805
Ph: (562)428-7733
Toll Free: 800-360-7943

Atkinson, Mary-Margaret, President
Association of Professional
Chaplains [19925]
2800 W Higgins Rd., Ste. 295
Schaumburg, IL 60173
Ph: (847)240-1014
Fax: (847)240-1015

Atkinson, Patrick, Founder, Exec.
Dir.
God's Child Project [11005]
721 Memorial Hwy.
Bismarck, ND 58504-5398
Ph: (701)255-7956
  (612)351-8020

Atlas, John, President
National Housing Institute [11981]
60 S Fullerton Ave., Ste. 202
Montclair, NJ 07042
Ph: (973)509-1600

Atlee, John S., PhD, President,
Director
Institute for Economic Analysis
[6389]
360 Mt. Auburn St., Ste. 001
Cambridge, MA 02138-5596

Atnip, Robert G., President
Alpha Omega Alpha Honor Medical
Society [23816]
525 Middlefield Rd., Ste. 130
Menlo Park, CA 94025
Ph: (650)329-0291
Fax: (650)329-1618

Atre, Nisha, Chairwoman
North Star Fund [12405]
520 8th Ave., Ste. 1800
New York, NY 10018-6656
Ph: (212)620-9110
Fax: (212)620-8178

Attar, Ani, Mem.
Armenian Relief Society of Eastern
U.S.A. [12622]

80 Bigelow Ave., Ste. 200
Watertown, MA 02472
Ph: (617)926-3801
Fax: (617)924-7238

Attaway, Pat, Act. Chm.
Helicopter Safety Advisory Conference [139]
c/o Pat Attaway, Acting Chairman
PHI, Inc.
2001 SE Evangeline Thruway
Lafayette, LA 70508

Attawia, Mohamed Amr, MD, Contact
Islamic Relief U.S.A. [12690]
PO Box 22250
Alexandria, VA 22304
Ph: (703)370-7202
Toll Free: 855-447-1001
Fax: (866)917-0667

Attebery, Stina, Rep.
International Association for the
Fantastic in the Arts [10203]
1279 W Palmetto Park Rd., Unit
  272285
Boca Raton, FL 33427

Attebery, Tim, President
Cardiology Advocacy Alliance
[14105]
PO Box 26588
Birmingham, AL 35260
Ph: (202)505-2221
Fax: (205)978-3106

Attieh, Aman, Exec. Dir.
American Association of Teachers of
Arabic [8168]
3416 Primm Ln.
Birmingham, AL 35216
Ph: (205)822-6800
Fax: (205)823-2760

Atwater, Danielle, DVM, Contact
Suenos International [10699]
255 McKinley Dr.
Bennett, CO 80102
Ph: (720)350-2199

Atwater, Janet, Chmn. of the Bd.
Food Allergy Research and Educa-
tion [13577]
7925 Jones Branch Dr., Ste. 1100
McLean, VA 22102
Ph: (703)691-3179
Toll Free: 800-929-4040
Fax: (703)691-2713

Atwater, Mary M., President
National Association for Research in
Science Teaching [8550]
12100 Sunset Hills Rd., Ste. 130
Reston, VA 20190-3221
Ph: (703)234-4138
Fax: (703)435-4390

Atwood, Nancy, Exec. Dir., Founder
Children's Hemiplegia and Stroke
Association [17296]
4101 W Green Oaks Blvd., Ste. 305,
No. 149
Arlington, TX 76016

Atwood, Roger, President
Pope and Young Club [22506]
PO Box 548
Chatfield, MN 55923-0548
Ph: (507)867-4144

Au Allen, Susan, CEO, President
U.S. Pan Asian American Chamber
of Commerce [23634]
1329 18th St. NW
Washington, DC 20036
Ph: (202)296-5221
Toll Free: 800-696-7818
Fax: (202)296-5225

Aubrey, Curtis, CFO
Heart to Heart International [12670]
13250 W 98th St.
Lenexa, KS 66215
Ph: (913)764-5200
Fax: (913)764-0809

Auch, Lynette, President
Lutherans For Life [12780]
1101 5th St.
Nevada, IA 50201-1816
Ph: (515)382-2077
Toll Free: 888-364-LIFE
Fax: (515)382-3020

Audas, JP, Assoc. VP
Oklahoma University Alumni As-
sociation [19342]
900 Asp Ave., Rm. 427
Norman, OK 73019-5142
Ph: (405)325-1710

Audrain, David, Exec. Dir.
Society of Independent Show
Organizers [1178]
2700 Cumberland Pky. SE, Ste. 580
Atlanta, GA 30339
Ph: (310)450-8831
Toll Free: 877-937-7476
Fax: (310)450-9305

Auerbach, Bruce, Chmn. of the Bd.
Albert Schweitzer Fellowship
[10351]
330 Brookline Ave.
Boston, MA 02215
Ph: (617)667-5111
Fax: (617)667-7989

Augat, Thomas J., Mem.
Council on Chiropractic Guidelines
and Practice Parameters [14265]
PO Box 2542
Lexington, SC 29071-2542
Ph: (803)356-6809
Fax: (803)356-6826

Augsbury, Larry A., Commissioner
Clan Cunningham Society of
America [20804]

August, Frank, Secretary
Mobile Satellite Users Association
[7112]
1350 Beverly Rd., Ste. 115, No. 341
McLean, VA 22101
Ph: (650)839-0376

August, J. W., President
Bilateral Safety Corridor Coalition
[12025]
2050 Wilson Ave., Ste. C
National City, CA 91950
Ph: (619)336-0770
  (619)666-2757
Fax: (619)336-0791

Augusta, Lauren, Exec. Dir.,
Founder
Multinational Exchange for Sustain-
able Agriculture [4698]
2362 Bancroft Way, No. 202
Berkeley, CA 94704
Ph: (510)654-8858
Toll Free: 888-834-7461

Augustine, Keith, Exec. Dir., Editor
Internet Infidels [10098]
711 S Carson St., Ste. 4
Carson City, NV 89701
Toll Free: 877-501-5113

Augustine, Ruth, Treasurer
Peanut Pals [21710]
c/o Ruth Augustine, Treasurer
6052 Canter Glen Ave.
Las Vegas, NV 89122
Ph: (301)604-5858

Augustus, Dr. Amelia, Director,
Founder
Women's Economic Round Table
[19010]
The Journalism School, Columbia
University
Knight-Bagehot Fellowship Program
2950 Broadway, MC 3850
New York, NY 10027
Ph: (914)922-1747
Fax: (914)922-1747

Auker, Jim, President
Kustoms of America [22399]
5126 E ST RT 26
Portland, IN 47371

Auld, Elaine, CEO
Society for Public Health Education
[17022]
10 G St. NE, Ste. 605
Washington, DC 20002-4242
Ph: (202)408-9804
Fax: (202)408-9815

Auld, Ruth Gabig, EdD, Chairperson
Society for Middle Ear Disease
[16541]
c/o Charles D. Bluestone, MD,
Founder
Children's Hospital of Pittsburgh
Faculty Pavilion, 7th Fl.
One Children's Hospital Dr.
4401 Penn Ave.
Pittsburgh, PA 15224
Ph: (412)924-1026

Ault, Ron, President
AFL-CIO - Metal Trades Department
[23479]
815 16th St. NW
Washington, DC 20006
Ph: (202)508-3705
Fax: (202)508-3706

Aumiller, Gary S., PhD, Exec. Dir.
Society for Police and Criminal
Psychology [16939]
c/o JoAnne Brewster, PhD.,
Membership Chair
Department of Graduate Psychology,
MSC 7704, Miller 1151
James Madison University
Harrisonburg, VA 22807
Ph: (540)568-6107

Ausili, Gene, Mem.
Professional Picture Framers As-
sociation [8883]
83 South St., Ste. 303
Freehold, NJ 07728
Ph: (732)536-5160
Fax: (732)536-5161

Auslander, Mr. Louis, President
International Kennel Club of Chicago
[21900]
20 S Clark, Ste. 1830
Chicago, IL 60603
Ph: (773)237-5100
Fax: (773)237-5126

Austin, Bob, Exec. Dir.
Rolls-Royce Owners' Club [21486]
191 Hempt Rd.
Mechanicsburg, PA 17050-2605
Ph: (717)697-4671
Fax: (717)697-7820

Austin, Charles P., Sr., Chairman
Milton S. Eisenhower Foundation
[11508]
1875 Connecticut Ave. NW, Ste. 410
Washington, DC 20009
Ph: (202)234-8104
Fax: (202)234-8484

Austin, Dave, President
American Ecological Engineering
Society [3987]

c/o Anand Jayakaran, Treasurer
2606 W Pioneer
Puyallup, WA 98371-4900
Ph: (253)445-4523
Fax: (253)445-4571

Austin, Dennis, VP
American Guild of Town Criers
[10172]
121 S Division Ave.
Holland, MI 49424
Ph: (616)396-1043

Austin, Gail, President, Treasurer
The Pig Preserve Association
[10682]
PO Box 555
Jamestown, TN 38556

Austin, Glenn D., President
American Seed Research Founda-
tion [4640]
1701 Duke St., Ste. 275
Alexandria, VA 22314
Ph: (703)837-8140
Fax: (703)837-9365

Austin, Jonathan, Exec. Dir.
American Association of Veterinary
Clinicians [17602]
125 N Main St., Ste. 500-403
Blacksburg, VA 24060
Ph: (614)358-0417
Fax: (540)242-3385

Austin, Leila Golestaneh, Dr., Exec.
Dir.
Public Affairs Alliance of Iranian
Americans [18577]
1001 Connecticut Ave. NW
Washington, DC 20036-5504
Ph: (202)828-8370
Fax: (202)828-8371

Austin, Robin, Comm. Spec.
National Council on Folic Acid
[16230]
4590 MacArthur Blvd. NW, Ste. 250
Washington, DC 20007
Toll Free: 800-621-3141

Austin, Scott, Contact
International Golf Associates [22884]
1040 Genter St., No. 103
La Jolla, CA 92037-5550
Ph: (858)546-4737
Fax: (619)615-2083

Austin, William F., Founder
Starkey Hearing Foundation [15210]
6700 Washington Ave. S
Eden Prairie, MN 55344
Toll Free: 866-354-3254
Fax: (952)828-6900

Austria, Thereza, Dir. of Fin.
Hudson Institute [18982]
1201 Pennsylvania Ave. NW, Ste.
400
Washington, DC 20004
Ph: (202)974-2400
Fax: (202)974-2410

Ausubel, Kenny, CEO, Founder
Bioneers [4490]
1014 Torney Ave.
San Francisco, CA 94129
Ph: (505)986-0366
Toll Free: 877-246-6337
Fax: (505)986-1644

Auter, Phil, Exec. Dir.
American Communication Associa-
tion [7257]
104 E University Cir.
Lafayette, LA 70503
Ph: (337)482-1000

Autin, Diana, Coord.
Family Voices [14189]
3701 San Mateo Blvd. NE, Ste. 103

Albuquerque, NM 87110
Ph: (505)872-4774
Toll Free: 888-835-5669
Fax: (505)872-4780

Autry, Alex, President
Federal Government Distance
Learning Association [7767]
166 Bledsoe Dr.
Bellbrook, OH 45305
Ph: (937)904-5480

Auxier, Sam, President
United States Figure Skating As-
sociation [23157]
20 1st St.
Colorado Springs, CO 80906
Ph: (719)635-5200
Fax: (719)635-9548

Auyang, Bernie, Chairman
Young Presidents' Organization
[676]
600 E Las Colinas Blvd., Ste. 1000
Irving, TX 75039
Ph: (972)587-1500
Toll Free: 800-773-7976
Fax: (972)587-1611

Avallone, Ralph, President
International Green Energy Council
[5887]
1701 Pennsylvania Ave. NW, Ste.
300
Washington, DC 20006
Ph: (202)349-7138

Avenell, Bruce K., Director, Founder
Eureka Society [20654]
PO Box 222
Mount Shasta, CA 96067

Avent, Gail, Founder, Exec. Dir.
Total Family Care Coalition [11833]
1214 I St. SE, Ste. 11
Washington, DC 20003
Ph: (202)758-3281

Averhart, Mr. James, President
National Montford Point Marine As-
sociation, Inc. [5611]
PO Box 1070
Sharon Hill, PA 19079

Averhoff, Shad, Officer
Youth in Model Railroading [22194]
12990 Prince Ct.
Broomfield, CO 80020-5419
Ph: (303)466-2857

Averill, Sue, RN, President, Founder
One Nurse At A Time [16176]
7747 38th Ave. NE
Seattle, WA 98115

Avery, Susan, CAE, CEO
Copper and Brass Servicenter As-
sociation [2346]
6734 W 121st St.
Overland Park, KS 66209
Ph: (913)396-0697
Fax: (913)345-1006

Avery, Virginia, VP
Dream Factory [11225]
410 W Chestnut St., Ste. 530
Louisville, KY 40202
Ph: (502)561-3001
Toll Free: 800-456-7556
Fax: (502)561-3004

Avila, Lydia, Exec. Dir.
Energy Action Coalition [6478]
1875 Connecticut Ave. NW, 10th Fl.
Washington, DC 20009-5728

Avila, Maria del Pilar, CEO
New America Alliance [1007]

c/o Maria del Pilar Avila, Chief
Executive Officer
1050 Connecticut Ave. NW, 10th Fl.
Washington, DC 20036
Ph: (202)772-1044
Fax: (214)466-6415

Avila, Merle, VP
National Token Collectors Associa-
tion [22276]
PO Box 281
Ormond Beach, FL 32175
Ph: (386)677-4206

Avilla, Shirley, Bd. Member
Pacific Islanders' Cultural Associa-
tion [10059]
409 Tenant Sta., No. 230
Morgan Hill, CA 95037
Ph: (415)281-0221

Avitsian, Rafi, MD, Secretary,
Treasurer
Society for Neuroscience in
Anesthesiology and Critical Care
[16069]
2209 Dickens Rd.
Richmond, VA 23230-2005
Ph: (804)565-6360
Fax: (804)282-0090

Aviv, Diana, CEO
Feeding America [12086]
35 E Whacker Dr., Ste. 2000
Chicago, IL 60601
Ph: (312)263-2303
Fax: (312)263-5626

Aviv, Diana, CEO, President
Independent Sector [12484]
1602 L St. NW, Ste. 900
Washington, DC 20036
Ph: (202)467-6100
   (202)467-6161
Fax: (202)467-6101

Avkiran, Dr. Metin, President
International Society for Heart
Research [14128]
c/o Dr. Leslie Anderson Lobaugh,
Executive Secretary
PO Box 52643
Durham, NC 27717-2643
Ph: (919)493-4418

Avner, Lindsay, Founder, CEO
Bright Pink [17754]
670 N Clark St., Ste. 2
Chicago, IL 60654
Ph: (312)787-4412

Avni, Ronit, Founder
Just Vision [18008]
1616 P St. NW, Ste. 340
Washington, DC 20036

Avtzon, Eliezer, Exec. Dir.
Global Jewish Assistance and Relief
Network [12037]
1485 Union St.
Brooklyn, NY 11213
Ph: (212)868-3636
   (718)774-6497

Aw, Fanta, President, Chmn. of the
Bd.
NAFSA: Association of International
Educators [7934]
1307 New York Ave. NW, 8th Fl.
Washington, DC 20005-4701
Ph: (202)737-3699
Fax: (202)737-3657

Awad, Nihad, Exec. Dir., Bd.
Member
Council on American-Islamic Relations [9604]
453 New Jersey Ave. SE

Washington, DC 20003
Ph: (202)488-8787
Fax: (202)488-0833

Awh, Mark H., MD, President
Clinical Magnetic Resonance Society
[14292]
5620 W Sligh Ave.
Tampa, FL 33634-4490
Ph: (813)806-1080
Toll Free: 888-350-CMRS
Fax: (813)806-1081

Axelrod, Susan, Chairperson,
Founder
Citizens United for Research in
Epilepsy [14738]
430 W Erie St., Ste. 210
Chicago, IL 60654
Ph: (312)255-1801
Toll Free: 800-765-7118

Axlund, Todd, President
Veterinary Neurosurgical Society
[17673]
5671 Crooked Stick Dr.
Wadsworth, OH 44281

Axtell, Mr. David, Contact
SCI - International Voluntary Service
[13307]
5505 Walnut Level Rd.
Crozet, VA 22932
Ph: (206)350-6585
Fax: (206)350-6585

Ayala, Dr. Plinio, CEO, President
Per Scholas [7796]
804 E 138th St., 2nd Fl.
Bronx, NY 10454
Ph: (718)991-8400
Fax: (718)991-0362

Ayaz, Dr. Sandi, Exec. Dir.
National Tutoring Association [8721]
PO Box 6840
Lakeland, FL 33807
Ph: (863)529-5206
Fax: (863)937-3390

Ayeliya, Dr. Abio, Founder, Exec. Dir.
Sabu Help International [12809]
743 N Wilton Dr.
North Salt Lake, UT 84054
Ph: (801)834-4992

Ayer, Lynsay, President
Families for Private Adoption
[10452]
PO Box 6375
Washington, DC 20015-0375

Ayers, Blaine, Exec. Dir.
Sigma Alpha Epsilon [23924]
1856 Sheridan Rd.
Evanston, IL 60201-3837
Ph: (847)475-1856
Fax: (847)475-2250

Ayers, Charletta, Chairperson
International Healthcare Volunteers
[15025]
PO Box 8231
Trenton, NJ 08650
Ph: (609)259-8807

Ayers, Gail, PhD, CEO, President
CREW Network [2858]
1201 Wakarusa Dr., Ste. D
Lawrence, KS 66049
Ph: (785)832-1808
Fax: (785)832-1551

Ayers, Jill, President
Society for Environmental Graphic
Design [1557]
1900 L St. NW, Ste. 710
Washington, DC 20036
Ph: (202)638-5555

Ayers, Linda, CEO
American College of Osteopathic
 Surgeons **[16507]**
123 N Henry St.
Alexandria, VA 22314-2903
Ph: (703)684-0416
Toll Free: 800-888-1312
Fax: (703)684-3280

Ayers, Wendy, Secretary, Treasurer
Lippitt Morgan Breeders Association
 [4377]
c/o Grace Yaglou, President
728 Walnut Hill Rd.
Barre, MA 01005
Ph: (978)355-2539
 (802)558-8144

Aylesworth, Ryan, President, CEO
Audubon International **[3817]**
120 Defreest Dr.
Troy, NY 12180
Ph: (518)767-9051
Toll Free: 844-767-9051
Fax: (518)767-9076

Ayres, Bill, Founder, Amb.
Why Hunger **[18459]**
505 8th Ave., Ste. 2100
New York, NY 10018
Ph: (202)629-8850
Toll Free: 800-548-6479

Azar, Frederick M., VP
American Academy of Orthopaedic
 Surgeons **[16460]**
9400 W Higgins Rd.
Rosemont, IL 60018-4262
Ph: (847)823-7186
Toll Free: 800-346-2267
Fax: (847)823-8125

Azarian, Michael, Exec. Dir.
Chi Phi **[23892]**
1160 Satellite Blvd.
Suwanee, GA 30024
Ph: (404)231-1824
Toll Free: 800-849-1824

Azim, Erica, Director, President
MBIRA **[9952]**
Box 7863
Berkeley, CA 94707-0863
Ph: (510)548-6053

Aziz, Malik, Chairman
National Black Police Association
 [5495]
3100 Main St., No. 256
Dallas, TX 75226
Ph: (214)942-2022
Toll Free: 855-879-6272
Fax: (855)879-6272

Aziz, Nikhil, Exec. Dir.
Grassroots International **[12158]**
179 Boylston St., 4th Fl.
Boston, MA 02130
Ph: (617)524-1400
Fax: (617)524-5525

Aziz, Shahid R., MD, President,
 Founder
Smile Bangladesh **[14344]**
PO Box 1403
Mountainside, NJ 07092
Ph: (908)400-1226
Fax: (866)558-4311

Azizi, Ayub, Director
Solace International **[13398]**
629 S K St.
Lake Worth, FL 33460
Ph: (520)270-5916

Azuine, Dr. Magnus A., President
TransWorld Development Initiatives
 [12073]

PO Box 105
Brentwood, MD 20722
Ph: (301)793-7551
Fax: (301)779-8892

Azuma, Glenn, Chairperson
Hostelling International-American
 Youth Hostels **[12577]**
8401 Colesville Rd., Ste. 600
Silver Spring, MD 20910
Ph: (240)650-2100
Fax: (240)650-2094

Azuma, Julie, Chairperson
Asian Women in Business **[611]**
42 Broadway, Ste. 1748
New York, NY 10004-3876
Ph: (212)868-1368
Toll Free: 877-686-6870

B

B., Abigail, Founder
A.R.T.S. Anonymous **[12868]**
PO Box 230175
New York, NY 10023
Ph: (718)251-3828

Ba Thong, Martino Nguyen, Founder
One Body Village **[11104]**
PO Box 162933
Atlanta, GA 30321
Ph: (706)825-3032

Baade, Trudy, President
American Association of Certified
 Wedding Planners **[441]**
210 W College St., Ste. 400
Grapevine, TX 76051
Toll Free: 844-202-2297

Baars, Suzanne, President
Catholic Psychotherapy Association
 [16967]
7251 W 20th St., M-2
Greeley, CO 80634
Ph: (402)885-9272

Baas, John, President
Society of Outdoor Recreation
 Professionals **[5669]**
PO Box 221
Marienville, PA 16239
Ph: (814)927-8212
Fax: (814)927-6659

Babay, Karim, Chairman
Friendship Ambassadors Foundation
 [18541]
299 Greenwich Ave.
Greenwich, CT 06830
Ph: (203)542-0652
 (203)622-7420
Toll Free: 800-526-2908
Fax: (203)542-0661

Babayi, Robert, Founder
Iranian American Bar Association
 [5016]
5185 MacArthur Blvd. NW, Ste. 624
Washington, DC 20016

Babbitt, Angie, VP
Grassland Heritage Foundation
 [3878]
PO Box 394
Shawnee Mission, KS 66201
Ph: (785)691-9748

Babbitt, Carol, Chairperson, Exec.
 Dir.
Project Linus **[11134]**
PO Box 5621
Bloomington, IL 61702-5621
Ph: (309)585-0686
Fax: (309)585-0745

Babbitt, Jim, Exec. Dir.
Decorative Plumbing and Hardware
 Association **[2636]**

7508 Wisconsin Ave., 4th Fl.
Bethesda, MD 20814-3561
Ph: (301)657-3642
Toll Free: 888-871-6520
Fax: (301)907-9326

Babcock, Jeannette, Administrator
National Marriage Encounter **[12257]**
c/o Jeannette Babcock, Administrator
3922 77th St.
Urbandale, IA 50322
Ph: (515)278-8458

Babich, Babette E., Exec. Dir.
Nietzsche Society **[10104]**
Fordham University
Graduate School of Arts and Sci-
 ences
441 E Fordham Rd.
Bronx, NY 10458
Ph: (212)636-6297

Babin, Allison, Administrator,
 Secretary
Intervention & Coiled Tubing As-
 sociation **[7036]**
PO Box 1082. 8
Montgomery, TX 77356
Ph: (936)520-1549
Fax: (832)201-9977

Babjak, Patricia M., CEO
Academy of Nutrition and Dietetics
 [16198]
120 S Riverside Plz, Ste. 2000
Chicago, IL 60606-6995
Ph: (312)899-0040
Toll Free: 800-877-1600

Baca, Leroy, Chmn. of the Bd.
Fight Crime: Invest in Kids **[17845]**
1212 New York Ave. NW, Ste. 300
Washington, DC 20005
Ph: (202)776-0027
Fax: (202)776-0110

Bachinski, Julia, Admin. Ofc.
JILA **[7027]**
440 UCB
Boulder, CO 80309-5004
Ph: (303)492-7789
Fax: (303)492-5235

Bachman, Ms. Ann, Director
American Association of Physician
 Offices and Laboratories **[15514]**
c/o Doctors Management
10401 Kingston Pke.
Knoxville, TN 37922
Toll Free: 800-635-4040
Fax: (865)531-0722

Bachman, Dan, President
National Gymnastics Judges As-
 sociation **[22902]**
c/o Dan Bachman, President
Guide Financial Group
2830 100th, No. 108
Urbandale, IA 50322
Ph: (515)974-4561

Bachman, Donald M., MD, President
Society for the Advancement of
 Women's Imaging **[17062]**
PO Box 885
Schererville, IN 46375
Ph: (219)588-2119

Bachman, Judy, Chairperson
Citizens Equal Rights Alliance
 [12028]
PO Box 0379
Gresham, WI 54128

Bachman, Randall, Chmn. of the Bd.
Autism Recovery Foundation
 [13750]

401 Groveland Ave.
Minneapolis, MN 55403
Ph: (612)879-1817

Bachmann, Mr. Brett, CEO, Exec.
 Dir.
International Commission of Peace
 [18007]
20669 Martinez St.
Woodland Hills, CA 91364

Bachrach, Dr. Richard M., DO,
 President
Center for Sports and Osteopathic
 Medicine **[16801]**
317 Madison Ave., Ste. 400
New York, NY 10017
Ph: (212)685-8113
Fax: (212)697-4541

Backer, Carl L., President
Congenital Heart Surgeons' Society
 [17386]
500 Cummings Ctr., Ste. 4550
Beverly, MA 01915
Ph: (978)927-8330
Fax: (978)524-0498

Bacon, Brenda J., Chmn. of the Bd.
Argentum **[11963]**
1650 King St., Ste. 602
Alexandria, VA 22314
Ph: (703)894-1805
Fax: (703)894-1831

Bacon, Ellen, President
Ernst Bacon Society **[9905]**
8 Drovers Ln.
Syracuse, NY 13214-1805

Bacote, Dr. Vincent, Director
Center for Applied Christian Ethics
 [19948]
501 College Ave.
Wheaton, IL 60187-5593
Ph: (630)752-5890

Badcock, Tracy A., Act. Pres.
Shelter Alliance **[11434]**
2201 SW 145th Ave., No. 209
Miramar, FL 33027
Toll Free: 866-744-1003

Bade, Donald D., Treasurer
Brotherhood of the Knights of the
 Vine **[4928]**
3343 Industrial Dr., Ste. 2
Santa Rosa, CA 95403-2060
Ph: (707)579-3781
Fax: (707)579-3996

Badeau, Sue, President
North American Council on Adopt-
 able Children **[10461]**
970 Raymond Ave., Ste. 106
Saint Paul, MN 55114
Ph: (651)644-3036
Fax: (651)644-9848

Baden, John A., PhD, Chairman
Foundation for Research on
 Economics and the Environment
 [3868]
16380 Cottonwood Rd.
Gallatin Gateway, MT 59730
Ph: (406)585-1776

Bader, Bill, Mem.
International Electronics Manufactur-
 ing Initiative **[6796]**
2214 Rock Hill Rd., Ste. 110
Herndon, VA 20170-4214
Ph: (703)834-0330
Fax: (703)834-2735

Badesch, Scott, COO, President,
 CEO
Autism Society **[13756]**
4340 East-West Hwy., Ste. 350

Bethesda, MD 20814
Toll Free: 800-328-8476

Badio, Bernadette, Dir. of Operations
Grantmakers for Children, Youth,
and Families [12481]
12138 Central Ave., Ste. 422
Bowie, MD 20721
Ph: (301)589-4293
Fax: (301)589-4289

Badri, Hala, President
Sudan-American Foundation for
Education [7595]
1700 Westwind Way
McLean, VA 22102
Ph: (571)297-4099

Badzek, Laurie, Director
Center for Ethics and Human Rights
[14745]
c/o American Nurses Association
8515 Georgia Ave., Ste. 400
Silver Spring, MD 20910-3492
Ph: (301)628-5000
Toll Free: 800-274-4262
Fax: (301)628-5001

Baer, Ellen, Dir. of Admin.
Telluride Association [7803]
217 West Ave.
Ithaca, NY 14850-3911
Ph: (607)273-5011
Fax: (607)272-2667

Baer-Sinnott, Sara, President
Whole Grains Council [16243]
266 Beacon St.
Boston, MA 02116
Ph: (617)421-5500
Fax: (617)421-5511

Baez, Aurora, President, Founder
Aurora's Promise - 4 Kids [10860]
198 S Myrtle Ave.
Monrovia, CA 91016
Ph: (626)233-9391

Baeza, Della Britton, CEO, President
Jackie Robinson Foundation [13454]
1 Hudson Sq., 2nd Fl.
75 Varick St.
New York, NY 10013-1917
Ph: (212)290-8600
Fax: (212)290-8081

Bagby, Ihsan, Gen. Sec.
Muslim Alliance in North America
[10030]
PO Box 910375
Lexington, KY 40591
Ph: (859)296-0206
Fax: (859)257-3743

Bagin, Richard D., APR, Exec. Dir.
National School Public Relations As-
sociation [8472]
15948 Derwood Rd.
Rockville, MD 20855-2123
Ph: (301)519-0496
Fax: (301)519-0494

Bagwell, Beth, MPA, Exec. Dir.
International Town & Gown Associa-
tion [11387]
1250 Tiger Blvd.
Clemson, SC 29631
Ph: (864)624-1148
Fax: (864)653-2032

Bahr, Prof. Ruth Huntley, PhD,
President
International Society of Phonetic Sci-
ences [9743]
c/o Prof. Ruth Huntley Bahr, PhD
University of South Florida
4202 E Fowler Ave., PCD 1017
Tampa, FL 33647
Ph: (813)974-3182
Fax: (813)974-0822

Baier, James, Exec. Sec.
National Sweet Sorghum Producers
and Processors Association [3769]
c/o James Baier, Executive
Secretary
PO Box 1356
Cookeville, TN 38503-1356
Ph: (931)644-7764

Baier, Johnny, Editor
ALL FRETS [9847]
2501 Saddleback Dr.
Edmond, OK 73034
Ph: (405)819-3883

Baigelman, Louise, Founder, Exec.
Dir.
Story Shares [8493]
1313 Boylston St.
Boston, MA 02215

Bail, Dr. Richard, Founder, President
Communities Without Borders
[10947]
PO Box 111
Newton, MA 02468
Ph: (617)965-4713

Baile, David, CEO
International Society for the Perform-
ing Arts Foundation [8982]
630 9th Ave., Ste. 213
New York, NY 10036-4752
Ph: (212)206-8490
Fax: (212)206-8603

Bailey, Arthur, President
Dream Jamaica [13442]
PO Box 14424
Seattle, WA 98114

Bailey, Brent, Exec. Dir.
Coordinating Research Council
[2517]
5755 N Point Pky., Ste. 265
Alpharetta, GA 30022-1175
Ph: (678)795-0506
Fax: (678)795-0509

Bailey, Jarad, Director
Professional Lighting and Sign
Management Companies of
America [2105]
1100-H Brandywine Blvd.
Zanesville, OH 43701-7303
Ph: (740)452-4541

Bailey, Kathleen M., President
American Association for Applied
Linguistics [9735]
Bldg. 14, Ste. 100
1827 Powers Ferry Rd.
Atlanta, GA 30339
Ph: (678)229-2892
Toll Free: 866-821-7700
Fax: (678)229-2777

Bailey, Laura, President
Association of Ignition Interlock
Program Administrators [280]
5030 N May Ave., Ste. 212
Oklahoma, OK 73112

Bailey, Marsha, Chairperson
Association of Women's Business
Centers [3488]
1629 K St. NW, Ste. 300
Washington, DC 20006
Ph: (202)552-8732

Bailey, Matt, President
Independent Glass Association
[1505]
14747 N Northsight Blvd., Ste. 111-
387
Scottsdale, AZ 85260
Ph: (480)535-8650
Fax: (480)522-3104

Bailey, Matthew R., Exec. VP
National Association for Biomedical
Research [13720]
1100 Vermont Ave. NW, Ste. 1100
Washington, DC 20006-2733
Ph: (202)857-0540
Fax: (202)659-1902

Bailey, Michael, Secretary
Southeast Desalting Association
[4774]
2409 SE Dixie Hwy.
Stuart, FL 34996
Ph: (772)781-7698
Fax: (772)463-0860

Bailey, Pamela G., President, CEO
Grocery Manufacturers Association
[1334]
1350 I St. NW
Washington, DC 20005
Ph: (202)639-5900
Fax: (202)639-5932

Bailey, Rolinda, Secretary, Treasurer
National Association of Birth Centers
of Color [14238]
213 S Dillard St., Ste. 340
Winter Garden, FL 34787
Ph: (706)901-7508

Bailey, Scott, Director
Arabian Horse Breeders Alliance
[4337]
9777 S Las Vegas Blvd.
Las Vegas, NV 89101

Bailey, Steve, CM, Exec. Dir.
National Management Association
[2187]
2210 Arbor Blvd.
Dayton, OH 45439
Ph: (937)294-0421

Bailey, Vicky A., Chairman
United States Energy Association
[6515]
1300 Pennsylvania Ave. NW, Ste.
550
Mailbox 142
Washington, DC 20004-3022
Ph: (202)312-1230
Fax: (202)682-1682

Bailey, Victoria, Exec. Dir.
Theatre Development Fund [10275]
520 8th Ave., Ste. 801
New York, NY 10018-6507
Ph: (212)912-9770

Bailey-Hainer, Brenda, Exec. Dir.
American Theological Library As-
sociation [9677]
300 S Wacker Dr., Ste. 2100
Chicago, IL 60606-6701
Ph: (312)454-5100
Toll Free: 888-665-2852
Fax: (312)454-5505

Bailey-Hainer, Brenda, Treasurer
National Federation of Advanced
Information Services [6749]
801 Compass Way, Ste. 201
Annapolis, MD 21401
Ph: (443)221-2980

Bailey-Ndiaye, Stacy, Founder, Exec.
Dir.
Bridge Kids International [13434]
501 W Kenwood Dr.
Louisville, KY 40214
Ph: (502)457-1910

Bain, Heather L., Chairman
American-Scottish Foundation
[19635]
575 Madison Ave., 10th Fl.
New York, NY 10022-2511
Ph: (212)605-0338
Fax: (212)605-0222

Bainwol, Mitch, President, CEO
Alliance of Automobile Manufactur-
ers [305]
803 7th St. NW, Ste. 300
Washington, DC 20001
Ph: (202)326-5500

Baird, Andrew, President
Wound Healing Society [15074]
9650 Rockville Pke.
Bethesda, MD 20814-3998
Ph: (301)634-7600

Baird, Daniel D., Chmn. of the Bd.
National Surgical Assistant Associa-
tion [17396]
1775 Eye St. NW, Ste. 1150
Washington, DC 20006
Ph: (206)266-9951
Toll Free: 855-270-6722
Fax: (202)587-5610

Baird, Lisa, Exec. Dir.
World Molecular Imaging Society
[15752]
6162 Bristol Pky.
Culver City, CA 90230
Ph: (310)215-9730
Fax: (310)215-9731

Baish, Mary Alice, Contact
Americans for Fair Electronic Com-
merce Transactions [995]
111 G St. NW
Washington, DC 20001
Ph: (202)662-9200

Baitani, Smart P., Exec. Dir.,
Founder
Community Solutions for Africa's
Development [11342]
7111 Merrimac Ln. N
Osseo, MN 55311-3829
Ph: (612)644-9905

Bajek, Mike, President
Aquatic Animal Life Support Opera-
tors [6810]
1032 Irving St., No. 902
San Francisco, CA 94122
Ph: (702)503-6472
    (952)431-9539

Bak, Kelita Svoboda, CEO
National Youth Leadership Council
[8200]
1667 Snelling Ave. N, Ste. D300
Saint Paul, MN 55108
Ph: (651)631-3672
Fax: (651)631-2955

Baker, Alex, CIO
Tau Kappa Epsilon [23935]
7439 Woodland Dr., Ste. 100
Indianapolis, IN 46278
Ph: (317)872-6533
Fax: (317)875-8353

Baker, Amy, Exec. Dir.
2Seeds Network [3533]
920 U St. NW
Washington, DC 20001
Ph: (202)697-9565

Baker, Andrew M., Chairman
Forensic Sciences Foundation
[5246]
410 N 21st St.
Colorado Springs, CO 80904
Ph: (719)636-1100
Fax: (719)636-1993

Baker, Anjanette, Mgr.
American Genetic Association [6664]
c/o Anjanette Baker, Manager
2030 SE Marine Science Dr.
Newport, OR 97365
Ph: (541)264-5612

Baker, Aspen, Exec. Dir., Founder
Exhale **[10429]**
1714 Franklin St., No. 100-141
Oakland, CA 94612
Ph: (510)446-7900
Fax: (309)410-1127

Baker, Brook, Analyst
Health Global Access Project
[10544]
540 President St., 3rd Fl.
Brooklyn, NY 11215
Ph: (347)263-8438
Fax: (347)263-8439

Baker, Carl P., President
American Bicycle Polo Association
[23068]
305 Magnolia Lake Ct.
Aiken, SC 29803-2654
Ph: (803)648-4993

Baker, Carol J., MD, Chairperson
Childhood Influenza Immunization
Coalition **[15376]**
7201 Wisconsin Ave., Ste. 750
Bethesda, MD 20814-4850
Ph: (301)656-0003
Fax: (301)907-0878

Baker, Chuck, President
National Railroad Construction and
Maintenance Association, Inc.
[2839]
500 New Jersey Ave. NW, Ste. 400
Washington, DC 20001
Ph: (202)715-1264
Fax: (202)318-0867

Baker, David, Exec. Dir.
Council for Art Education **[7510]**

Baker, David H., Gen. Counsel
Lighter Association **[1571]**
5614 Connecticut Ave. NW, No. 292
Washington, DC 20015
Ph: (202)253-4347
Fax: (202)330-5092

Baker, David H., Gen. Counsel
Plastic Shipping Container Institute
[841]
5614 Connecticut Ave. NW, No. 284
Washington, DC 20015
Ph: (202)253-4347
Fax: (202)330-5092

Baker, David H., Exec. Dir.
Writing Instrument Manufacturers
Association **[3179]**
1701 Pennsylvania Ave. NW, Ste.
300
Washington, DC 20006

Baker, David P., Chairperson
Comparative and International
Education Society **[8112]**
19 Mantua Rd.
Mount Royal, NJ 08061-1006
Ph: (856)423-3629

Baker, David, V. Chmn. of the Exec.
Committee
Swedish Council of America **[19664]**
3030 W River Pky.
Minneapolis, MN 55406
Ph: (612)871-0593

Baker, Dean, Director
Center for Economic and Policy
Research **[18165]**
1611 Connecticut Ave. NW, Ste. 400
Washington, DC 20009
Ph: (202)293-5380
Fax: (202)588-1356

Baker, Don, Director
Electronic Components Certification
Corporation **[1042]**

1002 Shell Ave.
Midland, TX 79705

Baker, Dona Cosgrove, Founder,
President
Feral Cat Caretakers' Coalition
[3624]
PO Box 491244
Los Angeles, CA 90049
Ph: (310)820-4122

Baker, Doris, President
Women Writing the West **[3521]**
8547 E Arapahoe Rd., No. J-541
Greenwood Village, CO 80112-1436

Baker, Edward, Secretary, Treasurer
Association for Living History, Farm
and Agricultural Museums **[9824]**
8774 Route 45 NW
North Bloomfield, OH 44450
Ph: (440)685-4410
Fax: (440)685-4410

Baker, Elgan, PhD, President
American Board of Psychological
Hypnosis **[15356]**
1509 Richie Hwy., Ste. F
Spectrum Behavioral Health
1509 Ritchie Hwy., Ste. F
Arnold, MD 21012
Ph: (410)757-2077

Baker, Dr. Elsworth F., Founder
American College of Orgonomy
[16450]
PO Box 490
Princeton, NJ 08542
Ph: (732)821-1144
Fax: (732)821-0174

Baker, Dr. Eva, Director
National Center for Research on
Evaluation, Standards, and
Student Testing **[7788]**
UCLA CSE/CRESST
GSE&IS Bldg., 3rd Fl.
300 Charles E. Young Dr. N
Los Angeles, CA 90095-1522
Ph: (310)206-1101
Fax: (310)825-3883

Baker, Jack, President
Trail of Tears Association **[10048]**
1100 N University Ave., Ste. 143
Little Rock, AR 72207
Ph: (501)666-9032
Fax: (501)666-5875

Baker, Jeff, PhD, Exec. Dir.
Association of Psychology
Postdoctoral and Internship
Centers **[8312]**
Onyx One, Ste. 170
17225 El Camino Real
Houston, TX 77058-2748
Ph: (832)284-4080
Fax: (832)284-4079

Baker, John, Contact
Discovery Owners Association, Inc.
[22421]
PO Box 95
Saint George, UT 84771-0095
Toll Free: 888-594-6818

Baker, Ms. M. Angela, Director
Association for Gerontology in
Higher Education **[7940]**
1220 L St. NW, Ste. 901
Washington, DC 20005-4001
Ph: (202)289-9806
Fax: (202)289-9824

Baker, Margery F., Exec. VP
People for the American Way
[17924]
1101 15th St. NW, Ste. 600

Washington, DC 20005
Ph: (202)467-4999

Baker, Mark, President, CEO
Aircraft Owners and Pilots Associa-
tion **[124]**
421 Aviation Way
Frederick, MD 21701
Ph: (301)695-2000
Toll Free: 800-872-2672
Fax: (301)695-2375

Baker, Mark, President
International Council of Aircraft
Owner and Pilot Associations **[142]**
421 Aviation Way
Frederick, MD 21701
Ph: (301)695-2220
Fax: (301)695-2375

Baker, Hon. Nannette A.,
Chairperson
National Conference of Federal Trial
Judges **[5394]**
American Bar Association, Judicial
Division
321 N Clark St., 19th Fl.
Chicago, IL 60654
Toll Free: 800-238-2667

Baker, Norman L., Asst. Treas.
Fourth Marine Division Association
[21195]
3 Black Skimmer Ct.
Beaufort, SC 29907

Baker, Peggy, President
Operation First Response **[10750]**
20037 Dove Hill Rd.
Culpeper, VA 22701
Toll Free: 888-289-0280
Fax: (888)505-2795

Baker, Dr. Phillip J., Exec. Dir.
American Lyme Disease Foundation
[14558]
PO Box 466
Lyme, CT 06371

Baker, Rob, Exec. Dir.
The League of Young Voters **[18912]**
540 President St., 3rd Fl.
Brooklyn, NY 11215
Ph: (347)464-8683

Baker, Ron, Co-Pres.
Gale Storm Appreciation Society
[23993]
PO Box 212
Coalton, OH 45621-0212

Baker, Sally J., Dir. of Public Rel.
American Association of Equine
Practitioners **[17593]**
4033 Iron Works Pky.
Lexington, KY 40511
Ph: (859)233-0147
Toll Free: 800-443-0177
Fax: (859)233-1968

Baker, Stephen, Chairman
Theta Xi **[23938]**
745 Craig Rd., Ste.222
Saint Louis, MO 63141
Toll Free: 800-783-6294
Fax: (314)993-8760

Baker, Steve, Treasurer
National Association of Presbyterian
Scouters **[12854]**
c/o Steve Baker, Treasurer
5620 Charlott St.
Fort Worth, TX 76112
Ph: (301)948-7121
(512)458-9889

Baker, Walter E., Administrator
Storage Performance Council **[7238]**
643 Bair Island Rd., Ste. 103

Redwood City, CA 94063
Ph: (650)556-9384
Fax: (650)556-9385

Baker, Will, Advisor
International Organization of Black
Security Executives **[3061]**
2340 Powell St., No. 327
Emeryville, CA 94608
Ph: (510)648-4292

Bakke, Dennis, Co-Ch., Treasurer
Mustard Seed Foundation **[20443]**
7115 Leesburg Pke., Ste. 304
Falls Church, VA 22043
Ph: (703)524-5620

Bakken, Ms. Vickie, Treasurer
National Council of the United
States, International Organization
of Good Templars **[19449]**
PO Box 202238
Minneapolis, MN 55420-7238
Ph: (952)210-0382

Baksa, Barbara, Exec. Dir.
National Association of Stock Plan
Professionals **[1285]**
PO Box 21639
Concord, CA 94521-0639
Ph: (925)685-9271
Fax: (925)930-9284

Bal, Kevin, President
Alpha Delta Gamma **[23880]**
1100 Rockhurst Rd.
Kansas City, MO 64110

Balachandran, S., Treasurer
Alpha Pi Mu **[23736]**
3005 Lancaster Dr.
Blacksburg, VA 24060
Ph: (540)553-2043

Balakgie, Carla, President, CEO
National Automatic Merchandising
Association **[3431]**
20 N Wacker Dr., Ste. 3500
Chicago, IL 60606
Ph: (312)346-0370
Fax: (312)704-4140

Balakrishnan, Usha R., Chairman,
CEO, President
CARTHA **[913]**
85 Leamer Ct.
Iowa City, IA 52246

Balas, Calaneet H., CEO
Ovarian Cancer National Alliance
[14038]
1101 14th St. NW, Ste. 850
Washington, DC 20005
Ph: (202)331-1332
Toll Free: 866-399-6262
Fax: (202)331-2292

Balazinska, Magdalena, Treasurer
Association for Computing
Machinery - Special Interest Group
on Management of Data **[6238]**
c/o Magdalena Balazinska,
Treasurer
Computer Science & Engineering
University of Washington, Box
352350
Seattle, WA 98195-2350
Ph: (206)616-1069

Balcells, Cristy, RN, Exec. Dir.
MitoAction **[15828]**
PO Box 51474
Boston, MA 02205
Toll Free: 888-648-6228

Balcomb, Janissa, President
Laptops to Lesotho **[11066]**
55 Eagle Creek Rd.

Wayan, ID 83285
Ph: (208)574-2990

Baldacchino, Joseph, President
National Humanities Institute [8007]
PO Box 1387
Bowie, MD 20718-1387
Ph: (301)464-4277

Baldacci, Karen, Chairperson
Leadership to Keep Children Alcohol
Free [13150]
2933 Lower Bellbrook Rd.
Spring Valley, OH 45370
Ph: (937)848-2993

Baldauf, Jim, Founder
Association for the Study of Peak Oil
and Gas U.S.A. [6999]
1725 Eye St. NW, Ste. 300
Washington, DC 20006
Ph: (202)470-4809

Balderrama, Arturo, Founder
National Puro Conjunto Music As-
sociation [9978]
9200 Lockwood Springs Rd.
Manor, TX 78653
Ph: (512)853-0034

Balducci, Lodovico, MD, Director
Geriatric Oncology Consortium
[16344]
672 E Old Mill Rd., No. 187
Millersville, MD 21108
Ph: (410)941-9744
Toll Free: 888-437-4662
Fax: (410)467-4100

Balduino, William, President
Credit Research Foundation [1230]
1812 Baltimore Blvd., Ste. H
Westminster, MD 21157
Ph: (443)821-3000
Fax: (443)821-3627

Baldwin, Charles, CFO
Distance Education Accrediting
Commission [7994]
1101 17th St. NW, Ste. 808
Washington, DC 20036
Ph: (202)234-5100
Fax: (202)332-1386

Baldwin, Cris, President
Women on Wheels Motorcycle As-
sociation [23043]
PO Box 83076
Lincoln, NE 68501-3076
Ph: (402)477-1280

Baldwin, Hayden B., Exec. Dir.
International Crime Scene Investiga-
tors Association [5248]
PMB 385
15774 S LaGrange Rd.
Orland Park, IL 60462
Ph: (708)460-8082

Baldwin, Jason, Founder
Proclaim Justice [18074]
2303 RR 620 S
Lakeway, TX 78734
Ph: (512)605-7525

Baldwin, Melissa, Program Mgr.
SAVE International [6724]
19 Mantua Rd.
Mount Royal, NJ 08061
Ph: (856)423-3215
Fax: (856)423-3420

Baldwin, Phillip N., Chmn. of the Bd.
United Way Worldwide [11863]
701 N Fairfax St.
Alexandria, VA 22314-2045
Ph: (703)836-7112

Baldwin, Tom, President
American Association of Veterinary
Laboratory Diagnosticians [17604]

PO Box 6396
Visalia, CA 93290-6396
Ph: (559)781-8900
Fax: (559)781-8989

Bale, Peter, CEO
Center for Public Integrity [18315]
910 17th St. NW, Ste. 700
Washington, DC 20006
Ph: (202)466-1300
    (202)481-1232

Bales, Kevin, Founder, President
Free the Slaves [12034]
1320 19th St. NW, Ste. 600
Washington, DC 20036
Ph: (202)775-7480
Fax: (202)775-7485

Balestrery, Jean E., Fac. Memb.
Council on Sexual Orientation and
Gender Identity and Expression
[8570]
Council on Social Work Education
1701 Duke St., Ste. 200
Alexandria, VA 22314-3457
Ph: (703)683-8080
Fax: (703)683-8099

Balian, Rita, CEO, President
Armenian American Cultural As-
sociation, Inc [8823]
1300 Crystal Dr., Ste. 1504
Arlington, VA 22202
Ph: (703)416-2555

Baliozian, Kevin, Exec. Dir.
American Academy of Medical
Administrators [15566]
330 N Wabash 2000
Chicago, IL 60611

Baliozian, Kevin, Exec. Dir.
Medical Library Association [9716]
65 E Wacker Pl., Ste. 1900
Chicago, IL 60601-7246
Ph: (312)419-9094
Fax: (312)419-8950

Balk, Dr. Melvin W., Exec. Dir.
American College of Laboratory
Animal Medicine [17613]
96 Chester St.
Chester, NH 03036
Ph: (603)887-2467
Fax: (603)887-0096

Balko, Gregg, Secretary
Society for the Advancement of
Material and Process Engineering
[6587]
1161 Park View Dr., Ste. 200
Covina, CA 91724-3759
Ph: (626)331-0616
Toll Free: 800-562-7360
Fax: (626)332-8929

Ball, Andrea, Exec. Dir.
American Mothers [11812]
1701 K St. NW, Ste. 650
Washington, DC 20006
Toll Free: 877-242-4264

Ball, Antoinette, CEO, Founder
Women's Entrepreneurial Op-
portunity Project, Inc. [19248]
250 Georgia Ave., Ste. 213
Atlanta, GA 30312
Ph: (404)681-2497
Fax: (404)681-2499

Ball, Joe, President
Society of the Third Infantry Division,
United States Army [20726]
510 W York St.
Blue Hill, NE 68930

Ball, Karen L., President, CEO
Sturge-Weber Foundation [15993]
1240 Sussex Tpke., Ste. 1

Randolph, NJ 07869
Ph: (973)895-4445
Toll Free: 800-627-5482
Fax: (973)895-4846

Ball, Stephen, Coord.
Dance Educators of America [7700]
PO Box 740387
Boynton Beach, FL 33474
Ph: (914)636-3200

Ball, Trent, Chairman
Council for Opportunity in Education
[7819]
1025 Vermont Ave. NW, Ste. 900
Washington, DC 20005-3516
Ph: (202)347-7430
Fax: (202)347-0786

Ballantyne, Larry, Secretary
United States Stamp Society
[22378]
c/o Nicholas Lombardi, President
PO Box 1005
Mountainside, NJ 07092-0005

Ballard, Terri, Exec. Dir.
Scott Joplin International Ragtime
Foundation [10000]
111 W 5th St.
Sedalia, MO 65301
Ph: (660)826-2271
Toll Free: 866-218-6258

Ballas, Stephen, President
North American Shippers Association
[3099]
1600 St. Georges Ave., Ste. 301
Rahway, NJ 07065
Ph: (732)850-7610
Fax: (732)340-9133

Ballen, Kenneth, President
Terror Free Tomorrow [19187]
5335 Wisconsin Ave. NW, Ste. 440
Washington, DC 20015-2052
Ph: (202)274-1800
Fax: (202)274-1821

Ballenger, Buzz, President
International Flying Dutchman Class
Association of the U.S. [22630]
c/o Chris Liberti, Secretary-
Treasurer, 60 Spring Hill Rd.
60 Spring Hill Rd.
Kingston, RI 02881-1806
Ph: (401)487-3062

Ballentine, Debbie, Director
International Ticketing Association
[1146]
5868 E 71st St., Ste. E-367
Indianapolis, IN 46290
Ph: (212)629-4036

Balliett, Suzy, Founder
Biomagnetic Therapy Association
[17439]
PO Box 394
Lyons, CO 80540
Ph: (303)823-0307

Ballweg, Mary Lou, Exec. Dir.,
President
Endometriosis Association [16283]
8585 N 76th Pl.
Milwaukee, WI 53223
Ph: (414)355-2200
Fax: (414)355-6065

Balmaseda, Clarissa M., President
National Association of Asian
American Law Enforcement Com-
manders [5486]
PO Box 70581
Oakland, CA 94612

Baloche, Lynda, Co-Pres.
International Association for the
Study of Cooperation in Education
[7679]

11 South Rd.
Readfield, ME 04355
Ph: (207)685-3171

Balsam, Kimberly, President
Society for the Psychological Study
of Lesbian, Gay, Bisexual and
Transgender Issues [16941]
c/o Brenda J. Marston, Curator
Cornell University
Human Sexuality Collection and
Library Women's Studies Selector
2B Carl A Kroch Library
Ithaca, NY 14853

Bancheri, Salvatore, President
American Association of Teachers of
Italian [8172]
c/o Colleen M. Ryan
626 Ballantine Hall
Department of French and Italian
Indiana University
Bloomington, IN 47405
Ph: (815)855-1429

Banchik, Dr. Mark E., President
American Philatelic Congress
[22300]
c/o Dr. Michael D. Dixon, Second
Vice President
7321 SE Taylor St.
Portland, OR 97215-2262
Ph: (415)861-0515

Bancroft, Betzy, Bd. Member
United Plant Savers [13662]
PO Box 147
Rutland, OH 45775
Ph: (740)742-3455

Bancroft, Ms. Connie, Exec. Dir.
Teachers Saving Children Inc.
[19073]
PO Box 125
Damascus, OH 44619-0125
Ph: (330)821-2747

Bancroft, Elizabeth A., Exec. Dir.
Association of Former Intelligence
Officers [5357]
7700 Leesburg Pke., Ste. 324
Falls Church, VA 22043
Ph: (703)790-0320
Fax: (703)991-1278

Bandera, Memory, Founder
Tariro: Hope and Health for
Zimbabwe's Orphans [11164]
PO Box 50273
Eugene, OR 97405
Ph: (541)729-2972

Bandstra, Richard, Exec. Dir.
Association for a More Just Society
[17877]
PO Box 888631
Grand Rapids, MI 49588
Toll Free: 800-897-1135

Banerjee, Paula, President
International Association for the
Study of Forced Migration [9797]
c/o Institute for the Study of
International Migration
Georgetown University
3300 Whitehaven St. NW, Ste. 3100
Washington, DC 20007
Ph: (202)687-2258
Fax: (202)687-2541

Bang, Avery Louise, CEO
Bridges to Prosperity [12798]
1031 33rd St., Ste. 170
Denver, CO 80205
Ph: (757)784-5071

Banga, Ajaypal S., Chairman
Financial Services Roundtable [398]
600 13th St. NW, Ste. 400

Washington, DC 20005
Ph: (202)289-4322
Fax: (202)628-2507

Bankhead, Jordan, Chairman
Citizens for Global Solutions [18776]
420 7th St. SE
Washington, DC 20003-2707
Ph: (202)546-3950

Banks, Brenda, President
Society of American Archivists
[8822]
17 N State St., Ste. 1425
Chicago, IL 60602-4061
Ph: (312)606-0722
Toll Free: 866-722-7858
Fax: (312)606-0728

Banks, Caroline, President
Million Dollar Round Table [1885]
325 W Touhy Ave.
Park Ridge, IL 60068-4265
Ph: (847)692-6378
Fax: (847)518-8921

Banks, Sonja L., COO, President
Sickle Cell Disease Association of
America [15244]
3700 Koppers St., Ste. 570
Baltimore, MD 21227-1019
Ph: (410)528-1555
Toll Free: 800-421-8453
Fax: (410)528-1495

Bannerman, Alexander N., President
Flagon and Trencher Descendants
of Colonial Tavern Keepers
[20752]
1716 Bigley Ave.
Charleston, WV 25302-3938
Ph: (304)340-0200

Banning, Kobina, Founder, President
Fusion Architecture [5968]
PO Box 66853
Phoenix, AZ 85082-6853

Bannister, James R., Exec. Dir.
Association for Financial Technology
[66]
c/o Jeannine Windbigler, Managing
Director
96 Northwoods Blvd., Ste. B2
Columbus, OH 43235
Ph: (614)895-1208
Fax: (614)436-6181

Bannon, Dr. Kris, President
American Veterinary Dental Society
[17628]
PO Box 803
Fayetteville, TN 37334
Ph: (931)438-0238
Toll Free: 800-332-2837
Fax: (931)433-6289

Bannura, Ramzi, Treasurer
J/80 Class Association [22642]
c/o Chris Chadwick, President
433 Fairmont Ln.
Weston, FL 33326
Ph: (860)539-3938

Bannwarth, Amanda, Exec. Dir.
Aviation Insurance Association
[1841]
7200 W 75th St.
Overland Park, KS 66204
Ph: (913)627-9632
Fax: (913)381-2515

Banuelos, Cristina, President
Latinas Promoviendo Comunidad/
Lambda Pi Chi Sorority [23801]
PO Box 1522
New York, NY 10028

Banzer, Cindy, President
Alfa Romeo Owners Club [21314]
c/o Barbara Clark, Administrator

PO Box 92155
Portland, OR 97292
Ph: (816)459-7462

Bao, Dr. Shuming, Exec. Dir.
Chinese Economists Society [6386]
330 Packard St.
Ann Arbor, MI 48104-2910
Ph: (734)647-9610
Fax: (734)763-0335

Bapna, Manish, Exec. VP, Managing
Dir.
World Resources Institute [3973]
10 G St. NE, Ste. 800
Washington, DC 20002
Ph: (202)729-7600
(202)729-7602
Fax: (202)729-7610

Baptista, Prof. Carlos A.C., PhD,
President
International Society for Plastination
[16587]
Dept. of Neurosciences
College of Medicine and Life Sci-
ences
University of Toledo
3000 Arlington Ave.
Toledo, OH 43614-2598
Ph: (419)383-4283
Fax: (419)383-3008

Baquerizo, Maria Rosa, CEO
Venezuelan American Association of
the United States [23668]
641 Lexington Ave., Ste. 1430
New York, NY 10022
Ph: (212)233-7776

Barak, Gregg, Editor
Global Options [18980]
PO Box 40601
San Francisco, CA 94140-0601
Ph: (415)550-1703

Barak, Dr. Jacob, MBA, CEO,
President
Postgraduate Center for Mental
Health [16987]
Westside Rehabilitation Ctr.
344 W 36th St.
New York, NY 10018-1843
Ph: (212)889-5500

Barallon, Matthew, President
Pediatric Association of Naturopathic
Physicians [15866]
PO Box 20665
Juneau, AK 99802

Baranoski, Andrew, Exec. Dir.
American Civic Association [12122]
131 Front St.
Binghamton, NY 13905-3101
Ph: (607)723-9419
Fax: (607)723-0023

Baranski-Walker, Donna, Exec. Dir.,
Founder
Rebuilding Alliance [11990]
1818 Gilbreth Rd.
Burlingame, CA 94010
Ph: (650)325-4663
(650)651-7156

Baras, Regina, Exec. Dir.
Healthcare Laundry Accreditation
Council [2078]
PO Box 1306
Plainfield, IL 60544
Ph: (815)436-1404
Toll Free: 855-277-4522
Fax: (815)436-1403

Baravik, Jeff, President
American Association of Public
Health Veterinarians [17598]

PO Box 66419
Albuquerque, NM 87193

Barazandeh, Vajeh, Contact
Society of Iranian-American Women
for Education [8123]
PO Box 572371
Houston, TX 77257
Ph: (713)532-6666

Barba, Martha M., Founder,
President
International Institute of
Photographic Arts [2584]
1690 Frontage Rd.
Chula Vista, CA 91911
Ph: (619)628-1466

Barbara, Rosina, VP of Fin. &
Admin.
Ms. Foundation for Women [18219]
12 MetroTech Ctr., 26th Fl.
Brooklyn, NY 11201
Ph: (212)742-2300
Fax: (212)742-1653

Barbarone, Toni, Officer
Print Services and Distribution As-
sociation [3177]
330 N Wabash Ave., Ste. 2000
Chicago, IL 60611
Toll Free: 800-230-0175
Fax: (312)673-6880

Barbato, Steven, Exec. Dir.
International Technology and
Engineering Educators Association
[8669]
1914 Association Dr., Ste. 201
Reston, VA 20191-1539
Ph: (703)860-2100
Fax: (703)860-0353

Barbee, Mike, President
National Association of Scale Aero-
modelers [22202]
c/o Tina Patton, Secretary-Treasurer
572 Cedar Pointe Dr.
Somerset, KY 42501

Barbee, Mike, Officer
U.S. Scale Masters Association
[22206]
c/o Mitchell Baker
2878 Mariposa Dr.
Terre Haute, IN 47803
Ph: (760)807-5519
(812)236-5351

Barber, Arthur H., III, Liaison
National Association of Rocketry
[22201]
PO Box 407
Marion, IA 52302-0407
Toll Free: 800-262-4872
Fax: (319)373-8910

Barber, David G., President
American Canal Society [9369]
117 Main St.
Freemansburg, PA 18017-7231
Ph: (610)691-0956

Barber, Donna, Exec. Dir., Founder
Global Orphan Outreach [11002]
PO Box 193
Ladysmith, WI 54848
Ph: (715)415-4401

Barber, Karla R., President
Women for Winesense [22479]
3121 Park Ave., Ste. C
Soquel, CA 95073
Ph: (831)464-4893

Barber, Lois, Exec. Dir.
Alliance for Renewable Energy
[6448]

PO Box 63
Amherst, MA 01004
Ph: (413)549-8118

Barber, Lois, Exec. Dir., President
EarthAction International [4054]
44 N Prospect St.
Amherst, MA 01002
Ph: (413)427-8827
Fax: (413)256-8871

Barber, Mary E., MD, President
Association of Women Psychiatrists
[16828]
PO Box 570218
Dallas, TX 75357-0218
Ph: (972)613-0985
Fax: (972)613-5532

Barbera, Robert J., Chmn. of the
Bd., President
Americanism Educational Leaders
[18278]
610 W Foothill Blvd.
Monrovia, CA 91016
Ph: (626)357-7733

Barberio, Doug, Chairman
Ontario and Western Railway
Historical Society [10187]
22 Cottage St.
Middletown, NY 10940
Ph: (845)283-2637

Barbier, Keith, President
American Association of State
Troopers [5453]
1949 Raymond Diehl Rd.
Tallahassee, FL 32308
Toll Free: 800-765-5456
Fax: (850)385-8697

Barbiers, Robyn, President
Anti-Cruelty Society [10588]
157 W Grand Ave.
Chicago, IL 60654
Ph: (312)644-8338
Fax: (312)644-3878

Barboriak, Daniel P., MD, President
American Society of Functional Neu-
roradiology [17045]
800 Enterprise Dr., Ste. 205
Oak Brook, IL 60523
Ph: (630)574-0220
Fax: (630)574-0661

Barbour, Fr. Hugh, Director
Aid to the Church in Need [19788]
725 Leonard St.
Brooklyn, NY 11222-2350
Ph: (718)609-0939
Toll Free: 800-628-6333

Barcan, Cristian, VP
The Vinyl Institute [2633]
1747 Pennsylvania Ave. NW, Ste.
825
Washington, DC 20006
Ph: (202)765-2200
Fax: (202)765-2275

Barchiesi, Robert C., President
International Anticounterfeiting Coali-
tion [18052]
1730 M St. NW, Ste. 1020
Washington, DC 20036
Ph: (202)223-6667

Barck, Patrick, Secretary
Society for Ear, Nose, and Throat
Advances in Children [16540]
32 West 200 South, No. 105
Salt Lake City, UT 84101
Ph: (407)650-7440
Fax: (407)650-7955

Barclay, Gregory P., Contact
American Society for Adolescent
Psychiatry [16823]

PO Box 570218
Dallas, TX 75357-0218
Ph: (972)613-0985
　　(866)672-9060
Fax: (972)613-5532

Barclay, Tony, Treasurer
National Peace Corps Association
　[18848]
1900 L St. NW, Ste. 610
Washington, DC 20036
Ph: (202)293-7728
Fax: (202)293-7554

Bardach, Emily, Exec. Dir.
Women in Government Relations
　[18323]
8400 Westpark Dr., 2nd Fl.
McLean, VA 22102
Ph: (703)610-9030
Fax: (703)995-0528

Bardi, Amy, Founder
Clothed in Hope [13036]
314 Bonniewood Dr.
Cary, NC 27518

Bardo, Stacy, Co-Chmn. of the Bd.
National Association of Consumer
　Advocates [18053]
1215 17th St. NW, 5th Fl.
Washington, DC 20036-3021
Ph: (202)452-1989
Fax: (202)452-0099

Barfield, Steve, Editor
Iron Overload Diseases Association
　[15826]
525 Mayflower Rd.
West Palm Beach, FL 33405
Ph: (561)586-8246

Barfield, Thomas, President
American Institute for Afghanistan
　Studies [19285]
Boston University
232 Bay State Rd., Rm. 426
Boston, MA 02215
Ph: (617)358-4649
Fax: (617)358-4650

Barford, Mark, CEO
National Hardwood Lumber Associa-
　tion [1443]
6830 Raleigh LaGrange Rd.
Memphis, TN 38134
Ph: (901)377-1818
Toll Free: 800-933-0318

Bargerstock, Burton, Chmn. of the
　Exec. Committee
International Association for
　Research on Service-Learning and
　Community Engagement [7647]
Tulane University Ctr. for Public
　Service
Alcee Fortier Hall
6823 St. Charles Ave.
New Orleans, LA 70118
Ph: (504)862-3366

Barikzai, M. Ilias, Director
Afghans4Tomorrow [11306]
4699 Apple Way
Boulder, CO 80301

Barineau, Leslie, Secretary
National Conference of Bar Founda-
　tions [5441]
Division for Bar Services
321 N Clark St., Ste. 1600
Chicago, IL 60654
Ph: (312)988-5344
Fax: (312)988-5492

Baris, David H., Esq., President
American Association of Bank Direc-
　tors [377]

1250 24th St. NW, Ste. 700
Washington, DC 20037-1222
Ph: (202)463-4888
Fax: (202)349-8080

Barkan, Elazar, Director
Columbia University I Institute for the
　Study of Human Rights [18385]
Riverside Church Twr., 7th Fl.
91 Claremont Ave.
New York, NY 10027
Ph: (212)854-2479

Barker, Hal, Founder
Korean War Project [5837]
PO Box 180190
Dallas, TX 75218-0190
Ph: (214)320-0342

Barker, Jennifer, Exec. Dir., Founder
Per Diems Against Poverty [12106]
3315 Glen Flora Way
Fort Smith, AR 72908

Barker, John, President
T-Ten Class Association [22672]
2655 S Belvoir Blvd.
University Heights, OH 44118
Ph: (330)592-5243

Barker, Jonathan, Secretary
Giant Screen Cinema Association
　[3277]
624 Holly Springs Rd., Ste. 243
Holly Springs, NC 27540
Ph: (919)346-1123
Fax: (919)573-9100

Barker, Marc, President
National Association of Veterans
　Program Administrators [21131]
c/o Marc Barker, President
Colorado State University
Asst. Registrar, Military & Veterans
　Benefits
1063 Campus Delivery
Fort Collins, CO 80523-1063
Ph: (970)491-1342
Fax: (970)491-2283

Barker, Marcia S., Exec. Dir.,
　Founder
Adoption Information Services
　[10439]
1840 Old Nocross Rd., Ste. 400
Lawrenceville, GA 30044
Ph: (770)339-7236
Fax: (770)456-5961

Barker, Mike, President
Professional Ropes Course Associa-
　tion [2470]
6260 E Riverside Blvd., No. 104
Loves Park, IL 61111
Ph: (815)986-7776
Fax: (815)637-2964

Barkman, Brent, Chairperson
National Honey Board [1359]
11409 Business Park Cir., Ste. No.
　210
Firestone, CO 80504-9200
Ph: (303)776-2337

Barlera, Paolo, Officer
Istituto Italiano di Cultura [9613]
686 Park Ave.
New York, NY 10065-5009
Ph: (212)879-4242
Fax: (212)861-4018

Barlerin, Michael, Exec. Dir.
Leading Jewelers of the World
　[2057]
500 7th Ave., Ste. 12B
New York, NY 10018-4502
Ph: (212)398-6401
Fax: (212)398-6406

Barley, David D., CEO
National Ovarian Cancer Coalition
　[14030]
2501 Oak Lawn Ave., Ste. 435
Dallas, TX 75219
Ph: (214)273-4200
Toll Free: 888-682-7426
Fax: (214)273-4201

Barlow, Julie, Trustee
Institute of Current World Affairs
　[19263]
1779 Massachusetts Ave. NW, Ste.
　615
Washington, DC 20036
Ph: (202)364-4068

Barlow, Roger, President
The Catfish Institute [3639]
6311 Ridgewood Rd., Ste. W404
Jackson, MS 39211
Ph: (601)977-9559

Barlow, Zenobia, Exec. Dir.
Center for Ecoliteracy [3994]
The David Brower Ctr.
2150 Allston Way, Ste. 270
Berkeley, CA 94704-1377
Ph: (510)845-4595

Barmash, Mona, President
Congenital Heart Information
　Network [14110]

Barna, Blair, President
Association of Alternative Newsme-
　dia [2658]
116 Cass St.
Traverse City, MI 49684
Ph: (231)487-2261

Barnaby, Charles, President
International Building Performance
　Simulation Association [536]
c/o Michael Wetter, Treasurer
Lawrence Berkeley National Labora-
　tory
1 Cyclotron Rd.
Berkeley, CA 94720
Ph: (902)486-4000

Barnard, Linda Garcia, Dir. of Opera-
　tions
9 to 5 Working Women Education
　Fund [18200]
207 E Buffalo St., Ste. 211
Milwaukee, WI 53202
Ph: (414)274-0925
Fax: (414)272-2870

Barnard, Neal D., MD, President
Physicians Committee for
　Responsible Medicine [14960]
5100 Wisconsin Ave. NW, Ste. 400
Washington, DC 20016
Ph: (202)686-2210
Toll Free: 866-416-PCRM
Fax: (202)686-2216

Barndt, Kristen, Contact
Bluefaced Leicester Union of North
　America [4667]
PO Box 2304
Frisco, TX 75034
Ph: (610)905-1136

Barnes, Brandy, CEO, Founder
DiabetesSisters [14532]
2530 Meridian Pkwy., Ste. 2123
Durham, NC 27713
Ph: (919)361-2012
Toll Free: 855-361-2012

Barnes, Doug, Leader
Freedom Socialist Party [19141]
4710 University Way NE, No. 102
Seattle, WA 98105
Ph: (206)985-4621
Fax: (206)985-8965

Barnes, Greg, Director
American Safe Climbing Association
　[21596]
PO Box 3691
Boulder, CO 80307

Barnes, Ian, President
Project Kesho [11208]
PO Box 677
Bellevue, WA 98009
Ph: (206)501-0758

Barnes, Jim, Managing Dir.
Institute for Supply Management
　[2817]
2055 E Centennial Cir.
Tempe, AZ 85284
Ph: (480)752-6276
Toll Free: 800-888-6276
Fax: (480)752-7890

Barnes, Kenneth, Exec. Dir.
Omega Psi Phi Fraternity [23909]
3951 Snapfinger Pky.
Decatur, GA 30035
Ph: (404)284-5533
Fax: (404)284-0333

Barnes, Patrick J., FLMI, President
Fraternal Field Managers' Associa-
　tion [1856]
c/o Patrick J. Barnes, FLMI
Modern Woodmen of America
1701 1st Ave.
Rock Island, IL 61201-8724
Ph: (309)786-6481

Barnes, Susan, Treasurer
Center for Governmental Research
　[18966]
1 S Washington St., Ste. 400
Rochester, NY 14614
Ph: (585)325-6360
Toll Free: 888-388-8521

Barnes, Teresa, Co-Ch.
Association of Concerned Africa
　Scholars [17774]
c/o Michael Walker, Treasurer
538 Pacific St., Apt. 5-6
Brooklyn, NY 11217-2280

Barnes, Teveia Rose, Exec. Dir.,
　President
Lawyers For One America [5538]
4136 Redwood Hwy., Ste. 9
San Rafael, CA 94903
Ph: (415)479-3636
Fax: (415)479-3621

Barnett, Lauren
Society for Healthcare Strategy and
　Market Development [15335]
155 N Wacker Dr., Ste. 400
Chicago, IL 60606
Ph: (312)422-3888
Fax: (312)278-0883

Barnett, Melissa, President
Scleral Lens Education Society
　[14299]
c/o Mindy Toabe, Secretary
MetroHealth Medical Ctr.
2500 MetroHealth Dr.
Cleveland, OH 44109

Barnett, Ray, Founder, President
African Children's Choir [8774]
PO Box 29690
Bellingham, WA 98228-1690
Toll Free: 877-532-8651
Fax: (360)752-2402

Barnette, Carrie, Exec. Dir.
American Orff-Schulwerk Association
　[9865]
147 Bell St., Ste. 300
Chagrin Falls, OH 44022
Ph: (440)600-7329
Fax: (440)600-7332

Barney, Dr. Gerald O., Exec. Dir.,
Founder
Our Task **[4094]**
1900 N Harvard St.
Arlington, VA 22201

Barney, William C., President,
Founder
Barney Family Historical Association
[20783]

Barnhart, Carolyn, President
American Association of Family and
Consumer Sciences **[11810]**
400 N Columbus St., Ste. 202
Alexandria, VA 22314
Ph: (703)706-4600
Toll Free: 800-424-8080
Fax: (703)706-4663

Barnhart, Jeffrey E., Exec. Dir.,
Founder
International Card Manufacturers
Association **[2626]**
191 Clarksville Rd.
Princeton Junction, NJ 08550-5391
Ph: (609)799-4900
Fax: (609)799-7032

Barnikow, Al, President
Midstates Jeepster Association
[21432]
7721 Howick Rd.
7721 Howick Rd.
Celina, OH 45822

Barnoti, Pierre, Founder, President
SPCA International **[10697]**
PO Box 8682
New York, NY 10001
Ph: (212)244-7722
Toll Free: 888-690-7722

Barnum, Greg, Chairman, President
Beef4Hunger **[12077]**
PO Box 464
Lake Forest, IL 60045

Barocas, Charles, Exec. Dir.
American Society of Orthopedic
Professionals **[16468]**
PO Box 7440
Seminole, FL 33775
Ph: (727)394-1700

Baron, Caroline, Founder
FilmAid International **[12590]**
234 5th Ave., Ste. 206
New York, NY 10001
Ph: (212)920-3663

Baron, Daniel, Exec. Dir.
School Project Foundation **[7904]**
349 S Walnut St.
Bloomington, IN 47401
Ph: (812)558-0041

Baron, Glenn, Contact
Libros for Learning **[11068]**
7614 Sims Rd.
Waxhaw, NC 28173
Ph: (704)562-4596

Baron, Jessica, Exec. Dir.
Guitars in the Classroom **[8369]**
1911 Shady Acre Cir.
Encinitas, CA 92024
Ph: (760)452-6123

Baron, Krystyna, Librarian
Polish Institute of Arts and Sciences
of America **[10167]**
208 E 30th St.
New York, NY 10016
Ph: (212)686-4164
Fax: (212)545-1130

Baron, Marc, President
The Lambs, Inc. **[10256]**
3 W 51st St.

New York, NY 10019
Ph: (212)586-0306

Baron, Richard J., President, CEO
American Board of Internal Medicine
[15425]
510 Walnut St., Ste. 1700
Philadelphia, PA 19106-3699
Toll Free: 800-441-ABIM
Fax: (215)446-3590

Baroncelli, Brenda, Admin. Asst.
National Center on Deaf-Blindness
[17731]
345 N Monmouth Ave.
Monmouth, OR 97361
Ph: (503)838-8754
Fax: (503)838-8150

Barone, Diane, President
International Literacy Association
[8485]
800 Barksdale Rd.
Newark, DE 19711-3204
Ph: (302)731-1600
Toll Free: 800-336-7323
Fax: (302)731-1057

Baros, Jonathan, VP
Food Distribution Research Society
[6646]
c/o Jonathan Baros, Vice President
for Membership
600 Laureate Way
Kannapolis, NC 28081
Ph: (704)250-5458
Fax: (704)250-5427

Barq, Mirna, President
Syrian-American Council **[18529]**
1875 I St. NW, No. 500
Washington, DC 20006
Ph: (202)429-2099
Fax: (202)429-9574

Barquin, Ramon, President
Computer Ethics Institute **[8496]**
1775 Massachusetts Ave. NW
Washington, DC 20036
Ph: (202)797-6183

Barr, Elizabeth, Mem.
Grailville **[19840]**
932 O Bannonville Rd.
Loveland, OH 45140-9705
Ph: (513)683-2340

Barrasso, Judy, VP
International Society of Barristers
[5825]
210 Science Dr.
Durham, NC 27708-0360
Ph: (919)613-7085

Barratt, John, Chairman
Industrial Designers Society of
America **[6721]**
555 Grove St., Ste. 200
Herndon, VA 20170
Ph: (703)707-6000
Fax: (703)787-8501

Barrere, John, President
Force 5 Class Association **[22614]**
3438 Scupper Run SE
Southport, NC 28461

Barreto, Hector V., Chairman
The Latino Coalition **[9663]**
PO Box 55086
Irvine, CA 92619
Toll Free: 855-852-1995
Fax: (866)496-1944

Barrett, Craig, Chairman
Carnegie Institution for Science
[7088]
1530 P St. NW

Washington, DC 20005
Ph: (202)387-6400
Fax: (202)387-8092

Barrett, David J., Chairman
Center for Communication **[7536]**
195 Plymouth St., Ste. 320
Brooklyn, NY 11201
Ph: (212)686-5005

Barrett, Heidi, Mgr.
Greater Yellowstone Coalition **[3880]**
215 S Wallace Ave.
Bozeman, MT 59715
Ph: (406)586-1593
Toll Free: 800-775-1834

Barrett, James, Chairman
Redefining Progress **[18159]**
1904 Franklin St., Ste. 600
Oakland, CA 94612
Ph: (510)444-3041
Fax: (510)444-3191

Barrett, Dr. Janet R., Editor
Council for Research in Music
Education **[8365]**
University of Illinois Press
1325 S Oak St.
Champaign, IL 61820
Ph: (217)244-0626
Toll Free: 866-244-0626
Fax: (217)244-9910

Barrett, Jerome A., Exec. Dir.
Sleep Research Society **[17221]**
2510 N Frontage Rd.
Darien, IL 60561
Ph: (630)737-9702
Fax: (630)737-9790

Barrett, John, Exec. Dir.
International Sanitary Supply As-
sociation **[2133]**
3300 Dundee Rd.
Northbrook, IL 60062
Ph: (847)982-0800
Toll Free: 800-225-4772
Fax: (847)982-1012

Barrett, Mary Brigid, President,
Exec. Dir.
National Children's Book and
Literacy Alliance **[8249]**
PO Box 1479
Brewster, MA 02631
Ph: (508)533-5851

Barrett, Ron, President
Air Force Navigators Observer Association **[20681]**
c/o James Faulkner, Director
4109 Timberlane
Enid, OK 73703-2825
Ph: (580)242-0526

Barrett, Stephen, Director
Certified Audit of Circulations **[116]**
155 Willowbrook Blvd.
Wayne, NJ 07470
Ph: (973)785-3000

Barrett, Stephen, Bd. Member, Editor
National Council Against Health
Fraud **[18329]**
11312 US 15-501 N, Ste. 107/108
Chapel Hill, NC 27517
Ph: (919)533-6009

Barrett, Stu, President
Tripoli Rocketry Association **[8557]**
PO Box 87
Bellevue, NE 68005
Ph: (402)884-9530
Fax: (402)884-9531

Barrett, Susann, Secretary
American School Band Directors Association **[8360]**

227 N 1st St.
Guttenberg, IA 52052-9010
Ph: (563)252-2500

Barrett, Terry L., Secretary
Independent Order of Odd Fellows
[19599]
422 Trade St.
Winston Salem, NC 27101
Ph: (336)725-5955
Toll Free: 800-235-8358
Fax: (336)722-7317

Barrett, Terry L., Secretary
International Association of Rebekah
Assemblies, IOOF **[19600]**
422 Trade St.
Winston Salem, NC 27101
Ph: (336)725-5955
Toll Free: 800-235-8358
Fax: (336)722-7317

Barrett, Mr. Terry, Secretary
Theta Rho Girls' Club **[13484]**
3440 W 2nd Ave.
Corsicana, TX 75110
Ph: (903)872-7438
Fax: (903)872-7277

Barrette, Margaret Pilaro, Exec. Dir.
Pacific Coast Shellfish Growers As-
sociation **[3035]**
120 State Ave. NE, No. 142
Olympia, WA 98501
Ph: (360)754-2744
Fax: (360)754-2743

Barrientos, June J., Exec. Sec.
American Institute of Oral Biology
[14411]
PO Box 1338
Loma Linda, CA 92354
Ph: (909)558-4671
Fax: (909)558-0285

Barrios, Carlos, Editor
The Adhesion Society **[6176]**
7101 Wisconsin Ave., Ste. 9901
Bethesda, MD 20814
Ph: (301)986-9700
Fax: (301)986-9795

Barron, Jim, Exec. Dir.
Refrigerating Engineers and Techni-
cians Association **[6583]**
1035 2nd Ave. SE
Albany, OR 97321
Ph: (541)497-2955
Fax: (541)497-2966

Barron, Paul B., Dir., Archives, Dir.
of Lib. Svcs.
George C. Marshall Foundation
[10338]
1600 VMI Parade
Lexington, VA 24450-1600
Ph: (540)463-7103
Fax: (540)464-5229

Barron, Dr. Pepe, Founder
Luz Social Services, Inc. **[13151]**
2797 N Cerrada de Beto Dr.
Tucson, AZ 85745-8617
Ph: (520)882-6216
Fax: (520)623-9291

Barrow, Clyde W., Contact
Caucus for a New Political Science
[7045]

Barrus, Pamela, Bd. Member
Travelers' Century Club **[22470]**
8939 S Sepulveda Blvd., Ste. 102
Los Angeles, CA 90045
Toll Free: 888-822-0228

Barry, Ms. Alethia, Chairperson
Clearing the Fog About Autism
[13761]

3695F Cascade Rd., No. 2172
Atlanta, GA 30331
Toll Free: 888-803-6046
Fax: (404)585-5687

Barry, Joanne S., Exec. Dir.
Foundation for Accounting Education
[30]
PO Box 10490
Uniondale, NY 11555-0490
Toll Free: 866-495-1354

Barry, Kevin, President
Professional and Organizational
Development Network in Higher
Education [7970]
PO Box 3318
Nederland, CO 80466
Ph: (303)258-9521
Fax: (303)258-7377

Barry, Michael, CAE, Exec. Dir.
American College of Preventive
Medicine [16798]
455 Massachusetts Ave. NW, Ste.
200
Washington, DC 20001
Ph: (202)466-2044
Fax: (202)466-2662

Barry, Michael J., MD, President
Informed Medical Decisions Founda-
tion [15686]
40 Court St., Ste. 300
Boston, MA 02108
Ph: (617)367-2000

Barry, Michael P., VP of Corp. &
Member Svcs.
Stutz Club [21497]
PO Box 2031
Dublin, OH 43017
Ph: (330)730-9498

Barry, Nancy, Secretary
College Music Society [8364]
312 E Pine St.
Missoula, MT 59802
Ph: (406)721-9616
Fax: (406)721-9419

Barry, Nancy, Founder, President
Pierre Robin Network [14850]
3604 Biscayne St.
Quincy, IL 62305-4740

Barry, Thomas C., Founder, CEO
Trickle Up Program [12192]
104 W 27th St., 12th Fl.
New York, NY 10001-6210
Ph: (212)255-9980
Toll Free: 866-246-9980
Fax: (212)255-9974

Barsky, Robert, Director
W.T. Bandy Center for Baudelaire
and Modern French Studies [9041]
419 21st Ave. S
Nashville, TN 37203-2405
Ph: (615)343-0372

Barstnar, Kathie A., Exec. Dir.
Environmental and Engineering
Geophysical Society [6686]
1720 S Bellaire St., Ste. 110
Denver, CO 80222-4308
Ph: (303)531-7517
Fax: (303)820-3844

Barstow, Bob, Contact
Automotive Distribution Network
[310]
3085 Fountainside Dr., No. 210
Germantown, TN 38138
Toll Free: 800-727-8112
Fax: (901)682-9098

Barta, Bill, Chmn. of the Bd.
Giving Children Hope [10998]
8332 Commonwealth Ave.

Buena Park, CA 90621
Ph: (714)523-4454
Fax: (714)523-4474

Bartasavich, Gerard, President
International Thunderbird Club
[21407]
PO Box 24041
Pepper Pike, OH 44124-9998
Ph: (216)375-2808
(205)938-7494

Bartecchi, David, MA, Exec. Dir.
Village Earth: CSVBD [11456]
PO Box 797
Fort Collins, CO 80522
Ph: (970)237-3002
Fax: (970)237-3026

Bartek, Mr. Ronald J., Director,
Founder, President
Friedreich's Ataxia Research Alliance
[14775]
533 W Uwchlan Ave.
Downingtown, PA 19335-1763
Ph: (484)879-6160
Fax: (484)872-1402

Bartelink, Eric J., President
American Board of Forensic
Anthropology [14771]
c/o Joan E. Baker, Secretary
Defense POW/MIA Accounting
Agency
2600 Defence Pentagon
Washington, DC 20301-2600
Ph: (703)699-1428

Bartfield, Ira, VP
Center for Community Action of
B'Nai B'rith International [11330]
1120 20th St. NW, Ste. 300N
Washington, DC 20036
Ph: (212)490-3290

Barth, Cathy L., Mgr.
Academy of Criminal Justice Sci-
ences [11514]
7339 Hanover Pky., Ste. A
Greenbelt, MD 20770
Ph: (301)446-6300
Toll Free: 800-757-2257
Fax: (301)446-2819

Barth, Roy, President
Professional Tennis Registry [23305]
4 Office Way, Ste. 200
Hilton Head Island, SC 29928
Ph: (843)785-7244
Toll Free: 800-421-6289
Fax: (843)686-2033

Barth, Scott, Chairman
Independent Bakers Association
[374]
PO Box 3731
Washington, DC 20027-0231
Ph: (202)333-8190

Barthel, Bill, President
Surface Mount Technology Associa-
tion [1773]
6600 City W Pky., Ste. 300
Eden Prairie, MN 55344
Ph: (952)920-7682
Fax: (952)926-1819

Barthelmess, Don, Treasurer
Association of Commercial Diving
Educators [23341]
c/o Santa Barbara City College
721 Cliff Dr.
Santa Barbara, CA 93109
Ph: (805)965-0581
Fax: (805)560-6059

Bartholomew, John R., MD, MSVM,
President
Society for Vascular Medicine
[17580]

One ParkView Plz., Ste. 100
Oakbrook Terrace, IL 60181
Ph: (847)686-2232
Fax: (847)686-2251

Bartles, Dean L., PhD, President
North American Manufacturing
Research Institution of SME [6797]
1 SME Dr.
Dearborn, MI 48128
Ph: (313)425-3000
Toll Free: 800-733-4763
Fax: (313)425-3400

Bartlett, Doug, President
International Aerobatic Club [22488]
PO Box 3086
Oshkosh, WI 54903
Ph: (920)426-4800

Bartlett, Terri L., President
Marketing EDGE [8271]
1333 Broadway, Rm. 301
New York, NY 10018
Ph: (212)768-7277
Fax: (212)790-1561

Bartley, Ben, Exec. Dir.
National Intercollegiate Running
Club Association [23118]
121 N College Ave.
Bloomington, IN 47404

Bartol, Mike, 1st VP
Casting Industry Suppliers Associa-
tion [1719]
14175 W Indian School Rd., Ste.
B4-504
Goodyear, AZ 85395
Ph: (623)547-0920
Fax: (623)536-1486

Bartold, Prof. P. Mark, Officer
International Academy of Periodon-
tology [14445]
c/o Alecha Pantaleon
The Forsyth Institute
245 First St.
Cambridge, MA 02142
Ph: (617)892-8536
Fax: (617)262-4021

Bartoldus, Ellen, Bd. Member
The Transition Network [13401]
505 8th Ave., Ste. 1212
New York, NY 10128
Ph: (347)735-6035

Bartoletti, JoAnn D., Exec. Dir.
National Association of Student
Councils [8623]
1904 Association Dr.
Reston, VA 20191-1537
Ph: (703)860-0200

Bartolini, Vicki, Contact
Teachers Resisting Unhealthy
Children's Entertainment [11165]
160 Lakeview Ave.
Cambridge, MA 02138-3367

Barton, Bill, President
Professional Construction Estimators
Association of America, Inc. [899]
PO Box 680336
Charlotte, NC 28216
Ph: (704)489-1494
Toll Free: 877-521-7232

Barton, Doug, President
Advertising and Marketing
International Network [80]
3587 Northshore Dr.
Wayzata, MN 55391
Ph: (952)471-7752

Barton, Erin, President
Division for Early Childhood of the
Council for Exceptional Children
[8583]

3415 S Sepulveda Blvd., Ste. 1100
Los Angeles, CA 90034
Ph: (310)428-7209
Fax: (855)678-1989

Barton, James, President, Coord.,
Member Svcs.
National Federation of State Poetry
Societies [10153]
c/o James Barton
PO Box 263
Huttig, AR 71747-0263

Barton, Prof. Larry L., Secretary
International Biometals Society
[6838]
c/o Prof. Larry L. Barton, Secretary
Dept. of Biology, MSC03 2020
University of New Mexico
Albuquerque, NM 87131
Ph: (505)277-2537
Fax: (505)277-0304

Bartz, Claudia C., President
Army Nurse Corps Association
[15838]
8000 IH-10
San Antonio, TX 78218-1235
Ph: (210)650-3534
Fax: (210)650-3494

Bartz, Elizabeth, Bd. Member
Kent State University Alumni As-
sociation [19330]
PO Box 5190
Kent, OH 44242-0001
Ph: (330)672-5368
Toll Free: 888-320-5368
Fax: (330)672-4723

Barwick, Timi Agar, CEO
Physician Assistant Education As-
sociation [16724]
655 K St. NW, Ste. 700
Washington, DC 20001-2385
Ph: (703)548-5538

Barwis, John, President
U.S. Philatelic Classics Society
[22377]
2913 Fulton St.
Everett, WA 98201-3733

Barwuah, Adwoa K., President, CEO
International Child Empowerment
Network [11239]
8605-B Engleside Office Park Dr.
Alexandria, VA 22309-4130
Ph: (571)332-1179

Barzansky, Barbara, PhD, MHPE,
Secretary
American Medical Association -
Liaison Committee on Medical
Education [8292]
330 N Wabash Ave., Ste. 39300
Chicago, IL 60611-5885
Ph: (312)464-4933

Basa, Eniko, Exec. Dir.
American Hungarian Educators Association [19465]
4515 Willard Ave., Apt. 2210
Chevy Chase, MD 20815

Basch-Harod, Heidi, Exec. Dir.
Women's Voices Now [19257]
46-E Peninsula Ctr.
Rolling Hills Estates, CA 90274-3562
Ph: (310)748-1929

Basciano, Danielle, VP
International Association of Animal
Behavior Consultants [7402]
565 Callery Rd.
Cranberry Township, PA 16066

Basco, Buenaventura, Exec. Dir.
Asian Pacific American Librarians
Association [9681]

PO Box 677593
Orlando, FL 32867-7593

Baseil, Rich, Exec. Dir.
IEEE - Signal Processing Society
[5853]
445 Hoes Ln.
Piscataway, NJ 08854-4141
Ph: (732)562-3888
Fax: (732)235-1627

Basham, Janelle, Director
Liberty Godparent Home [12776]
124 Liberty Mountain Dr.
Lynchburg, VA 24502
Ph: (434)845-3466
Toll Free: 800-542-4453
Fax: (434)845-1751

Bashore, Harvey, Director
Rough and Tumble Engineers'
  Historical Association [22439]
PO Box 9
Kinzers, PA 17535-0009
Ph: (717)442-4249

Bashore, Lisa, President
Shine Therapy [15563]
1450 8th Ave.
Fort Worth, TX 76104
Ph: (817)372-8998

Basile, Josh, Founder
Determined2heal Foundation
  [17254]
8112 River Falls Dr.
Potomac, MD 20854
Ph: (703)795-5711

Basile, Matthew, Founder, Director
Building Bridges Worldwide, Inc.
  [11323]
509 48th Ave., Apt. 8E
Long Island City, NY 11101-5622

Basin, Geetu, Dir. of Public Rel.
Caring Hand for Children [11199]
6901 McLaren Ave.
West Hills, CA 91307-2527
Ph: (818)620-1206

Baskerville, Dr. Lezli, CEO,
  President
National Association for Equal Op-
  portunity in Higher Education
  [7637]
209 3rd St. SE
Washington, DC 20003
Ph: (202)552-3300
Fax: (202)552-3330

Baskin, Bob, President
Peace Alliance [18814]
1616 P St. NW, Ste. 100
Washington, DC 20036
Ph: (202)684-2553
Fax: (202)204-5712

Bass, Jessica, Exec. Sec.
International Association of Equine
  Dentistry [14448]
PO Box 1141
Seguin, TX 78156
Ph: (830)268-5005

Bass, Rev. Monsignor Ricardo E.,
  Chap.
International Order of Alhambra
  [19407]
4200 Leeds Ave.
Baltimore, MD 21229-5421
Ph: (410)242-0660
Toll Free: 800-478-2946
Fax: (410)536-5729

Basse, Hanno, President, Chmn. of
  the Bd.
UHD Alliance [6015]
48377 Fremont Blvd., Ste. 117

Fremont, CA 94538
Ph: (510)492-4025
Fax: (510)492-4001

Bassett, Gene, President
National Association of Wastewater
  Technicians [3452]
2800 W Higgins Rd., Ste. 440
Hoffman Estates, IL 60169
Toll Free: 800-236-NAWT
Fax: (866)220-1055

Bassett, Martin, Chairman
Vision Council Lab Division [2460]
225 Reinekers Ln., Ste. 700
Alexandria, VA 22314
Ph: (703)548-4560
Toll Free: 866-826-0290

Bassey, Offiong, Secretary
One Hen, Inc. [10821]
PO Box 920048
Needham, MA 02492-0001
Ph: (650)400-0987

Bassler, Max, Chairman
1394 Trade Association [3204]
315 Lincoln, Ste. E
Mukilteo, WA 98275
Ph: (425)870-6574
Fax: (425)320-3897

Bast, Gail L., Director
Federation of Clinical Immunology
  Societies [15378]
N83 W13410 Leon Rd.
Menomonee Falls, WI 53051
Ph: (414)359-1670
Fax: (414)359-1671

Bast, Gail L., President
Society for Vascular Nursing [16188]
N83 W13410 Leon Rd.
Menomonee Falls, WI 53051
Ph: (414)376-0001
Fax: (414)359-1671

Bast, Joseph L., CEO, President
Heartland Institute [12977]
3939 N Wilke Rd.
Arlington Heights, IL 60004
Ph: (312)377-4000
Fax: (312)377-5000

Basta, Daniel, Advisor
Women's Aquatic Network [6808]
c/o Daniel Basta, Advisor
NOAA National Marine Sanctuary
1305 E West Hwy., 11th Fl.
Silver Spring, MD 20910

Bastable, Caroline, President
Original Hobo Nickel Society [22281]
c/o Becky Jirka, Secretary
5111 Illinois Ave.
Lisle, IL 60532-2015

Basu, Jaya, President
Promise World Wide [12179]
46170 Paseo Padre Pky.
Fremont, CA 94539-6930
Ph: (408)605-0495

Batajoo, Ayodhya, Treasurer
Nepali American Friendship Associa-
  tion [19592]
408 Midland Ln.
Monona, WI 53716
Ph: (608)222-0646

Bataraga, Anita, President
American Latvian Association
  [19533]
400 Hurley Ave.
Rockville, MD 20850-3121
Ph: (301)340-1914

Batcha, Laura, CEO, Exec. Dir.
Organic Trade Association [4483]
444 N Capitol St. NW, Ste. 445A

Washington, DC 20001
Ph: (202)403-8520

Batchik, John, V. Chmn. of the Bd.
Automotive Industry Action Group
  [284]
26200 Lahser Rd., Ste. 200
Southfield, MI 48033-7100
Ph: (248)358-3570
    (248)358-3003
Toll Free: 877-275-2424
Fax: (248)358-3253

Batdorff, Donna, Founder, Exec. Dir.
National Necrotizing Fasciitis
  Foundation [17346]
2731 Porter SW
Grand Rapids, MI 49519-2140
Ph: (862)213-5213

Bateman, C. Fred, Exec. Dir.
Urban Superintendent's Association
  of America [8726]
PO Box 1248
Chesapeake, VA 23327-1248
Ph: (757)436-1032

Bateman, Paul, Secretary
Green Seal [18050]
1001 Connecticut Ave. NW, Ste. 827
Washington, DC 20036-5525
Ph: (202)872-6400
Fax: (202)872-4324

Bater, D. Craig, MD, President
Association of Specialty Professors
  [15428]
c/o Alliance for Academic Internal
  Medicine
330 John Carlyle St., Ste. 610
Alexandria, VA 22314
Ph: (703)341-4540
Fax: (703)519-1893

Bates, Albert K., Chairman
Global Village Institute [5732]
184 Schoolhouse Ridge Rd.
Summertown, TN 38483-0090
Ph: (931)964-4474
Fax: (931)964-2200

Bates, Craig
Lambda Pi Alumni Association
  [23758]
PO Box 36
Chico, CA 95927

Bates, Laura, Gen. Mgr.
Learning Light Foundation [9541]
1212 E Lincoln Ave.
Anaheim, CA 92805-4249
Ph: (714)533-2311
Fax: (714)533-1458

Bates, Lyn, Bd. Member, Inst.
We Are AWARE [13403]
PO Box 242
Bedford, MA 01730

Bates, Sylvia, Dir. of Res.
Land Trust Alliance [3892]
1660 L St. NW, Ste. 1100
Washington, DC 20036
Ph: (202)638-4725
Fax: (202)638-4730

Bates, Tammy, Liaison
Pediatric Brain Tumor Foundation -
  Georgia [14210]
6065 Roswell Rd. NE, Ste. 505
Atlanta, GA 30328
Ph: (404)252-4107
Fax: (404)252-4108

Bateson, Rick, Chmn. of the Bd.
Freshwater Society [4547]
2424 Territorial Rd., Ste. B
Saint Paul, MN 55114
Ph: (651)313-5800
Fax: (651)666-2569

Batey, Mr. Boyce, Exec. Dir.
Academy of Religion and Psychical
  Research [6982]
PO Box 84
Loxahatchee, FL 33470
Ph: (561)714-1423

Batluck, Rev. Joseph S., Sr.,
  President, CEO
Teen Challenge International [20663]
5250 N Towne Centre Dr.
Ozark, MO 65721
Ph: (417)581-2181

Batres, Manuel, President
Mission2Guatemala [13071]
301 Sutton Rd.
Xenia, OH 45385
Ph: (937)830-1478

Batson, Ruth, RJ, CEO
American Gem Society [2039]
8881 W Sahara Ave.
Las Vegas, NV 89117

Batstone, Dave, Founder
Not For Sale [12053]
2225 3rd St.
San Francisco, CA 94107
Ph: (650)560-9990

Battaglia, Dr. Carmen, President
German Shepherd Dog Club of
  America [21882]
c/o Dania Karloff, Recording
  Secretary
2136 Mt. Pleasant Rd.
Chesapeake, VA 23322-1215
Ph: (757)482-3966

Battaglia, Loretta, Sec. Gen.,
  Membership Chp.
Society of Wetland Scientists [3945]
22 N Carroll St., Ste. 300
Madison, WI 53703-2798
Ph: (608)310-7855
Fax: (608)251-5941

Battaglino, Beth, Founder
HealthyWomen [17757]
PO Box 430
Red Bank, NJ 07701
Ph: (732)530-3425
Toll Free: 877-986-9472
Fax: (732)865-7225

Battalion, John Lenihan, Comm.
  Chm.
National Public Safety Telecom-
  munications Council [3235]
8191 Southpark Ln., Unit 205
Littleton, CO 80120-4641
Toll Free: 866-807-4755
Fax: (303)649-1844

Battey, James F., Jr., MD, Director
National Institute on Deafness and
  Other Communication Disorders
  Information Clearinghouse [15206]
1 Communication Ave.
Bethesda, MD 20892-3456
Toll Free: 800-241-1044

Battista, Mark, CEO, President
Medical Care Development
  International [15483]
8401 Colesville Rd., Ste. 425
Silver Spring, MD 20910-3391
Ph: (301)562-1920
Fax: (301)562-1921

Battle, DuWayne, President
Association of Baccalaureate Social
  Work Program Directors [8568]
1701 Duke St., Ste. 200
Alexandria, VA 22314
Ph: (703)519-2045
Fax: (703)683-8493

Battle, Pamela L., Exec. Dir.
Manufacturers Representatives of
America [2478]
4604 Ringold Dr.
Fort Worth, TX 76133
Ph: (817)690-4308

Battrell, Ann, Exec. Dir.
American Dental Hygienists' As-
sociation [14406]
444 N Michigan Ave., Ste. 3400
Chicago, IL 60611
Ph: (312)440-8900
    (312)440-8913

Batzer, Mary, Exec. Dir.
American Society of Trial
Consultants [6028]
10534 York Rd., Ste. 102
Hunt Valley, MD 21030
Ph: (410)560-7949
Fax: (410)560-2563

Bau, Tom, Director
Gull Wing Group International
[21392]
776 Cessna Ave.
Chico, CA 95928-9571
Ph: (949)364-6035

Bauer, Aaron, President
Society for the Study of Amphibians
and Reptiles [6708]
c/o Ann Paterson, Treasurer
60 W Fulbright Ave.
Walnut Ridge, AR 72476

Bauer, Ann, LPN, President
National Association for Practical
Nurse Education and Service
[8332]
2071 N Bechtle Ave., No. 307
Springfield, OH 45504-1583
Ph: (703)933-1003
Fax: (703)940-4089

Bauer, Cynthia, Exec. Dir., Founder
Kupenda for the Children [11065]
PO Box 473
Hampton, NH 03843
Ph: (978)626-1625

Bauer, Gary, Founder
Campaign for Working Families
[18862]
PO Box 1222
Merrifield, VA 22116-1222
Ph: (703)671-8800

Bauer, Dr. John E., CEO, President
Bethesda Lutheran Communities
[12319]
600 Hoffmann Dr.
Watertown, WI 53094
Ph: (920)261-3050
Toll Free: 800-369-4636
Fax: (920)261-8441

Bauer, Kate E., MBA, Exec. Dir.
American Association of Birth
Centers [16267]
3123 Gottschall Rd.
Perkiomenville, PA 18074
Ph: (215)234-8068
Toll Free: 866-542-4784
Fax: (215)234-8829

Bauer, Ken, President
DROKPA [11347]
95 Stowell Rd.
Norwich, VT 05055

Bauer, Scotia, Exec. Dir.
United States Windsurfing Associa-
tion [22688]
8211 Sun Spring Cir., Apt. 73
Orlando, FL 32825
Toll Free: 877-386-8708

Bauer, Steve, Exec. Dir.
Federal Employee Education and
Assistance Fund [19574]
3333 S Wadsworth Blvd., Ste. 300
Lakewood, CO 80227
Ph: (303)933-7580
Toll Free: 800-323-4140
Fax: (303)933-7587

Baughn, Joyce, Director
International Child Amputee Network
[11606]
PO Box 13812
Tucson, AZ 85732

Baum, Gordon, CEO
Council of Conservative Citizens
[19155]
PO Box 221683
Saint Louis, MO 63122
Ph: (636)940-8474

Baum, Hadassah, CPA
Beta Alpha Psi [23669]
220 Leigh Farm Rd.
Durham, NC 27707
Ph: (919)402-4044
Fax: (919)402-4040

Baum, Karen, Secretary
International Lama Registry [3601]
11 1/2 Meridian Rd.
Kalispell, MT 59901
Ph: (406)755-3438
Fax: (406)755-3439

Baum, Rabbi Shalom, President
Rabbinical Council of America
[20276]
305 7th Ave., 12th Fl.
New York, NY 10001
Ph: (212)807-9000
    (212)741-7522
Fax: (212)727-8452

Bauman, Chad, President
Society for Hindu-Christian Studies
[20578]
232 Malloy Hall
University of Notre Dame
Notre Dame, IN 46556
Ph: (574)631-7128

Bauman, Margaret L., Director
Friends of LADDERS [12235]
193 Oak St., Ste. 1
Newton, MA 02464-1453
Ph: (781)860-1700

Bauman, Mark, Chairman
Antarctic and Southern Ocean Coali-
tion [7039]
1320 19th St. NW, 5th Fl.
Washington, DC 20036
Ph: (202)234-2480

Bauman, Stephan, President
World Relief [20123]
7 E Baltimore St.
Baltimore, MD 21202-1602
Ph: (443)451-1900
Toll Free: 800-535-5433

Baumann, Micki, Officer
Coalition of Visionary Resources
[2951]
PO Box 100866
Denver, CO 80250
Ph: (303)758-0007

Baumel, Judith, President
Association of Writers & Writing
Programs [10361]
George Mason University
4400 University Dr.
MSN 1E3
Fairfax, VA 22030-4444
Ph: (703)993-4301
Fax: (703)993-4302

Baumgart, Chris, Chairman
Hollywood Sign Trust [9401]
PO Box 48361
Los Angeles, CA 90048-9998
Ph: (213)300-0108

Baumgartner, Jo Ann, Exec. Dir.
Wild Farm Alliance [4172]
406 Main St., Ste. 316
Watsonville, CA 95076
Ph: (831)761-8408
Fax: (831)761-8103

Baumgartner, William A., MD, Exec.
Dir.
American Board of Thoracic Surgery
[17470]
633 N St. Clair St., Ste. 2320
Chicago, IL 60611
Ph: (312)202-5900
Fax: (312)202-5960

Bavisi, Sanjay, President
EC-Council [997]
101C Sun Ave. NE
Albuquerque, NM 87109
Ph: (505)341-3228
Fax: (505)341-0050

Baxter, Ann, Chairperson
International Guild of Glass Artists
[251]
27829 365th Ave.
Platte, SD 57369
Ph: (313)886-0099

Baxter, Ms. Lorrie, Coord.
Rubinstein-Taybi Parent Group
U.S.A. [13835]
24081 G Ln.
Cedar, KS 67628
Toll Free: 888-447-2989

Baxter, Mrs. Sybil, Secretary,
Administrator
International Association of Currency
Affairs [403]
PO Box 821
Colleyville, TX 76034
Ph: (613)985-5723
Fax: (972)692-8186

Baybrook, Loren, Editor
Center for the Study of Film and His-
tory [9301]
Lawrence University
Memorial Hall B5
711 E Boldt Way
Appleton, WI 54911
Ph: (920)832-6649

Baydo, Jerry, Exec. Dir.
National Social Science Association
[7169]
2020 Hills Lake Dr.
El Cajon, CA 92020
Ph: (619)448-4709
Fax: (619)258-7636

Bayles, James, Director
Helping Orphans and Widows
[11026]
3413 Sungate Dr.
Palmdale, CA 93551
Ph: (661)273-4249

Bayless, J. Mark, DMD, Founder
International Health Emissaries
[15148]
8 Sommerset Rise
Monterey, CA 93940

Bayliff, William H., Mem.
Comision Interamericana del Atún
Tropical [1298]
8901 La Jolla Shores Dr.
La Jolla, CA 92037-1509
Ph: (858)546-7100
Fax: (858)546-7133

Bayouth, John, President
Society of Directors of Academic
Medical Physics Programs [16766]
1 Physics Ellipse
College Park, MD 20740
Ph: (301)209-3377
Fax: (301)209-0862

Bayston, Darwin, CEO, President
Life Insurance Settlement Associa-
tion [1880]
280 W Canton Ave., Ste. 430
Winter Park, FL 32789
Ph: (407)894-3797

Baz, Chris, President, Owner
Friends of Health [13624]
Box 906
Kula, HI 96790
Ph: (808)878-6762

Bazerjian, Linda, Director
Institute for Children, Poverty and
Homelessness [11044]
44 Cooper Sq.
New York, NY 10003
Ph: (212)358-8086
Fax: (212)358-8090

Bazyn, Ardis, President
Independent Visually Impaired
Entrepreneurs [17713]
2121 Scott Rd., No. 105
Burbank, CA 91504-2448
Ph: (818)238-9321

Bazzarone, Anne, Founder
La Vallee Alliance [11207]
PO Box 75
Vienna, VA 22183

Bazzy, Michael, Mktg. Mgr.
The Minerals, Metals, and Materials
Society [6849]
184 Thorn Hill Rd.
Warrendale, PA 15086
Ph: (724)776-9000
Toll Free: 800-759-4867
Fax: (724)776-3770

Beach, Rev. Bruce, Chairman
COME International Baptist
Ministries [20136]
c/o Mark Gervais, Web Administrator
937 9th St.
Phillipsburg, KS 67661
Ph: (651)470-2454

Beach, Chris, President
B.K.S. Iyengar Yoga National As-
sociation of the U.S. [10422]
PO Box 538
Seattle, WA 98111
Ph: (206)623-3562

Beach, Gary, Founder, V. Ch.
TECH CORPS [13308]
6600 Busch Blvd., Ste. 210
Columbus, OH 43229-8259
Ph: (614)583-9211
Fax: (614)340-9840

Beach, Thomas E., Chairman
The Reason Foundation [5645]
5737 Mesmer Ave.
Los Angeles, CA 90230
Ph: (310)391-2245
Fax: (310)391-4395

Beacham, R. Brad, Exec. Dir.
Sigma Nu Fraternity, Inc. [23928]
9 N Lewis St.
Lexington, VA 24450
Ph: (540)463-1869
Fax: (540)463-1669

Beal, Becky, Treasurer
Mountain Pleasure Horse Association [4379]

PO Box 33
Wellington, KY 40387
Ph: (606)768-3847

Beal, Deron, Exec. Dir., Founder,
  Chairperson
Freecycle Network [4630]
PO Box 294
Tucson, AZ 85702-0294

Beal, Doug, CEO
USA Volleyball [23350]
4065 Sinton Rd., Ste. 200
Colorado Springs, CO 80907
Ph: (719)228-6800
Fax: (719)228-6899

Beale, Bobbi, President
Association for Experiential Educa-
  tion [7910]
1435 Yarmouth Ave., Ste. 104
Boulder, CO 80304
Ph: (303)440-8844
Toll Free: 866-522-8337

Beale, Charles L., President
International Association of Counsel-
  ing Services [7688]
101 S Whiting St., Ste. 211
Alexandria, VA 22304-3416
Ph: (703)823-9840
Fax: (703)823-9843

Beall Gruits, Rev. Patricia, DD, CEO,
  Founder
RHEMA International [12723]
PO Box 82085
Rochester, MI 48308
Ph: (248)652-2450
Fax: (248)652-9894

Beall, Melissa, Comm. Chm.
International Listening Association
  [7776]
Dr. Nan Johnson-Curiskis, Executive
  Director
943 Park Dr.
Belle Plaine, MN 56011
Ph: (952)594-5697

Beall, Randy, Bd. Member
PRISMS: Parents and Researchers
  Interested In Smith-Magenis
  Syndrome [14853]
21800 Town Center Plz., Ste. No.
  266A-633
Sterling, VA 20164
Ph: (972)231-0035
Fax: (972)499-1832

Beals, Kimberly, Exec. Dir.
International Pharmaceutical Excipients Council of the Americas
  [2560]
3138 N 10th St., Ste. 500
Arlington, VA 22201
Ph: (571)814-3449
    (571)814-3451

Beam, Dr. Stephen, Chairman
National Conference on Interstate
  Milk Shipments [3980]
PO Box 108
Monticello, IL 61856
Ph: (217)762-2656

Beaman, Rick, Chairman
SourceAmerica [11639]
8401 Old Courthouse Rd., Ste. 200
Vienna, VA 22182-3820
Ph: (571)226-4660
Toll Free: 800-411-8424
Fax: (703)849-8916

Beame, Paul, Chairman
Association for Computing
  Machinery - Special Interest Group
  on Algorithms and Computation
  Theory [7056]

c/o Paul Beame, Chairman
University of Washington
PO Box 352350
Seattle, WA 98195

Beamer, Barbara, President
Rocky Mountain Horse Association
  [4406]
71 S Main St.
Winchester, KY 40391
Ph: (859)644-5244
Fax: (859)644-5245

Beamon, Betsy, Founder
Women of Hope Project [13405]
4876-118 Princess Anne Rd., No.
  203
Virginia Beach, VA 23462

Bean, Arch. Carl, DM, Founder
Unity Fellowship Church Movement
  [20191]
c/o Archbishop Carl Bean, DM,
  Founder
PO Box 78342
Los Angeles, CA 90016-0342
Ph: (323)938-8322

Bean, Cathy Bao, Chairperson
Society for Values in Higher Education [20090]
c/o Western Kentucky University
1906 College Heights Blvd., No.
  8020
Bowling Green, KY 42101-1041
Ph: (270)745-2907
Fax: (270)745-5374

Bean, Frank, Exec. Dir.
American Armsport Association
  [22509]
176 Dean Rd.
Mooresburg, TN 37811
Ph: (423)272-6162
Fax: (423)272-6162

Beane, Laura, Chairman
Climate Trust [4543]
65 SW Yamhill St., Ste. 400
Portland, OR 97204
Ph: (503)238-1915

Beard, Elisa Villanueva, CEO
Teach For America [7802]
25 Broadway, 12th Fl.
New York, NY 10004-1056
Toll Free: 800-832-1230

Beard, Heather, Exec. Dir.
EarthShare [7888]
7735 Old Georgetown Rd., Ste. 900
Bethesda, MD 20814
Ph: (240)333-0300
Toll Free: 800-875-3863
Fax: (240)333-0301

Beard, Jeffrey, Chairperson
Construction History Society of
  America [802]
PO Box 93461
Atlanta, GA 30377
Ph: (404)378-3779

Beard, Mike, President
Coalition to Stop Gun Violence
  [18249]
805 15th St. NW, Ste. 700
Washington, DC 20005
Ph: (202)408-0061

Bearden, Dan, Treasurer
Metabolomics Society [15653]
331 Ft. Johnson Rd.
Charleston, SC 29412

Bearden, Stephen, Mem.
Import Vehicle Community [321]
7101 Wisconsin Ave., Ste. 1300

Bethesda, MD 20814
Ph: (301)654-6664
Fax: (301)654-3299

Beardsley, Karen, Officer
Society for Conservation GIS [3944]
c/o Healy Hamilton, President
NatureServe
4600 N Fairfax Dr., 7th Fl.
Arlington, VA 22203
Ph: (703)908-1889

Bearer, Robert, Treasurer
Orthodox Christian School Association [7613]
c/o Ro Kallail, Business Manager
13213 E Bridlewood Ct.
Wichita, KS 67230
Ph: (316)734-6286

Bearse, Jamie, CEO, President
ZERO-The Project to End Prostate
  Cancer [14084]
515 King St., Ste. 420
Alexandria, VA 22314-3137
Ph: (202)463-9455
Toll Free: 888-245-9455
Fax: (571)257-8559

Beary, Lori, President
Council of Infrastructure Financing
  Authorities [5731]
316 Pennsylvania Ave. SE, Ste. 201
Washington, DC 20003
Ph: (202)547-7886
Fax: (202)547-1867

Beasley, Bill, Exec. Dir., Founder
Green Home Council [534]
PO Box 51008
Durham, NC 27717-1008
Ph: (919)624-7903
Fax: (919)493-1240

Beasley, Mark, President
International Cornish Breeders Association [3665]
c/o Mark Beasley, President
1264 Old Allendale Hwy.
Barnwell, SC 29812
Ph: (803)259-3752

Beasley, Noel, President
Eugene V. Debs Foundation [9387]
451 N 8th St.
Terre Haute, IN 47807
Ph: (812)232-2163

Beaton, Dianne, Chairman
Panelized Building Systems Council
  [2201]
National Association of Home Build-
  ers
1201 15th St. NW
Washington, DC 20005
Ph: (202)266-8200
Toll Free: 800-368-5242
Fax: (202)266-8400

Beattie, Michael, Exec. Dir.
American Wagyu Association [3715]
PO Box 3235
Coeur d Alene, ID 83816
Ph: (208)262-8100
Fax: (208)292-2670

Beattie, William, Chmn. of the Bd.
Council on Quality and Leadership
  [12321]
100 West Rd., Ste. 300
Towson, MD 21204
Ph: (410)583-0060
    (410)961-8124

Beaty, Lisa, Exec. Dir.
Institute of Navigation [6907]
8551 Rixlew Ln., Ste. 360
Manassas, VA 20109
Ph: (703)366-2723
Fax: (703)366-2724

Beauchamp, Curtis, Chairman
Soldiers' Angels [19383]
2700 NE Loop 410, Ste. 310
San Antonio, TX 78217
Ph: (210)629-0020
Fax: (210)629-0024

Beauchamp, John, President
Plymouth Rock Fanciers Club of
  America [4570]
2724 Cedarville Rd.
2724 Cedarville Rd.
Millville, NJ 08332
Ph: (856)265-7278

Beauchere, Jacqueline, President
Coalition Against Domain Name
  Abuse [6764]
1000 Potomac St. NW, Ste. 350
Washington, DC 20007
Ph: (202)503-8649

Beaudoin, Mary, Editor
Women Against Military Madness
  [18699]
4200 Cedar Ave. S, Ste. 3
Minneapolis, MN 55407
Ph: (612)827-5364
Fax: (612)827-6433

Beaumont, Devon, VP
Caribbean-American Netball As-
  sociation Inc. [23046]
Empire Blvd., Lefferts Sta.
Brooklyn, NY 11225

Beauvais, Jessica, Mgr.
United Barrel Racing Association
  [22933]
960 Bunyan Ave.
Balsam Lake, WI 54810
Ph: (715)857-6343

Beauvois, Nan Marchand, VP
National Council of State Tourism
  Directors [23662]
c/o US Travel Association
1100 New York Ave. NW, Ste. 450
Washington, DC 20005-3934

Bebar, Mark R., President
International Hydrofoil Society
  [22632]
PO Box 157
Hume, VA 22639

Beber, Diane, Director
Diabetes Research Institute Founda-
  tion [14529]
200 S Park Rd., Ste. 100
Hollywood, FL 33021
Ph: (954)964-4040
Toll Free: 800-321-3437
Fax: (954)964-7036

Becar, Michael N., Exec. Dir.
International Association of Directors
  of Law Enforcement Standards
  and Training [5469]
1330 N Manship Pl.
Meridian, ID 83642
Ph: (517)857-3828
    (208)288-5491

Becher, Carolyn Yashari, Esq., Exec.
  Dir.
Neuromuscular Disease Foundation
  [15976]
269 S Beverly Dr., No. 1206
Beverly Hills, CA 90212
Ph: (310)736-2978

Becher, John W., President
American Osteopathic Association
  [16508]
142 E Ontario St.
Chicago, IL 60611-2864
Ph: (312)202-8000
Toll Free: 800-621-1773
Fax: (312)202-8200

Becherer, John, CEO
United Soybean Board [4254]
16305 Swingley Ridge Rd., Ste. 150
Chesterfield, MO 63017
Toll Free: 800-989-USB1
Fax: (636)530-1560

Beck, Dan, Trustee
Music Performance Trust Fund
[9960]
1501 Broadway, Ste. 600
New York, NY 10036
Ph: (212)391-3950
Fax: (212)221-2604

Beck, James, Treasurer, VP,
Secretary
Anita Borg Institute for Women and
Technology [12508]
1501 Page Mill Rd., MS 1105
Palo Alto, CA 94304
Ph: (212)897-2157

Beck, Lindsay Nohr, Exec. Dir.,
Founder
Fertile Hope [14756]
c/o Livestrong Foundation
2201 E 6th St.
Austin, TX 78702
Toll Free: 877-236-8820

Beck, Lisa, RN, President
Academy of Spinal Cord Injury
Nurses Section [16080]
Academy of Spinal Cord Injury
Professionals
206 S 6th St.
Springfield, IL 62701
Ph: (217)753-1190
Fax: (217)525-1271

Beck, Matthew, Contact
Investment Company Institute [3045]
1401 H St. NW, Ste. 1200
Washington, DC 20005
Ph: (202)326-5800

Beck, Melissa, Exec. Dir.
The Educational Foundation of
America [3853]
55 Walls Dr., Ste. 302
Fairfield, CT 06824
Ph: (845)765-2670
Toll Free: 800-839-1821

Beck, Paul, Treasurer
Azalea Society of America [22086]
c/o Leslie Nanney, Secretary
8646 Tuttle Rd.
Springfield, VA 22152-2243

Beck, Peter M., President
Korea Stamp Society [22338]
PO Box 6889
Oak Ridge, TN 37831-3588

Beck, Ralph S., President
Independent Order of Vikings
[19487]
5250 S 6th St.
Springfield, IL 62705-5147
Toll Free: 877-241-6006

Beck, Roy, Founder, CEO
NumbersUSA [18995]
1400 Crystal Dr., Ste. 240
Arlington, VA 22202
Ph: (703)816-8820

Beck, Ms. Tracey R., Exec. Dir.
American Swedish Historical
Museum [10229]
1900 Pattison Ave.
Philadelphia, PA 19145-5901
Ph: (215)389-1776

Beckenbach, William C., President
Intermuseum Conservation Association [9830]

2915 Detroit Ave.
Cleveland, OH 44113
Ph: (216)658-8700
Fax: (216)658-8709

Becker, Ms. Angie, President
Antiques and Collectibles National
Association [195]
PO Box 4389
Davidson, NC 28036
Toll Free: 800-287-7127
Fax: (704)895-0230

Becker, Carolyn, PhD, President
Academy for Eating Disorders
[14631]
12100 Sunset Hills Rd., Ste. 130
Reston, VA 20190
Ph: (703)234-4079
Fax: (703)435-4390

Becker, Catherine, Secretary
American Council for Southern Asian
Art [8831]
Dept. of Art History
University of Illinois at Chicago
211A Henry Hall
935 W Harrison St.
Chicago, IL 60607
Ph: (312)996-3303
Fax: (312)413-2460

Becker, Chris, President
Crane Manufacturers Association of
America [1725]
c/o MHI
8720 Red Oak Blvd., Ste. 201
Charlotte, NC 28217-3996
Ph: (704)676-1190
Fax: (704)676-1199

Becker, Don, President
Classic Jaguar Association [21358]
Reed Van Rozeboom, 11321 Loch
Lomond Rd., Rossmoor
11321 Loch Lomond Rd.
Los Alamitos, CA 90720

Becker, John, Director
American Moving and Storage As-
sociation [3081]
1611 Duke St.
Alexandria, VA 22314-3406
Ph: (703)683-7410
Toll Free: 888-849-2672
Fax: (703)683-7527

Becker, Lora, PhD, President
Nu Rho Psi [23836]
Baldwin Wallace University
275 Eastland Rd.
Berea, OH 44017-2088
Ph: (440)826-8526

Becker, Maureen, Exec. Dir.
International Police Mountain Bike
Association [5475]
583 Frederick Rd., Ste. 5B
Baltimore, MD 21228
Ph: (410)744-2400
Fax: (410)744-5504

Becker, Milt, Coord., Member Svcs.
Canadian Corkscrew Collectors Club
[21631]
1 Madison St., Ste. 5B
East Rutherford, NJ 07073-1605
Ph: (973)773-9224

Beckett, John, Bd. Member
Intercessors for America [19984]
PO Box 915
Purcellville, VA 20134
Toll Free: 800-872-7729

Beckham, Wayne, President, Chair-
man
Commission on Accreditation of
Medical Physics Education
Programs [8317]

1 Physics Ellipse
College Park, MD 20740
Ph: (301)209-3346
Fax: (301)209-0862

Beckler, Greg, VP
National Caves Association [1154]
PO Box 625
Cobleskill, NY 12043
Ph: (270)749-2228
Toll Free: 866-552-2837
Fax: (270)749-2428

Beckman, Eric, Operations Mgr.
Pro Energy Alliance [1120]
1665 N 1200 W
Lehi, UT 84043-3573
Ph: (801)935-4360
Toll Free: 888-316-8285

Beckmann, David, President
Bread for the World [18453]
425 3rd St. SW, Ste. 1200
Washington, DC 20024
Ph: (202)639-9400
Toll Free: 800-822-7323
Fax: (202)639-9401

Beckmann, Derek, Secretary
Hispanic Alliance for Career
Enhancement [18338]
29 E Madison
Chicago, IL 60606
Ph: (312)435-0498
Fax: (312)454-7448

Beckner, Debbie, Exec. Sec.
Delta Omicron International Music
Fraternity [23826]
910 Church St.
Jefferson City, TN 37760
Ph: (865)471-6155
Fax: (865)475-9716

Beckner, Gary, Chairman, President
Association of American Educators
[7847]
27405 Puerta Real, Ste. 230
Mission Viejo, CA 92691
Ph: (949)595-7979
Toll Free: 800-704-7799
Fax: (949)595-7970

Becks, Gary, Chairman
World Emergency Relief [12738]
425 W Allen Ave., No. 111
San Dimas, CA 91773-1485
Ph: (909)593-7140
Toll Free: 888-484-4543
Fax: (909)593-3100

Beckwith, Mark, Exec. Dir.
Nevus Outreach, Inc [14608]
600 SE Delaware Ave., Ste. 200
Bartlesville, OK 74003
Ph: (918)331-0595
Toll Free: 877-426-3887
Fax: (281)417-4020

Bedau, Mark, Bd. Member
International Society of Artificial Life
[6086]

Bedford, Robert, Exec. VP
Foundation for the Advancement of
Sephardic Studies and Culture
[19517]
34 W 15th St., 3rd Fl.
New York, NY 10011

Bedil, Susan J., Exec. Dir.
International Education Research
Foundation [8102]
6133 Bristol Pky., Ste. 300
Culver City, CA 90230
Ph: (310)258-9451
Fax: (310)342-7086

Bedker, Shari, Exec. Dir.
American College of Bankruptcy
[5084]

PO Box 249
Stanardsville, VA 22973
Ph: (434)939-6004
Fax: (434)939-6030

Bedker, Shari, Exec. Dir.
Association of Independent
Consumer Credit Counseling
Agencies [941]
10332 Main St.
Fairfax, VA 22030
Ph: (434)939-6006
Toll Free: 866-703-8787
Fax: (434)939-6030

Bednarczyk, Bro. Paul, CSC, Exec.
Dir.
National Religious Vocation Confer-
ence [19889]
5401 S Cornell Ave., Ste. 207
Chicago, IL 60615
Ph: (773)363-5454
Fax: (773)363-5530

Bednarski, Karen, Exec. Dir.
Golf Collectors Society [21657]
c/o Karen Bednarski, Executive
Director
PO Box 2386
Florence, OR 97439
Ph: (541)991-7313
Fax: (541)997-3871

Beebe, Linda, Director
American Psychological Association
[16861]
750 1st St. NE
Washington, DC 20002-4242
Ph: (202)336-5500
Toll Free: 800-374-2721

Beech, Jill, Director
Walking Horse Owners' Association
[4424]
PO Box 4007
Murfreesboro, TN 37129
Ph: (615)494-8822

Beecher, Janice A., PhD, Director
Institute of Public Utilities [3418]
Michigan State University
Owen Graduate Hall
735 E Shaw Ln., Rm. W157
East Lansing, MI 48825-1109
Ph: (517)355-1876
Fax: (517)355-1854

Beecroft, Alexander, Secretary,
Treasurer
American Comparative Literature
Association [9748]
University of South Carolina
Dept. of Languages, Literatures &
Cultures
1620 College St., Rm. 813A
Columbia, SC 29208

Beekmann, Susan, RN, Program
Mgr.
Infectious Diseases Society of
America Emerging Infections
Network [15403]
Carver College of Medicine
University of Iowa
200 Hawkins Dr., SW-34JGH
Iowa City, IA 52242
Ph: (319)384-8622
Fax: (319)384-8860

Beeks, Graydon, President
American Handel Society [9178]
c/o Marjorie Pomeroy, Secretary/
Treasurer
49 Christopher Hollow Rd.
Sandwich, MA 02563-2227
Ph: (909)607-3568

Beer, Michael, Exec. Dir.
Nonviolence International [18724]
4000 Albemarle St. NW, Ste. 401

Washington, DC 20016
Ph: (202)244-0951
Fax: (202)244-6396

Beers, Dean A., President
The National Council of Investigation
and Security Services, Inc. [3064]
7501 Sparrows Point Blvd.
Baltimore, MD 21219-1927
Toll Free: 800-445-8408

Beers, Tom, Exec. Dir.
National Association for Business
Economics [6396]
1920 L St. NW, Ste. 300
Washington, DC 20036
Ph: (202)463-6223
Fax: (202)463-6239

Beery, Janet, Officer
Association for Women in Mathemat-
ics [6818]
11240 Waples Mill Rd., Ste. 200
Fairfax, VA 22030
Ph: (703)934-0163
Fax: (703)359-7562

Begay, Jefferson, Bd. Member
American Indian Council of
Architects and Engineers [5952]
c/o Beverly Diddy, President
Beverly Diddy Designs, LLC
PO Box 36647
Albuquerque, NM 87176
Ph: (505)884-4815
Fax: (505)884-4914

Begert, Bret, President
North American Limousin Foundation
[3745]
6 Inverness Ct. E, Ste. 260
Englewood, CO 80112-5595
Ph: (303)220-1693
Toll Free: 888-320-8747
Fax: (303)220-1884

Begley, Ann M., Secretary, Gen.
Counsel
Enzyme Technical Association
[1167]
1111 Pennsylvania Ave. NW
Washington, DC 20004-2541
Ph: (202)739-5613
Fax: (202)739-3001

Begner, Steve, Treasurer
Antique Tribal Art Dealers Associa-
tion [236]
c/o Larry Cornelius, Treasurer
PO Box 45628
Rio Rancho, NM 87174
Ph: (505)823-4560
    (415)863-3173
Fax: (415)431-1939

Begner, Steve, Treasurer
Antique Tribal Art Dealers Associa-
tion [8837]
c/o Larry Cornelius, Treasurer
PO Box 45628
Rio Rancho, NM 87174
Ph: (505)823-4560
    (415)863-3173
Fax: (415)431-1939

Behling, Susan Haugen, Treasurer
International Association for
Computer Information Systems
[6251]
c/o Gary DeLorenzo, Vice President
California University of Pennsylvania
250 University Ave.
California, PA 15419-1341

Behney, Clyde J., Exec. Dir.
Food and Nutrition Board [16220]
Keck Ctr., W700
500 5th St. NW

Washington, DC 20001
Ph: (202)334-1732
Fax: (202)334-2316

Behney, Clyde J., Exec. Dir.
National Academies of Sciences,
Engineering, and Medicine I
Institute of Medicine [15737]
500 5th St. NW
Washington, DC 20001
Ph: (202)334-2352
Fax: (202)334-1694

Behnke, Robert, Bd. Member
National Association of Publicly
Funded Truck Driving Schools
[3339]
1324 S 220 W Ave.
Sand Springs, OK 74063
Ph: (918)770-6446

Behrend, Cheryl, Secretary
The Curtis/s Family Society [20851]
c/o Cheryl Behrend, Secretary
17924 SE 89th Rothway Ct.
The Villages, FL 32162-4840

Behrstock, David, Director
Alexander Technique International
[13583]
1692 Massachusetts Ave., 3rd Fl.
Cambridge, MA 02138
Ph: (617)497-5151
Toll Free: 888-668-8996
Fax: (617)497-2615

Beightol, Rob, President
Monorail Manufacturers Association
[1751]
c/o MHI
8720 Red Oak Blvd., Ste. 201
Charlotte, NC 28217
Ph: (704)676-1190
Fax: (704)676-1199

Beigi, Richard, MD, President
Infectious Diseases Society for
Obstetrics and Gynecology
[15404]
230 W Monroe St., Ste. 710
Chicago, IL 60606
Ph: (312)676-3928

Beirich, Heidi, Director
Intelligence Project [17902]
Southern Poverty Law Ctr.
400 Washington Ave.
Montgomery, AL 36104
Ph: (334)956-8200
Toll Free: 888-414-7752

Bekalo, Isaac B., President
International Institute of Rural
Reconstruction U.S. Chapter
[12802]
601 W 26th St., Ste. 325-1
New York, NY 10001
Ph: (908)347-5585

Belafsky, Peter C., MD, Officer
Dysphagia Research Society
[14572]
International Meeting Managers, Inc.
4550 Post Oak Place Dr., Ste. 342
Houston, TX 77027-3167
Ph: (713)965-0566
Fax: (713)960-0488

Belanger, Julie, Exec. Dir.
Professional Aerial Photographers
Association International [2591]
12069 Cessna Pl.
Brookshire, TX 77423
Ph: (713)721-6523
    (713)721-6593
Toll Free: 800-373-2135
Fax: (713)721-6586

Belar, Cynthia D., CEO
American Psychological Association
of Graduate Students [16864]

750 1st St. NE
Washington, DC 20002-4242
Ph: (202)336-5500
Toll Free: 800-374-2721
Fax: (202)336-5997

Belasco, Jill, Chairman
Sense of Smell Institute [1454]
c/o The Fragrance Foundation
621 2nd Ave., 2nd Fl.
New York, NY 10016
Ph: (212)725-2755
Fax: (212)786-3260

Belassai, John King, President
Council of Scottish Clans and As-
sociations [19639]
Bldg. 2, Ste. 10
315 N Page Rd.
Pinehurst, NC 28370
Ph: (980)333-4686

Belcastro, David, President
International Thomas Merton Society
[9060]
2001 Newburg Rd.
Louisville, KY 40205
Ph: (502)272-8177
Fax: (502)272-8452

Belden, John, Bd. Member
Give Kids the World Village [11233]
210 S Bass Rd.
Kissimmee, FL 34746
Ph: (407)396-1114
Fax: (407)396-1207

Beletsky, Misha, Exec. VP
The Typophiles [9351]
PO Box 36-20594
New York, NY 10129
Toll Free: 800-996-2556

Belfanti, Andrea, Exec. Dir.
International Society of Hospitality
Consultants [821]
c/o David Neff, President
131 S Dearborn St., Ste.1700
Chicago, IL
Ph: (312)324-8689
Fax: (312)324-9689

Belger, Monte, Contact
Air Traffic Control Association [122]
1101 King St., Ste. 300
Alexandria, VA 22314
Ph: (703)299-2430
Fax: (703)299-2437

Belinda, Steve, Exec. Dir.
North American Grouse Partnership
[4858]
10630 North 135th St.
Waverly, NE 68462-1256
Fax: (402)786-5547

Belinson, Jerome L., President
Preventive Oncology International
[16352]
2762 Fairmount Blvd.
Cleveland Heights, OH 44118
Ph: (216)312-3663

Belk, Mary, Exec. Dir.
The Crustacean Society [7400]
1320 Winding Way
New Braunfels, TX 78132
Ph: (210)842-9152

Belknap, Robert, President
National Tuberculosis Controllers
Association [14606]
2452 Spring Rd. SE
Smyrna, GA 30080-3828
Ph: (678)503-0503
    (678)503-0804
Toll Free: 877-503-0806
Fax: (678)503-0805

Bell, Andrew F., President, CEO
American Sommelier Association
[178]
580 Broadway, Ste. 714
New York, NY 10012
Ph: (212)226-6805
Fax: (212)226-6407

Bell, Ann, Mktg. Mgr., Mgr., Comm.
International Microelectronic and
Packaging Society [6437]
611 2nd St. NE
Washington, DC 20002-4909
Ph: (202)548-4001
    (202)548-8707
Toll Free: 888-464-1066
Fax: (202)548-6115

Bell, Charles, V. Ch.
National Jobs for All Coalition
[18188]
PO Box 96
Lynbrook, NY 11563
Ph: (203)856-3877

Bell, Craig, President
Company of Military Historians
[22182]
PO Box 910
Rutland, MA 01543-0910
Ph: (508)799-9229

Bell, David E., VP of Fin. Admin.
American Iron and Steel Institute
[2343]
25 Massachusetts Ave. NW, Ste.
800
Washington, DC 20001
Ph: (202)452-7100

Bell, David E., President
Clan Bell North America [20798]
1513 Anterra Dr.
Wake Forest, NC 27587
Ph: (919)528-7959

Bell, David, Chairman
Plasma Protein Therapeutics As-
sociation [13842]
147 Old Solomons Island Rd., Ste.
100
Annapolis, MD 21401
Ph: (202)789-3100
Fax: (410)263-2298

Bell, Dwight, President
United States Luge Association
[22978]
57 Church St.
Lake Placid, NY 12946-1805
Ph: (518)523-2071
Fax: (518)523-4106

Bell, Frances M., Exec. Dir.
American Association of Psychiatric
Administrators [15303]
c/o Frances M. Bell, Executive
Director
PO Box 570218
Dallas, TX 75357-0218
Ph: (972)613-0985
Fax: (972)613-5532

Bell, Kathy, Coord., Ed. Resources
National Association of Elevator
Contractors [877]
1298 Wellbrook Cir.
Conyers, GA 30012
Ph: (770)760-9660
Toll Free: 800-900-6232
Fax: (770)760-9714

Bell, Linda, Secretary
Historic Iris Preservation Society
[22101]
c/o Linda Bell, Secretary
608 Beckwood
Little Rock, AR 72205
Ph: (501)580-0183

Bell, Melanie, Exec. VP
American Association of Professional
  Landmen [2507]
800 Fournier St.
Fort Worth, TX 76102
Ph: (817)847-7700
Fax: (817)847-7704

Bell, Peter H., President, CEO
National Reverse Mortgage Lenders
  Association [2096]
1400 16th St. NW, Ste. 420
Washington, DC 20036
Ph: (202)939-1760
Fax: (202)265-4435

Bell, Peter, President, CEO
National Housing and Rehabilitation
  Association [11982]
1400 16th St. NW, Ste. 420
Washington, DC 20036-2244
Ph: (202)939-1750
Fax: (202)265-4435

Bell, Robert, Exec. Dir.
World Teleport Association [3249]
250 Park Ave., 7th Fl.
New York, NY 10177
Ph: (212)825-0218
Fax: (212)825-0075

Bell, Ron, President
International Plastic Modelers
  Society - United States Branch
  [22199]
PO Box 56023
Saint Petersburg, FL 33732-6023
Ph: (727)537-6886

Bell, Sarah, Director
World T.E.A.M. Sports [22806]
4250 Veterans Memorial Hwy., Ste.
  420 E
Holbrook, NY 11741-4020
Toll Free: 855-987-8326
Fax: (855)288-3377

Bell, Valerie, CEO
Awana Clubs International [20658]
1 E Bode Rd.
Streamwood, IL 60107-6658
Ph: (630)213-2000
Toll Free: 866-292-6227
Fax: (877)292-6232

Bellaman, Michael D., CEO,
  President
Associated Builders and Contractors
  [853]
440 1st St. NW, Ste. 200
Washington, DC 20001

Bellamkonda, Ravi V., PhD,
  President
American Institute for Medical and
  Biological Engineering [6665]
1400 I St. NW, Ste. 235
Washington, DC 20005
Ph: (202)496-9660

Bellamy, Don, Contact
Traditional Cowboy Arts Association
  [8805]
PO Box 2002
Salmon, ID 83467
Ph: (208)865-2006

Belland, Chris, CEO
National Park Hospitality Association
  [1156]
1200 G St. NW, Ste. 650
Washington, DC 20005
Ph: (202)682-9530
Fax: (202)682-9529

Bellanti, Claire, President
Jane Austen Society of North
  America [9039]

c/o Carole Stokes, Membership
  Secretary
3140 S Temperance Way
Boise, ID 83706
Toll Free: 800-836-3911

Bellantone, Paul, CAE, V. Ch.
Incentive Federation [2282]
c/o Melissa Van Dyke, Co-Chair
The Incentive Research Foundation
100 Chesterfield Business Pky., Ste.
  200
Chesterfield, MO 63005-1271
Ph: (636)549-3193

Bellantone, Paul, CAE, CEO,
  President
Promotional Products Association
  International [107]
3125 Skyway Cir. N
Irving, TX 75038-3526
Ph: (972)252-0404
Toll Free: 888-426-7724
Fax: (972)258-3004

Belle, Linda B., Exec. Dir.
Jane Addams Peace Association
  [18798]
777 United Nations Plz., 6th Fl.
New York, NY 10017
Ph: (212)682-8830

Beller, Floyd O., President, CEO
Alliance for Education and Com-
  munity Development [11721]
9452 Telephone Rd., No. 274
Ventura, CA 93004-2600
Ph: (805)861-0010
Fax: (805)477-9883

Beller, Jeff, Treasurer
Renew the Earth [7204]
428 Sand Creek Rd.
Albany, NY 12205
Ph: (518)797-3377

Bellesi, Karen, President
Women in Housing and Finance
  [1271]
400 N Washington St., Ste. 300
Alexandria, VA 22314
Ph: (703)683-4742
Fax: (703)683-0018

Belli, Barbara, Secretary
National Association of Government
  Web Professionals, Inc. [6325]
6311 W Gross Point Rd.
Niles, IL 60714
Ph: (847)647-7226

Bellini, Lisa M., MD, Comm. Chm.
Association of Program Directors in
  Internal Medicine [15427]
Alliance for Academic Internal
  Medicine
330 John Carlyle St., Ste. 610
Alexandria, VA 22314-5946
Ph: (703)341-4540
Fax: (703)519-1893

Bello, Antonio, Officer
American Prosthodontic Society
  [14413]
225 W Wacker Dr., Ste. 650
Chicago, IL 60606
Ph: (312)981-6780
Fax: (312)265-2908

Bellonci, Christopher, President
American Association of Children's
  Residential Centers [13424]
11700 W Lake Park Dr.
Milwaukee, WI 53224
Toll Free: 877-332-2272

Belmont, Donald P., Chmn. of the
  Bd.
Paper Shipping Sack Manufacturers'
  Association, Inc. [840]

5050 Blue Church Rd.
Coopersburg, PA 18036
Ph: (610)282-6845
Fax: (610)282-1577

Belmore, Carolyn, President
National Boating Federation [22648]
PO Box 4111
Annapolis, MD 21403-4111
Toll Free: 866-239-2070

Below, Stephany, Mgr., Comm.
Society For Industrial Organizational
  Psychology [16936]
440 E Poe Rd., Ste. 101
Bowling Green, OH 43402-2756
Ph: (419)353-0032
Fax: (419)352-2645

Belshe, Mark, Exec. Dir.
Rubber Pavements Association
  [576]
3420 W Danbury Dr.
Phoenix, AZ 85053
Ph: (480)517-9944

Belski, Thomas, CEO
Guild for Human Services [17711]
411 Waverley Oaks Rd., Ste.104
Waltham, MA 02452-8468
Ph: (781)893-6000
Fax: (781)893-1171

Belt, Maynard H., President
Fellowship of Missions [20417]
1608 Aberdeen St. NE
Grand Rapids, MI 49505-3910
Ph: (616)361-2396

Beltrano, Bob, President
Swan Owners Association of
  America [22671]
PO Box 347
Jamestown, RI 02835
Ph: (401)423-0600

Belzer, Dena, President
Community Economics, Inc. [11966]
538 9th St., Ste. 200
Oakland, CA 94607
Ph: (510)832-8300
Fax: (510)832-2227

Belzer, Jason, Exec. Dir.
Jewish Coaches Association [22732]
PO Box 167
Tennent, NJ 07763
Ph: (732)322-5145

Bemis, Reneé, President
Society of Animal Artists [8942]
5451 Sedona Hills Dr.
Berthoud, CO 80513-8987
Ph: (970)532-3127
Fax: (970)532-2537

Benard, Marc A., DPM, Exec. Dir.
American Board of Podiatric
  Medicine [16779]
3812 Sepulveda Blvd., Ste. 530
Torrance, CA 90505
Ph: (310)375-0700
Fax: (310)375-1386

BenAvram, Ms. Debra, CEO
American Society for Parenteral and
  Enteral Nutrition [16207]
8630 Fenton St., Ste. 412
Silver Spring, MD 20910-3805
Ph: (301)587-6315
Fax: (301)587-2365

Benbrook, Rod, President
International Formalwear Association
  [205]
244 E Main St.
Galesburg, IL 61401
Ph: (309)721-5450
Fax: (309)342-5921

Benchley, Wendy W., President
Shark Savers [4887]
744 Montgomery St., Ste. 300
San Francisco, CA 94111
Ph: (415)834-3174
Fax: (415)834-1759

Bender, Doug, President
Fairlane Club of America [21378]
340 Clicktown Rd.
Church Hill, TN 37642-6622
Ph: (423)245-6678
Fax: (423)245-2456

Bender, James K., II, Asst. Pres.
International Union of Elevator
  Constructors [23447]
7154 Columbia Gateway Dr.
Columbia, MD 21046
Ph: (410)953-6150
Fax: (410)953-6169

Bender, Leslie
ACA International [981]
4040 W 70th St.
Minneapolis, MN 55435
Ph: (952)926-6547
Fax: (952)926-1624

Bender, Rich, Exec. Dir.
U.S.A. Wrestling [23374]
6155 Lehman Dr.
Colorado Springs, CO 80918-3456
Ph: (719)598-8181
Fax: (719)598-9440

Bendixen, Prof. Alfred, Exec. Dir.
American Literature Association
  [9750]
Dept. of English
Princeton University
Princeton, NJ 08544

BenDor, Jan, Chairman
Gray Panthers [10508]
10 G St. NE, Ste. 600
Washington, DC 20002
Ph: (202)737-6637
Toll Free: 800-280-5362

Bendroth, Ms. Margaret, Exec. Dir.
American Congregational Associa-
  tion [20034]
14 Beacon St., 2nd Fl.
Boston, MA 02108-3704
Ph: (617)523-0470
Fax: (617)523-0491

Benedict, Beth, Ph.D., President
American Society for Deaf Children
  [15174]
800 Florida Ave. NE, No. 2047
Washington, DC 20002-3695
Toll Free: 800-942-2732
Fax: (410)795-0965

Benedict, Dr. Mary I., Director
Welsh Pony & Cob Society of
  America [4426]
720 Green St.
Stephens City, VA 22655
Ph: (540)868-7669

Benedict, Tony, President
Association of Business Process
  Management Professionals [2150]
100 East Washington St.
Springfield, IL 62701
Ph: (217)753-4007
Fax: (217)528-6545

Benedict, Wes, Exec. Dir.
Libertarian National Committee
  [18892]
1444 Duke St.
Alexandria, VA 22314-3403
Ph: (202)333-0008
Toll Free: 800-ELECT-US
Fax: (202)333-0072

Benefiel, Phil, President
99th Infantry Division Association
[20715]
PO Box 99
Marion, KS 66861-0099

Benet, Dr. Les, Founder
American Association of
Pharmaceutical Scientists [7005]
2107 Wilson Blvd., Ste. 700
Arlington, VA 22201-3042
Ph: (703)243-2800

Bengloff, Rich, Mem.
American Association of
Independent Music [2900]
132 Delancey St.
New York, NY 10002
Ph: (646)692-4877

Bengston, Prof. William, President
Society for Scientific Exploration
[7017]
c/o Stephen E. Braude, Ph.D.
University of Maryland - Baltimore
County
8022 S Rainbow Blvd., Ste. 236
Las Vegas, NV 89139

Bengtson, Carol, President
Scrollsaw Association of the World
[22481]
116 E Lynn St.
Botkins, OH 45306
Ph: (937)693-3309

Benham, Frances, PhD, Chairman,
President
National Association for Pseudox-
anthoma Elasticum [14504]
8760 Manchester Rd.
Saint Louis, MO 63144-2724
Ph: (314)301-7345
Fax: (314)301-7345

Ben-Horin, Daniel, Founder,
Secretary
TechSoup Global [6732]
435 Brannan St., Ste. 100
San Francisco, CA 94107
Ph: (415)633-9300

Benincasa, Joseph P., CEO,
President
Actors' Fund [11793]
729 7th Ave., 10th Fl.
New York, NY 10019
Ph: (212)221-7300
Toll Free: 800-825-0911

Bening, Stephen L., Chairman
World Salt Foundation [20479]
6810 Lee St.
Hollywood, FL 33024
Ph: (954)600-6381

Benisch, Johnny, Mem.
American Association of Code
Enforcement [5452]
114 Lakeshore Loop
Tow, TX 78672-4900
Ph: (830)613-4268

Benjamin, David A., Exec. Dir.
InterCollegiate Tennis Association
[23300]
174 Tamarack Cir.
Skillman, NJ 08558-2021
Ph: (609)497-6920
Fax: (609)497-9586

Benjamin, Maynard H., CAE, CEO,
President
Envelope Manufacturers Association
[3171]
500 Montgomery St., Ste. 550
Alexandria, VA 22314
Ph: (703)739-2200
Fax: (703)739-2209

Benjamin, Renee, Director
Association of Corporate Counsel
[5108]
1025 Connecticut Ave. NW, Ste. 200
Washington, DC 20036
Ph: (202)293-4103
Fax: (202)293-4701

Benjamin, Roger, PhD, President,
CEO
Council for Aid to Education [7833]
215 Lexington Ave., 16th Fl.
New York, NY 10016-6056
Ph: (212)661-5800
Fax: (212)661-9766

Benjamin, Stephen, Comm. Chm.
National Conference on Weights and
Measures [5771]
1135 M St., Ste. 110
Lincoln, NE 68508
Ph: (402)434-4880
Fax: (402)434-4878

Benjaminson, Rabbi Yerachmiel,
Exec. Dir.
Tzivos Hashem [9643]
792 Eastern Pkwy.
Brooklyn, NY 11213
Ph: (718)907-8855
    (718)467-6630

Benjelloun, Karim, Secretary
Moroccan-American Society for Life
Sciences [6896]
PO Box 324
Dunn Loring, VA 22027-0324
Ph: (202)413-6025
    (860)944-7934

Benn, Ruth, Coord.
National War Tax Resistance
Coordinating Committee [19174]
PO Box 150553
Brooklyn, NY 11215
Ph: (718)768-3420
Toll Free: 800-269-7464

Benner, Christine, VP
Sacro Occipital Technique Organiza-
tion U.S.A. [14282]
PO Box 1357
Sparta, NC 28675
Ph: (336)793-6524
Fax: (336)372-1541

Bennet, Marilyn, President
Women Band Directors International
[8392]
c/o Carol Nendza, Treasurer
10611 Ridgewood Dr.
Palos Park, IL 60464

Bennett, Amy, President
American Society of Access Profes-
sionals [5299]
1444 I St. NW, Ste. 700
Washington, DC 20005
Ph: (202)712-9054
Fax: (202)216-9646

Bennett, Brad, President
Wilderness Medical Society [15750]
2150 South 1300 East, Ste. 500
Salt Lake City, UT 84106-4375
Ph: (801)990-2988
Fax: (801)990-4601

Bennett, Brandon, President
Back to the Basics Please [13530]
10329 S Del Rey Dr.
Yuma, AZ 85367
Ph: (928)550-3999

Bennett, Craig, President
American Society of Military
Comptrollers [5591]
415 N Alfred St.

Alexandria, VA 22314
Ph: (703)549-0360
Toll Free: 800-462-5637
Fax: (703)549-3181

Bennett, Dave, Sr. VP
Independent Grocers Alliance [1337]
8745 W Higgins Rd., Ste. 350
Chicago, IL 60631
Ph: (773)693-4520
Fax: (773)693-4533

Bennett, Irving, Treasurer, Secretary
Vision USA [16440]
243 N Lindbergh Blvd., Fl. 1
Saint Louis, MO 63141
Ph: (314)983-4200
Toll Free: 800-365-2219
Fax: (314)991-4101

Bennett, Jane, Exec. VP
Building Stone Institute [3182]
Bldg. 2
5 Riverside Dr.
Chestertown, NY 12817
Ph: (518)803-4336
Toll Free: 866-786-6313
Fax: (518)803-4338

Bennett, Kathleen, President
American Academy of Dental Sleep
Medicine [17207]
2510 N Frontage Rd.
Darien, IL 60561
Ph: (630)737-9755
    (630)737-9705
Fax: (630)737-9790

Bennett, Lisa, Office Mgr.
Rhine Research Center [6991]
Bldg. 500
2741 Campus Walk Ave.
Durham, NC 27705
Ph: (919)309-4600

Bennett, Pat, Comm. Chm.
Concerned Persons for Adoption
[10449]
PO Box 179
Whippany, NJ 07981
Ph: (973)293-2621

Bennett, Russell, Exec. Dir.
National AIDS Housing Coalition
[11976]
727 15th St. NW, 11th Fl.
Washington, DC 20005
Ph: (202)347-0333
Fax: (202)347-3411

Bennett, Severine, CGMP, PMP,
Exec. Dir.
International Society of Political
Psychology [16921]
126 Ward St., Ste. 1213
Columbus, NC 28722
Ph: (828)894-5422
Fax: (828)894-5422

Bennett, Sharon, Exec. Dir.
American Academy of Implant
Dentistry [14380]
211 E Chicago Ave., Ste. 750
Chicago, IL 60611
Ph: (312)335-1550
Toll Free: 877-335-2243

Bennett, Stephen, CEO, President
United Cerebral Palsy [14158]
1825 K St. NW, Ste. 600
Washington, DC 20006
Ph: (202)776-0406
Toll Free: 800-872-5827

Bennett, Steven, COO, VP
Brookings Institution [18963]
1775 Massachusetts Ave. NW
Washington, DC 20036
Ph: (202)797-6210
Fax: (202)797-6133

Bennett, Sue, President
American Lawyers Alliance [4990]
2756 Patterson Rd. SW
Pataskala, OH 43062-7704

Bennett, Vaneeda, CRO
American Diabetes Association
[14518]
1701 N Beauregard St.
Alexandria, VA 22311
Ph: (800)342-2383
    (202)331-8303
Toll Free: 800-342-2383

Benney, James C., CAE, CEO
National Fenestration Rating Council
[557]
6305 Ivy Ln., Ste. 140
Greenbelt, MD 20770
Ph: (301)589-1776
Fax: (301)589-3884

Benoit, Dana, President
ADED, Inc. [7722]
200 1st Ave. NW, Ste. 505
Hickory, NC 28601-6113
Toll Free: 866-672-9466
Fax: (828)855-1672

Benoit, Jeff, CEO, President
Restore America's Estuaries [4762]
2300 Clarendon Blvd., Ste. 603
Arlington, VA 22201-3392
Ph: (703)524-0248

Benoit, Mike, Exec. Dir.
Cement Kiln Recycling Coalition
[4627]
PO Box 7553
Arlington, VA 22207
Ph: (703)624-4513

Benor, Daniel J., M.D., Founder
Council for Healing [13618]
c/o Daniel J. Benor, MD, Founder
PO Box 76
Bellmawr, NJ 08099
Ph: (609)714-1885

Benor, Sarah, VP
Association for the Social Scientific
Study of Jewry [8136]
c/o Prof. Leonard Saxe, Treasurer
Cohen Center for Modern Jewish
Studies
Brandeis University
415 South St.
Waltham, MA 02453

Bens, Catherine M., President
Society of Quality Assurance [2824]
154 Hansen Rd., Ste. 201
Charlottesville, VA 22911
Ph: (434)297-4772
Fax: (434)977-1856

Bensinger, Roger, Secretary
National Council on Alcoholism and
Drug Dependence, Inc. [13168]
217 Broadway, Ste. 712
New York, NY 10007
Ph: (212)269-7797

Ben-Sira, Aviva, Director
Association of Israel's Decorative
Arts [8965]
c/o Dale & Doug Anderson
100 Worth Ave., Apt. 713
Palm Beach, FL 33480

Benslimane, Mr. Aomar, PhD,
President
Amazigh Cultural Association in
America [8777]
75 Washington Rd., CN753 PMB163
Bedminster, NJ 07921

Benson, Chuck, Chairman
Tee it up for the Troops [13248]
515 W Travelers Trl.

Burnsville, MN 55337
Ph: (952)646-2490

Benson, Deborah, Officer
Grateful American Coin [10743]
15207 Hammock Chase Ct.
Odessa, FL 33556
Ph: (813)404-2568

Benson, Jeremy, Contact
Free the Grapes! [4952]
2700 Napa Valley Corporate Dr.,
Ste. H
Napa, CA 94558
Ph: (707)254-1107

Benson, Peter, Chief Tech. Ofc.,
Exec. Dir.
Electronic Commerce Code Manage-
ment Association [998]
2980 Linden St., Ste. E2
Bethlehem, PA 18017-3283
Ph: (610)861-5990
Fax: (610)625-4657

Benson, Ray, President, Chairman
Asleep at the Wheel Fan Club
[24024]
PO Box 463
Austin, TX 78767
Ph: (512)444-9885
Fax: (512)444-4699

Bent, Graham, CEO
National Commission for the
Certification of Crane Operators
[810]
2750 Prosperity Ave., Ste. 505
Fairfax, VA 22031
Ph: (703)560-2391
Fax: (703)560-2392

Bentley, Andy, President
Society for the Preservation of
Natural History Collections [9436]
PO Box 526
New York, NY 10044-0526

Bentley, Annette, BA, President
American Celiac Society Dietary
Support Coalition [16202]
New Orleans, LA 70123
Ph: (504)305-2968

Bentley, Robert, President
Roller Skating Association
International [23153]
6905 Corporate Dr.
Indianapolis, IN 46278
Ph: (317)347-2626
Fax: (317)347-2636

Bentley, Dr. Sean, Director
Sigma Pi Sigma [23850]
1 Physics Ellipse
College Park, MD 20740
Ph: (301)209-3007
Fax: (301)209-0839

Bentley, Woody, President
The Bolling Family Association
[20785]
PO Box 591
Vienna, VA 22183-0591

Benton, Janice, Exec. Dir.
Council on Intellectual and
Developmental Disability [20137]
415 Michigan Ave. NE, Ste. 95
Washington, DC 20017-4501
Ph: (202)529-2933
Fax: (202)529-4678

Benton, Janice, Exec. Dir.
National Catholic Partnership on Dis-
ability [19880]
415 Michigan Ave. NE, Ste. 95
Washington, DC 20017-4501
Ph: (202)529-2933
Fax: (202)529-4678

Benton, Joe, Mem.
National Association of Black Social
Workers [13111]
2305 Martin Luther King, Jr. Ave. SE
Washington, DC 20020-5813
Ph: (202)678-4570
Fax: (202)678-4572

Benton, Julius L., Jr., Director
Association of Lunar and Planetary
Observers [21306]
c/o Matthew L. Will, Secretary
PO Box 13456
Springfield, IL 62791

Benton, Susan, President, CEO
Urban Libraries Council [9733]
1333 H St. NW, Ste. 1000W
Washington, DC 20005
Ph: (202)750-8650

Bentti, Robert, Director
National Adult Education Honor
Society [7454]
4953 Madison Pke.
Independence, KY 41051
Ph: (859)685-8559

Bentz, Brian, Officer
Glenkirk [11599]
3504 Commercial Ave.
Northbrook, IL 60062
Ph: (847)272-5111
Fax: (847)272-7350

Bentz, Michael L., President
American Association of Plastic
Surgeons [14304]
500 Cummings Ctr., Ste. 4550
Beverly, MA 01915
Ph: (978)927-8330
Fax: (978)524-0498

Benus, John, Director, Founder
Venezuelan Tourism Association
[3407]
PO Box 3010
Sausalito, CA 94966-3010
Ph: (415)331-0100

Benz, Dr. Edward J., Jr., CEO,
President
Dana-Farber Cancer Institute
[13958]
450 Brookline Ave.
Boston, MA 02215-5450
Ph: (617)632-3000
Toll Free: 866-408-3324

Benzer, Brian, Chairman
World Bicycle Relief [12736]
1000 W Fulton Market, 4th Fl.
Chicago, IL 60607
Ph: (312)664-3836

Benzer, Jo Ann, Exec. Dir.
Information Technology Alliance
[7272]
23940 N 73rd Pl.
Scottsdale, AZ 85255
Ph: (480)515-2003

Benzil, Deborah L., VP
American Association of Neurologi-
cal Surgeons [16058]
5550 Meadowbrook Dr.
Rolling Meadows, IL 60008-3852
Ph: (847)378-0500
Toll Free: 888-566-2267
Fax: (847)378-0600

Beral, Valerie, President
International Epidemiological As-
sociation [14731]
1500 Sunday Dr., Ste. 102
Raleigh, NC 27607
Ph: (919)861-5586
Fax: (919)787-4916

Beranek, Randy, President, CEO
National Psoriasis Foundation USA
[14506]
6600 SW 92nd Ave., Ste. 300
Portland, OR 97223-7195
Ph: (503)244-7404
Toll Free: 800-723-9166
Fax: (503)245-0626

Bercu, Dr. Daniel, Founder,
President
Doctors at War Against Trafficking
Worldwide [12921]
PO Box 681364
Franklin, TN 37068
Toll Free: 888-552-8927

Berdell, John, Mem.
History of Economics Society [9485]
c/o Marianne Johnson, Secretary
Dept. of Economics
University of Wisconsin Oshkosh
800 Algoma Blvd.
Oshkosh, WI 54901
Ph: (920)424-2230
Fax: (920)424-1441

Berecz, Ms. Illya, Exec. Dir.
North American Association of
Subway Franchisees [1464]
PO Box 320955
Fairfield, CT 06825
Ph: (203)579-7779
Toll Free: 866-590-9865

Berenbach, Shari, CEO, President
United States African Development
Foundation [18505]
1400 I St. NW, Ste. 1000
Washington, DC 20005-2248
Ph: (202)673-3916
Fax: (202)673-3810

Berenbeim, Jane Rosen, President
Jewish Genealogical Society [20981]
PO Box 631
New York, NY 10113-0631
Ph: (212)294-8318

Berg, Bradley R., MD, Founder
Humanity for Children [16608]
2101 W Broadway, No. 103-131
Columbia, MO 65203-7632
Toll Free: 866-406-2006
Fax: (206)420-5353

Berg, Dave, Exec. Dir.
Inland Lake Yachting Association
[22621]
PO Box 662
Fontana, WI 53125-0311
Ph: (847)675-6434

Berg, Don, CEO
IHG Owners Association [1662]
3 Ravinia Dr., Ste. 100
Atlanta, GA 30346
Ph: (770)604-5555
Fax: (770)604-5684

Berg, Jim, President
People's Lobby [18918]
810 N Milwaukee Ave.
Chicago, IL 60642
Ph: (312)676-2805

Berg, Leslie J., PhD, Chairman
American Association of Immunolo-
gists [15369]
1451 Rockville Pke., Ste. 650
Bethesda, MD 20814
Ph: (301)634-7178
Fax: (301)634-7887

Berg, Ms. Miriam, President
Council on Size and Weight
Discrimination [12395]
PO Box 305

Mount Marion, NY 12456
Ph: (845)679-1209
Fax: (845)679-1206

Berg, Nancy S., CEO, President
International Society for
Pharmaceutical Engineering [7006]
600 N Westshore Blvd., Ste. 900
Tampa, FL 33609-1114
Ph: (813)960-2105
Fax: (813)264-2816

Berg, Mr. Peter, Director
Planet Drum Foundation [17810]
PO Box 31251
San Francisco, CA 94131-0251
Ph: (415)285-6556
Fax: (415)285-6563

Bergaminiinc, William, President, VP
Heating Airconditioning and
Refrigeration Distributors
International [1620]
445 Hutchinson Ave., Ste. 550
Columbus, OH 43235
Ph: (614)345-4328
Toll Free: 888-253-2128
Fax: (614)345-9161

Bergdall, Terry, PhD, CEO
Institute of Cultural Affairs in the
U.S.A. [12003]
4750 N Sheridan Rd.
Chicago, IL 60640
Ph: (773)769-6363
Fax: (773)944-1582

Bergemann, Lori, Exec. Dir.,
Founder
Amara Conservation [4780]
1531 Packard St., No. 12
Ann Arbor, MI 48104
Ph: (734)761-5357

Bergen, Jerri, President
American Aviation Historical Society
[21212]
15211 Springdale St.
Huntington Beach, CA 92649
Ph: (714)549-4818

Berger, Dan, President
National Association of Media and
Technology Centers [2317]
PO Box 9844
Cedar Rapids, IA 52409-9844
Ph: (319)654-0608
Fax: (319)654-0609

Berger, Ernest, Founder, President
Santa America, Inc. [11267]
308 Belrose Ave., Ste. 200 E
Daphne, AL 36526
Ph: (251)626-6609

Berger, Helena, President, CEO
American Association of People with
Disabilities [11568]
2013 H St. NW, 5th Fl.
Washington, DC 20006
Ph: (202)521-4316
Toll Free: 800-840-8844

Berger, Jason, Director
National Association of Ticket
Brokers [1152]
214 N Hale St.
Wheaton, IL 60187
Ph: (630)510-4594
Fax: (630)510-4501

Berger, Jay, Exec. Dir.
Earthquake Engineering Research
Institute [7155]
499 14th St., Ste. 320
Oakland, CA 94612-1934
Ph: (510)451-0905
Fax: (510)451-5411

Berger, Jennifer, Exec. Dir.
About-Face [13367]
PO Box 191145
San Francisco, CA 94119
Ph: (415)839-6779

Berger, Dr. Karl Hans, Director,
Founder
Creative Music Foundation [9898]
PO Box 671
Woodstock, NY 12498
Ph: (845)679-8847
(845)679-5616

Berger, Ron, President
Desert Tortoise Preserve Committee
[3848]
4067 Mission Inn Ave.
Riverside, CA 92501
Ph: (951)683-3872
Fax: (951)683-6949

Berger, Scott, Exec. Dir.
Center for Chemical Process Safety
[6193]
120 Wall St., 23rd Fl.
New York, NY 10005-4020
Ph: (203)702-7660
Toll Free: 800-242-4363
Fax: (203)775-5177

Bergeron, Larry, Exec. Dir., Founder
A Child's Hope International [10937]
2430 E Kemper Rd.
Cincinnati, OH 45241
Ph: (513)771-2244

Bergeron, Margaret, Exec. Dir.
American Military Retirees Associa-
tion [21107]
5436 Peru St., No. 1
Plattsburgh, NY 12901
Ph: (518)563-9479
Toll Free: 800-424-2969
Fax: (518)324-5204

Bergeson, Dave, Exec. Dir.
Association of Pediatric Hematology/
Oncology Nurses [16122]
8735 W Higgins Rd., Ste. 300
Chicago, IL 60631
Ph: (847)375-4724
(855)202-9760
Fax: (847)375-6478

Bergeson, Dave, Exec. Dir.
PRISM International [1806]
8735 W Higgins Rd., Ste. 300
Chicago, IL 60631
Ph: (847)375-6344
Toll Free: 800-336-9793
Fax: (847)375-3643

Bergfeld, Ellen G.M., PhD, CEO
American Society of Agronomy
[3544]
5585 Guilford Rd.
Madison, WI 53711-5801
Ph: (608)273-8080

Bergfeld, Wilma F., MD, Chairperson
Cosmetic Ingredient Review [1585]
1620 I St. NW, Ste. 1200
Washington, DC 20036
Ph: (202)331-0651
Fax: (202)331-0088

Bergfeld, Wilma F., MD, Officer
North American Hair Research
Society [14903]
303 W State St.
Geneva, IL 60134-2156
Ph: (630)578-3991
Fax: (630)262-1520

Bergfeld, Wilma F., MD, Founder
Women's Dermatologic Society
[14516]

700 N Fairfax St., Ste. 510
Alexandria, VA 22314
Ph: (856)423-7222
Toll Free: 877-937-7673
Fax: (856)423-3420

Berggren, Erin, Exec. Dir.
The Giving Institute [1469]
225 W Wacker Dr., Ste. 650
Chicago, IL 60606-3396
Ph: (312)981-6794
Fax: (312)265-2908

Berghahn, Mr. Walt, Exec. Dir.
HealthCare Compliance Packaging
Council [16661]
2711 Buford Rd., No. 268
Bon Air, VA 23235-2423
Ph: (804)338-5778
Toll Free: 888-812-4272

Bergman, Christer, Secretary
International Biometric Identification
Association [7277]
1090 Vermount Ave. NW, 6th Fl.
Washington, DC 20005
Ph: (202)789-4452
Fax: (202)289-7097

Bergman, Edward, Exec. Dir.
Africa Travel Association [3366]
1100 17th St. NW, Ste. 1000
Washington, DC 20036
Ph: (202)835-1115
Toll Free: 888-439-0478
Fax: (202)835-1117

Bergman, Edward, President,
Founder
Miracle Corners of the World
[13458]
152 Madison Ave., Ste. 1702
New York, NY 10016
Ph: (212)453-5811
Fax: (212)213-4890

Bergquist, Robbie, Founder,
President
Cell Phones for Soldiers [10740]
5665 N Commerce Ct.
Alpharetta, GA 30004
Ph: (678)580-1976

Bergstrand, Jeffrey, President
International Economics and Finance
Society [6395]
c/o Florida International University
Dept. of Economics
11200 SW 8th St.
Miami, FL 33199-2516
Ph: (305)348-2316
Fax: (305)348-1524

Bergt, Michael, Contact
Society of Tempera Painters [8944]
c/o Michael Bergt, Tutor
PO Box 30766
Santa Fe, NM 87592-0766
Ph: (505)473-9654

Berhinig, Robert, Chairman
Steel Door Institute [582]
30200 Detroit Rd.
Westlake, OH 44145
Ph: (440)899-0010
Fax: (440)892-1404

Berich, Ms. Peg, Registrar
Swedish Colonial Society [10232]
916 S Swanson St.
Philadelphia, PA 19147-4332

Beringer, Dennis, President, Exec.
Sec., Treasurer
Association for Aviation Psychology
[5859]
PO Box 671393
Marietta, GA 30066

Berkheimer, Beth, Mgr. of Mtgs. &
Exhibits
American Chemical Society - Rubber
Division [2984]
411 Wolf Ledges, Ste. 201
Akron, OH 44311
Ph: (330)595-5531
Fax: (330)972-5269

Berkley, Bert, Chmn. of the Bd.
Global Envelope Alliance [3172]
700 S Washington St., Ste. 260
Alexandria, VA 22314
Ph: (703)739-2200
Fax: (703)739-2209

Berkley, Seth, CEO
GAVI Alliance [15142]
1776 I St. NW, Ste. 600
Washington, DC 20006
Ph: (202)478-1050
Fax: (202)478-1060

Berkman, Harold W., Director, Exec.
VP
Academy of Marketing Science
[8267]
PO Box 3072
Ruston, LA 71272
Ph: (318)257-2612
Fax: (318)257-4253

Berkoff, Mr. Bruce, Chairman
LCD TV Association [3251]
16055 SW Walker Rd., Ste. 264
Beaverton, OR 97006
Ph: (215)206-6506

Berkowitz, Joanne, Exec. Dir.
International Society of Worldwide
Stamp Collectors [22336]
c/o Joanne Berkowitz, Executive
Director
PO Box 19006
Sacramento, CA 95819

Berkowitz, Scott, Founder, President
Rape, Abuse and Incest National
Network [12571]
1220 L St. NW, Ste. 505
Washington, DC 20005
Ph: (202)544-3064
(202)544-1034
Toll Free: 800-656-4673

Berlant, Dan, Mgr.
North American Skull Base Society
[16033]
11300 W Olympic Blvd., Ste. 600
Los Angeles, CA 90064
Ph: (310)424-3326
Fax: (310)437-0585

Berlin, Dr. Robert H., Exec. Dir.
Society for Military History [9809]
George C. Marshall Library
Virginia Military Institute
Lexington, VA 24450-1600
Ph: (540)464-7468
(928)237-1289
Fax: (540)464-7330

Berlin, Dr. Steven, Treasurer
Wreck and Crash Mail Society
[22381]
c/o Ken Sanford
613 Championship Dr.
Oxford, CT 06478-128
Ph: (203)888-9237
Fax: (203)888-9237

Berliner, Don, Chairman
Fund for UFO Research [7010]
PO Box 7501
Alexandria, VA 22307

Berman, Al, CEO, President
DRI International [5075]
1115 Broadway, 12th Fl.

New York, NY 10010
Toll Free: 866-542-3744

Berman, Amy, Founder
Mother Bear Project [11080]
PO Box 62188
Minneapolis, MN 55426

Berman, Brian E., President
National Gaucher Foundation
[15829]
61 General Early Dr.
Harpers Ferry, WV 25425
Toll Free: 800-504-3189
Fax: (770)934-2911

Berman, Ellen, CEO
CECA Solutions [18190]
2737 Devonshire Pl. NW, Ste. 102
Washington, DC 20008

Berman, Henry L., CEO
Exponent Philanthropy [18852]
1720 N St. NW
Washington, DC 20036
Ph: (202)580-6560
Toll Free: 888-212-9922
Fax: (202)580-6579

Berman, Ms. Jean C., Esq., Advisor
International Senior Lawyers Project
[5014]
96 Morton St., 7th Fl.
New York, NY 10014
Ph: (646)798-3289

Berman, Steven, Treasurer
Science Fiction Research Associa-
tion [10206]
c/o Steven Berman, Treasurer
PO Box 214441
Auburn Hills, MI 48321

Bernacchio, Paul, President
National Amputation Foundation
[11621]
c/o Paul Bernacchio, President
40 Church St.
Malverne, NY 11565
Ph: (516)887-3600
Fax: (516)887-3667

Bernard, Harold, Contact
Gyro International [12890]
1096 Mentor Ave.
Painesville, OH 44077-0489
Ph: (440)352-2501

Bernard, John, President
Latin America Mission [20430]
United World Mission
205 Regency Executive Park Dr.,
Ste. 430
Charlotte, NC 28217
Ph: (704)357-3355
Toll Free: 800-825-5896

Bernard, Rev. John, President
United World Mission [20472]
205 Regency Executive Park Dr.,
Ste. 430
Charlotte, NC 28217
Ph: (704)357-3355
Toll Free: 800-825-5896
Fax: (704)357-6389

Bernard, Sallie, President
Coalition for SafeMinds [15918]
PO Box 285
Huntington Beach, CA 92648
Ph: (404)934-0777
(202)780-9821

Bernardo, Meg, Gen. Mgr.
World Surf League [23280]
149 Bay St.
Santa Monica, CA 90405
Ph: (310)450-1212

Bernat, Patrick, Director
Association for the Advancement of
Medical Instrumentation [6109]
4301 N Fairfax Dr., Ste. 301
Arlington, VA 22203-1633
Ph: (703)525-4890
Fax: (703)276-0793

Bernath, Eric, Bd. Member
Reusable Industrial Packaging As-
sociation [843]
51 Monroe St., Ste. 812
Rockville, MD 20850
Ph: (301)577-3786
Fax: (301)577-6476

Bernett, David, Administrator
National Energy Management
Institute [6497]
8403 Arlington Blvd., Ste. 100
Fairfax, VA 22031
Ph: (703)739-7100
Fax: (703)683-7615

Bernetti, Capt. Al, President
National Teen Anglers [22043]
1177 Bayshore Dr., No. 207
Fort Pierce, FL 34949
Ph: (772)519-0482

Bernhard, Berl, V. Chmn. of the Bd.
Middle East Investment Initiative
[1251]
500 Eighth St. NW
Washington, DC 20004
Ph: (202)799-4345
Fax: (202)799-5000

Bernhard, Dianne, Exec. Dir.
Concerns of Police Survivors [5461]
846 Old South 5
Camdenton, MO 65020-3199
Ph: (573)346-4911
Fax: (573)346-1414

Bernhardt, Emily, President
Society for Freshwater Science
[4015]
5400 Bosque Blvd., Ste. 680
Waco, TX 76710-4446
Ph: (254)399-9636
Fax: (254)776-3767

Bernhardt, Emily, President
Society for Freshwater Science
[6375]
5400 Bosque Blvd., Ste. 680
Waco, TX 76710-4446
Ph: (254)399-9636
Fax: (254)776-3767

Berns, Peter V., CEO
The Arc [12315]
1825 K St. NW, Ste. 1200
Washington, DC 20006-1266
Ph: (202)534-3700
Toll Free: 800-433-5255
Fax: (202)534-3731

Berns, Peter V., CEO
National Conference of Executives
of the Arc [2185]
1825 K St. NW, Ste. 1200
Washington, DC 20006
Ph: (202)534-3700
Toll Free: 800-433-5255
Fax: (202)534-3731

Bernstein, Alan, Bd. Member
Family Equality Council [11880]
225 Franklin St., Ste.2660
Boston, MA 02110
Ph: (617)502-8700
Fax: (617)502-8701

Bernstein, Andy, Exec. Dir.
HeadCount [18181]
104 W 29th St., 11th Fl.

New York, NY 10001

Bernstein, David E., MD, VP
Bockus International Society of
Gastroenterology [14783]
220 W Rittenhouse Sq., No. 18C
Philadelphia, PA 19103
Ph: (215)732-5468
Fax: (215)732-4989

Bernstein, David, President
Jewish Council for Public Affairs
[12224]
116 E 27th St.
New York, NY 10016-8942
Ph: (212)684-6950

Bernstein, Edward, President
Industrial Research Institute [7091]
2300 Clarendon Blvd., Ste. 400
Arlington, VA 22201
Ph: (703)647-2580
Fax: (703)647-2581

Bernstein, Jeffrey, President
National Kidney Foundation [15882]
30 E 33rd St.
New York, NY 10016-5337
Toll Free: 800-622-9010
Fax: (212)689-9261

Bernstein, Jon
National Coalition for Technology in
Education and Training [8672]
2724 Kenwood Ave.
Alexandria, VA 22302
Ph: (202)263-2577

Bernstein, Dr. Robert
American Academy of Dental Group
Practice [14373]
2525 E Arizona Biltmore Cir., Ste.
127
Phoenix, AZ 85016
Ph: (602)381-1185

Bernstein, Robert, President
Commercial Law League of America
[5085]
1000 N Rand Rd., Ste. 214
Wauconda, IL 60084
Ph: (312)240-1400
Fax: (847)526-3993

Bernstein, Scott, President, Founder
Center for Neighborhood Technology
[17969]
2125 W North Ave.
Chicago, IL 60647
Ph: (773)278-4800
Fax: (773)278-3840

Bernstein, Tom A., Chairman
U.S. Holocaust Memorial Council
[18353]
100 Raoul Wallenberg Pl. SW
Washington, DC 20024-2126
Ph: (202)488-0400

Berry, Prof. David, Exec. Dir.
Community College Humanities As-
sociation [8004]
Essex County College
303 University Ave.
Newark, NJ 07102
Ph: (973)877-3577
Fax: (973)877-3578

Berry, James H., Assoc. Pub.
American Dental Association [14404]
211 E Chicago Ave.
Chicago, IL 60611-2678
Ph: (312)440-2500
Toll Free: 800-947-4746
Fax: (312)440-3542

Berry, Jim, President
Retailers of Art Glass and Supplies
[1509]

c/o Margie Bolton, Treasurer
109 Main St. S
Minot, ND 58701-3913
Ph: (701)837-8555

Berry, Ken, Editor
Napoléonic Age Philatelists [22348]
c/o Don Smith, President
PO Box 576
Johnstown, PA 15907-0576

Berry, Mr. Kim, President
Programmers Guild [7290]
PO Box 1250
Summit, NJ 07902-1250

Berry, Dr. Lemuel, Jr., Exec. Dir.,
Founder
International Association of Asian
Studies [7523]
850 Main St.
Westbrook, ME 04092
Ph: (207)839-8004
Fax: (207)839-3776

Berry, Dr. Lemuel, Jr., Exec. Dir.,
Founder
National Association of African
American Studies [7467]
PO Box 6670
Scarborough, ME 04070
Ph: (207)839-8004
Fax: (207)839-3776

Berry, Dr. Lemuel, Jr., Exec. Dir.,
Founder
National Association of Hispanic and
Latino Studies [9292]
850 Main St.
Westbrook, ME 04092
Ph: (207)839-8004
Fax: (207)856-2800

Berry, Dr. Lemuel, Jr., Founder
National Association of Native
American Studies [8396]
850 Main St.
Westbrook, ME 04092
Ph: (207)839-8004
Fax: (207)839-3776

Berry, Maya, Exec. Dir.
Arab American Institute [18903]
1600 K St. NW, Ste. 601
Washington, DC 20006
Ph: (202)429-9210
Fax: (202)429-9214

Berry, Michael, Treasurer, Trustee
General Grand Chapter, Order of the
Eastern Star [19555]
1618 New Hampshire Ave. NW
Washington, DC 20009-2549
Ph: (202)667-4737
Fax: (202)462-5162

Berry, Michael, President
National Ski Areas Association
[1674]
133 S Van Gordon St., Ste. 300
Lakewood, CO 80228
Ph: (303)987-1111
Fax: (303)986-2345

Berry, Nick, CEO
International Youth Conditioning As-
sociation [23377]
PO Box 1539
Elizabethtown, KY 42702-1539
Toll Free: 888-366-4922

Berry, Scott, Program Mgr.
National Association of Black
Journalists [2693]
1100 Knight Hall, Ste. 3100
College Park, MD 20742
Ph: (301)405-0248
Fax: (301)314-1714

Berry, Selisse, Founder, CEO
Out and Equal Workplace Advocates
[11903]
155 Sansome St., Ste. 450
San Francisco, CA 94104
Ph: (415)694-6500

Berry, Thomas, Arch.
Historical Construction Equipment
Association [9579]
16623 Liberty Hi Rd.
Bowling Green, OH 43402
Ph: (419)352-5616
Fax: (419)352-6086

Berryhill, Vivian, Founder, President
National Coalition of Pastors'
Spouses [13073]
950 Mt. Moriah Rd., Ste. 100
Memphis, TN 38117
Ph: (901)517-6537
Toll Free: 866-901-5044

Berryman, Matt, Exec. Dir.
Reconciling Ministries Network
[20187]
123 W Madison St., Ste. 2150
Chicago, IL 60602
Ph: (773)736-5526

Bertagna, Joe, Exec. Dir.
American Hockey Coaches Association [22906]
7 Concord St.
Gloucester, MA 01930

Bertelsen, Val, III, VP
Association of Waldorf Schools of
North America [8002]
515 Kimbark, Ste. 106
Longmont, CO 80501
Ph: (612)870-8310

Bertke, Andrew, Web Adm.
Gaylactic Network [10202]
PO Box 7587
Washington, DC 20044-7587
Ph: (612)387-8265

Bertolino, Brett, VP
The Haunted Attraction Association
[1137]
2885 Stanford Ave. SW, No. 28015
Grandville, MI 49418
Ph: (616)439-4220
Toll Free: 866-490-9603

Bertone, Charles, Exec. Dir.
Society of Photo-Technologists
[2594]
11112 S Spotted Rd.
Cheney, WA 99004
Ph: (509)710-4464

Bertram, Susan, Secretary
Animal Behavior Society [7396]
2111 Chestnut Ave., Ste. 145
Glenview, IL 60025
Ph: (312)893-6585
Fax: (312)896-5619

Bertsch, Leann, President
Association of State Correctional
Administrators [11521]
1110 Opal Ct., Ste. 5
Hagerstown, MD 21740
Ph: (301)791-2722
Fax: (301)393-9494

Bertschmann, Mary, Exec. Dir.
Huguenot Society of America
[20972]
20 W 44th St., Ste. 510
New York, NY 10036-6603
Ph: (212)755-0592
Fax: (212)317-0676

Bertschy, Timothy, President
American Counsel Association
[4988]

3770 Ridge Pike
Collegeville, PA 19426
Ph: (610)489-3300

Beruldsen, Diane, President
International Women's Flag Football
Association [22859]
25 A 7th Ave.
Key West, FL 33040
Ph: (305)293-9315
Toll Free: 888-464-9332
Fax: (305)293-9315

Bervell, Rachel, Founder
Hugs for Ghana [11041]
PO Box 694
Mukilteo, WA 98275

Bervera, Xochitl S., Director
We Interrupt This Message [18666]
1215 York St.
San Francisco, CA 94110

Besch, Kate, President
Rewrite Beautiful [14651]
397 La Perle Ln., Ste. A
Costa Mesa, CA 92627
Ph: (949)903-4784

Besen, Wayne, Exec. Dir., Founder
Truth Wins Out [11911]
5315 N Clark St., No. 634
Chicago, IL 60640

Besonen, Jim, Treasurer, Secretary
Woodworking Machinery Industry
Association [1780]
225 Reinekers Ln., Ste. 410
Alexandria, VA 22314
Ph: (571)279-8340
Fax: (571)279-8343

Bess, Stacy D., Exec. Dir.
Global Advertising Lawyers Alliance
[5425]
c/o Stacy D. Bess, Executive Director
488 Madison Ave., 10th Fl.
New York, NY 10022
Ph: (212)705-4895
Fax: (347)438-2185

Besser, Dr. Mitch, Founder, Medical
Dir.
mothers2mothers International
[13553]
7441 W Sunset Blvd., Ste. 205
Los Angeles, CA 90046
Ph: (323)969-0445
Fax: (323)796-8152

Bessette, Robert D., President
Council of Industrial Boiler Owners
[1724]
6801 Kennedy Rd., Ste. 102
Warrenton, VA 20187
Ph: (540)349-9043
Fax: (540)349-9850

Bessey, Samuel C., Exec. Dir.
Chi Psi [23893]
Jeffrey Hall
45 Rutledge St.
Nashville, TN 37210
Ph: (615)736-2520
Fax: (615)736-2366

Best, Jane R., PhD, Director
Arts Education Partnership [7506]
1 Massachusetts Ave. NW, Ste. 700
Washington, DC 20001-1431
Ph: (202)326-8693
Fax: (202)408-8081

Best, Rev. Thomas F, VP
North American Academy of Ecumenists [20070]
3838 W Cypress St.

Tampa, FL 33607
Ph: (813)435-5335

Beswick, Terry, Exec. Dir.
Gay, Lesbian, Bisexual, Transgender
Historical Society [9393]
4127 18th St.
San Francisco, CA 94114
Ph: (415)621-1107

Bethers, Bruce R., President
Martial Arts International Federation
[23002]
3816 Bellingham Dr.
Reno, NV 89511
Ph: (775)851-8875

Bett, BJ, Founder
Nevus Network [17347]
c/o Congenital Nevus Support Group
PO Box 305
West Salem, OH 44287-0305
Ph: (419)853-4525
   (405)377-3403

Bettiga, Bart, Exec. Dir.
National Tile Contractors Association
[892]
626 Lakeland East Dr.
Jackson, MS 39232
Ph: (601)939-2071
Fax: (601)932-6117

Betts, George, President
National Association for Gifted
Children [7943]
1331 H St. NW, Ste. 1001
Washington, DC 20005
Ph: (202)785-4268
Fax: (202)785-4248

Betts, Mike, President
Spring Manufacturers Institute
[1577]
2001 Midwest Rd., Ste. 106
Oak Brook, IL 60523-1335
Ph: (630)495-8588
Fax: (630)495-8595

Betzner, Claudia J., Exec. Dir.
Service Industry Association [3079]
2164 Historic Decatur Rd., Villa 19
San Diego, CA 92106
Ph: (619)458-9063

Beutlich, Scott, Secretary, Treasurer
U.S. Psychotronics Association
[6992]
525 Juanita Vista
Crystal Lake, IL 60014
Ph: (815)355-8030

Bevacqua, Frank, Officer
International Joint Commission
[4494]
2000 L St. NW, Ste. 615
Washington, DC 20036-4930
Ph: (202)736-9000
Fax: (202)632-2006

Bevan, Sue, Director
Society for Epidemiologic Research
[14734]
PO Box 990
Clearfield, UT 84089
Ph: (801)525-0231
Fax: (801)525-6549

Bever, Ken, President, Founder
Hope for Haiti's Children [11039]
12020 Southwick Ln.
Cincinnati, OH 45241
Toll Free: 866-314-9330
Fax: (888)316-9646

Beverage, Dick, Secretary, Treasurer
Association of Professional Ball
Players of America [22545]

101 S Kraemer Ave., Ste. 112
Placentia, CA 92870-6109
Ph: (714)528-2012
Fax: (714)528-2037

Beverage, Jim, Membership Chp.
Antique Glass Salt and Sugar
Shaker Club [21622]
29 Autumn River Ln.
Ogunquit, ME 03907

Beveridge, Richard, President
Alliance of Cardiovascular Profes-
sionals [14086]
PO Box 2007
Midlothian, VA 23113
Ph: (804)632-0078
Fax: (804)639-9212

Bevington, Kay, Founder
Alive Alone [10770]
PO Box 182
Van Wert, OH 45891

Bewley, Kirk, Bd. Member
American Spice Trade Association
[1314]
1101 17th St. NW, Ste. 700
Washington, DC 20036
Ph: (202)331-2460
Fax: (202)463-8998

Beydoun, Fouad, PhD, CEO,
President
International Association for Organ
Donation [17510]
PO Box 545
Dearborn, MI 48121
Ph: (313)745-2379
Fax: (313)745-4509

Beyer, Jessica, President
National Association of County
Information Officers [5114]
c/o Rita McGee, Membership
Coordinator
102 Minden Ln.
Raleigh, NC 27607-4989
Ph: (919)715-7336

Beyer, Marygale, Mgr.
Inner Light Foundation [7092]
PO Box 750265
Petaluma, CA 94975
Ph: (707)765-2200

Beyer, Mick, President
Twentieth Century Society USA
[8895]
PO Box 110148
Cleveland, OH 44111
Ph: (828)778-6425

Bezdjian, Joseph, President
Armenian Rugs Society [8838]
PO Box 21104
Glendale, CA 91201
Ph: (650)343-8585
Fax: (650)343-0960

Bezold, Clement, PhD, Chairman
Institute for Alternative Futures
[6656]
2331 Mill Rd., Ste. 100
Alexandria, VA 22314
Ph: (703)684-5880

Bhagat, Mohan, President
Association for India's Development
[12141]
5011 Tecumseh St.
College Park, MD 20740
Ph: (304)825-5243

Bhagwandin, Bryon, Chmn. of the
Bd.
The Malawi Project, Inc. [10481]
3314 Van Tassel Dr.

Indianapolis, IN 46240-3555

Bhajan, Yogi, Founder
3HO Foundation [20651]
PO Box 1560
Santa Cruz, NM 87567
Toll Free: 888-346-2420
Fax: (424)731-8348

Bhargava, Deepak, Exec. Dir.
Center for Community Change
[12532]
1536 U St. NW
Washington, DC 20009
Ph: (202)339-9300

Bhatia, Anjali, CEO, President
Discover Worlds [12969]
908 B2 Pompton Ave.
Cedar Grove, NJ 07009

Bhattacharyya, Dibakar, President
North American Membrane Society
[6837]
Dept. of Chemical Engineering
University of Arkansas
3202 Bell Engineering Ctr.
Fayetteville, AR 72701-1201
Ph: (479)575-3419
Fax: (479)575-7926

Bhattacharyya, Pushpak, President
Association for Computational
Linguistics [9738]
209 N 8th St.
Stroudsburg, PA 18360
Ph: (570)476-8006
Fax: (570)476-0860

Bhattiprolu, Nandita, Exec. Dir.
Indo-American Chamber of Com-
merce USA [696]
PO Box 250125
Franklin, MI 48025
Ph: (248)506-7555

Bhend, Dave, Mktg. Mgr.
Organization of Regulatory and Clini-
cal Associates [6123]
PO Box 3490
Redmond, WA 98073
Ph: (206)464-0825

Bhutada, Ramesh, Director
Sewa International U.S.A. [12187]
PO Box 820867
Houston, TX 77082-0867
Ph: (708)872-7392

Biacchi, Mr. Anthony, Exec. Dir.
American Risk and Insurance As-
sociation [8038]
716 Providence Rd.
Malvern, PA 19355-3402
Ph: (610)640-1997
Fax: (610)725-1007

Bialick, Jim, Exec. Dir., Founder
Newborn Coalition [14208]
750 9th St. NW, Ste. 750
Washington, DC 20001
Ph: (858)353-3581
Fax: (858)353-3581

Bialkin, Kenneth J., Chairman,
President
America-Israel Friendship League
[9609]
1430 Broadway, Ste. 1804
New York, NY 10018
Ph: (212)213-8630
   (646)892-9142

Bianchi, Alison, Director
Center for the Study of Group
Processes [7164]
c/o Alison Bianchi, Director
W28D Seashore Hall

Dept. of Sociology
University of Iowa
Iowa City, IA 52242-1401
Ph: (319)335-2495

Bianchi, Liz, Corr. Sec.
American Shetland Sheepdog As-
   sociation [21821]
500 Millstone Rd.
Chesapeake, VA 23322-4367
Ph: (757)436-4868

Biane, Andre, President, CEO
Baking Industry Sanitation Standards
   Committee [370]
PO Box 3999
Manhattan, KS 66505-3999
Ph: (785)537-4750
Toll Free: 866-342-4772
Fax: (785)537-1493

Bias, Val, CEO
National Hemophilia Foundation
   [15241]
116 W 32nd St., 11th Fl.
New York, NY 10001
Ph: (212)328-3700
Fax: (212)328-3777

Bibb, Marcia M., President
International Practice Management
   Association [5430]
Bldg. 5, Ste. 300
3525 Piedmont Rd. NE
Atlanta, GA 30305
Ph: (404)467-6757

Bibb, Sandra, President
Navy Nurse Corps Association
   [16166]
PO Box 3289
Newport, RI 02840
Ph: (401)619-4432

Bibeau, Philip A., Exec. Dir.
Wood Products Manufacturers As-
   sociation [1448]
PO Box 761
Westminster, MA 01473-0761
Ph: (978)874-5445
Fax: (978)874-9946

Bicha, Reggie, Exec.
American Public Human Services
   Association [13029]
1133 19th St. NW, Ste. 400
Washington, DC 20036-3631
Ph: (202)682-0100
Fax: (202)289-6555

Bidabe, D. Linda, Founder
MOVE International [11619]
5555 California Ave., Ste. 302
Bakersfield, CA 93309
Toll Free: 800-397-6683

Biddle, Steve, Consultant
American Society of Pediatric
   Hematology/Oncology [15221]
8735 W Higgins Rd., Ste. 300
Chicago, IL 60631-2738
Ph: (847)375-4716
Fax: (847)375-6483

Bidwell, Dennis, Chairman
National Priorities Project [18313]
243 King St., Ste. 246
Northampton, MA 01060
Ph: (413)584-9556

Biedenbach, Amy, Rep.
American Association of Surgical
   Physician Assistants [17361]
PO Box 781688
Sebastian, FL 32978
Ph: (772)388-0498
Fax: (772)388-3457

Bielecki, Joseph, President
SOKOL U.S.A. [19651]
276 Prospect St.

East Orange, NJ 07017-2889
Ph: (973)676-0281
Fax: (973)676-3348

Bieliauskas, Linas A., PhD, Exec.
   Dir.
American Academy of Clinical Neu-
   ropsychology [16001]
Dept. of Psychiatry
University of Michigan Health
   System
1500 E Medical Center Dr.
Ann Arbor, MI 48109-5295
Ph: (734)936-8269
Fax: (734)936-9761

Biemesderfer, David, CEO,
   President
Forum of Regional Associations of
   Grantmakers [12474]
1020 19th St. NW, Ste. 360
Washington, DC 20036
Ph: (202)888-7533
   (202)457-8784
Toll Free: 888-391-3235

Bien-Aime, Taina, Exec. Dir.
Coalition Against Trafficking in
   Women [18384]
PO Box 7160, JAF Sta.
New York, NY 10116
Fax: (212)643-9895

Bier, Deborah, PhD, Founder
World Wide Essence Society
   [15272]
PO Box 285
Concord, MA 01742
Ph: (978)369-8454

Bier, Marilyn, Director, Exec. Dir.
ARMA International [1792]
11880 College Blvd., Ste. 450
Overland Park, KS 66210
Toll Free: 800-422-2762
Fax: (913)341-3742

Bierlein, Allan, President
Force Recon Association [21054]
PO Box 111000
Carrollton, TX 75011-1000

Bierman, Steve, MD, Founder,
   President
National Alliance for the Primary
   Prevention of Sharps Injuries
   [17174]
PO Box 10
Milner, GA 30257
Ph: (770)358-7860
Fax: (770)358-6793

Biers, Carl, VP
Stafford Canary Club of America
   [21551]
c/o John Ferreira
207 Rodman St.
Fall River, MA 02721
Ph: (508)493-3311

Biesenbach, Klaus, Director
MoMA PS1 [8985]
22-25 Jackson Ave.
Long Island City, NY 11101
Ph: (718)784-2084

Bieterman, Karen, Mgr.
American Society of Anesthesiolo-
   gists [13694]
1061 American Ln.
Schaumburg, IL 60173-4973
Ph: (847)825-5586
Fax: (847)825-1692

Big, Susan, VP
Pomegranate Guild of Judaic
   Needlework [21777]
PO Box 60953

Longmeadow, MA 01116-5953

Biggs, Robert A., CAE, Exec. VP
Phi Delta Theta International
   Fraternity [23910]
2 S Campus Ave.
Oxford, OH 45056-1801
Ph: (513)523-6345
Toll Free: 877-563-1848
Fax: (513)523-9200

Bighorn, Prairie, Exec. Dir.
American Indian Business Leaders
   [608]
Gallagher Business Bldg., Ste. 366
Missoula, MT 59812
Fax: (406)243-2298

Bihun, Andrew, President
The Washington Group [19683]
Washington, DC

Bilezikian, John P., MD, Chairman
Endocrine Fellows Foundation
   [14703]
342 N Main St., Ste. 301
West Hartford, CT 06117-2507
Fax: (860)586-7500

Billeb, Ms. Jan, Exec. Sec.
The International Cessna 170 As-
   sociation [21231]
22 Vista View Ln.
Cody, WY 82414
Ph: (307)587-6397
Fax: (307)587-8296

Biller, Mr. Gary, President
National Motorists Association
   [13233]
402 W 2nd St.
Waunakee, WI 53597
Toll Free: 800-882-2785
Fax: (888)787-0381

Billias, Athan, Contact
MIDI Manufacturers Association
   [2226]
PO Box 3173
La Habra, CA 90632-3173
Ph: (714)736-9774

Billinger, George, President
Society of Camera Operators [3434]
PO Box 2006
Toluca Lake, CA 91610
Ph: (818)563-9110
Fax: (818)563-9117

Billison, Dr. Samuel, President
Navajo Code Talkers Association
   [21198]
PO Box 1266
Window Rock, AZ 86515-1266
Ph: (928)688-5202
Fax: (928)688-5204

Bills, Danny, Bd. Member
Association of Directory Publishers
   [2770]
116 Cass St.
Traverse City, MI 49684
Toll Free: 800-267-9002
Fax: (231)486-2182

Bills, Lisa E., Exec. Dir.
United States Christian Chamber of
   Commerce [23629]
2201 Main St., Ste. 501
Dallas, TX 75201
Ph: (214)801-5419

Bills, Robert, Secretary, Editor
Socialist Labor Party of America
   [18896]
PO Box 218
Mountain View, CA 94042-0218
Ph: (650)938-8359
Fax: (650)938-8392

Bills, Ron, Chmn. of the Bd., CEO
Envirofit International [4137]
109 N College Ave., Ste. 200
Fort Collins, CO 80524
Ph: (970)372-2874
Fax: (970)221-1550

Billups, Christie, Founder
Note Karacel Uganda [11415]
3338 S Aberdeen St.
Chicago, IL 60608

Billups, Mr. Clinton Ford, Jr.,
   President
National Conference of Personal
   Managers, Inc. [163]
PO Box 50008
Henderson, NV 89016-0008
Toll Free: 866-916-2676

Billups, Darrel, Exec. Dir.
National Coalition of Ministries to
   Men [19998]
180 Wilshire Blvd.
Casselberry, FL 32707
Ph: (407)472-2188
Fax: (407)331-7839

Billy, Carrie L., JD, CEO, President
American Indian Higher Education
   Consortium [8393]
121 Oronoco St.
Alexandria, VA 22314
Ph: (703)838-0400
Fax: (703)838-0388

Bilodeau, Timothy W., Exec. Dir.
Medicines for Humanity [14203]
800 Hingham St., Ste. 200N
Rockland, MA 02370-1067
Ph: (781)982-0274

Bimblick, Warren N., Treasurer
Gay Men's Health Crisis [13539]
446 W 33rd St.
New York, NY 10001-2601
Ph: (212)367-1000
   (212)807-6655

Binder, Alexandra M., Exec. Dir.
National Academy of Building
   Inspection Engineers [550]
PO Box 860
Shelter Island, NY 11964

Binder, Leah, MA, CEO, President
Leapfrog Group [15029]
1660 L St. NW, Ste. 308
Washington, DC 20036
Ph: (202)292-6713
Fax: (202)292-6813

Bing, Catherine Mercer, CEO
ITAP International Alliance [683]
353 Nassau St., 1st Fl.
Princeton, NJ 08540

Bingham, Debra, President
Controlled Release Society [6196]
3340 Pilot Knob Rd.
Saint Paul, MN 55121
Ph: (651)454-7250
Fax: (651)454-0766

Bingham, Mike, President
Toyota Owner's and Restorer's Club
   [21503]

Bingham, Tony, CEO, President
Association for Talent Development
   [7546]
1640 King St.
Alexandria, VA 22314-2746
Ph: (703)683-8100
Toll Free: 800-628-2783
Fax: (703)683-1523

Binstock, Dan, Director
National Association of Legal Search
   Consultants [2013]

1525 N Park Dr., Ste. 102
Weston, FL 33326-3225
Ph: (954)349-8081
Toll Free: 866-902-6587
Fax: (954)349-1979

Binstock, Stuart, President, CEO
Construction Financial Management
Association [862]
100 Village Blvd., Ste. 200
Princeton, NJ 08540
Ph: (609)452-8000
Toll Free: 888-421-9996
Fax: (609)452-0474

Biordi, Michele, Exec. Dir.
International Energy Credit Associa-
tion [1244]
1120 Route 73, Ste. 200
Mount Laurel, NJ 08054
Ph: (856)380-6854
Fax: (856)439-0525

Birch, J., Officer
Kuza Project [13012]
PO Box 529
Wheaton, IL 60187
Ph: (630)220-0101

Birch, Tom, Rep.
Friends of Morocco [19572]
PO Box 2579
Washington, DC 20013-2579
Ph: (703)470-3166

Birch, Woody, President
Tea Leaf Club International [21585]
21275 E 900 St.
Geneseo, IL 61254

Birchard, Bob, President
Society for Cinephiles/Cinecon
[9313]
3727 W Magnolia Blvd., No. 760
Burbank, CA 91505

Bird, Marsha, CEO
North American Truck Stop Network
[2973]
PO Box 337
Sullivan, MO 63080
Ph: (573)468-6288
Toll Free: 800-771-6016
Fax: (573)468-5885

Bird, Michael, President
American Indian Graduate Center
[7922]
3701 San Mateo Blvd. NE, No. 200
Albuquerque, NM 87110
Ph: (505)881-4584
Toll Free: 800-628-1920
Fax: (505)884-0427

Birdsell, Chris, President
Cookie Cutter Collectors Club
[21641]
PO Box 22518
Lexington, KY 40522-2518

Birdsong, James R., CEO, Exec. VP
RCI, Inc. [900]
1500 Sunday Dr., Ste. 204
Raleigh, NC 27607
Ph: (919)859-0742
Toll Free: 800-828-1902
Fax: (919)859-1328

Birenbaum, Mark S., Administrator
American Association of Bioanalysts
[15513]
906 Olive St., Ste. 1200
Saint Louis, MO 63101-1448
Ph: (314)241-1445
Fax: (314)241-1449

Biring, Amarjot Singh, Contact
Punjabi-American Cultural Association [9571]

5055 Business Center Dr., Ste. 108,
No. 165
Fairfield, CA 94534

Biris, Anne, LAc, President
American Association of Acupuncture
and Oriental Medicine [13502]
PO Box 96503
Washington, DC 20090-6503
Ph: (916)451-6950
Toll Free: 866-455-7999
Fax: (916)451-6952

Birks, Heather, Exec. Dir.
Broadcast Education Association
[7535]
1771 N St. NW
Washington, DC 20036-2800
Ph: (202)602-0584
Fax: (202)609-9940

Birnbaum, Robby H., President
American Fair Credit Council [1217]
100 W Cypress Creek Rd., Ste. 700
Fort Lauderdale, FL 33309
Toll Free: 888-657-8272
Fax: (954)343-6960

Birns, Larry, Director
Council on Hemispheric Affairs
[17796]
1250 Connecticut Ave. NW, Ste. 1C
Washington, DC 20036
Ph: (202)223-4975
Fax: (202)223-4979

Birsh, Hope, Contact
American Equestrian Trade Associa-
tion [4306]
2207 Forest Hills Dr.
Harrisburg, PA 17112
Ph: (717)724-0204
Fax: (717)238-9985

Bisanzo, Mark, President, Exec. Dir.,
Founder
Global Emergency Care Collabora-
tive [15451]
PO Box 4404
Shrewsbury, MA 01545

Bisceglia, Lisa, Officer
ACTS Honduras [11304]
PO Box 433
Norwich, VT 05055

Bisceglie, Rob, CEO
Action for Healthy Kids [14163]
600 W Van Buren St., Ste. 720
Chicago, IL 60607
Toll Free: 800-416-5136
Fax: (312)212-0098

Biscone, Mark J., V. Chmn. of the
Bd.
The Living Bank [14622]
4545 Post Oak Pl., Ste. 340
Houston, TX 77027
Ph: (713)961-9431
Toll Free: 800-528-2971

Bishop, Beth, VP
United Doberman Club [21974]
c/o Bonnie Guzman, Membership
Secretary
367 Chickadee Ln.
Bailey, CO 80421
Ph: (303)733-4220

Bishop, Donna, President, Founder
Alliance for Animals [10564]
232 Silver St.
South Boston, MA 02127-2206
Ph: (617)268-7800

Bishop, Jewel, RN, President
National Alaska Native American
Indian Nurses Association [16143]

c/o Pelagie Snesrud, RN, Treasurer
418 Russell Dr. S
Holmen, WI 54636

Bishop, Joan, Exec. Dir.
Oley Foundation for Home Parent-
eral and Enteral Nutrition [15281]
c/o Albany Medical Center
43 New Scotland Ave., MC-28
Albany, NY 12208-3478
Ph: (518)262-5079
Toll Free: 800-776-6539
Fax: (518)262-5528

Bishop, John, Exec. Dir.
Organ Clearing House [9991]
PO Box 231127
Boston, MA 02123-1127
Ph: (617)688-9290

Bishop, Ken L., President, CEO
National Association of State Boards
of Accountancy [4940]
150 4th Ave. N, Ste. 700
Nashville, TN 37219-2417
Ph: (615)880-4200
Fax: (615)880-4290

Bishop, Nicci, Secretary
National MIS User Group [6751]
c/o Nicci Bishop, Secretary
899 Riverside St.
Portland, ME 04103
Ph: (207)871-1200
Fax: (207)797-6457

Bishop, Pam, President
Fox Terrier Network [21880]

Bishop, Paul D., CAE, CEO
Association of Boards of Certification
[5831]
2805 SW Snyder Blvd., Ste. 535
Ankeny, IA 50023
Ph: (515)232-3623
Fax: (515)965-6827

Bishwakarma, Dil, President,
Founder
International Commission for Dalit
Rights [18414]
PO Box 11191
Washington, DC 20008
Ph: (202)538-1435

Bissell, Mary Sue, VP, Trustee,
Exec. Dir.
U.S.-Asia Institute [17815]
232 E Capitol St. NE
Washington, DC 20003
Ph: (202)544-3181
Fax: (202)747-5889

Bissett, Jennifer, Exec. Dir.
College Democrats of America
[18109]
c/o Democratic National Committee
430 S Capitol St. SE
Washington, DC 20003

Bissonnette, Chad W., Exec. Dir.,
Founder
Roots of Development [12808]
1325 18th St. NW, Unit 303
Washington, DC 20036-6505
Ph: (202)466-0805

Biswal, Mr. Hemant, Chairman
Jagannath Organization for Global
Awareness [20576]
PO Box 152
Glenelg, MD 21737-0152

Biswell, Jeremy, President
National Chimney Sweep Guild
[2137]
2155 Commercial Dr.
Plainfield, IN 46168
Ph: (317)837-1500
Fax: (317)837-5365

Bitkower, Jay, President
Action to Cure Kidney Cancer
[13869]
150 W 75th St., Ste. 4
New York, NY 10023
Ph: (212)714-5341

Bittenbender, Emily L., Chmn. of the
Bd.
General Building Contractors As-
sociation [530]
36 S 18th St.
Philadelphia, PA 19103
Ph: (215)568-7015
Fax: (215)568-3115

Bittner, Brett, Exec. Dir.
Advocates for Self-Government
[18638]
405 Massachusetts Ave.
Cartersville, GA 30120-8528
Ph: (770)386-8372
Toll Free: 800-932-1776
Fax: (770)386-8373

Bittner, Dick, Membership Chp.
International Nippon Collectors Club
[21582]
8 Geoley Ct.
Thurmont, MD 21788

Bittner, Stephen E., VP
Catholic Cemetery Conference
[2401]
Bldg. No. 3
1400 S Wolf Rd.
Hillside, IL 60162-2197
Ph: (708)202-1242
Toll Free: 888-850-8131
Fax: (708)202-1255

Bivalacqua, Trinity J., Comm. Chm.
Sexual Medicine Society of North
America, Inc. [17202]
c/o Status Plus
PO Box 1233
Lakeville, MN 55044
Ph: (218)428-7072
Fax: (910)778-2586

Bixby, Robert, Exec. Dir.
Concord Coalition [18147]
1011 Arlington Blvd., Ste. 300
Arlington, VA 22209-2299
Ph: (703)894-6222
Fax: (703)894-6231

Bizo, Lewis, Director, President
Society for Quantitative Analyses of
Behavior [6049]
c/o Derek Reed, Executive Director
Department of Applied Behavioral
Science
University of Kansas
100 Sunnyside Ave.
Lawrence, KS 66045

Bjelland, Jenae, Exec. Dir.
National Association for State Com-
munity Services Programs [5779]
111 K St. NE, Ste. 300
Washington, DC 20001-1569
Ph: (202)624-5866
    (202)624-5850

Bjorling, Debra, Treasurer
International Association of Pet
Cemeteries and Crematories
[2542]
390 Amwell Rd., Ste. 402
Hillsborough, NJ 08844
Toll Free: 800-952-5541
Fax: (908)450-1398

Bjornlund, Eric, Founder, Principal,
President
Democracy International [18866]
7600 Wisconsin Ave., Ste. 1010

Bethesda, MD 20814
Ph: (301)961-1660
Fax: (301)961-6605

Blache-Cohen, Brandon, Exec. Dir.
Amizade Global Service-Learning
  [13282]
305 34th St.
Pittsburgh, PA 15201
Ph: (412)586-4986
Fax: (757)257-8358

Black, Amber, Dir. of Comm.
Rosenberg Fund for Children
  [11266]
116 Pleasant St., Ste. 348
Easthampton, MA 01027-2759
Ph: (413)529-0063
Fax: (413)529-0802

Black, Amy, Exec. Dir.
American Supply Association [2634]
1200 N Arlington Heights Rd., Ste.
  150
Itasca, IL 60143
Ph: (630)467-0000
Fax: (630)467-0001

Black, Andrew J., President, CEO
Association of Oil Pipe Lines [2514]
1808 Eye St. NW, Ste. 300
Washington, DC 20006
Ph: (202)408-7970
Fax: (202)280-1949

Black, Borden, Exec. Dir.
American Association of Private
  Railroad Car Owners, Inc. [2830]
PO Box 6307
Columbus, GA 31917-6307
Ph: (706)326-6262

Black, David, Founder
American Mindfulness Research Association [7061]
99 W California Blvd.
Pasadena, CA 91105

Black, Donald W., MD, President
American Academy of Clinical
  Psychiatrists [16808]
PO Box 458
Glastonbury, CT 06033
Ph: (860)633-6023
Toll Free: 866-668-9858

Black, Edward J., President, CEO
Computer and Communications
  Industry Association [3223]
900 17th St. NW, Ste. 1100
Washington, DC 20006
Ph: (202)783-0070
Fax: (202)783-0534

Black, Faye Malarkey, President
Regional Airline Association [157]
2025 M St. NW, Ste. 800
Washington, DC 20036-3309
Ph: (202)367-1170
Fax: (202)367-2170

Black, Jason, Mem.
American Geographical Society
  [6671]
32 Court St., Ste. 201
Brooklyn Heights, NY 11201
Ph: (917)745-8354

Black, Kevin P., President
The American Orthopaedic Associa-
  tion [16465]
9400 W Higgins Rd., Ste. 205
Rosemont, IL 60018-4975
Ph: (847)318-7330
Fax: (847)318-7339

Black, Maureen, PhD, Chairperson
Child Health Foundation [14173]
110 E Ridgely Rd.

Timonium, MD 21093
Ph: (410)992-5512

Black, Parnell, CEO
National Association of Certified
  Valuators and Analysts [46]
5217 S State St., Ste. 400
Salt Lake City, UT 84107-4812
Ph: (801)486-0600
Toll Free: 800-677-2009
Fax: (801)486-7500

Black, Rachel E., President
Society for the Anthropology of Food
  and Nutrition [5917]

Black, Samuel W., President
Association of African American
  Museums [9820]
PO Box 23698
Washington, DC 20026
Ph: (202)633-1134

Black, Scott Hoffman, Exec. Dir.
Xerces Society [4922]
628 NE Broadway, Ste. 200
Portland, OR 97232
Ph: (503)232-6639
Toll Free: 855-232-6639
Fax: (503)233-6794

Black, Valerie, VP
Berger Picard Club of America
  [21839]
1071 S Lakeside Dr.
Hesperus, CO 81326
Ph: (970)749-5540

Black, Dr. Vince, Founder
North American Tang Shou Tao As-
  sociation [13645]
PO Box 36235
Tucson, AZ 85740-6235
Ph: (520)498-0678

Blackburn, Capt. Percy, Director
National Association of Charterboat
  Operators [2250]
PO Box 1070
Hurley, MS 39555
Toll Free: 866-981-5136

Blackburn, Zacciah, Director
World Sound Healing Organization
  [12448]
PO Box 389
Ascutney, VT 05030-0389
Ph: (802)674-9585
Fax: (802)674-9585

Blackburn-Moreno, Ronald,
  President, CEO
ASPIRA Association [7743]
1444 I St. NW, Ste. 800
Washington, DC 20005
Ph: (202)835-3600
Fax: (202)853-3613

Blackman, Bill, Founder, President
Hearts and Minds Network [19180]
165 W 105th St.
New York, NY 10025
Ph: (212)280-0333
Fax: (212)280-0336

Blackmer, Carl, Comm. Chm.
National Hay Association [4179]
24064 SW Rd. L
Mattawa, WA 99349
Ph: (615)854-5574
Fax: (509)932-4514

Blackmon, Fredron Dekarlos, Chmn.
  of the Bd., CEO
Knights of Peter Claver [19405]
1825 Orleans Ave.
New Orleans, LA 70116-2825
Ph: (504)821-4225
Fax: (504)821-4253

Blackmon, Fredron Dekarlos, CEO,
  Chmn. of the Bd.
Junior Knights of Peter Claver
  [19408]
1825 Orleans Ave.
New Orleans, LA 70116-2825
Ph: (504)821-4425
Fax: (504)821-4253

Blackmore, Doug, President
American Cat Fanciers Association
  [21565]
PO Box 1949
Nixa, MO 65714-1949
Ph: (417)725-1530
Fax: (417)725-1533

Black-Nasta, Wendy, Founder, Exec.
  Dir.
Artists for World Peace [12432]
PO Box 95
Middletown, CT 06457
Ph: (860)685-1789

Blackshaw, G. Lansing, President
Council on Naturopathic Medical
  Education [15859]
PO Box 178
Great Barrington, MA 01230
Ph: (413)528-8877

Blackstone, Jann, Founder
Bonus Families [11814]
PO Box 1238
Discovery Bay, CA 94505
Ph: (925)516-2681
Fax: (925)308-4715

Black-Weisheit, Roxanne, Founder,
  Exec. Dir.
Friends' Health Connection [21736]
PO Box 114
New Brunswick, NJ 08903
Ph: (732)418-1811
Toll Free: 800-483-7436
Fax: (732)249-9897

Blackwell, Angela Glover, CEO,
  Founder
PolicyLink [11719]
1438 Webster St., Ste. 303
Oakland, CA 94612
Ph: (510)663-2333
Fax: (510)663-9684

Blackwell, Morton C., Director,
  Treasurer
Free Congress Foundation [18868]
901 N Washington, Ste. 206
Alexandria, VA 22314-1535
Ph: (703)837-0030

Blackwell, Morton C., President
Leadership Institute [8199]
Steven P.J. Wood Bldg.
1101 N Highland St.
Arlington, VA 22201-2807
Ph: (703)247-2000
Fax: (703)247-2001

Blackwood, Wade, Exec. Dir.
American Canoe Association
  [23360]
503 Sophia St., Ste. 100
Fredericksburg, VA 22401
Ph: (540)907-4460
Toll Free: 888-229-3792

Blackwood, Wade, CEO
U.S.A. Canoe/Kayak [23366]
503 Sophia St., Ste. 100
Fredericksburg, VA 22401
Ph: (540)907-4460

Blacquiere, William J., CEO,
  President
Bethany Christian Services
  International [10865]

901 Eastern Ave. NE
Grand Rapids, MI 49501-0294
Ph: (616)224-7550
Toll Free: 800-238-4269

Blades, Catherine, Chmn. of the Bd.
Operation Homefront [12348]
1355 Central Pky. S, Ste. 100
San Antonio, TX 78232-5056
Ph: (210)659-7756
Toll Free: 800-722-6098
Fax: (210)566-7544

Blaine, Barbara, President
Survivors Network of Those Abused
  by Priests [13266]
PO Box 6416
Chicago, IL 60680-6416
Ph: (312)455-1499
Toll Free: 877-762-7432
Fax: (312)455-1498

Blair, Dan G., President, CEO
National Academy of Public
  Administration [5696]
1600 K St. NW, Ste. 400
Washington, DC 20006
Ph: (202)347-3190
Fax: (202)223-0823

Blair, Heather, Contact
Society for the Study of Japanese
  Religions [20579]
USC School of Religion, ACB 233
Los Angeles, CA 90089-1481

Blair, Karen McCurtain, President
Taos Watercolor Society [8893]
PO Box 282
Taos, NM 87571
Ph: (575)224-3166

Blair, Martin, Exec. Dir.
Rural Institute: Center for Excellence
  in Disability Education, Research
  and Service [11636]
52 Corbin Hall
University of Montana
Missoula, MT 59812
Ph: (406)243-5467
Toll Free: 800-732-0323
Fax: (406)243-4730

Blair, Michele, CEO
Heart Failure Society of America
  [14113]
6707 Democracy Blvd., Ste. 925
Bethesda, MD 20817
Ph: (301)312-8635
Toll Free: 888-213-4417

Blair, Dr. Ralph, Founder
Evangelicals Concerned [20179]
311 E 72nd St., Ste. 1G
New York, NY 10021

Blair, Robert B., President
National Business Education As-
  sociation [7563]
1914 Association Dr.
Reston, VA 20191-1596
Ph: (703)860-8300
Fax: (703)620-4483

Blair, Tracy, President, Treasurer
Columbia College of Nursing Alumni
  Association [19319]
4425 N Port Washington Rd.
Glendale, WI 53212
Ph: (414)326-2330
Fax: (414)326-2331

Blake, Bob, VP
National Fireworks Association
  [6629]
8224 NW Bradford Ct.
Kansas City, MO 64151
Ph: (816)741-1826

Blake, Chad, President
National Mobility Equipment Dealers
  Association [11627]
3327 W Bearss Ave.
Tampa, FL 33618
Ph: (813)264-2697
Toll Free: 866-948-8341
Fax: (813)962-8970

Blake, Bishop Charles E., Co-Ch.
Pentecostal Charismatic Churches of
  North America [20518]
8408 131st St., Ct. E
Puyallup, WA 98373-5402
Ph: (253)446-6475

Blake, Bishop Charles E., CEO,
  President
Save Africa's Children [11268]
3045 Crenshaw Blvd.
Los Angeles, CA 900016
Ph: (323)733-1048
Fax: (323)778-8168

Blake, Diane, President
Raoul Wallenberg Committee of the
  United States [18143]
37 W 26th St., Ste. 403
New York, NY 10010
Ph: (646)678-3711

Blake, Jay, Founder, President
Follow A Dream [11596]
381 Old Falmouth Rd.
Marstons Mills, MA 02648
Ph: (508)420-8319

Blake, Richard, President
National American Indian Court
  Judges Association [5388]
1942 Broadway, Ste. 215
Boulder, CO 80302
Ph: (303)449-4112
Fax: (303)449-4038

Blakely, Mack, Exec. Dir.
International Society of Certified
  Electronics Technicians [1051]
3000-A Landers St.
Fort Worth, TX 76107-5642
Ph: (817)921-9101
Toll Free: 800-946-0201
Fax: (817)921-3741

Blakely, Mack, Exec. Dir.
National Electronics Service Dealers
  Association [1055]
3000-A Landers St.
Fort Worth, TX 76107-5642
Ph: (817)921-9061
Fax: (817)921-3741

Blakely, Shirley Williams,
  Chairperson
Federation of Southern Cooperatives
  [12801]
2769 Church St.
East Point, GA 30344-3258
Ph: (404)765-0991
Fax: (404)765-9178

Blakey, Kevin M., President, CEO
Risk Management Association [416]
1801 Market St., Ste. 300
Philadelphia, PA 19103-1613
Ph: (215)446-4000
Toll Free: 800-677-7621
Fax: (215)446-4101

Blakey, Patch, Exec. Dir.
Association of Classical and
  Christian Schools [8529]
205 E 5th St.
Moscow, ID 83843
Ph: (208)882-6101
Fax: (208)882-9097

Blakey, Victoria D., Exec. Dir.
It's Nice to be Nice International
  [11389]

2715 W 85th Pl.
Chicago, IL 60652
Ph: (773)673-7528

Blalock, Phil, Exec. Dir.
National Association of Farmers'
  Market Nutrition Programs [4158]
PO Box 9080
Alexandria, VA 22304-0080
Ph: (703)837-0451
Fax: (919)471-0137

Blancato, Robert B., Coord.
Elder Justice Coalition [11748]
1612 K St. NW, Ste. 400
Washington, DC 20006
Ph: (202)682-4140
Fax: (202)223-2099

Blancato, Robert, Exec. Dir.
National Association of Nutrition and
  Aging Services Programs [16228]
1612 K St. NW, Ste. 400
Washington, DC 20006
Ph: (202)682-6899
Fax: (202)223-2099

Blanchard, Kelly, President
Ibis Reproductive Health [17107]
17 Dunster St., Ste. 201
Cambridge, MA 02138
Ph: (617)349-0040
Fax: (617)349-0041

Blanchard, Ted, President
Insulation Contractors Association of
  America [868]
1321 Duke St., Ste. 303
Alexandria, VA 22314
Ph: (703)739-0356
Fax: (703)739-0412

Blanchette, Karen, Director
Professional Association of Health
  Care Office Management [15592]
1576 Bella Cruz Dr., Ste. 360
Lady Lake, FL 32159
Toll Free: 800-451-9311
Fax: (407)386-7006

Blanco, Maria Alejandra, EdD,
  President
Society of Directors of Research in
  Medical Education [8337]
136 Harrison Ave., Sackler 321
Office of Educational Affairs
Tufts University School of Medicine
136 Harrison Ave., Sackler 321
Boston, MA 02111
Ph: (617)636-6588
Fax: (617)636-0894

Bland, Bubba, President
Mexico-Elmhurst Philatelic Society
  International [22345]
PO Box 29040
Denver, CO 80229-0040

Bland, F. Paul, Jr., Exec. Dir.
Public Justice [5724]
1620 L St. NW, Ste. 630
Washington, DC 20006-1220
Ph: (202)797-8600
Fax: (202)232-7203

Bland, Robert M., Founder, Director
Teen Missions International [20468]
885 E Hall Rd.
Merritt Island, FL 32953
Ph: (321)453-0350
Fax: (321)452-7988

Blaney, Desane, Exec. Dir.
Association of Golf Merchandisers
  [3135]
PO Box 7247
Phoenix, AZ 85011-7247
Ph: (602)604-8250
Fax: (602)604-8251

Blaney, Tammie DeVooght, Exec.
  Dir.
International Association of
  Structural Movers [3088]
PO Box 2104
Neenah, WI 54956-2104
Ph: (803)951-9304
Fax: (920)486-1519

Blank, Martin J., President
Institute for Educational Leadership
  [7772]
4301 Connecticut Ave. NW, Ste. 100
Washington, DC 20008-2304
Ph: (202)822-8405
Fax: (202)872-4050

Blankenhorn, David, Founder,
  President
Institute for American Values [11821]
1841 Broadway, Ste. 211
New York, NY 10023
Ph: (212)246-3942

Blankenship, Arthur, Director
Utility Management and Conservation Association [3427]
7607 Equitable Dr.
Eden Prairie, MN 55344

Blanks, Jack, Exec. Dir.
Seva Foundation [12186]
1786 5th St.
Berkeley, CA 94710
Ph: (510)845-7382
Fax: (510)845-7410

Blanton, R. Daniel, Chairman
American Bankers Association [378]
1120 Connecticut Ave. NW
Washington, DC 20036
Ph: (202)663-5071
Toll Free: 800-226-5377
Fax: (202)828-4540

Blaser, Dave, Cmdr.
STARFLEET [24081]
c/o Wayne Killough, President
1053 E Palestine Ave., Apt. 204
Palestine, TX 75801
Toll Free: 888-734-8735

Blashek, Carolyn, President
Operation Gratitude [4975]
21100 Lassen St.
Chatsworth, CA 91311
Ph: (818)469-0448

Blatzer, Bruce T., Exec. Dir.
Iron Casting Research Institute, Inc.
  [1741]
2802 Fisher Rd.
Columbus, OH 43204
Ph: (614)275-4201
Fax: (614)275-4203

Blauvelt, George A., President
Association of Blauvelt Descendants
  [20781]
3367 W 113th Ave.
Westminster, CO 80031

Blazejewski, Arek, President
Dual Laminate Fabrication Associa-
  tion [2623]
PO Box 582
Berwyn, PA 19312-0582
Ph: (609)636-0826
Fax: (610)695-8446

Blazek, David G., FIC, President,
  CEO
National Slovak Society of the
  United States of America [19646]
351 Valley Brook Rd.
McMurray, PA 15317-3337
Ph: (724)731-0094
Toll Free: 800-488-1890
Fax: (724)731-0145

Blease, Robert R., DVM, President
Common Sense for Animals [10605]
2420 Route 57
Broadway, NJ 08808
Ph: (908)859-3060
Fax: (908)859-3738

Bledig, Joan, Chairperson
Burroughs Bibliophiles [9045]
318 Patriot Way
Yorktown, VA 23693-4639

Bledsoe, Doug, President
American British White Park As-
  sociation [3689]
PO Box 409
Myerstown, PA 17067
Toll Free: 877-900-BEEF
Fax: (208)979-2008

Bledsoe, Dr. Tyrone, CEO, Founder
Student African American Brother-
  hood [19697]
PO Box 350842
Toledo, OH 43635
Ph: (419)530-3221
Fax: (419)530-3223

Bleicher, Robert A., President, Chair-
  man
San Francisco Maritime National
  Park Association [9840]
PO Box 470310
San Francisco, CA 94147-0310
Ph: (415)561-6662
    (415)775-1943
Fax: (415)561-6660

Blekys, Irena, Dir. of Admin.
Association for the Advancement of
  Baltic Studies [9205]
University of Washington, Box
  353420
Seattle, WA 98195-3420
Ph: (301)977-8491
Fax: (301)977-8492

Blessing, Matt, President
Council of State Archivists [8821]
Cultural Education Ctr., Rm. 9B70
222 Madison Ave.
Albany, NY 12230
Ph: (608)264-6480
    (518)473-9098
Fax: (518)473-7058

Blethen, Chuck, Contact
Squire SS-100 Registry [21494]
c/o Chuck Blethen
PO Box 4
Marshall, NC 28753
Ph: (828)606-3130

Blick, Dr. Gary, Founder
World Health Clinicians [13567]
618 West Ave.
Norwalk, CT 06850-4008
Ph: (203)852-9525
Toll Free: 855-205-7535
Fax: (203)854-0371

Blick, Kristy, Chairman
Elimu Africa [11201]
6480 Balsam Ln. N
Maple Grove, MN 55369

Blievernicht, John A., Exec. Dir.
Native American Fitness Council
  [16711]
PO Box K
Flagstaff, AZ 86002
Ph: (928)774-3048
Fax: (928)774-3049

Bligh, Ms. Judy, President
American Fuchsia Society [22071]
c/o Judy Salome, Membership
  Secretary

6979 Clark Rd.
Paradise, CA 95969-2210
Ph: (530)876-8517

Blint, Rich, Director
Center for LGBTQ Studies [11877]
365 5th Ave., Rm. 7115
New York, NY 10016
Ph: (212)817-1955
Fax: (212)817-1567

Bliss, Bob, President
Aerostar Owners Association [21211]
2608 W Kenosha St., No. 704
Broken Arrow, OK 74012
Ph: (918)258-2346
Fax: (918)258-2346

Bliss, Christine, President
Coalition of Service Industries [3071]
1707 L St. NW, Ste. 1000
Washington, DC 20036
Ph: (202)289-7460

Bliss, Martha, Secretary
Catalina 400 International Association [22604]
PO Box 9207
Fayetteville, AR 72703
Ph: (717)225-5325

Bliss, Mary, President
Association of Occupational Health Professionals in Healthcare [16317]
125 Warrendale Bayne Rd., Ste. 375
Warrendale, PA 15086
Toll Free: 800-362-4347
Fax: (724)935-1560

Bliss, Thomas, Site Mgr.
International Association of Architectural Photographers [2581]
2901 136th St. NW
Gig Harbor, WA 98332-9111
Toll Free: 877-845-4783

Blissard, Laureen, Tech. Dir.
Green Builder Coalition [532]
PO Box 7507
Gurnee, IL 60031-7000

Blissett, Roger, Chairman
Institute of International Bankers [401]
299 Park Ave., 17th Fl.
New York, NY 10171
Ph: (212)421-1611
Fax: (212)421-1119

Bloch, Frank, Exec. Sec.
Global Alliance for Justice Education [8214]

Bloch, Sam E., Bd. Member
Conference on Jewish Material Claims Against Germany [12221]
1359 Broadway, Rm. 2000
New York, NY 10018
Ph: (646)536-9100
Fax: (212)685-5299

Bloch, Sam, Exec. Dir., Founder
Haiti Communitere [13056]
PO Box 966
Kings Beach, CA 96143
Ph: (530)563-8076

Block, Carolyn, Dir. of Fin.
Property Management Association [2887]
7508 Wisconsin Ave., 4th Fl.
Bethesda, MD 20814
Ph: (301)657-9200
Fax: (301)907-9326

Block, Marsha S., CAE, CEO
American Group Psychotherapy Association [16960]

25 E 21st St., 6th Fl.
New York, NY 10010
Ph: (212)477-2677
Fax: (212)979-6627

Block, Nadine, Co-Ch., Co-Chmn. of the Bd.
Center for Effective Discipline [7720]
327 Groveport Pke.
Canal Winchester, OH 43110
Ph: (614)834-7946
Fax: (614)321-6308

Block, Pamela, President, Exec. Dir.
Association for the Bladder Exstrophy Community [14564]
6737 W Washington St., Ste. 3265
West Allis, WI 53214
Ph: (425)941-1475

Block, Valerie, Chairperson
Glazing Industry Code Committee [531]
800 SW Jackson St., Ste. 1500
Topeka, KS 66612-1200
Ph: (785)271-0208
Fax: (785)271-0166

Block, William C., Exec. Dir.
Social Science History Association [7172]
391 Pine Tree Rd.
905 W Main St., Ste. 18-B
Ithaca, NY 14850

Blocker, Bobby, Bd. Member
American Albacore Fishing Association [1296]
4364 Bonita Rd.
Bonita, CA 91902
Ph: (619)941-2307
Fax: (619)863-5046

Blogin, Nancy, Director, President
National Council on Fireworks Safety [6628]
1701 Pennsylvania Ave. NW, Ste. 300
Washington, DC 20006

Blois, Michael, VP
Mining and Metallurgical Society of America [6881]
PO Box 810
Boulder, CO 80306-0810
Ph: (303)444-6032

Bloise, John R., President
Advancing the Gospel in Angola [12605]
25 Maple St.
Addison, NY 14801-1009

Blomquist, Janet, Administrator
Association for Child Psychoanalysis [16844]
900 Ranch Rd. 620 S, Ste. C101
Austin, TX 78734
Ph: (512)261-3422
Fax: (866)534-7555

Blondin, Patrick, President
International Embryo Transfer Society [17649]
1800 S Oak St., Ste. 100
Champaign, IL 61820-6974
Ph: (217)398-4697
Fax: (217)398-4119

Blood, Margaret, Founder, Exec. Dir.
Mil Milagros [11078]
400 Atlantic Ave.
Boston, MA 02110
Ph: (617)330-7382

Bloom, Darryl, Bd. Member
Planting Hope [11422]
1 Granite St., 3rd Fl.

Montpelier, VT 05601
Ph: (802)778-0344

Bloom, David J, V. Chmn. of the Bd.
Children's Literacy Initiative [8238]
2314 Market St., 3rd Fl.
Philadelphia, PA 19103
Ph: (215)561-4676
Toll Free: 888-408-3388
Fax: (215)561-4677

Bloom, Gary, Exec. Dir.
Thyroid Cancer Survivors' Association [17482]
PO Box 1545
New York, NY 10159-1545
Toll Free: 877-588-7904
Fax: (630)604-6078

Bloom, Steven, President
American Automotive Leasing Association [2923]
675 N Washington St., Ste. 410
Alexandria, VA 22314
Ph: (703)548-0777
Fax: (703)548-1925

Bloomfield, Dr. Clara D., Sec. Gen.
International Association for Comparative Research on Leukemia and Related Diseases [15534]
c/o Clara D. Bloomfield, MD, Secretary-General
1216 James Cancer Hospital
300 W 10th Ave.
Columbus, OH 43210
Ph: (614)293-7518
Fax: (614)366-1637

Bloomfield, Lincoln, Jr., Chmn. of the Bd.
Henry L. Stimson Center [18481]
1211 Connecticut Ave. NW, 8th Fl.
Washington, DC 20036
Ph: (202)223-5956
Fax: (202)238-9604

Bloomfield, Mr. Mark A., CEO, President
American Council for Capital Formation [18062]
1001 Connecticut Ave. NW, Ste. 620
Washington, DC 20036
Ph: (202)293-5811
Fax: (202)785-8165

Bloomfield, Steven B., Exec. Dir.
Harvard University | Weatherhead Center for International Affairs [18523]
1737 Cambridge St.
Cambridge, MA 02138
Ph: (617)495-4420
Fax: (617)495-8292

Blouin, Edmour, Secretary, Treasurer
Society for Tropical Veterinary Medicine [17661]
250 McElroy Hall
Center for Veterinary Health Sciences
Department of Veterinary Pathobiology
Oklahoma State University
Stillwater, OK 74078
Ph: (405)744-6726
(405)744-7271

Bloys, Ben, Chairman
Drilling Engineering Association [2519]
International Association of Drilling Contractors
10370 Richmond Ave., Ste. 760
Houston, TX 77042
Ph: (713)292-1945
Fax: (713)292-1946

Bludworth, Aaron, Chmn. of the Bd.
Center for Exhibition Industry Research [1170]
12700 Park Central Dr., Ste. 308
Dallas, TX 75251
Ph: (972)687-9242
Fax: (972)692-6020

Blugerman, Michael, President
Association for Treatment and Training in the Attachment of Children [15762]
310 E 38th St., Ste. 215
Minneapolis, MN 55409
Ph: (612)861-4222
Fax: (612)866-5499

Blum, Jared O., President
Polyisocyanurate Insulation Manufacturers Association [570]
529 14th St. NW, Ste. 750
Washington, DC 20045
Ph: (202)591-2473

Blumberg, Thomas A., Gov.
Hillel: The Foundation for Jewish Campus Life [20251]
800 8th St. NW
Washington, DC 20001-3724
Ph: (202)449-6500
Fax: (202)449-6600

Blume, Nancy, Rec. Sec.
Czechoslovak Genealogical Society International [20964]
PO Box 16225
Saint Paul, MN 55116-0225
Ph: (651)964-2322

Blumel, Philip, President
U.S. Term Limits Foundation [18883]
c/o US Term Limits - Palm Beach Office
2875 S Ocean Blvd., No. 200
Palm Beach, FL 33480-5593
Ph: (561)578-8636
Fax: (561)578-8660

Blumenstein, Penny, Chmn. of the Bd.
American Jewish Joint Distribution Committee [12217]
New York, NY
Ph: (212)687-6200
Fax: (212)370-5467

Blumenthal, David, M.D., President
The Commonwealth Fund [17001]
1 E 75th St.
New York, NY 10021
Ph: (212)606-3800
Fax: (212)606-3500

Blumenthal, Mark, Exec. Dir., Founder
American Botanical Council [6127]
6200 Manor Rd.
Austin, TX 78723
Ph: (512)926-4900
Toll Free: 800-373-7105
Fax: (512)926-2345

Blumstein, Mr. Albert, Ph.D, Mem.
SEARCH: The National Consortium for Justice Information and Statistics [11547]
7311 Greenhaven Dr., Ste. 270
Sacramento, CA 95831-3595
Ph: (916)392-2550
Fax: (916)392-8440

Blunt, Matt, President
American Automotive Policy Council [276]
1401 H St. NW, Ste. 780
Washington, DC 20005
Ph: (202)789-0030
Fax: (202)789-0054

Blyth, Trevor, CEO
Kamut Association of North America
[3764]
PO Box 4903
Missoula, MT 59806
Ph: (406)251-4903

Blythe, Patricia, Director
Society of Communications Technology Consultants International
[6352]
PO Box 70
Old Station, CA 96071
Ph: (530)335-7313
Toll Free: 866-782-7670
Fax: (530)335-7370

Blythe-Perry, Sandra, Exec. Dir.
Integrated Family Community Services **[12546]**
3370 S Irving St.
Englewood, CO 80110-1816
Ph: (303)789-0501
Fax: (303)789-3808

Boak, Alison, MPH, Founder, Exec. Dir.
International Organization for Adolescents **[11049]**
53 W Jackson Blvd., Ste. 857
Chicago, IL 60604
Ph: (773)404-8831
Fax: (773)257-9128

Boak, Brian P., Contact
Risk Strategies Company **[1924]**
1086 Teaneck Rd., Ste. 5B
Teaneck, NJ 07666
Ph: (201)837-1100
    (212)826-9744
Fax: (201)837-5050

Boal, Clint, President
Raptor Research Foundation **[4876]**
c/o Rick Watson, Conservation Committee Co-Chairman
5668 W Flying Hawk Ln.
Boise, ID 83709
Ph: (208)362-8272

Boaz, Joyce, Exec. Dir., Founder
Gift From Within **[12523]**
16 Cobb Hill Rd.
Camden, ME 04843-4341
Ph: (207)236-8858
Fax: (207)236-2818

Bob, Kenneth, President
Ameinu **[19514]**
424 W 33rd St., Ste. 150
New York, NY 10001
Ph: (212)366-1194
Fax: (212)675-7685

Bob, Kenneth, Chairman
American Zionist Movement **[20230]**
40 Wall St.
New York, NY 10005
Ph: (212)318-6100
Fax: (212)935-3578

Bobango, John A., President
Pi Kappa Alpha **[23920]**
8347 W Range Cove
Memphis, TN 38125
Ph: (901)748-1868
Fax: (901)748-3100

Bobanick, David, President
Rotarian Action Group for the Alleviation of Hunger and Malnutrition **[12111]**
4015 Boulder Ave.
Odessa, TX 79762
Fax: (432)550-0538

Bockman, Jon, Exec. Dir.
Animal Charity Evaluators **[10572]**
PO Box 5482

San Diego, CA 92165
Ph: (619)363-1402

Bodaken, Michael, Exec. Dir.
Institute for Community Economics
[17981]
1101 30th St. NW, Ste. 100A
Washington, DC 20007
Ph: (202)333-8931

Bodarky, George, President
Public Radio News Directors Incorporated **[480]**
PO Box 838
Sturgis, SD 57785

Bode, Lars, President
The International Society for Research in Human Milk and Lactation **[13856]**
c/o Dr. Shelley McGuire, Secretary-Treasurer
1908 E D St.
Moscow, ID 83843

Bodeving, Karen, Corr.
Saint Bernard Club of America
[21954]

Bodine, Ronny O., President
Owsley Family Historical Society
[20911]
6185 Oilskin Dr.
Ooltewah, TN 37363
Ph: (423)910-0058

Bodington, Jeffrey, Chairman
Facial Pain Association **[15930]**
408 W University Ave., Ste. 602
Gainesville, FL 32601
Ph: (352)384-3600
Toll Free: 800-923-3608
Fax: (352)384-3606

Bodkin, Larry E., Jr., Exec. Dir.
American Society of Cosmetic Dermatology and Aesthetic Surgery **[14309]**
1876-B Eider Ct.
Tallahassee, FL 32308
Ph: (850)531-8330
Toll Free: 888-531-8330
Fax: (850)531-8344

Bodmer, Leonardo, Director
Aerospace Industries Association of America **[119]**
1000 Wilson Blvd., Ste. 1700
Arlington, VA 22209-3928
Ph: (703)358-1000
Fax: (703)358-1011

Bodner, Celeste, CEO, Founder
FosterClub **[13443]**
753 1st Ave.
Seaside, OR 97138
Ph: (503)717-1552
Fax: (503)717-1702

Bodnovich, John D., Exec. Dir.
American Beverage Licensees **[175]**
5101 River Rd., Ste. 108
Bethesda, MD 20816-1560
Ph: (301)656-1494
Fax: (301)656-7539

Boea, Monique, Founder, President
African-American Women in Technology **[7255]**

Boeckmann, Laverne, Founder
World Research Foundation **[14968]**
PO Box 20828
Sedona, AZ 86341
Ph: (928)284-3300

Boehm, John, Chmn. of the Bd.
Bio-Process Systems Alliance **[2554]**
1850 M St. NW, Ste. 700

Washington, DC 20036
Ph: (212)721-4100
Fax: (212)296-8120

Boehm, Ken, Chairman
National Legal and Policy Center
[18319]
107 Park Washington Ct.
Falls Church, VA 22046
Ph: (703)237-1970
Fax: (703)237-2090

Boehm, Teddy, Advisor
German-Texan Heritage Society
[19445]
PO Box 684171
Austin, TX 78768-4171
Ph: (512)467-4569
Toll Free: 855-892-6691
Fax: (512)467-4574

Boehmer, Jennifer, President
National Council for Marketing and Public Relations **[8471]**
5901 Wyoming Blvd. NE, No. J-254
Albuquerque, NM 87109
Ph: (505)349-0500

Boehmer, Judson L., Chairman
Southern Textile Association, Inc.
[3269]
PO Box 66
Gastonia, NC 28053-0066
Ph: (704)215-4543
Fax: (704)215-4160

Boender, Ron, Founder
Passiflora Society International
[4440]
PO Box 350
Elmira, CA 95625

Bogardus, Mr. William, Founder
Anneke Jans and Everardus Bogardus Descendants Association
[20888]
c/o Mr. William Bogardus
1121 Linhof Rd.
Wilmington, OH 45177-2917

Bogdan, Thomas J., President
University Corporation for Atmospheric Research **[6860]**
3090 Center Green Dr.
Boulder, CO 80301
Ph: (303)497-1000

Boghosian, Heidi, Exec. Dir.
A. J. Muste Memorial Institute
[18808]
339 Lafayette St.
New York, NY 10012
Ph: (212)533-4335
Fax: (212)228-6193

Bogle, Hon. Ronald, CEO, President
American Architectural Foundation
[5951]
740 15th St. NW, Ste. 225
Washington, DC 20005
Ph: (202)787-1001
Fax: (202)787-1002

Bognanno, Thomas G., President, CEO
Community Health Charities **[11858]**
1240 N Pitt St., 3rd Fl.
Alexandria, VA 22314
Ph: (703)528-1007
Toll Free: 800-654-0845
Fax: (703)528-5975

Bogues, Tyrone, Founder
Always Believe, Inc. **[11743]**
PO Box 1884
Matthews, NC 28106
Ph: (704)430-6149

Bohan, Chara Haeussler, President
American Association for Teaching and Curriculum **[8640]**

c/o Lynne Bailey, Executive Secretary
5640 Seminole Blvd.
Seminole, FL 33772

Bohannon-Kaplan, Margaret, Director, Founder
Harry Singer Foundation **[19005]**
PO Box 223159
Carmel, CA 93922-3159
Ph: (831)625-4223
Fax: (831)624-7994

Bohl, Anne, Founder
Clean Water for the World **[13318]**
PO Box 20416
Kalamazoo, MI 49019-1416
Ph: (269)342-1354

Bohle, Suzanne, Exec. Dir.
Research Chefs Association **[964]**
1100 Johnson Ferry Rd., Ste. 300
Atlanta, GA 30342
Ph: (678)298-1178

Bohlen, Stacy A., Exec. Dir.
National Indian Health Board
[12380]
926 Pennsylvania Ave. SE
Washington, DC 20003
Ph: (202)507-4085

Bohlinger, Peter, Contact
Child Hope International **[10898]**
1225 Coast Village Rd., Ste. C
Santa Barbara, CA 93108
Ph: (805)845-1946

Bohlke, Terry, President
Ambulatory Surgery Center Association **[17358]**
1012 Cameron St.
Alexandria, VA 22314-2427
Ph: (703)836-8808
Fax: (703)549-0976

Bohm, Mr. Carl, President
International Corrugated Case Association **[837]**
500 Park Blvd., Ste. 985
Itasca, IL 60143
Ph: (847)364-9600
Fax: (847)364-9639

Bohnert, Victor, Exec. Dir.
International Avaya Users Group
[3229]
330 N Wabash Ave.
Chicago, IL 60611
Ph: (312)321-5126

Bohrer, Jason, President, CEO
Lignite Energy Council **[738]**
1016 E Owens Ave.
Bismarck, ND 58502
Ph: (701)258-7117
Toll Free: 800-932-7117
Fax: (701)258-2755

Boice, John D., Jr., President
National Council on Radiation Protection and Measurements
[5740]
7910 Woodmont Ave., Ste. 400
Bethesda, MD 20814-3095
Ph: (301)657-2652
Fax: (301)907-8768

Boice, Nicole, Founder, CEO
Global Genes **[14579]**
28 Argonaut, Ste. 150
Aliso Viejo, CA 92656
Ph: (949)248-7273

Boies, Vicki, Chairman
Solve ME/CFS Initiative **[14613]**
5455 Wilshire Blvd., Ste. 806
Los Angeles, CA 90036-0007
Ph: (704)364-0016

Boire, Martin C., Chairman
Support Our Troops **[10761]**
PO Box 70
Daytona Beach, FL 32115-0070
Ph: (386)767-8882

Boisen, Caryn, Director
Women Construction Owners and
  Executives U.S.A. **[903]**
1004 Duke St.
Alexandria, VA 22314
Toll Free: 800-788-3548
Fax: (202)330-5151

Boland, Betsy, Exec. Dir.
American Copper Council **[2341]**
475 Broadway
Saratoga Springs, NY 12866-6735
Ph: (518)871-1062

Boland, Bob, President
American Association of Directors of
  Psychiatric Residency Training
  [16811]
c/o Sara Brewer, Administrative
  Director
PO Box 30618
Indianapolis, IN 46230
Ph: (317)407-1173

Boland, Hal, President
American Association of Teachers of
  German **[8171]**
112 Haddontowne Ct., Ste. 104
Cherry Hill, NJ 08034-3662
Ph: (856)795-5553
Fax: (856)795-9398

Boles, Anita, CEO
National Organizations for Youth
  Safety **[13467]**
901 N Washington St., Ste. 703
Alexandria, VA 22314
Ph: (571)367-7171
Toll Free: 866-559-9398

Boles, Jerry C., Secretary, Treasurer
Brotherhood of Railroad Signalmen
  [23515]
917 Shenandoah Shores Rd.
Front Royal, VA 22630
Ph: (540)622-6522
Fax: (540)622-6532

Boles, Steve, President
American Shagya Arabian Verband
  [4326]
PO Box 169
Finchville, KY 40022

Bolger, Tisha, President
American Camp Association **[22718]**
5000 State Road 67 N
Martinsville, IN 46151-7902
Ph: (765)342-8456
Toll Free: 800-428-2267
Fax: (765)342-2065

Bolin, Barbara, PhD, President
National Organization for Career
  Credentialing **[7571]**
c/o Barbara Bolin, President
1133 May St.
Lansing, MI 48906
Ph: (804)310-2552

Bolinger, Terry, President, Web Adm.
Zane Grey's West Society **[9116]**
c/o Sheryle Hodapp, Secretary-
  Treasurer
15 Deer Oaks Dr.
Pleasanton, CA 94588-8236
Ph: (925)485-1325

Bolinger, Vickie, President
Advertising Media Credit Executives
  Association **[1215]**
24600 Detroit Rd., Ste. 100

Bay Village, OH 44140-0036
Ph: (410)992-7609
Fax: (410)740-5574

Boliver, Bruce, President
Resort and Commercial Recreation
  Association **[2915]**
PO Box 16449
Fernandina Beach, FL 32035

Bollinger, Dan, Exec. Dir.
International Coalition for Genital
  Integrity **[11284]**
1970 N River Rd.
West Lafayette, IN 47906

Bollinger, Daniel H., Officer
Intact America **[11283]**
PO Box 8516
Tarrytown, NY 10591

Bollinger, Lee C., Chmn. of the Bd.
Center for United States-China Arts
  Exchange **[9151]**
423 W 118th St., No. 1E
New York, NY 10025
Ph: (212)280-4648
Fax: (212)662-6346

Bollon, Vincent J., Contact
National Fire Protection Association
  [12832]
1 Batterymarch Pk.
Quincy, MA 02169-7471
Ph: (617)770-3000
Fax: (617)770-0700

Bolme, Sarah, Director, Founder
Christian Small Publishers Associa-
  tion **[2777]**
PO Box 481022
Charlotte, NC 28269
Ph: (704)277-7194
Fax: (704)717-2928

Bolonkin, Alexander, PhD, President
International Association of Former
  Soviet Political Prisoners and
  Victims of the Communist Regime
  [18412]
1310 Avenue R, Ste. 6-F
Brooklyn, NY 11229
Ph: (718)339-4563

Bolotin, Laurence A., Exec. Dir.
Zeta Beta Tau **[23939]**
3905 Vincennes Rd., Ste. 100
Indianapolis, IN 46268
Ph: (317)334-1898
Fax: (317)334-1899

Bolser, Clint, President, CEO
Logan Community Resources
  [11616]
2505 E Jefferson Blvd.
South Bend, IN 46615
Ph: (574)289-4831
Fax: (574)234-2075

Bolte, Brig. Gen. (Ret.) Philip L.,
  Chairman
U.S. Cavalry Association and Memo-
  rial Research Library **[9810]**
7107 W Cheyenne St.
El Reno, OK 73036
Ph: (405)422-6330

Bolu Omodele, Agba-Akin, President
Egbe Omo Yoruba, North America
  [19594]
173 Hagaman Pl.
Staten Island, NY 10302
Ph: (646)209-5158

Bolz, Shihan Mary H., VP
International Okinawa Kobudo Association **[22993]**
2354 Ackley Pl.

Woodland, CA 95776
Ph: (707)428-7266

Bomberger, Irvin E., Exec. Dir.
American Orthopaedic Society for
  Sports Medicine **[17276]**
9400 W Higgins Rd., Ste. 300
Rosemont, IL 60018
Ph: (847)292-4900
Toll Free: 877-321-3500
Fax: (847)292-4905

Bomia, Robert, President
National Federation of Flemish Giant
  Rabbit Breeders **[4603]**
c/o Wayne Bechdel, Secretary/
  Treasurer
117 Hollow Rd.
Lock Haven, PA 17745

Bonaparte, David J., President, CEO
Jewelers of America **[2050]**
120 Broadway, Ste. 2820
New York, NY 10271
Ph: (646)658-5806
Toll Free: 800-223-0673

Bonauto, Mary L., Director
Gay and Lesbian Advocates and
  Defenders **[17898]**
30 Winter St., Ste. 800
Boston, MA 02108
Ph: (617)426-1350
Toll Free: 800-455-GLAD
Fax: (617)426-3594

Bond, Craig, President
Paint and Decorating Retailers As-
  sociation **[1958]**
1401 Triad Center Dr.
Saint Peters, MO 63376-7353
Ph: (636)326-2636

Bond, Jason, President
Association of Forensic Quality Assurance Managers **[5243]**
c/o Lise A. Swacha, Secretary
NH State Police Forensic Laboratory
33 Hazen Dr.
Concord, NH 03305

Bond, Leslie, Jr., CEO
National Association of Securities
  Professionals **[3047]**
1000 Vermont Ave. NW, Ste. 810
Washington, DC 20005
Ph: (202)371-5535
Fax: (202)371-5536

Bond, Sandra, President
Homer Laughlin China Collectors
  Association **[21661]**
PO Box 721
North Platte, NE 69103-0721
Fax: (308)534-7015

Bonde, Debra, Director, Founder
Seedlings Braille Books for Children
  [13278]
14151 Farmington Rd.
Livonia, MI 48154-5422
Ph: (734)427-8552
Toll Free: 800-777-8552
Fax: (734)427-8552

Bonderson, Paul, Jr., President
Ducks Unlimited **[4808]**
1 Waterfowl Way
Memphis, TN 38120
Ph: (901)758-3825
Toll Free: 800-453-8257

Bonderson, Roxana, Founder,
  Developer, Exec. Dir.
Worldhealer, Inc. **[12201]**
PO Box 62121
Santa Barbara, CA 93160
Ph: (805)253-2324

Bonds, Leslie, Exec. Dir.
Diversity Information Resources
  [2392]
2300 Kennedy St. NE, Ste. 230
Minneapolis, MN 55413
Ph: (612)781-6819
Fax: (612)781-0109

Bonds, Roger G., Exec. Dir.
American Academy of Medical
  Management **[15620]**
560 W Crossville Rd., Ste. 104
Roswell, GA 30075
Ph: (770)649-7150
Fax: (770)649-7552

Bone, David, Exec. Dir.
Fellowship of United Methodists in
  Music and Worship Arts **[20342]**
PO Box 24787
Nashville, TN 37202-4787
Toll Free: 800-952-8977
Fax: (615)749-6874

Bone, David, Exec. Dir.
United States Racquet Stringers As-
  sociation **[3166]**
310 Richard Arrington Jr. Blvd. N,
  Ste. 400
Birmingham, AL 35203
Ph: (760)536-1177
Fax: (760)536-1171

Bone, Sarah, Contact
Extra Miler Club **[22466]**
PO Box 73
Death Valley, CA 92328

Boney, Maurice W., Founder
Irish Black Cattle Association **[3734]**
PO Box 7
Arlee, MT 59821
Ph: (406)696-5977

Bonfield, Susan, Exec. Dir.
Environment for the Americas **[3660]**
5171 Eldorado Springs Dr., Ste. N
Boulder, CO 80303-9672
Ph: (303)499-1950
Toll Free: 866-334-3330
Fax: (303)499-9567

Boni, Chris, VP
Waves of Health **[15506]**
206 Bergen Ave., Ste. 203
Kearny, NJ 07032

Bonino, Emma, Founder
No Peace Without Justice **[18809]**
866 Union Plz., No. 408
New York, NY 10017
Ph: (212)980-2558
Fax: (212)980-1072

Bonneau, Josiane, Director
Wildlife Habitat Council **[3967]**
8737 Colesville Rd., Ste. 800
Silver Spring, MD 20910
Ph: (301)588-8994

Bonner, John, President
Weimaraner Club of America
  [21988]
c/o Ellen Dodge, Executive
  Secretary
PO Box 489
Wakefield, RI 02880-0489
Ph: (401)782-3725
Fax: (401)789-8279

Bonner, Dr. Linda Hanifin, Opera-
  tions Mgr.
Water Design-Build Council **[599]**
PO Box 1924
Edgewater, MD 21037
Ph: (410)798-0842
Fax: (410)798-5741

Bonner, Monica, Contact
Society for the Experimental
  Analysis of Behavior **[6047]**

Indiana University
Psychological and Brain Sciences
1101 E 10th St.
Bloomington, IN 47405-7007
Ph: (812)336-1257
Fax: (812)855-4691

Bonner, Wayne, VP of Fin. & Admin.
National Energy Foundation [7881]
4516 South 700 East, Ste. 100
Salt Lake City, UT 84107
Ph: (801)327-9500
Toll Free: 800-616-8326
Fax: (801)908-5400

Bonoff, Steve, Sr. VP of Mktg.
Idealliance [1537]
1800 Diagonal Rd., Ste. 320
Alexandria, VA 22314
Ph: (703)837-1070
    (703)837-1066
Fax: (703)837-1072

Bonosaro, Carol A., President
SEA Professional Development
League [5200]
Senior Executives Association
77 K St. NE, Ste. 2600
Washington, DC 20002
Ph: (202)971-3300
Fax: (202)971-3317

Bonosaro, Carol A., President
Senior Executives Association
[5201]
77 K St. NE, Ste. 2600
Washington, DC 20002
Ph: (202)971-3300
Fax: (202)971-3317

Bonowitz, Abraham J., Director,
Founder
Citizens United for Alternatives to
the Death Penalty [5130]
177 US Highway No. 1
Tequesta, FL 33469
Toll Free: 800-973-6548

Bonpasse, Morrison, Director
Single Global Currency Association
[417]
PO Box 390
Newcastle, ME 04553
Ph: (207)586-6078

Bonsey, David, President
American Federation of Violin and
Bow Makers [9856]
1035 S Josephine Ave.
Rosalia, WA 99170-9551

Bonvoisin, Fabrice, President
International Trade Club of Chicago
[1968]
134 N LaSalle St., Ste. 1300
Chicago, IL 60602
Ph: (312)423-5250

Boo, Michael, Chief Strat. Ofc.
National Marrow Donor Program
[14624]
500 N 5th St.
Minneapolis, MN 55401-1206
Ph: (612)627-5800
Toll Free: 800-627-7692

Book, Dr. Wayne J., Chairman
ServeHAITI [11432]
999 Peachtree St. NE, Ste. 2300
Atlanta, GA 30309
Ph: (404)407-5023

Bookman, Terri, Editor
IEEE - Society on Social Implica-
tions of Technology [7271]
c/o Terri Bookman, Managing Editor
PO Box 7465
Princeton, NJ 08543

Bookout, Bill, President, Chmn. of
the Bd.
National Animal Supplement Council
[3618]
PO Box 2568
Valley Center, CA 92082
Ph: (760)751-3360

Bookson, Shoshana T., President
Jewish Lawyers Guild [20256]
c/o Shoshana T. Bookson, President
570 Lexington Ave., Ste. 1600
New York, NY 10022
Ph: (646)300-8100

Boone, Deborah, President
Spalding University Alumni Associa-
tion [19349]
845 S 3rd St.
Louisville, KY 40203
Ph: (502)585-7111
    (502)585-9911
Toll Free: 800-896-8941

Boone, Doug, President
NTCA, The Rural Broadband As-
sociation [3423]
4121 Wilson Blvd., Ste. 1000
Arlington, VA 22203
Ph: (703)351-2000
Fax: (703)351-2001

Boone, Elverta, President
African American Mutual Assistance
Network [11307]
2709 South Ave., Ste. E
La Crosse, WI 54601
Toll Free: 800-765-4050

Boone, Dr. Oliver C., Founder, Exec.
Dir.
High School Band Directors National
Association [8370]
4166 Will Rhodes Dr.
Columbus, GA 31909
Ph: (706)568-0760

Boone, Dr. Oliver C., Exec. Dir.
National High School Band Directors
Hall of Fame [8386]
4166 Will Rhoades Dr.
Columbus, GA 31909

Boone, Prof. Tommy, PhD, Founder
American Society of Exercise
Physiologists [16695]
503 8th Ave. W
Osakis, MN 56360

Boone, Xenia, Exec. Dir.
DMA Nonprofit Federation [255]
1615 L St. NW, Ste. 1100
Washington, DC 20036
Ph: (202)861-2427
    (202)861-2498

Boote, Mary, CEO
Global Farmer Network [6121]
309 Court Ave., Ste. 214
Des Moines, IA 50309
Ph: (515)274-0800
Fax: (240)201-8451

Booth, Heather, President
Midwest Academy [11294]
27 E Monroe St., 11th Fl.
Chicago, IL 60603
Ph: (312)427-2304
Fax: (312)379-0313

Booth, Heather, Chairman
USAction [19121]
1825 K St. NW, Ste. 210
Washington, DC 20006-1220
Ph: (202)263-4520
Fax: (202)263-4530

Booth, Hillary Arrow, VP
Transportation Lawyers Association
[5820]

PO Box 15122
Lenexa, KS 66285-5122
Ph: (913)895-4615
Fax: (913)895-4652

Booth, Robert, Exec. Dir.
American Board of Examiners in
Clinical Social Work [13101]
214 Humphrey St.
Marblehead, MA 01945
Ph: (781)639-5270
Toll Free: 800-694-5285
Fax: (781)639-5278

Boothroyd, Kaaren, CEO
Aging Life Care Association [16194]
3275 W Ina Rd., Ste. 130
Tucson, AZ 85741-2198
Ph: (520)881-8008
Fax: (520)325-7925

Boots, Kent E., President
Professional Society of Forensic
Mapping [5251]
4964 Ward Rd.
Wheat Ridge, CO 80033

Boquet, Fr. Shenan J., President
Human Life International [12773]
4 Family Life Ln.
Front Royal, VA 22630
Toll Free: 800-549-5433
Fax: (540)622-6247

Borans, Mr. Andrew S., Exec. Dir.
Alpha Epsilon Pi [19663]
8815 Wesleyan Rd.
Indianapolis, IN 46268-1185
Ph: (317)876-1913
Fax: (317)876-1057

Borans, Mr. Andrew S., Exec. Dir.
Alpha Epsilon Pi [23883]
8815 Wesleyan Rd.
Indianapolis, IN 46268-1185
Ph: (317)876-1913
Fax: (317)876-1057

Borch, Colonel (Retired) Fred,
President
Orders and Medals Society of
America [22184]
PO Box 540
Claymont, DE 19703-0540

Borch, Marianne, President
Certification Board for Urologic
Nurses and Associates [17550]
E Holly Ave.
Pitman, NJ 08071-0056
Ph: (856)256-2351

Borchardt, Ms. Marilyn, Dir. of Dev.
Food First Books [18455]
398 60th St.
Oakland, CA 94618
Ph: (510)654-4400
Fax: (510)654-4551

Bordeaux, Dr. Roger, Exec. Dir.
Association of Community Tribal
Schools [8394]
220 Omaha St.
Mission, SD 57555
Ph: (605)838-0424
Fax: (605)838-0424

Borden, Joan, Rec. Sec.
International Benchrest Shooters
[23130]
c/o Jeff Stover, President
84 Susquehanna Ave.
Lock Haven, PA 17745
Ph: (570)660-6102

Bordenick, Jennifer Covich, CEO
eHealth Initiative [14997]
818 Connecticut Ave. NW, Ste. 500

Washington, DC 20006
Ph: (202)624-3270
Fax: (202)429-5553

Borders, Denise, Chairman
AdvancED [8526]
9115 Westside Pky.
Alpharetta, GA 30009
Toll Free: 888-413-3669

Borders, Emma, Comm. Chm.
American Medical Association Alli-
ance [15709]
550 M Ritchie Highway 271
Severna Park, MD 21146
Toll Free: 800-549-4619

Bordignon, Kristen, Administrator
American Neurotology Society
[17236]
c/o Kristen Bordignon, Administrator
4960 Dover St. NE
Saint Petersburg, FL 33703
Ph: (217)638-0801
Fax: (217)679-1677

Borello, Federico, Exec. Dir.
Center for Civilians in Conflict
[17999]
1210 18th St. NW, 4th Fl.
Washington, DC 20036
Ph: (202)558-6958

Borer, Jeffrey S., MD, President
Heart Valve Society of America
[14116]
PO Box 1365
New York, NY 10021

Borgen, Clint, President
The Borgen Project [12530]
1416 NW 46th St., Ste. 105, PMB
145
Seattle, WA 98107
Ph: (206)414-1032

Borglum, Dale, PhD, Founder, Exec.
Dir.
Living/Dying Project [13217]
PO Box 357
Fairfax, CA 94978-0357
Ph: (415)456-3915

Borgstede, James P., President
International Society of Radiology
[17059]
1891 Preston White Dr.
Reston, VA 20191
Ph: (703)648-8360
Fax: (703)648-8361

Borgstrom, Marna P., Chairman
Coalition to Protect America's Health
Care [15320]
PO Box 30211
Bethesda, MD 20824-0211
Toll Free: 877-422-2349

Borich, Alexis, Exec. Sec.
American College of Veterinary
Dermatology [17616]
c/o Alexis Borich, Executive Secr-
etary
11835 Forest Knolls Ct.
Nevada City, CA 95959
Ph: (530)272-7334
Fax: (530)272-8518

Borishade, James, Exec. Dir.
Association for Challenge Course
Technology [2467]
PO Box 47
Deerfield, IL 60015
Ph: (773)966-2503
Toll Free: 800-991-0286
Fax: (800)991-0287

Borja, Anie, Exec. Dir.
National Women's Business Council
[3498]

409 3rd St. SW, 5th Fl.
Washington, DC 20416
Ph: (202)205-3850
Fax: (202)205-6825

Borja, Armando, Director
Jesuit Refugee Service/U.S.A.
[12592]
1016 16th St. NW, Ste. 500
Washington, DC 20036
Ph: (202)629-5939

Bork, Mr. Christopher, Secretary
Mu Beta Psi [23828]

Borlaug, Nicolette, President
University of Mary Alumni Associa-
tion [19360]
7500 University Dr.
Bismarck, ND 58504
Ph: (701)355-8030
Toll Free: 800-408-6279
Fax: (701)255-7687

Borman, Keith T., VP, Gen. Counsel
American Short Line and Regional
Railroad Association [2834]
50 F St. NW, Ste. 7020
Washington, DC 20001
Ph: (202)628-4500
    (202)585-3442
Fax: (202)628-6430

Borne, Bill, President, Chairman
Alliance for Home Health Quality
and Innovation [15274]
PO Box 7319
Washington, DC 20044
Ph: (202)239-3983

Borne, Tom, VP
Association of Consulting Chemists
and Chemical Engineers [6189]
PO Box 902
New Providence, NJ 07974
Ph: (908)464-3182
Fax: (908)464-3182

Borneman, Carol, Contact
Healing the Children [11235]
c/o Carol Borneman
PO Box 9065
Spokane, WA 99209-9065
Ph: (509)327-4281
Fax: (509)327-4284

Bornmann, Carl F., Jr., Managing
Ed.
Artisans Order of Mutual Protection
[19482]
8100 Roosevelt Blvd.
Philadelphia, PA 19152
Ph: (215)708-1000
Toll Free: 800-551-1873

Borochoff, Mr. Daniel, Founder,
President
CharityWatch [12468]
3450 N Lake Shore Dr., Ste. 2802
Chicago, IL 60657-2862
Ph: (773)529-2300
Fax: (773)529-0024

Boron, Walter, Sec. Gen.
International Union of Physiological
Sciences [7034]
c/o Steven Webster, Manager
Dept. of Physiology and Biophysics
Case Western Reserve University
10900 Euclid Ave.
Cleveland, OH 44106-4970
Ph: (216)368-5520
Fax: (216)368-5586

Borovilos, George, President
North American Agricultural Marketing Officials [4481]
c/o Amy Pettit, 1800 Glenn Hwy.,
Ste. 12

1800 Glenn Hwy., Ste. 12
Palmer, AK 99645
Ph: (907)761-3864

Borowich, Sivan, Founder, CEO
Innovation: Africa [5884]
520 8th Ave., 15th Fl.
New York, NY 10018-6507
Ph: (646)472-5380

Borrello, Joe, CEO, President
Tasters Guild International [191]
1515 Michigan NE
Grand Rapids, MI 49503
Ph: (616)454-7815
Fax: (616)459-9969

Borrero, Francisco, President
Colombian-American Chamber of
Commerce of Greater Miami
[23575]
2305 NW 107 Ave., Ste. 1M14, Box
No. 105
Miami, FL 33172
Ph: (305)446-2542

Borrero, Roberto, President, Chair-
man
United Confederation of Taino
People [19399]
PO Box 4515
New York, NY 10163
Ph: (123)456-7890

Borrmann, Harald, President, Chair-
man
Catholic United Financial [19404]
3499 Lexington Ave. N
Saint Paul, MN 55126
Ph: (651)490-0170

Borschke, Dan, Exec. VP
National Association of Conces-
sionaires [1394]
180 N Michigan Ave., Ste. 2215
Chicago, IL 60601
Ph: (312)236-3858
Fax: (312)236-7809

Borstein, Rick, President
Federation of American Aquarium
Societies [6715]
c/o Hedy Padgett, Membership Chair
4816 E 64th St.
Indianapolis, IN 46220-4728
Ph: (847)478-8110
    (847)732-0526

Borthwick, Dr. Mark, Exec. Dir.
United States National Committee
for Pacific Economic Cooperation
[18162]
1819 L St. NW, 6th Fl.
Washington, DC 20036
Ph: (202)293-3995
Fax: (202)293-1402

Bortner, John, Chairman, Bd.
Member
Afghan Friends Network [19284]
PO Box 170368
San Francisco, CA 94117
Toll Free: 800-831-2339

Bortner, Robert, Founder, President
Community Empowerment Network
[12799]
1685 Grandview Pl.
Ferndale, WA 98248
Ph: (206)329-6244
Fax: (617)344-7868

Borwick, Susan, President
International Alliance for Women in
Music [9923]
c/o Susan Borwick, President
Dept. of Music
Wake Forest University

PO Box 7345
Winston Salem, NC 27109-7345

Boschert, Jeff, President
National Clay Pipe Institute [2609]
N6369 US Highway 12, Ste. A
Elkhorn, WI 53121
Ph: (262)742-2904
Fax: (360)242-9094

Bosco, Mary Lou, COO
AIM [271]
20399 Route 19, Ste. 203
Cranberry Township, PA 16066
Ph: (724)742-4470
Fax: (724)742-4476

Boshier, Peter, President
Association of Family and Concilia-
tion Courts [23575]
6525 Grand Teton Plz.
Madison, WI 53719
Ph: (608)664-3750
Fax: (608)664-3751

Boslego, Jordan, President
Coalition to Cure Calpain 3 [15847]
15 Compo Pkwy.
Westport, CT 06880

Boss, Derk, CSP, President
International Association of Certified
Surveillance Professionals [3057]
8438 Langhorne Creek St.
Las Vegas, NV 89139
Ph: (270)724-4368

Bossard, Steve, Mgr.
Interdisciplinary Biblical Research
Institute [20082]
PO Box 423
Hatfield, PA 19440-0423
Ph: (215)368-7002

Bostian, Julie, President
Association of Donor Relations
Professionals [12461]
2150 N 107th St., No. 205
Seattle, WA 98133-9009
Toll Free: 800-341-0014
Fax: (206)367-8777

Bostinto, Mr. Andrew, Founder,
President
National Gym Association [23064]
PO Box 970579
Coconut Creek, FL 33097-0579
Ph: (954)344-8410
Fax: (954)344-8412

Boston, Terry W., Exec. Dir.,
Secretary, Treasurer
Association of Edison Illuminating
Companies [3412]
600 N 18th St. N
Birmingham, AL 35203
Ph: (205)257-3839
Fax: (205)257-2540

Boswell, Cecelia, President
The Association for the Gifted [7942]
PO Box 316
De Leon, TX 76444
Ph: (270)745-5991

Boswell, Nancy, Co-Chmn. of the
Bd.
Ethics Research Center [17856]
2345 Crystal Dr., Ste. 201
Arlington, VA 22202-4807
Ph: (703)647-2185
Fax: (703)647-2180

Botbol, Mindy Moline, President
Jewish Funeral Directors of America
[2409]
107 Carpenter Dr., Ste. 100
Sterling, VA 20164
Toll Free: 800-645-7700
Fax: (703)391-8416

Bott, Richard P., Director
National Religious Broadcasters
[19769]
9510 Technology Dr.
Manassas, VA 20110-4149
Ph: (703)330-7000
Fax: (703)330-7100

Bottomley, John T., Exec. Dir.
The Fuller Foundation, Inc. [12973]
PO Box 479
Rye Beach, NH 03871
Ph: (603)964-6998

Bouchane, Kolleen, Director
ACTION [17131]
RESULTS Educational Fund
1101 15th St. NW, Ste. 1200
Washington, DC 20005
Ph: (202)783-4800
Fax: (202)783-2818

Boucher, Bradley A., President
The Rho Chi Society [23847]
c/o UNC Eshelman School of
Pharmacy
University of North Carolina
3210 Kerr Hall, CB 7569
Chapel Hill, NC 27514
Ph: (919)843-9001
Fax: (919)962-0644

Boulpaep, Prof. Emile L., CEO,
President
Belgian American Educational
Foundation [9118]
195 Church St.
New Haven, CT 06510
Ph: (203)777-5765
    (203)785-4055
Fax: (203)777-5765

Boulton, Lyndie, Exec. Dir.
American Society for Enology and
Viticulture [4923]
PO Box 1855
Davis, CA 95617-1855
Ph: (530)753-3142
Fax: (530)753-3318

Bounds, Alan, President
National Narcotic Detector Dog As-
sociation [5504]
379 County Road 105
Carthage, TX 75633
Toll Free: 888-289-0070

Bounds, Ken, Director
Early Ford V-8 Club of America
[21372]
PO Box 1715
Maple Grove, MN 55311
Ph: (763)420-7829
Toll Free: 866-427-7583

Bourg, Lorna, President, CEO
Southern Mutual Help Association,
Inc. [11443]
3602 Old Jeanerette Rd.
New Iberia, LA 70563
Ph: (337)367-3277
Fax: (337)367-3279

Bourgeois, Marie-Claude, President
Junior Optimist Octagon
International [12892]
4494 Lindell Blvd.
Saint Louis, MO 63108
Ph: (314)371-6000
Toll Free: 800-500-8130
Fax: (314)371-6006

Bourgeois, Fr. Roy, Founder
School of the Americas Watch
[18949]
5525 Illinois Ave. NW
Washington, DC 20011-2937
Ph: (202)234-3440
Fax: (202)636-4505

Bourgerie, Dana Scott, Dept. Chm.
Cantonese Language Association
[20297]
Brigham Young University
A-41 ASB
Provo, UT 84602
Ph: (801)422-4636
    (801)422-1211

Bourne, Peter G., MD, Chairman
Medical Education Cooperation with
Cuba [15625]
1814 Franklin St., Ste. 820
Oakland, CA 94612
Ph: (678)904-8092

Bourque, Debra, Exec. Dir.
International Pedicure Association
[921]
36 Washburn Ave.
Fairhaven, MA 02719
Toll Free: 866-326-7573

Bova, Steve, Exec. Dir.
Financial & Insurance Conference
Planners [2329]
330 N Wabash Ave., Ste. 2000
Chicago, IL 60611-7621
Ph: (312)245-1023

Bowar-Ferres, Susan, PhD,
President
Nurses Educational Funds, Inc.
[16168]
137 Montague St.
Brooklyn, NY 11201
Ph: (212)590-2443
    (917)524-8051
Fax: (212)590-2446

Bowden, Cindy, President
World Crafts Council North America
[9191]
c/o Cindy Bowden, President
1246 Fork Creek Trl.
Decatur, GA 30033
Ph: (404)213-1864

Bowden, Kirk, PhD, President
NAADAC: The Association for Addic-
tion Professionals [17317]
1001 N Fairfax St., Ste. 201
Alexandria, VA 22314
Toll Free: 800-548-0497
Fax: (703)377-1136

Bowden, Mwata, Chairman
AACM Chicago [9844]
Chicago, IL
Ph: (312)555-5555

Bowen, Deborah J., CEO, President
American College of Healthcare
Executives [15304]
1 N Franklin St., Ste. 1700
Chicago, IL 60606-3529
Ph: (312)424-2800
    (312)424-9400
Fax: (312)424-0023

Bowen, Eric, Bd. Member
Biofuel Recycling [4626]
5758 Geary Blvd., No. 421
San Francisco, CA 94121
Ph: (415)747-2771
Fax: (415)962-2372

Bowen, Gene, Founder
Road Recovery Foundation [17327]
PO Box 1680
New York, NY 10101-1680
Ph: (212)489-2425

Bowen, Gordon, CEO
LifeBanc [14621]
4775 Richmond Rd.
Cleveland, OH 44128-5919
Ph: (216)752-5433
Toll Free: 888-558-5433
Fax: (216)292-8191

Bowen, Jenny, Founder, CEO
Half the Sky [11011]
715 Hearst Ave., Ste. 200
Berkeley, CA 94710
Ph: (510)525-3377
Fax: (510)525-3611

Bowen, Mrs. Marie, Exec. Dir.
Presbyterians Pro-Life [12788]
PO Box 461
Glenshaw, PA 15116
Ph: (412)487-1990
Fax: (412)487-1994

Bowen, Shelia, Rec. Sec.
American National CattleWomen
[3706]
15954 Jackson Creek Pky., Ste. B
225
Monument, CO 80132
Ph: (303)850-3441
Fax: (303)694-2390

Bowen, Tracy, Exec. Dir.
Center for a New American Dream
[18016]
PO Box 797
Charlottesville, VA 22902
Ph: (301)891-3683

Bower, Tim, CAE, Managing Dir.
National Association of
Environmental Professionals
[4083]
PO Box 460
Collingswood, NJ 08108
Ph: (856)283-7816
Fax: (856)210-1619

Bowers, Jan, Exec. Dir.
Family and Consumer Sciences
Education Association [7917]
Dept. of Family and Consumer Sci-
ences
Central Washington University
400 E University Way, MS 7565
Ellensburg, WA 98926-7565
Ph: (509)963-2766

Bowers, Wayne, Exec. Dir.
Citizens United for the Rehabilitation
of Errants-Sex Offenders Restored
through Treatment [12920]
c/o Wayne Bowers, Executive Director
PO Box 1022
Norman, OK 73070-1022
Ph: (405)639-7262

Bowersox, Jerry Sue, Secretary,
Treasurer
Addington Association [20774]
100 Oak Beech Ct.
Holly Springs, NC 27540

Bowler, Kevin, CEO
New Zealand Tourism Board [23607]
501 Santa Monica Blvd., Ste. 300
Santa Monica, CA 90401
Ph: (310)395-7480
Fax: (310)395-5453

Bowles, Cheryl, Contact
Association of Executive and
Administrative Professionals [65]
900 S Washington St., Ste. G-13
Falls Church, VA 22046
Ph: (703)237-8616
Fax: (703)533-1153

Bowles, Sandra, Ed.-in-Chief, Exec.
Dir.
Handweavers Guild of America, Inc.
[21760]
1255 Buford Hwy., Ste. 211
Suwanee, GA 30024-8421
Ph: (678)730-0010
Fax: (678)730-0836

Bowman, Betsi, President
Incentive Gift Card Council [1499]
4248 Park Glen Rd.
Minneapolis, MN 55416
Ph: (952)928-4649

Bowman, Dorothy, Vol., Exec. Dir.
Embrace Uganda [11351]
PO Box 742
Wake Forest, NC 27588

Bowman, John, Gov.
State Revenue Society [22372]
27 Pine St.
Lincroft, NJ 07738-1827

Bowman, Richard, President
WPC Club [21524]
Box 3504
Kalamazoo, MI 49003-3504
Fax: (269)694-2818

Bowzer, Melanie, Exec. Dir.
National Academies of Practice
[15037]
201 E Main St., Ste. 1405
Lexington, KY 40507
Ph: (859)514-9184
Fax: (859)514-9188

Boxer Wachler, Brian S., Founder,
Director
Giving Vision [17702]
Box 206A
9663 Santa Monica Blvd.
Beverly Hills, CA 90210
Ph: (310)860-1900
Fax: (310)860-1902

Boxwill, Helen, Exec. Dir.
H2 Empower [11371]
PO Box 493
Huntington Station, NY 11746
Ph: (631)549-9346

Boyadjian, Jacklin, Exec. Dir.
Armenian Bar Association [4992]
c/o Lisa Boyadjian, Administrative
Assistant
PO Box 29111
Los Angeles, CA 90029
Ph: (626)584-0043
    (818)905-6484

Boyce, Aaron, Founder
Team Success [13483]
5050 Laguna Blvd., Ste. 112-415
Elk Grove, CA 95758-4151
Ph: (916)629-4229

Boyd, Jean, President
National Association of Academic
Advisors for Athletics [7690]
24651 Detroit Rd.
Westlake, OH 44145
Ph: (440)892-4000
Fax: (440)892-4007

Boyd, Mr. John, III, President
American Boxwood Society [22067]
PO Box 85
Boyce, VA 22620

Boyd, John, President, CEO
Mission Aviation Fellowship [20437]
112 N Pilatus Ln.
Nampa, ID 83687
Ph: (208)498-0800
Toll Free: 800-359-7623
Fax: (208)498-0801

Boyd, John R., President
Workers' Injury Law and Advocacy
Group [5752]
1701 Pennsylvania Ave. NW, Ste.
300
Washington, DC 20006
Ph: (202)349-7150
Fax: (202)249-4191

Boyd, Dr. John W., Jr., Founder,
President
National Black Farmers Association
[4159]
68 Wind Rd.
Baskerville, VA 23915
Ph: (804)691-8528

Boyd, Lynn, Exec. Dir.
National Association Medical Staff
Services [15588]
2025 M St. NW, Ste. 800
Washington, DC 20036
Ph: (202)367-1196
Fax: (202)367-2196

Boyd, Nicki, President
Animal Behavior Management Alliance [7395]
c/o San Diego Zoo Safari Pk.
15500 San Pasqual Valley Rd.
Escondido, CA 92027

Boyd, Nicki, Chairperson
Red Panda Network [4877]
1859 Powell St., Ste. 100
San Francisco, CA 94133
Ph: (541)228-1902

Boyd, Tim, President
Theosophical Society in America
[20624]
1926 N Main St.
Wheaton, IL 60187
Ph: (630)668-1571
Toll Free: 800-669-9425

Boyer, David S., Bd. Member
Retina Vitreous Foundation [17742]
1127 Wilshire Blvd., Ste. 304
Los Angeles, CA 90017
Ph: (310)644-3863

Boyer, Jan, Exec. Dir.
Cast Stone Institute [783]
c/o Jan Boyer, Executive Director
813 Chesnut St.
Lebanon, PA 17042-0068
Ph: (717)272-3744
Fax: (717)272-5147

Boyer, Luann, Dir. of Fin.
International Federation for Home
Economics USA [7991]
c/o Luann Boyer, Director of Finance
238 County Road 21
Fort Morgan, CO 80701-9337

Boyer, Valerie, Editor
National Student Speech Language
Hearing Association [17246]
2200 Research Blvd., No. 322
Rockville, MD 20850-3289
Ph: (301)296-5700
Toll Free: 800-498-2071
Fax: (301)296-8580

Boykin, Raymond, VP
Barzona Breeders Association of
America [3718]
c/o Alecia Heinz, Executive
Secretary
604 Cedar St.
Adair, IA 50002
Fax: (641)743-6611

Boylan, Jennifer K., Exec. Dir.
The Society for Pediatric Radiology
[17070]
1891 Preston White Dr.
Reston, VA 20191-4397
Ph: (703)648-0680

Boyle, Farley, Exec. Dir., Founder,
President
C.H.A.S.E. for Life [14661]
PO Box 443
Little Silver, NJ 07739
Toll Free: 888-547-4460

Boyle, Marcia, Founder, President
Immune Deficiency Foundation
[15379]
110 West Rd., Ste. 300
Towson, MD 21204
Toll Free: 800-296-4433
Fax: (410)321-9165

Boyle, Miriam, President
Fenton Art Glass Collectors of
America [22132]
702 W 5th St.
Williamstown, WV 26187-0384
Ph: (304)375-6196

Boyne, Gil, Founder
American Council of Hypnotist
Examiners [15357]
3435 Camino del Rio S, Ste. 316
San Diego, CA 92108
Ph: (619)280-7200

Boyum, Ben, V. Chmn. of the Bd.
American Refugee Committee
[12584]
615 1st Ave. NE, Ste. 500
Minneapolis, MN 55413-2681
Ph: (612)872-7060
Toll Free: 800-875-7060
Fax: (612)607-6499

Bozarth, George S., Bd. Member
American Brahms Society [9176]
Music Dept.
University of New Hampshire
30 Academic Way
Durham, NH 03824
Ph: (206)543-0400
Fax: (206)284-0111

Bozarth, Stephanie, President
National MPS Society [15830]
PO Box 14686
Durham, NC 27713
Ph: (919)806-0101
Toll Free: 877-MPS-1001

Bozell, L. Brent, III, Founder,
President
Media Research Center [12262]
1900 Campus Commons Dr., Ste.
600
Reston, VA 20191
Ph: (571)267-3500
Toll Free: 800-672-1423
Fax: (571)375-0099

Bozella, Ralph, Chairman
American Legion [20687]
700 N Pennsylvania St.
Indianapolis, IN 46206
Ph: (317)630-1200
Fax: (317)630-1223

Bozeman, Rev. Anthony, President
National Black Catholic Clergy
Caucus [19873]
2815 Forbes Dr.
Montgomery, AL 36110
Ph: (334)230-1910
    (505)234-8735

Bozof, Lynn, President
National Meningitis Association
[14604]
PO Box 60143
Fort Myers, FL 33906
Toll Free: 866-366-3662

Bozzo, Marion, Director
International Chinese Snuff Bottle
Society [21556]
2601 N Charles St.
Baltimore, MD 21218-4514
Ph: (410)467-9400
Fax: (410)243-3451

Bozzone, Janet, DMD, President
National Network for Oral Health Access [14467]

181 E 56th Ave., Ste. 501
Denver, CO 80216
Ph: (303)957-0635
Fax: (866)316-4995

Braatz, George O., Exec. Sec.
Masonic Service Association of
North America [19563]
3905 National Dr., Ste. 280
Burtonsville, MD 20866
Ph: (301)476-7330
    (301)588-4010
Toll Free: 855-476-4010
Fax: (301)476-9440

Brabenec, Robert, Exec. Sec.
Association of Christians in the
Mathematical Sciences [19945]
Dept. of Mathematics
Wheaton College
501 College Ave.
Wheaton, IL 60187
Ph: (630)752-5869

Braber, Curtis, President
Cleaning Equipment Trade Associa-
tion [2127]
11450 US Highway 380, Ste. 130
Crossroads, TX 76227-8322
Ph: (704)635-7362
Toll Free: 800-441-0111
Fax: (704)635-7363

Bracewell, Debbie, Exec. Dir.
National Council for Spirit Safety and
Education [22726]
c/o Debbie Bracewell, Executive
Director
PO Box 311192
Enterprise, AL 36331-1192
Toll Free: 866-456-2773
Fax: (334)393-6799

Bracey, Arthur W., MD, President
Society for the Advancement of
Blood Management [15245]
2209 Dickens Rd.
Richmond, VA 23230-2005
Ph: (804)565-6399
Fax: (804)282-0090

Brackett, Robert E., PhD, VP
Institute for Food Safety and Health
[1338]
Illinois Institute of Technology
Moffett Campus
6502 S Archer Rd.
Bedford Park, IL 60501-1957
Ph: (708)563-1576
    (708)563-8175
Fax: (708)563-1873

Brackmann, Derald E., MD,
President
American Laryngological, Rhinologi-
cal and Otological Society [16535]
13930 Gold Cir., Ste. 103
Omaha, NE 68144
Ph: (402)346-5500
Fax: (402)346-5300

Brada, Josef C., Exec. Sec.
Association for Comparative
Economic Studies [6379]
c/o Josef C. Brada, Executive
Secretary
333 N Pennington Dr., No. 57
Chandler, AZ 85224-8269

Bradbery, Angela, Dir. of Comm.
Freedom of Information
Clearinghouse [18957]
1600 20th St. NW
Washington, DC 20009
Ph: (202)588-7741

Braddock, David, VP, Treasurer
National ATM Council [411]
9802-12 Baymeadows Rd., No. 196

Jacksonville, FL 32256
Ph: (904)683-6533
Fax: (904)425-6010

Braddock, Mike, Director
German Wirehaired Pointer Club of
America [21885]
c/o Erika Brown, Treasurer
236 Park Ave.
Woodstock, GA 30188-4274
Ph: (770)591-4329

Brade, Condencia, Exec. Dir.
National Organization of Sisters of
Color Ending Sexual Assault
[12929]
PO Box 625
Canton, CT 06019

Braden, Laurie, President
NIRSA [23246]
4185 SW Research Way
Corvallis, OR 97333-1067
Ph: (541)766-8211
Fax: (541)766-8284

Braden, Mrs. Sharon, President
National Grigsby Family Society
[20906]
c/o Phyllis J. Bryant, Administrator
69 Plymouth St.
Medina, OH 44256-2418

Braden, Suzanne, Director
Pandas International [4867]
PO Box 620335
Littleton, CO 80162
Ph: (303)933-2365

Bradford, Alec, President
Large Black Hog Association [4710]
c/o Felicia Krock, Secretary
16383 County Road 75
Kenton, OH 43326
Toll Free: 800-687-1942
Fax: (800)687-2089

Bradford, Brian, Secretary
Alliance for Digital Equality [6729]
Piedmont Ctr.
3525 Piedmont Rd.
Atlanta, GA 30305
Ph: (404)262-0188

Bradford, Carol, President
Society of University Otolaryngolo-
gists - Head and Neck Surgeons
[16542]
c/o Anand Devaiah, MD, Secretary/
Treasurer
Dept. of Otolaryngology – Head and
Neck Surgery
Boston University School of
Medicine/Boston Medical Ctr.
FGH Bldg., 4th Fl.
820 Harrison Ave.
Boston, MA 02118
Ph: (312)202-5674
Fax: (312)268-6280

Bradham, Stefan R., Administrator
International Association for Vegeta-
tion Science [6144]
9650 Rockville Pke.
Bethesda, MD 20814
Ph: (301)634-7255
    (301)634-7453

Bradie, Alice, President
American Belgian Malinois Club
[21796]
c/o Sara Andersen
308 Scott Rd.
Rocky Point, NC 28457
Ph: (717)487-3323

Bradley, Carol, Chairperson
World Institute on Disability [11648]
3075 Adeline St., Ste. 155

Berkeley, CA 94703
Ph: (510)225-6400
Fax: (510)225-0477

Bradley, David A., CEO
National Workforce Association
[5263]
1 Massachusetts Ave. NW, Ste. 310
Washington, DC 20001
Ph: (202)842-2092

Bradley, David, Exec. Dir.
National Community Action Founda-
tion [11296]
PO Box 78214
Washington, DC 20013
Ph: (202)842-2092
Fax: (202)842-2095

Bradley, Heather, President
Down Syndrome Diagnosis Network
[14625]
PO Box 140
Stillwater, MN 55082
Ph: (612)460-0765

Bradley, John, Founder
Lamia Afghan Foundation [12694]
4014 Skyline Dr.
Nashville, TN 37215
Ph: (615)783-2899

Bradley, John, Legal Counsel
National Association of the Holy
Name Society [19870]
6939 Sevenoaks Ave.
Baton Rouge, LA 70806
Ph: (225)925-8921
    (225)266-8654

Bradley, Karen, Exec. Dir., Dir. of
Res.
Laban/Bartenieff Institute of Move-
ment Studies [9266]
138 S Oxford St., Ste. 2D
Brooklyn, NY 11217
Ph: (212)643-8888
Fax: (347)422-0948

Bradley, Orton, Founder
British Schools and Universities Club
of New York [7628]
PO Box 4116
New York, NY 10163
Ph: (212)465-3270

Bradley, Paquita, Officer
National Black Coalition of Federal
Aviation Employees [5061]
PO Box 87216
Atlanta, GA 30337

Bradley, Patrick, Specialist
American Foreign Service Associa-
tion [23426]
2101 E St. NW
Washington, DC 20037
Ph: (202)338-4045
Fax: (202)338-6820

Bradley, Patrick, Chairman,
President
International Crisis Aid [12683]
PO Box 510167
Saint Louis, MO 63151
Ph: (314)487-1400
Toll Free: 888-740-7779
Fax: (314)487-1409

Bradley, Richard, V. Chmn. of the
Bd.
Mystery Shopping Providers As-
sociation North America [2294]
328 E Main St.
Louisville, KY 40202-1216
Ph: (502)574-9033

Bradley, Robert E., President
Euler Society [8279]
c/o Erik R. Tou, Secretary-Treasurer

School of Interdisciplinary Arts and
Sciences
University of Washington - Tacoma
1900 Commerce St.
Tacoma, WA 98402

Bradley, Sharron, CEO, Exec. Dir.
Home Furnishings Association
[1482]
500 Giuseppe Ct., Ste. 6
Roseville, CA 95678
Toll Free: 800-422-3778
Fax: (916)784-7697

Bradley, Troy, Director
Balloon Federation of America
[21529]
PO Box 400
Indianola, IA 50125-1484

Bradner, Curt, Founder
Thirst-Aid [13357]
12478 W 70th Pl.
Arvada, CO 80004

Brado, John Frank, Director
Combat Martial Art Practitioners Association [22990]
2277 E Elm St.
Lima, OH 45804

Bradshaw, Cindy, MS, ACC, Exec.
Dir.
National Certification Council for
Activity Professionals [1591]
PO Box 62589
Virginia Beach, VA 23466
Ph: (757)552-0653
Fax: (757)552-0491

Bradshaw, Sean, Membership Chp.
Clan MacDuff Society of America
[20820]
8105 Rainfall Rd.
Alvarado, TX 76009-4505
Ph: (817)783-2942

Bradshaw, Teresa J., Exec. Dir.
Pan-American Association of
Ophthalmology [16405]
1301 S Bowen Rd., No. 450
Arlington, TX 76013
Ph: (817)275-7553
Fax: (817)275-3961

Brady, Carole, President
Parents-Coaches Association
[22707]
PO Box 224
Odenton, MD 21113
Ph: (410)207-1570
Fax: (301)912-1039

Brady, Gene, Chairman
National Center for Appropriate
Technology [17808]
PO Box 3838
Butte, MT 59702
Ph: (406)494-4572
Toll Free: 800-275-6228
Fax: (406)494-2905

Brady, Lynn, President
Kuvasz Club of America [21910]
c/o Doreen MacPherson Hardt,
Treasurer
3132 Snoblin Rd.
North Branch, MI 48461-8244

Brady, Mr. Paul W., Exec. Dir.
National Organization of Forensic
Social Work [8573]
460 Smith St., Ste. K
Middletown, CT 06457
Ph: (860)613-0254
Toll Free: 866-668-9858

Brady, Peter, President
National Tax Association [5801]
725 15th St. NW, No. 600

Washington, DC 20005-2109
Ph: (202)737-3325
Fax: (202)737-7308

Brady, Thomas, Director
Ceramic Tile Institute of America
[860]
12061 Jefferson Blvd.
Culver City, CA 90230
Ph: (310)574-7800
Fax: (310)821-4655

Brady, Timothy J., Membership Chp.
American Livebearer Association
[22029]
5 Zerbe St.
Cressona, PA 17929-1513
Ph: (570)385-0573

Brady, Vicki, President
Doberman Assistance Network
[11688]
c/o Heidi Merriman
3852 La Colina Rd.
El Sobrante, CA 94803

Braga, Francesco, CEO
International Food and Agribusiness
Management Association [1342]
1010 Vermont Ave. NW, Ste. 201
Washington, DC 20005
Ph: (202)429-1610
Fax: (202)628-9044

Braga, Julio, VP
International Interior Design Associa-
tion [1951]
222 Merchandise Mart, Ste. 567
Chicago, IL 60654
Ph: (312)467-1950
Toll Free: 888-799-4432

Bragg, Amy F., RD, President
Collegiate and Professional Sports
Dietitians Association [16212]
38 E Lucas Dr.
Palos Hills, IL 60465
Ph: (708)974-3153
Fax: (708)974-3174

Bragg, Lynn M., President
Glass Packaging Institute [834]
1220 N Fillmore St., Ste. 400
Arlington, VA 22201
Ph: (703)684-6359
Fax: (703)546-0588

Bragg, Ryan T., Chairman, Founder
Students for the Second Amendment
[18258]
9624 Braun Run
San Antonio, TX 78254
Ph: (210)674-5559

Bragg, Capt. Terry A., Exec. Dir.
USS North Carolina Battleship As-
sociation [21203]
1 Battleship Rd.
Wilmington, NC 28401
Ph: (910)251-5797
Fax: (910)251-5807

Bragg-Grant, Ira, Exec. Dir.
American Sickle Cell Anemia As-
sociation [17206]
DD Bldg.
10900 Carnegie Ave., Ste. DD1-201
Cleveland, OH 44106
Ph: (216)229-8600
Fax: (216)229-4500

Braginsky, Philip, Esq., Secretary
Lymphatic Education and Research
Network [15544]
261 Madison Ave., 9th Fl.
New York, NY 10016
Ph: (516)625-9675
Fax: (516)625-9410

Braico, Charlie, President
National Association Broadcast
Employees and Technicians
[23396]
501 3rd St. NW
Washington, DC 20001
Ph: (202)434-1254
Fax: (202)434-1426

Brainerd, Mathew A., Chairman
National Association of Chemical
Distributors [723]
1560 Wilson Blvd., Ste. 1100
Arlington, VA 22209
Ph: (703)527-6223
Fax: (703)527-7747

Braithwaite, Steve, President
Transload Distribution Association of
North America [3106]
1980 Willamette Falls Dr., No. 120-
282
West Linn, OR 97068
Ph: (503)656-4282
Fax: (888)347-9933

Brakensiek, Jay, Treasurer
Campus Safety, Health and
Environmental Management As-
sociation [4125]
One City Centre, Ste. 204
120 W 7th St.
Bloomington, IN 47404
Ph: (812)245-8084
Fax: (812)245-6710

Braley, Bethany, Chairperson, Exec.
Dir., Publisher
National Day of the Cowboy [8802]
822 W Monte Way
Phoenix, AZ 85041
Ph: (928)759-0951

Bram, Jim, President
National Association of Underwater
Instructors [23343]
9030 Camden Field Pky.
Riverview, FL 33578
Ph: (813)628-6284
Toll Free: 800-553-6284
Fax: (813)628-8253

Bramante, Christina, Chairperson
Synthetic Amorphous Silica and
Silicates Industry Association [731]
c/o David A. Pavlich, Association
Manager
116 Countryside Dr.
Chagrin Falls, OH 44022
Ph: (440)897-8780

Bramble, Sen. Curt, President
National Conference of State
Legislatures [5783]
7700 E 1st Pl.
Denver, CO 80230
Ph: (303)364-7700
Fax: (303)364-7800

Bramble, Sylma Brown, Director
Caribbean Tourism Organization,
American Branch [23548]
80 Broad St., Ste. 3302
New York, NY 10004
Ph: (212)635-9530
Fax: (212)635-9511

Bramley, Aaron, Exec. Dir.
Lights. Camera. Help. [6014]
PO Box 270069
Austin, TX 78727
Ph: (512)524-7227

Brancati, Annette, Secretary,
Treasurer
American Board of Perianesthesia
Nursing Certification [16103]
475 Riverside Dr., 6th Fl.

New York, NY 10115-0089
Toll Free: 800-6-ABPANC
Fax: (212)367-4256

Branch, Brian, President, CEO
World Council of Credit Unions [959]
5710 Mineral Point Rd.
Madison, WI 53705-4454
Ph: (608)395-2000
Fax: (608)395-2001

Branchcomb, Shane, Treasurer
Association of Coffee Mill
Enthusiasts [21625]
c/o Shane Branchcomb, Treasurer
12031 George Farm Dr.
Lovettsville, VA 20180

Brand, Betsy, Exec. Dir., Treasurer
American Youth Policy Forum
[13425]
1836 Jefferson Pl. NW
Washington, DC 20036
Ph: (202)775-9731
Fax: (202)775-9733

Brand, Betsy, Exec. Dir.
Pathways to College Network [7969]
c/o American Institute for Research
1000 Thomas Jefferson St. NW
Washington, DC 20007

Brand, David, CEO
Alliance for Global Good [12458]
445 Dolley Madison Rd., Ste. 208
Greensboro, NC 27410
Ph: (336)376-7710

Brand, Margie, Founder
EcoVentures International [4115]
2016 Mt. Vernon Ave., Ste. 203
Alexandria, VA 22301

Brand, Mike, Dir. of Programs
Jewish World Watch [18309]
5551 Balboa Blvd.
Encino, CA 91316
Ph: (818)501-1836
Fax: (818)501-1835

Brand, Tim, Founder
Many Hands for Haiti [13014]
PO Box 204
Pella, IA 50219
Ph: (641)629-1243

Brandas, E., President
International Society for Theoretical
Chemical Physics [7026]
c/o Dr. K. Rupnik
Dept. of Chemistry
Louisiana State University
Baton Rouge, LA 70803

Brandel, Ms. Norma Dusty,
President
American Auto Racing Writers and
Broadcasters Association [22520]
922 N Pass Ave.
Burbank, CA 91505-2703
Ph: (818)842-7005
Fax: (818)842-7020

Brandenberger, Joel, President
National Turkey Federation [4569]
1225 New York Ave., Ste. 400
Washington, DC 20005
Ph: (202)898-0100
Fax: (202)898-0203

Brandenburg, Bert, Exec. Dir.
Justice at Stake [19128]
717 D St. NW, Ste. 203
Washington, DC 20004
Ph: (202)588-9700
Fax: (202)588-9485

Brandenstein, Daniel, Chairman
Astronaut Scholars Honor Society
[23858]

Astronaut Scholarship Foundation
Kennedy Space Center, SR 405
Titusville, FL 32780
Ph: (321)449-4876
Fax: (321)264-9176

Brandhorst, Carl G., President
Atlantic Seaboard Wine Association
[4927]
PO Box 11332
Burke, VA 22009
Ph: (703)323-6873
Fax: (703)323-1271

Brandon, Adam, President, CEO
FreedomWorks **[18869]**
400 N Capitol St. NW, Ste. 765
Washington, DC 20001
Ph: (202)783-3870
Toll Free: 888-564-6273

Brandon, Laura, Exec. Dir.
GALA: Globalization and Localiza-
tion Association **[1005]**
4000 NE 41st St., Ste. 201
Seattle, WA 98105
Ph: (206)494-4686
Fax: (815)346-2361

Brandon, Robert M., Founder,
President
Fair Elections Legal Network **[5004]**
1825 K St. NW, Ste. 450
Washington, DC 20006
Ph: (202)331-1550

Brandow, Chap. Stephen, President
National Association of Veterans'
Affairs Chaplains **[19934]**
c/o Stephen Brandow, President
PO Box 69004
Alexandria, LA 71306
Ph: (318)473-0010

Brandt, Annie, Exec. Dir.
Best Answer for Cancer Foundation
[13899]
8127 Mesa, B-206, No. 243
Austin, TX 78759
Ph: (512)342-8181
Fax: (512)276-6678

Brandt, Rebecca, Exec. Dir.
American College of Mohs Surgery
[16330]
555 E Wells St., Ste. 1100
Milwaukee, WI 53202-3823
Ph: (414)347-1103
Toll Free: 800-500-7224
Fax: (414)276-2146

Branen, Tom, Exec. Dir.
American Association of State
Service Commissions **[5692]**
455 Massachusetts Ave. NW, Ste.
153
1625 K St. NW, 5th Fl.
Washington, DC 20001
Ph: (202)729-8179

Branfman, Steven, Officer
Potters Council **[6173]**
Ceramic Publications Co.
600 N Cleveland Ave., Ste. 210
Westerville, OH 43082
Toll Free: 800-424-8698
Fax: (818)487-2054

Brannan, Jeanette, Founder, Exec.
Dir.
Together for Tanzania **[11452]**
PO Box 395
Powhatan, VA 23139

Brannen, Dan, Exec. Dir.
American Ultrarunning Association
[23116]

Branon, Brian, President
North American Ring Association
[21931]

c/o Brian Branon, President
PO Box 760967
Melrose, MA 02176-0006
Ph: (781)307-6540

Bransford, Patricia, Founder,
President
National Urban Technology Center
[7287]
80 Maiden Ln., Ste. 606
New York, NY 10038
Ph: (212)528-7350

Branson, Bill, Coord.
Vietnam Veterans Against the War
[19225]
PO Box 355
Champaign, IL 61824-0355
Ph: (773)569-3520

Branson, Daryl, Treasurer, VP
National Association of State 911
Administrators **[7316]**
c/o Dorothy Spears-Dean, Secretary
11751 Meadowville Ln.
Chester, VA 23836-6315
Ph: (804)416-6201
Fax: (804)416-6353

Brantley, Andy, CEO, President
College and University Professional
Association for Human Resources
[8414]
1811 Commons Point Dr.
Knoxville, TN 37932-1989
Ph: (865)637-7673
Toll Free: 877-287-2474
Fax: (865)637-7674

Brantley, John Kenneth, President
Brantley Association of America
[20788]
4750 Oakleigh Manor Dr.
Powder Springs, GA 30127
Ph: (770)428-4402

Brantner, Paula, Exec. Dir.
Workplace Fairness **[11792]**
920 U St. NW
Washington, DC 20001
Ph: (202)683-6114
Fax: (240)282-8801

Branzell, Russ, CEO
Association for Executives in Health-
care Information Security **[14982]**
710 Avis Dr., Ste. 200
Ann Arbor, MI 48108
Ph: (734)665-0000
Fax: (734)665-4922

Brasch, Pamela, Exec. Dir., CEO
Suzuki Association of the Americas
[8390]
PO Box 17310
Boulder, CO 80308
Ph: (303)444-0948
Toll Free: 888-378-9854
Fax: (303)444-0984

Brase, Twila J., RN, President
Citizens' Council for Health Freedom
[18332]
161 St. Anthony Ave., Ste. 923
Saint Paul, MN 55103
Ph: (651)646-8935
Fax: (651)646-0100

Brasher, Bobby, Officer
Christian Hunters and Anglers As-
sociation **[22165]**
PO Box 132379
Tyler, TX 75712-0072
Ph: (903)312-7390

Brasuell, David, President
National Association of State Directors of Veterans Affairs **[5839]**

107 S West St., Ste. 550
Alexandria, VA 22314
Ph: (208)780-1300
Fax: (208)780-1301

Bratter, Rebecca, Exec. Dir.
United States Dry Bean Council
[4256]
c/o Jeane Wharton, Executive Direc-
tor
PO Box 9224
Jackson, WY 83002
Ph: (307)201-1894

Bratton, Adam, COO
Public Employees Roundtable
[5081]
500 N Capitol St., Ste. 1204
Washington, DC 20001
Ph: (202)927-4926
Fax: (202)927-4920

Braun, Eileen, Exec. Dir.
Angelman Syndrome Foundation
[17335]
75 Executive Dr., Ste. 327
Aurora, IL 60504
Ph: (630)978-4245
Toll Free: 800-432-6435
Fax: (630)978-7408

Braun, Patrick, Contact
Society of Mineral Analysts **[6876]**
Lewiston, ID 83501
Ph: (775)313-4229

Braun, Sharon, VP
Sunsweet Growers **[4251]**
901 N Walton Ave.
Yuba City, CA 95993
Ph: (530)674-5010
Toll Free: 800-417-2253
Fax: (530)751-5395

Braunschweiger, Paul, PhD, VP
Scientists Center for Animal Welfare
[10695]
2660 NE Highway 20, Ste. 610-115
Bend, OR 97701
Ph: (301)345-3500
Fax: (541)383-4655

Braunstein, Clyde, Exec. Dir.
Confrerie de la Chaîne des Rotis-
seurs, Bailliage des U.S.A. **[22146]**
285 Madison Ave.
Madison, NJ 07940
Ph: (973)360-9200
Fax: (973)360-9330

Braus, Judy, Exec. Dir.
North American Association for
Environmental Education **[7882]**
2000 P St. NW, Ste. 540
Washington, DC 20036
Ph: (202)419-0412

Bravo, Jose T., Exec. Dir.
Just Transition Alliance **[23458]**
2810 Camino Del Rio S, Ste. 116
San Diego, CA 92108-3819
Ph: (619)573-4934
Fax: (619)546-9910

Bravo, Ken, VP
International Association of Jewish
Genealogical Societies **[20974]**
PO Box 3624
Cherry Hill, NJ 08034-0556

Brawders, Bob, Director
Portuguese Podengo Club of
America **[21946]**
2051 Elm St.
Denver, CO 80207

Bray, Ann, President, CEO
Phoenix House **[13173]**
164 W 74th St., 4th Fl.

New York, NY 10023-2301
Ph: (646)505-2080
Toll Free: 888-671-9392
Fax: (212)595-6365

Bray, Darlene, President
Women in Mining **[2390]**
PO Box 260246
Lakewood, CO 80226
Toll Free: 866-537-9694

Bray, Faustin, Events Coord.
Association for Cultural Evolution
[9225]
PO Box 2382
Mill Valley, CA 94942
Ph: (415)409-3220
Fax: (415)931-0948

Brazier, April, Sr. VP
Little People of America **[12955]**
250 El Camino Real, Ste. 218
Tustin, CA 92780
Ph: (714)368-3689
Toll Free: 888-LPA-2001
Fax: (714)368-3367

Brazunas, Michael, RN, BSN,
President
Association for Vascular Access
[17571]
5526 West 13400 South, Ste. 229
Herriman, UT 84096
Ph: (801)792-9079
Toll Free: 877-924-2821
Fax: (801)601-8012

Brebner, Nancy, Exec. Dir.
Insurance Consumer Affairs
Exchange **[1864]**
PO Box 746
Lake Zurich, IL 60047
Ph: (847)991-8454

Breece, George W., Exec. Dir.
National Association for the
Advancement of Orthotics and
Prosthetics **[16496]**
1501 M St. NW, 7th Fl.
Washington, DC 20005-1700
Ph: (202)624-0064
Toll Free: 800-622-6740
Fax: (202)785-1756

Breece, Sharon L., President
All Navy Women's National Alliance
[5587]
PO Box 147
Goldenrod, FL 32733-0147

Breed, Michael, Ed.-in-Chief
International Union for the Study of
Social Insects **[6614]**
c/o Karen Kapheim
Dept. of Biology
Utah State University
Logan, UT 84322-5305
Ph: (630)915-1738

Breen, Jennifer Moss, President
Association of Leadership Educators, Inc. **[8192]**
c/o Jennifer Moss Breen, President
2500 California Plz.
Omaha, NE 68178
Ph: (402)280-3952

Breen, Michael, President, CEO
Truman Center for National Policy
[19006]
1250 I St. NW, Ste. 500
Washington, DC 20005
Ph: (202)216-9723
Fax: (202)682-1818

Breeze, Erin, Bd. Member
Building Bridges **[13435]**
PO Box 101958

Denver, CO 80250
Ph: (303)691-2393
Fax: (303)691-2394

Breeze-Harris, Heidi, Founder, CEO
One By One [15087]
2622 NW Market St., Ste. C
Seattle, WA 98107
Ph: (206)297-1418
Fax: (206)374-3010

Bregman, Peter, DPM, President
Association of Extremity Nerve
   Surgeons [16062]
15577 Ranch Rd. 12, Ste. 103
Wimberley, TX 78676
Toll Free: 888-708-9575
Fax: (888)394-1123

Brehany, John, PhD, Contact
Catholic Medical Association [16746]
29 Bala Ave., Ste. 205
Bala Cynwyd, PA 19004-3206
Ph: (484)270-8002
Fax: (866)666-2319

Breitlow, Jay, Director, Founder
Journey to Solidarity [14276]
301 Cottage Grove Ave. SE
Cedar Rapids, IA 52403
Fax: (888)860-9263

Brekken, MS, RN, Shirley, President
National Council of State Boards of
   Nursing [16160]
111 E Wacker Dr., Ste. 2900
Chicago, IL 60601-4277
Ph: (312)525-3600
Fax: (312)279-1032

Brelsford, Ms. Ginna, Exec. Dir.
Ayni Education International [7583]
PO Box 17672
Seattle, WA 98127
Ph: (206)331-3786

Brendtro, Kari, Exec. Dir., Founder
North American NeuroEndocrine
   Tumor Society [14709]
800 NE Tenney Rd., Ste. 110-412
Vancouver, WA 98685
Ph: (360)314-4112

Brennan, Chris, President
Association for Young Astrologers
   [5990]
2019 NW 31st Ter.
Gainesville, FL 32605

Brennan, Garett, Bd. Member
Focus the Nation [18191]
240 N Broadway, Ste. 212
Portland, OR 97227-1881
Ph: (503)224-9440

Brennan, Jennifer, President
Perennial Plant Association [4441]
3383 Schirtzinger Rd.
Hilliard, OH 43026
Ph: (614)771-8431
Fax: (614)876-5238

Brennan, Dr. Pauline, President
Association of Doctoral Programs in
   Criminology & Criminal Justice
   [7691]
c/o Amanda L. Burris, Secretariat
   Administrator
College of Criminal Justice
Sam Houston State University
Box 2296
Huntsville, TX 77341-2296
Ph: (936)294-3799
   (936)294-1658

Brennan, Richard, Exec. Dir.
Home Care Technology Association
   of America [15277]

228 7th St. SE
Washington, DC 20003
Ph: (202)547-2871
Fax: (202)547-3540

Brennan, Ms. Sheila, Director
September 11 Digital Archive
   [19186]
Center for History and New Media
Dept. of History and Art History,
   MSN 1E7
George Mason University
4400 University Dr.
Fairfax, VA 22030
Ph: (703)993-9277
   (212)817-1970

Brennan, William J., Jr., Chmn. of
   the Bd.
American Society of Radiologic
   Technologists [15680]
15000 Central Ave. SE
Albuquerque, NM 87123-3909
Ph: (505)298-4500
Toll Free: 800-444-2778
Fax: (505)298-5063

Brenner, August K., President
Patrol Craft Sailors Association
   [21060]
c/o Jim Heywood, Membership Officer
7005 Bridge Rd.
Cincinnati, OH 45230
Ph: (513)233-2775

Brenner, David, Exec. Dir.
Dysautonomia Foundation, Inc.
   [15925]
315 W 39th St., Ste. 701
New York, NY 10018
Ph: (212)279-1066
Fax: (212)279-2066

Brenner, Mark, Director
Labor Notes [23468]
7435 Michigan Ave.
Detroit, MI 48210
Ph: (313)842-6262
Fax: (313)842-0227

Brenner, Peggy, Mem.
International Women Fly Fishers
   [22042]
c/o Fanny Krieger, Founder
Krieger Enterprises
790 27th Ave.
San Francisco, CA 94121
Ph: (415)752-0192

Brennick, Charles, Director, Founder
InterConnection [11480]
3415 Stone Way N
Seattle, WA 98103
Ph: (206)633-1517

Brent, Jonathan, Exec. Dir.
YIVO Institute for Jewish Research
   [9645]
15 W 16th St.
New York, NY 10011-6301
Ph: (212)246-6080
   (212)294-6139
Fax: (212)292-1892

Brent, Dr. Linda, PhD, Trustee
Chimp Haven, Inc [10599]
13600 Chimpanzee Pl.
Keithville, LA 71047
Ph: (318)925-9575
Toll Free: 888-982-4467
Fax: (318)925-9576

Breschi, Dr. Lorenzo, Secretary
Academy of Dental Materials
   [14363]
21 Grouse Ter.
Lake Oswego, OR 97035
Ph: (503)636-0861
Fax: (503)675-2738

Breslof, Lisa, Secretary
John Burroughs Association [6895]
261 Floyd Ackert Rd.
West Park, NY 12493
Ph: (845)384-6320

Bresnahan, Linda R., Exec. Dir.
Federation of State Physician Health
   Programs, Inc. [16750]
860 Winter St.
Waltham, MA 02451-1414
Ph: (781)434-7343
Fax: (781)464-4802

Bress, Joshua, President
Global Strategies for HIV Prevention
   [13543]
828 San Pablo Ave., Ste. 260
Albany, CA 94706
Ph: (415)451-1814

Bresson, Cindy McAlister, President
Clan McAlister of America [20830]
c/o Robert W. McAlister, Membership Chairman
208 Annapolis Ln.
Rotonda West, FL 33947
Ph: (941)698-1112

Bretz, Joan, Contact
Platt Family Association [20914]
4081 Greystone Dr.
Harrisburg, PA 17112

Brew, Wayne, Exec. Dir.
International Society for Landscape,
   Place, & Material Culture [9405]
c/o Timothy G. Anderson, Treasurer
Dept. of Geography
Ohio University
122 Clippinger Laboratories
Athens, OH 45701

Brewer, Chip, Chairman
National Golf Foundation [3162]
501 N Highway A1A
Jupiter, FL 33477
Ph: (561)744-6006
Toll Free: 888-275-4643
Fax: (561)744-6107

Brewer, Jeffrey, President, CEO
Juvenile Diabetes Research Founda-
   tion International [14539]
26 Broadway
New York, NY 10004
Toll Free: 800-533-CURE
Fax: (212)785-9595

Brewer, Kathy, President
EGD Global Alliance [14573]
PO Box 775
Deridder, LA 70634
Ph: (337)515-6987

Brewer, Leanna, Founder, CEO
SPARK Worldwide [11155]
PO Box 1349
Joshua, TX 76058
Ph: (817)645-6200
Fax: (817)645-2208

Brewer, Michael, Director
United States PostgreSQL Associa-
   tion [6289]
9220 SW Barbur Blvd., Ste. 119-230
Portland, OR 97219
Ph: (503)778-5428
Fax: (503)276-5813

Brewer, Sue, Secretary
Pacific International Trapshooting
   Association [23141]
Ph: (541)258-8766

Brewer, Susan, Founder, President
America's Heroes of Freedom
   [20702]

PO Box 18984
Washington, DC 20036-8984

Brewster, Richard P., Exec. Dir.
National Center on Nonprofit
   Enterprise [12391]
10717 Oldfield Dr.
Reston, VA 20195
Ph: (757)214-5084

Brey, Ann, Exec. Dir.
Pan-American Allergy Society
   [13580]
c/o Ann Brey, Executive Director
1317 Wooded Knoll
San Antonio, TX 78258
Ph: (210)495-9853
Fax: (210)495-9852

Breyault, John, Director
Fraud.org [18049]
1701 K St. NW, Ste. 1200
Washington, DC 20006
Ph: (202)835-3323
Fax: (202)835-0747

Breyer, Dr. Walter H., Secretary
Antique Telescope Society [21287]
c/o Walter Breyer, PhD, Secretary
1878 Robinson Rd.
Dahlonega, GA 30533

Bria, William, MD, Chairman
Association of Medical Directors of
   Information Systems [6737]
682 Peninsula Dr.
Westwood, CA 96137
Ph: (719)548-9360

Brian, Kathleen, Treasurer
Disability History Association [7715]
c/o Sara Scalenghe, Treasurer
Humanities Bldg., Rm. 322A
4501 N Charles St.
Loyola University Maryland
Baltimore, MD 21210

Briant, Thomas A., Exec. Dir.
National Association of Tobacco
   Outlets [3285]
15560 Boulder Pointe Rd.
Minneapolis, MN 55437
Toll Free: 866-869-8888
Fax: (952)934-7442

Brice, Carline, Founder
HavServe Volunteer Service Network
   [10722]
PO Box 4173
Silver Spring, MD 20914-4173
Ph: (301)490-2368

Brice, Lee, President
Association of Ancient Historians
   [9459]
c/o Lee Brice, President
Morgan Hall 438
Western Illinois University
1 University Cir.
Macomb, IL 61455-1390

Brick, Neil, President
Survivorship [13274]
Family Justice Center
470 27th St.
Oakland, CA 94612

Bricker, Dr. Kelly S., Chairperson
The International Ecotourism Society
   [3292]
427 N Tatnall St.
Wilmington, DE 19801-2230
Ph: (202)506-5033
Fax: (202)789-7279

Bricker, Scott, Exec. Dir.
America Walks [17751]
PO Box 10581

Portland, OR 97296
Ph: (503)757-8342
 (414)241-3805

Brickley, Michael, President
The Pocket Testament League
[19762]
PO Box 800
Lititz, PA 17543-7026
Toll Free: 844-376-2538

Brickner, David, Director
Jews for Jesus [20337]
60 Haight St.
San Francisco, CA 94102-5802
Ph: (415)864-2600
Fax: (415)552-8325

Brickner, David W., President
Honda Sport Touring Association
[22224]
4040 E 82nd St., Ste. C9
PMB 331
Indianapolis, IN 46250-4209
Ph: (317)890-8858
 (615)758-3734
Fax: (317)841-0111

Bridge, Dawn Averitt, Founder, Bd.
Member
The Well Project [13564]
PO Box 220410
Brooklyn, NY 11222

Bridge, Dr. Julia, President
International Society of Bone and
Soft Tissue Pathology [16585]
800 Spruce St.
Philadelphia, PA 19107
Ph: (215)829-3541
Fax: (215)829-7564

Bridgeman, Pete, Contact
Association of Technical and
Supervisory Professionals [5222]
c/o Larry Hortert, Treasurer
153 Nettie Ln.
McDonough, GA 30252

Bridges, Jeff, Founder
End Hunger Network [18454]
3819 Hunt Manor Dr.
Fairfax, VA 22033
Ph: (703)731-6109

Bridges, Dr. Joseph L., CEO,
President
The Seniors Coalition [10529]
1250 Connecticut Ave. NW, Ste. 200
Washington, DC 20036-2643
Ph: (202)261-3594

Briel, Don, President
National Insulator Association
[21695]
c/o Don Briel, President
PO Box 188
Providence, UT 84332

Brienen, Lisa, President
Academy of Veterinary Homeopathy
[17587]
PO Box 232282
Leucadia, CA 92023-2282
Toll Free: 866-652-1590
Fax: (866)652-1590

Brienzo, Frank, Director
Professional Awning Manufacturers
Association [3267]
1801 County Road B W
Roseville, MN 55113
Ph: (651)225-6944

Brierton, Gary, Chairman
Austin-Healey Club of America
[21332]
c/o Fred Dabney, 2327 Christensens
Ct.

2327 Christensens Ct.
Charlotte, NC 28270
Ph: (704)366-9808

Briggs, Dr. Deborah, Bd. Member
Global Alliance for Rabies Control
[14578]
529 Humboldt St., Ste. 1
Manhattan, KS 66502

Briggs, Dorothy, President
College Reading and Learning As-
sociation [8484]
7044 S 13th St.
Oak Creek, WI 53154
Ph: (414)908-4961

Briggs, Jean, VP
Tibetan Spaniel Club of America
[21969]
c/o William Chaffee, President
469 Langford Creek Rd.
Van Etten, NY 14889-9752
Ph: (607)589-6868
 (419)352-1176

Briggs, John, President
Association of Literary Scholars,
Critics, and Writers [9751]
Marist Hall
The Catholic University of America
620 Michigan Ave. NE
Washington, DC 20064
Ph: (202)319-5650
Fax: (202)319-5650

Briggs, Josephine P., MD, Director
U.S. Department of Health and Hu-
man Services | National Institutes
of Health | National Center for
Complementary and Intergrative
Health [13663]
9000 Rockville Pke.
Bethesda, MD 20892
Toll Free: 888-644-6226

Briggs, Joyce, President
Alliance for Contraception in Cats
and Dogs [12452]
11145 NW Old Cornelius Pass Rd.
Portland, OR 97231
Ph: (503)358-1438

Brigham, Lorri, Exec. VP, Treasurer
National Paddleball Association
[22534]
7642 Kingston Dr.
Portage, MI 49002-4370
Ph: (269)779-6615
Fax: (269)279-6275

Bright, Bob, CEO
National Beta Club [23866]
151 Beta Club Way
Spartanburg, SC 29306
Toll Free: 800-845-8281
Fax: (864)542-9300

Bright Faust, Wendy, Exec. Dir.
Alpha Gamma Delta [23943]
8710 N Meridian St.
Indianapolis, IN 46260
Ph: (317)663-4200
Fax: (317)663-4210

Bright, Ron, Secretary
World Fast-Draw Association
[23146]
6000 Wilkins Ave.
Oakdale, CA 95361-9797
Ph: (209)847-0483

Bright, Stephen B., President
Southern Center for Human Rights
[17834]
83 Poplar St. NW
Atlanta, GA 30303
Ph: (404)688-1202
Fax: (404)688-9440

Brightwell, David, Secretary
International Transportation Manage-
ment Association [5814]
PO Box 670228
Houston, TX 77267-0228
Ph: (832)399-1032

Brill, Laurie, Exec. Dir. (Actg.)
Lutheran Educational Conference of
North America [8259]
2601 S Minnesota Ave., Ste. 105
Sioux Falls, SD 57105
Ph: (605)271-9894

Brimelow, Deborah Ann, Exec. Dir.,
Secretary, Treasurer
Sigma Sigma Phi [23842]
c/o Deborah Ann Brimelow, Execu-
tive Director/Secretary-Treasurer
PO Box 4096
Cedar Park, TX 78613
Ph: (512)553-1705

Brimmer, J. David, President
Society of American Fight Directors
[8701]
1350 E Flamingo Rd., No. 25
Las Vegas, NV 89119

Brimsek, Tobi, Exec. Dir.
Society for American Archaeology
[5947]
1111 14th St. NW, Ste. 800
Washington, DC 20005-5622
Ph: (202)789-8200
Fax: (202)789-0284

Brinegar, Richard, Exec. Dir.
HTML Writers Guild [6315]
119 E Union St., Ste. A
Pasadena, CA 91103
Ph: (626)449-3709
Fax: (866)607-1773

Brinkema, Corey, President
Forest Stewardship Council - United
States [4202]
212 3rd Ave. N, Ste. 445
Minneapolis, MN 55401-1446
Ph: (612)353-4511

Brinkmann, Rev. Frederick C.,
President
Holy Shroud Guild [19843]

Brinson, Mr. A. Ray, Exec. Ofc.
Bethune-Cookman University
National Alumni Association
[19308]
PO Box 11646
Daytona Beach, FL 32120
Ph: (386)226-2131
Fax: (386)226-2131

Brinton, Eliot A., MD, Bd. Member
Cardiovascular and Metabolic Health
Foundation [14152]
Educational Concepts in Medicine
163 Madison Ave., Ste. 401
Morristown, NJ 07960
Toll Free: 800-732-2161
Fax: (973)525-1891

Briscoe, Eric, Director
Open Air Campaigners U.S.A.
[20157]
PO Box D
Nazareth, PA 18064
Ph: (610)746-0508
Toll Free: 888-886-5661

Briseno, Michael A., President
504th Parachute Infantry Regiment
Association [21183]
c/o Ronald H. Rath, Treasurer
22 Club Hill Dr.
Garner, NC 27529-6528
Ph: (919)803-4554
Fax: (919)803-2400

Briski, Zana, Founder
Kids with Cameras [10141]
122 S Main St.
Salt Lake City, UT 84101
Ph: (801)746-7600

Brislawn, Josie, President
Spanish Mustang Registry [4411]
c/o Josie Brislawn, President
2740 D Rd.
Moorcroft, WY 82721

Brislin, Prof. Tom, Administrator
Carol Burnett Fund for Responsible
Journalism [8150]
c/o Prof. Tom Brislin, Administrator
School of Communications
University of Hawaii
2550 Campus Rd.
Honolulu, HI 96822-2250

Bristo, Marca, President
United States International Council
on Disabilities [11643]
1012 14th St. NW, Ste. 105
Washington, DC 20005-3429
Ph: (202)347-0102
Fax: (202)347-0351

Brito, Janete A., Director
Organization of Nematologists of
Tropical America [6909]
1911 SW 34th St.
Nematology Section
Division of Plant Industry, DPI-
FDACS
1911 SW 34th St.
Gainesville, FL 32614
Ph: (352)395-4752
Fax: (352)395-4714

Brittan, Dana Rasis, MBA, Exec. Dir.
American Board of Obesity Medicine
[16246]
2696 S Colorado Blvd., St.e 340
Denver, CO 80222
Ph: (303)770-9100
Fax: (303)770-9104

Brittingham, Don, V. Chmn. of the
Bd.
Industry Council for Emergency
Response Technologies [768]
PO Box 42563
Washington, DC 20015-2604
Ph: (240)398-3065

Broach, Mary, President
Tabitha USA [11449]
PO Box 449
Wynnewood, PA 19096

Broad, Steven, Exec. Dir.
Traffic North America [4894]
c/o WWF-US
1250 24th St. NW
Washington, DC 20037
Ph: (202)293-4800
Fax: (202)775-8287

Broadbent, Happy, President
Thoroughbred Club of America
[22929]
3555 Rice Rd.
Lexington, KY 40510-9643
Ph: (859)254-4282
Fax: (859)231-6131

Broadway, Ashley, President
American Military Partner Associa-
tion [5589]
1725 I St. NW, Ste. 300
Washington, DC 20006
Ph: (202)695-2672

Broadway, Julie, Exec. Dir.
American Morgan Horse Association
[4316]

4066 Shelburne Rd., Ste. 5
Shelburne, VT 05482
Ph: (802)985-4944
Fax: (802)985-8897

Broadwell, Christopher, Exec. Dir.
English-Speaking Union of the
United States **[9651]**
144 E 39th St.
New York, NY 10016
Ph: (212)818-1200
Fax: (212)867-4177

Broadwell, George Aaron, Secretary,
Treasurer
International Lexical Functional
Grammar Association **[8185]**
University at Albany, State University
of New York
Arts and Sciences Bldg., Rm. 239
1400 Washington Ave.
Albany, NY 12222

Broatch, James W., MSW, Exec. VP,
Director
Reflex Sympathetic Dystrophy
Syndrome Association **[15990]**
99 Cherry St.
Milford, CT 06460
Ph: (203)877-3790
Toll Free: 877-662-7737
Fax: (203)882-8362

Brock, Greg, Exec. Dir.
Alliance for School Choice **[8527]**
1660 L St. NW, Ste. 1000
Washington, DC 20036
Ph: (202)280-1990
Fax: (202)280-1989

Brock, Greg, Exec. Dir.
American Federation for Children
[11722]
1660 L St. NW, Ste. 1000
Washington, DC 20036
Ph: (202)280-1990
Fax: (202)280-1989

Brock, Heidi Biggs, President
Aluminum Association **[2339]**
1400 Crystal Dr., Ste. 430
Arlington, VA 22202
Ph: (703)358-2960

Brock, John, Treasurer
Disciples Peace Fellowship **[18781]**
PO Box 1986
Indianapolis, IN 46206-1986
Ph: (317)713-2666

Brock, John, PhD, President
Global Economic Education Alliance
[7731]
307 Lowden Hall
Northern Illinois University
DeKalb, IL 60115

Brock Jr., William, President
International Order of the Golden
Rule **[2408]**
3520 Executive Center Dr., Ste. 300
Austin, TX 78731
Ph: (512)334-5504
Toll Free: 800-637-8030
Fax: (512)334-5514

Brockey, Liam Matthew, President
American Catholic Historical As-
sociation **[9452]**
Dealy Hall, Rm. 637
441 E Fordham Rd.
Bronx, NY 10458
Ph: (718)817-3830
Fax: (718)817-5690

Brockway, Sandi, Editor, President
Macrocosm USA **[2799]**
PO Box 185

Cambria, CA 93428
Ph: (805)927-2515

Brod, Bruce, President
American Contact Dermatitis Society
[14480]
2323 N State St., Unit 30
Bunnell, FL 32110-4395
Ph: (386)437-4405
(386)206-8215
Fax: (386)437-4427

Brodbeck, Kay, President
National Association of Women
Highway Safety Leaders, Inc.
[12830]
c/o KAy Brodbeck, President
PO Box 1379
Clinton, MS 39060
Ph: (601)924-7815
Fax: (601)924-7747

Brodbelt, Jennifer S., President
American Society for Mass
Spectrometry **[7223]**
Bldg. I-1
2019 Galisteo St.
Santa Fe, NM 87505
Ph: (505)989-4517
Fax: (505)989-1073

Broder, Arthur I., MD, Chairman
American Board of Quality Assur-
ance and Utilization Review Physi-
cians **[17026]**
6640 Congress St.
New Port Richey, FL 34653
Ph: (727)569-0195
Toll Free: 800-998-6030
Fax: (727)569-0195

Broderick, Tim, Director, Editor
People for Life **[12786]**
1625 W 26th St.
Erie, PA 16508-1262
Ph: (814)459-1333
(814)882-1333

Brodeur, Rick, Membership Chp.
Austin-Healey Sports and Touring
Club **[21334]**
309 E Broad St.
Quakertown, PA 18951-1703
Ph: (215)536-6912

Brodnax, Shell, CEO
Real Estate Staging Association
[2893]
2274 Partridge Dr.
Valley Springs, CA 95252
Toll Free: 888-201-8687
Fax: (916)273-7736

Brodrick, Michael, PhD, Treasurer
Josiah Royce Society **[10117]**
150 Charleston Dr.
Oxford, OH 45056

Brody, Barbara, Liaison
American Driver and Traffic Safety
Education Association **[7723]**
Highway Safety Services, LLC
1434 Trim Tree Rd.
Indiana, PA 15701
Ph: (724)801-8246
Toll Free: 877-485-7172
Fax: (724)349-5042

Brody, Roger, President
American Philatelic Research Library
[22301]
100 Match Factory Pl.
Bellefonte, PA 16823-1367
Ph: (814)933-3803
Fax: (814)933-6128

Broeker, Judith, Founder, President,
Prog. Dir.
Adventures in Preservation **[9364]**
1557 North St.

Boulder, CO 80304
Ph: (303)444-0128

Broene, Mr. G. Richard, Exec. Dir.
Dynamic Youth Ministries **[19973]**
Calvinist Cadet Corps
1333 Alger St. SE
Grand Rapids, MI 49507
Ph: (616)241-5616
Fax: (616)241-5558

Brogie, Ed M., Exec. Dir.
National Association of Academies of
Science **[7140]**
c/o Academy of Science of St. Louis
5050 Oakland Ave.
Saint Louis, MO 63110-1404
Ph: (314)533-8083
Fax: (314)533-8885

Broke Stokely, Hannah, President
Pharmacy Technician Educators
Council **[16683]**
c/o Lisa McCartney
7366 FM 672
Dale, TX 78616-2526

Brokke, Daniel, President
Bethany International Missions
[20387]
6820 Auto Club Rd., Ste. M
Bloomington, MN 55438

Bromm, Rick, Chairman
Wiring Harness Manufacturer's As-
sociation **[1034]**
15490 101st Ave. N, Ste. 100
Maple Grove, MN 55369
Ph: (763)235-6467
Fax: (763)235-6461

Bronk, Robin, CEO
The Creative Coalition **[18864]**
360 Park Ave. S, 11th Fl.
New York, NY 10010-1717
Ph: (646)717-9908

Brons, Gloria J., Officer
International Butterfly Breeders As-
sociation **[3677]**
c/o Dale McClung
3025 70th Ln. N
Saint Petersburg, FL 33710
Ph: (727)381-1932
Fax: (727)381-5046

Bronson, Andrew, CAE, Exec. Dir.
The Society for Education in
Anesthesia **[13711]**
6737 W Washington St., Ste. 4210
Milwaukee, WI 53214
Ph: (414)389-8614
Fax: (414)276-7704

Bronznick, Shifra, Founder,
President
Advancing Women Professionals
and the Jewish Community
[13368]
520 8th Ave., 4th Fl.
New York, NY 10018
Ph: (212)542-4280

Brook, Dr. Yaron, Exec. Dir.,
President
Ayn Rand Institute **[10081]**
2121 Alton Pky., Ste. 250
Irvine, CA 92606
Ph: (949)222-6550
Fax: (949)222-6558

Brooke, Bryant, Dir. of Programs
VIA **[13310]**
870 Market St., No. 656
San Francisco, CA 94102
Ph: (415)904-8033

Brooke, Rachel, Exec. Dir.
International Anaplastology Association **[14338]**

PO Box 8685
Delray Beach, FL 33482
Ph: (202)642-2053

Brooke, Tal, President
Spiritual Counterfeits Project **[20050]**
PO Box 40015
Pasadena, CA 91114-7015
Ph: (510)540-0300
Fax: (510)540-1107

Brookins, Peggy, President, CEO
National Board for Professional
Teaching Standards **[8653]**
1525 Wilson Blvd., Ste. 700
Arlington, VA 22209
Ph: (703)465-2700

Brooks, A. Oakley, President
National Air Carrier Association **[146]**
1000 Wilson Blvd., Ste. 1700
Arlington, VA 22209
Ph: (703)358-8060
Fax: (703)358-8070

Brooks, Allison, President, CEO
Reconnecting America **[13234]**
436 14th St., Ste. 1005
Oakland, CA 94612
Ph: (510)268-8602
Fax: (510)268-8673

Brooks, Becky, Exec. Dir.
Alliance for Women in Media **[452]**
1250 24th St. NW, Ste. 300
Washington, DC 20037
Ph: (202)750-3664

Brooks, Carolyn B., Exec. Dir.
Association of Research Directors
[7087]
c/o Moses Kairo, Chairman
University of Maryland Eastern
Shore
30665 Student Services Center
Princess Anne, MD 21853
Ph: (410)651-6072

Brooks, Connie, Bd. Member
American Blue Cattle Association,
Inc. **[3685]**
PO Box 633404
Nacogdoches, TX 75963
Ph: (936)652-2550

Brooks, Cornell William, President,
CEO
National Association for the
Advancement of Colored People
[17915]
4805 Mt. Hope Dr.
Baltimore, MD 21215
Ph: (410)580-5777
Toll Free: 877-NAACP-98

Brooks, Jonathan, President
Voice of China and Asia Missionary
Society **[20473]**
PO Box 702015
Tulsa, OK 74170-2015
Ph: (918)392-0560
Toll Free: 877-392-0560

Brooks, Michelle, Director
Global Network for Neglected Tropical Diseases **[14580]**
2000 Pennsylvania Ave. NW, Ste.
7100
Washington, DC 20006
Ph: (202)842-5025

Brooks, Rod, President, CEO
Stop Hunger Now **[12116]**
615 Hillsborough St., Ste. 200
Raleigh, NC 27603
Ph: (919)839-0689
Toll Free: 888-501-8440
Fax: (919)839-8971

Brooks, Susan, Exec. Dir.
IEEE - Communications Society
[7307]
3 Park Ave., 17th Fl.
New York, NY 10016
Ph: (212)705-8900
Fax: (212)705-8999

Brooks, Suzanne, MA, CEO,
President, Founder
International Association for Women
of Color Day **[18214]**
3325 Northrop Ave.
Sacramento, CA 95864
Ph: (916)483-9804
Fax: (916)483-9805

Brooks, Tony, President
Military Postal History Society
[22346]
PO Box 15927
Seattle, WA 98115-0927

Brookshire, Brian, Exec. Dir.
American Walnut Manufacturers As-
sociation **[1427]**
c/o Brian Brookshire, Executive
Director
505 E State St.
Jefferson City, MO 65101
Ph: (573)635-7877
Fax: (573)636-2591

Brookshire, James E., Esq., Exec.
Dir.
Federal Circuit Bar Association
[5006]
1620 I St. NW, Ste. 801
Washington, DC 20006-4033
Ph: (202)466-3923
    (202)558-2421
Fax: (202)833-1061

Brookshire, Lance, President
Antique Auto Racing Association
[21326]
5295 S Linden Rd.
Swartz Creek, MI 48473-8200
Ph: (810)655-2219

Brookshire, Shannon, Founder
Toyota Territory Off-Roaders As-
sociation **[22435]**
1715 Earl Porter Dr.
Mont Belvieu, TX 77580
Ph: (281)414-1645
Fax: (281)576-5413

Broome, Mr. David, Chairman
Driver Employer Council of America
[3327]
815 Connecticut Ave. NW, Ste. 400
Washington, DC 20006-4046
Ph: (202)842-3400
Fax: (202)842-0011

Brophy, Edward P., Exec. Dir.
International Boxing Hall of Fame
Museum **[22712]**
1 Hall of Fame Dr.
Canastota, NY 13032
Ph: (315)697-7095
Fax: (315)697-5356

Brophy, Jaki, Contact
Hop Growers of America **[3762]**
301 W Prospect Pl.
Moxee, WA 98936
Ph: (509)453-4749
Fax: (509)457-8561

Brose, Judy, Chairperson
Rising International **[10732]**
300 Potrero St.
Santa Cruz, CA 95060-2769
Ph: (831)429-7473
Toll Free: 888-574-7464

Brosi, Sunshine, Secretary
Society for Economic Botany **[6155]**
PO Box 299

Saint Louis, MO 63166-0299
Fax: (314)577-9515

Brosnan, Susan H., Arch., Librarian
Knights of Columbus **[19409]**
1 Columbus Plz.
New Haven, CT 06510
Ph: (203)752-4000
Toll Free: 800-380-9995

Brost, James A., Mem.
Intermediaries & Reinsurance
Underwriters Association, Inc.
[1872]
c/o The Beaumont Group, Inc.
3626 E Tremont Ave., Ste. 203
Throggs Neck, NY 10465
Ph: (718)892-0228

Brostow, Prof. Witold, President
International Council on Materials
Education **[7775]**
3940 N Elm St.
Denton, TX 76207
Ph: (940)565-3262
    (940)565-4337

Brother, Millie, Founder
Children of Deaf Adults **[15181]**
7370 Formal Ct.
San Diego, CA 92120

Brotman, Martin, MD, Chairman
American Gastroenterological Association Research Foundation
[14778]
c/o American Gastroenterological
Association
4930 Del Ray Ave.
Bethesda, MD 20814
Ph: (301)222-4002

Brott Buss, Judy J., PhD, Exec. Dir.
American Quilt Study Group **[21748]**
1610 L St.
Lincoln, NE 68508-2509
Ph: (402)477-1181
Fax: (402)477-1181

Brouillette, Don, President
Irish Terrier Club of America **[21902]**
c/o Susan Bednar, Secretary
7170 N Seneca Ave.
Glendale, WI 53217-3870
Ph: (414)228-0268

Brous, David, VP of Sales
School and Office Products Network
[2446]
PO Box 751705
Dayton, OH 45475-1705
Ph: (937)610-3333

Browde, Levi, Exec. Dir.
Falun Dafa Information Center
[18397]
PO Box 577
New City, NY 10956-9998
Ph: (845)418-4870

Browder, Bob, Div. Dir.
Southern Pine Inspection Bureau
[1420]
PO Box 10915
Pensacola, FL 32524-0915
Ph: (850)434-2611
Fax: (850)434-1290

Browdie, Richard, Chmn. of the Bd.,
Chairman
National Council on Aging **[10522]**
251 18th St. S, Ste. 500
Arlington, VA 22202
Ph: (571)527-3900

Brown, Allan, Exec. Dir.
Compasio Relief and Development
[12648]

9111 N Oregon Ave.
Kansas City, MO 64154
Ph: (612)216-5565

Brown, Allyson Criner, Project Mgr.
Teaching for Change **[7846]**
1832 11th St. NW
Washington, DC 20009-4436
Ph: (202)588-7204
Toll Free: 800-763-9131
Fax: (202)238-0109

Brown, Amy, RN, President
Society of Gynecologic Nurse
Oncologists **[16355]**
c/o Erica Lumpkin, Secretary-
Treasurer
5067 Skylar Way
Birmingham, AL 35235

Brown, Ann, Comm. Spec.
Alliance to End Slavery and Traffick-
ing **[18367]**
1700 Pennsylvania Ave. NW, Ste.
520
Washington, DC 20006
Ph: (202)503-3200
Fax: (202)503-3201

Brown, Becky, Founder
Women in the Wind **[22238]**
PO Box 8392
Toledo, OH 43605

Brown, Betty, VP
Eskridge Family Association **[20864]**
PO Box 102
Ocean View, DE 19970
Ph: (804)270-7841

Brown, Bill, Treasurer
Association for Rehabilitation
Marketing **[2268]**
118 Julian Pl.
Syracuse, NY 13210

Brown, Bill, President
National Association of Realtors
[2880]
430 N Michigan Ave.
Chicago, IL 60611-4087
Toll Free: 800-874-6500

Brown, Brian S., President
National Organization for Marriage
[12258]
2029 K St. NW, Ste. 300
Washington, DC 20006
Toll Free: 888-894-3604

Brown, Bridget, Exec. Dir.
National Association of Workforce
Development Professionals
[11770]
1155 15th St. NW, Ste. 350
Washington, DC 20005
Ph: (202)589-1790
Fax: (202)589-1799

Brown, Bruce D., Exec. Dir.
Reporters Committee for Freedom of
the Press **[17955]**
1156 15th St. NW, Ste. 1250
Washington, DC 20005-1779
Ph: (202)795-9300
Toll Free: 800-336-4243

Brown, Bruce, Chairman
Junior Order, Knights of Pythias
[19523]
Supreme Lodge Knights of Pythias
458 Pearl St.
Stoughton, MA 02072-1655
Ph: (781)436-5966
Fax: (781)341-0496

Brown, Bruce, Treasurer
URANTIA Association of the United
States **[20557]**

533 Diversey Pky.
Chicago, IL 60614
Ph: (773)525-3319
Fax: (773)525-7739

Brown, Carey, Secretary, Treasurer
Livestock Publications Council
[2796]
200 W Exchange Ave.
Fort Worth, TX 76164
Ph: (817)247-1200

Brown, Catherine, Chairperson
Jack Russell Terrier Club of America
[21906]
PO Box 4527
Lutherville, MD 21094-4527
Ph: (410)561-3655
Fax: (410)560-2563

Brown, Cecilia, President
Pro-Life Alliance of Gays and
Lesbians **[12789]**
PO Box 3005
York, PA 17402
Ph: (202)223-6697

Brown, Celia, President
MindFreedom International **[18426]**
454 Willamette, Ste. 216
Eugene, OR 97401-2643
Ph: (541)345-9106
Toll Free: 877-623-7743
Fax: (480)287-8833

Brown, Cherie R., Exec. Dir.
National Coalition Building Institute
[17988]
Metro Plaza Bldg.
8403 Colesville Rd., Ste. 1100
Silver Spring, MD 20910
Ph: (202)785-9400
Fax: (202)785-3385

Brown, Chris, Secretary
River Network **[3935]**
2400 Spruce St., Ste. 200
Boulder, CO 80302
Ph: (503)241-3506
Fax: (503)241-9256

Brown, Christine, Exec. Dir.
National PKU Alliance **[16690]**
PO Box 501
Tomahawk, WI 54487
Ph: (715)437-0477

Brown, Christopher, President
Seafood Harvesters of America
[1303]
PO Box 66365
Washington, DC 20035
Ph: (202)888-2733

Brown, Clayola, President
A. Philip Randolph Institute **[19100]**
815 16th St. NW, 4th Fl.
Washington, DC 20006-4101
Ph: (202)508-3710
Fax: (202)508-3711

Brown, Clinton, Exec. Dir.
Seventh Day Baptist Missionary
Society **[19739]**
19 Hillside Ave.
Ashaway, RI 02804
Ph: (401)596-4326
Fax: (401)348-9494

Brown, Craig, Founder, Editor
Common Dreams **[12957]**
PO Box 443
Portland, ME 04112-0443
Ph: (207)775-0488
Fax: (207)775-0489

Brown, Craig, V. Chmn. of the Bd.
Hydrocephalus Association **[15943]**
4340 East-West Hwy., Ste. 905

Bethesda, MD 20814-4447
Ph: (301)202-3811
Toll Free: 888-598-3789
Fax: (301)202-3913

Brown, Crystal, Chairperson
NEA Foundation [7793]
1201 16th St. NW
Washington, DC 20036-3201
Ph: (202)822-7840
Fax: (202)822-7779

Brown, Curtis M., President
Alpha Nu Omega [23708]
PO Box 39033
Baltimore, MD 21212
Toll Free: 866-337-1988

Brown, Dan, Director
Educators Rising [7849]
1525 Wilson Blvd., Ste. 705
Arlington, VA 22209
Toll Free: 800-766-1156

Brown, Dana, Exec. Dir.
Witness for Peace [18840]
1616 P St. NW, Ste. 100
Washington, DC 20036
Ph: (202)547-6112
Fax: (202)536-4708

Brown, Daniel R., Treasurer
Society of Critical Care
  Anesthesiologists [13710]
44 Montgomery St., Ste. 1605
San Francisco, CA 94104-4703
Ph: (415)296-6952
Fax: (415)296-6901

Brown, David E., CIIP, Chairman
Society for Imaging Informatics in
  Medicine [17067]
19440 Golf Vista Plz., Ste. 330
Leesburg, VA 20176-8264
Ph: (703)723-0432
Fax: (703)723-0415

Brown, David L., Exec. Dir.
America Outdoors Association
  [23091]
PO Box 10847
Knoxville, TN 37939
Ph: (865)558-3595
Toll Free: 800-524-4814
Fax: (865)558-3598

Brown, David W., President
Massachusetts Bay Railroad
  Enthusiasts [10183]
PO Box 4245
Andover, MA 01810-0814
Ph: (617)489-5277
  (978)470-2066

Brown, David W., President
National Association for Media
  Literacy Education [8290]
10 Lauren Hill Dr.
Cherry Hill, NJ 08003
Toll Free: 888-775-2652

Brown, Dee, President, Curator
Fairy Lamp Club [21652]
PO Box 438
Pine, CO 80470-0438

Brown, Don, President
Blind LGBT Pride International
  [11874]
PO Box 19561
Minneapolis, MN 55419
Ph: (612)695-6991

Brown, Dudley, Exec. VP
National Association for Gun Rights
  [17916]
PO Box 7002
Fredericksburg, VA 22404
Toll Free: 877-405-4570
Fax: (202)351-0528

Brown, Edmund G., Jr., Leader
We the People [18738]
200 Harrison St.
Oakland, CA 94607
Ph: (510)836-3273
Fax: (510)836-3063

Brown, Ernest H., Exec. Dir.
Kappa Alpha Psi Fraternity [23902]
2322-24 N Broad St.
Philadelphia, PA 19132-4590
Ph: (215)228-7184
Fax: (215)228-7181

Brown, Esther, Exec. Dir.
Project Hope to Abolish the Death
  Penalty [17833]
c/o Esther Brown, Executive Director
PO Box 1362
Lanett, AL 36863

Brown, Fritzie, Exec. Dir.
CEC ArtsLink [18077]
291 Broadway, 12th Fl.
New York, NY 10007
Ph: (212)643-1985
Fax: (212)643-1996

Brown, Gail, President
Pure Puerto Rican Paso Fino
  Federation of America, Inc. [4403]
PO Box 2027
Leesville, SC 29070
Fax: (803)657-7780

Brown, Gary S., Acct. Mgr.
U.S. National Committee for
  International Union of Radio Sci-
  ence [7150]
c/o David Jackson, Chairman
Dept. of Electrical and Computer
  Engineering
University of Houston
4800 Calhoun Rd.
Houston, TX 77004
Ph: (713)743-4426
Fax: (713)743-4444

Brown, Genevieve, Exec. Dir.
International Volunteer Programs
  Association [13301]
PO Box 811012
Los Angeles, CA 90081
Ph: (646)505-8209

Brown, Geoffrey, CEO
National Association of Personal
  Financial Advisors [1284]
8700 W Bryn Mawr Ave., Ste. 700N
Chicago, IL 60630
Ph: (847)483-5400
Toll Free: 888-333-6659
Fax: (847)483-5415

Brown, Dr. Gregory E., Director
Black Holocaust Society [17779]
6622 N Bourbon St., Rm. 16
Milwaukee, WI 53224
Ph: (414)446-4377

Brown, Gwendolyn, Exec. Dir.,
  President
National Trailer Dealers Association
  [3347]
9864 E Grand River Ave., Ste. 110-
  290
Brighton, MI 48116
Toll Free: 800-800-4552
Fax: (810)229-5961

Brown, Harriet, Bd. Member
Maudsley Parents [14644]
c/o National Eating Disorder Association
165 W 46th St., No. 402
New York, NY 10036

Brown, Heather, Secretary
National Association of Myofascial
  Trigger Point Therapists [17453]

88 Union Ave.
Pittsburgh, PA 15205-2724

Brown, Howard F., Secretary,
  Treasurer
43rd Infantry Division Veterans Association [20710]
c/o Howard F. Brown, Assistant
  Secretary-Treasurer
150 Lakedell Dr.
East Greenwich, RI 02818-4716

Brown, Janet, President, CEO
Grantmakers in the Arts [12480]
4055 21st Ave. W, Ste. 100
Seattle, WA 98199-1247
Ph: (206)624-2312
Fax: (206)624-5568

Brown, Janet H., Exec. Dir.
Commission on Presidential Debates
  [18908]
Box 445
1200 New Hampshire Ave. NW
Washington, DC 20036
Ph: (202)872-1020

Brown, Mr. Jay, Exec. Dir.
Combat Helicopter Pilots Association
  [20668]
PO Box 42
Divide, CO 80814-0042
Toll Free: 800-832-5144

Brown, Jena, Dir. of Dev.
Concern Foundation [13950]
11111 W Olympic Blvd., Ste. 214
Los Angeles, CA 90064
Ph: (310)360-6100
Fax: (310)473-8300

Brown, Jerry, V. Chmn. of the Bd.
Crazy Horse Memorial Foundation
  [10038]
12151 Avenue of the Chiefs
Crazy Horse, SD 57730-8900
Ph: (605)673-4681

Brown, Rev. Jesse W., Jr., Exec. Dir.
National Association of African
  Americans for Positive Imagery
  [17781]
1231 N Broad St.
Philadelphia, PA 19122
Ph: (215)235-6488
Fax: (215)235-6491

Brown, Mr. John, CEO, President
Communications Supply Service As-
  sociation [3413]
5700 Murray St.
Little Rock, AR 72209
Ph: (501)562-7666
Toll Free: 800-252-2772

Brown, John, President
National Firearms Act Trade and
  Collectors Association [1293]
20603 Big Wells Dr.
Katy, TX 77449-6269
Ph: (281)492-8288
Toll Free: 866-897-0182

Brown, Judie, President
American Life League [12760]
PO Box 1350
Stafford, VA 22555
Ph: (540)659-4171
Fax: (540)659-2586

Brown, June, Registrar
American Council of Spotted Asses
  [3590]
2933 Silvercrest Ln.
Grapevine, TX 76051

Brown, Kathleen S., PhD, President
APA Division 22: Rehabilitation
  Psychology [16874]

c/o American Psychological Association
750 1st St. NE
Washington, DC 20002-4242
Ph: (202)216-7602
  (202)218-3599
Fax: (202)820-0291

Brown, Ken, Exec. Dir.
National Association of Local
  Government Environmental Profes-
  sionals [5640]
1001 Connecticut Ave., Ste. 405
Washington, DC 20036
Ph: (202)337-4503
Fax: (202)429-5290

Brown, Kerwin, President, CEO
BEMA [371]
10740 Nall Ave., Ste. 230
Overland Park, KS 66211
Ph: (913)338-1300
Fax: (913)338-1327

Brown, Kevin H., Exec. Dir., Sr. VP
CPCU Society [1853]
720 Providence Rd.
Malvern, PA 19355
Ph: (610)251-2716
  (610)644-2100
Toll Free: 800-932-2728
Fax: (610)725-5969

Brown, Kim, CEO, President
Alliance for Smiles [14327]
2565 3rd St., Ste. 237
San Francisco, CA 94107-3160
Ph: (415)647-4481
Fax: (415)647-7041

Brown, Kristin, President, Founder
Grow Learn Give [15082]
1495 N 450 E
Orem, UT 84097

Brown, Kristina, Exec. Dir.
Integrity: Arts & Culture Association
  [8862]
PO Box 6491
Rock Island, IL 61204-6491
Ph: (309)721-6155

Brown, Kuba J., Chairman
International Union of Operating
  Engineers [23398]
1125 17th St. NW
Washington, DC 20036
Ph: (202)429-9100

Brown, Mr. Kyle, Exec. Dir.
Bridal Association of America [443]
1901 Chester Ave., Ste. 201
Bakersfield, CA 93301-4477
Ph: (661)633-9200
Toll Free: 866-699-3334
Fax: (661)633-9199

Brown, Landon, Chairman
National Pollution Prevention
  Roundtable [4554]
50 F St. NW, Ste. 350
Washington, DC 20001-1770
Ph: (202)299-9701

Brown, Linda, Bus. Mgr.
American Society of Plant
  Taxonomists [6136]
University of Wyoming
Laramie, WY 82071
Ph: (307)766-2556

Brown, Linda, President
RVing Women [22432]
PO Box 1940
Apache Junction, AZ 85117-4074
Ph: (480)671-6226
Fax: (480)671-6230

Brown, Lori A., President
Associated Schools of Construction
  [7664]

PO Box 29
Windsor, CO 80550-0029
Ph: (970)988-1130
Fax: (970)282-0396

Brown, Lovie, Contact
Society of Black Academic Surgeons
  [17401]
c/o Lovie Brown
825 Fairfax Ave., 6th Fl.
Norfolk, VA

Brown, Mac, President
Association of Halfway House
  Alcoholism Programs of North
  America, Inc. [13125]
963 S 2nd St.
Louisville, KY 40203-2211
Ph: (502)581-0765
Fax: (502)581-1748

Brown, Mark, President
National Water Safety Congress
  [12837]
PO Box 4132
Frankfort, KY 40604-4132
Ph: (502)352-8771

Brown, Mark, President
Pediatric Chaplains Network [19937]
PO Box 561071
Orlando, FL 32856

Brown, Michael J., President
National Chicken Council [4568]
1152 15th St. NW, Ste. 430
Washington, DC 20005-2622
Ph: (202)296-2622
Fax: (202)293-4005

Brown, Michelle, Exec. Dir.
Transportation Safety Equipment
  Institute [3007]
4021 SW 10th Ave., No. 323
Topeka, KS 66604-1916
Ph: (785)220-4062
Fax: (866)286-3641

Brown, Dr. Noel J., President, CEO
Friends of the United Nations
  [19211]
866 UN Plz., Ste. 544
New York, NY 10017
Ph: (212)355-4192

Brown, Pamila, Chairman
National Conference of Specialized
  Court Judges [5395]
c/o American Bar Association
321 N Clark St., 19th Fl.
Chicago, IL 60654
Toll Free: 800-238-2667
Fax: (321)988-5709

Brown, Pat, Contact
For Mother Earth [18471]
1101 Bryden Rd.
Columbus, OH 43205
Ph: (614)252-9255

Brown, Paulette, President
American Bar Association [4981]
321 N Clark St.
Chicago, IL 60654
Ph: (312)988-5000
Toll Free: 800-285-2221

Brown, Paulette, President
American Bar Association - Commis-
  sion on Women in the Profession
  [5406]
321 N Clark St., 18th Fl.
Chicago, IL 60654
Ph: (312)988-5715
Fax: (312)988-5790

Brown, Peggy, Exec. Dir.
National Sexual Violence Resource
  Center [12930]

123 N Enola Dr.
Enola, PA 17025
Ph: (717)909-0710
Toll Free: 877-739-3895
Fax: (717)909-0714

Brown, Randall, President
Tan Son Nhut Association [21158]
PO Box 236
Penryn, PA 17564-0236
Ph: (803)463-7555
    (870)932-8085

Brown, Randy, Exec. Dir.
Clean Islands International [4042]
8219 Elvaton Dr.
Pasadena, MD 21122-3903
Ph: (410)647-2500

Brown, Randy, Chmn. of the Bd.
Helping Orphans Worldwide [11027]
10736 Jefferson Blvd., Ste. 808
Culver City, CA 90230
Ph: (971)400-4100

Brown, Randy, Dir. of Comm.
National Coalition for Homeless
  Veterans [21132]
333 1/2 Pennsylvania Ave. SE
Washington, DC 20003-1148
Ph: (202)546-1969
Toll Free: 800-233-8582
Fax: (202)546-2063

Brown, Robert, Founder
Food Animal Concerns Trust [4454]
3525 W Peterson Ave., Ste. 213
Chicago, IL 60659-3314
Ph: (773)525-4952

Brown, Robert G. W., CEO
American Institute of Physics [7022]
1 Physics Ellipse
College Park, MD 20740
Ph: (516)576-2200
    (301)209-3100
Toll Free: 888-491-8833
Fax: (516)349-7669

Brown, Robert H., Jr., President
ALS Therapy Alliance [13680]
16 Oakland Ave.
Needham, MA 02492
Ph: (603)664-5005

Brown, Robert, Div. Mgr.
Restaurant Loss Prevention and
  Security Association [2942]
885 Woodstock Rd., Ste. 430
Roswell, GA 30075-2274
Ph: (240)252-5542

Brown, Robert, Director
The Tax Council [5802]
600 13th St. NW, Ste. 1000
Washington, DC 20005
Ph: (202)822-8062
Fax: (202)315-3413

Brown, Ron, Mgr. of Fin.
Air & Waste Management Associa-
  tion [4535]
1 Gateway Ctr., 3rd Fl.
420 Fort Duquesne Blvd.
Pittsburgh, PA 15222-1435
Ph: (412)232-3444
Toll Free: 800-270-3444
Fax: (412)232-3450

Brown, Sara, Secretary
Company of Fifers and Drummers
  [9891]
62 N Main St.
Ivoryton, CT 06442-0277
Ph: (860)767-2237
Fax: (860)767-9765

Brown, Sarita E., President
Excelencia in Education [8347]
1156 5th St. NW, Ste. 1001

Washington, DC 20005
Ph: (202)785-7350
Fax: (202)785-7351

Brown, Scott, Officer
National Society of Professional
  Insurance Investigators [1911]
PO Box 88
Delaware, OH 43015
Toll Free: 888-677-4498
Fax: (740)369-7155

Brown, Mr. Stephan C., President
Commemorative Air Force [21219]
PO Box 764769
Dallas, TX 75376-4769
Ph: (214)330-1700
Toll Free: 877-767-7175
Fax: (214)623-0014

Brown, Stephen, President
Western International Walking Horse
  Association [4427]
c/o Kim Swingley, Secretary
9101 NE LaView St.
La Center, WA 98629

Brown, Steve A., Advisor, Chmn. of
  the Bd.
National FFA Organization [7479]
6060 FFA Dr.
Indianapolis, IN 46278-1370
Ph: (317)802-6060
Toll Free: 888-332-2668

Brown, Suzanne, Treasurer
Kappa Delta Epsilon [23729]
c/o Dr. Lesley Sheek, Vice President
302 Bibb St.
Marion, AL 36756
Ph: (334)683-5133

Brown, Terry, President
Private Practice Section of the
  American Physical Therapy As-
  sociation [17461]
1055 N Fairfax St., Ste. 204
Alexandria, VA 22314
Ph: (703)299-2410
Toll Free: 800-517-1167
Fax: (703)299-2411

Brown, Therese, Exec. Dir.
Association of Catholic Publishers
  [2769]
4725 Dorsey Hall Dr., Ste. A
Ellicott City, MD 21042
Ph: (410)988-2926
Fax: (410)571-4946

Brown, Mr. Tracy J., Founder
Urban Awareness USA [20011]
601 Dinwiddie St.
Portsmouth, VA 23704
Toll Free: 866-975-8722

Brown, Troy, Secretary, Treasurer
Stadium Managers Association
  [23268]
6919 Vista Dr.
West Des Moines, IA 50266
Ph: (515)282-8192
Fax: (515)282-9117

Brown, Walter, Jr., Bd. Member
Urban Financial Services Coalition
  [418]
1200 G St. NW, Ste. 800
Washington, DC 20005
Ph: (202)434-8970
Fax: (202)434-8704

Brown, Warren, President
Association of Public Data Users
  [6738]
PO Box 100155
Arlington, VA 22210
Ph: (703)522-4980
Fax: (480)393-5098

Brown, Warren K., President
Veterans of Safety [12847]
22 Logan St.
New Bedford, MA 02740-7324

Browne, Des, V. Ch.
Nuclear Threat Initiative [18755]
1747 Pennsylvania Ave. NW, 7th Fl.
Washington, DC 20006
Ph: (202)296-4810
Fax: (202)296-4811

Browne, Lorna, Editor
National Association of Teacher
  Educators for Family and
  Consumer Sciences [7993]
c/o Mari Borr, Treasurer/Membership
  Chairperson
PO Box 6050
Fargo, ND 58108-6050
Ph: (701)231-7968

Browne, Saideh, President, CEO
National Council of Women of the
  United States [19256]
777 United Nations Plz.
New York, NY 10017
Ph: (212)697-1278

Brownell, Larry, CEO
Marketing Research Association
  [2291]
1156 15th St. NW, Ste. 302
Washington, DC 20005
Ph: (202)800-2545
Toll Free: 888-512-1050
Fax: (888)512-1050

Brownell, Peter, Chairman
National Association of Sporting
  Goods Wholesalers [3141]
1 Parkview Plz.
Oakbrook Terrace, IL 60181
Ph: (630)596-9006
Fax: (630)544-5055

Browning, Adam, Exec. Dir.
Vote Solar Initiative [7215]
360 22nd St., Ste. 730
Oakland, CA 94612
Ph: (415)817-5061

Browning, Butch, President
National Association of State Fire
  Marshals [5212]
315 S Main St., Ste. 1
Burns, WY 82053
Ph: (202)737-1226
Fax: (307)547-2260

Browning, Robyn M., CFRE, Exec.
  Dir.
Herbalife Family Foundation [11030]
800 W Olympic Blvd., Ste. 406
Los Angeles, CA 90015
Ph: (213)745-0569
Fax: (213)765-9812

Brownlee, Cathy, Exec. Dir.
Association of Professional Design
  Firms [1554]
1448 E 52nd St., No. 201
Chicago, IL 60615
Ph: (773)643-7052

Brownlee, Denise, Exec. Dir.
Cystic Fibrosis Foundation [17138]
6931 Arlington Rd., Ste. B
Bethesda, MD 20814
Ph: (301)657-8444
Toll Free: 877-657-8444
Fax: (301)652-9571

Brownlee, Kenny, Treasurer
National Peanut Buying Points As-
  sociation [4509]
115 W 2nd St.
Tifton, GA 31793-0314
Ph: (229)386-1716
Fax: (229)386-8757

Brownstein, Clifford, Exec. Dir.
National Association of Therapeutic
  Schools and Programs [13800]
5272 River Rd., Ste. 600
Bethesda, MD 20816
Ph: (301)986-8770
Fax: (301)986-8772

Brownstein, David, Exec. Dir.
Wild Earth [3964]
29 S Chestnut St., Ste. 201
New Paltz, NY 12561
Ph: (845)256-9830

Brownwell, Patricia, PhD, President
National Committee for the Preven-
  tion of Elder Abuse [10521]
1730 Rhode Island Ave. NW, Ste.
  1200
Washington, DC 20036-3109
Ph: (202)464-9481
  (855)500-3537
Toll Free: 800-677-1116
Fax: (202)872-0057

Bruce, Gail, Founder
Unreserved American Indian Fashion
  and Art Alliance [9006]
55 Bethune St., 13th Fl.
New York, NY 10014
Ph: (212)206-6580

Bruce, Jeffrey N., Chairman
American Board of Neurological
  Surgery [16059]
245 Amity Rd., Ste. 208
Woodbridge, CT 06525
Ph: (203)397-2267
Fax: (203)392-0400

Bruce, Dr. Joy, Chairperson,
  President
National Alliance to Nurture the Aged
  and the Youth [12011]
659 NE 125th St.
North Miami, FL 33161-5503
Ph: (305)981-3232

Bruce, LeAnn, President
Association of VA Social Workers
  [13105]
9451 Petit Ave.
Northridge, CA 91343

Bruce, Pamela, Project Mgr.
International Thymic Malignancy
  Interest Group [13995]
6 Cold Spring Ct.
Mount Kisco, NY 10549

Bruce, Richard, Exec. Dir.
National Truck & Heavy Equipment
  Claims Council [1912]
c/o Richard Bruce, Executive Direc-
  tor
PO Box 5928
Fresno, CA 93755-5928
Ph: (559)431-3774
Fax: (559)436-4755

Bruce, Sasha, Sr. VP
NARAL Pro-Choice America [19034]
1156 15th St. NW, Ste. 700
Washington, DC 20005
Ph: (202)973-3000
  (202)973-3032
Fax: (202)973-3096

Bruce, Shawn, Officer
Piano Technicians Guild [2437]
4444 Forest Ave.
Kansas City, KS 66106-3750
Ph: (913)432-9975
Fax: (913)432-9986

Bruce, Zola Z., Contact
Unified for Global Healing [15502]
106 Waverly Ave.

Brooklyn, NY 11205
Ph: (212)555-0123

Bruckner, Scott, Chmn. of the Bd.
God's Love We Deliver [10542]
166 Avenue of the Americas
New York, NY 10013
Ph: (212)294-8100
  (212)294-8102
Toll Free: 800-747-2023
Fax: (212)294-8101

Brueggemann, Ingar, Chairman
Rotarian Action Group for Population
  and Development [12520]
344 W Pike St.
Lawrenceville, GA 30046
Ph: (770)407-5633
Fax: (770)822-9492

Brugger, Michael, Secretary
Gamma Sigma Delta [23674]
c/o Edward Rister, President
Texas A & M University
College Station, TX 77843-2124
Ph: (979)845-3801

Brumfield, Martha A., Chmn. of the
  Bd.
Regulatory Affairs Professionals
  Society [14963]
5635 Fishers Ln., Ste. 550
Rockville, MD 20852
Ph: (301)770-2920
Fax: (301)841-7956

Brumfield, Thomas, Jr., VP
Folk Art Society of America [9326]
PO Box 17041
Richmond, VA 23226-7041
Toll Free: 800-355-6709

Brummel, Fr. Mark, CMF, Director
St. Jude League [19903]
205 W Monroe St.
Chicago, IL 60606
Ph: (312)544-8230

Brumskine, Winifred, Accountant
National Communication Association
  [8597]
1765 N St. NW
Washington, DC 20036
Ph: (202)464-4622
Fax: (202)464-4600

Brunch, Dr. Ron, Officer
World Sturgeon Conservation
  Society U.S.A. [3974]
Wisconsin Dept. of Natural
  Resources
PO Box 7921
Madison, WI 53707-7921
Ph: (608)267-7591
Fax: (608)266-2244

Brune, Christine W., Exec. Dir.
American Horse Publications [2763]
49 Spinnaker Cir.
South Daytona, FL 32119-8552
Ph: (386)760-7743
Fax: (386)760-7728

Brune, Michael, Exec. Dir.
Sierra Club [4012]
2101 Webster St., Ste. 1300
Oakland, CA 94612
Ph: (415)977-5500
Fax: (510)208-3140

Bruner, Darl, Director
Northwest Nazarene University
  Alumni Association [19339]
Office of Alumni Relations
524 E Dewey St.
Nampa, ID 83686
Ph: (208)467-8841
Toll Free: 800-654-2411
Fax: (208)467-8838

Brungardt, Stacy, CAE, Exec. Dir.
Society of Teachers of Family
  Medicine [14751]
11400 Tomahawk Creek Pky., Ste.
  240
Leawood, KS 66211
Ph: (913)906-6000
Toll Free: 800-274-7928
Fax: (913)906-6096

Brunk, Nadene S., CNM, Founder,
  Exec. Dir.
Midwives for Haiti [15125]
7130 Glen Forest Dr., Ste. 101
Richmond, VA 23226
Ph: (804)662-6060

Brunner, Thomas, Director
Lincoln Zephyr Owner's Club
  [21420]
c/o Cornerstone Registration, Ltd.
PO Box 1715
Maple Grove, MN 55311-6715
Ph: (763)420-7829
Toll Free: 866-427-7583
Fax: (763)420-7849

Brunner, Thomas M., CEO,
  President
Glaucoma Research Foundation
  [16384]
251 Post St., Ste. 600
San Francisco, CA 94108
Ph: (415)986-3162
Toll Free: 800-826-6693
Fax: (415)986-3763

Bruno, Beth, MA, Exec. Dir.
A Face to Reframe [11997]
PO Box 273112
Fort Collins, CO 80527
Ph: (970)213-9457

Bruno, Duane R., Treasurer
Veterans of the Battle of the Bulge
  [21204]
PO Box 27430
Philadelphia, PA 19118
Ph: (703)528-4058

Bruno, Joseph F., President, CEO
Helen Keller National Center for
  Deaf-Blind Youths and Adults
  [15199]
141 Middle Neck Rd.
Sands Point, NY 11050
Ph: (516)944-8900
Fax: (516)944-7302

Bruno, Sarah, Exec. Dir.
Public Leadership Education
  Network [8754]
1875 Connecticut Ave. NW, 10th Fl.
Washington, DC 20009
Ph: (202)872-1585

Bruno-Reitzner, Joyce, MBA, Exec.
  Dir.
Association of Pulmonary and Criti-
  cal Care Medicine Program Direc-
  tors [14350]
559 W Diversey Pky.
Chicago, IL 60614
Toll Free: 877-301-6800

Brunsman, August E., IV, Exec. Dir.
Secular Student Alliance [20212]
1550 Old Henderson Rd., Ste. W200
Columbus, OH 43220
Ph: (614)441-9588
Toll Free: 877-842-9474

Brunson, Neal E., Esq., Director
Afro-American Historical Society
  Museum [8782]
1841 Kennedy Blvd.
Jersey City, NJ 07305
Ph: (201)547-5262
Fax: (201)547-5392

Brunswick, Shelli, Chairperson
Women in Aerospace [5879]
204 E St. NE
Washington, DC 20002
Ph: (202)547-0229
Fax: (202)547-6348

Brunt, Jane, DVM, Exec. Dir.
CATalyst Council [10598]
PO Box 3064
Annapolis, MD 21403

Brusacoram, Gary, Contact
Manufacturers' Representatives
  Educational Research Foundation
  [2207]
5460 Ward Rd., Ste. 125
Arvada, CO 80002
Ph: (303)463-1801
Fax: (303)379-6024

Brush, Sam, Director
American Poultry Association [4563]
PO Box 306
Burgettstown, PA 15021-0306
Ph: (724)729-3459
Fax: (724)729-1003

Bruskewitz, Eileen, Exec. Dir.
American Dream Coalition [17870]
3711 NW 59th Pl.
Gainesville, FL 32653
Ph: (352)281-5817
Fax: (352)381-7026

Brussat, Mary Ann, Director,
  Founder
Spirituality & Practice [7674]
15 W 24th St., 10th Fl.
New York, NY 10010

Brusseau, Jerilyn, Bd. Member
Earthstewards Network [11996]
PO Box 10697
Bainbridge Island, WA 98110
Ph: (206)842-7986
Fax: (206)842-8918

Brust, Haley J., Exec. Dir.
Association of Women in the Metal
  Industries [3487]
19 Mantua Rd.
Mount Royal, NJ 08061
Ph: (856)423-3201
Fax: (856)423-3420

Brust, Joel, President
American Ostrich Association [3597]
PO Box 218
Scurry, TX 75158
Ph: (972)968-8546

Brust, Mike, Chairman
North American Bowhunting Coali-
  tion [22167]
PO Box 493
Chatfield, MN 55923-0493

Brutus, Emmanuel, Founder
Haiti Verte Foundation [11372]
169 Arlington Ave.
Staten Island, NY 10303

Bruursema, Tom, Director
NSF International [17015]
789 N Dixboro Rd.
Ann Arbor, MI 48113
Ph: (734)769-8010
Toll Free: 800-673-6275
Fax: (734)769-0109

Bruzzese, Len, Exec. Dir.
Association of Health Care Journal-
  ists [2663]
10 Neff Hall
Missouri School of Journalism
Columbia, MO 65211
Ph: (573)884-5606
Fax: (573)884-5609

Bry, John, President
Gene Stratton-Porter Memorial
Society [9099]
1205 Pleasant Pt.
Rome City, IN 46784
Ph: (260)854-3790
Fax: (260)854-9102

Bryan, Alex, President
National Young Farmers Coalition
[4165]
PO Box 1074
Hudson, NY 12534
Ph: (518)643-3564

Bryan, Charles, President
Independent Research Libraries As-
sociation [9706]
c/o Charles Bryan, President
Virginia Historical Society
428 N Blvd.
Richmond, VA 23221-0311
Ph: (804)358-4901

Bryan, Fleur, President
Irish Draught Horse Society of North
America [4373]
1279 Bates Ln.
Smithfield, KY 40068
Ph: (502)649-2037

Bryan, J.W., Director
National Conference of State Social
Security Administrators [5760]
501 High St., 4th Fl.
Frankfort, KY 40601
Ph: (502)564-3952
Fax: (502)564-2124

Bryan, Robert A., Chairman
Quebec-Labrador Foundation [4097]
55 S Main St.
Ipswich, MA 01938
Ph: (978)356-0038
Fax: (978)356-7322

Bryant, Cedric, Director
Associated Services for the Blind
[17687]
919 Walnut St.
Philadelphia, PA 19107
Ph: (215)627-0600
Toll Free: 800-732-0999
Fax: (215)922-0692

Bryant, Cindy, Editor, President
Purple Flower Gang [24058]
1803 Lucas St.
Muscatine, IA 52761

Bryant, Daniel, Prop.
Association of African American
Vintners [179]
4225 Solano Ave.
Napa, CA 94558
Ph: (707)334-6048

Bryant, Geoff, President, Founder
United States Golf Teachers Federa-
tion [22896]
1295 SE Port St. Lucie Blvd.
Port Saint Lucie, FL 34952
Ph: (772)335-3216
Toll Free: 888-346-3290
Fax: (772)335-3822

Bryant, Jennifer, Exec. Dir.
National Association of Negro Busi-
ness and Professional Women's
Clubs, Inc. [12900]
1806 New Hampshire Ave. NW
Washington, DC 20009-3206
Ph: (202)483-4206
Fax: (202)462-7253

Bryant, John Hope, CEO, Founder,
Chairman
Operation HOPE, Inc. [11420]
707 Wilshire Blvd., 30th Fl.

Los Angeles, CA 90017
Ph: (213)891-2900
Fax: (213)489-7511

Bryant, Michael D., President
National Marine Lenders Association
[414]
1 Melvin Ave.
Annapolis, MD 21401
Ph: (410)980-1401
Fax: (410)268-3755

Bryant, Naomi, President
Christian Women Connection
[20019]
PO Box 2328
Anderson, IN 46018
Ph: (765)648-2102
Toll Free: 866-778-0804
Fax: (765)608-3094

Bryant, Phil, Chairman
Jobs for America's Graduates
[11766]
1729 King St., Ste. 100
Alexandria, VA 22314
Ph: (703)684-9479
Fax: (703)684-9489

Bryant, Tracee, Mem.
Black Mental Health Alliance [15764]
200 E Lexington St., Ste. 803
Baltimore, MD 21202
Ph: (410)338-2642

Bryce, Shauna C., President
National Resume Writers' Associa-
tion [3514]
5113 Monona Dr.
Madison, WI 53716
Toll Free: 877-843-6792

Bryer, Jackson R., President
F. Scott Fitzgerald Society [9050]
c/o Prof. Kirk Curnutt, Vice President
Troy University, Montgomery
Campus
English Dept.
Montgomery, AL 36103-4419

Brynteson, Richard, Managing Dir.
National Association for Proficiency
Testing [7327]
4445 W 77th St., Ste. 212
Edina, MN 55435
Ph: (952)303-6126
Fax: (305)425-5728

Bryon, Bill, Chmn. of the Bd.
ChildVoice International [10938]
202 Kent Pl.
Newmarket, NH 03857
Ph: (603)842-0132

Bucalo, Patricia, Founder, President
Laity for Life [19850]
PO Box 111478
Naples, FL 34108
Ph: (239)352-6333

Buch, Dr. Harikesh, Officer
International Ostomy Association
[16527]
PO Box 512
Northfield, MN 55057
Toll Free: 800-826-0826
Fax: (507)645-5168

Buch, Shilpa, PhD, Secretary
Society on Neuroimmune
Pharmacology [16055]
University of Nebraska Medical
Center
Department of Pharmacology and
Experimental Neuroscience
985880 Nebraska Medical Ctr., DRC
8011
Omaha, NE 68198-5880
Ph: (402)559-3165
Fax: (402)559-3744

Buchan, Kimberly, Coord., Admin.
Progressive Democrats of America
[18117]
PO Box 150064
Grand Rapids, MI 49515-0064
Toll Free: 877-239-2093

Buchanan, Buck
EIFS Industry Members Association
[521]
513 W Broad St., Ste. 210
Falls Church, VA 22046-3257
Toll Free: 800-294-3462
Fax: (703)538-1736

Buchanan, Calvin, President
Hudson Essex Terraplane Historical
Society [21396]
c/o Cheri Holz
13270 McKanna Rd.
Minooka, IL 60447
Ph: (815)263-3827

Buchanan, Homer L., Leader
Ancient Egyptian Arabic Order
Nobles of the Mystic Shrine
[19552]
2239 Democrat Rd.
Memphis, TN 38132-1802
Ph: (901)395-0150
Fax: (901)395-0115

Buchanan, John C., Esq., Founder,
President
International Society of Primerus
Law Firms [5015]
171 Monroe Ave. NW, Ste. 750
Grand Rapids, MI 49503
Ph: (616)454-9939
Toll Free: 800-968-2211
Fax: (616)458-7099

Buchanan, Patrick J., Chairman
The American Cause [18293]
PO Box 7
Vienna, VA 22183
Ph: (703)255-9224
Fax: (703)255-2219

Buchanan, Sara, VP
American Cavy Breeders Association
[3589]
1157 E San Angelo Ave.
Gilbert, AZ 85234
Ph: (519)834-2110
(831)630-0480

Buche, Tim, President, CEO
Motorcycle Safety Foundation [3000]
2 Jenner St., Ste. 150
Irvine, CA 92618
Toll Free: 800-446-9227

Buchholz, Monica, Contact
International Automotive Technicians
Network [296]
640 W Lambert Rd.
Brea, CA 92821
Ph: (714)257-1335

Buchholz, Noah D., Founder
Deaf International [11936]
PO Box 3838
Olathe, KS 66063-3838
Ph: (913)390-9010
Fax: (913)390-9011

Buchner, Brian, President
National Association for Civilian
Oversight of Law Enforcement
[5489]
PO Box 87227
Tucson, AZ 85754-7227
Ph: (317)721-8133

Buchner, Chris, President
Comicbook Artists' Guild [9169]
PO Box 38

Moodus, CT 06469

Buck, Alison, Assoc. Dir.
Women's Global Connection [13409]
University of the Incarnate Word
4503 Broadway St.
San Antonio, TX 78209
Ph: (210)828-2224

Buck, Bob, Exec. Dir.
Eastern Amputee Golf Association
[22878]
2015 Amherst Dr.
Bethlehem, PA 18015-5606
Ph: (610)867-9295
Fax: (610)867-9295

Buck, Deanne, Secretary
American Alpine Club [22727]
710 10th St., Ste. 100
Golden, CO 80401
Ph: (303)384-0110
(303)384-0112
Fax: (303)384-0111

Buck, Deanne, Exec. Dir.
Outdoor Industries Women's Coali-
tion [2468]
PO Box 7203
Boulder, CO 80306
Ph: (513)202-6492
Toll Free: 877-686-6492

Buck, Jill, Exec. Dir., Founder
Go Green Initiative Association
[7891]
4307 Valley Ave., Ste. 2
Pleasanton, CA 94566
Ph: (925)289-0145
Fax: (925)226-3942

Buck, Joy, PhD, President
Hospice and Palliative Nurses As-
sociation [16135]
1 Penn Ctr. W, Ste. 425
Pittsburgh, PA 15276
Ph: (412)787-9301

Buck, Kathryn, President
Pictorial Photographers of America
[10145]
147-10 41st Ave.
Flushing, NY 11355-1266
Ph: (212)243-0273

Buck, Kay, Exec. Dir.
Coalition to Abolish Slavery and
Trafficking [12029]
5042 Wilshire Blvd., No. 586
Los Angeles, CA 90036
Ph: (213)365-1906
Toll Free: 888-539-2373
Fax: (213)341-4439

Buck, Matthew, Director
Food Alliance [6645]
PO Box 86457
Portland, OR 97286
Ph: (503)267-4667

Buckalew, Michelle, Founder,
President
Animal World USA [3622]
PO Box 11126
Memphis, TN 38111
Ph: (901)791-2455
(703)625-1392
Fax: (901)249-3253

Buckberg, Phil, President
Alpha Rho Chi [23677]
PO Box 4671
Olathe, KS 66062

Buckland, Kelly, Exec. Dir.
National Council on Independent
Living [11624]
2013 H St. NW, 6th Fl.

Washington, DC 20006
Ph: (202)207-0334
Toll Free: 877-525-3400
Fax: (202)207-0341

Buckle, Marcie, Treasurer
State Instructional Materials Review
Association [8695]
PO Box 94064
Baton Rouge, LA 70804-9064
Ph: (225)342-1848
Fax: (225)342-0178

Buckley, John, Contact
American Association of Blind
Teachers [8638]
c/o John Buckley
1025 Ree Way
Knoxville, TN 37909
Ph: (865)692-4888

Buckley, John, VP
United States Kuo Shu Federation
[23020]
PO Box 927
Reisterstown, MD 21136-0927
Ph: (443)394-9200
Fax: (443)394-9202

Buckley, Maurice A., CEO, Founder,
President
Ireland Chamber of Commerce
U.S.A. [23595]
219 South St., Ste. 203
New Providence, NJ 07974
Ph: (908)286-1300
Fax: (908)286-1200

Buckley, Mona F., MPA, CEO
Professional Insurance Marketing
Association [1917]
35 E Wacker Dr., Ste. 850
Chicago, IL 60601-2106
Ph: (817)569-7462
Fax: (312)644-8557

Buckman, Michael, President
International Association of Butterfly
Exhibitors and Suppliers [1174]
Houston Museum of Natural Science
Cockerell Butterfly Ctr.
5555 Hermann Park Dr.
Houston, TX 77030
Ph: (713)639-4750
Fax: (713)639-4788

Bucknam, Heidi, Exec. Dir.
Birds of Prey Foundation [4797]
2290 S 104th St.
Broomfield, CO 80020
Ph: (303)460-0674

Buckner, Bill, President, CEO
The Samuel Roberts Noble Founda-
tion [3529]
2510 Sam Noble Pky.
Ardmore, OK 73401
Ph: (580)223-5810

Buckwalter, Samuel, Exec. Sec.
Avionics Maintenance Conference
[131]
Aeronautical Radio, Inc.
2551 Riva Rd.
Annapolis, MD 21401
Ph: (240)334-2576

Bucura, David, Coord.
African Great Lakes Initiative
[13023]
1001 Park Ave.
Saint Louis, MO 63104
Ph: (314)647-1287

Buczynski, Ruth, PhD, President
National Institute for the Clinical Application of Behavioral Medicine
[13801]

PO Box 523
Mansfield Center, CT 06250-0523
Ph: (860)456-1153
Fax: (860)477-1454

Bud, Matthew R., Chairman
The Financial Executives Networking
Group [1234]
32 Gray's Farm Rd.
Weston, CT 06883
Ph: (203)227-8965
Fax: (203)227-8984

Budak, Taylor, Asst.
German Marshall Fund of the United
States [18543]
1744 R St. NW
Washington, DC 20009
Ph: (202)683-2650
Fax: (202)265-1662

Budgell, Jeffrey, President
Association of Licensed Architects
[232]
1 E Northwest Hwy., Ste. 200
Palatine, IL 60067
Ph: (847)382-0630
Fax: (847)382-8380

Budgen, Betty, Dir. of Member Svcs.,
Treasurer
American Hair Loss Council [14482]
30 S Main St.
Shenandoah, PA 17976
Ph: (615)721-8085

Budke, Dr. Ken, CEO, President
Champions of Autism and ADHD
[13760]
3025 Kimball Ave.
Waterloo, IA 50702
Ph: (319)233-0380

Buechele, Paul, President
Melanoma Awareness [14008]
PO Box 5512
Hopkins, MN 55343-7502

Buehler, George, Treasurer
American Bonsai Society [22066]
PO Box 6
Lynnville, IN 47619
Ph: (812)922-5451

Buergermeister, Jennifer, Founder
Breathe the Cure [13613]
Houston, TX

Buffenbarger, R. Thomas, President
Machinists Non-Partisan Political
League [23448]
c/o International Association of
Machinists and Aerospace Workers
9000 Machinists Pl.
Upper Marlboro, MD 20772-2687
Ph: (301)967-4500

Buffington, Kathy
American Board of Certification for
Gastroenterology Nurses [16098]
330 N Wabash Ave., Ste. 2000
Chicago, IL 60611
Toll Free: 855-252-2246
Fax: (312)673-6723

Buford, Brian, PhD, Treasurer
Society of Consulting Psychology
[16935]
c/o Debra Nolan, CAE
631 US Highway 1, Ste., 400
North Palm Beach, FL 33408
Toll Free: 800-440-4066

Buford, Bryan, Exec. Dir.
Associated Mail and Business
Centers [2114]
5411 E State St., No. 599
Rockford, IL 61108
Ph: (815)316-8255
Fax: (866)314-2672

Bugaj, Mike, Editor, Publisher
Worldwide Television-FM DX As-
sociation [21274]
PO Box 501
Somersville, CT 06072

Buggeln, Gretchen, President
Vernacular Architecture Forum
[5982]
c/o William Littmann, Secretary
PO Box 225158
San Francisco, CA 94122

Buhler, Jeff, President
Pi Lambda Phi Fraternity, Inc.
[23922]
60 Newtown Rd., No. 118
Danbury, CT 06810
Ph: (203)740-1044
Fax: (203)740-1644

Buhlis, Roger, President
Police Society for Problem Based
Learning [5516]
PO Box 362
Oakley, CA 94561
Toll Free: 800-862-6307

Buhrow, William C., Jr., President
Christian Association for Psychologi-
cal Studies [16912]
PO Box 365
Batavia, IL 60510-0365
Ph: (630)639-9478
Fax: (630)454-3799

Buikstra, Dr. Jane, President
Center for American Archeology
[5935]
PO Box 366
Kampsville, IL 62053
Ph: (618)653-4316

Bujol, K. Angelle, Exec. Dir.
Sigma Alpha Sorority [23875]
Po Box 570
Muskego, WI 53150-0570
Ph: (262)682-4690

Bujosa, John, Founder, President
The Emergency Vehicle Owners &
Operators Association [21377]
PO Box 1149
Airway Heights, WA 99001-1149

Bukhari, Dr. Zahid, President
Islamic Circle of North America
[20499]
166-26 89th Ave.
Queens, NY 11432
Ph: (718)658-1199
Fax: (718)658-1255

Buksa, Daniel, Assoc. Dir.
Academy of General Dentistry
[14365]
560 W Lake St., 6th Fl.
Chicago, IL 60661-6600
Toll Free: 888-243-DENT

Bulat, Cheryl, President
Associate Degree Early Childhood
Teacher Educators [7580]
14 Freedom Ter.
14 Freedom Terr.
Easton, PA 18045
Ph: (610)861-4162

Bulcher, Sandy, Director
Maple Syrup Urine Disease Family
Support Group [15827]
9517 Big Bear Ave.
Powell, OH 43065

Bulgarelli, David M., Exec. Dir.
National Examining Board of Ocularists [16396]
David M. Bulgarelli, Executive Director

625 1st Ave., Ste. 220
Coralville, IA 52241-2101
Ph: (319)339-1125
Fax: (319)354-3465

Bulger, John B., DO, Comm. Chm.
Association of Osteopathic Directors
and Medical Educators [16520]
142 E Ontario St., 4th Fl.
Chicago, IL 60611-2874
Ph: (312)202-8211
Toll Free: 800-621-1773

Bulger, Nan, Exec. Dir., CEO
Strategic and Competitive Intel-
ligence Professionals [6754]
7550 IH 10 W, Ste. 400
San Antonio, TX 78229
Ph: (703)739-0696
Fax: (703)739-2524

Bulkley, Dr. Ed, President
International Association of Biblical
Counselors [20042]
11500 Sheridan Blvd.
Westminster, CO 80020
Toll Free: 844-843-4222

Bull, James, Chairman
Official Red Dwarf Fan Club [24088]
c/o Jupiter Mining Co.
PO Box 3152
East Falmouth, MA 02536

Bull, Jonathan, President
Ethylene Oxide Sterilization Associa-
tion, Inc. [718]
PO Box 33361
Washington, DC 20033-0361
Toll Free: 866-235-5030
Fax: (202)557-3836

Bulla, Randi, President
North American Brass Band Associa-
tion [9985]
PO Box 113
Miamiville, OH 45147

Bullard, Dr. Joanna E., President
International Society for Aeolian
Research [6693]
c/o Dr. Jeff Lee, Secretary/Treasurer
Dept. of Geosciences
Texas Tech University
Lubbock, TX 79409-1053

Bullington, Allan, Founder
The True Nature Network, Inc.
[10704]
PO Box 20672
Columbus Cir. Sta.
New York, NY 10023-1487

Bullington-McGuire, Richard,
President
Obscure Organization [7288]
300 S Jackson St.
Arlington, VA 22204
Ph: (703)979-4380

Bullitt-Jonas, Margaret, Co-Chmn. of
the Bd.
Religious Witness for the Earth
[4144]
PO Box 642
Littleton, MA 01460

Bullock, Scott, President, Gen.
Counsel
Institute for Justice [5427]
901 N Glebe Rd., Ste. 900
Arlington, VA 22203
Ph: (703)682-9320
Fax: (703)682-9321

Bulmash, Robert, President
Private Citizen [17926]
PO Box 233

Naperville, IL 60566-0233
Ph: (630)393-2370

Bulthuis, Dave, Certified Public Accountant
FishAmerica Foundation [3863]
1001 N Fairfax St., Ste. 501
Alexandria, VA 22314
Ph: (703)519-9691
Fax: (703)519-1872

Bunce, Peter J., CEO, President
General Aviation Manufacturers Association [136]
1400 K St. NW, Ste. 801
Washington, DC 20005-2485
Ph: (202)393-1500
Fax: (202)842-4063

Bunch, Ted, Founder, Director
A Call To Men [12305]
250 Merrick Rd., Ste. 813
Rockville Centre, NY 11570
Ph: (917)922-6738

Bunker, Mr. Gil, President
Bunker Family Association [20790]
c/o Gil Bunker, President
9 Sommerset Rd.
Turnersville, NJ 08012-2122
Ph: (856)589-6140
     (520)940-7225

Bunker, James A., Exec. Dir.
National Gulf War Resource Center
[21133]
1725 SW Gage Blvd.
Topeka, KS 66604
Ph: (785)221-0162
Toll Free: 866-531-7183
Fax: (785)235-6531

Bunn, G. Peter, III, Gen. Counsel
International Wheat Gluten Association [1348]
9393 W 110th St., Ste. 200
Overland Park, KS 66212-6319
Ph: (913)381-8180
Fax: (913)381-8836

Bunn, Kamilah, CEO
Adoption Exchange Association
[10438]
605 Global Way, Ste. 100
Linthicum, MD 21090
Ph: (410)636-7030
Toll Free: 888-200-4005
Fax: (410)636-7039

Bunn, Paul A., Jr., Mem.
International Association for the
Study of Lung Cancer [13989]
13100 E Colfax Ave., Unit 10
Aurora, CO 80011
Toll Free: 855-464-2752
Fax: (720)505-2176

Bunnag, Usa, DDS, Founder,
President
Smiles on Wings [15161]
6501 Democracy Blvd.
Bethesda, MD 20817
Ph: (301)896-0064
Fax: (301)758-7401

Bunzel, David, Exec. Dir.
Physical Security Interoperability Alliance [6581]
65 Washington St., Ste. 170
Santa Clara, CA 95050
Ph: (650)938-6945
Fax: (408)516-3950

Buono, Anthony F., Treasurer
Graduation Pledge Alliance [19111]
Bentley University
175 Forest St.
Waltham, MA 02452
Ph: (781)891-2529
Fax: (781)891-2896

Burak, Asi, Director
Games for Change [22052]
205 E 42nd St., 20th Fl.
New York, NY 10017
Ph: (212)242-4922

Burandt, Mr. Gary, Contact
International Communications
Agency Network [771]
PO Box 490
Rollinsville, CO 80474
Ph: (808)965-8240
Fax: (303)484-4087

Burant, Connie, President
Silver Marten Rabbit Club [4612]
c/o Katie Peltier, Secretary/Treasurer
9599 E Highway 2
Poplar, WI 54864
Ph: (715)364-6801

Burbank, Sandee, Exec. Dir.
Mothers Against Misuse and Abuse
[17316]
5217 SE 28th Ave.
Portland, OR 97202
Ph: (503)233-4202
Toll Free: 866-559-3369

Burbidge, Richard, President
International Academy of Trial
Lawyers [5009]
5841 Cedar Lake Rd., Ste. 204
Minneapolis, MN 55416
Ph: (952)546-2364
Fax: (952)545-6073

Burch, Kevin, V. Chmn. of the Bd.
Professional Truck Driver Institute
[3354]
555 E Braddock Rd.
Alexandria, VA 22314
Ph: (703)647-7015
Fax: (703)836-6610

Burch, Monte, President
National Association of Home and
Workshop Writers [2695]
PO Box 12
Baker, NV 89311
Toll Free: 866-457-2582

Burch, Peter, MD, President
International Wooden Bow Tie Club
[206]
5112 Ashlar Village
Wallingford, CT 06492
Ph: (203)265-3001

Burch, Ruth, Secretary, Treasurer
Karl Jaspers Society of North
America [10099]
c/o Helmut Wautischer
Dept. of Philosophy
Sonoma State University
1801 E Cotati Ave.
Rohnert Park, CA 94928
Ph: (707)664-2270
Fax: (707)644-4400

Burchard, Brenda, Exec. Dir.
Safer Society Foundation [11546]
PO Box 340
Brandon, VT 05733-0340
Ph: (802)247-3132
Fax: (802)247-4233

Burchard, Peter, President
United States Fencing Coaches Association [22835]
514 NW 164th St.
Edmond, OK 73013-2001

Burchell, Leigh, Chairperson
HIMSS Electronic Health Record
Association [15634]
33 W Monroe St., Ste. 1700
Chicago, IL 60603-5616
Ph: (312)664-4467
Fax: (312)664-6143

Burchfield, Larry A., PhD, CEO,
President, Founder
Radiochemistry Society [6212]
PO Box 3091
Richland, WA 99354
Ph: (509)460-7474

Burcroff, LeRoy, President
Power Transmission Distributors Association [1760]
230 W Monroe St., Ste. 1410
Chicago, IL 60606-4703
Ph: (312)516-2100
Fax: (312)516-2101

Burdelski, Vince, Chmn. of the Bd.
Marine Corps Interrogator Translator
Teams Association [19548]
1900 S Ocean Blvd., Apt. 14L
Pompano Beach, FL 33062-8030

Burden, Jeffry C., Cmdr.
Military Order of the Loyal Legion of
the United States [20743]
121 S Broad St., Ste. 1910
Philadelphia, PA 19107

Burden, Keith, Exec. Sec.
National Association of Free Will
Baptists [19734]
5233 Mount View Rd.
Antioch, TN 37013-2306
Ph: (615)731-6812
Toll Free: 877-767-7659
Fax: (615)731-0771

Burdick, Frederick, President
Thomas Minor Society [20901]
c/o Ray Howell, Secretary
38 West 1600 South
Orem, UT 84058

Burg, Ronald G., Exec. VP
American Concrete Institute [6344]
38800 Country Club Dr.
Farmington Hills, MI 48331-3439
Ph: (248)848-3700
Fax: (248)848-3701

Burge, Susan, President
Poodle Club of America [21945]

Burger, Lisa, President
Independent Arts and Media [8860]
PO Box 420442
San Francisco, CA 94142-0442
Ph: (415)738-4975

Burges, Eric, Founder
National Black Home Educators
[7996]
13434 Plank Rd.
Baker, LA 70714
Ph: (225)778-0169

Burgess, Angela, Exec. Dir.
International Imaging Industry Association [2583]
2001 L St., NW Ste. 700
Washington, DC 20036
Ph: (202)371-0101
Toll Free: 800-272-6657
Fax: (202)728-9614

Burgess, Angela R., Exec. Dir.
IEEE - Computer Society [6246]
2001 L St. NW, Ste. 700
Washington, DC 20036-4928
Ph: (202)371-0101
Toll Free: 800-678-4333
Fax: (202)728-9614

Burgess, Ruby, Ed.D, President
AHEAD-INC. [14922]
PO Box 2049
Rockville, MD 20847-2049
Ph: (301)530-3697
Fax: (301)530-3697

Burggraeve, Chris, President
Belgian American Chamber of Commerce [23564]
1177 Avenue of the Americas, 7th Fl.
New York, NY 10036
Ph: (212)541-0771

Burghart, Steven, PhD, President
College of Psychiatric and
Neurologic Pharmacists [16658]
8055 O St., Ste. S113
Lincoln, NE 68510
Ph: (402)476-1677
Fax: (888)551-7617

Burgman, Lynda, Founder, Exec. Dir.
Kindness in a Box [11063]
5955 Grayling View Ct.
Villa Ridge, MO 63089

Burgos, Dr. Nilda R., VP
International Weed Science Society
[3550]
c/o Dr. Nilda R. Burgos, Vice
President
Dept. of Crop, Soil, and
Environmental Sciences
University of Arkansas
1366 W Altheimer Dr.
Fayetteville, AR 72704
Ph: (479)575-3984
     (479)575-3955
Fax: (479)575-3975

Burgoyne, Paul J., President
National Organization of Bar
Counsel [5444]
275 N York St., Ste. 401
Elmhurst, IL 60126
Ph: (630)617-5153
     (215)560-6296

Burk, Brett J., Exec. Dir.
Society for Integrative and Comparative Biology [7403]
1313 Dolley Madison Blvd., Ste. 402
McLean, VA 22101
Ph: (703)790-1745
Toll Free: 800-955-1236
Fax: (703)790-2672

Burk, Brett, Exec. Dir.
Semiconductor Environmental,
Safety and Health Association
[6439]
1313 Dolley Madison Blvd., Ste. 402
McLean, VA 22101-3926
Ph: (703)790-1745
Fax: (703)790-2672

Burke, Amy Lestition
Special Libraries Association [9728]
7918 Jones Branch Dr., Ste. 300
McLean, VA 22102
Ph: (703)647-4900
Fax: (703)506-3266

Burke, Ed, VP
Federation of Metal Detector and
Archaeological Clubs [22151]
c/o Mark Schuessler, President
1464 Graft Rd.
Attica, NY 14011
Ph: (585)591-0010

Burke, John, PhD, President, CEO
Accreditation Association for
Ambulatory Health Care [13674]
5250 Old Orchard Rd., Ste. 200
Skokie, IL 60077-4461
Ph: (847)853-6060
Fax: (847)853-9028

Burke, John, President
Amateur Trapshooting Association
[23124]
1105 E Broadway
Sparta, IL 62286
Ph: (618)449-2224
Toll Free: 866-454-5198

Burke, Kathleen, President
Military Family and Veterans Service
  Organizations of America [21027]
1100 Larkspur Landing, Ste. 340
Larkspur, CA 94939
Ph: (415)925-2673
Fax: (415)925-2650

Burke, Kevin, Director
National Association for Court
  Management [5118]
National Center for State Courts
300 Newport Ave.
Williamsburg, VA 23185-4147
Ph: (757)259-1841
Toll Free: 800-616-6165
Fax: (757)259-1520

Burke, Kevin S., Treasurer
American Judges Association [5375]
300 Newport Ave.
Williamsburg, VA 23185-4147
Ph: (757)259-1841
Fax: (757)259-1520

Burke, Lon, President
International Shrine Clown Association [21602]
c/o Lon Burke, President
19859 Country Road 200 E
Dahlgren, IL 62828
Ph: (618)736-2763

Burke, Margaret Barton, PhD, RN,
  FAAN, President
Oncology Nursing Society [16174]
125 Enterprise Dr.
Pittsburgh, PA 15275
Ph: (412)859-6100
Toll Free: 877-369-5497
Fax: (412)859-6162

Burke, Mary, Mgr.
American Conference for Irish Stud-
  ies [9597]
Theatre and Drama Dept.
University of Wisconsin-Madison
821 University Ave., 6192 Vilas Hall
Madison, WI 53706-1497
Ph: (212)180-3590

Burke, Nancy M., VP
Direct Selling Association [3010]
1667 K St. NW, Ste. 1100
Washington, DC 20006
Ph: (202)452-8866
Fax: (202)452-9010

Burke, Thomas, Chairman
International Association of Drilling
  Contractors [2525]
10370 Richmond Ave., Ste. 760
Houston, TX 77042
Ph: (713)292-1945
Fax: (713)292-1946

Burke, Thomas J., President
Irish American Unity Conference
  [18580]
PO Box 55573
Washington, DC 20040
Toll Free: 888-295-5077

Burkes, Ted, Secretary
American Board of Forensic Docu-
  ment Examiners [5234]
7887 San Felipe St., Ste. 122
Houston, TX 77063
Ph: (713)784-9537
Fax: (713)784-3985

Burkey, Bob, President
Hoist Manufacturers Institute [1733]
c/o MHI
8720 Red Oak Blvd., Ste. 201
Charlotte, NC 28217-3996
Ph: (704)676-1190
Fax: (704)676-1199

Burkgren, Dr. Tom, Exec. Dir.
American Association of Swine
  Veterinarians [17601]
830 26th St.
Perry, IA 50220
Ph: (515)465-5255
Fax: (515)465-3832

Burkhart, Janice, Librarian, President
American-French Genealogical
  Society [20953]
78 Earle St.
Woonsocket, RI 02895
Ph: (401)765-6141
Fax: (401)597-6290

Burleigh, William R., Chmn. of the
  Bd.
Ethics and Public Policy Center
  [18975]
1730 M St. NW, Ste. 910
Washington, DC 20036
Ph: (202)682-1200
Fax: (202)408-0632

Burlingame, Kevin, Chairman
Tile Roofing Institute [592]
2150 N 107th St., Ste. 205
Seattle, WA 98133
Ph: (206)209-5300

Burlison, Angie, Exec. Dir.,
  Secretary, Treasurer
Retail Confectioners International
  [1371]
2053 S Waverly, Ste. C
Springfield, MO 65804
Toll Free: 800-545-5381

Burnell, Craig, Treasurer
International Thunderbird Class As-
  sociation [22641]
PO Box 1033
Mercer Island, WA 98040

Burnett, Joan, Chairman
National Corvette Restorers Society
  [21451]
6291 Day Rd.
Cincinnati, OH 45252-1334
Ph: (513)385-8526
    (513)385-6367
Fax: (513)385-8554

Burnett, Michael J., Secretary
CPA Associates International [23]
Meadows Office Complex
301 Route 17
Rutherford, NJ 07070
Ph: (201)804-8686
Fax: (201)804-9222

Burnett, Nancy A., Program Mgr.
International Panel on Fissile Materi-
  als [18749]
Princeton University
221 Nassau St., 2nd Fl.
Princeton, NJ 08542
Ph: (609)258-4677
Fax: (609)258-3661

Burnett, Pat, Jr., President
World Watusi Association [3759]
PO Box 201
Walnut Springs, TX 76690
Ph: (254)797-3032

Burnham, Gracia, Rep.
New Tribes Mission [20446]
1000 E 1st St.
Sanford, FL 32771-1441
Ph: (407)323-3430

Burnham, Linda Frye, Director, Edi-
  tor
Art in the Public Interest [8958]
NC

Burnham, Margaret, Co-Chmn. of
  the Bd.
National Center of Afro-American
  Artists [8786]

300 Walnut Ave.
Roxbury, MA 02119
Ph: (617)442-8614

Burns, Bill, CAE
Association for Play Therapy
  [17438]
401 Clovis Ave., Ste. 107
Clovis, CA 93612
Ph: (559)298-3400
Fax: (559)238-3410

Burns, Duncan, VP
Internet Corporation for Assigned
  Names and Numbers [6321]
12025 Waterfront Dr., Ste. 300
Los Angeles, CA 90094-2536
Ph: (310)301-5800
Fax: (310)823-8649

Burns, Gary, President
National Association of Container
  Distributors [838]
800 Roosevelt Rd., Bldg. C-312
Glen Ellyn, IL 60137
Ph: (630)942-6585
Fax: (630)790-3095

Burns, Gina, President
Group B Strep Association [14192]
PO Box 16515
Chapel Hill, NC 27516

Burns, Jordan, President
Children's Humanitarian International
  [10929]
PO Box 1735
Sebastopol, CA 95473
Ph: (707)596-8398

Burns, Mike, President
College Gymnastics Association
  [22900]
306 Cooke Hall
1900 University Ave. SE
Minneapolis, MN 55455
Ph: (612)625-9567
Fax: (612)626-9922

Burow, Kirsty, Dir. of Comm.
Women's Funding Network [13408]
156 2nd St.
San Francisco, CA 94105
Ph: (415)441-0706
Fax: (415)441-0827

Burrell, Douglas K., Director
Defense Research Institute [5559]
55 W Monroe St., Ste. 2000
Chicago, IL 60603
Ph: (312)795-1101
    (312)698-6218
Fax: (312)795-0749

Burrell, Tony, President
National Black State Troopers Coali-
  tion [5496]
PO Box 18192
Milwaukee, WI 53218

Burroughs, Frank, Founder
Abigail Alliance [13868]
8881 White Orchid Pl.
Lorton, VA 22079
Ph: (703)646-5306

Burroughs, John, Exec. Dir.
Lawyers Committee on Nuclear
  Policy [18751]
866 UN Plz., Ste. 4050
New York, NY 10017-1830
Ph: (212)818-1861
Fax: (212)818-1857

Burrow, Gayle, President
American Correctional Health
  Services Association [15133]

Burrow, Ian, VP of Government Rel.
American Cultural Resources Association [8951]

2101 L St. NW, Ste. 800
Washington, DC 20037
Ph: (202)367-9094
Toll Free: 866-875-6492

Burrows, Barbara, Director
North American Wensleydale Sheep
  Association [4680]
4589 Fruitland Rd.
Marysville, CA 95901
Ph: (530)743-5262

Burrows, Roberta, Exec. Dir.
Institute of Environmental Sciences
  and Technology [7093]
2340 S Arlington Heights Rd., Ste.
  620
Arlington Heights, IL 60005-4510
Ph: (847)981-0100
Fax: (847)981-4130

Burstein, Mark, Chairman
Lewis Carroll Society of North
  America [9074]
11935 Beltsville Dr.
Beltsville, MD 20705

Burt, Lindsay, MD, Chairperson
Association of Residents in Radia-
  tion Oncology [16339]
8280 Willow Oaks Corporate Dr.,
  Ste. 500
Fairfax, VA 22031
Ph: (703)502-1550
Toll Free: 800-962-7876
Fax: (703)502-7852

Burton, Chris, President
New England Trail Rider Association
  [23328]
PO Box 1235
Derry, NH 03038
Ph: (508)306-1410

Burton, Debby, Exec. Dir.
National Podiatric Medical Associa-
  tion [16791]
1706 E 87th St.
Chicago, IL 60617
Ph: (773)374-5300
Fax: (773)374-5860

Burton, Edward, CEO, President
U.S.-Saudi Arabian Business Council
  [2004]
8081 Wolftrap Rd., Ste. 300
Vienna, VA 22182
Ph: (703)962-9300
Toll Free: 888-638-1212
Fax: (703)204-0332

Burton, LaVarne A., CEO, President
American Kidney Fund [15870]
11921 Rockville Pke., Ste. 300
Rockville, MD 20852
Ph: (301)984-5055
Toll Free: 800-638-8299

Burton, Paula, Chmn. of the Bd.,
  Founder
Celebration U.S.A. [8444]
18482 Valley Dr.
Villa Park, CA 92861-2849
Ph: (714)974-3691
Fax: (714)974-3691

Burton, Tim, President
National Council for Print Industry
  Certifications [1543]
W232 N2950 Roundy Cir. E, Ste.
  200
Pewaukee, WI 53072
Ph: (262)522-2215

Burwell, Tod, President, CEO
Banker Association for Foreign and
  Trade [387]
1120 Connecticut Ave. NW

Washington, DC 20036
Ph: (202)663-7575
Fax: (202)663-5538

Burzynski, Cherri, RN, President
National Association of Long Term
Hospitals [15333]
342 N Main St.
West Hartford, CT 06117-2507
Ph: (860)586-7579

Busby, Mr. Dan, President
Evangelical Council for Financial Ac-
countability [20138]
440 W Jubal Early Dr., Ste. 100
Winchester, VA 22601-6319
Ph: (540)535-0103
Toll Free: 800-323-9473
Fax: (540)535-0533

Busby-Whitehead, Jan, MD, Chair-
man
Association of Directors of Geriatric
Academic Programs [14889]
American Geriatrics Society
40 Fulton St., 18th Fl.
New York, NY 10038
Ph: (212)308-1414
Fax: (212)832-8646

Busch, Virginia, Exec. Dir.
Endangered Wolf Center [4814]
PO Box 760
Eureka, MO 63025
Ph: (636)938-5900
Fax: (636)938-6490

Bush, Barbara, Founder
Barbara Bush Foundation for Family
Literacy [8236]
516 N Adams St.
Tallahassee, FL 32301
Ph: (850)562-5300

Bush, Barbara, Founder, CEO
Global Health Corps [15454]
5 Penn Plz., 3rd Fl.
New York, NY 10001

Bush, Colleen, Exec. Dir.
Phi Sigma Rho [23741]
PO Box 58304
Cincinnati, OH 45258

Bush, Douglas M., Bd. Member
U.S. National Oral Health Alliance
[14473]
465 Medford St.
Boston, MA 02129

Bush, Milton, CEO
American Council of Independent
Laboratories [6775]
1875 I St. NW, Ste. 500
Washington, DC 20006
Ph: (202)887-5872
Fax: (202)887-0021

Bush, Milton, CEO
Independent Laboratories Institute
[6778]
1875 I St. NW, Ste. 500
Washington, DC 20006
Ph: (202)887-5872
Fax: (202)887-0021

Bush, Milton, Exec. Dir.
International Federation of Inspec-
tion Agencies - Americas Commit-
tee, Inc. [1818]
1600 N Oak St., No. 1710
Arlington, VA 22209
Ph: (703)528-2737
Fax: (703)533-1612

Bush, Robert D., Secretary
National Association of Hispanic
Publications, Inc. [2803]

National Press Bldg.
529 14th St. NW, Ste. 923
Washington, DC 20045
Ph: (202)662-7250

Bush, Shery, President
Southwest Celtic Music Association
[9150]
2528 Elm St., Ste. B
Dallas, TX 75226-1472
Ph: (214)821-4173

Bushey, Wayne, Founder
National Nostalgic Nova [21458]
PO Box 29177
York, PA 17402-0109
Ph: (717)252-4192
(717)252-2383
Fax: (717)252-1666

Bushkie, Scott, Chmn. of the Bd.
International Business Brokers As-
sociation, Inc. [2865]
7100 E Pleasant Valley Rd., Ste.
160
Independence, OH 44131
Toll Free: 888-686-4222
Fax: (800)630-2380

Bushnell, Rick, Contact
Integrated Business Communica-
tions Alliance [274]
81 Cottage St.
Doylestown, PA 18901
Ph: (215)489-1722

Bushnell, Tom, Director
National Challenged Homeschoolers
Associated Network [7997]
PO Box 310
Moyie Springs, ID 83845
Ph: (208)267-6246
Toll Free: 800-266-9837

Bushnik, Tamara, PhD. FACRM,
Contact
American Congress of Rehabilitation
Medicine [17079]
11654 Plaza America Dr., Ste. 535
Reston, VA 20190-4700
Ph: (703)435-5335
Fax: (866)692-1619

Busiek, Pam, President, CEO
Independent Cosmetic Manufactur-
ers and Distributors [919]
21925 W Field Pky., Ste. 205
Deer Park, IL 60010
Toll Free: 800-334-2623
Fax: (847)991-8161

Buskirk, George A., Treasurer
National American Legion Press Association [20689]
3 Morton St.
Norwood, NY 13668-1100

Busler, Sam, Treasurer
UHL Collectors Society [21729]
398 S Star Dr.
Santa Claus, IN 47579
Ph: (812)544-2987

Buss, James Joseph, Secretary
American Society for Ethnohistory
[9289]
c/o James Joseph Buss, Secretary
1101 Camden Ave.
Salisbury, MD 21801
Ph: (410)546-6902

Bussey, Stuart A., President
Union of American Physicians and
Dentists [23445]
180 Grand Ave., Ste. 1380
Oakland, CA 94612
Ph: (510)839-0193
Toll Free: 800-622-0909
Fax: (510)763-8756

Bussey, Tadson, Exec. Dir.
University and College Designers
Association [8037]
199 Enon Springs Rd. W, Ste. 400
Smyrna, TN 37167
Ph: (615)459-4559
Fax: (615)459-5229

Butash, Mike, President
Circus Model Builders International
[22197]
c/o Armando Ortiz, Membership
Secretary
1649 Park Ave.
Hanover Park, IL 60133-3610

Butcher, Sherry, President
United States Parachute Association
[23057]
5401 Southpoint Centre Blvd.
Fredericksburg, VA 22407
Ph: (540)604-9740
Fax: (540)604-9741

Butera, Michael A., CEO, Exec. Dir.
National Association for Music
Education [8380]
1806 Robert Fulton Dr.
Reston, VA 20191
Ph: (703)860-4000
Toll Free: 800-336-3768

Buthidi, Willie, President
Help Congo Network [12672]
PO Box 650
Wheaton, IL 60187

Buthker, Bonnie, President
Association of State and Territorial
Solid Waste Management Officials
[5844]
1101 17th St. NW, Ste. 707
Washington, DC 20036
Ph: (202)640-1060
Fax: (202)331-3254

Butin, Danielle, MPH, Exec. Dir.
Afya Foundation [15596]
140 Saw Mill River Rd.
Yonkers, NY 10701
Ph: (914)920-5081
Fax: (914)920-5082

Butler, Anne, Receptionist
Garden Club of America [22094]
14 E 60th St., 3rd Fl.
New York, NY 10022
Ph: (212)753-8287
Fax: (212)753-0134

Butler, Charles E., President
The Plastic Surgery Foundation
[14320]
444 E Algonquin Rd.
Arlington Heights, IL 60005-4664
Ph: (847)228-9900
Toll Free: 800-766-4955

Butler, Cindy, VP
Craniofacial Foundation of America
[14332]
975 E 3rd St.
Chattanooga, TN 37403
Ph: (423)778-9176
Toll Free: 800-418-3223
Fax: (423)778-8172

Butler, Cindy, Exec. Dir.
Unmarried Equality [12260]
7149 Rivol Rd.
West Hills, CA 91307
Ph: (347)987-1068

Butler, Craig D., Exec. Dir.
Cooley's Anemia Foundation Inc.
[15229]
330 7th Ave., No. 200
New York, NY 10001
Ph: (212)279-8090

Butler, David L., PhD, Exec. Dir.
National Association of Call Centers
[772]
100 S 22nd Ave.
Hattiesburg, MS 39401
Ph: (480)922-5949
(601)447-8300

Butler, David, Dir. of Fin. & Admin.
National Steinbeck Center [9085]
1 Main St.
Salinas, CA 93901
Ph: (831)775-4721
Fax: (831)796-3828

Butler, David P., Treasurer, Director
Safe Haven Project [10552]
6 University Dr., Ste. 206-181
Amherst, MA 01002-3820
Ph: (252)295-9073

Butler, Edward, Chmn. of the Bd.
AirFuel Alliance [7051]
3855 SW 153rd Dr.
Beaverton, OR 97003
Ph: (503)619-0666
Fax: (503)644-6708

Butler, Erik, Chmn. of the Bd.
National Child Labor Committee
[13465]
1501 Broadway, Ste. 1908
New York, NY 10036-5600
Ph: (212)840-1801
Fax: (212)768-0963

Butler, Gaines, President
Amusement & Music Operators As-
sociation [1133]
600 Spring Hill Ring Rd., Ste. 111
West Dundee, IL 60118
Ph: (847)428-7699
Toll Free: 800-937-2662
Fax: (847)428-7719

Butler, Grace L., PhD, Founder,
Chmn. of the Bd.
Hope Through Grace [13982]
4660 Beechnut St., Ste. 102
Houston, TX 77096
Ph: (713)668-4673
Fax: (713)668-6040

Butler, Jon, Exec. Dir.
Pop Warner Little Scholars, Inc.
[22864]
586 Middletown Blvd., Ste. C-100
Langhorne, PA 19047-1867
Ph: (215)752-2691
Fax: (215)752-2879

Butler, Kathleen, Exec. Dir.
American Society of Notaries [5655]
PO Box 5707
Tallahassee, FL 32314-5707
Ph: (850)671-5164
Fax: (850)671-5165

Butler, Lisa, Exec. Dir.
Guillain-Barre Syndrome/Chronic
Inflammatory Demyelinating Poly-
neuropathy Foundation
International [15938]
The Holly Bldg.
104 1/2 Forrest Ave.
Narberth, PA 19072
Ph: (610)667-0131
Toll Free: 866-224-3301
Fax: (610)667-7036

Butler, Malcolm, President
Association for Science Teacher
Education [8643]
c/o Dr. Bob Hollon, Executive Direc-
tor
9324 27th Ave.
Eau Claire, WI 54703
Ph: (715)838-0893
Fax: (715)838-0893

Butler, Patrick, President, CEO
Association of Public Television Sta-
tions [455]
2100 Crystal Dr., Ste. 700
Arlington, VA 22202
Ph: (202)654-4200
Fax: (202)654-4236

Butler, Scott, President
Neurosurgery Executives' Resource
Value and Education Society
[16066]
1300 Baxter St., Ste. 360
Charlotte, NC 28204
Ph: (704)940-7386
Fax: (704)365-3678

Butler, Sean, Chairperson
International Criminal Court Alliance
[5149]
11835 W Olympic Blvd., Ste. 1090
Los Angeles, CA 90064
Ph: (310)473-0777

Butler, Susan, Contact
Society of the Companions of the
Holy Cross [20115]
Adelynrood Retreat & Conference
Ctr.
46 Elm St.
Byfield, MA 01922-2812

Butlin, Jennifer, Exec. Dir.
Commission on Collegiate Nursing
Education [8318]
1 Dupont Cir. NW, Ste. 530
Washington, DC 20036
Ph: (202)887-6791
Fax: (202)887-8476

Butman, Rabbi Shmuel M., Director
Lubavitch Youth Organization
[20264]
770 Eastern Pky.
Brooklyn, NY 11213-3409
Ph: (718)953-1000
Fax: (718)771-6315

Butterfield, G. K., Chairman
Congressional Black Caucus
[18012]
2305 Rayburn House Office Bldg.
Washington, DC 20515
Ph: (202)226-9776

Butterfield, Jason, President,
Founder
Afflicted War Heroes [20764]
PO Box 95794
South Jordan, UT 84095

Butterworth, Prof. Charles E.,
Secretary
American Academy for Liberal
Education [8225]
1200 G St. NW, Ste. 883
Washington, DC 20005
Ph: (202)434-8971

Buttfield, Dr. Ian, Chairman
International Association for Pain
and Chemical Dependency
[16557]
101 Washington St.
Morrisville, PA 19067-7111
Fax: (215)337-0959

Butts, Ryan, Officer
Registry of Interpreters for the Deaf,
Inc. [15208]
333 Commerce St.
Alexandria, VA 22314
Ph: (703)838-0030
Fax: (703)838-0454

Buxton, Robert, President
International Harvester Collectors
[22455]

c/o Emmett Webb, Membership
Chairperson
PO Box 35
Dublin, IN 47335-0035
Ph: (765)478-6179

Buzby, Mark, President, COO
National Defense Transportation As-
sociation [5608]
50 S Pickett St., Ste. 220
Alexandria, VA 22304-7296
Ph: (703)751-5011
Fax: (703)823-8761

Byard, Eliza, PhD, Exec. Dir.
Gay, Lesbian, and Straight Educa-
tion Network [11885]
110 William St., 30th Fl.
New York, NY 10003
Ph: (212)727-0135

Bybee, David B., CPA, CEO,
President
National Association of Certified
Public Bookkeepers [45]
238 North 300 West, Ste. 504
Kaysville, UT 84037
Toll Free: 866-444-9989
Fax: (801)451-4688

Bycel, Josh, Founder, Exec. Dir.
OneKid OneWorld [11108]
1109 S Clark Dr.
Los Angeles, CA 90035
Ph: (323)806-9294

Byer, Barbara, Exec. Dir.
ALS Worldwide [13681]
5808 Dawley Dr
Madison, WI 53711-7209
Ph: (608)663-0920

Byerley, Patti, President
American Harlequin Rabbit Club
[4589]
c/o Pamela Granderson, Secretary/
Treasurer
14991 Opera Rd.
Leopold, IN 47551

Byerman, Keith, President
African American Literature and
Culture Society [9747]
Indiana State University
English and Women's Studies
200 N 7th St.
Terre Haute, IN 47809

Byers, Gail, Dept. Mgr.
International Institute of Reflexology,
Inc. [17450]
5650 1st Ave. N
Saint Petersburg, FL 33710
Ph: (727)343-4811
Fax: (727)381-2807

Byers, Onnie, Dr., Chairman
Conservation Breeding Specialist
Group [3836]
12101 Johnny Cake Ridge Rd.
Apple Valley, MN 55124-8151
Ph: (952)997-9800
Fax: (952)997-9803

Byfield, Margaret H., Exec. Dir.
American Stewards of Liberty
[18929]
624 S Austin Ave., Ste. 101
Georgetown, TX 78626
Ph: (512)591-7843
Fax: (512)365-7931

Byk, Prof. Christian, Sec. Gen.
International Association of Law, Ethics and Science [5428]
c/o American University of Sovereign
Nations
8840 E Chaparral Rd., Ste. 285

Scottsdale, AZ 85250-2611
Ph: (602)396-5788

Byler, J. Ron, Exec. Dir.
Mennonite Central Committee
[20327]
21 S 12th St.
Akron, PA 17501-0500
Ph: (717)859-1151
Toll Free: 888-563-4676

Byrd, John, Mgr.
Management Association for Private
Photogrammetric Surveyors [7019]
1856 Old Reston Ave., Ste. 205
Reston, VA 20190
Ph: (703)787-6996
Fax: (703)787-7550

Byrne, Jeffrey, Chairman
Giving U.S.A. Foundation [12477]
225 W Wacker Dr., Ste. 650
Chicago, IL 60606
Ph: (312)981-6794

Byrne, Peter, Founder
International Wildlife Conservation
Society [4833]
PO Box 34
Pacific Palisades, CA 90272
Ph: (310)476-9305

Byrne, Thomas J., President
The Korea Society [23648]
950 3rd Ave., 8th Fl.
New York, NY 10022
Ph: (212)759-7525
Fax: (212)759-7530

Byrnes, Betty, Contact
Consumer Data Industry Association
[1228]
1090 Vermont Ave. NW, Ste. 200
Washington, DC 20005-4905
Ph: (202)371-0910
Fax: (202)371-0134

Bystricky, Bill, Exec. Dir.
National Youth Rights Association
[19276]
PO Box 516
Rockville, MD 20848-0516
Ph: (301)738-6769

C

C., Bill, Founder
Crystal Meth Anonymous [11716]
4470 W Sunset Blvd., Ste. 107
Los Angeles, CA 90027
Toll Free: 855-638-4373

Caballero, Axel, Exec. Dir.
National Association of Latino
Independent Producers [1201]
3415 S Sepulveda Blvd., Ste. 1100
Los Angeles, CA 90034
Ph: (310)470-1061
Fax: (310)470-1091

Caballero, Jeffrey B., Exec. Dir.
Association of Asian Pacific Com-
munity Health Organizations
[15137]
101 Callan Ave., Ste. 400
San Leandro, CA 94577
Ph: (510)272-9536
Fax: (510)272-0817

Caballero, Ma. Cristina C., CEO,
President
Dialogue on Diversity [8346]
1629 K St. NW, Ste. 300
Washington, DC 20006
Ph: (703)631-0650
Fax: (703)631-0617

Cabañas, Alex, President
International Association of Conference Centres [2320]

35 E Wacker Dr., Ste. 850
Chicago, IL 60601-2106
Ph: (312)224-2580
Fax: (312)644-8557

Cabasso, Jacqueline, Exec. Dir.
Western States Legal Foundation
[5657]
c/o Jacqueline Cabasso, Executive
Director
Preservation Pk.
655 13th St., Ste. 201
Oakland, CA 94612
Ph: (510)839-5877
Fax: (510)839-5397

Cable, Nancy J., PhD, President
Arthur Vining Davis Foundations
[11725]
225 Water St., Ste. 1510
Jacksonville, FL 32202-5185
Ph: (904)359-0670
Fax: (904)359-0675

Cable, Susan, Program Mgr.
Public Technology Institute [5700]
1420 Prince St., Ste. 200
Alexandria, VA 22314
Ph: (202)626-2400

Cabo, Ralph, Treasurer
Association of Retired Hispanic
Police, Inc. [5456]
PO Box 722
Tallman, NY 10982-0722
Ph: (845)521-4716

Cabral, Samuel A., President
International Union of Police As-
sociations [23471]
1549 Ringling Blvd., Ste. 600
Sarasota, FL 34236
Toll Free: 800-247-4872
Fax: (941)487-2570

Cabrera, Ana, Officer
Pueblo a Pueblo [17992]
PO Box 303
Neenah, WI 54957-0303
Ph: (920)209-0488

Cabrera, Cynthia, President
Smoke Free Alternatives Trade As-
sociation [3131]
1155 F St. NW, Ste. 1050
Washington, DC 20004
Ph: (202)251-1661

Cabrera, Jessica, Contact
Tropical Flowering Tree Society
[4442]
Fairchild Tropical Botanical Garden
10901 Old Cutler Rd.
Coral Gables, FL 33156

Cabrera, John P., Contact
Philippine American Chamber of
Commerce [23613]
Washington, DC

Cabrera, Marcelo, President
Amateur Astronomers Association
[5995]
PO Box 150253
Brooklyn, NY 11215
Ph: (212)535-2922

Caccamo, Paul, Founder, CEO
Up2Us [13486]
520 8th Ave., 2nd Fl.
New York, NY 10018
Ph: (212)563-3031
    (212)563-4046

Caccavale, John, PhD, Exec. Dir.
National Alliance of Professional
Psychology Providers [16926]
PO Box 6263

Garden Grove, CA 92846

Cacchione, Robert, Exec. Dir.
Intercollegiate Horse Shows Association [22943]
c/o Eddie Federswich, Director
Savannah College of Art & Design
342 Bull St.
Savannah, GA 31402
Ph: (315)682-1933
Fax: (315)682-9416

Cacciatore, Dr. Joanne, Founder,
President
Amazon Conservation Association
[3796]
1012 14th St. NW, Ste. 625
Washington, DC 20005
Ph: (202)234-2356
    (202)234-2357
Fax: (202)234-2358

Cacciatore, Marianna, Exec. Dir.
Bread for the Journey International
[12463]
101 Coronado Ln., Ste. 732
Santa Fe, NM 87505

Cade, Dale, Secretary
Civil War Token Society [22264]

Cader, Naushard, Exec. Dir.
Child Literacy [10901]
201 N Charles St., Ste. 2406
Baltimore, MD 21201
Ph: (212)531-1111

Cades, Stewart R., Treasurer
Conservation Center for Art and
Historic Artifacts [8852]
264 S 23rd St.
Philadelphia, PA 19103
Ph: (215)545-0613
Fax: (215)735-9313

Cadet, Dr. Joseph Pierre-Paul,
Contact
Association of Haitian Physicians
Abroad [15714]
1166 Eastern Pky.
Brooklyn, NY 11213
Ph: (718)245-1015
Fax: (718)735-8015

Cadle, Chuck, CEO
Destination ImagiNation [8410]
1111 S Union Ave.
Cherry Hill, NJ 08002
Toll Free: 888-321-1503
Fax: (856)881-3596

Cadorette, David, President
Military Vehicle Preservation Association [22183]
3305 Blue Ridge Cutoff
Independence, MO 64055
Ph: (816)833-6872
Toll Free: 800-365-5798
Fax: (816)833-5115

Cadwallader, Ken, President
Oil Painters of America [8936]
PO Box 2488
Crystal Lake, IL 60039-2488
Ph: (815)356-5987
Fax: (815)356-5987

Cadwell, Steve, Exec. Dir.
Academy of Integrative Health and
Medicine [15260]
5313 Colorado St.
Duluth, MN 55804
Ph: (218)525-5651
Fax: (218)525-5651

Cady, Barb, President
TOPS Club Inc. [12399]
4575 S Fifth St.

Milwaukee, WI 53207-0360
Ph: (414)482-4620
Toll Free: 800-932-8677
Fax: (414)482-1655

Cafaro, Kit, President
Fire and Emergency Manufacturers
and Services Association [14694]
PO Box 147
Lynnfield, MA 01940-0147
Ph: (781)334-2771
Fax: (781)334-2771

Caftel, Brad, Chief Legal Ofc.
Insight Center for Community
Economic Development [18150]
1999 Harrison St., Ste. 1800
Oakland, CA 94612-4700
Ph: (510)251-2600
Fax: (510)251-0600

Cage, Patrick, Director
Tropical Forest Group [3959]
1125 Fort Stockton Dr.
San Diego, CA 92103

Caggiano, Lee, Exec. Dir., Founder
Friends: The National Association of
Young People Who Stutter [17240]
38 S Oyster Bay Rd.
Syosset, NY 11791
Toll Free: 866-866-8335

Cagigas, Xavier E., Ph.D., President
Hispanic Neuropsychological Society
[16015]
151 E 31st St., No. 22C
New York, NY 10016

Cahill, George F., Chairman
Patriotic Education Inc. [7616]
107 Heritage Ln.
Madison, AL 35758-7974
Ph: (256)461-0612
Toll Free: 800-248-1787

Cahill, Maureen, Exec. Dir.
Smile Network International [14345]
PO Box 3986
Minneapolis, MN 55403
Ph: (612)377-1800

Cahn, Edgar, Founder, CEO, Chmn.
of the Bd.
TimeBanks USA [13219]
5500 39th St. NW
Washington, DC 20015
Ph: (202)686-5200
Fax: (202)537-5033

Caicedo-Selinger, Juana, President
Ecuadorean American Association
[19424]
641 Lexington Ave., Ste. 1430
New York, NY 10022
Ph: (212)233-7776

Cailteux, Scott, President
American Milking Shorthorn Junior
Society [3703]
800 Pleasant St.
Beloit, WI 53511
Ph: (608)365-3332
Fax: (608)365-6644

Cain, Amy, VP
American Buckskin Registry Association [4300]
320 S Boston Ave., Ste. 808
Tulsa, OK 74103
Ph: (918)936-4707

Cain, Andrew, President
United States Bowling Congress
[22709]
621 Six Flags Dr.
Arlington, TX 76011
Toll Free: 800-514-2695

Cain, Doug, President
Coin Operated Collectors Association [21638]
4804 Clubview Ct.
Fuquay Varina, NC 27526-8681
Ph: (330)837-2265
    (419)350-0477

Cain, John, Director
United States Fastpitch Association
[23207]
7814 Laird St.
Panama City Beach, FL 32408
Ph: (850)234-2839

Cain, Linda, VP
Valley Fig Growers [4259]
2028 S 3rd St.
Fresno, CA 93702
Ph: (559)237-3893
Fax: (559)237-3898

Caine, Christine, Founder
The A21 Campaign [12021]
427 E 17th St., No. F223
Costa Mesa, CA 92627
Ph: (949)202-4681
Fax: (949)612-0827

Caine, Nancy, Sec. Gen.
International Primatological Society
[5914]
c/o Steve Schapiro, Treasurer
650 Cool Water Dr.
Bastrop, TX 78602
Ph: (512)321-3991
Fax: (512)332-5208

Calabrese, Denise, Exec. Dir.
Association of Professional
Landscape Designers [2067]
2207 Forest Hills Dr.
Harrisburg, PA 17112
Ph: (717)238-9780
Fax: (717)238-9985

Calabrese, Denise, Exec. Dir.
Perlite Institute [2388]
2207 Forest Hills Dr.
Harrisburg, PA 17112
Ph: (717)238-9723

Calambokidis, Joan Baggett,
President
International Masonry Institute [871]
17101 Science Dr.
Bowie, MD 20715
Ph: (301)291-2124
Toll Free: 800-803-0295

Calamia, Maureen, Secretary
International Feng Shui Guild [9278]
705 B SE Melody Ln., Ste. 166
Lees Summit, MO 64063
Ph: (816)246-1898

Calandra, Frank, Secretary
The Photographic Historical Society
[10144]
PO Box 10342
Rochester, NY 14610
Ph: (585)475-2411

Calcinardi, Fulvio, Exec. Dir.
Italian-American Chamber of Commerce [23596]
500 N Michigan Ave., Ste. 506
Chicago, IL 60611

Caldara, Jon, President
Independence Institute [17901]
727 E 16th Ave.
Denver, CO 80203
Ph: (303)279-6536
Fax: (303)279-4176

Calderon, Vicente, Founder
National Latino Peace Officers Association [19530]

PO Box 23116
Santa Ana, CA 92711
Ph: (702)204-6383

Caldicott, Helen, President, Founder
Beyond Nuclear [18742]
6930 Carroll Ave., Ste. 400
Takoma Park, MD 20912
Ph: (301)270-2209
Fax: (301)270-4000

Caldwell, Chris, Dir. of Comm., Dir.
of Mktg.
International Foodservice Distributors Association [1391]
1410 Spring Hill Rd., Ste. 210
McLean, VA 22102
Ph: (703)532-9400
Fax: (703)538-4673

Caldwell, Clarke A., CEO, President
Harmony Foundation International
[9917]
110 7th Ave. N, Ste. 200
Nashville, TN 37203
Ph: (615)823-5611
Toll Free: 866-706-8021
Fax: (615)823-5612

Caldwell, Dodd, President
Rice Bowls [12109]
951 S Pine St., Ste. 252
Spartanburg, SC 29302
Toll Free: 866-312-5791

Caldwell, John S., Jr., President
Cause - Comfort for America's
Uniformed Services [10739]
4114 Legato Rd., Ste. B
Fairfax, VA 22033-4002
Ph: (703)591-4965

Caldwell, Larry, President
Association of Professors of Mission
[20385]
University of Northwestern
3003 Snelling Ave. N
Saint Paul, MN 55113
Ph: (651)631-5229
Fax: (651)628-3258

Caldwell, Rob, President
American Polocrosse Association
[22774]
PO Box 158
Bonneau, SC 29431-0158
Ph: (843)825-2686

Cale, Erica, Founder
Helping Hearts Helping Hands
[12544]
6250 Chinn Ct.
Holly, MI 48442
Ph: (248)980-5090
    (248)830-6871

Calhoon, John H., MD, President
Thoracic Surgery Foundation for
Research and Education [17477]
633 N St. Clair St., 23rd Fl.
Chicago, IL 60611
Ph: (312)202-5868
Fax: (773)289-0871

Calhoun, David R., President
Association of Theatrical Press
Agents and Managers [23494]
14 Penn Plz., Ste. 1703
225 W 34th St.
New York, NY 10122
Ph: (212)719-3666
Fax: (212)302-1585

Calhoun, Glen, COO
International Association for
Identification [5247]
2131 Hollywood Blvd., Ste. 403
Hollywood, FL 33020
Ph: (954)589-0628
Fax: (954)589-0657

Cali, Francisco, President
International Indian Treaty Council
[18474]
2940 16th St., Ste. 305
San Francisco, CA 94103-3664
Ph: (415)641-4482
Fax: (415)641-1298

Caliari, Aldo, Director
Center of Concern [18382]
1225 Otis St. NE
Washington, DC 20017
Ph: (202)635-2757
Fax: (202)832-9494

Calica, Carl, MD, President
Society of Philippine Surgeons in
America, Inc. [17404]
c/o Edward E. Quiros, MD, Website
Editor
PO Box 5284
Borger, TX 79008

Calico, Marla, President, CEO
International Association of Fairs and
Expositions [2331]
3043 E Cairo St.
Springfield, MO 65802-6204
Ph: (417)862-5771
Toll Free: 800-516-0313

Caligiuri, Dr. Michael A., President
Society for Natural Immunity [15386]
c/o Dr. Michael A. Caligiuri,
President
Ohio State University
460 W 10th Ave.
Columbus, OH 43210

Calio, Nicholas E., CEO, President
Airlines for America [125]
Communications Dept.
1301 Pennsylvania Ave. NW, Ste.
1100
Washington, DC 20004-7017
Ph: (202)626-4000

Calixte, Mr. Jacques Albert,
President
Haitian American Association Against
Cancer, Inc. [13980]
225 NE 34th St., Ste. 208
Miami, FL 33137-3800
Ph: (305)572-1825
Fax: (305)572-1827

Call, Jerry, CEO
American Foundry Society [8659]
1695 N Penny Ln.
Schaumburg, IL 60173
Ph: (847)824-0181
Toll Free: 800-537-4237
Fax: (847)824-7848

Call, Kathy, Exec. Dir., Founder
China Connection [12146]
458 S Pasadena Ave.
Pasadena, CA 91105-1838
Ph: (626)793-3737
Fax: (626)793-3362

Callaham, William C., President
American Board of Professional Li-
ability Attorneys [5558]
4355 Cobb Pky., Ste. J-208
Atlanta, GA 30339
Ph: (404)919-4009
Fax: (866)531-9643

Callahan, Barbara, Exec. Dir.
International Bird Rescue [4828]
4369 Cordelia Rd.
Fairfield, CA 94534
Ph: (707)207-0380
Fax: (707)207-0395

Callahan, Brendan, Founder,
President
Achieve in Africa [10829]
1104 Woodridge Ave.

Thousand Oaks, CA 91362

Callahan, Christopher, Secretary,
Treasurer
International Courtly Literature
Society - North American Branch
[9761]
c/o Leslie Zarker Morgan, President
Maryland Hall 461
Loyola University Maryland
4501 N Charles St.
Baltimore, MD 21210

Callahan, Holly, Office Mgr.
Americans for Nonsmokers' Rights
[17225]
2530 San Pablo Ave., Ste. J
Berkeley, CA 94702
Ph: (510)841-3032
Fax: (510)841-3071

Callahan, Kateri, President
Alliance to Save Energy [6449]
1850 M St. NW, Ste. 610
Washington, DC 20036
Ph: (202)857-0666
Fax: (202)331-9588

Callahan, Kevin J., President
Peace History Society [9504]
c/o Kevin J. Callahan, President
University of Saint Joseph
1678 Asylum Ave.
West Hartford, CT 06117

Callahan, Nora, Exec. Dir.
November Coalition [17325]
282 W Astor
Colville, WA 99114
Ph: (509)680-4679

Callahan, Sharon, Officer
Planetary Citizens [19264]
PO Box 1056
Mount Shasta, CA 96067
Ph: (530)926-6424
Fax: (530)926-1245

Callander, Meryn, President
Alliance for Transforming the Lives
of Children [10848]
901 Preston Ave., Ste. 400
Charlottesville, VA 22903
Ph: (206)666-4145

Callaway, Rev. Canon James G.,
Gen. Sec.
Colleges and Universities of the
Anglican Communion [19700]
Association of Episcopal Colleges
815 2nd Ave.
New York, NY 10017
Ph: (212)716-6149
Fax: (212)986-5039

Callaway, Kristy, Exec. Dir.
Art Schools Network [7505]
c/o Kristy Callaway, Executive Direc-
tor
PO Box 5534
Key West, FL 33045
Ph: (970)300-4650
Fax: (970)797-9116

Callejas, Rafael, Exec. Dir.
Millennium Water Alliance [13331]
1001 Connecticut Ave. NW, Ste. 710
Washington, DC 20036
Ph: (202)296-1832
Fax: (202)296-1786

Callender, Alana, EdD, Exec. Dir.
Association for the History of
Chiropractic [14257]
4430 8th St.
Rock Island, IL 61201-6608
Ph: (309)788-0799
    (309)781-9903

Callison, Kenneth P., Contact
Allied Beauty Experts [918]
6551 S Revere Pky., Ste. 120
Centennial, CO 80111-6410
Ph: (303)662-9075
Toll Free: 800-444-7546
Fax: (303)662-9845

Callori, Kathy, Mem.
Straight Spouse Network [12259]
PO Box 4985
Chicago, IL 60680
Ph: (773)413-8213

Calloway, Kim, President
American Beveren Rabbit Club
[22396]
c/o Meg Whitehouse, Secretary-
Treasurer
480 Colts Neck Rd.
Farmingdale, NJ 07727
Ph: (732)919-0909

Calnan, Jacqueline, MPA, President
Americans for Medical Progress
[13716]
444 N Capitol St. NW, Ste. 417
Washington, DC 20001
Ph: (202)624-8810

Calvert, Donna, Mem.
Institute of Industrial and Systems
Engineers [6558]
3577 Parkway Ln., Ste. 200
Norcross, GA 30092
Ph: (770)449-0460
    (770)449-0461
Toll Free: 800-494-0460
Fax: (770)441-3295

Calvo, Roque J., Exec. Dir.
Electrochemical Society [6198]
Bldg. D
65 S Main St.
Pennington, NJ 08534-2827
Ph: (609)737-1902
Fax: (609)737-2743

Camac, Clint, President
Leadership Development Network
[17983]
3941 Park Dr., Ste. 20-311
El Dorado Hills, CA 95762-4549
Ph: (916)514-7655
Fax: (916)514-8650

Camarena, Fermin, Founder,
President
International Coalition for the
Advancement of Neurology
[16018]
PO Box 1708
San Juan Capistrano, CA 92693
Ph: (760)213-5320

Camblor, Dr. Christi, Director
Compassion Without Borders
[10607]
537 4th St., Ste. F
Santa Rosa, CA 95401
Ph: (707)474-3345

Camera, Lou, Treasurer
Delphi Foundation [23728]
c/o Lou Camera, Treasurer
1017 L St., PMB 274
Sacramento, CA 95814

Cameron, Jared S., President
USS Pyro AE-1 and AE-24 Association [21072]
3808 Brighton Ct.
Alexandria, VA 22305-1571

Cameron, Dr. Paul, Chairman
Family Research Institute [18327]
PO Box 62640
Colorado Springs, CO 80962-2640
Ph: (303)681-3113

Cameron, Prof. Rich, Dir. of Comm.
Journalism Association of Com-
munity Colleges [8155]
2701 K St.
Sacramento, CA 95816
Fax: (916)288-6002

Cameron, Rick, President
Island Aid [11673]
450 Taraval St., No. 110
San Francisco, CA 94116-2530
Ph: (415)992-7517

Cameron, Tim, Managing Dir.
Asset Managers Forum [1221]
c/o SIFMA
120 Broadway, 35th Fl.
New York, NY 10017
Ph: (212)313-1389

Cameron, Tim, Director
Little Hearts [14199]
PO Box 171
Cromwell, CT 06416
Ph: (860)635-0006
Toll Free: 866-435-HOPE

Camlin, William C., President
National Association of Traffic Ac-
cident Reconstructionists and
Investigators [5366]
PO Box 2588
West Chester, PA 19382
Ph: (610)696-1919

Cammack, Mary Ellen, VP
Women Involved in Farm Economics
[17793]
c/o Linda Newman, President
442 4 Rd.
Roundup, MT 59072-6404
Ph: (406)323-8299
    (406)462-5597

Camp, Sherri, President
Afro-American Historical and
Genealogical Society [20950]
PO Box 73067
Washington, DC 20056-3067
Ph: (202)234-5350

Campbell, Cindy, Specialist
International Parking Institute [2496]
1330 Braddock Pl., Ste. 350
Alexandria, VA 22314
Ph: (571)699-3011
Fax: (703)566-2267

Campbell, David, Founder, Chairman
All Hands Volunteers [11651]
6 County Rd., Ste. 6
Mattapoisett, MA 02739
Ph: (508)758-8211

Campbell, David; Treasurer
International Maple Syrup Institute
[1346]
647 Bunker Hill Rd.
Salem, NY 12865
Ph: (518)854-7669

Campbell, David, President, Founder
MarineBio Conservation Society
[3899]
1995 Fairlee Dr.
Encinitas, CA 92024-4227
Ph: (713)248-2576

Campbell, Deanna, Exec. Dir.
Antahkarana Society International
[12621]
PO Box 1543
Bozeman, MT 59771-1543
Ph: (406)581-5963

Campbell, Douglas P., President
Automotive Safety Council [313]
c/o Douglas Campbell, President

5572 Arbor Bay Ct.
Brighton, MI 48116
Ph: (586)201-8653
Fax: (810)225-8567

Campbell, Duncan, Founder
Friends of the Children [10983]
44 NE Morris
Portland, OR 97212
Ph: (503)281-6633

Campbell, Duncan, President
Library Binding Council [1540]
4440 PGA Blvd., Ste. 600
Palm Beach Gardens, FL 33410
Ph: (561)745-6821
Toll Free: 800-837-7321

Campbell, Ernestina R., President
Association for Episcopal Deacons
[20094]
PO Box 1516
Westborough, MA 01581-6516
Ph: (508)873-1881

Campbell, J. Bart, OD, Chairman
Accreditation Council on Optometric
Education [16418]
American Optometric Association
243 N Lindbergh Blvd., 1st Fl.
Saint Louis, MO 63141-7881
Toll Free: 800-365-2219

Campbell, James, VP
Lawyers for Civil Justice [18600]
1140 Connecticut Ave. NW, Ste. 503
Washington, DC 20036
Ph: (202)429-0045
Fax: (202)429-6982

Campbell, Janice, Director
National Association of Independent
Writers and Editors [2696]
PO Box 549
Ashland, VA 23005-0549
Ph: (804)767-5961

Campbell, Jim, Director
American Literacy Council [8233]
1441 Mariposa Ave.
Boulder, CO 80302
Ph: (303)440-7385

Campbell, Jim, Director
Professional Service Association
[3077]
71 Columbia St.
Cohoes, NY 12047
Toll Free: 888-777-8851
Fax: (518)237-0418

Campbell, Joan
Urban Land Institute [5099]
2001 L St. NW
Washington, DC 20036
Ph: (202)624-7000
Fax: (202)624-7140

Campbell, Kenneth, Trustee
Clan Campbell Society - North
America [20800]
118 Eagle Dr.
Daphne, AL 36526
Ph: (251)621-0079
(910)864-4231

Campbell, Martha, PhD, Founder,
President
Venture Strategies for Health and
Development [15068]
962 Arlington Ave.
Berkeley, CA 94707
Ph: (510)524-4320

Campbell, Mary-Mitchell, Exec. Dir.,
Founder
Artists Striving to End Poverty
[12526]

165 W 46th St., Ste. 1303
New York, NY 10036
Ph: (212)921-1227
Fax: (212)840-0551

Campbell, Melanie L., President,
CEO
Black Women's Roundtable on Voter
Participation [18906]
c/o National Coalition on Black Civic
Participation
1050 Connecticut Ave. NW, 10th Fl.,
Ste. No. 1000
Washington, DC 20036
Ph: (202)659-4929
Fax: (202)659-5025

Campbell, Melanie L., President,
CEO
National Coalition on Black Civic
Participation [18913]
1050 Connecticut Ave. NW, 5th Fl.,
Ste. 500
Washington, DC 20036
Ph: (202)659-4929
Fax: (202)659-5025

Campbell, Nancy Duff, Co-Pres.
National Women's Law Center
[18230]
11 Dupont Cir. NW, No. 800
Washington, DC 20036
Ph: (202)588-5180
Fax: (202)588-5185

Campbell, Rebecca, Founder
Children of Fallen Soldiers Relief
Fund [10916]
PO Box 3968
Gaithersburg, MD 20885-3968
Ph: (301)685-3421
Toll Free: 866-96C-FSRF

Campbell, Rich, President
American Hackney Horse Society
[4307]
4059 Iron Works Pky., A-3
Lexington, KY 40511-8462
Ph: (859)255-8694
Fax: (859)255-0177

Campbell, Rishona, Contact
Delta Gamma Pi Multicultural Soror-
ity [23968]
PO Box 1414
New York, NY 10113-1414

Campbell, Robert, President
Phylaxis Society [19567]
PO Box 5675
Albuquerque, NM 87185-5675

Campbell, Robin, President
Costume Society of America [9189]
PO Box 852
Columbus, GA 31902-0852
Ph: (706)615-2851
Toll Free: 800-CSA-9447

Campbell, Robin, Dir. of Comm.
Pretrial Justice Institute [5550]
305 Main St., Ste. 200
Gaithersburg, MD 20878
Ph: (240)477-7152

Campbell, Samantha, Chairperson
Ocean Champions [18018]
c/o David Wilmot, President and Co-
Founder
202 San Jose Ave.
Capitola, CA 95010
Ph: (831)462-2539
Fax: (831)462-2542

Campbell, Scott, Exec. Dir.
Elton John AIDS Foundation [10532]
584 Broadway, Ste. 906
New York, NY 10012
Ph: (212)219-0670

Campbell, Scott, CEO
American Occupational Therapy
Foundation [16315]
4720 Montgomery Ln., Ste. 202
Bethesda, MD 20814-3449
Ph: (240)292-1079
Fax: (240)396-6188

Campbell, Scott, VP
Council for Adult and Experiential
Learning [7911]
55 E Monroe St., Ste. 2710
Chicago, IL 60603
Ph: (312)499-2600

Campbell, Scott, Director
Inland Press Association [2791]
701 Lee St., Ste. 925
Des Plaines, IL 60016
Ph: (847)795-0380
Fax: (847)795-0385

Campbell, Sherri, Exec. Sec.
International Laser Class Association
- North American Region [22634]
One Design Management
2812 Canon St.
San Diego, CA 92106
Ph: (619)222-0252

Campbell, Steve, Secretary
International Association for Property
and Evidence, Inc. [5471]
PO Box 652
Hot Springs, SD 57747
Ph: (818)846-2926
Toll Free: 800-449-4273
Fax: (818)846-4543

Campbell, Tom, CFO
Association for College and
University Technology Advance-
ment [8022]
152 W Zandale Dr., Ste. 200
Lexington, KY 40503
Ph: (859)278-3338
Fax: (859)278-3268

Campbell, Ms. Trista, Officer
Ludwick Family Foundation [11860]
203 S Glendora Ave., Ste. B
Glendora, CA 91741
Ph: (626)852-0092
Fax: (626)852-0776

Campbell, Wayne, Rep.
National Bench Rest Shooters As-
sociation [23135]
PO Box 6770
Sheridan, WY 82801-6770
Ph: (307)655-7415

Campe, Joanna, Exec. Dir., Founder
Remineralize the Earth [4687]
152 South St.
Northampton, MA 01060

Camper, Anne, President
American Working Dog Federation
[21830]
c/o Michelle Testa, Secretary
31 Mohawk St.
Sharon, MA 02067

Camper, Anne, President
American Working Malinois Associa-
tion [21281]
c/o Angie Stark, Membership Chair
PO Box 9183
Chicago, IL 60609
Ph: (708)359-4113

Campi, Dr. Alicia, President
Mongolia Society [9813]
703 Eigenmann Hall
1900 E 10th St.
Indiana University
Bloomington, IN 47406-7512
Ph: (812)855-4078
Fax: (812)855-4078

Campos, Alexander, Exec. Dir.,
Curator
Center for Book Arts [9124]
28 W 27th St., 3rd Fl.
New York, NY 10001
Ph: (212)481-0295

Campos, Joseph M., Secretary
American Society for Microbiology
[6071]
1752 N St. NW
Washington, DC 20036-2904
Ph: (202)942-9207
(202)737-3600
Fax: (202)942-9333

Camus, Julien, President
Wine Scholar Guild [3482]
1777 Church St. NW, Ste. B
Washington, DC 20036
Ph: (202)600-8022
Fax: (202)449-8331

Canada, Geoffrey, President
Harlem Children's Zone Inc. [11374]
35 E 125th St.
New York, NY 10035
Ph: (212)534-0700

Canadas, Frédéric, President
Association of French Schools in
North America [8530]
c/o Philippe Dietz, Treasurer
151 Laura Ln.
Palo Alto, CA 94303

Canal, Adolfo, President
Give a Child Hope [10996]
12021 SW 97th Terr.
Miami, FL 33186

Canalia, Peter B., JD, Exec. Dir.
American Board of Hair Restoration
Surgery [14898]
8840 Calumet Ave., Ste 205
Munster, IN 46321
Ph: (219)836-5858
Fax: (219)836-5525

Canby, Anne P., President
Alliance for a New Transportation
Charter [5807]
Surface Transportation Policy Project
1100 17th St. NW, 10 Fl.
Washington, DC 20036
Ph: (202)466-2636
Fax: (202)466-2247

Canby, Sheila, President
Historians of Islamic Art Association
[8899]
c/o Glaire D. Anderson, Treasurer
UNC-Chapel Hill
115 S Columbia St., CB 3405
Chapel Hill, NC 27514
Fax: (919)962-0722

Candella, Camille, Dir. of Mktg.
Affordable Shopping Destination
[3190]
6255 W Sunset Blvd., 19th Fl.
Los Angeles, CA 90028
Ph: (323)817-2200
Toll Free: 800-421-4511
Fax: (310)481-1900

Cannan, Kevin, President
Environmental Information Associa-
tion [525]
6935 Wisconsin Ave., Ste. 306
Chevy Chase, MD 20815-6112
Ph: (301)961-4999
Toll Free: 888-343-4342
Fax: (301)961-3094

Cannell, Dr. John Jacob, Medical
Dir., Founder
Vitamin D Council [16242]
1241 Johnson Ave., No. 134

San Luis Obispo, CA 93401-3306
Ph: (805)439-1075

Canniff, Teri, Mgr.
Hearing Loss Association of America
[15195]
7910 Woodmont Ave., Ste. 1200
Bethesda, MD 20814
Ph: (301)657-2248

Cannon, Aise, Secretary
National Association of Medical
Minority Educators [8331]
1500 Sunday Dr., Ste. 102
Raleigh, NC 27607
Ph: (919)573-1309
Toll Free: 855-201-6247
Fax: (919)573-1310

Cannon, Brian Q., President
Mormon History Association [20299]
175 South 1850 East
Heber City, UT 84032
Ph: (801)521-6565
Fax: (801)521-8686

Cannon, Jim, CEO, Founder,
President
Sustainable Fisheries Partnership
[3647]
4348 Waialae Ave., No. 692
Honolulu, HI 96816-5767
Ph: (202)580-8187

Cannon, Joseph, President
National Liquor Law Enforcement
Association [5503]
11720 Beltsville Dr., Ste. 900
Beltsville, MD 20705-3102
Ph: (301)755-2795
Fax: (301)755-2799

Cannon, Sarita, Bd. Member
Humanities Education and Research
Association [8005]
PO Box 715
Pacifica, CA 94044-0715

Cannon, Susan, Chairperson
India Partners [12679]
PO Box 5470
Eugene, OR 97405-0470
Ph: (541)683-0696
Toll Free: 877-874-6342

Canny, William, Exec. Dir.
United States Conference of
Catholic Bishops Migration and
Refugee Services [12600]
3211 4th St. NE
Washington, DC 20017-1194
Ph: (202)541-3352

Canoll, Tim, President
Air Line Pilots Association
International [23381]
1625 Massachusetts Ave. NW
Washington, DC 20036
Ph: (703)689-2270

Cantelon, Jim, President, Founder
Visionledd USA [10555]
PO Box 20158
Mesa, AZ 85277
Toll Free: 866-664-4673

Canter, Thomas C., Exec. Dir.
National Coal Transportation Association [739]
4 W Meadow Lark Ln., Ste. 100
Littleton, CO 80127-5718

Canterbury, Chuck, President
Fraternal Order of Police [19535]
701 Marriott Dr.
Nashville, TN 37214
Ph: (614)224-1856

Canterbury-Counts, Jaya, MEd,
Exec. Dir.
River Fund [10551]
11155 Roseland Rd., Unit 16

Sebastian, FL 32958
Ph: (772)589-5076

Cantino, Philip, President
International Society for
Phylogenetic Nomenclature [6669]
c/o Michael Keesey, Treasurer
2450 Colorado Ave., Ste. 3000 W
Santa Monica, CA 90404

Cantor, David, Exec. Dir., Founder,
President
Responsible Policies for Animals,
Inc. [10688]
PO Box 891
Glenside, PA 19038
Ph: (215)886-7721

Cantrell, Hugh, CEO
National Softball Association [23203]
PO Box 7
Nicholasville, KY 40340
Ph: (859)887-4114
Fax: (859)887-4874

Cantrell, Susan, CEO
Academy of Managed Care
Pharmacy [16629]
100 N Pitt St., Ste. 400
Alexandria, VA 22314-3141
Ph: (703)683-8416
Toll Free: 800-827-2627
Fax: (703)683-8417

Capece, Laurie, Exec. Sec.,
Treasurer
Weather Modification Association
[6861]
PO Box 845
Riverton, UT 84065
Ph: (801)598-4392

Caperton, Gaston, President
The College Board [8682]
45 Columbus Ave.
New York, NY 10023-6917
Ph: (212)713-8000

Capes, Ms. Diana, Exec. VP
Securities and Insurance Licensing
Association [1925]
PO Box 498
Zionsville, IN 46077-0498
Toll Free: 800-428-8329
Fax: (866)253-6026

Capobianco, John, President
National Chrysanthemum Society
[22110]
c/o Anette M. Lloyd, Secretary
PO Box 20456
Roanoke, VA 24018-0046
Ph: (516)263-2717

Capobianco, Tina, Bd. Member
International Factoring Association
[1245]
6627 Bay Laurel Pl., Ste. C
Avila Beach, CA 93424
Ph: (805)773-0011
Toll Free: 800-563-1895
Fax: (805)773-0021

Capodanno, John, Chmn. of the Bd.
REACT International [5751]
PO Box 21064
Glendale, CA 91221
Ph: (301)316-2900
Fax: (800)608-9755

Caporale, Wende, President
Artists' Fellowship, Inc. [19573]
47 5th Ave.
New York, NY 10003-4679
Ph: (212)255-7740

Capote, Juan, Dr., President
International Goat Association [4277]
c/o Christian De Vries

12709 Grassy Dr.
Little Rock, AR 72210-2708
Ph: (501)454-1641
Fax: (501)251-9391

Capote, Melody, Dep. Dir.
Caribbean Cultural Center African
Diaspora Institute [9226]
1825 Park Ave., Ste. 602
New York, NY 10035
Ph: (212)307-7420

Capote, Nicholas, President
APhA Academy of Student
Pharmacists [16650]
American Pharmacists Association
2215 Constitution Ave. NW
Washington, DC 20037
Ph: (202)628-4410
Toll Free: 800-237-2742
Fax: (202)783-2351

Capp, Stephen, Treasurer
Laser Institute of America [6782]
13501 Ingenuity Dr., Ste. 128
Orlando, FL 32826
Ph: (407)380-1553
Toll Free: 800-345-2737
Fax: (407)380-5588

Cappellino, Thomas, Exec. Dir.
Western Dredging Association
[2259]
c/o Thomas P. Cappellino, Executive
Director
PO Box 1393
Bonsall, CA 92003
Ph: (949)422-8231

Capps, Duane, Officer
Civitan International [12887]
PO Box 130744
Birmingham, AL 35213-0744
Ph: (205)591-8910
Toll Free: 800-CIVITAN

Capps, Stew, President
Charted Designers Association
[22253]
c/o Designs with TLC
7310 W Roosevelt St., Ste. 6
Phoenix, AZ 85043
Ph: (623)936-9900
Fax: (623)936-9981

Caprio, Vincent, Chairman
NanoBusiness Commercialization
Association [7284]
4 Research Dr., Ste. 402
Shelton, CT 06484
Ph: (203)733-1949

Caprio, Vincent, Founder, Exec. Dir.
Water Innovations Alliance [7379]
4 Research Dr., Ste. 402
Shelton, CT 06484-6242
Ph: (203)733-1949

Capron, Mark, VP
Chess Journalists of America [2671]
c/o Stan Booz, Secretary-Treasurer
511 Solliday Ct.
Perkasie, PA 18944

Caputo, Dr. Lucio, President,
Founder
Italian Wine and Food Institute
[1350]
1 Grand Central Pl.
60 E 42nd St., Ste. 2214
New York, NY 10165
Ph: (212)867-4111
Fax: (212)867-4114

Caputo, Paul, Dep. Dir.
National Association for Interpreta-
tion [6897]
230 Cherry St., Ste. 200

Fort Collins, CO 80521
Ph: (970)484-8283
Toll Free: 888-900-8283
Fax: (970)484-8179

Caputo, Peter, Act. Pres.
American Society of Cost Segrega-
tion Professionals [3200]
1101 Pennsylvania Ave. NW, 6th Fl.
Washington, DC 20004
Ph: (203)671-7372
Fax: (203)745-0724

Caputo, Sally, President, COO
Association of Management Consult-
ing Firms [2154]
370 Lexington Ave., Ste. 2209
New York, NY 10017
Ph: (212)262-3055
Fax: (212)262-3054

Caradec, Philippe, Bd. Member
International Bottled Water Associa-
tion [425]
1700 Diagonal Rd., Ste. 650
Alexandria, VA 22314
Ph: (703)683-5213
Fax: (703)683-4074

Caralla, Nancy C., Founder, Exec.
Dir., President
C Diff Foundation [15395]
6931 Ian Ct., Ste. 14
New Port Richey, FL 34653
Ph: (919)201-1512

Caramanico, Thomas, President
National Liberty Museum [18351]
321 Chestnut St.
Philadelphia, PA 19106
Ph: (215)925-2800
Fax: (215)925-3800

Carbaugh, Rick, Chairman
American Society for the Alexander
Technique [13601]
11 W Monument Ave., Ste. 510
Dayton, OH 45402-1233
Ph: (937)586-3732
Toll Free: 800-473-0620

Carberry, Christine, Chairperson
Association of Strategic Alliance
Professionals [2157]
960 Turnpike St., Ste. 3A
Canton, MA 02021-2818
Ph: (781)562-1630

Carbone, William J., CEO
American Association of Physician
Specialists, Inc. [16503]
5550 W Executive Dr., Ste. 400
Tampa, FL 33609
Ph: (813)433-2277
Fax: (813)830-6599

Carbott, Tom, VP
Material Handling Institute of
American - Lift Manufacturers
Product Section [1749]
8720 Red Oak Blvd., Ste. 201
Charlotte, NC 28217-3996
Ph: (704)676-1190
Fax: (704)676-1199

Card, Vice Adm. James C., Chairman
Marine Board [6802]
c/o Transportation Research Board
500 5th St. NW
Washington, DC 20001

Cardello, Paul, Chairman
iPods for Wounded Veterans
[13066]
4 Heather Dr.
Wilmington, MA 01887
Ph: (603)770-5765

Carden, Kelly, MD, President
American Board of Sleep Medicine
[17211]
2510 N Frontage Rd.
Darien, IL 60561
Ph: (630)737-9701
Fax: (630)737-9790

Carden, Skip, Web Adm.
Ercoupe Owners Club [21224]
c/o Larry Snyder, Executive Director
PO Box 220
Pleasant Grove, AR 72567-0220
Ph: (870)652-3925

Cardenas, Rick, Contact
Advocating Change Together
[11567]
1821 University Ave. W, Ste. 306-S
Saint Paul, MN 55104
Ph: (651)641-0297
Toll Free: 800-641-0059
Fax: (651)641-4053

Cardillo, Dr. Mark, Exec. Dir.
Camille and Henry Dreyfus Founda-
tion, Inc. [7759]
555 Madison Ave., 20th Fl.
New York, NY 10022-3301
Ph: (212)753-1760
Fax: (212)593-2256

Cardin, RJ, Director
National Association of County Park
and Recreation Officials [5663]
c/o Daniel Betts, President
69 W Washington, Ste. 290
Chicago, IL 60602
Ph: (312)603-0310
Fax: (312)603-9971

Cardinal, David, President
American Federation of New
Zealand Rabbit Breeders [4588]
c/o Bruce Himmelberger, Director,
Box 173
PO Box 173
Bethel, PA 19507
Ph: (717)865-5803

Cardona, Jeanne L., Exec. Dir.,
Secretary
Association of Ship Brokers and
Agents, Inc. [2239]
510 Sylvan Ave., Ste. 201
Englewood Cliffs, NJ 07632
Ph: (201)569-2882

Cardoza, Dr. Freddy, Director
Society of Professors in Christian
Education [7615]
c/o Freddy Cardoza, Director
Biola University
Feinberg Ste. 119
13800 Biola Ave.
La Mirada, CA 90639
Ph: (310)779-5224
    (562)944-0351
Fax: (949)748-7006

Cardoza, Rod, Exec. Dir., Founder
Abrahamic Alliance International
[20213]
1930 Camden Ave., Ste. 3A
San Jose, CA 95124
Ph: (408)728-8943
Fax: (408)641-7545

Carell, Mr. Alan J., Secretary
Jon-Erik Hexum Fan Club [23994]
32 Lee Ave.
Ferguson, MO 63135

Carey, Jim, VP
Belgian Draft Horse Corporation of
America [4339]
125 Southwood Dr.
Wabash, IN 46992
Ph: (260)563-3205
Fax: (260)563-3205

Carey, Laura, Director
Cosmetic Industry Buyers and Suppliers [1584]
c/o Jenifer Brady, Recording
Secretary
124 South Ave.
Garwood, NJ 07027

Carey, Martha Ann, Treasurer
APA Division 52: International
Psychology [16895]
750 1st St. NE
Washington, DC 20002-4242
Ph: (202)336-6013
    (202)336-5500
Toll Free: 800-374-2721

Carey, Meghan, Exec. Dir.
National Society of Genetic
Counselors [14883]
330 N Wabash Ave., Ste. 2000
Chicago, IL 60611
Ph: (312)321-6834
Fax: (312)673-6972

Carey, Michael, Exec. VP
Phi Sigma Kappa [23916]
2925 E 96th St.
Indianapolis, IN 46240
Ph: (317)573-5420
Toll Free: 888-846-6851
Fax: (317)573-5430

Carey-Grant, Cynthia, Exec. Dir.
Women Organized to Respond to
Life-Threatening Diseases [13566]
389 30th St.
Oakland, CA 94609-3402
Ph: (510)986-0340
Fax: (510)986-0341

Cargill, Noreen, Mgr. of Admin.
Bread Loaf Writers Conference
[10366]
204 College St.
Middlebury, VT 05753-1054
Ph: (802)443-5286
Fax: (802)443-2087

Carhee, Winston, President
American Black Chiropractic As-
sociation [14249]
3915 Cascade Rd., Ste. 220
Atlanta, GA 30331
Ph: (404)647-2225
Fax: (404)699-0988

Caricato, Carissa, Founder
Hoola for Happiness [13062]
3225 S MacDill Ave., Ste. 129-343
Tampa, FL 33629

Carignan, Joe, President
Law Enforcement Thermographers'
Association [5482]
PO Box 6485
Edmond, OK 73083
Ph: (405)330-6988

Carithers, Doug, Secretary,
Treasurer
American Association of Veterinary
Parasitologists [17605]
c/o Doug Carithers, Secretary-
Treasurer
Merial Limited
3239 Satellite Blvd.
Duluth, GA 30096
Ph: (678)638-3837

Carlat, Charlotte, Secretary
American Cormo Sheep Association
[4649]
c/o Charlotte Carlat, Treasurer/
Registrar
100 E River Rd.
Broadus, MT 59317
Ph: (406)427-5449

Carleson, Susan A., Chairman, CEO
American Civil Rights Union [17869]
3213 Duke St., No. 625
Alexandria, VA 22314
Ph: (703)217-2660
Toll Free: 877-730-2278

Carley, Karon, CEO, President
Operation Interdependence [12347]
2695 Patterson, No. 2-147
Grand Junction, CO 81506
Ph: (760)468-8001

Carlile, Rev. Wilson, Founder
Church Army USA [20096]
380 Franklin Ave.
Aliquippa, PA 15001
Ph: (724)375-5659

Carlin, Roberta, MS, Exec. Dir.
American Association on Health and
Disability [14544]
110 N Washington St., Ste. 328-J
Rockville, MD 20850
Ph: (301)545-6140
Fax: (301)545-6144

Carlisle, David, President
Rachel Carson Homestead Associa-
tion [10318]
613 Marion Ave.
Springdale, PA 15144
Ph: (724)274-5459

Carlisle, Debbie, President
Organization of Facial Plastic
Surgery Assistants [14318]
c/o Debbie Carlisle, President
533 E County Line Rd., Ste. 104
Greenwood, IN 46143
Ph: (317)859-3810
Fax: (317)851-3817

Carll, Dr. Elizabeth, President
Communications Coordination Committee for the United Nations
[19209]
1140 Avenue of the Americas, 9th Fl.
New York, NY 10036

Carlson, Dave, Chmn. of the Bd.
United States Curling Association
[22742]
5525 Clem's Way
Stevens Point, WI 54482-8841
Ph: (715)344-1199
Toll Free: 888-287-5377
Fax: (715)344-2279

Carlson, Deborah, PhD, Comm.
Chm.
American Academy of Audiology
[17234]
11480 Commerce Park Dr., Ste. 220
Reston, VA 20191
Ph: (703)790-8466
Toll Free: 800-222-2336
Fax: (703)790-8631

Carlson, Deborah, PhD, President
Institute of Nautical Archaeology
[5940]
PO Box HG
College Station, TX 77841-5137
Ph: (979)845-6694
Fax: (979)847-9260

Carlson, Ed, 1st VP
Treatment Communities of America
[13186]
1875 I St. NW, Rm. 574
Washington, DC 20006
Ph: (202)296-3503

Carlson, Karen J., Exec. Dir.
Foundation for Women's Cancer
[13972]
230 W Monroe St., Ste. 2528

Chicago, IL 60606-4902
Ph: (312)578-1439
Fax: (312)235-4059

Carlson, Kevin, Chairperson
National Coalition for Sexual
Freedom [12948]
Box 127
822 Guilford Ave.
Baltimore, MD 21202-3707
Ph: (410)539-4824

Carlson, Larry, Mgr.
Art Greenhaw Official International
Fan Club [24023]
105 Broad St.
105 Broad St.
Mesquite, TX 75149-4201
Ph: (214)739-2664

Carlson, Larry, VP
National Defender Investigator As-
sociation [5368]
PO Box 169
Kohler, WI 53044
Ph: (920)395-2330
Fax: (866)668-9858

Carlson, Lisa, Exec. Dir.
Funeral Ethics Organization [11799]
87 Upper Access Rd.
Hinesburg, VT 05461
Ph: (802)482-6021

Carlson, Mark, Chairman
National Association of Personnel
Services [1097]
78 Dawson Village Way, Ste. 410-
201
Dawsonville, GA 30534
Ph: (706)531-0060
Fax: (866)739-4750

Carlson, Matt, CEO, President
National Sporting Goods Association
[3144]
1601 Feehanville Dr., Ste. 300
Mount Prospect, IL 60056
Ph: (847)296-6742
Toll Free: 800-815-5422
Fax: (847)391-9827

Carlson, Michael S., Secretary
U.S. Life-Saving Service Heritage
Association [9442]
PO Box 1031
Eastham, MA 02642
Toll Free: 844-875-7742

Carlson, Michelle, President
Sigma Delta Tau [23962]
714 Adams St.
Carmel, IN 46032
Ph: (317)846-7747

Carlson, Mr. Scott A., CPA, CEO,
Secretary
Alpha Chi Rho [23879]
109 Oxford Way
Neptune, NJ 07753
Ph: (732)869-1895
Fax: (732)988-5357

Carlson, Thea Maria, Director
Biodynamic Association [4150]
1661 N Water St., Ste. 307
Milwaukee, WI 53202
Ph: (262)649-9212
Fax: (262)649-9213

Carlson-Khorsand, Ms. Susan,
Founder
Glories Happy HATS, Inc. [13448]
PO Box 624
Merrifield, VA 22116-0624
Ph: (703)506-1415

Carlton, Christopher E., President
The Coleopterists Society [6609]
c/o Insect Biodiversity Lab

South Dakota State University
Box 2207A, SAG 361
Brookings, SD 57007
Ph: (605)688-4438
Fax: (605)688-4602

Carlton, J. Steven, Director
Teens Fighting Hunger [12117]
PMB 410
3 Monroe Pky., Ste. P
Lake Oswego, OR 97035
Ph: (971)285-5588

Carlton Loftis, Deborah, Exec. Dir.
Hymn Society in the United States
and Canada [20492]
8040 Villa Park Dr.
Henrico, VA 23228
Toll Free: 800-843-4966

Carman, Ray, President
The Duke Ellington Society [9902]
Church Street Sta.
New York, NY 10008-0031

Carmona, Richard H., Chairperson
Strategies to Overcome and Prevent
Obesity Alliance [16264]
George Washington University
School of Public Health and Health
Services
2021 K St. NW, Ste. 850
Washington, DC 20006
Ph: (202)609-6003

Carneiro, Ana, President
History of Earth Sciences Society
[9484]
c/o David Spanagel, Treasurer
PO Box 70
Lancaster, MA 01523

Carner, Ron, President
Maccabi USA/Sports for Israel
[23233]
1511 Walnut St., Ste. 401
Philadelphia, PA 19102
Ph: (215)561-6900
Fax: (215)561-5470

Carnes, Rick, President
Songwriters Guild of America [5342]
5120 Virginia Way, Ste. C22
Brentwood, TN 37027-7594
Ph: (615)742-9945
Toll Free: 800-524-6742
Fax: (615)630-7501

Carney, Carole, Exec. Sec.
National Junior Horticultural Association [22113]
c/o Carole Carney, Executive
Secretary
15 Railroad Ave.
Homer City, PA 15748-1378

Caro, Danie, Dir. of Comm.
Intercollegiate Women's Lacrosse
Coaches Association [22973]
PO Box 1124
Grand Lake, CO 80447
Ph: (443)951-9611
Fax: (970)432-7058

Carolan, John J., President
Vespa Club of America [22235]
PO Box 23806
New Orleans, LA 70183
Ph: (719)473-4692

Caron, Cathleen, Exec. Dir., Founder
Global Workers Justice Alliance
[12338]
789 Washington Ave.
Brooklyn, NY 11238
Ph: (646)351-1160

Caron, Fr. Marcel, Dir. Gen.
Pius X Secular Institute [19896]
c/o Fr. Marcel Caron

27 Cove St.
Goffstown, NH 03045
Ph: (418)626-5882

Carosso, Dr. John, Exec. Dir.
Autism Link [13748]
900 John St.
New York, NY 10038
Ph: (412)364-1886

Carpenter, Barry, President, CEO
North American Meat Institute [2311]
1150 Connecticut Ave. NW, 12th Fl.
Washington, DC 20036
Ph: (202)587-4200
Fax: (202)587-4300

Carpenter, Bob, President, CEO
GS1 US [273]
Princeton Pike Corporate Ctr.
1009 Lenox Dr., Ste. 202
Lawrenceville, NJ 08648
Ph: (609)620-0200

Carpenter, Carolyn Hoff, President
Zeta Tau Alpha [23967]
3450 Founders Rd.
Indianapolis, IN 46268
Ph: (317)872-0540
Fax: (317)876-3948

Carpenter, Christopher, DVM, MBA,
Exec. Dir.
Companion Animal Parasite Council
[17643]
6331 Walina Ct. SE
Salem, OR 97317

Carpenter, David R., Director
International Association of Color
Manufacturers [756]
1101 17th St. NW, Ste. 700
Washington, DC 20036
Ph: (202)293-5800
Fax: (202)463-8998

Carpenter, Glenn, President
University Photographers Association of America [8427]
c/o Glenn Carpenter, President
Moraine Valley Community College
9000 W College Pky.
Palos Hills, IL 60465

Carpenter, Jay, President
1-800 American Free Trade Associa-
tion [3410]
PO Box 1049
Burlington, VT 05402-1049
Ph: (802)383-0816
Fax: (802)860-4821

Carpenter, Mark, President
International Association of Law
Enforcement Planners [5136]
PO Box 11437
Torrance, CA 90510-1437
Ph: (310)225-5148

Carpenter, Stephen, Dep. Dir.
Farmers' Legal Action Group [5530]
6 W 5th St., Ste. 650
Saint Paul, MN 55102
Ph: (651)223-5400

Carpenter, Todd, Exec. Dir., Manag-
ing Dir.
National Information Standards
Organization [6750]
3600 Clipper Mill Rd., Ste. 302
Baltimore, MD 21211
Ph: (301)654-2512
Fax: (410)685-5278

Carpenter-Palumbo, Karen,
Treasurer
National Association for Children of
Alcoholics [13162]

10920 Connecticut Ave., Ste. 100
Kensington, MD 20895
Ph: (301)468-0985
Toll Free: 888-554-COAS
Fax: (301)468-0987

Carpentier, Martha C., President,
Web Adm.
International Susan Glaspell Society
[10381]
c/o Dr. Doug Powers
555 Jefferson St.
Northumberland, PA 17857-9634

Carr, Cathie, President
Escapees [22422]
100 Rainbow Dr.
Livingston, TX 77351-9340
Ph: (936)327-8873
Toll Free: 888-757-2582
Fax: (936)327-4388

Carr, Christine, Exec. Dir.
Computers for Children Inc. [8666]
701 Seneca St., Ste. 601
Buffalo, NY 14210
Ph: (716)823-7248

Carr, Greg Kimathi, VP
Association for the Study of Classi-
cal African Civilizations [8778]
PO Box 2128
Silver Spring, MD 20915

Carr, Jim, Treasurer
American Council for Construction
Education [7662]
1717 N Loop 1604 E, Ste. 320
San Antonio, TX 78232-1570
Ph: (210)495-6161
Fax: (210)495-6168

Carr, Jim, VP
Developing Hands [10955]
1602 E 100th Pl.
Thornton, CO 80229
Ph: (303)949-2363

Carr, Jim, CEO, President
National Association of Intercol-
legiate Athletics [23239]
1200 Grand Blvd.
Kansas City, MO 64106
Ph: (816)595-8000
Fax: (816)595-8200

Carr, Jim, Chairman
Technology and Manufacturing As-
sociation [2232]
1651 Wilkening Rd.
Schaumburg, IL 60173
Ph: (847)825-1120
Fax: (847)825-0041

Carr, Kate S., President, CEO
Safe Kids Worldwide [11144]
1301 Pennsylvania Ave. NW, Ste.
1000
Washington, DC 20004-1707
Ph: (202)662-0600
Fax: (202)393-2072

Carr, Mary, Exec. Dir.
Petroleum Technology Transfer
Council [2535]
c/o Kathy Chapman, Operations
Director
PO Box 710942
Herndon, VA 20171
Ph: (703)928-5020
Fax: (571)485-8255

Carr, Matt, Exec. Dir.
Algae Biomass Organization [6446]
125 St. Paul St.
Preston, MN 55965-1092
Toll Free: 877-531-5512

Carr, Peggy G., PhD, Commissioner
Institute of Education Sciences |
National Center for Education

Statistics | National Assessment of
Educational Progress [8686]
Assessment Division, 8th Fl.
1990 K St. NW
Washington, DC 20006
Ph: (202)502-7400
Fax: (202)502-7440

Carr, Peggy, CEO, Founder
Vacations for Veterans [13250]
9435 Lorton Market St., No. 105
Lorton, VA 22079
Ph: (202)731-0109

Carr, Sally, President
Old English Sheepdog Club of
America [21937]
c/o Marilyn Marshall, Corresponding
Secretary
2541 Bent Spur Dr.
Acton, CA 93510-2105
Ph: (661)269-5716

Carr, Tom, Bd. Member
Rebuilding Together [11991]
1899 L St. NW, Ste. 1000
Washington, DC 20036-3810
Toll Free: 800-473-4229

Carrabba, Mary W., PhD, Treasurer
The Coblentz Society [7224]
c/o Mark Druy, President
41 Wellman St.
Lowell, MA 01851

Carragher, Michael, President
Irish Family History Forum [20977]
PO Box 67
Plainview, NY 11803-0067

Carrasco, Emma, Chief Mktg. Ofc.
National Public Radio [9145]
1111 N Capitol St. NE
Washington, DC 20002
Fax: (202)513-3329

Carreiro, Jane, Chairman
Osteopathic International Alliance
[16525]
142 E Ontario St.
Chicago, IL 60611

Carreras, Jose, President
Friends of the Jose Carreras
International Leukemia Foundation
[13976]
1100 Fairview Ave. N
Seattle, WA 98109-1024
Ph: (206)667-7108
Fax: (206)667-6498

Carrillo, Sr. Elizabeth, OSB, Exec.
Sec.
American Benedictine Academy
[19790]
Monastery of St. Benedict
104 Chapel Ln.
Saint Joseph, MN 56374

Carrin, Patricia, President
Nonverbal Learning Disorders As-
sociation [12240]
507 Hopmeadow St.
Simsbury, CT 06070
Ph: (860)658-5522
Fax: (860)658-6688

Carroll, Austin David, PhD, Bd.
Member
Catholic Academy of Sciences in the
United States of America [20075]
c/o Lee T. Grady, PhD, Secretary
1205 Carol Raye St.
McLean, VA 22101-2620

Carroll, Bonnie, Founder, President
Tragedy Assistance Program for
Survivors [10762]

3033 Wilson Blvd., Ste. 630
Arlington, VA 22201
Ph: (202)588-8277
Toll Free: 800-959-8277
Fax: (571)385-2524

Carroll, David, Contact
American Mushroom Institute [4226]
1284 Gap Newport Pke.
Avondale, PA 19311
Ph: (610)268-7483
Fax: (610)268-8015

Carroll, Francis R., Chairman,
  Founder
Small Business Service Bureau
  [3129]
554 Main St.
Worcester, MA 01615-0014
Toll Free: 800-343-0939

Carroll, Matthew, Exec. Dir.
International Association for Society
  and Natural Resources [4493]
c/o Sam Houston State University
Sociology Dept.
1901 Avenue I, Ste. 270
Huntsville, TX 77341
Ph: (936)294-4446
     (936)294-4143

Carroll, Michael, President
National Association of Black
  Geoscientists [6694]
4212 San Felipe St., Ste. 420
Houston, TX 77027

Carroll, Molly, Contact
International Council of Toy
  Industries [3293]
c/o Toy Industry Association
1115 Broadway, Ste. 400
New York, NY 10010-3466
Ph: (212)675-1141
     (202)459-0355

Carroll, Richard, Treasurer
Child Aid [15180]
917 SW Oak St., Ste. 208
Portland, OR 97205
Ph: (503)223-3008
Fax: (503)223-4017

Carruthers, Marcia, Chmn. of the Bd.
Disability Management Employer
  Coalition [1089]
5173 Waring Rd., Ste. 134
San Diego, CA 92120-2705
Toll Free: 877-789-3632

Carson, Amy, President, Founder
Moms Against Mercury [13223]
55 Carson's Trl.
Leicester, NC 28748
Ph: (828)776-0082
Fax: (828)683-6866

Carson, Glenn Thomas, PhD, Mem.
Disciples of Christ Historical Society
  [20022]
1101 19th Ave. S
Nashville, TN 37212-
Ph: (615)327-1444

Carson, Joel G., Exec. Dir.
Geoprofessional Business Associa-
  tion [6221]
1300 Piccard Dr., No. LL14
Rockville, MD 20850-4303
Ph: (301)565-2733
Fax: (301)589-2017

Carson, Laura, Treasurer
United States Border Collie Club
  [21979]
1712 Hertford St.
Greensboro, NC 27403

Carstarphen, Nike, Consultant,
  Founder, Director
Alliance for Conflict Transformation
  [17998]

PO Box 9117
Alexandria, VA 22304
Ph: (703)879-7039

Carstens, Peter, Founder
Lifeline to Africa [15482]
407 N Hebard St.
Knoxville, IL 61448
Ph: (845)661-8465

Cartagena, Juan, President, Gen.
  Counsel
LatinoJustice PRLDEF [17905]
99 Hudson St., 14th Fl.
New York, NY 10013-2815
Ph: (212)219-3360
Toll Free: 800-328-2322
Fax: (212)431-4276

Carteaux, William R., President,
  CEO
SPI: The Plastics Industry Trade As-
  sociation [2632]
1425 K St. NW, Ste. 500
Washington, DC 20005
Ph: (202)974-5200
Fax: (202)296-7005

Carter, Ms. Barbara, Secretary,
  Exec. Asst.
Society for Human Ecology [14725]
c/o Barbara Carter, Secretary
105 Eden St.
Bar Harbor, ME 04609
Ph: (207)801-5632

Carter, Prof. C. Barry, VP
International Federation of Societies
  for Microscopy [6866]
c/o C. Barry Carter, Vice President
Chemical, Materials & Biomolecular
  Engineering Department, Unit 3222
University of Connecticut
191 Auditorium Rd.
Storrs, CT 06269-3222
Ph: (860)486-4020
Fax: (860)486-2959

Carter, Catherine, Exec. Dir.
American Board for Certification in
  Orthotics, Prosthetics and Pedorth-
  ics [16493]
330 John Carlyle St., Ste. 210
Alexandria, VA 22314
Ph: (703)836-7114
Fax: (703)836-0838

Carter, Charlie, Officer
Research Council on Structural Con-
  nections [7246]
1 E Wacker Dr., Ste. 700
Chicago, IL 60601
Ph: (312)670-5414

Carter, Dr. Craig N., Exec. Dir.
World Association of Veterinary
  Laboratory Diagnosticians [17678]
College of Agriculture
University of Kentucky
Livestock Disease Diagnostic Ctr.
1490 Bull Lea Rd.
Lexington, KY 40512-4125
Ph: (859)253-0571
Fax: (859)255-1624

Carter, Diane, RN, CEO, President
American Association of Nurse As-
  sessment Coordination [14975]
400 S Colorado Blvd., Ste. 600
Denver, CO 80246
Ph: (303)758-7647
Toll Free: 800-768-1880
Fax: (303)758-3588

Carter, Erika Ruebensaal, Dir. of
  Comm., Dir. of Dev.
Osteogenesis Imperfecta Foundation
  [16490]

804 W Diamond Ave., Ste. 210
Gaithersburg, MD 20878
Ph: (301)947-0083
Toll Free: 844-889-7579
Fax: (301)947-0456

Carter, Dr. Frances Tunnell, Exec.
  Dir., Founder
American Rosie the Riveter Associa-
  tion [21191]
c/o Stephanie Davis
8336 Valley Oak Dr.
North Richland Hills, TX 76182
Ph: (205)822-4106
Toll Free: 888-557-6743

Carter, Janet, Exec. Dir.
American Board of Clinical
  Optometry [16420]
23679 Calabasas Rd., No. 1010
Calabasas, CA 91302
Ph: (818)714-1350
Fax: (818)337-2226

Carter, Jerry T., CEO
National Council of Examiners for
  Engineering and Surveying [6574]
PO Box 1686
Clemson, SC 29633
Ph: (864)654-6824
Toll Free: 800-250-3196
Fax: (864)654-6033

Carter, Joanne, Exec. Dir.
RESULTS [18458]
1101 15th St. NW, Ste. 1200
Washington, DC 20005
Ph: (202)783-7100
Fax: (202)466-1397

Carter, Joyce, Chairperson
Conference on College Composition
  and Communication [7867]
1111 W Kenyon Rd.
Urbana, IL 61801-1010
Ph: (217)328-3870
Toll Free: 877-369-6283

Carter, Julie, Secretary
Association of Philanthropic Counsel
  [818]
136 Everett Rd.
Albany, NY 12205-1418
Ph: (518)694-5525
Fax: (518)677-1668

Carter, McCall, Director
Ashburn Institute [18878]
198 Okatie Village Dr., Ste. 103
PMB No. 301
Bluffton, SC 29909
Ph: (703)728-6482
Fax: (843)705-7643

Carter, Michael L., VP
National Association of Black Owned
  Broadcasters [469]
1201 Connecticut Ave. NW, Ste. 200
Washington, DC 20036
Ph: (202)463-8970
Fax: (202)429-0657

Carter, Ronald, President, CEO
Children Inc. [11220]
PO Box 72848
North Chesterfield, VA 23235
Ph: (804)359-4562
Toll Free: 800-538-5381

Carter, Shannon S., MA, CEO
Competency and Credentialing
  Institute [15322]
2170 S Parker Rd., Ste. 120
Denver, CO 80231
Ph: (303)369-9566
Toll Free: 888-257-2667
Fax: (303)695-8464

Carter, Rabbi Suzanne H., President
International Federation of Rabbis
  [20252]

5600 Wisconsin Ave., No. 1107
Chevy Chase, MD 20815
Fax: (561)499-6316

Carter, Terry, VP
Polish Genealogical Society of
  America [20992]
984 N Milwaukee Ave.
Chicago, IL 60642-4101

Carter, Wendell L., President
Association for Iron and Steel
  Technology [6842]
186 Thorn Hill Rd.
Warrendale, PA 15086-7528
Ph: (724)814-3000
Fax: (724)814-3001

Carvalho, Cassia, Exec. Dir.
Brazil-U.S. Business Council [23566]
1615 H St. NW
Washington, DC 20062
Ph: (202)463-5729

Carver, Kendall, Chairman
International Cruise Victims [19221]
4747 E Elliot Rd., No. 29598
Phoenix, AZ 85044
Ph: (602)852-5896
     (818)655-5711

Cary, John, Dir. of Operations,
  Founder
ArchVoices [5960]
1014 Curtis St.
Albany, CA 94706
Ph: (510)757-6213

Cary, Neal, Chmn. of the Bd.
American Atheists [19708]
225 Cristiani St.
Cranford, NJ 07016
Ph: (908)276-7300

Casas, J. Manuel, President
Society for the Psychological Study
  of Ethnic Minority Issues [16940]
c/o J. Manuel Casas, President
317 E Padre St.
Santa Barbara, CA 93105-3609
Ph: (805)983-3375
Fax: (805)983-7264

Casazza, Dr. Larry, Director
African Communities Against Malaria
  [15390]
3644 36th Ave. S, Unit A
Seattle, WA 98144

Cascino, Terrence L., President
American Academy of Neurology
  [16002]
201 Chicago Ave.
Minneapolis, MN 55415-1126
Ph: (612)928-6000
Toll Free: 800-879-1960
Fax: (612)454-2746

Casey, Chris, Exec. Dir.
World's Window [11742]
40 Van Schoick Ave.
Albany, NY 12208

Casey, Donald E., Jr., VP
American College of Medical Quality
  [17027]
5272 River Rd., Ste. 630
Bethesda, MD 20816
Ph: (301)718-6516
Fax: (301)656-0989

Casey, George, Chairman
USO World Headquarters [19384]
PO Box 96860
Washington, DC 20077-7677
Ph: (703)908-6400
Toll Free: 888-484-3876

Casey, Joanne F., CEO, President
Intermodal Association of North
  America [3332]

11785 Beltsville Dr., Ste. 1100
Calverton, MD 20705
Ph: (301)982-3400

Casey, Joe, Exec. Dir.
National Association of Equipment
    Leasing Brokers [2928]
100 N 20th St., Ste. 400
Philadelphia, PA 19103
Toll Free: 800-996-2352
Fax: (215)564-2175

Casey, Joe, Exec. Dir.
National Council on Measurement in
    Education [8690]
100 N 20th St., Ste. 400
Philadelphia, PA 19103
Ph: (215)461-6263
Fax: (215)564-2175

Casey, Ralph, Exec. Dir.
Brotherhood of Working Farriers As-
    sociation [1179]
14013 E Highway 136
La Fayette, GA 30728-5660
Ph: (706)397-8047
Fax: (706)397-8047

Casey, Ray, CEO
Hagar USA [12038]
1609 E 5th St., Ste. 2
Charlotte, NC 28204
Ph: (803)322-2221
    (980)272-0114

Casey, Teresa M., Exec. Dir.
Association of Financial Guaranty
    Insurers [1837]
c/o Teresa M. Casey, Executive
    Director
Mackin & Casey, LLC
139 Lancaster St.
Albany, NY 12210-1903
Ph: (518)449-4698

Cason-Reed, Dr. Shirley, President
Women's Missionary Society, AME
    Church [20649]
1134 11th St. NW
Washington, DC 20001
Ph: (202)371-8886
Fax: (202)371-8820

Caspari, Rachel, Chairperson
Biological Anthropology Section
    [5911]
c/o Rachel Caspari, Chairperson
Centeal Michigan University
Anspach Hall 142
Mount Pleasant, MI 48859
Ph: (574)631-0299

Cass, Craig, President
International Premium Cigar & Pipe
    Retailers Association [2959]
513 Capital Ct. NE
Columbus, GA 31904-3637
Ph: (202)621-8064

Casserly, Michael D., Exec. Dir.
Council of the Great City Schools
    [8727]
1301 Pennsylvania Ave. NW, Ste.
    702
Washington, DC 20004
Ph: (202)393-2427
Fax: (202)393-2400

Cassette, Philip M., VP
American Dairy Goat Association
    [3591]
161 W Main St.
Spindale, NC 28160
Ph: (828)286-3801
Fax: (828)287-0476

Cassidy, Frances M., President
American Australian Association
    [9200]

50 Broadway, Ste. 2003
New York, NY 10004
Ph: (212)338-6860
Fax: (212)338-6864

Cassidy, Richard T., President
National Conference of Commission-
    ers on Uniform State Laws [5782]
111 N Wabash Ave., Ste. 1010
Chicago, IL 60602
Ph: (312)450-6600

Cassidy, Steve, Founder, President
Orphan's Hope [11120]
10190 B Suncrest Dr.
Leavenworth, WA 98826
Ph: (952)941-1546
Toll Free: 888-251-2871

Cassidy, Thomas E., President, Edi-
    tor
World Ocean and Cruise Liner
    Society [22471]
PO Box 329
Northport, NY 11768-0329
Toll Free: 866-631-0611

Cassimatis, Emmanuel G., MD,
    Chmn. of the Bd.
Foundation for Advancement of
    International Medical Education
    and Research [8321]
3624 Market St.
Philadelphia, PA 19104
Fax: (215)966-3121

Cassimatis, N. Emmanuel G., MD,
    CEO, President
Educational Commission for Foreign
    Medical Graduates [16748]
3624 Market St.
Philadelphia, PA 19104-2685
Ph: (215)386-5900
Fax: (215)386-9196

Cassity, Colleen, Exec. Dir.
Oracle Education Foundation [8117]
c/o Colleen Cassity, Executive Direc-
    tor
500 Oracle Pkwy., 5OP-8
Redwood City, CA 94065

Castagna, Dr. Daniel M., Officer
Pierre Fauchard Academy [14432]
PO Box 3718
Mesquite, NV 89024-3718
Ph: (702)345-2950
Toll Free: 800-232-0099
Fax: (702)345-5031

Castaldo, Anthony, President
United States Hereditary An-
    gioedema Association [14863]
500 Ala Moana Blvd., Ste. 400
7 Waterfront Plz.
Honolulu, HI 96813
Toll Free: 866-798-5598
Fax: (508)437-0303

Castañeda, Rudy, President
Aquarium and Zoo Facilities As-
    sociation [7397]
3900 Wildlife Way
Cleveland, OH 44109

Castellano, John, President
Bright Steps Forward [10875]
4026 N Ocean Blvd.
Fort Lauderdale, FL 33308
Ph: (954)491-6611
Toll Free: 877-NOW-ICAN

Castellanos, Noel, CEO
Christian Community Development
    Association [20362]
3851 W Ogden Ave.
Chicago, IL 60623
Ph: (773)475-7370
Fax: (773)475-6303

Caster, Sam, Founder
MannaRelief [12100]
PO Box 540669
Grand Prairie, TX 75054-0669
Ph: (817)557-8700
Fax: (817)557-8750

Castiello, Andrea, Coord.
Partnership for Drug-Free Kids
    [13172]
352 Park Ave. S, 9th Fl.
New York, NY 10010
Ph: (212)922-1560
Toll Free: 855-378-4373
Fax: (212)922-1570

Castillo, Ms. Laura, Exec. Dir.
Five P Minus Society [17340]
PO Box 268
Lakewood, CA 90714-0268
Ph: (562)804-4506
Toll Free: 888-970-0777
Fax: (562)920-5240

Castillo, Mauricio, MD, President
American Roentgen Ray Society
    [17043]
44211 Slatestone Ct.
Leesburg, VA 20176-5109
Ph: (703)729-3353
Toll Free: 866-940-2777
Fax: (703)729-4839

Castle, Gregory, CEO
Best Friends Animal Society [10593]
5001 Angel Canyon Rd.
Kanab, UT 84741-5000
Ph: (435)644-2001
Fax: (435)644-2078

Castle, Marie Alena, Dir. of Comm.
Atheists For Human Rights [18376]
5146 Newton Ave. N
Minneapolis, MN 55430-3459
Ph: (612)529-1200
    (612)326-6925
Toll Free: 866-ATH-EIST

Casto, Mr. Bill, Commissioner, Exec.
    Dir.
United States Collegiate Athletic As-
    sociation [23259]
150 Boush St., Ste. 603
Norfolk, VA 23510
Ph: (757)706-3756
Fax: (757)706-3758

Castro, Ceasar, Contact
Psi Sigma Phi Multicultural Fraternity
    Inc. [23868]
PO Box 3613
Jersey City, NJ 07303-3062

Castro Cortes, Raul, President
Cuban American Alliance Education
    Fund, Inc. [9195]
PO Box 5113
San Luis Obispo, CA 93403
Ph: (805)627-1959
Fax: (805)627-1959

Castro, Karina, Assoc. Dir.
Sigma Lambda Alpha Sorority Inc.
    [23976]
PO Box 424613
Denton, TX 76204-4296

Castro, Martin, CEO, President
Mexican American Opportunity
    Foundation [11944]
401 N Garfield Ave.
Montebello, CA 90640
Ph: (323)890-9600
Fax: (323)890-9637

Castro, Ralph, Founder, President
International Shaolin Kenpo Associa-
    tion [22995]

69 Washington St.
Daly City, CA 94014
Ph: (650)755-8996

Castro, Ricardo, President
National Institute of Ceramic
    Engineers [6172]
American Ceramic Society
600 N Cleveland Ave., Ste. 210
Westerville, OH 43082-6921
Ph: (614)794-5821
Fax: (614)794-5881

Caswell, Kathleen, Exec. Dir.
Orthopaedic Trauma Association
    [16488]
9400 W Higgins Rd., Ste. 305
Rosemont, IL 60018-4226
Ph: (847)698-1631
Fax: (847)430-5140

Caswell, Lyman, Director
Society for Hungarian Philately
    [22366]
4889 76th St. SW, Unit A403
Mukilteo, WA 98275
Ph: (770)840-8766
Toll Free: 888-868-8293

Catalon, Dr. Katie B., President
National Beauty Culturists' League,
    Inc. [924]
25 Logan Cir. NW
Washington, DC 20005-3725
Ph: (202)332-2695
Fax: (202)223-0940

Cates, James, Chairman
National Native American Veterans
    Association [21135]
3903 County Rd. 382
San Antonio, TX 78253

Cates-Wessel, Ms. Kathryn, Exec.
    Dir.
American Academy of Addiction
    Psychiatry [16806]
400 Massasoit Ave., 2nd Fl., Ste.
    307
East Providence, RI 02914-2012
Ph: (401)524-3076
Fax: (401)272-0922

Cathcart, Christopher, CEO,
    President
Consumer Specialty Products As-
    sociation [715]
1667 K St. NW, Ste. 300
Washington, DC 20006
Ph: (202)872-8110
Fax: (202)223-2636

Cathcart, Kevin M., Exec. Dir.
Lambda Legal [11896]
120 Wall St., 19th Fl.
New York, NY 10005-3919
Ph: (212)809-8585
Fax: (212)809-0055

Cathcart, Sherrie, Exec. Dir.
American Association for the Study
    of Liver Diseases [15248]
1001 N Fairfax St., Ste. 400
Alexandria, VA 22314-1587
Ph: (703)299-9766

Catherall, Dr. Tom, Consultant
Marklin Digital Special Interest
    Group [22188]
PO Box 510559
New Berlin, WI 53151-0559
Fax: (262)522-7288

Cathey, Christopher D., President
Student National Dental Association
    [7711]
3517 16th St. NW
Washington, DC 20010
Ph: (202)806-0065
    (202)588-1697
Fax: (202)518-7471

Cathy, Angela, President
Anxiety Disorders Special Interest
Group [12504]
c/o Laurel Sarfan, Treasurer
90 N Patterson Ave.
Oxford, OH 45056

Catizone, Carmen A., MS, RPh,
DPh, Exec. Dir., Secretary
Foreign Pharmacy Graduate
Examination Committee [16660]
National Association of Boards of
Pharmacy
1600 Feehanville Dr.
Mount Prospect, IL 60056
Ph: (847)391-4406
Fax: (847)391-4502

Cator, Karen, President
Digital Promise [7302]
1001 Connecticut Ave. NW, Ste. 830
Washington, DC 20036
Ph: (202)450-3675

Cattani, Mary, Co-Chmn. of the Bd.,
Co-Ch.
Folk Education Association of
America [7768]
73 Willow St.
Florence, MA 01062
Ph: (413)489-1012

Catura, Nate, President
Federal Law Enforcement Officers
Association [5359]
7945 MacArthur Blvd., Ste. 201
Cabin John, MD 20818
Ph: (202)870-5503
Toll Free: 866-553-5362

Caughron, Tony, President
Controlled Environment Testing As-
sociation [7324]
1500 Sunday Dr., Ste. 102
Raleigh, NC 27607-5151
Ph: (919)861-5576
Fax: (919)787-4916

Cauhorn, Jennifer A., Exec. Dir.
Handbell Musicians of America
[9915]
201 E 5th St., Ste. 1900-1025
Cincinnati, OH 45202
Ph: (937)438-0085
Fax: (937)438-0085

Cauley, Gerry W., CEO, President
North American Electric Reliability
Corporation [1032]
North Twr., Ste. 600
3353 Peachtree Rd. NE
Atlanta, GA 30326
Ph: (404)446-2560
Fax: (404)446-2595

Caulfield, Cheryl, President
American Bearing Manufacturers
Association [1704]
2025 M St. NW, Ste. 800
Washington, DC 20036-3309
Ph: (202)367-1155

Caulfield, Cheryl, Exec. Dir.
National Demolition Association
[886]
2025 M St. NW, Ste. 800
Washington, DC 20036
Ph: (202)367-1152
Toll Free: 800-541-2412
Fax: (202)367-2152

Caulfield, Joshua, Liaison, CEO
American Institute of Architecture
Students [230]
1735 New York Ave. NW, Ste. 300
Washington, DC 20006-5209
Ph: (202)626-7472
Fax: (202)626-7414

Caulfield, Joshua, Exec. Dir.
American Medical Student Associa-
tion [8303]
45610 Woodland Rd., Ste. 300
Sterling, VA 20166
Ph: (703)620-6600
Toll Free: 800-767-2266
Fax: (703)620-6445

Cavalier, Crystal, President, Founder
Support Our Arthritic Kids [17169]
PO Box 624
Spring Lake, NC 28390
Ph: (919)842-3484

Cavanagh, John, Chairperson
Fund for Constitutional Government
[18317]
122 Maryland Ave. NE
Washington, DC 20002
Ph: (202)546-3799
Fax: (202)543-3156

Cavanagh, John, Director
U.S. Labor Education in the
Americas Project [18614]
1634 I St. NW, Ste. 1001
Washington, DC 20006
Ph: (202)347-4100
Fax: (202)347-4885

Cavanagh, Mike, Exec. Dir.
Council for Electronic Revenue
Communication Advancement
[3224]
600 Cameron St., Ste. 309
Alexandria, VA 22314
Ph: (703)340-1655
Fax: (703)340-1658

Cavanaugh, Bob, Managing Dir.
Calorie Restriction Society [16211]
187 Ocean Dr.
Newport, NC 28570
Ph: (252)241-3079
Toll Free: 877-511-2702

Cavanaugh, Greg, CEO, President
Charity Music [12368]
40736 Hayes Rd.
Clinton Township, MI 48038-2545
Ph: (586)247-7444
Fax: (586)247-7443

Cavender, Carrie, Office Mgr.
National Peanut Festival Association
[4510]
5622 Highway 231 S
Dothan, AL 36301
Ph: (334)793-4323
Fax: (334)793-3247

Cavender, Mike, Exec. Dir.
Radio-Television Digital News As-
sociation [481]
529 14th St. NW, Ste. 1240
Washington, DC 20045
Fax: (202)223-4007

Cavendish, James C., Exec. Ofc.
Association for the Sociology of
Religion [7182]
University of South Florida
Dept. of Sociology
4202 E Fowler Ave.
Tampa, FL 33620
Ph: (813)974-2758
Fax: (813)974-6455

Cavlovic, Mike, Contact
Hailey's Wish [14581]
25422 Trabuco Rd., Ste. 105-436
Lake Forest, CA 92630
Ph: (949)878-2122

Cawood, Steve, President
National Scrip Collectors Association
[22275]

c/o Garrett Salyers, Secretary
86 McKenzie Ln.
Olive Hill, KY 41164
Ph: (606)337-6622

Cayse, Dan, VP of Fin., VP of Dev.
Cooperative Education and Intern-
ship Association [7677]
PO Box 42506
Cincinnati, OH 45242
Ph: (513)793-2342
Fax: (513)793-0463

Ceballos, Jacqui, Founder
Veteran Feminists of America
[18236]
18 Aberdeen Pl.
Saint Louis, MO 63105

Cebula, Ray, VP
National Association of Benefits and
Work Incentive Specialists [1074]
5025 E Washington St., Ste. 200
Phoenix, AZ 85034
Ph: (602)443-0722

Cech, John, Dep. Comm.
National Council of State Directors
of Community Colleges [7644]
1 Dupont Cir. NW, Ste. 410
Washington, DC 20036
Ph: (202)728-0200
Fax: (202)833-2467

Cedar, Dr. Paul A., Chairman, CEO
Mission America Coalition [19993]
PO Box 13930
Palm Desert, CA 92255
Ph: (760)200-2707
Fax: (760)200-8837

Cedar, Dr. Paul A., Chairman, CEO
Pioneer Clubs [20661]
PO Box 788
Wheaton, IL 60187-0788
Toll Free: 800-694-2582

Cederstav, Anna, Exec. Dir.
Interamerican Association for
Environmental Defense [4130]
50 California St., Ste. 500
San Francisco, CA 94111
Ph: (415)217-2156
Fax: (415)217-2040

Celebi, Mehmet, Bd. Member
Assembly of Turkish American As-
sociations [19673]
1526 18th St. NW
Washington, DC 20036
Ph: (202)483-9090
Fax: (202)483-9092

Celentano, Amanda, Associate
National Consumer Voice for Quality
Long-Term Care [18054]
1001 Connecticut Ave. NW, Ste. 632
Washington, DC 20036
Ph: (202)332-2275
Fax: (866)230-9789

Celeste, Jordan, MD, Bd. Member
Emergency Medicine Residents' As-
sociation [14679]
1125 Executive Cir.
Irving, TX 75038
Ph: (972)550-0920
Toll Free: 866-566-2492
Fax: (972)692-5995

Celestino, Linda, Bd. Member
Airline Passenger Experience As-
sociation [358]
355 Lexington Ave., 15th Fl.
New York, NY 10017
Ph: (212)297-2177
Fax: (212)370-9047

Celik, Emre, President
Rumi Forum [18827]
750 1st St. NE, Ste. 1120

Washington, DC 20002-8013
Ph: (202)429-1690
Fax: (202)747-2919

Celik, Emre, CEO, President
SAFE-BioPharma Association [2571]
82 N Summit St., Ste. 2
Tenafly, NJ 07670-1018
Ph: (201)925-2173

Cellar, Dr. Doug, Contact
Center for Community and Organiza-
tion Development [11291]
DePaul University
1 E Jackson Blvd.
Chicago, IL 60604
Ph: (773)325-4250
   (312)362-8000
Fax: (773)325-4249

Cena, Mr. Jay, Chairman
ReformAMT [19162]
PO Box 915
Cupertino, CA 95015
Ph: (408)482-2400
   (650)207-3940

Cendana, Gregory A., Exec. Dir.
Asian Pacific American Labor Alli-
ance [23453]
815 16th St. NW
Washington, DC 20009
Ph: (202)508-3733

Cendana, Gregory A., VP
Youth Pride Alliance [11913]
PO Box 12196
Washington, DC 20005

Centrone, Dr. Wayne, President
Health Bridges International [15466]
PO Box 8813
Portland, OR 97207
Ph: (608)354-7567

Cernich, Andrea, Director
Champions for America's Future
[10815]
1212 New York Ave. NW, Ste. 300
Washington, DC 20005
Ph: (202)684-8865

Cervantes, Arlaine, Founder, Exec.
Dir.
Ninos del Lago [11100]
PO Box 1005
Silverton, OR 97381

Cervone, Barbara, Founder,
President
What Kids Can Do [19279]
PO Box 603252
Providence, RI 02906
Ph: (401)247-7665
Fax: (401)245-6428

Cesare, Dennis, Contact
JEM Cure for CLL [15535]
140 S Broadway
Pitman, NJ 08071
Ph: (856)256-1490

Cespedes, Javier de, Founder,
President
Directorio Democratico Cubano
[18076]
730 NW 170 Ave., Ste. 177
Miami, FL 33155
Ph: (305)220-2713

Cha, Susan Scanlan, Contact
National Council of Women's
Organizations [18225]
1050 17th St. NW, Ste. 250
Washington, DC 20036
Ph: (202)293-4505
Fax: (202)293-4507

Chabin, Jim, President
International 3D and Advanced
Imaging Society [6719]

1801 Century Pk. E, Ste. 1040
Los Angeles, CA 90067
Ph: (310)203-9733

Chabrian, Dr. Peggy, President
Women in Aviation International
[3502]
Morningstar Airport
3647 State Route 503 S
West Alexandria, OH 45381-9354
Ph: (937)839-4647
Fax: (937)839-4645

Chacón, Hilda, Vice Cmdr.
Feministas Unidas [9356]
c/o Mayte De Lama, Professor
919 Creek Crossing Trl.
Whitsett, NC 27377

Chadabe, Benjamin, Exec. Dir.
Electronic Music Foundation [9904]
176 3rd St.
Troy, NY 12180
Ph: (518)434-4110
    (212)206-1505
Toll Free: 888-749-9998
Fax: (518)434-0308

Chadabe, Joel, President
New Wilderness Foundation [9984]
307 7th Ave., Ste. 1402
New York, NY 10001
Ph: (646)912-7990

Chadwick, Kirstie, President, CEO
International Business Innovation
Association [638]
12703 Research Pky., Ste. 100
Orlando, FL 32826
Ph: (407)965-5653

Chadwick, Kirstie, President, CEO
National Business Incubation As-
sociation [653]
12703 Research Pky., Ste. 100
Orlando, FL 32826
Ph: (407)965-5653

Chadwick, Phil, President
Bioelectromagnetics Society [6062]
c/o James C. Lin. Editor-in-Chief
University of Illinois
851 S Morgan St.
Chicago, IL 60607-7053
Fax: (312)413-0024

Chadwick, Wallace, Exec. Dir.
Law Enforcement United Inc. [5483]
PO Box 2126
Chesapeake, VA 23327-2126

Chafetz, Adam, CEO, President
TIPS Program [11513]
c/o Health Communications, Inc.
1400 Key Blvd., Ste. 700
Arlington, VA 22209
Toll Free: 800-438-8477
Fax: (703)524-1487

Chaffee, Mark J., Chairman
Radiant Professionals Alliance
[1635]
18927 Hickory Creek Dr., Ste. 220
Mokena, IL 60448
Toll Free: 877-427-6601
Fax: (708)479-6023

Chaffin, Eugene F., Chmn. of the Bd.
Creation Research Society [20595]
6801 N Highway 89
Chino Valley, AZ 86323
Ph: (928)636-1153
Toll Free: 877-277-2665
Fax: (928)636-8444

Chafin, Darren, President
Vintage Motor Bike Club [22237]
c/o Kaitlyn Edelbrock, Secretary

419 W Ervin Rd.
Van Wert, OH 45891-3403
Ph: (419)605-5336

Chagnon, Christiane, Mem.
Daughters of Isabella, International
Circle [19406]
PO Box 9585
New Haven, CT 06535
Ph: (203)865-2570

Chakrabarti, Dr. Chandana, VP
Society for Indian Philosophy and
Religion [9572]
PO Box 79
Elon, NC 27244

Chakraborty, Rini, Co-Ch.
SweatFree Communities [23462]
c/o Liana Foxvog
2 Conz St., Ste. 2B
Northampton, MA 01060
Ph: (413)586-0974
Fax: (413)584-8987

Chalfie, Martin, Chairman
Committee on Human Rights of
National Academies of Sciences,
Engineering and Medicine [18387]
500 5th St. NW
Washington, DC 20001
Ph: (202)334-3043
Fax: (202)334-2225

Chalker, Bob, CEO
NACE International [6571]
15835 Park Ten Pl.
Houston, TX 77084
Ph: (281)228-6200
Fax: (281)228-6300

Challinor, Mark, President
International News Media Associa-
tion [18654]
PO Box 740186
Dallas, TX 75374
Ph: (214)373-9111
Fax: (214)373-9112

Chamanara, Soudy, Chairperson
World Cultural Heritage Voices
[9238]
PO Box 3584
Littleton, CO 80161
Ph: (720)352-5092

Chamberlain, Henry, COO, President
Building Owners and Managers As-
sociation International [2852]
1101 15th St. NW, Ste. 800
Washington, DC 20005
Ph: (202)408-2662
Fax: (202)326-6377

Chamberlain, John, President
United States Twirling Association
[22581]
c/o Julie Jenkins, Business Manager
244 Overland Dr.
Sidney, OH 45365

Chamberlain, Robert S., Secretary,
Treasurer
Corn Items Collectors Association
[21642]
9288 Poland Rd.
Warrensburg, IL 62573
Ph: (217)674-3334

Chamberlin, Donald L., VP
World Chamberlain Genealogical
Society [21001]
c/o Patricia Sugg, Corresponding
Secretary
13305 Cloverdale Pl.
Germantown, MD 20874

Chamberlin, Nat, President
Merck Family Fund [4081]
PO Box 870245

Milton Village, MA 02187
Ph: (617)696-3580
Fax: (617)696-7262

Chamberlin, Peter Klotz, Coord.
Resource Center for Nonviolence
[18726]
612 Ocean St.
Santa Cruz, CA 95060-4006
Ph: (831)423-1626

Chamberlin, Wendy J., President
Middle East Institute [18687]
1761 N St. NW
Washington, DC 20036
Ph: (202)785-1141
    (202)785-1141
Fax: (202)331-8861

Chambers, Andrea, Contact
Process Gas Consumers Group
[18056]
1909 K St. NW, 12th Fl.
Washington, DC 20006
Ph: (202)661-7607

Chambers, Anthony, President
APA Division 43: Society for Family
Psychology [16888]
Division Services Office
750 1st St. NE
Washington, DC 20002
Ph: (202)336-6013

Chambers, Denise, Admin. Asst.
International Bronchoesophagological Society [13861]
1720 2nd Ave. S, BDB 563
Birmingham, AL 35203

Chambers, Greg, Chairman
National Institute for Metalworking
Skills [6850]
10565 Fairfax Blvd., Ste. 10
Fairfax, VA 22030
Ph: (703)352-4971
Toll Free: 844-839-6467
Fax: (703)352-4991

Chambers, Janet Favero, President
National Fibromyalgia and Chronic
Pain Association [14769]
31 Federal Ave.
Logan, UT 84321-4640
Ph: (801)200-3627

Chambers, John E., Founder
Martial Arts U.S.A. [23004]
c/o Patricia Hill, 1619 Fairway Dr.,
SW
1619 Fairway Dr. SW
Jacksonville, AL 36265
Ph: (256)782-3045
    (256)714-8270

Chambers, Liza, Founder
Soliya [19278]
261 Madison Ave., 9th Fl.
New York, NY 10016
Ph: (718)701-5855
Fax: (718)701-5856

Chambers, Louise, Dir. of Comm.
Purple Martin Conservation Associa-
tion [4873]
301 Peninsula Dr., Ste. 6
Erie, PA 16505
Ph: (814)833-7656
Fax: (814)833-2451

Chambers, Monica, Chmn. of the
Bd.
National Association of Victim
Service Professionals in Correc-
tions [13262]
212 S Market St.
Wichita, KS 67202
Ph: (316)613-7263

Chambers, Richard F., CIA, CGAP,
CCSA, CRMA, President, CEO
Institute of Internal Auditors [32]
247 Maitland Ave.
Altamonte Springs, FL 32701-4201
Ph: (407)937-1111
Fax: (407)937-1101

Chambers, Rick, Exec. Dir.
Association of Mailing, Shipping and
Office Automation Specialists
[2116]
11310 Wornall Rd.
Kansas City, MO 64114
Toll Free: 888-750-6245
Fax: (888)836-9561

Chamiec-Case, Rick, PhD, Exec.
Dir.
North American Association of
Christians in Social Work [13115]
PO Box 121
Botsford, CT 06404-0121
Toll Free: 888-426-4712

Chamness, Charles, President
National Association of Mutual Insur-
ance Cos [1898]
3601 Vincennes Rd.
Indianapolis, IN 46268
Ph: (317)875-5250
Fax: (317)879-8408

Champney, Dawn Kristof, President
Water and Wastewater Equipment
Manufacturers Association [1777]
PO Box 17402
Washington, DC 20041
Ph: (703)444-1777
Fax: (703)444-1779

Chan, Chris, President
Association of Asian American
Investment Managers [2018]
50 California St., Ste. 2320
San Francisco, CA 94111

Chan, Michael A., Director
National Federation of Community
Development Credit Unions [958]
39 Broadway, Ste. 2140
New York, NY 10006-3063
Ph: (212)809-1850
Toll Free: 800-437-8711
Fax: (212)809-3274

Chanay, Dr. Marcus A., President
National Association of Student Af-
fairs Professionals [7437]
c/o Gwinetta L. Trice, Recording
Secretary
504 College Drive
Albany, GA 31705
Ph: (540)831-6297
    (229)903-3606

Chandler, B. Glenn, VP
Chandler Family Association [20792]
c/o Helen Chandler, Secretary-
Treasurer, 5020 Monk House Rd.
5020 Monk House Rd.
Somerville, TN 38068
Ph: (901)355-5614

Chandler, Evelyn, President
National Association of Women's
Gymnastics Judges [22901]
c/o Barbara Tebben, Secretary
6913 Rosemary Rd.
Eden Prairie, MN 55346

Chandler, Mary, President
International Society for Educational
Planning [8441]
2903 Ashlawn Dr.
Blacksburg, VA 24060-8101

Chandler, Stephanie, Founder, CEO
Nonfiction Authors Association
[9086]

11230 Gold Express Dr., Ste. 310-413
Gold River, CA 95670
Toll Free: 877-800-1097

Chandler, Terry, President, CEO
Diamond Council of America [2042]
3212 W End Ave., Ste. 400
Nashville, TN 37203
Ph: (615)385-5301
Toll Free: 877-283-5669
Fax: (615)385-4955

Chandler, Terry, President
German Shorthaired Pointer Club of
America [21884]
c/o Cynthia McCracken, Membership
Chairperson
3026 Tidwell Rd.
Burke, TX 75941-6173
Ph: (814)421-2946

Chandra, Damyenti, Founder
Fiji Aid International [13049]
5800 Balfor Rd.
Rocklin, CA 95765
Ph: (916)663-6578

Chandran, Joyce, Exec. Dir.
Women's Council on Energy and the
Environment [6518]
816 Connecticut Ave. NW, Ste. 200
Washington, DC 20006
Ph: (202)997-4512
Fax: (202)478-2098

Chanen, Andrew, President
International Society for the Study of
Personality Disorders [15780]
c/o Ashley Stauffer
341 Science Complex
Eastern Michigan University
Psychology Dept.
Ypsilanti, MI 48197-6229
Ph: (734)487-0047
Fax: (734)487-6553

Chaney, Bill, Director
Inland Seas Education Association
[2243]
100 Dame St.
Suttons Bay, MI 49682
Ph: (231)271-3077
Fax: (231)271-3088

Chaney, Gary, President
American Bop Association [9239]

Chaney, Dr. Verne E., Jr., Founder
Intermed International [15479]
125-28 Queens Blvd., Ste. 538
Kew Gardens, NY 11415
Ph: (646)820-7360

Chang, Anthony C., Group VP, Intl.
Pediatric Cardiac Intensive Care
Society [16612]
2209 Dickens Rd.
Richmond, VA 23230-2005
Ph: (804)565-6398
Fax: (804)282-0090

Chang, Cheryl S., Esq, President
Taiwanese American Lawyers Association [5051]
1661 Hanover Rd., Ste. 215
City of Industry, CA 91748
Ph: (626)839-3800

Chang, Christina K., President
Organization of Chinese American
Women [18232]
PO Box 815
Great Falls, VA 22066
Ph: (301)907-3898
Fax: (301)907-3899

Chang, Christine Minji, Exec. Dir.
Kollaboration [13456]
1933 S Broadway, Ste. 745

Los Angeles, CA 90007

Chang, Claire
Asian Business League of San
Francisco [610]
PO Box 191345
San Francisco, CA 94119-1345

Chang, David, MD, Sec. Gen.
World Society for Reconstructive
Microsurgery [17421]
20 N Michigan Ave., Ste. 700
Chicago, IL 60602
Ph: (312)263-7150
Fax: (312)782-0553

Chang, Edward, President
Asian American Advertising Federation [87]
6230 Wilshire Blvd., No. 1216
Los Angeles, CA 90048

Chang, Esther, PhD, Act. Pres.
American Society for Nanomedicine
[15712]
Georgetown University Medical Ctr.
3970 Reservoir Rd. NW
Washington, DC 20057
Ph: (202)687-8418

Chang, Gigi Lee, CEO
Healthy Child Healthy World [14193]
8383 Wilshire Blvd. Fl., 8
Los Angeles, CA 900211
Ph: (424)343-0020

Chang, Jim, Officer
ReSurge International [14322]
145 N Wolfe Rd.
Sunnyvale, CA 94086
Ph: (408)737-8743
Fax: (408)737-8000

Chang, Paul Wen-liang, Amb.
Taipei Economic and Cultural Office
in New York [9157]
1 E 42nd St., 4th Fl.
New York, NY 10017
Ph: (212)486-0088
Fax: (212)421-7866

Chang, Ms. Tsu-Wei, Director
United Nations Women's Guild
[12910]
DC-1, Rm. 0775
1 United Nations Plz.
New York, NY 10017
Ph: (212)963-4149

Changchit, Chuleeporn, VP
Association of Thai Professionals in
America and Canada [19671]
4398 Ellinwood Blvd.
Palm Harbor, FL 34685

Chan-Ling, Tailoi, Secretary
International Society for Eye
Research [6092]
655 Beach St.
San Francisco, CA 94119
Ph: (415)561-8569
Fax: (415)561-8531

Channel, Tommy, Mem.
International Gay Rodeo Association
[23095]
PO Box 460504
Aurora, CO 80046-0504

Chanoff, Sasha, Exec. Dir., Founder
RefugePoint [12717]
689 Massachusetts Ave., 2nd Fl.
Cambridge, MA 02139
Ph: (617)864-7800
Fax: (617)864-7802

Chan-Padgett, Vicki, Treasurer
Refugee Relief International [12299]
2995 Woodside Rd., No. 400-244

Woodside, CA 94062

Chanthyasack, Sirch, CEO
Laotian American National Alliance,
Inc. [19527]
1628 16th St. NW
Washington, DC 20009
Ph: (202)370-7841
(415)680-4027
Fax: (202)462-2774

Chao, Gene, CEO, President, Chairman
National Captioning Institute [15201]
3725 Concorde Pky., Ste. 100
Chantilly, VA 20151
Ph: (703)917-7600
Fax: (703)917-9853

Chapa, Anthony, Exec. Dir.
Hispanic American Police Command
Officers Association [5464]
PO Box 29626
Washington, DC 20017
Ph: (202)664-4461

Chaparro, Jennifer, Founder, Director
International Street Painting Society
[8869]
9285 SE Delafield St.
Hobe Sound, FL 33455
Ph: (561)315-0243

Chapin, Krissane, PhD, President
Gait and Clinical Movement Analysis
Society [14934]
Naperville, IL

Chapman, Mrs. Beth, Chmn. of the
Bd., President
Professional Bail Agents of the
United States [5064]
801 N Magnolia Ave., Ste. 418
Orlando, FL 32803
Ph: (202)783-4120
Toll Free: 800-883-7287
Fax: (202)783-4125

Chapman, Cindy, Exec. Dir.
Commission on Rehabilitation
Counselor Certification [11488]
1699 E Woodfield Rd., Ste. 300
Schaumburg, IL 60173-4957
Ph: (847)944-1325
Fax: (847)944-1346

Chapman, Clayton, Director
Intercollegiate Rowing Association
[23110]
1311 Craigville Beach Rd.
Centerville, MA 02632-4129
Ph: (857)257-3728
Fax: (508)771-9481

Chapman, Julie, President
American Miniature Llama Association [3595]
PO Box 8
Kalispell, MT 59903-0008
Ph: (406)755-3438

Chapman, Lloyd, President
American Small Business League
[3113]
3910 Cypress Dr., Ste. B
Petaluma, CA 94954
Ph: (707)789-9575
Fax: (707)789-9580

Chapman, Marvin, President
United Fathers of America [11687]
1651 E 4th St., Ste. 107
Santa Ana, CA 92701
Ph: (714)558-7949

Chapman, Nancy, MPH, RD,
Principal
Advocates for Better Children's Diets
[16199]

1050 17th St. NW, Ste. 600
Washington, DC 20036
Ph: (202)659-1858
Fax: (202)659-3522

Chapman, Nancy E., President
United Board for Christian Higher
Education in Asia [8106]
475 Riverside Dr., Ste. 1221
New York, NY 10115
Ph: (212)870-2600
Fax: (212)870-2322

Chapman, Richard F., President
International Sunfish Class Association [22640]
2812 Canon St.
San Diego, CA 92106-2742
Ph: (619)222-0252

Chapman-Henderson, Leslie, CEO,
President
Federal Alliance For Safe Homes
[14693]
1427 E Piedmont Dr., Ste. 2
Tallahassee, FL 32308
Toll Free: 877-221-7233
Fax: (850)201-1067

Chappell, Dave, Commodore
Annapolis Naval Sailing Association
[22597]
6807 Crofton Colony Ct.
Crofton, MD 21114-3276

Chappell, Patricia, Exec. Dir.
Pax Christi U.S.A. [18725]
415 Michigan Ave. NE, Ste. 240
Washington, DC 20017-4503
Ph: (202)635-2741

Characklis, Gregory W., President
Association of Environmental
Engineering & Science Professors
[8465]
1211 Connecticut Ave. NW, Ste. 650
Washington, DC 20036
Ph: (202)640-6591

Charash, Bruce, MD, Founder
Doc2Doc [15599]
1299 Corporate Dr., Ste. 703
Westbury, NY 11590

Charchian, Paul, President
Fantasy Sports Trade Association
[3155]
600 N Lake Shore Dr.
Chicago, IL 60611
Ph: (312)771-7019

Chard, Dr. Joshua, PhD, Chairman
Manufacturers of Aerial Devices &
Digger Derricks Council [1744]
c/o Dr. Joshua Chard, PhD, Chairman
33 Inverness Center Pky.
Birmingham, AL 35242
Ph: (414)272-0943
Fax: (414)272-1170

Chardella, Anthony, Chairman
369th Fighter Squadron Association
[20677]
511 Crest Haven Dr.
Pittsburgh, PA 15239
Ph: (412)793-7619

Charette, Everett, President
Charette/Charest Family Association
[20794]
c/o Ray Thomas, Treasurer
22 Ludlow Rd.
Windsor, CT 06095

Charles, Cheryl, PhD, Consultant
Children and Nature Network [4039]
808 14th Ave. SE

Minneapolis, MN 55414

Charles, David, MD, Chairman
Mending Faces [14341]
422 Humboldt St.
Denver, CO 80218

Charles, Earl, President
United States Sign Council [114]
211 Radcliffe St.
Bristol, PA 19007-5017
Ph: (215)785-1922
Fax: (215)788-8395

Charles, Elizabeth C., Secretary
Society for History in the Federal
Government [9519]
PO Box 14139
Washington, DC 20044

Charles, George S., Jr., President
William Penn Association [19499]
709 Brighton Rd.
Pittsburgh, PA 15233
Ph: (412)231-2979
Toll Free: 800-848-7366
Fax: (412)231-8535

Charles, J. Kenneth, III, Managing
Dir.
Steel Joist Institute [583]
234 W Cheves St.
Florence, SC 29501
Ph: (843)407-4091

Charles, Jodel Stanley, Founder
Renewal 4 Haiti [12300]
18625 E Dorado Dr.
Aurora, CO 80015
Ph: (720)530-6975

Charles, Kristi, Assoc. Dir.
National Resource Center for Youth
Services [11096]
Bldg. 4W
Schusterman Ctr.
4502 E 41st St.
Tulsa, OK 74135-2512
Ph: (918)660-3700
Fax: (918)660-3737

Charles, Dr. Marie, MD,
Chairperson, CEO
Global Medic Force [15461]
101 W 23rd St., Ste. 179
New York, NY 10011
Toll Free: 866-232-4954

Charles, Mark, VP
National Mini Rex Rabbit Club
[4606]
c/o Doug King, Secretary
2719 Terrace Ave.
Sanger, CA 93657

Charlton, Mr. Knight, Exec. Dir.
American Dental Society of
Anesthesiology [14408]
211 E Chicago Ave.
Chicago, IL 60611
Ph: (312)664-8270
Fax: (312)224-8624

Charney, Alyssa, Specialist
National Sustainable Agriculture
Coalition [4699]
110 Maryland Ave. NE, Ste. 209
Washington, DC 20002
Ph: (202)547-5754

Charney, Amanda, Exec. Dir.
Small Steps in Speech [14296]
PO Box 134
Collingswood, NJ 08108
Toll Free: 888-577-3256
Fax: (856)632-7741

Charnik, Jo Ann, President
Akita Club of America [21793]

Charno, Chrysa, Director
Association of Plastic Surgery Physi-
cian Assistants [14314]
5790 Farnsworth Dr.
Tallahassee, FL 32312-4881
Ph: (850)385-4596
Fax: (585)383-4051

Charron, Kenneth G., President
Association of Transportation Law
Professionals [5811]
c/o Lauren Michalski, Executive
Director
PO Box 5407
Annapolis, MD 21403
Ph: (410)268-1311
Fax: (410)268-1322

Chase, Devin, President
Peace Officers for Christ
International [20005]
3000 W MacArthur Blvd., Ste. 426
Santa Ana, CA 92704-6962
Ph: (714)426-7632

Chase, Fred, President
Antique Truck Club of America
[22473]
85 S Walnut St.
Boyertown, PA 19512
Ph: (610)367-2567
Fax: (610)367-9712

Chase, Jonathan, President
Golden Retriever Club of America
[21887]
c/o Jolene Carey, Administrative Assistant
PO Box 20434
Oklahoma City, OK 73156

Chase, Mark, President
United States Boxer Association
[21980]
c/o Jowhar Karim, Secretary
PO Box 5991
Goodyear, AZ 85338-0617

Chase, Mike, Director, Founder
Elephants Without Borders [4812]
500 Linwood Ave.
Buffalo, NY 14209
Ph: (716)884-1548

Chase, Paul, VP, CFO
Financial Executives International
[1233]
West Twr., 7th Fl.
1250 Headquarters Plz.
Morristown, NJ 07960
Ph: (973)765-1000
Toll Free: 877-359-1070
Fax: (973)765-1018

Chase, Robert, CEO, President
Sales Exchange for Refugee
Rehabilitation and Vocation [3305]
500 Main St.
New Windsor, MD 21776-0365
Toll Free: 800-422-5915
Fax: (888)294-6376

Chase, Sue, Dir. of Fin.
National Fluid Power Association
[1754]
6373 W Washington St., Ste. 2350
Milwaukee, WI 53214
Ph: (414)778-3344
Fax: (414)778-3361

Chasin, Denise, Director
Personal Ponies Ltd. [11631]
c/o Cindy Pullen, National Director
368 River Rd.
Lakeland, GA 31635
Ph: (229)503-9964

Chasin, Laura, Bd. Member
Public Conversations Project
[17953]

186 Alewife Brook Pky., Ste. 212
Cambridge, MA 02138
Ph: (617)923-1216
Fax: (617)923-2757

Chasin, Laura, Advisor
Trust for Mutual Understanding
[12193]
1 Rockefeller Pl., Rm. 2500
New York, NY 10020
Ph: (212)649-5776
Fax: (212)649-5777

Chasse, Beatrice, President
International Oak Society [4730]

Chasse, Jaclyn, ND, President
American Association of Natur-
opathic Physicians [15855]
818 18th St., Ste. 250
Washington, DC 20006
Ph: (202)237-8150
Toll Free: 866-538-2267
Fax: (202)237-8152

Chastain, Merritt B., III, Managing
Dir.
National Association of Pipe Coating
Applicators [745]
500 Dallas St., Ste. 3000
Houston, TX 77002
Ph: (713)655-5761
Fax: (713)655-0020

Chastain, Scott, Chairman
PROMAXBDA [478]
5700 Wilshire Blvd., Ste. 275
Los Angeles, CA 90036-3687
Ph: (310)788-7600
Fax: (310)788-7616

Chatara, Nathela, CAE, Exec. Dir.
American Society for Pharmacy Law
[15529]
3085 Stevenson Dr., Ste. 200
Springfield, IL 62703-4270
Ph: (217)529-6948
Fax: (217)529-9120

Chatara, Nathela, Dir. of Admin.
Association for Preservation
Technology International [9377]
3085 Stevenson Dr., Ste. 200
Springfield, IL 62703
Ph: (217)529-9039
Fax: (888)723-4242

Chatfield, Steven J., PhD, CFO, Dir.
of Member Svcs.
International Association for Dance
Medicine and Science [15728]
Dept. of Dance
1214 University of Oregon
Eugene, OR 97403-1214
Ph: (541)465-1763
Fax: (541)465-1763

Chatlos, Mr. William J., Founder
The Chatlos Foundation, Inc.
[20622]
PO Box 915048
Longwood, FL 32791-5048
Ph: (407)862-5077

Chatterjee, Choi, President
Association for Women in Slavic
Studies [10216]
c/o Sarah D. Phillips, Treasur-
er,Bloomington
Student Bldg. 130
Dept. of Anthropology
Indiana University
701 E Kirkwood Ave.
Bloomington, IN 47405
Ph: (812)855-0216

Chatterjee, Pratap, Exec. Dir.
CorpWatch [18389]
PO Box 29198

San Francisco, CA 94129
Ph: (415)226-6226

Chaudhary, Ved, Advisor
80-20 Initiative [17818]
5 Farm House Rd.
Newark, DE 19711
Ph: (858)472-5558

Chaudhry, Humayon J., FACP, CEO,
President
Federation of State Medical Boards
[15724]
400 Fuller Wiser Rd.
Euless, TX 76039
Ph: (817)868-4000
(817)868-4041
Toll Free: 888-ASK-FCVS
Fax: (817)868-4099

Chaudhry, Humayun, Dr., Chairman,
Secretary
International Association of Medical
Regulatory Authorities [15730]
400 Fuller Wiser Rd., Ste. 300
Euless, TX 76039
Ph: (817)868-4006
Fax: (817)868-4097

Chaudry, Dr. Muhammad Munir,
President
Islamic Food and Nutrition Council of
America [1349]
777 Busse Hwy.
Park Ridge, IL 60068
Ph: (847)993-0034
Fax: (847)993-0038

Chaulsett, Eric, Director
American Plate Number Single
Society [22303]
PO Box 1023
Palatine, IL 60078-1023

Chauncy, Charles Bud, Coord.
Driving School Association of the
Americas [7724]
Communications Office
3125 Wilmington Pke.
Kettering, OH 45429-4003
Toll Free: 800-270-3722
Fax: (937)290-0696

Chavez, Anna Maria, CEO
Girl Scouts of the U.S.A. [12852]
420 5th Ave.
New York, NY 10018-2798
Ph: (212)852-8000
Toll Free: 800-478-7248

Chavez, Arturo, PhD, President,
CEO
Mexican American Catholic College
[20373]
3115 W Ashby Pl.
San Antonio, TX 78228-5104
Ph: (210)732-2156
Toll Free: 866-893-6222
Fax: (210)732-9072

Chavez, Brian, President
National Wheelchair Softball Association [22792]
c/o Brian Chavez, President
10004 Fallgold
Brooklyn Park, MN 55443
Ph: (402)305-5020

Chavez, Jim, Exec. Dir.
Latin American Educational Founda-
tion [7972]
561 Santa Fe Dr.
Denver, CO 80204
Ph: (303)446-0541
Fax: (303)446-0526

Chavez, Linda, Chairman
Center for Equal Opportunity
[12124]

7700 Leesburg Pike, Ste. 231
Falls Church, VA 22043
Ph: (703)442-0066
Fax: (703)442-0449

Chavez-Metoyer, Sylvia, Exec.,
CEO, President
National Image Inc. [19464]
374 E H St., Ste. A, PMB 419
Chula Vista, CA 91913

Chavez-Ramirez, Felipe, President
North American Crane Working
Group [4856]
c/o Barry Hartup
E-11376 Shady Lane Rd.
Baraboo, WI 53913

Chazan, Naomi, Director
New Israel Fund [18587]
6 E 39th St., Ste. 301
New York, NY 10016-0112
Ph: (212)613-4400
Fax: (212)714-2153

Chazdon, Dr. Robin L., Exec. Dir.
Association for Tropical Biology and
Conservation [6076]
c/o Robin L. Chazdon, Executive
Director
Dept. of Ecology and Evolutionary
Biology, U-3043
75 N Eagleville Rd.
Storrs, CT 06269-3042

Chazkel, Amy, Chairman
MARHO: The Radical Historians'
Organization [9493]
New York University
Tamiment Library, 10th Fl.
70 Washington Sq. S
New York, NY 10012

Cheadle, Barbara, Officer
National Organization of Parents of
Blind Children [17735]
1800 Johnson St.
Baltimore, MD 21230
Ph: (410)659-9314

Cheadle, Don, Founder
Not On Our Watch [18433]
162 5th Ave., 8th Fl.
New York, NY 10010

Check, Fr. Paul N., Exec. Dir.
Courage International [20177]
8 Leonard St.
Norwalk, CT 06850
Ph: (203)803-1564

Cheek, Dr. Jimmy, Chmn. of the Bd.
International Fertilizer Development
Center [3568]
PO Box 2040
Muscle Shoals, AL 35662
Ph: (256)381-6600
Fax: (256)381-7408

Chekel, Martin J., President
Talking Page Literacy Organization
[8254]
1500 King William Woods Rd.
Midlothian, VA 23113
Ph: (949)510-1804

Chelf, Lauren, Dir. of Mtgs.
AOAC International [6187]
2275 Research Blvd., Ste. 300
Rockville, MD 20850-3250
Ph: (301)924-7077
Toll Free: 800-379-2622
Fax: (301)924-7089

Chell, Jeffrey W., MD, CEO
Be The Match Registry [13845]
National Marrow Donor Program
3001 Broadway St. NE, Ste. 100

Minneapolis, MN 55413-2196
Ph: (612)627-5800
Toll Free: 800-627-7692

Cheltenham, Faith, President
BiNet U.S.A. [11873]
4201 Wilson Blvd., No. 110-311
Arlington, VA 22203-1859
Toll Free: 800-585-9368

Chen, Albert, COO
Pi Lambda Theta [23734]
320 W 8th St., Ste. 216
Bloomington, IN 47404
Ph: (812)339-1156
Toll Free: 800-766-1156
Fax: (812)339-0018

Chen, Christine, Exec. Dir.
Asian and Pacific Islander American
Vote [18904]
1612 K St. NW, Ste. 510
Washington, DC 20006
Ph: (202)223-9170

Chen, Christine, President
Association for Childhood Education
International [7581]
1200 18th St. NW, Ste. 700
Washington, DC 20036
Ph: (202)372-9986
Toll Free: 800-423-3563
Fax: (202)372-9989

Chen, David, Treasurer
Asian American Real Estate As-
sociation [2849]
PO Box 1762
Alief, TX 77411
Ph: (281)799-4939

Chen, John, Mgr. Dir.
Public Media Business Association
[479]
7918 Jones Branch Dr., Ste. 300
McLean, VA 22102
Ph: (703)506-3292
Fax: (703)506-3266

Chen, Ken, Exec. Dir.
Asian American Writers' Workshop
[3513]
110-112 W 27th St., Ste. 600
New York, NY 10001
Ph: (212)494-0061

Chen, Lillien, Exec. Dir.
Christian Communications, Inc. of
USA [19954]
9600 Bellaire Blvd., No. 111
Houston, TX 77036
Ph: (713)778-1155
   (713)778-1144

Chen, Nan, Director, President
Metro Ethernet Forum [7282]
6033 W Century Blvd., Ste. 1107
Los Angeles, CA 90045
Ph: (310)642-2800
Fax: (310)642-2808

Chen, Tsute, President
International Association for Biological and Medical Research [15646]
140 Fenway
Boston, MA 02115

Cheney, Dr. Liana De Girolami,
President, Treasurer
Association for Textual Scholarship
in Art History [8847]
Beacon Hill
112 Charles St.
Boston, MA 02114-3201
Ph: (617)367-1670
Fax: (617)557-2962

Cheng, Eric Siu-kei, Secretary
North American Taiwan Studies Association [9214]

c/o Hong, Gou-Juin, Advisor
Campus Box 90414
2204 Erwin Rd., Rm. 220
Durham, NC 27708
Ph: (919)660-4396
Fax: (919)981-7871

Cheng, Dr. Jiangang, Officer
Society of International Chinese in
Educational Technology [8676]
c/o Dr. Hong Zhan, Treasurer
7200 E Pioneer Ln.
Prescott Valley, AZ 86314
Ph: (928)523-0408
Fax: (928)523-1929

Cheng, Paul, Mgr.
National Team Cheng Martial Arts
Association [23007]
2269 Garrett Rd.
Drexel Hill, PA 19026
Ph: (610)622-5260

Cheng, Qiuming, President
International Association for
Mathematical Geosciences [6692]
5868 Westheimer Rd., No. 537
Houston, TX 77057
Ph: (832)380-8833

Cheng, Wendy, President
Association of Adult Musicians with
Hearing Loss, Inc. [15175]
PO Box 522
Rockville, MD 20848

Chereso, Tony, President, CEO
Investment Program Association
[2026]
PO Box 480
Ellicott City, MD 21041-0480
Ph: (212)812-9799

Cherian, Dr. Joy, PhD, Founder,
President
Association of Americans for Civic
Responsibility [17858]
13316 Foxhall Dr.
Silver Spring, MD 20906-5308
Ph: (301)933-1494

Chernetsky, Vitaly, President
American Association for Ukrainian
Studies [8107]
34 Kirkland St.
Cambridge, MA 02138

Cherry, Charles L., Editor
Friends Historical Association
[20170]
Haverford College
370 Lancaster Ave.
Haverford, PA 19041-1336
Ph: (610)896-1161
Fax: (610)896-1102

Cherry, James L., President
National Smokejumper Association
[5213]
c/o John McDaniel, Membership
Coordinator
PO Box 105
Falun, KS 67442-0105

Cherry, Mr. Lee O., CEO, President
African Scientific Institute [7114]
PO Box 20810
Piedmont, CA 94620
Ph: (510)653-7027

Cherry, Robert, President
Health Physics Society [16765]
1313 Dolley Madison Blvd., Ste. 402
McLean, VA 22101
Ph: (703)790-1745
Fax: (703)790-2672

Chervin, Ronald, President
American Academy of Sleep
Medicine [17208]

2510 N Frontage Rd.
Darien, IL 60561
Ph: (630)737-9700
Fax: (630)737-9790

Chestnut, Maj. Melissa, Secretary
National Naval Officers Association
[5612]
PO Box 10871
Alexandria, VA 22310-0871
Ph: (703)828-7308

Chestnutt, Rod, Chairman
Kappa Kappa Psi [23827]
401 E 9th Ave.
Stillwater, OK 74074-4704
Ph: (405)372-2333
Fax: (405)372-2363

Cheung, Paul, President
Asian American Journalists Associa-
tion [2656]
5 3rd St., Ste. 1108
San Francisco, CA 94103
Ph: (415)346-2051
Fax: (415)346-6343

Chevez-Barrios, Patricia, President
American Association of Ophthalmic
Oncologists and Pathologists
[16363]
655 Beach St.
San Francisco, CA 94109
Ph: (415)561-8516
Fax: (415)561-8531

Chia, Douglas K., Chmn. of the Bd.
Society of Corporate Secretaries and
Governance Professionals [78]
240 W 35th St., Ste. 400
New York, NY 10001
Ph: (212)681-2000
Fax: (212)681-2005

Chiaia, Nicholas, President
United Press International, Inc.
[2728]
1133 19th St. NW, Ste. 800
Washington, DC 20036-3655
Ph: (202)898-8000

Chiang, Rev. Samuel, Gen. Sec.
Chinese Christian Mission [20394]
1269 N McDowell Blvd.
Petaluma, CA 94954-1133
Ph: (707)762-1314
Fax: (707)762-1713

Chiaro, Delia, President
International Society for Humor
Studies [9562]
c/o Martin Lampert, Ph.D., Executive
Secretary
Holy Names University
3500 Mountain Blvd.
Oakland, CA 94619
Ph: (510)436-1532

Chikhoune, Dr. Ismael, CEO,
President
U.S.-Algeria Business Council
[1996]
2001 Jefferson Davis Hwy., Ste. 208
Arlington, VA 22202
Ph: (703)418-4150
Fax: (703)418-4151

Child, Lee, Co-Pres.
International Thriller Writers [10382]
PO Box 311
Eureka, CA 95502

Childre, Sara, CEO, President
HeartMath Institute [9536]
14700 W Park Ave.
Boulder Creek, CA 95006
Ph: (831)338-8500
Toll Free: 800-711-6221
Fax: (831)338-8504

Childs, Barry, Founder
Africa Bridge [10835]
PO Box 115
Marylhurst, OR 97036-0115
Ph: (503)699-6162

Childs, Greg, CEO
Nissan Infiniti Car Owners Club
[21461]
237 Fernwood Blvd., Ste. 111
Fern Park, FL 32730-2116
Ph: (407)828-8908

Childs, Mary Ellen, Chmn. of the Bd.
American Composers Forum [9177]
75 W 5th St., Ste. 522
Saint Paul, MN 55102-1439
Ph: (651)228-1407
Fax: (651)291-7978

Chilian, William M., President
Microcirculatory Society [17576]
18501 Kingshill Rd.
Germantown, MD 20874
Ph: (301)760-7745

Chilton, Jim, Founder
The Society for Financial Awareness
[1265]
3914 Murphy Canyon Rd., Ste. A125
San Diego, CA 92123
Toll Free: 800-689-4851

Chin, Felix M., President, CEO
Myanmar Community USA [11406]
1178 Southgate Ave.
Daly City, CA 94015
Ph: (650)303-1800

Chin, Warren W., MD, Chairman
Federation of Chinese American and
Chinese Canadian Medical Societ-
ies [15723]
445 Grant Ave., 2nd Fl.
San Francisco, CA 94108-3208
Ph: (415)677-2464
Fax: (415)677-2489

Ching, June, President
APA Division 42: The Community for
Psychologists in Independent
Practice [16886]
919 W Marshall Ave.
Phoenix, AZ 85013
Ph: (602)284-6219

Chinnappan, Benjamin, President
Dalit Solidarity, Inc. [18392]
PO Box 112
Hines, IL 60141-0112
Ph: (708)612-4248

Chipman, John, Dir. Gen., CEO
International Institute for Strategic
Studies - Americas [18945]
2121 K St. NW, Ste. 801
Washington, DC 20037
Ph: (202)659-1490
Fax: (202)296-1499

Chisholm, Kenneth, Secretary
Clan Chisholm Society - United
States [20802]
19 Green Meadow Dr.
Acushnet, MA 02743-1603

Chisom, Ronald, Exec. Dir., Founder
People's Institute for Survival and
Beyond [19115]
601 N Carrollton Ave.
New Orleans, LA 70119
Ph: (504)301-9292
Fax: (504)301-9291

Chiu, John C., MD, Secretary,
Treasurer
International Society for Minimal
Intervention in Spinal Surgery
[17257]

c/o John Chiu, Secretary-Treasurer
1001 Newbury Rd.
Newbury Park, CA 91320
Fax: (805)375-7975

Chizmadia, Richard, President
American Guild of Music [9858]
PO Box 599
Warren, MI 48090-0599
Ph: (248)686-1975

Chlipala, Liz, Treasurer
Digital Pathology Association
[16582]
10293 N Meridian St., Ste. 175
Indianapolis, IN 46290
Ph: (317)816-1630
Toll Free: 877-824-4085
Fax: (317)816-1633

Chmura, Jason, Dir. of Member
Svcs.
Society for Nonprofit Organizations
[258]
PO Box 510354
Livonia, MI 48151
Ph: (734)451-3582
Fax: (734)451-5935

Cho, Rev. James, 1st VP
Great Commission Research
Network [20024]
13800 Biola Ave.
La Mirada, CA 90639

Cho, Man, V. Ch.
Korean American Sharing Movement
[12692]
7004 Little River Tpke., Ste. O
Annandale, VA 22003
Ph: (703)867-0846
Fax: (703)354-0427

Chobin, Nancy, RN, Bd. Member
Certification Board for Sterile
Processing and Distribution
[15663]
148 Main St., Ste. C-1
Lebanon, NJ 08833
Ph: (908)236-0530
Toll Free: 800-555-9765
Fax: (908)236-0820

Chockley, Nancy, CEO, President
National Institute for Health Care
Management Research and
Educational Foundation [15048]
1225 19th St. NW, Ste. 710
Washington, DC 20036-2454
Ph: (202)296-4426
Fax: (202)296-4319

Choi, Bill, VP of Res.
Equipment Leasing and Finance As-
sociation [2927]
1825 K St. NW, Ste. 900
Washington, DC 20006
Ph: (202)238-3400
Fax: (202)238-3401

Choi, Gun, MD, PhD, President
International Intradiscal Therapy
Society [17256]
1635 E Myrtle Ave., Ste. 400
Phoenix, AZ 85020
Ph: (310)279-3159
Fax: (602)944-0064

Choi, Mr. Ji Ho, President
Pan American Taekwondo Union
[23010]
c/o Rick W. Shin, Secretary General
8001 SE Powell Blvd., Ste. O
Portland, OR 97206
Ph: (503)970-8928

Choi, Dr. Mun Young, President
Pi Tau Sigma [23742]
c/o Mun Young Choi, President

University of Connecticut
352 Mansfield Rd., Unit 1086
Storrs, CT 06269
Ph: (860)486-6399

Choi, Susan, Exec. Dir.
Asians for Miracle Marrow Matches
[17507]
244 S San Pedro St., No. 503
Los Angeles, CA 90012
Toll Free: 888-236-4673
Fax: (213)625-2802

Chol, Eric, VP
Reporters Without Borders [18441]
Southern Railway Bldg., Ste. 600
15th & K St. NW
Washington, DC 20005

Chontos, Ms. Diana, Founder,
President
Wild Burro Rescue and Preservation
Project [10715]
PO Box 10
Olancha, CA 93549-0010
Ph: (760)384-8523

Chopp, Joanna, Arch.
Finnish American Historical Archives
[9321]
c/o Joanna Chopp
435 Quincy St.
Hancock, MI 49930
Ph: (906)487-7347
Fax: (906)487-7557

Choquette, Kent, President
IEEE - Photonics Society [6430]
445 Hoes Ln.
Piscataway, NJ 08854-1331
Ph: (732)562-3926
Fax: (732)562-8434

Chow, Alan, Founder, Director
Chinese-American Arts Council
[8970]
456 Broadway, 3rd Fl.
New York, NY 10013
Ph: (212)431-9740
Fax: (212)431-9789

Chow, Dr. Effie, Founder, President
East West Academy of Healing Arts
[16456]
117 Topaz Way
San Francisco, CA 94131
Ph: (415)285-9401

Chow, Prof. Peter C.Y., Exec. Dir.
American Association for Chinese
Studies [7598]
The City College of New York -
CUNY
NAC R4/116
Convent Ave. & 138th St.
New York, NY 10031
Ph: (212)650-6206
    (212)650-8268
Fax: (212)650-8287

Chowdhury, Sayedur Rahman, Dir.
Ed.
Muslim Ummah of North America
[9607]
1033 Glenmore Ave.
Brooklyn, NY 11208
Ph: (646)683-2174
Fax: (718)277-7901

Choy, Daniel S.J., MD, Exec. Dir.
North American Association for
Laser Therapy [15524]
142 Whitbeck Rd.
Coeymans Hollow, NY 12046

Chrisler, Jennifer, VP
Alumnae Association of Smith College [19298]

33 Elm St.
Northampton, MA 01060
Ph: (413)585-2040
Toll Free: 800-526-2023

Chrisley, Michael, Exec. Dir.
Ruritan National, Inc. [12907]
5451 Lyons Rd.
Dublin, VA 24084
Ph: (540)674-5431
Toll Free: 877-787-8727
Fax: (540)674-2304

Chriss, Richard, Exec. Dir.
American Institute for International
Steel [2342]
701 W Broad St., Ste. 301
Falls Church, VA 22046
Ph: (703)245-8075
Fax: (703)610-0215

Christ, Grace, PhD, Chairperson
Social Work Hospice and Palliative
Care Network [15299]
1521 2nd Ave., Ste. 609
Seattle, WA 98101
Ph: (412)701-1192

Christ, Michael, Exec. Dir.
International Physicians for the
Prevention of Nuclear War [18750]
66-70 Union Sq., No. 204
Somerville, MA 02143
Ph: (617)440-1733
Fax: (617)440-1734

Christakis, Michael, President,
Trustee
Omicron Delta Kappa Society
[23788]
224 McLaughlin St.
Lexington, VA 24450-2002
Ph: (540)458-5336
Toll Free: 877-635-6437
Fax: (540)458-5342

Christakis, Michael, Bd. Member
Orthodox Christian Association of
Medicine, Psychology and Religion
[16931]
50 Goddard Ave.
Brookline, MA 02445-7415

Christen, Tim, Chairman
American Institute of Certified Public
Accountants [10]
1211 Avenue of the Americas
New York, NY 10036-8775
Ph: (212)596-6200
Fax: (212)596-6213

Christensen, Alice, Founder, Director
American Yoga Association [10417]
PO Box 19986
Sarasota, FL 34276

Christensen, John, VP of Operations
Utilities Service Alliance [3425]
9200 Indian Creek Pky., Ste. 201
Overland Park, KS 66210
Ph: (913)451-5641

Christensen, Lynne, Dir. of Opera-
tions
Cedar Shake and Shingle Bureau
[1432]
PO Box 1178
Sumas, WA 98295-1178

Christensen, Dr. Michael, Founder,
CEO
WorldHope Corps [11465]
1984 Sunset Cliffs Blvd.
San Diego, CA 92167
Ph: (619)886-7854

Christensen, Randy, President
World Clown Association [21603]
PO Box 12215

Merrillville, IN 46411-2215
Ph: (219)487-5317
Toll Free: 800-336-7922
Fax: (765)807-8649

Christensen, Scott R., CEO,
President
The Glaucoma Foundation [16383]
80 Maiden Ln., Ste. 700
New York, NY 10038-4965
Ph: (212)285-0080

Christensen, Scott, President
World Glaucoma Patient Association
[16410]
The Glaucoma Foundation
80 Maiden Ln., Ste. 1206
New York, NY 10038
Ph: (212)651-1900
Fax: (212)651-1888

Christensen, Ms. Valerie, Exec. Sec.
Association of Educators in Imaging
and Radiologic Sciences [17052]
PO Box 90204
Albuquerque, NM 87199-0204
Ph: (505)823-4740

Christesen, Dr. John D., CEO
Alpha Beta Gamma International
[23700]
1160 Midland Ave., Ste. 4C
Bronxville, NY 10708
Ph: (914)771-9987

Christian, Bill, President
National Conference of State Societ-
ies [19660]
PO Box 70175
Washington, DC 20024

Christian, Donna, Associate
Center for Applied Linguistics [9739]
4646 40th St. NW
Washington, DC 20016-1859
Ph: (202)362-0700
Fax: (202)362-3740

Christian, Gladys DeVonne,
President
International Association of Peer
Supporters [15772]
PO Box 19265
Cincinnati, OH 45219
Ph: (585)797-4641

Christiansen, Lisa M., President
North American Gaming Regulators
Association [5258]
1000 Westgate Dr., Ste. 252
Saint Paul, MN 55114
Ph: (651)203-7244
Fax: (651)290-2266

Christianson, John, President
Pedro Rescue Helicopter Association
[20672]
16610 14th Ave. SW
Burien, WA 98166
Ph: (503)653-7727

Christianson, Uta, Founder
InterExchange [8076]
100 Wall St., Ste. 301
New York, NY 10005
Ph: (212)924-0446
Fax: (212)924-0575

Christie, Jeanne, Exec. Dir.
Association of State Wetland
Managers [3816]
32 Tandberg Trl., Ste. 2A
Windham, ME 04062
Ph: (207)892-3399
Fax: (518)892-3089

Christie, Michelle, Exec. Dir.,
Founder
No Limits [15207]
9801 Washington Blvd., 2nd Fl.

Culver City, CA 90232
Ph: (310)280-0878
Fax: (310)280-0872

Christman, Abigail, CVT, Director
Galgo Rescue International Network
[10627]
17784 N County Road 15
Wellington, CO 80549-2030

Christman, Ian, VP
National Association of Motor
Vehicle Boards and Commissions
[5564]
1507 21st St., Ste. 330
Sacramento, CA 95811
Ph: (916)445-1888

Christopher, Jim, Founder, Exec. Dir.
Secular Organizations for Sobriety
[13181]
4773 Hollywood Blvd.
Hollywood, CA 90027
Ph: (323)666-4295
Fax: (323)666-4271

Christopher, Maia, Exec. Dir.
Association for the Treatment of
Sexual Abusers [6036]
4900 SW Griffith Dr., Ste. 274
Beaverton, OR 97005
Ph: (503)643-1023
Fax: (503)643-5084

Christophersen, Julia, President
GreaterGood.org [12975]
1 Union Sq., Ste. 1000
600 University St.
Seattle, WA 98101-4107
Toll Free: 888-811-5271

Christou, Andreas, VP
Sons of Pericles [19458]
1909 Q St. NW, Ste. 500
Washington, DC 20009-1050
Ph: (202)232-6300
Fax: (202)232-2140

Chromek, Paul, Secretary, Gen.
Counsel
Gas Technology Institute [4263]
1700 S Mount Prospect Rd.
Des Plaines, IL 60018-1804
Ph: (847)768-0500
Toll Free: 866-484-5227
Fax: (847)768-0501

Chu, David, President
Institute for Defense Analyses [5755]
4850 Mark Center Dr.
Alexandria, VA 22311-1882
Ph: (703)845-2000

Chu, Stephen J., President
Society for Color and Appearance in
Dentistry [14470]
5116 Bissonnet St., No. 394
Bellaire, TX 77401
Ph: (281)687-8752
Fax: (877)255-6075

Chu, Vincent, Contact
Gin Soon Tai Chi Chuan Federation
[23014]
33 Harrison Ave., Ground Fl.
Boston, MA 02111
Ph: (617)542-4442

Chuang, Rueyling, Ph.D., Exec. Dir.,
Reg.
Phi Beta Delta [23790]
c/o Dr. Salaam Yousif, Interim PBD
Executive Director & CEO
Administration Bldg., Rms. 148 &
150
California State University
5500 University Pky.
San Bernardino, CA 92407
Ph: (909)537-3250
Fax: (909)537-7458

Chukwuemeka, Odili P., President
Ogbaru National Association [12054]
PO Box 832701
Richardson, TX 75083
Ph: (214)734-1343

Chukwumerije, Nkem, President
Association of Nigerian Physicians in
the Americas [16742]
506 Summer Storm Dr.
Durham, NC 27704
Ph: (919)230-1488
(913)402-7102
Fax: (928)496-7006

Chumley, Pamela A, Exec. Dir.
International Jelly and Preserve As-
sociation [1345]
5775 Peachtree-Dunwoody Rd., Ste.
500-G
Atlanta, GA 30342
Ph: (404)252-3663
Fax: (404)252-0774

Chun, Soon Ae, President
Digital Government Society [5261]
USC-ISI
4676 Admiralty Way
Marina del Rey, CA 90292
Ph: (570)476-8006
Fax: (570)476-0860

Chunduri, Durga, President
Hand in Hand USA [12667]
710 St. Josephs Dr.
Oak Brook, IL 60523

Chung, Ms. Hee-Sun, President
International Association of Forensic
Toxicologists [7340]
3701 Welsh Rd.
Willow Grove, PA 19090

Chung, Jeffrey, Exec. Dir.
National Safety Management Society
[12836]
PO Box 4460
Walnut Creek, CA 94596-0460
Ph: (925)944-7094

Chung, Prof. Jin S., PhD, Exec. Dir.
International Society of Offshore and
Polar Engineers [6565]
495 N Whisman Rd., Ste. 300
Mountain View, CA 94043-5711
Ph: (650)254-1871
Fax: (650)254-2038

Chung, Ulric K., CEO
American Board of Industrial
Hygiene [16311]
6015 W St. Joseph, Ste. 102
Lansing, MI 48917
Ph: (517)321-2638
Fax: (517)321-4624

Church, Gail, Exec. Dir.
Tree Musketeers [3957]
305 Richmond St.
El Segundo, CA 90245
Ph: (310)322-0263
Fax: (310)322-4482

Church, Jeff, Exec. Dir.
Pressure Vessel Manufacturers As-
sociation [1761]
Bldg. C, Ste. 312
800 Roosevelt Rd.
Glen Ellyn, IL 60137
Ph: (630)942-6590
Fax: (630)790-3095

Church, Jerilyn J., CAE, Exec. Dir.
Thermoset Resin Formulators As-
sociation [750]
Bldg. C, Ste. 312
800 Roosevelt Rd.
Glen Ellyn, IL 60137
Ph: (630)942-6596
Fax: (630)790-3095

Church, Michael, Exec. Dir.
Movers and Shakers [15954]
880 Grand Rapids Blvd.
Naples, FL 34120
Ph: (239)919-8287

Church, Michael, Exec. Dir.
Sigma Chi Fraternity [23927]
1714 Hinman Ave.
Evanston, IL 60201
Ph: (847)869-3655
Fax: (847)869-4906

Church, Rick, Exec. Dir.
Association of Rotational Molders
[2620]
800 Roosevelt Rd., Ste. C-312
Glen Ellyn, IL 60137
Ph: (630)942-6589
Fax: (630)790-3095

Church, Rick, Exec. Dir.
Ceramic Tile Distributors Association
[511]
800 Roosevelt Rd., Bldg. C, Ste.
312
Glen Ellyn, IL 60137
Ph: (630)545-9415
Fax: (630)790-3095

Churchill, John, Secretary
The Phi Beta Kappa Society [23681]
1606 New Hampshire Ave. NW
Washington, DC 20009
Ph: (202)265-3808
Fax: (202)986-1601

Churchman, Emily, MPH, Chmn. of
the Bd.
Support for International Change
[15499]
PO Box 25803
Los Angeles, CA 90025

Chvany, Elena, Exec. Dir., Founder
One Voice of Peace [8406]
522 S Sunrise Way, Ste. 32
Palm Springs, CA 92264
Ph: (760)424-8811

Chwat, John, President
American Friends of the
Shakespeare Birthplace Trust
[10357]
1423 Powhatan St., Ste.1
Alexandria, VA 22314
Ph: (703)566-3805
Fax: (703)566-3806

Chylinski-Polubinski, Roger, Chairman
Polish Nobility Association Foundation [19612]
Villa Anneslie
529 Dunkirk Rd.
Baltimore, MD 21212-2014

Ciabattari, Jane, VP
National Book Critics Circle [9133]
160 Varick St., 11th Fl.
New York, NY 10013

Cialone, Dr. Henry J., CEO,
President
Edison Welding Institute [7383]
1250 Arthur E Adams Dr.
Columbus, OH 43221-3585
Ph: (614)688-5000
Fax: (614)688-5001

Cibulka, James G., President
National Council for Accreditation of
Teacher Education [7414]
1140 19th St., Ste. 400
Washington, DC 20036
Ph: (202)223-0077
Fax: (202)296-6620

Ciccariello, Priscilla, MA, Co-Pres.
Coalition for Heritable Disorders of
Connective Tissue [14816]

4301 Connecticut Ave. NW, Ste. 404
Washington, DC 20008
Ph: (202)362-9599
Fax: (202)966-8553

Ciccariello, Priscilla, President
International Federation of Marfan
Syndrome Organizations **[14830]**
c/o National Marfan Foundation
22 Manhasset Ave.
Port Washington, NY 11050

Ciccone, Anthony, President
International Society for the Scholarship of Teaching and Learning
[8515]
c/o Anthony Ciccone, President
University of Wisconsin-Milwaukee
Milwaukee, WI

Cicerani, Nikki, Exec. Dir., President
Upwardly Global **[2745]**
582 Market St., Ste. 1207
San Francisco, CA 94104
Ph: (415)834-9901
Fax: (415)840-0334

Cichon, Charlie, Exec. Dir.
National Association of Drug Diver-
sion Investigators **[5490]**
1810 York Rd., No. 435
Lutherville, MD 21093
Ph: (410)321-4600

Cicio, Paul N., President
Industrial Energy Consumers of
America **[1114]**
1776 K St. NW, Ste. 720
Washington, DC 20006
Ph: (202)223-1661
    (202)223-1420
Fax: (202)530-0659

Cid, Ximena, Secretary
National Society of Hispanic
Physicists **[7029]**
c/o Jesus Pando, President
Dept. of Physics
2219 N Kenmore Ave., Ste. 211
Chicago, IL 60614-3504
Ph: (773)325-4942

Cieri, Dr. Christopher, Exec. Dir.
Linguistic Data Consortium **[9745]**
3600 Market St., Ste. 810
Philadelphia, PA 19104-2653
Ph: (215)898-0464
Fax: (215)573-2175

Ciesinski, Michael, CEO, President
FlexTech Alliance **[3208]**
3081 Zanker Rd.
San Jose, CA 95134
Ph: (408)577-1300
Fax: (408)577-1301

Ciesla, Maria, President
Polish Museum of America **[10168]**
984 N Milwaukee Ave.
Chicago, IL 60622-4101
Ph: (773)384-3352
Fax: (773)384-3799

Cihon, Michael, Exec. Dir.
U.S. Flag & Touch Football League
[22869]
6946 Spinach Dr.
Mentor, OH 44060
Ph: (440)974-8735
Fax: (440)974-8441

Cinar, Ali, President
Federation of Turkish American As-
sociations **[19674]**
821 United Nations Plz.
New York, NY 10017
Ph: (212)682-7688
Toll Free: 888-352-9886
Fax: (646)290-6171

Cini, Marie, President
Online Learning Consortium **[7795]**
PO Box 1238
Newburyport, MA 01950-8238
Ph: (617)716-1414
Fax: (888)898-6209

Ciocca, Joseph R., CLU, President
National Association of Prudential
Retirees and Vested Terminators,
Inc. **[12757]**
2018 Bergen St.
Philadelphia, PA 19152
Toll Free: 888-730-6090
Fax: (215)722-1017

Ciocci, Linda Church, Exec. Dir.
National Hydropower Association
[6499]
25 Massachusetts Ave. NW, Ste.
450
Washington, DC 20001
Ph: (202)682-1700
Fax: (202)682-9478

Cioffi-Revilla, Claudio, President
North American Computational
Social and Organization Sciences
[6259]
Carnegie Mellon University
Wean Hall 1325
5000 Forbes Ave.
Pittsburgh, PA 15213
Ph: (412)268-3163

Cionni, Robert J., President
American Society of Cataract and
Refractive Surgery **[16369]**
4000 Legato Rd., Ste. 700
Fairfax, VA 22033
Ph: (703)591-2220

Ciorra, Anthony, Officer
Center for Christian and Jewish
Understanding **[20057]**
5151 Park Ave.
Fairfield, CT 06825-1000
Ph: (203)371-7999
    (203)371-7912

Cipolla, Prof. Gaetano, President
Arba Sicula **[19643]**
c/o Prof. Gaetano Cipolla, President
PO Box 149
Mineola, NY 11501

Cipollone, Peter, Rep.
USRowing **[23113]**
2 Wall St.
Princeton, NJ 08540
Ph: (609)751-0700
Toll Free: 800-314-4769
Fax: (609)924-1578

Cipov, Pat, Chairperson
National Association of Tower Erec-
tors **[6165]**
8 2nd St. SE
Watertown, SD 57201-3624
Ph: (605)882-5865
Toll Free: 888-882-5865

Cisneros, Gilbert M., Chairman,
CEO
Chamber of the Americas **[23571]**
720 Kipling St., Ste. 13
Denver, CO 80215
Ph: (303)462-1275
Fax: (303)462-1560

Cisneros, Mary Alice P., Founder,
President
American Sunrise **[11961]**
2007 W Commerce St.
San Antonio, TX 78207-3836
Ph: (210)212-2227

Cisternino, Mark, President
Flexographic Technical Association
[1533]

3920 Veterans Memorial Hwy., Ste.
9
Bohemia, NY 11716-1074
Ph: (631)737-6020
Fax: (631)737-6813

Citrhyn, Tony, President
American Emu Association **[4450]**
510 W Madison St.
Ottawa, IL 61350
Ph: (541)332-0675

Clack, Sharon, Founder, President
Lily of the Valley Endeavor **[10546]**
PO Box 1007
Agoura Hills, CA 91376-1007
Ph: (805)277-1827

Cladoosbys, Brian, President
National Congress of American
Indians **[18709]**
1516 P St. NW
Washington, DC 20005-1910
Ph: (202)466-7767
Fax: (202)466-7797

Claiborne, Susan, Receptionist
National Corn Growers Association
[3766]
632 Cepi Dr.
Chesterfield, MO 63005
Ph: (636)733-9004
Fax: (636)733-9005

Clancy, Eileen, Officer
Salmagundi Club **[8999]**
47 5th Ave.
New York, NY 10003-4679
Ph: (212)255-7740
Fax: (212)229-0172

Clancy, Ms. Marianne, Exec. Dir.
HHT Foundation International, Inc.
[14827]
PO Box 329
Monkton, MD 21111
Ph: (410)357-9932
Fax: (410)357-0655

Clancy, Tom, President
Business Architecture Guild **[2461]**

Clapp, Katherine, Founder, President
FRAXA Research Foundation
[17341]
10 Prince Pl., Ste. 203
Newburyport, MA 01950
Ph: (978)462-1866

Clark, Bruce A., Coord.
Six of One Club: The Prisoner Appreciation Society **[24089]**
871 Clover Dr.
North Wales, PA 19454-2749

Clark, Caroline, Officer
Montreat College Alumni Association
[19335]
310 Gaither Cir.
Montreat, NC 28757
Ph: (828)669-8012
Toll Free: 800-849-3347

Clark, Chris, Founder
Children of the Nations International
[10918]
11992 Clear Creek Rd. NW
Silverdale, WA 98383
Ph: (360)698-7227

Clark, Doug, Exec. Dir.
Fathers for Equal Rights **[11684]**
1314 Texas St., Ste. 609
Houston, TX 77002-3521
Ph: (512)588-7900

Clark, Doug, Treasurer
Security Traders Association **[3052]**
1115 Broadway, Ste. 1110

New York, NY 10010
Ph: (646)699-5995

Clark, Rev. Douglas, Exec. Dir.
Association of North American Mis-
sions **[20384]**
PO Box 610
Salem, MO 65560
Ph: (573)261-0057

Clark, Douglas N., President
Mobile Post Office Society **[22347]**
PO Box 1058
Poulsbo, WA 98370-0048
Ph: (508)428-9132

Clark, Gregory, Officer
Rhetoric Society of America **[10198]**
c/o Kathie Cesa, Member Services
Officer
1143 Tidewater Ct.
Westerville, OH 43082
Ph: (702)895-4825

Clark, Guy C., DDS, Chairman
Stop Predatory Gambling Founda-
tion **[11869]**
100 Maryland Ave. NE, Rm. 310
Washington, DC 20002
Ph: (202)567-6996

Clark, Helen, Administrator
United Nations Development
Programme **[18503]**
1 United Nations Plz.
New York, NY 10017
Ph: (212)963-1234
    (212)906-5382
Fax: (212)906-5364

Clark, Jackie, Exec. Dir., President
Share and Care Cockayne
Syndrome Network **[14856]**
PO Box 282
Waterford, VA 20197-0282
Ph: (703)727-0404

Clark, James, President, CEO
Boys and Girls Clubs of America
[13430]
1275 Peachtree St. NE
Atlanta, GA 30309-3506
Ph: (404)487-5700

Clark, James D., President
IUE-CWA **[23414]**
2701 Dryden Rd.
Dayton, OH 45439
Ph: (937)298-9984
Fax: (937)298-2636

Clark, Jamie Rappaport, President,
CEO
Defenders of Wildlife **[4805]**
1130 17th St. NW
Washington, DC 20036
Ph: (202)682-9400
Toll Free: 800-385-9712

Clark, Jane Forbes, Chairperson,
Director
National Baseball Hall of Fame and
Museum **[22559]**
25 Main St.
Cooperstown, NY 13326
Ph: (607)547-7200
Toll Free: 888-425-5633
Fax: (607)547-2044

Clark, Janie, MA, President
American Senior Fitness Association
[16694]
PO Box 2575
New Smyrna Beach, FL 32170
Ph: (386)423-6634
Toll Free: 888-689-6791
Fax: (877)365-3048

Clark, Jean, President
Supreme Emblem Club of the United
States of America [19426]
Ph: (479)394-1372
(501)525-8348

Clark, Jim, Founder
The Andy Griffith Show Rerun
Watchers Club [24084]
118 16th Ave. S
Nashville, TN 37203-3100

Clark, John D., Jr., CEO, Exec. Dir.
BICSI [3219]
8610 Hidden River Pky.
Tampa, FL 33637-1000
Ph: (813)979-1991
Toll Free: 800-242-7405
Fax: (813)971-4311

Clark, John R., President, CEO
Center for Plant Conservation [3826]
15600 San Pasqual Valley Rd.
Escondido, CA 92027-7000
Ph: (760)796-5686

Clark, Dr. J.R., Secretary, Treasurer
Association of Private Enterprise
Education [8461]
c/o Probasco Chair of Free
Enterprise
University of Tennessee at Chat-
tanooga
313 Fletcher Hall, Dept. 6106
615 McCallie Ave.
Chattanooga, TN 37403-2598

Clark, J.R., Secretary, Treasurer
Southern Economic Association
[6403]
313 Fletcher Hall, Dept. 6106
615 McCallie Ave.
Chattanooga, TN 37403-2598
Ph: (423)425-4118
Fax: (423)425-5218

Clark, Julie, Director
BVU: The Center for Nonprofit
Excellence [13289]
1300 E 9th St., Ste. 1805
Cleveland, OH 44114-1509
Ph: (216)736-7711
Fax: (216)736-7710

Clark, Julie, Director
T-34 Association Inc. [21528]
880 N County Rd., 900-E
Tuscola, IL 61953

Clark, Karen, Chairman
American Association of Police
Polygraphists [5232]
3223 Lake Ave., Unit 15c-168
Wilmette, IL 60091-1069
Ph: (847)635-3980

Clark, Karen, Dir. of Fin. & Admin.
United States Pony Clubs [22952]
4041 Iron Works Pky.
Lexington, KY 40511
Ph: (859)254-7669
Fax: (859)233-4652

Clark, Lee Ann, Exec. Dir.
American Pediatric Surgical Associa-
tion [16601]
1 Parkview Plz., Ste. 800
Oakbrook Terrace, IL 60181
Ph: (847)686-2237
Fax: (847)686-2253

Clark, Prof. Mark T., President
Association for the Study of the
Middle East and Africa [8339]
2100 M St. NW, No. 170-291
Washington, DC 20037
Ph: (202)429-8860

Clark, Michael A., CAE, COO
National Institute for Certification in
Engineering Technologies [6576]

1420 King St.
Alexandria, VA 22314-2794
Ph: (703)548-1518
Toll Free: 888-476-4238

Clark, Michael E., Chairman
American Bar Association - Health
Law Section [5272]
321 N Clark St.
Chicago, IL 60654-7598
Fax: (312)988-5814

Clark, Mike, President
The International Amphicar Owners
Club [21400]
c/o Pat DePasquale, Treasurer
9938 Forest St.
Lakeview, OH 43331

Clark, Capt. Paul, President
Save Our Seas [3940]
PO Box 223508
Princeville, HI 96722
Ph: (808)651-3452

Clark, Phil, ScD, President
National Association of Geriatric
Education Centers [14894]
c/o Phil Clark, ScD, President
University of Rhode Island
55 Lower College Rd.
Kingston, RI 02881

Clark, Ramsey, Founder
International Action Center [18695]
147 W 24th St., 2nd Fl.
New York, NY 10011
Ph: (212)633-6646
Fax: (212)633-2889

Clark, Rick, President
National Reining Horse Association
[4386]
3000 NW 10th St.
Oklahoma City, OK 73107-5302
Ph: (405)946-7400
Fax: (405)946-8425

Clark, Rick, Founder, VP
Native American Cancer Research
Corporation [14031]
PO Box 27494
Denver, CO 80227
Ph: (303)838-9359
Toll Free: 800-537-8295

Clark, Rick, President
Used Truck Association [357]
325 Country Club Dr., Ste. A
Stockbridge, GA 30281
Toll Free: 877-438-7882

Clark, Robert W., CEO, President
Cooperative Business International
Inc. [905]
507 Executive Campus Dr., Ste. 120
Westerville, OH 43082
Ph: (614)839-2700
Fax: (614)839-2709

Clark, Ron, CEO, Founder
National Federation of Professional
Trainers [23336]
PO Box 4579
Lafayette, IN 47903-4579
Toll Free: 800-729-6378
Fax: (765)471-7369

Clark, Sallie, President
National Association of Counties
[5113]
25 Massachusetts Ave. NW, Ste.
500
Washington, DC 20001
Ph: (202)393-6226
Toll Free: 888-407-6226
Fax: (202)393-2630

Clark, Sherry, Exec. Dir.
World Senior Golf Federation
[22899]

PO Box 350667
Westminster, CO 80035-0667
Ph: (303)920-4206
Fax: (303)920-8206

Clark, Thomas R., RPh, Exec. Dir.
Commission for Certification in
Geriatric Pharmacy [16659]
1321 Duke St., Ste. 400
Alexandria, VA 22314-3563
Ph: (703)535-3036
Fax: (703)739-1500

Clark, Tommy, MD, CEO, Founder
Grassroot Soccer [10543]
198 Church St.
Norwich, VT 05055
Ph: (802)649-2900
Fax: (802)649-2910

Clark, Tony, Exec. Dir.
Major League Baseball Players As-
sociation [23392]
12 E 49th St., 24th Fl.
New York, NY 10017
Ph: (212)826-0808
Fax: (212)752-4378

Clark, Vaughn, Chairman
National Association of State Energy
Officials [5172]
2107 Wilson Blvd., Ste. 850
Arlington, VA 22201
Ph: (703)299-8800
Fax: (703)299-6208

Clark, Velva, Chairperson
Auxiliary to the National Medical As-
sociation [15717]
8403 Colesville Rd., Ste. 820
Silver Spring, MD 20910
Ph: (301)495-3779
Fax: (301)495-0037

Clark, Wes, Contact
Glass Paperweight Foundation
[22295]
644 E Deerpath Rd.
Lake Forest, IL 60045
Ph: (312)419-0403

Clarke, Andy D., President
League of American Bicyclists
[22750]
1612 K St. NW, Ste. 308
Washington, DC 20006-2849
Ph: (202)822-1333

Clarke, Barbara, Director
DreamCatcher Wild Horse and Burro
Sanctuary [10612]
PO Box 9
Ravendale, CA 96123
Ph: (530)260-0148
(530)260-0377
Fax: (530)625-3364

Clarke, David J., President
Joshua's Journey of Hope [14833]
30141 Antelope Rd.
Menifee, CA 92584
Ph: (951)719-5277

Clarke, Dick, President
National Board of Diving &
Hyperbaric Medical Technology
[15344]
9 Medical Pk., Ste. 330
Columbia, SC 29203
Ph: (803)434-7802
Toll Free: 866-451-7231

Clarke, Jane, CEO, Managing Dir.
Coalition for Innovative Media
Measurement [2315]
1115 Broadway, 12th Fl.
New York, NY 10010
Ph: (212)590-2431

Clarke, Lindsay, Chmn. of the Bd.
Breaking Ground [11320]
104 Neal St.
Portland, ME 04102
Fax: (207)772-7487

Clarke, Ron, Director
North American Falconers Association [22829]
c/o Scott McNeff, President
64 High St.
Kennebunk, ME 04043
Ph: (207)604-6283

Clarke, Scott, Founder, Exec. Dir.
Amandla Development [7807]
42 Water St., 4th Fl.
New York, NY 10004

Clarke, Thomas M., VP of Res.
National Center for State Courts
[5392]
300 Newport Ave.
Williamsburg, VA 23185
Ph: (757)259-1525
Toll Free: 800-616-6164

Clark-Flynn, Mary, Contact
Lambda Iota Tau [23808]
Ball State University
Dept. of English
2000 W University Ave.
Muncie, IN 47306-0460
Ph: (765)285-8370
Fax: (765)285-3765

Clarkson, John G., MD, Exec. Dir.,
CEO
American Board of Ophthalmology
[16365]
111 Presidential Blvd., Ste. 241
Bala Cynwyd, PA 19004-1075
Ph: (610)664-1175
Fax: (610)664-6503

Claro, Maria Cristina, Asst. VP of
Fin.
Cuban American National Council
[13044]
1223 SW 4th St.
Miami, FL 33135
Ph: (305)642-3484
Fax: (305)642-9122

Clasper, Barry, Mem.
Callerlab - International Association
of Square Dance Callers [9245]
200 SW 30th St., Ste. 104
Topeka, KS 66611
Ph: (785)783-3665
Toll Free: 800-331-2577
Fax: (785)783-3696

Clausen, Matthew, Chairman
Building Bridges Coalition [13288]
129 N Second St., Ste. 102
Minneapolis, MN 55401

Claussen, Hon. Eileen, President
Center for Climate and Energy Solu-
tions [4126]
2101 Wilson Blvd., Ste. 550
Arlington, VA 22201
Ph: (703)516-4146
Fax: (703)516-9551

Clawson, Kevin, President
Reach the Children [11137]
14 Chesham Way
Fairport, NY 14450
Ph: (585)223-3344

Clay, Gordon, President, Editor
National Men's Resource Center
[18670]
PO Box 12
Brookings, OR 97415

Clay, Jennifer, Secretary, Treasurer
Association for Veterinary Family
Practice [17638]

c/o Jen Clay, Secretary-Treasurer
1157 Madison Ave.
Memphis, TN 38104-2202

Clay, Landon T., Chairman
Sea Turtle Conservancy [4885]
4424 NW 13th St., Ste. B-11
Gainesville, FL 32609
Ph: (352)373-6441
Toll Free: 800-678-7853
Fax: (352)375-2449

Clay, Mr. Lawrence E., President
Scouts on Stamps Society
International [22362]
c/o Jay Rogers
15 Hickory Court Ln.
Hendersonville, NC 28792-1229
Ph: (803)466-4783

Clayback, Don, Exec. Dir.
National Coalition for Assistive and
Rehab Technology [15695]
54 Towhee Ct.
East Amherst, NY 14051
Ph: (716)839-9728
Fax: (716)839-9624

Clayton, Doug, President
National Bowhunter Education
Foundation [22503]
PO Box 2934
Rapid City, SD 57709-2934
Ph: (605)716-0596
Fax: (309)401-6096

Clayton, Jeffrey J., Director
American Bail Coalition [5063]
225 Union Blvd., Ste. 150
Lakewood, CO 80228
Ph: (303)885-5872
Toll Free: 855-718-3006

Clayton, Joseph, President
National Yogurt Association [977]
2000 Corporate Ridge, Ste. 1000
McLean, VA 22102
Ph: (703)245-7698
    (703)821-0770

Clear, Allan, Exec. Dir.
Harm Reduction Coalition [13141]
22 W 27th St., 5th Fl.
New York, NY 10001
Ph: (212)213-6376

Cleary, Pat, CEO, President
National Association of Professional
Employer Organizations [1098]
707 N St. Asaph St.
Alexandria, VA 22314
Ph: (703)836-0466
Fax: (703)836-0976

Cleary, Tim, President
American Station Wagon Owners
Association [21324]
PO Box 914
Matthews, NC 28106
Ph: (704)847-7510

Cleave, Barbara, President
Society of Commercial Seed
Technologists [4646]
653 Constitution Ave. NE
Washington, DC 20002
Ph: (202)870-2412
    (605)688-4606

Cleaveland, Brent, Exec. Dir.
Fashion Jewelry & Accessories
Trade Association [2045]
25 Sea Grass Way
North Kingstown, RI 02852
Ph: (401)667-0520
Fax: (401)267-9096

Cleaves, Bob, CEO, President
Biomass Power Association [7052]
100 Middle St.

Portland, ME 04104-9729
Ph: (207)228-7376

Clegg, Justine, Chairperson
Association of Midwifery Educators
[14221]
24 S High St.
Bridgton, ME 04009
Ph: (207)615-2566

Clegg, Philip, Exec. Dir.
American Student Association of
Community Colleges [8611]
2250 N University Pky., No. 4865
Provo, UT 84604
Ph: (801)785-9784
Toll Free: 888-240-4993
Fax: (801)406-4385

Cleghorn, Tracy, President
Hemophilia Federation of America
[15231]
820 1st St. NE, Ste. 720
Washington, DC 20002
Ph: (202)675-6984
Toll Free: 800-230-9797
Fax: (202)675-6983

Clemans, Terry, Exec. Dir.
National Consumer Reporting As-
sociation [944]
701 E Irving Park Rd., Ste. 306
Roselle, IL 60172-2358
Ph: (630)539-1525
Fax: (630)539-1526

Clemens, Lynne, President
Cushing's Understanding Support
and Help Organization [16769]
PO Box 1424
Florence, AL 35631

Clemens, Roy, President
National Organization of Vascular
Anomalies [17577]
PO Box 38216
Greensboro, NC 27438-8216

Clement, Audrey, Co-Ch.
Green Party of the United States
[18890]
PO Box 75075
Washington, DC 20013
Ph: (202)319-7191

Clement, Cari, Director, Founder
Rwanda Knits [11425]
122 Ward Brook Rd.
Montpelier, VT 05602
Ph: (518)791-0212

Clement, Paul, Treasurer
All-American Indian Motorcycle Club
[22208]
c/o Teri Clement
140 N Centennial Rd.
Holland, OH 43528

Clements, David, Exec. Dir., CEO
International Association of Electrical
Inspectors [1023]
901 Waterfall Way, Ste. 602
Richardson, TX 75080
Ph: (972)235-1455
Toll Free: 800-786-4234

Clements, Fred, VP
National Bicycle Dealers Association
[3142]
3176 Pullman St., No. 117
Costa Mesa, CA 92626
Ph: (949)722-6909

Clements, Fred, Treasurer
PeopleForBikes [10781]
1966 13th St., Ste. 250
Boulder, CO 80302
Ph: (303)449-4893

Clements, Holly, Dir. of HR
Working Families Party [18899]
1 Metrotech Ctr. N, 11th Fl.
Brooklyn, NY 11217
Ph: (718)222-3796

Clements, Irene, Exec. Dir.
National Foster Parent Association
[12418]
1102 Prairie Ridge Trl.
Pflugerville, TX 78660
Toll Free: 800-557-5238
Fax: (888)925-5634

Clements, John, Director
Association for Renaissance Martial
Arts [22986]
105 Gainesborough Walk
Dallas, GA 30157

Clements, Richard A., President
National Association of Professional
Insurance Agents [1900]
400 N Washington St.
Alexandria, VA 22314
Ph: (703)836-9340
    (703)518-1360
Fax: (703)836-1279

Clemons, Mr. Cal, CAE, Exec. Dir.
National Association of Sign Supply
Distributors [3473]
1001 N Fairfax St., Ste. 301
Alexandria, VA 22314-1587
Ph: (703)836-4013
Fax: (703)836-8353

Clerkin, Tom, V. Chmn. of the Bd.
Finishing Contractors Association
International [528]
1 Parkview Plz., Ste. 610
Oakbrook Terrace, IL 60181
Ph: (630)537-1042
Toll Free: 866-322-3477
Fax: (630)590-5272

Cleveland, Lt. Gen. Charles,
President
American Fighter Aces Association
[20666]
9404 E Marginal Way S
Seattle, WA 98108-4907
Ph: (206)764-5700

Cleveland, Kenneth, Exec. Dir.
American Academy of Orofacial Pain
[14385]
174 S New York Ave.
Oceanville, NJ 08231
Ph: (609)504-1311
Fax: (609)573-5064

Cleveland, Paul M., Trustee
DACOR [5229]
1801 F St. NW
Washington, DC 20006
Ph: (202)682-0500
Fax: (202)842-3295

Clevenger, Rose, President
Christian Cheerleaders of America
[22725]
PO Box 49
Bethania, NC 27010-0049
Toll Free: 877-243-3722
Fax: (866)222-1093

Clifford, Allen, V. Chmn. of the Bd.
Containerization and Intermodal
Institute [831]
960 Holmdel Rd., Bldg. 2, Ste. 201
Holmdel, NJ 07733
Ph: (732)817-9131
Fax: (732)817-9133

Clifford, Deborah L., Exec. Dir.
One to World [8087]
285 W Broadway, Ste. 450

New York, NY 10013
Ph: (212)431-1195
Fax: (212)941-6291

Clifford, Garry, Director
Public Education Center [18948]
1830 Connecticut Ave. NW
Washington, DC 20009
Ph: (202)466-4310
Fax: (202)466-4344

Clifford, Peg, Comm. Chm.
National Association of State
Controlled Substances Authorities
[5158]
72 Brook St.
Quincy, MA 02170-1616
Ph: (617)472-0520
Fax: (617)472-0521

Clift, Roland, CBE, FREng,
FIChemE, HonFCIWEM, FRSA,
Comm. Chm.
International Society for Industrial
Ecology [4075]
Yale School of Forestry and
Environmental Studies
Yale University
195 Prospect St.
New Haven, CT 06511-2189
Ph: (203)432-6953
Fax: (203)432-5556

Clinard, Kay N., President
UCA International Users Group
[7357]
10604 Candler Falls Ct.
Raleigh, NC 27614
Ph: (919)847-2944
Fax: (919)869-2700

Clinchy, Richard A., Chairman
Coalition for Tactical Medicine
[16319]
3337 Duke St.
Alexandria, VA 22314
Ph: (703)370-7436
Fax: (703)342-4311

Cline, Allison, Dep. Dir.
American Association of School
Librarians [9666]
50 E Huron St.
Chicago, IL 60611-2729
Ph: (312)280-4382
Toll Free: 800-545-2433
Fax: (312)280-5276

Cline, Bobbee, Exec. Dir.
Michael Crawford International Fan
Association [23997]
2272 Colorado Blvd.
Los Angeles, CA 90041
Fax: (562)683-2677

Cline, Phil, Officer
Holiday Rambler Recreational
Vehicle Club [22427]
PO Box 3028
Elkhart, IN 46515
Ph: (574)295-9800
Toll Free: 877-702-5415

Cline, Robert, Secretary
Circus Historical Society [9162]
c/o Les Smout CHS Treasurer
PO Box 15742
Clearwater, FL 33766

Clinton, Catherine, President
Southern Historical Association
[8799]
c/o Stephen Berry, Secretary-
Treasurer
LeConte Hall, Rm. 111A
Dept. of History
University of Georgia
Athens, GA 30602-1602
Ph: (706)542-8848

Clinton, Timothy E., EdD, President
American Association of Christian
    Counselors [20036]
PO Box 739
Forest, VA 24551
Toll Free: 800-526-8673

Clinton, William J., Founder
William J. Clinton Foundation
    [18506]
1200 President Clinton Ave.
Little Rock, AR 72201
Ph: (501)748-0471
    (646)775-9175

Clippinger, Marni Zea, COO
Marketing Science Institute [2292]
1000 Massachusetts Ave.
Cambridge, MA 02138-5396
Ph: (617)491-2060
Fax: (617)491-2065

Cloninger, Chuck, President
Trees for Tomorrow [4221]
519 Sheridan E St.
Eagle River, WI 54521
Ph: (715)479-6456
Fax: (715)479-2318

Cloonan, James B., PhD, Founder,
    Chairman
American Association of Individual
    Investors [7918]
625 N Michigan Ave.
Chicago, IL 60611
Ph: (312)280-0170
Toll Free: 800-428-2244
Fax: (312)280-9883

Cloppas, Dan, CEO, Sec. Gen.
U.S.A. Badminton [22531]
1 Olympic Plz.
Colorado Springs, CO 80909
Ph: (719)866-4808
Fax: (719)866-4507

Close, Leroy S., Founder, President
1000 Jobs [12524]
316 W Main Rd.
Little Compton, RI 02837
Fax: (401)635-1838

Close, Sandy, Director, Editor
New America Media [18662]
209 9th St., Ste. 200
San Francisco, CA 94103
Ph: (415)503-4170
Fax: (415)503-0970

Clott, Abe, Chairman
Society for the Advancement of
    Judaism [20281]
15 W 86th St.
New York, NY 10024
Ph: (212)724-7000

Cloud, David, MBA, CEO
National Sleep Foundation [17220]
1010 N Glebe Rd., Ste. 310
Arlington, VA 22201
Ph: (703)243-1697

Clough, Brier, President
National Junior Classical League
    [9166]
860 NW Washington Blvd., Ste. A
Hamilton, OH 45013
Ph: (513)529-7741

Clough, John W., President
John Clough Genealogical Society
    [20847]
21 Lowell Rd.
Pembroke, MA 02359

Clouse, Doug, President
Type Directors Club [6700]
347 W 36th St., Ste. 603

New York, NY 10018
Ph: (212)633-8943
Fax: (212)633-8944

Clouser, Sue F., RN, MSN, CRNO,
    Officer
American Society of Ophthalmic
    Registered Nurses [16112]
655 Beach St.
San Francisco, CA 94109
Ph: (415)561-8513
Fax: (415)561-8531

Clow, Mrs. Mary, Chairperson
Tyndale Society [20580]
c/o Mary Clow, Chairman
3 E 85th St., Apt. 7a
New York, NY 10028

Clugston, Amy, President, Treasurer
Syndromes Without a Name USA
    [14614]
1745 Lorna Ln.
Otsego, MI 49078
Ph: (269)692-2090
Toll Free: 888-880-7926

Clugston, Richard M., Exec. Dir.
Center for Respect of Life &
    Environment [4112]
2100 L St. NW
Washington, DC 20037
Ph: (202)778-6133
Fax: (202)778-6138

Clune, Dr. David, President, CEO
Educational Records Bureau [8683]
470 Park Ave. S, 2nd Fl., South
    Tower
New York, NY 10016
Toll Free: 800-989-3721

Clyde, April, President
Airedale Terrier Club of America
    [21792]
c/o Richard Schlicht, Coordinator
9762 230th St. E
Lakeville, MN 55044-8292
Ph: (952)461-5597

Clymer, George, Mem.
Rosicrucian Fraternity [19627]
PO Box 220
Quakertown, PA 18951

Coakley, Michael, President
Manufacturing CPAs [40]
1801 West End Ave., Ste. 800
Nashville, TN 37203
Ph: (615)373-9880
Toll Free: 800-231-2524
Fax: (615)377-7092

Cobb, Al, Bd. Member
Structural Insulated Panel Associa-
    tion [586]
PO Box 39848
Fort Lauderdale, FL 33339
Ph: (253)858-7472

Cobb, Coralie, President
National Military Fish and Wildlife
    Association [4845]
103 W Highway 33
Lake Jackson, TX 77566
Ph: (831)656-2850
    (720)542-3085

Cobb, Rev. David C., Chairman
The Society for the Increase of the
    Ministry [20376]
120 Sigourney St.
Hartford, CT 06105
Ph: (860)233-1732
Fax: (860)233-2644

Cobb, James C., Rep.
Association of American State
    Geologists [6678]

903 W Tennessee St.
Tallahassee, FL 32304-7716
Ph: (850)617-0320
    (701)328-8000

Cobb, Dr. Matthew, President
Assembly of Episcopal Healthcare
    Chaplains [20092]
c/o Susan Roberts, Secretary
The University of Utah
50 N Medical Dr., Rm. 1C351
Salt Lake City, UT 84132
Ph: (801)587-9064

Cobb, Max, President, CEO
U.S. Biathlon Association [23168]
49 Pineland Dr., Ste. 301A
New Gloucester, ME 04260-5132
Ph: (207)688-6500
Fax: (207)688-6505

Cobb, Suzanne, Dir. of Member
    Svcs.
International Bird Dog Association
    [21229]
c/o Suzanne Cobb, Membership
    Director
2829 Aviation Loop
Fredericksburg, TX 78624

Coble, Dave, Dir. of Member Svcs.
American Christian Fiction Writers
    [10356]
PO Box 101066
Palm Bay, FL 32910-1066

Coble, John, VP
Society for Japanese Irises [22123]
c/o Patrick Spence, President
PO Box 1062
Lake Stevens, WA 98258

Coborn, J.Michael, Dir. of Dev.
CBM U.S. [14547]
228 Adley Way
Greenville, SC 29607
Toll Free: 800-937-2264

Cobran, Philip L., Chmn. of the Bd.
American Friends of the National
    Gallery of Australia [9818]
50 Broadway, Ste. 2003
New York, NY 10004
Ph: (212)338-6860
Fax: (212)338-6864

Cocciolone, Denise F., Founder,
    President
National Life Center [12783]
686 N Broad St.
Woodbury, NJ 08096-1607
Ph: (856)848-1819
    (856)848-5683
Toll Free: 800-848-5683

Cochener, Nancy McArthur,
    President, Exec. Sec.
Clan Arthur Association USA [20797]
10821 E Glengate Cir.
Wichita, KS 67206-8902

Cochran, Amalia, MD, FACS, FCCM,
    President
Association of Women Surgeons
    [17381]
35 E Wacker Dr., Ste. 850
Chicago, IL 60601
Ph: (312)224-2575
Fax: (312)644-8557

Cochran, Angela, President
Council of Science Editors [2675]
10200 W 44th Ave., Ste. 304
Wheat Ridge, CO 80033
Ph: (720)881-6046
Fax: (720)881-6101

Cochran, Tom, CEO, Exec. Dir.
United States Conference of Mayors
    [5647]

1620 Eye St. NW
Washington, DC 20006
Ph: (202)293-7330
Fax: (202)293-2352

Cochrane, Kylie, Secretary
International Association for Public
    Participation Practitioners [5733]
PO Box 270723
Louisville, CO 80027-5012

Cockrell, Al, Act. Pres.
Association of Baptists for World
    Evangelism [19716]
522 Lewisberry Rd.
New Cumberland, PA 17070
Ph: (717)774-7000
Fax: (717)774-1919

Coconis, Michel, Chairman
Association for Community
    Organization and Social
    Administration [13102]
20560 Bensley Ave.
Lynwood, IL 60411
Ph: (708)757-4187
Fax: (708)757-4234

Cocroft, Robert A., CEO, President
Center for Veterans Issues [21115]
315 W Court St.
Milwaukee, WI 53212
Ph: (414)345-3917
    (414)345-4272
Fax: (414)342-1073

Code, Cindy, Exec. Dir.
Project EverGreen [4448]
8500 Station St., Ste. 230
Mentor, OH 44060
Toll Free: 877-758-4835

Code, Cindy, Director
Turf and Ornamental Communica-
    tors Association [2074]
605 Columbus Ave. S
New Prague, MN 56071-1935
Ph: (952)758-6340
Fax: (952)758-5813

Codikow, Stacy, Exec. Dir., Founder
POWER UP: Professional Organiza-
    tion of Women in Entertainment
    Reaching UP! [18302]
419 N Larchmont Blvd., No. 283
Los Angeles, CA 90004
Ph: (323)463-3154

Codispoti, Noelle, Exec. Dir.
Gamma Iota Sigma [23695]
PO Box 356
Yardley, PA 19067
Ph: (484)991-4471

Cody, Alison, Exec. Dir.
Manufacturers' Agents Association
    for the Foodservice Industry [1384]
1199 Euclid Ave.
Atlanta, GA 30307
Ph: (404)214-9474
Fax: (404)522-0133

Cody, Kathleen M., Exec. Dir.
American Bone Health [13843]
1814 Franklin St., Ste. 620
Oakland, CA 94612
Ph: (510)832-2663
Toll Free: 888-266-3015
Fax: (510)208-7174

Coe, Wendy, Exec. Dir.
American College of Veterinary
    Pathologists [17620]
2424 American Ln.
Madison, WI 53704
Ph: (608)443-2466
Fax: (608)443-2474

Coffee, Craig F., President
Association of Real Estate License
    Law Officials [5742]

150 N Wacker Dr., Ste. 920
Chicago, IL 60606-1682
Ph: (312)300-4800
     (312)300-4807

Coffee, Larry, DDS, Founder, CEO
Dental Lifeline Network [14430]
1800 15th St., Ste. 100
Denver, CO 80202-7134
Ph: (303)534-5360
Fax: (303)534-5290

Coffelt, Doug, VP
Newspaper Target Marketing Coalition [2297]
351 W Camden St., 6th Fl.
Baltimore, MD 21201-2473
Ph: (202)386-6357

Coffer, Rony, President, Founder
Save A Generation [12724]
PO Box 370
Carolina Beach, NC 28428

Coffey, D. Wayne, Founder, President
No More Stolen Childhoods [10797]
PO Box 1553
Cockeysville, MD 21030
Toll Free: 877-666-6735

Coffey, Nora W., President
Hysterectomy Educational Resources and Services Foundation [16286]
422 Bryn Mawr Ave.
Bala Cynwyd, PA 19004
Ph: (610)667-7757
Toll Free: 888-750-4377
Fax: (610)667-8096

Coffey, Steve, President
CHRISTAR [20396]
1500 International Pky., Ste. 300
Richardson, TX 75081
Ph: (214)838-3800
Toll Free: 800-755-7955
Fax: (214)237-7515

Coffin, Charles, Secretary
Navy Seabee Veterans of America [21059]
c/o Charles Coffin, Secretary
16 Graham Ave.
West Haven, CT 06516
Ph: (203)843-5513
Toll Free: 800-SEA-BEE5

Coffin, Linda, Exec. Dir.
Association of Personal Historians [9462]
3208 E 25th St.
Minneapolis, MN 55406-1411

Coffman, Jennifer, Officer
Association for Africanist Anthropology [5905]
American Anthropological Association
2200 Wilson Blvd., Ste. 600
Arlington, VA 22201-3357
Ph: (703)528-1902
Toll Free: 800-545-4703
Fax: (703)528-3546

Coffman, Linda, Owner
American Mammoth Jackstock Registry [3594]
PO Box 9062
Pahrump, NV 89060
Ph: (830)330-0499

Coffman, Madonna W., President
Locks of Love [14200]
234 Southern Blvd.
West Palm Beach, FL 33405-2701
Ph: (561)833-7332
Toll Free: 888-896-1588
Fax: (561)833-7962

Cofoni, Paul, Director
AFCEA International [5583]
4400 Fair Lakes Ct.
Fairfax, VA 22033-3899
Ph: (703)631-6100
Toll Free: 800-336-4583
Fax: (703)631-6169

Cogan, Barry, President
Dodge Brothers Club [21371]
PO Box 1648
Cambridge, OH 43725
Ph: (740)439-5102

Coggins, Celine, Founder, CEO
Teach Plus [11739]
27-43 Wormwood St.
Tower Point, Ste. 410
Boston, MA 02210
Ph: (617)533-9900

Cogswell, Howard, President
Cogswell Family Association [20848]
c/o Edward R. Cogswell, Secretary
214 140th St. NW
Tulalip, WA 98271-8105
Ph: (360)652-4615

Cohan, Steven, President
Society for Cinema and Media Studies [9312]
Wallace Old Science Hall, Rm. 300
640 Parrington Oval
Norman, OK 73019
Ph: (405)325-8075
Fax: (405)325-7135

Cohen, Aaron, Founder, President
.Abolish Slavery Coalition [17860]
8620 W 3rd St.
Los Angeles, CA 90048
Toll Free: 800-821-2009

Cohen, Andrea, Chairperson
International Planned Parenthood Federation - Western Hemisphere Region [11844]
125 Maiden Ln., 9th Fl.
New York, NY 10038-4730
Ph: (212)248-6400
Fax: (212)248-4221

Cohen, Armond, Exec. Dir.
Clean Air Task Force [4539]
18 Tremont St., Ste. 530
Boston, MA 02108
Ph: (617)624-0234
Fax: (617)624-0230

Cohen, Bruce, President
American Foundation for Equal Rights [18371]
6565 Sunset Blvd., Ste. 400
Los Angeles, CA 90028

Cohen, Dan
Council on Library and Information Resources [9702]
1707 NW L St., Ste. 650
Washington, DC 20036
Ph: (202)939-4750
Fax: (202)939-4765

Cohen, Dan, Exec. Dir.
Music & Memory Inc. [12370]
160 1st St.
Mineola, NY 11501

Cohen, Gary, Acting CEO
GBCHealth [10539]
1 Rockefeller Plz., 28th Fl.
New York, NY 10020
Ph: (212)584-1600
Fax: (212)584-1699

Cohen, Gary, Founder, President
Health Care Without Harm [15009]
12355 Sunrise Valley Dr., Ste. 680

Reston, VA 20191
Ph: (703)860-9790
Fax: (703)860-9795

Cohen, Genie, CEO
International Association of Jewish Vocational Services [8737]
1845 Walnut St., Ste. 640
Philadelphia, PA 19103
Ph: (215)854-0233
Fax: (215)854-0212

Cohen, Greg, President, CEO
American Highway Users Alliance [12814]
1920 L St. NW, Ste. 525
Washington, DC 20036
Ph: (202)857-1200
Fax: (202)857-1220

Cohen, Greg, President
Electronic Transactions Association [394]
1101 16th St. NW, No. 402
Washington, DC 20036
Ph: (202)828-2635
Toll Free: 800-695-5509

Cohen, Jeff, Chmn. of the Bd.
Association of Jewish Aging Services [10500]
2519 Connecticut Ave. NW
Washington, DC 20008
Ph: (202)543-7500

Cohen, Larry, Chairman
American Seniors Housing Association [11960]
5225 Wisconsin Ave. NW, Ste. 502
Washington, DC 20015
Ph: (202)237-0900
Fax: (202)237-1616

Cohen, Marc, President
United States Judo Association [22966]
2005 Merrick Rd., No. 313
Merrick, NY 11566
Toll Free: 877-411-3409
Fax: (888)276-3432

Cohen, Marilyn A., President
American Cleft Palate-Craniofacial Association [14328]
1504 E Franklin St., Ste. 102
Chapel Hill, NC 27514-2820
Ph: (919)933-9044
Toll Free: 800-242-5338
Fax: (919)933-9604

Cohen, Marsha, Comm. Chm.
Food and Drug Law Institute [5223]
1155 15th St. NW, Ste. 910
Washington, DC 20005-2706
Ph: (202)371-1420
Toll Free: 800-956-6293
Fax: (202)371-0649

Cohen, Megan, Exec. Dir.
American Association of Cardiovascular and Pulmonary Rehabilitation [14087]
330 N Wabash Ave., Ste. 200
Chicago, IL 60611
Ph: (312)321-5146
Fax: (312)673-6924

Cohen, Rabbi Michael, Dir. of Operations, Founder
Green Zionist Alliance, Inc. [4067]
PO Box 1176
Long Beach, NY 11561
Ph: (347)559-4492

Cohen, Michael R., RPh, President
Institute for Safe Medication Practices [15021]
200 Lakeside Dr., Ste. 200

Horsham, PA 19044-2321
Ph: (215)947-7797
Fax: (215)914-1492

Cohen, Michael R., RPh, Chairperson
International Medication Safety Network [16666]
c/o Institute for Safe Medication Practices
200 Lakeside Dr., Ste. 200
Horsham, PA 19044
Ph: (215)947-7797
Fax: (215)914-1492

Cohen, Moshe, Founder
Clowns Without Borders - U.S.A. [12306]
705 Rockcreek Rd.
Charlottesville, VA 22903
Ph: (707)363-5513

Cohen, Dr. Nancy, Chairperson
Association of Nutrition Departments and Programs [16208]
c/o Dr. Nancy Cohen, Chairperson
University of Massachusetts-Amherst, Chenoweth Lab
100 Holdsworth Way
Amherst, MA 01003

Cohen, Philippe S., Treasurer
Organization of Biological Field Stations [6094]
PO Box 20492
Stanford, CA 94309

Cohen, Rabbi Mitchell, Director
National Ramah Commission [8143]
3080 Broadway
New York, NY 10027
Ph: (212)678-8881
Fax: (845)358-6284

Cohen, Richard J., Treasurer
American Public Health Association [16993]
800 I St. NW
Washington, DC 20001
Ph: (202)777-2742
Fax: (202)777-2534

Cohen, Richard, President, CEO
Southern Poverty Law Center [17932]
400 Washington Ave.
Montgomery, AL 36104-4344
Ph: (334)956-8200
Fax: (334)956-8481

Cohen, Ron, Chairman
Biotechnology Industry Organization [6120]
1201 Maryland Ave. SW, Ste. 900
Washington, DC 20024
Ph: (202)962-9200
Fax: (202)488-6301

Cohen, Stephanie, Founder, President
Kids Making a Difference [3628]
1527 W State Highway 114, Ste. 500, No. 106
Grapevine, TX 76051-8647

Cohen-Joppa, Felice, Editor
Nuclear Resister [18754]
PO Box 43383
Tucson, AZ 85733-3383
Ph: (520)323-8697

Cohn, Felicia, PhD, MA, President
American Society for Bioethics and Humanities [8305]
O'Hare Plz. Office Complex
8735 W Higgins Rd., Ste. 300
Chicago, IL 60631
Ph: (847)375-4745
Fax: (847)375-6482

Cohn, Kendra, President
American Computer Barrel Racing
Association [22912]
PO Box 322
French Camp, CA 95231
Ph: (209)481-8042

Cohn, Marilyn, Director
Chosen Children International
[10939]
PO Box 97112
Raleigh, NC 27624
Ph: (719)634-5437

Cohn, Peter, President
Christopher Morley Knothole Association [9081]
c/o The Bryant Library
2 Paper Mill Rd.
Roslyn, NY 11576-2133

Cohon, Charles, President
Manufacturers' Agents National Association [2206]
6321 W Dempster St., Ste. 110
Morton Grove, IL 60053
Ph: (949)859-4040
Toll Free: 877-626-2776
Fax: (949)855-2973

Cohoon, Leila, Contact
Victorian Hairwork Society [21787]
c/o Marlys Fladeland, Founder
PO Box 806
Pleasant Grove, UT 84062
Ph: (816)833-2955

Coimbra, Beth, President, Treasurer
The Erythromelalgia Association
[14575]
200 Old Castle Ln.
Wallingford, PA 19086-6027
Ph: (610)566-0797

Cokley-Dunlap, Nicole, Co-Pres.
Black Retail Action Group [2948]
68 E 131st St., Ste. 704
New York, NY 10037
Ph: (212)234-3050
Fax: (212)234-3053

Coku, Lindita, MD, Mem.
Albanian American Medical Society
[15702]
58 E Springfield St., Ste. 2
Boston, MA 02118
Ph: (617)236-0113
Fax: (617)236-0113

Colabaugh, Kathy, Specialist
IEEE - Robotics and Automation
Society [7104]
445 Hoes Ln.
Piscataway, NJ 08854
Ph: (732)562-3906
(732)562-6585

Colaco, Robert, Chairman, Founder
Citizens for a Better America
[17885]
PO Box 1949
Littlerock, CA 93543-5949
Ph: (818)574-8911

Colannino, Joseph, President
Knowledge & Information Professional Association [1801]
PO Box 4107
Tulsa, OK 74159-4107

Colaresi, Fr. Robert E., Mem.
Society of the Little Flower [19907]
1313 Frontage Rd.
Darien, IL 60561
Ph: (630)968-9400
Toll Free: 800-621-2806
Fax: (630)968-9542

Colbert, Kenny L., SPHR, President,
CEO
The Employers Association [1068]
3020 W Arrowood Rd.

Charlotte, NC 28273
Ph: (704)522-8011
Fax: (704)522-8105

Colburn, Loren, Exec. Dir.
Association of Free Community
Papers [2771]
7445 Morgan Rd., Ste. 203
Liverpool, NY 13090
Toll Free: 877-203-2327
Fax: (781)459-7770

Colburn, Sherry, Exec. Dir.
ConnectMed International [14992]
7040 Avenida Encinas, Ste. 104
Carlsbad, CA 92011
Ph: (619)800-5349

Cole, Alicia, Founder
Alliance for Safety Awareness for
Patients [15391]
14622 Ventura Blvd., No. 102-827
Sherman Oaks, CA 91403
Ph: (818)379-9679

Cole, Angel, President
American Nigerian Dwarf Dairy Association [4274]
c/o Angel Cole, President
72 Highway 92
Boydton, VA 23917
Ph: (434)738-8527

Cole, Bill, MS, Founder, President
International Mental Game Coaching
Association [22731]
PO Box 8151
San Jose, CA 95155
Ph: (408)440-2398
Toll Free: 888-445-0291
Fax: (408)440-2339

Cole, Ms. Cortney A., Founder,
President
Pink Door Nonprofit Organization
[14045]
PO Box 6990
Houston, TX 77265-6990
Ph: (832)727-3121

Cole, Dana Lee, Exec. Dir.
Hardwood Federation [1439]
1101 K St. NW, Ste. 100
Washington, DC 20005
Ph: (202)463-2705
(202)463-2452
Fax: (202)463-4702

Cole, David, President
The Masquers Playhouse, Inc.
[10260]
105 Park Pl.
Richmond, CA 94801-3922
Ph: (510)232-3888
(510)232-4031

Cole, Debra, Comm. Chm.
CREW New York [2859]
1201 Wakarusa Dr., Ste. D
Lawrence, KS 66049
Ph: (785)832-1808
Fax: (785)832-1551

Cole, Dr. Donald W., President
Organization Development Institute
[2463]
11234 Walnut Ridge Rd.
Chesterland, OH 44026
Ph: (440)729-7419
Fax: (440)729-9319

Cole, Eric, Exec. Dir.
Dandy-Walker Alliance [15922]
10325 Kensington Pkwy., Ste. 384
Kensington, MD 20895
Toll Free: 877-326-3992

Cole, Geneva Clark, President
National United Church Ushers Association of America [20633]

c/o Geneva Clark-Cole, President
6231 W Spencer Pl.
Milwaukee, WI 53218
Ph: (414)462-4997

Cole, Jerryne, President
The Public Lands Alliance [4580]
2401 Blueridge Ave., Ste. 303
Wheaton, MD 20902
Ph: (301)946-9475
Fax: (301)946-9478

Cole, John Y., Director
Center for the Book in the Library of
Congress [9754]
101 Independence Ave. SE
Washington, DC 20540-4920
Ph: (202)707-5221
Fax: (202)707-0269

Cole, Johnnetta Betsch, PhD,
President
Association of Art Museum Directors
[9822]
120 E 56th St., Ste. 520
New York, NY 10022-3673
Ph: (212)754-8084
Fax: (212)754-8087

Cole, Kathleen, President
Richard Burgi Fan Club [23989]
c/o Kathleen Cole, President
11155 Aqua Vista St., No. 302
Studio City, CA 91602-3700

Cole, Kenneth, Chmn. of the Bd.
amfAR, The Foundation for AIDS
Research [13528]
120 Wall St., 13th Fl.
New York, NY 10005-3908
Ph: (212)806-1600
Fax: (212)806-1601

Cole, Lance, Treasurer
Friends of Malawi [9208]
c/o Lance Cole, Treasurer
7940 SW 11th Ave.
Portland, OR 97219

Cole, Lya, Contact
Cancer Federation [13922]
PO Box 1298
Banning, CA 92220-0009
Ph: (951)849-4325

Cole, Ms. Melissa, Administrator
Foster Family-based Treatment Association [10982]
294 Union St.
Hackensack, NJ 07601-4303
Ph: (201)343-2246
Toll Free: 800-414-3382
Fax: (201)489-6719

Cole, Milford, President
Clumber Spaniel Club of America
[21858]
c/o Jack Poole
874 Orchard Terrace Dr.
New Wilmington, PA 16142-4222

Cole, Randy, President
National Hot Rod Diesel Association
[23084]
14702 Smokey Point Blvd.
Marysville, WA 98271
Ph: (360)658-4353
Fax: (360)322-3334

Cole, Robert H., Jr., Officer
MC Sailing Association [22647]
W257 S10550 Horseshoe Ln.
Mukwonago, WI 53149
Ph: (847)255-0210
Toll Free: 866-457-2582

Cole, Robert, Commodore
National Class E Scow Association
[22651]

337 Woodland Cir.
Madison, WI 53704
Ph: (608)347-1480

Cole, Sarah, CEO
CHAN Healthcare Auditors [7752]
231 S Bemiston Ave., Ste. 300
Clayton, MO 63105-1914
Ph: (314)802-2000
Fax: (314)802-2020

Cole, Sue, President
Man from U.N.C.L.E. Fan Club
[24087]
PO Box 1733
Oshkosh, WI 54903

Cole, William, Chairman
Crop Insurance Professionals Association [1854]
316 Pennsylvania Ave. SE, Ste. 401
Washington, DC 20003
Ph: (202)544-5873
Fax: (202)544-5874

Coleman, Barry, Exec. Dir.
Riders for Health [15061]
88 Pine St., 26th Fl.
New York, NY 10005

Coleman, Clare, President, CEO
National Family Planning and
Reproductive Health Association
[11845]
1627 K St. NW, 12th Fl.
Washington, DC 20006
Ph: (202)293-3114

Coleman, Jacquelyn T., Exec. Dir.
American Academy of Psychiatry
and the Law [5270]
1 Regency Dr.
Bloomfield, CT 06002-2310
Ph: (860)242-5450
Toll Free: 800-331-1389
Fax: (860)286-0787

Coleman, Jacquelyn T., CAE, Exec.
Dir.
American Academy of
Psychoanalysis and Dynamic
Psychiatry [16840]
1 Regency Dr.
Bloomfield, CT 06002
Toll Free: 888-691-8281
Fax: (860)286-0787

Coleman, John J., PhD, President
Drug Watch International [18137]
PO Box 45218
Omaha, NE 68145-0218
Ph: (402)384-9212

Coleman, Kelly, Director
Save the Rain [13336]
PO Box 1510
Mount Shasta, CA 96067
Ph: (530)926-9999
Fax: (530)926-5050

Coleman, Louise, President
American-European Greyhound Alliance [4286]
Ph: (508)435-5969

Coleman, Louise, Exec. Dir.
Greyhound Friends, Inc. [10631]
167 Saddle Hill Rd.
Hopkinton, MA 01748
Ph: (508)435-5969

Coleman, Mel, President
National Rural Electric Cooperative
Association [1031]
4301 Wilson Blvd.
Arlington, VA 22203
Ph: (703)907-5500
(703)907-5732

Coleman, Michael John, Exec. Dir.,
Founder, President
Migraine Awareness Group: A
National Understanding for Mi-
graineurs [14918]
100 N Union St., Ste. B
Alexandria, VA 22314
Ph: (703)349-1929

Coleman, Patricia M., President
Society for Intercultural Education,
Training and Research U.S.A.
[8122]
PO Box 1382
Crown Point, IN 46308
Toll Free: 877-796-9700

Coleman, R. Brooke, Exec. Dir.
New Fuels Alliance [6501]
101 Tremont St., Ste. 700
Boston, MA 02108
Ph: (617)275-8215

Coleman, Richard, President
Space Transportation Association
[5876]
4305 Underwood St.
University Park, MD 20782
Ph: (703)855-3917

Coleman, Shay, Exec. Dir.
Global Learning [8114]
PO Box 1011
Chatham, NJ 07928
Ph: (201)317-8796

Coles, Matthew, Chairman
Guttmacher Institute [11841]
125 Maiden Ln., 7th Fl.
New York, NY 10038
Ph: (212)248-1111
Toll Free: 800-355-0244
Fax: (212)248-1951

Coles, Roger, Chairman
World Leisure Organization [22415]
Central Michigan University
Warriner Hall 210
Mount Pleasant, MI 48859-0001
Ph: (989)774-6099

Coletti, Cinthia, Chmn. of the Bd.,
CEO
Literate Nation [8247]
870 Market St., Ste. 962
San Francisco, CA 94102
Ph: (415)789-5574

Coletti, Louis J., CEO, President
Building Trades Employers' Associa-
tion [509]
1430 Broadway, Ste. 1106
New York, NY 10018
Ph: (212)704-9745
Fax: (212)704-4367

Coley, Hillary, CFO, Asst. VP of
Admin.
Trout Unlimited [4895]
1777 N Kent St., Ste. 100
Arlington, VA 22209
Ph: (703)522-0200
Toll Free: 800-834-2419
Fax: (703)284-9400

Coley, Liz, Director
El Ayudante Nicaragua [13006]
PO Box 10805
Jackson, TN 38308

Colford, Michael, President
Chlotrudis Society for Independent
Film [9302]
PO Box 301237
Jamaica Plain, MA 02130
Ph: (781)526-5384

Colicchio, Heather, Founder,
President
American Association of Dental Of-
fice Managers [15568]

125 Half Mile Rd., Ste. 200
Red Bank, NJ 07701
Ph: (732)842-9977

Coll, Steve, Contact
New America Foundation [18994]
740 15th St. NW, Ste. 900
Washington, DC 20005
Ph: (202)986-2700
Fax: (202)986-3696

Collen, Jodi, President
International Special Events Society
[1145]
330 N Wabash Ave., Ste. 2000
Chicago, IL 60611
Ph: (312)321-6853
Toll Free: 800-688-4737
Fax: (312)673-6953

Collette, Robert L., President
Institute of Shortening and Edible
Oils [2449]
1319 F St. NW, Ste. 600
Washington, DC 20004
Ph: (202)783-7960
Fax: (202)393-1367

Colley, Dennis, President
Fibre Box Association [2491]
500 Park Blvd., Ste. 985
Itasca, IL 60143
Ph: (847)364-9600
Fax: (847)364-9639

Colley, Micaela, Exec. Dir.
Organic Seed Alliance [4644]
PO Box 772
Port Townsend, WA 98368
Ph: (360)385-7192

Collie, Asher, Founder, Exec. Dir.
Sole Hope [13018]
605 E Innes St., Ste. 3263
Salisbury, NC 28145
Toll Free: 855-516-4673

Collier, Kevin L., Cmdr.
Sons of the American Legion
[21044]
700 N Pennsylvania St.
Indianapolis, IN 46206
Ph: (317)630-1205
Fax: (317)630-1223

Collier, Robin, President
Natural Dyes International [7726]
HCR74, Box 21912
El Prado, NM 87529
Toll Free: 800-665-9786

Collings, Patty, President
Concerned United Birthparents, Inc.
[10450]
PO Box 5538
Sherman Oaks, CA 91413
Toll Free: 800-822-2777
Fax: (858)712-3317

Collingsworth, Terry, Exec. Dir.
International Rights Advocates
[18417]
1156 15th St. NW, Ste. 502
Washington, DC 20005
Ph: (202)527-7997
Toll Free: 866-594-4001

Collins, Ardis, Treasurer
Hegel Society of America [9053]
PO Box 7147
Charlottesville, VA 22906-7147
Ph: (804)220-3300
Toll Free: 800-444-2419
Fax: (804)220-3301

Collins, Beth, Exec. Dir.
Food Family Farming Foundation
[15090]

PO Box 20708
Boulder, CO 80308

Collins, Bill, Founder
Children's Medical Ministries [14182]
PO Box 3382
Crofton, MD 21114
Ph: (301)536-3173
Fax: (410)721-6261

Collins, Bill, Director
Mining Electrical Maintenance and
Safety Association [2387]
PO Box 7163
Lakeland, FL 33807

Collins, Bill, Chmn. of the Bd.
National Court Appointed Special
Advocate Association [11092]
North Twr., Ste. 500
100 W Harrison St.
Seattle, WA 98119
Toll Free: 800-628-3233

Collins, Bob, Chairman
National Dropout Prevention Center/
Network [7823]
Clemson University
209 Martin St.
Clemson, SC 29631-1555
Ph: (864)656-2599
Fax: (864)656-0136

Collins, Carolyn, President
Art Therapy Connection [13728]
PO Box 146462
Chicago, IL 60614
Ph: (773)791-7865

Collins, Emily, Founder
Esperanza - Hope for the Children
[10963]
27 Captain Miles Ln.
Concord, MA 01742
Ph: (978)808-8967

Collins, Erma, Founder
Compassion Care for Disabled
Children [16473]
PO Box 4712
Crofton, MD 21114
Ph: (301)261-3211
Fax: (410)721-4647

Collins, Francis, Contact
Human Heredity and Health in Africa
[13514]
National Human Genome Research
Institute
National Institutes of Health
5635 Fishers Ln., Ste. 4076
Bethesda, MD 20892-9305
Ph: (301)496-7531
Fax: (301)480-2770

Collins, George R., President
United States Distance Learning As-
sociation [8000]
76 Canal St., Ste. 400
Boston, MA 02114
Ph: (617)399-1770
Fax: (617)399-1771

Collins, Grenville, Chairman
Muhyiddin Ibn 'Arabi Society [20610]
38 Miller Ave., No. 486
Mill Valley, CA 94941-1927

Collins, Jeannette, Dir. of Operations
International Center for Assault
Prevention [11704]
107 Gilbreth Pky., Ste. 200
Mullica Hill, NJ 08062
Ph: (856)582-7000
Toll Free: 800-258-3189
Fax: (856)582-3588

Collins, Kathryn K., MD, President
Pediatric & Congenital Electrophysiology Society [16768]

9650 Rockville Pke.
Bethesda, MD 20814
Ph: (301)634-7401
Fax: (301)634-7099

Collins, Kelli, President
Railway Industrial Clearance As-
sociation [3355]
8900 Eastloch Dr., Ste. 215
Spring, TX 77379
Ph: (281)826-0009
Toll Free: 888-203-5580

Collins, Lee, President
Vietnamese Nom Preservation
Foundation [9770]
229 Beachers Brook Ln.
Cary, NC 27511

Collins, Martha, MD, Director,
President
Organization for Medical and
Psychological Assistance for
Children Overseas [14209]
14 Curve St.
Lexington, MA 02420

Collins, Mary, President, CEO
Broadcast Cable Credit Association
[456]
550 W Frontage Rd., Ste. 3600
Northfield, IL 60093
Ph: (847)881-8757
Fax: (847)784-8059

Collins, Mary M., President, CEO
Media Financial Management As-
sociation [1250]
550 W Frontage Rd., Ste. 3600
Northfield, IL 60093
Ph: (847)716-7000
Fax: (847)716-7004

Collins, Max Allan, Founder,
President, VP
International Association of Media
Tie-in Writers [10378]
PO Box 8212
Calabasas, CA 91372

Collins, Meg, Mktg. Mgr.
Council of American Survey
Research Organizations [18923]
170 N Country Road, Ste. 4
Port Jefferson, NY 11777
Ph: (631)928-6954
Fax: (631)928-6041

Collins, Michael, Secretary
Coalition of Irish Immigration
Centers [12125]
PO Box 210
Bronx, NY 10470
Ph: (914)837-2007

Collins, Michael, Secretary
The Players [10269]
16 Gramercy Park S
New York, NY 10003
Ph: (212)475-6116

Collins, Mike, Secretary
Batten Disease Support and
Research Association [15909]
1175 Dublin Rd.
Columbus, OH 43215
Toll Free: 800-448-4570
Fax: (800)648-8718

Collins, Mike, Secretary
International Society for Aviation
Photography, Inc. [2585]
c/o Bonnie Kratz, Treasurer
N4752 Valley Rd.
Luxemburg, WI 54217

Collins, Pamela Y., MD, Founder
Society for Emotional Well-Being
Worldwide [15807]

PO Box 41
New York, NY 10024

Collins, Ray R., President
International Space Exploration and
Colonization Co. [5864]
PO Box 60885
Fairbanks, AK 99706-0885
Ph: (907)488-1001

Collins, Dr. Richard, Director
National Association of Private
Special Education Centers [8587]
South Bldg.
601 Pennsylvania Ave. NW, Ste. 900
Washington, DC 20004
Ph: (202)434-8225
Fax: (202)434-8224

Collins, Susan V., President
Container Recycling Institute [4629]
4361 Keystone Ave.
Culver City, CA 90232
Ph: (310)559-7451

Collins, Woody M., President
Congo Helping Hands [10475]
8170 Hague Rd.
Indianapolis, IN 46256-1649

Collopy, Michael, Founder
Architects of Peace Foundation
[12431]
119 E Weber Ave.
Stockton, CA 95219
Ph: (209)608-5455

Collura, Barbara, Director
National Health Council [14955]
1730 M St. NW, Ste. 500
Washington, DC 20036-4561
Ph: (202)785-3910
Fax: (202)785-5923

Collura, Barbara, President, CEO
RESOLVE: The National Infertility
Association [14764]
7918 Jones Branch Dr., Ste. 300
McLean, VA 22102
Ph: (703)556-7172
Fax: (703)506-3266

Colman, Jennifer, Exec. Dir.
Automotive Trade Association
Executives [286]
8400 Westpark Dr.
McLean, VA 22102
Ph: (703)821-7072
Fax: (703)556-8581

Colman, Victor, Director
Childhood Obesity Prevention Coali-
tion [16252]
419 3rd Ave. W
Seattle, WA 98119
Ph: (206)859-2500

Colon Valle, Miriam, Director
Pregones Theater Puerto Rican
Traveling Theater [10270]
304 W 47th St.
New York, NY 10036
Ph: (212)354-1293

Colorafi, Robert, VP, Secretary
Electric Railroaders' Association
[10181]
PO Box 3323
New York, NY 10163-3323

Colson, Dorothy, President
United Negro College Fund -
National Alumni Council [19353]
1805 7th St. NW
Washington, DC 20001
Toll Free: 800-331-2244

Colson, Robert, President
Academy of Accounting Historians
[9447]

Case Western Reserve University
Weatherhead School of Manage-
ment
10900 Euclid Ave.
Cleveland, OH 44106-7235
Ph: (216)368-2058

Colton, Prof. Samuel, Sr., Founder
Welders Without Borders [7384]
PO Box 1597
Yuma, AZ 85364
Ph: (928)344-7570

Colucci, Margaret, Officer
National Board of Chiropractic
Examiners [14278]
901 54th Ave.
Greeley, CO 80634
Toll Free: 800-964-6223

Colucci, Marlene M., Exec. Dir.
Business Council [18951]
1901 Pennsylvania Ave. NW, Ste.
701
Washington, DC 20006
Ph: (202)298-7650
Fax: (202)785-0296

Colucci, Mary, Exec. Dir.
Craft Yarn Council of America
[21754]
3740 N Josey Ln., Ste. 102
Carrollton, TX 75007
Ph: (972)325-7232
Fax: (972)215-7333

Colucci, Paul, Treasurer
Red Devon USA [3753]
c/o Sarah Wilkerson, Administrative
Secretary
2983 US Hwy. 84
Dixie, GA 31629
Ph: (229)516-0394

Colvin, JoAnn, Chairperson
American Chesapeake Club [21805]
c/o Joanne Silver, Membership
Chairperson
412 Woodbury Dr.
Wyckoff, NJ 07481-1514

Coly, Lisette, VP, Exec. Dir.
Parapsychology Foundation [6990]
PO Box 1562
New York, NY 10021-0043
Ph: (212)628-1550
Fax: (212)628-1559

Combes, John R., President
Health Research and Educational
Trust [15327]
155 N Wacker, Ste. 400
Chicago, IL 60606
Ph: (312)422-2600
Fax: (312)422-4568

Combest, Hannes, CEO
National Auctioneers Association
[261]
8880 Ballentine St.
Overland Park, KS 66214
Ph: (913)541-8084
Fax: (913)894-5281

Combs, Glen E., President
Association of Physician Assistants
in Psychiatry [16827]
732 Eden Way N, No. 261, Ste. E
Chesapeake, VA 23320
Ph: (678)606-9418
Toll Free: 888-973-9477

Combs, Roberta, President, CEO
Christian Coalition of America
[18034]
PO Box 37030
Washington, DC 20013
Ph: (202)479-6900

Comeau, Stephen, Exec. Asst.
National Catholic Educational As-
sociation [7577]
1005 N Glebe Rd., Ste. 525
Arlington, VA 22201
Ph: (571)257-0010
Toll Free: 800-711-6232
Fax: (703)243-0025

Comenote, Janeen, Director
National Urban Indian Family Coalition [12381]
2626 Eastlake Ave. E, Ste. D
Seattle, WA 98102

Comer, Dawn, President
Society for the Study of Midwestern
Literature [9767]
c/o Mr. Roger J. Bresnahan, PhD,
Secretary/Treasurer
Michigan State University
Bessey Hall, Rm. 235
434 Farm Ln.
East Lansing, MI 48824

Comer, Douglas C., V. Chmn. of the
Bd.
International Council on Monuments
and Sites - United States National
Committee [9404]
1307 New Hampshire Ave. NW
Washington, DC 20036-1531
Ph: (202)463-1291
Fax: (202)463-1299

Comer, Jenise M., President
Association of Social Work Boards
[13104]
400 S Ridge Pky., Ste. B
Culpeper, VA 22701
Ph: (540)829-6880
Toll Free: 800-225-6880
Fax: (540)829-0562

Comer, Jim, Comm. Chm.
Association for Career and Technical
Education [8733]
1410 King St.
Alexandria, VA 22314
Toll Free: 800-826-9972
Fax: (703)683-7424

Comer, Jim, Trustee
VIP Mentoring [11550]
7700 2nd Ave., Ste. 617
Detroit, MI 48202-2411
Ph: (313)964-1110

Comer, Lisa, Dir. (Actg.)
National Association of Mammogra-
phers [17060]
PO Box 792011
Paia, HI 96779

Comerford, Tony, PhD, CEO,
President
New Hope Foundation [13171]
80 Conover Rd.
Marlboro, NJ 07746
Ph: (732)946-3030
Toll Free: 800-705-4673
Fax: (732)946-3541

Comins, Prof. Daniel, President
International Society of Heterocyclic
Chemistry [6204]
c/o Dr. Frederick Luzzio, Treasurer
Dept. of Chemistry
University of Louisville
2320 S Brook St.
Louisville, KY 40208
Ph: (502)852-7323
(502)295-3469

Comis, Robert L., MD, Chairman,
President
Coalition of Cancer Cooperative
Groups [13946]

1818 Market St., Ste. 1100
Philadelphia, PA 19103
Ph: (215)789-3600
Fax: (215)789-3655

Comolli, Loic, Co-CEO
NESsT International [12998]
995 Market St., Ste. 1115
San Francisco, CA 94103
Ph: (415)644-0509

Compeau, Prof. Larry D., PhD,
Exec. Ofc.
APA Division 23: Society for
Consumer Psychology [16875]
c/o Larry D. Compeau, Executive
Officer
Clarkson University School of Busi-
ness
Snell Hall
Potsdam, NY 13699

Comperini, Bob, Inst.
United States Ultralight Association
[21255]
16192 Coastal Hwy.
Lewes, DE 19958
Ph: (717)339-0200

Compton, Don, Officer
Society for the Scientific Study of
Reading [8492]
c/o Carol M. Connor, Treasurer
16 Coltrane Ct.
Irvine, CA 92617

Compton, Sam, President
Boone Society [20787]
1303 Hunter Ace Way
Cedar Park, TX 78613

Comsky, Bryna, Rec. Sec.
Canaan Dog Club of America
[21850]
565 Illinois Blvd.
Hoffman Estates, IL 60169-3360

Comstack, Mark, VP
Highpointers Club [22467]
PO Box 1496
Golden, CO 80402

Conant, John, President
Inter-Society Color Council [755]
7820B Wormans Mill Rd., Ste. 115
Frederick, MD 21701
Toll Free: 866-876-4816

Conant, Sara Ellis, Contact
Young Women Social Entrepreneurs
[677]
1218 Green St.
San Francisco, CA 94109
Ph: (707)272-0066
(415)716-6409

Conatser, Glenn, Officer
National Swine Improvement
Federation [4715]
102 McCord Hall
Dept. of Animal Science
University of Tennessee
2640 Morgan Cir.
Knoxville, TN 37996-4588
Ph: (865)974-7238
Fax: (865)974-9043

Concotelli, Ms. Shelby, Dir. of Admin.
National Association of Chamber
Ambassadors [23602]
PO Box 1198
Seminole, TX 79360
Toll Free: 800-411-6222
Fax: (432)758-6698

Conde, Eric, MSA, CFAAMA, Bd.
Member
American Academy of Medical
Administrators Research and
Educational Foundation [15567]

330 N Wabash Ave., Ste. 2000
Chicago, IL 60611
Ph: (312)321-6815
Fax: (312)673-6705

Condon, Linda, President
American Society of Group
  Psychotherapy and Psychodrama
  [16964]
301 N Harrison St., No. 508
Princeton, NJ 08540
Ph: (609)737-8500
Fax: (609)737-8510

Condrick, Diane, Exec. Asst.
AMSUS - The Society of the Federal
  Health Professionals [15837]
9320 Old Georgetown Rd.
Bethesda, MD 20814-1653
Ph: (301)897-8800
Toll Free: 800-761-9320
Fax: (301)530-5446

Condrill, Joe, President
Overseas Brats [19661]
PO Box 47112
Wichita, KS 67201
Ph: (316)269-9610
Fax: (316)269-9610

Coneghen, Cathleen, Asst. Dir.
American Academy of Pain Manage-
  ment [16546]
975 Morning Star Dr., Ste. A
Sonora, CA 95370-9249
Ph: (209)533-9744
Fax: (209)533-9750

Coneset, Phyllis M., VP
Institute of Real Estate Management
  [2864]
430 N Michigan Ave.
Chicago, IL 60611
Toll Free: 800-837-0706
Fax: (800)338-4736

Conetta, Carl, Director
Project on Defense Alternatives
  [18089]
Center for International Policy
2000 M St. NW, Ste. 720
Washington, DC 20036-3327
Ph: (202)232-3317

Conforti, St. Guido, Founder
Xaverian Missionaries of the United
  States [20483]
12 Helene Ct.
Wayne, NJ 07470
Ph: (973)942-2975
Fax: (973)492-5012

Conger, Brenda, Exec. Dir.,
  President
Cardio-Facio-Cutaneous
  International [14811]
183 Brown Rd.
Vestal, NY 13850
Ph: (607)772-9666
Fax: (607)748-0409

Conklin, Charlie, President
U.S. Trout Farmers Association
  [3649]
PO Box 61342
Raleigh, NC 27661
Ph: (919)909-1943

Conklin, Pete, Director
American Association of Daily
  Money Managers [1272]
174 Crestview Dr.
Bellefonte, PA 16823-8516
Toll Free: 877-326-5991
Fax: (814)355-2452

Conkling, Susan, Chairperson
Society for Music Teacher Education
  [8389]

c/o Susan Conkling, Chairperson
Boston University
233 Bay State Rd.
Boston, MA 02215

Conley, Stephen, Director
American School Health Association
  [15136]
7918 Jones Branch, Ste. 500
McLean, VA 22102
Ph: (703)506-7675
Fax: (703)506-3266

Conley, Tom, President, CEO
High Point Market Authority [1481]
164 S Main St., Ste. 700
High Point, NC 27260
Ph: (336)869-1000
Toll Free: 800-874-6492

Conlin, Sue, President
Therapeutic Touch International As-
  sociation [15270]
PO Box 130
Delmar, NY 12054
Ph: (518)325-1185
Fax: (509)693-3537

Conn, Michael, Exec. Dir.
International Institute for Building-
  Biology and Ecology [4005]
PO Box 8520
Santa Fe, NM 87504
Toll Free: 866-960-0333

Connell, Lori, Founder
Mi Esperanza [13383]
PO Box 1575
Mandeville, LA 70470
Ph: (205)533-8725

Connell, Wayne, Founder, President
Invisible Disabilities Association
  [14551]
PO Box 4067
Parker, CO 80134

Connell-Freund, Anne, President
International Community Corrections
  Association [11532]
2100 Stella Ct.
Columbus, OH 43215
Ph: (614)252-8417
Fax: (614)252-7987

Connelly, Dan, Chairman
Dunkin' Donuts Independent
  Franchise Owners [1459]
2 1st Ave., Ste. 127 - 3
Peabody, MA 01960
Ph: (978)587-2581

Connelly, David, CEO
Open Applications Group [6280]
PO Box 4897
Marietta, GA 30061-4897
Ph: (404)402-1962
Fax: (801)740-0100

Connelly, Edward F., President
New Ecology, Inc. [11412]
15 Court Sq., Ste. 420
Boston, MA 02108
Ph: (617)557-1700
Fax: (617)557-1770

Connelly, Gail, Exec. Dir.
National Association of Elementary
  School Principals [8458]
1615 Duke St.
Alexandria, VA 22314
Ph: (703)684-3345
Toll Free: 800-386-2377
Fax: (703)549-5568

Connelly, John, President
National Fisheries Institute [3033]
7918 Jones Branch Dr., Ste. 700

McLean, VA 22102-3319
Ph: (703)752-8880
Fax: (703)752-7583

Connelly, Michael, Exec. Dir.
United States Justice Foundation
  [5726]
932 D St., Ste. 2
Ramona, CA 92065
Ph: (760)788-6624
Fax: (760)788-6414

Conner, Coye, Jr., Chmn. of the Bd.
Kids Matter International [11059]
535 S Nolen Dr., Ste. 300
Southlake, TX 76092
Ph: (817)488-7679
Fax: (817)488-7685

Conner, Frances Clay, Exec. Dir.
American Academy of Equine Art
  [8828]
160 E Main St.
Georgetown, KY 40324
Ph: (502)570-8567

Conner, Frances, President
Staffordshire Terrier Club of America
  [21966]
c/o Stephanie Rogers, Secretary
70 Pamela Dr.
Ward, AR 72176

Conner, Gary, Exec. Dir.
National Association of Independent
  Real Estate Brokers [2870]
7102 Mardyke Ln.
Indianapolis, IN 46226
Ph: (317)547-4679

Conner, Jennifer, President
Society of Dermatology Physician
  Assistants [16726]
8400 Westpark Dr., 2nd Fl.
McLean, VA 22102
Toll Free: 800-380-3992
Fax: (703)563-9263

Conner, Preston L., President
National Association of Part-Time
  and Temporary Employees [1096]
5800 Barton, Ste. 201
Shawnee, KS 66203
Ph: (913)962-7740
Fax: (913)631-0489

Conner, Tracey, President
Estrela Mountain Dog Association of
  America [21876]
c/o Tracey Conner, President
102 Cherokee Dr.
Shickshinny, PA 18655
Ph: (570)592-8784

Connerly, Ward, Founder, President
American Civil Rights Institute
  [17868]
PO Box 188350
Sacramento, CA 95818-8350
Ph: (916)444-2278

Connett, Michael, Exec. Dir.
Fluoride Action Network [14433]
104 Walnut St.
Binghamton, NY 13905
Ph: (802)338-5577

Connolly, Aidan, Exec. Dir.
Irish Arts Center [9601]
553 W 51st St.
New York, NY 10019
Ph: (212)757-3318
Toll Free: 866-811-4111
Fax: (212)247-0930

Connolly, Dave, VP
Sailors' Union of the Pacific [23476]
450 Harrison St.

San Francisco, CA 94105
Ph: (415)777-3400
    (415)777-3616
Fax: (415)777-5088

Connolly, Jim, President, CEO
Aeras [14726]
1405 Research Blvd.
Rockville, MD 20850
Ph: (301)547-2900
Fax: (301)547-2901

Connor, Keli, Chairman
Gamma Sigma Sigma [23874]
PO Box 248
Rindge, NH 03461
Ph: (603)674-4931
Fax: (603)899-3225

Connors, J. Michael, MD, President
Society for Pediatric Sedation
  [13713]
2209 Dickens Rd.
Richmond, VA 23230-2005
Ph: (804)565-6354
Fax: (804)282-0090

Connors, Susan H., President, CEO
Brain Injury Association of America
  [14909]
1608 Spring Hill Rd., Ste. 110
Vienna, VA 22182
Ph: (703)761-0750
Toll Free: 800-444-6443
Fax: (703)761-0755

Conrad, Cecilia, VP, Chmn. of the
  Bd.
International Association for Feminist
  Economics [6391]
371 CBA
Dept. of Economics
College of Business Administration
University of Nebraska-Lincoln
Lincoln, NE 68588-0479
Ph: (402)472-3372
Fax: (866)257-8304

Conrad, Chris, Director
Business Alliance for Commerce in
  Hemp [18860]
PO Box 1716
El Cerrito, CA 94530
Ph: (510)215-8326

Conrad, Chris, Director
Family Council on Drug Awareness
  [13140]
PO Box 1716
El Cerrito, CA 94530
Ph: (510)215-8326
Fax: (510)215-8326

Conrad, Chris, Director
Friends and Families of Cannabis
  Consumers [18646]
PO Box 1716
El Cerrito, CA 94530
Ph: (510)215-8326
Fax: (510)215-8326

Conrad, Gregory E., Exec. Dir.
Interstate Mining Compact Commis-
  sion [5634]
445 Carlisle Dr.
Herndon, VA 20170
Ph: (703)709-8654
Fax: (703)709-8655

Conrad, Amb. Kevin M., Exec. Dir.
Coalition for Rainforest Nations
  [4613]
52 Vanderbilt Ave., 14th Fl.
New York, NY 10017-3808
Ph: (646)448-6870
Fax: (646)448-6889

Conrad, Sara, Director
American Council of Blind Students
  [17683]

American Council of the Blind
2200 Wilson Blvd., Ste. 650
Arlington, VA 22201-3354
Ph: (202)467-5081
Toll Free: 800-424-8666
Fax: (202)465-5085

Conroy, Kathy, VP, COO
National Association of Theatre
Owners [1151]
750 1st St. NE, Ste. 1130
Washington, DC 20002
Ph: (202)962-0054
Fax: (202)962-0370

Consalo, Frank A., VP
Bank Insurance and Securities Association [1842]
2025 M St. NW, Ste. 800
Washington, DC 20036-2422
Ph: (202)367-1111
Fax: (202)367-2111

Consoli, Melissa Morgan,
Chairperson
American Psychological Association
Committee on International Relations in Psychology [16862]
Office of International Affairs
750 1st St. NE
Washington, DC 20002-4242
Ph: (202)336-6025
Fax: (202)312-6499

Constant, Amelie F., President
Society of Government Economists
[5160]
PO Box 23010
Washington, DC 20026-3010
Ph: (202)643-1743

Constantine, John, President
American Miniature Schnauzer Club
[21815]
c/o Jacquelyn Ebersbach
424 45th St.
West Palm Beach, FL 33407

Constantino, Kris, Treasurer
Chromosome 9p- Network [14812]
PO Box 71
Tillson, NY 12486
Ph: (920)931-2644

Conti, Matt, Founder
Our Hearts to your Soles [13015]
PO Box 243
Ingomar, PA 15127

Contos, George, CEO
YAI Network [12334]
460 W 34th St., 11th Fl.
New York, NY 10001-2382
Ph: (212)273-6100
(212)273-6199
Toll Free: 877-924-4438

Contreras-Vidal, Jose, President
International Graphonomics Society
[10414]
c/o Dr. Hans-Leo Teulings, Website
Manager and Treasurer
NeuroScript
435 E Carson Dr.
Tempe, AZ 85282

Convertino, Fr. David I., OFM, Exec.
Dir.
St. Anthony's Guild [20458]
144 W 32nd St.
New York, NY 10001-3202
Ph: (212)564-8799
Toll Free: 800-848-4538

Convissor, Rena, Exec. Dir.
American Jewish Society for Service
[12218]
10319 Westlake Dr., Ste. 193

Bethesda, MD 20817
Ph: (301)664-6400

Conway, Chris, President
Education Credit Union Council
[951]
PO Box 426
Corning, NY 14830
Toll Free: 855-888-5851
Fax: (866)861-8132

Conway, Jim, Exec. Dir.
Express Delivery and Logistics Association [3085]
400 Admiral Blvd.
Kansas City, MO 64106
Ph: (816)221-0254
Toll Free: 888-838-0761
Fax: (816)472-7765

Conway, Monica, Exec. Asst.
The Fertilizer Institute [1182]
425 3rd St. SW, Ste. 950
Washington, DC 20024
Ph: (202)962-0490
Fax: (202)962-0577

Conway, Stuart, President
Trees, Water and People [4106]
633 Remington St.
Fort Collins, CO 80524
Toll Free: 877-606-4TWP
Fax: (970)224-1726

Conway, Tony, Contact
Lorrie Morgan International Fan Club
[24055]
PO Box 213
White Creek, TN 37189
Ph: (615)724-1818

Cook, Betty, VP
Women Marines Association [21022]
PO Box 377
Oaks, PA 19456-0377
Toll Free: 888-525-1943

Cook, Brad, Bd. Member
International Precious Metals
Institute [6847]
5101 N 12th Ave., Ste. C
Pensacola, FL 32504
Ph: (850)476-1156
Fax: (850)476-1548

Cook, Clint, Exec. Dir.
General Association of General
Baptists [19730]
100 Stinson Dr.
Poplar Bluff, MO 63901
Ph: (573)785-7746
Fax: (573)785-0564

Cook, David, Chairman
Association for Computing
Machinery - Special Interest Group
on Ada [7055]
c/o Clyde Roby, Secretary-Treasurer
Institute for Defense Analyses
4850 Mark Center Dr.
Alexandria, VA 22311
Ph: (703)845-6666
Fax: (703)845-6848

Cook, David, Chairperson
Special Interest Group on Ada
[7059]
c/o David Cook, Chairperson
PO Box 13063
Nacogdoches, TX 75962
Ph: (936)468-2508
Fax: (936)468-7086

Cook, Dennis, Chairman
Young Republican National Federation [19053]
PO Box 15293
Washington, DC 20003-0293

Cook, Diana, Coord.
Mennonite Voluntary Service [20332]
3145 Benham Ave., Ste. 3
Elkhart, IN 46517
Ph: (574)523-3000
Toll Free: 866-866-2872
Fax: (316)283-0454

Cook, Ernest, President
The Conservation Campaign [18017]
10 Milk St., Ste. 810
Boston, MA 02108
Ph: (617)371-0526

Cook, Guy R., Director, President
Internet Business Alliance [7303]
PO Box 11518
Seattle, WA 98110-5518

Cook, James
Children International [20393]
2000 E Red Bridge Rd.
Kansas City, MO 64121
Ph: (816)942-2000
Toll Free: 800-888-3089
Fax: (816)942-3714

Cook, James, Chmn. of the Bd.
National Criminal Enforcement Association [5500]
PO Box 807
Jackson, LA 70748-0807
Ph: (700)314-4543
Toll Free: 877-468-2392
Fax: (770)679-8671

Cook, Jim, Secretary
Federation of Fire Chaplains [19926]
c/o Ed Stauffer, Executive Director
PO Box 437
Meridian, TX 76665
Ph: (254)435-2256
Fax: (254)435-2256

Cook, Joan, President
APA Division 56: Trauma Psychology
[16897]
750 1st St. NE
Washington, DC 20002-4242
Ph: (607)722-5857
Toll Free: 800-429-6784

Cook, Joan, Exec. Dir.
Roofing Industry Committee on
Weather Issues, Inc. [575]
6314 Kungle Rd.
Clinton, OH 44216
Ph: (330)671-4569
Fax: (330)825-7172

Cook, Kaye, PhD, President
Association for Moral Education
[7744]
c/o Kaye Cook PhD., President
Dept. of Psychology
Gordon College
255 Grapevine Rd.
Wenham, MA 01984-1813

Cook, Kris, CAE, Exec. Dir.
National Affordable Housing
Management Association [1690]
400 N Columbus St., Ste. 203
Alexandria, VA 22314
Ph: (703)683-8630

Cook, Kristin, Founder, Director
Faces of Loss, Faces of Hope
[12352]
PO Box 26131
Minneapolis, MN 55426

Cook, Melanie K., Chmn. of the Bd.
Association of Home Appliance
Manufacturers [212]
1111 19th St. NW, Ste. 402
Washington, DC 20036
Ph: (202)872-5955
Fax: (202)872-9354

Cook, Nick, Officer
American Association of Woodturners [21744]
222 Landmark Ctr.
75 5th St. W
Saint Paul, MN 55102-7704
Ph: (651)484-9094
Toll Free: 877-595-9094

Cook, R. Scott, President
American-Osteopathic Academy of
Sports Medicine [17277]
2424 American Ln.
Madison, WI 53704
Ph: (608)443-2477
Fax: (608)443-2474

Cook, Richard, CFO
Social Accountability International
[18443]
15 W 44th St., 6th Fl.
New York, NY 10036
Ph: (212)684-1414
Fax: (212)684-1515

Cook, Steven H., President
National Association of Assistant
United States Attorneys [5025]
5868 Mapledale Plz., Ste. 104
Woodbridge, VA 22193
Toll Free: 800-455-5661

Cook, Tim, President
Alpine Coach Association [22416]
5808 A Summitview Ave., No. 337
Yakima, WA 98908-3042
Ph: (509)457-4133

Cook, Tim, Secretary
Marine Corps Mustang Association,
Inc. [21016]
PO Box 12
Chalfont, PA 18914-0012
Toll Free: 866-937-6262

Cooke, Laurie, CEO
Healthcare Businesswomen's Association [15015]
Bldg. E, Ste. 215
373 Route 46 West
Fairfield, NJ 07004
Ph: (973)575-0606
Fax: (973)575-1445

Cooke, Susan, Dir. of Programs
Catalogue Raisonne Scholars Association [7503]
c/o Suzi Villiger, Director
294 E 7th St.
Brooklyn, NY 11218

Cookenham, Edward, President
USS Wainwright Veterans Association [21145]
210 Greenwood Ave.
Lehigh Acres, FL 33936

Coolahan, James, President
Simulation Interoperability Standards
Organization [7292]
3100 Technology Pkwy.
Orlando, FL 32826
Ph: (407)882-1378
Fax: (407)882-1304

Coolidge, Laurie, Contact
Colonial Coverlet Guild of America
[21639]
536 Arizona Ave.
Glenwood, IL 60425-1006

Coolidge, Tony, Exec. Dir.
ATAYAL [9574]
900 E Pecan St., Ste. 300
Pflugerville, TX 78660
Ph: (407)459-7766

Coombs, Ms. Emily, Exec. Sec.
Association of Mormon Counselors
and Psychotherapists [16966]

PO Box 540385
North Salt Lake, UT 84054
Ph: (801)425-3490
Fax: (801)931-2010

Coons, Marnie, Contact
Together Against Malaria [15416]
220 Broadway
Cambridge, MA 02139-1904

Cooper, Arthur G., Chairman
Marine Mammal Conservancy [4841]
102200 Overseas Hwy.
Key Largo, FL 33037
Ph: (405)451-4774
Fax: (405)451-4730

Cooper, Becky, Exec. Dir.
Friends for Youth [13445]
1741 Broadway St.
Redwood City, CA 94063
Ph: (650)368-4444
     (650)368-4464
Fax: (650)368-4467

Cooper, Claude, Chmn. of the Bd.
Association of Major City Building
  Officials [5066]
505 Huntmar Park Dr., Ste. 210
Herndon, VA 20170-5139
Ph: (703)481-2038
Toll Free: 800-DOC-CODE
Fax: (703)481-3596

Cooper, George, Contact
Kids Fund [11244]
416 Benninghaus Rd.
Baltimore, MD 21212
Ph: (410)532-9330
Toll Free: 877-532-9330

Cooper, Harry, Founder, President
Sharkhunters International, Inc.
  [9808]
PO Box 1539
Hernando, FL 34442
Ph: (352)637-2917
Toll Free: 866-258-2188
Fax: (352)637-6289

Cooper, Amb. Henry F., Chairman
High Frontier Organization [18478]
500 N Washington St.
Alexandria, VA 22314
Ph: (703)535-8774

Cooper, Jeff, Bd. Member
National Recycling Coalition [3453]
1220 L St. NW, Ste. 100-155
Washington, DC 20005
Ph: (202)618-2107

Cooper, Jennifer, Bd. Member
Amazing Little Hearts CHD Support
  Group [15212]
1314 W McDermott Dr., Ste. 106,
  No. 818
Allen, TX 75013

Cooper, Jill, Exec. Dir.
Israel Cancer Association USA
  [13996]
2751 S Dixie Hwy., Ste. 3A
West Palm Beach, FL 33405
Ph: (561)832-9277
Fax: (561)832-9337

Cooper, Joel, Founder
1970 Dart Swinger 340s Registry
  [21311]
PO Box 9
Wethersfield, CT 06129-0009
Ph: (860)257-8434

Cooper, Joel, Editor, Founder
DARTS Club [21367]
PO Box 9
Wethersfield, CT 06129-0009
Ph: (860)257-8434

Cooper, Kenneth H., MD, Founder
Cooper Institute [16697]
12330 Preston Rd.
Dallas, TX 75230
Ph: (972)341-3200
Toll Free: 800-635-7050
Fax: (972)341-3227

Cooper, Kier, President
Electrical Equipment Representa-
  tives Association [1018]
638 W 39th St.
Kansas City, MO 64111
Ph: (816)561-5323
Fax: (816)561-1991

Cooper, Michael, Rep.
National Plant Board [4950]
c/o Aurelio Posadas, Executive
  Secretary
10022 Calvine Rd.
Sacramento, CA 95829
Ph: (916)709-3484
Fax: (916)689-2385

Cooper, Patricia, V. Ch.
Satellite Industry Association [776]
1200 18th St. NW, Ste. 1001
Washington, DC 20036
Ph: (202)503-1560
Fax: (202)503-1590

Cooper, Paul, President
The Hydrographic Society of
  America [7251]
PO Box 841361
Houston, TX 77284
Ph: (774)773-8470

Cooper, Rachel, Founder
Optometrists Network [16438]
58 Mohonk Rd.
High Falls, NY 12440
Ph: (212)923-0496

Cooper Ramo, Roberta, President
American Law Institute [5414]
4025 Chestnut St.
Philadelphia, PA 19104
Ph: (215)243-1600
Fax: (215)243-1636

Cooper, Richard, Co-Pres.
National Association for Adults with
  Special Learning Needs [7718]
PO Box 716
Bryn Mawr, PA 19010

Cooper, Sandra, Director
National Oldtime Fiddlers' Associa-
  tion, Inc. [9975]
PO Box 447
Weiser, ID 83672
Ph: (208)414-0255
Fax: (208)414-0256

Cooper, Shelley B., President
Jack and Jill Foundation [11243]
1930 17th St. NW
Washington, DC 20009
Ph: (202)232-5290
Fax: (202)232-1747

Cooper, Thomas A., Exec. Dir.
International Anesthesia Research
  Society [13702]
44 Montgomery St., Ste. 1605
San Francisco, CA 94104-4703
Ph: (415)296-6900
Fax: (415)296-6901

Cooper, Toby, Chairman
Mountain Lion Foundation [4844]
PO Box 1896
Sacramento, CA 95812
Ph: (916)442-2666

Cooperman, Dr. Harry N., DDS,
  President
International Academy of Myodontics
  [14443]

777 Ferry Rd., P-6
Doylestown, PA 18901
Ph: (215)345-1149

Cooper-Nelson, Joli, VP
Jack and Jill of America, Inc. [11242]
1930 17th St. NW
Washington, DC 20009
Ph: (202)667-7010
Fax: (202)667-6133

Coopwood, Reginald, Chairman
American Hospital Association - Section for Metropolitan Hospitals
  [15307]
155 N Wacker Dr., Ste. 400
Chicago, IL 60606
Ph: (312)422-3000
     (312)422-3317

Cope, Larry W., Chairman
American Frozen Food Institute
  [1313]
2000 Corporate Ridge, Ste. 1000
McLean, VA 22102
Ph: (703)821-0770
Fax: (703)821-1350

Copeland, Christy, Treasurer
Association for International
  Agriculture and Rural Development
  [7473]
c/o Christy Copeland, Treasurer
213D Mumford Hall
Columbia, MO 65211

Copeland, Greg, Contact
Boykin Spaniel Club and Breeders
  Association of America [21847]
PO Box 42
Gilbert, SC 29054
Ph: (713)501-1661

Copeland, J. Joseph, Exec. Dir.
National AMBUCS [11620]
4285 Regency Dr.
Greensboro, NC 27410
Ph: (336)852-0052
Toll Free: 800-838-1845
Fax: (336)852-6830

Copeland, Nancy J., President
Dream Catchers USA [11593]
PO Box 701
Killen, AL 35645
Ph: (256)272-0286
Fax: (256)272-0286

Coplin, Nathan, Program Mgr.,
  Coord.
New Rules for Global Finance Coali-
  tion [18156]
2000 M St. NW, Ste. 720
Washington, DC 20036-3327
Ph: (202)277-9390
Fax: (202)280-1141

Copp, Mr. Doug, Exec. Dir.
American Rescue Team International
  [11948]
236 W Portal Ave.
San Francisco, CA 94127-1423
Ph: (415)533-2231

Coppinger, Jim, Exec. Sec.
International Association of Torch
  Clubs [2741]
2917 Duchess Dr.
Kalamazoo, MI 49008
Ph: (269)312-8026
Toll Free: 888-622-4101
Fax: (866)873-3690

Coppock, Daren, CEO, President
Agricultural Retailers Association
  [2943]
1156 15th St. NW, Ste. 500
Washington, DC 20005
Ph: (202)457-0825
Fax: (202)457-0864

Copps, Mike, Exec. Dir.
Vacation Rental Managers Associa-
  tion [2896]
2025 M St. NW, Ste. 800
Washington, DC 20036
Ph: (202)367-1179
     (202)321-5138
Fax: (202)367-2179

Cora, Cat, Founder, President
Chefs for Humanity [12081]
c/o Jaime Wolf, Esq.
The Woolworth Bldg.
233 Broadway, Ste. 2208
New York, NY 10279

Corbeil, Susan, President
Hugs Project [10748]
720 W Wilshire Blvd., Ste. 105
Oklahoma City, OK 73116-7737
Ph: (405)651-8359

Corben, Allen, Co-Ch.
National Organization for Men
  Against Sexism [18432]
3500 E 17th Ave.
Denver, CO 80206
Ph: (720)466-3882

Corbett, Kevin, President
University of Kansas Alumni As-
  sociation [19358]
1266 Oread Ave.
Lawrence, KS 66045
Ph: (785)864-4760
Toll Free: 800-584-2957
Fax: (785)864-5397

Corbett, Michael F., Chairman,
  Founder
International Association of
  Outsourcing Professionals [2472]
2600 S Rd., Ste. 44-240
Poughkeepsie, NY 12601
Ph: (845)452-0600
Fax: (845)452-6988

Corbin, Bill, Chairman
National Archery Association of the
  United States [22502]
4065 Sinton Rd., Ste. 110
Colorado Springs, CO 80907-5093
Ph: (719)866-4576
Fax: (719)632-4733

Corbin, John, Chairman
National Traffic Incident Management Coalition [5806]
c/o American Association of State
  Highway and Transportation Officials
444 N Capitol St. NW, Ste. 249
Washington, DC 20001
Ph: (608)266-0459

Corby, Christine, Exec. Dir.
Broadband Forum [1795]
48377 Fremont Blvd., Ste. 117
Fremont, CA 94538
Ph: (510)492-4020
Fax: (510)492-4001

Corcillo, Judy, Exec. Dir.
National Association for Alternative
  Certification [7853]
PO Box 5750
Washington, DC 20016
Ph: (202)277-3600
Fax: (202)403-3545

Corcillo, Libby, President
Group Underwriters Association of
  America [1858]
PO Box 735
Northbrook, IL 60065-0735
Ph: (205)427-2638
Fax: (205)981-2901

Corcoran, John J., CPA, Exec. Dir.
Construction Industry CPAs/
  Consultants Association [21]

15011 E Twilight View Dr.
Fountain Hills, AZ 85268
Ph: (480)836-0300
Fax: (480)836-0400

Corcoran, Kevin P., President, CEO
Eye Bank Association of America
[14618]
1015 18th St. NW, Ste. 1010
Washington, DC 20036
Ph: (202)775-4999
Fax: (202)429-6036

Corcoran, William, President, CEO
American Near East Refugee Aid
[12583]
1111 14th St. NW, Ste. 400
Washington, DC 20005-5604
Ph: (202)266-9700
Fax: (202)266-9701

Cordeiro, Carlos, Exec. VP
U.S. Soccer Federation [23196]
1801 S Prairie Ave.
Chicago, IL 60616
Ph: (312)808-1300
Fax: (312)808-1301

Cordeiro, Jon R., Director
Reform Sex Offender Laws [12934]
PO Box 400838
Cambridge, MA 02140
Toll Free: 888-997-RSOL

Cordell, Kirk A., Exec. Dir.
National Center for Preservation
Technology and Training [9415]
645 University Pky.
Natchitoches, LA 71457
Ph: (318)356-7444
Fax: (318)356-9119

Cordero, Barry, Chairman
Society of Hispanic Professional
Engineers [6592]
13181 Crossroads Pky. N, Ste. 450
City of Industry, CA 91746
Ph: (323)725-3970
Fax: (323)725-0316

Cordero, Tony, Chairman
Sons and Daughters In Touch
[21045]
PO Box 1596
Arlington, VA 22210
Toll Free: 800-984-9994

Cordor, Jeannette, Founder, CEO
Faces of HOPE [12396]
PO Box 35229
Richmond, VA 23235
Ph: (804)592-4751
Fax: (804)592-4752

Cordova, France A., Director
National Science Foundation [7142]
4201 Wilson Blvd.
Arlington, VA 22230
Ph: (703)292-5111
Toll Free: 800-877-8339

Cordts, David, Assoc. Dir.
National Honor Society [23786]
1904 Association Dr.
Reston, VA 20191-1537
Ph: (703)860-0200
Toll Free: 866-647-7253
Fax: (703)476-5432

Cordts, David, Assoc. Dir.
National Junior Honor Society
[23787]
1904 Association Dr.
Reston, VA 20191-1537
Ph: (703)860-0200
Fax: (703)476-5432

Corea, Ravi, CEO, President
Sri Lanka Wildlife Conservation
Society [4892]

127 Kingsland St.
Nutley, NJ 07110
Ph: (973)667-0576

Corell, Phil, Treasurer
Adirondack Forty-Sixers [23317]
PO Box 180
Cadyville, NY 12918-0180
Ph: (518)293-6401

Corelli, Dave, President
Vibration Institute [6834]
2625 Butterfield Rd., Ste. 128 N
Oak Brook, IL 60523-3415
Ph: (630)654-2254
Fax: (630)654-2271

Corenman, Jim, Director
SailMail Association [6445]
39270 Paseo Padre Pky., No. 850
Fremont, CA 94538
Ph: (619)980-6215
Toll Free: 877-282-1485

Corina, Ilene, Rep.
Persons United Limiting Substan-
dards and Errors in Health Care
[15056]
PO Box 353
Wantagh, NY 11793-0353
Ph: (516)579-4711
Toll Free: 800-96P-ULSE
Fax: (516)520-8105

Corkin, Michael
National Brain Tumor Society
[14598]
55 Chapel St., Ste. 200
Newton, MA 02458
Ph: (617)924-9997
Toll Free: 800-770-8287
Fax: (617)924-9998

Corless, James, Director
Transportation for America [19200]
1707 L St. NW, Ste. 250
Washington, DC 20036
Ph: (202)955-5543

Corley, Scott, Exec. Dir.
Compete America [11760]
1615 H St. NW
Washington, DC 20062

Corn, William, CCE, Chairman
Forius Business Credit Resources
[1237]
8441 Wayzata Blvd., Ste. 270
Golden Valley, MN 55426
Ph: (763)253-4300
Toll Free: 800-279-6226

Cornelius, Danny, President
National Depression Glass Associa-
tion [22138]
PO Box 8264
Wichita, KS 67208

Cornell, Mr. James, Consultant
International Science Writers As-
sociation [2689]
6666 N Mesa View Dr.
Tucson, AZ 85718
Ph: (520)529-6835

Cornell, Jim, Officer
The American Scientific Glassblow-
ers Society [3024]
PO Box 453
Machias, NY 14101-0453
Ph: (716)353-8062
Toll Free: 866-880-3216

Cornell, Laura, Founder
Green Yoga Association [10420]
2340 Powell St., No. 141
Emeryville, CA 94608
Ph: (415)655-1081

Cornell, Lois Dehls, President
American Health Lawyers Associa-
tion [5273]
1620 Eye St. NW, 6th Fl.
Washington, DC 20006-4010
Ph: (202)833-1100
Fax: (202)833-1105

Cornely, John, Advisor
The Trumpeter Swan Society [4896]
c/o Rivers Pk. District - French
Regional Pk.
12615 Rockford Rd.
Minneapolis, MN 55441-1248
Ph: (715)441-1994
Fax: (763)557-4943

Cornett, Sandy, President
Health Care Education Association
[7769]
2424 American Ln.
Madison, WI 53704-3102
Ph: (608)441-1054
Fax: (608)443-2474

Corns, Randee, President
North American Limousin Junior As-
sociation [3746]
N American Limousin Foundation
6 Inverness Ct. E, Ste. 260
Englewood, CO 80112-5595
Ph: (303)220-1693
Fax: (303)220-1884

Corpora, Corine R., President
Worldwide Employee Benefits
Network [1079]
11520 N Central Expy., Ste. 201
Dallas, TX 75243-6608
Toll Free: 888-795-6862
Fax: (214)382-3038

Corrado, Mary, President, CEO
American Society of Employers
[1084]
19575 Victor Pky., Ste. 100
Livonia, MI 48152
Ph: (248)353-4500
Fax: (734)402-0462

Corrales, Carmen A., Gen. Counsel
Academy of Political Science [7040]
475 Riverside Dr., Ste. 1274
New York, NY 10115-1274
Ph: (212)870-2500
Fax: (212)870-2202

Correa, Juan Luis, 1st VP
Sociedad Interamericana de Prensa
[17956]
Jules Dubois Bldg.
1801 SW 3rd Ave.
Miami, FL 33129
Ph: (305)634-2465
Fax: (305)635-2272

Correll, Krystle G., Exec. Dir.
Safety Pharmacology Society
[16685]
1821 Michael Faraday Dr., Ste. 300
Reston, VA 20190
Ph: (703)547-0874
Fax: (703)438-3113

Corridan, Betsy Sierk, Exec. Dir.
Kappa Alpha Theta [23956]
8740 Founders Rd.
Indianapolis, IN 46268
Toll Free: 800-526-1870
Fax: (317)876-1925

Corrigan, Kathy, Coord.
National Cancer Registrars Associa-
tion [16349]
1330 Braddock Pl., Ste. 520
Alexandria, VA 22314
Ph: (703)299-6640
Fax: (703)299-6620

Corrigan, Kimberly E., Exec. Dir.
Facing the Future [7809]
516 High St., MS 9102
Bellingham, WA 98225
Toll Free: 844-284-2151

Corry, Maureen P., MPH, Advisor
Childbirth Connection [16280]
1875 Connecticut Ave. NW, Ste. 650
Washington, DC 20009
Ph: (202)986-2600
Fax: (202)986-2539

Corson, Dr. Michael, President
Corson/Colson Family History Association [20849]
c/o Brian Corson
105 Diane Dr.
Streamwood, IL 60107

Corson, Tom, Exec. Dir.
Servants in Faith and Technology
[17812]
2944 County Road 113
Lineville, AL 36266
Ph: (256)396-2015
Fax: (256)396-2501

Cortie, Mr. Joseph, President
Safe and Vault Technicians Associa-
tion [3067]
3500 Easy St.
Dallas, TX 75247
Ph: (214)819-9733
Toll Free: 800-532-2562

Corwin, Cheryl, President
Friends of the Cassidys [24037]
1647 Crystal Downs St.
Banning, CA 92220

Corwin, Jennifer, Exec. Dir.
American Committee for Kiyosato
Educational Experiment Project
[12138]
825 Green Bay Rd., Ste. 122
Wilmette, IL 60091-2500
Ph: (847)853-2500
Fax: (847)853-8901

Coryer, Bill, Founder
Reiki Education and Research
Institute [17102]
725 Providence Rd., Ste. 200
Charlotte, NC 28207
Ph: (704)644-3644

Coscetta, Holly, Exec. Dir.
National Conference of CPA
Practitioners [49]
22 Jericho Tpke., Ste. 110
Mineola, NY 11501
Ph: (516)333-8282
Toll Free: 888-488-5400
Fax: (516)333-4099

Cossu, Catherine, Secretary,
Treasurer
Professional Liability Underwriting
Society [1918]
5353 Wayzata Blvd., Ste. 600
Minneapolis, MN 55416-1335
Ph: (952)746-2580
Toll Free: 800-845-0778
Fax: (952)746-2599

Cost, Diana, President
National Middle Level Science
Teachers Association [8553]
c/o Kathy Brooks, Membership
Chairperson
258 River St.
Guilford, CT 06437

Costa, Annie, Exec. Dir.
Association of Synthetic Grass
Installers [501]
17487 Penn Valley Dr., Ste. B103

Penn Valley, CA 95946
Ph: (530)432-5851
Toll Free: 888-378-4581
Fax: (530)432-1098

Costanza, Kira, Founder, Exec. Dir.
SunPower Afrique [7213]
188 Moorman Ln.
Bowling Green, KY 42101
Ph: (610)489-1105

Costanzo, Susan, President, Chmn.
of the Bd.
The American Bouvier des Flandres
Club [21798]
c/o Karen Florentine, Secretary
79 W Indian Springs Dr.
Glenmoore, PA 19343-3989
Ph: (610)458-7179

Costello, Christina, Commissioner
United States of America Deaf
Basketball [22576]
5313 Windwood Cir.
McFarland, WI 53558-9676

Costello, Jerry, Contact
Inland Rivers Ports and Terminals,
Inc. [2242]
1 Confluence Way
East Alton, IL 62024
Ph: (618)468-3010

Costello, Megan, VP
Global Cold Chain Alliance [1616]
1500 King St., Ste. 201
Alexandria, VA 22314-2730
Ph: (703)373-4300
Fax: (703)373-4301

Costello, Patti, Exec. Dir.
Association for the Healthcare
Environment [15312]
155 N Wacker Dr., Ste. 400
Chicago, IL 60606
Ph: (312)422-3860
Fax: (312)422-4578

Costello, Tim, Coord., Founder
North American Alliance for Fair
Employment [1099]
33 Harrison Ave., 5th Fl.
Boston, MA 02111
Ph: (617)482-6300
Fax: (617)482-7300

Costello, Walter A., Director
Underfashion Club, Inc. [113]
326 Field Rd.
Clinton Corners, NY 12514
Ph: (845)758-6405
Fax: (845)758-2546

Costello, Walter, Secretary
Intimate Apparel Square Club
[11859]
326 Field Rd.
Clinton Corners, NY 12514
Ph: (845)758-5752
Fax: (845)758-2546

Coster, Rob, President
American Platform Tennis Associa-
tion [23297]
109 Wesport Dr.
Pittsburgh, PA 15238
Toll Free: 888-744-9490

Cota, Tammy, Exec. Dir.
Internet Alliance [645]
1615 L St. NW, Ste. 1100
Washington, DC 20036-5624
Ph: (202)861-2407
   (802)279-3534

Cote, Alan, President
Inlandboatmen's Union of the Pacific
[2244]

1711 W Nickerson St., Ste. D
Seattle, WA 98119-1663
Ph: (206)284-6001
Fax: (206)284-5043

Cote, Joyce S., President
International Order of the King's
Daughters and Sons [19991]
34 Vincent Ave.
Chautauqua, NY 14722
Ph: (716)357-4951
Fax: (716)357-3762

Coto, Susanna, Director
The Media Institute [17950]
2300 Clarendon Blvd., Ste. 602
Arlington, VA 22201
Ph: (703)243-5700
Fax: (703)243-8808

Cotroneo, Bergitta E., CEO, Exec.
VP
Alliance for Academic Internal
Medicine [15424]
330 John Carlyle St., Ste. 610
Alexandria, VA 22314
Ph: (703)341-4540
Fax: (703)519-1893

Cotroneo, Rick, President
Accreditation Commission for
Homeopathic Education in North
America [15285]
105 State Route 151
East Greenbush, NY 12061
Ph: (518)477-1416

Cotter, Christine, Exec. Dir.
American Society of Psychoanalytic
Physicians [16842]
13528 Wisteria Dr.
Germantown, MD 20874
Ph: (301)540-3197
Fax: (301)540-3511.

Cotter, David, CEO
Textile Care Allied Trades Associa-
tion [2080]
271 Route 46 W, Ste. C205
Fairfield, NJ 07004
Ph: (973)244-1790
Fax: (973)244-4455

Cotter, Edmond J., Jr., Founder,
Exec. Dir.
Dead Theologians Society [19831]
PO Box 368
Black Earth, WI 53515-0368
Ph: (608)767-4063
Fax: (608)767-4064

Cotter, James, Project Mgr.
National Association of State
Workforce Agencies [5166]
444 N Capitol St. NW, Ste. 142
Washington, DC 20001
Ph: (202)434-8020
Fax: (202)434-8033

Cotterman, Col. JoAnn, OP,
President
Dominican Volunteers USA [20410]
1914 S Ashland Ave.
Chicago, IL 60608
Ph: (312)226-0919
Fax: (312)226-0919

Cottingham, Linda, Coord.
Donna Fargo International Fan Club
[24034]
PO Box 210877
Nashville, TN 37221

Cottington, Robert B.
Pipe Fabrication Institute [2611]
511 Avenue of the Americas, No.
601
New York, NY 10011-8436
Ph: (514)634-3434
Fax: (514)634-9736

Cotton, Dr. Ira, President
National Duck Stamp Collectors
Society [22349]
PO Box 43
Harleysville, PA 19438-0043

Cotton, Julie, Chairman
Sustainable Agriculture Education
Association [7482]
c/o Krista Jacobsen, Treasurer
College of Agriculture, Food and
Environment
University of Kentucky
Lexington, KY 40506

Cottongnim, Anissa, Secretary
American Trakehner Association
[4330]
663 Hopewell Dr.
Heath, OH 43056
Ph: (740)344-1111
Fax: (740)344-3225

Cottrill, Carol, MD, Bd. Member
Children of the Americas [10914]
PO Box 25046
Lexington, KY 40524
Ph: (859)422-4278

Cottrill, Carol, MD, Secretary
Eastern Apicultural Society of North
America [3636]
c/o Erin M. Forbes, Chairman
188 Capisic St.
Portland, ME 04102
Ph: (207)772-3380

Cotugno, Charlie, President
Stories of Autism [13778]
13110 NE 177th Pl., No. 237
Woodinville, WA 98072
Ph: (425)501-9725

Couch, Steve, VP of Admin.
International Plant Nutrition Institute
[4686]
3500 Parkway Ln., Ste. 550
Norcross, GA 30092-2844
Ph: (770)447-0335
Fax: (770)448-0439

Coueignoux, Catherine, President
Western Association for Art
Conservation [249]
c/o Denise Migdail, Secretary
200 Larkin St.
San Francisco, CA 94102
Ph: (415)581-3544

Coulibaly, Darius, MA, CEO,
Founder, President
Empowering the Poor [12152]
PO Box 42031
Fredericksburg, VA 22404
Ph: (540)735-6806

Coulter, John, President
Horticultural Research Institute
[4503]
525 9th St. NW, Ste. 800
Washington, DC 20004
Ph: (202)789-2900
Fax: (202)789-1893

Coulter, Karin, Exec. Dir., Founder,
President
Saving Little Hearts [14141]
PO Box 52285
Knoxville, TN 37950
Ph: (865)748-4605

Coulter, Robert T., Exec. Dir.,
President
Indian Law Resource Center [18708]
602 N Ewing St.
Helena, MT 59601-3603
Ph: (406)449-2006
Fax: (406)449-2031

Coulton, Claudia, Director
Center on Urban Poverty and Com-
munity Development [12533]
Jack, Joseph and Morton Mandel
School of Applied Social Sciences
Case Western Reserve University
10900 Euclid Ave.
Cleveland, OH 44106-7167
Ph: (216)368-6946
Fax: (216)368-8592

Coultress, Susie, President
National Association of State Directors of Migrant Education [12342]
1001 Connecticut Ave. NW, Ste. 915
Washington, DC 20036

Counsil, Dick, Treasurer
Opel Motorsports Club [21469]
c/o Dick Counsil, Treasurer
3824 Franklin St.
La Crescenta, CA 91214

Coupe, Anita W., Director
Doris Day Animal League [10611]
2100 L St. NW
Washington, DC 20037
Ph: (202)452-1100

Couraud, Gretchen, Exec. Dir., CEO
National Association of College and
University Food Services [1393]
2525 Jolly Rd., Ste. 280
Okemos, MI 48864-3681
Ph: (517)332-2494
Fax: (517)332-8144

Couric, Katie, Founder
Stand Up to Cancer [14066]
1801 W Olympic Blvd.
Pasadena, CA 91199-1224
Toll Free: 888-204-5809

Coursin, Kevin, Chmn. of the Bd.
Porcelain Enamel Institute [571]
PO Box 920220
Norcross, GA 30010
Ph: (770)676-9366
Fax: (770)409-7280

Courson, John A., President, CEO
Home Builders Institute [535]
1201 15th St. NW, Ste. 600
Washington, DC 20005
Ph: (202)371-0600
Toll Free: 800-795-7955

Courtade, Ginevra, Chairman
American Council on Rural Special
Education [8576]
West Virginia University
509 Allen Hall
Morgantown, WV 26506-6122
Ph: (304)293-3450

Courter, Maj Gen Amy S., President
Women in Defense, a National
Security Organization [18090]
2111 Wilson Blvd., Ste. 400
Arlington, VA 22201-3061
Ph: (703)522-1820
   (703)247-2551
Fax: (703)522-1885

Courtney, Dennis, President
Capital PC User Group [6296]
19209 Mt. Airey Rd.
Brookeville, MD 20833
Ph: (301)560-6442
Fax: (301)760-3303

Courtney, Fara, Exec. Dir.
United States Offshore Wind Col-
laborative [7390]
1 Broadway, 14th Fl.
Cambridge, MA 02142
Ph: (617)401-3145

Courtney, Jeremy, President,
Founder
Preemptive Love Coalition [14139]
1300 Darbyton Dr.

Hewitt, TX 76643
Ph: (254)400-2033

Courtney, John E., PhD, Exec. Ofc.
American Society for Nutrition
[16206]
9211 Corporate Blvd., Ste. 300
Rockville, MD 20850
Ph: (301)634-7050
(240)428-3650
Fax: (301)634-7894

Courtney, William, Directo
American Academy of D
[5228]
1200 18th St. NW, S
Washington, DC 2
Ph: (202)331-37
Fax: (202)833-

Courtney, W
U.S.-Kazz
tion [2
1625]
Was
Ph

78

Exec. Dir
[17471]

ent
4]

01
88

, Philippe, Jr., Founder,
dent
Echo International [3849]
01 L St. NW, Ste. 800
Washington, DC 20037
Ph: (202)350-3190
Fax: (202)857-3977

Covall, Mark J., CEO, President
National Association of Psychiatric
Health Systems [16834]
900 17th St. NW, Ste. 420
Washington, DC 20006-2507
Ph: (202)393-6700
Fax: (202)783-6041

Covarrubias, Irene, Treasurer
National Latina Business Women
Association [656]
1100 S Flower St., Ste. 3300
Los Angeles, CA 90015
Toll Free: 888-696-5292

Cove, Tom, CEO, President
Soccer Industry Council of America
[3146]
c/o Sports & Fitness Industry Association
8505 Fenton St., Ste. 211
Silver Spring, MD 20910
Ph: (301)495-6321
Fax: (301)495-6322

Cove, Tom, CEO, President
Sports and Fitness Industry Associa-
tion [3147]
8505 Fenton St., Ste. 211
Silver Spring, MD 20910
Ph: (301)495-6321
Fax: (301)495-6322

ey, Matthew, Director
izdat [9216]
Jay St., Ste. 308
oklyn, NY 11201-8322
: (718)254-0022
x: (413)513-1157

ovington, Chris, President
lpha Sigma Tau [23947]
3334 Founders Rd.
Indianapolis, IN 46268
Ph: (317)613-7575
Toll Free: 877-505-1899
Fax: (317)613-7111

Covington, Julie, President
American Hemerocallis Society
[22073]
c/o Julie Covington, President
4909 Labradore Dr.
Roanoke, VA 24012
Ph: (540)977-1704

Covino, Susan, Officer
Association for Demand Response
and Smart Grid [6415]
1220 19th St. NW
Washington, DC 20036
Ph: (202)857-0898

Cowan, Daniel, Mem.
Builders Exchange Network [858]
c/o Kristin Loney, Executive Director
1 Regency Dr.
Bloomfield, CT 06002
Ph: (860)243-3977
Fax: (860)286-0787

Cowan, Houston, CEO, Founder
Challenge Aspen at Snowmass
[22779]
PO Box 6639
Snowmass Village, CO 81615
Ph: (970)923-0578
Fax: (970)923-7338

Cowan, Penney, Contact
Alliance for Balanced Pain Manage-
ment [16544]
Washington, DC
Ph: (202)499-4114

Cowan, Penney, CEO, Founder
American Chronic Pain Association
[16550]
PO Box 850
Rocklin, CA 95677
Toll Free: 800-533-3231
Fax: (916)652-8190

Cowan, Rich, Founder, Project Mgr.
Organizers' Collaborative [17997]
33 Harrison Ave., Fl. 5
Boston, MA 02111
Ph: (617)720-6190
Fax: (617)848-9513

Cowan, Wendy, Exec. Dir., Secretary
American Association of Engineering
Societies [6527]
1801 Alexander Bell Dr.
Reston, VA 20191
Ph: (202)296-2237
Toll Free: 888-400-2237
Fax: (202)296-1151

Cowart, Kim, President
North American Trail Ride Confer-
ence [23330]
PO Box 224
Sedalia, CO 80135
Ph: (303)688-1677
Fax: (303)688-3022

Cowdery, John, President
Association of AE Business Leaders
[2149]
PO Box 330152

San Francisco, CA 94133
Ph: (415)659-9973
(415)350-9213

Cowell, Carole, Leader
Scleroderma Support Group [17183]
Roger Williams Meeical Ctr., 1st Fl.,
825 Chalkstone Ave.
825 Chalkstone Ave.
Providence, RI 02908
Ph: (401)781-5013

Cowell, Karen, Co-Ch.
Association of Pediatric Therapists
[17437]
PO Box 194191
San Francisco, CA 94119-4191

Cowen, Joshua Lionel, Founder
Lionel Railroader Club [22187]
6301 Performance Dr.
Concord, NC 28027-3426
Ph: (586)949-4100
Toll Free: 800-454-6635

Cowles, Nancy A., President
International Consumer Product
Health and Safety Organization
[2997]
c/o Nancy A. Cowles, President
Kids in Danger
116 W Illinois St., Ste. 4E
Chicago, IL 60654
Ph: (312)595-0649

Cowles, Nancy, Exec. Dir.
Kids In Danger [11058]
116 W Illinois St., Ste. 4E
Chicago, IL 60654
Ph: (312)595-0649
Fax: (312)595-0939

Cowles, Page Knudsen, Chmn. of
the Bd.
Trust for Public Land [3960]
101 Montgomery St., Ste. 900
San Francisco, CA 94104
Ph: (415)495-4014
Toll Free: 800-714-LAND

Cowley, Terrie, Founder, President
TMJ Association [16565]
PO Box 26770
Milwaukee, WI 53226-0770
Ph: (262)432-0350

Cox, Chapman B., Chairman
Alliance Defending Freedom [18080]
15100 N 90th St.
Scottsdale, AZ 85260-2769
Ph: (480)444-0020
Toll Free: 800-835-5233
Fax: (480)444-0025

Cox, Chris, President
Architectural Precast Association
[782]
325 John Knox Rd., Ste. L103
Tallahassee, FL 32303
Ph: (850)205-5637
Fax: (850)222-3019

Cox, Cynthia, President
American Woman's Society of Certi-
fied Public Accountants [11]
701 N Post Oak Rd., Ste. 635
Houston, TX 77024
Ph: (937)222-1872
(713)893-5685
Toll Free: 800-297-2721
Fax: (937)222-5794

Cox, Darren, President
American Honey Producers Associa-
tion [3633]
c/o Cassie Cox, Executive Secretary
PO Box 435
Mendon, UT 84325
Ph: (281)900-9740

Cox, David A., Treasurer
Society for Cardiovascular Angiogra-
phy and Interventions [14142]
1100 17th St. NW, Ste. 330
Washington, DC 20036
Ph: (202)741-9854
Toll Free: 800-992-7224
Fax: (800)863-5202

Cox, Debra L., President
American Academy of Ambulatory
Care Nursing [16083]
E Holly Ave.
Pitman, NJ 08071-0056
Toll Free: 800-262-6877

Cox, Duncan, Director
Accredited Certifiers Association,
Inc. [4516]
PO Box 472
Port Crane, NY 13833
Ph: (607)648-3259
Fax: (607)648-3259

Cox, James L., MD, President, CEO
World Heart Foundation [17420]
1828 L St. NW, Ste. 1100
Washington, DC 20036
Ph: (502)222-9003
Fax: (502)222-9555

Cox, Jean, President
International Catholic Deaf Association United States Section [19845]
c/o T.K. Hill, Treasurer
5608 Lavender Ct.
Rolling Meadows, IL 60008

Cox, Jennifer, Founder
National Network of Embroidery
Professionals [2440]
4693 Kent Rd.
Kent, OH 44240
Toll Free: 800-866-7396

Cox, Jim, CEO
American Association of Cosmetol-
ogy Schools [7681]
9927 E Bell Rd., Ste. 110
Scottsdale, AZ 85260
Ph: (480)281-0431
Toll Free: 800-831-1086
Fax: (480)905-0993

Cox, Jim, Secretary
Burton Island Association [21051]
c/o Ralf Mauthe, Treasurer
13190 Cedarwood Dr.
Saint George, KS 66535
Ph: (785)494-2502

Cox, John H., Exec. Dir.
Flavor and Extract Manufacturers
Association of the United States
[1325]
1101 17th St. NW, Ste. 700
Washington, DC 20036
Ph: (202)293-5800
Fax: (202)463-8998

Cox, Kathleen, Controller
American Institute of Graphic Arts
[1526]
223 Broadway, 17th Fl.
New York, NY 10279
Ph: (212)807-1990

Cox, Kathleen, Exec. Dir., COO
National Cathedral Association
[20068]
3101 Wisconsin Ave. NW
Washington, DC 20016-5015
Ph: (202)537-6200
Fax: (202)364-6600

Cox, Laura, Contact
Echo Dogs White Shepherd Rescue
[10613]

PO Box 63
Sherman, IL 62684

Cox, Mike, President
Clowns of America International
[21601]
PO Box 122
Eustis, FL 32727-0122
Ph: (352)357-1676
Toll Free: 877-816-6941

Cox, Shirley, Exec. Dir.
Chemotherapy Foundation [16340]
183 Madison Ave., Ste. 403
New York, NY 10016
Ph: (212)213-9292
Fax: (212)213-3831

Cox, Thomas D., President
Adult Higher Education Alliance
[7452]
c/o Fred Prasuhn, Treasurer
350 Will Wynne Rd.
Rayle, GA 30660-2515

Cox, Warren L., Membership Chp.
CID Agents Association [21048]
c/o Warren L. Cox, Membership
Chairperson
165 Birch Creek Cir.
McDonough, GA 30253-7253
Ph: (770)363-1188

Coxe, Sally, President, Founder
Bonobo Conservation Initiative
[4798]
2701 Connecticut Ave. NW, No. 702
Washington, DC 20008
Ph: (202)332-1014

Coy, Bob, Exec. Dir.
United States Classic Racing As-
sociation [22234]
441 Athol Rd.
Winchester, NH 03470
Ph: (413)341-6780

Coy, Jacquelyn, Membership Chp.
106th Infantry Division Association
[21179]
PO Box 140535
PO Box 140535
Dallas, TX 75214
Ph: (214)823-3004

Coy, Patricia, MS, Exec. Dir.
Step Out USA [12242]
8926 Greenwood Ave.
Niles, IL 60714
Ph: (847)289-4480

Coyhis, Don, Founder, President
White Bison [10050]
5585 Erindale Dr., Ste. 203
Colorado Springs, CO 80918
Ph: (877)871-1495
Toll Free: 877-871-1495
Fax: (719)548-9407

Coyle, Patrick X., Exec. Dir.
Young Americans for Freedom
[18029]
c/o Patrick X. Coyle, Executive
Director
11480 Commerce Park Dr.
Reston, VA 20191
Toll Free: 800-USA-1776
Fax: (703)318-9122

Coyle, Patrick X., VP
Young America's Foundation [18030]
11480 Commerce Park Dr., Ste. 600
Reston, VA 20191-1556
Ph: (703)318-9608
Toll Free: 800-USA-1776
Fax: (703)318-9122

Coyle, Rebecca, Exec. Dir.
American Immunization Registry Association [15371]

1155 F St. NW, Ste. 1050
Washington, DC 20004
Ph: (202)552-0208

Coyne, Brian, President
Clinical Exercise Physiology Association [16767]
401 W Michigan St.
Indianapolis, IN 46202

Coyne, Jac, Director
Men's Collegiate Lacrosse Associa-
tion [22974]
PO Box 93531
Atlanta, GA 30377

Coyne, Kathryn, CEO
Animal Medical Center [10579]
510 E 62nd St.
New York, NY 10065
Ph: (212)838-8100
    (212)838-7053
Fax: (212)752-2592

Cozzens, Alisa, Exec. Dir.
Serve a Village [11431]
11732 Thomas Ave.
Great Falls, VA 22066
Ph: (571)213-1978

Cozzens, Bishop Andrew, Chmn. of
the Bd.
National Evangelization Teams
[19885]
110 Crusader Ave. W
Saint Paul, MN 55118
Ph: (651)450-6833
Fax: (651)450-9984

Cozzetto, Charlotte, President
Animal Rights Coalition [10580]
317 W 48th St.
Minneapolis, MN 55419
Ph: (612)822-6161

Crabtree, Barbara, Dir. of Operations
Metropolitan Community Churches
[20185]
PO Box 50488
Sarasota, FL 34232-0304
Ph: (310)360-8640
Fax: (310)388-1252

Craft, James, President
Nigerian Dairy Goat Association
[4280]
1927 E 500 N
Ossian, IN 46777
Ph: (260)307-1984

Craft, Ron, President
National Cotton Ginners' Association
[938]
7193 Goodlett Farms Pky.
Cordova, TN 38016-4909
Ph: (901)274-9030
Fax: (901)725-0510

Crago, Mark, Director
Columbia Sheep Breeders Associa-
tion of America [4668]
PO Box 722
Lakefield, MN 56150
Ph: (507)360-2160
Fax: (507)662-6294

Craig, Bob, President
Genealogical Society of Hispanic
America [20970]
PO Box 3040
Pueblo, CO 81005-3040

Craig, Carol A., Exec. Asst.
Congregation of Sisters of Saint
Agnes [19828]
320 County Road K
Fond du Lac, WI 54937-8158
Ph: (920)907-2300

Craig, Catherine L., PhD, Preside
Founder
Conservation through Poverty Al-
leviation International [3839]
712 S Palouse St.
Walla Walla, WA 99362

Craig, Charles R., Chairman
American Management Association
[2146]
1601 Broadway
New York, NY 10019
Ph: (212)586-8100
Toll Free: 877-566-9441
Fax: (212)903-8168

Craig, Fiona, President
International Clinical Cytometry
Society [16584]
2111 Chestnut Ave., Ste. 145
Glenview, IL 60025
Ph: (847)550-3080
Fax: (312)896-5614

Craig, Judy, Founder
Eliminate Poverty Now [10720]
PO Box 67
Mendham, NJ 07945

Craig, Mathias, Exec. Dir.
blueEnergy [6463]
1595 Walnut St.
Eugene, OR 97403
Ph: (415)509-0155

Craig, Ryan, President
American Corriedale Association
[4650]
c/o Marcia Craig, Executive
Secretary
PO Box 391
Clay City, IL 62824
Ph: (618)676-1046
Fax: (618)676-1133

Crain, Stephen A., Officer
John Reich Collectors Society
[22284]
c/o Stephen A. Crain, Secretary
PO Box 1680
Windham, ME 04062

Cramb, Heidi, Exec. Dir.
American Culinary Federation [697]
180 Center Place Way
Saint Augustine, FL 32095
Toll Free: 800-624-9458
Fax: (904)824-4468

Cramer, Lorri, Director
New York Turtle and Tortoise Society
[4851]
1214 W Boston Post Rd.
Mamaroneck, NY 10543
Toll Free: 800-847-7332

Cramer, Dr. Steven R., President
Missionary Church Historical Society
[20027]
Bethel College
1001 Bethel Cir.
Mishawaka, IN 46545
Ph: (574)807-7000
Toll Free: 800-422-4101

Crampton, Janice, Exec. Dir.
Association of Independent School
Admission Professionals [7445]
PO Box 709
Madison, CT 06443
Ph: (203)421-7051

Crandall, Dr. David, President
NETWORK [7794]
23 NE Morgan St.
Portland, OR 97211
Toll Free: 800-877-5400
Fax: (503)336-1014

Crandall, Derrick A., President, CEO
American Recreation Coalition
[12574]
1200 G St. NW, Ste. 650
Washington, DC 20005-3832
(202)682-9530
(202)682-9529

...thy
... ...
P...ciation of Tissue
Fa..., Ste. 320

Cran...
Ameri...
...tion [...
41 Buen...
Hanover, ...

Crane, Dale...
Antique Sma...
Club [22010...
5655 US Highw...
Bedford, IN 474...

Crane, Janet, Pres...
Organization of Wo...
and Design Profes...
PO Box 10078
Berkeley, CA 94709-50...

Crane, Stephen C., PhD,...
American Thoracic Society...
25 Broadway
New York, NY 10004
Ph: (212)315-8600
Fax: (212)315-6498

Crane, Teresa Yancey, President...
Founder
Issue Management Council [2179]
207 Loudoun St. SE
Leesburg, VA 20175-3115
Ph: (703)777-8450

Crane, Thomas R., Dep. Dir.
Great Lakes Commission [5652]
2805 S Industrial Hwy., Ste. 100
Ann Arbor, MI 48104-6791
Ph: (734)665-9135
Fax: (734)665-9150

Cranley, Diane, President, Chmn. of
the Bd.
TAALK: Talk About Abuse to Liberate
Kids [11279]
30251 Golden Lantern, E283
Laguna Niguel, CA 92677-5993
Ph: (949)495-4553
Toll Free: 888-808-6558

Cranmer, John D., Director
American Nystagmus Network
[17685]
303-D Beltline Pl., No. 321
Decatur, AL 35603

Cranston, Kim, Chmn. of the Bd.
Global Security Institute [18747]
866 United Nations Plz., Ste. 4050
New York, NY 10017
Ph: (646)289-5170
Fax: (646)289-5171

Cranston, Laura, Exec. Dir.
Pharmacy Quality Alliance [16682]
6213 Old Keene Mill Ct.
Springfield, VA 22152
Ph: (703)690-1987
Fax: (703)842-8150

Craparo, John S., Contact
International Aeronauts League
[21530]
PO Box 200931

Austin, TX 78720-0931
Ph: (512)740-2506

Craven, John, CEO, Founder, Ed.
Dir.
Beverage Network [423]
44 Pleasant St., Ste. 110
Watertown, MA 02472
Ph: (617)231-8800

Cravens, Stephen, Founder, Exec.
Dir.
Young Professionals in Energy
[6521]
1601 Elm St., Ste. 3130
Dallas, TX 75201
Ph: (214)550-8991

Crawford, Alvin H., MD, President
J. Robert Gladden Orthopaedic
Society [16475]
9400 W Higgins Rd., Ste. 500
Rosemont, IL 60018-4238
Ph: (847)698-1633
Fax: (847)823-4921

Crawford, DaChea, CEO
Power of Pink! Foundation [14047]
6368 Coventry Way, No. 347
Clinton, MD 20735
Ph: (240)389-4767

Crawford, David, President
American Rainwater Catchment
Systems Association [7362]
7650 S McClintock Dr., Ste. 103, No.
134
Tempe, AZ 85284-1673
Ph: (512)617-6528

Crawford, David, Treasurer
International Rainwater Catchment
Systems Association [7368]
875 Komohana St.
Hilo, HI 96720

Crawford, Diane, CEO, President
National Phlebotomy Association
[15242]
1901 Brightseat Rd.
Landover, MD 20785
Ph: (301)386-4200
Fax: (301)386-4203

Crawford, Gregory L., Exec. Dir.
Cool Metal Roofing Coalition [517]
680 Andersen Dr.
Pittsburgh, PA 15220
Ph: (412)922-2772
Fax: (412)922-3213

Crawford, Joan, President
Alliance of Jamaican and American
Humanitarians [11313]
8549 Wilshire Blvd., Ste. 1004
Beverly Hills, CA 90211
Ph: (424)249-8135
    (909)851-9359

Crawford, Rachel, Prog. Dir.
The Amarun Organization [3795]
9505 Seany Dr. NE
Leland, NC 28451
Ph: (910)508-3630

Crawford, Scott, President
American Rambouillet Sheep Breed-
ers' Association [4660]
c/o Robbie G. Eckhoff, Executive
Secretary
PO Box 214
Hawley, TX 79525
Ph: (409)256-3687

Crawford, Todd, Chairperson
National Reined Cow Horse Association [22155]
1017 N Highway 377

Pilot Point, TX 76258
Ph: (940)488-1500
Fax: (940)488-1499

Crawford, Tom, President
Native American Water Association
[3461]
1662 Highway 395, Ste. 212
Minden, NV 89423
Ph: (775)782-6636
Toll Free: 866-632-9992
Fax: (775)782-1021

Crawford, Tom, CEO
U.S.A. Ultimate [22809]
5825 Delmonico Dr., Ste. 350
Colorado Springs, CO 80919
Ph: (719)219-8322
Toll Free: 800-872-4384

Crawford, Walter, Exec. Dir.
World Bird Sanctuary [4919]
125 Bald Eagle Ridge Rd.
Valley Park, MO 63088
Ph: (636)225-4390
Fax: (636)861-3240

Crawford-Spinelli, John R., President
International Council of Fine Arts
Deans [7512]
PO Box 331
West Palm Beach, FL 33402
Ph: (561)514-0810

Craycraft, Michael, RPh, President
Testicular Cancer Society [14074]
792 Woodlyn Dr. S
Cincinnati, OH 45230
Ph: (513)696-9827

Crea, Mark, Exec. Dir., CEO
Feed My Starving Children [12085]
401 93rd Ave. NW
Coon Rapids, MN 55433
Ph: (763)504-2919

Creagan, Dan, President
Pyrotechnics Guild International
[2822]
c/o Dan Creagan, President
1501 Cobblestone Lane Cir.
Bellevue, NE 68005
Ph: (402)212-9200
Toll Free: 877-223-3552

Creamer, Jan, President, Founder,
CEO
Animal Defenders International
U.S.A. [10573]
6100 Wilshire Blvd., No. 1150
Los Angeles, CA 90048
Ph: (323)935-2234

Creamer, Kellie, Officer
Clear Path International [18122]
1700 N Northlake Way, Ste. 201
Seattle, WA 98103
Ph: (754)444-8885

Creech, Dennis, Exec. Dir.
Southface Energy Institute [6513]
241 Pine St. NE
Atlanta, GA 30308
Ph: (404)872-3549
Fax: (404)872-5009

Creedon, James, President
National Security and Law Society
[5757]
c/o American University Washington
College of Law
4801 Massachusetts Ave. NW
Washington, DC 20016
Ph: (202)274-4000

Creek, John R., Jr., President
6th Bomb Group Association [20674]
29277 Garrard Ave.

Frontenac, MN 55026

Cregier, Jan, President
Interior Design Society [1946]
164 S Main St., Ste. 404
High Point, NC 27260
Ph: (336)884-4437
Fax: (336)885-3291

Creighton, Colleen, Exec. Dir.
Alliance for Consumer Education
[4121]
1667 K St. NW, Ste. 300
Washington, DC 20006
Ph: (202)862-3902
Fax: (202)872-8114

Cremer, Dr. Miriam, Founder
Basic Health International [17752]
25 Broadway, 5th Fl.
New York, NY 10004
Ph: (646)593-8694

Crenshaw, Diallo, Treasurer
Association of Intellectual Property
Firms [5674]
2125 Center Ave., Ste. 406
Fort Lee, NJ 07024-5874
Ph: (201)403-0927
Fax: (201)461-6635

Crerar, Ken A., President
Council of Insurance Agents and
Brokers [1852]
701 Pennsylvania Ave. NW, Ste. 750
Washington, DC 20004-2608
Ph: (202)783-4400
Fax: (202)783-4410

Crespo, Orlando Perez, President
American Association of Spanish
Timbrado Breeders [21532]
c/o Orlando Perez, President
4100 N Tampania Ave.
Tampa, FL 33607
Ph: (813)781-4153

Cretin, Shan, Gen. Sec.
American Friends Service Commit-
tee [13027]
1501 Cherry St.
Philadelphia, PA 19102
Ph: (215)241-7000
    (215)241-7104

Crews, Kay Allison, President
American Institute of Parliamentar-
ians [5670]
618 Church St., Ste. 220
Nashville, TN 37219
Ph: (615)522-5269
Toll Free: 888-664-0428
Fax: (615)248-9253

Cridennda, Diane, Secretary
American Board of Oriental
Reproductive Medicine [17124]
910 Hampshire Rd., Ste. A
Westlake Village, CA 91361
Ph: (805)497-1335

Cridland, Janelle, Exec. Dir.
Real Diaper Industry Association
[991]
1017 L St., Ste. 338
Sacramento, CA 95814
Ph: (678)224-1801

Cripps, Kathy, President
PR Council [2756]
32 E 31st St., 9th Fl.
New York, NY 10016
Ph: (646)588-0139
Fax: (646)651-4770

Crisci, Alice, Founder
Fertile Action [14755]
PO Box 3526

Manhattan Beach, CA 90266
Toll Free: 877-276-5951

Crisco, J. Keith, Chmn. of the Bd.
GLOBIO [7890]
5544 N Burrage Ave.
Portland, OR 97217
Ph: (503)367-2874

Crispen, Cheryl, Exec. VP
Securities Industry and Financial
Markets Association [3050]
120 Broadway, 35th Fl.
New York, NY 10271
Ph: (212)313-1200
Fax: (212)313-1301

Criss, Amy, President
Society for Mathematical Psychology
[7073]
c/o Richard Golden, Secretary-
Treasurer
University of Texas at Dallas
School of Behavioral and Brain Sci-
ences, GR41
800 W Campbell Rd.
Richardson, TX 75080

Crittenden, Patricia M., PhD,
President
International Association for the
Study of Attachment [15773]
c/o Patricia M. Crittenden, PhD,
Honorary and Founding President
Family Relations Institute
9481 SW 147th St.
Miami, FL 33176
Ph: (305)256-9110
Fax: (305)251-0806

Croce, Nicholas, Jr., Exec. Dir.
American Psychiatric Nurses As-
sociation [16111]
3141 Fairview Park Dr., Ste. 625
Falls Church, VA 22042
Ph: (571)533-1919
Toll Free: 855-863-2762
Fax: (855)883-2762

Crocker, Collamore, President
Shields National Class Association
[22668]
PO Box 152
Wareham, MA 02571-0152
Ph: (508)295-3550
Fax: (508)295-3551

Crocker, Amb. Ryan, Co-Ch.
Alliance in Support of the Afghan
People [10466]
1225 Eye St. NW
Washington, DC 20005

Crockett, Kim, Exec. VP, COO, Gen.
Counsel
Center of the American Experiment
[18021]
8441 Wayzata Blvd., Ste. 350
Golden Valley, MN 55426
Ph: (612)338-3605
Fax: (612)338-3621

Crockett, Lisa, President
Society for Research on
Adolescence [13479]
2950 S State St., Ste. 401
Ann Arbor, MI 48104
Ph: (734)926-0700
Fax: (734)926-0701

Crockett, Michelle, President
Federally Employed Women [18206]
455 Massachusetts Ave. NW
Washington, DC 20001
Ph: (202)898-0994

Croen, Caroline C., VP, CFO,
Treasurer
Educational Broadcasting Corp.
[9143]

c/o THIRTEEN
825 8th Ave.
New York, NY 10019
Ph: (212)560-1313
Fax: (212)560-1314

Croft, Earl J., III, President
International Bridge, Tunnel and
Turnpike Association [5813]
1146 19th St. NW, Ste. 600
Washington, DC 20036
Ph: (202)659-4620
Fax: (202)659-0500

Crolla, Susan, Exec. Dir.
Power-Motion Technology
Representatives Association [1759]
5353 Wayzata Blvd., Ste. 350
Minneapolis, MN 55416-1300
Toll Free: 888-817-7872
Fax: (949)252-8096

Cromartie, William J., President
American Entomological Society
[6606]
1900 Benjamin Franklin Pky.
Philadelphia 19103-1101
Ph: (215)561-3978
Fax: (215)299-1028

Crombé, Gilberto, Chairman
Entrepreneurs' Organization [628]
500 Montgomery St., Ste. 700
Alexandria, VA 22314
Ph: (703)519-6700
Fax: (703)519-1864

Cromer, Andy, President
North American Truffle Growers' Association [4485]
c/o Koru Farm/CMTGMT Farm
1541 Little Russell Creek Rd.
Stuart, VA 24171-2553

Crompton, Joanne, Founder
We Improve Tomorrow [11184]
1054 Lehman St.
Houston, TX 77018

Cron, Amber, Coord.
Ambassadors for Children [11212]
500 W Battlefield St., Ste. B
Springfield, MO 65807-4294
Ph: (417)708-0565
Fax: (417)708-0566

Cronan, Jessie, Exec. Dir.
Gardens for Health International
[13538]
9 Waterhouse St.
Cambridge, MA 02138
Ph: (845)204-5263

Croneberger, Lynn M., CEO
SOS Children's Villages-USA
[11153]
1620 I St. NW, Ste. 900
Washington, DC 20006
Toll Free: 888-767-4543

Cronig, Jeremy, President
North American Federation of
Temple Youth [19521]
c/o Union for Reform Judaism
633 3rd Ave., 7th Fl.
New York, NY 10017
Ph: (212)650-4070
Fax: (212)650-4064

Cronin, Brian, CEO
Professional Association of Diving
Instructors [23345]
30151 Tomas St.
Rancho Santa Margarita, CA 92688-
2125
Ph: (949)858-7234
Toll Free: 800-729-7234
Fax: (949)267-1267

Cronin, Carolyn, Exec. Dir.
Research Down Syndrome Founda-
tion [14628]
225 Cedar Hill St.
Marlborough, MA 01752
Ph: (508)630-2177
Fax: (508)630-2101

Cronin, Jim, President
Council of Protocol Executives
[2324]
101 W 12th St., Ste. PH-H
New York, NY 10011
Ph: (212)633-6934

Crook, Larry, MD, President
Thai Burma Border Health Initiative
[17024]
1127 Boggio Dr.
Gallup, NM 87301

Cropp, Michael, M.D., Officer
Alliance of Community Health Plans
[15093]
1825 Eye St. NW, Ste. 401
Washington, DC 20006
Ph: (202)785-2247
Fax: (202)785-4060

Crosbie, Dr. Kim, Exec. Dir.
International Association of
Antarctica Tour Operators [3379]
c/o Janeen Haase, Administrative
Officer
320 Thames St., Ste. 264
Newport, RI 02840
Ph: (401)841-9700
Fax: (401)841-9704

Crosby, Brett, President
Y's Men International [13422]
101 YMCA Dr.
Kannapolis, NC 28081

Crosby, Kathryn, President
International Crosby Circle [24046]
c/o Wig Wiggins
5608 N 34th St.
Arlington, VA 22207
Ph: (703)241-5608

Crosby, Mark E., Secretary,
Treasurer
Land Mobile Communications
Council [3231]
c/o Mark Crosby, Secretary-
Treasurer
2121 Cooperative Way, Ste. 225
Herndon, VA 20171
Ph: (703)528-5115

Croskey, Raymond Bazemore,
President
American College of Counselors
[11811]
273 Glossip Ave.
Highlandville, MO 65669-8133
Ph: (417)885-7632
Fax: (417)443-3002

Croson, Matt, President
Adhesive and Sealant Council [60]
7101 Wisconsin Ave., Ste. 990
Bethesda, MD 20814
Ph: (301)986-9700
Fax: (301)986-9795

Croson, Matthew, President
American Gear Manufacturers As-
sociation [1706]
1001 N Fairfax St., Ste. 500
Alexandria, VA 22314-1587
Ph: (703)684-0211
Fax: (703)684-0242

Cross, James, Exec. Dir.
National Association for Public
Safety Infection Control Officers
[15410]

9250 Mosby St., Ste. 100
Manassas, VA 20110
Ph: (703)365-8388

Cross, JaNeen, DSW, President
National Association of Perinatal
Social Workers [17228]
3319 N Youngs Blvd.
Oklahoma City, OK 73112-7835

Cross, Jim, Memb. Ofc.
Association of Certified Marine
Surveyors [2237]
19 Nooseneck Hill Rd.
West Greenwich, RI 02817
Ph: (401)397-1888
Toll Free: 800-714-5040

Cross, Mr. Terry, Advisor
National Indian Child Welfare As-
sociation [19583]
5100 SW Macadam Ave., Ste. 300
Portland, OR 97239
Ph: (503)222-4044
Fax: (503)222-4007

Crosse, Ann Mehan, CAE, Exec. Dir.
Society for Scholarly Publishing
[2813]
10200 W 44th Ave., Ste. 304
Wheat Ridge, CO 80033
Ph: (303)422-3914
Fax: (720)881-6101

Crossfield, Roger, President
Synthetic Yarn and Fiber Association
[3272]
c/o Diane Bayatafshar, Managing
Director
3033 Wilson Blvd., Ste. 700
Arlington, VA 22201

Crossley, Lisa, Exec. Dir.
National Society of Compliance
Professionals [1515]
22 Kent Rd.
Cornwall Bridge, CT 06754
Ph: (860)672-0843
Fax: (860)672-3005

Crossman, Dr. Steve, Contact
Honduras Outreach Medical Brigada
Relief Effort [15471]
c/o Dr. Steve Crossman
West Hospital, 14th Fl.
1200 E Broad St.
Richmond, VA 23298-0251

Crossno, Barry, Gen. Sec.
Friends General Conference [20169]
1216 Arch St., Ste. 2B
Philadelphia, PA 19107
Ph: (215)561-1700
Toll Free: 800-966-4556

Croston, Damion, Dir. of Operations
Planting Empowerment [4214]
Washington, DC 20009

Crotty, Columban, Contact
National Enthronement Center
[19884]
Box 111
Fairhaven, MA 02719
Ph: (508)999-2680
Fax: (508)993-8233

Crotty, Francis, Trustee
National Association of Private
Catholic and Independent Schools
[7413]
2640 3rd Ave.
Sacramento, CA 95818
Ph: (916)451-4963

Crotz, Keith, Chmn. of the Bd.
Seed Savers Exchange [22122]
3094 N Winn Rd.

Decorah, IA 52101-7776
Ph: (563)382-5990

Crouch, Harry, President
National Coalition for Men [18668]
932 C St., Ste. B
San Diego, CA 92101
Ph: (619)231-1909
Toll Free: 888-223-1280

Crouch, Madeleine, Gen. Mgr.
American Viola Society [9871]
14070 Proton Rd., Ste. 100, LB 9
Dallas, TX 75244
Ph: (972)233-9107

Crouch, Madeleine, Officer
National Association of School Music
Dealers, Inc. [2433]
14070 Proton Rd., Ste. 100
Dallas, TX 75244
Ph: (972)233-9107
Fax: (972)490-4219

Croucher, LaDessa, Secretary
National Association for Community
Mediation [4967]
PO Box 5246
Louisville, KY 40255
Ph: (602)633-4213

Crouse, Cindy C., CEO
International Association of Diecut-
ting and Diemaking [1736]
651 W Terra Cotta Ave., Ste. 132
Crystal Lake, IL 60014-3406
Ph: (815)455-7519
Toll Free: 800-828-4233
Fax: (815)455-7510

Crouse, Don, VP
Multiple System Atrophy Coalition
[15958]
9935-D Rea Rd., Ste. 212
Charlotte, NC 28277
Toll Free: 866-737-5999

Crowder, Chaquita, VP
Delta Sigma Chi Multicultural Soror-
ity, Inc. [23970]
New York City Technical College
300 Jay St.
Brooklyn, NY 11201-1909

Crowe, Dean, Founder, CEO
Rally Foundation [14054]
5775 Glenridge Dr., Bldg. B, Ste.
370
Sandy Springs, GA 30328
Ph: (404)847-1270
Fax: (678)251-4067

Crowley, Bob, Exec. Dir.
U.S.A. Water Ski [23357]
1251 Holy Cow Rd.
Polk City, FL 33868
Ph: (863)324-4341
Toll Free: 800-533-2972
Fax: (863)325-8259

Crowley, Dominic, Chmn. of the Bd.
International NGO Safety and
Security Association [12685]
PO Box 7236
Silver Spring, MD 20907
Ph: (202)643-6435

Crowley, Nadia, President, Founder
Another Joy Foundation [13002]
2629 E Craig Rd., Ste. F
North Las Vegas, NV 89030
Ph: (702)808-3967

Crowley, Sheila, Chairperson
Technical Assistance Collaborative
[13019]
31 St. James Ave., Ste. 950
Boston, MA 02116
Ph: (617)266-5657

Crown, Steven A., President
Association of American Rhodes
Scholars [19633]
8229 Boone Blvd., Ste. 240
Vienna, VA 22182-2623
Ph: (703)821-7377
Toll Free: 866-746-0283
Fax: (703)821-2770

Crowson, Seresa, Founder,
President
American APS Association [13783]
6942 FM 1960 E, No. 363
Humble, TX 77346
Ph: (281)812-3384

Crozier, Peter A., Treasurer
Microscopy Society of America
[6868]
12100 Sunset Hills Rd., Ste. 130
Reston, VA 20190
Ph: (703)234-4115
Toll Free: 800-538-3672
Fax: (703)435-4390

Cruden, John, President
Environmental Law Institute [5180]
2000 L St. NW, Ste. 620
Washington, DC 20036
Ph: (202)939-3824

Crugnola, Dr. Aldo, Exec. Dir.
Plastics Institute of America [7037]
Ball Hall
Plastics Engineering Department
University of Massachusetts Lowell
1 University Ave., Rm. 204
Lowell, MA 01854
Ph: (978)934-2575
Fax: (978)934-3089

Crum, Dr. Glen, President
United States Helice Association
[23143]
7750 N MacArthur Blvd., Ste. 120-
324
Irving, TX 75063
Ph: (817)296-3104

Crumb, Steve, Exec. Dir.
WiMedia Alliance [6342]
2400 Camino Ramon, Ste. 375
San Ramon, CA 94583
Ph: (925)275-6604
Fax: (925)886-3809

Crummett, Maria de los Angeles,
Exec. Dir.
Council for International Exchange of
Scholars [8065]
1400 K St. NW, Ste. 700
Washington, DC 20005
Ph: (202)686-4000
Fax: (202)686-4029

Crump, Charlene, President
American Deafness and Rehabilita-
tion Association [15170]
PO Box 480
Myersville, MD 21773-0480
Fax: (301)293-8969

Crump, Karen, Director
Information Services on Latin
America [18620]
PO Box 6103
Albany, CA 94706
Ph: (510)845-4922

Crumpton, Rex B., Chairman
Automotive Engine Rebuilders As-
sociation [311]
500 Coventry Ln., Ste. 180
Crystal Lake, IL 60014
Ph: (815)526-7600
Toll Free: 888-326-2372
Fax: (815)526-7601

Crutchfield, Kevin, Chairman
National Mining Association [740]

101 Constitution Ave. NW, Ste. 500
E
Washington, DC 20001
Ph: (202)463-2600
    (202)463-2639
Fax: (202)463-2666

Cruz, Debra Renee, Editor
National News Bureau [2702]
PO Box 43039
Philadelphia, PA 19129
Ph: (215)849-9016
Fax: (215)754-4488

Cruz, Ms. Yanira L., MPH, CEO,
President
National Hispanic Council on Aging
[10523]
734 15th St. NW, Ste. 1050
Washington, DC 20005
Ph: (202)347-9733
Fax: (202)347-9735

Crystal, Dr. David, Exec. Sec.
American Society for the Advancement of Anesthesia and Sedation
in Dentistry [13693]
6 E Union Ave.
Bound Brook, NJ 08805
Ph: (732)469-9050

Csuka, Anne G., Exec. VP
North American Bar-Related Title
Insurers [1914]
101 Corporate Pl.
Rocky Hill, CT 06067
Ph: (860)257-0606
Fax: (860)563-4833

Cucurny, Denise, Founder, President
Women for World Health [15072]
16291 Fantasia Ln.
Huntington Beach, CA 92649
Ph: (714)846-4524

Cudahy, John, President
International Council of Air Shows
[21232]
748 Miller Dr. SE, Ste. G-3
Leesburg, VA 20175-8919
Ph: (703)779-8510
Fax: (703)779-8511

Cuddy, Rebecca, Chairman
National Council of Postal Credit
Unions [956]
PO Box 160
Del Mar, CA 92014
Ph: (760)745-3883
Fax: (858)792-3884

Cueroni, Nancy, Exec. Dir.
Outdoor Power Equipment and
Engine Service Association [1127]
37 Pratt St.
Essex, CT 06426-1159
Ph: (860)767-1770
Fax: (860)767-7932

Cuerrier, Alain, President
International Society of Ethnobiology
[6091]
PO Box 303
Bristol, VT 05443
Ph: (802)453-6996
Fax: (802)453-3420

Culbertson, Hal, Exec. Dir.
Joan B. Kroc Institute for
International Peace Studies
[18801]
100 Hesburgh Center for
International Studies
University of Notre Dame
Notre Dame, IN 46556-5677
Ph: (574)631-6970
Fax: (574)631-6973

Culbertson, Steven A., President,
CEO
Youth Service America [12912]
1101 15th St. NW, No. 200

Washington, DC 20005
Ph: (202)296-2992

Cull, Bruce, President
National Field Archery Association
[22505]
800 Archery Ln.
Yankton, SD 57078-4119
Ph: (605)260-9279

Cullen, Linda, Exec. Dir.
Fifty Lanterns International [7199]
47399 Anchor Ave.
Stanchfield, MN 55080
Ph: (612)747-9516

Cullifer, Bill, Exec. Dir.
World Organization of Webmasters
[1809]
PO Box 584
Washington, IL 61571
Ph: (916)989-2933
Fax: (916)989-2933

Cullom, Elaine, President
DigitalEve [6835]
1902 NE 98th St.
Seattle, WA 98115

Cullyer, Helen, Exec. Dir.
Society for Classical Studies [9657]
New York University
20 Cooper Sq., 2nd Fl.
New York, NY 10003
Ph: (215)992-7828

Culver, Alicia, Exec. Dir.
Responsible Purchasing Network
[4132]
1440 Broadway, Ste. 901
Oakland, CA 94612
Ph: (510)547-5475
Toll Free: 866-776-1330

Culver, Bill, President
Mining History Association [9494]
323 Daniels Pl.
Canon City, CO 81212
Ph: (573)290-2453

Culver, Mr. Jim, Coord.
United States Consortium of Soil
Science Associations [4690]
c/o Mr. Jim Culver, Coordinator
611 Jeffrey Dr.
Lincoln, NE 68505
Ph: (402)483-0604

Cummer, John, Chmn. of the Bd.
U.S.S. LCI National Association
[21144]
101 Rice Bent Way, No. 6
Columbia, SC 29229
Ph: (803)865-5665

Cummings, Joe, CEO
National Soccer Coaches Associa-
tion of America [23189]
30 W Pershing Rd., Ste. 350
Kansas City, MO 64108-2463
Ph: (816)471-1941
Fax: (816)474-7408

Cummings, Judy, Secretary
American Working Collie Association
[21829]
c/o Judy Cummings, Secretary
26695 Snell Ln.
Los Altos Hills, CA 94022

Cummings, Kathy, President
International Labor Communications
Association [2792]
815 16th St. NW
Washington, DC 20006
Ph: (202)637-5068
Fax: (202)637-3931

Cummings, Sean, President
Fermata Arts Foundation [8854]
24 Brentwood Dr.

Avon, CT 06001
Ph: (860)404-1781
Fax: (860)404-1781

Cummings, Sherry, PhD, Bd.
Member
Association for Gerontology Educa-
tion in Social Work [7939]
PO Box 198136
Nashville, TN 37219-8136

Cummings, Toby, Exec. Dir.
National Association for Campus
Activities [8606]
13 Harbison Way
Columbia, SC 29212-3401
Ph: (803)732-6222

Cummins, Bob, Dir. (Actg.)
American Brahmousin Council
[3687]
PO Box 88
Whitesboro, TX 76273
Ph: (903)564-3995

Cummins, Mr. Fred A., Co-Ch.
Business Modeling and Integration
Domain Task Force [617]
Object Management Group
109 Highland Ave.
Needham, MA 02494
Ph: (781)444-0404
Fax: (781)444-0320

Cummins, Tim, CEO, President
International Association for Contract
& Commercial Management [682]
90 Grove St.
Ridgefield, CT 06877
Ph: (203)431-8741

Cuneo, Cesar, President, Founder
American Obesity Treatment As-
sociation [16247]
117 Anderson Ct., Ste. 1
Dothan, AL 36301
Ph: (334)651-0821

Cuneo, Jonathan W., Gen. Counsel
Committee to Support the Antitrust
Laws [18282]
c/o Joe Sauder, Treasurer
1 Haverford Centre
361 W Lancaster Ave.
Haverford, PA 19041
Ph: (202)789-3960
    (610)645-4717

Cuneo, Richard A., President
Catholic Traditionalist Movement
[19817]
210 Maple Ave.
Westbury, NY 11590-3117
Ph: (516)333-6470
Fax: (516)333-7535

Cunningham, Aaron, President
International Tactical Training As-
sociation [5601]
PO Box 59833
Chicago, IL 60659
Ph: (872)221-4882
Fax: (872)221-5882

Cunningham, Annalisa, Advisor
North American Studio Alliance
[13644]
2313 Hastings Dr.
Belmont, CA 94002-3317
Toll Free: 877-626-2782
Fax: (530)482-2311

Cunningham, Beth A., Exec. Ofc.
American Association of Physics
Teachers [7020]
1 Physics Ellipse
College Park, MD 20740-3841
Ph: (301)209-3311
Fax: (301)209-0845

Cunningham, Beth, President
American Center for Physics [7021]
1 Physics Ellipse
College Park, MD 20740
Ph: (301)209-3000
Toll Free: 866-773-2274

Cunningham, Carlos, ND, CEO,
   Founder
Naturopathic Medicine for Global
   Health [15863]
PO Box 483
Princeton, NJ 08540
Ph: (609)310-1340

Cunningham, Darlene, Founder
Youth With a Mission [20484]
c/o Darlene Cunningham, Founder
75-5851 Kuakini Hwy.
Kailua Kona, HI 96740
Ph: (808)326-7228
   (808)326-4400

Cunningham, Derek, President
National Association for Healthcare
   Recruitment [15586]
18000 W 105th St.
Olathe, KS 66061-7543
Ph: (913)895-4627
Fax: (913)895-4652

Cunningham, Diane, Founder,
   President
National Association of Christian
   Women Entrepreneurs [3496]
2140 E Southlake Blvd., Ste. L-643
Southlake, TX 76092
Ph: (940)247-0090

Cunningham, Gregg, Esq., Exec. Dir.
Center for Bio-Ethical Reform
   [19056]
PO Box 219
Lake Forest, CA 92609
Ph: (949)206-0600

Cunningham Hall, Kathryn, Founder
Power Up Gambia [7203]
4724 Kingsessing Ave.
Philadelphia, PA 19143

Cunningham, Janet, PhD, President
International Board for Regression
   Therapy [17448]
3746 Mount Diablo Blvd., Ste. 200
Lafayette, CA 94549
Ph: (925)283-3941

Cunningham, L. Greg, CEO
National Institute for Case Manage-
   ment [15590]
11701 W 36th St.
Little Rock, AR 72211
Ph: (501)227-2262
Fax: (501)227-4247

Cunningham, Mike, Exec. Dir.
American Nephrology Nurses' As-
   sociation [15871]
E Holly Ave.
Pitman, NJ 08071-0056
Ph: (856)256-2320
Fax: (856)589-7463

Cunningham, Ralph, Secretary
International Association of Accident
   Reconstruction Specialists [5465]
c/o Ralph Cunningham, Secretary
1804 Thornhill Pass, SE
Conyers, GA 30013-6321
Ph: (770)918-0973

Cunningham, Robin, Founder
Cure Alliance for Mental Illness
   [15767]
470 Lloyd Ave.
Providence, RI 02906

Cunningham, Terrence M., President
International Association of Chiefs of
   Police - Law Enforcement Informa-
   tion Management Section [5304]

44 Canal Center Plz., Ste. 200
Alexandria, VA 22314
Ph: (800)843-4227
   (703)836-6767

Cuppy, Ms. Michele, CFO,
   President, Founder
Sew Much Comfort [10759]
c/o Michele Cuppy, President/Chief
   Financial Officer/Co-Founder
13805 Frontier Ln.
Burnsville, MN 55337
Ph: (952)431-6233
   (952)236-7300

Curl, Pat, Coord.
Spine Technology and Educational
   Group Organization [17266]
PO Box 420942
San Diego, CA 92142-0942
Ph: (858)279-9955
Fax: (858)279-1130

Curley, Maureen F.
Campus Compact [7749]
45 Temple Pl.
Boston, MA 02111
Ph: (617)357-1881
Fax: (617)357-1889

Curling, Lauren Lynn, Coord.,
   Admin.
North American Reggio Emilia Alli-
   ance [11102]
1131 Canton St.
Roswell, GA 30075
Ph: (770)552-0179
Fax: (770)552-0767

Curling, Michael, VP
Amigos for Christ [12387]
1845 S Lee Ct., Ste. A
Buford, GA 30518
Ph: (770)614-9250
Fax: (770)614-9850

Curran, Pattie, Director
Shwachman Diamond America
   [14857]
931-B S Main St., No. 332
Kernersville, NC 27284
Ph: (336)423-8158

Curran, Prof. Ricky, Mem.
International Society for Productivity
   Enhancement [6566]
c/o CERA Institute
PO Box 60650
Irvine, CA 92602
Ph: (714)396-9424

Curran, Stuart, President
Keats-Shelley Association of
   America [9068]
New York Public Library, Rm. 226
476 5th Ave.
New York, NY 10018-2788

Curran, Sullivan D., PE, Exec. Dir.
Fiberglass Tank and Pipe Institute
   [832]
14323 Heatherfield Dr.
Houston, TX 77079-7407

Curran, Tim, CEO
Global Technology Distribution
   Council [3210]
141 Bay Point Dr. NE
Saint Petersburg, FL 33704-3805
Ph: (813)412-1148

Currie, Candace, Secretary
Green Burial Council [2405]
PO Box 851
Ojai, CA 93024-0851
Toll Free: 888-966-3330

Currie, John V., Administrator, Chief
   Tech. Ofc.
Council on Safe Transportation of
   Hazardous Articles, Inc. [3082]

10 Hunter Brook Ln.
Queensbury, NY 12804
Ph: (518)761-0389
Fax: (518)792-7781

Currie, Robert, President
Clan Currie Society [20805]
PO Box 541
Summit, NJ 07902-0541

Currie, Robert, Chairman
Defense Orientation Conference As-
   sociation [19090]
9245 Old Keene Mill Rd., Ste. 100
Burke, VA 22015
Ph: (703)451-1200

Currier, Bradford, MD, President
Lumbar Spine Research Society
   [17259]
1685 Highland Ave.
Madison, WI 53705-2281
Ph: (608)770-8992

Currier, Nuchhi, VP of Admin.
Woman's National Democratic Club
   [18118]
1526 New Hampshire Ave. NW
Washington, DC 20036
Ph: (202)232-7363
Fax: (202)328-8772

Curry, Linda, Chairperson
John Clare Society [7981]
c/o James McKusick, Dean
The Davidson Honors College
University of Montana
Missoula, MT 59812

Curry Mathis, Maj. Jillyen, VP
Military Audiology Association
   [13734]

Curry, Pam, Exec. Dir.
Center for Economic Options
   [11759]
910 Quarrier St., Ste. 206
Charleston, WV 25301
Ph: (304)345-1298
Fax: (304)342-0641

Curry Rodriguez, Dr. Julia E., Exec.
   Dir.
National Association for Chicana and
   Chicano Studies [7974]
PO Box 720052
San Jose, CA 95172-0052
Ph: (408)924-5310

Curry, Tom, President
Adenoid Cystic Carcinoma Organiza-
   tion International [13870]
PO Box 112186
Tacoma, WA 98411
Toll Free: 888-223-7983

Curry, Zanna, Contact
Women, Children and Family
   Service Charities of America
   [11864]
1100 Larkspur Landing Cir., Ste. 340
Larkspur, CA 94939
Ph: (415)925-2662

Curtas, Paul M., Director
Fellowship of Christian Airline
   Personnel [20140]
136 Providence Rd.
Fayetteville, GA 30215
Ph: (770)461-9320

Curtin, Sr. Joan, Advisor
American Bible Society [19746]
101 N Independence Mall E, 8th Fl.
Philadelphia, PA 19106-2155
Ph: (215)309-0900
Fax: (215)689-4308

Curtis, Alex, VP
The Heads Network [8457]

c/o Dr. Margaret Wade, Executive
   Director
2140 Chickering Ln.
Nashville, TN 37215
Ph: (615)533-6022
Fax: (615)523-1952

Curtis, Brad, Chairman
Metal Building Manufacturers As-
   sociation [544]
1300 Sumner Ave.
Cleveland, OH 44115-2851
Ph: (216)241-7333
Fax: (216)241-0105

Curtis, Darwin, Director, Founder
Solar Household Energy [7209]
3327 18th. St. NW
Washington, DC 20010

Curtis, Maj. Gen. Glenn H.,
   President
Adjutants General Association of the
   United States [5581]
6400 St. Claude Ave.
New Orleans, LA 70117
Ph: (504)278-8357

Curtis, Graham, Treasurer
Treasures for Little Children [22451]
20581 E CR 1100 N
Kilbourne, IL 62655-6529

Curtis, Kerry, Exec. Dir.
American Society for Colposcopy
   and Cervical Pathology [16275]
1530 Tilco Dr., Ste. C
Frederick, MD 21704-6726
Ph: (301)733-3640
Toll Free: 800-787-7227
Fax: (240)575-9880

Curtis, Liane, President
Rebecca Clarke Society, Inc. [9181]
Brandeis University
Women's Studies Research Ctr.
Mailstop 079
Waltham, MA 02454-9110
Ph: (617)776-1809
Fax: (781)736-8117

Curtis, Richard E., President
Institute for Health Policy Solutions
   [15098]
1444 Eye St. NW, Ste. 900
Washington, DC 20005
Ph: (202)789-1491
Fax: (202)789-1879

Cuschieri, Joseph M., Exec. Dir.
Institute of Noise Control Engineer-
   ing [6923]
12100 Sunset Hills Rd., Ste. 130
Reston, VA 20190
Ph: (703)234-4124
Fax: (703)435-4390

Cushinberry, Dr. Catherine, Exec.
   Dir.
Parents for Public Schools [11734]
125 S Congress St., Ste. 1218
Jackson, MS 39201
Ph: (601)969-6936
Toll Free: 800-880-1222
Fax: (601)397-6132

Cushing, Mary, Advisor
American Sokol Organization
   [19417]
9126 Ogden Ave.
Brookfield, IL 60513-1943
Ph: (708)255-5397

Cushing, Renny, Exec. Dir.
Murder Victims' Families for Human
   Rights [18428]
89 South St., Ste. 601
Boston, MA 02111
Ph: (617)443-1102

Cushing, Victor, Founder, CEO
International Modern Hapkido
  Federation [22992]
210 Homestead Dr.
Moscow, PA 18444
Ph: (570)842-1558
Fax: (570)842-3741

Cushman, Charles, Exec. Dir.,
  Founder
American Land Rights Association
  [5690]
30218 NE 82nd Ave.
Battle Ground, WA 98604
Ph: (360)687-3087
Fax: (360)687-2973

Cushman, Diane L., Exec. Dir.
National Council on Family Relations
  [14749]
1201 W River Pky., Ste. 200
Minneapolis, MN 55454-1115
Ph: (763)781-9331
Toll Free: 888-781-9331
Fax: (763)781-9348

Cushman, Diane L., Exec. Dir.
National Council on Family Relations
  Education and Enrichment Section
  [11825]
1201 W River Pky., Ste. 200
Minneapolis, MN 55454
Ph: (763)781-9331
Toll Free: 888-781-9331
Fax: (763)781-9348

Cushman, Diane L., Exec. Dir.
National Council on Family Relations
  Feminism and Family Studies Sec-
  tion [11826]
1201 W River Pky., Ste. 200
Minneapolis, MN 55454-1115
Ph: (763)781-9331
Toll Free: 888-781-9331
Fax: (763)781-9348

Cushman, John L., President
Sportsmen's Association for
  Firearms Education, Inc. [18255]
PO Box 343
Commack, NY 11725S
Ph: (631)475-8125

Cusick, Terry, Chairman
Goldfish Society of America [22032]
PO Box 551373
Fort Lauderdale, FL 33355-1373

Cusson, Pauline, Editor
American-Canadian Genealogical
  Society [20951]
PO Box 6478
Manchester, NH 03108-6478
Ph: (603)622-1554

Cutcher, Rev. Anthony, President
National Federation of Priests'
  Councils [19887]
333 N Michigan Ave., Ste. 1114
Chicago, IL 60601-4001
Ph: (312)442-9700
Toll Free: 888-271-6372

Cutler Jr., John M.
National Shippers Strategic
  Transportation Council [3096]
330 N Wabash Ave., Ste. 2000
Chicago, IL 60611
Ph: (202)367-1174
Fax: (952)442-3941

Cutshaw, Stacey McCarroll, Editor
Society for Photographic Education
  [8426]
2530 Superior Ave., Ste. 403
Cleveland, OH 44114
Ph: (216)622-2733
Fax: (216)622-2712

Cutting, Dorothy, Office Mgr.
Athletic Equipment Managers As-
  sociation [23215]
460 Hunt Hill Rd.
Freeville, NY 13068-9643
Ph: (607)539-6300
Fax: (607)539-6340

Cuttriss, Nicolas, Founder, Chmn. of
  the Bd.
American Youth Understanding
  Diabetes Abroad [14519]
1700 N Moore St., Ste. 2000
Arlington, VA 22209
Ph: (703)527-3860

Cutts, Shannon, Founder, Exec. Dir.,
  Chmn. of the Bd.
MentorCONNECT [14645]
1302 Waugh Dr., No. 660
Houston, TX 77019

Cycyota, Thomas A., CEO,
  President
AlloSource [17500]
6278 S Troy Cir.
Centennial, CO 80111
Ph: (720)873-0213
Toll Free: 800-557-3587
Fax: (720)873-0212

Cypess, Raymond, PhD, Chairman,
  CEO
American Type Culture Collection
  [6073]
10801 University Blvd.
Manassas, VA 20110
Ph: (703)365-2700
Toll Free: 800-638-6597
Fax: (703)365-2750

Cyril, Malkia, Exec. Dir.
Media Action Grassroots Network
  [18657]
c/o Center for Media Justice
436 14th St., 5th Fl.
Oakland, CA 94612
Ph: (510)698-3800

Cyrus, Sylvia, Exec. Dir.
Association for the Study of African-
  American Life and History [8783]
Howard Ctr.
2225 Georgia Ave. NW, Ste. 331
Washington, DC 20059
Ph: (202)238-5910
Fax: (202)986-1506

Czarnecki, Dr. Barbara, President
National Medical and Dental As-
  sociation [19604]
Philadelphia, PA
Ph: (484)431-0111
Fax: (610)566-6888

Czarnecki, Mark T., Owner,
  President
The Benchmarking Network, Inc.
  [2441]
4606 FM 1960 W, Ste. 300
Houston, TX 77069-9949
Ph: (281)440-5044
Toll Free: 888-323-6246
Fax: (281)440-6677

Czarnik-Laurin, Darcy, President
National Cooperative of Health
  Networks Association [15046]
400 S Main St.
Hardinsburg, KY 40143
Ph: (970)712-0732
Fax: (970)417-4186

Czuhajewski, Stephanie, Exec. Dir.
Academy of Doctors of Audiology
  [15164]
446 E High St., Ste. 10
Lexington, KY 40517
Toll Free: 866-493-5544

D

da Cruz, Eduardo, MD, President
Surgeons of Hope [17409]
1675 Broadway, 8th Fl.
New York, NY 10019
Ph: (212)474-5994
Fax: (212)474-5996

da Cruz, Maria, Exec. Dir.
U.S.- Angola Chamber of Commerce
  [23625]
1100 17th St. NW, Ste. 1000
Washington, DC 20036
Ph: (202)857-0789
Fax: (202)223-0551

Dabby, Firoza Chic, Director
Asian Pacific Institute on Gender-
  Based Violence [11696]
500 12th St., Ste. 330
Oakland, CA 94607
Ph: (415)568-3315
Fax: (415)954-9999

Dabney, Dennis, President
Logistics Officer Association [18696]
PO Box 2264
Arlington, VA 22202

Dabral, Hari Shankar, Director
Association of Himalayan Yoga
  Meditation Societies International
  [10419]
631 University Ave. NE
Minneapolis, MN 55413
Ph: (612)379-2386

Dabrishus, Michael, President
Manuscript Society [21684]
14003 Rampart Ct.
Baton Rouge, LA 70810-8101

Dackerman, Rosemarie E., Exec.
  Dir.
The Single Parent Resource Center,
  Inc. [12429]
228 E 45th St., 5th Fl.
New York, NY 10017
Ph: (212)951-7030
Fax: (212)951-7037

D'Adamo, Charles, Sen. Ed.
Alternative Press Center [2645]
PO Box 13127
Baltimore, MD 21203-3127
Ph: (312)451-8133

Dadd, Robert F., President
Christian Missions in Many Lands
  [20401]
PO Box 13
Spring Lake, NJ 07762-0013
Ph: (732)449-8880
Fax: (732)974-0888

Dagget, Claudia, President
Independent Schools Association of
  the Central States [8011]
55 W Wacker Dr., Ste. 701
Chicago, IL 60601
Ph: (312)750-1190
Fax: (312)750-1193

Daggett, Christopher, CEO,
  President
Geraldine R. Dodge Foundation
  [12970]
14 Maple Ave., Ste. 400
Morristown, NJ 07960
Ph: (973)540-8442
Fax: (973)540-1211

Dagher, Ali, Mem., Founder
American Arab Chamber of Com-
  merce [23551]
12740 W Warren Ave.
Dearborn, MI 48126
Ph: (313)945-1700
Fax: (313)945-6697

D'Agostino, Bruce, CEO, President
Construction Management Associa-
  tion of America [2164]
7926 Jones Branch Dr., Ste. 800
McLean, VA 22102-3303
Ph: (703)356-2622
Fax: (703)356-6388

D'Agostino, Charles, President
Association of University Research
  Parks [8495]
6262 N Swan Rd., Ste. 100
Tucson, AZ 85718
Ph: (520)529-2521
Fax: (520)529-2499

Dahl, Bill, Exec. Dir.
Botanical Society of America [6138]
4475 Castleman Ave.
Saint Louis, MO 63110-3201
Ph: (314)577-9566
Fax: (314)577-9515

Dahl, Eric, CEO
World Trade Centers Association
  [3308]
120 Broadway, Ste. 3350
New York, NY 10271
Ph: (212)432-2626

Dahl, Ophelia, Founder, Chairman,
  Trustee
Partners in Health [12297]
888 Commonwealth Ave., 3rd Fl.
Boston, MA 02215
Ph: (617)998-8922
Fax: (617)998-8973

Dahl, Susie, Exec. Dir.
National Association of Public Pen-
  sion Attorneys [5030]
2410 Hyde Park Rd., Ste. B
Jefferson City, MO 65109
Ph: (573)616-1895
Fax: (573)616-1897

Dahlia, Gianna, Exec. Dir.
Together We Rise [11170]
580 W Lambert Rd., No. A
Brea, CA 92821
Ph: (714)784-6760

Daigle, Jerrell, Treasurer
Dragonfly Society of the Americas
  [6610]
c/o Jerrell Daigle, Treasurer
2067 Little River Ln.
Tallahassee, FL 32311

Dailey, Betsy, President
Help Kids India [11021]
PO Box 12
Topsham, VT 05076

Dailey, Cheryl, CFO
National Council of Juvenile and
  Family Court Judges [5396]
PO Box 8970
Reno, NV 89507
Ph: (775)507-4777
Fax: (775)507-4855

Dailey, Derick, Chairperson
National Black Law Students As-
  sociation [8220]
1225 11th St. NW
Washington, DC 20001-4217
Ph: (202)618-2572

Daines, John, Contact
Charley Pride Fan Club [24028]
3198 Royal Ln.
Dallas, TX 75229
Ph: (214)350-8477
Fax: (214)350-0534

Dainty, Gladstone, President, Chairman
U.S.A. Cricket Association [23262]
8461 Lake Worth Rd., Ste. B-1-185

Lake Worth, FL 33467
Ph: (561)839-1888

Dakduk, Michael, Exec. VP
Association of Private Sector Colleges and Universities **[8735]**
1101 Connecticut Ave. NW, Ste. 900
Washington, DC 20036
Ph: (202)336-6700
Toll Free: 866-711-8574
Fax: (202)336-6828

Dal Bello, Pete, President, Founder
International Chiari Association
[15944]
27 W Anapamu St., No. 340
Santa Barbara, CA 93101
Ph: (805)570-0484
Fax: (815)301-6541

Dale, Alexander, Exec. Dir.
Engineers for a Sustainable World
[11354]
3715 Beechwood Blvd.
Pittsburgh, PA 15217

Dale, Casey, President, Founder
North American Bungee Association
[23247]
32016 NE Healy Rd.
Amboy, WA 98601
Ph: (503)520-0303

Dale, Terry, President, CEO
United States Tour Operators Association **[3404]**
345 7th Ave., Ste. 1801
New York, NY 10001
Ph: (212)599-6599
Fax: (212)599-6744

Daley, Horace A., Founder,
President, CEO
Professional Jamaicans for Jamaica
[12216]
PO Box 320058
Fairfield, CT 06825
Toll Free: 866-285-9312

Daley, Mike, Director
ArtWatch International Inc. **[8961]**
Ruth Osborne
47 5th Ave.
New York, NY 10003-4396

Daley, Mike, CEO
The Vision Council **[1606]**
225 Reinekers Ln., Ste. 700
Alexandria, VA 22314
Ph: (703)548-4560
Toll Free: 866-826-0290
Fax: (703)548-4580

Daley, Sheila, Director, Curator
Noah Webster House **[9424]**
227 S Main St.
West Hartford, CT 06107
Ph: (860)521-5362
Fax: (860)521-4036

Dalke, Katie Baratz, President
InterAct Advocates for Intersex Youth
[17903]
PO Box 676
Cotati, CA 94931
Ph: (707)793-1190

Dalsky, Dianne, Exec. Dir.
American Society for Laser Medicine
and Surgery **[15522]**
2100 Stewart Ave., Ste. 240
Wausau, WI 54401-1709
Ph: (715)845-9283
Toll Free: 877-258-6028
Fax: (715)848-2493

Dalton, Robert K., President
Society of Reliability Engineers
[6598]

c/o Joel A. Nachlas, PhD, Committee Chairman
Virginia Tech
250 Durham Hall
Blacksburg, VA 24061-0118
Ph: (540)231-5357
Fax: (540)231-3322

Daluvoy, Sanjay, MD, Founder,
President
World Children's Initiative **[11189]**
1328 American Way
Menlo Park, CA 94025
Ph: (408)554-4188

Daly, Frank, President
Airflow Club of America **[21312]**
1651 209th Pl. NE
Sammamish, WA 98074-4212
Ph: (425)868-7448

Daly, Kay, President
Dinah Shore Memorial Fan Club
[23991]
3552 Federal Ave.
Los Angeles, CA 90066

Daly, Kenneth, CEO
National Association of Corporate
Directors **[2183]**
2001 Pennsylvania Ave. NW, Ste.
500
Washington, DC 20006
Ph: (202)775-0509
Fax: (202)775-4857

Daly, V. Adm. (Ret.) Peter H., CEO
United States Naval Institute **[5630]**
291 Wood Rd.
Annapolis, MD 21402
Ph: (410)268-6110
Toll Free: 800-223-8764
Fax: (410)571-1703

Daly, Timothy, Dir. of Admin.
National Council for the Social Studies **[8566]**
8555 16th St., Ste. 500
Silver Spring, MD 20910
Ph: (301)588-1800
Toll Free: 800-683-0812
Fax: (301)588-2049

D'Amato, Alfonse, Chmn. of the Bd.
Poker Players Alliance **[22388]**
705 8th St. SE, Ste. 300
Washington, DC 20003
Ph: (202)621-6936

D'Ambra, Nora, Coord., Member
Svcs.
Investment Casting Institute **[1740]**
136 Summit Ave.
Montvale, NJ 07645
Ph: (201)573-9770
Fax: (201)573-9771

D'Ambrosia, Becky, Contact
Pacific Northwest Region of the
Lincoln and Continental Owners
Club **[21471]**
c/o Roger Clements
16630 SE 235th St.
Kent, WA 98042
Toll Free: 866-427-7583

D'Ambrosia, John, Chmn. of the Bd.
Ethernet Alliance **[7266]**
3855 SW 153rd Dr.
Beaverton, OR 97003-5105
Ph: (503)619-0564
Fax: (503)644-6708

D'Ambrosio, Joseph J., President,
Founder
Eye-Bank for Sight Restoration
[14619]
120 Wall St.

New York, NY 10005-3902
Ph: (212)742-9000
Fax: (212)269-3139

Damm, Paul, PA-C, President
Association of Neurosurgical Physician Assistants **[16722]**
PO Box 17781
Tampa, FL 33682
Ph: (813)799-8807
Fax: (813)856-3533

Dammrich, Thomas, President
National Marine Manufacturers Association **[437]**
231 S LaSalle St., Ste. 2050
Chicago, IL 60604
Ph: (312)946-6200

Damon, Betsy, Director, Founder
Keepers of the Waters **[4760]**
191 22nd St.
Brooklyn, NY 11232
Ph: (917)977-1411

Damon, Dr. Dwight F., President
National Guild of Hypnotists **[15366]**
PO Box 308
Merrimack, NH 03054-0308
Ph: (603)429-9438
Fax: (603)424-8066

Damon-Bach, Lucinda, Founder,
President
Sedgwick Society **[10398]**
c/o Deborah Gussman
619 Wayne Ave.
Haddonfield, NJ 08033

Damour, Yvon, MD, President
Alliance For Relief Mission in Haiti
[12613]
PO Box 250028
Brooklyn, NY 11225
Ph: (516)499-7452

Dampier, David, PhD, Director
American Society of Digital
Forensics and eDiscovery **[6652]**
2451 Cumberland Pky., Ste. 3382
Atlanta, GA 30339-6157
Toll Free: 866-534-9734

Damrosch, Prof. Lori, VP
American Society of International
Law **[5349]**
2223 Massachusetts Ave. NW
Washington, DC 20008
Ph: (202)939-6000
Fax: (202)797-7133

Dana, Rodger, Mem.
National Association of Fleet Tug
Sailors **[21055]**

Dandrea, Joel, Exec. VP
Specialized Carriers and Rigging
Association **[3103]**
5870 Trinity Pky., Ste. 200
Centreville, VA 20120
Ph: (703)698-0291
Fax: (703)698-0297

Dandridge, Dr. Joyce A., Corr. Sec.
Chow Chow Club **[21856]**
c/p Dr. Joyce A. Dandridge, Corresponding Secretary
8132 Eastern Ave. NW
Washington, DC 20012-1312
Ph: (202)726-9155
Fax: (202)726-9155

Dang, Cathy, Exec. Dir.
Committee Against Anti-Asian
Violence **[17813]**
55 Hester St., Storefront
New York, NY 10002
Ph: (212)473-6485

Dang, Cathy, Exec. Dir.
Racial Justice 911 **[17927]**
c/o CAAAV: Organizing Asian Communities
55 Hester St.
New York, NY 10002
Ph: (718)473-6485

d'Angelo, George, President
Conflict Solutions International
[18004]
1629 K St. NW, Ste. 300
Washington, DC 20006

D'Angelo, Michael, Director
The Maryheart Crusaders **[19860]**
531 W Main St.
Meriden, CT 06451
Ph: (203)238-9735
Toll Free: 800-879-1957
Fax: (203)235-0059

d'Angelo, Raphael, M.D., President
Alliance of International Aromatherapists **[13584]**
9956 W Remington Pl., Unit A10,
Ste. 323
Littleton, CO 80128-6733
Ph: (303)531-6377
Toll Free: 877-531-6377
Fax: (303)979-7135

D'Angelo, Richard A., Counsel
North American Shortwave Association **[21271]**
45 Wildflower Rd.
Levittown, PA 19057-3209

Dangerfield, Deborah, Chairperson
Black Methodists for Church
Renewal **[20340]**
653 Beckwith St. SW
Atlanta, GA 30314
Ph: (470)428-2251
Fax: (470)428-3353

Dangoor, David E. R., President
American Sephardi Federation
[20229]
15 W 16th St.
New York, NY 10011-6301
Ph: (212)548-4486

Daniel, Mary, Founder
African Children's Mission **[10837]**
PO Box 26470
Birmingham, AL 35260
Ph: (205)620-4937

Daniel, Stacee, Exec. Dir.
American College of Veterinary
Ophthalmologists **[17619]**
PO Box 1311
Meridian, ID 83680
Ph: (208)466-7624
Fax: (208)895-7872

Daniel, Stephen, Mem.
International Berkeley Society
[10091]
26 E Main St.
Dept. of Philosophy
Wheaton College
Norton, MA 02766

Daniels, Diana, Exec. Dir.
National Council on Educating Black
Children **[7468]**
3737 N Meridian St., Ste. 102
Indianapolis, IN 46208
Ph: (317)283-9081

Daniels, Dr. Eric S., Exec. Dir.
Emulsion Polymers Institute **[6199]**
Lehigh University
111 Research Dr.
Bethlehem, PA 18015
Ph: (610)758-3602
Fax: (610)758-5880

Daniels, Fred, President
Haviland Collectors International
Foundation [21580]
PO Box 5163
Buffalo Grove, IL 60089

Daniels, John Y., Exec. VP
Association of Textile, Apparel and
Materials Professionals [6191]
1 Davis Dr.
Research Triangle Park, NC 27709-
2215
Ph: (919)549-8141
Fax: (919)549-8933

Daniels, Lisa, Exec. Dir., Founder
Windustry [7392]
201 Ridgewood Ave.
Minneapolis, MN 55403
Ph: (612)200-0331
Toll Free: 800-818-0936

Daniels, Margery Berg, Exec. Dir.
International Society for Third-Sector
Research [12402]
Hampton House, No. 356
624 N Broadway
Baltimore, MD 21205-1900
Ph: (410)614-4678
Fax: (410)502-0397

Daniels, Neil T., Founder, President
Dean Martin Fan Center [24014]
PO Box 660212
Arcadia, CA 91066-0212

Daniels, R. Scott, President
National Organization of State Of-
fices of Rural Health [17011]
44648 Mound Rd., No. 114
Sterling Heights, MI 48314-1322
Ph: (586)739-9940
      (586)336-4627
Fax: (586)739-9941

Daniels, Ron, Exec. Dir.
Blacks in Law Enforcement [5458]
591 Vanderbilt Ave., Ste. 133
Brooklyn, NY 11238
Ph: (718)455-9059

Daniels, Susan, CEO, President
Leader Dogs for the Blind [17721]
1039 S Rochester Rd.
Rochester Hills, MI 48307
Ph: (248)651-9011
Toll Free: 888-777-5332

Daniels, Theodore R., CEO,
President
Society for Financial Education and
Professional Development [7572]
500 Montgomery St., Ste. 400
Alexandria, VA 22314
Ph: (703)920-3807
Fax: (703)920-3809

Daniels, Wes, President
National Association of Farm Service
Agency County Office Employees
[5269]
PO Box 598
Floydada, TX 79235
Ph: (724)853-5555

Danielson, Ann, President
Alpaca Breeders of the Rockies
[3584]
PO Box 1965
Estes Park, CO 80517
Ph: (970)586-5589
Toll Free: 888-993-9898

Danis, Peter, President
American Academy of Fertility Care
Professionals [11835]
11700 Studt Ave., Ste. C
Saint Louis, MO 63141
Ph: (402)489-3733
Fax: (402)488-6525

Danish, Susan, Exec. Dir.
Association of Junior Leagues
International [13284]
80 Maiden Ln., Ste. 305
New York, NY 10038
Ph: (212)951-8300
Toll Free: 800-955-3248
Fax: (212)481-7196

Danley, Robert J., Secretary,
Treasurer
United Union of Roofers Waterproof-
ers and Allied Workers [23403]
1660 L St. NW, Ste. 800
Washington, DC 20036-5646
Ph: (202)463-7663
Fax: (202)463-6906

Dannenhoffer, Michelle, Secretary
American Model Yachting Associa-
tion [22196]
c/o Michelle Dannenhoffer, Secretary
PO Box 360374
Melbourne, FL 32936-0374
Toll Free: 888-237-9524

Danson, Casey Coates, Founder,
Director
Global Possibilities [7200]
1955 Mandeville Canyon Rd.
Los Angeles, CA 90049-2200

Danylchuk, Lynette S., PhD, Chair-
man
International Society for the Study of
Trauma and Dissociation [15781]
8400 Westpark Dr., 2nd Fl.
McLean, VA 22102
Ph: (703)610-9037
Fax: (703)610-0234

Daoud, Dana Zureikat, Director
Jordan Information Bureau [23647]
c/o Embassy of the Hashemite
Kingdom of Jordan
3504 International Dr. NW
Washington, DC 20008
Ph: (202)265-1606
Fax: (202)966-3110

D'Aponte, Mimi Gisolfi, President
Pirandello Society of America [9089]
c/o Casa Italiana Zerilli-Marimo
24 W 12th St.
New York, NY 10011

Dapp, Veronica, Contact
American Ivy Society [22079]
PO Box 163
Deerfield Street, NJ 08313

Dapsis, Susan, President
International Society for Animal
Rights [10651]
PO Box F
Clarks Summit, PA 18411
Ph: (570)586-2200
Fax: (570)586-9580

Dapson, Richard, Trustee
Biological Stain Commission [6077]
c/o Chad Fagan
University of Rochester Medical Ctr.
601 Elmwood Ave.
Rochester, NY 14642-0001
Ph: (585)275-2751
Fax: (585)442-8993

Dar, Ami, Exec. Dir.
Action Without Borders/Idealist.org
[18291]
302 5th Ave., 11th Fl.
New York, NY 10001-3604
Ph: (646)786-6886
Fax: (212)695-7243

Darack, Ms. Sharon, Dir. of
Programs
Jewish Alcoholics, Chemically
Dependent Persons and Significant
Others [13149]

135 W 50th St.
New York, NY 10020
Ph: (212)632-4600
Fax: (212)399-3525

Darby, Karl, Chmn. of the Bd.
Horseless Carriage Club of America
[21394]
1301 N Manship Pl.
Meridian, ID 83642-5072
Ph: (626)287-4222

Darby, Maria, President
Association of Change Management
Professionals [2152]
3625 E 16th Ave.
Spokane, WA 99223
Ph: (301)200-2362

Darcy, Bill, CEO
National Kitchen and Bath Associa-
tion [1955]
687 Willow Grove St.
Hackettstown, NJ 07840
Toll Free: 800-843-6522
Fax: (908)852-1695

Darcy, Gina, President
Chevrolet Nomad Association
[21351]
1720 Laurie Dr.
Haw River, NC 27258

Dardik, Alan, MD, PhD, President
International Society for Vascular
Surgery [17392]
10062 SE Osprey Point Dr.
Hobe Sound, FL 33455
Ph: (631)993-4321

Darensburg, Oletha, Secretary,
Exec. Dir.
Society for Modeling & Simulation
International [6264]
2598 Fortune Way, Ste. I
Vista, CA 92081
Ph: (858)277-3888
Fax: (858)277-3930

Darin, John A., CEO, President
National Association on Drug Abuse
Problems [13163]
355 Lexington Ave., 2nd Fl.
New York, NY 10017
Ph: (212)986-1170
Fax: (212)697-2939

Darity, William, President
Association of Black Sociologists
[7180]
3473 S Martin Luther King Dr.
Chicago, IL 60616-4108
Ph: (312)342-7618
Fax: (773)955-8890

Darko, Philip, Dir. of Programs
World Partners for Development
[13098]
14658 Gap Way, Ste. 165
Haymarket, VA 20168
Ph: (571)435-2657

Darling, Helen, President, CEO
National Quality Forum [15051]
1030 15th St. NW, Ste. 800
Washington, DC 20005
Ph: (202)783-1300
Fax: (202)783-3434

Darling, Sharon, Founder, President
National Center for Families Learn-
ing [8248]
325 W Main St., Ste. 300
Louisville, KY 40202
Ph: (502)584-1133

Darlington, John, President
National Indy 500 Collectors Club
[21456]

PO Box 24105
Speedway, IN 46224

D'Arminio, Richard, President
Unico National [19509]
271 US Highway 46, Ste. F-103
Fairfield, NJ 07004-2447
Ph: (973)808-0035
Toll Free: 800-877-1492
Fax: (973)808-0043

Darmody, Robert, Exec. Sec.
American Society of Mining and
Reclamation [5632]
1305 Weathervane
Champaign, IL 61821
Ph: (217)333-9489

Darmohraj, Andrew, Exec. VP, COO
American Pet Products Association
[2540]
255 Glenville Rd.
Greenwich, CT 06831
Ph: (203)532-0000
Toll Free: 800-452-1225
Fax: (203)532-0551

Daronatsy, Laura, President
Public Relations Student Society of
America [8473]
33 Maiden Ln., 11th Fl.
New York, NY 10038-5150
Ph: (212)460-1474
Fax: (212)995-0757

Darr, Bud, Sr. VP
Cruise Lines International Associa-
tion [3376]
1201 F St. NW, Ste. 250
Washington, DC 20004
Ph: (202)759-9370
Fax: (202)759-9344

Darr, Stephen, Exec. Dir.
Peacework Volunteer Organization
[18821]
620 N Main St., Ste. 306
Blacksburg, VA 24060
Ph: (540)953-1376

Darrell, Karin, Director
Bermuda Department of Tourism
[23659]
675 3rd Ave., 20th Fl.
New York, NY 10017
Toll Free: 800-223-6106

Darrow, Duncan N., Founder
Cancer Simplified [13930]
No. 34 Bay St., Ste. 202
Sag Harbor, NY 11963
Ph: (631)725-4646

Darrow, Joanna, Officer
American Accordion Musicological
Society [9849]
322 Haddon Ave.
Westmont, NJ 08108
Ph: (856)854-6628

Darstein, Marie W., Exec. Dir.
National Child Care Association
[10810]
1325 G St. NW, Ste. 500
Washington, DC 20005-3136
Toll Free: 800-543-7161

Dart, Dave, Founder, Exec. Dir.
Dart Music International [9899]
2704 E 2nd St.
Austin, TX 78702
Ph: (707)836-3278

Dart, Patty, Treasurer
Cushman Club of America [22219]
c/o Patty Dart, Treasurer
PO Box 102
Indian Hills, CO 80454
Ph: (303)697-4436

Darvish, Babak, MD, Founder, President
Advancement of Research for Myopathies [14802]
PO Box 261926
Encino, CA 91426-1926
Toll Free: 800-276-2000
Fax: (818)609-7350

Darwick, Kristi, President
Society for Calligraphy [10415]
PO Box 64174
Los Angeles, CA 90064-0174

Dasgupta, Santwana, Exec. Dir.
Partnership for Education of Children in Afghanistan [11260]
7121 W 113th St.
Bloomington, MN 55438
Ph: (612)821-8759

Dashoff, Joni Brill, VP
Association of Science Fiction and Fantasy Artists [241]
PO Box 60933
Harrisburg, PA 17106-0933

Dassow, Kelly, Operations Mgr.
Quixote Center [19898]
7307 Baltimore Ave.
College Park, MD 20740
Ph: (301)699-0042

Datri, James Edmund, CEO, President
American Advertising Federation [84]
1101 Vermont Ave. NW, Ste. 500
Washington, DC 20005-6306
Ph: (202)898-0089

Daucher, Rachelle, Mgr.
ABET [6522]
415 N Charles St.
Baltimore, MD 21201
Ph: (410)347-7700
Fax: (410)625-2238

Daudi, Mr. Jamil, President
Sindhi Association of North America [9235]
12881 Knott St., Ste. 219
Garden Grove, CA 92841-3925
Ph: (714)271-9947
Fax: (714)373-3702

Daugherty, Dianne M., Exec. Dir.
Malignant Hyperthermia Association of the United States [14841]
PO Box 1069
Sherburne, NY 13460
Ph: (607)674-7901
Fax: (607)674-7910

Daugherty, Dianne, Exec. Dir.
Neuroleptic Malignant Syndrome Information Service [15975]
Box 1069
Sherburne, NY 13460-1069
Ph: (607)674-7920
Toll Free: 888-667-8367
Fax: (607)674-7910

Daugherty, Steve, Exec. Ofc.
O'Dochartaigh Clann Association [20989]
c/o Cameron Dougherty, Interim Executive Committee
4078 Bruce Ct. SW
Grandville, MI 49418
Ph: (616)534-8032

Daughton, Dr. William, Exec. Dir.
American Society for Engineering Management [6535]
200 Sparkman Dr., Ste. 2
Huntsville, AL 35805

Daum, Matt, Chairman
International Safe Transit Association [3091]

1400 Abbott Rd., Ste. 160
East Lansing, MI 48823-1900
Ph: (517)333-3437
Fax: (517)333-3813

Dauzier, Jennifer, Treasurer
International Association of Law Enforcement Intelligence Analysts [5362]
PO Box 13857
Richmond, VA 23225
Fax: (804)565-2059

Dave, Ronda, Contact
Association for Support of Graduate Students [7956]
PO Box 4698
Incline Village, NV 89450-4698
Ph: (775)831-1399
Fax: (775)831-1221

Davenport, Deborah, President
Society of Insurance Trainers and Educators [8039]
1821 University Ave. W, Ste. S256
Saint Paul, MN 55104
Ph: (651)999-5354
Fax: (651)917-1835

Davenport, George, Contact
Super Coupe Club of America [21500]
4322 Hamilton Rd.
Medina, OH 44256
Ph: (330)242-1122

Davenport, Jane, President
American Bell Association International [21607]
26 Hunting Lodge Dr.
Miami Springs, FL 33166-5100

Davenport, Robert W., President
National Development Council [18155]
24 Whitehall St., Ste. 710
New York, NY 10004
Ph: (212)682-1106
    (859)578-4850
Fax: (212)573-6118

Davenport-Ennis, Nancy, CEO, President
Patient Advocate Foundation [15054]
421 Butler Farm Rd.
Hampton, VA 23666
Toll Free: 800-532-5274
Fax: (757)873-8999

Daversa, Chad, Exec. Dir.
International Society for Bipolar Disorders [13722]
PO Box 7168
Pittsburgh, PA 15213
Ph: (412)624-4407
Fax: (412)624-4484

Davey, Tara, Exec. Dir.
Council of Hotel and Restaurant Trainers [1654]
PO Box 2835
Westfield, NJ 07091
Ph: (908)389-9277
Toll Free: 800-463-5918

David, Amos, Secretary
International Society for Knowledge Organization [6745]
Mary Gates Hall, Ste. 370
The Information School
Seattle, WA 98195-2840

David, Gabrielle, Exec. Dir., Chmn. of the Bd.
Intercultural Alliance of Artists and Scholars, Inc. [8925]
PO Box 4378, Grand Central Sta.

New York, NY 10163-4378
Ph: (646)801-4227
Fax: (646)998-1314

David, Hal, Chairman
National Academy of Popular Music [9964]
330 W 58th St., Ste. 411
New York, NY 10019-1827

David, Lauren K., Founder
Keep Dentistry Alive [14454]
4825 Sanford St.
Metairie, LA 70006

David, Narsai M., Chairman
Assyrian Aid Society of America [12623]
350 Berkeley Park Blvd.
Berkeley, CA 94707
Ph: (510)527-9997
Fax: (510)527-6633

David, Pam, Exec. Dir.
National LGBTQ Task Force [11901]
1325 Massachusetts Ave. NW, Ste. 600
Washington, DC 20005-4164
Ph: (202)393-5177
Fax: (202)393-2241

David, Paul G., Exec. VP, Founder
Multicultural Golf Association of America [22886]
Long Island, NY
Ph: (631)288-8255

Davidheiser, Dr. James, President
Delta Phi Alpha [23769]
c/o Michael Shaughnessy, Secretary-Treasurer
Washington & Jefferson College
60 S Lincoln St.
Washington, PA 15301
Ph: (724)223-6170

Davidoo, Albert, Chairman, Founder
Assyrian Medical Society [15716]
16055 Ventura Blvd., Ste. 1225
Encino, CA 91436-2625
Ph: (818)501-8867

Davids, Peter H., Bd. Member
Anglican Association of Biblical Scholars [19699]
c/o Rev. Frank Hughes, Treasurer
1107 Broadway St.
Minden, LA 71055
Ph: (318)377-1259

Davidsen, Amy, Exec. Dir.
The Climate Group [3832]
145 W 58th St., Ste. 2A
New York, NY 10019
Ph: (646)233-0550

Davidson, Betsy, Exec. Dir.
Shakespeare Society [9097]
191 7th Ave., Ste. 2S
New York, NY 10011
Fax: (267)381-5283

Davidson, Bob, Founder
Davidson Institute for Talent Development [11914]
9665 Gateway Dr., Ste. B
Reno, NV 89521
Ph: (775)852-3483

Davidson, Carl, Co-Chmn. of the Bd.
Committees of Correspondence for Democracy and Socialism [5765]
522 Valencia St.
San Francisco, CA 94110
Ph: (415)863-6637

Davidson, Ms. Christie, Exec. Dir.
National Association of Probation Executives [5142]

c/o Christie Davidson, Executive Director
National Association of Probation Executives
Correctional Management Institute
George J. Beto Criminal Justice Center
Sam Houston State University
Huntsville, TX 77341-2296
Ph: (936)294-3757
Fax: (936)294-1671

Davidson, Dr. Dan E., President
American Councils for International Education [7739]
1828 L St. NW, Ste. 1200
Washington, DC 20036-5136
Ph: (202)833-7522
Fax: (202)833-7523

Davidson, Daryl, Exec. Dir.
Association for Unmanned Vehicle Systems International [7101]
2700 S Quincy St., Ste. 400
Arlington, VA 22206
Ph: (703)845-9671
Fax: (703)845-9679

Davidson, Don, Director, Founder
Institute of Singles Dynamics [20368]
PO Box 27222
Overland Park, KS 66225

Davidson, Dwight, President
United States Marine Corps Motor Transport Association, Inc. [5628]
PO Box 1372
Jacksonville, NC 28541-1372
Ph: (910)450-1841

Davidson, Gordon, President
Center for Visionary Leadership [18629]
369B 3rd St., No. 563
San Rafael, CA 94901-3581
Ph: (415)472-2540
    (480)595-4709

Davidson, Jean, CEO
New York Live Arts [8992]
219 W 19th St.
New York, NY 10011
Ph: (212)691-6500
Fax: (212)633-1974

Davidson, Joan, President
Alliance of Supplier Diversity Professionals [2815]
PO Box 782049
Orlando, FL 32878-2049
Toll Free: 877-405-6565

Davidson, June, Contact
American Seminar Leaders Association [7667]
2405 E Washington Blvd.
Pasadena, CA 91104-2040
Ph: (626)791-1211
Toll Free: 800-801-1886
Fax: (626)791-0701

Davidson, Linda, Exec. Dir., Founder
Our Military Kids [12349]
6861 Elm St., Ste. 2A
McLean, VA 22101
Ph: (703)734-6654
Toll Free: 866-691-6654
Fax: (703)734-6503

Davidson, Peggy, Exec. Dir.
Pilot International Founders Fund [12904]
102 Preston Ct.
Macon, GA 31210-5768
Ph: (478)477-1208
Fax: (478)477-6978

Davidson, Rev. Ronald T., COO, Founder, President
Gleaning for the World [12663]
7539 Stage Rd.

Concord, VA 24538-3590
Ph: (434)993-3600
Toll Free: 877-913-9212
Fax: (434)993-2300

Davidson, Russell A., President
American Institute of Architects
[5953]
1735 New York Ave. NW
Washington, DC 20006
Toll Free: 800-AIA-3837
Fax: (202)626-7547

Davidson, Wendy, President
Pinto Horse Association of America
Inc. [4401]
7330 NW 23rd St.
Bethany, OK 73008
Ph: (405)491-0111
Fax: (405)787-0773

Davidson, Wendy, President
Women's Foodservice Forum [1399]
6730 LBJ Fwy., Bldg. B
Dallas, TX 75240
Ph: (972)770-9100
Fax: (972)770-9150

Davies, Jude, President
International Theodore Dreiser
Society [9059]
c/o Roark Mulligan, Secretary-
Treasurer
Christopher Newport University
Dept. of English
1 Avenue of the Arts
Newport News, VA 23606

Davies, Marcia, COO
Mortgage Bankers Association [405]
1919 M St. NW, 5th Fl.
Washington, DC 20036
Ph: (202)557-2700
Toll Free: 800-793-6222

Davies, Mark, Chairman
Global Integrity [916]
1110 Vermont Ave. NW, Ste. 500
Washington, DC 20005
Ph: (202)449-4100
Fax: (202)888-3172

Davies, Marshall, PhD, Exec. Dir.
Public Risk Management Association
[5320]
700 S Washington St., Ste. 218
Alexandria, VA 22314
Ph: (703)528-7701
Fax: (703)739-0200

Davies, Moses, President
Rebuild A Nation [10731]
866 E 175th St., Ste. 1
Bronx, NY 10460
Ph: (718)207-7142

Davies, Rae, Dir. of Admin.
International MotherBaby Childbirth
Organization [14234]
PO Box 2346
Ponte Vedra Beach, FL 32004
Ph: (904)285-0028

Davies, Rrivre, VP
Wedding Industry Professionals As-
sociation [448]
8711 E Pinnacle Peak Rd., No. 227
Scottsdale, AZ 85255
Ph: (844)444-9300
Fax: (480)513-3207

Davies, Sandi, Exec. Dir.
International Foundation for Protec-
tion Officers [3059]
1250 Tamiami Trl. N, Ste. 206
Naples, FL 34102
Ph: (239)430-0534
Fax: (239)430-0533

Davis, Alan, Chairman
National Council on Child Abuse and
Family Violence [11707]
1025 Connecticut Ave. NW, Ste.
1000
Washington, DC 20036
Ph: (202)429-6695
Fax: (202)521-3479

Davis, Annette, President
National Association for Holistic
Aromatherapy [15269]
PO Box 27871
Raleigh, NC 27611-7871
Ph: (919)894-0298
Fax: (919)894-0271

Davis, Avi, Exec. Dir.
American Freedom Alliance [19023]
11500 W Olympic Blvd., Ste. 400
Los Angeles, CA 90064
Ph: (310)444-3085
Fax: (310)444-3086

Davis, Bill, VP
InfraGard National Members Alliance
[5754]

Davis, Bob, Founder
Heart Bandits American Eskimo Dog
Rescue [10634]
PO Box 4322
Fresno, CA 93744-4322
Ph: (559)787-2459

Davis, Brenda, Treasurer
National Alliance for Medication As-
sisted Recovery [17320]
435 2nd Ave.
New York, NY 10010-3101
Ph: (212)595-6262
Fax: (212)595-6262

Davis, Bruce, Treasurer
American Association for Paralegal
Education [8206]
222 S Westmonte Dr., Ste. 101
Altamonte Springs, FL 32714
Ph: (407)774-7880
Fax: (407)774-6440

Davis, Bruce, Exec. Dir.
National Association of Orthopaedic
Technologists [15693]
8365 Keystone Crossing, Ste. 107
Indianapolis, IN 46240
Ph: (317)205-9484
Fax: (317)205-9481

Davis, Bruce, Assistant Vice
President
New York Stock Exchange Inc.
[3048]
11 Wall St.
New York, NY 10005-1905
Ph: (212)656-3000

Davis, Bruce, Exec. Dir.
The Noah Worcester Dermatological
Society [14509]
8365 Keystone Crossing, Ste. 107
Indianapolis, IN 46240
Ph: (317)257-5907
Fax: (317)205-9481

Davis, Chester, Jr., President, CEO
Generic Pharmaceutical Association
[2558]
777 6th St. NW, Ste. 510
Washington, DC 20001-4498
Ph: (202)249-7100
Fax: (202)249-7105

Davis, Chris, Exec. Dir., Founder
Home School Sports Network
[23226]
153 Old Linden Rd.
Linden, VA 22642
Ph: (540)631-5683
(540)636-3713

Davis, Christopher, Comm. Chm.
National Shellfisheries Association
[6788]
c/o Karolyn Mueller Hansen,
President
300 College Park Ave.
Dayton, OH 45469-0001
Ph: (937)229-2141
Fax: (937)229-2021

Davis, Daniel R., Exec. Dir.
International Association for World
Englishes Inc. [9283]
c/o Aya Matsuda, Secretary/
Treasurer
Arizona State University
Tempe, AZ 85280

Davis, David D., Jr., Director
Friends Outside [11527]
7272 Murray Dr.
Stockton, CA 95210-3339
Ph: (209)955-0701
Fax: (209)955-0735

Davis, Denyvetta, President
Black Caucus of the American
Library Association [9695]
c/o Denyvetta Davis, President
PO Box 13367
Oklahoma City, OK 73113

Davis, Don, Sr. VP, Director
World Impact [20478]
2001 S Vermont Ave.
Los Angeles, CA 90007
Ph: (323)735-1137
Fax: (323)735-2576

Davis, Donald, Dir. of Dev.
BethanyKids [17382]
PO Box 1297
Abingdon, VA 24212-1297
Toll Free: 800-469-1512

Davis, Floyd, Treasurer
Travelers Aid International [13091]
5000 Sunnyside Ave., Ste. 103
Beltsville, MD 20705-2327
Ph: (202)546-1127

Davis, Frank, VP of Public Affairs
Ecological Society of America [4000]
1990 M St. NW, Ste. 700
Washington, DC 20036
Ph: (202)833-8773
Fax: (202)833-8775

Davis, Frank, President
Spastic Paraplegia Foundation
[15992]
7700 Leesburg Pike, Ste. 123
Falls Church, VA 22043
Toll Free: 877-773-4483

Davis, Garry, Coord., Founder
World Service Authority [18884]
5 Thomas Cir. NW
Washington, DC 20005-4104
Ph: (202)638-2662
Fax: (202)638-0638

Davis, Gary, President, CEO
National Center for American Indian
Enterprise Development [12378]
953 E Juanita Ave.
Mesa, AZ 85204
Ph: (480)545-1298
Fax: (480)545-4208

Davis, Glen, VP
International Functional Electrical
Stimulation Society [16019]
1854 Los Encinos Ave.
Glendale, CA 91208-2240

Davis, Gregory E., President
Superstition Mountain Historical
Society [8804]

4087 N Apache Trl.
Apache Junction, AZ 85119
Ph: (480)983-4888

Davis, Gregory W., Contact
National Tree Society [4088]
PO Box 10808
Bakersfield, CA 93389
Ph: (805)589-6912

Davis, Heather, Office Mgr.,
Secretary
National Society of the Sons of Utah
Pioneers [21085]
3301 E Louise Ave.
Salt Lake City, UT 84109
Ph: (801)484-4441
Toll Free: 866-724-1847
Fax: (801)484-2067

Davis, J. Madison, President
International Association of Crime
Writers - North American Branch
[10377]
243 5th Ave., No. 537
New York, NY 10016

Davis, Janet L., MD, Membership
Chp.
American Uveitis Society [16371]
700 18th St. S, Ste. 601
Birmingham, AL 35233
Ph: (205)325-8507
Fax: (205)325-8200

Davis, Jeff, Chairman
Contractors Pump Bureau [1721]
c/o Juan Quiros
Multiquip Inc.
18910 Wilmington Ave.
Carson, CA 90746
Ph: (414)272-0943
Fax: (414)272-1170

Davis, Jeremy, President
Acacia Fraternity [23878]
8777 Purdue Rd., Ste. 225
Indianapolis, IN 46268
Ph: (317)872-8210
Fax: (317)872-8213

Davis, Jim, President
Fostoria Glass Society of America
[22133]
511 Tomlinson Ave.
Moundsville, WV 26041
Ph: (304)845-9188

Davis, John, Controller
CoreNet Global [2854]
133 Peachtree St. NE, Ste. 3000
Atlanta, GA 30303-1815
Ph: (404)589-3200
Toll Free: 800-726-8111
Fax: (404)589-3201

Davis, Jon, Bd. Member
International Dairy Foods Associa-
tion [975]
1250 H St. NW, Ste. 900
Washington, DC 20005
Ph: (202)737-4332
Fax: (202)331-7820

Davis, Joslin, President
American Academy of Matrimonial
Lawyers [5187]
150 N Michigan Ave., Ste. 1420
Chicago, IL 60601
Ph: (312)263-6477
Fax: (312)263-7682

Davis, Karen, CPhT, President
Society for the Education of
Pharmacy Technicians [16687]
PO Box 1176
Lyons, GA 30436
Toll Free: 800-811-7214
Fax: (800)811-7214

Davis, Karen, PhD, President
United Poultry Concerns **[10708]**
PO Box 150
Machipongo, VA 23405
Ph: (757)678-7875
Fax: (757)678-5070

Davis, Kathie, Exec. Dir.
IDEA Health and Fitness Association
[16701]
10190 Telesis Ct.
San Diego, CA 92121
Ph: (858)535-8979
Toll Free: 800-999-4332
Fax: (858)535-8234

Davis, Kenneth, President, CEO
International Center for Fabry
Disease **[17343]**
c/o Dana Doheny
One Gustave L. Levy Pl.
Mt. Sinai School of Medicine
New York, NY 10029-6574
Ph: (212)241-6500
(212)241-6696

Davis, Mr. Kenneth, Director
Society of Environmental
Understanding and Sustainability
[4764]
716 Kent Rd.
Kenilworth, IL 60043
Ph: (847)251-2079

Davis, LaRonda, President
Black Rock Coalition **[9285]**
PO Box 1054
New York, NY 10276

Davis, LeCount R., Chairman,
Founder
Association of African American
Financial Advisors **[1273]**
PO Box 4853
Capitol Heights, MD 20791
Ph: (240)396-2530
Toll Free: 888-392-5702

Davis, Mark, Coord.
North American Meteor Network
[6859]
101 Margate Cir.
Goose Creek, SC 29445

Davis, Mark S., Director
Inner Circle of Advocates **[5560]**
c/o Richard H. Friedman, Director
1126 Highland Ave.
Bremerton, WA 98337
Ph: (360)782-4300

Davis, Dr. Mark, President, Founder
Unicode Consortium **[19154]**
PO Box 391476
Mountain View, CA 94039-1476
Ph: (650)693-2793
Fax: (650)693-3010

Davis, Mary, VP
American Legion Auxiliary **[21037]**
8945 N Meridian St., Ste. 200
Indianapolis, IN 46260
Ph: (317)569-4500
Fax: (317)569-4502

Davis, Mary Ellen K., Exec. Dir.
Association of College and Research
Libraries **[9684]**
50 E Huron St.
Chicago, IL 60611
Ph: (312)280-2523
Toll Free: 800-545-2433
Fax: (312)280-2520

Davis, Michael Cory, Founder
Artists United for Social Justice
[19125]
5042 Wilshire Blvd., No.131

Los Angeles, CA 90036

Davis, Michael, VP
The Retired Enlisted Association
[21139]
1111 S Abilene Ct.
Aurora, CO 80012
Ph: (303)752-0660
Toll Free: 800-338-9337
Fax: (303)752-0835

Davis, Mikell, President
Fullblood Simmental Fleckvieh
Federation **[3726]**
PO Box 321
Cisco, TX 76437
Toll Free: 855-353-2584
Fax: (855)638-2582

Davis, Patricia Libbey, President
John Libby Family Association
[20893]
c/o Pat Libbey Davis, President
195 Deacon Haynes Rd.
Concord, MA 01742
Ph: (978)369-6250

Davis, Paul, Treasurer
Historical Writers of America **[10375]**
PO Box 4238
Middletown, RI 02842
Ph: (401)847-6832
Fax: (401)537-9159

Davis, Paula, Exec. Dir.
IdeasAmerica **[1091]**
PO Box 210863
Auburn Hills, MI 48321
Ph: (248)961-2674
Fax: (248)253-9252

Davis, Pauline, Div. Mgr.
The National Bowling Association
[22705]
9944 Reading Rd.
Cincinnati, OH 45241
Ph: (513)769-1985
Fax: (513)769-3596

Davis, R. Daniel, President
American Podiatric Medical Associa-
tion **[16783]**
9312 Old Georgetown Rd.
Bethesda, MD 20814-1621
Ph: (301)581-9200

Davis, Dr. Richard A., Exec. Sec.
Omega Chi Epsilon **[23738]**
c/o Dr. Douglas K. Ludlow, President
Chemical & Biological Engineering
Dept.
Missouri University of Science and
Technology
132 Schrenk Hall
Rolla, MO 65409-1230
Ph: (573)341-6477
Fax: (573)341-4377

Davis, Richard, President
Institute of Mathematical Statistics
[7242]
PO Box 22718
Beachwood, OH 44122
Ph: (216)295-2340
Toll Free: 877-557-4674
Fax: (216)295-5661

Davis, Rick, Director
Darkride and Funhouse Enthusiasts
[21276]
PO Box 484
Vienna, OH 44473-0484

Davis, Rick, Founder, President
Dream Pursuit **[11226]**
205 Holmes Dr.
Sikeston, MO 63801
Ph: (573)421-5580

Davis, Rob, Founder
Hedge Funds Care **[10795]**
330 7th Ave., Ste. 2B
New York, NY 10001
Ph: (212)991-9600
Fax: (646)214-1079

Davis, Robin C., RN, Officer
Global Health Action **[15453]**
1190 W Druid Hills, Ste. 145
Atlanta, GA 30329
Ph: (404)634-5748
Fax: (404)634-9685

Davis, Rocco, Chairman
National Alliance for Fair Contracting
[23400]
905 16th St. NW
Washington, DC 20006-1703
Toll Free: 866-523-6232
Fax: (202)942-2228

Davis, Sara L.M., PhD, Founder, Bd.
Member
Asia Catalyst **[12389]**
1270 Broadway, Suite 1109
New York, NY 10001
Ph: (212)967-2123

Davis, Sara McCormick, President
National Association of Early Childhood Teacher Educators **[8652]**
3017 Tilton St.
Philadelphia, PA 19134

Davis, Stephanie S., Treasurer
Association of PeriOperative
Registered Nurses **[16123]**
2170 S Parker Rd., Ste. 400
Denver, CO 80231
Ph: (303)755-6300
Toll Free: 800-755-2676
Fax: (800)847-0045

Davis, Stephen, Chairman
Global Market Development Center
[3470]
1275 Lake Plaza Dr.
Colorado Springs, CO 80906
Ph: (719)576-4260
Fax: (719)576-2661

Davis, Terry, CEO, President
American Association for State and
Local History **[9451]**
1717 Church St.
Nashville, TN 37203-2991
Ph: (615)320-3203
Fax: (615)327-9013

Davis, Timothy S., President, CEO
Close Up Foundation **[17855]**
1330 Braddock Pl., Ste. 400
Alexandria, VA 22314
Ph: (703)706-3300
Toll Free: 800-CLOSE UP

Davis, Tinsley, Exec. Dir.
National Association of Science Writ-
ers **[2698]**
PO Box 7905
Berkeley, CA 94707
Ph: (510)647-9500

Davis, Wendy, PhD, Exec. Dir.
Postpartum Support International
[12425]
6706 SW 54th Ave.
Portland, OR 97219
Ph: (503)894-9453
Toll Free: 800-944-4773
Fax: (503)894-9452

Davis, Will, President
MAES: Latinos in Science and
Engineering **[6569]**
2437 Bay Area Blvd., No. 100
Houston, TX 77058
Ph: (281)557-3677
Fax: (281)715-5100

Davis, Will, President
Society of Mexican American
Engineers and Scientists **[6593]**
2437 Bay Area Blvd., No. 100
Houston, TX 77058
Ph: (281)557-3677
Fax: (281)715-5100

Davison, Dawn M., Treasurer
Just Detention International **[11534]**
3325 Wilshire Blvd., Ste. 340
Los Angeles, CA 90010
Ph: (213)384-1400
Fax: (213)384-1411

Davison, Susan Jean, Treasurer
National Fenton Glass Society
[22140]
PO Box 4008
Marietta, OH 45750
Ph: (740)374-3345
Fax: (740)374-3345

Davison, William M., Treasurer
Athenaeum of Philadelphia **[9693]**
219 S 6th St.
Philadelphia, PA 19106-3794
Ph: (215)925-2688
Fax: (215)925-3755

Davisson, Donna, Exec. Dir.
NASBITE International **[7555]**
c/o Donna Davisson, Executive
Director
Monte Ahuja College of Business
1860 E 18th St., BU327
Cleveland, OH 44115
Ph: (216)802-3381

Davoodpour, Shiva, VP
Children of Persia **[10922]**
PO Box 2602
Montgomery Village, MD 20886
Ph: (301)315-0750

Daw, Paul, Treasurer
American Literary Translators As-
sociation **[8713]**
900 E 7th St
Bloomington, IN 47405-3201
Ph: (415)735-4546

Dawes, Robert V., President
Clan Moncreiffe Society **[20833]**
1405 Plaza St. SE
Decatur, AL 35603-1521

Dawkins, Brig. Gen. Peter, Chairman
American-Kuwaiti Alliance **[1978]**
2550 M St. NW
Washington, DC 20037
Ph: (202)429-4999

Dawley, Jeff, Secretary
North American One-Armed Golfer
Association **[22793]**
8406 Cloverport Dr.
Louisville, KY 40228
Ph: (502)964-7734

Dawood, Nazeera, President
South Asian Public Health Association **[17023]**
9408 Holbrook Ln.
Potomac, MD 20854

Dawson, Deb, President
African Soul, American Heart
[10839]
300 NP Ave., Ste. 308
Fargo, ND 58102
Ph: (701)478-7800

Dawson, Eric, President
Peace First **[12440]**
25 Kingston St., 6th Fl.
Boston, MA 02111
Ph: (617)261-3833

Dawson, Jan, President
American Association for Horseman-
ship Safety **[22954]**
4125 Fish Creek Rd.
Estes Park, CO 80517
Toll Free: 866-485-6800

Dawson, John D., President
Clan Davidson Society **[20806]**
235 Fairmont Dr.
North Wilkesboro, NC 28659-9050

Dawson, Stephanie A., President
National Association of Black Military
Women **[21028]**
5695 Pine Meadows Ct.
Morrow, GA 30260-1053
Ph: (404)675-0195

Dawson, Steve, MD, Chairman
Advanced Initiatives in Medical
Simulation **[15672]**
1500 K St. NW, Ste. 1100
Washington, DC 20005-3317
Ph: (202)230-5091
Fax: (202)842-8465

Dawson Taggart, Amy, Director
Mission: Readiness **[5756]**
1212 New York Ave. NW, Ste. 300
Washington, DC 20005
Ph: (202)464-5224
Fax: (202)464-5357

Dawson, Tom, President
52 Plus Joker **[21604]**
12290 W 18th Dr.
Lakewood, CO 80215

Dawson, Victoria A., Librarian
Ford Foundation **[18943]**
320 E 43rd St.
New York, NY 10017-4801
Ph: (212)573-5000
Fax: (212)351-3677

Day, Alfred T., III, Gen. Sec.
General Commission on Archives
and History of the United Method-
ist Church **[20343]**
36 Madison Ave.
Madison, NJ 07940
Ph: (973)408-3189
Fax: (973)408-3909

Day, Frankie, President
Alpha Psi Omega **[23723]**
1601 E Market St.
North Carolina A&T University
1601 E Market St.
Greensboro, NC 27411-0002

Day, Jeanelle, Treasurer
Council for Elementary Science
International **[8544]**
c/o James T. McDonald, President
EHS 134C
Department of Teacher Education
Central Michigan University
Mount Pleasant, MI 48859

Day, Jeffrey D., Chairperson
American Association of Drilling
Engineers **[6997]**
PO Box 107
Houston, TX 77001
Ph: (281)293-9800
Fax: (281)293-9800

Day, Kristen, Exec. Dir.
Democrats for Life of America
[19057]
10521 Judicial Dr., Unit 200
Fairfax, VA 22030
Ph: (703)424-6663

Day, Maurine, Exec. Dir.
Government Investment Officers Association **[5373]**

10655 Park Run Dr., Ste. 120
Las Vegas, NV 89144
Ph: (702)489-8993
Fax: (702)575-6670

Day, Robert A., Chairman
W.M. Keck Foundation **[15650]**
550 S Hope St., Ste. 2500
Los Angeles, CA 90071
Ph: (213)680-3833

Day, Robert, Contact
Cyclone Montego Torino Registry
[21366]
19 Glyn Dr.
Newark, DE 19713-4016
Ph: (302)737-4252

Day, Robert D., Exec. Dir.
Renewable Natural Resources
Foundation **[3931]**
3010 Executive Blvd., 5th Fl.
Rockville, MD 20852-3827
Ph: (301)493-9101
Fax: (301)770-9104

Day, Terry, Contact
American Head and Neck Society
[16533]
11300 W Olympic Blvd., Ste. 600
Los Angeles, CA 90064
Ph: (310)437-0559
Fax: (310)437-0585

Daye, Sheri, President
International Underwater Spearfishing Association **[22847]**
2515 NW 29th Dr.
Boca Raton, FL 33434

de Alabona-Ostrogojsk, William,
Master
Order of the Noble Companions of
the Swan **[9336]**
PO Box 404
Milltown, NJ 08850

de Bernardo, Mark A., Exec. Dir.
Institute for a Drug-Free Workplace
[13144]
10701 Parkridge Blvd., Ste. 300
Reston, VA 20191
Ph: (703)391-7222
Fax: (703)391-7223

De Bruyne, Leila, Founder, Exec.
Dir.
Flying Kites **[10978]**
51 Melcher St.
Boston, MA 02210
Ph: (401)575-0009

De Cesaris, Robert, President
The Oughtred Society **[21708]**
9 Stephens Ct.
Roseville, CA 95678

de Ferranti, David, President
Center on Budget and Policy Priori-
ties **[18953]**
820 1st St. NE, Ste. 510
Washington, DC 20002
Ph: (202)408-1080
Fax: (202)408-1056

De Funiak, David, Exec. Dir.
Tree House Humane Society
[10703]
1212 W Carmen Ave.
Chicago, IL 60640
Ph: (773)784-5488
Fax: (773)784-2332

De Guise, Sylvain, President
Sea Grant Association **[6807]**
703 E Beach Dr.
Ocean Springs, MS 39564
Ph: (228)818-8842

de Habsburgo-Lorena, Immaculada,
President, CEO
Queen Sofia Spanish Institute
[10220]
684 Park Ave.
New York, NY 10065
Ph: (212)628-0420
Fax: (212)734-4177

De Kuany, Michael Ayuen,
President, CEO
Rebuild Sudan **[13084]**
2820 22nd St.
San Francisco, CA 94110
Ph: (415)226-9879

De La Cruz, Jennifer, Treasurer
National Association of Judiciary
Interpreters and Translators **[5119]**
2002 Summit Blvd., Ste. 300
Atlanta, GA 30319
Ph: (404)566-4705
Fax: (404)566-2301

De La Garza, Mary, Officer
National Association of State
Archaeologists **[5943]**
University of Iowa
Office of the State Archaeologist
700 S Clinton St.
Iowa City, IA 52242-1030
Ph: (319)384-0732
Fax: (319)384-0768

de Laforcade, Dr. Armelle, DVM,
Exec. Sec.
American College of Veterinary
Emergency and Critical Care
[17617]
Tufts Cummings School of
Veterinary Medicine
200 Westboro Rd.
North Grafton, MA 01536
Ph: (508)839-5395
Fax: (508)887-4634

De Leon, Maria Lopez, Exec. Dir.
National Association of Latino Arts
and Culture **[8989]**
1208 Buena Vista St.
San Antonio, TX 78207
Ph: (210)432-3982
Fax: (210)432-3934

De Lima, Liliana, MHA, Exec. Dir.
International Association for Hospice
and Palliative Care **[15279]**
5535 Memorial Dr., Ste. F, PMB 509
Houston, TX 77007
Ph: (936)321-9846
Toll Free: 866-374-2472
Fax: (713)589-3657

De Lucca, Donald W., VP
International Association of Chiefs of
Police **[5468]**
44 Canal Center Plz., Ste. 200
Alexandria, VA 22314
Ph: (703)836-6767

De Maio, Stephen, President
Gerda Lissner Foundation **[9950]**
15 E 65th St., 4th Fl.
New York, NY 10065-6501
Ph: (212)826-6100
Fax: (212)826-0366

De Meij, Annie, Founder
Aid to Orphans of Madagascar
[10842]
13670 Lone Bear Rd.
Bozeman, MT 59715

De Michiel, Helen, Director
National Alliance for Media Arts and
Culture **[8986]**
145 9th St., Ste. 230
San Francisco, CA 94103
Ph: (510)336-2555

de Moor, Tine, President
International Association for the
Study of the Commons **[3886]**
513 N Park Ave.
Bloomington, IN 47408-3895
Ph: (317)608-3067

De Peppo, Vin, Membership Chp.
1953-54 Buick Skylark Club **[21309]**
c/o Gary Di Lillo, Newsletter Editor
27315 Hemlock Dr.
Westlake, OH 44145
Fax: (440)871-5484

de Raad, Lydia, Co-Chmn. of the
Bd.
La Leche League International
[11249]
35 E Wacker Dr., Ste. 850
Chicago, IL 60601
Ph: (312)646-6260
Toll Free: 800-525-3243
Fax: (312)644-8557

de Roucy, Fr. Thierry, Founder
Heart's Home USA **[20366]**
108 St. Edwards St.
Brooklyn, NY 11205
Ph: (718)522-2121

De Rozario, Fabian, President, CEO
National Association of Asian
American Professionals **[9029]**
4850 Sugarloaf Pky., Ste. 209-289
Lawrenceville, GA 30044
Ph: (404)409-2471

de Santos, Rob, Chairman
Australian Football Association of
North America **[22856]**
PO Box 27623
Columbus, OH 43227-0623
Ph: (614)571-8986
Fax: (866)334-9884

De Schutter, Dr. Erik, President
Organization for Computational
Neurosciences **[6919]**
2885 Sanford Ave. SW, No. 15359
Grandville, MI 49418

De Serrano, Jodi, Founder,
President
Alport Syndrome Hope for the Cure
Foundation **[14806]**
2560 King Arthur Blvd., Ste. 124-76
Lewisville, TX 75056
Ph: (469)951-6533

De Toledo, Sylvie, MSW, LCSW,
BCD, Founder
Grandparents as Parents **[11917]**
22048 Sherman Way, Ste. 217
Canoga Park, CA 91303
Ph: (818)264-0880
Fax: (818)264-0882

de la Vega, Connie, Director
Human Rights Advocates **[12040]**
PO Box 5675
Berkeley, CA 94705

De Vet, Chuck, President
Humanitarian Services for Children
of Vietnam **[11042]**
2965 Spring Lake Rd. SW
Prior Lake, MN 55372
Ph: (952)447-3502
Fax: (952)447-3573

De Vlieger, Michael, Director
Dozenal Society of America **[7230]**
5106 Hampton Ave., Ste. 205
Saint Louis, MO 63109-3115

de Vogel, Willem, Chairman
Jamestown Foundation **[18140]**
1111 16th St. NW, Ste. 320

Washington, DC 20036
Ph: (202)483-8888
Fax: (202)483-8337

De Vries, Geert J., Contact
Organization for the Study of Sex
Differences [17201]
c/o Dr. Arbi Nazarian, Treasurer
College of Pharmacy
Western University of Health Sciences
309 E 2nd St.
Pomona, CA 91766-1854

de Vries, Lt. Col. Sherry, USMCR,
President
Alliance for National Defense [5848]
PO Box 184
Alexandria, VA 22313
Ph: (703)445-4263

De Vries, Yvette, President
Association for the Promotion of
Tourism to Africa [3289]
Norwalk, CT
Ph: (203)858-0444

de Waal, Alex, Exec. Dir.
World Peace Foundation [18567]
Tufts University
169 Holland St., Ste. 209
Somerville, MA 02144
Ph: (617)627-2255
Fax: (617)627-3712

de Wardt, Susan, Treasurer,
Secretary, Comm. Chm.
International Federation for Biblio/
Poetry Therapy [16977]
1625 Mid Valley Dr., No. 1, Ste. 126
Steamboat Springs, CO 80487

Deakin, Spencer, Contact
Coalition of Higher Education Associations for Substance Abuse
Prevention [13131]
c/o Spencer Deakin
Frostburg State University
101 Braddock Rd.
111 Sandspring Hall
Frostburg, MD 21532-1099
Ph: (301)687-4234

Deal, Evelyn, President
Jana Jae Fan Club [24048]
PO Box 35726
Tulsa, OK 74153
Ph: (918)786-8896

Deal, Jennifer J., Scientist
Center for Creative Leadership
[2159]
1 Leadership Pl.
Greensboro, NC 27410-9427
Ph: (336)288-7210
     (336)545-2810
Fax: (336)282-3284

Dean, Arthur T., Chairman, CEO
Community Anti-Drug Coalitions of
America [13133]
625 Slaters Ln., Ste. 300
Alexandria, VA 22314
Toll Free: 800-54-CADCA
Fax: (703)706-0565

Dean, Don, President
American Hosta Society [22076]
PO Box 7539
Kill Devil Hills, NC 27948-7539

Dean, Eric, Gen., President
International Association of Bridge,
Structural, Ornamental and
Reinforcing Iron Workers [23480]
1750 New York Ave. NW, Ste. 400
Washington, DC 20006
Ph: (202)383-4800
Fax: (202)638-4856

Dean, Eric, Chairman
Pharmaceutical Industry Labor-
Management Association [2568]
101 N Union St., No. 305
Alexandria, VA 22314
Ph: (703)548-4721

Dean, Frank, President, CEO
Yosemite Conservancy [6903]
PO Box 230
El Portal, CA 95318-0230
Ph: (209)379-2317
Fax: (209)379-2486

Dean, Jim, Chairman
Democracy for America [18865]
PO Box 1717
Burlington, VT 05402
Ph: (802)651-3200
Fax: (802)651-3299

Dean, Amb. (Ret.) Jonathan,
President
Institute for Defense and Disarmament Studies [18128]
675 Massachusetts Ave.
Cambridge, MA 02139
Ph: (617)354-4337
Fax: (617)354-1450

Dean, Stephen O., President
Fusion Power Associates [6486]
2 Professional Dr., Ste. 249
Gaithersburg, MD 20879
Ph: (301)258-0545
Fax: (301)975-9869

Deane, Gordon, President
National Organization of Legal
Services Workers [23436]
256 W 38th St., Ste. 705
New York, NY 10018
Ph: (212)228-0992
Fax: (212)228-0097

DeAngelis, Dominick, Chairperson
Ultrasonic Industry Association
[3032]
11 W Monument Ave., Ste. 510
Dayton, OH 45402
Ph: (937)586-3725
Fax: (937)586-3699

Dear, Stephen, Exec. Dir.
People of Faith Against the Death
Penalty [17832]
PO Box 61943
Durham, NC 27701
Ph: (919)933-7567

Dearing, Bill, President
North American Laminate Flooring
Association [569]
1747 Pennsylvania Ave. NW, Ste.
1000
Washington, DC 20006-4636
Ph: (202)785-9500
Fax: (202)835-0243

Deas, Thomas C., Sr., Chairman
National Association of Corporate
Treasurers [1252]
12100 Sunset Hills Rd., Ste. 130
Reston, VA 20190-3221
Ph: (703)437-4377
Fax: (703)435-4390

D'Eath, Michael, President
Society for the Preservation and
Advancement of the Harmonica
[10010]
PO Box 551381
Dallas, TX 75355-1381

Deats, Edward, Secretary, Treasurer
USS Nimitz (CVN-68) Association
[21071]
c/o Ed Deats, Secretary-Treasurer

8324 Triad Cir.
Sacramento, CA 95828-6642
Ph: (630)575-7572

Deaver, John, MD, President, Director
Siempre Salud [11436]
9839 Crest Meadow Dr.
Dallas, TX 75230
Ph: (214)363-0362

Debatin, Gloria, Contact
Mu Phi Epsilon International [23829]
PO Box 1369
Fort Collins, CO 80522-1369
Toll Free: 888-259-1471

DeBernardis, Richard, Secretary,
Director
Blue Marble Institute [23219]
3481 E Michigan St.
Tucson, AZ 85714-2221
Ph: (520)382-4847

Debnath, Dr. Narayan, Contact
International Society for Computers
and their Applications [6319]
64 White Oak Ct.
Winona, MN 55987
Ph: (507)458-4517

DeBoer, Kathy, Exec. Dir.
American Volleyball Coaches Association [23349]
2365 Harrodsburg Rd., Ste. A325
Lexington, KY 40504
Toll Free: 866-544-2822

DeBroff, Dr. Brian M., President
Distressed Children and Infants
International [10956]
195 S Main St.
Cheshire, CT 06410
Ph: (203)272-3869
Toll Free: 866-516-7495
Fax: (203)272-3869

DeBruin, Debra, PhD, Director
University of Minnesota Center for
Bioethics [6065]
N504 Boynton Health Ctr.
410 Church St. SE
Minneapolis, MN 55455
Ph: (612)624-9440
Fax: (612)624-9108

DeCaprio, Bob, Exec. Dir.
Customized Logistics and Delivery
Association [3083]
750 National Press Bldg.
529 14th St. NW
Washington, DC 20045
Ph: (202)591-2460
Fax: (202)591-2445

DeCarlo, John, Jr., President
National Pigeon Association [21546]
C/o Lennie Mefferd, Secretary
17128 Colima Dr., Unit 603
Hacienda Heights, CA 91745
Ph: (626)820-8080

Decatur, Sean, Treasurer
Association of American Colleges
and Universities [7621]
1818 R St. NW
Washington, DC 20009
Ph: (202)387-3760

Dechant, Bobbie, Officer
National High School Rodeo Association [23099]
12011 Tejon St., Ste. 900
Denver, CO 80234
Ph: (303)452-0820
Toll Free: 800-466-4772
Fax: (303)452-0912

Dechert, Alan, CEO, President
Open Voting Consortium [18186]
4941 Forest Creek Way

Granite Bay, CA 95746
Ph: (916)209-6620

Decker, J. Edward, Founder
Saints Alive in Jesus [20161]
PO Box 1347
Issaquah, WA 98027
Toll Free: 800-861-9888

Decker, Penny, Advisor
Creative Floral Arrangers of the
Americas [1307]
PO Box 237
Mims, FL 32754-0237

DeCook, Joseph, Mem.
American Association of Pro Life
Obstetricians and Gynecologists
[19054]
PO Box 395
Eau Claire, MI 49111-0395
Ph: (202)230-0997

DeCoster, Tim, Chief of Staff
United States Department of
Agriculture - Forest Service
Volunteers Program [4222]
1400 Independence Ave. SW
Washington, DC 20250-1111
Toll Free: 800-832-1355

Decrappeo, Tony, President
Council on Governmental Relations
[8498]
1200 New York Ave. NW, Ste. 460
Washington, DC 20005
Ph: (202)289-6655
Fax: (202)289-6698

Decuire, Yasmin K., Treasurer
International Expressive Arts
Therapy Association [13730]
PO Box 40707
San Francisco, CA 94110-9991
Ph: (415)522-8959

DeDecker, Todd, Administrator
Bishop Hill Heritage Association
[20959]
103 Bishop Hill St.
Bishop Hill, IL 61419-0092
Ph: (309)927-3899

DeDonatis, Don, Chairman, CEO,
Exec. Dir.
United States Specialty Sports Association [23261]
611 Line Dr.
Kissimmee, FL 34744
Toll Free: 800-741-3014

Dee, Beverlee, Exec. Dir.
Bright Futures Farm [4340]
238 Old Franklin Pke.
Cochranton, PA 16314
Ph: (724)496-4960

Deeds, Dr. Jan, Dir. of Comm.
American Men's Studies Association
[11995]
1080 S University Ave.
Ann Arbor, MI 48109-1106
Ph: (470)333-AMSA

Deegan-Krause, Dr. Kevin, President
Slovak Studies Association [19650]
c/o Kevin Deegan-Krause, President
Dept. of Political Science
Wayne Station University
2040 F/AB
Detroit, MI 48220
Ph: (313)577-2630
Fax: (313)993-3435

Deeley, Martin, Exec. Dir.
International Association of Canine
Professionals [3986]
PO Box 928

Lampasas, TX 76550
Ph: (512)564-1011
Fax: (512)556-4220

Deems, Joe, Exec. Dir.
National Risk Retention Association
[1909]
16133 Ventura Blvd., Ste. 1055
Encino, CA 91436
Ph: (818)995-3274
Toll Free: 800-421-5981
Fax: (818)995-6496

Deery, Gordon, Director
Holy Face Association [19842]
PO Box 821
Champlain, NY 12919-0821
Ph: (518)320-8570

DeFatta, Jerry, Exec. Dir.
University of Southern Mississippi
Alumni Association [19366]
118 College Dr., No. 5013
Hattiesburg, MS 39406-0001
Ph: (601)266-5013
Fax: (601)266-4214

DeFelice, Stephen L., MD, Chair-
man, Founder
Foundation for Innovation in
Medicine [15725]
PO Box 1220
Mountainside, NJ 07092
Ph: (908)233-2448

DeFeo, Nicole L., Exec. Dir.
Delta Phi Epsilon Sorority [23952]
251 S Camac St.
Philadelphia, PA 19107
Ph: (215)732-5901
Fax: (215)732-5906

DeFlorian, Terri, Exec. Dir.
American Physical Therapy Associa-
tion - Orthopaedic Section [17435]
2920 East Ave. S, Ste. 200
La Crosse, WI 54601
Ph: (608)788-3982
Toll Free: 800-444-3982
Fax: (608)788-3965

DeFrance, Charles S., Editor
Association for Crime Scene
Reconstruction [11500]
c/o Amy Jagmin, Membership Chair-
man
Forensic Analytical Sciences, Inc.
2203 Airport Way S, Ste. 250
Seattle, WA 98134
Ph: (206)262-6067

DeFranco, Denise W., President
American Intellectual Property Law
Association [5321]
241 18th St. S, Ste. 700
Arlington, VA 22202
Ph: (703)415-0780
Fax: (703)415-0786

DeFrehn, Randy G., Exec. Dir.
National Coordinating Committee for
Multi-employer Plans [1075]
815 16th St. NW
Washington, DC 20006
Ph: (202)737-5315
Fax: (202)737-1308

DeFries, Diane, Exec. Dir.
American College Dance Association
[9240]
326 N Stonestreet Ave., Ste. 204
Rockville, MD 20850
Ph: (240)428-1736

DeFries, Michael, MBA, Chmn. of
the Bd.
Kids Konnected [11246]
26071 Merit Cir., Ste. 103

Laguna Hills, CA 92653
Ph: (949)582-5443

Degennaro, Louis J., PhD, CEO,
President
Leukemia and Lymphoma Society
[14001]
3 International Dr., Ste. 200
Rye Brook, NY 10573
Ph: (914)949-5213
Fax: (914)949-6691

DeGerome, James, MD, Officer
Digestive Disease National Coalition
[14788]
507 Capitol Ct. NE, Ste. 200
Washington, DC 20002
Ph: (202)544-7497
Fax: (202)546-7105

DeGloria, Stephen D., President
ASPRS, The Imaging and Geospa-
tial Information Society [7018]
5410 Grosvenor Ln., Ste. 210
Bethesda, MD 20814-2160
Ph: (301)493-0290
Fax: (301)493-0208

Degnon, Laura, CAE, Exec. Dir.
Association of Medical School
Pediatric Department Chairs
[16602]
6728 Old McLean Village Dr.
McLean, VA 22101
Ph: (703)556-9222
Fax: (703)556-8729

Degnon, Laura, CAE, Exec. Dir.
Council on Medical Student Educa-
tion in Pediatrics [8320]
c/o Sherilyn Smith, President
4800 Sand Point Way NE
Seattle, WA 98105
Ph: (206)987-2008
Fax: (206)987-2890

Degnon, Laura E., CAE, Exec. Dir.
Association of Pediatric Program
Directors [8310]
6728 Old McLean Village Dr.
McLean, VA 22101
Ph: (703)556-9222
Fax: (703)556-8729

Degnon, Laura, CAE, Exec. Dir.
Society for Developmental and
Behavioral Pediatrics [16618]
6728 Old McLean Village Dr.
McLean, VA 22101
Ph: (703)556-9222
Fax: (703)556-8729

DeGolia, Bill, VP
Alfa Romeo Association [21313]
PO Box 1458
Alameda, CA 94501

DeGolia, Rachel, Exec. Dir.
Universal Health Care Action
Network [15067]
2800 Euclid Ave., No. 520
Cleveland, OH 44115-2418
Ph: (216)241-8422
Toll Free: 800-634-4442
Fax: (216)241-8423

DeGolia, Ruth, Exec. Dir.
Mercado Global [3495]
33 Nassau Ave., Ste. 54
Brooklyn, NY 11222
Ph: (718)838-9908
Fax: (203)772-4493

DeGrazia-DiTucci, Mary-Angela,
Founder, President
Association of Gastrointestinal Motility Disorders, Inc. [14782]
12 Roberts Dr.

Bedford, MA 01730
Ph: (781)275-1300
Fax: (781)275-1304

Degroot, David, Secretary
Bonsai Clubs International [22087]
PO Box 40463
Bay Village, OH 44140-0463

Dehlin, Jill, Chairperson
American Headache and Migraine
Association [14915]
19 Mantua Rd.
Mount Royal, NJ 08061
Ph: (856)423-0043
Fax: (856)423-0082

Dehrmann, Gerard, President
State Government Affairs Council
[18321]
515 King St., Ste. 325
Alexandria, VA 22314
Ph: (703)684-0967

Dei, Randall I., Chairman
Council of Teaching Hospitals
[15323]
15850 Crabbs Branch Way, Ste. 320
Rockville, MD 20855
Ph: (301)948-9764

Deichmann, Dr. Wendy J., President
Center for the Evangelical United
Brethren Heritage [20117]
4501 Denlinger Rd.
Dayton, OH 45426
Ph: (937)529-2201

Deike, Ruth, Exec. Dir., Founder
Rock Detective Geoscience Educa-
tion [7937]
14655 Betz Ln.
Red Bluff, CA 96080
Ph: (530)529-4890
Fax: (530)529-6441

Deitle, John O., 1st VP
Second Marine Division Association
[21020]
PO Box 8180
Camp Lejeune, NC 28547
Ph: (910)451-3176

Deitrick, Scott, Mgr. of Admin.
American Vineyard Foundation
[4924]
PO Box 5779
Napa, CA 94581
Ph: (707)252-6911
Fax: (707)252-7672

DeJong, Cheri Morrell, President
Sigma Kappa Sorority [23964]
695 Pro-Med Ln., Ste. 300
Carmel, IN 46032-5323
Ph: (317)872-3275
Fax: (317)872-0716

DeJong, Tina, President
International Midas Dealers Associa-
tion [346]
400 Admiral Blvd.
Kansas City, MO 64106
Ph: (816)285-0811
Toll Free: 877-543-6203
Fax: (816)472-7765

Dejonge, Katie, Exec. Dir.
Logistics and Transportation As-
sociation of North America [3092]
PO Box 426
Union, WA 98592
Toll Free: 877-858-8627

deJori, Charlene, Founder
NOAH Nature Alliance [4852]
PO Box 6768
San Antonio, TX 78209
Ph: (210)826-0599
Fax: (210)824-3161

Del Castillo, Mercedes, Exec. Dir.
Infant Massage USA [15557]
34760 Center Ridge Rd., No. 39006
North Ridgeville, OH 44039
Toll Free: 800-497-5996
Fax: (440)385-0197

Del Gandio, Frank S., President
International Society of Air Safety
Investigators [12824]
c/o Ann Schull, International Office
Manager
107 E Holly Ave., Ste. 11
Sterling, VA 20164
Ph: (703)430-9668
Fax: (703)430-4970

del Junco, Dr. Tirso, Jr., Founder,
Medical Dir.
Institute for Female Alternative
Medicine [17125]
14860 Roscoe Blvd., Ste. 200
Panorama City, CA 91402
Ph: (818)997-5000
Toll Free: 800-505-4326
Fax: (818)997-5005

Del Mastro, Mark P., Exec. Dir.
Sigma Delta Pi [23979]
c/o Mark P. Del Mastro, Executive
Director
College of Charleston
66 George St.
Charleston, SC 29424-0001
Ph: (843)953-6748
Toll Free: 866-920-7011

Del Polito, Gene A., PhD, President
Association for Postal Commerce
[2117]
1100 Wyne St., Unit 1268
Alexandria, VA 22313
Ph: (703)524-0096
Fax: (703)997-2414

Del Villar, Dr. Carmencita, Bd.
Member
World Communication Association
[7538]
Dept. of Communication and Culture
Indiana University
800 E 3rd St.
Bloomington, IN 47405-3657
Ph: (812)855-0524
Fax: (812)855-6014

DeLaCruz, James T., Sr., V. Chmn.
of the Bd.
National Indian Council on Aging,
Inc. [10524]
10501 Montgomery Blvd. NE, Ste.
210
Albuquerque, NM 87111
Ph: (505)292-2001
Fax: (505)292-1922

DeLancey, Renee, Mgr.
African Studies Association [8776]
Rutgers University Livingston
Campus
54 Joyce Kilmer Ave.
Piscataway, NJ 08854
Ph: (848)445-8173
Fax: (732)445-1366

Delaney, Anne, Chairperson
Rotaplast International [14343]
3317 26th St.
San Francisco, CA 94110
Ph: (415)252-1111
Fax: (415)252-1211

Delaney, Tim, CEO, President
National Council of Nonprofits [257]
1001 G St. NW, Ste. 700E
Washington, DC 20001
Ph: (202)962-0322
Fax: (202)962-0321

Delany, James E., Commissioner
Big Ten Conference **[23217]**
5440 Park Pl.
Rosemont, IL 60018-3732
Ph: (847)696-1010
Fax: (847)696-1150

DeLapp, Greg, CEO
Employee Assistance Professionals
   Association **[13109]**
4350 N Fairfax Dr., Ste. 740
Arlington, VA 22203
Ph: (703)387-1000
Fax: (703)522-4585

DeLauro, Al, Chmn. of the Bd.
Ferrari Club of America **[21380]**
PO Box 2488
Fort Lauderdale, FL 33303-2488
Toll Free: 800-328-0444

Delemar, Natalie, President
Oracle Development Tools User
   Group **[6285]**
2601 Iron Gate Dr., Ste. 101
Wilmington, NC 28412
Ph: (910)452-7444
Toll Free: 855-853-0491
Fax: (910)523-5504

Delener, Dr. Nejdet, Founder,
   President
Global Business and Technology
   Association **[633]**
PO Box 8021
New York, NY 10116
Ph: (631)662-1336
Fax: (215)628-2436

Delgado, Dr. Hector L., Exec. Ofc.
Society for the Study of Social
   Problems **[12992]**
University of Tennessee
901 McClung Twr.
Knoxville, TN 37996-0490
Ph: (865)689-1531
Fax: (865)689-1534

Delgado, Jairo, CEO
World Solutions Against Infectious
   Diseases **[15417]**
PO Box 49042
Jacksonville Beach, FL 32240-9042
Fax: (786)513-5762

Delgado, Dr. Jane L., President,
   CEO
National Alliance for Hispanic Health
   [13072]
1501 16th St. NW
Washington, DC 20036-1401
Ph: (202)387-5000

Delgaudio, Eugene A., Mem.
Public Advocate of the U.S. **[19156]**
PO Box 1360
Merrifield, VA 22116
Ph: (703)845-1808
Toll Free: 800-293-8436

Delisle, Rachel, President
Worcester Polytechnic Institute
   Alumni Association **[19375]**
100 Institute Rd.
Worcester, MA 01609-2280
Ph: (508)831-5600
Fax: (508)831-5791

Della Giustina, Jo-Ann, Ph.D., J.D.,
   President
Justice Studies Association **[12962]**
c/o Jo-Ann Della Giustina, President
Dept. of Criminal Justice
Bridgewater State University
Maxwell Library, Rm. 311E
Bridgewater, MA 02325

Delman, Farrell, President
Tobacco Merchants Association
   [3287]

PO Box 8019
Princeton, NJ 08543-8019
Ph: (609)275-4900
Fax: (609)275-8379

DeLorenzo, Joseph F., Founder,
   President
Organization of Bricklin Owners
   [21470]
PO Box 24775
Rochester, NY 14624-0775
Ph: (585)247-1575

DeLorme, Eugene, JD, Director
Indians Into Medicine **[8325]**
c/o School of Medicine and Health
   Sciences
501 N Columbia Rd., Stop 9037
Grand Forks, ND 58202-9037
Ph: (701)777-3037
Fax: (701)777-3277

DeLoyola, Arlyse, Secretary,
   Treasurer
National Rex Rabbit Club **[4607]**
c/o Arlyse DeLoyola, Secretary-
   Treasurer
PO Box 1465
Cave Junction, OR 97523
Ph: (541)592-4865

d'Elsa, Laura, Reg. Dir.
German Convention Bureau **[23546]**
122 E 42nd St., Ste. 2000
New York, NY 10168
Ph: (212)661-4582
Fax: (212)661-6192

Deltoro, Ubaldo, President,
   Secretary, Treasurer
Haiti Philatelic Society **[22332]**
5709 Marble Archway
Alexandria, VA 22315-4013

DeMar, Dr. Gary, Sr. Partner
American Vision **[19943]**
PO Box 611
Braselton, GA 30517
Ph: (770)222-7266
Toll Free: 800-628-9460
Fax: (770)222-7269

DeMarco, Joseph J., Exec. Dir.,
   Founder, President
Association of Marine Technicians
   [2238]
513 River Estates Pky.
Canton, GA 30115-3019
Ph: (770)720-4324
Toll Free: 800-467-0982
Fax: (770)720-4329

DeMare, Sheila Rogers, MS, Director, Founder
Association for Comprehensive NeuroTherapy **[16010]**
c/o Sheila Rogers DeMare, Director
PO Box 159
Grosse Ile, MI 48138-0159

DeMaria, Alfred, VP
Council of State and Territorial
   Epidemiologists **[14729]**
2872 Woodcock Blvd., Ste. 250
Atlanta, GA 30341
Ph: (770)458-3811
Fax: (770)458-8516

DeMay, Denny, President
National Council of Field Labor
   Locals **[23434]**
8 N 3rd St., Rm. 207
Lafayette, IN 47901
Ph: (765)423-2152
Fax: (765)423-2194

DeMayo, Neda, Founder, President
Return to Freedom **[10689]**
PO Box 926

Lompoc, CA 93438
Ph: (805)737-9246
Fax: (805)800-0868

Demchak, Kimberly, President
Giant Schnauzer Club of America
   [21886]
c/o Cindy Wallace, Membership
   Chairperson
PO Box 967
Divide, CO 80814

DeMeis, Jonathan, Chairman
Independent Laboratory Distributors
   Association **[3026]**
827 Maple Ave.
North Versailles, PA 15137
Ph: (412)829-5190
Toll Free: 888-878-4532
Fax: (412)829-5191

DeMello, Margo, Exec., Prog. Dir.
Animals & Society Institute **[10585]**
2512 Carpenter Rd., Ste. 202-A
Ann Arbor, MI 48108-1188
Ph: (734)677-9240
Fax: (734)677-9242

DeMello, Margo, President
House Rabbit Society **[10640]**
148 Broadway
Richmond, CA 94804
Ph: (510)970-7575
Fax: (510)970-9820

Deming, Austin Jay
Society of the Founders and Friends
   of Norwich, Connecticut **[9435]**
348 Washington St.
Norwich, CT 06360
Ph: (860)889-9440

DeMio, Phillip C., MD, Chairman,
   Exec. Dir.
American Medical Autism Board
   [13739]
320 Orchardview Ave., Ste. 2
Seven Hills, OH 44131
Ph: (216)901-0441

DeMio, Phillip C., MD, Director
International Lyme and Associated
   Diseases Society **[14587]**
PO Box 341461
Bethesda, MD 20827-1461
Ph: (301)263-1080
Fax: (301)263-0776

Demir, Khalil, Exec. Dir.
Zakat Foundation of America
   [11467]
PO Box 639
Worth, IL 60482
Ph: (708)233-0555
   (773)363-4230
Toll Free: 888-925-2887

Demisse, Dr. Yonas, President
Ethiopian Geophysical Union -
   International **[6687]**
261 Glenbrook Rd., Unit 2037
Storrs Mansfield, CT 06269-2037
Ph: (204)989-2254

Demman, Reid, Mem.
National Association of County
   Surveyors **[5116]**
526 S East St.
Santa Rosa, CA 95404
Ph: (707)578-1130
Fax: (707)578-4406

Demmellash, Alfa, CEO, Founder
Rising Tide Capital **[1008]**
334 Martin Luther King Dr.
Jersey City, NJ 07305
Ph: (201)432-4316
Fax: (201)432-3504

Demmy, David W., Sr., Exec. Dir.
Sons of Union Veterans of the Civil
   War **[20746]**
National Civil War Museum
1 Lincoln Circle at Reservoir Park,
   Ste. 240
Harrisburg, PA 17103-2411
Ph: (717)232-7000
Fax: (717)412-7492

DeMoor, Steve, Director
International Miniature Zebu As-
   sociation **[3732]**
17500 Hamilton Arms Ct.
Dewitt, VA 23840
Ph: (407)717-0084

DeMore, Mike, Managing Dir.
UnitedAg **[3532]**
54 Corporate Pk.
Irvine, CA 92606-5105
Ph: (949)975-1424
Toll Free: 800-223-4590
Fax: (949)975-1573

Dempsey, Tom, President
National Commission for the Ac-
   creditation of Special Education
   Services **[8590]**
South Bldg., Ste. 900
601 Pennsylvania Ave. NW
Washington, DC 20004
Ph: (202)434-8225
Fax: (202)434-8224

Demsas, Jerusalem
American Parliamentary Debate As-
   sociation **[8593]**
1 Whig Hall
Princeton University
Princeton, NJ 08544

Demulling, Judi, Secretary
Defense Intel Alumni Association
   [19320]
PO Box 354
Charlotte Court House, VA 23923
Ph: (571)426-0098

Demyanovich, Michael A., President
The Maserati Club **[21425]**
325 Walden Ave.
Harriman, TN 37748-2738
Ph: (865)882-9230

Denenga, Sandra, Exec. Dir.,
   Founder
Heart4Kids Society, Inc. **[11018]**
2801 Park Center Dr.
Alexandria, VA 22302
Ph: (404)957-9014

Denepitiya, Lakshman, DDS,
   President
Sri Lanka Medical Association of
   North America **[15066]**
2500 Nesconset Hwy., Bldg. 16A
Stony Brook, NY 11790-2563
Ph: (631)246-5454
Fax: (631)246-5902

Dengel, Dennis M., Treasurer
American Topical Association,
   Americana Unit **[22307]**
17 Peckham Rd.
Poughkeepsie, NY 12603
Ph: (845)452-2126
Fax: (817)274-1184

Dengel, Victoria A., Exec. Dir.
General Society of Mechanics and
   Tradesmen of the City of New York
   [8661]
20 W 44th St.
New York, NY 10036
Ph: (212)840-1840

Denhart, Matthew, Exec. Dir.
Calvin Coolidge Presidential
   Foundation, Inc. **[10321]**

PO Box 97
Plymouth, VT 05056
Ph: (802)672-3389
Fax: (802)672-3289

Denholm, David Y., President
Americans Against Union Control of
Government [18615]
Public Service Research Council
320D Maple Ave. E
Vienna, VA 22180-4742
Ph: (703)242-3575
Fax: (703)242-3579

Denholm, David Y., President
Public Service Research Council
[18613]
320-D Maple Ave. E
Vienna, VA 22180-4742
Ph: (703)242-3575
Fax: (703)242-3579

Denipoti, Massimo, President
Italian American Alliance for Busi-
ness and Technology [646]
41000 Woodward Ave., Office 231
Bloomfield Hills, MI 48304
Ph: (248)258-1428

Denis, David, President
Financial Management Association
International [1278]
College of Business Administration
University of South Florida
4202 E Fowler Ave., BSN 3416
Tampa, FL 33620-5500
Ph: (813)974-2084
Fax: (813)974-3318

Denis, Jean Claude, Founder
Konbit pou Rebati Bele [11206]
2804 Church Ave.
Brooklyn, NY 11226

Denis-Luque, Marie F., Founder
Caring for Haitian Orphans with
AIDS [10885]
PO Box 145
Statesboro, GA 30459-0145
Ph: (813)843-0038

Denison, Karl, President
National Association of Public Insur-
ance Adjusters [1902]
21165 Whitfield Pl., No. 105
Potomac Falls, VA 20165
Ph: (703)433-9217
Fax: (703)433-0369

Denison, Steve, President
United States Powerlifting Associa-
tion [23072]
PO Box 1090
Placentia, CA 92871
Ph: (661)333-9800

Dennehy, Siobhan, Exec. Dir.
Emerald Isle Immigration Center
[18463]
59-26 Woodside Ave.
Woodside, NY 11377
Ph: (718)478-5502
Fax: (718)446-3727

Denney, Mike, Editor
Road Race Lincoln Register [21485]
5847 E 201st St. S
5847 E 201st St. S
Mounds, OK 74047

Dennis, Lane T., President,
Publisher
American Tract Society [20125]
1300 Crescent St.
Wheaton, IL 60187
Ph: (630)682-4300
Toll Free: 800-543-1659

Dennison Himmelfarb, Cheryl R.,
RN, ANP
Preventive Cardiovascular Nurses
Association [16181]

613 Williamson St., Ste. 200
Madison, WI 53703-3515
Ph: (608)250-2440

Denniston, George C., MD, CEO,
President
Doctors Opposing Circumcision
[11282]
2442 NW Market St., S-42
Seattle, WA 98107-4137
Ph: (415)647-2687
    (225)383-8067

Denny, Beth, Exec. Dir.
American Society for Cytotechnology
[14358]
1500 Sunday Dr., Ste. 102
Raleigh, NC 27607-5151
Ph: (919)861-5571
Toll Free: 800-948-3947
Fax: (919)787-4916

Denny, Gayle, Exec. Dir.
Evangelical Lutheran Education As-
sociation [8258]
500 N Estrella Pky., Ste. 601
Goodyear, AZ 85338-4135
Toll Free: 800-500-7644
Fax: (623)882-8770

Denoix, Jean-Marie, President
International Society of Equine
Locomotor Pathology [16586]
2716 Landmark School Rd.
The Plains, VA 20198
Toll Free: 800-363-2034

Dent, Jim, Bus. Mgr.
Railroad Station Historical Society
[10189]
c/o Jim Dent, Business Manager
26 Thackeray Rd.
Oakland, NJ 07436-3312
Ph: (212)818-8085

Dentali, Steven, Chairperson
International Aloe Science Council
[1604]
8630 Fenton St., Ste. 918
Silver Spring, MD 20910
Ph: (301)476-9690
Fax: (301)588-1174

DeParis, Lawrence C., President
Retail Marketing Society [2300]
PO Box 3376
Teaneck, NJ 07666
Ph: (201)692-8087
Fax: (201)692-1291

DePass, Linval, President
Hispanic Organization of Toxicologists [7339]
c/o Ranulfo Lemus-Olalde, Treasurer
2131 Annandale Pl.
Xenia, OH 45385
Ph: (804)852-4439

Depew, Brian, Exec. Dir.
Center for Rural Affairs [17787]
145 Main St.
Lyons, NE 68038
Ph: (402)687-2100

DePinto, Jessica, President
Justinian Society of Lawyers [5018]
PO Box 3217
Oak Brook, IL 60522
Ph: (708)338-0760
Fax: (708)401-0360

DePouli, Brian, President
Buick Club of America [21344]
PO Box 360775
Columbus, OH 43236-0775
Ph: (614)472-3939
Fax: (614)472-3222

Deprest, Jan, President
International Fetal Medicine and
Surgery Society [16620]

c/o Dr. Frank Craparo, Secretary-
Treasurer
2406 April Dr.
Jamison, PA 18929

Deputy, Keith B., Chairman
Supima [3772]
4141 E Broadway Rd.
Phoenix, AZ 85040-8831
Ph: (602)792-6002
Fax: (602)792-6004

Dequito, April, CEO, Founder
Omnilogy, Inc. [12175]
22 Camp Fire Ln.
Coram, NY 11727

Der, Channing J., PhD, President
Cancer Biology Training Consortium
[13916]
834 Madison Ave.
Winston Salem, NC 27103
Ph: (520)222-8722
Fax: (480)393-4589

Der Matossian, Bedross, VP
Society for Armenian Studies [8827]
c/o Armenian Studies Program
California State University
5245 N Backer Ave., PB4
Fresno, CA 93740-8001
Ph: (559)278-2669
Fax: (559)278-2129

Der Simonian, Varoujan, MA, Exec.
Dir.
Armenian Technology Group [3535]
550 E Shaw Ave.
Fresno, CA 93755-5969
Ph: (559)224-1000
Fax: (559)224-1002

Derks, Paula, President
Aircraft Electronics Association [123]
3570 NE Ralph Powell Rd.
Lees Summit, MO 64064
Ph: (816)347-8400
Fax: (816)347-8405

Derks, Steven M., President, CEO
Muscular Dystrophy Association
[15959]
222 S Riverside Plz., Ste. 1500
Chicago, IL 60606
Toll Free: 800-572-1717

Deroche, Gerry, CEO
National Education for Assistance
Dog Services [15203]
305 Redemption Rock Trl. S
Princeton, MA 01541
Ph: (978)422-9064

DeRoin, DeeAnn, Chairman
Association on American Indian Af-
fairs [18707]
966 Hungerford Dr., Ste. 12-B
Rockville, MD 20850
Ph: (240)314-7155
Fax: (240)314-7159

DeRose, Chris, President, Founder
Last Chance for Animals [10656]
8033 Sunset Blvd., No. 835
Los Angeles, CA 90046
Ph: (310)271-6096
Toll Free: 888-882-6462
Fax: (310)271-1890

Derrick, Deb, President
Friends of the Global Fight Against
AIDS, Tuberculosis and Malaria
[15399]
1730 Rhode Island Ave. NW, Ste.
912
Washington, DC 20036
Ph: (202)789-0801
Fax: (202)789-0802

Derrick, Lisa L., President
National Healthy Start Association
[16298]
1325 G St. NW, Ste. 500
Washington, DC 20005
Ph: (202)296-2195
Toll Free: 877-437-8126
Fax: (202)296-2197

Derry, John, President
Hope International University Alumni
Association [19326]
2500 Nutwood Ave.
Fullerton, CA 92831
Ph: (714)879-3901
Toll Free: 888-352-HOPE
Fax: (714)681-7450

DeRusso, Dean, Contact
American Disabled for Attendant
Programs Today [11569]
1208 S Logan St.
Denver, CO 80210

Desai, Meena, President
Society for Ambulatory Anesthesia
[13707]
330 N Wabash Ave., Ste. 2000
Chicago, IL 60611
Ph: (312)321-6872
Fax: (312)673-6620

Desai, Viresh, CFO
Population Reference Bureau [6369]
1875 Connecticut Ave. NW, Ste. 520
Washington, DC 20009-5728
Toll Free: 800-877-9881
Fax: (202)328-3937

DeSantis, Charles, Chairperson
USA for the United Nations High
Commissioner for Refugees
[12601]
1775 K St. NW, Ste. 580
Washington, DC 20006
Ph: (202)296-1081
Toll Free: 855-808-6427

Desbenoit, Jean-Pierre, V. Chmn. of
the Bd.
ZigBee Alliance [3250]
508 2nd St., Ste. 206
Davis, CA 95616
Ph: (530)564-4565
Fax: (530)564-4721

Deschamps, Jeff, VP
Izaak Walton League of America
[3962]
707 Conservation Ln.
Gaithersburg, MD 20878
Ph: (301)548-0150

Deshaies, Richard, 1st VP
American Correctional Chaplains
Association [19924]
ACCA Chaplains Office
Auburn Correctional Facility
135 State St.
Auburn, NY 13021
Ph: (347)783-7684
Fax: (315)253-8401

Deshais, Janice B., President
National Association of Hearing Of-
ficials [5389]
PO Box 330865
Fort Worth, TX 76163-0865

DeShazo, Peter, Exec. Dir.
LASPAU: Academic and Profes-
sional Programs for the Americas
[7635]
25 Mt. Auburn St., Ste. 300
Cambridge, MA 02138-6095
Ph: (617)495-5255
Fax: (617)495-8990

DeSiano, Fr. Frank, CSP, President
Paulist Evangelization Ministries
[19895]

3031 4th St. NE
Washington, DC 20017
Ph: (202)832-5022
Fax: (202)269-0209

Desimone, Nick, Director
Plymouth Owners Club [21477]
PO Box 416
Cavalier, ND 58220-0416

Desir, Mr. Philocles, Founder
All the Children are Children [10845]
PO Box 153012
Cape Coral, FL 33915
Ph: (239)878-2104

Desmond, Marilyn, Director
State University of New York at
   Binghamton | Center for Medieval
   and Renaissance Studies [9791]
PO Box 6000
Binghamton, NY 13902-6000
Ph: (607)777-2130
Fax: (607)777-2408

Desmond-Hellmann, Sue, CEO
Bill and Melinda Gates Foundation
   [12529]
500 5th Ave. N
Seattle, WA 98109
Ph: (206)709-3400
   (206)709-3100

Desplaines, Sharon, Secretary
Renault Owners Club of North
   America [21482]
c/o Sharon Desplaines, Secretary
7467 Mission Gorge Rd., No. 81
Santee, CA 92071
Ph: (619)334-1711

D'Esposito, Stephen, President
RESOLVE [19003]
1255 23rd St. NW, Ste. 275
Washington, DC 20037
Ph: (202)944-2300
Fax: (202)338-1264

Desrosiers, Chuck, Contact
Crime Prevention Coalition of
   America [11503]
1201 Connecticut Ave. NW, Ste. 200
Washington, DC 20036
Ph: (202)466-6272

Desrosiers, Keith, Exec. Dir.
Thorne Nature Experience [4016]
1466 N 63rd St.
Boulder, CO 80303
Ph: (303)499-3647
Fax: (720)565-3873

Desrosiers, Philip, President
National Catholic Band Association
   [9971]
Villanova University
800 E Lancaster Ave.
Villanova, PA 19085

DeStigter, Dr. Kristen, Founder
Imaging the World [15146]
PO Box 25
Charlotte, VT 05445
Ph: (802)734-1440

Destino, Ralph, Chairman
International Watch Collectors
   Society [22445]
257 Adams Ln.
Hewlett, NY 11557
Ph: (516)295-2516
Fax: (516)374-5060

Detchon, Reid, Exec. Dir.
Energy Future Coalition [6480]
1750 Pennsylvania Ave. NW, Ste.
   300
Washington, DC 20006
Ph: (202)463-1947

DeTemple, Matthew, President
National Association of Towns and
   Townships [5641]
1130 Connecticut Ave. NW, Ste. 300
Washington, DC 20036
Ph: (202)454-3954
Toll Free: 866-830-0008
Fax: (202)331-1598

Detsky, Mark, Officer
Energy Efficiency Business Coalition
   [1111]
Bldg. 52, 3rd Fl.
14062 Denver West Pky.
Golden, CO 80401
Ph: (720)274-9764

Detterman, Paul, Director
The Fellowship Community [20521]
8134 New LaGrange Rd., Ste. 227
Louisville, KY 40222
Ph: (502)425-4630

Detwiler, Bob, Contact
US ProMiniGolf Association [22897]
3210 Highway 17 S
North Myrtle Beach, SC 29582
Ph: (843)458-2585
   (843)272-7812
Fax: (843)361-7922

Deumic, Vehid, VP
Advisory Council for Bosnia and
   Herzegovina [18475]
1510 H St. NW, Ste. 900
Washington, DC 20005
Ph: (202)347-6742

Deutsch, Ayala, Treasurer
International Trademark Association
   [5333]
655 3rd Ave., 10th Fl.
New York, NY 10017
Ph: (212)642-1700
Fax: (212)768-7796

Deutsch, Dr. Curtis K., Contact
Society for Craniofacial Morphometry
   [14347]
Shriver Center
Harvard Medical School
200 Trapelo Rd.
Waltham, MA 02452-6332
Ph: (781)642-0163
Fax: (781)642-0196

Deutschlander, Dr. Mark, VP
Wilson Ornithological Society [6966]
5400 Bosque Blvd., Ste. 680
Waco, TX 76710
Ph: (254)399-9636
Fax: (254)776-3767

DeVan, Lawrence S., President
Harness Racing Museum and Hall of
   Fame [22916]
240 Main St.
Goshen, NY 10924
Ph: (845)294-6330
Fax: (845)294-3463

Devarennes, Jim, Founder,
   President
Sober Living America [13183]
2530 Peachwood Cir.
Atlanta, GA 30345
Toll Free: 877-430-0086
Fax: (404)639-9887

DeVault, Kenneth R., President
American Gastroenterological As-
   sociation [14777]
4930 Del Ray Ave.
Bethesda, MD 20814
Ph: (301)654-2055
Fax: (301)654-5920

DeVault, Lynn, Comm. Chm.
Community Financial Services Association of America [1227]

515 King St., Ste. 300
Alexandria, VA 22314
Toll Free: 888-572-9329
Fax: (703)684-1219

Devaux, Odile, Mgr.
Saint Lucia Tourist Board [23549]
800 2nd Ave., Rm. 910
New York, NY 10017
Ph: (212)867-2950
Toll Free: 800-456-3984

Devers, Thomas, President
German Gun Collectors' Association
   [21656]
PO Box 429
Mayfield, UT 84643-0429
Ph: (435)979-9723
Fax: (435)528-7966

Devi, Gayatri, MD, President
National Council on Women's Health
   [17761]
1300 York Ave.
New York, NY 10021

Devine, Mercedes, Managing Dir.
Society of California Pioneers
   [21086]
300 4th St.
San Francisco, CA 94107-1272
Ph: (415)957-1849
Fax: (415)957-9858

DeVisser, Don, PE, Exec. VP
American Institute of Timber
   Construction [1425]
7012 S Revere Pky., Ste. 140
Centennial, CO 80112
Ph: (503)639-0651
Fax: (503)684-8928

DeVito, Dennis, President
Lionel Collectors Club of America
   [22185]
PO Box 529
Peru, IL 61354-0529
Fax: (815)223-0791

Devitt, John, Chairman, Founder
Vietnam Combat Veterans [21170]
PO Box 715
White Pine, MI 49971
Ph: (906)885-5599

DeVon, Holli, RN, Chairperson
The Council for the Advancement of
   Nursing Science [16128]
c/o American Academy of Nursing
1000 Vermont Ave. NW, Ste. 910
Washington, DC 20005
Ph: (202)777-1166

DeVore, Dr. Steven, Founder
Medicine for Mali [12290]
4605 80th Pl.
Urbandale, IA 50322-7340

DeVore, Susan, President
Healthcare Leadership Council
   [15145]
750 9th St. NW, Ste. 500
Washington, DC 20001
Ph: (202)452-8700
Fax: (202)296-9561

Devoti, Andrea, Chairperson
National Association for Home Care
   and Hospice [15280]
228 7th St. SE
Washington, DC 20003
Ph: (202)547-7424
Fax: (202)547-3540

Devrick, Jill, President
Association for Healthcare
   Documentation Integrity [15618]
4120 Dale Rd., Ste. J8-233

Modesto, CA 95356
Ph: (209)527-9620
Toll Free: 800-982-2182
Fax: (209)527-9633

Devries, Dawn, DHA, MPA, CTRS,
   President
American Therapeutic Recreation
   Association [17083]
629 N Main St.
Hattiesburg, MS 39401
Ph: (601)450-2872
Fax: (601)582-3354

DeWaal, Klaas, Chairman
American Filtration and Separations
   Society [7258]
618 Church St., Ste. 220
Nashville, TN 37219
Fax: (615)254-7047

Dewalt, Dr. Mark, VP
Country School Association of
   America [9384]
210 N Kansas Ave.
League City, TX 77573
Ph: (281)554-2994

Dewey, Elizabeth, Director
New Perimeter [5549]
500 8th St. NW
Washington, DC 20004
Ph: (202)799-4505

Dewispelaere, Jay, CEO, President
PRIDE Youth Programs [13175]
707 W Main St.
Fremont, MI 49412-1414
Ph: (231)924-1662
Toll Free: 800-668-9277

DeWitt, Ed, Exec. Dir.
Association to Preserve Cape Cod
   [3814]
482 Main St.
Dennis, MA 02638
Ph: (508)362-4226

DeWitt, John, Chmn. of the Bd.
American Board of Physical Therapy
   Residency and Fellowship Educa-
   tion [16716]
c/o American Physical Therapy As-
   sociation
1111 N Fairfax St.
Alexandria, VA 22314-1488
Ph: (703)706-3152
Fax: (703)706-8186

DeWitt, Robert E., Chairman
National Multi Housing Council
   [2883]
1850 M St. NW, Ste. 540
Washington, DC 20036-5803
Ph: (202)974-2300
Fax: (202)775-0112

DeWitt, Scott, Founder
International Steel Guitar Convention
   [9935]
9535 Midland Blvd.
Saint Louis, MO 63114-3314
Ph: (314)427-7794
Fax: (314)427-0516

DeWitt, Sean, Exec. Dir.
Alliance for Southern African
   Progress [12137]
1424 31st Ave., Ste. 3R
Astoria, NY 11106
Toll Free: 877-375-5778
Fax: (877)375-5778

DeWolf, Dawn, VP
American Association for Women in
   Community Colleges [8744]
PO Box 3098
Gaithersburg, MD 20885
Ph: (301)442-3374

Dews, Morris, President
Correctional Education Association
[11523]
PO Box 3430
Laurel, MD 20709
Ph: (443)459-3080
Fax: (443)459-3088

Dey, Sheila, Exec. Dir., Gen.
Counsel
Western Manufactured Housing
Communities Association [2202]
455 Capitol Mall, Ste. 800
Sacramento, CA 95814-4420
Ph: (916)448-7002
Fax: (916)448-7085

Deyak Voelk, Mary Lou, President
Slovenian Union of America [19654]
431 N Chicago St.
Joliet, IL 60432-1703
Ph: (815)727-1926

DeYoung, Barry R., MD, President
Association of Directors of Anatomic
and Surgical Pathology [16576]
c/o Nilda Barrett
American Society for Clinical Pathol-
ogy
33 W Monroe St., Ste. 1600
Chicago, IL
Toll Free: 800-267-2727
Fax: (312)541-4998

Dezarn, Ms. Christine G., CEO,
Founder
Polycystic Ovarian Syndrome As-
sociation [16302]
4230 N Oakland Ave., Ste. 204
Shorewood, WI 53211

Dezert, Jean, President
International Society of Information
Fusion [6744]
PO Box 4631
Mountain View, CA 94040

d'Haiti, Pierre F., MBS, President
Haiti Works! [12159]
PO Box 55483
Bridgeport, CT 06610-5483
Ph: (203)526-3542
    (203)908-4007

Dhaliwal, Harvinder S., Chairman
Sikh Sports Association of USA
[23149]
4430 Deer Field Way
Danville, CA 94506
Ph: (510)501-2263
Toll Free: 866-499-0032

Dhami, Sukhman, Founder, Director
Ensaaf [19126]
PO Box 11682
Pleasanton, CA 94588-1682
Ph: (206)866-5642
Fax: (270)916-7074

Dhammasiri, Venerable Maha-
ragama, President, Founder
Washington Buddhist Vihara [19784]
5017 16th St. NW
Washington, DC 20011
Ph: (202)723-0773

Dharmananda, Subhuti, PhD, Direc-
tor
Institute for Traditional Medicine and
Preventive Health Care [13630]
2017 SE Hawthorne Blvd.
Portland, OR 97214
Ph: (503)233-4907
Fax: (503)233-1017

D'Hondt, Nancy, Officer
American Association of Diabetes
Educators [14517]

200 W Madison St., Ste. 800
Chicago, IL 60606
Toll Free: 800-338-3633
Fax: (312)424-2427

Dhoot, Dalwinder Singh, Chairman
North American Punjabi Association
[19478]
1250 Ames Ave., Ste. 101
Milpitas, CA 95035
Ph: (408)221-5732
Fax: (408)547-0522

Dhurandhar, Nikhil V., PhD,
President
The Obesity Society [16263]
8757 Georgia Ave., Ste. 1320
Silver Spring, MD 20910-3757
Ph: (301)563-6526
Toll Free: 800-974-3084
Fax: (301)563-6595

Di Cerbo, Michael, President
Society of American Graphic Artists
[9350]
32 Union Sq. E, Rm. 1214
New York, NY 10003-3225

Di Giovanni, Anthony, Treasurer
United States Deaf Ski and
Snowboard Association [22801]
76 Kings Gate N
Rochester, NY 14617-5409

Di Yeso, Michael E., CEO, President
Freedoms Foundation at Valley
Forge [18296]
1601 Valley Forge Rd.
Valley Forge, PA 19481
Ph: (610)933-8825
Fax: (610)935-0522

Diak, Wanda, Exec. Dir., COO
Cancer Hope Network [13923]
2 North Rd., Ste. A
Chester, NJ 07930
Ph: (908)879-4039
Toll Free: 800-552-4366
Fax: (908)879-6518

Diamond, Michael, Treasurer
Building Service Contractors As-
sociation International [2125]
330 N Wabash Ave., Ste. 2000
Chicago, IL 60611
Ph: (312)321-5167
Toll Free: 800-368-3414
Fax: (312)673-6735

Diamond, Robbie, President, CEO
Electrification Coalition [3328]
1111 19th St. NW, Ste. 406
Washington, DC 20036-3627
Ph: (202)448-9300
Fax: (202)461-2379

Diamond, Robbie, CEO, President,
Founder
Securing America's Future Energy
[6512]
1111 19th St. NW, Ste. 406
Washington, DC 20036
Ph: (202)461-2360
Fax: (202)461-2379

Diamond, Rochelle, Chairperson
National Organization of Gay and
Lesbian Scientists and Technical
Professionals [7141]
PO Box 91803
Pasadena, CA 91109
Ph: (626)791-7689
Fax: (626)791-7689

Diana, Janine, VP
Experimental Aircraft Association
[5862]
EAA Aviation Ctr.

3000 Poberezny Rd.
Oshkosh, WI 54902-8939
Ph: (920)426-4800
Toll Free: 800-564-6322
Fax: (920)426-6865

Dianda, Jane, Officer
Italian Catholic Federation Central
Council [19506]
8393 Capwell Dr., Ste. 110
Oakland, CA 94621
Ph: (510)633-9058
Toll Free: 888-ICF-1924
Fax: (510)633-9758

Dias, Robette, President
Oyate [19587]
330 E Thomson Ave.
Sonoma, CA 95476-3957
Ph: (707)996-6700
Fax: (707)935-9961

Diaz, Jimmy, Chairman
Professional Windsurfers Association
[22661]
PO Box 791656
Paia, HI 96779

Diaz, Luis J., Esq., CEO, President
United States Hispanic Advocacy
Association [18342]
601 Pennsylvania Ave. NW, Ste. 900
Washington, DC 20004

Diaz, Nelson, Chairman
National Foundation for Credit
Counseling [2094]
2000 M St. NW, Ste. 505
Washington, DC 20036
Ph: (202)677-4300
Toll Free: 800-388-2227
Fax: (202)677-4333

Diaz-Granados, Jim, Exec. Dir.
American Psychological Association
Education Directorate [16863]
750 1st St. NE
Washington, DC 20002-4242
Ph: (202)336-5970
Toll Free: 800-374-2721

Diaz-Obregon, Emmanuel, Dir. of
Operations
Intrax Cultural Exchange [7933]
Intrax Global Headquarters
600 California St., 10th Fl.
San Francisco, CA 94108
Ph: (415)434-1221

Dib, Dr. Nabil, President
International Society for
Cardiovascular Translational
Research [14126]
3104 E Camelback Rd., No. 564
Gilbert, AZ 85297
Ph: (480)438-5015

DiBartolo, Anthony, Director
Italian Genealogical Group [20980]
PO Box 626
Bethpage, NY 11714-0626

Dibie-Violante, Maia, Treasurer
FACE Foundation [8031]
972 5th Ave.
New York, NY 10075
Ph: (212)439-1439

Dicampli, Edward F., COO,
Secretary
Helicopter Association International
[137]
1920 Ballenger Ave.
Alexandria, VA 22314-2898
Ph: (703)683-4646
Toll Free: 800-435-4976
Fax: (703)683-4745

Dicampli, Edward F., Secretary,
COO
Helicopter Foundation International
[138]

1920 Ballenger Ave.
Alexandria, VA 22314-2898
Ph: (703)683-4646
    (703)360-1521

DiCarlo, Rosemary A., President,
CEO
National Committee on American
Foreign Policy [18271]
320 Park Ave., 3rd Fl.
New York, NY 10022-6815
Ph: (212)224-1120
Fax: (212)224-2524

Dice, Rick, President
National Wildfire Suppression As-
sociation [4212]
PO Box 330
Lyons, OR 97358
Ph: (541)389-3526
Toll Free: 877-676-6972
Fax: (866)854-8186

Dicker, Eli J., Exec. Dir.
Tax Executives Institute [5803]
1200 G St. NW, Ste. 300
Washington, DC 20005
Ph: (202)638-5601

Dickerhoof, Edward, Exec. VP
Organization of Professional
Employees of the United States
Department of Agriculture [4951]
PO Box 23762
Washington, DC 20026-3762
Ph: (202)720-4898

Dickerson, Bob, Chairman
National Community Reinvestment
Coalition [17990]
727 15th St. NW, Ste. 900
Washington, DC 20005
Ph: (202)628-8866
Fax: (202)628-9800

Dickerson, Dave, VP
Personal Watercraft Industry Association [2919]
650 Massachusetts Ave. NW, Ste.
520
Washington, DC 20001

Dickerson, Ken, Exec. Dir.
Ecological Farming Association
[3548]
2901 Park Ave., Ste. D-2
Soquel, CA 95073
Ph: (831)763-2111

Dickey, Forest, VP
Furniture Society [1479]
4711 Hope Valley Rd., Ste. 4F, No.
512
Durham, NC 27707-5651
Ph: (828)581-9663

Dickinson, Charlotte, Founder
American Impressionist Society
[8909]
PO Box 27818
Omaha, NE 68127
Ph: (402)592-3399

Dickinson, Mary Ann, CEO,
President
Alliance for Water Efficiency [4749]
33 N LaSalle St., Ste. 2275
Chicago, IL 60602
Ph: (773)360-5100
Toll Free: 866-730-A4WE
Fax: (773)345-3636

Dickinson, Susan, Exec. Dir.
Association for Frontotemporal
Degeneration [15905]
Radnor Station Bldg. 2, Ste. 320
290 King of Prussia Rd.
Radnor, PA 19087
Ph: (267)514-7221
Toll Free: 866-507-7222

Dickman, Karen, Exec. Dir.
Global Water [13325]
1901 N Fort Myer Dr., Ste. 405
Arlington, VA 22209
Ph: (703)528-3863
Fax: (703)528-5776

Dickson, Mrs. Robin, Bd. Member
Dogs for the Deaf [15188]
10175 Wheeler Rd.
Central Point, OR 97502
Ph: (541)826-9220
Toll Free: 800-990-DOGS

Dickson-Gilbert, Deirdre, Director,
   Founder
National Medical Malpractice
   Advocacy Association [12052]
9119 Hwy. 6, Ste. 230
Missouri City, TX 77459
Toll Free: 800-379-1054

Dickstein, Jason, President
Modification and Replacement Parts
   Association [173]
2233 Wisconsin Ave., NW, Ste. 503
Washington, DC 20007
Ph: (202)628-6777
Fax: (202)628-8948

Dickstein, Michele L., President
Aviation Suppliers Association
   [2215]
2233 Wisconsin Ave. NW, Ste. 503
Washington, DC 20007-4124
Ph: (202)347-6899
Fax: (202)347-6894

Didriksen, Judie, President
National Autumn Leaf Collectors
   Club [21692]
8426 Clint Dr.
Belton, MO 64012

Diederich, Ken, Exec. Dir.
National Ice Carving Association
   [8874]
PO Box 109
Aurora, OH 44202
Ph: (630)871-8431

Diehl, Larry, Director
North American Lily Society [22117]
PO Box W
Bonners Ferry, ID 83805-1287

Diehl, Mary Grace, President
National Conference of Bankruptcy
   Judges [5393]
c/o Jeanne Sleeper, Executive Direc-
   tor
954 La Mirada St.
Laguna Beach, CA 92651-3751
Ph: (949)497-3673
Fax: (949)497-2523

Dieper, Ms. Susanne, Dir. of Admin.
American Institute for Contemporary
   German Studies [9338]
1755 Massachusetts Ave. NW, Ste.
   700
Washington, DC 20036-2121
Ph: (202)332-9312
Fax: (866)307-6691

Dieringer, Larry, Exec. Dir.
Engaging Schools [18539]
23 Garden St.
Cambridge, MA 02138
Ph: (617)492-1764
Toll Free: 800-370-2515
Fax: (617)864-5164

Dierker, Charmayne, Bd. Member
Mothers Supporting Daughters with
   Breast Cancer [14015]
25235 Fox Chase Dr.
Chestertown, MD 21620-3409
Ph: (410)778-1982
Fax: (410)778-1411

Dierks, Neil, CEO
National Pork Producers Council
   [4713]
122 C St. NW, Ste. 875
Washington, DC 20001
Ph: (202)347-3600
Fax: (202)347-5265

Dierks, Steve, Director
Mercedes-Benz Club of America
   [21429]
1907 Lelaray St.
Colorado Springs, CO 80909-2872
Ph: (719)633-6427
Toll Free: 800-637-2360
Fax: (719)633-9283

Dieterich, Bob, Advisor
Lincoln Highway Association [9407]
136 N Elm St.
Franklin Grove, IL 61031
Ph: (815)456-3030

Diethrich, Edward B., MD, Chairman
International Society of Endovascular Specialists [17575]
3639 Ambassador Caffery Pky., Ste.
   605
Lafayette, LA 70503
Ph: (337)993-7920

Dietrich, Kyle, Exec. Dir., Founder
Peace in Focus [18817]
281 Summer St.
Boston, MA 02210

Dietz, Harry C., MD, President
American Society of Human Genet-
   ics [6666]
9650 Rockville Pke.
Bethesda, MD 20814
Ph: (301)634-7300
Toll Free: 866-HUM-GENE
Fax: (301)634-7079

Dietz, Timothy J., President, CEO
Self Storage Association [3441]
1901 N Beauregard St., Ste. 106
Alexandria, VA 22311
Ph: (703)575-8000
Toll Free: 888-735-3784
Fax: (703)575-8901

Dietzler, Deborah, Exec. Dir.
University of Louisville Alumni As-
   sociation [19359]
University Club and Alumni Ctr.
200 E Brandeis Ave.
Louisville, KY 40208
Ph: (502)852-6186
Toll Free: 800-813-8635
Fax: (502)852-6920

Diez, Daniel V., Chairman
Cocoa Merchants' Association of
   America [1321]
55 E 52nd St., 40th Fl.
New York, NY 10055
Ph: (212)748-4193

DiFilipo, Thomas, CEO, President
Joint Council on International
   Children's Services [10456]
117 S St. Asaph St.
Alexandria, VA 22314
Ph: (703)535-8045
Fax: (703)535-8049

DiFilippo, Frank, Ph.D, VP
American Board of Science in
   Nuclear Medicine [16074]
c/o Gregory Beavers, PhD
3098 Creek Point Rd.
Graham, NC 27253
Ph: (336)508-5148

DiFiore, Kristine, CFO
Flashes of Hope [10787]
6009 Landerhaven Dr., Ste. I

Cleveland, OH 44124
Ph: (440)442-9700

DiFiori, John, MD, Bd. Member
American Medical Society for Sports
   Medicine [17275]
4000 W 114th St., Ste. 100
Leawood, KS 66211-2622
Ph: (913)327-1415
   (626)445-1983
Fax: (913)327-1491

DiGangi, Brian A., DVM, MS,
   DABVP, President
Association of Shelter Veterinarians
   [17637]
3225 Alphawood Dr.
Apex, NC 27539
Ph: (919)803-6113

Diggs, David, Exec. Dir.
Beyond Borders [12143]
5016 Connecticut Ave. NW
Washington, DC 20008
Ph: (202)686-2088

Diggs, Lawrence, Contact
Vinegar Connoisseurs International
   [22150]
The Vinegar Man
PO Box 41
Roslyn, SD 57261

Diggs, Tia, Exec. Dir.
Aviation Distributors and Manufactur-
   ers Association [130]
100 N 20th St., Ste. 400
Philadelphia, PA 19103-1462
Ph: (215)320-3872
Fax: (215)564-2175

DiGregorio, Domenico, Chmn. of the
   Bd., President
Plumbers Without Borders [13332]
PO Box 16082
Seattle, WA 98116
Ph: (206)390-5000
   (206)384-3222

DiGregorio, Kevin, Exec. Dir.
National Institute for Chemical Stud-
   ies [13224]
3200 Kanawha Tpke.
South Charleston, WV 25303
Toll Free: 800-611-2296
Fax: (800)611-2296

Diing, Dominic, Founder
Aid and Care [11311]
338 Auburn Ave.
Buffalo, NY 14213

Dik, David A., Exec. Dir.
Young Audiences Arts for Learning
   [9010]
171 Madison Ave., Ste. 200
New York, NY 10016-5110
Ph: (212)831-8110
Fax: (212)289-1202

Dike, Ejim, Exec. Dir.
US Human Rights Network [18450]
250 Georgia Ave. SE, Ste. 330
Atlanta, GA 30312
Ph: (404)588-9761
Fax: (404)588-9763

Dikter, David, CEO
Accessibility Interoperability Alliance
   [6733]
330 N Wabash Ave., Ste. 2000
Chicago, IL 60611
Ph: (312)321-5172
Toll Free: 877-687-2842
Fax: (312)673-6659

DiLauro, Vin, President
National Amateur Baseball Federation [22555]

PO Box 705
Bowie, MD 20718
Ph: (410)721-4727
Fax: (410)721-4940

Dilcher, Karl, Mem.
Fibonacci Association [6820]
c/o Ashley DeFazio, Subscription
   Manager
PO Box 1740
Sun City, AZ 85372

Dillane, Dominic, Chmn. of the Bd.
International Society of Travel and
   Tourism Educators [3382]
23220 Edgewater St.
Saint Clair Shores, MI 48082
Ph: (586)294-0208
Fax: (586)294-0208

Diller, Chris, President
National States Geographic Informa-
   tion Council [6326]
9 Newport Dr., Ste. 200
Forest Hill, MD 21050
Ph: (443)640-1075
Fax: (443)640-1031

Diller, Rita, Director
STOPP International [19072]
c/o American Life League
PO Box 1350
Stafford, VA 22555-1350
Ph: (540)659-4171
Fax: (540)659-2586

Dillhyon, Michael D., Exec. Dir.
National Association of Police
   Athletic/Activities Leagues, Inc.
   [13462]
1662 N US Highway 1, Ste. C
Jupiter, FL 33469
Ph: (561)745-5535
Fax: (561)745-3147

Dillinger, Phyllis, Bd. Member
Women in Bio [6125]
PO Box 31493
Sea Island, GA 31561-1493
Ph: (240)204-0719

Dillingham, Tim, Exec. Dir.
American Littoral Society [3800]
18 Hartshorne Dr., Ste. 1
Highlands, NJ 07732
Ph: (732)291-0055
Fax: (732)291-3551

Dillon, Karena K., President
Consultants Association for the
   Natural Products Industry [680]
PO Box 4014
Clovis, CA 93613-4014
Ph: (559)325-7192

Dillon, Kristine, President
Consortium on Financing Higher
   Education [8497]
c/o Dr. Kristine Dillon, President
238 Main St., Ste. 402
Cambridge, MA 02142
Ph: (617)253-5030
Fax: (617)258-8280

Dillow, Katharine, Officer
Marquette University Alumni As-
   sociation [19334]
PO Box 1881
Milwaukee, WI 53201-1881
Ph: (414)288-7448
Toll Free: 800-344-7544

DiLorenzo, Michael J., Mgr.
Forging Industry Association [2348]
1111 Superior Ave., Ste. 615
Cleveland, OH 44114
Ph: (216)781-6260
Fax: (216)781-0102

DiLouie, Craig, Contact
Lighting Controls Association [2101]
c/o National Electrical Manufacturers
Association
1300 N 17th St., Ste. 1752
Arlington, VA 22209
Ph: (403)802-1809

Dilworth, Stephanie, President
Iota Phi Lambda [23696]
1325 G St. NW, Ste. 500
Washington, DC 20005
Ph: (202)462-4682
Fax: (202)234-4682

Dimaggio, John A., DPM, President
American Society of Forensic
Podiatry [14773]
PO Box 549
Bandon, OR 97411

Dimencescu, Dr. Mihai, Contact
Institutes for the Achievement of Hu-
man Potential [11237]
8801 Stenton Ave.
Wyndmoor, PA 19038
Ph: (215)233-2050
Fax: (215)233-9312

DiMeo, Sonny, VP
Pacific Coast Cichlid Association
[22035]
PO Box 28145
San Jose, CA 95159-8145
Ph: (408)243-0434

Dimondstein, Mark, President
American Postal Workers Union
[23504]
1300 L St. NW
Washington, DC 20005
Ph: (202)842-4250

Din, Aung, Exec. Dir., Founder
United States Campaign for Burma
[18448]
1444 N St. NW, Ste. A2
Washington, DC 20005
Ph: (202)234-8022

Dineen, Martin K., President
American Association of Clinical
Urologists, Inc. [17543]
1100 E Woodfield Rd., Ste. 350
Schaumburg, IL 60173
Ph: (847)517-1050
Fax: (847)517-7229

Dinerman, David, Director
Fitness Industry Suppliers Associa-
tion - North America [2599]
3525 Del Mar Heights Rd.
San Diego, CA 92130
Ph: (858)509-0034
Fax: (858)792-1251

Dinerman, Hayley, Exec. Dir. (Actg.)
Triple Negative Breast Cancer
Foundation [13853]
PO Box 204
Norwood, NJ 07648
Ph: (646)942-0242

Ding, Michelle, President
Angel Heart International [15213]
PO Box 17486
Irvine, CA 92623-7486
Ph: (949)310-8181

Dinger, June, President
The Tanygnathus Society [3672]
4510 Buckingham Rd.
Fort Myers, FL 33905

Dinh, Quyên, Chairman
National Council of Asian Pacific
Americans [17820]
1629 K St. NW, Ste. 400

Washington, DC 20006
Ph: (202)706-6768

Dinneen, Bob, CEO, President
Renewable Fuels Association [6507]
425 3rd St. SW, Ste. 1150
Washington, DC 20024
Ph: (202)289-3835
Fax: (202)289-7519

Dino, Rev. Gerald N., President
Catholic Golden Age [19811]
PO Box 249
Olyphant, PA 18447-0249
Toll Free: 855-586-1091

Dinovitz, Paul, Exec. Dir.
Hearst Foundation [12976]
90 New Montgomery St., Ste. 1212
San Francisco, CA 94105
Ph: (415)908-4500
Fax: (415)348-0887

Dinshah, Darius, President
Dinshah Health Society [13619]
PO Box 707
Malaga, NJ 08328-0707
Ph: (856)692-4686

Dinshah, Freya, President
American Vegan Society [10291]
56 Dinshah Ln.
Malaga, NJ 08328
Ph: (856)694-2887
Fax: (856)694-2288

DioGuardi, Joseph J., Founder,
President
Albanian American Civic League
[19295]
PO Box 70
Ossining, NY 10562
Ph: (914)762-5530
Fax: (914)762-5102

Dion, Jane, Director
Churg Strauss Syndrome Associa-
tion [13786]
82 Pine Ridge Rd.
Westfield, MA 01085
Ph: (413)862-3636

Dion, Jeffrey R., Director
National Crime Victim Bar Associa-
tion [5843]
National Center for Victims of Crime
2000 M St. NW, Ste. 480
Washington, DC 20036
Ph: (202)467-8700
(202)467-8753
Fax: (202)467-8701

Dionne, Carla, Founder, Exec. Dir.
National Uterine Fibroids Foundation
[17112]
PO Box 9688
Colorado Springs, CO 80932
Ph: (719)633-3454

DiPasquale, John, Chairman,
President
USA National Karate-do Federation
[23025]
1631 Mesa Ave., Ste. A1
Colorado Springs, CO 80906-2956
Ph: (719)477-6925

DiPeri, Frances, Founder
Brain and Body Alternatives [15597]
290 Community Dr.
Great Neck, NY 11021
Ph: (631)807-6819
(631)873-6366
Fax: (516)686-0641

DiPerna, James C., PhD, President
APA Division 16: School Psychology
[16871]

750 1st St. NE
Washington, DC 20002-4242
Ph: (202)336-5500

Dirago, Joe, Exec. Ofc.
National Council of Social Security
Management Associations [5761]
3303 S Wakefield St.
Arlington, VA 22206
Ph: (202)547-8530
Fax: (202)547-8532

Director, Mark, Chairman
Everybody Wins! USA [7587]
1920 N St. NW
Washington, DC 20036
Ph: (202)216-9467
Fax: (202)216-9552

DiSaia, Dr. Philip J., Chairman
Gynecologic Oncology Group
[16345]
4 Penn Ctr., Ste. 1020
1600 John F. Kennedy Blvd.
Philadelphia, PA 19103
Ph: (215)854-0770
Toll Free: 800-225-3053

Discher, Blake J., President
Vintage Triumph Register [21517]
PO Box 655
Howell, MI 48844

Dischler, Patricia, President
National Association for Family Child
Care [5189]
1743 W Alexander St., Ste. 201
Salt Lake City, UT 84119-2000
Ph: (801)886-2322
Toll Free: 800-359-3817
Fax: (801)886-2325

Discipio, Laura, LCSW, Exec. Dir.
National Association of Anorexia
Nervosa and Associated Disorders
[14646]
750 E Diehl Rd., No. 127
Naperville, IL 60563
Ph: (630)577-1330
(630)577-1333

Disney, Kathy, President
Professional Loadmaster Association
[5621]
PO Box 4351
Tacoma, WA 98438
Toll Free: 800-239-4524

Ditlow, Clarence, Exec. Dir.
Center for Auto Safety [12817]
1825 Connecticut Ave. NW, Ste. 330
Washington, DC 20009-5708
Ph: (202)328-7700

Dittrich, Charles, Exec. Dir.
U.S.-Libya Business Association
[2001]
1625 K St. NW, Ste. 200
Washington, DC 20006
Ph: (202)464-2038

Dituri, Joseph, MS, CEO
Association for Marine Exploration
[4464]
91-1056 A'awa Dr.
Ewa Beach, HI 96706
Ph: (858)337-9418

DiVincenzo, Brenda, Director
Independent Photo Imagers [2580]
2518 Anthem Village Dr., Ste. 104
Henderson, NV 89052-5554
Ph: (702)617-1141
Fax: (702)617-1181

Divine, Ann, Exec. Dir.
Fischoff National Chamber Music
Association [9908]

303 Brownson Hall
Notre Dame, IN 46556
Ph: (574)631-0984

Divine, Deborah, President
The Quilters Hall of Fame [21781]
926 S Washington St.
Marion, IN 46953
Ph: (765)664-9333

DiVirgilio, Debbie, President
Grant Professionals Association
[12479]
1333 Meadowlark Ln., Ste. 105
Kansas City, KS 66102-1200
Ph: (913)788-3000
Fax: (913)788-3398

Dix Smith, Marilyn, RPh, Exec. Dir.
International Society for Pharmaco-
economics and Outcomes
Research [16667]
505 Lawrence Square Blvd. S
Lawrenceville, NJ 08648-2675
Ph: (609)586-4981
Toll Free: 800-992-0643
Fax: (609)586-4982

Dixon, Jackie, Dir. of Admin., Dir. of
HR
VolunteerMatch [13311]
550 Montgomery St., 8th Fl.
San Francisco, CA 94111
Ph: (415)241-6868
Fax: (415)241-6869

Dixon, Philip G., Director, Gen.
International Order of St. Vincent
[20110]
126 Coming St.
Charleston, SC 29403
Ph: (843)722-7345
Fax: (843)722-2105

Dixon, Steve, Web Adm.
70th Infantry Division Association
[21177]
c/o Diane Kessler, Secretary
73 Providence Hill Rd.
Atkinson, NH 03811

Dixon, William, Founder, President
Relief Labs International [12720]
109 Windsor St., Ste. 4
Cambridge, MA 02139

do Lago, Carlos Bessa, Sec. Gen.
International Alliance of Furnishing
Publications [1483]
7025 Albert Pick Rd.
Greensboro, NC 27409
Ph: (336)605-1033

Do, Thien, Founder, CEO, Director
World Health Ambassador [15073]
7611 Little River Tpke., Ste. 108W
Annandale, VA 22003
Ph: (703)658-7060

Doak, Dr. Gordon A., Secretary,
Treasurer, President
National Association of Animal
Breeders [4459]
PO Box 1033
Columbia, MO 65205
Ph: (573)445-4406
Fax: (573)446-2279

Doan, David R, Officer
Red Cross of Constantine I United
Grand Imperial Council [19568]
PO Box 1606
El Cajon, CA 92022-1606
Ph: (619)456-4652

Doan, Lesia Foerster, President
Northamerican Association of
Masters In Psychology [8468]

PO Box 721270
Norman, OK 73070
Ph: (405)329-3030
Toll Free: 800-919-9330

Doan-Crider, Dr. Diana, Mem.
International Association for Bear
Research and Management [4827]
15542 County Road 72
Warba, MN 55793
Ph: (218)259-6686
(830)324-6550
Fax: (865)974-3555

Doane, Kenneth M., President
Doane Family Association of
America [20854]
c/o Jane MacDuff, Membeship Chair
2618 Occidental Dr.
Vienna, VA 22180

Dobbin, Ronald, President
Society for Occupational and
Environmental Health [16321]
1010 Vermont Ave. NW, No. 513
Washington, DC 20005
Ph: (202)347-4976

DoBell, Paul S., Exec. Dir.
Petrified Forest Museum Association
[10064]
1 Park Rd.
Petrified Forest National Park, AZ
86028
Ph: (928)524-6228

Doblin, Rick, PhD, Founder, Exec.
Dir.
Multidisciplinary Association for
Psychedelic Studies [16671]
1115 Mission St.
Santa Cruz, CA 95060-3528
Ph: (831)429-6362
Fax: (831)429-6370

Dobo, Krista, Officer
Genetic Toxicology Association
[7337]
c/o Leon Stankowski, Treasurer
1712 DaVinci Ln.
Clarks Summit, PA 18411

Dobosz, Mark, Exec. Dir.
National Creditors Bar Association
[5038]
8043 Cooper Creek Blvd., Ste. 206
University Park, FL 34201
Ph: (202)861-0706

Dobson, Barbara, Treasurer
National Association of College and
University Mail Services [2644]
6 Boston Rd., Ste. 202
Chelmsford, MA 01824-3075
Toll Free: 877-NAC-UMS1

Dockett, Shirley, Associate
American Association of State Col-
leges and Universities [7619]
1307 New York Ave. NW, 5th Fl.
Washington, DC 20005-4701
Ph: (202)293-7070
(202)478-4647
Fax: (202)296-5819

Dockray, J. Parker, President, Exec.
Dir.
Backline [11487]
PO Box 28284
Oakland, CA 94604-8284
Ph: (503)287-4344
(510)817-0781
Toll Free: 888-493-0092

Dockter, Darrell, Bd. Member
American Shropshire Registry Association [4664]
c/o Becky Peterson, Secretary

41 Bell Rd.
Bernardston, MA 01337
Ph: (413)624-9652

Doctors, Shelley, PhD, President
International Association for
Psychoanalytic Self Psychology
[16916]
4907 Morena Blvd., Ste. 1402
San Diego, CA 92117
Ph: (858)270-3503
Toll Free: 888-280-1476
Fax: (858)270-3513

Dodd, Bobby, CEO, President
Amateur Athletic Union [23209]
PO Box 22409
Lake Buena Vista, FL 32830-2409
Ph: (407)934-7200
Toll Free: 800-AAU-4USA
Fax: (407)934-7242

Dodd, Christopher J., CEO, Chair-
man
Motion Picture Association of
America, Inc. [1199]
1600 Eye St. NW
Washington, DC 20006
Ph: (202)293-1966
Fax: (202)296-7410

Dodd, Donna, Mgr., Dir. of Conf.
Association of Collegiate Schools of
Planning [8722]
6311 Mallard Trace Dr.
Tallahassee, FL 32312
Ph: (850)385-2054
Fax: (850)385-2084

Dodge, Justin, Exec. Dir.
World Allergy Organization [13582]
555 E Wells St., Ste. 1100
Milwaukee, WI 53202-3823
Ph: (414)276-1791
Fax: (414)276-3349

Dodge, Norman E., President
Dodge Family Association [20855]
10105 W 17th Pl.
Lakewood, CO 80215-2863
Ph: (303)237-4947

Dodge, Rev. Robin, President
American Friends of St. David's
Cathedral [9370]
c/o St. David's Episcopal Church
5150 Macomb St. NW
Washington, DC 20016

Dodson, Eric, CEO
Audubon Lifestyles [3992]
35246 US Highway 19 N, No. 299
Palm Harbor, FL 34684
Ph: (727)733-0762
Fax: (727)683-9153

Dodson, Judi, President
Peruvian Hearts [11130]
24918 Genesee Trail Rd.
Golden, CO 80401
Ph: (303)526-2756

Dodson, Ronald, Chairman
International Sustainability Council
[4007]
35246 US Highway 19, No. 299
Palm Harbor, FL 34684
Ph: (727)733-0762
Fax: (727)683-9153

Doebert, Sandra, President
National Association of Federally
Impacted Schools [7835]
444 N Capitol St. NW, Ste. 419
Washington, DC 20001
Ph: (202)624-5455
Fax: (202)624-5468

Doepker, Jacquelyn, Secretary
Association of U.S. Catholic Priests
[19800]

200 St. Francis Ave.
Tiffin, OH 44883-3458
Ph: (872)205-5862

Doerfler, Jill, President
Association for the Study of
American Indian Literatures
[10035]
c/o Jeff Berglund, Treasurer
PO Box 6032
Flagstaff, AZ 86011-6032

Doering, Erika, Founder
Association of Women Industrial
Designers [6720]
Old Chelsea St.
New York, NY 10008-0461

Doerr, Bob, VP
Military Writers Society of America
[22484]
PO Box 1768
Cranberry Township, PA 16066

Doheny, Kay, President
NASSCO [3419]
2470 Longstone Ln., Ste. M
Marriottsville, MD 21104
Ph: (410)442-7473
Fax: (410)442-7788

Doherty, James
Business for Orphans [10878]
8 Hickory Oak Dr.
The Woodlands, TX 77381
Ph: (832)693-9185

Doherty, Mark G., Exec. Dir.
EMDR International Association
[16970]
5806 Mesa Dr., Ste. 360
Austin, TX 78731-3785
Toll Free: 866-451-5200
Fax: (512)451-5256

Doherty, Will, Founder
Online Policy Group [17996]
1800 Market St., No. 123
San Francisco, CA 94102-6227
Fax: (928)244-2347

Doherty-Mason, Enitan, Exec. Dir.,
Founder
Eduwatch [8070]
8817 Swallow Ct.
Gaithersburg, MD 20879
Ph: (301)869-4720

Dohm, Paul, Exec. Dir.
Furniture Bank Association of North
America [13052]
c/o Dallas Furniture Bank
1417 Upfield Dr., Ste. 104
Carrollton, TX 75006

Dohrmann, Deb, Office Mgr.
National Wildlife Rehabilitators As-
sociation [4849]
2625 Clearwater Rd.
Saint Cloud, MN 56301
Ph: (320)230-9920

Doiron, John, President
Professional Grounds Management
Society [4289]
720 Light St.
Baltimore, MD 21230
Ph: (410)223-2861
Fax: (410)752-8295

Doiron, Roger, Founder
Kitchen Gardeners International
[4237]
3 Powderhorn Dr.
Scarborough, ME 04074
Ph: (207)956-0606

Doka, Kenneth J., Consultant
Hospice Foundation of America
[15295]

1707 L St. NW, Ste. 220
Washington, DC 20036-3123
Ph: (202)457-5811
Toll Free: 800-854-3402

Dokras, Anuja, MD, PhD, President
Androgen Excess and PCOS
Society [14700]
12520 Magnolia Blvd., Ste. 212
North Hollywood, CA 91607

Dolan, Gregory A., CEO
Methanol Institute [6662]
124 S West St., Ste. 203
Alexandria, VA 22314-2872
Ph: (703)248-3636

Dolan, Patrick, Founder
Haiti Air Ambulance [12279]
1 Media Crossways
Woodbury, NY 11797

Dolan, Pete, Treasurer
Australian Shepherd Club of America
[21833]
6091 E State Highway 21
Bryan, TX 77808
Ph: (979)778-1082
Fax: (979)778-1898

Dolan, Peter R., MBA, Chairman
ChildObesity180 [16253]
Tufts University
150 Harrison Ave.
Boston, MA 02111

Dolce, Gillian, Program Mgr.
Global Youth Coalition on HIV/AIDS
[10541]
155 Water St.
Brooklyn, NY 11201-1040
Ph: (917)677-9927

Doleva, John, President
Naismith Memorial Basketball Hall of
Fame [22572]
1000 Hall of Fame Ave.
Springfield, MA 01105
Toll Free: 877-4HO-OPLA

Dolezal, Jeffrey, President
National Wheelchair Poolplayers As-
sociation [22791]
90 Flemons Dr.
Somerville, AL 35670
Ph: (703)817-1215
Fax: (703)817-1215

Doliente, Dino, III, President
Philippine Nurses Association of
America [16180]
656 Canton St.
Westwood, MA 02090

Dolim, Mike, Exec. Dir.
Association of Old Crows [6416]
1000 N Payne St., Ste. 200
Alexandria, VA 22314-1652
Ph: (703)549-1600
Fax: (703)549-2589

Dollak, Joseph, OD, President, CEO
Interprofessional Fostering of
Ophthalmic Care for Underserved
Sectors [17717]
18555 Kuykendahl Rd.
Spring, TX 77379
Ph: (281)547-7477
Toll Free: 866-398-7525
Fax: (877)302-6385

Dollar, Deb, Treasurer
National Cockatiel Society [21542]
c/o Deb Dollar, Treasurer
PO Box 12058
Brooksville, FL 34603-2058

Dollar, Maj. Gen. (Ret.) Douglas O.,
Exec. Dir.
National Society of Scabbard and
Blade [23824]

Dollus, John, Exec.
American Society of Architectural
Illustrators [231]
c/o Tina Bryant, Executive Director
294 Merrill Hill Rd.
Hebron, ME 04238
Ph: (207)966-2062

Dolphus, Rev. Warren H., Founder
National Religious Affairs Association
[20548]
712 18th St. NE
Washington, DC 20002

Domadia, Ashok, 1st VP
Federation of Jain Associations in
North America [20539]
722 S Main St.
Milpitas, CA 95035
Ph: (510)730-0204

Doman, Janet, Director
International Academy for Child
Brain Development [16016]
c/o Institutes for the Achievement of
Human Potential
8801 Stenton Ave.
Wyndmoor, PA 19038
Ph: (215)233-2050
Fax: (215)233-9312

Domby, Gary, D.C., DIBAK, Chair-
man
International College of Applied Ki-
nesiology U.S.A. [15266]
6405 Metcalf Ave., Ste. 503
Shawnee Mission, KS 66202
Ph: (913)384-5336
Fax: (913)384-5112

Domenech, Daniel A., Exec. Dir.
American Association of School
Administrators [7416]
1615 Duke St.
Alexandria, VA 22314
Ph: (703)528-0700
Fax: (703)841-1543

Domenico, Joe, VP
Association of Northwest Steelhead-
ers [22840]
6641 SE Lake Rd.
Milwaukie, OR 97222
Ph: (503)653-4176

Domenico, Prof. Roy, Exec. Sec.,
Treasurer
Society for Italian Historical Studies
[9620]
c/o Prof. Roy Domenico, Executive
Secretary/Treasurer
University of Scranton
800 Linden St.
Scranton, PA 18510

Dominelli, Debra L., Founder
Dysautonomia Youth Network of
America [15927]
1301 Greengate Ct.
Waldorf, MD 20601
Ph: (301)705-6995

Domingo, Cindy, Director
U.S. Women and Cuba Collaboration [18535]
6508 27th Ave. NW
Seattle, WA 98117

Dominguez, Joe, Founder
New Road Map Foundation [12013]
PO Box 1363
Langley, WA 98260

Don, Megan Gordon, Contact
Deadliest Cancers Coalition [13959]
c/o Megan Gordon Don
Pancreatic Cancer Action Network
Government Affairs & Advocacy Of-
fice

1050 Connecticut Ave. NW, Ste. 500
Washington, DC 20036
Ph: (202)742-6776

Donadio, Brian J., Exec. Dir.
American College of Osteopathic
Internists [16505]
11400 Rockville Pke., No. 801
Rockville, MD 20852
Ph: (301)231-8877
Toll Free: 800-327-5183
Fax: (301)231-6099

Donahoo, Pamela L., CAE, Exec.
Dir.
American Mensa [9342]
1229 Corporate Dr. W
Arlington, TX 76006-6103
Ph: (817)607-0060
Fax: (817)649-5232

Donahue, Dan, Comm. Chm.
North-American Association of
Uniform Manufacturers and
Distributors [208]
4400 Belmont Park Ter., No. 195
Nashville, TN 37215
Ph: (516)393-5838
  (615)480-8420

Donahue, Jed, Ed.-in-Chief
Intercollegiate Studies Institute
[18026]
3901 Centerville Rd.
Wilmington, DE 19807-1938
Ph: (302)652-4600
Toll Free: 800-526-7022
Fax: (302)652-1760

Donahue, Marla, President
Flexible Packaging Association
[2476]
185 Admiral Cochrane Dr., Ste. 105
Annapolis, MD 21401
Ph: (410)694-0800
Fax: (410)694-0900

Donaldson, Ana, Comm. Chm.
Association for Educational Com-
munications and Technology
[8023]
320 W 8th St., Ste. 101
Bloomington, IN 47404-3745
Ph: (812)335-7675
Toll Free: 877-677-2328

Donaldson, Hal, Founder, President
Convoy of Hope [12652]
330 S Patterson Ave.
Springfield, MO 65802
Ph: (417)823-8998
Fax: (417)823-8244

Donaldson, Dr. Lydia, Exec. Sec.
American College of Veterinary
Anesthesia and Analgesia [17615]
c/o Dr. Lydia Donaldson, Executive
Secretary
22499 Polecat Hill Rd.
Middleburg, VA 20118
Ph: (540)687-5270

Donaldson, Martyn, Director
Tucker Automobile Club of America
[21506]
PO Box 6177
Lindenhurst, IL 60046

Donaldson, Prof. Steven L.,
Treasurer
American Society for Composites
[6161]
University of Dayton
Dept. of Civil and Environmental
Engineering
422 Kettering Laboratory
300 College Park Ave.
Dayton, OH 45469-0243
Ph: (937)229-3847
Fax: (937)229-3491

Donaldson, Tom, President
National Organization on Fetal
Alcohol Syndrome [17324]
1200 Eton Court NW, 3rd Flr.
Washington, DC 20007
Ph: (202)785-4585
Toll Free: 800-66N-OFAS
Fax: (202)466-6456

Donaldson, William H., Chairman
Financial Services Volunteer Corps
[18489]
10 E 53rd St., 36th Fl.
New York, NY 10022
Ph: (212)771-1429
Fax: (212)771-1462

Donch, Tom Arie, President
Community Built Association [11335]
4217 Montgomery St.
Oakland, CA 94611

Donchin, Anne, Advisor
International Feminist Approaches to
Bioethics [11801]
PO Box 1712
Dearborn, MI 48121-1712

Doney, Tom, Chairman
Society of Professional Benefit
Administrators [1077]
2 Wisconsin Cir., Ste. 670
Chevy Chase, MD 20815
Ph: (301)718-7722
Fax: (301)718-9440

Donghia, Sherri, Officer
Color Association of the United
States [752]
33 Whitehall St., Ste. M3
New York, NY 10004
Ph: (212)947-7774

Donhofer, Norbert, President
International League of Antiquarian
Booksellers [2957]
310 Delaware St.
New Castle, DE 19720-5038

Donlan, Josh, Founder, Director
Advanced Conservation Strategies
[3787]
c/o Josh Donlan, Founder and Director
PO Box 1201
Midway, UT 84049-1201
Ph: (435)200-3031
  (607)227-9768

Donnatelli, Guy, Commodore
National One Design Racing Association [22653]
1225 E Bronson St.
South Bend, IN 46615

Donnell, Kyra, VP
National Association of Ordnance
Contractors [880]
c/o Kyra Donell, Membership
Chairperson
2095 Lakeside Center Way, Ste. 200
Knoxville, TN 37922
Ph: (865)560-2883
Fax: (865)560-2802

Donnelly, David, President, CEO
Every Voice Center [18941]
1211 Connecticut Ave. NW, Ste. 600
Washington, DC 20036
Ph: (202)640-5600
Fax: (202)521-0605

Donnelly, John E., Exec. Dir.
National Schools Committee for
Economic Education [7733]
250 E 73rd St., Apt. 12G
New York, NY 10021-4310
Ph: (212)535-9534
Fax: (212)535-4167

Donnelly, John, President
Global Healing [15452]
2140 Shattuck Ave., Ste. 203
Berkeley, CA 94704-1211
Ph: (510)898-1859
Fax: (510)280-5365

Donnelly, Maureen A., Secretary
American Society of Ichthyologists
and Herpetologists [6706]
PO Box 1897
Lawrence, KS 66044-8897
Ph: (785)843-1235
Toll Free: 800-627-0326
Fax: (785)843-1274

Donner, Jacki, Exec. Dir., CEO
Home Ventilating Institute [1621]
4915 Arendell St., Ste. J
Morehead City, NC 28557
Toll Free: 855-484-8368
Fax: (480)559-9722

Donner, Lisa, Exec. Dir.
Americans for Financial Reform
[18242]
1629 K St. NW, 10th Fl.
Washington, DC 20006
Ph: (202)466-1885

Donnes, John, President
U.S. Cancellation Club [22376]
1715 Valley Vista Dr.
Houston, TX 77077-4938

Donofrio, Jim, Exec. Dir.
Recreational Fishing Alliance [4186]
PO Box 3080
New Gretna, NJ 08224
Toll Free: 888-564-6732
Fax: (609)294-3812

Donohue, Colin, Exec. Dir.
National Network of Forest
Practitioners [4211]
8 N Court St., Ste. 411
Athens, OH 45701
Ph: (740)593-8733

Donohue, Danny, President
Civil Service Employees Association
[23429]
143 Washington Ave.
Albany, NY 12210
Ph: (518)257-1000
Toll Free: 800-342-4146

Donohue, Jay, President, CEO
International Association of
Administrative Professionals [72]
10502 N Ambassador Dr., Ste. 100
Kansas City, MO 64153
Ph: (816)891-6600
Fax: (816)891-9118

Donohue, Thomas J., President
Center for International Private
Enterprise [620]
1211 Connecticut Ave. NW, Ste. 700
Washington, DC 20036
Ph: (202)721-9200
Fax: (202)721-9250

Donohue, Thomas J., President
U.S. Chamber of Commerce [23628]
1615 H St. NW
Washington, DC 20062-2000
Ph: (202)659-6000
Toll Free: 800-638-6582
Fax: (202)463-3190

Donohue, Thomas J., CEO,
President
U.S.-Hungary Business Council
[673]
701 8th St. NW, Ste. 500
Washington, DC 20001
Ph: (202)659-8201
Toll Free: 800-638-6582

Donohue, Mr. Tom, Exec. Dir.,
Founder
Who's Positive **[10556]**
c/o Tom Donohue, Executive Director
2200 Prout St. SE, Ste. 1
Washington, DC 20020

Donovan, Paula, Director
AIDS-Free World **[13521]**
501 Northern Pky.
Uniondale, NY 11553
Ph: (212)729-5084

Donzelli, Steve, Chairman
World Alliance for Retail Excellence
& Standards **[2981]**
1100 Johnson Ferry Rd. NE
Atlanta, GA 30342
Ph: (678)303-2959
Fax: (404)591-6811

Dooley, Andy, VP
Amateur Softball Association of
America **[23199]**
ASA Hall of Fa,e Studio Complex
2801 NE 50th St.
Oklahoma City, OK 73111
Ph: (405)424-5266
Fax: (405)424-3855

Dooley, Calvin M., CEO, President
American Chemistry Council **[709]**
700 2nd St. NE
Washington, DC 20002
Ph: (202)249-7000
    (202)249-6623
Fax: (202)249-6100

Dooley, Calvin M., President, CEO
Plastics Division of the American
Plastics Council **[2629]**
700 2nd St. NE
Washington, DC 20002
Ph: (202)249-7000
    (202)249-6100

Dooley, Dennis, RCI, VP
American Construction Inspectors
Association **[798]**
530 S Lake Ave., No. 431
Pasadena, CA 91101
Ph: (626)797-2242
Fax: (626)797-2214

Dooley, Jeffrey, President
National Association of Black Scuba
Divers **[23362]**
PO Box 91630
Washington, DC 20090
Toll Free: 800-521-NABS

Dooley, Mr. Paul, Founder, CEO
MatchingDonors **[14623]**
766 Turnpike St.
Canton, MA 02021
Ph: (781)821-2204
Fax: (800)385-0422

Dooms, Tami, President, CEO
Youth Evangelism Association
[20166]
13000 US Highway 41 N
Evansville, IN 47725
Ph: (812)867-2418
Fax: (812)867-8933

Dorfman, Margot, CEO
U.S. Women's Chamber of Com-
merce **[23636]**
700 12th St. NW, Ste. 700
Washington, DC 20005
Toll Free: 888-418-7922

Doris, Gene, Comm. Chm.
Intercollegiate Association of
Amateur Athletes of America
[23228]

39 Old Ridgebury Rd.
Matrix Corporate Ctr.
39 Old Ridgebury Rd.
Danbury, CT 06810

Dorman, Todd, President
Society of Critical Care Medicine
[14353]
500 Midway Dr.
Mount Prospect, IL 60056
Ph: (847)827-6869
Fax: (847)827-6886

Dornan, Hon. Florence R.,
Secretary, Director
United States Marine Raider As-
sociation **[5629]**
704 Cooper Ct.
Arlington, TX 76011-5550
Ph: (817)275-1552
    (940)580-0298

Dornbos, Vicki, President
Parents of Infants and Children with
Kernicterus **[15981]**
PO Box 10744
White Bear Lake, MN 55110-0744

Dorosh, Michael, Bd. Member
AIDS Treatment Activists Coalition
[10533]
PO Box 9153
Denver, CO 80209-0153

Dorre, Theresa, Exec. Dir.
Air Charity Network **[14164]**
Toll Free: 877-621-7177

Dorsa, Robert, President
American Credit Union Mortgage
Association **[945]**
PO Box 400955
Las Vegas, NV 89140-0955
Toll Free: 877-442-2862
Fax: (702)823-3950

Dorsey, Bill, Chairman, Founder
Association of Luxury Suite Directors
[3151]
10017 McKelvey Rd.
Cincinnati, OH 45231
Ph: (513)674-0555
Fax: (513)674-0577

Dorsey, Judy, President
Blue Star Mothers of America
[21039]
c/o Carla Brodacki, Financial
Secretary
PO Box 443
Saint Clair, MI 48079

Dorsey, Mark, Exec. Dir., CEO
Construction Specifications Institute
[6349]
110 S Union St., Ste. 100
Alexandria, VA 22314
Toll Free: 800-689-2900

Dorsey, Mark, Exec. Dir., CEO
Professional Ski Instructors of
America and American Association
of Snowboard Instructors **[23167]**
133 S Van Gordon St., Ste. 200
Lakewood, CO 80228
Toll Free: 844-340-7669

Dort, Illens, President, Founder
International Aid Serving Kids
[11045]
1135 N 650 E
Orem, UT 84097

Dortch, Richard, Project Mgr.
Energy Farm **[6479]**
PO Box 1834
Jackson, MS 39215-1834

Doshier, Joe, President
11th Airborne Division Association
[20707]

c/o Charles J Magro, Treasurer
301 S Dabney Ln.
Rogersville, AL 35652
Ph: (256)247-7390

Dossman, Mr. Curley M., Jr., Chmn.
of the Exec. Committee
100 Black Men of America **[19292]**
141 Auburn Ave.
Atlanta, GA 30303
Ph: (404)688-5100
Fax: (404)522-5652

Doster, Sue, Co-Pres.
InterPride **[11895]**
Boston, MA 02118

Dotson, David, President
Dollywood Foundation **[24033]**
Dolly Parton's Imagination Library
1020 Dollywood Ln.
Pigeon Forge, TN 37863
Ph: (865)428-9606
Fax: (865)428-9612

Dotson, Heather, Secretary
International Order of E.A.R.S.
[10222]
7712 Briarwood Dr.
Crestwood, KY 40014-9094
Ph: (502)553-3406

Doty, Ed, Chairman
Council of Religious Volunteer Agen-
cies **[13291]**
Brethren Volunteer Service
1451 Dundee Ave.
Elgin, IL 60120

Doty, Steven, Founder, President
DirectConnect Humanitarian Aid
[12656]
PO Box 37
Bellevue, MI 49021
Ph: (269)763-3687
Toll Free: 800-708-0296
Fax: (269)763-3689

Doubet, Sherry, Exec. VP
American Salers Association **[3710]**
19590 E Main St., Ste. 202
Parker, CO 80138
Ph: (303)770-9292
Fax: (303)770-9302

Double, Ken, CEO, President
American Theatre Organ Society,
Inc. **[9870]**
7800 Laguna Vega Dr.
Elk Grove, CA 95758
Ph: (503)372-6987

Doublet, Barbara Ann H., 1st VP
Eta Phi Beta Sorority, Inc. **[23693]**
19983 Livernois Ave.
Detroit, MI 48221-1299
Ph: (313)862-0600
Fax: (313)862-6245

Doud, Gregg, President
Commodity Markets Council **[1517]**
1300 L St. NW, Ste. 1020
Washington, DC 20005
Ph: (202)842-0400

Dougan, William R., President
National Federation of Federal
Employees **[23435]**
1225 New York Ave., Ste. 450
Washington, DC 20005
Ph: (202)216-4420
Fax: (202)898-1861

Dougherty, Aaron, Exec. Dir.
Historic Winslow House Association
[9400]
634 Careswell St.
Marshfield, MA 02050
Ph: (781)837-5753

Dougherty, Dave, Exec. Dir.
National High School Athletic
Coaches Association **[22734]**
c/o Dave Dougherty, Executive
Director
PO Box 10277
Fargo, ND 58106
Ph: (701)570-1008

Dougherty, Rev. Edward, Gen.
Maryknoll Fathers and Brothers
[19861]
55 Ryder Rd.
Ossining, NY 10562
Ph: (914)941-7590
Toll Free: 888-627-9566

Dougherty, Ms. Nancy J., President
Special Care Dentistry Association
[14471]
330 N Wabash Ave., Ste. 2000
Chicago, IL 60611
Ph: (312)527-6764
Fax: (312)673-6663

Dougherty, Richard H., President,
Founder
BasicNeeds US **[15763]**
9 Meriam St., Ste. 4
Lexington, MA 02420
Ph: (781)869-6990

Douglas, Cindy, President
North American Spotted Draft Horse
Association **[4396]**
17594 US Highway 20
Goshen, IN 46528
Ph: (574)821-4226

Douglas, Clifford, President
The Center for Social Gerontology,
Inc. **[10503]**
2307 Shelby Ave.
Ann Arbor, MI 48103
Ph: (734)665-1126
Fax: (734)665-2071

Douglas, Jeffrey, Chmn. of the Bd.
Free Speech Coalition **[17835]**
PO Box 10480
Canoga Park, CA 91309
Ph: (818)348-9373
Fax: (818)348-8893

Douglas, Ulester, Exec. Dir.
Men Stopping Violence **[18723]**
2785 Lawrenceville Hwy., Ste. 112
Decatur, GA 30033
Ph: (404)270-9894
Toll Free: 866-717-9317
Fax: (404)270-9895

Douglas-Ntagha, Pamela, DNP,
President
National Association of Healthcare
Transport Management **[14952]**
c/o Pamela Douglas-Ntagha, DNP,
1400 Holcombe Blvd. Ste. 0422
1400 Holcombe Blvd., Unit 0422
Houston, TX 77030-4009
Ph: (713)563-7700

Douglass, Adele, President
Center for Food Safety **[6643]**
660 Pennsylvania Ave. SE, Ste. 302
Washington, DC 20003
Ph: (202)547-9359
Fax: (202)547-9429

Douglass, Adele, CEO
Humane Farm Animal Care **[10641]**
PO Box 727
Herndon, VA 20172
Ph: (703)435-3883

Douglass, Stephen B., President,
Chmn. of the Bd.
Campus Crusade for Christ
International **[20131]**

100 Lake Hart Dr.
Orlando, FL 32832
Toll Free: 888-278-7233

Douin, David A., Exec. Dir.
National Board of Boiler and Pressure Vessel Inspectors [5309]
1055 Crupper Ave.
Columbus, OH 43229-1183
Ph: (614)888-8320
Fax: (614)888-0750

Doumeng, Richard, Chairman
Caribbean Hotel and Tourism Association [3374]
2655 Le Jeune Rd., Ste. 910
Coral Gables, FL 33134
Ph: (305)443-3040
Fax: (305)675-7977

Dourson, Michael L., PhD, President
CEO
Toxicology Excellence for Risk Assessment [7344]
2300 Montana Ave., Ste. 409
Cincinnati, OH 45211
Ph: (513)542-7475
Fax: (513)542-7487

Dove, Susan H., Exec. Dir.
Nurses Organization of Veterans Affairs [16171]
47595 Watkins Island Sq.
Sterling, VA 20165
Ph: (703)444-5587
Fax: (703)444-5597

Dove, Tangila, PhD, President
Community College Business Officers [7549]
3 Boar's Head Ln., Ste. B
Charlottesville, VA 22903-4604
Ph: (434)293-2825
Fax: (434)245-8453

Dove, William E., President
International Society for Cow Protection [10652]
7016 SE 92 Ter.
Gainesville, FL 32641
Ph: (352)792-6777

Dowd, Maria, VP, Exec. Dir.
Event Planners Association [2326]
4390 Piedmont Ave.
Oakland, CA 94611
Ph: (510)426-5818

Dowd, Thomas C., President
Earth Society Foundation [4053]
238 E 58th St., Ste. 2400
New York, NY 10022
Ph: (212)832-3659

Dowdell, Jamie, Director
Investigative Reporters and Editors, Inc. [2691]
Missouri School of Journalism
141 Neff Annex
Columbia, MO 65211
Ph: (573)882-2042

Dowden, C. James, Exec. Dir.
Alliance of Area Business Publishers [2760]
2512 Artesia Blvd., Ste. 200
Redondo Beach, CA 90278
Ph: (310)379-8261
Fax: (310)379-8283

Dowden, C. James, Exec. Dir.
City and Regional Magazine Association [2778]
2512 Artesia Blvd., Ste. 200
Redondo Beach, CA 90278
Ph: (310)379-8261
Fax: (310)379-8283

Dowell, Ed, Secretary, Treasurer
American Train Dispatchers Association [23513]

4239 W 150th St.
Cleveland, OH 44135
Ph: (216)251-7984
Fax: (216)251-8190

Dowell, Kelly, Exec. Dir.
Credit Union Information Security Professionals Association [6757]
1717 W 6th St., Ste. 112
Austin, TX 78703
Ph: (512)465-9711
Toll Free: 888-475-4440

Down, Beverly, CEO, President
Creativity Coaching Association [22729]
PO Box 328
Lake George, NY 12845
Ph: (518)798-6933

Downey, David T., CAE, President, CEO
International Downtown Association [640]
910 17th St. NW, Ste. 1050
Washington, DC 20006
Ph: (202)204-1385
Fax: (202)393-6869

Downey, Hugh, Founder
Lalmba Association [12693]
1000 Corey St.
Longmont, CO 80501
Ph: (303)485-1810

Downey, Stephen S., Exec. Dir.
American Osteopathic Foundation [16518]
142 E Ontario St., Ste. 1450
Chicago, IL 60611
Ph: (312)202-8234
Toll Free: 866-455-9383
Fax: (312)202-8216

Downham, Max C., Exec. Dir.
International College of Surgeons [17390]
1516 N Lakeshore Dr.
Chicago, IL 60610
Ph: (312)642-3555
Fax: (312)787-1624

Downing, Denise, Exec. Dir., Secretary
International Hard Anodizing Association [2350]
PO Box 5
Mount Laurel, NJ 08054-0005
Ph: (856)234-0330

Downing, J. D., Director
American Cross Country Skiers [23161]
PO Box 604
Bend, OR 97709
Ph: (541)317-0217

Downing, John, Chairman
Council of Scientific Society Presidents [7130]
1155 16th St. NW
Washington, DC 20036
Ph: (202)872-6230

Downing, John, Director
World Masters Cross-Country Ski Association [23174]
c/o John Downing, Director
PO Box 604
Bend, OR 97709
Ph: (541)317-0217
Fax: (541)317-0217

Downing, RBP, CBSP, SM, Marian M., Officer
ABSA International [2987]
1200 Allanson Rd.
Mundelein, IL 60060-3808
Ph: (847)949-1517
Toll Free: 866-425-1385
Fax: (847)566-4580

Downs Jr., John H., President, CEO
National Confectioners Association [1355]
1101 30th St. NW, Ste. 200
Washington, DC 20007
Ph: (202)534-1440
Fax: (202)337-0637

Downs, Linda, Exec. Dir.
College Art Association [7509]
50 Broadway, 21st Fl.
New York, NY 10004
Ph: (212)691-1051
Fax: (212)627-2381

Downs, Paul, President
American Foreign Law Association [5347]
c/o Paul Downs, President
222 E 41st St.
New York, NY 10017

Doyle, Francis J., III, President
IEEE - Control Systems Society [6556]
c/o Francis J. Doyle III, President
Dept. of Chemical Engineering
University of California - Santa Barbara
333 Engineering II
Santa Barbara, CA 93106

Doyle, J. Andrew, Officer
American Coatings Association [2487]
1500 Rhode Island Ave. NW
Washington, DC 20005
Ph: (202)462-6272
Fax: (202)462-8549

Doyle, Jim, VP
Alpaca Llama Show Association [21278]
17102 Mueschke Rd.
Cypress, TX 77433
Ph: (281)516-1442
Fax: (281)516-1449

Doyle, Dr. Laurance, President
PlanetQuest [6009]
PO Box 211
Sausalito, CA 94966

Doyle-Kimball, Mary, Exec. Dir.
National Association of Real Estate Editors [2697]
1003 NW 6th Ter.
Boca Raton, FL 33486-3455
Ph: (561)391-3599
Fax: (561)391-0099

Doyle-Propst, Elizabeth, Contact
Breath of Hope, Inc. [13826]
PO Box 6627
Charlottesville, VA 22906-6627
Toll Free: 888-264-2340

Dozoretz, Linda, Exec. Dir., Founder
Children's Wish Foundation International [11224]
8615 Roswell Rd.
Atlanta, GA 30350
Ph: (770)393-9474
Toll Free: 800-323-9474
Fax: (770)393-0683

Draeger, Justin, CEO, President
National Association of Student Financial Aid Administrators [7836]
1101 Connecticut Ave. NW, Ste. 1100
Washington, DC 20036-4303
Ph: (202)785-0453
Fax: (202)785-1487

Drager, Ron, CEO, President
Automobile Racing Club of America [22523]

PO Box 5217
Toledo, OH 43611
Ph: (734)847-6726

Drago, Ms. Young, Registrar, Treasurer
Leschetizky Association [9948]
37-21 90th St., Apt. 2R
Jackson Heights, NY 11372-7838

Dragone, Mr. Christopher, Director
Godolphin Society [23081]
National Museum of Racing and Hall of Fame
191 Union Ave.
Saratoga Springs, NY 12866
Ph: (518)584-0400
Toll Free: 800-562-5394
Fax: (518)584-4574

Dragone, Christopher, Director
National Museum of Racing and Hall of Fame [22924]
191 Union Ave.
Saratoga Springs, NY 12866-3566
Ph: (518)584-0400
Toll Free: 800-562-5394
Fax: (518)584-4574

Drake, Adam, Treasurer
American Association of the Deaf-Blind [15167]
PO Box 24493
Federal Way, WA 98093
Ph: (770)492-8646

Drake, Bryan, Chairman
Computer Measurement Group [6244]
3501 Route 42, Ste. 130, No. 121
Turnersville, NJ 08012-1734
Ph: (856)401-1700
(303)773-7985

Drake, Carrie L., Contact
Antipsychiatry Coalition [16824]
2040 Polk St.
San Francisco, CA 94109

Drake, Diane, President
National Academy of Opticianry [16414]
8401 Corporate Dr., Ste. 605
Landover, MD 20785
Toll Free: 800-229-4828
Fax: (301)577-3880

Drake, Paul, Director
American College of Heraldry [20952]
1818 N Taylor St., Ste. B, No. 312
Little Rock, AR 72207

Drake, Raymond E., President
American Society for the Defense of Tradition, Family and Property [18032]
PO Box 341
Hanover, PA 17331
Ph: (717)225-7147
Toll Free: 888-317-5571
Fax: (717)225-7382

Drame, Papa, President
Act for Africa International [12796]
9040 Falcon Glen Ct.
Bristow, VA 20136
Ph: (804)994-4962
(571)212-6167

Draper, Mike, Secretary
Nautical Research Guild [22656]
237 S Lincoln St.
Westmont, IL 60559-1917
Ph: (585)968-8111

Draper, Timothy D., Secretary
Immigration and Ethnic History Society [9489]

Div. of Social Science and Education
Waubonsee Community College
Waubonsee Dr., Route 47
Sugar Grove, IL 60554-9454
Ph: (630)466-7900

Draves, William A., CAE, President
Learning Resources Network [7670]
PO Box 9
River Falls, WI 54022
Ph: (715)426-9777
Toll Free: 800-678-5376
Fax: (888)234-8633

Drayer, Burton P., MD, Chairman
Radiological Society of North
    America [17061]
820 Jorie Blvd.
Oak Brook, IL 60523-2251
Ph: (630)571-2670
Toll Free: 800-381-6660
Fax: (630)571-7837

Drayton, Bill, Founder, CEO, Chair-
man
Ashoka Innovators for the Public
    [12139]
1700 N Moore St., Ste. 2000
Arlington, VA 22209
Ph: (703)527-8300
Fax: (703)527-8383

Drea, Patricia, Chairman
Private Duty Homecare Association
    [15282]
228 7th St. SE
Washington, DC 20003
Ph: (202)547-7424
Fax: (202)547-3660

Drege, Pastor Marsh Luther, Exec.
    Dir., Pastor
Seafarers and International House
    [20318]
123 E 15th St.
New York, NY 10003
Ph: (212)677-4800

Dreifuss, Shelly, VP
ORT America [12230]
75 Maiden Ln., 10th Fl.
New York, NY 10038
Ph: (212)505-7700
Toll Free: 800-519-2678
Fax: (212)674-3057

Drenkard, Karen, PhD, RN, NEA-
    BC, FAAN, Exec. Dir.
American Nurses Association
    [16106]
8515 Georgia Ave., Ste. 400
Silver Spring, MD 20910-3492
Ph: (301)628-5000
Toll Free: 800-284-2378
Fax: (301)628-5001

Dreslin, John E., DMD., MAES,
    Chairman
American Endodontic Society
    [14409]
PO Box 545
Glen Ellyn, IL 60138-0545
Ph: (773)519-4879
Fax: (630)858-0525

Dressman, Jim, Chmn. of the Bd.
Free Store Food Bank [12540]
112 E Liberty St.
Cincinnati, OH 45202-6510
Ph: (513)241-1064

Drewes, Lester R., President
International Brain Barriers Society
    [16017]
c/o Lester R. Drewes, President
University of Minnesota - Medical
    School Duluth
1035 University Dr., 251 SMed

Duluth, MN 55812

Drews-Botsch, Carolyn, President
Society for Pediatric and Perinatal
    Epidemiologic Research [14736]
PO Box 160191
Clearfield, UT 84016
Ph: (617)432-3942

Dreyfus, Susan, President, CEO
Alliance for Strong Families and
    Communities [11809]
1020 19th St. NW, Ste. 500
Washington, DC 20036
Ph: (414)359-1040
Toll Free: 800-221-3726

Driegert, Robert S., Director
American Academy of Attorney-
    CPAs [8]
PO Box 706
Warrendale, PA 15095
Ph: (703)352-8064
Toll Free: 888-272-2889
Fax: (703)352-8073

Driggs, Daniel, Mem.
Globus Relief [12278]
1775 West 1500 South
Salt Lake City, UT 84104
Ph: (801)977-0444
Fax: (801)977-3999

Driscoll, Carl F., President
American College of Prosthodontists
    [14402]
211 E Chicago Ave., Ste. 1000
Chicago, IL 60611
Ph: (312)573-1260

Driscoll, John, Officer
Hazelden Betty Ford Foundation
    [13142]
PO Box 11
Center City, MN 55012-0011
Ph: (651)213-4200
Toll Free: 800-257-7810

Driscoll, Rich, President
Marine Corps Air Transport Associa-
    tion [21012]
PO Box 1134
Millington, TN 38083

Driskill, Wayne, President
Miniature Arms Collectors/Makers
    Society [21296]
c/o Alice McGinnis, Treasurer
2109 Spring St.
Cross Plains, WI 53528

Dristas, Victor, VP of Operations
National Association of Real Estate
    Investment Trusts [2879]
1875 I St. NW, Ste. 600
Washington, DC 20006-5413
Ph: (202)739-9400
Fax: (202)739-9401

Drobnich, Darrel, President
American Sleep Apnea Association
    [17212]
1717 Pennsylvania Ave. NW, Ste.
    1025
Washington, DC 20006
Toll Free: 888-293-3650
Fax: (888)293-3650

Drobnis, Ann, Director
Computing Research Association
    [6245]
1828 L St. NW, Ste. 800
Washington, DC 20036-5104
Ph: (202)234-2111
Fax: (202)667-1066

Drobot, Joseph A., Jr., President
Polish Roman Catholic Union of
    America [19613]

984 N Milwaukee Ave.
Chicago, IL 60642-4101
Ph: (773)782-2600
Toll Free: 800-772-8632
Fax: (773)278-4595

Droll, Paul, Founder
Hydroponic Society of America
    [4443]
PO Box 1183
El Cerrito, CA 94530
Ph: (510)926-2908

Drollinger, Darrin, Exec. Dir.
American Society of Agricultural and
    Biological Engineers [6533]
2950 Niles Rd.
Saint Joseph, MI 49085-8607
Ph: (269)429-0300
Toll Free: 800-371-2723
Fax: (269)429-3852

Drost, Tod, Exec. Dir.
American College of Veterinary
    Radiology [17621]
777 E Park Dr.
Harrisburg, PA 17105
Ph: (717)558-7865
Fax: (717)558-7841

D'Loss, Rick, Secretary, Treasurer
Social Democrats USA [18874]
PO Box 16161
Pittsburgh, PA 15242-0161
Ph: (412)894-1799

Drucker, Chuck, President
Association of Commercial Profes-
    sionals - Life Sciences [1597]
1691 Holly Rd.
North Brunswick, NJ 08902
Ph: (908)824-0318

Drudy, Michael A., Exec. Dir.,
    Secretary, Treasurer
Railway Systems Suppliers, Inc.
    [2842]
13133 Professional Dr., Ste. 100
Jacksonville, FL 32225-4178
Ph: (904)379-3366
Fax: (904)379-3941

Drupa, David A., Exec. Sec.
Society for Risk Analysis [1932]
1313 Dolley Madison Blvd., Ste. 402
McLean, VA 22101
Ph: (703)790-1745

D'Souza, Dr. Joseph, President
Dalit Freedom Network [18391]
PO Box 3459
Virginia Beach, VA 23454
Ph: (202)233-9110
Fax: (202)280-1340

Dual, Patricia, Secretary
National Black Sisters' Conference
    [19875]
1200 Varnum St. NE
Washington, DC 20017
Ph: (202)529-9250
Fax: (202)529-9370

DuBasky, Valentina, Director,
    Founder
Art in a Box [10764]
463 W St., Ste. G-122
New York, NY 10014
Ph: (212)691-2543

Dubaybo, Dr. Basim, President
National Arab American Medical As-
    sociation [15126]
2265 Livernois Rd., Ste. 720
Troy, MI 48083
Ph: (248)646-3661
Fax: (248)646-0617

Dubin, Corey S., President
Committee of Ten Thousand [13537]

236 Massachusetts Ave. NE, Ste.
    609
Washington, DC 20002-4971
Ph: (202)543-0988
    (202)681-2351
Toll Free: 800-488-2688

Dubin, Marc, Exec. Dir., Founder
Communities Against Violence
    Network [13271]
2711 Ordway St. NW, No. 111
Washington, DC 20008
Ph: (305)896-3000

Dubinsky, James, Exec. Dir.
Association for Business Com-
    munication [7543]
355 Shanks Hall
181 Turner St. NW
Blacksburg, VA 24061
Ph: (540)231-1939
    (540)231-8460

DuBois, David, President
DuBois Family Association [20856]
c/o Pamela Bailey, Treasurer
726 Loveville Rd., Cottage 60
Hockessin, DE 19707

Dubois, David, President, CEO
International Association of Exhibi-
    tions and Events [1175]
12700 Park Central Dr., Ste. 308
Dallas, TX 75251
Ph: (972)458-8002
Fax: (972)458-8119

DuBois, Joan, Dir. of Public Rel.
U.S. Chess Federation [21593]
137 O'Brien Dr.
Crossville, TN 38555
Ph: (931)787-1234
Fax: (931)787-1200

DuBois, Rev. Joleen D., Founder,
    President
White Mountain Education Associa-
    tion [20620]
PO Box 11975
Prescott, AZ 86304
Ph: (928)778-0638

Dubois, Deacon Thomas R., MPS,
    Exec. Dir.
National Association of Diaconate
    Directors [19868]
7625 N High St.
Columbus, OH 43235
Ph: (614)985-2276

Dubost, Joy, Officer
Beer Institute [180]
440 1st. St. NW, Ste. 350
Washington, DC 20001
Ph: (202)737-2337
Fax: (202)737-7004

Dubrule, Mike, Chairman
Marine Corps Counterintelligence
    Association [19546]
PO Box 1948
Seminole, OK 74818-1948

Dubsky, Dawn, President
America Against Malaria [15392]
PO Box 4
Frankfort, IL 60423
Ph: (815)693-1657
    (773)640-1347
Fax: (815)464-3531

Duca, John V., VP, Assoc. Dir.
International Banking, Economics
    and Finance Association [6393]
c/o John V. Duca, Vice President
Federal Reserve Bank of Dallas
2200 N Pearl St.
Dallas, TX 75201
Ph: (214)922-5154

Ducca, Mary, President
Amateur Astronomers, Inc. [21305]
PO Box 111
Garwood, NJ 07027-0111

Duckett, Helen, Founder
Angels With Special Needs [11571]
PO Box 25555
Columbia, SC 29224-5555
Ph: (803)419-5136
Fax: (803)788-3236

Ducommun, Debbie, Contact
Rat Assistance and Teaching Society
  [22242]
857 Lindo Ln.
Chico, CA 95973
Ph: (530)899-0605

Ducommun, Debbie, Founder
Rat Fan Club [22243]
857 Lindo Ln.
Chico, CA 95973-0914
Ph: (530)899-0605

Duda, Doug, Dir. of Strat. Plan.
International Association of Culinary
  Professionals [1388]
45 Rockefeller Plz., Ste. 2000
New York, NY 10111
Ph: (646)358-4957
Toll Free: 866-358-4951
Fax: (866)358-2524

Duda, Sherry, Chairperson
Organization Development Network
  [2464]
2025 M St. NW, Ste. 800
Washington, DC 20036
Ph: (202)367-1127
Fax: (202)367-2127

Dudley, Julie, Founder, Advisor
Grey Muzzle Organization [10629]
14460 Falls of Neuse Rd., Ste. 149-
  269
Raleigh, NC 27614
Ph: (919)529-0309

Dudley, Dr. Susan, Exec. Dir.
Society for the Psychological Study
  of Social Issues [16942]
208 I St. NE
Washington, DC 20002-4340
Ph: (202)675-6956
Toll Free: 877-310-7778
Fax: (202)675-6902

Dudzik, Dennis, Founder, President
International Association for the
  Advancement of Steam Power
  [7245]
Box 106
3323 Watt Ave.
Sacramento, CA 95821
Ph: (916)473-1240

Duevel, Linda, President
Association for the Advancement of
  International Education [8100]
Maliman Hollywood Bldg. No. 314
3301 College Ave.
Fort Lauderdale, FL 33314-7721
Ph: (954)262-6937

Dufault, Randy, Director
COMMON [6298]
8770 W Bryn Mawr Ave., Ste. 1350
Chicago, IL 60631
Ph: (312)279-0192
Toll Free: 800-777-6734
Fax: (312)279-0227

Duff, Ms. Diane, Exec. Dir.
Southern Governors' Association
  [5787]
Hall of the States
444 N Capitol St. NW, Ste. 200

Washington, DC 20001
Ph: (202)624-5897
Fax: (202)624-7797

Duffy, Deb, Exec. Dir.
Women in Insurance and Financial
  Services [1935]
136 Everett Rd.
Albany, NY 12205
Ph: (518)694-5506
Toll Free: 866-264-9437
Fax: (518)935-9232

Duffy, Jean Macpherson, Chairman
Clan Macpherson Association
  [20827]
c/o Jean Macpherson Duffy, Chairman
6438 Stone Bridge Rd.
Santa Rosa, CA 95409

Duffy, Jonathan, President
Adventist Development and Relief
  Agency International [12606]
12501 Old Columbia Pke.
Silver Spring, MD 20904
Toll Free: 800-424-2372

Duffy, Rebecca, President
Professional Disc Golf Association
  [22808]
International Disc Golf Ctr.
3828 Dogwood Ln.
Appling, GA 30802-3012
Ph: (706)261-6342
Toll Free: 888-840-7342
Fax: (706)261-6347

Duffy, Sandy, Contact
Consumers for Dental Choice
  [14425]
316 F St. NE, Ste. 210
Washington, DC 20002
Ph: (202)544-6333
Fax: (202)544-6331

Duffy, Stephen C., Exec. VP, CEO
American Academy of Facial Plastic
  and Reconstructive Surgery
  [14301]
310 S Henry St.
Alexandria, VA 22314-3524
Ph: (703)299-9291
Toll Free: 800-332-FACE
Fax: (703)299-8898

Duffy Stewart, Barbara, MPH, Exec.
  Dir.
Association of American Cancer
  Institutes [13890]
Medical Arts Bldg., Ste. 503
3708 5th Ave.
Pittsburgh, PA 15213
Ph: (412)647-6111

DuFran, Zac, Mem.
International Aroid Society [22104]
PO Box 43-1853
South Miami, FL 33143

Dufurrena, Dr. Quinn, Exec. Dir.
Association of Dental Support
  Organizations [14420]
19751 E Mainstreet, Ste. 340
Parker, CO 80138
Ph: (720)379-5342
Fax: (720)379-5409

Dugan, Kevin, Director, Founder
Fields of Growth International
  [11358]
PO Box 2
Avon by the Sea, NJ 07717-0002
Toll Free: 888-318-8541

Duggal, Elizabeth, Co-Chmn. of the
  Bd.
International Council of Museums -
  U.S. National Committee [9832]

1025 Thomas Jefferson St. NW, Ste.
  500 E
Washington, DC 20007
Ph: (202)452-1200
Fax: (202)833-3636

Dugger, Ronnie, Founder
Alliance for Democracy [18935]
21 Main St.
Hudson, MA 01749
Ph: (978)333-7971
Fax: (978)333-7972

Dugoni, Dr. Steven A., Secretary,
  Treasurer
American Board of Orthodontics
  [14398]
401 N Lindbergh Blvd., Ste. 300
Saint Louis, MO 63141-7839
Ph: (314)432-6130
Fax: (314)432-8170

Duhon-Sells, Rose, Founder
National Association for Multicultural
  Education [8045]
2100 M St., Ste. 170-245
Washington, DC 20037
Ph: (202)679-6263

Duke, Arnold, President
Gem and Lapidary Dealers Associa-
  tion [2046]
120 Derwood Cir.
Rockville, MD 20850
Ph: (301)294-1640

Duke, David, PhD, President
European-American Unity and
  Rights Organization [17894]
PO Box 5941
Thibodaux, LA 70302-5941
Ph: (985)209-9937

Duke, Mike, Treasurer
American Council of the Blind Radio
  Amateurs [21264]
c/o Robert R Rogers
1121 Morado Dr.
Cincinnati, OH 45238

Duke, Natalie, Secretary, Treasurer
United States Elite Coaches' Association for Women's Gymnastics
  [22739]
c/o Natalie Duke
10 Quail Point Pl.
Carmichael, CA 95608
Ph: (916)487-3559
Fax: (916)487-3706

Duke, Richard B., President
Electrical Manufacturing and Coil
  Winding Association [1020]
PO Box 278
Imperial Beach, CA 91933
Ph: (619)435-3629
Fax: (619)435-3639

Dukovich, Theresa, Exec. Dir.
Alliance of Families Fighting
  Pancreatic Cancer [16566]
PO Box 2023
Lower Burrell, PA 15068
Toll Free: 800-704-9080

Dulli, Zachary R., CEO
National Council for Geographic
  Education [7935]
1775 Eye St. NW, Ste. 1150
Washington, DC 20006-2435
Ph: (202)587-5727
Fax: (202)618-6249

Dumais, Céline, Chairperson
SOCAP International [2758]
625 N Washington St., Ste. 304
Alexandria, VA 22314
Ph: (703)519-3700
Fax: (703)549-4886

Dumesnil, Robert, Jr., Trustee
Construction Employers' Association
  [515]
2175 N California Blvd., Ste. 420
Walnut Creek, CA 94596
Ph: (925)930-8184
Fax: (925)930-9014

Dumm, Sue, Chmn. of the Bd.
Retinoblastoma International [14056]
18030 Brookhurst St.
Fountain Valley, CA 92708

Dummer, Greg, CAE, CEO
Society for Laboratory Automation
  and Screening [6217]
100 Illinois St., Ste. 242
Saint Charles, IL 60174
Ph: (630)256-7527
Toll Free: 877-990-SLAS
Fax: (630)741-7527

Dumont, Jacques, President
Association of Caribbean Historians
  [9460]
c/o Michelle Craig McDonald,
  Secretary/Treasurer
Dept. of History
Richard Stockton College
101 Vera King Farris Dr.
Galloway, NJ 08205-9441

Dumont, Robert J., President, CEO
Tooling, Manufacturing and
  Technologies Association [1774]
28237 Orchard Lake Rd., Ste. 101
Farmington Hills, MI 48334
Ph: (248)488-0300
Toll Free: 800-969-9682
Fax: (248)488-0500

Dumphy, Shawn, VP
National Bulk Vendors Association
  [3432]
1202 E Maryland Ave., Ste. 1K
Phoenix, AZ 85014-1342
Toll Free: 888-628-2872
Fax: (480)302-5108

Dunay, Darren, President
National Association of Publishers'
  Representatives, Inc. [2805]
2800 W Higgins Rd., Ste. 440
Hoffman Estates, IL 60169
Toll Free: 877-263-9640
Fax: (847)885-8393

Dunbar, Dr. Gary L., President
American Society for Neural Therapy
  and Repair [16006]
c/o Paul R. Sanberg, Executive
  Director
MDC-78
12901 Bruce B. Downs Blvd.
Tampa, FL 33612
Ph: (813)974-3154
Fax: (813)974-3078

Dunbar, Melanie, President
HOPE Animal-Assisted Crisis
  Response [12742]
1292 High St., No. 182
Eugene, OR 97401
Toll Free: 877-467-3597

Dunbar, William K., Exec., Officer
International Blue Jay Class Association [22626]
12 Sandpiper Pt. Rd.
12 Sandpiper Point Rd.
Old Lyme, CT 06371
Ph: (860)434-5125

Duncan, Bryan, V. Chmn. of the Bd.
Community Action Partnership
  [12534]
1140 Connecticut Ave. NW, Ste.
  1210

Washington, DC 20036
Ph: (202)265-7546
Fax: (202)265-5048

Duncan, Matthew, Chairman
Soil Science Society of America -
   Consulting Soil Scientists Division
   [4689]
c/o Matthew Duncan, Chair
10379 E 1000th St.
Macomb, IL 61455-8111
Ph: (309)333-0535
   (406)581-5066

Duncan, Mike, President
Board Retailers Association [2949]
PO Box 1170
Wrightsville Beach, NC 28480
Ph: (910)509-0109

Duncan, PhD, CRC, CPO, J. Chad,
   Officer
National Council on Rehabilitation
   Education [17093]
1099 E Champlain Dr., Ste. A, No.
   137
Fresno, CA 93720
Ph: (559)906-0787
Fax: (559)412-2550

Duncan, William A., President
International Hyperbaric Medical As-
   sociation [15342]
6155 Beachway Dr.
Falls Church, VA 22041-1431
Ph: (703)339-0900

Duncan-Smith, Billie, Founder
CADASIL Together We Have Hope
   [14567]
3605 Monument Dr.
Round Rock, TX 78681-3707
Ph: (512)255-0209
Toll Free: 877-519-4673

Duncanson, Pete, Chairman, Act.
   Pres.
Institute of Inspection, Cleaning and
   Restoration Certification [1945]
4043 S Eastern Ave.
Las Vegas, NV 89119
Ph: (775)553-5458
Fax: (775)553-5458

Dundas, William, President
Society for the Preservation and Ap-
   preciation of Antique Motor Fire
   Apparatus in America [22015]
c/o Candy Bennett, Membership
   Secretary
8035 Bird Pond Rd.
Adams Run, SC 29426-5545

Dunfee, Matt, Program Mgr.
Wildlife Management Institute [4914]
1440 Upper Bermudian Rd.
Gardners, PA 17324
Ph: (802)563-2087
   (717)677-4480

Dunham, Cathy, President
Access Project [14970]
89 South St., 7th Fl.
Boston, MA 02111

Dunham, Luanne K., Corr. Sec.
American Cavalier King Charles
   Spaniel Club [21804]
c/o Lun Dunham, Corresponding
   Secretary
2 Bud Davis Rd.
Newnan, GA 30263

Dunham, Robert, Exec. Dir.
Death Penalty Information Center
   [17829]
1015 18th St. NW, Ste. 704
Washington, DC 20036
Ph: (202)289-2275

Dunipace, David, Director
American Academy of Anesthesiolo-
   gist Assistants [13690]
1231 Collier Rd. NW, Ste. J
Atlanta, GA 30318-2322
Ph: (678)222-4221
Fax: (404)249-8831

Dunklee, Kelli F., Liaison
National Junior Holstein Association
   [3742]
1 Holstein Pl.
Brattleboro, VT 05302-0808
Ph: (802)254-4551
Toll Free: 800-952-5200
Fax: (802)254-8251

Dunlap, Ellen S., President
American Antiquarian Society [9368]
185 Salisbury St.
Worcester, MA 01609-1634
Ph: (508)755-5221
Fax: (508)753-3311

Dunlap, Michaele, President
American Mental Health Alliance
   [15757]
c/o Michaele P. Dunlap, PsyD,
   President
Mentor Professional Corporation
818 NW 17th Ave., No. 11
Portland, OR 97209
Ph: (503)227-2027

Dunlop, Mr. Peter, President
Dunlop - Dunlap Family Society
   [20857]
PO Box 652
East Aurora, NY 14052
Ph: (716)655-2521

Dunn, Alexandra Dapolito, Officer
The Environmental Council of the
   States [4138]
50 F St. NW, Ste. 350
Washington, DC 20001
Ph: (202)266-4920
Fax: (202)266-4937

Dunn, Art, President
Bigfoot Owners Club International
   [21337]
PO Box 18282
San Jose, CA 95158

Dunn, Bruce, President
National Swimming Pool Foundation
   [2914]
4775 Granby Cir.
Colorado Springs, CO 80919
Ph: (719)540-9119
Fax: (719)540-2787

Dunn, Jeffrey D., President, CEO
Sesame Workshop [11269]
1 Lincoln Plz.
New York, NY 10023
Ph: (212)595-3456
   (212)595-3457

Dunn, Kirby, President
National Shared Housing Resource
   Center [11987]
c/o Pam Reed
2004 E Sherwood Rd.
Arlington Heights, IL 60004
Ph: (847)823-0453

Dunn, Robert H., Advisor
Synergos [12566]
3 E 54th St., 14th Fl.
New York, NY 10022
Ph: (646)963-2100
Fax: (646)201-5220

Dunn, Sharon L., President
American Physical Therapy Association [16718]

1111 N Fairfax St.
Alexandria, VA 22314-1488
Ph: (703)684-2782
Toll Free: 800-999-2782
Fax: (703)684-7343

Dunn, Sidney N., Exec. Dir.
The Osteopathic Cranial Academy
   [16524]
3535 E 96th St., Ste. 101
Indianapolis, IN 46240
Ph: (317)581-0411
Fax: (317)580-9299

Dunn Soeby, Lisa, President
Hope for Hypothalamic Hamartomas
   [15941]
PO Box 721
Waddell, AZ 85355

Dunn, Tom, Secretary
Automotive Parts Remanufacturers
   Association [340]
7250 Heritage Village Plz., Ste. 201
Gainesville, VA 20155
Ph: (703)968-2772
Fax: (703)753-2445

Dunnam, Jennifer, Chairperson
Braille Authority of North America
   [17693]
c/o National Federation of the Blind
200 E Wells St., Jernigan Pl.
Baltimore, MD 21230
Ph: (612)767-5658

Dunning, Mark, Chmn. of the Bd.
Usher Syndrome Coalition [14864]
2 Mill and Main Place, Ste. 418
Maynard, MA 01754
Ph: (978)637-2625
Fax: (978)637-2618

Duong, Quang, Exec. Ofc.
VietHope [13270]
133 Clarendon St., No. 170649
Boston, MA 02217-4128

Duplantier, F.R., Ed. Dir.
America's Future [18279]
7800 Bonhomme Ave.
Saint Louis, MO 63105
Ph: (314)725-6003
Fax: (314)721-3373

Duplay, David S., Chairman
Vital Options International [14080]
17328 Ventura Blvd., No. 161
Encino, CA 91316
Ph: (818)508-5657

Dupont, Jean-Claude, President
World Confederation of Billiard
   Sports [22591]
4345 Beverly St., Ste. D
Colorado Springs, CO 80918
Ph: (719)264-8300
Fax: (719)264-0900

Dupree, Dr. Mary Helen, Secretary,
   Treasurer
Lessing Society [9073]
c/o Dr. Monika Nenon, President
University of Memphis
Dept. of Foreign Languages and
   Literatures
Memphis, TN 38152
Ph: (901)678-4094
Fax: (901)678-5338

Dupuis, Alain H., President
Federation of French War Veterans
   [21206]
39-45 51st St., Ste. 6F
Woodside, NY 11377-3165
Ph: (718)426-1474

Dupuis, Josée, President
International Genetic Epidemiology
   Society [14732]

c/o Mariza de Andrade, PhD,
   Treasurer
Mayo Clinic
200 1st St. SW
Rochester, MN 55905-0002

Durante, Douglas A., Exec. Dir.
Clean Fuels Development Coalition
   [4541]
c/o Douglas Durante, Executive
   Director
4641 Montgomery Ave., Ste. 350
Bethesda, MD 20814
Ph: (301)718-0077
Fax: (301)718-0606

Durante, Kim, President
Western Association of Map Libraries [9734]
c/o Greg Armento
California State University
1250 Bellflower Blvd.
Long Beach, CA 90840-1901

Durbin, Joanna, Director
Climate, Community and Biodiversity
   Alliance [3829]
c/o Joanna Durbin, Director
2011 Crystal Dr., Ste. 500
Arlington, VA 22202-3787
Ph: (703)341-2461

Durchslag, Jimmy, Exec. Dir.
Mainstream Media Project [18656]
854 9th St., Ste. B
Arcata, CA 95521
Ph: (707)826-9111
Fax: (707)826-9112

Durham, Clarice, Co-Ch.
National Alliance Against Racist and
   Political Repression [17914]
1325 S Wabash Ave., Ste. 105
Chicago, IL 60614
Ph: (312)939-2750

Durham, David, President
Quiet Valley Living Historical Farm
   [9508]
347 Quiet Valley Rd.
Stroudsburg, PA 18360
Ph: (570)992-6161
Fax: (570)992-9587

Durham, Mario Garcia, President,
   CEO
Association of Performing Arts
   Presenters [7508]
1211 Connecticut Ave. NW, Ste. 200
Washington, DC 20036-2716
Ph: (202)833-2787
Toll Free: 888-820-2787
Fax: (202)833-1543

Durham, Mario Garcia, Chairman
Performing Arts Alliance [8996]
1211 Connecticut Ave. NW, Ste. 200
Washington, DC 20036
Ph: (202)207-3850
Fax: (202)833-1543

Durham, Susan, VP
Neuro-Optometric Rehabilitation Association International, Inc. [16030]
28514 Costellation Rd.
Valencia, CA 91355
Ph: (949)250-0176
   (253)661-6005

Duric, Marko, President
Serbian Bar Association of America
   [5048]
20 S Clark St., Ste. 700
Chicago, IL 60603
Ph: (312)782-8500

Durkee, David B., President
Bakery, Confectionery, Tobacco
   Workers and Grain Millers
   International Union [23454]

10401 Connecticut Ave.
Kensington, MD 20895
Ph: (301)933-8600

Durley, Cynthia C., Exec. Dir.
Dental Assisting National Board, Inc.
[14429]
444 N Michigan Ave., Ste. 900
Chicago, IL 60611
Ph: (312)642-3368
Toll Free: 800-367-3262
Fax: (312)642-8507

Durning, David, President, CEO
CRE Finance Council [2857]
900 7th St. NW, Ste. 501
Washington, DC 20001
Ph: (202)448-0850
Fax: (202)448-0865

Durrant, Karen, President, Founder
Autoinflammatory Alliance [14566]
PO Box 590354
San Francisco, CA 94159
Ph: (415)831-8782

Durso, Pam, Exec. Dir.
Baptist Women in Ministry [19725]
3001 Mercer University Dr.
Atlanta, GA 30341-4115
Ph: (404)513-6022

Durst, Elizabeth, Ph.D., Exec. Dir.
American Association of Teachers of
Slavic and East European
Languages [8174]
c/o Elizabeth Durst, PhD, Executive
Director
University of Southern California
3501 Trousdale Pky., THH 255L
Los Angeles, CA 90089
Ph: (213)740-2734
Fax: (213)740-8550

Durst, Steve, Founder, Director
International Lunar Observatory As-
sociation [6005]
65-1230 Mamalahoa Highway D20
Kamuela, HI 96743
Ph: (808)885-3474
Fax: (808)885-3475

Durtka, Alexander, Jr., Counsel
Global Ties U.S. [18545]
1250 H St. NW, Ste. 305
Washington, DC 20005
Ph: (202)842-1414
Fax: (202)289-4625

Dusek, Robin, President, Exec. Dir.
Educating Africa's Children [11200]
2633 N Wilton Ave., Unit 1
Chicago, IL 60614
Ph: (773)991-2812

Duss, Matthew, President
Foundation for Middle East Peace
[18681]
1761 N St. NW
Washington, DC 20036
Ph: (202)835-3650
Fax: (202)835-3651

Duston, Rob, Chairman
Helping Children Worldwide [11022]
14101 Parke Long Ct., Ste. T
Chantilly, VA 20151
Ph: (703)793-9521
Fax: (703)956-6866

Dut, Salva, Founder
Water for South Sudan [13345]
PO Box 25551
Rochester, NY 14625-0551
Ph: (585)383-0410

Dutschke, Dwight A., President
Native Sons of the Golden West
[19394]

414 Mason St., Ste. 300
San Francisco, CA 94102
Ph: (415)392-1223
Toll Free: 800-337-1875

Dutson, Greg, President
Vizsla Club of America [21987]
379 Costa Mesa St.
Costa Mesa, CA 92627

Dutt, Mallika, CEO, President,
Founder
Breakthrough [18379]
4 W 43rd St., Ste. 715
New York, NY 10036
Ph: (212)868-6500
Fax: (212)868-6501

Dutton, Leslie C., President
American Association of Women
[18960]
337 Washington Blvd., Ste. 1
Marina del Rey, CA 90292
Ph: (310)822-4449
Fax: (310)919-2890

Duval, Robert, Director
L'Athletique d'Haiti [13429]
13799 Park Blvd. N, No. 284
Seminole, FL 33776

DuVall, Randy, President
Hebron USA [20422]
12375 Kinsman Rd., Ste. H11
Newbury, OH 44065
Ph: (440)804-5733
Toll Free: 888-598-8276
Fax: (440)564-1273

Duvall, Zippy, Chairman
American Farm Bureau Foundation
for Agriculture [3543]
600 Maryland Ave. SW, Ste. 1000W
Washington, DC 20024
Toll Free: 800-443-8456
Fax: (202)314-5121

Duvic, Philip, Exec. VP
Architectural Woodwork Institute
[491]
46179 Westlake Dr., Ste. 120
Potomac Falls, VA 20165
Ph: (571)323-3636
Fax: (571)323-3630

Dvorak, Jane, APR, Officer
Public Relations Society of America
[2757]
33 Maiden Ln., 11th Fl.
New York, NY 10038-5150
Ph: (212)460-1400

Dvorak, Mitchell, Exec. Dir.
International Association of Oral and
Maxillofacial Surgeons [16447]
8618 W Catalpa Ave., Ste. 1116
Chicago, IL 60656
Ph: (224)232-8737
Fax: (224)735-2965

Dvorak, Mitchell L.
Council of Medical Specialty Societ-
ies [15664]
35 E Wacker Dr., Ste. 850
Chicago, IL 60601-2106
Ph: (312)224-2585
Fax: (312)644-8557

Dvorak, Prof. Steven L., Contact
Center for Electronic Packaging
Research [6967]
Dept. of Electrical and Computer
Engineering
University of Arizona
Tucson, AZ 85721-0104
Ph: (520)621-6193
Fax: (520)621-8076

Dvorin, Diane, Managing Dir.,
Founder
Women Work Together [11747]
3232 6th St.

Boulder, CO 80304
Ph: (303)444-8193

Dwinell-Yardley, Dana, Dir. of
Comm.
Interweave Continental: Unitarian
Universalists for Lesbian, Gay,
Bisexual and Transgender
Concerns [20183]
156 Massapoag Ave.
Sharon, MA 02067-2749

Dworkin, Aaron P., Founder,
President
Sphinx Organization [10015]
400 Renaissance Ctr., Ste. 2550
Detroit, MI 48243
Ph: (313)877-9100
Fax: (313)887-0164

Dwyer, Bob, Contact
Carbon Monoxide Safety Association
[17495]
12500 1st St., Ste. 5
Thornton, CO 80241
Toll Free: 800-394-5253
Fax: (800)546-3726

Dwyer Gunn, Barbara, CEO,
President
Structured Employment Economic
Development Corporation [18160]
22 Cortlandt St., 33rd Fl.
New York, NY 10007-3107
Ph: (212)473-0255

Dwyer, Jeanette P., President
National Rural Letter Carriers' As-
sociation [23510]
1630 Duke St.
Alexandria, VA 22314-3465
Ph: (703)684-5545

Dwyer, Joe, President
Association for Pet Loss and
Bereavement [12453]
PO Box 55
Nutley, NJ 07110
Ph: (718)382-0690

Dwyer, Mary M., PhD, CEO,
President
Institute for the International Educa-
tion of Students [8616]
33 W Monroe St., Ste. 2300
Chicago, IL 60603-5405
Ph: (312)944-1750
Toll Free: 800-995-2300
Fax: (312)944-1448

Dwyer, Michael, President
Juvenile Products Manufacturers
Association [2064]
1120 Route 73, Ste. 200
Mount Laurel, NJ 08054
Ph: (856)638-0420
Fax: (856)439-0525

Dyak, Brian L., Bd. Member,
Secretary, Founder, Exec.
Producer
Entertainment Industries Council Inc.
[13138]
4206 Technology Ct., Ste. E
Chantilly, VA 20151
Ph: (703)481-1414
Fax: (703)481-1418

Dyak, Brian, Membership Chp., Advi-
sor
Sun Safety Alliance [14069]
1856 Old Reston Ave., Ste. 215
Reston, VA 20190
Ph: (703)481-1414

Dyck, Thomas Van, Chairman,
Secretary
As You Sow Foundation [18064]
1611 Telegraph Ave., Ste. 1450

Oakland, CA 94612
Ph: (510)735-8158
Fax: (510)735-8143

Dyer, C.H., President, CEO
Bright Hope International [12531]
2060 Stonington Ave.
Hoffman Estates, IL 60169
Ph: (224)520-6100
Fax: (866)530-3489

Dyer, D.Alexandra, Exec. Dir.
Healing Arts Initiative, Inc. [10253]
33-02 Skillman Ave. 1st Fl.
Long Island City, NY 11101
Ph: (212)575-7676
Fax: (212)575-7669

Dyer, Dr. Esther R., CEO, President
National Medical Fellowships [8333]
347 5th Ave., Rm. 510
New York, NY 10016-5007
Ph: (212)483-8880
Fax: (212)483-8897

Dyer, Jenny Eaton, PhD, Exec. Dir.
Hope Through Healing Hands
[15473]
2908 Poston Ave.
Nashville, TN 37203
Ph: (615)320-7888
     (615)818-5579

Dyer, Lynn, President
Foodservice and Packaging Institute
[2477]
7700 Leesburg Pke., Ste. 421
Falls Church, VA 22043
Ph: (703)592-9889
Fax: (703)592-9864

Dykema, Sue M., Exec. Dir.
American Society for Aesthetic
Plastic Surgery [14307]
11262 Monarch St.
Garden Grove, CA 92841
Ph: (562)799-2356
Toll Free: 800-364-2147
Fax: (562)799-1098

Dykes, Mark, President
Apiary Inspectors of America [3634]
Virginia Department of Agriculture
and Consumer Services
PO Box 1163
Richmond, VA 23218

Dyson, Lily, Bd. Member
North America Taiwanese Professors' Association [19669]
c/o Dr. Mao Lin, Membership Committee Chairperson
5250 Soledad Mountain Rd.
San Diego, CA 92109-1529

Dyson, Robert R., Chairman
Dyson Foundation [12471]
25 Halcyon Rd.
Millbrook, NY 12545-9611
Ph: (845)677-0644
Fax: (845)677-0650

Dziekanowski, Alex, Founder, Exec.
Dir.
Dance 4 Health [16698]
1072 S DeAnza Blvd., Ste. A107-
317
San Jose, CA 95129
Ph: (408)253-4673
Fax: (408)253-4673

Dzienkowski, Karla, Exec. Dir.
Restless Legs Syndrome Foundation
[17349]
3006 Bee Caves Rd., Ste. D206
Austin, TX 78746
Ph: (512)366-9109
Fax: (512)366-9189

Dzu, Heng, Master
Buddhist Text Translation Society
[19772]
International Translation Institute
1777 Murchison Dr.
Burlingame, CA 94010-4504
Ph: (415)332-6221

Dzwonkowski, Megan, Exec. Dir.
National School Foundation Associa-
tion [8540]
509 Aurora Ave., Ste. 406
Naperville, IL 60540
Toll Free: 866-824-8513

E

Eade, John, President
Investorside Research Association
[2027]
61 Broadway, Ste. 1910
New York, NY 10006-2701
Toll Free: 877-834-4777
Fax: (877)834-4777

Eaglefeathers, Moke, Exec. Dir., Bd.
Member
National Council of Urban Indian
Health [18710]
924 Pennsylvania Ave. SE
Washington, DC 20003
Ph: (202)544-0344
Fax: (202)544-9394

Eakin, Max, President
Blue/White Pottery Club [21288]
C/o Priscilla Lindstrom, Treasurer
PO Box 297
Saint Joseph, IL 61873

Eakin, Max, Co-Pres.
Blue & White Pottery & Old Sleepy
Eye Collectors Club [21577]
c/o Susie Reicheneker
402 N Laurel St.
Elmwood, IL 61529

Eames, Michael, President
Association of Independent Music
Publishers [2419]
PO Box 10482
Marina del Rey, CA 90295
Ph: (818)771-7301

Eames, Toni, President
International Association of As-
sistance Dog Partners [14550]
PO Box 638
Sterling Heights, MI 48311
Ph: (586)826-3938
Toll Free: 888-544-2237
Fax: (248)357-6209

Eanes, Gordon, Treasurer
Sanitary Supply Wholesaling As-
sociation [2141]
1432 Riverwalk Ct.
Waterville, OH 43566
Ph: (419)878-2787
Fax: (614)340-7938

Earing, Amy, Treasurer
STRIDE [7719]
476 N Greenbush Rd., Ste. 9
Rensselaer, NY 12144
Ph: (518)598-1279
Fax: (518)391-2563

Earl, Mia, President
Reflexology Association of America
[13653]
PO Box 220
Achilles, VA 23001
Ph: (980)234-0159

Earle, Sylvia, Bd. Member
Ocean Futures Society [4771]
513 De La Vina St.

Santa Barbara, CA 93101
Ph: (805)899-8899

Earle, William T., President
National Association of Beverage
Importers Inc. [187]
National Press Bldg.
529 14th St. NW, Ste. 1183
Washington, DC 20045
Ph: (202)393-6224
Toll Free: 877-393-6224
Fax: (202)393-6595

Earley, Matt, President
Outside the Bean [18623]
PO Box 1565
Madison, WI 53701-1565

Earley, Terry, President
Specialty Tools and Fasteners
Distributors Association [1769]
500 Elm Grove Rd., Ste. 210
Elm Grove, WI 53122
Ph: (262)784-4774
Toll Free: 800-352-2981
Fax: (262)784-5059

Earp, Jamie, President
United States Sweet Potato Council
[4258]
12 Nicklaus Ln., Ste. 101
Columbia, SC 29229-3363

Earwood, Dr. Glenda, Exec. Dir.
National Alpha Lambda Delta
[23784]
328 Orange St.
Macon, GA 31201
Toll Free: 800-925-7421

East, Bill, Exec. Dir.
National Association of State Direc-
tors of Special Education [8589]
225 Reinekers Ln., Ste. 420
Alexandria, VA 22314
Ph: (703)519-3800
Fax: (703)519-3808

Easter, Karen Butler, President
National Association of Crisis
Organization Directors [11553]
c/o Karen Butler Easter, President
PO Box 5051
Potsdam, NY 13676
Ph: (315)265-2422

Easterling, Letson E., Sr., President
Easterling Family Genealogical
Society [20859]
1124 Pearl Valley Rd.
Wesson, MS 39191-9361

Eastman, Brent, President
Partners for Peace [18812]
Bldg. H
855 E Laurel Dr.
Salinas, CA 93905
Ph: (831)754-3888

Eastman, Hope B., Esq.,
Chairperson
American Employment Law Council
[4989]
4800 Hampden Ln., 7th Fl.
Bethesda, MD 20814
Ph: (301)951-9326
Fax: (301)654-7354

Easton, Linda, Exec. Dir.
International Professional Groomers
[2544]
6475 Wallace Rd. NW
Salem, OR 97304
Ph: (503)551-2397

Eaton, Michael, Exec. Dir.
National Model United Nations
[8116]

2945 44th Ave. S, Ste. 600
Minneapolis, MN 55406
Ph: (612)353-5649
Fax: (651)305-0093

Ebberts, Ann M., CEO
Association of Government Ac-
countants [4938]
2208 Mt. Vernon Ave.
Alexandria, VA 22301-1314
Ph: (703)684-6931
Toll Free: 800-AGA-7211
Fax: (703)548-9367

Ebenezer, Job S., PhD, President
Technology for the Poor [4703]
877 Pelham Ct.
Westerville, OH 43081

Eberhart, Ralph E., Chairman,
President
AFBA [19377]
909 N Washington St.
Alexandria, VA 22314
Ph: (703)549-4455
Toll Free: 800-776-2322
Fax: (703)706-5961

Ebert, Jeff, Exec. Sec.
American Cheviot Sheep Society
[4648]
PO Box 231
Wamego, KS 66547
Ph: (785)456-8500
Fax: (785)456-8599

Eberts, Shari, Chairman
Hearing Health Foundation [15193]
363 7th Ave., 10th Fl.
New York, NY 10001-3904
Ph: (212)257-6140
Toll Free: 866-454-3924

Eblen, Ruth A., Founder, President
Rene Dubos Center for Human
Environments [4047]
The Rene Dubos Center, Ste. 387
Bronxville, NY 10708-3818
Ph: (914)337-1636
Fax: (914)771-5206

Ebrahimi, Sharifa, CCEP, Treasurer
Association of Collegiate Conference
and Events Directors International
[2322]
2900 S College Ave., Ste. 3B
Fort Collins, CO 80525
Ph: (970)449-4960
Fax: (970)449-4965

Eby, Bill, President
H.H. Franklin Club, Inc. [21385]
Cazenovia College
Cazenovia, NY 13035
Ph: (201)384-1530
    (518)883-5765
Fax: (518)773-7742

Eby, Debbie, Mgr.
International Society of Automation
[6762]
67 TW Alexander Dr.
Research Triangle Park, NC 27709
Ph: (919)549-8411
Fax: (919)549-8288

Echeverri, Juan Diego Villegas, MD,
President
International Pelvic Pain Society
[16560]
1100 E Woodfield Rd., Ste. 350
Schaumburg, IL 60173
Ph: (847)517-8712
Fax: (847)517-7229

Echodu, Calvin, Founder, V. Chmn.
of the Bd.
Pilgrim Africa [12712]
2200 6th Ave., No. 804

Seattle, WA 98121
Ph: (206)706-0350

Echohawk, Sarah, CEO
American Indian Science and
Engineering Society [6531]
2305 Renard Pl. SE, Ste. 200
Albuquerque, NM 87106
Ph: (505)765-1052
Fax: (505)765-5608

Echohawk, Sarah, President
Red Feather Development Group
[11992]
PO Box 907
Bozeman, MT 59771-0907
Ph: (406)585-7188
    (928)440-5119

Echols, Karolynn, MD, President
Medicine in Action [15736]
8101 Skyline Blvd.
Oakland, CA 94611
Ph: (510)339-7579
Fax: (510)339-6012

Eckberg, Bill, President
Early American Coppers [22268]

Eckel, Fred, President
Christian Pharmacists Fellowship
International [16657]
PO Box 1154
Bristol, TN 37621-1154
Ph: (423)844-1043

Ecker, Robert H., Exec. Dir.
Aircraft Locknut Manufacturers As-
sociation [1561]
c/o Robert H. Ecker, Executive
Director
994 Old Eagle School Rd., Ste.
1019
Wayne, PA 19087
Ph: (610)971-4850
Fax: (610)971-4859

Ecker, Robert H., Exec. Dir.
Vibration Isolation and Seismic
Control Manufacturers Association
[7159]
994 Old Eagle School Rd., Ste.
1019
Wayne, PA 19087-1866
Ph: (610)971-4850

Eckerle, Mark, President
Goals 4 Ghana [11003]
5830 N Glenwood Ave.
Chicago, IL 60660
Ph: (773)307-8848

Eckert, Emilie, Exec. Asst., Office
Mgr.
Pediatric Brain Tumor Foundation
[14043]
302 Ridgefield Ct.
Asheville, NC 28806
Ph: (828)665-6891
Toll Free: 800-253-6530
Fax: (828)665-6894

Eckert, Mimi, Exec. Dir.
American Board of Spine Surgery
[17364]
1350 Broadway, 17th Fl., Ste. 1705
New York, NY 10018
Ph: (212)356-0682
Fax: (212)356-0678

Eckhart, Chris, Chairman
Binding Industries Association [1529]
301 Brush Creek Rd.
Warrendale, PA 15086
Ph: (412)259-1736
    (317)347-2665
Fax: (412)749-9890

Eckstein, Peter A., President
Institute of Electrical and Electronics
Engineers USA [6557]

2001 L St. NW, Ste. 700
Washington, DC 20036-4910
Ph: (202)785-0017
Fax: (202)785-0835

Eckstein, Rabbi Yechiel Z., Founder,
President
International Fellowship of Christians
and Jews [20543]
30 N LaSalle St., Ste. 4300
Chicago, IL 60602-2584
Toll Free: 800-486-8844

Eddins, Lt. Col. Tim, Treasurer
International Black Aerospace
Council [140]
7120 Sugar Maple Dr.
Irving, TX 75063-5522
Ph: (972)373-9551
Fax: (972)373-9551

Eddy, Dan, Exec. Dir.
National Association of Crime Victim
Compensation Boards [13261]
PO Box 16003
Alexandria, VA 22302
Ph: (703)780-3200

Eddy, Patricia, Founder
Renew Haiti [12722]
821 South Dale Mabry Hwy.
Tampa, FL 33609
Ph: (813)876-5841

Edelheit, Jonathan, CEO
Medical Tourism Association [15735]
10130 Northlake Blvd., Ste. 214-315
West Palm Beach, FL 33412
Ph: (561)791-2000

Edelman, Catherine, President
Association of International
Photography Art Dealers [10136]
2025 M St. NW, Ste. 800
Washington, DC 20036
Ph: (202)367-1158
Fax: (202)367-2158

Edelman, Diane Penneys, President
Lawyers' Committee for Cultural
Heritage Preservation [9232]
2600 Virginia Ave. NW, Ste. 1000
Washington, DC 20037

Edelman, Mrs. Marian Wright,
Founder, President
Black Community Crusade for
Children [10867]
c/o Children's Defense Fund
25 E St. NW
Washington, DC 20001-1522
Toll Free: 800-233-1200

Edelman, Marian Wright, President
Children's Defense Fund [11223]
25 E St. NW
Washington, DC 20001
Toll Free: 800-233-1200

Edelman, Peter B., President
National Center for Youth Law
[5190]
405 14th St., 15th Fl.
Oakland, CA 94612
Ph: (510)835-8098
Fax: (510)835-8099

Edelman, Phil, President
Paperweight Collectors' Association
[21709]
PO Box 334
Fairless Hills, PA 19030

Edelman, Steven V., MD, Director,
Founder
Taking Control of Your Diabetes
[14543]
1110 Camino Del Mar, Ste. B

Del Mar, CA 92014-2649
Ph: (858)755-5683
Toll Free: 800-998-2693
Fax: (858)755-6854

Edelson, Stephen M., PhD,
President
Global Autism Collaboration [13766]
Autism Research Institute
4182 Adams Ave.
San Diego, CA 92116
Toll Free: 866-366-3361

Edelstein, David R., Chairman
American Academy of Otolaryngol-
ogy - Head and Neck Surgery
[16531]
1650 Diagonal Rd.
Alexandria, VA 22314-2857
Ph: (703)836-4444
Fax: (703)683-5100

Edelstein, Edward, Exec. Dir.
Jewish Educators Assembly [8139]
Broadway & Locust Ave.
Cedarhurst, NY 11516
Ph: (516)569-2537
Fax: (516)295-9039

Eden, Ami, CEO, Exec. Ed.
Jewish Telegraphic Agency [18592]
24 W 30th St., 4th Fl.
New York, NY 10001
Ph: (212)643-1890
Fax: (212)643-8499

Edens, Jason, Director, Founder
Rural Renewable Energy Alliance
[6511]
2330 Dancing Wind Rd. SW, Ste. 2
Pine River, MN 56474
Ph: (218)947-3779

Eder, Mike
Equipment Managers Council of
America [806]
PO Box 794
South Amboy, NJ 08879-0794
Ph: (732)354-7264

Eder, Stefen, Exec. VP
U.S. Austrian Chamber of Com-
merce [23626]
165 W 46th St., Ste. 1113
New York, NY 10036
Ph: (212)819-0117

Edgar, C. Ernest, LTC, Chairperson
The Infrastructure Security Partnership [3056]
607 Prince St.
Alexandria, VA 22314
Ph: (703)549-3800
(703)373-7981

Edgar, Patrick B., President
Association for the Rights of
Catholics in the Church [19799]
PO Box 6512
Helena, MT 59604-6512
Ph: (870)235-5209

Edgecombe, John, Jr., Officer
National Newspaper Association
[2703]
900 Community Dr.
Springfield, IL 62703
Ph: (217)241-1400
Fax: (217)241-1301

Edgerton, Dani, President
Greyhound Club of America [21891]
c/o Helen Hamilton
2443 Chardonnay Way
Livermore, CA 94550-6160

Edington, William, Founder, Exec.
Dir.
USA Athletes International [22514]
13095 S Brentwood St.

Olathe, KS 66061
Ph: (913)397-9024
Toll Free: 800-413-6418
Fax: (913)782-5556

Edleman, Keith, Membership Chp.
Love on a Leash [17452]
PO Box 4548
Oceanside, CA 92052-4548
Ph: (760)740-2326

Edlund, Martin, CEO
Malaria No More [14592]
432 Park Ave. S, 4th Fl.
New York, NY 10016

Edlund, Thomas, President
Foundation of East European Family
History Studies [20968]
PO Box 321
Springville, UT 84663

Edmark, Dave, Dir. of Comm.
Food Safety Consortium [1328]
University of Arkansas
110 Agriculture Bldg.
Fayetteville, AR 72701
Ph: (479)575-5647
Fax: (479)575-7531

Edmiaston, Mark, President
Children's Brain Tumor Foundation
[14177]
1460 Broadway
New York, NY 10016-0715
Toll Free: 866-228-4673

Edmonds, Gary L., President
Breakthrough Partners [20360]
110 3rd Ave. N, Ste. 101
Edmonds, WA 98020
Ph: (425)775-3362
Fax: (425)640-3671

Edmonds, Sibel, Founder, President
National Security Whistleblowers
Coalition [19093]
PO Box 320518
Alexandria, VA 22320

Edmondson, Dianne, Exec. Dir.
Republican National Coalition for
Life [19070]
PO Box 618
Alton, IL 62002
Ph: (618)462-5415
Fax: (618)462-8909

Edmunds, Amy, Founder, CEO
YoungStroke, Inc. [17301]
PO Box 692
Conway, SC 29528
Ph: (843)655-2835

Edmunds, Anton E., Consultant
Caribbean - Central American Action
[12144]
1625 K St. NW, Ste. 200
Washington, DC 20006
Ph: (202)464-2031

Edward, Beth, Secretary
Magnolia Society International
[6150]
3000 Henneberry Rd.
Jamesville, NY 13078-9640

Edward, Sanjiv, Chairman
The International Air Cargo Associa-
tion [3333]
5600 NW 36th St., Ste. 620
Miami, FL 33166
Ph: (786)265-7011
Fax: (786)265-7012

Edwards, Beatrice, Prog. Dir.
Government Accountability Project
[18318]

1612 K St. NW, Ste. 1100
Washington, DC 20006
Ph: (202)457-0034

Edwards, Dr. Betty J., President
Daughters of the Republic of Texas
[20965]
510 E Anderson Ln.
Austin, TX 78752
Ph: (512)339-1997
Fax: (512)339-1998

Edwards, Brennan, Exec. Dir.
National Collegiate Roller Hockey
Association [22910]
4733 Torrance Blvd., No. 618
Torrance, CA 90503
Ph: (310)753-7285
Fax: (310)347-4001

Edwards, Connie, President
Newborns in Need [11197]
3323 Transou Rd.
Pfafftown, NC 27040
Ph: (336)469-8953

Edwards, Gary, Chairman
Association of TeleServices
International [3218]
222 S Westmonte Dr., Ste. 101
Altamonte Springs, FL 32714
Toll Free: 866-896-ATSI
Fax: (407)774-6440

Edwards, Prof. Gene, CEO
Christian Jujitsu Association [22989]
PO Box 7174
Kalispell, MT 59904-0174
Ph: (406)257-3245

Edwards, Dr. Germaine, Chmn. of
the Bd.
African-American Female
Entrepreneurs Alliance [3484]
45 Scottdale Ave.
Lansdowne, PA 19050
Ph: (215)747-9282
Fax: (610)394-0264

Edwards, Greg, Treasurer
United Methodist Association of
Ministers with Disabilities [20347]
3645 Toronto Ct.
Indianapolis, IN 46268

Edwards, Jane, PhD, President
International Association for Music &
Medicine [16976]
c/o Dr. Fred Schwartz, Treasurer
314 Woodward Way NW
Atlanta, GA 30305-4039

Edwards, Jason, Exec. Dir.
Hemochromatosis Information
Society [15247]
3017 Princeton Dr.
Plano, TX 75075
Ph: (214)702-2698

Edwards, Jeff, VP
Progressive Gardening Trade As-
sociation [4272]
7809 FM 179
Shallowater, TX 79363-3637
Ph: (806)832-5306
Fax: (806)832-5244

Edwards, John, Bd. Member
Energy and Environmental Building
Alliance [524]
9900 13th Ave. N, Ste. 200
Plymouth, MN 55441
Ph: (952)881-1098
Fax: (952)881-3048

Edwards, Lawrence, PhD, Contact
Kundalini Research Network [15267]
c/o Lawrence Edwards, Ph.D.

PO Box 541166
Cincinnati, OH 45254

Edwards, Lee, VP of Mktg., VP,
Comm.
Data Management Association
International [6740]
c/o Dama Education & Research
Foundation
PO Box 9937
Wyoming, MI 49508
Ph: (813)778-5495
Fax: (813)464-7864

Edwards, Michael, President
National Federation of Music Clubs
[9972]
1646 Smith Valley Rd.
Greenwood, IN 46142
Ph: (317)882-4003
Fax: (317)882-4019

Edwards, Scott, VP
National Conference of State Fleet
Administrators [5817]
301 W High St., Rm. 760
Jefferson City, MO 65101

Edwards, Shari, President
Ouachita Baptist University Alumni
Association [19343]
410 Ouachita St.
Arkadelphia, AR 71998
Ph: (870)245-5506
(870)245-5111

Edwards, Simon, Chairman
Anti-Malware Testing Standards
Organization [6269]
1 Ferry Bldg., Ste. 200
San Francisco, CA 94111-4213
Ph: (415)963-3563

Edwards, Stephanie, Secretary,
Treasurer
Pi Mu Epsilon [23814]
c/o Angela Spalsbury, President
Dept. of Mathematics and Statistics
Youngstown State University
Youngstown, OH 44555
Ph: (330)941-1803

Edwards, Dr. Steve, CEO, Bd.
Member
Ignitus Worldwide [13451]
1199 Haywood Dr.
College Station, TX 77845
Ph: (800)316-4311

Edwards, Terry, Fac. Memb.
National Crime Prevention Institute
[11512]
University of Louisville
2301 S 3rd St.
Louisville, KY 40208-1838
Ph: (800)334-8635

Edwards, Tracey, Exec. VP
National Exchange Club [12901]
3050 Central Ave.
Toledo, OH 43606-1700
Ph: (419)535-3232
Toll Free: 800-924-2643
Fax: (419)535-1989

Edwards, Tracey, Exec. VP
National Exchange Club Foundation
[11093]
3050 Central Ave.
Toledo, OH 43606-1700
Ph: (419)535-3232
Fax: (419)535-1989

Edwards, Trish, Director
Shibumi International Reiki Associa-
tion [17104]
PO Box 1776
Berthoud, CO 80513

Edwards, Virginia B., President, Edi-
tor
Editorial Projects in Education
[7760]
6935 Arlington Rd., Ste. 100
Bethesda, MD 20814
Ph: (301)280-3100
Toll Free: 800-346-1834
Fax: (301)280-3200

Eells, Tracy D., PhD, Exec. Ofc.
Society for Psychotherapy Research
[16952]
University of Louisville
401 E Chestnut St., Unit 610
Louisville, KY 40202-5711

Effiong, Clare, Founder
Esther's Aid for Needy and
Abandoned Children [10964]
271 N Ave.
New Rochelle, NY 10801
Ph: (914)365-1544
(914)365-1545

Effner, Harold, Secretary, Treasurer
Meter Stamp Society [22343]
c/o Rick Stambaugh, President
100 Elder Ct.
Prescott, AZ 86303-5364

Efrati, Eran, Exec. Dir.
Israeli Committee Against House
Demolitions - USA [18797]
PO Box 8118
New York, NY 10150-8101
Ph: (646)308-1322

Eftimiades, Mr. Nicholas, Chairman,
Founder
Federation of Galaxy Explorers
[7459]
6404 Ivy Ln., Ste. 810
Greenbelt, MD 20770-1420
Fax: (610)981-8511

Egan, Lorraine W., CEO, President
Damon Runyon Cancer Research
Foundation [13957]
1 Exchange Plz.
55 Broadway, Ste. 302
New York, NY 10006-3720
Ph: (212)455-0500

Egan, Nora, Director
Help Hospitalized Veterans [13240]
36585 Penfield Ln.
Winchester, CA 92596
Ph: (951)926-4500

Egan, Tom, VP
Packaging Machinery Manufacturers
Institute [2479]
1191 Freedom Dr., Ste. 600
Reston, VA 20190
Ph: (571)612-3200
Fax: (703)243-8556

Egbe, Daniel, Officer
National Organization for Manyu
Advancement [19288]
186 Olin Ave.
Fitchburg, MA 01420
Ph: (617)388-8992

Egbert, Steve, VP
United Four Wheel Drive Associa-
tions [21510]
PO Box 316
Swartz Creek, MI 48473-0316
Toll Free: 800-448-3932

Egbulem, Fatmata, Officer
Action Africa [17769]
2903 Mills Ave. NE
Washington, DC 20018
Ph: (202)529-8350
Fax: (202)529-1912

Egeler, Dr. Dan, President
Association of Christian Schools
International [7607]
731 Chapel Hills Dr.
Colorado Springs, CO 80920-3949
Ph: (719)528-6906
Toll Free: 866-793-8162
Fax: (719)531-0631

Egeler, Jon, President
International Association of Mission-
ary Aviation [20425]
6922 Davis Rd.
Waxhaw, NC 28173
Ph: (704)562-2481

Egge, Dennis, President
American Retirees Association
[21024]
700 E Redlands Bvld., Ste. U-307
Redlands, CA 92373-6152
Ph: (909)557-0107
(703)527-3065
Fax: (909)335-2711

Eggensammer, Chuck, Secretary
National Institute of Red Orange
Canaries and All Other Cage Birds
[21545]
c/o Chuck Eggenseammer, Membership Secretary
3318 Wirth Ter.
Crystal Lake, IL 60012
Ph: (815)455-4439

Eggert, Roy, President
National Heisey Glass Museum
[22141]
169 W Church St.
Newark, OH 43055-4945
Ph: (740)345-2932
Fax: (740)345-9638

Eggleston, Gillian, President
Sweet Sorghum Association [5891]
8912 Brandon Station Rd.
Raleigh, NC 27613
Ph: (919)870-0782

Eggleston, Margaret, PhD, President
American Association for Adult and
Continuing Education [7666]
Bldg. 14, Ste. 100
1827 Powers Ferry Rd.
Atlanta, GA 30339
Ph: (678)271-4319
Fax: (678)229-2777

Eggleston, Victor, Exec. Dir.
Belted Galloway Society [3720]
c/o Victor Eggleston, DVM, Execu-
tive Director
N8603 Zentner Rd.
New Glarus, WI 53574
Ph: (608)220-1091
Fax: (608)527-4811

Egnoski, Christine, Exec. Dir.
Portrait Society of America [8881]
1349 E Lafayette St.
Tallahassee, FL 32301
Toll Free: 877-772-4321
Fax: (850)222-7890

Egwuonwu, Dr. Uchenna, Founder,
President
Complementary and Alternative
Medicine Initiative [13616]
75 Winchell Dr.
Rock Tavern, NY 12575
Ph: (718)877-0292

Ehabe, Ernest, President
Bread for Life International [12078]
PO Box 291307
Kerrville, TX 78029
Ph: (830)896-8326
Fax: (830)866-5262

Ehlers, Suzanne, CEO, President
Population Action International
[12512]
1300 19th St. NW, Ste. 200
Washington, DC 20036-1624
Ph: (202)557-3400
Fax: (202)728-4177

Ehrenberg, Dr. Erica, Exec. Dir.
American Institute of Iranian Studies
[9201]
c/o Dr. Erica Ehrenberg, Executive
Director
118 Riverside Dr.
New York, NY 10024

Ehrig, John, Exec. Dir.
International Peoplemedia Telecom-
munications Consortium [7313]
2400 Camino Ramon, Ste. 375
San Ramon, CA 94583
Ph: (925)275-6600
Fax: (925)275-6691

Ehrlich, Alan, President
Veteran Wireless Operators Associa-
tion [3246]
Peck Slip
New York, NY 10272-1003

Ehrlich, Lois, Administrator
International Forum for
Psychoanalytic Education [16847]
PO Box 961
Culver City, CA 90232-0961
Ph: (310)694-3463

Ehrlich, Marc B., Secretary,
Treasurer
American Academy of the History of
Dentistry [14379]
c/o Marc B. Ehrlich, Secretary
1371 Beacon St.
Brookline, MA 02446

Eibling, David, MD, President
American Society of Geriatric
Otolaryngology [16538]
c/o Dr. Brian J. McKinnon, Treasurer
Shea Ear Clinic
6133 Poplar Pke.
Memphis, TN 38119

Eibner, Dr. John, CEO
Christian Solidarity International
[20571]
870 Hampshire Rd., Ste. T
Westlake Village, CA 91361-6038
Ph: (805)777-7107
Toll Free: 888-676-5700
Fax: (805)777-7508

Eichel, Steve K. D., PhD, ABPP,
President
International Cultic Studies Associa-
tion [20048]
PO Box 2265
Bonita Springs, FL 34133
Ph: (239)514-3081
Fax: (305)393-8193

Eicher, Penelope, Exec. Dir.
Heart Walk Foundation [9172]
437 S Bluff St., Ste. 202
Saint George, UT 84770-3590
Ph: (435)619-0797

Eichler, Caroline, Secretary
National Beagle Club of America
[21920]
22265 Oatlands Rd.
Aldie, VA 20105

Eichler, Steve, JD, President
State Department Watch [18276]
PO Box 65398
Washington, DC 20035

Eichner, Rev. Philip, Chairman
Catholic League for Religious and
Civil Rights [19813]

450 7th Ave.
New York, NY 10123
Ph: (212)371-3191
Fax: (212)371-3394

Eidbo, Elling, CEO
Association of Organ Procurement
Organizations [14616]
8500 Leesburg Pke., Ste. 300
Vienna, VA 22182-2409
Ph: (703)556-4242
Fax: (703)556-4852

Eidelman, Prof. Arthur I, Chmn. of
the Bd.
Center for Jewish Community Stud-
ies [18590]
7 Church Ln., Ste. 9
Baltimore, MD 21208
Ph: (410)653-7779
Fax: (410)653-8889

Eidelman, Steven M., Exec. Dir.
Joseph P. Kennedy, Jr. Foundation
[12325]
1133 19th St. NW, 12th Fl.
Washington, DC 20036-3604
Ph: (202)393-1250

Eidman-Aadahl, Elyse, Exec. Dir.
National Writing Project [8765]
University of California
2105 Bancroft Way, No. 1042
Berkeley, CA 94720-1042
Ph: (510)642-0963
Fax: (510)642-4545

Eidson, Pam, MEd, Exec. Dir.
National Physical Activity Society
[16709]
1100 Peachtree St., Ste. 200
Atlanta, GA 30309
Ph: (404)692-5396

Eiken, Mary C., MS, RN, Exec. Dir.
Society of Gynecologic Oncology
[16356]
230 W Monroe St., Ste. 710
Chicago, IL 60606-4703
Ph: (312)235-4060
Fax: (312)235-4059

Eimer, Mary Jane, CAE, Exec. Dir.
Association for Behavioral and
Cognitive Therapies [13794]
305 7th Ave., 16th Fl.
New York, NY 10001-6008
Ph: (212)647-1890
Fax: (212)647-1865

Eise, Martha, Contact
Aiding Mothers and Fathers
Experiencing Neonatal Death
[11554]
c/o Martha Eise
1559 Ville Rosa
Hazelwood, MO 63042
Ph: (314)291-0892
(314)487-7582

Eisen, Maryellen Maguire, RN,
Founder, Exec. Dir.
Children's Melanoma Prevention
Foundation [13942]
PO Box 254
Hingham, MA 02043
Ph: (781)875-1773

Eisenbrey, Ross, VP
Economic Policy Institute [18973]
1225 Eye St. NW, Ste. 600
Washington, DC 20005
Ph: (202)775-8810
Toll Free: 800-374-4844
Fax: (202)775-0819

Eisenhower, Dwight D., President
Crosscurrents International Institute
[18537]

7122 Hardin-Wapak Rd.
Sidney, OH 45365
Ph: (937)492-0407

Eisenhower, Susan, Chairman
Gettysburg College | Eisenhower
Institute [18979]
818 Connecticut Ave. NW, Ste. 800
Washington, DC 20006
Ph: (202)628-4444
Fax: (202)628-4445

Eisenhower, Susan, Director
Gettysburg Foundation [9394]
1195 Baltimore Pke.
Gettysburg, PA 17325-7034
Ph: (717)338-1243
Toll Free: 866-889-1243
Fax: (717)338-1244

Eitel, Maria, CEO
Corporation for National & Com-
munity Service | Senior Corps
[13290]
250 E St. SW
Washington, DC 20525

Ejikeme, Anene, PhD, Exec. Dir.
Africa Network [18365]
c/o Jim Pletcher, Chairman
Denison University
100 W College St.
Granville, OH 43023

Ekstein, Rick
North American Wholesale Lumber
Association [1413]
330 N Wabash, Ste. 2000
Chicago, IL 60611
Ph: (312)321-5133
Toll Free: 800-527-8258
Fax: (312)673-6838

Ekus, Bryan, Exec. Dir.
SolarUnited [1123]
PO Box 771507
Orlando, FL 32877
Ph: (747)777-2081

El Gamal, Abbas, President
IEEE Information Theory Society
[7308]
3 Park Ave., 17th Fl.
New York, NY 10016-5997

Elam, Joyce, Director
Royal Neighbors of America [19493]
230 16th St.
Rock Island, IL 61201-8645
Toll Free: 800-627-4762

Elbin, Susan B., Chairperson
Ornithological Council [6964]
c/o Ellen Paul, Executive Director
6512 E Halbert Rd.
Bethesda, MD 20817
Ph: (301)986-8568
Fax: (301)986-5205

Elder, Dr. Linda, Exec. Dir.
Center for Critical Thinking [7694]
PO Box 196
Tomales, CA 94971
Toll Free: 800-833-3645
Fax: (707)878-9111

Elder, Richard D., President
Theta Chi Fraternity [23936]
PO Box 503
Carmel, IN 46082
Ph: (317)848-1856
Fax: (317)824-1908

Eldredge, Bruce, CEO, Exec. Dir.
Buffalo Bill Center of the West
[10316]
720 Sheridan Ave.
Cody, WY 82414-3428
Ph: (307)587-4771
(307)578-4008

Eldurubi, Imad Y., President
World Organization of Building Officials [603]
c/o National Fire Protection Association
1 Batterymarch Pk.
Quincy, MA 02169-7471
Ph: (617)984-7464
Fax: (617)984-7110

Elersich, Rich, Treasurer
MRFAC [467]
c/o BAC and Associates LLC
616 E 34th St. N
Wichita, KS 67219
Ph: (316)832-9213

Elfers, Barb, Contact
National Morgan Reining Horse Association [4382]
c/o Barb Elfers
7701 Olivas Ln.
Vacaville, CA 95688

Elgarico, David, MHA, Officer
Asian Health Care Leaders Association [15577]
566 W Adams St., Ste. 750
Chicago, IL 60661

Elhihi, Maher, President
Bethlehem Association [18677]
1192 N Garey Ave.
Pomona, CA 91767
Ph: (610)353-2010
(650)740-3119

Eliason, Krista, President
International Design Guild [1949]
670 N Commercial St.
Manchester, NH 03101
Toll Free: 800-450-7595
Fax: (603)626-3444

Elifrits, Kathy, President
American Classical League [8176]
860 NW Washington Blvd., Ste. A
Hamilton, OH 45013
Ph: (513)529-7741
Toll Free: 800-670-8346
Fax: (513)529-7742

Eliopoulos, Charlotte, Exec. Dir.
American Association for Long Term
Care Nursing [16090]
11104 Glen Arm
Glen Arm, MD 21057
Toll Free: 888-458-2687
Fax: (888)741-0942

El-Issa, Ali, Rep.
Rigoberta Menchu Tum Foundation
[17929]
c/o Ali El-Issa, Representative
11 Broadway, 2nd Fl.
New York, NY 10004-1300
Ph: (212)982-5358
Fax: (212)982-5346

Elizondo, Sondra, Director
Vida Volunteer [11455]
PO Box 856499
Minneapolis, MN 55485
Toll Free: 888-365-VIDA

Elkind, Arthur H., MD, President
National Headache Foundation
[14919]
820 N Orleans St., Ste. 411
Chicago, IL 60610
Ph: (312)274-2650
Toll Free: 888-NHF-5552

Elkins, Lt. Comdr. David G.,
Secretary
Navy Anesthesia Society [13704]
Dept. of Anesthesiology
Naval Medical Ctr.

34800 Bob Wilson Dr.
San Diego, CA 92134-5000
Ph: (619)532-8943
Fax: (619)532-8945

Elkins, Scot, VP
International Motor Sports Associa-
tion [22526]
International Motorsports Ctr.
1 Daytona Blvd.
Daytona Beach, FL 32114
Ph: (386)310-6500
Fax: (386)310-6505

Ellenberg, Kristy Thomson, Exec.
Dir.
American Agricultural Law Associa-
tion [4941]
c/o Kristy Thomason Ellenberg,
Executive Director
PO Box 5861
Columbia, SC 29250
Ph: (803)728-3200

Ellert, Kent, Director
Men for Missions International
[20435]
PO Box A
Greenwood, IN 46142-6599
Ph: (317)881-6752
Fax: (317)865-1076

Elliff, Tom, President
International Mission Board [20426]
3806 Monument Ave.
Richmond, VA 23230-0767
Toll Free: 800-999-3113

Ellinger, Carol, Chmn. of the Bd.
Gold Star Wives of America [21040]
PO Box 361986
Birmingham, AL 35236
Toll Free: 888-751-6350

Ellinger, Marc H., Treasurer
International Masters of Gaming Law
[5259]
PO Box 27106
Las Vegas, NV 89126
Ph: (702)375-5812

Ellingson, Stephanie, Secretary
Health Professions Network [15119]
PO Box 2007
Midlothian, VA 23113
Ph: (804)639-9211
Fax: (804)639-9212

Ellington, Chad, Secretary, Treasurer
International Occultation Timing As-
sociation [6006]
c/o Chad K. Ellington, Secretary/
Treasurer
PO Box 7152
Kent, WA 98042

Elliott, Bill, VP
Elliot Clan Society USA [20862]
c/o Patricia Tennyson Bell, Treasurer
2984 Siskiyou Blvd.
Medford, OR 97504-8161

Elliott, Carol Silver, Secretary
LeadingAge [10514]
2519 Connecticut Ave. NW
Washington, DC 20008-1520
Ph: (202)783-2242
Fax: (202)783-2255

Elliott, Jennifer, RDH, President
Big Smiles Big Hearts [14422]
PO Box 3388
Cumming, GA 30028-6520

Elliott, Karin, Exec. Dir.
National Partnership for Educational
Access [7966]
155 Federal St., Ste. 800

Boston, MA 02110
Ph: (617)423-6300
Fax: (617)423-6303

Elliott, Scott, Editor
Council of Societies for the Study of
Religion [8708]
Rice University
PO Box 1892
Houston, TX 77251-1892
Ph: (713)348-5721
Fax: (713)348-5725

Elliott, Scott, President
Education Writers Association [2679]
3516 Connecticut Ave. NW
Washington, DC 20008
Ph: (202)452-9830

Elliott, Victoria, RPh, MBA, CAE,
Exec. Dir.
American Neurological Association
[16004]
1120 Route 73, Ste. 200
Mount Laurel, NJ 08054
Ph: (856)380-6892
Fax: (856)439-0525

Elliott, William S., Exec. Dir.
Initiatives of Change [18360]
2201 W Broad St., Ste. 200
Richmond, VA 23220-2022
Ph: (804)358-1764
Fax: (804)358-1769

Elliott, Yolanda, President
Seventh Day Adventist Kinship
International [20189]
PO Box 244
Orinda, CA 94563-0244

Ellis, Brenda, Exec. Dir.
Professional Football Chiropractic
Society [14280]
PO Box 552
Puyallup, WA 98371
Ph: (253)948-6039
Fax: (253)435-1053

Ellis, Bishop Charles H., III, Bishop
Pentecostal Assemblies of the World
[20517]
3939 N Meadows Dr.
Indianapolis, IN 46205-3113
Ph: (317)547-9541
Fax: (317)543-0513

Ellis, Curt, Exec. Dir.
FoodCorps [16221]
281 Park Ave. S
New York, NY 10010
Ph: (212)596-7045
Fax: (347)244-7213

Ellis, Dr. David, Exec. Dir.
National Foreign Language Center
[8191]
Severn Bldg. 810
5245 Greenbelt Rd.
College Park, MD 20742
Ph: (301)405-9828
Fax: (301)405-9829

Ellis, Lynn, Rep.
Affirmation: United Methodists for
Lesbian, Gay, Bisexual, Transgen-
der and Queer Concerns [20174]
PO Box 1021
Evanston, IL 60204

Ellis, Mark, President
Industrial Minerals Association-North
America [2380]
2011 Pennsylvania Ave. NW, Ste.
301
Washington, DC 20006
Ph: (202)457-0200
Fax: (202)457-0287

Ellis, Mark, President
National Industrial Sand Association
[2381]
2011 Pennsylvania Ave. NW, Ste.
301
Washington, DC 20006
Ph: (202)457-0200
Fax: (202)457-0287

Ellis, Mark, COO
Rainbow/PUSH Coalition [13083]
930 E 50th St.
Chicago, IL 60615
Ph: (773)373-3366
Fax: (773)373-3571

Ellis, Mr. Matthew, Exec. Dir.
National Episcopal AIDS Coalition
[10548]
6050 N Meridian St.
Indianapolis, IN 46208-1549
Toll Free: 800-588-6628

Ellis, Matthew, CEO
National Episcopal Health Ministries
[14954]
9120 Fredrick Rd.
Ellicott City, MD 21042
Ph: (203)451-9134

Ellis, Patricia, President
Women's Foreign Policy Group
[19249]
1615 M St. NW, Ste. 210
Washington, DC 20036-3235
Ph: (202)429-2692
Fax: (202)429-2630

Ellis, Randall, President
American Society of Health
Economists [1010]
725 15th St. NW, Ste. 600
Washington, DC 20005
Ph: (202)737-6608
Fax: (202)737-7308

Ellis, Renee G., President
Black Women of Essence, Inc.
[10494]
Baltimore, MD 21201

Ellis, Deacon Robert F., Coord.
World Apostolate of Fatima - USA
[19923]
674 Mountain View Rd. E
Asbury, NJ 08802-1400
Ph: (908)689-1700
(908)689-3590

Ellis, Ronald, Finance Ofc.
Americal Division Veterans Associa-
tion [21188]
4493 Highway 64 W
Henderson, TX 75652
Ph: (830)377-8115

Ellis, Ross, CEO, Founder
Love Our Children USA [11071]
220 E 57th St.
New York, NY 10022
Ph: (212)629-2099
Toll Free: 888-347-KIDS

Ellis, Sarah Kate, CEO, President
GLAAD [11887]
5455 Wilshire Blvd., Ste. 1500
Los Angeles, CA 90036
Ph: (212)629-3322

Ellis, Tony, VP
National Association of College
Stores [2967]
500 E Lorain St.
Oberlin, OH 44074
Ph: (440)775-7777
Toll Free: 800-622-7498

Ellis, Wanda J., Exec. Dir.
American Floorcovering Alliance
[1937]

210 W Cuyler St.
Dalton, GA 30720
Ph: (706)278-4101
Toll Free: 800-288-4101
Fax: (706)278-5323

Ellis, Willem, Co-Chmn. of the Bd.,
President
South African Chamber of Com-
merce in America [23617]

Ellis-Brearey, Terri Lynn, Founder,
CEO
Infant and Children Sleep Apnea
Awareness Foundation [17216]
PO Box 2328
New Smyrna Beach, FL 32170
Ph: (386)423-5430
Fax: (386)428-2001

Ellison, Riki, Chmn. of the Bd.,
Founder
Missile Defense Advocacy Alliance
[18087]
515 King St., Ste. 320
Alexandria, VA 22314
Ph: (703)299-0060

Ellrod, Dr. Frederick, III, Chairman
Philosophy Education Society
[10113]
The Catholic University of America
223 Aquinas Hall
Washington, DC 20064
Ph: (202)635-8778
Toll Free: 800-255-5924
Fax: (202)319-4484

Ellsworth, Skip, Founder
Log Home Builders Association
[874]
14241 NE Woodinville-Duvall Rd.,
No. 345
Woodinville, WA 98072
Ph: (360)794-4469

Elm, Dawn, Exec. Dir.
Society for Business Ethics [5186]
820 N Michigan Ave.
Chicago, IL 60611

Elm, Susanna, President
North American Patristics Society
[20515]
Johns Hopkins University
Press Journals Division
2715 N Charles St.
Baltimore, MD 21218
Toll Free: 800-548-1784

ElMasri, Marwan, President
International Isotope Society [6054]
c/o David Hesk, Executive Secretary
Merck Research Laboratories
126 E Lincoln Ave.
Rahway, NJ 07065

Elmen, Jim, Editor
Russian Numismatic Society [22285]
PO Box 3684
Santa Rosa, CA 95402
Ph: (707)527-1007
Fax: (707)527-1204

Elmore, DG, Chmn. of the Bd.
The Navigators [19999]
3820 N 30th St.
Colorado Springs, CO 80904-5001
Ph: (719)598-1212
Fax: (719)260-0479

Elmore, Eugene, President
Society for In Vitro Biology [6101]
514 Daniels St., Ste. 411
Raleigh, NC 27605
Ph: (919)562-0600
Fax: (919)562-0608

Elmore, Mark, Sports Dir.
United States Snowshoe Association
[23180]

678 County Route 25
Corinth, NY 12822
Ph: (518)654-7648
(518)420-6961

Elmquist, Marion, President
Ski for Light [22796]
1455 W Lake St.
Minneapolis, MN 55408-2648
Ph: (612)827-3232

Elnashar, Dr. Adel M., President
International Council for Health,
Physical Education, Recreation,
Sport, and Dance [8428]
1900 Association Dr.
Reston, VA 20191-1502
Ph: (703)476-3462
Fax: (703)476-9527

Elneus, Louis, Founder, President
Haiti Lumiere de Demain [11204]
PO Box 1114
Fairfield, CT 06825
Ph: (203)612-7860

Elrick, Doug, Chmn. of the Bd.
International Association of
Computer Investigative Specialists
[7656]
PO Box 2411
Leesburg, VA 20177
Ph: (304)915-0555
Toll Free: 888-884-2247

Elrod, Louis, President
Young Democrats of America
[18120]
PO Box 77496
Washington, DC 20013-8496

Elsberry, David, President
Triumph Wedge Owners Association
[21505]
c/o Gary Klein, Treasurer
8153 Quarterfield Farms Dr.
Severn, MD 21144

Elser, Jim, President
Association for the Sciences of Lim-
nology and Oceanography [6937]
5400 Bosque Blvd., Ste. 680
Waco, TX 76710-4446
Ph: (254)399-9635
Toll Free: 800-929-2756
Fax: (254)776-3767

Elsheikh, Tarik, President
Papanicolaou Society of Cytopathol-
ogy [14360]
2295 Vallejo St., No. 508
San Francisco, CA 94123
Ph: (415)833-3871

Elsner, Tim
Mended Hearts, Inc. [14133]
8150 N Central Expy., M2248
Dallas, TX 75206
Ph: (214)206-9259
Toll Free: 888-432-7899
Fax: (214)295-9552

Elston, Nikki Carol, President
Association for Specialists in Group
Work [11485]
c/o Nikki Carol Elston, President
Georgia State University
Atlanta, GA 30302-3980
Ph: (202)491-9561

Elton, Serona, Bd. Member
Music and Entertainment Industry
Educators Association [8376]
1900 Belmont Blvd.
Nashville, TN 37212-3758
Ph: (615)460-6946

Elvrum, Tillie, President
PublicSchoolOptions.org [8480]
2100 M St. NW, Ste. 170-257

Washington, DC 20037-1233
Toll Free: 866-558-2874

Elwell, Anne, Bd. Member
United States Icelandic Horse
  Congress [4419]
c/o Kari Pietsch-Wangard
300 S Sawyer Rd.
Oconomowoc, WI 53066
Toll Free: 866-929-0009

Ely, Mark, Founder, Exec. Dir.
Pura Vida [11209]
9609 S University Blvd.
Littleton, CO 80163
Ph: (303)215-0994
Toll Free: 888-845-8963
Fax: (303)215-0995

Embleton, Sheila, Chairman
Linguistic Association of Canada and
  the United States [9744]
2900 Bedford Ave.
Brooklyn, NY 11210
Ph: (713)348-2820
Fax: (713)348-5846

Embrey, Lauren, Chmn. of the Bd.
Women's Media Center [19250]
1825 K St. NW, Ste. 400
Washington, DC 20006
Ph: (212)563-0680
Fax: (212)563-0688

Emburg, Kate, President
Society of Phantom Friends [9136]
40 S Vine St.
Mount Carmel, PA 17851

Emdin, Ben, Exec. Dir.
HighScope Educational Research
  Foundation [7696]
600 N River St.
Ypsilanti, MI 48198-2821
Toll Free: 800-587-5639
Fax: (734)485-0704

Emery, Susan, Exec. Dir.
Circle of Rights [14154]
5802 Augusta Ln.
Bethesda, MD 20816
Ph: (301)229-1355
     (301)948-5818

Emig, Carol, President
Child Trends [11219]
7315 Wisconsin Ave., Ste. 1200W
Bethesda, MD 20814
Ph: (240)223-9200
Fax: (240)200-1238

Emiru, Gizachew, Esq. Exec. Dir.
Torture Abolition and Survivors Sup-
  port Coalition International [18445]
4121 Harewood Rd. NE, Ste. B
Washington, DC 20017
Ph: (202)529-2991

Emko, Tod, President, Founder
Darwin Animal Doctors [3623]
222 E 89th St., No. 8
New York, NY 10128-4309

Emmerich, Susanne Bross, Founder,
  Exec. Dir.
Incontinentia Pigmenti International
  Foundation [14828]
30 E 72nd St., Ste. No. 16
New York, NY 10021-4265
Ph: (212)452-1231
Fax: (212)452-1231

Emmerling, Rev. Christine, President
Divine Science Ministers Association
  [20053]
1540 Hicks Ave.
San Jose, CA 95125
Ph: (408)293-3838

Emmert, Dr. Mark A., President
National Collegiate Athletic Associa-
  tion [23241]
700 W Washington St.
Indianapolis, IN 46206
Ph: (317)917-6222
Fax: (317)917-6888

Emmons, Debra Lynn, President
National Space Club and Foundation
  [5865]
204 E St. NE
Washington, DC 20002
Ph: (202)547-0060

Emmons, Jim, President
Water Sports Industry Association
  [3149]
PO Box 568512
Orlando, FL 32856-8512
Ph: (407)251-9039
     (407)835-1363

Emory, Bobby Yates, President
Libertarian Nation Foundation
  [18642]
335 Mulberry St.
Raleigh, NC 27604

Empson, Ray, Chmn. of the Bd.
Arbor Day Foundation [19148]
100 Arbor Ave.
Nebraska City, NE 68410
Ph: (402)474-5655
Toll Free: 888-448-7337
Fax: (402)474-0820

Ems, Kathy, VP of Fin.
Parent Cooperative Preschools
  International [7594]
National Cooperative Business Ctr.
1401 New York Ave. NW, Ste. 1100
Washington, DC 20005

Enberg, Dick, Chmn. of the Bd.
American Sportscasters Association
  [453]
225 Broadway, Ste. 2030
New York, NY 10007
Ph: (212)227-8080
Fax: (212)571-0556

Endean, John, President
American Business Conference
  [1977]
1828 L St. NW, Ste. 280
Washington, DC 20036-5114
Ph: (202)822-9300
Fax: (202)467-4070

Enders, David G., President
Enders Family Association [20863]
c/o David G. Enders, President
56 Marie Dr.
Halifax, PA 17032
Ph: (717)877-9214

Endicott, Bill, Editor
33rd Infantry Division Association
  [20700]
617 143rd St. NW
Marysville, WA 98271

Endicott, Steve, President
Perfins Club [22352]
6500 Upper Applegate Rd.
Jacksonville, OR 97530-9314

Endza, Lisa, Dir. of Comm.
International Association of Certified
  Home Inspectors [1817]
1750 30th St., Ste. 301
Boulder, CO 80301
Ph: (303)502-6214
Toll Free: 877-346-3467
Fax: (650)429-2057

Enegess, Karen, President
American Association of State
  Counseling Boards [14325]

305 N Beech Cir.
Broken Arrow, OK 74012
Ph: (918)994-4413
Fax: (918)663-7058

Eng, Loren A., President
Spinal Muscular Atrophy Foundation
  [17271]
888 7th Ave., Ste. 400
New York, NY 10019
Ph: (646)253-7100
Toll Free: 877-386-3762
Fax: (212)247-3079

Engber, Andrea, Director, Founder
National Organization of Single
  Mothers [12956]
PO Box 68
Midland, NC 28107

Engblom-Bradley, Claudette,
  Secretary
North American Study Group on Eth-
  nomathematics [6825]
c/o Fredrick L. Silverman, Treasurer
1459 S St. Vrain Ave.
Estes Park, CO 80517-7318

Engel, Thom, Director
National Speleological Society
  [7228]
6001 Pulaski Pke.
Huntsville, AL 35810-1122
Ph: (256)852-1300

Engelen, Leen, Sec. Gen.
International Association for Media
  and History [268]
c/o Cynthia Miller, Treasurer
484 Bolivar St.
Canton, MA 02021

Engelman, Robert, Contact
Worldwatch Institute [19268]
1400 16th St. NW, Ste. 430
Washington, DC 20036-2239
Ph: (202)745-8092

Engelward, Bevin P., President
Environmental Mutagenesis and
  Genomics Society [6080]
1821 Michael Faraday Dr., Ste. 300
Reston, VA 20190
Ph: (703)438-8220
Fax: (703)438-3113

Engerer, Malinda, MBA, Exec. Dir.
Cardiovascular Disease Foundation
  [14151]
3088 Pio Pico Dr., Ste. 202
Carlsbad, CA 92008
Ph: (760)730-1471
Toll Free: 888-249-9575
Fax: (760)730-0165

Engh, Fred C., CEO, President
International Alliance for Youth
  Sports [23376]
2050 Vista Pky.
West Palm Beach, FL 33411
Toll Free: 800-688-KIDS
Fax: (561)712-9887

Engh, Fred, Founder
National Alliance for Youth Sports
  [22733]
2050 Vista Pky.
West Palm Beach, FL 33411
Ph: (561)684-1141
Toll Free: 800-729-2057
Fax: (561)684-2546

England, Janice, Prog. Dir.
Lay Mission-Helpers Association
  [19853]
3435 Wilshire Blvd., Ste. 1940
Los Angeles, CA 90010
Ph: (213)368-1870
Fax: (213)368-1871

Engle, Joe, Mgr.
Adopt a Special Kid [10436]
8201 Edgewater Dr., Ste. 103
Oakland, CA 94621

Engler, John, President
Business Roundtable [18952]
300 New Jersey Ave. NW, Ste. 800
Washington, DC 20001
Ph: (202)872-1260

Engler, Maggie, Treasurer
Spanish Barb Horse Association
  [4410]
PO Box 30
Mule Creek, NM 88051-0030

Engler, Theresa, Exec. Dir.
Deep Foundations Institute [863]
326 Lafayette Ave.
Hawthorne, NJ 07506
Ph: (973)423-4030
Fax: (973)423-4031

English, Marietta, President
National Alliance of Black School
  Educators [8649]
310 Pennsylvania Ave. SE
Washington, DC 20003
Ph: (202)608-6310
Toll Free: 800-221-2654
Fax: (202)608-6319

Engo, Ruth Bamela, President
African Action on AIDS [13517]
511 Ave. of the Americas, No. 302
New York, NY 10011

Ennis, Catherine D., PhD,
  Chairperson
National Academy of Kinesiology
  [8429]
PO Box 5076
Champaign, IL 61825-5076
Fax: (217)351-1549

Ennis, James F., Exec. Dir.
Catholic Rural Life [19815]
2115 Summit Ave.
Saint Paul, MN 55105-1078
Ph: (651)962-5955
Fax: (651)962-5957

Ennis, Lori, Exec. Dir.
American Neurogastroenterology
  and Motility Society [14779]
45685 Harmony Ln.
Belleville, MI 48111
Ph: (734)699-1130
Fax: (734)699-1136

Ennis, Mike, Director
Cool Roof Rating Council [518]
449 15th St., Ste. 400
Oakland, CA 94612
Toll Free: 866-465-2523
Fax: (510)482-4421

Enright, Cathleen, President, CEO
Pet Food Institute [2547]
1020 19th St. NW, Ste. 225
Washington, DC 20036
Ph: (202)791-9440

Ensz, Shelley, Founder, President
International Scleroderma Network
  [17179]
7455 France Ave. S, No. 266
Edina, MN 55435-4702
Ph: (952)831-3091
Toll Free: 800-564-7099

Enteman, John, President
Kappa Alpha Society [23903]
3109 N Triphammer Rd.
Lansing, NY 14882
Toll Free: 877-895-1825

Epelbaum, Dr. Gerard, President
Committee of French Speaking
  Societies [19437]

c/o Gerard Epelbaum, President
30 E 40th St., Ste. 906
New York, NY 10016

Epps, Chad, President
Society for Simulation in Healthcare
[15700]
2021 L St. NW, Ste. 400
Washington, DC 20036
Toll Free: 866-730-6127

Epstein, Bob, Founder
Environmental Entrepreneurs [3857]
111 Sutter St., 21st Fl.
San Francisco, CA 94104-4540

Epstein, Eric, Chmn. of the Bd.,
Chairman
Three Mile Island Alert [18736]
315 Peffer St.
Harrisburg, PA 17102-1834
Ph: (717)233-7897

Epstein, Dr. Jonathan H., Assoc. VP
EcoHealth Alliance [4810]
460 W 34th St., 17th Fl.
New York, NY 10001-2320
Ph: (212)380-4460
Fax: (212)380-4465

Epstein, Mark Alan, Treasurer
National Health Association [15853]
PO Box 477
Youngstown, OH 44501-0477
Ph: (330)953-1002
Fax: (330)953-1030

Epstein, Mark H., ScD, Exec. Sec.
International Society for Pharma-
coepidemiology [16668]
5272 River Rd., Ste. 630
Bethesda, MD 20816
Ph: (301)718-6500
Fax: (301)656-0989

Epstein, Mark H., Exec. Dir.
Society for Radiation Oncology
Administrators [17071]
5272 River Rd., Ste. 630
Bethesda, MD 20816
Ph: (301)718-6510
Fax: (301)656-0989

Epstein, Mary, President
Organization of American Kodaly
Educators [8372]
10801 National Blvd., Ste. 590
Los Angeles, CA 90064
Ph: (310)441-3555
Fax: (310)441-3577

Epstein, Michael, President
Vintage Volkswagen Club of America
[21518]
PO Box 8559
Prairie Village, KS 66208
Ph: (641)421-0965

Epstein, Miriam Stannard, Director,
Founder
Books to Dreams [12243]
312 Ferguson Rd.
Manchester, CT 06040
Ph: (860)646-5934

Epstein, Dr. Samuel S., MD, Chair-
man, Founder
Cancer Prevention Coalition [13927]
1735 W Harrison St., Ste. 206
School of Public Health
2121 W Taylor St.
MC 922
Chicago, IL 60612

Erb, Donna, VP
Society of Plastic Surgical Skin Care
Specialists [14324]
11262 Monarch St.

Garden Grove, CA 92841
Ph: (562)799-0466
Toll Free: 800-486-0611
Fax: (562)799-1098

Erceg, Linda Ebner, RN, Author
Association of Camp Nurses [16117]
19006 Hunt County Ln.
Fisherville, KY 40023-7704
Ph: (502)232-2945

Erdem, Mehmet, PhD, President
International Hospitality Information
Technology Association [7279]
c/o Mehmet Erdem, PhD, President
Box 456021
Harrah College of Hotel Administra-
tion
University of Nevada
4505 Maryland Pky.
Las Vegas, NV 89154-6021
Ph: (702)895-5811
Fax: (702)895-4872

Erdman, Lynn, CEO
Association of Women's Health,
Obstetric and Neonatal Nurses
[16125]
2000 L St. NW, Ste. 740
Washington, DC 20036-4912
Ph: (202)261-2400
Toll Free: 800-673-8499
Fax: (202)728-0575

Erickson, Aimee, Exec. Dir.
Citizens Coal Council [4023]
125 W Pike St., Ste. B
Canonsburg, PA 15317
Ph: (724)338-4629

Erickson, Audrae, President
Corn Refiners Association [1323]
1701 Pennsylvania Ave. NW, Ste.
950
Washington, DC 20006
Ph: (202)331-1634
Fax: (202)331-2054

Erickson, David, President, CEO
Educational Concerns for Hunger
Organization [12082]
17391 Durrance Rd.
North Fort Myers, FL 33917
Ph: (239)543-3246

Erickson, Edward, Treasurer
Institute of Turkish Studies [10285]
Georgetown University
Intercultural Ctr. 305R
Washington, DC 20057-1033
Ph: (202)687-0292
Fax: (202)687-3780

Erickson, Jane, Officer
Kiwanis International [12894]
3636 Woodview Trace
Indianapolis, IN 46268-3196
Ph: (317)875-8755
Toll Free: 800-549-2647
Fax: (317)879-0204

Erickson, Milton H., Founder
American Society of Clinical
Hypnosis [15360]
140 N Bloomingdale Rd.
Bloomingdale, IL 60108-1017
Ph: (630)980-4740
Fax: (630)351-8490

Erickson, Robbyn, President
Now I Lay Me Down to Sleep
[12505]
7500 E Arapahoe Rd., Ste. 101
Centennial, CO 80112
Ph: (720)283-3339
Toll Free: 877-834-5667
Fax: (720)283-8998

Ericson, Dr. Kris, Exec. Dir.
ACMHA: The College for Behavioral
Health Leadership [15753]

7804 Loma del Norte Rd. NE
Albuquerque, NM 87109-5419
Ph: (505)822-5038

Eriksson, John, President
Global Peace Services [18790]
PO Box 27922
Washington, DC 20038-7922
Ph: (202)216-9886

Ernest, Terry, President
National Association of Automobile
Museums [9838]
PO Box 271
Auburn, IN 46706
Ph: (260)925-1444
Fax: (260)925-6266

Ernst, Karen, Administrator
Voices for Vaccines [14217]
325 Swanton Way
Decatur, GA 30030

Ernst, Robert, Asst. Sec.
National Railway Historical Society
[10186]
100 N 20th St., Ste. 400
Philadelphia, PA 19103-1462
Ph: (215)557-6606
Fax: (215)963-9785

Eroglu, Dogan, PhD, President
American Turkish Friendship Council
[18515]
1266 W Paces Ferry Rd., No. 257
Atlanta, GA 30327-2306
Ph: (404)884-8666
Fax: (404)393-9301

Erskine, Pamela, President
IT Service Management Forum USA
[6746]
20333 State Highway 249, Ste. 200
Houston, TX 77070-2613
Ph: (626)963-1900
Toll Free: 888-959-0673

Erusha, Kimberly S., PhD, Managing
Dir.
USGA Green Section [22898]
77 Liberty Cor. Rd.
Far Hills, NJ 07931-2570
Ph: (908)234-2300
Fax: (908)781-1736

Erven, Marlene, Exec. Dir.
Alpha-1 Foundation [14804]
3300 Ponce de Leon Blvd.
Coral Gables, FL 33134
Ph: (305)567-9888
Toll Free: 877-228-7321
Fax: (305)567-1317

Ervin, Roger, President, CEO
International Relief & Development
[11386]
1621 N Kent St., 4th Fl.
Arlington, VA 22209
Ph: (703)248-0161
Fax: (703)248-0194

Esch, Dr. Emily, Exec. Dir.
American Association of Philosophy
Teachers [8416]
Cominican College
470 Westen Hwy.
Orangeburg, NY 10962
Ph: (434)220-3300
Toll Free: 800-444-2419
Fax: (434)220-3301

Esch, Gerald W., President
American Society of Parasitologists
[6993]
c/o Lee Couch, Secretary/Treasurer
76 Homesteads Rd.
Placitas, NM 87043
Ph: (505)867-9480

Escobosa, Laura, Exec. Dir.
Operation Rainbow [15610]
4200 Park Blvd., PMB 157
Oakland, CA 94602
Ph: (510)273-2485
    (510)655-4598

Esguerra, Jorge, CFO
Society of American Foresters
[4216]
5400 Grosvenor Ln.
Bethesda, MD 20814-2198
Toll Free: 866-897-8720
Fax: (301)897-3691

Eshak, David, MD, President
Committee of Interns and Residents
[23443]
520 8th Ave., Ste. 1200
New York, NY 10018
Ph: (212)356-8100
    (212)356-8180
Toll Free: 800-247-8877
Fax: (212)356-8111

Esher, Cynthia A., President
Measurement, Control, and Automa-
tion Association [3028]
200 City Hall Ave., Ste. D
Poquoson, VA 23662
Ph: (757)258-3100

Eshetu, Mahnaz K., Exec. Dir.
Refugee Women's Alliance [19020]
4008 Martin Luther King, Jr. Way S
Seattle, WA 98108
Ph: (206)721-0243
Fax: (206)721-0282

Eskandari-Qajar, Dr. Manoutchehr
M., Founder, President
International Qajar Studies Associa-
tion [9594]
PO Box 31107
Santa Barbara, CA 93130
Ph: (805)687-1148
Fax: (805)687-1148

Eslinger, Ron, MA, President,
Treasurer
American Association of Moderate
Sedation Nurses [16092]
322 Commerce St.
Clinton, TN 37716
Ph: (865)230-9995
Fax: (865)269-4613

Esmail, Hafeez, Bd. Member
Baraka Africa [10863]
425 1st St., Ste. 1103
San Francisco, CA 94105-4623
Ph: (415)690-0601
    (415)425-5194
Fax: (415)520-0930

Esp, Jim, Exec. Dir., Secretary
Professional School Photographers
Association International [2592]
3000 Picture Pl.
Jackson, MI 49201
Ph: (517)788-8100
Toll Free: 800-762-9287
Fax: (517)788-8371

Espenoza, Cecelia M., Chairperson
National Hispana Leadership
Institute [18340]
PO Box 70061
Washington, DC 20024
Ph: (703)527-6007

Espinoza, Manny, Contact
Association of Latino Professionals
in Finance and Accounting [15]
801 S Grand Ave., Ste. 650
Los Angeles, CA 90017
Ph: (213)243-0004
Fax: (213)243-0006

Espinoza, Rev. Melesio Peter,
President
Pro-Moskitia Foundation of
Nicaragua [12130]
2435 Oak Crest
Austin, TX 78704
Ph: (512)444-8640
Fax: (512)443-1212

Espiritu, Russ, Chmn. of the Bd.
American Cuemakers Association
[22582]
2231 Galloway Blvd.
Trophy Club, TX 76262
Ph: (817)683-5652

Esposito, Donna Kaye, MCC,
President
National Association of Cruise-
Oriented Agencies Inc. [3385]
7378 W Atlantic Blvd., Ste. 115
Margate, FL 33063
Ph: (305)663-5626
Fax: (866)816-7143

Esquivel, Jesus, MD, Bd. Member
American Society of Peritoneal
Surface Malignancies [13887]
11806 Wollingford Ct.
Clarksville, MD 21029
Ph: (410)368-2743
Fax: (410)951-4007

Esser, Jeffrey L., CEO, Exec. Dir.
Government Finance Officers As-
sociation of United States and
Canada [5706]
203 N LaSalle St., Ste. 2700
Chicago, IL 60601-1210
Ph: (312)977-9700
Fax: (312)977-4806

Estades, Javier, Chairman
Cigar Association of America, Inc.
[3284]
1100 G St. NW, Ste. 1050
Washington, DC 20005-7405
Ph: (202)223-8204
Fax: (202)833-0379

Estep, Andrew, Exec. Dir.
Association of Workplace Investiga-
tors [5358]
2150 N 107th St., Ste. 205
Seattle, WA 98133
Ph: (206)209-5278

Estep, Ms. Carolyn, Treasurer
Stein Collectors International
[21725]
8002 NE Highway 99
Vancouver, WA 98665
Ph: (708)323-9283

Estep, Janet O., CEO, President
NACHA: The Electronic Payments
Association [406]
2550 Wasser Ter., Ste. 400
Herndon, VA 20171
Ph: (703)561-1100
Fax: (703)787-0996

Estep, Sarah, Founder
Association TransCommunication
[7008]
PO Box 13111
Reno, NV 89507

Estes, Chris, President, CEO
National Housing Conference
[11980]
1900 M St. NW, Ste. 200
Washington, DC 20036
Ph: (202)466-2121
Fax: (202)466-2122

Estes, Jim, Founder
Salute Military Golf Association
[22894]

Argyle Country Club
14600 Argyle Club Rd.
Silver Spring, MD 20906-1999
Ph: (301)500-7449
    (301)525-1639

Estevez, pablo, President
IEEE Computational Intelligence
Society [6555]
c/o Jo-Ellen B. Snyder, Senior
Administrator
445 Hoes Ln.
Piscataway, NJ 08855
Ph: (732)465-5892
Fax: (732)465-6435

Estwanik, Joe, Bd. Member
Association of Ringside Physicians
[16744]
2424 American Ln.
Madison, WI 53704

Etegran, Lars, Contact
George H. Buck Jr. Jazz Foundation
[22246]
61 French Market Pl.
New Orleans, LA 70116
Ph: (504)525-5000
Fax: (504)525-1776

Etienne, Dr. Carissa, Director
Pan American Health Organization
Foundation [15611]
1889 F St. NW, Ste. 312
Washington, DC 20006
Ph: (202)974-3416
    (202)974-3000
Fax: (202)974-3636

Etienne, Jina, President, CEO
National Association of Black Ac-
countants, Inc. [44]
7474 Greenway Center Dr., Ste.
1120
Greenbelt, MD 20770
Ph: (301)474-6222
Toll Free: 888-571-2939
Fax: (301)474-3114

Etkin, Steven A., Exec. VP, CEO
Association of the Wall and Ceiling
Industries International [502]
513 W Broad St., Ste. 210
Falls Church, VA 22046
Ph: (703)538-1600
Fax: (703)534-8307

Ettarp, Lars, President
International Federation of Psoriasis
Associations [14496]
6600 SW 92nd, Ste. 300
Portland, OR 97223
Ph: (503)244-7404
Toll Free: 800-723-9166
Fax: (503)245-0626

Etzioni, Dr. Amitai, Director, Founder
Communitarian Network [18971]
1922 F St. NW, Rm. 413
Washington, DC 20052
Ph: (202)994-8190
Fax: (202)994-1606

Eubanks, Bill, Contact
Bicycle Stamps Club [22311]
c/o Bill Eubanks
21304 2nd Ave. SE
Bothell, WA 98021-7550

Eugene, Patrick, Founder
Organization Chemen Lavi [8252]
PO Box 1952
Staunton, VA 24402
Ph: (540)480-4852
    (540)607-1212

Eugster, Fr. Josef, Chairman
Father Josef's Method of Reflexology [13622]

1441 High Ridge Rd.
Stamford, CT 06903-4906
Ph: (203)968-6824

Eulberg, Del, President
Professional Housing Management
Association [5284]
154 Ft. Evans Rd. NE
Leesburg, VA 20176
Ph: (703)771-1888
Fax: (703)771-0299

Euwema, John, VP
Consumer Credit Industry Association [1851]
6300 Powers Ferry Rd., Ste. 600-
286
Atlanta, GA 30339
Ph: (678)858-4001

Evanko, Dolores M., Secretary,
Treasurer
Slovak Catholic Federation [19648]
173 Berner Ave.
Hazleton, PA 18201
Ph: (570)454-5547

Evans, Bethany, Exec. VP
International Association of
Trampoline Parks [3309]
PO Box 594
Hershey, PA 17033
Ph: (717)910-4534

Evans, Dr. Beverly J., PhD, Exec.
Dir.
Pi Delta Phi [23765]
c/o Dr. Beverly J. Evans, Executive
Director
State University of New York at
Geneseo
Dept. of Languages and Literatures
Welles 211
1 College Cir.
Geneseo, NY 14454
Ph: (585)245-5247
Fax: (585)245-5399

Evans, Bill, Exec. Sec.
American Cut Glass Association
[22131]
c/o Bill Evans, Executive Secretary
PO Box 1147
Elizabeth, CO 80107-1147

Evans, Blaine
United Duroc Swine Registry [4718]
2639 Yeager Rd.
West Lafayette, IN 47996-2417
Ph: (765)463-3594

Evans, Brian, President
International Trumpet Guild [9937]
PO Box 2688
Davenport, IA 52809-2688
Ph: (563)676-2435
Fax: (413)403-8899

Evans, Brooke DiGiovanni, President
Museum Education Roundtable
[9835]
PO Box 15727
Washington, DC 20003

Evans, Catherine, President,
Founder
Orphanages for Africa [11118]
PO Box 44294
Washington, DC 20026

Evans, Connie, CEO, President
Association for Enterprise Op-
portunity [3115]
1310 L St NW, Ste. 830
Washington, DC 20005
Ph: (202)650-5580

Evans, Diane Carlson, RN, Founder,
President
Vietnam Women's Memorial
Foundation [21174]

c/o Eastern National
470 Maryland Dr., Ste. 1
Fort Washington, PA 19034
Toll Free: 877-463-3647

Evans Gayle, Margaret, Exec. Dir.
American Association for Gifted
Children [7941]
Erwin Mill Bldg.
2024 W Main St.
Durham, NC 27705
Ph: (919)684-8459

Evans, Hugh, CEO
The Global Poverty Project [12543]
594 Broadway, Ste. 207
New York, NY 10012

Evans, Ian, Founder
Konbit Mizik [13457]
2658 Griffith Park Blvd., Ste. 276
Los Angeles, CA 90039
Ph: (917)450-2413

Evans, Joanie, Co-Pres.
Federation of Gay Games [23225]
584 Castro St., Ste. 343
San Francisco, CA 94114-2512
Toll Free: 866-459-1261

Evans, Jodie, Founder, Director
Code Pink Women's Pre-Emptive
Strike for Peace [18778]
2010 Linden Ave.
Venice, CA 90291
Ph: (310)827-4320
Fax: (310)827-4547

Evans, Jodie, Bd. Member
Rainforest Action Network [3930]
425 Bush St., Ste. 300
San Francisco, CA 94108
Ph: (415)398-4404
Fax: (415)398-2732

Evans, John, Sr. VP, CFO
American Hospital Association
[15305]
155 N Wacker Dr.
Chicago, IL 60606
Ph: (312)422-3000

Evans, John T., II, President
Council of International Restaurant
Real Estate Brokers [2935]
8350 N Central Expy., Ste. 1300
Dallas, TX 75206-1620
Toll Free: 866-247-2123
Fax: (866)247-2329

Evans, Julie, CEO
Project Tomorrow [7813]
15707 Rockfield Blvd., Ste. 250
Irvine, CA 92618
Ph: (949)609-4660
Fax: (949)609-4665

Evans, Kathy, Officer
International Research and
Exchanges Board [8081]
1275 K St. NW, Ste. 600
Washington, DC 20005
Ph: (202)628-8188
Fax: (202)628-8189

Evans, Leon, Bd. Member
National Association of County
Behavioral Health and
Developmental Disability Directors
[15127]
25 Massachusetts Ave. NW, Ste.
500
Washington, DC 20001
Ph: (202)661-8816
Fax: (202)478-1659

Evans, Paula M., Chairman
Foundation for Angelman Syndrome
Therapeutics [15932]

PO Box 608
Downers Grove, IL 60515-0608
Ph: (630)852-3278
Toll Free: 866-783-0078
Fax: (630)852-3270

Evans, Peter, President
U.S. Travel Insurance Association
[3406]
9707 Key West Ave., Ste. 100
Rockville, MD 20850
Ph: (240)342-3816

Evans, Rhett, CEO
Golf Course Superintendents Association of America [3157]
1421 Research Park Dr.
Lawrence, KS 66049-3859
Ph: (785)841-2240
Toll Free: 800-472-7878
Fax: (785)832-3643

Evans, Ron, Exec. Dir.
Independent Textile Rental Association [3260]
202 Commerce St.
Hogansville, GA 30230-1120
Ph: (706)637-6552
        (706)637-8875

Evans, Ruth, Exec. Dir.
New Chaucer Society [9763]
Adorjan Hall, Rm. 127
St. Louis University
3800 Lindell Blvd.
Saint Louis, MO 63108
Ph: (314)520-7067
Fax: (314)977-1514

Evans, Samuel C., MD, Director
Reach International Healthcare and
Training [15491]
PO Box 152
Caulfield, MO 65626

Evans, Scott, President
Federation of Employers and Workers of America [1090]
2901 Bucks Bayou Rd.
Bay City, TX 77414
Ph: (979)245-7577
Toll Free: 877-422-3392
Fax: (979)245-8969

Evans, Stephen R. T., Chairman
American Board of Surgery [17365]
1617 John F. Kennedy Blvd., Ste.
860
Philadelphia, PA 19103
Ph: (215)568-4000
Fax: (215)563-5718

Evans, Wilma J., Chairperson
Frontiers International, Inc. [11360]
6301 Crittenden St.
Philadelphia, PA 19138-1031
Ph: (215)549-4550
Fax: (215)549-4209

Evans, Zander, Dir. of Res.
Forest Guild [3865]
2019 Galisteo St., Ste. N7
Santa Fe, NM 87505
Ph: (505)983-8992
Fax: (505)986-0798

Evans-Lombe, Monica, Exec. Dir.
International Nurses Society on Addictions [16137]
3416 Primm Ln.
Birmingham, AL 35216
Ph: (205)823-6106

Evans-Lombe, Monica, Exec. Dir.
National Association of Graduate
Admissions Professionals [7450]
18000 W 105th St.
Olathe, KS 66061-7543
Ph: (913)895-4616
Fax: (913)895-4652

Evans-Richey, Elfriede, President,
Secretary, Treasurer
Music Teachers Association
International [8377]
11111 Maricopa Ln.
Dewey, AZ 86327

Evenson, Becky, VP
Baromedical Nurses Association
[16126]
PO Box 53
Gotha, FL 34734
Ph: (407)361-4715

Evered, Emine, Secretary
Ottoman and Turkish Studies Association [10286]
c/o Heather Ferguson, Treasurer
850 Columbia Ave.
Claremont, CA 91711

Everett, Lisa O., President
International Women's Fishing Association [22848]
PO Box 31507
Palm Beach Gardens, FL 33420-1507

Everhart, Robert, CEO
National Traditional Country Music
Association [9980]
650 Main St.
Anita, IA 50020
Ph: (712)762-4363

Everingham, J. Theodore, Chairman
Grosse Pointe War Memorial Association [21122]
32 Lake Shore Dr.
Grosse Pointe Farms, MI 48236-3726
Ph: (313)881-7511
Fax: (313)884-6638

Eversole, Eric, President, Advisor
U.S. Chamber of Commerce
Foundation [19007]
1615 H St. NW
Washington, DC 20062
Ph: (202)463-5500

Everson, Sharon, President
National Intercollegiate Women's
Fencing Association [22833]
c/o Denise C. O'Connor, Secretary/
Treasurer
224C Buckingham Ct.
Lakewood, NJ 08701-7802

Evert, Frank, President
Water Without Borders [13363]
10 Cole Rd., Ste. A
Pleasant Valley, NY 12569

Evert, Dr. Jessica, Exec. Dir.
Child Family Health International
[14172]
995 Market St., Ste. 1104
San Francisco, CA 94103
Ph: (415)957-9000
Toll Free: 866-345-4674
Fax: (415)840-0486

Evins, Louise, Treasurer
Fashion Group International, Inc.
[203]
8 W 40th St., 7th Fl.
New York, NY 10018
Ph: (212)302-5511
Fax: (212)302-5533

Evnin, Luke, PhD, Chairman
Scleroderma Research Foundation
[17182]
220 Montgomery St., Ste. 1411
San Francisco, CA 94104
Toll Free: 800-441-2873

Evola, Vito M., Exec. Dir.
Delta Theta Phi Law Fraternity
International [23803]

Campbell University
Wiggins School of Law
225 Hillsborough St., Ste. 432
Raleigh, NC 27603
Ph: (919)866-4667
        (919)865-4667
Toll Free: 800-783-2600

Ewald, Eric, Exec. Dir.
American Society for Theatre
Research [10239]
1000 Westgate Dr., Ste. 252
Saint Paul, MN 55114
Ph: (651)288-3429
Fax: (651)290-2266

Ewald, Eric, Exec. Dir.
Association for Theatre in Higher
Education [8696]
1000 Westgate Dr., Ste. 252
Saint Paul, MN 55114
Ph: (651)288-3430
Toll Free: 800-918-9216
Fax: (800)809-6374

Ewalt, David, MD, President
American Association of Pediatric
Urologists [17545]
c/o Dominic Frimberger, MD,
Secretary and Treasurer
The Children's Hospital of Oklahoma
1200 Children's Ave.
Oklahoma City, OK 73104
Ph: (405)271-6900
Fax: (405)271-3118

Ewart, Ron, President
National Association of Rural
Landowners [18933]
PO Box 1031
Issaquah, WA 98027
Ph: (425)837-5365
Toll Free: 800-682-7848
Fax: (425)837-5365

Ewing, Bob, Contact
Attunement Guild [13608]
c/o Bob Ewing, Practitioner
100 Sunrise Ranch Rd.
Loveland, CO 80538

Ewing, Jamie, Secretary
Transgender American Veterans Association [21141]
574 E Cuyahoga Falls Ave., Unit
4513
Akron, OH 44310
Ph: (516)828-2911
        (616)427-5724

Ewing, John, President
Math for America [8281]
915 Broadway, 16th Fl.
New York, NY 10010
Ph: (646)437-0904
Fax: (646)437-0935

Ewing, Wade, Director
Africa Inland Mission International
[20379]
PO Box 3611
Peachtree City, GA 30269-7611
Ph: (845)735-4014
Toll Free: 800-254-0010
Fax: (770)631-3213

Ewing, Wallace K., Chancellor
Ewing Family Association [19640]
1330 Vaughn Ct.
Aurora, IL 60504

Exman, Delphine, VP
North American Conference of
Separated and Divorced Catholics
[11686]
PO Box 568
Waldorf, MD 20604-0568
Toll Free: 855-727-2269
Fax: (855)729-8751

Exum, Jane Slade, President
Puli Club of America [21950]
1616 E Calumet St.
Appleton, WI 54915-4222
Ph: (920)730-1885

Eyerly, Sarah, President
Society for Eighteenth-Century
Music [10005]
School of Music
Texas Tech University
Lubbock, TX 79409-2033
Fax: (806)742-2294

Eyeson-Akiwowo, Nana, Founder,
President
African Health Now [15433]
PO Box 3243
New York, NY 10163
Ph: (347)389-2461

Eykamp, Susan, President
Association for Distance Education
and Independent Learning [7483]
c/o Susan Eykamp, 820 N
Washington Ave.
Dakota State University
Madison, SD 57042
Ph: (605)256-5798

Eyles, Marynell, Secretary
American Connemara Pony Society
[4302]
PO Box 100
Middlebrook, VA 24459

Eyring, Teresa, Exec. Dir.
Theatre Communications Group
[10274]
520 8th Ave., 24th Fl.
New York, NY 10018-4156
Ph: (212)609-5900
Fax: (212)609-5901

Ezell, Dr. Barry C., President
Security Analysis and Risk Management Association [3068]
PO Box 100284
Arlington, VA 22210
Ph: (703)635-7906
Fax: (703)635-7935

Ezell, Brian, Chairman
Peanut & Tree Nut Processors Association [1366]
PO Box 2660
Alexandria, VA 22301
Ph: (301)365-2521

F

Faber, Scott, VP of Gvt. Affairs
Environmental Working Group
[4061]
1436 U St. NW, Ste. 100
Washington, DC 20009
Ph: (202)667-6982
Fax: (202)232-2592

Faberman, Edward P., Exec. Dir.
Air Carrier Association of America
[121]
421 Watts Branch Pky.
Rockville, MD 20854
Ph: (202)236-1018

Fabiani, Christine, Exec. Dir.
Knots of Love [13998]
2973 Harbor Blvd., No. 822
Costa Mesa, CA 92626
Ph: (949)229-5668

Fabricant, Dr. Daniel, Exec. Dir.,
CEO
Natural Products Association [2972]
1773 T St. NW
Washington, DC 20009
Ph: (202)223-0101
Toll Free: 800-966-6632
Fax: (202)223-0250

Facinelli, James, Chairman
Modern Car Society [21440]
Rolls-Royce Owners Club
191 Hempt Rd.
Mechanicsburg, PA 17050

Facione, Francis P., Exec. Dir.
American Catholic Union [19791]
1207 Potomac Pl.
Louisville, KY 40214
Ph: (502)368-0871
Fax: (502)361-9782

Factor, Ms. Judith, Exec. Dir.
Friends of Karen [11231]
118 Titicus Rd.
North Salem, NY 10560
Ph: (914)277-4547
Toll Free: 800-637-2774
Fax: (914)277-4967

Factor, Richard, President
SETI League [6011]
433 Liberty St.
Little Ferry, NJ 07643
Ph: (201)641-1770
Toll Free: 800-TAU-SETI
Fax: (201)641-1771

Fagen, Adam, PhD, Exec. Dir.
Genetics Society of America [6667]
9650 Rockville Pke.
Bethesda, MD 20814-3998
Ph: (301)634-7300
Toll Free: 866-486-GENE
Fax: (301)634-7079

Fager, Hayley, Dir. of Programs, Dir.
of Operations
International Network for Urban
Agriculture [3569]
Chicago, IL

Fahey, Bruce, Administrator
Brothers and Sisters of Penance of
St. Francis [19805]
65774 County Road 31
Northome, MN 56661
Ph: (218)897-5974

Fahey, Dan, Leader
Veterans for Common Sense
[21148]
900 2nd St. NE, Ste. 216
Washington, DC 20002
Ph: (202)558-4553

Fahner, Thomas, President
National Fellowship of Child Care
Executives [13466]
c/o Robert Miller, Executive
Secretary
PO Box 1195
Somerset, PA 15501

Fahy, Barbara, President
Mail Systems Management Associa-
tion [2118]
PO Box 1145
North Riverside, IL 60546-1145
Toll Free: 800-714-6762

Faigel, Douglas O., President
American Society for Gastrointestinal
Endoscopy [14781]
3300 Woodcreek Dr.
Downers Grove, IL 60515
Ph: (630)573-0600
(630)570-5605
Toll Free: 866-353-2743
Fax: (630)963-8332

Fair, Rob, President
Chris LeDoux International Fan Club
[24029]
c/o Rob Fair, President
PO Box 41052
San Jose, CA 95160

Fair, Shirley, Treasurer
American Baptist Historical Society
[19712]
3001 Mercer University Dr.,
Atlanta, GA 30341
Ph: (678)547-6680
(610)768-2269
Toll Free: 800-222-3872
Fax: (678)547-6682

Fairbanks, Casie, President
American Mule Association [3596]
260 Neilson Rd.
Reno, NV 89521
Ph: (775)849-9437
(916)390-1861

Fairbanks, Dick, Contact
Automotive Warehouse Distributors
Association [314]
7101 Wisconsin Ave., Ste. 1300
Bethesda, MD 20814-3415
Ph: (301)654-6664
Fax: (301)654-3299

Fairbanks, Jonathan, Chairman
The Decorative Arts Trust [8973]
20 S Olive St., Ste. 304
Media, PA 19063
Ph: (610)627-4970

Faires, Barbara, Secretary
Mathematical Association of America
[6823]
1529 18th St. NW
Washington, DC 20036-1358
Ph: (202)387-5200
Toll Free: 800-741-9415
Fax: (202)265-2384

Fairfax, Jane Ellen, Chmn. of the
Bd., Treasurer
Society for the Second Self [12952]
PO Box 20785
Houston, TX 77225
Ph: (832)431-7104

Fairfax, Jennifer, VP
American Academy of Adoption At-
torneys [4978]
PO Box 33053
Washington, DC 20033-0053
Ph: (202)832-2222

Fairman, Ronald M., President
Society for Vascular Surgery [17581]
633 N St. Clair St., 22nd Fl.
Chicago, IL 60611-5098
Ph: (312)334-2300
Toll Free: 800-258-7188
Fax: (312)334-2320

Fairtile, Linda B., Director
American Institute for Verdi Studies
[9861]
Music Dept., Rm. 268
New York University
24 Waverly Pl.
New York, NY 10003-6757
Ph: (212)998-2587
Fax: (212)995-4147

Fajgenbaum, David, MSc, Founder,
Chmn. of the Bd.
Actively Moving Forward [10769]
3344 Hillsborough St., Ste. 260
Raleigh, NC 27607
Ph: (919)803-6728
Toll Free: 877-830-7442

Fakely, Carolyn, Officer
Edsel Owner's Club [21375]
c/o Lois Roth
1740 NW 3rd St.
Gresham, OR 97030
Ph: (503)492-0878

Fales, Sgt. John, Jr., President
Blinded American Veterans Foundation [20765]

PO Box 65900
Washington, DC 20035-5900
Ph: (202)257-5446
Fax: (301)622-3330

Falick, Jeffrey L., President
Association of Humanistic Rabbis
[20232]

Falks, Laval D., Director
Archery Shooters Association
[22499]
PO Box 399
Kennesaw, GA 30156-0399
Ph: (770)795-0232
Fax: (770)795-0953

Fall, Amadou, CEO
National Renewables Cooperative
Organization [6500]
4140 W 99th St.
Carmel, IN 46032-7731
Ph: (317)344-7900
Fax: (317)344-7901

Fall, Jeff, VP
International Association of Medical
Equipment Remarketers and Ser-
vicers [15687]
85 Edgemont Pl.
Teaneck, NJ 07666-4605
Ph: (201)357-5400
Fax: (201)833-2021

Fallah-Fini, Saeideh, Secretary
Association of Professors and
Scholars of Iranian Heritage [9592]
PO Box 4175
Diamond Bar, CA 91765-0175
Ph: (909)869-2569
Fax: (909)869-2564

Falley, Nanci, President
American Indian Horse Registry
[4313]
9028 State Park Rd.
Lockhart, TX 78644-4310
Ph: (512)398-6642

Fallon, Robert E., Chairman
Council on International Educational
Exchange USA [8064]
300 Fore St.
Portland, ME 04101
Ph: (207)553-4000
Fax: (207)553-4299

Fallon, Tim, Treasurer
Catboat Association, Inc. [22605]
262 Forest St.
Needham, MA 02492-1326

Fallon, William J., Chairman
Naval Historical Foundation [9804]
Washington Navy Yard
1306 Dahlgren Ave. SE
Washington, DC 20374-5109
Ph: (202)678-4333
Toll Free: 888-880-0102
Fax: (703)580-5280

Falls, Bob, President
International Meteorite Collectors
Association [21675]

Falls, Susan, President
Society for the Anthropology of North
America [5919]
c/o American Anthropological As-
sociation
2300 Clarendon Blvd., Ste. 1301
Arlington, VA 22201-3386
Ph: (703)528-1902
Fax: (703)528-3546

Fan, Shenggen, Dir. Gen.
International Food Policy Research
Institute [18457]

2033 K St. NW
Washington, DC 20006-1002
Ph: (202)862-5600
Fax: (202)467-4439

Fanaie, Delfarib, Founder
Moms Against Poverty [12554]
PO Box 4212
Burlingame, CA 94011
Ph: (650)271-7178

Fanis, Linda, Mktg. & Sales Mgr.
Institute for Chemical Education
[6202]
Dept. of Chemistry
University of Wisconsin-Madison
1101 University Ave.
Madison, WI 53706-1322
Ph: (608)262-3033
Toll Free: 888-220-9822
Fax: (608)265-8094

Fankhauser, Davina, President,
Founder
Fertility Within Reach [14758]
1005 Boylston St., No. 332
Newton Highlands, MA 02461
Ph: (857)636-8674

Fanning, Suzanne, President
Word of Mouth Marketing Associa-
tion [2305]
200 E Randolph St., Ste. 5100
Chicago, IL 60601
Ph: (312)577-7610

Fansler, Greg, President
Council of Alumni Marketing and
Membership Professionals [2276]
211 Emmet St. S
Charlottesville, VA 22903-2431
Ph: (434)243-9020

Fant, Peter, President
Water Engineers for the Americas
[13359]
1201 Parkway Dr.
Santa Fe, NM 87507
Ph: (505)473-9211
Toll Free: 800-460-5366
Fax: (505)471-6675

Fantaci, Kim, President
CPA Firm Management Association
[24]
136 S Keowee St.
Dayton, OH 45402
Ph: (937)222-0030
Fax: (937)222-5794

Fantauzzi, Rafael A., CEO,
President
National Puerto Rican Coalition
[9234]
1220 L St. NW, Ste. 701
Washington, DC 20005
Ph: (202)223-3915

Fantozzi, Jeff, President
Pacific Lumber Inspection Bureau
[1417]
909 S 336th St., Ste. 203
Federal Way, WA 98003
Ph: (253)835-3344
Fax: (253)835-3371

Farah, George, Exec. Dir.
Open Debates [18185]
Ph: (202)688-1340

Faraj, Dr. Walid, Director
American Druze Society [20215]
PO Box 781628
San Antonio, TX 78278

Faraldo, Joe, President
Standardbred Owners Association of
New York [22928]

733 Yonkers Ave., Ste. 102
Yonkers, NY 10704-2659
Ph: (914)968-3599
Fax: (914)968-3943

Faraone, Barbara, Exec. Dir.
International Neuro-Linguistic
  Programming Association [16979]
NY

Faraz, Ahmed, Gen. Sec.
Pakistan Chamber of Commerce
  USA [23611]
11110 Bellaire Blvd., Ste. 202
Houston, TX 77072-2610
Ph: (832)448-0520
Toll Free: 888-712-5111

Farb Hernandez, Prof. Jo, Director
Saving and Preserving Arts and
  Cultural Environments [8887]
9053 Soquel Dr., Ste. 205
Aptos, CA 95003
Ph: (831)662-2907
Fax: (831)662-2918

Farber, Erica, President, CEO
Radio Advertising Bureau [108]
1320 Greenway Dr., Ste. 500
Irving, TX 75038-2587
Toll Free: 800-232-3131

Farbman, Dr. Andrea, Exec. Dir.
American Music Therapy Association
  [16961]
8455 Colesville Rd., Ste. 1000
Silver Spring, MD 20910
Ph: (301)589-3300
Fax: (301)589-5175

Farer, David B., President
American College of Environmental
  Lawyers [5175]
1730 M St. NW Ste. 700
Washington, DC 20036
Ph: (617)832-1203
Fax: (617)832-7000

Fargnoli, A. Nicholas, President
James Joyce Society [9066]
80 E Hartsdale Ave., No. 414
Hartsdale, NY 10530-2805
Ph: (516)764-3119

Farguharson, Phil, Treasurer
Association of Earth Science Editors
  [2661]
c/o Mary Ann Schmidt
554 Chess St.
Pittsburgh, PA 15205-3212

Faris, Hanna, Contact
American Federation of Ramallah,
  Palestine [8812]
27484 Ann Arbor Trl.
Westland, MI 48185
Ph: (734)425-1600
Fax: (734)425-3985

Farkas, Beth, Coord.
International Association of Animal
  Massage and Bodywork [15558]
c/o Beth Farkas, Coordinator
2950 Douglas Rd.
Toledo, OH 43606
Toll Free: 800-903-9350

Farkas, Bill, CEO
Lambda Chi Alpha [23907]
404 Pell Ave.
Troy, AL 36081

Farley, Frank, Officer
APA Division 48: Society for the
  Study of Peace, Conflict and
  Violence [16891]
c/o Caitlin Mahoney, Secretary
Dept. of Psychology

Metropolitan State University
1450 Energy Park Dr.
Saint Paul, MN 55108
Ph: (651)999-5823

Farley, Jason, President
Association of Nurses in AIDS Care
  [13529]
3538 Ridgewood Rd.
Akron, OH 44333
Ph: (330)670-0101
Toll Free: 800-260-6780
Fax: (330)670-0109

Farley, Shawn, Contact
Mammography Saves Lives [15688]
American College of Radiology
1891 Preston White Dr.
Reston, VA 20191
Toll Free: 800-227-5463
Fax: (703)295-6773

Farley, Judge William, VP
Federal Administrative Law Judges
  Conference [5382]
PO Box 1772
Washington, DC 20013
Ph: (202)523-5750
Fax: (202)566-0042

Farman, Tonia, Founder
Athletes for Cancer [13896]
216 Cascade Ave., No. 227
Hood River, OR 97031

Farmer, Christine, President
Healthcare Convention and Exhibi-
  tors Association [1173]
7918 Jones Branch Dr., Ste. 300
McLean, VA 22102
Ph: (703)935-1961
Fax: (703)506-3266

Farmer, David, VP
Restaurant Marketing and Delivery
  Association [1396]
3636 Menaul Blvd. NE, Ste. 323
Albuquerque, NM 87110

Farmer, Gabby Penn, President, Edi-
  tor
Amputees in Motion International
  [11570]
PO Box 19236
San Diego, CA 92159
Ph: (858)454-9300

Farmer, Martha P., Founder, Exec.
  Dir.
Leadership America [8198]
c/o Selection Committee
25 Highland Park Village, Ste. 100-
  371
Dallas, TX 75205
Ph: (214)421-5566

Farnsworth, Brad, Asst. VP
Center for Internationalization and
  Global Engagement [8193]
American Council on Education
1 Dupont Cir. NW
Washington, DC 20036
Ph: (202)939-9300

Farnum, Evayon, Bd. Member
Beta Pi Sigma Sorority [23690]
256 Waterville St.
San Francisco, CA 94124
Ph: (415)467-0717

Farquhar, Mark, President
Union Youth Football Association
  [22868]
10026-A S Mingo Rd., No. 124
Tulsa, OK 74133
Ph: (918)289-8916

Farrar, Troy, President
United States Adventure Racing Association [23085]

PO Box 514
Wellborn, TX 77881-0514
Ph: (979)703-5018

Farrell, Dennis, Commissioner
Big West Conference [23218]
2 Corporate Pk., Ste. 206
Irvine, CA 92606
Ph: (949)261-2525
Fax: (949)261-2528

Farrell, Edward J, Chairman
United States-New Zealand Council
  [2002]
DACOR Bacon House
1801 F St. NW, 3rd Fl.
Washington, DC 20006
Ph: (202)638-8601

Farrell, LM, CPM, Marinah Valenzu-
  ela, President
Midwives Alliance of North America
  [16294]
PO Box 373
Montvale, NJ 07645
Toll Free: 844-626-2674

Farrell, Robert P., Contact
Regional and Distribution Carriers
  Conference [3100]
c/o Robert Farrell
950 N Glebe Rd., Ste. 210
Arlington, VA 22203-4181

Farrell, Robyn Hussa, MFA,
  Founder, CEO
NORMAL In Schools [14649]
339 E 19th St., Ste. 2B
New York, NY 10003
Ph: (917)771-4977

Farrell, Soke Ray, President
American Kempo-Karate Association
  [22981]
5760 Oak Dr.
Charlotte, NC 28216
Ph: (704)393-1077
Toll Free: 800-320-2552

Farrey, Patrick, Exec. Dir.
Institute of Packaging Professionals
  [6968]
1 Parkview Plz., Ste. 800
Naperville, IL 60563
Ph: (630)544-5050
Fax: (630)544-5055

Farrington, Jennifer, VP
Association of Children's Museums
  [9823]
2711 Jefferson Davis Hwy., Ste. 600
Arlington, VA 22202
Ph: (703)224-3100
Fax: (703)224-3099

Farrington, Thomas A., Founder,
  President
Prostate Health Education Network
  [14052]
500 Victory Rd., Ste. 4
Quincy, MA 02171
Ph: (617)481-4020
Fax: (617)481-4021

Farris, Melinda, CAE, Exec. VP
International Association of Opera-
  tive Millers [2377]
12351 W 96th Ter., Ste. 100
Lenexa, KS 66215
Ph: (913)338-3377
Fax: (913)338-3553

Farro, Anne, VP
Professional Association for Investment Communications Resources
  [2036]
10020 Monroe Rd., Ste. 170
Matthews, NC 28105
Ph: (704)724-5753

Farrukh, Raza, President, CEO
Helping Hand for Relief and
  Development [11668]
12541 McDougall St., Ste. 100
Detroit, MI 48212
Ph: (313)279-5378
Toll Free: 877-521-6291
Fax: (313)366-0200

Farver, Michael, President, Founder
End Childhood Hunger [12083]
c/o Michael Farver, President and
  Founder
1080 W Tropical Way
Plantation, FL 33317-3358
Ph: (954)792-3852
Fax: (954)678-3004

Fasching, Larry, President
Carver-Scott Humane Society
  [10597]
210 N Chesnut St.
Chaska, MN 55318-0215
Ph: (952)368-3553

Fassett, Edward, Chairman
Magis Americas [10726]
1016 16th NW, Ste. 400
Washington, DC 20036
Ph: (212)777-8930

Fatheree, James W., President,
  COO
U.S.-Japan Business Council
  [23646]
1615 H St. NW
Washington, DC 20062
Ph: (202)463-5772

Fatt, Michell Hoo, Secretary
Tire Society [3283]
810 E 10th St.
Lawrence, KS 66044
Ph: (785)865-9403
Toll Free: 800-627-0326
Fax: (785)843-6153

Fattahi, Behrooz, President
Society of Petroleum Engineers
  [6595]
222 Palisades Creek Dr.
Richardson, TX 75080-2040
Ph: (972)952-9393
Toll Free: 800-456-6863
Fax: (972)952-9435

Faubus, Stoney, President
Air Weather Reconnaissance As-
  sociation [21104]
c/o Bernie Barris, Membership
  Chairman
11019 Oaktree Park
San Antonio, TX 78249-4440
Ph: (760)793-4733

Faulk, Emma, President
Pi Omega Pi [23702]
BITE Dept., Bate 2318A
East Carolina University
Greenville, NC 27858
Ph: (252)328-6983

Faulkner, Bonita, Chairman
International Pediatric Hypertension
  Association [15347]
c/o Melinda Andrews, Assistant
Cincinnati Children's Hospital Medi-
  cal Ctr.
3333 Burnet Ave.
MLC 7002
Cincinnati, OH 45229
Ph: (513)636-8265
Fax: (513)636-0162

Faulkner, Kiersten, Exec. Dir.
Historic Hawaii Foundation [9397]
Dole Office Building Twr.
680 Iwilei Rd., Ste. 690

Honolulu, HI 96817
Ph: (808)523-2900
Fax: (808)523-0800

Faulkner, Larry R., MD, CEO,
President
American Board of Psychiatry and
Neurology [16817]
2150 E Lake Cook Rd., Ste. 900
Buffalo Grove, IL 60089
Ph: (847)229-6500
Fax: (847)229-6600

Faulkner, Patricia A., Chairperson
Diabetes Action Research and
Education Foundation [14522]
6701 Democracy Blvd., Ste. 300
Bethesda, MD 20817
Ph: (202)333-4520
Fax: (202)558-5240

Faulkner, Sharon, Exec. Dir.
American Car Rental Association
[2924]
PO Box 584
Long Lake, NY 12847
Toll Free: 888-200-2795

Fausnaught, Wayne D., Exec. Dir.
National Association of Pupil
Services Administrators [7436]
PO Box 113
Williamsport, PA 17701
Ph: (570)323-2050
Fax: (570)323-2051

Fauss, Brad, President, CEO
Network Branded Prepaid Card As-
sociation [1260]
10332 Main St., Ste. 312
Fairfax, VA 22030
Ph: (202)548-7200

Faust, Kate, VP
American Artists Professional
League [8908]
47 5th Ave.
New York, NY 10003
Ph: (212)645-1345

Fay, Calvina L., Exec. Dir.
Save Our Society From Drugs
[11718]
5999 Central Ave., Ste. 301
Saint Petersburg, FL 33710
Ph: (727)828-0211

Fay, Jake, Treasurer, Secretary
Association of State Energy
Research & Technology Transfer
Institutions [6460]
455 Science Dr., Ste. 200
Madison, WI 53711
Ph: (703)395-1076

Fazeli, Mandy, President, Founder
A More Balanced World [11729]
25149 Smokewood Way
Stevenson Ranch, CA 91381
Ph: (805)587-1897

Fazelian, Jaleh, President
Middle East Librarians Association
[9717]
c/o Jaleh Fazelian, President
Grasselli Library and Breen Learning
Center
John Carroll University
1 John Carroll Blvd.
University Heights, OH 44118
Ph: (216)397-1509

Fazio, Lauren, Founder, President
Hold the Door for Others [10774]
PO Box 755
Closter, NJ 07624
Ph: (732)851-3667

Fazio, Sara B., Chairman
Clerkship Directors in Internal
Medicine [15429]

330 John Carlyle St., Ste. 610
Alexandria, VA 22314-5946
Ph: (703)341-4540
Fax: (703)519-1893

Feagan, Marlene, President
Health Ministries Association [20540]
c/o Michelle Randall, Office Manager
PO Box 60042
Dayton, OH 45406
Toll Free: 800-723-4291
Fax: (937)558-0453

Feal, Rosemary G., Exec. Dir.
Modern Language Association of
America [8187]
85 Broad St., Ste. 500
New York, NY 10004-1789
Ph: (646)576-5000
Fax: (646)458-0030

Feather, Alexander White Tail, Exec.
Dir.
National Native American AIDS
Prevention Center [10549]
1031 33rd St.
Denver, CO 80205
Ph: (720)382-2244
Fax: (720)382-2248

Feather, John, PhD, CEO
Grantmakers In Aging [12482]
2001 Jefferson Davis Hwy., Ste. 504
Arlington, VA 22202

Featherston, Lisa, President
Association for Healthcare
Administrative Professionals [67]
328 E Main St.
Louisville, KY 40202
Ph: (502)574-9040
Toll Free: 888-320-0808
Fax: (502)589-3602

Feda, Ghulam, President, Chairman
Afghan Education for a Better
Tomorrow [13022]
PO Box 2054
Discovery Bay, CA 94505
Ph: (916)505-2364

Fedder, Alan, President
UniForum Association [6305]
PO Box 3177
Annapolis, MD 21403-0177
Ph: (410)715-9500
Toll Free: 800-333-8649
Fax: (240)465-0207

Fedderly, Bradley J., Chairman
COLA [15722]
9881 Broken Land Pky., Ste. 200
Columbia, MD 21046-3016
Toll Free: 800-981-9883
Fax: (410)381-8611

Fedeli, Sean, Chairman
Good Shepherd Volunteers [13295]
25-30 21st Ave.
Astoria, NY 11105
Ph: (718)943-7488
    (718)943-7489
Fax: (718)408-2332

Feder, Dr. Theodore H., President
Artists Rights Society [239]
536 Broadway, 5th Fl.
New York, NY 10012
Ph: (212)420-9160
Fax: (212)420-9286

Federici, Dr. Ronald Steven, CEO,
President
Care for Children International
[10884]
Neuropsychological and Family
Therapy Associates
13310 Compton Rd.

Clifton, VA 20124-1512
Ph: (703)830-6052

Federoff, Howard J., MD, President
American Society for Experimental
Neuro Therapeutics [16005]
342 N Main St.
West Hartford, CT 06117
Ph: (860)586-7570
Fax: (860)586-7550

Fedorenko, Eugene, President
Ukrainian Educational Council
[10288]
Cooper Sta.
New York, NY 10276-0391
Ph: (212)477-1200
Fax: (212)777-7201

Fedoroff, Nina V., Chairperson
American Association for the
Advancement of Science [7116]
1200 New York Ave. NW
Washington, DC 20005
Ph: (202)326-6400

Fedorova, Tatiana, CEO
American Business Association of
Russian-speaking Professionals
[2738]
555 Bryant St., Ste. 392
Palo Alto, CA 94301
Ph: (650)278-0431

Fedrizzi, S. Richard, Chairman,
CEO, Founder
U.S. Green Building Council [596]
2101 L St. NW, Ste. 500
Washington, DC 20037-1599
Ph: (202)742-3792
Toll Free: 800-795-1747

Feehan, Brian J., President
Industrial Truck Association [322]
1750 K St. NW, Ste. 460
Washington, DC 20006
Ph: (202)296-9880
Fax: (202)296-9884

Feeler, Greg, Director
BMW Motorcycle Owners of America
[22215]
640 S Main St., Ste. 201
Greenville, SC 29601
Ph: (864)438-0962

Feeley, Derek, CEO, President
Institute for Healthcare Improvement
[15020]
20 University Rd., 7th Fl.
Cambridge, MA 02138
Ph: (617)301-4800
Toll Free: 866-787-0831
Fax: (617)301-4848

Feeney, Diane, Bd. Member
National Committee for Responsive
Philanthropy [12490]
1331 H St. NW, Ste. 200
Washington, DC 20005-4706
Ph: (202)387-9177
Fax: (202)332-5084

Feeney, Don, Bd. Member
National Council on Problem
Gambling [11868]
730 11th St. NW, Ste. 601
Washington, DC 20001
Ph: (202)547-9204
Toll Free: 800-522-4700
Fax: (202)547-9206

Feffer, John, Director
Foreign Policy in Focus [18267]
1112 16th St. NW, Ste. 600
Washington, DC 20036
Ph: (202)787-5271

Fefferman, Mr. Dan, President
International Coalition for Religious
Freedom [19028]

3600 New York Ave. NE, 3rd Fl.
Washington, DC 20002
Ph: (202)558-5462

Feher, Leslie, PhD, Exec. Dir.
Association for Birth Psychology
[16900]
9115 Ridge Blvd.
Brooklyn, NY 11209-5748
Ph: (347)517-4607

Feierstein, Prof. Daniel, President
International Association of
Genocide Scholars [18308]
c/o Borislava Manojlovic, Secretary-
Treasurer
Seton Hall University
400 S Orange Ave.
South Orange, NJ 07079

Feight, Scott, Exec. Dir.
Foundation for Hospital Art [13729]
4238 Highborne Dr.
Marietta, GA 30066
Ph: (678)324-1705

Fein, David, Contact
Czech Collector's Association
[21647]
c/o Davin Fein
810 - 11th St., Ste. 201
Miami Beach, FL 33139-4834

Fein, Helen, Chmn. of the Bd.
Institute for the Study of Genocide
[18410]
c/o Joyce Apsel, President
New York University
726 Broadway, 6th Fl.
New York, NY 10003

Fein, Leonard, Founder
National Jewish Coalition for Literacy
[8251]
134 Beach St., No. 2A
Boston, MA 02111
Ph: (617)423-0063

Feinberg, Melissa, President
Czechoslovak Studies Association
[9474]
c/o Gregory Ference, Secretary-
Treasurer
Department of History
Salisbury University
Salisbury, MD 21801

Feinberg, Scott, Exec. Dir.
Karma Krew [10423]
4300 S US Highway 1, Ste. 203-144
Jupiter, FL 33477

Feinstein, Carla, Mgr., Comm.
Feldenkrais Guild of North America
[9545]
401 Edgewater Pl., Ste. 600
Wakefield, MA 01880

Feinstein, Ms. Roberta E., Exec. Dir.
Congress of Secular Jewish
Organizations [9636]
320 Claymore Blvd.
Cleveland, OH 44143
Ph: (216)481-0850
Toll Free: 866-874-8608

Feinstein, Steven B., MD, Co-Pres.
International Contrast Ultrasound
Society [17539]
East Tower, Ste. 600
1301 K St. NW
Washington, DC 20005
Ph: (202)408-6199

Feinstein, Wayne, Chmn. of the Bd.
Gastric Cancer Foundation [13977]
c/o The V Foundation for Cancer
Research

106 Towerview Ct.
Cary, NC 27513

Feist, Mary Ann, Secretary
Society of Herbarium Curators
[6156]
3380 University Dr. E
College Station, TX 77845
Ph: (979)845-4328
Fax: (979)889-9898

Feist, Shelley, Exec. Dir.
Partnership for Food Safety Education [16234]
2345 Crystal Dr., Ste. 800
Arlington, VA 22202
Ph: (202)220-0651

Feit, Mel, Exec. Dir.
The National Center For Men
[18667]
117 Pauls Path, No. 531
Coram, NY 11727
Ph: (613)476-2115

Fekula, Mick, VP, Exec. Dir.
Association for Business Simulation and Experiential Learning [7544]
c/o Chris Scherpereel, President
WA Franke College of Business
Northern Arizona University
PO Box 15066
Flagstaff, AZ 86011
Ph: (928)523-7831

Fekula, Vladimir P., Mem.
Russian Children's Welfare Society
[11143]
16 W 32nd St., No. 405
New York, NY 10001
Ph: (212)473-6263
Fax: (212)473-6301

Felder, Dr. Cain Hope, Chairman, CEO, Founder
Biblical Institute for Social Change
[20534]
1400 Shepherd Street Ne Ste. 264 & 266
Cain Hope Felder, PhD
Washington, DC 20017
Ph: (202)269-4311
Fax: (202)269-0051

Felder, Tamika L., Founder
Tamika and Friends, Inc. [14072]
PO Box 2942
Upper Marlboro, MD 20773-2942
Toll Free: 866-595-2448

Feldges, Melanie, President
United States Kerry Blue Terrier Club [21982]
c/o Mary McGreevy, Membership Chairman
25 New Castle Dr.
Charles Town, WV 25414
Ph: (681)252-0816

Feldman, Alexander C., President, CEO
U.S. ASEAN Business Council
[3306]
1101 17th St. NW, Ste. 411
Washington, DC 20036-4720
Ph: (202)289-1911

Feldman, Allison, CEO
Acoustic Neuroma Association
[16530]
600 Peachtree Pky., Ste. 108
Cumming, GA 30041-6899
Ph: (770)205-8211
Toll Free: 877-200-8211
Fax: (770)205-0239

Feldman, Jay, Exec. Dir.
Beyond Pesticides [13220]
701 E St. SE, Ste. 200

Washington, DC 20003
Ph: (202)543-5450
Fax: (202)543-4791

Feldman, Joseph L., MD, President
Lymphology Association of North America [15545]
PO Box 16183
Saint Louis, MO 63105
Ph: (773)756-8971

Feldman, Judy Scott, PhD, Chairperson
National Coalition to Save Our Mall
[9416]
PO Box 4709
Rockville, MD 20849
Ph: (301)340-3938

Feldman, Larry, President
Messianic Jewish Alliance of America [20338]
PO Box 274
Springfield, PA 19064
Toll Free: 800-225-6522
Fax: (610)338-0471

Feldman, Larry, President
Volunteers for Israel [18589]
330 W 42nd St., Ste. 1618
New York, NY 10036
Ph: (212)643-4848
Toll Free: 866-514-1948

Feldman, Laurie B., Officer
Women in Cognitive Science [7078]
c/o Laurie B. Feldman, Officer
University at Albany - State University of New York
Department of Psychology
1400 Washington Ave.
Albany, NY 12222
Ph: (518)442-4820
Fax: (518)442-4867

Feldman, Lee, President
International City/County Management Association [5638]
777 N Capitol St. NE, Ste. 500
Washington, DC 20002-4201
Ph: (202)289-4262
Toll Free: 800-745-8780
Fax: (202)962-3500

Feldman, Marc, MD, President
Ophthalmic Anesthesia Society
[16400]
N83 W13410 Leon Rd.
Menomonee Falls, WI 53051
Ph: (414)359-1628
Fax: (414)359-1671

Feldman, Rabbi Marla J., Exec. Dir.
Women of Reform Judaism [20290]
633 3rd Ave.
New York, NY 10017-6778
Ph: (212)650-4050

Feldman, Michael D., FMP, CM, Chairperson
International Facility Management Association [2747]
800 Gessner Rd., Ste. 900
Houston, TX 77024-4257
Ph: (713)623-4362
Fax: (713)623-6124

Feldman, Shaul, Director
Bnei Akiva of the United States and Canada [20238]
520 W 8th Ave., 15th Fl.
New York, NY 10018
Ph: (212)465-9536
Fax: (212)216-9578

Feldner, David, Exec. Dir.
Association of Professional Dog Trainers [3984]

2365 Harrodsburg Rd., A325
Lexington, KY 40504
Toll Free: 800-738-3647
Fax: (864)331-0767

Feldstein, Martin, President
Economics of National Security Association [5753]
c/o John Whitley, Secretary
4850 Mark Center Dr.
Alexandria, VA 22311

Felix, Chris, President
American Amusement Machine Association [1131]
450 E Higgins Rd., Ste. 201
Elk Grove Village, IL 60007
Ph: (847)290-9088

Felix, Jeanette, Founder, VP
Children in Need Haitian Project
[10919]
PO Box 604846
Bayside, NY 11360

Felix, Robert, President
Organization of Teratology Information Specialists [13833]
5034A Thoroughbred Ln.
Brentwood, TN 37027
Ph: (615)649-3082
Toll Free: 866-626-6847
Fax: (615)523-1715

Felker, Beth, Exec. Dir.
SpineHope [16070]
PO Box 684261
Austin, TX 78768
Ph: (512)750-0788

Fellman, Glenn, Exec. Dir.
Indoor Environmental Standards Organization [4142]
12339 Carroll Ave.
Rockville, MD 20852
Ph: (301)230-9636
Toll Free: 800-406-0256
Fax: (301)230-9648

Fellows, Raymond, Founder, Exec. Dir.
Children Across America [10913]
23 Pine St.
Milford, MA 01757
Ph: (508)381-8107

Felton, Cheri, Treasurer
American Hydrangea Society
[22077]
PO Box 53234
Atlanta, GA 30355-1234

Felton, David, Director
LittleLight International [12550]
2061 Deer Park Ave.
Deer Park, NY 11729
Ph: (631)940-9966
Fax: (631)940-9960

Felton, Sandra, Founder
Messies Anonymous [12876]

Felts, Vera, Exec. Dir., Director
American Topical Association
[22306]
100 N Division St., Fl. 2
Carterville, IL 62918
Ph: (618)985-5100
     (817)274-1181
Fax: (618)985-5100

Femister, Arthur, Founder, President
National Association Citizens on Patrol [12828]
PO Box 727
Corona, CA 92878-0727
Ph: (951)279-6893
Fax: (951)279-1915

Fenili, Leo, VP
International Association of Elevator Consultants [1737]
448 W 19th St., No. 484
Houston, TX 77008
Ph: (713)426-1662
Fax: (713)690-0004

Fenly, Leigh, Founder, President
Women's Empowerment International [12568]
PO Box 501406
San Diego, CA 92150-1406
Ph: (619)333-0026

Fennel, Sarah, CEO, Founder
Restore Humanity [12182]
1655 Woolsey Ave.
Fayetteville, AR 72703
Ph: (479)841-2841

Fennell, Janette E., Founder, President
KidsAndCars.org [19079]
7532 Wyoming St.
Kansas City, MO 64114
Ph: (816)216-7085
     (913)732-2792

Fennema, Bud, Secretary, Treasurer
Society for Judgment and Decision Making [7569]
c/o Bud Fennema, Secretary-Treasurer
College of Business
Florida State University
Tallahassee, FL 32306-1110
Ph: (850)644-8231
Fax: (850)644-8234

Fensterheim, Robert, Contact
Acrylonitrile Group [705]
1250 Connecticut Ave. NW, Ste. 700
Washington, DC 20036
Ph: (202)419-1500

Fensterheim, Robert J., Exec. Dir.
Chlorinated Paraffins Industry Association [713]
1250 Connecticut Ave. NW, Ste. 700
Washington, DC 20036
Ph: (202)419-1500

Fenstermacher, Rob, President, CEO
Cultural Vistas [8067]
440 Park Ave. S, 2nd Fl.
New York, NY 10016-8012
Ph: (212)497-3500

Fenton, Eileen G., Exec. Dir.
American Pediatric Society [16600]
3400 Research Forest Dr., Ste. B-7
The Woodlands, TX 77381
Ph: (281)419-0052
Fax: (281)419-0082

Fenton, Tom, VP
Ayrshire Breeders' Association
[3717]
1224 Alton Darby Creek Rd., Ste. B
Columbus, OH 43228
Ph: (614)335-0020
Fax: (614)335-0023

Fenwick, Jack, Contact
Association of University Architects
[5964]
1277 University of Oregon
Eugene, OR 97403-1277
Ph: (541)346-3537
Toll Free: 800-280-6218
Fax: (541)346-3545

Feral, Priscilla, President
Friends of Animals [10624]
777 Post Rd., Ste. 205
Darien, CT 06820
Ph: (203)656-1522
Fax: (203)656-0267

Feral, Priscilla, President,
Chairperson
Primarily Primates, Inc. **[10684]**
26099 Dull Knife Trl.
San Antonio, TX 78255
Ph: (830)755-4616
Fax: (830)755-4618

Ferch, Roger E., President
National Steel Bridge Alliance **[6158]**
1 E Wacker Dr., Ste. 700
Chicago, IL 60601-1802
Ph: (312)670-2400
Fax: (312)670-5403

Ferchaud, Lorena, President
Rhinelander Rabbit Club of America
[4611]
c/o Frank Gale, Vice President
802 N Division
Creston, IA 50801
Ph: (515)782-2998

Ferenc, Sue, DVM, PhD, President
International Society of Regulatory
Toxicology and Pharmacology
[14944]
6546 Belleview Dr.
Columbia, MD 21046-1054
Ph: (410)992-9083
Fax: (410)740-9181

Ferenc, Dr. Susan, President
Council of Producers & Distributors
of Agrotechnology **[716]**
1730 Rhode Island Ave. NW, Ste.
812
Washington, DC 20036
Ph: (202)386-7407
Fax: (202)386-7409

Feresten, Nancy, Director
Children's Book Council **[9125]**
54 W 39th St., 14th Fl.
New York, NY 10018-7480
Ph: (212)966-1990

Fergerson, Julie, Chairman
Identity Theft Resource Center
[5533]
3625 Ruffin Rd., No. 204
San Diego, CA 92123
Toll Free: 888-400-5530

Ferguson, Billy J., President
Clan Fergusson Society of North
America **[20809]**
c/o Billy J. Ferguson, President
192 Hawthorne Hill Rd.
Jasper, GA 30143

Ferguson, Bruce, President, Asst.
Ed.
American Association of Traditional
Chinese Veterinary Medicine
[13590]
PO Box 141324
Gainesville, FL 32614
Ph: (352)672-6400

Ferguson, Charles D., President
Federation of American Scientists
[18976]
1725 DeSales St. NW, 6th Fl.
Washington, DC 20036
Ph: (202)546-3300

Ferguson, Dwayne, VP, Dep. Dir.
Men Against Destruction - Defending
Against Drugs and Social Disorder
[13152]
3026 4th Ave. S
Minneapolis, MN 55408
Ph: (612)822-0802
Fax: (612)253-0663

Ferguson, Fall, MA, President
Association for Size Diversity and
Health **[16249]**

PO Box 3093
Redwood City, CA 94064
Toll Free: 877-576-1102

Ferguson, Jeffrey, President
International Association for Obsid-
ian Studies **[5941]**
Archaeometry Laboratory
University of Missouri Research
Reactor
1513 Research Park Dr.
Columbia, MO 65211
Ph: (573)882-5241
Fax: (573)882-6360

Ferguson, John, President
National Association of Breweriana
Advertising **[21689]**
1585 W Tiffany Woods Dr.
La Porte, IN 46350-7599
Ph: (219)325-8811

Ferguson, Karen, Director
Pension Rights Center **[12451]**
1350 Connecticut Ave. NW, Ste. 206
Washington, DC 20036-1739
Ph: (202)296-3776
Toll Free: 888-420-6550

Ferguson, Paul, President
American Singers Club **[21538]**
c/o Ed Medrano, Secretary &
Treasurer
8908 S Yates Blvd.
Chicago, IL 60617-3863
Ph: (773)717-6506

Ferguson, Rich, Secretary
Divco Club of America **[21649]**
c/o Rich Ferguson, Secretary
309 Beverly Ave.
San Leandro, CA 94577
Ph: (510)568-0887

Ferguson, Roger W., Jr., Chairman
The Conference Board **[6387]**
845 3rd Ave.
New York, NY 10022-6600
Ph: (212)759-0900

Ferguson, Roger W., Jr., CEO,
President
TIAA **[8507]**
730 3rd Ave.
New York, NY 10017-3206
Ph: (212)490-9000
(212)913-2803
Toll Free: 866-842-2442

Ferguson, Stephen, Secretary
Samaritans International **[20460]**
c/o Stephen Ferguson, Secretary
370 E Cedar St.
Mooresville, NC 28115-2806
Ph: (704)663-7951

Ferguson, Vic, Exec. Dir., Founder
World Federation for Coral Reef
Conservation **[3972]**
PO Box 311117
Houston, TX 77231
Ph: (281)309-1201

Ferini-Strambi, Luigi, President
World Association of Sleep Medicine
[17223]
3270 19th St. NW, Ste. 109
Rochester, MN 55901-2950
Ph: (507)316-0084
Toll Free: 877-659-0760

Ferko, Bill, President
Association for Bridge Construction
and Design **[5963]**
c/o Todd Carroll, Secretary
117 Industry Dr.
Pittsburgh, PA 15275
Ph: (412)788-0472
Fax: (412)787-3588

Ferland, David, Exec. Dir.
United States Police Canine Association **[5521]**
c/o Melinda Ruopp, Secretary
1575 Wallace Ave.
Marshalltown, IA 50158
Ph: (651)592-7874
(540)226-4265

Ferlenda, Tony, CEO
National Fragile X Foundation
[14846]
2100 M St. NW, Ste. 170
Washington, DC 20037-1233
Toll Free: 800-688-8765
Fax: (202)747-6208

Fermin, Marci, Dir. of Dev.
Les Clefs d'Or U.S.A. **[1666]**
68 Laurie Ave.
Boston, MA 02132
Ph: (617)469-5397
Fax: (617)469-4397

Fernandes, John J., President, CEO
Association to Advance Collegiate
Schools of Business **[7542]**
777 S Harbour Island Blvd., Ste. 750
Tampa, FL 33602
Ph: (813)769-6500
Fax: (813)769-6559

Fernandez, Bonney, President
North American Danish Warmblood
Association **[4391]**
c/o Jane Hayes, Treasurer
32781 Chadlyn Ct.
Wildomar, CA 92595
Ph: (951)609-3787

Fernandez, Fabio, Exec. Dir.
Society of Arts and Crafts **[9000]**
100 Pier 4 Blvd., Ste. 200
Boston, MA 02210
Ph: (617)266-1810
Fax: (617)266-5654

Fernandez, Mai, Exec. Dir.
National Center for Victims of Crime
[13263]
2000 M St. NW, Ste. 480
Washington, DC 20036
Ph: (202)467-8700
Fax: (202)467-8701

Fernandez-Gonzalez, Alfredo,
President
Society of Building Science Educa-
tors **[7856]**
c/o Alfredo Fernandez-Gonzalez,
President
Paul B. Sogg Architecture Bldg.
4505 Maryland Pky.
Las Vegas, NV 89154-4018

Ferrara, Christopher A., Counsel,
President
American Catholic Lawyers Associa-
tion **[5411]**
420 US Highway Route 46, Ste. 7
Fairfield, NJ 07004
Ph: (973)244-9895
Fax: (973)244-9897

Ferrara, Peter D., Mem.
Supreme Council of the Royal Arca-
num **[19495]**
61 Batterymarch St.
Boston, MA 02110-3208
Toll Free: 888-272-2686

Ferrarello, Debi Page, President
United States Lactation Consultant
Association **[13859]**
4410 Massachusetts Ave. NW, No.
406
Washington, DC 20016
Ph: (202)738-1125

Ferrari, Hal, Chairman
American Microchemical Society
[6184]
c/o Herk Felder, Treasurer
2 June Way
Middlesex, NJ 08846

Ferrari, Philip, President
World Bocce League **[22696]**
14 Tiverton Ct.
Algonquin, IL 60102-6290
Ph: (847)669-9444
Toll Free: 855-652-6223
Fax: (847)669-2613

Ferrarini, Tawni, President
National Association of Economic
Educators **[7732]**
c/o Dr. Kim Sosin, Executive
Secretary
PO Box 27925
Omaha, NE 68127

Ferraro, C. Michael, Chairman
Bite Me Cancer **[13903]**
4094 Majestic Ln., Ste. 335
Fairfax, VA 22033

Ferrell, Brian, Officer
Association of Destination Management Executives International
[3371]
11 W Monument Ave., Ste 510
Dayton, OH 45402
Ph: (937)586-3727

Ferrer, Amy, Exec. Dir.
American Philosophical Association
[10076]
University of Delaware
31 Amstel Ave.
Newark, DE 19716
Ph: (302)831-1112
Fax: (302)831-8690

Ferrer, Leanne, Exec. Dir.
Pacific Islanders in Communications
[9785]
615 Pikoii St., Ste. 1504
Honolulu, HI 96814
Ph: (808)591-0059
Fax: (808)591-1114

Ferrick, Joe, President
American Blind Skiing Foundation
[22772]
609 Crandell Ln.
Schaumburg, IL 60193
Ph: (312)409-1605

Ferriola, Melissa ', Secretary
Society of Permanent Cosmetic
Professionals **[929]**
69 N Broadway St.
Des Plaines, IL 60016
Ph: (847)635-1330
Fax: (847)635-1326

Ferro, Anne, CEO, President
American Association of Motor
Vehicle Administrators **[5054]**
4401 Wilson Blvd., Ste. 700
Arlington, VA 22203
Ph: (703)522-4200

Ferro, Jean, Exec. Dir., President
Women in Photography International
[2598]
569 N Rossmore Ave., No. 604
Los Angeles, CA 90004
Ph: (323)462-1444

Ferry, Michael, President
National Consumer Law Center
[5106]
7 Winthrop Sq.
Boston, MA 02110-1245
Ph: (617)542-8010
Fax: (617)542-8028

Ferry, Ruth, Director, Sr. VP
Au Pair in America [8059]
1 High Ridge Pk.
Stamford, CT 06905
Ph: (203)399-5000
Toll Free: 800-928-7247

Fertel, Marvin S., CEO, President
Nuclear Energy Institute [6505]
1201 F St. NW, Ste. 1100
Washington, DC 20004-1218
Ph: (202)739-8000
Fax: (202)785-4019

Fesler, Douglas, Assoc. Exec.
American Society for Bone and
Mineral Research [16498]
2025 M St. NW, Ste. 800
Washington, DC 20036-3309
Ph: (202)367-1161
Fax: (202)367-2161

Festa, John P., President
Knights of Life Motorcycle Club
[12826]
53 Jefferson Ave.
Pompton Lakes, NJ 07442

Fetchet, Mary, Founder
Voices of September 11th [19188]
161 Cherry St.
New Canaan, CT 06840
Ph: (203)966-3911
Toll Free: 866-505-3911
Fax: (203)966-5701

Fete, Mary, MSN,RN,CCM, Exec.
Dir.
National Foundation for Ectodermal
Dysplasias [14845]
6 Executive Dr., Ste. 2
Fairview Heights, IL 62208-1360
Ph: (618)566-2020

Fetgatter, James A., CEO
Association of Foreign Investors in
Real Estate [2019]
1300 Pennsylvania Ave. NW
Washington, DC 20004
Ph: (202)312-1400

Fetter, Nina, President
Professional Handlers' Association
[21948]
17017 Norbrook Dr.
Olney, MD 20832
Ph: (301)924-0089

Fetteroll, Steven J., Exec. Dir.
The Wire Association International,
Inc. [6852]
71 Bradley Rd., Ste. 9
Madison, CT 06443-2662
Ph: (203)453-2777
Fax: (203)453-8384

Feuer, Ethan, President
United Synagogue Youth [20288]
120 Broadway, Ste. 1540
New York, NY 10271
Ph: (212)533-7800
Fax: (212)353-9439

Fey, Kristine, COMT, Bd. Member
Commission on Accreditation of
Ophthalmic Medical Programs
[8294]
2025 Woodlane Dr.
Saint Paul, MN 55125
Ph: (651)731-0410
Fax: (651)731-2944

Fey, Margo
National Niemann Pick Disease
Foundation [15831]
401 Madison Ave., Ste. B
Fort Atkinson, WI 53538
Ph: (920)563-0930
Toll Free: 877-287-3672
Fax: (920)563-0931

Fiaz, Ali, President
Muslim Students Association of the
United States and Canada [8620]
4400 S Saginaw St., Ste. 1250
Flint, MI 48507
Ph: (810)893-6011

Fichtenbaum, Rudy H., President
American Association of University
Professors [8464]
1133 19th St. NW, Ste. 200
Washington, DC 20036
Ph: (202)737-5900
Fax: (202)737-5526

Fickle, Ramona, Founder
Special Wish Foundation [11273]
1250 Memory Ln. N, Ste. B
Columbus, OH 43209
Ph: (614)258-3186
Toll Free: 800-486-WISH
Fax: (614)258-3518

Ficklin, Jordan, Exec. Dir.
American Watchmakers-
Clockmakers Institute [2041]
701 Enterprise Dr.
Harrison, OH 45030
Ph: (513)367-9800
Toll Free: 866-367-2924
Fax: (513)367-1414

Fidenci, Pierre, Founder, President
Endangered Species International
[3855]
2112 Hayes St.
San Francisco, CA 94117

Fiedelholtz, Liisa Pierce, Chmn. of
the Bd.
Surfrider Foundation [3951]
942 Calle Negocio, Ste. 350
San Clemente, CA 92673
Ph: (949)492-8170
Fax: (949)492-8142

Field, Ann Thornton, Treasurer,
Secretary
International Aviation Womens As-
sociation [362]
c/o Jennifer Miller, Executive Direc-
tor
9 Newport Dr., Ste. 200
Forest Hill, MD 21050
Ph: (443)640-1056
Fax: (443)640-1031

Field, Carmen, Founder
International Bird Beer Label As-
sociation [21263]
PO Box 2551
Homer, AK 99603

Field, Donna L., Contact
American Horse Trials Foundation
[22938]
7913 Colonial Ln.
Clinton, MD 20735-1908
Ph: (301)856-3064
Fax: (301)856-3065

Field, Joe, Director
Comics Professional Retailers
Organization [758]
PO Box 16804
Irvine, CA 92623-6804
Ph: (714)446-8871
Toll Free: 866-457-2582

Field, Richard, Secretary
International Biogeography Society
[6672]
2133 Basswood Ct.
Westlake Village, CA 91361

Fields, Dr. Andy, VP
Professional Climbing Instructors
Association [22728]

PO Box 200
Bangor, ME 04402
Ph: (541)704-7242

Fields, Carmen, Chairman
Museum of African American History
[8785]
14 Beacon St., Ste. 401
Boston, MA 02108
Ph: (617)725-0022
Fax: (617)720-5225

Fields, Cindy, Treasurer
Foreign Press Association [2681]
333 E 46th St., Ste. 1-K
New York, NY 10017
Ph: (212)370-1054
Fax: (212)370-1058

Fields, Debbi, Exec. Dir.
National Hydrocephalus Foundation
[14603]
12413 Centralia Rd.
Lakewood, CA 90715-1653
Ph: (562)924-6666
Toll Free: 888-857-3434

Fields, Gary, Exec. Dir., Founder
Career Gear [8409]
40 Fulton St., Ste. 701
New York, NY 10038
Ph: (212)577-6190

Fields, Taylor, Chairperson
Black Archives of Mid-America
[8820]
1722 E 17th Ter.
Kansas City, MO 64108
Ph: (816)221-1600

Fields-Cruz, Leslie, Exec. Dir. (Actg.)
National Black Programming
Consortium [9144]
68 E 131st St., 7th Fl.
New York, NY 10037
Ph: (212)234-8200

Fieler, Sean, Chairman
National Bible Association [20296]
488 Madison Ave., 24th Fl.
New York, NY 10022
Ph: (212)658-0365
Fax: (212)898-1147

Fiels, Keith Michael, Exec. Dir.
American Library Association [9668]
50 E Huron St.
Chicago, IL 60611-2795
Ph: (312)944-6780
Toll Free: 800-545-2433
Fax: (312)440-9374

Fierstein, Sharon Sabba,
Chairperson
Mom-mentum [12416]
4940 Merrick Rd., No. 300
Massapequa Park, NY 11762
Ph: (516)750-5365
Toll Free: 877-939-MOMS

Fiesta, Richard, Exec. Dir.
Alliance for Retired Americans
[12753]
815 16th St. NW, 4th Fl.
Washington, DC 20006
Ph: (202)637-5399
    (202)637-5275
Toll Free: 800-333-7212

Fifer, Joseph J., FHFMA, CEO,
President
Healthcare Financial Management
Association [15016]
3 Westbrook Corporate Ctr., Ste.
600
Westchester, IL 60154
Ph: (708)531-9600
Toll Free: 800-252-HFMA

Fiffick, Andrew, Chairman
Mobile Air Conditioning Society
[1631]
225 S Broad St.
Lansdale, PA 19446
Ph: (215)631-7020
Fax: (215)631-7017

Figart, Deborah M., President
Association for Evolutionary
Economics [6380]
c/o Eric R. Hake, Secretary-
Treasurer
Catawba College
2300 W Innes St.
Salisbury, NC 28144-2488
Ph: (704)637-4293
Fax: (704)637-4491

Fighetti, Carlos, President
International Phalaenopsis Alliance
[4434]
c/o Lynn Fuller, Membership
Secretary
1401 Pennsylvania Ave., No. 1604
Wilmington, DE 19806
Fax: (302)425-4660

Figman, Elliot, Exec. Dir.
Poets and Writers [10159]
90 Broad St., Ste. 2100
New York, NY 10004
Ph: (212)226-3586
Fax: (212)226-3963

Figueroa, Edgar, CEO, President
Wi-Fi Alliance [6341]
10900-B Stonelake Blvd., Ste. 126
Austin, TX 78759-5748
Ph: (512)498-9434
Fax: (512)498-9435

Fiksdal, Shari, Founder, President
International Post Polio Support
Organization [16792]
2252 Table Rock Rd., SPC 40
Medford, OR 97501-1426
Ph: (541)772-1102
Fax: (541)772-1102

Filian, Mr. Levon, Exec. Dir.
Armenian Missionary Association of
America [19706]
31 W Century Rd.
Paramus, NJ 07652
Ph: (201)265-2607
Fax: (201)265-6015

Filipic, Anne, President
Enroll America [14998]
1001 G St. NW, 8th Fl.
Washington, DC 20001
Ph: (202)737-6340

Filliette, Edith, Founder
Society of Saint Mary Magdalene
[19912]
PO Box 28423
Saint Petersburg, FL 33709

Fillion, Larry, President
United Nations Philatelists Inc.
[22374]
c/o Blanton Clement, Jr., Secretary
PO Box 146
Boyertown, PA 19512-0146

Fillmore, Kari, Exec. Dir.
Angel Covers [10853]
PO Box 6891
Broomfield, CO 80021
Ph: (303)947-5215
    (303)552-6129

Filson, Cindy, President
Cody's Wheels of Hope [10942]
PO Box 8735
Erie, PA 16505
Ph: (814)460-8228

Finan, Chris, Director
American Booksellers Foundation for
Free Expression [18292]
c/o American Book Seller Associa-
tion
333 Westchester Ave., Ste. S202
White Plains, NY 10604
Ph: (914)406-7576
(917)509-0340
Toll Free: 800-727-4203
Fax: (212)587-2436

Finan, Chris, Chmn. of the Bd.
Media Coalition [17910]
19 Fulton St., Ste. 407
New York, NY 10038
Ph: (212)587-4025

Finch, Frank, Corr. Sec., Exec. Dir.
L.C. Smith Collectors Association
[22024]
c/o Frank Finch, Executive Director
1322 Bay Ave.
Mantoloking, NJ 08738

Finch, Jerry, President
Habitat for Horses [10632]
PO Box 213
Hitchcock, TX 77563
Ph: (409)935-0277
Toll Free: 866-434-5737
Fax: (409)515-0657

Finch, LaDonna, Exec. Dir.
Inflammatory Skin Disease Institute
[14583]
PO Box 1074
Newport News, VA 23601
Ph: (757)223-0795
Fax: (757)595-1842

Finch, Liz, VP
Accordionists and Teachers Guild,
International [8355]
10349 Century Ln.
Overland Park, KS 66215
Ph: (913)888-4706

Fincke, Ola, President
Worldwide Dragonfly Association
[6618]
c/o Jessica Ware, Secretary
206 Boyden Hall
Dept. of Biological Sciences
Rutgers University
195 University Ave.
Newark, NJ 07102

Findley, Paul, Founder
Council for the National Interest
[18680]
1350 Beverly Rd., Ste. 115-100
McLean, VA 22101
Ph: (202)863-2951

Fine, Jordan, President
Natural Color Diamond Association
[2060]
22 W 48th St., 4th Fl.
New York, NY 10036
Ph: (212)644-9747
Fax: (212)840-0607

Fine, Robert C, Exec. Dir.
American Nuclear Society [6926]
555 N Kensington Ave.
La Grange Park, IL 60526
Ph: (708)352-6611
Toll Free: 800-323-3044
Fax: (708)352-0499

Finefrock, Kyle, President
Thistle Class Association [22675]
PO Box 741
Loveland, OH 45140
Ph: (513)461-3845

Finegan, Joanne, President
Council on Brain Injury [14911]
16 Industrial Blvd., Ste. 203

Paoli, PA 19301-1609

Fineman, Elliot, President, CEO
National Gun Victims Action Council
[18253]
PO Box 10657
Chicago, IL 60610-0657

Fineran, Diana, Founder
The Traditional Cat Association, Inc.
[21574]
PO Box 178
Heisson, WA 98622

Finger, Amanda, MA, Exec. Dir.
Laboratory to Combat Human Traf-
ficking [18421]
3455 Ringsby Ct., No. 101
Denver, CO 80216
Ph: (303)295-0451

Fink, David J., MD, President
Association of University Professors
of Neurology [16011]
5841 Cedar Lake Rd., Ste. 204
Minneapolis, MN 55416
Ph: (952)545-6724
Fax: (952)545-6073

Finke, Roger, Director
The Association of Religion Data
Archives [20533]
211 Oswald Twr.
Dept. of Sociology
Pennsylvania State University
University Park, PA 16802-6207
Ph: (814)865-6258
Fax: (814)863-7216

Finkel, Deborah, President
Association of Graduate Liberal
Studies Programs [8227]
Duke University
2114 Campus Dr.
Durham, NC 27708-9940
Ph: (919)684-1987
Fax: (919)681-8905

Finkel, Dr. Gerald, Chairman
Joint Industry Board of the Electrical
Industry [873]
158-11 Harry Van Arsdale Jr. Ave.
Flushing, NY 11365
Ph: (718)591-2000
Fax: (718)380-7741

Finkel, James C., Sr., Cmdr.
Catholic War Veterans of the U.S.A.
[21114]
441 N Lee St.
Alexandria, VA 22314
Ph: (703)549-3622
Fax: (703)684-5196

Finkel, Muriel, President
Amyloidosis Support Groups [14560]
232 Orchard Dr.
Wood Dale, IL 60191
Ph: (630)350-7539
Toll Free: 866-404-7539

Finkelstein, Lauren Haas, Exec. Dir.
American Indian Youth Running
Strong, Inc. [12373]
8301 Richmond Hwy., Ste. 200
Alexandria, VA 22309-2324
Ph: (703)317-9881
Toll Free: 888-491-9859
Fax: (703)317-9690

Finley, Cynthia, President
Christian Aid Mission [20398]
1201 5th St.
Charlottesville, VA 22902
Ph: (434)977-5650

Finley, Daryl, Founder
Well Done Organization [11461]
10813 27th St. SE

Lake Stevens, WA 98258-5179

Finley, Katherine, Exec. Dir.
Organization of American Historians
[9503]
112 N Bryan Ave.
Bloomington, IN 47408-4141
Ph: (812)855-7311
Fax: (812)855-0696

Finley, Michael, President, Treasurer
Turner Foundation, Inc. [4107]
133 Luckie St. NW, 2nd Fl.
Atlanta, GA 30303
Ph: (404)681-9900
Fax: (404)681-0172

Finley, Patrick D., President
Operative Plasterers and Cement
Masons International [23401]
11720 Beltsville Dr., Ste. 700
Beltsville, MD 20705
Ph: (301)623-1000
Fax: (301)623-1032

Finley, Saundra, Exec. Dir.
Phi Chi Theta [23697]
1508 E Belt Line Rd., Ste. 104
Carrollton, TX 75006
Ph: (972)245-7202

Finley-Croswhite, Annette, Exec. Dir.
Society for the History of Navy
Medicine [9520]
Old Dominion University
Norfolk, VA 23529-0091

Finn, Brian, V. Ch.
CityKids Foundation [13437]
601 W 26th St., Ste. 325
New York, NY 10001
Ph: (212)925-3320

Finn, Don
Chain Link Fence Manufacturers
Institute [512]
10015 Old Columbia Rd., Ste. B-215
Columbia, MD 21046
Ph: (301)596-2583
Fax: (301)596-2594

Finn, Kelsey H., CEO
National Association of College
Auxiliary Services [3022]
3 Boar's Head Ln., Ste. B
Charlottesville, VA 22903
Ph: (434)245-8425
Fax: (434)245-8453

Finn, Laura Seckbach, Founder
Fly By Night: The Bat Specialists
[4817]
PO Box 562
Osteen, FL 32764-0562
Ph: (407)414-2142

Finnegan, Jerry, President
International Society of Weighing
and Measurement [3465]
13017 Wisteria Dr., No. 341
Germantown, MD 20874
Ph: (240)753-4397
Toll Free: 866-285-3512

Finnegan, Joseph P., Jr., Exec. Dir.
Conference of Educational
Administrators of Schools and
Programs for the Deaf [15183]
PO Box 1778
Saint Augustine, FL 32085-1778
Ph: (904)810-5200
Fax: (904)810-5525

Finnegan, Ms. Linda, Founder
Kids With A Cause [11060]
10736 Jefferson Blvd., No. 401
Culver City, CA 90230
Ph: (310)880-6780

Finnegan, Michael H., President
American Catholic Historical Society
[9453]
263 S 4th St.
Philadelphia, PA 19106
Ph: (717)632-3535

Finnerty, Maureen, Chairperson
Coalition to Protect America's
National Parks [4520]
5625 N Wilmot Rd.
Tucson, AZ 85750-1216
Ph: (520)615-9417
Fax: (520)615-9474

Finney, Mike, Exec. Dir.
Travel Journalists Guild [2726]
4701 S Lakeshore Dr., Ste. 1
Tempe, AZ 85282
Ph: (480)897-3331
Fax: (480)897-3332

Finser, Torin, Gen. Sec.
Anthroposophical Society in America
[19704]
1923 Geddes Ave.
Ann Arbor, MI 48104
Ph: (734)662-9355
(718)644-7913
Fax: (734)662-1727

Finsterbusch, Marty, Treasurer
National Coalition for Literacy [8250]
PO Box 2932
Washington, DC 20013-2932
Fax: (866)738-3757

Finsterbusch, Marty, Exec. Dir.
VALUEUSA [8255]
1 W 2nd St.
Media, PA 19063
Ph: (484)443-8457
Fax: (484)443-8458

Fiorito, Susan S., Treasurer
American Collegiate Retailing As-
sociation [8268]
c/o Robert Jones, Secretary
University of Texas at Tyler
Business Bldg. 122
3900 University Blvd.
Tyler, TX 75799

Fiorletta, Carlo, President
Guild of Italian American Actors
[23495]
PO Box 123
New York, NY 10013-0123
Ph: (201)344-3411

Firman, James, President
National Institute of Senior Housing
[11983]
National Council on Aging
1901 L St. NW, 4th Fl.
Washington, DC 20036
Ph: (202)479-1200
Fax: (202)479-0735

Fischer, Bill, Exec. Dir.
EAA Warbirds of America [21223]
PO Box 3086
Oshkosh, WI 54903-3086
Ph: (920)426-4800

Fischer, Harlan J., President
Art Alliance for Contemporary Glass
[8839]
11700 Preston Rd., Ste. 660, No.
327
Dallas, TX 75230
Ph: (214)890-0029
Fax: (214)890-0029

Fischer, John, President
International Messianic Jewish Alliance [20147]
c/o Paul Wilbur, Executive Director

Jacksonville, FL

Fischer, Megann Anderson, President
National Organization of State Associations for Children **[11095]**
c/o Michigan Federation for Children and Families
320 N Washington Sq., Suite 100
Lansing, MI 48933

Fischetti, Mrs. Marie, Founder
Guardians of Hydrocephalus Research Foundation **[15937]**
2618 Avenue Z
Brooklyn, NY 11235
Ph: (718)743-4473
Fax: (718)743-1171

Fischgrund, Joseph E., Exec. Dir.
Council on Education of the Deaf **[15185]**
Gallaudet University
800 Florida Ave. NE
Washington, DC 20002

Fise, Tom, Exec. Dir., Secretary
American Orthotic and Prosthetic Association **[1596]**
330 John Carlyle St., Ste. 200
Alexandria, VA 22314
Ph: (571)431-0876
Fax: (571)431-0899

Fiser, Randy, CEO
American Society of Interior Designers **[1938]**
1152 15th St. NW, Ste. 910
Washington, DC 20005
Ph: (202)546-3480
Fax: (202)546-3240

Fish, Lt. Dan, President
Polly Klaas Foundation **[12357]**
PO Box 800
Petaluma, CA 94953
Toll Free: 800-587-4357
Fax: (707)769-4019

Fish, Jim, President
National Association of Professional Allstate Agents **[1899]**
22 N Carroll St., Ste. 300
Madison, WI 53703
Toll Free: 877-627-2248
Fax: (866)627-2232

Fishback, Price, Exec. Dir.
Economic History Association **[7982]**
McClelland Hall, 401GG
Dept. of Economics
University of Arizona
Tucson, AZ 85721
Ph: (520)621-4421
Fax: (520)621-8450

Fishbein, Rabbi Irwin H., Director
Rabbinic Center for Research and Counseling **[16989]**
PO Box 897
Westfield, NJ 07091-0897
Ph: (908)233-0419

Fisher, Crit, President
National Board of Surgical Technology and Surgical Assisting **[13497]**
6 W Dry Creek Cir., Ste. 100
Littleton, CO 80120
Toll Free: 800-707-0057
Fax: (303)325-2536

Fisher, David, President
Society for Melanoma Research **[14065]**
c/o Site Solution Worldwide
PO Box 113
Clifton Park, NY 12065
Toll Free: 866-374-6338

Fisher, Diane J., Director
National Association for Business Teacher Education **[7557]**
1914 Association Dr.
Reston, VA 20191-1538
Ph: (703)860-8300
Fax: (703)620-4483

Fisher, Dr. Donald W., CAE, CEO, President
American Medical Group Association **[15135]**
1 Prince St.
Alexandria, VA 22314-3318
Ph: (703)838-0033
Fax: (703)548-1890

Fisher, Donna, Administrator
Unitarian Universalist Musicians' Network **[20496]**
c/o Donna Fisher, Executive Administrator
2208 Henery Tuckers Ct.
Charlotte, NC 28270
Toll Free: 800-969-8866

Fisher, Doug, President
Highlander Class International Association **[22620]**
2280 US 68 S
Xenia, OH 45385
Ph: (937)271-8658

Fisher, Jay M., Director, Founder
Plymouth Barracuda/Cuda Owners Club **[21476]**
c/o Ann M. Curfman, Secretary, 36 Woodland Rd.
36 Woodland Rd.
East Greenwich, RI 02818-3430

Fisher, Joe, III, President
Philadelphia Flyers Fan Club **[24077]**
3601 S Broad St.
Philadelphia, PA 19148

Fisher, John, Dir. of Admin.
Metropolitan Opera Association **[9954]**
Lincoln Center for the Performing Arts
30 Lincoln Center Plz.
New York, NY 10023
Ph: (212)870-7457
(212)362-6000

Fisher, Lee, CEO, President
CEOs for Cities **[19216]**
1717 Euclid Ave., UR 130
Cleveland, OH 44115
Ph: (216)687-4704

Fisher, Lucy, Founder
CuresNow **[15684]**
10100 Santa Monica Blvd., Ste. 1300
Los Angeles, CA 90067

Fisher, Martin, CEO
KickStart International **[12547]**
123 10th St.
San Francisco, CA 94102
Ph: (415)346-4820
Fax: (415)935-5116

Fisher, Nicole Lennon, Secretary
Federal Court Clerks Association **[5117]**
c/o John Hermann, Treasurer
312 N Spring St., Rm. 815
Los Angeles, CA 90012-4701
Ph: (213)894-5451
Fax: (213)894-3105

Fisher, Paul, President
Institute of the Great Plains **[9352]**
601 NW Ferris Ave.

Lawton, OK 73507
Ph: (580)581-3460

Fisher, Rand, President
National Rural Economic Developers Association **[19076]**
1255 SW Prairie Trail Pky.
Ankeny, IA 50023-7068
Ph: (515)284-1421
Fax: (515)334-1167

Fisher, Randy, Exec. Dir.
Hip-Hop Summit Youth Council, Inc. **[9256]**
PO Box 300925
Jamaica, NY 11430
Ph: (212)316-7639
Fax: (805)800-1459

Fisher, Rick, President
Society of Depreciation Professionals **[58]**
6 Boston Rd., Ste. 202
Chelmsford, MA 01824
Ph: (978)364-5195
Fax: (978)250-1117

Fisher, Todd, Exec. Dir.
Napoleonic Historical Society **[10342]**
6000A W Irving Park Rd.
Chicago, IL 60634
Ph: (773)794-1804
Fax: (773)794-1769

Fisher, Vickie, Dir. of Fin. & Admin.
American Railway Engineering and Maintenance-of-Way Association **[2833]**
4501 Forbes Blvd., Ste. 130
Lanham, MD 20706
Ph: (301)459-3200
Fax: (301)459-8077

Fishman, Steven J., President
International Society for the Study of Vascular Anomalies **[15948]**
Arkansas Children's Hospital
1 Children's Way, Slot 836
Little Rock, AR 72202
Ph: (501)364-2656
Fax: (501)364-4790

Fishwick, Paul, Chairman
Association for Computing Machinery - Special Interest Group on Simulation and Modelling **[6241]**
2 Penn Plz., Ste. 701
New York, NY 10121-0701
Ph: (212)626-0605

Fisk, Hayward D., Chairman, Act. Pres.
Atlantic Legal Foundation **[5419]**
2039 Palmer Ave., Ste. 104
Larchmont, NY 10538
Ph: (914)834-3322
Fax: (914)833-1022

Fiske, Dan, Contact
United States Girls Wrestling Association **[23373]**
3000 Newell Dr.
American Canyon, CA 94503

Fissell, William, MD, President
ASAIO **[13732]**
7700 Congress Ave., Ste. 3107
Boca Raton, FL 33487-1356
Ph: (561)999-8969
Fax: (561)999-8972

Fisslinger, Johannes R., Bookcrafter
International Meta-Medicine Association **[13635]**
578 Washington Blvd., No. 716
Marina del Rey, CA 90292
Ph: (310)906-0366

Fitch, Bradford, President, CEO
Congressional Management Foundation **[18013]**
710 East St. SE
Washington, DC 20003
Ph: (202)546-0100
Fax: (202)547-0936

Fitch, Jane C.K., MD, President
Society of Academic Anesthesiology Associations **[13705]**
520 N Northwest Hwy.
Park Ridge, IL 60068
Ph: (847)825-5586

Fite, James F., Librarian
White Lung Association **[17489]**
PO Box 1483
Baltimore, MD 21203-1483
Ph: (410)243-5864

Fithian, Peter, Founder
Hawaiian International Billfish Tournament **[22040]**
PO Box 29638
Honolulu, HI 96820
Ph: (808)836-3422
(808)383-6701
Fax: (808)833-7756

Fitschen, Steven W., President
National Legal Foundation **[5723]**
PO Box 64427
Virginia Beach, VA 23467-4427
Ph: (757)463-6133
Fax: (757)463-6055

Fitterer, Amy, Exec. Dir.
Dance USA **[9254]**
1029 Vermont Ave. NW, Ste. 400
Washington, DC 20005
Ph: (202)833-1717
Fax: (202)833-2686

Fitzgerald, Armaiti, Founder
International Oral Cancer Association **[13992]**
424 Maplelawn Dr.
Plano, TX 75075
Ph: (972)612-7886
Fax: (972)612-7842

Fitzgerald, Brian K., Officer
Business-Higher Education Forum **[7547]**
2025 M St. NW, Ste. 800
Washington, DC 20036
Ph: (202)367-1189

Fitzgerald, Kristen, Founder, President
Brave Kids **[14170]**
c/o United Cerebral Palsy
1825 K St. NW, Ste. 600
Washington, DC 20006
Ph: (202)776-0406
Toll Free: 800-872-5827

Fitzgerald, MaryClare, CEO, President
Women's High Tech Coalition **[7301]**
100 M St. SE, No. 500
Washington, DC 20003
Ph: (202)479-7141

Fitzgerald, Steve, President
National Hydrologic Warning Council **[7370]**
2480 W 26th Ave., Ste. 156-B
Denver, CO 80211-5304
Ph: (303)455-6277
Fax: (303)455-7880

Fitzmier, John R., Exec. Dir.
American Academy of Religion **[7736]**
825 Houston Mill Rd. NE, Ste. 300
Atlanta, GA 30329-4205
Ph: (404)727-3049

Fitzpatrick, Mr. Francis L., Founder
Survivor Connections [12938]
52 Lyndon Rd.
Cranston, RI 02905-1121
Ph: (401)941-2548
Fax: (401)941-2335

Fitzpatrick, Jim, President
National Investment Company
  Service Association [2032]
8400 Westpark Dr., 2nd Fl.
McLean, VA 22102
Ph: (508)485-1500
Fax: (508)485-1560

Fitzpatrick, Dr. John W., Exec. Dir.
Cornell Lab of Ornithology [6957]
159 Sapsucker Woods Rd.
Ithaca, NY 14850
Ph: (607)254-2165
Toll Free: 800-843-2473
Fax: (607)254-2415

Fitzpatrick, Kathleen, Liaison
Modern Language Association of
  America Committee on Scholarly
  Editions [10386]
85 Broad St., Ste. 500
New York, NY 10004-2434
Ph: (646)576-5000
Fax: (646)458-0030

Fiumara, Georganne, Founder
Mothers' Home Business Network
  [1644]
PO Box 423
East Meadow, NY 11554
Ph: (516)997-7394
Fax: (516)997-0839

Flach, Freddie, Director
American Angora Goat Breeder's
  Association [3587]
PO Box 195
Rocksprings, TX 78880
Ph: (830)683-4483
Fax: (830)683-2559

Flack, Brandon, President
National Marine Representatives As-
  sociation [2254]
PO Box 360
Gurnee, IL 60031
Ph: (847)662-3167
Fax: (847)336-7126

Flagg, Michael, Contact
Merchants Payment Coalition [2960]
325 7th St. NW, Ste. 1100
Washington, DC 20004

Flagg, Ronald S., Chairman
National Veterans Legal Services
  Program [21136]
PO Box 65762
Washington, DC 20035
Ph: (202)265-8305

Flaherty, Dennis, President
Council of Vedic Astrology [5991]
PO Box 84312
Seattle, WA 98124-5612

Flaherty, Paul, President
Ovations for the Cure [14040]
79 Main St., Ste. 202
Framingham, MA 01702-2945
Ph: (508)655-5412
Toll Free: 866-920-6382
Fax: (508)655-5414

Flaherty, Paul, President, Director
Ovations for the Cure of Ovarian
  Cancer [14041]
251 W Central St., Ste. 35
Natick, MA 01760
Ph: (508)655-5412
Toll Free: 866-920-6382
Fax: (508)655-5414

Flaherty, Richard M., President
International Corrugated Packaging
  Foundation [12485]
113 SW St., 3rd. Fl
Alexandria, VA 22314
Ph: (703)549-8580
Fax: (703)549-8670

Flanagan, Fr. James, Founder
Society of Our Lady of the Most
  Holy Trinity [19909]
1200 Lantana St.
Corpus Christi, TX 78407
Fax: (361)387-8800

Flanagan, John, Treasurer
UNITE [12430]
c/o Riddle Hospital
1068 W Baltimore Pke.
Media, PA 19063
Ph: (610)296-2411
Toll Free: 888-488-6483

Flanary, Lisa, CEO
Degree of Honor Protective Associa-
  tion [19483]
287 W Lafayette Frontage Rd., Ste.
  200
Saint Paul, MN 55107-3464
Ph: (651)228-7600
Toll Free: 800-947-5812
Fax: (651)224-7446

Flando, Andrew, VP
Precision Metalforming Association
  [2368]
6363 Oak Tree Blvd.
Independence, OH 44131
Ph: (216)901-8800
Fax: (216)901-9190

Flanigan, Rosie, Exec. Dir.
National Criminal Defense College
  [5151]
Mercer Law School
343 Orange St.
Macon, GA 31207
Ph: (478)746-4151

Flannery, Ellen J., VP
American Bar Foundation [5410]
750 N Lake Shore Dr.
Chicago, IL 60611-4403
Ph: (312)988-6500
Fax: (312)988-6579

Flannery, Ellen M., Founder, Exec.
  Dir.
CancerFree KIDS [13934]
PO Box 575
Loveland, OH 45140
Ph: (513)575-5437

Flannery, Kevin, President
American Catholic Philosophical As-
  sociation [8417]
Ctr. for Thomistic Studies
University of St. Thomas
3800 Montrose Blvd.
Houston, TX 77006-4626
Ph: (713)942-3483
Toll Free: 800-444-2419
Fax: (713)525-6964

Flatley, Carl J., Chairman, Founder
Sepsis Alliance [15415]
1855 First Ave., Ste. 102
San Diego, CA 92101
Ph: (619)232-0300
    (813)874-2552

Flatt, Gregory, Director
Ecova Mali [3561]
69 Cherry St.
Swampscott, MA 01907
Ph: (978)818-0751

Fleagle, Jerry, Exec. Dir.
Hoover Presidential Foundation
  [10332]

302 Parkside Dr.
West Branch, IA 52358
Ph: (319)643-5327
Fax: (319)643-2391

Fleischmann, Samuel, VP
International Association for College
  Admission Counseling [7448]
PO Box 41348
Arlington, VA 22204
Ph: (678)827-1622

Fleisher, Lee A., MD, Contact
Association of University
  Anesthesiologists [13698]
44 Montgomery St., Ste. 1605
San Francisco, CA 94104-4703
Ph: (415)296-6950
Fax: (415)296-6901

Fleisher, Dr. Thomas A., President
American Academy of Allergy
  Asthma & Immunology [13568]
555 E Wells St., Ste. 1100
Milwaukee, WI 53202-3823
Ph: (414)272-6071

Fleiss, Mr. Peter H., Exec. Dir.
Corporate Angel Network [13951]
Westchester County Airport
1 Loop Rd.
White Plains, NY 10604-1215
Ph: (914)328-1313
Fax: (914)328-3938

Fleming, Dr. A.V., Exec. Dir.
Ford Minority Dealers Association
  [342]
c/o Dee Suber, Executive Assistant
PO Box 760386
Southfield, MI 48076
Ph: (248)557-2500
Toll Free: 800-247-0293

Fleming, Mick, President
Alliance for Regional Stewardship
  [18625]
c/o American Chamber of Commerce Executives
1330 Braddock Pl., Ste. 300
Alexandria, VA 22314-6400
Ph: (703)998-0072
Fax: (888)577-9883

Fleming, Mick, President
Association of Chamber of Com-
  merce Executives [23561]
1330 Braddock Pl., Ste. 300
Alexandria, VA 22314
Ph: (703)998-0072
Toll Free: 888-577-9883

Fleming, Robert E., MD, President
International BioIron Society [14585]
Two Woodfield Lake
1100 E Woodfield Rd., Ste. 350
Schaumburg, IL 60173-5121
Ph: (847)517-7225
Fax: (847)517-7229

Fleming, Robert, CEO-
eMarketing Association [999]
40 Blue Ridge Dr.
Charlestown, RI 02813
Toll Free: 800-496-2950
Fax: (408)884-2461

Fleming, Steve, CPMR, Chairman
Association of Independent
  Manufacturers'/Representatives,
  Inc. [2203]
800 Roosevelt Rd., Suite C-312
Glen Ellyn, IL 60137
Ph: (630)942-6581
Fax: (630)790-3095

Fleming, Susan, President
National Search Dog Alliance
  [12747]

1302 Waugh Dr., Ste. 121
Houston, TX 77019
Ph: (360)808-0894

Fleming, Tarah, Director
Interracial-InterCultural Pride [11823]
1581 LeRoy Ave.
Berkeley, CA 94708
Ph: (510)644-1000
Fax: (510)525-4106

Fleming, Terry, Director
Risk and Insurance Management
  Society [1923]
5 Bryant Park, 13th Fl.
New York, NY 10018
Ph: (212)286-9292

Flescher, Dr. Sharon, Exec. Dir.
International Foundation for Art
  Research [8866]
500 5th Ave., Ste. 935
New York, NY 10110
Ph: (212)391-6234
Fax: (212)391-8794

Fletcher, Angela, CFO
4 Real Women International [13366]
299 Broadway, Ste. 1508
New York, NY 10007-2061
Toll Free: 866-494-4794

Fletcher, Greg, Contact
Jensen Healey Preservation Society
  [21410]
4 Estrade Ln.
Foothill Ranch, CA 92610

Fletcher, Marian, Exec. Dir.
USA Jump Rope [23107]
2431 Crosstimbers Dr.
Huntsville, TX 77320
Ph: (936)295-3332
Fax: (936)295-3309

Fletcher, Mary, Administrator
Order of the Daughters of the King
  [20113]
101 Weatherstone Dr., Ste. 870
Woodstock, GA 30188
Ph: (770)517-8552
Fax: (770)517-8066

Fletcher, Dr. Robert J., CEO
National Association for the Dually
  Diagnosed [14555]
132 Fair St.
Kingston, NY 12401
Ph: (845)331-4336
Toll Free: 800-331-5362
Fax: (845)331-4569

Fletty, Eric, Exec. Dir.
Association of Suppliers to the
  Paper Industry [1715]
15 Technology Pky. S
Peachtree Corners, GA 30092
Ph: (770)209-7521
Fax: (770)209-7581

Flickinger, Jim, President
International Brotherhood of DuPont
  Workers [23404]
PO Box 10
Waynesboro, VA 22980
Fax: (540)337-5442

Flier, Prof. Michael S., Chairman
American Committee of Slavists
  [10214]
Dept. of Slavic Languages and
  Literatures, Barker Ctr., 3rd Fl.
Harvard University
12 Quincy St.
Cambridge, MA 02138
Ph: (617)495-4065
Fax: (617)496-4466

Flimlin, Gef, President
United States Aquaculture Society
  [3648]

c/o David Cline, President-Elect
203 Swingle Hall
Auburn University, AL 36849
Ph: (334)844-2874
Fax: (334)844-0830

Flinn, Kathleen, Chairperson
The Culinary Trust [7692]
PO Box 5485
Portland, OR 97228-5485

Flint, Anthony, Dir. Pub. Aff.
Lincoln Institute of Land Policy
[5402]
113 Brattle St.
Cambridge, MA 02138-3407
Ph: (617)661-3016
Toll Free: 800-526-3873
Fax: (617)661-7235

Flint, Christopher, President
AACTION Autism [13735]
1861 Manor Ln.
Park Ridge, IL 60068
Ph: (773)456-3655

Flint, Douglas J., Chairman
Institute of International Finance
[402]
1333 H St. NW, Ste. 800E
Washington, DC 20005-4770
Ph: (202)857-3600
Fax: (202)775-1430

Flint, Terri, President
Elevator U [522]
4751 N Olcott Ave.
Harwood Heights, IL 60706

Flionis, Nikki, Exec. Dir.
MissionSAFE [13459]
PO Box 290799
Charlestown, MA 02129

Floersch, Ms. Natasha, Officer
National Center for American Indian
and Alaska Native Mental Health
Research [15792]
c/o Colorado School of Public Health
13001 E 17th Pl.
Aurora, CO 80045
Ph: (303)724-4585

Flood, Kathleen, CEO
American Society of Nuclear Cardiol-
ogy [14094]
4340 East-West Hwy., Ste. 1120
Bethesda, MD 20814-4578
Ph: (301)215-7575
Fax: (301)215-7113

Flood, Thomas W., Contact
Surgical Volunteers International
[17412]
65712 E Mesa Ridge Ct.
Tucson, AZ 85739
Ph: (832)434-1593
Fax: (832)415-2814

Flora, Debi, President, Owner
About Books [2759]
1001 Taurus Dr.
Colorado Springs, CO 80906
Ph: (719)632-8226
Fax: (719)213-2602

Flora, Gloria, Director
Sustainable Obtainable Solutions
[4583]
PO Box 1424
Helena, MT 59624
Ph: (406)495-0738
Fax: (406)495-9703

Flora, John, Founder, President
Create A Smile Dental Foundation
[14426]
607 W Idaho Ave.

Carterville, IL 62918
Ph: (618)925-2140

Flora, Scott, Consultant
Association of Publishers for Special
Sales [2772]
PO Box 9725
Colorado Springs, CO 80932-0725
Ph: (719)924-5534
Fax: (719)213-2602

Florek, Ms. Donna, Specialist
IEEE - Power Electronics Society
[6431]
445 Hoes Ln.
Piscataway, NJ 08855-1331

Flores, Dr. Antonio R., President,
CEO
Hispanic Association of Colleges and
Universities [7633]
8415 Datapoint Dr., Ste. 400
San Antonio, TX 78229
Ph: (210)692-3805
Fax: (210)692-0823

Flores, Brendan, Chairman
National Federation of Filipino
American Associations [10073]
1322 18th St. NW
Washington, DC 20036-1803
Ph: (347)669-8764

Flores, Ernie, President
Association of Farmworker Op-
portunity Programs [12335]
1120 20th St. NW, Ste 300 S
Washington, DC 20036
Ph: (202)828-6006

Flores, Leonardo, Treasurer
Electronic Literature Organization
[2783]
Massachusetts Institute of Technol-
ogy
77 Massachusetts Ave., 14N-234
Cambridge, MA 02139-4307
Ph: (617)324-4845

Flores, Paula, President
Institute of Transportation Engineers
[7348]
1627 Eye St. NW, Ste. 600
Washington, DC 20006
Ph: (202)785-0060
Fax: (202)785-0609

Flores, Syl, President
A Future Without Poverty, Inc.
[12542]
PO Box 73
Ripley, OH 45167-9715

Flores-Quilty, Alexandra, President
United States Student Association
[8631]
1211 Connecticut Ave. NW, Ste. 406
Washington, DC 20036
Ph: (202)640-6570
Fax: (202)223-4005

Flory, Chip, Editor
Professional Farmers of America
[4168]
6612 Chancellor Dr., Ste. 300
Cedar Falls, IA 50613
Toll Free: 800-772-0023

Flosi, Sherri, President
National American Pit Bull Terrier
Association [21918]
c/o Sherri Flosi, President
PO Box 296
La Grange, CA 95329
Ph: (209)404-3077

Flounders, Sara, Contact
Workers World Party [19146]
147 W 24th St., 2nd Fl.

New York, NY 10011
Ph: (212)627-2994
Fax: (212)675-7869

Flowers, Brian, Gen. Mgr.
Chess Collectors International
[21589]
PO Box 166
Commack, NY 11725
Ph: (631)543-1330
Fax: (516)543-7901

Flowers, Jon, President
National Association of Left-Handed
Golfers [22887]
c/o jim Bradley, Treasurer
PO Box 640
Leland, NC 28451
Ph: (910)383-0339

Flowers, Linda, Contact
Clan Leslie Society International
[20817]
302 SW 3rd St.
Tuttle, OK 73089-8927
Ph: (405)381-3577

Flowers, Simon Talma, Secretary
Ecumenical and Interreligious Lead-
ers Network [20060]
Bldg. D, Ste. 3
2921 E 17th St.
Austin, TX 78702
Ph: (512)386-9145
Fax: (512)385-1430

Floyd, Craig W., President, CEO
National Law Enforcement Officers
Memorial Fund [5502]
901 E St. NW, Ste. 100
Washington, DC 20004-2025
Ph: (202)737-3400
Fax: (202)737-3405

Floyd, Devin, Director
Educate Tomorrow [8767]
1717 N Bayshore Dr., No. 203
Miami, FL 33132
Ph: (305)374-3751

Flynn, Bob, CEO, President
Christian Military Fellowship [19962]
PO Box 1207
Englewood, CO 80150-1207
Ph: (303)761-1959
Toll Free: 800-798-7875
Fax: (303)761-4577

Flynn, Chris, Treasurer
Autism Research Institute [13752]
4182 Adams Ave.
San Diego, CA 92116
Ph: (619)281-7165
Toll Free: 866-366-3361
Fax: (619)563-6840

Flynn, Deirdre, Exec. VP
North American Association of Food
Equipment Manufacturers [1385]
161 N Clark St., Ste. 2020
Chicago, IL 60601
Ph: (312)821-0201
Fax: (312)821-0202

Flynn, Jennifer, President
Association for Continuing Legal
Education [8211]
1000 Westgate Dr., Ste. 252
Saint Paul, MN 55114
Ph: (651)366-6082
Fax: (651)290-2266

Flynn, Kathryn A., Exec. Dir.
National New Deal Preservation As-
sociation [10068]
PO Box 602
Santa Fe, NM 87504-0602
Ph: (505)473-3985

Flynn, Kevin, Chmn. of the Bd.
Council for Affordable and Rural
Housing [11967]
1112 King St.
Alexandria, VA 22314
Ph: (703)837-9001
Fax: (703)837-8467

Flynn, Dr. Marilyn, President
The Network for Social Work
Management [13114]
Special Service for Groups
905 E 8th St.
Los Angeles, CA 90021
Ph: (213)553-1870
Fax: (213)553-1822

Flynn, Mark, Contact
Uniformed Services Academy of
Family Physicians [15843]
1503 Santa Rosa Rd., Ste. 207
Richmond, VA 23229
Ph: (804)968-4436
Fax: (804)968-4418

Flynn, Steve, President, CEO
Graves Disease and Thyroid
Foundation [17481]
PO Box 2793
Rancho Santa Fe, CA 92067
Toll Free: 877-643-3123
Fax: (877)643-3123

Fobes, Natalie, President
Blue Earth Alliance [10137]
4557 51st Pl SW
Seattle, WA 98116
Ph: (206)569-8754

Fodor, Peter, MD, Liaison
American Society of Plastic Surgery
Administrators [14313]
6324 Fairview Ave. N
Crystal, MN 55428
Ph: (717)249-2424
Fax: (717)249-4534

Fogarty, W. Tom, President,
Treasurer
Concentra Occupational Health
Research Institute [16322]
5080 Spectrum Dr., Ste. 1200
Addison, TX 75001

Fogel, Maggie, Administrator
Association of Medical Laboratory
Immunologists [15375]
40 Prospect St.
Portsmouth, NH 03801
Ph: (603)610-7766
Fax: (603)610-7288

Fogelberg, Paul A., Director
Pulmonary Fibrosis Advocates
[17146]
c/o Paul A. Fogelberg, Director
700 Twelve Oaks Center Dr., Ste.
716
Wayzata, MN 55391-4450
Ph: (952)933-9990
Toll Free: 800-229-2531

Fogerty, Sally, MEd, Director
Children's Safety Network [10935]
Education Development Center, Inc.
43 Foundry Ave.
Waltham, MA 02453-8313
Ph: (617)618-2918

Foggs, Michael B., MD, President
American College of Allergy, Asthma
and Immunology [13572]
85 W Algonquin Rd., Ste. 550
Arlington Heights, IL 60005-4460
Ph: (847)427-1200
Fax: (847)427-1294

Fogleman, Guy C., Exec. Dir.
Federation of American Societies for
Experimental Biology [6081]

9650 Rockville Pke.
Bethesda, MD 20814
Ph: (301)634-7000
Fax: (301)634-7001

Folen, Raymond A., PhD, Chairman,
President
National Register of Health Service
Psychologists [16929]
1200 New York Ave. NW, Ste. 800
Washington, DC 20005
Ph: (202)783-7663
Fax: (202)347-0550

Foley, Laura, President
Theta Phi Alpha [23966]
27025 Knickerbocker Rd.
Bay Village, OH 44140-2300
Ph: (440)899-9282

Foley, Mark, President, Secretary
Jhamtse International [13011]
25 Duggan Rd.
Acton, MA 01720
Ph: (978)502-6452

Foley, Mary E., Exec. Dir.
Medicaid-CHIP State Dental As-
sociation [14455]
4411 Connecticut Ave. NW, No. 104
Washington, DC 20008
Ph: (202)248-3993
Fax: (202)248-2315

Foley, Mike, VP
Saleen Club of America [21488]
PO Box 274
Odenville, AL 35120
Ph: (714)400-2121

Foley, Mike, President
United States Practical Shooting As-
sociation [23144]
827 N Hill Blvd.
Burlington, WA 98233
Ph: (360)855-2245
Fax: (360)855-0380

Foley, Terry, President
National Association of Professional
Canine Handlers [5493]
24800 Hayes St.
Taylor, MI 48180
Ph: (313)291-2902
Fax: (313)291-2783

Followell, Ken, President
MaleSurvivor: The National
Organization Against Male Sexual
Victimization [12926]
4768 Broadway, No. 527
New York, NY 10034

Fong, Danny, MD, VP
Chinese American Medical Society
[15721]
265 Canal St., Ste. 515
New York, NY 10013
Ph: (212)334-4760
Fax: (646)304-6373

Fong, Gisele, PhD, Exec. Dir.
EndOil [6477]
c/o Gisele Fong, Executive Director
4000 Long Beach Blvd., Ste. 249
Long Beach, CA 90807

Fong, Serena, VP
Catalyst, Inc. [10303]
120 Wall St., 15th Fl.
New York, NY 10005-3904
Ph: (212)514-7600
Fax: (212)514-8470

Fong, Wenda, Founder
Coalition of Asian Pacifics in
Entertainment [1134]
Los Angeles, CA

Fonkalsrud, Lisa, President
Society of Gastroenterology Nurses
and Associates [14798]
330 N Wabash Ave., Ste. 2000
Chicago, IL 60611-7621
Ph: (312)321-5165
Toll Free: 800-245-7462
Fax: (312)673-6694

Fontaine, Paul, President
Harness Tracks of America [22917]
AZ
Ph: (520)529-2525
Fax: (520)529-3235

Fontaine, Pierre, President
Randolph for Haiti [12714]
41 S Main St.
Randolph, MA 02368
Ph: (781)961-9779
     (781)308-0458

Fontana, Chris, CEO
Global Visionaries [12974]
2524 16th Ave. S, Rm. 206 and 305
Seattle, WA 98144
Ph: (206)322-9448
Fax: (206)322-9719

Fontana, Giuseppe, President
Association for Social Economics
[6383]
c/o Sanjukta Chaudhuri, Secretary
University of Wisconsin
Department of Economics
463 Schneider Hall
Eau Claire, WI 54701
Ph: (715)836-6046

Fontes, Brian, CEO
National Emergency Number As-
sociation [14668]
1700 Diagonal Rd., Ste. 500
Alexandria, VA 22314-2846
Ph: (202)466-4911
Fax: (202)618-6370

Foor, Carrie, Exec. Dir.
American Association of Railroad
Superintendents [2831]
PO Box 200
Lafox, IL 60147-0200

Foor, Carrie, Exec. Dir.
North American Rail Shippers As-
sociation [3349]
40W815 S Bridle Creek Dr.
Saint Charles, IL 60175
Ph: (630)386-1366

Foote, Melvin P., President
Constituency for Africa [17775]
1350 Connecticut Ave., NW, Ste.
850
Washington, DC 20036
Ph: (202)255-8893
Fax: (202)371-9017

Foote, Neil, President
National Black Public Relations
Society [2754]
14636 Runnymede St.
Van Nuys, CA 91405
Toll Free: 888-976-0005

Foote, Dr. Sally, President
American Veterinary Society of
Animal Behavior [17631]
c/o Kari Krause, Treasurer
45298 Indian Creek Dr.
Canton, MI 48187
Ph: (734)454-7470

Foote, Virginia B., President
New Forests Project [12173]
PO Box 41720
Arlington, VA 22204
Ph: (202)285-4328

Foote, Virginia B., President
U.S.-Vietnam Trade Council [17816]
737 8th St. SE, Ste. 202
Washington, DC 20003
Ph: (202)464-9380
Fax: (202)544-4065

Foote, Virginia B., President
U.S.-Vietnam WTO Coalition [18536]
1101 17th St. NW, Ste. 411
Washington, DC 20036
Ph: (202)289-1912
Fax: (202)289-0519

Foote, William F., CEO, Founder
Root Capital [1264]
130 Bishop Allen Dr., 2nd Fl.
Cambridge, MA 02139
Ph: (617)661-5792

Forbes, Kathryn A., Chmn. of the
Bd.
American Lung Association in the
District of Columbia [17134]
1301 Pennsylvania Ave. NW
Washington, DC 20004
Ph: (202)785-3355
     (202)747-5541
Toll Free: 800-548-8252
Fax: (202)452-1805

Forbus, Brian, President
Coastal Carolina University Alumni
Association [19315]
PO Box 261954
Conway, SC 29528
Ph: (843)349-2846
     (843)349-2586

Forbus, Tonia, Exec. Dir.
Professional and Technical
Consultants Association [822]
PO Box 2261
Santa Clara, CA 95055
Ph: (408)971-5902
Toll Free: 800-747-2822

Ford, Dr. Anabel, President
Exploring Solutions Past: The Maya
Forest Alliance [5938]
PO Box 3962
Santa Barbara, CA 93130
Ph: (805)893-8191

Ford, Carol, Bd. Member
Society for Adolescent Health and
Medicine [14215]
1 Parkview Pl., Ste. 800
Deerfield, IL 60015-4943
Ph: (847)753-5226
Fax: (847)480-9282

Ford, Cindy, President
Welsh Springer Spaniel Club of
America [21989]
c/o Carla Vooris, Secretary
284 Welshie Way Ln.
Henderson, NC 27537

Ford, Duane B., President
North American Boxing Federation
[22715]
c/o Duane B. Ford, President
5255 S Decatur Blvd., Ste. 110
Las Vegas, NV 89118
Ph: (702)382-8360

Ford, Duane B., President
North American Boxing Federation
[22716]
911 Kimbark St.
Longmont, CO 80501
Ph: (303)442-0258
Fax: (303)442-0380

Ford, John E., Exec. Dir.
National Junior Santa Gertrudis Association [3743]

PO Box 1257
Kingsville, TX 78364
Ph: (361)592-9357
Fax: (361)592-8572

Ford, John E., Exec. Dir.
Santa Gertrudis Breeders
International [3755]
PO Box 1257
Kingsville, TX 78364
Ph: (361)592-9357
Fax: (361)592-8572

Ford, Mr. Lawrence, Dir. of Comm.
Institute for Creation Research
[20585]
1806 Royal Ln.
Dallas, TX 75229
Toll Free: 800-337-0375

Ford, Mark L., President, Exec. Dir.
Professional Football Researchers
Association [22866]
257 Joslyn Rd.
Guilford, NY 13780-3138

Ford, Nelson M., Chairman
Center for Strategic and Budgetary
Assessments [18694]
1667 K St. NW, Ste. 900
Washington, DC 20006
Ph: (202)331-7990
Fax: (202)331-8019

Ford, Tim, CEO
Association of Defense Communities
[5296]
2020 K St. NW, Ste. 650
Washington, DC 20006
Ph: (202)822-5256
Fax: (202)289-8326

Forde, J. Winston, Exec. Dir.
International Society of Explosives
Engineers [6564]
30325 Bainbridge Rd.
Cleveland, OH 44139
Ph: (440)349-4400
Fax: (440)349-3788

Ford-Gilboe, Marilyn, PhD, President
Nursing Network on Violence
Against Women International
[11712]
2401 E Orangeburg Ave., Ste. 675
Modesto, CA 95355-3379
Toll Free: 800-933-6679

Ford-Wagner, Amy, V. Chmn. of the
Bd.
Alliance for Biking and Walking
[19194]
PO Box 65150
Washington, DC 20035
Ph: (202)449-9692
     (202)621-5442

Forest, Don, President
National Center for Advanced
Technologies [7285]
1000 Wilson Blvd., Ste. 1700
Arlington, VA 22209-3901
Ph: (703)358-1000
Fax: (703)358-1012

Foreste, Suze, President, Chmn. of
the Bd.
Organizing for Haiti [12055]
879 E 93rd St.
Brooklyn, NY 11236
Ph: (718)496-5103

Forestieri, Christina, Exec. Dir.,
President, Treasurer
The Fight Against Hunger Organiza-
tion [12089]
PO Box 2250
Monroe, NY 10949
Ph: (845)232-1420

Forgey, William W., Director
International Association for Medical
Assistance to Travellers [13238]
1623 Military Rd., No. 279
Niagara Falls, NY 14304-1745
Ph: (716)754-4883

Forman, Mr. John, VP of Res.
International Society for Mannosidosis and Related Diseases [14832]
c/o The International Advocate for
Glycoprotein Storage Diseases
20880 Canyon View Dr.
Saratoga, CA 95070

Formenti, Inge, Librarian
American Printing House for the
Blind, Inc. [17686]
1839 Frankfort Ave.
Louisville, KY 40206-3148
Ph: (502)895-2405
Toll Free: 800-223-1839
Fax: (502)899-2284

Formidoni, Kathleen Bagley, Dir. of
Public Rel.
Email Sender and Provider Coalition
[6444]
PO Box 478
Kennebunk, ME 04043
Ph: (207)351-5770

Fornelli, Cynthia M., Exec. Dir.
Center for Audit Quality [19]
1155 F St. NW, Ste. 450
Washington, DC 20004
Ph: (202)609-8120

Forney, Mrs. Georgette, President
Anglicans for Life [12763]
405 Frederick Ave.
Sewickley, PA 15143
Toll Free: 800-707-6635

Forney, James, Treasurer
The Gardeners of America [22095]
PO Box 241
Johnston, IA 50131-6245
Ph: (515)278-0295
Fax: (515)278-6245

Fornito, Jill, Dir. of Operations
Global Interdependence Center
[19261]
Federal Reserve Bank of
Philadelphia
100 N 6th St., 5th Fl. SE
Philadelphia, PA 19106
Ph: (215)238-0990
Fax: (215)238-0966

Forrest, Wayne, President, Secretary
American Indonesian Chamber of
Commerce [23552]
521 5th Ave., Ste. 1700
New York, NY 10175
Ph: (212)687-4505
Fax: (212)867-5844

Forrester, Ben, Membership Chp.
Clan Forrester Society [20810]
c/o Ben Forrester, Membership
Director
1034 Blue Heron Dr.
Commerce, GA 30529-4210

Forrester, Don, Chairman
CORE: Coalition for Residential
Education [8536]
1001 G St. NW, Ste. 800
Washington, DC 20001
Ph: (202)627-6832
Fax: (240)510-9456

Forsberg, Philip, Dir. of Programs
North American Lake Management
Society [6781]
PO Box 5443

Madison, WI 53705-0443
Ph: (608)233-2836
Fax: (608)233-3186

Forschler-Tarrasch, Anne, President
American Ceramic Circle [21576]
PO Box 224
Williamsburg, VA 23187

Forsman, Rodney W., Treasurer
Clinical Laboratory Management As-
sociation [15517]
330 N Wabash Ave., Ste. 2000
Chicago, IL 60611
Ph: (312)321-5111

Forstchen, Ann, President
Organization of Wildlife Planners
[4862]
c/o Michele Beucler
600 S Walnut St.
Boise, ID 83707
Ph: (208)287-2856

Forster-Smith, Rev. Lucy, Contact
Association of College and
University Religious Affairs [8605]
Macalester College
Center for Religious and Spiritual
Life
1600 Grand Ave.
Saint Paul, MN 55105
Ph: (651)696-6293
Fax: (651)696-6580

Forsyth, Ms. Nicole, CEO, President
RedRover [10686]
3800 J St., Ste. 100
Sacramento, CA 95816
Ph: (916)429-2457
Fax: (916)378-5098

Fortenberry, James, Chairman
Extracorporeal Life Support
Organization [14351]
Bldg. 300, Rm. 303
2800 Plymouth Rd.
Ann Arbor, MI 48109-2800
Ph: (734)998-6600
Fax: (734)998-6602

Fortenberry, Norman, Exec. Dir.
American Society for Engineering
Education [7857]
1818 N St. NW, Ste. 600
Washington, DC 20036-2479
Ph: (202)331-3500
(202)331-3511

Fortenberry, Norman L., ScD, Exec.
Dir.
Commission on Professionals in Sci-
ence and Technology [7128]
1200 New York Ave. NW, Ste. 113
Washington, DC 20005

Fortenberry, Norman, Exec. Dir.
Tau Alpha Pi [23744]
c/o ASEE
1818 North St. NW, Ste. 600
Washington, DC 20036
Ph: (202)350-5764
Fax: (202)265-8504

Fortier, Kenneth J., Secretary
International Maintenance Institute
[2132]
c/o Joyce Rhoden, Executive
Secretary
PO Box 751896
Houston, TX 77275
Ph: (281)481-0869
Toll Free: 888-207-1773
Fax: (281)481-8337

Fortin, Gerry, President
Liberty Seated Collectors Club
[22272]

c/o Dennis Fortier
PO Box 1841
Pawtucket, RI 02862

Fortino, Paul, Chmn. of the Bd.
Native Fish Society [4850]
813 7th St., Ste 200A
Oregon City, OR 97045
Ph: (503)344-4218

Fortune, James, President
Agoraphobics in Motion [12502]
PO Box 725363
Berkley, MI 48072
Ph: (248)547-0400

Fosburgh, Whit, CEO, President
Theodore Roosevelt Conservation
Partnership [3956]
1660 L St. NW, Ste. 208
Washington, DC 20036
Ph: (202)639-8727
Fax: (202)639-8728

Foscarinis, Maria, Exec. Dir.,
Founder
National Law Center on Homeless-
ness and Poverty [11958]
2000 M St. NW, Ste. 210
Washington, DC 20036-3382
Ph: (202)638-2535
Fax: (202)628-2737

Foshee, Emily, Exec. Dir.
National Investment Banking As-
sociation [413]
422 Chesterfield Rd.
Bogart, GA 30622
Ph: (706)208-9620
Fax: (706)993-3342

Fosnight, Aleece, MSPAS, PA-C,
President
Association of Physician Assistants
in Obstetrics and Gynecology
[16276]
563 Carter Ct., Ste. B
Kimberly, WI 54136-2201
Ph: (920)560-5620
Toll Free: 800-545-0636
Fax: (920)882-3655

Foss, Vanessa, Dir. of Mtgs., Dir. of
Member Svcs.
American Society for Information
Science and Technology [6735]
8555 16th St., Ste. 850
Silver Spring, MD 20910
Ph: (301)495-0900
Fax: (301)495-0810

Foss-Brugger, Valerie, Exec. Dir.,
President
International Hearing Dog [15197]
5901 E 89th Ave.
Henderson, CO 80640
Ph: (303)287-3277
Fax: (303)287-3425

Foster, Allison, Exec. Dir.
Association of Schools and
Programs of Public Health [16998]
1900 M St. NW, Ste. 710
Washington, DC 20036
Ph: (202)296-1099
Fax: (202)296-1252

Foster, Prof. Andrew D., PhD,
Founder
Christian Mission for the Deaf
[20399]
PO Box 1651
Aledo, TX 76008

Foster, Ann, Exec. Dir.
National Network for Educational
Renewal [7844]
2125 1st Ave., No. 2305

Seattle, WA 98121
Ph: (206)850-2017
Fax: (206)441-5697

Foster, C. Stephen, MD, Founder,
President
Ocular Immunology and Uveitis
Foundation [16399]
348 Glen Rd.
Weston, MA 02493
Ph: (617)494-1431
Fax: (617)621-2953

Foster, Dacia, Acct. Mgr.
Softwood Export Council [1419]
720 NE Flanders, Ste. 207
Portland, OR 97232
Ph: (503)620-5946

Foster, Jan, President
Annie Sims International Fan Club
[24022]
PO Box 218478
Nashville, TN 37221-8478

Foster, John, Consultant
National Association of Subrogation
Professionals [2744]
3 Robinson Plz., Ste. 130
6600 Steubenville Pke.
Pittsburgh, PA 15205
Toll Free: 800-574-9961
Fax: (412)706-7164

Foster, Johnny, Chmn. of the Bd.
National Aircraft Resale Association
[149]
PO Box 92013
Southlake, TX 76092
Toll Free: 866-447-1777

Foster, Nancy, President
National Renderers Association
[2455]
500 Montgomery St., Ste. 310
Alexandria, VA 22314
Ph: (703)683-0155
Fax: (571)970-2279

Foster, Robert, Exec. Dir.
American Optometric Student As-
sociation [16425]
243 N Lindbergh, Ste. 311
Saint Louis, MO 63141
Ph: (314)983-4231

Foster, Robert, President
Association for Federal Information
Resources Management [5300]
400 N Washington St., Ste. 300
Alexandria, VA 22314
Ph: (703)778-4646
Fax: (703)683-5480

Foster, Serrin M., President
Feminists for Life of America [19058]
PO Box 320667
Alexandria, VA 22320
Ph: (703)836-3354

Foster-Scott, Denise, President
International Association of
Structural Integrators [13633]
PO Box 31381
Raleigh, NC 27622
Toll Free: 855-253-4274
Fax: (919)787-8081

Foti, Margaret, PhD, CEO
American Association for Cancer
Research [16329]
615 Chestnut St., 17th Fl.
Philadelphia, PA 19106-4406
Ph: (215)440-9300
Toll Free: 866-423-3965
Fax: (215)440-9313

Fotis, James J., Director, Exec. Dir.
Law Enforcement Alliance of
America [5478]

12427 Hedges Run Dr., Ste. 113
Lake Ridge, VA 22192-1715
Ph: (202)706-9218

Foulk, Dan, President
Model A Ford Club of America
[21435]
250 S Cypress St.
La Habra, CA 90631-5515
Ph: (562)697-2712
Fax: (562)690-7452

Fountain, Sharon, President
National Association for Self-Esteem
[15790]
PO Box 597
Fulton, MD 20759-0597

Fournier, Jim, Founder, President
Planetwork [4009]
29 Grove St., Ste. 517
San Francisco, CA 94102
Ph: (415)721-1591

Fournier, Wendy, President
National Autism Association [13773]
1 Park Ave., Ste. 1
Portsmouth, RI 02871
Ph: (401)293-5551
Toll Free: 877-622-2884
Fax: (401)293-5342

Foutch, Marty, President
National Bucking Bull Association
[23097]
PO Box 867
Canton, TX 75103
Ph: (903)848-4150
Toll Free: 800-878-1454

Fowle, Edward, President
63rd Infantry Division Association
[20711]
c/o Judith Schaefer, Secretary
6152 George Fox Dr.
Galloway, OH 43119
Ph: (614)818-6440

Fowle, Kate, Director
Independent Curators International
[8861]
401 Broadway, Ste. 1620
New York, NY 10013
Ph: (212)254-8200
Fax: (212)477-4781

Fowler, Craig, President
National Association of Physician
Recruiters [16757]
222 S Westmonte Dr., Ste. 101
Altamonte Springs, FL 32714
Ph: (407)774-7880
Toll Free: 800-726-5613
Fax: (407)774-6440

Fowler, Sir Edward H., Jr., Secretary
Royal Order of Scotland [19569]
400 Fallowfield Ave.
Charleroi, PA 15022
Ph: (724)489-0670
Fax: (724)489-0688

Fowler, Ms. Kris, Treasurer
The Wodehouse Society [9113]
236 Davis Rd.
Bedford, MA 01730-1500

Fowler LaBerge, Rev. Carmen S.,
Editor, President
Presbyterian Lay Committee [20526]
PO Box 682247
Franklin, TN 37068-2247
Ph: (615)591-4388
Toll Free: 800-368-0110

Fowler, Thomas, President
Tau Sigma Delta [23678]
c/o Maria Jeffrey, Administrartive Assistant

College of Architecture, Box 42091
Texas Tech University
Lubbock, TX 79409

Fowlkes, Earl D., Jr., CEO,
President
Center For Black Equity [11876]
PO Box 77313
Washington, DC 20013
Ph: (202)641-8527

Fox, Camilla H., Founder, Exec. Dir.
Project Coyote [4872]
PO Box 5007
Larkspur, CA 94977
Ph: (415)945-3232

Fox, Cedering, Art Dir.
WordTheatre [10228]
PO Box 1981
Studio City, CA 91614
Ph: (323)822-0823

Fox, Charles D., IV, VP
American College of Trust and
Estate Counsel [5684]
901 15th St. NW, Ste. 525
Washington, DC 20005
Ph: (202)684-8460
Fax: (202)684-8459

Fox, Christine Banvard, President
Goodenow Family Association
[20872]
163 Landham Rd.
Sudbury, MA 01776-3156

Fox, Christopher H., Exec. Dir.
American Association for Dental
Research [14390]
1619 Duke St.
Alexandria, VA 22314-3406
Ph: (703)548-0066
Fax: (703)548-1883

Fox, Christopher H., Exec. Dir.
International Association for Dental
Research [14446]
1619 Duke St.
Alexandria, VA 22314-3406
Ph: (703)548-0066
Fax: (703)548-1883

Fox, David, Officer
AHRA: The Association for Medical
Imaging Management [17037]
490B Boston Post Rd., Ste. 200
Sudbury, MA 01776
Ph: (978)443-7591
Toll Free: 800-334-2472

Fox, Dennis, Arch., Founder
Radical Psychology Network [16934]
c/o Roberta F. Sprague, Co-
Moderator
University of Illinois at Springfield
1 William Maxwell Ln.
Springfield, IL 62703

Fox, Donald T., Chmn. of the Bd.
American Association for the
International Commission of Jurists
[18370]
280 Madison Ave., Ste. 1102
New York, NY 10016
Ph: (212)972-0883
Fax: (212)972-0888

Fox, Frank, Exec. Dir.
Professional Association of Resume
Writers and Career Coaches
[11781]
1388 Brightwaters Blvd. NE
Saint Petersburg, FL 33704
Ph: (727)821-2274
Toll Free: 800-822-7279
Fax: (727)894-1277

Fox, Gina, Assoc. Dir.
Alpha Chi Omega [23941]
5939 Castle Creek Pky.

North Dr.
Indianapolis, IN 46250
Ph: (317)579-5050
Fax: (317)579-5051

Fox, Dr. Herbert, Director
Center for Energy, Environment and
Economics [6464]
New York Institute of Technology
Northern Blvd.
Old Westbury, NY 11568-8000
Ph: (516)686-1000

Fox, Jean, CEO, Founder
Aid to Incarcerated Mothers [11515]
434 Massachusetts Ave. 5th Fl., Ste.
503
Boston, MA 02118
Ph: (617)536-0058

Fox, Jean, Treasurer
User Experience Professionals As-
sociation [1808]
140 N Bloomingdale Rd.
Bloomingdale, IL 60108-1017
Ph: (630)980-4997
    (470)333-8972

Fox, John, Treasurer
USS Wisconsin Association [21073]
PO Box 227
Marion, MS 39342

Fox, Julie M., Secretary
National Association of Community
Development Extension Profes-
sionals [11407]
600 Cleveland St., Ste 780
Clearwater, FL 33755
Ph: (561)477-8100

Fox, Katie, President
American Friends of "For Survival"
[13205]
5333 42nd St. NW
Washington, DC 20015

Fox, Lee, President
National Dance Teachers Associa-
tion of America [22763]
2309 E Atlantic Blvd.
Pompano Beach, FL 33062
Ph: (954)782-7760

Fox, Martin E., President
National Pro-Life Alliance [19063]
5211 Port Royal Rd., Ste. 500
Springfield, VA 22151
Ph: (703)321-9200

Fox, Michael, President
Association for Computer Aided
Design in Architecture [6236]

Fox, Michael J., Exec. Dir.
Gasoline and Automotive Service
Dealers Association [343]
29 Thornhill Rd.
Riverside, CT 06878-1322
Ph: (203)327-4773
Fax: (203)323-6935

Fox, Nancy M., Contact
One Child at a Time [11105]
AIAA/Corporate Office
2151 Livernois Rd., Ste. 200
Troy, MI 48083
Ph: (248)362-1207
Fax: (248)362-8222

Fox, Nancy, Officer
Midori & Friends [7514]
352 7th Ave., Ste. 301
New York, NY 10001
Ph: (212)767-1300

Fox, Radhika, CEO
U.S. Water Alliance [4765]
1816 Jefferson Pl. NW

Washington, DC 20036
Ph: (202)263-3677
    (202)263-3671

Fox, Ronald L., Exec. Dir.
Society of Allied Weight Engineers
[7236]
5734 E Lucia Walk
Long Beach, CA 90803-4015
Ph: (562)596-2873
Fax: (562)596-2874

Fox, Thomas J., Exec. Dir.
Psi Upsilon [23923]
3003 E 96th St.
Indianapolis, IN 46240
Ph: (317)571-1833

Fox, William, President
Photo Chemical Machining Institute
[2366]
11 Robert Toner Blvd., No. 234
North Attleboro, MA 02763
Ph: (508)385-0085
Fax: (508)232-6005

Foxman, Abraham H., Director
Braun Holocaust Institute [18346]
Anti-Defamation League
605 3rd Ave.
New York, NY 10158
Ph: (212)885-7700
Toll Free: 866-386-3235

Foxman, Boris, Chmn. of the Bd.
American Association for Russian
Language, Culture and Education
[19628]
451 Hungerford Dr., Ste. 300
Rockville, MD 20850
Ph: (240)372-3343
Fax: (405)625-5349

Foy, Sharon, Director
Exercise Safety Association [16699]
PO Box 547916
Orlando, FL 32854-7916
Ph: (407)246-5090

Fra, Juan, President
American Greyhound Track Opera-
tors Association [22824]
Palm Beach Kennel Club
1111 N Congress Ave.
West Palm Beach, FL 33409
Ph: (561)688-5799
Fax: (801)751-2404

Fraas, Lynn, V. Chmn. of the Bd.,
Chairman, Chairperson
Association for Information and Im-
age Management International
[1794]
1100 Wayne Ave., Ste. 1100
Silver Spring, MD 20910
Ph: (301)587-8202
Toll Free: 800-477-2446
Fax: (301)587-2711

Fracyon, Noelle M., President
Raskob Foundation for Catholic
Activities, Inc. [19899]
10 Montchanin Rd.
Wilmington, DE 19807
Ph: (302)655-4440
Fax: (302)655-3223

Frado, Chris, Exec. Dir., President
Cross Country Ski Areas Association
[3153]
88 S Lincoln St., No. 1
Keene, NH 03431
Ph: (603)239-4341

Fragomen, Austin T., Jr., Chairman
Council for Global Immigration
[1088]
1800 Duke St.

Alexandria, VA 22314
Ph: (703)535-6365
Toll Free: 855-686-4777

Fraker, Hon. Ford M., President
Middle East Policy Council [18688]
1730 M St. NW, Ste. 512
Washington, DC 20036
Ph: (202)296-6767
Fax: (202)296-5791

Frampton, Cory, Exec. Dir.
U.S. Mexican Numismatic Association [22289]
PO Box 5270
Carefree, AZ 85377
Ph: (480)921-2562
Fax: (480)575-1279

Frampton, Ed, President
International Board of Jewish Missions [20146]
5106 Genesis Ln.
Hixson, TN 37343
Ph: (423)876-8150
Fax: (423)876-8156

Frampton, Susan, PhD, President
Planetree [14961]
130 Division St.
Derby, CT 06418
Ph: (203)732-1365

France, Brian, Chairman, CEO
National Association for Stock Car Auto Racing [22527]
PO Box 2875
Daytona Beach, FL 32120
Toll Free: 800-CARCASH

France, Ms. Leslie, CO, Exec. Dir.
American Orthoptic Council [16368]
3914 Nakoma Rd.
Madison, WI 53711
Ph: (608)233-5383
Fax: (608)263-4247

France, Nancey E.M., President
International Association for Human Caring [15024]
PO Box 6703
Grand Rapids, MI 49516-6703

Francis, David, President
National Association of Plant Breeders [4436]
c/o Dr. Rita Mumm, Awards Panel Chairperson
University of Illinois
1102 S Goodwin Ave.
Urbana, IL 61801
Ph: (217)244-9497

Francis, Donald P., MD, Exec. Dir., Founder
Global Solutions for Infectious Diseases [15400]
830 Dubuque Ave.
South San Francisco, CA 94080
Ph: (650)228-7900
Fax: (650)228-7901

Francis, Dr. G. James, President
Sigma Iota Epsilon [23809]
c/o Dr. G. James Francis, President
Colorado State University
213 Rockwell Hall
Fort Collins, CO 80521
Ph: (970)491-6265
    (970)491-7200
Fax: (970)491-3522

Francis, Keith A., Contact
American Society of Church History [20202]
PO Box 2793
Santa Rosa, CA 95405-2793
Ph: (707)538-6005
Fax: (707)538-2166

Francis, Peter, Treasurer
Africare [11309]
440 R St. NW
Washington, DC 20001
Ph: (202)462-3614
Fax: (202)464-0867

Francis, Shaun, Exec. Dir.
Association of Minor League Umpires [22544]
80 8th Ave., Ste. 205
New York, NY 10011

Francisco, Ms. Linda, Dir. of Operations
Cocaine Anonymous World Services [13132]
21720 S Wilmington Ave., Ste. 304
Long Beach, CA 90810-1641
Ph: (310)559-5833
Fax: (310)559-2554

Francisco, Mike, President
Bereaved Parents of the USA [10771]
PO Box 622
Saint Peters, MO 63376
Ph: (636)947-9403

Franco, Antonia O., Ed.D, Exec. Dir.
Society for Advancement of Chicanos/Hispanics and Native Americans in Science [7145]
1121 Pacific Ave.
Santa Cruz, CA 95060
Ph: (831)459-0170
Toll Free: 877-722-6271
Fax: (831)459-0194

Franco, Pedro F., DDS, President
American College of Oral and Maxillofacial Surgeons [16443]
2025 M St. NW, Ste. 800
Washington, DC 20036
Ph: (202)367-1182
Fax: (202)367-2182

Francz, Sharon, RN, Exec. Dir., President
National Coalition of Oncology Nurse Navigators [16159]
PO Box 1688
Rockville, MD 20849-1688
Toll Free: 800-581-0175

Frangopol, Prof. Dan M., President
International Association for Bridge Maintenance and Safety [6157]
c/o Professor Dan M. Frangopol, President
Lehigh University
ATLSS Research Ctr.
117 ATLSS Dr.
Bethlehem, PA 18015-4729
Ph: (610)758-6103
Fax: (610)758-5902

Frank, Allan Dodds, Chairperson
Society of the Silurians [2724]
PO Box 1195, Madison Square Sta.
New York, NY 10159

Frank, Carl, Founder, President
Freedom is Not Free [12344]
11760 Sorrento Valley Rd., Ste. G
San Diego, CA 92121

Frank, Chris, Treasurer
International Association of Lighting Management Companies [2100]
1255 SW Prairie Trail Pky.
Ankeny, IA 50023-7068
Ph: (515)243-2360
Fax: (515)334-1173

Frank, John M., Jr., Exec. Dir., Founder
Cessna Pilots Association [21218]
3409 Corsair Cir.

Santa Maria, CA 93455
Ph: (805)934-0493
Toll Free: 800-343-6416

Frank, Karen, President
Academy of Clinical Laboratory Physicians and Scientists [16729]
c/o Becky Lubbers, Administrative Assistant
500 Chipeta Way
Salt Lake City, UT 84108
Ph: (801)583-2787
Fax: (801)584-5207

Frank, Martin, PhD, Exec. Dir.
American Physiological Society [7033]
9650 Rockville Pke.
Bethesda, MD 20814-3991
Ph: (301)634-7164
Fax: (301)634-7241

Frank, Dr. Paul D., Exec. Dir., CEO
Information Storage Industry Consortium [6316]
6920 Miramar Rd., Ste. 301
San Diego, CA 92121
Ph: (619)392-0895

Frank, Rob, CEO, President
Bible League International [19753]
3801 Eagle Nest Dr.
Crete, IL 60417
Toll Free: 866-825-4636
Fax: (708)367-8600

Frank, Robin, Mgr.
National Council of Jewish Women [20270]
475 Riverside Dr., Ste. 1901
New York, NY 10115
Ph: (212)645-4048
Fax: (212)645-7466

Frank, Scot, CEO, Founder
One Earth Designs [4092]
PO Box 382559
Cambridge, MA 02238
Ph: (617)671-0727
Fax: (617)849-5661

Frankenberry, Nancy K., President
Metaphysical Society of America [10102]
c/o Brian G. Henning
Dept. of Philosophy
Gonzaga University
502 E Boone Ave.
Spokane, WA 99258-1774
Ph: (509)313-5885

Frankenfield, Lynne, Exec. Dir.
Cleaning for a Reason [10786]
211 S Stemmons, Ste. G
Lewisville, TX 75067
Toll Free: 877-337-3348

Franklin, Douglas G., CEO, President
Multiple Sclerosis Association of America [15955]
375 Kings Hwy. N
Cherry Hill, NJ 08034
Ph: (856)488-4500
Toll Free: 800-532-7667
Fax: (856)661-9797

Franklin, Jim, Exec. Dir.
Red Tag News Publications Association [2122]
1415 N Dayton St.
Chicago, IL 60622
Ph: (312)274-2215
Fax: (312)266-3363

Franklin, Joe, Rep.
Vintage Garden Tractor Club of America [22459]

c/o Doug Tallman, President
804 N Trimble Rd.
Mansfield, OH 44906
Ph: (419)545-2609

Franklin, Kelly, CEO, President
Sustainable Smiles [3952]
Box 148
Alberton, MT 59820
Ph: (406)370-0226

Franklin, Margaret E., Bd. Member
CFA Institute [2021]
915 E High St.
Charlottesville, VA 22902
Ph: (434)951-5499
Fax: (434)951-5262

Franklin, Neill, Exec. Dir.
Law Enforcement Against Prohibition [5477]
121 Mystic Ave., Ste. 9
Medford, MA 02155
Ph: (781)393-6985
Fax: (781)393-2964

Franklin, Patricia, President
National Art Education Association [7515]
901 Prince St.
Alexandria, VA 22314
Ph: (703)860-8000
Toll Free: 800-299-8321
Fax: (703)860-2960

Frantz, Sarah S.G., President
International Association for the Study of Popular Romance [9760]
887 Flintwood Rd.
Fayetteville, NC 28314

Franz, Charles F., DVM, Contact
American College of Theriogenologists [17614]
PO Box 3065
Montgomery, AL 36109-3065
Ph: (334)395-4666
Fax: (334)270-3399

Franzen, Jay, VP
American Oxford Sheep Association [4658]
9305 Zollman Rd.
Marysville, IN 47141
Ph: (812)256-3478
Fax: (812)256-3478

Franzese, Heather, Exec. Dir., Founder
Good World Solutions [12157]
1500 Broadway, Ste. 400
Oakland, CA 94612-2079
Ph: (510)844-1693

Fraser, Denise, Director
National Pygmy Goat Association [3606]
1932 149th Ave. SE
Snohomish, WA 98290
Ph: (425)334-6506
Fax: (425)334-5447

Fraser, Ms. Jane, President
Stuttering Foundation of America [17248]
1805 Moriah Woods Blvd., Ste. 3
Memphis, TN 38117-0749
Fax: (901)761-0484

Fraser, Leslye M., President
African American Federal Executive Association [5266]
6701 Democracy Blvd., Ste. 300
Bethesda, MD 20817
Toll Free: 866-600-4894
Fax: (413)778-2563

Fraser, Lucy, Exec. Dir.
Limbs for Life Foundation [14554]
218 E Main St.

Oklahoma City, OK 73104
Ph: (405)605-5462
Toll Free: 888-235-5462
Fax: (405)823-5123

Fraser, Ron, Founder, CEO
Starve Poverty International [10733]
6 Norwick Dr.
Forked River, NJ 08731
Ph: (609)249-5392
Fax: (609)971-6827

Fratt, Justin, Dir. of Operations
Gospel Music Association [9910]
4012 Granny White Pke.
Nashville, TN 37204-3924
Ph: (615)242-0303
Fax: (615)254-9755

Frausto, Keith, Exec. Dir.
Namlo International [12171]
8790 W Colfax Ave., Ste. 100
Lakewood, CO 80215
Ph: (303)399-3649
Fax: (303)399-1995

Frawley, Irene, Prog. Dir.
Association for Computing
   Machinery Special Interest Group
   on Artificial Intelligence [5984]
2 Penn Plz., Ste. 701
New York, NY 10121-0701
Ph: (212)626-0605
   (212)302-5826

Frawley, Irene, Coord.
Special Interest Group on Applied
   Computing [6336]
c/o Irene Frawley, Program
   Coordinator
Association for Computing
   Machinery
2 Penn Plaza, Ste. 701
New York, NY 10121-0701

Frazee, Jeff, Exec. Dir.
Young Americans for Liberty [19281]
PO Box 2751
Arlington, VA 22202-0751

Frazier, Hal A., MD, President
Society of Government Service
   Urologists [17561]
c/o DeSantis Management Group
1950 Old Tustin Ave.
Santa Ana, CA 92705
Ph: (714)550-9155
Fax: (714)550-9234

Frazier, Kimberly N., Ph.D., LPC,
   LMFT, NCC, President
Association for Multicultural Counsel-
   ing and Development [11484]
VA

Frazier, Pat, President
Josephine Porter Institute for Applied
   Bio-Dynamics [3554]
201 E Main St., Ste. 14
Floyd, VA 24091
Ph: (540)745-7030
Fax: (540)745-7033

Frazier, Scott, Contact
International Jet Sports Boating As-
   sociation [23354]
330 Purissima St., Ste. C
Half Moon Bay, CA 94019
Ph: (714)751-8695
Fax: (714)751-8609

Fream, Julie A., President, CEO
Original Equipment Suppliers As-
   sociation [661]
25925 Telegraph Rd., Ste. 350
Southfield, MI 48033-2553
Ph: (248)952-6401
Fax: (248)952-6404

Frederick, Amy Noone, Treasurer
National Foundation for Women
   Legislators [5849]
1727 King St., Ste. 300
Alexandria, VA 22314
Ph: (703)518-7931

Frederick, Brenda, Exec. Dir.
Orthopaedic Research Society
   [16487]
9400 W Higgins Rd., Ste. 225
Rosemont, IL 60018-4976
Ph: (847)823-5770
   (847)430-5020
Fax: (847)823-5772

Frederick, Carrie, President
Phi Beta Fraternity [23680]

Frederick, Gale Park, Director
National Chincoteague Pony As-
   sociation [4380]
2595 Jensen Rd.
Bellingham, WA 98226
Ph: (360)671-8338
Fax: (360)671-7603

Frederick, Margaretta, Secretary
William Morris Society in the United
   States [9082]
PO Box 53263
Washington, DC 20009

Frederick, Mr. Michael, Exec. Dir.
Thoreau Society [9104]
341 Virginia Rd.
Concord, MA 01742
Ph: (978)369-5310
Fax: (978)369-5382

Fredericks, Mr. Daniel P., Exec. Dir.
United Indian Missions International
   [20471]
6419 W Maryland Ave.
Glendale, AZ 85301-3718
Ph: (623)847-9227
Fax: (623)934-5996

Frederickson, Sara, President
Deaf Overcoming Violence through
   Empowerment [11937]
PO Box 150449
Denver, CO 80215
Ph: (303)831-7932
Fax: (303)831-4092

Frederiksen, Peter, Chairman
Danish American Chamber of Commerce [23580]
1 Dag Hammarskjold Plz.
885 2nd Ave., 18th Fl.
New York, NY 10017-2201
Ph: (646)790-7169

Fredricksen, Jane, Exec. Dir.
FaithTrust Institute [11702]
2900 Eastlake Ave. E, Ste. 200
Seattle, WA 98102
Ph: (206)634-1903
Toll Free: 877-860-2255
Fax: (206)634-0115

Fredrickson, Barbara, President
International Positive Psychology
   Association [16918]
14607 Felton Ct., Ste. 116
Apple Valley, MN 55124
Toll Free: 888-389-9687
Fax: (888)389-9687

Fredrickson, Ella M., Coord.
Major Orchestra Librarians' Association, Inc. [9715]
c/o Karen Schnackenberg
Dallas Symphony Orchestra
2301 Flora St., Ste. 300
Dallas, TX 75201

Free, Barbara, VP
Operation Identity [10462]
1818 Somervell St. NE

Albuquerque, NM 87112
Ph: (505)350-1344

Freedman, Brett D., President
ClearWater Initiative [13353]
PO Box 1684
New Haven, CT 06507
Toll Free: 866-585-6078

Freedman, Helen, Exec. Dir.
Americans for a Safe Israel [18675]
1751 2nd Ave., 91st St.
New York, NY 10128-5363
Ph: (212)828-2424
Toll Free: 800-235-3658
Fax: (212)828-4538

Freeland, Cynthia, President
American Society for Aesthetics
   [8956]
PO Box 915
Pooler, GA 31322
Ph: (912)748-9524

Freeman, Barbara Nicholson, MEd,
   Exec. Dir.
National Association of University-
   Model Schools [7638]
103 N 1st St.
Midlothian, TX 76065
Ph: (972)525-7005
Toll Free: 888-485-8525
Fax: (888)506-6597

Freeman, Geoff, President, CEO
American Gaming Association
   [22059]
799 9th St. NW, Ste. 700
Washington, DC 20001
Ph: (202)552-2675
Fax: (202)552-2676

Freeman, Herbert L., VP
National Town Builders' Association
   [563]
9655 24th Bay St.
Norfolk, VA 23518
Ph: (914)715-5576

Freeman, Ken, President
Last Harvest - The Outreach [12774]
1813 Eldorado Dr.
Garland, TX 75042
Ph: (214)703-0505
   (908)926-2607

Freeman, Kenneth, President
National Insulation Association [890]
12100 Sunset Hills Rd., Ste. 330
Reston, VA 20190
Ph: (703)464-6422
Fax: (703)464-5896

Freeman, Lakisha, VP
Western Public Radio [2827]
1308 Clear Fork Rd.
Crawford, CO 81415
Ph: (970)279-3411

Freeman, Mark, President
Outdoor Writers Association of
   America [2714]
615 Oak St., Ste. 201
Missoula, MT 59801
Ph: (406)728-7434

Freeman, Dr. Marsha A., Director
International Women's Rights Action
   Watch [18420]
University of Minnesota Human
   Rights Ctr.
229 19th Ave. S
Minneapolis, MN 55455
Ph: (612)625-4985
Fax: (612)625-2011

Freeman, Robert, Dir. of Admin.
One Dollar for Life [12963]
783 Kendall Ave.

Palo Alto, CA 94306
Ph: (661)203-8750
Fax: (650)856-1017

Freeman, Scott, President
American Membrane Technology
   Association [7361]
2409 SE Dixie Hwy.
Stuart, FL 34996
Ph: (772)463-0820
Fax: (772)463-0860

Frees, David, President
American Bandstand Fan Club
   [24083]
c/o David Frees, President
52 Stauffer Park Ln.
Mohnton, PA 19540-7751

Freeston, John, V. Ch.
London Vintage Taxi Association -
   American Section [21421]
PO Box 445
Windham, NH 03087
Ph: (603)893-8919

Freeth, Pam, President
Zellweger Baby Support Network
   [14870]
c/o Pam Freeth, Pres.
9310 Groundhog Dr.
Richmond, VA 23235
Ph: (919)741-9778

Freid, Alex, Founder, Director
Post-Landfill Action Network [4745]
1 Depot Ln.
Lee, NH 03861
Ph: (603)608-9859

Freier, Russel E., CET, Chmn. of the
   Bd.
American Society of Certified
   Engineering Technicians [6534]
PO Box 95
Cape May Court House, NJ 08210
Ph: (609)600-2097
Fax: (609)600-2097

Freitag, Scott, President
International Academies of
   Emergency Dispatch [14697]
110 S Regent St., Ste. 800
Salt Lake City, UT 84111
Ph: (801)359-6916
Toll Free: 800-960-6236
Fax: (801)359-0996

Freitas-Astua, Juliana, Chairperson
International Organization of Citrus
   Virologists [6146]
University of California
900 University Ave.
Riverside, CA 92521
Ph: (951)827-1012

French, Dan, Act. Pres., Editor
Mailer's Postmark Permit Club
   [22340]
c/o Robert Johnston, Secretary
PO Box 902
East Windsor, CT 06088-0902

French, Dennis, Comm. Chm.
American Board of Veterinary
   Practitioners [17609]
5003 SW 41st Blvd.
Gainesville, FL 32608-4930
Ph: (352)431-2843
Toll Free: 800-697-3583
Fax: (352)354-9046

French, Dorothy, Exec. Dir., Founder
Education-A-Must, Inc. [11594]
PO Box 216
East Derry, NH 03041
Ph: (603)437-6286
Fax: (603)434-0371

French, Jennifer, Founder, Exec. Dir.
Neurotech Network **[16053]**
PO Box 27386
Tampa, FL 33623
Ph: (727)321-0150

French, Lynda P., CFO, Treasurer
Table Shuffleboard Association, Inc.
[23148]
c/o Lynda French, Chief Finanacial
Officer/Treasurer
8155 Meadow Lark Dr.
Wynnewood, OK 73098-8949
Ph: (512)619-6030
Fax: (512)597-0609

French, Mary, Director
Dictionary Project **[12245]**
PO Box 1845
Charleston, SC 29402-1845
Ph: (843)388-8375
    (843)856-2706

French, Ms. Melanie, Exec. Dir.
American Institute for Foreign Study
Foundation **[8109]**
1 High Ridge Pk.
Stamford, CT 06905
Ph: (203)399-5414
Toll Free: 800-322-4678
Fax: (203)724-1536

French, Rod, Chmn. of the Bd.
Painting and Decorating Contractors
of America **[896]**
2316 Millpark Dr.
Maryland Heights, MO 63043
Ph: (314)514-7322
Toll Free: 800-332-7322
Fax: (314)890-2068

Fresco, Jacque, Founder
Venus Project **[19122]**
21 Valley Ln.
Venus, FL 33960-2327
Ph: (863)465-0321

Freshman, Phil, President
Association of Art Editors **[2766]**
3912 Natchez Ave. S
Minneapolis, MN 55416
Ph: (952)922-1374
Fax: (952)922-1374

Frett, Deborah L., CEO
Business and Professional Women/
U.S.A. **[18201]**
1620 Eye St. NW, Ste. 210
Washington, DC 20006
Ph: (202)293-1100
Toll Free: 888-491-8833
Fax: (202)861-0298

Freudenberger, Mr. John, President
National Reye's Syndrome Founda-
tion **[17151]**
426 N Lewis St.
Bryan, OH 43506
Toll Free: 800-233-7393

Freund, David, Director
Ephemera Society of America
[22012]
PO Box 95
Cazenovia, NY 13035-0095
Ph: (315)655-9139
Fax: (315)655-9139

Freund, Ron, Chairman
Electric Auto Association **[6018]**
323 Los Altos Dr.
Aptos, CA 95003
Ph: (831)688-8669

Frevert, Kenneth D., Contact
Epidermoid Brain Tumor Society
[16343]
c/o Kenneth D. Frevert

12573 Wedd St.
Overland Park, KS 66213-1845

Frey, Barry, President
Digital Place Based Advertising As-
sociation **[93]**
205 E 42nd St., 20th Fl.
New York, NY 10017
Ph: (212)371-8961

Frey, John, Founder
National Coalition of Healthcare
Recruiters **[15589]**
1742 N Willow Woods Dr.
Anaheim, CA 92807
Ph: (304)699-5426

Frey, Neal, President
Educational Research Analysts
[8692]
PO Box 7518
Longview, TX 75607-7518
Ph: (903)753-5993
Fax: (903)753-8424

Freyd, Pamela, PhD, Exec. Dir.
False Memory Syndrome Foundation
[16914]
PO Box 30044
Philadelphia, PA 19103-8044
Ph: (215)940-1040
Fax: (215)940-1042

Freyer, Dana H., Chairman, Founder
Global Partnership for Afghanistan
[10469]
PO Box 1237
New York, NY 10276-1237
Ph: (212)735-2080

Freysinger, Carol, Exec. Dir.
Juice Products Association **[427]**
529 14th St. NW
Washington, DC 20045
Ph: (202)591-2438

Frick, Rachel L., Director
Digital Library Federation **[9703]**
1707 L St. NW, Ste. 650
Washington, DC 20036-4228
Ph: (202)939-4758

Frick, Roy, Director
Accreditation Council for Ac-
countancy and Taxation **[4]**
1330 Braddock Pl., Ste. 540
Alexandria, VA 22314-1574
Toll Free: 888-289-7763
Fax: (703)549-2984

Fricton, James, President
International MYOPAIN Society
[16559]
PO Box 268
Nine Mile Falls, WA 99026-0268
Ph: (714)423-4863

Fried, Brandon, Exec. Dir.
Airforwarders Association **[2112]**
750 National Press Bldg.
529 14th St. NW, Ste. 750
Washington, DC 20045
Ph: (202)591-2456
Fax: (202)591-2445

Fried, Warren, Exec. Dir., Founder
Dyspraxia Foundation USA **[15928]**
84 Westover Rd.
Highwood, IL 60040
Ph: (847)780-3311

Friedberg, Aaron L., Founder,
President
The Alexander Hamilton Society
[5679]
11 Dupont Cir. NW, Ste. 325
Washington, DC 20036
Ph: (202)559-7389

Friedberg, Fred, PhD, President
International Association for Chronic
Fatigue Syndrome/Myalgic
Encephalomyelitis **[14584]**
9650 Rockville Pke.
Bethesda, MD 20814
Ph: (301)634-7701
Fax: (301)634-7099

Friedberg, Josh, Exec. Dir.
International Association of
Skateboard Companies **[23089]**
315 S Coast Highway 101, Ste.
U-253
Encinitas, CA 92024
Ph: (949)455-1112
Fax: (949)455-1112

Friedberg, Rena, Officer
JARC **[12324]**
30301 Northwestern Hwy., Ste. 100
Farmington Hills, MI 48334
Ph: (248)538-6611

Friedberg, Richard C., MD, PhD,
President
College of American Pathologists
[16581]
325 Waukegan Rd.
Northfield, IL 60093-2750
Ph: (847)832-7000
Toll Free: 800-323-4040
Fax: (847)832-8000

Friedell, Morris, Director, Treasurer
Dementia Advocacy and Support
Network International **[15923]**
PO Box 1645
Mariposa, CA 95338

Frieders, Bryan, President
Firefighter Cancer Support Network
[13969]
2600 W Olive Ave., 5th Fl., PMB 608
Burbank, CA 91505
Ph: (866)994-3276

Friedland, Nancy, President
Theatre Library Association **[9730]**
The New York Public Library for the
Performing Arts
40 Lincoln Center Plz.
New York, NY 10023

Friedman, David, Mem.
Association of Biomolecular
Resource Facilities **[6776]**
9650 Rockville Pke.
Bethesda, MD 20814-3999
Ph: (301)634-7306
Fax: (301)634-7455

Friedman, Elias, OCD, Founder
Association of Hebrew Catholics
[19796]
4120 W Pine Blvd.
Saint Louis, MO 63108-2802

Friedman, Ellen, Exec. Dir.
Compton Foundation **[12967]**
101 Montgomery St., Ste. 850
San Francisco, CA 94104-4126
Ph: (415)391-9001
Fax: (415)391-9005

Friedman, Gary, Chairman
Jewish Prisoner Services
International **[20259]**
PO Box 85840
Seattle, WA 98145-1840
Ph: (206)985-0577
Fax: (206)526-7113

Friedman, James M., MD, Exec. Dir.
American Academy of HIV Medicine
[13527]
1705 DeSales St. NW, Ste. 700
Washington, DC 20036
Ph: (202)659-0699
Fax: (202)659-0976

Friedman, Lawrence, President
Customs and International Trade Bar
Association **[5156]**
204 E St. NE
Washington, DC 20002
Ph: (212)549-0149
Fax: (212)883-0068

Friedman, Mr. Martin, Exec. Dir.,
Founder
EducationWorks **[7645]**
3149 Germantown Ave.
Philadelphia, PA 19133
Ph: (215)221-6900
Fax: (215)221-6901

Friedman, Michael, ND, Founder,
Exec. Dir.
Association for the Advancement of
Restorative Medicine **[13605]**
PO Box 874
Montpelier, VT 05601
Toll Free: 866-962-2276

Friedman, Rabbi Mordechai Yitz-
chok, President
American Board of Rabbis **[20223]**
276 5th Ave., Ste. 704
New York, NY 10001-4527
Ph: (212)714-3598
    (646)996-4040
Toll Free: 800-539-4743

Friedman, Nat, Editor, Founder
International Society of the Arts,
Mathematics, and Architecture
[8047]
University at Albany
1400 Washington Ave.
Albany, NY 12222

Friedman, Robert, Chmn. of the Bd.,
Founder, Gen. Counsel
Corporation for Enterprise Develop-
ment **[18148]**
1200 G St. NW, Ste. 400
Washington, DC 20005
Ph: (202)408-9788
Fax: (202)408-9793

Friedman, Sarah, Exec. Dir.
SEAMS Association **[2230]**
1908 Richland Ave. E
Aiken, SC 29801
Ph: (803)772-5861
    (803)642-1111
Fax: (803)731-7709

Friedmann, Peter, Exec. Dir.
Agriculture Transportation Coalition
[3317]
1120 G St. NW, Ste. 1020
Washington, DC 20005
Ph: (202)783-3333
Fax: (202)783-4422

Friedrich, Jessa, Specialist
Realtors Land Institute **[2894]**
430 N Michigan Ave., 11th Fl.
Chicago, IL 60611
Toll Free: 800-441-5263
Fax: (312)329-8633

Friend, Donna M., Treasurer
Friend Family Association of America
[20866]
261 Maple St.
Friendsville, MD 21531-2131
Ph: (301)746-4690

Friend, Stephen, Secretary
International Association for the
Study of Maritime Mission **[9782]**
c/o Rev. Clint Padgitt
123 E 15th St.
New York, NY 10003

Frierson, John, Founder
A Bone Marrow Wish **[13847]**
PO Box 21554

Detroit, MI 48221

Frilow-Steenhoek, Michelle, CMP, Director
Help Desk Institute [3074]
121 S Tejon, Ste. 1100
Colorado Springs, CO 80903-2254
Ph: (719)955-8146
   (719)955-8180
Toll Free: 800-248-5667
Fax: (719)955-8114

Frisbie, Fred, President
Frisbie - Frisbee Family Association of America [20867]
c/o Margaret Zimny, Secretary
5417 61st Ave. SE
Rochester, MN 55904

Frisbie, Thomas, President
Society of Midland Authors [3520]
PO Box 10419
Chicago, IL 60610

Frisch, Marianne Brunson, Secretary
International Motor Press Association [2687]
783 Old Queen Anne Rd.
Chatham, MA 02633
Ph: (508)945-2400

Frisina, Cynthia, Founder, Exec. Dir.
Reaching for the Stars [14157]
3000 Old Alabama Rd., Ste. 119-300
Alpharetta, GA 30022
Toll Free: 855-240-RFTS

Fritts, David, VP, Chairman
Singles in Agriculture [21741]
PO Box 51
Lincoln, KS 67455-0051
Ph: (815)947-3559

Fritz, Harold A., President
Congressional Medal of Honor Society [20731]
40 Patriots Point Rd.
Mount Pleasant, SC 29464-4377
Ph: (843)884-8862
Fax: (843)884-1471

Fritz, Janie Harden, Exec. Sec., Exec. Dir.
Religious Communication Association [20033]
c/o Janie Harden Fritz, Executive Secretary
340 College Hall
Dept. of Communication & Rhetorical Studies
Duquesne University
600 Forbes Ave.
Pittsburgh, PA 15282

Fritz, Dr. Noah, President
International Association of Crime Analysts [5155]
9218 Metcalf Ave., No. 364
Overland Park, KS 66212
Toll Free: 800-609-3419

Fritz, Scott, President
Society for the Prevention of Teen Suicide [13198]
110 W Main St.
Freehold, NJ 07728

Fritz, Wendy, CEO
Category Management Association [2158]
7900 Xerxes Ave. S, Ste. 980
Minneapolis, MN 55431
Ph: (210)587-7203

Fritzer, Dr. Penelope, Secretary, President
Angela Thirkell Society [9102]
c/o Lynne Crowley, Treasurer

PO Box 203
Larchmont, NY 10538

Fritzman, J. M., Contact
The Society for German Idealism [9341]
c/o J.M. Fritzman
Dept. of Philosophy
Lewis and Clark College
615 SW Palatine Hill Rd.
Portland, OR 97219-7879
Ph: (503)768-7477

Froehlich, Steve, Director
Direct Marketing Fundraisers Association [1468]
PO Box 51
Tenafly, NJ 07670
Ph: (646)675-7314
Fax: (201)266-4006

Frogel, Michael, M.D., Contact
American Physicians and Friends for Medicine in Israel [12207]
2001 Beacon St., Ste. 210
Boston, MA 02135
Ph: (617)232-5382

Fromyer, Mary O., Exec. Dir.
Global Offset and Countertrade Association [1984]
818 Connecticut Ave. NW, 12th Fl.
Washington, DC 20006
Ph: (202)887-9011
Fax: (202)872-8324

Fronek, Steve, Chairman
American Architectural Manufacturers Association [488]
1827 Walden Office Sq., Ste. 550
Schaumburg, IL 60173
Ph: (847)303-5664
Fax: (847)303-5774

Fronimos, Mike, Officer
National Information Officers Association [2755]
PO Box 10125
Knoxville, TN 37939-0125
Ph: (865)389-8736

Fronk, Susan, President
MRA - The Management Association [2181]
N19 W24400 Riverwood Dr.
Waukesha, WI 53188
Ph: (262)523-9090
Toll Free: 800-488-4845

Froom, Robert Keith, Founder
4 the World [11300]
404 Butler Dr.
Garner, NC 27529

Frost, Eric, Bd. Member
Wilderness Classroom [8401]
4605 Grand Ave.
Western Springs, IL 60558
Ph: (312)505-9973

Frost, Mark D., Exec. Dir.
Clean Technology Trade Alliance [5882]
441 NE Silver Pine Dr.
Bremerton, WA 98311
Ph: (360)824-5417

Frost, Michael, Founder
International Autograph Dealer Alliance & Collectors Club [21667]
11435 Lake Shore Dr.
Hollywood, FL 33026-1120

Fruchter, Jason, President
Cartoonists Northwest [8969]
PO Box 31122
Seattle, WA 98103

Fruchter, Y., Mgr.
Torah Umesorah - The National Society for Hebrew Day Schools [20197]

620 Foster Ave.
Brooklyn, NY 11230-1399
Ph: (212)227-1000
Fax: (212)406-6934

Fruedenthaler, Tatianna, Exec. Dir.
World Investigators Network [2015]
875 6th Ave., Ste. 206
New York, NY 10001
Ph: (212)779-2000
Toll Free: 888-946-6389
Fax: (212)779-2545

Fruth, Dr. Larry L., II, CEO, Exec. Dir.
Schools Interoperability Framework Association [6261]
1090 Vermont Ave. NW, 6th Fl.
Washington, DC 20005
Ph: (202)789-4460
Fax: (202)289-7097

Fry, Douglas, Exec. Dir.
Independent Free Papers of America [2789]
104 Westland Dr.
Columbia, TN 38401
Ph: (931)224-8151

Fry, Jack, Comm. Chm.
International Playground Contractors Association [872]
2207 Forest Hills Dr.
Harrisburg, PA 17112
Ph: (717)724-0594
Fax: (717)238-9985

Fry, John, Chairman
International Skiing History Association [23163]
PO Box 1064
Manchester Center, VT 05255
Ph: (802)366-1158

Frydland, Michael, Exec.
Global Action to Prevent War [18720]
866 UN Plz., Ste. 4050
New York, NY 10017
Ph: (212)818-1815
Fax: (212)818-1857

Frye, Irene, Exec. Dir.
Retirement Research Foundation [10528]
8765 W Higgins Rd., Ste. 430
Chicago, IL 60631-4172
Ph: (773)714-8080
Fax: (773)714-8089

Frye, Laurel, Administrator
Golden Rule Foundation [9548]
PO Box 658
Camden, ME 04843-0658
Ph: (207)338-1866

Frye, Lisa, Exec. Dir.
Association of Outdoor Lighting Professionals [2099]
2207 Forest Hills Dr.
Harrisburg, PA 17112
Ph: (717)238-2504
Fax: (717)238-9985

Frye, Steven, President
The Cormac McCarthy Society [10368]
13850 SW 100th Ave.
Miami, FL 33176-6717

Frye, Dr. Veryl F., Secretary, Treasurer
American Medical Fly Fishing Association [3801]
PO Box 768
Lock Haven, PA 17745
Ph: (570)769-7375

Fteha, Elie F., MD, President
Historical Society of Jews from Egypt [9638]

PO Box 230445
Brooklyn, NY 11223
Fax: (718)998-2497

Fuchs, Susan, Secretary
Commission on Accreditation of Allied Health Education Programs [8293]
25400 US Highway 19 N, Ste. 158
Clearwater, FL 33763
Ph: (727)210-2350
Fax: (727)210-2354

Fuchs, Tibor, VP
Indoor Gardening Society of America [22103]
NY

Fudenberg, Mr. John, Chairman
International Association of Coroners and Medical Examiners [15629]
c/o Nicole Coleman, Executive Administrator
1704 Pinto Ln.
Las Vegas, NV 89106
Ph: (702)455-1937
Fax: (702)380-9669

Fuentes, Julio A., CEO, President
Hispanic Council for Reform and Educational Options [7770]
Ste. L, No. 151
4095 State Road 7
Wellington, FL 33449

Fuentes, Phil, Chairman
McDonald's Hispanic Owner-Operators Association [2940]
Ph: (951)698-1245
   (951)973-4851

Fugita, Shane, Director, President
National Adult Baseball Association [22554]
5944 S.Kipling St., Ste. 200
Littleton, CO 80127
Toll Free: 800-621-6479

Fujii, Stacie, Founder, President
American Council of Young Political Leaders [18626]
2131 K St. NW, Ste. 400
Washington, DC 20037-1870
Ph: (202)857-0999
Fax: (202)857-0027

Fujiko Willgerodt, Penny, Exec. Dir.
Prospect Hill Foundation [10822]
99 Park Ave., Ste. 2220
New York, NY 10016-1601
Ph: (212)370-1165
Fax: (212)599-6282

Fujimoto, Junko, Director
Japanese National Honor Society [23793]
c/o American Association of Teachers of Japanese
1424 Broadway
Boulder, CO 80309-0366
Ph: (303)492-5487
Fax: (303)492-5856

Fujiyama, Shin, Exec. Dir.
Students Helping Honduras [11161]
1213 Dandridge St.
Fredericksburg, VA 22401
Ph: (703)445-5497

Fulcher, Carlos, Exec. Dir.
International Association of Business Communicators [770]
155 Montgomery St., Ste. 1210
San Francisco, CA 94104
Ph: (415)544-4700
Toll Free: 800-776-4222
Fax: (415)544-4747

Fulghum, Christian, President, Chairman
Wild Entrust International [4902]
5140 Ballard Ave. NW, Ste. A

Seattle, WA 98107
Ph: (206)687-7956

Fuller, Ben, Treasurer
Qajaq U.S.A. [23363]
88 Mason Cove Ln.
Cushing, ME 04563

Fuller, Bill, Founder
Transmission Rebuilders Network
International [331]
4757 E Greenway Rd., Ste. 107B-54
Phoenix, AZ 85032-8512
Ph: (602)404-0299
Toll Free: 888-582-8764
Fax: (602)404-7650

Fuller, Bob, President
Lloyd Shaw Foundation [7703]
2124 Passolt St.
Saginaw, MI 48603

Fuller, David, Treasurer
National Theatre Conference
[10265]

Fuller, Howard, Bd. Member
Black Alliance for Educational Op-
tions [7817]
1001 G St. NW, Ste. 800
Washington, DC 20001
Ph: (202)429-2236

Fuller, Ivonne Perlaza, MPA, NRPP,
CEO, President
Hepatitis Foundation International
[15256]
8121 Georgia Ave., Ste. 350
Silver Spring, MD 20910
Ph: (301)565-9410
Toll Free: 800-891-0707

Fuller, Paul, Secretary
National Council of State Sociologi-
cal Associations [7186]
Medaille College
Buffalo, NY 14214-2695

Fuller, Sarah, President, Chmn. of
the Bd.
Cultural Survival [9533]
2067 Massachusetts Ave.
Cambridge, MA 02140
Ph: (617)441-5400
Fax: (617)441-5417

Fullmer, Glen, Dir. of Comm.
National Spiritual Assembly of the
Baha'is of the U.S. [20549]
1233 Central St.
Evanston, IL 60201
Ph: (847)733-3400

Fullmer, Jim, Exec. Dir.
Demeter Association, Inc. [4151]
PO Box 1390
Philomath, OR 97370
Ph: (541)929-7148

Fulmer, Sherry, Exec. Dir.
National Barrel Horse Association
[22922]
725 Broad St.
Augusta, GA 30901
Ph: (706)722-7223

Fulmer, Terry, PhD, President
The John A. Hartford Foundation
[10509]
55 E 59th St., 16th Fl.
New York, NY 10022-1713
Ph: (212)832-7788
Fax: (212)593-4913

Fultz, D. Mark, President
American Brush Manufacturers Association [1680]
736 Main Ave., Ste. 7

Durango, CO 81301
Ph: (720)392-2262
Fax: (866)837-8450

Funaro, Elaine, President
Historical Keyboard Society of North
America [22248]
c/o David C. Kelzenberg, Secretary
2801 Highway 6 E, Ste. 344
Iowa City, IA 52240

Funch, Flemming, Founder
New Civilization Network [12012]
PO Box 260433
Encino, CA 91316
Ph: (818)725-3775

Funder, David, President
Association for Research in
Personality [7062]
c/o Rebecca Shiner, Executive Of-
ficer
Dept. of Psychology
13 Oak Dr.
Hamilton, NY 13346
Ph: (217)333-3486
Fax: (217)244-5876

Funk, Debbie, VP
Oregon Horsemen's Benevolent and
Protective Association [22927]
10350 N Vancouver Way, No. 351
Portland, OR 97217
Ph: (503)285-4941
Fax: (503)285-4942

Funk, Pat, Editor
Association of Retail Travel Agents
[3372]
4320 N Miller Rd.
Scottsdale, AZ 85251-3606
Toll Free: 866-369-8969
Fax: (866)743-8969

Funt, Peter, President
Laughter Therapy Enterprises
[17451]
c/o Enda Junkins
PO Box 684
Ouray, CO 81427
Ph: (970)325-0050

Furbush, Lori, Chairperson
National Qigong Association [13642]
PO Box 270065
Saint Paul, MN 55127
Toll Free: 888-815-1893

Furchgott, David, President
International Arts and Artists [8978]
9 Hillyer Ct. NW
Washington, DC 20008
Ph: (202)338-0680

Furlong, Douglas J., CEO
Tissue Banks International [17519]
815 Park Ave.
Baltimore, MD 21201
Ph: (410)752-3800
Toll Free: 800-756-4824
Fax: (410)783-0183

Furlong, Pat, President
Parent Project Muscular Dystrophy
[15980]
401 Hackensack Avenue, 9th Floor
Hackensack, NJ 07601
Ph: (201)250-8440
Toll Free: 800-714-5437
Fax: (201)250-8435

Furnas, Kelly, Exec. Dir.
Journalism Education Association
[8156]
105 Kedzie Hall
828 Mid-Campus Dr. S
Manhattan, KS 66506-0008
Ph: (785)532-5532
Toll Free: 866-532-5532
Fax: (785)532-5563

Furrey, Mike, President
Basket of Hope [10784]
PO Box 510860
Saint Louis, MO 63151
Ph: (314)268-1515

Fuschillo, Charles J., Jr., CEO,
President
Alzheimer's Foundation of America
[13670]
322 8th Ave., 7th Fl.
New York, NY 10001
Ph: (646)638-1542
Toll Free: 866-232-8484
Fax: (646)638-1546

Fusell, Kevin, MD, President
World Water Relief [13352]
931 Monroe Dr., Ste. 102-593
Atlanta, GA 30308
Ph: (678)661-9982
Fax: (770)993-9770

Fussel, Larry, Officer
Ice Screamers [21664]
PO Box 465
Warrington, PA 18976
Ph: (215)343-2676

Fussell, Alison, Exec. Dir.
Childspring International [14184]
1328 Peachtree St. NE
Atlanta, GA 30309-3209
Ph: (404)228-7770
    (404)228-7744

Fustero, Steven J., Dir. of Opera-
tions
International Association for
Counterterrorism and Security
Professionals [19181]
PO Box 100688
Arlington, VA 22210-3688
Ph: (201)224-0588
Fax: (202)315-3459

Futrell, Prof. Alison, Secretary,
Treasurer
Women's Classical Caucus [9168]
c/o Prof. Alison Futrell, Secretary-
Treasurer
Dept. of History, Social Sciences
215
University of Arizona
1145 E South Campus Dr.
Tucson, AZ 85721

G

Gaarde, Mike, Officer
Mission: Wolf [4843]
PO Box 1211
Westcliffe, CO 81252
Ph: (719)859-2157

Ga'avah, Keshet, Treasurer
World Congress of Gay, Lesbian,
Bisexual, and Transgender Jews
[20192]
PO Box 23379
Washington, DC 20026-3379

Gaba, Nancy, MD, President
Society for Academic Specialists in
General Obstetrics and Gynecol-
ogy [16304]
817 Ogden Ave., No. 4537
Lisle, IL 60532
Toll Free: 844-472-7464

Gabaudan, Michel, President
Refugees International [12597]
2001 S St. NW, Ste. 700
Washington, DC 20009
Ph: (202)828-0110
    (202)361-6131
Toll Free: 800-733-8433
Fax: (202)828-0819

Gabel, Marianne, Contact
Population Connection [12514]
2120 L St. NW, Ste. 500
Washington, DC 20037
Ph: (202)332-2200
Toll Free: 800-767-1956
Fax: (202)332-2302

Gables, Lisa, Chief Dev. Ofc., Exec.
Dir.
American Academy of Physician As-
sistants [16721]
2318 Mill Rd., Ste. 1300
Alexandria, VA 22314
Ph: (703)836-2272
Fax: (703)684-1924

Gabner, Cindy, President
Angels for Hope [13031]
708 Falls Creek Dr.
West Melbourne, FL 32904

Gabrenya, William, Sec. Gen.
International Association for Cross-
Cultural Psychology [16915]
c/o William Gabrenya, Secretary
General
Florida Institute of Technology
School of Psychology
150 W University Blvd.
Melbourne, FL 32901
Ph: (310)825-7526
    (310)825-2961

Gabriel, John, Comm. Chm.
National Association of Unclaimed
Property Administrators [5688]
c/o National Association of State
Treasurers
The Council of State Governments
2760 Research Park Dr.
Lexington, KY 40578-1910
Ph: (859)244-8150
Fax: (859)244-8053

Gabrielson, Dr. Bruce, Founder
National Surf Schools and Instruc-
tors Association [23278]
PO Box 550
Chesapeake Beach, MD 20732

Gabrielson, Paul, President
Phycological Society of America
[6152]
PO Box 90001
Blacksburg, VA 24062-9001
Ph: (540)231-6170

Gaby, Elizabeth, ND, V. Ch.
Birth Without Boundaries [14222]
8 Riddle Rd.
Camp Hill, PA 17011
Ph: (717)654-9810

Gacos, Nicky, President
National Association of Blind
Merchants [2966]
7450 Chapman Hwy., Ste. 319
Knoxville, TN 37920
Ph: (719)527-0488
Toll Free: 866-543-6808

Gadd, Ian, President
Society for the History of Authorship,
Reading and Publishing [9135]
PO Box 19966
Baltimore, MD 21211-0966
Ph: (410)516-6987
Toll Free: 800-548-1784
Fax: (410)516-3866

Gaddie, Ben, President
Optometric Glaucoma Society
[16402]
900 NW 17th St.
Miami, FL 33136
Toll Free: 800-329-7000
Fax: (305)326-6113

Gaddis, Evan R., President, CEO
National Electrical Manufacturers
    Association [1029]
1300 N 17th St., Ste. 1752
Rosslyn, VA 22209
Ph: (703)841-3200
    (703)841-3272

Gaddis, Gay, Chairperson
Committee of 200 [624]
980 N Michigan Ave., Ste. 1575
Chicago, IL 60611
Ph: (312)255-0296
Fax: (312)255-0789

Gadenne, Francois, Chairman, Exec.
    Dir.
Retirement Income Industry Associa-
    tion [2983]
101 Federal St., Ste. 1900
Boston, MA 02110
Ph: (617)342-7390
Fax: (617)342-7080

Gadomski, Brent, President
American Veterinary Exhibitors' As-
    sociation [17629]
712 N Broadway
Menomonie, WI 54751-1511

Gaede, Dr. Stan D., President
Christian College Consortium [7609]
255 Grapevine Rd.
Wenham, MA 01984-1813
Ph: (978)468-1716
Fax: (978)867-4650

Gaertner, Kate, Exec. Dir.
Alpha Sigma Nu [23775]
707 N 11th St., No. 330
Milwaukee, WI 53201
Ph: (414)288-7542
Fax: (414)288-3259

Gaffney, Jonathan, President, CEO
National Aeronautic Association
    [145]
Reagan Washington National Airport
Hangar 7, Ste. 202
Washington, DC 20001-6015
Ph: (703)416-4888
Toll Free: 800-644-9777
Fax: (703)416-4877

Gagel, Robert F., M.D., President
National Osteoporosis Foundation
    [16485]
251 18th St. S, Ste. 630
Arlington, VA 22202
Ph: (703)647-3000
Toll Free: 800-231-4222
Fax: (703)414-3742

Gagliano, James L., President, COO
The Jockey Club [22920]
821 Corporate Dr.
Lexington, KY 40503
Ph: (859)224-2700
    (859)514-6616
Fax: (859)224-2710

Gagliardi, Kristine, Corp. Dev. Ofc.
the Radiosurgery Society [17413]
PO Box 5631
San Mateo, CA 94402
Ph: (408)385-9411

Gagliardi, Lily, Founder, CEO
Lily's Kids [15218]
589 East St.
Middletown, CT 06457

Gagnon, Bruce K., Coord., Secretary
Global Network Against Weapons
    and Nuclear Power in Space
    [18746]
PO Box 652
Brunswick, ME 04011
Ph: (207)443-9502

Gahlon, Dan E., Chairman
World Press Institute [17963]
3415 University Ave.
Saint Paul, MN 55114

Gailey, Patty, Corr. Sec.
Pembroke Welsh Corgi Club of
    America [21943]
c/o Patty Gailey, Secretary
94 South 250 East
Blackfoot, ID 83221-5982
Ph: (208)782-2510

Gaillard, Ulrick, JD, CEO, Founder
Batey Relief Alliance [12627]
PO Box 300565
Brooklyn, NY 11230-5656
Ph: (917)627-5026

Gaine, P. Courtney, Act. Pres., CEO
Sugar Association [1374]
1300 L St. NW, Ste. 1001
Washington, DC 20005
Ph: (202)785-1122
Fax: (202)785-5019

Gaines, Barry, Administrator
American Theatre Critics Association
    [10240]
12809 Northern Sky NE
Albuquerque, NM 87111-8089
Ph: (505)856-2101

Gaines, Clem, Chmn. of the Bd.
Air Force Public Affairs Alumni As-
    sociation [5585]
PO Box 447
Locust Grove, VA 22508-0447

Gaines, Sheryl, President
Spanish Water Dog Club of America
    [21965]
308 Granite Rd.
Guilford, CT 06437-4318

Gainey, Cheryl A., Exec. Dir.,
    Founder
SISTAS [13397]
PO Box 2845
Vacaville, CA 95687-9998
Ph: (707)317-9478
Toll Free: 888-SISTAS-8

Gainey, Judy, Officer
Navy Club of the United States of
    America Auxiliary [5617]
c/o Andrew Murphy, Liason Officer
194 Lepore Dr.
Lancaster, PA 17602-2646
Ph: (717)392-4479

Gaither, Commissioner Israel L.,
    Cmdr.
Salvation Army [13087]
615 Slaters Ln.
Alexandria, VA 22314-1112
Toll Free: 800-728-7825

Gaither, James, ThD, President
International Society for the Study of
    Subtle Energies and Energy
    Medicine [7661]
PO Box 297
Bolivar, MO 65613
Toll Free: 888-272-6109
Fax: (417)777-7711

Gaither, Kathy, Founder, President
Juvenile Scleroderma Network, Inc.
    [17180]
1204 W 13th St.
San Pedro, CA 90731
Ph: (310)519-9511
Toll Free: 866-338-5892

Gajano, Jean, Exec. Dir.
New Eyes for the Needy [12293]
549 Millburn Ave.

Short Hills, NJ 07078-3330
Ph: (973)376-4903

Gajdosik, Stephen, President
Catholic Radio Association [19814]
PO Box 172051
Spartanburg, SC 29301
Ph: (864)438-4801
Fax: (509)479-1186

Galaher, Bob, Exec. Dir., CEO
National Association of Presort Mail-
    ers [2119]
c/o Bob Galaher, Executive Director
PO Box 3552
Annapolis, MD 21403-3552
Toll Free: 877-620-6276

Galat, Joe, President
American Youth Football and Cheer
    [22855]
1000 S Point Dr., TH-9
Miami Beach, FL 33139
Toll Free: 800-622-7370

Galbraith, James K., Chairman
Economists for Peace and Security
    [18127]
PO Box 5000
Annandale on Hudson, NY 12504-
    5000
Ph: (845)758-0917
Fax: (845)758-1149

Galbreath, Dana, Convention Mgr.
Japan Convention Bureau [23643]
1 Grand Central Pl.
60 E 42nd St., Ste. 448
New York, NY 10165
Ph: (212)757-5640
Fax: (212)307-6754

Galbreth, Alan, President
Association of Official Seed Certify-
    ing Agencies [4946]
1601 52nd Ave., Ste. 1
Moline, IL 61265
Ph: (309)736-0120
Fax: (309)736-0115

Galderisi, Silvana, MD, President
EEG and Clinical Neuroscience
    Society [16046]
East Tennessee State University
Department of Psychology
807 University Pkwy.
Johnson City, TN 37614
Toll Free: 888-531-5335
Fax: (888)531-5335

Gale, Bonnie, Founder
American Willow Growers Network
    [4727]
412 County Rd. 31
Norwich, NY 13815-3149
Ph: (607)336-9031
Fax: (607)336-9031

Gale, Sid, Secretary, Treasurer
Love Token Society [22273]
c/o Sid Gale, Secretary & Treasurer
PO Box 2351
Denham Springs, LA 70727
Ph: (225)664-0718

Galea, Joe, Chairman
National Coalition of Associations of
    7-Eleven Franchisees [1462]
740 Front St., Ste. 170
Santa Cruz, CA 95060
Ph: (831)426-4711
Fax: (831)426-4713

Galedo, Lillian, Exec. Dir.
Filipino Advocates for Justice
    [17896]
310 8th St., Ste. 308
Oakland, CA 94607
Ph: (510)465-9876

Galignano, Fr. Eugenio, President
Militia of the Immaculata Movement
    [19862]
1600 W Park Ave.
Libertyville, IL 60048
Ph: (847)367-7800

Galindo, Lorena, XI, President
Gamma Alpha Omega [23873]
PO Box 427
Tempe, AZ 85280

Galinsky, Ellen, Founder, President
Families and Work Institute [11817]
245 5th Ave., Ste. 1002
New York, NY 10016
Ph: (212)465-2044
Fax: (212)465-8637

Gallagher, Brian, Exec. Dir.
Reach Out and Read [8489]
89 South St., Ste. 201
Boston, MA 02111
Ph: (617)455-0600
Fax: (617)455-0601

Gallagher, Christopher, Exec. Dir.,
    Director
French-American Chamber of Com-
    merce [23587]
1375 Broadway, Ste. 504
New York, NY 10018
Ph: (212)867-0123
Fax: (212)867-9050

Gallagher, Edward P., CEO,
    President
The American-Scandinavian Founda-
    tion [10199]
58 Park Ave. 38th St.
New York, NY 10016
Ph: (212)779-3587
    (212)847-9716

Gallagher, Kevin, Founder
Allergic To Hunger [10847]
244 Del Gado Rd.
San Clemente, CA 92672

Gallagher, Michael D., President,
    CEO
Entertainment Software Association
    [6274]
575 7th St. NW, Ste. 300
Washington, DC 20004

Gallagher, Patrick, President
Yuki Teikei Haiku Society [10162]
c/o Toni Homan, Membership
    Secretary
9457 Mereoak Cir.
Elk Grove, CA 95758

Gallaher, Ann, COO
Technology First [1810]
714 E Monument Ave., Ste. 106
Dayton, OH 45402
Ph: (937)229-0054

Gallanis, Peter G., President
National Organization of Life and
    Health Insurance Guaranty As-
    sociations [1593]
13873 Park Center Rd., Ste. 329
Herndon, VA 20171-3247
Ph: (703)481-5206
Fax: (703)481-5209

Gallant, Alison, President
International Polymer Clay Associa-
    tion [22152]
162 Lake St.
Haverhill, MA 01832

Gallardo, Abel, President
Gold Wing Road Riders Association
    [22221]
21423 N 11th Ave.

Phoenix, AZ 85027-2813
Ph: (623)581-2500
Toll Free: 800-843-9460
Fax: (877)348-9416

Gallardo, Jennifer, President
MamaBaby Haiti [14235]
PO Box 3061
Newberg, OR 97132

Gallegos, Mr. Al, President
National Association of Hispanic
Federal Executives [5198]
PO Box 23270
Washington, DC 20026
Ph: (202)315-3942

Galletly, Pete, President
Casket and Funeral Supply Associa-
tion of America [2400]
49 Sherwood Ter., Ste. Y
Lake Bluff, IL 60044
Ph: (847)295-6630
Fax: (847)295-6647

Galletta, Salvatore, PE, Chairperson
American Engineering Alliance
[6529]
Bowling Green Sta.
New York, NY 10004-1415
Ph: (212)606-4053

Galli, Marlo, C.O, Secretary
American Association of Certified
Orthoptists [16362]
655 Beach St.
San Francisco, CA 94109
Ph: (415)561-8522
Fax: (415)561-8531

Galligan, Catherine, MS, Mgr.
Sustainable Hospitals Project
[15338]
Lowell Center for Sustainable
Production
1 University Ave.
Lowell, MA 01854
Ph: (978)934-3386
Fax: (978)452-5711

Galligan-Stierle, Michael, PhD, CEO,
President
Association of Catholic Colleges and
Universities [7573]
1 Dupont Cir. NW, Ste. 650
Washington, DC 20036
Ph: (202)457-0650
Fax: (202)728-0977

Gallinati, Janet, President
Parents Without Partners, Inc.
[12424]
1100-H Brandywine Blvd.
Zanesville, OH 43701-7303
Toll Free: 800-637-7974
Fax: (740)452-2552

Gallinetti, Jon, Deputy
Marine Corps Aviation Association
[5569]
715 Broadway St.
Quantico, VA 22134
Ph: (703)630-1903
Toll Free: 800-280-3001
Fax: (703)630-2713

Gallivan, Elysia Balster, Exec. Dir.
Alpha Xi Delta Women's Fraternity
[23948]
8702 Founders Rd.
Indianapolis, IN 46268
Ph: (317)872-3500
Fax: (317)872-2947

Gallo, Ernie, President
USS Liberty Veterans Association
[21069]
PO Box 680275

Marietta, GA 30068

Gallo, Fred P., PhD, DCEP,
President
Association for Comprehensive
Energy Psychology [16902]
233 E Lancaster Ave., Ste. 104
Ardmore, PA 19003
Ph: (619)861-2237
Fax: (484)418-1019

Gallo, Maria, President
American Peanut Research and
Education Society [4507]
PO Box 15825
College Station, TX 77841
Ph: (979)845-8278
    (229)329-2949

Galloway, Alan, VP
National Association of County
Agricultural Agents [4948]
6584 W Duroc Rd.
Maroa, IL 61756
Ph: (217)794-3700
Fax: (217)794-5901

Galloway, Libba, Exec. Dir.
Professional Association of Athlete
Development Specialists [22517]
41 Crossroads Plz., No. 127
West Hartford, CT 06117

Galloway, Mozella, Founder,
President
National Black Herstory Task Force
[10307]
PO Box 55021
Atlanta, GA 30308
Ph: (404)749-6994

Galloway, Pat, President
National Ice Cream Mix Association
[1703]
2101 Wilson Blvd., Ste. 400
Arlington, VA 22201
Ph: (703)243-5630
Fax: (703)841-9328

Galm, Amy, President, Exec. Dir.
Craniosynostosis and Positional Pla-
giocephaly Support [14333]
208 NY-190 No. 205
Farmingdale, NY 11735
Toll Free: 888-572-5526

Galpin, Shannon, President,
Founder
Mountain2Mountain [11404]
PO Box 7399
Breckenridge, CO 80424
Ph: (970)376-0754

Galves, Albert, Ph.D., Director
International Society for Ethical
Psychology and Psychiatry [16830]
5884 Joshua Pl.
Welcome, MD 20693

Galvin, Dale, Managing Dir.
RARE [4498]
1310 N Courthouse Rd., Ste. 110
Arlington, VA 22201
Ph: (703)522-5070
Fax: (703)522-5027

Galvin, Mike, President
Ductile Iron Society [6843]
15400 Pearl Rd., Ste. 238
Strongsville, OH 44136
Ph: (440)665-3686
Fax: (440)878-0070

Galyen, Cindy, Director
Morse Telegraph Club, Inc. [22442]
PO Box 192
Buchanan, MI 49107
Ph: (269)548-8219

Gambert, Mitch, President
Custom Tailors and Designers As-
sociation [202]
229 Forest Hills Rd.
Rochester, NY 14625
Toll Free: 888-248-2832
Fax: (866)661-1240

Gambill, Brenda, Director
American Silkie Bantam Club [4564]
c/o Carina Moncrief, Secretary/
Treasurer, 23754 Spenser Butte
Dr.
23754 Spenser Butte Dr.
Perris, CA 92570
Ph: (951)240-2939

Gambill, Kathy, Mem.
Clan Carmichael U.S.A. [20801]
c/o Benjamin DeRosia, Membership
Chairman
333 Clarine Dr.
Goose Creek, SC 29445

Gamble, Chuck, Secretary,
Treasurer
Farm Show Council [3563]
c/o Chuck Gamble, Secretary-
Treasurer
232 Ag Engineering Bldg.
590 Woody Hayes Dr.
Columbus, OH 43210
Ph: (614)292-4278
Fax: (614)292-9448

Gambs, Edwin P., President
James A. Michener Society [9064]
c/o Kay A. Ferrell, Treasurer
1536 - 12th Ave.
Greeley, CO 80631-4734

Gambuzza, Frank, President
Intercoiffure America/Canada [920]
1645 Downtown W Blvd.
Knoxville, TN 37919
Toll Free: 800-442-3007

Gamelli, Richard L., Contact
International Society for Burn Injuries
[13863]
584 Arbor View
Adkins, TX 78101

Gamlin, Karen, Contact
Philip Boileau Collectors' Society
[21303]
1025 Redwood Blvd.
Redding, CA 96003-1905

Gammad, Engelberto, President
National Association of Filipino
Priests - USA [19869]
c/o Rev. Engelberto Gammad
1150 N First St.
San Jose, CA 95112

Gammel, C. David, CAE, Exec. Dir.
Entomological Society of America
[6612]
3 Park Pl., Ste. 307
Annapolis, MD 21401-3722
Ph: (301)731-4535
Fax: (301)731-4538

Gammonley, Kevin, Exec. VP
North American Association of Floor
Covering Distributors [565]
330 N Wabash Ave., Ste. 2000
Chicago, IL 60611-4267
Ph: (312)321-6836
Toll Free: 800-383-3091
Fax: (312)673-6962

Gammonley, Kevin, Executive Vice
President
North American Building Material
Distribution Association [566]
330 N Wabash Ave., Ste. 2000

Chicago, IL 60611
Ph: (312)321-6845
Toll Free: 888-747-7862
Fax: (312)644-0310

Gamse, Roy, Act. Pres.
Youth Venture [13490]
1700 N Moore St., Ste. 2000
Arlington, VA 22209
Ph: (703)527-8300
Fax: (703)527-8383

Gan, Barry, Exec. Dir.
Concerned Philosophers for Peace
[10084]
c/o Arnold Farr
1415 Patterson Office Twr.
Department of Philosophy
University of Kentucky
Lexington, KY 40506-0027

Ganapathy-Coleman, Hemalatha,
President
Society for Cross-Cultural Research
[9583]
c/o Lisa Oliver, Treasurer
Dept. of Counselor Education
San Jose State University
Sweeney Hall 420
San Jose, CA 95192

Gandorf, Jim, CAE, CEO, Exec. Dir.
Child Life Council [14174]
1820 N Fort Myer Dr., Ste. 520
Arlington, VA 22209
Ph: (571)483-4500
Toll Free: 800-252-4515
Fax: (571)483-4482

Gandy, Edith, 1st VP
North American Peruvian Horse As-
sociation [4394]
PO Box 2187
Santa Rosa, CA 95405
Ph: (707)544-5807

Gandy, Kim A., President, CEO
National Network to End Domestic
Violence [11710]
1400 16th St. NW, Ste. 330
Washington, DC 20036
Ph: (202)543-5566
Fax: (202)543-5626

Gangone, Angelo, CEM, Exec. VP
Association of Woodworking and
Furnishings Suppliers [1475]
2400 E Katella Ave., Ste. 340
Anaheim, CA 92806-5963
Ph: (323)838-9440
Toll Free: 800-946-2937
Fax: (323)838-9443

Gangone, Lynn, VP
American Council on Education -
Inclusive Excellence Group [8745]
1 Dupont Cir. NW
Washington, DC 20036
Ph: (202)939-9390

Gangone, Lynn, Director
Women's College Coalition [8761]
PO Box 3983
Decatur, GA 30031
Ph: (404)913-9492

Gann, Carl, Founder, President
Orphans Africa [11421]
2612 N 8th St.
Tacoma, WA 98406-7207
Ph: (253)252-3544

Gannon, Christa, CEO, Founder
Fresh Lifelines for Youth [13444]
568 Valley Way
Milpitas, CA 95035
Ph: (408)263-2630
Fax: (408)263-2631

Gannon, James, Exec. Dir., Secretary, Treasurer
Japan Center for International Exchange USA [18549]
135 W 29th St., Rm. 303
New York, NY 10001
Ph: (212)679-4130

Gannon, John L., Exec. Dir.
International Association for Correctional and Forensic Psychology [11530]
897 Oak Park Blvd., No. 124
Pismo Beach, CA 93449-3293
Ph: (910)799-9107

Gano, Geneva, President
Robinson Jeffers Association [10395]
c/o Charles Rodewald, Treasurer
5140 Cutty Way
Las Vegas, NV 89130

Gantenberg, James B., Exec. Dir., CEO
American Society of Neuroradiology [17048]
800 Enterprise Dr., Ste. 205
Oak Brook, IL 60523
Ph: (630)574-0220
Fax: (630)574-0661

Gantenberg, James, Exec. Dir.
World Federation of Neuroradiological Societies [17075]
c/o James B Gantenberg, Executive Director
800 Enterprise Dr., Ste. 205
Oak Brook, IL 60523
Ph: (630)574-0220
Fax: (630)574-0661

Gantzer, Mary Lou, PhD, Contact
Clinical and Laboratory Standards Institute [15518]
950 W Valley Rd., Ste. 2500
Wayne, PA 19087
Ph: (610)688-0100
Toll Free: 877-447-1888
Fax: (610)688-0700

Ganulin, Stewart, Director
Hope for Sderot [12675]
303 Gurley St., Ste. 240
Prescott, AZ 86301
Ph: (530)918-4929

Ganz, Jim, President
Print Council of America [8882]
Fine Arts Museums of San Francisco
Legion of Honor
100 34th Ave.
San Francisco, CA 94121-1677

Ganz, Patricia, Co-Ch.
Cancer Quality Alliance [13928]
2318 Mill Rd., Ste. 800
Alexandria, VA 22314
Ph: (571)483-1300

Ganzi, Marc, Chmn. of the Bd.
PCIA - The Wireless Infrastucture Association [3236]
500 Montgomery St., Ste. 500
Alexandria, VA 22314
Ph: (703)535-7492
Fax: (703)836-1608

Garbharran, Hari, Founder, Chairman
Humans in Crisis International Corporation [12678]
9417 NW 39th Pl.
Sunrise, FL 33351
Ph: (615)305-5796

Garbini, Robert A., PE, President
National Ready Mixed Concrete Association [793]

900 Spring St.
Silver Spring, MD 20910
Ph: (301)587-1400

Garbini, Robert, Exec. Sec.
Truck Mixer Manufacturers Bureau [333]
900 Spring St.
Silver Spring, MD 20910
Ph: (301)587-1400

Garced, Rick, DVS, CEO, President
United States Sommelier Association, Inc. [192]
1111 Lincoln Rd., Ste. 400
Miami Beach, FL 33139
Ph: (786)497-1854
    (954)437-0449

Garcia, Alex, Secretary
National Pan-American Junior Golf Association [22888]
1700 Seaspray, Ste. 1213
1700 Seaspray, No. 1213
Houston, TX 77008
Ph: (713)862-1911

Garcia, Alex, Secretary, Treasurer
Transport Workers Union of America [23527]
501 3rd St. NW, 9th Fl.
Washington, DC 20001
Ph: (202)719-3900
Fax: (202)347-0454

Garcia Granados, Aracely, Exec. Dir.
Mexicans and Americans Thinking Together [1965]
329 Old Guilbeau St.
San Antonio, TX 78204
Ph: (210)270-0300

Garcia, Helio Fred, Chairman
Interfaith Alliance [20542]
1250 24th St. NW, Ste. 300
Washington, DC 20037
Ph: (202)466-0567
    (202)466-0520

Garcia, Joe, Secretary
National Association of Hispanic Firefighters [5211]
PO Box 225037
Dallas, TX 75222-5037
Ph: (972)814-6766

Garcia, Joey, President
Rise Up Belize! [7814]
PO Box 19841
Sacramento, CA 95819-0841

Garcia, Luis Manuel, Dir. of Fin.
Action Against Hunger [12075]
1 Whitehall St., 2nd Fl.
New York, NY 10004
Ph: (212)967-7800
Toll Free: 877-777-1420
Fax: (212)967-5480

Garcia, Magda, VP of Fin.
Society for the Study of American Women Writers [10401]
c/o Heidi Hanrahan, Vice President
PO Box 5000
Dept. of English
Shepherd University
Shepherdstown, WV 25443-5000

Garcia, Miguel A., Jr., President, CEO
National Urban Fellows [19218]
1120 Avenue of the Americas, 4th Fl.
New York, NY 10036
Ph: (212)730-1700
Fax: (212)730-1823

Garcia, Nikki Atwell, Director
American Warmblood Society [4332]
PO Box 1561

Higley, AZ 85236
Ph: (480)251-0348
Fax: (520)568-3318

Garcia, Rodrigo, Chmn. of the Bd.
Student Veterans of America [21140]
1012 14th St. NW, 2nd Fl.
Washington, DC 20005
Ph: (202)223-4710

Garcia, Sylvia, 1st VP
Society of Professional Women in Petroleum [2538]

Garcia, Vicente M., President
U.S. ICE Hispanic Agents Association [5295]
10 Causeway St.
Boston, MA 02114

Garcia-Alonso, Monica, Secretary
International Society for Biosafety Research [6089]
c/o ILSI Research Foundation
1156 15th St. NW, Ste. 200
Washington, DC 20005-1743

Gardner, Benton, President
Sewn Products Equipment and Suppliers of the Americas [1767]
9650 Strickland Rd., Ste. 103-324
Raleigh, NC 27615-1902
Ph: (919)872-8909
Fax: (919)872-1915

Gardner, Bill, President
Council on International Nontheatrical Events [9304]
1003 K St. NW, Ste. 208
Washington, DC 20001
Ph: (507)400-2463

Gardner, Bob, Exec. Dir.
NFHS Speech, Debate and Theatre Association [8601]
PO Box 690
Indianapolis, IN 46206
Ph: (317)972-6900
Fax: (317)822-5700

Gardner, Bob, Exec. Dir.
NFHS Spirit Association [22737]
National Federation of State High School Associations
PO Box 690
Indianapolis, IN 46206
Ph: (317)972-6900
Fax: (317)822-5700

Gardner, Cecilia L., Esq., CEO, Gen. Counsel, President
Jewelers Vigilance Committee [2054]
801 2nd Ave., Ste. 303
New York, NY 10017
Ph: (212)997-2002
Fax: (212)997-9148

Gardner, Chris, Exec. Dir.
AASA Technology Council [63]
10 Laboratory Dr.
Research Triangle Park, NC 27709
Ph: (919)406-8830

Gardner, Christine, Exec. Sec., Treasurer
International Vocational Education and Training Association [8738]
186 Wedgewood Dr.
Mahtomedi, MN 55115-2702
Ph: (651)770-6719

Gardner, Dallas, Chmn. of the Bd.
National Hot Rod Association [22528]
2035 Financial Way
Glendora, CA 91741
Ph: (626)914-4761
Fax: (626)963-5360

Gardner, David, President
Nationwide Insurance Independent Contractors Association [1913]
c/o Bob McLean, Executive Director
PO Box 3146
Norfolk, VA 23514-3146
Ph: (703)416-4422
Fax: (703)416-0014

Gardner, Deborah Dushku, Founder, President
One Heart Bulgaria [11106]
165 N Main St.
Providence, UT 84332
Ph: (435)764-3093

Gardner, Mr. Den, Exec. Dir.
Agricultural Relations Council [2751]
605 Columbus Ave. S
New Prague, MN 56071
Ph: (952)758-5811
Fax: (952)758-5813

Gardner, Den, Exec. Dir.
American Agricultural Editors' Association [2646]
PO Box 156
New Prague, MN 56071
Ph: (952)758-6502
Fax: (952)758-5813

Gardner, Den, Exec. Dir.
NMC [17656]
421 S Nine Mound Rd.
Verona, WI 53593
Ph: (608)848-4615
Fax: (608)848-4671

Gardner, Ms. Jackie, Exec. Dir.
Vitiligo Support International [14515]
PO Box 3565
Lynchburg, VA 24503-0565
Ph: (434)326-5380

Gardner, James R., PhD, Chairman
The Neuropathy Association, Inc. [16031]
60 E 42nd St., Ste. 942
New York, NY 10165
Ph: (212)692-0662
Fax: (212)692-0668

Gardner, Jerry, Exec. Dir.
Tribal Court Clearinghouse [5448]
8235 Santa Monica Blvd., Ste. 211
West Hollywood, CA 90046
Ph: (323)650-5467
Fax: (323)650-8149

Gardner, Keith, Chairman
Geosynthetics Materials Association [6222]
1801 County Road B W
Roseville, MN 55113-4061
Ph: (651)225-6920

Gardner, Kenneth, Director
Council of Supplier Diversity Professionals [681]
PO Box 70226
Rochester, MI 48307-0005

Gardner, Kent, Secretary
Governmental Research Association [18981]
c/o Center for Governmental Research
1 S Washington St., Ste. 400
Rochester, NY 14614
Ph: (205)870-2482
    (205)726-2482
Fax: (205)726-2900

Gardner, Page S., Founder, President
Voter Participation Center [19246]
1707 L St. NW, Ste. 300
Washington, DC 20036
Ph: (202)659-9570
Fax: (202)659-9585

Gardner, Scott, President
International Hot Rod Association
[22524]
300 Cleveland Rd.
Norwalk, OH 44857
Ph: (419)663-6666
Fax: (419)663-4472

Gardner, Tim, Chmn. of the Bd.
Ford Owners' Association [21384]
3875 Thornhill Dr.
Lilburn, GA 30047

Gardner-Huggett, Joanna, Secretary
Radical Art Caucus [8884]
Dept. of Art and Art History
Depaul University
1150 W Fullerton Ave.
Chicago, IL 60614
Ph: (773)325-4890

Garello, Rene, President
IEEE - Oceanic Engineering Society
[6940]
c/o Stephen Holt, Web Administrator
National Aeronotics and Space
Administration
Code 444 Bldg. 3, Rm. 144
8800 Greenbelt Rd.
Greenbelt, MD 20771

Garfield, Dean, CEO, President
Information Technology Industry
Council [6317]
1101 K St. NW, Ste. 610
Washington, DC 20005
Ph: (202)737-8888
Fax: (202)638-4922

Garfield, Jason, Founder, President
World Juggling Federation [22969]
7511 Greenwood Ave. N, No. 315
Seattle, WA 98103

Garfinkle, Suzy, President, Founder
Prepare Tomorrow's Parents [13475]
454 NE 3rd St.
Boca Raton, FL 33432
Ph: (561)620-0256
Fax: (561)391-9711

Gargan, Lynda, Exec. Dir.
National Federation of Families for
Children's Mental Health [12309]
15883 Crabbs Branch Way
Rockville, MD 20855-2635
Ph: (240)403-1901
Fax: (240)403-1909

Gargano, Ray, President
International Performing Arts for
Youth [10067]
c/o CultureWorks
The Philadelphia Bldg.
1315 Walnut St., Ste. 320
Philadelphia, PA 19107
Ph: (267)690-1325
Fax: (267)519-3343

Garicoche, Tamara, Administrator
OAS Staff Association [23487]
1889 F St. NW, No. 622
Washington, DC 20006
Ph: (202)370-4643
   (202)370-4645

Garland, Jerry, Chairman
Food Marketing Institute [2954]
2345 Crystal Dr., Ste. 800
Arlington, VA 22202
Ph: (202)452-8444
Fax: (202)429-4519

Garland, Kristine, Exec. VP
Composite Can and Tube Institute
[830]
50 S Pickett St., Ste. 110
Alexandria, VA 22304-7206
Ph: (703)823-7234
Fax: (703)823-7237

Garland, Tracy, Secretary
National Association of Health
Services Executives [14950]
1050 Connecticut Ave. NW, 10th Fl.
Washington, DC 20036
Ph: (202)772-1030
Fax: (202)772-1072

Garlick, Saul, Founder
ThinkImpact [12190]
50 S Steele St., No. 328
Denver, CO 80209
Ph: (303)377-3776

Garlitz, Lois Ann, Dep. Chief
American Clan Gregor Society
[20779]
c/o Jeanne Lehr, Registrar
11 Ballas Ct.
Saint Louis, MO 63131-3038
Ph: (801)899-6157
   (314)432-2842

Garmo, Nidhal, Founder
One World Medical Mission [12295]
PO Box 2784
Farmington Hills, MI 48333

Garmon, Ann, President
Combined Council of America's
Credit Unions [947]
7101 E 56th St.
Indianapolis, IN 46226

Garnant, Beverly, Exec. Dir.
American Society of Concrete
Contractors [850]
2025 S Brentwood Blvd., Ste. 105
Saint Louis, MO 63144
Ph: (314)962-0210
Toll Free: 866-788-2722
Fax: (314)968-4367

Garnar, Martin, VP
Freedom to Read Foundation
[17836]
50 E Huron St.
Chicago, IL 60611
Ph: (312)280-4226
Toll Free: 800-545-2433

Garner, Aaron, Exec. Dir.
Corrections Technology Association
[18070]
c/o Conference Management Solutions, Inc.
1732 Copperfield Cir.
Tallahassee, FL 32312

Garner, Christina, President
National Hair Society [1586]
1672 Van Dorn St.
Lincoln, NE 68502
Ph: (402)302-0822

Garner, Jac B., Director
Book Manufacturers' Institute [1530]
PO Box 731388
Ormond Beach, FL 32173
Ph: (386)986-4552
Fax: (386)986-4553

Garner, Ken, COO, President
Epicomm [94]
1800 Diagonal Rd., Ste. 320
Alexandria, VA 22314-2806
Ph: (703)836-9200
Fax: (703)548-8204

Garner, Ken, President
Optimist International [12903]
4494 Lindell Blvd.
Saint Louis, MO 63108-2404
Ph: (314)371-6000
Toll Free: 800-500-8130
Fax: (314)735-4100

Garner, Margaret, President
Sacred Cat of Burma Fanciers
[21573]

c/o Kent Thompson, Secretary
5395 Ridge Ave. SW
East Sparta, OH 44626-2332
Ph: (330)484-4739

Garner, Mitchell, President
Road Runners Club of America
[23119]
1501 Lee Hwy., Ste. 140
Arlington, VA 22209
Ph: (703)525-3890

Garner, Takeia, Dir. of Member Svcs.
Taxpayers Against Fraud Education
Fund [19176]
1220 19th St. NW, Ste. 501
Washington, DC 20036-2497
Ph: (202)296-4826

Garner, Wanda L., Exec. Dir.
American Mathematical Association
of Two-Year Colleges [8275]
Southwest Tennessee Community
College
5983 Macon Cove
Memphis, TN 38134
Ph: (901)333-5643

Garnett, Justin, Treasurer
World Atlatl Association [22173]
c/o Justin Garnett, Executive
Treasurer
905 E 76th Ter.
Kansas City, MO 64131

Garnett, Terry W., Officer
Association of Civilian Technicians
[23428]
12620 Lake Ridge Dr.
Woodbridge, VA 22192
Ph: (703)494-4845
Fax: (703)494-0961

Garon, Philip S., Exec. Dir.
United States Law Firm Group
[5052]
c/o Philip S. Garon, Executive Director
2200 Wells Fargo Ctr.
90 S 7th St.
Minneapolis, MN 55402
Ph: (612)766-8101

Garoufalis, Leon, V. Chmn. of the
Bd.
American Composites Manufacturers
Association [489]
3033 Wilson Blvd., Ste. 420
Arlington, VA 22201-3843
Ph: (703)525-0511
Fax: (703)525-0743

Garoza, Ilze, Secretary
World Federation of Free Latvians
[18299]
400 Hurley Ave.
Rockville, MD 20850
Ph: (301)340-7646

Garrett, Betty, Contact
Caregivers4Cancer [13936]
PO Box 153448
Irving, TX 75015
Ph: (972)513-0668

Garrett, Deborah, President
Council for the Advancement of
Standards in Higher Education
[8613]
PO Box 1369
Fort Collins, CO 80522
Ph: (202)862-1400

Garrett, Robb, President
ADHD Coaches Organization
[15891]
701 Hunting Pl.
Baltimore, MD 21229
Toll Free: 888-638-3999
Fax: (410)630-6991

Garrett-Akinsanya, BraVada, PhD,
President
APA Division 35: Society for the
Psychology of Women [16882]
c/o APA Division Services
750 1st St. NE
Washington, DC 20002-4242
Ph: (202)336-6013
Fax: (202)218-3599

Garriott, Gale, Exec. Dir.
Federation of Tax Administrators
[5791]
444 N Capitol St. NW
Washington, DC 20001
Ph: (202)624-5890

Garrison, James, President
Checker Car Club of America
[21350]
Herndon, VA

Garrison, James, President
State of the World Forum [19266]
PO Box 29434
San Francisco, CA 94129
Ph: (415)561-2345
Fax: (415)561-2323

Garrison, Jenny, RN, President
Imagery International [15341]
1574 Coburg Rd., No. 555
Eugene, OR 97401-4802
Ph: (541)632-4197
   (514)938-6131
Toll Free: 866-494-9985

Garrity, Rose, President
National Coalition Against Domestic
Violence [11706]
1 Broadway, Ste. B210
Denver, CO 80203
Ph: (303)839-1852
Fax: (303)831-9251

Garst, Jennifer, Director
Adventure Cycling Association
[22743]
150 E Pine St.
Missoula, MT 59807
Ph: (406)721-1776
Toll Free: 800-755-2453
Fax: (406)721-8754

Gartell, Alice Finn, President
Books for a Better World [7745]
PO Box 9053
Phoenix, AZ 85068

Gartenfeld, Mr. Mark, Operations
Mgr.
National Senior Golf Association
[22889]
200 Perrine Rd., Ste. 201
Old Bridge, NJ 08857-2842
Toll Free: 800-282-6772
Fax: (732)525-9590

Gartley, Cheryle B., President,
Founder
Simon Foundation for Continence
[17556]
PO Box 815
Wilmette, IL 60091
Ph: (847)864-3913
Toll Free: 800-237-4666
Fax: (847)864-9758

Garton-Good, Julie, Founder,
President
National Association of Real Estate
Consultants [2877]
404 4th Ave.
Lewiston, ID 83501
Ph: (208)746-7963
Toll Free: 800-445-8543
Fax: (208)746-4760

Garvey, James, President
Association of Anglican Musicians
[20486]

PO Box 7530
Little Rock, AR 72217
Ph: (501)661-9925
Fax: (501)661-9925

Garvin, Mark, President
Tree Care Industry Association
  [4735]
136 Harvey Rd., Ste. 101
Londonderry, NH 03053
Ph: (603)314-5380
Toll Free: 800-733-2622
Fax: (603)314-5386

Garvin, Peter, President
Association of Visual Packaging
  Manufacturers [2473]
PO Box 758
Glenview, IL 60025-0758
Ph: (224)330-7470

Garwin, Arthur H., Director
American Bar Association Center for
  Professional Responsibility [4982]
321 N Clark St.
Chicago, IL 60654
Ph: (312)988-5000
Toll Free: 800-988-2221

Gary, Denise, Exec. Dir.
Kids Need to Read [12247]
33 S Mesa Dr.
Mesa, AZ 85210
Ph: (480)256-0115

Garza, Anita, Founder
Painted Desert Sheep Society
  [4681]
11819 Puska Rd.
Needville, TX 77461
Ph: (979)793-4207

Garza, Beatrice G., President, CEO
Association for the Advancement of
  Mexican Americans [11316]
Bldg. E
6001 Gulf Fwy.
Houston, TX 77023-5423
Ph: (713)967-6700
Fax: (713)926-8035

Gasaway, Laura N., Secretary,
  Treasurer
The Order of the Coif [23789]
University of North Carolina
CB No. 3385
Chapel Hill, NC 27599-3385

Gascon, Dave, Director
U.S.A Team Handball [22538]
1 Olympic Plz.
Colorado Springs, CO 80909-5780
Ph: (719)866-2203

Gash, Dennis N., President
International Assembly for Collegiate
  Business Education [7551]
11374 Strang Line Rd.
Lenexa, KS 66215
Ph: (913)631-3009
Fax: (913)631-9154

Gash, Jen, Founder
Sweet Sleep [11163]
PO Box 40486
Nashville, TN 37204-9998
Ph: (615)730-7671

Gasior, Pawel, President
Polish American Golf Association
  [22890]
616 Manhattan Ave.
Brooklyn, NY 11222
Ph: (718)389-8536

Gaskins, H. Rex, PhD, Officer
Society for Experimental Biology and
  Medicine [6100]

3220 N St. NW, No. 179
Washington, DC 20007-2829
Ph: (201)962-3519
Fax: (201)962-3522

Gasparich, Gail, Treasurer
International Organization for Mycoplasmology [6084]
c/o Gail Gasparich, Treasurer
Towson University
8000 York Rd.
Towson, MD 21252

Gasparovic, Walt, Officer
National Association of Service
  Managers [3076]
PO Box 250796
Milwaukee, WI 53225-6512
Ph: (414)466-6060

Gass, Jennifer, MD, President
National Consortium of Breast
  Centers [13851]
PO Box 1334
Warsaw, IN 46581-1334
Ph: (574)267-8058
Fax: (574)267-8268

Gassman, Larry, President
Society to Preserve and Encourage
  Radio Drama, Variety and Comedy
  [22405]
PO Box 7
Alachua, FL 32616

Gaston, Diana, Director
Tamarind Institute [7948]
2500 Central Ave. SE
Albuquerque, NM 87106-3562
Ph: (505)277-3901
Fax: (505)277-3920

Gatacre, Jim, President
Handicapped Scuba Association
  [22781]
1104 El Prado
San Clemente, CA 92672-4637
Ph: (949)498-4540

Gathercoal, Allan, DD, Founder,
  President
Flying Doctors of America [12273]
212 W Ironwood Dr., Ste. D-129
Coeur d Alene, ID 83814
Ph: (404)273-8348

Gatlin, Marna, Founder, CEO
Parents Via Egg Donation Organiza-
  tion [14761]
PO Box 597
Scappoose, OR
Ph: (503)987-1433

Gattari, Lynn, Director
National Miniature Donkey Associa-
  tion [4461]
6450 Dewey Rd.
Rome, NY 13440-8006
Ph: (315)336-0154
Fax: (315)339-4414

Gatti, John, President
Society for Fetal Urology [17559]
1000 Corporate Blvd.
Linthicum, MD 21090
Ph: (410)689-3950
Fax: (410)689-3825

Gatti, Mike, Exec. Dir.
Retail Advertising and Marketing As-
  sociation [109]
325 7th St. NW, Ste. 1100
Washington, DC 20004-2818
Ph: (202)783-7971
Toll Free: 800-673-4692
Fax: (202)737-2849

Gatzke, Nick, VP
Evangelical Homiletics Society
  [20206]

130 Essex St.
South Hamilton, MA 01982-2325

Gaudette, Gary, Chairperson
National Association of Credit
  Management [1253]
8840 Columbia 100 Pky.
Columbia, MD 21045
Ph: (410)740-5560
Fax: (410)740-5574

Gaudino, James L., Chairman
Council for Higher Education Ac-
  creditation [7756]
1 Dupont Cir. NW, Ste. 510
Washington, DC 20036
Ph: (202)955-6126
Fax: (202)955-6129

Gauger, Meghan, Exec. Dir.
No Stomach for Cancer [14034]
PO Box 46070
Madison, WI 53711
Ph: (608)692-5141
Toll Free: 855-355-0241

Gault, Iain, President
Society of Professional Rope Access
  Technicians [1768]
994 Old Eagle School Rd., Ste.
  1019
Wayne, PA 19087-1866
Ph: (610)971-4850
Fax: (610)971-4859

Gault, Paul H., Secretary
China Stamp Society [22316]
c/o H. James Maxwell, President
1050 West Blue Ridge Blvd.
Kansas City, MO 64145-1216
Ph: (816)210-1234

Gaunt, Ron, Founder
National Association of Canine Scent
  Work [22817]
7510 Sunset Blvd., No. 1180
Los Angeles, CA 90046

Gauntt, Jim, Exec. Dir.
Railway Tie Association [2843]
115 Commerce Dr., Ste. C
Fayetteville, GA 30214-7335
Ph: (770)460-5553
Fax: (770)460-5573

Gaus, Dr. David, Exec. Dir., Founder
Andean Health and Development
  [15439]
UW Dept. of Family Medicine
1100 Delaplaine Ct.
Madison, WI 53715
Ph: (619)788-6833

Gauthier, Jean-Paul, Sec. Gen.
World Economic Processing Zones
  Association [3307]
3 Bullet Hill Rd.
Danbury, CT 06811-2906
Ph: (203)798-9394
Fax: (203)798-9394

Gautschy, Ms. Sharon, Exec. Dir.
American Association for the
  Surgery of Trauma [17523]
633 N St. Clair St., Ste. 2600
Chicago, IL 60611
Toll Free: 800-789-4006
Fax: (312)202-5064

Gauvry, Glenn, President
Ecological Research and Develop-
  ment Group [3851]
190 Main St.
Dover, DE 19901-4801
Ph: (302)236-5383

Gavilan, Horacio, CMP, Exec. Dir.
Association of Hispanic Advertising
  Agencies [88]

8280 Willow Oaks Corporate Dr.,
  Ste. 600
Fairfax, VA 22031
Ph: (703)745-5531

Gavula, Mark S., Exec. Dir.
U.S. Cavalry & Armor Association
  [5627]
3100 Gentian Blvd., Ste. 17B
Columbus, GA 31907
Ph: (706)563-5714

Gaydos, Dr. Charlotte, Reg. Dir.
International Union Against Sexually
  Transmitted Infections North
  America [17199]
c/o Charlotte A Gaydos, Regional
  Director
Division of Infectious Diseases
Johns Hopkins University
530 Rangos Bldg.
855 N Wolfe St.
Baltimore, MD 21205-1503
Ph: (410)614-0932
Fax: (410)614-9775

Gaye, Pape Amadou, President,
  CEO
IntraHealth International [15123]
6340 Quadrangle Dr., Ste. 200
Chapel Hill, NC 27517-7891
Ph: (919)313-9100
  (919)433-5720
Fax: (919)313-9108

Gaylinn, Daniel, Exec. Dir.
Association for Transpersonal
  Psychology [9532]
PO Box 50187
Palo Alto, CA 94303
Ph: (650)424-8764

Gaylord, Rick, President
United Abrasives Manufacturers' As-
  sociation [2307]
30200 Detroit Rd.
Cleveland, OH 44145-1967
Ph: (440)899-0010
Fax: (440)892-1404

Gaynor, Charlene F., CEO
Association of Educational Publish-
  ers [8452]
325 Chestnut St., Ste. 1110
Philadelphia, PA 19106
Ph: (267)351-4310
Fax: (267)351-4317

Gazi, Sarah, Exec. Dir.
National Limousine Association
  [3344]
49 S Maple Ave.
Marlton, NJ 08053
Ph: (856)596-3344
Toll Free: 800-652-7007
Fax: (856)596-2145

Gazzale, Bob, CEO, President
American Film Institute [9294]
2021 N Western Ave.
Los Angeles, CA 90027-1657
Ph: (323)856-7600
Toll Free: 800-774-4234
Fax: (323)467-4578

Ge, Yufeng, Treasurer
Association of Overseas Chinese
  Agricultural, Biological and Food
  Engineers [6547]
c/o Dr. Liangcheng Yang
Illinois State University
Dept. of Health Sciences
324 Felmley Hall Annex
Normal, IL 61790
Ph: (309)438-7133

Geacintov, Dr. Cyril E., President
Russian Nobility Association in
  America [20994]

c/o Roberta Maged
DRG International, Inc.
841 Mountain Ave.
Springfield, NJ 07081

Gearhart, Judy, Exec. Dir.
International Labor Rights Forum
[18610]
1634 I St. NW, No. 1001
Washington, DC 20006
Ph: (202)347-4100
Fax: (202)347-4885

Geary, Bill, Chairman
Cold Finished Steel Bar Institute
[2345]
Washington, DC
Ph: (708)735-8000
Toll Free: 800-323-2750
Fax: (708)735-8100

Geary, Michael V., CEO
Society for Marketing Professional
Services [2303]
123 N Pitt St., Ste. 400
Alexandria, VA 22314
Ph: (703)549-6117
Toll Free: 800-292-7677
Fax: (703)549-2498

Gebbia, Robert T., CEO
American Foundation for Suicide
Prevention [13192]
120 Wall St., 29th Fl.
New York, NY 10005
Ph: (212)363-3500
(212)826-3577
Toll Free: 888-333-AFSP
Fax: (212)363-6237

Gebeily, Joseph, MD, President
American Lebanese Coalition
[18633]
4900 Leesburg Pke., Ste. 203
Alexandria, VA 22302
Ph: (703)578-4214
Fax: (703)578-4615

Gebeily, Joseph, MD, President
Lebanese Information Center
[18686]
1101 Pennsylvania Ave. NW, Ste.
600
Washington, DC 20004
Ph: (202)505-4542
Fax: (202)318-8409

Gebre-Mariam, Zewge, Founder
Partners for Rural Improvement and
Development in Ethiopia [12806]
2828 Kenyon Cir.
Boulder, CO 80305
Ph: (303)543-0515

Gee, Betty, Officer
Asian/Pacific American Heritage As-
sociation [9025]
6220 Westpark, Ste. 245BC
Houston, TX 77057
Ph: (713)784-1112

Geffen, David I., OD, President
Optometric Council on Refractive
Technology [16434]
8910 University Center Ln., Ste. 800
San Diego, CA
Ph: (858)455-9950
Fax: (858)455-9954

Gehani, Dr. Chad P., Exec. Dir.
Indian Dental Association (USA)
[14441]
140 Tulip Ave.
Floral Park, NY 11001
Ph: (516)345-8261

Gehring, Ronette, President
American Academy of Veterinary
Pharmacology and Therapeutics
[17589]

PO Box 103
Timnath, CO 80547-0103

Geidel, Gwen, Secretary, Treasurer
Council of Environmental Deans and
Directors [7886]
National Council for Science and the
Environment
1101 17th St. NW, Ste. 250
Washington, DC 20036
Ph: (202)530-5810
Fax: (202)628-4311

Geier, Elizabeth, Exec. Dir.
Health Horizons International
[15468]
1 Regency Dr.
Bloomfield, CT 06002
Ph: (860)243-3977
Fax: (860)286-0787

Geiger, Angela, President, CEO
Autism Speaks [13757]
1 E 33rd St., 4th Fl.
New York, NY 10016
Ph: (212)252-8584
Fax: (212)252-8676

Geiger, Dr. Jo A., Exec. Dir.,
Founder
Adventures in Movement for the
Handicapped [17428]
945 Danbury Rd.
Dayton, OH 45420
Ph: (937)294-4611
Toll Free: 800-332-8210
Fax: (937)294-3783

Geigle, Ron, Contact
Diabetes Advocacy Alliance [14523]
Novo Nordisk Inc.
100 College Rd. W
Princeton, NJ 08540

Geisel, Ritchie, Chmn. of the Bd.
Heaven on Earth Society for Animals
[10636]
7342 Fulton Ave.
North Hollywood, CA 91605
Ph: (818)474-2700

Geiselman, Cullen, Chairman
Bat Conservation International
[4791]
PO Box 162603
Austin, TX 78716
Ph: (512)327-9721
Toll Free: 800-538-BATS

Geisler, Connie, President
American Vaulting Association
[23348]
1443 E Washington Blvd., No. 289
Pasadena, CA 91104
Ph: (323)654-0800
Fax: (323)654-4306

Gelfound, Craig, DC, President
Academy of Forensic and Industrial
Chiropractic Consultants [14248]
1629 W Avenue J, Ste. 101
Lancaster, CA 93534-2850
Ph: (661)942-2273
Fax: (661)274-1590

Gellatley, Juliet, Founder, President
Viva! USA [10713]
1123 Broadway, Ste. 912
New York, NY 10010
Ph: (212)989-8482
Fax: (212)627-6037

Geller, Eileen, President
True Compassion Advocates
[15300]
PO Box 27514
Seattle, WA 98165
Ph: (206)366-2715

Geller, Jeffrey, Director
World Federation for Mental Health
[15811]
PO Box 807
Occoquan, VA 22125
Fax: (703)490-6926

Geller, Laurence S., Chairman
Churchill Centre [10319]
c/o Lee Pollock, Executive Director
131 S Dearborn St., Ste. 1700
Chicago, IL 60603
Ph: (312)263-5637

Geller, Marilyn Grunzweig, CEO
Celiac Disease Foundation [14784]
20350 Ventura Blvd., Ste. 240
Woodland Hills, CA 91364
Ph: (818)716-1513
Fax: (818)267-5577

Geller, Sandra R., Exec. VP
Practising Law Institute [8224]
1177 Avenue of the Americas, 2nd
Fl.
New York, NY 10036
Ph: (212)824-5700
Toll Free: 800-260-4754

Geller, Stephanie, Ed.M,
Researcher, Director
Volunteers in Health Care [15069]
111 Brewster St.
Pawtucket, RI 02860
Toll Free: 877-844-8442

Gelormino, Anthony, President,
Comm. Chm.
World Federation of Therapeutic
Communities [13667]
54 W 40th St.
New York, NY 10018

Gendler, Tamar Szabo, President
Society for Philosophy and Psychol-
ogy [10127]
206 McMicken Hall
Dept. of Philosophy
University of Cincinnati
Cincinnati, OH 45221
Ph: (513)556-6324
Fax: (513)556-2939

Gendron, Heather, President
Art Libraries Society of North
America [9680]
7044 S 13th St.
Oak Creek, WI 53154
Ph: (734)764-3166
Toll Free: 800-817-0621

Genetti, Marianne, Exec. Dir.,
Founder
In Need of Diagnosis [15549]
PO Box 536456
Orlando, FL 32853-6456
Ph: (407)894-9190
Toll Free: 888-894-9190
Fax: (407)898-4234

Genheimer, Stephen R., Ph.D,
Chairman
American Leprosy Missions [15531]
1 Alm Way
Greenville, SC 29601
Toll Free: 800-543-3135
Fax: (866)881-9769

Genick, Michael J., Secretary
National Postal Forum [5682]
3998 Fair Ridge Dr., Ste. 150
Fairfax, VA 22033-2907
Ph: (703)218-5015
Fax: (703)218-5020

Geno, Beth, Exec. Dir.
Athletes with Disabilities Network
[22776]

2845 Crooks Rd.
Rochester Hills, MI 48309-3661
Ph: (248)829-8353

Genova, Gina, Exec. Dir., Gen. Mgr.
American Composers Alliance
[9855]
PO Box 1108
New York, NY 10040
Ph: (212)568-0036

Gentry, Jake, Founder, President
Orphans to Ambassadors [11119]
4742 42nd Ave. SW, No. 479
Seattle, WA 98116

Gentry, Marilyn, President
American Institute for Cancer
Research [13886]
1759 R St. NW
Washington, DC 20009
Ph: (202)328-7744
Toll Free: 800-843-8114
Fax: (202)328-7226

Geoffrey, Kevin, President
Messianic Jewish Movement
International [20339]
PO Box 41071
Phoenix, AZ 85080
Ph: (515)999-6564
Toll Free: 800-493-7482

George, David, Exec. Dir.
Water for Life International [13342]
514 Via de la Valle, Ste. 207
Solana Beach, CA 92075-2717
Ph: (858)509-9445
Fax: (858)509-0708

George, Joan, Contact
Egg Cup Collectors' Corner [21651]
c/o Joan George
67 Stevens Ave.
Old Bridge, NJ 08857

George, Melinda, President
National Commission on Teaching
and America's Future [8654]
1525 Wilson Blvd., Ste. 705
Arlington, VA 22209
Ph: (202)429-2570

George, Peter, Comm. Chm.
North American Rock Garden
Society [4271]
c/o Bobby J. Ward, Membership
Director
PO Box 18604
Raleigh, NC 27619-8604
Ph: (919)781-3291
(914)762-2948

George, Peter, Comm. Chm.
North American Rock Garden
Society [22118]
c/o Bobby J. Ward, Membership
Director
PO Box 18604
Raleigh, NC 27619-8604
Ph: (919)781-3291
(914)762-2948

George, Robley Evans, Director
Center for the Study of Democratic
Societies [18093]
PO Box 475
Manhattan Beach, CA 90267-0475

Georgitis, Nathan, Exec. Dir.
Association for Recorded Sound
Collections [9688]
c/o Nathan Georgitis, Executive
Director
Knight Library
1299 University of Oregon
Eugene, OR 97403-1299

Gephart, George W., Jr., CEO,
President
Academy of Natural Sciences of
Drexel University [6891]

1900 Benjamin Franklin Pky.
Philadelphia, PA 19103
Ph: (215)299-1000

Geraci, Joseph J., President
Postal History Society [22356]
c/o Joseph J. Geraci, President
PO Box 4129
Merrifield, VA 22116-4129

Gerard, Jack, President, CEO
American Petroleum Institute [2511]
1220 L St. NW
Washington, DC 20005
Ph: (202)682-8000

Gerard, Dr. Jason, President, CEO
ChiroMission, Inc. [14259]
255 Highway 97, Ste. 2A
Forest Lake, MN 55025

Gerard, Leo W., President
United Steelworkers [23482]
60 Boulevard of the Allies
Pittsburgh, PA 15222-1214
Ph: (412)562-2400
Fax: (412)562-2445

Gerbasi, Francis, PhD, Exec. Dir.
Council on Accreditation of Nurse
  Anesthesia Educational Programs
  [8296]
222 S Prospect Ave.
Park Ridge, IL 60068-4001
Ph: (847)655-1160
Fax: (847)692-7137

Gerber, Bego, Founder, Chairman
Chemists Without Borders [12269]
745 S Bernardo Ave., No. A121
Sunnyvale, CA 94087-1051
Ph: (707)750-5945

Gerber, David J., President
American Society of Comparative
  Law [5348]
1420 N Charles St.
Baltimore, MD 21201
Ph: (410)837-4689
Fax: (410)837-4560

Gerber, Russ, Mgr.
Christian Science Publishing Society
  [2776]
210 Massachusetts Ave.
Boston, MA 02115
Ph: (617)450-2000

Gerdes, Jessica, President
National Association of State School
  Nurse Consultants [16155]
1181 Wyndham Hills Dr.
Lexington, KY 40514
Ph: (502)564-5279

Gere, Joanne, Exec. Dir.
BioPharma Research Council [6111]
1 Sheila Dr.
Tinton Falls, NJ 07724
Ph: (732)403-3137

Gere, Richard, Chairman
International Campaign for Tibet
  [19189]
1825 Jefferson Pl. NW
Washington, DC 20036
Ph: (202)785-1515
Fax: (202)785-4343

Gergen, Ann, Exec. Dir.
Association of Governmental Risk
  Pools [5311]
9 Cornell Rd.
Latham, NY 12110
Ph: (518)389-2782

Gerhardt, Charles H., III, Bd.
  Member
National Down Syndrome Society
  [15816]

666 Broadway, 8th Fl.
New York, NY 10012
Toll Free: 800-221-4602

Gerhardt, Dana, M.A., Contact
Mooncircles [20609]
c/o Dana Gerhardt, MA
397 Arnos St.
Talent, OR 97540

Gerhart, Mr. Thomas J., President,
  Bd. Member
Pennsylvania German Society
  [10065]
PO Box 118
Ephrata, PA 17522
Ph: (717)597-7940

Gerhke, Karissa, Director
Sierra Student Coalition [4013]
50 F St. NW, 8th Fl.
Washington, DC 20001
Ph: (202)547-1141
Fax: (202)547-6009

Gerl, Peter J., Exec. Dir.
Whitetails Unlimited [4899]
2100 Michigan St.
Sturgeon Bay, WI 54235
Ph: (920)743-6777
Toll Free: 800-274-5471
Fax: (920)743-4658

Gerlach, Alvin, President
AMOA National Dart Association
  [22767]
9100 Purdue Rd., Ste. 200
Indianapolis, IN 46268
Toll Free: 800-808-9884

Gerlinger, Col. Tad, MD, Rep.
The Society of Military Orthopaedic
  Surgeons [15841]
110 West Rd., Ste. 227
Towson, MD 21204
Toll Free: 866-494-1778
Fax: (410)494-0515

Germek, Paul, Contact
Suntanning Association for Educa-
  tion [2916]
c/o Paul Germek
PO Box 1181
Gulf Breeze, FL 32562
Ph: (850)939-3388
Toll Free: 800-536-8255
Fax: (801)348-9571

Geroni, Dr. Jennifer, Treasurer
International Mine Water Association
  [6880]
c/o Itasca Denver, Inc.
143 Union Blvd., Ste. 525
Lakewood, CO 80228
Ph: (303)969-8033

Gerow, John E., Exec. Dir.
American Murray Grey Association
  [3705]
PO Box 1222
Shelbyville, KY 40066
Ph: (502)384-2335
Toll Free: 866-571-2554

Gerritsen, Jim, President
Organic Seed Growers and Trade
  Association [4645]
PO Box 362
Washington, ME 04574
Ph: (207)809-7530

Gerry, Frank, President
Flying Scot Sailing Association
  [22613]
1 Windsor Cove, Ste. 305
Columbia, SC 29223
Ph: (803)252-5646

Gerry, Kristy, Director
International Newspaper Group
  [2688]
Ph: (770)263-3805

Gershanik, Oscar S., President
International Parkinson and Move-
  ment Disorder Society [15027]
555 E Wells St., Ste. 1100
Milwaukee, WI 53202-3823
Ph: (414)276-2145
Fax: (414)276-3349

Gershman, Carl, President
National Endowment for Democracy
  [18104]
1025 F St. NW, Ste. 800
Washington, DC 20004-1432
Ph: (202)378-9700
Fax: (202)378-9407

Gershoff, Jeff, Coord.
Narcotics Anonymous [13157]
PO Box 9999
Van Nuys, CA 91409
Ph: (818)773-9999
Fax: (818)700-0700

Gershwin, Dr. Laurel J., President
Conference of Research Workers in
  Animal Diseases [17644]
Ohio State University
Research Services Bldg., Rm. 209e
Wooster, OH 44691
Ph: (330)263-3703
Fax: (330)263-3688

Gerson, Charlotte, Founder
Gerson Institute [13625]
4631 Viewridge Ave.
San Diego, CA 92123
Ph: (858)694-0707
Toll Free: 888-443-7766
Fax: (858)694-0757

Gerstenberger, Richard, VP
American Sugarbeet Growers As-
  sociation [4694]
1156 15th St. NW, Ste. 1101
Washington, DC 20005
Ph: (202)833-2398
Fax: (240)235-4291

Gessert, Bill, President
International Customer Service As-
  sociation [3075]
1110 South Ave., Ste. 50
Staten Island, NY 10314
Toll Free: 888-900-8503

Gessler, Mark D., President
Historic Vehicle Association [9117]
7960 Cessna Ave.
Gaithersburg, MD 20879
Ph: (301)407-1911

Gessmann, Leroy, President, Chmn.
  of the Bd.
National Horsemen's Benevolent
  and Protective Association [22923]
870 Corporate Dr., Ste. 300
Lexington, KY 40503-5419
Ph: (859)259-0451
Toll Free: 866-245-1711
Fax: (859)259-0452

Gesualdo, Pat, Founder
Drums and Disabilities [12234]
1360 Clifton Ave., Unit No. 231
Clifton, NJ 07012-1453
Ph: (973)725-5150

Getchell, Michelle, Exec. Dir.
Twinless Twins Support Group
  International [12366]
PO Box 980481
Ypsilanti, MI 48198-0481
Toll Free: 888-205-8962

Getler, Al, President, Publicist
Free Press Media [18652]
100 Bank St., Ste. 700
Burlington, VT 05401
Ph: (802)660-1896

Getnick, Neil V., Chairman,
  President
International Association of
  Independent Private Sector Inspec-
  tors General [5308]
PO Box 5017
New York, NY 10185-5017
Toll Free: 888-70I-PSIG

Getz, Bonnie, Founder
Fight Staph Infections [15397]
624 Station West Ln.
Roebuck, SC 29376
Ph: (864)431-1411

Getz, Charles W., President
National Model Railroad Association
  [22189]
PO Box 1328
Soddy Daisy, TN 37384-1328
Ph: (423)892-2846
Fax: (423)899-4869

Getz, Deborah, Founder
Never Forget Our Fallen [10749]
PO Box 695
Roseville, CA 95661
Ph: (916)223-6816

Getz, George F., Jr., Founder
National Historical Fire Foundation
  [22014]
c/o Hall of Flame Fire Museum
6101 E Van Buren St.
Phoenix, AZ 85008-3421
Ph: (602)275-3473
Fax: (602)275-0896

Getz, Kelli, Secretary
North American Serials Interest
  Group [9719]
1902 Ridge Rd., PMB 305
West Seneca, NY 14224-3312

Gevirtz, Dr. Karen, President
Aphra Behn Society [10363]
Seton Hall University
Dept. of English
400 S Orange Ave.
South Orange, NJ 07079

Gewert, Jadwiga, Exec. Dir.
Chopin Foundation of the United
  States [9888]
1440 79th Street Cswy., Ste. 117
Miami, FL 33141
Ph: (305)868-0624
Fax: (305)865-5150

Ghantous, Hanan, PhD, President
American College of Toxicology
  [7335]
1821 Michael Farady Dr., Ste. 300
Reston, VA 20190
Ph: (703)547-0875
Fax: (703)438-3113

Gharakhanian, Razmik D., President
Armenian Engineers and Scientists
  of America [7120]
117 S Louise St., No. 306
Glendale, CA 91205-1076
Ph: (818)547-3372

Ghesquiere, Francis, Exec. Dir.
Global Facility for Disaster Reduc-
  tion and Recovery [11662]
1818 H St. NW
Washington, DC 20433
Ph: (202)473-6253
Fax: (202)522-3227

Ghetti, Bernardino, MD, President
International Society for Frontotemporal Dementias [15947]
1124 Frederick Dr. S
Indianapolis, IN 46260

Ghisini, Elisabetta, Director
Business Association Italy America
  [1980]

625 2nd St., Ste. 280, 2nd Fl.
San Francisco, CA 94107
Ph: (415)992-7454

Ghodasara, Kiran, President
Patidar Cultural Association of USA
[9570]
32 Stevenson Dr.
Marlboro, NJ 07746
Ph: (732)761-9829

Ghosh, Amal, President
Society for Information Display
[6263]
1475 S Bascom Ave., Ste. 114
Campbell, CA 95008-0628
Ph: (408)879-3901
Fax: (408)879-3833

Ghosh, Somnath, President
U.S. Association for Computational
Mechanics [6832]
PO Box 8137
Austin, TX 78713
Ph: (512)743-3273

Giacobbe, Ray, President
World Bulldog Alliance [21996]
1700 Ridgewood Ave., Ste. D
Holly Hill, FL 32117-1782
Ph: (386)437-4762

Giacobozzi, Samantha, Exec. Dir.
Break Away: The Alternative Break
Connection [12575]
112 N Avodale Rd., Ste. 280
Avondale Estates, GA 30002
Ph: (404)919-7482

Giaier, Thomas, Secretary, Treasurer
American Boiler Manufacturers As-
sociation [1705]
8221 Old Courthouse Rd., Ste. 380
Vienna, VA 22182
Ph: (703)356-7172

Giaimo, Frank, Chairman
American Institute of Wine and Food
[22145]
PO Box 4961
Louisville, KY 40204
Toll Free: 800-274-2493
Fax: (502)456-1821

Giambalvo, Pete, Rep.
USS Intrepid Association of Former
Crew Members [21067]
c/o Robert Dunne, President
PO Box 654
Bingham, ME 04920-0654
Ph: (207)672-3455

Giampietro, Mr. Wayne, Gen.
Counsel
First Amendment Lawyers Associa-
tion [5103]
c/o Wayne B. Giampietro
123 W Madison St., Ste. 1300
Chicago, IL 60602
Ph: (312)236-0606
Fax: (312)236-9264

Giannelli, Antonio, President
Society of Physician Assistants in
Rheumatology [17167]
PO Box 492
Dimondale, MI 48821
Ph: (517)646-9337

Giannini, Richard A., Chairperson
Aircraft Carrier Industrial Base Coali-
tion [985]
700 13th St. NW
Washington, DC 20005
Ph: (202)585-2141
Fax: (202)383-0079

Giannone, Garry, VP
Alcoholics Anonymous World
Services, Inc. [13120]

475 Riverside Dr., 11th Fl.
W 120th St.
New York, NY 10115
Ph: (212)870-3400

Giarrizzo, Pastor John, Coord.
Association of Reformed Baptist
Churches of America [19717]
401 E Louther St., Ste. 303
Carlisle, PA 17013-2652
Ph: (717)249-7473

Giarrusso, Sam, President
Kidney & Urology Foundation of
America [15880]
63 W Main St., Ste. G
Freehold, NJ 07728
Ph: (732)866-4444
Toll Free: 800-633-6628

Gibber, Jere, Exec. Dir.
National Preservation Institute
[9420]
PO Box 1702
Alexandria, VA 22313
Ph: (703)765-0100

Gibbons, Christopher, MD, President
American Autonomic Society [16043]
c/o Christopher Gibbons, MD,
President
Beth Israel Deaconess Medical Ctr.
1 Deaconess Rd., Palmer 111
Boston, MA 02215
Ph: (952)469-5837

Gibbons, Jim, CEO, President
Goodwill Industries International
[11600]
15810 Indianola Dr.
Rockville, MD 20855
Toll Free: 800-741-0186

Gibbons, Michael, Exec. Dir.
Babe Ruth Birthplace and Museum
[22547]
216 Emory St.
Baltimore, MD 21230
Ph: (410)727-1539
Fax: (410)727-1652

Gibbons, Russell W., Editor, Exec.
Dir.
Frederick A. Cook Society [10320]
PO Box 247
Hurleyville, NY 12747
Ph: (845)434-8044
Fax: (845)434-8056

Gibbs, Dr. David C., Jr., Founder,
President
Christian Law Association [19960]
PO Box 8600
Mason, OH 45040
Toll Free: 888-252-1969
Fax: (888)600-9899

Gibbs, Gary, President
National Assembly of State Arts
Agencies [8988]
1200 18th St. NW, Ste. 1100
Washington, DC 20036
Ph: (202)347-6352
Fax: (202)737-0526

Gibbs, Linda Chiarelli, President
Honest Ballot Association [18182]
27246 Grand Central Pky.
Floral Park, NY 11005
Toll Free: 800-541-1851

Gibbs, Lois Marie, Founder
Center For Health, Environment and
Justice [4738]
105 Rowell Ct., 1st Fl.
Falls Church, VA 22046
Ph: (703)237-2249

Gibbs, Randy, Founder, Exec. Dir.
Jenny's Light [17759]
5021 Vernon Ave., Ste. 107

Minneapolis, MN 55436

Gibel, Larry, Secretary, Treasurer
National Drilling Association [887]
4036 Center Rd., Ste. B
Brunswick, OH 44212
Toll Free: 877-632-4748
Fax: (216)803-9900

Giberson, Karen, President
Accessories Council [197]
224 W 30th St., Ste. 201
New York, NY 10001
Ph: (212)947-1135
Fax: (646)674-0205

Gibson, Anna, CEO
Equine Land Conservation Resource
[3859]
4037 Iron Works Pky., Ste. 120
Lexington, KY 40511-8508
Ph: (859)455-8383
Fax: (859)455-8381

Gibson, Bill, Officer
International Door Association [537]
PO Box 246
West Milton, OH 45383
Ph: (937)698-8042
Toll Free: 800-355-4432
Fax: (937)698-6153

Gibson, Brent, President, Founder
HaitiCorps International [11665]
4 Washington Square Village, Apt.
2-ORT
New York, NY 10012
Ph: (347)674-4241

Gibson, Chiann, DMD, President
American Academy of Cosmetic
Dentistry [14372]
402 W Wilson St.
Madison, WI 53703
Ph: (608)222-8583
Toll Free: 800-543-9220
Fax: (608)222-9540

Gibson, Cindy, President
Guinea Fowl International Association [3662]
2812 FM 987
Kaufman, TX 75142

Gibson, Cortney, President
International Nanny Association
[10808]
PO Box 18126
Charlotte, NC 28218
Toll Free: 888-878-1477
Fax: (508)638-6462

Gibson, Liz, Exec. Dir., President
Golden Crown Literary Society
[9337]
PO Box 720154
Dallas, TX 75372

Gibson, Milo, Founder
North American Fruit Explorers
[22114]

Gibson, Patricia, Chmn. of the Bd.
National Association of Real Estate
Investment Managers [2878]
410 N Michigan Ave., Ste. 330
Chicago, IL 60611
Ph: (312)884-5180

Gibson, Susan, Account Exec.
Culligan Dealers Association of
North America [1458]
Bldg. 1600-B
14101 Highway 290 W
Austin, TX 78737
Ph: (512)894-4106
Fax: (512)858-0486

Gibson, Susan, President
Motor Maids [23039]
PO Box 9418

Catonsville, MD 21228

Gibson, Tom, CEO
Psychiatric Rehabilitation Association
[17097]
7918 Jones Branch Dr., Ste. 300
McLean, VA 22102
Ph: (703)422-2078
Fax: (703)506-3266

Gibson, Victoria, BSN, Founder,
President, Chmn. of the Bd.
Helping Ugandans Grow Stronger
[11029]
PO Box 731312
Ormond Beach, FL 32173
Ph: (386)492-7624

Gibson, William E., PhD, President
Children's Eye Foundation [16379]
1631 Lancaster Dr., Ste. 200
Grapevine, TX 76051-2116
Ph: (817)310-2641
Fax: (817)423-6672

Giddo, Suliman A., CEO, President
Darfur Peace and Development
Organization [12150]
PO Box 10384
Alexandria, VA 22310

Gierhahn, Rebecca, Director
American Medical Association
[15708]
AMA Plaza
330 N Wabash Ave.
Chicago, IL 60611
Ph: (312)464-4430
Toll Free: 800-621-8335
Fax: (312)464-5226

Gierhart, Roger, President
Bicycle Product Suppliers Associa-
tion [3136]
740 34th St.
Boulder, CO 80303
Ph: (303)442-2466
Fax: (303)552-2060

Giesbrecht, Rev. Vernon, Coord.
Double Harvest [3537]
55 S Main St.
Oberlin, OH 44074
Ph: (440)714-1694

Giesen, James C., PhD, Exec. Sec.
Agricultural History Society [9448]
PO Box H
Mississippi State, MS 39762
Ph: (662)268-2247

Giess, Dar, President
North American South Devon As-
sociation [3749]
19590 E Main St., Ste. 104
Parker, CO 80138
Ph: (303)770-3130
Fax: (303)770-9302

Giffoniello, Rosalie, Founder
Empower the Children [10961]
PO Box 1412
Jackson, NJ 08527

Gifford, Dr. James M., CEO
Jesse Stuart Foundation [9100]
4440 13th St.
Ashland, KY 41102-5432
Ph: (606)326-1667
Toll Free: 855-407-6243
Fax: (606)325-2519

Gifford, Kimberly A., MBA, Exec. Dir.
American Society of Transplant
Surgeons [17504]
2461 S Clark St., Ste. 640
Arlington, VA 22202
Ph: (703)414-7870
Fax: (703)414-7874

Gifford, Mike, Founder, Exec. Dir.
OnBehalf.org **[13247]**
223 E 88th St., No. 3A
New York, NY 10128

Giffords, Gabrielle, Founder
Americans for Responsible Solutions
[18245]
PO Box 15642
Washington, DC 20003

Gigl, Michael, Director
Austrian Tourist Office **[23543]**
PO Box 1142
New York, NY 10108-1142
Ph: (212)575-7723
    (212)944-6885
Fax: (212)730-4568

Gigliotti, Leslie, President, CEO
Italian Folk Art Federation of
America **[9615]**
5275 Robinwood Ln.
Hales Corners, WI 53130

Giguere, Paul, Bd. Member
National Association of Public Affairs
Networks **[472]**
21 Oak St., Ste. 605
Hartford, CT 06106
Ph: (860)246-1553
Fax: (860)246-1547

Gilanshah, Ellie, VP of Fin., VP of
Admin.
The National Industrial Transporta-
tion League **[3343]**
1700 N Moore St., Ste. 1900
Arlington, VA 22209
Ph: (703)524-5011
Fax: (703)524-5017

Gilbane, Thomas F., Jr., Chairman
Construction Industry Round Table
[803]
8115 Old Dominion Dr., Ste. 210
McLean, VA 22102-2325
Ph: (202)466-6777

Gilbert, Gary, Chairman
International Etchells Class Associa-
tion **[22629]**
2812 Canon St.
San Diego, CA 92106
Ph: (619)222-0252

Gilbert, Joyce, President
Association of Nutrition and Food-
service Professionals **[16209]**
406 Surrey Woods Dr.
Saint Charles, IL 60174
Ph: (630)587-6336
Toll Free: 800-323-1908
Fax: (630)587-6308

Gilbert, Kellie, Administrator
IEEE - Electron Devices Society
[6427]
IEEE Operations Ctr.
445 Hoes Ln.
Piscataway, NJ 08854
Ph: (732)562-3926
Fax: (732)235-1626

Gilbert, Lisa, Director
Public Citizen's Congress Watch
[18059]
215 Pennsylvania Ave. SE
Washington, DC 20003
Ph: (202)546-4996

Gilbert, Ronald R., Chairman
Foundation for Aquatic Injury
Prevention **[12821]**
631 Warner Dr.
Linden, MI 48451-9659
Toll Free: 800-342-0330

Gilbert, Sally, Dir. of Admin., Director
The TLT Group **[7299]**
PO Box 5643

Takoma Park, MD 20913-5643
Ph: (301)270-8312

Gilbert, Sheila, President
National Council of the United States
Society of St. Vincent de Paul
[13074]
58 Progress Pky.
Maryland Heights, MO 63043-3706
Ph: (314)576-3993
Fax: (314)576-6755

Gilbert, Steven G., President
Basel Action Network **[4291]**
206 1st Ave. S, Ste. 410
Seattle, WA 98104
Ph: (206)652-5555
Fax: (206)652-5750

Gilbertson, David, President
Conference of Chief Justices **[5379]**
c/o Association and Conference
Services
300 Newport Ave.
Williamsburg, VA 23185-4147
Ph: (757)259-1841
Fax: (757)259-1520

Gilbride, Kevin, Exec. Dir.
Accredited Snow Contractors As-
sociation **[848]**
5811 Canal Rd.
Valley View, OH 44125
Ph: (216)393-0303
Toll Free: 800-456-0707

Gildea, Adrienne L., Dep. Dir.
Commercial Vehicle Safety Alliance
[291]
6303 Ivy Ln., Ste. 310
Greenbelt, MD 20770-6319
Ph: (301)830-6143
Fax: (301)830-6144

Gildhouse, Vern, President
Quaker Parakeet Society **[3670]**
PO Box 343
Valley Park, MO 63088

Giles, Bob, Treasurer
National Association of State Elec-
tion Directors **[18184]**
21946 Royal Montreal Dr., Ste. 100
Katy, TX 77450
Ph: (281)396-4314
Fax: (281)396-4315

Giles, Dr. Deborah, Dir. of Res.
Center for Whale Research **[6791]**
PO Box 1577
Friday Harbor, WA 98250
Toll Free: 866-ORC-ANET

Giliberti, Mary, J.D., Exec. Dir.
National Alliance on Mental Illness
[15785]
3803 N Fairfax Dr., Ste. 100
Arlington, VA 22203
Ph: (703)524-7600
Toll Free: 800-950-6264

Gill, Barbara E., Exec. Dir.
Dana Alliance for Brain Initiatives
[16014]
505 5th Ave., 6th Fl.
New York, NY 10017
Ph: (212)223-4040
Fax: (212)593-7623

Gill, Chuck, President
United States Professional Tennis
Association **[23308]**
3535 Briarpark Dr., Ste. 202
Houston, TX 77042-5233
Ph: (713)978-7782
Fax: (713)978-7780

Gill, Ms. Marie, President, CEO
Jamaica USA Chamber of Commerce **[23598]**

4770 Biscayne Blvd., Ste. 1050
Miami, FL 33137-3247
Ph: (305)573-3235
Toll Free: 866-577-3236
Fax: (305)576-0089

Gillan, Jackie, President
Advocates for Highway and Auto
Safety **[12811]**
750 1st St. NE, Ste. 1130
Washington, DC 20002
Ph: (202)408-1711
Fax: (202)408-1699

Gillen, Cathy, Managing Dir.
Roadway Safety Foundation **[12842]**
1101 14th St. NW, Ste. 750
Washington, DC 20005
Ph: (202)857-1208
Fax: (202)857-1220

Gillens, Harold, President
International Association of Profes-
sional Security Consultants **[3058]**
575 Market St., Ste. 2125
San Francisco, CA 94105
Ph: (415)536-0288
Fax: (415)764-4915

Giller, Esther, Director, President
Sidran Institute for Traumatic Stress
Education and Advocacy **[12313]**
PO Box 436
Brooklandville, MD 21022-0436
Ph: (410)825-8888
Fax: (410)560-0134

Gillespie, Fred, President
Swiss American Historical Society
[9440]
c/o Ernest Thurston, Membership
Secretary
65 Town Mountain Rd.
Asheville, NC 28804

Gillespie, Robert, President
Population Communication **[12513]**
1250 E Walnut St., Ste. 160
Pasadena, CA 91106-1833
Ph: (626)793-4750

Gillick, Kevin, Exec. Dir.
GlobalPlatform **[7270]**
544 Hillside Rd.
Redwood City, CA 94062

Gillies, John, Co-Ch.
Basic Education Coalition **[8234]**
1400 16th St. NW, Ste. 210
Washington, DC 20036
Ph: (202)729-6712
Fax: (202)729-6713

Gillies, Susan, Officer
American Baptist Churches USA
[19711]
588 N Gulph Rd.
King of Prussia, PA 19406
Ph: (610)768-2000
Toll Free: 800-222-3872
Fax: (610)768-2309

Gillies, Suzy Benson, Founder,
President
African Promise Foundation **[13001]**
25545 SE 274th Pl.
Maple Valley, WA 98038
Ph: (630)947-2805

Gillig, Tim, President
FPDA Motion and Control Network
[1730]
105 Eastern Ave., Ste. 104
Annapolis, MD 21403-3300
Ph: (410)940-6347
Fax: (410)263-1659

Gilligan, Michael, President
Henry Luce Foundation **[11728]**
51 Madison Ave., 30th Fl.

New York, NY 10010
Ph: (212)489-7700
Fax: (212)581-9541

Gilligan, Paige, Sr. VP, Director
American Society of Agricultural
Consultants **[3523]**
605 Columbus Ave. S
New Prague, MN 56071
Ph: (952)758-5811
Fax: (952)758-5813

Gilligan, Toni, VP
Association for the Advancement of
Gestalt Therapy **[16899]**
PO Box 42221
Portland, OR 97242
Ph: (971)238-2248
Fax: (212)202-3974

Gillikin, Derrick, President
Antique and Amusement
Photographers International **[2575]**
PO Box 3094
McDonough, GA 30253
Ph: (860)578-2274
Fax: (877)865-1052

Gillin, Dr. Colin, Chairman, Web
Adm.
American Association of Wildlife
Veterinarians **[17607]**
c/o Dr. Megin Nichols, Treasurer
1616 Piedmont Ave. NE, Apt. S5
Atlanta, GA 30324

Gillis, Arlene, Chairperson
National Commission on Orthotic
and Prosthetic Education **[16497]**
Ste. 200
330 John Carlyle St.
Alexandria, VA 22314
Ph: (703)836-7114
Fax: (703)836-0838

Gillman, Theodore J., Chairman
Ubuntu Africa **[11175]**
PO Box 7906
Greenwich, CT 06836-7906

Gillmor, Carroll, Secretary, Treasurer
De Re Militari: The Society for
Medieval Military History **[9801]**
PO Box 2211
Olathe, KS 66051

Gilman, Diane, Founder
Context Institute **[19104]**
PO Box 946
Langley, WA 98260

Gilmore, Dian, Exec. Dir.
American Board of Certification
[4984]
4403 1st Ave. SE, Ste. 113
Cedar Rapids, IA 52402-3221
Ph: (319)365-2222
Toll Free: 877-365-2221
Fax: (319)363-0127

Gilpin, Melinda, Exec. Dir.
Surveyors Historical Society **[9523]**
6465 Reflections Dr., Ste. 100
Dublin, OH 43017-2353
Ph: (614)798-5257
Fax: (614)761-2317

Gilroy, Kelly, Exec. Dir.
American Legal Finance Association
[1219]
818 Connecticut Ave. NW, Ste. 1100
Washington, DC 20006
Ph: (202)552-2793

Gilsdorf, Janet R., President
Pediatric Infectious Diseases Society
[15414]
1300 Wilson Blvd., Ste. 300

Arlington, VA 22209
Ph: (703)299-6764
Fax: (703)299-0473

Gilstrap, Dr. Larry C., III, Exec. Dir.
American Board of Obstetrics and
Gynecology, Inc. [16269]
2915 Vine St.
Dallas, TX 75204
Ph: (214)871-1619
    (214)721-7520
Fax: (214)871-1943

Gilstrap, Marcus D., Contact
Gilstrap Family Association [20870]
1921 N Harrison
San Angelo, TX 76901-1335
Ph: (325)949-0792

Gimbel, Joseph B., DPM, President,
    Treasurer
American Board of Lower Extremity
    Surgery [16777]
PO Box 5373
Evanston, IL 60204-5373
Ph: (248)855-7740
Fax: (248)855-7743

Gimpel, John R., President, CEO
National Board of Osteopathic Medi-
    cal Examiners [16523]
8765 W Higgins Rd., Ste. 200
Chicago, IL 60631-4174
Ph: (773)714-0622
Toll Free: 866-479-6828
Fax: (773)714-0631

Gin, Catherine, Asst. Sec.
Deadline Club [2676]
c/o The Salmagundi Club
47 5th Ave.
New York, NY 10003
Ph: (646)481-7584

Ginger, Ann Fagan, Exec. Dir.
Meiklejohn Civil Liberties Institute
    [12050]
PO Box 673
Berkeley, CA 94701-0673
Ph: (510)848-0599

Gingerich, Dan, Treasurer
Council for Agricultural Science and
    Technology [7474]
4420 W Lincoln Way
Ames, IA 50014-3447
Ph: (515)292-2125
Fax: (515)292-4512

Ginn, Clay, President, Chmn. of the
    Bd.
Reach Out Honduras [11139]
PO Box 2993
McKinney, TX 75070

Ginn, Sherry R., Secretary,
    Treasurer
International Society for the History
    of the Neurosciences [6916]
c/o Sherry R. Ginn, Secretary
Rowan-Cabarrus Community Col-
    lege
1531 Trinity Church Rd.
Concord, NC 28027
Ph: (704)216-3799
Fax: (704)216-0992

Ginn, William D., President
Basal Cell Carcinoma Nevus
    Syndrome Life Support Network
    [14809]
14525 N Cheshire St.
Burton, OH 44021
Ph: (440)834-0011
Toll Free: 866-834-1895
Fax: (440)834-0132

Ginnan, Shannon, MD, Director
Alliance for the Adoption of Innova-
    tions in Medicine [14971]

1000 Potomac St. NW, Ste. 150-A
Washington, DC 20007
Ph: (202)559-0380
Fax: (202)459-9611

Gino, Alex, Secretary
National Organization for Lesbians
    of Size [11902]
PO Box 5475
Oakland, CA 94605

Ginter, Gary, Chairman, Founder
Paraclete [20453]
PO Box 63450
Colorado Springs, CO 80962
Ph: (719)302-2500

Gintert, Mark, Exec. Dir.
Future Fisherman Foundation
    [22845]
5998 N Pleasant View Rd.
Ponca City, OK 74601
Ph: (580)716-4251

Giordano, Amanda, Treasurer
Association for Spiritual, Ethical and
    Religious Values in Counseling
    [20039]
c/o American Counseling Association
6101 Stevenson Ave., Ste. 600
Alexandria, VA 22304-3580

Giordano, Richard, Trustee
Carnegie Endowment for
    International Peace [18519]
1779 Massachusetts Ave. NW
Washington, DC 20036-2103
Ph: (202)483-7600
Fax: (202)483-1840

Gippe, Annette, Exec. Dir.
American Osteopathic Association of
    Medical Informatics [16509]
142 E Ontario St.
Chicago, IL 60611-2864
Ph: (312)202-8142
Toll Free: 800-621-1773
Fax: (312)202-8449

Gipper, Jerry, Exec. Dir.
VITA [6339]
9100 Paseo del Vita
Oklahoma City, OK 73131

Gipson, Genevieve, RN, Director
National Network of Career Nursing
    Assistants [16163]
3577 Easton Rd.
Norton, OH 44203-5661
Ph: (330)825-9342
Fax: (330)825-9378

Gipson, Roy, CEO, Founder
Youth Media Minds of America
    [8680]
206 N Clarendon Ave.
Avondale Estates, GA 30002
Ph: (404)292-1265
    (404)848-5000

Gira, Robert, Exec. VP
Advancement Via Individual
    Determination [7950]
9246 Lightwave Ave., Ste. 200
San Diego, CA 92123
Ph: (858)380-4800
Fax: (858)268-2265

Girard, Karen, Chairman
Directors of Health Promotion and
    Education [5716]
1432 K St. NW, Ste. 400
Washington, DC 20005-2539
Ph: (202)659-2230
Fax: (202)478-0884

Giribet, Prof. Dr. Gonzalo, President
The Willi Hennig Society [6108]
c/o Mark E. Siddall, Treasurer

Division of Invertebrate Zoology
American Museum of Natural History
Central Park W at 79th St.
New York, NY 10024
Ph: (212)769-5638
Fax: (212)769-5277

Giroux, Randy, President
Toy Train Operating Society [22192]
PO Box 6710
Fullerton, CA 92834-6710
Ph: (714)449-9391
Fax: (714)449-9631

Giroux, William, Exec. VP
Truckload Carriers Association
    [3360]
555 E Braddock Rd.
Alexandria, VA 22314
Ph: (703)838-1950
Fax: (703)836-6610

Giseke, Ken, Chairman
National Frame Builders Association
    [889]
8735 W Higgins Rd., Ste. 300
Chicago, IL 60631
Toll Free: 800-557-6957
Fax: (847)375-6495

Gish, Bob, Chairman
North American Gun Dog Associa-
    tion [21928]
1404 Willow Dr.
Berthoud, CO 80513
Ph: (719)342-0776

Gisser, Keith, Project Mgr.
Harness Horse Youth Foundation
    [22915]
16575 Carey Rd.
Westfield, IN 46074-8925
Ph: (317)867-5877
Fax: (317)867-1886

Giuliani, Dr. George, President
National Association of Parents with
    Children in Special Education
    [8586]
3642 E Sunnydale Dr.
Chandler Heights, AZ 85142
Toll Free: 800-754-4421
Fax: (800)424-0371

Giuliano, Patti, Co-Pres.
League of Chiropractic Women
    [14277]
PO Box 21772
York, PA 17402
Ph: (413)353-4636
Fax: (678)669-2786

Giusti, Kathy, Chairman, Founder
Multiple Myeloma Research Founda-
    tion [14017]
383 Main Ave., 5th Fl.
Norwalk, CT 06851
Ph: (203)229-0464
Fax: (203)229-0572

Given, Gale, Director
National Association of State Chief
    Information Officers [5306]
c/o AMR Management Services
201 E Main St., Ste. 1405
Lexington, KY 40507
Ph: (859)514-9217
Fax: (859)514-9166

Givens, Beth, Director, Founder
Privacy Rights Clearinghouse [2734]
3033 5th Ave., Ste. 223
San Diego, CA 92103
Ph: (619)298-3396
Fax: (619)298-5681

Givner, Joel, President
Auburn-Cord-Duesenberg Club
    [21330]

24218 E Arapahoe Pl.
Aurora, CO 80016
Ph: (303)748-3579

Gizzi, Amanda, Contact
Jewelry Information Center [2056]
120 Broadway, Ste. 2820
New York, NY 10271
Ph: (646)658-0246
Toll Free: 800-223-0673
Fax: (646)658-0256

Gjellstad, Melissa, President
Norwegian Researchers and Teach-
    ers Association of North America
    [8398]
c/o Gergana May, Treasurer
Global and International Studies
    Bldg., No. 3111
Indiana University
Bloomington, IN 47405-1105

Gjernes, Marylou, President
Council on America's Military Past
    [9383]
PO Box 4209
Charlottesville, VA 22905

Glading, Laura, President
Association of Professional Flight
    Attendants [23386]
1004 W Euless Blvd.
Euless, TX 76040
Ph: (817)540-0108
Fax: (817)540-2077

Gladstone, Frank, Exec. Dir.
International Animated Film Society
    [1194]
2114 W Burbank Blvd.
Burbank, CA 91506
Ph: (818)842-8330

Gladstone, Steve, President
Cardigan Welsh Corgi Club of
    America [21851]
c/o Barbara Peterson, Membership
    Chairperson
6263 Seville Rd.
Saginaw, MN 55779-9510
Ph: (218)729-4527

Gladysz, Thomas, Director
Louise Brooks Society [23987]
1518 Church St.
San Francisco, CA 94131-2018

Glandon, Gerald, PhD, President,
    CEO
Association of University Programs
    in Health Administration [8315]
1730 M St. NW, Ste. 407
Washington, DC 20036
Ph: (202)763-7283
Fax: (202)894-0941

Glantzberg, Hughes, President
461st Bombardment Group Associa-
    tion [20680]
c/o Hughes J. Glantzberg, President
PO Box 926
Gunnison, CO 81230

Glas, Kim, Exec. Dir.
BlueGreen Alliance [4135]
1300 Godward St. NE, Ste. 2625
Minneapolis, MN 55413

Glasberg, Prof. Ronald, President
International Society for the Study of
    Human Ideas on Ultimate Reality
    and Meaning [10097]
c/o David J. Leigh
English Dept.
Seattle University
901 12th Ave.
Seattle, WA 98122
Ph: (206)296-5414
    (403)220-7124
Fax: (403)282-6716

Glaser, Josh, Exec. Dir.
Regeneration [20044]
PO Box 9830
Baltimore, MD 21284-9830
Ph: (410)661-0284
Fax: (443)275-7918

Glaser, Kelli, President
DOCARE International [12271]
142 E Ontario St., 18th Fl.
Chicago, IL 60611
Ph: (312)202-8163
Fax: (312)202-8316

Glass, Bill, Founder
Bill Glass Champions for Life
[20129]
1101 S Cedar Ridge Dr.
Duncanville, TX 75137
Ph: (972)298-1101
Fax: (972)298-1104

Glass, Martha, Exec. Dir.
National Agritourism Professionals
Association [3573]
c/o Martha Glass, Executive Director
108 Forest Holls Ct.
Cary, NC 27511
Ph: (919)467-5809

Glass, Renee, Founder, President
Jaw Joints and Allied Musculo-
Skeletal Disorders Foundation, Inc.
[16483]
790 Boylston St., Ste. 17-G
Boston, MA 02199
Ph: (617)266-2550

Glassberg, Jeffrey, President
North American Butterfly Association
[6783]
4 Delaware Rd.
Morristown, NJ 07960-5725
Ph: (973)285-0907

Glasser, Roberta, Exec. Dir.
Holistic Dental Association [14440]
1825 Ponce de Leon Blvd., No. 148
Coral Gables, FL 33134
Ph: (305)356-7338
Fax: (305)468-6359

Glassman, Jeffrey, Founder
RainforestMaker [4617]
1 Beacon St., Ste. 3333
Boston, MA 02108
Toll Free: 877-763-6778

Glawe, Amber, Treasurer
Healthcare Hospitality Network
[15328]
PO Box 1439
Gresham, OR 97030
Toll Free: 800-542-9730

Glaze, Mitch, Office Mgr.
Astronomical League [6001]
9201 Ward Pky., Ste. 100
Kansas City, MO 64114
Ph: (816)333-7759

Glazer, Bob, Exec. Dir.
Gulf and Caribbean Fisheries
Institute [4185]
Florida Fish and Wildlife Conserva-
tion Commission
Marine Research Institute
2796 Overseas Hwy., Ste. 119
Marathon, FL 33050
Ph: (305)289-2330
Fax: (305)289-2334

Glazer, Carol, President
National Organization on Disability
[11629]
77 Water St., Ste. 204
New York, NY 10005
Ph: (646)505-1191
Fax: (646)505-1184

Glazer, Cheryl, President
Association of Divorce Financial
Planners [1274]
6 Boston Rd., Ste. 202
Chelmsford, MA 01824
Ph: (978)364-5035

Gleason, Deborah, Bd. Member
Association of Staff Physician
Recruiters [16745]
1000 Westgate Dr., Ste. 252
Saint Paul, MN 55114
Toll Free: 800-830-2777

Gleason, Jim, President
Transplant Recipients International
Organization [17520]
13705 Currant Loop
Gainesville, VA 20155-3031
Ph: (202)293-0980
Toll Free: 800-TRIO-386

Gleason, Thomas R., President
National Council of State Housing
Agencies [5282]
444 N Capitol St. NW, Ste. 438
Washington, DC 20001
Ph: (202)624-7710
Fax: (202)624-5899

Gleba, Michael W., Chairman,
Treasurer
Sarah Scaife Foundation [19004]
1 Oxford Ctre.
301 Grant St., Ste. 3900
Pittsburgh, PA 15219-6402
Ph: (412)392-2900

Gleick, Dr. Peter H., President
Pacific Institute for Studies in
Development, Environment, and
Security [12958]
Preservation Pk.
654 13th St.
Oakland, CA 94612
Ph: (510)251-1600
Fax: (510)251-2203

Glen, Bob, President
American Single Shot Rifle Associa-
tion [23126]
c/o Keith Foster, Membership
Administrator
15770 Road 1037
Oakwood, OH 45873
Ph: (630)898-4229

Glenn, Capt. Albert, Advisor
Organization of Black Aerospace
Professionals [154]
1 Westbrook Corporate Ctr., Ste.
300
Westchester, IL 60154
Toll Free: 800-JET-OBAP

Glenn, Emily, Librarian
Association of College and
University Housing Officers
International [8604]
1445 Summit St.
Columbus, OH 43201-2105
Ph: (614)292-0099
Fax: (614)292-3205

Glenn, Gary, President
Society of Cleaning and Restoration
Technicians [2142]
142 Handsome Jack Rd.
Abilene, TX 79602
Toll Free: 800-949-4728
Fax: (325)692-1823

Glenn, Tasha, President
ChronoRecord Association [13810]
PO Box 3501
Fullerton, CA 92834
Ph: (714)773-0301
Fax: (714)773-1037

Gletow, Danielle, Founder, Exec. Dir.
One Simple Wish [11107]
1977 N Olden Ave., No. 292
Trenton, NJ 08618
Ph: (609)883-8484

Gliessman, Stephen, Chairman
Community Agroecology Network
[4695]
PO Box 7653
Santa Cruz, CA 95061-7653
Ph: (831)459-3619

Glissman, Inge, Treasurer, Secretary
The International Osprey Foundation
[4830]
PO Box 250
Sanibel, FL 33957

Gliva-McConvey, Gayle, Comm.
Chm.
Association of Standardized Patient
Educators [15623]
222 S Westmonte Dr., Ste. 101
Altamonte Springs, FL 32714
Ph: (407)774-7880
Fax: (407)774-6440

Gloria, Soli Deo, Contact
Xslaves.org [17934]
PO Box 2672
Rancho Santa Fe, CA 92067

Glover, Dr. Beverly W., President
International Association of Ministers
Wives and Ministers Widows
[20064]
105 River Knoll
Macon, GA 31211
Ph: (478)743-5126
Fax: (478)745-5504

Glover, Vivette, Treasurer
Marce Society [15782]
5034-A Thoroughbred Ln.
Brentwood, TN 37027
Ph: (615)324-2362

Glowa-Kollisch, Anya, Coord.
Students Active For Ending Rape
[12573]
222 Broadway, 19th Fl.
New York, NY 10004
Ph: (347)465-7233

Glowinski, Robert W., President,
CEO
American Wood Council [3510]
222 Catoctin Cir. SE, Ste. 201
Leesburg, VA 20175
Ph: (202)463-2766
Toll Free: 800-890-7732

Gluck, Pam, Exec. Dir.
American Trails [23321]
PO Box 491797
Redding, CA 96049-1797
Ph: (530)605-4395
Fax: (530)547-2035

Glucksmann, Alexandra,
Chairperson
Women Entrepreneurs in Science
and Technology [3505]
1 Broadway, 14th Fl.
Cambridge, MA 02142-1187
Ph: (617)682-3703
Fax: (617)588-1765

Gmiter, Cheri D., Exec. Dir.
Marketing and Advertising Global
Network [101]
c/o Cheri D. Gmiter, Executive Direc-
tor
MAGNET Global
226 Rostrevor Pl.
Pittsburgh, PA 15202

Gnass, Stephen Paul, Exec. Dir.
National Congress of Inventor
Organizations [6771]

8306 Wilshire Blvd., Ste. 391
Beverly Hills, CA 90211
Toll Free: 866-466-0253

Gómez, María Mercedes, Coord.
OutRight Action International [11904]
80 Maiden Ln., Ste. 1505
New York, NY 10038
Ph: (212)430-6054
Fax: (212)430-6060

Goble, Dr. Phillip, President
Artists for Israel International [8844]
PO Box 2056
New York, NY 10163-2056
Ph: (212)245-4188
Fax: (646)607-0667

Goble, Terry L., Sr., Liaison
Palomino Horse Breeders of
America [3611]
15253 E Skelly Dr.
Tulsa, OK 74116-2637
Ph: (918)438-1234
Fax: (918)438-1232

Goddard, Carol A., Exec. Dir.
American Hernia Society [17368]
4582 S Ulster St., Ste. 201
Denver, CO 80237
Toll Free: 866-798-5406
Fax: (303)771-2550

Goddard, Debbie, Director
Center for Inquiry [18294]
PO Box 741
Amherst, NY 14226
Ph: (716)636-4869
Fax: (716)636-1733

Goddu, Bill, VP
Planning and Visual Education
Partnership [2974]
4651 Sheridan St., Ste. 470
Hollywood, FL 33021-3437
Ph: (954)893-7225
Fax: (954)893-8375

Godfrey, Kimberly, Reg. Dir.
American Society of PeriAnesthesia
Nurses [16114]
90 Frontage Rd.
Cherry Hill, NJ 08034-1424
Toll Free: 877-737-9696
Fax: (856)616-9601

Godfrey, Robin, Exec. Dir.
GALA Choruses [9909]
PO Box 99998
Pittsburgh, PA 15233
Ph: (412)418-7709

Godinez, Fernando S., CEO,
President
Mexican American Unity Council
[11945]
2300 W Commerce St., Ste. 200
San Antonio, TX 78207
Ph: (210)978-0500

Godlewski, Matthew, President
Natural Gas Vehicles for America
[6020]
400 N Capitol St. NW
Washington, DC 20001
Ph: (202)824-7360

Godley, Alan, Director
Blue Dolphin Alliance [4465]
PO Box 312
Watsonville, CA 95077
Ph: (831)761-1477
Toll Free: 888-694-2537

Godley, Frederick, MD, President
Association of Migraine Disorders
[14917]
PO Box 870

North Kingstown, RI 02852

Godsey, Van, Chairperson
Association of Law Enforcement
Intelligence Units [5455]
1825 Bell St., Ste. 205
Sacramento, CA 95825
Ph: (916)263-1187
Fax: (916)263-1180

Godsman, Bonnie, CEO
GAMA International [1857]
2901 Telestar Ct., Ste. 140
Falls Church, VA 22042
Toll Free: 800-345-2687
Fax: (571)499-4311

Goedelman, M. Kurt, Exec. Dir.,
Founder
Personal Freedom Outreach [20049]
PO Box 26062
Saint Louis, MO 63136-0062
Ph: (314)921-9800

Goehl, George, Exec. Dir.
National People's Action [11297]
810 N Milwaukee Ave.
Chicago, IL 60642
Ph: (312)243-3035

Goel, Mahesh, Founder
Hands to Clinical Labs of Third
World Countries [15519]
5 Compton Ln.
Princeton Junction, NJ 08550
Ph: (609)468-5673
Fax: (609)301-8737

Goenka, Animesh, Mem.
Association of Indians in America
[19471]
26 Pleasant Ln.
Oyster Bay, NY 11771
Ph: (516)624-2460

Goering, Curt, Exec. Dir.
Center for Victims of Torture [13258]
St. Paul Healing Ctr.
649 Dayton Ave.
Saint Paul, MN 55104-6631
Ph: (612)436-4840
    (612)436-4800
Toll Free: 877-265-8775

Goering, Peter, President
Society of Toxicology [7343]
1821 Michael Faraday Dr., Ste. 300
Reston, VA 20190
Ph: (703)438-3115
Toll Free: 800-826-6762
Fax: (703)438-3113

Goertz, Susan, Treasurer
Tandem Club of America [22754]

Goertzen, Ryan, President
Aviation Technician Education
Council [7458]
117 North Henry St.
Alexandria, VA 22314-2903
Ph: (703)548-2030

Goes, Mark, President
American Gelbvieh Association
[3692]
10900 Dover St.
Westminster, CO 80021
Ph: (303)465-2333

Goessling, Shannon L., Counsel,
Exec. Dir.
Southeastern Legal Foundation
[5447]
2255 Sewell Mill Rd., Ste. 320
Marietta, GA 30062-7218
Ph: (770)977-2131
Fax: (770)977-2134

Goetsch, Jim, Administrator
Friends of the Third World [12541]
611 W Wayne St.

Fort Wayne, IN 46802-2167
Ph: (260)422-6821
Fax: (260)422-1650

Goetz, Tom, Exec. VP
Associated Construction Distributors
International [499]
1605 SE Delaware Ave., Ste. B
Ankeny, IA 50021
Ph: (515)964-1335
Fax: (515)964-7668

Goff, Debbie, Membership Chp.
Brazilian Dimensional Embroidery
International Guild, Inc. [21300]
13013 89th Ave. N
Seminole, FL 33776-2706
Ph: (727)391-9207

Goff, Phil, President
Goff/Gough Family Association
[20871]
5704 Riverboat Cir. SW
Vero Beach, FL 32968

Goff, Stacy, Dir. of Mktg.
International Project Management
Association [2178]
6547 N Academy, No. 404
Colorado Springs, CO 80918-8342
Ph: (719)488-3850

Goffinet, Bernard, President
International Association of Bryolo-
gists [6143]
c/o Matt von Konrat, Secretary-
Treasurer
1400 S Lake Shore Dr.
Chicago, IL 60605
Ph: (312)665-7864

Gogis, Mike, CFO
Willow Creek Association [20030]
67 E Algonquin Rd.
South Barrington, IL 60010-6132
Toll Free: 800-570-9812

Goh, Anthony, President
United States of America Wushu-
Kungfu Federation [23017]
7710 Harford Rd.
Baltimore, MD 21234
Ph: (443)808-0048

Gohde, William, President
AE/AOE Sailors Association [5582]
603 S Market St.
Martinsburg, PA 16662
Ph: (772)340-2709

Goin, Charles, Founder, President
Opel Association of North America
[21468]
630 Watch Hill Rd.
Midlothian, VA 23113
Ph: (804)379-9737

Goin, Jeff, President
United States Powered Paragliding
Association [23052]
500 Westover Dr., No. 2384
Sanford, NC 27330
Toll Free: 866-378-7772

Goins, Marnel Niles, VP
Organization for Research on
Women and Communication
[10309]
Box 7381
Dept. of Communication Studies
Southwestern University
1001 E University Ave.
Georgetown, TX 78626

Golbuu, Yimnang, VP
International Society for Reef Studies [4076]
c/o Schneider Group Meeting and
Marketing Services

5400 Bosque Blvd., Ste. 680
Waco, TX 76710-4446
Ph: (254)776-3550

Gold, E.J., Founder
Institute for the Development of the
Harmonious Human Being, Inc.
[12004]
PO Box 370
Nevada City, CA 95959
Ph: (530)271-2239
Toll Free: 800-869-0658
Fax: (530)687-0317

Gold, Jeff, Founder
World Environmental Organization
[3971]
2020 Pennsylvania Ave. NW, Ste.
2001
Washington, DC 20006
Toll Free: 800-800-2099
Fax: (202)351-6867

Gold, Jeffrey, President
Integrative Touch for Kids [14196]
8340 N Thornydale Rd., No. 110-153
Tucson, AZ 85741
Ph: (520)303-4992

Goldacker, Wilfried, President
International Cryogenic Materials
Conference [6357]
908 Main St., Ste. 230
Louisville, CO 80027
Ph: (303)499-2299
Fax: (303)499-2599

Goldberg, Bob, Exec. Dir.
The Myositis Association [15962]
1737 King St., Ste. 600
Alexandria, VA 22314-2764
Ph: (703)299-4850
Toll Free: 800-821-7356
Fax: (703)535-6752

Goldberg, Brad, Director, President
Animal Welfare Advocacy [10582]
141 Halstead Ave., Ste. 301
Mamaroneck, NY 10543
Ph: (914)381-6177
Fax: (914)381-6176

Goldberg, David, Assoc. Dir.
Association of Departments of
Foreign Languages [8178]
85 Broad St., Ste. 500
New York, NY 10004-2434
Ph: (646)576-5140

Goldberg, Ira, Exec. Dir.
Art Students League of New York
[8915]
215 W 57th St.
New York, NY 10019
Ph: (212)247-4510
Fax: (212)541-7024

Goldberg, Joan R., Exec. Dir. (Actg.)
International Association for the
Study of Pain [16558]
1510 H St. NW, Ste. 600
Washington, DC 20005-1020
Ph: (202)524-5300
Fax: (202)524-5301

Goldberg, Linda Lee, Exec. Dir.,
Founder
National Association of Buyers'
Agents [298]
4040 Civic Center Dr., Ste. 200
Terra Linda, CA 94903
Ph: (415)721-7741
Toll Free: 800-517-2277

Goldberg, Max, President
National Association of Marine
Services [2251]
5458 Wagon Master Dr.

Colorado Springs, CO 80917-2235
Ph: (719)573-5946
Fax: (719)573-5952

Goldberg, Mitchell B., VP
Decalogue Society of Lawyers
[5002]
134 N LaSalle St., Ste. 1430
Chicago, IL 60602
Ph: (312)263-6493

Goldberg, Richard M., MD, Co-Ch.
Society for Translational Oncology
[16359]
318 Blackwell St., Ste. 270
Durham, NC 27701
Ph: (919)433-0489

Goldbetter, Larry, President
National Writers Union [23541]
256 W 38th St., Ste. 703
New York, NY 10018
Ph: (212)254-0279
Fax: (212)254-0673

Golden, Carolyn C., Vice Chlr.
Auburn University Montgomery
Alumni Association [19306]
7400 East Dr.
Montgomery, AL 36117
Ph: (334)244-3344
Fax: (334)394-5937

Golden, Dr. Gregory S., Contact
American Board of Forensic Odon-
tology [14772]
Forensic Sciences Foundation, Inc.
410 N 21st St.
Colorado Springs, CO 80904-2798
Ph: (734)697-4400

Golden, Michael, Chairman
International Center for Journalists
[2684]
2000 M St., Ste. 250
Washington, DC 20036
Ph: (202)737-3700
    (202)349-7636

Golden, Michael, Director
Newspaper Association of America
[2807]
4401 Wilson Blvd., Ste. 900
Arlington, VA 22203-1867
Ph: (571)366-1000
Fax: (571)366-1195

Golden, Russell G., Chairman
Financial Accounting Standards
Board [27]
401 Merritt 7
Norwalk, CT 06856-5116
Ph: (203)847-0700
Fax: (203)849-9714

Golden, Tammy, Secretary,
Treasurer
In-Plant Printing and Mailing As-
sociation [2787]
455 S Sam Barr Dr., Ste. 203
Kearney, MO 64060
Ph: (816)919-1691
Fax: (816)902-4766

Goldfield, Matthew, Chairman
National Havurah Committee
[20272]
7135 Germantown Ave., 2nd Fl.
Philadelphia, PA 19119
Ph: (215)248-1335
Fax: (215)248-9760

Goldfield, Norbert, MD, Exec. Dir.
Healing Across the Divides [15465]
72 Laurel Pk.
Northampton, MA 01060

Goldhaber, Dan, President
Association for Education Finance
and Policy [7830]

226 Middlebush Hall
Columbia, MO 65211
Ph: (573)814-9878
Fax: (573)884-4872

Goldin, Kimberly, Gen. Mgr.
International Society for Medical
Publication Professionals [2795]
520 White Plains Rd., Ste. 500
Tarrytown, NY 10591
Toll Free: 888-252-7904
Fax: (914)618-4453

Goldman, Jack, President, CEO
Hearth, Patio and Barbecue Associa-
tion [1617]
1901 N Moore St., Ste. 600
Arlington, VA 22209
Ph: (703)522-0086
Fax: (703)522-0548

Goldman, Jack, President, CEO
Hearth, Patio and Barbecue Educa-
tion Foundation [1618]
1901 N Moore St., Ste. 600
Arlington, VA 22209
Ph: (703)522-0086
Fax: (703)522-0548

Goldman, Jonathan, Director,
Founder
Sound Healers Association [13658]
PO Box 2240
Boulder, CO 80306
Ph: (303)443-8181
Fax: (303)443-6023

Goldman, Ken, President
National Watercolor Society [8876]
915 S Pacific Ave.
San Pedro, CA 90731
Ph: (310)831-1099
(424)225-4966

Goldman, Mark, President
American Conference of Cantors
[20224]
1375 Remington Rd., Ste. M
Schaumburg, IL 60173-4844
Ph: (847)781-7800
Fax: (847)781-7801

Goldman, Mitchel P., MD, Bd.
Member
American Society for Dermatologic
Surgery [14485]
5550 Meadowbrook Dr., Ste. 120
Rolling Meadows, IL 60008
Ph: (847)956-0900
Fax: (847)956-0999

Goldman, Robert, Founder, Chmn.
of the Bd.
American Academy of Anti-Aging
Medicine [15673]
1801 N Military Trail, Ste. 200
Boca Raton, FL 33431
Ph: (561)997-0112
Toll Free: 888-997-0112
Fax: (561)997-0287

Goldman, Ronald, PhD, Exec. Dir.
Anaerobe Society of the Americas
[6074]
PO Box 452058
Los Angeles, CA 90045
Ph: (310)216-9265
Fax: (310)216-9274

Goldman, Theodore D., President,
Treasurer
Chemical Development and Market-
ing Association [6194]
c/o Product Development and
Management Association
401 N Michigan Ave., Ste. 2200
Chicago, IL 60611
Ph: (312)321-5145
Toll Free: 800-232-5241
Fax: (312)673-6885

Goldrich, Sybil Niden, Founder,
Exec. Dir.
Command Trust Network [17755]
11301 W Olympic Blvd., Ste. 332
Los Angeles, CA 90064

Goldsmith, Cindy, Office Mgr.
Antique Telephone Collectors As-
sociation [22443]
PO Box 1252
McPherson, KS 67460
Ph: (620)245-9555

Goldsmith, Michelle, Director
International Brotherhood of
Motorcycle Campers [23038]
PO Box 24
South Fork, CO 81154
Ph: (435)650-3290
(719)873-5466

Goldsmith, Ryan, President
World Wide Opportunities on
Organic Farms - USA [17794]
654 Fillmore St.
San Francisco, CA 94117
Ph: (415)621-3276

Goldstein, Abby, Secretary
Public Radio Program Directors As-
sociation [2826]
150 Hilliard Ave.
Asheville, NC 28801
Ph: (828)424-7510

Goldstein, Avram, Dir. of Comm., Dir.
of Res.
Health Care for America Now
[18333]
1825 K St. NW, Ste. 400
Washington, DC 20006
Ph: (202)454-6200

Goldstein, Bruce, President
Farmworker Justice [12337]
1126 16th St. NW, Ste. 270
Washington, DC 20036
Ph: (202)293-5420

Goldstein, David B., PhD, President
New Buildings Institute [5070]
623 SW Oak St.
Portland, OR 97205
Ph: (503)761-7339
Fax: (503)968-6160

Goldstein, David, Secretary
Workmen's Circle [19502]
247 W 37th St., 5th Fl.
New York, NY 10018
Ph: (212)889-6800
Toll Free: 800-922-2558
Fax: (212)532-7518

Goldstein, Eric, Exec. Dir., Founder
One World Education [8628]
1752 Columbia Rd. NW, 3rd Fl.
Washington, DC 20009

Goldstein, Irwin, MD, President
International Society for the Study of
Women's Sexual Health [17198]
PO Box 1233
Lakeville, MN 55044
Ph: (218)461-5115
Fax: (612)808-0491

Goldstein, Dr. Judith S., Founder,
Exec. Dir.
Humanity in Action [12042]
601 W 26th St., Rm. 325
New York, NY 10001
Ph: (212)828-6874
Fax: (212)704-4130

Goldstein, Justin, Administrator
Web Offset Association [1551]
Printing Industries of America

301 Brush Creek Rd.
Warrendale, PA 15086
Ph: (412)741-6860
Toll Free: 800-910-4283
Fax: (412)741-2311

Goldstein, Mitchell, MD, Medical Dir.
National Coalition for Infant Health
[16622]
1275 Pennsylvania Ave. NW, Ste.
1100
Washington, DC 20004
Ph: (202)499-4114

Goldtooth, Tom, Exec. Dir.
Indigenous Environmental Network
[4116]
PO Box 485
Bemidji, MN 56619
Ph: (218)751-4967

Goldwater, Janice, Founder, Exec.
Dir.
Adoptions Together [10440]
4061 Powder Mill Rd., Ste. 320
Beltsville, MD 20705
Ph: (301)439-2900
Fax: (301)937-2147

Golgart, Jim, President
National Association of County
Veterans Service Officers [21130]
25 Massachusetts Ave. NW, Ste.
500
Washington, DC 20001

Golightly, Steven, President
National Child Support Enforcement
Association [5191]
7918 Jones Branch Dr., Ste. 300
McLean, VA 22102
Ph: (703)506-2880
Fax: (703)506-3266

Golub, Stan, Exec. Dir.
Reel Recovery [10792]
160 Brookside Rd.
Needham, MA 02492
Toll Free: 800-699-4490
Fax: (781)449-9031

Golubovich, Zoran, Director
Serbian-American Chamber of Com-
merce [23616]
448 W Barry Ave.
Chicago, IL 60657
Toll Free: 877-686-7222

Gomez, Allan, Prog. Dir.
Prometheus Radio Project [18664]
PO Box 42158
Philadelphia, PA 19101
Ph: (215)727-9620

Gomez, Kimberley, Mem.
Carnegie Foundation for the
Advancement of Teaching [8646]
51 Vista Ln.
Stanford, CA 94305-8703
Ph: (650)566-5100
Fax: (650)326-0278

Gomez, Leo, PhD, Rep.
National Association for Bilingual
Education [7534]
c/o Ana G. Mendez University
System
1106 Veirs Mills Rd., No. L-1
Wheaton, MD 20902
Ph: (240)450-3700
Fax: (240)450-3799

Gomez, Rosamon, President
National Association of The
Bahamas [19396]
Parish Hall
16711 W Dixie Hwy.
North Miami Beach, FL 33160
Ph: (954)673-0980
Fax: (954)673-0980

Gomez, Teresa C., President, CEO
Futures for Children [11232]
9600 Tennyson St. NE
Albuquerque, NM 87122
Toll Free: 800-545-6843

Gomez-Acuña, Dr. Beatriz, President
Alpha Mu Gamma Honor Society
[23797]
855 N Vermont Ave.
Los Angeles, CA 90029
Ph: (323)644-9752
Fax: (323)644-9752

Gomez-Jelalian, Esperanza,
President
U.S.-Pakistan Business Council
[674]
1615 H St. NW
Washington, DC 20062
Ph: (202)463-5732
Fax: (202)822-2491

Gomulinski, Curtis D., Exec. Dir.,
Editor
Tau Beta Pi Association, Inc. [23745]
508 Dougherty Engineering Bldg.
1512 Middle Dr.
Knoxville, TN 37996
Ph: (865)546-4578
Fax: (865)546-4579

Gonaver, Chris, President
Municipal Waste Management As-
sociation [5845]
United States Conference of Mayors
1620 Eye St. NW
Washington, DC 20006

Gondles, James A., Jr., Exec. Dir.
American Correctional Association
[11517]
206 N Washington St.
Alexandria, VA 22314
Ph: (703)224-0000
Fax: (703)224-0179

Gong, Changzhen, PhD, President
American Academy of Acupuncture
and Oriental Medicine [13586]
1925 County Road B2 W
Roseville, MN 55113-2703
Ph: (651)631-0204
Fax: (651)631-0361

Gong, Stephen, Exec. Dir.
Center for Asian American Media
[17939]
145 9th St., Ste. 350
San Francisco, CA 94103-2641
Ph: (415)863-0814
Fax: (415)863-7428

Gonitzke, Connie, President, CEO
National Foundation for Transplants
[17517]
5350 Poplar Ave., Ste. 430
Memphis, TN 38119
Ph: (901)684-1697
Toll Free: 800-489-3863
Fax: (901)684-1128

Gonlag, Mari, VP
Wesleyan/Holiness Women Clergy
[20377]
305 W 10th St.
Anderson, IN 46016-1323
Ph: (260)241-2993

Gonyeau, Thom, Chairman
Creative Education Foundation
[7758]
46 Watch Hill Dr.
Scituate, MA 02066
Ph: (508)960-0000

González, Antonio, President
William C. Velasquez Institute
[19532]

1426 El Paso St., Ste. A
San Antonio, TX 78207
Ph: (210)223-2918
Fax: (210)922-7095

González-Rojas, Jessica, Exec. Dir.
National Latina Institute for
    Reproductive Health [17111]
50 Broad St., Ste. 1937
New York, NY 10004
Ph: (212)422-2553
Fax: (212)422-2556

Gonzales, Jorge, President
Earth Care [7887]
Bldg. A
6600 Valentine Way
Santa Fe, NM 87507
Ph: (505)983-6896

Gonzales, J.R., President
National Hispanic Professional
    Organization [7975]
PO Box 41780
Austin, TX 78704
Ph: (512)662-0249

Gonzales, Yvette, President
National Association of Professional
    Pet Sitters [2545]
1120 Route 73, Ste. 200
Mount Laurel, NJ 08054
Ph: (856)439-0324
Fax: (856)439-0525

Gonzalez, Mr. Anthony, Director
Child Quest International [10903]
1177 Branham Ln., No.280
San Jose, CA 95118-3766

Gonzalez, Danny, Dir. of Comm.
Move America Forward [19185]
8795 Folsom Blvd., Ste. 103
Sacramento, CA 95826-3720
Ph: (916)441-6197
Fax: (916)383-6608

Gonzalez, Darlene, President
BISH Foundation [13902]
20770 US 281 N, No. 108-114
San Antonio, TX 78258
Ph: (210)287-9881

Gonzalez, Elvia, Mgr., Member Svcs.
Hollywood Radio and Television
    Society [462]
16530 Ventura Blvd.
Encino, CA 91436
Ph: (818)789-1182
Fax: (818)789-1210

Gonzalez, Elvia, Asst. Dir.
Society for Neuroscience [6921]
1121 14th St. NW, Ste. 1010
Washington, DC 20005
Ph: (202)962-4000

Gonzalez, Henry, VP
United States Lighthouse Society
    [9443]
9005 Point No Point Rd. NE
Hansville, WA 98340-8759
Ph: (415)362-7255
Fax: (415)362-7464

Gonzalez, Manny, President
National Latino Officers Association
    [5443]
27-14 Kearney St.
East Elmhurst, NY 11369
Toll Free: 866-579-5806
Fax: (347)426-2188

Gonzalez, Manny, CEO
Scrum Alliance, Inc. [6334]
7401 Church Ranch Blvd., No. 210
Westminster, CO 80021-5539

Gonzalez, Margaret, Founder,
    President
International Association of Hispanic
    Meeting Professionals [2332]

2600 S Shore Blvd., Ste. 300
League City, TX 77573-2944
Ph: (281)245-3330
Fax: (281)668-9199

Gonzalez, Rick, Contact
Association of Residential Construc-
    tion Workers [801]
3680 Wheeler Ave., Ste. 100
Alexandria, VA 22304
Ph: (703)212-8294
Fax: (703)386-6444

Gonzalez-del-Valle, Luis T., Fac.
    Memb.
Society of Spanish and Spanish-
    American Studies [10221]
Anderson Hall, 4th Fl.
Dept. of Spanish and Portuguese
Temple University
1114 W Berks St.
Philadelphia, PA 19122
Ph: (215)204-8285
    (215)204-1706

Good, Byron, President
Society for Psychological Anthropol-
    ogy [7076]
Dept. of Global Health and Social
    Medicine
Harvard Medical School
641 Huntington Ave.
Boston, MA 02115
Ph: (617)432-2612

Good, Megan, Director
Independence Seaport Museum
    [21095]
211 S Columbus Blvd.
Philadelphia, PA 19106
Ph: (215)413-8655
Fax: (215)925-6713

Good, Meriam, Exec. Dir.
Mind Science Foundation [6988]
117 W El Prado Dr.
San Antonio, TX 78212
Ph: (210)821-6094
Fax: (210)821-6199

Good, Nikole, Exec. Dir.
Air and Surface Transport Nurses
    Association [16081]
13918 E Mississippi Ave., Ste. 215
Aurora, CO 80012
Ph: (303)344-0457
Toll Free: 800-897-6362
Fax: (800)937-9890

Good, Richard, President
National Band Association [9970]
c/o Bruce Moss, Music Education
    Committee Chair
537 Monroe Ct.
Bowling Green, OH 43402-1541

Good, William, Exec. VP
National Roofing Contractors As-
    sociation [891]
10255 W Higgins Rd., Ste. 600
Rosemont, IL 60018-5607
Ph: (847)299-9070
Fax: (847)299-1183

Goodall, Ashley, Founder, President
Rock Out To Knock Out RSD
    [15991]
PO Box 5332
Bakersfield, CA 93388-5332
Ph: (661)399-0502

Goodall, Jane, Founder
Jane Goodall Institute [4835]
1595 Spring Hill Rd., Ste. 550
Vienna, VA 22182
Ph: (703)682-9220
Fax: (703)682-9312

Goode, Carl, Jr., Cmdr.
Army & Navy Union U.S.A. [21110]
PO Box 686

Niles, OH 44446

Goodell, Roger, Commissioner
National Football League [22861]
345 Park Ave.
New York, NY 10017
Ph: (212)450-2000

Goodfellow, Bill, Exec. Dir.
Center for International Policy
    [18383]
2000 M St. NW, Ste. 720
Washington, DC 20036
Ph: (202)232-3317
Fax: (202)232-3440

Goodin, Barbara, Secretary,
    Treasurer
Comanche Language and Cultural
    Preservation Committee [10037]
1375 NE Cline Rd.
Elgin, OK 73538-3086
Ph: (580)492-4988
Toll Free: 877-492-4988
Fax: (580)492-5119

Goodman, Dr. Allan E., CEO,
    President
Institute of International Education
    [8075]
IIE New York City
809 United Nations Plz.
New York, NY 10017-3503
Ph: (212)883-8200
Fax: (212)984-5452

Goodman, Craig, President
National Energy Marketers Associa-
    tion [1117]
3333 K St. NW, Ste. 110
Washington, DC 20007
Ph: (202)333-3288
Fax: (202)333-3266

Goodman, Donna L., Founder
Earth Child Institute [4048]
777 United Nations Plz.
New York, NY 10017

Goodman, Gail S., President
APA Division 7: Developmental
    Psychology [16868]
750 1st St. NE
Washington, DC 20002-4242
Ph: (202)336-5500

Goodman, Dr. Joel, Director,
    Founder
HUMOR Project [9561]
10 Madison Ave.
Saratoga Springs, NY 12866
Ph: (518)587-8770

Goodman, John, Officer
The Independent Institute [18983]
100 Swan Way
Oakland, CA 94621-1428
Ph: (510)632-1366
Fax: (510)568-6040

Goodman, John, Chairman
Professional Services Council
    [18289]
4401 Wilson Blvd., Ste. 1110
Arlington, VA 22203
Ph: (703)875-8059
Fax: (703)875-8922

Goodman, Julie, Comm. Chm.
National Association of Student
    Anthropologists [7494]
c/o Suzanne Marie Barber, President
Indiana University
107 S Indiana Ave.
Bloomington, IN 47405

Goodman, Kathy Landau, AuD,
    Chairperson
Audiology Awareness Campaign
    [13733]

1 Windsor Cove, Ste. 305
Columbia, SC 29223
Toll Free: 800-445-8629
Fax: (803)765-0860

Goodman, Meg, Mem.
Business Marketing Association
    [2270]
708 3rd Ave.
New York, NY 10017
Ph: (212)697-5950

Goodman, Ruth, Mgr.
Israeli Dance Institute [9264]
225 W 34th St., Ste. 1607
New York, NY 10122
Ph: (212)983-4806
Fax: (212)983-4084

Goodman-Collins, Darcie, PhD,
    Exec. Dir.
League to Save Lake Tahoe [3895]
2608 Lake Tahoe Blvd.
South Lake Tahoe, CA 96150
Ph: (530)541-5388
Fax: (530)541-5454

Goodnight, Randy, Founder,
    President
United States Football Alliance
    [22870]
c/o Danial Marshall, League Com-
    missioner
Morgantown, WV 26505
Ph: (724)866-1714

Goodrich, Jennifer J., Exec. Dir.
National Field Hockey Coaches As-
    sociation [22836]
3352 E Virgil Dr.
Gilbert, AZ 85298
Ph: (480)789-1136

Goodrich, Kristopher, President
Association for Lesbian, Gay,
    Bisexual and Transgender Issues
    in Counseling [11872]
c/o Joy Whitman, Representative
Walden University
100 Washington Ave. S, Ste. 900
Minneapolis, MN 55401-2455
Ph: (773)230-1789

Goodrich, Nina, Director
Sustainable Packaging Coalition
    [2484]
600 E Water St., Ste. C
Charlottesville, VA 22902-5361
Ph: (434)817-1424

Goodman, Benny, Exec. Dir.
International Narcotics Interdiction
    Association [5227]
PO Box 1757
Spring Hill, TN 37174
Toll Free: 866-780-4642

Goodwein, Mark, Director
Wirehaired Vizsla Club of America
    [21993]
100 Gill Field Ct.
Lexington, SC 29072

Goodwin, Barry, President
Agricultural and Applied Economics
    Association [6376]
555 E Wells St., Ste. 1100
Milwaukee, WI 53202
Ph: (414)918-3190
    (919)515-4620

Goodwin, Celeste, President
National Pediatric Blood Pressure
    Awareness Foundation [15349]
38261 Brown Rd.
Prairieville, LA 70769
Ph: (225)955-2770
Fax: (225)677-8702

Goodwin, Corin Barsily, President, Exec. Dir.
Gifted Homeschoolers Forum **[11915]**
1467 Siskiyou Blvd., No. 174
Ashland, OR 97520

Goodwin, Frank, President
SATS/EAF Association **[21019]**
2514 Hickory St.
New Bern, NC 28562

Goodwin, Dr. Michele Bratcher, President
Defence for Children International-USA **[10953]**
2215 Pillsbury Ave. S
Minneapolis, MN 55404
Ph: (612)626-9305

Goodwin, Peter, Treasurer, COO
Josiah Macy Jr. Foundation **[14945]**
44 E 64th St.
New York, NY 10065-7306
Ph: (212)486-2424
Fax: (212)644-0765

Goodwin, Peter, President
Orienteering USA **[23051]**
c/o Glen Schorr, Executive Director
PO Box 505
Riderwood, MD 21139
Ph: (410)802-1125

Goodwin, Richard C., Chairman
Middle East Peace Dialogue Network, Inc. **[12437]**
PO Box 943
Atco, NJ 08004
Ph: (856)768-0938
Fax: (856)768-1444

Goodwin, Robert, Founder
Executives Without Borders **[631]**
281 Summer St., 5th Fl.
Boston, MA 02210
Toll Free: 800-790-6134

Goolsby, Susan M., Mgr.
Job's Daughters International **[19562]**
233 W 6th St.
Papillion, NE 68046-2210
Ph: (402)592-7987
Fax: (402)592-2177

Goonight, Bill, President
National Country Ham Association **[1356]**
PO Box 948
Conover, NC 28613
Ph: (828)466-2760
Toll Free: 800-820-4426
Fax: (828)466-2770

Goosman, Gary, Dir. of Comm.
ACCSES **[17965]**
1501 M St. NW, 7th Fl.
Washington, DC 20005
Ph: (202)349-4259
Fax: (202)785-1756

Gopalak, Sangeetha, President
International Association for Language Learning Technology **[8184]**
c/o Sangeetha Gopalakrishnan, President
Wayne State University
385 Manoogian Hall
906 W Warren
Detroit, MI 48202

Gopalakrishnan, Geetha, MD, President
Association of Program Directors in Endocrinology, Diabetes and Metabolism **[14701]**

2055 L St. NW, Ste. 600
Washington, DC 20036
Ph: (202)971-3706
Fax: (202)736-9705

Gopalakrishnan, Gopi, Founder, President
World Health Partners **[15508]**
1875 Connecticut Ave. NW
Washington, DC 20008

Gor, Edmond J., President
Chinese American Citizens Alliance **[19413]**
1044 Stockton St.
San Francisco, CA 94108

Gorbsky, Gary J., Treasurer
American Society for Cell Biology **[6069]**
8120 Woodmont Ave., Ste. 750
Bethesda, MD 20814
Ph: (301)347-9300
Fax: (301)347-9310

Gordils, Wanda, President
National Conference of Puerto Rican Women **[18223]**
1220 L St. NW, Ste. 100-177
Washington, DC 20005
Ph: (773)405-3535

Gordley, John, Exec. Dir.
U.S. Canola Association **[1379]**
600 Pennsylvania Ave. SE, Ste. 320
Washington, DC 20003
Ph: (202)969-8113
Fax: (202)969-7036

Gordon, Audrey, Esq., President, Exec. Dir.
Progeria Research Foundation **[17348]**
PO Box 3453
Peabody, MA 01961-3453
Ph: (978)535-2594
Fax: (978)535-5849

Gordon, Barbara Ribakove, Exec. Dir., Founder
North American Conference on Ethiopian Jewry **[18593]**
255 W 36th St., Rm. 701
New York, NY 10018
Ph: (212)233-5200

Gordon, Bruce, Founder, Exec. Dir.
EcoFlight **[3998]**
307 L Aspen Airport Business Ctr.
Aspen, CO 81611
Ph: (970)429-1110
Fax: (970)429-1110

Gordon, Bruce, Chairperson
Nuclear Information Technology Strategic Leadership **[6933]**
c/o Mary Lou Furtek
30 Thayer Way
Phoenixville, PA 19460

Gordon, Dean, Bd. Member
NAHAD - Association for Hose and Accessories Distribution **[1752]**
105 Eastern Ave., Ste. 104
Annapolis, MD 21403
Ph: (410)940-6350
Toll Free: 800-624-2227
Fax: (410)263-1659

Gordon, Doris, Founder, Coord.
Libertarians for Life **[18643]**
13424 Hathaway Dr.
Wheaton, MD 20906
Ph: (301)460-4141

Gordon, Duane, President
Attention Deficit Disorder Association **[15907]**

PO Box 103
Denver, PA 17517-0103
Toll Free: 800-939-1019
Fax: (800)939-1019

Gordon, Gabrielle, VP
Cleveland Bay Horse Society of North America **[4343]**
PO Box 483
Goshen, NH 03752
Ph: (703)401-4054
(817)431-8775

Gordon, Jason, President
Ceilings and Interior Systems Construction Association **[859]**
1010 Jorie Blvd., Ste. 30
Oak Brook, IL 60523
Ph: (630)584-1919
Fax: (866)560-8537

Gordon, John R., Chairman
myFace **[14342]**
Lobby Office
333 E 30th St.
New York, NY 10016
Ph: (212)263-6656
Fax: (212)263-7534

Gordon, Joi, CEO
Dress for Success Worldwide **[13375]**
32 E 31st St., 7th Fl.
New York, NY 10016
Ph: (212)532-1922
Fax: (212)684-9563

Gordon, Dr. Joseph, Chairman
International Association for Intelligence Education **[8041]**
PO Box 10508
Erie, PA 16514-0508
Ph: (814)824-2131
Fax: (814)824-2008

Gordon, Patricia Trudell, Founder
Indian Youth of America **[12376]**
PO Box 2786
Sioux City, IA 51106-0786
Ph: (712)252-3230
Fax: (712)252-3712

Gordon, Randall C., President
National Grain and Feed Association **[4178]**
1250 I St. NW, Ste. 1003
Washington, DC 20005
Ph: (202)289-0873
Fax: (202)289-5388

Gordon, Rich, COO
International Rett Syndrome Foundation **[15946]**
4600 Devitt Dr.
Cincinnati, OH 45246
Ph: (513)874-3020
Toll Free: 800-818-7388
Fax: (513)874-2520

Gordon, Richard, President
Cosmopolitan International **[12888]**
PO Box 7351
Lancaster, PA 17604
Ph: (717)295-7142
Toll Free: 800-648-4331
Fax: (717)295-7143

Gordon, Robin, Director
American Society for the Protection of Nature in Israel **[3806]**
c/o Robin Gordon, Director
28 Arrandale Ave.
Great Neck, NY 11024
Toll Free: 800-411-0966

Gordy, Jennifer, President
Melorheostosis Association **[14842]**
410 E 50th St.

New York, NY 10022

Gore, Belinda, VP
International Enneagram Association **[8411]**
4010 Executive Park Dr., Ste. 100
Cincinnati, OH 45241
Ph: (513)232-5054
Fax: (513)563-9743

Gore, Mary, VP of Admin.
Association of Resort and Leisure Ministers **[20359]**
c/o Mary Gore
3840 Carter's Ferry Rd.
Zwolle, LA 71486

Gore, Richard D., Sr., CEO
Marine Corps League **[5572]**
8626 Lee Hwy., Ste. 201
Fairfax, VA 22031
Ph: (703)207-9588
Toll Free: 800-625-1775
Fax: (703)207-0047

Gore, Sally, Director
Kidney Community Emergency Response Coalition **[15879]**
3000 Bayport Dr., Ste. 300
Tampa, FL 33607
Toll Free: 866-901-3773

Goreau, Dr. Thomas J., President
Global Coral Reef Alliance **[3876]**
37 Pleasant St.
Cambridge, MA 02139
Ph: (617)864-4226
(617)864-0433

Gorecki, Robert, Chairman
Dawn Bible Students Association **[19756]**
199 Railroad Ave.
East Rutherford, NJ 07073-1915
Toll Free: 888-440-3296

Goren, Dave, Exec. Dir.
National Sports Media Association **[2707]**
307 Summit Ave.
Salisbury, NC 28144
Ph: (704)633-4275

Goretsk, Winston J., President
African Violet Society of America **[22064]**
2375 N St.
Beaumont, TX 77702-1722
Ph: (409)839-4725
Toll Free: 844-400-2872

Gorga, Greg, President
Council of American Maritime Museums **[9828]**
c/o Paul Fontenoy, Treasurer
North Carolina Maritime Museum
315 Front St.
Beaufort, NC 28516

Gorham, Millicent, Exec. Dir.
National Black Nurses Association **[16156]**
8630 Fenton St., Ste. 330
Silver Spring, MD 20910-3803
Ph: (301)589-3200
Fax: (301)589-3223

Gorley, Jerry, President
Contemporary Historical Vehicle Association **[21361]**
PO Box 493398
Redding, CA 96049-3398

Gorman, Alicia, Contact
Making a Difference in Infectious Diseases Pharmacotherapy **[16669]**
PO Box 1604

Fairfield, CT 06825
Ph: (203)373-0599
Toll Free: 866-373-0599

Gorman, Christelle, Exec. Asst.
National Alliance of State and Ter-
ritorial AIDS Directors [10547]
444 N Capitol St. NW, Ste. 339
Washington, DC 20001
Ph: (202)434-8090
Fax: (202)434-8092

Gorman, Pat, President
Utility Supply Management Alliance
[3428]
c/o Alan Morris, Treasurer
2800 Quail Run Dr., Ste. 100
Corinth, TX 76208

Gormley, Tom, Mgr.
American Iris Society [22078]
c/o Tom Gormley, Membership
Secretary
PO Box 177
De Leon Springs, FL 32130
Ph: (386)277-2057
Fax: (386)277-2057

Gorn, Dr. Cathy, Exec. Dir.
National History Day [7989]
4511 Knox Rd., Ste. 205
College Park, MD 20740
Ph: (301)314-9739

Gorny, Toby, Founder, President
Crown Victoria Association [21365]
PO Box 6
Bryan, OH 43506-0006
Ph: (419)636-2475
Fax: (419)636-8449

Gorsegner Ehlinger, Betty, Exec. Dir.
Association for Information Media
and Equipment [263]
PO Box 9844
Cedar Rapids, IA 52409-9844

Gorton, Mark, President, Founder
OpenPlans [6283]
148 Lafayette St., 12th Fl.
New York, NY 10013
Ph: (917)388-9033
Fax: (646)390-2624

Gorzkowski, Ed, Secretary
Ceramic Educational Council [6171]
600 N Cleveland Ave., Ste. 210
Westerville, OH 43082
Ph: (240)646-7054
   (866)721-3322
Fax: (240)396-5637

Goscinski, Lt. Comdr. Rosie,
President
Sea Service Leadership Association
[21077]
PO Box 40371
Arlington, VA 22204

Gosiewski, Sean, Exec. Dir.
Alliance for Sustainability [4148]
2801 21st Ave. S, Ste. 100
Minneapolis, MN 55407
Ph: (612)250-0389

Gosper, Bruce, CEO
Australian Trade and Investment
Commission [3297]
150 E 42nd St., 34th Fl.
New York, NY 10017-5612
Ph: (646)344-8111
Fax: (212)867-7710

Goss, Elizabeth, Contact
Cancer Leadership Council [13925]
2446 39th St. NW
Washington, DC 20007
Ph: (202)333-4041
Fax: (202)333-4081

Goss, Martin, VP
National Sunroom Association [562]
1300 Sumner Ave.
Cleveland, OH 44115-2851
Ph: (216)241-7333
Fax: (216)241-0105

Goss, Victoria, President
Last Chance Corral [10657]
5350 US-33 S
Athens, OH 45701
Ph: (740)594-4336

Goss, Wayne L., President
International Right of Way Associa-
tion [5743]
19210 S Vermont Ave.
Bldg. A, Ste. 100
Gardena, CA 90248
Ph: (310)538-0233
Toll Free: 888-340-4792
Fax: (310)538-1471

Gosselin, Rev. Bradley, President
National Spiritualist Association of
Churches [20510]
13 Cottage Row
Lily Dale, NY 14752
Ph: (716)595-2000
Fax: (716)595-2020

Gossett, A. C., III, Chmn. of the Bd.
American Concrete Pipe Association
[2601]
8445 Freeport Pky., Ste. 350
Irving, TX 75063-2595
Ph: (972)506-7216
Fax: (972)506-7682

Gossiaux, Gen. Dale, President
Knights of Saint John International
[19849]
c/o Bruce Stowers, Membership
Chairman
29 Cranberry Ln.
Delran, NJ 08075
Ph: (856)764-3147

Gosta, Predrag, PGCE, Founder,
President
Early Music Network Inc. [9903]
PO Box 854
Atlanta, GA 30301-0854
Ph: (770)638-7574

Gothard, Bill, Founder, President
Institute in Basic Life Principles
[13452]
Box 1
Oak Brook, IL 60522-3001
Ph: (630)323-9800

Goto, Glen S., CEO
Raisin Bargaining Association [4249]
2444 Main St., No. 160
Fresno, CA 93721
Ph: (559)221-1925
Fax: (559)221-0725

Gotta, Roy, Chairman
International Association of Round
Dance Teachers [9260]
2803 Louisiana St.
Longview, WA 98632-3536
Ph: (360)423-7423
Toll Free: 877-943-2623

Gottesfeld, Mr. Perry, President
Occupational Knowledge
International [4555]
4444 Geary Blvd., Ste. 208
San Francisco, CA 94118
Ph: (415)221-8900
Fax: (415)221-8903

Gottlieb, Alan, Director
Jews for the Preservation of
Firearms Ownership [17904]

12500 NE 10th Pl.
Bellevue, WA 98005
Toll Free: 800-869-1884
Fax: (425)451-3959

Gottlieb, Alan M., Chairman
Citizens Committee for the Right to
Keep and Bear Arms [17886]
Liberty Park
12500 NE 10th Pl.
Bellevue, WA 98005
Ph: (425)454-4911
Toll Free: 800-486-6963
Fax: (425)451-3959

Gottlieb, Alan, Founder
Second Amendment Foundation
[17930]
12500 NE 10th Pl.
Bellevue, WA 98005
Ph: (425)454-7012

Gottlieb, Cass, Chairman
Jewish Education Service of North
America [8138]
247 W 37th St., 5th Fl.
New York, NY 10018
Ph: (212)284-6877
Fax: (212)532-7518

Gottlieb, Eng. Martin S., President
American Institute of Engineers
[6532]
5420 San Martin Way
Antioch, CA 94531-8506
Ph: (510)758-6240
Fax: (510)758-6240

Gottschalk, John, Director
Quail Forever [4874]
1783 Buerkle Cir.
Saint Paul, MN 55110
Ph: (651)773-2000
Toll Free: 877-773-2070

Gottstein, James B., President, CEO
Law Project for Psychiatric Rights
[12049]
406 G St., Ste. 206
Anchorage, AK 99501
Ph: (907)274-7686
Fax: (907)274-9493

Goudeseune, Scott, CEO, President
American Council on Exercise
[16692]
4851 Paramont Dr.
San Diego, CA 92123-1449
Ph: (858)576-6500
Toll Free: 888-825-3636
Fax: (858)576-6564

Goudie, John C., President
American Alliance of Paralegals, Inc.
[5658]
4023 Kennett Pke., Ste. 146
Wilmington, DE 19807-2018

Gough, Karen, Coord.
Health Action Council [15143]
6133 Rockside Rd., Ste. 210
Cleveland, OH 44131
Ph: (216)328-2200

Gould, Deb Lee, Director
Fatty Oxidation Disorders Family
Support Group [17338]
1745 Hamilton Rd., Ste. 330
Okemos, MI 48864
Ph: (517)381-1940
Fax: (866)290-5206

Gould, Deb Lee, Director, President
FOD Family Support Group [15823]
1745 Hamilton Rd., Ste. 330
Okemos, MI 48864
Ph: (517)381-1940
Fax: (866)290-5206

Gould, Earl, Founder
Association of Certified Background
Investigators [5354]
c/o Donald Johnson, Secretary
6873 Auckland Dr.
Austin, TX 78749

Gould, Larry, Exec. Dir.
Western Social Science Association
[7174]
2307 Chof Trl.
Flagstaff, AZ 86005

Gould, Marc, Exec. Dir.
Real Estate Buyer's Agent Council
[2889]
430 N Michigan Ave.
Chicago, IL 60611
Ph: (312)329-8656
Toll Free: 800-648-6224
Fax: (312)329-8632

Gould, Mark R., Director
American Library Association Public
Awareness Office [9674]
50 E Huron St.
Chicago, IL 60611
Ph: (312)280-4393
   (312)280-1546

Gould-Earley, Mary Jean, Rep.
Fell Pony Society of North America,
Inc. [4350]
c/o Kim Owens, General Secretary
1041 Scott Rd.
Coldwater, MS 38618-3070
Ph: (662)622-0267
Fax: (901)212-2034

Goulding, Tressa, CAE, Exec. Dir.
Scoliosis Research Society [17186]
555 E Wells St., Ste. 1100
Milwaukee, WI 53202-3823
Ph: (414)289-9107
Fax: (414)276-3349

Gousse, Ralph, MD, President
Haiti Help Med Plus, Inc. [11921]
3145 Cecelia Dr.
Apopka, FL 32703
Ph: (407)928-8317
Fax: (407)964-1189

Gow, Andrew, President
Nitric Oxide Society [6209]
2604 Elmwood Ave., No. 350
Rochester, NY 14618

Gow, Monica, Exec. Dir., Founder
Wake Up Narcolepsy [13791]
PO Box 60293
Worcester, MA 01606
Ph: (978)751-3693

Gowdy, Kathy, Secretary, Treasurer
National Association of Decorative
Fabric Distributors [3264]
1 Windsor Cove, Ste. 305
Columbia, SC 29223
Ph: (803)765-0860
Toll Free: 800-445-8629

Gowen, Alex, Founder, Director
The Fishermen [10977]
PO Box 17171
Raleigh, NC 27619
Ph: (919)452-2405

Gowens, Pat, Editor
Welfare Warriors [18766]
2711 W Michigan Ave.
Milwaukee, WI 53208
Ph: (414)342-6662

Gower, Dan, Exec. Dir.
DUSTOFF Association [20719]
PO Box 8091, Wainwright Sta.
San Antonio, TX 78208

Gowey, Dr. Brandie, NMD, Founder, President
Naturopaths International [15864]
3011 N West St.
Flagstaff, AZ 86004
Ph: (928)214-8793

Goyal, Sushil, Director
International Colored Gemstone Association [3185]
30 W 47th St., Ste. 201
New York, NY 10036
Ph: (212)620-0900
Fax: (212)352-9054

Goyer, Anne, Exec. VP
Industrial Heating Equipment Association [1622]
5040 Old Taylor Mill Rd.
Latonia, KY 41015
Ph: (859)356-1575
Fax: (859)356-0908

Grabbe, Heather, Director
Open Society Foundations [18526]
224 W 57th St.
New York, NY 10019-3212
Ph: (212)548-0600
Fax: (212)548-4600

Grabowicz, George, President
Shevchenko Scientific Society [19678]
63 4th Ave.
New York, NY 10003
Ph: (212)254-5130
Fax: (212)254-5239

Grabowski, Eric, President
Thrombosis and Hemostasis Societies of North America [15246]
2111 Chestnut Ave., Ste. 145
Glenview, IL 60025
Ph: (847)978-2001

Gracey, Kyle, Chmn. of the Bd.
SustainUS [13482]
1718 21st St. NW
Washington, DC 20009

Gracie, Tanya, President
Association of Cooperative Educators [7676]
1057 Parkview Ln.
Victoria, MN 55386-3709
Ph: (763)432-2032

Gradeless, Rex L., Treasurer
National Huguenot Society [21004]
7340 Blanco Rd., Ste. 104
San Antonio, TX 78216
Ph: (210)366-9995

Graden, John, Founder, Exec. Dir.
Martial Arts Teachers' Association [23003]
800 S Gulfview Blvd., Ste. 804
Clearwater Beach, FL 33767

Gradwohl, Prof. Richard, Director, Founder
International Miniature Cattle Breeders Society and Registry [3731]
16000 SE 252nd Pl.
Covington, WA 98042
Ph: (253)631-1911
Fax: (253)631-5774

Grady, Brian, Exec.
North American Thermal Analysis Society [7330]
c/o Greg Jewell, Executive Director
PO Box 4961
Louisville, KY 40204
Ph: (502)456-1851
Fax: (502)456-1821

Grady, Justin, President
Miniature Hereford Breeders Association [3735]

c/o Fran MacKenzie, Treasurer
60885 Salt Creek Rd.
Collbran, CO 81624
Ph: (970)487-3182

Graening, Joyce, President
Missouri Fox Trotting Horse Breed Association [4378]
1 Mile N Highway 5
Ava, MO 65608
Ph: (417)683-2468
Fax: (417)683-6144

Graetz, Rabbi Tzvi, Exec. Dir.
World Council of Conservative/Masorti Synagogues [20292]
3080 Broadway
New York, NY 10027
Ph: (212)280-6039
Fax: (212)678-5321

Graf, Kristen, Exec. Dir.
Women of Wind Energy [7393]
155 Water St.
Brooklyn, NY 11201
Ph: (718)210-3666

Graf, Marie, Chairman
FutureChurch [19838]
17307 Madison Ave.
Lakewood, OH 44107
Ph: (216)228-0869
Fax: (216)228-4872

Graff, Stuart I., President, CEO
Frank Lloyd Wright Foundation [7502]
12621 N Frank Lloyd Wright Blvd.
Scottsdale, AZ 85259
Ph: (480)860-2700

Grafton, Steve, CEO, President
Alumni Association of the University of Michigan [19302]
200 Fletcher St.
Ann Arbor, MI 48109-1007
Ph: (734)764-0384
Toll Free: 800-847-4764

Gragg, Steven, President
Lambda Alpha International [23725]
PO Box 72720
Phoenix, AZ 85050
Ph: (480)719-7404
Fax: (602)532-7865

Grago, David M., Sr., Chairman
International Chinese Boxing Association Worldwide [22713]
3465 Blackhawk St.
Helena, MT 59602
Ph: (214)796-4039

Graham, Alexander T., Exec. Dir.
Council for Exceptional Children [8667]
2900 Crystal Dr., Ste. 1000
Arlington, VA 22202-3557
Toll Free: 888-232-7733

Graham, Anita, President
Association of Pediatric Oncology Social Workers [16603]
c/o Anita Graham, MSW, LCSW, President
Dept. of Pediatrics, Section of Hematology/Oncology
WVU Healthcare Children's Hospital
Morgantown, WV 26506-9214
Ph: (304)293-1205
Fax: (304)293-1216

Graham, Billy, Chairman
Billy Graham Evangelistic Association [20130]
1 Billy Graham Pkwy.
Charlotte, NC 28201-0001
Ph: (704)401-2432
Toll Free: 877-247-2426

Graham, Bob, Chairperson
AMBUCS [12883]
4285 Regency Dr.
Greensboro, NC 27410-8101
Toll Free: 800-838-1845
Fax: (336)852-6830

Graham, Bob, Chmn. of the Bd.
International Automotive Remarketers Alliance [295]
257 N Calderwood St., No. 316
Alcoa, TN 37701
Ph: (865)805-5954
Toll Free: 866-277-6996

Graham, Dr. Charles, President
American Breeds Coalition [3688]
3003 S Loop W, Ste. 520
Houston, TX 77054

Graham, David E., Chairperson
TRI Princeton [3274]
601 Prospect Ave.
Princeton, NJ 08542
Ph: (609)430-4820

Graham, David W., Chairman, Founder
Association of Certified Green Technology Auditors [6457]
1802 N University Dr., Ste. 112
Plantation, FL 33322
Ph: (954)594-3584
Fax: (754)551-5354

Graham, Franklin, Co-Ch.
Presidential Prayer Team [20300]
PO Box 69010
Tucson, AZ 85737-9010
Toll Free: 866-433-7729
Fax: (480)347-2691

Graham, Franklin, Chmn. of the Bd., President
Samaritan's Purse [12301]
PO Box 3000
Boone, NC 28607
Ph: (828)262-1980
Fax: (828)266-1056

Graham, Gloria, President
Association of Healthcare Value Analysis Professionals [14983]
1000 Westgate Dr., Ste. 252
Saint Paul, MN 55114
Ph: (651)290-6288
Fax: (651)290-2266

Graham, Dr. James, President
Alpha Tau Alpha [7470]
c/o Rebekah Barnes Epps
The University of Kentucky
College of Agriculture, Food, and Environment
708 Garrigus Bldg.
Lexington, KY 40546

Graham, John, President
American Backflow Prevention Association [7354]
3016 Maloney Ave.
Bryan, TX 77801-3121
Ph: (979)846-7606
Toll Free: 877-227-2127
Fax: (979)846-7607

Graham, Karen, Exec. Dir.
International Neuroethics Society [16052]
PO Box 34252
Bethesda, MD 20827
Ph: (301)229-1660

Graham, Norma, Treasurer
Vision Sciences Society [7151]
19 Richardson Rd.
Novato, CA 94949
Ph: (415)883-3301
Fax: (415)593-7606

Graham, Peter W., President
Byron Society of America [9046]
Univ. of English, Dept. of English
219 Bryan Hall
PO Box 400121
Charlottesville, VA 22904

Graham, Robert, MD, Chairman
Alliance for Health Reform [18326]
1444 Eye St. NW, Ste. 910
Washington, DC 20005-6573
Ph: (202)789-2300
Fax: (202)789-2233

Graham, Sharon, Consultant
National Association for Continuing Education [7671]
300 NW 70th Ave., Ste. 102
Plantation, FL 33317
Ph: (954)723-0057
Toll Free: 866-266-6223
Fax: (954)723-0353

Graham, Susan, Exec. Dir.
Project RACE [19431]
PO Box 2366
Los Banos, CA 93635
Fax: (209)826-2510

Graham, Susan, VP
The Transformer Association [1578]
1300 Sumner Ave.
Cleveland, OH 44115
Ph: (216)241-7333
Fax: (216)241-0105

Graham, Thomas M., PhD, Founder, President
Center for Organizational and Ministry Development [19950]
PO Box 49488
Colorado Springs, CO 80949-9488
Ph: (719)590-8808

Graham, W. Franklin, III, President, Chairman
World Medical Mission [15751]
c/o Samaritan's Purse
PO Box 3000
Boone, NC 28607
Ph: (828)262-1980
Fax: (828)266-1056

Graham, Ms. Zehra Schneider, CHMM, Advisor, Director
Alliance of Hazardous Materials Professionals [4290]
9707 Key W Ave., Ste. 100
Rockville, MD 20850
Ph: (301)329-6850
Fax: (301)990-9771

Grahl, Timothy M., Founder
Mustang II Network [21445]
115 McDonald Dr.
Houghton Lake, MI 48629
Ph: (313)653-1516

Grajales, José, President
Lambda Theta Phi Latin Fraternity [23759]
181 New Rd., Ste. 304
Parsippany, NJ 07054-5625
Toll Free: 866-4-A-LAMBDA

Gran, Brian, Mem.
American Association for the Advancement of Science - Science and Human Rights Coalition [18369]
1200 New York Ave. NW
Washington, DC 20005-3928
Ph: (202)326-6400

Granahan, Sean T., Esq, Gen. Counsel, President
The Floating Hospital [15326]
41-43 Crescent St.

Long Island City, NY 11101
Ph: (718)784-2240

Granich, Debra, CEO
The Red Hat Society Inc. [10310]
431 S Acacia Ave.
Fullerton, CA 92831
Ph: (714)738-0001
Toll Free: 866-386-2850
Fax: (714)738-0005

Granieri, Marie, Chief of Staff
Crohn's and Colitis Foundation of
America [14786]
733 3rd Ave., Ste. 510
New York, NY 10017
Ph: (212)685-3440
Toll Free: 800-932-2423
Fax: (212)779-4098

Grann, Douglas H., CEO, President
Wildlife Forever [4913]
2700 Freeway Blvd., No. 1000
Brooklyn Center, MN 55430-1779
Ph: (763)253-0222

Grannan, David W., President
International Claim Association
[1877]
1155 15th St. NW, Ste. 500
Washington, DC 20005
Ph: (202)452-0143
Fax: (202)530-0659

Grannell, Barbara, Exec. Dir.,
Founder
A Promise of Health [15060]
PO Box 247
Hiawatha, IA 52233
Ph: (719)547-1995
    (719)873-5450

Grannis, Renee, Director
Association of Bridal Consultants
[442]
56 Danbury Rd., Ste. 11
New Milford, CT 06776
Ph: (860)355-7000
Fax: (860)354-1404

Granpeesheh, Dr. Doreen, President
Autism Care and Treatment Today!
[13746]
21600 Oxnard St., Ste. 1800
Woodland Hills, CA 91367
Ph: (818)340-4010
Toll Free: 877-922-8863

Grant, Christine, President
Casey's Cause [13839]
PO Box 1305
Trussville, AL 35173
Ph: (205)281-3037

Grant, Gary R., President
Black Farmers and Agriculturists As-
sociation [3559]
PO Box 61
Tillery, NC 27887-0061
Ph: (252)826-3017
Fax: (252)826-3244

Grant, Dr. Gerald T., President
American Academy of Maxillofacial
Prosthetics [14381]
c/o Dr. Jeffery C. Markt, Vice
President
Dept. of Otolaryngology - Head &
Neck Surgery
University of Nebraska Medical Ctr.
981225 Nebraska Medical Ctr.
Omaha, NE 68198-1225

Grant, Jacquelyn, PhD, Director,
Founder
The Office of Black Women in
Church and Society [20645]
700 Martin Luther King Jr. Dr.

Atlanta, GA 30314
Ph: (404)527-5710
Fax: (404)525-5715

Grant, Jo, President
Bikes for the Philippines, Inc.
[10779]
PO Box 43
Westminster, MA 01473
Ph: (978)621-2599

Grant, Jodi, Exec. Dir.
Afterschool Alliance [10801]
1616 H St. NW, Ste. 820
Washington, DC 20006
Ph: (202)347-2030
Toll Free: 866-543-7863
Fax: (202)347-2092

Grant, Kate, CEO
Fistula Foundation [14229]
1922 The Alameda, Ste. 302
San Jose, CA 95126
Ph: (408)249-9596
Toll Free: 866-756-3700

Grant, Laura, Exec. Dir.
American Rhododendron Society
[22083]
c/o Laura Grant, Executive Director
PO Box 525
Niagara Falls, NY 14302

Grant, Marcus, President
International Center for Alcohol Poli-
cies [186]
The Jefferson Bldg., Ste. 500
1225 19th St. NW
Washington, DC 20036
Ph: (202)986-1159
Fax: (202)986-2080

Grantland, Brenda, Esq., President
Forfeiture Endangers American
Rights [5086]
20 Sunnyside Ave., Ste. A-419
Mill Valley, CA 94941
Ph: (415)381-6105
Toll Free: 888-332-7001

Graper, Mary L., President
Wilson Disease Association
International [14615]
5572 N Diversey Blvd.
Milwaukee, WI 53217
Ph: (414)961-0533
Toll Free: 866-961-0533

Graper, Mary L., President
Wilson's Disease Association
[15836]
5572 N Diversey Blvd.
Milwaukee, WI 53217
Ph: (414)961-0533
Toll Free: 866-961-0533

Grasinger, Todd, Chmn. of the Bd.
National Coalition of Anti-Violence
Programs [19230]
116 Nassau St., 3rd Fl.
New York, NY 10038
Ph: (212)714-1184
    (212)714-1141

Grass, Peter T., President
Asphalt Institute [493]
2696 Research Park Dr.
Lexington, KY 40511-8480
Ph: (859)288-4960
Fax: (859)288-4999

Grate, Shifu/Sensei Koré, Exec. Dir.
Association of Women Martial Arts
Instructors [22987]
PO Box 28166
Las Vegas, NV 89126

Grau, John, CEO
National Electrical Contractors Association [888]

3 Bethesda Metro Ctr., Ste. 1100
Bethesda, MD 20814
Ph: (301)657-3110
Fax: (301)215-4500

Grauds, Constance, RPh, President
Association of Natural Medicine
Pharmacists [15858]
PO Box 150727
San Rafael, CA 94915
Ph: (415)847-8192

Graue, Jim, President
American Air Mail Society [22297]
PO Box 110
Mineola, NY 11501-0110

Gravani, Robert, Treasurer
Institute of Food Technologists
[6648]
525 W Van Buren St., Ste. 1000
Chicago, IL 60607
Ph: (312)782-8424
Toll Free: 800-438-3663
Fax: (312)782-8348

Graves, Bill, CEO, President
American Trucking Associations
Technology and Maintenance
Council [3323]
950 N Glebe Rd., Ste. 210
Arlington, VA 22203-4181
Ph: (703)838-1763
Toll Free: 800-333-1759
Fax: (703)838-1701

Graves, Chris, Chmn. of the Exec.
Committee
Council of PR Firms [2752]
32 E 31st St., 9th Fl.
New York, NY 10016
Ph: (646)588-0139
Toll Free: 877-773-4767

Graves, Deborah C., Founder,
President, Chairman, Sec. (Actg.)
Promised Land International [19397]
13509 Martha Jefferson Pl.
Herndon, VA 20171
Ph: (703)723-0089
Toll Free: 877-754-7137
Fax: (703)723-0089

Graves, Kenneth V., President
Graves Family Association [20873]
20 Binney Cir.
Wrentham, MA 02093
Ph: (508)384-8084

Graves, Lisa, President
Bill of Rights Defense Committee
[17879]
8 Bridge St., Ste. A
Northampton, MA 01060
Ph: (413)582-0110
Fax: (413)582-0116

Graves, Mark, Web Adm.
American College of Obstetricians
and Gynecologists - Council on
Resident Education in Obstetrics
and Gynecology [16270]
409 12th St. SW
Washington, DC 20024-2188
Ph: (202)638-5577
Toll Free: 800-673-8444

Graves, Steve, President
World Aquatic Babies and Children
Network [23292]
838 20th Ave. N
Saint Petersburg, FL 33704
Ph: (727)804-3399

Graves, Whitney C., Asst.
Community Voices: Healthcare for
the Underserved [11344]
c/o National Center for Primary Care

Morehouse School of Medicine
720 Westview Dr. SW
Atlanta, GA 30310
Ph: (404)756-8914
Fax: (404)752-1198

Gravitz, Alisa, CEO
Green America [907]
1612 K St. NW, Ste. 600
Washington, DC 20006-2810
Toll Free: 800-584-7336
Fax: (202)331-8166

Gray, Acia, President
International Tap Association [9263]
PO Box 150574
Austin, TX 78715
Ph: (303)443-7989

Gray, Albert C., PhD, CEO, Exec.
Dir.
Accrediting Council for Independent
Colleges and Schools [7411]
750 1st St. NE, Ste. 980
Washington, DC 20002-4241
Ph: (202)336-6780
Fax: (202)842-2593

Gray, Anita, Secretary
Association of Christian Librarians
[9683]
PO Box 4
Cedarville, OH 45314-0004
Ph: (937)766-2255
Fax: (937)766-5499

Gray, Anita, President
Ishmael and Isaac [18685]
1 Bratenahl Pl., Ste. 1302
Cleveland, OH 44108-1156
Ph: (216)233-7333
    (216)751-6446

Gray, Charlie, Mem.
Wofford College National Alumni As-
sociation [19374]
429 N Church St.
Spartanburg, SC 29303
Ph: (864)597-4208
    (864)597-4192

Gray, Donna M., Administrator
American Insurance Marketing and
Sales Society [1832]
PO Box 35718
Richmond, VA 23235
Ph: (804)674-6466
Toll Free: 877-674-2742
Fax: (703)579-8896

Gray, Geneva M., PhD, LPC, NCC,
Treasurer
International Association of Addic-
tions and Offender Counselors
[11490]
5999 Stevenson Ave.
Alexandria, VA 22304-3300
Ph: (703)823-9800
Toll Free: 800-347-6647
Fax: (703)461-9260

Gray, Janet, President
English Setter Association of
America [21872]
c/o Dr. Rhonda Dillman
62 Dillman Rd.
Roundup, MT 59072
Ph: (256)435-9652

Gray, John, President
American Peanut Shellers Associa-
tion [4508]
2336 Lake Park Dr.
Albany, GA 31707
Ph: (229)888-2508
Fax: (229)888-5150

Gray, John, Sr. VP
Association of American Railroads
[2835]

425 3rd St. SW
Washington, DC 20024
Ph: (202)639-2100

Gray, Larry, Gen. Sec., Principal
General Grand Chapter of Royal
  Arch Masons International [19556]
PO Box 128
Greenfield, IN 46140-0128
Ph: (317)467-3600
Fax: (317)467-3899

Gray, Linda, Rec. Sec.
International Association of Master
  Penmen, Engrossers, and Teachers of Handwriting [10412]
c/o Kathleen Markham, Treasurer
609 Marcellus Rd., 2nd Fl.
Williston Park, NY 11596

Gray, Linda, Director
Linda Gray's Official Fan Club
  [23996]
PO Box 5064
Sherman Oaks, CA 91413-5064

Gray, Mary W., Chairwoman
America-MidEast Educational and
  Training Services [18671]
2025 M St. NW, Ste. 600
Washington, DC 20036-3363
Ph: (202)776-9600
Fax: (202)776-7000

Gray, Ron, Chairman
U.S. Grains Council [4180]
20 F St. NW, Ste. 600
Washington, DC 20001
Ph: (202)789-0789
Fax: (202)898-0522

Graybeal, James, Liaison
National Association of State Boating
  Law Administrators [5065]
1648 McGrathiana Pky., Ste. 360
Lexington, KY 40511-1385
Ph: (859)225-9487

Graybeal, John, President
American Dutch Rabbit Club [4586]
c/o Janet Bowers, Secretary/
  Treasurer
3520 Baker Hwy.
Olivet, MI 49076
Ph: (517)449-8341

Graz, Dr. John, Sec. Gen.
International Religious Liberty As-
  sociation [19029]
12501 Old Columbia Pke.
Silver Spring, MD 20904
Ph: (301)680-6683
Fax: (301)680-6695

Grazel, Regina, President
National Association of Neonatal
  Nurses [16149]
8735 W Higgins Rd., Ste. 300
Chicago, IL 60631
Ph: (847)375-3660
Fax: (866)927-5321

Greaves, Richard W., President
SAE International [6584]
400 Commonwealth Dr.
Warrendale, PA 15096-0001
Ph: (724)776-4841
Toll Free: 877-606-7323
Fax: (724)776-0790

Greaves, William W., MD, Exec. Dir.
American Board of Preventive
  Medicine [16796]
111 W Jackson Blvd., Ste. 1340
Chicago, IL 60604
Ph: (312)939-2276
Fax: (312)939-2218

Greco, Greg, President
International Graphoanalysis Society
  [10413]

842 5th Ave.
New Kensington, PA 15068
Ph: (724)472-9701
Fax: (509)271-1149

Greco, Krista A., Contact
American Society for Reconstructive
  Microsurgery [17375]
20 N Michigan Ave., Ste. 700
Chicago, IL 60602-4822
Ph: (312)456-9579
Fax: (312)782-0553

Greek, Dr. Ray, President, Founder
Americans for Medical Advancement
  [15639]
2251 Refugio Rd.
Goleta, CA 93117
Ph: (805)685-6812

Greeley, Christy, Exec. Dir.
Cystinosis Research Network
  [15821]
302 Whytegate Ct.
Lake Forest, IL 60045-4705
Ph: (847)735-0471
Toll Free: 866-276-3669
Fax: (847)235-2773

Green, Cam, Contact
Intermarket Agency Network [2285]
c/o Alicia Wadas, President
LAVIDGE
2777 E Camelback Rd., Ste. 300
Phoenix, AZ 85016

Green, Carol, President
American Fuzzy Lop Rabbit Club
  [22397]
c/o Paula Grady, Secretary
PO Box 267
Elbert, CO 80106

Green, Claire S., President
Parents' Choice Foundation [12422]
201 W Padonia Rd., Ste. 303
Timonium, MD 21093
Ph: (410)308-3858
Fax: (410)308-3877

Green, Dr. Daniel W.E., VP
Central Bureau for Astronomical
  Telegrams [6003]
Harvard University, Dept. of Earth
  and Planetary Sciences
Hoffman Lab 209
20 Oxford St.
Cambridge, MA 02138

Green, Eleanor M., President
Association of American Veterinary
  Medical Colleges [17633]
1101 Vermont Ave. NW, Ste. 301
Washington, DC 20005
Ph: (202)371-9195
Fax: (202)842-0773

Green, Gary, Exec. Dir.
American Association of Kidney
  Patients [15869]
1440 Bruce B. Downs Blvd.
Tampa, FL 33613
Toll Free: 800-749-2257
Fax: (813)636-8122

Green, Heather, President
Down Syndrome Information Alliance
  [14626]
400 Capitol Mall, 22nd Fl.
Sacramento, CA 95814
Ph: (916)658-1686
Fax: (916)914-1875

Green, Henry L., AIA, President
BuildingSMART Alliance [6348]
National Institute of Building Sciences
1090 Vermont Ave. NW, Ste. 700

Washington, DC 20005
Ph: (202)289-7800
Fax: (202)289-1092

Green, Henry L., President
National Institute of Building Sci-
  ences [6350]
1090 Vermont Ave. NW, Ste. 700
Washington, DC 20005
Ph: (202)289-7800
Fax: (202)289-1092

Green, Henry L., AIA, President
Sustainable Buildings Industry
  Council [7214]
1090 Vermont Ave. NW, Ste. 700
Washington, DC 20005-4950
Ph: (202)289-7800
Fax: (202)289-1092

Green, Janet, Exec. Dir.
Accord Alliance [17189]
531 Route 22 E, No. 244
Whitehouse Station, NJ 08889
Ph: (908)349-0534
Fax: (801)349-0534

Green, Jen, President
Visual Resources Association [269]
c/o Jen Green, President
6025 Baker, Office 180
Dartmounth Library
Darmounth College
Hanover, NH 03755
Ph: (603)646-2132

Green, Dr. Jerrold D., CEO,
  President
Pacific Council on International
  Policy [18274]
725 S Figueroa St., Ste. 450
Los Angeles, CA 90017
Ph: (213)221-2000
Fax: (213)221-2050

Green, Joanne, Director
Wide Smiles [17354]
PO Box 5153
Stockton, CA 95205-0153
Ph: (209)942-2812
Fax: (209)464-1497

Green, Jody L., PhD, President
Society of Clinical Research Associ-
  ates [15657]
530 W Butler Ave., Ste. 109
Chalfont, PA 18914-3209
Ph: (215)822-8644
Toll Free: 800-762-7292

Green, Judy L., PhD, President
Family Firm Institute [3118]
200 Lincoln St., No. 201
Boston, MA 02111-2418
Ph: (617)482-3045
Fax: (617)482-3049

Green, Karen, VP
Society of Illustrators [8943]
128 E 63rd St.
New York, NY 10065-7303
Ph: (212)838-2560
Fax: (212)838-2561

Green, Karen, President
Women's Regional Publications of
  America [3509]
c/o J.M. Gaffney
San Antonio Woman
8603 Botts Ln.
San Antonio, TX 78217
Ph: (210)826-5375

Green, Kidada, MAT, Founder, Exec.
  Dir.
Black Mothers' Breastfeeding Association [13854]
9641 Harper Ave.

Detroit, MI 48213
Toll Free: 800-313-6141

Green, Kimberly A., Exec. Dir.
National Association of State Direc-
  tors of Career Technical Education
  Consortium [8739]
8484 Georgia Ave., Ste. 320
Silver Spring, MD 20910
Ph: (301)588-9630
  (301)588-9635
Fax: (301)588-9631

Green, Kylanne, President, CEO
URAC [13498]
1220 L St. NW, Ste. 400
Washington, DC 20005
Ph: (202)216-9010
Fax: (202)216-9006

Green, Leah, Exec. Dir., Founder
The Compassionate Listening
  Project [11477]
PO Box 17
Indianola, WA 98342

Green, Linda, Treasurer
Women in Health Care Management
  [15071]
PO Box 150
Sharon, MA 02067-0150

Green, Mary, Exec. Dir.
Real Diaper Association [11560]
3401 Adams Ave., Ste. A
San Diego, CA 92116-2490

Green, MD, Allen, President
American College for Advancement
  in Medicine [16797]
380 Ice Center Ln., Ste. C
Bozeman, MT 59718
Toll Free: 800-532-3688
Fax: (406)587-2451

Green, Michael, Exec. Dir.
Generation Green [14190]
c/o Center for Environmental Health
2201 Broadway, Ste. 302
Oakland, CA 94612
Ph: (510)655-3900
Fax: (510)655-9100

Green, Neville, Chairman
National Society of Black Engineers
  [6577]
205 Daingerfield Rd.
Alexandria, VA 22314
Ph: (703)549-2207
Fax: (703)683-5312

Green, Paul, Founder
Never Surrender to Parkinson's
  [15977]
15 Old Mill Rd.
Westport, CT 06880
Ph: (203)227-6500
Fax: (203)227-6500

Green, Rob, Exec. Dir.
National Council of Chain
  Restaurants [1671]
c/o National Retail Federation
PO Box 781081
Philadelphia, PA 19178-1081
Ph: (202)626-8183

Green, Sara M., Exec. Dir., Founder
Art for Refugees in Transition
  [12585]
100 Bank St., 5G
New York, NY 10014
Ph: (917)757-6191

Green, Seth, Founder
Americans for Informed Democracy
  [18091]
1220 L St. NW, Ste. 100-161

Washington, DC 20005
Ph: (202)709-6172

Green, Sonya, President
National Federation of Community
Broadcasters [476]
1308 Clear Fork Rd.
Crawford, CO 81415-8501
Ph: (970)279-3411

Green, Susan, Counsel
National Capital Lyme Disease As-
sociation [14599]
PO Box 8211
McLean, VA 22106-8211
Ph: (703)821-8833

Green, Susan, Bd. Member
National Family Association for Deaf-
Blind [15204]
141 Middle Neck Rd.
Sands Point, NY 11050
Toll Free: 800-255-0411
Fax: (516)883-9060

Green, Tom, President
CorStone [15766]
250 Camino Alto, Ste. 100A
Mill Valley, CA 94941
Ph: (415)388-6161
Fax: (415)388-6165

Green, Tom, Secretary, Dep. Dir.
Marine Corps Reserve Association
[5573]
8626 Lee Hwy., Ste. 205
Fairfax, VA 22031-2135
Ph: (703)289-1204

Green, Victoria L., Counsel
American College of Legal Medicine
[15527]
9700 W Bryn Mawr Ave., Ste. 210
Rosemont, IL 60018
Ph: (847)447-1713
Fax: (847)447-1150

Greenawait, Kent S., President,
Chairman, Founder
Foundation for Chiropractic Educa-
tion [8322]
PO Box 560
Carmichael, CA 95609-0560
Ph: (703)868-2420
Toll Free: 866-901-3427

Greenawalt, Kent S., Founder,
Chairman
Foundation for Chiropractic Progress
[14270]
PO Box 560
Carmichael, CA 95609-0560
Ph: (703)868-2420
Toll Free: 866-901-3427

Greenaway, Rev. Douglas A., CEO,
President
National WIC Association [5763]
2001 S St. NW, Ste. 580
Washington, DC 20009-1165
Ph: (202)232-5492
Fax: (202)387-5281

Green-Barnhill, Shelia, Founder,
CEO
Bikers Against Breast Cancer
[13900]
PO Box 3183
Newark, NJ 07103
Ph: (973)819-3519

Greenberg, Josh, CEO
Progressive Health Partnership
[15489]
3040 Fresno Ln.
Homewood, IL 60430
Ph: (708)365-9747

Greenberg, Melanie, President, CEO
Alliance for Peacebuilding [18769]

1800 Massachusetts Ave. NW, Ste.
401
Washington, DC 20036
Ph: (202)822-2047
Fax: (202)822-2049

Greenberg, Pamela, MPP, CEO,
President
Association for Behavioral Health
and Wellness [14979]
1325 G St. NW, Ste. 500
Washington, DC 20005-3136
Ph: (202)449-7660
Fax: (202)449-7659

Greenberg, Sally, Co-Ch.
Child Labor Coalition [10900]
National Consumers League
1701 K St. NW, Ste. 1200
Washington, DC 20006

Greenberg, Sally, Exec. Dir.
National Consumers League [18055]
1701 K St. NW, Ste. 1200
Washington, DC 20006
Ph: (202)835-3323
Fax: (202)835-0747

Greenberg, Stephen M., Chairman
Conference of Presidents of Major
American Jewish Organizations
[20243]
633 3rd Ave.
New York, NY 10017
Ph: (212)318-6111
Fax: (212)644-4135

Greenberg, Wendy, Chairperson
Association for Women Soil
Scientists [7192]
c/o Kelly Counts
PO Box 8264
Kirkland, WA 98034

Greenberger, Jim, Exec. Dir.
National Alliance for Advanced
Technology Batteries [1115]
122 S Michigan Ave., Ste. 1700
Chicago, IL 60603
Ph: (312)588-0477

Greenberger, Phyllis, MSW, CEO,
President
Society for Women's Health
Research [17766]
1025 Connecticut Ave. NW, Ste. 601
Washington, DC 20036
Ph: (202)223-8224
Fax: (202)833-3472

Green-Carpenter, Heidi, Contact
American Appaloosa Association
[4296]
PO Box 429
Republic, MO 65738-0429
Ph: (417)466-3633

Greene, David, Counsel, Exec. Dir.
(Actg.)
First Amendment Project [18942]
1736 Franklin St., 9th Fl.
Oakland, CA 94612-3442
Ph: (510)208-7744
Fax: (510)208-4562

Greene, Fred, Chairman
American Parkinson Disease As-
sociation [15900]
135 Parkinson Ave.
Staten Island, NY 10305
Ph: (718)981-8001
Toll Free: 800-223-2732
Fax: (718)981-4399

Greene, George C., III, CEO,
Founder
Water Missions International [13344]
PO Box 71489

North Charleston, SC 29415
Ph: (843)769-7395
Toll Free: 866-280-7107
Fax: (843)763-6082

Greene, Jeff, President
National Society of Mural Painters
[8933]
450 W 31st St., 7th Fl.
New York, NY 10001
Ph: (212)244-2800

Greene, Kellie, Founder
Speaking Out About Rape [12572]
3208 E Colonial Dr., Unit 243
Orlando, FL 32803
Ph: (321)278-5246

Greene, Maryann, Exec. Asst.
ISRI [1053]
1615 L St. NW, Ste. 600
Washington, DC 20036-5664
Ph: (202)662-8500
Fax: (202)626-0900

Greene, Merle R., Jr., President
Pontiac-Oakland Club International
[21479]
PO Box 68
Maple Plain, MN 55359
Ph: (763)479-2111
Toll Free: 877-368-3454
Fax: (763)479-3571

Greene, Richard, CFO
Scholarship America [8520]
7900 International Dr., Ste. 500
Minneapolis, MN 55425
Ph: (952)830-7300
Toll Free: 800-279-2083

Greene, Dr. Richard, Exec. Dir.
Society for Skeptical Studies [10129]
c/o Dr. Richard Greene, Executive
Director
Dept. of Political Science and
Philosophy
Weber State University
1203 University Cir.
Ogden, UT 84408-1203

Greene, Shana, Exec. Dir., Founder
Village Volunteers [12197]
5100 S Dawson St., Ste. 202
Seattle, WA 98118
Ph: (206)577-0515

Greene, Terry, Director
September Eleventh Families for
Peaceful Tomorrows [12442]
Park West Finance Sta.
New York, NY 10025
Ph: (212)598-0970

Greenfield, William, Chairman
Connected Warriors [13617]
900 Broken Sound Pky., Ste. 125
Boca Raton, FL 33487
Ph: (954)278-3764

Greening, Rev. John, Rep.
General Association of Regular
Baptist Churches [19731]
3715 N Ventura Dr.
Arlington Heights, IL 60004-7678
Ph: (847)843-1600
Toll Free: 888-588-1600
Fax: (847)843-3757

Greenland, Micah, Director
National Conference of Synagogue
Youth [20269]
11 Broadway
New York, NY 10004
Ph: (212)613-8233
Fax: (212)613-0793

Greeno, Joel, President
Family Farm Defenders [4153]
122 State St., No. 405A

Madison, WI 53703
Ph: (608)260-0900
Fax: (608)260-0900

Greenrose, Karen, CEO, President
American Association of Preferred
Provider Organizations [15094]
974 Breckenridge Ln., No. 162
Louisville, KY 40207
Ph: (502)403-1122
Fax: (502)403-1129

Greenstein, Bob, Director
Industry Council for Tangible Assets
[3196]
PO Box 3253
Annapolis, MD 21403
Ph: (410)626-7005

Greenstein, Bob, Founder, President
Urban-Brookings Tax Policy Center
[19177]
2100 M St. NW
Washington, DC 20037
Ph: (202)797-6000
   (202)833-7200

Greenstein, Susan, President
Wenzi kwa Afya [15089]
24 Wildwood Dr.
West Lebanon, NH 03784

Greenwald, Jeffrey H., CAE, Liaison
Institute of Hazardous Materials
Management [4292]
11900 Parklawn Dr., Ste. 450
Rockville, MD 20852-2624
Ph: (301)984-8969
Fax: (301)984-1516

Greenway, Suzi, President
International Norton Owners' Association [22226]
c/o Tari Norum, 276 Butterworth Ln.
276 Butterworth Ln.
Langhorne, PA 19047-2616
Ph: (215)741-0110

Greenwood, Hank, President, Chmn.
of the Bd.
American Dog Breeders Association
[21807]
PO Box 1771
Salt Lake City, UT 84110
Ph: (801)936-7513
Fax: (801)936-4229

Greenwood, James C., Chmn. of the
Bd.
BIO Ventures for Global Health
[15440]
401 Terry Ave. N
Seattle, WA 98109

Greenwood, Karen, Exec. VP, COO
American Medical Informatics As-
sociation [14361]
4720 Montgomery Ln., Ste. 500
Bethesda, MD 20814
Ph: (301)657-1291
Fax: (301)657-1296

Greenwood, Karen, Exec. VP, COO
Global Health Informatics Partner-
ship [15457]
American Medical Informatics As-
sociation
4720 Montgomery Ln., Ste. 500
Bethesda, MD 20814-3683
Ph: (301)657-1291
Fax: (301)657-1296

Greenwood, Robert, VP of Public
Affairs
National PACE Association [10526]
675 N Washington St., Ste. 300
Alexandria, VA 22314
Ph: (703)535-1565
Fax: (703)535-1566

Greer, Diana, President
Center for Teaching About China
[8024]
c/o Kathleen Trescott, Manager
1214 W Schwartz St.
Carbondale, IL 62901
Ph: (618)549-1555

Greer, Diana, President
US China Peoples Friendship Association **[17850]**
105 Treva Rd.
Sandston, VA 23150
Ph: (804)737-2704
(561)747-9487

Greer, Dr. Marty, DVM, JD, Chmn. of the Bd.
National Animal Interest Alliance
[10663]
PO Box 66579
Portland, OR 97290
Ph: (503)761-8962
(503)227-8450

Greer, Peter, President, CEO
HOPE International **[13379]**
227 Granite Run Dr., Ste. 250
Lancaster, PA 17601-6826
Ph: (717)464-3220
Fax: (717)255-0306

Gregerson, Mary, Div. Pres.
APA Division 46: Society for Media Psychology and Technology
[16889]
750 1st St. NE
Washington, DC 20002-4242
Ph: (202)336-5500

Gregg, David, President
American Fence Association **[799]**
6404 International Pky., Ste. 2048-A
Plano, TX 75093
Toll Free: 800-822-4342
Fax: (314)480-7118

Gregorcich, Sr. Jan, SSND, Exec. Dir.
Global Partners Running Waters, Inc. **[11367]**
13105 Watertown Plank Rd.
Elm Grove, WI 53122
Ph: (262)787-1010

Gregorian, Dr. Hrach, President
Institute of World Affairs **[8119]**
1255 23rd St. NW, Ste. 275
Washington, DC 20037
Ph: (202)944-2300
Fax: (202)338-1264

Gregorian, Vartan, President
Carnegie Corporation of New York
[7750]
437 Madison Ave.
New York, NY 10022
Ph: (212)371-3200
Fax: (212)754-4073

Gregory, Alexis, Officer
American Friends of the Israel Museum **[9817]**
545 5th Ave., Ste. 920
New York, NY 10017
Ph: (212)997-5611
Fax: (212)997-5536

Gregory, Bryan, President
Basenji Club of America **[21835]**
c/o Janet Ketz, Secretary
34025 W River Rd.
Wilmington, IL 60481-9599

Gregory, Chad, President, CEO
United Egg Processors **[4572]**
1720 Windwind Concourse, Ste. 230
Alpharetta, GA 30005
Ph: (770)360-9220
Fax: (770)360-7058

Gregory, Chad, President
United Egg Producers **[4573]**
1720 Windward Concourse, Ste. 230
Alpharetta, GA 30005
Ph: (770)360-9220
Fax: (770)360-7058

Gregory, James, President
Labor and Working Class History Association **[8165]**
Duke University
226 Carr Bldg.
Durham, NC 27708
Ph: (919)688-5134
Toll Free: 888-651-0122

Gregory, JayaMae, CEO, Founder
Spirit Quilts **[11156]**
PO Box 3268
Paradise, CA 95967
Ph: (530)873-2765

Gregory, Kama, Director, Consultant
Hope Imaging **[17232]**
14248 F Manchester Rd., No. 187
Manchester, MO 63011
Ph: (206)588-9931
Fax: (636)527-7700

Gregory, Maughn, Director
Montclair State University I Institute for the Advancement of Philosophy for Children **[10103]**
1 Normal Ave.
College of Education & Human Services
1 Normal Ave.
Montclair, NJ 07043
Ph: (973)655-4000

Gregory, Mindy, Bd. Member
Spinal Health International **[17264]**
2221 NW 3rd Pl.
Gainesville, FL 32603-1406

Grehan, Mike, Chairperson
Search Engine Marketing Professional Organization **[2301]**
401 Edgewater Pl., Ste. 600
Wakefield, MA 01880-6200
Ph: (781)876-8866

Greiner, Marley, Exec. Chmn. of the Bd., Founder
Bastard Nation: The Adoptee Rights Organization **[10446]**
PO Box 9959
Spokane, WA 99209-0959
Ph: (415)704-3166
Fax: (415)704-3166

Greiner, Scott, CEO
North American Sports Federation
[22512]
311 Race St.
Sunbury, PA 17801
Ph: (717)278-2474

Greitens, Eric, CEO
Mission Continues **[13243]**
1141 S 7th St.
Saint Louis, MO 63104
Ph: (314)588-8805
Fax: (314)571-6227

Greiwe, Peg, Exec. Sec.
Back Country Horsemen of America
[22940]
PO Box 1367
Graham, WA 98338-1367
Ph: (360)832-2461
Toll Free: 888-893-5161
Fax: (360)832-1564

Grenny, Joseph, Chairman
Unitus Labs **[12196]**
435 South 660 West
Orem, UT 84058-6078
Ph: (206)926-3700

Gresham, Robert, Chairman
Engineering Ministries International
[19974]
130 E Kiowa St., Ste. 200
Colorado Springs, CO 80903-1722
Ph: (719)633-2078
Fax: (719)633-2970

Gresser, Ruth, President
Women Chefs and Restaurateurs
[703]
115 S Patrick St., Ste. 101
Alexandria, VA 22314
Toll Free: 877-927-7787

Gressley, Trudy, Office Mgr.
International Disk Drive Equipment and Materials Association **[6252]**
1226 Lincoln Ave., Ste. 100
San Jose, CA 95125
Ph: (408)294-0082
(408)649-3415
Fax: (408)294-0087

Gretchko, Fr. Ed, Contact
League of St. Dymphna **[19855]**
206 Cherry Rd. NE
Massillon, OH 44646
Ph: (330)833-8478
Fax: (330)833-5193

Gretz, Sharon, Exec. Dir.
Childhood Apraxia of Speech Association **[17239]**
416 Lincoln Ave., 2nd Fl.
Pittsburgh, PA 15209
Ph: (412)343-7102

Grey, Jacqui, President
Society for Pentecostal Studies
[20519]
1435 N Glenstone Ave.
Springfield, MO 65802
Ph: (417)268-1084

Grider, Jody, Dir. of Operations
American Society of Brewing Chemists **[6186]**
3340 Pilot Knob Rd.
Saint Paul, MN 55121-2097
Ph: (651)454-7250
Fax: (651)454-0766

Grider, Mr. Ron, President
Immigrant Genealogical Society
[20973]
1310-B W Magnolia Blvd.
Burbank, CA 91506
Ph: (818)848-3122
Fax: (818)716-6300

Griebling, Kim, President
National Independent Flag Dealers Association **[20948]**
7984 S South Chicago Ave.
Chicago, IL 60617-1010
Ph: (961)798-5730

Grief, Gary, Director
North American Association of State and Provincial Lotteries **[5565]**
1 S Broadway
Geneva, OH 44041
Ph: (440)466-5630
(440)361-7962

Griepentrog, Paul, VP
National Organization for Raw Materials **[17791]**
680 E 5 Point Hwy.
Charlotte, MI 48813
Ph: (517)543-0111

Grier, John A., Editor
American Breweriana Association
[21259]
c/o Darrell Smith, Executive Director
PO Box 269

Manitowish Waters, WI 54545-0269
Ph: (715)604-2774

Griesinger, Jan, Officer
Old Lesbians Organizing for Change
[10527]
PO Box 5853
Athens, OH 45701
Toll Free: 888-706-7506

Griesser, Christina, President
German Professional Women's Association **[3490]**
PO Box 476
Lake Orion, MI 48361-0476
Ph: (248)693-9341
Fax: (248)693-9341

Griff, Martin, President
North American Snowsports Journalists Association **[2712]**
11728 SE Madison St.
Portland, OR 97216
Ph: (503)255-3771
Fax: (503)255-3771

Griffin, Amy, President
North American Cartographic Information Society **[6168]**
American Geographical Society Library
2311 E Hartford Ave.
Milwaukee, WI 53211
Ph: (414)229-6282
Fax: (414)229-3624

Griffin, Berna, Specialist
Association for Community Health Improvement **[16995]**
155 N Wacker Dr., Ste. 400
Chicago, IL 60606
Fax: (312)422-2609

Griffin, Chad, President
Human Rights Campaign **[11893]**
1640 Rhode Island Ave. NW
Washington, DC 20036-3278
Ph: (202)628-4160
Toll Free: 800-777-4723
Fax: (202)347-5323

Griffin, G. Edward, Founder, President
Cure Research Foundation **[13955]**
PO Box 3782
Westlake Village, CA 91359
Ph: (805)498-0185
Toll Free: 800-282-2873
Fax: (805)498-4868

Griffin, Gerald, President
International Betta Congress **[22033]**
c/o Steve Van Camp, Secretary
923 Wadsworth St.
Syracuse, NY 13208

Griffin, Jane, President
The Groundwater Foundation **[4758]**
3201 Pioneers Blvd., Ste. 105
Lincoln, NE 68502-5963
Ph: (402)434-2740
Toll Free: 800-858-4844
Fax: (402)434-2742

Griffin, Jeanne, Director
Deaf Friends International **[11935]**
PO Box 13192
Hamilton, OH 45013-0192
Ph: (513)658-4879

Griffin, Marcia, Founder, President
HomeFree - U.S.A. **[1689]**
6200 Baltimore Ave.
Riverdale, MD 20737-1054
Ph: (301)891-8400
Toll Free: 855-493-4002

Griffin, Mike, President
National One Coat Stucco Association **[559]**

1615 W Abram St. Ste. U
Arlington, TX 76012-1325

Griffin, Patricia, Founder, President
Green Hotels Association **[1656]**
1611 Mossy Stone Dr.
Houston, TX 77077-4109
Ph: (713)789-8889
Fax: (713)789-9786

Griffin, Peter Burley, President
Walter Burley Griffin Society of
America **[5969]**
1152 Center Dr.
Saint Louis, MO 63117
Ph: (314)644-4546

Griffin-Rossi, Theresa, Exec. Dir.
American Association for Accredita-
tion of Ambulatory Surgery Facili-
ties **[17359]**
5101 Washington St., Ste. 2F
Gurnee, IL 60031
Ph: (847)775-1970
Toll Free: 888-545-5222
Fax: (847)775-1985

Griffith, Gwen, D.V.M., Bd. Member
Alliance of Veterinarians for the
Environment **[4122]**
c/o Gwen Griffith, Board Member,
836 W Hillwood Dr.
836 W Hillwood Dr.
Nashville, TN 37205
Ph: (615)353-0272
Fax: (615)353-8904

Griffith, Melinda, CEO
Thrive Networks **[18502]**
1611 Telegraph Ave., Ste. 1420
Oakland, CA 94612
Ph: (510)763-7045
Fax: (510)763-6545

Griffith, Michael J., Esq., Contact
International Legal Defense Counsel
[5352]
405 Lexington Ave., 26th Fl.
New York, NY 10174
Toll Free: 888-534-9106

Griffith, Richard O., President
International Council of Community
Churches **[20026]**
21116 Washington Pky.
Frankfort, IL 60423
Ph: (815)464-5690

Griffiths, Ann Mills, Chmn. of the Bd.
National League of Families of
American Prisoners and Missing in
Southeast Asia **[18697]**
5673 Columbia Pke., Ste. 100
Falls Church, VA 22041
Ph: (703)465-7432

Griffiths, Christopher, President
International Psoriasis Council
[14497]
1034 S Brentwood Blvd., Ste. 600
Saint Louis, MO 63117-1206
Ph: (972)861-0503
Fax: (214)242-3391

Griffiths, R. Wayne, Contact
National Organization of Restoring
Men **[11287]**
3205 Northwood Dr., Ste. 209
Concord, CA 94520-4506
Ph: (925)827-4077
Fax: (925)827-4119

Griggs, Karen, Exec. Dir.
Lawyer-Pilots Bar Association **[5059]**
PO Box 1510
Edgewater, MD 21037
Ph: (410)571-1750
Fax: (410)571-1780

Griggs, Regina, Exec. Dir.
Parents and Friends of Ex-Gays and
Gays **[11906]**
PO Box 510
Reedville, VA 22539
Ph: (804)453-4737

Griggs, Ruth Ann, President
Alpha Delta Kappa **[23727]**
1615 W 92nd St.
Kansas City, MO 64114
Ph: (816)363-5525
Toll Free: 800-247-2311
Fax: (816)363-4010

Grigori, Natasha, Chairperson
Anti-Child Pornography Organization
[18926]
PO Box 22338
Eagan, MN 55122-0388

Grigsby, Garrett, Exec. Dir.
Christian Connections for
International Health **[14932]**
1329 Shepard Dr., Ste. 6
Sterling, VA 20164
Ph: (703)444-8250

Grill, Howard A., VP of Fin.
Gastro-Intestinal Research Founda-
tion **[14789]**
70 E Lake St.
Chicago, IL 60601
Ph: (312)332-1350

Grilli, Tracy, Mgr., Member Svcs.
United States Masters Swimming
[23288]
1751 Mound St., Ste. 201
Sarasota, FL 34236
Ph: (941)256-8767
Toll Free: 800-550-7946
Fax: (941)556-7946

Grillone, Gregory A., President
American Broncho-Esophagological
Association **[13860]**
c/o American College of Surgeons
633 N St. Clair St., 27th Fl.
Chicago, IL 60611
Toll Free: 855-876-2232
Fax: (312)278-0793

Grim, Dr. John A., Director
American Teilhard Association
[9036]
c/o John Grim, Director
29 Spoke Dr.
Woodbridge, CT 06525

Grimm, Rick, CEO, Secretary
NIGP: The Institute for Public
Procurement **[5737]**
2411 Dulles Corner Pk., Ste. 350
Herndon, VA 20171
Ph: (703)736-8900
Toll Free: 800-367-6447
Fax: (703)736-9644

Grimord, Karen, Founder, President
Landstuhl Hospital Care Project
[12284]
29 Greenleaf Ter.
Stafford, VA 22556

Grimsrud, Knut, President
Serial ATA International Organization
[6335]
3855 SW 153rd Dr.
Beaverton, OR 97006
Ph: (503)619-0572
Fax: (503)644-6708

Grinder, N. Scott, President
Christian Sports International
[23221]
PO Box 254
Zelienople, PA 16063
Ph: (724)453-1400
Fax: (724)240-1617

Grindlay, Kate, Exec. Dir.
Cervical Barrier Advancement
Society **[17195]**
17 Dunster St., Ste. 201
Cambridge, MA 02138
Fax: (617)349-0041

Grinzi, Joan, RN, Exec. Dir.
Price-Pottenger Nutrition Foundation
[16237]
7890 Broadway
Lemon Grove, CA 91945
Ph: (619)462-7600
Toll Free: 800-366-3748
Fax: (619)433-3136

Grippo, Gary, VP
Treasury Historical Association
[9524]
PO Box 28118
Washington, DC 20038-8118
Ph: (202)298-0550

Griswold, John, Chairman
BoardSource **[12400]**
750 9th St. NW, Ste. 650
Washington, DC 20001
Ph: (202)349-2500
Toll Free: 877-892-6273
Fax: (202)349-2599

Grizzard, Karen, President
National Costumers Association
[207]
PO Box 3406
Englewood, CO 80155
Ph: (303)758-9611
Toll Free: 800-NCA-1321
Fax: (303)758-9616

Grob, John, Chairperson
International Housewares
Representatives Association **[1684]**
1755 Lake Cook Rd., No. 318
Highland Park, IL 60035
Ph: (847)748-8269
Fax: (847)748-8273

Grodzinski, Piotr, PhD, Director
U.S. Department of Health and Hu-
man Services | National Institutes
of Health | National Cancer
Institute | Alliance for Nanotechnol-
ogy in Cancer **[15659]**
Bldg. 31, Rm. 10A52
31 Center Dr.
Bethesda, MD 20892-2580
Ph: (301)451-8983

Groelinger, James F., Exec. Dir.
Clean Energy Alliance **[1108]**
c/o Suzanne Roberts, Director
1155 University Blvd. SE
Albuquerque, NM 87106
Ph: (505)843-4091

Groeper, Michelle, Secretary
Women in Management Fox Valley
[2196]
PO Box 6690
Elgin, IL 60121-6690

Groff, Scott W., Chmn. of the Bd.
Surgical Eye Expeditions
International **[17747]**
5638 Hollister Ave., Ste. 210
Santa Barbara, CA 93117
Ph: (805)963-3303
Toll Free: 877-937-3133
Fax: (805)965-3564

Grogan, Jane, President
International Spenser Society **[9058]**
Dept. of English
Emory University
Callaway Ste. N302
537 Kilgo Cir.
Atlanta, GA 30322

Grogan, Shareen, President
International Writing Centers As-
sociation **[8764]**
c/o Shareen Grogan, President
National University
705 Palomar Airport Rd.
Carlsbad, CA 92011
Ph: (760)268-1567

Gronert, Gary, President
Global Health Ministries **[15005]**
7831 Hickory St. NE
Minneapolis, MN 55432-2500
Ph: (763)586-9590
Fax: (763)586-9591

Groothuis, Austin, Director
American Bar Association - Law
Student Division **[8207]**
321 N Clark St.
Chicago, IL 60654
Ph: (312)988-5624
Toll Free: 800-285-2221
Fax: (312)988-6033

Groover, Dr. Mark, Exec. Sec.
Lambda Alpha **[23676]**
Dept. of Anthropology
Ball State University
Burkhardt Bldg., Rm. 315
2000 W University Ave.
Muncie, IN 47306
Ph: (765)285-1575
Fax: (765)285-2163

Gropper, Adrian, MD, Chief Tech.
Ofc.
Patient Privacy Rights **[15636]**
1006 Mopac Cir., Ste. 102
Austin, TX 78746
Ph: (512)732-0033
Fax: (512)732-0036

Grose, Rachel, Assoc. Dir.
Jewish Free Loan Association
[20255]
6505 Wilshire Blvd., Ste. 715
Los Angeles, CA 90048
Ph: (323)761-8830
Fax: (323)761-8841

Gross, Bill, Founder, President
Farm Rescue **[4155]**
PO Box 28
Horace, ND 58047
Ph: (701)252-2017
Fax: (708)221-6488

Gross, Dan, President
Brady Center to Prevent Gun
Violence **[18248]**
840 1st St. NE, Ste. 400
Washington, DC 20002
Ph: (202)370-8101

Gross, Daniel, President
Brady Campaign to Prevent Gun
Violence **[18247]**
840 1st St. NE, Ste. 400
Washington, DC 20002
Ph: (202)370-8100

Gross, Jo-Ann, Director
Association for the Study of Persian-
ate Societies **[9593]**
Stony Brook-Manhattan
387 Park Ave. S, 3rd Fl.
New York, NY 10016
Ph: (631)632-7746
Fax: (631)632-8203

Gross, Larry, Exec. Dir.
Coalition for Economic Survival
[13037]
514 Shatto Pl., Ste. 270
Los Angeles, CA 90020
Ph: (213)252-4411
Fax: (213)252-4422

Gross, Paul, Founder
MX for Children [11084]
PO Box 141
Woodinville, WA 98072
Ph: (425)301-0527

Gross, Richard, Editor
Stained Glass Association of
America [1511]
9313 E 63rd St.
Raytown, MO 64133
Ph: (816)737-2090
Toll Free: 800-438-9581
Fax: (816)737-2801

Gross, Robin D., Exec. Dir.
IP Justice [5335]
1192 Haight St.
San Francisco, CA 94117
Ph: (415)553-6261
Fax: (415)462-6451

Grossberg, Michael, Secretary
Libertarian Futurist Society [18641]
650 Castro St., Ste. 120-433
Mountain View, CA 94041

Grosser, Dr. T.J., EdD, Bd. Member
AngelCare Programs of Americans
Care & Share [11213]
3295 Meade Ave., Ste. 102
San Diego, CA 92116-4557
Toll Free: 888-264-5227
Fax: (619)481-3089

Grossman, David, President
National Association of Patent
Practitioners [5675]
1629 K St. NW, Ste. 300
Washington, DC 20006
Ph: (919)230-9635

Grossman, Debbie, Exec. Dir.
Blind Service Association [17691]
17 N State St., Ste. 1050
Chicago, IL 60602-3510
Ph: (312)236-0808

Grossman, Jennifer, CEO
The Atlas Society [10080]
800 Rockmead Dr., Ste. 200
Kingwood, TX 77339-9958
Ph: (202)296-7263
Fax: (202)296-0771

Grossman, Jerry, Exec. Dir.
Photoimaging Manufacturers and
Distributors Association [2589]
7600 Jericho Tpke., Ste. 301
Woodbury, NY 11797
Ph: (516)802-0895
Fax: (516)364-0140

Grossman, Jim, Exec. Dir.
American Historical Association
[9455]
400 A St. SE
Washington, DC 20003-3889
Ph: (202)544-2422
Fax: (202)544-8307

Grossman, Karen Doyle, Exec. Dir.
WorldTeach [7806]
1 Brattle Sq., Ste. 550
Cambridge, MA 02138-3723
Ph: (857)259-6646
Fax: (857)259-6638

Grossman, Marilyn, President
National Saanen Breeders Association [3607]
c/o Amy Keach, President
4701 Lebanon Rd.
Bagdad, KY 40003
Ph: (502)227-1044

Grossman, Mr. Matthew, CEO
BBYO, Inc. [20235]
800 8th St. NW

Washington, DC 20001
Ph: (202)857-6633
    (202)857-6580
Fax: (202)857-6568

Grossmann, Atina, VP of Admin.
Central European History Society
[9470]
c/o Benjamin Marschke, Administrator
1 Harpst St.
Department of History
Humboldt State University
Arcata, CA 95521

Grosso, Frank, Exec. Dir., CEO
American Society of Consultant
Pharmacists [16644]
1321 Duke St.
Alexandria, VA 22314-3563
Ph: (703)739-1300
Toll Free: 800-355-2727
Fax: (703)739-1321

Grost, Gregg, CEO
Golf Coaches Association of America
[22880]
1225 W Main St., Ste. 110
Norman, OK 73069
Ph: (405)329-4222
Fax: (405)573-7888

Grote, Christopher, PhD, President
Association of Postdoctoral
Programs in Clinical Neuropsychol-
ogy [16904]
Dept. of Neurosurgery
12631 E 17th Ave., C307
Aurora, CO 80045
Ph: (303)724-5957

Groupp, Jason, Dir. Ed.
Wedding and Portrait Photographers
International [2596]
Emerald Expositions
85 Broad St., 11th Fl.
New York, NY 10004

Grout, Trudy, Director
Contact Lens Society of America
[1599]
2025 Woodlane Dr.
Saint Paul, MN 55125-2998
Ph: (703)437-5100
Toll Free: 800-296-9776
Fax: (703)437-0727

Grove, Gloria, Exec. Dir.
Insurance Marketing & Communica-
tions Association [1869]
4248 Park Glen Rd.
Minneapolis, MN 55416-4758
Ph: (952)928-4644
Fax: (952)929-1318

Grow, Mary Lewis, Coord., Founder
Student Pledge Against Gun
Violence [18256]
112 Nevada St.
Northfield, MN 55057
Ph: (507)664-9494
Fax: (507)573-1775

Grubbe, Fred, CEO
Appraisal Institute [218]
200 W Madison St., Ste. 1500
Chicago, IL 60606
Ph: (312)335-4401
    (312)335-4111
Toll Free: 888-756-4624
Fax: (312)335-4415

Grubbs, Richard, President
Biblical Ministries Worldwide [20128]
1595 Herrington Rd.
Lawrenceville, GA 30043
Ph: (770)339-3500
Fax: (770)513-1254

Gruber, Mr. Jeremy, Exec. Dir.,
President
Council for Responsible Genetics
[19084]
5 Upland Rd., Ste. 3
Cambridge, MA 02140-2717
Ph: (617)868-0870
Fax: (617)491-5344

Gruber, Rev. Linda, President
Evangelical and Reformed Historical
Society [20632]
555 W James St.
Lancaster, PA 17603
Ph: (717)290-8734

Grubich, Mr. Donald N., Chairman
International Peat Society - United
States National Committee [6996]
10105 White City Rd.
Britt, MN 55710
Ph: (218)741-2813
Fax: (218)741-2813

Gruchow, Emilie, Dir., Archives
Morris-Jumel Mansion [10340]
65 Jumel Ter.
New York, NY 10032
Ph: (212)923-8008

Grudzinski, Phil, CEO, President
Professional Association for
Customer Engagement [2299]
8500 Keystone Crossing, Ste. 480
Indianapolis, IN 46240-2460
Ph: (317)816-9336

Gruenwald, Dr. Oskar, President
International Christian Studies As-
sociation [19986]
1065 Pine Bluff Dr.
Pasadena, CA 91107-1751
Ph: (626)351-0419

Grumm, Christine, Chmn. of the Bd.
Lutheran Immigration and Refugee
Service [12593]
700 Light St.
Baltimore, MD 21230
Ph: (410)230-2700
Fax: (410)230-2890

Grunberger, George, MD, FACP,
President
American Association of Clinical
Endocrinologists [14698]
245 Riverside Ave., Ste. 200
Jacksonville, FL 32202
Ph: (904)353-7878
Fax: (904)353-8185

Grundahl, Kirk, PE, Officer
Structural Building Components As-
sociation [585]
6300 Enterprise Ln.
Madison, WI 53719
Ph: (608)274-4849
Fax: (608)274-3329

Grungras, Neil, Founder, Exec. Dir.
Organization for Refuge Asylum and
Migration [12595]
39 Drumm St., 4th Fl.
San Francisco, CA 94111
Ph: (415)399-1701
Fax: (415)373-9191

Grupp, Virginia, President
Pacific Railroad Society [10188]
210 W Bonita Ave.
San Dimas, CA 91773
Ph: (909)394-0616
    (714)637-4676

Grusak, Michael A., President
Crop Science Society of America
[3547]
5585 Guilford Rd.

Madison, WI 53711-5801
Ph: (608)273-8080

Gruskin, Bob, President
National Amateur Body Builders As-
sociation U.S.A. [22697]
PO Box 531
Bronx, NY 10469
Ph: (718)882-6413

Grygny, Joseph, Exec. Dir.
International Molded Fiber Associa-
tion [2492]
355 Lexington Ave., 15 Fl.
New York, NY 10017
Ph: (630)544-5056
Fax: (630)544-5055

Gryskiewicz, Joe, MD, President
The Rhinoplasty Society [14323]
PO Box 441745
Jacksonville, FL 32222
Ph: (904)786-1377
Fax: (904)786-9939

Grzych, Wendy, Director
Unicycling Society of America
[22756]
35011 Munger
Livonia, MI 48154-2412

Grzymkowski, Karlyn, VP
Doll Artisan Guild [22000]
233 Cherokee Trl.
Pensacola, FL 32506-3513
Ph: (607)432-4977
Fax: (607)441-0460

Gsell, Brad, President
Independent Board for Presbyterian
Foreign Missions [20522]
PO Box 1346
Blue Bell, PA 19422-0435
Ph: (610)279-0952
Fax: (610)279-0954

Guadagno, Joseph, VP
International.NET Association [6278]
PO Box 6713
Bellevue, WA 98008-0713

Guadagno, Lou, President
Stamps on Stamps Collectors Club
[22371]
c/o Michael Merritt
73 Mountainside Rd.
Mendham, NJ 07945-2014

Guajardo, Francisco J., PhD, V. Ch.
Rural School and Community Trust
[8511]
4301 Connecticut Ave. NW, Ste. 100
Washington, DC 20008
Ph: (202)822-3919
Fax: (202)872-4050

Gualtieri, Ann, V. Chmn. of the Bd.
National Park Trust [4521]
401 E Jefferson St., Ste. 203
Rockville, MD 20850-2617
Ph: (301)279-7275
Fax: (301)279-7211

Guarasci, Richard, President
Coalition of Urban and Metropolitan
Universities [7630]
8000 York Rd.
Towson, MD 21252
Ph: (410)704-3700

Guardino, Mary, Exec. Dir., Founder,
President
Freedom From Fear [15770]
308 Seaview Ave.
Staten Island, NY 10305-2246
Ph: (718)351-1717

Guarrine, John, Chairperson
Play for Peace [12441]
500 N Michigan Ave., Ste. 600

Chicago, IL 60611-3754
Ph: (312)675-8568

Gubins, Samuel, Treasurer
Society for Industrial and Applied
Mathematics **[6826]**
3600 Market St., 6th Fl.
Philadelphia, PA 19104-2688
Ph: (215)382-9800
Toll Free: 800-447-7426
Fax: (215)386-7999

Gucciardi, Ben, Director, Founder
Soccer Without Borders **[23191]**
9 Waterhouse St.
Cambridge, MA 02138
Ph: (857)264-0097

Guccione, Gary, Advisor
National Greyhound Association
[21922]
PO Box 543
Abilene, KS 67410-0543
Ph: (785)263-7272

Gudmundsson, BJ, President
Pearl S. Buck Birthplace Museum
[9044]
PO Box 126
Hillsboro, WV 24946-0126
Ph: (304)653-4430

Guenette, Paul, Sr. VP
ACDI/VOCA **[3976]**
50 F St. NW, Ste. 1000
Washington, DC 20001
Ph: (202)469-6000
Toll Free: 800-929-8622
Fax: (202)469-6257

Guerci, Ingrid, Treasurer
Encephalitis Global **[14574]**
1 Franklin Ave., Apt. 4C
White Plains, NY 10601

Guerdat, Dr. Todd C., President
Aquacultural Engineering Society
[6541]
8969 Mountain View Dr.
Copper Hill, VA 24079

Guerette, Sarah, President
Ecuador Children's Hope Organiza-
tion **[10958]**
94 Beckett St., No. 3
Portland, ME 04101-4473
Ph: (207)615-7788

Guerra, Jose O., Web Adm.
Hispanic Genealogical Society
[20971]
PO Box 231271
Houston, TX 77223-1271
Fax: (281)449-4020

Guerra, Ruben, Chmn. of the Bd.,
CEO
Latin Business Association **[648]**
120 S San Pedro St., Ste. 530
Los Angeles, CA 90012
Ph: (213)628-8510
Fax: (213)628-8519

Guerra, Stephen, Secretary
National Beep Baseball Association
[22787]
1501 41st St. NW, Apt. G1
Rochester, MN 55901
Ph: (507)208-8383
Toll Free: 866-400-4551

Guerrieri, Dexter, President, Founder
Preservation Volunteers **[9429]**
1995 Broadway, Ste. 605
New York, NY 10023
Ph: (212)769-2900

Guess, Dr. Michael, Officer
College of Diplomates of the
American Board of Orthodontics
[14424]

401 N Lindbergh Blvd.
Saint Louis, MO 63141
Toll Free: 888-217-2988
Fax: (314)997-1745

Guettich, Bruce, Founder
World Footbag Association **[23266]**
2673 Jacob Cir., Unit 400
Steamboat Springs, CO 80487
Ph: (970)870-9898
Toll Free: 800-878-8797

Guevara, Beatriz, President
REFORMA: National Association to
Promote Library & Information
Services to Latinos and the Span-
ish Speaking **[9725]**
PO Box 832
Anaheim, CA 92815-0832

Guevara, Matt, Exec. Dir.
International Network of Children's
Ministry **[19990]**
PO Box 190
Castle Rock, CO 80104
Toll Free: 855-933-6466

Gueye, Dr. Tiffany Cooper, CEO
Building Educated Leaders for Life
[8235]
60 Clayton St.
Dorchester, MA 02122
Ph: (617)282-1567
Fax: (617)282-2698

Guffey, Jean, President
American Kiko Goat Association
[4273]
8222 Kay Rd.
Wakita, OK 73771
Ph: (254)423-5914

Guggenheim, Dr. David E., President
Ocean Doctor **[3922]**
PO Box 53090
Washington, DC 20009
Ph: (202)695-2550
Fax: (202)888-3329

Guggolz, Richard A., Exec. Dir.
Sports Lawyers Association **[5769]**
12100 Sunset Hills Rd., Ste. 130
Reston, VA 20190
Ph: (703)437-4377
Fax: (703)435-4390

Guggolz, Rick, Exec. Dir.
American Brachytherapy Society
[13879]
12100 Sunset Hills Rd., Ste. 130
Reston, VA 20190-5202
Ph: (703)234-4078
Fax: (703)435-4390

Guha, Dr. Amala, Director
International Society for Ayurveda
and Health **[13636]**
PO Box 271737
West Hartford, CT 06127-1737
Ph: (860)561-4857

Guidong, Zhu, VP
Association of Chinese Scientists
and Engineers U.S.A. **[6543]**
PO Box 59715
Schaumburg, IL 60159

Guilbeau, Merlin, Exec. Dir.
Electronic Security Association
[3054]
6333 N State Highway 161, Ste. 350
Irving, TX 75038
Ph: (972)807-6800
Toll Free: 888-447-1689
Fax: (972)807-6883

Guilford, Francisca, President
Veterans of Foreign Wars of the
United States, Ladies Auxiliary
[21150]

406 W 34th St., 10th Fl.
Kansas City, MO 64111
Ph: (816)561-8655
Fax: (816)931-4753

Guiliano, Jennifer, President
Association for Computers and the
Humanities **[8003]**
c/o Vika Zafrin, Executive Secretary
Boston University Libraries
771 Commonwealth Ave.
Boston, MA 02215
Ph: (617)358-6370

Guillies, Wendy, President, CEO
Ewing Marion Kauffman Foundation
[647]
4801 Rockhill Rd.
Kansas City, MO 64110
Ph: (816)932-1000

Guiltinan, Jane, President
Association of Accredited Natur-
opathic Medical Colleges **[15857]**
818 18th St. NW, Ste. 250
Washington, DC 20006
Toll Free: 800-345-7454

Guimaraes, George, CEO, President
Project Concern International
[15490]
5151 Murphy Canyon Rd., Ste. 320
San Diego, CA 92123-4339
Ph: (858)279-9690
Toll Free: 877-PCI-HOPE
Fax: (858)694-0294

Guinee, Dr. Donald G., Jr., President
Pulmonary Pathology Society
[16590]
Virginia Mason Medical Center
Department of Pathology, C6-PTH
1100 9th Ave.
Seattle, WA 98101

Guitierrez, Linda Mazon, President,
CEO
Hispanic Women's Corporation
[9359]
PO Box 20725
Phoenix, AZ 85018-0725
Ph: (602)954-7995
Fax: (602)954-7563

Gula, Janet, President
United Federation of Doll Clubs
[22009]
10900 N Pomona Ave.
Kansas City, MO 64153-1256
Ph: (816)891-7040

Gulina, Gulnara, President
Atheists United **[19710]**
4773 Hollywood Blvd.
Hollywood, CA 90027-5333
Ph: (323)666-4258
Toll Free: 866-GOD-LESS

Gulit, Nadine, Founder
Operation Support Our Troops -
America **[10757]**
1807 S Washington St., No. 100
Naperville, IL 60565
Ph: (630)971-1150

Gulla, John C., Exec. Dir.
The Edward E. Ford Foundation
[12972]
26 Court St., Ste. 2200
Brooklyn, NY 11242-1122
Ph: (718)596-1950
Fax: (718)596-1988

Gulliford, Jim, Exec. Dir.
Soil and Water Conservation Society
[3947]
945 SW Ankeny Rd.
Ankeny, IA 50023-9723
Ph: (515)289-2331
Toll Free: 800-843-7645
Fax: (515)289-1227

Gulyas, Carol, Coord.
American Library Association -
Alternatives Media Task Force
[9669]
Alternatives Media Task Force
50 E Huron St.
Chicago, IL 60611
Toll Free: 800-545-2433

Gumbonzvanda, Nyaradzayi, Chmn.
of the Bd., Chmn. of the Exec.
Committee
CIVICUS: World Alliance for Citizen
Participation **[18901]**
355 Lexington Ave.
New York, NY 10017

Gunderson, Arlene, MEd, President
American Sign Language Teachers
Association **[15173]**
10413 E Spring Creek Rd.
Chandler, AZ 85248

Gundlach, Tina, Secretary
Lyman Boat Owners Association
[22645]
PO Box 40052
Cleveland, OH 44140
Ph: (440)241-4290

Gundram, Bob, Chmn. of the Bd.
SnowSports Industries America
[3163]
8377B Greensboro Dr.
McLean, VA 22102-3587
Ph: (703)556-9020
Fax: (703)821-8276

Gunn, Allen, Secretary
Ruckus Society **[19130]**
PO Box 28741
Oakland, CA 94604
Ph: (510)931-6339
Toll Free: 866-778-6374

Gunn, Dr. Donna, President
Africa's Promise Village **[12023]**
15 Monarch Oaks Ln.
The Hills, TX 78738
Ph: (512)291-3593

Gunn, Teresa, President
International Mammalian Genome
Society **[6668]**
c/o Darla Miller
Dept. of Genetics
University of North Carolina at
Chapel Hill
5047 Genetic Medicine Bldg.
Chapel Hill, NC 27599

Gunter, Dale, President
Association of Conservation
Engineers **[3810]**
c/o Howard David Thomas,
Treasurer
PO Box 180
Jefferson City, MO 65102-0180
Ph: (573)522-4115
Fax: (573)522-2324

Gunther, Ed, Director
National Association of Land Title
Examiners and Abstractors **[2872]**
7490 Eagle Rd.
Waite Hill, OH 44094
Fax: (440)256-2404

Gunther, Mark, Officer
Equal Access **[7902]**
1212 Market St., Ste. 200
San Francisco, CA 94102
Ph: (415)561-4884
Fax: (415)561-4885

Gupta, Jyothi, Chairman
Society for the Study of Occupation:
U.S.A. **[7532]**

University of Oklahoma Health Sciences Ctr.
1200 N Stonewall Ave.
Oklahoma City, OK 73117
Ph: (734)487-2280

Gupta, Neeru, MD, PhD, MBA, VP
International Council of Ophthalmology [16387]
711 Van Ness Ave., Ste. 445
San Francisco, CA 94102
Ph: (415)521-1651
Fax: (415)521-1649

Gupta, Neha, Founder
Empower Orphans [10962]
1415 Hidden Pond Dr.
Yardley, PA 19067
Ph: (610)909-1778

Gupta, Dr. Paul R., Director, President
Hindustan Bible Institute [20081]
PO Box 584
Forest, VA 24551
Ph: (434)525-5847
Toll Free: 877-424-4634

Gupta, Rina, President
India American Cultural Association [9566]
1281 Cooper Lake Rd.
Smyrna, GA 30082
Ph: (770)436-3719
Fax: (770)436-4272

Gupta, Sarita, Exec. Dir.
Jobs With Justice [19258]
1616 P St. NW, Ste. 150
Washington, DC 20036-1427
Ph: (202)393-1044
Fax: (202)822-2168

Gupta, Prof. Sushil, PhD, Exec. Dir.
Production and Operations Management Society [2190]
The University of Texas at Dallas
800 W Campbell Rd., SM 30
Richardson, TX 75080
Ph: (972)883-4834
Fax: (972)883-5834

Gupta, V Nagendra, President
NRI Vasavi Association [9569]
PO Box 2492
Reston, VA 20195
Toll Free: 855-936-7482

Gupta-Brietzke, Shailey, Treasurer
National Network of Abortion Funds [10432]
PO Box 170280
Boston, MA 02117

Guralnick, David, President, Treasurer
International E-Learning Association [7488]
Kaleidoscope Learning
304 Park Ave. S, 11th Fl.
New York, NY 10010
Ph: (646)397-3710

Gurel, Michelle, RN, President
Endocrine Nurses Society [14704]
c/o Molly Solares Yeardley, Treasurer
2991 E Beechnut Pl.
Chandler, AZ 85249

Gurley, Cathy, Exec. Dir.
You Have the Power [18731]
2814 12th Ave. S
Nashville, TN 37204-2513
Ph: (615)292-7027
Fax: (615)292-4088

Gurtler, Gary Michael, President
International Society for Neoplatonic Studies [10096]

c/o Michael Wagner, General Secretary
Dept. of Philosophy
University of San Diego
5998 Alcala Park
San Diego, CA 92110-2492
Ph: (619)260-4600
Fax: (619)260-4227

Gurung, Jeannette, PhD, Exec. Dir.
Women Organizing for Change in Agriculture & Natural Resource Management [3583]
1775 K St. NW, Ste. 410
Washington, DC 20006
Ph: (202)331-9099

Gustafson, Dian, Bd. Member
Chapman Family Association [20793]
c/o Robert L. Sonfield, Executive Director
770 S Post Oak Ln., Ste 435
Houston, TX 77056-1913
Ph: (713)877-8333

Gustafson, Eric, Exec. Dir.
Alumni Association - Framingham State College [19300]
100 State St.
Framingham, MA 01701-9101
Ph: (508)626-4012
Fax: (508)626-4036

Gustafson, Erik, Exec. Dir.
Education for Peace in Iraq Center [18396]
900 2nd St. NE, Ste. 216
Washington, DC 20002
Ph: (202)682-0208

Gusterson, Hugh, Asst. Pres.
American Ethnological Society [5902]
c/o Carol Greenhouse, President
125 Aaron Burr Hall
Princeton, NJ 08544
Ph: (609)258-7369

Guthrie, Carol, Officer
Organization for Economic Cooperation and Development [18157]
1776 Eye St. NW, Ste. 450
Washington, DC 20006
Ph: (202)785-6323
Fax: (202)315-2508

Guthrie, Davonna, Treasurer
The Dameron-Damron Family Association [20852]
1326 N Audubon Rd.
Indianapolis, IN 46219

Gutiérrez, Germán, President
International Society for Comparative Psychology [16919]
University of Southern Mississippi
Dept. of Psychology
118 College Dr., No. 5025
Hattiesburg, MS 39406

Gutierrez, Carlos A., Founder, Exec. Dir.
Cinema Tropical [9303]
611 Broadway, Ste. 836
New York, NY 10012
Ph: (212)254-5474

Gutierrez, Denise, Administrator
U.S. Branch of the World Association for Psychosocial Rehabilitation [17099]
c/o The Bridge
248 W 108th St.
New York, NY 10025
Ph: (212)663-3000
Fax: (212)663-3181

Gutierrez, Frank, President, Bd. Member
Dominicans on Wall Street [1231]
41 Kew Gardens Rd., Apt. 6A

Kew Gardens, NY 11415

Gutierrez, Teresa, President
Neuro-Developmental Treatment Association [16029]
1540 S Coast Hwy., Ste. 204
Laguna Beach, CA 92651
Toll Free: 800-869-9295
Fax: (949)376-3456

Gutmann, David, PhD, President
International Association for Group Psychotherapy and Group Processes [16975]
c/o Bonnie Buchele, PhD, President-Elect
411 Nichols Rd., Ste. 194
Kansas City, MO 64112
Ph: (816)531-2600

Gutow, Rabbi Steve, Bd. Member
Coalition on the Environment and Jewish Life [20242]
1775 K St. NW
Washington, DC 20006
Ph: (202)579-6800

Gutt, Mr. Phillip, CAE, Exec. Dir.
B-26 Marauder Historical Society [21192]
3900 E Timrod St.
Tucson, AZ 85711
Ph: (520)322-6226

Guttadauro, L.T., Contact
Fab Owners Association [1047]
19925 Stevens Creek Blvd., Ste. 100
Cupertino, CA 95014-2358
Ph: (408)725-7127
Fax: (408)725-8885

Guttermuth, Ken, Chairman, Treasurer
Boardgame Players Association [22047]
1541 Redfield Rd.
Bel Air, MD 21015

Guy, Elmer, Chairman
American Indian College Fund [8512]
8333 Greenwood Blvd.
Denver, CO 80221-4488
Ph: (303)426-8900
Toll Free: 800-776-3863
Fax: (303)426-1200

Guy, Jan, President
International Magnesium Association [2351]
1000 Westgate Dr., Ste. 252
Saint Paul, MN 55114
Ph: (847)526-2010
    (651)379-7305
Fax: (847)526-3993

Guyton, Bill, President
World Cocoa Foundation [4173]
1411 K St. NW, Ste. 500
Washington, DC 20005
Ph: (202)737-7870
Fax: (202)737-7832

Guzior, Betsey, Chairperson
Society for Features Journalism [2721]
c/o Lisa Glowinski, Preident
More Content Now
9001 IH-35 N, Ste. 102
Austin, TX 78753
Ph: (217)816-3343

Guzman, Angela M., Secretary
International Commission for Optics [6947]
c/o Angela M. Guzman, Secretary
College of Optics and Photonics

University of Central Florida
4000 Central Florida Blvd.
Orlando, FL 32816-2700
Ph: (561)313-8204

Guzman, Jessica, Mem.
College for Creative Studies Alumni Association [19316]
201 E Kirby St.
Detroit, MI 48202-4034
Ph: (313)664-7400
Toll Free: 800-952-2787

Guzman, Jessica, Dir. of Comm.
World Pet Association [2551]
135 W Lemon Ave.
Monrovia, CA 91016
Ph: (626)447-2222
Fax: (626)447-8350

Gwal, Anne, President
South Asian Bar Association of North America [5446]
c/o Faisal Charania
Prime Communications
3006 Arrowhead Dr.
Sugar Land, TX 77479

Gyure, Michael, Exec. Dir.
Friars Club [10252]
57 E 55th St.
New York, NY 10022
Ph: (212)751-7272
Fax: (212)355-0217

H

H., Joe, Exec. Dir.
Sex Addicts Anonymous [12915]
PO Box 70949
Houston, TX 77270-0949
Ph: (713)869-4902
Toll Free: 800-477-8191

Haack, Susan, Dir. of Member Svcs.
Counselors of Real Estate [2856]
430 N Michigan Ave.
Chicago, IL 60611-4089
Ph: (312)329-8427

Hámos, László, President
American Hungarian Library and Historical Society [19468]
215 E 82nd St.
New York, NY 10028
Ph: (212)744-5298

Haake, David, President
International Leptospirosis Society [15405]
c/o David Haake, President
11301 Wilshire Blvd.
Los Angeles, CA 90073
Ph: (310)268-3814
Fax: (310)268-4928

Haaland, Kathleen Y., President
The International Neuropsychological Society [16022]
2319 S Foothill Dr., Ste. 260
Salt Lake City, UT 84109
Ph: (801)487-0475

Haaland, Paul, COO
National Association of Affordable Housing Lenders [407]
1667 K St. NW, Ste. 210
Washington, DC 20006
Ph: (202)293-9850
Fax: (202)293-9852

Haas, Charles A., President
Titanic International Society [9779]
c/o Robert Bracken, Treasurer
47 Van Blarcom Ave.
Midland Park, NJ 07432

Haas, Michael, Chmn. of the Bd., Founder
Alliance for Climate Education [4111]
4696 Broadway St., Ste. 2

Boulder, CO 80304
Ph: (510)251-5990
Fax: (510)419-0383

Haas, Yvette, President
Association for Continuing Dental
Education [7709]
c/o Yvette Haas, President
The University of Texas
School of Dentistry at Houston
7500 Cambridge St., Ste. 6130
Houston, TX 77054
Ph: (713)486-4028
Fax: (713)486-4037

Haase, Betty, CFO
Adventist World Aviation [19696]
8023 County Road L (Hangar S-3)
East Troy, WI 53120
Ph: (414)226-5196
Fax: (414)231-9430

Haataja, Dave, Exec. Dir.
Water Quality Association [3462]
4151 Naperville Rd.
Lisle, IL 60532-3696
Ph: (630)505-0160
Fax: (630)505-9637

Haberaecker, Charlotte, President,
CEO
Lutheran Services in America
[20312]
100 Maryland Ave. NE, Ste. 500
Washington, DC 20002
Ph: (202)499-5836
Toll Free: 800-664-3848
Fax: (202)544-0890

Haberstro, Philip, Exec. Dir.
National Association for Health and
Fitness [16706]
10 Kings Mill Ct.
Albany, NY 12205-3632
Ph: (518)456-1058

Habib, Amid, MD, Founder,
President
United People in Christ, Inc. [20010]
789 Douglas Ave., Ste. 137
Altamonte Springs, FL 32714
Ph: (407)862-0107
Fax: (407)862-1283

Habiby, Mrs. Nadira F., Dir. of
Admin.
American Bahraini Friendship
Society [18509]
3502 International Dr. NW
Washington, DC 20008-3035
Ph: (202)342-1111

Hace, Gerald, V. Chmn. of the Bd.
Pharmaceutical Printed Literature
Association [2569]
c/o Nosco, Inc.
2199 N Delany Rd.
Gurnee, IL 60031

Hachtman, Steve, Comm. Chm.
Academy of Surgical Research
[15638]
15490 101st Ave. N, Ste. 100
Maple Grove, MN 55369
Ph: (763)235-6464
Fax: (763)235-6461

Hacke, Kevin, VP
National Association of Independent
Fee Appraisers [228]
330 N Wabash Ave., Ste. 2000
Chicago, IL 60611
Ph: (312)321-6830
Fax: (312)673-6652

Hacker, Chris, President
Wood Machinery Manufacturers of
America [1779]

9 Newport Dr., Ste. 200
Forest Hill, MD 21050
Ph: (443)640-1052
Fax: (443)640-1031

Hackett, James T., Chairman
National Petroleum Council [5173]
1625 K St. NW, Ste. 600
Washington, DC 20006
Ph: (202)393-6100
Fax: (202)331-8539

Hackley, Paul, Membership Chp.
The Society for Organic Petrology
[7002]
US Geological Survey
956 National Ctr.
Reston, VA 20192
Ph: (703)648-6458
Fax: (703)648-6419

Hackney, Arthur, Chairman
American Association of Political
Consultants [18902]
8400 Westpark Dr.
McLean, VA 22102
Ph: (703)245-8020

Hackworth, Eilhys England,
Chairperson
Stand for the Troops [20706]
PO Box 11179
Greenwich, CT 06831
Ph: (203)629-0288

Hada, Jayjeev, Chairman, Exec. Dir.,
Founder
Community Members Interested
[11340]
205 Yoakum Pky., Unit 807
Alexandria, VA 22304
Ph: (301)273-5679

Haddad, Danny, MD, Director
International Trachoma Initiative
[17716]
325 Swanton Way
Decatur, GA 30030
Ph: (404)371-0466
Toll Free: 800-765-7173
Fax: (404)371-1087

Haddad, Prof. Heskel M., MD, Chair-
man
International Society on Metabolic
Eye Disease [16392]
1125 Park Ave.
New York, NY 10128
Ph: (212)427-1246
Fax: (212)360-7009

Haddigan, Hilary
Heifer International [3727]
1 World Ave.
Little Rock, AR 72202
Ph: (501)907-2902
Toll Free: 855-948-6437

Haden, Kelly, President
Kappa Gamma Pi [23782]
7250 Overcliff Rd.
Cincinnati, OH 45233-1038
Ph: (305)525-3744
Fax: (305)718-9362

Hadley, Jessica, Director
College of Healthcare Information
Management Executives [1796]
710 Avis Dr., Ste. 200
Ann Arbor, MI 48108
Ph: (734)665-0000
Fax: (734)665-4922

Hadley, Dr. Phillip, Chairman
Los Ninos [11400]
717 3rd Ave.
Chula Vista, CA 91910
Ph: (619)426-9110
Toll Free: 866-922-8984
Fax: (619)426-6664

Hadley, Sam, VP
U.S. Log Rolling Association [23365]
c/o Polly Pappadopoulos, Secretary
3111 S Pleasant Dr.
Holmen, WI 54636

Hadsell, Heidi, President
International Institute of Islamic
Thought [9605]
500 Grove St., Ste. 200
Herndon, VA 20170
Ph: (703)471-1133
    (703)230-2850
Fax: (703)471-3922

Haecker, Nancy, President
Location Managers Guild
International [2180]
8033 Sunset Blvd., No. 1017
Los Angeles, CA 90046
Ph: (310)967-2007
Fax: (310)967-2013

Haefner, Hope, MD, Exec. Dir.
Childhood Gynecologic Cancer As-
sociation [14175]
PO Box 3130
Ann Arbor, MI 48106
Ph: (734)663-7251

Haemmerle, Larry, President
USA Racquetball [23088]
2812 W Colorado Ave., Ste. 200
Colorado Springs, CO 80904-2906
Ph: (719)635-5396
Fax: (719)635-0685

Haessner, Elaine C., Exec. Dir.
International Society for Vehicle
Preservation [21406]
PO Box 50046
Tucson, AZ 85703-1046

Haff, G. Gregory, President
National Strength and Conditioning
Association [23337]
1885 Bob Johnson Dr.
Colorado Springs, CO 80906
Ph: (719)632-6722
Toll Free: 800-815-6826
Fax: (719)632-6367

Hafner, Madeline M., PhD, Exec. Dir.
Minority Student Achievement
Network [7903]
Wisconsin Center for Education
Research
467 Education Sciences Bldg.
1025 W Johnson St.
Madison, WI 53706
Ph: (608)263-1565
Fax: (608)263-6448

Hagan, Beth, Exec. Dir.
Community College Baccalaureate
Association [7642]
25216 Pelican Creek Cir., No. 103
Bonita Springs, FL 34134-1979
Ph: (239)947-8085
Fax: (239)947-8870

Hagan, Kate, Exec. Dir.
American Association of Law Librar-
ies [5562]
105 W Adams St., Ste. 3300
Chicago, IL 60603
Ph: (312)939-4764
Fax: (312)431-1097

Hagan, Marie, Exec. Sec.
Association for Interdisciplinary
Research in Values and Social
Change [12764]
512 10th St. NW
Washington, DC 20004
Ph: (202)626-8800

Hagans, Lori Renegar, Exec. Dir.
Oklahoma Baptist University Alumni
Association [19340]

500 W University
500 W University St.
Shawnee, OK 74804
Ph: (405)275-2850
    (405)585-5413
Toll Free: 800-654-3285

Hagele, Glenn, Exec. Dir.
Council for Refractive Surgery Qual-
ity Assurance [17387]
8543 Everglade Dr.
Sacramento, CA 95826-3616
Ph: (916)381-0769

Hagerman, Bonnie, Founder
Care Wear Volunteers, Inc. [14171]
c/o Bonnie Hagerman, Founder
102 Mercer Ct., Ste. 23-5
Frederick, MD 21701
Ph: (301)620-2858

Hagg, Ida, Exec. Dir.
AdoptaPlatoon [10735]
PO Box 1457
Seabrook, NH 03874
Ph: (956)748-4206

Haggart, Sandy, Founder
Feed the Dream Guatemala [10970]
PO Box 2642
Glenview, IL 60025

Haggis, Paul, Founder
Artists for Peace and Justice
[12994]
87 Walker St., No. 6B
New York, NY 10013
Ph: (646)398-7804
Fax: (646)398-8343

Hagiwara, Tuesday, Exec. Dir.
Phi Gamma Nu [23698]
213 E King Rd.
Ithaca, NY 14850
Ph: (630)412-1746

Hagle, Paul D., Exec. Dir.
National Association of ADA
Coordinators [11622]
PO Box 958
Rancho Mirage, CA 92270
Toll Free: 888-679-7227
Fax: (877)480-7858

Haglin, Mark, President
English Springer Spaniel Field Trial
Association [21874]
c/o Danelle Oliver, Secretary
8312 Old Moro Rd.
Dorsey, IL 62021

Haglund, Kristine, Editor
Dialogue Foundation [20298]
PO Box 381209
Cambridge, MA 02238-1209
Ph: (857)600-1620

Hagood, Taylor, VP
William Faulkner Society [10370]
c/o Ted Atkinson, President
PO Box 5272
Mississippi State, MS 39762

Hagy, Sarah, Exec. Dir.
International Kitchen Exhaust Clean-
ing Association [1290]
100 N 20th St., Ste. 400
Philadelphia, PA 19103-1462
Ph: (215)320-3876
Fax: (215)564-2175

Hahn, Al, Exec. Dir.
Association of Support Professionals
[3070]
38954 Proctor Blvd., Ste. 396
Sandy, OR 97055
Ph: (503)668-9004

Hahn, Barbara, Director
Educate Tanzania [7761]
858 Oriole Ln.

Chaska, MN 55318
Ph: (952)250-9740

Hahn, Mr. Bruce, CAE, President
American Homeowners Grassroots
Alliance [18357]
6776 Little Falls Rd.
Arlington, VA 22213-1213

Hahn, Cindy L., Exec. Dir.
Alagille Syndrome Alliance [14803]
10500 SW Starr Dr.
Tualatin, OR 97062-8411
Ph: (503)885-0455

Hahn, Gail Bennett, Gov., Rec. Sec.
Descendants of Founders of New
Jersey [20750]
c/o Evelyn Ogden, Registrar
816 Grove St.
Point Pleasant Beach, NJ 08742

Hahn, Kenneth, Founder
Global Routes [9209]
1 World Way
Hillsborough, NH 03244
Ph: (413)585-8895
Fax: (413)585-8810

Hahn, Kimiko, President
Poetry Society of America [10158]
15 Gramercy Park
New York, NY 10003
Ph: (212)254-9628
Fax: (212)673-2352

Hahn, Dr. Lorna, Exec. Dir.
Association on Third World Affairs,
Inc. [18484]
c/o Dr. Lorna Hahn
1717 K St. NW, Ste. 600
Washington, DC 20036
Ph: (202)973-0157
Fax: (202)775-7465

Hahn, Mike, Founder, President
His Little Feet [11032]
1555 Main St., Ste. A3-290
Windsor, CO 80550
Toll Free: 866-252-3988

Hahn, Peter L., Exec. Dir.
Society for Historians of American
Foreign Relations [9515]
Dept. of History
Middle Tennessee State University
1301 E Main St.
Murfreesboro, TN 37132
Ph: (617)458-6156
Fax: (615)898-5881

Hahn, Theodore, Contact
Society for Software Quality [6286]
PO Box 27634
San Diego, CA 92198

Haigler, Evan, Exec. Dir.
Impact Carbon [4027]
582 Market St., Ste. 1204
San Francisco, CA 94104
Ph: (415)968-9087

Hail, Janelle, CEO, Chmn. of the
Bd., Founder
National Breast Cancer Foundation
[14021]
2600 Network Blvd., Ste. 300
Frisco, TX 75034

Haile, Dan, President
American Y-Flyer Yacht Racing As-
sociation [22596]
7349 Scarborough Blvd., E Dr.
Indianapolis, IN 46256-2052
Ph: (518)831-1321

Hailey, Tammy, CAE, Exec. Dir.
NALS [5545]
8159 E 41st St.

Tulsa, OK 74145-3313
Ph: (918)582-5188
Fax: (918)582-5907

Haima, Scott, Director
CSB Ministries [20659]
PO Box 1010
Hamburg, NY 14075
Ph: (716)526-0026
(716)951-5515
Toll Free: 800-815-5573

Haines, Mrs. Ann, Coord.
Hoover Historical Center [21293]
1875 E Maple St.
North Canton, OH 44720-3331
Ph: (330)499-0287
(330)490-7435
Fax: (330)494-4725

Haines, Carolyn, VP
Cornish American Heritage Society
[9139]
c/o Kathryn Herman, President
222 Park Pl., No. 476
Waukesha, WI 53186-4815
Ph: (608)342-1719

Haines, Kathleen, Treasurer
Women's International Shipping and
Trading Association [3110]
Total Marine Solutions Inc.
4350 Oakes Rd., Ste. 502
Fort Lauderdale, FL 33314

Haines, Matt, President
Integrity USA [20182]
770 Massachusetts Ave., No.
390170
Cambridge, MA 02139
Toll Free: 800-462-9498

Hair, Ray, President
American Federation of Musicians
[23492]
1501 Broadway, Ste. 600
New York, NY 10036

Hairston, Rod, CEO, Chmn. of the
Bd.
National Association of Sales Profes-
sionals [3017]
555 Friendly St.
Bloomfield, MI 48302

Haitz, Linn, Founder
Children of Promise International
[10923]
6844 Loop Rd.
Centerville, OH 45459-2159
Ph: (937)436-5397
Toll Free: 888-667-7426
Fax: (937)438-4972

Hajdu-Nemeth, Gergely, Exec. Dir.
American Hungarian Foundation
[19467]
300 Somerset St.
New Brunswick, NJ 08901-2248
Ph: (732)846-5777
Fax: (732)249-7033

Hakansson, Susie, President
TODOS: Mathematics for ALL [8286]
PO Box 25482
Tempe, AZ 85285-5482

Hake, Jim, Founder
Spirit of America [19015]
12021 Wilshire Blvd., No. 507
Los Angeles, CA 90025
Ph: (310)230-5476
Fax: (310)826-4542

Hake, Kater D., PhD, VP
Cotton Inc. [934]
6399 Weston Pky.
Cary, NC 27513
Ph: (919)678-2220
Fax: (919)678-2230

Hakemian, John, Exec. Dir.
National Employment Counseling
Association [11773]
c/o Seneka Arrington, President
Adapt Behavioral Services, Inc.
1000 St. Georges Rd.
Ormond Beach, FL 32174
Ph: (386)259-0154

Hakovirta, Marko, Assoc. Dir.
Renewable Bioproducts Institute
[6978]
500 10th St. NW
Atlanta, GA 30332-0620
Ph: (404)894-5700
Fax: (404)894-4778

Halamandaris, Val J., President
World Homecare and Hospice
Organization [15284]
228 7th St. SE
Washington, DC 20003
Ph: (202)547-7424
Fax: (202)547-3540

Halas, Dr. F. Peter, Chairman
Irish American Cultural Institute
[9599]
PO Box 1716
Morristown, NJ 07962
Ph: (973)605-1991

Halbach, Jeff, Comm. Chm.
American Bantam Association [4560]
PO Box 127
Augusta, NJ 07822
Ph: (419)234-4427
(716)592-0766

Haldeman, Dr. Scott, President
World Spine Care [17269]
801 N Tustin Ave., Ste. 202
Santa Ana, CA 92705

Hale, Chris, President
National Veteran-Owned Business
Association [5842]
420 Rouser Rd., Ste. 101
Moon Township, PA 15108
Ph: (412)269-1663

Hale, Dr. Cynthia L., Pastor
Ray of Hope [13197]
2778 Snapfinger Rd.
Decatur, GA 30034
Ph: (770)696-5100
Fax: (770)696-5111

Hale, Heather, President
Australian Labradoodle Association
of America [3985]
c/o Butch Charlton, Treasurer and
Registrar
10729 Grassy Creek Pl.
Raleigh, NC 27614
Fax: (309)418-9916

Hale, Sunny, Founder, President
American Polo Horse Association,
Inc. [23069]
4095 State Road 7, Ste. L
Lake Worth, FL 33449

Hales, Daniel B., Director
Americans for Effective Law
Enforcement [5146]
PO Box 75401
Chicago, IL 60675-5401
Ph: (847)685-0700
Fax: (847)685-9700

Hales, Daniel B., Asst. Sec.
Philadelphia Society [18998]
11620 Rutan Cir.
Jerome, MI 49249
Ph: (517)688-5111
Fax: (517)688-5113

Hales, Sarah, Founder, Treasurer
Ekissa [12031]
PO Box 370

Clemmons, NC 27012
Ph: (336)971-4855

Haley, Boyd, PhD, Director
International Academy of Oral
Medicine and Toxicology [14444]
8297 Champions Gate Blvd., No.
193
Champions Gate, FL 33896
Ph: (863)420-6373
Fax: (863)419-8136

Haley, David C., President
Managed Funds Association [2028]
600 14th St. NW, Ste. 900
Washington, DC 20005
Ph: (202)730-2600

Haley, Dianne, Chairperson
GISCorps [13292]
701 Lee St., Ste. 680
Des Plaines, IL 60016
Ph: (847)824-6300
Fax: (847)824-6363

Haliday, Rae Lynn, CRM, Chairman
Institute of Certified Records Manag-
ers [1799]
1450 Western Ave., Ste. 101
Albany, NY 12203
Ph: (518)694-5362
Toll Free: 877-244-3128
Fax: (518)463-8656

Hall, Beth, Exec. Dir., Founder
Pact, An Adoption Alliance [10463]
5515 Doyle St., Ste. 1
Emeryville, CA 94608-2510
Ph: (510)243-9460
Toll Free: 800-750-7590
Fax: (510)243-9970

Hall, Bill, President
Fire Museum Network [9324]
c/o Bob Vallero, Treasurer
2912 S Otis St.
Denver, CO 80227-3530

Hall, C-Ray, President
National Championship Racing As-
sociation [23083]
7700 N Broadway St.
Wichita, KS 67219
Ph: (316)755-1781
Fax: (316)755-0665

Hall, Charlie, PhD, Contact
America in Bloom [3780]
2130 Stella Ct.
Columbus, OH 43215
Ph: (614)453-0744
Fax: (614)487-1216

Hall, Daron, Treasurer
National Sheriffs' Association [5511]
1450 Duke St.
Alexandria, VA 22314
Toll Free: 800-424-7827
Fax: (703)838-5349

Hall, David, Director
WEC International [20164]
PO Box 1707
Fort Washington, PA 19034
Ph: (215)646-2322
Toll Free: 888-646-6202

Hall, Doug, Officer
Association for Automatic Identification and Mobility North America
[272]
1 Landmark N
20399 Route 19, Ste. 203
Cranberry Township, PA 16066
Ph: (724)742-4473
Fax: (724)742-4476

Hall, Doug, VP
National Association of Competitive
Mounted Orienteering [23050]

c/o Jim Klein, Treasurer/National
Pointskeeper
24305 98th St. NW
Zimmerman, MN 55398
Ph: (763)856-6735

Hall, Drew, DC, President
Blair Chiropractic Society [14258]
550 E Carson Plaza Dr., Ste. 122
Carson, CA 90746

Hall, Jann, President
National Silver Rabbit Club [4609]
c/o Patty Beamer, Secretary/
Treasurer
1239 NW Dogwood Ave.
Redmond, OR 97756
Ph: (541)815-8160

Hall, Dr. Jim, Exec. Dir.
Sigma Zeta [23862]
Our Lady of the Lake University
411 SW 24th St.
San Antonio, TX 78207-4689

Hall, John L., III, President,
Treasurer
American Milking Devon Cattle Association [3702]
c/o Raymond Clark, Director
1429 Red Village Rd.
Lyndonville, VT 05851

Hall, John, Bd. Member
Trollope Society [9105]
c/o Midge Fitzgerald
6 Pier Pointe
New Bern, NC 28562
Ph: (212)683-4023

Hall, Ken, Gen. Sec., Treasurer
Brewery and Soft Drink Conference
[23394]
25 Louisiana Ave., NW
25 Louisiana Ave. NW
Washington, DC 20001
Ph: (202)624-6800

Hall, Ken, Director
Fellowship of Christian Firefighters
International [5203]
249 Rochiri Dr.
Boydton, VA 23917
Ph: (443)336-9859

Hall, Kurt, V. Chmn. of the Bd.
American Logistics Association
[5588]
1101 Vermont Ave. NW, Ste. 1002
Washington, DC 20005
Ph: (202)466-2520
Fax: (240)823-9181

Hall, L. Michael, PhD, Founder
International Society of Neuro-
Semantics [17187]
PO Box 8
Clifton, CO 81520-0008
Ph: (970)523-7877

Hall, Manly P., Founder
Philosophical Research Society
[10111]
3910 Los Feliz Blvd.
Los Angeles, CA 90027
Toll Free: 800-548-4062
Fax: (323)663-9443

Hall, Maryann, President
Prune Belly Syndrome Network
[14854]
PO Box 16071
Philadelphia, PA 19154
Toll Free: 855-275-7276

Hall, Meghan, Founder, CEO
Avery's Angels Gastroschisis
Foundation [13824]

PO Box 58312
Raleigh, NC 27658
Toll Free: 855-692-8379
Fax: (919)400-4595

Hall, Mike, President
American Ambulance Association
[14659]
8400 Westpark Dr., 2nd Fl.
McLean, VA 22102
Ph: (703)610-9018
Toll Free: 800-523-4447
Fax: (703)610-0210

Hall, Mike, President
National Association of Rhythm and
Blues Dee Jay's [9969]
c/o Sue Kestner, Secretary
5375 Ridge Rd.
Joelton, TN 37080
Ph: (615)876-2343

Hall, Mike, Dir. of Member Svcs.
Society of Naval Architects and
Marine Engineers [6906]
99 Canal Center Plz., Ste. 310
Alexandria, VA 22314
Ph: (703)997-6701

Hall, Neil, President
Bowen USA [13612]
710 Butternut St., Ste. B
Abilene, TX 79602

Hall, Reggie, Exec. Dir.
International Art Materials Associa-
tion [245]
20200 Zion Ave.
Cornelius, NC 28031
Ph: (704)892-6244
Fax: (704)892-6247

Hall, Reggie, Exec. Dir.
National Art Materials Trade Associa-
tion [1541]
20200 Zion Ave.
Cornelius, NC 28031
Ph: (704)892-6244

Hall, Russ, Consultant
Wilderness International [3965]
PO Box 491
Canby, OR 97013-0491
Ph: (503)593-0199

Hall, Stephanie, President, Chmn. of
the Bd.
National Equipment Finance As-
sociation [2929]
PO Box 69
Northbrook, IL 60065
Ph: (847)380-5050
Fax: (847)380-5055

Hall, Stevan A., Exec. Dir.
Pile Driving Contractors Association
[897]
33 Knight Boxx Rd., Ste. 1
Orange Park, FL 32065
Ph: (904)215-4771
Toll Free: 888-311-7322
Fax: (904)215-2977

Hall, Steve, Exec. Dir.
International Hunter Education As-
sociation [22961]
800 E 73rd Ave., Unit 2
Denver, CO 80229
Ph: (303)430-7233
Fax: (303)430-7236

Hall, Susan, Mktg. Mgr.
Turfgrass Producers International
[4285]
2 E Main St.
East Dundee, IL 60118
Ph: (847)649-5555
Toll Free: 800-405-8873
Fax: (847)649-5678

Hall, Tim, President
Monster Truck Racing Association
[23082]
c/o Brenda Noelke, Secretary, 947
Crider Ln.
947 Crider Ln.
Union, MO 63084
Ph: (636)234-6162
Fax: (636)583-1660

Hall, Tony P., Exec. Dir.
Alliance to End Hunger [12076]
425 3rd St. SW, Ste. 1200
Washington, DC 20024
Ph: (202)688-1157

Hallack, Nick, President, CEO
MediSend International [12291]
9244 Markville Dr.
Dallas, TX 75243
Ph: (214)575-5006
Fax: (214)570-9284

Hallak, Eli, Founder, President
National Honors Society of Sports
Medicine [17286]
13636 Ventura Blvd., No. 387
Sherman Oaks, CA 91423
Ph: (641)715-3900

Hallauer, Jake, Secretary
Neighbor to Neighbor [17842]
1550 Blue Spruce Dr.
Fort Collins, CO 80524
Ph: (970)484-7498

Hall-Clifford, Rachel, Secretary
National Association for the Practice
of Anthropology [5916]
c/o Kathleen Terry-Sharp
American Anthropological Association
2200 Wilson Blvd., Ste. 600
Arlington, VA 22201
Ph: (703)528-1902

Hallenbeck, Scott, Exec. Dir.
USA Football [22871]
45 N Pennsylvania St., Ste. 700
Indianapolis, IN 46204
Ph: (317)614-7750
Toll Free: 877-536-6822

Haller, Cindy, Editor
Guild of Book Workers [9129]
521 5th Ave.
New York, NY 10175
Ph: (212)292-4444

Haller, MD, Julia A., President
Association of University Professors
of Ophthalmology [16376]
655 Beach St.
San Francisco, CA 94109
Ph: (415)561-8548
Fax: (415)561-8531

Haller, Stacy Pagos, CEO, President
BrightFocus Foundation [15641]
22512 Gateway Center Dr.
Clarksburg, MD 20871
Toll Free: 800-437-2423
Fax: (301)258-9454

Hallerman, Dr. Eric, President
National Association of University
Fisheries and Wildlife Programs
[7880]
c/o Dr. Keith Owens, President-Elect
Dept. of Natural Resource Ecology
and Management
Oklahoma State University
008C Agricultural Hall
Stillwater, OK 74078
Ph: (405)744-5438

Hallett, Jill, Secretary, Treasurer
International Naples Sabot Association [22637]

2812 Canon St.
San Diego, CA 92106
Ph: (949)275-2636
     (619)222-0252
Fax: (619)222-0528

Hallett, Lisa, President
Wear Blue: Run to Remember
[13255]
PO Box 76
DuPont, WA 98327

Hallisy, Dr. Julia, Founder
The Empowered Patient Coalition
[15637]
595 Buckingham Way, No. 305
San Francisco, CA 94132

Hallman, Eric, Exec. Dir.
Livestock Conservancy [4458]
33 Hillsborough St.
Pittsboro, NC 27312
Ph: (919)542-5704

Hallman, Linda D., CAE, CEO
AAUW Legal Advocacy Fund [5403]
1111 16th St. NW
Washington, DC 20036
Ph: (202)785-7700
Toll Free: 800-326-2289
Fax: (202)872-1425

Hallman, Ms. Linda D., Exec. Dir.
American Association of University
Women [8742]
1111 16th St. NW
Washington, DC 20036-4809
Ph: (202)785-7700
     (202)728-7602
Toll Free: 800-326-2289
Fax: (202)872-1425

Hallsmith, Gwendolyn, Exec. Dir.,
Founder
Global Community Initiatives [11366]
12 Parkside Dr.
Montpelier, VT 05602
Ph: (802)851-7697

Hallum, Anne, Founder, President
Alliance for International Reforestation [3793]
4514 Chamblee Dunwoody Rd., Unit
496
Atlanta, GA 30338
Ph: (770)543-9529

Halper, June, MSN, Exec. Dir.
International Organization of Multiple
Sclerosis Nurses [16139]
359 Main St., Ste. A
Hackensack, NJ 07601-5806
Ph: (201)487-1050
Fax: (201)678-2291

Halpin, Hal, Founder, President
Entertainment Consumers Associa-
tion [18047]
64 Danbury Rd., Ste. 700
Wilton, CT 06897-4406
Ph: (203)761-6183

Halstead, Heather, Exec. Dir.
Reach the World [7915]
222 Broadway, 21st Fl.
New York, NY 10007
Ph: (212)288-6987
Toll Free: 866-411-5090

Halverson, Julie, Exec. Dir.
National Association of Service Dogs
[11692]
2549 Eastbluff Dr., Ste. 430
Newport Beach, CA 92660
Toll Free: 888-669-6273
Fax: (877)329-6273

Ham, Gen. Carter F., Leader
Military Order of the Carabao
[20705]

PO Box 987
Millersville, MD 21108
Ph: (703)946-7777

Hamann, Diane, President
American Rock Art Research Association [5929]
c/o Jack Wedgwood, Treasurer
1884 The Alameda
San Jose, CA 95126-1733

Hamblen, Jessica, Exec. Dir.
U.S. Department of Veterans Affairs
| National Center for Post-
Traumatic Stress Disorder [17293]
1234 VA Cut Off Rd.
White River Junction, VT 05009
Ph: (802)296-6300

Hamblin, Ms. Jane, JD, Exec. Dir.
Mortar Board, Inc. [23783]
c/o Motor Board National College
Senior Honor Society
1200 Chambers Rd., Ste. 201
Columbus, OH 43212
Ph: (614)488-4094
Toll Free: 800-989-6266
Fax: (614)488-4095

Hamblin, Stephen A., Exec. Dir.
American Junior Golf Association
[22873]
1980 Sports Club Dr.
Braselton, GA 30517
Ph: (770)868-4200
Toll Free: 877-373-2542
Fax: (770)868-4211

Hamburg, Steven, Scientist
Environmental Defense Fund [4058]
257 Park Ave. S
New York, NY 10010
Toll Free: 800-684-3322

Hamed, Prof. Awatef, Exec. Sec.
International Society of Airbreathing
Engines [6605]
c/o Prof. Awatef Hamed, Executive
Secretary
745 Baldwin Hall
Dept. of Aerospace Engineering and
Engineering Mechanics
University of Cincinnati
Cincinnati, OH 45221-0070

Hamel, Dr. Willem Arthur, Founder,
President
Association of Management/
International Association of
Management [6034]
PO Box 72894
Richmond, VA 23235
Ph: (757)482-2273
Fax: (757)482-0325

Hameline, Thomas, PhD, President,
CEO
HELP USA [11952]
5 Hanover Sq., 17th Fl.
New York, NY 10004
Ph: (212)400-7000
Toll Free: 800-311-7999
Fax: (212)400-7005

Hames, John, Exec. Dir.
American Wine Society [4926]
PO Box 279
Englewood, OH 45322
Toll Free: 888-297-9070

Hamid, Allan H., Founder
Spanish-Norman Horse Registry
[4412]
c/o Linda Osterman Hamid,
Registrar
PO Box 985
Woodbury, CT 06798
Ph: (203)266-4048
Fax: (203)263-3306

Hamill, John, Secretary
Atheist Alliance International [19709]
1777 T St. NW
Washington, DC 20009-7102

Hamill, Joseph, Contact
International Society of Biomechan-
ics in Sports [6087]
c/o East Tennessee State University
PO Box 70300
Johnson City, TN 37614
Ph: (423)439-1000

Hamill, Richard, Founder, President
Will2Walk Foundation [17268]
1909 E Ray Rd., No. 9-238
Chandler, AZ 85225
Fax: (480)634-7867

Hamilton, Carrie, President
North American Teckel Club [21932]
536 Orchard Rd.
Reinholds, PA 17569-9632
Ph: (610)285-2469

Hamilton, Craig, Editor
National Puzzlers' League [22055]
2507 Almar St.
Jenison, MI 49428

Hamilton, Frank H., III, President
Independent Lubricant Manufactur-
ers Association [2523]
400 N Columbus St., Ste. 201
Alexandria, VA 22314-2264
Ph: (703)684-5574
Fax: (703)836-8503

Hamilton, George, President
Institute for Sustainable Communi-
ties [11385]
535 Stone Cutters Way
Montpelier, VT 05602-3795
Ph: (802)229-2900
Fax: (802)229-2919

Hamilton, Dr. Henry, Founder,
President
MedLend [15035]
1820 Ogden Dr., 2nd Fl.
Burlingame, CA 94010
Ph: (650)375-1800

Hamilton, Jared, Founder, President
Child Aid International [10893]
125 Washington St., Ste. 201
Salem, MA 01970
Ph: (978)338-4240
Fax: (978)236-7272

Hamilton, Jim, President
Radiology Business Management
Association [15593]
9990 Fairfax Blvd.
Fairfax, VA 22030
Ph: (703)621-3355
Toll Free: 888-224-7262
Fax: (703)621-3356

Hamilton, Katherine, Exec. Dir.
Advanced Energy Management Alli-
ance [1105]
1155 15th St. NW, Ste. 500
Washington, DC 20005
Ph: (202)524-8832

Hamilton, Larry, Jr., President
Hamilton National Genealogical
Society [20876]
116 W Vine St.
Vicksburg, MI 49097

Hamilton, Paul, PhD, Founder, Exec.
Dir.
The Biodiversity Group [4795]
10980 W Rudasill Rd.
Tucson, AZ 85743
Ph: (520)647-1434

Hamilton, Paul, Capt.
Cruising Club of America [22610]
298 Winslow Way W
Bainbridge Island, WA 98110

Hamilton, Peggy, President
North American Saddle Mule As-
sociation [21283]
PO Box 1108
Boyd, TX 76023

Hamilton, Scott, Exec. Dir.
American Society of Sanitary
Engineering [7111]
18927 Hickory Creek Dr., Ste. 220
Mokena, IL 60448
Ph: (708)995-3019
Fax: (708)479-6139

Hamilton, Thomas J., Director
International Association of Com-
mercial Collectors, Inc. [984]
4040 W 70th St.
Minneapolis, MN 55435
Ph: (952)925-0760
Toll Free: 800-859-9526
Fax: (952)926-1624

Hamilton, Vonda, President
Champagne Horse Breeders' and
Owners' Association [4342]
619 Raiford Rd.
Erwin, NC 28339
Ph: (910)891-5022

Hamilton-LaFortune, Minna,
President, Secretary
Society for the Advancement of the
Caribbean Diaspora [19398]
PO Box 24556
Brooklyn, NY 11202
Ph: (917)771-7935

Hamlett, James, Chairman
Church Benefits Association [20516]
1120 Rte., Ste. 200
Mount Laurel, NJ 08054
Ph: (856)439-0500
Fax: (856)439-0525

Hamlin, Deborah M., CAE, CEO
Irrigation Association [169]
8280 Willow Oaks Corporate Dr.,
Ste. 400
Fairfax, VA 22031
Ph: (703)536-7080
Fax: (703)536-7019

Hamlin-Smith, Stephan J.
Society for Disability Studies [11638]
University at Buffalo
538 Park Hall
Buffalo, NY 14260
Ph: (716)645-0276
Fax: (716)645-5954

Hamlow, Eric, Commissioner
United States Flag Football for the
Deaf [22802]
Pendelton, IN
Ph: (317)288-3590

Hamm, Harold, Chairman
Domestic Energy Producers Alliance
[1110]
PO Box 18359
Oklahoma City, OK 73154-0359
Ph: (405)424-1699

Hamm, Julia, CEO, President
Solar Electric Power Association
[7206]
1220 19th St. NW, Ste. 800
Washington, DC 20036-2405
Ph: (202)857-0898

Hamm, Rita R., CEO
International Association for Impact
Assessment [7273]

1330 23rd St. S, Ste. C
Fargo, ND 58103-3705
Ph: (701)297-7908
Fax: (701)297-7917

Hammatt, Hank, Exec. Dir., Founder
Elephant Care International [4811]
166 Limo View Ln.
Hohenwald, TN 38462
Ph: (931)796-7102

Hammel, Allan, President
Automation Association [2214]
c/o Allan Hammel, President
7300 Hudson Blvd. N, Ste. 285
Oakdale, MN 55128
Ph: (651)264-9841

Hammer, Cathy, Chairperson
American Eskimo Dog Club of
America [21809]
c/o Cathy Hammer, Membership
Chairman
423 Center St. N
Vienna, VA 22180
Ph: (703)999-7300

Hammer, Floyd, President
Outreach [11123]
301 Center St.
Union, IA 50258
Ph: (641)486-2550
Toll Free: 800-513-0935
Fax: (641)486-2570

Hammer, Paul, VP
Academy of Organizational and Oc-
cupational Psychiatry [16309]
402 E Yakima Ave., No. 1080
Yakima, WA 98901-2760
Ph: (509)457-4611
Fax: (509)454-3295

Hammer, Richard O., Act. Pres.,
Founder
Free Nation Foundation [18295]
c/o Robert T. Long, Director
Auburn University
6080 Haley Ctr.
Auburn, AL 36830
Ph: (334)844-3782

Hammer, Steven, President
Acres Land Trust [3785]
1802 Chapman Rd.
Huntertown, IN 46748
Ph: (260)637-2273
Fax: (260)637-2273

Hammerberg, Thomas P., Director
Automatic Fire Alarm Association
[2991]
81 Mill St., Ste. 300
Gahanna, OH 43230
Ph: (614)416-8076
Toll Free: 844-438-2322
Fax: (614)453-8744

Hammock, Dr. John, Co-Chmn. of
the Bd.
Episcopalians for Global Reconciliation [20104]
2202 Wildwood Hollow Dr.
Valrico, FL 33594
Ph: (813)333-1832

Hammond, Clyde, Chairman
American Health and Beauty Aids
Institute [1582]
PO Box 19510
Chicago, IL 60619-0510
Ph: (708)633-6328
Fax: (708)633-6329

Hammond, Mr. Darrell, Founder
KaBOOM! [12506]
4301 Connecticut Ave. NW, Ste.
ML-1

Washington, DC 20008
Ph: (202)659-0215
Fax: (202)659-0210

Hammond, Marie, Treasurer
Society for Vocational Psychology
[7077]
Kimberly Howard, PhD, Associate
Professor
Dept. of Educational Foundations,
Leadership, & Counseling
School of Education
Boston University
2 Silber Way
Boston,.MA 02215
Ph: (617)353-3378

Hammond, Tim, Founder, Exec. Dir.
National Organization to Halt the
Abuse and Routine Mutilation of
Males [11286]
PO Box 460795
San Francisco, CA 94146
Ph: (415)826-9351
Fax: (305)768-5967

Hamner, Charles E., V. Chmn. of the
Bd.
The Hamner Institutes for Health
Sciences [7338]
6 Davis Dr.
Research Triangle Park, NC 27709
Ph: (919)558-1200
Fax: (919)558-1400

Hamod, Mr. David, CEO, President
National United States-Arab
Chamber of Commerce [23605]
1101 17th St., NW, Ste. 1220
Washington, DC 20036
Ph: (202)289-5920
Fax: (202)289-5938

Hamparian, Aram S., Exec. Dir.
Armenian National Committee of
America [19386]
1711 N St. NW
Washington, DC 20036-2801
Ph: (202)775-1918
Fax: (202)223-7964

Hampton, Brian, Founder
Circle of Friends for American
Veterans [21116]
210 E Broad St., Ste. 202
Falls Church, VA 22046
Ph: (703)237-8980
Fax: (703)237-8976

Hampton, David, Chairman
World Forestry Center [4225]
4033 SW Canyon Rd.
Portland, OR 97221
Ph: (503)228-1367
(503)488-2111
Fax: (503)228-4608

Hampton, Michael, Jr., Exec. Dir.
National Skeet Shooting Association
[23138]
5931 Roft Rd.
San Antonio, TX 78253
Ph: (210)688-3371
Toll Free: 800-877-5338
Fax: (210)688-3014

Hampton, Michael, Exec. Dir.
National Sporting Clays Association
[23139]
5931 Roft Rd.
San Antonio, TX 78253
Ph: (210)688-3371
Toll Free: 800-877-5338
Fax: (210)688-3014

Hampton, Talitha, President
National Organization for the Professional Advancement of Black
Chemists and Chemical Engineers
[6207]

PO Box 255
Blue Bell, PA 19422
Toll Free: 866-599-0253

Hamre, John J., CEO, President
Center for Strategic and International
Studies [18939]
1616 Rhode Island Ave. NW
Washington, DC 20036
Ph: (202)887-0200
(202)775-3242
Fax: (202)775-3199

Hamrin, Dr. Robert, Founder, Chair-
man
Great Dads [12414]
PO Box 7537
Fairfax Station, VA 22039
Ph: (571)643-4526
Toll Free: 888-478-3237

Han Moon, Dr. Hak Ja, President
International Relief Friendship
Foundation [13065]
39 N Jefferson Rd.
Red Hook, NY 12571
Ph: (917)319-6202
Fax: (845)835-8214

Hanania, Ray, Contact
National Arab American Journalists
Association [2692]
c/o Ray Hanania
PO Box 2127
Orland Park, IL 60462
Fax: (708)575-9078

Hancock, Amy E., Secretary
American Beverage Association
[421]
1275 Pennsylvania Ave. NW, Ste.
1100
Washington, DC 20004
Ph: (202)463-6732
(202)463-6770
Fax: (202)659-5349

Hancock, Carol, CEO
International Chili Society [22148]
32244 Paseo Adelanto, Ste. D3
San Juan Capistrano, CA 92675
Ph: (949)496-2651
Toll Free: 877-777-4427
Fax: (949)496-7091

Hancock, Curtis, President
Farm Credit Council [396]
50 F St. NW, No. 900
Washington, DC 20001
Ph: (202)626-8710
(202)879-0843
Fax: (202)626-8718

Hancock, Dahlen K., President
Cotton Council International [932]
1521 New Hampshire Ave. NW
Washington, DC 20036
Ph: (202)745-7805
Fax: (202)483-4040

Hancock, Dell, Chairman
Grayson-Jockey Club Research
Foundation [4355]
821 Corporate Dr.
Lexington, KY 40503
Ph: (859)224-2850
Fax: (859)224-2853

Hancock, George, Director
National Center for Homeless
Education [11956]
5900 Summit Ave., No. 201
Browns Summit, NC 27214
Toll Free: 800-308-2145
Fax: (336)315-7457

Hancock, Marsali S., President, CEO
Internet Keep Safe Coalition [18569]
97 S 2nd St., 100 No. 244

San Jose, CA 95113
Ph: (703)717-9066
Fax: (703)852-7100

Hancock, Ms. Rose, Chairman
Guard a Heart [15216]
5405 Alton Pkwy., Ste. A-213
Irvine, CA 92604

Hancock, Russell, CEO, President
Joint Venture: Silicon Valley Network
[7280]
100 W San Fernando St., Ste. 310
San Jose, CA 95113
Ph: (408)298-9330

Hand, Ivan L., Jr., CEO, President
Money Management International
[1280]
14141 Southwest Fwy., Ste. 1000
Sugar Land, TX 77478-3494
Toll Free: 866-889-9347

Hand, Marc, CEO, Founder
Public Media Company [2825]
5277 Manhattan Cir., Ste. 210
Boulder, CO 80303-8201
Ph: (720)304-7274
Fax: (720)304-8923

Handcock, Ben, Exec. VP
Wheat Quality Council [3776]
5231 Tall Spruce St.
Brighton, CO 80601
Ph: (303)558-0101
Fax: (303)558-0100

Hands, Barry Lee, President
Firearms Engravers Guild of America
[21757]
6120 David Dr.
Wisconsin Rapids, WI 54494
Ph: (616)929-6146

Handschuh, Steve, President, CEO
Motor and Equipment Manufacturers
Association [326]
10 Laboratory Dr.
Research Triangle Park, NC 27709
Ph: (919)549-4800
Fax: (919)406-1465

Hanegraaff, Hank, Chairman,
President
Christian Research Institute [19965]
PO Box 8500
Charlotte, NC 28271
Toll Free: 888-700-0274

Hanen, Laura, Chairperson
Adult Vaccine Access Coalition
[15368]
1150 17th St. NW, Ste. 400
Washington, DC 20036
Ph: (202)540-1070

Hanes, Dr. Jonathan M., Secretary
International Society of Biometeorol-
ogy [6088]
c/o Dr. Jonathan M. Hanes,
Secretary
Dept. of Geography
University of Wisconsin-Milwaukee
Milwaukee, WI 53201
Ph: (414)229-6611
Fax: (414)229-3981

Haness, Rabbi Mayer Baal, Contact
Kolel Chibas Jerusalem [20262]
4802-A 12th Ave.
Brooklyn, NY 11219
Ph: (718)633-7112
Toll Free: 866-787-4520
Fax: (718)633-5783

Haney, Bill, Founder
World Connect [14247]
681 Main St., Ste. 3-37

Waltham, MA 02451
Ph: (347)563-7452
Fax: (781)894-8050

Haney, Dawn, Director
Buddhist Peace Fellowship [18773]
PO Box 3470
Berkeley, CA 94703
Ph: (510)239-3764

Haney, Jim, Exec. Dir.
National Association of Basketball
Coaches [22573]
1111 Main St., Ste. 1000
Kansas City, MO 64105-2136
Ph: (816)878-6222
Fax: (816)878-6223

Haney, Michael L., PhD, Exec. Dir.
American Professional Society on
the Abuse of Children [10851]
1706 E Broad St.
Columbus, OH 43203
Ph: (614)827-1321
Toll Free: 877-402-7722
Fax: (614)251-6005

Haney, Ralph A., Founder
United Street Machine Association
[21511]
430 N Batchewana St.
Clawson, MI 48017
Ph: (248)435-3091

Haney, Dr. Regina M., Exec. Dir.
Department of Boards and Councils
of Catholic Education [7575]
National Catholic Educational As-
sociation
1005 N Glebe Rd., Ste. 525
Arlington, VA 22201
Ph: (202)337-6232
Toll Free: 800-711-6232
Fax: (703)243-0025

Haney, Dr. Regina M., Exec. Dir.
National Association of Church
Personnel Administrators [20564]
2050 Ballenger Ave., Ste. 200
Alexandria, VA 22314
Ph: (703)746-8315

Hanft, Noah J., President, CEO
International Institute for Conflict
Prevention and Resolution [4962]
30 E 33rd St., 6th Fl.
New York, NY 10016
Ph: (212)949-6490
Fax: (212)949-8859

Hang, Sifu Ng Fu, Founder
Choy Lee Fut Martial Arts Federation
of America [23000]
500 1/2E Live Oak Ave.
Arcadia, CA 91006
Ph: (626)574-1523

Hanin, Laurie, PhD, Exec. Dir.
Center for Hearing and Communica-
tion [15179]
50 Broadway, 6th Fl.
New York, NY 10004
Ph: (917)305-7766

Hanink, James G., President
American Maritain Association
[10075]
c/o James G. Hanink, President
Independent Scholar
443 W Hillsdale St.
Inglewood, CA 90302-1123

Hanisch, Jim, Chairman
Electronic Funds Transfer Association [393]
4000 Legato Rd., Ste. 1100
Fairfax, VA 22033
Ph: (571)318-5556
(571)318-5555

Hankes, Doug, President
American Association of Meat
Processors [2308]
1 Meating Pl.
Elizabethtown, PA 17022
Ph: (717)367-1168
Fax: (717)367-9096

Hankin, Robert A., PhD, CEO,
President
Health Industry Business Com-
munications Council [14362]
2525 E Arizona Biltmore Cir., Ste.
127
Phoenix, AZ 85016
Ph: (602)381-1091
Fax: (602)381-1093

Hankins, Jamie, VP
Walking Horse Trainers Association
[4425]
PO Box 61
Shelbyville, TN 37162
Ph: (931)684-5866
Fax: (931)684-5895

Hankins, Leslie Kathleen
International Virginia Woolf Society
[9061]
c/o Jeanne Dubino, Secretary-
Treasurer
Appalachian State University
131 Living Learning Ctr.
Boone, NC 28608
Ph: (828)262-7598
Fax: (828)262-6400

Hankins, Rose, Founder
Worlds Apart One Heart [11466]
402 Country Club Dr.
Greensboro, NC 27408

Hankoff, Norm, Founder
International Association of People
Who Dine Over the Kitchen Sink
[22161]

Hanks, Leslie, President
American Right To Life [12761]
PO Box 1145
Wheat Ridge, CO 80034
Ph: (303)753-9341
Toll Free: 888-888-2785

Hanley, Delinda C., Dir. of Advertis-
ing, Editor
American Educational Trust [18672]
1902 18th St. NW
Washington, DC 20009
Ph: (202)939-6050
Toll Free: 800-368-5788
Fax: (202)265-4574

Hanley, Jack, Exec. Dir.
Network of Employers for Traffic
Safety [19081]
344 Maple Ave. W, No. 357
Vienna, VA 22180
Ph: (703)755-5350

Hanley, Lawrence J., President
Amalgamated Transit Union [23525]
1000 New Hampshire Ave.
Silver Spring, MD 20903
Ph: (301)431-7100
Toll Free: 888-240-1196
Fax: (301)431-7117

Hanley, Prof. Ryan Patrick
International Adam Smith Society
[10088]
Dept. of Political Science
Marquette University
Milwaukee, WI 53201-1881
Ph: (414)288-6842

Hanna, Betty
International Association of Health-
care Central Service Materiel
Management [15329]

55 W Wacker Dr., Ste. 501
Chicago, IL 60601
Ph: (312)440-0078
Toll Free: 800-962-8274
Fax: (312)440-9474

Hanna, Craig, Dir. Pub. Aff.
American Academy of Actuaries
[1822]
1850 M St. NW, Ste. 300
Washington, DC 20036
Ph: (202)223-8196
Fax: (202)872-1948

Hanna, Libby, President
American Gerbil Society [21280]
18893 Lawrence 2100
Mount Vernon, MO 65712

Hannah, Dave, Founder
Athletes in Action [20127]
651 Taylor Dr.
Xenia, OH 45385-7246
Ph: (937)352-1000
Fax: (937)352-1001

Hannah, Kent, Jr., President
National Association of Timetable
Collectors [22462]
PO Box 1266
Hendersonville, TN 37077-1266

Hannan, Claire, MPH, Treasurer
Every Child By Two [14188]
1233 20th St. NW, Ste. 403
Washington, DC 20036-2304
Ph: (202)783-7034
Fax: (202)783-7042

Hannan, John, Exec. Dir.
Bridges to Community [13287]
95 Croton Ave.
Ossining, NY 10562
Ph: (914)923-2200
Fax: (914)923-8396

Hanne, Gio, Contact
Hazardous Materials Training and
Research Institute [6704]
ATEEC
201 N Harrison St., Ste. 101
Davenport, IA 52801-1918
Ph: (563)441-4081
Toll Free: 866-419-6761
Fax: (563)441-4080

Hannen, Margie, Exec. Sec.
American Association of Endodon-
tists [14391]
211 E Chicago Ave., Ste. 1100
Chicago, IL 60611-2691
Ph: (312)266-7255
Toll Free: 800-872-3636
Fax: (312)266-9867

Hannenburg, Alexander A., MD,
Chairman
Council on Surgical and Periopera-
tive Safety [17388]
633 N St. Clair
Chicago, IL 60611
Ph: (312)202-5700
Fax: (312)267-1782

Hanni, M. John, Jr., Exec. Dir.
American Society of Dermatology
[14486]
2721 Capital Ave.
Sacramento, CA 95816-8335
Ph: (916)446-5054
Fax: (916)446-0500

Hans, Valerie, President
Law and Society Association [5432]
383 S University St.
Salt Lake City, UT 84112
Ph: (801)581-3219
Fax: (888)292-5515

Hansbury, Vivien, Chairwoman
National Association of Colored
Women's Clubs [12898]
1601 R St. NW
Washington, DC 20009
Ph: (202)667-4080
Fax: (202)667-2574

Hansel, David, Treasurer
National Weighing and Sampling
Association [3466]
c/o David Hansel, Treasurer
1013 Shaffner Dr.
Bel Air, MD 21014
Ph: (484)645-1464
Fax: (610)765-7753

Hansel, John P., Officer
Elm Research Institute [4199]
c/o Liberty Tree Society
11 Kit St.
Keene, NH 03431
Ph: (603)358-6198
Fax: (603)358-6305

Hansen, Christian, President
IEEE - Reliability Society [6433]
3 Park Ave., 17th Fl.
New York, NY 10016-5997
Ph: (212)419-7900
Fax: (212)752-4929

Hansen, Ed, CEO, CFO
American Association of Zoo Keep-
ers [7394]
8476 E Speedway Blvd., Ste. 204
Tucson, AZ 85710-1728
Ph: (520)298-9688

Hansen, Evie, Director, Founder
National Seafood Educators [3034]
PO Box 93
Skamokawa, WA 98647

Hansen, Glenn J., CEO, President
BPA Worldwide [91]
100 Beard Sawmill Rd., 6th Fl.
Shelton, CT 06484
Ph: (203)447-2800
Fax: (203)447-2900

Hansen, Jennie Chin, CEO
American Geriatrics Society [14888]
40 Fulton St., 18th Fl.
New York, NY 10038-5082
Ph: (212)308-1414
Fax: (212)832-8646

Hansen, Joseph T., President
United Food and Commercial Workers International Union [23419]
1775 K St. NW
Washington, DC 20006

Hansen, Josh, Director
Inflatable Advertising Dealers As-
sociation [95]
c/o Bruce Cohen, President
Skyline International
PO Box 152641
Tampa, FL 33684-2641
Toll Free: 888-923-8652

Hansen, Keith, Contact
Bichon Frise Club of America
[21841]
c/o Karen Chesbro, Membership
Administrator
140 Pine Ave.
North Adams, MA 01247
Ph: (413)663-7109

Hansen, Robert, Exec. Dir.
National Opera Association [9976]
PO Box 60869
Canyon, TX 79016-0869
Ph: (806)651-2843
Fax: (806)651-2958

Hansen, Robert, CEO
University Professional and Continu-
ing Education Association [7675]
1 Dupont Cir., Ste. 615
Washington, DC 20036
Ph: (202)659-3130
Fax: (202)785-0374

Hansen, Roland C., Officer
American Library Association - Gay,
Lesbian, Bisexual and Transgender
Round Table [9670]
50 E Huron St.
Chicago, IL 60611-2795
Ph: (312)944-6780
Toll Free: 800-545-2433

Hansen, Steve, Chairman
Auto Haulers Association of America
[3409]
Bldg. 500, Ste. 503
4080 McGinnis Ferry Rd.
Alpharetta, GA 30005
Ph: (678)264-8610

Hanskat, Charles S., P.E., Exec. Dir.
American Shotcrete Association
[781]
38800 Country Club Dr.
Farmington Hills, MI 48331
Ph: (248)848-3780
Fax: (248)848-3740

Hanson, Brian, Chairman
GlobeMed [15463]
Scott Hall, Rm. 14, 16, 16A
601 University Pl.
Evanston, IL 60208
Ph: (847)786-5716

Hanson, Chuck, Contact
American Chevelle Enthusiasts
Society [21319]
4636 Lebanon Pike, Ste. 195
Hermitage, TN 37076-1316
Ph: (615)773-2237

Hanson, Craig Ashley, President
Historians of British Art [8897]
c/o Craig Ashley Hanson, President
Calvin College
3201 Burton St., SE
Grand Rapids, MI 49546

Hanson, Craig, Director
Global Forest Watch [4203]
10 G St. NE, Ste. 800
Washington, DC 20002
Ph: (202)729-7600
Fax: (202)729-7610

Hanson, David, President
National Council for Interior Design
Qualification [1954]
1602 L St. NW, Ste. 200
Washington, DC 20036-2581

Hanson, Jan M., Exec. Dir., Founder
200 Orphanages Worldwide [10826]
704 228th Ave. NE, No. 236
Sammamish, WA 98074

Hanson, Michelle, President
National Association of Bionutrition-
ists [16227]
c/o Sarah Rusnak
Ohio State University
376 W 10th Ave., Ste. 260
Columbus, OH 43210

Hanson, Mike, President
National Flood Determination As-
sociation [4488]
PO Box 82642
Austin, TX 78708
Ph: (512)977-3007

Hanson, Roseann, Founder
ConserVentures [3842]

3400 E Speedway Blvd., Ste. 118-
138
Tucson, AZ 85716
Ph: (520)591-1410

Hanson, Scott, Exec. Dir.
International Tuba-Euphonium As-
sociation [9938]
PO Box 1296
Gilbert, AZ 85299-1296
Ph: (480)200-9765

Hanson, Steve, President
Alveolar Capillary Dysplasia Association [13821]
c/o Donna Hanson, Treasurer
5902 Marcie Ct.
Garland, TX 75044-4958

Hanson, Steven J., CPA, Officer
National Society of Accountants [52]
1330 Braddock Pl., Ste. 540
Alexandria, VA 22314
Ph: (703)549-6400
Toll Free: 800-966-6679
Fax: (703)549-2984

Hanstein, Jack, Sr. VP
Brotherhood of Saint Andrew
[20095]
PO Box 632
Ambridge, PA 15003
Ph: (724)266-5810

Hapke, Patrice, President
Maternity Acupuncture Association
[13504]
c/o Patrice Hapke, President
340 15th Ave. E, No. 304
Seattle, WA 98122
Ph: (206)851-0228

Happ, Ms. Pamela R., CAE, Exec.
Dir.
College of Optometrists in Vision
Development [16428]
215 W Garfield Rd., Ste. 200
Aurora, OH 44202
Ph: (330)995-0718
Fax: (330)995-0719

Happy, Bonnie, President
United Stuntwomen's Association
[1208]
26893 Bouquet Cyn Rd., Ste. C
Saugus, CA 91350
Ph: (818)508-4651

Haque, Maryam, VP of Res.
National Venture Capital Association
[2035]
25 Massachusetts Avenue NW, Ste.
730
Washington, DC 20001
Ph: (202)864-5920
Fax: (202)864-5930

Harader, Joyce, RCST, President
Biodynamic Craniosacral Therapy
Association of North America
[14349]
115 Williamston Ridge Dr.
Youngsville, NC 27596
Ph: (708)837-8090

Harbaugh, Dr. Robert E., President
Society of Neurological Surgeons
[16068]
c/o Nicholas M. Barbaro, MD,
Secretary
Dept. of Neurosurgery
Goodman Campbell Brain & Spine
Indiana University
355 W 16th St., GH 5100
Indianapolis, IN 46202
Ph: (317)396-1234

Harbison, Victoria, President
Turn the Page Uganda [12250]
3723 Dixon St.

Santa Barbara, CA 93105
Ph: (805)569-0709

Harbolt, Elizabeth, President
Legal Secretaries International [75]
2951 Marina Bay Dr., Ste. 130-641
League City, TX 77573-2735
Ph: (713)651-2933
Fax: (713)651-2908

Harburg, Ernie, Bd. Member
Freedom From Religion Foundation
[20014]
PO Box 750
Madison, WI 53701
Ph: (608)256-8900
Fax: (608)204-0422

Harder, Harold C., PhD, Mem.
Blessings International [12266]
1650 N Indianwood Ave.
Broken Arrow, OK 74012-1284
Ph: (918)250-8101
Fax: (918)250-1281

Harder, Robert, ARM, President
Society of Risk Management
Consultants [1933]
330 S Executive Dr., Ste. 301
Brookfield, WI 53005-4275
Toll Free: 800-765-7762

Hardiman, Tom, CAE, Exec. Dir.
Modular Building Institute [2445]
944 Glenwood Station Ln., Ste. 204
Charlottesville, VA 22901
Ph: (434)296-3288
Toll Free: 888-811-3288
Fax: (434)296-3361

Hardin, Stan, President
Association of Peyronie's Disease
Advocates [17194]
PO Box 62865
Colorado Springs, CO 80962

Hardin, William, Director
Harden - Hardin - Harding Family
Association [20877]
c/o Colleen Taylor, Membership
Coordinator
380 Powell Grove Rd.
Lebanon, TN 37090-8275
Ph: (615)449-4806

Hardin, William S., Chairman
AMG International [20381]
6815 Shallowford Rd.
Chattanooga, TN 37421
Ph: (423)894-6060
Toll Free: 800-251-7206
Fax: (423)894-6863

Harding, Alan D., President
International Council on Systems
Engineering [6561]
7670 Opportunity Rd., Ste. 220
San Diego, CA 92111-2222
Ph: (858)541-1725
Toll Free: 800-366-1164

Harding, Alex, Founder
Agua Ecuador [13313]
183 Marlborough St., Apt. 2
Boston, MA 02116
Ph: (443)858-5869

Harding, Alton, Founder, President
Hands for Africa [12668]
14511 Myford Rd., Ste. 250
Tustin, CA 92780
Ph: (714)426-2245
      (714)249-4773

Harding, Ingrid, Founder, Exec. Dir.
Girl Power 2 Cure [15935]
1881 S 14th St., No. 1
Amelia Island, FL 32034
Ph: (904)277-2628
Fax: (904)212-0587

Harding, R. Scott, CEO, Founder
National Relief Network [12703]
PO Box 125
Greenville, MI 48838-0125
Ph: (616)225-2525

Harding, Richard, Chairman,
President
End Malaria Now [15396]
9461 Charleville Blvd., Ste. 558
Beverly Hills, CA 90212
Ph: (310)860-6073
Fax: (310)773-1730

Hardison, Kenneth L., Founder,
President
Personal Injury Lawyers Marketing
and Management Association
[5047]
802 41st Ave. S
North Myrtle Beach, SC 29582
Ph: (843)361-1700
Toll Free: 800-497-1890
Fax: (866)859-8126

Hardman, Patricia K., PhD, Director
Dyslexia Research Institute [14629]
5746 Centerville Rd.
Tallahassee, FL 32309
Ph: (850)893-2216
Fax: (850)893-2440

Hardy, Carol, Administrator
International Guild of Miniature
Artisans [21761]
PO Box 629
Freedom, CA 95019-0629
Ph: (831)724-7974
Toll Free: 800-711-4462

Hardy, Cary, Chairman
Family Promise, Inc. [11950]
71 Summit Ave.
Summit, NJ 07901
Ph: (908)273-1100
Fax: (908)273-0030

Hardy, David, MD, Chmn. of the Bd.
AIDS Research Alliance [13524]
1400 S Grand Ave., Ste. 701
Los Angeles, CA 90015-3011
Ph: (310)358-2423
     (310)358-2429
Fax: (310)358-2431

Hardy, John, Jr., President
Coalition for Employment through
Exports [1982]
1625 K St. NW, Ste. 200
Washington, DC 20006
Ph: (202)296-6107
Fax: (202)296-9709

Hardy, Maureen, Bd. Member
American Society of Hand
Therapists [14907]
1120 Route 73, Ste. 200
Mount Laurel, NJ 08054-2212
Ph: (856)380-6856
Fax: (856)439-0525

Hardy, Michael C., Director
Institute of Outdoor Theatre [10254]
East Carolina University
201 Erwin Bldg., MS 528
Greenville, NC 27858-4353
Ph: (252)328-5363
Fax: (252)328-0968

Hardy-Holley, Don, President
American Academy of Medical Hyp-
noanalysts [15352]
PO Box 365
Winfield, IL 60190-0365
Ph: (720)975-4485
Toll Free: 888-454-9766

Hare, Carly, Exec. Dir.
Native Americans in Philanthropy
[12491]

2801 21st Ave. S, Ste. 132 D
Minneapolis, MN 55407
Ph: (612)724-8798
Fax: (612)879-0613

Harger, Justin, President
United Lightning Protection Associa-
tion [3008]
426 North Ave.
Libertyville, IL 60048
Toll Free: 800-668-8572
Fax: (847)362-6443

Hargrave, Prof. Carter, President,
Founder
World Jeet Kune Do Federation
[23028]
8086 S Yale Ave., No. 133
Tulsa, OK 74136

Hargrave, Kathleen, President
Society of Medicolegal Death
Investigators [5370]
124 Elm St.
Big Rapids, MI 49307

Hargreaves, David, Chairman
Toy Industry Association, Inc. [3294]
1115 Broadway, Ste. 400
New York, NY 10010
Ph: (212)675-1141

Harken, Bonnie, Managing Dir.
International Association of Eating
Disorders Professionals [14641]
PO Box 1295
Pekin, IL 61555-1295
Toll Free: 800-800-8126

Harker, Roy, Exec. Dir.
AGLP: The Association of LGBTQ
Psychiatrists [11870]
4514 Chester Ave.
Philadelphia, PA 19143-3707
Ph: (215)222-2800
Fax: (215)222-3881

Harkin, Lynn, Exec. Dir.
Federation of Exchange Accommo-
dators [3202]
1255 SW Prairie Trail Pky.
Ankeny, IA 50023
Ph: (515)244-6515
Fax: (515)334-1174

Harkins, Ann M., President, CEO
National Crime Prevention Council
[11511]
1201 Connecticut Ave. NW, Ste. 200
Washington, DC 20036
Ph: (202)466-6272
Fax: (202)296-1356

Harkins, James Stanley, Sr.,
President
Conservative Majority for Citizen's
Rights [18023]
c/o Jim Harkins, Sr.
American Gospel Ministries
302 Briarwood Cir. NW
Fort Walton Beach, FL 32548-3904
Ph: (850)862-6211
     (850)862-4429

Harlan, Bob, President
National Lamb Feeders Association
[4673]
1270 Chemeketa St. NE
Salem, OR 97301-4145
Ph: (503)370-7024
Fax: (503)585-1921

Harley, Carol, President
Interhelp [19112]
PO Box 111
Greenwich, NY 12834-0111
Ph: (518)475-1929

Harman, Jane, CEO, President,
Director
Woodrow Wilson International
Center for Scholars [9559]

1 Woodrow Wilson Plz.
1300 Pennsylvania Ave. NW
Washington, DC 20004-3027
Ph: (202)691-4000
Fax: (202)691-4001

Harman, Ron, Contact
Jeannie Seely's Circle of Friends
[24062]
c/o Ron Harman
101 Cottage Pl.
Nashville, TN 37214

Harmon, David, Exec. Dir.
George Wright Society [4110]
PO Box 65
Hancock, MI 49930-0065
Ph: (906)487-9722

Harmon, Dianne, President
Elvis' Angels Fan Club [24012]
621 Dodd Dr.
Shreveport, LA 71107
Ph: (318)424-5000

Harmon, Linda L., MPH, CEO, Exec.
Dir.
Lamaze International [16292]
2025 M St. NW, Ste. 800
Washington, DC 20036-3309
Ph: (202)367-1128
Toll Free: 800-368-4404
Fax: (202)367-2128

Harmon-Dodge, Linda, VP
Clydesdale Breeders of the U.S.A.
[4344]
17346 Kelley Rd.
Pecatonica, IL 61063
Ph: (815)247-8780
Fax: (815)247-8337

Harmony, Barbara, Contact
National Water Center [7372]
5473 Highway 23 N
Eureka Springs, AR 72631
Ph: (479)244-0985

Harmsen, Dr. Betty Jean, Exec. Dir.
Haiti Share [11922]
PO Box 9208
Horseshoe Bay, TX 78657
Ph: (830)598-2172

Harne, Rick, Exec. Dir.
Military Police Regimental Associa-
tion [21049]
Bldg. 1607
495 S Dakota Ave.
Fort Leonard Wood, MO 65473
Ph: (573)329-6772
Fax: (573)596-0603

Harned, Patricia J., Ph.D., CEO
Ethics and Compliance Initiative
[630]
2345 Crystal Dr., Ste. 201
Arlington, VA 22202
Ph: (703)647-2185
Fax: (703)647-2180

Harold, Elliotte, Membership Chp.
Still Bank Collectors Club of America
[21726]
13239 Bundoran Ct.
Orland Park, IL 60462

Harp, Becky, Contact
Orphan Coalition [11115]
1880 Office Club Pointe, Ste. 1000
Colorado Springs, CO 80920
Ph: (719)481-3700
Fax: (303)253-8972

Harper, Barbara, Founder
Waterbirth International [14243]
PO Box 5578
Lighthouse Point, FL 33074-5578
Ph: (954)821-9125

Harper, Deborah, President
American Pointer Club [21816]
c/o Paul Wessberg, Membership
Chairman
4485 N Lake Dr.
Sarasota, FL 34232
Ph: (412)343-9169

Harper, Doug, President
International Visual Sociology Association [7185]
c/o Doug Harper, President
504 College Hall
Duquesne University
1100 Locust St.
Pittsburgh, PA 15219
Ph: (412)396-6490

Harper, Mr. Forest T., CEO,
President
INROADS [8195]
10 S Broadway, Ste. 300
Saint Louis, MO 63102
Ph: (314)241-7488
Fax: (314)241-9325

Harper, George, Director
Examination Board of Professional
Home Inspectors [1815]
53 Regional Dr., Ste. 1
Concord, NH 03301-8500
Ph: (847)298-7750

Harper, Dr. Howard, Exec. Dir.
Society for Sedimentary Geology
[6974]
4111 S Darlington Ave., Ste. 100
Tulsa, OK 74135-6373
Ph: (918)610-3361
Toll Free: 800-865-9765
Fax: (918)621-1685

Harper, Jane, President, CEO
National Network for Youth [12793]
741 8th St. SE
Washington, DC 20003
Ph: (202)783-7949

Harper, Joel, Exec. Dir.
United States Junior Chamber
[23632]
15645 Olive Blvd., Ste. A
Chesterfield, MO 63017
Ph: (636)778-3010
Fax: (636)449-3107

Harper, Mary, Contact
Operation ShoeBox [10755]
8360 E Highway 25
Belleview, FL 34420
Ph: (352)307-6723

Harper, Virginia, Director, Founder
U.S. Surveyors Association [7254]
13430 McGregor Blvd.
Fort Myers, FL 33919-5924
Ph: (239)481-5150
Toll Free: 800-245-4425

Harpham, Geoffrey, Director,
President
National Humanities Center [9556]
7 TW Alexander Dr.
Research Triangle Park, NC 27709
Ph: (919)549-0661
Fax: (919)990-8535

Harpster, Joyce, President
United States Women of Today
[12911]
c/o Jane Hanson, Secretary
31078 790th Ave.
Madelia, MN 56062

Harralson, Heidi H., President
National Association of Document
Examiners [5249]
c/o Heidi H. Harralson, President

PO Box 65095
Tucson, AZ 85728
Toll Free: 866-569-0833

Harriman, Dr. Hubert, President
World Gospel Mission [20477]
3783 E State Road 18
Marion, IN 46952-0948
Ph: (765)664-7731
Fax: (765)671-7230

Harriman, Jake, CEO, Founder
Nuru International [10729]
5405 Alton Pky., Ste. A-474
Irvine, CA 92604
Ph: (949)667-0796

Harrington, Nancy, Founder
Books for the Barrios [11723]
1125 Wiget Ln.
Walnut Creek, CA 94598
Ph: (925)934-6718

Harrington, Page, Exec. Dir.
National Woman's Party [18229]
Sewall-Belmont House and Museum
144 Constitution Ave. NE
Washington, DC 20002-5608
Ph: (202)546-1210

Harrington, Tony, President
McCoy Pottery Collectors' Society
[21584]
420 Quail Run Cir.
Fountain Inn, SC 29644

Harris, Adrienne, VP
Slavic, East European, and Eurasian
Folklore Association [9331]
c/o Shannon Spasova
Dept. of Linguistics and Germanic,
Slavic, Asian and African
Languages, Michigan State
University
B-331 Wells Hall
619 Red Cedar Rd.
East Lansing, MI 48824-3402

Harris, Alfred L., Sr., President
Lincoln University Alumni Association
[19333]
820 Chestnut St.
Jefferson City, MO 65101
Ph: (573)681-5573
    (573)681-5572
Fax: (573)681-5892

Harris, Alice, President
Linguistic Society of America [9746]
Archibald A. Hill
522 21st St. NW, Ste. 120
Washington, DC 20006-5012
Ph: (202)835-1714
Fax: (202)835-1717

Harris, AnDee, President
American Escrow Association [1216]
1000 Q St., Ste. 200
Sacramento, CA 95811-6518
Ph: (916)446-5165
Fax: (916)443-6719

Harris, Bev, Director
Black Box Voting [18179]
330 SW 43rd St., Ste. K
Renton, WA 98057
Ph: (206)335-7747

Harris, Bo, Exec. Dir.
Helps International Ministries
[20423]
1340-J Patton Ave.
Asheville, NC 28806
Ph: (828)277-3812
Fax: (828)274-7770

Harris, Bruce, CEO
U.S. Taekwondo [23022]
1 Olympic Plz.

Colorado Springs, CO 80909
Ph: (719)866-4632
Fax: (719)866-4642

Harris, Chad, Exec. Dir.
FarmHouse Fraternity, Inc. [23899]
7306 NW Tiffany Spring Pky., Ste.
210
Kansas City, MO 64153
Ph: (816)891-9445
Fax: (816)891-0838

Harris, Charles W., Chairman
National Biplane Association [21241]
7215 E 46th St.
Tulsa, OK 74145
Ph: (918)665-0755

Harris, Dan, President
Livestock Marketing Association
[4477]
10510 NW Ambassador Dr.
Kansas City, MO 64153
Toll Free: 800-821-2048

Harris, Danny, CAE, Exec. Dir., CEO
National Association of Fire Equip-
ment Distributors [3001]
180 N Wabash Ave., Ste. 401
Chicago, IL 60603
Ph: (312)461-9600
Fax: (312)461-0777

Harris, David J., Founder
Health Optimizing Institute [15265]
PO Box 1233
Del Mar, CA 92014
Ph: (858)481-7751

Harris, David J., Founder
Mandala Society [12009]
c/o David J. Harris
PO Box 1233
Del Mar, CA 92014
Ph: (858)481-7751

Harris, Deborah, Bd. Member
ArtTable [8916]
1 E 53rd St., 5th Fl.
New York, NY 10022
Ph: (212)343-1735
Fax: (866)363-4188

Harris, George, VP of Bus. Dev.
Computing Technology Industry As-
sociation [6312]
3500 Lacey Rd., Ste. 100
Downers Grove, IL 60515
Ph: (630)678-8300
Fax: (630)678-8384

Harris, George, Chairman
Hydraulic Institute [1734]
6 Campus Dr., 1st Fl. N
Parsippany, NJ 07054-4405
Ph: (973)267-9700
Fax: (973)267-9055

Harris, Georgia L., President
NCSL International [7233]
2995 Wilderness Pl., Ste. 107
Boulder, CO 80301-5404
Ph: (303)440-3339
Fax: (303)440-3384

Harris, Helen, Founder, President
Retinitis Pigmentosa International
[17743]
PO Box 900
Woodland Hills, CA 91365-0900
Toll Free: 800-344-4877
Fax: (818)992-3265

Harris, James E., Founder
African Blackwood Conservation
Project [3790]
PO Box 26
Red Rock, TX 78662

Harris, Jerry, Secretary
Global Studies Association North
America **[8043]**
1250 N Wood St.
Chicago, IL 60622

Harris, John, President
Enlisted Association of National
Guard of the United States **[5599]**
3133 Mount Vernon Ave.
Alexandria, VA 22305-2640
Toll Free: 800-234-3264
Fax: (703)519-3849

Harris, John, President, Founder
Professional Air Sports Association
[23250]
PO Box 1839
Nags Head, NC 27959

Harris, Karen, President
International Association of Speakers
Bureaus **[10175]**
4015 S McClintock Dr., Ste. 110
Tempe, AZ 85282
Ph: (480)839-1423

Harris, Kathryn M., VP
Abraham Lincoln Association
[10336]
1 Old State Capitol Plz.
Springfield, IL 62701-1507
Toll Free: 866-865-8500

Harris, Kimberly, CEO
America Needs You **[11744]**
589 8th Ave., 5th Fl.
New York, NY 10018
Ph: (212)571-0202

Harris, Laura, Exec. Dir.
Americans for Indian Opportunity
[12374]
1001 Marquette Ave. NW
Albuquerque, NM 87102-1937
Ph: (505)842-8677
Fax: (505)842-8658

Harris, Malia E., Founder, VP
Growing Liberia's Children **[11203]**
PO Box 125065
San Diego, CA 92112
Ph: (619)961-0287

Harris, Ms. Pamela, Chairperson,
President, Founder
Caring Voice Coalition **[12465]**
8249 Meadowbridge Rd.
Mechanicsville, VA 23116
Ph: (804)427-6468
Toll Free: 888-267-1440

Harris, Randall, President
North American Case Research As-
sociation **[3516]**
c/o Deborah Ettington, Editor
Smeal College of Business
Pennsylvania State University
University Park, PA 16802
Ph: (306)585-5647

Harris, Richard, President
Lawyers for Children America **[5536]**
151 Farmington Ave., RW61
Hartford, CT 06156-3124
Ph: (860)273-0441
Fax: (860)273-8340

Harris, Richard, Founder
Road to Hope **[11141]**
PO Box 210
Littleton, CO 80160

Harris, Rick, Exec. Dir.
Association of Proposal Management Professionals **[2156]**
c/o Rick Harris, Executive Director
20 F St. NW, 7th Fl.

Washington, DC 20001
Ph: (240)646-7075
Toll Free: 866-466-APMP

Harris, Rico E., Exec. Dir.
Community for Creative Non-
Violence **[11949]**
425 2nd St. NW
Washington, DC 20001
Ph: (202)393-1909
Fax: (202)783-3254

Harris, Ms. Robin, Exec. Dir.
Council of Ivy League Presidents
[23224]
228 Alexander St., 2nd Fl.
Princeton, NJ 08540-7121
Ph: (609)258-6426
Fax: (609)258-1690

Harris, Rosanna, Editor
Musical Box Society International
[22251]
PO Box 10196
Springfield, MO 65808-0196
Ph: (417)886-8839
Fax: (417)886-8839

Harris, Ruby Dell, Exec. Dir.
African American Advocates for
Victims of Clergy Sexual Abuse
[12918]
4020 E Madison St., Ste. 205
Seattle, WA 98112
Ph: (425)232-0504

Harris, Scott, President
Outdoor Power Equipment
Aftermarket Association **[1126]**
341 S Patrick St.
Alexandria, VA 22314
Ph: (703)549-7608
Fax: (703)549-7609

Harris, Sheryl, Mgr. of Admin.
National Advertising Division **[103]**
112 Madison Ave., 3rd Fl.
New York, NY 10016

Harris, Stan, President
Council of State Restaurant Associa-
tions **[2936]**
2055 L St. NW
Washington, DC 20036
Ph: (410)931-8100
    (202)973-5377
Fax: (410)931-8111

Harris, Tony, Chmn. of the Bd.
National Advisory Group **[2965]**
19111 Detroit Rd., Ste. 201
Rocky River, OH 44116
Ph: (440)250-1583
Fax: (440)333-1892

Harris, Will, President
American Grassfed Association
[4451]
469 S Cherry St., Ste. 220
Denver, CO 80246
Toll Free: 877-774-7277

Harris, Will, President
Working Capital for Community
Needs **[18564]**
517 N Segoe Rd., Ste. 209
Madison, WI 53705-3172
Ph: (608)257-7230

Harris, William G., PhD, CEO
Association of Test Publishers
[2773]
South Bldg., Ste. 900
601 Pennsylvania Ave. NW
Washington, DC 20004-3647
Ph: (717)755-9747
Toll Free: 866-240-7909

Harrison, Dr. C. Scott, MD, Founder
CURE International **[14186]**
701 Bosler Ave.

Lemoyne, PA 17043
Ph: (717)730-6706
Fax: (717)730-6747

Harrison, Charles, Trustee
American Killifish Association
[22028]
c/o Bob Meyer
733 County Road 600 E
Tolono, IL 61880
Ph: (508)643-4603
    (717)266-3453

Harrison, Connie, President
Association of Desk and Derrick
Clubs **[2513]**
5321 S Sheridan Rd., Ste. 24
Tulsa, OK 74145
Ph: (918)622-1749
Fax: (918)622-1675

Harrison, David, President
American Real Estate Society **[2846]**
300 Sirrine Hall
Clemson University
Clemson, SC 29634
Ph: (864)656-1373
Fax: (864)656-4982

Harrison, Donna, Dir. of Res.
Americans United for Life **[12762]**
655 15th St. NW, Ste. 410
Washington, DC 20005
Ph: (202)289-1478
    (202)696-4632

Harrison, Joel, Art Dir., CEO,
President
American Pianists Association
[22245]
4603 Clarendon Rd., Ste. 030
Indianapolis, IN 46208
Ph: (317)940-9945

Harrison, Joel, President
ARRL **[21265]**
225 Main St.
Newington, CT 06111-1494
Ph: (860)594-0200
Toll Free: 888-277-5289
Fax: (860)594-0259

Harrison, John, Exec. Dir., CEO
Alternative & Direct Investment
Securities Association **[1688]**
Two Meridian Plz.
10401 N Meridian St., Ste. 202
Indianapolis, IN 46290
Toll Free: 866-353-8422

Harrison, Kathleen, Secretary
Marine Corps Intelligence Associa-
tion, Inc. **[19547]**
PO Box 1028
Quantico, VA 22134

Harrison, Mary, Secretary
The Caspian Horse Society of the
Americas **[4341]**
29056 East 1200 North Rd.
Ellsworth, IL 61737
Ph: (309)724-8373

Harrison, Mary, President
Women's International League for
Peace and Freedom **[18842]**
11 Arlington St.
Boston, MA 02116
Ph: (617)266-0999
Fax: (617)266-1688

Harrison, Peg, CEO
Pediatric Nursing Certification Board
[16178]
9605 Medical Center Dr., Ste. 250
Rockville, MD 20850
Ph: (301)330-2921
Toll Free: 888-641-2767
Fax: (301)330-1504

Harrison, Scott, Founder, President
charity: water **[13317]**
40 Worth St., Ste. 330
New York, NY 10013
Ph: (646)688-2323
Fax: (646)883-3456

Harrison-Ross, Dr. Phyllis, President
All Healers Mental Health Alliance
[15755]
c/o United Social Services, Inc.
2 W 64th St., Ste. 505
New York, NY 10023
Ph: (212)874-5210
Fax: (212)721-4407

Harry, Debra, Exec. Dir.
Indigenous Peoples Council on Bio-
colonialism **[12129]**
PO Box 72
Nixon, NV 89424
Ph: (775)574-0248
Fax: (775)574-0345

Harsh, Ed, CEO, President
New Music USA **[9982]**
90 Broad St. Ste. 1902
New York, NY 10004
Ph: (212)645-6949
Fax: (646)490-0998

Harsh, Laurie, Founder
The Fabric Shop Network, Inc.
[3257]
PO Box 820128
Vancouver, WA 98682-0003

Harshbarger, Rich, CEO
Running USA **[23120]**
3450 N Ridgewood St., No. 311
Wichita, KS 67220
Ph: (313)408-3655

Harshbarger, Ted L., Chairman
Future Business Leaders of America
- Phi Beta Lambda **[23694]**
1912 Association Dr.
Reston, VA 20191-1591
Toll Free: 800-325-2946

Hart, Archie, Director
Rural Advancement Foundation
International-USA **[3555]**
274 Pittsboro Elementary School Rd.
Pittsboro, NC 27312
Ph: (919)542-1396

Hart, Guy, Exec. Dir.
Weatherby Collectors Association
[22026]
PO Box 1217
Washington, MO 63090-8217
Ph: (636)239-0348

Hart, Jan, President
Society for Transplant Social Workers **[17229]**
c/o Patricia Voorhes, Treasurer
2273 E Tara Ln., No. 3
Salt Lake City, UT 84117

Hart, Kimberly A., Exec. Dir.
National Child Abuse Defense and
Resource Center **[13264]**
PO Box 638
Holland, OH 43528
Ph: (419)865-0513
Fax: (419)865-0526

Hart, Richard H., MD, President
Adventist Health International
[15432]
11060 Anderson St.
Loma Linda, CA 92350
Ph: (909)558-4540
Fax: (909)558-0242

Hart, Richard T., President
Biomedical Engineering Society
[6110]

8201 Corporate Dr., Ste. 1125
Landover, MD 20785-2224
Ph: (301)459-1999
Toll Free: 877-871-2637
Fax: (301)459-2444

Hart, Rochelle L, Treasurer
National Shelley China Club [21699]
591 W 67th Ave.
Anchorage, AK 99518-1555

Hart, Scott D., CEO, Dir. Gen.
Moose International [19435]
155 S International Dr.
Mooseheart, IL 60539-1169
Ph: (630)906-3658

Hart, Stuart L., Founder, President
Enterprise for a Sustainable World
[1004]
1609 Shadford Rd.
Ann Arbor, MI 48104-4464
Ph: (734)369-8060

Hart, Ted, AFCRE, CEO
CAF America [13003]
King Street Sta.
1800 Diagonal Rd., Ste. 150
Alexandria, VA 22314-2840
Ph: (202)793-2232
Fax: (703)549-8934

Hart, Terry, Dir. of Legal Svcs.
Copyright Alliance [5327]
1224 M St. NW, Ste. 101
Washington, DC 20005
Ph: (202)540-2243

Hart, William T., President
Independent Turf and Ornamental
Distributors Association [2069]
174 Crestview Dr.
Bellefonte, PA 16823-8516
Ph: (814)357-9197
Fax: (814)355-2452

Harte, Ms. Carri, Contact
Conservation and Preservation
Charities of America [3840]
1100 Larkspur Landing Cir., Ste. 340
Larkspur, CA 94939
Ph: (415)925-2654

Hartford, Mr. Dale E., Director,
President
Guide Dogs of America [17708]
13445 Glenoaks Blvd.
Sylmar, CA 91342-2049
Ph: (818)362-5834

Hartgrove, Mary, Exec. Dir.
Mohair Council of America [3604]
233 W Twohig Ave.
San Angelo, TX 76903
Ph: (325)655-3161
Toll Free: 800-583-3161

Hartl, Martin, President
American Society of Alternative
Therapists [13602]
PO Box 303
Topsfield, MA 01983
Ph: (978)561-1639

Hartley, James, President
American Lumberjack Association
[23211]
c/o Chrissy Ramsey, Secretary
11800 US Highway 12
Naches, WA 98937

Hartley, Kimberly, Exec. Dir.
National Lubricating Grease Institute
[2531]
249 SW Noel St., Ste. 249
Lees Summit, MO 64063-2241
Ph: (816)524-2500
Fax: (816)524-2504

Hartman, Chester, Founder
Planners Network [18999]
106 W Sibley Hall
Cornell University
Ithaca, NY 14853

Hartman, Chester, Dir. of Res.
Poverty and Race Research Action
Council [12561]
1200 18th St. NW, No. 200
Washington, DC 20036-2529
Ph: (202)906-8023
Fax: (202)842-2885

Hartman, Christian, Founder
Medication Safety Officers Society
[15124]
200 Lakeside Dr., Ste. 200
Horsham, PA 19044
Ph: (215)947-7797
Fax: (215)914-1492

Hartman, Dr. Katie, President
Mu Kappa Tau [23810]
5217 S 51st St.
Greenfield, WI 53220
Ph: (414)328-1952
Fax: (414)235-3425

Hartman, Robert, CEO
American Contract Bridge League
[21559]
6575 Windchase Blvd.
Horn Lake, MS 38637-1523
Ph: (662)253-3100
Fax: (662)253-3187

Hartman, Timothy J., President,
Tech. Dir.
World Modern Arnis Alliance [23031]
PO Box 5
West Seneca, NY 14224
Ph: (716)247-5254

Hartmayer, Bishop Gregory, Mem.
National Organization for Continuing
Education of Roman Catholic
Clergy [20088]
110 E West St.
Baltimore, MD 21230
Ph: (410)978-3676
Fax: (410)752-2703

Hartong, Ernie, Exec. Dir.
Association of Residential Cleaning
Services International [2124]
7870 Olentangy River Rd., Ste. 301
Columbus, OH 43235
Ph: (614)547-0887
Fax: (614)505-7136

Hartsell, Brandon, Chmn. of the Bd.
Yoga Alliance [10425]
1560 Wilson Blvd., Ste. 700
Arlington, VA 22209
Ph: (571)482-3355
Toll Free: 888-921-9642

Hartsell, Matt, Founder, Exec. Dir.
Forgotten Children Worldwide
[10980]
650 N Main St.
Bluffton, IN 46714
Ph: (260)353-1580
Toll Free: 888-353-1580
Fax: (260)824-1955

Hartshorn, Peggy, PhD, Chmn. of
the Bd.
Heartbeat International [12769]
5000 Arlington Center Blvd., Ste.
2277
Columbus, OH 43220-2913
Toll Free: 888-550-7577
Fax: (614)885-8746

Hartung, Thomas, MD, Director
Johns Hopkins Center for Alternatives to Animal Testing [10654]

615 N Wolfe St., W7032
Baltimore, MD 21205
Ph: (410)614-4990
Fax: (410)614-2871

Hartvigsen, John M., President
North American Vexillological As-
sociation [10298]
PO Box 55701
Boston, MA 02205-5071

Hartwell, David, Chairman
Island Conservation [3889]
2161 Delaware Ave., Ste. A
Santa Cruz, CA 95060
Ph: (831)359-4787

Hartwell, Jessica, Chairman
Augustan Society [20958]
PO Box 771267
Orlando, FL 32877-1267
Ph: (407)745-0848
Fax: (321)206-6313

Hartwell, Lori, Founder, President
Renal Support Network [15887]
1146 N Central Ave., No. 121
Glendale, CA 91202-2506
Ph: (818)543-0896
Toll Free: 866-903-1728
Fax: (818)244-9540

Hartwig Moorhead, Holly J., CEO
Chi Sigma Iota [14326]
PO Box 1829
Thomasville, NC 27360
Ph: (336)841-8180
Fax: (336)844-4323

Hartwig, Dr. Robert P., President
Insurance Information Institute
[1866]
110 William St.
New York, NY 10038
Ph: (212)346-5500
Fax: (212)267-9591

Hartwig, Ron, Exec. Dir.
North America Indigenous Ministries
[20448]
PO Box 499
Sumas, WA 98295
Ph: (604)850-3052
Toll Free: 888-942-5468
Fax: (604)504-0178

Harty, Melinda, President
Pittsburgh Penguins Booster Club
[24078]
PO Box 903
Pittsburgh, PA 15230

Hartz, Jill, President
Association of Academic Museums
and Galleries [9819]
c/o Joseph S. Mella, Director
Vanderbilt University Fine Arts Gallery
230 Appleton Pl.
Nashville, TN 37203
Ph: (765)658-6556
(402)882-2264

Hartzog, Martha, President
Hood's Texas Brigade Association
[20741]
605 Pecan Grove Rd.
Austin, TX 78704-2507

Hartzok, David, OD, Exec. Dir.
Vision Surgery Rehab Network
[17415]
1643 N Alpine Rd., Ste. 104
PMB 180
Rockford, IL 61107
Toll Free: 877-666-8776

Harvey, Dave, President, Exec. Dir.
Cowboys for Christ [19971]
PO Box 7557

Fort Worth, TX 76111
Ph: (817)236-0023

Harvey, Mr. John W., Director
National Monte Carlo Owners Association [21457]
204 Shelby Dr.
Greensburg, PA 15601-4974

Harvey, Katie G., VP
Arabian Professional & Amateur
Horseman's Association [4338]
c/o Johnny Ryan, President
216 Irish Dr.
New Oxford, PA 17350
Ph: (609)558-4616
(507)867-2981

Harvey, Morris, VP
American Merchant Marine Veterans
[21190]
2722 Maynes Ct.
Santa Rosa, CA 95405

Harvey, Nancy A., VP
Arabian Horse Association [4336]
10805 E Bethany Dr.
Aurora, CO 80014
Ph: (303)696-4500
Fax: (303)696-4599

Harvey, Yvonne, President
Loners on Wheels [22429]

Harvieux, Anne, LCSW, President
Association of SIDS and Infant
Mortality Programs [17332]
c/o The KIDS Network, Inc.
1148 S Hillside St., Ste. 10
Wichita, KS 67211
Toll Free: 800-930-7437

Harvill, Denise E., Chmn. of the Bd.
Ovarian Cancer Symptom Aware-
ness [14039]
875 N Michigan Ave., No. 1525
Chicago, IL 60611
Ph: (312)280-0457

Harvis, Joe, President
National Ski Council Federation
[23165]
c/o Joe Harvis, President
4 Green Rd.
Mine Hill, NJ 07803-2908

Harwick, Dennis P., President
Captive Insurance Companies As-
sociation [1843]
4248 Park Glen Rd.
Minneapolis, MN 55416
Ph: (952)928-4655
Fax: (952)929-1318

Hasbrouck, LaMar, Exec. Dir.
National Association of County and
City Health Officials [5717]
1100 17th St. NW, 7th Fl.
Washington, DC 20036
Ph: (202)783-5550
Fax: (202)783-1583

Hasbrouck, Robert W., Jr., President
Hasbrouck Family Association
[20878]
PO Box 176
New Paltz, NY 12561
Ph: (845)255-3223
Fax: (845)255-0624

Hascall, Vincent, Trustee
International Society for Hyaluronan
Sciences [6056]
c/o Mary K. Cowman, President
433 1st Ave., Rm. 910
New York, NY 10010
Ph: (212)992-5971
Fax: (405)271-3092

Hascup, David, President
American Darts Organization
[22766]
PO Box 209
Stanton, CA 90680-0209
Toll Free: 844-883-2787

Hasegawa, Lisa, Exec. Dir.
National Coalition for Asian Pacific
American Community Development
[11409]
1628 16th St. NW, 4th Fl.
Washington, DC 20009
Ph: (202)223-2442
Fax: (202)223-4144

Hasegawa, Paul, Secretary,
Treasurer
International Academy of
Gnathology-American Section
[14442]
1322 Ave. D, Ste. A
Snohomish, WA 98290
Ph: (210)567-3644
Fax: (210)493-7046

Haseltine, William A., PhD, Founder,
President, Chairman
ACCESS Health International, Inc.
[14969]
1016 5th Ave., Ste. 11A
New York, NY 10028

Hashmi, Sohail, President
Society for the Study of Muslim Eth-
ics **[7906]**
PO Box 5126
Saint Cloud, MN 56302
Ph: (320)253-5407

Haskell, David, CEO
Dreams InDeed International
[12959]
PO Box 211006
Denver, CO 80221
Ph: (303)953-0426

Haslett, Jon, Founder
Ninos de la Luz **[11101]**
PO Box 7686
Capistrano Beach, CA 92624
Ph: (949)481-8355

Hassan, Ilshat, President
Uyghur American Association
[18451]
1420 K St. NW, Ste. 350
Washington, DC 20005
Ph: (202)478-1920
Fax: (202)478-1910

Hasselbrink, Arthur R., Founder,
President
Homefront America **[10745]**
27375 Paseo La Serna
San Juan Capistrano, CA 92675
Ph: (949)248-9468

Hastad, Nick, VP
American Chiropractic Association
Council on Sports Injuries and
Physical Fitness **[14251]**
c/o Carly May, Secretary
1720 S Bellaire St., Ste. 406
Denver, CO 80222
Ph: (303)758-1100

Haste, Amanda, Act. Pres., VP
National Coalition of Independent
Scholars **[7965]**
PO Box 120182
San Antonio, TX 78212

Haster, Jeanne, Exec. Dir.
Jesuit Volunteer Corps Northwest
[19848]
2780 SE Harrison St.
Milwaukie, OR 97222
Ph: (503)335-8202
Fax: (503)249-1118

Hastick, Roy A., Sr., Founder,
President, CEO
Caribbean American Chamber of
Commerce and Industry, Inc.
[23570]
Bldg. No. 5, Unit 239
Brooklyn Navy Yard
63 Flushing Ave.
Brooklyn, NY 11205
Ph: (718)834-4544
Fax: (718)834-9774

Hastings, Christopher Devin,
Founder
Diabetes Research Association of
America **[14528]**
10560 Wayzata Blvd., Ste. 19
Minnetonka, MN 55305
Ph: (612)730-2789

Hastings, Joan, President
National Angora Rabbit Breeders
Club **[4602]**
c/o Margaret Bartold, Secretary
909 Highway E
Silex, MO 63377
Ph: (573)384-5866

Hastings, Jonathan, President
Business Today **[7548]**
48 University Pl.
Princeton, NJ 08544
Ph: (609)258-1111

Haston, Carissa, President
Gastroparesis Patient Association for
Cures and Treatments, Inc.
[14791]
185-132 Newberry Commons
Etters, PA 17319
Toll Free: 888-874-7228

Hatch, George W., Jr., Exec. Dir.
Committee on Accreditation for
Educational Programs for the
Emergency Medical Services
Professions **[8295]**
8301 Lakeview Pky., Ste. 111-312
Rowlett, TX 75088
Ph: (214)703-8445
Fax: (214)703-8992

Hatch, Robert, President
American Society of Sugar Beet
Technologists **[6640]**
800 Grant St., Ste. 300
Denver, CO 80203
Ph: (303)832-4460

Hatch, Robert W., Chmn. of the Bd.
Foundation for International Com-
munity Assistance **[17976]**
1201 15th St. NW, 8th Fl.
Washington, DC 20005
Ph: (202)682-1510
Fax: (202)682-1535

Hatcher, Chris, President
National Association of Catastrophe
Adjusters **[1889]**
PO Box 499
Alvord, TX 76225
Ph: (817)498-3466

Hatcher, Donald, Treasurer
Association for Informal Logic and
Critical Thinking **[10079]**
Center for Critical Thinking
Baker University
618 8th St.
Baldwin City, KS 66006

Hatcher, Judy, Exec. Dir.
Pesticide Action Network North
America Regional Center **[13226]**
1611 Telegraph Ave., Ste. 1200
Oakland, CA 94612-2130
Ph: (510)788-9020

Hatchett-Teske, Rivers, President,
Founder
Hidden Choices **[12770]**
PO Box 194
Greens Farms, CT 06838
Toll Free: 877-488-9537

Hatfield, Ron, Chairman
In Our Own Quiet Way **[13328]**

Hatfield, Tom, PhD, Dir. of Programs
National Environmental Health Sci-
ence and Protection Accreditation
Council **[14720]**
PO Box 66057
Seattle, WA 98105
Ph: (206)522-5272
Fax: (206)985-9805

Hathaway, Allen, President
11th Armored Cavalry's Veterans of
Vietnam and Cambodia **[21163]**
PO Box 956
Colleyville, TX 76034-0956

Hathaway, Marjie, Exec. Dir.
American Academy of Husband-
Coached Childbirth **[16266]**
PO Box 5224
Sherman Oaks, CA 91413-5224
Ph: (818)788-6662
Toll Free: 800-422-4784
Fax: (818)788-1580

Hathaway, Oscar, III, Secretary
Escort Carrier Sailors and Airmen
Association **[21025]**
c/o Anthony Looney, President
1215 N Military Hwy., No. 128
Norfolk, VA 23502
Toll Free: 855-505-2469

Hathaway, William S., Jr., President
Hathaway Family Association
[20879]
2231 Riverside Ave.
Somerset, MA 02726-4104
Ph: (508)889-6584

Hatherill, William, CEO
Federation of State Boards of Physi-
cal Therapy **[16719]**
124 West St. S, 3rd Fl.
Alexandria, VA 22314
Ph: (703)299-3100
Fax: (703)299-3110

Hatlie, Martin J., JD, CEO, President
Partnership for Patient Safety
[15053]
405 N Wabash Ave., Ste. P2W
Chicago, IL 60611
Ph: (312)464-0600
Fax: (312)277-3307

Hattis, Ronald, MD, President
Beyond AIDS **[13532]**
2200 Wilson Blvd., No. 102-232
Arlington, VA 22201
Fax: (888)BEY-AIDS

Hauck, Dennis William, Coord.
Ghost Research Society **[7011]**
PO Box 205
Oak Lawn, IL 60454-0205
Ph: (708)425-5163

Hauck, Graham, Exec. Dir.
DFK International/USA **[26]**
1025 Thomas Jefferson St. NW, Ste.
500 E
Washington, DC 20007
Ph: (202)452-1588
Fax: (202)833-3636

Hauer, Cynthia, President
Association for Configuration and
Data Management **[6736]**

PO Box 58888
Salt Lake City, UT 84158-0888

Haugaard, Lisa, Exec. Dir.
Latin America Working Group
[18621]
2029 P St. NW, Ste. 301
Washington, DC 20036
Ph: (202)546-7010

Haugen, Gary A., CEO, President
International Justice Mission **[12046]**
PO Box 58147
Washington, DC 20037
Ph: (703)465-5495
Fax: (703)465-5499

Haupert, Michael, Exec. Dir.
Cliometric Society **[18145]**
c/o Michael Haupert, Executive
Director
Dept. of Economics
University of Wisconsin - La Crosse
1725 State St.
La Crosse, WI 54601
Ph: (608)785-6863
Fax: (608)785-8549

Haus, Erhard, PhD, President
American Association for Medical
Chronobiology and Chronothera-
peutics **[13820]**
c/o Erhard Haus, President
Dept. of Pathology
University of Minnesota
640 Jackson St.
Saint Paul, MN 55101
Ph: (651)254-9630
Fax: (651)254-2741

Hauser, Melanie, Secretary,
Treasurer
Golf Writers Association of America
[22882]
10210 Greentree Rd.
Houston, TX 77042
Ph: (713)782-6664
Fax: (713)781-2575

Hauser, Dr. Rita E., Chairwoman
International Peace Institute **[18361]**
777 United Nations Plz.
New York, NY 10017-3521
Ph: (212)687-4300
Fax: (212)983-8246

Hauser, Valerie, Director
Advisory Council on Historic
Preservation **[9365]**
401 F St. NW, Ste. 308
Washington, DC 20001-2637
Ph: (202)517-0200

Hausler, Dr. Elizabeth, CEO,
Founder
Build Change **[11964]**
535 16th St., Ste. 605
Denver, CO 80202
Ph: (303)953-2563

Hausner, Petr, MD, President
Czechoslovak Society of Arts and
Sciences **[9016]**
PO Box 34617
Bethesda, MD 20827
Ph: (301)881-7222

Hauss, Linda, Exec. Dir.
United Shoe Retailers Association
[1405]
PO Box 4931
West Hills, CA 91308
Ph: (818)703-6062
Fax: (866)929-6068

Hauter, Wenonah, Exec. Dir.
Food and Water Watch **[18262]**
1616 P St. NW, Ste. 300

Washington, DC 20036
Ph: (202)683-2500
Fax: (202)683-2501

Havele, Anita, Exec. Dir.
Web3D Consortium [6340]
650 Castro St., Ste. 120-490
Mountain View, CA 94041
Ph: (248)342-7662
Fax: (844)768-6886

Havens, Scott, Exec. Dir.
Open Arms International [12709]
PO Box 343
Portland, OR 97207
Ph: (503)296-9989
Fax: (503)297-0193

Havenstein, Walter P., Director
For Inspiration and Recognition of
Science and Technology [7810]
200 Bedford St.
Manchester, NH 03101
Ph: (603)666-3906
Toll Free: 800-871-8326
Fax: (603)666-3907

Haviland, Lyndon, CEO
Darkness to Light [10952]
1064 Gardner Rd., Ste. 210
Charleston, SC 29407
Ph: (843)965-5444
Toll Free: 866-FOR-LIGHT
Fax: (843)965-5449

Havis, Lee, Director
International Montessori Accredita-
tion Council [8351]
International Montessori Society
9525 Georgia Ave., No. 200
Silver Spring, MD 20910
Ph: (301)589-1127
Fax: (301)920-0764

Havis, Lee, Exec. Dir.
International Montessori Society
[8352]
9525 Georgia Ave., No. 200
Silver Spring, MD 20910
Ph: (301)589-1127
Fax: (301)920-0764

Haviv, Melissa, Exec. Dir.
Take Root [12358]
PO Box 930
Kalama, WA 98625
Ph: (360)673-3720
Toll Free: 800-ROOT-ORG
Fax: (360)673-3732

Havlin, Victor, President
National Mossberg Collectors As-
sociation [22021]
PO Box 487
Festus, MO 63028
Ph: (636)937-6401

Hawk, Caryn, Director
American Bar Association - Section
of Science and Technology Law
[5409]
321 N Clark St., 18th Fl.
Chicago, IL 60654-4740
Ph: (312)988-5599
Fax: (312)988-6797

Hawkes, Jesse, Exec. Dir., Prog. Dir.
Global Youth Connect [19274]
PO Box 1342
New York, NY 10159-1342
Ph: (845)657-3273

Hawkins, John, President
Brazil Philatelic Association [22312]
c/o William V. Kriebel, Secretary-
Treasurer, 1923 Manning St.
1923 Manning St.
Philadelphia, PA 19103-5728

Hawkins, Ms. Kristan, President
Students for Life of America [12790]
9900 Courthouse Rd.
Spotsylvania, VA 22553
Ph: (540)834-4600
Fax: (866)582-6420

Hawkins, Perry, Chairman
American Institute of Inspectors
[1813]
PO Box 7243
South Lake Tahoe, CA 96158
Ph: (530)577-1407
Toll Free: 800-877-4770

Hawkins, Richard J., Exec. Dir.
U.S.A. Roller Sports [23159]
4730 South St.
Lincoln, NE 68506
Ph: (402)483-7551
Fax: (402)483-1465

Hawkins, Dr. Ross, Exec. Dir.,
Founder
Hummingbird Society [3664]
6560 State Route 179, Ste. 124
Sedona, AZ 86351
Ph: (928)284-2251
Toll Free: 800-529-3699

Hawks, Rob, President
Randonneurs USA [22752]
c/o Rob Hawks, President
5630 Santa Cruz Ave.
Richmond, CA 94804
Ph: (510)526-2653

Hawley, Pamela, Founder, CEO
UniversalGiving [13309]
901 Mission St., Ste. 205
San Francisco, CA 94103
Ph: (415)296-9193
Fax: (415)296-9195

Hawley, Paul, Secretary
Society of the Hawley Family
[20929]
c/o Linda D. Hawley, Interim
President
63 Shelbourne Ct.
Wayne, PA 19087-5723

Hawthorne, Josetta, Exec. Dir.
Council for Environmental Education
[7873]
5555 Morningside Dr., Ste. 212
Houston, TX 77005
Ph: (713)520-1936
Fax: (713)520-8008

Hawthorne, Dr. Tonya, Founder,
President
New Frontiers Health Force [12706]
PO Box 1059
Indian Rocks Beach, FL 33785
Ph: (727)544-3555
Fax: (727)546-0106

Hay, Jeff, Chairman
Global Brigades [11365]
220 2nd Ave. S
Seattle, WA 98104
Ph: (206)489-4798

Hay, Paul Melvin, Registrar
National Society Sons of Colonial
New England [20758]
c/o Paul Melvin Hays, Registrar
General
147 12th St. SE
Washington, DC 20003-1420

Hayashi, Leslie A., President
National Council of Lawyer Disciplinary Boards [5037]
1414 Colorado St., Ste. 610
Austin, TX 78701

Hayden, Kristin, Advisor, Founder
OneWorld Now! [8629]
220 2nd Ave. S, Ste. 102

Seattle, WA 98104
Ph: (206)223-7703
Fax: (206)223-0371

Hayden, Vincent, PhD, Chairman
National Black Alcoholism and Ad-
diction Council [13166]
1500 Golden Valley Rd.
Minneapolis, MN 55411
Toll Free: 877-622-2674
Fax: (407)532-2815

Hayden-Lemmons, R. Mary, PhD,
President
University Faculty for Life [8657]
Georgetown University
120 New North
Washington, DC 20057
Ph: (718)817-3291
Fax: (718)817-3300

Hayes, Brian, President
Tire Retread & Repair Information
Bureau [3281]
1013 Birch St.
Falls Church, VA 22046
Ph: (703)533-7677
Fax: (703)533-7678

Hayes, Cheryl D., Contact
The Finance Project [18243]
1150 18th St. NW, Ste. 325
Washington, DC 20036
Ph: (202)628-4200
Fax: (202)628-1293

Hayes, Dr. Cyndy, President,
Founder
Aging with Autism [13738]
704 Marten Rd.
Princeton, NJ 08540
Ph: (908)904-9319

Hayes, Jim, President
Association of Emergency Physi-
cians [14676]
911 Whitewater Dr.
Mars, PA 16046-4221
Toll Free: 866-772-1818
Fax: (866)422-7794

Hayes, Jonathan, Chairman
Richard III Society - American
Branch [10347]
c/o Sally Keil, Membership Chair
1219 Route 171
Woodstock, CT 06281-2126
Fax: (504)822-7599

Hayes, Linda J., President
Society for the Advancement of
Behavior Analysis [6045]
550 W Centre Ave.
Portage, MI 49024
Ph: (269)492-9310
Fax: (269)492-9316

Hayes, Lisa, President, CEO
Accokeek Foundation | National
Colonial Farm [9362]
3400 Bryan Point Rd.
Accokeek, MD 20607
Ph: (301)283-2113

Hayes, Patty McIntire, President
Clan MacIntyre Association [20821]
c/o Patty McIntire Hayes, President
306 Kent Oaks Way
Gaithersburg, MD 20878

Hayes, Mr. Pete, Exec. Dir.
ASSE International Student
Exchange Programs [8058]
228 N Coast Hwy.
Laguna Beach, CA 92651
Ph: (949)494-4100
Toll Free: 800-333-3802
Fax: (949)494-3579

Hayes, Peter, PhD, Exec. Dir.,
Founder
Nautilus Institute [19094]
2342 Shattuck Ave., No. 300
Berkeley, CA 94704
Ph: (510)423-0372

Hayes, Reed, Membership Chp.
Scientific Association of Forensic
Examiners [5252]
c/o Reed Hayes, Membership
Chairperson
PO Box 235213
Honolulu, HI 96823

Hayes, Stephen A., President
Rutherford B. Hayes Presidential
Center [10330]
Spiegel Grove
1337 Hayes Ave.
Fremont, OH 43420-2796
Ph: (419)332-2081
Toll Free: 800-998-PRES
Fax: (419)332-4952

Hayes, Stephen, CEO, President
Corporate Council on Africa [625]
1100 17th St. NW, Ste. 1000
Washington, DC 20036
Ph: (202)835-1115
Fax: (202)835-1117

Hayes, Steven, Owner
Cult Awareness Network [20046]
3055 Wilshire Blvd., Ste. 900
Los Angeles, CA 90010

Hayes, William T., President
IEEE - Broadcast Technology
Society [7306]
445 Hoes Ln.
Piscataway, NJ 08854
Ph: (732)562-6061
Fax: (732)981-1769

Haylock, David, Founder, Director
Vision Earth Society [4019]
c/o David Haylock, Director
1825 NE 149 St.
Miami, FL 33181
Ph: (305)945-2727
Fax: (305)945-0300

Haynes, Alicia K., President
National Employment Lawyers As-
sociation [5040]
2201 Broadway, Ste. 402
Oakland, CA 94612
Ph: (415)296-7629
Toll Free: 866-593-7521

Haynes, David, President
Association of Opinion Journalists
[2665]
c/o The Poynter Institute
801 3rd St. S
Saint Petersburg, FL 33701

Haynes, J. Charles, JD, Exec. Dir.
Society for Neuro-Oncology [16054]
PO Box 273296
Houston, TX 77277
Ph: (281)554-6589
Fax: (713)583-1345

Haynes, Milton O., Chmn. of the Bd.
Caribbean American Medical and
Scientific Association [15114]
410 Lakeville Rd., Ste. 202
New Hyde Park, NY 11042
Toll Free: 866-648-2620

Haynes, Rhonda, Dep. Dir.
National Association of Urban
Debate Leagues [8595]
200 S Michigan Ave., Ste. 1040
Chicago, IL 60604-2421
Ph: (312)427-0175
Fax: (312)427-6130

Haynes, Richard, President
Border Patrol Supervisors' Association **[5459]**
3755 Avocado Blvd., No. 404
La Mesa, CA 91941

Haynes, Veronica, Exec. Dir.
Radiation Research Society **[7083]**
380 Ice Center Ln., Ste. C
Bozeman, MT 59718
Toll Free: 877-216-1919

Hays, George, Dir. Gen.
World Corrosion Organization **[3978]**
PO Box 2544
New York, NY 10116-2544

Hays, Laura, Exec. Dir.
Fanconi Anemia Research Fund
[14822]
1801 Willamette St., Ste. 200
Eugene, OR 97401
Ph: (541)687-4658
Toll Free: 888-326-2664

Hays, Steve, President
National Fishing Lure Collectors
Club **[21694]**
PO Box 509
Mansfield, TX 76063
Ph: (817)473-6748

Hays, Sue, Contact
Wild Bird Feeding Institute **[4181]**
PO Box 502
West End, NC 27376
Ph: (855)233-6362
Toll Free: 888-839-1237

Hayward, Catherine, President
International Society for Laboratory
Hematology **[15238]**
2111 Chestnut Ave., Ste. 145
Glenview, IL 60025
Ph: (847)737-1584
Fax: (312)896-5614

Hayward, Chad, Exec. Dir.
ACCORD Network **[12602]**
PO Box 15815
Washington, DC 20003

Hayward, Jeffrey, President
Earth's Physical Features Study Unit
[22325]
c/o Jeffrey Hayward, President
163 Baden Pl.
Staten Island, NY 10306-6048

Haywood, Arleene, Treasurer
Los Californianos **[19392]**
PO Box 1633
Ventura, CA 93002-1633

Haywood, J.R., PhD, Secretary
Association of Medical School
Pharmacology Chairs **[16653]**
University of Utah
Department of Pharmacology and
Toxicology
30 S 2000 E, Rm. 201
Salt Lake City, UT 84112
Ph: (801)581-6287
Fax: (801)585-5111

Haywood-Sullivan, Liz, President
International Association of Pastel
Societies **[8863]**
PO Box 512
Marshfield Hills, MA 02051

Hazard, Bruce, President
BMW Car Club of America **[21338]**
640 S Main St., Ste. 201
Greenville, SC 29601-2564
Ph: (864)250-0022
Toll Free: 800-878-9292
Fax: (864)250-0038

Hazelton, Thomas, President
D.A.R.E. America **[13135]**
PO Box 512090
Los Angeles, CA 90051-0090
Ph: (310)215-0575
Toll Free: 800-223-DARE
Fax: (310)215-0180

Hazen, Bob, Mem.
International Association of Gay
Square Dance Clubs **[9259]**
PO Box 9176
Denver, CO 80209-0176

He, Sheng Yang, President
International Society for Molecular
Plant-Microbe Interactions **[6148]**
3340 Pilot Knob Rd.
Saint Paul, MN 55121
Ph: (651)454-7250
Fax: (651)454-0766

He, Zili, Dr., CEO
Association of Chinese American
Physicians **[16741]**
33-70 Prince St., Ste. 703
Flushing, NY 11354
Ph: (718)321-8798
Fax: (718)321-8836

Head, Terry R., President
International Association of Movers
[3087]
5904 Richmond Hwy., Ste. 404
Alexandria, VA 22303
Ph: (703)317-9950
Fax: (703)317-9960

Head, Thomas M., Founder
Childhood Cancer Society **[13939]**
189 Berdan Ave., No. 221
Wayne, NJ 07470

Headlee-Miner, Kathy, Founder
Mothers Without Borders **[11083]**
125 E Main St., Ste. 402
American Fork, UT 84003
Ph: (801)607-5641

Heagerty, Brooke, Editor
League of Revolutionaries for a New
America **[18871]**
PO Box 477113
Chicago, IL 60647
Ph: (773)486-0028

Healey, Jason, Secretary
Cyber Conflict Studies Association
[7698]
c/o Karl Grindal
4600 N Fairfax Dr., Ste. 906
Arlington, VA 22203

Healey, Patrick, President
Friction Materials Standards Institute
[319]
23 Woodland Rd., Apt. B3
Madison, CT 06443
Ph: (203)245-8425
Fax: (203)245-8537

Healey, Paul, Chairman
Compatible Technology International
[3536]
800 Transfer Rd., Ste. 6
Saint Paul, MN 55114-1414
Ph: (651)632-3912
Fax: (651)204-9033

Healy, Becky, President
The Communication Leadership
Exchange **[762]**
65 Enterprise
Aliso Viejo, CA 92656
Toll Free: 866-463-6226

Healy, Hall, Director
International Crane Foundation
[4829]

E-11376 Shady Lane Rd.
Baraboo, WI 53913-0447
Ph: (608)356-9462
Fax: (608)356-9465

Healy, Mariah, Assoc. Dir.
Safe Passage **[11145]**
81 Bridge St., Ste. 104
Yarmouth, ME 04096
Ph: (207)846-1188
Fax: (207)846-1688

Heaney, Jess, Dir. of Dev.
Critical Resistance **[18390]**
1904 Franklin St., Ste. 504
Oakland, CA 94612
Ph: (510)444-0484
Fax: (510)444-2177

Heaney, Kevin, President
International Association of Golf
Administrators **[22883]**
1974 Sproul Rd., Ste. 400
Broomall, PA 19008-9998
Ph: (610)687-2340
Fax: (610)687-2082

Heard, Robert, CAE, Exec. Dir.
Emergency Medicine Foundation
[14678]
1125 Executive Cir.
Irving, TX 75038-2522
Toll Free: 800-798-1822

Hearing, Steve, President
Benefit4Kids **[10864]**
21660 23 Mile Rd.
Macomb, MI 48044-1307
Toll Free: 877-245-5430

Heary, Robert F., MD, President
Cervical Spine Research Society
[17253]
9400 W Higgins Rd., Ste. 500
Rosemont, IL 60018-4976
Ph: (847)698-1628
Fax: (847)268-9699

Heath, Beverly, Contact
Art Aids Art **[10486]**
PO Box 6438
Altadena, CA 91003

Heath, Craig, President
ProSkaters **[23152]**
1844 N Larrabee St.
Chicago, IL 60614-5208
Ph: (312)296-7864
Fax: (312)896-9119

Heath, Rebecca, Editor
Descendants of Mexican War
Veterans **[21023]**
PO Box 461941
Garland, TX 75046-1941

Heath, Roger, President
American Helvetia Philatelic Society
[22299]
c/o Richard T. Hall, Secretary
PO Box 15053
Asheville, NC 28813-0053

Heaton, Terri, CIPMA, President
National Association of Municipal
Advisors **[1283]**
19900 MacArthur Blvd., Ste. 100
Irvine, CA 92612
Ph: (703)395-4896
Toll Free: 844-770-NAMA

Hebenstreit, Lyn, President
Global Resource Alliance **[4492]**
963 Oso Rd.
Ojai, CA 93023
Ph: (805)646-4439

Hebert, David E., CEO
American Association of Nurse
Practitioners **[16096]**

Bldg. II, Ste. 450
911 S MoPac Expy.
Austin, TX 78711-2846
Ph: (512)442-4262
(703)740-2529
Fax: (512)442-6469

Hebert, Elaine, Chairman
American Solar Energy Society
[7197]
2525 Arapahoe Ave., Ste. E4-253
Boulder, CO 80302
Ph: (303)443-3130

Hebert, Marc, Chairman, President
Leonardo, The International Society
for the Arts, Sciences and Technology **[9017]**
1440 Broadway, Ste. 422
Oakland, CA 94612

Hebert, Paul, President
American Collegiate Hockey Association **[22905]**
7638 Solution Ctr.
Chicago, IL 60677-7006
Ph: (330)221-4411

Hecht, Joan, President, Founder
Alliance for the Lost Boys of Sudan
[12024]
8241 Wallingford Hills Ln.
Jacksonville, FL 32256
Ph: (904)363-9821

Hecht, Michael, President
Universal Autograph Collectors Club
[21730]
PO Box 1392
Mount Dora, FL 32756

Hecht, Rabbi Sholem Ber, Director
National Committee for Furtherance
of Jewish Education **[8142]**
824 Eastern Pky.
Brooklyn, NY 11213
Ph: (718)735-0200
Fax: (718)735-4455

Hecht, Prof. Stuart J., Secretary
American Theatre and Drama
Society **[10241]**

Heck, Kim, Exec. Dir.
Foundation for Safer Athletic Field
Environments **[22516]**
805 New Hampshire St., Ste. E
Lawrence, KS 66044-2774
Toll Free: 800-323-3875
Fax: (785)843-2977

Hecker, Debbie, Exec. Dir.
National Alliance of Wound Care and
Ostomy **[15039]**
717 St. Joseph Dr., Ste. 297
Saint Joseph, MI 49085
Ph: (877)922-6292
Toll Free: 888-352-4575
Fax: (800)352-8339

Heckman, Ms. Julie L., Exec. Dir.
American Pyrotechnics Association
[2821]
7910 Woodmont Ave., Ste. 1220
Bethesda, MD 20814
Ph: (301)907-8181
Fax: (301)907-9148

Heckman, Trathen, President
Transition United States **[4146]**
970 Gravenstein Hwy. S
Sebastopol, CA 95472
Ph: (707)824-1554

Hedberg, Blaine, Treasurer
Norwegian-American Historical Association **[10052]**
1510 St. Olaf Ave.

Northfield, MN 55057-1097
Ph: (507)786-3221
        (507)786-3229
Fax: (507)786-3734

Hedden, Harvey V., Exec. Dir.
International Law Enforcement
    Educators and Trainers Association
    [5474]
4742 79 St.
Kenosha, WI 53142
Ph: (262)767-1406
Fax: (262)767-1813

Hedgecock, Jim, President
Spuria Iris Society [22128]
c/o Jim Hedgecock, President
12421 SE State Route 116
Gower, MO 64454-8613

Hedges, Arthur, President
American Automobile Touring Alli-
    ance [3367]
PO Box 24980
San Jose, CA 95154
Ph: (480)371-5635

Hedges, Ms. Carrie, President
International Wizard of Oz Club
    [9062]
2443 Fillmore St., No. 347
San Francisco, CA 94115

Hedges, Larry V., PhD, President
Society for Research on Educational
    Effectiveness [7801]
2040 Sheridan Rd.
Evanston, IL 60208
Ph: (202)495-0920
Fax: (202)640-4401

Hedl, Lynn, President
Friends-in-Art of American Council of
    the Blind [8920]
c/o Lynn Hedl, President
521 Oxford Cir.
Birmingham, AL 35209
Ph: (205)942-1987

Hedlund, Mitch, Founder, Exec. Dir.
Recycle Across America [4634]
Minneapolis, MN
Toll Free: 855-424-5266

Hedren, Tippi, President
American Sanctuary Association
    [10570]
9632 Christine View Ct.
Las Vegas, NV 89129
Ph: (702)804-8562
Fax: (702)804-8561

Heed, Peter, President
United States Canoe Association
    [23364]
581 W St.
581 West St.
Keene, NH 03431
Ph: (603)209-2299

Heeg, Günther, VP
Sociedad Internacional Brecht
    [9098]
c/o Paula Hanssen, Secretary-
    Treasurer
Webster University
470 E Lockwood Ave.
Saint Louis, MO 63119-3141
Ph: (314)968-6900
Fax: (314)963-6926

Hefferan, Jennifer, President
Association of Pedestrian and
    Bicycle Professionals [19196]
PO Box 93
Cedarburg, WI 53012-0093
Ph: (262)228-7025
Fax: (866)720-3611

Heffernan, Judy, Secretary
Organization for Competitive
    Markets [3530]
PO Box 6486
Lincoln, NE 68506
Ph: (402)817-4443

Heffington, Joan, CEO, Founder
Association for Honest Attorneys
    [4996]
7145 Blueberry Ln.
Derby, KS 67037
Ph: (316)788-0901

Hefley, Alexis, Founder, President
Empower African Children [10960]
3333 Lee Pkwy., Ste. 110
Dallas, TX 75219
Ph: (214)828-9323

Hegarty, John F., President
National Postal Mail Handlers Union
    [23509]
1101 Connecticut Ave. NW, Ste. 500
Washington, DC 20036
Ph: (202)833-9095

Hegmann, Bill, CEO, President
National Exchange Carrier Associa-
    tion [3420]
c/o Kathy McNary, Director
80 S Jefferson Rd.
Whippany, NJ 07981-1009
Toll Free: 800-228-8563

Hegstrand, Linda, PhD, Bd. Member
American Manual Medicine Associa-
    tion [13596]
2040 Raybrook SE, Ste. 103
Grand Rapids, MI 49546
Toll Free: 888-375-7245
Fax: (616)575-9066

Heidary, Don, President
American Swimming Coaches As-
    sociation [23281]
5101 NW 21st Ave., Ste. 530
Fort Lauderdale, FL 33309
Ph: (954)563-4930
Toll Free: 800-356-2722
Fax: (954)563-9813

Heidorn, Randy R., President
Natural Areas Association [3913]
PO Box 1504
Bend, OR 97709
Ph: (541)317-0199

Heidrich, Greg, Exec. Dir.
Society of Actuaries [1928]
475 N Martingale Rd., Ste. 600
Schaumburg, IL 60173
Ph: (847)706-3500
Fax: (847)706-3599

Heierbacher, Sandy, Director,
    Founder
National Coalition for Dialogue and
    Deliberation [8482]
PO Box 150
Boiling Springs, PA 17007
Ph: (717)243-5144

Heighton, Rachel, Office Mgr.
American Farrier's Association [433]
4059 Iron Works Pkwy., Ste. No. 1
Lexington, KY 40511
Ph: (859)233-7411
Toll Free: 877-268-4505
Fax: (859)231-7862

Heilman, Paul, Exec. Sec.
American Banjo Fraternity [9852]
c/o Paul Heilman, Executive
    Secretary
6929 Tuckahoe Rd.
Williamson, NY 14589

Heim, Alan, President
American Cinema Editors, Inc.
    [1185]

Bldg. 9128, Ste. 260
100 Universal City Plz.
Universal City, CA 91608
Ph: (818)777-2900

Heimburg, Shannon, President
Nichiren Buddhist Association of
    America [19782]
PO Box 5156
Buena Vista, CO 81211-5156

Heimes, Amy, Admin. Asst.
Mt. Marty College Alumni Associa-
    tion [19336]
1105 W 8th St.
Yankton, SD 57078-3725
Ph: (605)668-1545
Toll Free: 855-686-2789
Fax: (605)668-1508

Hein, James R., Officer
International Marine Minerals Society
    [4467]
c/o Karynne Morgan
University of Hawaii
1000 Pope Rd., MSB 303
Honolulu, HI 96822
Ph: (808)956-6036
Fax: (808)956-9772

Hein, Susan, Publisher, Administra-
    tor
Association for Psychohistory [9463]
140 Riverside Dr., Ste. 14H
New York, NY 10024-2605
Ph: (212)799-2294
Fax: (212)799-2294

Heinbokel, Raymond J., Jr.,
    President
National Association of Photo Equip-
    ment Technicians [2586]
3000 Picture Pl.
Jackson, MI 49201
Ph: (517)788-8100

Heindel, Lisa
United States Amateur Tug of War
    Association [23340]
W504 State Road 92
Brooklyn, WI 53521
Toll Free: 800-TUG-O-WAR

Heindel, Max, Owner
Rosicrucian Fellowship [19626]
2222 Mission Ave.
Oceanside, CA 92058-2329
Ph: (760)757-6600
Fax: (760)721-3806

Heininger, Jeffrey V., Chairman
American Motorcycle Heritage
    Foundation [23035]
13515 Yarmouth Dr.
Pickerington, OH 43147
Ph: (614)856-1924
        (614)856-1900

Heinonen, Therese, DVM, Founder
International Partnership for Critical
    Markers of Disease [14123]
24 Frank Lloyd Wright Dr., Ste.
    H1200
Ann Arbor, MI 48106
Ph: (734)930-4400
Fax: (734)930-4414

Heinrich, Dan, Director
US Squash [23274]
555 8th Ave., Ste. 1102
New York, NY 10018-4311
Ph: (212)268-4090
Fax: (212)268-4091

Heinrichs, Dr. E. A., Sec. Gen.
International Association for the
    Plant Protection Sciences [3567]
6517 S 19th St.

Lincoln, NE 68512
Ph: (402)805-4748
Fax: (402)472-4687

Heinrichs, Kris, Bd. Member
One in Four, Inc. [12931]
10 Shirlawn Dr.
Short Hills, NJ 07078
Ph: (405)338-8046

Heins, Marjorie, Director, Founder
Free Expression Policy Project
    [17897]
170 W 76th St., No. 301
New York, NY 10023

Heinsdorf, Michael, President
U.S. Albacore Association [22679]
c/o Kay Marsh, Membership
    Secretary
1031 Graham St.
Bethlehem, PA 18015-2520

Heintz, Stephen B., President
Rockefeller Brothers Fund [12494]
475 Riverside Dr., Ste. 900
New York, NY 10115
Ph: (212)812-4200
Fax: (212)812-4299

Heinz, Kimber, Contact
War Resisters League [18729]
339 Lafayette St.
New York, NY 10012
Ph: (212)228-0450
Fax: (212)228-6193

Heinze, Bernd G., Esq., Exec. Dir.
American Association of Managing
    General Agents [1827]
610 Freedom Business Ctr., Ste. 110
King of Prussia, PA 19406
Ph: (610)992-0022
Fax: (610)992-0021

Heischman, Rev. Daniel R.,
    President
Council for American Private Educa-
    tion [8462]
13017 Wisteria Dr., No. 457
Germantown, MD 20874-2621
Ph: (301)916-8460
Fax: (301)916-8485

Heischman, Rev. Daniel R., Exec.
    Dir.
National Association of Episcopal
    Schools [20112]
815 2nd Ave., 3rd Fl.
New York, NY 10017-4509
Ph: (212)716-6134
Toll Free: 800-334-7626
Fax: (212)286-9366

Heisel, Scott E., VP
American Malting Barley Association
    [3761]
740 N Plankinton Ave., Ste. 830
Milwaukee, WI 53203
Ph: (414)272-4640

Heiser, Barbara, RN, Exec. Dir.
National Alliance for Breastfeeding
    Advocacy [13857]
c/o Barbara Heiser, Executive Direc-
    tor
9684 Oak Hill Dr.
Ellicott City, MD 21042-6321

Heisey, Emie, VP
Heisey Collectors of America
    [22135]
169 W Church St.
Newark, OH 43055
Ph: (740)345-2932
Fax: (740)345-9638

Heit, Gary, PhD, Contact
Americare Neurosurgery
    International [16061]

PO Box 4041
Los Altos, CA 94024
Ph: (650)387-8647

Heiting, James O., Chairman
International Lawyers in Alcoholics
  Anonymous [13148]
c/o Laurie Besden, Treasurer
55 Central Blvd.
Camp Hill, PA 17011
Toll Free: 800-335-2572

Heitmann, John, President
Society of Automotive Historians
  [21491]
PO Box 1715
Maple Grove, MN 55311-6715

Heitzman, Linda N., Exec. VP
Project HOPE [14962]
255 Carter Hall Ln.
Millwood, VA 22646
Ph: (540)837-2100
Toll Free: 800-544-4673

Hejinian, Daniel Varoujan, Founder,
  President
Peace of Art, Inc. [8994]
PO Box 52416
Boston, MA 02205
Ph: (617)435-7608

Helderman, Phyllis, Contact
North American Society for Dialysis
  and Transplantation [15884]
c/o Phyllis Helderman
1113 Chickering Park Dr.
Nashville, TN 37215-4507
Ph: (615)665-0566
Fax: (615)665-2951

Heldman, Jessica, JD, President
Postpartum Health Alliance [14240]
PO Box 927231
San Diego, CA 92192-7231
Ph: (619)254-0023
Toll Free: 800-479-3339

Helen, Ruth, Administrator
APA Division 39: Psychoanalysis
  [16885]
c/o Ruth Helein, Administrator
2615 Amesbury Rd.
Winston Salem, NC 27103
Ph: (336)768-1113
   (336)448-4198
Fax: (336)464-2974

Helfand, Ivan, Exec. Dir.
American Committee for Shenkar
  College [8129]
307 7th Ave., No.1805
New York, NY 10001
Ph: (212)947-1597

Helfand, Mark, President
Society for Medical Decision Making
  [15746]
390 Amwell Rd., Ste. 402
Hillsborough, NJ 08844
Ph: (908)359-1184
Fax: (908)450-1119

Hellem, Steve, Exec. Dir.
Global Environmental Management
  Initiative [4128]
1156 15th St. NW, Ste. 800
Washington, DC 20005
Ph: (202)296-7449

Heller, Thomas C., Exec. Dir.
Climate Policy Initiative [4127]
235 Montgomery St., 13th Fl.
San Francisco, CA 94104
Ph: (415)202-5846

Hellinger, Douglas, Exec. Dir.,
  Founder
Development Group for Alternative
  Policies [18488]

3179 18th St. NW
Washington, DC 20010
Ph: (202)321-0822

Hellinger, Douglas, Founder, Exec.
  Dir.
Gender Action [19254]
925 H St. NW, Ste. 410
Washington, DC 20001-4978
Ph: (202)234-7722

Hellman, John, VP
Allied Trades of the Baking Industry
  [366]
PO Box 688
Maysville, OK 73057
Ph: (405)664-8762

Hellman, Richard A., Founder,
  President
Christians' Israel Public Action
  Campaign [18584]
1300 Pennsylvania Ave. NW, Ste.
  700
Washington, DC 20004
Ph: (202)234-3600

Hellwig, Beth, President
International Association of Jim
  Beam Bottle and Specialties Club
  [21554]
2965 Waubesa Ave.
Madison, WI 53711-5964
Ph: (608)663-9661
Fax: (608)663-9664

Helme, Ned, Advisor
Center for Clean Air Policy [4537]
750 1st St. NE, Ste. 940
Washington, DC 20002
Ph: (202)408-9260
Fax: (202)408-8896

Helmes, C. Tucker, PhD, Managing
  Dir.
Society of Chemical Manufacturers
  and Affiliates [728]
1850 M St. NW, Ste. 700
Washington, DC 20036-5810
Ph: (202)721-4100
Fax: (202)296-8120

Helmes, Tucker C., PhD, Exec. Dir.
Institute for Polyacrylate Absorbents
  [720]
1850 M St. NW, Ste. 700
Washington, DC 20036-5810
Ph: (202)721-4100
Fax: (202)296-8120

Helmick, Ken, President
Steam Automobile Club of America
  [21495]
c/o David Lewis, Membership
  Secretary
602 S Fancher St.
Mount Pleasant, MI 48858-2619
Ph: (586)214-4795

Helms, Amalie A., Exec. Dir.
American Tolkien Society [9037]
PO Box 97
Highland, MI 48357

Helms, Elizabeth, CEO, President
TMJ and Orofacial Pain Society of
  America [15849]
1020 12th St., Ste. 303
Sacramento, CA 95814
Ph: (916)444-1985
Fax: (916)444-1501

Helms, Mr. Harry, Secretary
94th Infantry Division Association
  [20712]
c/o Harry Helms, Secretary
609 Dogwood Dr.
Downingtown, PA 19335-3907
Ph: (484)288-2778

Helms, Matthew R., CAE, Exec. Dir.
Pediatric Pharmacy Advocacy Group
  [16615]
5865 Ridgeway Center Pky., Ste.
  300
Memphis, TN 38120
Ph: (901)820-4434
Fax: (901)767-0704

Helms-Gaddie, Ms. Michelle,
  Founder
Global Vaccine Awareness League
  [14936]
25422 Trabuco Rd., Ste. 105-230
Lake Forest, CA 92630-2797

Helsel, Bob, Director
IVI Foundation [6322]
PO Box 1016
Niwot, CO 80544-1016
Ph: (303)652-2585
Fax: (303)652-1444

Helsel, Bob, Exec. Dir.
PXI Systems Alliance [6331]
PO Box 1016
Niwot, CO 80544-1016
Ph: (303)652-2585
Fax: (303)652-1444

Helsel, Bob, Exec. Dir.
VXIbus Consortium [7329]
PO Box 1016
Niwot, CO 80544-1016
Ph: (303)652-2585
Fax: (303)652-1444

Helton, Bill, VP
National-Interstate Council of State
  Boards of Cosmetology [926]
c/o Debra Norton, Coordinator
7622 Briarwood Cir.
Little Rock, AR 72205
Ph: (501)227-8262

Helvarg, David, Exec. Dir.
Blue Frontier Campaign [4134]
PO Box 19367
Washington, DC 20036
Ph: (202)387-8030
Fax: (202)234-5176

Hemann, Rev. Mel, Treasurer
National Association of Priest Pilots
  [19871]
c/o Rev. John Hemann, Treasurer
481 N Shore Dr., Apt. 301
Clear Lake, IA 50428

Hemenway, Nancy, Exec. Dir.
International Council on Infertility
  Information Dissemination [14759]
5765 F Burke Center Pky.
Box 330
Burke, VA 22015
Ph: (703)379-9178
Fax: (703)379-1593

Heminger, Gordon F., CEO,
  President
Alpha Sigma Phi [23887]
710 Adams St.
Carmel, IN 46032
Ph: (317)843-1911

Hemphill, Jean, Contact
National District Attorneys Associa-
  tion [5039]
99 Canal Center Plz., Ste. 330
Alexandria, VA 22314
Ph: (703)549-9222

Henagan, Mr. Mike, Chairman
Society of the Plastics Industry, Flex-
  ible Film and Bag Division [844]
1667 K St. NW, Ste. 1000
Washington, DC 20006
Ph: (202)974-5216

Henderson, Adriana, Founder,
  President, Bd. Member
Start Thinking About Romanian
  Children Relief [11158]
100 Traylee Dr.
Wake Forest, NC 27587
Ph: (919)521-5851

Henderson, Allen, Exec. Dir.
National Association of Teachers of
  Singing [8384]
9957 Moorings Dr., Ste. 401
Jacksonville, FL 32257
Ph: (904)992-9101
Fax: (904)262-2587

Henderson, Casey, Exec. Dir.
USENIX Association [6306]
2560 9th St., Ste. 215
Berkeley, CA 94710
Ph: (510)528-8649
Fax: (510)548-5738

Henderson, Charles P., Jr., Exec.
  Ed.
Association for Religion and Intel-
  lectual Life [20074]
475 Riverside Dr., Ste. 1945
New York, NY 10115
Ph: (212)870-2544
Fax: (212)870-2539

Henderson, John, President
North American Geosynthetics
  Society [6224]
c/o L. Davis Suits, Executive Direc-
  tor
PO Box 12063
Albany, NY 12212-2063
Ph: (518)869-2917
Fax: (518)869-2917

Henderson, Johny, VP
American Polarity Therapy Associa-
  tion [13597]
122 N Elm St., Ste. 504
Greensboro, NC 27401-2818
Ph: (336)574-1121
Fax: (336)574-1151

Henderson, Kalen, Chmn. of the Bd.
American Society of Photographers
  [10135]
3120 N Argonne Dr.
Milwaukee, WI 53222
Ph: (414)871-6600

Henderson, Marsha B., Chairperson
YWCA U.S.A. [13493]
2025 M St. NW, Ste. 550
Washington, DC 20036
Ph: (202)467-0801
Fax: (202)467-0802

Henderson, Miquia, Contact
Medical Students for Choice [17110]
PO Box 40188
Philadelphia, PA 19106
Ph: (215)625-0800
Fax: (215)625-4848

Henderson, Phillip, President
Surdna Foundation [12497]
330 Madison Ave., 30th Fl.
New York, NY 10017
Ph: (212)557-0010

Henderson, Shirell, Founder
BrittiCares International [13912]
PO Box 43504
Los Angeles, CA 90043
Ph: (323)393-0778
Fax: (323)292-8528

Henderson, Susan, Exec. Dir.
Disability Rights Education and
  Defense Fund [11588]
3075 Adeline St., Ste. 210

Berkeley, CA 94703-2578
Ph: (510)644-2555
Toll Free: 800-348-4232
Fax: (510)841-8645

Henderson, Wade, Esq., CEO,
President
Leadership Conference on Civil and
Human Rights [17906]
1629 K St. NW, 10th Fl.
Washington, DC 20006-1602
Ph: (202)466-3311
Fax: (202)466-3434

Henderson, Wade, CEO, President
Leadership Conference Education
Fund [17907]
1629 K St. NW, 10th Fl.
Washington, DC 20006
Ph: (202)466-3311
    (202)466-3434

Hendin, Herbert, CEO
Suicide Prevention Initiatives
[13200]
1045 Park Ave., Ste. 3C
New York, NY 10028

Hendley, Doc, Founder, President
Wine to Water [13350]
747 W King St., Ste. 200, 2nd Fl.
Boone, NC 28607
Ph: (828)355-9655

Hendrick, Peter, Exec. Dir.
American Association of Radon
Scientists and Technologists
[6659]
4989 Hendersonville Rd.
Fletcher, NC 28732
Fax: (828)214-6299

Hendricks, Daniel, Contact
American Crossbow Federation
[22959]
PO Box 251
Glenwood, MN 56334

Hendricks, Fred, President
National Dairy Shrine [3981]
PO Box 725
Denmark, WI 54208
Ph: (920)863-6333
Fax: (920)863-6333

Hendricks, Kelly, President
National Association of Professional
Mortgage Women [410]
c/o Agility Resources Group LLC
705 N Mountain Business Ctr., Ste.
E-104
Newington, CT 06111
Toll Free: 800-827-3034

Hendrickson, Jed, Exec. Dir.
American Institute of Commemora-
tive Art [2399]
3 N Milpas St.
Santa Barbara, CA 93103
Ph: (805)886-8384
Fax: (805)564-8296

Hendrickson, Lon, Exec. Dir.
CCNG International [2272]
2201 Long Prairie Rd., Ste. 107-365
Flower Mound, TX 75022
Toll Free: 855-599-2264
Fax: (972)539-9661

Hendrickson, Portasue, Dir. of
Admin.
Paws With a Cause [11630]
4646 S Division
Wayland, MI 49348
Toll Free: 800-253-7297
Fax: (616)877-0248

Hendrixson, Karen, Chairperson
Bikes for the World [10780]
1408 N Fillmore St., Ste. 11

Arlington, VA 22201
Ph: (703)740-7856

Hendron, Michael, President
Reed Organ Society, Inc. [9999]
c/o Charlie Robison, Treasurer/
Membership Secretary
PO Box 47
Independence, MO 64051-0047
Ph: (816)461-7300

Hendry, Krista, Mem.
Fund for Peace [19260]
1101 14th St. NW, Ste. 1020
Washington, DC 20005
Ph: (202)223-7940

Hendry, Krista, Chairperson
Liberty's Promise [5293]
2900-A Jefferson Davis Hwy.
Alexandria, VA 22305
Ph: (703)549-9950
Fax: (703)549-9953

Heney, Daniel F., Exec. Dir.
Maple Flooring Manufacturers As-
sociation [542]
1 Parkview Plz., Ste. 800
Oakbrook Terrace, IL 60181
Ph: (847)480-9138
Toll Free: 888-480-9138
Fax: (847)686-2251

Heng, Wei, PhD, Bd. Member
Chinese Overseas Transportation
Association [3325]
c/o Dr. Heng Wei
University of Cincinnati
792 Rhodes Hall
2850 Campus Way
Cincinnati, OH 45221-0071

Henk, Skip, CEO, President
Xplor International [1552]
24156 State Rd., Ste. 4
Lutz, FL 33559
Ph: (813)949-6170
Fax: (813)949-9977

Henke, Henry, Contact
Electrical Rebuilder's Association
[317]
PO Box 906
Union, MO 63084
Ph: (636)584-7400
Fax: (636)584-7401

Henkel, Kathleen, Exec. Dir.
American Endurance Ride Confer-
ence [23319]
1373 Lincoln Way
Auburn, CA 95603
Ph: (530)823-2260
Toll Free: 866-271-2372
Fax: (530)823-7805

Henken, Ted, VP
Association for the Study of the
Cuban Economy [7727]
5931 Beech Ave.
Bethesda, MD 20817

Henley, Don, Chairman, Founder
Walden Woods Project [9444]
44 Baker Farm Rd.
Lincoln, MA 01773-3004
Ph: (781)259-4700
Fax: (781)259-4710

Henley, Douglas E., MD, CEO,
Exec. VP
American Academy of Family Physi-
cians [14746]
11400 Tomahawk Creek Pkwy.
Leawood, KS 66211-2680
Ph: (913)906-6000
Toll Free: 800-274-2237
Fax: (913)906-6075

Henmi, Rod, VP
National Organization of Minority
Architects [5974]
1735 New York Ave. NW, No. 357
Washington, DC 20006
Ph: (202)586-6682

Henmueller, Joseph M., President,
COO
Automotive Maintenance and Repair
Association [338]
725 E Dundee Rd., Ste. 206
Arlington Heights, IL 60004-1538
Ph: (847)947-2650
Fax: (202)318-0378

Henn, Jack, President
Religious Brothers Conference
[19900]
233 S Wacker Dr., 84th Fl.
Chicago, IL 60606
Toll Free: 866-339-0371
Fax: (866)339-0371

Hennesey, Meg, President
Dalmatian Club of America [21865]
864 Ettin Ave.
Simi Valley, CA 93065-4209
Ph: (805)583-5914

Hennessey, David, President
Harley Hummer Club [22222]
13 Sylvan Rd.
High Bridge, NJ 08829

Hennessy, Thomas F., Jr., Asst. Cur.,
President
Lock Museum of America [21769]
230 Main St.
Terryville, CT 06786
Ph: (860)480-4408
Fax: (860)589-6359

Hennick, Barry, Omb.
Japanese Sword Society of the
United States [21295]
427 W Dussel, No. 128
Maumee, OH 43537-4208

Henning, Tim, Exec. Dir.
Association of Sites Advocating
Child Protection [10859]
5042 Wilshire Blvd., No. 540
Los Angeles, CA 90036-4305
Ph: (323)908-7864

Hennon, Paula, Mem.
Jet 14 Class Association [22643]
6176 Winding Creek Ln.
North Olmsted, OH 44070
Ph: (440)716-1859

Henrion, Connie, Coord.
Society of Saint Peter Apostle
[19913]
20 Archbishop May Dr.
Saint Louis, MO 63119
Ph: (314)792-7655

Henry, Bruce B., President
Cavalier King Charles Spaniel Club
of America [21853]
2301 E Emory Rd.
Knoxville, TN 37938-4518
Ph: (865)688-2484
Fax: (865)219-0363

Henry, Dr. Byron, Founder
Free to Smile Foundation [14336]
75 E Gay St., Ste. 300
Columbus, OH 43215
Ph: (614)778-5344

Henry, Charles, President
National Initiative for a Networked
Cultural Heritage [9233]
21 Dupont Cir. NW
Washington, DC 20036-1109
Ph: (202)296-5346
Fax: (202)872-0886

Henry, Corey
National Frozen Pizza Institute
[1357]
2000 Corporate Ridge, Ste. 1000
McLean, VA 22102
Ph: (703)245-7696
Fax: (703)821-1350

Henry, Edward P., President
Doris Duke Charitable Foundation
[12971]
650 5th Ave., 19th Fl.
New York, NY 10019
Ph: (212)974-7000
Fax: (212)974-7590

Henry, Fran, Founder
Stop it Now! [11160]
351 Pleasant St., Ste. B-319
Northampton, MA 01060
Ph: (413)587-3500
Toll Free: 888-PREVENT

Henry, G. Steven, Founder, Exec.
Dir., Gen. Counsel
Litigation Counsel of America [5022]
641 Lexington Ave., 15th Fl.
New York, NY 10022
Ph: (212)724-4128
Fax: (212)918-9144

Henry, James L., Chairman,
President
Transportation Institute [3107]
5201 Auth Way
Camp Springs, MD 20746-4211
Ph: (301)423-3335

Henry, Jeff, Exec. Dir.
International Staple, Nail and Tool
Association [1570]
8735 W Higgins Rd., Ste. 300
Chicago, IL 60631
Ph: (847)375-6454
Fax: (847)375-6455

Henry, Kevin P., Web Adm.
International and American Associa-
tions of Clinical Nutritionists
[16224]
15280 Addison Rd., Ste. 130
Addison, TX 75001
Ph: (972)407-9089
Fax: (972)250-0233

Henry, Kristin F., President
GalaxyGoo [7588]
4104 24th St., No. 349
San Francisco, CA 94114

Henry, Mary Kay, President
Service Employees International
Union [23461]
1800 Massachusetts Ave. NW
Washington, DC 20036
Ph: (202)730-7000
    (202)730-7684
Toll Free: 800-424-8592

Henry, Mitchell L., MD, President
Vascular Access Society of the
Americas [15888]
19 North St.
Salem, MA 01970
Ph: (978)745-8331
    (978)745-8334

Henry, Ronald, Founder
Men's Health Network [14946]
PO Box 75972
Washington, DC 20013
Ph: (202)543-6461

Henry-Crowe, Rev. Susan, Gen.
Sec.
United Methodist Church I General
Board of Church and Society
[20348]

100 Maryland Ave. NE
Washington, DC 20002
Ph: (202)488-5600

Hensley, Lyman, Secretary
American Society of Check Collectors [22258]
c/o Lyman Hensley, Secretary
473 E Elm St.
Sycamore, IL 60178-1934

Hensley, Mr. Max, President
International Bond and Share
Society [21668]
116 Parklane Dr.
San Antonio, TX 78212-1748

Hensley, Wayne, VP
Knifemakers' Guild [21767]
121 Mount Pisgah Church Rd.
Statesboro, GA 30458
Ph: (912)682-8103

Henson, Gwen, Exec. Dir.
American Society for Indexing
[9676]
1628 E Southern Ave., No. 9-223
Tempe, AZ 85282
Ph: (480)245-6750

Henson, Jay, President
National Versatility Ranch Horse As-
sociation [22946]
5925 Omaha Blvd.
Colorado Springs, CO 80915
Ph: (719)550-0189
Fax: (719)550-0194

Henz, Siegfried, President
American Aid Society of German
Descendants [19440]
6540 N Milwaukee Ave.
Chicago, IL 60631-1750

Henzi, Pia, President
National Association of Flavors and
Food-Ingredient Systems [1352]
3301 Route 66, Bldg. C, Ste. 205
Neptune, NJ 07753
Ph: (732)922-3218
Fax: (732)922-3590

Hepburn, Brian, Exec. Dir.
National Association of State Mental
Health Program Directors [15791]
66 Canal Center Plz., Ste. 302
Alexandria, VA 22314
Ph: (703)739-9333
Fax: (703)548-9517

Hepinstall-Cymerman, Jeffrey,
Secretary
United States Regional Association
of the International Association for
Landscape Ecology [4017]
c/o Janet Franklin, President
PO Box 875302
Tempe, AZ 85287-5302
Ph: (480)965-9884

Heppenheimer, Sue, Exec. Dir.
American Society of Master Dental
Technologists [14417]
146-21 13th Ave.
Whitestone, NY 11357-2420
Fax: (718)746-8355

Hepper, Colin, Secretary, Treasurer,
President
Nepal and Tibet Philatelic Study
Circle [22351]
c/o Roger Skinner, Representative
1020 Covington Rd.
Los Altos, CA 94024-5003

Heppes, Jerry, CEO
DHI [1567]
14150 Newbrook Dr., Ste. 200

Chantilly, VA 20151
Ph: (703)222-2010
Fax: (703)222-2410

Heppes, Jerry, Chairman
Small Business Legislative Council
[3128]
4800 Hampden Ln., 6th Fl.
Bethesda, MD 20814
Ph: (301)652-8302

Herb, Lisa, Exec. Dir.
Alliance for International Women's
Rights [19253]
PO Box 165
East Chatham, NY 12060
Ph: (518)632-4797

Herbas, Ericson, Contact
Gay Asian Pacific Support Network
[11882]
PO Box 461104
Los Angeles, CA 90046
Ph: (213)368-6488
     (323)596-7574

Herbers, Wendy, RN, VP
Developmental Disabilities Nurses
Association [16131]
1501 S Loop 288, Ste. 104 - 381
Denton, TX 76205
Toll Free: 800-888-6733
Fax: (844)336-2329

Herbert, Barry, President
International Star Riders Association
[22227]
848 N Rainbow Blvd., No. 793
Las Vegas, NV 89107

Herbison, Barton, Exec. Dir.
Nashville Songwriters Association
International [9963]
1710 Roy Acuff Pl.
Nashville, TN 37203
Ph: (615)256-3354
Toll Free: 800-321-6008
Fax: (615)256-0034

Herbst, Bob, President
International Association of Larynge-
ctomees [11605]
925B Peachtree St. NE, Ste. 316
Atlanta, GA 30309
Toll Free: 866-425-3678

Herbst, Michael, President
International Alliance of Law Firms
[5010]
527 Marquette Ave. S, Ste. 1925
Minneapolis, MN 55402
Ph: (612)454-5242

Herd, David, President
American Chiropractic Association
[14250]
1701 Clarendon Blvd., Ste. 200
Arlington, VA 22209
Ph: (703)276-8800
Fax: (703)243-2593

Herdman, Dr. T. Heather, Exec. Dir.,
CEO
NANDA International [16142]
PO Box 157
Kaukauna, WI 54130

Herdrich, Marty, Exec. Asst.
American Scientific Affiliation
[20594]
218 Boston St., Ste. 208
Topsfield, MA 01983-2210
Ph: (978)887-8833
Fax: (978)887-8755

Herguth, Robert, Director
Better Government Association
[18859]

223 W Jackson Blvd., Ste. 900
Chicago, IL 60606
Ph: (312)427-8330

Herischi, Ali, President
US Iran People Friendship Society
[9586]
215 Depot Ct. SE, Ste. 201
Leesburg, VA 20175

Hermach, Timothy G., Director
Native Forest Council [3910]
PO Box 2190
Eugene, OR 97402
Ph: (541)688-2600
Fax: (541)461-2156

Herman, Carole, Chmn. of the Bd.,
President
Foundation Aiding the Elderly
[18048]
3430 American River Dr., Ste. 105
Sacramento, CA 95864
Ph: (916)481-8558
Toll Free: 877-481-8558
Fax: (916)481-2239

Herman, Howard, Chairman
American Bar Association - Section
of Dispute Resolution [4956]
1050 Connecticut NW, Ste. 400
Washington, DC 20036
Ph: (202)662-1680
Fax: (202)662-1683

Herman, Jeffrey, Founder, Exec. Dir.
Society of American Silversmiths
[3195]
PO Box 786
West Warwick, RI 02893
Ph: (401)461-6840
Toll Free: 800-339-0417
Fax: (401)828-0162

Herman, Jonathan, Exec. Dir.
National Guild for Community Arts
Education [7518]
520 8th Ave., Ste. 302
New York, NY 10018
Ph: (212)268-3337
Fax: (212)268-3995

Herman, Lisa Redding, Contact
Bikers Battling Breast Cancer
[13901]
2035 N Hwy. 113
Carrollton, GA 30117
Ph: (678)378-5653

Herman, Lloyd E., Director
Friends of Fiber Art International
[8856]
PO Box 468
Western Springs, IL 60558
Ph: (708)710-0644

Herman, Nate, VP
American Apparel and Footwear Association [198]
2200 Wilson Blvd.
Falls Church, VA 22040

Herman, Roberta, CEO
American College of Veterinary
Internal Medicine [17618]
1997 Wadsworth Blvd.
Lakewood, CO 80214-5293
Ph: (303)231-9933
Toll Free: 800-245-9081
Fax: (303)231-0880

Herman, Susan N., President
ACLU Capital Punishment Project
[17827]
201 W Main St., Ste. 402
Durham, NC 27701-3228
Ph: (919)682-5659
Fax: (919)682-5961

Herman, Susan N., President
American Civil Liberties Union
National Prison Project [11516]
915 15th St. NW, 7th Fl.
Washington, DC 20005
Ph: (202)393-4930
Fax: (202)393-4931

Herman, Susan T., MD, Mem.
American Clinical Neurophysiology
Society [14655]
555 E Wells St., Ste. 1100
Milwaukee, WI 53202-3800
Ph: (414)918-9803
Fax: (414)276-3349

Herman-Betzen, Marsha, Exec. Dir.
Association of College Unions
International [8603]
1 City Centre Ste. 200
120 W 7th St.
Bloomington, IN 47404-3925
Ph: (812)245-2284
Fax: (812)245-6710

Hermans, Hubert, President
International Society for Dialogical
Science [7063]
Psychology Dept.
Le Moyne College
1419 Salt Springs Rd.
Syracuse, NY 13214

Hermatz, Lisa, Officer
Deaf Women United [11938]
PO Box 91563
Austin, TX 78709-1563

Hermening, Kevin, Treasurer
Marine Embassy Guard Association
[21018]
PO Box 6226
Wausau, WI 54402-6226

Hernández, Dr. Francisco José
(Pepe), President
Cuban American National Founda-
tion [18075]
2147 SW 8th St.
Miami, FL 33135
Ph: (305)592-7768

Hernan, Richard A., Jr., President
Greenlaw Family Association
[20874]
c/o Barbara Britton, Treasurer
104 W Upper Ferry Rd.
West Trenton, NJ 08628

Hernandez, Antonio, President
Hispanic Public Relations Associa-
tion [17948]
PO Box 86760
Los Angeles, CA 90086-0760

Hernandez, Helen, CEO
North American Travel Journalists
Association [3388]
3579 E Foothill Blvd., No. 744
Pasadena, CA 91107
Ph: (626)376-9754
Fax: (626)628-1854

Hernandez, Lisa Justine, Treasurer
Mujeres Activas en Letras Y Cambio
Social [7973]
1404 66th St.
Berkeley, CA 94702

Hernandez, Manny, Founder,
President
Diabetes Hands Foundation [14526]
1962 University Ave., No. 1
Berkeley, CA 94704
Ph: (510)898-1301

Hernandez, Mimi, Exec. Dir.
American Herbalists Guild [13595]
PO Box 3076

Asheville, NC 28802-3076
Ph: (617)520-4372

Hernandez, Mr. Raul, President
Society for Costa Rica Collectors
[22365]
c/o Raul Hernandez, President
4204 Haring Rd.
Metairie, LA 70006

Hernandez, Virginia Rondero, PhD,
Contact
Association of Latina and Latino
Social Work Educators [8569]
California State University, Fresno
Department of Social Work Educa-
tion
5310 Campus Dr., M/S PH102
Fresno, CA 93740-8019

Hernstat, Jan, President
International Al Jolson Society
[24045]
c/o Sandra K. Gerloff
419 Glenwood Dr.
Douglassville, PA 19518-1125

Herrell, Vicki, Exec. Dir.
Society for Workforce Planning
Professionals [1699]
6508 Grayson Ct.
Nashville, TN 37205
Ph: (615)352-4292
Fax: (615)352-4204

Herren, Dr. Hans R., President
Millennium Institute [18495]
1634 Eye St. NW, Ste. 300
Washington, DC 20006
Ph: (202)383-6200
Fax: (202)383-6209

Herrera, Ed, President
American Commodity Distribution
Association [3760]
3085 Stevenson Dr., Ste. 200
Springfield, IL 62703
Ph: (217)241-6747
Fax: (217)529-9120

Herrera, J. Manuel, Chmn. of the
Bd.
Youth for Environmental Sanity
[4120]
3240 King St.
Berkeley, CA 94703
Ph: (510)922-8556

Herrick, Mary Anne, President,
Chairman
Foster Care Alumni of America
[10981]
5810 Kingstowne Center Dr., Ste.
120-730
Alexandria, VA 22315
Ph: (703)299-6767
Toll Free: 888-ALU-MNI0

Herrin, Haven, Exec. Dir.
Soulforce [11909]
PO Box 2499
Abilene, TX 79604
Toll Free: 800-810-9143

Herrmann, Dr. Siegfried, Founder
Care Through Education
International [11218]
13810 Sutton Park Dr. N, No. 137
Jacksonville, FL 32224
Ph: (904)992-0977

Herrmann-Lingen, Christoph,
President
American Psychosomatic Society
[16954]
6728 Old McLean Village Dr.
McLean, VA 22101-3906
Ph: (703)556-9222
Fax: (703)556-8729

Herron, Keith, Sr., Coord.
The Child Connection [12355]
2210 Meadow Dr., Ste. 28
Louisville, KY 40218-1335
Ph: (502)459-6888
Fax: (502)459-8899

Hersey, Jane, Director
Feingold Association of the United
States [16219]
11849 Suncatcher Dr.
Fishers, IN 46037
Ph: (631)369-9340

Hershberger, Ann Graber, Chmn. of
the Bd.
Mennonite Central Committee
Overseas Peace Office [18804]
121 E 30th St.
North Newton, KS 67117
Ph: (717)859-1151
Toll Free: 888-563-4676

Hershey, Jim, Exec. Dir.
World Initiative for Soy in Human
Health [3777]
12125 Woodcrest Executive Dr., Ste.
100
Saint Louis, MO 63141
Ph: (314)576-1770
Fax: (314)576-2786

Hershey, Lyle, Chairman
Mennonite Economic Development
Associates - Lancaster Chapter
[20329]
1891 Santa Barbara Dr., Ste. 201
Lancaster, PA 17601-4106
Ph: (717)560-6546
Toll Free: 800-665-7026
Fax: (717)560-6549

Hertling, Bill, Dir. of Member Svcs.
International CBX Owners Association [22225]

Herz, William C., Exec. Dir.
National Lime Association [724]
200 N Glebe Rd., Ste. 800
Arlington, VA 22203
Ph: (703)243-5463
Fax: (703)243-5489

Herzberg, Roberta Q., President
Public Choice Society [7049]
224C Forsyth Hall
College of Business
Western Carolina University
1 University Way
Cullowhee, NC 28723
Ph: (608)363-2775

Herzig, Ralph M., Director
Laymen's Home Missionary Movement [20149]
1156 St. Matthews Rd.
Chester Springs, PA 19425-2700

Herzog, Eric L., PhD, President
Center for Management Effective-
ness [2160]
PO Box 1202
Pacific Palisades, CA 90272-1202
Ph: (310)459-6052

Herzog, Kelly A., Director
National Emergency Medicine As-
sociation [14687]
PO Box 1039
Edgewood, MD 21040
Ph: (443)922-7533
Toll Free: 888-682-7947

Hess, Lucinda, Contact
International Percy Grainger Society
[9539]
c/o Susan Edwards Colson
6 Benedict Ave.

White Plains, NY 10603

Hess, Marlene, Chairman
International Women's Health Coali-
tion [17758]
333 7th Ave., 6th Fl.
New York, NY 10001
Ph: (212)979-8500

Hess, Robert, Bd. Member
Hearts for the Hungry [12098]
PO Box 10701
Erie, PA 16514-0701
Ph: (814)873-1397

Hess, Rosanna F., Founder,
President
Research for Health [15492]
4321 Northampton Rd.
Cuyahoga Falls, OH 44223

Hess, Tony, President
TVR Car Club North America
[21507]
c/o Terry Telke, Membership
Chairperson
267 Ocean Dr.
Clayton, NC 27520

Hessek, Scott, President
American Guild for Infant Survival
[17330]
301 Eastwood Cir.
Virginia Beach, VA 23454
Ph: (757)463-3845

Hession, David M., Founder,
President
Hands Across the Water [11012]
29 Deacon Cir.
Southington, CT 06489
Ph: (860)620-3735
     (860)620-3705
Fax: (860)620-3700

Hessler-Radelet, Carrie, Director
United States Peace Corps [18850]
1111 20th St. NW
Washington, DC 20526
Toll Free: 855-855-1961

Hester, D. Micah, Contact
William James Society [10354]
Philosophy Dept.
The College of Wooster
1189 Beall Ave.
Wooster, OH 44691
Ph: (330)263-2548

Hester, Michelle, President
Oikonos [4008]
PO Box 1918
Kailua, HI 96734
Ph: (808)228-4463

Hester, Mike, President
The Hardware Companies Kollectors
Klub [21660]
c/o Barbara Keener, Secretary-
Treasurer
PO Box 325
Pacific, MO 63069-0325
Ph: (636)257-2926

Hesterlee, Edward J., Exec. VP
American College of Apothecaries
[16635]
2830 Summer Oaks Dr.
Bartlett, TN 38134
Ph: (901)383-8119
Fax: (901)473-8187

Hesterman, Oran B., PhD,
President, CEO
Fair Food Network [4190]
205 E Washington St., Ste. B
Ann Arbor, MI 48104
Ph: (734)213-3999

Heston, Jann, President
National Eosinophilia-Myalgia
Syndrome Network [17498]
767 Tower Blvd.
Lorain, OH 44052-5213

Hetherington, Kregg, Secretary
Society for Cultural Anthropology
[5921]
c/o Yarimar Bonilla, Secretary
Rutgers University
Dept. of Anthropology
131 George St.
New Brunswick, NJ 08901-1414

Hetke, Richard, Exec. Dir.
American Association of Dental
Boards [14389]
211 E Chicago Ave., Ste. 760
Chicago, IL 60611
Ph: (312)440-7464
Fax: (312)440-3525

Hettrick, Jane Schatkin, Secretary
Mozart Society of America [9183]
c/o Suzanne Forsberg
865 W End Ave., Apt. 8C
New York, NY 10025-8405

Heuser, Gunnar, PhD, Advisor
International Hyperbarics Associa-
tion, Inc. [15343]
15810 E Gale Ave., No. 178
Hacienda Heights, CA 91745
Toll Free: 877-442-8721

Heusslein, Klaus, Mem.
International Gay and Lesbian
Football Association [23187]

Hevener, Ron, CEO, Founder,
President
Greyhound Racing Association of
America [22825]
2207 Concord Pike, No. 335
Wilmington, DE 19803
Ph: (717)274-3097

Hewett, Sandra, Phd, Secretary
American Society for Neurochemis-
try [6914]
9037 Ron Den Ln.
Windermere, FL 34786
Ph: (407)909-9064
Fax: (407)876-0750

Hewitt, Brad, CEO, President
Thrivent Financial for Lutherans
[20320]
4321 N Ballard Rd.
Appleton, WI 54919-0001
Toll Free: 800-847-4836

Hewitt, Steve, Exec. Dir., Director
International Marking and Identifica-
tion Association [3174]
PO Box 49649
Charlotte, NC 28277

Heydrick, Kenneth W., EdD, Exec.
Dir.
National Alliance of State Science
and Mathematics Coalitions [8549]
Ingenuity Ctr., The University of
Texas at Tyler
3900 University Blvd.
Tyler, TX 75799-6600
Ph: (903)617-6813
Fax: (903)617-6814

Heying, Dr. Jerry, Exec. Dir.
Nine Lives Associates [3065]
c/o Executive Protection Institute
16 Penn Pl., Ste. 1570
New York, NY 10001

Heyison, Marc, Founder, President
Men Against Breast Cancer [14013]
PO Box 150

Adamstown, MD 21710-0150
Toll Free: 866-547-MABC
Fax: (301)874-8657

Heyliger, Arjarn Clint, President, Founder
United States Muay Thai Association [23021]
6535 Broadway, Ste. 1K
Riverdale, NY 10471
Fax: (718)549-6122

Heywood, Nicole, President
Humanity Corps [11379]
PO Box 1543
Meridian, ID 83680
Ph: (720)239-2858

Heywood, Pat, Dir. of Operations
American Exploration & Mining Association [2385]
10 N Post St., Ste. 305
Spokane, WA 99201
Ph: (509)624-1158

Hiatt, Richard S., PE, Exec. Dir., President
Rural Electricity Resource Council [6510]
2333 Rombach Ave.
Wilmington, OH 45177
Ph: (937)383-0001
Fax: (937)383-0003

Hiatt, Shobha, President, Founder
NARIKA [13386]
PO Box 14014
Berkeley, CA 94712
Ph: (510)444-6068
Fax: (510)444-6025

Hiatt, Thomas, Chairman
World Learning [8093]
1 Kipling Rd.
Brattleboro, VT 05301
Toll Free: 800-257-7751
Fax: (802)258-3248

Hiatt, Thomas, Chmn. of the Bd.
World Learning Visitor Exchange Program [18565]
1 Kipling Rd.
Brattleboro, VT 05302-0676
Ph: (800)257-7751

Hiatte, Mary, Coord.
National Association of State Retirement Administrators [5078]
449 Lewis Hargett Cir., Ste. 290
Lexington, KY 40503-3669
Ph: (202)624-1418

Hibbs, Maria, Chmn. of the Bd.
Institute of Women Today [18211]
7315 S Yale Ave.
Chicago, IL 60621
Ph: (773)651-8372
Fax: (773)783-2673

Hibbs, Mary, President
International Machine Quilters Association, Inc. [21762]
PO Box 419
Higginsville, MO 64037-0419
Ph: (660)584-8171
Fax: (660)584-3841

Hickey, Bill, Exec. Dir.
U.S. Naval Cryptologic Veterans Association [21143]
PO Box 16009
Pensacola, FL 32507-6009
Ph: (850)452-6990

Hickey, Connor, Founder
Got Agua [13354]
23 E Colorado Blvd., Ste. 203
Pasadena, CA 91105
Ph: (626)657-2255

Hickey, David L., President
International Union, Security, Police and Fire Professionals of America [23521]
25510 Kelly Rd.
Roseville, MI 48066
Ph: (586)772-7250
Fax: (586)772-9644

Hickey, Marcia, Dir. of Mtgs., Dir. of Member Svcs.
Pet Industry Distributors Association [2548]
3465 Box Hill Corporate Center Dr., Ste. H
Abingdon, MD 21009
Ph: (443)640-1060
Fax: (443)640-1086

Hickey, Patrick M., President
U.S.A. Karate Federation [23023]
1550 Ritchie Rd.
Stow, OH 44224
Ph: (330)388-3115

Hickey, Roger, Director
Campaign for America's Future [18937]
1825 K St. NW, Ste. 400
Washington, DC 20006-1254
Ph: (202)955-5665
Fax: (202)955-5606

Hickey, Roger, Director
Institute for America's Future [18910]
1825 K St. NW, Ste. 400
Washington, DC 20006-1254
Ph: (202)955-5665
Fax: (202)955-5606

Hickling, Diana, Secretary
Wagner and Griswold Society [22158]
c/o Diana Hickling
5409 State Highway 23
Norwich, NY 13815
Ph: (512)282-3924

Hicks, Bandy, Keeper
Sanctuary Workers and Volunteers Association [10691]
PO Box 637
Boyd, TX 76023
Ph: (940)433-5091
Fax: (940)433-5092

Hicks, Dawn Alexandra, Exec. Dir.
Stand Among Friends [11640]
777 Glades Rd., Bldg. NU84, Ste. 120
Boca Raton, FL 33431
Ph: (561)297-4400
Fax: (561)297-4405

Hicks, Jim Davis, Founder, President
Thirst Relief International [13339]
PO Box 2266
Bend, OR 97709
Toll Free: 866-584-4778

Hicks, Joel, President
National Institute of Steel Detailing [2362]
2600 Kitty Hawk Rd., Ste. 117
Livermore, CA 94551
Ph: (925)294-9626
Fax: (925)294-9621

Hicks, John W., Jr., President
Black Pilots of America, Inc. [360]
c/o Les Morris, Treasurer
PO Box 1295
Green Valley, AZ 85622
Ph: (520)625-4745

Hicks, Steve, President
National Center for the Study of Collective Bargaining in Higher Education and the Professions [5082]

425 E 25th St., No. 615
New York, NY 10010-2547
Ph: (212)481-7550

Hicks, Theresa, Coord.
SMA Lay Missionaries [20463]
256 Manor Cir.
Takoma Park, MD 20912
Ph: (301)891-2037
Fax: (301)270-6370

Hiden, Taylor, Advisor
Policy and Taxation Group [19161]
1775 Pennsylvania Ave. NW, Ste. 350
Washington, DC 20006
Ph: (202)505-4255

Hieb, James A., CEO
Marble Institute of America [3186]
380 E Lorain St.
Oberlin, OH 44074
Ph: (440)250-9222
Fax: (440)250-9223

Hiebert, Jeff, President
Search and Rescue Dogs of the United States [11695]
46848 Highway 61
Otis, CO 80743

Hienzsch, Stephan, Exec. Dir.
United States Dressage Federation [22948]
4051 Iron Works Pky.
Lexington, KY 40511
Ph: (859)971-2277,
Fax: (859)971-7722

Hieshetter, Janet, Certified Public Accountant
American Brain Coalition [15898]
6257 Quantico Ln. N
Maple Grove, MN 55311-3281
Ph: (763)557-2913
Fax: (860)586-7550

Hieshetter, Janet, Exec. Dir.
Dystonia Medical Research Foundation [15929]
1 E Wacker Dr., Ste. 2810
Chicago, IL 60601-1905
Ph: (312)755-0198
Toll Free: 800-377-3978
Fax: (312)803-0138

Higdon, Capt. James N, President
National Sojourners Inc. [19565]
7942R Cluny Ct.
Springfield, VA 22153-2810
Ph: (703)765-5000
Fax: (703)765-8390

Higdon, Janice M., Treasurer
Higdon Family Association [20880]
c/o Janice M. Higdon, Treasurer
Box 315
Moon, VA 23119-0315

Higgens, Barbara C., CEO, Exec. Dir.
Plumbing Manufacturers International [2640]
1921 Rohlwing Rd., Unit G
Rolling Meadows, IL 60008
Ph: (847)481-5500
Fax: (847)481-5501

Higginbotham, Susan, Exec. Dir.
Society of Family Planning [11848]
255 S 17th St., Ste. 2709
Philadelphia, PA 19103
Toll Free: 866-584-6758

Higginbotham, Susan, Exec. Dir.
Society of Family Planning [14752]
255 S 17th St., Ste. 2709
Philadelphia, PA 19103
Toll Free: 866-584-6758

Higgins, David, Chairman
International Colored Appaloosa Association [4363]
PO Box 99
Shipshewana, IN 46565
Ph: (574)238-4280

Higgins, Jan, VP
International Society of Managing and Technical Editors [2794]
275 N York St., Ste. 401
Elmhurst, IL 60126-2752
Ph: (630)433-4513
Fax: (630)563-9181

High, David M., President
Homeless Children International [11034]
PO Box 416
Reidville, SC 29375-0416

High, Mark R., President
Canada-United States Business Association [1981]
c/o Clayton & McKervey, P.C.
2000 Town Ctr., Ste. 1800
Southfield, MI 48075

Highfill, Dr. Deborah M., PhD, Director
HealthCare Ministries [20365]
521 W Lynn St.
Springfield, MO 65802-1829
Ph: (417)866-6311
Fax: (417)866-4711

Hightower, Chris, Director
International Cuemakers Association [22586]
444 Flint Hill Rd.
Aragon, GA 30104
Ph: (770)684-7004

Hightower, Stephanie, V. Chmn. of the Bd., President
U.S.A. Track and Field [23315]
132 E Washington St., Ste. 800
Indianapolis, IN 46204
Ph: (317)261-0500
Fax: (317)261-0481

Hightower, Tristin, Dir. of Operations
International Game Developers Association [6253]
19 Mantua Rd.
Mount Royal, NJ 08061

Higinbotham, Sarah, Treasurer
Association for the Study of Law, Culture and the Humanities [8046]
Dept. of Political Science
San Francisco State University
1600 Holloway Ave.
San Francisco, CA 94132

Hilbert, John W., III, President
Vanadium Producers and Reclaimers Association [2375]
1001 G St. NW, Ste. 500 W
Washington, DC 20001-4545
Ph: (202)251-3200
(202)842-3203

Hilgartner, Richard, President
National Association of Pastoral Musicians [8381]
962 Wayne Ave., Ste. 210
Silver Spring, MD 20910-4461
Ph: (240)247-3000
Fax: (240)247-3001

Hilger, Bill, VP
International Kart Federation [22970]
1609 S Grove Ave., Ste. 105
Ontario, CA 91761
Ph: (909)923-4999
Fax: (909)923-6940

Hill, Alec D., CEO, President
InterVarsity Christian Fellowship [20428]

635 Science Dr.
Madison, WI 53707-7895
Ph: (608)274-9001
Fax: (608)274-7882

Hill, Becky, Administrator
CHWMEG, Inc. **[3447]**
470 William Pitt Way
Pittsburgh, PA 15238-1330
Ph: (412)826-3055
Fax: (586)461-1856

Hill, Brian R., Founder, Exec. Dir.
Oral Cancer Foundation **[14037]**
3419 Via Lido, No. 205
Newport Beach, CA 92663
Ph: (949)646-8000

Hill, Charles E., MD, PhD, President
Association for Molecular Pathology
  [16578]
9650 Rockville Pke., Ste. E133
Bethesda, MD 20814-3993
Ph: (301)634-7939
Fax: (301)634-7995

Hill, Connie, Secretary
Cyclic Vomiting Syndrome Associa-
  tion **[14787]**
PO Box 270341
Milwaukee, WI 53227
Ph: (414)342-7880
Fax: (414)342-8980

Hill, Edwin D., President
International Brotherhood of Electri-
  cal Workers **[23413]**
900 Seventh St. NW
Washington, DC 20001-3886
Ph: (202)833-7000
Fax: (202)728-7676

Hill, Fred, Treasurer
Hobby Manufacturers Association
  [1642]
1410 E Erie Ave.
Philadelphia, PA 19124
Ph: (267)341-1604
Fax: (215)744-4699

Hill, Gerald, President
Association of American Indian
  Physicians **[16737]**
1225 Sovereign Row, Ste. 103
Oklahoma City, OK 73108-1854
Ph: (405)946-7072
Fax: (405)946-7651

Hill, James, President
International Association of Black
  Professional Fire Fighters **[5206]**
1200 G St. NW, Ste. 800
Washington, DC 20005
Ph: (202)434-4526
Toll Free: 877-213-2170
Fax: (202)434-8707

Hill, John, Sec. Gen.
Intergovernmental Renewable
  Energy Organization **[6490]**
Dag Hammarskjold UN Ctr.
884 2nd Ave., No. 20050
New York, NY 10017
Ph: (917)862-6444

Hill, Dr. John, Director
National Rural Education Association
  [8510]
100 N University St.
West Lafayette, IN 47907-2098
Ph: (765)494-0086
Fax: (765)496-1228

Hill, Jonathan, President
Society for the Anthropology of
  Lowland South America **[5918]**
c/o Jeremy Campbell, Secretary-
  Treasurer

Roger Williams University
1 Old Ferry Rd.
Bristol, RI 02809

Hill, Kenneth B. N., Secretary
United States Army Warrant Officers
  Association **[5625]**
462 Herndon Pky., Ste. 207
Herndon, VA 20170-5235
Ph: (703)742-7727
Toll Free: 800-587-2962
Fax: (703)742-7728

Hill, Larry, Exec. Dir.
American Association for Community
  Dental Programs **[14388]**
635 W 7th St., Ste. 309
Cincinnati, OH 45203
Ph: (513)621-0248
Fax: (513)621-0288

Hill, Michael E., President, CEO
Youth For Understanding USA
  [8096]
641 South St. NW, Ste. 200
Washington, DC 20001
Ph: (202)774-5200
Toll Free: 800-833-6243

Hill, Nancy, Scientist
Ad Council **[18934]**
815 2nd Ave., 9th Fl.
New York, NY 10017
Ph: (212)922-1500
Fax: (212)922-1676

Hill, Nancy, President, CEO
American Association of Advertising
  Agencies **[85]**
1065 Avenue of Americas, 16th Fl.
New York, NY 10018
Ph: (212)682-2500

Hill, Nancy, Secretary
ChildFund International **[10911]**
2821 Emerywood Pky.
Richmond, VA 23294
Toll Free: 800-776-6767

Hill, Rick, President
Antique Fan Collectors Association
  [21621]
c/o Dick Boswell, Treasurer
2245 Harrison Ave.
Lincoln, NE 68502

Hill, Rick, Treasurer
Winchester Arms Collectors Associa-
  tion **[21299]**
PO Box 10427
Bozeman, MT 59719
Ph: (541)526-5929
Fax: (971)285-9046

Hill, Samuel E., President
The Gideons International **[20144]**
PO Box 140800
Nashville, TN 37214-0800
Ph: (615)564-5000

Hill, Tessa, President
Kids for Saving Earth **[7879]**
37955 Bridge Rd.
North Branch, MN 55056-5398
Ph: (763)559-1234
Fax: (651)674-5005

Hill, Tim, Director
Church of God World Missions
  [20404]
2490 Keith St. NW
Cleveland, TN 37311
Toll Free: 800-345-7492

Hill, Willie J., Dr., President
Benedict College National Alumni
  Association **[19307]**
1600 Harden St.

Columbia, SC 29204
Ph: (803)705-4600
Toll Free: 800-868-6598
Fax: (803)705-6654

Hilliard, Herbert H., Chairman
Tennessee Regulatory Authority
  [5836]
502 Deaderick St.
Nashville, TN 37243
Ph: (615)741-2904
Toll Free: 800-342-8359

Hillier, Polexeni Maouris, Director
Saint Photios Foundation **[20196]**
41 St. George St.
Saint Augustine, FL 32085-1960
Ph: (904)829-8205
Toll Free: 800-222-6727
Fax: (904)829-8707

Hillman, Alma, Contact
Society for Old Ivory and Ohme
  Porcelains **[22389]**
1650 SE River Ridge Dr.
Milwaukie, OR 97222

Hillman, Bill, CEO
Clean Water Council **[4752]**
c/o National Utility Contractors As-
  sociation
3925 Chain Bridge Rd., Ste. 300
Fairfax, VA 22030
Ph: (703)358-9300
Fax: (703)358-9307

Hillman, Bill, CEO
National Utility Contractors Associa-
  tion **[893]**
3925 Chain Bridge Rd., Ste. 300
Fairfax, VA 22030
Ph: (703)358-9300
Fax: (703)358-9307

Hillmen, Peter, PhD, Chairman
International PNH Interest Group
  [15236]
521 5th Ave., 6th Fl.
New York, NY 10175

Hills, Carla A., Chairwoman
Council on Foreign Relations
  [18265]
The Harold Pratt House
58 E 68th St.
New York, NY 10065
Ph: (212)434-9400
Fax: (212)434-9800

Hills, Carla A., Chairwoman
National Committee on United
  States-China Relations **[17849]**
6 E 43rd St., 24th Fl.
New York, NY 10017-4650
Ph: (212)645-9677
Fax: (212)645-1695

Hills, Lisa, President
Newspaper Association Managers
  [2711]
PO Box 458
Essex, MA 01929-0008
Ph: (978)338-2555

Hillsman, Sally, Exec. Ofc.
American Sociological Association -
  Status of Women in Sociology
  [7177]
1430 K St. NW, Ste. 600
Washington, DC 20005-2529
Ph: (202)383-9005
Fax: (202)638-0882

Hilly, Jed, Exec. Dir.
Americana Music Association **[9872]**
PO Box 628
Franklin, TN 37065
Ph: (615)386-6936
Fax: (615)386-6937

Hilsenroth, Dr. Robert, Exec. Dir.
American Association of Zoo
  Veterinarians **[17608]**
581705 White Oak Rd.
Yulee, FL 32097
Ph: (904)225-3275
Fax: (904)225-3289

Hilton, Jennifer, Chairperson
National Council for Therapeutic
  Recreation Certification **[17456]**
7 Elmwood Dr.
New City, NY 10956
Ph: (845)639-1439
Fax: (845)639-1471

Hilton, Lawrence D., Esq., Gen.
  Counsel
United Precious Metals Association
  [2374]
270 N Main St., Ste. B
Alpine, UT 84004
Toll Free: 888-210-8488

Hilton, Ronald, Founder
World Association of International
  Studies **[9591]**
Goldsmith Hall
Dept. of Modern Languages and
  Cultures
Adrian College
Adrian, MI 49221

Hime, Dr. Leslie Campbell,
  Chairperson
Ethnic and Multicultural Information
  Exchange Round Table of the
  American Library Association
  [9704]
50 E Huron St.
Chicago, IL 60611
Toll Free: 800-545-5433

Hinchman, Kristen, Director
American Belarussian Relief
  Organization **[12614]**
PO Box 25303
Winston Salem, NC 27114-5303
Ph: (336)407-6062

Hinckley, Dr. Richard, CEO,
  President
Center for Occupational Research
  and Development **[7840]**
4901 Bosque Blvd., 2nd Fl.
Waco, TX 76710
Ph: (254)772-8756
Toll Free: 800-972-2766
Fax: (254)772-8972

Hinckley, Stewart, Exec. Dir.
American Society of ExtraCorporeal
  Technology **[15678]**
330 N Wabash Ave., Ste. 2000
Chicago, IL 60611
Ph: (312)321-5156
Fax: (312)673-6656

Hinckley, Stewart, Exec. Dir.
Clinical Orthopaedic Society **[16472]**
2209 Dickens Rd.
Richmond, VA 23230-2005
Ph: (804)565-6366
Fax: (804)282-0090

Hinderberger, Peter, MD, Mem.
Physicians' Association for Anthropo-
  sophic Medicine **[13648]**
4801 Yellowwood Ave.
Baltimore, MD 21209
Ph: (734)930-9462
Fax: (410)367-1961

Hindes, Tim, Exec. Dir.
University Economic Development
  Association **[8740]**
PO Box 97930
Pittsburgh, PA 15227
Ph: (216)200-8332
Toll Free: 877-583-8332

Hindman, Heather, President, Web Adm.
Association of Nepal and Himalayan Studies [9588]
Dept. of Anthropology
Dartmouth College
6047 Silsby Hall
Hanover, NH 03755
Ph: (603)646-9356
Fax: (603)646-1140

Hindy, Shawn, Chairman
U.S. Field Hockey Association [22837]
5540 N Academy Blvd., Ste. 100
Colorado Springs, CO 80918
Ph: (719)866-4567
Fax: (719)632-0979

Hines, Carrie, President, CEO
American Small Manufacturers Coalition [2212]
PO Box 15289
Washington, DC 20003
Ph: (202)341-7066
Fax: (202)315-3906

Hines, Linda, President
Songea's Kids [11152]
3020 Issaquah Pine Lake Rd. SE, No. 539
Sammamish, WA 98075
Ph: (425)961-0623

Hines, Susan, Director
Gypsum Association [2379]
6525 Belcrest Rd., Ste. 480
Hyattsville, MD 20782
Ph: (301)277-8686
Fax: (301)277-8747

Hingson, Luke L., President
Brother's Brother Foundation [12630]
1200 Galveston Ave.
Pittsburgh, PA 15233-1604
Ph: (412)321-3160
Fax: (412)321-3325

Hinkle, Bob, Exec. Dir.
Institute for Briquetting and Agglomeration [2498]
PO Box 205
Portersville, PA 16051
Ph: (724)368-4004
Fax: (715)368-4014

Hinkle, Jim, Bd. Member
National Wild Turkey Federation [4846]
770 Augusta Rd.
Edgefield, SC 29824-0530
Ph: (803)637-3106
Toll Free: 800-843-6983

Hinnebusch, Thomas J., Project Mgr.
Language Materials Project [8186]
1337 Rolfe Hall,
University of California
Los Angeles, CA 90095-1487
Ph: (310)267-4720
Fax: (310)206-5183

Hinterman, Dr. John V., Registrar
International College of Dentists [14450]
G3535 Beecher Rd., Ste. G
Flint, MI 48532-2700
Ph: (810)820-3087
Fax: (810)265-7047

Hinton, Jean, Secretary
National Association of Division Order Analysts [2528]
PO Box 2300
Lees Summit, MO 64063-7300

Hinton, Kevin, Bd. Member
Convention Industry Council [3290]
700 N Fairfax St., Ste. 510

Alexandria, VA 22314
Ph: (571)527-3116
Fax: (571)527-3105

Hinton, Kevin M., CIS, CEO
Society for Incentive Travel Excellence [3394]
330 N Wabash Ave.
Chicago, IL 60611
Ph: (312)321-5148
Fax: (312)527-6783

Hinton, Kevin M., CIS, CEO
Society of Incentive and Travel Executives [3395]
330 N Wabash
Chicago, IL 60611
Ph: (312)321-5148

Hinton, Mike, Contact
National Association of Rural Rehabilitation Corporations [12804]
c/o Mike Hinton
USDA-FSA, Loan Servicing Division
1400 Independence Ave. SW, Stop 0522
Washington, DC 20250-0522
Ph: (202)720-1472

Hinton, Skip, President
National Educational Telecommunications Association [7827]
939 S Stadium Rd.
Columbia, SC 29201
Ph: (803)799-5517
     (803)978-1581
Fax: (803)771-4831

Hintzke, Mark, Founder, Managing Dir.
Restoration Works International [9431]
PO Box 6803
Albany, CA 94706

Hipes, Charlene, COO
Alliance of Information and Referral Systems [6734]
c/o Moayad Zahralddin, Membership Director
11240 Waples Mill Rd., Ste. 200
Fairfax, VA 22030
Ph: (703)218-2477
Fax: (703)359-7562

Hippard, William, Exec. Dir.
Metal Roofing Alliance [2357]
12430 Tesson Ferry Rd., No. 112
Saint Louis, MO 63128
Ph: (314)495-5906

Hirano, Irene, President
U.S.-Japan Council [18534]
1819 L St. NW, Ste. 200
Washington, DC 20036
Ph: (202)223-6840
Fax: (202)280-1235

Hirmes, Fran, Chmn. of the Bd.
Emunah of America [12208]
363 7th Ave., 2nd Fl.
New York, NY 10001
Ph: (212)564-9045
Fax: (212)643-9731

Hirmes, Fran, Chmn. of the Bd.
Emunah Women of America [20245]
7 Penn Plz.
New York, NY 10001
Ph: (212)564-9045
Toll Free: 800-368-6440
Fax: (212)643-9731

Hirsch, Daniel, President
Committee to Bridge the Gap [18743]
PO Box 4

Ben Lomond, CA 95005-0004
Ph: (831)336-8003

Hirsch, David, Bd. Member
U.S. Boomerang Association [22700]
c/o Betsylew Miale-Gix, Treasurer
3351 236th St. SW
Brier, WA 98036-8421
Ph: (425)485-1672

Hirsch, Joshua A., MD, President
American Society of Spine Radiology [17051]
800 Enterprise Dr., Ste. 205
Oak Brook, IL 60523-4216
Ph: (630)574-0220
Fax: (630)574-0661

Hirsch, Michael, President
Society for Commercial Archeology [8905]
PO Box 2500
Little Rock, AR 72203

Hirsch, Sanford, Exec. Dir.
Adolph and Esther Gottlieb Foundation [8922]
380 W Broadway
New York, NY 10012
Ph: (212)226-0581
Fax: (212)274-1476

Hirschberg, Mike, Exec. Dir.
AHS International [120]
2701 Prosperity Ave., Ste. 210
Fairfax, VA 22031
Ph: (703)684-6777
Toll Free: 855-247-4685
Fax: (703)739-9279

Hirschfeld, Amy, Exec. Dir.
International Catacomb Society [9402]
71 Prince St.
Boston, MA 02113-1827

Hirschfeld, Stephen J., Esq., CEO, Founder
Employment Law Alliance [5003]
505 Montgomery St., 13th Fl.
San Francisco, CA 94111-6529
Ph: (415)835-9011
Fax: (415)834-0443

Hirschfield, Rabbi Brad, President
CLAL - The National Jewish Center for Learning and Leadership [20241]
440 Park Ave. S, 4th Fl.
New York, NY 10016-8012
Ph: (212)779-3300
Fax: (212)779-1009

Hirschmann, David, CEO, President
Coalition Against Counterfeiting and Piracy [5325]
US Chamber of Commerce
Global Intellectual Property Ctr.
1615 H St. NW
Washington, DC 20062-0001
Ph: (202)463-5601
Fax: (202)463-3114

Hirsh, Anne E., Director
Job Accommodation Network [11609]
PO Box 6080
Morgantown, WV 26506-6080
Toll Free: 800-526-7234

Hirsh, Dr. Richard N., Founder
Radiology Mammography International [13852]
1037 Robinwood Hills Dr.
Akron, OH 44333-1553
Ph: (330)666-1967

Hirsh, Stephanie, Exec. Dir.
Learning Forward [7430]
504 S Locust St.

Oxford, OH 45056
Toll Free: 800-727-7288
Fax: (513)523-0638

Hissong, Hon. Candace, Exec. Dir., Treasurer
National Judges Association [5397]
222 Gilbert Ave.
Glendale, OR 97442
Fax: (541)832-2647

Hitchcock, Helen Hull, Editor
ADOREMUS - Society for the Renewal of the Sacred Liturgy [19787]
PO Box 385
La Crosse, WI 54602-0385
Ph: (608)521-0385

Hitchcock, Mrs. Helen Hull, President
Women for Faith and Family [19921]
PO Box 300411
Saint Louis, MO 63130
Ph: (314)863-8385
Fax: (314)863-5858

Hitchcock, Reed, Exec. Dir.
Aircraft Fleet Recycling Association [12579]
529 14th St. NW, Ste. 750
Washington, DC 20045
Ph: (202)591-2478
Fax: (202)223-9741

Hitchcock, Reed, Exec. VP, Director
Asphalt Roofing Manufacturers Association [496]
750 National Press Bldg.
529 14th St. NW
Washington, DC 20045
Ph: (202)591-2450
Fax: (202)591-2445

Hitchcock, Reed, Exec. Dir.
Hotel Electronic Distribution Network Association [1660]
750 National Press Bldg.
529 14th St. NW
Washington, DC 20045
Ph: (202)204-8400
Fax: (202)591-2445

Hite, Tracy, Treasurer
American Tarot Association [22441]
1020 Liberty Rd.
Lexington, KY 40505-4035
Toll Free: 888-211-1572
Fax: (859)514-9799

Hite, William P., President
United Association of Journeymen and Apprentices of the Plumbing and Pipe Fitting Industry of the United States, Canada [23503]
3 Park Pl.
Annapolis, MD 21401
Ph: (410)269-2000
Fax: (410)267-0262

Hitzig, Marc, Exec. Dir.
Japan-America Society of Washington, D.C. [9622]
1819 L St. NW, B2
Washington, DC 20036
Ph: (202)833-2210
Fax: (202)833-2456

Hively, Barb, President
White German Shepherd Dog Club of America [21992]
c/o Barb Hively, President, 8837 N Mountain Dr.
8837 N Mountain Dr.
Mercersburg, PA 17236

Hjalmquist, Jennifer, Contact
Heavy-Duty Business Forum [294]

c/o Heavy Duty Manufacturers Association
10 Laboratoty Dr.
Research Triangle Park, NC 27709-3966

Hlava, Margie, President
Hubbell Family Historical Society [20883]
c/o Jan Fulton, Treasurer
4933 Stetzer Rd.
Bucyrus, OH 44820

Hmurovich, James M., CEO, President
Prevent Child Abuse America [11132]
228 S Wabash Ave., 10th Fl.
Chicago, IL 60604
Ph: (312)663-3520
Toll Free: 800-244-5373
Fax: (312)939-8962

Hnatiuk, Harve D., President
National Society of Professional Engineers [6578]
1420 King St.
Alexandria, VA 22314
Toll Free: 888-285-6773
Fax: (703)836-4875

Ho, Cindy, Founder
Saving Antiquities for Everyone [21292]
PO Box 231172, Ansonia Sta.
New York, NY 10023-0020

Ho, Patricia Fae, President
American Association of University Women - Women Educational Foundation [8743]
1111 16th St. NW
Washington, DC 20036
Ph: (202)785-7700
Toll Free: 800-326-2289
Fax: (202)785-7777

Ho, Vi, PhD, Founder, Chairman
Vietnamese-American Nurses Association [16190]
PO Box 691994
Houston, TX 77269-1994

Hoag, Mary, Asst.
Window Coverings Association of America [1963]
PO Box 731
Wake Forest, NC 27588
Ph: (919)263-9850
Fax: (919)426-2047

Hoagland, Deena, LCSW, Exec. Dir.
Island Dolphin Care [11607]
150 Lorelane Pl.
Key Largo, FL 33037
Ph: (305)451-5884
Fax: (305)453-5399

Hoal, Brian G., Exec. Dir.
Society of Economic Geologists [6682]
7811 Shaffer Pky.
Littleton, CO 80127-3732
Ph: (720)981-7882
Fax: (720)981-7874

Hoang, Chau, Founder, CEO, Director
Orphans' Futures Alliance [11731]
244 5th Ave., Ste. 2247
New York, NY 10001
Ph: (212)726-2247

Hoard, Michael G., President
The Tube Council [2485]
114 S Tamie Cir.
Kathleen, GA 31047

Hoarle, Kimberly, MBA, Exec. Dir.
American Society for Healthcare Risk Management [15310]

155 N Wacker Dr., Ste. 400
Chicago, IL 60606
Ph: (312)422-3980
Fax: (312)422-4580

Hoban, Roseanne, Exec. Dir.
Wire Fabricators Association [1581]
PO Box 304
Montgomery, IL 60538-0304
Ph: (630)896-1469
Fax: (209)633-6265

Hobart, Tom, Contact
Food Service Enablers [3013]
4256 Ridge Lea Rd., Ste. 100
Amherst, NY 14226
Ph: (716)819-6600
Toll Free: 866-377-8833

Hobbs, Chris, Web Adm.
Q Users Experience [6753]
c/o Kathy Wetherell, Treasurer
4750 1st St.
Pleasanton, CA 94566

Hobbs, Paul, VP
Spokane, Portland and Seattle Railway Historical Society [10192]
c/o Bill Baker, Treasurer
6345 Peppermill Pl. SE
Port Orchard, WA 98366

Hobby, Kenneth, President
Cure SMA [15921]
925 Busse Rd.
Elk Grove Village, IL 60007
Toll Free: 800-886-1762

Hobson, David, Exec. Dir.
National Organization of Veterans' Advocates [5841]
1425 K St. NW, Ste. 350
Washington, DC 20005-3514
Ph: (202)587-5708

Hoch, Steven G., Chairman
American Swiss Foundation [19666]
271 Madison Ave., Ste. 1403
New York, NY 10016
Ph: (212)754-0130
Fax: (212)754-4512

Hochhalter, Andrew, Exec. Dir.
Quest for Peace [18440]
c/o Quixote Center
7307 Baltimore Ave., Ste. 214
College Park, MD 20740
Ph: (301)699-0042

Hochman, Steven H., PhD, Dir. of Res.
Carter Center [18938]
1 Copenhill
453 Freedom Pkwy.
Atlanta, GA 30307
Ph: (404)420-5100
Toll Free: 800-550-3560
Fax: (404)331-0283

Hochschild, Jennifer, President
American Political Science Association [7042]
1527 New Hampshire Ave. NW
Washington, DC 20036-1206
Ph: (202)483-2512
Fax: (202)483-2657

Hochstetler, Daniel E., VP
Jacob Hochstetler Family Association [20881]
PO Box 154
Goshen, IN 46527-0154

Hockenstein, Jeremy, CEO, Founder
Digital Divide Data [7263]
115 W 30th St., Ste. 400
New York, NY 10001
Ph: (212)461-3700
Fax: (212)813-3209

Hocking, Jim, Founder, CEO
Water for Good [13360]
PO Box 247
Winona Lake, IN 46590
Ph: (574)306-2810

Hodapp, Theodore, Director
Physics Teacher Education Coalition [8656]
1 Physics Ellipse
College Park, MD 20740-3843
Ph: (301)209-3263
(301)209-3273

Hodel, Paul L., President
Promoting Enduring Peace [18824]
323 Temple St.
New Haven, CT 06511-6602
Ph: (203)584-5224

Hodel, Rolande R., PhD, Founder, President
AIDSfreeAFRICA [13526]
125 S Highland Ave., No. 3-B1
Ossining, NY 10562
Ph: (914)236-0658

Hodge, Bill, Chairperson
National Wilderness Stewardship Alliance [3907]
PO Box 5293
Reno, NV 89513

Hodge, Victoria L., President
North American Hazardous Materials Management Association [6705]
12011 Tejon St., Ste. 700
Westminster, CO 80234
Ph: (303)451-5945
Toll Free: 877-292-1403
Fax: (303)458-0002

Hodgert, Mike, President
Electrathon America [23080]
2495 Cleveland St.
Eugene, OR 97405
Ph: (541)915-9834

Hodges, Debbie, Exec. Dir.
Eastern Surfing Association [23275]
PO Box 4736
Ocean City, MD 21843
Ph: (302)988-1953
Fax: (302)258-0735

Hodges, Deborah J., Exec. Dir.
Construction Writers Association [2672]
PO Box 14784
Chicago, IL 60614-0784
Ph: (773)687-8726
Fax: (773)687-8627

Hodges, Eddie, Chmn. of the Bd.
Master's Men of the National Association of Free Will Baptists [19732]
5233 Mount View Rd.
Antioch, TN 37013-2306
Ph: (615)731-6812
Toll Free: 877-767-7659
Fax: (615)731-0771

Hodges, Elizabeth, Exec. Dir.
Women Nationally Active for Christ [19744]
PO Box 5002
Antioch, TN 37011-5002
Ph: (615)731-6812
Toll Free: 877-767-7662
Fax: (615)727-1157

Hodges, Jean, President
Parents, Families and Friends of Lesbians and Gays, Inc. [11905]
1828 L St. NW, Ste. 660
Washington, DC 20036
Ph: (202)467-8180
Fax: (202)467-8194

Hodges, Joanna, Founder
Fondation Hopital Bon Samaritain [15141]
PO Box 32446
West Palm Beach, FL 33420
Ph: (561)246-3360

Hodgson, Gregor, PhD, Exec. Dir., Founder
Reef Check [4470]
17575 Pacific Coast Hwy., Ste. B
Pacific Palisades, CA 90272-1057
Ph: (310)230-2371
(310)230-2360
Fax: (310)230-2376

Hodson, Colleen, Exec. Dir.
Dude Ranchers' Association [1655]
1122 12th St.
Cody, WY 82414
Ph: (307)587-2339
Toll Free: 866-399-2339

Hoekstra, Robert, Director
International Prison Ministry [11533]
PO Box 2868
Costa Mesa, CA 92628-2868
Toll Free: 800-527-1212
Fax: (714)972-0557

Hoelter, Matt, Exec. Dir.
American Electrophoresis Society [6407]
Kendrick Laboratories, Inc.
1202 Ann St.
Madison, WI 53713-2410

Hoeme, Mike, VP
National Conference of State Transportation Specialists [5818]
c/o Larry Herold, Treasurer
1560 Broadway, Ste. 250
Denver, CO 80202
Ph: (303)894-2859

Hoerber, Janice, Treasurer
Nuclear Information and Records Management Association [6932]
c/o Julie Hannum, Administrator
245 Sunnyridge Ave., No. 34
Fairfield, CT 06824
Ph: (203)388-8795

Hoerle, Heather, Exec. Dir.
Secondary School Admission Test Board [8691]
862 Route 518
Skillman, NJ 08558
Ph: (609)683-5558
Fax: (609)683-4507

Hoerle, Jeff, President
Foundation for Ichthyosis and Related Skin Types [14494]
2616 N Broad St.
Colmar, PA 18915
Ph: (215)997-9400
Toll Free: 800-545-3286
Fax: (215)997-9403

Hoeter, Eileen, Chmn. of the Bd.
Women in Film & Television International [3506]
c/o WIFV-DC
4000 Albermarle St. NW
Washington, DC 20016

Hofacre, Charles, Exec. VP
American Association of Avian Pathologists [17591]
12627 San Jose Blvd., Ste. 202
Jacksonville, FL 32223-8638
Ph: (904)425-5735
Fax: (281)664-4744

Hoff, Kate, VP
Institute for Agriculture and Trade Policy [17789]

2105 1st Ave. S
Minneapolis, MN 55404
Ph: (612)870-0453
Fax: (612)870-4846

Hoff, Laura, Dir. of Lib. Svcs.
Association for Research and
Enlightenment [6984]
215 67th St.
Virginia Beach, VA 23451
Ph: (757)428-3588
Toll Free: 800-333-4499

Hoffa, James P., Chairperson
Change to Win [23529]
1900 L St. NW, Ste. 900
Washington, DC 20036
Ph: (202)721-0660
Fax: (202)721-0661

Hoffecker, Paul S., CEO
National Hyperbaric Association
[15345]
PO Box 438
Westtown, PA 19395
Ph: (484)886-4272

Hoffee, James, Mem.
United States Power Squadrons
[22683]
1504 Blue Ridge Rd.
Raleigh, NC 27607
Ph: (919)821-0281
Toll Free: 888-367-8777

Hoffheimer, Lawrence S., Chairman,
Founder
Macular Degeneration Association
[17725]
PO Box 20256
Sarasota, FL 34276
Ph: (941)870-4399
Fax: (866)317-0593

Hoffman, Alan, President
American Friends of Lafayette
[10312]
PO Box 9463
Easton, PA 18042-1798

Hoffman, D. Douglas, CEO
National Organization of Remedia-
tors and Mold Inspectors [1166]
22174 Prats Rd.
Abita Springs, LA 70420-2250
Toll Free: 877-251-2296
Fax: (866)211-4324

Hoffman, Daniel, Office Mgr.
John Howard Association of Illinois
[11529]
PO Box 10042
Chicago, IL 60610-0042
Ph: (312)291-9183
Fax: (312)526-3714

Hoffman, Daryl, Exec. Dir.
Elephant Managers Association
[10614]
1513 Cambridge St.
Houston, TX 77030
Ph: (407)938-1988

Hoffman, David, Founder
Internews Network [18655]
PO Box 4448
Arcata, CA 95518-4448
Ph: (707)826-2030
Toll Free: 877-247-8819
Fax: (707)826-2136

Hoffman, David, VP, Managing Dir.
Society for New Communications
Research [6231]
845 3rd Ave.
New York, NY 10022-6600
Ph: (212)759-0900

Hoffman, Eric, Contact
Americans Well-informed on
Automobile Retailing Economics
[279]

919 18th St. NW, Ste. 300
Washington, DC 20006
Ph: (202)585-2808
Toll Free: 888-400-7577

Hoffman, Fred G., Treasurer
Clan Munro Association [20835]
6895 Hundred Acre Dr.
Cocoa, FL 32927-2981
Ph: (321)632-2118

Hoffman, Jonathan I., Director,
Founder
Direct Aid International [12655]
PO Box 394
Northfield, VT 05663

Hoffman, Lee M., President
American Association of Insurance
Management Consultants [815]
Ph: (713)664-6424

Hoffman, Marcelle, President
Bondurant Family Association
[20786]
c/o Amy B. Sanders
2143 Lansing St.
Melbourne, FL 32935-2176

Hoffman, Marsha, President
National Federation of Press Women
[2700]
PO Box 5556
Arlington, VA 22205
Ph: (804)746-1033

Hoffman, Martha, President
Call to Care Uganda [10879]
PO Box 1075
Madison, CT 06443
Ph: (203)245-3932

Hoffman, Mary C., Founder
Coffin-Lowry Syndrome Foundation
[14817]
675 Kalmia Pl. NW
Issaquah, WA 98027
Ph: (425)427-0939

Hoffman, Perry D., PhD, President
National Education Alliance for
Borderline Personality Disorder
[15796]
10 Quarry Ct.
Saint Albans, VT 05478

Hoffman, R. Lynn, Chairman
World Flower Council [1312]
1608 Tyler St.
Hollywood, FL 33020
Ph: (954)444-6445
Fax: (888)506-7808

Hoffman, Ron, Founder, Exec. Dir.
Compassionate Care ALS [13683]
PO Box 1052
West Falmouth, MA 02574
Ph: (508)444-6775

Hoffman-Lee, Nicky, Mgr. Dir.
The Naturist Society, LLC [10057]
627 Bay Shore Dr., Ste. 100
Oshkosh, WI 54901
Ph: (920)426-5009
Toll Free: 800-886-7230

Hoffmann, Rev. John W., Chairman
Air Compassion for Veterans [21102]
4620 Haygood Rd., Ste. 1
Virginia Beach, VA 23455

Hoffmann, Richard R., Exec. Dir.
Interstate Natural Gas Association of
America [4264]
20 F St. NW, Ste. 450
Washington, DC 20001
Ph: (202)216-5900

Hoffmann, Susie, Director
Washburn Alumni Association
[19370]

1700 SW College Ave.
Topeka, KS 66621
Ph: (785)670-1641
   (785)670-1643

Hoffmann, Tom, President
Order of United Commercial Travel-
ers of America [19491]
1801 Watermark Dr., Ste. 100
Columbus, OH 43215
Ph: (614)487-9680
Toll Free: 800-848-0123
Fax: (614)487-9675

Hofheins-Wackerfuss, Gretchen,
President
Miniature Pinscher Club of America
[21916]
c/o Joanne Wilds-Snell, Secretary
1800 Coral Ivy Ct.
Chesapeake, VA 23323-6370

Hofmann, Laurie, MPH, CEO
Institute for Functional Medicine
[13629]
505 S 336th St., Ste. 600
Federal Way, WA 98003
Ph: (253)661-3010
Toll Free: 800-228-0622
Fax: (253)661-8310

Hofmann, Rick, President
American Amputee Soccer Associa-
tion [23184]
1033 Creekside Dr.
Wilmington, DE 19804
Ph: (302)683-0997

Hofmeister, Dr. Karen, Bd. Member
Citizens for Affordable Energy [6466]
1302 Waugh Dr., No. 940
Houston, TX 77019-3908
Ph: (713)523-7333
Fax: (888)318-7878

Hofmeyer, Bonnie, Exec. Dir.
Jamestowne Society [20753]
PO Box 6845
Richmond, VA 23230
Ph: (804)353-1226

Hofsommer, Don L., Treasurer, Edi-
tor
Lexington Group in Transportation
History [10182]
c/o Byron Olsen, Vice President/
Secretary
1543 Grantham St.
Saint Paul, MN 55108-1449

Hofwolt, Capt. Jerry, President
Historic Naval Ships Association
[9773]
626-C Admiral Dr.
Annapolis, MD 21401
Ph: (443)949-8341

Hogan, Rachel, Director
Ape Action Africa [4786]
555 Bryant St., No. 862
Palo Alto, CA 94301

Hogg, Mark, Founder, CEO
WaterStep [13364]
625 Myrtle St.
Louisville, KY 40208
Ph: (502)568-6342

Hoggatt, Brad, VP
Weather Risk Management Associa-
tion [6862]
529 14th St. NW, Ste. 750
Washington, DC 20045
Ph: (202)289-3800
Fax: (202)591-2445

Hogue, Bill, Treasurer
EDUCAUSE [8029]
282 Century Pl., Ste. 5000

Louisville, CO 80027
Ph: (303)449-4430
Fax: (303)440-0461

Hogue, Bill, Director
National Roof Certification and
Inspection Association [560]
2232 E Wilson Ave.
Orange, CA 92867
Toll Free: 866-210-7464

Hohenhaus, Susan M., Exec. Dir.
Emergency Nurses Association
[14680]
915 Lee St.
Des Plaines, IL 60016-6569
Ph: (847)460-4123
Toll Free: 800-900-9659

Hohimer, Colette Iocca, Exec. Dir.
The Association of Bone and Joint
Surgeons [16470]
300 S Northwest Hwy., Ste. 203
Park Ridge, IL 60068
Ph: (847)720-4186
Fax: (847)720-4013

Hohn, Marty, President
The Rock Poster Society [8886]
PO Box 20309
Oakland, CA 94620-0309

Hohnstreiter, Shawn, Chairman
Texas Search and Rescue [12749]
PO Box 171258
Austin, TX 78717
Ph: (512)956-6727

Hoke, Robert, Secretary, Treasurer
American Spelean History Associa-
tion [9458]
6304 Kaybro St.
Laurel, MD 20707
Ph: (301)725-5877

Holbeck, Natasha, VP
Association of Chartered Ac-
countants in the United States [13]
347 5th Ave., Ste. 1406
New York, NY 10016
Ph: (212)481-7950

Holbrook, Anna Maria, VP, Director
Honduras Relief Effort [12674]
4400 Cranston Pl.
Orlando, FL 32812
Ph: (407)277-9920
Fax: (407)277-9920

Holbrook, Les, Secretary
The Elongated Collectors [22269]
4010 Foothills Blvd., Ste. 103
Roseville, CA 95747-7241

Holbrook, Scott, CEO, President
Avant Ministries [20386]
10000 N Oak Trafficway
Kansas City, MO 64155
Ph: (816)734-8500
Toll Free: 800-468-1892
Fax: (816)734-4601

Holcomb Krafft, Ms. Cynthia, PhD,
President
Aquatic & Fitness Professional As-
sociation International [23062]
547 WCR 18
Longmont, CO 80504
Fax: (303)678-9989

Hold, William T., PhD, CEO,
President
National Alliance for Insurance
Education and Research [1888]
3630 N Hills Dr.
Austin, TX 78731
Toll Free: 800-633-2165
Fax: (512)349-6194

Holdaway, Tamara, Exec. Dir.
National Quarter Horse Registry
[4384]
PO Box 513
La Verkin, UT 84745
Ph: (435)915-6747
Fax: (734)917-6747

Holder, Carl, President
Dachshund Club of America **[21864]**
c/o Neal Hamilton, Membership
   Administrator
59 Cloverhill Rd.
Flemington, NJ 08822-9801
Ph: (908)782-4724

Holder, Carlyle I., President
National Association of Blacks in
   Criminal Justice **[11536]**
Whiting Criminal Justice Bldg.
1801 Fayetteville St.
Durham, NC 27707
Ph: (919)683-1801
Toll Free: 866-846-2225
Fax: (919)683-1903

Holdman, Travis, President
National Conference of Insurance
   Legislators **[5318]**
2317 Route 34, Ste. 2B
Manasquan, NJ 08736
Ph: (732)201-4133
Fax: (609)989-7491

Holguín, Sandie, Gen. Sec.
Association for Spanish and
   Portuguese Historical Studies
   [9464]
c/o A. Katie Harris, General
   Secretary
1 Shields Ave.
Department of History
University of California, Davis
Davis, CA 95616-8611

Holguin, Robert, CEO, President
Saturn Awards **[9311]**
334 W 54th St.
Los Angeles, CA 90037
Ph: (323)752-5811

Holl, Joyce, Exec. Dir.
National Orientation Directors As-
   sociation **[7439]**
2829 University Ave., Ste. 415
Minneapolis, MN 55414
Ph: (612)301-6632
Toll Free: 866-521-6632
Fax: (612)624-2628

Holl, Shawn A., Dir. of Dev.
Omohundro Institute of Early
   American History and Culture
   [9501]
PO Box 8781
Williamsburg, VA 23187-8781
Ph: (757)221-1114
Fax: (757)221-1047

Holland, Ann, Dir. of Operations
National Alliance of Families for the
   Return of America's Missing
   Servicemen **[21091]**
2528 Poly Dr.
Billings, MT 59102-1442
Ph: (406)652-3528

Holland Barnes, Donna, PhD,
   President, Founder, Exec. Dir.
National Organization for People of
   Color Against Suicide **[13196]**
PO Box 75571
Washington, DC 20013-0571
Ph: (202)549-6039
      (202)806-7706

Holland, Billy, Contact
Sammy Kershaw Fan Club **[24051]**
833 Todd Preis Dr.

Nashville, TN 37221
Ph: (615)564-2580
Fax: (615)646-4721

Holland, Brad, Co-Chmn. of the Bd.
American Society of Illustrators
   Partnership **[910]**
536 Broadway, 5th Fl.
New York, NY 10012
Ph: (212)420-9160

Holland, Christy K., President
Acoustical Society of America **[5852]**
c/o Elaine Moran, Office Manager
1305 Walt Whitman Rd., Ste. 300
Melville, NY 11747-4300
Ph: (516)576-2360
Fax: (516)576-2377

Holland, Daniel J., Chairman
BlazeSports America **[22777]**
1670 Oakbrook Dr., Ste. 331
Norcross, GA 30093
Ph: (404)270-2000
Fax: (404)270-2039

Holland, John, President
Equine Welfare Alliance **[10619]**
PO Box 6161
Naperville, IL 60567
Ph: (630)961-9292

Holland, Kenneth, President
Association for Canadian Studies in
   the United States **[9206]**
1740 Massachusetts Ave. NW, Nitze
   516
Washington, DC 20036
Ph: (202)670-1424
Fax: (202)663-5717

Holland, Susan, Exec. Dir.
Cancer Schmancer Movement
   [13929]
22837 Pacific Coast Hwy.
Malibu, CA 90265
Toll Free: 888-621-2001

Holland, Tex, Mgr.
Lone Ranger Fan Club **[24086]**
PO Box 1253
Salisbury, MD 21802-1253

Hollander, Kim, Exec. Dir.
Oxalosis and Hyperoxaluria Founda-
   tion **[15885]**
201 E 19th St., Ste. 12E
New York, NY 10003
Ph: (212)777-0470
Toll Free: 800-OHF-8699

Hollander, Richard, Exec. VP
Society of Industrial and Office Real-
   tors **[2895]**
1201 New York Ave. NW, Ste. 350
Washington, DC 20005-6126
Ph: (202)449-8200
Fax: (202)216-9325

Hollebrands, Karen, Chairperson
North American Chapter of the
   International Group for the
   Psychology of Mathematics Educa-
   tion **[6824]**
c/o Ji-Eun Lee, Treasurer
470A Pawley Hall
Oakland University
2200 N Squirrel Rd.
Rochester, MI 48309

Hollenbach, David, President
Catholic Theological Society of
   America **[19816]**
John Carroll University
1 John Carroll Blvd.
University Heights, OH 44118
Ph: (216)397-4980
Fax: (216)397-1804

Hollenbeck, Brian, VP
Kappa Mu Epsilon **[23812]**
c/o Dr. Rhonda McKee, President
Dept. of Mathematics and Computer
   Science
University of Central Missouri
Warrensburg, MO 64093
Ph: (660)543-8929
Fax: (417)865-9599

Holler, Mr. Richard, Exec. Dir.
Association of Software Profession-
   als **[6272]**
PO Box 1522
Martinsville, IN 46151
Ph: (765)349-4740
Fax: (815)301-3756

Holleran, Edward, Chairman
National Cable Television Cooperative, Inc. **[692]**
11200 Corporate Ave.
Lenexa, KS 66219-1392

Holley, Cary, President
Downed Bikers Association **[22220]**
PO Box 21713
Oklahoma City, OK 73156
Ph: (405)789-5565

Holley, Dr. Mary, Founder, President
Mothers Against Methamphetamine
   [13154]
PO Box 8
Arab, AL 35016
Ph: (256)498-6262
Toll Free: 866-293-8901

Holliday, Barry, Exec. Dir.
Dredging Contractors of America
   [2241]
503 D St. NW, Ste. 150
Washington, DC 20001
Ph: (202)737-2674
Fax: (202)737-2677

Holliday, Doug, President
Open Door Haiti **[13079]**
5070 Orange Blvd.
Sanford, FL 32771
Ph: (407)221-4386

Holliday, Stuart W., CEO, President
Meridian International Center
   [18550]
1630 Crescent Pl. NW
Washington, DC 20009
Ph: (202)667-6800
Toll Free: 800-424-2974
Fax: (202)667-1475

Holliday, Stuart W., CEO, President
Meridian International Center
   Programming Division **[18551]**
1630 Crescent Pl. NW
Washington, DC 20009
Ph: (202)667-6800
Toll Free: 800-424-2974
Fax: (202)667-1475

Hollingshead, Mark, Secretary,
   Treasurer
American College of Eye Surgeons
   [17366]
334 E Lake Rd., No. 135
Palm Harbor, FL 34685-2427
Ph: (727)366-1487
Fax: (727)836-9783

Hollingworth, Steve, President, CEO
Freedom from Hunger **[12095]**
1460 Drew Ave., Ste. 300
Davis, CA 95618
Ph: (530)758-6200
Toll Free: 800-708-2555
Fax: (530)758-6241

Hollins, Jessica, Founder, CEO
My Very Own Blanket **[11085]**
PO Box 2691

Westerville, OH 43086
Ph: (614)530-3327

Hollinsworth, Leah, Contact
International Federation of Bike Mes-
   senger Associations **[3335]**
PO Box 191443
San Francisco, CA 94119-1443

Hollis, Lyn, Comm. Chm.
WTCARES **[21998]**
c/o Lyn Hollis
164 N Forrest Ave.
Camden, TN 38320-1217

Hollis, Nicholas E., Exec. Dir.
Agri-Energy Roundtable **[18482]**
PO Box 5565
Washington, DC 20016
Ph: (202)887-0528

Hollis, Nicholas E., CEO, President
Agribusiness Council **[3522]**
PO Box 5565
Washington, DC 20016
Ph: (202)296-4563

Hollis, Thomas, Jr., President
American Measuring Tool
   Manufacturers Association **[7229]**
8562 East Ave.
Mentor, OH 44060
Ph: (440)974-6829
Fax: (440)974-6828

Hollis, Tim, Secretary
National Lum and Abner Society
   [22402]
81 Sharon Blvd.
Dora, AL 35062

Holloway, Albert, CEO, Founder,
   President
The IPA Association of America
   [16753]
12850 Highway 9, No. 600-334
Alpharetta, GA 30004
Ph: (510)967-7305
Fax: (510)217-2241

Holloway, Carson, Exec. Dir.
Association for the Study of Free
   Institutions **[7954]**
c/o Stephen H. Balch, Chairman
Institute for the Study of Western
   Civilization
Box 41017
Lubbock, TX 79409-1017
Ph: (806)834-8289

Holloway, Mr. Gary, Exec. Dir.
World Convention of Churches of
   Christ **[20031]**
Vine Street Christian Church
4101 Harding Pke.
Nashville, TN 37205
Ph: (615)298-1824

Holmer, Steve, Director
Bird Conservation Alliance **[3658]**
PO Box 249
The Plains, VA 20198-0249
Ph: (202)234-7181

Holmes, Anastasia, MPA, Exec. Dir.
Families of September 11 **[19179]**
1560 Broadway, Ste. 305
New York, NY 10036
Ph: (212)575-1878
Fax: (212)575-1877

Holmes, Anne, Chairperson
National Association of Baby
   Boomer Women **[13387]**
9672 W US Highway 20
Galena, IL 61036
Toll Free: 877-266-6379

Holmes, David R., MD
American College of Cardiology
   [14089]

2400 N St. NW
Washington, DC 20037
Ph: (202)375-6000
Toll Free: 800-253-4636
Fax: (202)375-7000

Holmes, Douglas J., President
National Foundation for Unemploy-
ment Compensation and Workers
Compensation [5167]
910 17th St., Ste. 1070
Washington, DC 20006
Ph: (202)223-8902
    (202)223-8904
Fax: (202)783-1616

Holmes, Douglas J., President
UWC: Strategic Services on
Unemployment and Workers'
Compensation [13239]
910 17th St. NW, Ste. 1070
Washington, DC 20006
Ph: (202)223-8904
Fax: (202)783-1616

Holmes, George, Secretary,
Treasurer
Congress of Racial Equality [17780]
817 Broadway, 3rd Fl.
New York, NY 10003
Ph: (212)598-4000
Toll Free: 800-439-2673
Fax: (212)982-0184

Holmes, Irv, President
American Butter Institute [968]
2101 Wilson Blvd., Ste. 400
Arlington, VA 22201
Ph: (703)243-5630
Fax: (703)841-9328

Holmes, James, President
International Homicide Investigators
Association [5363]
2310 Falkenburg Rd. N
Tampa, FL 33619
Ph: (540)898-7898

Holsinger, Russelle, Contact
Angels of Hope [11196]
1043 Ferrari Dr.
Coal City, IL 60416

Holt, Brittany, President
Youth M.O.V.E. National [13489]
PO Box 215
Decorah, IA 52101
Toll Free: 800-580-6199

Holt, David, President
Consumer Energy Alliance [6471]
2211 Norfolk St., Ste. 410
Houston, TX 77098
Ph: (713)337-8800

Holt, David, President
Mine Warfare Association [19092]
6551 Loisdale Ct., Ste. 222
Springfield, VA 22150-1808
Ph: (703)960-6804
Fax: (703)960-6807

Holt, Rev. Earl, President
Unitarian Universalist History and
Heritage Society [20628]
70 High St.
Dedham, MA 02026

Holt, Sid, CEO
American Society of Magazine Edi-
tors [2654]
757 3rd Ave., 11th Fl.
New York, NY 10017-2194
Ph: (212)872-3700
Fax: (212)906-0128

Holt, Valerie, Exec. Asst.
Parkinson's Disease Foundation
[15984]

1359 Broadway, Ste. 1509
New York, NY 10018
Ph: (212)923-4700
Fax: (212)923-4778

Holterman, Ai-Xuan, MD, President
International Pediatric Specialists
Alliance for the Children of
Vietnam [16610]
1425 W Forrest Hill Ave.
Peoria, IL 61604

Holthus, Paul, President, CEO
World Ocean Council [4775]
3035 Hibiscus Dr., Ste. 1
Honolulu, HI 96815
Ph: (808)277-9008

Holtmann, Peter, President, CEO
International Association for Radio,
Telecommunications and Electro-
magnetics [7311]
600 N Plankinton Ave.
Milwaukee, WI 53201
Ph: (414)272-3937
Toll Free: 888-722-2440
Fax: (414)765-8661

Holtrop, Joel, Chmn. of the Bd.
The Corps Network [13438]
1275 K St. NW, Ste. 1050
Washington, DC 20005
Ph: (202)737-6272
Fax: (202)737-6277

Holtzman, Aimee, Founder,
President
rock CAN roll [12110]
PO Box 700
Jericho, NY 11753
Ph: (516)822-3457

Holway, David J., President
International Association of EMTs
and Paramedics [14681]
159 Thomas Burgin Pky.
Quincy, MA 02169
Ph: (617)376-0220
Toll Free: 866-412-7762

Holway, David J., President
International Brotherhood of Police
Officers [23470]
159 Burgin Pky.
Quincy, MA 02169
Ph: (617)376-0220
Toll Free: 866-412-7762
Fax: (617)984-5695

Holway, David J., President
National Association of Government
Employees [23432]
159 Burgin Pky.
Quincy, MA 02169
Ph: (617)376-0220
Fax: (617)984-5695

Holzenberg, Eric, Director
Grolier Club [9128]
47 E 60th St.
New York, NY 10022
Ph: (212)838-6690
Fax: (212)838-2445

Holzmann, Pete, Exec. Dir., Founder
International Christian Technologists
Association [20369]
5555 Erindale Dr., Ste. 205
Colorado Springs, CO 80918-6965
Ph: (719)785-0120

Holzweiss, Robert, President
Railway and Locomotive Historical
Society [10190]
PO Box 2913
Pflugerville, TX 78691-2913
Ph: (512)989-2480

Hom, Sharon, Exec. Dir.
Human Rights in China [12041]
450 7th Ave., Ste. 1301

New York, NY 10123
Ph: (212)239-4495
Fax: (212)239-2561

Homan, David, Exec. Dir.
America-Israel Cultural Foundation,
Inc. [9199]
1140 Broadway, Ste. No. 304
New York, NY 10001
Ph: (212)557-1600
Fax: (212)557-1611

Homan-Sandoval, Elizabeth, MD,
Exec. Dir.
Latino Medical Student Association
[8326]
113 S Monroe St., 1st Fl.
Tallahassee, FL 32301
Ph: (904)999-4690

Homayun, Dr. Tahira, President
Organization for Advancement of
Afghan Women [10470]
PO Box 946
New York, NY 10024
Ph: (212)998-8994

Homer, Charles J., MD, Founder
National Initiative for Children's
Healthcare Quality [14206]
30 Winter St., 6th Fl.
Boston, MA 02108
Ph: (617)391-2700
Fax: (617)391-2701

Honaker, Meranda, VP
United States Adult Cystic Fibrosis
Association [17149]
PO Box 1618
Gresham, OR 97030-0519
Ph: (248)349-4553

Honeycutt, Gina, Exec. Dir.
National Correctional Industries As-
sociation [11539]
800 N Charles St., Ste. 550B
Baltimore, MD 21201-5343
Ph: (410)230-3972
Fax: (410)230-3981

Honeycutt, Nancy, Exec. Dir.
American Student Dental Association
[7708]
211 E Chicago Ave., Ste. 700
Chicago, IL 60611-2663
Ph: (312)440-2795
Toll Free: 800-621-8099
Fax: (312)440-2820

Honeywell, Chrissy, Contact
Operation Paperback [10753]
PO Box 347
Dunstable, MA 01827
Ph: (641)715-3900

Hong, Dukjin, Rev., Sec. Gen.
National Association of Korean
Americans [17917]
3883 Plaza Dr.
Fairfax, VA 22030-2512
Ph: (703)267-2388
Fax: (703)267-2396

Honnigford, Laurie, Managing Dir.
International Association of Geosyn-
thetic Installers [869]
8357 N Rampart Range Rd., Unit
106
Roxborough, CO 80125
Ph: (720)353-4977
Fax: (612)235-6484

Honnigford, Laurie L., Exec. Dir.
Erosion Control Technology Council
[4685]
8357 N Rampart Range Rd., Unit
106, PMB 154
Roxborough, CO 80125-9365
Ph: (720)353-4977
Fax: (612)235-8454

Honor, Bill, Administrator
Abbott and Costello International
Fan Club [24007]
PO Box 5566
Fort Wayne, IN 46895-5566

Hood, David S., President
Association of Deans and Directors
of University Colleges &
Undergraduate Studies [7624]
PO Box 3948
Parker, CO 80134-1443
Ph: (720)496-4974
Toll Free: 844-705-3293

Hood, Linda, President
Association of Traumatic Stress
Specialists [11486]
5000 Old Buncombe Rd., Ste. 27-11
Greenville, SC 29617
Ph: (864)294-4337

Hood, Rita, Exec. Dir.
AGN North America [6]
2851 S Parker Rd., Ste. 850
Aurora, CO 80014
Ph: (303)743-7880
Fax: (303)743-7660

Hood, Rita J., Reg. Dir.
Accountants Global Network [1]
2851 S Parker Rd., Ste. 850
Aurora, CO 80014
Ph: (303)743-7880
Toll Free: 800-782-2272
Fax: (303)743-7660

Hood, Virginia L., Specialist
American College of Physicians
[15426]
190 N Independance Mall W
Philadelphia, PA 19106-1572
Ph: (215)351-2400
    (215)351-2600
Toll Free: 800-523-1546

Hood, Wendy, President
Comparative Nutrition Society
[16215]
c/o Wendy Hood, President-Elect
315 Rouse Life Sciences Bldg.
Auburn University
Auburn, AL 36849

Hooker, Deborah, Director
Public Media Foundation [18665]
Campus Box 7016
Office of Development
College of humanities and Social
Sciences
Raleigh, NC 27695-7016
Ph: (919)515-5973

Hooper, Bruce, Director
American Blind Golf [22872]
c/o Bruce Hooper, Co-Director
7410 Quail Run Dr.
San Antonio, TX 78209-3129
Ph: (210)822-6366

Hooper, Kenneth W., President
National Electrical Manufacturers
Representatives Association [1030]
28 Deer St., Ste. 302
Portsmouth, NH 03801
Ph: (914)524-8650
Toll Free: 800-446-3672
Fax: (914)524-8655

Hooper, Steven, President
Pacific Arts Association [8879]
c/o Christina Hellmich, Acting
Treasurer
Fine Arts Museums of San Francisco
Golden Gate Pk.
Hagiwara Garden Tea Dr.
San Francisco, CA 94118

Hooppaw, James, President
B-52 Stratofortress Association
[5861]

498 Carthage Dr.
Beavercreek, OH 45434-5865
Fax: (937)426-1289

Hootman, Steve, Exec. Dir., Curator
Rhododendron Species Foundation
[6154]
PO Box 3798
Federal Way, WA 98063
Ph: (253)838-4646
Fax: (253)838-4686

Hope, Amy, Exec. VP
Master Brewers Association of the
Americas [428]
3340 Pilot Knob Rd.
Saint Paul, MN 55121
Ph: (651)454-7250
Fax: (651)454-0766

Hopen, Thomas, Advisor
International Sand Collectors Society
[21677]
PO Box 1786
Lilburn, GA 30048-1786

Hopfenbeck, Jill, Dr., Director
American Whippet Club [21827]
c/o Kathy Rasmussen, Membership
Chairperson
11714 Harmony Ln.
Olathe, KS 66062
Ph: (913)526-5702

Hopkins, Ernest, Chairman
National Black Gay Men's Advocacy
Coalition [11898]
3636 Georgia Ave. NW
Washington, DC 20010-1646
Ph: (202)455-8441

Hopkins, George, CEO, Exec. Dir.
Youth Education in the Arts [9011]
601 W Hamilton St.
Allentown, PA 18101
Ph: (610)821-0345
Fax: (610)821-1451

Hopkins, Joe, President
Forest Landowners Association
[4200]
900 Circle 75 Pky., Ste. 205
Atlanta, GA 30339
Ph: (404)325-2954
Toll Free: 800-325-2954
Fax: (404)325-2955

Hopkins, Matthew M., President
Congenital Hyperinsulinism
International [16567]
PO Box 135
Glen Ridge, NJ 07028
Ph: (973)544-8372

Hopkins, Prof. Paul N., MD, Director,
Investigator
Make Early Diagnosis to Prevent
Early Death [14840]
School of Medicine, Rm. 1160
University of Utah
420 Chipeta Way
Salt Lake City, UT 84108
Toll Free: 888-244-2465

Hopkins, Polly, President
American Border Leicester Associa-
tion [4647]
c/o Polly Hopkins, President
Maybe Tomorrow Farm
494 Evans Rd.
Chepachet, RI 02814
Ph: (401)949-4619

Hopkins, Raymond E., President
National Council of State Agencies
for the Blind, Inc. [17732]
397 Azalea Ave.
Richmond, VA 23227
Ph: (804)371-3145
Fax: (804)371-3157

Hopkins, Ronald L., President
National Association of Fire
Investigators [1890]
857 Tallevast Rd.
Sarasota, FL 34243-3257
Ph: (941)359-2800
Toll Free: 877-506-NAFI
Fax: (941)351-5849

Hopkins, Sheila, President
National Council of Catholic Women
[19882]
200 N Glebe Rd., Ste. 725
Arlington, VA 22203
Ph: (703)224-0990
Toll Free: 800-506-9407
Fax: (703)224-0991

Hopkins, Wanda, Director
Germans From Russia Heritage
Society [19446]
1125 W Turnpike Ave.
Bismarck, ND 58501-8115
Ph: (701)223-6167
Fax: (701)223-4421

Hopper, Dr. David, Director
American Academy of Somnology
[17209]
PO Box 27077
Las Vegas, NV 89126-1077
Ph: (702)371-0947

Hopper, Regina, President, CEO
Intelligent Transportation Society of
America [3331]
1100 New Jersey Ave. SE, Ste. 850
Washington, DC 20003
Ph: (202)484-4847
Toll Free: 800-374-8472

Hoppert, Don, President
Coalition for Health Funding [16999]
c/o Cavarocchi Ruscio Dennis As-
sociates, L.L.C.
600 Maryland Ave. SW, Ste. 835W
Washington, DC 20024
Ph: (202)484-1100
Fax: (202)484-1244

Hopping, Ronald L., O.D., President
American Optometric Association
[16422]
243 N Lindbergh Blvd., 1st Fl.
Saint Louis, MO 63141-7881
Ph: (314)991-4100
   (314)983-4136
Toll Free: 800-365-2219
Fax: (314)991-4101

Hopton, Melissa, VP
National Public Records Research
Association [1804]
2501 Aerial Center Pky., Ste. 103
Morrisville, NC 27560
Ph: (919)459-2078
Fax: (919)459-2075

Hopwood, Chris, PhD, VP
North American Society for the
Study of Personality Disorders
[15801]
c/o Marianne Goodman, Treasurer
Icahn School of Medicine at Mount
Sinai
130 W Kingsbridge Rd.
Bronx, NY 10468

Horan, Bill, VP
North American Pet Health Insur-
ance Association [15105]
PO Box 37940
Raleigh, NC 27627
Toll Free: 877-962-7442

Horan, Bill, COO, President
Operation Blessing International
[20003]

977 Centerville Tpke.
Virginia Beach, VA 23463-1001
Ph: (757)226-3401
   (757)226-3440
Toll Free: 800-730-2537
Fax: (757)226-3657

Horan, Kathy, Director
Friends of the National Arboretum
[6140]
3501 New York Ave. NE
Washington, DC 20002
Ph: (202)544-8733
Fax: (202)544-5398

Horazdovsky, Mr. David J., CEO,
President
Evangelical Lutheran Good
Samaritan Society [13048]
4800 W 57th St.
Sioux Falls, SD 57108
Ph: (605)362-3100
Toll Free: 866-928-1635
Fax: (605)362-3240

Hord, Dr. Fred, Founder, Exec. Dir.
Association for Black Culture
Centers [9196]
c/o Dr. Fred Hord, Founder and
Executive Director
312 Altgeld Hall
Northern Illinois University
DeKalb, IL 60115
Ph: (815)753-5275

Horell, Harold (Bud), President
Religious Education Association: An
Association of Professors,
Practitioners, and Researchers in
Religious Education [20089]
Yale Divinity School
409 Prospect St.
New Haven, CT 06511
Ph: (765)225-8836
Fax: (203)432-5356

Hork, Dana, President, Founder
Change for Change [12467]
PO Box 230426
New York, NY 10023
Ph: (212)918-9303
Fax: (212)918-9220

Horn, Deborah Bade, DO, President
Obesity Medicine Association
[16262]
101 University Blvd., Ste. 330
Denver, CO 80206
Ph: (303)770-2526
Fax: (303)779-4834

Horn, Ms. Esther, Mgr.
Computer Assisted Language
Instruction Consortium [8025]
Texas State University
214 Centennial Hall
San Marcos, TX 78666
Ph: (512)245-1417
Fax: (512)245-9089

Horn, Jeffrey A., CEO, President
BOMI International Independent
Institute for Property and Facility
Management Education [2851]
1 Park Pl., Ste. 475
Annapolis, MD 21401-3479
Ph: (410)974-1410
Toll Free: 800-235-2664
Fax: (410)974-0544

Horn, Judy, Contact
The Barbara Pym Society [9093]
c/o Judy Horn
4 Summit Dr., Apt. 005
Reading, MA 01867-4050

Hornak, David, Exec. Dir.
National Association for Year-Round
Education [7785]

PO Box 711386
San Diego, CA 92171-1386

Hornbeck, Mary, President
Association for Early Learning Lead-
ers [10803]
8000 Center Park Dr., Ste. 170
Austin, TX 78754
Toll Free: 800-537-1118

Hornberger, Jacob G., President,
Founder
Future of Freedom Foundation
[18025]
11350 Random Hills Rd., Ste. 800
Fairfax, VA 22030
Ph: (703)934-6101
Fax: (703)352-8678

Hornung, Susan, Exec. Dir.
Association of Specialized and
Cooperative Library Agencies
[9691]
50 E Huron St.
Chicago, IL 60611-2729
Ph: (312)280-4395

Hornung, Susan, Exec. Dir.
Reference and User Services As-
sociation of the American Library
Association [9724]
50 E Huron St.
Chicago, IL 60611
Ph: (312)280-4395
Toll Free: 800-545-2433
Fax: (312)280-5273

Horobin, Lynn, Administrator
Accellera Systems Initiative [6412]
8698 Elk Grove Blvd., Ste. 1, No.
114
Elk Grove, CA 95624
Ph: (916)670-1056

Horowitz, Earl R., DPM, President
American Board of Multiple Special-
ties in Podiatry [16778]
555 8th Ave., Ste. 1902
New York, NY 10018
Ph: (646)779-8438
Toll Free: 888-852-1442
Fax: (646)786-4488

Horowitz, Prof. Gary, President
International Society on General
Relativity and Gravitation [6703]
PO Box 3388
Livermore, CA 94551-3388
Ph: (805)893-2742
   (925)371-8979

Horowitz, Jeff, Founder, Partner
Avoided Deforestation Partners
[4196]
c/o Jeff Horowitz, Founding Partner
Avoided Deforestation Partners
134 The Uplands
Berkeley, CA 94705

Horowitz, Jeffrey, Exec. Dir.,
Founder
Urbanists International [5981]
134 The Uplands
Berkeley, CA 94705
Ph: (510)547-5500
Fax: (510)654-5807

Horowitz, Roger, Secretary,
Treasurer
Business History Conference [9468]
c/o Hagley Museum and Library
PO Box 3630
Wilmington, DE 19807-0630
Ph: (302)658-2400
Fax: (302)655-3188

Horowitz, Sara, Founder, Exec. Dir.
Freelancers Union [23421]
20 Jay St., Ste. 700

Brooklyn, NY 11201
Toll Free: 800-856-9981

Horras, Jud, President, CEO
North-American Interfraternity
   Conference [23763]
3901 W 86th St., Ste. 390
Indianapolis, IN 46268
Ph: (317)872-1112
Fax: (317)872-1134

Horras, Judson A., CAE, Admin.
   Sec.
Beta Theta Pi [23891]
5134 Bonham Rd.
Oxford, OH 45056
Toll Free: 800-800-2382
Fax: (513)523-2381

Horsak, Cathy, Director
Alpha-1 Kids [14805]
PO Box 132
Coltons Point, MD 20626
Ph: (410)243-4499
Toll Free: 877-346-3212

Horsley, Victor, Dr., President
Academy of Ambulatory Foot and
   Ankle Surgery [16773]
3707 S Grand Blvd., Ste. A
Spokane, WA 99203
Ph: (509)624-1452
Toll Free: 800-433-4892
Fax: (509)624-1128

Horst, Irene B., Exec. Dir.
Foundation for International
   Cooperation [8072]
1237 S Western Ave.
Park Ridge, IL 60068

Horsting, John, President
American Pencil Collectors Society
   [21613]
c/o Aaron Bartholmey, Secretary-
   Treasurer
18 N Maple St., Apt 4
Colfax, IA 50054

Horton, Juana, President
International Medical Interpreters
   Association [3314]
c/o William Colangeli
33 Bedford St., Ste. 9
Lexington, MA 02420
Ph: (617)636-1798
Fax: (866)406-4642

Horton, Lemeul, President
National African-American RV'ers
   Association [22430]
614 Chipley Ave.
Charlotte, NC 28205
Ph: (704)333-3070
Fax: (704)333-3071

Horton, Mackie, Contact
CEO Netweavers [914]
3535 Peachtree Rd. NE, Ste. 520-
   231
Atlanta, GA 30326
Ph: (773)914-1735

Horton, RCS, RCIS, FASE, Ken,
   President
Cardiovascular Credentialing
   International [14106]
1500 Sunday Dr., Ste. 102
Raleigh, NC 27607
Toll Free: 800-326-0268
Fax: (919)787-4916

Horton, Renee, President
National Society of Black Physicists
   [7028]
3303 Wilson Blvd., Ste. 700
Arlington, VA 22201
Ph: (703)617-4176
Fax: (703)536-4203

Horton-Deutsch, Sara, Mem.
International Society of Psychiatric-
   Mental Health Nurses [16140]
2424 American Ln.
Madison, WI 53704-3102
Ph: (608)443-2463
Fax: (608)443-2478

Horvath, Michael J, President
Slovak Catholic Sokol [19649]
205 Madison St.
Passaic, NJ 07055
Toll Free: 800-886-7656
Fax: (973)779-8245

Horvath, Peter W., President
Quality Chekd Dairies [978]
901 Warrenville Rd., Ste. 405
Lisle, IL 60532
Toll Free: 800-222-6455
Fax: (630)717-1126

Horvath, Thomas, PhD, President
Alcohol and Drug Abuse Self-Help
   Network [17304]
7304 Mentor Ave., Ste. F
Mentor, OH 44060
Ph: (440)951-5357
Toll Free: 866-951-5357
Fax: (440)951-5358

Horwitz, Alexander E., MD, Exec.
   Ofc.
American Board of Disability
   Analysts [17077]
Belle Mead Office Pk.
4525 Harding Rd., 2nd Fl.
Nashville, TN 37205

Horwitz, Joshua, Exec. Dir.
Educational Fund to Stop Gun
   Violence [18251]
805 15th St. NW, Ste. 700
Washington, DC 20005
Ph: (202)408-7560

Hosken, Fran P., Editor
Women's International Network
   [18239]
187 Grant St.
Lexington, MA 02420-2126
Ph: (781)862-9431

Hosking, Rachel, VP
United States Neapolitan Mastiff
   Club [21984]
c/o Mike McDonald, Treasurer
40 Sam Carroll Rd.
Lecompte, LA 71364

Hoskins, Brent, Exec. Dir.
Business Technology Association
   [2442]
12411 Wornall Rd., Ste. 200
Kansas City, MO 64145
Ph: (816)941-3100
Toll Free: 800-325-7219
Fax: (816)941-4843

Hoskins, Harvey, President
National Association of Nonprofit Ac-
   countants and Consultants [48]
1801 West End Ave., Ste. 800
Nashville, TN 37203
Ph: (615)373-9880
Toll Free: 800-231-2524

Hoskins, Kathy, Exec. Dir.
Association of Investment Manage-
   ment Sales Executives [2020]
12100 Sunset Hills Rd., Ste. 130
Reston, VA 20190
Ph: (703)234-4098
Fax: (703)435-4390

Hoskins, Linda, Exec. Dir.
American Pie Council [368]
PO Box 368

Lake Forest, IL 60045
Ph: (847)371-0170
Fax: (847)371-0199

Hosni, Yasser, President
International Association for the
   Management of Technology [7274]
248294 College of Engineering
University of Miami
Coral Gables, FL 33124-0623
Ph: (305)284-2344
Fax: (305)284-4040

Hosten, Melissa, President
Women and Mathematics Education
   [8287]
c/o Lorraine Howard, Treasurer
PO Box 88
Wynnewood, PA 19096

Hostetter, Carl F., Editor
Elvish Linguistic Fellowship [9740]
2509 Ambling Cir.
Crofton, MD 21114

Hotaling, Brock, BSc, Exec. Dir.
Alfred Adler Institute of New York
   [16854]
372 Central Pk. W
New York, NY 10025
Ph: (212)254-1048

Hotelling, Barbara, Co-Ch.
Coalition for Improving Maternity
   Services [16281]
PO Box 33590
Raleigh, NC 27636-3590
Toll Free: 866-424-3635

Hoter-Ishay, Arnon, President
Israel Humanitarian Foundation -
   New York [12209]
2 W 46th St., Ste. 1500
New York, NY 10036

Hotop, Arthur R., Comm. Chm.
VII Corps Desert Storm Veterans
   Association [21155]
2425 Wilson Blvd.
Arlington, VA 22201
Ph: (703)562-4163

Hotz, Jean, President
Cystinosis Foundation [15820]
58 Miramonte Dr.
Moraga, CA 94556
Ph: (925)631-1588
Toll Free: 888-631-1588

Hotz, Michael, President
First Zen Institute of America
   [19777]
113 E 30th St.
New York, NY 10016
Ph: (212)686-2520

Hou, Master FaXiang, Founder,
   Director
QiGong Research Society [13650]
3802 Church Rd.
Mount Laurel, NJ 08054-1106
Ph: (856)234-3056

Houchin, Pat, Coord., Founder
Stickler Involved People [14859]
15 Angelina Dr.
Augusta, KS 67010-2207
Ph: (316)259-5194

Houck, Amy, Director, Founder
World Wins International [11464]
5812 W Cavendale Dr.
Eagle, ID 83616
Ph: (208)585-7370

Houck, Anita, Secretary, Treasurer
Society for the Study of Christian
   Spirituality [20007]

The Johns Hopkins University Press
PO Box 19966
Baltimore, MD 21211-0966
Toll Free: 800-548-1784
Fax: (410)516-3866

Hough, Richard H., Exec. VP
American Purchasing Society [2816]
8 E Galena Blvd., Ste. 203
Aurora, IL 60506
Ph: (630)859-0250
Fax: (630)859-0270

Houghton, David, Legal Counsel
National Association of Pipe Fabrica-
   tors [2606]
2061 Brae Trl.
Birmingham, AL 35242
Ph: (205)706-0886

Houghton, Helen, Secretary
Academy of American Poets [10148]
75 Maiden Ln., Ste. 901
New York, NY 10038
Ph: (212)274-0343
Fax: (212)274-9427

Houghton, Melissa, Exec. Dir.
Women in Film and Video [1213]
4000 Albemarle St. NW, Ste. 305
Washington, DC 20016
Ph: (202)429-9438
Fax: (202)429-9440

Houghton, Peter, PhD, President
Cancer Molecular Therapeutics
   Research Association [13926]
1670 University Blvd.
Birmingham, AL 35294
Ph: (205)934-4569
Fax: (205)934-8240

Houk, Lane, Founder, Exec. Dir.
Herocare [13010]
235 W Brandon Blvd., Ste. 241
Brandon, FL 33511
Toll Free: 877-437-6411
Fax: (877)437-6411

Houlette, Judy Kasey, Exec. Dir.
Friend for Life Cancer Support
   Network [13974]
4003 Kresge Way, Ste. 100
Louisville, KY 40207
Ph: (502)893-0643
Toll Free: 866-374-3634
Fax: (502)896-3010

Hourihan, Jeremy, President
Keuka College Alumni Association
   [19331]
Office of Alumni and Family Relations
141 Central Ave., Ball 122
Keuka Park, NY 14478
Ph: (315)279-5238
   (315)279-5338

Housberg, Steven, Bd. Member
American Medical Billing Association
   [15575]
2465 E Main St.
Davis, OK 73030
Ph: (580)369-2700
Fax: (580)369-2703

House, Brian, Founder
Hope for Haiti [11377]
PO Box 496
Westminster, MD 21158-0496
Ph: (410)635-4348

House, Paul R., Mem.
Evangelical Theological Society
   [20120]
2825 Lexington Rd.
Louisville, KY 40280-0001
Ph: (502)897-4388
Fax: (502)897-4386

House, Scott, Operating Ofc.
Cave Research Foundation [7227]
c/o Bob Hoke, Treasurer
6304 Kaybro St.
Laurel, MD 20707
Ph: (301)725-5877

House, Tiffany, President
Acid Maltase Deficiency Association
[13499]
PO Box 700248
San Antonio, TX 78270-0248
Ph: (210)494-6144
Fax: (210)490-7161

House, Tom, Founder
National Pitching Association
[22563]
Vanguard University
55 Fair Dr.
Costa Mesa, CA 92626

Houser, Susan, Officer
National Council of Teachers of
English [7869]
1111 W Kenyon Rd.
Urbana, IL 61801-1010
Ph: (217)328-3870
Toll Free: 877-369-6283
Fax: (217)328-9645

Houseweart, Connie, President
Sixth Marine Division Association
[21201]
704 Cooper Ct.
Arlington, TX 76011-5550

Housley, Ryan, Exec. Dir.
HeroBox [10744]
237 Senoia Rd.
Peachtree City, GA 30269
Toll Free: 866-999-4376

Houston, Aaron, Exec. Dir.
Students for Sensible Drug Policy
[19158]
1317 F St. NW, Ste. 501
Washington, DC 20004
Ph: (202)393-5280

Houston, Betsy, Exec. Dir.
Federation of Materials Societies
[6813]
910 17th St. NW, Ste. 800
Washington, DC 20006-2606
Ph: (301)325-2494

Houston, Carol, Exec. Dir.
American Osteopathic College of
Radiology [17042]
119 E 2nd St.
Milan, MO 63556-1331
Ph: (660)265-4011
Fax: (660)265-3494

Houston, Marsha, Contact
Teacup Dogs Agility Association
[21968]
14543 State Route 676
Waterford, OH 45786
Ph: (740)749-3597

Houten, Becky, Secretary
Otterhound Club of America [21938]
c/o Becky Van Houten, Secretary
3846 Juddville Rd.
Fish Creek, WI 54212
Ph: (570)739-7074

Hoven, Pat, Chairperson
World Savvy [8773]
917 Irving St., No. 4
San Francisco, CA 94122
Ph: (415)292-7421
Fax: (888)452-0993

Hovis, Joanne, President
National Association of Telecommunications Officers and Advisors
[3234]

3213 Duke St., Ste. 695
Alexandria, VA 22314
Ph: (703)519-8035
Fax: (703)997-7080

Howard, Cassandra, Col., VP
Alliance of Air National Guard Flight
Surgeons [17357]
3653 Larchmont Dr.
Ann Arbor, MI 48105

Howard, Dean, President
Metal Powder Producers Association
[2356]
Metal Powder Institute Federation
105 College Rd. E
Princeton, NJ 08540-6692
Ph: (609)452-7700
Fax: (609)987-8523

Howard, Deborah, President, Chmn.
of the Bd.
Companion Animal Protection
Society [12454]
759 CJC Highway No. 332
Cohasset, MA 02025
Ph: (339)309-0272

Howard, Glen, President
American Committee for Peace in
the Caucasus [18770]
1301 Connecticut Ave. NW, 6th Fl.
Washington, DC 20036
Ph: (202)296-5101

Howard, Joe, Mgr.
National Accounting and Finance
Council [43]
c/o Joe Howard, Manager
950 N Glebe Rd., Ste. 210
Arlington, VA 22203-4181
Ph: (703)838-1763
Fax: (703)838-1701

Howard, John, President
Antique and Classic Boat Society
[22598]
422 James St.
Clayton, NY 13624
Ph: (315)686-2628
Fax: (315)686-2680

Howard, Linda, Treasurer
National Wellness Institute [16802]
1300 College Ct.
Stevens Point, WI 54481-0827
Ph: (715)342-2969
Fax: (715)342-2979

Howard, Matt, Dir. of Comm.
Iraq Veterans Against the War
[19236]
PO Box 3565
New York, NY 10008-3565
Ph: (646)723-0989
Fax: (646)723-0996

Howard, Mike, President
International Security Management
Association [3062]
PO Box 623
Buffalo, IA 52728-0623
Ph: (563)381-4008
Fax: (563)381-4283

Howard, Phil, President
Agriculture, Food & Human Values
Society [3542]
480 Wilson Rd., Rm 316
East Lansing, MI 48824

Howard, Randye, Director
Famous Fone Friends [11229]
9101 Sawyer St.
Los Angeles, CA 90035

Howard, Sara, President
International Clinical Phonetics and
Linguistics Association [9741]

Dept. of Communicative Disorders
University of Louisiana at Lafayette
Lafayette, LA 70504-3170

Howard, Susan, Chairperson, Coord.
Waldorf Early Childhood Association
of North America [8451]
285 Hungry Hollow Rd.
Spring Valley, NY 10977
Ph: (845)352-1690
   (413)549-5930
Fax: (845)352-1695

Howard-Weigel, Maggie, Secretary,
Treasurer
Cinnamon Rabbit Breeders Associa-
tion [4596]
N59 W22476 Silver Spring Dr.
W248 N7411 Beverly Ln.
Sussex, WI 53089
Ph: (765)463-4616
   (262)894-3647

Howden, Tim, Treasurer
Grays Harbor Historical Seaport
Authority [8265]
500 N Custer St.
Aberdeen, WA 98520
Ph: (360)532-8611
Toll Free: 800-200-5239
Fax: (360)533-9384

Howe, Anne, Exec. Dir.
Next Generation Nepal [11098]
527 3rd Ave., Ste. 196
New York, NY 10016
Ph: (646)820-0696

Howe, Phil, President
Lionel Operating Train Society
[22186]
6376 W Fork Rd.
Cincinnati, OH 45247-5704
Ph: (513)598-8240
Fax: (866)286-6416

Howell, Andrew, VP of Operations
Multicultural Foodservice and
Hospitality Alliance [1392]
1144 Narragansett Blvd.
Providence, RI 02905
Ph: (401)461-6342
Fax: (401)461-9004

Howell, Cynthia D., Exec. Dir.
Alpha Kappa Alpha [23869]
5656 S Stony Island Ave.
Chicago, IL 60637
Ph: (773)684-1282

Howell, Darliene, Chmn. of the Bd.
National Association to Advance Fat
Acceptance [12397]
PO Box 4662
Foster City, CA 94404-0662
Ph: (916)558-6880

Howell, Fran, Contact
DES Action USA [13960]
PO Box 7296
Jupiter, FL 33468-7296
Toll Free: 800-337-9288

Howell, Joe M., DVM, President
Western Veterinary Conference
[17675]
2425 E Oquendo Rd.
Las Vegas, NV 89120
Ph: (702)739-6698
Toll Free: 866-800-7326
Fax: (702)739-6420

Howell, Leann, Exec. Dir., President
American Lead Poisoning Help As-
sociation [17494]
PO Box 403
Riverside, NJ 08075

Howell, Stewart, President
Dutch Bantam Society [4565]
c/o Jerrod Alcaida, Secretary

10814 131st St. NW
Gig Harbor, WA 98329
Ph: (310)991-5799

Howery, Larry D., 1st VP
Society for Range Management
[4620]
6901 S Pierce St., Ste. 225
Littleton, CO 80128
Ph: (303)986-3309
Fax: (303)986-3892

Howes, Rupert, CEO
Marine Stewardship Council [4638]
2110 N Pacific St., Ste. 102
Seattle, WA 98103
Ph: (206)691-0188
Fax: (206)691-0190

Howick, Andrew, Chairman
Amigos de las Americas [13281]
5618 Star Ln.
Houston, TX 77057
Ph: (713)782-5290
Toll Free: 800-231-7796

Howland, Jim, Director
Gravely Tractor Club of America
[22454]
PO Box 194
Avondale, PA 19311

Howland, Susan, Founder
Sky Help, Inc. [17530]
218 Evergreen Dr.
Moorestown, NJ 08057
Toll Free: 877-SKY-HELP

Howse, Dr. Jennifer L., President
March of Dimes Foundation [13831]
1275 Mamaroneck Ave.
White Plains, NY 10605
Ph: (914)997-4488

Howse, Jennifer L., PhD, Comm.
Chm.
Partnership for Prevention [14959]
1015 18th St. NW, Ste. 300
Washington, DC 20036
Ph: (202)833-0009
Fax: (202)833-0113

Hoxie, Lance O., Contact
American Board of Oral and Maxillo-
facial Surgery [16442]
625 N Michigan Ave., Ste. 1820
Chicago, IL 60611-3177
Ph: (312)642-0070

Hoyer, Dr. Hans J., Sec. Gen.
International Federation of Engineer-
ing Education Societies [7858]
College of Engineering
Marquette University
Milwaukee, WI 53201-1881
Ph: (414)288-0736
Fax: (414)288-1516

Hoying, Cheryl, RN, Treasurer
The Nursing Organizations Alliance
[16172]
201 E Main St., Ste. 1405
Lexington, KY 40507
Ph: (859)514-9157
Fax: (859)514-9166

Hoynacki, Jan, Exec. Dir.
United States Pilots Association
[160]
1652 Indian Point Rd.
Branson, MO 65616
Ph: (417)338-2225

Hoyt, David B., MD, Exec. Dir.
American College of Surgeons
[17367]
633 N St. Clair St.
Chicago, IL 60611-3211
Ph: (312)202-5000
Toll Free: 800-621-4111
Fax: (312)202-5001

Hoyt, James, President, CEO
Esperança [14999]
1911 W Earll Dr.
Phoenix, AZ 85015-6041
Ph: (602)252-7772
Toll Free: 888-701-5150
Fax: (602)340-9197

Hoyt, Jane Hansen, President, CEO
Aglow International [20639]
123 2nd Ave., Ste. 100
Edmonds, WA 98020-8457
Ph: (425)775-7282
Fax: (425)778-9615

Hoyt, Jason, President, COO
Beta Upsilon Chi [23709]
12650 N Beach St., Ste. 114, No. 305
Fort Worth, TX 76244
Toll Free: 877-250-4512

Hoyt, Lynn, President
Natural Fibers Group [21301]
c/o Lynn Hoyt, President
549 Bluebird Trl.
Blounts Creek, NC 27814

Hribek, Donald, Chmn. of the Bd.
Path2Parenthood [14762]
315 Madison Ave., Ste. 901
New York, NY 10017
Toll Free: 888-917-3777

Hron, Ihor, Cmdr.
Ukrainian American Veterans [21142]
3535 Fox Run Dr.
Allentown, PA 18103

Hroza, Robbie, VP of Operations
Options for Animals International [17658]
PO Box 3682
Cartersville, GA 30120
Ph: (309)658-2920

Hrycelak, George, MD, Exec. Dir.
Ukrainian Medical Association of
    North America [15748]
2247 W Chicago Ave.
Chicago, IL 60622-8957
Ph: (773)278-6262
Fax: (773)278-6962

Hsiao, Teresa, Founder
Smart Women Securities [7568]
1530 W Boynton Beach Blvd., Ste. 3834
Boynton Beach, FL 33436

Hsu, Chao-Hsiung, President
North American Taiwanese Medical
    Association [15130]
c/o Chao-Hsiung Hsu, M.D.,
    President
790 E Latham Ave.
Hemet, CA 92543
Ph: (951)658-3254
Fax: (951)766-7236

Hsu, Dr. James, Div. Dir.
Burmese Medical Association of
    North America [15720]
PO Box 20052
Baltimore, MD 21284

Hsu, Madeline Y, Rep.
Association for Asian American Stud-
    ies [7521]
PO Box 19966
Baltimore, MD 21211-0966
Ph: (800)548-1784
Fax: (410)516-3866

Hu, Jianhua, Exec. Sec.
International Association of Chinese
    Linguistics [8182]

Dept. of East Asian Studies
University of Arizona
1512 1st St.
Tucson, AZ 85721-0105
Fax: (520)621-1149

Hua, Hsuan, Founder
Dharma Realm Buddhist Association [19776]
2001 Talmage Rd.
Ukiah, CA 95482
Ph: (707)462-0939
Fax: (707)462-0949

Hua, Jingdong, VP
International Finance Corporation [18152]
2121 Pennsylvania Ave. NW
Washington, DC 20433
Ph: (202)473-1000
    (202)473-3800
Fax: (202)974-4384

Huang, Chien Liang, Chairman
The World Kuo Shu Federation [23029]
PO Box 927
Reisterstown, MD 21136
Ph: (443)394-9222
Fax: (443)394-9202

Huang, Margaret, Exec. Dir.
Amnesty International of the USA [18373]
5 Penn Plz.
New York, NY 10001
Ph: (212)807-8400
Fax: (212)627-1451

Huang, Dr. Ngan, Chairperson
International Institute for Scientific
    and Academic Collaboration [12167]
15 Honiss Pl., Ste. 1
Newark, NJ 07104
Ph: (973)699-2550

Huang, Yonggang, VP
Association of Chinese Professors of
    Social Sciences in the United
    States [7162]
c/o Yunqiu Zhang, Treasurer
210 Heritage Creek Way
Greensboro, NC 27405

Hubacher, Christine, Exec. Dir.
Swiss Benevolent Society of New
    York [19667]
500 5th Ave., Rm. 1800
New York, NY 10110
Ph: (212)246-0655
Fax: (212)246-1366

Hubbard, Bill, Exec. Sec.
Association of Natural Resource
    Extension Professionals [4489]
c/o Bill Hubbard, Executive
    Secretary
4-402 Forest Resources Bldg.
Warnell School of Forestry & Natural
    Resources
University of Georgia
Athens, GA 30602-2152
Ph: (706)542-7813
Fax: (706)542-3342

Hubbard, Darrin, Exec. Dir.
American Association of Medical
    Society Executives [15704]
1000 Westgate Dr., Ste. 252
Saint Paul, MN 55114
Ph: (651)288-3432
Fax: (651)290-2266

Hubbard, Bishop Howard, VP
Interfaith Worker Justice [20214]
1020 W Bryn Mawr Ave.
Chicago, IL 60660
Ph: (773)728-8400

Hubbart, Larry, Founder
Canadian Poolplayers Association [22585]
1000 Lake St. Louis Blvd., Ste. 325
Lake Saint Louis, MO 63367
Ph: (636)625-8611
Fax: (636)625-2975

Hubbell, Samantha, CEO
Disorders of Chromosome 16
    Foundation [14820]
PO Box 230448
Encinitas, CA 92023-0448

Hubbs, Heather, Director
New Art Dealers Alliance [8877]
55-59 Chrystie St., Ste. 410
New York, NY 10002
Ph: (212)594-0883
Fax: (212)594-0884

Huber, John, Exec. Dir.
Aplastic Anemia and MDS
    International Foundation [15223]
100 Park Ave., Ste. 108
Rockville, MD 20850
Ph: (301)279-7202
Toll Free: 800-747-2820
Fax: (301)279-7205

Huber, John J., President
National Oilheat Research Alliance [1118]
600 Cameron St., Ste. 206
Alexandria, VA 22314
Ph: (703)340-1660
Fax: (703)340-1642

Huber, Laurent, Exec. Dir.
Action on Smoking and Health [17224]
701 4th St. NW
Washington, DC 20001
Ph: (202)659-4310
Fax: (202)289-7166

Huber, Stephen, Project Mgr.
Water Harvest International [13361]
3131 W 7th St., Ste. 400
Fort Worth, TX 76107
Ph: (817)632-5200

Huber, Valerie, President, CEO
National Abstinence Education As-
    sociation [8564]
1701 Pennsylvania Ave. NW, Ste. 300
Washington, DC 20006
Ph: (202)248-5420
Toll Free: 866-935-4850

Huberman, Mark A., Secretary,
    Treasurer
International Association of Hygienic
    Physicians [15852]
c/o Mark A. Huberman, Secretary/
    Treasurer
4620 Euclid Blvd.
Youngstown, OH 44512
Ph: (330)788-5711
Fax: (330)788-0093

Hubert, Jaimee, President
American Mini Pig Association [4708]
PO Box 735
Aurora, MO 65605

Hucker, Douglas, CEO
American Gem Trade Association [2040]
3030 LBJ Fwy., Ste. 840
Dallas, TX 75234
Ph: (214)742-4367
Toll Free: 800-972-1162
Fax: (214)742-7334

Hudasek, Ms. Kristin, Coord.
International Biopharmaceutical As-
    sociation [16665]

PMB 143
11521 N FM 620, No. 250
Austin, TX 78726
Ph: (713)366-8062
Fax: (713)366-8062

Huddleston, Lew, VP
North American Wildlife Enforcement
    Officers Association [4859]
c/o Steve Beltran, Treasurer
PO Box 7
Leaf River, IL 61047
Ph: (815)243-7777
    (250)442-5643
Fax: (250)442-4312

Huddleston, West, CEO
National Association of Drug Court
    Professionals [13164]
1029 N Royal St., Ste. 201
Alexandria, VA 22314
Ph: (703)575-9400

Hudgins, Tamara, Exec. Dir.
Girlstart [7946]
1400 W Anderson Ln.
Austin, TX 78757
Ph: (512)916-4775
Toll Free: 888-852-6481

Hudis, Clifford, MD, President
American Society of Clinical Oncol-
    ogy [16335]
2318 Mill Rd., Ste. 800
Alexandria, VA 22314
Ph: (571)483-1300
Toll Free: 888-282-2552

Hudlin, Warrington, Founder
Black Filmmaker Foundation [9299]
131 Varick St., Ste. 937
New York, NY 10013
Ph: (212)253-1690

Hudnall, Gary, President
Aeronautical Repair Station Associa-
    tion [118]
121 N Henry St.
Alexandria, VA 22314-2903
Ph: (703)739-9543
Fax: (703)299-0254

Hudnut-Beumler, James, VP
Association of Theological Schools [8704]
10 Summit Park Dr.
Pittsburgh, PA 15275-1110
Ph: (412)788-6505
Fax: (412)788-6510

Hudson, Bobbi, Exec. Dir.
Pacific Shellfish Institute [3646]
120 State Ave. NE, No. 1056
Olympia, WA 98501
Ph: (360)754-2741
Fax: (360)754-2246

Hudson, Gary C., President, Trustee
Space Studies Institute [5875]
16922 Airport Blvd., No. 24
Mojave, CA 93501
Ph: (661)750-2774

Hudson, Julie, President
Gesneriad Hybridizers Association [22096]
1122 E Pike St., PMB 637
Seattle, WA 98122-3916

Hudson Jr., Eugene, Secretary,
    Treasurer
American Federation of Government
    Employees [23424]
80 F St. NW
Washington, DC 20001
Ph: (202)737-8700

Hudson, Lisa, Founder
Boarding for Breast Cancer Founda-
    tion [13906]

1650 Mateo St.
Los Angeles, CA 90021
Ph: (323)467-2663

Hudson, Marianne, Exec. Dir.
Angel Capital Association [2017]
10977 Granada Ln., Ste. 103
Overland Park, KS 66211
Ph: (913)894-4700

Hudson, Mark, Coord.
Progressive Librarians Guild [9722]
St. Catherine University
2004 Randolph Ave., No. 4125
Saint Paul, MN 55105

Hudson, Matt, President
Geoscience Information Society
[6689]
Emily Wild, President
US Geological Survey, Denver
Library
Denver Federal Ctr.
Denver, CO 80225-0046
Ph: (303)236-1003
(303)357-1020

Hudson, Patricia A., President
Melos Institute [256]
1071 Yosemite Dr.
Pacifica, CA 94044
Ph: (650)355-4094
Fax: (650)359-3611

Hudson, Rick, President
Turtle Survival Alliance [4897]
1989 Colonial Pky.
Fort Worth, TX 76110
Ph: (817)759-7262
Fax: (817)759-7501

Hudson, Teresa, President, Chmn. of
the Bd.
National Christian Forensics and
Communications Association
[7998]
200 Broad St., 3rd Fl., Ste. B
Gadsden, AL 35901
Ph: (205)500-0081

Hudson, Tim, CEO
Phi Kappa Tau [23913]
5221 Morning Sun Rd.
Oxford, OH 45056
Ph: (513)523-4193
Toll Free: 800-PKT-1906
Fax: (513)523-9325

Hudsont, Paul, President
Flyersrights.org [19197]
4411 Bee Ridge Rd., No. 274
Sarasota, FL 34233-2514
Toll Free: 800-662-1859

Huebel, Keith, President
National Society of Tax Profession-
als [54]
11700 NE 95th St., Ste. No. 100
Vancouver, WA 98682
Ph: (360)695-8309
Toll Free: 800-367-8130
Fax: (360)695-7115

Huezo, Jeannette, Exec. Dir.
United for a Fair Economy [18169]
62 Summer St.
Boston, MA 02110
Ph: (617)423-2148

Huff, Charles, Contact
International Association of Milk
Control Agencies [5225]
c/o Charles Huff, Contact
28 SHS
Augusta, ME 04333
Ph: (518)457-5731

Huff, Jason, President
Pug Dog Club of America [21949]

c/o Joella Collier-Flory, Membership
Chairperson
3920 Raintree Dr.
Flower Mound, TX 75022-6323

Huff, Jim, President
Health and Science Communications
Association [14295]
PO Box 31323
Omaha, NE 68132
Ph: (402)915-5373

Huff, John M., President
National Association of Insurance
Commissioners [5316]
1100 Walnut St., Ste. 1500
Kansas City, MO 64106-2277
Ph: (816)842-3600
Fax: (816)783-8175

Huff, Mickey, Director
Project Censored [17838]
PO Box 750940
Petaluma, CA 94975
Ph: (707)874-2695

Huff, Samuel, Exec. Dir., President
National Rosacea Society [14507]
196 James St.
Barrington, IL 60010
Toll Free: 888-662-5874

Huffaker, Bradley, Tech. Mgr.
Cooperative Association for Internet
Data Analysis [6765]
9500 Gilman Dr.
La Jolla, CA 92093
Ph: (858)534-5000

Huffhines, Craig, Exec. VP
American Quarter Horse Association
[4320]
1600 Quarter Horse Dr.
Amarillo, TX 79104
Ph: (806)376-4811

Huffhines, Craig, Exec. VP
American Quarter Horse Youth As-
sociation [4321]
1600 Quarter Horse Dr.
Amarillo, TX 79104
Ph: (806)376-4811
Fax: (806)349-6411

Huffman, Anne, President
National Cued Speech Association
[17245]
1300 Pennsylvania Ave. NW, Ste.
190-713
Washington, DC 20004
Toll Free: 800-459-3529

Huggins, Marvin A., Secretary
Lutheran Historical Conference
[20310]
c/o Richard O. Johnson, Treasurer
PO Box 235
Grass Valley, CA 95945
Ph: (530)273-9631

Hughes, Barbara Ann, President
National Association of Local Boards
of Health [17008]
563 Carter Ct., Ste. B
Kimberly, WI 54136
Ph: (920)560-5644
Fax: (920)882-3655

Hughes, Cheryl, VP
North American Celtic Trade As-
sociation [9149]
27 Addison Ave.
Rutherford, NJ 07070-2303
Ph: (201)842-9922
Fax: (201)804-9143

Hughes, Danna, Founder, President
Vietnam Veteran Wives [21154]
12 Trout Creek Rd.

Republic, WA 99166
Ph: (509)775-8893

Hughes, Donna Rice, CEO,
President
Enough Is Enough [18568]
746 Walker Rd., Ste. 116
Great Falls, VA 22066
Toll Free: 888-744-0004

Hughes, J. Trevor, CIPP, CEO,
President
International Association of Privacy
Professionals [1800]
75 Rochester Ave., Ste. 4
Portsmouth, NH 03801
Ph: (603)427-9200
(209)351-1500
Toll Free: 800-266-6501
Fax: (603)427-9249

Hughes, Joseph E.M., Chairman,
CEO
Shipowners Claims Bureau, Inc.
[1927]
1 Battery Park Plz., 31st Fl.
New York, NY 10004
Ph: (212)847-4500
Fax: (212)847-4599

Hughes, Julia, President
United States Fashion Industry As-
sociation [3275]
1140 Connecticut Ave., Ste. 950
Washington, DC 20036
Ph: (202)419-0444
Fax: (202)783-0727

Hughes, Kathryn, Program Mgr.
U.S. National Committee for the
International Union of Pure and
Applied Chemistry [6218]
Bldg. 4201, Ste. 260
79 TW Alexander Dr.
Research Triangle Park, NC 27709
Ph: (202)334-2807
Fax: (202)334-2231

Hughes, Lily, Director
Campaign to End the Death Penalty
[17822]
PO Box 25730
Chicago, IL 60625
Ph: (773)955-4841

Hughes, Patrick, President
Aldea Development [12797]
1485 S Getty St.
Muskegon, MI 49442

Hughes, Peter, President
Wheelchair Athletes Worldwide
[11645]
7615 N Soledad Ave.
Tucson, AZ 85741
Ph: (619)249-1885

Hughes, Robert, President
American Fisheries Society [6713]
425 Barlow Pl., Ste. 110
Bethesda, MD 20814
Ph: (301)897-8616
Fax: (301)897-8096

Hughes, Robert, Chairperson
National Association of Real Estate
Brokers [2874]
9831 Greenbelt Rd.
Lanham, MD 20706
Ph: (301)552-9340
Fax: (301)552-9216

Hughes, Ronald, Chairman
National Council on Crime and
Delinquency [11510]
1970 Broadway, Ste. 500
Oakland, CA 94612
Toll Free: 800-306-6223

Hughes, Steven R., Exec. Dir.
Oracle Applications Users Group
[6284]
Bldg. 5, Ste. 300
3525 Piedmont Rd. NE
Atlanta, GA 30305-1509
Ph: (404)240-0897
Fax: (404)240-0998

Hughes, Tom, Treasurer
Association of Family Practice Physi-
cian Assistants [15112]
77 Wollcott Ave.
Dartmouth, MA 02747
Ph: (774)206-6774
Fax: (508)998-6001

Hughes White, Karen, Exec. Dir.
Delta Delta Delta [23950]
2331 Brookhollow Plaza Dr.
Arlington, TX 76006
Ph: (817)633-8001
Fax: (817)652-0212

Hughes-Wert, Melinda, Founder,
President
Nature Abounds [4090]
PO Box 506
Dubois, PA 15801-0506
Ph: (814)765-1453
Fax: (855)629-7329

Hughey, Katherine, Assoc. Mgr.
American Board of Genetic Counsel-
ing [14872]
PO Box 14216
Lenexa, KS 66285
Ph: (913)895-4617
Fax: (913)895-4652

Hughlett, Janice, President
National Opossum Society [10673]
PO Box 21197
Catonsville, MD 21228

Hugo, Fr. Bill, Director
Capuchin-Franciscans [19807]
3407 S Archer Ave.
Chicago, IL 60608
Ph: (773)475-6206

Huhn, Wanda, President
National Kappa Kappa Iota [23731]
1875 E 15th St.
Tulsa, OK 74104-4610
Ph: (918)744-0389
Toll Free: 800-678-0389
Fax: (918)744-0578

Hui, James, President
Phi Kappa Upsilon Fraternity
[23740]
21000 W 9 Mile Rd.
Southfield, MI 48075

Huisman, Bill, Exec. Dir.
Aviation Development Council [129]
14107 20th Ave., Ste. 404
Whitestone, NY 11357
Ph: (718)746-0212
Fax: (718)746-1006

Huizar, Teresa, Exec. Dir.
National Children's Alliance [11090]
516 C St. NE
Washington, DC 20002
Ph: (202)548-0090

Hukill, Jim, Exec. Dir.
Lift Disability Network [11615]
PO Box 770607
Winter Garden, FL 34777
Ph: (407)228-8343
Fax: (407)403-6528

Hulbert, Steve, Dir. of Lib. Svcs.
Center for Process Studies [10083]
1325 N College Ave.

Claremont, CA 91711
Ph: (909)621-5330
Fax: (909)621-2760

Huling, Mike, Officer
American Society of Naval
Engineers [6904]
1452 Duke St.
Alexandria, VA 22314
Ph: (703)836-6727
Fax: (703)836-7491

Hulkow, Lynn, VP
Society of Stukely Westcott
Descendants of America [20930]
c/o Lyle Wescott, Editor
180 Pleasant Valley Dr.
Holly Springs, MS 38635
Ph: (847)304-1755

Hull, Don, President
Packards International Motor Car
Club [21473]
302 French St.
Santa Ana, CA 92701-4845
Ph: (714)541-8431
Fax: (714)836-4014

Hull, Jennifer, Mgr.
American Association for Pediatric
Ophthalmology and Strabismus
[16364]
655 Beach St.
San Francisco, CA 94109
Ph: (415)561-8505
Fax: (415)561-8531

Hull, S., Contact
National Starwind/Spindrift Class
Association [22654]
PO Box 21262
Columbus, OH 43221

Hulsey, Timothy L., President
Phi Kappa Phi [23791]
7576 Goodwood Blvd.
Baton Rouge, LA 70806
Ph: (225)388-4917
Toll Free: 800-804-9880
Fax: (225)388-4900

Hulsoor, Jean, Administrator
Association Global View [7545]
PO Box 3324
Chico, CA 95927-3324
Ph: (530)228-5886
    (530)892-9696

Hultman, Ms. Alberta E., CAE, CEO,
Exec. Dir.
USFN-America's Mortgage Banking
Attorneys [5053]
625 The City Dr., Ste. 310
Orange, CA 92868
Ph: (714)838-7167
Toll Free: 800-635-6128
Fax: (714)573-2650

Humbert, Laurel, Exec. Dir.
Association for the Behavioral Sci-
ences and Medical Education
[6031]
PO Box 368
Harrison City, PA 15636
Ph: (724)590-9187
Fax: (724)744-0146

Humble, Mike, President
Beaver Ambassador Club [22419]
c/o Iris Schmidt, Membership Director
3916 N Potsdam Ave.
Sioux Falls, SD 57104-7048
Ph: (541)953-3595

Humes, Kevin, Exec. Dir.
American Veterans Alliance [21108]
13899 Biscayne Blvd.

Miami, FL 33181
Ph: (305)200-7492

Humesky, Gr. Mast. Eugene A.,
PhD, Chairman, CEO, Founder
Universal Martial Arts Brotherhood
[23024]
2427 Buckingham Rd.
Ann Arbor, MI 48104-4913
Ph: (734)971-7040

Humphrey, Carol Sue, Admin. Sec.
American Journalism Historians As-
sociation [7978]
Arlington, TX
Ph: (662)325-0983
    (405)585-4158

Humphrey, J. Steven, Exec. Dir.
National Association of Watch and
Clock Collectors [22446]
514 Poplar St.
Columbia, PA 17512-2124
Ph: (717)684-8261
Fax: (717)684-0878

Humphrey, Scott, CEO
World Floor Covering Association
[2982]
2211 E Howell Ave.
Anaheim, CA 92806
Ph: (714)978-6440
Toll Free: 800-624-6880
Fax: (714)978-6066

Humphreys, Eve, MBA, CAE, Exec.
Dir.
Society for Healthcare Epidemiology
of America [14735]
1300 Wilson Blvd., Ste. 300
Arlington, VA 22209
Ph: (703)684-1006
Fax: (703)684-1009

Humphreys, Ian, Director
Network of Sacred Heart Schools
[8014]
821 Varnum St. NE
Washington, DC 20017
Ph: (202)636-9300
Fax: (202)636-9306

Humphreys, Margaret, MD,
President
American Association for the History
of Medicine [15259]
c/o Jodi Koste, Secretary
509 N 12th St.
Richmond, VA 23298
Ph: (804)828-9898
Fax: (804)828-6098

Humphris, Susan, Chairperson
Sea Education Association [8264]
PO Box 6
Woods Hole, MA 02543-0006
Ph: (508)540-3954
Toll Free: 800-552-3633
Fax: (800)977-8516

Humphry, Derek, President, Founder
Euthanasia Research and Guidance
Organization [11806]
24829 Norris Ln.
Junction City, OR 97448-9559
Ph: (541)998-1873
Fax: (541)998-1873

Humphrys, Andrea, Exec. Dir.
International Association of Women
Police [5137]
12600 Kavanaugh Ln.
Bowie, MD 20715
Ph: (301)464-1402
Fax: (301)560-8836

Hundert, Prof. Gershon, President
American Academy for Jewish
Research [9630]

202 S Thayer St., Ste. 211
Ann Arbor, MI 48104-1608

Hundley, Reggie, Exec. Dir.
Mission Services Association
[20438]
2004 E Magnolia Ave.
Knoxville, TN 37917
Ph: (865)525-7010
Fax: (865)525-7012

Huneycutt, Delphine, Mem.
Polish Women's Alliance of America
[19616]
6643 N Northwest Hwy., 2nd Fl.
Chicago, IL 60631-1300
Ph: (847)384-1200
Toll Free: 888-522-1898
Fax: (847)384-1494

Hung, Eric, Inst.
Cheng Ming USA [22988]
3916 McDermott Dr., Ste. 160
Plano, TX 75025
Ph: (972)740-8458

Hunt, Elaine, President
International Wood Collectors
Society [22480]
2300 W Rangeline Rd.
Greencastle, IN 46135-7875
Ph: (765)653-6483

Hunt, Elizabeth K., Exec. Dir.
Methacrylate Producers Association,
Inc. [722]
17260 Vannes Ct.
Hamilton, VA 20158

Hunt, Gail Gibson, CEO, President
National Alliance for Caregiving
[11824]
4720 Montgomery Ln., Ste. 205
Bethesda, MD 20814
Ph: (301)718-8444
Fax: (301)951-9067

Hunt, Geoffrey, Secretary
American Association of Electronic
Reporters and Transcribers [2737]
PO Box 9826
Wilmington, DE 19809
Ph: (302)765-3510
Toll Free: 800-233-5306
Fax: (302)241-2177

Hunt, John, Exec. Dir.
Legatus [19856]
5072 Annunciation Cir., Ste. 202
Ave Maria, FL 34142
Ph: (239)867-4900
Fax: (239)867-4198

Hunt, Julie Mayer, DC, President
Society of Chiropractic Orthospinol-
ogy [14283]
c/o Dr. Steve Humber, Treasurer
Humber Clinic, P.C.
2336 Wisteria Dr., Ste. 110
Snellville, GA 30078-6162
Ph: (770)979-8327
Fax: (770)979-8338

Hunt, Kelly, President
National Student Nurses' Association
[8335]
45 Main St., Ste. 606
Brooklyn, NY 11201
Ph: (718)210-0705
Fax: (718)797-1186

Hunt, Kim, President
Public Agency Risk Managers Association [5319]
c/o Kim Hunt, President
707 3rd St. 1-330
West Sacramento, CA 95605
Ph: (916)376-5271

Hunt, Ms. Mary E., PhD, Founder,
Director
Women's Alliance for Theology, Eth-
ics and Ritual [20648]
8121 Georgia Ave., Ste. 310
Silver Spring, MD 20910
Ph: (301)589-2509
Fax: (301)589-3150

Hunt, Priscilla, Exec. Dir.
Better Marriages [12254]
PO Box 21374
Winston Salem, NC 27120
Toll Free: 800-634-8325

Hunt, Richard, President, CEO
Consumer Bankers Association
[392]
1225 Eye St. NW, Ste. 550
Washington, DC 20005

Hunt, Robert A., Chmn. of the Bd.
United States Telecom Association
[3424]
607 14th St. NW, Ste. 400
Washington, DC 20005
Ph: (202)326-7300
Fax: (202)326-7333

Hunt, Capt. Terry, Contact
American Reef Coalition [3802]
PO Box 844
Kihei, HI 96753
Ph: (808)870-5817

Hunt, William E.
National Association of Industrial and
Office Properties [2871]
2201 Cooperative Way, Ste. 300
Herndon, VA 20171-3034
Ph: (703)904-7100
Fax: (703)904-7942

Hunt, William Randolph, Founder,
President
International Tinnitus Awareness As-
sociation [17241]
8408 Markethouse Ln.
Charlotte, NC 28227
Ph: (704)567-6860

Hunter, Dave, Exec. Dir.
Zeta Psi Fraternity, Inc. [23940]
15 S Henry St.
Pearl River, NY 10965
Ph: (845)735-1847
Toll Free: 800-477-1847
Fax: (845)735-1989

Hunter, David, Exec. Dir.
Orthopterists' Society [6616]
c/o Pamm Mihm, Treasurer
2417 Fields South Dr.
Champaign, IL 61822

Hunter, David, Chairman
Project on Government Oversight
[18698]
1100 G St. NW, Ste. 500
Washington, DC 20005-3806
Ph: (202)347-1122
Fax: (202)347-1116

Hunter, Douglas, Chairman
American Public Power Association
[5830]
2451 Crystal Dr., Ste. 1000
Arlington, VA 22202-4804
Ph: (202)467-2900

Hunter, Gary, Secretary
International Ultraviolet Association
[6494]
7720 Wisconsin Ave., Ste. 208
Bethesda, MD 20814
Ph: (240)437-4615
Fax: (240)209-2340

Hunter, Gilda Cobb, VP
National Black Caucus of State
Legislators [5781]

444 N Capitol St. NW, Ste. 622
Washington, DC 20001
Ph: (202)624-5457
Fax: (202)508-3826

Hunter, Gregg, President
Christian Camp and Conference As-
sociation [22719]
405 W Rockrimmon Blvd.
Colorado Springs, CO 80919
Ph: (719)260-9400

Hunter, Jackie, President
Marine Corps League Auxiliary
[21015]
8626 Lee Hwy., Ste. 207
Fairfax, VA 22031-2135
Ph: (703)207-0626
Fax: (703)207-0264

Hunter, Shelly, President
Society for the Technological
Advancement of Reporting [5122]
222 S Westmonte Dr., Ste. 101
Altamonte Springs, FL 32714-4268
Toll Free: 800-565-6054
Fax: (407)774-6440

Hunter, Stephen, President
National Association of Rehabilitation
Providers and Agencies [17091]
701 8th St. NW, Ste. 500
Washington, DC 20001
Toll Free: 866-839-7710
Fax: (800)716-1847

Hunter, Dr. Tim, Founder
International Dark-Sky Association
[6004]
3223 N 1st Ave.
Tucson, AZ 85719
Ph: (520)293-3198
Fax: (520)293-3192

Hunter, William C., President
Beta Gamma Sigma [23688]
125 Weldon Pky.
Maryland Heights, MO 63043
Ph: (314)432-5650
Toll Free: 800-337-4677
Fax: (314)432-7083

Huntington, Derek, President
International Pet and Animal
Transportation Association [2543]
2129 S FM 2869, Ste. 4
Hawkins, TX 75765
Ph: (903)769-2267
Fax: (903)769-2867

Huntoon, Jacqueline, Chairperson
Graduate Record Examinations
Board [8685]
225 Phillips Blvd.
Ewing, NJ 08618-1426
Ph: (609)771-7670
Toll Free: 866-473-4373
Fax: (610)290-8975

Huntsman, Jon M., Jr., Chairman
Atlantic Council of the United States
[19087]
1030 15th St. NW, 12th Fl.
Washington, DC 20005
Ph: (202)463-7226
Fax: (202)463-7241

Hunyor, Susan, Comm. Chm.
National Agri-Marketing Association
[105]
11020 King St., Ste. 205
Overland Park, KS 66210
Ph: (913)491-6500
Fax: (913)491-6502

Hunziker, Jim, President
Relief and Education for Afghan
Children [11265]

PO Box 304
Redmond, WA 98073
Ph: (206)463-3839
(425)844-8591
Fax: (206)463-2832

Huppe, Michael J., President, CEO
SoundExchange [2439]
733 10th St. NW, 10th Fl.
Washington, DC 20001
Ph: (202)640-5858

Hurd, Jeff, Commissioner
Western Athletic Conference [23264]
9250 E Costilla Ave., Ste. 300
Englewood, CO 80112
Ph: (303)799-9221
Fax: (303)799-3888

Hurlburt, Carol, Administrator
Graphic Communications Council
[1535]
c/o Graphic Arts Education and
Research Foundation
1899 Preston White Dr.
Reston, VA 20191-4367
Toll Free: 866-381-9839
Fax: (703)620-3165

Hurley, Art, President
International Metal Decorators As-
sociation [1538]
9574 Deereco Rd.
Timonium, MD 21093
Ph: (410)252-5205
Fax: (410)628-8079

Hurley, Candace, Exec. Dir.,
Founder
Sidelines National High-Risk
Pregnancy Support Network
[16303]
PO Box 1808
Laguna Beach, CA 92652
Toll Free: 888-447-4754

Hurley, Diane, Chairman
Touro Synagogue Foundation [9441]
85 Touro St.
Newport, RI 02840
Ph: (401)847-4794

Hurley, John, President, CEO
CRDF Global [7131]
1776 Wilson Blvd., Ste. 300
Arlington, VA 22209
Ph: (703)526-9720
Fax: (703)526-9721

Hurley, Mary, Contact
Chronic Granulomatous Disease Association [14570]
c/o Mary Hurley
2616 Monterey Rd.
San Marino, CA 91108-1646
Ph: (626)441-4118

Hurley, Wilson, Secretary
Burma-America Buddhist Association
[19773]
1708 Powder Mill Rd.
Silver Spring, MD 20903
Ph: (301)439-4035

Hurowitz, Glenn, Director
Tropical Forest and Climate Coali-
tion [4618]
1616 P St. NW, Ste. 403
Washington, DC 20036
Ph: (202)552-1828

Hursh, Shannon, Prog. Dir.
American Academy of Health Care
Providers in the Addictive
Disorders [15895]
314 W Superior St., Ste. 508
Duluth, MN 55802
Ph: (218)727-3940
Toll Free: 888-429-3701
Fax: (218)722-0346

Hurt, Richard D., MD, Chairman
Global Bridges [17313]
200 1st St. SW
Rochester, MN 55905

Hurteau, Paul, Exec. Dir.
OneWorld Classrooms [8673]
180 Main St.
Andover, MA 01810
Ph: (518)618-0571

Hurula, Barbara, Exec. Dir.
Federation of Environmental
Technologists, Inc. [4546]
W175 N11081 Stonewood Dr., Ste.
203
Germantown, WI 53022
Ph: (262)437-1700
Fax: (262)437-1702

Hurwitz, Eric L., President
Delta Omega [23857]
1900 M St. NW, Ste. 710
Washington, DC 20036

Huss, Alexandra, Mktg. Coord.
National School Transportation As-
sociation [3346]
122 S Royal St.
Alexandria, VA 22314
Ph: (703)684-3200

Hussar, William J., Economist
National Center for Education
Statistics [7787]
Institute of Education Sciences
550 12th St. SW
Washington, DC 20202
Ph: (202)245-6940

Hustad, Leon, President, Membership Chp.
Norwegian Lundehund Association
of America, Inc. [21935]
c/o Leon Hustad, President/Member-
ship Chairperson
744 Via Toscana
Wellington, FL 33414-7984
Ph: (561)385-4642

Huston, Andy, Exec. Dir.
Sigma Alpha Mu [23925]
8701 Founders Rd.
Indianapolis, IN 46268
Ph: (317)789-8338
Fax: (317)824-1505

Huston, Ms. Jayne H., Director
Seton Hill University's E-magnify
[7567]
Seton Hill University
1 Seton Hill Dr.
Greensburg, PA 15601
Toll Free: 800-826-6234

Huta, Leda, Exec. Dir.
Endangered Species Coalition
[4813]
PO Box 65195
Washington, DC 20035
Ph: (240)353-2765

Hutchens, Sher. Sandra, President
Major County Sheriffs' Association
[5484]
1450 Duke St.
Alexandria, VA 22314
Ph: (202)237-2001
Toll Free: 855-625-2689

Hutcherson, Dimitrius, Chairman
National Black Child Development
Institute [10820]
1313 L St. NW, Ste. 110
Washington, DC 20005-4110
Ph: (202)833-2220
Toll Free: 800-556-2234
Fax: (202)833-8222

Hutchins, Dr. Carleen M., Exec. Dir.,
Founder
The New Violin Family Association,
Inc. [9983]
Hutchins Consort
701 3rd St.
Encinitas, CA 92024
Ph: (760)632-0554

Hutchins, Dave, Exec. Dir., Founder
Genesis Institute [20596]
1220 N Howard St.
Spokane, WA 99201
Ph: (509)467-7913
Fax: (509)467-0344

Hutchins, Emmett, Fac. Memb., VP
Guild for Structural Integration
[13627]
150 S State St.
Salt Lake City, UT 84111
Ph: (800)447-0150
Toll Free: 800-447-0150
Fax: (801)906-8157

Hutchins, Michael, Exec. Dir., CEO
The Wildlife Society [4917]
5410 Grosvenor Ln., Ste. 200
Bethesda, MD 20814-2144
Ph: (301)897-9770
Fax: (301)530-2471

Hutchinson, Dr. Barbara, Managing
Dir.
International Arid Lands Consortium
[4071]
1955 E 6th St.
Tucson, AZ 85719
Ph: (520)626-0329
Fax: (520)621-7196

Hutchinson, Brian, Director
Oceanic Society [6942]
PO Box 844
Ross, CA 94957
Ph: (415)256-9604
Toll Free: 800-326-7491

Hutchinson, Brian, Officer
State of the World's Sea Turtles
[4893]
30 Sir Francis Drake Blvd.
Ross, CA 94957
Ph: (202)642-5830

Hutchinson, Estelle, President
American Board of Vocational
Experts [8732]
3121 Park Ave., Ste. C
Soquel, CA 95073
Ph: (831)464-4890
Fax: (831)576-1417

Hutchinson, Gertrude B., President
Interagency Council on Information
Resources in Nursing [9707]
c/o Richard Barry
American Nurses Association Library
8515 Georgia Ave., Ste. 400
Silver Spring, MD 20910-3492

Hutchinson, Robert, Founder,
President
Wireless Industry Association [3248]
9746 Tappenbeck Dr.
Houston, TX 77055
Ph: (713)467-0077

Hutchinson, Ted, Exec. Dir., Pub.
Dir.
American Society of Law, Medicine
and Ethics [15528]
765 Commonwealth Ave., Ste. 1634
Boston, MA 02215-1401
Ph: (617)262-4990
Fax: (617)437-7596

Hutchison, Coleman, President
Society for the Study of Southern
Literature [9768]

PO Box 1848
University, MS 38677-1848

Hutchison, Whit, Director
Ecumenical Program on Central
America and the Caribbean
[18619]
102 Park Ave.
Takoma Park, MD 20912
Ph: (240)770-8405

Huth, Myra Martz, PhD, Comm.
Chm.
Society of Pediatric Nurses [16185]
330 N Wabash Ave., Ste. 2000
Chicago, IL 60611-7621
Ph: (312)321-5154
Fax: (312)673-6754

Huttler, Adam, Exec. Dir.
Fractured Atlas [8918]
248 W 35th St., 10th Fl.
New York, NY 10001
Toll Free: 888-692-7878
Fax: (212)277-8025

Hutwagner, Jackie, President
Club de l'Epagneul Breton of the
United States [21857]
c/o Fatmi Anders, Secretary
25900 Poland Rd.
Chantilly, VA 20152

Huyck, Margaret Hellie, President
OWL - The Voice of Midlife and
Older Women [13392]
1627 K St. NW, Ste. 600
Washington, DC 20006
Fax: (202)450-8986

Hwang, Jessie Nia, President
Student National Pharmaceutical
Association [8415]
PO Box 761388
San Antonio, TX 78245
Ph: (210)383-7381
Fax: (210)579-1059

Hwang, Roland, VP
American Citizens for Justice
[17866]

Hwang, Steve, Exec. Dir.
A Bridge for Children [10872]
PO Box 1054
New York, NY 10268

Hwang, Dr. Sun Jo, Chairman
World Association of Non-
Governmental Organizations
[10767]
200 White Plains Rd., 1st Fl.
Tarrytown, NY 10591

Hyatt, David, President
American Budgerigar Society
[21533]
c/o Luemma McWilliams, Secretary
1407 Southport Rd.
Mount Pleasant, TN 38474-1987
Ph: (931)626-2230

Hyatt, Jay, Director
Missionary Gospel Fellowship
[20440]
PO Box 1535
Turlock, CA 95381-1535
Ph: (209)634-8575

Hybarger, John, Cmte. Mgmt. Ofc.
Society for the Conservation of
Bighorn Sheep [4890]
PO Box 94182
Pasadena, CA 91109-4182
Ph: (310)339-4677

Hyde, Lindsay, Founder
Strong Women, Strong Girls [13400]
262 Washington St., Ste. 602

Boston, MA 02108
Ph: (617)338-4833

Hyde, Mark, SDB, Director
Salesian Missions [20459]
2 Lefevre Ln.
New Rochelle, NY 10801-5710
Ph: (914)633-8344
Fax: (914)633-7404

Hyde, Montana, Exec. Asst.
American Legislative Exchange
Council [18961]
2900 Crystal Dr., 6th Fl.
Arlington, VA 22202
Ph: (703)373-0933
Fax: (703)373-0927

Hyett, Becky, Secretary
National Hereford Hog Record Association [4711]
c/o Becky Hyett, Secretary
2056 50th Ave.
Aledo, IL 61231
Ph: (309)299-5122

Hyland, Roberta, 1st VP
National Catholic Forensic League
[8596]
c/o Michael Colletti, Executive
Secretary-Treasurer
PO Box 31785
Chicago, IL 60631

Hyland, Sarah, Mgr.
Narrow Fabrics Institute [3263]
1801 County Rd. B W
Roseville, MN 55113
Ph: (651)222-6920

Hyman, Michael B., President
Scribes - The American Society of
Legal Writers [5093]
c/o Michael B. Hyman, President
50 W Washington St., Chambers
415
Chicago, IL 60602
Ph: (312)603-7582

Hyman, Peter, Chap.
The National Jewish Committee on
Scouting [12859]
Boy Scouts of America
PO Box 152079
Irving, TX 75015-2091
Ph: (972)580-2000

Hyppolite, Francinor, President
Haiti Needs My Help [13057]
1131 Alabama Ave.
Fort Lauderdale, FL 33312
Ph: (954)302-7422
Fax: (954)302-2041

Hyslop, Marsha, RN, Secretary
National Association of Healthcare
Advocacy Consultants [15040]
2625 Alcatraz Ave., Ste. 228
Berkeley, CA 94705

HyunSuk Oh, Dr. Harold, Chairman
World Water Organization [13351]
866 United Nations Plz.
New York, NY 10017
Ph: (212)759-1639
Fax: (646)666-4349

I

Iacuzzi, Judith Q., Exec. Dir.
U.S.A. Toy Library Association
[10824]
2719 Broadway Ave.
Evanston, IL 60201-1503
Ph: (847)612-6966
Fax: (847)864-8473

Iannettoni, Mark, MD, President
Thoracic Surgery Directors Association [17476]

633 N St. Clair St., 23rd Fl.
Chicago, IL 60611
Ph: (312)202-5854
Fax: (773)289-0871

Ibach, Greg, President
National Association of State Depart-
ments of Agriculture [4949]
4350 N Fairfax Dr., No. 910
Arlington, VA 22203
Ph: (202)296-9680
Fax: (703)880-0509

Ibrahim, Mr. Tod, Exec. Dir.
American Society of Nephrology
[15873]
1510 H St. NW, Ste. 800
Washington, DC 20005
Ph: (202)640-4660
Fax: (202)637-9793

Ibri, Ivo, President
Charles S. Peirce Society [9088]
University of West Georgia
Philosophy Program
1601 Maple St.
Carrollton, GA 30118

Icaza, Emilio Alvarez, Exec. Sec.
Inter-American Commission on Hu-
man Rights [18411]
1889 F St. NW
Washington, DC 20006-4401
Ph: (202)370-9000
Fax: (202)458-3992

Ichazo, Oscar, Founder, Owner
Arica Institute [9531]
27 N Main St., Ste. 6
Kent, CT 06757-1512
Ph: (860)927-1006
Fax: (860)201-1003

Ida, DJ, PhD, Exec. Dir.
National Asian American Pacific
Islander Mental Health Association
[15787]
1215 19th St., Ste. A
Denver, CO 80202
Ph: (303)298-7910
Fax: (303)298-8081

Iddi-Gubbels, Alice Azumi, Founder,
Exec. Dir.
PAMBE Ghana [11732]
PO Box 18813
Oklahoma City, OK 73154-0813

Idell, Ed, President
Project Cuddle [11133]
2973 Harbor Blvd., No. 326
Costa Mesa, CA 92626
Ph: (714)432-9681
Fax: (714)433-6815

Iden, Jeff, President
Web Sling and Tie Down Association
[1778]
9 Newport Dr., Ste. 200
Forest Hill, MD 21050
Ph: (443)640-1070
Fax: (443)640-1031

Idris, Mohamed, Exec. Dir.
American Relief Agency for the Horn
of Africa [12619]
PO Box 141117
Minneapolis, MN 55414
Ph: (612)781-7646
Toll Free: 866-992-7242
Fax: (612)781-7653

Idriss, Shamil, President, CEO
Search for Common Ground [18528]
1601 Connecticut Ave. NW, Ste. 200
Washington, DC 20009-1035
Ph: (202)265-4300
Fax: (202)232-6718

Ielpi, Lee, President
September 11th Families' Association [11678]
22 Cortlandt St., Rm. 801
New York, NY 10007-3128

Iglesia, Enrique, President
North American Catalysis Society
[7143]
c/o C.Y. Chen, Treasurer
100 Chevron Way, Rm. 10-2320
Richmond, CA 94802
Ph: (510)242-1860

Iglitzin, Lara, Exec. Dir.
Henry M. Jackson Foundation
[18170]
1501 4th Ave., Ste. 1580
Seattle, WA 98101-1653
Ph: (206)682-8565
Fax: (206)682-8961

Ignace, Fredo, Rep.
Light Path 4 Haiti [11399]
210 Park Ave., Ste. 261
Worcester, MA 01609
Ph: (774)262-0603

Ignacio, Jose, Director
Mobility Outreach International
[17395]
192 Nickerson St., Ste. 201
Seattle, WA 98109
Ph: (206)726-1636
Fax: (206)726-1637

Igrejas, Andy, Director
Safer Chemicals, Healthy Families
[17019]
641 S St. NW, 3rd Fl.
Washington, DC 20001

Ikeda, Mr. Daisaku, President
Soka Gakkai International-United
States of America [19783]
606 Wilshire Blvd.
Santa Monica, CA 90401
Ph: (310)260-8900
Fax: (310)260-8917

Iken, Monika, Chairperson, Founder
September's Mission [13212]
548 Broadway, 3rd Fl.
New York, NY 10012-3950
Ph: (212)312-8800
Toll Free: 888-424-4685

Ilagan, Ms. Venus, Sec. Gen.
Rehabilitation International [17098]
866 United Nations Plz., Office 422
New York, NY 10017
Ph: (212)420-1500
Fax: (212)505-0871

Iliasu, Iddrisu, Director
Ghana Relief Organization [10994]
PO Box 1722
Baltimore, MD 21203-1722

Illari, Jason, President
Small Museum Association [9841]
Historic Ships
301 E Pratt St.
Baltimore, MD 21202

Illian, Mark, President
Nature Healing Nature [11410]
514 Byrne St.
Houston, TX 77009
Ph: (832)423-8425

Illions, Kim, President
Pediatric Hydrocephalus Foundation
[15986]
2004 Green Hollow Dr.
Iselin, NJ 08830
Ph: (732)634-1283
Fax: (847)589-1250

Im, Hyepin, President, CEO
Korean Churches for Community
Development [11394]
3550 Wilshire Blvd., Ste. 736
Los Angeles, CA 90010
Ph: (213)985-1500

Immordino, Phil, President, Founder
Golf Tournament Association of
America [22881]
16605 N, 56th Pl.
Scottsdale, AZ 85254
Ph: (602)524-7034
Toll Free: 888-810-4822

Imparato, Andrew J., Exec. Dir.
Association of University Centers on
Disabilities [12317]
1100 Wayne Ave., Ste. 1000
Silver Spring, MD 20910
Ph: (301)588-8252
Fax: (301)588-2842

Impellizeri, Mary, Exec. Dir.
Catholic Daughters of the Americas
[19401]
10 W 71st St.
New York, NY 10023-4201
Ph: (212)877-3041

Indelicato, Dr. Joseph, Dir. of Res.
American Association of Bariatric
Counselors [16245]
9901 Brodie Ln., Ste. 160-278
Austin, TX 78748
Toll Free: 866-284-3682

Indig, Zalman, Director
All4Israel [12204]
53 Dewhurst St.
Staten Island, NY 10314
Toll Free: 877-812-7162

Ingalsbee, Timothy, PhD, Exec. Dir.
Firefighters United for Safety, Ethics
and Ecology [5204]
2852 Willamette St., No. 125
Eugene, OR 97405-8200
Ph: (541)338-7671

Inge, M. Thomas, VP
Poe Foundation [9090]
c/o Poe Museum
1914-16 E Main St.
Richmond, VA 23223
Ph: (804)648-5523

Ingenthron, Robin, President
World Reuse, Repair and Recycling
Association [4637]
PO Box 1010
Middlebury, VT 05753

Ingham, Stella, President
American Junior Rodeo Association
[23094]
c/o Mary McMullan, Secretary and
Manager
PO Box 398
Bronte, TX 76933-0298
Ph: (325)277-5824
    (530)662-8246

Ingram, Paul, Exec. Dir.
British American Security Information
Council [18082]
1725 DeSales St. NW, Ste. 600
Washington, DC 20036
Ph: (202)546-8055

Ingram, Tom, Exec. Dir.
Diving Equipment and Marketing As-
sociation [3138]
3750 Convoy St., Ste. 310
San Diego, CA 92111-3741
Ph: (858)616-6408
Toll Free: 800-862-3483
Fax: (858)616-6495

Ingrassia, Phil, CAE, President
National RV Dealers Association
[2918]
3930 University Dr.
Fairfax, VA 22030
Ph: (703)591-7130

Ingvarsson, Keri, CEO
Gen Art [8857]
1617 Cosmo St. Ste., 412
Los Angeles, CA 90028
Ph: (319)551-6157

Inikori, Solomon, PhD, President
Association of Nigerian Petroleum
Professionals Abroad [6998]
PO Box 218865
Houston, TX 77218

Inlow, Brand, President
Jessie's Wish [14642]
742 Colony Forest Dr.
Midlothian, VA 23114
Ph: (804)378-3032
Fax: (804)378-3032

Inman, Dennis, President
Teton Club International [22434]
c/o TCI Secretary-Treasurer
3916 N Potsdam Ave., No. 2590
Sioux Falls, SD 57104-7048

Inman, Pam, President
National Tour Association [3387]
101 Prosperous Pl., Ste. 350
Lexington, KY 40509
Ph: (859)264-6540
Toll Free: 800-682-8886
Fax: (859)264-6570

Inman, Sam, President
Jeffco Schools Foundation [18037]
Bldg. No. 1
809 Quail St.
Lakewood, CO 80215
Ph: (303)982-2210

Inman, Tom, President
Appalachian Hardwood Manufactur-
ers [1430]
816 Eastchester Dr.
High Point, NC 27262
Ph: (336)885-8315
Fax: (336)886-8865

Innes, Diane D., Officer
Innes Clan Society [20885]
c/o Carole A. Innes, Membership
129 Ravenna Dr.
Long Beach, CA 90803

Innis, Larry, Treasurer
VOR [12333]
836 S Arlington Heights Rd., No.
351
Elk Grove Village, IL 60007
Toll Free: 877-399-4867
Fax: (605)399-1631

Inns, David, V. Ch.
Consumer Electronics Association,
TechHome Division [1039]
1919 S Eads St.
Arlington, VA 22202
Ph: (703)907-7600
Toll Free: 866-858-1555
Fax: (703)907-7675

Insel, Thomas, MD, Director
National Institute of Mental Health
[15797]
6001 Executive Blvd.
Rockville, MD 20852
Ph: (301)443-4536
Toll Free: 866-615-6464
Fax: (301)443-4279

Inturrisi, Charles E., Ph.D., President
American Pain Society [16551]
8735 W Higgins Rd., Ste. 300

Chicago, IL 60631-2738
Ph: (847)375-4715

Iorio, Pam, President
Big Brothers Big Sisters of America
[11216]
2202 N Westshore Blvd., Ste. 455
Tampa, FL 33607
Ph: (469)351-3100
    (813)720-8778
Fax: (972)717-6507

Ipiotis, Ms. Celia, Director
Arts Resources in Collaboration
[9243]
70 E 10th St., Rm. 19D
New York, NY 10003
Ph: (212)206-6492

Iqbal, Meher, Chmn. of the Bd.
Circle of Women: Reach and Teach
Across Borders [8534]
PO Box 381365
Cambridge, MA 02238-1365

Iqbal, Naiel, President
Muslim Urban Professionals [10171]
244 Fifth Ave., Ste. N-270
New York, NY 10001

Iranmanesh, Dr. Ali A., Chairman,
Founder
International Society for Quality
Electronic Design [6371]
PO Box 607
Los Altos, CA 94023-0607
Ph: (408)573-0100
Fax: (408)573-0200

Ireland, Evelyn F., CAE, Exec. Dir.
National Association of Dental Plans
[15421]
12700 Park Central Dr., Ste. 400
Dallas, TX 75251
Ph: (972)458-6998
Fax: (972)458-2258

Ireland, Michael, Mem.
International Gas Turbine Institute
[6563]
6525 The Corners Pky., Ste. 115
Norcross, GA 30092
Ph: (404)847-0072
Fax: (404)847-0151

Irion, Jean, Chairperson
American Board of Physical Therapy
Specialties [16717]
c/o American Physical Therapy As-
sociation
1111 N Fairfax St.
Alexandria, VA 22314-1488
Ph: (703)706-8520
Toll Free: 800-999-2782
Fax: (703)706-8186

Irion, Peter, Secretary
American Vecturist Association
[22460]

Irion, Peter, Librarian
Token and Medal Society, Inc.
[22288]
c/o Kathy Freeland, Secretary
PO Box 195
Mayville, MI 48744-0195
Ph: (989)843-5247

Irish, Michael, Secretary
Farm Equipment Manufacturers As-
sociation [167]
1000 Executive Pky., Ste. 100
Saint Louis, MO 63141-6369
Ph: (314)878-2304
Fax: (314)732-1480

Irvin, Ms. Alice, Ed.-in-Chief
Austrian Press and Information
Service [23542]

3524 International Ct. NW
Washington, DC 20008
Ph: (202)895-6700
Fax: (202)895-6750

Irvin, Guy C., Chairman
Clan Irwin Association [20814]
226 1750th Ave.
Mount Pulaski, IL 62548-6635
Ph: (217)792-5226

Irvine, Don, Chairman
Accuracy in Media [17935]
4350 E West Hwy., Ste. 555
Bethesda, MD 20814
Ph: (202)364-4401
Fax: (202)364-4098

Irvine, Lori, Chairman
National Association for Rural Mental
Health [15789]
25 Massachusetts Ave. NW, Ste.
500
Washington, DC 20001
Ph: (202)942-4276

Irwin, Gilbert, MD, President
Medical Missionaries [15605]
9590 Surveyor Ct.
Manassas, VA 20110
Ph: (703)361-5116

Irwin, Mary Kay, EdD, Chairperson
Association of Pediatric Hematology
Oncology Educational Specialists
[15224]
c/o Karen DeMairo, Treasurer
5 Eileen Ave.
Plainview, NY 11803
Ph: (631)370-7532
Fax: (631)370-7560

Isaac, Debbie, President
AMIT [20231]
817 Broadway, 3rd Fl.
New York, NY 10003
Ph: (212)477-4720
Toll Free: 800-989-2648
Fax: (212)353-2312

Isaacs, John, Officer
Council for a Livable World [18124]
322 4th St. NE
Washington, DC 20002-5824
Ph: (202)543-4100

Isaacs, Rebecca, Exec. Dir.
Equality Federation [18301]
818 SW 3rd Ave., No. 141
Portland, OR 97204-2405
Ph: (415)252-0510

Isaacson, Jeff, President, CEO
Universities Space Research As-
sociation [5878]
7178 Columbia Gateway Dr.
Columbia, MD 21046
Ph: (410)730-2656

Isaacson, Walter, CEO, President
Aspen Institute [20209]
1 Dupont Cir. NW, Ste. 700
Washington, DC 20036-1133
Ph: (202)736-5800
Fax: (202)467-0790

Isayama, Maki, Info. Technology
Mgr.
Copper Development Association
Inc. [6879]
260 Madison Ave.
New York, NY 10016-2401
Ph: (212)251-7200
Fax: (212)251-7234

Isemann, Dr. William, CEO,
President
KidsPeace [11062]
4085 Independence Dr.

Schnecksville, PA 18078-2574
Toll Free: 800-257-3223
Fax: (610)799-8001

Isenberg, Michelle, Principal
Association of Professional Art Advisors [240]
433 3rd St., Ste. 3
Brooklyn, NY 11215
Ph: (718)788-1425

Isenburg, Matthew, Founder
Daguerreian Society [10138]
PO Box 306
Cecil, PA 15321-0306
Ph: (412)221-0306

Isgreen, Cheri
United States Lipizzan Federation [4420]
8414 W Farm Rd., Ste. 180
Las Vegas, NV 89143-1235
Ph: (503)589-3172

Ishak, Sherry, Mem.
National Association of Professional Women [3497]
1325 Franklin Ave., Ste. 160
Garden City, NY 11530
Ph: (516)877-5500
Toll Free: 866-540-6279

Isham, Mic, Chairman
Great Lakes Indian Fish and Wildlife Commission [4824]
72682 Maple St.
Odanah, WI 54861
Ph: (715)682-6619

Isherwood, Mike, Chairman
Burma Humanitarian Mission [11326]
3395 E Deer Hollow Cir.
Sandy, UT 84092
Ph: (435)487-9244

Ishihara, Wayne, President
Honolulu Japanese Chamber of Commerce [23591]
2454 S Beretania St., Ste. 201
Honolulu, HI 96826
Ph: (808)949-5531
Fax: (808)949-3020

Ishii, Dr. Naoko, Chairperson, CEO
Global Environment Facility [4062]
1818 H St. NW
Washington, DC 20433
Ph: (202)473-0508
Fax: (202)522-3240

Iskenderian, Ms. Mary Ellen, CEO, President
Women's World Banking - USA [13412]
122 E 42nd St., 42nd Fl.
New York, NY 10168
Ph: (212)768-8513
Fax: (212)768-8519

Islam, Dr. Saiful, President, Director
Bangladeshi American Charitable Organization [10862]
155 N Lake Ave., Ste. 600
Pasadena, CA 91101

Isler, Dr. Ellen, CEO, President
JBI International [17718]
110 E 30th St.
New York, NY 10016
Ph: (212)889-2525
Toll Free: 800-433-1531
Fax: (212)689-3692

Isles, John, Secretary, Treasurer
Webb Deep-Sky Society [6013]
c/o John Isles, Secretary/Treasurer
10575 Darrel Dr.

Hanover, MI 49241

Ismail, Amid, Chairman
Alliance for Oral Health Across Borders [14371]
135 Duryea Rd., No. E-310
Melville, NY 11747
Ph: (631)777-5275

Israel, Tim, President
American Industrial Extension Alliance [2211]
Georgia Institute of Technology
Enterprise Innovation Institute
75 5th St. NW, Ste. 300
Atlanta, GA 30308-2272
Ph: (404)894-2272
Fax: (404)894-1192

Israelite, David M., CEO, President
National Music Publishers' Association [2434]
975 F St. NW, Ste. 375
Washington, DC 20004
Ph: (202)393-6672

Israelsen, Loren D., President
United Natural Products Alliance [15079]
1075 E Hollywood Ave.
Salt Lake City, UT 84105-3446
Ph: (801)474-2572
Fax: (801)474-2571

Issing, David, Exec. Dir.
Association of Independent Research Institutes [7086]
c/o David A. Issing, Executive Director
PO Box 844
Westminster, MD 21157

Istrate, Daniela, President
Union and League of Romanian Societies [19624]
Cleveland, OH

Iszak, Frank, Founder
Silver Age Yoga [10424]
PO Box 160
Del Mar, CA 92014
Ph: (858)693-3110
Toll Free: 877-313-3110

Italiano, Ronnie, President, Founder
United in Group Harmony Association [10019]
PO Box 185
Clifton, NJ 07011
Ph: (973)365-0049

Ito, Ellyn M., Exec. Dir., Trustee
Seeds to Sew International, Inc. [11429]
PO Box 22
Hopewell, NJ 08525
Ph: (609)564-0441

Iv, Mr. Tin, Founder, President
Cambodia America Mobile Clinic [14245]
PO Box 1913
Clackamas, OR 97015
Ph: (725)333-2262

Ivancic, Joanne M., Exec. Dir., President
Advanced Biofuels USA [5880]
507 N Bentz St.
Frederick, MD 21701
Ph: (301)644-1395

Iversen, Prof. Paul, VP
American Society of Greek and Latin Epigraphy [10411]
1201 Euclid Ave.
11201 Euclid Ave.
Cleveland, OH 44106-7111
Ph: (261)368-2348
Fax: (261)368-4681

Iverson, Ron, Contact
National Association of Medicare Supplement Advisors [15041]
PO Box 4459
Helena, MT 59604
Ph: (406)442-4016

Ives, H. Russell, President
National Pest Management Association [2504]
10460 N St.
Fairfax, VA 22030
Ph: (703)352-6762
Toll Free: 800-678-6722
Fax: (703)352-3031

Ives, Kim, Director
Haiti Support Network [11923]
International Action Ctr.
39 W 14th St., Ste. 206
New York, NY 10011
Ph: (212)633-6646

Ivester, Hermann, VP
American Revenue Association [22304]
PO Box 74
Grosse Ile, MI 48138-0074
Ph: (734)676-2649
Fax: (734)676-2959

Ivie, George, CEO, Exec. Dir.
Media Rating Council [466]
420 Lexington Ave., Ste. 343
New York, NY 10170
Ph: (212)972-0300
Fax: (212)972-2786

Ivy, Joanne, President, CEO
American Egg Board [4561]
1460 Renaissance Dr., Ste. 301
Park Ridge, IL 60068
Ph: (847)296-7043
Fax: (847)296-7007

Iwaskiw, Leo, Editor
Providence Association of Ukrainian Catholics in America [19676]
817 N Franklin St.
Philadelphia, PA 19123-2004
Toll Free: 877-857-2284
Fax: (215)238-1933

Iwere, Dr. Fabian, President
Ugbajo Itsekiri USA [18079]
PO Box 11465
Washington, DC 20008-0665

Iwuanyanwu, Eucharia, President
Africa Cancer Care Inc. [13871]
6011 Telephone Rd.
Houston, TX 77087
Ph: (713)995-8000
Fax: (713)645-5588

Iyer, Deepa, Chairman
Race Forward: The Center for Racial Justice Innovation [12989]
900 Alice St., Ste. 400
Oakland, CA 94607
Ph: (510)653-3415
Fax: (510)986-1062

Iyer, Deepa, Advisor
South Asian Americans Leading Together [19131]
6930 Carroll Ave., Ste. 506
Takoma Park, MD 20912-4480
Ph: (301)270-1855
Fax: (301)270-1882

J

Jabateh, Voffee, Exec. Dir.
African Cultural Alliance of North America [10485]
5530 Chester Ave.

Philadelphia, PA 19143-5328
Ph: (215)729-8225

Jaber, Hassan, Exec. Dir.
Arab Community Center for Economic and Social Services [8813]
2651 Saulino Ct.
Dearborn, MI 48120
Ph: (313)842-7010
Fax: (313)842-5150

Jablonski, Jarrod, Founder, President, Chairman
Global Underwater Explorers [4466]
18487 High Springs Main St.
High Springs, FL 32643
Ph: (386)454-0820
Toll Free: 800-762-3483
Fax: (386)454-0654

Jablonski, Tiffany, VP
International Association of Colon Hydrotherapy [16805]
11103 San Pedro Ave., Ste. 117
San Antonio, TX 78216-3117
Ph: (210)366-2888
Fax: (210)366-2999

Jabs, Ethylin Wang, MD, Director
John Hopkins Cleft and Craniofacial Center [14339]
4940 Eastern Ave.
Baltimore, MD 21224
Ph: (410)955-7337

Jacecko, Kathleen, Founder, Director
TeachingGreen [4119]
PO Box 754
Hermosa Beach, CA 90254
Ph: (310)372-7484
Fax: (310)372-7484

Jack, Maia, Secretary
International Council of Grocery Manufacturer Associations [1339]
1350 I St. NW, Ste. 300
Washington, DC 20005
Ph: (202)337-9400
Fax: (202)337-4508

Jackley, Marty, President
National Association of Attorneys General [5776]
2030 M St. NW, 8th Fl.
Washington, DC 20036
Ph: (202)326-6000

Jacklin, Don, President
American Mule Racing Association [23078]
1600 Exposition Blvd.
Sacramento, CA 95815

Jackman, Dr. Jay, CAE, Exec. Dir.
National Association of Agricultural Educators [7476]
300 Garrigus Bldg.
University of Kentucky
Lexington, KY 40546-0215
Ph: (859)257-2224
Toll Free: 800-509-0204

Jackman, Dr. Jay, CAE, Treasurer
National Association of Supervisor of Agricultural Education [7477]
c/o Jay Jackman, NASAE Executive Treasurer
300 Garrigus Bldg.
Lexington, KY 40546-0215
Ph: (859)257-2224
Toll Free: 800-509-0204
Fax: (859)323-3919

Jackman, Jennifer, Officer
American Gold Star Mothers [21036]
2128 Leroy Pl. NW
Washington, DC 20008-1847
Ph: (202)265-0991

Jacks, Dorthy, VP
International Association of Assessing Officers [5795]
314 W 10th St.
Kansas City, MO 64105
Ph: (816)701-8100
Toll Free: 800-616-4226
Fax: (816)701-8149

Jackson, Ann, Exec. Dir.
International Atherosclerosis Society [14120]
6535 Fannin St.
Houston, TX 77030-2703
Ph: (713)797-0401
Fax: (713)796-8853

Jackson, Bill, CEO, Founder, President
GreatSchools [7589]
1999 Harrison St., Ste. 1100
Oakland, CA 94612-4708

Jackson, Brian, President
Helping Autism through Learning and Outreach [13768]
PO Box 303399
Austin, TX 78703-0057
Ph: (512)465-9595
Toll Free: 866-465-9595
Fax: (512)465-9598

Jackson, Clint, President
National Federation of Professional Bullriders [23098]
2222 Highway F
Mansfield, MO 65704
Ph: (417)924-3591
      (417)259-3361

Jackson, Deborah A., Ph.D, Editor
National Conference of Black Lawyers [5035]
PO Box 25162
Brooklyn, NY 11202
Toll Free: 866-266-5091

Jackson, Eric, President
American Fats and Oils Association [2447]
PO Box 11035
Columbia, SC 29211
Ph: (803)252-7128
Fax: (803)252-7799

Jackson, Herb, Treasurer
Regional Reporters Association [2716]
PO Box 254, Ben Franklin Sta.
Washington, DC 20005

Jackson, Prof. James S., PhD, Director
Institute for Social Research [7166]
426 Thompson St.
Ann Arbor, MI 48104-2321
Ph: (734)764-8354
      (734)647-8043
Fax: (734)647-4575

Jackson, Janet T., Co-Pres.
Clinical Legal Education Association [8212]
c/o Janet T. Jackson, Co-President
1700 SW College Ave.
Topeka, KS 66621
Ph: (785)670-1637

Jackson, Janine, Prog. Dir.
Fairness and Accuracy in Reporting [17945]
124 W 30th St., Ste. 201
New York, NY 10001
Ph: (212)633-6700

Jackson, Mr. Joseph M., CAE, Exec. Dir.
American Academy of Esthetic Dentistry [14375]

225 W Wacker Dr., Ste. 650
Chicago, IL 60606
Ph: (312)981-6770

Jackson, Joseph M., Exec. Dir.
International Society of Appraisers [227]
225 W Wacker Dr., Ste. 650
Chicago, IL 60606
Ph: (312)981-6778
Fax: (312)265-2908

Jackson, Karen E., CEO, Founder
Sisters Network, Inc. [14062]
2922 Rosedale St.
Houston, TX 77004
Ph: (713)781-0255
Toll Free: 866-781-1808
Fax: (713)780-8998

Jackson, Kent L., PhD, Exec. Dir.
Outpatient Ophthalmic Surgery Society [16404]
c/o Kent L. Jackson, Executive Director
4671 E Phillips Pl.
Centennial, CO 80122
Ph: (720)550-7667

Jackson, Laurie, President, CEO
National Safe Place Network [12834]
2429 Crittenden Dr.
Louisville, KY 40217
Ph: (502)635-3660
Toll Free: 888-290-7233
Fax: (502)635-3678

Jackson, Linda, MFA, Exec. Dir., Founder
Helping Hand for Nepal [12673]
2930 Brittany Dr.
Anchorage, AK 99504-3982
Ph: (907)338-8128

Jackson, Lisa, Chief Adm. Ofc.
Business Executives for National Security [19088]
1030 15th St. NW, Ste. 200 E
Washington, DC 20005-1505
Ph: (202)296-2125
Fax: (202)296-2490

Jackson, Mamie V., Founder
National Organization for Renal Disease [15883]
11018 Aqua Vista St., No. 19
Studio City, CA 91602

Jackson, Miguel M., Founder, President
World Bible Project, Inc. [19766]
PO Box 1606, FDR Sta.
New York, NY 10150
Toll Free: 888-576-2210

Jackson, Pamela M., Exec. Dir.
Intercultural Cancer Council [13988]
1 Baylor Plz., MS 620
Houston, TX 77030-3411
Ph: (713)798-4614
Fax: (713)798-3990

Jackson, Rich, V. Chmn. of the Bd.
MultiState Tax Commission [5796]
444 N Capitol St. NW, Ste. 425
Washington, DC 20001
Ph: (202)650-0300

Jackson, Sarah, Secretary
Preservation Trades Network [573]
75 Holt Rd.
Lyndeborough, NH 03082-5815
Toll Free: 866-853-9336

Jackson, Shirley A., PhD, Mem.
Sociologists for Women in Society [7191]

1415 Jayhawk Blvd.
University of Kansas
Department of Sociology, Rm. 716
Lawrence, KS 66045
Ph: (785)864-9405

Jackson, Stephen, Pol. Dir.
Ripon Society [19051]
1155 15th St. NW, Ste. 550
Washington, DC 20005
Ph: (202)216-1008

Jackson, Steve, Chairman
American Concrete Pavement Association [779]
9450 W Bryn Mawr, Ste. 150
Rosemont, IL 60018
Ph: (847)966-2272

Jackson, Steve, VP
Freight Rail Customer Alliance [18870]
300 New Jersey Ave. NW, Ste. 900
Washington, DC 20001
Ph: (202)469-3471
Fax: (202)347-0130

Jackson, Tom, Secretary, Treasurer
Critical Messaging Association [766]
441 N Crestwood Dr.
Wilmington, NC 28405-2609
Toll Free: 866-301-2272
Fax: (910)792-9733

Jackson, Tom, Treasurer
International Palm Society [6147]
9300 Sandstone St.
Austin, TX 78737-1135
Ph: (512)301-2744
Fax: (512)870-9366

Jackson, Valerie P., Exec. Dir.
The American Board of Radiology [17039]
5441 E Williams Cir.
Tucson, AZ 85711-7412
Ph: (520)790-2900
Fax: (520)790-3200

Jackson, Victoria, Coord.
Lifelong Fitness Alliance [23313]
2682 Middlefield Rd., Ste. Z
Redwood City, CA 94063
Toll Free: 855-361-8282
Fax: (650)361-8885

Jackson, Dr. Yvette, CEO
National Urban Alliance for Effective Education [8729]
33 Queens St., Ste. 100
Syosset, NY 11791
Ph: (516)802-4192
Toll Free: 800-682-4556
Fax: (516)921-0298

Jackson, Yvonne R., Chmn. of the Bd.
Association of Governing Boards of Universities and Colleges [7424]
1133 20th St. NW, Ste. 300
Washington, DC 20036
Ph: (202)296-8400
Fax: (202)223-7053

Jacobs, Charlene, President
United States Freshwater Prawn and Shrimp Growers Association [3038]
c/o Dolores Fratesis, Secretary-Treasurer
655 Napanee Rd.
Leland, MS 38756
Ph: (662)686-2894
      (662)390-3528

Jacobs, Christiane, Exec. Asst.
Association of Military Banks of America [383]

PO Box 3335
Warrenton, VA 20188-1935
Ph: (540)347-3305
Fax: (540)347-5995

Jacobs, Mr. David W., Chairman
American Revolution Round Table of New York [8793]
8 Spencer Ave.
Niantic, CT 06357-3015
Ph: (860)739-5505

Jacobs, Debbie, President
Lowe Syndrome Association [14838]
PO Box 864346
Plano, TX 75086-4346
Ph: (972)733-1338

Jacobs, Mr. Francis Brinton, II, President
Brinton Association of America [20963]
William Brinton 1704 House and Historic Site
21 Oakland Rd.
West Chester, PA 19382
Ph: (610)399-0913

Jacobs, Garry, Chmn. of the Bd., CEO
World Academy of Art and Science [9018]
4225 Solano Ave., Ste. 631
Napa, CA 94558

Jacobs, Jill, Exec. Dir.
T'ruah: The Rabbinic Call for Human Rights [18446]
333 7th Ave., 13th Fl.
New York, NY 10001
Ph: (212)845-5201

Jacobs, Mary, President
International Disciples Women's Ministries [20643]
1099 N Meridian St., Ste. 700
Indianapolis, IN 46206-1986
Ph: (317)635-3100

Jacobs, Matthew, President
Thomas Paine National Historical Association [10343]
983 North Ave.
New Rochelle, NY 10804-3609
Ph: (914)434-7270
Fax: (914)632-5376

Jacobs, Michael, Chairman
Robotic Industries Association [7105]
900 Victors Way, Ste. 140
Ann Arbor, MI 48108
Ph: (734)994-6088
Fax: (734)994-3338

Jacobs, Myra, MA, Founder
National Bone Marrow Transplant Link [17516]
20411 W 12 Mile Rd., Ste. 108
Southfield, MI 48076
Ph: (248)358-1886
Toll Free: 800-546-5268
Fax: (248)358-1889

Jacobs, Paul, Chairman
Greater Public [461]
401 N 3rd St., Ste. 370
Minneapolis, MN 55401
Toll Free: 888-454-2314

Jacobs, Pete, President
Musical Missions of Peace [18806]
1930 Central Ave., Ste. E
Boulder, CO 80301
Ph: (303)449-4196
Fax: (303)440-9592

Jacobs, Rabbi Rick, President
Union for Reform Judaism [20285]
633 3rd Ave.

New York, NY 10017-6778
Ph: (212)650-4000
Toll Free: 855-URJ-1800

Jacobs, Terrance, Director
Industrial Auctioneers Association
[259]
3213 Ayr Ln.
Dresher, PA 19025
Ph: (215)366-5450
Toll Free: 800-805-8359
Fax: (215)657-1964

Jacobsen, David, President
Morgan 3/4 Group [21441]
388 High Head Rd.
Harpswell, ME 04079
Ph: (207)721-3206

Jacobsen, Linda, Chairperson
Council of Professional Associations
on Federal Statistics [5301]
20 F St. NW, Ste. 700
Washington, DC 20001
Ph: (202)507-6254

Jacobsen, Paul, VP
International Psycho-Oncology
Society [13993]
244 5th Ave., Ste. L296
New York, NY 10001
Ph: (416)968-0260
Fax: (416)968-6818

Jacobsen-Tews, Lorilyn, Exec. Dir.
Hemostasis and Thrombosis
Research Society [15232]
8733 Watertown Plank Rd.
Milwaukee, WI 53226-3548
Ph: (414)937-6569

Jacobson, Brian M., Contact
National Aircraft Appraisers Associa-
tion [148]
7 W Square Lake Rd.
Bloomfield Hills, MI 48302
Ph: (248)758-2333
Fax: (248)769-6084

Jacobson, Carlotta, President
Cosmetic Executive Women [1583]
159 W 25th St., 8th Fl.
New York, NY 10001
Ph: (212)685-5955
    (646)929-8000
Fax: (212)685-3334

Jacobson, Guy, Exec. Dir., Founder
RedLight Children [10798]
75 Rockefeller Plz., 17th Fl.
New York, NY 10019-6927

Jacobson, James B., President,
Founder
Christian Freedom International
[20570]
986 John Marshall Hwy.
Front Royal, VA 22630-0011
Toll Free: 800-323-2273

Jacobson, John, Founder, President
America Sings! [9848]
PO Box 990
Ocoee, FL 34761
Ph: (321)209-0097

Jacobson, Kenneth M., President
American College of Real Estate
Lawyers [4987]
11300 Rockville Pke., Ste. 903
Rockville, MD 20852-3034
Ph: (301)816-9811
Fax: (301)816-9786

Jacobson, Lisa, President
Business Council for Sustainable
Energy [1107]
805 15th St., NW Ste. 708

Washington, DC 20005
Ph: (202)785-0507
Fax: (202)785-0514

Jacobson, Sheldon H., Treasurer
Institute for Operations Research
and the Management Sciences
[2174]
5521 Research Park Dr., Ste. 200
Catonsville, MD 21228
Ph: (443)757-3500
Toll Free: 800-446-3676
Fax: (443)757-3515

Jacobstein, Neil, Chairman
Institute for Molecular Manufacturing
[6794]
555 Bryant St., Ste. 354
Palo Alto, CA 94301
Ph: (650)917-1120
Fax: (650)917-1120

Jaeger, A. Robert, President
Partners for Sacred Places [20552]
1700 Sansom St., 10th Fl.
Philadelphia, PA 19103
Ph: (215)567-3234
Fax: (215)567-3235

Jaeger, Trent, Chairman
Association for Computing
   Machinery - Special Interest Group
   on Security, Audit and Control
   [6240]
c/o Trent Jaeger, Chairman
Pennsylvania State University
Dept. of Computer Science and
   Engineering
346A IST Bldg.
University Park, PA 16802
Ph: (814)865-1042
Fax: (814)865-3176

Jaffe, Alexandra, Ed.-in-Chief
Society for Linguistic Anthropology
[5924]
c/o Prof. Brigittine M. French, Editor
Dept. of Anthropology
Grinnell College
306 Goodnow Hall
1118 Park St.
Grinnell, IA 50112

Jaffe, David, Exec. Dir.
International Association for
   Quantitative Finance [1241]
555 8th Ave., Rm. 1902
New York, NY 10018-4349
Ph: (646)736-0705

Jaffe, David, Exec. Dir.
Software and Technology Vendors'
   Association [6288]
555 8th Ave., Ste. 1902
New York, NY 10019
Ph: (646)233-0167

Jaffe, Kenneth, Exec. Dir., President
International Child Resource Institute
[11046]
2nd Fl., Southwest Ste.
125 University Ave.
Berkeley, CA 94710
Ph: (510)644-1000
Fax: (510)644-1115

Jaffe, Richard P., Chmn. of the Bd.
Association for Corporate Growth
[612]
125 S Wacker Dr., Ste. 3100
Chicago, IL 60606
Toll Free: 877-358-2220

Jagdfeld, Fr. Lawrence, Administrator
CUSA: An Apostolate of Persons
   with Chronic Illness or Disability
   [19830]

4856 W 29th St.
Cicero, IL 60804-3611

Jaggar, Karuna, Exec. Dir.
Breast Cancer Action [13908]
657 Mission St., Ste. 302
San Francisco, CA 94105
Ph: (415)243-9301
Toll Free: 877-278-6722
Fax: (415)243-3996

Jahnke, Roger, Officer
American Tai Chi and Qigong Association [17422]
2465 J-17 Centreville Rd., No. 150
Herndon, VA 20171

Jain, Bawa, Sec. Gen.
World Council of Religious Leaders
[20568]
Empire State Bldg.
350 5th Ave., 59th Fl.
New York, NY 10118-5999
Ph: (212)967-2891
Fax: (212)967-2898

Jain, Mukesh K., Chairman
American Society for Clinical
   Investigation [14288]
2015 Manchester Rd.
Ann Arbor, MI 48104
Ph: (734)222-6050
Fax: (734)222-6058

Jakpor, Viktor, Exec. Dir., Founder
Mission Africa [11402]
11002 S 48th St.
Phoenix, AZ 85044
Ph: (480)788-3832
Fax: (480)893-8318

Jakub, Paula S., Exec. VP, CEO
American Foreign Service Protective
   Association [19480]
1620 L St. NW, Ste. 800
Washington, DC 20036-2902
Ph: (202)833-4910
Fax: (202)833-4918

James, Adam, Secretary
Army Sniper Association [20718]
2525 Auburn Ave.
Columbus, GA 31906

James, Christine, President
Shwachman-Diamond Syndrome
   Foundation [17351]
2334 Rolling Ridge Dr.
Avon, NY 14414-9642
Toll Free: 888-825-7373

James, Elizabeth, MD, Officer
A Call to Serve International [11329]
610 West Blvd.
Columbia, MO 65203

James, Jennifer, Librarian
Institute of American Indian Arts
[10042]
83 Avan Nu Po Rd.
Santa Fe, NM 87508-1300
Ph: (505)424-2300
Fax: (505)424-0050

James, John, Secretary
National Association of Construction
   Contractors Cooperation [553]
6301 Rockhill Rd., Ste 316
Kansas City, MO 64130
Ph: (816)923-5399
Fax: (816)444-3226

James, Jonathan, President, Exec.
Dir.
Hope for Hemophilia [15234]
PO Box 77728
Baton Rouge, LA 70879
Toll Free: 888-529-8023

James, Judith M, Asst. VP
Catholic Order of Foresters [19403]
355 Shuman Blvd.
Naperville, IL 60563
Ph: (630)983-4900
Toll Free: 800-552-0145

James, Kay, Founder
Black Americans for Life [12765]
512 10th St. NW
Washington, DC 20004
Ph: (202)378-8855

James Mackie, Mrs. Deadra, Exec.
Sec.
Beta Kappa Chi [23859]
244 William James Hall
Baton Rouge, LA 70813
Ph: (225)771-4854

James, Mary Ann, Mem.
Railroadiana Collectors Association
   Inc. [22411]
c/o Mary Ann James, Secretary
17675 W 113th St.
Olathe, KS 66061

James, Matthew B., MA, Founder
Association for Integrative Psychol-
   ogy, Inc. [16903]
75-6099 Kuakini Hwy.
Kailua Kona, HI 96740
Ph: (808)930-8707
Toll Free: 877-935-0247
Fax: (808)930-8701

James, Nathaniel, President
369th Veterans' Association Inc.
[21100]
369th Armory 2366 5th Ave., - 1
   369th Plz.
2366 5th Ave.
New York, NY 10037
Ph: (516)378-5328

James, Robert, President
Presbyterian Men [20527]
100 Witherspoon St.
Louisville, KY 40202-1396
Toll Free: 800-728-7228

James, Rolita, Exec. Dir.
PASSION: Pursuing A Successful
   Seed In-spite of Negativity [13473]
110 Lenox Ave., Ste. D
Stamford, CT 06911-2069
Ph: (203)577-5744

James, Taj, Exec. Dir.
Funders' Collaborative on Youth
   Organizing [12475]
330 7th Ave., Ste. 1902
New York, NY 10001
Ph: (212)725-3386

James, Vickie L., Director
Healthy Kids Challenge [14194]
2 W Road 210
Dighton, KS 67839
Toll Free: 888-259-6287
Fax: (620)397-5979

James-Brown, Christine, President,
CEO
Child Welfare League of America
[10908]
1726 M St. NW, Ste. 500
Washington, DC 20036-4522
Ph: (202)688-4200
Fax: (202)833-1689

James-Townes, Lori, MSW, Chairman
National Alliance of Sentencing
   Advocates and Mitigation Specialists [5138]
c/o Edwin A. Burnette
1140 Connecticut Ave. NW, Ste. 900

Washington, DC 20036
Ph: (202)452-0620

Jamgochian, Hrant, CEO
Dialysis Patient Citizens **[15877]**
1012 14th St. NW, Ste. No. 905
Washington, DC 20005-3403
Toll Free: 866-877-4242
Fax: (888)423-5002

Jamil, Prof. Hikmet, MD, President
International Society of Iraqi
  Scientists **[7138]**
PO Box 4445
Dearborn, MI 48126
Fax: (248)538-6034

Jamison, Dr. Albert L., Sr., Chairman
Gospel Music Workshop of America
  [9911]
3908 W Warren Ave.
Detroit, MI 48208
Ph: (313)898-6900

Jamison, Kevin, Founder, Director
Community Development
  International **[11338]**
PO Box 3417
New York, NY 10163

Jamison, Martha Hill, President
American Judicature Society **[5376]**
Center Bldg.
2014 Broadway, Ste. 100
Nashville, TN 37203-2425
Ph: (615)873-4675
Toll Free: 800-626-4089
Fax: (615)873-4671

Jammal, Oussama, Sec. Gen.
US Council of Muslim Organizations
  [20503]
1155 F St. NW, Ste. 1050
Washington, DC 20004
Ph: (202)683-6557

Jamu, Lisa, Founder, Exec. Dir.
Stepping Stones International
  [11159]
693 17th Ave.
Salt Lake City, UT
Ph: (801)359-2746
     (801)651-1771

Jane, Amanda, Chairman
Sudan Sunrise **[12443]**
11404 Summer House Ct.
Reston, VA 20194-2006
Ph: (202)499-6984

Janecek, Lenore, CEO, President
Save the Patient **[14964]**
260 E Chestnut St., No. 1712
Chicago, IL 60611
Ph: (312)440-0630
Fax: (312)440-0631

Janik, John J., President
National Flag Day Foundation
  [20947]
PO Box 55
Waubeka, WI 53021-0055
Ph: (262)692-9111
     (262)692-2811

Janiszewski, Claudia, Founder,
  President
Organization for the Support of
  Albania's Abandoned Babies
  [11114]
PO Box 1672
Dubois, WY 82513
Ph: (303)989-7260

Janko, Scott, President
National Association of Financial and
  Estate Planning **[1254]**
515 E 4500 S, No. G-200

Salt Lake City, UT 84107
Toll Free: 800-454-2649
Fax: (877)890-0929

Janney, Caroline E., President
Society of Civil War Historians
  [9512]
c/o UNC Press Journals Dept.
116 S Boundary St.
Chapel Hill, NC 27514
Ph: (814)863-0151
     (919)962-4201

Janov, Barbara, Exec. Dir.
Hineni **[9637]**
232 W End Ave.
New York, NY 10023-3604
Ph: (212)496-1660

Janowitz, Karl, President
American Professional Partnership
  for Lithuanian Education **[9587]**
PO Box 179017
San Diego, CA 92177

Jansen, Eric, Coord.
Christian Comic Arts Society **[8850]**
c/o FrontGate Media
22342 Avenida Empresa, Ste. 260
Rancho Santa Margarita, CA 92688

Jansen, Rene, President
Rexx Language Association **[7058]**
7028 W Waters Ave.
Tampa, FL 33634-2292

Janson, Heidi, Founder
Brides Across America **[10783]**
28 W Main St.
Georgetown, MA 01833

Janssen, Alan, Chairman
American Osteopathic Board of
  Emergency Medicine **[14675]**
c/o Jennifer Hausman, Certification
  Director
142 E Ontario
Chicago, IL 60611
Ph: (312)202-8293
Fax: (312)202-8402

Janssen, Brian, President
Allied Purchasing **[967]**
PO Box 1249
Mason City, IA 50402-1249
Toll Free: 800-247-5956
Fax: (800)635-3775

Janssen, Phil, Contact
World Umpires Association **[23393]**
PO Box 394
Neenah, WI 54957
Ph: (920)969-1580

Janzen, Judith, Administrator
Church and Synagogue Library As-
  sociation **[9699]**
10157 SW Barbur Blvd., No. 102C
Portland, OR 97219
Ph: (503)244-6919
Toll Free: 800-542-2752
Fax: (503)977-3734

Janzen, Warren, Chairman
Missio Nexus **[20436]**
655 Village Square Dr., Ste. A
Stone Mountain, GA 30083
Ph: (770)457-6677
     (630)682-9270

Jaramillo, Alex, Jr., President
Cracker Jack Collectors Association
  [21644]
c/o Linda Farris, Membership
  Chairperson
4908 N Holborn Dr.
Muncie, IN 47304

Jarbah, Joseph Fatinyan, President,
  Founder
Children's Welfare International
  [10936]

223 Pacific Ave. S
Pacific, WA 98047-1214
Ph: (206)317-3545

Jarboe, Kenan Patrick, President
Athena Alliance **[18164]**
231 Harvard Ave.
Half Moon Bay, CA 94019
Ph: (202)547-7064

Jardinaso, Ruth Ann, Founder,
  President, CEO
Renew Our Minds and Hearts
  Foundation **[13017]**
PO Box 18521
Encino, CA 91416
Ph: (323)247-9581
Fax: (206)888-0328

Jardosh, Snehal, Officer
International Real Estate Institute
  [2866]
810 N Farrell Dr.
Palm Springs, CA 92262
Toll Free: 877-327-5284
Fax: (760)327-5631

Jarrett, Robert M., MD, President
Hearts Around the World **[14117]**
PO Box 5336
Brookfield, CT 06804
Ph: (203)733-3222

Jarrow, Paul, President
Motorcycle Touring Association
  [23040]
PO Box 2394
Loveland, CO 80539
Ph: (970)663-2044

Jarvis, David, President
National Aircraft Finance Association
  [2091]
PO Box 1570
Edgewater, MD 21037
Ph: (410)571-1740

Jasim, Azhar, CEO
Al-Rafidain Humanitarian Aid for
  Women and Children **[12611]**
PO Box 45906
Philadelphia, PA 19149

Jasinski, Jerry, Chairman
American Institute of Chemists
  [6182]
315 Chestnut St.
Philadelphia, PA 19106-2702
Ph: (215)873-8224
Fax: (215)629-5224

Jasso, Roy, Chmn. of the Exec.
  Committee
Bilingual Foundation of the Arts
  [10243]
201 N Los Angeles St., Ste. 12
Los Angeles, CA 90012
Ph: (213)437-0500

Javornik, Emy Neuman, President
National Grants Management As-
  sociation **[2186]**
2100 M St. NW, Ste. 170
Washington, DC 20037
Ph: (202)308-9443

Jawad, Said Tayeb, President
Foundation for Afghanistan **[10468]**
1212 New York Ave. NW, Ste. 825
Washington, DC 20005
Ph: (202)289-2515
Fax: (202)289-2516

Jay, Dennis, Exec. Dir.
Coalition Against Insurance Fraud
  [1846]
1012 14th St. NW, Ste. 200
Washington, DC 20005
Ph: (202)393-7330

Jay, Katie, Founder, Director
National Association for Weight Loss
  Surgery **[16260]**
609A Piner Rd., No. 319
Wilmington, NC 28409
Toll Free: 877-746-5759

Jay, Larsen, Founder, CEO
Random Acts of Flowers **[11850]**
3500 Workman Rd., Ste. 101A
Knoxville, TN 37921
Ph: (865)248-3045
Fax: (865)240-2933

Jayasuriya, Catherine, Exec. Dir.,
  Founder
Coalition Duchenne **[15917]**
1300 Quail St., Ste. 100
Newport Beach, CA 92660
Fax: (949)721-9359

Jayweh, Frederick A.B., Exec. Dir.
Association of Liberian Lawyers in
  the Americas **[5418]**
1582 S Parker Rd., Ste. 110
Denver, CO 80231
Ph: (720)535-5237
Fax: (720)535-4681

Jean-Jacques, Vasquez, CEO
Brave International **[17967]**
5338 SW 183rd Ave.
Miramar, FL 33029
Ph: (954)964-2362
     (786)486-0897

Jean-Louis, Dr. Franco, President,
  Founder
Generations of Hope, Haiti **[13053]**
210 Dogwood Ln.
Meriden, CT 06450
Ph: (305)458-1098

Jean-Louis, Jimmy, Founder,
  President
Hollywood Unites For Haiti **[11926]**
5338 Hillcrest Dr., Ste. 2
Los Angeles, CA 90043
Ph: (323)244-2712
Toll Free: 866-533-1859
Fax: (323)290-9000

Jefferies, Steve, President
National Association for Sport and
  Physical Education **[8431]**
1900 Association Dr.
Reston, VA 20191-1598
Ph: (703)476-3410
Toll Free: 800-213-7193
Fax: (703)476-8316

Jeffers, Jeff, Comm. Chm.
Association of Fruit and Vegetable
  Inspection and Standardization
  Agencies **[4229]**
1557 Reeves St.
Dothan, AL 36302
Ph: (334)792-5185
Fax: (334)671-7984

Jefferson, Kelley, M.D., Administrator
Society for Assisted Reproductive
  Technology **[17126]**
1209 Montgomery Hwy.
Birmingham, AL 35216-2809
Ph: (205)978-5000
Fax: (205)978-5018

Jefford, Janet, President
American Legion Auxiliary Girls Na-
  tion **[17851]**
8945 N Meridian St., Ste. 200
Indianapolis, IN 46260
Ph: (317)569-4500
Fax: (317)569-4502

Jeffreys, Greg, President
InfoComm International **[267]**
11242 Waples Mill Rd., Ste. 200

Fairfax, VA 22030
Ph: (703)273-7200
Toll Free: 800-659-7469
Fax: (703)991-8259

Jeffries, Erin, Mgr. of Public Rel.
Arcosanti, A Project of the Cosanti
Foundation [3988]
13555 S Cross L Rd.
Mayer, AZ 86333
Ph: (928)632-7135
Fax: (928)632-6229

Jeffries, Hon. Tim, Contact
National Organization for Victim As-
sistance [13265]
510 King St., Ste. 424
Alexandria, VA 22314-3132
Ph: (703)535-6682
Toll Free: 800-879-6682
Fax: (703)535-5500

Jeker, Bjoern A., President
Swiss-American Chamber of Com-
merce [23621]
PO Box 26007
San Francisco, CA 94126-6007
Ph: (415)433-6679

Jelinek, James, Co-Ch.
Submarine Industrial Base Council
[986]
1825 Eye St. NW, Ste. 600
Washington, DC 20006-5415
Ph: (202)207-3633
Fax: (202)575-3400

Jenkin, Rev. Bill, III, President
Continental Baptist Missions [19728]
11650 Northland Dr. NE
Rockford, MI 49341
Ph: (616)863-2226

Jenkins, Chanel, President
Pi Nu Epsilon [23832]
2159 White St., Ste. 3, No. 104
York, PA 17404

Jenkins, Dr. Dave, Founder, Director
SurfAid International [11446]
345 S Coast Hwy. 101, Ste. K
Encinitas, CA 92024
Ph: (760)753-1103
Fax: (760)487-1943

Jenkins, Elizabeth, Exec. Dir.
American Society of Cytopathology
[14357]
100 W 10th St., Ste. 605
Wilmington, DE 19801-6604
Ph: (302)543-6583
Fax: (302)543-6597

Jenkins, Forrest (Joe) N, V. Chmn.
of the Bd., Treasurer
Foundations and Donors Interested
in Catholic Activities [19836]
4201 Connecticut Ave. NW, Ste. 505
Washington, DC 20008
Ph: (202)223-3550

Jenkins, Jennifer, Exec. Dir.
Distributed Wind Energy Association
[7387]
c/o Jennifer Jenkins, Executive
Director
1065 Main Ave., No. 209
Durango, CO 81301-5297
Ph: (928)380-6012

Jenkins, Jim, Founder
Children with AIDS Project of
America [10447]
PO Box 23778
Tempe, AZ 85285-3778
Ph: (602)405-2196
Fax: (602)454-9092

Jenkins, Mr. Joe, Exec. Dir.
Slate Roofing Contractors Association of North America [580]

143 Forest Ln.
Grove City, PA 16127
Ph: (814)786-7015
Fax: (814)786-8209

Jenkins, John, Exec. Dir.
Judge Advocates Association [5602]
c/o The Army Navy Club
901 17th St.
Washington, DC 20006

Jenkins, Kevin, CEO, President
World Vision International [12740]
800 W Chestnut Ave.
Monrovia, CA 91016
Ph: (626)303-8811
Fax: (626)301-7786

Jenkins, Mary, President, CEO
Christians Overcoming Cancer
[13945]
PO Box 307133
Gahanna, OH 43230
Ph: (614)985-3750

Jenkins, Michael, CEO, President
Forest Trends [3866]
1203 19th St. NW, 4th Fl.
Washington, DC 20036
Ph: (202)298-3000
Fax: (202)298-3014

Jenkins, Michael W., Chairman
American Clergy Leadership Confer-
ence [20532]
3224 16th St. NW
Washington, DC 20010
Ph: (202)319-3200

Jenkins, Nancy, Exec. Dir., Editor,
Secretary
American Reusable Textile Associa-
tion [3254]
PO Box 1142
Shawnee Mission, KS 66202
Ph: (863)660-5350
    (913)709-0229

Jenkins, Peter, Founder
Tree Climbers International [21598]
PO Box 5588
Atlanta, GA 31107
Ph: (404)377-3150
    (404)458-4303

Jenkins, Scott R., Chmn. of the Bd.
Southern Sudan Humanitarian
[12731]
9959 S 3200 W
South Jordan, UT 84095
Ph: (801)323-2007

Jenkins-Perez, Jenni, LVT, President
Veterinary Laboratory Association
[17672]
PO Box 433
Cream Ridge, NJ 08514
Ph: (732)492-8019

Jennings, Bryan Scott, Director,
Founder
Walking on Water [20012]
5928 Balfour Ct., Ste. C
Carlsbad, CA 92008
Ph: (760)438-1111

Jennings, Clay, Membership Chp.
Heritage Roses Group [22100]
22 Gypsy Ln.
Camarillo, CA 93010

Jennings, Doug, President
International Association of Silver Art
Collectors [21666]
PO Box 5202
Lakeland, FL 33807-5202

Jennings, Kevin, Chairman
Association of Film Commissioners
International [1188]

9595 Wilshire Blvd., Ste. 900
Beverly Hills, CA 90211
Ph: (323)461-2324
Fax: (413)375-2903

Jennings, Ross, President
American International Recruitment
Council [7444]
4710 Rosedale Ave.
Bethesda, MD 20814
Ph: (240)547-6400
Fax: (240)547-6400

Jennings, Wayne, Chairman
International Association for Learning
Alternatives [7487]
112103 Haering Cir.
Chaska, MN 55318-1378
Ph: (612)716-5620

Jenny, J. Peter, President
The Peregrine Fund [4869]
5668 W Flying Hawk Ln.
Boise, ID 83709
Ph: (208)362-3716
Fax: (208)362-2376

Jens, Virginia, President
American Begonia Society [22065]
PO Box 471651
San Francisco, CA 94147-1651

Jensen, Anabel, PhD, President
Six Seconds [7068]
PO Box 1985
Freedom, CA 95019
Ph: (831)763-1800

Jensen, Dick, President
First Foundations Inc. [13050]
PO Box 991
Travelers Rest, SC 29690
Ph: (864)834-2300

Jensen, Jerry F., VP
American Suffolk Horse Association
[4329]
c/o Mary Margaret Read, Secretary
4240 Goehring Rd.
Ledbetter, TX 78946-5004
Ph: (979)249-5795

Jensen, Jessica, Chief of Staff
National Journalism Center [18288]
11480 Commerce Park Dr., Ste. 600
Reston, VA 20191
Toll Free: 800-USA-1776
Fax: (702)318-9122

Jensen, Patty, Chairman
Project Harmony [8089]
11949 Q St.
Omaha, NE 68137
Ph: (402)595-1326

Jensen, Sharon, Exec. Dir.
Alliance for Inclusion in the Arts
[10234]
1560 Broadway, Ste. 709
New York, NY 10036
Ph: (212)730-4750

Jensen, Timothy, President
Danish America Heritage Society
[9475]
1717 Grant St.
Blair, NE 68008
Ph: (402)426-9610

Jenya, Judith, Founder
Global Children's Organization
[11234]
3580 Wilshire Blvd., Ste. 1800
Los Angeles, CA 90010
Ph: (213)368-8385

Jeon, Danny, Chairperson
Japan-America Student Conference
[8082]

International Student Conferences
1211 Connecticut Ave. NW, Ste. 420
Washington, DC 20036
Ph: (202)289-9088

Jepson, Paul, Director
Integrated Plant Protection Center
[3566]
2040 Cordley Hall
Dept. of Environmental and
Molecular Toxicology
Oregon State University
Corvallis, OR 97331-2915
Ph: (541)737-3541
Fax: (541)737-3080

Jeremiah, Bill, President
Deep Draft Lubricant Association
[2107]
PO Box 40788
Mobile, AL 36640

Jernigan, Jerry, VP
Braunvieh Association of America
[3721]
c/o Patti Teeler, Frances Miller
5750 Epsilon, Ste. 200
San Antonio, TX 78249-3407
Ph: (210)561-2892
Fax: (210)696-5031

Jerome, Ann, PhD, CCH, RSHom,
President
National Center for Homeopathy
[15290]
7918 Jones Branch Dr., Ste. 300
McLean, VA 22102
Ph: (703)506-7667
Fax: (703)506-3266

Jesse, Terry, Exec. Dir.
National Association of Legal Fee
Analysis [5438]
1712 W Greeanleaf Ave., No. 2
Chicago, IL 60626
Ph: (312)907-7275

Jessee, Gary, President
National Association of States United
for Aging and Disabilities [10519]
1201 15th St. NW, Ste. 350
Washington, DC 20005
Ph: (202)898-2578
Fax: (202)898-2583

Jessop, Sandy, President
Siberian Husky Club of America, Inc.
[21961]
c/o Delbert Thacker, Membership
Chairman
3413 67th Dr.
Union Grove, WI 53182-9405

Jester, Molly, Founder, President
Stop Exploitation Now! [10799]
15100 SE 38th St., Ste. 101, No.
753
Bellevue, WA 98006

Jeter, Katherine F., EdD, Founder
National Association for Continence
[17553]
1415 Stuart Engals Blvd.
Mount Pleasant, SC 29464
Ph: (843)377-0900
Toll Free: 800-252-3337

Jewell, Mr. Greg, Exec. Dir.
Les Dames d'Escoffier International
[963]
PO Box 4961
Louisville, KY 40204-0961
Ph: (502)456-1851
Fax: (502)456-1821

Jewell, Lucinda, V. Chmn. of the Bd.
Depression and Bipolar Support Alliance [15768]

55 E Jackson Blvd., Ste. 490
Chicago, IL 60604
Toll Free: 800-826-3632
Fax: (312)642-7243

Jewell, Mark L., Mem.
Physicians Coalition for Injectable
 Safety [14319]
11262 Monarch St.
Garden Grove, CA 92841
Ph: (562)799-2356
Toll Free: 800-364-2147
Fax: (562)799-1098

Jewell, Rebecca, Dir. of Programs
International Volunteer Program
 [13300]
7106 Sayre Dr.
Oakland, CA 94611
Ph: (415)477-3667
Fax: (415)477-3669

Jewell, Sally, Chairman
National Park Foundation [5665]
1110 Vermont Ave. NW, Ste. 200
Washington, DC 20005
Ph: (202)796-2500
Fax: (202)796-2509

Jex, Rod, Treasurer
National Softball Association of the
 Deaf [23204]
c/o Rod Jex, Treasurer
1039 E Wyndom Way
Layton, UT 84040

Jeyalingam, Brintha, Bd. Member
People for Equality and Relief in
 Lanka [18434]
PO Box 292
Glenn Dale, MD 70769
Ph: (301)805-2465

Jeyarajah, Dr. Elias, President
United States Tamil Political Action
 Council [19151]
PO Box 35536
Washington, DC 20033-5536
Ph: (202)595-3123

Jezierski, Eduardo, CEO, Bd.
 Member
Innovative Support to Emergencies
 Diseases and Disasters [11672]
955 Benecia Ave.
Sunnyvale, CA 94085
Ph: (408)471-5758

Jezycki, Michelle, Project Mgr.,
 Director
Team HOPE: Help Offering Parents
 Empowerment [12359]
699 Prince St.
Charles B. Wang International
 Children's Bldg.
699 Prince St.
Alexandria, VA 22314
Toll Free: 800-843-5678

Jezzard, Peter, Ph.D, Mem.
Section for Magnetic Resonance
 Technologists [15698]
2030 Addison St., 7th Fl.
Berkeley, CA 94704
Ph: (510)841-1899
Fax: (510)841-2340

Jha, Santosh, President
Bihar Association of North America
 [9565]
3618 Battle Creek Dr.
Missouri City, TX 77459
Ph: (281)892-9187

Jia, Ji-Dong, President
Association Internationale pour
 l'Etude du Foie [15251]
230 S Clark St., No. 315

Chicago, IL 60604-1406

Jiang, Haobo, Ph.D., Secretary
Overseas Chinese Entomologists
 Association [6617]
136 Ag Hall
Stillwater, OK 74078-6015
Ph: (405)744-5395

Jiang, Tao, President
Chinese American Chromatography
 Association [6195]
c/o Tao Jiang, President
Covidien/Mallinckrodt
3600 N 2nd St.
Saint Louis, MO 63147
Ph: (314)654-1744

Jillaow, Ugas, Chairman
Baitulmaal, Inc. [12625]
PO Box 166911
Irving, TX 75016-6911
Ph: (972)257-2564
Toll Free: 800-220-9554
Fax: (972)258-1396

Jimas, George, Bd. Member
Society of Kastorians Omonoia
 [19457]
150-28 14th Ave.
Whitestone, NY 11357
Ph: (718)746-4505
 (718)747-3246
Fax: (718)746-4506

Jimenez, Sandy, Dir. of Info. Svcs.
MPA - The Association of Magazine
 Media [2802]
757 3rd Ave., 11th Fl.
New York, NY 10017
Ph: (212)872-3700

Jimenez, Vanessa, Exec. Dir.
Sigma Lambda Gamma National
 Sorority [23977]
125 E Zeller St., Ste. D
North Liberty, IA 52317
Ph: (319)774-5370

Jimeno-Nieto, July, Founder
Amanda Jimeno Foundation [13876]
1155 Dairy Ashford, Ste. 610
Houston, TX 77079
Ph: (281)920-2668

Jin, Feiyan, Treasurer
Chinese Biopharmaceutical Association, U.S.A. [16656]
111 Rockville Pke., Ste. 800
Rockville, MD 20850

Jing-hua Yin, John, Exec. Dir.
Chinese Language Teachers As-
 sociation [7601]
c/o Dept. of Asian Langauges &
 Literatures
University of Vermont
479 Main St.
Burlington, VT 05405
Ph: (802)656-5764
Fax: (802)656-8472

Joaquin, Linton, Gen. Counsel
National Immigration Law Center
 [18466]
PO Box 70067
Los Angeles, CA 90070
Ph: (213)639-3900
Fax: (213)639-3911

Jocius, Kelly, Exec. Dir.
National Flute Association [9973]
70 E Lake St., No. 200
Chicago, IL 60601
Ph: (312)332-6682
Fax: (312)332-6684

Johannigman, Roger, Exec. Dir.
Food Ingredient Distributors Association [1326]

3206 Columbia Pky.
Cincinnati, OH 45226
Ph: (513)235-6786

Johanns, Patrick J., Leader
Alpha Chi Sigma Fraternity, Inc.
 [23703]
6296 Rucker Rd., Ste. B
Indianapolis, IN 46220
Ph: (317)357-5944
Toll Free: 800-252-4369
Fax: (317)351-9702

Johansen, Connie, President
BioCommunications Association
 [13818]
c/o Connie Johansen, President
1394 Redwood Cir.
Laplata, MD 20646
Ph: (571)557-1971

Johanson, Ms. Cindy, Exec. Dir.
Edutopia - The George Lucas
 Educational Foundation [7766]
PO Box 3494
San Rafael, CA 94912-3494

John, Susan D., MD, FACR, Exec.
American Society of Emergency
 Radiology [17044]
4550 Post Oak Pl., Ste. 342
Houston, TX 77027
Ph: (713)965-0566
Fax: (713)960-0488

John, Tony, VP
Malayalee Engineers Association in
 North America [6570]
c/o Abraham Joseph, President
2214 N Williamsburg St.
Arlington Heights, IL 60004

Johns, Brian, President
Whooping Crane Conservation Association [4900]
11411 SW 49th Pl.
Davie, FL 33330

Johns, Marie C., Chairman
Council for Court Excellence [5380]
1111 14th St. NW, Ste. 500
Washington, DC 20005
Ph: (202)785-5917

Johns, Michael N., VP
Monument Builders of North America
 [2410]
136 S Keowee St.
Dayton, OH 45402
Toll Free: 800-233-4472
Fax: (937)222-5794

Johnson, Allan, President
517th Parachute Regimental Combat
 Team Association [21186]
c/o K. Allan Johnson, President
215 Mission Rd.
Hackettstown, NJ 07840

Johnson, Allan, III, Chairman
Drycleaning and Laundry Institute
 International [2077]
14700 Sweitzer Ln.
Laurel, MD 20707
Ph: (301)622-1900
Toll Free: 800-638-2627

Johnson, Amy, Exec. Dir.
Phi Beta Chi [23959]
PO Box 65426
West Des Moines, IA 50265

Johnson, Amy, Exec. Dir.
United States Federation of Worker
 Cooperatives [23538]
1904 Franklin St., Ste. 400
Oakland, CA 94612
Ph: (415)392-7277

Johnson, Anne Doherty, Exec. Dir.
Society for Clinical and Experimental
 Hypnosis [15367]
Commoncove, Ste. 100
305 Commandants Way
Chelsea, MA 02150-4057
Ph: (617)744-9857
Fax: (413)451-0668

Johnson, Barbara L., Chairman
Joint Center for Political and
 Economic Studies [7047]
2000 H St. NW, Ste. 422
Washington, DC 20052
Ph: (202)789-3500
Fax: (202)789-6390

Johnson, Mr. Bern, Exec. Dir.
Environmental Law Alliance
 Worldwide [5179]
1412 Pearl St.
Eugene, OR 97401
Ph: (541)687-8454
Fax: (541)687-0535

Johnson, Bill, Founder, President
American Decency Association
 [18031]
203 E Main St.
Fremont, MI 49412
Ph: (231)924-4050

Johnson, Bill, Exec. Dir.
American Truck Historical Society
 [22472]
PO Box 901611
Kansas City, MO 64190-1611
Ph: (816)891-9900
 (816)891-9903
Fax: (816)891-9903

Johnson, Bo, Founder
Addi's Cure [15538]
c/o Bo Johnson, Founder
19520 W Catawba Ave., Ste. 200
Cornelius, NC 28031

Johnson, Bob, Contact
World Union of Deists [20581]
PO Box 4052
Clearwater, FL 33758

Johnson, Brandon, Contact
Gold Prospectors Association of
 America [22392]
43445 Business Park Dr., Ste. 113
Temecula, CA 92590-3671
Ph: (951)699-4749
Toll Free: 800-551-9707
Fax: (951)699-4062

Johnson, Bryan, Chairman
International Council for Machinery
 Lubrication [2108]
2208 W Detroit St., Ste. 101
Broken Arrow, OK 74012-3630
Ph: (918)259-2950
Fax: (918)259-0177

Johnson, Carl V., President
International Society of Bible Collec-
 tors [19760]
PO Box 26654
Minneapolis, MN 55426

Johnson, Carol A., MA, Founder,
 President
Largely Positive [16257]
PO Box 170223
Milwaukee, WI 53217-8021

Johnson, Catherine, Exec. Dir.
Spellbinders [10226]
520 S 3rd St.
Carbondale, CO 81623
Ph: (970)544-2389

Johnson, Catie, Exec. Dir.
World Council of Elders [9223]
PO Box 7915

Boulder, CO 80306
Ph: (303)444-9263

Johnson, Charles, President, CEO
National Council for Adoption
[10460]
225 N Washington St.
Alexandria, VA 22314-2561
Ph: (703)299-6633
Fax: (703)299-6004

Johnson, Charlie, Mem.
Steel Erectors Association of
America [6351]
401 E 4th St., No. 204
Winston Salem, NC 27101-4171
Ph: (336)294-8880
Fax: (413)208-6936

Johnson, Chuck, Web Adm.
International Rivers [7369]
2054 University Ave., Ste. 300
Berkeley, CA 94704-2644
Ph: (510)848-1155
Fax: (510)848-1008

Johnson, Craig, Chairman
ClimateTalk Alliance [5883]
2400 Camino Ramon, Ste. 375
San Ramon, CA 94583-4373
Ph: (925)275-6641
Fax: (925)275-6691

Johnson, Dale, Treasurer
Council of Institutional Investors
[3041]
888 17th St. NW, Ste. 500
Washington, DC 20006
Ph: (202)822-0800
Fax: (202)822-0801

Johnson, Dan, Chmn. of the Bd.,
President
Light Aircraft Manufacturers Associa-
tion [363]
2001 Steamboat Ridge Ct.
Port Orange, FL 32128-6918
Ph: (651)592-7565
   (651)226-1825

Johnson, Mr. Dana, Contact
Toy Car Collectors Association
[22450]
c/o Dana Johnson
PO Box 1824
Bend, OR 97709-1824
Ph: (541)318-7176

Johnson, David C, President
Association for Clinical Pastoral
Education [20073]
1 W Court Sq., Ste. 325
Decatur, GA 30030-2576
Ph: (404)320-1472
Fax: (404)320-0849

Johnson, David, President
Classic Car Club of America [21356]
PO Box 346160
Chicago, IL 60634
Ph: (847)390-0443
Fax: (847)916-2674

Johnson, David, Comm. Chm.
Gulf Yachting Association [22617]
c/o Sarah Ashton, Regional
Administrative Judge
79 Pitt St.
Charleston, SC 29403

Johnson, David, CFO
International Rescue Committee
USA [12687]
122 E 42nd St.
New York, NY 10168-1289
Ph: (212)551-3000
Toll Free: 855-9RE-SCUE
Fax: (212)551-3179

Johnson, David R., Director
National Alliance for Secondary
Education and Transition [8559]
6 Pattee Hall
150 Pillsbury Dr. SE
Minneapolis, MN 55455
Ph: (612)624-2097

Johnson, David, Founder, Director
Silent Images [12991]
100 W John St., Ste. H
Matthews, NC 28105
Ph: (704)999-5010

Johnson, Dean, Exec. Dir.
National Association of Church
Facilities Managers [20563]
Ph: (616)956-9377

Johnson, Deborah, Contact
Western Society of Periodontology
[14474]
PO Box 458
Artesia, CA 90702-0458
Ph: (562)493-4080
Toll Free: 800-367-8386
Fax: (562)493-4340

Johnson, Denise, Bus. Mgr.
International Society of Limnology
[6780]
c/o Denise Johnson, Business
Manager
5020 Swepsonville-Saxapahaw Rd.
Graham, NC 27253

Johnson, Don C., Director
National Association of Legal
Investigators [5365]
235 N Pine St.
Lansing, MI 48933
Ph: (517)702-9835
Toll Free: 866-520-6254
Fax: (517)372-1501

Johnson, Don, President
National Association for Civil War
Brass Music, Inc. [9966]
124 Maiden Choice Ln.
Baltimore, MD 21228
Ph: (410)744-7708

Johnson, Donna, Treasurer
International Brick Collectors' Association [21670]
c/o Donna Johnson, Treasurer
3141 S Fork Rd.
Cody, WY 82414-8009
Ph: (307)587-5061

Johnson, Donna, President, CEO
Unity Worldwide Ministries [20029]
PO Box 610
Lees Summit, MO 64063
Ph: (816)524-7414
Fax: (816)525-4020

Johnson, Doug, Chmn. of the Bd.
National Association of Exotic Pest
Plant Councils [4530]
University of Georgia
Center for Invasive Species and
Ecosystem Health
2360 Rainwater Rd.
Tifton, GA 31793
Ph: (229)386-3298
Fax: (229)386-3352

Johnson, Douglas W., President
Flying Physicians Association
[16751]
11626 Twain Dr.
Montgomery, TX 77356
Ph: (936)588-6505
Fax: (832)415-0287

Johnson, Dwain Anthony, Founder
Saving Soles Foundation [12564]
PO Box 1475

Bear, DE 19701-7475
Ph: (708)218-8945

Johnson, Eric, Treasurer
Council on Anthropology and Education [5912]

Johnson, Ethan, President
American Conifer Society [4725]
PO Box 1583
Maple Grove, MN 55311
Ph: (763)657-7251

Johnson, Fred, President
All One People [10473]
460 East 100 North
Manti, UT 84642
Ph: (435)851-1548

Johnson, Fred M., President
AAA Charity Investment Fund
[13020]
300 E State St., No. 531
Redlands, CA 92373
Ph: (909)793-2009
Fax: (909)793-6880

Johnson, Fred M., President
World-Wide Missions [20481]
300 E State St., Ste. 531
Redlands, CA 92373-5235
Ph: (909)793-2009
Fax: (909)793-6880

Johnson, Fred, VP of Admin.
National Cotton Council of America
[937]
7193 Goodlett Farms Pky.
Cordova, TN 38016-4909
Ph: (901)274-9030
Fax: (901)725-0510

Johnson, Gary, Contact
Cancer Adventures [13915]
PO Box 7353
Bend, OR 97708-7353
Ph: (541)610-7278

Johnson, Gary, VP
Model A Restorers Club [21437]
6721 Merriman Rd.
Garden City, MI 48135-1956
Ph: (734)427-9050
Fax: (734)427-9054

Johnson, Gay, CEO
National Association of Nurse
Practitioners in Women's Health
[16151]
505 C St. NE
Washington, DC 20002
Ph: (202)543-9693

Johnson, Ginger, President
Pontius Family Association [20915]
21810 Fairmount Blvd.
Shaker Heights, OH 44118-4816

Johnson, Glenda, Founder,
President
Medical Wings International [15034]
PO Box 16812
Chicago, IL 60616
Ph: (817)800-0080

Johnson, Harold, Director
Hands and Voices [15191]
PO Box 3093
Boulder, CO 80307
Ph: (303)492-6283
Toll Free: 866-422-0422

Johnson, Harold
Presbyterian Hunger Program
[12108]
100 Witherspoon St.
Louisville, KY 40202-1396
Ph: (502)569-8080
Toll Free: 800-728-7228

Johnson, J., Founder
Fabry Support and Information
Group [14576]
108 NE 2nd St., Ste. C
Concordia, MO 64020-8324
Ph: (660)463-1355
Fax: (660)463-1356

Johnson, Jacquelyn Clark, PHR,
Exec. Dir.
Beauty 4 Ashes International
[13370]
3713 Lexham Dr.
High Point, NC 27265
Ph: (336)209-7405
Fax: (336)574-0277

Johnson, Jady, Exec. Dir.
Reading Recovery Council of North
America [8491]
500 W Wilson Bridge Rd., Ste. 250
Worthington, OH 43085-2238
Ph: (614)310-7323
Toll Free: 877-883-READ
Fax: (614)310-7345

Johnson, Dr. James D., President
American Board of Endodontics
[14396]
211 E Chicago Ave., Ste. 1100
Chicago, IL 60611-2691
Ph: (312)266-7255
Toll Free: 800-872-3636
Fax: (312)266-9867

Johnson, James, Chairman
International Cotton Advisory Com-
mittee [3763]
1629 K St. NW, Ste. 702
Washington, DC 20006-1636
Ph: (202)463-6660
Fax: (202)463-6950

Johnson, James, President
United States Beet Sugar Associa-
tion [1378]
1156 15th St. NW, Ste. 1019
Washington, DC 20005
Ph: (202)296-4820
Fax: (202)331-2065

Johnson, Jeffery M., PhD, CEO,
President
National Partnership for Community
Leadership [11478]
1629 K St. NW, Ste. 300
Washington, DC 20006

Johnson, Jennifer, Treasurer
American Society for Veterinary
Clinical Pathology [17626]
2424 American Ln.
Madison, WI 53704
Ph: (608)443-2479
Fax: (608)443-2474

Johnson, Jennifer, Director
Society for Industrial Microbiology
and Biotechnology [6102]
3929 Old Lee Hwy., Ste. 92A
Fairfax, VA 22030
Ph: (703)691-3357
Fax: (703)691-7991

Johnson, Chief Jim, Chairperson
National Law Enforcement Partnership to Prevent Gun Violence
[5219]
c/o Police Foundation
1201 Connecticut Ave. NW, No. 200
Washington, DC 20036
Ph: (202)833-1460

Johnson, John, Ph.D, Chairman
National Certification Board for
Diabetes Educators [14540]
330 E Algonquin Rd., Ste. 4
Arlington Heights, IL 60005
Ph: (847)228-9795
Toll Free: 877-239-3233
Fax: (847)228-8469

Johnson, Judy M., Editor
Original Paper Doll Artists Guild
[22008]
PO Box 14
Kingfield, ME 04947
Ph: (207)265-2500
Toll Free: 800-290-2928

Johnson, Ken, Mem.
Society of American Period Furniture
Makers [1487]
c/o Connecticut Valley School of
Woodworking, 249 Spencer St.,
249 Spencer St.
Manchester, CT 06040

Johnson, Kersten, Exec. Dir.
University of South Dakota Alumni
Association [19365]
414 E Clark St.
Vermillion, SD 57069-2390
Ph: (605)677-6734
Toll Free: 800-655-2586

Johnson, Kevin, COO
Geochemical Society [6688]
5241 Broad Branch Rd. NW
Washington, DC 20015-1305
Ph: (202)545-6946

Johnson Kipreos, Jaci, President
American Academy of Professional
Coders [15107]
2233 S Presidents Dr., Ste. F
Salt Lake City, UT 84120
Ph: (801)236-2200
Toll Free: 800-626-2633
Fax: (801)236-2258

Johnson, Kristina, Program Mgr.
Society of Jewish Ethics [20283]
1531 Dickey Dr.
Atlanta, GA 30322
Ph: (404)712-8550
Fax: (404)727-7399

Johnson, Lanier, Exec. Dir.
American Sports Medicine Institute
[17278]
2660 10th Ave. S, Ste. 505
Birmingham, AL 35205
Ph: (205)918-0000
Fax: (205)918-2177

Johnson, Larry D., President
National Association of School
Safety and Law Enforcement Of-
ficials [8524]
c/o Larry D. Johnson, President
1331 Franklin St.
Grand Rapids, MI 49504
Ph: (616)819-2100
Fax: (616)819-2017

Johnson, Leilani, Exec. Dir.
Circle of Health International [15598]
c/o Sera Bonds
1905 Paramount Ave.
Austin, TX 78704
Ph: (347)712-1721
    (512)210-7710

Johnson, Leon A., President
Tuskegee Airmen Inc. [20673]
PO Box 830060
Tuskegee, AL 36083-0060
Ph: (334)725-8200
Fax: (334)725-8205

Johnson, Luci Baines, Chairperson
Nurses for a Healthier Tomorrow
[16169]
Honor Society of Nursing, Sigma
Theta Tau International
550 W North St.
Indianapolis, IN 46202

Johnson, M. Scout, VP
National Association of Graduate-
Professional Students [8622]

1050 K St. NW, No. 400
Washington, DC 20001-4448
Ph: (202)643-8043

Johnson, Mark R., DVM, Exec. Dir.
Global Wildlife Resources [4822]
PO Box 10248
Bozeman, MT 59719
Ph: (406)586-4624

Johnson, Marlene, Exec. Dir., CEO
National Association of State Facili-
ties Administrators [5697]
1776 Avenue of the States
Lexington, KY 40511
Ph: (859)244-8181
Fax: (859)244-8001

Johnson, Maryann, BSN, RN,
President
Pediatric Endocrinology Nursing
Society [16614]
18000 W 105th St.
Olathe, KS 66061
Ph: (913)895-4628
Toll Free: 877-936-7367
Fax: (913)895-4652

Johnson, Michele, Exec. Dir.
International Society of Arthroscopy,
Knee Surgery and Orthopaedic
Sports Medicine [16480]
2410 Camino Ramon, Ste. 215
San Ramon, CA 94583
Ph: (925)807-1197
Fax: (925)807-1199

Johnson, Mike W., President, CEO
National Stone, Sand and Gravel
Association [3188]
1605 King St.
Alexandria, VA 22314
Ph: (703)525-8788

Johnson, Minnie Fells, Chairwoman
Project for Public Spaces [17993]
419 Lafayette, 7th Fl.
New York, NY 10003
Ph: (212)620-5660
Fax: (212)620-3821

Johnson, Monika, Mgr.
United Nations Association of the
United Nations of America - Council
of Organizations [19213]
801 2nd Ave., 9th Fl.
New York, NY 10017
Ph: (212)697-3315
Fax: (212)697-3316

Johnson, Nancy J., Prog. Dir., Exec.
Sec.
American Board of Health Physics
[16764]
c/o Nancy J. Johnson, Program
Director/Executive Secretary
1313 Dolley Madison Blvd., Ste. 402
McLean, VA 22101
Ph: (703)790-1745
Fax: (703)790-2672

Johnson, Nancy, Secretary,
Treasurer
National Gypsy Moth Management
Board [4531]
Northeastern Center for Forest
Health Research
51 Mill Pond Rd.
Hamden, CT 06514-1703
Ph: (203)230-4321
Fax: (203)230-4315

Johnson, Nicholas, President
Institute on Taxation and Economic
Policy [18167]
Washington Office
1616 P St. NW, Ste. 200
Washington, DC 20036
Ph: (202)299-1066
Fax: (202)299-1065

Johnson, Orlan, President
North American Religious Liberty
Association [20573]
PO Box 7505
Riverside, CA 92513
Ph: (805)955-7683

Johnson, Pam, Editor
Orangeburgh German Swiss
Genealogical Society [20990]
PO Box 974
Orangeburg, SC 29116-0974

Johnson, Pamela Gail, Founder
Secret Society of Happy People
[9563]
240 N Denton Tap Rd., PMB 112
Coppell, TX 75019
Ph: (972)459-7031

Johnson, Patty, Founder
SunnyTravelers [22433]
58800 Executive Dr.
Mishawaka, IN 46544
Ph: (574)258-0571
Toll Free: 800-262-5178
Fax: (574)259-7105

Johnson, Q. Richards, President
Phi Delta Psi Fraternity [23671]
PO Box 3088
Southfield, MI 48037-2105

Johnson, R. Steven, President
International Association of Law
Enforcement Firearms Instructors
[5470]
25 Country Club Rd., Ste. 707
Gilford, NH 03249
Ph: (603)524-8787
Fax: (603)524-8856

Johnson, Rebecca Grooms,
President
Music Teachers National Association
[8378]
1 W 4th St., Ste. 1550
Cincinnati, OH 45202
Ph: (513)421-1420
Toll Free: 888-512-5278

Johnson, Rebecca, President
International Association of Human-
Animal Interaction Organizations
[17447]
2005 W Broadway, Ste 100
Columbia, MO 65203

Johnson, Rebecca L., MD, CEO
American Board of Pathology
[16572]
4830 W Kennedy Blvd., Ste. 690
Tampa, FL 33609-2571
Ph: (813)286-2444
Fax: (813)289-5279

Johnson, Renee, President
Federal Managers Association
[5196]
1641 Prince St.
Alexandria, VA 22314-2818
Ph: (703)683-8700
Fax: (703)683-8707

Johnson, Richard, President
International Federation of Stamp
Dealers' Associations [22335]
c/o Sam Malamud, Vice President
161 Helen St.
South Plainfield, NJ 07080
Ph: (908)548-8088
Fax: (908)822-7379

Johnson, Richard, President, CEO
Parenteral Drug Association [2565]
Bethesda Towers, Ste. 150
4350 E West Hwy.
Bethesda, MD 20814-4485
Ph: (301)656-5900
Fax: (301)986-0296

Johnson, Richard, CEO
Spark Ventures [11154]
134 N LaSalle St., 5th Fl.
Chicago, IL 60602
Ph: (773)293-6710
Fax: (773)293-6920

Johnson, Rob, CEO
Billiard Congress of America [22584]
10900 W 120th Ave., Ste. B7
Broomfield, CO 80021
Ph: (303)243-5070

Johnson, Robert, Treasurer
Independent Association of Publish-
ers' Employees [23511]
5 Schalks Crossing Rd., Ste. 220
Plainsboro, NJ 08536
Ph: (609)275-6020
Toll Free: 800-325-4273
Fax: (609)275-6023

Johnson, Robert, CEO
National Association for Information
Destruction [1803]
3030 N 3rd St., Ste. 940
Phoenix, AZ 85012-3059
Ph: (602)788-6243
Fax: (480)658-2088

Johnson, Robert W., II, VP
International Sugar Trade Coalition
[3189]
401 9th St. NW, Ste. 640
Washington, DC 20004
Ph: (202)531-4028

Johnson, Robert W., President
Outdoor Amusement Business As-
sociation [1158]
1035 S Semoran Blvd., Ste. 1045A
Winter Park, FL 32792
Ph: (407)681-9444
Toll Free: 800-517-OABA
Fax: (407)681-9445

Johnson, Ruth Sieber, Exec. Dir.
Sigma Alpha Iota International Music
Fraternity [23833]
1 Tunnel Rd.
Asheville, NC 28805
Ph: (828)251-0606
Fax: (828)251-0644

Johnson, Sally S., CSA, Exec. Dir.
National Council of Youth Sports
[23242]
7185 SE Seagate Ln.
Stuart, FL 34997-2160
Ph: (772)781-1452
Fax: (772)781-7298

Johnson, Sara G., President
Society of Nuclear Medicine and
Molecular Imaging Technologist
Section [16078]
1850 Samuel Morse Dr.
Reston, VA 20190
Ph: (703)708-9000
Fax: (703)708-9015

Johnson, Scott, President, CEO,
Founder
Myelin Repair Foundation [15961]
18809 Cox Ave., Ste. 190
Saratoga, CA 95070
Ph: (408)871-2410
Toll Free: 877-863-4967
Fax: (408)871-2409

Johnson, Scott, Secretary, Treasurer
National Association of State Boards
of Education [8521]
333 John Carlyle St., Ste. 530
Alexandria, VA 22314
Ph: (703)684-4000

Johnson, Scott, Leader
Positive Music Association [9997]
c/o Scott Johnson

4593 Maple Ct.
Boulder, CO 80301-5829

Johnson, Scott, PhD, President
Veterinary Emergency and Critical
 Care Society [17669]
6335 Camp Bullis Rd., Ste. 12
San Antonio, TX 78257
Ph: (210)698-5575
Fax: (210)698-7138

Johnson, Shelly
American Massage Therapy As-
 sociation [15551]
500 Davis St., Ste. 900
Evanston, IL 60201-4695
Toll Free: 877-905-0577

Johnson, Starlene, Exec. Dir.
Better Future International [10866]
PO Box 20196
New York, NY 10014

Johnson, Steve, Exec. Dir.
Associated Equipment Distributors
 [1711]
600 22nd St., Ste. 220
Oak Brook, IL 60523
Ph: (630)574-0650

Johnson, Steve, Secretary
North American Squirrel Association
 [22293]
PO Box 186
Holmen, WI 54636
Ph: (608)234-5988

Johnson, Steve, CEO, President
USA Cycling [22759]
210 USA Cycling Pt., Ste. 100
Colorado Springs, CO 80919
Ph: (719)434-4200

Johnson, Stuart F., President
Aaron Burr Association [10317]
c/o Stuart Johnson, President
1004 Butterworth Ln.
Upper Marlboro, MD 20774-2205
Fax: (301)350-5700

Johnson, Susan E., President
Real Estate Services Providers
 Council [2892]
2101 L St. NW, Ste. 800
Washington, DC 20037
Ph: (202)862-2051
Fax: (202)862-2052

Johnson, Terri, Exec. Dir.
Center for New Community [17970]
47 W Division St., No. 514
Chicago, IL 60610
Ph: (312)266-0319
Fax: (312)266-0278

Johnson, Tom, Jr., Founder
Africa Surgery [17356]
70 Macculloch Ave.
Morristown, NJ 07960
Ph: (973)292-3320

Johnson, Vicki, Exec. Dir.
North American Piedmontese Cattle
 Association [3748]
1740 County Road 185
Ramah, CO 80832
Ph: (306)329-8600

Johnson, Wallace, Officer
National Corrugated Steel Pipe As-
 sociation [2610]
14070 Proton Rd., Ste. 100, LB 9
Dallas, TX 75244
Ph: (972)850-1907
Fax: (972)490-4219

Johnson, Whitney, Coord.
Comprehensive Health Education
 Foundation [8319]

419 3rd Ave. W
Seattle, WA 98119
Ph: (206)824-2907
Toll Free: 800-323-2433
Fax: (206)824-3072

Johnson, William A., Secretary,
 Treasurer
American Society of Papyrologists
 [10063]
233 Allen Bldg.
Dept. of Classical Studies
Duke University
Durham, NC 27708-0103
Fax: (919)681-4262

Johnson, Dr. William C., Exec. Dir.
Sigma Tau Delta [23747]
711 N 1st St.
DeKalb, IL 60115
Ph: (815)981-9974

Johnson-Brown, Stephanie, Officer
National Optometric Association
 [16432]
1801 N Tryon St., Ste. 315
Charlotte, NC 28206
Ph: (704)918-1809
Toll Free: 877-394-2020

Johnsrud, Ann, President
National Association of County
 Recorders, Election Officials, and
 Clerks [5115]
2501 Aerial Center Pky., Ste. 103
Morrisville, NC 27560
Ph: (919)459-2080
Fax: (919)459-2075

Johnston, Alan T., CEO, President
Machinery Information Management
 Open Systems Alliance [2224]
2200 Jack Warner Pky., Ste. 300
Tuscaloosa, AL 35406
Ph: (949)625-8616
Fax: (949)625-8616

Johnston, Denise, President
National Cat Protection Society
 [10667]
6904 W Coast Hwy.
Newport Beach, CA 92663-1306
Ph: (949)650-1232
Fax: (949)650-7367

Johnston, Gordon, VP
Historical Harp Society [9919]
PO Box 662
Havertown, PA 19083-0662

Johnston, J. Bennett, Jr., Chairman
American Iranian Council [18574]
PO Box 707
Princeton, NJ 08542-0707
Ph: (609)252-9099
Fax: (609)252-9698

Johnston, Jeremiah, Bd. Member
Internet Commerce Association
 [2007]
1155 F St. NW
Washington, DC 20004-1312
Ph: (202)255-6172

Johnston, Jim, President
Owner-Operator Independent Drivers
 Association [3353]
1 NW OOIDA Dr.
Grain Valley, MO 64029-7903
Ph: (816)229-5791
Toll Free: 800-444-5791
Fax: (816)229-0518

Johnston, Jim, Treasurer
Sigma Tau Gamma Fraternity, Inc.
 [23933]
101 Ming St.
Warrensburg, MO 64093
Ph: (660)747-2222
Fax: (660)747-9599

Johnston, J.J., President
Clan Johnston/e in America [20815]
c/o J. J. Johnston, President
4207 Leona River
San Antonio, TX 78253
Ph: (210)560-2639

Johnston, John, Exec. Dir.
Production Equipment Rental As-
 sociation [1204]
101 W 31st St.
Manhattan, NY 10001-3507
Ph: (646)839-0430

Johnston, Mike, CPhT, Chairman
National Pharmacy Technician As-
 sociation [16680]
PO Box 683148
Houston, TX 77268-3148
Toll Free: 888-247-8700
Fax: (888)247-8706

Johnston, Pat, Exec. Dir.
National Association for Children's
 Behavioral Health [16833]
1025 Connecticut Ave. NW, Ste.
 1012
Washington, DC 20036-5417
Ph: (202)857-9735
Fax: (202)362-5145

Johnston, Sara, Exec. Dir.
Society for Shamanic Practitioners
 [20507]
PO Box 100007
Denver, CO 80250
Ph: (303)757-0908

Johnston, Rev. Scott Black, Pastor
Center for Christian Studies [19949]
7 W 55th St.
New York, NY 10019
Ph: (212)247-0490

Johnston-Robeldo, Ingrid, President
Society for Menstrual Cycle
 Research [16306]
c/o Ingrid Johnston-Robeldo,
 President
Castleton State College
Castleton, VT 05735

Joines, Vann, PhD, Director,
 President
Southeast Institute for Group and
 Family Therapy [19119]
659 Edwards Ridge Rd.
Chapel Hill, NC 27517-9201
Ph: (919)929-1171
Fax: (919)929-1174

Jonas, Bob, Founder
Wild Gift [4904]
PO Box 1151
Hailey, ID 83333
Ph: (208)471-5091

Jonas, Richard, Contact
Children of Nowhere [10921]
601 W 26th St., Rm. 1105
New York, NY 10001-1133

Joner, Dan, Officer
Carpet Cleaners Institute of the
 Northwest [711]
2661 N Pearl St.
Tacoma, WA 98407
Ph: (360)687-6156
Toll Free: 877-692-2469

Jones, Alan E., MD, President
Society for Academic Emergency
 Medicine [14690]
2340 S River Rd., Ste. 208
Des Plaines, IL 60018
Ph: (847)813-9823
Fax: (847)813-5450

Jones, Alan, Chmn. of the Bd.
International Plant Propagators
 Society [4435]

174 Crestview Dr.
Bellefonte, PA 16823
Fax: (814)355-2467

Jones, Dr. Bill, Exec. Dir.
Surfer's Medical Association [15747]
PO Box 51881
Pacific Grove, CA 93950

Jones, Brian Jay, President
Biographers International Organiza-
 tion [10364]
PO Box 33020
Santa Fe, NM 87594

Jones, Caroline, Chairman
American Council of State Savings
 Supervisors [379]
1129 20th St. NW, 9th Fl.
Washington, DC 20036
Ph: (512)475-1038
Fax: (512)475-1505

Jones, Cathy, Director
Concerned Educators Against
 Forced Unionism [18608]
c/o Cathy Jones, Director
8001 Braddock Rd.
Springfield, VA 22160
Ph: (703)321-8519
Toll Free: 800-336-3600
Fax: (703)321-9319

Jones, Chris, President
Association for Governmental Leas-
 ing and Finance [5704]
19 Mantua Rd.
Mount Royal, NJ 08061
Ph: (856)423-3259
Fax: (856)423-3420

Jones, Chris, President
Wales North America Business
 Chamber [23640]
69 Closter Rd.
Palisades, NY 10964
Ph: (845)398-0619

Jones, David R., Chmn. of the Bd.
Nation Institute [18989]
116 E 16th St., 8th Fl.
New York, NY 10003
Ph: (212)822-0250
Fax: (212)253-5356

Jones, David, Exec. Dir., Counselor
Restoration Path [20045]
PO Box 343418
Bartlett, TN 38184
Ph: (901)751-2468
Toll Free: 877-320-5217

Jones, Debbie, Registrar
Reynolds Family Association [20919]
c/o Larry Reynolds, President
1007 Stone Shore St.
Mount Pleasant, TX 75455
Ph: (903)717-8608

Jones, Debbie, Production Mgr.
Society of St. Andrew [12115]
3383 Sweet Hollow Rd.
Big Island, VA 24526
Ph: (434)299-5956
Toll Free: 800-333-4597
Fax: (434)299-5949

Jones, Douglas S., PhD, President
Association of Science Museum
 Directors [9825]
Illinois State Museum
502 S Spring St.
Springfield, IL 62706-5000
Ph: (217)782-5969
Fax: (217)557-9226

Jones, Evan, Web Adm.
National Association for Rehabilitation Leadership [17090]

c/o National Rehabilitation Association
PO Box 150235
Alexandria, VA 22315
Ph: (703)836-0850
Fax: (703)836-0848

Jones, Fred, Gen. Mgr., VP
Vagabundos Del Mar RV, Boat and
Travel Club [22436]
190 Main St.
Rio Vista, CA 94571
Ph: (707)374-5511
Toll Free: 800-474-2252
Fax: (707)374-6843

Jones, Gerard A., President
National Organization of Industrial
Trade Unions [23449]
148-06 Hillside Ave.
Jamaica, NY 11435
Ph: (718)291-3434

Jones, Glen, Treasurer
American Polypay Sheep Associa-
tion [4659]
305 Lincoln St.
Wamego, KS 66547
Ph: (785)456-8500
Fax: (785)456-8599

Jones, Gloria, Secretary
International Professional Pond
Companies Association [3641]
4045 N Arnold Mill Rd.
Woodstock, GA 30188
Ph: (770)592-9790
Fax: (770)924-9589

Jones, Grace L., President
Audience Development Committee
[10242]
Manhattanville Sta.
New York, NY 10027
Ph: (212)368-6906

Jones, Greg, Secretary
Association of Fertilizer and
Phosphate Chemists [6190]
PO Box 1645
Bartow, FL 33831-1645

Jones, Greg, VP
Association for Manufacturing
Technology [6793]
7901 W Park Dr.
McLean, VA 22102-4206
Ph: (703)893-2900
Toll Free: 800-524-0475
Fax: (703)893-1151

Jones, Greg, President
Friends of Nigeria [19595]
c/o Warren Keller, Treasurer
PO Box 8032
Berkeley, CA 94707
Ph: (319)466-3119

Jones, Hal, CEO, President
Global Hope Network International
[12665]
934 N Magnolia Ave.
Orlando, FL 32801
Ph: (407)207-3256

Jones, Hardy, Exec. Dir.
BlueVoice.org [3821]
10 Sunfish Dr.
Saint Augustine, FL 32080-6386

Jones, Iris, Gen. Counsel
World Jurist Association [5353]
7910 Woodmont Ave., Ste. 1440
Bethesda, MD 20814
Ph: (202)466-5428
Fax: (202)452-8540

Jones, Jack R., Editor
USS St. Louis CL-49 Association
[9780]

1112 N 18th St.
Cambridge, OH 43725
Ph: (740)432-5305

Jones, Jacqueline, President, CEO
Foundation for Child Development
[10818]
295 Madison Ave., 40th Fl.
New York, NY 10017
Ph: (212)867-5777
Fax: (212)867-5844

Jones, James, President
Cloud Family Association [20846]
508 Crestwood Dr.
Eastland, TX 76448

Jones, James L., Chairman
American-Turkish Council [19203]
1111 14th St. NW, Ste. 1050
Washington, DC 20005
Ph: (202)783-0483
Fax: (202)783-0511

Jones, James, VP
National Association of Parliamentar-
ians [5671]
213 S Main St.
Independence, MO 64050-3808
Ph: (816)833-3892
Toll Free: 888-627-2929
Fax: (816)833-3893

Jones, Jennifer, Exec. Dir.
International Furnishings and Design
Association [1950]
610 Freedom Business Ctr., Ste. 110
King of Prussia, PA 19406
Ph: (610)992-0011
Fax: (610)992-0021

Jones, Jennifer M., President
National Pan-Hellenic Council
[23761]
3951 Snapfinger Pky., Ste. 218
Decatur, GA 30035
Ph: (404)942-3257
Fax: (404)806-9943

Jones, Jeremy, CEO, Founder
Protect Our Winters [4096]
PO Box 38
Pacific Palisades, CA 90272
Ph: (310)909-7941

Jones, Jerry, President
Antique Poison Bottle Collectors Association [21623]
312 Summer Ln.
Huddleston, VA 24104

Jones, Jerry, Exec. Dir.
National Coalition for the Homeless
[11957]
2201 P St. NW
Washington, DC 20037-1033
Ph: (202)462-4822
Fax: (202)462-4823

Jones, Jo Anne, Officer
Transferware Collectors Club
[21586]
c/o Jo Anne Jones, Membership
Chair
207 Paseo Bernal
Moraga, CA 94556

Jones, Joe, Publisher
Piper Owner Society [21243]
N7450 Aanstad Rd.
Iola, WI 54945
Ph: (715)445-5000
Toll Free: 800-331-0038
Fax: (715)445-4053

Jones, John, President
International Fantasy Gaming
Society [22053]

PO Box 36555
Cincinnati, OH 45236

Jones, Jordan, President
National Genealogical Society
[20985]
3108 Columbia Pke., Ste. 300
Arlington, VA 22204-4370
Ph: (703)525-0050
Toll Free: 800-473-0060
Fax: (703)525-0052

Jones, Dr. Jude, Director
Society for the Study of Process
Philosophies [10131]
c/o Jude Jones
Collins Hall
Dept. of Philosophy
Fordham University
441 E Fordham Rd.
Bronx, NY 10458
Ph: (718)817-4721

Jones, Karyne, CEO, President
National Caucus and Center on
Black Aging, Inc. [10520]
1220 L St. NW, Ste. 800
Washington, DC 20005
Ph: (202)637-8400
Fax: (202)347-0895

Jones, Keith, Exec. Dir.
Biopesticide Industry Alliance [4528]
PO Box 313
Oakton, VA 22124
Ph: (202)570-1411

Jones, Kim, Founder, CEO
Testicular Cancer Awareness
Foundation [14073]
202 North Ave., No. 305
Grand Junction, CO 81501
Toll Free: 888-610-8223

Jones, Larry, Mem.
Wycliffe Bible Translators [19767]
11221 John Wycliffe Blvd.
Orlando, FL 32832
Ph: (407)852-3600
Toll Free: 800-992-5433
Fax: (407)852-3601

Jones, Lisa Dale, President
Capitol Hill Restoration Society
[9379]
420 10th St. SE
Washington, DC 20003-0264
Ph: (202)543-0425

Jones, Michael, Exec. VP
Public Broadcasting Service [9147]
2100 Crystal Dr.
Arlington, VA 22202
Ph: (703)739-5000

Jones, Millie, Bd. Member
Association of Maternal and Child
Health Programs [14167]
2030 M St. NW, Ste. 350
Washington, DC 20036
Ph: (202)775-0436
Fax: (202)775-0061

Jones, Newton B., President
International Brotherhood of
Boilermakers [23457]
753 State Ave., Ste. 570
Kansas City, KS 66101
Ph: (913)371-2640
Fax: (913)281-8104

Jones, Paul, Officer
Truck-Frame and Axle Repair Association [356]
c/o Ken Dias, Consultant
364 W 12th St.
Erie, PA 16501

Jones, Peter, President, Founder
American Council for International
Studies [8053]

343 Congress St., Ste. 3100
Boston, MA 02210
Ph: (617)236-2051
Toll Free: 800-888-ACIS
Fax: (617)450-5601

Jones, Dr. Robin, President,
Founder
Children's International Health Relief
[14181]
c/o Dr. Robin Jones, President
4218 S Steele St., Ste. 220
Tacoma, WA 98409
Ph: (253)476-0556

Jones, Robyn A., Contact
Automobile Competition Committee
for the United States FIA [22522]
7800 S Elati St., Ste. 303
Littleton, CO 80120-4456
Ph: (303)730-8100
Fax: (303)730-8108

Jones, Ross, President
Rhodesian Ridgeback Club of the
United States [21953]
1185 Alleghenyville Rd.
Mohnton, PA 19540

Jones, Sam Louis, Jr., President
Negro Airmen International [5868]
PO Box 23911
Savannah, GA 31403
Ph: (912)232-7524

Jones, Sarah, Founder
Tanzania Health and Education Mis-
sion [11450]
151 Stratford St.
Redwood City, CA 94062
Ph: (650)368-9454

Jones, Sheldon R., VP
Farm Foundation [3549]
1301 W 22nd St., Ste. 906
Oak Brook, IL 60523-2197
Ph: (630)571-9393
Fax: (630)571-9580

Jones, Dr. Stephen, President
American Heartworm Society
[17623]
PO Box 8266
Wilmington, DE 19803-8266

Jones, Steve G., MEd, Founder
American Alliance of Hypnotists
[15353]

Jones, Mr. Steven R., Exec. Dir.
Association of Cable Communicators
[5089]
9259 Old Keene Mill Rd., Ste. 202
Burke, VA 22015
Ph: (703)372-2215
Toll Free: 800-210-3396
Fax: (703)782-0153

Jones, Susan, Director
International Association of Sickle
Cell Nurses and Physician As-
sistants [15121]
c/o Patricia Bailey, RN
PO Box 3235
Oak Park, IL 60303

Jones, Susan, Chairman
International Association of Women
in Fire and Emergency Services
[5208]
4025 Fair Ridge Dr., Ste. 300
Fairfax, VA 22033
Ph: (703)896-4858
Fax: (703)273-9363

Jones, Thomas M., Chairman
American-Russian Chamber of Commerce & Industry [23554]

Aon Ctr.
200 E Randolph St., Ste. 2200
Chicago, IL 60601
Ph: (312)494-6562
Fax: (312)494-9840

Jones, Van, President
Green for All [17804]
1611 Telegraph Ave., Ste. 600
Oakland, CA 94612
Ph: (510)663-6500

Jones, Wells B., CAE, CEO
Guide Dog Foundation for the Blind
[17706]
371 E Jericho Tpke.
Smithtown, NY 11787-2976
Ph: (631)930-9000
Fax: (631)930-9009

Jones, William, Treasurer
National Council of Exchangors
[2882]
11 W Main St., Ste. 223
Belgrade, MT 59714
Ph: (858)222-1608

Jonkel, Chuck, Founder, Act. Pres.
Great Bear Foundation [4823]
PO Box 9383
Missoula, MT 59807-9383
Ph: (406)829-9378
Fax: (406)829-9379

Joon, Oh, President
United Nations Economic and Social
Council [18161]
Office for ECOSOC Support and
Coordination
1 United Nations Plz.
New York, NY 10017
Ph: (212)963-8415
Fax: (212)963-1712

Joosten, Jan, President
International Organization for
Septuagint and Cognate Studies
[19759]
c/o Jay C. Treat, Editor
University of Pennsylvania
255 S 36th St.
Philadelphia, PA 19104-6305

Jordan, Dr. Abigail, Founder
Consortium of Doctors [11761]

Jordan, Christie Batterman, Founder
Alliance for Water Education [7883]
120 Village Sq., Ste. 137
Orinda, CA 94563
Ph: (925)386-0515
Fax: (925)386-0501

Jordan, Donald K., Exec. VP
Alumni Association of City College of
New York [19299]
Shepard Hall, Rm. 162
160 Convent Ave.
138th St.
New York, NY 10027
Ph: (212)234-3000
Fax: (212)368-6576

Jordan, Edwards, Officer
Baptist Joint Committee for Religious
Liberty [19723]
200 Maryland Ave. NE
Washington, DC 20002
Ph: (202)544-4226
Fax: (202)544-2094

Jordan, Heather, Contact
Osteoarthritis Action Alliance [17162]
PO Box 7669
Atlanta, GA 30357-0669
Ph: (202)887-2916

Jordan, Kenny, Exec. Dir.
Association of Energy Service
Companies [1106]

121 E Magnolia St., Ste. 103
Friendswood, TX 77546
Ph: (713)781-0758
Fax: (713)781-7542

Jordan, Linda K., Exec. Sec.
Council of State Science Supervisors [8545]
c/o C. J. Evans, Treasurer
614 Indian Hills Dr.
Saint Charles, MO 63301-0561
Ph: (314)614-7701

Jordan, Mick, Chairman
Overseas Automotive Council [301]
c/o Automotive Aftermarket Suppliers
Association
10 Laboratory Dr.
Research Triangle Park, NC 27709
Ph: (919)406-1464

Jordan, Nicole, President
International Lilac Society [22106]
c/o Karen McCauley, Treasurer
325 W 82nd St.
Chaska, MN 55318

Jordan, Reita, Secretary
Aril Society International [22085]
c/o Reita Jordan, Secretary
3500 Avenida Charada NW
Albuquerque, NM 87107-2604

Jordan, Susannah, President
National Button Society [21693]
c/o Susan Porter, Membership
Coordinator
1564 Wilson Rd.
Ramona, CA 92065-3539

Jordan, William, President
Association of Program Directors in
Vascular Surgery [17379]
633 N St. Clair St., 22nd Fl.
Chicago, IL 60611
Toll Free: 800-258-7188
Fax: (312)334-2320

Jorgensen, Adam, President
Professional Association for SQL
Server [6330]
203 N LaSalle St., Ste. 2100
Chicago, IL 60601
Ph: (604)899-6009
Fax: (604)899-1269

Jorgensen, Chris, Founder,
President
International Association of Attune-
ment Practitioners [13631]
PO Box 28574
Kansas City, MO 64188-8574
Ph: (816)221-7123

Jorgensen, Daren E., President
Battery Recycling Association of
North America [4625]
12505 N Main St., Ste. 212
Rancho Cucamonga, CA 91739

Jorgensen, Eric, Contact
American Truck Dealers, a Division
of NADA [278]
8400 Westpark Dr.
McLean, VA 22102
Ph: (703)821-7230
Toll Free: 800-352-6232
Fax: (703)749-4700

Jorgensen, Sven E., President
International Society for Ecological
Modelling [4006]
550 M Ritchie Hwy.
Severna Park, MD 21146

Jorkasky, James, Exec. Dir.
National Alliance for Eye and Vision
Research [17728]

1801 Rockville Pike, Ste. 400
Rockville, MD 20852
Ph: (240)221-2905
Fax: (240)221-0370

Jortner, Jeff, President
ACM SIGGRAPH [6232]
2 Penn Plz., Ste. 701
New York, NY 10121
Ph: (212)626-0500
Fax: (212)944-1318

Jose, A.S., President
World Malayalee Council [19479]
PO Box 823
Sugar Land, TX 77487-0823

Joseph, Angelina M., MA, Founder
Health For All Missions [12281]
9101 W Sahara Ave., Ste. 105-F11
Las Vegas, NV 89117
Ph: (702)795-6776
Fax: (702)838-8436

Joseph, Gregory P., President
Supreme Court Historical Society
[9522]
Opperman House
224 E Capitol St. NE
Washington, DC 20003
Ph: (202)543-0400
Toll Free: 888-539-4438
Fax: (202)547-7730

Joseph, Heather, Exec. Dir.
Scholarly Publishing and Academic
Resources Coalition [2811]
21 Dupont Cir. NW, Ste. 800
Washington, DC 20036
Ph: (202)296-2296
Fax: (202)872-0884

Joseph, James, Co-Chmn. of the
Bd.
Lawyers' Committee for Civil Rights
Under Law [5537]
1401 New York Ave. NW, Ste. 400
Washington, DC 20005
Ph: (202)662-8600
Toll Free: 888-299-5227
Fax: (202)783-0857

Joseph, J.W., President
Society for Historical Archaeology
[5949]
13017 Wisteria Dr., No. 395
Germantown, MD 20874
Ph: (301)972-9684
Fax: (866)285-3512

Joseph, Michael, Chairman
Lewa Wildlife Conservancy U.S.A.
[4840]
495 Miller Ave., Ste. 301
Mill Valley, CA 94941
Ph: (415)627-8187

Joseph, Michael, President
Oriental Rug Retailers of America
[1957]
PO Box 53
Landrum, SC 29356-0053
Ph: (864)895-6544

Joseph, Patrick, President
National Foundation for Infectious
Diseases [15411]
7201 Wisconsin Ave., Ste. 750
Bethesda, MD 20814-5278
Ph: (301)656-0003
Fax: (301)907-0878

Joseph, Dr. Robert, Chairman
Native American Leadership Alliance
[20511]
3600 New York Ave. NE, 3rd Fl.
Washington, DC 20002
Ph: (202)841-9061

Joseph, Tommy, Chairman
National Council for Air and Stream
Improvement [4210]
1513 Walnut St., Ste. 200
Cary, NC 27511
Ph: (919)941-6400
Fax: (919)941-6401

Josephson, Philip, Bus. Mgr.
Alpha Gamma Rho [23672]
10101 NW Ambassador Dr.
Kansas City, MO 64153-1395
Ph: (816)891-9200
Fax: (816)891-9401

Joshi, Anupama, Exec. Dir., Founder
National Farm to School Network
[3541]
8770 W Bryn Mawr Ave., Ste. 1300
Chicago, IL 60631
Ph: (847)917-7292

Joshi, Paramjit T., M.D., President
American Academy of Child and
Adolescent Psychiatry [16807]
3615 Wisconsin Ave. NW
Washington, DC 20016-3007
Ph: (202)966-7300
Fax: (202)966-2891

Joskow, Paul L., President
Alfred P. Sloan Foundation [18950]
630 5th Ave., Ste. 2200
New York, NY 10111
Ph: (212)649-1649
Fax: (212)757-5117

Jourdain, Christine, Exec. Dir.
American Council of Snowmobile
Associations [23175]
c/o Christine Jourdain, Executive
Director
271 Woodland Pass, Ste. 216
East Lansing, MI 48823-2060
Ph: (517)351-4362
Fax: (517)351-1363

Jourdain, Patrick, President
International Bridge Press Association [21560]
611 Pleasant
Miles City, MT 59301

Jovanovich, Linda, Exec. VP
Hardwood Manufacturers Associa-
tion [1440]
665 Rodi Rd., Ste. 305
Pittsburgh, PA 15235
Ph: (412)244-0440
Fax: (412)244-9090

Jowell, Russell, Mgr., Comm.
Worldwide Responsible Accredited
Production [209]
2200 Wilson Blvd., Ste. 601
Arlington, VA 22201-3357
Ph: (703)243-0970
Fax: (703)243-8247

Joyal, Suzanne, Exec. Dir.
Give a Jumpstart [12036]
414 Redwood Ave.
Corte Madera, CA 94925
Ph: (414)595-6757

Joyce, Sherman, President
American Tort Reform Association
[5415]
1101 Connecticut Ave. NW, Ste. 400
Washington, DC 20036
Ph: (202)682-1163
Fax: (202)682-1022

Joyce-Grendahl, Dr. Kathleen, Exec.
Producer
World Flute Society [10024]
3351 Mintonville Point Dr.
Suffolk, VA 23435
Ph: (757)651-8328
Fax: (757)538-2937

Joyner, Carolyn, Director
Labor Project for Working Families
[23469]
1101 15th St. NW, Ste., 1212
Washington, DC 20005
Ph: (202)288-4762

Joyner, Mildred C., VP
National Association of Social Work-
ers [13113]
750 1st St. NE, Ste. 800
Washington, DC 20002-4241
Ph: (202)408-8600
Toll Free: 800-742-4089
Fax: (202)336-8313

Joyrich, Richard, 1st VP
Shakespeare Oxford Fellowship
[9096]
PO Box 66083
Auburndale, MA 02466

Jozwiak, Mrs. Mary Ann, Bd.
Member
The Discussion Club [17891]
c/o Racquet Club Ladue
1600 Log Cabin Ln.
Saint Louis, MO 63124
Ph: (314)416-7722
Fax: (314)416-7760

Juarez, Teresa, President
Peace Development Fund [18816]
3221 22nd St.
San Francisco, CA 94110-3006
Ph: (415)642-0900
Fax: (415)642-8200

Juba, George N., CEO, President
Greek Catholic Union of the U.S.A.
[19454]
5400 Tuscarawas Rd.
Beaver, PA 15009
Ph: (800)722-4428
Fax: (724)495-3421

Juceam, Robert E., Secretary
American Immigration Council
[5288]
1331 G St. NW, Ste. 200
Washington, DC 20005-3141
Ph: (202)507-7500
Fax: (202)742-5619

Juchno, Wayne, Exec. Dir.
National Automotive Radiator
Service Association [349]
3000 Village Run Rd., Ste. 103, No.
221
Wexford, PA 15090-6315
Ph: (724)799-8415
Fax: (724)799-8416

Judd, Robert, Exec. Dir.
American Musicological Society
[9863]
6010 College Sta.
Brunswick, ME 04011-8451
Ph: (207)798-4243
Toll Free: 877-679-7648
Fax: (207)798-4254

Judd, Robert P., Div. Dir.
American Automatic Control Council
[270]
Department of Chemical and Biologi-
cal Engineering
Rensselaer Polytechnic Institute
110 8th St.
Troy, NY 12180-3590
Ph: (512)471-3061

Judeh, Jumana, President
Arab American Business Women's
Council [3485]
22952 Outer Dr.
Dearborn, MI 48124-4279
Ph: (313)277-1986

Judex, Angeline, Exec. Dir.
Global Sourcing Council [2471]
750 3rd Ave., 11th Fl.
New York, NY 10017
Ph: (914)645-0605

Judge, Kate, Exec. Dir.
American Nurses Foundation
[16107]
8515 Georgia Ave., Ste. 400
Silver Spring, MD 20910-3492
Ph: (301)628-5227
Fax: (301)628-5354

Judge, Lisa M., M.D., Treasurer
Association of Anesthesia Clinical
Directors [16739]
c/o Kimberly R. Corey
3757 Indianola Ave.
Columbus, OH 43214-3753
Ph: (614)784-9772
Fax: (614)784-9771

Judge, Rob, Exec. Dir.
National Shrine of St. Elizabeth Ann
Seton [19891]
339 S Seton Ave.
Emmitsburg, MD 21727-9297
Ph: (301)447-6606
Fax: (301)447-6061

Judson, Bennett, Exec. Dir.
Roofing Industry Alliance for
Progress [811]
10255 W Higgins, Ste. 600
10255 W Higgins Rd., Ste. 600
Rosemont, IL 60018-5607
Toll Free: 800-323-9545
Fax: (847)493-7959

Judy, Dr. Kenneth W.M., Co-Chmn.
of the Bd.
International Congress of Oral Im-
plantologists [14452]
55 Lane Rd., Ste. 305
Fairfield, NJ 07004
Ph: (973)783-6300
Toll Free: 800-442-0525
Fax: (973)783-1175

Juergens, Dr. John P., Chairman
American Wine Alliance for
Research and Education [4925]
PO Box 765
Washington, DC 20004-0765
Toll Free: 800-700-4050

Julian, David R., Founder
Epilepsy Connection [14739]
1344 Cabrillo Park Dr., Unit H
Santa Ana, CA 92701
Ph: (714)943-2567

Julian, Rev. Frank, RN, Founder
Fighting AIDS with Nutrition [10538]
PO Box 394
Allen Park, MI 48101
Ph: (313)977-0259

Julius, Bonnie, President
Crickett's Answer for Cancer [13952]
1110 Skyview Dr.
York, PA 17406
Ph: (717)843-7903

Junco, Kirk, Comm. Chm.
The Moles [19659]
577 Chestnut Ridge Rd.
Woodcliff Lake, NJ 07677
Ph: (201)930-1923
Fax: (201)930-8501

Junemann, Gregory J., President
International Federation of Profes-
sional and Technical Engineers
[6562]
501 3rd St. NW, Ste. 701
Washington, DC 20001
Ph: (202)239-4880
Fax: (202)239-4881

Jung, Tae, President
World Hapkido Association [23026]
1789 Thousand Oaks Blvd.
Thousand Oaks, CA 91362
Ph: (805)495-9622
Fax: (805)494-4554

Jungmeyer, Mr. Lance, President
Fresh Produce Association of the
Americas [1330]
590 E Frontage Rd.
Nogales, AZ 85621-9753
Ph: (520)287-2707
Fax: (520)287-2948

Juntunen, Kathi, President
Chances for Children [10889]
20343 N Hayden Rd., Ste. 105-114
Scottsdale, AZ 85255
Ph: (480)513-3373
Fax: (480)323-2343

Jupiter, Jesse, MD, President
American Shoulder and Elbow
Surgeons [17369]
9400 W Higgins Rd., Ste. 500
Rosemont, IL 60018
Ph: (847)698-1629
Fax: (847)268-9499

Juren, Joanne E., BA, Director,
Founder
Eta Sigma Alpha National Home
School Honor Society [7485]
11665 Fuqua St., Ste. A-100
Houston, TX 77034
Ph: (281)922-0478

Juric, Radmilla, VP
Society for Design and Process Sci-
ence [6372]
3824 Cedar Springs Rd., Ste. 368
Dallas, TX 75219
Ph: (214)253-9025
Fax: (214)520-0227

Jurus, William L., Rep.
American Chain of Warehouses
[3436]
156 Flamingo Dr.
Beecher, IL 60401
Ph: (708)946-9792
Fax: (708)946-9793

Justice, Tom, Comm. Chm.
National Air Filtration Association
[1632]
PO Box 68639
Virginia Beach, VA 23471
Ph: (757)313-7400
Fax: (757)313-7401

Justin, Sandi, Contact
World Arnold Chiari Malformation
Association [17355]
31 Newtown Woods Rd.
Newtown Square, PA 19073
Ph: (610)353-4737

Jyotirmayananda, Swami, Founder
Yoga Research Foundation [20656]
6111 SW 74th Ave.
Miami, FL 33143
Ph: (305)666-2006
Fax: (305)666-4443

K

K., Pamela, President
Compulsive Eaters Anonymous-
HOW [11851]
3371 Glendale Blvd., Ste. 104
Los Angeles, CA 90039
Ph: (323)660-4333
Fax: (323)660-4334

Kaatz, Kraig, Rep.
National Trappers Association [4724]
2815 Washington Ave.

Bedford, IN 47421
Ph: (812)277-9670
Toll Free: 866-680-8727
Fax: (812)277-9672

Kaatz, Petra C., President
National Ladies Auxiliary of the Jew-
ish War Veterans of the United
States of America Inc. [21041]
1811 R St. NW
Washington, DC 20009-1603
Ph: (202)667-9061

Kabad, Kanchan, MBA, President
Indian American Cancer Network
[10789]
PO Box 741886
Houston, TX 77274
Ph: (713)370-3489

Kabbani, Jim, CEO, Exec. Dir.
Tortilla Industry Association [1376]
1600 Wilson Blvd., Ste. 650
Arlington, VA 22209
Toll Free: 800-944-6099
Fax: (800)944-6177

Kabnick, Lowell S., President
American Venous Forum [17570]
6800 Gulfport Blvd., Ste. 201-212
South Pasadena, FL 33707-2163
Ph: (414)918-9880
    (727)202-6213
Fax: (414)276-3349

Kacandes, Tom, Bd. Member
Reuse Development Organization,
Inc. [4746]
The Loading Dock
2 N Kresson St.
Baltimore, MD 21224
Ph: (410)558-3625
Fax: (410)558-1888

Kacic, George, Secretary
Gift and Home Trade Association
[3014]
Box 214
2550 Sandy Plains Rd., Ste. 225
Marietta, GA 30066
Toll Free: 877-600-4872

Kaczaraj, Stefan, President
Ukrainian National Association
[19680]
2200 Route 10
Parsippany, NJ 07054
Toll Free: 800-253-9862
Fax: (973)292-0900

Kaczinski, Mark, Exec. Dir.
Bridge Grid Flooring Manufacturers
Association [504]
300 E Cherry St.
North Baltimore, OH 45872-1227
Toll Free: 877-257-5499

Kadel, Jon, Exec. Dir.
Kappa Delta Phi [23904]
373 S Willow St., Ste. 111
Manchester, NH 03103

Kaden, Lewis B., Chmn. of the Bd.
Markle Foundation [6229]
10 Rockefeller Plz., 16th Fl.
New York, NY 10020-1903
Ph: (212)713-7600
Fax: (212)765-9690

Kader, Ralph, CEO
U.S. Federation for Middle East
Peace [18834]
777 United Nations Plz.
44th St. & 1st Ave., Ste. 7H
New York, NY 10017-3521
Ph: (973)568-8384
    (917)331-4699
Fax: (646)688-5582

Kadereit, Bill, President
National Retiree Legislative Network
[12751]
South Bldg., Ste. 900
601 Pennsylvania Ave. NW
Washington, DC 20004-2601
Ph: (202)220-3172
Toll Free: 866-360-7197

Kadlec, Gary, Chairman
American Foundation for
Pharmaceutical Education [16639]
6076 Franconia Rd., Ste. C
Alexandria, VA 22310-1758
Ph: (703)875-3095
Toll Free: 855-624-9526
Fax: (703)875-3098

Kadow, Joe, Chairman
National Restaurant Association
[1672]
2055 L St. NW, Ste. 700
Washington, DC 20036
Ph: (202)331-5900
Toll Free: 800-424-5156
Fax: (202)331-2429

Kaestner, Mr. Eric, CEO, President
Bible Believers Fellowship [19752]
PO Box 0065
Baldwin, NY 11510-0065
Ph: (516)739-7746

Kafin, Robert J., Chairman
Adirondack Council [3786]
103 Hand Ave., No. 3
Elizabethtown, NY 12932
Ph: (518)873-2240
Toll Free: 877-873-2240
Fax: (518)873-6675

Kafle, KP, Exec. Dir., Founder
Nepal SEEDS: Social Educational
Environmental Development
Services in Nepal [11411]
800 Kansas St.
San Francisco, CA 94107-2607
Ph: (415)813-3331

Kagan, Ute W., Exec. Dir.
American Numismatic Society
[22257]
75 Varick St., 11th Fl.
New York, NY 10013
Ph: (212)571-4470
Fax: (212)571-4479

Kaganoff Stern, Rachel, President
Junior State of America [8196]
111 Anza Blvd., Ste. 109
Burlingame, CA 94010
Ph: (650)347-1600
Toll Free: 800-334-5353
Fax: (650)347-7200

Kaganoff Stern, Rachel, President
Junior Statesmen Foundation [8197]
111 Anza Blvd., Ste. 109
Burlingame, CA 94010
Ph: (650)347-1600
Toll Free: 800-334-5353
Fax: (650)347-7200

Kahana, Doron, MD, Secretary,
Treasurer
American Board of Physician Nutri-
tion Specialists [16201]
National Board of Physician Nutrition
Specialists
8630 Fenton St., Ste. 412
Silver Spring, MD 20910
Ph: (301)587-6315
Toll Free: 800-727-4567
Fax: (301)587-2365

Kahangi, Linda, Exec. Dir.
Alpha Phi International Fraternity
[23945]

1930 Sherman Ave.
Evanston, IL 60201
Ph: (847)475-0663
(847)475-4786
Fax: (847)475-6820

Kahn, Anne, VP
Society for Asian Art [8890]
Asian Art Museum
200 Larkin St.
San Francisco, CA 94102
Ph: (415)581-3701
Fax: (415)861-2358

Kahn, David, Exec. Dir.
Adirondack Historical Association
[9363]
c/o Adirondack Museum
Route 28N & 30
Blue Mountain Lake, NY 12812
Ph: (518)352-7311
Fax: (518)352-7653

Kahn, Jody, Admin. Sec.
Association of Authors' Representatives, Inc. [161]
302A W 12th St., No. 122
New York, NY 10014

Kahn, Patrick, Treasurer
Barbados Blackbelly Sheep Associa-
tion International [4666]
801 County Road 243
Hondo, TX 78861
Ph: (301)440-4808

Kahn, René, M.D., President
Schizophrenia International
Research Society [15804]
5034-A Thoroughbred Ln.
Brentwood, TN 37027
Ph: (615)324-2370

Kahraman, Semra, President
Preimplantation Genetic Diagnosis
International Society [14884]
2910 MacArthur Blvd.
Northbrook, IL 60062
Ph: (773)472-4900
(847)400-1515
Fax: (773)871-5221

Kahre, Joe, President
American Miniature Horse Associa-
tion [4315]
5601 S Interstate 35 W
Alvarado, TX 76009
Ph: (817)783-5600
Fax: (817)783-6403

Kahveci, Nihat Gurel, PhD, Gen.
Sec.
International Association of Educa-
tors [7851]
320 Fitzelle Hall
Ravine Pky.
Oneonta, NY 13820

Kai, Brenda, Exec. Dir.
Electronic Document Systems
Foundation [1797]
1845 Precinct Line Rd., Ste. 212
Hurst, TX 76054
Ph: (817)849-1145
Fax: (817)849-1185

Kaikobad, Mahmudul H., Exec. Sec.
North American Bangladeshi As-
sociation for Bangladesh [7531]
PO Box 55103
Kansas City, MO 64138

Kain, Rev. Greg, President
Children's Bible Ministries [20133]
160 Bear Lodge Dr.
Townsend, TN 37882
Ph: (865)448-1200
Fax: (865)448-1233

Kaiser, Kathleen, President
Small Publishers, Artists and Writers
Network [2812]
1129 Maricopa Highway 142
Ojai, CA 93023

Kaiser, Linda, Founder
Parents for Window Blind Safety
[11127]
PO Box 205
Barnhart, MO 63012
Ph: (314)494-7890

Kaiser, Michael, Exec. Dir.
National Cyber Security Alliance
[7153]
1101 Pennsylvania Ave. NW, Ste.
600
Washington, DC 20004
Ph: (756)756-2278

Kaiser, Michael, Dir. Pub. Aff.
WineAmerica: The National Association of American Wineries [3483]
818 Connecticut Ave. NW, Ste. 1006
Washington, DC 20006
Ph: (202)783-2756
(202)223-5172

Kaiser, Timothy G., Exec. Dir.
Public Housing Authorities Directors
Association [5285]
511 Capitol Ct. NE
Washington, DC 20002-4937
Ph: (202)546-5445
Fax: (202)546-2280

Kajosevic, Indira, Contact
Women in Black [18841]
PO Box 20554
New York, NY 10021
Ph: (212)560-0905

Kajunju, Amini, CEO, President
The Africa-America Institute [17770]
420 Lexington Ave., Ste. 1706
New York, NY 10170-0002
Ph: (212)949-5666
Fax: (212)682-6174

Kalamas, Maria, Exec. Dir.
Society for Marketing Advances
[2302]
c/o Cynthia Rodriguez Cano,
Treasurer, 836 SW Munjack Cir.
Northwood University
836 SW Munjack Cir.
Port Saint Lucie, FL 34986-3459
Ph: (772)380-2667

Kalas, Andrea, President, Director
Association of Moving Image
Archivists [9298]
1313 N Vine St.
Hollywood, CA 90028
Ph: (323)463-1500
Fax: (323)463-1506

Kalasho, Tahrir S., CEO, Founder
National Organization of Iraqi
Christians [12438]
PO Box 833
Hazel Park, MI 48030
Ph: (586)939-2554

Kalayjian, Ani, Dr., Founder
Armenian American Society for Studies on Stress and Genocide
[15760]
185 E 85th St., Mezzanine No. 4
New York, NY 10028
Ph: (201)723-9578

Kalechofsky, Roberta, Contact
Jews for Animal Rights [10653]
Micah Publications, Inc.
255 Humphrey St.
Marblehead, MA 01945
Ph: (781)631-7601

Kalfas, Tom, Secretary
Independent Pilots Association
[23387]
3607 Fern Valley Rd.
Louisville, KY 40219
Ph: (502)968-0341
Fax: (502)753-3252

Kalikow, Mary, V. Chmn. of the Bd.
National Center for Learning Disabilities [12239]
32 Laight St., 2nd Fl.
New York, NY 10013-2152

Kalina, Greg, President
A Wish With Wings [11281]
3751 West Fwy.
Fort Worth, TX 76107
Ph: (817)469-9474

Kallan, Henry, President
American Fund for Czech and
Slovak Leadership Studies [12582]
Bohemian National Hall
321 E 73rd St.
New York, NY 10021-3705

Kallembach, Rex, Treasurer
Policy Studies Organization [19000]
1527 New Hampshire Ave. NW
Washington, DC 20036
Fax: (202)483-2657

Kaller, Seth, VP
Professional Autograph Dealers Association [21716]
c/o Stuart Lutz, Membership Chairman
784 Morris Tpke.
Short Hills, NJ 07078-2698
Toll Free: 877-428-9362

Kallies, Kirsten, V. Chmn. of the Bd.
Perfusion Program Directors' Council
[14138]
c/o Thomas Rath, Chairman
University of Iowa Hospitals and
Clinics
Perfusion Technology Education
Program
200 Hawkins Dr.
Iowa City, IA 52242
Ph: (319)356-8496
Fax: (319)353-7174

Kallis, Lynn, Exec. Dir.
Pilot Parents of Southern Arizona
[12332]
2600 N Wyatt Dr.
Tucson, AZ 85712
Ph: (520)324-3150
Toll Free: 877-365-7220
Fax: (520)324-3152

Kallmeyer, Dick, VP
Cat Fanciers' Association [21566]
260 E Main St.
Alliance, OH 44601-2423
Ph: (330)680-4070
Fax: (330)680-4633

Kallstrom, Tom, Exec. Dir., CEO
American Association for Respiratory
Care [17431]
9425 N MacArthur Blvd., Ste. 100
Irving, TX 75063-4706
Ph: (972)243-2272
Fax: (972)484-2720

Kalmanson, Dr. Martin L., President
American Jewish League for Israel
[20228]
400 N Flagler Drive, PH D4
West Palm Beach, FL 33401
Ph: (212)371-1583
Fax: (561)659-0402

Kalmbach, Hilary, President
Syrian Studies Association [8340]

c/o Geoffrey D. Schad, Treasurer
and Secretary
312 Maplewood Rd.
Merion Station, PA 19066-10331

Kaltenegger, Jörg, VP
North American Deutsch Kurzhaar
Club [21927]
c/o Rick Medina, Membership
Coordinator
17W050 Woodland Ave.
Bensenville, IL 60106

Kalter, Alan, Chairman
AKC Reunite [10561]
8051 Arco Corporate Dr., Ste. 200
Raleigh, NC 27617-3900
Toll Free: 800-252-7894
Fax: (919)233-1290

Kalter, Alan, Director
American Bullmastiff Association
[21802]

Kamara-Bangura, Mrs. Bernadette,
Founder
Sierra Leone Relief and Develop-
ment Outreach, Inc. [12728]
4231-B Duke St.
Alexandria, VA 22304-2485
Ph: (703)507-5576

Kamath, Janine, President
Association of Internal Management
Consultants [2153]
720 N Collier Blvd., Unit 201
Marco Island, FL 34145
Ph: (239)642-0580
Fax: (239)642-1119

Kambin, Sheila, MD, Chairperson
International 22q11.2 Deletion
Syndrome Foundation [14829]
PO Box 2269
Cinnaminson, NJ 08077
Toll Free: 877-739-1849

Kamens, Joanne, PhD, Exec. Dir.
Addgene [6863]
75 Sidney St., Ste. 550A
Cambridge, MA 02139
Ph: (617)225-9000
Fax: (617)300-8688

Kaminski, Patricia A., Director
Flower Essence Society [13623]
PO Box 459
Nevada City, CA 95959
Ph: (530)265-9163
Toll Free: 800-736-9222
Fax: (530)265-0584

Kaminski, Stephen T., CEO, Exec.
Dir.
American Association of Poison
Control Centers [17491]
515 King St., Ste. 510
Alexandria, VA 22314
Ph: (703)894-1858
Toll Free: 800-222-1222
Fax: (703)683-2812

Kaminsky, Greg, Chairman
American International Automobile
Dealers Association [335]
500 Montgomery St., Ste. 800
Alexandria, VA 22314
Toll Free: 800-462-4232
Fax: (703)519-7810

Kaminsky, Joan, Secretary,
Treasurer
National Association of State Farm
Agents [1903]
14070 Proton Rd., Ste. 100
Dallas, TX 75244
Ph: (972)233-9107
Fax: (972)490-4219

Kamiya, Masamichi, Treasurer
NGO Committee on Disarmament,
Peace and Security [18130]
The Church Ctr., 7th Fl.
777 United Nations Pl.
New York, NY 10017
Ph: (212)986-5165

Kammer, Chris, President
American Academy for Oral
Systemic Health [14384]
8911 W Grandridge Blvd., Ste. D
Kennewick, WA 99336
Toll Free: 855-246-9133

Kamp, John, Exec. Dir.
Coalition for Healthcare Communica-
tion [14987]
405 Lexington Ave.
New York, NY 10174-1801
Ph: (212)850-0708

Kamp, Michael, Chairperson
Global Applied Disability Research
and Information Network on
Employment and Training [14549]
201 Dolgen Hall
Yang-Tan Institute
Cornell University
Ithaca, NY 14853

Kamper, Ken, Hist.
Daniel Boone and Frontier Families
Research Association [9466]
c/o Ken Kamper
1770 Hickory Hill Dr.
Hermann, MO 65041

Kampia, Rob, Exec. Dir.
Marijuana Policy Project [18647]
PO Box 77492
Washington, DC 20013
Ph: (202)462-5747

Kamuda, Edward S., President
Titanic Historical Society, Inc. [9778]
PO Box 51053
Indian Orchard, MA 01151-0053
Ph: (413)543-4770
Fax: (413)583-3633

Kan, Athena, Founder
Coalition Halting Obesity in Children
Everywhere [16255]
8630-M Guilford Rd., No. 168
Columbia, MD 21046
Ph: (410)868-9286

Kanagy, David, Exec. Dir.
Society for Mining, Metallurgy, and
Exploration [6884]
12999 E Adam Aircraft Cir.
Englewood, CO 80112
Ph: (303)948-4200
Toll Free: 800-763-3132
Fax: (303)973-3845

Kanalis, John, Administrator
Business Espionage Controls and
Countermeasures Association
[1785]
Box 55582
Shoreline, WA 98155-0582

Kandaras, Kenneth, President
National Anti-Vivisection Society
[10664]
53 W Jackson Blvd., Ste. 1552
Chicago, IL 60604
Ph: (312)427-6065
Toll Free: 800-888-NAVS
Fax: (312)427-6524

Kane, Dan, President
National Association of Produce
Market Managers [4478]
PO Box 1617
Garner, NC 27529
Ph: (919)779-5258

Kane, Katherine, Exec. Dir.
Harriet Beecher Stowe Center
[10403]
77 Forest St.
Hartford, CT 06105
Ph: (860)522-9258
Fax: (860)522-9259

Kane, Linda M., Officer
Hope and a Future [15940]
PO Box 13646
Ogden, UT 84412
Ph: (801)395-1979
Fax: (801)627-1831

Kane, Mary D., President, CEO
Sister Cities International [18558]
915 15th St. NW, 4th Fl.
Washington, DC 20005
Ph: (202)347-8630
Fax: (202)393-6524

Kane, Terry M., Exec. Dir.
Industrial Diamond Association
[1735]
PO Box 29460
Columbus, OH 43229
Ph: (614)797-2265
Fax: (614)797-2264

Kaneko, Ree, Chairman
International Sculpture Center
[10209]
14 Fairgrounds Rd., Ste. B
Hamilton, NJ 08619-3447
Ph: (609)689-1051
Fax: (609)689-1061

Kang, Sahie, Dr., President
American Association of Teachers of
Korean [8163]
c/o Dr. Sahie Khang, The School of
Korean,Middlebury College
The School of Korean
Middlebury College
Middlebury, VT 05753
Ph: (802)443-5215

Kang, Sewon, MD, President
Photomedicine Society [15668]
c/o Jo Urquhart, Administrative
Coordinator
Dept. of Dermatology
UT Southwestern Medical Center
5323 Harry Hines Blvd.
Dallas, TX 75390-9069
Fax: (214)648-5556

Kania, Ryan, Founder
Advocates for World Health [15595]
13650 N 12th St.
Tampa, FL 33613

Kanick, Steve, VP, Secretary
Association of Stained Glass Lamp
Artists [242]
5070 Cromwell Dr. NW
Gig Harbor, WA 98335

Kaniuk, Anthony R., President
International Memorialization Supply
Association [2407]
PO Box 425
West Bend, WI 53095-0425
Toll Free: 800-375-0335

Kann, Karl, VP
American Board of Funeral Service
Education [2397]
3414 Ashland Ave., Ste. G
Saint Joseph, MO 64506-1333
Ph: (816)233-3747
Fax: (816)233-3793

Kanneberg, Matthew, Chairman
Pulp and Paper Safety Association
[6977]
15 Technology Pky. S

Peachtree Corners, GA 30092-8200
Ph: (770)209-7300

Kannel, Susan, Exec. Dir.
National Coalition for Telecommunications Education and Learning [7317]
c/o Council for Adult and Experiential
Learning
55 E Monroe St., Ste. 2710
Chicago, IL 60603

Kannenje, Ramadhan, President
Relief for Africa [12718]
3914 Trade Center Dr.
Ann Arbor, MI 48104
Ph: (734)975-7200

Kannusamy, Priya, Director
Pediatric Neurotransmitter Disease
Association [15987]
28 Prescott Pl.
Old Bethpage, NY 11804

Kanowitz, Richard, President
Families Fighting Flu [17141]
4201 Wilson Blvd., No. 110-702
Arlington, VA 22203
Toll Free: 888-236-3358

Kansky, Gail R., President
National CFIDS Foundation [15964]
103 Aletha Rd.
Needham, MA 02492
Ph: (781)449-3535
Fax: (781)449-8606

Kanter, Mitch, PhD, Exec. Dir.
Egg Nutrition Center [16218]
PO Box 738
Park Ridge, IL 60068
Ph: (847)296-7055
Fax: (847)768-7973

Kantos, Anthony P., President
APA Division 47: Exercise and Sport
Psychology [16890]
c/o American Psychological Associa-
tion
750 1st St. NE
Washington, DC 20002-4242
Ph: (202)336-6121
Fax: (202)218-3599

Kanyoro, Ms. Musimbi, CEO,
President
Global Fund for Women [18210]
800 Market St., 7th Fl.
San Francisco, CA 94108-4456
Ph: (415)248-4800
Fax: (415)248-4801

Kao, Mark L., PhD, President
Formosan Association for Public Af-
fairs [18400]
552 7th St. SE
Washington, DC 20003
Ph: (202)547-3686
Fax: (202)543-7891

Kaplan, David, President
Cetacean Society International
[4802]
65 Redding Road 0953
Georgetown, CT 06829-0953
Ph: (203)770-8615
Fax: (860)561-0187

Kaplan, Kate, President
Tufts University Alumni Association
[19352]
Office Of Alumni Relations
80 George St., Ste. 100-3
Medford, MA 02155
Ph: (617)627-3532
Toll Free: 800-843-2586
Fax: (617)627-3938

Kaplan, Keith, Exec. Dir.
Fur Information Council of America
[204]

1921 Stevens Ave., No. 210
Bedford, IN 47421
Ph: (323)782-1700
Fax: (323)651-1417

Kaplan, Lawrence P., PhD, Chairman, CEO
U.S. Autism and Asperger Association [13781]
PO Box 532
Draper, UT 84020-0532
Ph: (801)816-1234
Toll Free: 888-928-8476

Kaplan, Michael, CEO, President
AIDS United [18856]
1424 K St. NW, Ste. 200
Washington, DC 20005-2411
Ph: (202)408-4848
Fax: (202)408-1818

Kaplan, Nancy, MSW, Exec. Dir.
CRU Institute [18000]
16301 NE 8th St., Ste. 231
Bellevue, WA 98008
Ph: (425)869-4041
Toll Free: 800-922-1988
Fax: (425)867-0491

Kaplan, Robert N., President, CEO
Inter-American Foundation [19075]
1331 Pennsylvania Ave. NW, Ste. 1200 N
Washington, DC 20004-1766
Ph: (202)360-4530
    (703)306-4301
Fax: (703)306-4365

Kaplan, Sally, Coord.
Student Peace Alliance [18830]
1616 P St. NW, Ste. 100
Washington, DC 20036
Ph: (202)684-2553

Kaplan, Thomas S., PhD, Chairman, Founder
Panthera [4868]
8 W 40th St., 18th Fl.
New York, NY 10018-2218
Ph: (646)786-0400
Fax: (646)786-0401

Kapoor, Aman, Founder
Immigration Voice [5291]
1177 Branham Ln., No. 321
San Jose, CA 95118
Ph: (202)386-6250
Fax: (202)403-3853

Kapoor, Neeraj, Founder, CEO
Learn to be Foundation [8720]
1268 N Lakeview Ave., Ste. 201
Anaheim, CA 92807

Kappas, Arvid, President
International Society for Research on Emotion [7065]
La Salle University
1900 W Olney Ave., Wister 219
Philadelphia, PA 19141

Kappas, George J., Director
American Hypnosis Association [15359]
18607 Ventura Blvd., Ste. 310
Tarzana, CA 91356-4158
Ph: (818)758-2730

Kappel, Michael L., CEO, Act. Pres.
National Coalition for Cancer Survivorship [14024]
1010 Wayne Ave., Ste. 315
Silver Spring, MD 20910
Toll Free: 877-622-7937

Kapral, Nancy K., Bookkeeper
Environmental Management Association [2129]

c/o Lauren Marosi, Executive Director
38575 Mallast St.
Harrison Township, MI 48045
Toll Free: 866-999-4EMA
Fax: (586)463-8075

Kaprow, Moe, President
Neshama: Association of Jewish Chaplains [19936]
50 Eisenhower Dr.
Paramus, NJ 07652
Ph: (973)929-3168

Kapur, Raj, Director
Society for Pediatric Pathology [16593]
355 Lexington Ave., 15th Fl.
New York, NY 10017
Ph: (706)364-3375
    (212)297-2196
Fax: (706)733-8033

Karabel, Lance, President
U.S. Powerlifting Federation [23073]
c/o Lance Carabel, President
Lance's Gym
3636 S Iron St.
Chicago, IL 60609
Ph: (773)927-0009

Karacostas, Nicholas A., Chairman
American Hellenic Educational Progressive Association [19450]
1909 Q St. NW, Ste. 500
Washington, DC 20009-1050
Ph: (202)232-6300
Fax: (202)232-2140

Karadimos, Charles, Director
Brewster Kaleidoscope Society [21629]
PO Box 95
Damascus, MD 20872

Karakatsanis, Neovi, President
Modern Greek Studies Association [9354]
c/o Gonda Van Steen, Executive Director
PO Box 117435
Gainesville, FL 32611-7435
Ph: (352)273-3796

Karam, Ed, Treasurer
Drama Desk [10246]
New York, NY

Karam, Dr. Nadim, Exec. Dir.
World Rehabilitation Fund [11649]
16 E 40th St., Ste. 704
New York, NY 10016
Ph: (212)532-6000
Fax: (212)532-6012

Karas, Kristin, Coord.
DanceSafe [13134]
800 Grant St., Ste. 110
Denver, CO 80203
Toll Free: 888-MDMA-411

Karasek, Tom, President
Hobby Greenhouse Association [22102]
922 Norwood Dr.
Norwalk, IA 50211-1329
Ph: (724)744-7082

Kardiasmenos, Katrina, Secretary
Protection Sports Association [23251]
7719 Leigh Rd.
Glen Burnie, MD 21060-8505
Ph: (240)475-3637

Karen, Jay, CEO
National Golf Course Owners Association [3161]

291 Seven Farms Dr.
Charleston, SC 29492
Ph: (843)881-9956
Toll Free: 800-933-4262
Fax: (843)881-9958

Karen, Jay, CEO, President
Professional Association of Innkeepers International [1676]
108 South Cleveland St.
Merrill, WI 54452-2435
Ph: (715)257-0128

Karesh, James W., MD, Advisor
American Society of Ophthalmic Plastic and Reconstructive Surgery [14311]
5841 Cedar Lake Rd. Ste. 204
Minneapolis, MN 55416-5657
Ph: (952)646-2038
Fax: (952)545-6073

Kareus, Matt, Exec. Dir.
International Galapagos Tour Operators Association [23667]
PO Box 1043
Winchester, MA 01890-8443
Ph: (781)729-6262
Fax: (781)729-6262

Karl, Chris, Exec. Dir.
Z Car Club Association [21525]
6 Jason Dr.
Londonderry, NH 03053
Ph: (603)425-2270
Fax: (603)218-6149

Karl, Jim, Act. Pres.
Purdue Alumni Association [19346]
Dick and Sandy Dauch Alumni Ctr.
403 W Wood St.
West Lafayette, IN 47907
Ph: (765)494-5175
Toll Free: 800-414-1541
Fax: (765)494-9179

Karlan, Prof. Dean, President, Founder
Innovations for Poverty Action [17805]
101 Whitney Ave.
New Haven, CT 06510-1256
Ph: (203)772-2216
Fax: (203)772-2428

Karlsson, Calle, President
United States Floorball Association [22535]
10037 Scenic Blvd.
Cupertino, CA 95014

Karp, Erin, Chairperson
American Society of Contemporary Artists [8912]
150 W 96th St., No. 14G
New York, NY 10025

Karras, Dr. Louis, Exec. Dir.
Hellenic American Dental Society [14438]
PO Box 2505
Glenview, IL 60025-2505

Karstadt, Bruce, CEO, President
American Swedish Institute [10230]
2600 Park Ave.
Minneapolis, MN 55407-1090
Ph: (612)871-4907

Kartiala, Eero, Chmn. of the Bd.
Scientists, Engineers, and Technicians Leadership Association [6585]
2101 E Palmdale Blvd.
Palmdale, CA 93550
Ph: (661)267-1505

Kasabian, Robert J., MBA, Exec. Dir.
American Jail Association [11519]
1135 Professional Ct.

Hagerstown, MD 21740-5853
Ph: (301)790-3930
Fax: (301)790-2941

Kasbaum, Diana, Coord.
Association of State Supervisor of Mathematics [8277]
c/o Dewey Gottlieb, Vice President
475 22nd Ave., Rm. 116
Honolulu, HI 96816

Kaseman, Dr. Julius, Founder
Association of Faith Churches and Ministers [20356]
PO Box 1918
Willmar, MN 56201
Ph: (320)235-3838
Fax: (320)235-1802

Kasendorf, Christina, Exec. Dir.
Association for Academic Surgery [17377]
11300 W Olympic Blvd., Ste. 600
Los Angeles, CA 90064
Ph: (310)437-1606
Fax: (310)437-0585

Kasendorf, Christina, Exec. Dir.
Minimally Invasive Robotic Association [17394]
11300 W Olympic Blvd., Ste. 600
Los Angeles, CA 90064
Ph: (310)424-3353
Fax: (310)437-0585

Kashani, Ali, Secretary, Treasurer
Association of American Feed Control Officials [4942]
1800 S Oak St., Ste. 100
Champaign, IL 61820-6974
Ph: (217)356-4221
Fax: (217)398-4119

Kashmiri, Sayyid Mohammad Baqir, Chairman
Imam Mahdi Association of Marjaeya [20497]
22000 Garrison St.
Dearborn, MI 48124-2306
Ph: (313)562-4626
Toll Free: 888-SISTANI

Kasirsky, Gilbert, PhD, President
Medical Care International [15484]
PO Box 69
New Hope, PA 18938-0069

Kasischke, Betty, Treasurer
EPIC, the Electronic Publishing Industry Coalition [2784]

Kasner, Sara-ann G., Founder, CEO
National Concierge Association [1670]
2920 Idaho Ave. N
Minneapolis, MN 55427
Ph: (612)317-2932

Kasnic, David M., Exec. Dir.
Pediatric Congenital Heart Association [15219]
14 Ellis Potter Ct., Ste. 100
Madison, WI 53711
Ph: (608)370-3739

Kasoff, Barbara, President
Women Impacting Public Policy [19009]
PO Box 31279
San Francisco, CA 94131
Ph: (415)434-4314
Toll Free: 888-488-9477
Fax: (415)434-4331

Kasper, John, Exec. Dir.
American Dental Assistants Association [14403]
140 N Bloomingdale Rd.

Bloomingdale, IL 60108-1017
Ph: (630)994-4247
Toll Free: 877-874-3785
Fax: (630)351-8490

Kasper, Nate, Dir. of Operations
American College of Addiction Treat-
ment Administrators [13122]
11380 Prosperity Farms Rd., Ste.
209A
Palm Beach Gardens, FL 33410
Ph: (561)429-4527
Fax: (561)429-4650

Kass, Fritz, CEO
Intercollegiate Broadcasting System
Inc. [7537]
367 Windsor Hwy.
New Windsor, NY 12553-7900
Ph: (845)565-0003
Fax: (845)565-7446

Kassab, Joseph T., Exec. Dir.
Chaldean Federation of America
[8816]
29850 Northwestern Hwy., Ste. 250
Southfield, MI 48034
Ph: (248)996-8384
Fax: (248)996-8342

Kassalen, Ms. Beth, MBA, Exec. Dir.
International Society of Nurses in
Genetics [14880]
461 Cochran Rd.
Pittsburgh, PA 15228
Ph: (412)344-1414
Fax: (412)344-0599

Kassell, Neal F., MD, Chairman,
Founder
Focused Ultrasound Foundation
[17537]
1230 Cedars Ct., Ste. F
Charlottesville, VA 22903
Ph: (434)220-4993
Fax: (434)220-4978

Kassell, Neal F., MD, Founder,
Chairman
Focused Ultrasound Surgery
Foundation [17538]
1230 Cedars Ct., Ste. F
Charlottesville, VA 22903
Ph: (434)220-4993
Fax: (434)220-4978

Kastner, Michael, Managing Dir.
National Truck Equipment Associa-
tion [328]
37400 Hills Tech Dr.
Farmington Hills, MI 48331-3414
Ph: (248)489-7090
Fax: (248)489-8590

Kaswell, Robert, Chmn. of the Bd.
Boys Town Jerusalem Foundation of
America [13433]
1 Penn Plz., Ste. 6250
New York, NY 10119
Toll Free: 800-469-2697
Fax: (866)730-2697

Katanick, Sandra, CAE, CEO
IAC Vascular Testing [17573]
6021 University Blvd., Ste. 500
Ellicott City, MD 21043
Ph: (443)973-3239
Toll Free: 800-838-2110
Fax: (888)927-2637

Kateb, Babak, Chairman, CEO
Society for Brain Mapping and
Therapeutics [16035]
8159 Santa Monica Blvd., Ste. 200
West Hollywood, CA 90046
Ph: (310)500-6196
Fax: (323)654-3511

Katona, Roger, Treasurer
International Borzoi Council [21897]
c/o Roger Katona, Treasurer

7617 Pelham Dr.
Chesterland, OH 44026-2011

Katz, Daniel R., Chmn. of the Bd.
Rainforest Alliance [4497]
233 Broadway, 28th Fl.
New York, NY 10279
Ph: (212)677-1900
Fax: (212)677-2187

Katz, Dave, Chief of Staff
The Patriots [18756]
1494 Patriot Dr.
Melbourne, FL 32940
Ph: (321)752-5955

Katz, Douglas J., Chairman
U.S. Naval Sailing Association
[21063]
PO Box 4702
Annapolis, MD 21403
Ph: (443)510-1421

Katz, Dr. Elliot M., DVM, Founder
In Defense of Animals [10645]
3010 Kerner Blvd.
San Rafael, CA 94901
Ph: (415)448-0048
Fax: (415)454-1031

Katz, Irv, CEO, President
National Human Services Assembly
[13304]
1101 14th St. NW, Ste. 600
Washington, DC 20005-5639
Ph: (202)347-2080

Katz, Jonathan David, PhD,
President
Leslie-Lohman Museum of Gay and
Lesbian Art [8870]
26 Wooster St.
New York, NY 10013
Ph: (212)431-2609
Fax: (212)431-2666

Katz, Karen, CEO
Phi Delta Epsilon International Medi-
cal Fraternity [23819]
1005 N Northlake Dr.
Hollywood, FL 33019
Ph: (786)302-1120
Fax: (786)472-7133

Katz, Linda, VP, Treasurer, Secretary
Polyurethane Manufacturers As-
sociation [2631]
6737 W Washington St., Ste. 1300
Milwaukee, WI 53214
Ph: (414)431-3094
Fax: (414)276-7704

Katz, Dr. Stephen I., Director
U.S. Department of Health and Hu-
man Services | National Institutes
of Health | National Institute of
Arthritis and Musculoskeletal and
Skin Diseases Information
Clearinghouse [17171]
1 AMS Cir.
Bethesda, MD 20892
Ph: (301)495-4484
Toll Free: 877-226-4267
Fax: (301)718-6366

Katz, Steve, Contact
Disabled Drummers Association
[11592]
18901 NW 19th Ave.
Miami Gardens, FL 33056-2808
Ph: (305)621-9022

Katz, Terry, Exec. Dir.
Society of Jewish Science [20284]
109 E 39th St.
New York, NY 10016
Ph: (212)682-2626

Katzman, Harlene, JD, VP
Reproductive Health Access Project
[17117]

PO Box 21191
New York, NY 10025
Ph: (212)206-5247
Fax: (314)584-3260

Katznelson, Ira, President
Social Science Research Council
[7173]
300 Cadman Plz. W, 15th Fl.
Brooklyn, NY 11201-2701
Ph: (212)377-2700
Fax: (212)377-2727

Katz-Schwartz, Judith, President
Association of Online Appraiser
[222]
PO Box 1292
Frederick, MD 21702-0292
Ph: (301)228-2279

Kauffman, Craig L., Comm. Chm.
Safari Club International [4879]
4800 W Gates Pass Rd.
Tucson, AZ 85745-9490
Ph: (520)620-1220
Toll Free: 888-486-8724
Fax: (520)622-1205

Kauffman, Reese R., President
Child Evangelism Fellowship [20132]
17482 Hwy. M
Warrenton, MO 63383-3414
Ph: (636)456-4321
Toll Free: 800-748-7710
Fax: (636)456-9935

Kaufman, Bruce, President, Founder
United States Lawn Mower Racing
Association [23086]
PO Box 628
Northbrook, IL 60065
Ph: (847)272-2120
(251)645-2942
Fax: (847)272-2120

Kaufman, Howard, President
Society for Immunotherapy of
Cancer [14064]
555 E Wells St., Ste. 1100
Milwaukee, WI 53202-3823
Ph: (414)271-2456
Fax: (414)276-3349

Kaufman, Jim, Contact
Dedham Pottery Collectors Society
[21648]
248 Highland St.
Dedham, MA 02026-5833
Toll Free: 800-283-8070

Kaufman, Mr. Lawrence, Chairman
National Stereoscopic Association
[10142]
PO Box 86708
Portland, OR 97286
Ph: (503)771-4440

Kaufman, Reuven, President
Diamond Dealers Club [2043]
580 5th Ave., 10th Fl.
New York, NY 10036
Ph: (212)790-3600
Fax: (212)869-5164

Kaufman, Stephen R., MD, Chair-
man
Christian Vegetarian Association
[20635]
PO Box 201791
Cleveland, OH 44120
Ph: (216)283-6702
Toll Free: 866-202-9170
Fax: (216)283-6702

Kaufman, Stephen R., MD, Co-Ch.
Medical Research Modernization
Committee [15652]
3200 Morley Rd.

Shaker Heights, OH 44122
Ph: (216)283-6702
Fax: (216)283-6702

Kaufmann, Jacquelyn, MS, HS-BCP,
VP
Council for Standards in Human
Service Education [13041]
3337 Duke St.
Alexandria, VA 22314
Ph: (571)257-3959

Kaufmann, Janey, President
National Science Education Leader-
ship Association [8554]
55466 Forrester Valley Ln.
Glenwood, IA 51534
Ph: (919)561-3612
Fax: (801)659-3351

Kaufmann, Jeff, President
Home Fashion Products Association
[1944]
355 Lexington Ave.
New York, NY 10017
Ph: (212)297-2122

Kaufmann, Nancy, President,
Founder
Multiple Myeloma Opportunities for
Research & Education [14016]
117 E Louisa St., No. 554
Seattle, WA 98102
Toll Free: 888-486-4240

Kaufmann, William J., Chairman
Scandinavian Seminar [8090]
24 Dickinson St.
Amherst, MA 01002-2310
Ph: (413)253-9737

Kaur, Ravneet, Chairperson
Alliance for Preventive Health
[15106]
817 Broadway, 5th Fl.
New York, NY 10003
Ph: (212)257-6105
Fax: (212)631-3619

Kaur, Sapreet, Exec. Dir.
Sikh Coalition [19099]
50 Broad St., Ste. 1537
New York, NY 10004
Ph: (212)655-3095

Kavanagh, Colleen, Founder, Exec.
Dir.
A Better Course [16210]
30 Woodland Ave.
San Francisco, CA 94117
Ph: (415)706-8094

Kavanagh, Dr. Kevin T., Chmn. of
the Bd.
Health Watch USA [15014]
3396 Woodhaven Dr.
Somerset, KY 42503

Kavelaars, Annemieke, President
Psychoneuroimmunology Research
Society [13802]
c/o Susan Keran Solomon, Executive Director
10724 Wilshire Blvd., No. 602
Los Angeles, CA 90024

Kaveny, M. Cathleen, Mem.
Society of Christian Ethics [11804]
PO Box 5126
Saint Cloud, MN 56302-5126
Ph: (320)253-5407
Fax: (320)252-6984

Kavinoky, Janet, VP
Americans for Transportation Mobility [5810]
US Chamber of Commerce
1615 H St. NW

Washington, DC 20062-2000
Ph: (202)463-5600

Kawano, Emily, PhD, Exec. Dir.
Center for Popular Economics
[6385]
PO Box 785
Amherst, MA 01004-0785
Ph: (413)545-0743

Kawata, Paul A., Exec. Dir.
National Minority AIDS Council
[13556]
1000 Vermont Ave., NW, Ste. 200
Washington, DC 20005-4903
Ph: (202)853-1846

Kay, Beryl, President
Action for Nature, Inc. [4032]
2269 Chestnut St., No. 263
San Francisco, CA 94123
Ph: (415)922-6155
Fax: (415)922-5717

Kay, Debby, Exec. Dir.
Diabetes Alert Dog Alliance [14524]
719 Mission Rd.
Harpers Ferry, WV 25425

Kay, Sara, Founder
Professional Organization for
  Women in the Arts [8998]
New York, NY

Kayama, Ikumi, Secretary
Guild of Natural Science Illustrators
[6698]
Ben Franklin Sta.
Washington, DC 20044-0652
Ph: (301)309-1514
Fax: (301)309-1514

Kayinamura, Yohani, PhD, President
Rwandan International Network As-
  sociation [11426]
901 15th St. NW
Washington, DC 20005
Ph: (301)259-1792

Kayler, J. Allan, Treasurer
Global Alliance for Africa [17776]
703 W Monroe St.
Chicago, IL 60661
Ph: (312)382-0607
Fax: (312)382-8850

Kaynak, Erdener, PhD, Ed.-in-Chief
International Management Develop-
  ment Association [643]
PO Box 216
Hummelstown, PA 17036-0216
Ph: (717)566-3054

Kayser, Casey, President
The Carson McCullers Society
[10367]
Dept. of English
Columbus State University
4225 University Ave.
Columbus, GA 31907-5679

Kayserian, Andrew, President
Pi Delta Psi Fraternity, Inc. [9334]
176-25 Union Tpke.
Fresh Meadows, NY 11366

Kazakos, Sophia, Secretary
Evrytanian Association of America
[19453]
121 Greenwich Rd., Ste. 212
Charlotte, NC 28211
Ph: (704)366-6571
Fax: (704)366-6678

Kazar, Bob, Chmn. of the Bd.
Society for Maintenance and Reliability Professionals [2143]
1100 Johnson Ferry Rd., Ste. 300

Atlanta, GA 30342
Toll Free: 800-950-7354
Fax: (404)591-6811

Kazarians, Lily, President
Armenian Professional Society
[9203]
117 S Louise St.
Glendale, CA 91205
Ph: (818)685-9946

Kazeminy, Nasser J., Chairman,
CEO
National Ethnic Coalition of
  Organizations [19430]
16 W 36th St., Ste. 801
New York, NY 10018
Ph: (212)755-1492
Fax: (212)755-3762

Kazim, Ayesha, President
Kappa Phi Gamma Sorority, Inc.
[23974]

Kazim, Michael, President
International Thyroid Eye Disease
  Society [13787]
Columbia University
635 W 165th St.
New York, NY 10032
Ph: (212)305-5477

Kea, Perry, Chairman
Westar Institute [20558]
PO Box 346
Farmington, MN 55024
Ph: (651)200-2372

Kealey, Paul, COO
National Low Income Housing Coali-
  tion [11985]
1000 Vermont Ave., Ste. 500
Washington, DC 20005
Ph: (202)662-1530
Fax: (202)393-1973

Kean, Hamilton, Chairman
Center for War/Peace Studies
[18520]
866 United Nations Plz., Rm. 4050
New York, NY 10017
Ph: (646)553-3464

Kean, Thomas H., Chairman
National Campaign to Prevent Teen
  and Unplanned Pregnancy [13464]
1776 Massachusetts Ave. NW, Ste.
  200
Washington, DC 20036
Ph: (202)478-8500
Fax: (202)478-8588

Keane, Eileen, VP
The Appliqué Society [21750]
PO Box 89
Sequim, WA 98382-0089
Toll Free: 800-597-9827

Keane, Patrice, Exec. Dir., Director
American Society for Psychical
  Research [6983]
5 W 73rd St.
New York, NY 10023
Ph: (212)799-5050
Fax: (212)496-2497

Kearney, Stephen, Exec. Dir.
Alliance of Nonprofit Mailers [2113]
1211 Connecticut Ave. NW, Ste. 610
Washington, DC 20036-2705
Ph: (202)462-5132
Fax: (202)462-0423

Kearns, Kevin L., President, Ed.-in-
Chief
United States Business and Industry
  Council [18290]
512 C St. NE

Washington, DC 20002-5810
Ph: (202)266-3980
Fax: (202)266-3981

Kearns, Suzanne, President
University Aviation Association
[7462]
2415 Moore's Mill Rd., Ste. 265-216
Auburn, AL 36830
Ph: (334)528-0300

Keathley, Karen, PMAC, Exec. Dir.
American Society of Podiatric Medi-
  cal Assistants [16785]
1000 W St. Joseph Hwy., Ste. 200
Lansing, MI 48915
Toll Free: 888-882-7762
Fax: (517)485-9408

Keating, Frank, V. Chmn. of the Bd.
character.org [11724]
1634 I St. NW, Ste. 550
Washington, DC 20036
Ph: (202)296-7743

Keating, J. Patrick, President
452nd Bomb Group Association
[21182]
c/o Cally A. Boatwright, Secretary/
  Editor
PO Box 72
Pacific Junction, IA 51561

Keating, Neal J., Chairman
Manufacturers Alliance for Productiv-
  ity and Innovation [1745]
1600 Wilson Blvd., 11th Fl.
Arlington, VA 22209-2594
Ph: (703)841-9000
Fax: (703)841-9514

Keating, Prof. Patricia A., PhD,
President
International Phonetic Association
[8423]
c/o Patricia Keating, President
3125 Campbell Hall
Dept. of Linguistics
University of California, Los Angeles
Los Angeles, CA 90095-1543
Ph: (310)794-6316
Fax: (310)206-5743

Keating, Sonja, Sr. VP
United States Equestrian Federation
[22949]
4047 Iron Works Pky.
Lexington, KY 40511
Ph: (859)258-2472
Fax: (859)231-6662

Keating, Tim, Exec. Dir.
Rainforest Relief [4616]
PO Box 8451
Jersey City, NJ 07308
Ph: (917)543-4064

Keay, Lou Carter, President
INTERTEL [9344]
c/o Linda Woodhead, Acting
  Secretary
PO Box 5518
Douglasville, GA 30154
Ph: (678)426-8379

Kecskemethy, Tom, Exec. Dir.
American Academy of Political and
  Social Science [7041]
Annenberg Public Policy Ctr.
202 S 36th St.
Philadelphia, PA 19104-3806
Ph: (215)746-6500
Fax: (215)573-2667

Keefe, Pamela J., CFO, Sr. VP,
Treasurer
Electric Power Research Institute
[6474]

3420 Hillview Ave.
Palo Alto, CA 94304
Ph: (650)855-2121
Toll Free: 800-313-3774

Keefe, Tom, Founder
International Medical Equipment Col-
  laborative [14943]
1620 Osgood St.
North Andover, MA 01845
Ph: (978)557-5510
Fax: (978)557-5525

Keegan, Bill, Founder, President
HEART 9/11: Healing Emergency
  Aid Response Team 9/11 [11667]
614 Frelinghuysen Ave.
Newark, NJ 07114

Keegan, Tom, President
American Institute of Fishery
  Research Biologists [6714]
7909 Sleaford Pl.
Bethesda, MD 20814-4625

Keehan, Sr. Carol, DC, CEO,
President
Catholic Health Association of the
  United States [15317]
4455 Woodson Rd.
Saint Louis, MO 63134-3701
Ph: (314)427-2500
Fax: (314)427-0029

Keeley, Rep. Helene, Chairperson
National Order of Women Legisla-
  tors [5556]
National Foundation for Women
  Legislators
1727 King St., Ste. 300
Alexandria, VA 22314
Ph: (703)518-7931

Keeley, Wayne J., Director
Children's Advertising Review Unit
[92]
112 Madison Ave., 3rd Fl.
New York, NY 10016
Ph: (212)705-0100
Fax: (212)705-0134

Keeling, J. Michael, President
ESOP Association [1080]
1200 18th St. NW, Ste. 1125
Washington, DC 20036-2506
Ph: (202)293-2971
Toll Free: 866-366-3832
Fax: (202)293-7568

Keeling, Kara, President
Children's Literature Association
[9755]
1301 W 22nd St., Ste. 202
Oak Brook, IL 60523
Ph: (630)571-4520
Fax: (708)876-5598

Keen, Jane, Director
South African Education and
  Environment Project U.S.A.
[12188]
2116 Chesapeake Harbour Dr. E,
  Unit 102
Annapolis, MD 21403
Ph: (410)295-5544
  (410)626-1747

Keenan, Debra, President
National Alliance of Independent
  Crop Consultants [3525]
349 E Nolley Dr.
Collierville, TN 38017
Ph: (901)861-0511
Fax: (901)861-0512

Keenan, James P., Director
American Society of Bookplate Collectors and Designers [21615]

5802 Bullock Loop, Ste. C1.No.
84404
Laredo, TX 78041-8807

Keenan, Mal, Founder
A to Z Literacy Movement [10827]
PO Box 2483
Crystal Lake, IL 60039
Ph: (815)477-8187

Keene, Beverly, Chairperson
PeaceJam [8408]
11200 Ralston Rd.
Arvada, CO 80004
Ph: (303)455-2099
Fax: (303)455-3921

Keene, Larry, CEO
Traffic Directors Guild of America
[483]
Bldg. 114
26000 Avenida Aeropuerto
San Juan Capistrano, CA 92675-
4713
Ph: (949)429-7063
Fax: (509)471-5765

Keene, Paulette, President
National Independent Conces-
sionaires Association, Inc. [1395]
1043 E Brandon Blvd.
Brandon, FL 33511-5515
Ph: (813)438-8926
Fax: (813)438-8928

Keener, Jackie, Events Coord.
National Association of Landscape
Professionals [2070]
950 Herndon Pky., Ste. 450
Herndon, VA 20170-5528
Ph: (703)736-9666
Toll Free: 800-395-2522
Fax: (703)736-9668

Keener, Dr. Patricia A., Founder
Safe Sitter [10813]
8604 Allisonville Rd., Ste. 248
Indianapolis, IN 46250-1597
Ph: (317)596-5001
Fax: (317)596-5008

Keener, Stephen D., President, CEO
Little League Baseball and Softball
[22550]
539 US Route 15 Hwy.
Williamsport, PA 17701-0485
Ph: (570)326-1921
Fax: (570)326-1074

Keeney, David, Administrator
Software Contractors' Guild [980]
7151 E US Highway 60, No. 704
Gold Canyon, AZ 85118-9769

Keeny, Yvonne, Exec. Dir., Founder
Fibromyalgia Coalition International
[14766]
5201 Johnson Dr., Ste. 210
Mission, KS 66205-2920
Ph: (913)384-4673
Fax: (913)384-8998

Keese, Bill, Exec. Dir.
Association of Progressive Rental
Organizations [2926]
1504 Robin Hood Trl.
Austin, TX 78703
Toll Free: 800-204-2776
Fax: (512)794-0097

Keesey, Ben, Chmn. of the Bd.
Invisible Children [17846]
641 S St. NW
Washington, DC 20001-5196
Ph: (619)562-2799

Keeslar, Joe, Chairman
American Bladesmith Society
[21745]

c/o Cindy Sheely, Office Manager
PO Box 160
Grand Rapids, OH 43522-0160
Ph: (419)832-0400

Kehl-Rose, Karen, President
Leading Edge Alliance [39]
621 Cedar St.
Saint Charles, IL 60174
Ph: (630)513-9814
Fax: (630)524-9014

Keiper, Sam, CEO, President
Specialty Crop Trade Council [4250]
8050 N Palm Ave., Ste. 300
Fresno, CA 93711
Ph: (559)389-5895
(559)287-1837

Keirn, Tim, President
Society for History Education [7990]
California State University, Long
Beach
1250 Bellflower Blvd.
Long Beach, CA 90840-0101
Ph: (562)985-2573

Keiser, Arnold, President, Project
Mgr.
Organization for International
Cooperation [18552]
Bldg. C, Ste. 196
100 Conestoga Dr.
Marlton, NJ 08053
Ph: (856)596-6679
Fax: (856)282-1184

Keiser, Lauren, VP
Music Publishers' Association of the
United States [2429]
243 5th Ave., Ste. 236
New York, NY 10016

Keisling, Mara, Exec. Dir.
National Center for Transgender
Equality [13227]
1325 Massachusetts Ave. NW, Ste.
700
Washington, DC 20005
Ph: (202)903-0112

Keith, Alan, Chairman
Green Electronics Council [6421]
227 SW Pine St., Ste. 300
Portland, OR 97204
Ph: (503)279-9383
Fax: (503)279-9381

Keith, Dr. Louis G., Founder
Center for the Study of Multiple Birth
[15845]
333 E Superior St., Ste. 464
Chicago, IL 60611
Ph: (312)695-1677
Fax: (312)908-8777

Keith, Penny, Coord.
Community of Caring [10949]
1721 Campus Center Dr.
Salt Lake City, UT 84112
Ph: (801)581-8221

Keith, Timothy, Secretary, Treasurer
International Society for Intelligence
Research [6763]
12340 Morning Creek Rd.
Glen Allen, VA 23059-7100
Ph: (804)727-0209

Keithline, Judy, Exec. Asst.
American Industrial Hygiene As-
sociation [16314]
3141 Fairview Park Dr., Ste. 777
Falls Church, VA 22042
Ph: (703)849-8888
Fax: (703)207-3561

Kelemu, Mekdes, Founder
Aerie Africa, Inc. [10834]
1249 Hazelwood Dr.

Fort Washington, PA 19034

Kell, James, President
American Dove Association [21536]
7334 Highway 15
Sparta, GA 31087-3567

Kell, Tanya, President
North American Society of
Homeopaths [15291]
PO Box 115
Troy, ME 04987
Ph: (206)720-7000
Fax: (208)248-1942

Kellas, Costas, Director
Hellenic American Bankers Associa-
tion [399]
PO Box 7244
New York, NY 10150
Ph: (212)421-1057

Kelleher, Dennis P., Chairman
American Irish Historical Society
[9598]
991 5th Ave.
New York, NY 10028
Ph: (212)288-2263
Fax: (212)628-7927

Kelleher, Margaret, Chairperson
International Association for the
Study of Irish Literatures [9759]
c/o Dawn Duncan, Secretary
Dept. of English
Concordia College
901 8th St. S
Moorhead, MN 56562

Kelleher, Robin, CEO, President
Hope for the Warriors [10746]
5101C Backlick Rd.
Annandale, VA 22003
Toll Free: 877-246-7349

Kelleher, Rory, Chairman
Catholic Guardian Services [10887]
1011 1st Ave. 10th Fl.
New York, NY 10022
Ph: (212)371-1011
Fax: (212)758-5892

Keller, Brigitt, Esq., Exec. Dir.
National Police Accountability Project
[5507]
499 7th Avenue 12N
New York, NY 10018-7058
Ph: (212)630-9939
Fax: (212)659-0695

Keller, Frederique, President
American Apitherapy Society
[13588]
14942 S Eagle Crest Dr.
Draper, UT 84020
Ph: (631)470-9446
Fax: (631)693-2528

Keller, Hal, VP
National Association of State and
Local Equity Funds [1256]
1970 Broadway, Ste. 250
Oakland, CA 94612
Ph: (510)444-1101

Keller, Kurt, Exec. Dir., Treasurer
Les Amis d'Escoffier Society of New
York [1351]
787 Ridgewood Rd.
Millburn, NJ 07041
Ph: (212)414-5820
(973)564-7575
Fax: (973)379-3117

Keller, Dr. Mary M., CEO, President
Military Child Education Coalition
[8344]
909 Mountain Lion Cir.

Harker Heights, TX 76548-5709
Ph: (254)953-1923
Fax: (254)953-1925

Keller, Michael E., Ed.-in-Chief,
Exec. Dir., Treasurer
American Society of Test Engineers
[7322]
PO Box 389
Nutting Lake, MA 01865-0389

Keller, Peter, Exec. Dir.
Aid Africa [12525]
3916 Pennsylvania Ave.
La Crescenta, CA 91214
Ph: (818)249-2398

Keller, Seth M., MD, President
American Academy of
Developmental Medicine and
Dentistry [15894]
PO Box 681
Prospect, KY 40059

Keller, Thomas, VP
Friends of Old St. Ferdinand [19837]
1 rue St. Francois
Florissant, MO 63031
Ph: (314)837-2110

Kellerman, Dana F., Secretary
Black Russian Terrier Club of
America [21842]
PO Box 291815
Phelan, CA 92329

Kellermann, Ms. Alessandra,
Founder, President
Homefront Hugs U.S.A. [13241]
1881 W Liberty St.
Ann Arbor, MI 48103
Ph: (734)330-8203

Kelley, Allison, CAE, Exec. Dir.
Romance Writers of America
[10396]
14615 Benfer Rd.
Houston, TX 77069
Ph: (832)717-5200

Kelley, Brady, Exec. Dir.
National Association of Professional
Surplus Lines Offices [1901]
4131 N Mulberry Dr., Ste. 200
Kansas City, MO 64116
Ph: (816)741-3910

Kelley, Bret, Chmn. of the Bd.
United States Industrial Fabrics
Institute [3276]
1801 County Road B W
Roseville, MN 55113-4061
Ph: (651)225-6956

Kelley, Bruce, EMC, Chairman
Property and Liability Resource
Bureau [1921]
3025 Highland Pky., Ste. 800
Downers Grove, IL 60515-1291
Ph: (630)724-2200
Fax: (630)724-2260

Kelley, Colleen M., President
National Treasury Employees Union
[23437]
1750 H St. NW
Washington, DC 20006
Ph: (202)572-5500

Kelley, Cynthia S., Treasurer
National Association of Community
College Teacher Education
Programs [8651]
2323 W 14th St.
Tempe, AZ 85281-6942

Kelley, Mrs. Danielle, Founder, Exec.
Dir.
Jump Start Your Heart [14155]
17732 Highland Rd., Ste. G150

Baton Rouge, LA 70810
Ph: (225)751-8684
Fax: (225)751-9664

Kelley, Jeff, President
Triumph Register of America **[21504]**
c/o Jeff Kelley, President
443 Edgewater Ct.
Coldwater, MI 49036
Ph: (269)251-1996

Kelley, John J., President
United States Mangalarga Mar-
chador Association **[4421]**
10487 E Rising Sun Dr.
Scottsdale, AZ 85262
Ph: (480)595-2559

Kelley, Kelli D., Founder, Exec. Dir.
Hand to Hold **[14232]**
13492 Research Blvd., Ste. 120
Austin, TX 78750
Ph: (512)293-0165
Toll Free: 855-424-6428

Kelley, Loretta, President
Hardanger Fiddle Association of
America **[9916]**
PO Box 23046
Minneapolis, MN 55423-0046
Ph: (612)568-7448

Kelley, Matthew W., PhD, President
Association for Research in
Otolaryngology **[16539]**
19 Mantua Rd.
Mount Royal, NJ 08061-1006
Ph: (856)423-0041
Fax: (856)423-3420

Kelley, Mr. Peter, President
National Association of Japan-
America Societies **[19511]**
1819 L St. NW, Ste. 800
Washington, DC 20036
Ph: (202)429-5545
Fax: (202)429-0027

Kelley, Richard Allan, Chairperson
Network Professional Association
[6258]
3157 Carmino Del Rio S, Ste. 115
San Diego, CA 92108-4098
Toll Free: 888-NPA-NPA0

Kellgren, Tore, Master
Vasa Order of America **[19498]**
c/o Bruce Elfvin, Membership Chairman
2924 E Overlook Rd.
Cleveland Heights, OH 44118-2434

Kelli, Heval Mohammad, MD,
President
Kurdish American Medical Associa-
tion **[15734]**
6117 Marlboro Pke.
District Heights, MD 20747

Kelliher, Donna, CTC, GLP,
President, CEO
Global Business Travel Association
[3378]
123 N Pitt St.
Alexandria, VA 22314
Ph: (703)684-0836
Fax: (703)342-4324

Kellman, Jack, President
Better Boys Foundation **[11215]**
1512 S Pulaski Rd.
Chicago, IL 60623
Ph: (773)542-7300
Fax: (773)521-4153

Kellum, Stan, Exec. Dir.
National Duckpin Bowling Congress
[22706]

4991 Fairview Ave.
Linthicum, MD 21090
Ph: (410)636-2695
Fax: (410)636-3256

Kelly, Andrea M., CEO
International Association of Infant
Massage **[15559]**
PO Box 2447
Ventura, CA 93002
Ph: (805)644-8524
Fax: (805)299-4563

Kelly, Anna C., MD, FAAMA, VP
American Academy of Medical
Acupuncture **[16452]**
2512 Artesia Blvd., Ste. 200
Redondo Beach, CA 90278
Ph: (310)379-8261
Fax: (310)379-8283

Kelly, Bill, President
Scruggs Family Association **[20924]**
c/o Mary Beth Scruggs Rephlo,
Secretary-Treasurer
6130 Sherborn Ln.
Springfield, VA 22152
Ph: (703)451-9473

Kelly, Brian G., Founder
Juvenile Diabetes Cure Alliance
[14538]
14 E 60th St., Ste. 208
New York, NY 10022

Kelly, Debbie, President
Comparative Cognition Society
[5893]
c/o Michael Brown, Treasurer
Dept. of Psychology
Villanova University
800 Lancaster Ave.
Villanova, PA 19085

Kelly, Denise, Director
Avian Welfare Coalition **[10592]**
PO Box 40212
Saint Paul, MN 55104

Kelly, Diane, Chairperson
Special Interest Group on Informa-
tion Retrieval **[6758]**
c/o Diane Kelly, Chairperson
School of Information Sciences
University of Tennessee
1345 Circle Park Dr., Ste. 451
Knoxville, TN 37996-0341

Kelly, Dorien, Administrator
Authors Coalition of America **[9040]**
PO Box 929
Pentwater, MI 49449
Ph: (231)869-2011

Kelly, Rev. Douglas F., President
Scottish Heritage U.S.A. **[19641]**
Bldg. 2, Ste. 10
315 N Page Rd.
Pinehurst, NC 28374-8751
Ph: (910)295-4448

Kelly, Edmund, CEO, President
American Association of Insurance
Services **[1825]**
701 Warrenville Rd.
Lisle, IL 60532
Ph: (630)681-8347
Toll Free: 800-564-AAIS
Fax: (630)681-8356

Kelly, Edward W., MFH, Director
Masters of Foxhounds Association of
America **[22962]**
PO Box 363
Millwood, VA 22646
Ph: (540)955-5680
Fax: (540)955-5682

Kelly, Elizabeth, Specialist
National Association of State Ap-
proving Agencies **[5838]**

120 Penmarc Dr., Ste. 103
Raleigh, NC 27603-2434
Ph: (919)733-7535
Fax: (919)733-1284

Kelly, Frances, Exec. Dir.
Chimney Safety Institute of America
[2126]
2155 Commercial Dr.
Plainfield, IN 46168
Ph: (317)837-5362
Fax: (317)837-5365

Kelly, Ginna, Founder
Climb for Conservation **[3833]**
PO Box 4971
Aspen, CO 81612
Ph: (970)948-2991
Fax: (757)548-2345

Kelly, John F., President
Lymphangiomatosis and Gorham's
Disease Alliance **[15543]**
19919 Villa Lante Pl.
Boca Raton, FL 33434
Toll Free: 844-588-5771

Kelly, John, President
JEDEC **[1054]**
3103 N 10th St., Ste. 240-S
Arlington, VA 22201-2107
Ph: (703)907-7515

Kelly, Kathryn, President
Tau Beta Sigma **[23835]**
PO Box 849
Stillwater, OK 74076-0849
Ph: (405)372-2333
Toll Free: 800-543-6505
Fax: (405)372-2363

Kelly, Ken, President
Wooden Canoe Heritage Association
[22693]
PO Box 117
Tamworth, NH 03886
Ph: (603)323-8992

Kelly, Kevin, CFO
Society of Independent Gasoline
Marketers of America **[2537]**
3930 Pender Dr., Ste. 340
Fairfax, VA 22030
Ph: (703)709-7000

Kelly, L. Michael, Chairman
Forest History Society **[9477]**
701 William Vickers Ave.
Durham, NC 27701
Ph: (919)682-9319
Fax: (919)682-2349

Kelly, Laura, Dir. of Operations
Wainwright House **[20619]**
260 Stuyvesant Ave.
Rye, NY 10580-3115
Ph: (914)967-6080

Kelly, Laureen A., Founder
Save One Life, Inc. **[15243]**
65 Central St., Ste. 204
Georgetown, MA 01833
Ph: (978)352-7652
Fax: (978)225-3492

Kelly, Linda, Dir. of Comm.
Fellowship of Reconciliation - USA
[18783]
PO Box 271
Nyack, NY 10960
Ph: (845)358-4601
Fax: (845)358-4924

Kelly, Linda, President
Operation Never Forgotten **[10752]**
PO Box 1229
Manhattan, MT 59741

Kelly, Lisa, President
Laboratory Animal Welfare Training
Exchange **[3629]**

885 Strongtown Rd.
Southbury, CT 06488

Kelly, Lori, President
Scottish Terrier Club of America
[21959]
c/o Kelli Edell, Membership Chairman
2727 Cheryl Ct.
Missouri City, TX 77459-2930
Ph: (281)261-6031

Kelly, Luke, V. Chmn. of the Bd.
Wild Steelhead Coalition **[4905]**
117 E Louisa St., No. 329
Seattle, WA 98102

Kelly, Megan, President, Founder
Tailored for Education **[11738]**
PO Box 171236
Boston, MA 02117

Kelly, Mike, President
Fairchild Club **[21226]**
c/o Mike Kelly, President
92 N Circle Dr.
Coldwater, MI 49036

Kelly, Mike
IEEE - Solid-State Circuits Society
[6411]
445 Hoes Ln.
Piscataway, NJ 08854
Ph: (732)981-3400
(732)981-3410
Fax: (732)981-3401

Kelly, Nancy, Exec. Dir.
Health Volunteers Overseas **[12282]**
1900 L St. NW, No. 310
Washington, DC 20036
Ph: (202)296-0928
Fax: (202)296-8018

Kelly, Nancy, Exec. Dir.
Orthopaedics Overseas **[16489]**
1900 L St. NW, No. 310
Washington, DC 20036
Ph: (202)296-0928
Fax: (202)296-8018

Kelly, Pat, Director
Future Corvette Owners Association
[21386]
c/o Pat Kelly, Director
S68W17323 Rossmar Ct.
Muskego, WI 53150-8575
Ph: (262)971-5046

Kelly, Richard, President
Eire Philatelic Association **[22326]**
1559 Grouse Ln.
1559 Grouse Ln.
Mountainside, NJ 07092-1340

Kelly, Richard, Director
Plug In America **[5889]**
2370 Market St., No. 419
San Francisco, CA 94114
Ph: (415)323-3329

Kelly, Robert J., Chairman
Sales Management Association
[3018]
1440 Dutch Valley Pl. NE, Ste. 990
Atlanta, GA 30324
Ph: (404)963-7992

Kelly, Stacy, Chairman
Automatic Guided Vehicle Systems
[1717]
c/o MHI
8720 Red Oak Blvd., Ste. 201
Charlotte, NC 28217
Ph: (704)676-1190
Fax: (704)676-1199

Kelly, Terri, Bus. Dev. Mgr.
International Council of Shopping
Centers **[2956]**

1221 Avenue of the Americas, 41st Fl.
New York, NY 10020-1099
Ph: (646)728-3800
Fax: (732)694-1755

Kelly, Thomas F., PhD, Chairman
Link Foundation [7304]
c/o Binghamton University Foundation
PO Box 6005
Binghamton, NY 13902-6005

Kelly, Tiffani, Contact
National Exercise Trainers Association [22485]
5955 Golden Valley Rd., Ste. 240
Minneapolis, MN 55422
Ph: (763)545-2505
Toll Free: 800-AEROBIC
Fax: (763)545-2524

Kelly, Tim T., President
National Geographic Society [6673]
1145 17th St. NW
Washington, DC 20036-4688
Ph: (202)862-8638
Toll Free: 800-373-1717

Kelly, William J., CEO
Chartered Alternative Investment Analyst Association [2022]
100 University Dr.
Amherst, MA 01002-2357
Ph: (413)253-7373
Fax: (413)253-4494

Kelly-Frey, Brenda, Chairperson
National Association for State Relay Administration [3232]
c/o Brenda Kelly-Frey, Chair
Telecommunications Access of Maryland
301 W Preston St., Ste. 1008A
Baltimore, MD 21201
Ph: (443)453-5970
Toll Free: 800-552-7724

Kelsey, Jarman J., President
Kelsey Kindred of America [20890]
c/o Jarman Kelsey, President
37 Ackerman St.
Salem, NH 03079
Ph: (603)893-6814

Kelsey, Sarah, CEO
National Alliance for Model State Drug Laws [5157]
420 Park St.
Charlottesville, VA 22902
Ph: (703)836-6100
Fax: (662)892-8660

Kelsh, Janice E., Founder
Miniature Piano Enthusiast Club [21688]
633 Pennsylvania Ave.
Hagerstown, MD 21740
Ph: (301)797-7675
Fax: (301)827-7029

Kelso, Brian, Exec. Dir.
Great Commission Alliance [11663]
4700 SW 188th Ave.
Fort Lauderdale, FL 33332
Ph: (954)434-4500

Kemmer, Mr. Corby, Dir. of Dev.
University of Minnesota Crookston Alumni Association [19362]
Office of Development & Alumni Relations, Kiehle 115
2900 University Ave.
Crookston, MN 56716-5001
Ph: (218)281-8439
Toll Free: 800-862-6466
Fax: (218)281-8440

Kemner, Chuck, Exec. Dir.
National Association of Show Trucks [3340]

2425 Seymour Rd.
Eau Claire, WI 54703
Ph: (715)832-6666

Kemnitz, D'Arcy, Exec. Dir.
National LGBT Bar Association [5043]
1875 I St. NW, Ste. 1100
Washington, DC 20006
Ph: (202)637-7661

Kemp, John D., President, CEO
National Business and Disability Council [11771]
201 I.U. Willets Rd.
Albertson, NY 11507
Ph: (516)465-1400

Kemp, John D., Esq., CEO, President
The Viscardi Center [11644]
201 I.U. Willets Rd.
Albertson, NY 11507-1516
Ph: (516)465-1400
   (516)465-1450

Kemp, Mark, Comm. Chm.
Mason Contractors Association of America [875]
1481 Merchant Dr.
Algonquin, IL 60102
Ph: (224)678-9709
Toll Free: 800-536-2225
Fax: (224)678-9714

Kemp, Mark, President
Police and Firemen's Insurance Association [19492]
101 E 116th St.
Carmel, IN 46032
Ph: (317)581-1913
Toll Free: 800-221-7342
Fax: (317)571-5946

Kemp, Steven C., CAE
National Association of Healthcare Access Management [15332]
2025 M St. NW, Ste. 800
Washington, DC 20036-2422
Ph: (202)367-1125
Fax: (202)367-2125

Kemp, Tom, Treasurer
OV-10 Bronco Association [5869]
3300 Ross Ave.
Fort Worth, TX 76106-3646
Toll Free: 800-575-0535

Kempe, Ursula A., CEO, President
Therapy Dogs International [17466]
88 Bartley Rd.
Flanders, NJ 07836
Ph: (973)252-9800
Fax: (973)252-7171

Kempfer, George, VP
American Brahman Breeders Association [3686]
3003 S Loop W, Ste. 520
Houston, TX 77054
Ph: (713)349-0854
Fax: (713)349-9795

Kempthorne, Dirk, CEO, President
American Council of Life Insurers [1829]
101 Constitution Ave. NW, Ste. 700
Washington, DC 20001-2133
Ph: (202)624-2000
Toll Free: 877-674-4659

Kendall, Jim, President
International Association of Employee Assistance Professionals in Education [11750]
c/o Scott Embley, Treasurer
Clinical Education Bldg.
1542 Tulane Ave., 8th Fl., Office 866

New Orleans, LA 70112
Ph: (504)568-8888
Fax: (504)568-3892

Kendall, Rex, Exec. Dir.
Indiana State University Alumni Association [19327]
30 N 5th St.
Terre Haute, IN 47807
Ph: (812)514-8400
Toll Free: 800-258-6478
Fax: (812)237-8157

Kendell, Kate, Esq., Exec. Dir.
National Center for Lesbian Rights [11899]
870 Market St., Ste. 370
San Francisco, CA 94102
Ph: (415)392-6257
Fax: (415)392-8442

Kendi, Ayo Handy, Director, Founder
African American Holiday Association [22437]
Positive Energy Ctr.
Capitol Heights, MD 20743
Ph: (202)667-2577

Kendrick, Bob, President
Negro Leagues Baseball Museum [22564]
1616 E 18th St.
Kansas City, MO 64108-1610
Ph: (816)221-1920
Toll Free: 888-221-NLBM
Fax: (816)221-8424

Kendzior, Russell J., Chairman, President
National Floor Safety Institute [3003]
PO Box 92607
Southlake, TX 76092
Ph: (817)749-1700
Fax: (817)749-1702

Keneipp, Brian, Exec. Sec.
Aetherius Society [20604]
6202 Afton Pl.
Los Angeles, CA 90028-8205
Ph: (323)465-9652
Toll Free: 800-800-1354

Kenigsberg, Rositta E., President
The Holocaust Documentation and Education Center, Inc. [18347]
2031 Harrison St.
Hollywood, FL 33020
Ph: (954)929-5690

Kennedy, Brian T., Director
Claremont Institute [17854]
1317 W Foothill Blvd., Ste. 120
Upland, CA 91786
Ph: (909)981-2200
Fax: (909)981-1616

Kennedy, Craig, Exec. Dir.
Association of Clinicians for the Underserved [14980]
1420 Spring Hill Rd., Ste. 600
McLean, VA 22102
Toll Free: 844-442-5318
Fax: (703)562-8801

Kennedy, Evelyn S., Founder, President
PRIDE Foundation - Promote Real Independence for the Disabled and Elderly [11633]
c/o Sewtique, Inc.
391 Long Hill Rd.
Groton, CT 06340-1293
Ph: (860)445-7320
Toll Free: 800-332-9122
Fax: (860)445-1448

Kennedy, Gerard J., Jr., Exec. VP
Plumbing-Heating-Cooling Contractors Association [2639]

180 S Washington St., Ste. 100
Falls Church, VA 22046
Ph: (703)237-8100
Toll Free: 800-533-7694
Fax: (703)237-7442

Kennedy, Jason, President
American Association for Employment in Education [8437]
PO Box 173
Slippery Rock, PA 16057
Ph: (614)485-1111
Fax: (360)244-7802

Kennedy, John J., President
Jewelers' Security Alliance [2052]
6 E 45th St.
New York, NY 10017
Toll Free: 800-537-0067
Fax: (212)808-9168

Kennedy, Joseph, Chairman, CEO
U.S.-China Education Foundation [8091]
970 W Valley Pky., No. 220
Escondido, CA 92025

Kennedy, Kerry, President
Robert F. Kennedy Center for Justice and Human Rights [13455]
1300 19th St. NW, Ste. 750
Washington, DC 20036
Ph: (202)463-7575
Fax: (202)463-6606

Kennedy, Rich, Secretary
Antique Doorknob Collectors of America [21620]
PO Box 803
Hackettstown, NJ 07840
Ph: (908)684-5253

Kennedy, Robert, Exec. Dir., Exec. VP
American Association for Technology in Psychiatry [16816]
PO Box 11
Bronx, NY 10464-0011
Ph: (718)502-9469

Kennedy, Taylor, President
National Agricultural Communicators of Tomorrow [8157]
c/o Dr. Emily Buck, Adviser
208 Agricultural Administration Bldg.
Department of Agricultural Communication, Education, and Leadership
The Ohio State University
2120 Fyffe Rd.
Columbus, OH 43210

Kennedy, Teresa, President
International Council of Associations for Science Education [8548]
c/o Prof. Teresa Kennedy, President
3900 University Blvd.
Tyler, TX 75799

Kennedy, Tom, Exec. Dir.
American Society of Media Photographers [2573]
150 N 2nd St.
Philadelphia, PA 19106-1912
Ph: (215)451-2767
Fax: (215)451-0880

Kennedy, Victoria Reggie, President
Common Sense about Kids and Guns [5216]
1225 I St. NW, Ste. 1100
Washington, DC 20005-3914
Ph: (202)546-0200
Toll Free: 877-955-KIDS

Kennedy-Sutherland, Elaine, President
Tree-Ring Society [4220]
4624 Foothills Dr.

Loveland, CO 80537

Kenneke, Jon, Editor
North American Truffling Society
[6889]
3200 Jefferson Way
Corvallis, OR 97339-0296

Kennelly, Barbara, President
United States Association of Former
Members of Congress [18015]
1401 K St. NW, Ste. 503
Washington, DC 20005
Ph: (202)222-0972
Fax: (202)222-0977

Kennelly, Ed, President
American Society of Pharmacognosy
[16646]
3149 Dundee Rd., No. 260
Northbrook, IL 60062-2402
Ph: (773)995-3748
Fax: (847)656-2800

Kenney, Linda, Exec. Dir., President,
Founder
Medically Induced Trauma Support
Services [17527]
830 Boylston St., Ste. 206
Chestnut Hill, MA 02467
Ph: (617)232-0090
Toll Free: 888-366-4877
Fax: (617)232-7181

Kenniff, Thomas, Director
National Press Photographers Association [2587]
120 Hooper St.
Athens, GA 30602

Kensicki, Nancy E.
Deaf Seniors of America [15187]
5619 Ainsley Ct.
Boynton Beach, FL 33437-1503

Kent, Barbara, Fac. Memb.
American Center for the Alexander
Technique Inc. [13591]
39 W 14th St., Ste. 507
New York, NY 10011
Ph: (212)633-2229

Kent, Jeffrey S., Director
U.S. Senate Press Photographers'
Gallery [2595]
S-317, United States Capitol
Washington, DC 20510
Ph: (202)224-6548

Kent, Kenneth Craig, MD, President
Society of Surgical Chairs [17407]
c/o Ellen Waller, Administrator
633 N St. Clair St.
Chicago, IL 60611
Ph: (312)202-5447

Kent, Norman Elliott, V. Ch.
National Organization for the Reform
of Marijuana Laws [17921]
1100 H St. NW, Ste. 830
Washington, DC 20005-5485
Ph: (202)483-5500
Fax: (202)483-0057

Kent, Stacy, Exec. Dir.
American Association of Endocrine
Surgeons [14699]
11300 W Olympic Blvd., Ste. 600
Los Angeles, CA 90064
Ph: (310)986-6452
Fax: (310)437-0585

Kent, Tanya, Contact
Autism Angels Network [13743]
1693 E Desert Rose Trail
San Tan Valley, AZ 85143

Kenworthy, John, Exec. Dir.,
Founder
Brick by Brick for Tanzania! [8447]
539 Braatz Dr.

Kewaskum, WI 53040
Ph: (262)573-9032

Keny-Guyer, Neal, CEO
Global Envision [18284]
c/o Mercy Corps
45 SW Ankeny St.
Portland, OR 97204

Keny-Guyer, Neal, Chairman
InterAction [12165]
1400 16th St. NW, Ste. 210
Washington, DC 20036
Ph: (202)667-8227

Keny-Guyer, Neal, CEO
Mercy Corps [18494]
45 SW Ankeny St.
Portland, OR 97204
Ph: (503)896-5000
Toll Free: 800-292-3355

Kenyon, Michael, President, CEO
Partnership for Philanthropic Plan-
ning [1472]
233 McCrea St., Ste. 300
Indianapolis, IN 46225
Ph: (317)269-6274
Fax: (317)269-6268

Keohohou, Nicki, CEO, Founder
Direct Selling Women's Alliance
[3012]
111 Hekili St., Ste. A-139
Kailua, HI 96734
Ph: (808)230-2427
Toll Free: 888-417-0743

Kepner, Susan, MEd, Exec. Dir.
Association for Surgical Education
[8314]
3085 Stevenson Dr., Ste. 200
Springfield, IL 62703
Ph: (217)529-6503

Kerby, Zane, President, CEO
American Society of Travel Agents
[3369]
675 N Washington St., Ste. 490
Alexandria, VA 22314
Ph: (703)739-2782
Toll Free: 800-275-2782

Kerby, Zane, Treasurer
National Association of Career
Travel Agents [3384]
675 N Washington St., Ste. 490
Alexandria, VA 22314
Ph: (703)739-6826
Toll Free: 877-22-NACTA
Fax: (703)739-6861

Kerdel, Francisco, MD, Bd. Member
International Society of Dermatology
[14499]
2323 N State St., No. 30
Bunnell, FL 32110
Ph: (386)437-4405
Fax: (386)437-4427

Kerester, Alison, Exec. Dir.
Gasification and Syngas Technolo-
gies Council [1497]
3030 Clarendon Blvd., Ste. 330
Arlington, VA 22201-6518
Ph: (703)276-0110
Fax: (703)276-0141

Keritsis, Maria, Chairman
National Forum of Greek Orthodox
Church Musicians [20494]
9030 Kings Crown Rd.
Richmond, VA 23236-1302
Ph: (804)745-8606
Fax: (804)745-9726

Kern, Francis, Exec. Dir.
Snowball Express [12351]
611 S Main St., Ste. 400

Grapevine, TX 76051
Ph: (817)410-4673

Kern, Friedrich Heinrich, Officer
International Society for
Contemporary Music USA [9932]
24 Waverly Pl., Rm. 268
New York, NY 10003
Ph: (347)559-5376
Fax: (516)694-1340

Kernaghan, Charles, Director
Institute for Global Labour and Hu-
man Rights [17841]
5 Gateway Ctr., 6th Fl.
Pittsburgh, PA 15222
Ph: (412)562-2406
Fax: (412)562-2411

Kernan, Beatrice, Exec. Dir.
Project Sunshine [11135]
211 E 43rd St., Ste. 401
New York, NY 10017
Ph: (212)354-8035
Fax: (212)354-8052

Kerner, Marc, MD, Founder,
President, CEO
Foundation for Airway and Maxillofa-
cial Surgery [16446]
696 Hampshire Rd., Ste. 110
Westlake Village, CA 91361
Ph: (805)230-1111

Kerney, Brian, Exec. Dir.
Unchartered International [12195]
400 S Green River Rd.
Evansville, IN 47715
Ph: (812)402-1886

Kernick, Stevie Hughes, Chief of
Staff
Property Records Industry Associa-
tion [2750]
2501 Aerial Center Pky., Ste. 103
Morrisville, NC 27560
Ph: (919)459-2081
Fax: (919)459-2075

Kerns, Madeline Abel, Mem.
Professional Women Singers As-
sociation [9998]
PO Box 29
Deer Park, NY 11729

Kerr, Autumn, Exec. Dir.
Visiting Orphans [11181]
449 Metroplex Dr.
Nashville, TN 37211
Toll Free: 866-683-7554
Fax: (866)683-5087

Kerr, Christine, Exec.
Themed Entertainment Association
[1161]
150 E Olive Ave., Ste. 306
Burbank, CA 91502
Ph: (818)843-8497
Fax: (818)843-8477

Kerr, David, Chairman
Deaf Bilingual Coalition [11934]
c/o Chriz Dally, Treasurer
11541 S Penrose St.
Olathe, KS 66061

Kerr, David, Director
Kerr Family Association of North
America [20891]
c/o Katharine R. Kerr, Treasurer
6540 Greyledge Ct.
Alexandria, VA 22310

Kerr, Glenn D., Exec. Dir.
American Association of State
Climatologists [6853]
c/o Hope Mizzell, PhD, President
South Carolina State Climatologist

South Carolina State Climatology
Office
SC Department of Natural
Resources
PO Box 167
Columbia, SC 29202
Ph: (803)734-9568

Kerr, Jerry, Founder, President
Disability Rights Advocates for
Technology [11587]
500 Fox Ridge Rd.
Saint Louis, MO 63131
Toll Free: 800-401-7940
Fax: (314)965-4956

Kerr, Nancy, President
Children's Reading Foundation
[12244]
515 W Entiat Ave.
Kennewick, WA 99336
Ph: (509)735-9405
Fax: (509)396-7730

Kerr, Paul, CEO
Small Luxury Hotels of the World
[1679]
12 E 49th St., Ste. 1211
New York, NY 10017
Ph: (212)953-2064
Toll Free: 877-234-7033

Kerr, Scott, President
Collins Collectors Association
[21267]
c/o Scott Kerr, President
2500 Chantilly Ct.
Heath, TX 75032
Ph: (972)772-9750

Kerrigan, Karen, CEO, President
Small Business and Entrepreneur-
ship Council [3126]
301 Maple Ave. W, Ste. 690
Vienna, VA 22180-4320
Ph: (703)242-5840

Kerrigan, Peter, Dep. Dir., Dir. of
Mktg.
Deutscher Akademischer Austausch
Dienst [8068]
871 United Nations Plz.
New York, NY 10017
Ph: (212)758-3223
Fax: (212)755-5780

Kerstein, Bob, President
Professional Scripophily Trade As-
sociation [666]
PO Box 223795
Chantilly, VA 20153
Ph: (703)579-4209
Toll Free: 888-786-2576
Fax: (703)995-4422

Kersten, Mr. Nicholas J., Hist.,
Librarian
Seventh Day Baptist Historical
Society [19738]
PO Box 1678
Janesville, WI 53547-1678
Ph: (608)752-5055
Fax: (608)752-7711

Kerwin, Donald M., Jr., Exec. Dir.
Center for Migration Studies [9796]
37 E 60th St., 4th Fl.
New York, NY 10022
Ph: (212)337-3080

Kerwood, Terry, Managing Dir.
Engineered Wood Technology As-
sociation [1437]
7011 S 19th St.
Tacoma, WA 98466
Ph: (253)620-7237

Kerzner, Robert A., CLU, CEO,
President
Life Insurers Council [1881]
6190 Powers Ferry Rd., Ste. 600

Atlanta, GA 30339-8443
Ph: (770)951-1770

Kerzner, Robert A., CEO, President
LIMRA International [1882]
300 Day Hill Rd.
Windsor, CT 06095
Ph: (860)688-3358
    (860)285-7789
Toll Free: 800-235-4672
Fax: (860)298-9555

Kerzner, Robert A., CEO, President
LOMA [1883]
6190 Powers Ferry Rd., Ste. 600
Atlanta, GA 30339
Ph: (770)951-1770
    (770)984-3720
Toll Free: 800-ASK-LOMA
Fax: (770)984-6422

Keslar, carol, President
National Association of Mobile
   Entertainers [1150]
PO Box 144
Willow Grove, PA 19090
Toll Free: 800-434-8274

Kesnow, Robyn, RVT, President
International Association of Animal
   Hospice and Palliative Care
   [17647]
2143 Cheviot Ct.
Greenwood, IN 46143
Ph: (317)966-0096

Kesselbrenner, Dan, Exec. Dir.
National Immigration Project [5294]
14 Beacon St., Ste. 602
Boston, MA 02108
Ph: (617)227-9727
Fax: (617)227-5495

Kessen, Clifford, President
National Association of the 6th
   Infantry Div. [20721]
9733 Still Meadow Ct.
Union, KY 41091-6914

Kessen, Clifford, President
National Association of the Sixth
   Infantry Division [20722]
c/o Thomas E. Price
317 Court St. NE, Ste. 203
Salem, OR 97301
Ph: (503)363-7334
Fax: (503)581-2260

Kessler, Brett, President
American North Country Cheviot
   Sheep Association [4657]
PO Box 9275
Brooks, OR 97305
Ph: (503)792-3448
Fax: (503)792-4416

Kessler, Ryan, Contact
Motorcycle Events Association
   [22228]
3221 Tyrone Blvd. N
Saint Petersburg, FL 33710
Ph: (727)343-1049
Toll Free: 866-203-4485
Fax: (727)344-0327

Kesten, Robert, Consultant
Bnai Zion Foundation [19515]
1430 Broadway, Ste. 1804
New York, NY 10018
Ph: (212)725-1211
Fax: (212)684-6327

Kesten, Robert, Exec. Dir.
People's Movement for Human
   Rights Learning [18435]
526 W 111th St., Ste. 4E
New York, NY 10025
Ph: (212)749-3156
Fax: (212)666-6325

Kestenbaum, Rick, President
American Jewish Press Association
   [2650]
c/o KCA Association Management
107 S Southgate Dr.
Chandler, AZ 85226-3222
Ph: (480)403-4602
Fax: (480)893-7775

Kesty, Katarina, Bd. Member
Cataract Pack Organization [17696]
331 Hanover Arms Ct.
Winston Salem, NC 27104
Ph: (813)476-2704

Ketchum, Dr. Daniel D., Director
Nazarene Missions International
   [20444]
17001 Prairie Star Pkwy.
Lenexa, KS 66220
Ph: (913)577-2970
Fax: (913)577-0861

Ketchum, Richard G., Chairman,
   CEO, Chmn. of the Bd.
Financial Industry Regulatory Author-
   ity [3043]
1735 K St.
Washington, DC 20006
Ph: (301)590-6500

Ketner, Saundra, Librarian
Joslin Diabetes Center [14537]
1 Joslin Pl.
Boston, MA 02215
Ph: (617)732-2400
    (617)226-5815

Ketterlinus, Jack, CPA, Treasurer
MHP Salud [12341]
2111 Golfside Dr., Ste. 2B
Ypsilanti, MI 48197
Toll Free: 800-461-8394

Kewl-Durfey, Grace, Chairperson
The Association of American
   Cultures [8964]
1635 S 15th St.
Lincoln, NE 68502
Ph: (402)472-0208

Key, Abraham, CEO, President
Pony Baseball and Softball [22565]
1951 Pony Pl.
Washington, PA 15301-5889
Ph: (724)225-1060
Fax: (724)225-9852

Key, John R., Asst.
Photographic Society of America
   [22384]
8421 S Walker Ave., Ste. 104
Oklahoma City, OK 73139
Ph: (405)843-1437
Toll Free: 855-772-4636

Key, Louie, Director
Aircraft Mechanics Fraternal As-
   sociation [23382]
14001 E Iliff Ave., Ste. 217
Aurora, CO 80014
Ph: (303)752-2632
Fax: (303)362-7736

Key, Stan, President
Francis Asbury Society [19757]
1580 Lexington Rd.
Wilmore, KY 40390
Ph: (859)858-4222
Fax: (859)858-4155

Keyes, David, Exec. Dir.
Advancing Human Rights [18364]
PO Box 85
New York, NY 10008
Ph: (646)678-5626
Fax: (212)207-5047

Keyes, Elizabeth K., Chairman
National Council on Patient Information and Education [16677]

200-A Monroe St., Ste. 212
Rockville, MD 20850-4448
Ph: (301)340-3940
Fax: (301)340-3944

Keyes, Vanetta S., Exec. Dir.,
   President, Founder
Center Helping Obesity in Children
   End Successfully [16251]
1275 Shiloh Rd., Ste. 2660
Kennesaw, GA 30144
Ph: (678)819-3663
Fax: (770)850-1236

Keys, Alicia, Founder
Keep a Child Alive [13551]
11 Hanover Sq., 14th Fl.
New York, NY 10005
Ph: (646)762-8100
Fax: (646)762-8201

Keyser, Jenny, PhD, Exec. Dir.
Higher Education Consortium for
   Urban Affairs [8724]
2233 University Ave. W, Ste. 210
Saint Paul, MN 55114
Ph: (651)287-3300
Fax: (651)659-9421

Keyser, Sharon Hyland, Founder
A Hero's Welcome [20703]
PO Box 14
Frederick, PA 19435-0014
Ph: (484)679-1717

Kezios, Susan P., President
American Franchisee Association
   [1456]
53 W Jackson Blvd., Ste. 1256
Chicago, IL 60604
Ph: (312)431-0545
Fax: (312)431-1469

Kezirian, Eric J., MD, President
International Surgical Sleep Society
   [17218]
c/o Mary Ellen Hernandez
Dept. of Otolaryngology - Head &
   Neck Surgery
University of Southern California
1540 Alcazar St., Ste. 204-U
Los Angeles, CA 90089

Khachatryan, Alexander R., PhD,
   CEO, President, Founder
Reasoning Mind [8285]
2000 Bering Dr., Ste. 300
Houston, TX 77057-3774
Ph: (281)579-1110
Toll Free: 800-994-1306

Khachaturian, Zaven, President
Prevent Alzheimer's Disease 2020
   [13673]
451 Hungerford Dr.
PMB 119-355
Rockville, MD 20850
Ph: (301)294-7201
Fax: (301)294-7203

Khalid, Aryana, Exec. VP of Fin.,
   Exec. VP of HR
America's Health Insurance Plans
   [15095]
South Bldg., Ste. 500
601 Pennsylvania Ave. NW
Washington, DC 20004
Ph: (202)778-3200
Fax: (202)331-7487

Khalifa, Rose, RN, President
National American Arab Nurses As-
   sociation [16144]
615 Griswold St., Ste. 925
Detroit, MI 48226
Ph: (313)680-5049

Khalilian, Michael, Chairman,
   President
IMS Forum [7309]
PO Box 10000

Silverthorne, CO 80498-1000
Ph: (970)262-6100
Fax: (407)641-9595

Khamvongsa, Channapha, Exec. Dir.
Legacies of War [7986]
1312 9th St. NW
Washington, DC 20001
Ph: (202)841-7841

Khan, Awal, PhD, President
North American Alliances for Social
   Relief [12174]
PO Box 468
Tucker, GA 30085
Ph: (770)330-3897

Khan, Daisy, Exec. Dir., Founder
American Society for Muslim
   Advancement [9602]
475 Riverside Dr., Ste. 248
New York, NY 10115

Khan, Dr. Murad, VP
International Association for Suicide
   Prevention [13194]
5221 Washington Ave. NW
Washington, DC 20015

Khan, Ms. Shazia, Esq., Exec. Dir.
Eco Energy Finance [6473]
129 Pleasant St., NW
Vienna, VA 22180-4419
Ph: (202)262-0412

Khanal, Dr. Netra, President
Association of Nepalese Mathematicians in America [8276]
4106 Skipper Rd., Apt. 221
Tampa, FL 33613

Kharrazi, Mana, Exec. Dir.
Iranian Alliances Across Borders
   [9595]
154 Grand St.
New York, NY 10013

Khatamee, Dr. Masood A., Exec. Dir.
Society for Prevention of Human
   Infertility [17127]
877 Park Ave.
New York, NY 10075-0341
Ph: (212)744-5500
Toll Free: 888-439-2999
Fax: (212)744-6536

Khatamee, Dr. Masood, Exec. Dir.
Fertility Research Foundation
   [14757]
877 Park Ave.
New York, NY 10021
Ph: (212)744-5500
Toll Free: 888-439-2999
Fax: (212)744-6536

Khatami, Haleh, President
Children's Hope International
   Literacy and Development [10927]
1526 Brookhollow Dr., Ste. 82
Santa Ana, CA 92705
Ph: (714)545-3050
Fax: (714)545-3030

Khateeb, Mr. Shaheen, President
Indian American Muslim Council
   [19475]
6321 W Dempster St., Ste. 295
Morton Grove, IL 60053-2848
Toll Free: 800-839-7270

Khosrow-Pour, Dr. Mehdi, Exec. Dir.
Information Resources Management
   Association [1798]
701 E Chocolate Ave., Ste. 200
Hershey, PA 17033-1240
Ph: (717)533-8845
Fax: (717)533-8661

Khoury, Kim, President
Machinery Dealers National Association [1743]

315 S Patrick St.
Alexandria, VA 22314-3501
Ph: (703)836-9300
Toll Free: 800-872-7807
Fax: (703)836-9303

Kibat, Elizabeth, Controller
Ice Skating Institute [23150]
6000 Custer Rd., Bldg. 9
Plano, TX 75023
Ph: (972)735-8800
Fax: (972)735-8815

Kibugu-Decuir, Philippa, Founder
Breast Cancer Initiative East Africa
  [13909]
8903 Emerald Heights Ln.
Houston, TX 77083
Ph: (281)564-0974

Kidd, Jim, President
American Association of Orthopaedic
  Executives [16461]
6602 E 17th St., Ste. 112
Indianapolis, IN 46250
Toll Free: 800-247-9699
Fax: (317)805-0340

Kidder, Dr. Rushworth M., Founder
Institute for Global Ethics [6621]
10 E Doty St., Ste. 825
Madison, WI 53703
Ph: (608)204-5902
Toll Free: 888-607-0883

Kidwell-Ross, Ranger, Exec. Dir.,
  Founder
World Sweeping Association [2145]
PO Box 667
Bellingham, WA 98227
Ph: (360)724-7355
Toll Free: 866-635-2205
Fax: (866)890-0912

Kiefer, Matthew, Mgr.
Lions-Quest [7712]
Lions Clubs International Foundation
300 W 22nd St.
Oak Brook, IL 60523-8842
Toll Free: 844-567-8378

Kieft, Janis, President
National Garden Bureau [4437]
1311 Butterfield Rd., Ste. 310
Downers Grove, IL 60515-5625
Ph: (630)963-0770
Fax: (630)963-8864

Kiehl, Kimberlee, President
Visitor Studies Association [8719]
2885 Sanford Ave. SW, No. 18100
Grandville, MI 49418
Ph: (740)872-0566
Fax: (301)637-3312

Kielczewski, John J., President
CSA Fraternal Life [19418]
2050 Finley Rd., Ste. 70
Lombard, IL 60148
Ph: (630)472-0500
Toll Free: 800-543-3272
Fax: (630)472-1100

Kiely, Jason, Contact
Natural Trails and Waters Coalition
  [4579]
PO Box 7516
Missoula, MT 59807-7516
Ph: (406)543-9551

Kierulff, Charles Taylor, Contact
Kjaerulf Family Association [20892]
c/o Charles Taylor Kierulff
358 S Bentley Ave.
Los Angeles, CA 90049-3219

Kiesewetter, Cynthia, President
North American Cockatiel Society
  [21547]

PO Box 143
Bethel, CT 06801-0143

Kiesling, Dr. Ernst W., Exec. Dir.
National Storm Shelter Association
  [3464]
c/o TTU Student Media Bldg.
1009 Canton Ave., Rm. 117
Lubbock, TX 79409
Toll Free: 877-700-6772
Fax: (806)742-3446

Kiev, Ari, MD, Founder, President
Social Psychiatry Research Institute
  [16835]
3044 Coney Island Ave., Ste. 201
Brooklyn, NY 11235
Toll Free: 888-345-7774

Kifle, Selamawit, Founder
Blue Nile Children's Organization
  [10871]
PO Box 28658
Seattle, WA 98118-8658
Ph: (206)633-1508

Kiggins, Karen, President
National Slag Association [561]
PO Box 1197
Pleasant Grove, UT 84062
Ph: (801)785-4535
Fax: (801)785-4539

Kilanko, Glory, Director, Founder,
  CEO
Women Watch Afrika [19247]
PO Box 208
Avondale Estates, GA 30002
Ph: (404)759-6419
Fax: (404)300-3505

Kilbourn, Aldean, Secretary
Atmospheric Science Librarians
  International [8230]
NOAA Center for Weather Prediction
Betty Peterson Memorial Library
5830 University Research Ct.
College Park, MD 20740
Ph: (301)683-1307
    (310)825-3983
Fax: (301)683-1308

Kildall, Sheryl, Mgr.
Aerospace Medical Association
  [13506]
320 S Henry St.
Alexandria, VA 22314-3579
Ph: (703)739-2240
Fax: (703)739-9652

Kildee, Dale, Co-Ch.
Congressional Automotive Caucus
  [18011]
Longworth House Office Bldg., Rm.
  1519
15 Independence Ave. SE
Washington, DC 20515
Ph: (202)225-5406
Fax: (202)225-3103

Kilgannon, Thomas P., President
Freedom Alliance [8790]
22570 Markey Ct., Ste. 240
Dulles, VA 20166
Ph: (703)444-7940
Toll Free: 800-475-6620
Fax: (703)444-9893

Kilgore, Victoria, Dir. of Res.
Insurance Research Council [1871]
718 Providence Rd.
Malvern, PA 19355

Kilkenny, Sara, Director
Academy of Physicians in Clinical
  Research [8299]
6816 Southpoint Pky., Ste. 1000
jacksonville, FL 32216
Ph: (703)254-8100
    (904)309-6271
Fax: (703)254-8101

Killam, Wendy, Ph.D., President
Association for Adult Development
  and Aging [10499]
c/o Andrew Daire, President-Elect
214 Farish Hall, Rm. 466G
College of Education
University of Houston
Houston, TX 77204-5023
Ph: (713)743-5443

Killen, Audrey Fisher, Exec. Dir.
Operation Shooting Star [13788]
32711 Fisher Pl.
Frankford, DE 19945
Ph: (302)542-2393

Kilm, Toomas, Chairman, President
Estonian Relief Committee [12660]
243 E 34th St.
New York, NY 10016-4852

Kilmurry, Simon, Exec. Dir.
International Documentary Associa-
  tion [1197]
3470 Wilshire Blvd., Ste. 980
Los Angeles, CA 90010
Ph: (213)232-1660
Fax: (213)232-1669

Kim, Anthony, President
Cambodian American Business As-
  sociation [678]
1902 E Anaheim St.
Long Beach, CA 90813
Ph: (424)226-2289

Kim, Baxon, Dir. of Bus. Dev.
Korea IT Network [6255]
3003 N 1st St.
San Jose, CA 95134
Ph: (408)232-5475

Kim, Rev. Daniel, President
ARISE International Mission [20382]
PO Box 1014
College Park, MD 20741-1014
Ph: (301)395-2385

Kim, Dongchan, President
Korean American Civic Empower-
  ment [18602]
35-20 147th St., No. 2D
Flushing, NY 11354
Ph: (718)961-4117
Fax: (718)961-4603

Kim, Jim Yong, Ph.D, President
International Development Associa-
  tion [18492]
The World Bank
1818 H St. NW
Washington, DC 20433
Ph: (202)473-1000
Fax: (202)477-6391

Kim, Dr. Jim Yong, President
World Bank Group [18507]
1818 H St. NW
Washington, DC 20433
Ph: (202)473-1000
    (202)477-1234
Toll Free: 800-831-0463
Fax: (202)477-6391

Kim, Joseph, President
National Association of Medical
  Education Companies [8330]
3416 Primm Ln.
Birmingham, AL 35216
Ph: (205)824-7612
Fax: (205)823-2760

Kim, Judy H., V. Chmn. of the Bd.
Korean American League for Civic
  Action [18604]
149 W 24th St., 6th Fl.
New York, NY 10011
Ph: (212)633-2000

Kim, Dr. Ki-Chan, President
International Council for Small Busi-
  ness [3119]
Funger Hall, Ste. 315
2201 G St. NW
Washington, DC 20052
Ph: (202)994-0704
Fax: (202)994-4930

Kim, KyungMann, President
Society for Clinical Trials [14293]
100 N 20th St., 4th Fl.
Philadelphia, PA 19103
Ph: (215)320-3878
Fax: (215)564-2175

Kim, Linda, Chairperson
Women and Youth Supporting Each
  Other [8760]
PO Box 712189
Los Angeles, CA 90071
Ph: (714)390-8363

Kim, Dr. Nanyoung, Treasurer
United States Society for Education
  Through Art [7519]
c/o Nanyoung Kim, Treasurer
East Carolina University
Jenkins Fine Arts Ctr.
Greenville, NC 27858-4353
Ph: (252)328-1298

Kim, Paul J., Founder, President
National Council for Taekwondo
  Masters Certification [23006]
501 W Glenoaks Blvd., Ste. 336
Glendale, CA 91202
Ph: (213)503-3302

Kim, S. Samuel, President
International Society for Fertility
  Preservation [14760]
University of Kansas, School of
  Medicine
Division of REI, Department of OB/
  GYN
3901 Rainbow Blvd.
Kansas City, KS 66160

Kim, Dr. Stanley Y., VP, Treasurer
Korean American Medical Associa-
  tion [15733]
200 Sylvan Ave., Ste. 22
Englewood Cliffs, NJ 07632
Ph: (201)567-1434
Fax: (201)567-1753

Kim, Vivian C., MA, Chairperson
National Association of Professional
  Asian American Women [650]
304 Oak Knoll Ter.
Rockville, MD 20850
Ph: (301)785-8585

Kimani-Chomba, Jane, Bd. Member
UHAI for Health, Inc. [15501]
PO Box 3603
Worcester, MA 01613

Kimball, Randy, President, Chmn. of
  the Bd., Owner
American Ski-Bike Association
  [23212]
PO Box 65220
Albuquerque, NM 87193
Ph: (505)350-9835
    (505)350-3844

Kimber, Evelyn, Bd. Member
Citizens to End Animal Suffering and
  Exploitation [10600]
PO Box 67278
Chestnut Hill, MA 02467
Ph: (617)379-0535

Kimble, Prof. Joseph, Treasurer
Clarity [5529]
c/o Joseph Kimble

Box 13038
Lansing, MI 48901-3038
Ph: (517)371-5140
Fax: (517)334-5748

Kimbrell, Andrew, Exec. Dir.
True Food Network [6651]
660 Pennsylvania Ave. SE, No. 302
Washington, DC 20003
Ph: (202)547-9359
Fax: (202)547-9429

Kimbrough-Melton, Robin, Exec.
Ofc.
American Orthopsychiatric Associa-
tion [16821]
PO Box 202798
Denver, CO 80220
Ph: (720)708-0187
Fax: (303)366-3471

Kimmel, Kathryn, Sr. VP, Chief Mktg.
Ofc.
Gemological Institute of America Inc.
[2047]
The Robert Mouawad Campus
5345 Armada Dr.
Carlsbad, CA 92008
Ph: (760)603-4000
Toll Free: 800-421-7250
Fax: (760)603-4080

Kimmelman, Elbrun E., Dir. Gen.
Society of Daughters of Holland
Dames [20762]
PO Box 536
Essex, CT 06426

Kimmel-Schary, Carol, President
Foundation of the Wall and Ceiling
Industry [529]
513 W Broad St., Ste. 210
Falls Church, VA 22046
Ph: (703)538-1600
Fax: (703)538-1728

Kimmich, Allison, Exec. Dir.
National Women's Studies Associa-
tion [8752]
11 E Mount Royal Ave., Ste. 100
Baltimore, MD 21202-5504
Ph: (410)528-0355
Fax: (410)528-0357

Kimmitt, Robert M., Chairman
American Council on Germany
[19441]
14 E 60th St., Ste. 1000
New York, NY 10022
Ph: (212)826-3636
Fax: (212)758-3445

Ki-Moon, Ban, Sec. Gen.
United Nations Association of the
United States of America [19212]
801 2nd Ave.
New York, NY 10017
Ph: (212)697-3315
Fax: (212)697-3316

Kimpton, Jeffrey S., President
Interlochen Center for the Arts
[8977]
9900 Diamond Park Rd.
Interlochen, MI 49643
Ph: (231)276-7200
(231)276-7230
Toll Free: 800-681-5912

Kimpton, Michele, CEO
DuraSpace [6362]
28 Church St., Unit 2
Winchester, MA 01890
Ph: (607)216-4548

Kimsey, Bob, President
North American Forensic Entomology Association [6615]

c/o Rachel Mohr, Treasurer
103 Open Ridge Rd.
Morgantown, WV 26508

Kincaid, Cliff, President
America's Survival [17873]
PO Box 146
Owings, MD 20736-0146
Ph: (443)964-8208

Kincaid, Diane, Dep. Dir.
American Probation and Parole As-
sociation [5672]
1776 Ave. of the States, Bldg. B
Lexington, KY 40511
Ph: (859)244-8203
Fax: (859)244-8001

Kincaid, Marti, VP
National Association of Dog Obedi-
ence Instructors [21919]
7910 Picador Dr.
Houston, TX 77083-4918
Ph: (972)296-1196

Kind, Amy, Co-Pres.
Southern Society for Philosophy and
Psychology [10133]
c/o Lauren A. Taglialatela, Treasurer
Dept. of Psychology
Kennesaw State University
1000 Chastain Rd. NW
Kennesaw, GA 30144-5588

Kind, Jerrie Lynn, Exec. Dir.
National Association of EMS Physi-
cians [14684]
18000 W 105th St.
Olathe, KS 66061
Ph: (913)895-4611
Toll Free: 800-228-3677
Fax: (913)895-4652

Kindel, Susan, MD, President
Melanoma Know More [14010]
PO Box 9155
Cincinnati, OH 45209
Ph: (513)364-6653

Kindred, Brent, President
SkillsUSA Inc. [8018]
14001 Skills USA Way
Leesburg, VA 20176-5494
Ph: (703)777-8810
Toll Free: 800-321-8422
Fax: (703)777-8999

King, Ann Marie, Founder
Hyperemesis Education and
Research Foundation [16285]
932 Edwards Ferry Rd., No. 23
Leesburg, VA 20176-3324
Ph: (703)399-1272

King, Betsy, President, CEO
Golf Fore Africa [13512]
32531 N Scottsdale Rd., Ste. 105
Scottsdale, AZ 85266-1519
Ph: (480)284-5818
Fax: (480)292-8805

King, Bob, Director
Tomiki Aikido of the Americas
[23015]
1835-A S Centre City Pky., Ste. 300
Escondido, CA 92025
Ph: (510)459-4079

King, Bruce, Director, Founder
Ecological Building Network [3676]
PO Box 6397
San Rafael, CA 94903
Ph: (415)491-4802

King, Bruce, President
United States Animal Health Association [17666]
4221 Mitchell Ave.

Saint Joseph, MO 64507
Ph: (816)671-1144
Fax: (816)671-1201

King, Cathy, DVM, CEO, Founder
World Vets [10718]
802 1st Ave. N
Fargo, ND 58102-4906
Toll Free: 877-688-8387
Fax: (701)282-9324

King, Dan L., CEO, President
American Association of University
Administrators [7418]
10 Church Rd.
Wallingford, PA 19086
Ph: (814)460-6498
Fax: (610)565-8089

King, H. Elizabeth, PhD, Bd.
Member
KIDSCOPE [10791]
2045 Peachtree Rd., Ste. 150
Atlanta, GA 30309

King, Jackie, Exec. Dir.
American Veterinary Distributors As-
sociation [2541]
3465 Box Hill Corporate Center Dr.,
Ste. H
Abingdon, MD 21009
Ph: (443)640-1040
Fax: (443)640-1086

King, Jackie, Exec. Dir.
Council for Textile Recycling [3449]
3465 Box Hill Corporate Center Dr.,
Ste. H
Abingdon, MD 21009
Ph: (443)640-1050
Fax: (443)640-1086

King, Jackie, Exec. Dir.
Secondary Materials and Recycled
Textiles [1766]
3465 Box Hill Corporate Center Dr.,
Ste. H
Abingdon, MD 21009
Ph: (443)640-1050
Fax: (443)640-1086

King, James, Chairman
Stable Value Investment Association
[2037]
1025 Connecticut Ave. NW, Ste.
1000
Washington, DC 20036-5417
Ph: (202)580-7620
Fax: (202)580-7621

King, Jim, Exec. Dir.
AMVETS [21109]
4647 Forbes Blvd.
Lanham, MD 20706-4380
Ph: (301)459-9600
Toll Free: 877-726-8387
Fax: (301)459-7924

King, Julie, President
Into Your Hands [8508]
PO Box 3981
Evergreen, CO 80437
Ph: (720)491-1901

King, Kenny, CEO
Global ADE [11469]
8094 N Burlington Ave.
Portland, OR 97203
Ph: (425)346-0921

King, Kevin, Exec. Dir.
Mennonite Disaster Service [12698]
583 Airport Rd.
Lititz, PA 17543-9339
Ph: (717)735-3536
Toll Free: 800-241-8111
Fax: (717)735-0809

King, Kevin, Director
Water and Sewer Distributors of
America [3429]

100 N 20th St., Ste. 400
Philadelphia, PA 19103-1462
Ph: (215)320-3882
Fax: (215)564-2175

King, Larry R., President, CEO
Woodmen of the World/Omaha
Woodmen Life Insurance Society
[19694]
1700 Farnam St.
Omaha, NE 68102-2025
Toll Free: 800-225-3108

King, Laura Rasar, MPH, Exec. Dir.
Council on Education for Public
Health [17002]
1010 Wayne Ave., Ste. 220
Silver Spring, MD 20910
Ph: (202)789-1050
Fax: (202)789-1895

King, Linda, Exhibits Dir.
1904 World's Fair Society [22482]
2605 Causeway Dr.
Saint Louis, MO 63125

King, Linda, Managing Dir.
SPRI [812]
465 Waverley Oaks Rd., Ste. 421
Waltham, MA 02452
Ph: (781)647-7026
Fax: (781)647-7222

King, MacDara, Dir. of Comm.
Foreign Policy Association [18266]
470 Park Ave. S
New York, NY 10016-6819
Ph: (212)481-8100
Toll Free: 800-477-5836
Fax: (212)481-9275

King, Mr. Martin Luther, III, President
Martin Luther King, Jr. Center for
Nonviolent Social Change [18722]
449 Auburn Ave. NE
Atlanta, GA 30312
Ph: (404)526-8900
(404)526-8983

King, Maureen Pecht, Chairperson
Museum Trustee Association [9837]
211 E Lombard St., Ste. 179
Baltimore, MD 21202-6102
Ph: (410)402-0954

King, Michael, President, CEO
Volunteers of America [13093]
1660 Duke St.
Alexandria, VA 22314
Ph: (703)341-5000
Toll Free: 800-899-0089

King, Mr. Richard, Exec. Dir.
Chosen International Medical As-
sistance [12270]
3638 W 26th St.
Erie, PA 16506-2037
Ph: (814)833-3023
Fax: (814)833-4091

King, Sarah, President, CEO
Project Sweet Peas [12132]
45 Boylston St.
Warwick, RI 02889
Ph: (724)268-0465

King, Shirley J., Director, Founder
Gramma's Hugs International
[11009]
c/o Shirley J. King, Director/Founder
8652 Elk Way
Elk Grove, CA 95624
Ph: (916)685-9660

King, Wayne, Sr., VP
U.S. Composting Council [5847]
5400 Grosvenor Ln.
Bethesda, MD 20814-2122
Ph: (301)897-2715
Fax: (301)530-5072

Kingfisher, Alli, President
Building Materials Reuse Association
[508]
PO Box 47776
Chicago, IL 60647
Ph: (773)340-2672

Kingman, Winnie, Director
Jack London Research Center
[9063]
PO Box 337
Glen Ellen, CA 95442-0337
Ph: (707)996-2888

Kingsley, Dr. David, Chairman
World Trichology Society [14904]
2550 Victory Blvd., Ste. 305
Staten Island, NY 10314
Ph: (718)698-4700

Kini, Manjunatha, VP
International Proteolysis Society
[6055]
6105 Scott Hall
School of Medicine
Wayne State University
Detroit, MI 48201
Ph: (313)577-0514
    (313)577-4451
Fax: (313)577-6739

Kinkle, Suzanne, Treasurer
National Organization of Alternative
Programs [17175]
3416 Primm Ln.
Birmingham, AL 35216-5602
Ph: (205)823-6106

Kinnas, Cynthia, President
National Association of Travel
Healthcare Organizations [15156]
558 8th Ave., Ste. 1902
New York, NY 10018
Ph: (646)350-4083

Kinnear, Meg, Sec. Gen.
International Centre for Settlement of
Investment Disputes [4961]
1818 H St. NW
Washington, DC 20433
Ph: (202)458-1534
Fax: (202)522-2615

Kinney, Arthur F., Director
Massachusetts Center for
Interdisciplinary Renaissance Stud-
ies [10195]
650 E Pleasant St.
Amherst, MA 01002
Ph: (413)577-3600

Kinney, Bill, President
Lisle Intercultural Project [8084]
PO Box 1932
Leander, TX 78646
Ph: (512)259-4404
Toll Free: 800-477-1538

Kinney, John, President
Pacific Marine Mammal Center
[4863]
20612 Laguna Canyon Rd.
Laguna Beach, CA 92651
Ph: (949)494-3050

Kinney, Paul T., Exec. Dir.
National Retail Tenants Association
[2930]
60 Shaker Rd.
East Longmeadow, MA 01028-2760
Ph: (413)525-4565
Fax: (413)525-4590

Kinowski, Anne, President
Association of Residency Coordinators in Orthopaedic Surgery
[16471]
3965 W 83rd St.

Box 157
Prairie Village, KS 66208
Ph: (816)404-5406

Kinsella, Brian, Founder, CEO
Stop Soldier Suicide [13199]
318 Blackwell St., Ste. 130
Durham, NC 27701

Kinsella, Cynthia, President, CEO
American Bladder Cancer Society
[13878]
399 Main St., Ste. 2B
Dalton, MA 01226
Ph: (413)684-2344
Toll Free: 888-413-2344

Kinsella, Susan, Chancellor
Pi Gamma Mu [23863]
1001 Millington St., Ste. B
Winfield, KS 67156
Ph: (620)221-3128
Fax: (620)221-7124

Kint, Brian, President
International Beverage Dispensing
Equipment Association [424]
PO Box 248
Reisterstown, MD 21136
Ph: (410)602-0616
Toll Free: 877-404-2332
Fax: (410)486-6799

Kinzelman, Cara, Assoc. Dir.
American College of Nurse-Midwives
[16104]
8403 Colesville Rd., Ste. 1550
Silver Spring, MD 20910
Ph: (240)485-1800
Fax: (240)485-1818

Kipa, Albert, President
Ukrainian Academy of Arts and Sci-
ences in the U.S. [10287]
206 W 100th St.
New York, NY 10025
Ph: (212)222-1866
Fax: (212)864-3977

Kirby, Angela, Coord.
Stolen Horse International [10698]
PO Box 1341
Shelby, NC 28151
Ph: (704)484-2165

Kirch, Darrell G., MD, CEO,
President
Association of American Medical
Colleges [8307]
655 K St. NW, Ste. 100
Washington, DC 20001-2399
Ph: (202)828-0400

Kirckpatrick, Amb. Barbro Owens,
Chairman
Health and Development
International [14937]
318 Seth Pl.
Rockville, MD 20850
Ph: (858)245-2410
Fax: (858)764-0604

Kiritz, Cathleen E., President
The Grantsmanship Center [1470]
350 S Bixel St., Ste. 110
Los Angeles, CA 90017
Ph: (213)482-9860
Toll Free: 800-421-9512
Fax: (213)802-2240

Kirk, Justin, Treasurer
Association of Fraternity/Sorority
Advisors [23754]
PO Box 1369
Fort Collins, CO 80522-1369
Ph: (970)797-4361
Toll Free: 888-855-8670

Kirk, Stephen J., VP
Miles Value Foundation [6723]
5505 Connecticut Ave. NW, No. 149

Washington, DC 20015-2601
Ph: (202)253-5550

Kirkland, Katherine H., Exec. Dir.
Association of Occupational and
Environmental Clinics [16316]
1010 Vermont Ave. NW, Ste. 513
Washington, DC 20005
Ph: (202)347-4976
Toll Free: 888-347-2632
Fax: (202)347-4950

Kirkland, Stephen, VP
International Linear Algebra Society
[6821]
c/o Leslie Hogben, Secretary-
Treasurer
Carver Hall
Dept. of Mathematics
Iowa State University
Ames, IA 50011
Fax: (515)294-5454

Kirkpatrick, Charles, Exec. Dir.
(Actg.)
National Association of Barber
Boards of America [923]
2886 Airport Dr.
Columbus, OH 43219
Ph: (614)523-0203

Kirkpatrick, Jean, Mgr.
Women for Sobriety, Inc. [13189]
PO Box 618
Quakertown, PA 18951
Ph: (215)536-8026
Fax: (215)538-9026

Kirkpatrick, Jim, Treasurer
Carpet and Rug Institute [1941]
100 S Hamilton St.
Dalton, GA 30720
Ph: (706)278-3176
Fax: (706)278-8835

Kirkpatrick, John, Exec. Dir.
American Medical Tennis Association
[23296]
2414 43rd Ave. E, B-1
Seattle, WA 98112
Toll Free: 800-326-2682

Kirlin, Joseph P., III, President
Civil Affairs Association [5596]
6689 Kodiak Dr.
Fayetteville, NC 28304
Ph: (910)835-1314

Kirr, Lori, President
Violin Society of America [10021]
14070 Proton Rd., Ste. 100
Dallas, TX 75244
Ph: (972)233-9107

Kirsch, Dr. Dan, CKM, MKMP, CEO,
President
Knowledge Management Profes-
sional Society [1802]
PO Box 68549
Virginia Beach, VA 23471
Ph: (206)395-2556

Kirsch, Joel, President
American Sports Institute [7742]
PO Box 1837
Mill Valley, CA 94942
Ph: (415)383-5750

Kirschen, OD, PhD, FAAO, David
G., President
American Optometric Foundation
[16423]
2909 Fairgreen St.
Orlando, FL 32803
Ph: (321)710-3936
Toll Free: 800-368-6263
Fax: (407)893-9890

Kirschner, Celeste, CEO
Large Urology Group Practice Association [17552]

1100 E Woodfield Rd., Ste. 350
Schaumburg, IL 60173
Ph: (847)517-7225

Kirschner, Stephanie L., Exec. Dir.
Society for Design Administration
[5978]
8190-A Beechmont Ave., No. 276
Cincinnati, OH 45255
Ph: (513)268-5302
Toll Free: 800-711-8199
Fax: (513)448-1921

Kirtley, Olivia, President
International Federation of Ac-
countants [37]
529 5th Ave., 6th Fl.
New York, NY 10017
Ph: (212)286-9344
Fax: (212)286-9570

Kirwan, Kerry, President
BioEnvironmental Polymer Society
[6192]
Lead Scientist USDA-ARS
800 Buchanan St.
Albany, CA 94710

Kirwan, Steve, Exec. Dir.
American Screenwriters Association
[10358]
269 S Beverly Dr., Ste. 2600
Beverly Hills, CA 90212-3807

Kirwan, Tony, President, Founder
Destiny Rescue [10954]
PO Box 752
North Webster, IN 46555
Ph: (574)457-2470

Kirwin, Liza, Dep. Dir.
Smithsonian Institution Archives of
American Art [8889]
750 9th St. NW
Victor Bldg., Ste. 2200
Washington, DC 20013-7012
Ph: (202)633-7940
Fax: (202)633-7994

Kiser, Joseph, Founder
Children's HeartLink [14108]
5075 Arcadia Ave.
Minneapolis, MN 55436
Ph: (952)928-4860
Toll Free: 888-928-6678
Fax: (952)928-4859

Kish, Daniel, Founder, President
World Access for the Blind [17749]
650 N Rose Dr., No. 208
Placentia, CA 92870
Toll Free: 866-396-7035

Kislak, Paula, Bd. Member
Humane Society Veterinary Medical
Association [10644]
700 Professional Dr.
Gaithersburg, MD 20879
Ph: (202)452-1100
    (301)258-1478

Kiss, Teri Lynn, President
American Association of Critical-
Care Nurses [16088]
101 Columbia
Aliso Viejo, CA 92656-4109
Ph: (949)362-2000
    (206)340-1275
Fax: (949)362-2020

Kissam, Linda, President
International Food, Wine and Travel
Writers Association [2685]
39252 Winchester Rd., Ste. 107, No.
418
Murrieta, CA 92563
Toll Free: 877-439-8929
Fax: (877)439-8929

Kissel, Laura, Secretary
Polar Libraries Colloquy [9721]
c/o Laura Kissel, Secretary
Byrd Polar Research Center Archival
    Program
134 University Archives
2700 Kenny Rd.
Columbus, OH 43210
Ph: (614)688-8173

Kissinger, J. Peter, CEO, President
AAA Foundation for Traffic Safety
    [12810]
607 14th St. NW, Ste. 201
Washington, DC 20005
Ph: (202)638-5944
Fax: (202)638-5943

Kist, Nadia, Chmn. of the Bd.,
    Founder
Seeds For Hope [11677]
PO Box 145
Plainview, NY 11803

Kitajewski, Jan, President
North American Vascular Biology
    Organization [17578]
18501 Kingshill Rd.
Germantown, MD 20874-2211
Ph: (301)760-7745
Fax: (301)540-6903

Kitchens, Lance, President
ADSC: The International Association
    of Foundation Drilling [849]
8445 Freeport Pky., Ste. 325
Irving, TX 75063
Ph: (469)359-6000
Fax: (469)359-6007

Kith, Sarah R., Contact
Southeast Asia Resource Action
    Center [12598]
1628 16th St. NW
Washington, DC 20009-3064
Ph: (202)601-2960
Fax: (202)667-6449

Kitila, Dinknesh, Director
International Oromo Women's
    Organization [12047]
PO Box 34144
Washington, DC 20043-4144

Kittell, Howard J., President, CEO
Andrew Jackson Foundation [10333]
4580 Rachel's Ln.
Hermitage, TN 37076-1331
Ph: (615)889-2941
Fax: (615)889-9909

Kittredge, Dan, Exec. Dir.
Bionutrient Food Association [4189]
24 Hillsville Rd.
North Brookfield, MA 01535
Ph: (978)257-2627
Fax: (978)277-6400

Kittrell, Kari, Exec. Dir.
Kappa Kappa Gamma [23958]
530 E Town St.
Columbus, OH 43215
Ph: (614)228-6515
Toll Free: 866-KKG-1870
Fax: (614)228-7809

Kittrie, Prof. Nicholas, Chairperson
Social Integration and Community
    Development Association [11440]
3 Church Cir., Ste. 294
Annapolis, MD 21401
Ph: (443)569-3578

Kitts, Tracy, Chief Adm. Ofc.
International Economic Development
    Council [5297]
734 15th St. NW, Ste. 900
Washington, DC 20005
Ph: (202)223-7800
Fax: (202)223-4745

Kitzmiller, W. John, M.D., President
American Council of Academic
    Plastic Surgeons [14306]
500 Cummings Ctr., Ste. 4550
Beverly, MA 01915
Ph: (978)927-8330
Fax: (978)524-0498

Kivette, Rad, CEO, Founder, Direc-
    tor
Hannah's Promise International Aid
    [12669]
120 Juniper Dr.
Boone, NC 28607

Kiyak, Dr. Tunga, Managing Dir.
Academy of International Business
    [7539]
Eppley Ctr.
Michigan State University
645 N Shaw Ln., Rm. 7
East Lansing, MI 48824
Ph: (517)432-1452
Fax: (517)432-1009

Kjellson, Emily, Contact
Beyond Tears Worldwide [12628]
123 Saratoga Ln.
Swedesboro, NJ 08085
Ph: (570)309-0324

Klaber, Andrew, President
Association of Marshall Scholars
    [8514]
1120 Chester Ave., Ste. 470
Cleveland, OH 44114
Toll Free: 866-276-0741
Fax: (216)696-2582

Klarfeld, Simon, Exec. Dir.
Young Judaea [20293]
575 8th Ave., 11th Fl.
New York, NY 10018
Ph: (917)595-2100

Klassen, Ben, Founder
The Creativity Movement [19238]
c/o Rev. Chappel
PO Box 8044
Brookings, SD 57006

Klassen, Henry J., MD, Founder,
    Chairman
Foundation for Retinal Regeneration
    [17701]
PO Box 10452
Newport Beach, CA 92658
Ph: (714)551-6400

Klatt, Bryan, Secretary
Benevolent and Protective Order of
    Elks [19425]
2750 N Lakeview Ave.
Chicago, IL 60614-1889
Ph: (773)755-4700
Fax: (773)755-4790

Klatzker, Dale K., PH.D., Chairman
Mental Health Corporations of
    America [13798]
1876 Eider Ct., Ste. A
Tallahassee, FL 32308
Ph: (850)942-4900
Fax: (850)942-0560

Klauber, Avery, Exec. Dir., Founder
Disability Resources, Inc. [11586]
4 Glatter Ln.
Centereach, NY 11720-1032
Ph: (631)585-0290
Fax: (631)585-0290

Klaunig, James, President
Toxicology Forum [7345]
1821 Michael Faraday Dr., Ste. 300
Reston, VA 20190
Ph: (703)547-0876
Fax: (703)438-3113

Klay, Karla, Exec. Dir.
Artist Boat [3809]
2627 Ave. O
Galveston, TX 77550
Ph: (409)770-0722

Klebe, Mrs. Joerg, Mem.
French-American Aid for Children
    [19438]
150 E 58th St., 27th Fl.
New York, NY 10155
Ph: (212)486-9593
Fax: (212)486-9594

Klee, Susie, Info. Technology Mgr.
Compassion and Choices [11805]
PO Box 101810
Denver, CO 80250-1810
Toll Free: 800-247-7421

Kleen, Vernon, President
Inland Bird Banding Association
    [6962]
c/o Mike Eickman, Treasurer/
    Membership Secretary
11114 Harrison Rd.
Rockton, IL 61072

Kleeschulte, Dave, VP
Eastern Winter Sports Reps As-
    sociation [3154]
PO Box 88
White Haven, PA 18661
Ph: (570)443-7180
Fax: (570)443-0388

Klein, Anne, President, CEO
Support Dogs, Inc. [11641]
10995 Linpage Pl.
Saint Louis, MO 63132
Ph: (314)997-2325
Fax: (314)997-7202

Klein, Mrs. Arlene, Chairwoman
Fund for an OPEN Society [17978]
3403 Palace Ct., Ste. C
Pennsauken, NJ 08109
Ph: (856)910-9210

Klein, Donna M., Chairman, CEO
Corporate Voices for Working
    Families [18065]
1020 19th St. NW, Ste. 750
Washington, DC 20036
Ph: (202)467-8130
Fax: (202)467-8140

Klein, Eric, CEO, Founder
Compassion into Action Network -
    Direct Outcome Organization
    [11654]
578 Washington Blvd., Ste. 390
Marina del Rey, CA 90292
Toll Free: 877-226-3697

Klein, Dr. Hans E., President, Exec.
    Dir.
World Association for Case Method
    Research and Application [7099]
23 Mackintosh Ave.
Needham, MA 02492-1218
Ph: (781)444-8982
Fax: (781)444-1548

Klein, James A., President
American Benefits Council [5677]
1501 M St. NW, Ste. 600
Washington, DC 20005-1775
Ph: (202)289-6700
Fax: (202)289-4582

Klein, Jason, Exec.
Reconstructionist Rabbinical As-
    sociation [20277]
1299 Church Rd.
Wyncote, PA 19095
Ph: (215)576-5210
Fax: (215)576-8051

Klein, Melissa, VP, Director
Assisting Children in Need [10802]
c/o Frank O. Klein II, President
600 Cameron St.
Alexandria, VA 22314-2506
Ph: (703)340-1677

Klein, Michael, Chairman
Auto Care Association [281]
7101 Wisconsin Ave., Ste. 1300
Bethesda, MD 20814-3415
Ph: (301)654-6664
Fax: (301)654-3299

Klein, Morton A., President
Zionist Organization of America
    [20294]
4 E 34th St.
New York, NY 10016
Ph: (212)481-1500
Fax: (212)481-1515

Klein, Capt. Richard, President
Council of American Master Mariners
    Inc. [2240]
30623 Chihuahua Valley Rd.
Warner Springs, CA 92086-9220

Klein, Rick, Exec. Dir.
Ancient Forest International [3807]
PO Box 1850
Redway, CA 95560
Ph: (707)923-4475
Fax: (707)923-4475

Klein, Robert, President
National Stamp Dealers Association
    [22350]
430 E Southern Ave.
Tempe, AZ 85282-5216
Ph: (248)709-8940
Toll Free: 800-875-6633

Klein, Ron, CACC, Exec. Dir.
National Board for Certified Clinical
    Hypnotherapists [15365]
1110 Fidler Ln., Ste. 1218
Silver Spring, MD 20910
Ph: (301)608-0123
Toll Free: 800-449-8144
Fax: (301)588-9535

Klein, Sabine, President
New England Theatre Conference
    [10267]
215 Knob Hill Dr.
Hamden, CT 06518
Ph: (617)851-8535

Klein, Terry, President
Register of Professional Archaeolo-
    gists [5946]
3601 E Joppa Rd.
Baltimore, MD 21234
Ph: (410)931-8100
Fax: (410)931-8111

Klein, Virgil A., President
381st Bomb Group Memorial As-
    sociation [20678]
145 Kimel Park Dr., Ste. 370
Winston Salem, NC 27103-6972

Klein, Virginia, Exec. Dir.
Partners in Sustainable Develop-
    ment International [12558]
PO Box 16505
Saint Louis, MO 63105-1005
Ph: (314)993-5599

Kleinberger, Paul, President
Red Nose Response [12074]
2660 Peachtree Rd., Ste. 25F
Atlanta, GA 30305

Kleinfelter, Janet, Dep. Atty. Gen.
National Association of State Charity
    Officials [5254]

c/o Janet M. Kleinfelter, Deputy At-
torney General
PO Box 20207
Nashville, TN 37202
Ph: (615)741-7403

Klemp, Harold, Leader
ECKANKAR [20538]
PO Box 2000
Chanhassen, MN 55317-2000
Ph: (952)380-2222
     (952)380-2200
Fax: (952)380-2295

Kleunen, Andy Van, Exec. Dir.
National Skills Coalition [11776]
1730 Rhode Island Ave. NW, Ste.
712
Washington, DC 20036
Ph: (202)223-8991
Fax: (202)318-2609

Klever, Scott, President
Air and Expedited Motor Carriers
Association [3318]
9532 Liberia Ave., No. 705
Manassas, VA 20110
Ph: (703)361-5208
Fax: (703)361-5274

Klien, Eric, Chairman, President,
Founder
Lifeboat Foundation [19184]
1638 Esmeralda Ave.
Minden, NV 89423
Ph: (775)853-5212
Fax: (775)853-5214

Klimek, John, Sr. VP
National Council for Prescription
Drug Programs [16678]
9240 E Raintree Dr.
Scottsdale, AZ 85260
Ph: (480)477-1000
Fax: (480)767-1042

Kliment, Brian, Contact
Subaru 360 Drivers' Club [21498]
c/o Brian Kliment
23251 Hansen Rd.
Tracy, CA 95304

Klindt, Sara, Director
Californian Rabbit Specialty Club
[4595]
c/o Jerry Hicks, Secretary/Treasurer
10698 Prairie Creek Rd.
New Berlin, IL 62670
Ph: (217)626-1811

Kline, Malcolm A., Exec. Dir.
Accuracy in Academia [7838]
4350 EW Hwy., Ste. 555
Bethesda, MD 20814
Ph: (202)364-4403
Fax: (202)364-4098

Kline, Richard, President
AFL-CIO-Union Label and Service
Trades Department [23528]
815 16th St. NW
Washington, DC 20006
Ph: (202)508-3700

Kline, Sean, Exec. Dir., Founder
Reach Global [12990]
1611 Telegraph Ave., Ste. 1420
Oakland, CA 94612
Ph: (510)763-7045
Fax: (510)763-6545

Klingel, Stephen J., CEO, President
National Council on Compensation
Insurance [1905]
901 Peninsula Corporate Cir.
Boca Raton, FL 33487
Ph: (561)893-1000
Toll Free: 800-622-4123
Fax: (561)893-1191

Klingenstein, Mr. Andrew D.,
President
Esther A. and Joseph Klingenstein
Fund, Inc [15651]
125 Park Ave., Ste. 1700
New York, NY 10017-5529
Ph: (212)492-6195

Klingenstein Martell, Sally, Exec. Dir.
Klingenstein Third Generation
Foundation [14198]
125 Park Ave., Ste. 1700
New York, NY 10017-5529
Ph: (212)492-6179

Klinginsmith, Ray, Trustee
Rotary International [12906]
1 Rotary Ctr.
1560 Sherman Ave.
Evanston, IL 60201-3698
Toll Free: 866-976-8279

Kloda, Harry, President
Cash Registers Collectors Club
[21635]
PO Box 20534
Dayton, OH 45429-0534

Klonoff, David C.
Diabetes Technology Society
[14531]
1157 Chess Dr., Ste. 100
Foster City, CA 94404
Ph: (650)357-7140
Toll Free: 800-397-7755
Fax: (650)349-6497

Klonoff, Elizabeth, PhD, Rep.
APA Division 38: Health Psychology
[16884]
PO Box 1838
Ashland, VA 23005-2544
Ph: (804)752-4987

Klos, Diana Mitsu, Exec. Dir.
National Scholastic Press Associa-
tion [8456]
2221 University Ave. SE, Ste. 121
Minneapolis, MN 55414-3074
Ph: (612)625-8335

Klosterman, Michelle, President
National Amateur Press Association
[22391]
184 Reinhard Ave.
Columbus, OH 43206-2635

Klug, Jim, Dir. of Operations
American Fly Fishing Trade Associa-
tion [3133]
321 E Main St., Ste. 300
Bozeman, MT 59715
Ph: (406)522-1556
Fax: (406)522-1557

Klugman, Keith, Officer
International Society for Infectious
Diseases [15406]
9 Babcock St., 3rd Fl.
Brookline, MA 02446
Ph: (617)277-0551
Fax: (617)278-9113

Kluttz, Jean Swink, Bd. Member
National Hospice Regatta Alliance
[22652]
PO Box 1054
McLean, VA 22101

Klutznick, James, Chairman
Americans for Peace Now [18583]
2100 M St. NW, Ste. 619
Washington, DC 20037
Ph: (202)408-9898
Fax: (202)408-9899

Knackstedt, Kurt, President
Association of Corporate Travel
Executives [3370]

510 King St., Ste. 220
Alexandria, VA 22314
Ph: (262)763-1902
Toll Free: 800-375-2283

Knapp, Jan, President
Ladies Auxiliary of the Military Order
of the Purple Heart United States
of America [20735]
c/o Jan Knapp, President
PO Box 150
Six Lakes, MI 48886
Ph: (231)881-0735

Knapp, Stephen, President,
Treasurer
Vedic Friends Association [20618]
PO Box 15082
Detroit, MI 48215

Knapp, Steven, President
HEATH Resource Center at the
National Youth Transitions Center
[7717]
2134 G St. NW
Washington, DC 20052-0001

Knauer, Amanda, President
National Association of Junior
Auxiliaries, Inc. [12899]
845 S Main St.
Greenville, MS 38701-5871
Ph: (662)332-3000
Fax: (662)332-3076

Knauer, Judy, Founder
National Toothpick Holder Collectors'
Society [21700]
PO Box 852
Archer City, TX 76351-0852

Knaus, Dr. Ron, Founder
American Asperger's Association
[15896]
1301 Seminole Blvd., Ste. B-112
Largo, FL 33770
Ph: (727)518-7294

Knausz, Maria, Founder
Kids in Flight [14197]
PO Box 5234
Willowick, OH 44095-0234

Knechtle, Sharon, Founder
Pura Vida for Children [11136]
PO Box 1692
New Canaan, CT 06840
Ph: (203)644-4404

Kneeland, Charlotte, Director
American Riding Instructors Associa-
tion [22939]
28801 Trenton Ct.
Bonita Springs, FL 34134-3337
Ph: (239)948-3232
Fax: (239)948-5053

Kneller, Lars, Director
Cadillac-LaSalle Club [21346]
PO Box 360835
Columbus, OH 43236-0835
Ph: (614)478-4622
Fax: (614)472-3222

Knese, Bill, Bd. Member
Institute of Management Ac-
countants, Inc. [33]
10 Paragon Dr., Ste. 1
Montvale, NJ 07645-1774
Ph: (201)573-9000
Toll Free: 800-638-4427

Knief, Annette, President
Society of Financial Examiners
[5711]
12100 Sunset Hills Rd., Ste. 130
Reston, VA 20190
Ph: (703)234-4140
Toll Free: 800-787-7633
Fax: (703)435-4390

Knight, Bob, President
North American Railcar Operators
Association [3350]
PO Box 9035
Cincinnati, OH 45209

Knight, Deirdre, Admin. Asst.
International Castor Oil Association,
Inc. [2450]
PO Box 595
Mohegan Lake, NY 10547

Knight, Don, Act. Pres.
Veteran Motor Car Club of America
[21512]
c/o Don Knight, Acting President
1610 Knight Circle
Grand Prairie, TX 75050-2848
Ph: (972)641-4517

Knights, Peter, Exec. Dir.
WildAid [4906]
333 Pine St., Ste. 300
San Francisco, CA 94104
Ph: (415)834-3174
Fax: (415)834-1759

Knoll, Dominik, CEO, President
World Trade Center of New Orleans
[1973]
1 Canal Pl.
365 Canal St., Ste. 1120
New Orleans, LA 70130-1195
Ph: (504)529-1601
Fax: (504)529-1691

Knoll, Monica, Founder
Cancer101 [13932]
304 Park Ave. S, 11th Fl.
New York, NY 10010
Ph: (646)638-2202
Fax: (646)349-3035

Knoll, Robin, Chap.
Inspiration Ministries [11604]
N2270 State Road 67
Walworth, WI 53184
Ph: (262)275-6131

Knollmann, Bjorn C., President
Cardiac Muscle Society [14104]
c/o Bjorn Knollmann
2215B Garland Ave.
Nashville, TN 37232-0575
Ph: (615)343-6493
Fax: (615)343-4522

Knopke, Harry, President
Aqua Clara International [13316]
88 Sun Ridge Dr.
Holland, MI 49424

Knorr, Marci, CPht, President
American Association of Pharmacy
Technicians [16633]
PO Box 1447
Greensboro, NC 27402
Ph: (336)333-9356
Toll Free: 877-368-4771
Fax: (336)333-9068

Knosp, Suzanne, Contact
International Guild of Musicians in
Dance [23497]
c/o John Toenjes, Administrator
University of Illinois
Dance Administration Bldg.
907 1/2 W Nevada St.
Urbana, IL 61801

Knoster, Tim, Exec. Dir.
Association for Positive Behavior
Support [6035]
PO Box 328
Bloomsburg, PA 17815
Ph: (570)441-5418

Knott, Bruce, President
Council for Qualification of
Residential Interior Designers
[1943]

Interior Design Society
164 S Main St., Ste. 404
High Point, NC 27260
Ph: (336)884-4437
Toll Free: 888-884-4469
Fax: (336)885-3291

Knott, Ray, Director, Editor
Riviera Owners Association **[21484]**
PO Box 261218
Denver, CO 80226-9218
Ph: (303)233-2987
Fax: (303)984-0909

Knott, Stephen, Secretary, Treasurer
International Longshoremen's As-
   sociation **[23474]**
5000 W Side Ave.
North Bergen, NJ 07047
Ph: (212)425-1200
Fax: (212)425-2928

Knotts, Jim, President, CEO
Vietnam Veterans Memorial Fund
   [21173]
1235 S Clark St., Ste. 910
Arlington, VA 22202
Ph: (202)393-0090

Knouse, Dr. Nola Reed, Director
Moravian Music Foundation **[9957]**
457 S Church St.
Winston Salem, NC 27101-5314
Ph: (336)725-0651
Fax: (336)725-4514

Knowdell, Richard, Contact
Career Planning and Adult Develop-
   ment Network **[11756]**
PO Box 611930
San Jose, CA 95161-1930
Ph: (408)828-3858

Knowles, Alice, VP
Dignity U.S.A. **[20178]**
PO Box 376
Medford, MA 02155-0004
Ph: (202)861-0017
Toll Free: 800-877-8797
Fax: (781)397-0584

Knowles, Brian, Chairperson
Media & Content Marketing Associa-
   tion **[2800]**
225 W 34th St., Ste. 946
New York, NY 10122
Ph: (818)487-2090
Fax: (818)487-4501

Knowles, Charles, President,
   Founder, Chmn. of the Bd.
Wildlife Conservation Network
   [4909]
209 Mississippi St.
San Francisco, CA 94107
Ph: (415)202-6380
Fax: (415)202-6381

Knowles, Ralph I., Director
Legal Momentum **[18217]**
5 Hanover Sq., Ste. 1502
New York, NY 10004
Ph: (212)925-6635

Knowlton, Peter, President
United Electrical, Radio and Machine
   Workers of America **[23415]**
1 Gateway Ctr., Ste. 1400
Pittsburgh, PA 15222
Ph: (412)471-8919

Knowlton, Tiffany, MBA, Exec. Dir.
Association of Academic Physiatrists
   [17084]
10461 Mill Run Cir., Ste. 730
Owings Mills, MD 21117
Ph: (410)654-1000
Fax: (410)654-1001

Knox, John A., Exec. Dir.
Earth Island Institute **[4051]**
2150 Allston Way, Ste. 460
Berkeley, CA 94704-1375
Ph: (510)859-9100
Fax: (510)859-9091

Knox, Meg, Chmn. of the Bd.
National Affordable Housing Network
   [11975]
PO Box 632
Butte, MT 59703-0632
Ph: (406)782-8579
Fax: (406)782-5539

Knox, Tom, President
National Automatic Pistol Collectors
   Association **[21297]**
PO Box 15738
Saint Louis, MO 63163-0738

Knox, Wendy, Chairman
National Alliance of Highway
   Beautification Agencies **[5734]**
PO Box 191
Columbia, SC 29202

Knudson, David, Founder
National Historic Route 66 Federa-
   tion **[9419]**
374 Klamath Dr.
Lake Arrowhead, CA 92352-1848
Ph: (909)336-6131
Fax: (909)336-1039

Knue, Alan, Chairman
Association of Assistive Technology
   Act Programs **[14546]**
1020 S Spring St.
Springfield, IL 62704

Knurowski, Frank, President
Association of the Sons of Poland
   [19602]
333 Hackensack St.
Carlstadt, NJ 07072
Ph: (201)935-2807
Fax: (201)935-2752

Knutson, Kate S., President
American Animal Hospital Associa-
   tion **[17590]**
12575 W Bayaud Ave.
Lakewood, CO 80228-2021
Ph: (303)986-2800
Toll Free: 800-252-2242
Fax: (303)986-1700

Knutzen, Robert, Chairman, CEO
Pituitary Network Association
   [16771]
PO Box 1958
Thousand Oaks, CA 91358-1958
Ph: (805)499-9973
Fax: (805)480-0633

Ko, Austin, President
Intercollegiate Taiwanese American
   Students Association **[19668]**
PO Box 654
New York, NY 10163

Kobayashi, Alan, Chairman
Video Electronics Standards As-
   sociation **[6440]**
1754 Technology Dr., Ste. 238
San Jose, CA 95110
Ph: (408)982-3850
Fax: (408)669-0976

Kobenan, Mrs. Brigitte, Founder
Autism Community of Africa **[13747]**
PO Box 502
Charles Town, WV 25414-0504
Ph: (443)718-1824

Kobetz, Dr. Richard W., CST,
   Founder
Executive Protection Institute **[8560]**
16 Penn Plz., Ste. 1130

New York, NY 10001
Ph: (212)268-4555
Toll Free: 800-947-5827
Fax: (212)563-4783

Kobler, William, MD, President
American Medical Association
   Foundation **[8302]**
AMA Plz.
330 N Wabash Ave., Ste. 39300
Chicago, IL 60611-5885
Ph: (312)464-4200
Fax: (312)464-4142

Kobus, Diana, Exec. Dir.
Institute of Professional
   Environmental Practice **[4070]**
339 Fisher Hall
600 Forbes Ave.
Pittsburgh, PA 15282
Ph: (412)396-1703
Fax: (412)396-1704

Kobza, Kelly, Founder
Greater Good Haiti **[11369]**
1230 Market St., No. 129
San Francisco, CA 94102

Kobziar, Dr. Leda, President
Association for Fire Ecology of the
   Tropics **[3991]**
PO Box 50412
Eugene, OR 97405-0412
Ph: (541)852-7903

Koch, Bob, Secretary, Treasurer
National Lilac Rabbit Club of
   America **[4605]**
c/o Bob Koch, Secretary-Treasurer
N3650 Oak Ridge Rd.
Waupaca, WI 54981
Ph: (715)281-3106

Koch, Bob, Memb. Ofc.
Vietnam Era Seabees **[21161]**
PO Box 5177
Midlothian, VA 23112-0020

Koch, Jay, Founder
Diabetic Supply Rescue **[14533]**
3060 Los Lentes Rd. SE
Los Lunas, NM 87031
Ph: (505)565-8526

Koch, Kim, Chairperson
American Oil Chemists' Society
   Agricultural Microscopy Division
   [4175]
c/o Kim Koch, Chairperson
National Crops Institute
PO Box 6050
Fargo, ND 58108
Ph: (701)235-3662

Koch, Laura, Editor, Founder
Hospital-Based Massage Network
   [15556]
612 S College Ave., No. 1
Fort Collins, CO 80524
Ph: (970)407-9232
Toll Free: 800-754-9790

Koch, Natalie, Secretary
Central Eurasian Studies Society
   [8111]
2873 W Broad St.
Columbus, OH 43204-2673

Koch, Robert, Treasurer
Dodge Pilothouse Era Truck Club of
   America **[22474]**
3778 Hoen Ave.
Santa Rosa, CA 95405

Koch, Robert, CEO, President
Wine Institute **[4936]**
425 Market St., Ste. 1000
San Francisco, CA 94105
Ph: (415)512-0151
Fax: (415)356-7569

Kocharian, Bella, Chairperson
Armenian Bone Marrow Donor
   Registry **[13844]**
c/o Frieda Jordan, President
3111 Los Feliz Ave. No. 206
Los Angeles, CA 90039
Ph: (323)663-3609
Fax: (323)662-3648

Kochevar, Deborah, DVM, PhD,
   Dean
Tufts University I Cummings School
   of Veterinary Medicine I Center for
   Animals and Public Policy **[10705]**
200 Westboro Rd.
North Grafton, MA 01536
Ph: (508)839-7991
Fax: (508)839-3337

Kochkin, Sergei, PhD, Exec. Dir.
Better Hearing Institute **[15178]**
1444 I St. NW, Ste. 700
Washington, DC 20005
Ph: (202)449-1100
Fax: (202)216-9646

Kochman, Caroline, Exec. Dir.
National Association for Shoplifting
   Prevention **[12877]**
225 Broadhollow Rd., Ste. 400E
Melville, NY 11747
Ph: (631)923-2737
Toll Free: 800-848-9595
Fax: (631)923-2743

Kodjak, Drew, Exec. Dir.
International Council on Clean
   Transportation **[3334]**
1225 I St. NW, Ste. 900
Washington, DC 20005
Ph: (202)534-1600

Koebel, George, President
Tobacconists' Association of America
   [3288]
PO Box 81152
Conyers, GA 30013
Ph: (770)597-6264

Koeber, Chuck, President
Association for Humanist Sociology
   [7181]
Esch Hall, Rm. 230
University of Indianapolis
1400 E Hanna Ave.
Indianapolis, IN 46227
Ph: (317)788-3365

Koehler, Dr. Brian, Exec. Ofc.
International Society for Psychologi-
   cal and Social Approaches to
   Psychosis - United States Chapter
   [15779]
PO Box 491
Narberth, PA 19072

Koehler, Matthew, Exec. Dir.
Native Forest Network **[3911]**
PO Box 8251
Missoula, MT 59807
Ph: (406)542-7343
Fax: (406)542-7347

Koelling, Preston, President
American Criminal Justice Associa-
   tion - Lambda Alpha Epsilon
   [11518]
PO Box 601047
Sacramento, CA 95860-1047
Ph: (916)484-6553
Fax: (916)488-2227

Koenig, Dr. George J., DO,
   President
National Collegiate Emergency
   Medical Services Foundation
   [14686]
PO Box 93

West Sand Lake, NY 12196
Toll Free: 877-623-6731
Fax: (877)623-6731

Koenig, Gerry, Chmn. of the Bd.
Iron Disorders Institute [15825]
PO Box 675
Taylors, SC 29687

Koenig, Stephen E., Exec. Dir.
Poultry Science Association [4571]
1800 S Oak St., Ste. 100
Champaign, IL 61820-6974
Ph: (217)356-5285
Fax: (217)398-4119

Koenings, Todd, Exec. Dir.
Global Parks [3877]
Ph: (703)317-1669

Koeningsberg, Karen, Founder,
President
Cherished Feet [13004]
115 E 34th St., No. 1870
New York, NY 10156
Ph: (646)770-6892

Koepfer, Stephen R., President
American Sambo Association
[22983]
PO Box 5773
Long Island City, NY 11105
Ph: (718)728-8054

Koepke, Rick, Exec. Dir.
International Ombudsman Associa-
tion [644]
1 Parkview Plz., Ste. 800
17W110 22nd St.
Oakbrook Terrace, IL 60181
Ph: (847)686-2242
Fax: (847)686-2253

Koepke, Rick, Exec. Dir.
International Society for Traumatic
Stress Studies [17292]
1 Parkview Plz., Ste. 800
Oakbrook Terrace, IL 60181
Ph: (847)686-2234
Fax: (847)686-2251

Koepp, Bernhard, President
Opera Foundation [9990]
712 5th Ave., 32nd Fl.
New York, NY 10019
Ph: (212)664-8843

Koeppel, Gary, Delegate
Parson Russell Terrier Association of
America [21940]
c/o Lance Nobriga, Secretary
91-1650 Laupai St.
Ewa Beach, HI 96706-4902
Ph: (808)652-7877

Koepsell, Mark, Exec. Dir.
Association of Fraternal Leadership
& Values [23753]
PO Box 1576
Fort Collins, CO 80522-1576
Ph: (970)372-1174

Koetzle, Thomas, Editor
American Crystallographic Associa-
tion [6359]
PO Box 96
Buffalo, NY 14205-0096
Ph: (716)898-8690
Fax: (716)898-8695

Koffman, Steven, Director, Founder
Malawi Children's Mission [11074]
274 Redwood Shores Pky., Box 313
Redwood City, CA 94065

Kofmehl, Dr. William E., Jr., Founder,
President
Christian Literacy Associates [8239]
541 Perry Hwy.

Pittsburgh, PA 15229-1857
Ph: (412)364-3777

Kogan, Barry Allan, MD, President
Society of University Urologists
[17563]
1100 E Woodfield Rd., Ste. 350
Schaumburg, IL 60173
Ph: (847)517-7225
Fax: (847)517-7229

Kogen, Lisa, Dir. Ed.
Women's League for Conservative
Judaism [20291]
475 Riverside Dr., Ste. 820
New York, NY 10115
Ph: (212)870-1260
Toll Free: 800-628-5083
Fax: (212)870-1261

Kogevinas, Manolis, President
International Society for
Environmental Epidemiology
[14733]
c/o Infinity Conference Group, Inc.
1035 Sterling Rd., Ste. 202
Herndon, VA 20170
Ph: (703)925-0178
Toll Free: 844-369-4121
Fax: (703)925-9453

Kogovsek, John, Chmn. of the Bd.
WSA Fraternal Life [19503]
11265 Decatur St., Ste. 100
Westminster, CO 80234
Ph: (303)451-1494
Toll Free: 800-451-7528
Fax: (303)451-5112

Kohan, Richard, Chairman
National YoungArts Foundation
[8991]
2100 Biscayne Blvd.
Miami, FL 33137
Ph: (305)377-1140
Toll Free: 800-970-2787
Fax: (305)377-1149

Kohlenbach, Ulrich, VP
Association for Symbolic Logic
[6817]
Vassar College
124 Raymond Ave.
Poughkeepsie, NY 12604
Ph: (845)437-7080
Fax: (845)437-7830

Kohler, Betsy, Exec. Dir.
North American Association of
Central Cancer Registries [14035]
2050 W Iles, Ste. A
Springfield, IL 62704-7412
Ph: (217)698-0800
Fax: (217)698-0188

Kohles, Micah, DVM, President
Association of Exotic Mammal
Veterinarians [17635]
618 Church St., Ste. 220
Nashville, TN 37219

Kohn, Stephen M., Exec. Dir., Chair-
man
National Whistleblower Center
[12838]
PO Box 25074
Washington, DC 20027
Ph: (202)342-1903

Kohno, Hikedi, President
PACON International [4469]
Oceanography Mail Room
MSB 2nd Fl.
1000 Pope Rd.
Honolulu, HI 96822
Ph: (808)956-6163
Fax: (808)956-2580

Kohomban, Lisa, President, Exec.
Dir.
Aiding Children Together [10843]
1055 W Dover Rd.

Pawling, NY 12564
Ph: (845)832-7594
Fax: (845)832-7594

Kohout, Keith, President
American Bonanza Society [21213]
PO Box 12888
Wichita, KS 67277
Ph: (316)945-1700
Fax: (316)945-1710

Kohr, Howard, CEO
American Israel Public Affairs Com-
mittee [18673]
251 H St. NW
Washington, DC 20001
Ph: (202)639-5200

Kohring, John, Exec. Dir.
United Council for Neurologic Subspecialties [16040]
201 Chicago Ave.
Minneapolis, MN 55415

Kohring, John, Exec. Dir.
United Council for Neurological Sub-
specialties [16041]
201 Chicago Ave.
Minneapolis, MN 55415
Ph: (612)928-6106
Fax: (612)454-2750

Kohse-Hoinghaus, Katharina,
President
Combustion Institute [7024]
5001 Baum Blvd., Ste. 664
Pittsburgh, PA 15213-1851
Ph: (412)687-1366
Fax: (412)687-0340

Koken, Juline, PhD, Mem.
Society for the Scientific Study of
Sexuality [17204]
881 3rd St., Ste. B5
Whitehall, PA 18052
Ph: (610)443-3100
Fax: (610)443-3105

Kokolus, Cait C., Bd. Member
Catholic Library Association [9696]
205 W Monroe St., Ste. 314
Chicago, IL 60606-5061
Ph: (312)739-1776
Toll Free: 855-739-1776
Fax: (312)739-1778

Kolacny, Dave, President
International Society of Folk Harpers
and Craftsmen [9933]
Alice Williams, Secretary
1614 Pittman Dr.
Missoula, MT 59803
Ph: (406)542-1976

Kolar, Mary Jane, CAE, Exec. Dir.
National Council on Qualifications for
the Lighting Professions [2103]
PO Box 142729
Austin, TX 78714-2729
Ph: (512)973-0042
Fax: (512)973-0043

Kolarik, Randall, FIC, President
National Association of Fraternal
Insurance Counsellors [1892]
211 Canal Rd.
Waterloo, WI 53594
Toll Free: 866-478-3880

Kolb, Justin, Exec. Sec.
American Liszt Society [9179]
c/o Alexander Djordjevic, Member-
ship Secretary
PO Box 1020
Wheaton, IL 60187-6777
Ph: (845)586-4457

Kolb, Michael T., Exec. Dir.
National Public Employer Labor
Relations Association [5400]

1012 S Coast Hwy., Ste. M
Oceanside, CA 92054
Ph: (760)433-1686
Toll Free: 877-673-5721
Fax: (760)433-1687

Kolb, Steven, President, CEO
CFDA Foundation [201]
65 Bleecker St., 11th Fl.
New York, NY 10012
Ph: (212)302-1821
Fax: (212)768-0515

Kolbo, Russell, President
International Association for Colon
Hydrotherapy [14942]
11103 San Pedro, Ste. 117
San Antonio, TX 78216
Ph: (210)366-2888
Fax: (210)366-2999

Koliatsos, Dr. Vassilis, Chairperson
Society for the Preservation of the
Greek Heritage [9355]
PO Box 53341
Washington, DC 20009
Ph: (757)692-4701

Kolibaba, Sharon, Mem.
National Antique Doll Dealers Association [22005]
c/o Lynette Gross, Secretary
13710 Smokey Ridge Trace
Carmel, IN 46033-9297
Ph: (623)266-2926

Kolker, Justine L., President
American Board of Operative
Dentistry [14397]
c/o Dr. Jeanette Gorthy, Secretary
PO Box 1276
Anacortes, WA 98221
Ph: (310)794-4387
Fax: (310)825-2536

Kollantai, Jean, Founder
Center for Loss in Multiple Birth, Inc.
[12409]
PO Box 91377
Anchorage, AK 99509
Ph: (907)222-5321

Kollar, Kipp, President
North American Grappling Associa-
tion [23372]
36 Saner Rd.
Marlborough, CT 06447
Ph: (860)295-0403
Fax: (860)295-0447

Kollman, Rand, VP
Pet Care Trust [10679]
3465 Box Hill Corporate Center Dr.,
Ste. H
Abingdon, MD 21009
Ph: (443)921-2825
Fax: (443)640-1086

Kolodziej, Bernard, President
Polish Union of the United States of
North America [19615]
53-59 N Main St.
Wilkes Barre, PA 18701
Ph: (570)823-1611
Fax: (570)829-7849

Kolodziej, Richard R., Officer
National Center for Missing and
Exploited Children [11088]
Charles B Wang International
Children's Bldg.
699 Prince St.
Alexandria, VA 22314-3175
Ph: (703)224-2150
Toll Free: 800-843-5678
Fax: (703)224-2122

Koltai, Mikael, Esq., Founder
Swedish-American Bar Association
[5050]

5020 Campus Dr.
Newport Beach, CA 92660
Ph: (949)706-9111
    (760)436-9600

Komisar, Marie, Exec. Dir.
National Association of Women
   Judges [5391]
1001 Connecticut Ave. NW, Ste.
   1138
Washington, DC 20036
Ph: (202)393-0222
Fax: (202)393-0125

Komives, Stephen, Exec. Dir.
Society for News Design [2722]
424 E Central Blvd., Ste. 406
Orlando, FL 32801
Ph: (407)420-7748
Fax: (407)420-7697

Komoski, P. Kenneth, Exec. Dir.,
   President
EPIE Institute [8030]
PO Box 590
Hampton Bays, NY 11946-0509
Ph: (631)728-9100

Kompelien, Kevin, President
Evangelical Free Church of America
   [20412]
901 E 78th St.
Minneapolis, MN 55420
Ph: (952)854-1300
Toll Free: 800-745-2202

Kong, Dr. June, President
American Chinese Medical
   Exchange Society [15434]
15 New England Executive Pk.
Burlington, MA 01803-5202
Ph: (781)791-5066
Fax: (781)402-0284

Kong, Dr. Laura S.L., Director
United Nations Educational,
   Scientific and Cultural Organization
   | Intergovernmental Oceanographic
   Commission [7158]
Bldg. 176
1845 Wasp Blvd.
Honolulu, HI 96818
Ph: (808)725-6050
Fax: (808)725-6055

Konkel, Rev. Dennis, Director
Lutheran Deaf Mission Society
   [20307]
9907 Sappington Rd.
Saint Louis, MO 63128

Konkel, Joseph L., President
Paper Industry Management As-
   sociation [2494]
15 Technology Pkwy. S
Norcross, GA 30092
Ph: (770)209-7230
Fax: (770)209-7359

Konkle, Dr. Lincoln, Exec. Dir.
Thornton Wilder Society [10405]
c/o College of New Jersey
PO Box 7718
Ewing, NJ 08628-0718
Ph: (609)771-2346

Konn, Dr. Terry, Founder, Chairman
World Healthcare Educational
   Resources, Etc. [15510]
17 Sun Ray Dr.
Toms River, NJ 08753
Ph: (732)255-4738

Konosky, Carolyn, Co-CEO,
   Secretary
Kidney Cancer Association [13997]
PO Box 803338, No. 38269
Chicago, IL 60680-3338
Ph: (847)332-1051
    (503)215-7921
Toll Free: 800-850-9132

Kontos, Michael C., MD, President
Society of Cardiovascular Patient
   Care [16564]
6161 Riverside Dr.
Dublin, OH 43017
Ph: (614)442-5950
Toll Free: 877-271-4176
Fax: (614)442-5953

Koob, Steve, Exec. Dir., Founder
One More Soul [19066]
1846 N Main St.
Dayton, OH 45405-3832
Ph: (937)279-5433
Toll Free: 800-307-7685
Fax: (937)275-3902

Koonce, Kevin, Exec. Dir.
Vinyl Building Council [597]
1747 Pennsylvania Ave. NW, Ste.
   825
Washington, DC 20006
Ph: (202)765-2200

Koontz, Shelly Brady, Founder
Global Organization for Organ Dona-
   tion [14620]
PO Box 52757
Tulsa, OK 74105
Ph: (918)605-1994
Fax: (918)745-6637

Kopelan, Brett, Exec. Dir., Bd.
   Member
Dystrophic Epidermolysis Bullosa
   Research Association of America
   [14493]
75 Broad St., Ste. 300
New York, NY 10004
Ph: (212)868-1573
Toll Free: 855-287-3432
Fax: (212)868-9296

Koplan, Jeffrey P., President
International Association of National
   Public Health Institutes [17005]
Emory University
Global Health Institute
1599 Clifton Rd. NE
Atlanta, GA 30322
Ph: (404)727-1416

Koplon, Lane, Consul Gen.
Tau Epsilon Phi Fraternity, Inc.
   [23934]
1000 White Horse Rd., Ste. 512
Voorhees, NJ 08043-4411

Koplovitz, Kay, Chairperson
Springboard Enterprises [3500]
2100 Foxhall Rd. NW
Washington, DC 20007
Ph: (202)242-6282
Fax: (202)242-6284

Koplow, Amy, Exec. Dir.
Hebrew Free Burial Association
   [20250]
224 W 35th St., Rm. 300
New York, NY 10001
Ph: (212)239-1662
Fax: (212)239-1981

Kopp, Joanne, Treasurer
American Musical Instrument Society
   [9862]
c/o Joanne Kopp, Treasurer
1106 Garden St.
Hoboken, NJ 07030
Ph: (201)656-0107

Kopp, Ronn, President
North American Fastpitch Associa-
   tion [23205]
c/o Benjie Hedgecock, Executive
   Director
PO Box 566
Dayton, OR 97114
Ph: (503)864-3939
Fax: (503)864-3939

Kopp, Sandra, MD, President
Anesthesia History Association
   [13696]
c/o Martin Giesecke, M.D., Treasurer
5010 Crawford St.
Houston, TX 77004-5735

Koppa, Jim, President
Fishing Has No Boundaries Inc.
   [22844]
15453 County Highway B
Hayward, WI 54843
Ph: (715)634-3185
Toll Free: 800-243-3462
Fax: (715)634-1305

Koppel, Lora Stege, RN, Chair-
   woman
Children's Surgery International
   [17384]
Medical Arts Bldg.
825 Nicollet Mall, Ste. 706
Minneapolis, MN 55402
Ph: (612)746-4082
Fax: (612)746-4083

Koprulu, Mr. Murat, Chairman
American Turkish Society [19672]
1460 Broadway Ste. 10023
New York, NY 10036
Ph: (646)434-4409
Fax: (646)434-4405

Koral, Richard, President
American Ethical Union [20207]
2 W 64th St.
New York, NY 10023-7183
Ph: (212)873-6500
Fax: (212)624-0203

Korbel, KImberly A., Exec. Dir.
American Wire Producers Associa-
   tion [1710]
PO Box 151387
Alexandria, VA 22315-1387
Ph: (703)299-4434
Fax: (703)299-4434

Korenman, Victor, VP
International Book Bank [8078]
4000 Buena Vista Ave.
Baltimore, MD 21211
Ph: (410)685-2665
Fax: (410)362-0336

Korga, Dr. Iwona, Exec. Dir.,
   Treasurer
Jozef Pilsudski Institute of America
   for Research in the Modern History
   of Poland [10165]
138 Greenpoint Ave.
Brooklyn, NY 11222
Ph: (212)505-9077
Fax: (347)763-9469

Korin, Anne, Chairperson
Set America Free [18194]
7811 Montrose Rd., Ste. 505
Potomac, MD 20854-3368
Toll Free: 866-713-7527

Korkow, John, Chairman
International Coalition for Addiction
   Studies Education [13146]
PO Box 224
Vermillion, SD 57069-0224
Ph: (605)677-5520

Korn, Leslie E., Ph.D., MPH, Dir. of
   Res.
Center for World Indigenous Studies
   [18470]
1001 Cooper Point Rd. SW, Ste. 140
Olympia, WA 98502-1107
Ph: (360)529-4896

Kornbluh, Harvey L., Chairman,
   CEO, Founder
Associated Owners and Developers
   [800]

PO Box 4163
McLean, VA 22103-4163
Ph: (703)405-5324

Kornblum, William, Director
Association for Union Democracy
   [23466]
104 Montgomery St.
Brooklyn, NY 11225
Ph: (718)564-1114

Korner, Roger T., Exec. Dir.
United Seamen's Service [12862]
104 Broadway, Ground Fl.
Jersey City, NJ 07306
Ph: (201)369-1100
Fax: (201)369-1105

Kornhaber, Arthur, MD, Founder,
   President
Foundation for Grandparenting
   [11916]
108 Farnham Rd.
Ojai, CA 93023-1759

Kornreich, Dr. Bruce, DVM, Assoc.
   Dir.
Cornell Feline Health Center [17645]
235 Hungerford Hill Rd.
Ithaca, NY 14853
Ph: (607)253-3414
    (607)253-3000
Toll Free: 800-548-8937
Fax: (607)253-3419

Koroshetz, M.D., Walter J., Dir.
   (Actg.)
U.S. Department of Health and Hu-
   man Services | National Institutes
   of Health | National Institute of
   Neurological Disorders and Stroke
   [15999]
Bldg. 31, Rm 8A52
31 Center Dr.
Bethesda, MD 20892
Ph: (301)496-5751
Toll Free: 800-352-9424

Korsmo, Michelle L., CEO
American Land Title Association
   [2845]
1800 M St. NW, Ste. 300S
Washington, DC 20036-5828
Ph: (202)296-3671
Toll Free: 800-787-ALTA
Fax: (202)223-5843

Korte, Paulette, Secretary
Motorcycle Riders Foundation
   [22230]
1325 G St. NW, Ste. 500
Washington, DC 20005
Ph: (202)546-0983
Fax: (202)546-0986

Kortenhorst, Jules, CEO
Rocky Mountain Institute [4499]
22830 Two Rivers Rd.
Basalt, CO 81621
Ph: (970)927-3851
Fax: (970)927-3420

Korth, Peggy G., President
Water Assurance Technology Energy
   Resources [6517]
40 Sun Valley Dr.
Spring Branch, TX 78070
Fax: (830)885-4827

Kortum, Katherine, Chairperson
Young Professionals in Transporta-
   tion [3364]
PO Box 77783
Washington, DC 20013

Kos, Eric, President, Secretary,
   Treasurer
Michael Oakeshott Association
   [10110]

Political Sciences Dept.
Colorado College
14 E Cache La Poudre St.
Colorado Springs, CO 80903

Kos, Karleen, Exec. Dir.
Portable Sanitation Association
International **[4744]**
2626 E 82nd St., Ste. 175
Bloomington, MN 55425
Ph: (952)854-8300
Toll Free: 800-822-3020
Fax: (952)854-7560

Kosakowski, Jack E., President,
CEO
Junior Achievement **[7554]**
1 Education Way
Colorado Springs, CO 80906
Ph: (719)540-8000

Kosich, Andi, Exec. Dir.
Optical Internetworking Forum
[3212]
48377 Fremont Blvd., Ste. 117
Fremont, CA 94538
Ph: (510)492-4040
Fax: (510)492-4001

Kosner, John, Advisor
Digital Content Next **[2781]**
1350 Broadway, Rm. 606
New York, NY 10018-7205
Ph: (646)473-1000
Fax: (646)473-0200

Kosnik, Dr. David, Chairman
Acoustic Emission Working Group
[5851]
c/o Mark Carlos, Secretary-
Treasurer
MISTRAS Group Inc.
195 Clarksville Rd.
Princeton Junction, NJ 08550
Ph: (609)716-4030

Kosogof, Alexandra, VP
Ukrainian Children's Aid and Relief
Effort, Inc. **[11176]**
6123 Hidden Oak Dr.
Crystal Lake, IL 60012

Kosseff, Alex, Exec. Dir.
American Mountain Guides Associa-
tion **[21595]**
207 Canyon Blvd., Ste. 201N
Boulder, CO 80302-4932
Ph: (303)271-0984
Fax: (303)271-1377

Kosson, David, PhD, President
Aftermath: Surviving Psychopathy
Foundation **[16949]**
PO Box 267
Yorkville, IL 60560

Kosson, David, PhD, President
Society for the Scientific Study of
Psychopathy **[15808]**
University of South Florida
Louis de la Parte Florida Mental
Health Institute
13301 Bruce B. Downs Blvd., MHC
2639
Tampa, FL 33612
Ph: (813)974-8612
Fax: (813)974-6411

Kost, Mr. Keith, CEO, Exec. Dir.
STEER, Inc. **[20467]**
1025 N 3rd St.
Bismarck, ND 58502
Ph: (701)258-4911
Fax: (701)258-7684

Kostant, Amy, Exec. Dir.
Science Communication Network
[17020]

4833 West Ln.
Bethesda, MD 20814
Ph: (301)654-6665

Kostecki, Paul, PhD, Editor, Exec.
Dir.
The Association for Environmental
Health and Sciences **[4684]**
150 Fearing St.
Amherst, MA 01002-1941
Ph: (413)549-5170
Fax: (413)549-0579

Kostelny, Elizabeth, Exec. Dir.
Preservation Virginia **[9428]**
204 W Franklin St.
Richmond, VA 23220-5012
Ph: (804)648-1889
Fax: (804)775-0802

Koster, Janet Bandows, Exec. Dir.,
CEO
Association for Women in Science
[7123]
1321 Duke St., Ste. 210
Alexandria, VA 22314
Ph: (703)894-4490
Fax: (703)894-4489

Koster, Dr. Klaas, President
Society of Exploration Geophysicists
[6695]
8801 S Yale, Ste. 500
Tulsa, OK 74137-3575
Ph: (918)497-5500
    (918)497-5581
Fax: (918)497-5557

Koster, Rich, Coord.
Christian Universalist Association
[19967]
14 Fairfield Pl.
Fort Thomas, KY 41075
Ph: (269)352-4457

Kosto, Adam J., Officer
American Academy of Research
Historians of Medieval Spain
[9449]
c/o Miguel Gomez, Treasurer
Dept. of History
University of Dayton
300 College Pk.
Dayton, OH 45469

Koszorus, Frank, Jr., President
American Hungarian Federation
[19466]
c/o Tamas Teglassy, Treasurer
1805 Snow Meadow Ln., No. 103
Baltimore, MD 21209

Koten, Mustafa, Program Mgr.
United States-Azerbaijan Chamber
of Commerce **[23627]**
1212 Potomac St. NW
Washington, DC 20007
Ph: (202)333-8702
Fax: (202)333-8703

Kotiadis, Peter, President
Composite Lumber Manufacturers
Association **[1433]**
750 National Press Bldg.
529 14th St. NW
Washington, DC 20045
Ph: (202)591-2451
Fax: (202)591-2445

Kotler, Mindy L., Director
Asia Policy Point **[9621]**
1730 Rhode Island Ave. NW, Ste.
414
Washington, DC 20036
Ph: (202)822-6040
Fax: (202)822-6044

Kotrla, Stacey, President
Women in Corporate Aviation **[6026]**
4450 Nicholas Ln.

Southaven, MS 38672
Ph: (901)277-7078

Kotterman, Mr. Jeff, LMSN, Director
National Association of Sports Nutri-
tion **[16229]**
8898 Clsiremont Mesa Blvd., Ste. J
San Diego, CA 92111
Ph: (858)694-0317

Kotting, Christopher, Exec. Dir.
Energy Information Standards Alli-
ance **[1113]**
275 Tennant Ave., Ste. 202
Morgan Hill, CA 95037
Ph: (408)778-8370
    (614)657-6483
Fax: (408)852-3496

Kotzian, Melinda, CEO
Meso Foundation **[14595]**
1317 King St.
Alexandria, VA 22314
Toll Free: 877-363-6376
Fax: (703)299-0399

Kouidri, David, Exec. Dir.
Swiss-American Business Council
[1995]
PO Box 64975
Chicago, IL 60664-0975
Ph: (312)508-3340

Kountz, David, M.D, Trustee
International Society on Hyperten-
sion in Blacks **[15348]**
2111 Wilson Blvd., Ste. 700
Arlington, VA 22201
Ph: (703)351-5023
Fax: (703)351-9292

Kouri, Janne, Founder, Chmn. of the
Bd.
NextStep Fitness **[17096]**
4447 Redondo Beach Blvd.
Lawndale, CA 90260
Ph: (310)546-5666
Fax: (310)542-8868

Koury, Mike, Chairman
Order of the Indian Wars **[9806]**
PO Box 1650
Johnstown, CO 80534-1650

Kovach, Marge, President
Fellowship of Orthodox Christians in
America **[20591]**
892 Scott St.
Wilkes Barre, PA 18705-3630
Ph: (570)824-0562
Fax: (516)922-0954

Kovacs, Luciano, Secretary
World Student Christian Federation-
North America **[11462]**
475 Riverside Dr., Ste. 700
New York, NY 10115
Ph: (212)870-2470
Fax: (212)870-3220

Kovelan, Linda, Exec. Dir.
National Crop Insurance Services
[1907]
8900 Indian Creek Pky., Ste. 600
Overland Park, KS 66210-1567
Ph: (913)685-2767
Fax: (913)685-3080

Kovesci, Kim, Exec. Dir.
Military Aviation Preservation Society
[20670]
2260 International Pky.
North Canton, OH 44720
Ph: (330)896-6332

Kowal, Rebekah J., VP
Society of Dance History Scholars
[9513]

3416 Primm Ln.
Birmingham, AL 35216
Ph: (205)978-1404
Fax: (205)823-2760

Kowalczyk, Sara, Bd. Member
Narcolepsy Network **[17219]**
46 Union Dr., No. A212
North Kingstown, RI 02852
Ph: (401)667-2523
Toll Free: 888-292-6522
Fax: (401)633-6567

Kowalenko, Don, Chairman
The Evangelical Alliance Mission
[20411]
400 S Main Pl.
Carol Stream, IL 60188
Ph: (630)653-5300
Toll Free: 800-343-3144
Fax: (630)653-1826

Kowalik, Amy, Registrar
American Goat Society **[3593]**
PO Box 63748
Pipe Creek, TX 78063
Ph: (830)535-4247
Fax: (830)535-4561

Kowalke, Kim H., President
Kurt Weill Foundation for Music
[10022]
7 E 20th St., 3rd Fl.
New York, NY 10003
Ph: (212)505-5240
Fax: (212)353-9663

Kowalske, Karen J., MD, Chairman
American Board of Physical
Medicine and Rehabilitation
[17078]
3015 Allegro Park Ln. SW
Rochester, MN 55902-4139
Ph: (507)282-1776
Fax: (507)282-9242

Kowalski, Dennis, President, CEO
Cryonics Institute **[14356]**
24355 Sorrentino Ct.
Clinton Township, MI 48035
Ph: (586)791-5961
Toll Free: 866-288-2796
Fax: (586)792-7062

Kowalski, Gloria, Director
Wireless Technology Association
[6267]
PO Box 680
Hood River, OR 97031-0021
Ph: (541)490-5140
Fax: (413)410-8447

Kowalski, Marina Fischer, Officer
International Society for Ecological
Economics **[1015]**

Kowen, Ken, Treasurer
International Willow Collectors
[21680]
c/o Brenda Nottingham, Membership
Chairperson
969 County Road 3357
Saltillo, TX 75478

Kowlzan, Mark W., Chmn. of the Bd.
American Forest and Paper Associa-
tion **[4193]**
1101 K St., NW, Ste. 700
Washington, DC 20005
Ph: (202)463-2700
Fax: (202)463-2785

Koyamada, Shin, Founder, Chairman
Shin Koyamada Foundation **[13478]**
5532 N Figueroa St., Ste. 220
Los Angeles, CA 90042
Ph: (818)588-9754

Koyle, Jay, President
Associated Parishes for Liturgy and
Mission **[20093]**

3405 Alman Dr.
Durham, NC 27705

Kozar, John E., President, Secretary
Catholic Near East Welfare Associa-
tion [18678]
1011 1st Ave.
New York, NY 10022-4195
Ph: (212)826-1480
Fax: (212)838-1344

Kozar, John E., President
Pontifical Mission for Palestine
[12596]
c/o Catholic Church of the Holy Land
1011 1st Ave.
New York, NY 10022-4195
Ph: (212)826-1480
Fax: (212)838-1344

Kozmetsky, Gregory A., Chairman,
President, Treasurer
RGK Foundation [15656]
1301 W 25th St., Ste. 300
Austin, TX 78705-4248
Ph: (512)474-9298
Fax: (512)474-7281

Kracker, Thomas, VP, Director
Human Resources Research
Organization [6038]
66 Canal Center Plz., Ste. 700
Alexandria, VA 22314-1578
Ph: (703)549-3611
Fax: (703)549-9025

Kraemer, Carol, CCCE, Registrar
Institute of Tax Consultants [5794]
7500 - 212th St. SW, Ste. 205
Edmonds, WA 98026
Ph: (425)774-3521

Krafchik, Warren, Exec. Dir.
International Budget Partnership [36]
820 1st St. NE, Ste. 510
Washington, DC 20002
Ph: (202)408-1080
Fax: (202)408-8173

Krafft, Charles, President
International Penguin Class Dinghy
Association [22638]
1812 Highland Terr.
Glenview, IL 60025

Kraft, Dave, Director
Nuclear Energy Information Service
[18733]
3411 W Diversey Ave., No. 16
Chicago, IL 60647
Ph: (773)342-7650

Kraft, Ethan, President
National Senior Classical League
[9167]
422 Wells Mills Dr.
Oxford, OH 45056
Ph: (701)799-1210

Kraft, Ira, Founder, Treasurer
One Hour for Life [11929]
678 E 3rd Ave., Unit 5
Salt Lake City, UT 84103
Ph: (435)565-1663

Kraft, Phillip R., President, Treasurer
National Veterans Services Fund
[13246]
PO Box 2465
Darien, CT 06820-0465
Toll Free: 800-521-0198

Kraining, Chuck, President
International Association of Confer-
ence Center Administrators [1663]
PO Box 1012
Seabeck, WA 98380

Krajewski, Andrew, Contact
National Association of State
Motorcycle Safety Administrators
[5750]

1434 Trim Tree Rd.
Indiana, PA 15701
Ph: (724)801-8075
Fax: (724)349-5042

Krajicek, Marilyn J., EdD, Director
National Resource Center for Health
and Safety in Child Care and Early
Education [10812]
13120 E 19th Ave., Mail Stop F541
Aurora, CO 80045
Toll Free: 800-598-5437
Fax: (303)724-0960

Krakow, Doron, Exec. VP
American Associates Ben-Gurion
University of the Negev [8128]
1001 Avenue of the Americas, 19th
Fl.
New York, NY 10018-5460
Ph: (212)687-7721
Toll Free: 800-962-2248
Fax: (212)302-6443

Kralka, Peter, Exec. Dir.
American College of Epidemiology
[14727]
1500 Sunday Dr., Ste. 102
Raleigh, NC 27607
Ph: (919)861-5573
Fax: (919)787-4916

Kram, Joan, Exec. Dir.
American Association of Neurosci-
ence Nurses [16093]
8735 W Higgins Rd., Ste. 300
Chicago, IL 60631
Ph: (847)375-4733
Fax: (847)375-6430

Kram, Joan, Exec. Dir.
American Board of Neuroscience
Nursing [16100]
8735 W Higgins Rd., Ste. 300
Chicago, IL 60631
Ph: (847)375-4733
Toll Free: 888-557-2266
Fax: (847)375-6430

Kram, Joan, Exec. Dir.
International Transplant Nurses
Society [16141]
8735 W Higgins Rd., Ste. 300
Chicago, IL 60631
Ph: (847)375-6340
    (847)375-4877
Fax: (847)375-6341

Kramer, Glenn, Director
Lincoln and Continental Owners
Club [21419]
PO Box 1715
Maple Grove, MN 55311-6715
Ph: (763)420-7829
Fax: (763)420-7849

Kramer, Larry D., President
William and Flora Hewlett Founda-
tion [13060]
2121 Sand Hill Rd.
Menlo Park, CA 94025
Ph: (650)234-4500
Fax: (650)234-4501

Kramer, Linda, Liaison
Carriage Operators of North America
[693]
1648 N Hancock St.
Philadelphia, PA 19122-3120
Ph: (215)923-8516

Kramer, Liz, Exec. Dir.
Society for the Study of Psychiatry
and Culture [16838]
c/o Dan Savin, Treasurer
6737 E 5th Ave.
Denver, CO 80220
Ph: (717)848-2978

Kramer, Melinda, Director, Founder
Women's Earth Alliance [3969]
2150 Allston Way, Ste. 460
Berkeley, CA 94704
Ph: (510)859-9106

Kramer, Rob, President
International Game Fish Association
[22846]
IGFA Fishing Hall of Fame and
Museum
300 Gulf Stream Way
Dania Beach, FL 33004
Ph: (954)927-2628
Fax: (954)924-4299

Kramer, Russ, President
American Society of Marine Artists
[8913]
PO Box 557
Carrollton, VA 23314
Ph: (314)241-2339

Kramer, Sasha, Exec. Dir., Founder
Sustainable Organic Integrated
Livelihoods [11448]
124 Church Rd.
Sherburne, NY 13460

Kramer, Thomas, President
International Society for Fall Protec-
tion [16324]
2500 Newmark Dr.
Miamisburg, OH 45342-5407
Ph: (937)259-6350
Toll Free: 877-472-8483
Fax: (937)259-5100

Kramer, Wayne, Founder
Jail Guitar Doors USA [12570]
840 N Fairfax Ave.
Los Angeles, CA 90046

Krank, Lindsey Sterling, Director
Prairie Dog Coalition [10683]
c/o Humane Society of the United
States
2100 L St. NW
Washington, DC 20037
Ph: (301)258-8276

Kranz, Patrica, Exec. Dir.
Overseas Press Club of America
[2715]
40 W 45th St.
New York, NY 10036

Kratochvil, Errean, Secretary,
Treasurer
American Himalayan Rabbit Associa-
tion [4590]
c/o Errean Kratochvil, Secretary-
Treasurer
2159 Bendway Dr.
Port Charlotte, FL 33948
Ph: (727)686-9075

Kraus, Bill, Founder
Cruise Club of America [3375]
PO Box 318
North Pembroke, MA 02358
Toll Free: 800-982-2276
Fax: (781)826-6156

Kraus, D. Bambi, President
National Association of Tribal
Historic Preservation Officers
[9413]
1320 18th St. NW, 2nd Fl.
Washington, DC 20036
Ph: (202)628-8476
Fax: (202)628-2241

Kraus, Jill, Chairman
Public Art Fund [17994]
1 E 53rd St.
New York, NY 10022
Ph: (212)223-7800
Fax: (212)223-7801

Kraus, Rev. Paul D., President
International Association of Christian
Chaplains [19927]
5804 Babcock Rd.
San Antonio, TX 78240-2134
Ph: (210)696-7313

Kraus, Sibella, Founder, President
Sustainable Agriculture Education
[4702]
2150 Allston Way, Ste. 320
Berkeley, CA 94704-1381
Ph: (510)526-1793
Fax: (510)524-7153

Kraus, Timothy R., COO, President
Heavy Duty Manufacturers Associa-
tion [2221]
10 Laboratory Dr.
Research Triangle Park, NC 27709-
3966
Ph: (919)549-4800
    (919)549-4824
Fax: (919)506-1465

Krause, Al, President
International Human Powered
Vehicle Association [7349]
PO Box 357
Cutten, CA 95534-0357
Ph: (707)443-8261
Toll Free: 877-333-1029
Fax: (707)444-2579

Krause, Jeffrey M., CEO
Society of Manufacturing Engineers
[6798]
1 SME Dr.
Dearborn, MI 48128-2408
Ph: (313)425-3000
Toll Free: 800-733-4763
Fax: (313)425-3400

Krausmann, Jim, President
Chrysler 300 Club International
[21353]
PO Box 40
Benson, MD 21018

Krauss, Kate, Managing Dir.
Slow Food USA [3576]
1000 Dean St., Ste. 222
Brooklyn, NY 11238
Ph: (718)260-8000
Toll Free: 877-SLOWFOOD
Fax: (718)260-8068

Krauss, Philip, II, Chairman
International Lutheran Laymen's
League [20304]
660 Mason Ridge Center Dr.
Saint Louis, MO 63141
Ph: (314)317-4100
Toll Free: 800-876-9880

Krausz, Dr. Steve, PhD, Asst. Dir.
Jewish Children's Adoption Network
[10455]
PO Box 147016
Denver, CO 80214-7016
Ph: (303)573-8113
Fax: (303)893-1447

Krautblatt, Chuck, CEO, President
International Fitness Association
[16703]
12472 Lake Underhill Rd., No. 341
Orlando, FL 32828-7144
Ph: (407)579-8610
Toll Free: 800-227-1976

Kravetz, Dan, President, Editor
Gilbert & Sullivan Society of New
York [9182]
c/o Samuel Silvers, Membership
Secretary
117 Broadway, Apt. 28
New York, NY 10027

Kravitz, Rabbi Bentzion, Exec. Dir.
Jews for Judaism [20545]
PO Box 351235
Los Angeles, CA 90035-1235
Ph: (310)556-3344
Toll Free: 800-477-6631
Fax: (310)556-3304

Kravitz, Jeffrey, President
Joseph A. Holmes Safety Associa-
tion [23483]
PO Box 9375
Arlington, VA 22219
Ph: (304)256-3223
Fax: (304)256-3319

Kravitz, Roberta A., Exec. Dir.
International Society for Magnetic
Resonance in Medicine [17058]
2300 Clayton Rd., Ste. 620
Concord, CA 94520
Ph: (510)841-1899
Fax: (510)841-2340

Krcmar, Zuzana, President
Slovak-American Cultural Center
[19647]
PO Box 5395
New York, NY 10185

Krebs, Dee, President
International Association of Forensic
Nurses [16136]
6755 Business Pky., Ste. 303
Elkridge, MD 21075-6740
Ph: (410)626-7805
Fax: (410)626-7804

Krebs, Mitchell, President
Silver Institute [2370]
1400 I St. NW, Ste. 550
Washington, DC 20005
Ph: (202)835-0185
Fax: (202)835-0155

Krebsbach, Sandra, Exec. Dir.
American Technical Education As-
sociation [8660]
Dunwoody College of Technology
818 Dunwoody Blvd.
Minneapolis, MN 55403
Ph: (612)381-3315
(701)671-2301
Fax: (701)671-2260

Kreeger, Daniel, Exec. Dir.
Association of Climate Change Of-
ficers [4035]
1921 Florida Ave. NW
Washington, DC 20009
Ph: (202)496-7390

Kreider, Robert Q., CEO, President
Devereux National [13795]
444 Devereux Dr.
Villanova, PA 19085
Toll Free: 800-345-1292

Kreider, Ryan, Exec. Dir.
Association for the Study of
Nationalities [9290]
420 W 118th St., 12th Fl.
The Harriman Institute
Columbia University
New York, NY 10027

Kreiensieck, Charlene, President
Urological Association of Physician
Assistants [17567]
Two Woodfield Lake
1100 E Woodfield Rd., Ste. 350
Schaumburg, IL 60173

Kreiter, Kathy, Exec. Dir.
American Board of Foot and Ankle
Surgery [16780]
445 Fillmore St.
San Francisco, CA 94117-3404
Ph: (415)553-7800
Fax: (415)553-7801

Krejci, David, Exec. VP, Secretary
Grain Elevator and Processing
Society [1519]
4800 Olson Memorial Hwy.
Golden Valley, MN 55422
Ph: (763)999-4300
Fax: (763)710-5328

Krell, Pam, President
Multiples of America [12365]
2000 Mallory Ln., Ste. 130-600
Franklin, TN 37067-8231
Ph: (248)231-4480

Krenglicki, Mrs. Teresa, President
Polish Singers Alliance of America
[9996]
208 Caesar Blvd.
Williamsville, NY 14221

Krenn, Ms. Susan, Exec. Dir.
Center for Communication Programs
[12509]
111 Market Pl., Ste. 310
Baltimore, MD 21202
Ph: (410)659-6300

Kresin, Susan, Editor
International Association of Teachers
of Czech [9652]
Dept. of Slavic Languages
Brown University
20 Manning Walk, Box E
Providence, RI 02912

Kress, W. John, Director
Heliconia Society International
[4432]
3530 Papalina Rd.
Kalaheo, HI 96741-9599
Ph: (808)332-7324

Kret, Dot, President
Association for Rehabilitation
Programs in Computer Technology
[11575]
Sangren Hall
Educational Leadership, Research
and Technology Dept.
Western Michigan University
Kalamazoo, MI 49008-5275
Ph: (269)387-2053
Fax: (269)387-3696

Kretzmann, Stephen, Exec. Dir.,
Founder
Oil Change International [4029]
714 G St. SE, No. 202
Washington, DC 20003
Ph: (202)518-9029

Kreuzburg, Paula, Exec. VP
Business Solutions Association
[3169]
3601 E Joppa Rd.
Baltimore, MD 21234
Ph: (410)931-8100
Fax: (410)931-8111

Krevans, Sarah, Chmn. of the Bd.
Families Empowered and Supporting
Treatment of Eating Disorders
[14640]
PO Box 331
Warrenton, VA 20188
Ph: (540)227-8518

Krever, Thomas, CEO
Hetrick-Martin Institute [11890]
2 Astor Pl.
New York, NY 10003
Ph: (212)674-2400

Krichbaum, John A., JD, Exec. Dir.,
CEO
American Burn Association [13862]
311 S Wacker Dr., Ste. 4150
Chicago, IL 60606-6671
Ph: (312)642-9260
Fax: (312)642-9130

Krichevsky, Micah I., Director
Bionomics International [7124]
3023 Kramer St.
Silver Spring, MD 20902

Krick, Cecil, Cmdr.
Navy Club of the United States of
America [5616]
PO Box 6051
De Pere, WI 54115-6051
Ph: (765)447-2766
(317)473-5087

Krieger, David, President
Nuclear Age Peace Foundation
[18811]
1622 Anacapa St.
Santa Barbara, CA 93101
Ph: (805)965-3443

Krieger, Lynette, President
The Willa Cather Foundation [9047]
413 N Webster St.
Red Cloud, NE 68970-2466
Ph: (402)746-2653
Toll Free: 866-731-7304
Fax: (402)746-2652

Krig, Matt, President
Cabinet Makers Association [1477]
47 W Polk St., Ste. 100-145
Chicago, IL 60605-2085
Toll Free: 866-562-2512
Fax: (866)645-0468

Kriger, Dr. Kerry M., President
Save the Frogs! [3939]
PO Box 78758
Los Angeles, CA 90016
Ph: (415)878-6525

Krikorian, Mark, Exec. Dir.
Center for Immigration Studies
[18462]
1629 K St. NW, Ste. 600
Washington, DC 20006
Ph: (202)466-8185
Fax: (202)466-8076

Krill, Jennifer, Exec. Dir.
Earthworks [5633]
1612 K St. NW, Ste. 808
Washington, DC 20006
Ph: (202)887-1872
Fax: (202)887-1875

Krimsky, Beth-Ann, President
I Care I Cure Childhood Cancer
Foundation [13986]
PO Box 291386
Davie, FL 33329
Toll Free: 800-807-8013

Kring, Lisa, Treasurer
Association of University Interior
Designers [1939]
c/o Lisa Kring, Treasurer
University of Kansas
1301 Jayhawk Blvd., Rm. 476
Lawrence, KS 66045
Ph: (765)494-9603
Fax: (765)496-1579

Krinsky, Rabbi Yehuda, Chairman
Machne Israel Development Fund
[12227]
770 Eastern Pky.
Brooklyn, NY 11213
Ph: (718)774-4000
Fax: (718)774-2718

Kriss, Holden, President
National Association of Shooting
Ranges [23133]
11 Mile Hill Rd.
Newtown, CT 06470-2359
Ph: (203)426-1320
Fax: (203)426-1087

Krissoff, Mike, Exec. Dir.
Asphalt Emulsion Manufacturers As-
sociation [492]
3 Church Cir., PMB 250
Annapolis, MD 21401
Ph: (410)267-0023
Fax: (410)267-7546

Krissoff, Mike, Exec. Dir.
Asphalt Recycling and Reclaiming
Association [3444]
3 Church Cir.
Annapolis, MD 21401-1933
Ph: (410)267-0023
Fax: (410)267-7546

Kristensen, Hans, President
International Municipal Signal As-
sociation [5748]
597 Haverty Ct., Ste. 100
Rockledge, FL 32955
Ph: (321)392-0500
Toll Free: 800-723-4672
Fax: (321)806-1400

Kristiansen, Marit, Mem.
Sons of Norway [10053]
1455 W Lake St.
Minneapolis, MN 55408-2666
Ph: (612)827-3611
Toll Free: 800-945-8851
Fax: (612)827-0658

Krivda, James, Secretary
American Society of Perfumers
[1449]
PO Box 1256
Piscataway, NJ 08855-1256
Ph: (201)500-6101
Fax: (877)732-0090

Krizek, Eugene L., Exec. Dir., Gen.
Counsel
Christian Relief Services [12642]
8301 Richmond Hwy., Ste. 900
Alexandria, VA 22309
Ph: (703)317-9086
(703)317-9690
Toll Free: 800-33-RELIEF

Krocka, Randall A., Administrator
Sheet Metal Occupational Health
Institute Trust [12844]
8403 Arlington Blvd., Ste. 100
Fairfax, VA 22031
Ph: (703)739-7130

Kroeze, Andrea, Contact
Touch the World [20163]
1 Maple St.
Allendale, NJ 07401
Ph: (201)760-9925
Fax: (201)760-9926

Krofchok, Lorraine, Director
Grandmothers for Peace
International [18748]
PO Box 1292
Elk Grove, CA 95759-1292
Ph: (916)730-6476

Krolikowski, Anne, Exec. Dir.
Certification Board of Infection
Control and Epidemiology [15116]
555 E Wells St., Ste. 1100
Milwaukee, WI 53202
Ph: (414)918-9796
Fax: (414)276-3349

Krolikowski, Anne, Exec. Dir.
Clinical Immunology Society [15377]
555 E Wells St., Ste. 1100
Milwaukee, WI 53202-3823
Ph: (414)224-8095
Fax: (414)272-6070

Kromm, Chris, Exec. Dir., Publisher
Institute for Southern Studies [8798]
PO Box 531

Durham, NC 27702
Ph: (919)419-8311
Fax: (919)419-8315

Kronenberg, Henry H., MD,
  President
Endocrine Society [14705]
2055 L St. NW, Ste. 600
Washington, DC 20036
Ph: (202)971-3636
Toll Free: 888-363-6274
Fax: (202)736-9705

Kroshinsky, Daniela, President
Medical Dermatology Society
  [14501]
526 Superior Ave. E, Ste. 540
Cleveland, OH 44114-1900
Ph: (216)579-9300
Fax: (216)579-9333

Kroupa, Cheryl, Dir. of Mktg.
National Cherry Growers and
  Industries Foundation [4241]
2667 Reed Rd.
Hood River, OR 97031
Ph: (541)386-5761
Fax: (541)386-3191

Krow, Julie, President
National Association of Public Child
  Welfare Administrators [11087]
c/o American Public Human Services
  Association
1133 19th St. NW, Ste. 400
Washington, DC 20036
Ph: (202)682-0100
Fax: (202)204-0071

Krueger, Jack, President
Veterans and Military Families for
  Progress [21151]
PO Box 66353
Washington, DC 20035
Ph: (202)841-1687
   (563)451-9919

Krueger, Jon, Exec. Dir.
Association of Fund-Raising Distribu-
  tors and Suppliers [1467]
1100 Johnson Ferry Rd., Ste. 300
Atlanta, GA 30342
Ph: (404)252-3663
Fax: (404)252-0774

Krueger, Jon, Exec. Dir.
Recreational Vehicle Aftermarket As-
  sociation [2922]
One ParkView Plaza, Ste. 800
Oakbrook Terrace, IL 60181
Ph: (630)596-9004
Fax: (630)544-5055

Krueger, Keith R., CEO
Consortium for School Networking
  [8027]
1025 Vermont Ave. NW, Ste. 1010
Washington, DC 20005-3599
Ph: (202)861-2676
Toll Free: 800-727-1227
Fax: (202)393-2011

Krueger, Steven, President
Catholic Democrats [18108]
PO Box 6262
Boston, MA 02114-0016
Ph: (617)817-8617

Krug, Larry L., President
Association of Collecting Clubs
  [21626]
18222 Flower Hill Way, No. 299
Gaithersburg, MD 20879
Ph: (301)926-8663

Krug, Susan, CAE, Exec. Dir.
American Medical Writers Association [2651]

30 W Gude Dr., Ste. 525
Rockville, MD 20850-4347
Ph: (240)238-0940
Fax: (301)294-9006

Kruger, Kevin, President
NASPA - Student Affairs Administra-
  tors in Higher Education [7431]
111 K St. NE, 10th Fl.
Washington, DC 20002
Ph: (202)265-7500

Kruger, Nancy, Dep. Dir.
National Association of Clean Air
  Agencies [5183]
444 N Capitol St. NW, Ste. 307
Washington, DC 20001
Ph: (202)624-7864
Fax: (202)624-7863

Kruger, Ruth, President
FIABCI-USA [2860]
1050 Connecticut Ave. NW, Ste.
  1000
Washington, DC 20036
Ph: (202)772-3308

Krule, Lawrence J., President
Jewish Book Council [9130]
520 8th Ave., 4th Fl.
New York, NY 10018
Ph: (212)201-2920
Fax: (212)532-4952

Krumholz, Sheila, Exec. Dir.
Center for Responsive Politics
  [18907]
1101 14th St. NW, Ste. 1030
Washington, DC 20005-5635
Ph: (202)857-0044
Fax: (202)857-7809

Krumich, Mr. John, Art Dir.
American Children of SCORE [9853]
PO Box 3423
Warrenton, VA 20188
Ph: (540)428-2313

Krusack, Sue, President
Prairie Club [12578]
12 E Willow St., Unit A
Lombard, IL 60148-2681
Ph: (630)620-9334
Fax: (630)620-9335

Kruse, Caroline, Exec. Dir.
Platelet Disorder Support Associa-
  tion [13789]
8751 Brecksville Rd., Ste. 150
Cleveland, OH 44141
Ph: (440)746-9003
Toll Free: 877-528-3538
Fax: (844)270-1277

Kruse, Karissa, President
Sonoma County Winegrape Com-
  mission [4934]
400 Aviation Blvd., Ste. 500
Santa Rosa, CA 95403
Ph: (707)522-5860

Kubic, Micah, Chairman
People to People International
  [18554]
2405 Grand Blvd., Ste. 500
Kansas City, MO 64105-5305
Ph: (816)531-4701
Toll Free: 800-676-7874
Fax: (816)561-7502

Kubicki, Rev. James M., SJ, Director
Apostleship of Prayer [19792]
1501 S Layton Blvd.
Milwaukee, WI 53215-1924
Ph: (414)486-1152
Fax: (414)486-1159

Kuchern, Dana, President
National Association of Fellowships
  Advisors [8516]

c/o Alicia Hayes, Secretary
University of California, Berkeley
5 Durant Hall, No.2940
Berkeley, CA 94720-2940

Kueppers, Mark, Asst. Dir.
National Center for Student Leader-
  ship [8624]
2718 Dryden Dr.
Madison, WI 53704
Toll Free: 800-433-0499
Fax: (608)246-3597

Kugler, Ellen, Esq., Exec. Dir.
National Association of Urban
  Hospitals [15334]
21351 Gentry Dr., Ste. 210
Sterling, VA 20166
Ph: (703)444-0989
Fax: (703)444-3029

Kuhar, Bogomir M., Bd. Member,
  Exec. Dir.
Pharmacists for Life International
  [12787]
PO Box 1281
Powell, OH 43065-1281
Ph: (740)881-5520
Toll Free: 800-227-8359
Fax: (740)206-1260

Kuhlmann, Hank, President
CAS Collectors [21578]
2000 Wisconsin Ave. N
Golden Valley, MN 55427-3363

Kuhn, Heidi, Chairperson, Founder
Roots of Peace [18826]
990 A St., Ste. 402
San Rafael, CA 94901
Ph: (415)455-8008
Toll Free: 888-766-8731
Fax: (415)455-9086

Kuhn, Jennifer, President
Break the Cycle [11697]
PO Box 811334
Los Angeles, CA 90081
Ph: (310)286-3383
Toll Free: 888-988-TEEN
Fax: (310)286-3386

Kuhns, Martha, President
Women's Overseas Service League
  [21156]
PO Box 124
Cedar Knolls, NJ 07927-0124

Kuijsten, Marcel, Exec. Dir.
Julian Jaynes Society [16922]
PO Box 778153
Henderson, NV 89077-8153

Kujanson, Jude, Admin. Sec.
U.S. Soling Association [22686]
Ph: (704)264-0996

Kulakowski, Elliott, CEO
Society of Research Administrators
  [7097]
500 N Washington St., Ste. 300
Falls Church, VA 22046
Ph: (703)741-0140
Fax: (703)741-0142

Kuletz, Kathy, Chairman
Pacific Seabird Group [4864]
PO Box 61493
Honolulu, HI 96839-1493

Kulish, Tim, VP
Desert German Shorthaired Pointer
  Club [21868]
2026 N 7th St.
Phoenix, AZ 85006
Ph: (480)862-6896

Kullman, Joyce A., Exec. Dir.
Vasculitis Foundation [17352]
PO Box 28660

Kansas City, MO 64188-8660
Ph: (816)436-8211
Toll Free: 800-277-9474
Fax: (816)656-3838

Kullman, Maureen Mack, President
American Tarentaise Association
  [3714]
9150 N 216th St.
Elkhorn, NE 68022
Ph: (402)639-9808

Kulukulualani, Anthony, President
Student National Medical Association
  [8338]
5113 Georgia Ave. NW
Washington, DC 20011-3921
Ph: (202)882-2881
Fax: (202)882-2886

Kulwatdanaporn, Somchai, MD,
  Comm. Chm.
Thai Physicians Association of
  America [16762]
c/o Chintana Paramagul, MD,
  President
4972 Starak Ln.
Ann Arbor, MI 48105
Ph: (734)604-6211

Kum, Kyenan, Founder
International Aid for Korean Animals
  [10646]
PO Box 20600
Oakland, CA 94620
Ph: (510)271-6795

Kumanyika, Shiriki K., PhD,
  Founder, Chairperson
African American Collaborative
  Obesity Research Network [16244]
University of Pennsylvania
Perelman School of Medicine
415 Curie Blvd.
Philadelphia, PA 19104

Kumar, Sachit, President
Council of International Investigators
  [2009]
PO Box 565
Elmhurst, IL 60126-0565
Ph: (630)501-1880
Toll Free: 888-759-8884

Kumar, Dr. Satish, President
International Society of Coating Sci-
  ence and Technology [6226]
Dept. of Chemical Engineering and
  Materials Science
University of Minnesota
151 Amundson Hall
421 Washington Ave. SE
Minneapolis, MN 55455-0132

Kummerow, Jean M.
Center for Applications of
  Psychological Type [16910]
2815 NW 13th St., Ste. 401
Gainesville, FL 32609-2878
Ph: (352)375-0160
Toll Free: 800-777-2278
Fax: (352)378-0503

Kumpikas, Giedre M., PhD, Bd.
  Member
Lithuanian National Foundation
  [18423]
307 W 30th St.
New York, NY 10001-2703
Ph: (212)868-5860
Fax: (212)868-5815

Kungys, Salvijus, Administrator
Lithuanian Catholic Religious Aid
  [19857]
64-25 Perry Ave.
Maspeth, NY 11378-2441
Ph: (718)326-5202
Fax: (718)326-5206

Kunin, Gr. Mast. Alexey, Advisor
All Japan Ju-Jitsu International
   Federation [22979]
11677 San Vicente Blvd., Ste. 202
Los Angeles, CA 90049

Kunin, Richard A., MD, President
Society for Orthomolecular Health
   Medicine [13657]
3637 Sacramento St., Ste. C
San Francisco, CA 94118-1726
Ph: (415)922-6462
Fax: (415)346-2519

Kunkle, Randall, VP
National Council on Agricultural Life
   and Labor Research Fund [11979]
363 Saulsbury Rd.
Dover, DE 19904
Ph: (302)678-9400
Fax: (302)678-9058

Kunstadter, Geraldine S., Chairman
Network 20/20, Inc. [18632]
850 7th Ave., Ste. 1101
New York, NY 10019
Ph: (212)582-1870
Fax: (212)586-3291

Kunz, Elizabeth, CEO
Girls on the Run International
   [23117]
801 E Morehead St., Ste. 201
Charlotte, NC 28202
Ph: (704)376-9817
Toll Free: 800-901-9965
Fax: (704)376-1039

Kupper, Cynthia, CEO
Gluten Intolerance Group [16223]
31214 124th Ave. SE
Auburn, WA 98092-3667
Ph: (253)833-6655
Fax: (253)833-6675

Kuprys, Saulius V., Esq., President
Lithuanian American Council [19542]
6500 S Pulaski Rd., Ste. 200
Chicago, IL 60629
Ph: (773)735-6677
Fax: (773)735-3946

Kupsick, Phyllis, President
Wound, Ostomy and Continence
   Nurses Society [16192]
1120 Route 73, Ste. 200
Mount Laurel, NJ 08054
Toll Free: 888-224-9626
Fax: (856)439-0525

Kurica, Ken, Founder
Finding Refuge [10974]
5390 Academy Bldg.
Colorado Springs, CO 80918
Ph: (480)442-6219
Fax: (719)227-0238

Kurland, Norman G., President
Center for Economic and Social
   Justice [18166]
PO Box 40711
Washington, DC 20016
Ph: (703)243-5155
Fax: (703)243-5935

Kurps, Rev. Jack, Director
Sacred Heart League [19902]
6050 Highway 161
Walls, MS 38680
Toll Free: 800-232-9079

Kurrle, Diane, Sr. VP
U.S. Apple Association [4255]
8233 Old Courthouse Rd., Ste. 200
Vienna, VA 22182
Ph: (703)442-8850
Fax: (703)790-0845

Kurtz, Rev. Joseph, President
United States Conference of
   Catholic Bishops [19917]

3211 4th St. NE
Washington, DC 20017
Ph: (202)541-3000

Kurtz, Paul, Founder
Committee for Skeptical Inquiry
   [6985]
Box 703
Amherst, NY 14226
Ph: (716)636-1425
Toll Free: 800-634-1610

Kurtz, Polly, Exec. Dir.
Collaborative Family Healthcare As-
   sociation [14989]
PO Box 23980
Rochester, NY 14692-3980
Ph: (585)482-8210
Fax: (585)482-2901

Kurtzberg, Joanne, MD, President
Cord Blood Association [13840]
211 Garfield St.
Geneva, IL 60134-2313
Ph: (630)463-9040

Kury, Linda, President
American German Shepherd Rescue
   Association, Inc. [10568]
c/o Linda Kury, President
PO Box 7113
Clearlake, CA 95422
Ph: (707)994-5241

Kury, Nader, President
Birzeit Society [8815]
PO Box 1822
Norwalk, CA 90651
Ph: (714)991-1943
   (510)786-8247

Kurzak, Mary Beth, Exec. Dir.
International Association of Defense
   Counsel [5011]
303 W Madison St., Ste. 925
Chicago, IL 60606
Ph: (312)368-1494
Fax: (312)368-1854

Kusel, Hilary, Exec. Dir.
Green Business Alliance [4066]
925 S Federal Hwy., Ste. 750
Boca Raton, FL 33432
Ph: (561)361-6766
Fax: (561)431-7835

Kushiner, James M., Exec. Ed.
Fellowship of Saint James [19980]
PO Box 410788
Chicago, IL 60641
Ph: (773)481-1090

Kushner, Marina, Founder
Caffeine Awareness Association
   [17309]
93 S Jackson St.
Seattle, WA 98104
Ph: (888)710-5870

Kushner, Melissa, Exec. Dir.,
   Founder
Goods for Good [11007]
45 Main St., Ste. 518
Brooklyn, NY 11201
Ph: (646)963-6076

Kushnick, Bruce, Chairman
TeleTruth: The Alliance for Customers' Telecommunications Rights
   [18061]
568 Broadway, Ste. 404
New York, NY 10012
Toll Free: 800-780-1939

Kutcipal, Rick, President
SCSI Trade Association [1807]
Presidio of San Francisco
572-B Ruger St.

San Francisco, CA 94129
Ph: (415)561-6273
Fax: (415)561-6120

Kuter, Lois, President
American Association for Museum
   Volunteers [9816]
PO Box 9494
Washington, DC 20016-9494
Ph: (215)299-1029

Kuter, Lois, Editor, Secretary,
   Treasurer
International Committee for the
   Defense of the Breton Language,
   US Branch [9653]
c/o Lois Kuter, Secretary
605 Montgomery Rd.
Ambler, PA 19002
Ph: (215)886-6361

Kutsch, Dr. James A., Jr., CEO,
   President
Seeing Eye [17744]
10 Washington Valley Rd.
Morristown, NJ 07960-3412
Ph: (973)539-4425
Fax: (973)539-0922

Kutsko, John, Exec. Dir.
Society of Biblical Literature [19765]
Luce Ctr.
825 Houston Mill Rd.
Atlanta, GA 30329
Ph: (404)727-3100
Fax: (404)727-3101

Kutzik, Jordan, Chairman
Yugntruf - Youth for Yiddish [9646]
419 Lafayette St., 2nd Fl.
New York, NY 10003
Ph: (212)796-5782

Kuykendall, Ron, Contact
Coalition to Insure Against Terrorism
   [1847]
1875 I St. NW, Ste. 600
Washington, DC 20006-5413
Ph: (202)739-9454

Kuyper, Mark W., CEO, President
Evangelical Christian Publishers As-
   sociation [2785]
9633 S 48th St., Ste. 195
Phoenix, AZ 85044
Ph: (480)966-3998
Fax: (480)966-1944

Kuzma, Timothy L., CEO, President
Polish Falcons of America [19609]
381 Mansfield Ave.
Pittsburgh, PA 15220
Ph: (412)922-2244
Toll Free: 800-535-2071
Fax: (412)922-5029

Kuzmanovich, Zoran, Editor, VP
International Vladimir Nabokov
   Society [9083]
Davidson College
English Dept.
Davidson, NC 28036

Kwast, Karla B., CEO, Exec. Dir.
Blind Children's Fund [17690]
PO Box 187
Grand Ledge, MI 48837
Ph: (989)779-9966
Fax: (269)756-3133

Kwaterski, Mr. Jeffrey, Director
Impact Alliance [12162]
1350 610 8th St. NE
Washington, DC 20002
Ph: (202)470-5566

Kwemain, Roland, President
Junior Chamber International, Inc.
   [12891]

15645 Olive Blvd., Ste. A
Chesterfield, MO 63017-1722
Ph: (636)778-3010
Fax: (636)449-3107

Kwentua, Victor, Secretary
Asaba National Association, USA,
   Inc. [19286]
PO Box 1627
Sugar Land, TX 77487-1627
Ph: (678)860-9602

Kwon, Daniel J., Contact
A Cup of Water International, Inc.
   [4755]
PO Box 9809
Kansas City, MO 64134
Ph: (267)242-1798

Kwon, Steven, Founder, President
Nutrition and Education International
   [12105]
2500 E Foothill Blvd., Ste. 407
Pasadena, CA 91107
Ph: (626)744-0270
Fax: (626)316-6067

Kwon, Sung, Exec. Dir.
Adventist Community Services
   [20600]
12501 Old Columbia Pke.
Silver Spring, MD 20904
Ph: (301)680-6438
Toll Free: 877-ACS-2702
Fax: (301)680-6125

Kyger, Alliena, President
Miracle Wings Foundation [10775]
PO Box 9841
Springfield, MO 65801
Ph: (417)576-5471

Kyi, Sandar, MD, President
Burmese American Medical Associa-
   tion [15719]
339 Sharon Rd.
Arcadia, CA 91007
Ph: (626)244-4744

Kyj, Larissa, President
United Ukrainian American Relief
   Committee Inc. [19682]
1206 Cottman Ave.
Philadelphia, PA 19111
Ph: (215)728-1630
Fax: (215)728-1631

Kynaston, Shar, Treasurer
The Bulldog Club of America Rescue
   Network, Inc. [10596]
c/o Shar Kynaston
PO Box 1049
Kaysville, UT 84037
Ph: (801)546-0265

L

L., Shannon, Founder, President
Pandora's Project [12932]
3109 W 50th St., Ste. 320
Minneapolis, MN 55410-2102
Ph: (612)234-4204

La Forgia, Barry, Exec. Dir., Founder
International Relief Teams [12686]
4560 Alvarado Canyon Rd., Ste. 2G
San Diego, CA 92120
Ph: (619)284-7979
Fax: (619)284-7938

La, Kirk, Chairman
Boat Owners Association of the
   United States [22601]
880 S Pickett St.
Alexandria, VA 22304-4606
Toll Free: 800-395-2628

Laabs, Mrs. Heidi, President
Irish Setter Club of America [21901]

c/o Mary Goeke, Membership Chairman
31557 Lookout Rd.
Paola, KS 66071-4900
Ph: (913)271-7554

Laabs, Jonathan C., EdD, Exec. Dir.
Lutheran Education Association
[20308]
7400 Augusta St.
River Forest, IL 60305
Ph: (708)209-3343
Fax: (708)209-3458

Laatsch, Ann, Chairperson
Heshima Kenya, Inc. [11031]
1111 N Wells St., Ste. 306
Chicago, IL 60610
Ph: (312)985-5667

Laatsch, Shawn, President
International Planetarium Society
[6007]
c/o Ann Bragg, Treasurer
Marietta College
215 5th St.
Marietta, OH 45750
Ph: (407)376-4589

LaBahn, David, President, CEO
Association of Prosecuting Attorneys
[4999]
1615 L St. NW, Ste. 1100
Washington, DC 20036
Ph: (202)861-2480
Fax: (202)223-4688

Labeau, Fabrice, VP
IEEE - Vehicular Technology Society
[6434]
3 Park Ave., 17th Fl.
New York, NY 10016-5997
Ph: (212)419-7900
Fax: (212)752-4929

Laberge, Guy, Chairman
Organic Crop Improvement Association [4167]
1340 N Cotner Blvd.
Lincoln, NE 68505-1838
Ph: (402)477-2323
Fax: (402)477-4325

LaBert, Dan, Exec. Dir.
National Association of Consumer
Bankruptcy Attorneys [5028]
2200 Pennsylvania Ave. NW, 4th Fl.
Washington, DC 20037
Toll Free: 800-499-9040
Fax: (866)408-9515

LaBlonde, Charles J., Secretary
Civil Censorship Study Group
[22320]
c/o Charles J. LaBlonde, Secretary
15091 Ridgefield Ln.
Colorado Springs, CO 80921

LaBombard, Jodi, Secretary
Mastiff Club of America [21913]
c/o Jodi LaBombard, Recording
Secretary
189 Miranda Ln.
Roxboro, NC 27574-6602

Laborde, Patricia, President
National Association of Settlement
Purchasers [1255]
720 Collier Dr.
Dixon, CA 95620

Labov, Teresa G.
Sociologists' AIDS Network [13561]
c/o Neal Carnes, Treasurer
3813 Cooper Ln.
Indianapolis, IN 46228

LaBrie, Terri, President
National Council of State Agricultural
Finance Programs [4182]

c/o Terri LaBrie, President
South Dakota Department of
Agriculture
523 E Capitol Ave.
Pierre, SD 57501
Ph: (605)773-4026
Fax: (605)773-3481

Labun, Carolyn, Secretary
IEEE - Professional Communication
Society [6432]
445 Hoes Ln.
Piscataway, NJ 08854-6804
Ph: (732)981-0060
Toll Free: 800-678-4333
Fax: (732)981-0225

LaCagnin, Stephen Michael, Chairman
Wellness Council of America [15163]
17002 Marcy St., Ste. 140
Omaha, NE 68118-2933
Ph: (402)827-3590
Fax: (402)827-3594

Lacayo, Dr. Carmela G., President,
CEO
National Association for Hispanic
Elderly [19462]
234 E Colorado Blvd., Ste. 300
Pasadena, CA 91101
Ph: (626)564-1988

LaCelle-Peterson, Mark, Sr. VP
American Association of Colleges for
Teacher Education [8635]
1307 New York Ave. NW, Ste. 300
Washington, DC 20005-4721
Ph: (202)293-2450
Fax: (202)457-8095

Lacey, Catherine, VP
American Resort Development Association [2848]
1201 15th St. NW, Ste. 400
Washington, DC 20005
Ph: (202)371-6700
Fax: (202)289-8544

Lacey, Christine, Founder
Autism Alert [13741]
PO Box 282
Deerfield, WI 53531
Ph: (608)628-7852

Lacey, Eileen, President
American Society of Mammalogists
[6790]
c/o Christy Classi, CAE
PO Box 4973
Topeka, KS 66604
Ph: (785)550-6904

Lacey, Marilyn, Chairperson, Exec.
Dir.
Mercy Beyond Borders [12552]
1885 De La Cruz Blvd., Ste. 101
Santa Clara, CA 95050-3000
Ph: (650)815-1554

Lachance, Janice, VP
American Society for Public
Administration [5693]
1370 Rhode Island Ave. NW, Ste.
500
Washington, DC 20036
Ph: (202)393-7878
Fax: (202)638-4952

Lachapelle, Pete, Publisher
National Association of Pizzeria
Operators [1669]
c/o Pizza Today
908 S 8th St., Ste. 200
Louisville, KY 40203
Ph: (502)736-9500

Lachs, Joshua, Exec. Dir.
Breakthrough Collaborative [7746]
180 Grand Ave., Ste. 1225

Oakland, CA 94612
Ph: (415)442-0600
Fax: (415)442-9371

Lackey, Sam, Secretary, Treasurer
William Gilmore Simms Society
[10399]
c/o Dr. Todd Hagstette, Secretary-
Treasurer
South Caroliniana Library
University of South Carolina
910 Sumter St.
Columbia, SC 29208-1760

LaCorte, John N., PhD, Exec. Dir.
Italian Historical Society of America
[9617]
410 Park Ave., Ste. 1530
New York, NY 10022

Lacritz, Laura, Ph.D., President
National Academy of Neuropsychology [16925]
7555 E Hampden Ave., Ste. 525
Denver, CO 80231- 4836
Ph: (303)691-3694
Fax: (303)691-5983

LaCroix, Nancy, President
International Handgun Metallic
Silhouette Association [23132]

Lacy, Scott M., PhD, Exec. Dir.
African Sky [11308]
PO Box 203
Munroe Falls, OH 44262

Ladd, Holly, JD, Exec. Dir.
SATELLIFE Global Health Information Network [15062]
30 California St.
Watertown, MA 02472-2539
Ph: (617)926-9400
Fax: (617)926-1212

Ladd, Paula Aruputhasamy, Esq.,
President
Lambda Psi Delta Sorority, Inc.
[23975]
PO Box 734
Old Saybrook, CT 06475

Ladd, Virginia, RT, Exec. Dir.,
President
American Autoimmune Related
Diseases Association, Inc. [15370]
22100 Gratiot Ave.
Eastpointe, MI 48021
Ph: (586)776-3900
Toll Free: 800-598-4668
Fax: (586)776-3903

LaDuke, Winona, Exec. Dir.
Honor the Earth [19579]
607 Main Ave.
Callaway, MN 56521
Ph: (218)375-3200
Fax: (218)375-2603

Laepple, Klaus, Chmn. of the Bd.
German National Tourist Office
[3377]
122 E 42nd St., Ste. 2000
New York, NY 10168-0072
Ph: (212)661-4796
Fax: (212)661-7174

Lafever, Howard B., President
American Academy of Environmental
Engineers and Scientists [6526]
147 Old Solomons Rd., Ste. 303
Annapolis, MD 21401
Ph: (410)266-3311
Fax: (410)266-7653

Lafferty, James, President
Office of the Americas [17843]
2016 Hill St.

Santa Monica, CA 90405
Ph: (310)450-1185

Lafferty, Marty, CEO
Distributed Computing Industry Association [6313]
2838 Cox Neck Rd., Ste. 200
Chester, MD 21619
Ph: (410)476-7965
Fax: (410)643-3585

LaFianza, Javier, CEO
Hugh O'Brian Youth Leadership
[8203]
31255 Cedar Valley Dr., Ste. 327
Westlake Village, CA 91362-7140
Ph: (818)851-3980
Fax: (818)851-3999

Laflamme, Louis, President
First Issues Collectors Club [22328]
c/o Kurt Streepy, Secretary and
Treasurer
3128 Mattatha Dr.
Bloomington, IN 47401

LaFlamme, Pete, VP
Association of Clean Water
Administrators [5176]
1634 Eye St. NW, Ste. No. 750
Washington, DC 20006
Ph: (202)756-0605
Fax: (202)756-0600

LaFleur, Amanda, Exec. Dir.
National Association for
Premenstrual Dysphoric Disorder
[16296]
PO Box 102361
Denver, CO 80250
Toll Free: 800-609-7633

LaFrance, David B., Secretary, CEO
American Water Works Association
[3457]
6666 W Quincy Ave.
Denver, CO 80235
Ph: (303)794-7711
Toll Free: 800-926-7337
Fax: (303)347-0804

Lagan, Paul, President
Alliance for Life Ministries [19940]
PO Box 5102
Madison, WI 53705

Lagas, Sharon, President
Alport Syndrome Foundation [15868]
1608 E Briarwood Terr.
Phoenix, AZ 85048-9414
Ph: (480)800-3510

LaGasse, Alfred, CEO
Taxicab, Limousine & Paratransit
Association [3357]
3200 Tower Oaks Blvd., Ste. 220
Rockville, MD 20852
Ph: (301)984-5700
Fax: (301)984-5703

Lage, Susan, President
American College of Osteopathic
Neurologists and Psychiatrists
[16003]
28595 Orchard Lake Rd., Ste. 200
Farmington Hills, MI 48334
Ph: (248)553-6207
Fax: (248)553-6222

Lahdenpera, V. Kay, RN, Exec. Dir.
American Qigong Association
[13598]
117 Topaz Way
San Francisco, CA 94131
Ph: (415)285-9400
Fax: (415)647-5745

Lai, Lambert, Exec.
United States J/24 Class Association
[22681]

12900 Lake Ave., No. 2001
Lakewood, OH 44107
Ph: (617)285-9455

Laine, Steven, Chairman
TechServe Alliance [823]
1420 King St., Ste. 610
Alexandria, VA 22314
Ph: (703)838-2050
Fax: (703)838-3610

Laird, Holly
D.H. Lawrence Society of North
   America [9072]
c/o Matthew Leone, Treasurer
45 Broad St.
Hamilton, NY 13346

Lais, Greg, Exec. Dir.
Wilderness Inquiry [22722]
808 14th Ave. SE
Minneapolis, MN 55414-1516
Ph: (612)676-9400
Fax: (612)676-9401

Laister, Mary Ellen, Mem.
General Federation of Women's
   Clubs [19691]
1734 N St. NW
Washington, DC 20036-2990
Ph: (202)347-3168
Fax: (202)835-0246

Laitner, John, President
Association for Environmental Stud-
   ies and Sciences [7885]
1101 17th St. NW, Ste. 250
Washington, DC 20036
Fax: (202)628-4311

LaJoie, Randy, Founder
The Safer Racer Tour [12843]
4537 Orphanage Rd.
Concord, NC 28027
Ph: (704)795-7474

Lajoye, Dane, President
Boston Terrier Club of America
   [21846]
c/o Margaret Noble, Corresponding
   Secretary
233 E 69th St., Unit 7D
New York, NY 10021-5447
Ph: (212)452-2324

Lake, Anthony, Exec. Dir.
UNICEF [12733]
125 Maiden Ln., 11th Fl.
New York, NY 10038
Ph: (212)686-5522
Fax: (212)779-1679

Lake, Sara, Exec. Dir.
International Board of Lactation
   Consultant Examiners [13855]
10301 Democracy Ln., Ste. 400
Fairfax, VA 22030
Ph: (703)560-7330
Fax: (703)560-7332

Lakhan, Shaheen E., Exec. Dir.
Global Neuroscience Initiative
   Foundation [16047]
9776 Peavine Dr.
Beverly Hills, CA 90210
Ph: (206)339-8274
Fax: (206)339-8274

Lallier, Janette M., Dir. of Admin.
Unitarian Universalist Ministers As-
   sociation [20629]
24 Farnsworth St.
Boston, MA 02210-1409
Ph: (617)848-0498
Fax: (617)848-0973

Lam, Jonathan Hoang, MD,
   President
Vietnamese Medical Association of
   the U.S.A. [15749]

1926 SW Green Oaks Blvd.
Arlington, TX 76017
Ph: (687)667-1016

Lam, Shau-Wai, Co-Chmn. of the
   Bd.
Coalition of Asian American Busi-
   ness Organizations [679]
Ronald Reagan Bldg. & International
   Trade Ctr.
1300 Pennsylvania Ave. NW, No.
   700
Washington, DC 20004
Ph: (202)204-3019

Lamar, Judy, President
Filipino American Real Estate
   Professionals Association [2861]
PO Box 261083
Milpitas, CA 95035
Ph: (408)934-8202

Lamar, Nancy, Treasurer, Secretary
Crossdressers International [12943]
404 W 40th St., Apt. 2
New York, NY 10018
Ph: (212)564-4847

LaMarche, Mary, President
Women in Municipal Government
   [5649]
c/o National League of Cities
1301 Pennsylvania Ave. NW, Ste.
   550
Washington, DC 20004-1747
Ph: (202)626-3169

Lamarra, Norberto Fernandez, VP
World Council of Comparative
   Education Societies [7649]
Moore Hall 2018
405 Hilgard Ave.
Los Angeles, CA 90095-1521

Lamb, Joann, Secretary
National Birman Fanciers [21572]
c/o Joann Lamb, Secretary
7 Cornwall Ct.
Hamburg, NJ 07419-1359

Lamb, Lori L., Mem.
National Alternative Education As-
   sociation [7489]
PO Box 22185
Chattanooga, TN 37422

Lamberson, Zeta, President
Association of Presbyterian Church
   Educators [20018]
404 BNA Dr., Ste. 650
Nashville, TN 37217
Ph: (615)953-4648
Toll Free: 855-566-5657

Lambert, David, Treasurer
Environmental Bankers Association
   [395]
Bldg. 14, Ste. 100
1827 Powers Ferry Rd.
Atlanta, GA 30339
Ph: (678)619-5045
Fax: (678)229-2777

Lambert, David, Exec. Sec.
Phi Beta Mu [23830]
c/o David Lambert, Executive
   Secretary
3323 Meadowcreek Dr.
Missouri City, TX 77459

Lambert, Kent, President
American Academy of Health Phys-
   ics [17429]
c/o Nancy Johnson
1313 Dolley Madison Blvd., Ste. 402
McLean, VA 22101
Ph: (703)790-1745
Fax: (703)790-2672

Lambert, Lanneau W., Jr., President
National Conference of Bar
   Presidents [5034]
Division for Bar Services
321 N Clark St., 16th Fl.
Chicago, IL 60654
Ph: (803)227-4248
Fax: (803)400-1523

LAMBERT MESSERLIAN, GERA-
   LYN, Secretary, Treasurer
Women in Endocrinology [14710]
c/o Dana Gaddy, PhD, President
University of Arkansas for Medical
   Sciences
4301 W Markham St., Slot 505
Little Rock, AR 72205
Ph: (501)686-5918
Fax: (501)686-8167

Lamberth, David, Exec. Dir.
American Historic Racing Motorcycle
   Association [22210]
c/o David Lamberth, Executive
   Director
309 Buffalo Run
Goodlettsville, TN 37072
Ph: (615)420-6435
Fax: (615)420-6438

Lamberton, Jack C., President
U.S.A. Deaf Sports Federation
   [22803]
PO Box 22011
Lexington, KY 40591-0338

Lamborn, Jason, Comm. Chm.
Air Diffusion Council [1612]
1901 N Roselle Rd., Ste. 800
Schaumburg, IL 60195
Ph: (847)706-6750
Fax: (847)706-6751

Lamesch, Fernand, Chairman
Luxembourg-American Chamber of
   Commerce [23601]
17 Beekman Pl.
New York, NY 10022
Ph: (212)888-6701
Fax: (212)935-5896

Lamie, David, President
Community Development Society
   [17973]
17 S High St., Ste. 200
Columbus, OH 43215
Ph: (614)221-1900
Fax: (614)221-1989

Lamiell, James, President
APA Division 26: Society for the History of Psychology [16878]
c/o Cathy Faye, Council Representative
University of Akron
73 College St.
Akron, OH 44325-4302
Ph: (202)336-6121

Lamielle, Mary, Exec. Dir.
National Center for Environmental
   Health Strategies [14718]
c/o Mary Lamielle, Executive Direc-
   tor
1100 Rural Ave.
Voorhees, NJ 08043-2234
Ph: (856)429-5358

Lamm, Carolyn B., Chmn. of the Bd.
American-Uzbekistan Chamber of
   Commerce [23555]
1030 15th St. NW, Ste. 555W
Washington, DC 20005
Ph: (202)223-1770
   (202)509-3744

Lamm, Dr. Maurice, Founder,
   President
National Institute for Jewish Hospice
   [15298]

732 University St.
North Woodmere, NY 11581
Ph: (516)791-9888
Toll Free: 800-446-4448

Lammert, Catherine, RN, President
Pregnancy Loss and Infant Death
   Alliance [10776]
PO Box 658
Parker, CO 80134
Toll Free: 888-693-1435
Fax: (866)705-9251

Lamond, Joe, CEO, President
NAMM Foundation [9962]
5790 Armada Dr.
Carlsbad, CA 92008

Lamond, Joe, CEO, President
NAMM, the International Music
   Products Association [2431]
5790 Armada Dr.
Carlsbad, CA 92008
Ph: (760)438-8001
Toll Free: 800-767-6266
Fax: (760)438-7327

LaMonica, John, President
Congress of Chiropractic State As-
   sociations [14262]
12531 E Meadow Dr.
Wichita, KS 67206
Ph: (316)613-3386
Fax: (316)633-4455

Lamstein, Joel H., President
World Education [7456]
44 Farnsworth St.
Boston, MA 02210
Ph: (617)482-9485
Fax: (617)482-0617

Lancaster, Giovanna, Administrator
Association of Clinical Research
   Professionals [16652]
99 Canal Center Plz., Ste. 200
Alexandria, VA 22314
Ph: (703)254-8100
Fax: (703)254-8101

Lancaster, Janice, Secretary
National Alliance of Burmese Breeders [3681]
c/o Janice Lancaster, Secretary
91 Maner Rd.
Rockmart, GA 30153

Lancaster, Joyce, Exec. Sec.
Weed Science Society of America
   [3556]
810 E 10th St.
Lawrence, KS 66044
Ph: (785)865-9520
Toll Free: 800-627-0326

Lance, Peter M., Exec. Dir.
Gasket Fabricators Association
   [1732]
994 Old Eagle School Rd., Ste.
   1019
Wayne, PA 19087-1866
Ph: (610)971-4850

Land, Ronnie, Exec. Dir.
International Association for Truancy
   and Dropout Prevention [7822]
c/o Ronnie Land, Executive Director
409 Mockingbird Ln.
Logansport, LA 71049
Ph: (318)697-5003

Landacre, Jessica K., Deputy
Intellectual Property Owners As-
   sociation [5330]
1501 M St. NW, Ste. 1150
Washington, DC 20005
Ph: (202)507-4500
Fax: (202)507-4501

Landahl, Rev. Paul R., Director
Tithing and Stewardship Foundation
[20626]
1100 E 55th St.
Chicago, IL 60615-5112
Ph: (773)256-0679
Fax: (773)256-0692

Landau, Kathy, Exec. Dir.
National Dance Institute [7706]
217 W 147th St.
New York, NY 10039-3427
Ph: (212)226-0083
Fax: (212)226-0761

Lander, Janet, CSJ, Facilitator
Manna House of Prayer [11954]
323 E 5th St.
Concordia, KS 66901
Ph: (785)243-4428

Landers, Jim, VP
Reblooming Iris Society [22120]
c/o Riley Probst, President
2701 Fine Ave.
Modesto, CA 95355-9773

Landes, Ann, President
APA Division 19: Society for Military
Psychology [16873]
c/o APA Division Services
750 1st St. NE
Washington, DC 20002-4242
Ph: (202)216-7602
(202)336-6013

Landesman, Yosef, PhD, Dir. of
Res., President
Cure Alveolar Soft Part Sarcoma
International [13953]
260 Tappan St.
Brookline, MA 02445
Ph: (617)731-1143

Landi, Giacomo, Exec. VP
Norwegian-American Chamber of
Commerce [23610]
655 3rd Ave., Ste. 1810
New York, NY 10017
Ph: (212)885-9737

Landig, Rhea, Exec. Dir.
Species Alliance [4891]
PO Box 54
Annandale, NJ 08801
Ph: (973)207-5457

Landis, Gail, Chairman
Pro Mujer [13394]
253 W 35th St., 11th Fl.
New York, NY 10001
Ph: (646)626-7000
Fax: (212)904-1038

Landou, Bernard, President
Association for Macular Diseases
[16372]
210 E 64th St.
New York, NY 10065
Ph: (212)605-3719
Fax: (212)605-3795

Landram, Mike, Exec. Dir.
Family Literacy Alliance [12246]
801 E Wayne St.
Fort Wayne, IN 46802

Landreneau, Karl, CCIM, President
CCIM Institute [2853]
430 N Michigan Ave., Ste. 800
Chicago, IL 60611
Ph: (312)321-4460
Toll Free: 800-621-7027
Fax: (312)321-4530

Landrith, George C., CEO, President
Frontiers of Freedom [18024]
4094 Majestic Blvd., No. 380

Fairfax, VA 22033-2104
Ph: (703)246-0110
Fax: (703)246-0129

Landrum, John T., President
International Carotenoid Society
[6145]
c/o Kevin Gellenbeck, Secretary
Amway Corporation
Nutrilite Research Institute
5600 Beach Blvd.
Buena Park, CA 90621-2007
Ph: (714)562-4875

Landry, Coleen Perilloux,
Chairperson
Live Oak Society [4207]
17832 River Rd.
Montz, LA 70068

Landsman, David, Exec. Dir.
National Money Transmitters As-
sociation [1258]
12 Welwyn Rd., Ste. C
Great Neck, NY 11021
Ph: (516)829-2742

Landwehr, Kurt, President
Hardwood Distributor's Association
[1438]
PO Box 1921
Fort Worth, TX 76101

Lane, Ann Reiss, Founder
Women Against Gun Violence
[19233]
8800 Venice Blvd., Ste. 304
Los Angeles, CA 90034
Ph: (310)204-2348
Fax: (310)204-6643

Lane, Dr. Carla, EdD, Exec. Dir.
The Education Coalition [7820]
31 Segovia
San Clemente, CA 92672
Ph: (949)369-3867
Fax: (949)369-3865

Lane, Clayton, CEO
Institute for Transportation and
Development Policy [18491]
9 E 19th St., 7th Fl.
New York, NY 10003
Ph: (212)629-8001
Fax: (646)380-2360

Lane, George, President
International Association of Civil
Aviation Chaplains [19928]
c/o Beverly McNeely, Treasurer
2571 Oak Dr.
Clayton, IN 46118
Ph: (317)491-5089
Fax: (317)244-9362

Lane, Gloria J., PhD, Founder
Women's International Center
[13410]
PO Box 669
Rancho Santa Fe, CA 92067-0669
Ph: (858)759-3567
Fax: (619)296-1633

Lane, Hilary, Secretary, Treasurer
American Treibball Association
[22532]
PO Box 33780
Northglenn, CO 80233-0780
Ph: (303)718-7705

Lane, Jacob, Director
Collegiate Network [8152]
3901 Centerville Rd.
Wilmington, DE 19807
Ph: (302)652-4600
Toll Free: 800-526-7022
Fax: (302)652-1760

Lane, Nancy, President
Local Media Association [2797]
116 Cass St.

Traverse City, MI 49684
Toll Free: 888-486-2466

Lane, Ned, 1st VP
Gases and Welding Distributors As-
sociation [1731]
1 Oakwood Blvd., Ste. 195
Hollywood, FL 33020
Ph: (954)367-7728
Toll Free: 844-251-3219
Fax: (954)367-7790

Lane, Pamela, Exec. Dir.
National Association of Emergency
Medical Technicians [14683]
132-A E Northside Dr.
Clinton, MS 39056
Ph: (601)924-7744
Toll Free: 800-34-NAEMT
Fax: (601)924-7325

Lane, Robert, VP, Secretary
Guitar Foundation of America [9914]
PO Box 2900
Palos Verdes Peninsula, CA 90274
Toll Free: 877-570-1651

Lanfermann, Sr. Agnes, MMS,
Coord.
Medical Mission Sisters [20434]
8400 Pine Rd.
Philadelphia, PA 19111-1385
Ph: (215)742-6100

Lanfronza, Vincent, MS, EdD, Chmn.
of the Bd.
Education, Training and Research
Associates [8028]
100 Enterprise Way, Ste. G300
Scotts Valley, CA 95066
Ph: (831)438-4284
Toll Free: 800-620-8884

Lang, Andy, Exec. Dir.
United Church of Christ Coalition for
Lesbian, Gay, Bisexual and Trans-
gender Concerns [20190]
700 Prospect Ave.
Cleveland, OH 44115
Ph: (216)736-3228

Lang, Eric, Chairman
Pension Real Estate Association
[2886]
100 Pearl St., 13th Fl.
Hartford, CT 06103
Ph: (860)692-6341
Fax: (860)692-6351

Lang, Kurt, President
National Society of Insurance
Premium Auditors [1910]
PO Box 936
Columbus, OH 43216-0936
Toll Free: 888-846-7472
Fax: (877)835-5798

Lang, Marechiel Santos, Exec. Dir.
Environmental Design Research As-
sociation [5967]
22 N Caroll St., Ste. 300
Madison, WI 53703
Ph: (608)310-7540
Fax: (608)251-5941

Lang, Tom, President, CEO
Breeder's Registry [22031]
5541 Columbia Dr. N
Fresno, CA 93727

Langbecker, Kim, Exec. Dir.,
Founder
Journey to the Heart [9576]
10828 Whitburn St.
Culver City, CA 90230
Toll Free: 800-540-0471

Lange, Barbara, Exec. Dir.
Society of Motion Picture and Television Engineers [6594]

3 Barker Ave., 5th Fl.
White Plains, NY 10601
Ph: (914)761-1100
Fax: (914)761-3115

Lange, Dr. G. Max, Founder,
President, Chmn. of the Bd.
Childcare Worldwide [10910]
1971 Midway Ln., Ste. N
Bellingham, WA 98226-7682
Ph: (360)647-2283
Toll Free: 800-553-2328
Fax: (360)647-2392

Lange, Janet, Exec. Sec.
North American Association of Sum-
mer Sessions [8634]
Bradley University
Continuing Education
1501 W Bradley Ave.
Peoria, IL 61625
Ph: (309)677-2523
Toll Free: 866-880-9607
Fax: (309)677-3321

Lange, Richard A., MD, Secretary,
Treasurer
American Clinical and Climatological
Association [14286]
c/o Richard A. Lange, MD,
Secretary-Treasurer
507 Blackjack Oak
San Antonio, TX 78230
Ph: (210)567-4812
Fax: (210)567-4654

Lange, Robert, President
North American Normande Associa-
tion [3747]
748 Enloe Rd.
Rewey, WI 53580
Ph: (608)943-6091
Toll Free: 800-573-6254

Langeman, Jane, President
Association of Independent Informa-
tion Professionals [1793]
8550 United Plaza Blvd., Ste. 1001
Baton Rouge, LA 70809
Ph: (225)408-4400

Langenburg, Dianna, VP of HR
W.K. Kellogg Foundation [18946]
1 Michigan Ave. E
Battle Creek, MI 49017
Ph: (269)968-1611
Fax: (269)968-0413

Langenderfer, Mike, Exec. Dir.
International Surface Fabricators As-
sociation [2223]
2400 Wildwood Rd.
Gibsonia, PA 15044
Ph: (412)487-3207
Fax: (412)487-3269

Langenohl, Marc William,
Administrator
Waste-to-Energy Research and
Technology Council [4747]
Mudd Bldg., Rm. 926
Earth Engineering Ctr.
Columbia University
500 W 120th St.
New York, NY 10027
Ph: (212)854-9136
Fax: (212)854-5213

Langer, Kathy, President
National Senior Women's Tennis Association [23304]
c/o Sue Bramlette
96 Sugarberry Cir.
Houston, TX 77024

Langford, Michael, President
Utility Workers Union of America
[23464]

1300 L St. NW No. 1200
Washington, DC 20005
Ph: (202)899-2851
Fax: (202)974-8201

Langham, Gary, President
Neotropical Grassland Conservancy
[3916]
6274 Heathcliff Dr.
Carmichael, CA 95608

Langhauser, Beth, President
American Concrete Pumping Association [780]
606 Enterprise Dr.
Lewis Center, OH 43035
Ph: (614)431-5618

Langheier, Jason, Chairman,
Founder, Exec. Dir.
Fitness Forward [16700]
202 Remington Cir.
Durham, NC 27705
Ph: (919)309-4446

Langland, Johnny, Founder,
President
FOOTPRINTS in the Sky [12275]
7375 S Peoria St., Ste. 209, B-10
Centennial, CO 80112-4157
Ph: (303)799-0461
Fax: (303)799-8020

Langley, F. Phillip, President
United States Trotting Association
[22935]
6130 S Sunbury Rd.
Westerville, OH 43081
Ph: (614)224-2291
    (614)224-3281
Toll Free: 877-800-8782

Langley, Leon, President
National Association of State Directors of Pupil Transportation
Services [3341]
c/o Charlie Hood, Executive Director
8205 Bristol Ct.
Tallahassee, FL 32311
Ph: (850)274-4308

Langman, Loralie, President
International Association of
Therapeutic Drug Monitoring and
Clinical Toxicology [17496]
2604 Elmwood Ave., No. 350
Rochester, NY 14618
Ph: (613)531-8166
Fax: (866)303-0626

Langman, Loralie, PhD, FACB,
President
National Academy of Clinical
Biochemistry [13813]
American Association for Clinical
Chemistry
900 7th St. NW, Ste. 400
Washington, DC 20001
Ph: (202)857-0717
Toll Free: 800-892-1400
Fax: (202)887-5093

Langrige, Florence, Membership
Chp.
American Council for Polish Culture
[19601]
c/o Florence Langrige, Membership
Chair
78 Meadow Ln.
West Hartford, CT 06107
Ph: (860)521-4034

Langston, Ken Brooker, Director
Disciples Justice Action Network
[19972]
1040 Harbor Dr.
Annapolis, MD 21403-4251
Ph: (410)212-7964

Lanier, Dena, President
National Association of Dental
Laboratories [14457]
325 John Knox Rd., No. L103
Tallahassee, FL 32303
Toll Free: 800-950-1150
Fax: (850)222-0053

Laning, Bill, President
American Meat Goat Association
[2309]
PO Box 333
Junction, TX 76849-0333
Ph: (915)446-3921

Lanke, Eric, CEO
National Conference on Fluid Power
[6636]
6737 W Washington St., Ste. 2350
Milwaukee, WI 53214
Ph: (414)778-3344
Fax: (414)778-3361

Lannen, John, Exec. Dir.
Truck Safety Coalition [12846]
2020 14th St. N, Ste. 710
Arlington, VA 22201
Ph: (703)294-6404
Fax: (703)294-6406

Lannone, Susan, VP
Life Sciences Trainers & Educators
Network [3016]
4423 Pheasant Ridge Rd., Ste. 100
Roanoke, VA 24014-5274
Ph: (540)725-3859
Fax: (540)989-7482

Lansbury, Emily Bickford, Chairman
Ziegfeld Club [10280]
593 Park Ave.
New York, NY 10065
Ph: (212)751-6688

Lansky, Aaron, Founder, President
Yiddish Book Center [9644]
Harry and Jeanette Weinberg Bldg.
1021 West St.
Amherst, MA 01002
Ph: (413)256-4900
Fax: (413)256-4700

Lanson, Susan Clark, President
43rd Bomb Group Association
[20675]
c/o Louise V. Terrell, Secretary
207 Huron St.
Houghton, MI 49931

Lantz, Richard, 1st VP
National Air Duct Cleaners Association [2136]
1120 Route 73, Ste. 200
Mount Laurel, NJ 08054
Ph: (856)380-6810
Fax: (856)439-0525

Lanyard, Cathy M., Exec. Dir.
American Friends of ALYN Hospital
[10850]
122 E 42nd St., No. 1519
New York, NY 10168
Ph: (212)869-8085
Toll Free: 877-568-3259
Fax: (212)768-0979

Lanyon, Scott M., President
American Ornithologists' Union
[6953]
c/o Scott Lanyon, President
University of Minnesota
1987 Upper Buford Cir.
Corvallis, OR 97331
Ph: (612)624-6291

Lanza, Dana, CEO, Founder
Confluence Philanthropy [12470]
475 Riverside Dr., Ste. 900

New York, NY 10115
Ph: (212)812-4367

Lanza, Terri Glendon, President
CAMUS International [2216]
45738 Northport Loop W
Fremont, CA 94538

Lanzano, Steve, CEO, President
Television Bureau of Advertising
[111]
120 Wall St., 15th Fl.
New York, NY 10005-3908
Ph: (212)486-1111
Fax: (212)935-5631

Lanzaratta, Tony, Exec. Dir.
NASCA International [12947]
PO Box 6978
Buena Park, CA 90622-6978

Lapidus, Sidney, Chmn. of the Bd.
American Jewish Historical Society
[9632]
15 W 16th St.
New York, NY 10011-6301
Ph: (212)294-6160
Fax: (212)294-6161

Lapidus, Sidney, Treasurer
Center for Jewish History [19516]
15 W 16th St.
New York, NY 10011
Ph: (212)294-8301

LaPierre, Mr. Rick, President,
Founder
National Association for Moisture
Management [1164]
76 D St.
Hull, MA 02045
Ph: (781)925-0354
Fax: (781)925-0650

Lapin, Phil, Bd. Member
Alliance for Responsible
Atmospheric Policy [707]
2111 Wilson Blvd., 8th Fl.
Arlington, VA 22201
Ph: (703)243-0344
Fax: (703)243-2874

LaPorte, Courtney, Exec. Dir.
The Autism Research Foundation
[13751]
School of Medicine
Boston University
72 E Concord St., R-1014
Boston, MA 02118
Ph: (617)414-7012
Fax: (617)414-7207

Lapp, Tina, Officer
Real Estate Educators Association
[2890]
7739 E Broadway, No. 337
Tucson, AZ 85710
Ph: (520)609-2380

Lara, Alice A., Chairperson
Sudden Cardiac Arrest Coalition
[14149]
Sudden Arrhythmia Death Sydromes
Foundation
508 E South Temple, Ste. 202
Salt Lake City, UT 84102
Ph: (801)531-0937

Lara, Alice, RN, CEO, President
Sudden Arrhythmia Death
Syndromes Foundation [14860]
4527 South 2300 East, Ste. 104
Salt Lake City, UT 84117-4448
Ph: (801)272-3023

Lara, Carmen, President
Pan-American Alumni Association
[19344]

1201 W University Dr., UC108
Edinburg, TX 78541
Ph: (956)381-2500
    (956)665-2005
Fax: (956)381-2385

Larabee, Mark, Treasurer, Exec. Ed.
Joseph Conrad Society of America
[9065]
c/o Christopher GoGwilt, President
Fordham University
Dealy 512W
Bronx, NY 10458-9993
Ph: (718)817-4020

Large, Ed, President
Society for Music Perception and
Cognition [10008]

Largent, Bette, President
National Carousel Association
[21562]
c/o Norma Pankratz, Executive
Secretary
PO Box 1256
Castle Rock, CO 80104-1256

Larigakis, Nick, President
American Hellenic Institute [23642]
1220 16th St. NW
Washington, DC 20036
Ph: (202)785-8430
Fax: (202)785-5178

Lariviere, James, Exec. Dir.
International Stability Operations Association [18796]
2025 M St. NW, Ste. 800
Washington, DC 20036
Ph: (202)367-1153
Fax: (202)367-2153

Larkin, Amy, Dir. of Mktg.
United States Sailing Foundation
[22685]
15 Maritime Dr.
Portsmouth, RI 02871-0907
Ph: (401)683-0800
Toll Free: 800-877-2451
Fax: (401)683-0840

Larkin, Douglas, Dir. of Comm.
Asbestos Disease Awareness
Organization [17486]
1525 Aviation Blvd., Ste. 318
Redondo Beach, CA 90278

Larmett, Kathleen, Exec. Dir.
National Council of University
Research Administrators [8504]
1015 18th St. NW, Ste. 901
Washington, DC 20036-5273
Ph: (202)466-3894
Fax: (202)223-5573

LaRocca, Suzanne, President
Women's Army Corps Veterans' Association [20728]
PO Box 663
Weaver, AL 36277
Ph: (256)820-6824

LaRose, CHPA,CPP, David,
President
International Association for Healthcare Security and Safety [15330]
PO Box 5038
Glendale Heights, IL 60139
Ph: (630)529-3913
Fax: (630)529-4139

LaRose, Lisa, Treasurer
Kinder Goat Breeders Association
[4278]
PO Box 63406
Colorado Springs, CO 80962

Larosiliere, Steven, President
Stoked [13480]
10 Jay St., Ste. 908

Brooklyn, NY 11201
Ph: (646)710-3600
Fax: (212)859-7357

Larracas, Anne, Secretary
Global Alliance for Incinerator
Alternatives **[4742]**
1958 University Ave.
Berkeley, CA 94704
Ph: (510)883-9490
Fax: (510)883-9493

Larrea, Ma. Carolina J., VP,
Secretary
International Association of Hand
Papermakers and Paper Artists
[10062]
c/o Nicole Donnelly, President
2120 E Westmoreland St.
Philadelphia, PA 19133

Larsen, Brian, PE, President
Plastic Lumber Trade Association
[2628]
PO Box 211
Worthington, MN 56187
Ph: (507)372-5558
Fax: (507)372-5726

Larsen, David, President
Gamewardens Association, Vietnam
to Present **[21166]**
PO Box 83
Parsons, KS 67357
Toll Free: 866-220-7477

Larsen, Donna, CEO
Forensic CPA Society **[29]**
PO Box 31060
Spokane, WA 99223
Ph: (509)448-9318
Toll Free: 800-923-2797
Fax: (509)448-9302

Larsen, Kristine, President
American Association of Variable
Star Observers **[5996]**
49 Bay State Rd.
Cambridge, MA 02138
Ph: (617)354-0484
Fax: (617)354-0665

Larsen, Sarah, Secretary, Treasurer
Nourish America **[16231]**
PO Box 1567
Morro Bay, CA 93443
Ph: (805)715-2693

Larson, Amy W., Esq., President
National Waterways Conference
[3098]
1100 N Glebe Rd., Ste. 1010
Arlington, VA 22201
Ph: (703)224-8007
Fax: (866)371-1390

Larson, David, VP
Nuttall Ornithological Club **[6963]**
c/o David Larson, Vice President
736 Salem St.
Bradford, MA 01835

Larson, Deb, Bd. Member
National Association on Alcohol,
Drugs and Disability **[17321]**
2165 Bunker Hill Dr.
San Mateo, CA 94402-3801
Ph: (650)578-8047
Fax: (650)286-9205

Larson, Eric C., Publisher
Horn and Whistle Enthusiasts Group
[21662]
c/o Eric C. Larson, Publisher
2 Abell Ave.
Ipswich, MA 01938

Larson, Janice, Director
Association for Linen Management
[2075]

138 N Keeneland Dr., Ste. D
Richmond, KY 40475
Ph: (859)624-0177
Toll Free: 800-669-0863
Fax: (859)624-3580

Larson, John, Exec. Dir.
American Farmland Trust **[17786]**
1150 Connecticut Ave. NW, Ste. 600
Washington, DC 20036
Toll Free: 800-431-1499

Larson, John, CEO
National Association of Conservation
Districts **[3901]**
509 Capitol Ct. NE
Washington, DC 20002
Ph: (202)547-6223
Fax: (202)547-6450

Larson, Kim, VP
Thanks to Scandinavia **[7927]**
366 Amsterdam Ave., Ste. 205
New York, NY 10024
Ph: (347)855-4109

Larson, Mr. Larry A., CFM, Pol. Dir.
Association of State Floodplain
Managers **[3815]**
575 D'Onofrio Dr., Ste. 200
Madison, WI 53719
Ph: (608)828-3000
Fax: (608)828-6319

Larson, Marta, Mgr.
Association for Gender Equity
Leadership in Education **[7900]**
317 S Division St. Pmb 54
Ann Arbor, MI 48104
Ph: (734)769-2456

Larson, Matt, President
National Council of Teachers of
Mathematics **[8284]**
1906 Association Dr.
Reston, VA 20191-1502
Ph: (703)620-9840
Toll Free: 800-235-7566
Fax: (703)476-2970

LaRue, James, Director
American Library Association - Office
for Intellectual Freedom **[9672]**
50 E Huron St.
Chicago, IL 60611
Ph: (312)280-4220
Toll Free: 800-545-2433
Fax: (312)280-4227

Lash, Kelley, President
College Media Association **[8151]**
355 Lexington Ave., 15th Fl.
New York, NY 10017-6603
Ph: (212)297-2195

Lashaway, Steve, President
National Threshers Association
[8904]
c/o Steve Lashaway, President
20550 Carter Rd.
Bowling Green, OH 43402

Laskawy, Tom, Founder, Exec. Dir.
Food & Environment Reporting
Network **[2062]**
576 5th Ave., Ste. 903
New York, NY 10036

Laskow, Mark, Chairman
Carnegie Hero Fund Commission
[12885]
436 7th Ave., Ste. 1101
Pittsburgh, PA 15219-1841
Ph: (412)281-1302
Toll Free: 800-447-8900
Fax: (412)281-5751

Laskowski, Sixtus, Mem.
Catholic Life Insurance **[19402]**
1635 NE Loop 410

San Antonio, TX 78209-1625
Ph: (210)828-9921
    (210)828-5529
Toll Free: 800-262-2548
Fax: (210)828-4629

Lasky, George, Chairman
Accounting Group International **[3]**
10830 N Central Expy., Ste. 300
Dallas, TX 75231
Ph: (214)378-8111
Fax: (214)378-8118

Lasorsa, Rob, Contact
National Throws Coaches Associa-
tion **[22735]**
PO Box 14114
Palm Desert, CA 92255-4114
Toll Free: 888-527-6772

Lasota, Irena, Director, Founder
Institute for Democracy in Eastern
Europe **[18139]**
1718 M St. NW, No. 147
Washington, DC 20036
Ph: (202)361-9346

LaSpina, John, Chairman
Bowlers to Veterans Link **[22701]**
11350 Random Hills Rd., Ste. 800
Fairfax, VA 22030
Ph: (703)934-6039
Fax: (703)591-3049

Lass, Carmina, Director
Credit Builders Alliance **[942]**
1701 K St. NW, Ste. 1000
Washington, DC 20006
Ph: (202)730-9390
Fax: (202)350-9430

Lassalle, Honor, President
Norman Foundation, Inc. **[12985]**
147 E 48th St.
New York, NY 10017
Ph: (212)230-9830
Fax: (212)230-9849

Lassanske, Donna, President
Purebred Morab Horse Association
[4404]
PO Box 802
Georgetown, KY 40324
Ph: (502)535-4803

Lassin, Gary, Curator
Three Stooges Fan Club **[24011]**
904 Sheble Ln.
Ambler, PA 19002
Ph: (267)468-0810

Lassiter, Luke Eric, PhD, President
American Anthropological Association - General Anthropology Division **[5899]**
Marshall University Graduate College
100 Angus E Peyton Dr.
South Charleston, WV 25303
Ph: (304)746-1923

Latessa, Phil, Exec. Dir.
Empower Tanzania, Inc. **[12800]**
5414 Cervantes Dr.
Ames, IA 50014

Lathrop, Prof. Dr. Gordon, Mem.
Societas Liturgica **[20072]**
c/o Peter C. Bower, Editor
587 Moorhead Pl.
Pittsburgh, PA 15232-1426

Lathrop, Rick, Exec. Dir., Founder
Global Service Corps **[13293]**
1306 NW Hoyt St., Ste. 310
Portland, OR 97209
Ph: (503)954-1659

Latimer, Megan, Exec. Dir.
JumpStart International **[11391]**
112 Krog St., Ste. 17

Atlanta, GA 30307
Ph: (678)383-9618

Latin, Prof. Howard A., President
EcoVitality **[3852]**
224 Centre St., 2nd Fl.
New York, NY 10013
Ph: (212)966-8803
Fax: (212)966-8803

Latterell, Julie, President
Bernese Mountain Dog Club of
America **[21840]**
c/o Dee McDuffee, Membership
Chairperson
4N156 Country View Ln.
Elburn, IL 60119
Ph: (630)365-0190

Lattimer, Cheri A., RN, BSN, Exec.
Dir.
Case Management Society of
America **[15583]**
6301 Ranch Dr.
Little Rock, AR 72223
Ph: (501)225-2229
Toll Free: 800-216-2672
Fax: (501)221-9068

Lattimer, Cheri A., RN, BSN, Exec.
Dir.
National Transitions of Care Coali-
tion **[15052]**
10 G St. NE, Ste. 605
Washington, DC 20002
Toll Free: 888-562-9267

Lattimer, Suzanne, Treasurer
Near East Archaeological Society
[5944]
Andrews University
Horn Archaeological Museum
9047 Old US 31
Berrien Springs, MI 49104-0990
Ph: (269)471-3273

Latus, Timothy D., DPMP, Founder
Academy of Psychic Arts and Sci-
ences **[6981]**
PO Box 191129
Dallas, TX 75219-8129
Ph: (214)219-2020

Latz, Dr. Gil, President
Association of International Educa-
tion Administrators **[7425]**
2204 Erwin Rd., Rm. 030
Durham, NC 27708-0404
Ph: (919)668-1928
Fax: (919)684-8749

Lau, Frederick, President
Society for Asian Music **[10004]**
PO Box 7819
Austin, TX 78713-7819
Ph: (512)232-7621
Fax: (512)232-7178

Lau, Jennifer, Secretary
American Society of Naturalists
[6893]
PO Box 37005
Chicago, IL 60637-0005
Ph: (773)753-3347
Toll Free: 877-705-1878

Laub, Carolyn, Founder, Exec. Dir.
GSA Network **[18402]**
1550 Bryant St., Ste. 600
San Francisco, CA 94103
Ph: (415)552-4229
Fax: (415)552-4729

Lauder, Ronald, Chairman
Jewish National Fund **[20257]**
42 E 69th St.
New York, NY 10021
Toll Free: 800-542-8733
Fax: (212)409-8548

Lauder, Ronald, Chairman
National Association for Temple
    Administration **[20268]**
3060 El Cerrito Plz., No. 331
El Cerrito, CA 94530
Ph: (360)887-0464
Toll Free: 800-966-NATA

Lauder, Ronald S., President
World Jewish Congress, American
    Section **[18595]**
501 Madison Ave.
New York, NY 10022
Ph: (212)755-5770

Lauderdale, Jana, PhD, Trustee
Transcultural Nursing Society
    [16189]
Madonna University
36600 Schoolcraft Rd.
Livonia, MI 48150
Toll Free: 888-432-5470
Fax: (734)793-2457

Laudon, Matthew, Chairman,
    President
Clean Technology and Sustainable
    Industries Organization **[3675]**
3925 W Braker Ln.
Austin, TX 78759
Ph: (925)886-8461

Laue, Bruce A., President
Order of Lafayette **[21208]**
243 W 70th St., Apt. 6f
New York, NY 10023
Ph: (212)873-9162

Laugharn, Peter, President, CEO
Conrad N. Hilton Foundation **[13061]**
30440 Agoura Rd.
Agoura Hills, CA 91301
Ph: (818)851-3700

Laughlin, Keith, President
Rails-to-Trails Conservancy **[23331]**
Duke Ellington Bldg., 5th Fl.
2121 Ward Ct. NW
Washington, DC 20037
Ph: (202)331-9696
Fax: (202)223-9257

Laughlin, Sherburne, VP
Association of Arts Administration
    Educators **[7507]**
PO Box 721031
McAllen, TX 78504
Ph: (312)469-0795

Laughon, Carisa, Director
USA Gymnastics **[22903]**
132 E Washington St., Ste. 700
Indianapolis, IN 46204-3674
Ph: (317)237-5050
    (317)829-5667
Toll Free: 800-345-4719

Laumeister, Bruce, President
Hormone Refractory Prostate
    Cancer Association **[13984]**
PO Box 260
Bennington, VT 05201
Ph: (802)879-1131

Lässig, Prof. Simone, PhD, Director
German Historical Institute **[9479]**
1607 New Hampshire Ave. NW
Washington, DC 20009-2562
Ph: (202)387-3355
Fax: (202)387-6437

Laurence, David, Director
Association of Departments of
    English **[7865]**
c/o David Laurence, Director
26 Broadway, 3rd Fl.
New York, NY 10004-1789
Ph: (646)576-5137
    (646)576-5130
Fax: (646)835-4056

Laursen, Finn, Exec. Dir.
Christian Educators Association
    International **[20077]**
PO Box 45610
Westlake, OH 44145
Toll Free: 888-798-1124

Laushman, Judy, Exec. Dir.
Association of Specialty Cut Flower
    Growers **[1306]**
MPO Box 268
Oberlin, OH 44074
Ph: (440)774-2887

Lauter, Sr. Larraine, Founder
Water With Blessings **[13362]**
11714 Main St., Ste. B
Middletown, KY 40243
Ph: (502)356-9281

Lauve, Janie Ward, Exec. Dir.
People Against Rape **[12933]**
PO Box 1723
Charleston, SC 29402
Ph: (843)745-0144
    (843)577-9882

LaVanchy, Master Charlie, Exec. Dir.
Traditional Tae Kwon Do Chung Do
    Association **[23016]**
1209 Gilmore Ln.
Louisville, KY 40213
Ph: (502)964-3800

Laven, Charles, President
Urban Homesteading Assistance
    Board **[11994]**
120 Wall St., 20th Fl.
New York, NY 10005
Ph: (212)479-3300

LaVenture, Susan, Exec. Dir.
National Association for Parents of
    Children With Visual Impairments
    [17729]
c/o Susan LaVenture, Executive
    Director
15 W 65th St.
New York, NY 10023
Toll Free: 800-562-6265

LaVigne, Andrew W., President,
    CEO
American Seed Trade Association
    [4641]
1701 Duke St., Ste. 275
Alexandria, VA 22314-3415
Ph: (703)837-8140
Toll Free: 888-890-7333
Fax: (703)837-9365

LaVigne, Andrew W., VP
National Coalition for Food and
    Agricultural Research **[3551]**
1800 S Oak St., Ste. 100
Champaign, IL 61820-6974
Ph: (217)356-3182
Fax: (217)398-4119

LaVigne, Andrew W., Exec. VP
National Council of Commercial
    Plant Breeders **[4643]**
1701 Duke St., Ste. 275
Alexandria, VA 22314
Ph: (703)837-8140
Fax: (703)837-9365

Lavin, Jack, Director
National Petroleum Management
    Association **[2532]**
10908 Courthouse Rd., Ste. 102-301
Fredericksburg, VA 22408-2658
Ph: (540)507-4371
Fax: (540)507-4372

Lavin, James, Jr., Chairman
Northern Haiti Hope Foundation
    [11414]

332 W Lee Hwy., Ste. 119
Warrenton, VA 20186

Lavin, James Kevin, Chairman, Edi-
    tor, Treasurer
Air Weather Association **[21103]**
1697 Capri Way
Charlottesville, VA 22911-3534

LaViolet, Raye, Dir. of Fin.
American Public Works Association
    [5730]
1275 K St. NW, Ste. 750
Washington, DC 20005
Ph: (202)408-9541
Fax: (202)408-9542

Law, Col. Denise, Chairman
USAF Medical Service Corps As-
    sociation **[15844]**
4008 Plantation House Rd.
Summerville, SC 29485-6239
Ph: (404)500-6722

Law, Kristin Hartness, Contact
Canines for Disabled Kids **[11578]**
255 Park Ave., Ste. 601
Worcester, MA 01609
Ph: (978)422-5299
Fax: (978)422-7380

Lawaetz, Mr. Hans, VP
Senepol Cattle Breeders Association
    [3756]
2321 Chestnut St.
Wilmington, NC 28405
Ph: (910)444-0234
Toll Free: 800-SEN-EPOL
Fax: (704)919-5871

Lawler, Lawrence M., CPA, Director
American Society of Tax Problem
    Solvers **[5789]**
2250 Wehrle Dr., Ste. 3
Williamsville, NY 14221
Ph: (716)630-1650
Fax: (716)630-1651

Lawlor, Kevan P., Chmn. of the Bd.
American National Standards
    Institute **[5770]**
1899 L St. NW, 11th Fl.
Washington, DC 20036
Ph: (202)293-8020
Fax: (202)293-9287

Lawlor, Mary, CPM, Exec. Dir.
National Association of Certified
    Professional Midwives **[16295]**
PO Box 340
Keene, NH 03431
Ph: (603)358-3322

Lawrence, Alan, President
American Primrose Society **[22082]**
c/o Jon Kawaguchi, Treasurer
3524 Bowman Ct.
Alameda, CA 94502-7607

Lawrence, Donna, President, CEO
I Have a Dream Foundation **[13450]**
330 7th Ave., 20th Fl.
New York, NY 10001
Ph: (212)293-5480
Fax: (212)293-5478

Lawrence, Geoffrey, AON, President
International Rural Sociology As-
    sociation **[7184]**
c/o Ray Jussaume, Jr., Secretary-
    Treasurer
Michigan State University
317B Berkey Hall
East Lansing, MI 48824
Ph: (517)353-6790

Lawrence, Guy B.
Bideawee **[10594]**
410 E 38th St.

New York, NY 10016
Toll Free: 866-262-8133

Lawrence, Hal C, III, MD, Exec. VP,
    CEO
American Congress of Obstetricians
    and Gynecologists **[16272]**
409 12th St. SW
Washington, DC 20024-2188
Ph: (202)638-5577
Toll Free: 800-673-8444

Lawrence, Joanne, Founder,
    Chairperson
Disabled Americans Have Rights
    Too **[11591]**
616 SW 152nd St.
Burien, WA 98166
Ph: (206)241-1697
Fax: (206)241-1697

Lawrence, John, VP
Doctors Without Borders USA
    [12657]
333 7th Ave., 2nd Fl.
New York, NY 10001-5004
Ph: (212)679-6800
Toll Free: 888-392-0392
Fax: (212)679-7016

Lawrence, Kriste, Officer
International Function Point Users
    Group **[642]**
191 Clarksville Rd.
Princeton Junction, NJ 08550
Ph: (609)799-4900
Fax: (609)799-7032

Lawrence, Melissa, Officer
Aesthetics International Association
    [917]
310 E Interstate 30, Ste. B107
Garland, TX 75043
Toll Free: 877-968-7539

Lawrence, Rev. Stephen, Officer
Commission on Religious Counsel-
    ing and Healing **[13615]**
456 Nimick St.
Sharon, PA 16146
Ph: (724)308-6218

Lawrie-Munro, L. Michele, Exec. Dir.
American Institute of Mining, Metal-
    lurgical, and Petroleum Engineers
    [6878]
12999 E Adam Aircraft Cir.
Englewood, CO 80112
Ph: (303)325-5185
Fax: (888)702-0049

Laws, Carol Britton, PhD, MSW,
    President
National Alliance for Direct Support
    Professionals **[1701]**
240 Washington Avenue Ext., Ste.
    501
Albany, NY 12203
Ph: (518)449-7551

Laws, Charlotte Anne, Chairperson,
    President
League for Earth & Animal Protec-
    tion **[3894]**
21781 Ventura Blvd., Ste. 633
Woodland Hills, CA 91364
Ph: (818)346-5280

Lawson, Don, Dir. (Actg.)
Yamaha 650 Society **[22240]**
FL

Lawson, Gerard, PhD, Rep.
Association for Counselor Education
    and Supervision **[7685]**
PO Box 862
Lake Worth, FL 33460
Toll Free: 800-347-6647

Lawson, Karen, PhD, Founder
Reach Grenada [11138]
575 Madison Ave., 10th Fl.
New York, NY 10022
Ph: (212)605-0281

Lawson, Karyl McCurdy, Founder
Women's Energy Network [6519]
Two Woodfield Lake
1100 E Woodfield Rd., Ste. 350
Schaumburg, IL 60173
Toll Free: 855-390-0650
Fax: (847)517-7229

Lawson, Kirk, Exec. Dir.
Business Professionals of America
[8736]
5454 Cleveland Ave.
Columbus, OH 43231-4021
Ph: (614)895-7277
Toll Free: 800-334-2007
Fax: (614)895-1165

Lawson, Meko L., Founder
Professional Women of Color
Network [3499]
PO Box 22367
Seattle, WA 98122
Ph: (206)659-6356

Lawson, Mike, Exec. Dir.
Technology Institute for Music
Educators [8391]
7503 Kingwood Ct.
Fairview, TN 37062
Ph: (615)870-9333

Lawson, Richard, Exec. Dir., Director
Marine Technology Society [6804]
1100 H St. NW, Ste. LL100
Washington, DC 20005
Ph: (202)717-8705
Fax: (202)347-4302

Lawson, Steve, Exec. Dir.
Advent Christian General Confer-
ence [19695]
14601 Albemarle Rd.
Charlotte, NC 28227
Ph: (704)545-6161
Toll Free: 800-676-0694
Fax: (704)573-0712

Lawton, Jennifer S., MD, President
Women in Thoracic Surgery [17479]
633 N Saint Clair St., 23rd Fl.
Chicago, IL 60611
Ph: (312)202-5835
Fax: (773)289-0871

Lawton, Dr. Orville, Asst. Treas.
National Association of Negro Musi-
cians [9968]
PO Box 51669
Durham, NC 27717
Ph: (919)489-4139

Lawton, Wendy, Founder
Lawton Collector's Guild [22004]
PO Box 1227
Hilmar, CA 95324
Ph: (209)632-3655
Fax: (209)632-6788

Lay, Andy, Chairman
Help the Children [12671]
Bldg.1B
5600 Rickenbacker Rd.
Bell, CA 90201-6437
Ph: (323)980-9870
Toll Free: 888-818-4483
Fax: (323)980-9878

Lay, Prof. Thorne, President
International Association of Seismol-
ogy and Physics of the Earth's
Interior [7156]
Earth and Marine Science Bldg.

Dept. of Earth and Planetary Sci-
ence
University of California - Santa Cruz
Santa Cruz, CA 95064
Ph: (831)459-3164
Fax: (831)459-3074

Layman, Colleen M., President
Society of Women Engineers [6601]
203 N La Salle St., Ste. 1675
Chicago, IL 60601
Toll Free: 877-793-4636

Layman, Dawn, President
National Association of Women Law
Enforcement Executives [5494]
12500 W 87th Street Pky.
Lenexa, KS 66215
Ph: (847)404-8189
Fax: (913)477-7249

Layne, R. Davis, Advisor
Voluntary Protection Programs
Participants' Association [16327]
7600E Leesburg Pke., Ste. 100
Falls Church, VA 22043-2004
Ph: (703)761-1146
Fax: (703)761-1148

Layne, Scott, Chairperson
Association for Learning Environ-
ments [7825]
11445 E Via Linda, Ste. 2-440
Scottsdale, AZ 85259
Ph: (480)391-0840

Layne, Tim, President
Pilots for Christ International [20159]
9130 Vinto St.
Sparta, MI 49345
Ph: (616)884-6241
Fax: (616)884-6079

Layton, Denise, COO
Soaring Society of America [22491]
PO Box 2100
Hobbs, NM 88241-2100
Ph: (575)392-1177

Le Du, Emma, President, Founder
Technology and Information for All
[8678]
333 18th Ave. E
Seattle, WA 98112

Le Poole, Caroline, President
PanAmerican Society for Pigment
Cell Research [15654]
c/o Prashiela Manga, PhD,
Secretary and Treasurer
Ronald O. Perelman Department of
Dermatology
NYU Langone Medical Ctr., Smilow
401
522 First Ave.
New York, NY 10016
Ph: (212)263-9086
Fax: (212)263-5819

Lea, Jon, Secretary, Treasurer, Mgr.
Western Snow Conference [7381]
PO Box 485
Brush Prairie, WA 98606
Ph: (530)414-3267

Leab, Daniel, Gen. Sec.
Historians of American Communism
[7984]
PO Box 1216
Washington, CT 06793

Leach, Danielle, Chairperson
Alliance for Childhood Cancer
[13875]
2318 Mill Rd., Ste. 800
Alexandria, VA 22314
Fax: (571)366-9595

Leach, Jim, Treasurer
Data Interchange Standards Association [19153]

8300 Greensboro Dr., Ste. 800
McLean, VA 22102
Ph: (703)970-4480
Fax: (703)970-4488

Leach, Richard K., Director
American Society for Precision
Engineering [6539]
PO Box 10826
Raleigh, NC 27605-0826
Ph: (919)839-8444
Fax: (919)839-8039

Leach, Richard, CEO, President
World Food Program USA [12120]
1725 I St. NW, Ste. 510
Washington, DC 20006
Ph: (202)627-3737
Fax: (202)530-1698

Leach, Ruth, Founder
Single Booklovers [21740]
2205 Oak Ridge Rd.
Oak Ridge, NC 27310
Ph: (336)298-1767

Leahey, Mark B., CEO, President
Medical Device Manufacturers As-
sociation [3029]
1333 H St. NW, Ste. 400 W
Washington, DC 20005
Ph: (202)354-7171

Leaman, Dr. Bruce M., Exec. Dir.
International Pacific Halibut Commis-
sion [1300]
2320 W Commodore Way, Ste. 300
Seattle, WA 98199
Ph: (206)634-1838
Fax: (206)632-2983

Leaman, Crystal, Gen. Mgr.
For the Love of Horses [18354]
605 Oak St.
Lathrop, MO 64465
Ph: (814)474-5382
Toll Free: 866-537-7336

Leaman, George, Director
Philosophy Documentation Center
[10112]
701 Charlton Ave.
Charlottesville, VA 22903-5203
Ph: (434)220-3300
Toll Free: 800-444-2419
Fax: (434)220-3301

Leanna, DeeAnn, President, Chmn.
of the Bd.
Heavenly Hats Foundation [13059]
1813 Coach Ln.
Suamico, WI 54173
Ph: (920)362-2668

Leap, J. Kenneth, Comm. Chm.
American Glass Guild [1500]
c/o Carol Slovikosky, Treasurer
612 S Queen St.
Martinsburg, WV 25401

Leaper, Eric, President, Exec. Dir.
National Organization for Rivers
[23093]
212 W Cheyenne Mountain Blvd.
Colorado Springs, CO 80906
Ph: (719)579-8759

Learned, Mike, Editor
Lesbian, Gay, Bisexual, Transgender
Returned Peace Corps Volunteers
[18846]
PO Box 14332
San Francisco, CA 94114-0332
Toll Free: 800-424-8580

Leary, Mal, President
National Freedom of Information
Coalition [18958]

University of Missouri-Columbia
Journalism Institute
101 Reynolds
Columbia, MO 65211
Ph: (573)882-4856

Leary, Meg, Dir. of Programs
United States Artists [8946]
980 N Michigan Ave., Ste. 1300
Chicago, IL 60611-4513
Ph: (312)470-6325
Fax: (312)470-6335

Leas, Alyson, Director
Museum of the Fur Trade [9496]
6321 Highway 20
Chadron, NE 69337
Ph: (308)432-3843
Fax: (308)432-5963

Lease, Dr. Loren, Secretary,
Treasurer
Dental Anthropology Association
[14428]
c/o Dr. Loren R. Lease, Secretary
and Treasurer
Dept. of Sociology and Anthropology
Youngstown State University
1 University Plz.
Youngstown, OH 44555

Leavitt, Kate, President
Soyfoods Association of North
America [3771]
1050 17th St. NW, Ste. 600
Washington, DC 20036
Ph: (202)659-3520

Leavitt, Michael, President
American Society for Jewish Music
[9868]
Center for Jewish History
15 W 16th St.
New York, NY 10011
Ph: (212)874-3990
Fax: (212)874-8605

Leavy, Hannelore R., Exec. Dir.,
Founder
International Medical Spa Associa-
tion [15149]
1551 Sandbar Cir.
Waconia, MN 55387
Ph: (952)283-1252
Toll Free: 877-851-8998
Fax: (952)767-0742

Lebamoff, Jordan, President
Macedonian Patriotic Organization of
United States and Canada [9772]
124 W Wayne St.
Fort Wayne, IN 46802-2500
Ph: (260)422-5900
Fax: (260)422-1348

Leber, Michele, Chairman
National Committee on Pay Equity
[18222]
c/o AFT
555 New Jersey Ave. NW
Washington, DC 20001-2029
Ph: (703)920-2010
Fax: (703)979-6372

LeBlanc, Kim Edward, MD, Exec.
Dir.
Accreditation Council for Continuing
Medical Education [15701]
515 N State St., Ste. 1801
Chicago, IL 60654
Ph: (312)527-9200

LeBlond, Lawrence, Secretary,
Treasurer
Phi Chi Medical Fraternity [23818]
2039 Ridgeview Dr.
Floyds Knobs, IN 47119
Ph: (812)923-7270
Toll Free: 800-800-7442

Leblond, Norm, FALU, President
Association of Home Office
Underwriters [1838]
1155 15th St. NW, Ste. 500
Washington, DC 20005
Ph: (202)962-0167
Fax: (202)530-0659

LeBoeuf, Mr. Jeffrey J., CAE, Exec.
Dir.
American Osteopathic College of
Occupational and Preventive
Medicine [16514]
PO Box 3043
Tulsa, OK 74101
Ph: (253)968-3423
Toll Free: 800-558-8686

LeBov, Mr. Ray, Exec. Dir.
Association for Professional
Basketball Research [22570]
PO Box 35771
Phoenix, AZ 85069-5771

Lebow, Mark D., Chairman
American Friends of Magen David
Adom [12604]
352 7th Ave., Ste. 400
New York, NY 10001-5012
Ph: (212)757-1627
Toll Free: 866-632-2763
Fax: (212)757-4662

Lebowitz, Joel L., Co-Ch.
Committee of Concerned Scientists
[18386]
222 W 135th St., Ste. 3A
New York, NY 10030

Lebron, Maria L., Mem.
American Mathematical Society
[6816]
201 Charles St.
Providence, RI 02904-2294
Ph: (401)455-4000
Toll Free: 800-321-4267
Fax: (401)331-3842

Lebwohl, Mark, President
American Academy of Dermatology
[14477]
930 E Woodfield Rd.
Schaumburg, IL 60173
Ph: (847)240-1280
    (202)842-3555
Toll Free: 866-503-7546
Fax: (847)240-1859

LeChevalier, Robert, President
Logical Language Group [9656]
2904 Beau Ln.
Fairfax, VA 22031
Ph: (703)385-0273

Leclair, Ms. Denise, Exec. Dir.
International Foundation for Gender
Education [12944]
272 Carroll St. NW
Waltham, MA 02454
Ph: (202)207-8364

LeCody, Peter J., Chairman
National Association of Railroad
Passengers [2837]
505 Capitol Ct. NE, Ste. 300
Washington, DC 20002-7706
Ph: (202)408-8362
Fax: (202)408-8287

Ledbetter, Beth, President
PEO International [8753]
3700 Grand Ave.
Des Moines, IA 50312-2806
Ph: (515)255-3153
Fax: (515)255-3820

Ledbetter, D. Orlando, President
Professional Football Writers of
America [22867]

c/o Howard Blazer, Secretary
The Sports Xchange
4632 Windsong St.
Sacramento, CA 95834

Leddy, John C., Founder, President
United States Water and Power
[5892]
1179 Nelrose Ave.
Venice, CA 90291

Lederer, Laura J., President
Global Centurion [10999]
PO Box 17107
Arlington, VA 22216-7107
Ph: (703)919-6828

Lederhausen, Mats, Founder
Business for Social Responsibility
[618]
88 Kearny St., 12th Fl.
San Francisco, CA 94108
Ph: (415)984-3200
Fax: (415)984-3201

Lederman, Stephanie, EdM, Exec.
Dir.
American Federation for Aging
Research [14887]
55 W 39th St., 16th Fl.
New York, NY 10018-0541
Ph: (212)703-9977
Toll Free: 888-582-2327
Fax: (212)997-0330

Ledford, Lewis, Exec. Dir.
National Association of State Park
Directors [5664]
PO Box 91567
Raleigh, NC 27675

Ledgerwood, Anna M., Counselor
American Surgical Association
[17376]
500 Cummings Ctr., Ste. 4550
Beverly, MA 01915
Ph: (978)927-8330
Fax: (978)524-0498

Ledogar, Mark, President
Seven Generations Ahead [11433]
1049 Lake St., Ste. 200
Oak Park, IL 60301
Ph: (708)660-9909
Fax: (708)660-9913

Lee, Anne, Coord.
World Kouk Sun Do Society [18844]
45 S Main St., Ste. 90
West Hartford, CT 06107-2402
Ph: (860)523-5260

Lee, Ben, President
Law Enforcement Association of
Asian Pacifics [19536]
905 E 2nd St., Ste. 200
Los Angeles, CA 90012

Lee, Beth, President
Teethsavers International [14472]
3306 34th St.
Lubbock, TX 79410
Ph: (806)368-7513

Lee, Bonnie, President, Founder
Learn for Life Kenya [11395]
2477 N 91st St.
Wauwatosa, WI 53226

Lee, Brenda, President
National Society of Artists [8932]
PO Box 1885
Dickinson, TX 77539

Lee, Brendan H., President
Society for Pediatric Research
[16619]
3400 Research Forest Dr., Ste. B-7

The Woodlands, TX 77381
Ph: (281)419-0052
Fax: (281)419-0082

Lee, Cori, RDH, Exec. Dir.
United States Dental Tennis Associa-
tion [23306]
1096 Wilmington Ave.
San Jose, CA 95129-3242
Toll Free: 800-445-2524

Lee, Dr. Cornelia, President
Angioma Alliance [15902]
520 W 21st St., Ste. G2-411
Norfolk, VA 23517-1950
Ph: (571)306-2873
Fax: (757)623-0616

Lee, Don, President
American Association of
Acupuncture and Oriental Medicine
[16453]
PO Box 96503, No. 44144
Washington, DC 20090-6503
Toll Free: 866-455-7999
Fax: (866)455-7999

Lee, Don, President
United States Mondioring Associa-
tion [22822]
PO Box 4432
Carson City, NV 89702
Ph: (775)848-0041

Lee, Donna A., President
American College Personnel As-
sociation [8413]
1 Dupont Cir. NW, Ste. 300
Washington, DC 20036-1137
Ph: (202)835-2272
Fax: (202)296-3286

Lee, Dwaine E., President
Global Action International [12664]
7356 Altiva Pl.
Carlsbad, CA 92013
Ph: (760)438-3979
Fax: (760)602-0383

Lee, George, President
American Society of Neurophysi-
ological Monitoring [16007]
275 N York St., Ste. 401
Elmhurst, IL 60126
Ph: (630)832-1300

Lee, Gina Mennett, MEd, Founder,
President
Food Allergy Education Network
[13576]
1 Wildwood Dr.
Branford, CT 06405
Ph: (203)206-3141

Lee, Gordon, President
Psychologists for Social Responsibil-
ity [18761]
c/o Brad Olson, Treasurer
National Louis University
122 S Michigan Ave.
Chicago, IL 60603
Ph: (707)797-7016
Fax: (312)261-3464

Lee, Ilchi, Founder, President
International Brain Education As-
sociation [16050]
866 United Nations Plz., Ste. 479
New York, NY 10017
Ph: (212)319-0848
Fax: (212)319-8671

Lee, Insook, PhD, President
Society for Pastoral Theology
[20623]
c/o Dr. Roslyn Karaban
St. Bernard's School of Theology
and Ministry

120 French Rd.
Rochester, NY 14618
Ph: (585)750-6693
Fax: (585)271-2045

Lee, J. Scott, Exec. Dir.
Association for Core Texts and
Courses [7815]
St. Mary's College of California
1928 St. Marys Rd.
Moraga, CA 94556
Ph: (925)631-8597

Lee, Jae Kyu, President
Association for Information Systems
[6242]
Computer Information Systems Dept.
J. Mack Robinson College of Busi-
ness
Georgia State University
35 Broad St., Ste. 917
Atlanta, GA 30303
Ph: (404)413-7445

Lee, Jean, President, CEO
Minority Corporate Counsel Associa-
tion [5110]
1111 Pennsylvania Ave. NW
Washington, DC 20004
Ph: (202)739-5901
Fax: (202)739-5999

Lee, John, Director
Russell Sage Foundation [7171]
112 E 64th St.
New York, NY 10065
Ph: (212)750-6000

Lee, Ken, CEO
Asian Pacific American Advocates
[17847]
1322 18th St. NW
Washington, DC 20036-1803
Ph: (202)223-5500
Fax: (202)296-0540

Lee, Kenton, CEO, President,
Founder
Because International [12527]
216 12th Ave. N
Nampa, ID 83686
Ph: (208)697-4417

Lee, Kym, President
Bullseye Class Association [22602]
37 High St.
Rockport, MA 01966

Lee, Linda, President
Audio Publishers Association [2901]
100 N 20th St., Ste. 400
Philadelphia, PA 19103
Ph: (215)564-2729

Lee, Dr. Lois, Founder, President
Children of the Night [12792]
14530 Sylvan St.
Van Nuys, CA 91411-2324
Ph: (818)908-4474
Toll Free: 800-551-1300
Fax: (818)908-1468

Lee, Mary M., MD, President
American Society of Andrology
[17547]
1100 E Woodfield Rd., Ste. 350
Schaumburg, IL 60173-5125
Ph: (847)619-4909
Fax: (847)517-7229

Lee, May O., Founder
Asian Resources [11755]
5709 Stockton Blvd.
Sacramento, CA 95824
Ph: (916)454-1892
Fax: (916)454-1895

Lee, Michael, Managing Dir.
International Advertising Association
[98]

747 3rd Ave., 2nd Fl.
New York, NY 10017
Ph: (646)722-2612
Fax: (646)722-2501

Lee, Mike, CEO
ATM Industry Association [384]
PO Box 88433
Sioux Falls, SD 57109-8433
Ph: (605)271-7371
    (605)271-7371

Lee, Missy, President
United White Shepherd Club [21986]
128 Cavalier Dr.
Raeford, NC 28376
Ph: (253)468-6673

Lee, Nathan, CEO, President
Frontier Nursing Service [16133]
Frontier Nursing University
195 School St.
Hyden, KY 41749
Ph: (606)672-2312

Lee, NTanya, Exec. Dir.
POWER: People Organized to Win
    Employment Rights [11780]
2145 Keith St.
San Francisco, CA 94124
Ph: (415)864-8372
Fax: (415)864-8373

Lee, Patricia M., Exec. Dir.
Wallace Genetic Foundation [3581]
4910 Massachusetts Ave. NW, Ste.
    221
Washington, DC 20016
Ph: (202)966-2932
Fax: (202)966-3370

Lee, Paul, Exec. Dir.
Fellowship of Christian Peace Of-
    ficers U.S.A. [19978]
105 Lee Parkway Dr., Ste. C
Chattanooga, TN 37421
Ph: (423)553-8806
Fax: (423)553-8846

Lee, Paul, Counselor
Men's Resource Center [12010]
12 SE 14th Ave.
Portland, OR 97214-1404
Ph: (503)235-3433
Fax: (503)235-4762

Lee, Rex, Director
Action International Ministries
    [20124]
PO Box 398
Mountlake Terrace, WA 98043-0398
Ph: (425)775-4800
Fax: (425)775-0634

Lee, Robert, Exec. Dir., Curator
Asian American Arts Centre [8963]
111 Norfolk St.
New York, NY 10002
Ph: (212)233-2154
Fax: (360)283-2154

Lee, Dr. Robert V., III, Chairman,
    CEO, Founder
Be The Change International
    [12142]
1131 N Laura St.
Jacksonville, FL 32206
Ph: (904)355-0000

Lee, Roger Y., CEO, Treasurer
International Association for
    Computer and Information Science
    [6250]
735 Meadowbrook Dr.
Mount Pleasant, MI 48858
Ph: (989)774-3811

Lee, Scott, PhD, President
Common Hope for Health [14990]
212 Highland St., Unit A

Roxbury, MA 02119

Lee, Steve, President
Lewis and Clark Trail Heritage
    Foundation [9492]
4201 Giant Springs Rd.
Great Falls, MT 59405
Ph: (406)454-1234
Toll Free: 888-701-3434

Lee, Sue, Exec. Dir.
Chinese Historical Society of
    America [9154]
965 Clay St.
San Francisco, CA 94108
Ph: (415)391-1188
Fax: (415)391-1150

Lee, Teresa, CEO
Alpha Zeta [23673]
16020 Swingley Ridge Rd., Ste. 300
Chesterfield, MO 63017
Ph: (636)449-5090
Fax: (636)449-5051

Lee, Tyjaun, President
National Council on Student
    Development [8607]
301 Largo Rd.
Largo, MD 20774
Toll Free: 866-972-0717
Fax: (303)755-7363

Lee, Yong Sung, CEO, President,
    Founder
World Mudo Federation [23032]
7137 Old Alexandria Ferry Rd.
Clinton, MD 20735
Ph: (301)868-8880
Fax: (301)868-0805

Lee, Dr. Yuan Yuan, Contact
Chinese Music Society of North
    America [9887]
PO Box 5275
Woodridge, IL 60517

Leebrick, Meradith, Founder
Abriendo Mentes [12795]
Guanacaste Literacy Inc.
3310 Crosspark Ln.
Houston, TX 77007
Ph: (832)548-4493

Leech, Elvin W. D., Chmn. of the Bd.
Our World-Underwater Scholarship
    Society [23344]
PO Box 6157
Woodridge, IL 60517
Ph: (630)969-6690
Fax: (630)969-6690

Leech, Irene, President
Consumer Federation of America
    [18046]
1620 I St. NW, Ste. 200
Washington, DC 20006
Ph: (202)387-6121
    (202)737-0766

Leemaster, Scott, President
American Technion Society [8132]
55 E 59th St.
New York, NY 10022-1112
Ph: (212)407-6300
Fax: (212)753-2925

Leeming, Jann, Bd. Member
Women's Project Theater [19124]
55 W End Ave.
New York, NY 10023
Ph: (212)765-1706
Fax: (212)765-2024

Leeson, Shirley, President
American Lands Access Association
    [22412]
PO Box 54398

San Jose, CA 95154

Lee-White, Marsha, President
International Association of Orofacial
    Myology [16583]
PO Box 2352
Sequim, WA 98382
Ph: (360)683-5794
Fax: (503)345-6858

Lefcourt, David, President
Society of Municipal Arborists [4217]
PO Box 3129
Champaign, IL 61826-3129

Lefever, Shirley, President
Association of Teacher Educators
    [8644]
11350 Random Hills Rd., Ste. 800
PMB 6
Fairfax, VA 22030
Ph: (703)659-1708
Fax: (703)595-4792

Lefever, Sue, Liaison
Red Wing For'em Club [24079]
PO Box 66456
Roseville, MI 48066

Lefevre, Christine, Secretary
International Council for Archaeozo-
    ology [5942]
c/o Pam J. Crabtree, Treasurer
25 Waverly Pl.
New York, NY 10003

Leff, Laura, President
International Jack Benny Fan Club
    [24009]
PO Box 11288
Piedmont, CA 94611

Lefkowicz, Todd, Founder, Exec. Dir.
Mobility Builders [11617]
Washington Assistive Technology
    Foundation
100 S King St., Ste. 280
Seattle, WA 98104
Ph: (206)328-5116

Lefler, Bill B., President
Association of Army Dentistry
    [14418]
10 Cordoba Way
Hot Springs Village, AR 71909

Leftwich, Sarah, CEO, President
Humane Water [4769]
PO Box 782916
wichita, KS 67278
Ph: (316)788-1150

Leger, George, Founder, Exec. Dir.
Only a Child [11109]
PO Box 990885
Boston, MA 02199-0885
Ph: (781)642-9317

LeGrant, Randy, Exec. Dir.
GeoVisions [8074]
PO Box 167
Chesterfield, NH 03443
Ph: (603)363-4187
Toll Free: 888-830-9455

Legutki, Gregg, Contact
Skinner Family Association [20928]
c/o Gregg Legutki
PO Box 2594
Rancho Cucamonga, CA 91729

Lehman, Adam H., TNP, President
Energy Kinesiology Awareness
    Council [13621]
c/o Adam H. Lehman, TNP,
    President
Institute of BioEnergetic Arts and
    Sciences

19210 Sonoma Hwy.
Sonoma, CA 95476

Lehman, Cheryl A., PhD, RN,
    President
Association of Rehabilitation Nurses
    [16124]
8735 W Higgins Rd., Ste. 300
Chicago, IL 60631-2738
Toll Free: 800-229-7530

Lehman, Karen A., Exec. Dir.
The Episcopal Actors' Guild of
    America, Inc. [10249]
1 E 29th St.
New York, NY 10016-7405
Ph: (212)685-2927

Lehman, Mark, Director
Ancient Coins for Education [22261]
PO Box 90193
Springfield, MA 01139-0193

Lehmann, Lawrence M., President
National Association of Estate Plan-
    ners & Councils [1282]
1120 Chester Ave., Ste. 470
Cleveland, OH 44114
Toll Free: 866-226-2224
Fax: (216)696-2582

Lehmkuhl, Vance, Mgr.
North American Vegetarian Society
    [10293]
PO Box 72
Dolgeville, NY 13329
Ph: (518)568-7970

Lehmuth, Sr. Georgette, CEO,
    President
National Catholic Development
    Conference [19878]
734 15th St. NW Ste.,700
Washington, DC 20005-1013
Ph: (202)637-0470
Fax: (202)637-0471

Lehnen, Leila, Secretary
American Portuguese Studies As-
    sociation [10169]
University of New Mexico
Dept. of Spanish and Portuguese
MSC03-2100
Albuquerque, NM 87131-0001

Lehrman, Margie A. S., Exec. Dir.
American Craft Spirits Association
    [176]
PO Box 701414
Louisville, KY 40270
Ph: (502)299-0238

Leibhart, Allison, President
American Salers Junior Association
    [3711]
American Salers Association
19590 E Main St., No. 104
Parker, CO 80138
Ph: (303)770-9292
Fax: (303)770-9302

Leibman, Abby J., President
MAZON [12101]
10495 Santa Monica Blvd., Ste. 100
Los Angeles, CA 90025
Ph: (310)442-0020
Toll Free: 800-813-0557
Fax: (310)442-0030

Leicht, Mary Ellen, Exec. Dir.
National Junior College Athletic As-
    sociation [23245]
1631 Mesa Ave., Ste. B
Colorado Springs, CO 80906-2956
Ph: (719)590-9788
Fax: (719)590-7324

Leichtling, Michael, Chairman
Friends of Israel Disabled Veterans
    [21006]

1133 Broadway, Ste. 232
New York, NY 10010
Ph: (212)689-3220

Leiderman, Sally H., President
Center for Assessment and Policy
Development [12965]
268 Barren Hill Rd.
Conshohocken, PA 19428
Ph: (610)828-1063

Leighton, Carolyn, Chairperson,
Founder, Chmn. of the Bd.
Women in Technology International
[7300]
11500 Olympic Blvd., Ste. 400
Los Angeles, CA 90064
Ph: (818)788-9484
Fax: (818)788-9410

Leighty, Craig, President
International Scouting Collectors Association [21678]
c/o Craig Leighty, President
724 Kineo Ct.
Oakley, CA 94561-3541
Ph: (925)548-9966

Leinberger, Robert C., Jr., President
National Animal Care and Control
Association [10662]
40960 California Oaks Rd., No. 242
Murrieta, CA 92562
Ph: (913)768-1319
Fax: (913)768-1378

Leinen, Margaret, President
American Geophysical Union [6684]
2000 Florida Ave. NW
Washington, DC 20009-1277
Ph: (202)462-6900
Toll Free: 800-966-2481
Fax: (202)328-0566

Leininger, Robert, Managing Dir.
Music Critics Association of North
America, Inc. [9959]
722 Dulaney Valley Rd., Ste. 259
Baltimore, MD 21204
Ph: (410)435-3881

Leino, Victor E., Dir. of Res.
American College Health Association
[15132]
1362 Mellon Rd., Ste. 180
Hanover, MD 21076-3198
Ph: (410)859-1500
Fax: (410)859-1510

Leinwand, Janis, Contact
Crayons4Kids [13042]
601 John St., Ste. M-351
Kalamazoo, MI 49007
Ph: (269)377-1860

Leinwand, Dr. Nancy, Exec. Dir.
American Research Institute in
Turkey [10284]
3260 S St.
Philadelphia, PA 19104-6324
Ph: (215)898-3474

Leipold, John A., Jr., Director,
President
National Confectionery Sales As-
sociation [2968]
Spitfire House
3135 Berea Rd.
Cleveland, OH 44111
Ph: (216)631-8200
Fax: (216)631-8210

Leitch, David G., Director
U.S. Chamber Litigation Center
[5725]
1615 H St. NW
Washington, DC 20062
Ph: (202)463-5337
Fax: (202)463-5346

Leith, Sandy, President
Vintage Sports Car Club of America
[21515]
39 Woodland Dr.
New Britain, PA 18901

Leitis, Imants, Director, Editor
Baltic American Freedom League
[17822]
PO Box 65056
Los Angeles, CA 90065-0056
Ph: (323)255-4215

Leitner, Elaine, President
Kite Trade Association International
[3140]
PO Box 6898
Bend, OR 97708
Ph: (541)994-9647
Toll Free: 800-243-8548
Fax: (503)419-4369

Leitz, Fred, President
National Council of Agricultural
Employers [3528]
525 9th St. NW, Ste. 800
Washington, DC 20004
Ph: (202)629-9320

Leitzel, Karl Eric, Director, Founder
Landscape Artists International
[8928]
c/o Karl Eric Leitzel, Founder
155 Murray School Ln.
Spring Mills, PA 16875
Ph: (814)422-8461

LeJeune, B.J., Director
Care Ministries [17694]
PO Box 1830
Starkville, MS 39760-1830
Ph: (662)323-4999
Toll Free: 800-336-2232

Leland, James, President
International Commission on Il-
lumination - U.S. National Commit-
tee [6785]
Virginia Tech Transportation Institute
3500 Transportation Research Plz.
Blacksburg, VA 24061
Ph: (540)231-1581
Fax: (540)231-1555

Lelei, Macrina, Chairman
Association of African Studies
Programs [7465]
c/o African Studies Program
Anthropology Dept.
Bridgewater State University
Hart Hall, Rm. 237
Bridgewater, MA 02325-0001
Ph: (508)531-2166

Lelek, Jeremy, President
Association of Biblical Counselors
[20038]
209 N Industrial Blvd., Ste. 237
Bedford, TX 76021-6128
Toll Free: 877-222-4551

Lemaire, Tom, President
International 210 Association
[22624]
59 Water St.
Hingham, MA 02043
Ph: (781)985-5460

Lemak, Dr. Lawrence J., Founder
National Center for Sports Safety
[17285]
2316 1st Ave. S
Birmingham, AL 35233
Ph: (205)329-7535
Toll Free: 866-508-6277
Fax: (205)329-7526

Leman, Talia, CEO, Founder
RandomKid [13477]
PO Box 102

Waukee, IA 50263-0102
Ph: (646)926-0778

LeMar, Chelsea, Exec. Dir.
National Association of Professional
Women in Construction, Inc. [881]
1001 Avenue of the Americas, Ste.
405
New York, NY 10018
Ph: (212)486-7745
Fax: (212)486-0228

LeMay, Brian J., Exec. Dir.,
President
Bostonian Society [9467]
Old State House Museum
206 Washington St.
Boston, MA 02109
Ph: (617)720-1713
Fax: (617)720-3289

Lemay, Helen Schneider, Exec. Dir.
Ornithological Societies of North
America [6965]
c/o Helen Schneider Lemay, Execu-
tive Director
USNA Business Office
5400 Bosque Blvd., Ste. 680
Waco, TX 76710
Ph: (254)399-9636
Fax: (254)776-3767

Lembeck, William, Director
Society of Wine Educators [22478]
1612 K St. NW, Ste. 700
Washington, DC 20006
Ph: (202)408-8777
Fax: (202)408-8677

LeMelle, Therese, Contact
Hall of Fame for Great Americans
[10329]
Bronx Community College
2155 University Ave.
Bronx, NY 10453
Ph: (718)289-5160

Lemer, Patricia S., Exec. Dir.,
Founder
Developmental Delay Resources
[14159]
5801 Beacon St.
Pittsburgh, PA 15217
Toll Free: 800-497-0944
Fax: (412)422-1374

Lemke, Lee, Exec. VP
China Clay Producers Association
[2386]
113 Arkwright Landing
Macon, GA 31210
Ph: (478)757-1211
Fax: (478)757-1949

Lemle, Mr. Michael, Chairman
The Tibet Fund [10281]
241 E 32 St.
New York, NY 10016
Ph: (212)213-5011
Fax: (212)213-1219

Lemmon, Brita, President
Danish/Swedish Farmdog Club of
America [21867]
PO Box 819
Seal Beach, CA 90740

Lemon, Joel, Mgr.
Sports Car Club of America [21493]
PO Box 19400
Topeka, KS 66619-0400
Ph: (785)357-7222
Toll Free: 800-770-2055
Fax: (785)232-7228

Lempert, Ted, President
Children Now [10920]
1404 Franklin St., Ste. 700

Oakland, CA 94612-3232
Ph: (510)763-2444
Fax: (510)763-1974

LeMunyan Newberry, Lauren, Exec.
Dir.
National Institute of Oilseed
Products [2453]
750 National Press Bldg.
529 14th St. NW
Washington, DC 20045
Ph: (202)591-2461
Fax: (202)223-9741

Lenaghan, Michael J., Chmn. of the
Bd.
Service for Peace [18829]
360 Fairfield Ave.
Bridgeport, CT 06604
Ph: (203)339-0064
Fax: (203)339-0874

Lendoire, Javier C., MD, President
Americas Hepato-Pancreato-Biliary
Association [15250]
PO Box 410454
Kansas City, MO 64141
Ph: (913)402-7102
Fax: (913)273-1140

Lenhart, Amy M., President
American College Counseling As-
sociation [7682]
c/o Amy M. Lenhart, President
Collin College - PRC Campus
9700 Wade Blvd.
Frisco, TX 75035
Ph: (972)377-1008

Lenihan, Daniel J., MD, President
International Cardioncology Society,
North America [14121]
602 S Audubon Ave., Ste. B
Tampa, FL 33609

Lennard, Mr. Ian J., President
National Cargo Bureau [3094]
17 Battery Pl., Ste. 1232
New York, NY 10004-1110
Ph: (212)785-8300
Fax: (212)785-8333

Lennon, J. Michael, President
Norman Mailer Society [10389]
c/o David Light, Treasurer
75 Jennings Ln.
Windham, CT 06280

Lennox, James G., Co-Ch.
Ayn Rand Society [10082]
Dept. of History and Philosophy of
Science
University of Pittsburgh
4200 5th Ave.
Pittsburgh, PA 15260

Lenoci, Terri, President
International Fainting Goat Associa-
tion [4276]
c/o John Savage, Registrar
1039 State Rte. 168
Darlington, PA 16115
Ph: (724)843-2084
Fax: (724)891-1440

Lenocker, Jodi, VP
American Hatpin Society [21611]
c/o Jodi Lenocker, Vice President
PO Box 2672
Lake Arrowhead, CA 92352

LeNoir, Barry, President
United Black Fund [11862]
2500 Martin Luther King, Jr. Ave. SE
Washington, DC 20020
Ph: (202)783-9300
Fax: (202)347-2564

Lenoir, Michael A., MD, Contact
National Medical Association [15741]
8403 Colesville Rd., Ste. 920

Silver Spring, MD 20910
Ph: (202)347-1895

Lent, Donna, President
National Women's Political Caucus
[18231]
PO Box 50476
Washington, DC 20091
Ph: (202)785-1100
Fax: (202)370-6306

Lentini, Rev. James, Secretary
Alpha Phi Delta Fraternity [23885]
257 E Camden Wyoming Ave., Unit
A
Camden, DE 19934
Ph: (302)531-7854

Lenz, Ashley, COO
Project HEAL [14650]
38-18 W Dr.
Douglaston, NY 11363
Fax: (718)709-7787

León, Oscar, Exec. Sec.
Inter-American Telecommunication
Commission [3228]
1889 F St. NW, 6th Fl.
Washington, DC 20006
Ph: (202)370-4713
    (202)370-4953

Leon, Rachel, Exec. Dir.
Environmental Grantmakers Associa-
tion [4533]
475 Riverside Dr., Ste. 960
New York, NY 10115
Ph: (212)812-4310
Fax: (212)812-4311

Leon, Sharon, Exec. Dir.
National Foundation for Autism
Research [13774]
PO Box 502177
San Diego, CA 92150-2177
Ph: (858)679-8800

Leonard, Catherine, Chmn. of the
Bd.
Enterprise Wireless Alliance [3226]
2121 Cooperative Way, Ste. 225
Herndon, VA 20171
Toll Free: 800-482-8282
Fax: (703)524-1074

Leonard, Dan, President
National Pharmaceutical Council
[2563]
1717 Pennsylvania Ave. NW, Ste.
800
Washington, DC 20006
Ph: (202)827-2100
Fax: (202)827-0314

Leonard, John, Jr., Dir. of Accred.
International Association of Campus
Law Enforcement Administrators
[5467]
342 N Main St.
West Hartford, CT 06117-2507
Ph: (860)586-7517
Fax: (860)586-7550

Leonard, Michael, Chmn. of the Bd.
The Conservation Fund [3837]
1655 N Fort Myer Dr., Ste. 1300
Arlington, VA 22209
Ph: (703)525-6300
Fax: (703)525-4610

Leonard, Mike, Secretary
Wilderness Volunteers [22294]
PO Box 22292
Flagstaff, AZ 86002
Ph: (928)255-1128
Fax: (928)222-1912

Leonardi, Anthony D., President
National Association of Postmasters
of the United States [5681]

8 Herbert St.
Alexandria, VA 22305
Ph: (703)683-9027
Fax: (703)683-0923

Leong, Benjamin, President
International Association of Asian
Crime Investigators and Specialists
[5153]
PO Box 612
North Scituate, MA 02060-0612

Leong, Benjamin, Exec. Dir.,
President
International Organization of Asian
Crime Investigators and Specialists
[5126]
PO Box 612
North Scituate, MA 02060-0612

Leong, Lawrence H., Exec. Dir.
Society of Atherosclerosis Imaging
and Prevention [17579]
26804 Ridge Rd.
Damascus, MD 20872
Ph: (301)253-4155
Fax: (301)414-7535

Leong, Tim, President
Society of Publication Designers
[1558]
27 Union Sq. W, Ste. 207
New York, NY 10003
Ph: (212)223-3332
Fax: (212)223-5880

Leparulo, Willy, President
National Collegiate Table Tennis As-
sociation [23293]
154 Mill Run Ln.
Saint Peters, MO 63376-7106
Toll Free: 800-581-6770

Lepczyk, Billie, Chairperson
International Council of Kinetography
Laban [9261]
c/o Susan Gingrasso, Treasurer
4308 Heffron St.
Stevens Point, WI 54481-5338

Lependorf, Jeffrey, Exec. Dir.
Council of Literary Magazines and
Presses [2674]
154 Christopher St., Ste. 3C
New York, NY 10014-9110
Ph: (212)741-9110
Fax: (212)741-9112

Lerner, Georgia, Exec. Dir.
Women's Prison Association [11552]
110 2nd Ave.
New York, NY 10003
Ph: (646)292-7740
Fax: (646)292-7763

Lerner, Jeffrey C., PhD, President,
CEO
ECRI Institute [15685]
5200 Butler Pke.
Plymouth Meeting, PA 19462-1298
Ph: (610)825-6000
Fax: (610)834-1275

Lerner, Lawrence, President
Union of Councils for Jews in the
Former Soviet Union [18142]
East Tower, 4th Fl.
2200 Pennsylvania Ave. NW
Washington, DC 20037
Ph: (202)567-7572
Fax: (888)825-8314

LeRoy, Greg, Exec. Dir. (Actg.)
Americans for Transit [19195]
1616 P St. NW, Ste. 210
Washington, DC 20036
Ph: (202)232-1616

Lesan, Rob, President
Connect Worldwide [6299]
PO Box 204086

Austin, TX 78720-4086

Lesavich, Stephen, PhD, President
International Society for Law and
Technology [5431]
1811 W Katella Ave., Ste. 101
Anaheim, CA 92804-6657
Ph: (714)778-3230
Fax: (714)778-5463

Lesh, Frank, Exec. Dir.
American Society of Home Inspec-
tors [490]
932 Lee St., Ste. 101
Des Plaines, IL 60016
Ph: (847)759-2820
Fax: (847)759-1620

Leslie, Catherine A., Exec. Dir.
Engineers Without Borders-U.S.A.
[6553]
1031 33rd St., Ste. 210
Denver, CO 80205
Ph: (303)772-2723
Fax: (303)772-2699

Leslie, David, President, CEO
MedicAlert Foundation International
[14665]
5226 Pirrone Ct.
Salida, CA 95368
Toll Free: 800-432-5378

Leslie, Laura, President
Association of Capitol Reporters and
Editors [2660]
c/o Alan Johnson, Treasurer
34 S 3rd St.
Columbus, OH 43215-4201

Leslie, Seaver, President
Americans for Customary Weight
and Measure [19152]
PO Box 248
Wiscasset, ME 04578
Ph: (207)882-5554

Leslie, William D., MD, MSc,
President
International Society for Clinical
Densitometry [16499]
Bldg. C
955 S Main St.
Middletown, CT 06457-5153
Ph: (860)259-1000
Fax: (860)259-1030

Lessin, Nancy, Founder
Military Families Speak Out [19237]
1716 Clark Ave.
Long Beach, CA 90815
Ph: (562)597-3980

Lester, Anne, Chairman
The Medieval Academy of America
Committee on Centers and
Regional Associations [9788]
17 Dunster St., Ste. 202
Cambridge, MA 02138
Ph: (617)491-1622
Fax: (617)492-3303

Lester, Damon, President
National Association of Minority
Automobile Dealers [2394]
9745 Lottsford Rd., Ste. 150
Largo, MD 20774
Ph: (301)306-1614
Fax: (301)306-1493

Lester, Thomas, President
American Blind Bowling Association
[22771]
c/o Thomas Lester, President
19146 Ardmore St.
Detroit, MI 48235-1701
Ph: (313)864-0448

Leszcz, Michael, President
Professional Managers Association
[5199]

PO Box 77235
Washington, DC 20013
Ph: (202)803-9597
Fax: (202)803-9044

Lethin, Linda, President
Miniature Bull Terrier Club of
America [21915]
c/o Kathleen Coffman
11200 Newman Ct.
Fredericksburg, VA 22407
Ph: (540)219-3751

Letizia, John J., Chairman
American Association for Homecare
[15076]
1707 L St. NW, Ste. 350
Washington, DC 20036
Ph: (202)372-0107
Fax: (202)835-8306

Leto, Julie, President
Novelists Inc. [3517]
PO Box 2037
Manhattan, KS 66505
Fax: (785)537-1877

Letocha, Phoebe Evans, Secretary
Archivists and Librarians in the History of the Health Sciences [9679]
c/o Barbara Niss, Treasurer
14 Elmwood Ave.
Rye, NY 10580
Ph: (310)825-6940

Letterman, Judy, CEO
Pesticide Applicators Professional
Association [2505]
PO Box 80095
Salinas, CA 93912-0095
Ph: (831)442-3536
Fax: (831)442-2351

Letterman, Tracie, Exec. Dir.
American Anti-Vivisection Society
[10565]
801 Old York Rd., Ste. 204
Jenkintown, PA 19046
Toll Free: 800-729-2287

Lettman-Hicks, Sharon J., CEO,
Exec. Dir.
National Black Justice Coalition
[19129]
PO Box 71395
Washington, DC 20024
Ph: (202)319-1552
Fax: (202)319-7365

Leung, Som-lok, Exec. Dir.
International Association of Credit
Portfolio Managers [943]
360 Madison Ave., 17th Fl.
New York, NY 10017-7111
Ph: (646)289-5430
Fax: (646)289-5429

Leupold, Nancy E., Founder,
President
Support for People with Oral and
Head and Neck Cancer [14071]
PO Box 53
Locust Valley, NY 11560-0053
Toll Free: 800-377-0928
Fax: (516)671-8794

Leuthauser, Kishawn, VP, Director
Louis and Harold Price Foundation
[13069]
1371 E Hecla Dr., Ste. B-1
Louisville, CO 80027
Ph: (303)665-9201
Fax: (303)665-1027

Leuthold, Doug, President,
Treasurer, Director
Cellulose Insulation Manufacturers
Association [510]

S Keowee St.
Dayton, OH 45402
Ph: (937)222-2462
Toll Free: 888-881-2462
Fax: (937)222-5794

Leven, Stuart, Chairperson
Friends of the Western Philatelic
Library [10071]
PO Box 2219
Sunnyvale, CA 94087-0219
Ph: (408)733-0336

Levene, Nate, Secretary, Treasurer
American Glovebox Society [6925]
526 S East St.
Santa Rosa, CA 95404
Toll Free: 800-530-1022
Fax: (707)578-4406

Levengood, Lynn, VP
Mannlicher Collectors Association
[21683]
1000 Jacklin Rd.
Milpitas, CA 95035

Levengood, Paul, Chmn. of the Bd.
EnterpriseWorks/VITA [17807]
818 Connecticut Ave. NW, Ste. 600
Washington, DC 20006
Ph: (202)639-8660
Fax: (202)639-8664

Levens, Esther, CEO, Founder
Unity Coalition for Israel [8134]
3965 W 83rd St., No. 292
Shawnee Mission, KS 66208-5308
Ph: (913)648-0022
Fax: (913)648-7997

Leventhal, John, President
The Ray E. Helfer Society [14211]
350 Poplar Ave.
Elmhurst, IL 60126
Ph: (630)359-4273
Fax: (630)359-4274

Leverenz, Larry J., President
World Federation of Athletic Training
& Therapy [17287]
c/o Larry J. Leverenz, President
Dept. of Health & Kinesiology
Purdue University
800 W Stadium Ave.
West Lafayette, IN 47907
Ph: (765)494-3167

Levey, Dan, Exec. Dir.
Parents of Murdered Children, Inc.
[12423]
4960 Ridge Ave., Ste. 2
Cincinnati, OH 45209-1075
Ph: (513)721-5683
Toll Free: 888-818-7662
Fax: (513)345-4489

Levi, Jeffrey, PhD, Exec. Dir.
Trust for America's Health [17025]
1730 M St. NW, Ste. 900
Washington, DC 20036
Ph: (202)223-9870
Fax: (202)223-9871

Levi, Moshe, Chairman, Director
American Physician Scientists Association [8304]
6 Boston Rd., Ste. 202
Chelmsford, MA 01824

Levin, Andrea, President, Exec. Dir.
Committee for Accuracy in Middle
East Reporting in America [18679]
PO Box 35040
Boston, MA 02135-0001
Ph: (617)789-3672
Fax: (617)787-7853

Levin, Debra J., CEO, President
Center for Health Design [14986]
1850 Gateway Blvd., Ste. 1083

Concord, CA 94520
Ph: (925)521-9404
Fax: (925)521-9405

Levin, Edward D., PhD, President
International Neurotoxicology As-
sociation [7342]
c/o Edward D. Levin, PhD, President
Psychiatry and Behavioral Sciences
School of Medicine
Duke Institute for Brain Sciences
Durham, NC 27708
Ph: (919)681-6273

Levin, Jules, Exec. Dir.
National AIDS Treatment Advocacy
Project [13555]
580 Broadway, Ste. 1010
New York, NY 10012
Ph: (212)219-0106
Toll Free: 888-26N-ATAP
Fax: (212)219-8473

Levin, Mark B., Exec. Dir.
National Coalition Supporting
Eurasian Jewry [18141]
1120 20th St. NW, Ste. 300N
Washington, DC 20036
Ph: (202)898-2500
Fax: (202)898-0822

Levin, Mark, Managing Dir.
National Elementary Schools Press
Association [8455]
c/o Meredith Cummings, CJE
Box 870172
Tuscaloosa, AL 35487-0172
Ph: (205)348-2772

Levin, Mike, Exec. Dir.
International Concrete Repair
Institute [789]
1000 Westgate Dr., Ste. 252
Saint Paul, MN 55114
Ph: (651)366-6095
Fax: (651)290-2266

Levin, Saul, MD, CEO
American Psychiatric Association
[16822]
1000 Wilson Blvd., Ste. 1825
Arlington, VA 22209-3901
Ph: (703)907-7300
Toll Free: 888-357-7924
Fax: (703)907-1097

Levin, Susan, President, Founder
Lung Cancer Circle of Hope [14005]
7 Carnation Dr., Ste. A
Lakewood, NJ 08701
Ph: (732)363-4426
Fax: (732)370-9180

Levinas, Randi, Exec. VP
U.S.-Russia Business Council [2003]
1110 Vermont Ave. NW, Ste. 350
Washington, DC 20005
Ph: (202)739-9180
Fax: (202)659-5920

Levine, David, Founder, CEO
American Sustainable Business
Council [1002]
1401 New York Ave. NW, Ste. 1225
Washington, DC 20005
Ph: (202)595-9302

Levine, Deb, MA, Founder
Internet Sexuality Information
Services, Inc. [8563]
409 13th St., 14th Fl.
Oakland, CA 94612-2607
Ph: (510)835-9400

Levine, Don, VP
World Airline Historical Society
[21257]
PO Box 489

Ocoee, FL 34761
Fax: (407)522-9352

Levine, Felice, Chmn. of the Bd.
Consortium of Social Science As-
sociations [7165]
1701 K St. NW, Ste. 1150
Washington, DC 20006
Ph: (202)842-3525
Fax: (202)842-2788

Levine, Felice J., PhD, Exec. Dir.
American Educational Research As-
sociation [8494]
1430 K St. NW, Ste. 1200
Washington, DC 20005-2504
Ph: (202)238-3200
Fax: (202)238-3250

Levine, Gail Brett, Exec. Dir.
National Association of Jewelry Ap-
praisers [2059]
c/o Gail Brett Levine, GG, Executive
Director
PO Box 18
Rego Park, NY 11374-0018
Ph: (718)896-1536
Fax: (718)997-9057

Levine, Jenny, Exec. Dir.
Library and Information Technology
Association [9713]
50 E Huron St.
Chicago, IL 60611-2795
Ph: (312)944-6780
Toll Free: 800-545-2433
Fax: (312)280-3257

Levine, Joyce, Secretary
American Gathering of Jewish
Holocaust Survivors and Their
Descendants [18343]
c/o The American Gathering
122 W 30th St., Ste. 304A
New York, NY 10001
Ph: (212)239-4230

Levine, Laura, CEO, President
JumpStart Coalition for Personal
Financial Literacy [7921]
919 18th St. NW, Ste. 300
Washington, DC 20006
Toll Free: 888-45-EDUCATE
Fax: (202)223-0321

Levine, Marie, Exec. Dir.
Shark Research Institute [6811]
PO Box 40
Princeton, NJ 08540
Ph: (609)921-3522
Fax: (609)921-1505

Levine, Nicole, President
Firefly, Inc. [10975]
1405 S Fern St., No. 552
Arlington, VA 22202
Ph: (917)359-7207
Fax: (240)396-2107

Levine, Paul, Exec. Dir.
National Motor Freight Traffic As-
sociation, Inc. [3095]
1001 N Fairfax St., Ste. 600
Alexandria, VA 22314-1798
Ph: (703)838-1810
Toll Free: 866-411-6632
Fax: (703)683-6296

Levine, Robert, DPM, President
Federation of Podiatric Medical
Boards [16788]
12116 Flag Harbor Dr.
Germantown, MD 20874-1979
Ph: (202)810-3762
Fax: (202)318-0091

Levine, Shalom, Dir. of Lib. Svcs.
Chabad Lubavitch [20240]
Lubavich World Headquarters

770 Eastern Pky.
Brooklyn, NY 11213
Ph: (718)774-4000
Fax: (718)774-2718

Levine, Susan Goldwater, Exec. Dir.
Hospice Association of America
[15278]
228 7th St. SE
Washington, DC 20003
Ph: (202)546-4759
Fax: (202)547-9559

Levine, Susan V., Creative Dir.
American Alliance of Museums
[9815]
2451 Crystal Dr., Ste. 1005
Arlington, VA 22202
Ph: (202)289-1818
Toll Free: 866-226-2150
Fax: (202)289-6578

Levinson, Martin H., President
Institute of General Semantics
[10212]
72-11 Austin St., No. 233
Forest Hills, NY 11375
Ph: (212)729-7973
Fax: (718)793-2527

Levinson, Sandra, Exec. Dir.
Center for Cuban Studies [9194]
231 W 29th St., 4th Fl.
New York, NY 10001
Ph: (212)242-0559
Fax: (212)242-1937

Levitan, Ken, Contact
Hank Williams Jr. Fan Club [24070]
c/o Ken Levitan
Vector Management
PO Box 120479
Nashville, TN 37212

Levitt, Jacob, MD, President, Medi-
cal Dir., Bd. Member
Periodic Paralysis Association
[15666]
c/o Jacob Levitt, MD, FAAD,
President/Medical Director
Periodic Paralysis Association
155 W 68th St., Ste. 1732
New York, NY 10023
Ph: (407)339-9499

Levitt, Joseph, Director
Food and Drug Administration
Alumni Association [18261]
c/o Karen Carson, Membership
Chair
540 N St. SW, No. S104
Leesburg, VA 20176

Levy, Chris, President
Hungarian Pumi Club of America
Inc. [21894]
c/o Tammy Hall, Vice President
211 SE Maplewood Ln.
Shelton, WA 98584
Ph: (360)427-8918

Levy, Deb, President, Founder
Association of Professional Animal
Waste Specialists [3445]
c/o Timothy Stone, Treasurer/
Founder
PO Box 2325
Santa Clarita, CA 91386-2325
Ph: (409)422-7297

Levy, Debra, President
Auto Glass Safety Council [1502]
20 PGA Dr., Ste. 201
Stafford, VA 22554
Ph: (540)720-7484
Fax: (540)720-5687

Levy, Rabbi Don Yoel, President
OK Kosher Certification [20273]
391 Troy Ave.

Brooklyn, NY 11213
Ph: (718)756-7500
Fax: (718)756-7503

Levy, Emanuel, Exec. Dir.
Systems Building Research Alliance
 [1692]
1776 Broadway, Ste. 2205
New York, NY 10019-2016
Ph: (212)496-0900
Fax: (212)496-5389

Levy, Jared R., President
ChemoClothes [13938]
Five Greentree Center
525 Lincoln Dr., Ste. 104, Rte. 73
Marlton, NJ 08053
Ph: (609)706-3896
Toll Free: 888-852-5858

Levy, Justin, Exec. Dir.
Conscious Alliance [11345]
2525 Arapahoe Ave., Ste. E4 - 182
Boulder, CO 80302
Ph: (720)406-7871
Toll Free: 866-259-9455

Levy, Markus, President
Multicore Association [6256]
PO Box 4794
El Dorado Hills, CA 95762
Ph: (530)672-9113

Levy, Michael H., Contact
Plastics Foodservice Packaging
 Group [2482]
American Chemistry Council
700 2nd St. NE
Washington, DC 20002
Ph: (202)249-7000
Fax: (202)249-6100

Levy, Paul, VP
Professional Golfers' Association of
 America [22892]
100 Avenue of the Champions
Palm Beach Gardens, FL 33418-
 3653
Ph: (561)624-8400

Levy, Richard M., Founder, CEO
Lift Up Africa [11398]
PO Box 3112
Woburn, MA 01888
Toll Free: 888-854-3887

Levy, Robert A., Chairman
Cato Institute [18964]
1000 Massachusetts Ave. NW
Washington, DC 20001-5403
Ph: (202)842-0200
Fax: (202)842-3490

Levy-Fisch, Jill, President
Save Babies Through Screening
 Foundation [14213]
PO Box 42197
Cincinnati, OH 45242
Toll Free: 888-454-3383

Lew, Rod, MPH, Exec. Dir.
Asian Pacific Partners for Empowerment, Advocacy and Leadership
 [11315]
424 3rd St., Ste. 220
Oakland, CA 94607
Ph: (510)844-4147

Lewallen, David G., MD, President
Orthopaedic Research and Educa-
 tion Foundation [16486]
9400 W Higgins Rd., Ste. 215
Rosemont, IL 60018-4975
Ph: (847)698-9980
Fax: (847)698-7806

Lewin, Bruno, MD, Founder
Integrative Clinics International
 [15147]

3871 Piedmont Ave., No. 34
Oakland, CA 94611

Lewin, David N.B., President
American Society for Clinical Pathol-
 ogy [16574]
33 W Monroe St., Ste. 1600
Chicago, IL 60603
Ph: (312)541-4999
Fax: (312)541-4998

Lewin, Leslie Adelson
Seeds of Peace [18828]
370 Lexington Ave., Ste. 1201
New York, NY 10017
Ph: (212)573-8040
Fax: (212)573-8047

Lewin, Paul, VP
IEEE - Dielectrics and Electrical
 Insulation Society [6409]
Auburn University
Electrical and Computer Engineering
200 Broun Hall
Auburn, AL 36849-5201
Ph: (334)844-1822
Fax: (334)844-1809

Lewins, Thomas, Exec. Dir.
New Avenues to Independence
 [12331]
17608 Euclid Ave.
Cleveland, OH 44112
Ph: (216)481-1907
Fax: (216)481-2050

Lewis, Adam, President
Association Montessori International
 USA [8350]
206 N Washington St., Ste. 330
Alexandria, VA 22314
Ph: (703)746-9919

Lewis, Allison L., Exec. Dir.
Association for Prevention Teaching
 and Research [16800]
1001 Connecticut Ave. NW, Ste. 610
Washington, DC 20036
Ph: (202)463-0550
Toll Free: 866-520-2787
Fax: (202)463-0555

Lewis, Ann, President
Ronald Reagan Home Preservation
 Foundation [10345]
816 S Hennepin Ave.
Dixon, IL 61021
Ph: (815)288-5176
Fax: (815)288-3642

Lewis, Bill, Mem.
TechAssure Association [3213]
c/o Mark Ware, Chairman Elect
IMA
1705 17th St., Ste 100
Denver, CO 80202
Ph: (888)208-8670

Lewis, Bob, President
International Fancy Guppy Association [22034]
c/o Ramino Carbonell, Treasurer,
 744 Flowers St.
744 Flowers St.
Saint Augustine, FL 32092
Ph: (561)414-0057

Lewis, Bonnie Sue, Dr., V. Ch.
Presbyterian Frontier Fellowship
 [20454]
7132 Portland Ave., Ste. 136
Richfield, MN 55423-3264
Ph: (612)869-0062

Lewis, Dr. Brad, President
American Waldensian Society
 [20637]
208 Rodoret St. S

Valdese, NC 28690-0398
Ph: (828)874-3500
Toll Free: 866-825-3373
Fax: (828)874-0880

Lewis, Brian, CEO
International Society for Technology
 in Education [7657]
1530 Wilson Blvd., Ste. 730
Arlington, VA 22209
Ph: (703)348-4784
Toll Free: 800-336-5191
Fax: (703)348-6459

Lewis, Carma, Exec. Dir.
Armed Females of America [18246]
2702 E University Dr., Ste. 103
Mesa, AZ 85213
Ph: (480)924-8202

Lewis, Darcy, Contact
Touch for Health Kinesiology As-
 sociation [13660]
4917 Waters Edge Dr., Ste. 125
Raleigh, NC 27606
Ph: (919)637-4938

Lewis, David P., Chairman
Tax Foundation [5804]
1325 G St. NW, Ste. 950
Washington, DC 20005
Ph: (202)464-6200
     (202)464-5120
Fax: (202)464-6201

Lewis, Prof. Herbert S., President
Association of Senior Anthropolo-
 gists [5909]
2300 Clarendon Blvd., Ste. 1301
Arlington, VA 22201
Ph: (703)528-1902
Fax: (703)528-3546

Lewis, Hunter, President
Alliance for Natural Health USA
 [16795]
Bldg. 6, Ste. 110
3525 Piedmont Rd. NE
Atlanta, GA 30305
Ph: (202)803-5123
Toll Free: 800-230-2762
Fax: (202)315-5837

Lewis, Janine, PhD, Chairperson
National Healthy Mothers, Healthy
 Babies Coalition [16297]
PO Box 3360
Alexandria, VA 22302-3360
Ph: (703)838-7552

Lewis, Jason, Exec. Dir. (Actg.),
 CFO
Association for Institutional Research
 [8440]
1435 E Piedmont Dr., Ste. 211
Tallahassee, FL 32308
Ph: (850)385-4155
Fax: (850)385-5180

Lewis, Jennifer, Exec. Dir.
Society for Prevention Research
 [17328]
11240 Waples Mill Rd., Ste. 200
Fairfax, VA 22030-6078
Ph: (703)934-4850
Fax: (703)359-7562

Lewis, Jenniffer, Founder, CEO
Foundation for Children with Micro-
 cephaly [15933]
PO Box 12134
Glendale, AZ 85318
Ph: (623)476-7494
Toll Free: 877-476-5503
Fax: (623)241-4543

Lewis, Jeremy, Exec. Dir.
International Association of Human
 Trafficking Investigators [5286]

PO Box 2185
Oldsmar, FL 34677
Ph: (727)504-7203
Fax: (865)851-9141

Lewis, Jerome R., Director
Institute of Public Administration
 USA [5695]
University of Delaware
180 Graham Hall
Newark, DE 19716
Ph: (302)831-8971
Fax: (302)831-3488

Lewis, Jim, Director
American Association of Electrodiag-
 nostic Technologists [15675]
PO Box 2770
Cedar Rapids, IA 52406
Toll Free: 877-333-2238

Lewis, Jim, Bd. Member
University of Iowa Alumni Associa-
 tion [19357]
PO Box 1970
Iowa City, IA 52244-1970
Ph: (319)335-3294
Toll Free: 800-469-2586
Fax: (319)335-1079

Lewis, Dr. Jimmy, Bd. Member
HIS Nets [13513]
PO Box 721701
Norman, OK 73070-8301
Ph: (405)443-4014
     (828)782-0705

Lewis, Joe, President
Angels of America's Fallen [10854]
10010 Devonwood Ct.
Colorado Springs, CO 80920
Ph: (719)377-7352

Lewis, Joe, President
VietNow National [13254]
1835 Broadway
Rockford, IL 61104
Ph: (815)227-5100
Toll Free: 800-837-8669

Lewis, John, Exec. Dir.
American CueSports Alliance
 [22583]
101 S Military Ave., Ste. P, No. 131
Green Bay, WI 54303
Ph: (920)662-1705
Fax: (920)662-1706

Lewis, Karen S., Exec. Dir.
Forging Industry Educational and
 Research Foundation [6844]
1111 Superior Ave., Ste. 615
Cleveland, OH 44114-2568
Ph: (216)781-5040
Fax: (216)781-0102

Lewis, Karissa, Exec. Dir.
Center for Third World Organizing
 [17882]
900 Alice St., Ste. 300
Oakland, CA 94607
Ph: (510)201-0080
Fax: (510)433-0908

Lewis, Lisa, Media Spec.
Fully Informed Jury Association
 [18598]
PO Box 5570
Helena, MT 59604-5570
Ph: (406)442-7800
Toll Free: 800-TEL-JURY

Lewis, Lisa, President, CEO
University of Minnesota Alumni As-
 sociation [19361]
McNamara Alumni Ctr.
200 Oak St. SE, Ste. 200
Minneapolis, MN 55455-2040
Ph: (612)624-2323
Toll Free: 800-862-5867
Fax: (612)626-8167

Lewis, Lynn, Exec. Dir.
Picture the Homeless [11959]
104 E 126th St.
New York, NY 10468
Ph: (646)314-6423

Lewis, Michael, MD, President
Society for the Advancement of
Geriatric Anesthesia [13706]
c/o Michael Lewis, MD
University of Florida
College of Medicine
655 W 8th St.
Jacksonville, FL 32209
Ph: (904)244-5431

Lewis, Paul, VP of Fin.
Eno Transportation Foundation
[7347]
1710 Rhode Island Ave. NW, Ste.
500
Washington, DC 20036
Ph: (202)879-4700

Lewis, Robin D., President
Optometric Extension Program
Foundation [16435]
2300 York Rd., Ste. 113
Timonium, MD 21093
Ph: (410)561-3791
Fax: (410)252-1719

Lewis, Roderick, Director
American Bus Association [3320]
111 K St. NE, 9th Fl.
Washington, DC 20002
Ph: (202)842-1645
Toll Free: 800-283-2877
Fax: (202)842-0850

Lewis, Shireen K., Sen. Ed.
Black World Foundation [8779]
c/o The Black Scholar
Dept. of English
University of Washington
Padelford A-101, Box 354330
Seattle, WA 98105-4412

Lewis, Tim, President
Wild Ones [4449]
2285 Butte des Morts Beach Rd.
Neenah, WI 54956
Ph: (920)730-3986
Toll Free: 877-394-9453

Lewis, Vincent P., Founder,
President
All Roads Ministry [19789]
55 Palen Rd., No. 3
Hopewell Junction, NY 12533
Ph: (845)226-4172

Lewis-Nwosu, Rhonda, Founder
Sparkles of Life [14242]
11569 Hwy. 6 S, Ste. 148
Sugar Land, TX 77498
Ph: (281)397-3260

Lezama, Michele, Exec. Dir.
National GEM Consortium [7862]
1430 Duke St.
Alexandria, VA 22314-3403
Ph: (703)562-3646
Fax: (202)207-3518

Iezzi Mezzera, Carmen, Exec. Dir.
Association of Professional Schools
of International Affairs [8110]
1615 L St., NW 8th Flt.
Washington, DC 20036
Ph: (202)559-5831

Lezzi, S. Nicholas, Chmn. of the Bd.
Life Laboratory [15030]
1244 Fort Washington Ave., Ste. N1
Fort Washington, PA 19034
Ph: (215)646-6504

Lhamo, Jetsunma Ahkon, Director
Kunzang Palyul Choling [19780]
18400 River Rd.

Poolesville, MD 20837
Ph: (301)710-6259

Li, Ge, President
Council of Overseas Chinese
Services, Inc. [19415]
430 E 6th St., Apt. 13A
New York, NY 10009-6432
Ph: (415)860-6932

Li, Grace, Founder
We Care Act [11681]
2722 Garden Falls Dr.
Manvel, TX 77578
Ph: (832)298-5888

Li, Guo-Min, Secretary
Chinese Biological Investigators
Society [6079]
c/o Yingzi Yang, PhD, Treasurer
8102 Woodhaven Blvd.
Bethesda, MD 20817

Li, Jianming, President
Chinese American Heart Association
[14109]
120 Liberty St.
North Andover, MA 01845

Li, Liliana, Exec. Dir.
Vision New America [19008]
100 N Winchester Blvd., Ste. 368
Santa Clara, CA 95050
Ph: (408)260-0116
Fax: (408)260-0180

Liautaud, Tom, President
Mission Doctors Association [15607]
3435 Wilshire Blvd., Ste. 1940
Los Angeles, CA 90010
Ph: (213)368-1872
Fax: (213)368-1871

Libby, Landon, DDS, President
National Association of Seventh-day
Adventist Dentists [14458]
PO Box 101
Loma Linda, CA 92354
Ph: (909)558-8187
Fax: (909)558-0209

Libby, Lauren, President, CEO
Trans World Radio [20469]
PO Box 8700
Cary, NC 27512
Ph: (919)460-3700
Toll Free: 800-456-7897
Fax: (919)460-3702

Licht, Jane, V. Chmn. of the Bd.
International Morab Breeders' As-
sociation [4367]
c/o Wendy Konichek, Chairperson/
Registrar
S101 W 34628 Hwy. LO
Eagle, WI 53119
Ph: (262)594-3667

Lichtenberg, James, President
APA Division 17: Society of Counseling Psychology [16872]
c/o Ashley Randall, PhD, Membership Chair
APA Membership Department
750 1st St. NE
Washington, DC 20002-4242
Toll Free: 800-374-2721

Lichtenberg, Mark R., President
Phi Mu Alpha Sinfonia Fraternity of
America [23831]
10600 Old State Rd.
Evansville, IN 47711
Ph: (812)867-2433
Toll Free: 800-473-2649

Lichtenstein, Albert, Contact
American Balint Society [16856]
912 E Burk Rd.

Colbert; WA 99005

Lichtenstein, Dr. Michael, Comm.
Chm.
Association for Clinical and
Translational Science [14291]
2025 M St. NW, Ste. 800
Washington, DC 20036
Ph: (202)367-1119
Fax: (202)367-2119

Lichter, David A., D.Min, Exec. Dir.
National Association of Catholic
Chaplains [19933]
4915 S Howell Ave., Ste. 501
Milwaukee, WI 53207
Ph: (414)483-4898
Fax: (414)483-6712

Licitra, Karen, Chairwoman
Campaign to End Obesity [16250]
805 15th St. NW, Ste. 650
Washington, DC 20005
Ph: (202)466-8100

Licitra, Tim, Exec. Dir.
Market Technicians Association
[1249]
61 Broadway, Ste. 514
New York, NY 10006
Ph: (646)652-3300
Fax: (646)652-3322

Liddell, Iona, Exec. Dir.
Tibet Justice Center [19192]
440 Grand Ave., Ste. 425
Oakland, CA 94610
Ph: (510)486-0588

Lidiak, Peter, VP of Government Rel.
International Liquid Terminals As-
sociation [3437]
1005 N Glebe Rd., Ste. No. 600
Arlington, VA 22201
Ph: (703)875-2011
Fax: (703)875-2018

Lieber, Kurt, Exec. Dir., Founder
Ocean Defenders Alliance [3921]
19744 Beach Blvd.
Huntington Beach, CA 92648
Ph: (714)875-5881

Liebers, Howard, Founder, CEO
MarbleRoad [15152]
PO Box 34176
Washington, DC 20043-4176
Ph: (415)562-7253

Liebno, Albert, President
A.L.E.R.T. International [14691]
PO Box 74
Pickerington, OH 43147
Toll Free: 866-402-5378

Liebson, Matthew E., President
Machine Cancel Society [22339]
c/o Gary Carlson
3097 Frobisher Ave.
Dublin, OH 43017-1652

Lieby, Joseph, Ed.D, President
Palatines to America German
Genealogy Society [20991]
4601 N High St., Ste. C
Columbus, OH 43214
Ph: (614)267-4700

Liechty, Skyler, President
Medal Collectors of America [22274]
c/o Barry D. Tayman, Treasurer
3115 Nestling Pine Ct.
Ellicott City, MD 21042

Lieser, Dina, MD, Director
Docs for Tots [14187]
128 Breeley Blvd.
Melville, NY 11747
Ph: (856)362-4868

Liestman, Linda L., President,
Founder
North American Horsemen's As-
sociation [4393]
310 Washburne Ave.
Paynesville, MN 56362-1645
Ph: (320)243-7250
Toll Free: 800-328-8894
Fax: (320)243-7224

Liflieri, Glenn, Exec. Chmn. of the
Bd.
National Chemical Credit Association
[1257]
500 Seneca St., Ste. 400
Buffalo, NY 14204-1963
Ph: (716)885-4444
Toll Free: 844-937-3268

Lifshitz, Jonathan, Ph.D, VP
National Neurotrauma Society
[16028]
9037 Ron Den Ln.
Windermere, FL 34786
Ph: (407)876-0750

Liggett, Lauren, President
Eller Family Association [20861]
c/o Edward K. Eller, Secretay/
Treasurer
3009 E Walnut Ave.
Dalton, GA 30721

Liggett, Martha, Esq., Exec. Dir.
American Society of Hematology
[15220]
2021 L St. NW, Ste. 900
Washington, DC 20036-4929
Ph: (202)776-0544
Fax: (202)776-0545

Liggett, Shelly, President
International Side Saddle Organiza-
tion [22944]
75 Lamington Rd.
Branchburg, NJ 08876-3314
Ph: (706)871-4776

Light, Brent A., Secretary
Chief Warrant and Warrant Officers
Association [5595]
12 Brookley Ave. SW
Washington, DC 20032
Ph: (202)554-7753

Light, Mark, Exec. Dir., CEO
International Association of Fire
Chiefs [5207]
4025 Fair Ridge Dr., Ste. 300
Fairfax, VA 22033-2868
Ph: (703)273-0911
Fax: (703)273-9363

Light, Rick, Secretary
American Academy of Craniofacial
Pain [16459]
12100 Sunset Hills Rd., Ste. 130
Reston, VA 20190
Ph: (703)234-4142
Toll Free: 800-322-8651
Fax: (703)435-4390

Light, Rev. Rick J., Exec. Dir.
Presbyterian Evangelistic Fellowship
[20524]
100 5th St., Ste. 330
Bristol, TN 37620
Ph: (423)573-5308
Toll Free: 800-225-5733
Fax: (423)573-5309

Lighterman, Mark, President
Combined Organizations of
Numismatic Error Collectors of
America [22266]
c/o Mark Lighterman, President
PO Box 471518
Lake Monroe, FL 32747-1518
Ph: (407)688-7006

Lighthizer, James, President
Civil War Trust **[9381]**
1156 15th St. NW, Ste. 900
Washington, DC 20005
Ph: (202)367-1861
Fax: (202)367-1865

Lightwalker, Mr. Charles, PhD,
Treasurer
International Association of Medical
Intuitives **[15729]**
PO Box 30752
Spokane, WA 99223-3021
Ph: (509)389-7290

Likins, Jamesene E., President
United Daughters of the
Confederacy **[20747]**
328 N Blvd.
Richmond, VA 23220-4009
Ph: (804)355-1636
Fax: (804)353-1396

Likins, Dr. Marilyn, Exec. Dir.
National Resource Center for Para-
educators **[8591]**
2865 Old Main Hill
Logan, UT 84322-2865
Ph: (435)797-7272

Liles, Allison, Exec. Dir.
Episcopal Peace Fellowship **[19106]**
c/o Allison Liles, Executive Director
PO Box 15
Claysburg, PA 16625
Ph: (312)922-8628

Lilienthal, Philip, Founder, President
Global Camps Africa **[10540]**
1606 Washington Plz.
Reston, VA 20190
Ph: (703)437-0808

Lillard, Susan, Contact
Mold Help Organization **[14947]**
1255 Broadway St. NE, Ste. 410
Salem, OR 97301
Ph: (503)763-0808

Lilleker, Ross, President
Model T Ford Club International
[21439]
PO Box 355
Hudson, NC 28638-0355
Ph: (828)728-5758

Lilly, Jane, President
Roy Rogers - Dale Evans Collectors
Association **[24061]**
PO Box 1166
Portsmouth, OH 45662
Ph: (740)259-1195
    (740)727-4444

Lilly, Joan, President
Art and Creative Materials Institute
[1527]
99 Derby St., Ste. 200
Hingham, MA 02043
Ph: (781)556-1044
Fax: (781)207-5550

Lilly, Patricia A., Exec. VP
Wholesale Florist and Florist Sup-
plier Association **[1311]**
Horn Point Harbor Marina
105 Eastern Ave., Ste. 104
Annapolis, MD 21403-3300
Ph: (410)940-6580
Toll Free: 888-289-3372
Fax: (410)263-1659

Lily, Maureen, Exec. Dir.
Americans for Better Care of the Dy-
ing **[13215]**
1700 Diagonal Rd., Ste. 635
Alexandria, VA 22314-2866
Ph: (703)647-8505
Fax: (703)837-1233

Lim, Ty, President
Gay Asian Pacific Alliance Founda-
tion **[11881]**
PO Box 22482
San Francisco, CA 94142
Ph: (415)857-4272

Limberakis, Anthony J., MD, Cmdr.
Order of Saint Andrew the Apostle
[20195]
8 E 79th St.
New York, NY 10075-0192
Ph: (212)570-3550
Fax: (212)774-0214

Limon, Lavinia, CEO, President
United States Committee for
Refugees and Immigrants **[19022]**
2231 Crystal Dr., Ste. 350
Arlington, VA 22202
Ph: (703)310-1130
Toll Free: 800-307-4712
Fax: (703)769-4241

Lin, Eric, Officer
Council for Chemical Research
[6197]
1120 Route 73, Ste. 200
Mount Laurel, NJ 08054
Ph: (856)439-0500
Fax: (856)439-0525

Lin, Hsin-Hui, President
Association of Chinese-American
Professionals **[19412]**
10303 Westoffice Dr.
Houston, TX 77042-5306

Lin, Janet, Chief of Staff
U.S. Department of the Interior |
Bureau of Land Management |
National Wild Horse and Burro
Program **[4417]**
BLM Washington Office
1849 C St. NW, Rm. 5665
Washington, DC 20240
Ph: (202)208-3801
Fax: (202)208-5242

Lin, Joseph, Exec. Chmn. of the Bd.
AIR Commercial Real Estate As-
sociation **[2844]**
500 N Brand Blvd., Ste. 900
Glendale, CA 91203-3315
Ph: (213)687-8777
Fax: (213)687-8616

Lin, Kant Y., Contact
American Society of Maxillofacial
Surgeons **[16444]**
500 Cummings Ctr., Ste. 4550
Beverly, MA 01915
Ph: (978)927-8330
Fax: (978)524-0498

Lin, Peter K.R., President
Chinese-American Golf Association
[22876]
2 Doloree Dr.
East Brunswick, NJ 08816
Ph: (732)422-9558
Fax: (732)422-9558

Lin, Tatiana, President
Society of Practitioners of Health
Impact Assessment **[15065]**
304 12th St., Ste. 2B
Oakland, CA 94607
Ph: (510)452-9442

Lin, Dr. Yu-Lan, Exec. Dir.
Chinese Language Association of
Secondary-Elementary Schools
[7600]
PO Box 2348
Livingston, NJ 07039

Linares, Jesus, Chairman
National Hispanic Business Group
[654]

45 W 21st St., Ste. 6D
New York, NY 10010
Ph: (212)265-2664
Fax: (212)265-2675

Lincer, James D., MD, President
American Board of Pain Medicine
[16549]
85 W Algonquin Rd., No. 550
Arlington Heights, IL 60005
Ph: (847)981-8905
Fax: (847)427-9656

Lincoln, John, Chmn. of the Bd.
Maniilaq Association **[12377]**
733 2nd Ave.
Kotzebue, AK 99752
Ph: (907)442-7660
    (907)442-3311
Toll Free: 800-478-3312
Fax: (907)442-7830

Lincoln, Maj. (Ret.) Walt, CFP,
President, Treasurer
American Armed Forces Mutual Aid
Association **[19379]**
102 Sheridan Ave.
Fort Myer, VA 22211-1110
Ph: (703)707-4600
Toll Free: 800-522-5221
Fax: (888)210-4882

Lincoln-Smith, Dorothy, President
National Society of Arts and Letters
[9557]

Lindamood, Cherry, President
North American Association of
Wardens and Superintendents
[11541]
PO Box 3573
Dublin, OH 43016

Lindberg, Brian W., Exec. Dir.
Consumer Coalition for Quality
Health Care **[14993]**
1612 K St. NW, Ste. 400
Washington, DC 20006
Ph: (202)789-3606
Fax: (202)898-2389

Lindborg, Nancy, President, CEO
United States Institute of Peace
[18835]
2301 Constitution Ave. NW
Washington, DC 20037-2900
Ph: (202)457-1700
Fax: (202)429-6063

Linde, Therese, Contact
Swedish-American Chambers of
Commerce, U.S.A. **[23620]**
2900 K St. NW, Ste. 403
Washington, DC 20007
Ph: (202)536-1520

Lindell, Brad, PhD, President
American Academy of Experts in
Traumatic Stress **[17522]**
203 Deer Rd.
Ronkonkoma, NY 11779
Ph: (631)543-2217
Fax: (631)543-6977

Lindeman, Kent, Exec. Dir.
Association for Applied Sport
Psychology **[17279]**
8365 Keystone Crossing, Ste. 107
Indianapolis, IN 46240
Ph: (317)205-9225
Fax: (317)205-9481

Lindeman, Kent, Exec. Dir.
Society for Free Radical Biology and
Medicine **[6118]**
8365 Keystone Crossing, Ste. 107
Indianapolis, IN 46240-2685
Ph: (317)205-9482
Fax: (317)205-9481

Lindeman, Kent, Exec. Dir.
Society for Pediatric Dermatology
[14514]
8365 Keystone Crossing, Ste. 107
Indianapolis, IN 46240
Ph: (317)202-0224
Fax: (317)205-9481

Linden, Julie H., PhD, Bd. Member
International Society of Hypnosis
[15364]
PO Box 602
Berwyn, PA 19312
Toll Free: 800-550-4741

Linden, Mark Vander, VP
Association of Problem Gambling
Service Administrators **[11865]**
PO Box 135
PO Box 135
Newburyport, MA 01950-6619
Ph: (617)548-8057

Linden, Saphira, Director
Omega Theatre and the Omega Arts
Network **[8993]**
41 Greenough Ave.
Boston, MA 02130
Ph: (617)522-8300

Lindenmeyer, Kriste, Secretary,
Treasurer
Society for the History of Children
and Youth **[9517]**
c/o Kriste Lindenmeyer, Secretary-
Treasurer
Armitage Hall, Rm. 379
311 N 5th St.
Rutgers University
Camden, NJ 08102-1405

Linder, Donna, Exec. Dir.
Child Find of America **[10896]**
PO Box 277
New Paltz, NY 12561-0277
Ph: (845)883-6060
Fax: (845)883-6614

Lindgren, Rob, President
Association of College and
University Clubs **[7623]**
185 Providence St., Unit A315
West Warwick, RI 02893
Ph: (239)687-8819

Lindholm, Douglas L., Esq., Exec.
Dir., President
Council On State Taxation **[19169]**
122 C St. NW, Ste. 330
Washington, DC 20001-2109
Ph: (202)484-5222
Fax: (202)484-5229

Lindholm, Rev. William C., Chairman
National Committee for Amish
Religious Freedom **[19698]**
15343 Susanna Cir.
Livonia, MI 48154
Ph: (734)464-3908

Lindner, Randy, President, CEO
National Association Long Term
Care Administrator Boards **[16197]**
1444 I St. NW
Washington, DC 20005-6542
Ph: (202)712-9040

Lindner, Ulrich, Regional Mgr.
Goethe-Institut **[9339]**
30 Irving Pl.
New York, NY 10003
Ph: (212)439-8700
Fax: (212)439-8705

Lindow, Sandra J., VP
Science Fiction Poetry Association
[10205]
PO Box 907

Winchester, CA 92596

Lindquist, Eric, President
International Veterinary Ultrasound
  Society [17653]
PO Box 524
Birdsboro, PA 19508

Lindqvist, Ursula, VP
Swedish Translators in North
  America [8715]

Lindsay, C.L., III, Exec. Dir., Founder
Coalition for Student and Academic
  Rights [7406]
PO Box 491
Solebury, PA 18963-0491
Ph: (215)862-9096
Fax: (215)862-9557

Lindsay, Dennis, CEO, President
Christ for the Nations [20395]
3404 Conway St.
Dallas, TX 75224
Ph: (214)376-1711
Toll Free: 800-933-2364

Lindsay, James, Exec. Dir.
Catholic Volunteer Network [19818]
6930 Carroll Ave., Ste. 820
Takoma Park, MD 20912
Ph: (301)270-0900
Toll Free: 800-543-5046
Fax: (301)270-0901

Lindsay, Melissa, Chairman
Radix Institute [13652]
3212 Monte Vista Blvd. NE
Albuquerque, NM 87106-2120
Ph: (310)570-2439
      (808)256-3347

Lindsay, Mr. Ronald, PhD, CEO,
  President
Council for Secular Humanism
  [20210]
PO Box 664
Amherst, NY 14226-0664
Ph: (716)636-7571
Toll Free: 800-458-1366
Fax: (716)636-1733

Lines, Daniel, President
Correspondence Chess League of
  America [21591]
PO Box 142
Livingston, NJ 07039-0142

Ling, Denise P., President
National Association of Federal
  Education Program Administrators
  [7435]
c/o Bobby Burns, Executive Director
PO Box 880
Jacksonville, AL 36265
Ph: (256)310-9293
Toll Free: 844-623-3721

Ling, Moses D.F., PE, RA, President
Architectural Engineering Institute of
  ASCE [5958]
c/o American Society of Civil
  Engineers
1801 Alexander Bell Dr.
Reston, VA 20191-4400
Ph: (703)295-6300
Toll Free: 800-548-2723

Lingenfelter, Dwight, Comm. Chm.
Northeastern Weed Science Society
  [4447]
PO Box 25
Woodstown, NJ 08098
Ph: (315)209-7580

Lingle, Kathie, Director
Alliance for Work-Life Progress
  [2736]

14040 N Northsight Blvd.
Scottsdale, AZ 85260-3601
Ph: (480)951-9191
Toll Free: 877-951-9191

Link, Dr. Eric Carl, President
The Frank Norris Society [10371]
c/o Dr. Eric Carl Link, President
Liberal Arts Bldg., Rm. 153D
College of Arts and Sciences
Indiana University-Purdue University
  Fort Wayne
2101 E Coliseum Blvd.
Fort Wayne, IN 46805-1499
Ph: (260)481-5750

Link, Steven J., Chmn. of the Bd.
Self-Insurance Institute of America
  [1926]
PO Box 1237
Simpsonville, SC 29681
Toll Free: 800-851-7789
Fax: (864)962-2483

Linkous, Jonathan, CEO
American Telemedicine Association
  [17425]
1100 Connecticut Ave. NW, Ste. 540
Washington, DC 20036
Ph: (202)223-3333
Fax: (202)223-2787

Linley, Laura, President
American Association of Sleep
  Technologists [17210]
2510 N Frontage Rd.
Darien, IL 60561
Ph: (630)737-9704
Fax: (630)737-9788

Linn, Michael, CPP, CEO
National Independent Automobile
  Dealers Association [350]
2521 Brown Blvd.
Arlington, TX 76006-5203
Ph: (817)640-3838
Toll Free: 800-682-3837
Fax: (817)649-5866

Linn, Mott, President
Academy of Certified Archivists
  [8819]
1450 Western Ave., Ste. 101
Albany, NY 12203-3539
Ph: (518)463-8644
Fax: (518)463-8656

Linn, Sherry, Cmte. Mgmt. Ofc.
North American Bluebird Society
  [4855]
PO Box 7844
Bloomington, IN 47407
Ph: (812)200-5700

Linn, Susan, Director
Campaign for a Commercial-Free
  Childhood [10881]
89 South St., Ste. 403
Boston, MA 02111-2651
Ph: (617)896-9368
Fax: (617)896-9397

Linneman, Dean, President
Association of Health Facility Survey
  Agencies [5712]
5105 Solemn Grove Rd.
Garner, NC 27529

Linsday, Richard, President
Devil Pups [21009]
PO Box 6607
Westlake Village, CA 91359
Ph: (805)470-8340
Fax: (805)435-1767

Linthicum, Dorothy, Coord.
Center for the Ministry of Teaching
  [20076]

3737 Seminary Rd.
Alexandria, VA 22304
Ph: (703)370-6600
Toll Free: 800-941-0083

Linville, Dr. Greg, Exec. Dir.
Association of Church Sports and
  Recreation Ministries [20017]
5350 Broadmoor Cir. NW
Canton, OH 44709
Ph: (330)493-4824

Liodice, Robert D., CEO, President
Association of National Advertisers
  [90]
708 3rd Ave., 33rd Fl.
New York, NY 10017
Ph: (212)697-5950
Fax: (212)687-7310

Lioi, Margaret M., CEO
Chamber Music America [9886]
12 W 32nd St., 7th Fl.
New York, NY 10001-0802
Ph: (212)242-2022
Fax: (212)967-9747

Lione, Armand, PhD, President
The National Flossing Council
  [14464]
533 4th St. SE
Washington, DC 20003
Ph: (202)544-0711

Liotta, Alicia Marantz, CEO, Founder
Beauty Bus Foundation [13208]
2716 Ocean Park Blvd., Ste. 1062
Santa Monica, CA 90405
Ph: (310)392-0900
Fax: (310)392-0907

Lipetz, Robert Weisenburger, Exec.
  Dir.
Glass Manufacturing Industry
  Council [1504]
600 N Cleveland Ave., Ste. 210
Westerville, OH 43082
Ph: (614)818-9423
Fax: (614)818-9485

Lipinski, Ann Marie, Curator
Nieman Foundation for Journalism at
  Harvard [8158]
Harvard University
Walter Lippmann House
1 Francis Ave.
Cambridge, MA 02138
Ph: (617)495-2237

Lipka, Cyndie, President
Society of Flavor Chemists [6216]
Bldg. C, Ste. 205
3301 Route 66
Neptune, NJ 07753
Ph: (732)922-3393
Fax: (732)922-3590

Lipkin, John, President
Children Beyond Our Borders
  [17844]
PO Box 568411
Orlando, FL 32856

Lipkis, Andy, President, Founder
TreePeople [3958]
12601 Mulholland Dr.
Beverly Hills, CA 90210
Ph: (818)753-4600
      (818)623-4848
Fax: (818)753-4635

Lipner, Rabbi Pinchas, Dean,
  Founder
The San Francisco Institute for Jew-
  ish Medical Ethics [20280]
645 14th Ave.
San Francisco, CA 94118
Ph: (415)752-7333

Lippel, Naomi, Managing Dir.
Overeaters Anonymous World
  Service Office [12398]
6075 Zenith Ct. NE
Rio Rancho, NM 87144-6424
Ph: (505)891-2664
Fax: (505)891-4320

Lipper, Laurie, Founder, President
The Children's Partnership [10932]
2013 H St. NW, 6th Fl.
Washington, DC 20036
Ph: (202)429-0033
Fax: (202)429-0974

Lippincott, John, President
Council for Advancement and Sup-
  port of Education [7754]
1307 New York Ave. NW, Ste. 1000
Washington, DC 20005-4701
Ph: (202)328-2273
Toll Free: 800-554-8536

Lipps, Jeff, CFO
American Sighthound Field Association [21823]
c/o Jeff Lipps, Chief Financial Officer
3052 Mann Rd.
Blacklick, OH 43004
Ph: (614)855-5067
      (724)586-6158

Lipps, Jere H., President
Cushman Foundation for Foramin-
  iferal Research [6970]
PO Box 37012
Washington, DC 20560-0121
Ph: (202)633-1333
Fax: (202)786-2832

Lipson, Mr. David, Chairman
British Schools and Universities
  Foundation [7629]
575 Madison Ave., Ste. 1006
New York, NY 10022-8511
Ph: (212)662-5576

Liquori, Toni, Exec. Dir.
School Food FOCUS [12113]
40 Worth St., 5th Fl.
New York, NY 10013
Ph: (616)619-6449
Fax: (646)619-6777

Lisak, David, President
1in6, Inc. [12917]
PO Box 222033
Santa Clarita, CA 91322

Liscio, Eugene, President
International Association of Forensic
  and Security Metrology [7231]
3416 Primm Ln.
Birmingham, AL 35216
Ph: (205)823-6106
Fax: (205)824-7700

Liske, Jim, President, CEO
Prison Fellowship Ministries [11544]
44180 Riverside Pky.
Lansdowne, VA 20176
Toll Free: 877-478-0100

Lissack, Michael, President
American Society for Cybernetics
  [6234]
c/o Stuart A. Umpleby, Professor
204 Funger Hall
Dept. of Management
The George Washington University
2201 G St. NW
Washington, DC 20052
Ph: (617)475-0514

Lissade, Herby, President
Haiti Engineering [11664]
9384 Boulder River Way
Elk Grove, CA 95624
Ph: (916)296-8586

Listak, Anissa, Exec. Dir.
Urban Teacher Residency United **[8658]**
1332 N Halsted St., Ste. 304
Chicago, IL 60642-2694
Ph: (312)397-8878

Listwin, Don, Founder
Canary Foundation **[13914]**
3155 Porer Dr.
Palo Alto, CA 94304
Ph: (650)646-3200
Fax: (650)251-9758

Litjens, Stephan, Chmn. of the Bd.
MulteFire Alliance **[6886]**
48377 Fremont Blvd., Ste. 117
Fremont, CA 94538
Ph: (510)492-4026
Fax: (510)492-4001

Litovsky, Silvio H., MD, Treasurer
Society for Cardiovascular Pathology
[14143]
UAB Pathology
PD6A 175
Birmingham, AL 35294

Litt, Barrett S., Chmn. of the Bd.
Justice in Aging **[10511]**
1444 Eye St. NW, Ste. 1100
Washington, DC 20005
Ph: (202)289-6976

Littky, Dennis, Director, Founder
Big Picture Learning **[7839]**
325 Public St.
Providence, RI 02905
Ph: (401)752-3442
Fax: (919)573-0787

Little, Craig S., DC, President
Council on Chiropractic Education
[14264]
8049 N 85th Way
Scottsdale, AZ 85258-4321
Ph: (480)443-8877
Toll Free: 888-443-3506
Fax: (480)483-7333

Little, Mr. Harvey, Chairman
Voice of the Martyrs **[20474]**
PO Box 443
Bartlesville, OK 74005-0443
Ph: (918)337-8015
Toll Free: 877-337-0302
Fax: (918)338-0189

Little, Joleigh, Advisor
National Teens for Life **[12785]**
c/o Derrick Jones, Advisor
512 10th St. NW
Washington, DC 20004
Ph: (202)626-8800
   (202)626-8825

Little, Margaret Olivia, Ph.D., Direc-
   tor
Joseph P. and Rose F. Kennedy
   Institute of Ethics **[11803]**
Healy Hall, 4th Fl.
Georgetown University
37th & O Sts. NW
Washington, DC 20057
Ph: (202)687-8099

Little, Gr. Mast. Phil E., President
United States Isshinryu Karate As-
   sociation **[23019]**
2202 Surfside Dr.
Anderson, SC 29625
Ph: (864)225-8610

Little, Walter E., PhD, President
Society for Latin American and
   Caribbean Anthropology **[5923]**
c/o American Anthropological Association

4350 N Fairfax Dr., Ste. 640
Arlington, VA 22203-1620

Littleton, Jeff H., Exec. VP
American Society of Heating,
   Refrigerating and Air-Conditioning
   Engineers **[6536]**
1791 Tullie Cir. NE
Atlanta, GA 30329
Ph: (404)636-8400
Toll Free: 800-527-4723
Fax: (404)321-5478

Littleton, Phillip A., CEO, President
Holt International Children's Services
[11236]
250 Country Club Rd.
Eugene, OR 97401
Ph: (541)687-2202
Toll Free: 888-355-4658
Fax: (541)683-6175

Littlewood, Chris, VP
Association of Late-Deafened Adults
[15176]
8038 MacIntosh Ln., Ste. 2
Rockford, IL 61107
Ph: (815)332-1515
Toll Free: 866-402-2532

Littman, Brett, Exec. Dir.
The Drawing Center **[8853]**
35 Wooster St.
New York, NY 10013
Ph: (212)219-2166
Fax: (888)380-3362

Littman, Karl, CPO, OHC, Chairman
National Association of RV Parks &
   Campgrounds **[2912]**
9085 E Mineral Cir., Ste. 200
Centennial, CO 80112
Ph: (303)681-0401
Fax: (303)681-0426

Litts, David, OD, Exec. Sec.
National Action Alliance for Suicide
   Prevention **[13195]**
1025 Thomas Jefferson St. NW, Ste.
   700
Washington, DC 20007
Ph: (202)572-3784

Litz, Michael, Bd. Member
Gypsy Vanner Horse Society **[4357]**
PO Box 65
Waynesfield, OH 45896
Toll Free: 888-520-9777

Litzenberg, Homer L., III, President
Litzenberger-Litzenberg Association
[20895]
3233 Simberlan Dr.
San Jose, CA 95148-3128
Ph: (408)270-7227

Liu, Dr. Hanmin, CEO, President,
   Founder
Wildflowers Institute **[9158]**
1144 Pacific Ave.
San Francisco, CA 94133
Ph: (415)775-1151

Liu, Margaret, President
International Society for Vaccines
[15382]

Liu, Shujie, VP
Society of Petrophysicists and Well
   Log Analysts **[7004]**
8866 Gulf Fwy., Ste. 320
Houston, TX 77017
Ph: (713)947-8727
Fax: (713)947-7181

Liu, Wing Kam, Chairman
U.S. National Committee on
   Theoretical and Applied Mechanics
[6833]

Board on International Scientific
   Organizations
The National Academies
500 5th St.
Washington, DC 20001
Ph: (202)334-2807
Fax: (202)334-2231

Lively, John, President
National Association of Lively
   Families **[20904]**
c/o Polly Lively, Treasurer
411 Claxton-Lively Rd.
Waynesboro, GA 30830

Livermore, Arthur, Director
American Alliance for Medical Can-
   nabis **[15550]**
44500 Tide Ave.
Arch Cape, OR 97102
Ph: (503)436-1882

Livesay, Richard, Treasurer
Jewelry Industry Distributors As-
   sociation **[2055]**
c/o Diehl Accounting and Financial
   Services, P.C.
703 Old Route 422 W
Butler, PA 16001
Ph: (203)254-4492

Livezeanu, Irina, President
Society for Romanian Studies
[21094]
c/o William Crowther, Treasurer
Dept. of Political Science
University of North Carolina-
   Greensboro
Greensboro, NC 27402-6170
Ph: (480)965-4658

Livingston, Dr. David, Founder
Associates for Biblical Research
[19749]
PO Box 144
Akron, PA 17501
Ph: (717)859-3443
Toll Free: 800-430-0008
Fax: (717)859-3393

Livingston, Nancy, Chmn. of the Bd.
American Conservatory Theater
[10237]
30 Grant Ave., 7th Fl.
San Francisco, CA 94108-5834
Ph: (415)834-3200
   (415)439-2350

Livney, Patrick A., CEO
Charcot-Marie-Tooth Association
[15913]
PO Box 105
Glenolden, PA 19036
Ph: (610)499-9264
Toll Free: 800-606-2682
Fax: (610)499-9267

Liwanga, Roger-Claude, Exec. Dir.,
   Founder
Promote Congo **[18438]**
87 Madison St., Unit 2L
Malden, MA 02148
Ph: (781)321-3060

Lizotte, David, Jr., President
Association of Physician Assistants
   in Cardiovascular Surgery **[14100]**
500 Cummings Ctr., Ste. 4550
Beverly, MA 01915
Ph: (978)927-8330
Fax: (978)927-8330

Llorca, Heather, Chairperson
Professional Women in Healthcare
[15059]

Lloyd, Brian, Bd. Member
Water Alliance for Africa **[13341]**
3267 East 3300 South, No. 535

Salt Lake City, UT 84109

Lloyd, Jonathan, Exec. Dir.
Brethren in Christ World Missions
[20389]
431 Grantham Rd.
Mechanicsburg, PA 17055-5812
Ph: (717)697-2634
Fax: (717)691-6053

Lloyd, Larry, Treasurer
Free Geek **[12580]**
1731 SE 10th Ave.
Portland, OR 97214
Ph: (503)232-9350

Lloyd, Rachel, CEO, Founder
Girls Educational and Mentoring
   Services **[12923]**
298B W 149th St.
New York, NY 10039
Ph: (212)926-8089
Fax: (212)491-2696

Lloyd, Robin, Chairman, Publisher
Toward Freedom **[18298]**
PO Box 468
Burlington, VT 05402
Ph: (802)657-3733

Lloyd, Sterrett, Director
National Elevator Industry **[1753]**
1677 County Route 64
Salem, NY 12865-0838
Ph: (518)854-3100
Fax: (518)854-3257

Lloyd, Timothy, Exec. Dir.
American Folklore Society **[9325]**
Indiana University
1900 E 10th St.
Bloomington, IN 47406
Ph: (812)856-2379
Fax: (812)856-2483

Lo, Robert, V. Chmn. of the Bd.
ASIAN, Inc. **[9024]**
1167 Mission St., 4th Fl.
San Francisco, CA 94103
Ph: (415)928-5910
Fax: (415)921-0182

López, Carlos, President
Federacion Interamericana de
   Abogados **[5423]**
1889 F St. NW, Ste. 335, 3rd Fl.
Washington, DC 20036
Ph: (202)466-5944
Fax: (202)466-5946

López, Rómulo, Dir. of Fin.
Atlas Network **[6384]**
1201 L St. NW
Washington, DC 20005
Ph: (202)449-8449
Fax: (202)280-1259

Loar, Granville, Exec. Dir.
Scaffold and Access Industry As-
   sociation **[578]**
400 Admiral Blvd.
Kansas City, MO 64106
Ph: (816)595-4860
Fax: (816)472-7765

Lobban, Trudie C.A., Founder, CEO
Atrial Fibrillation Association - USA
[14102]
PO Box 5507
Hilton Head Island, SC 29938
Ph: (843)785-4101

Lobel, Martin, Chmn. of the Bd.
Tax Analysts **[19175]**
400 S Maple Ave., Ste. 400
Falls Church, VA 22046
Ph: (703)533-4400
Toll Free: 800-955-2444
Fax: (703)533-4444

Lobel-Weiss, Nick, Exec. Dir.,
    Founder
Global Emergency Relief [14696]
107 Suffolk St.
New York, NY 10002-3300
Ph: (212)213-0213

Lobley, Joseph B., VP
Society of Accredited Marine
    Surveyors, Inc. [7253]
7855 Argyle Forest Blvd., No. 203
Jacksonville, FL 32244-5598
Ph: (904)384-1494
Toll Free: 800-344-9077
Fax: (904)388-3958

Loch, Tom, President
Graphic Communications Education
    Association [9348]
1899 Preston White Dr.
Reston, VA 20191-4367
Ph: (417)690-2511

Lochner, Betty, Chairperson
College Savings Plans Network
    [7925]
2760 Research Park Dr.
Lexington, KY 40511

Lochstampfor, Dr. Mark, Exec. Dir.
Society of Pi Kappa Lambda [23834]
Capital University, 1 College & Main
Conservatory of Music
1 College and Main
Columbus, OH 43209
Ph: (614)236-7211
Fax: (614)236-6935

Lockett, Matt, Director
Bound4LIFE [19055]
205 3rd St. SE
Washington, DC 20003
Ph: (202)681-7729

Locklear, David, President
American Association of SNAP
    Directors [5762]

Lockmann, Paulo, President
World Methodist Council [20351]
545 N Lakeshore Dr.
Lake Junaluska, NC 28745
Ph: (828)456-9432

Lockwood, Bill, Exec. Dir.
American Society for Automation in
    Pharmacy [2552]
492 Norristown Rd., Ste. 160
Blue Bell, PA 19422
Ph: (610)825-7783
Fax: (610)825-7641

Lockwood, Karen, Exec. Dir.
National Institute for Trial Advocacy
    [5828]
1685 38th St., Ste. 200
Boulder, CO 80301-2735
Ph: (303)953-6845
    (720)890-4860
Toll Free: 800-225-6482
Fax: (720)890-7069

Lockwood, Peter, President
Clean Water Fund [4753]
1444 Eye St. NW, Ste. 400
Washington, DC 20005
Ph: (202)895-0420
Fax: (202)895-0438

Lockwood, Sue, CST, Exec. Dir.,
    Founder
American Latex Allergy Association
    [13573]
63334 Lohmann LN
Eastman, WI 54626
Ph: (608)874-4044
Toll Free: 888-972-5378

Locust, Eloise, Treasurer
National Indian Child Care Associa-
    tion [12379]

c/o Eloise Locust, Treasurer
PO Box 2146
Tahlequah, OK 74465
Ph: (918)453-5051

Lodal, Kirsten, CEO, Founder
LIFT [10724]
1620 I St. NW, Ste. 820
Washington, DC 20006
Ph: (202)289-1151

Lodge, Liz, Exec. Dir.
Penobscot Marine Museum [9777]
5 Church St.
Searsport, ME 04974
Ph: (207)548-2529
Toll Free: 800-268-8030
Fax: (207)548-2520

Lodhie, Pervaiz, Chairman
Pakistani American Business Execu-
    tives Association [664]
23105 Kashiwa Ct.
Torrance, CA 90505
Ph: (310)534-1505
Fax: (310)534-1424

LoDuca, Gerry, President
Healthcare Manufacturers Manage-
    ment Council [15077]
191 Clarksville Rd.
Princeton Junction, NJ 08550
Ph: (609)297-2211
Fax: (609)799-7032

Loeb, Jerod M.
Joint Commission [15331]
1515 W 22nd St., Ste. 1300W
Oakbrook Terrace, IL 60181-4294
Ph: (630)792-5000
Toll Free: 800-746-6578
Fax: (630)792-5005

Loeb, Matthew D., President
International Alliance of Theatrical
    Stage Employees, Moving Picture
    Technicians, Artists and Allied
    Crafts of the United States, Its Ter-
    ritories and Canada [23496]
207 W 25th St., 4th Fl.
New York, NY 10001
Ph: (212)730-1770
Fax: (212)730-7809

Loehndorf, Steve, President
Refrigerated Foods Association
    [1370]
3823 Roswell Rd., Ste. 208
Marietta, GA 30062
Ph: (770)303-9905
    (770)303-9906
Fax: (678)550-4504

Loehr, Kim, Dir. of Comm.
Lightning Protection Institute [2999]
25475 Magnolia Dr.
Maryville, MO 64468
Toll Free: 800-488-6864
Fax: (660)582-0430

Loew, Ann T., EdM, CEO
American College of Veterinary
    Surgeons [17622]
19785 Crystal Rock Dr., Ste. 305
Germantown, MD 20874
Ph: (301)916-0200
Toll Free: 877-217-2287
Fax: (301)916-2287

Loewe, B., Dir. of Comm.
National Day Laborer Organizing
    Network [23460]
675 S Park View St., Ste. B
Los Angeles, CA 90057
Ph: (213)380-2783
Fax: (213)380-2787

Loewy, Jeffrey M., Chairman
American Federation of Arts [8952]
305 E 47th St., 10th Fl.

New York, NY 10017
Ph: (212)988-7700
Toll Free: 800-232-0270
Fax: (212)861-2487

Lofaro, Frank, CEO
Prison Fellowship International
    [11543]
PO Box 17434
Washington, DC 20041
Ph: (703)481-0000

Lofas, Jeannette, PhD, Founder,
    President
Stepfamily Foundation, Inc. [11831]
310 W 85th St.
New York, NY 10024
Ph: (212)877-3244
    (631)725-0911

LoFaso, Marcella A., President
Pediatric Digestion and Motility
    Disorders Society, Inc. [16613]
701 Washington St.
Buffalo, NY 14205

Lofland, Doug, President
Over the Hill Gang, International
    [23249]
2121 N Weber St.
Colorado Springs, CO 80907
Ph: (719)471-0222
Fax: (719)389-0024

Loflin, Stephen E., Founder, CEO
National Society of Collegiate
    Scholars [8518]
2000 M St. NW, Ste. 600
Washington, DC 20036
Ph: (202)265-9000
Fax: (202)265-9200

Lofquist, Dr. Les, Exec. Dir.
IFCA International [20025]
3520 Fairlane Ave. SW
Grandville, MI 49418
Ph: (616)531-1840
Fax: (616)531-1814

Logan, Art, President
National Mole Day Foundation
    [6206]

Logan, Brad, Director
Hands4Africa [12280]
13046 Race Track Rd., Ste. 242
Tampa, FL 33626
Ph: (813)343-8899

Logan, Richard, President
Society for Humanistic Judaism
    [20282]
28611 W 12 Mile Rd.
Farmington Hills, MI 48334
Ph: (248)478-7610
Fax: (248)478-3159

Logan, Sharon D., Mem.
Native Daughters of the Golden
    West [19393]
543 Baker St.
San Francisco, CA 94117-1405
Ph: (415)563-9091
Fax: (415)563-5230

Logan, Willis, Coord.
Operation Crossroads Africa [17778]
PO Box 5570
New York, NY 10027
Ph: (212)289-1949
Fax: (212)289-2526

Logsdon, David, Exec. Dir.
Space Enterprise Council [159]
1525 Wilson Blvd., Ste. 540
Arlington, VA 22209-2444
Ph: (202)682-9110
Fax: (202)682-9111

Logus, Maria, Esq., President
Greek Orthodox Ladies Philoptochos
    Society [20193]
126 E 37th St.
New York, NY 10016
Ph: (212)977-7770
Fax: (212)977-7784

Logvin, Rachel Sottile, Exec. Dir.
Project YES [8770]
5275 Sunset Dr.
Miami, FL 33143-5914
Ph: (305)663-7195
Fax: (305)663-7197

Lohin, Susan, Director
Wellesley College Alumnae Associa-
    tion [19371]
Green Hall, Rm. 246
106 Central St.
Wellesley, MA 02481-8203
Ph: (781)283-2331
Toll Free: 800-358-3543
Fax: (781)283-3638

Lohman, Nancy R.
International Cemetery, Cremation
    and Funeral Association [2406]
107 Carpenter Dr., Ste. 100
Sterling, VA 20164
Ph: (703)391-8400
Toll Free: 800-645-7700
Fax: (703)391-8416

Lohmann, Courtney Carmignani,
    Director
St. Mary's College of California
    Alumni Association [19347]
1928 St. Mary's Rd.
Moraga, CA 94575
Ph: (925)631-4200
    (925)631-4803
Toll Free: 800-800-ALUM
Fax: (925)631-0764

Lohnes, Robin C., Secretary
Arabian F.O.A.L. Association [10589]
PO Box 198
Parksville, NY 12768-0198
Ph: (845)392-7797
    (845)292-7797
Fax: (845)292-7797

Lohnes, Robin C., Exec. Dir.
Equine Protection Network [4815]
c/o Horse Cruelty Fund
PO Box 232
Friedensburg, PA 17933

Lohr, Jeffry, Founder, President,
    Treasurer
Moringa Community [11403]
242 N Limerick Rd.
Schwenksville, PA 19473
Ph: (610)287-7802

Lomax, Mark, Exec. Dir.
National Tactical Officers Association
    [5512]
PO Box 797
Doylestown, PA 18901
Toll Free: 800-279-9127
Fax: (215)230-7552

Lomax, Michael L., PhD, CEO,
    President
United Negro College Fund [7929]
1805 7th St. NW
Washington, DC 20001
Toll Free: 800-331-2244

Lomax, William, President
Native American Finance Officers
    Association [1259]
1101 30th St. NW, Ste. 500
Washington, DC 20007
Ph: (202)631-2003

Lombard, Gail, President
American Boxer Rescue Association
    [10567]

PO Box 184
Carmel, IN 46082
Ph: (334)272-2590

Lombard, Matthew, President
International Society for Presence
    Research [7095]
Media Interface and Network Design
    Lab.
Dept. of Broadcasting, Telecom-
    munications, and Mass Media
Temple University
Philadelphia, PA 19122
Ph: (215)204-7182
Fax: (215)204-5402

Lombardini, Carol, President
Alliance of Motion Picture and
    Television Producers [1184]
Bldg. E
15301 Ventura Blvd.
Sherman Oaks, CA 91403
Ph: (818)935-5938

LoMonte, Frank, Exec. Dir.
Student Press Law Center [17958]
1608 Rhode Island Ave. NW, Ste.
    211
Washington, DC 20036
Ph: (202)785-5450
Fax: (202)822-5045

Lonac, Robert, CEO
World Concern [12569]
19303 Fremont Ave. N
Seattle, WA 98133
Ph: (206)546-7201
Toll Free: 800-755-5022
Fax: (206)546-7269

London, Bob, Exec. Dir.
Alpha Phi Omega National Service
    Fraternity [23865]
14901 E 42nd St.
Independence, MO 64055-7347
Ph: (816)373-8667
Fax: (816)373-5975

Lonero, Larry, President
International Texas Longhorn As-
    sociation [3733]
1600 Texas Dr.
Glen Rose, TX 76043
Ph: (254)898-0157
Fax: (254)898-0165

Long, Bill, President
Classic Thunderbird Club
    International [21359]
1308 E 29th St.
Signal Hill, CA 90755-1842
Ph: (562)426-2709
Toll Free: 800-488-2709
Fax: (562)426-7023

Long, Rev. Brad, Exec. Dir.
Presbyterian-Reformed Ministries
    International [20528]
3227 N Fork Left Fork Rd.
Black Mountain, NC 28711-0429
Ph: (828)669-7373
Fax: (828)669-4880

Long, Candace, President
National League of American Pen
    Women [8990]
1300 17th St. NW
Washington, DC 20036
Ph: (202)785-1997
Fax: (202)452-8868

Long, Prof. Charles A., Chairman
World Scientific and Engineering
    Academy and Society [6604]
c/o Charles A. Long, Chairman
University of Wisconsin
2100 Main St.
Stevens Point, WI 54481-3897

Long, Chuck, President
American Independent Cockpit Alli-
    ance [23384]
PO Box 220670
Saint Louis, MO 63122-0670
Ph: (603)528-2552

Long, Danny, President
American Checkered Giant Rabbit
    Club [4585]
c/o David Freeman, Secretary
1119 Klondyke Rd.
Milford, OH 45150-9659
Ph: (513)576-0804

Long, David, VP
Pierre Chastain Family Association
    [20795]
c/o David Long, Vice President
2796 Vine St.
Orlando, FL 32806
Ph: (407)894-8454
    (931)388-9289

Long, David, Secretary, Treasurer
National Association of Independent
    Life Brokerage Agencies [1896]
11325 Random Hills Rd., Ste. 110
Fairfax, VA 22030
Ph: (703)383-3081
Fax: (703)383-6942

Long, David, President
One Mission Society [20452]
941 Fry Rd.
Greenwood, IN 46142-1821
Ph: (317)888-3333
Fax: (317)888-5275

Long, Garrett, President
United States Telemark Ski Associa-
    tion [23173]
PO Box 844
Putney, VT 05346
Ph: (406)862-3303

Long, Dr. Jeff, Bd. Member
After Death Communication
    Research Foundation [15340]
PO Box 20238
Houma, LA 70360

Long, Dr. Lynette, President
Equal Visibility Everywhere [12032]
1400 Church St. NW, No. 201
Washington, DC 20005

Long, Marie, MD, Founder, Chair-
    man
Global Nutrition Empowerment
    [16222]
3205 NW Elmwood Dr.
Corvallis, OR 97330

Long, Michael R., Chairman
Conservative Party [18888]
486 78th St.
Brooklyn, NY 11209-3404
Ph: (718)921-2158
Fax: (718)921-5268

Long, Michelle, Exec. Dir.
Business Alliance for Local Living
    Economies [11328]
2323 Broadway
Oakland, CA 94612
Ph: (510)587-9417

Long, Thayer, Exec. VP, CEO
Independent Electrical Contractors
    [866]
4401 Ford Ave., Ste. 1100
Alexandria, VA 22302
Ph: (703)549-7351
Toll Free: 800-456-4324
Fax: (703)549-7448

Long, Thayer, President
NPES: Association for Suppliers of
    Printing, Publishing and Converting
    Technologies [1544]

1899 Preston White Dr.
Reston, VA 20191
Ph: (703)264-7200
Fax: (703)620-0994

Long, Therese M., MBA, Exec. Dir.
Organization for Safety, Asepsis and
    Prevention [14468]
Bldg. 5, Ste. 300
3525 Piedmont Rd.
Atlanta, GA 30305
Ph: (410)571-0003
Toll Free: 800-298-6727
Fax: (404)264-1956

Long, Victoria L., Exec. Dir.
Society for Music Theory [10009]
Dept. of Music
University of Chicago
1010 E 59th St.
Chicago, IL 60637
Ph: (773)834-3821

Longhini, Liza, Director
Center for Consumer Affairs [18042]
UWM School of Continuing Educa-
    tion
161 W Wisconsin Ave., Ste. 6000
Milwaukee, WI 53203-2602
Ph: (414)227-3252

Longhorn, Roger, Sec. Gen.
Global Spatial Data Infrastructure
    Association [7269]
PMB 194
946 Great Plain Ave.
Needham, MA 02492-3030

Longman, Tremper, III, President
Institute for Biblical Research
    [19758]
PO Box 305
Princeton, IL 61356

Longmire, Kaitlin, Administrator
Samuel Rubin Foundation [13086]
50 Church St., 5th Fl.
Cambridge, MA 02138
Ph: (617)547-0444

Longo, Daniel J., President
Order Sons of Italy in America
    [19508]
219 E St. NE
Washington, DC 20002
Ph: (202)547-2900
    (202)547-8115
Toll Free: 800-552-OSIA
Fax: (202)546-8168

Longrigg, William, President
International Academy of Matrimonial
    Lawyers [5577]
1 N Lexington Ave.
White Plains, NY 10601

Longwell, Sarah, Managing Dir.
American Beverage Institute [422]
Washington, DC 20005
Ph: (202)463-7110

Longwell, Sarah, V. Chmn. of the
    Bd.
Log Cabin Republicans [19038]
1090 Vermont Ave. NW, Ste. 850
Washington, DC 20005
Ph: (202)420-7873

Lonser, Russell R., President
Congress of Neurological Surgeons
    [16063]
10 N Martingale Rd., Ste. 190
Schaumburg, IL 60173
Ph: (847)240-2500
Toll Free: 877-517-1CNS
Fax: (847)240-0804

Lonseth, Andrew, Founder
Extend the Day [13007]
710 John Nelson Ln. NE

Bainbridge Island, WA 98110

Lonstein, Avi, Exec. Dir.
Association for Peace and
    Understanding in the Middle East
    [18676]
2029 Verdugo Blvd.
Montrose, CA 91020

Looby, Richard, President
United Brachial Plexus Network, Inc.
    [16039]
32 William Rd.,
Reading, MA 01867
Ph: (718)315-6161

Loomans, Marcel, President
International Society of Indoor Air
    Quality and Climate [4074]
c/o Infinity Conference Group, Inc.
1035 Sterling Rd., Ste. 202
Herndorn, VA 20170-3838
Ph: (703)925-9455
Fax: (703)925-9453

Loonan, Peggy, Exec. Dir., Founder
Life and Liberty for Women [10430]
PO Box 271778
Fort Collins, CO 80527-1778
Ph: (970)217-7577

Looney, Jeff, President
Horatio Alger Society [9033]
1004 School St.
Shelbyville, IN 46176

Loos, Barbara, President
American Action Fund for Blind
    Children and Adults [17681]
1800 Johnson St.
Baltimore, MD 21230
Ph: (410)659-9315

Lopes, Tommy, Exec. Dir.
International Association of Approved
    Basketball Officials [22571]
PO Box 355
Carlisle, PA 17013-0344
Ph: (717)713-8129
Fax: (717)718-6164

Lopez, Anthony, Chairman
National Society of Hispanic MBAs
    [659]
450 E John Carpenter Fwy., Ste.
    200
Irving, TX 75062
Ph: (214)596-9338
Toll Free: 877-467-4622
Fax: (214)596-9325

Lopez, Belinda, Secretary
Association for Humanistic Counsel-
    ing [8001]
5999 Stevenson Ave.
Alexandria, VA 22304

Lopez, Carolyn, Chairperson
Interstate Postgraduate Medical As-
    sociation of North America [14748]
PO Box 5474
Madison, WI 53705
Ph: (608)231-9045
Toll Free: 877-292-4489

Lopez, Cindy, Office Mgr.
Institute of Makers of Explosives
    [6626]
1120 19th St. NW, Ste. 310
Washington, DC 20036-3605
Ph: (202)429-9280
Fax: (202)293-2420

Lopez, Fe, President
OneAmerica [18105]
1225 S Weller St., Ste. 430
Seattle, WA 98144
Ph: (206)723-2203
Fax: (206)826-0423

Lopez, Jose, President
Catholic Migrant Farmworker
Network **[12336]**
701 Walnut Ave. NE
Canton, OH 44702
Ph: (330)454-6754

Lopez, Matt, CEO
National Stroke Association **[17297]**
9707 E Easter Ln., Ste. B
Centennial, CO 80112
Toll Free: 800-787-6537

Lopez, Ralph, President
Energy Traffic Association **[2520]**
935 Eldridge Rd., No. 604
Sugar Land, TX 77478-2809

Lopez, Sonia, Medical Dir.
START Treatment and Recovery
Centers **[13184]**
22 Chapel St.
Brooklyn, NY 11201
Ph: (718)260-2900
Fax: (718)875-2817

Lopilato, Mike, Exec. Dir.
CrimeWatch USA **[11505]**
6671 W Indiantown Rd.
Jupiter, FL 33458-3991
Ph: (561)247-5113

Lorance, Michael, Treasurer
Wabash, Frisco and Pacific Associa-
tion **[10194]**
101 Grand Ave.
Glencoe, MO 63038
Ph: (636)587-3538

Lord, Blyth, Founder
Courageous Parents Network
[12411]
21 Rochester Rd.
Newton, MA 02458

Lord, Jim, Exec. Dir.
American Association of Cheerleading Coaches and Administrators
[22724]
6745 Lenox Center Ct., Ste. 318
Memphis, TN 38115
Toll Free: 800-533-6583

Lord, Gen. (Ret.) Lance, President
Association of Air Force Missileers
[20683]
PO Box 5693
Breckenridge, CO 80424-5693
Ph: (970)453-0500
Fax: (970)453-0500

Lord, Richard, President
Assistance Dogs International
[11574]
PO Box 5174
Santa Rosa, CA 95402

Lorefice, Chris, Chairman
Wrestlers WithOut Borders **[23375]**
63 Whitney St.
San Francisco, CA 94131

Lorentz, Dr. Christopher, President
Delta Epsilon Sigma **[23779]**
c/o Dr. Claudia Marie Kovach,
Secretary-Treasurer
1 Neumann Dr.
Aston, PA 19014-1298

Lorenz, Birgit, President
International Society for Genetic Eye
Diseases and Retinoblastoma
[16390]
9500 Euclid Ave., I32
Cleveland, OH 44195

Lorenz, Greg, VP
National Society for Experiential
Education **[7913]**

c/o Talley Management Group, Inc.
19 Mantua Rd.
Mount Royal, NJ 08061-1006
Ph: (856)423-3427
Fax: (856)423-3420

Lorigan, Kim, President
United States Coast Guard Chief
Petty Officers Association **[20749]**
5520 Hempstead Way, Ste. G
Springfield, VA 22151
Fax: (703)941-0397

Lory, David, Treasurer, Secretary
Ferguson Enthusiasts of North
America **[22452]**
5604 Southwest Rd.
Platteville, WI 53818-8923
Ph: (608)348-6344

Losch, Dale, President
CrossWorld **[20407]**
10000 N Oak Trafficway
Kansas City, MO 64155
Ph: (816)479-7300
Toll Free: 888-785-0087
Fax: (816)734-4601

LoSchiavo, Joe, President
American Society for Scleroderma
Research **[17178]**
31 Patmar Terr.
Monroe, CT 06468
Ph: (203)273-2034

Losey, Marshall, President
International Nubian Breeders As-
sociation **[3602]**
c/o Caroline Lawson, Secretary/
Treasurer
5124 FM 1940
Franklin, TX 77856
Ph: (979)828-4158

Losey, Marshall, President
National Toggenburg Club **[4279]**
2100 Painted Desert Dr.
Winslow, AZ 86047
Ph: (928)289-4868

Losos, Elizabeth, CEO, President
Organization for Tropical Studies -
North American Office **[7353]**
410 Swift Ave.
Durham, NC 27705-4831
Ph: (919)684-5774
Fax: (919)684-5661

Lothamer, M. Thomas, President
Life Matters Worldwide **[12779]**
5075 Clay Ave. SW, Ste. C
Grand Rapids, MI 49548
Ph: (616)257-6800
Toll Free: 800-968-6086

Loto, Judith Livingston, Exec. Dir.
Antiques Dealers Association of
America **[21624]**
PO Box 218
Northwood, NH 03261
Ph: (603)942-6498
Fax: (603)942-5035

Lott, Christine, Founder, Director
Tanzania School Foundation **[11451]**
2 Canton St., Ste. 222
Stoughton, MA 02072-2878
Ph: (781)718-4307

Lotz, Dr. Barry, President
Professional Golf Teachers Associa-
tion of America **[22891]**
PO Box 912
La Quinta, CA 92247
Ph: (760)777-1925
Toll Free: 888-90-PGTAA
Fax: (760)406-9898

Louaillier, Kelle, President
Corporate Accountability
International **[18745]**

10 Milk St., Ste. 610
Boston, MA 02108
Ph: (617)695-2525

Loubier, Andrea, Operations Mgr.
International Newsmedia Marketing
Association **[2793]**
PO Box 740186
Dallas, TX 75374
Ph: (214)373-9111
Fax: (214)373-9112

Louda, Dale, Exec. Dir.
CHP Association **[7355]**
718 7th St. NW, 2nd Fl.
Washington, DC 20001
Ph: (202)888-0708

Lougaris, Betty I., Exec. Dir.,
Treasurer
Media Guilds International **[2316]**
9651 Trailwood Dr.
Las Vegas, NV 89164
Ph: (702)255-1179

Lough, Donald H., Jr., Exec. Dir.
Word of Life Fellowship **[20165]**
PO Box 600
Schroon Lake, NY 12870
Ph: (518)494-6000

Loughlin, Thomas G., Exec. Dir.
ASME International **[6831]**
2 Park Ave.
New York, NY 10016-5990
Ph: (973)882-1170
Toll Free: 800-843-2763
Fax: (973)882-1717

Louie, Andrea, Exec. Dir.
Asian American Arts Alliance **[8962]**
20 Jay St., Ste. 740
Brooklyn, NY 11201
Ph: (212)941-9208
Fax: (212)366-1778

Lounds-Brooks, Ashley, President,
Founder
Christian Ladies All together Stand-
ing against Social Injustice
Corporation **[13373]**
PO Box 3795
Cartersville, GA 30120
Ph: (404)326-8619

Lounsbury, Lee, Exec. Dir.
Welfare Research, Inc. **[13094]**
14 Columbia Cir., Ste. 104
Albany, NY 12203
Ph: (518)713-4726
Fax: (518)608-5435

Louttit, Dana, President
Irish Water Spaniel Club of America
[21903]
c/o Gregory L Johnson, Membership
Director
2316 NE 5th St.
Minneapolis, MN 55418-3504
Ph: (612)205-0075

Lovatt, Dr. Carol, Secretary,
Treasurer
International Society of Citriculture
[4235]
University of California
Dept. of Botany and Plant Sciences
Riverside, CA 92521-0124

Lovatt-Smith, Lisa, Founder
OAfrica **[11103]**
268 Bush St., No. 3100
San Francisco, CA 94104
Ph: (917)477-3822

Love, Arthur, Mem.
International M-100 Group **[21403]**
c/o Francis Abate

PO Box 880283
Steamboat Springs, CO 80488

Love, Denise, Exec. Dir.
National Association of Health Data
Organizations **[14949]**
124 S 400 E, Ste. 220
Salt Lake City, UT 84111-5312
Ph: (801)532-2299
Fax: (801)532-2228

Love, James, Director
Knowledge Ecology International
[7281]
1621 Connecticut Ave. NW, Ste. 500
Washington, DC 20009
Ph: (202)332-2670
Fax: (202)332-2673

Love, Rhonda, VP
B'nai B'rith International's Center for
Jewish Identity **[8137]**
1120 20th St. NW, Ste. 300 N
Washington, DC 20036
Ph: (212)490-3290
(202)857-6600
Toll Free: 888-388-4224

Lovejoy, Riki F., President
National Association of Women in
Construction **[885]**
327 S Adams St.
Fort Worth, TX 76104
Ph: (817)877-5551
Toll Free: 800-552-3506
Fax: (817)877-0324

Lovelace, James, President
Academy for Sports Dentistry
[17272]
PO Box 364
Farmersville, IL 62533
Ph: (217)227-3431
Fax: (217)227-3438

Loveland, Gail, Exec. Dir.
National Ability Center **[22784]**
1000 Ability Way
Park City, UT 84060
Ph: (435)649-3991
Fax: (435)658-3992

Lovell, Cindy, Exec. Dir.
Mark Twain Memorial **[9076]**
351 Farmington Ave.
Hartford, CT 06105-6400
Ph: (860)247-0998
(860)280-3127
Fax: (860)278-8148

Lovell, Rick, Gen. Mgr.
Producers Livestock Marketing As-
sociation **[4484]**
PO Box 540477
North Salt Lake, UT 84054-0477
Ph: (801)936-2424

Loving, Allen, Advisor
SAFE Association **[5872]**
300 N Mill St., Unit B
Creswell, OR 97426
Ph: (541)895-3012
Fax: (541)895-3014

Loving, Robert, CFO
Indoor Football League **[22858]**
3123 W Stolley Park Rd.
Grand Island, NE 68801
Ph: (804)643-7277
Fax: (804)643-7278

Low, Gina, Contact
Association Promoting Education
and Conservation in Amazonia
[4788]
21338 Dumetz Rd.
Woodland Hills, CA 91364

Low, Ms. Melissa, VP
National Alliance for Accessible Golf
[22785]

1 World Golf Pl.
Saint Augustine, FL 32092-2724
Ph: (904)940-4204

Lowdermilk, Dale, Founder
National Organization Taunting
  Safety and Fairness Everywhere
  [22164]
PO Box 5743
Montecito, CA 93150

Lowe, Christopher, President
American Elasmobranch Society
  [6809]
c/o Cathy J. Walsh, Treasurer
1600 Ken Thompson Pkwy.
Sarasota, FL 34236

Lowenstein, Prof. Ariela, PhD,
  Contact
Gift Sales Manager Association
  [3015]
c/o Ari D. Lowenstein
105 Atlantic Ave.
Brooklyn, NY 11201
Ph: (718)243-9492

Lowers, Heather A., Secretary
Microanalysis Society [6867]
c/o Thomas F. Kelly, President
5500 Nobel Dr., Ste. 100
Madison, WI 53711-4951

Lowery, John, VP
Phi Sigma Nu American Indian
  Fraternity [23917]
PO Box 2040
Pembroke, NC 28372

Lowery, John, Sr., President
National High School Baseball
  Coaches Association [22561]
PO Box 12843
Tempe, AZ 85284-0048
Ph: (602)615-0571
Fax: (480)838-7133

Lowery, Lawrence F., President
Big Little Book Collector's Club
  [21627]
PO Box 1242
Danville, CA 94526

Lowes, Susan, Assoc. Dir.
Columbia University I Institute for
  Learning Technologies [7841]
Teachers College
525 W 120th St.
New York, NY 10027-6605
Ph: (212)678-3000

Lowinger, Rabbi, Chairman
International Alliance of Messianic
  Congregations and Synagogues
  [20335]
PO Box 1570
Havertown, PA 19083
Ph: (215)452-5590
Toll Free: 866-426-2766

Lowry, Doug, President
National Police Bloodhound Association [5508]
c/o Coby Webb, Treasurer
38540 Alva Dr.
Cherry Valley, CA 92223

Lowry, Fred, Jr., VP
National Association of Independent
  Insurance Auditors and Engineers
  [1895]
PO Box 794
Clifton Park, NY 12065
Toll Free: 800-232-2342

Lowry, Glenn D., Director
International Council of the Museum
  of Modern Art [8865]

11 W 53rd St.
New York, NY 10019
Ph: (212)708-9400
Toll Free: 888-999-8861

Lowry, Rachel, President
International Zoo Educators Association [7852]
3605 E Bougainvillea Ave.
Tampa, FL 33612

Lowy, Dr. Douglas R., Dir. (Actg.)
Cancer Information Service [13924]
9609 Medical Center Dr.
Rockville, MD 20850
Toll Free: 800-422-6237

Lowy, Stephan, Exec. Dir., Founder
Move For Hunger [12103]
Bldg. 1, Ste. 1
1930 Heck Ave.
Neptune, NJ 07753
Ph: (732)774-0521
Fax: (732)774-6683

Loza, Moises, Exec. Dir.
Housing Assistance Council [11973]
1025 Vermont Ave. NW, Ste. 606
Washington, DC 20005
Ph: (202)842-8600
Fax: (202)347-3441

Lozada, Edwin Agustin, Director
Philippine American Writers and Art-
  ists, Inc. [10394]
PO Box 31928
San Francisco, CA 94131-0928

Lozada, Herman, Contact
American Council for Drug Educa-
  tion [13124]
164 W 74th St.
New York, NY 10023
Ph: (646)505-2061
    (212)595-5810
Toll Free: 800-488-3784
Fax: (212)595-2553

Lozier, Mr. John, Exec. Dir.
National Health Care for the Home-
  less Council [15158]
PO Box 60427
Nashville, TN 37206-0427
Ph: (615)226-2292
Fax: (615)226-1656

Lu, Jian-yu, President
IEEE - Ultrasonics, Ferroelectrics,
  and Frequency Control Society
  [5854]
1800 S Oak St., Ste 100
Champaign, IL 61820
Ph: (217)356-3182

Luanghy, Sylvie, VP, Founder
Fashion Fights Poverty [12537]
1101 Wilson Blvd., Ste. 932
Arlington, VA 22209
Ph: (571)969-3121

Lubber, Mindy S., President
Ceres [4038]
99 Chauncy St., 6th Fl.
Boston, MA 02111
Ph: (617)247-0700
Fax: (617)267-5400

Lubell, David, Exec. Dir.
Welcoming America [18469]
PO Box 2554
Decatur, GA 30031
Ph: (404)631-6593

Lubin, Barbara, Exec. Dir., Founder
Middle East Children's Alliance
  [18424]
1101 8th St., Ste. 100
Berkeley, CA 94710
Ph: (510)548-0542
Fax: (510)548-0543

Lubin, Marc Jean, Exec. Dir.
Mission of Hope [12701]
PO Box 171500
Austin, TX 78717
Ph: (239)791-8125
Fax: (239)791-8133

Lublink, Leslie, Administrator
Society for Inherited Metabolic
  Disorders [15835]
c/o Leslie Lublink, Administrator
18265 Lower Midhill Dr.
West Linn, OR 97068
Ph: (503)636-9228
Fax: (503)210-1511

Lucas, Col. Charles Clement, M.D.,
  Gov.
National Society Sons of the
  American Colonists [20757]
c/o Robert Darrell Pollock, Registrar
  General
PO Box 86
Urbana, OH 43078-0086

Lucas, Ed, President
National Alliance of HUD Tenants
  [18358]
42 Seaverns Ave.
Boston, MA 02130
Ph: (617)522-4523
    (617)233-1885
Fax: (617)522-4857

Lucas, Frank, Chairman
U.S.A. Rice Federation [1523]
2101 Wilson Blvd., Ste. 610
Arlington, VA 22201-3040
Ph: (703)236-2300
Fax: (703)236-2301

Lucas, Jami, Exec. Dir., CEO
American Academy of Otolaryngic
  Allergy [13569]
11130 Sunrise Valley Dr., Ste. 100
Reston, VA 20191
Ph: (202)955-5010
    (202)955-5016

Lucas, Jami, CEO, Exec. Dir.
American Academy of Otolaryngic
  Allergy and Foundation [13570]
11130 Sunrise Valley Dr., Ste. 100
Reston, VA 20191
Ph: (202)955-5010
Fax: (202)955-5016

Lucas, Lisa, Exec. Dir.
National Book Foundation [9134]
90 Broad St., Ste. 604
New York, NY 10004
Ph: (212)685-0261
Fax: (212)213-6570

Lucas, Mark A., Exec. Dir.
U.S. Association for Blind Athletes
  [22798]
1 Olympic Plz.
Colorado Springs, CO 80909
Ph: (719)866-3224
Fax: (719)866-3400

Lucas, Susanne, President
American Bamboo Society [6126]
315 S Coast Highway 101, Ste. U
Encinitas, CA 92024-3555

Lucas, Susanne, CEO
World Bamboo Organization [4500]
9 Bloody Pond Rd.
Plymouth, MA 02360

Luce, Jim, President, Founder
Orphans International Worldwide,
  Inc. [11258]
55 Exchange Pl., 4th Fl.
New York, NY 10005

Luckas, Matt, Chairman
International Refrigerated
  Transportation Association [3336]

Global Cold Chain Alliance
1500 King St., Ste. 201
Alexandria, VA 22314-2730
Ph: (703)373-4300
Fax: (703)373-4301

Lucker, Jay R., President
National Coalition on Auditory
  Processing Disorders [15202]
PO Box 494
Rockville Centre, NY 11571-0494

Luckhardt, Shirley, Secretary
American Turners [23213]
1127 E Kentucky St.
Louisville, KY 40204
Ph: (502)636-2395
Fax: (502)636-1935

Ludeke, Larry, VP
American-International Charolais As-
  sociation [3696]
11700 NW Plaza Cir.
Kansas City, MO 64153
Ph: (816)464-5977
Fax: (816)464-5759

Ludlum, Mike, President
North American Shetland Sheep-
  breeders Association [4679]
305 Lincoln
Wamego, KS 66547
Ph: (260)672-9623

Ludwig, Andy, VP
Crane Certification Association of
  America [805]
1608 S Ashland Ave., No. 83408
Chicago, IL 60608
Toll Free: 800-447-3402
Fax: (407)598-2902

Ludwig, Dave, President
Family Campers and RVers [22720]
Bldg. 2
4804 Transit Rd.
Depew, NY 14043
Ph: (716)668-6242
Toll Free: 800-245-9755

Ludwig, Deborah, Treasurer
American Electrology Association
  [14657]
c/o Pearl G. Warner, President
4711 Midlothian Tpke. 13
Crestwood, IL 60445
Ph: (708)293-1400
Fax: (708)293-1405

Ludwig, Terri, President, CEO
Enterprise Community Partners, Inc.
  [11968]
11000 Broken Land Pky., Ste. 700
Columbia, MD 21044
Toll Free: 800-624-4298

Lueck, Beth L., President
Harriet Beecher Stowe Society
  [10374]
c/o Nancy Lusignan Schultz,
  Treasurer
Dept. of English
Salem State University
352 Lafayette St.
Salem, MA 01970-5333

Luedeka, Robert J., Exec. Dir.
Polyurethane Foam Association, Inc.
  [2630]
334 Lakeside Plz.
Loudon, TN 37774-4165
Ph: (865)657-9840
Fax: (865)381-1292

Luest, Helga, MA, CEO, Founder,
  President
Witness Justice [19232]
PO Box 2516

Rockville, MD 20847-2516
Ph: (301)846-9110
Toll Free: 800-394-2255

Luettgen, Chris, Chairperson
Technical Association of the Pulp
and Paper Industry [2495]
15 Technology Pky. S, Ste. 115
Peachtree Corners, GA 30092
Ph: (770)446-1400

Lugar, Katherine, President, CEO
American Hotel and Lodging Association [1647]
1250 I St. NW, Ste. 1100
Washington, DC 20005
Ph: (202)289-3100
Fax: (202)289-3199

Lugt, Lee Vander, DO, Exec. Dir.
American Osteopathic Academy of
Orthopedics [16467]
2209 Dickens Rd.
Richmond, VA 23230-2005
Ph: (804)565-6370
Toll Free: 800-741-2626
Fax: (804)282-0090

Luick, Barbara A., CEO
Country Music Showcase
International [9897]
PO Box D
Carlisle, IA 50047-0368
Ph: (515)989-3748

Luick, Sarah, Chairwoman
Animal Legal Defense Fund [10578]
525 E Cotati Ave.
Cotati, CA 94931
Ph: (707)795-2533
Fax: (707)795-7280

Lujan, James, President
Catching the Dream [7923]
8200 Mountain Rd. NE, Ste. 203
Albuquerque, NM 87110-7856
Ph: (505)262-2351
Fax: (505)262-0534

Luk, John, Chairman
Silicon Valley Chinese Engineers
Association [6586]
PO Box 642
Mountain View, CA 94042

Luk, Joseph, Director
U.S.-China Business Council [1998]
1818 N St. NW, Ste. 200
Washington, DC 20036
Ph: (202)429-0340
Fax: (202)775-2476

Lukas, Katherine, President
Fan Association of North America
[21653]
2 Sterling Hill Ln., No. 228
Exeter, NH 03833

Luke, Anne Forristall, President,
CEO
Rubber Manufacturers Association
[2986]
1400 K St. NW, Ste. 900
Washington, DC 20005
Ph: (202)682-4800

Luke, Jenni, CEO
Step Up [13399]
510 S Hewitt St., No. 111
Los Angeles, CA 90013-2268
Ph: (213)382-9161

Lukens, Amb. Alan W., Bd. Member
American Friends of Turkey [19202]
1025 Connecticut Ave. NW, Ste.
1000
Washington, DC 20036
Ph: (202)327-5450

Luketich, Bernard M., President
Junior Tamburitzans [9193]
100 Delaney Dr.
Pittsburgh, PA 15235-5416
Ph: (412)843-0380
Fax: (412)823-1594

Lukken, Walter L., President, CEO
Futures Industry Association [1493]
2001 Pennsylvania Ave. NW, Ste.
600
Washington, DC 20006
Ph: (202)466-5460

Lum, Heidi, President
Advocates for Africa's Children
[10833]
PO Box 283233
Honolulu, HI 96828
Ph: (808)391-9777

Lum, Lisa M., Exec. Dir.
Asia America MultiTechnology Association [7260]
555 Bryant St., No. 332
Palo Alto, CA 94301-1704
Ph: (650)773-2293

Lum, Wesley, President, CEO
National Asian Pacific Center on Aging [10517]
1511 3rd Ave., Ste. 914
Seattle, WA 98101
Ph: (206)624-1221
Toll Free: 800-336-2722
Fax: (206)624-1023

Luna, Thomas R., President
Council of Chief State School Officers [7755]
1 Massachusetts Ave. NW, Ste. 700
Washington, DC 20001-1431
Ph: (202)336-7000
Fax: (202)408-8072

Lund, Adrian, President
Insurance Institute for Highway
Safety [12822]
1005 N Glebe Rd., Ste. 800
Arlington, VA 22201
Ph: (703)247-1500
Fax: (703)247-1588

Lund, Sena P., Secretary
Afghan Hindu Association, Inc.
[20198]
45-32 Bowne St.
New York, NY 11355
Ph: (718)961-8838

Lundberg, Laurie, Founder,
President, Exec. Dir.
Bridge of Love [10873]
PO Box 1869
West Jordan, UT 84084-8869

Lundblad, Jennifer, PhD, CEO,
President
Stratis Health [14965]
2901 Metro Dr., Ste. 400
Bloomington, MN 55425-1525
Ph: (952)854-3306
Toll Free: 877-787-2847
Fax: (952)853-8503

Lundgaard, Rev. Spencer L., Exec.
Dir.
A Christian Ministry in the National
Parks [19963]
9185 E Kenyon Ave., Ste. 230
Denver, CO 80237
Ph: (303)220-2808
Toll Free: 800-786-3450
Fax: (303)220-0128

Lundgren, Dr. Elizabeth, Exec. Sec.
Ankole Watusi International Registry
[3716]

22484 W 239 St.
Spring Hill, KS 66083-9306
Ph: (913)592-4050

Lundholm, Renee, President
Swedish-American Chamber of
Commerce Inc. [23619]
570 Lexington Ave., 20th Fl.
New York, NY 10022
Ph: (212)838-5530
Fax: (212)755-7953

Lundy, Rachel, President
Dysautonomia Information Network
[15926]
PO Box 55
Brooklyn, MI 49230

Lunn, Nick, Chairman
Society for Marine Mammalogy
[4474]
c/o Jay Barlow, President
8901 La Jolla Shores Dr.
La Jolla, CA 92037-1508
Ph: (858)546-7178

Lunn, Rev. Robin R., Exec. Dir.
Association of Welcoming & Affirming Baptists [19718]
PO Box 60008
Chicago, IL 60660
Ph: (240)242-9220

Lunsmann, Sr. Kathleen, IHM,
President
Support Our Aging Religious [10530]
3025 4th St. NE
Washington, DC 20017
Ph: (202)529-7627
Fax: (202)529-7633

Luongo, Kenneth N., President,
Founder
Partnership for Global Security
[19096]
1911 Pine St.
Philadelphia, PA 19103
Ph: (202)332-1412
Fax: (202)332-1413

Lupant, Michel R., President
Federation Internationale des associations vexillologiques [10296]
c/o Charles A. Spain, Secretary
General
504 Branard St.
Houston, TX 77006-5018
Ph: (713)249-0416
Fax: (713)752-2304

Lurie, Joseph, President, Founder
Peggy Browning Fund [5524]
100 S Broad St., Ste. 1208
Philadelphia, PA 19110
Ph: (267)273-7990
Fax: (267)273-7688

Lusby, Frank, Exec. Dir., Founder
Action for Enterprise [11303]
4600 N Fairfax Dr., Ste. 304
Arlington, VA 22203-1553
Ph: (703)243-9172
Fax: (703)243-9123

Lust, Tim, CEO
National Sorghum Producers [3767]
4201 N Interstate 27
Lubbock, TX 79403-7507
Ph: (806)749-3478
Toll Free: 800-658-9808
Fax: (806)749-9002

Lustig, Andy, Contact
Society of U.S. Pattern Collectors
[22287]
PO Box 806
Nyack, NY 10960

Lutgendorf, Philip, President
American Institute of Indian Studies
[9564]

1130 E 59th St.
Chicago, IL 60637
Ph: (773)702-8638

Luthi, Randall, Treasurer
National Energy Education Development Project [18192]
8408 Kao Cir.
Manassas, VA 20110
Ph: (703)257-1117
Toll Free: 800-875-5029
Fax: (703)257-0037

Luthi, Randall, President
National Ocean Industries Association [6941]
1120 G St. NW, Ste. 900
Washington, DC 20005
Ph: (202)347-6900
Fax: (202)347-8650

Lutter, John, President
American Kitefliers Association
[22971]
PO Box 22365
Portland, OR 97269
Ph: (609)755-5483

Lutton, Wayne, PhD, Editor
Social Contract Press [12406]
445 E Mitchell St.
Petoskey, MI 49770
Ph: (231)347-1171
Toll Free: 800-352-4843
Fax: (231)347-1185

Luttrell, Barbara Ann, President
Refugee Women's Network [13396]
1431-A McLendon Dr., Ste. A
Decatur, GA 30033
Ph: (404)437-7767
Fax: (404)806-1440

Luttrell, Ed, President
National Grange [4163]
1616 H St. NW
Washington, DC 20006
Ph: (202)628-3507
Toll Free: 888-447-2643
Fax: (202)347-1091

Lutz, Dennis, President
International Bank Note Society
[22270]
c/o Roger Urce, General Secretary
PO Box 289
Saint James, NY 11780-0289

Luu, Jennie, President
American Women's Hospitals
Service Committee of AMWA
[15311]
12100 Sunset Hills Rd.
Reston, VA 20190
Ph: (703)234-4069

Luurs, Ken, Exec. Dir.
American Society for Blood and Marrow Transplantation [17503]
85 W Algonquin Rd., Ste. 550
Arlington Heights, IL 60005-4460
Ph: (847)427-0224
Fax: (847)427-9656

Luwis, Brian Andrew, CEO
America World Adoption Association
[10442]
6723 Whittier Ave.
McLean, VA 22101
Ph: (703)356-8447
Toll Free: 800-429-3369

Lux, Alexis, VP, Director
HIKE Fund [15196]
530 Elliott St.
Council Bluffs, IA 51503-0202
Ph: (712)325-0812

Luz, Rev. David W., President
Society of the Descendants of the
Schwenkfeldian Exiles [10066]

105 Seminary St.
Pennsburg, PA 18073
Ph: (215)679-3103
Fax: (215)679-8175

Lyfoung, Pacyinz, Prog. Dir.
Public Interest Intellectual Property
Advisors [5340]
PO Box 65245
Washington, DC 20035

Lyle, David, Counsel
American Constitution Society for
Law and Policy [5100]
1333 H St. NW, 11th Fl.
Washington, DC 20005
Ph: (202)393-6181
Fax: (202)393-6189

Lyle, David, Chmn. of the Bd.
Quest International Users Group
[6365]
2365 Harrodsburg Rd., Ste. A325
Lexington, KY 40504-3366
Ph: (859)425-5081
Toll Free: 800-225-0517

Lyle, Ian, Director
National Water Resources Associa-
tion [7373]
4 E St. SE
Washington, DC 20003
Ph: (202)698-0693

Lyles, Marjorie, President
Strategic Management Society
[2194]
Rice Bldg., Ste. 215
815 W Van Burren St.
Chicago, IL 60607-3567
Ph: (312)492-6224
Fax: (312)492-6223

Lyles, Mary M., PhD, Exec. Dir.
Children's Grief Education Associa-
tion [10773]
6883 Wyman Way
Westminster, CO 80030
Ph: (303)246-3826

Lyman, Eugene W., Treasurer
Medieval Academy of America
[9787]
17 Dunster St., Ste. 202
Cambridge, MA 02138
Ph: (617)491-1622
Fax: (617)492-3303

Lyman, James, President
Lakes Region Sled Dog Club
[22827]
PO Box 341
Laconia, NH 03247
Ph: (603)524-4314

Lyman, Ms. Mary, Exec. Dir.
Master Limited Partnership Associa-
tion [2029]
4350 N Fairfax Dr., Ste. 815
Arlington, VA 22203
Ph: (703)822-4995
Fax: (703)842-8333

Lymbertos, Chris, Director
Generation Five [12922]
1015 M.L.K. Jr. Way
Oakland, CA 94607
Ph: (510)251-8552

Lynch, Bill, President
Digital Screenmedia Association
[3072]
13100 Eastpoint Park Blvd.
Louisville, KY 40223
Ph: (502)489-3915
Toll Free: 877-441-7545
Fax: (502)241-2795

Lynch, Brian P., VP
National Grocers Association [2969]
1005 N Glebe Rd., Ste. 250

Arlington, VA 22201-5758
Ph: (703)516-0700
Fax: (703)516-0115

Lynch, Clifford A., Exec. Dir.
Coalition for Networked Information
[6739]
21 Dupont Cir., Ste. 800
Washington, DC 20036
Ph: (202)296-5098
Fax: (202)872-0884

Lynch, Evan, Exec. Dir. (Actg.)
International Clarinet Association
[9925]
829 Bethel Rd., No. 216
Columbus, OH 43214

Lynch, Harry, CEO, Exec. Dir.
Farm Sanctuary [10623]
3100 Aikens Rd.
Watkins Glen, NY 14891
Ph: (607)583-2225
Fax: (607)583-2041

Lynch, Henry T., MD, Founder
Lynch Syndrome International
[14839]
PO Box 19
Madison, CT 06443-0019
Ph: (203)779-5034

Lynch, Jeffrey, MD, CEO, Founder
ReSpectacle [16406]
c/o Jeffrey Lynch, MD, Chief Executive Officer and Founder
1719 Tower Dr.
Stillwater, MN 55082

Lynch, Fr. John P., Director
Society of Missionaries of Africa
[19908]
1622 21st St. NW
Washington, DC 20009-1089
Ph: (202)232-5995
Toll Free: 877-523-4662
Fax: (303)232-0120

Lynch, Kevin A., CEO, President
National Industries for the Blind
[17734]
1310 Braddock Pl.
Alexandria, VA 22314-1691
Ph: (703)310-0500

Lynch, Mike, Mem.
National Cartoonists Society [8931]
PO Box 592927
Orlando, FL 32859-2927
Ph: (407)994-6703
Fax: (407)442-0786

Lynch, Mike, Sr. VP of Sales & Mktg.
U.S. Tobacco Cooperative, Inc.
[4722]
1304 Annapolis Dr.
Raleigh, NC 27608
Ph: (919)821-4560
Fax: (919)821-4564

Lynch, Robert L., President, CEO
Americans for the Arts [8957]
1000 Vermont Ave. NW, 6th Fl.
Washington, DC 20005
Ph: (202)371-2830
Fax: (202)371-0424

Lynch, Robert, VP
United States Personal Chef As-
sociation [702]
7680 Universal Blvd., Ste. 550
Orlando, FL 32819-8959
Toll Free: 800-995-2138

Lynch, Terry, Founder, President
American Patriots Association
[21078]
6701 Winton Blont Blvd.

Montgomery, AL 36124-1035

Lynch, Zack, Exec. Dir., Founder
Neurotechnology Industry Organiza-
tion [16032]
2339 3rd St., Ste. 56
San Francisco, CA 94131
Ph: (415)341-0193
Fax: (415)358-5888

Lynn, Barry W., Exec. Dir.
Americans United for Separation of
Church and State [20013]
1901 L St. NW, Ste. 400
Washington, DC 20036-3564
Ph: (202)466-3234
Fax: (202)466-2587

Lynn, Bob, President
Massey Collectors Association
[22456]
c/o Bob Lynn, President
4273 280th St.
Shenandoah, IA 51601

Lynn, Colleen, Founder
DogsBite.org [12819]
PO Box 12443
Austin, TX 78711

Lyon, Anne, Dir. of Comm.
Design Management Institute [1555]
38 Chauncy St., Ste. 800
Boston, MA 02111
Ph: (617)338-6380

Lyon, Chris, Exec. Dir.
Fibre Channel Industry Association
[3227]
5353 Wayzata Blvd., Ste. 350
Minneapolis, MN 55416
Ph: (415)561-6270
     (425)359-3326

Lyon, Desiree H., Exec. Dir.
American Porphyria Foundation
[15817]
4900 Woodway, Ste. 780
Houston, TX 77056-1837
Ph: (713)266-9617
Toll Free: 866-273-3635
Fax: (713)840-9552

Lyon, Jasmine C., Exec. Dir.
Veterinary Botanical Medicine Association [17667]
c/o Jasmine C. Lyon, Executive
Director
6410 Highway 92
Acworth, GA 30102

Lyon, John, President, CEO
World Hope International [20378]
1330 Braddock Pl., Ste. 301
Alexandria, VA 22314-6400
Ph: (703)594-8527
Toll Free: 888-466-4673

Lyons, Betty, President, Exec. Dir.
American Indian Law Alliance
[18372]
PO Box 3036
Hoboken, NJ 07030

Lyons, Charles, CEO, President
Elizabeth Glaser Pediatric AIDS
Foundation [13540]
1140 Connecticut Ave. NW, Ste. 200
Washington, DC 20036
Ph: (202)296-9165
Fax: (202)296-9185

Lyons, Eddie, President
Baptist Bible Fellowship International
[19720]
720 E Kearney St.
Springfield, MO 65803
Ph: (417)862-5001
Fax: (417)865-0794

Lyons, Jesse, President
Fraternity Communications Association [23712]
c/o KB Parrish
6840 Eagle Highlands Way
Indianapolis, IN 46254

Lyons, Shiela, Contact
Bicycle Ride Directors' Association
of America [22745]
755 N Leafwood Ct.
Brea, CA 92821
Ph: (562)690-9693

Lyons, Tom, VP
Combatant Craft Crewmembers As-
sociation [21052]
PO Box 6912
San Diego, CA 92166

Lysoby, Linda, Exec. Dir.
National Commission for Health
Education Credentialing [15084]
1541 Alta Dr., Ste. 303
Whitehall, PA 18052-5642
Ph: (484)223-0770
Toll Free: 888-624-3248
Fax: (800)813-0727

Lytle, David, Director
American Hampshire Sheep As-
sociation [4654]
305 Lincoln St.
Wamego, KS 66547
Ph: (785)456-8500
Fax: (785)456-8599

Lytle, Glen E., Contact
104th Infantry Division National Timberwolf Association [20716]
c/o National Timberwolf Pups Association
1749 9th Ave.
San Francisco, CA 94122

Lytle, Jessica, Exec. Dir.
The International Childbirth Educa-
tion Association [16288]
2501 Aerial Center Pky., Ste. 103
Morrisville, NC 27560
Ph: (919)863-9487
     (919)674-4183
Toll Free: 800-624-4934
Fax: (919)787-4916

Lytle, Jessica, Dir. of Operations
International Lactation Consultant
Association [11240]
2501 Aerial Center Pky., Ste. 103
Morrisville, NC 27560
Ph: (919)861-5577
Toll Free: 888-452-2478
Fax: (919)459-2075

Lytle, Rosemary, Chmn. of the Bd.
Murder Victims' Families for
Reconciliation [17830]
PO Box 27764
Raleigh, NC 27611-7764
Toll Free: 877-896-4702

Lyttle, Bradford, Founder
United States Pacifist Party [18898]
5729 S Dorchester Ave.
Chicago, IL 60637
Ph: (773)324-0654
Fax: (773)324-6426

M

Maatz, Lisa, Chairperson
National Coalition for Women and
Girls in Education [8751]
American Association of University
Women
1111 16th St. NW
Washington, DC 20036
Ph: (202)785-7793

Mabie, Steve, VP
Maybee Society [20897]
718 Pachester Dr.
Houston, TX 77079

Mac Adam, Barbara, Bd. Member
International Association of Art Crit-
ics - United States Section [8979]
PO Box 20533, London Terrace Sta.
New York, NY 10011

Mac Swain, William F., Officer
Korean War Veterans Association
[21007]
430 W Lincoln Ave.
Charleston, IL 61920-3021
Ph: (863)859-1384
    (682)518-1040

Macallair, Daniel, MPA, Exec. Dir.
Center on Juvenile and Criminal
Justice [5129]
40 Boardman Pl.
San Francisco, CA 94103
Ph: (415)621-5661
Fax: (415)621-5466

Macbain, Mark, VP
International Gay Bowling Organization [22704]

MacCaskill, Laurie, Chairman
Pancreatic Cancer Action Network
[14042]
1500 Rosecrans Ave., Ste. 200
Manhattan Beach, CA 90266
Ph: (310)725-0025
Toll Free: 877-272-6226
Fax: (310)725-0029

Maccioni, Dr. Hugo J. F., Chairman
Pan-American Association for
Biochemistry and Molecular Biol-
ogy [6059]
Michigan State University
Dept. of Biochemistry and Molecular
East Lansing, MI 48824-1319

MacDonagh, Catherine Alman, Esq.,
Founder, CEO
Legal Sales and Services Organiza-
tion [5540]
c/o Beth Marie Cuzzone, Founder
Goulston & Storrs
400 Atlantic Ave.
Boston, MA 02110
Ph: (617)574-6525

MacDonald, Cami, Exec. Dir.
Our Family in Africa [10483]
PO Box 626
Camas, WA 98607
Ph: (602)330-6337

Macdonald, Donald Ian, MD, Chair-
man, Founder
ChildAlive [15443]
14505 Gilpin Rd.
Silver Spring, MD 20906
Ph: (301)598-1163

MacDonald, Ken, Chairperson
Desert Tortoise Council [3847]
4654 East Ave. S, No. 257B
Palmdale, CA 93552

MacDonald, Mia, Exec. Dir.
Brighter Green [3822]
165 Court St., No. 171
Brooklyn, NY 11201
Ph: (212)414-2339

MacDonald, Robert A., Director
All Services Postal Chess Club
[21588]
c/o Robert A. MacDonald, Director
38 Louise Ct.
Rising Sun, MD 21911
Ph: (410)378-5859

MacDonald, Shawn, Coord.
Christian Lesbians Out [19961]
3653-F Flakes Mill Rd., No. 306
Decatur, GA 30034-5255

MacDonald, Walt, President, CEO
Educational Testing Service [8684]
225 Phillips Blvd.
Ewing, NJ 08628
Ph: (609)921-9000
Fax: (609)734-5410

MacDougall, PhD, Pauleena, Direc-
tor
Maine Folklife Center [9328]
University of Maine
5773 S Stevens Ste. 112 B
Orono, ME 04469-5773
Ph: (207)581-1891
Fax: (207)581-1823

Mace, Carissa, President
Fresh Produce and Floral Council
[1331]
2400 E Katella Ave., Ste. 330
Anaheim, CA 92806
Ph: (714)739-0177
Fax: (714)739-0226

Mace, Pamela, Exec. Dir.
Fibromuscular Dysplasia Society of
America, Inc. [15931]
20325 Center Ridge Rd., Ste. 360
Rocky River, OH 44116
Ph: (216)834-2410
Toll Free: 888-709-7089

Mace, William M., Officer
International Society for Ecological
Psychology [7064]
c/o William M. Mace
Dept. of Psychology
Trinity College
300 Summit St.
Hartford, CT 06106-3100
Ph: (860)297-2343
Fax: (860)297-2538

MacEachern, Steven, President
International Society for Bayesian
Analysis [6822]
Box 90251
Duke University
Durham, NC 27708-0251

Maceno, Witlet, President
Stand Up 4 Haiti [12732]
PO Box 3314
New York, NY 10008

Macfarland, Randy, Chmn. of the
Bd.
WorldVenture [19745]
1501 W Mineral Ave.
Littleton, CO 80120
Ph: (720)283-2000
Fax: (720)283-9383

MacFarlane, Glenn, President, CEO
Association for Community Affiliated
Plans [14981]
1015 15th St. NW, Ste. 950
Washington, DC 20005
Ph: (202)204-7508
Fax: (202)204-7517

MacGregor, Ms. Molly Murphy, Exec.
Dir., Founder
National Women's History Project
[10308]
730 2nd St., Ste. 469
Santa Rosa, CA 95402
Ph: (707)636-2888
Fax: (707)636-2909

MacGuineas, Maya, President
Committee for a Responsible
Federal Budget [18954]

1900 M St. NW, Ste. 850
Washington, DC 20036
Ph: (202)596-3597
Fax: (202)478-0681

Machacek, Larry, Coord.
Model A Ford Cabriolet Club [21434]
PO Box 1487
Conroe, TX 77305
Ph: (936)441-8209

Machiorlatti, Jennifer, Exec. VP
University Film and Video Associa-
tion [9317]
3800 Barham Blvd.
Los Angeles, CA 90068
Toll Free: 866-647-8382

Machlin, Gia, Chmn. of the Bd.
The Blue Card, Inc. [12220]
171 Madison Ave., Ste. 1405
New York, NY 10016
Ph: (212)239-2251
Fax: (212)594-6881

Machtay, Dr. Mitchell, Deputy Chmn.
Radiation Therapy Oncology Group
[16353]
1818 Market St., Ste. 1720
Philadelphia, PA 19103-3609
Ph: (215)574-3189
Toll Free: 800-227-5463

Maciag, Gregory A., CEO, President
ACORD [1820]
1 Blue Hill Plz., 15th Fl.
Pearl River, NY 10965-3104
Ph: (845)620-1700
Fax: (845)620-3600

Macias, Steven J., Chairman
Association of American Law
Schools - Section on Sexual
Orientation and Gender Identity
Issues [8210]
1614 20th St. NW
Washington, DC 20009-1001

Macikas, Barb, Exec. Dir.
Public Library Association [9723]
50 E Huron St.
Chicago, IL 60611
Ph: (312)280-5752
    (312)280-5047
Toll Free: 800-545-2433
Fax: (312)280-5029

Mack, Bernadette, Exec. Dir.
Women's Jewelry Association [2061]
82 Washington St., Ste. 203A
Poughkeepsie, NY 12601
Ph: (212)687-2722
Fax: (646)355-0219

Mack, Charles, Editor, Owner
Matchbox U.S.A. [21685]
62 Saw Mill Rd.
Durham, CT 06422
Ph: (860)349-1655
Fax: (860)349-3256

Mack, Stephen, President
Joubert Syndrome and Related
Disorders Foundation [14834]
1415 W Ave.
Cincinnati, OH 45215
Ph: (614)864-1362

Mackay, Christine Torrison, Founder,
Exec. Dir.
Crooked Trails [8717]
PO Box 94034
Seattle, WA 98124
Ph: (206)383-9828

Mackay, Gail Mercer, President
International Association of Microsoft
Channel Partners [6276]

c/o The TransSynergy Group
909 Lake Carolyn Pky., Ste. 320
Irving, TX 75039
Ph: (425)746-1572

MacKay, Michael, President
Children and Adults With Attention
Deficit/Hyperactivity Disorder
[15915]
4601 Presidents Dr., Ste. 300
Lanham, MD 20706
Ph: (301)306-7070
Fax: (301)306-7090

Mackay, Mike, President
An Comunn Gaidhealach Ameirea-
ganach [19638]
PO Box 103069
Denver, CO 80250

MacKenzie, Budd E., Founder
Trust in Education [11453]
985 Moraga Rd., Ste. 207
Lafayette, CA 94549
Ph: (925)299-2010

Mackenzie, Joneen, V. Ch.
National Association for Relationship
and Marriage Education [12256]
PO Box 14946
Tallahassee, FL 32317

Mackes, Marilyn, Exec. Dir.
National Association of Colleges and
Employers [8438]
62 Highland Ave.
Bethlehem, PA 18017-9481
Ph: (610)868-1421

Mackey, Chris, Bus. Mgr.
Episcopal Women's Caucus [20103]
1103 Magnolia St.
South Pasadena, CA 91030

Mackey, Elayne
Associates of Vietnam Veterans of
America [21165]
8719 Colesville Rd., Ste. 100
Silver Spring, MD 20910
Ph: (301)585-4000
Toll Free: 800-882-1316
Fax: (301)585-0519

MacKey, J., VP of Mktg.
Wine Appreciation Guild [4935]
450 Taraval St., Ste. 201
San Francisco, CA 94116
Ph: (650)866-3020
Toll Free: 800-231-9463

Mackey, John, Chairman
Farm Forward [10622]
PO Box 4120
Portland, OR 97208
Toll Free: 877-313-3276
Fax: (877)313-3276

MackFall, John, President
Clan Phail Society in North America
[20836]
Box 16
403 Garfield St. S
Tacoma, WA 98444
Ph: (253)531-4112
Fax: (253)539-0921

MacKie, Robb, CEO, President
American Bakers Association [367]
601 Pennsylvania Ave. NW, Ste. 230
Washington, DC 20004
Ph: (202)789-0300
Fax: (202)898-1164

Mackie, Sue, Exec. Dir.
United States Swim School Associa-
tion [23289]
13215 N Verde River Dr., Ste. 10
Fountain Hills, AZ 85268
Ph: (480)837-5525
Fax: (480)836-8277

Mackintosh, Stuart P.M., Exec. Dir.
Group of Thirty [1013]
1701 K St. NW, Ste. 950
Washington, DC 20006
Ph: (202)331-2472

Mackler, Jeff, Secretary
Socialist Action [19144]
PO Box 10328
Oakland, CA 94610
Ph: (510)268-9429

Macko, John, Director
NTID's Center on Employment
  [11778]
Rochester Institute of Technology
Lyndon Baines Johnson Bldg.
52 Lomb Memorial Dr.
Rochester, NY 14623-5604
Ph: (585)475-6219
Fax: (585)475-7570

MacLane-Baeder, Doreen, Exec. Dir.
Association for Medical Education
  and Research in Substance Abuse
  [8309]
135 Lyndon Rd.
Cranston, RI 02905
Ph: (401)243-8460
Toll Free: 877-418-8769

MacLean, Reverend Canon Patrick,
  President
Clan Gillean U.S.A. [20812]
PO Box 61066
Raleigh, NC 27661-1066
Ph: (919)334-8977
Fax: (919)881-5228

MacLennan, Alexandra M., Treasurer
National Association of Bond
  Lawyers [5437]
601 13th St. NW, Ste. 800 S
Washington, DC 20005-3807
Ph: (202)503-3300
Fax: (202)637-0217

Maclennan, Sherry, President
Australian Cattle Dog Club of
  America [21832]
c/o Lib Nichols, Membership
  Secretary
1861 Central Valley Rd.
Murfreesboro, TN 37129-7618

MacLeod, Prof. Catriona, VP
Goethe Society of North America
  [9052]
c/o Professor Birgit Tautz, Executive
  Secretary
Bowdoin College
Dept. of German
7700 College Sta.
Brunswick, ME 04011-8477

MacLeod, Prof. Catriona, Secretary
International Association of Word
  and Image Studies [8501]
c/o Prof. Catriona MacLeod,
  Secretary
745 Williams Hall
University of Pennsylvania
Philadelphia, PA 19104-6305
Ph: (215)898-7332
Fax: (215)573-7794

MacMakin, Mary, Founder
Afghanistan Zendabad [10465]
PO Box 1064
Bisbee, AZ 85603
Ph: (520)366-7007

MacMillan, Sandra, Bd. Member
The Billfish Foundation [4794]
5100 N Federal Hwy., Ste. 200
Fort Lauderdale, FL 33308
Ph: (954)938-0150
Toll Free: 800-438-8247
Fax: (954)938-5311

MacNab, Ron, Coord.
Trail Riders of Today [22947]
PO Box 506
Highland, MD 20777
Ph: (301)906-6089

MacNamara, Elisabeth, President
League of Women Voters Education
  Fund [18988]
1730 M St. NW, Ste. 1000
Washington, DC 20036-4508
Ph: (202)429-1965
Fax: (202)429-0854

MacNamara, Elisabeth, President
League of Women Voters of the
  United States [18911]
1730 M St. NW, Ste. 1000
Washington, DC 20036-4570
Ph: (202)429-1965
Fax: (202)429-0854

MacRae-Hall, Capt. John M., VP
Clan MacRae Society of North
  America [20828]
c/o Stuart Macrae
12623 Terrymill Dr.
Herndon, VA 20170-2874

MacSems, Michael, Director
North American English and
  European Ford Registry [21462]
PO Box 11415
Olympia, WA 98508
Ph: (360)754-9585

MacSithigh, Prof. Gearoid P.,
  Treasurer
Society for Natural Philosophy
  [6828]
c/o Professor Gearoid P. MacSithigh,
  Treasurer
Toomey Hall
Dept. of Mechanical and Aerospace
  Engineering
Missouri University of Science and
  Technology
400 W 13th St.
Rolla, MO 65409-0500

MacSlarrow, Heather, Exec. Dir.
Society for Wilderness Stewardship
  [3946]
3225 Fort Missoula Rd., B30
Missoula, MT 59804
Ph: (435)962-9453

MacSwain, Debby Griffith, President
American Red Cross Overseas Association [12618]
c/o Dorris Heaston, Treasurer
27118 Eagle Ridge Pl.
Harrisburg, SD 57032

Madan, Praveen, Founder
Jeena, Inc. [11608]
1510 Centre Pointe Dr.
Milpitas, CA 95035
Ph: (408)957-0481

Maday, Michelle L., President
Alpha Psi Lambda National [23886]
PO Box 804835
Chicago, IL 60680
Ph: (847)361-4378

Madden, Rev. Denis J., Mem.
U.S. Conference of Catholic Bishops
  - Ecumenical and Interreligious
  Affairs [19919]
3211 4th St. NE
Washington, DC 20017-1104
Ph: (202)541-3000

Madden, Francine, Exec. Dir.
Human-Wildlife Conflict Collaboration [4826]
c/o The Columbus Zoo

9990 Riverside Dr.
Powell, OH 43065-0400
Ph: (202)746-4421

Madden, Rachelle, Exec. Dir.
Association of Independent Creative
  Editors [2664]
3 W 18th St., 5th Fl.
New York, NY 10011
Ph: (212)665-2679

Maddox, Bill, President, Founder
National Fastdance Association
  [9268]
c/o Bill Maddox, President
3371 Debussy Rd.
Jacksonville, FL 32277
Ph: (904)744-2424
Toll Free: 877-632-2582

Maddox, Richard, Chairman
Fire Department Safety Officers As-
  sociation [5747]
33365 Raphael Rd.
Farmington Hills, MI 48336
Ph: (248)880-1864
Fax: (248)479-0491

Maddux, Daniel J., Exec. Dir.
American Payroll Association - San
  Antonio [1083]
660 N Main Ave., Ste. 100
San Antonio, TX 78205-1217
Ph: (210)226-4600
    (210)224-6406
Fax: (210)226-4027

Maddux, Michael, Exec. Dir.
American College of Clinical
  Pharmacy [16637]
13000 W 87th Street Pky.
Lenexa, KS 66215-4530
Ph: (913)492-3311
Fax: (913)492-0088

Madery, Tara Aveson, Treasurer
Prism Comics [759]
c/o Ted Abenheim, Pres.
3624 Westwood Blvd., No. 202
Los Angeles, CA 90034
Ph: (714)258-6457

Madhavaram, Karunakar R.,
  President
American Telugu Association [9202]
PO Box 4496
Naperville, IL 60567
Ph: (630)783-2250
Fax: (630)783-2251

Madrid, Jorge, Contact
Edutechnia [6741]
4849 S Darrow Dr., No. L138
Tempe, AZ 85282
Ph: (602)434-1778

Madrigal, Damaris, President
Delta Tau Lambda Sorority, Inc.
  [23971]
PO Box 7714
Ann Arbor, MI 48107-7714

Madrigal, Liliana, President
OSA Conservation [3926]
1012 14th St. NW, Ste. 625
Washington, DC 20005
Ph: (202)765-2266
Fax: (202)765-2228

Madrigal, Orlando S., PhD, Exec.
  Dir.
Upsilon Pi Epsilon Association
  [23714]
158 Wetlands Edge Rd.
American Canyon, CA 94503
Ph: (530)518-8488
Fax: (707)647-3560

Madrigal-Dersch, Juliette, President
Association of American Physicians
  and Surgeons [16738]

1601 N Tucson Blvd., No. 9
Tucson, AZ 85716
Ph: (520)323-3110
Toll Free: 800-635-1196
Fax: (520)326-3529

Madry, Randy, Exec. Dir.
Preventing Colorectal Cancer
  [14049]
326 1st St., Ste. 29
Annapolis, MD 21403
Ph: (410)777-5310
Fax: (410)777-8490

Madsen, Nikki, Exec. Dir.
Abortion Care Network [10426]
PO Box 16323
Minneapolis, MN 55416
Ph: (202)419-1444

Madsen, Stephanie, Exec. Dir.
At-sea Processors Association
  [1297]
c/o Stephanie Madsen, Executive
  Director
222 Seward St., Ste. 201
Juneau, AK 99801
Ph: (907)523-0970
    (206)285-5139
Fax: (907)523-0798

Mady, Ashley, President
Women in Toys [3295]
300 Winston Dr., Ste. 1509
Cliffside Park, NJ 07010
Ph: (201)224-2190

Maestrone, Mark C., President
Sports Philatelists International
  [22370]
1320 Bridget Ln.
Twinsburg, OH 44087-2729

Magalong, Michelle, Chairperson
Asian & Pacific Islander Americans
  in Historic Preservation [9375]
1628 16th St. NW, Ste. 4
Washington, DC 20009

Magaram, Kate, VP
Spoons Across America [16240]
630 9th Ave., Ste. 418
New York, NY 10036-4750
Ph: (212)245-1145

Magaziner, Ira C., CEO, V. Ch.
Clinton Health Access Initiative
  [13536]
383 Dorchester Ave., Ste. 400
Boston, MA 02127
Ph: (617)774-0110

Magdangal, Pastor Wally, Founder,
  President
Christians in Crisis [20602]
PO Box 293627
Sacramento, CA 95829-3627
Ph: (916)682-0376

Magder, Rick, Exec. Dir.
Groundwork USA [11370]
22 Main St., 2nd Fl.
Yonkers, NY 10701
Ph: (914)375-2151
Fax: (914)375-2153

Magee, Dion, President
National Black Bridal Association
  [446]
68 Abbond Ct.
Plainfield, NJ 07063
Toll Free: 888-299-2250

Magee, Mr. Earl, Exec. Dir.
Society of Professors of Child and
  Adolescent Psychiatry [16837]
3615 Wisconsin Ave. NW
Washington, DC 20016
Ph: (202)966-1994
Fax: (202)966-2037

Magee, Gayle Sherwood, President
Charles Ives Society [9940]
c/o Donald Berman, Vice President
  and Treasurer
Granoff Music Ctr.
Tufts University
20 Talbot Ave.
Medford, MA 02155

Magee, Jodi, President, CEO
Physicians for Reproductive Health
  [17116]
55 W 39th St., Ste. 1001
New York, NY 10018-3889
Ph: (646)366-1890
Fax: (646)366-1897

Magee, Kathleen S., M.S.W., M.Ed.,
  President, Founder
Operation Smile [15159]
3641 Faculty Blvd.
Virginia Beach, VA 23453
Ph: (757)321-7645
Toll Free: 888-677-6453

Magers, Diane M., Chairperson
Customer Experience Professionals
  Association [767]
401 Edgewater Pl., Ste. 600
Wakefield, MA 01880
Ph: (781)876-8838
Fax: (781)623-0538

Maggi, Osvaldo, President
International Racquetball Federation
  [23087]
1631 Mesa Ave.
Colorado Springs, CO 80906
Ph: (719)433-2017

Maggio, Wendy, President
Thornton W. Burgess Society [4036]
6 Discovery Hill Rd.
East Sandwich, MA 02537
Ph: (508)888-6870
Fax: (508)888-1919

Magid, Mohamed, President
Islamic Society of North America
  [9606]
6555 S County Road 750 E
Plainfield, IN 46168
Ph: (317)839-8157

Magill, Sherry P., PhD, President
Jessie Ball duPont Fund [12462]
40 E Adams St. E, Ste. 300
Jacksonville, FL 32202-3302
Ph: (904)353-0890
Toll Free: 800-252-3452
Fax: (904)353-3879

Maglaris, Dean C., CEO
AmeriCares Foundation Inc. [12620]
88 Hamilton Ave.
Stamford, CT 06902-3111
Ph: (203)658-9500
Toll Free: 800-486-4357
Fax: (203)327-5200

Maglio, Altom M., President
United States Court of Federal
  Claims Bar Association [5449]
Ben Franklin Sta.
Washington, DC 20044-7614
Ph: (202)220-8638
  (202)357-6400

Magpantay, Glenn D., Exec. Dir.
National Queer Asian Pacific
  Islander Alliance [12954]
233 5th Ave., Ste. 4A
New York, NY 10016
Ph: (917)439-3158

Magrino, Arlene, President
International Desert Lynx Cat Association [3680]

PO Box 511
Selma, OR 97538

Magruder, Jim, Exec. Dir.
Board of Registered Polysomno-
  graphic Technologists [15683]
8400 Westpark Dr., 2nd Fl.
McLean, VA 22102
Ph: (703)610-9020
Fax: (703)610-0229

Maguire, Bruce, President
Norrie Disease Association [14609]
PO Box 3244
Munster, IN 46321-0244

Maguire, Gerald, MD, Chmn. of the
  Bd.
National Stuttering Association
  [17247]
119 W 40th St., 14th Fl.
New York, NY 10018
Ph: (212)944-4050
Toll Free: 800-937-8888
Fax: (212)944-8244

Mahaffey, J.C., CAE, Exec. Dir.
American College of Foot and Ankle
  Surgeons [16782]
8725 W Higgins Rd., Ste. 555
Chicago, IL 60631-2724
Ph: (773)693-9300
Toll Free: 800-421-2237
Fax: (773)693-9304

Mahan, Dr. Melissa, Director
National Clearinghouse for Com-
  muter Programs [8625]
Western Illinois University - Quad
  Cities
3300 River Dr.
Moline, IL 61265
Ph: (309)762-8843

Mahanna, Justin J., President
American Precision Optics
  Manufacturers Association [3023]
PO Box 20001
Rochester, NY 14602

Mahar, Caren, Exec. Dir.
Xeroderma Pigmentosum Society
  [14868]
437 Snydertown Rd.
Craryville, NY 12521-5224
Ph: (518)851-3466

Maher, Chris, VP
National Co+op Grocers [908]
14 S Linn St.
Iowa City, IA 52240
Toll Free: 866-709-COOP

Maher, D'Arcy, Exec. Dir.
Evangelical Press Association
  [20139]
PO Box 20198
El Cajon, CA 92021
Toll Free: 888-311-1731

Maher, Robert, President, Founder
American History Forum I Civil War
  Education Association [7977]
PO Box 78
Winchester, VA 22604
Ph: (540)678-8598
Toll Free: 800-298-1861
Fax: (540)667-2339

Maher, Teresa, President
Electronics Technicians Association
  International [1046]
5 Depot St.
Greencastle, IN 46135
Ph: (765)653-8262
Toll Free: 800-288-3824
Fax: (765)653-4287

Mahlay, Rev. Ihor, President
Saint Andrew's Ukrainian Orthodox
  Society [19205]

c/o Vitali Vizir
1023 Yorkshire Dr.
Los Altos, CA 94024
Ph: (440)582-1051

Mahmoud, Khaled M., PhD, Chair-
  man
Bridge Engineering Association
  [6549]
11 Broadway, 21st Fl.
New York, NY 10004
Ph: (212)286-8014
Fax: (435)203-1166

Mahoney, Elizabeth, President
Nurses House, Inc. [16170]
2113 Western Ave., Ste. 2
Guilderland, NY 12084-9559
Ph: (518)456-7858

Mahoney, Jennifer, VP
Society for Chemical Hazard Com-
  munication [727]
PO Box 1392
Annandale, VA 22003-9392
Ph: (703)658-9246
Fax: (703)658-9247

Mahoney, Jim, PhD, Exec. Dir.
Battelle for Kids [7584]
1160 Dublin Rd., Ste. 500
Columbus, OH 43215-1085
Ph: (614)481-3141
Toll Free: 866-543-7555

Mahoney, Mary, Secretary, Treasurer
Office and Professional Employees
  International Union [77]
80 8th Ave., 20th Fl.
New York, NY 10011
Ph: (212)367-0902
Toll Free: 800-346-7348

Mahoney, Meredith, Treasurer
Herpetologists' League [6707]
c/o Meredith Mahoney, Treasurer
ISM Research and Collections Ctr.
1011 E Ash St.
Springfield, IL 62703
Ph: (217)785-4843
  (215)895-2627

Mahoney, Pat, Director
Weddings Beautiful Worldwide [449]
2225 Grove Ave.
Richmond, VA 23220
Ph: (804)342-6061
Fax: (804)342-6062

Mahoney, Simon, President
Marketing Agencies Association
  Worldwide [2289]
60 Peachcroft Dr.
Bernardsville, NJ 07924
Ph: (908)428-4300
Fax: (908)766-1277

Mahrt, William P., President
Church Music Association of
  America [20488]
12421 New Point Dr.
Richmond, VA 23233

Maickel, Bob, President
Pedal Steel Guitar Association
  [9994]
PO Box 20248
Floral Park, NY 11002-0248
Ph: (516)616-9214
Fax: (516)616-9214

Maignan, Jemps, Exec. Dir.,
  Founder
God's Planet for Haiti [13055]
PO Box 4462
Maryville, TN 37802
Ph: (865)257-7680

Maile, Larry J., PhD, President
U.S.A. Powerlifting [23074]
1120 Huffman Rd., Ste. 24, No. 223

Anchorage, AK 99515
Ph: (260)248-4889

Maile, Dr. Lawrence, President
North American Powerlifting Federa-
  tion [23071]
c/o Lawrence Maile, President
PO Box 668
Columbia City, IN 46725
Ph: (907)334-9977

Main, Barbara, Operations Mgr.
Advanced Media Workflow Associa-
  tion [3205]
436 N Westfield Rd.
Madison, WI 53717
Ph: (608)513-5992

Maine, Lucinda L., CEO, Exec. VP
American Association of Colleges of
  Pharmacy [16632]
1727 King St.
Alexandria, VA 22314
Ph: (703)739-2330
Fax: (703)836-8982

Maisch, Chris, President
National Association of State Forest-
  ers [4209]
444 N Capitol St. NW, Ste. 540
Washington, DC 20001
Ph: (202)624-5415
Fax: (202)624-5407

Majde-Cottrell, Jeannine A., PhD,
  Exec. Dir., Treasurer
International Society for NeuroImmu-
  noModulation [16025]
PO Box 41269
Arlington, VA 22204-8269
Fax: (703)521-3462

Major, Bill, Exec. Dir.
Zarrow Families Foundation [13099]
401 S Boston, Ste. 900
Tulsa, OK 74103-4012
Ph: (918)295-8004

Mak, Anthony, Director
Hong Kong Trade Development
  Council [23547]
219 E 46th St.
New York, NY 10017
Ph: (212)838-8688
Fax: (212)838-8941

Makhijani, Arjun, PhD, President
Institute for Energy and
  Environmental Research [6489]
6935 Laurel Ave., Ste. 201
Takoma Park, MD 20912
Ph: (301)270-5500
Fax: (301)270-3029

Maki, Dr. Sonja L., Exec. Dir.
Plant Growth Regulation Society of
  America [6153]
1018 Duke St.
Alexandria, VA 22314
Ph: (703)836-4606
Fax: (703)836-4607

Makofske, Florence, Treasurer
National Tattoo Association, Inc.
  [3199]
485 Business Park Ln.
Allentown, PA 18109-9120
Ph: (610)433-7261

Makris, Sue, Liaison
Developmental Neurotoxicology
  Society [15924]
c/o Helen J. K. Salbe, PhD
Department of Psychology
University of Memphis
400 Innovation Dr.
Memphis, TN 38152

Malabey, Emily, Founder, VP
International Coalition for Autism and
  All Abilities [13770]

PO Box 781
Saint Peters, MO 63376-0014

Malashock, Sarah, Director
California College of the Arts Alumni
   Association [19312]
5212 Broadway
Oakland, CA 94618
Ph: (510)594-3600
   (415)703-9595
Toll Free: 800-447-1ART
Fax: (415)703-9539

Malcolm, Ellen R., Chmn. of the Bd.,
   Founder
EMILY's List [18867]
1800 M St. NW, Ste. 375N
Washington, DC 20036
Ph: (202)326-1400
Toll Free: 800-683-6459

Malcolm, Ellen R., Chairperson
National Partnership for Women &
   Families [18228]
1875 Connecticut Ave. NW, Ste. 650
Washington, DC 20009
Ph: (202)986-2600
Fax: (202)986-2539

Malcom, Cathy, Chmn. of the Bd.
Holiday and Decorative Association
   [1308]
2050 N Stemmons Fwy., Ste. 1F312
Dallas, TX 75207
Ph: (214)742-2747
Fax: (214)742-2648

Malcuit, Pam, President
American Dexter Cattle Association
   [3691]
1325 W Sunshine No. 519
Springfield, MO 65807
Ph: (970)858-1931
   (605)745-4755

Maldonado, Robert, President
Hispanic National Bar Association
   [5008]
1020 19th St. NW, Ste. 505
Washington, DC 20036
Ph: (202)223-4777

Maldonado, Thomas S., MD,
   President
Vascular and Endovascular Surgery
   Society [17414]
c/o Administrare, Inc.
100 Cummings Ctr., Ste. 124A
Beverly, MA 01915
Ph: (978)927-7800
Fax: (978)927-7872

Male, Ms. Jane, Exec. Dir.
Electric Utility Industry Sustainable
   Supply Chain Alliance [3415]
638 W 39th St.
Kansas City, MO 64111
Ph: (816)561-5323
Fax: (816)561-1991

Male, Jane, Exec. Dir.
Investment Recovery Association
   [3191]
638 W 39th St.
Kansas City, MO 64111
Ph: (816)561-5323
Toll Free: 800-728-2272
Fax: (816)561-1991

Malec, Elsie T., Officer
Czech Catholic Union [19419]
5349 Dolloff Rd.
Cleveland, OH 44127
Ph: (216)341-0444
Fax: (216)341-0711

Malec, Karen, Founder, President
Coalition on Abortion/Breast Cancer
   [13494]

PO Box 957133
Hoffman Estates, IL 60195
Ph: (847)421-4000
Toll Free: 877-803-0102

Malek, Fred, Chairman
American Friends of the Czech
   Republic [19416]
4410 Massachusetts Ave. NW, No.
   391
Washington, DC 20016-5572
Ph: (202)413-5528

Malers, Steve, Founder
Open Water Foundation [6282]
320 E Vine Dr., Ste. 315
Fort Collins, CO 80524
Ph: (970)286-7439
Fax: (970)286-7439

Maleski, Cynthia M., President
First Catholic Slovak Ladies Associa-
   tion [19644]
24950 Chagrin Blvd.
Beachwood, OH 44122-5634
Ph: (216)464-8015
Toll Free: 800-464-4642
Fax: (216)464-9260

Malfara, Robert, President, Founder
M.O.R.G.A.N. Project [15953]
4241 N Hwy. 1
Melbourne, FL 32935
Ph: (321)506-2707

Malfetti, Cheryl, Exec. Dir., Founder
International Ski Dancing Association
   [23162]
22 Fountain Dr.
Westerly, RI 02891
Ph: (401)596-8009

Malik, Hersh, President
Sigma Beta Rho Fraternity, Inc.
   [23926]
PO Box 4668
New York, NY 10163-4668

Mallardi, Vincent, Chairman
Printing Brokerage/Buyers Associa-
   tion International [1546]
1530 Locust St., Mezzanine 124
Philadelphia, PA 19102
Ph: (215)821-6581

Mallernee, Rollin, Gen. Counsel
National Basketball Athletic Trainers
   Association [22575]
c/o Rollin Mallernee
400 Colony Sq. NE, Ste. 1750
Atlanta, GA 30361

Mallett, Jetaun, CAE, Operations
   Mgr., Bus. Dev. Mgr.
Institute for Diversity in Health
   Management [15120]
155 N Wacker Ave.
Chicago, IL 60606
Ph: (312)422-2630

Mallison, Thomas, VP
Coast Guard Auxiliary Association
   [20748]
9449 Watson Industrial Pk.
Saint Louis, MO 63126
Toll Free: 877-875-6296

Mallman, James, President
Watchable Wildlife, Inc. [4898]
c/o James Mallman, President
PO Box 319
Marine on Saint Croix, MN 55047-
   0319
Ph: (651)433-4100
Fax: (651)433-4101

Mallobox, Joseph, President
Agricultural Personnel Management
   Association [4147]

512 Pajaro St., Ste. 7
Salinas, CA 93901
Ph: (831)422-8023
Fax: (831)422-7318

Mallon, Michael, Bd. Member
The Institute of Financial Operations
   [6301]
149 Terra Mango Loop, Ste. B
Orlando, FL 32835
Ph: (407)351-3322
Fax: (407)895-5031

Mallory, Georgeann, RD, Exec. Dir.
American Society for Metabolic and
   Bariatric Surgery [17374]
100 SW 75th St., Ste. 201
Gainesville, FL 32607-5776
Ph: (352)331-4900
Fax: (352)331-4975

Mallory, Lene, President
National Association of Extension
   4-H Agents [13461]
3801 Lake Boone Trl., Ste. 190
Raleigh, NC 27607
Ph: (919)232-0112
Fax: (919)779-5642

Mallory, Steve, CEO, President
Stroke Network [17300]
PO Box 492
Abingdon, MD 21009

Malm, Barbara, MBA, Exec. Dir.
Foundation for Physical Therapy
   [17441]
1111 N Fairfax St.
Alexandria, VA 22314
Toll Free: 800-875-1378

Malmon, Alison, Exec. Dir., Founder
Active Minds [15754]
2001 S St. NW, Ste. 450
Washington, DC 20009
Ph: (202)332-9595
Toll Free: 800-273-TALK

Malone, Eric, Founder
World Freestyle Watercraft Alliance
   [23367]
c/o Eric Malone Enterprises LLC
16432 Dunnings Hwy.
Duncansville, PA 16635
Ph: (814)207-9709

Malone, Patrick A., Treasurer
Pound Civil Justice Institute [5829]
777 6th St. NW, Ste. 200
Washington, DC 20001
Ph: (202)944-2841
Fax: (202)298-6390

Malone, Robert Jay, Exec. Dir.
History of Science Society [9487]
University of Notre Dame
440 Geddes Hall
Notre Dame, IN 46556
Ph: (574)631-1194
Fax: (574)631-1533

Malone, Sean, Director
Crisis Response International
   [11655]
PO Box 1122
Moravian Falls, NC 28654

Malone, Steve, President
Association of American Seed
   Control Officials [4944]
c/o Fawad Shah, Director
801 Summit Crossing Pl., Ste. C
Gastonia, NC 28054-2194
Ph: (704)810-8884

Maloney, Mr. Eddie, President
University of Mississippi Alumni Association [19363]

651 Grove Loop
651 Groove Loop
University, MS 38677
Ph: (662)915-7375
Fax: (662)915-7756

Maloney, Jeff, President
Directed Energy Professional
   Society [6472]
7770 Jefferson St. NE, Ste. 440
Albuquerque, NM 87109
Ph: (505)998-4910
Fax: (505)998-4917

Maloney, Laura, President
Parents Education Network [8405]
6050 Geary Blvd., Ste. 101A
San Francisco, CA 94121
Ph: (415)751-2237
Fax: (415)933-8772

Maloney, Michael V., Exec. Dir.,
   Secretary
Organization for Autism Research
   [13775]
2000 N 14th St., Ste. 240
Arlington, VA 22201
Ph: (703)243-9710

Maloney, Terrence M., Officer
Honorable Order of the Blue Goose,
   International [19486]
12940 Walnut Rd.
Elm Grove, WI 53122
Ph: (414)221-0341
Fax: (262)782-7608

Maloney, Toni, Bd. Member
Business Council for Peace [13372]
2576 Broadway, No. 317
New York, NY 10025
Ph: (212)696-9696

Malott, Maria E., CEO, Secretary,
   Treasurer, President
Association for Behavior Analysis
   International [6030]
550 W Centre Ave.
Portage, MI 49024
Ph: (269)492-9310
Fax: (269)492-9316

Malthouse, Brian, Director
CPAmerica International [25]
104 N Main St., 5th Flr.
Gainesville, FL 32601-5320
Ph: (352)727-4070
Fax: (352)727-4031

Malveaux, Floyd J., MD, Exec. VP,
   Exec. Dir.
Merck Childhood Asthma Network,
   Inc. [17143]
North Bldg., Ste. 1200
601 Pennsylvania Ave. NW
Washington, DC 20004
Ph: (202)326-5200

Mamiya, Tadatoshi, President
Japan National Tourist Organization
   [23644]
1 Grand Central Pl.
60 E 42nd St., Ste. 448
New York, NY 10165
Ph: (212)757-5640
Fax: (212)307-6754

Mammone, Diane, Chairperson
National Chinese Honor Society
   [23706]
10100 Finch Ave.
Cupertino, CA 95014-3411

Manahan, Nathan, Exec. Dir.
Women's Oncology Research and
   Dialogue [14082]
828 Hickory Dr.
Carmel, IN 46032
Ph: (317)489-4187

Mancebo, Mr. Christian, LLM, President
American Masters of Laws Association [4991]
PO Box 5466
Washington, DC 20016

Manchikanti, Laxmaiah, MD, Medical Dir.
American Society of Interventional Pain Physicians [16553]
81 Lakeview Dr.
Paducah, KY 42001
Ph: (270)554-9412
Fax: (270)554-5394

Mancini, John, Exec. Dir.
Italic Institute of America [9618]
PO Box 818
Floral Park, NY 11001
Ph: (516)488-7400
Fax: (516)488-4889

Mancini, Pete, Chairman
BP Amoco Marketers Association [2515]
4 Skidaway Village Sq., Ste. 201
Savannah, GA 31411
Ph: (912)598-7939
Fax: (912)598-7949

Mancini, Pierluigi, President
National Latino Behavioral Health Association [15798]
6555 Robin St.
Cochiti Lake, NM 87083
Ph: (505)980-5156

Manck, Katy, President
International Association of School Librarianship [9709]
PO Box 684
Jefferson City, MO 65102
Ph: (573)635-6044
Fax: (573)635-2858

Mancuso, Dawn M., CAE, Exec. Dir.
Association of Schools and Colleges of Optometry [16427]
6110 Executive Blvd., Ste. 420
Rockville, MD 20852
Ph: (301)231-5944
Fax: (301)770-1828

Mancuso, Rachel, Founder, CEO
Cleft Lip and Palate Foundation of Smiles [14331]
1270 Blanchard SW
Wyoming, WY 49509
Ph: (616)329-1335

Mandaville, Jon, President
North American Association of Islamic and Muslim Studies [7170]
PO Box 5502
Herndon, VA 20172

Mandel, Ms. Gerry, Founder
Children's Art Foundation [11221]
PO Box 567
Selmer, TN 38375
Toll Free: 800-447-4569

Mandel, Jed R., President
Truck and Engine Manufacturers Association [332]
333 W Wacker Dr., Ste. 810
Chicago, IL 60606-1249
Ph: (312)929-1970
Fax: (312)929-1975

Mandelbaum, Carola, Managing Dir.
Aid to Artisans [12136]
5225 Wisconsin Ave. NW, Ste. 104
Washington, DC 20015
Ph: (202)572-2628

Mandell, Missy, Exec. Dir.
Large Public Power Council [5171]
c/o Van Ness Feldman

1050 Thomas Jefferson St. NW, 5th Fl.
Washington, DC 20007-3877
Ph: (202)430-0101
Fax: (843)278-8351

Mandell, Missy, Secretary, Director
Spinal Cord Tumor Association, Inc. [17263]
PO Box 461
Jay, FL 32565
Ph: (850)675-6663
Toll Free: 866-893-1689

Mandrier, Brian J., Exec. Dir.
Association of Cancer Executives [13891]
1025 Thomas Jefferson St. NW, Ste. 500 E
Washington, DC 20007
Ph: (202)521-1886
Fax: (202)833-3636

Mandros, Dino, President
Motor Bus Society [21444]
PO Box 261
Paramus, NJ 07653-0261

Manduca, Dr. Cathryn, Exec. Dir.
National Association of Geoscience Teachers [7936]
c/o Carleton College W-SERC
1 N College St.
Northfield, MN 55057
Ph: (507)222-7096
    (507)222-4545
Fax: (507)222-5175

Mane, Purnima, President, CEO
Pathfinder International [17115]
9 Galen St., Ste. 217
Watertown, MA 02472
Ph: (617)924-7200
Fax: (617)924-3833

Manecke, Kirt, President
LandChoices [3893]
PO Box 181
Milford, MI 48381
Ph: (248)685-0483

Mangan, Andrew, Exec. Dir., Founder
U.S. Business Council for Sustainable Development [1009]
411 W Monroe St.
Austin, TX 78704-3025
Ph: (512)981-5417
Fax: (512)309-5456

Manganello, Rick, President
Pure Water for the World Inc. [13334]
PO Box 55
Rutland, VT 05702
Ph: (802)747-0778
Fax: (802)773-8575

Mangano, Joseph, Exec. Dir.
Radiation and Public Health Project [17036]
PO Box 1260
Ocean City, NJ 08226

Mango, Nabila, Exec. Dir.
Zawaya [8818]
311 41st Ave.
San Mateo, CA 94403
Ph: (650)504-5965

Mani, Ravi, Trustee
India Literacy Project [8243]
PO Box 361143
Milpitas, CA 95035-9998

Manion, Bernadette, Treasurer
Stroke Awareness for Everyone [17298]

PO Box 36186
Los Angeles, CA 90036-6186

Manis, Justin, Chmn. of the Bd.
National Spotted Saddle Horse Association [4389]
PO Box 898
Murfreesboro, TN 37133-0898
Ph: (615)890-2864

Manke, Mr. Jim, CAE, Exec. Dir.
Laboratory Animal Management Association [13718]
15490 101st Ave. N, Ste. 100
Maple Grove, MN 55369
Ph: (763)235-6483
Fax: (763)235-6461

Mankiewicz, Paul, PhD, Exec. Dir.
Gaia Institute [4002]
440 City Island Ave.
Bronx, NY 10464

Mankin, Richard, President
Foundation for Science and Disability [11597]
c/o Angela Lee Foreman, Treasurer
PO Box 3384
San Leandro, CA 94578

Manley, Rev. J. Stevan, President
Evangelistic Faith Missions [20414]
PO Box 609
Bedford, IN 47421
Ph: (812)275-7531

Mann, Donald, President
Negative Population Growth [12510]
2861 Duke St., Ste. 36
Alexandria, VA 22314
Ph: (703)370-9510
Fax: (703)370-9514

Mann, Hallie J., Exec. Dir.
Lawyers Associated Worldwide [5019]
Minneapolis, MN
Ph: (952)404-1546
Fax: (952)404-1796

Mann, Jason, President
United States Marine Corps Scout Sniper Association [21021]
PO Box 762
Quantico, VA 22134

Mann, Hon. Julian, III, Chairman
American Bar Association National Conference of the Administrative Law Judiciary [5408]
321 N Clark St.
Chicago, IL 60654
Toll Free: 800-285-2221

Mann, Robert, Exec. Sec.
Dance Masters of America [7702]
PO Box 610533
Bayside, NY 11361-0533
Ph: (718)225-4013
Fax: (718)225-4293

Manning, Archie, Chairman
National Football Foundation and College Hall of Fame [22860]
433 E Las Colinas Blvd., Ste. 1130
Irving, TX 75039
Ph: (972)556-1000
Fax: (972)556-9032

Manning, Brian, President
National Tay-Sachs and Allied Diseases Association [15973]
2001 Beacon St., Ste. 204
Boston, MA 02135
Ph: (617)277-4463
Toll Free: 800-906-8723
Fax: (617)277-0134

Manning, Cheryl, President
National Earth Science Teachers Association [8552]

PO Box 2716521
Fort Collins, CO 80527
Ph: (201)519-1071

Manning, PhD, CRNP, CIC, FAAN, Mary Lou, President
Association for Professionals in Infection Control and Epidemiology [15393]
1275 K St. NW, Ste. 1000
Washington, DC 20005-4006
Ph: (202)789-1890
Fax: (202)789-1899

Manno, Edward, President
Neurocritical Care Society [14352]
5841 Cedar Lake Rd., Ste. 204
Minneapolis, MN 55416
Ph: (952)646-2031
Fax: (952)545-6073

Mano, Barry, President
National Association of Sports Officials [23270]
2017 Lathrop Ave.
Racine, WI 53405
Ph: (262)632-5448
Fax: (262)632-5460

Mansbach, Peter, PhD, President
Circadian Sleep Disorders Network [17215]
4619 Woodfield Rd.
Bethesda, MD 20814

Mansfield, Mary, Chairperson
National Association of Development Companies [2092]
1725 Desales St. NW, Ste. 504
Washington, DC 20036
Ph: (202)349-0070
Fax: (202)349-0071

Manson, Rod, Chairman
National Office Products Alliance [3176]
3601 E Joppa Rd.
Baltimore, MD 21234-3314
Ph: (410)931-8100

Mansour, Joanne, Director
Nail Patella Syndrome Worldwide [14844]
14980 Stream Valley Ct.
Haymarket, VA 20169

Manthe, Laura, Director
Midwest Treaty Network [19582]
PO Box 43
Oneida, WI 54155
Ph: (920)496-5360
    (715)295-0018

Mantonya, Claire, MA, President
National Association of Councils on Developmental Disabilities [12328]
1825 K St. NW, Ste. 600
Washington, DC 20006
Ph: (202)506-5813

Manzer, Alison, President
Association of Commercial Finance Attorneys [4995]
c/o Paul Ricotta, Treasurer
1 Financial Ctr.
Boston, MA 02111
Ph: (617)542-6000

Manzione, Patricia, Exec. Dir., Secretary
Elder Craftsmen [10505]
307 7th Ave., Ste. 1401
New York, NY 10001

Manzullo, Donald, President, CEO
Korea Economic Institute [18601]
1800 K St. NW, Ste. 1010
Washington, DC 20006
Ph: (202)464-1982
Fax: (202)464-1987

Mao, Jun, MD, MSCE, President
Society for Integrative Oncology
[16357]
136 Everett Rd.
Albany, NY 12205
Ph: (347)676-1746

Maplethorp, F. Amanda, BSc, VP
World Federation of Orthodontists
[14476]
401 N Lindbergh Blvd.
Saint Louis, MO 63141-7816
Fax: (314)985-1036

Mara, Ricky L., President
North American Corriente Associa-
tion [3744]
PO Box 2698
Monument, CO 80132
Ph: (719)425-9151

Marak, Steve, Director
American Milking Shorthorn Society
[3704]
800 Pleasant St.
Beloit, WI 53511
Ph: (608)365-3332
Fax: (608)365-6644

Marangu, Makena, Founder
Answer Africa [14563]
203 E Avenida San Juan
San Clemente, CA 92672-2325
Ph: (949)498-5274
Fax: (949)498-5280

Marcanello, Steve, Director
Professional Manufacturing
Confectioners Association [1369]
2980 Linden St., Ste. E3
Bethlehem, PA 18017
Ph: (610)625-4655
Fax: (610)625-4657

Marcavitch, Aaron, President
Recent Past Preservation Network
[9430]
PO Box 383
Evansville, IN 47703-0383
Ph: (765)387-7776

Marchesella, John, Chairman
National Council for GeoCosmic
Research [6353]
c/o Alvin Burns, Executive Secretary
1351 Maryland Ave. NE, Apt. B
Washington, DC 20002-4439

Marchi, Ben, Mem.
Philomathean Society of the
University of Pennsylvania [9765]
3450 Woodland Walk
Philadelphia, PA 19104

Marchitelli, Claudia, MD, President
International Society for the Study of
Vulvovaginal Disease [16291]
PO Box 586
Waxhaw, NC 28173
Ph: (704)814-9493

Marcus-Newhall, Amy, President
Scripps Association of Families
[7639]
Scripps College
1030 Columbia Ave., No. 2009
Claremont, CA 91711
Ph: (909)621-8000

Mardas, Denny, President
Greek Olympic Society [23048]
555 N High St.
Columbus, OH 43215
Ph: (614)224-9020

Margaritis, John, Secretary
Independent Armored Car Operators
Association, Inc. [3086]

8000 Research Forest Dr., Ste. 115
The Woodlands, TX 77382
Ph: (281)292-8208
Fax: (281)292-9308

Margherio, Michael, President
SHARE: Pregnancy and Infant Loss
Support [12427]
c/o Patti Budnik, RN
National Share Office
402 Jackson St.
Saint Charles, MO 63301-3468
Ph: (636)947-6164

Margolies, Liz, Founder, Exec. Dir.
National LGBT Cancer Network
[14029]
136 W 16th St., No. 1E
New York, NY 10011
Ph: (212)675-2633

Margolies, Richard, VP
Project on Technology, Work and
Character [6712]
c/o The Maccoby Group
4825 Linnean Ave. NW
Washington, DC 20008
Ph: (202)895-8922
Fax: (202)895-8923

Margolis, Wendy, Dir. of Comm.
Law School Admission Council
[8216]
662 Penn St.
Newtown, PA 18940
Ph: (215)968-1001

Margot, Jean-Michel, VP
North American Jules Verne Society,
Inc. [10390]
c/o Mark Eckell
7106 Talisman Ln.
Columbia, MD 21045-4805

Marguleas, David, Chairman
California Table Grape Commission
[4230]
392 W Fallbrook Ave., Ste. 101
Fresno, CA 93711
Ph: (559)447-8350
Fax: (559)447-9184

Mariani, Doris, CEO
Nonviolent Peaceforce [18810]
2610 University Ave. W, Ste. 550
Saint Paul, MN 55114
Ph: (612)871-0005
Fax: (612)871-0006

Marincola, Elizabeth, President
Society for Science and the Public
[7146]
1719 N St. NW
Washington, DC 20036
Ph: (202)785-2255
Toll Free: 800-552-4412

Marini, Marc, Chairman
Automated Imaging Association
[7102]
900 Victors Way, Ste. 140
Ann Arbor, MI 48108
Ph: (734)994-6088

Marino, Gary, Founder
Generation Excel [15081]
87 Cambridge St.
Burlington, MA 01803
Ph: (617)448-8517

Marino, Monique, Managing Ed.
Association of Community Cancer
Centers [13893]
11600 Nebel St., Ste. 201
Rockville, MD 20852-2557
Ph: (301)984-9496
Fax: (301)770-1949

Marinoff, Prof. Lou, PhD, Director,
Editor
American Philosophical Practitioners
Association [8418]

PO Box 166
Monroe, NY 10949-0166

Mariotte, Michael, President
Nuclear Information and Resource
Service [18734]
6930 Carroll Ave., Ste. 340
Takoma Park, MD 20912
Ph: (301)270-6477
Fax: (301)270-4291

Mariotti, Margaret, President
Tom Jones "Tom Terrific" Fan Club
[24067]
136 Kyle's Way
Shelton, CT 06484-6614

Mariotti, Steve, Founder
Network for Teaching Entrepreneurship [7565]
120 Wall St., 18th Fl.
New York, NY 10005

Marjanovic, Michael Miroslav, Mem.
Serb National Federation [19642]
615 Iron City Drive Ste. 302
Pittsburgh, PA 15205
Ph; (412)458-5227
Fax: (412)875-5924

Mark, Lisa, Treasurer
National Association of Professional
Organizers [6711]
1120 Route 17, Ste. 200
Mount Laurel, NJ 08054
Ph: (856)380-6828
Fax: (856)439-0525

Markarian, Michael, President
The Fund for Animals [10625]
200 W 57th St.
New York, NY 10019
Toll Free: 866-482-3708

Markaverich, Larry, President
US Navy Beach Jumpers Associa-
tion [21065]
450-106 State Road 13N, No. 407
Saint Johns, FL 32259-3860
Ph: (727)487-6252

Markel, Richard, President
Association for Wedding Profession-
als International [1653]
PO Box 5598
Sacramento, CA 95817
Ph: (916)392-5000
Fax: (916)392-5222

Markens, Ben, President
Paperboard Packaging Council
[2480]
1350 Main St., Ste. 1508
Springfield, MA 01103-1628
Ph: (413)686-9191
Fax: (413)747-7777

Marker, Rita L., Exec. Dir.
Patients Rights Council [11807]
PO Box 760
Steubenville, OH 43952
Ph: (740)282-3810
Toll Free: 800-958-5678

Markert, Rebecca, Treasurer
Church Periodical Club [20097]
PO Box 1206
Manorville, NY 11949
Ph: (631)447-3996

Markham, Donna, President, CEO
Catholic Charities USA [13035]
2050 Ballenger Ave., Ste. 400
Alexandria, VA 22314
Ph: (703)549-1390
Toll Free: 800-919-9338
Fax: (703)549-1656

Markie, Tracy, Chairman
LonMark International [3193]
2901 Patrick Henry Dr.

Santa Clara, CA 95054
Ph: (408)938-5266
Fax: (408)790-3838

Markiewicz, Evan, Exec. Dir.,
Founder
ViviendasLeon [12388]
1585 Folsom St.
San Francisco, CA 94103
Ph: (415)255-2920

Markle, Robert, President
Radio Technical Commission for
Maritime Services [3237]
1611 N Kent St., Ste. 605
Arlington, VA 22209-2128
Ph: (703)527-2000
Fax: (703)351-9932

Markley, Dan, President, Exec. Dir.
National Music Theater Network
[10262]
36 W 44th St.
New York, NY 10019
Ph: (212)664-0979
Fax: (212)664-0978

Marko, Tammy, Dir. of Info. Technol-
ogy
American Institute of Aeronautics
and Astronautics [5857]
12700 Sunrise Valley Dr., Ste. 200
Reston, VA 20191-5807
Ph: (703)264-7500
Toll Free: 800-639-2422
Fax: (703)264-7551

Markovsky, Sharon, President
Society of Insurance Research
[1930]
4248 Park Glen Rd.
Minneapolis, MN 55416
Ph: (952)928-4641

Markowitz, Erika, Exec. Dir.
Thyroid, Head and Neck Cancer
Foundation [14075]
10 Union Sq. E, Ste. 5B
New York, NY 10003
Ph: (212)844-6832
Fax: (212)844-8465

Markowitz, Michael, Director
Institute for Retired Professionals
[12756]
6 E 16th St., Rm. 905
New York, NY 10011
Ph: (212)229-5682

Marks, Christopher, Chmn. of the
Bd.
Organ Historical Society [9992]
PO Box 26811
Richmond, VA 23261
Ph: (804)353-9226
Fax: (804)353-9266

Marks, Cliff, Chairman, President
Cinema Advertising Council [623]
122 E 42nd St., Ste. 511
New York, NY 10168
Ph: (212)931-8106

Marks, Hon. Dana Leigh, President
National Association of Immigration
Judges [5390]
c/o Judge Lawrence Burman,
Secretary-Treasurer
Arlington Immigration Court
1901 S Bell St., Ste. 200
Arlington, VA 22202
Ph: (703)603-1306

Marks, John H., MD, President
International Society of Laparoscopic
Colorectal Surgery [17391]
5019 W 147th St.
Leawood, KS 66224
Ph: (913)402-7102
Fax: (913)273-9940

Markwood, Priscilla S., Exec. Dir.
Association of Pathology Chairs
[16579]
9650 Rockville Pke., Ste. 4111
Bethesda, MD 20814-3993
Ph: (301)634-7880
Fax: (301)576-5156

Markwood, Sandy, CEO
National Association of Area Agen-
cies on Aging [10518]
1730 Rhode Island Ave. NW, Ste.
1200
Washington, DC 20036
Ph: (202)872-0888
Fax: (202)872-0057

Markwood, Sandy, V. Ch., Secretary,
Treasurer
Setting Priorities for Retirement
Years [12758]
3916 Rosemary St.
Chevy Chase, MD 20815
Ph: (301)656-3405
Fax: (301)656-6221

Marler, Pat, President
Society of Decorative Painters
[21784]
1220 E 1st st.
Wichita, KS 67203-5968
Ph: (316)269-9300
Fax: (316)269-9191

Marling, George, Chmn. of the Bd.
German Wine Society [3479]
5607 Huntington Pky.
Bethesda, MD 20814

Marlow, Lisa, Exec. Asst.
American Association of Blood
Banks [13836]
8101 Glenbrook Rd.
Bethesda, MD 20814-2749
Ph: (301)907-6977
Fax: (301)907-6895

Marlow, Vicky, Founder
DAST International Inc. [17389]
42611 Saratoga Park St.
Fremont, CA 94538

Marlowe, Kendall, Exec. Dir.
National Association of Counsel for
Children [11254]
13123 E 16th Ave. No. B390
Aurora, CO 80045
Toll Free: 888-828-NACC

Marlowe, Walter, Chmn. of the Bd.
Council of Engineering and Scientific
Society Executives [6551]
38800 Country Club Dr.
Farmington Hills, MI 48331
Ph: (734)972-3930
     (248)848-3191

Marmor, Max, President
Samuel H. Kress Foundation
[12980]
174 E 80th St.
New York, NY 10075
Ph: (212)861-4993
Fax: (212)628-3146

Maroundit, Sebastian, President,
Founder
Building Minds in South Sudan
[13034]
5880 Pittsford Palmyra Rd.
Pittsford, NY 14534
Ph: (585)350-4035

Marquette, Dr. Gayle, Founder
American Guild of Court Videogra-
phers [5526]
1437 S Border Ave., Ste. 170
Tulsa, OK 74119
Toll Free: 800-678-1990

Marquez Leon, Jose A., CEO,
President
Latinos in Information Sciences and
Technology Association [6747]
Ph: (770)765-3478

Marrapese, Jennifer, Comm. Chm.,
Exec. Dir.
Northeast Sustainable Energy As-
sociation [6504]
50 Miles St.
Greenfield, MA 01301
Ph: (413)774-6051
Fax: (413)774-6053

Marrin, Yvette, PhD, Founder,
President, Bd. Member
National Cristina Foundation [11625]
339 Lea Dr.
West Chester, PA 19382
Ph: (203)863-9100

Marriott, Tanya, President
National Institute of American Doll
Artists [22006]
c/o Donna May Robinson
109 Ladder Hill N
Weston, CT 06883
Ph: (203)557-3169

Marsden, Mike, President
Multi-Housing Laundry Association
[2079]
1500 Sunday Dr., Ste. 102
Raleigh, NC 27607
Ph: (919)861-5579
Fax: (919)787-4916

Marsden, R. Bruce, President
The Collectors Club [22321]
22 E 35th St.
New York, NY 10016-3806
Ph: (212)683-0559

Marsh, George, Exec. Dir.
Marine Corps Veterans Association
[21017]
2245 Park Towne Cir.
Sacramento, CA 95825-0415
Ph: (916)979-1862

Marsh, James, President
Association of Professors of
Medicine [8311]
330 John Carlyle St., Ste. 610
Alexandria, VA 22314
Ph: (703)341-4540

Marsh, Randie, Exec. Dir.
SOTENI International [10554]
1662 Blue Rock St., Ste. 3
Cincinnati, OH 45223
Ph: (513)729-9932
Fax: (513)961-2101

Marsh, Valerie L., Exec. Dir.
National Coalition for Mental Health
Recovery [15794]
611 Pennsylvania Ave. SE, No. 133
Washington, DC 20003
Toll Free: 877-246-9058

Marshall, Bill, Director
International Association of Arson
Investigators [5205]
2111 Baldwin Ave., Ste. 203
Crofton, MD 21114
Ph: (410)451-3473
Toll Free: 800-468-4224
Fax: (410)451-9049

Marshall, Charles, Chairman
Law Enforcement Technology
Information Exchange [5481]
155 Bovet Rd., Ste. 410
San Mateo, CA 94402
Ph: (415)297-1226

Marshall, Denise, MS, Exec. Dir.
Council of Parent Attorneys and
Advocates [8582]

PO Box 6767
Towson, MD 21285
Toll Free: 844-426-7224
Fax: (410)372-0209

Marshall, Raymond J., VP
National Association of Clean Water
Agencies [5735]
1816 Jefferson Pl. NW
Washington, DC 20036
Ph: (202)833-2672
Fax: (888)267-9505

Marshall, Robert P., Exec. Dir.
Alström Syndrome International
[14807]
14 Whitney Farm Rd.
Mount Desert, ME 04660
Toll Free: 800-371-3628

Marshall, Ruth, Director
Center for Human Services [12966]
7200 Wisconsin Ave., Ste. 600
Bethesda, MD 20814
Ph: (301)654-8338
Fax: (301)941-8427

Marshall, Stacey, Dir. of Fin. &
Admin.
Appalachian Trail Conservancy
[23322]
799 Washington St.
Harpers Ferry, WV 25425
Ph: (304)535-6331
Fax: (304)535-2667

Marshall, Will, III, Founder, President
Progressive Policy Institute [19001]
1200 New Hampshire Ave. NW, Ste.
575
Washington, DC 20036
Ph: (202)525-3926
Fax: (202)525-3941

Marshburn, Mr. Steve, Sr., Founder,
President
Lightning Strike and Electric Shock
Survivors International Inc. [14653]
PO Box 1156
Jacksonville, NC 28541-1156
Ph: (910)346-4708
Fax: (910)346-4708

Marston, Karen, President
NURTUREart Non-Profit, Inc. [8935]
56 Bogart St.
Brooklyn, NY 11206
Ph: (718)782-7755
Fax: (718)569-2086

Marstrand, Marianne, Exec. Dir.
Global Peace Initiative of Women
[18789]
301 E 57th St., 4th Fl.
New York, NY 10022

Mart, Charles, V. Ch.
Energy Frontiers International [4026]
1425 K St. NW
Washington, DC 20005
Ph: (202)587-5780

Martens, Priscilla, Exec. Dir.
National Family Preservation
Network [11828]
3971 North 1400 East
Buhl, ID 83316
Toll Free: 888-498-9047

Martin, Andrew, Contact
American Lunar Society [5998]
c/o Andrew Martin
722 Mapleton Rd.
Rockville, MD 20850

Martin, Ann, Officer
North American Guild of Change
Ringers [9987]

c/o A. Thomas Miller, Membership
Secretary
229 Howard Ave.
Woodstown, NJ 08098-1249

Martin, Antonia Cottrell, Founder,
President
Educational Equity Center [7901]
71 5th Ave., 6th Fl.
New York, NY 10003
Ph: (212)243-1110
Fax: (212)627-0407

Martin, Bill, Exec. Dir., Editor
Phi Delta Gamma [23852]
1201 Red Mile Rd.
Lexington, KY 40504-2648
Ph: (859)255-1848
Fax: (859)253-0779

Martin, Bill, Exec. Dir.
Phi Gamma Delta [23911]
1201 Red Mile Rd.
Lexington, KY 40544-4599
Ph: (859)255-1848

Martin, Carol, Exec. Dir.
EMDR Humanitarian Assistance
Programs [12522]
2911 Dixwell Ave., Ste. 201
Hamden, CT 06518
Ph: (203)288-4450
Fax: (203)288-4060

Martin, Christopher J., President
Woman's Life Insurance Society
[19500]
1338 Military St.
Port Huron, MI 48060-5423
Ph: (810)985-5191
Toll Free: 800-521-9292
Fax: (810)985-6970

Martin, Conrad, Co-Ch.
Help Abolish Legal Tyranny [18599]
1612 K St. NW, Ste. 1102
Washington, DC 20006
Ph: (202)887-8255

Martin, David F., M.D., Exec. Dir.
The American Board of Orthopaedic
Surgery [16464]
400 Silver Cedar Ct.
Chapel Hill, NC 27514
Ph: (919)929-7103
Fax: (919)942-8988

Martin, Dawn M., President
Seafood Choices Alliance [3037]
8401 Colesville Rd., Ste. 500
Silver Spring, MD 20910
Ph: (301)495-9570
Fax: (301)495-4846

Martin, Dawn M., President
SeaWeb [4473]
8401 Colesville Rd., Ste. 1100
Silver Spring, MD 20910
Ph: (301)495-9570
Toll Free: 888-473-2932
Fax: (301)495-4846

Martin, Edward, President
Association of Racing Commission-
ers International [5738]
1510 Newtown Pke., Ste. 210
Lexington, KY 40511
Ph: (859)224-7070

Martin, Elizabeth, Exec. Dir.
WomensLaw.org [19252]
c/o National Network to End
Domestic Violence
1400 16th St. NW, Ste. 330
Washington, DC 20036

Martin, Eric, CEO, President
Music for All, Inc. [9958]
39 W Jackson Pl., Ste. 150

Indianapolis, IN 46225
Ph: (317)636-2263
Toll Free: 800-848-2263
Fax: (317)524-6200

Martin, E.X., III, President
Cyberspace Bar Association [5422]
8828 Greenville Ave.
Dallas, TX 75243
Ph: (214)343-7400

Martin, Fonda, Exec. Ofc.
Association for Applied and Clinical
Sociology [7179]
c/o Fonda Martin, Executive Officer
Eastern Michigan University
Dept. of Sociology, Anthropology,
and Criminology
926 E Forest Ave.
Ypsilanti, MI 48198
Ph: (734)845-1206

Martin, Freddie, PhD, Gen. Sec.,
Treasurer
American Society of Sugar Cane
Technologists [4692]
c/o Freddie Martin, General
Secretary
LSU AgCenter
Sturgis Hall, No. 128
Baton Rouge, LA 70803
Ph: (225)578-6930
Fax: (225)578-1403

Martin, Gary C., President, CEO
North American Export Grain As-
sociation [1521]
1250 I St. NW, Ste. 1003
Washington, DC 20005
Ph: (202)682-4030
Fax: (202)682-4033

Martin, James L., Chairman,
President
60 Plus Association [10495]
515 King St., Ste. 315
Alexandria, VA 22314
Ph: (703)807-2070
Fax: (703)807-2073

Martin, Jaye, Exec. Dir.
Legal Services for the Elderly [5542]
5 Wabon St.
Augusta, ME 04330
Ph: (207)621-0087
Toll Free: 800-750-5353
Fax: (207)621-0742

Martin, Jean, PhD, President
National Association of Pediatric
Nurse Practitioners [16153]
5 Hanover Sq., Ste. 1401
New York, NY 10004
Ph: (917)746-8300
(856)857-9700
Toll Free: 877-662-7627
Fax: (212)785-1713

Martin, Jim, President
Council for Exceptional Children
Division on Career Development
and Transition [8580]
PO Box 79026
Baltimore, MD 21279-0026
Toll Free: 888-232-7733
Fax: (703)264-9494

Martin, John C., CEO, President
Children's Corrective Surgery
Society [17383]
PO Box 500578
San Diego, CA 92150
Toll Free: 800-803-9190

Martin, Joyce, Director
Environmental Policy Center [5181]
PO Box 670056
Cincinnati, OH 45267-0056
Ph: (513)558-5439
(513)558-0105
Fax: (513)558-4397

Martin, Julie, Director
Second Wind Lung Transplant Association, Inc. [17147]
c/o Cheryl Keeler, President
2781 Chateau Cir.
Columbus, OH 43221
Ph: (614)488-1149
(815)723-3622
Toll Free: 888-855-9463

Martin, Julie, Director
We Care of India Association
[11183]
13816 Parkhill
Overland Park, KS 66221

Martin, Kamry, President
American Collegiate Horsemen's
Association [4301]
PO Box 2088
Huntsville, TX 77341-2088
Ph: (936)294-1214

Martin, Kate, Director
Center for National Security Studies
[19089]
1730 Pennsylvania Ave. NW, 7th Fl.
Washington, DC 20006
Ph: (202)721-5650
Fax: (202)530-0128

Martin, Katie, President
Crigler-Najjar Association [15254]
c/o Cory Mauck
3134 Bayberry St.
Wichita, KS 67226

Martin, Kevin, Exec. Dir.
Peace Action [18757]
8630 Fenton St., Ste. 524
Silver Spring, MD 20910-3800
Ph: (301)565-4050
Fax: (301)565-0850

Martin, Kevin, Exec. Dir.
Peace Action Education Fund
[18758]
Montgomery Ctr., Ste. 524
8630 Fenton St.
Silver Spring, MD 20910
Ph: (301)565-4050
Fax: (301)565-0850

Martin, LeaAnn, President
United States Handball Association
[22904]
2333 N Tucson Blvd.
Tucson, AZ 85716
Ph: (520)795-0434
Toll Free: 800-289-8742
Fax: (520)795-0465

Martin, Lynn D., MD, Comm. Chm.
Society for Pediatric Anesthesia
[13712]
2209 Dickens Rd.
Richmond, VA 23230-2005
Ph: (804)282-9780
Fax: (804)282-0090

Martin, Margo, Exec. Dir.
American Sewing Guild [21749]
9660 Hillcroft, Ste. 510
Houston, TX 77096-3866
Ph: (713)729-3000
Fax: (713)721-9230

Martin, Mary, President
American Association of Women
Dentists [14394]
7794 Grow Dr.
Pensacola, FL 32514
Toll Free: 800-920-2293
Fax: (850)484-8762

Martin, Melinda, Dir. of Operations
Society of Interventional Pain
Management Surgery Centers
[17402]

81 Lakeview Dr.
Paducah, KY 42001
Ph: (270)554-9412
Fax: (270)554-5394

Martin, Melissa M., President,
Chairperson
American Health Information
Management Association [15633]
233 N Michigan Ave., 21st Fl.
Chicago, IL 60601-5809
Ph: (312)233-1100
Toll Free: 800-335-5535
Fax: (312)233-1090

Martin, Melissa, Exec. Dir.
Phi Upsilon Omicron, Inc. [23772]
PO Box 50970
Bowling Green, KY 42102-4270
Ph: (270)904-1340

Martin, Michael, V. Chmn. of the Bd.
Climate Counts [3830]
131 Main St., No. 107
Durham, NH 03824
Ph: (603)862-0121

Martin, Michael J., Exec. Dir.
National Association for Pupil
Transportation [5815]
1840 Western Ave.
Albany, NY 12203-4624
Ph: (518)452-3611
Toll Free: 800-989-6278
Fax: (518)218-0867

Martin, Michael, CEO, President
National Wood Flooring Association
[564]
111 Chesterfield Industrial Blvd., Ste.
B
Chesterfield, MO 63005
Ph: (636)519-9663
Toll Free: 800-422-4556
Fax: (636)519-9664

Martin, Mike, President
Alliance of Professional Tattooists,
Inc. [3197]
22052 W 66th St., Ste. 225
Shawnee, KS 66226
Ph: (816)979-1300

Martin, Natasha, Founder
Grassroots Alliance for Community
Education [7646]
PO Box 185
Half Moon Bay, CA 94019
Ph: (650)712-0561
Fax: (650)712-0562

Martin, Prof. Patrick, President
International Committee for the
Conservation of the Industrial
Heritage [9490]
c/o Prof. Patrick Martin, President
Michigan Technological University
1400 Townsend Dr.
Houghton, MI 49931-1200
Ph: (906)487-2070

Martin, Randi, Bd. Member
Academy of Aphasia [13724]
5130 W Suffield Ter.
Skokie, IL 60077

Martin, Rod, Director, President
Orphan Resources International
[11116]
550 W Trout Run Rd.
Ephrata, PA 17522-9604
Ph: (717)733-7444

Martin, Ted, Chmn. of the Bd.
Diverse Emerging Music Organiza-
tion [9900]
PO Box 50252
Minneapolis, MN 55405

Martin, Prof. Terry, Treasurer
IEEE - Industrial Electronics Society
[6428]
c/o Milos Manic, Secretary
Virginia Commonwealth University
401 W Main St., Rm. E2254
Richmond, VA 23284
Ph: (804)827-3999

Martin, Titus R., Chairman
Life Counseling Ministries [20184]
250 Meadow Ln.
Conestoga, PA 17516
Ph: (717)871-0540
Fax: (717)871-0547

Martin, Todd, CEO
International Tennis Hall of Fame
[23301]
194 Bellevue Ave.
Newport, RI 02840
Ph: (401)849-3990
Toll Free: 800-457-1144

Martin, Todd L., Exec. Dir., CEO
Independent Professional Seed As-
sociation [3565]
Box 139
2504 Alexander Dr.
Jonesboro, AR 72401
Ph: (870)336-0777
Toll Free: 888-888-5058
Fax: (888)888-5058

Martin, Tracey, Admin. Ofc.
Society for the Exploration of
Psychotherapy Integration [16990]
c/o Tracey Martin, Administrative Officer
6557 E Riverdale St.
Mesa, AZ 85215

Martin, W. David, Director
National Association of Public Auto
Auctions [260]
PO Box 41368
Raleigh, NC 27629
Ph: (919)876-0687

Martinage, Bernard, Chairman,
Founder, President
Federation of Dining Room Profes-
sionals [2938]
1417 Sadler Rd., No. 100
Fernandina Beach, FL 32034
Ph: (904)491-6690
Fax: (904)491-6689

Martineau, Cynthia J., Exec. Dir.
Towing and Recovery Association of
America, Inc. [355]
700 12th St. NW, Ste. 700
Washington, DC 20005
Toll Free: 888-392-9300
Fax: (888)392-9300

Martinelli, Amy, VP
Delta Sigma Rho - Tau Kappa Alpha
[23980]
c/o Mike Edmonds, Treasurer
Colorado College
14 E Cache La Poudre
Colorado Springs, CO 80903

Martinez, Andre, President
Professional Decorative Painters As-
sociation [2488]
PO Box 13427
Denver, CO 80201

Martinez, Astrid, President
National Organization of Professional Hispanic Natural Resources
Conservation Service Employees
[3906]
7098 Atlanta Cir.
Seaford, DE 19973

Martinez, Carlos, President
State Guard Association of the
United States [5623]

PO Box 2441
Clarksville, TN 37042
Ph: (931)624-0588

Martinez, John, Chairman, Dep. Dir.
National Youth Employment Coalition
[13469]
115 15th St. NW, Ste. 350
Washington, DC 20036
Ph: (202)780-5928

Martinez, Juan, Director
National Association of Hispanic
Real Estate Professionals [2869]
591 Camino de la Reina, Ste. 720
San Diego, CA 92108
Ph: (858)622-9046

Martinez, Jr., Robert, President
International Association of Machinists and Aerospace Workers
[23388]
9000 Machinists Pl.
Upper Marlboro, MD 20772-2687
Ph: (301)967-4500

Martinez, Mr. Luis, Chairman
International Schools Association
[8104]
1033 Diego Dr. S
Boca Raton, FL 33428
Ph: (561)883-3854
Fax: (561)483-2004

Martinez, Lydia N., VP
Hispanic Elected Local Officials
[5637]
c/o National League of Cities
1301 Pennsylvania Ave. NW, Ste.
550
Washington, DC 20004-1747
Ph: (202)626-3169

Martinez, Pat, CEO, President
National Hispanic Corporate Council
[655]
1050 Connecticut Ave. NW, 5 Fl.
Washington, DC 20036
Ph: (202)772-1100
Fax: (202)772-3101

Martinez, Samanthi, Exec. Dir.
Association of Professional Model
Makers [6548]
PO Box 165
Hamilton, NY 13346-0165
Ph: (315)750-0803
Toll Free: 877-765-6950

Martinez-Marmolejos, Claribel,
President
Dominican American National
Roundtable [19422]
PO Box 472
Washington, DC 20044
Toll Free: 800-647-1083

Martini, Carolyn, President
Napa Valley Wine Library Associa-
tion [22476]
PO Box 328
Saint Helena, CA 94574
Ph: (707)963-5145

Martini, Michael E., Chmn. of the Bd.
Automotive Hall of Fame [283]
21400 Oakwood Blvd.
Dearborn, MI 48124
Ph: (313)240-4000

Martino, Melinda, Treasurer
American Bashkir Curly Registry
[4298]
71 Cavalier Blvd., No. 124
Florence, KY 41042
Ph: (859)485-9700
Toll Free: 877-324-0956
Fax: (859)485-9777

Martino, Mike, Exec. Dir.
U.S.A. Boxing [22717]
1 Olympic Plz.
Colorado Springs, CO 80909
Ph: (719)866-2300
Toll Free: 888-222-2313
Fax: (719)866-2132

Martino, Tom, President
Bowling Proprietors' Association of
America [3152]
621 Six Flags Dr.
Arlington, TX 76011
Toll Free: 800-343-1329

Martins, Patrick, Founder, President
Heritage Foods USA [6647]
790 Washington Ave., PMB 303
Brooklyn, NY 11238
Ph: (718)389-0985
Fax: (718)389-0547

Martinson, Mark, VP
United States Durum Growers As-
sociation [3773]
1605 E Capitol Ave.
Bismarck, ND 58501
Ph: (701)214-3203
Fax: (701)223-4645

Martinu, Ludvik, Officer
Society of Vacuum Coaters [749]
71 Pinon Hill Pl. NE
Albuquerque, NM 87122
Ph: (505)856-7188
Fax: (505)856-6716

Martinussen, Jytte, Exec. Dir.
Institute for International Cooperation
and Development [12164]
1117 Hancock Rd.
Williamstown, MA 01267
Ph: (413)441-5126
(413)458-9466
Fax: (413)458-3323

Marty, Pete, President
1st Fighter Wing Association [21205]
c/o Steve Grass, Secretary/
Treasurer
11512 Henegan Pl.
Spotsylvania, VA 22551

Martyniuk, Andrew O., President
Ukrainian Philatelic and Numismatic
Society [22373]
157 Lucinda Ln.
Wyomissing, PA 19610

Marvel, Kevin B., Exec. Ofc.
American Astronomical Society
[5997]
2000 Florida Ave. NW, Ste. 400
Washington, DC 20009-1231
Ph: (202)328-2010
Fax: (202)234-2560

Marvin, Shellie, Director
Ridgeback Rescue of the United
States [10690]
c/o Kitty Morgan
1790 Valley Dr.
Highland, MI 48356
Ph: (786)309-7787

Marx, Joann, President
Phi Sigma Iota [23798]
Allegheny College, Box 30
520 N Main St.
Meadville, PA 16335-3902
Ph: (814)332-4886
Fax: (814)337-4445

Marx, Karen, Exec. Dir.
Mali Assistance Project [10482]
c/o Karen Marx, Executive Director
Box 221
3601 Arapahoe Ave.

Boulder, CO 80303
Ph: (303)449-4464

Marxen, Dic, President, CEO
Outside Sales Support Network
[3390]
320 Hemphill St.
Fort Worth, TX 76104
Ph: (941)322-9700
Fax: (941)981-1902

Masciana, Joe, President
Student Veterinary Emergency and
Critical Care Society [17665]
6335 Camp Bullis Rd., Ste. 12
San Antonio, TX 78257-9721
Ph: (210)698-5575

Masek, Joyce A., Exec. Dir.
National Catholic College Admission
Association [19876]
PO Box 267
New Albany, OH 43054
Ph: (614)633-5444
Fax: (614)839-9232

Mash, Paul, President
National Association of State
Procurement Officials [5736]
201 E Main St., Ste. 1405
Lexington, KY 40507
Ph: (859)514-9159
Fax: (859)514-9166

Masher, Joe, Treasurer
Theatre Historical Society of America
[10277]
461 Cochran Rd.
Pittsburgh, PA 15228-1253
Ph: (412)528-1801
(630)782-1800

Maslar, Mallory, Treasurer
Armenian Church Youth Organiza-
tion of America [19705]
630 2nd Ave.
New York, NY 10016-4806
Ph: (212)686-0710

Maslowsky, Michael, President,
Founder
World Spark [11192]
PO Box 83479
Portland, OR 97206-2378
Ph: (503)245-7899
Fax: (503)245-4639

Mason, Alan, President
Guild of Temple Musicians [20491]
2420 E Hillcrest Dr.
Thousand Oaks, CA 91362

Mason, Dr. Bob, Founder, President
Missions International [20155]
PO Box 93235
Southlake, TX 76092-0112

Mason, Dr. Debra L., Exec. Dir.
Religion Newswriters Association
[2718]
30 Neff Annex
Columbia, MO 65211-2600
Ph: (573)882-9257

Mason, Greg, President
Tennis Industry Association [3148]
117 Executive Ctr.
1 Corpus Christie Pl.
Hilton Head Island, SC 29928
Ph: (843)686-3036
Toll Free: 866-686-3036
Fax: (843)686-3078

Mason, James, Director, Founder
American Solar Action Plan [7196]
52 Columbia St.
Farmingdale, NY 11735-2606
Ph: (516)694-0759

Mason, Marianne, Exec. Dir.
Cordell Hull Foundation for
International Education [8113]
1745 Broadway, 17th Fl.
New York, NY 10019
Ph: (646)289-8620
Fax: (646)349-3455

Mason, Shirley, Exec. Dir.,
Secretary, Founder
Beach Education Advocates for
Culture, Health, Environment and
Safety Foundation Institute [10055]
PO Box 530702
Miami Shores, FL 33153
Ph: (305)620-7090

Mason, Virginia L., Manager
Family Support America [11819]
307 West 200 South, Ste. 2004
Salt Lake City, UT 84101-1261
Ph: (312)338-0900
Toll Free: 877-338-3722
Fax: (312)338-1522

Mason-Monheim, Joyce, President
American Institute of Floral Design-
ers [1305]
720 Light St.
Baltimore, MD 21230
Ph: (410)752-3318

Masri, Hani, Founder, President
Tomorrow's Youth Organization
[13485]
1356 Beverly Rd., Ste. 200
McLean, VA 22101-3640
Ph: (703)893-1143
Fax: (703)893-1227

Massaquoi, Bill, Founder, Exec. Dir.
Rebuild Africa [11424]
38 Porter Rd.
Cambridge, MA 02140
Ph: (617)491-3539

Massare, John S., PhD, Exec. Dir.
Contact Lens Association of
Ophthalmologists [16382]
2025 Woodlane Dr.
Saint Paul, MN 55125
Toll Free: 855-264-8818
Fax: (703)434-3003

Massaro, Julie, Exec. Dir.
Performing Arts Medicine Associa-
tion [16932]
PO Box 117
Englewood, CO 80151
Ph: (303)808-5643
Toll Free: 866-408-7069

Massey, Edwin, Director
National Association for Community
College Entrepreneurship [7558]
Bldg. 101, 1 Federal St.
Springfield, MA 01105
Ph: (413)306-3131
Fax: (413)372-4992

Massey, Jennifer, VP
American Rescue Dog Association
[12741]
PO Box 613
Bristow, VA 20136-0613
Toll Free: 888-775-8871

Massey, Mr. W. Kenny, CEO,
President
Modern Woodmen of America
[19693]
1701 1st Ave.
Rock Island, IL 61201-8724
Toll Free: 800-447-9811
Fax: (309)793-5547

Massik, Michael, Gen. Sec.
USA Weightlifting [23368]
1 Olympic Plz.

Colorado Springs, CO 80909
Ph: (719)866-4508
Fax: (719)866-4741

Massimino, Elisa, CEO, President
Human Right First [18404]
75 Broad St., 31st Fl.
New York, NY 10001-5108
Ph: (212)845-5200
Fax: (212)845-5299

Massimino, Elisa, President, CEO
Human Rights First [18405]
75 Broad St., 31st Fl.
New York, NY 10004
Ph: (212)845-5200
Fax: (212)845-5299

Massinga, Ruth, Co-Ch.
Economic Success Clearinghouse
[12535]
The Finance Project
1150 18th St. NW, Ste. 325
Washington, DC 20036
Ph: (202)628-4200
Fax: (202)628-1293

Massotto, Nancy, Chairperson, Exec.
Dir., Founder
Holistic Moms Network [12415]
PO Box 408
Caldwell, NJ 07006
Toll Free: 877-465-6667

Mast, JoAnn, Secretary, Treasurer
American Romney Breeders Association [4662]
c/o Chris Posbergh, President
381 Burnt Mill Rd.
Somerville, NJ 08876
Ph: (908)310-8548

Mastalski, Frank, Mem.
Center for the Study of Economics
[19166]
1501 Cherry St.
Philadelphia, PA 19102
Ph: (267)519-5312

Master, Lynne, President
International Federation for Secular
and Humanistic Judaism [20211]
175 Olde Half Day Rd., Ste. 123
Lincolnshire, IL 60069
Ph: (847)383-6330

Masters, Amb. Carl, Chmn. of the
Bd.
Institute of Caribbean Studies
[12163]
1629 K St. NW, Ste. 300
Washington, DC 20001
Ph: (202)638-0460

Masters, Roy, President
Foundation of Human Understanding
[9792]
PO Box 1000
Grants Pass, OR 97528
Ph: (541)956-6700
Toll Free: 800-877-3227
Fax: (541)956-6705

Masterson, Michael, President
American Society of Picture Profes-
sionals [2574]
12126 Hwy. 14 N, No. A-4
Cedar Crest, NM 87008
Ph: (505)281-3177
    (213)760-1176

Masterson, Patricia, Editor, President
Runkle Family Association [20922]
1281 Route 179
Lambertville, NJ 08530-3502

Mata, Mrinalini, President
Self-Realization Fellowship [20655]
3880 San Rafael Ave.

Los Angeles, CA 90065-3219
Ph: (818)549-5151
    (323)225-2471
Fax: (818)549-5100

Matallana, Lynne, Founder
National Fibromyalgia Association
[14768]
1000 Bristol St. N, Ste. 17-247
Newport Beach, CA 92660

Matchett, Barry, Chairman
United States Modern Pentathlon
    Association [23314]
1 Olympic Plz.
Colorado Springs, CO 80909
Ph: (305)332-8148

Matejek, Bob, Secretary
Jaguar Clubs of North America
[21409]
500 Westover Dr., No. 8354
Sanford, NC 27330
Toll Free: 888-258-2524

Mathbor, Dr. Golam, President
American Institute of Bangladesh
    Studies [7530]
B488 Medical Science Ctr.
1300 University Ave.
Madison, WI 53706
Ph: (608)261-1471

Matheis, Christian, Treasurer
Society for Philosophy in the
    Contemporary World [10126]
PO Box 7147
Charlottesville, VA 22906-7147
Ph: (434)220-3300
Toll Free: 800-444-2419
Fax: (434)220-3301

Mathers, James, Founder, President
Digital Cinema Society [1190]
PO Box 1973
Studio City, CA 91614-0973
Ph: (818)762-2214

Matheson, Malcolm, III, Lt.
Clan Matheson Society [20896]
2880 W 15th St.
Los Angeles, CA 90006-4239
Ph: (323)732-4737

Mathews, David, Chairman
National Issues Forums Institute
[18993]
100 Commons Rd.
Dayton, OH 45459-2777
Toll Free: 800-433-7834

Mathews, Mark, President
Lighthouse Station, Inc. [12549]
2215 Canton St., Unit 121
Dallas, TX 75201
Ph: (214)676-9999

Mathews, Terry, Mem.
Society of Air Force Physician As-
    sistants [20686]
2833 Gramercy Pl.
Beavercreek, OH 45431

Mathewson, Dave, Exec. Dir.
Academy of Model Aeronautics
[21210]
5161 E Memorial Dr.
Muncie, IN 47302
Toll Free: 800-435-9262
Fax: (765)289-4248

Mathis, Janice L., Exec. Dir.
National Council of Negro Women,
    Inc. [18224]
633 Pennsylvania Ave. NW
Washington, DC 20004-2605
Ph: (202)737-0120
Fax: (202)737-0476

Mathis, Marilyn, President
Academic Language Therapy As-
    sociation [12232]
14070 Proton Rd., Ste. 100, LB 9
Dallas, TX 75244-3601
Ph: (972)233-9107
Fax: (972)490-4219

Mathur, Balbir S., Founder
Trees for Life [12118]
3006 W St. Louis St.
Wichita, KS 67203
Ph: (316)945-6929
Fax: (316)945-0909

Matijasevic, Margaret, Exec. Dir.
National Conference for Catechetical
    Leadership [20087]
415 Michigan Ave., Ste. 110
Washington, DC 20017
Ph: (202)756-5512
Fax: (202)756-5519

Matlack, Larry, President
American Agriculture Movement
[17785]
c/o Larry Matlack, President
13118 E Stroud Rd.
Burrton, KS 67020
Ph: (620)463-3513

Matos, Paulo, Chmn. of the Bd.
Luso-American Fraternal Federation
[19489]
c/o Luso-American Life Insurance
    Society
7080 Donlon Way, Ste. 200
Dublin, CA 94568
Ph: (925)828-4884
Toll Free: 877-525-5876
Fax: (925)828-4554

Matras, Gwyneth, Exec. Dir.
Building Material Dealers Association
[507]
1006 SE Grand Ave., Ste. 301
Portland, OR 97214-2323
Ph: (503)208-3763
Toll Free: 888-960-6329
Fax: (971)255-0790

Matsuda, Kent, President
Buddhist Churches of America
[19771]
1710 Octavia St.
San Francisco, CA 94109
Ph: (415)776-5600
Fax: (415)771-6293

Matsumoto, Carol, Chairman
National Council of Supervisors of
    Mathematics [8283]
2851 S Parker Rd., No. 1210
Aurora, CO 80014
Ph: (303)758-9611
Fax: (303)200-7099

Matsunaga, Robin, President
United States Ombudsman Associa-
    tion [4969]
200 W 2nd Ave.
Indianola, IA 50125
Toll Free: 866-442-6751

Matsuoka, Tina R., Exec. Dir.
National Asian Pacific American Bar
    Association [5434]
1612 K St. NW, Ste. 1400
Washington, DC 20006
Ph: (202)775-9555
Fax: (202)775-9333

Matt, C. Diane, CAE, Exec. Dir.
Women in Engineering ProActive
    Network [3504]
1901 E Asbury St., Ste. 220
Denver, CO 80210
Ph: (303)871-4642

Matt, D. Fred, Exec. Dir.
Native American Fish and Wildlife
    Society [4089]
1055 17th Ave., Ste. 91
Longmont, CO 80501
Ph: (303)466-1725
Toll Free: 866-890-7258
Fax: (303)466-5414

Mattar, Dr. Mohammed Y., Exec. Dir.
Protection Project [12057]
1717 Massachusetts Ave. NW
Washington, DC 20036
Ph: (202)256-7520

Mattei, Norma Jean, President
American Society of Civil Engineers
[6219]
1801 Alexander Bell Dr.
Reston, VA 20191
Ph: (703)295-6300
Toll Free: 800-548-2723

Matter, John, Exec. Dir.
National Ballroom and Entertainment
    Association [1153]
c/o John Matter, Executive Director
PO Box 274
Decorah, IA 52101-7600
Ph: (563)382-3871

Mattes, Jane, Director, Founder
Single Mothers By Choice [12428]
PO Box 1642
New York, NY 10008-1642
Ph: (212)988-0993

Mattes, Tracy, Exec. Dir.
USA Water Ski Foundation [23358]
1251 Holy Cow Rd.
Polk City, FL 33868-8200
Ph: (863)324-2472
Fax: (863)324-3996

Matthes, Wanda Rawson, President
Majolica International Society
[21583]
c/o Amy C. Griffin
8912 Crestview Dr.
Denton, TX 76207

Matthew, Thampy, Contact
Children's Network International
[10931]
5449 Robin Hill Ct.
Norcross, GA 30093
Ph: (404)259-8818
Fax: (770)925-0580

Matthews, Becky, Chairperson
American Daffodil Society [22070]
3670 E Powell Rd.
Lewis Center, OH 43035-9530
Ph: (614)882-5720

Matthews, Bill, Exec. Dir.
National Association of Professional
    Band Instrument Repair Techni-
    cians, Inc. [2432]
2026 Eagle Rd.
Normal, IL 61761
Ph: (309)452-4257
Fax: (309)452-4825

Matthews, Ms. DJ, Chairperson
Association of Vision Science Librar-
    ians [9692]
Marshall B. Ketchum University
2575 Yorba Linda Blvd.
Fullerton, CA 92831-1699
Ph: (734)763-9468
Fax: (734)936-9050

Matthews, Gary, Treasurer
pureHOPE [18928]
110 Boggs Ln., Ste. 302
Cincinnati, OH 45246
Ph: (513)521-6227

Matthews, Dr. James, President
Society for the History of Discoveries
[9518]
c/o William Brandenburg, Treasurer
631 Masonic Way, Apt. 1
Belmont, CA 94002
Ph: (650)591-1601

Matthews, Jeffrey B., President
Society for Surgery of the Alimentary
Tract [17406]
500 Cummings Ctr., Ste. 4550
Beverly, MA 01915
Ph: (978)927-8330
Fax: (978)524-8890

Matthews, Pam, Exec. Dir.
International Entertainment Buyers
Association [1140]
412 E Iris Dr.
Nashville, TN 37204
Ph: (615)679-9601

Matthews, Russ, Managing Dir.
International Furniture Transportation
and Logistics Council [3089]
282 N Ridge Rd.
Brooklyn, MI 49230
Ph: (517)467-9355

Matthews, Tanya, FAIC, DBIA, Direc-
tor
American Institute of Constructors
[6345]
700 N Fairfax St., Ste. 510
Alexandria, VA 22314
Ph: (703)683-4999
Fax: (571)527-3105

Matthews, Walter, Exec. Dir.
National Service Committee/
Chariscenter USA [19890]
PO Box 628
Locust Grove, VA 22508-0628
Ph: (540)972-0225
Toll Free: 800-338-2445

Mattice, Sarah, Secretary, Treasurer
International Society for Comparative
Studies of Chinese and Western
Philosophy [8421]
c/o Sarah Mattice, Secretary &
Treasurer
Philosophy & Religious Studies
College of Arts & Sciences
University of North Florida
1 UNF Dr.
Jacksonville, FL 32224

Mattingly, Bob, Exec. Dir.
Center for Spiritual and Ethical
Education [8009]
910 M St. NW, No.722
Washington, DC 20001
Ph: (202)838-1099
Toll Free: 800-298-4599
Fax: (678)623-5634

Mattingly, Chris, Editor
Telephone Collectors International
[22444]
3805 Spurr Cir.
Brea, CA 92823
Ph: (714)528-3561

Mattingly, Terry, Director
Washington Journalism Center
[8162]
331 8th St. NE
Washington, DC 20002

Mattiola, Paul, Treasurer
Association for Computers and Taxa-
tion [3201]
PO Box 1093
Warwick, NY 10990
Ph: (845)987-9690

Mattison, Avon, President, Founder
Pathways to Peace [12439]
PO Box 1507

Larkspur, CA 94977
Ph: (415)461-0500
Fax: (415)925-0330

Mattison, Jay, Administrator, CEO
National Dairy Herd Improvement
Association [3738]
5940 Seminole Centre Ct., Ste. 200
Fitchburg, WI 53711
Ph: (608)848-6455
Fax: (608)260-7772

Mattison, Lindsay, Bd. Member
International Action [13329]
PO Box 15188
Washington, DC 20003
Ph: (202)488-0735
Fax: (202)488-0736

Mattocks, Jeff, Treasurer
American Pastured Poultry Produc-
ers Association [4562]
PO Box 85
Hughesville, PA 17737-0085
Ph: (570)584-2309
Toll Free: 888-662-7772

Mattox, Kuae Kelch, President
Mocha Moms, Inc. [13384]
PO Box 1995
Upper Marlboro, MD 20773
Toll Free: 877-456-7667

Mattson, Holly, Exec. Dir.
Council for Interior Design Accredita-
tion [8049]
206 Grandville Ave. SW, Ste. 350
Grand Rapids, MI 49503-4079
Ph: (616)458-0400
Fax: (616)458-0460

Matusiak, Ari A., Founder, Chairman
Young Invincibles [19282]
1411 K St. NW, 4th Fl.
Washington, DC 20005
Ph: (202)734-6519

Matz, Art C., President, Secretary,
Treasurer
Latin American Paper Money Society
[22271]
c/o Arthur C. Matz, President,
Secretary & Treasurer
1500 Bedford Ave., Apt. 209
Baltimore, MD 21206

Mauer, Marc, Exec. Dir.
Sentencing Project [11548]
1705 DeSales St. NW, 8th Fl.
Washington, DC 20036
Ph: (202)628-0871
Fax: (202)628-1091

Maulawizada, Matin, Founder
Afghan Hands [10464]
220 Treescape Dr.
East Hampton, NY 11937
Ph: (312)786-3309

Mauren, Kris Alan, Exec. Dir.
Action Institute for the Study of
Religion and Liberty [20531]
98 E Fulton St.
Grand Rapids, MI 49503
Ph: (616)454-3080
Toll Free: 800-345-2286
Fax: (616)454-9454

Maurer, Heather L., Founder
Mother Health International [15608]
8004 Trevor Pl.
Vienna, VA 22182

Maurer, Kristen, President, Founder
Mission K9 Rescue [10660]
14027 Memorial Dr., No. 185
Houston, TX 77079
Ph: (713)589-9362

Maurer, Dr. Marc, President
National Federation of the Blind
[17733]
200 E Wells St.
Baltimore, MD 21230-4850
Ph: (410)659-9314
Fax: (410)685-5653

Maust, John D., President
Media Associates International
[20121]
351 S Main Pl., Ste. 230
Carol Stream, IL 60188-2455
Ph: (630)260-9063
Fax: (630)260-9265

Mavreshko, Lana, CFO
Brand Activation Association [2269]
708 3rd Ave., 33rd Fl.
New York, NY 10017
Ph: (212)697-5950

Mawyer, Martin J., Founder
Christian Action Network [19951]
PO Box 606
Forest, VA 24551
Toll Free: 888-499-4226

Maxwell, Dr. Carleton B., President
National Pharmaceutical Association
[16679]
107 Kilmayne Dr., Ste. C
Cary, NC 27511
Toll Free: 877-215-2091
Fax: (919)469-5858

Maxwell, Ian, CEO, Founder
Heart for Africa [11015]
PO Box 1308
Roswell, GA 30077
Ph: (678)566-1589
Toll Free: 800-901-7585

Maxwell, James A., President
Clan Maxwell Society of the USA
[20829]
54 Pawcatuck Ave.
Pawcatuck, CT 06379-2417

Maxwell, Kim, President
U.S. Women in Nuclear [6936]
c/o Nuclear Energy Institute
1201 F St. NW, Ste. 1100
Washington, DC 20004-1218
Ph: (202)739-8000
Fax: (202)785-4019

Maxwell, Susan A., Exec. Dir.
National Association of Advisors for
the Health Professions, Inc. [8328]
108 Hessel Blvd., Ste. 101
Champaign, IL 61820-6574
Ph: (217)355-0063
Fax: (217)355-1287

Maxwell, Tom, President
United States Faceters Guild [6361]
c/o Sue Lichtenberger, Secretary-
Treasurer
6625 Skyline Dr.
Ashland, KY 41102

May, Dean, Chairman
American Specialty Toy Retailing
Association [2063]
432 N Clark St., Ste. 305
Chicago, IL 60654
Ph: (312)222-0984
Fax: (312)222-0986

May, John, Chairman, Founder
Imerman Angels [13987]
205 W Randolph, 19th Fl.
Chicago, IL 60606
Ph: (312)274-5529
Toll Free: 877-274-5529
Fax: (312)274-5530

May, John P., MD, President,
Founder
Health through Walls [15469]
12555 Biscayne Blvd., No. 955

North Miami, FL 33181

May, Kimberly, Gov.
Society of Air Force Physicians
[15839]
c/o JoAnn Honn, Administrative As-
sistant
PO Box 64
Devine, TX 78016
Ph: (830)665-4048

May, Marilyn, Mem.
National Conference of Appellate
Court Clerks [5120]
Association Services National Center
for State Courts
300 Newport Ave.
Williamsburg, VA 23185
Ph: (757)259-1841

May, Todd J., President
Securities Transfer Association
[3051]
PO Box 5220
Hazlet, NJ 07730
Ph: (732)888-6040
Fax: (732)888-2121

May, Wes, Exec. Dir.
Engineering Contractors Association
[864]
2190 S Towne Centre Pl., Ste. 310
Anaheim, CA 92806
Ph: (714)937-5000
Fax: (714)937-5030

Mayer, John, Exec. Dir.
Center for Computer-Assisted Legal
Instruction [6297]
565 W Adams St., Rm. 542
Chicago, IL 60661-3652
Ph: (312)906-5307

Mayer, Keith, CEO
American Home Life International
[8055]
2137 Embassy Dr., Ste. 202
Lancaster, PA 17603
Ph: (717)560-2840
Fax: (717)560-2845

Mayer, Lyle, President
Santana 20 Class Association
[22666]
c/o Zoe Gilstrap, 1266 Napa Creek
Dr.
1266 Napa Creek Dr.
Eugene, OR 97404

Mayer, Rochelle, EdD, Director
National Sudden and Unexpected
Infant/Child Death and Pregnancy
Loss Resource Center [17334]
Georgetown University, Box 571272
2115 Wisconsin Ave. NW, Ste. 601
Washington, DC 20007-2292
Ph: (202)687-7400
(202)784-9552
Toll Free: 866-866-7437
Fax: (202)784-9777

Mayer Sachs, Alison, President
Association of Oncology Social Work
[13103]
1 Parkview Plz., Ste. 800
Oakbrook Terrace, IL 60181
Ph: (847)686-2233
Fax: (847)686-2253

Mayer Todd, Donna, President
Ape Conservation Effort [4787]
800 Cherokee Ave. SE
Atlanta, GA 30315-1470

Mayes, Kevin, President
Instream Flow Council [3885]
c/o Kevin Mayes, President
Texas Parks and Wildlife Department

PO Box 1685
San Marcos, TX 78667

Mayes, Linda, MD, Bd. Member
Psychodynamic Psychoanalytic
  Research Society [16850]
Yale Child Study Center
230 S Frontage Rd.
New Haven, CT 06519
Ph: (203)785-7205
Fax: (203)785-7926

Mayeux, Mike, President
Recruitment Process Outsourcing
  Association [1698]
14621 Charter Walk Pl.
Midlothian, VA 23114
Ph: (804)897-1310

Mayfield, Dan, Secretary
Military Law Task Force of the
  National Lawyers Guild [5603]
730 N 1st St.
San Jose, CA 95122
Ph: (619)463-2369

Mayi, Dr. Bindu, Chmn. of the Bd.
Share a Pet [12457]
2881 E Oakland Park Blvd., Ste. 204
Fort Lauderdale, FL 33309-6302
Ph: (954)630-8763

Maynard, R.D., President
International Association of Industrial
  Accident Boards and Commissions
  [5164]
5610 Medical Cir., Ste. 24
Madison, WI 53719
Ph: (608)663-6355

Mayne, Bill, Exec. Dir.
Country Radio Broadcasters Inc.
  [459]
1009 16th Ave. S
Nashville, TN 37212
Ph: (615)327-4487
Fax: (615)329-4492

Mayne, Brad, Chairman
International Association of Venue
  Managers [2321]
635 Fritz Dr., Ste. 100
Coppell, TX 75019-4442
Ph: (972)906-7441
Toll Free: 800-935-4226
Fax: (972)906-7418

Mayo, E. Andrew, CEO
Medical Benevolence Foundation
  [15153]
10707 Corporate Dr., Ste. 220
Stafford, TX 77477-4001
Ph: (281)201-2043
Toll Free: 800-547-7627
Fax: (281)903-7627

Mayo, Kathy, Exec. Dir.
PODS Association [7234]
PO Box 1726
Sand Springs, OK 74063
Ph: (918)246-9343

Mayo, Paula M., President, Exec.
  Dir.
Interchurch Center [20063]
475 Riverside Dr.
New York, NY 10115
Ph: (212)870-2200
  (212)870-3804

Mayo, Pi-Yi, President
Special Needs Alliance [5552]
6341 E Brian Kent Dr.
Tucson, AZ 85710
Ph: (520)546-1005
Toll Free: 877-572-8472

Mayo-Smith, William W., MD,
  President
Society of Abdominal Radiology
  [17557]

4550 Post Oak Pl., Ste. 342
Houston, TX 77027
Ph: (713)965-0566
Fax: (713)960-0488

Mays, Elizabeth, Founder
American Partnership for Eosino-
  philic Disorders [14780]
PO Box 29545
Atlanta, GA 30359-0545
Ph: (713)493-7749

Mays, Fate, President
The International Cat Association
  [21570]
306 E Jackson
Harlingen, TX 78550-6892
Ph: (956)428-8046
Fax: (956)428-8047

Mays, William E., PhD, Exec. Dir.,
  President
Medical Relief International [12697]
12316 134th Ct. NE
Redmond, WA 98052
Ph: (425)284-2630

Mayton, Don M., Project Mgr.
GM Futurliner [21387]
4521 Majestic Vue
Zeeland, MI 49464
Ph: (616)875-3058

Mazour, James, Editor
Sunbeam Rapier Registry [21499]
c/o James Mazour, Editor
3212 Orchard Cir.
West Des Moines, IA 50266-2140
Ph: (515)226-9475

Mazria, Edward, CEO, Founder
Architecture 2030 [4133]
607 Cerrillos Rd.
Santa Fe, NM 87505
Ph: (505)988-5309

Mazur, Joseph, President, CEO
All-American Soap Box Derby
  [23181]
789 Derby Downs Dr.
Akron, OH 44306
Ph: (330)733-8723
Fax: (330)733-1370

Mazyck, Donna, MS, RN, NCSN,
  Exec. Dir.
National Association of School
  Nurses [16154]
1100 Wayne Ave., Ste. 925
Silver Spring, MD 20910
Ph: (240)821-1130
Toll Free: 866-627-6767
Fax: (301)585-1791

Mazzali, Claudio, Chairman
Optoelectronics Industry Develop-
  ment Association [2458]
2010 Massachusetts Ave. NW
Washington, DC 20036
Ph: (202)416-1982
Fax: (202)416-1408

Mazzola, Brady, CEO, Founder
Watering Seeds Organization
  [22804]
6303 Owensmouth Ave., 10th Fl.
Woodland Hills, CA 91367-2262
Ph: (818)936-3476

Mazzola, Guerino, President
Society for Mathematics and
  Computation in Music [6827]
c/o Robert Peck, Founder
281 M&DA Bldg.
School of Music
Louisiana State University
Baton Rouge, LA 70803-2504
Ph: (225)578-6830
Fax: (225)578-2562

Mazzola, Ms. Karen, Exec. Dir.
United Association Manufacturers'
  Representatives [2209]
PO Box 4216
Dana Point, CA 92629-9216
Ph: (949)481-5214
Fax: (417)779-1576

Mazzone, Dino, Officer
National Italian American Bar As-
  sociation [5442]
2020 Pennsylvania Ave. NW, PMB
  932
Washington, DC 20006-1846
Ph: (414)750-4404
Fax: (414)255-3615

Mazzone, Michael, MD, President
Association of Family Medicine
  Residency Directors [15578]
11400 Tomahawk Creek Pky., Ste.
  670
Leawood, KS 66211
Ph: (913)906-6000
Toll Free: 800-274-2237
Fax: (913)906-6105

Mbacke, Dr. Cheikh, Chmn. of the
  Bd.
Tostan-U.S. [12059]
2121 Decatur Pl. NW
Washington, DC 20008
Ph: (202)818-8851

Mbito, Dr. Michael Njoroge, Founder,
  President, Chairman, Exec. Dir.
Child Aid Africa [10892]
551 Roslaire Dr.
Hummelstown, PA 17036-9165
Ph: (877)288-9666
  (205)967-0441

McAdams, Michael J., President
Advanced Biofuels Association
  [1465]
800 17th St. NW, Ste. 1100
Washington, DC 20006-3962
Ph: (202)469-5140

McAdams, R. Michael, Director
McAdams Historical Society [20898]
711 17th Ave. N
Surfside Beach, SC 29575-4354
Ph: (818)789-1086

McAfee, Amber, President
International Society for Organ
  Preservation [16449]
PO Box 590013
Homewood, AL 35259

McAleer, Mary Sugrue, Exec. Dir.
Irish American Partnership [9600]
15 Broad St., Ste. 501
Boston, MA 02109
Ph: (617)723-2707
Toll Free: 800-722-3893
Fax: (617)723-5478

McAlister, Roy E., President
American Hydrogen Association
  [6454]
PO Box 4205
Mesa, AZ 85211
Ph: (480)234-5070

McAllister, Elan, Exec. Dir.
Choices in Childbirth [14225]
441 Lexington Ave., 19th Fl.
New York, NY 10017
Ph: (212)983-4122
Fax: (212)983-0281

McAllister, James, President
Society for Research into
  Hydrocephalus and Spina Bifida
  [17261]
c/o Dr. David Nash, Membership
  Secretary

Pediatric Rehab Clinic Mayo
200 1st St. SW
Rochester, MN 55905

McAllister, Ken, President
National Public Parks Tennis Association [23303]
c/o Ron Melvin, President
13925 FM 1346
Saint Hedwig, TX 78152

McAllister, Kevin G., Chairman
ORBIS International [16403]
520 8th Ave., 11th Fl.
New York, NY 10018
Toll Free: 800-ORBIS-US
Fax: (646)674-5599

McAllister, Michael F., Gen. Counsel
Art Services International [8841]
119 Duke St.
Alexandria, VA 22314
Ph: (703)548-4554
Fax: (703)548-3305

McAlpin, Kathleen, RSM, DMin,
  Chairman
Spiritual Directors International
  [20554]
PO Box 3584
Bellevue, WA 98009
Ph: (425)455-1565
Fax: (425)455-1566

McAlpin, Michael T., President
Clan MacAlpine Society [20818]
32682 Rosemont Dr.
Trabuco Canyon, CA 92679-3386

McAlvanah, Tom, Exec. Dir.
Association for the Advancement of
  Blind and Retarded [17688]
1508 College Point Blvd.
College Point, NY 11356
Ph: (718)321-3800

McAnany, Patricia, President
American Anthropological Associa-
  tion - Archeology Division [5928]
c/o Jane Eva Baxter, Secretary
DePaul University
2343 N Racine Ave.
Chicago, IL 60614
Ph: (773)325-4757
Fax: (773)325-4761

McAndrews, Paul J., MD, Advisor
International Alliance of Hair
  Restoration Surgeons [14901]
c/o Paul J. McAndrews, Senior
  Medical Advisor
50 Alessandro Pl., Ste. 115
Pasadena, CA 91105
Fax: (626)449-4558

McAninch, Jay, CEO, President
Archery Trade Association [3134]
PO Box 70
New Ulm, MN 56073-0070
Ph: (507)233-8130
Toll Free: 866-266-2776
Fax: (507)233-8140

McArdle, Camille, President
American Bloodhound Club [21797]
c/o Cindy Andrews, Membership
  Chairperson
129 Little Bear Trail
Elkton, VA 22827-3922
Ph: (540)298-9899
  (386)788-0137
Fax: (386)788-0137

McArthur, John, CEO, Exec. Dir.
Millennium Promise Alliance Inc.
  [10727]
475 Riverside Dr., Ste. 1040
New York, NY 10115
Ph: (212)870-2490

McAtee, J. Craig, Exec. Dir.
National Coalition of Advanced
Technology Centers [8671]
33607 Seneca Dr.
Cleveland, OH 44139-5578
Ph: (440)318-1558

McAuley, Sara R., Chmn. of the Bd.
WorldatWork [1103]
14040 N Northsight Blvd.
Scottsdale, AZ 85260
Ph: (480)922-2020
     (480)951-9191
Toll Free: 866-816-2962
Fax: (480)483-8352

McAuliff, John, Exec. Dir.
US-Cuba Reconciliation Initiative
[18322]
355 W 39th St.
New York, NY 10118
Ph: (212)760-9903
Fax: (212)760-9906

McAward, Jennifer Mason, Dir.
(Actg.)
Center for Civil and Human Rights
[12026]
2150 Eck Hall of Law
Notre Dame Law School
Notre Dame, IN 46556
Ph: (574)631-8555
Fax: (574)631-8702

McBay, Shirley, President
Quality Education for Minorities
Network [7798]
1818 N St. NW, Ste. 350
Washington, DC 20036
Ph: (202)659-1818
Fax: (202)659-5408

McBrady, Carol, Director, Founder
Action for Children - Zambia [10831]
20855 Kensington Blvd.
Lakeville, MN 55044

McBride, Elissa, President
United Association for Labor Educa-
tion [8166]
PO Box 598
Lanham, MD 20703
Ph: (202)585-4393

McBride, Jere W., PhD, President
American Society for Rickettsiology
[13792]
c/o Jere McBride, PhD, President
University of Texas Medical Branch
301 University Blvd., Keiller 1.136
Galveston, TX 77555-0609

McBride, Ms. Lori, Chairperson
Nursing Mothers Counsel [11257]
PO Box 5024
San Mateo, CA 94402-0024
Ph: (650)327-6455

McBride, Robert W., President, CEO
The Sulphur Institute [730]
1020 19th St. NW, Ste. 520
Washington, DC 20036
Ph: (202)331-9660
Fax: (202)293-2940

McBrien, Bob, President
Tai Chi for Health Community
[17423]
PO Box 481
Glastonbury, CT 06033

McBurney, Brent, CEO, President
Advocates International [5404]
2920 King St.
Alexandria, VA 22302-3512
Ph: (571)319-0100

McBurney, Robert, CEO, President
Accelerated Cure Project for Multiple
Sclerosis [15890]

460 Totten Pond Rd., Ste. 140
Waltham, MA 02451
Ph: (781)487-0008

McCabe, Cyndi, President
Automobile License Plate Collectors
Association [21335]
118 Quaker Rd.
Hampton, VA 23669-2024

McCabe, Don, President, Dir. of
Res.
AVKO Educational Research
Foundation [8577]
3084 Willard Rd.
Birch Run, MI 48415-9404
Ph: (810)686-9283
Fax: (810)686-1101

McCabe, Georgia, CEO
PMA-The Worldwide Community of
Imaging Associations [2590]
7918 Jones Branch Dr., Ste. 300
McLean, VA 22102
Ph: (703)665-4416
Toll Free: 800-762-9287
Fax: (703)506-3266

McCabe, Lisa, Officer
Bulletin of the Atomic Scientists
[7125]
1155 E 60th St.
Chicago, IL 60637
Ph: (707)481-9372

McCabe, Mary Ann, PhD, President
APA Division 37: Society for Child
and Family Policy and Practice
[16883]
750 1st St. NE
Washington, DC 20002-4242
Ph: (202)336-5500

McCabe, Philip T., President
NALGAP: The Association of
Lesbian, Gay, Bisexual, and Trans-
gender Addiction Professionals and
Their Allies [13155]
c/o Phil McCabe
Rutgers School of Public Health/
OPHP
683 Hoes Ln.
Piscataway, NJ 08854
Ph: (937)972-9537

McCabe, Steven, MD, Contact
American Association for Hand
Surgery [14905]
500 Cummings Ctr., Ste. 4550
Beverly, MA 01915
Ph: (978)927-8330
Fax: (978)524-8890

McCaffree, Konnie, President
American Association of Sexuality
Educators, Counselors and
Therapists [17190]
1444 I St. NW, Ste. 700
Washington, DC 20005-6542
Ph: (202)449-1099
Fax: (202)216-9646

McCaffrey, Eileen, Exec. Dir.
Foster Care to Success [11230]
21351 Gentry Dr., Ste. 130
Sterling, VA 20166
Ph: (571)203-0270
Fax: (571)203-0273

McCaffrey, Stephen, Chairperson
Plan Sponsor Council of America
[1101]
200 S Wacker Dr., Ste. 3164
Chicago, IL 60606
Ph: (312)419-1863
Fax: (312)419-1864

McCaig, Joshua, President
National Lawyers Association [5041]
3801 E Florida Ave., Ste. 400

Denver, CO 80210
Toll Free: 800-471-2994

McCain, John, Chairman
International Republican Institute
USA [18102]
1225 Eye St. NW, Ste. 700
Washington, DC 20005-5962
Ph: (202)408-9450
Fax: (202)408-9462

McCain, Shellie G., President
Cooperative Association of Tractor
Dealers, Inc. [904]
6075 Poplar Ave., Ste. 125
Memphis, TN 38119
Ph: (901)333-8600
Fax: (901)333-8640

McCaleb, Robert S., President
Herb Research Foundation [6141]
5589 Arapahoe Ave., Ste. 205
Boulder, CO 80303
Ph: (303)449-2265
Fax: (303)449-7849

McCall, Debra Pearce, Editor
Global Association for Interpersonal
Neurobiology Studies [6915]
PO Box 3605
Santa Monica, CA 90408

McCalla, Jocelyn, Exec. Dir.
National Coalition for Haitian Rights
[19018]
275 7th Ave.
New York, NY 10001

McCalley, Barbara S., Exec. Dir.
Ophthalmic Photographers' Society
[16401]
1887 W Ranch Rd.
Nixa, MO 65714-8262
Ph: (417)725-0181
Toll Free: 800-403-1677
Fax: (417)724-8450

McCallum, Mark, CEO
National Association of Surety Bond
Producers [1904]
1140 19th St., Ste. 800
Washington, DC 20036-5104
Ph: (202)686-3700
Fax: (202)686-3656

McCamant, Robert, Editor, Treasurer
Fine Press Book Association [2680]
c/o Russell Maret, Vice-Chair
140 E 71st St., Apt. 5B
New York, NY 10021

McCann, Barbara, Exec. Asst.
Army Aviation Association of
America [5592]
593 Main St.
Monroe, CT 06468-2830
Ph: (203)268-2450
Fax: (203)268-5870

McCann, Bryan, President
Brazilian Studies Association [8060]
Watson Institute for International and
Public Affairs
Brown University
111 Thayer St.
Providence, RI 02912-1970
Fax: (401)863-2928

McCarberg, Bill H., M.D., Director
American Academy of Pain Medicine
[16547]
8735 W Higgins Rd., Ste. 3000
Chicago, IL 60631-2738
Ph: (847)375-4731
Fax: (847)375-6477

McCarren, Patrick, Exec. Dir.
IEEE - Industry Applications Society
[6722]

445 Hoes Ln.
Piscataway, NJ 08854
Ph: (732)465-5804

McCarroll, Jesse C., President
National Association for the Study
and Performance of African-
American Music [8383]
c/o Martha C. Brown, Treasurer
809 E Gladwick St.
Carson, CA 90746-3818

McCarron, Douglas J., President
United Brotherhood of Carpenters
and Joiners of America [23402]
101 Constitution Ave. NW
Washington, DC 20001
Ph: (202)546-6206
Fax: (202)547-8979

McCartan, Dr. Anne-Marie, Exec. Dir.
Council of Colleges of Arts and Sci-
ences [7511]
c/o College of William & Mary
PO Box 8795
Williamsburg, VA 23187-8795
Ph: (757)221-1784
Fax: (757)221-1776

McCarthy, James A., President, CEO
North American Millers' Association
[2378]
600 Maryland Ave. SW, Ste. 825 W
Washington, DC 20024
Ph: (202)484-2200
Fax: (202)488-7416

McCarthy, James J., Chairman
Union of Concerned Scientists
[18737]
2 Brattle Sq.
Cambridge, MA 02138-3780
Ph: (617)547-5552
Fax: (617)864-9405

McCarthy, James, President
Pediatric Orthopedic Society of
North America [16491]
9400 W Higgins Rd., Ste. 500
Rosemont, IL 60018-4976
Ph: (847)698-1692
Fax: (847)268-9684

McCarthy, James, Director
Silver Wings Fraternity [21247]
PO Box 1694
Oldsmar, FL 34677

McCarthy, Jim, Chairman
National Fair Housing Alliance
[18359]
1101 Vermont Ave. NW, Ste. 710
Washington, DC 20005
Ph: (202)898-1661
Fax: (202)371-9744

McCarthy, JoBeth, VP
Association of State and Territorial
Local Health Liaison Officials
[5715]
PO Box 260451
Denver, CO 80226

McCarthy, John, President
OPSEC Professionals Society
[19095]
PO Box 150515
Alexandria, VA 22315-0515

McCarthy, Kevin, President
Forest Industries Telecommunica-
tions [1408]
1565 Oak St.
Eugene, OR 97401
Ph: (541)485-8441
Fax: (541)485-7556

McCarthy, Maureen, President, CEO
Association for Long Term Care
Financial Managers [15581]

c/o Jaclyn Farnham, Administrator
95 West St.
Rocky Hill, CT 06067-3546
Ph: (860)721-7400
Fax: (860)721-7406

McCarthy, Oscar, Secretary
Professional Risk Managers'
International Association [1919]
400 Washington St.
Northfield, MN 55057
Ph: (612)605-5370
Fax: (212)898-9076

McCarthy, Pat, Exec. VP
Transportation Research Forum
[7352]
PO Box 6050
Fargo, ND 58108-6050
Ph: (701)231-7766

McCarthy, Sean, President
Westminster Kennel Club [21991]
149 Madison Ave., Ste. 402
New York, NY 10016-6722
Ph: (212)213-3165
Fax: (212)213-3270

McCarthy, Tom C., President
Motion Picture Sound Editors [1200]
10061 Riverside Dr.
Toluca Lake, CA 91602-2550
Ph: (818)506-7731
Fax: (818)506-7732

McCarty, John E., Exec. Dir.
Accreditation Review Commission
on Education for the Physician As-
sistant [16720]
12000 Findley Rd., Ste. 150
Duluth, GA 30097
Ph: (770)476-1224
Fax: (770)476-1738

McCarty, Kathy, CEO
International Council on Hotel,
Restaurant, and Institutional
Education [1664]
2810 N Parham Rd., Ste. 230
Richmond, VA 23294
Ph: (804)346-4800
Fax: (804)346-5009

McCarty, Dr. Robert J., Exec. Dir.
National Federation for Catholic
Youth Ministry [19886]
415 Michigan Ave. NE, Ste. 40
Washington, DC 20017-4503
Ph: (202)636-3825
Fax: (202)526-7544

McCarty, William M., MD, Secretary,
Treasurer
Clan MacCarthy Society [20819]
c/o Robert P. McCarthy, 5 Fox Hollow Rd.
5 Fox Hollow Rd.
Troy, NY 12180-7224

McCaughey, Betsy, PhD,
Chairperson, Founder
Committee to Reduce Infection
Deaths [15321]
c/o Betsy McCaughey, PhD,
Founder and Chairperson
5 Partridge Hollow Rd.
Greenwich, CT 06831
Ph: (212)369-3329

McCaughey, Steve, Exec. Dir.
Seaplane Pilots Association [158]
3859 Laird Blvd.
Lakeland, FL 33811
Ph: (863)701-7979

McCauley, Margaret C., Exec. Dir.
Gamma Beta Phi Society [23780]
99 E Midway Ln.

Oak Ridge, TN 37830
Ph: (865)483-6212

McCauley, Rebecca, President
National Association of Computer-
ized Tax Processors [5797]

McCausland, Mike, Exec. Dir.
Sustainable Communities Worldwide
[12072]
PO Box 50347
Colorado Springs, CO 80949

McCaw, Craig O., Chmn. of the Bd.
The Nature Conservancy [3914]
4245 N Fairfax Dr., Ste. 100
Arlington, VA 22203-1606
Ph: (703)841-5300
Toll Free: 800-628-6860
Fax: (703)841-1283

McClain, Marcia, VP
Cottage Industry Miniaturists Trade
Association, Inc. [21643]
848 N Rainbow Blvd., No. 3459
Las Vegas, NV 89107
Ph: (702)997-2077

McClatchy, J. D., Mem.
American Academy of Arts and Let-
ters [9551]
633 W 155 St.
New York, NY 10032
Ph: (212)368-5900
Fax: (212)491-4615

McClelland, Carra, Mem.
North American Model Horse Shows
Association [22156]
PO Box 1271
Decatur, TX 76234

McClelland, Jamie, Founder, Director
May First/People Link [18570]
237 Flatbush Ave., No. 278
Brooklyn, NY 11217
Fax: (815)642-9756

McClelland, Martha, President
Bukovina Society of the Americas
[3724]
PO Box 81
Ellis, KS 67637

McClenahan, Ann, Exec. Dir.
Boston Theological Institute [8705]
675 MAssachusetts Ave., 8th Fl.
Cambridge, MA 02139
Ph: (617)527-4880
Fax: (617)527-1073

McClendon, John, Contact
Baptist Association of Christian
Educators [19719]
3151 Winfield Ct.
Murfreesboro, TN 37129
Ph: (615)274-1567

McCloskey, Kathryn, Secretary
Interfaith Center on Corporate
Responsibility [18067]
475 Riverside Dr., Ste. 1842
New York, NY 10115
Ph: (212)870-2295
(212)870-2318
Fax: (212)870-2023

McCloskey, Lennie, President
National Constables and Marshals
Association [5499]
1244 Texas Ave.
Shreveport, LA 71101
Ph: (318)673-6800

McCloskey, Peter F., Chairman
National Science and Technology
Education Partnership [12983]
PO Box 9644

McLean, VA 22102

McCloud, Ralph, Director
Catholic Campaign for Human
Development [12466]
c/o United States Conference of
Catholic Bishops
3211 4th St., NE
Washington, DC 20017
Ph: (202)541-3210
Toll Free: 800-946-4-CHD
Fax: (202)541-3329

McCluggage, Wilson Glenn,
President
International Society of Gynecologi-
cal Pathologists [16290]
c/o Esther Oliva, Secretary
55 Fruit St.
Boston, MA 02114
Fax: (617)724-6564

McClure, Jennifer, Mem.
Society for Research on Nicotine
and Tobacco [4721]
2424 American Ln.
Madison, WI 53704
Ph: (608)443-2462
Fax: (608)443-2474

McClure, Kristie, Assoc. Prof.
International Conference for the
Study of Political Thought [7046]
Dept. of Political Science
Yale University
115 Prospect St.
New Haven, CT 06520

McClure, Matt, President
ASCD [7693]
1703 N Beauregard St.
Alexandria, VA 22311-1714
Ph: (703)578-9600
Toll Free: 800-933-2723
Fax: (703)575-5400

McClymont, Mary E., President
Public Welfare Foundation [12988]
1200 U St. NW
Washington, DC 20009-4443
Ph: (202)965-1800

McCole, Jerry, Exec. Dir.
National Disability Sports Alliance
[22789]
25 W Independence Way
Kingston, RI 02881
Ph: (401)792-7130
Fax: (401)792-7132

McColloch, John C., Dir. of Member
Svcs.
International Association of Insur-
ance Professionals [1874]
Bldg. 5, Ste. 300
3525 Piedmont Rd.
Atlanta, GA 30305
Ph: (404)789-3153
Toll Free: 800-766-6249
Fax: (404)240-0998

McCollum, Michelle, Director
Alliance of National Heritage Areas
[9224]
c/o C. Allen Sachse, President
2750 Hugh Moore Park Rd.
Easton, PA 18042-7120
Ph: (610)923-3548
Fax: (610)923-0537

McComis, Michale S., Exec. Dir.
Accrediting Commission of Career
Schools and Colleges [7410]
2101 Wilson Blvd., Ste. 302
Arlington, VA 22201
Ph: (703)247-4212
(703)247-4520
Fax: (703)247-4533

McConico, Sylvia, President
International Foundation of Bio-
Magnetics [13634]
5634 E Pima St.
Tucson, AZ 85712
Ph: (520)751-7751
Toll Free: 888-473-3812

McConlogue, Joe, Officer
Tigers East/Alpines East [21502]
c/o Joe McConlogue
820 Fishing Creek Valley Rd.
Harrisburg, PA 17112-9227
Ph: (717)474-8311

McConnaughy, James, President
National Antique & Art Dealers As-
sociation of America, Inc. [247]
220 E 57th St.
New York, NY 10022
Ph: (212)826-9707

McConnell, Nadia K., President
U.S. - Ukraine Foundation [19207]
1660 L St. NW, Ste. 1000
Washington, DC 20036-5634
Ph: (202)524-6555
Fax: (202)280-1989

McConnell, Robbie, Office Mgr.
Cum Laude Society [23778]
4100 Springdale Rd.
Louisville, KY 40214
Ph: (502)216-3814
Fax: (502)423-0445

McCord, Janet, PhD, FT, President
Association for Death Education and
Counseling [11555]
1 Parkview Plz., Ste. 800
Oakbrook Terrace, IL 60181
Ph: (847)686-2240
Fax: (847)686-2251

McCord, Mark, Exec. Dir.
National Association of State
Technology Directors [3233]
2760 Research Park Dr.
Lexington, KY 40511

McCorkell, Jim, Founder, CEO
College Possible [7753]
450 N Syndicate St., Ste. 325
Saint Paul, MN 55104
Ph: (651)917-3525

McCorkindale, Dr. Tina, President,
CEO
Institute for Public Relations [8470]
2096 Weimer Hall
Gainesville, FL 32611-8400
Ph: (352)392-0280
Fax: (352)846-1122

McCorkle, Betty, VP
Oberhasli Breeders of America
[3610]
c/o Michelle Liga, Secretary/
Treasurer
4140 Dogtown Rd.
Kingwood, WV 26537

McCormack, Michael, President
Citizens for Health [13614]
1400 16th St., NW Ste.101
Washington, DC 20036
Ph: (202)462-8800

McCormick, Dean, President
Construction Owners Association of
America [516]
5000 Austell Powder Springs Rd.,
Ste. 217
Austell, GA 30106
Ph: (770)433-0820
Toll Free: 800-994-2622
Fax: (404)577-3551

McCormick, Edmund, Director
Association of Lifecasters
International [10208]

18 Bank St.
Summit, NJ 07901
Ph: (908)273-5600
Fax: (908)273-9256

McCormick, Marla, President
Miniature Australian Shepherd Club
of America, Inc. **[21914]**
PO Box 712
Custer, SD 57730

McCormick, Rick, President
Nuclear Suppliers Association **[6934]**
PO Box 1354
Westerly, RI 02891
Ph: (401)637-4224
Fax: (401)637-4822

McCormick, Rosemary, Founder,
President
Shop America Alliance LLC **[2977]**
1308 Westhampton Woods Ct.
Chesterfield, MO 63005-6324
Ph: (707)224-3795

McCormick, Dr. Tara, Founder
Global Occupational Therapy for
Orphans **[16323]**
820 Turnpike St., Ste. 104
North Andover, MA 01845
Ph: (978)681-6605

McCormick, Tracy, Exec. Dir.
Retail Energy Supply Association
[1122]
PO Box 6089
Harrisburg, PA 17112
Ph: (717)566-5405
    (301)717-2988

McCormick, Van, Director, Founder
International Economic Alliance
[1014]
1 Mifflin Pl., Ste. 400
Harvard Sq.
Cambridge, MA 02138-4946
Ph: (617)418-1981
Fax: (617)812-0499

McCornick, Joni, President
Coast to Coast Dachshund Rescue
[10603]
PO Box 147
Jacobus, PA 17407

McCorquodale, Charlotte, Chairman
National Association of Catholic
Youth Ministry Leaders **[19867]**
415 Michigan Ave. NE, Ste. 40
Washington, DC 20017
Ph: (202)636-3825
Fax: (202)526-7544

McCourt, James P., President
International Association of Heat and
Frost Insulators and Allied Workers
[1624]
9602 Martin Luther King Jr. Hwy.
Lanham, MD 20706-1839
Ph: (301)731-9101
Fax: (301)731-5058

McCown, Colin, Exec. VP
American Wood Protection Associa-
tion **[1428]**
100 Chase Park S, Ste. 116
Birmingham, AL 35236-1851
Ph: (205)733-4077
Fax: (205)733-4075

McCoy, Charles H., Jr., Treasurer
Hampton One-Design Class Racing
Association **[22618]**
c/o Charlie McCoy, Treasurer
1721 Cloncurry Rd.
Norfolk, VA 23505

McCoy, David L., Exec. Dir.
Global Alliance for Community
Development **[11364]**

PO Box 20511
New York, NY 10017

McCoy, Doug, President
Clan MacKay Society **[20822]**
c/o Doug McCoy, President
1898 Prince Dr.
Lawrenceville, GA 30043
Ph: (972)424-3304

McCoy, Kalli, President
Delta Phi Epsilon Professional
Foreign Service Sorority **[23749]**
3401 Prospect St. NW
Washington, DC 20007

McCoy, Kevin, Chmn. of the Bd.
Rolf Institute of Structural Integration
[13654]
5055 Chaparral Ct., Ste. 103
Boulder, CO 80301
Ph: (303)449-5903
Fax: (303)449-5978

McCoy, Martha L., Exec. Dir.
Everyday Democracy **[19657]**
75 Charter Oak Ave., Ste. 2-300
Hartford, CT 06106
Ph: (860)928-2616
Fax: (860)928-3713

McCoy, MaryAnn, Exec. Dir.,
Founder
Children of Grace **[10917]**
PO Box 2394
Danville, CA 94526-7394
Ph: (415)766-0981

McCoy, Michael, President
Military Chaplains Association of the
U.S.A. **[19932]**
PO Box 7056
Arlington, VA 22207-7056
Ph: (703)533-5890
Fax: (770)649-1972

McCoy, Pat, Bd. Member
National Wheelchair Basketball As-
sociation **[22790]**
1130 Elkton St., Ste. C
Colorado Springs, CO 80907
Ph: (719)266-4082
Fax: (719)266-4876

McCoy, W. David, President
Croquet Foundation of America
[22740]
700 Florida Mango Rd.
West Palm Beach, FL 33406-4461
Ph: (561)315-5226
Fax: (561)478-0709

McCracken, Todd, President, CEO
National Small Business Association
[3124]
1156 15th St. NW, Ste. 502
Washington, DC 20005
Toll Free: 800-345-6728

McCrackin, Leah, Exec. Dir.
American Society of Dermatopathol-
ogy **[14487]**
1 Parkview Plz., Ste. 800
Oakbrook Terrace, IL 60181
Ph: (847)686-2231
Fax: (847)686-2251

McCrae, Fran, Coord.
Committee for the Promotion and
Advancement of Cooperatives
[18486]
c/o International Co-operative Alliance
1401 New York Ave.
Washington, DC 20005

McCravy, Tucker, Founder, President
Serendib **[11430]**
PO Box 11081

Columbia, SC 29211
Fax: (877)799-3383

McCray, Kevin B., CEO
National Ground Water Association
[3460]
601 Dempsey Rd.
Westerville, OH 43081
Ph: (614)898-7791
Toll Free: 800-551-7379
Fax: (614)898-7786

Mccray, Robert, CEO, President
Wireless-Life Sciences Alliance
[17426]
6450 Lusk Blvd., Ste. E202
San Diego, CA 92121
Ph: (858)227-9409

McCrea, Edward J., CEO, President
Environmental Education and
Conservation Global **[7889]**
204 E Locust St.
Coudersport, PA 16915
Ph: (814)260-9138

McCrensky, Jay, Exec. Dir.
Romanian-American Chamber of
Commerce **[23654]**
2 Wisconsin Cir., Ste. 700
Chevy Chase, MD 20815-7007
Ph: (240)235-6060
Fax: (240)235-6061

McCubbin, David, President
Academy of Behavioral Medicine
Research **[13793]**
810 Scott Ave.
Glenshaw, PA 15116

Mccuistion, Jeanene, Director
Red Angus Association of America
[3752]
4201 N Interstate 35
Denton, TX 76207-3415
Ph: (940)387-3502
Toll Free: 888-829-6069

McCulley, Kaitlyn, Treasurer
American Paint Horse Association
[4318]
2800 Meacham Blvd.
Fort Worth, TX 76137
Ph: (817)834-2742
Fax: (817)834-3152

McCullough, Carol, President
Brooks Bird Club **[4801]**
PO Box 4077
Wheeling, WV 26003

McCullough, Cassandra A., MBA,
CEO, Exec. Dir.
Association of Black Cardiologists
[14097]
122 East 42nd St., 18th Fl.
New York, NY 10168-1898
Toll Free: 800-753-9222

McCullough, Rev. John L., CEO,
President
Church World Service **[12643]**
28606 Phillips St.
Elkhart, IN 46514-1239
Ph: (574)264-3102
Toll Free: 800-297-1516
Fax: (574)262-0966

McCullough, Rev. John L., CEO,
President
Church World Service - Immigration
and Refugee Program **[19017]**
475 Riverside Dr., Ste. 700
New York, NY 10115
Ph: (212)870-2061
    (212)870-3300
Fax: (212)870-3194

McCullough, Lori, CEO
Tread Lightly! **[4622]**
353 East 400 South, Ste. 100

Salt Lake City, UT 84111
Ph: (801)627-0077
Toll Free: 800-966-9900

McCullough, Lynn, Exec. Dir.
Event Service Professionals As-
sociation **[2327]**
191 Clarksville Rd.
Princeton Junction, NJ 08550
Ph: (609)799-3712
Fax: (609)799-7032

McCullough, Rod, Chairman
American Association of Community
Theatre **[10236]**
1300 Gendy St.
Fort Worth, TX 76107
Ph: (817)732-3177
Toll Free: 866-687-2228
Fax: (817)732-3178

McCurdy, Dave, President, CEO
American Gas Association **[4262]**
400 N Capitol St. NW
Washington, DC 20001
Ph: (202)824-7000

McCurdy, G. Lincoln, President
Turkish Coalition of America **[19204]**
1510 H St. NW, Ste. 900
Washington, DC 20005
Ph: (202)370-1399
Fax: (202)370-1398

McCurdy, G. Lincoln, Treasurer
Turkish Coalition U.S.A. Political Action Committee **[18875]**
1025 Connecticut Ave. NW, Ste.
1000
Washington, DC 20036-5417
Fax: (866)314-7977

McCutcheon, Kimble D., President
Aircraft Engine Historical Society
[5855]
4608 Charles Dr. NW
Huntsville, AL 35816-1206
Ph: (256)683-1458

McCutcheon, Russell T., President
North American Association for the
Study of Religion **[20550]**
c/o Craig Martin, Executive
Secretary/Treasurer
St. Thomas Aquinas College
125 Route 340
Sparkill, NY 10976

McDaniel, Eugene, President
American Defense Institute **[18081]**
1055 N Fairfax St., Ste. 200
Alexandria, VA 22314
Ph: (703)519-7000
Fax: (703)519-8627

McDaniel, Jesse, President
American Guinea Hog Association
[4706]
1830 P Ave.
Jefferson, IA 50129
Ph: (515)370-1021

McDaniel, Mic, President
Global Helps Network **[11293]**
PO Box 1238
Enumclaw, WA 98022

McDaniels, Lon, Bd. Member
International Certification Accredita-
tion Board **[59]**
6263 N McCormick Rd., Ste. 318
Chicago, IL 60659
Ph: (847)724-6631
Fax: (847)724-4223

McDermott, Damien, President
The Vermiculite Association **[2389]**
2207 Forest Hills Dr.

Harrisburg, PA 17112
Ph: (717)238-9902
Fax: (717)238-9985

McDevitt, Caitlin, Program Mgr.
National Federation of Independent
Business **[3123]**
53 Century Blvd., Ste. 250
Nashville, TN 37214
Ph: (615)872-5800
Toll Free: 800-634-2669

McDonah, Becky, Secretary
Society of North American
Goldsmiths **[21785]**
PO Box 1355
Eugene, OR 97440
Ph: (541)345-5689
(813)977-5326
Fax: (541)345-1123

McDonald, Bill, VP
Community Transportation Associa-
tion of America **[11343]**
1341 G St. NW, 10th Fl.
Washington, DC 20005
Toll Free: 800-891-0590
Fax: (202)737-9197

McDonald, Brian, President
National Dance Council of America
[7705]
PO Box 22018
Provo, UT 84602-2018
Ph: (801)422-8124
Fax: (801)422-0541

McDonald, Candace, Exec. Dir.
Generation Rescue **[13765]**
13636 Ventura Blvd., No. 259
Sherman Oaks, CA 91423
Toll Free: 877-98-AUTISM

McDonald, David, Secretary
Board for Certification of Genealo-
gists **[20962]**
PO Box 14291
Washington, DC 20044

McDonald, Dorothy Cahill, Exec. Dir.
American Podiatric Medical
Students' Association **[16784]**
9312 Old Georgetown Rd.
Bethesda, MD 20814
Ph: (301)581-9263
Toll Free: 800-275-2762

McDonald, Ian, Bus. Dev. Mgr.
Media Access Group **[11941]**
1 Guest St.
Boston, MA 02135
Ph: (617)300-3600
Fax: (617)300-1020

Mcdonald, Jim, President
National Translator Association **[477]**
6868 Vivian St.
Arvada, CO 80004
Ph: (303)378-8209
Fax: (303)465-4067

McDonald, Ms. Mimi M., Contact
Miles Merwin Association **[20900]**
c/o Mimi M. McDonald
8416 Power Dr.
Oscoda, MI 48750-2016
Ph: (989)739-9394

McDonald, Norris, President
African American Environmentalist
Association **[4033]**
1629 K St. NW, Ste. 300
Washington, DC 20006-1631

McDonald, Rebecca, Founder,
President
Women At Risk, International
[12848]

2790 44th St. SW
Wyoming, MI 49519
Ph: (616)855-0796
Toll Free: 877-363-7528

Mcdonald, Rick, President
United Beagle Gundog Federation
[21973]
1150 Millshed Rd.
Morgantown, KY 42261
Ph: (931)629-6117

McDonald, Scott, CEO
Wyman Worldwide Health Partners
[15512]
c/o Oliver Wyman
1166 Avenue of the Americas
New York, NY 10036-2708
Ph: (212)345-8000

McDonel, Jennifer, Exec. Dir.
Gordon Institute for Music Learning
[8368]
PO Box 3466
Radford, VA 24143

McDonnell, Jane, Exec. Dir.
Online News Association **[2713]**
1111 N Capitol St. NE, 6th Fl.
Washington, DC 20002
Ph: (646)290-7900

McDonnell, Sean, President
Architectural Heritage Foundation
[9374]
Old City Hall
45 School St.
Boston, MA 02108-3204
Ph: (617)523-7210
Fax: (617)523-3782

McDougall, Mark, Exec. Dir.
Health Level Seven International
[15012]
3300 Washtenaw Ave., Ste. 227
Ann Arbor, MI 48104-4261
Ph: (734)677-7777
Fax: (734)677-6622

McDougall, Walter A., Chairman
Foreign Policy Research Institute
[18268]
1528 Walnut St., Ste. 610
Philadelphia, PA 19102
Ph: (215)732-3774
Fax: (215)732-4401

McDow, Will, Chairman
Autoimmune Encephalitis Alliance
[15394]
920 Urban Ave.
Durham, NC 27701

McDuff, James M, President
American Society of Military Insignia
Collectors **[22180]**
c/o Garth Thompson, Secretary
7350 Green Clover Cove
Germantown, TN 38138

McEachern, Terri O., Exec. Dir.
Museum of Transportation **[10184]**
2967 Barrett Station Rd.
Saint Louis, MO 63122
Ph: (314)965-6885

McElligott, John, Dep. Dir.
United States Public Health Service |
Commissioned Officers Association
[5719]
8201 Corporate Dr., Ste. 200
Landover, MD 20785
Ph: (301)731-9080
Fax: (301)731-9084

McEllrath, Robert, President
International Longshore and
Warehouse Union **[23473]**

1188 Franklin St., 4th Fl.
San Francisco, CA 94109-6800
Ph: (415)775-0533
Fax: (415)775-1302

McElroy, Arvel
National InterScholastic Swimming
Coaches Association of America
[23286]
29 Fairview Ave.
Great Neck, NY 11023-1206
Ph: (843)637-4663

McElroy, Karen S., PP, PL-SC,
President
NALS The Association for Legal
Professionals **[76]**
8159 E 41st St.
Tulsa, OK 74145-3313
Ph: (918)582-5188
Fax: (918)582-5907

McElroy, Marjorie, Chairperson
Committee on the Status of Women
in the Economics Profession
[5159]
Duke University
Durham, NC 27708-0097
Ph: (850)562-1211
Fax: (919)684-8974

McElvain, Guy, VP
American Holsteiner Horse Associa-
tion **[4311]**
25195 SW Parkway Ave., Ste. 201
Wilsonville, OR 97070
Ph: (503)570-7779
Fax: (503)570-7781

McEnany, Craig A., Exec. Dir.
National Postsecondary Agricultural
Student Organization **[7480]**
1055 SW Praire Trail Pky.
Ankeny, IA 50023
Ph: (515)964-6866

McEnerney, Cathe, President
American Needlepoint Guild, Inc.
[21747]
2424 American Ln.
Madison, WI 53704-3102
Ph: (608)443-2476
Fax: (608)443-2474

McEntee, Ms. Sarah, Exec. Dir.
Commission on Accreditation of
Ambulance Services **[13496]**
1926 Waukegan Rd., Ste. 300
Glenview, IL 60025-1770
Ph: (847)657-6828
Toll Free: 877-457-2227
Fax: (847)657-6825

McEvoy, Carol, VP
National Association of Reunion
Managers **[2743]**
PO Box 335428
North Las Vegas, NV 89033-5428
Toll Free: 800-654-2776

Mcevoy, Chad, President
Sport Marketing Association **[3164]**
1972 Clark Ave.
Alliance, OH 44601
Ph: (330)829-8207

McFadden, Dan, Director
Brethren Volunteer Service **[13286]**
1451 Dundee Ave.
Elgin, IL 60120-1674
Ph: (847)742-5100
Toll Free: 800-323-8039
Fax: (847)429-4394

McFadden, Elizabeth, President
Manpower Education Institute **[8034]**
1835 Charles Ave.
Lancaster, SC 29720-1512
Ph: (718)548-4200

McFadden, Lisa, Mgr.
National Biosolids Partnership
[4552]
601 Wythe St.
Alexandria, VA 22314-1994
Ph: (800)666-0206
Fax: (703)684-2492

McFadden-Allen, Barbara, Exec. Dir.
Committee on Institutional Coopera-
tion **[7632]**
1819 S Neil St., Ste. D
Champaign, IL 61820-7271
Ph: (217)333-8475
(217)244-9240
Fax: (217)244-7127

McFarland, Colleen, Director
Mennonite Church USA Historical
Committee **[20328]**
1700 S Main St.
Goshen, IN 46526-4794
Ph: (574)523-3080
Toll Free: 866-866-2872
Fax: (574)535-7756

McFarland, Kimberly, President
Association of Celebrity Personal
Assistants **[64]**
907 Westwood Blvd., No. 363
Los Angeles, CA 90024-2905

McFarland, Laurel, Exec. Dir.
Network of Schools of Public Policy,
Affairs, and Administration **[5699]**
1029 Vermont Ave. NW, Ste. 1100
Washington, DC 20005-3517
Ph: (202)628-8965
Fax: (202)626-4978

McFarlane, James, President
American Watercolor Society **[8836]**
47 5th Ave.
New York, NY 10003-4679
Ph: (212)206-8986
Fax: (212)206-1960

McFate, Katherine, President, CEO
Center for Effective Government
[18314]
2040 S St. NW, 2nd Fl.
Washington, DC 20009
Ph: (202)234-8494
Fax: (202)234-8584

McFerren, Amanda, Exec. Dir.
National Association of Church
Design Builders **[552]**
1000 Ballpark Way, Ste. 306
Arlington, TX 76011
Ph: (817)200-2622
Toll Free: 866-416-2232
Fax: (817)275-4519

McFerron, Mike, Chmn. of the Exec.
Committee
Society of Composers, Inc. **[9185]**
PO Box 687
Mineral Wells, TX 76068-0687

McGahee, Selvin, Bd. Member
National Rural Housing Coalition
[11986]
1331 G St. NW, 10th Fl.
Washington, DC 20005
Ph: (202)393-5229
Fax: (202)393-3034

McGarr, Conche, Founder
Bambi Uganda Orphans **[10861]**
4400 Oak Creek Ct., No. 205
Fairfax, VA 22033

McGarry, Jim, CEO, President
Education Market Association **[3021]**
8380 Colesville Rd., Ste. 250
Silver Spring, MD 20910
Toll Free: 800-395-5550
Fax: (301)495-3330

McGarvey, Sean, President
AFL-CIO-Building and Construction
Trades Department **[23451]**
815 16th St., 6th Fl.
Washington, DC 20006
Ph: (202)347-1461

McGeary, Judith, Exec. Dir.
Farm and Ranch Freedom Alliance
[4154]
PO Box 809
Cameron, TX 76520-0809
Ph: (254)697-2661

McGee, Ann, Founder, President
Miracle Flights for Kids **[14666]**
2764 N Green Valley Pky., No. 115
Green Valley, NV 89014-2120
Ph: (702)261-0494
Toll Free: 800-359-1711
Fax: (702)261-0497

McGee, Daniel, Treasurer
International Hustle Dance Associa-
tion **[9262]**
PO Box 11655
Philadelphia, PA 19116

McGee, James M., President
National Alliance of Postal and
Federal Employees **[23505]**
1628 11th St. NW
Washington, DC 20001-5008
Ph: (202)939-6325
Fax: (202)939-6392

McGee, Lisa D., President
International Association of Security
and Investigative Regulators
[2010]
PO Box 93
Waterloo, IA 50704
Toll Free: 888-354-2747
Fax: (319)232-1488

McGee, Robert, Secretary, Treasurer
United States Mine Rescue Associa-
tion **[6885]**
PO Box 1010
Uniontown, PA 15401
Ph: (724)366-5272

McGee, Robin, Treasurer
American Voyager Association
[22211]
c/o Bronson Barth, Membership
Director
1418 Clark Rd.
Lapeer, MI 48446

McGee, Sterry, Treasurer
Jefferson Davis Association **[10322]**
2545 Bellwood Rd.
Richmond, VA 23237
Ph: (804)275-5190
Fax: (804)275-5192

McGehee, Diane, Founder, Exec.
Dir.
Together in Hope **[11169]**
1250 Wood Branch Park Dr., Ste.
625
Houston, TX 77079
Ph: (832)758-2971

McGhee, Jerdone, Founder
North American Stone Skipping As-
sociation **[22414]**
PO Box 2986
Wimberley, TX 78676-7886

McGill, Jennifer H., Exec. Dir.
Association for Education in Journal-
ism and Mass Communication
[8149]
234 Outlet Pointe Blvd., Ste. A
Columbia, SC 29210-5667
Ph: (803)798-0271
Fax: (803)772-3509

McGill, Jennifer H., Exec. Dir.
Association of Schools of Journalism
and Mass Communication **[7428]**
234 Outlet Pointe Blvd.
Columbia, SC 29210-5667
Ph: (803)798-0271
Fax: (803)772-3509

McGill, Joseph P., President
Incorporated Society of Irish
American Lawyers **[5426]**
c/o Joseph P. McGill, President
Foley, Baron, Metzger & Juip, PLLC
38777 6 Mile Rd., Ste. 300
Livonia, MI 48152

McGill, Matt, Founder
Crystal Ball Cruise Association
[13441]
PO Box 390
Brewerton, NY 13029
Ph: (315)668-2277
Fax: (315)676-5782

McGillicuddy, Dr. Linda, CEO
American Headache Society **[14916]**
19 Mantua Rd.
Mount Royal, NJ 08061
Ph: (856)423-0043
Fax: (856)423-0082

McGinnis, Betty, Founder, President
World Artists Experiences **[9009]**
PO Box 9753
Arnold, MD 21012
Ph: (410)647-4482

McGinnis, Charles, Secretary
National Association of Energy
Service Companies **[6496]**
1615 M St. NW, Ste. 800
Washington, DC 20036
Ph: (202)822-0950
Fax: (202)822-0955

McGinnis, Charles, Chairman
United States Aikido Federation
[22498]
c/o Yoshimitsu Yamada
142 W 18th St.
New York, NY 10011-5403
Ph: (212)242-6246
Fax: (212)242-9749

McGinnis, Jon, Secretary, Treasurer
Society for Medieval and Renais-
sance Philosophy **[9790]**
c/o Jon McGinnis, Secretary-
Treasurer
599 Lucas Hall, MC 73
Department of Philosophy
University of Missouri, St. Louis
1 University Blvd.
Saint Louis, MO 63121-4400
Ph: (314)516-5439

McGinnis, Kathleen, Exec. Dir.
Institute for Peace and Justice
[18793]
475 E Lockwood Ave.
Saint Louis, MO 63119
Ph: (314)918-2630
    (314)533-4445
Fax: (314)918-2643

McGinnis, Kevin, Chairman
American Ground Water Trust
[3456]
50 Pleasant St., Ste. 2
Concord, NH 03301
Ph: (603)228-5444
Toll Free: 800-423-7748
Fax: (603)228-6557

Mcginniss, Kevin, President, CEO
Eastern College Athletic Conference
[22908]
39 Old Ridgebury Rd.

Danbury, CT 06810
Ph: (203)745-0434
Fax: (203)745-0440

McGlothlin, Ms. Karen, Exec. Dir.
Electrocoat Association **[7264]**
PO Box 541083
Cincinnati, OH 45254-1083
Fax: (513)527-8801

McGlotten, Shaka, Co-Chmn. of the
Bd.
Association for Queer Anthropology
[5908]

McGlynn, Frank, Exec. Dir.
English First **[9282]**
8001 Forbes Pl., Ste. 102
Springfield, VA.22151

McGlynn, Frank, Chief Adm. Ofc.
Gun Owners Foundation **[5218]**
8001 Forbes Pl., Ste. 102
Springfield, VA 22151
Ph: (703)321-8585
Fax: (703)321-8408

McGoff, Dr. Michael F., Provost,
Treasurer
American Name Society **[10058]**
c/o Dr. Michael F. McGoff, Senior
Vice Provost
Binghamton University
State University of New York
Office of the Provost
Binghamton, NY 13902-6000
Ph: (607)777-2143
Toll Free: 866-297-5154
Fax: (607)777-4831

McGonigle, Dr. Tracy, Exec. Dir.
Hooved Animal Humane Society
[10638]
10804 McConnell Rd.
Woodstock, IL 60098
Ph: (815)337-5563
Fax: (815)337-5569

McGough, Robert J., Counselor
Society for Thermal Medicine
[17467]
c/o Allen Press
810 E 10th St.
Lawrence, KS 66044
Ph: (785)865-9403
Toll Free: 800-627-0326
Fax: (785)843-6153

McGovern, Gail J., CEO, President
American National Red Cross
[12616]
2025 E St. NW
Washington, DC 20006
Ph: (202)303-5214
    (202)303-4498
Toll Free: 800-733-2767

McGovern, Myra, Officer
National Association of Independent
Schools **[8013]**
1129 20th St. NW, Ste. 800
Washington, DC 20036-3425
Ph: (202)973-9700
Fax: (888)316-3862

McGowan, Judy, President
USA Synchro **[23391]**
132 E Washington St., Ste. 820
Indianapolis, IN 46204
Ph: (317)237-5700
Fax: (317)237-5705

McGowan, Ms. Kitty, President
U.S. Superyacht Association **[440]**
757 SE 17th St., No. 662
Fort Lauderdale, FL 33316
Ph: (954)792-8666
Toll Free: 800-208-5801
Fax: (954)523-0607

McGowan, Mary, Director
Society for Strings **[10012]**
Meadowmount School of Music
1424 County Route 10
Westport, NY 12993
Ph: (518)962-2400

McGowan, Michael, Exec. Dir.
National Organization for Albinism
and Hypopigmentation **[15832]**
PO Box 959
East Hampstead, NH 03826-0959
Ph: (603)887-2310
Toll Free: 800-648-2310
Fax: (800)648-2310

McGrady, Ryan, President
International Children's Anophthal-
mia & Microphthalmia Network
[17715]
c/o Center for Developmental
Medicine and Genetics
Genetics, Levy 2 W
5501 Old York Rd.
Philadelphia, PA 19141
Ph: (215)456-8722
Toll Free: 800-580-4226

McGrath, Charles A., CAE, Exec.
Dir.
Interlocking Concrete Pavement
Institute **[788]**
14801 Murdock St., Ste.230
Chantilly, VA 20151
Ph: (703)657-6900
Fax: (703)657-6901

McGrath, Scott, COO
Organization for the Advancement of
Structured Information Standards
[7289]
35 Corporate Dr., Ste. 150
Burlington, MA 01803-4238
Ph: (781)425-5073
Fax: (781)425-5072

McGraw, George, Founder, Exec.
Dir.
DIGDEEP Water **[13320]**
3308 Descanso Dr.
Los Angeles, CA 90026
Ph: (323)250-3844

McGraw, Harold, III, Chairman
United States Council for
International Business **[672]**
1212 Avenue of the Americas
New York, NY 10036
Ph: (212)354-4480
Fax: (212)575-0327

McGreal, Dr. Shirley, Founder, Exec.
Dir.
International Primate Protection
League **[10650]**
PO Box 766
Summerville, SC 29484-0766
Ph: (843)871-2280
Fax: (843)871-7988

McGreevy, Tim D., CEO
USA Dry Pea & Lentil Council **[3580]**
2780 W Pullman Rd.
Moscow, ID 83843
Ph: (208)882-3023
Fax: (208)882-6406

McGreevy-Nichols, Susan, Exec. Dir.
National Dance Education Organiza-
tion **[22762]**
8609 2nd Ave., Ste. 203-B
Silver Spring, MD 20910
Ph: (301)585-2880
Fax: (301)585-2888

McGrew, George S., President
Travelers Protective Association of
America **[19496]**

2041 Exchange Dr.
Saint Charles, MO 63303
Toll Free: 877-872-2638
Fax: (636)724-2457

McGuffin, Michael, President
American Herbal Products Association [1639]
8630 Fenton St., Ste. 918
Silver Spring, MD 20910
Ph: (301)588-1171
Fax: (301)588-1174

McGuigan, Cindy, Treasurer
American Adoption Congress [10443]
PO Box 7601
Washington, DC 20004
Ph: (202)483-3399

McGuinness, Tom, Co-Chmn. of the Bd.
Point of Care Communication Council [15058]
PO Box 4342
Salisbury, MD 21803
Ph: (410)344-7580

McGuire, Mr. Andrew, Exec. Dir.
Trauma Foundation at San Francisco General Hospital [17532]
San Francisco General Hospital
San Francisco, CA 94110
Ph: (415)215-8980
Fax: (415)884-9230

McGuire, Colleen, Exec. Dir.
Delta Gamma [23951]
3250 Riverside Dr.
Columbus, OH 43221
Ph: (614)481-8169
Toll Free: 800-644-5414

McGuire, Diane, Managing Dir.
National Association of Purchasing Card Professionals [2818]
12701 Whitewater Dr., Ste. 110
Minnetonka, MN 55343
Ph: (952)546-1880
Fax: (952)546-1857

McGuire, K. Christian, Treasurer
International Society for Hildegard Von Bingen Studies [10314]
787 Iowa Ave. W
Saint Paul, MN 55117
Ph: (651)487-6357

McGuire, Robert E., Founder
Bomber Legends [21193]
PO Box 1479
Tehachapi, CA 93581

McGuire-Schoeff, Margaret, Exec. Dir.
Nursery and Landscape Association Executives of North America [4504]
2130 Stella Ct.
Columbus, OH 43215
Ph: (614)487-1117
Fax: (614)487-1216

McGuirk, Dennis P., President, CEO
SEMI International [1061]
3081 Zanker Rd.
San Jose, CA 95134
Ph: (408)943-6900
Toll Free: 800-974-7364
Fax: (408)428-9600

McGurgan, Diane, Administrator
Council for the Advancement of Science Writing [2673]
PO Box 910
Hedgesville, WV 25427
Ph: (304)754-6786

McHale, Caitlin, Director
Project Esperanza [11423]
1291 Valley Mill Rd.
Winchester, VA 22602

McHale, Mick, President
National Association of Police Organizations [5492]
317 S Patrick St.
Alexandria, VA 22314
Ph: (703)549-0775
Fax: (703)684-0515

McHugh, Bill, Exec. Dir.
Firestop Contractors International Association [807]
4415 W Harrison St., Ste. 436
Hillside, IL 60162-1906
Ph: (708)202-1108
Fax: (708)449-0837

McIlhenny, Dr. Alan, CEO
Open Schools Worldwide [11110]
PO Box 972
Franklin, TN 37065
Ph: (615)599-2059

McIlvaine, Greg, President
National Coalition for Capital [1006]
1028 33rd St. NW, Ste. 200
Washington, DC 20007
Ph: (202)337-1661

McInnis, Mr. John, President
International Association of Clan MacInnes [20886]
c/o Eric MacGinnis Perry, Membership Director
14 Jakes Ln.
Dexter, ME 04930-2194

McInnis, Kent, Exec., Chairman, Bd. Member
Westerners International [8807]
c/o National Cowboy & Western Heritage Museum
1700 NE 63rd St.
Oklahoma City, OK 73111-7906
Ph: (405)478-8408
Toll Free: 800-541-4650

McIntire-Strasburg, Janice, PhD, Exec. Dir.
American Humor Studies Association [9560]
Averett University, 316 Frith Hall
Danville, VA 24541
Ph: (434)791-7242

McIntosh, David, President
Club for Growth [18281]
2001 L St. NW, Ste. 600
Washington, DC 20036
Ph: (202)955-5500
Toll Free: 855-432-0899

McIntosh, Rob, Treasurer
Clan Mackintosh of North America [20825]
c/o Randy Holbrook, Treasurer
1037 35th Avenue Ln. NE
Hickory, NC 28601-9601

McIntosh, Yvonne, Asst. Sec.
College Language Association [8180]
c/o Yakini B. Kemp, Treasurer
PO Box 38515
Tallahassee, FL 32315
Ph: (850)599-3737
    (850)561-2608
Fax: (850)561-2976

McIntyre, Bruce, President
Radio Club of America [22404]
170 Kinnelon Rd., No. 33
Kinnelon, NJ 07405
Ph: (973)283-0626
Fax: (973)838-7124

McIntyre, Doug, Exec. Dir.
Homosexuals Anonymous Fellowship Services [11892]
PO Box 176
Hancock, ME 04640
Ph: (207)669-4264

McIntyre, Scott, Chairman
Prevent Cancer Foundation [14048]
1600 Duke St., Ste. 500
Alexandria, VA 22314-3421
Ph: (703)836-4412
Toll Free: 800-227-2732
Fax: (703)836-4413

McKay, Donna, Exec. Dir.
Physicians for Human Rights [18436]
256 W 38th St., 9th Fl.
New York, NY 10018
Ph: (646)564-3720
Fax: (646)564-3750

McKay, Dr. Jack, Exec. Dir.
Horace Mann League of the U.S.A. [8476]
c/o Jack McKay, Executive Director
560 Rainier Ln.
Port Ludlow, WA 98365
Ph: (360)821-9877

McKay, James, VP
Ancient Order of Hibernians in America [19504]
PO Box 539
West Caldwell, NJ 07007
Ph: (315)252-3895
Fax: (315)252-6996

McKay, Pat, Founder, Secretary, Treasurer
Society for Animal Homeopathy [15292]
272 Lucille Dr.
Hawthorne, NV 89415
Ph: (775)945-2395
    (775)313-5884

McKeag, Yvonne, Secretary, Treasurer
U.S. Complete Shooting Dog Association [21981]
3329 Redlawn Rd.
Boydton, VA 23917
Ph: (434)738-9757

McKee, Michael, President
Association of Medical Professionals with Hearing Losses [15177]
10708 Nestling Dr.
Miamisburg, OH 45342

McKee, Sherry, President
APA Division 50: Society of Addiction Psychology [16893]
750 1st St. NE
Washington, DC 20002-4242
Ph: (202)216-7602

McKeever, Rebecca, President
American Drum Horse Association [4304]
6700 Kuykendall Rd.
Bellville, TX 77418
Ph: (832)558-1630

McKenna, Ray, Founder, President
Catholic Athletes for Christ [22510]
3703 Cameron Mills Rd.
Alexandria, VA 22305
Ph: (703)239-3070

McKenna, Robin Martin, Exec. VP
National Parks Conservation Association [5666]
777 6th St. NW, Ste. 700
Washington, DC 20036
Ph: (202)223-6722
Toll Free: 800-628-7275
Fax: (202)454-3333

McKenzie, Alyce, President
Academy of Homiletics [20205]

Mckenzie, Craig, Treasurer
American Association of Medical Dosimetrists [15660]
2201 Cooperative Way, Ste. 600
Herndon, VA 20171
Ph: (703)677-8071
Fax: (703)677-8071

McKenzie, Mark S., Exec. Dir.
Accreditation Commission for Acupuncture and Oriental Medicine [16451]
8941 Aztec Dr.
Eden Prairie, MN 55347
Ph: (952)212-2434
Fax: (952)657-7068

McKenzie, Robert, Contact
The Judge GTO International [21411]
c/o Robert J. McKenzie
114 Prince George Dr.
Hampton, VA 23669-3604
Ph: (757)838-2059

McKenzie, Steve, President
American Hippotherapy Association, Inc. [17432]
PO Box 2014
Fort Collins, CO 80522
Ph: (970)818-1322
Toll Free: 877-851-4592
Fax: (877)700-3498

McKeon, Annette, Founder
Aimee's Army [13874]
PO Box 37
Scranton, PA 18504

McKeown, Grainne, Exec. Dir., Founder
Mindful Medicine Worldwide [13638]
1011 W Wellington Ave., Ste. 220
Chicago, IL 60657

McKeown, Dr. Mick, President
Air Force Aid Society [19378]
241 18th St. S, Ste. 202
Arlington, VA 22202
Ph: (703)972-2650
Fax: (703)972-2646

McKercher, Patrick, PhD, President
Patient Access Network Foundation [11930]
PO Box 221858
Charlotte, NC 28222
Ph: (202)347-9271
Toll Free: 866-316-7263

McKernon, Dean, VP
Council for Amusement and Recreational Equipment Safety [5746]
PO Box 8236
Des Moines, IA 50301
Ph: (515)281-5387

McKibben, Bill, President, Founder
350.org [3783]
20 Jay St., Ste. 1010
Brooklyn, NY 11201
Ph: (518)635-0350

McKiernan, Ms. Patricia, Exec. Dir.
Graphic Artists Guild [8923]
31 W 34th St., 8th Fl.
New York, NY 10001
Ph: (212)791-3400
Fax: (212)791-0333

McKim, Melanie, Membership Chp.
The National Association of Railway Business Women [2838]
367 Hinsdale Dr.

Debary, FL 32713-4555

McKinley, Gen. Creg R., President, CEO
National Defense Industrial Association [5607]
2111 Wilson Blvd., Ste. 400
Arlington, VA 22201
Ph: (703)522-1820

McKinney, Joe, Secretary
Horror Writers Association [10376]
244 5th Ave., Ste. 2767
New York, NY 10001-7604
Ph: (818)220-3965

McKinney, Joe, Exec. Dir.
National Association of Development Organizations [11408]
400 N Capitol St. NW, Ste. 390
Washington, DC 20001
Ph: (202)624-7806
Fax: (202)624-8813

McKinney, Joe, Exec. Dir.
National Association of Development Organizations Research Foundation [17987]
400 N Capitol St. NW, Ste. 390
Washington, DC 20001
Ph: (202)624-7806
Fax: (202)624-8813

McKinney, Phil, CEO, President
Cable Television Laboratories, Inc. [691]
858 Coal Creek Cir.
Louisville, CO 80027-9750
Ph: (303)661-9100
Fax: (303)661-9199

McKinnon, John G., Chairman
Clan MacKinnon Society [20824]
c/o Sharon MacKinnon
518 Penstemon Trl.
San Antonio, TX 78256
Ph: (231)861-6453

McKittrick, Todd, Founder, Director
Hear See Hope Foundation [14825]
19655 1st Ave. S, Ste. 101
Normandy Park, WA 98148
Ph: (206)429-3884
Fax: (206)299-9519

McKnight, Dr. John, President
American Council of Christian Churches [19941]
PO Box 628
Orwell, OH 44076
Ph: (440)579-2416

Mcknight, Todd, Chmn. of the Bd.
Texas Longhorn Breeders Association of America [3757]
2315 N Main St., Ste. 402
Fort Worth, TX 76164
Ph: (817)625-6241
Fax: (817)625-1388

McKown, Barrett L., President
Society of Mareen Duvall Descendants [20858]
c/o Barrett L. McKown, President
3580 S River Terr.
Edgewater, MD 21037

McKown, Kelly, Coord.
Council on Licensure, Enforcement and Regulation [5773]
403 Marquis Ave., Ste. 200
Lexington, KY 40502
Ph: (859)269-1289
Fax: (859)231-1943

McLachlan, Lauren Boyd, President
House of Boyd Society [20882]
1609 Truscott Ct.

Roseville, CA 95661

McLaren, Capt. Alfred S., President
American Polar Society [7038]
PO Box 300
Searsport, ME 04974

McLarty, Christopher, Contact
NAHB Leading Suppliers Council [549]
1201 15th St. NW
Washington, DC 20005
Ph: (202)266-8247

McLauchlin, Jim, President
Hero Initiative [9170]
11301 Olympic Blvd., No. 587
Los Angeles, CA 90064
Ph: (626)676-6354

McLaughlin, Brenna, Dir. of Mktg.
Association of American University Presses [8021]
28 W 36th St., Ste. 602
New York, NY 10018
Ph: (212)989-1010
Fax: (212)989-0275

McLaughlin, Jeff, Exec. Dir.
Private Equity CFO Association [1262]
c/o Citizens Financial Group
28 State St., 15th Fl.
Boston, MA 02109

McLaughlin, Jim, Chmn. of the Bd.
Honor Flight Network [21125]
300 E Auburn Ave.
Springfield, OH 45505-4703
Ph: (937)521-2400
(614)558-6220

McLaughlin, Maribeth, RN, BSN, President
Council of Women's and Infants' Specialty Hospitals [15324]
National Perinatal Information Ctr.
225 Chapman St., Ste. 200
Providence, RI 02905-4533
Ph: (401)274-0650

McLaughlin, Michele, President
Knowledge Alliance [8502]
20 F St. NW, Ste. 700
Washington, DC 20001
Ph: (202)507-6370

McLaughlin, Valerie, Bus. Mgr.
Swedenborg Foundation [9101]
320 N Church St.
West Chester, PA 19380
Ph: (610)430-3222
Fax: (610)430-7982

McLaughlin, Willie, President
Friends of Shelter Children in Kenya [10989]
PO Box 2206
Bridgeview, IL 60455

McLaurin, Stewart, President
White House Historical Association [9527]
1610 H St. NW
Washington, DC 20006-4907
Ph: (202)218-4337
(202)737-8292

McLean, Bob, CAE, Exec. Dir.
Employee Assistance Society of North America [11489]
PO Box 3146
Norfolk, VA 23514-3146
Ph: (703)416-0060

McLean, Ed, President
Central Intercollegiate Athletic Association [23220]

22 Enterprise Pky., Ste. 210
Hampton, VA 23666-6416
Ph: (757)865-0071
Fax: (757)865-8436

McLean, George F., President
Council for Research in Values and Philosophy [10085]
Gibbons Hall, B-20
620 Michigan Ave. NE
Washington, DC 20064-0001
Ph: (202)319-6089

McLean, Gloria, President
American Dance Guild [9242]
240 W 14th St.
New York, NY 10011

McLean, Rebecca, Exec. Dir.
National Real Estate Investors Association [2034]
7265 Kenwood Rd., Ste. 368
Cincinnati, OH 45236-4412
Ph: (513)827-9563
Toll Free: 888-762-7342
Fax: (859)422-4916

McLean, Robert E., CAE, Exec. Dir.
Coal Trading Association [737]
PO Box 3146
Norfolk, VA 23514-3146
Ph: (703)418-0392
Fax: (703)416-0014

McLellan, Elizabeth, Founder, President
Partners for World Health [15487]
2112 Broadway
South Portland, ME 04106
Ph: (207)774-5555
Fax: (207)772-9963

McLendon, Kelly, Program Mgr.
International Flight Services Association [1389]
1100 Johnson Ferry Rd., Ste. 300
Atlanta, GA 30342
Ph: (678)298-1187
Fax: (404)591-6811

McLendon, Dr. Lennox L., Exec. Dir.
National Adult Education Professional Development Consortium [7455]
c/o Lennox McLendon, Executive Director
444 N Capitol St. NW, Ste. 422
Washington, DC 20001
Ph: (202)624-5250
Fax: (202)624-1497

McLeod, Barbara, Administrator
Society of Thoracic Radiology [17074]
c/o Matrix Meetings, Inc.
1202 1/2 7th St. NW, Ste. 209
Rochester, MN 55901
Ph: (507)288-5620
Fax: (507)288-0014

McLeod, LaTeef, President
United States Society for Augmentative and Alternative Communication [17960]
Toll Free: 800-232-5108

McLernon, Donna, Exec. Dir., President
International Bossons Collectors Society [21669]
8316 Woodlake Pl.
Tampa, FL 33615-1728
Ph: (813)885-2038

McLernon, Nancy, CEO, President
Organization for International Investment [18996]
1225 19th St. NW, Ste. 501

Washington, DC 20036
Ph: (202)659-1903
Fax: (202)659-2293

McIntyre, Amy, Mgr. Dir.
Association for the Study of Literature and Environment [9752]
PO Box 502
Keene, NH 03431-0502
Ph: (603)357-7411
Fax: (603)357-7411

McLoone, Tim, Founder
Holiday Express [13297]
968 Shrewsbury Ave.
Tinton Falls, NJ 07724
Ph: (732)544-8010
Fax: (732)544-8020

McLoughlin, Kieran, President, CEO
American Ireland Fund [18578]
c/o Steve Greeley, Director
211 Congress St.
Boston, MA 02110
Ph: (617)574-0720
Fax: (617)574-0730

McMahan, Kelli, PhD, President
Wilderness Education Association [8402]
PO Box 601
Dresden, OH 43821
Ph: (740)607-9759
Toll Free: 888-365-4639

McMahon, John, Exec. Dir.
National Ski Patrol System [23166]
133 S Van Gordon St., Ste. 100
Lakewood, CO 80228
Ph: (303)988-1111
Fax: (303)988-3005

Mcmahon, Leslie, Exec. Dir.
Professional Law Enforcement Association [5517]
PO Box 1197
Troy, MI 48099-1197
Toll Free: 800-367-4321
Fax: (248)641-1197

McMahon, Madeline Fullerton, Sr. VP of Fin.
Central Station Alarm Association [2993]
8150 Leesburg Pke., Ste. 700
Vienna, VA 22182-2721
Ph: (703)242-4670

McMahon, Matt, President
Aluminum Extruders Council [2340]
1000 N Rand Rd., Ste. 214
Wauconda, IL 60084
Ph: (847)526-2010
Fax: (847)526-3993

Mcmahon, PJ, President
National Vehicle Leasing Association [2932]
N83 W13410 Leon Rd.
Menomonee Falls, WI 53051
Ph: (414)533-3300
Fax: (414)359-1671

McManemy, Victor, Chairman
Citizens for Alternatives to Chemical Contamination [4538]
8735 Maple Grove Rd.
Lake, MI 48632-9511
Ph: (989)544-3318

McManigal, Jill, Exec. Dir., Founder
Kids for Peace [18800]
1302 Pine Ave.
Carlsbad, CA 92008
Ph: (760)730-3320

McMann, Dale, President
International Softball Federation [23202]

1900 S Park Rd.
Plant City, FL 33563
Ph: (813)864-0100
Fax: (813)864-0105

McManus, Ms. Dee, Exec. Dir.
Sigma Delta Epsilon, Graduate
Women in Science [23860]
PO Box 240607
Saint Paul, MN 55124-0607
Ph: (952)236-9112

McManus, Kathryn, Exec. Dir.
American Harp Society [9860]
624 Crystal Ave.
Findlay, OH 45840
Ph: (805)410-4277
Fax: (508)803-8383

McManus, M. Linda, President
Enrichment Educational Experi-
ences, Inc. [9534]
13425 Ventura Blvd., Ste. 304
Sherman Oaks, CA 91423
Ph: (818)989-7509
Fax: (818)989-1763

McManus, Fr. Sean, President,
Founder
Irish National Caucus [18581]
PO Box 15128
Washington, DC 20003-0849
Ph: (202)544-0568
Fax: (202)488-7537

McMichael, Amy, MD, President
Skin of Color Society [14512]
303 W State St.
Geneva, IL 60134
Ph: (630)578-3991
Fax: (630)262-1520

McMillan, Joseph, President
American Heraldry Society [20954]
PO Box 96503
Washington, DC 20090-6503

McMillan, Laura, COO
NetHope [12705]
10615 Judicial Dr., Ste. 402
Fairfax, VA 22030
Ph: (703)388-2845

McMillan, Mike, President, CEO
Trucking Management, Inc. [3359]
PO Box 860725
Shawnee, KS 66286-0725

McMillan, Stanford, Bd. Member,
Reg. Dir.
Delta Kappa Epsilon [23894]
The Shant
611 1/2 E William St.
Ann Arbor, MI 48104
Ph: (734)302-4210

Mcmillan, Stuart, Chairman
International Organic Inspectors As-
sociation [4517]
PO Box 6
Broadus, MT 59317
Ph: (406)436-2031

McMillin, Matt, VP
Global Culinary Innovators Associa-
tion [962]
PO Box 2005
Winter Park, FL 32790-2005
Ph: (407)539-1459
Fax: (407)985-4538

McMoneagle, Nancy, Exec. Dir.,
President
The Monroe Institute [6918]
365 Roberts Mountain Rd.
Faber, VA 22938
Ph: (434)361-1500
Toll Free: 866-881-3440
Fax: (434)361-1237

McMullen, Mr. Kerry, President
Maserati Information Exchange
[21426]
1620 Industry Dr. SW, No. F
Auburn, WA 98001
Ph: (253)833-2598
Fax: (253)735-0946

McMurray, Karli Sue, Founder, CEO
One Love Worldwide [12708]
1223 El Caminito Dr.
Hobbs, NM 88240-0961

McMurray, Pat, Secretary
World Science Fiction Society
[10207]
PO Box 426159, Kendall Square
Sta.
Cambridge, MA 02142

McMutrie, Jamie, Founder, President
Haitian Families First [11924]
PO Box 99834
Pittsburgh, PA 15233

McNair, Wallace, Chairman
Surgeons for Sight [17746]
113 Doctors Dr.
Greenville, SC 29605

McNally, Denise D., Exec. Dir.
National Association of Medical
Examiners [15630]
c/o Denise D. McNally, Executive
Director
National Association of Medical
Examiners
362 Bristol Rd.
Marceline, MO 64658
Ph: (660)734-1891

McNally, Nancy Macan, Exec. Dir.
National Endangered Species Act
Reform Coalition [5185]
1050 Thomas Jefferson St. NW, 6th
Fl.
Washington, DC 20007-3837
Ph: (202)333-7481
Fax: (202)338-2416

McNamara, Michelle, Exec. Dir., Sr.
VP
NAED Education and Research
Foundation [2182]
1181 Corporate Lake Dr.
Saint Louis, MO 63132-1716
Ph: (314)991-9000
Toll Free: 888-791-2512
Fax: (314)991-3060

McNamee, David, Secretary,
Treasurer
Society of Australasian Specialists/
Oceania [22364]
c/o Steven Zirinsky, President
PO Box 49
New York, NY 10008
Ph: (925)934-3847

McNaught, Tom, Exec. Dir.
John F. Kennedy Library Foundation
[9711]
Columbia Point
Boston, MA 02125
Ph: (617)514-1550
Toll Free: 866-JFK-1960

McNaughton, Bob, Chmn. of the Bd.
Fertilizer Industry Round Table
[1181]
1701 S Highland Ave.
Baltimore, MD 21224
Ph: (410)276-4466
Fax: (410)276-0241

McNaughton, John Wm., III, CEO
Ancient Accepted Scottish Rite of
Free-Masonry, Northern Masonic
Jurisdiction Supreme Council
[19549]

33 Marrett Rd.
Lexington, MA 02421
Ph: (781)862-4410
Toll Free: 800-814-1432
Fax: (781)863-1833

McNeely, Juli, CFP, CLU, LUTCF,
President
National Association of Insurance
and Financial Advisors [1897]
2901 Telestar Ct.
Falls Church, VA 22042-1205
Toll Free: 877-866-2432

McNeely, Kathleen, Treasurer
National Art Museum of Sport [8872]
PO Box 441155
Indianapolis, IN 46244
Ph: (317)931-8600

McNees, Ms. Lynne Walker,
President
International Spa Association [2910]
2365 Harrodsburg Rd., Ste. A325
Lexington, KY 40504
Ph: (859)226-4326
Toll Free: 888-651-4772
Fax: (859)226-4445

McNeill, Alex Patchin, Exec. Dir.
More Light Presbyterians [20186]
4737 County Rd. 101
Minnetonka, MN 55345-2634
Ph: (952)941-6494

McNeill, Ann, Founder, President
National Association of Black
Women in Construction, Inc. [809]
c/o Gladys Keith, Member
1910 NW 105th Ave.
Pembroke Pines, FL 33026-2365
Ph: (954)323-3587
Toll Free: 866-364-4998
Fax: (954)437-4998

Mcneill, David, Co-Pres.
International Society for Gesture
Studies [6228]
c/o David McNeill
Dept. of Psychology
University of Chicago
5848 S University Ave.
Chicago, IL 60637
Ph: (773)702-8833
Fax: (773)702-4186

McNeill, Terri, Editor, Web Adm.
Vintage Thunderbird Club
International [21516]
c/o Rod Wake, President
PO Box 75308
Wichita, KS 67275
Ph: (316)722-2028

McNeill-Emery, Michele, President
National Coalition of 100 Black
Women Inc. [18221]
300 New Jersey, NW, Ste. 900
Washington, DC 20001
Ph: (212)222-5660
Fax: (212)222-5675

McNiel, Andy, CFO
National Alliance for Grieving
Children [11253]
900 SE Ocean Blvd., Ste. 130D
Stuart, FL 34994
Toll Free: 866-432-1542

McNulty, Jim, Chairman
National Association of Security
Companies [3063]
444 N Capitol St. NW, Ste. 345
Washington, DC 20001
Ph: (202)347-3257
Fax: (202)393-7006

McNulty, Michael J., Exec. Dir.
Wire and Cable Industry Suppliers
Association [1063]

1741 Akron Peninsula Rd.
Akron, OH 44313
Ph: (330)864-2122
Fax: (330)864-5298

McNutt, Marcia K., President
The National Academies | National
Research Council [7139]
500 5th St. NW
Washington, DC 20001
Ph: (202)334-2000

McPartland, Don, President
Local Independent Charities of
America [12486]
1100 Larkspur Landing, Ste. 340
Larkspur, CA 94939
Ph: (415)925-2663
Toll Free: 800-876-0413
Fax: (415)925-2650

McPhail, Irving Pressley, President,
CEO
National Action Council for Minorities
in Engineering [7860]
1 N Broadway, Ste. 601
White Plains, NY 10601-2318
Ph: (914)539-4010
Fax: (914)539-4032

McPhearson, Michael, Exec. Dir.
Veterans for Peace [18837]
1404 N Broadway
Saint Louis, MO 63102
Ph: (314)725-6005
Fax: (314)227-1981

Mcphee, Justin, VP
American Mold Builders Association
[1707]
7321 Shadeland Station Way, No.
285
Indianapolis, IN 46256
Ph: (317)436-3102
Fax: (317)913-2445

McPherson, Bruce, CEO, President
The Alliance for Advancing Nonprofit
Health Care [14972]
PO Box 41015
Washington, DC 20018
Toll Free: 877-299-6497

McPherson, Ms. Judy, Exec. Dir.,
Chmn. of the Bd.
Play Soccer Nonprofit International
[10492]
PO Box 106
Princeton, NJ 08542-0106
Ph: (609)683-4941
(609)651-0854

McPherson, M. Peter, President
Association of Public and Land
Grant Universities - Commission
on International Programs [18483]
1307 New York Ave. NW, Ste. 400
Washington, DC 20005-4722
Ph: (202)478-6040
Fax: (202)478-6046

McPherson, Mary Lynn, Chairperson
American Society of Pain Educators
[16554]
6 Erie St.
Montclair, NJ 07042
Ph: (973)233-5570
Fax: (973)453-8246

McPherson, Michael S., President
Spencer Foundation [11737]
625 N Michigan Ave., Ste. 1600
Chicago, IL 60611
Ph: (312)337-7000
Fax: (312)337-0282

McPherson, Peter, President
Association of Public and Land-
Grant Universities [7627]

1307 New York Ave. NW, Ste. 400
Washington, DC 20005-4722
Ph: (202)478-6040
Fax: (202)478-6046

McPherson, Peter, Chairman
Partnership to Cut Hunger and
Poverty in Africa [12559]
1100 New Jersey Ave. SE, Ste. 735
Washington, DC 20003
Ph: (202)678-4000
Fax: (202)488-0590

McQuade, Laura, COO, Exec. VP
Center for Reproductive Rights
[19032]
199 Water St.
New York, NY 10038
Ph: (917)637-3600
Fax: (917)637-3666

McQuaid, David L., President
American Welding Society [7382]
8669 NW 36th St., Ste. 130
Miami, FL 33166-6672
Ph: (305)443-9353
Toll Free: 800-443-9353

McQuarrie, Michael, Officer
Erskine Alumni Association [19323]
309 Windsor Rd.
South China, ME 04358-5118
Ph: (207)445-4026
     (207)445-5945

McQueary, Richard L., President
International Police Work Dog As-
   sociation [5476]
PO Box 7455
Greenwood, IN 46142-6424

McQuilkin, Andrew, Chairman
Retail Design Institute [2975]
126A W 4th St., 2nd Fl.
Cincinnati, OH 45202
Ph: (513)751-5815
Fax: (513)961-1192

McReynolds, John, President
Forensic Expert Witness Association
   [5245]
575 Market St., Ste. 2125
San Francisco, CA 94105
Ph: (415)369-9614
Fax: (415)764-4933

McRobbie, Charles E., Jr., President
Clan Drummond Society of North
   America [20808]
c/o Charles McRobbie, President
6 Bernard Ln.
Methuen, MA 01844
Ph: (978)682-0130

McTernan, John, Chap.
International Cops for Christ [19988]
c/o John McTernan
PO Box 444
Liverpool, PA 17045
Ph: (717)329-0470

McVeigh, Rich, President
International Hobie Class Association [22631]
c/o Rich McVeigh, President
15800 Bond Mill Rd.
Laurel, MD 20707-3257
Ph: (301)435-7795

McWhorter, Ladelle, Secretary
International Association for
   Environmental Philosophy [10089]
c/o Steven Vogel, Co-Director
Dept. of Philosophy
Denison University
100 W College St.
Granville, OH 43023-1100

McWilliams, Terry, CEO
Midwest Old Settlers and Threshers
   Association [8903]

405 E Threshers Rd.
Mount Pleasant, IA 52641
Ph: (319)385-8937

Méndez, Néstor M., President
Foundation of the Federal Bar Association [5424]
1220 N Fillmore St., Ste. 444
Arlington, VA 22201

Mead, Heidi Wright, Treasurer
Wallcovering Installers Association
   [1960]
136 S Keowee St.
Dayton, OH 45402
Ph: (937)222-6477
Toll Free: 800-254-6477
Fax: (937)222-5794

Mead, Karen, Exec. Dir.
Emotions Anonymous International
   Service Center [12307]
PO Box 4245
Saint Paul, MN 55104-0245
Ph: (651)647-9712
Fax: (651)647-1593

Mead, Kevin, CEO, President
PrimeGlobal [55]
Bldg. 400, Ste. 300
3235 Satellite Blvd.
Duluth, GA 30096
Ph: (678)417-7730
Fax: (678)999-3959

Mead, Nancy Caldwell, President
Independent Charities of America
   [1471]
1100 Larkspur Landing Cir., Ste. 340
Larkspur, CA 94939-1880
Ph: (415)925-2600

Meade, Jim, President
American Association of Safety
   Councils [12812]
United/Florida Safety Council
1505 E Colonial Dr.
Orlando, FL 32803
Ph: (407)896-1894
Toll Free: 800-372-3335
Fax: (407)897-8945

Meadors, Marc, President
Goodguys Rod and Custom Associa-
   tion [21388]
PO Box 9132
Pleasanton, CA 94566
Ph: (925)838-9876

Meanes, Willam M., Sr., President
National Association of Bench and
   Bar Spouses Inc. [5027]
7422 Lonewolf Ct.
Fairview Heights, IL 62208
Ph: (618)741-3589

Mease, Donald, Treasurer
Eastern Bird Banding Association
   [6958]
c/o Donald Mease, Treasurer
2366 Springtown Hill Rd.
Hellertown, PA 18055
Ph: (610)346-7754

Mechael, Patricia, Exec. Dir.
mHealth Alliance [15486]
1800 Massachusetts Ave. NW, Ste.
   400
Washington, DC 20036

Mecklenburg, Bill, Chairman
Children's Craniofacial Association
   [14330]
13140 Coit Rd., Ste. 517
Dallas, TX 75240
Ph: (214)570-9099
Toll Free: 800-535-3643
Fax: (214)570-8811

Medefind, Jedd, President
Christian Alliance for Orphans
   [10941]
6723 Whittier Ave., Ste. 202
McLean, VA 22101

Medford, Jesse L., President
Challenge Coin Association [22263]
1375 Mistletoe Ridge Pl. NW
Concord, NC 28027
Ph: (704)723-1170
     (704)918-6992
Fax: (704)723-9202

Medina, Adelita Michelle, Exec. Dir.
National Latino Alliance for the
   Elimination of Domestic Violence
   [11709]
PO Box 2787
Espanola, NM 87532
Ph: (505)753-3334

Medina, Sandy, Customer Svc.
American Alliance Drug Testing
   [13121]
326 N Euclid Ave.
Upland, CA 91786-6031
Ph: (909)982-8409
Toll Free: 800-820-9314

Medland, Maurice, President
Salisbury Sound Association [21061]
c/o Maurice Medland, President
19842 Villager Cir.
Yorba Linda, CA 92886
Ph: (505)293-3841
     (714)970-2288

Medlen, Joan Guthrie, RD, VP
Down Syndrome Education USA
   [15814]
1451 Quail St., Ste. 104
Newport Beach, CA 92660-2747
Ph: (949)757-1877
Fax: (949)757-1877

Medley, Carlos, Treasurer
Associated Church Press [2764]
924 Woodcrest Way
Oviedo, FL 32762-1001
Ph: (407)341-6615
Fax: (407)386-3236

Medlin, Will, Chairman
Organic Reactions Catalysis Society
   [6211]
c/o Will Medlin, Chairman
University of Colorado, Boulder
596 UCB
Boulder, CO 80309-0596

Medrano, Juan Diez, Chairperson
Council for European Studies [7907]
Columbia University
420 W 118 St., MC 3307
New York, NY 10027
Ph: (212)854-4172
Fax: (212)854-8808

Medsker, Bekki, President
National Board for Colon
   Hydrotherapy [13641]
11103 San Pedro Ave., Ste. 117
San Antonio, TX 78216
Ph: (210)308-8288

Meduski, Mary
Women in Cable Telecommunica-
   tions [484]
2000 K St. NW, Ste. 350
Washington, DC 20006
Ph: (202)827-4794
Fax: (202)450-5596

Medvidovic, Nenad, Chairman
Association for Computing
   Machinery - Special Interest Group
   on Software Engineering [6271]

c/o Nenad Medvidovic, Chairperson
University of Southern California
941 Bloom Walk
Los Angeles, CA 90089-0134
Ph: (213)740-5579
Fax: (213)740-4927

Meehan, Cynthia Hawkes, President
Adam Hawkes Family Association
   [20773]
c/o Cynthia Hawkes Meehan,
   President
65 Center St.
Danvers, MA 01923

Meehan, Michael J., President
National Rowing Foundation [23111]
67 Mystic Rd.
North Stonington, CT 06359
Ph: (860)535-0634

Meek, Paige, Exec. Dir.
Asian America MultiTechnology As-
   sociation [1036]
3 W 37th Ave., Ste. 19
San Mateo, CA 94403
Ph: (650)773-2293

Meek, Robin, President
National Lincoln Sheep Breeders
   Association [4674]
305 Lincoln St.
Wamego, KS 66547
Ph: (269)623-2549
     (585)494-1069

Meeks, Elsie, Chairperson
Native Financial Education Coalition
   [7932]
1010 9th St., Ste. 3
Rapid City, SD 57701
Ph: (605)342-3770

Meeks, Stephanie, President, CEO
National Trust for Historic Preserva-
   tion [9422]
2600 Virginia Ave. NW, Ste. 1100
Washington, DC 20037
Ph: (202)588-6000
Toll Free: 800-944-6847
Fax: (202)588-6038

Meenan, Timothy J., Exec. Dir., Gen.
   Counsel
Service Contract Industry Council
   [3078]
PO Box 11247
Tallahassee, FL 32302
Ph: (850)681-1058
Fax: (850)425-4001

Meenen, Ms. Patricia, Administrator
International Service for the Acquisi-
   tion of Agri-biotech Applications
   [3570]
105 Leland Lab
Cornell University
Ithaca, NY 14853
Ph: (607)255-1724
Fax: (607)255-1215

Mehr, Linda Harris, Director
Academy of Motion Picture Arts and
   Sciences [1183]
8949 Wilshire Blvd.
Beverly Hills, CA 90211
Ph: (310)247-3000
Fax: (310)859-9619

Mehrara, Babak, Chairman
Plastic Surgery Research Council
   [14321]
500 Cummings Ctr., Ste. 4550
Beverly, MA 01915
Ph: (978)927-8330
Fax: (978)524-8890

Mehren, Dave, Exec. Dir.
Society of Registered Professional
   Adjusters [1931]

PO Box 512
Geneva, IL 60134
Ph: (630)262-2270
Toll Free: 800-949-5272
Fax: (630)262-2274

Mehren, Steve, Exec. Dir., Founder
Saving Wildlife International [4883]
PO Box 2626
Malibu, CA 90265
Toll Free: 800-945-3794

Mehrmann, Craig S., President
Naturopathic Medical Student As-
    sociation [15862]
'049 SW Porter St.
Portland, OR 97201
Ph: (503)334-4153

Mehta, Laurie, Officer
Guide Dog Users, Inc. [17707]
3603 Morgan Way
Imperial, MO 63052-4106
Ph: (636)942-5956
Toll Free: 866-799-8436

Mehta, Rajan, Director
AIDS Global Action [13522]
5185 MacArthur Blvd. NW, No. 607
Washington, DC 20016
Ph: (202)716-4000
Fax: (347)841-3126

Mehta, Shimmy, Founder, CEO
Angelwish [10856]
PO Box 186
Rutherford, NJ 07070
Ph: (201)672-0722

Mei, Ingrid, Office Mgr.
China Institute in America [9152]
100 Wasington St.
New York, NY 10006
Ph: (212)744-8181
Fax: (212)628-4159

Meibohm, PhD, FCP, Bernd,
    President
American College of Clinical
    Pharmacology [16636]
21750 Red Rum Dr., Ste. 137
Ashburn, VA 20147
Ph: (571)291-3493
Fax: (571)918-4167

Meier, Erica, Exec. Dir.
Compassion Over Killing [10606]
PO Box 9773
Washington, DC 20016
Ph: (301)891-2458

Meier, Julia, Director
Coalition of Communities of Color
    [12030]
5135 NE Columbia Blvd.
Portland, OR 97218
Ph: (503)288-8177

Meier, Mark, Founder, Exec. Dir.
Face It Foundation [12308]
2500 Hwy. 88, Ste. 114
Saint Anthony, MN 55418
Ph: (612)789-9897

Meier, Sara, MSEd, Exec. Dir.
International Association for Continu-
    ing Education and Training [7669]
12100 Sunset Hills Rd., Ste. 130
Reston, VA 20190
Ph: (703)234-4065
Fax: (703)435-4390

Meighan, Ann Marie, Exec. Dir.
Adaptive Sports Association [22769]
125 E 32nd St.
Durango, CO 81301
Ph: (970)259-0374

Meikel, Larry, President
Association for Ambulatory
    Behavioral Healthcare [16825]

247 Douglas Ave.
Portsmouth, VA 23707
Ph: (757)673-3741
Fax: (757)966-7734

Meinecke, Dana, Exec. Dir.
National Pawnbrokers Association
    [2095]
PO Box 508
Keller, TX 76248
Ph: (817)337-8830
Fax: (817)337-8875

Meininger, Heather, Founder,
    President
The Mommies Network [13385]
8116 S Tryon St., Ste. B-3, No. 202
Charlotte, NC 28273
Ph: (980)429-4666

Meinsler, Lucille F., Exec. Dir.
American Association of Chairs of
    Departments of Psychiatry [16809]
c/o Lucille F. Meinsler, Executive
    Director
20 Woodland Est
Lebanon, PA 17042
Ph: (717)270-1673
    (717)228-7687
Fax: (717)270-1673

Meis, Doug, Director
Vintage Drivers Club of America
    [21514]
13505 Running Water Rd.
Palm Beach Gardens, FL 33418-
    7933
Ph: (561)622-7554
Fax: (561)228-0552

Meisel, Dr. David, Exec. Dir.
American Meteor Society [5999]

Meisinger, Jessica, PhD, Dir. Ed.
Fats and Proteins Research Founda-
    tion, Inc. [2448]
500 Montgomery St., Ste. 310
Alexandria, VA 22314
Ph: (703)683-2914

Mekas, Jonas, President
Anthology Film Archives [9295]
32 2nd Ave., 2nd St.
New York, NY 10003-8631
Ph: (212)505-5181
Fax: (212)477-2714

Mekdeci, Betty, Exec. Dir.
Birth Defect Research for Children
    [13825]
976 Lake Baldwin Ln., Ste. 104
Orlando, FL 32814
Ph: (407)895-0802

Melander, John, Exec. Dir.
Slag Cement Association [797]
38800 Country Club
Farmington Hills, MI 48331
Ph: (847)977-6920

Melcher, David, Chairman
International Coordinating Council of
    Aerospace Industries Associations
    [141]
c/o Doug Farren, Executive
    Secretary
Aerospace Industries Association of
    America
1000 Wilson Blvd., Ste. 1700
Arlington, VA 22209-3928
Ph: (703)358-1064

Melcher, Melanie, Chairman
Global Dental Relief [14437]
4105 E Florida Ave., Ste. 200
Denver, CO 80222
Ph: (303)858-8857
Toll Free: 800-543-1171

Melcher, Sonya, Gen. Mgr.
International Society for Brachial
    Plexus and Peripheral Nerve Injury
    [16023]
2201 W Holcombe Blvd., Ste. 225
Houston, TX 77030
Ph: (713)592-9900

Meldrum, Vince, President, CEO
Earth Force [4050]
35 Park Ave. W
Denver, CO 80205
Ph: (303)433-0016
Fax: (888)899-5324

Melduni, Rowlens M., MD, CEO,
    President
Clinicians of the World [15445]
PO Box 116
Rochester, MN 55903
Ph: (507)208-4202

Mellegers, Marije, Founder
Wheel Wishers [13095]
Jersey City, NJ

Mellen, Neil, President
Habele [7590]
701 Gervais St., Ste. 150-244
Columbia, SC 29201

Melling, Jon, Chairman
Healthcare Information and Manage-
    ment Systems Society [1646]
33 W Monroe St., Ste. 1700
Chicago, IL 60603-5616
Ph: (312)664-4467
Fax: (312)664-6143

Mellor, Diane, President
Auxiliary to Sons of Union Veterans
    of the Civil War [20739]
c/o Rachelle Campbell, Vice-
    President
9110 Avezan Way
Gilroy, CA 95020
Ph: (408)489-0115

Mellott, John D., President
Plastic Loose Fill Council [4534]
1298 Cronson Blvd., Ste. 201
Crofton, MD 21114
Toll Free: 800-828-2214

Melmed, Matthew E., JD, Exec. Dir.
Zero to Three: National Center for
    Infants, Toddlers and Families
    [14162]
1255 23rd St. NW, Ste. 350
Washington, DC 20037
Ph: (202)638-1144
Fax: (202)638-0851

Melnick, Scott, VP of Corp. Comm.
American Institute of Steel Construc-
    tion [6346]
1 E Wacker Dr., Ste. 700
Chicago, IL 60601-1802
Ph: (312)670-2400
Fax: (312)670-5403

Melnyk, Marcia Iannizzi D.,
    President
Italian Genealogical Society of
    America [9616]
PO Box 3572
Peabody, MA 01961-3572

Melo, Diego, Officer
U.S. Office on Colombia [18449]
1350 Connecticut Ave. NW, Ste.
    1100
Washington, DC 20036
Ph: (202)232-8090
Fax: (202)232-7530

Melton, Dr. Judy, Director
North American Ohara Teachers As-
    sociation [8878]

c/o E-Ling Lou, President
717 Chesterfield Ave.
Naperville, IL 60540
Ph: (630)527-0663
Fax: (630)527-0663

Melton, Ron, Administrator
GridWise Architecture Council [7053]
902 Battelle Blvd.
Richland, WA 99352
Ph: (509)372-6410
    (509)372-6777

Melton, William, Exec. Dir.
American Society of Hypothermic
    Medicine [15711]
901 S Oregon Ave.
Tampa, FL 33606
Ph: (813)323-5448
Fax: (813)875-4149

Meltz, Lewis, DC, VP
Chiropractic Orthopedists of North
    America [14261]
2048 Montrose Ave.
Montrose, CA 91020-1605
Ph: (818)249-8326
    (916)933-2707

Meluso, Erin, President
RADD [12840]
4370 Tujunga Ave., Ste. 212
Studio City, CA 91604-2763
Ph: (818)752-7799
Fax: (818)752-7792

Meluzio, Don, President
Iso and Bizzarrini Owners Club
    [21408]
24042 Hillhurst Dr.
Laguna Niguel, CA 92677

Melville, Nigel, CEO
USA Rugby [23115]
2655 Crescent Dr., Unit A
Lafayette, CO 80026
Ph: (303)539-0300
Fax: (303)539-0311

Melville, Scott, President, CEO
Consumer Healthcare Products As-
    sociation [2556]
1625 Eye St. NW, Ste. 600
Washington, DC 20006
Ph: (202)429-9260
Fax: (202)223-6835

Melvin, Terry L., President
Coalition of Black Trade Unionists
    [23530]
1150 17th St. NW, Ste. 300
Washington, DC 20036
Ph: (202)778-3318
Fax: (202)419-1486

Melvin, Tiffany, JD, President
North American Strategy for
    Competitiveness [3351]
4347 W Northwest Hwy., Ste. 130-
    250
Dallas, TX 75220
Ph: (214)744-1042

Melzer, Sharon, Exec. Dir.
International Association for the
    Study of Organized Crime [11506]
1919 Connecticut Ave. NW
Washington, DC 20009

Memo, Richard A., MD, Chmn. of
    the Bd.
Urology Care Foundation [17568]
1000 Corporate Blvd.
Linthicum, MD 21090
Ph: (410)689-3700
Toll Free: 800-828-7866
Fax: (410)689-3998

Memon, Mushtaq, Exec. Dir., Bd.
Member
World Association of Traditional
Chinese Veterinary Medicine
[17676]
9700 W Highway 318
Reddick, FL 32686
Toll Free: 844-422-8286

Mena, Rey, President
American Canary Fanciers Associa-
tion [21534]
5349 Overing Dr.
Woodland Hills, CA 91367
Ph: (818)884-6338

Menczer, Karen, Founder, Exec. Dir.
Animal Kind International [10576]
PO Box 300
Jemez Springs, NM 87025

Mendel, John, Chairman
Global Automakers [292]
1050 K St. NW, Ste. 650
Washington, DC 20001
Ph: (202)650-5555

Mendell, Gary, Founder, CEO
Shatterproof [13182]
101 Merritt 7 Corporate Pk., 1st Fl.
Norwalk, CT 06851
Toll Free: 800-597-2557

Mendels, David B., President
Beta Gamma Sigma Alumni [23689]
PO Box 297-006
Brooklyn, NY 11229-7006
Ph: (585)542-9181

Mendenhall, Jack, President
Association of Machinery and Equip-
ment Appraisers [221]
315 S Patrick St.
Alexandria, VA 22314
Ph: (703)836-7900
Toll Free: 800-537-8629
Fax: (703)836-9303

Mendenhall, Wendy, Managing Dir.
BritishAmerican Business Inc. of
New York and London [23568]
52 Vanderbilt Ave., 20th Fl.
New York, NY 10017
Ph: (212)661-4060
Fax: (212)661-4074

Mendez, Alicia, Exec. Dir.
Contemporary Design Group [1478]
633 University Ave.
San Diego, CA 92103
Toll Free: 888-588-4426

Mendez, Dr. Hermann, Contact
Salvadoran American Medical
Society [15626]
2080 SW 59th Ave.
Plantation, FL 33317
Ph: (713)864-1150
    (954)583-9995
Toll Free: 800-360-SAMS
Fax: (713)864-1150

Mendez, Kenneth, Sr. VP
Advanced Medical Technology As-
sociation [15075]
701 Pennsylvania Ave. NW, Ste. 800
Washington, DC 20004-2654
Ph: (202)783-8700
Fax: (202)783-8750

Mendez, Robert, MD, Founder
Mendez National Institute of
Transplantation Foundation
[17514]
2200 W 3rd St., Ste. 390
Los Angeles, CA 90057
Ph: (213)457-7495

Mendhro, Umaimah, Founder
Dreamfly [18005]
1818 Great Hwy.

San Francisco, CA 94122

Mendoza, Alberto B., Exec. Dir.
National Association of Hispanic
Journalists [2694]
1050 Connecticut Ave. NW, 5th Fl.
Washington, DC 20036
Ph: (202)853-7760
Fax: (202)662-7144

Mendoza, Carol, Director
World Aquaculture Society [3650]
Louisiana State University
143 J.M Parker Coliseum
Baton Rouge, LA 70803
Fax: (225)578-3137

Mendoza, David, President
Manos de Esperanza [13070]
PO Box 4604
Antioch, CA 94531
Ph: (925)756-7029

Menendez, Albert J., Dir. of Res.
Americans for Religious Liberty
[17872]
PO Box 6656
Silver Spring, MD 20916-6656
Ph: (301)460-1111

Meng, Clifford, Treasurer
Cactus and Succulent Society of
America [22090]
PO Box 1000
Claremont, CA 91711-1000

Menges, Cynthia Winslow, Exec. Dir.
Delta Zeta [23954]
202 E Church St.
Oxford, OH 45056
Ph: (513)523-7597
Fax: (513)523-1921

Menighan, Thomas E., CEO
American Pharmacists Association
[16641]
2215 Constitution Ave. NW
Washington, DC 20037
Ph: (202)628-4410
Toll Free: 800-237-2742
Fax: (202)783-2351

Menighan, Thomas E., CEO, Exec.
VP
APhA Academy of Pharmacy
Practice and Management [16649]
2215 Constitution Ave. NW
Washington, DC 20037
Ph: (202)628-4410
Toll Free: 800-237-2742
Fax: (202)783-2351

Menio, Diane, Exec. Dir.
Center for Advocacy for the Rights
and Interests of the Elderly
[10502]
2 Penn Ctr.
1500 JFK Blvd., Ste. 1500
Philadelphia, PA 19102-1718
Ph: (215)545-5728
Toll Free: 800-356-3606
Fax: (215)545-5372

Menken, Rabbi Yaakov, Director
Project Genesis [8144]
2833 Smith Ave., Ste. 225
Baltimore, MD 21209
Ph: (410)602-1350
Toll Free: 888-WWW-TORA
Fax: (410)602-1351

Menkes, Jason, President
Association of Music Producers
[2421]
3 W 18th St., 5th Fl.
New York, NY 10011
Ph: (212)924-4100
Fax: (212)675-0102

Mennillo, Kathleen, MBA, Exec. Dir.
International Hearing Society
[15198]
16880 Middlebelt Rd., Ste. 4
Livonia, MI 48154
Ph: (734)522-7200
Fax: (734)522-0200

Menotti, Victor, Exec. Dir.
International Forum on Globalization
[18480]
1009 General Kennedy Ave., No. 2
San Francisco, CA 94129
Ph: (415)561-7650
Fax: (415)561-7651

Menscer, Darlyne, Chairperson
American Medical Association
Council on Medical Education
[8291]
AMA Plz.
330 N Wabash Ave.
Chicago, IL 60611-5885

Mentel, Eva, Office Mgr.
Hardwood Plywood and Veneer As-
sociation [1441]
1825 Michael Faraday Dr.
Reston, VA 20190
Ph: (703)435-2900
Fax: (703)435-2537

Mento, Lynn, Exec. Dir.
Friends of the National Zoo [7401]
3001 Connecticut Ave. NW
Washington, DC 20008
Ph: (202)633-3038
    (202)633-4888

Mentzer, Steven C., President
Central American Relief Efforts
[12268]
2117 Saddleridge Rd.
Lancaster, PA 17601
Ph: (717)299-4942

Menzer, Prof. Paul, President
Marlowe Society of America [9077]
c/o Prof. Sarah K. Scott
Dept. of English
Mount St. Mary's University
16300 Old Emmitsburg Rd.
Emmitsburg, MD 21727-7700

Merberg, Eileen, Exec. Dir.
Alpha Lambda Delta [23750]
328 Orange St.
Macon, GA 31201
Toll Free: 800-9AL-7491
Fax: (478)744-9924

Mercado, Ethel, Officer
Federation of Philippine American
Chambers of Commerce, Inc.
[23585]
2625 Alcatraz Ave., No. 324
Berkeley, CA 94705
Ph: (510)541-0964

Mercado, Stephanie, Exec. Dir.
National Association for Healthcare
Quality [17030]
8735 W Higgins Rd., Ste. 300
Chicago, IL 60631
Ph: (847)375-4720
Toll Free: 800-966-9392
Fax: (847)375-6320

Mercer, Gerald, President
Rushlight Club [9433]
4508 Elsrode Ave.
Baltimore, MD 21214-3107
Ph: (443)433-6071

Mercer, Mike, President
Compassion First [12649]
16055 SW Walker Rd., PMB 239
Beaverton, OR 97006
Ph: (503)207-1320
Fax: (503)614-1599

Mercer, William, Mem.
Divine Science Federation
International [20052]
Bldg. 18, Unit 303
Howe Ctr., Ste. 51
1 Scale Ave.
Rutland, VT 05701
Ph: (802)779-9019
Toll Free: 800-644-9680

Mercieca, Dr. Charles, Founder,
President
International Association of Educa-
tors for World Peace USA [18794]
Office of the President
2013 Orba Dr. NE
Huntsville, AL 35811-2414
Ph: (256)534-5501
Fax: (256)536-1018

Mercier, Anika, Officer
Operation Lifesaver [12839]
1420 King St., Ste. 201
Alexandria, VA 22314
Ph: (703)739-0308
Toll Free: 800-537-6224
Fax: (703)519-8267

Merconi, Arn, Exec. Dir., Founder
SOS Outreach [23176]
450 Miller Ranch Rd.
Edwards, CO 81632
Ph: (970)926-9292
Fax: (970)306-0269

Meredith, Helen, Founder, President
United Pegasus Foundation [18356]
20411 Pegasus Rd.
Tehachapi, CA 93561
Ph: (661)823-9672
Fax: (626)452-8620

Meredith, Dr. William, Exec. Dir.
American Beethoven Society [9175]
San Jose State University
Beethoven Ctr.
1 Washington Sq.
San Jose, CA 95192-0171
Ph: (408)808-2058
Fax: (408)808-2060

Merghoub, Tara, President
Algerian American Scientists As-
sociation [7115]
1825 Madison Ave., Apt. 6H
New York, NY 10035
Ph: (646)641-7615

Meric, Linda, Exec. Dir.
9 to 5, National Association of Work-
ing Women [18199]
207 E Buffalo St., Ste. 211
Milwaukee, WI 53202
Ph: (414)274-0925
    (404)222-0077
Toll Free: 800-522-0925
Fax: (414)272-2870

Meringolo, Christina, Chairman
Alliance for Audited Media [115]
48 W Seegers Rd.
Arlington Heights, IL 60005-3913
Ph: (224)366-6939
Toll Free: 800-285-2220
Fax: (224)366-6949

Merkel, Mrs. Diane, Founder
Little Bighorn History Alliance
[10337]
PO Box 1752
Niceville, FL 32588

Merken, Stefan, Chairman
Jewish Peace Fellowship [18799]
PO Box 271
Nyack, NY 10960-0271
Ph: (845)358-4601
Fax: (845)358-4924

Merkl, Andreas, CEO
Ocean Conservancy [3919]
1300 19th St. NW, 8th Fl.
Washington, DC 20036
Ph: (202)429-5609
Toll Free: 800-519-1541
Fax: (202)872-0619

Merkle, Horst, President, Chairman
Personal Connected Health Alliance
[15055]
3855 SW 153rd Dr.
Beaverton, OR 97003
Ph: (503)619-0867
Fax: (503)644-6708

Merlau, John, President
Natural Colored Wool Growers As-
sociation [4676]
PO Box 406
New Palestine, IN 46163
Ph: (317)861-4795

Merlino, James, MD, Chmn. of the
Bd., President
Association for Patient Experience
[14930]
PO Box 21875
Cleveland, OH 44121
Ph: (216)316-5787

Merlo, Ellen, Chairperson
American Committee for the Weiz-
mann Institute of Science [7117]
633 3rd Ave.
New York, NY 10017
Ph: (212)895-7900
Toll Free: 800-242-2947

Merrell, Bill, Officer
Association of Construction Inspec-
tors [1814]
PO Box 879
Palm Springs, CA 92263-0879
Toll Free: 877-743-6806

Merrell, Bill C., PhD, Dir. Ed.
Housing Inspection Foundation
[1816]
PO Box 879
Palm Springs, CA 92263-0879
Toll Free: 877-743-6806

Merrell, Bill, Advisor
International Society of Meeting
Planners [2333]
810 N Farell Dr.
Palm Springs, CA 92263
Ph: (760)327-5284
Toll Free: 877-743-6802
Fax: (760)327-5631

Merrell, Bill, Mem.
National Association of Real Estate
Appraisers [229]
PO Box 879
Palm Springs, CA 92263
Toll Free: 877-743-6806
Fax: (760)327-5631

Merrell, Dr. Bill, Advisor
National Association of Review Ap-
praisers and Mortgage Underwrit-
ers [2881]
810 N Farrell Dr.
Palm Springs, CA 92262
Ph: (760)327-5284
Toll Free: 877-743-6805
Fax: (760)327-5631

Merrill, Brittany, Founder, President
Ugandan American Partnership
Organization [12194]
3311 Elm St.
Dallas, TX 75226
Ph: (214)310-0964

Merrill, Christina, Exec. Dir.
Bone Marrow Foundation [13846]
515 Madison Ave., Ste. 1130

New York, NY 10022
Ph: (212)838-3029
Toll Free: 800-365-1336
Fax: (212)223-0081

Merrill, Clarence, President
Christian Labor Association [19959]
405 Centerstone Ct.
Zeeland, MI 49464
Toll Free: 877-CLA-1018
Fax: (616)772-9830

Merrill, David, President
United States-Indonesia Society
[687]
1625 Massachusetts Ave. NW, Ste.
550
Washington, DC 20036-2260
Ph: (202)232-1400
Fax: (202)232-7300

Merrill, Vicky, President
Cat Fanciers' Federation [21567]
PO Box 661
Gratis, OH 45330
Ph: (937)787-9009

Merrithew, Daniel, Commissioner,
Secretary
Gay and Lesbian Tennis Alliance
[23299]

Merritt, Chris, Exec. Dir.
International Alliance of Composers
[9922]
9701 Clearwater Dr.
Knoxville, TN 37923-2021
Ph: (323)306-3057
      (347)767-2952

Merritt, Mark, President, CEO
Pharmaceutical Care Management
Association [16681]
325 7th St. NW
Washington, DC 20004
Ph: (202)756-5700
Fax: (202)756-5708

Merry, Bill, Jr., Chairman
Healing Hands International [13009]
455 McNally Dr.
Nashville, TN 37211-3311
Ph: (615)832-2000
Fax: (615)832-2002

Merson, Melissa, Exec. Dir.
National Coalition for Promoting
Physical Activity [23063]
1150 Connecticut Ave. NW, Ste. 300
Washington, DC 20036

Mertens, Mike, President
National School Plant Management
Association [7440]
c/o Dr. John A. Bailey, President
1021 Great Bridge Blvd.
Chesapeake, VA 23320
Ph: (757)547-0139
Fax: (757)547-2091

Mertz, Alan, President
American Clinical Laboratory As-
sociation [15515]
1100 New York Ave. NW, Ste. 725
W
Washington, DC 20005
Ph: (202)637-9466

Meserve, Robert, President
Disabled Sports USA [22780]
451 Hungerford Dr., Ste. 100
Rockville, MD 20850
Ph: (301)217-0960
      (301)217-9838
Fax: (301)217-0968

Messac, Prof. Achille, Exec. Chmn.
of the Bd.
Aerospace Department Chair's Association [7457]

University of Maryland
Dept. of Aerospace Engineering
Martin Hall, Rm. 3179F
College Park, MD 20742
Ph: (315)443-2341
Fax: (315)443-9099

Messer, Mitch, Treasurer
Cystic Fibrosis Worldwide [17139]
474 Howe St.
East Brookfield, MA 01515
Ph: (774)230-1629

Messer, Todd, Exec. Dir.
Independent Organization of Little
Caesar Franchisees [1460]
2685 Lapeer Rd., Ste. 101
Auburn Hills, MI 48326
Ph: (248)377-1900
Fax: (248)377-1913

Messersmith, Jack, President
International Submariners Associa-
tion/USA [21010]
7770 Loos Dr.
Prescott Valley, AZ 86314-5520
Ph: (928)759-9544

Messier, Krysta, Contact
Automotive Aftermarket Suppliers
Association | Filter Manufacturers
Council [308]
10 Laboratory Dr.
Research Triangle Park, NC 27709-
3966
Ph: (919)406-8825
Fax: (919)549-4824

Messier, Matt, President
Volunteers for Peace [18563]
7 Kilburn St., Ste. 316
Burlington, VT 05401
Ph: (802)540-3060

Messing, Russell, Sec. Gen.
International Organisation for
Biological Control [4529]
c/o Dr. Russell Messing, Secretary
General
University of Hawaii at Manoa
Kauai Agricultural Research Center
7370 Kuamoo Rd.
Kapaa, HI 96746
Ph: (808)822-4984
Fax: (808)822-2190

Messinger, Ruth W., President
American Jewish World Service
[12615]
45 W 36th St.
New York, NY 10018-7641
Ph: (212)792-2900
Toll Free: 800-889-7146
Fax: (212)792-2930

Messuri, Nicholas, Chairman
National Health Care Anti-Fraud As-
sociation [15422]
1220 L St. NW, Ste. 600
Washington, DC 20005
Ph: (202)659-5955
Fax: (202)785-6764

Mest, Richard, VP
Water Systems Council [3463]
1101 30th St. NW, Ste. 500
Washington, DC 20007
Ph: (202)625-4387
Fax: (202)625-4363

Metalitz, Steven J., Counsel
International Intellectual Property
Alliance [5331]
1818 N St. NW, 18th Fl.
Washington, DC 20036
Ph: (202)355-7900
Fax: (202)355-7899

Metallo, Michael, Contact
National Gardening Association
[22112]

5452 County Road 1405
Jacksonville, TX 75766

Metcalf, Allan A., Exec. Sec.
American Dialect Society [9736]
PO Box 90660
Durham, NC 27708-0660
Ph: (919)688-5134
Toll Free: 888-651-0122

Metcalf, Kathy J., President, CEO
Chamber of Shipping of America
[5579]
1730 Rhode Island Ave., Ste. 702
Washington, DC 20036
Ph: (202)775-4399
Fax: (202)659-3795

Metcalf, Michael, Exec. Dir.
International Doctors in Alcoholics
Anonymous [13147]
8514 E Maringo Dr.
Spokane, WA 99212

Metcalf, Patty McCarthy, Exec. Dir.
Faces and Voices of Recovery
[19157]
840 1st St., NE, 3rd Fl.
Washington, DC 20002
Ph: (202)737-0690
Fax: (202)737-0695

Metric, John, President
National Electric Drag Racing Association [22828]
264 Plum Cir.
Lake Jackson, TX 77566

Metz, Gregory, VP
Association of Asthma Educators
[17135]
70 Buckwalter Rd., Ste. 900
Royersford, PA 19468
Toll Free: 888-988-7747

Metz, Megan, Exec. Dir.
Santa Cruz Mountains Winegrowers
Association [4932]
101 Cooper St.
Santa Cruz, CA 95060
Ph: (831)685-8463

Metzgar, Jayme, Founder, President
Romania Reborn [11142]
PO Box 2027
Purcellville, VA 20134-2027
Ph: (540)751-9490

Metzger, Dan, President
Thoroughbred Owners and Breeders
Association [22930]
3101 Beaumont Centre Cir., Ste. 110
Lexington, KY 40513
Ph: (859)276-2291
Toll Free: 888-606-TOBA
Fax: (859)276-2462

Metzler, Don, President
We Care Program [11551]
3493 Highway 21
Atmore, AL 36502
Ph: (251)368-8818
Fax: (251)368-0932

Metzner, Traci, President
Gamma Delta Pi [23973]
900 Asp Ave., Rm. 370
Norman, OK 73019

Meunier, Michael, President
U.S. Copts Association [12061]
5116 Arlington Blvd., Ste. 155
5116 Arlington Blvd., Ste. 155
Falls Church, VA 22042

Meuter, Jeffrey, Treasurer
StandUp for Kids [11157]
83 Walton St. NW, Ste. 500

Atlanta, GA 30303
Toll Free: 800-365-4KID
Fax: (404)954-6610

Meyer, Adele, Exec. Dir.
NARTS - The Association of Resale
  Professionals [2964]
PO Box 190
Saint Clair Shores, MI 48080
Ph: (586)294-6700
Toll Free: 800-544-0751
Fax: (586)588-7018

Meyer, Bill, Founder
Reach Now International [12715]
PO Box 35133
Tulsa, OK 74153
Ph: (918)361-0452

Meyer, Brenda, President
Flow Blue International Collectors
  Club [21655]
PO Box 5427
Naperville, IL 60567-5427

Meyer, Charles, Tech. Ofc.
Conference of Radiation Control
  Program Directors [5739]
1030 Burlington Ln., Ste. 4B
Frankfort, KY 40601
Ph: (502)227-4543
Fax: (502)227-7862

Meyer, Cheryl, President
Colored Angora Goat Breeder's Association [4275]
c/o Polly Holmes, Treasurer
2JP Ranch
150 Scenic Dr.
Mountain Home, TX 78058-2152
Ph: (817)675-9352

Meyer, Dan, President
Sword Swallowers Association
  International [10069]
18842 Maisons Dr.
Lutz, FL 33558-2878
Ph: (615)969-2568

Meyer, Don, Mgr.
Mid-Continent Railway Historical
  Society [22409]
E8948 Diamond Hill Rd.
North Freedom, WI 53951
Ph: (608)522-4261
Toll Free: 800-930-1385
Fax: (608)522-4490

Meyer, Donna, CEO
Organization for Associate Degree
  Nursing [16177]
7794 Grow Dr.
Pensacola, FL 32514
Toll Free: 877-966-6236
Fax: (850)484-8762

Meyer, Eugene B., President
Federalist Society for Law and
  Public Policy Studies [5383]
1776 I St. NW, Ste. 300
Washington, DC 20006
Ph: (202)822-8138
Fax: (202)296-8061

Meyer, Gail, President
Independent Educational
  Consultants Association [7771]
3251 Old Lee Hwy., Ste. 510
Fairfax, VA 22030-1504
Ph: (703)591-4850
Fax: (703)591-4860

Meyer, Gwen, Director
Friends of Kenya Schools and
  Wildlife [11359]
95363 Grimes Rd.
Junction City, OR 97448
Ph: (541)998-3724

Meyer, Imke, President
Austrian Studies Association [9031]
c/o Robert von Dassanowsky,
  President
1420 Austin Bluffs Pky.
Department of Visual and Perform-
  ing Arts
University of Colorado at Colorado
  Springs
Colorado Springs, CO 80918

Meyer, John, Secretary
Holstein Association U.S.A. [3728]
1 Holstein Pl.
Brattleboro, VT 05302-0808
Ph: (802)254-4551
Toll Free: 800-952-5200
Fax: (802)254-8251

Meyer, John, Director
Independent Community Bankers of
  America [400]
1615 L St. NW, Ste. 900
Washington, DC 20036
Ph: (202)659-8111
Toll Free: 800-422-8439
Fax: (202)659-3604

Meyer, Ken, President
Classic Yacht Association [22608]
5267 Shilshole Ave. NW
Seattle, WA 98107
Ph: (206)937-6211

Meyer, Lynne, PhD, Exec. Dir.
Accreditation Council for Graduate
  Medical Education [7409]
515 N State St., Ste. 2000
Chicago, IL 60654
Ph: (312)755-5000
Fax: (312)755-7498

Meyer, Mary D., Project Mgr.,
  Founder, President
Indigo Threads [11383]
1601 W Canal Ct.
Littleton, CO 80120
Ph: (760)564-2679

Meyer, Mike, Trustee
National Onion Association [4242]
822 7th St., No. 510
Greeley, CO 80631
Ph: (970)353-5895
Fax: (970)353-5897

Meyer, Richard, President
Energy Bar Association [5169]
2000 M St. NW, Ste. 715
Washington, DC 20036
Ph: (202)223-5625
Fax: (202)833-5596

Meyer, Mr. Scott, President
Concordia Historical Institute [20303]
804 Seminary Pl.
Saint Louis, MO 63105-3014
Ph: (314)505-7900
    (314)505-7911
Fax: (314)505-7901

Meyer, Thomas, Chairman
American Conference of Academic
  Deans [7419]
1818 R St. NW
Washington, DC 20009
Ph: (202)884-7419
Fax: (202)265-9532

Meyer V, Ferdinand, President
Federation of Historical Bottle Col-
  lectors [21555]
c/o Elizabeth Meyer, Business
  Manager
101 Crawford St., Studio 1A
Houston, TX 77002
Ph: (713)222-7979

Meyerhof, Dr. Nina, President,
  Founder
Children of the Earth [12434]
26 Baycrest Dr.

South Burlington, VT 05403
Ph: (802)862-1936

Meyerrose, Maj. Gen. Dale, USAF,
  President, Chmn. of the Bd.
Air Force Historical Foundation
  [9798]
1602 California Ave., Ste. F-162
JB Andrews, MD 20762
Ph: (301)736-1959

Meyers, Carole J., President
American Color Print Society [8830]
c/o Elizabeth MacDonald
205 Woodside Ave.
Narberth, PA 19072-2430

Meyers, Chris, Editor, President
MG Vintage Racers [22400]
c/o Chris Meyers, President
55 Belden Rd.
Burlington, CT 06013

Meyers, Chris, Dir. Ed.
Museum of American Finance [9834]
48 Wall St.
New York, NY 10005
Ph: (212)908-4110
Fax: (212)908-4601

Meyers, Michael, Dir. of Member
  Svcs.
Print Alliance Credit Exchange
  [1261]
1100 Main St.
Buffalo, NY 14209-2356
Fax: (716)878-2807

Meyers, Mike, Chief Dev. Ofc.
Food for the Hungry [12091]
1224 E Washington St.
Phoenix, AZ 85034-1102
Ph: (480)998-3100
    (602)258-3750
Toll Free: 800-248-6437

Meyers, Philip M., MD, Bd. Member
Society of NeuroInterventional
  Surgery [17069]
3975 Fair Ridge Dr., Ste. 200 N
Fairfax, VA 22033
Ph: (703)691-2272
Fax: (703)537-0650

Meyers, Susan, RN, President
National Association of Pro-Life
  Nurses [12782]
2200 Pennsylvania Ave., 4th Fl. E
Washington, DC 20037
Ph: (202)556-1240
Fax: (202)556-1240

Meyerson, Adam, President
Philanthropy Roundtable [12493]
1730 M St. NW, Ste. 601
Washington, DC 20036
Ph: (202)822-8333
Fax: (202)822-8325

Meza, Giselle, Founder, President
Puresa Humanitarian [18439]
5970 SW 18th St., Ste. 102
Boca Raton, FL 33433
Ph: (561)826-7527

Mezzanotte, Tom, President
NFHS Officials Association [23271]
PO Box 690
Indianapolis, IN 46206
Ph: (317)972-6900
Fax: (317)822-5700

Miceli, Carl, President
Equipment Appraisers Association of
  North America [223]
1270 State Route 30
Clinton, PA 15026
Toll Free: 800-790-1053
Fax: (724)899-2001

Micetic, Dale, Chmn. of the Bd.
One Challenge International [20451]
PO Box 36900
Colorado Springs, CO 80936
Ph: (719)592-9292
Toll Free: 800-676-7837
Fax: (719)592-0693

Michael, Pamela, Exec. Dir.,
  Founder
River of Words [4763]
1928 St. Mary's Rd.
Moraga, CA 94575
Ph: (925)631-4289

Michaelis, Mike, President
Ryan's Reach [17350]
35 Augusta
Coto de Caza, CA 92679
Ph: (949)733-0046
    (949)246-4328

Michaels, Ken, Director
Book Industry Study Group [2774]
145 W 45th St., Ste. 601
New York, NY 10036
Ph: (646)336-7141
Fax: (646)336-6214

Michaels, Ted, President
Energy Recovery Council [4740]
2200 Wilson Blvd., Ste. 310
Arlington, VA 22201
Ph: (202)467-6240

Michaelsen, Veronica, MD, President
International Association of Medical
  Science Educators [15624]
c/o JulNet Solutions, LLC
1404 1/2 Adams Ave.
Huntington, WV 25704
Ph: (304)522-1270
Fax: (304)523-9701

Michalopoulos, William, Chmn. of
  the Bd.
Periodical and Book Association of
  America [2809]
481 8th Ave., Ste. 526
New York, NY 10001
Ph: (212)563-6502
Fax: (212)563-4098

Michaud, Arlene, President
North American Shagya-Arabian
  Society [4395]
c/o Beverly Thompson, Treasurer
2345 S Washington Rd.
Columbia City, IN 46725

Michaud, Lucy, President
Hope for a Cure Guild [14534]
PO Box 365
La Habra, CA 90633-0365
Toll Free: 800-672-4673
Fax: (562)690-6091

Michel, Claudine, Advisor
Haitian Studies Association [11925]
University of Massachusetts Boston
McCormack Hall, Rm. 2-211
100 Morrissey Blvd.
Boston, MA 02125-3393

Michel, Jonathan, VP
Association of Ingersoll-Rand
  Distributors [1714]
1300 Sumner Ave.
Cleveland, OH 44115-2851
Ph: (216)241-7333
Fax: (216)241-0105

Michel, Marchelle, Comm. Spec.
American Heart Association - Dallas
  [14092]
7272 Greenville Ave.
Dallas, TX 75231
Ph: (214)441-4200
Fax: (214)441-4201

Michel, Mark, CEO, President
Archaeological Conservancy [5930]
1717 Girard Blvd. NE
Albuquerque, NM 87106
Ph: (505)266-1540

Michel, Michelle A., MD, Officer
American Society of Head and Neck
    Radiology [17046]
800 Enterprise Dr., Ste. 205
Oak Brook, IL 60523-4216
Ph: (630)574-0220
Fax: (630)574-0661

Michel, Nancy, Pub. Dir.
Justice Research and Statistics As-
    sociation [11535]
720 7th St. NW, 3rd Fl.
Washington, DC 20001
Ph: (202)842-9330
Fax: (202)448-1723

Michell, Frank, President
Cooling Technology Institute [519]
3845 Cypress Creek Pky., Ste. 420
Houston, TX 77068
Ph: (281)583-4087
Fax: (281)537-1721

Michels, Linda, Exec. Dir.
American Association of Gynecologic
    Laparoscopists [16268]
6757 Katella Ave.
Cypress, CA 90630-5105
Ph: (714)503-6200
Toll Free: 800-554-2245

Michels, Matt, Treasurer
National Lieutenant Governors As-
    sociation [5785]
71 Cavalier Blvd., Ste. 223
Florence, KY 41042
Ph: (859)283-1400
    (859)244-8111
Toll Free: 800-800-1910

Michler, Robert, MD, Chairman,
    Founder
Heart Care International [14112]
139 E Putnam Ave.
Greenwich, CT 06830-5612
Ph: (203)552-5343
Fax: (203)552-5344

Michlmayr, Martin, Secretary
Software in the Public Interest
    [6287]
PO Box 501248
Indianapolis, IN 46250-6248

Michon, Mishka, CEO
Coalition for Pulmonary Fibrosis
    [17137]
10866 W Washington Blvd., No. 343
Culver City, CA 90232
Toll Free: 888-222-8541

Mickle, Andrea, CEO, President
Minority Access, Inc. [8348]
5214 Baltimore Ave.
Hyattsville, MD 20781
Ph: (301)779-7100
Fax: (301)779-9812

Middlebrook, Lucas, VP
American Maritime Safety [2235]
445 Hamilton Ave., Ste. 1204
White Plains, NY 10601-1833
Ph: (914)997-2916
Fax: (914)997-6959

Middleton, Lydia, Exec. Dir.
American Academy of Orthotists and
    Prosthetists [16492]
1331 H St. NW, Ste. 501
Washington, DC 20005
Ph: (202)380-3663
Fax: (202)380-3447

Midness, Lydia Tooker, President
AACC International [6175]
3340 Pilot Knob Rd.
Saint Paul, MN 55121-2055
Ph: (651)454-7250
Fax: (651)454-0766

Midura, Rev. John E., President
The National Spiritual Alliance
    [20509]
2 Montague Ave.
Lake Pleasant, MA 01347
Ph: (413)367-0138

Miel, Jennifer, Exec. Dir.
U.S.-Bahrain Business Council
    [1997]
1615 H St. NW
Washington, DC 20062
Fax: (202)463-3114

Miele, Joe, President
Committee to Abolish Sport Hunting
    [10604]
PO Box 13815
Las Cruces, NM 88013
Ph: (575)640-7372

Miers, Hariiet E., Chairman
Center for American and
    International Law [5420]
5201 Democracy Dr.
Plano, TX 75024
Ph: (972)244-3400
Toll Free: 800-409-1090
Fax: (972)244-3401

Mies, Robert, Exec. Dir., Founder
Organization for Bat Conservation
    [4861]
Cranbrook Institute of Science
39221 Woodward Ave.
Bloomfield Hills, MI 48303
Ph: (248)645-3232

Mighetto, Lisa, Exec. Dir.
American Society for Environmental
    History [7872]
Interdisciplinary Arts & Sciences
    Program
University of Washington
1900 Commerce St.
Tacoma, WA 98402

Miguel, Melinda M., Director
Association of Inspectors General
    [5265]
524 W 59th St., 3400 N
New York, NY 10019
Ph: (212)237-8001
Fax: (718)732-2480

Mihailidis, Alex, Officer
Rehabilitation Engineering and As-
    sistive Technology Society of North
    America [11634]
1700 N Moore St., Ste. 1540
Arlington, VA 22209-1903
Ph: (703)524-6686
Fax: (703)524-6630

Mihalic, Tricia, Director
Pull-thru Network [14796]
c/o Lori Parker, Executive Director
1705 Wintergreen Pky.
Normal, IL 61761-5642

Mikel, Rebecca, President
National Finch and Softbill Society
    [21544]
c/o Sara Roberts, Treasurer
720 Live Oak Ln.
Pinole, CA 94564

Mikhail, Mary, MPH, Exec. Dir.
Global Health through Education,
    Training and Service [15456]
8 N Main St., Ste. 404

Attleboro, MA 02703

Miki, Sherry, Inst.
Japan Karate-Do Organization
    [22999]
3545 Midway Dr.
San Diego, CA 92110-4922
Ph: (858)414-7361

Mikita, Stan, Founder
American Hearing Impaired Hockey
    Association [22773]
c/o Jeff Sauer, Head Coach
6623 Columbus Dr.
Middleton, WI 53562

Mikitka, Michael J., CEO
Warehousing Education and
    Research Council [3442]
1100 Jorie Blvd., Ste. 170
Oak Brook, IL 60523-4413
Ph: (630)990-0001
Fax: (630)990-0256

Mikitzel, Loretta, President
Potato Association of America [4248]
c/o Lori Wing, Administrator
5719 Crossland Hall, Rm. 220
University of Maine
Orono, ME 04469-5719
Ph: (207)581-3042
Fax: (207)581-3015

Mikkelsen, Robert, VP
Soil and Plant Analysis Council
    [7193]
347 N Shores Cir.
Windsor, CO 80550
Ph: (970)686-5702
    (352)392-1951

Miklus, John A., President
American Institute of Marine
    Underwriters [1830]
14 Wall St., Ste. 820
New York, NY 10005-2101
Ph: (212)233-0550
Fax: (212)227-5102

Mikoski, Edward F., Jr., VP
The Society of Standards Profes-
    sionals [7237]
1950 Lafayette Rd., Ste. 200
Portsmouth, NH 03801
Ph: (603)926-0750
Fax: (603)610-7101

Mikosz, David, Chairman
National Show Horse Registry
    [4387]
PO Box 862
Lewisburg, OH 45338
Ph: (937)962-4336
Fax: (937)962-4332

Mikucki, Chester, Founder
Polonus Philatelic Society [22354]
PO Box 60438
Rossford, OH 43460-0438

Milanchus, Robert, Dir. of Bus. Dev.
Society of Nuclear Medicine and
    Molecular Imaging [16077]
1850 Samuel Morse Dr.
Reston, VA 20190
Ph: (703)708-9000
Fax: (703)708-9015

Milanese, Jody, VP of Government
    Rel.
Small Business Exporters Associa-
    tion of the United States [1993]
1156 15th St. NW, Ste. 1100
Washington, DC 20005
Ph: (202)552-2903
    (202)552-2904
Toll Free: 800-345-6728

Milani, Leila, JD, Founder
Iran Rooyan [19255]
6402 Arlington Blvd., Ste. 300

Falls Church, VA 22042
Ph: (571)282-6194

Milchen, Jeff, Founder
Reclaim Democracy! [18106]
222 S Black Ave.
Bozeman, MT 59715
Ph: (406)582-1224

Milcinovic, David, VP
Polish National Alliance of the United
    States of North America [19610]
6100 N Cicero Ave.
Chicago, IL 60646
Ph: (773)286-0500
Toll Free: 800-621-3723

Milcinovic, David, VP
Union of Poles in America [19617]
9999 Granger Rd.
Garfield Heights, OH 44125
Ph: (216)478-0120
Fax: (216)478-0122

Milczarek, John, President,
    Treasurer
The Bridge Line Historical Society
    [22407]
2476 Whitehall Ct.
Schenectady, NY 12309

Miles, Carolyn S., President, CEO
Save the Children US [11147]
501 Kings Hwy. E, Ste. 400
Fairfield, CT 06825
Ph: (203)221-4000
Toll Free: 800-728-3843

Miles, Mrs. Jack, Founder
Koinonia Foundation [20065]
6037 Franconia Rd.
Alexandria, VA 22310
Ph: (703)971-1991

Miles, Kylie, Founder, CEO
Kya's Krusade [14553]
947 E Johnstown Rd., Ste. 143
Gahanna, OH 43230
Ph: (614)750-2198
Fax: (614)478-3223

Miles, Mrs. Monika P., CPA, Contact
Accounting and Financial Women's
    Alliance [2]
2365 Harrodsburg Rd., Ste. A325
Lexington, KY 40504
Ph: (859)219-3532
Toll Free: 800-326-2163
Fax: (859)219-3577

Miles, Paul, President
Wheat Ridge Ministries [20321]
1 Pierce Pl., Ste. 250E
Itasca, IL 60143-2634
Ph: (630)766-9066
Toll Free: 800-762-6748
Fax: (630)766-9622

Miles, Robert G., Director
International Social Service - United
    States of America Branch, Inc.
    [13110]
22 Light St., Ste. 200
Baltimore, MD 21202
Ph: (443)451-1200
Fax: (443)451-1220

Miles, Tom, Director
Model T Ford Club of America
    [21438]
119 W Main St.
Centerville, IN 47330
Ph: (765)855-5248
Fax: (765)855-3428

Milford, Lewis, Founder, President
Clean Energy Group [6468]
50 State St., Ste. 1

Montpelier, VT 05602
Ph: (802)223-2554
Fax: (802)223-4967

Milford, Lewis, Founder
Clean Energy States Alliance **[6469]**
50 State St., Ste. 1
Montpelier, VT 05602
Ph: (802)223-2554
Fax: (802)223-4967

Milgram, Donna, Exec. Dir.
Institute for Women in Trades,
Technology and Science **[3493]**
1150 Ballena Blvd., Ste. 102
Alameda, CA 94501-3682
Ph: (510)749-0200
Fax: (510)749-0500

Militano, Tony, President
Association of Printing and Data
Solutions Professionals **[1528]**
PO Box 13347
Chicago, IL 60613
Ph: (708)218-7755
(708)571-4685
Toll Free: 800-325-5165
Fax: (708)571-4731

Militello, Betsy King, Exec. Dir.
National Alliance for Musical Theatre
[9965]
520 8th Ave., Ste. 301
New York, NY 10018
Ph: (212)714-6668
Fax: (212)714-0469

Millar, Nancy, Director
United with Hope **[11177]**
PO Box 1086
Palmetto, GA 30268

Millar, Robert, President
International Neuroendocrine
Federation **[16051]**
c/o William Armstrong, Treasurer
University of Tennessee Health Sci-
ence Ctr.
855 Monroe Ave.
Memphis, TN 38117
Ph: (901)448-5966
Fax: (901)448-4685

Millard, Bob, Gen. Mgr.
International Show Car Association
[21405]
1092 Centre Rd.
Auburn Hills, MI 48326
Ph: (248)371-1600
(586)703-2381

Miller, Beverly, President
United Scenic Artists Local USA 829
[23501]
29 W 38th St., 15th Fl.
New York, NY 10018
Ph: (212)581-0300
Toll Free: 877-728-5635
Fax: (212)977-2011

Miller, Bill, Exec. Dir.
North American Hunting Club
[22963]
Ph: (952)936-9333
Toll Free: 888-850-8202
Fax: (952)936-9755

Miller, Bradley S., President
Humane Farming Association
[10642]
PO Box 3577
San Rafael, CA 94912
Ph: (415)485-1495
Fax: (415)485-0106

Miller, Brian, Mgr.
American Numismatic Association
[22256]

818 N Cascade Ave.
Colorado Springs, CO 80903-3208
Toll Free: 800-367-9723
Fax: (719)634-4085

Miller, Brian, Exec. Dir.
Nonprofit VOTE **[12393]**
2464 Massachusetts Ave., Ste. 210
Cambridge, MA 02140
Ph: (617)357-8683

Miller, Carolyn, Director, Founder
Selective Mutism Foundation
[15806]
c/o Sue Newman
PO Box 25972
Tamarac, FL 33320

Miller, Constance, MA, Founder,
Author
Brain Injury Resource Center
[17085]
PO Box 84151
Seattle, WA 98124-5451
Ph: (206)621-8558

Miller, Dabney, Assoc. Dir.
Women's Law Project **[18240]**
125 S 9th St., Ste. 300
Philadelphia, PA 19107
Ph: (215)928-9801

Miller, David, PhD, President
American Association of Suicidology
[13191]
5221 Wisconsin Ave. NW
Washington, DC 20015
Ph: (202)237-2280
Fax: (202)237-2282

Miller, David E., Chairman, CEO
American Cancer Assistance
[13881]
5865 Ridgeway Center Pkwy., Ste.
300
Memphis, TN 38120-4014
Toll Free: 877-767-9948

Miller, David K., President
USS LSM-LSMR Association
[21070]
c/o David K. Miller, President
21850 Vista Dr.
Saegertown, PA 16433
Ph: (814)763-3090
(727)360-5718

Miller, Debbie, Director
American College of Forensic
Psychiatry **[5236]**
PO Box 130458
Carlsbad, CA 92013-0458
Ph: (760)929-9777
Fax: (760)929-9803

Miller, Debbie, Exec. Dir.
American College of Forensic
Psychology **[16860]**
PO Box 130458
Carlsbad, CA 92013-0458
Ph: (760)929-9777
Fax: (760)929-9803

Miller, Debbie, Bd. Member
Associates of the American Foreign
Service Worldwide **[23427]**
4001 N 9th St., Ste. 214
Arlington, VA 22203
Ph: (703)820-5420
Fax: (703)820-5421

Miller, Debra, President, CEO
CureDuchenne **[14819]**
1400 Quail St., Ste. 110
Newport Beach, CA 92660
Ph: (949)872-2552

Miller, Debra, VP
Wildlife Disease Association **[4912]**
PO Box 7065

Lawrence, KS 66044-7065
Ph: (785)865-9403
Toll Free: 800-627-0326
Fax: (785)843-6153

Miller, Ed, Cmte. Mgmt. Ofc.
American Chianina Association
[3690]
1708 N Prairie View Rd.
Platte City, MO 64079
Ph: (816)431-2808
Fax: (816)431-5381

Miller, Elise, MEd, Director
Collaborative on Health and the
Environment **[14714]**
c/o Commonweal
PO Box 316
Bolinas, CA 94924
Ph: (415)868-0970

Miller, Felisia, Office Mgr.
National Society Colonial Dames
XVII Century **[20754]**
1300 New Hampshire Ave. NW
Washington, DC 20036-1502
Ph: (202)293-1700

Miller, Fred, Managing Dir.
Home Improvement Research
Institute **[825]**
10117 Princess Palm Ave., Ste. 575
Tampa, FL 33610
Ph: (813)627-6750

Miller, Gabrielle E., EdD, Exec. Dir.
Raising a Reader **[8488]**
330 Twin Dolphin Dr., Ste. 147
Redwood City, CA 94065-1455
Ph: (650)489-0550
Fax: (650)489-0551

Miller, Greg, Director
Northern Nut Growers Association
[4512]
c/o Jeanne Romero-Severson,
Treasurer
PO Box 489
Notre Dame, IN 46556
Fax: (203)974-8502

Miller, Gregory A., President
American Hiking Society **[23320]**
1422 Fenwick Ln.
Silver Spring, MD 20910
Ph: (301)565-6704
Toll Free: 800-972-8608
Fax: (301)565-6714

Miller, Gregory, President
Paso Fino Horse Association **[4400]**
4047 Iron Works Pky., Ste. 1
Lexington, KY 40511
Ph: (859)825-6000
Fax: (859)258-2125

Miller, Hope, RN, President
Caribbean Health Outreach, Inc.
[15441]
PO Box 1092
Inglewood, CA 90308
Ph: (323)403-3579
Fax: (323)291-7806

Miller, Jeanne E., Dir. of Info. Svcs.,
Pub. Dir.
University of Michigan I Center for
the Education of Women **[8757]**
330 E Liberty St.
Ann Arbor, MI 48104-2274
Ph: (734)764-6005
(734)764-6360
Fax: (734)998-6203

Miller, Jeff, Secretary
CTIA - The Wireless Association
[3225]
1400 16th St. NW, Ste. 600

Washington, DC 20036-2225
Ph: (202)785-0081

Miller, Jeff, President, Exec. Dir.
Treated Wood Council **[594]**
1101 K St. NW, Ste. 700
Washington, DC 20005
Ph: (202)641-5427
Fax: (202)463-2059

Miller, Jennifer, PhD, President,
CEO, Founder
Bioethics International **[13815]**
733 3rd Ave., 15th Fl.
New York, NY 10017
Ph: (646)549-0233

Miller, Dr. Jerome G., Founder
National Center on Institutions and
Alternatives, Inc. **[11537]**
7205 Rutherford Rd.
Baltimore, MD 21244
Ph: (443)780-1300
Fax: (410)597-9656

Miller, Jim, Secretary, Treasurer
International Union of Industrial and
Independent Workers **[23534]**
5250 Highway 78, Ste. 750-227
Sachse, TX 75048

Miller, Jim, Treasurer
Society of Army Physician Assistants
[16725]
PO Box 4068
Waynesville, MO 65583-4068
Ph: (573)528-2307
Fax: (888)711-8543

Miller, Joan M., Exec. Dir.
Association for Healthcare Volunteer
Resource Professionals **[13283]**
155 N Wacker Dr., Ste. 400
Chicago, IL 60606-1725
Ph: (312)422-3939
Fax: (312)278-0884

Miller, Joel E., CEO, Exec. Dir.
American Mental Health Counselors
Association **[15758]**
675 N Washington, Ste. 470
Alexandria, VA 22314
Ph: (703)548-6002
Toll Free: 800-326-2642

Miller, John, Chairman
Canine Companions for
Independence **[11577]**
2965 Dutton Ave.
Santa Rosa, CA 95407
Ph: (707)577-1700
Toll Free: 866-224-3647

Miller, Rev. John Henry, Founder
Loving Hands for the Needy, Inc.
[11073]
LHFN, Unit 2163
3170 Airmans Dr.
Fort Pierce, FL 34946
Ph: (561)305-5268

Miller, John, Chief Executive Officer
Minneapolis Grain Exchange **[3779]**
400 S 4th St.
Minneapolis, MN 55415
Ph: (612)321-7101
Toll Free: 800-827-4746

Miller, John, V. Chmn. of the Bd.
Northwestern Lumber Association
[1414]
5905 Golden Valley Rd., No. 110
Minneapolis, MN 55422
Ph: (763)544-6822
Toll Free: 888-544-6822
Fax: (763)595-4060

Miller, John, Exec. Dir., Founder
One Vision International **[11419]**
2915 Alcoa Hwy.

Knoxville, TN 37920
Ph: (865)579-3353

Miller, John, President, CEO
Tourette Association of America
[15994]
42-40 Bell Blvd., Ste. 205
Bayside, NY 11361
Ph: (718)224-2999
Fax: (718)279-9596

Miller, Jonathan, President, CEO
Sports Financial Advisors Associa-
tion [1268]
10645 N Tatum Blvd., Ste. 200-608
Phoenix, AZ 85028
Ph: (602)820-2220
Fax: (602)297-6608

Miller, Keith, Chairman
Coalition of Franchisee Associations,
Inc. [1457]
1750 K St. NW, Ste. 200
Washington, DC 20006
Ph: (202)416-0277
Fax: (202)416-0269

Miller, Ken, VP
National Association of State
Treasurers [5710]
2760 Research Park Dr.
Lexington, KY 40511-8482

Miller, Kevin, CEO, President
United States Auto Club [22530]
4910 W 16th St.
Speedway, IN 46224-5703
Ph: (317)247-5151
Fax: (317)248-5584

Miller, Kimerly, Editor
American Council on Immersion
Education [8641]
University of Minnesota
Center for Advanced Research on
Language Acquisition
140 University International Ctr.
331 17th Ave. SE
Minneapolis, MN 55414

Miller, Linda, Coord.
National Association of
Congregational Christian Churches
[20035]
8473 S Howell Ave.
Oak Creek, WI 53154
Ph: (414)764-1620
Toll Free: 800-262-1620
Fax: (414)764-0319

Miller, Lydia, President
International Oleander Society
[22107]
PO Box 3431
Galveston, TX 77552

Miller, Lynn, President
International Wildlife Rehabilitation
Council [4834]
PO Box 3197
Eugene, OR 97403
Toll Free: 866-871-1869
Fax: (408)876-6153

Miller, Marcel, President
National Quilting Association [21775]
PO Box 12190
Columbus, OH 43212-0190
Ph: (614)488-8520
Fax: (614)488-8521

Miller, Mark, Founder
American Association for Lost
Children [12360]
PO Box 386
Youngstown, PA 15696
Ph: (724)537-6970
Toll Free: 800-375-5683
Fax: (724)537-6971

Miller, Mark F., Mem.
Building Commissioning Association
[505]
1600 NW Compton Dr., Ste. 200
Beaverton, OR 97006
Ph: (503)747-2903
Toll Free: 877-666-2292

Miller, Matt, CEO, President
Association of Independent Com-
mercial Producers [89]
3 W 18th St., 5th Fl.
New York, NY 10011
Ph: (212)929-3000
Fax: (212)929-3359

Miller, Merle, Contact
Sons and Daughters of Oregon
Pioneers [21088]
PO Box 6685
Portland, OR 97228

Miller, Michael H., President
Society of Indiana Pioneers [21087]
140 N Senate Ave.
Indianapolis, IN 46204-2207
Ph: (317)233-6588

Miller, Michelle, Exec. VP
Pressure Sensitive Tape Council
[61]
1 Parkview Plz., Ste. 800
Oakbrook Terrace, IL 60181
Ph: (630)544-5048
Fax: (630)544-5055

Miller, Mike, Chairman
African Love Bird Society [21531]
3831 Whitehall
Dallas, TX 75229-2757

Miller, Mike, Director
National Association of Casino Party
Operators [1149]
PO Box 5626
South San Francisco, CA 94083-
5626
Toll Free: 888-922-0777

Miller, Mike, Exec. Dir.
Organize Training Center [11473]
442 Vicksburg St.
San Francisco, CA 94114-3831
Ph: (415)648-6894

Miller, Mike, Secretary, Treasurer
U.S. Wheat Associates [3774]
3103 10th St. N, Ste. 300
Arlington, VA 22201
Ph: (202)463-0999
Fax: (703)524-4399

Miller, Nancy, President
Eastern Museum of Motor Racing
[21373]
100 Baltimore Rd.
York Springs, PA 17372
Ph: (717)528-8279

Miller, Dr. Pamela J., President,
Chmn. of the Bd.
American Optometric Society
[16424]
801 Volvo Pkwy., Ste. 133
Chesapeake, VA 23320
Ph: (805)768-4267
Fax: (805)456-3005

Miller, Paul, Founder, Exec. Dir.
African Kids In Need [10838]
Box 140
137 N Larchmont Blvd.
Los Angeles, CA 90020

Miller, Paul Chamness, President
The International Society for
Language Studies, Inc. [9654]
1968 S Coast Hwy., No. 142

Laguna Beach, CA 92651-3681

Miller, Rabbi Bennett, Chairman
AZRA/World Union for Progressive
Judaism North America [20234]
633 3rd Ave., 7th Fl.
New York, NY 10017-6778
Ph: (212)650-4280
Fax: (212)650-4289

Miller, Richard Alan, Consultant
Organization for the Advancement of
Knowledge [3770]
1212 SW 5th St.
Grants Pass, OR 97526-6104
Ph: (541)476-5588
Fax: (541)476-1823

Miller, Richard B., Secretary
Transportation Alternatives [7351]
111 John St., Ste. 260
New York, NY 10038
Ph: (212)629-8080
  (648)873-6008
Fax: (212)629-8334

Miller, Richard F., Director
MG Drivers Club of North America
[21431]
18 George's Pl.
Clinton, NJ 08809-1334
Ph: (908)713-6251
Fax: (908)713-6251

Miller, Rick, President, Founder
Kids at Hope [11245]
2400 W Dunlap Ave., Ste. 135
Phoenix, AZ 85021-2885
Ph: (602)674-0026
Toll Free: 866-275-HOPE
Fax: (602)674-0034

Miller, Rick, President
Missions Door [19733]
2530 Washington St.
Denver, CO 80205-3142
Ph: (303)308-1818
Fax: (303)295-9090

Miller, Robert, Dir. (Actg.)
Association for X and Y Chromo-
some Variations [17336]
PO Box 861
Mendenhall, PA 19357
Toll Free: 888-999-9428

Miller, Robert E., President, CEO
Our Family Orphan Communities,
Inc. [11259]
PO Box 158
Conifer, CO 80433-0158
Ph: (303)514-6858
Fax: (435)228-2298

Miller, Robert H., Exec. Dir.
American Board of Otolaryngology
[16532]
5615 Kirby Dr., Ste. 600
Houston, TX 77005
Ph: (713)850-0399
Fax: (713)850-1104

Miller, Robert, Treasurer
National Society of Professional
Surveyors [7252]
5119 Pegasus Ct., Ste. Q
Frederick, MD 21704
Ph: (240)439-4615
Fax: (240)439-4952

Miller, Rose, Treasurer
Administrative Personnel Association
of the Presbyterian Church (U.S.
A.) [20015]
c/o Rose Miller, Treasurer
First Presbyterian Church
PO Box 765
Lawrenceville, GA 30046
Ph: (770)963-9498

Miller, Sally A., President
American Phytopathological Society
[6133]
3340 Pilot Knob Rd.
Saint Paul, MN 55121
Ph: (651)454-7250
Fax: (651)454-0766

Miller, Sara E., President
Society for Ultrastructural Pathology
[16595]
c/o Guillermo A. Herrera MD.,
Treasurer
1501 Kings Hwy.
Shreveport, LA 71103
Ph: (318)675-4557
Fax: (318)675-4541

Miller, Scott, President
Society for Electro-Acoustic Music in
the United States [10006]

Miller, Shanon, Chairman
Preservation Action [9427]
1307 New Hampshire Ave. NW, 3rd
Fl.
Washington, DC 20036-1531
Ph: (202)463-0970
Fax: (202)463-1299

Miller, Shawn, Contact
Milestone Car Society [21433]
626 N Park Ave.
Indianapolis, IN 46204
Ph: (317)636-9900

Miller, Shirley, RSCJ, Director
Society of the Sacred Heart, United
States-Canada [19911]
4120 Forest Park Ave.
Saint Louis, MO 63108
Ph: (314)652-1500
Fax: (314)534-6800

Miller, Stephen, Deputy
American Society for Biochemistry
and Molecular Biology [6050]
11200 Rockville Pke., Ste. 302
Rockville, MD 20852-3110
Ph: (240)283-6600
Fax: (301)881-2080

Miller, Stephen, Treasurer
National Organization of Test,
Research, and Training Reactors
[6930]
Oak Ridge National Laboratory
1 Bethel Valley Rd.
Oak Ridge, TN 37831-6249
Ph: (765)496-3573

Miller, Steve, Chairman
Pugwash Conferences on Science
and World Affairs [18003]
Washington Office
1211 Connecticut Ave. NW, Ste. 800
Washington, DC 20036
Ph: (202)478-3440
Fax: (202)238-9604

Miller, Susan, CEO, President
Alliance for Telecommunications
Industry Solutions [3215]
1200 G St. NW, Ste. 500
Washington, DC 20005
Ph: (202)628-6380

Miller, Terry L., Director
National Pesticide Information
Center [13225]
c/o Oregon State University
310 Weniger Hall
Corvallis, OR 97331-6502
Toll Free: 800-858-7378

Miller, Terry, Exec. Dir.
Tin Can Sailors-The National Association of Destroyer Veterans
[21062]

PO Box 100
Somerset, MA 02726-0100
Ph: (508)677-0515
Toll Free: 800-223-5535
Fax: (508)676-9740

Miller, Thomas, President, CEO
Geekcorps [3209]
1900 M St. NW, Ste. 500
Washington, DC 20036
Ph: (202)589-2600
Fax: (202)326-0289

Miller, Thomas J., President, CEO
International Executive Service
   Corps. [641]
1900 M St. NW, Ste. 500
Washington, DC 20036
Ph: (202)589-2600
Fax: (202)326-0289

Miller, Will, President
Wallace Foundation [11740]
5 Penn Plz., 7th Fl.
New York, NY 10001
Ph: (212)251-9700
Fax: (212)679-6990

Miller, William, Sr. VP of Operations
Specialty Equipment Market As-
   sociation [329]
1575 S Valley Vista Dr.
Diamond Bar, CA 91765-0910
Ph: (909)610-2030
Fax: (909)860-0184

Millerchip, EA, CFP, Jean, President
National Association of Tax
   Consultants [5799]
321 W 13th Ave.
Eugene, OR 97401

Miller-Cochran, Susan, President
Council of Writing Program
   Administrators [8763]
c/o Michael McCamley, Secretary
212 Memorial Hall
University of Delaware
Newark, DE 19716

Millet, Bev, Director
Horse Protection League [4359]
17999 W 60th Ave.
Arvada, CO 80403
Ph: (303)216-0141

Millett, David P., MD, Exec. VP
Civil Aviation Medical Association
   [13509]
PO Box 2382
Peachtree City, GA 30269-2382
Ph: (770)487-0100
Fax: (770)487-0080

Milley, Frankie, Exec. Dir., Founder
Meningitis Angels [14594]
PO Box 448
Porter, TX 77365-0448
Ph: (281)572-1998

Millhone, Alan, President
American Checker Federation
   [22044]
34490 Ridge Rd., Apt. 115
Willoughby, OH 44094

Milligan, Michelle, President
Society of Government Meeting
   Professionals [2338]
PO Box 321025
Alexandria, VA 22320-5125
Ph: (703)549-0892
Fax: (703)549-0708

Milligan, Robert J., Mgr., Member
   Svcs.
Post Mark Collectors Club [22355]
c/o Andy Mitchell

PO Box 265
Poquonock, CT 06064

Milliken, William E., Founder, V. Ch.
Communities In Schools [7818]
2345 Crystal Dr., Ste. 700
Arlington, VA 22202
Ph: (703)519-8999
Toll Free: 800-247-4543

Million, Holly, Exec. Dir.
BioBricks Foundation [6119]
955 Massachusetts Ave., Ste. 330
Cambridge, MA 02139

Milliron, Randa, Contact
Pacific Rocket Society [5870]
PO Box 662
Mojave, CA 93502-0662
Ph: (661)824-1662

Millner, Dave, President
International Radio Controlled
   Helicopter Association [22200]
6104 Hunter Valley Rd.
Ooltewah, TN 37363
Ph: (765)287-1256
Toll Free: 800-435-9262

Mills, David, President
Society of the 3rd Infantry Division
   [21030]
c/o Kathleen M. Daddato, Membership Chairperson
22511 N River Rd.
Alva, FL 33920-3358
Ph: (239)728-2475

Mills, David W., Chairman
NAACP Legal Defense and
   Educational Fund [17912]
40 Rector St., 5th Fl.
New York, NY 10006
Ph: (212)965-2200

Mills, Kaye P., VP
Burleson Family Association [20791]
14343 Markham Glen
San Antonio, TX 78247

Mills, Michael, Exec. Dir., Founder
Drums No Guns [18250]
193 Lamson St.
West Haven, CT 06516
Ph: (203)675-4827
   (203)931-8750

Mills, Michael, Director
Maremma Sheepdog Club of
   America [21912]
c/o, Kristi Zwicker, Secretary
31606 NE 40th Ave.
La Center, WA 98629
Ph: (360)430-3430

Mills, Nancy, Exec. Dir.
Working for America Institute
   [11791]
815 16th St. NW
Washington, DC 20005
Ph: (202)509-3717

Mills, Mr. Paul, Founder, President
American Kenpo Karate International
   [22982]
PO Box 768
Evanston, WY 82931-0768
Ph: (307)789-4124

Mills, Penny S., MBA, CEO, Exec.
   VP
American Society of Addiction
   Medicine [17307]
Upper Arcade, Ste. 101
4601 N Park Ave.
Chevy Chase, MD 20815-4520
Ph: (301)656-3920
Fax: (301)656-3815

Mills, Ta'ice, Coord.
American Association of Anatomists
   [13687]
9650 Rockville Pke.
Bethesda, MD 20814-3999
Ph: (301)634-7910
Fax: (301)634-7965

Millstone, David, President
Country Dance and Song Society
   [9247]
116 Pleasant St., Ste. 345
Easthampton, MA 01027-2759
Ph: (413)203-5467
Fax: (413)203-5471

Millward, Susan, Exec. Dir.
Animal Welfare Institute [10583]
900 Pennsylvania Ave. SE
Washington, DC 20003-2140
Ph: (202)337-2332
Fax: (202)446-2131

Milne, Amy, Exec. Dir.
Quilt Alliance [21780]
67 Broadway St., Ste. 200
Asheville, NC 28801
Ph: (828)251-7073
Fax: (828)251-7073

Milne, Peter, President
Volunteer Committees of Art
   Museums of Canada and the
   United States [9842]
5139 Thorncroft Ct.
Royal Oak, MI 48073

Milota, Michele, Exec. Dir.
XP Family Support Group [14869]
8495 Folsom Blvd., No. 1
Sacramento, CA 95826
Ph: (916)628-3814
   (916)379-0741

Milstead, Keith, President
International Public Debate Associa-
   tion [8481]
c/o Joe Ganakos, Chairman of the
   Board
Lee College
200 Lee Dr.
Baytown, TX 77520

Milstein, Donna, VP
Craft Retailers Association for
   Tomorrow [21753]
11238 Home Place Ln.
Charlotte, NC 28227
Ph: (980)938-4574

Milstein, Greg, Exec. Dir.
National Circus Project [9164]
56 Lion Ln.
Westbury, NY 11590
Ph: (516)334-2123
Fax: (516)334-2249

Milstein, Howard P., Chairman
American Skin Association [14484]
6 E 43rd St., 28th Fl.
New York, NY 10017-4605
Ph: (212)889-4858
Toll Free: 800-499-SKIN
Fax: (212)889-4959

Milton, John P., Founder, President
Threshold, Inc. [4105]
PO Box 152
Moab, UT 84532
Ph: (435)259-0816

Milton, Marina, Treasurer
Asian American Government Execu-
   tives Network [5260]
1001 Connecticut Ave. NW, Ste. 320
Washington, DC 20036
Ph: (202)930-2024
Fax: (202)296-9236

Milum, Vince, Chairman
Cold War Veterans Association
   [21119]
PO Box 13042
Overland Park, KS 66282-3042

Min, James K., MD, President
Society of Cardiovascular Computed
   Tomography [17064]
415 Church St. NE, Ste. 204
Vienna, VA 22180-4751
Ph: (703)766-1706
Toll Free: 800-876-4195
Fax: (888)849-1542

Mincey, Christopher, President
Turbine Inlet Cooling Association
   [1130]
427 Prairie Knoll Dr., Ste. 102
Naperville, IL 60565
Ph: (630)357-3960
Fax: (630)357-1004

Minde, Jeffrey H., President
The National Special Needs
   Network, Inc. [14556]
6424 Overland Dr.
Delray Beach, FL 33484
Ph: (561)447-4152

Mineer, Amanda L., Director,
   Treasurer
Give Clean Water [13324]
PO Box 720953
San Diego, CA 92172
Toll Free: 888-429-6741
Fax: (775)923-7897

Miner, Dave, Director
Vintage Chevrolet Club of America
   [21513]
PO Box 609
Lemont, IL 60439-0609
Ph: (708)455-8222

Mingtang, Xu, Contact
North American ZY Qigong Associa-
   tion [13646]
Duvall, WA

Minkowitz, Lior Levy, Esq.,
   President, Founder
Bringing U Maternal Paternal Suc-
   cess [14754]
7744 Peters Rd., Ste. 305
Plantation, FL 33324
Ph: (954)472-2867

Minnich, Brian, Exec. VP
Freedom Foundation [5729]
PO Box 552
Olympia, WA 98507
Ph: (360)956-3482
Fax: (360)352-1874

Minnis, Jerry, Contact
Clan Menzies Society - North
   American Branch [20831]
c/o Jerry Minnis
PO Box 397
Vernon, AZ 85940-0397
Ph: (928)537-1902

Minnix, William L., Jr., Officer
Generations United [13054]
25 E St. NW, 3rd Fl.
Washington, DC 20001
Ph: (202)289-3979

Minor, Ernie, President
Food Recovery Network [11853]
4321 Hartwick Rd., Ste. 320
College Park, MD 20740

Minorini, Paul A., President, CEO
Boys Hope Girls Hope [13432]
12120 Bridgeton Square Dr.
Bridgeton, MO 63044
Ph: (314)298-1250
Toll Free: 877-878-HOPE
Fax: (314)298-1251

Minsky, Bruce D., Chairman
American Society for Radiation
  Oncology **[17050]**
251 18th St. S, 8th Fl.
Arlington, VA 22202
Ph: (703)502-1550
Toll Free: 800-962-7876
Fax: (703)502-7852

Minsky, Maura, Founder, Exec. Dir.
Scenarios U.S.A. **[19277]**
80 Hanson Pl., Ste. 305
Brooklyn, NY 11217
Ph: (718)230-5125
Toll Free: 866-414-1044
Fax: (718)230-4381

Mintcheva, Svetlana, Dir. of
  Programs
National Coalition Against Censor-
  ship **[17837]**
19 Fulton St., Ste. 407
New York, NY 10038
Ph: (212)807-6222
Fax: (212)807-6245

Minter, Rebecca M., President
Society of University Surgeons
  [17408]
11300 W Olympic Blvd., Ste. 600
Los Angeles, CA 90064
Ph: (310)986-6442
Fax: (310)437-0585

Minton, Jack, CEO, Founder
Hope Force International **[11669]**
7065 Moores Ln., Ste. 200
Brentwood, TN 37027
Ph: (615)371-1271
Fax: (615)371-1261

Minton, Melinda, Founder, Exec. Dir.
The Spa Association **[2979]**
1001 E Harmony Rd., Ste. A 167
Fort Collins, CO 80525
Ph: (970)682-6045

Mintz, Eliyohu, Director
JOY for Our Youth **[11053]**
1805 Swarthmore Ave.
Lakewood, NJ 08701
Toll Free: 866-GIV-EJOY

Mintz, Jerry, Director, Founder
Alternative Education Resource
  Organization **[7735]**
417 Roslyn Rd.
Roslyn Heights, NY 11577
Ph: (516)621-2195
Toll Free: 800-769-4171
Fax: (516)625-3257

Mintzer, Janet L., CEO, President
Pearl S. Buck International **[10877]**
520 Dublin Rd.
Perkasie, PA 18944
Ph: (215)249-0100
Fax: (215)249-9657

Minyard, Gary, President
American Alliance for Theatre and
  Education **[10235]**
4908 Auburn Ave.
Bethesda, MD 20814
Ph: (301)200-1944
Fax: (301)280-1682

Miranda, Kathy, Exec. Dir.
American Society for Histocompat-
  ibility and Immunogenetics **[15372]**
1120 Route 73, Ste. 200
Mount Laurel, NJ 08054
Fax: (856)439-0500

Mirando, Tony, MS, Exec. Dir.
National Accrediting Commission of
  Career Arts and Sciences **[7412]**
4401 Ford Ave., Ste. 1300

Alexandria, VA 22302-1432
Ph: (703)600-7600
Fax: (703)379-2200

Mirau, Tammy, Admin. Asst.
National Association of Church Busi-
  ness Administration **[20562]**
100 N Central Expy., Ste. 914
Richardson, TX 75080-5326
Ph: (972)699-7555
Toll Free: 800-898-8085
Fax: (972)699-7617

Mirzayantz, Nicolas, V. Chmn. of the
  Exec. Committee
Research Institute for Fragrance
  Materials **[1453]**
50 Tice Blvd.
Woodcliff Lake, NJ 07677
Ph: (201)689-8089

Misa, Thomas J., PhD, Director
Charles Babbage Institute for the
  History of Information Technology
  [9471]
211 Andersen Library
222 21st Ave. S
Minneapolis, MN 55455
Ph: (612)624-5050
Fax: (612)625-8054

Mische, Gerald F., President
Global Education Associates **[18544]**
475 Riverside Dr., Ste. 1848
New York, NY 10115-0033
Ph: (212)870-3290
Fax: (212)870-2729

Mischel, Emmebeth, Founder,
  Treasurer
Ethiopia's Tomorrow **[10966]**
28 Hoffman St.
Maplewood, NJ 07040
Ph: (973)951-8035
   (763)350-1115

Mishell, Dan, Chairman
Travel and Tourism Research As-
  sociation **[3402]**
5300 Lakewood Rd.
Whitehall, MI 49461-9626
Ph: (248)708-8872
Fax: (248)814-7150

Mishev, Dina, Founder
Never Too Weak to Wander **[15978]**
PO Box 4424
Jackson, WY 83001

Mishra, Charadutt, Exec. Dir.
Snow Leopard Network **[4888]**
4649 Sunnyside Ave. N
Seattle, WA 98103
Ph: (206)632-2421

Mishra, Charadutt, Exec. Dir.
Snow Leopard Trust **[4889]**
4649 Sunnyside Ave. N, Ste. 325
Seattle, WA 98103
Ph: (206)632-2421
Fax: (206)632-3967

Mishra, Mr. Sailesh, Chairman
Bhojpuri Association of North
  America **[9649]**
801 Hebron Pky., No. 7210
Lewisville, TX 75057

Misiano, Vince, VP
Directors Guild of America **[1191]**
7920 Sunset Blvd.
Los Angeles, CA 90046
Ph: (310)289-2000
Toll Free: 800-421-4173

Misleh, Mr. Dan, Exec. Dir.
Catholic Climate Covenant **[3824]**
415 Michigan Ave. NE, Ste. 260

Washington, DC 20017
Ph: (202)756-5545

Misler, Dennis, President
Polish/American/Jewish Alliance for
  Youth Action, Inc. **[13474]**
c/o Jay Pollack, Treasurer
13 Pipe Hill Ct., Unit B
Baltimore, MD 21209-1655
Ph: (410)486-0698

Misra, Vishal, President
Association for Computing
  Machinery - Special Interest Group
  on Measurement and Evaluation
  [6239]
PO Box 30777
New York, NY 10087
Ph: (212)869-7440
Toll Free: 800-342-6626

Misrok, Mark, President
National Working Positive Coalition
  [10550]
c/o ACT, 110 Bartholomew Ave., Ste
  3050
110 Bartholomew Ave., Ste. 3050
Hartford, CT 06106-2251

Missen, Cliff, MA, Director
WiderNet Project **[8679]**
104 S Estes Dr., Ste. 301A
Chapel Hill, NC 27514
Ph: (919)240-4622

Mister, Steven M., Esq., CEO,
  President
Council for Responsible Nutrition
  [16216]
1828 L St. NW, Ste. 510
Washington, DC 20036-5114
Ph: (202)204-7700
Fax: (202)204-7701

Misuriellio, Harry, Dir. of Member
  Svcs.
Souvenir Building Collectors Society
  [21722]
c/o Katherine Isbell, Treasurer
809 Jackson St.
Rockwall, TX 75087-6106
Ph: (703)532-4532
   (703)477-4781

Mitch, Joe, Exec. Dir.
U.S. Basketball Writers Association
  [22577]
1818 Chouteau Ave.
Saint Louis, MO 63103
Ph: (314)444-4325

Mitchel, Beth, Contact
International Network of Prison
  Ministries **[20371]**
Box 227475
Dallas, TX 75222

Mitchell, Andrea, Exec. Dir.
Substance Abuse Librarians and
  Information Specialists **[9729]**
PO Box 9513
Berkeley, CA 94709-0513
Ph: (510)865-6225

Mitchell, Bobby, Chmn. of the Bd.,
  Founder
Fellowship of Companies for Christ
  International **[19979]**
4201 N Peachtree Rd., Ste. 200
Atlanta, GA 30341
Ph: (770)685-6000
Fax: (770)685-6001

Mitchell, Carl, Treasurer
National Shaving Mug Collectors
  Association **[21698]**
c/o Carl Mitchell, Treasurer
7058 Ballybunion Ct.

Fayetteville, PA 17222-9443

Mitchell, Deann, President
Vetarans Voices Writing Project
  [17100]
406 W 34th St., Ste. 103
Kansas City, MO 64111
Ph: (816)701-6844

Mitchell, Deborah B., Exec. Dir.
International Sealing Distributors As-
  sociation **[3472]**
105 Eastern Ave., Ste. 104
Annapolis, MD 21403-3366
Ph: (410)940-6344
Fax: (410)263-1659

Mitchell, Faith M., Ph.D., Chairman
Population Resource Center **[12519]**
1725 K St. NW
Washington, DC 20006
Ph: (202)467-5030

Mitchell, John E., PA
American Association of Patholo-
  gists' Assistants **[16570]**
2345 Rice St., Ste. 220
Saint Paul, MN 55113
Ph: (651)697-9264
Toll Free: 800-532-AAPA
Fax: (651)317-8048

Mitchell, John E., VP
USS Leyte CV32 Association
  [21068]
c/o Angelo R. Maisi, Treasurer
127 Glen Eagle Cir.
Naples, FL 34104-5714
Ph: (239)348-0085

Mitchell, John, MD, Mem.
Health and Education Relief for
  Guyana **[15467]**
883 Flatbush Ave.
Brooklyn, NY 11226
Ph: (718)282-2262
Fax: (718)282-2263

Mitchell, John, MD, President
Health and Educational Relief
  Organization **[15144]**
883 Flatbush Ave.
Brooklyn, NY 11226
Ph: (718)282-2262
Fax: (718)282-2263

Mitchell, John R., Treasurer
Peter Warlock Society **[9188]**
c/o Richard Valentine, Representative
1109 2nd Ave.
Schenectady, NY 12303-1643
Ph: (518)209-8052

Mitchell, John W., President, CEO
IPC - Association Connecting
  Electronics Industries **[1052]**
3000 Lakeside Dr., 105 N
Bannockburn, IL 60015
Ph: (847)615-7100
Fax: (847)615-7105

Mitchell, Johnny, Jr., President
United States Croquet Association
  [22741]
700 Florida Mango Rd.
West Palm Beach, FL 33406-4461
Ph: (561)478-0760
Fax: (561)686-5507

Mitchell, Julie, President, Chmn. of
  the Bd.
American Cockatiel Society **[21535]**
c/o Julie Mitchell, Secretary
100 Bailey Dr.
Yorktown, VA 23692-3052
Ph: (757)898-8397

Mitchell, Kevin P., Chairman,
  Founder
Business Travel Coalition **[23666]**
214 Grouse Ln.

Radnor, PA 19087
Ph: (610)999-9247

Mitchell, Kevin, President
Professional Pricing Society [930]
3535 Roswell Rd., Ste. 59
Marietta, GA 30062
Ph: (770)509-9933

Mitchell, Linda, VP
Society for Medieval Feminist
   Scholarship [8755]
Ohio Wesleyan University
Sturges 208
61 S Sandusky St.
Department of Comparative
   Literature
Ohio Wesleyan University
Delaware, OH 43015

Mitchell, Liz, Bd. Member
Association for Professional Observ-
   ers [4183]
PO Box 933
Eugene, OR 97440
Ph: (541)344-5503

Mitchell, Lloyd M., President
Forestry Conservation Communica-
   tions Association [3867]
122 Baltimore St.
Gettysburg, PA 17325
Ph: (717)398-0815
Toll Free: 844-458-0298
Fax: (717)778-4237

Mitchell, Lynda, President
Kids with Food Allergies [13579]
5049 Swamp Rd., Ste. 303
Fountainville, PA 18923-9660
Ph: (215)230-5394
Fax: (215)340-7674

Mitchell, Dr. Olivia S., Exec. Dir.
Pension Research Council [12450]
The Wharton School at the
   University of Pennsylvania
3620 Locust Walk
3000 Steinberg Hall - Dietrich Hall
Philadelphia, PA 19104-6302
Ph: (215)898-7620
Fax: (215)573-3418

Mitchell, Robert, Dir. of Comm.
Association for Research in Busi-
   ness Education [23701]
c/o Lisa Gueldenzoph Synder,
   President
North Carolina A&T State University
1601 E Market St.
Greensboro, NC 27411
Ph: (501)219-1866

Mitchell, Robert, Exec. Dir.
USA Shooting [23145]
1 Olympic Plz.
Colorado Springs, CO 80909
Ph: (719)866-4670

Mitchell, Mr. Thomas R., President
Nathaniel Hawthorne Society [9084]
University of Cincinnati
2600 Clifton Ave.
Cincinnati, OH 45220
Ph: (513)556-6000

Mitchem, Kathy, Administrator
American Chemical Society [708]
1155 16th St. NW
Washington, DC 20036
Ph: (202)872-4600
Toll Free: 800-227-5558

Mitra, Shekhar, Founder, President
Society of Asian Scientists and
   Engineers [6589]
PO Box 147139
Edgewater, CO 80214

Mitrano, Chuck, President
United States Intercollegiate
   Lacrosse Association [22975]
3738 W Lake Rd.
Perry, NY 14530
Ph: (585)237-5886
Fax: (585)237-5886

Mitri, Tarek, Chairman
Institute for Palestine Studies [8817]
3501 M St. NW
Washington, DC 20007
Ph: (202)342-3990
Fax: (202)342-3927

Mitro, Matthew T., Chairman,
   Founder
Indego Africa [10479]
51 W 52nd St., Ste. 2300
New York, NY 10019
Ph: (212)506-3697

Mitstifer, Dr. Dorothy I., Exec. Dir.
Kappa Omicron Nu [23771]
1749 Hamilton Rd., Ste. 106
Okemos, MI 48864
Ph: (517)351-8335

Mitsu Klos, Diana, Exec. Dir.
Associated Collegiate Press [8148]
National Scholastic Press Associa-
   tion
2221 University Ave. SE, Ste. 121
Minneapolis, MN 55414
Ph: (612)625-8335
Fax: (612)605-0720

Mitteldorf, Darryl, LCSW, Founder
Malecare [14007]
419 Lafayette St., 2nd Fl.
New York, NY 10003
Ph: (212)673-4920

Mix, Ann Bennett, Founder
American World War II Orphans
   Network [10444]
5745 Lee Rd.
Indianapolis, IN 46216-2063
Ph: (540)310-0750

Mix, Mark A., President
National Right to Work Legal
   Defense and Education Foundation
   [18618]
8001 Braddock Rd.
Springfield, VA 22160
Ph: (703)321-8510
Toll Free: 800-336-3600
Fax: (703)321-9613

Mixon, Bill, Editor
Association for Mexican Cave Stud-
   ies [7226]
PO Box 7672
Austin, TX 78713

Mixon, Theresa, Officer
Water Environment Federation
   [4557]
601 Wythe St.
Alexandria, VA 22314-1994
Toll Free: 800-666-0206
Fax: (703)684-2492

Miyamoto, H. Kit, President
Miyamoto Global Disaster Relief
   [11674]
1450 Halyard Dr., Ste. 1
West Sacramento, CA 95691
Ph: (916)373-1995
Fax: (916)373-1466

Miyares, Urban, Founder, President
Challenged America [14548]
c/o Disabled Businesspersons Association
SDSU - Interwork Institute
6367 Alvarado Ct., Ste. 350

San Diego, CA 92120
Ph: (619)594-8805

Miyares, Mr. Urban, President
Disabled Businesspersons Associa-
   tion [11762]
6367 Alvarado Ct., Ste. 350
San Diego, CA 92120
Ph: (619)594-8805

Miyazawa, Teruo, President
International Maillard Reaction
   Society [6203]
c/o David R. Sell, Secretary-
   Treasurer
Dept. of Patholoy
Case Western Reserve University
10900 Euclid Ave.
Cleveland, OH 44106

Mizel, Larry A., Chairman
Simon Wiesenthal Center [18352]
1399 S Roxbury Dr.
Los Angeles, CA 90035
Ph: (310)553-9036
Toll Free: 800-900-9036
Fax: (310)553-4521

Mizrahi, Alberto, President
Cantors Assembly [20239]
55 S Miller Rd., Ste. 201
Fairlawn, OH 44333-4168
Ph: (330)864-8533
Fax: (330)864-8343

Mkam, Ms. Judith, Assoc. Dir.
Seven Seas Cruising Association
   [22667]
2501 E Commercial Blvd., Ste. 203
Fort Lauderdale, FL 33308
Ph: (954)771-5660
Fax: (954)771-5662

Mlambo-Ngcuka, Phumzile, Exec.
   Dir.
United Nations Commission on the
   Status of Women [19214]
405 East 42 St.
New York, NY 10017
Ph: (646)781-4400
Fax: (646)781-4444

Mlambo-Ngcuka, Phumzile, Exec.
   Dir.
United Nations Women [18235]
405 E 42nd St.
New York, NY 10017
Ph: (646)781-4400
Fax: (646)781-4444

Mnatsakanyan, Zohrab, President
United Nations Population Fund
   [17120]
605 3rd Ave.
New York, NY 10158-0180
Ph: (212)297-5000
Fax: (212)370-0201

Moberly, Heather, Secretary
Evidenced-Based Veterinary
   Medicine Association [17646]
c/o Northwest Registered Agent
270 Trace Colony Pk., Ste. B
Ridgeland, MS 39157

Mobley, Chuck, Contact
San Francisco Camerawork [9310]
1011 Market St., 2nd Fl.
San Francisco, CA 94103
Ph: (415)487-1011

Mobley, Randy, President, Treasurer
International League of Professional
   Baseball Clubs [22549]
55 S High St., Ste. 202
Dublin, OH 43017
Ph: (614)791-9300
Fax: (614)791-9009

Mock, Janet, Mem.
Leadership Conference of Women
   Religious [19854]
8808 Cameron St.
Silver Spring, MD 20910-4152
Ph: (301)588-4955
Fax: (301)587-4575

Mock, Paul E., Chairman
Employer Support of the Guard and
   Reserve [5598]
4800 Mark Center Dr., Ste. 3E25
Alexandria, VA 22350-1200
Toll Free: 800-336-4590
Fax: (571)372-0705

Mockenhaupt, Robin, Ph.D, Chair-
   man
Grantmakers in Health [17003]
1100 Connecticut Ave. NW, Ste.
   1200
Washington, DC 20036
Ph: (202)452-8331
Fax: (202)452-8340

Modell, Vicki, Founder
Jeffrey Modell Foundation [15383]
780 3rd Ave.
New York, NY 10017
Fax: (212)764-4180

Modiano, Richard, Director
Beyond Baroque Literary/Arts Center
   [8968]
681 Venice Blvd.
Venice, CA 90291
Ph: (310)822-3006
Fax: (310)821-0256

Moe, Bennett, President
International Map Industry Associa-
   tion [6167]
23052 Alicia Pky., Ste. H-602
Mission Viejo, CA 92692-1661
Ph: (949)458-8200
Fax: (949)458-0300

Moehling, Laura, Bd. Member
Gift of Water [13323]
1025 Pine Hill Way
Carmel, IN 46032-7701
Ph: (317)371-1656

Moen, Caitlin, President
American Library Association Learn-
   ing Round Table [9671]
50 E Huron St.
Chicago, IL 60611-2729
Ph: (312)944-6780
Toll Free: 800-545-2433
Fax: (312)440-9374

Moenter, Kent, President
Montadale Sheep Breeders Associa-
   tion [4672]
47 North 12th
Indianola, IA 50125
Ph: (701)541-1120

Moeser, Erica, CEO, President
National Conference of Bar Examin-
   ers [5440]
302 S Bedford St.
Madison, WI 53703
Ph: (608)280-8550
Fax: (608)280-8552

Moessner, Sue, President
American Satin Rabbit Breeders'
   Association [4593]
c/o Sue Moessner, President
3500 S Wagner Rd.
Ann Arbor, MI 48103
Ph: (734)668-6709

Moffatt, Sharon, RN, Chairperson
National Forum for Heart Disease
   and Stroke Prevention [17010]

1150 Connecticut Ave. NW, Ste. 300
Washington, DC 20036
Toll Free: 866-894-3500
Fax: (202)330-5080

Moffett, Ms. Danielle, Director
Western New Mexico University
Alumni Association [19372]
PO Box 680
Silver City, NM 88062
Ph: (575)538-6675
Toll Free: 800-872-9668

Moffett, John, President
Clan Moffat Society [20832]
c/o Roger Moffat, Membership
Chairperson
3020 76th St. SE
Caledonia, MI 49316-8398

Moffitt, Dr. Robert, Founder,
President
Harvest [20364]
701 N 1st St.
Phoenix, AZ 85004
Ph: (602)258-1083
Fax: (602)258-1318

Mogilyansky, Andrew, Chairman,
Founder
International Foundation for Terror
Act Victims [19183]
1300 Industrial Blvd., Ste. 204
Southampton, PA 18966
Ph: (321)213-0198
Fax: (206)333-0505

Mogler, Chene, President
Llama Association of North America
[3603]
3966 Estate Dr.
Vacaville, CA 95688
Ph: (707)447-5046
Fax: (707)471-4020

Mogstad, Joni, Treasurer
BlueRibbon Coalition [23090]
4555 Burley Dr., Ste. A
Pocatello, ID 83202-1945
Ph: (208)237-1008
Fax: (208)237-9424

Mogul, Jonathan, Chairperson
Association of Research Institutes in
Art History [8896]
The Wolfsonian-Florida International
University
1001 Washington Ave.
Miami Beach, FL 33139
Ph: (305)535-2613
Fax: (305)531-2133

Mohamed, Feisal, Secretary
Milton Society of America [9080]
c/o Angelica Duran, Treasurer
Purdue University, Heavilon Hall
500 Oval Dr.
West Lafayette, IN 47907

Mohammed, Osama, Treasurer
Applied Computational Electromag-
netics Society [6414]
Colorado School of Mines
310D Brown Bldg.
1610 Illinois St.
Golden, CO 80401
Ph: (408)646-1111
Fax: (408)646-0300

Mohammedi, Omar, Esq., President
Association of Muslim American
Lawyers [4997]
233 Broadway, Ste. 801
New York, NY 10279
Ph: (212)608-7776

Mohan, Charles A., CEO, Exec. Dir.
United Mitochondrial Disease
Foundation [17148]

8085 Saltsburg Rd., Ste. 201
Pittsburgh, PA 15239-1977
Ph: (412)793-8077
Toll Free: 888-317-8633
Fax: (412)793-6477

Mohan, Ram, President, Chairman
World Organization of Dredging As-
sociations [2260]
c/o Thomas M. Verna, Executive
Director
PO Box 2035
Spotsylvania, VA 22553
Ph: (619)839-9474

Mohler, Lee, President
Saigon Mission Association [19224]
1762 Clear River Falls Ln.
Henderson, NV 89012
Ph: (702)435-4055
    (731)967-1595

Mohn, Kimball, MD, Exec. Dir.
Association for Hospital Medical
Education [15316]
109 Brush Creek Rd.
Irwin, PA 15642
Ph: (724)864-7321

Mohr, Mary, Exec. Dir.
Retirement Industry Trust Association [415]
c/o Mary L. Mohr, MBA, JD, Executive Director
4251 Pasadena Cir.
Sarasota, FL 34233
Ph: (941)724-0900

Mohr, Michael, Chmn. of the Bd.
Catholics United for the Faith
[19820]
827 N 4th St.
Steubenville, OH 43952
Ph: (740)283-2484
Toll Free: 800-398-5470
Fax: (740)283-4011

Mohr, Pamela, Exec. Dir.
FACES [14741]
223 E 34th St.
New York, NY 10016
Ph: (646)558-0900
Fax: (646)385-7163

Mohr, Robin, Exec. Sec.
Friends World Committee for
Consultation [18788]
1506 Race St.
Philadelphia, PA 19102-1406
Ph: (215)241-7250
Fax: (215)241-7285

Mohr, Robin, Exec. Sec.
Wider Quaker Fellowship [20172]
1506 Race St.
Philadelphia, PA 19102-1406
Ph: (215)241-7250
Fax: (215)241-7285

Mohrenweiser, Liz, President
Standard Schnauzer Club of
America [21967]
c/o Lynne Schuneman, Membership
Chairperson
2903 Dry Hollow Dr.
Kerrville, TX 78028-8051

Moir, Ellen, Founder, CEO
New Teacher Center [7855]
725 Front St., Ste. 400
Santa Cruz, CA 95060
Ph: (831)600-2200
Fax: (861)427-9017

Mojado, Alexandra, Secretary
National Native American Law
Students Association [8221]
1001 Marquette Ave. NW

Albuquerque, NM 87102
Ph: (505)289-0810

Mokelke, Susan, JD, President
Foundation for Shamanic Studies
[20505]
PO Box 1939
Mill Valley, CA 94942
Ph: (415)897-6416
Fax: (415)897-4583

Mokros, Mr. William M., Exec. VP
International Fire Buff Associates
[22013]
Ph: (619)839-9474

Mokyr, Joel, President
International Atlantic Economic
Society [6392]
229 Peachtree St. NE, Ste. 650
Atlanta, GA 30303
Ph: (404)965-1555
Fax: (404)965-1556

Mold, Doris, President
American Agri-Women [17784]
PO Box 743
Colchester, VT 05446
Ph: (586)530-1771
Fax: (802)479-5414

Molenda, Adam, President
Timber Products Manufacturers
[1423]
951 E 3rd Ave.
Spokane, WA 99202
Ph: (509)535-4646
Fax: (509)534-6106

Molenda, Nancy, Contact
Aluminum Anodizers Council [742]
1000 N Rand Rd., No. 214
Wauconda, IL 60084
Ph: (847)526-2010
Fax: (847)526-3993

Molinari, Lisa Smith, President
National Society of Newspaper
Columnists [2706]
PO Box 411532
San Francisco, CA 94141
Ph: (415)488-6762
Fax: (484)297-0336

Molitor, Renee, Coord.
InterVarsity Link [8618]
635 Science Dr.
Madison, WI 53711
Ph: (608)443-4558

Molkenbur, John, President
Wood Duck Society [4918]
c/o Lloyd Knudson, Secretary-
Treasurer
5581 129th Dr. N
Hugo, MN 55038

Molloy, Mr. John J., Chairman
National Vietnam and Gulf War
Veterans Coalition [19223]
2020 Pennsylvania Ave., No. 961
Washington, DC 20006

Molnar, Louis A., CEO
Shriners Hospitals for Children
[14214]
2900 N Rocky Point Dr.
Tampa, FL 33607
Ph: (813)281-0300
Toll Free: 800-237-5055

Molnar, Michael F., President
Society of Manufacturing Engineers -
Rapid Technologies and Additive
Manufacturing Community [6799]
1 SME Dr.
Dearborn, MI 48128-2408
Ph: (313)425-3000
Toll Free: 800-733-4763
Fax: (313)425-3400

Molnar, Dr. Pal, President
International Academy for Quality
[7080]
c/o American Society for Quality
600 N Plankinton Ave.
Milwaukee, WI 53203-2914
Ph: (414)272-2241

Molnau, Myron P., Secretary
Ships on Stamps Unit [22363]
c/o Myron Molnau, Secretary
1616 E 32nd Ct.
Spokane, WA 99203-3918

Moloney, Michael, Director
National Academies of Sciences,
Engineering, and Medicine | Divi-
sion on Engineering and Physical
Sciences | Space Studies Board
[7220]
500 5th St. NW
Washington, DC 20001
Ph: (202)334-3477
Fax: (202)334-3701

Momeni, Reza, President
Oriental Rug Importers Association
[1956]
400 Tenafly Rd., No. 699
Tenafly, NJ 07670
Ph: (201)866-5054
Fax: (201)866-6169

Momjian, Raffi, Exec. Dir., Founder,
Chmn. of the Bd.
Genocide Education Project [18305]
51 Commonwealth Ave.
San Francisco, CA 94118
Ph: (415)264-4203

Monahan, Capt. James E., Exec.
Dir.
Naval Sea Cadet Corps [5615]
2300 Wilson Blvd., Ste. 200
Arlington, VA 22201-5435
Ph: (703)243-6910
Fax: (703)243-3985

Monahan, Jeanne F., President
March for Life Education and
Defense Fund [19061]
1317 8th St. NW
Washington, DC 20001
Ph: (202)234-3300
Fax: (202)234-3350

Monahan, Shawne, Exec. Dir.
Melpomene Institute [17760]
550 Rice St., Ste. 104
Saint Paul, MN 55103

Monahan, Sherry, President
Western Writers of America, Inc.
[10406]
271 CR 219
Encampment, WY 82325

Moncrief, L. Raymond, Chairman
Community Development Venture
Capital Alliance [11339]
424 W 33rd St., Ste. 320
New York, NY 10001-2618
Ph: (212)594-6747
Fax: (212)594-6717

Moncur, Gary L., Editor
303rd Bomb Group (H) Association
[21180]
303rd Bomb Group
237 Oasis Dr.
Saint George, UT 84770-0901

Mondejar, Marily, Founder, CEO
Filipina Women's Network [19245]
PO Box 192143
San Francisco, CA 94119
Ph: (415)935-4396

Mondros, Jacqueline B., President
National Association of Deans and
Directors of Schools of Social
Work [8572]

1701 Duke St., Ste. 200
Alexandria, VA 22314
Ph: (703)683-8080
Fax: (703)683-8099

Mone, Rev. John A., President
Paisley Family Society [20912]
c/o Martha Pasley M. Brown, USA
  Commissioner
2205 Pine Knoll Cir.
Conyers, GA 30013
Ph: (770)483-6949

Monell, Ambrose K., President,
  Treasurer, Director
G. Unger Vetlesen Foundation
  [12500]
1 Rockefeller Plz., Ste. 301
New York, NY 10020-2002
Ph: (212)586-0700
Fax: (212)245-1863

Monell, Nathan R., CAE, Exec. Dir.
National PTA [8403]
1250 N Pitt St.
Alexandria, VA 22314
Ph: (703)518-1200
Toll Free: 800-307-4782
Fax: (703)836-0942

Money, Ken, President
National Space Society [5866]
PO Box 98106
Washington, DC 20090-8106
Ph: (202)429-1600
Fax: (703)435-4390

Monkaba, Terry, Exec. Dir.
Williams Syndrome Association
  [14866]
570 Kirts Blvd., Ste. 223
Troy, MI 48084-4156
Ph: (248)244-2229
Toll Free: 800-806-1871
Fax: (248)244-2230

Monks, Janice C., LSW, President,
  CEO
American Association of Service
  Coordinators [1700]
499 Village Park Dr.
Powell, OH 43065-1178
Ph: (614)848-5958
Fax: (614)848-5954

Monroe, Charlie, Chairperson
International Association of Gay/
  Lesbian Country Western Dance
  Clubs [9258]
5380 W 34th St., No. 207
Houston, TX 77092-6626

Monroe, John J., President
American Coon Hunters Association
  [22958]
PO Box 2015
Media, PA 19063-9015
Ph: (484)234-0582
Toll Free: 855-WIN-ACHA

Monroe, Raymond W., Exec. VP
Steel Founders' Society of America
  [1770]
780 McArdle Dr., Unit G
Crystal Lake, IL 60014
Ph: (815)455-8240
Fax: (815)455-8241

Monseu, Betsy, CEO
American Coal Council [734]
1101 Pennsylvania Ave. NW, Ste.
  600
Washington, DC 20004
Ph: (202)756-4540
Fax: (202)756-7323

Monson, Marty, Exec. Dir., CEO
Barbershop Harmony Society [9880]
110 7th Ave. N

Nashville, TN 37203-3704
Ph: (615)823-3993
Toll Free: 800-876-7464

Montague, Peter, Exec. Dir.
Environmental Research Foundation
  [13575]
PO Box 160
New Brunswick, NJ 08903
Ph: (732)828-9995
Toll Free: 888-272-2435
Fax: (732)791-4603

Montalvo, D'Arcy, Mgr. of Public Rel.
American Fire Sprinkler Association
  [2988]
12750 Merit Dr., Ste. 350
Dallas, TX 75251-1273
Ph: (214)349-5965
Fax: (214)343-8898

Montanari, Lorenzo, Exec. Dir.
Property Rights Alliance [5691]
722 12th St. NW, 4th Fl.
Washington, DC 20005
Ph: (202)785-0266

Montanaro, Ann, Director
Movable Book Society [9132]
PO Box 9190
Salt Lake City, UT 84109-0190
Ph: (801)277-6700

Montanez, Roberto, President
Parachute Industry Association
  [23056]
6499 S Kings Ranch Rd., No. 6-1
Gold Canyon, AZ 85118
Ph: (480)982-6125

Montanus, George, President
Gospel Association for the Blind
  [17705]
PO Box 1162
Bunnell, FL 32110-1162
Ph: (386)586-5885
Fax: (386)586-5886

Montero, Jose, Jr., Chairman,
  President
Trekking for Kids Inc. [23332]
PO Box 25493
Washington, DC 20027
Ph: (202)651-1387

Monteverde, Susan, VP of Rel.
American Association of Port
  Authorities [23423]
1010 Duke St.
Alexandria, VA 22314-3589
Ph: (703)684-5700
Fax: (703)684-6321

Montez, Stacye, Exec. Dir.
Zeta Phi Beta Sorority, Inc. [23877]
1734 New Hampshire Ave. NW
Washington, DC 20009
Ph: (202)387-3103
Fax: (202)232-4593

Montgomery, Allen, CEO, Exec. Dir.,
  Founder
American Nutraceutical Association
  [14977]
5120 Selkirk Dr., Ste. 100
Birmingham, AL 35242-4165
Ph: (205)980-5710
Toll Free: 800-566-3622
Fax: (205)991-9302

Montgomery, Mike, CIO
Association of Concert Bands [9875]
6613 Cheryl Ann Dr.
Independence, OH 44131-3718
Toll Free: 800-726-8720

Monti, Michael J., PhD, Exec. Dir.
Association of Collegiate Schools of
  Architecture [7497]

1735 New York Ave. NW, 3rd Fl.
Washington, DC 20006
Ph: (202)785-2324
Fax: (202)628-0448

Monticciolo, Dr. Vincent, Founder
Dentistry from the Heart [14431]
8313 W Hillsborough Ave.
Tampa, FL 33615
Ph: (727)849-2002

Montine, Thomas J., President
American Association of Neuro-
  pathologists [16569]
5575 S Sycamore St., Ste. 235
Littleton, CO 80120
Ph: (440)793-6565
     (720)372-0888
Fax: (303)568-0406

Montross, Lisa, President
American Business Women's As-
  sociation [607]
9820 Metcalf Ave., Ste. 110
Overland Park, KS 66212
Toll Free: 800-228-0007
Fax: (913)660-0101

Montroy, William J., Founder
Calix Society [13128]
PO Box 9085
Saint Paul, MN 55109
Ph: (651)773-3117
Toll Free: 800-398-0524

Montz, Dr. Larry, Founder
International Society for Paranormal
  Research [6986]
4712 Admiralty Way, No. 541
Marina del Rey, CA 90292
Ph: (323)644-8866

Moo, Dr. Douglas, Chairman
Biblica [19755]
1820 Jet Stream Dr.
Colorado Springs, CO 80921
Ph: (719)488-9200
Toll Free: 800-524-1588

Moody, Deborah, Director
Association of Certified Professional
  Wedding Consultants [2306]
San Jose, CA
Ph: (408)227-2792
Fax: (408)226-0697

Moody, Karen, President
National Coalition of Pharmaceutical
  Distributors [2562]
20101 NE 16th Pl.
Miami, FL 33179
Ph: (305)690-4233
Fax: (305)760-7227

Moody, Kim, Exec. Dir.
Disability Rights Maine [11589]
24 Stone St., Ste. 204
Augusta, ME 04330
Ph: (207)626-2774
Toll Free: 800-452-1948
Fax: (207)621-1419

Moody, Kim, VP
National Disability Rights Network
  [11626]
820 1st St. NE, Ste. 740
Washington, DC 20002
Ph: (202)408-9514
Fax: (202)408-9520

Moody, Maximiliane, Exec. Dir.
International Association of Insur-
  ance Fraud Agencies [5314]
PO Box 10018
Kansas City, MO 64171
Ph: (816)756-5285
Fax: (816)756-5287

Moody, Ms. Peggy, Exec. Dir.
Story Circle Network [10227]
PO Box 1670

Estes Park, CO 80517-1670
Ph: (970)235-1477

Moody, Robert R., Chairman
Sommelier Society of America [190]
West Village Sta.
New York, NY 10014
Ph: (212)679-4190

Mook, Magdalena, Exec. Dir., CEO
International Coach Federation
  [22730]
2365 Harrodsburg Rd., Ste. A325
Lexington, KY 40504
Ph: (859)219-3580
Toll Free: 888-423-3131
Fax: (859)226-4411

Moon, Camilla, President
North American Border Terrier
  Welfare [11693]
c/o Cindy Peebles, Treasurer
822 George St.
Lynchburg, VA 24502
Ph: (434)239-4576

Moon, Dr. Hak Ja Han, Founder
Women's Federation for World
  Peace International [12446]
4 W 43rd St.
New York, NY 10036-7408
Ph: (203)661-5820
Fax: (203)360-5895

Moon, Lisa, President, CEO
Global FoodBanking Network
  [12097]
203 N LaSalle St., Ste. 1900
Chicago, IL 60601-1263
Ph: (312)782-4560
Fax: (312)782-4580

Moon, Princess Pale, Chairman,
  President
American Indian Heritage Founda-
  tion [10033]
PO Box 750
Pigeon Forge, TN 37868
Ph: (703)354-2270

Moon, Terry, Managing Ed.
News and Letters Committee
  [19143]
228 S Wabash, Ste. 230
Chicago, IL 60604-2383
Ph: (312)431-8242
Fax: (312)431-8252

Mooney, James, VP
Latin Liturgy Association [19851]
c/o Regina Morris, President
3526 Oxford Blvd.
Saint Louis, MO 63143-4209

Mooney, John E., Chairman
Thoroughbred Racing Protective
  Bureau [22932]
420 Fair Hill Dr., Ste. 2
Elkton, MD 21921
Ph: (410)398-2261

Mooney, Michael, President
National Association of Christian
  Ministers [20375]
2801 Wade Hampton Blvd., Ste.
  115-227
Taylors, SC 29687

Moore, Albert B., President
Mobile Riverine Force Association
  [21167]
c/o Albert B. Moore, President
106 Belleview Dr. NE
Conover, NC 28613
Ph: (828)464-7228

Moore, Allen, Treasurer
American Textile Machinery Association [1708]

201 Park Washington Ct.
Falls Church, VA 22046
Ph: (703)538-1789

Moore, Allen, Co-Pres.
CORPUS [19829]
2 Adamian Dr.
North Falmouth, MA 02556
Ph: (508)523-4032

Moore, Andrew D., Exec. Dir.
Women of the National Agricultural
  Aviation Association [3653]
c/o National Agricultural Aviation As-
  sociation
1440 Duke St.
Alexandria, VA 22314
Ph: (202)546-5722
Fax: (202)546-5726

Moore, Anne, Director
Appraisers Association of America
  [219]
212 W 35th St., 11th Fl. S
New York, NY 10001
Ph: (212)889-5404
Fax: (212)889-5503

Moore, Barbara J., PhD, CEO,
  President
Shape Up America [16713]
PO Box 149
Clyde Park, MT 59018-0149
Ph: (406)686-4844
Fax: (406)686-4424

Moore, Cathleen, Chairperson
Psychonomic Society [16933]
2424 American Ln.
Madison, WI 53704-3102
Ph: (608)441-1070
Fax: (608)443-2474

Moore, Charles, Director
Friends of the Earth [3869]
1101 15th St. NW, 11th Fl.
Washington, DC 20005
Ph: (202)783-7400
Fax: (202)783-0444

Moore, Christopher, CEO
United States Youth Soccer Associa-
  tion [23197]
9220 World Cup Way
Frisco, TX 75033
Toll Free: 800-4SOCCER
Fax: (972)334-9960

Moore, Curtis, Secretary, Treasurer
National Onsite Wastewater
  Recycling Association [4743]
1199 N Fairfax St., Ste. 410
Alexandria, VA 22314
Ph: (703)836-1950
Toll Free: 800-966-2942

Moore, David Moffett, President
Academy of Parish Clergy [20353]
2249 Florinda St.
Sarasota, FL 34231
Ph: (941)922-8633

Moore, Deb, President
Marketing Education Association
  [8272]
1512 E Cambridge Ave.
Phoenix, AZ 85006-1128

Moore, Detlef B., Exec. Dir.
American Association of Dental Edi-
  tors [2647]
750 N Lincoln Memorial Dr., Ste. No.
  422
Milwaukee, WI 53202
Ph: (414)272-2759
Fax: (414)272-2754

Moore, Detlef B., Exec. Dir.
International Association for
  Orthodontics [14449]

750 N Lincoln Memorial Dr., Ste.
  422
Milwaukee, WI 53202
Ph: (414)272-2757
Toll Free: 800-447-8770
Fax: (414)272-2754

Moore, Diane, Founder, President,
  Exec. Dir.
Striving for More [14067]
PO Box 97443
Raleigh, NC 27624
Ph: (919)339-1214

Moore, Donald R., Exec. Dir.
Designs for Change [8475]
29 East Madison, Ste. 950
Chicago, IL 60602
Ph: (312)236-7252
Fax: (312)236-7927

Moore, Jerry, CGE, Exec. Dir.
American Society of Gas Engineers
  [6455]
PO Box 66
Artesia, CA 90702

Moore, Joe, CEO, President
International Health, Racquet and
  Sportsclub Association [2600]
70 Fargo St.
Boston, MA 02210
Ph: (617)951-0055
Toll Free: 800-228-4772
Fax: (617)951-0056

Moore, John C., Chairman
Thoroughbred Retirement Founda-
  tion [10702]
10 Lake Ave.
Saratoga Springs, NY 12866
Ph: (518)226-0028
Fax: (518)226-0699

Moore, Prof. John Norton, Director
Center for Oceans Law and Policy
  [6938]
580 Massie Rd.
Charlottesville, VA 22903-1789
Ph: (434)924-7441
Fax: (434)924-7362

Moore, Dr. John R., Chairman
Trees for the Future [4736]
1400 Spring St., Ste. 150
Silver Spring, MD 20910-2750
Ph: (301)565-0630
Toll Free: 800-643-0001

Moore, Kathryn J., PhD, Chairman
American Heart Association-Council
  on Arteriosclerosis, Thrombosis
  and Vascular Biology [14091]
American Heart Association
7272 Greenville Ave.
Dallas, TX 75231
Toll Free: 800-242-8721

Moore, Linda A., Founder, President
PBCers Organization [15258]
1426 Garden Rd.
Pearland, TX 77581
Ph: (346)302-1620

Moore, Linie A., CEO, Founder
Primary Biliary Cirrhosis Organiza-
  tion [14611]
1426 Garden Rd.
Pearland, TX 77581
Ph: (346)302-1620

Moore, Malcolm, MD, Contact
International Society of
  Gastrointestinal Oncology [14794]
200 Broadhollow Rd., Ste. 207
Melville, NY 11747
Ph: (631)390-8390
Fax: (631)393-5026

Moore, Margaret M., Chmn. of the
  Bd.
Women in Federal Law Enforce-
  ment, Inc. [5522]
2200 Wilson Blvd., Ste. 102
PMB 204
Arlington, VA 22201-3324
Ph: (301)805-2180
Fax: (301)560-8836

Moore, Margaret, Director
National Center for Women and
  Policing [5497]
433 S Beverly Dr.
Beverly Hills, CA 90212
Ph: (310)556-2500
Fax: (310)556-2509

Moore, Ms. Melissa, Exec. Dir.
We Are Family [11912]
29 Leinbach Dr., Ste. D-3
Charleston, SC 29407
Ph: (843)637-3697

Moore, Michael, Treasurer
International Conference of
  Symphony and Opera Musicians
  [9926]
1609 Tammany Dr.
Nashville, TN 37206
Ph: (615)227-2379

Moore, Michael, Exec. Dir.
North American Carbon Capture &
  Storage Association [6580]
c/o Michael Moore, Executive Direc-
  tor
FearnOil, Inc.
12012 Wickchester Ln., Ste. 350
Houston, TX 77079
Ph: (281)759-0245

Moore, Mike, Treasurer
Truth Initiative [19159]
900 G St. NW, 4th Fl.
Washington, DC 20001
Ph: (202)454-5555

Moore, Neal, Cmdr.
Centennial Legion of Historic Military
  Commands [21079]
46 Highland Ave.
Jaffrey, NH 03452

Moore, Ned, Exec. Dir., VP
Council of Independent Colleges
  [8010]
1 Dupont Cir. NW, Ste. 320
Washington, DC 20036-1142
Ph: (202)466-7230
Fax: (202)466-7238

Moore, Patrick, President
National Council on Public History
  [9499]
127 Cavanaugh Hall
425 University Blvd.
Indianapolis, IN 46202
Ph: (317)274-2716

Moore, Rev. Paul S., Sr., Chmn. of
  the Bd.
CitiHope International [12644]
629 Main St., Ste. 2
Margaretville, NY 12455
Ph: (845)586-6202

Moore, Rachel S., CEO
Ballet Theatre Foundation [9244]
890 Broadway, 3rd Fl.
New York, NY 10003
Ph: (212)477-3030
Fax: (212)254-5938

Moore, Richard, Chairman
National Safe Boating Council
  [12833]
9500 Technology Dr., Ste. 104

Manassas, VA 20110
Ph: (703)361-4294

Moore, Rick, Exec. Dir.
National Association for PET
  Container Resources [3451]
7310 Turfway Rd., Ste. 550
Florence, KY 41042
Ph: (859)372-6635

Moore, Russell D., President
Ethics and Religious Liberty Com-
  mission of the Southern Baptist
  Convention [19729]
901. Commerce St., Ste. 550
Nashville, TN 37203-3600
Ph: (615)244-2495
Fax: (615)242-0065

Moore, Sandra L., President
National Association of Housing
  Counselors and Agencies [1691]
PO Box 91873
Lafayette, LA 70509-1873
Ph: (337)962-6600
Fax: (337)232-8834

Moore, Stephanie, Exec. Dir.
Center for Craft, Creativity and
  Design [9012]
67 Broadway St.
Asheville, NC 28801
Ph: (828)785-1357
Fax: (828)785-1372

Moore, Steve, Exec. Dir.
Association for Biblical Higher
  Education [7606]
5850 T.G. Lee Blvd., Ste. 130
Orlando, FL 32822
Ph: (407)207-0808
Fax: (407)207-0840

Moore, Warner, Comm. Chm.
The League of Professional System
  Administrators [6323]
PO Box 5161
Trenton, NJ 08638-0161
Ph: (202)567-7201
Fax: (609)219-6787

Moore, Wendy, President
Respiratory Nursing Society [16182]
c/o Gina Martin
1018 Jamison Ave. SE
Roanoke, VA 24013
Fax: (540)981-8643

Moore, William A., President
Society for Clinical and Medical Hair
  Removal [14658]
2424 American Ln.
Madison, WI 53704-3102
Ph: (608)443-2470
Fax: (608)443-2474

Moore, William, President
Clan Guthrie USA [20813]
c/o Carrie Guthrie-Whitlow,
  Treasurer
PO Box 121
Port Orchard, WA 98366

Moorehead, Paul, President
Strategies for International Develop-
  ment [12189]
330 Pennsylvania Ave. SE, Ste. 304
Washington, DC 20003
Ph: (202)544-1115
Fax: (202)543-5288

Moore-Merrell, Lori, Asst. Pres.
International Fire Service Training
  Association [8662]
930 N Willis
Stillwater, OK 74078
Ph: (405)744-5723
Toll Free: 800-654-4055
Fax: (405)744-8204

Moorhead, Tracey, President, CEO
Visiting Nurse Associations of
America [16191]
2121 Crystal Dr., Ste. 750
Arlington, VA 22202
Ph: (571)527-1520
Toll Free: 888-866-8773
Fax: (571)527-1521

Moose, Debbie, President
Association of Food Journalists
[2662]
7 Avenida Vista Grande, Ste. B7,
No. 467
Santa Fe, NM 87508-9198

Mooser, Stephen, President
Society of Children's Book Writers
and Illustrators [10400]
4727 Wilshire Blvd., Ste. 301
Los Angeles, CA 90010
Ph: (323)782-1010
Fax: (323)782-1892

Mora, Claudia I., President
Geological Society of America
[6680]
3300 Penrose Pl.
Boulder, CO 80301
Ph: (303)357-1000
Fax: (303)357-1070

Morán, Manuel, President
Union Internationale de la Marion-
nette [22395]
1404 Spring St. NW
Atlanta, GA 30309
Ph: (404)881-5110
Fax: (404)873-9907

Morahg, Prof. Gilead, Exec. VP
National Association of Professors of
Hebrew [8141]
907 Van Hise Hall
University of Wisconsin-Madison
1220 Linden Dr.
Madison, WI 53706-1525
Fax: (608)262-8570

Morales, Joanna Fawzy, Esq., CEO
Triage Cancer [14076]
c/o Navigating Cancer Survivorship
PO Box 4552
Culver City, CA 90231-4552
Ph: (424)258-4628
Fax: (424)258-7064

Morales, Rev. Peter, President
Unitarian Universalist Association
[20556]
24 Farnsworth St.
Boston, MA 02210-1262
Ph: (617)742-2100
Fax: (617)367-3237

Morales-Payan, Jose Pablo,
President
InterAmerican Society for Tropical
Horticulture [4433]
Fairchild Tropical Garden Research
Ctr.
11935 Old Cutler Rd.
Miami, FL 33156
Ph: (305)667-1651
Fax: (305)665-8032

Moran, Ms. Lena, Coord.
International Foundation for Teleme-
tering [7320]
5665 Oberlin Dr., Ste. 200
San Diego, CA 92121

Moran, Margaret, V. Chmn. of the
Bd.
SER National [11783]
100 E Royal Ln., Ste. 130
Irving, TX 75039
Ph: (469)549-3600
Fax: (469)549-3684

Moran, Rev. Martin O., III, Exec. Dir.
Catholic Campus Ministry Associa-
tion [19809]
330 W Vine St.
Cincinnati, OH 45215
Ph: (513)842-0167
Toll Free: 888-714-6631
Fax: (513)842-0171

Moran, Patti J., President, CEO
Pet Sitters International [2550]
201 E King St.
King, NC 27021
Ph: (336)983-9222
Fax: (336)983-5266

Moran, Peter J., CEO, Exec. VP
Society of American Florists [1310]
1001 N Fairfax St., Ste. 201
Alexandria, VA 22314
Toll Free: 800-336-4743
Fax: (703)836-8700

Moran, Thomas J., Chairman
Concern Worldwide [12651]
355 Lexington Ave., 16th Fl.
New York, NY 10017
Ph: (212)557-8000
Fax: (212)557-8004

Moran, Tim, Founder
PediaWorks [16617]
10000 Cedar Ave., Ste. 16
Cleveland, OH 44106
Ph: (216)223-8877

Morana, Janet A., Exec. Dir.
Priests for Life [19068]
PO Box 141172
Staten Island, NY 10314
Ph: (718)980-4400
Toll Free: 888-735-3448
Fax: (718)980-6515

Morange, Mitchel, President
International Society for the History,
Philosophy, and Social Studies of
Biology [7985]
c/o Laura Perini, Treasurer
Philosophy Dept.
130 Castleton Dr.
Claremont, CA 91711

Moranian, Suzanne, President
Armenian International Women's As-
sociation [13369]
65 Main St., No. 3A
Watertown, MA 02472
Ph: (617)926-0171

Morava, Bob, President
FISA [1382]
1207 Sunset Dr.
Greensboro, NC 27408
Ph: (336)274-6311
Fax: (336)691-1839

Morcuende, Jose, MD, Contact
Ponseti International Association
[13834]
University of Iowa Healthcare
International Office 118 CMAB
Iowa City, IA 52242

More, Kevin, Chairman
Society for Information Management
[2193]
1120 Route 73, Ste. 200
Mount Laurel, NJ 08054-5113
Ph: (856)380-6807
Toll Free: 800-387-9746

More, Col. Lucia, President
Society of American Federal Medical
Laboratory Scientists [15521]
PO Box 2549
Fairfax, VA 22031-0549

More, Max, PhD, CEO, President
Alcor Life Extension Foundation
[14354]

7895 E Acoma Dr., Ste. 110
Scottsdale, AZ 85260-6916
Ph: (480)905-1906
Toll Free: 877-462-5267
Fax: (480)922-9027

Moreau, Sandra, Exec. Dir.
International Debate Education As-
sociation [8594]
222 Broadway, 19th Fl.
New York, NY 10038
Ph: (212)300-6076

Morek, Michele, OSU, Coord.
UNANIMA International [19132]
845 3rd Ave., Rm. 671
New York, NY 10017
Ph: (917)426-8285
Fax: (646)290-5001

Moreland, Master Shelton R., Director, Founder
United States Hapki Hae [23018]
4826 Old National Hwy.
College Park, GA 30337

Morell, Ada, Chmn. of the Bd.
Holocaust Resource Center [18348]
Kean University
1000 Morris Ave.
Union, NJ 07083
Ph: (908)737-5326

Morell, Sally Fallon, President,
Treasurer
Weston A. Price Foundation [16236]
4200 Wisconsin Ave. NW, PMB 106-
380
Washington, DC 20016
Ph: (202)363-4394
Fax: (202)363-4396

Moreno, Prof. Armando, President
International Federation of Festival
Organizations [1141]
4230 Stansbury Ave., Ste. 105
Sherman Oaks, CA 91423
Ph: (818)789-7596
Fax: (818)784-9141

Moreno, Carmen, Exec. Sec.
Inter-American Commission of
Women [18213]
17th St. & Constitution Ave. NW
Washington, DC 20006-4499
Ph: (202)370-5000
Fax: (202)458-3967

Moreno, Javier, Founder
Animal Equality [10574]
8581 Santa Monica Blvd., Ste. 350
Los Angeles, CA 90069
Ph: (424)400-2860

Moreno, Susan J., Editor
OASIS @ MAPP [15979]
950 S Court St.
Crown Point, IN 46307
Ph: (219)662-1311

Moretti, Laura, Founder, President
The Animals Voice [10586]
1692 Mangrove Ave., No. 276
Chico, CA 95926

Morey, Jeff, Director
Garden Centers of America [4502]
2873 Saber Dr.
Clearwater, FL 33759
Toll Free: 800-721-0024

Morey, Timothy, President
Society of Experimental Test Pilots
[5873]
44814 North Elm Ave.
Lancaster, CA 93534
Ph: (661)942-9574
Fax: (661)940-0398

Morford, Jackie, President
FG Syndrome Family Alliance
[17339]
922 NW Circle Blvd., Ste. 160
Corvallis, OR 97330

Morgan, Alan, CEO
National Rural Health Association
[17013]
4501 College Blvd., No. 225
Leawood, KS 66211-1921
Ph: (816)756-3140
Fax: (816)756-3144

Morgan, Ben, Exec. VP, Secretary
National Cottonseed Products As-
sociation [2452]
866 Willow Tree Cir.
Cordova, TN 38018
Ph: (901)682-0800

Morgan, Beverly, President
National Federation of Licensed
Practical Nurses [16161]
3801 Lake Boone Trl., Ste. 190
Raleigh, NC 27607
Ph: (919)779-0046
Toll Free: 800-948-2511
Fax: (919)779-5642

Morgan, Christine, Chairman,
President
Lucis Trust [18362]
120 Wall St., 24th Fl.
New York, NY 10005
Ph: (212)292-0707
Fax: (212)292-0808

Morgan, Clydie J., COO
American Ex-Prisoners of War
[21090]
c/o Clydie J. Morgan, Executive
Director
3201 E Pioneer Pky., No. 40
Arlington, TX 76010
Ph: (817)649-2979
Fax: (817)649-0109

Morgan, Dale R., Founder
Disaster Response Communications
[11659]
10719 Kell Ave. S
Bloomington, MN 55437
Ph: (952)224-2045

Morgan, Deirdre, Exec. Dir.
Jew's Harp Guild [9943]
69954 Hidden Valley Ln.
Cove, OR 97824

Morgan, Edward H., CEO, President
Christian Herald Association [19957]
432 Park Ave. S
New York, NY 10016
Ph: (212)684-2800
Toll Free: 800-269-3791
Fax: (212)684-3740

Morgan, Rev. E.F. Michael, Ph.D.,
President
Children's Rights Council [11682]
9470 Annapolis Rd., Ste. 310
Lanham, MD 20706
Ph: (301)459-1220
Fax: (301)459-1227

Morgan, Elmo Terry, Director
Rites and Reason Theatre [10271]
Dept. of Africana Studies
Brown University
155 Angell St.
Providence, RI 02912
Ph: (401)863-3137
Fax: (401)863-3559

Morgan, Gary, President
National Cage Bird Show [21541]
c/o Barbara Rosario, Membership
Chairman

715 Avocado Ct.
Del Mar, CA 92014-3911
Ph: (858)259-0232

Morgan, Gary, Chairman, President
North American Parrot Society
[21548]
c/o Gary Morgan, Chairman/
President
15341 Kingston St.
Brighton, CO 80602-7439
Ph: (303)659-9544

Morgan, James C., Chairman
Association of Certified Adizes
Practitioners International [2151]
1212 Mark Ave.
Carpinteria, CA 93013
Ph: (805)565-2901

Morgan, Jeff, CEO
Club Managers Association of
America [732]
1733 King St.
Alexandria, VA 22314
Ph: (703)739-9500
Fax: (703)739-0124

Morgan, John, Exec. Dir.
Association of Coupon Professionals
[2946]
1051 Pontiac Rd.
Drexel Hill, PA 19026
Ph: (610)789-1478
Fax: (610)789-5309

Morgan, John, Officer
Options for Children in Zambia
[11113]
20 Dassance Dr.
Foxboro, MA 02035

Morgan, Joseph, President
Veterans of Modern Warfare [21152]
PO Box 96503
Washington, DC 20090
Toll Free: 888-273-8255

Morgan, Julie, Contact
American Naturopathic Medical As-
sociation [15856]
P O Box 96273
Las Vegas, NV 89193
Ph: (702)450-3477

Morgan, Karlynn, Dir. of Member
Svcs.
Conchologists of America [21640]
c/o Karlynn Morgan, Membership
Director
3098 Shannon Dr.
Winston Salem, NC 27106-3647

Morgan, Kerry, Chief Mktg. Ofc.
HR Certification Institute [2499]
1725 Duke St., Ste. 700
Alexandria, VA 22314
Ph: (571)551-6700
Toll Free: 866-898-4724

Morgan, Kevin, CEO, President
ProLiteracy [8253]
104 Marcellus St.
Syracuse, NY 13204
Ph: (315)422-9121
Toll Free: 888-528-2224
Fax: (315)422-6369

Morgan, Michael A., President
Chemistry and Physics on Stamps
Study Unit [22315]
960 Lakemont Dr.
Pittsburgh, PA 15243

Morgan, Ricky, President
American Society for Nondestructive
Testing [7321]
1711 Arlingate Ln.

Columbus, OH 43228
Ph: (614)274-6003
Toll Free: 800-222-2768
Fax: (614)274-6899

Morgan, Rosemarie, Editor,
President
The Thomas Hardy Association
[9103]
c/o Rosemarie Morgan, President
124 Bishop St.
New Haven, CT 06511

Morgan, Scott, CEO, Founder
Education Pioneers [8614]
360 22nd St., Ste. 220
Oakland, CA 94612
Ph: (510)893-4374
Fax: (510)338-6517

Morgan, Scott, Dep. Dir.
Treatment Action Group [13563]
261 5th Ave., Ste. 2110
New York, NY 10016-7701
Ph: (212)253-7922
Fax: (212)253-7923

Morgan, Steven, Secretary
Western Society of Naturalists
[6902]
PO Box 247
Bodega Bay, CA 94923

Morgan, Thomas, Systems Mgr.
Society for Applied Learning
Technology [8036]
50 Culpeper St.
Warrenton, VA 20186
Ph: (540)347-0055
Fax: (540)349-3169

Morgan, Tim, President
Equipment and Tool Institute [318]
37899 W 12 Mile Rd., Ste. 220
Farmington Hills, MI 48331-3050
Ph: (248)656-5080

Morgan, Winthrop, President
International Social Marketing Association [2287]
6414 Hollins Dr.
Bethesda, MD 20817-2343

Morgoslepov, Molly McMaster,
President, Founder
Colon Club [13948]
17 Peach Tree Ln.
Wilton, NY 12831

Mori, Art, PhD, President, Director
Hawaii Heptachlor Research and
Education Foundation [13222]
PO Box 3735
Honolulu, HI 96812

Mori, Jim, President
Seismological Society of America
[7157]
400 Evelyn Ave., Ste. 201
Albany, CA 94706-1375
Ph: (510)525-5474
Fax: (510)525-7204

Mori, Kaz, Exec. Dir.
Society for Applied Research in
Memory and Cognition [7069]
University of Alaska
223 Burnett Hall
Lincoln, NE 68588-0308

Morial, Marc H., President, CEO
National Urban League [17922]
120 Wall St.
New York, NY 10005
Ph: (212)558-5300
Fax: (212)344-5332

Moriarty, Fred, Exec. Dir.
Unfinished Furniture Association
[1490]

PO Box 520
Spofford, NH 03462
Toll Free: 800-487-8321

Moriarty, Lynda, Director
Great Dane Club of America, Inc.
[21889]
c/o Dianne Powers, President
PO Box 216
West Tisbury, MA 02575

Morin, Frederick R., President
Naval Airship Association [5867]
c/o Frederick R. Morin, President
PO Box 136
Norwell, MA 02061-0136

Morin, Michael, President
National Association of Power
Engineers [7054]
1 Springfield St.
Chicopee, MA 01013
Ph: (413)592-6273
Fax: (413)592-1998

Morisetty, Harini, President
Delta Phi Omega Sorority, Inc.
[23969]
2020 Bailey St.
Houston, TX 77006

Moritsugu, John, President
Society for Community Research
and Action [7071]
PO Box 6560
Macon, GA 31208
Ph: (770)545-6448

Morland, Lyn, MSW, Director
Bridging Refugee Youth and
Children's Services [11217]
United States Conference of
Catholic Bishops
3211 4th St. NE
Washington, DC 20017
Toll Free: 888-572-6500

Morlini, Dr. Vincenzo, CEO,
President
AFS Intercultural Programs [9198]
71 W 23rd St., 6th Fl.
New York, NY 10010-4102
Ph: (212)807-8686
Fax: (212)807-1001

Morlino, John, Director, Founder
The ETHIC - The Essence of True
Humanity is Compassion [18718]
PO Box 6640
Albany, CA 94706-0640
Toll Free: 866-THE-ETHIC

Morningstar, Chip, Secretary
Foresight Institute [7268]
Box 61058
Palo Alto, CA 94306
Ph: (650)289-0860
Fax: (650)289-0863

Morocco, Robert, Treasurer
notMYkid [13471]
5230 E Shea Blvd.
Scottsdale, AZ 85254
Ph: (602)652-0163

Morock, Frank, Director
Catholic Academy of Communication
Professionals [9141]
1645 Brook Lynn Dr., Ste. 2
Beavercreek, OH 45432-1944
Ph: (937)458-0265
Fax: (937)458-0263

Morrell, Michael E., President
Association for Political Theory
[7043]

Morrill, Brig. Gen. Arthur B., III, Chief
of Staff
Military Order of the World Wars
[21207]

435 N Lee St.
Alexandria, VA 22314
Ph: (703)683-4911
Toll Free: 877-320-3774
Fax: (703)683-4501

Morrill, Jackson, President
Composite Panel Association [1434]
19465 Deerfield Ave., Ste. 306
Leesburg, VA 20176
Ph: (703)724-1128
Fax: (703)724-1588

Morris, Aaron, Exec. Dir.
Immigration Equality [11894]
40 Exchange Pl., Ste. 1300
New York, NY 10005
Ph: (212)714-2904
Fax: (212)714-2973

Morris, Alan, Exec. Dir.
United States Snooker Association
[22589]
PO Box 4000F
Berkeley, CA 94704
Ph: (408)615-7479

Morris, Dr. Ann W., Exec. Sec.,
Treasurer
Alpha Kappa Mu [23774]
101 Longwood Ln.
Greenwood, SC 29646-9262

Morris, Charles W., Sr. VP
Pine Chemicals Association [725]
PO Box 17136
Fernandina Beach, FL 32035
Ph: (404)994-6267

Morris, Chris, President
Piedmontese Association of the
United States [3750]
6134 NW Theil Dr.
Kidder, MO 64649
Ph: (816)786-3155

Morris, Del, Exec. Dir.
International Society of Professional
Trackers [23325]
c/o Del Morris, Executive Director
PO Box 1162
Pioneer, CA 95666

Morris, Elizabeth A., MD, President
Society of Breast Imaging [17063]
1891 Preston White Dr.
Reston, VA 20191
Ph: (703)715-4390
Fax: (703)295-6776

Morris, Elizabeth, Dir. of Admin.
Christian Alliance for Indian Child
Welfare [10940]
PO Box 253
Hillsboro, ND 58045-0253

Morris, Greg, VP, Secretary
American Court and Commercial
Newspapers, Inc. [2762]
PO Box 5337
Arlington, VA 22205-0437
Ph: (703)237-9806
Fax: (703)237-9808

Morris, Jean, President
Median Iris Society [22109]
c/o Jean Morris, President
682 Huntley Heights Dr.
Ballwin, MO 63021-5878

Morris, Jon B., Mem.
Association of Program Directors in
Surgery [17378]
6400 Goldsboro Rd., Ste. 200
Bethesda, MD 20817-5846
Ph: (301)320-1200
Fax: (301)263-9025

Morris, Karen, President
National Forensic Association [8598]

Morris, Kate, President
Native American Art Studies Association [7504]
c/o Kathleen Ash-Milby, President
NMAI-George Gustav Heye Ctr.
1 Bowling Green
New York, NY 10004

Morris, Margie Ferris, Chairperson
World Hunger Education Service
[18460]
PO Box 29015
Washington, DC 20017
Ph: (202)269-6322

Morris, Marilyn, Founder, President
Aim For Success [8562]
PO Box 550336
Dallas, TX 75355
Ph: (972)422-2322

Morris, Monica, Chief Adm. Ofc.
Association of Paroling Authorities
International [5673]
Sam Houston State University
George J. Beto Criminal Justice Ctr.
Huntsville, TX 77341-2296
Ph: (936)294-1706
Toll Free: 877-318-2724
Fax: (936)294-1671

Morris, Patrick, Exec. Dir.
International Committee for Information Technology Standards [7278]
Information Technology Industry
Council
1101 K St. NW, Ste. 610
Washington, DC 20005
Ph: (202)737-8888
Fax: (202)638-4922

Morris, Paul, Contact
Cedar Tree Inc. [8237]
421 NW 52nd Ave.
Des Moines, IA 50313
Ph: (515)243-1845
Fax: (515)282-3151

Morris, Rachel, Exec. Dir.
Sigma Gamma Rho Sorority, Inc.
[23876]
1000 Southill Dr., Ste. 200
Cary, NC 27513
Ph: (919)678-9720
Toll Free: 888-747-1922
Fax: (919)678-9721

Morris, Rob, President, Founder
Love146 [11072]
PO Box 8266
New Haven, CT 06530
Ph: (203)772-4420

Morris, Robert C., Secretary,
Treasurer
Society of Professors of Education
[7800]
c/o Dr. Robert C. Morris, Secretary/
Treasurer
College of Education
University of West Georgia
1601 Maple St.
Carrollton, GA 30118-0001
Ph: (678)839-6132

Morris, Skip, Exec. Dir.
International League of Electrical
Associations [1025]
c/o Brook Walker
13563 SE 27th Pl.
Bellevue, WA 98005

Morris, Stephen, Dir. of Engg.
Internet Systems Consortium Inc.
[6279]
950 Charter St.
Redwood City, CA 94063
Ph: (650)423-1300
Fax: (650)423-1355

Morris, Vernon, President
Carriers and Locals Society, Inc.
[21634]
PO Box 74
Grosse Ile, MI 48138
Ph: (734)676-2649
Fax: (734)676-2959

Morris-Fello, M. Yassah, Founder,
President
Aid for the Children of Liberia
[10841]
3320 Fairdale Rd.
Philadelphia, PA 19154
Ph: (484)202-4082
Fax: (267)338-1016

Morrison, Barbara, President, CEO
Association for Manufacturing Excellence [2213]
3701 Algonquin Rd., Ste. 225
Rolling Meadows, IL 60008-3150
Ph: (224)232-5980
Fax: (224)232-5981

Morrison, Mr. Brian R., CEO,
Founder, President
Believe In Tomorrow National
Children's Foundation [11214]
6601 Frederick Rd.
Baltimore, MD 21228
Toll Free: 800-933-5470
Fax: (410)744-1984

Morrison, Charles E., President
East-West Center [18538]
1601 E West Rd.
Honolulu, HI 96848-1601
Ph: (808)944-7111
Fax: (808)944-7376

Morrison, Christopher, Director,
Founder
Care Highway International [12632]
PO Box 100986
San Antonio, TX 78201

Morrison, Dan, Founder
Society of American Bayonet Collectors [21298]
PO Box 5866
Deptford, NJ 08096

Morrison, Daniel, Gen. Sec.
North American Araucanian Royalist
Society [9425]
PO Box 211
Bryn Athyn, PA 19009-0211

Morrison, Dawn, President
National Association of Supervisor of
Business Education [7559]
c/o Melissa Scott, Treasurer
9890 S Maryland Pky., Ste. 221
Las Vegas, NV 89183
Ph: (702)486-6625

Morrison, Dawn, President
National Association of Supervisors
of Business Education [7560]
c/o Melissa Scott, Treasurer
Nevada Department of Education
9890 S Maryland Pky., Ste. 221
Las Vegas, NV 89183
Ph: (702)486-6625

Morrison, Dennis, Chairman
Jamaica Tourist Board [23661]
5201 Blue Lagoon Dr., Ste. 670
Miami, FL 33126
Ph: (305)665-0557
Fax: (305)666-7239

Morrison, Jeff, Exec. Dir.
Substance Abuse Program
Administrators Association [17329]
1014 Whispering Oak Dr.
Bardstown, KY 40004
Toll Free: 800-672-7229
Fax: (281)664-3152

Morrison, Julie, VP
Supreme Lodge of the Danish
Sisterhood of America [9276]
c/o Aase Hansen, Trustee
2025 N Manning St.
Burbank, CA 91505
Ph: (818)845-5726
    (707)545-6023

Morrison, Kristin, VP
Schipperke Club of America [21957]
c/o Deb Decker, Membership
Chairperson
5100 Andalusia Trl.
Arlington, TX 76017

Morrison, Mary Kay, President
Association for Applied and
Therapeutic Humor [17436]
220 E State St., Fl. G
Rockford, IL 61104
Ph: (815)708-6587

Morrison, Melanie S., Founder,
Exec. Dir.
Allies for Change [19101]
PO Box 4353
East Lansing, MI 48826

Morrison, Merrie, VP of Operations
American Bird Conservancy [4781]
4249 Loudoun Ave.
The Plains, VA 20198-2237
Ph: (540)253-5780
Toll Free: 888-247-3624
Fax: (540)253-5782

Morrison, Nan J., CEO, President
Council for Economic Education
[7728]
122 E 42nd St., Ste. 2600
New York, NY 10168
Ph: (212)730-7007
Fax: (212)730-1793

Morrison, Patricia, President
Freshwater Mollusk Conservation
Society [4818]
c/o Teresa Newton, President
Upper Midwest Environ. Science Ctr.
U.S. Geological Survey
2630 Fanta Reed Rd.
Lacrosse, WI 54603
Ph: (608)781-6217

Morrison, Robert, Exec. Dir.
National Association of State Alcohol
and Drug Abuse Directors [13165]
1025 Connecticut Ave. NW, Ste. 605
Washington, DC 20036
Ph: (202)293-0090
Fax: (202)293-1250

Morrison, Sherrie, Secretary,
Treasurer
526th Armored Infantry Battalion Association [21187]
PO Box 456
Yolo, CA 95697-0456
Ph: (530)662-8160

Morrison, Tom, CEO
Metal Treating Institute [2358]
8825 Perimeter Park Blvd., No. 501
Jacksonville, FL 32216
Ph: (904)249-0448
Fax: (904)249-0459

Morrison, Capt. Vance H., Cmdr.
Naval Order of the United States
[21057]
PO Box 2142
Springfield, VA 22152-0142
Ph: (703)323-0929

Morrissey, Dan, Chairman
Automotive Body Parts Association
[336]

400 Putnam Pke., Ste. J, No. 503
Smithfield, RI 02917-2442
Ph: (401)949-0912
Toll Free: 800-323-5832
Fax: (401)262-0193

Morrow, Edwin P., CEO
International Association of
Registered Financial Consultants
[1242]
2507 N Verity Pky.
Middletown, OH 45042-0506
Toll Free: 800-532-9060
Fax: (513)424-5752

Morrow, Peter, Chairman
Arts Council of Mongolia-US [9812]
2025 23rd Ave. E
Seattle, WA 98112

Morrow, Theresa, VP
Women Against Prostate Cancer
[14081]
1220 L St. NW, Ste. 100-271
Washington, DC 20005-4018
Ph: (202)805-3266
Fax: (202)543-2727

Morse, Alan R., CEO, President
Jewish Guild for the Blind [17719]
15 W 65th St.
New York, NY 10023-6601
Ph: (212)769-6200
    (212)769-6331
Toll Free: 800-284-4422
Fax: (212)769-6266

Morse, Alan R., President, CEO
Lighthouse International [17722]
15 W 65th St.
New York, NY 10023-6601
Toll Free: 800-284-4422

Morse, Chuck, President
World Folk Music Association
[10025]
PO Box 83583
Gaithersburg, MD 20883

Morse, Susan C., Director, Founder
Keeping Track [4837]
2209 Main Rd.
Huntington, VT 05462
Ph: (802)434-7000
Fax: (802)434-5383

Mortati, Fred, Chairman
Association of Food Industries
[1318]
3301 Route 66, Ste. 205, Bldg. C
Neptune, NJ 07753
Ph: (732)922-3008
Fax: (732)922-3590

Mortel, Dr. Rodrigue, President
High Hopes for Haiti - Mortel
Foundation [11470]
PO Box 405
Hershey, PA 17033
Toll Free: 888-355-6065

Mortensen, Randy, President
World Wide Village [11463]
616 Sims Ave.
Saint Paul, MN 55130
Ph: (651)777-6908

Mortilla, Lynn, Exec. Dir.
Association of Dental Implant
Auxiliaries [14419]
55 Lane Rd., Ste. 305
Fairfield, NJ 07004
Ph: (973)783-6300
Fax: (973)783-1175

Morton, Cynthia, Treasurer
American Academy of Advertising
[83]

c/o Pat Rose, Executive Director
831 Fearrington Post
Pittsboro, NC 27312

Morton, Cynthia, Exec. VP
National Association for the Support
of Long Term Care [15044]
1050 17th St. NW, Ste. 500
Washington, DC 20036-5558
Ph: (202)803-2385

Morton, Erin Will, Director
Global Health Technologies Coalition
[15460]
455 Massachusetts Ave. NW, Ste.
1000
Washington, DC 20001
Ph: (202)822-0033

Morton, Joseph, Secretary
The National Press Club [2704]
529 14th St. NW, 13th Fl.
Washington, DC 20045
Ph: (202)662-7500
(202)662-7505

Morton, Linda, Rep.
Western Winter Sports Representa-
tives Association [3167]
726 Tenacity Dr., Unit B
Longmont, CO 80504
Ph: (303)532-4002
Fax: (866)929-4572

Morton, Dr. Marsha, President
Historians of German and Central
European Art [8859]
c/o James A. Van Dyke, Treasurer
365 McReynolds Hall
Dept. of Art History and Archaeology
University of Missouri
Columbia, MO 65211-2015

Morton, Thomas D., President
Child Welfare Institute [10907]
111 E Wacker Dr., Ste. 325
Chicago, IL 60601
Ph: (312)949-5640
Fax: (312)922-6736

Morzy, Anna, President
Polish American Chamber of Com-
merce [23614]
5214 W Lawrence Ave., Ste. 1
Chicago, IL 60630
Ph: (773)205-1998

Mosca, Michelle, President
Angel Names Association [12131]
PO Box 423
Saratoga Springs, NY 12866
Ph: (518)654-2411

Moscarillo, Dr. Frank, MD, Exec. Dir.
International Society for ECT and
Neurostimulation [15777]
5454 Wisconsin Ave., Ste. 1220
Chevy Chase, MD 20815
Ph: (301)951-7220
Fax: (301)299-4918

Moscato, Cathie, Administrator
Society of American Registered
Architects [5977]
14 E 38th St.
New York, NY 10016
Ph: (920)395-2330
Fax: (866)668-9858

Mosedale, Susan, Exec. VP
International Association of Amuse-
ment Parks and Attractions [1138]
1448 Duke St.
Alexandria, VA 22314
Ph: (703)836-4800
Fax: (703)836-4801

Moseley, Allyn, President
National Ornamental & Miscellaneous Metals Association [2363]

PO Box 492167
Lawrenceville, GA 30049
Toll Free: 888-516-8585
Fax: (888)279-7994

Moseley, Fred, Coord.
Union for Radical Political Econom-
ics [6404]
c/o Frances Boyes
University of Massachusetts
418 N Pleasant St.
Amherst, MA 01002-1735
Ph: (413)577-0806
Fax: (413)577-0261

Moser, Christine, Director
Austrian Cultural Forum [9197]
11 E 52nd St.
New York, NY 10022
Ph: (212)319-5300
Fax: (212)644-8660

Moses, Bob, Exec. Dir.
Audio Engineering Society [6417]
551 5th Ave., Ste. 1225
New York, NY 10165-2520
Ph: (212)661-8528

Moses, James A., CEO, President
Road Scholar [7673]
11 Ave. de Lafayette
Boston, MA 02111-1746
Ph: (978)323-4141
Toll Free: 800-454-5768
Fax: (877)426-2166

Moses, Mioshi J., President, CEO
Conference of Minority Transporta-
tion Officials [3326]
1875 I St. NW, Ste. 500
Washington, DC 20006
Ph: (703)234-4072
Fax: (202)318-0364

Mosley, LaDonna, President
American Maltese Association
[21813]
c/o LaDonna Mosley, President
10029 N River Rd.
New Haven, IN 46774-9450
Ph: (260)493-3413

Moss, Bill, President
World Whale Police [4921]
PO Box 814
Olympia, WA 98506
Ph: (360)561-7492

Moss, Ed, President
American Blonde d'Aquitaine Association [3684]
57 Friar Tuck Way
Fyffe, AL 35971
Ph: (256)996-3142
(918)772-2844

Moss, Gregg, President
Communications Media Manage-
ment Association [264]
140 Island Way, Ste. 316
Clearwater Beach, FL 33767
Ph: (561)477-8100

Moss, Ryan, President
American Ladder Institute [1564]
330 N Wabash Ave., Ste. 2000
Chicago, IL 60611
Ph: (202)367-1136
Fax: (312)673-6929

Moss, Mr. Stephen, Program Mgr.
American Ophthalmological Society
[16367]
655 Beach St.
San Francisco, CA 94109
Ph: (415)561-8578
Fax: (415)561-8531

Mossad, Emad, President
Congenital Cardiac Anesthesia
Society [13701]

2209 Dickens Rd.
Richmond, VA 23230-2005
Ph: (804)282-9780
Fax: (804)282-0090

Mott, Gary, Comm. Chm.
Automotive Fleet and Leasing As-
sociation [337]
N83 W13410 Leon Rd.
Menomonee Falls, WI 53051
Ph: (414)386-0366
Fax: (414)359-1671

Mottese, Lorelei, President
Women Grocers of America [2980]
1005 N Glebe Rd., Ste. 250
Arlington, VA 22201-5758
Ph: (703)516-0700
Fax: (703)516-0115

Motza, Maryann, President
National Conference of State Social
Security Administrators [5759]
61 Forsyth St. SW, Ste. 22T64
Atlanta, GA 30303
Ph: (404)562-1315
Fax: (404)562-1313

Mougey, Rob, VP
Marine Aquarium Societies of North
America [3642]
PO Box 105603
Atlanta, GA 30348-5603

Moulds, Steve, President
Napa Valley Grapegrowers [4930]
1795 3rd St.
Napa, CA 94559
Ph: (707)944-8311
Fax: (707)224-8644

Moulthrop, Jim, Exec. Dir.
FP2 Inc. [808]
8100 West Ct.
Austin, TX 78759
Ph: (512)977-1854

Moulton, Mika, President
Surviving Parents Coalition [11278]
1414 22nd St. NW, Ste. 4
Washington, DC 20037
Toll Free: 888-301-4343

Mount, Delora L., MD, Chairperson
American Association of Pediatric
Plastic Surgeons [16772]
500 Cummings Ctr., Ste. 4550
Beverly, MA 01915
Ph: (978)927-8330
Fax: (978)524-0498

Mount, Tom, PhD, CEO, President
International Association of Nitrox
and Technical Divers [22812]
119 NW Ethan Pl., Ste. 101
Lake City, FL 32055
Ph: (386)438-8312
Fax: (509)355-1297

Mountain, Matt, President
Association of Universities for
Research in Astronomy [6000]
1212 New York Ave. NW, Ste. 450
Washington, DC 20005
Ph: (202)483-2101
Fax: (202)483-2106

Mourning, Jillian, Founder
All We Want Is LOVE [18366]
300 Rampart St.
Charlotte, NC 28203
Ph: (704)625-6263

Mousley, Keith, President
Council of American Instructors of
the Deaf [15184]
PO Box 377
Bedford, TX 76095-0377
Ph: (817)354-8414

Mousseau, Kristine, President
United States Court Reporters As-
sociation [5123]
8430 Gross Point Rd., Ste. 115
Skokie, IL 60077-2036
Ph: (847)470-9500
Toll Free: 800-628-2730
Fax: (847)470-9505

Mowat, Allan, MD, PhD, President
Society for Mucosal Immunology
[15385]
N83 W13410 Leon Rd.
Menomonee Falls, WI 53051
Ph: (414)359-1650
Fax: (414)359-1671

Mowl, Harold, President
Discovering Deaf Worlds [11940]
PO Box 10063
Rochester, NY 14610
Ph: (585)234-8144

Moxley, Chuck, Founder, President
EcoLogical Mail Coalition [4056]
6886 Fallsbrook Ct.
Granite Bay, CA 95746-6510
Toll Free: 800-620-3975
Fax: (925)397-3096

Moy, Get W., Chairman
High Performance Building Council
[6164]
3101 Wilson Blvd., Ste. 900
Arlington, VA 22201
Ph: (703)682-1630

Moy, Patricia, President
World Association for Public Opinion
Research [18925]
201 N 13th St.
Lincoln, NE 68588-0242
Ph: (402)472-7720
Fax: (402)472-7727

Moye, Johnny, Membership Chp.
International Technology and
Engineering Educators Association
- Council for Supervision and
Leadership [8670]
c/o ITEEA
1914 Association Dr., Ste. 201
Reston, VA 20191-1539
Ph: (703)860-2100
Fax: (703)860-0353

Moyer, Mike, Exec. Dir.
National Wrestling Coaches Associa-
tion [23371]
330 Hostetter St.
Manheim, PA 17545
Ph: (717)653-8009
Fax: (717)653-8270

Moynahan, Karen P., Exec. Dir.
National Association of Schools of
Dance [7704]
11250 Roger Bacon Dr., Ste. 21
Reston, VA 20190-5248
Ph: (703)437-0700
Fax: (703)437-6312

Moynahan, Karen P., Exec. Dir.
National Association of Schools of
Music [8382]
11250 Roger Bacon Dr., Ste. 21
Reston, VA 20190-5248
Ph: (703)437-0700
Fax: (703)437-6312

Moynahan, Karen P., Exec. Dir.
National Association of Schools of
Theatre [8699]
11250 Roger Bacon Dr., Ste. 21
Reston, VA 20190-5248
Ph: (703)437-0700
Fax: (703)437-6312

Mozen, Judy, President
National Association of the Remodeling Industry [555]

PO Box 4250
Des Plaines, IL 60016
Ph: (847)298-9200
Fax: (847)298-9225

Mozer, David, Director
International Bicycle Fund [13232]
4887 Columbia Dr. S
Seattle, WA 98108-1919
Ph: (206)767-0848

Mroz, John Edwin, Founder
EastWest Institute [18477]
11 E 26th St., 20th Fl.
New York, NY 10010
Ph: (212)824-4100

Msiza, Paul, President
Baptist World Alliance [19726]
405 N Washington St.
Falls Church, VA 22046
Ph: (703)790-8980
Fax: (703)893-5160

Muccioli, Ron, Director
Lawrence Technological University
Alumni Association [19332]
21000 W 10 Mile Rd.
Southfield, MI 48075-1058
Ph: (248)204-2309

Muchnik, Pablo, President
North American Kant Society
[10105]
c/o Pablo Muchnik, President
120 Boylston St.
Boston, MA 02116-4624

Mucklow, Rosemary, V. Chmn. of the
Bd.
International HACCP Alliance [4567]
120 Rosethal Ctr., 2471 TAMU
College Station, TX 77843-2471
Ph: (979)862-3643
Fax: (979)862-3075

Mudre, Roger, Bd. Member
Silvermine Arts Center [8888]
1037 Silvermine Rd.
New Canaan, CT 06840-4398
Ph: (203)966-9700

Muehlbauer, Eric, Exec. Dir.
North American Spine Society
[16034]
7075 Veterans Blvd.
Burr Ridge, IL 60527
Ph: (630)230-3600
Toll Free: 866-960-6277
Fax: (630)230-3700

Mueller, Cathy, Exec. Dir.
Mapping Your Future [7962]
PO Box 2578
Sugar Land, TX 77487

Mueller, Gabriella, Exec. Dir.
A Leg To Stand On [11614]
401 Park Ave. S, 10th Fl.
New York, NY 10016
Ph: (212)683-8805
Fax: (212)683-8813

Mueller, Jack, Hist.
Kaiser-Frazer Owners Club
International [21413]
PO Box 424
Thomasville, AL 36784
Ph: (334)636-5873

Mueller, Rick, Treasurer
California Association of Tiger-
Owners [21347]
2950 Calle Grande Vista
San Clemente, CA 92672

Mueller, Ryan, Exec. Dir.
Interstate Council on Water Policy
[5653]

505 N Ivy St.
Arlington, VA 22201-1707
Ph: (573)303-6644

Mueller, Shannon, Mgr.
American Society of Ophthalmic
Administrators [15576]
4000 Legato Rd., Ste. 700
Fairfax, VA 22033
Ph: (703)788-5777

Muench, Richard G., Chairman
American Hearing Research
Foundation [15172]
275 N York St., Ste. 401
Elmhurst, IL 60126
Ph: (630)617-5079
Fax: (630)563-9181

Muffett, Carroll, CEO, President
Center for International
Environmental Law [5177]
1350 Connecticut Ave. NW, Ste.
1100
Washington, DC 20036
Ph: (202)785-8700
Fax: (202)785-8701

Mugar, Carolyn, Exec. Dir.
Farm Aid [17788]
501 Cambridge St., 3rd Fl.
Cambridge, MA 02141
Ph: (617)354-2922
Toll Free: 800-327-6243
Fax: (617)354-6992

Mugford, J. Gerry, Dr., President
American Psychotherapy and Medi-
cal Hypnosis Association [16963]
11827 Button Willow Cove
San Antonio, TX 78213
Ph: (956)203-0608

Muglich, Mark, Chairman
National Parking Association [2497]
1112 16th St. NW, Ste. 840
Washington, DC 20036
Ph: (202)296-4336
Toll Free: 800-647-7275
Fax: (202)296-3102

Muha, Denise B., Exec. Dir.
National Leased Housing Associa-
tion [11984]
1900 L St. NW, Ste. 300
Washington, DC 20036-5027
Ph: (202)785-8888
Fax: (202)785-2008

Muhanji, John, Director
Friends United Meeting [20171]
101 Quaker Hill Dr.
Richmond, IN 47374-1926
Ph: (765)962-7573

Muilenberg, Michael L., Secretary,
Treasurer
Pan-American Aerobiology Associa-
tion [6095]
University of Massachusetts-Amherst
N239B Morril-I
639 N Pleasant St.
Amherst, MA 01003-9298
Ph: (413)545-3052
Fax: (413)545-0964

Muindi, Dr. Florence, CEO, Founder,
President
Life in Abundance International
[10480]
211 Townepark Cir., Ste. 201
Louisville, KY 40243
Ph: (502)749-7691
Toll Free: 877-439-5566

Mujica, Mr. Mauro E., Chairman,
CEO
U.S. English [18877]
5335 Wisconsin Ave. NW, Ste. 930

Washington, DC 20015
Ph: (202)833-0100
Toll Free: 800-787-8216
Fax: (202)833-0108

Mukantabana, Mathilde, President
Friends of Rwanda Association
[10988]
PO Box 1311
Elk Grove, CA 95759-1311
Ph: (916)683-3356

Mukerjee-Brown, Lucy, Officer
Outfest [9309]
3470 Wilshire Blvd., Ste. 935
Los Angeles, CA 90010
Ph: (213)480-7088
Fax: (213)480-7099

Mukobi, Asaba, President
Kasese Wildlife Conservation Aware-
ness Organization [4836]
PO Box 10664
Portland, OR 97296

Mulberry, Joe, President
National Association of Consumer
Credit Administrators [5105]
PO Box 20871
Columbus, OH 43220-0871
Ph: (614)326-1165
Fax: (614)326-1162

Mulcahey, Mary Jane, President
American Spinal Injury Association
[17251]
2209 Dickens Rd.
Richmond, VA 23230
Ph: (804)565-6396
Fax: (804)282-0090

Mulcahy, Denis, Chairman, Founder
Project Children [11263]
PO Box 933
Greenwood Lake, NY 10925

Mulcaire-Jones, Dr. George,
Founder, President
Maternal Life International [17109]
326A S Jackson St.
Butte, MT 59701
Ph: (406)782-1719

Mulder, Gary, Director
Protestant Church-Owned Publishers
Association [2810]
6631 Westbury Oaks Ct.
Springfield, VA 22152
Ph: (703)220-5989

Mulder, Randy, Treasurer
National Coalition of Creative Arts
Therapies Associations [16984]
PO Box 3403
Seal Beach, CA 90740

Muldoon, Krista Wilson, President
Mounted Games Across America
[23235]
c/o Matthew Brown, Membership
Chairman
120 Long Acre Ct.
Frederick, MD 21702
Ph: (240)500-4906

Mulholland, Jane, President
Women in the Visual and Literary
Arts [9008]
PO Box 130406
Houston, TX 77219-0406

Mulholland-Wozniak, Ken, PhD.,
Secretary
InterServe U.S.A. [20427]
PO Box 418
Upper Darby, PA 19082-0418
Toll Free: 800-809-4440
Fax: (610)352-4394

Mull, Ms. Lynda Diane, Exec. Dir.,
President
International Initiative on Exploitative
Child Labor [11048]
1016 S Wayne St., Apt. 702
Arlington, VA 22204
Ph: (703)920-0435
Fax: (703)328-3401

Mullaney, Brian, Founder, CEO
WonderWork [17419]
420 5th Ave., 27th Fl.
New York, NY 10018
Ph: (212)729-1855
Fax: (212)729-4541

Mullaney, Tom, President
National Association of State Budget
Officers [5709]
Hall of the States Bldg.
444 N Capitol St. NW, Ste. 642
Washington, DC 20001
Ph: (202)624-5382
Fax: (202)624-7745

Mullen, Denise, President
National Association of Schools of
Art and Design [7517]
11250 Roger Bacon Dr., Ste. 21
Reston, VA 20190-5248
Ph: (703)437-0700
Fax: (703)437-6312

Mullen, Janet, Dir. of Fin. & Admin.
Institute for Women's Policy
Research [18212]
1200 18th St. NW, Ste. 301
Washington, DC 20036
Ph: (202)785-5100
Fax: (202)833-4362

Mullen, Jeanniey, Founder
Email Experience Council [6443]
1615 L St. NW
Washington, DC 20036

Mullen, Jewel, MD, MPH, MPA,
President
Association of State and Territorial
Health Officials [5714]
2231 Crystal Dr., Ste. 450
Arlington, VA 22202
Ph: (202)371-9090
Fax: (571)527-3189

Mullen-Roth, Barbara, President
Executive Women in Government
[5194]
PO Box 4233
Washington, DC 20044-9233
Ph: (202)496-1293
Fax: (202)466-3226

Muller, Artie, Exec. Dir.
Rolling Thunder [21093]
PO Box 216
Neshanic Station, NJ 08853
Ph: (908)369-5439
Fax: (908)369-2072

Muller, Craig, CEO, President
Kinship United [11248]
5105 Tollview Dr., Ste. 155
Rolling Meadows, IL 60008
Ph: (847)577-1070
Toll Free: 877-577-1070
Fax: (877)577-1080

Muller, Eugene, Chairperson
Collision Industry Electronic Com-
merce Association [996]
c/o Fred Iantorno, Executive Director
3149 Dundee Rd., No. 181
Northbrook, IL 60062-2402
Ph: (847)498-6945
Fax: (847)897-2094

Mulligan, Bob, Contact
Organization for Professional Astrology [5994]

c/o Sarah Leigh Serio, Treasurer
574 Linden Park Ct.
Boulder, CO 80304

Mulligan, Clark, CAE, President
Laboratory Products Association
[3027]
PO Box 428
Fairfax, VA 22038
Ph: (703)836-1360
Fax: (703)836-6644

Mullin, Mr. John J., Exec. Chmn. of
the Bd.
World Traditional Karate Organization [23033]
c/o John Mullin, Executive Chairman
521 Jewett Ave.
Staten Island, NY 10314
Ph: (347)609-3608

Mullin, Peter, President
American Bugatti Club [21317]
c/o Paul Simms, Secretary
600 Lakeview Terr.
Glen Ellyn, IL 60137
Ph: (630)469-4920

Mullings, Lisa J., CEO, President
NATSO [2971]
1330 Braddock Pl., No. 501
Alexandria, VA 22314
Ph: (703)549-2100
Toll Free: 800-527-1666

Mullings, Lorna, RN, President
Dorcas Medical Mission, Inc.
[15447]
907 Utica Ave.
Brooklyn, NY 11203
Ph: (718)342-2928
Fax: (718)342-5721

Mullins, Betsy, President, CEO
Women's Campaign Fund [18237]
718 7th St. NW, 2nd Fl.
Washington, DC 20001
Ph: (202)796-8259

Mullins, Bill, President
Parker Gun Collectors Association
[22022]
477 Ocean Ave.
Wells, ME 04090

Mullins, DeAnn, Chairman
National Community Pharmacists
Association [16676]
100 Daingerfield Rd.
Alexandria, VA 22314
Ph: (703)683-8200
Toll Free: 800-544-7447
Fax: (703)683-3619

Mullins, Mack H., Exec. Dir.
Retired Military Police Officers As-
sociation [21050]
PO Box 5477
Springfield, VA 22150
Fax: (703)533-7207

Mullins, Marcia Morse, President
Morse Society [20984]
PO Box 984
Lakeland, FL 33802

Mullis, Brian Thomas, CEO, Founder
Sustainable Travel International
[3398]
222 Broadway
New York, NY 10010

Mullner, Ken, Exec. Dir.
National Adoption Center [10459]
1500 Walnut St., Ste. 701
Philadelphia, PA 19102
Ph: (215)735-9988
Toll Free: 800-TO-ADOPT
Fax: (215)735-9410

Mulqueen, John, MD, President,
Founder
Forward in Health [15002]
192 Lawrence St.
Gardner, MA 01440
Ph: (978)808-5234

Mulrooney, Margaret, President
Association for General and Liberal
Studies [8226]
c/o Joyce Lucke, Executive Director
428 5th St.
Columbus, IN 47201
Ph: (812)376-7468

Mulroy, Fr. Timothy, Reg. Dir.
Missionary Society of St. Columban
[19865]
PO Box 10
Saint Columbans, NE 68056
Ph: (402)291-1920
Toll Free: 877-299-1920
Fax: (402)291-4984

Mumma, Mr. Keith, Director
International Child Care U.S.A.
[11238]
240 W Michigan
Kalamazoo, MI 49007
Ph: (269)382-9960
Toll Free: 800-722-4453

Mundell, George, Exec. VP, COO
National Private Truck Council
[3345]
950 N Glebe Rd., Ste. 2300
Arlington, VA 22203-4183
Ph: (703)683-1300
Fax: (703)683-1217

Mundinger, Elizabeth, Esq., Exec.
Dir.
Emergency Department Practice
Management Association [14677]
8400 Westpark Dr., 2nd Fl.
McLean, VA 22102
Ph: (703)610-0314
Fax: (703)995-4678

Mundis, Cindy, M.A, CRC, LPC, Bd.
Member
National Association of Multicultural
Rehabilitation Concerns [17089]
c/o Robin Washington, PhD,
President
Governors State University
Department of Physical Therapy
University Park, IL
Ph: (708)534-3147

Mundschenk, Chris, Exec. Dir.
Product Development and Manage-
ment Association [2189]
330 N Wabash Ave., Ste. 2000
Chicago, IL 60611
Ph: (312)321-5145
Toll Free: 800-232-5241
Fax: (312)673-6885

Mundy, Betty, Contact
National Brussels Griffon Rescue,
Inc. [10666]
c/o Betty Mundy
181 Bonetti Dr.
San Luis Obispo, CA 93401

Mundy, Ray, Exec. Dir.
Airport Ground Transportation As-
sociation [3319]
1538 Powell Rd.
Powell, OH 43065
Ph: (314)753-3432
Fax: (314)667-3850

Munger, Kelly, FSA, Coord.
Managed Care Risk Association
[1607]
333 Washington Ave. N, Ste. 5000

Minneapolis, MN 55401-1331
Ph: (612)455-8324

Munici, Pam, President
North American Potbellied Pig As-
sociation [3609]
15525 E Via Del Palo
Gilbert, AZ 85298-9720
Ph: (480)899-8941

Munion, Ivy, President
American Society of Irrigation
Consultants [7363]
4700 S Hagadorn Rd., Ste. 195D
East Lansing, MI 48823-6808
Ph: (508)763-8140

Munjal, Naveen, Director
Light Electric Vehicle Association
[3338]
6900-29 Daniels Pky., No. 209
Fort Myers, FL 33912

Munn, Christine, President
Montessori Institute of America
[7782]
3482 Keith Bridge Rd., No. 340
Cumming, GA 30041
Toll Free: 844-642-9675

Munn, David C., CEO, President
Information Technology Services
Marketing Association [2284]
91 Hartwell Ave.
Lexington, MA 02421-3137
Ph: (781)862-8500
Fax: (781)674-1366

Muno, Ed, Mgr.
National Cowboy and Western
Heritage Museum [8801]
1700 NE 63rd St.
Oklahoma City, OK 73111
Ph: (405)478-2250
Fax: (405)478-4714

Munoz, Diana, Admin. Asst.
American Radium Society [16334]
11300 W Olympic Blvd., Ste. 600
Los Angeles, CA 90064
Ph: (310)437-0581
Fax: (310)437-0585

Munoz, Elisa Lees, Exec. Dir.
International Women's Media
Foundation [3494]
1625 K St. NW, Ste. 1275
Washington, DC 20006
Ph: (202)496-1992

Munoz, Oscar, President
International Brotherhood of Magi-
cians [22178]
13 Point West Blvd.
Saint Charles, MO 63301-4431
Ph: (636)724-2400
Fax: (636)724-8566

Munro, Robert J., President
Caledonian Foundation USA, Inc.
[9883]
PO Box 1242
Edgartown, MA 02539-1242

Muns, William R., Founder
Mozambique Conservation
Organization [3900]
PO Box 610623
Dallas, TX 75261
Fax: (888)810-3161

Munshi, Dr. Anwar, President
Association of Indian Muslims of
America [19470]
PO Box 10654
Silver Spring, MD 20914

Munson, Angela, Managing Dir.
Sporting Goods Shippers Association [3104]

3250 Spanish Springs Ct.
Sparks, NV 89434
Ph: (775)356-9931
Fax: (775)356-9932

Muppidi, Dr. Uma, VP
India Development Service [19074]
PO Box 980
Chicago, IL 60690

Murdoch, Chris, Dir. of Programs
Opportunity International [12071]
550 W Van Buren, Ste. 200
Chicago, IL 60607
Ph: (312)487-5000
Toll Free: 800-793-9455
Fax: (312)487-5656

Murdock, Susan, Dir. of Operations,
Dir. of Member Svcs.
Kidney Care Partners [15878]
601 13th St. NW, 11th Fl.
Washington, DC 20005
Ph: (703)830-9192

Mureithi, Robinson, President
Immanuel Orphans [11043]
PO Box 43716
Baltimore, MD 21236

Murekeyisoni, Juliette, President
Inyana - League for Rwandan
Children and Youth [11241]
c/o Thomas Kainamura, Treasurer/
Co-Founder
230 Sunset Ridge
Rocky Hill, CT 06067

Muri, Ina, Contact
Scandinavian Tourist Boards [23664]
655 3rd Ave., Ste. 1810
New York, NY 10017
Ph: (212)885-9700

Muri, Janet H., MPA, President
National Perinatal Information Center
[16624]
225 Chapman St., Ste. 200
Providence, RI 02905-3633
Ph: (401)274-0650
Fax: (401)455-0377

Muric, Maja, Founder, President
Humanitarian Wave [13063]
649 Beach St.
Encinitas, CA 92024
Ph: (760)436-6016
Fax: (760)230-6866

Murner, Doreen, CEO
National Association of Educational
Procurement [7434]
8840 Stanford Blvd., Ste. 2000
Columbia, MD 21045
Ph: (443)543-5540
Fax: (443)219-9687

Murphy, Allen, President
Ballew Family Association of
America [20782]
c/o Paul Ballew
PO Box 2808
Lawton, OK 73502
Ph: (580)595-1007

Murphy, Bruce D., President
Society for the Study of Reproduc-
tion [17130]
1619 Monroe St., Ste. 3
Madison, WI 53711-2063
Ph: (608)256-2777
Fax: (608)256-4610

Murphy, Christopher M., Exec. Dir.
American Board of Wound Manage-
ment [17524]
1800 M St. NW, Ste. 400S
Washington, DC 20036
Ph: (202)457-8408
Fax: (202)530-0659

Murphy, Corey, Exec. Dir.
Oncology Association of Naturopathic Physicians [15865]
c/o Corey Murphy, Executive Director
PO Box 20665
Juneau, AK 99802
Toll Free: 800-908-5175

Murphy, Cynthia Miller, Exec. Dir.
Oncology Nursing Certification Corporation [16173]
125 Enterprise Dr.
Pittsburgh, PA 15275
Ph: (412)859-6104
Toll Free: 877-769-ONCC
Fax: (412)859-6168

Murphy, David, Contact
Energy Training Council [6483]
PO Box 850359
Yukon, OK 73085

Murphy, Dennis P., Chairman
Every Person Influences Children [10817]
1000 Main St.
Buffalo, NY 14202
Ph: (716)332-4100
Fax: (716)332-4101

Murphy, John, VP
Association of Modified Asphalt Producers [500]
PO Box 305
Avon, OH 44011
Ph: (330)714-4117
    (440)249-0144

Murphy, John, Treasurer
Council for Resource Development [7834]
8720 Georgia Ave., Ste. 700
Silver Spring, MD 20910
Ph: (202)822-0750

Murphy, Karen, President
Quota International [12905]
1420 21st St. NW
Washington, DC 20036-5901
Ph: (202)331-9694
Fax: (202)331-4395

Murphy, Ken, President
Moon Society [7219]
5015 Addison Cir., No. 420
Addison, TX 75001
Ph: (214)507-7911

Murphy, Kevin, Bd. Member
International Association for Human Resource Information Management [73]
PO Box 1086
Burlington, MA 01803
Ph: (781)791-9488
Toll Free: 800-804-3983

Murphy, Laura, Bd. Member
Historians Against Slavery [12039]
c/o Laura Murphy, Board Member
Dept. of English
Loyola University New Orleans
6363 St. Charles Ave.
New Orleans, LA 70116
Ph: (504)865-2479

Murphy, Lisa A., VMD, DABT, President
International Association for Aquatic Animal Medicine [17648]
c/o Pam Tuomi, President-elect
Alaska SeaLife Ctr.
301 Railway Ave.
Seward, AK 99664
Ph: (907)229-5524

Murphy, Megan, Exec. Dir.
National Coalition of Girls' Schools [7790]

Po Box 5729
Charlottesville, VA 22905-5729
Ph: (434)205-4496

Murphy, Michael, Exec. Dir.
International Catholic Stewardship Council [19846]
26300 Ford Rd., No. 317
Dearborn Heights, MI 48127
Toll Free: 800-352-3452
Fax: (313)446-8316

Murphy, Patricia Anne, Chairperson
International Philosophers for Peace and Prevention of Nuclear Omnicide [18795]
c/o Professor Glen T. Martin, President
PO Box 6943
Radford, VA 24142

Murphy, Mr. Patrick, Exec. Dir.
International Laser Display Association [1143]
7062 Edgeworth Dr.
Orlando, FL 32819
Ph: (407)797-7654

Murphy, Priscilla, 1st VP
Chi Eta Phi Sorority [23838]
3029 13th St. NW
Washington, DC 20009
Ph: (202)232-3858
Fax: (202)232-3460

Murphy, Mr. Steven, Secretary
Sertoma Inc. [12908]
1912 E Meyer Blvd.
Kansas City, MO 64132
Ph: (816)333-8300
Fax: (816)333-4320

Murphy, Thomas A., Exec. Dir.
Phi Mu Delta [23915]
216 Haddon Ave., Ste. 602
Haddon Township, NJ 08108
Ph: (609)220-4975

Murphy, Tim, Treasurer
Association of Environmental Health Academic Programs [4124]
PO Box 66057
Burien, WA 98166
Ph: (206)522-5272
Fax: (206)985-9805

Murphy, Tim, Treasurer
Merchant Risk Council [1000]
1809 7th Ave., Ste. 1403
Seattle, WA 98101-4405
Ph: (206)364-2789
Fax: (206)367-1115

Murphy, Tim, Coord.
Orphan's Lifeline of Hope International [11121]
135 Kelly Rd.
Kalispell, MT 59901
Ph: (406)257-0868

Murphy, Wayne C.
International Society of Certified Employee Benefit Specialists [1073]
18700 W Bluemound Rd.
Brookfield, WI 53008-0209
Ph: (262)786-8771
Fax: (262)786-8670

Murr, Donna, President, Director
National Association of Health and Educational Facilities Finance Authorities [1590]
PO Box 906
Oakhurst, NJ 07755
Toll Free: 888-414-5713

Murray, Barbara E., MD, Exec.
Infectious Diseases Society of America [15402]

1300 Wilson Blvd., Ste. 300
Arlington, VA 22209
Ph: (703)299-0200
Fax: (703)299-0204

Murray, David, Chairman
Craft and Hobby Association [1641]
319 E 54th St.
Elmwood Park, NJ 07407
Ph: (201)835-1200

Murray, Eileen, Exec. Dir.
American Epilepsy Society [14737]
342 N Main St., Ste. 301
West Hartford, CT 06117-2507
Ph: (860)586-7505
Fax: (860)586-7550

Murray, Dr. Elizabeth A., Founder, President
Lonergan Philosophical Society [10100]
c/o Prof. Mark Doorley, Secretary-Treasurer
St. Augustine Ctr., Rm. 481
Dept. of Philosophy
Villanova University
800 Lancaster Ave.
Villanova, PA 19085

Murray, Evelyn M.E., FSA, Mem.
Murray Clan Society of North America [20903]
c/o Steve Murray-Wolf, President
5764 S Kline St.
Littleton, CO 80127

Murray, George, Adj.
86th Chemical Mortar Battalion Association [21178]
c/o George Murray, Adjutant
818 W 62nd St.
Anniston, AL 36206
Ph: (256)820-4415

Murray, Gregg R., PhD, Exec. Dir.
Association for Politics and the Life Sciences [7044]
c/o Gregg R. Murray, PhD, Executive Director
Texas Tech University
Political Science Dept.
Lubbock, TX 79409
Ph: (806)834-4017

Murray, Jamala, VP, Director
International Association of Black Actuaries [1873]
PO Box 270701
West Hartford, CT 06127
Ph: (860)906-1286
Fax: (860)906-1369

Murray, Jane, MD, Chairperson
Women in Balance Institute [17767]
049 SW Porter St.
Portland, OR 97201-4848
Ph: (503)552-1527

Murray, Jim, 1st VP
United Ostomy Associations of America, Inc. [16528]
PO Box 525
Kennebunk, ME 04043-0525
Toll Free: 800-826-0826

Murray, Karen, Chairman
Marfan Foundation [17484]
22 Manhasset Ave.
Port Washington, NY 11050
Ph: (516)883-8712
Toll Free: 800-8 MARFAN
Fax: (516)883-8040

Murray, Patty, JD, Chairman
Hope for Two.. The Pregnant With Cancer Network [13983]
PO Box 253

Amherst, NY 14226
Toll Free: 800-743-4471

Murray, William J., Chairman
Religious Freedom Coalition [12721]
601 Pennsylvania Ave. NW, Ste. 900
Washington, DC 20004-3647

Murray, William, VP
National Alliance of Forest Owners [4208]
122 C St. NW, Ste. 630
Washington, DC 20001
Ph: (202)747-0750
Fax: (202)824-0770

Murray, William, CEO, President
National Coffee Association of U.S. A., Inc. [429]
45 Broadway, Ste. 1140
New York, NY 10006
Ph: (212)766-4007
Fax: (212)766-5815

Murray, William, VP
National Weather Association [6857]
3100 Monitor Ave., Ste. 123
Norman, OK 73072
Ph: (405)701-5167
Fax: (405)701-5227

Murren, James J., Chairman
Corporate Responsibility Association [915]
123 S Broad St., Ste. 1930
Philadelphia, PA 19109
Ph: (215)606-9520
Fax: (267)800-2701

Murrle, Christian, President
Colombian American Association [23545]
641 Lexington Ave., Ste. 1430
New York, NY 10022
Ph: (212)233-7776
Fax: (212)233-7779

Murry, Lynn, President
National Tunis Sheep Registry, Inc. [4675]
305 Lincoln St.
Wamego, KS 66547
Ph: (785)456-8500
Fax: (785)456-8599

Murtari, Joseph, President
National Aviation and Space Education Alliance [7526]
23 Nutmeg Dr.
Enfield, CT 06082
Ph: (505)774-0029

Muru-Lanning, Marama, Chmn. of the Bd.
Association for Social Anthropology in Oceania [5910]
c/o Jerry Jacka, Secretary
Dept. of Anthropology
University of Colorado - Boulder
CB 233
Boulder, CO 80309-0233

Musante, Kathleen, President
Society for Applied Anthropology [5920]
PO Box 2436
Oklahoma City, OK 73101-2436
Ph: (405)843-5113
Fax: (405)843-8553

Musch, Bruno, Chmn. of the Bd.
Society for Worldwide Medical Exchange [15497]
1666 Kennedy Cswy., Ste. 71
North Bay Village, FL 33141
Ph: (305)407-9222
Fax: (305)433-7128

Muse, Tonya, Exec. Dir.
Council of Manufacturing Associations [2219]

733 10th St. NW, Ste. 700
Washington, DC 20001
Ph: (202)637-3000
Toll Free: 800-814-8468
Fax: (202)637-3182

Musheno, Kim, Chairman
Consortium for Citizens with Dis-
abilities [11582]
1825 K St. NW, Ste. 1200
Washington, DC 20006
Ph: (202)783-2229
Fax: (202)783-8250

Musil, Robert K., PhD, MPH,
President, CEO
Rachel Carson Council [13221]
8600 Irvington Ave.
Bethesda, MD 20817
Ph: (301)214-2400

Musil, Robert K., Chmn. of the Bd.
Council for a Livable World Educa-
tion Fund [18125]
322 4th St. NE
Washington, DC 20002
Ph: (202)543-4100

Musk, Dennis, Contact
Catholics United for Life [12766]
PO Box 10
New Hope, KY 40052-0010
Toll Free: 800-764-8444

Musk, Kimbal, Founder, CEO
The Kitchen Community [8400]
1980 8th St.
Boulder, CO 80302
Ph: (720)263-0501

Muskat, Paul, President
International Saw and Knife Association [2066]
c/o Paul Muskat, President
200 Valley Dr. No. 34
Brisbane, CA 94005
Ph: (949)480-1228
(425)289-0125
Fax: (866)751-4979

Musnicki, Jaime, Exec. Dir.
American Avalanche Association
[12813]
c/o Jaime Musnicki, Executive Direc-
tor
PO Box 248
Victor, ID 83455
Ph: (307)699-2049

Musonda, Anne, Exec. Dir.
Zambia Hope International [11195]
Hope Mountain Foundation
5235 Westview Dr., Ste. 100
Frederick, MD 21703
Ph: (301)624-0061

Mussato-Allen, Cristala, Exec. Dir.,
Founder
Native Workplace [12384]
PO Box 136757
Fort Worth, TX 76136

Musselman, Gary, President
NFHS Coaches Association [22736]
c/o National Federation of State
High Schools
PO Box 690
Indianapolis, IN 46206
Ph: (317)972-6900
Fax: (317)822-5700

Musso, John D., CAE, Exec. Dir.
Association of School Business Of-
ficials International [7427]
11401 N Shore Dr.
Reston, VA 20190-4232
Toll Free: 866-682-2729
Fax: (703)478-0205

Musulin, Sarah, President
Association of Veterinary Hematol-
ogy and Transfusion Medicine
[17639]
PO Box 1234
Sahuarita, AZ 85629-1004
Toll Free: 844-430-4300
Fax: (844)430-4300

Musuraca, Michael, Chairman
Verité [11787]
44 Belchertown Rd.
Amherst, MA 01002-2992
Ph: (413)253-9227
Fax: (413)256-8960

Mutebi, Solomon, President
Blessings of Joy [10869]
PO Box 701143
Tulsa, OK 74170
Ph: (918)282-3623

Muth, R.Timothy, President
Volunteer Missionary Movement -
U.S. Office [19920]
5980 W Loomis Rd.
Greendale, WI 53129-1824
Ph: (414)423-8660
Fax: (414)423-8964

Mutua, Muthoka, Chairman,
President
International Development Missions
[12166]
PO Box 5600
Reno, NV 89513-5600

Mutunga, Charles, Chairman
Kenyan Americans Community
Organization, Inc. [10489]
PO Box 1701
Duluth, GA 30096
Ph: (404)219-2098

Müller, Ulla E., President, CEO
Engenderhealth [11839]
440 9th Ave.
New York, NY 10001
Ph: (212)561-8000
Toll Free: 800-564-2872
Fax: (212)561-8067

Mwinzi-Edozie, Mwende, Exec. Dir.
Twana Twitu [11172]
Mwinzi Kaluva Bldg.
350 5th Ave. 59th Fl.
New York, NY 10022
Ph: (212)537-5927
Fax: (914)470-1320

Myer, Allan A., Chmn. of the Bd.
The Israel Project [18585]
2020 K St. NW, Ste. 7600
Washington, DC 20006
Ph: (202)857-6644
Fax: (202)540-4567

Myerburg, Robert J., MD, President
Cardiac Arrhythmias Research and
Education Foundation [14103]
PO Box 69
Seymour, WI 54165
Ph: (920)833-7000
(425)785-5836
Toll Free: 800-404-9500
Fax: (920)833-7005

Myerowitz, Dr. Zev J., D.C., Officer
Council of Chiropractic Acupuncture
[14263]
c/o A. Rand Olso, President
1360 Big Bend Sq.
Ballwin, MO 63021
Ph: (636)225-2121
Fax: (636)225-8122

Myers, Bill, Treasurer
Wood Engravers Network [21788]
3999 Waters Rd.

Ann Arbor, MI 48103
Ph: (734)665-6044

Myers, Bruce D., VP
PBR Forces Veterans Association
[21168]
14015 Spanish Point Rd.
Jacksonville, FL 32225
Ph: (812)636-4343
Fax: (812)636-4343

Myers, Cathy, Exec. Dir.
Family and Home Network [12412]
PO Box 492
Merrifield, VA 22116

Myers, Dan A., Chairman
University of North Carolina General
Alumni Association [19364]
CB No 9180, Stadium Dr.
Chapel Hill, NC 27514
Ph: (919)962-1208
Fax: (919)962-0010

Myers, David, CEO, President
American Institutes for Research in
the Behavioral Sciences [6027]
1000 Thomas Jefferson St. NW
Washington, DC 20007
Ph: (202)403-5000
Fax: (202)403-5001

Myers, Jeff, President, CEO
Medicaid Health Plans of America
[15100]
1150 18th St. NW, Ste. 1010
Washington, DC 20036
Ph: (202)857-5720
Fax: (202)857-5731

Myers, Joseph A., Exec. Dir.
National Indian Justice Center
[19584]
5250 Aero Dr.
Santa Rosa, CA 95403
Ph: (707)579-5507
Toll Free: 800-966-0662
Fax: (707)579-9019

Myers, Linda, President
Blackburn Family Association
[20784]
25474 Wareham Dr.
Huntington Woods, MI 48070
Ph: (248)677-7411

Myers, Linda James, PhD, Chairman
National Association for the Educa-
tion of African American Children
with Learning Differences [12238]
PO Box 09521
Columbus, OH 43209
Ph: (614)237-6021
Fax: (614)238-0929

Myers, Linda Joy, PhD, Founder,
President
National Association of Memoir Writ-
ers [10388]
1700 Solano Ave.
Berkeley, CA 94707
Ph: (510)859-4718

Myers, Dr. Martin G., MD, Ed.-in-
Chief, Exec. Dir.
National Network for Immunization
Information [15384]
301 University Blvd.
Galveston, TX 77555-0350
Ph: (702)200-0201
Fax: (409)772-5208

Myers, Matthew L., President
National Center for Tobacco-Free
Kids [17226]
1400 Eye St. NW, Ste. 1200
Washington, DC 20005
Ph: (202)296-5469
Fax: (202)296-5427

Myers, Mike, CFO
Winrock International Institute for
Agricultural Development [17792]
2101 Riverfront Dr.
Little Rock, AR 72202
Ph: (501)280-3000
Fax: (501)280-3090

Myers, Ray, Exec. Dir.
Asphalt Interlayer Association [494]
1811 Hampshire Pl.
El Dorado Hills, CA 95762
Ph: (916)933-9140
Fax: (916)933-9473

Myers, Robert, Mem.
Collie Club of America [21859]
c/o Susan Houser
12736 W Watson
Sunset Hills, MO 63127-1325
Ph: (314)842-4832

Myers, Roger, CFO
Certified Financial Planner Board of
Standards [1277]
1425 K St. NW, No. 800
Washington, DC 20005
Ph: (202)379-2200
Toll Free: 800-487-1497
Fax: (202)379-2299

Myers, Rev. Ronald V., MD, Chair-
man, Founder
National Juneteenth Observance
Foundation [17783]
PO Box 269
Belzoni, MS 39038
Ph: (662)392-2016
Fax: (662)247-1471

Myers, Shimon, Dir. of Dev.
Jerusalem Institute of Justice - USA
[12995]
PO Box 610
Milford, OH 45150

Myers, Todd, President
Power & Communication Contractors
Association [898]
1908 Mt. Vernon Ave., 2nd Fl.
Alexandria, VA 22301
Ph: (703)212-7734
Toll Free: 800-542-7222
Fax: (703)548-3733

Myers, Vickie Rideout, Exec. Dir.
American Sugar Alliance [1315]
2111 Wilson Blvd., Ste. 600
Arlington, VA 22201
Ph: (703)351-5055
Fax: (703)351-6698

Myers, Dr. William T., Treasurer
Society for the Advancement of
American Philosophy [10118]
BSC Box 549013
Birmingham Southern College
Birmingham, AL 35254
Ph: (205)226-4868

Myles, Bradley, CEO
Polaris Project [18437]
PO Box 65323
Washington, DC 20035
Ph: (202)745-1001
Fax: (202)745-1119

Myles, Mrs. Peggie, Supervisor
National Association of Youth Clubs
[13463]
National Association of Colored
Women's Clubs
1601 R St. NW
Washington, DC 20009-6420
Ph: (202)667-4080
Fax: (202)667-2574

Mylin, Wayne, Mgr. Dir.
American Organization for Bodywork
Therapies of Asia [15553]

PO Box 343
West Berlin, NJ 08091
Ph: (856)809-2953
Fax: (856)809-2958

Myose, Roy, VP
Sigma Gamma Tau [23743]
c/o Dr. Shawn Keshmiri, Officer
Aerospace Engineering Dept.
University of Kansas
1530 W 15th St., 2120 Learned Hall
Wichita, KS 67260-0044
Ph: (316)978-6328
    (785)864-4267
Fax: (316)978-3307

N

Naasz, Byrdi, Mem.
National Impala Association [21455]
PO Box 111
Atlantic Highlands, NJ 07716-0111
Ph: (732)291-7668

Naber, Tom, President, CEO
National Association of Electrical
   Distributors [1028]
1181 Corporate Lake Dr.
Saint Louis, MO 63132-1716
Ph: (314)991-9000
Toll Free: 888-791-2512
Fax: (314)991-3060

Nabors, Andre, Exec. Dir.
American Association of Retirement
   Communities [12754]
PO Box 10981
Southport, NC 28461
Toll Free: 866-531-5567

Nachtrieb, Cheryl, Chairperson
Spinning and Weaving Group [3270]
c/o The National NeedleArts As-
   sociation
1100-H Brandywine Blvd.
Zanesville, OH 43701-7303
Toll Free: 800-889-8662
Fax: (740)452-2552

Nadeau, Carolyn, Managing Dir.
Cervantes Society of America [9048]
c/o Carolyn Nadeau, Managing
   Director
Illinois Wesleyan University
Dept. of Hispanic Studies
Bloomington, IL 61702

Nadeau, Jenifer, President
American Youth Horse Council
   [4334]
1 Gainer Rd.
McDonald, NM 88262
Ph: (817)320-2005
Fax: (575)356-3721

Nadel, Steven, Exec. Dir.
American Council for an Energy-
   Efficient Economy [6452]
529 14th St. NW, Ste. 600
Washington, DC 20045
Ph: (202)507-4000
Fax: (202)429-2248

Nadelmann, Ethan, Exec. Dir.,
   Founder
Drug Policy Alliance [17892]
925 15th St. NW, 2nd Fl.
Washington, DC 20005
Ph: (202)683-2030
Fax: (202)216-0803

Nader, Ralph, Founder
Center for Study of Responsive Law
   [18043]
PO Box 19367
Washington, DC 20036

Nader, Ralph, Founder
Citizen Works [17853]
PO Box 18478

Washington, DC 20036
Ph: (202)265-6164

Nader, Ralph, Founder
Essential Information [17944]
PO Box 19405
Washington, DC 20036
Ph: (202)387-8030

Naderi, Manizha, Exec. Dir.
Women for Afghan Women [12064]
158-24 73rd Ave.
Fresh Meadows, NY 11366-1024
Ph: (718)591-2434
Fax: (718)591-2430

Nadglowski, Joseph, Jr., CEO,
   President
Obesity Action Coalition [16261]
4511 N Himes Ave., Ste. 250
Tampa, FL 33614
Toll-Free: 800-717-3117

Nadol, Dr. Joseph B., Jr., Director
NIDCD: National Temporal Bone,
   Hearing and Balance Pathology
   Resource Registry [15665]
243 Charles St.
Boston, MA 02114-3096
Ph: (617)573-3711
Toll Free: 800-822-1327
Fax: (617)573-3838

Naeem, Munum, Exec. Dir.
Humanity First USA [11670]
300 E Lombard St., Ste. 840
Baltimore, MD 21202
Toll Free: 877-994-3872

Naef, Heinz, Treasurer
American Shire Horse Association
   [4328]
PQ Box 336
Cedar Springs, MI 49319
Toll Free: 888-302-6643

Nagano, Gwen, President
National Ayurvedic Medical Associa-
   tion [13640]
8605 Santa Monica Blvd., No. 46789
Los Angeles, CA 90069-4109
Toll Free: 800-669-8914
Fax: (949)743-5432

Nagarkatte, Ajay, Managing Dir.
Bank Administration Institute [385]
115 S La Salle St., Ste. 3300
Chicago, IL 60603-3801
Toll Free: 800-224-9889
Fax: (312)683-2373

Nagel, Catherine, Exec. Dir.
City Parks Alliance [17971]
2121 Ward Ct. NW, 5th Fl.
Washington, DC 20037
Ph: (202)974-5120
Fax: (202)223-9257

Nagel, Ed, Coord., Chairman, CEO
National Association for Legal Support of Alternative Schools [7490]
c/o Ed Nagel, Coordinator/Chairman
1 Alceda Ct.
Moffat, CO 81143-9792
Ph: (719)298-3020

Naghavi, Morteza, Exec. Chmn. of
   the Bd., Founder
Society for Heart Attack Prevention
   and Eradication [14145]
2500 W Loop S, Ste. 360-A
Houston, TX 77027
Toll Free: 877-SHA-PE11

Nagle, Bernard, Exec. Dir.
Precision Machined Products Association [2111]
6880 W Snowville Rd., Ste. 200

Brecksville, OH 44141
Ph: (440)526-0300
Fax: (440)526-5803

Nai, Janoi Marn, Chairman
Mon American Association [17825]
1357 Worthington Centre Dr.
Columbus, OH 43085
Ph: (614)456-9136

Nair, Satheesan, Secretary
National Federation of Indian
   American Associations [19476]
319 Summit Hall Rd.
Gaithersburg, MD 20877
Ph: (301)926-3013
    (301)935-5321
Fax: (301)926-3378

Nair, Sreedhar, MD, President
National Emphysema Foundation
   [14135]
128 East Ave.
Norwalk, CT 06851
Ph: (203)866-5000

Najafi, Khalil, VP
Electrical and Computer Engineering
   Department Heads Association
   [6552]
Two Prudential Plz.
180 N Stetson, Ste. 3500
Chicago, IL 60601
Ph: (312)559-3724
Fax: (312)559-4111

Najar, Julieann, Founder
A Soldier's Wish List [10760]
11143 Larimore Rd.
Saint Louis, MO 63138

Najib, Rabih, President
Arab American Association of
   Engineers and Architects [5957]
PO Box 1536
Chicago, IL 60690
Ph: (312)409-8560

Najt, Beverly A., Exec. Dir., Founder
4Ekselans [10825]
PO Box 1407
New York, NY 10150

Nalavala, Nosh, Exec. Dir.
MediaGlobal [12170]
7 Whitney Pl.
Princeton Junction, NJ 08550
Ph: (609)716-1296
Fax: (609)716-1297

Nall, Michael, Founder
Alliance of Merger and Acquisition
   Advisors [605]
222 N LaSalle St., Ste. 300
Chicago, IL 60601
Ph: (312)856-9590
Toll Free: 877-844-2535

Nalle, Mr. Dave, Reg. Dir.
Republican Liberty Caucus [19047]
PO Box 64
Brookfield, CT 06804
Ph: (202)524-9581
Toll Free: 866-752-5423

Nam, Gina, Secretary
Ascend [12]
120 Wall St., 9th Fl.
New York, NY 10005
Ph: (212)248-4888

Naman, Stephen L., President
American Council for Judaism
   [20225]
PO Box 888484
Atlanta, GA 30356-0484
Ph: (904)280-3131

Namazie, Maryam, Contact
Committee for Humanitarian Assistance to Iranian Refugees
   [12587]

17 Battery Pl., Rm. 605N
New York, NY 10004
Ph: (212)747-1046
Fax: (212)425-7240

Nam-Hau, Doan Thi, EdD, Founder,
   President
CHEER for Viet Nam [13269]
PO Box 341
Culver City, CA 90232

Namias, Nicholas, President
Surgical Infection Society [17411]
PO Box 1278
East Northport, NY 11731
Ph: (631)368-1880
Fax: (631)368-4466

Namie, Gary, PhD, Director
Workplace Bullying Institute [16948]
PO Box 29915
Bellingham, WA 98228
Ph: (360)656-6630

Nammo, David, Exec. Dir., CEO
Christian Legal Society [5073]
8001 Braddock Rd., Ste. 302
Springfield, VA 22151-2110
Ph: (703)642-1070
    (312)853-8709
Fax: (703)642-1075

Namnath, Antonia, President
Weight Loss Surgery Foundation of
   America [17417]
417 Mace Blvd., Ste. J-236
Davis, CA 95618
Ph: (657)229-5732

Namou-Yatooma, Weam, Founder,
   Director
Iraqi Artists Association [8926]
c/o Amer Hanna Fatuhi, Founder
PO Box 171
Hazel Park, MI 48030

Nance, Penny Young, President,
   CEO
Concerned Women for America
   [19970]
1015 15th St. NW, Ste. 1100
Washington, DC 20005
Ph: (202)488-7000

Nanda, Dr. Navin, MD, President
International Society of
   Cardiovascular Ultrasound [14652]
4240 Kennesaw Dr.
Birmingham, AL 35213
Ph: (205)934-8256
Fax: (205)934-6747

Nanevie, Enyonam, CEO, Founder,
   Co-Ch., Exec. Dir.
Building Community Bridges, Inc.
   [11324]
244 5th Ave., Ste. E283
New York, NY 10001-7604
Toll Free: 888-834-8611
Fax: (888)397-3717

Nanfito, Michael, Exec. Dir.
National Institute for Technology in
   Liberal Education [8228]
1001 E University Ave.
McCook-Crain Bldg.
Georgetown, TX 78626
Ph: (512)863-1603
Fax: (512)819-7684

Nangia, Ajay K., MD, Officer
Society for Male Reproduction and
   Urology [17118]
1209 Montgomery Hwy.
Birmingham, AL 35216
Ph: (205)978-5000
Fax: (205)978-5005

Nanney, Timothy, President
International Association of Clerks,
   Recorders, Election Officials and
   Treasurers [5262]

c/o Brenda Bell, Chief Administrator
156 Old Pond Ln.
Statesville, NC 28625
Toll Free: 800-890-7368

Napadow, Vitaly, PhD, LAc, Co-Pres.
Society for Acupuncture Research
[13505]
130 Cloverhurst Ct.
Winston Salem, NC 27103-9503

Napoli, Maryann, Assoc. Dir.
Center for Medical Consumers
[14931]
239 Thompson St.
New York, NY 10012
Ph: (212)674-7105

Nappi, Ralph J., President
Graphic Arts Education and
  Research Foundation [1534]
1899 Preston White Dr.
Reston, VA 20191-4367
Ph: (703)264-7200
Toll Free: 866-381-9839
Fax: (703)620-3165

Narayanan, Vijaykrishnan, Chairman
Association for Computing
  Machinery - Special Interest Group
  for Design Automation [6237]
c/o Debra Venedam, Program Direc-
  tor
Office of SIG Services
2 Penn Plz., Ste. 701
New York, NY 10121
Ph: (212)626-0614
Fax: (212)302-5826

Narcise, Alex, Chairperson
American Concrete Pressure Pipe
  Association [2602]
4122 E Chapman Ave., Ste. 27
Orange, CA 92869-4011
Ph: (714)801-0298

Narcisi, Jean, Chairman
Workgroup for Electronic Data
  Interchange [1595]
1984 Isaac Newton Sq., Ste. 304
Reston, VA 20190
Ph: (202)618-8788

Nardella, Jena Lee, Founder, Chief
  Strat. Ofc.
Blood: Water [10474]
PO Box 60381
Nashville, TN 37206
Ph: (615)550-4296

Nardizzi, Steven, ESQ, CEO
Wounded Warrior Project [21157]
4899 Belfort Rd., Ste. 300
Jacksonville, FL 32256
Ph: (904)296-7350
Toll Free: 877-832-6997
Fax: (904)296-7347

Nardoci, Bruce, VP
United States Table Soccer Federa-
  tion [22058]
PO Box 14455
Washington, DC 20044

Nardone, Natalie, CMP, Exec. Dir.
Green Meeting Industry Council
  [2330]
Bldg. 14, Ste. 100
1827 Powers Ferry Rd.
Atlanta, GA 30339
Ph: (571)527-3116

Nardone, Vincent J., Chairperson,
  President
Audubon Artists [8848]
c/o Vincent J. Nardone, President/
  Admissions Chair
3 Lamb Rd.

Brick, NJ 08724
Ph: (732)903-7468

Narducci, Justin, President
Lifewater International [13355]
PO Box 3131
San Luis Obispo, CA 93403
Toll Free: 888-543-3426

Narieka, Eileen, Secretary
United States of America Coton de
  Tulear Club [21978]
c/o Eileen Narieka, Membership
  Secretary
1103 Snyder Dr.
Leesport, PA 19533
Ph: (610)926-1681

Narkevicius, Jen, Coord.
Scottish Harp Society of America
  [10001]
PO Box 681
Mechanicsville, MD 20659

Narog, Walt, President
Tall Clubs International [13207]
c/o Walter J. Narog Jr., President
Tall Club of Rochester
PO Box 20197
Rochester, NY 14602

Narramore, Dr. Bruce, President
Narramore Christian Foundation
  [19994]
250 W Colorado Blvd., Ste. 100
Arcadia, CA 91007
Ph: (626)821-8400
Fax: (626)821-8409

Narula, Amarjot, President
North American Sikh Medical and
  Dental Association [15742]
4310 English Morning Ln.
Ellicott City, MD 21043

Nash, Gordon, President
El Toro International Yacht Racing
  Association [22612]
91 Waldo Point S 40
Sausalito, CA 94965
Ph: (415)332-7269

Nash, James, VP
Veterinary Hospital Managers As-
  sociation [17670]
PO Box 2280
Alachua, FL 32616-2280
Ph: (518)433-8911
Toll Free: 888-795-4520

Nash, Julie, Director
Society of Trauma Nurses [16186]
446 E High St., Ste. 10
Lexington, KY 40507
Ph: (859)271-0607
Fax: (859)977-7456

Nash, Dr. Will, President
Charles Johnson Society [10383]
c/o Dr. Linda Selzer, Treasurer
Penn State University
116 Burrowes Bldg.
University Park, PA 16802

Nasir, Dr. Adnan, President
Nanodermatology Society [14502]
4414 Lake Boone Trail, Ste. 408
Raleigh, NC 27607
Ph: (919)781-4375
Fax: (919)781-3909

Nasir, Dr. Musa, Chrmn. of the Bd.
International Palestinian Cardiac
  Relief Organization [14122]
PO Box 1926
Kent, OH 44240
Ph: (330)678-2645
Fax: (330)678-2661

Nasson, Robert, Exec. Dir.
National History Club [7988]
PO Box 441812
Somerville, MA 02144
Ph: (781)248-7921

Natale, Patrick J., PE, Exec. Dir.
United Engineering Foundation
  [6603]
1650 Market St., Ste. 1200
Philadelphia, PA 19103

Natarajan, Mohan, Chairperson
ActionAid International USA [12133]
1420 K St. NW, Ste. 900
Washington, DC 20005
Ph: (202)835-1240

Natarajan, Vivek S., President
Association of Collegiate Marketing
  Educators Inc. [8269]
c/o Silvia Lozano Martin, Secretary
School of Business and Economics
Lynchburg College
1501 Lakeside Dr.
Lynchburg, VA 24501
Ph: (434)544-8177

Natelson, Nina, Exec. Dir.
Concern for Helping Animals in
  Israel [10608]
PO Box 3341
Alexandria, VA 22302
Ph: (703)658-9650

Nathan, Joe, Director
Center for School Change [7751]
Higher Ground Academy
1381 Marshall Ave.
Saint Paul, MN 55104
Ph: (612)309-6571

Nathan, Mark, President
Independent Automotive Damage
  Appraisers Association [225]
PO Box 12291
Columbus, GA 31917-2291
Toll Free: 800-369-IADA

Nathan, Marvin, Chairman
Anti-Defamation League [17874]
605 3rd Ave., Fl. 9
New York, NY 10158
Ph: (212)885-7700
  (212)885-7800
Fax: (212)867-0779

Nathan, Melissa A., Secretary
Stage Managers' Association
  [10233]
PO Box 275
New York, NY 10108-0275

Nathan, Rhoda, President
Bernard Shaw Society [9042]
PO Box 1159
Madison Square Sta.
New York, NY 10159-1159

Nathan, Terry, COO
Independent Book Publishers As-
  sociation [2788]
1020 Manhattan Beach Blvd., Ste.
  204
Manhattan Beach, CA 90266
Ph: (310)546-1818
Fax: (310)546-3939

Nathaniel, Netta, Exec. Dir.
Larger Than Life [11067]
54-15 35th St.
Long Island City, NY 11101
Ph: (201)567-8990
Toll Free: 888-644-4040
Fax: (201)567-8991

Nathanson, Nancy, Exec. Dir.
International Friesian Show Horse
  Association [4365]

PO Box 2839
Lompoc, CA 93438
Ph: (805)448-3027

Nathasingh, Jeff, President
Association for Management
  Information in Financial Services
  [382]
14247 Saffron Cir.
Carmel, IN 46032
Ph: (317)815-5857

Nation, Richard, Secretary,
  Treasurer
Energy Telecommunications and
  Electrical Association [1022]
5005 W Royal Ln., Ste. 291
Irving, TX 75063
Toll Free: 888-503-8700

Natoli, Jack, President
Lesley Gore International Fan Club
  [24053]
PO Box 1548
Ocean Pines, MD 21811

Natz, Betsy, CEO
Kitchen Cabinet Manufacturers As-
  sociation [1952]
1899 Preston White Dr.
Reston, VA 20191-5435
Ph: (703)264-1690
Fax: (703)620-6530

Natz, Kevin, VP
National Council of Farmer Coopera-
  tives [3977]
50 F St. NW, Ste. 900
Washington, DC 20001
Ph: (202)626-8700
Fax: (202)626-8722

Naumann, Cheryl D.
Concordia Deaconess Conference
  [20302]
c/o Kim Schave, Webmaster
5000 Romaine Spring Dr.
Fenton, MO 63026

Nauser, Ms. Lauren, Exec. Dir.
Fixed Income Analysts Society, Inc.
  [1279]
c/o Executive Director
244 5th Ave., Ste. L230
New York, NY 10001
Ph: (212)726-8100
Fax: (212)591-6534

Navajo, Jason Begay, President
Native American Journalists Associa-
  tion [2710]
395 W Lindsey St.
Norman, OK 73019
Ph: (405)325-1649
Fax: (405)325-6945

Navarette, Brian, Chairman
Church Planting International
  [20405]
5186 Cressingham Dr.
Fort Mill, SC 29707

Navarro, Suteja, Specialist
OmSpring [13647]
550 Wisconsin St.
San Francisco, CA 94107
Ph: (415)206-9920

Nawalinski, Beth, Dep. Dir.
United for Libraries [9731]
859 W Lancaster Ave., Unit 2-1
Bryn Mawr, PA 19010
Ph: (312)280-2161
Toll Free: 800-545-2433
Fax: (484)383-3407

Nawash, Kamal, President
Free Muslims Coalition [18096]
1050 17th St. NW, Ste. 1000

Washington, DC 20036
Ph: (202)776-7190
　　(202)907-5724

Nawrocki, Chereen, President
English Cocker Spaniel Club of
　America [21871]
c/o Shannon Loritz, Secretary
903 Lake St.
Fremont, WI 54940
Ph: (920)216-2855

Nayar, Jani, Coord.
Society for Accessible Travel and
　Hospitality [11637]
347 5th Ave., Ste. 605
New York, NY 10016-5010
Ph: (212)447-7284
Fax: (212)447-1928

Naylor, Audrey, CEO
Wellstart International [15070]
PO Box 602
Blue Jay, CA 92317-0602
Ph: (714)724-1675
Fax: (802)985-8794

Nayseap, Hong, Founder, President
Bridges Cambodia International, Inc.
　[10874]
2970 Almond Dr.
San Jose, CA 95148-2001
Ph: (408)472-3489
　　(408)759-7902

Nazario, Prof. Thomas, Founder,
　President
The Forgotten International [12539]
PO Box 192066
San Francisco, CA 94119
Ph: (415)517-6942

Ndaba, Obadias, President
World Youth Alliance [19280]
228 E 71st St.
New York, NY 10021
Ph: (212)585-0757
Fax: (917)463-1040

Ndimbie, Oliver, Chairperson
Wimbum Cultural and Development
　Association in the United States of
　America [8780]
PO Box 3108
Bellaire, TX 77402-3108

Nduna, John, Gen. Sec.
ACT Alliance-New York [12603]
Ecumenical UN Office
Church Centre for the United Na-
　tions
777 United Nations Plaza, Ste. D
New York, NY 10017
Ph: (212)867-5890

Neal, Barbara, President
American Society of Consulting Ar-
　borists [4726]
9707 Key W Ave., Ste. 100
Rockville, MD 20850
Ph: (301)947-0483
Fax: (301)990-9771

Neal, Joseph M., MD, President
American Society of Regional
　Anesthesia and Pain Medicine
　[13695]
4 Penn Center W, Ste. 401
Pittsburgh, PA 15222
Ph: (412)471-2718
Toll Free: 855-795-ASRA

Neal, Pam, VP
International Conference of Police
　Chaplains [19929]
PO Box 5590
Destin, FL 32540
Ph: (850)654-9736
Fax: (850)654-9742

Neal, Richard, Contact
Integrated Manufacturing Technology
　Initiative [6795]
PO Box 5296
Oak Ridge, TN 37831
Ph: (865)385-7002

Neal, Richard, President
Self-Help International [12185]
703 2nd Ave. NW
Waverly, IA 50677-2308
Ph: (319)352-4040

Neale-May, Donovan, Exec. Dir.
CMO Council [2274]
c/o Donovan Neale-May, Executive
　Director
1494 Hamilton Way
San Jose, CA 95125
Ph: (408)677-5300

Nealey, William J., Jr., Exec. Dir.
Mission to Haiti [11927]
PO Box 523157
Miami, FL 33152-3157
Ph: (305)823-7516

Nealon, Thomas F., III, Chmn. of the
　Bd.
American Liver Foundation [15249]
39 Broadway, Ste. 2700
New York, NY 10006
Ph: (212)668-1000
Toll Free: 800-465-4837
Fax: (212)483-8179

Nearmyer, Roger, CPA, President,
　Bd. Member
Forensic Accountants Society of
　North America [28]
6200 Aurora Ave., Ste. 600W
Urbandale, IA 50322-2871
Ph: (515)669-0415
Fax: (515)274-4807

Nearon, John, President
Power Washers of North America
　[2139]
PO Box 270634
Saint Paul, MN 55127
Ph: (651)213-0060
Toll Free: 800-393-7962
Fax: (651)213-0369

Nease, Linda, Exec. Dir.
Council for Learning Disabilities
　[12233]
11184 Antioch Rd.
Overland Park, KS 66210
Ph: (913)491-1011
Fax: (913)491-1011

Nedelcovych, Dr. Mima S.,
　President, CEO
Initiative for Global Development
　[12545]
1101 Pennsylvania Ave. NW, 6th Fl.
Washington, DC 20004
Ph: (202)454-3972

Neece, Steven, COO
National Association of Pharmaceuti-
　cal Sales Representatives [2561]
2020 Pennsylvania Ave., Ste. 5050
Washington, DC 20006
Toll Free: 800-672-9104

Neeley, Edward, President
Commercial Vehicle Solutions
　Network [316]
3943-2 Baymeadows Rd.
Jacksonville, FL 32217
Ph: (904)737-2900
Fax: (904)636-9881

Neely, Norma, Ph.D., Director
American Indian Institute [10034]
1639 Cross Center Dr.

Norman, OK 73019
Ph: (405)325-4127
　　(405)325-0473

Neely, Richard, President
American Amateur Baseball
　Congress [22540]
100 W Broadway
Farmington, NM 87401
Ph: (505)327-3120
Fax: (507)327-3132

Neely, Sol, President
North American Levinas Society
　[10106]
c/o Sol Neely, President, 11120
　Glacier Hwy., SOB 1
11120 Glacier Hwy., SOB 1
Juneau, AK 99801
Ph: (907)796-6411
Toll Free: 877-465-4827
Fax: (907)796-6406

Neely, Ms. Susan K., Chairperson
ASAE: The Center for Association
　Leadership [254]
1575 I St. NW
Washington, DC 20005-1103
Ph: (202)371-0940
Toll Free: 888-950-ASAE
Fax: (202)371-8315

Ne'eman, Ari, Founder, President
Autistic Self Advocacy Network
　[13758]
PO Box 66122
Washington, DC 20035
Ph: (202)596-1056

Neesan, Ramsen, Secretary
Assyrian Academic Society [9647]
8324 Lincoln Ave.
Skokie, IL 60077-2436

Neff, Michael W., Exec. Dir.
American Society for Horticultural
　Science [6134]
1018 Duke St.
Alexandria, VA 22314
Ph: (703)836-4606
Fax: (703)836-2024

Neff, Vicki, President
CorgiAid [21862]
2108 N 38th St.
Seattle, WA 98103
Fax: (208)693-8342

Negley, Marvin, President
Glenn Miller Birthplace Society
　[24043]
122 W Clark St.
Clarinda, IA 51632
Ph: (712)542-2461
Fax: (712)542-2868

Negrel, Philippe, VP
International Association of
　Geochemistry [7938]
c/o Chris Gardner, Office Manager
275 Mendenhall Laboratory
125 S Oval Mall
Columbus, OH 43210-1308
Ph: (614)688-7400
Fax: (614)292-7688

Negri, Brian, Director
Bearing Specialists Association
　[1718]
Bldg. C, Ste. 312
800 Roosevelt Rd.
Glen Ellyn, IL 60137
Ph: (630)858-3838
Fax: (630)790-3095

Negron, Barbara, President
North American Natural Casing As-
　sociation [1365]

494 8th Ave., Ste. 805
New York, NY 10001
Ph: (212)695-4980
Fax: (212)695-7153

Negroponte, John D., Chairman
Americas Society/Council of the
　Americas [17795]
680 Park Ave.
New York, NY 10065-5072
Ph: (212)249-8950
Fax: (212)249-5868

Negroponte, Nicholas, Chairman,
　Founder
One Laptop Per Child [11481]
848 Brickell Ave., Ste. 307
Miami, FL 33131-2943
Ph: (305)971-3755

Neher, Kathleen, Founder, President
Catholic Social Workers National
　Association [13106]
PO Box 498531
Cincinnati, OH 45249-8531
Ph: (317)416-8285

Nehls, Kim, PhD, Exec. Dir.
Association for the Study of Higher
　Education [7955]
4505 S Maryland Pky.
Las Vegas, NV 89154-9900
Ph: (702)895-2737
Fax: (702)895-4269

Neidleman, Jason, Secretary,
　Treasurer
Rousseau Association [9094]
c/o Jason Neidleman, Secretary-
　Treasurer
University of La Verne
114 Founders Hall
1950 3rd St.
La Verne, CA 91750

Neill, Dr. Monty, Exec. Dir.
National Center for Fair and Open
　Testing [8689]
PO Box 300204
Jamaica Plain, MA 02130
Ph: (617)477-9792

Neill, Steve, Exec. Dir., President
Community Aid Relief and Develop-
　ment [12647]
PO Box 632162
Littleton, CO 80163
Ph: (720)432-7027

Neimeier, Pete, President
Miniature Motorsports Racing As-
　sociation [22519]
PO Box 50906
Bowling Green, KY 42102-4206
Ph: (270)784-8231

Neish, Scott R., DMD, President
World Congress of Minimally Inva-
　sive Dentistry [14475]
865 11th St.
Imperial Beach, CA 91932
Toll Free: 800-973-8003

Nelligan, Jim, President
Salmon Unlimited Inc. [22852]
c/o Massard Foot and Ankle Clinic
321 W Railroad Ave.
Bartlett, IL 60103

Nelson, Adam, President
History of Education Society [9486]
c/o Ralph Kidder, Treasurer
2020 Chadds Ford Dr.
Reston, VA 20191

Nelson, Alyse, President, CEO
Vital Voices Global Partnership
　[13402]

1625 Massachusetts Ave. NW, Ste. 300
Washington, DC 20036
Ph: (202)861-2625

Nelson, Beth, President
National Alfalfa and Forage Alliance **[4176]**
4630 Churchill St., Ste. 1
Saint Paul, MN 55126
Ph: (651)484-3888
Fax: (651)638-0756

Nelson, Collette, Officer
American Subcontractors Association **[852]**
1004 Duke St.
Alexandria, VA 22314
Ph: (703)684-3450
Fax: (703)836-3482

Nelson, Conley, Secretary, Treasurer
U.S. Meat Export Federation **[2312]**
1660 Lincoln St., Ste. 2800
Denver, CO 80264
Ph: (303)623-6328
Fax: (303)623-0297

Nelson, Dale, Chairman
Metal Construction Association **[546]**
8735 W Higgins Rd., Ste. 300
Chicago, IL 60631
Ph: (847)375-4718
Fax: (847)375-6488

Nelson, Deb, Contact
Social Venture Network **[669]**
Thoreau Center for Sustainability
1016 Torney Ave. 3
San Francisco, CA 94129
Ph: (415)561-6501
Fax: (415)561-6435

Nelson, Deborah, President
American Highland Cattle Association **[3695]**
Historic City Hall
22 S 4th Ave., Ste. 201
Brighton, CO 80601-2042
Ph: (303)659-2399
Fax: (303)659-2241

Nelson, Dianne, Founder, President
Wild Horse Sanctuary **[10716]**
5796 Wilson Hill Rd.
Shingletown, CA 96088-0030
Ph: (530)474-5770
Fax: (530)474-1384

Nelson, Donald, President
American Osteopathic College of Pathologists **[16515]**
142 E Ontario St.
Chicago, IL 60611-8224
Ph: (312)202-8197
Fax: (312)202-8224

Nelson, Doug, VP, Dir. of Dev.
Fidelco Guide Dog Foundation **[17699]**
103 Vision Way
Bloomfield, CT 06002
Ph: (860)243-5200
    (860)243-4044
Fax: (860)769-0567

Nelson, Doug, President
National Association of State Chief Administrators **[5778]**
PO Box 708
Lexington, KY 40588
Ph: (859)514-9156
Fax: (859)514-9166

Nelson, G. Macy, Secretary, Treasurer
International 505 Yacht Racing Association, American Section **[22625]**

519 Old Orchard Rd.
Baltimore, MD 21229

Nelson, Gwen T., President
Embroiderers' Guild of America **[21755]**
1355 Bardstown Rd., Ste. 157
Louisville, KY 40204-1353
Ph: (502)589-6956
Fax: (502)584-7900

Nelson, Jack, Founder
Master Window Cleaners of America **[2135]**
PO Box 193
Rushville, IN 46173
Ph: (910)724-4442
    (812)614-8329

Nelson, James, Chairman
International Consortium for Organizational Resilience **[2177]**
PO Box 1171
Lombard, IL 60148
Ph: (630)705-0910
Toll Free: 866-765-8321

Nelson, Janet, Educator
Hawkwatch International **[6961]**
2240 South 900 East
Salt Lake City, UT 84106
Ph: (801)484-6808
Fax: (801)484-6810

Nelson, Jeff, President
Art with Heart **[13727]**
316 Broadway, Ste. 316
Seattle, WA 98122-5325
Ph: (206)362-4047

Nelson, Jeff, CEO
EarthSave International **[3997]**
20555 Devonshire St., Ste. 105
Chatsworth, CA 91311
Ph: (415)234-0829
Fax: (818)337-1957

Nelson, Justin G., Founder, President
National Gay and Lesbian Chamber of Commerce **[23604]**
729 15th St. NW, 9th Fl.
Washington, DC 20005
Ph: (202)234-9181
Fax: (202)234-9185

Nelson, Karen, President
Second Bombardment Association **[20685]**
c/o Matt R. Bryner, Treasurer
8386 Fenton Way
Arvada, CO 80003

Nelson, Lydia, Chairperson
National Business Honor Society **[23785]**
1914 Association Dr.
1914 Association Dr.
Reston, VA 20191-1596
Ph: (703)860-8300
Fax: (703)620-4483

Nelson, Mark R., Exec. Dir.
Computer Science Teachers Association **[7654]**
PO Box 30778
New York, NY 10117-3509
Ph: (212)626-0530
Toll Free: 800-342-6626
Fax: (212)944-1318

Nelson, Dr. Melissa, President
Cultural Conservancy **[10039]**
1016 Lincoln Blvd., Bldg. 1016, 1st Fl.
San Francisco, CA 94129
Ph: (415)561-6594
Fax: (415)561-6482

Nelson, Ray, CEO, Founder
Guitars Not Guns **[18721]**
PO Box 3562
Peachtree City, GA 30269
Ph: (770)861-2443

Nelson, Richard D., President
National Association of Bankruptcy Trustees **[5087]**
1 Windsor Cove, Ste. 305
Columbia, SC 29223
Ph: (803)252-5646
Toll Free: 800-445-8629
Fax: (803)765-0860

Nelson, Robert, President
National Association of State Utility Consumer Advocates **[5834]**
8380 Colesville Rd., Ste. 101
Silver Spring, MD 20910
Ph: (301)589-6313
Fax: (301)589-6380

Nelson, Ms. Samantha, CEO, VP
The Hope of Survivors **[12924]**
843 Broadway
Sonoma, CA 95476
Toll Free: 866-260-8958

Nelson, Sara, President
Association of Flight Attendants - CWA **[23385]**
501 3rd St. NW
Washington, DC 20001
Ph: (202)434-1300
Toll Free: 800-424-2401

Nelson, Sheila, VP
Catholic Association for Lesbian and Gay Ministry **[20176]**
1798 Scenic Ave.
Berkeley, CA 94709
Ph: (972)638-7648

Nelson, Stacy, Chairperson
Bread and Roses **[11794]**
233 Tamalpais Dr., Ste. 100
Corte Madera, CA 94925-1415
Ph: (415)945-7120
Fax: (415)945-7128

Nelson, Thomas Lee, Rec. Sec.
National Organization of Black Law Enforcement Executives **[5506]**
4609-F Pinecrest Office Park Dr.
Alexandria, VA 22312-1442
Ph: (703)658-1529
Fax: (703)658-9479

Nelson, Vicki, President
Delta Xi Phi Multicultural Sorority, Inc. **[23953]**
PO Box 151
Chicago Ridge, IL 60415-0151

Nelson, Wendy, Exec. Dir.
Urban and Regional Information Systems Association **[6756]**
701 Lee St., Ste. 680
Des Plaines, IL 60016
Ph: (847)824-6300
Fax: (847)824-6363

Nelson, Whitney, Dir. of Mtgs.
International Association of Plastics Distribution **[2624]**
6734 W 121st St.
Overland Park, KS 66209
Ph: (913)345-1005
Fax: (913)345-1006

Nelson, Zeldon, Chmn. of the Bd., CEO
National Center for Constitutional Studies **[18038]**
37777 W Juniper Rd.
Malta, ID 83342
Ph: (208)645-2625
Toll Free: 800-388-4512
Fax: (208)645-2667

Neltrup, Ester, President
Planet Aid **[13016]**
6730 Santa Barbara Ct.
Elkridge, MD 21075-6814
Ph: (410)796-1510

Nerby, Jill, Founder, Exec. Dir.
Aniridia Foundation International **[13822]**
c/o University of Virginia Ophthalmology
PO Box 800715
Charlottesville, VA 22908-0715
Ph: (434)243-3357

Nercessian, Y.T., Editor
Armenian Numismatic Society **[22262]**
8511 Beverly Park Pl.
Pico Rivera, CA 90660-1920
Ph: (562)695-0380

Nerelus, Simeon S., Founder, Exec. Dir.
Haiti Emergency Relief Organization **[12666]**
PO Box 5634
Huntsville, AL 35814
Ph: (256)665-6151

Nerothin, Peter H., President, Founder
Insulindependence, Inc. **[14536]**
249 S Hwy. 101, No. 8000
Solana Beach, CA 92075
Toll Free: 888-912-3837

Nershi, Mr. David, Exec. Dir.
Society for Industrial and Organizational Psychology **[16937]**
440 E Poe Rd., Ste. 101
Bowling Green, OH 43402-1355
Ph: (419)353-0032
Fax: (419)352-2645

Nesbitt, Bill, President
Brewmeisters Anonymous **[21260]**
20210 N 76th Way
Scottsdale, AZ 85255
Ph: (480)319-2227

Nesbitt, Nick, Treasurer
Nesbitt/Nisbet Society of North America **[20907]**
c/o Nick Nesbitt, Treasurer
4573 Colburn Rd.
Bemus Point, NY 14712

Nespoli, Matt, Founder, President
Water for Waslala **[13347]**
c/o Justin Knabb
2000 Friedensburg Rd.
Reading, PA 19606

Nestingen, Carolyn, Attorney
Sola Publishing/WordAlone **[20319]**
PO Box 521
Maple Lake, MN 55358
Ph: (612)216-2055

Nestor, Mark S., MD, President
American Cutaneous Oncology Society **[16331]**
6816 Southpoint Pky., No. 1000
Jacksonville, FL 32216

Netburn, Mitchell, President, CEO
Project Renewal **[13177]**
200 Varick St. 9th Fl.
New York, NY 10014
Ph: (212)620-0340

Netter, Barbara, President, Founder
Alliance for Cancer Gene Therapy **[14871]**
96 Cummings Point Rd.
Stamford, CT 06902
Ph: (203)358-8000

Nettesheim, Patrick, Founder
Guitars For Vets [20769]
PO Box 617
Milwaukee, WI 53201-0617
Toll Free: 855-448-4376

Neu, Mr. Pat, Exec. Dir.
National Professional Anglers Association [22850]
PO Box 117
West Milton, OH 45383
Ph: (937)698-4188
Fax: (937)698-6153

Neuffer, John, President, CEO
Semiconductor Industry Association [1062]
1101 K St. NW, Ste. 450
Washington, DC 20005
Ph: (202)446-1700
Toll Free: 866-756-0715
Fax: (202)216-9745

Neugent, Lan, Exec. Dir.
State Educational Technology Directors Association [8677]
PO Box 10
Glen Burnie, MD 21060
Ph: (202)715-6636

Neuhaus, Dr. John, Founder
Apostolic Association of Churches, Ministers & Leaders International [20016]
810 Saturn St., Ste. 16
Jupiter, FL 33477
Ph: (954)309-7388

Neuhauser, Melinda, Pharm.D., President
Society of Infectious Diseases Pharmacists [16688]
823 Congress Ave., Ste. 230
Austin, TX 78701-2435
Ph: (512)328-8632
Fax: (512)495-9031

Neuhold, Walter, Founder
Professional Chef's Association, Inc. [701]
PO Box 453
Frederick, CO 80530
Ph: (720)379-8759

Neumeyer, Tom
Field Spaniel Society of America [21877]
c/o Barbara Cox, Secretary - Corresponding
404 Santa Anna Ave
Coleman, TX 76834

Neurohr, Mark, President
Handicapped Travel Club [22425]
c/o Mark Neurohr
1465 N 32nd Rd.
Ottawa, IL 61350
Ph: (815)252-1868

Neuvelt, Carol Singer, Mem.
NAEM [4082]
1612 K St. NW, Ste. 1002
Washington, DC 20006-2843
Ph: (202)986-6616
Toll Free: 800-391-NAEM
Fax: (202)530-4408

Neville, Cara Lee T., Chairman
Fellows of the American Bar Foundation [5007]
750 N Lake Shore Dr., 4th Fl.
Chicago, IL 60611
Toll Free: 800-292-5065
Fax: (312)564-8910

New, Hansel, President
Sustainable Food Trade Association [1375]

49 Race St.
New Castle, VA 24127-6397
Ph: (413)624-6678

Newbern, T. Carla, RDH, Trustee
National Dental Hygienists' Association [14462]
c/o LaVerna Wilson, Treasurer
366 E Gorgas Ln.
Philadelphia, PA 19119

Newberry, Jerald, Director
NEA Healthy Futures [15086]
1201 16th St. NW, No. 216
Washington, DC 20036
Ph: (202)822-7570
Fax: (202)822-7775

Newberry, Seth, Gen. Mgr.
Open Mobile Alliance [7318]
4330 La Jolla Village Dr., Ste. 110
San Diego, CA 92122
Fax: (858)623-0743

Newcomb, Polly, President
American Society of Preventive Oncology [16337]
330 WARF Bldg.
610 Walnut St.
Madison, WI 53726
Ph: (608)263-9515
Fax: (608)263-4497

Newcombe, Nora, Chairperson
Cognitive Science Society [5985]
10200 W 44th Ave., Ste. 304
Wheat Ridge, CO 80033-2840
Ph: (303)327-7547
Fax: (720)881-6101

Newcomer, Dr. Christian E., Exec. Dir.
Association for Assessment and Accreditation of Laboratory Animal Care International [5896]
5283 Corporate Dr., Ste. 203
Frederick, MD 21703-2879
Ph: (301)696-9626
Fax: (301)696-9627

Newell, Prof. William H., Exec. Dir.
Association for Interdisciplinary Studies [9580]
44575 Garfield Rd.
Clinton Township, MI 48038
Ph: (513)529-2213
Fax: (513)529-5849

Newhall, Amy W., Exec. Dir.
Middle East Studies Association of North America [18690]
University of Arizona
1219 N Santa Rita Ave.
Tucson, AZ 85721
Ph: (520)621-5850
Fax: (520)626-9095

Newhouse, Barbara, President, CEO
Amyotrophic Lateral Sclerosis Association [13682]
1275 K St. NW, Ste. 250
Washington, DC 20005
Ph: (202)407-8580
Toll Free: 800-782-4747
Fax: (202)289-6801

Newhouse, Nancy L.
American Academy of Periodontology [14387]
737 N Michigan Ave., Ste. 800
Chicago, IL 60611-6660
Ph: (312)787-5518

Newkirk, Ingrid E., President
People for the Ethical Treatment of Animals [10677]
501 Front St.
Norfolk, VA 23510
Ph: (757)622-7382
Fax: (757)622-0457

Newkirk, Jimmy, Exec. Dir.
National Society of Physical Activity Practitioners in Public Health [16710]
102 Parkdale Pl.
Madison, MS 39110

Newman, Andrew, Secretary
Society for Urban, National and Transnational/Global Anthropology [5926]
American Anthropological Association
2200 Wilson Blvd., Ste. 600
Arlington, VA 22201-3357
Ph: (703)528-1902
Fax: (703)528-3546

Newman, Ann, President
Simian Society of America, Inc. [10696]
c/o Brenda Keller, Membership Chairman
16322 S Graham Rd.
Pleasant Hill, MO 64080

Newman, Barbara, President, CEO
The Blues Foundation [9881]
421 S Main St.
Memphis, TN 38103-4464
Ph: (901)527-2583
Fax: (901)529-4030

Newman, David, President
Film Music Society [9907]
1516 S Bundy Dr., Ste. 305
Los Angeles, CA 90025
Ph: (310)820-1909
Fax: (310)820-1301

Newman, Mr. Jeffry, Secretary
International Society for Fat Research [6945]
c/o AOCS
2710 S Boulder
Urbana, IL 61802-6996
Ph: (217)359-2344
Fax: (217)351-8091

Newman, Jessica, Exec. Dir.
JustWorld International [11054]
11924 W Forest Hill Blvd., Ste. 22-396
Wellington, FL 33414
Ph: (561)333-9391
Fax: (561)792-0757

Newman, Joel, President, Treasurer, CEO
American Feed Industry Association [4174]
2101 Wilson Blvd., Ste. 916
Arlington, VA 22201
Ph: (703)524-0810
Fax: (703)524-1921

Newman, Joel G., President, Treasurer
American Feed Industry Association - Equipment Manufacturers Council [165]
2101 Wilson Blvd., Ste. 916
Arlington, VA 22201
Ph: (703)524-0810
Fax: (703)524-1921

Newman, Maggie, President
Silver Ghost Association [21490]
c/o Jim Bannon, Membership Chairman
306 Cross Hill Rd.
Fountain Inn, SC 29644-9239
Ph: (864)862-5494
Fax: (864)862-5494

Newman, Michael J., Officer
American Orthodontic Society [14412]

11884 Greenville Ave., Ste. 112
Dallas, TX 75243
Toll Free: 800-448-1601

Newman, Ms. Monica, Exec. Dir.
International Association of Flight and Critical Care Paramedics [14682]
c/o Monica Newman, Executive Director
4835 Riveredge Cove
Snellville, GA 30039
Ph: (770)979-6372
Fax: (770)979-6500

Newman, Nathan, Officer
Urgent Care Association of America [13679]
387 Shuman Blvd., Ste. 235W
Naperville, IL 60563
Ph: (331)472-3739
Toll Free: 877-698-2262
Fax: (331)457-5439

Newman, Patrick, Exec. Dir.
Lady Bird Johnson Wildflower Center [6149]
4801 La Crosse Ave.
Austin, TX 78739
Ph: (512)232-0100
Fax: (512)232-0156

Newman, Steve, President
Fellowship of American Baptist Musicians [20490]
3300 Fairlawn Dr.
Columbus, IN 47203-2731
Ph: (317)635-3552
Fax: (317)635-3554

Newport, Nancy, Exec. Dir.
Norwegian Fjord Horse Registry [4397]
1801 W County Road 4
Berthoud, CO 80513
Ph: (303)684-6466
Fax: (888)646-5613

Newschaffer, Craig, VP
International Society for Autism Research [13771]
342 N Main St.
West Hartford, CT 06117-2507
Ph: (860)586-7575
Fax: (860)586-7550

Newsum, Phil, Exec. Dir.
Association of Diving Contractors International [856]
5206 FM 1960 W, Ste. 202
Houston, TX 77069
Ph: (281)893-8388
Fax: (281)893-5118

Newton, David, President
Fellowship in Prayer [20061]
291 Witherspoon St.
Princeton, NJ 08542-3227
Ph: (609)924-6863

Newton, Jason, PhD, Chairperson
Society of Sensory Professionals [7147]
3340 Pilot Knob Rd.
Saint Paul, MN 55121
Ph: (651)454-7250
Fax: (651)454-0766

Newton, Neill F., Chairman, Founder
Global Flying Hospitals [15004]
4440 PGA Blvd., Ste. 600
Palm Beach Gardens, FL 33410
Toll Free: 855-434-4747

Newton, Steve, Mem.
International Clubmakers Guild [3139]
38 Walden Pond Ave.

Saugus, MA 01906-1146

Newton, Steven, Dir. of Programs
National Center for Science Educa-
tion [8551]
1904 Franklin St., Ste. 600
Oakland, CA 94612-2922
Ph: (510)601-7203
Fax: (510)788-7971

Newton, Steven, Founder, CEO
Silver Star Families of America
[12350]
525 Cave Hollow Rd.
Clever, MO 65631-6313
Ph: (417)743-2508

Nezer, Melanie, Chairman
Refugee Council USA [19019]
1628 16th St. NW
Washington, DC 20009-3064
Ph: (202)319-2102
Fax: (202)319-2104

Nezhat, Ceana H., M.D., VP
Society of Reproductive Surgeons
[17129]
1209 Montgomery Hwy.
Birmingham, AL 35216-2809
Ph: (205)978-5000
Fax: (205)978-5005

Nforba, Dieudonne Tantoh, Founder
Save Your Future Association [4101]
2641 Trojan Dr., No. 309
Green Bay, WI 54304
Ph: (920)857-9520

Ng, Sgt. James, President
National Asian Peace Officers' As-
sociation [5485]
1776 I St. NW, Ste. 900
Washington, DC 20006
Ph: (202)632-5384
Fax: (202)756-1301

Nguyen, Chi, President
Society of Scribes [10416]
PO Box 933
New York, NY 10150
Ph: (212)452-0139

Nguyen, Khac-Quan, Founder, Exec.
Dir.
Viet Dreams [11180]
PO Box 360624
Milpitas, CA 95036
Ph: (408)410-4920

Nguyen, Phong, PhD, Exec. Dir.
Institute for Vietnamese Music
[9920]
2005 Willow Ridge Cir.
Kent, OH 44240
Fax: (330)673-4434

Nguyen, Quoc, CFO
Freedom House [18097]
1850 M St. NW, 11th Fl.
Washington, DC 20036
Ph: (202)296-5101
Fax: (212)293-2840

Nguyen, QuynhGiao N., PhD,
President
Iota Sigma Pi [23704]
c/o QuynhGiao Nguyen, President
21000 Brookpark Rd.
MS 49-3
Cleveland, OH 44135
Ph: (216)433-6073

Nguyen, Ross, Chairman, Exec. Dir.
Vietnamese American Armed Forces
Association [4977]
6200 Rolling Rd.
Springfield, VA 22152
Ph: (714)386-9896

Nguyen, Sophie, Treasurer
Christian Life Community of the
United States of America [19822]
3601 Lindell Blvd.
Saint Louis, MO 63108-3301
Ph: (202)425-2572

Nguyen, Vu T.H., Exec. Dir.
Porsche Club of America [21480]
9689 Gerwig Ln., Unit 4C/D
Columbia, MD 21046
Ph: (410)381-0911
Fax: (410)381-0924

Nias, Danita, Exec. Dir.
University of Florida Alumni Associa-
tion [19355]
1938 W University Ave.
Gainesville, FL 32603
Ph: (352)392-1905
Toll Free: 888-352-5866
Fax: (352)846-3636

Nicewander, Alan, President
Society of Multivariate Experimental
Psychology [7074]
821 S Main Str.,
James Madison University
821 S Main Street
Harrisonburg, VA 22801

Nichol, Heather, Secretary
Section for Women in Public
Administration [5701]
c/o Phin Xaypangna, Treasurer
2828 Mt. Isle Harbor Dr.
Charlotte, NC 28214

Nicholas, Kyle, President, Founder
Cancer Dancer [13921]
PO Box 7416
Richmond, VA 23221

Nichols, Bruce, Bd. Member
Friends of Peace Pilgrim [10327]
PO Box 2207
Shelton, CT 06484-1841
Ph: (203)926-1581

Nichols, Dave, Director
Tailhook Association [5624]
9696 Businesspark Ave.
San Diego, CA 92131-1643
Ph: (858)689-9223
Toll Free: 800-322-4665

Nichols, David G., MD., President,
CEO
American Board of Pediatrics
[16599]
111 Silver Cedar Ct.
Chapel Hill, NC 27514
Ph: (919)929-0461
Fax: (919)929-9255

Nichols, Fern, Founder, President
Moms in Prayer International
[20644]
13939 Poway Rd., Ste. 3
Poway, CA 92064
Toll Free: 855-769-7729
Fax: (858)486-5132

Nichols, Mr. Jeffrey L., President,
CEO
Thomas Jefferson's Poplar Forest
[9406]
PO Box 419
Forest, VA 24551-0419
Ph: (434)525-1806
Fax: (434)525-7252

Nichols, Jim, Director
Christian Restoration Association
[19966]
7133 Central Parke Blvd.
Mason, OH 45040
Ph: (513)229-8000
Fax: (513)229-8003

Nichols, Jon, Exec. Dir.
Association of Correctional Food
Service Affiliates [1386]
PO Box 10065
Burbank, CA 91510
Ph: (818)843-6608
Fax: (818)843-7423

Nichols, Joseph A., President
American Society of Pension Profes-
sionals and Actuaries [1065]
4245 N Fairfax Dr., Ste. 750
Arlington, VA 22203
Ph: (703)516-9300
Fax: (703)516-9308

Nichols, Marggie, President
Hispanic Professional Women's As-
sociation [3492]
PO Box 152344
Tampa, FL 33684-2344
Ph: (813)877-5880

Nichols, Pete, President
Fertile Crescent Foundation [3862]
PO Box 4835
Arcata, CA 95521

Nichols, Sandra, President
Society of Woman Geographers
[6674]
415 E Capitol St. SE
Washington, DC 20003-3810
Ph: (202)546-9228

Nichols, Steve, President
Antenna Measurement Techniques
Association [6413]

Nichols, Willard R., President
American Public Communications
Council, Inc. [3216]
3213 Duke St., Ste. 806
Alexandria, VA 22314
Ph: (703)739-1322
Fax: (703)739-1324

Nicholson, Bruce J., President
Association of Medical and Graduate
Departments of Biochemistry
[6052]
c/o Bruce J. Nicholson, President
University of Texas
7703 Floyd Curl Dr., MC 7760
San Antonio, TX 78229-3901
Ph: (210)567-3770
Fax: (210)567-6595

Nicholson, Bryan, Exec. Dir.
Sorptive Minerals Institute [2383]
1800 M St, Ste. 400S
Washington, DC 20036
Ph: (202)289-2760
Fax: (202)530-0659

Nicholson, Glen, President
Tire Industry Association [3280]
1532 Pointer Ridge Pl., Ste. G
Bowie, MD 20716-1883
Ph: (301)430-7280
Toll Free: 800-876-8372
Fax: (301)430-7283

Nicholson, Harold, President
Bounders United [22463]
c/o Pat Hoffman,Treasurer
1970 N Leslie St.
Pahrump, NV 89060-3678

Nickel, Matthew, VP
Elizabeth Madox Roberts Society
[10369]
16 Montgomery St.
Tivoli, NY 12583

Nickeleit, Volker, MD, Advisor
Renal Pathology Society [16591]
c/o Lois J. Arend, Treasurer

Pathology 709
600 N Wolfe
Baltimore, MD 21287

Nicola, Robert J., President
Society Farsarotul [9236]
PO Box 753
Trumbull, CT 06611

Nicolaou, Nicolas, President
Cyprus-US Chamber of Commerce
[23579]
805 3rd Ave., 10th Fl.
New York, NY 10017
Ph: (201)444-5609
Fax: (201)444-0445

Nicole, Kristen, Founder
Women in Solar Energy [7216]
225 Franklin St., 26th Fl.
Boston, MA 02110

Nicoll, Kate, LCSW, Exec. Dir.,
Founder
Soul Friends [17464]
300 Church St., Ste. 105
Wallingford, CT 06492
Ph: (203)679-0849
Fax: (203)679-0348

Nieblas, Victor D., President
American Immigration Lawyers As-
sociation [5289]
1331 G St. NW, Ste. 300
Washington, DC 20005-3142
Ph: (202)507-7600
Fax: (202)783-7853

Niebuhr, Bonnie, RN, MS, CAE,
CEO
American Board of Nursing Special-
ties [16101]
610 Thornhill Ln.
Aurora, OH 44202
Ph: (330)995-9172
Fax: (330)995-9743

Niebuhr, Bonnie, RN, MS, CAE,
CEO
American Board for Occupational
Health Nurses [16102]
201 E Ogden Ave., Ste. 114
Hinsdale, IL 60521-3652
Ph: (630)789-5799
Toll Free: 888-842-2646
Fax: (630)789-8901

Niebylski, Dr. Mark L., CEO
World Hypertension League [15351]
415 Bass Ln.
Corvallis, MT 59828

Niederberger, Mary, Secretary
Day Sailer Association [22611]
c/o Mary Niederberger, Secretary
3840 Arrowhead Dr.
El Dorado Hills, CA 95762-4505
Ph: (781)893-5030

Niehaus, H. Brandt, CHB, President
Hotel Brokers International [2862]
1420 NW Vivion Rd., Ste. 111
Kansas City, MO 64118
Ph: (816)505-4315
Fax: (816)505-4319

Niekerk, Joan Van, President
International Society for Prevention
of Child Abuse and Neglect
[11051]
13123 E 16th Ave. B390
Aurora, CO 80045
Ph: (303)864-5220
Fax: (303)964-5222

Nield, Naylene, Contact
American Sulphur Horse Association
[22154]

1245 South 6300 West
Cedar City, UT 84720-9206

Nielsen, April, Mem.
Association of Pool and Spa Profes-
sionals [2906]
2111 Eisenhower Ave., Ste. 500
Alexandria, VA 22314
Ph: (703)838-0083
Fax: (703)549-0493

Nielsen, Rev. Cody, President
National Campus Ministry Associa-
tion [20086]
2422 College St.
Cedar Falls, IA 50613
Ph: (704)588-0183

Nielsen, Eva, President
GAIA Movement USA [3873]
8918 S Green St.
Chicago, IL 60620
Ph: (773)651-7870
Toll Free: 877-787-4242

Nielsen, John Mark, Secretary
Danish American Heritage Society
[9275]
1717 Grant St.
Blair, NE 68008
Ph: (402)426-9610

Nielson, Dennis, Bd. Member
Drilling, Observation and Sampling
of the Earth's Continental Crust
[6373]
2075 S Pioneer Rd., Ste. B
Salt Lake City, UT 84104-4231
Ph: (801)583-2150
Fax: (801)583-2153

Niessen, Wiro, Chmn. of the Bd.,
President
Medical Image Computing and
Computer Assisted Intervention
Society [15690]
c/o Stephen Aylward, Treasurer
Kitware, Inc.
28 Corporate Dr.
Clifton Park, NY 12065

Nieto, Ernesto, Founder, President
National Hispanic Institute [9360]
PO Box 220
Maxwell, TX 78656
Ph: (512)357-6137
Fax: (512)357-2206

Nieto-Rodriguez, Antonio, Chairman
Project Management Institute [2191]
14 Campus Blvd.
Newtown Square, PA 19073-3299
Ph: (610)356-4600
Toll Free: 855-746-4849
Fax: (610)482-9971

Niewedde, Bob, Chairman
Egg Clearinghouse, Inc. [4566]
PO Box 817
Dover, NH 03821
Toll Free: 800-736-7286

Nifong, Todd, President
International Textile Market Associa-
tion [3262]
305 W High Ave.
High Point, NC 27260
Ph: (336)885-6842

Nifong, Wiley, Comm. Chm.
International Society for Minimally
Invasive Cardiothoracic Surgery
[14129]
500 Cummings Ctr., Ste. 4550
Beverly, MA 01915
Ph: (978)927-8330
Fax: (978)524-0498

Nigro, Joseph J., President
International Association of Sheet
Metal, Air, Rail and Transportation
Workers [23481]

1750 New York Ave. NW, 6th Fl.
Washington, DC 20006
Ph: (202)783-5880
   (202)662-0858

Nikolich-Zugich, Janko, MD,
Chairperson
American Aging Association [14886]
Dept. of Pathology, College of
Medicine
Drexel University
New College Bldg.
245 N 15th St.
Philadelphia, PA 19102

Nikpourfard, Nick, Exec. Dir.
National Certified Pipe Welding
Bureau [2608]
1385 Piccard Dr.
Rockville, MD 20850-4329
Ph: (301)869-5800
Toll Free: 800-556-3653
Fax: (301)990-9690

Niles, Jaimee, President
Insurance and Financial Com-
municators Association [96]
PO Box 515 E Grant Rd., Ste. 141
Tucson, AZ 85705
Ph: (602)350-0717
Fax: (866)402-7336

Nilsen, Scott, Director
Young Life [20664]
PO Box 520
Colorado Springs, CO 80901
Fax: (719)332-6732

Nilsestuen, Ken, President
France and Colonies Philatelic
Society [22329]
PO Box 102
Brooklyn, NY 11209

Nilsson, Magnus, Exec. Dir.
International Trombone Association
[9936]
PO Box 3241
Henrico, VA 23228
Toll Free: 888-236-6241
Fax: (206)600-5845

Nimerichter, Jodee, Director
American Dance Festival [9241]
715 Broad St.
Durham, NC 27705
Ph: (919)684-6402
Fax: (919)684-5459

Nimitz, Andrew MacNeely, Exec. VP
Clan Macneil Association of America
[20826]
PO Box 230693
Montgomery, AL 36123-0693
Ph: (334)834-0612

Ning, MingMing, M.D., President
American Federation for Medical
Research [14287]
500 Cummings Ctr., Ste. 4550
Beverly, MA 01915-6534
Ph: (978)927-8330
Fax: (978)524-8890

Ninivaggi, Michele, Advisor
International Association of CPAs,
Attorneys, and Management
[5686]
16192 Coastal Hwy.
Lewes, DE 19958
Toll Free: 800-518-0950

Niravel, Anandan, President
Federation of Malayalee Associa-
tions of Americas [19473]
1922 Cottman Ave.
Philadelphia, PA 19111
Ph: (267)549-1196
Fax: (267)742-4142

Niroomand, Farhang, Exec. Sec.,
Treasurer
Omicron Delta Epsilon [23726]
19 S Summit St., No. 9
Fairhope, AL 36532
Ph: (251)928-0001
Fax: (251)928-0015

Nissenberg, Merel Grey, President
National Alliance of State Prostate
Cancer Coalitions [14018]
10250 Constellation Blvd., Ste. 2320
Los Angeles, CA 90067
Toll Free: 877-627-7228
Fax: (310)525-3572

Nissley, Rev. Denny, President,
Founder
Christ In Action [20134]
PO Box 4200
Manassas, VA 20108
Ph: (703)368-6286
Fax: (703)368-6470

Niswander, Rick, Treasurer
ARRL Foundation [21266]
225 Main St.
Newington, CT 06111-1494
Ph: (860)594-0200
Fax: (860)594-0259

Niu, Candice, Exec. Dir.
China General Chamber of
Commerce-U.S.A. [23573]
19 E 48th St., 5th Fl.
New York, NY 10017
Ph: (646)918-7804
Fax: (917)639-3124

Nivia, Adriana, Exec. VP
Society of Insurance Financial
Management [1266]
61 Mountain Ave.
Caldwell, NJ 07006
Ph: (973)303-6297

Nixon, Jon, President
Medical Dental Hospital Business
Associates [41]
350 Poplar Ave.
Elmhurst, IL 60126
Ph: (630)359-4273
Fax: (630)359-4274

Niyiragira, Oscar, President
United Burundian-American Com-
munity Association [18531]
14339 Rosetree Ct.
Silver Spring, MD 20906
Ph: (240)669-6305
Fax: (240)669-6305

Niyonzima-Aroian, Jeanine, Founder,
Chairperson
Burundi Friends International
[11327]
PO Box 927356
San Diego, CA 92192-7356
Ph: (619)800-2340

Njungwe, Eric Ngonji, President
Cameroon Center for Democracy
and Human Rights [18380]
8504 16th St., No. 715
Silver Spring, MD 20910
Ph: (301)938-5221
Fax: (240)260-0766

Nnaemeka, Dr. Obioma, President
Association of African Women
Scholars [8513]
c/o Obioma Nnaemeka, President
Cavanaugh Hall, Rm. 001C
Indiana University
425 University Blvd.
Indianapolis, IN 46202
Ph: (317)278-2038
   (317)274-0062
Fax: (317)274-2347

Noakes, Kevin, Consultant
Society of Piping Engineers and
Designers [6596]
9668 Westheimer Rd., Ste. 200-242
Houston, TX 77063
Ph: (832)286-3404

Nobel, Mr. Claes, Chairman
National Society of High School
Scholars [8519]
1936 N Druid Hills Rd.
Atlanta, GA 30319
Ph: (404)235-5500
Toll Free: 866-343-1800

Nobel, Mr. Claes, Chairman
World Peace Prayer Society [18845]
26 Benton Rd.
Wassaic, NY 12592
Ph: (845)877-6093
Fax: (845)877-6862

Noble, Dave, President
World Internet Numismatic Society
[22291]
PO Box 220401
Saint Louis, MO 63122

Noble, Don, Chairman, President
Maranatha Volunteers International
[20153]
990 Reserve Dr., Ste. 100
Roseville, CA 95678-1387
Ph: (916)774-7700
Fax: (916)774-7701

Noble, Linda, PhD, President
Women in Neurotrauma Research
[16042]
c/o National Neurotrauma Society
9037 Ron Den Ln.
Windermere, FL 34786
Ph: (407)876-0750

Nobles, Karen, Treasurer
American Society of Questioned
Document Examiners [5239]
PO Box 6140
Lakewood, CA 90714

Nobles, Wade W., PhD, Exec. Dir.
Institute for the Advanced Study of
Black Family Life and Culture
[8784]
1012 Linden St.
Oakland, CA 94607
Ph: (510)836-3705

Nodrat, Nooria, President
Afghanistan Blind Women and
Children Foundation [17679]
40-10 12th St., Apt 1C
Long Island City, NY 11101
Ph: (718)784-4541

Noebel, Dr. David, President
Christian Anti-Communism Crusade
[17802]
PO Box 129
Manitou Springs, CO 80829-0129
Ph: (719)685-9043

Noel, Becky, Exec. Dir.
International Crime Free Association
[5125]
c/o Samantha Scheurn
El Cajon Police Dept.
100 Civic Center Way
El Cajon, CA 92020
Ph: (619)579-4227
Fax: (619)441-5534

Noel, Elana, Pub. Dir.
National Environmental Balancing
Bureau [1633]
8575 Grovemont Cir.
Gaithersburg, MD 20877
Ph: (301)977-3698
Toll Free: 866-497-4447
Fax: (301)977-9589

Noelker, Timothy F., Director
Council on Accreditation [13039]
45 Broadway, 29th Fl.
New York, NY 10006
Ph: (212)797-3000
Fax: (212)797-1428

Noerenberg, Chuck, President, Bd.
Member
National Alliance for Drug
Endangered Children [13159]
9101 Harlan St., Ste. 245
Westminster, CO 80031
Ph: (612)860-1599

Nofziger, Joel, Dir. of Comm.
Mennonite Historical Society [20331]
1700 Main St.
Goshen, IN 46526
Ph: (574)535-7433

Nogales, Alex, CEO, President
National Hispanic Media Coalition
[17952]
55 S Grand Ave.
Pasadena, CA 91105
Ph: (626)792-6462
Fax: (626)792-6051

Nogueira, Raul G., President
Society of Vascular and Interven-
tional Neurology [16036]
6737 W Washington St., Ste. 1300
Milwaukee, WI 53214
Ph: (414)389-8613
Fax: (414)276-7704

Noguera, Felipe, Chairman
International Association of Political
Consultants [18100]
c/o Goddard Gunster
701 8th St. NW, Ste. 400
Washington, DC 20001
Ph: (202)659-4300
Fax: (202)371-1467

Nohmi, Takehiko, President
International Association of
Environmental Mutagenesis and
Genomics Societies [6083]
1821 Michael Faraday Dr., Ste. 300
Reston, VA 20190
Ph: (703)438-3103
Fax: (703)438-3113

Nolan, Betty, Bd. Member
Sumi-e Society of America [8892]
c/o Veronica Lowe, Membership
Secretary
94-72 220th St.
Queens Village, NY 11428
Ph: (718)468-4061

Nolan, Deborah, Chmn. of the Bd.
Counterpart International [12149]
2345 Crystal Dr., Ste. 301
Arlington, VA 22202
Ph: (571)447-5700
Fax: (703)412-5035

Nolasco, Juan, President
American Association of Psychiatric
Technicians [16814]
1220 S St., Ste. 100
Sacramento, CA 95811-7138
Toll Free: 800-391-7589
Fax: (916)329-9145

Nold, Carl R., CEO, President
Historic New England [9398]
141 Cambridge St.
Boston, MA 02114
Ph: (617)227-3956
Fax: (617)227-9204

Noles, Robert B., Director
Knowles/Knoles/Noles Family Association [20982]

c/o Robert B. Noles, Director
133 Acadian Ln.
Mandeville, LA 70471
Ph: (985)845-4688

Noll, Janet, President
Saluki Tree of Life Alliance, Inc.
[11694]
3701 Sacramento St., No. 345
San Francisco, CA 94118-1705

Nollenberg, Joy, Exec. Dir.,
Secretary
Joy Project [14643]
PO Box 16488
Saint Paul, MN 55116

Nollman, Jim, Director, Founder
Interspecies [6768]
301 Hidden Meadows Ln.
Friday Harbor, WA 98250

Noltenius, Jeannette, MA, Director
National Latino Tobacco Control
Network [17485]
Indiana Latino Institute
1869 Park Rd. NW
Washington, DC 20010
Ph: (202)328-1313
Fax: (202)797-9856

Nommesen, Torrey, Contact
YLEM: Artists Using Science and
Technology [8948]
PO Box 31923
San Francisco, CA 94131-0923
Ph: (415)445-0196

Nonini, Gena, President
Demeter Biodynamic Trade Associa-
tion [4152]
PO Box 264
Talmage, CA 95481-0264

Nonog, Lisa, President
American Manchester Terrier Club
[21814]
Ph: (270)789-8649

Nonomaque, Curt, CEO, President
VHA [15339]
290 E John Carpenter Fwy.
Irving, TX 75062
Toll Free: 800-750-4972

Nooman, Kevin M., Exec. Dir.
Association for Interactive Marketing
[3217]
1430 Broadway, 8th Fl.
New York, NY 10018
Ph: (212)790-1408
Fax: (212)391-9233

Noon, Marita, Advisor
Center for the Defense of Free
Enterprise [18280]
12500 NE 10th Pl.
Bellevue, WA 98005
Ph: (425)455-5038

Noon, Marita, Exec. Dir.
Citizens' Alliance for Responsible
Energy [6467]
PO Box 52103
Albuquerque, NM 87181
Ph: (505)239-8998

Noonan, Gary, Exec. Sec., Treasurer
American Academy of Sanitarians,
Inc. [17176]
c/o Gary Noonan, Executive
Secretary/Treasurer
1568 LeGrand Cir.
Lawrenceville, GA 30043-8191
Ph: (678)518-4028

Noonan, Roger, Chairman
Experience Works [11764]
4401 Wilson Blvd., Ste. 1100

Arlington, VA 22203
Toll Free: 800-397-9757

Noone, Dr. R. Barrett, Officer
The American Board of Plastic
Surgery, Inc. [14305]
7 Penn Ctr., Ste. 400
1635 Market St.
Philadelphia, PA 19103-2204
Ph: (215)587-9322
Fax: (215)587-9622

Noor, Moina, Director
American Muslims Intent on Learn-
ing and Activism [10028]
PO Box 420 614
San Francisco, CA 94142

Noorani, Ali, Exec. Dir.
National Immigration Forum [18465]
50 F St. NW, Ste. 300
Washington, DC 20001-1552
Ph: (202)347-0040
Fax: (202)347-0058

Noppen, Trip Van, President
Earthjustice [5178]
50 California St., Ste. 500
San Francisco, CA 94111
Toll Free: 800-584-6460
Fax: (510)217-2040

Noppen, Trip Van, Treasurer
League of Conservation Voters
[18880]
1920 L St. NW, Ste. 800
Washington, DC 20036-5045
Ph: (202)785-8683
Fax: (202)835-0491

Norberg, Robert L., President
Americans for Middle East
Understanding [18674]
475 Riverside Dr., Rm. 245
New York, NY 10115-0245
Ph: (212)870-2053
Fax: (212)870-2050

Norbu, Khyentse, Chairman
Lotus Outreach [13013]
c/o Patty Waltcher, President
1104 N Signal St.
Ojai, CA 93023
Ph: (760)290-7190
Toll Free: 888-831-9990

Nordahl, Regina T., President
Association of NROTC Colleges and
Universities [8343]
c/o Lauren Heary
University of Rochester, 208 Latti-
more Hall
Rochester, NY 14627
Ph: (585)273-2425
Fax: (585)275-8531

Nordal, Katherine C., PhD, Exec.
Dir.
American Psychological Association
Practice Organization [13808]
750 1st St. NE
Washington, DC 20002-4241
Toll Free: 800-374-2723
Fax: (202)336-5797

Nordan, Rebecca, VP of Operations
Medical Fitness Association [16705]
90 Cherokee Rd., Ste. 3A
Pinehurst, NC 28374
Ph: (910)420-8610
Toll Free: 844-312-3541
Fax: (910)420-8733

Nordboe, Jerry, Treasurer
Falcon Club of America [21379]
PO Box 113
Jacksonville, AR 72078-0113

Nordbrock, Ms. Terry, MPH, Bd.
Member
National Disease Clusters Alliance
[14601]

Nordin, Kerstin, Chairperson
Finnish and American Women's
Network [13377]
PO Box 3623
New York, NY 10163-3623

Nordstrom, Kimberly D., MD,
President
American Association for Emergency
Psychiatry [16812]
PO Box 3948
Parker, CO 80134
Toll Free: 877-749-0737
Fax: (720)496-4974

Noren, Carol, Secretary
Swedish-American Historical Society
[10231]
3225 W Foster Ave.
Chicago, IL 60625
Ph: (773)583-5722
    (773)244-6224

Norick, Vickie L., Chairman
Red Earth [19588]
6 Santa Fe Plz.
Oklahoma City, OK 73102
Ph: (405)427-5228
Fax: (405)427-8079

Norley, Julian, VP
American Carbon Society [6180]
2540 Research Park Dr.
Lexington, KY 40511
Ph: (859)257-0322
Fax: (859)257-0220

Norlock, Kate, President
Society for Analytical Feminism
[10119]
c/o Carol Hay, Secretary/Treasurer
Dept. of Philosophy
University of Massachusetts Lowell
883 Broadway Ave.
Lowell, MA 01854

Norman, Dr. Bill, Exec. Dir.,
Secretary
The Cotton Foundation [933]
PO Box 783
Cordova, TN 38088
Ph: (901)274-9030
Fax: (901)725-0510

Norman, David, Bd. Member
Institute of Management Consultants
USA [2173]
631 US Highway 1, Ste. 400
North Palm Beach, FL 33408
Ph: (561)472-0833
Toll Free: 800-837-7321

Norman, Ruth E., Founder
Unarius Academy of Science
[12018]
145 S Magnolia Ave.
El Cajon, CA 92020
Ph: (619)444-7062
Toll Free: 800-475-7062

Norquist, Grover G., President
Americans for Tax Reform [19165]
722 12th St. NW, Ste. 400
Washington, DC 20005
Ph: (202)785-0266
Fax: (202)785-0261

Norris, Gary, Chmn. of the Bd.
Association for Catechumenal
Ministry [20354]
990 Reece Rd.
Alpharetta, GA 30004
Ph: (513)301-4826

Norris, Kathy, President
International Iridology Practitioners
Association [16389]
2100 Southbridge Pky., Ste. 650

Homewood, AL 35209
Ph: (205)226-3522
Toll Free: 888-682-2208
Fax: (205)226-3525

Norris, Kim, Founder, President
Lung Cancer Foundation of America
  [15539]
15 S Franklin St.
New Ulm, MN 56073
Ph: (507)354-1361

Norris, Teresa, Exec. Dir.
Sacred Circle [10047]
c/o Teresa Norris, Executive Director
PO Box 21451
Keizer, OR 97303
Ph: (971)239-5697

Norsigian, Judy, Director
Public Responsibility in Medicine
  and Research [19085]
PO Box 845203
Boston, MA 02284-5203
Ph: (617)423-4112
Fax: (617)423-1185

North, Jason, Chmn. of the Bd.
Save the Chimps [10693]
PO Box 12220
Fort Pierce, FL 34979-2220
Ph: (772)429-0403
Fax: (772)461-7147

Northrup, Jack, Founder
One-Arm Dove Hunt Association
  [22794]
PO Box 582
Olney, TX 76374

Northup, Prof. Brent, Treasurer
National Parliamentary Debate As-
  sociation [8599]
Carroll College
1601 N Benton Ave.
Helena, MT 59625-0001
Ph: (503)768-7729
Fax: (503)768-7620

Northup, Chris, Distributor
Certified Automotive Parts Associa-
  tion [290]
1000 Vermont Ave. NW, Ste. 1010
Washington, DC 20005-4908
Ph: (202)737-2212
Fax: (202)737-2214

Norton, Blake, VP, COO
Police Foundation [5515]
1201 Connecticut Ave. NW, Ste. 200
Washington, DC 20036-2636
Ph: (202)833-1460
Fax: (202)659-9149

Norton, Nancy J., President
International Foundation for
  Functional Gastrointestinal
  Disorders [14793]
700 W Virginia St., No. 201
Milwaukee, WI 53204
Ph: (414)964-1799
Toll Free: 888-964-2001
Fax: (414)964-7176

Norton, Natalie, President, CEO
Association of YMCA Professionals
  [13418]
Springfield College
Stitzer YMCA, 2nd Fl.
263 Alden St.
Springfield, MA 01109
Ph: (413)748-3884
Fax: (413)748-3872

Norton, Neg, President
Local Search Association [2798]
820 Kirts Blvd., Ste. 100
Troy, MI 48084-4836
Ph: (248)244-6200
Fax: (248)244-0700

Norton, Neil S., Ph.D., President
American Association of Clinical
  Anatomists [13688]
c/o Caitlin Hyatt, Executive Director
PO Box 2945
LaGrange, GA 30241-0061
Ph: (706)298-0287
Fax: (706)883-8215

Norton, Norman J., Chairman
AASP - The Palynological Society
  [6976]
University of N Carolina at Pem-
  broke
Geology, Old Main 213
Pembroke, NC 28372
Ph: (910)521-6478

Norton, Oswald, Exec. Dir.
Subud USA [20621]
4216 Howard Rd.
Beltsville, MD 20705
Ph: (301)595-0626

Norton, Ruth Ann, Exec. Dir.
Coalition to End Childhood Lead
  Poisoning [4044]
Green & Healthy Homes Initiative
2714 Hudson St.
Baltimore, MD 21224
Ph: (410)534-6447
Toll Free: 800-370-5323
Fax: (410)534-6475

Nortz, Kim, President
National Association of Service
  Providers in Private Rehabilitation
  [17092]
c/o National Rehabilitation Associa-
  tion
PO Box 150235
Alexandria, VA 22315
Ph: (703)836-0850
Fax: (703)836-0848

Norwood, Victoria F., President
American Society of Pediatric Neph-
  rology [15874]
3400 Research Forest Dr., Ste. B7
The Woodlands, TX 77381-4259
Ph: (346)980-9752
Fax: (346)980-9752

Notkin, Susan, Director
Parents Anonymous [11126]
250 W 1st St., Ste. 250
Claremont, CA 91711
Ph: (909)621-6184
Fax: (909)621-0614

Nottingham, Jennifer, Officer
National Association of Disability
  Examiners [14298]
PO Box 243
9404 N Manor Dr.
Raleigh, NC 27602
Ph: (919)212-3222
Toll Free: 800-443-9359
Fax: (919)212-3155

Novaes, Nancy, Contact
International Society of Women
  Airline Pilots [144]
723 S Casino Center Blvd., 2nd Fl.
Las Vegas, NV 89101-6716

Novak, Alex, President
Czech Heritage Preservation Society
  [9385]
PO Box 3
Tabor, SD 57063-0003
Ph: (605)463-2571

Novak Winer, Rabbi Laura, RJE,
  President
Association of Jewish Reform
  Educators [20233]
633 3rd Ave.

New York, NY 10017
Ph: (212)452-6510
Fax: (212)452-6512

Noverr, Mairi, VP
Medical Mycological Society of the
  Americas [15850]
c/o Mairi Noverr, Vice President
1100 Florida Ave.
New Orleans, LA 70119

Novick, Mr. Michael, Exec. Ofc.
Anti-Racist Action-Los Angeles/
  People Against Racist Terror
  [17875]
PO Box 1055
Culver City, CA 90232
Ph: (323)636-7388

Novis, Susie, President, Founder
International Myeloma Foundation
  [13990]
12650 Riverside Dr., Ste. 206
North Hollywood, CA 91607-3421
Ph: (818)487-7455
Toll Free: 800-452-2873
Fax: (818)487-7454

Novosel, Joseph R., Esq., President
Tamburitza Association of America
  [10017]
c/o Joseph R. Novosel, Esq.,
  President
3894 Spartan Dr.
Fort Gratiot, MI 48059
Ph: (810)385-9667

Novotny, Tamir, Exec. Dir.
Emerging Practitioners in
  Philanthropy [12473]
601 W 26th St., No. 325-7
New York, NY 10001
Ph: (212)584-8249

Nowack, David, President
Eighth Air Force Historical Society
  [21194]
PO Box 956
Pooler, GA 31322
Ph: (912)748-8884

Nowak, Ed, VP
American Mookee Association
  [3656]
c/o Steve Bieberich, President
22523 E 1020 Rd.
Clinton, OK 73601
Ph: (580)323-6259

Nowak, Jonathan, Exec. Sec.
InterCollegiate Outing Club Association [23324]
35-41 72 St.
35-41 72 St.
Jackson Heights, NY 11372

Nowak, Mark, President
Steel Framing Alliance [2372]
25 Massachusetts Ave. NW, Ste.
  800
Washington, DC 20001-7400
Ph: (202)452-1039
Fax: (202)452-1039

Nowicki Hnatiuk, Cynthia, CEO
Academy of Medical-Surgical Nurses
  [16079]
PO Box 56
Pitman, NJ 08071
Toll Free: 866-877-2676
Fax: (856)589-7463

Nowinski, Christopher, Founder
Concussion Legacy Foundation
  [17282]
PO Box 181225
Boston, MA 02118
Ph: (781)790-8922
    (781)790-1921

Ntowe, Dr. Francis, Exec. Dir.
Cameroon America AIDS Alliance
  [13534]
25 E Superior St., No. 3702
Chicago, IL 60611
Ph: (847)963-1664

Nuby, Glenn, President
National Construction Investigators
  Association Inc. [5367]
4328 Murillo St.
Las Vegas, NV 89121

Nuckles, K., President
Insulated Cable Engineers Associa-
  tion [6559]
PO Box 2694
Alpharetta, GA 30023
Ph: (770)830-0369
Fax: (770)830-8501

Nuckolls, Madonna, Editor, President
Three Dog Night Fan Club [24065]
c/o Madonna Nuckolls, President
PO Box 1975
Rowlett, TX 75030

Nuckols, Dan, Director, Chairman
Holistic Management International
  [3882]
5941 Jefferson St. NE, Ste. B
Albuquerque, NM 87109
Ph: (505)842-5252
Fax: (505)843-7900

Nuelle, Fr. John, Exec. Dir.
United States Catholic Mission As-
  sociation [19916]
415 Michigan Ave. NE, Ste. 102
Washington, DC 20017
Ph: (202)832-3112
Fax: (202)832-3688

Nuernberger, Andreas, VP
IEEE - Systems, Man, and
  Cybernetics Society [6247]
3 Park Ave., 17th Fl.
New York, NY 10016-5997
Ph: (212)419-7900
Fax: (212)752-4929

Nugent, Dr. James F., President
Prayers for Life [20071]
c/o Dr. James F. Nugent, President
Salve Regina University
100 Ochre Point Ave.
Newport, RI 02840-4149
Ph: (401)849-5421

Nugent, Ms. Madeline Pecora, Min.
Confraternity of Penitents [19826]
1702 Lumbard St.
Fort Wayne, IN 46803
Ph: (260)739-6882

Nugent, Rebecca, Contact
Classification Society [6994]
c/o Beth Ayers, Secretary/ Treasurer
American Institutes for Research
1000 Thomas Jefferson St. NW
Washington, DC 20007

Nullet, Joe, Exec. Dir.
Supervised Visitation Network
  [11162]
3955 Riverside Ave.
Jacksonville, FL 32205
Ph: (904)419-7861
Fax: (904)239-5888

Nunn, Dorsey, Exec. Dir.
All of Us or None [17863]
c/o Legal Services for Prisoners with
  Children
1540 Market St., Ste. 490
San Francisco, CA 94102-6049
Ph: (415)255-7036
Fax: (415)552-3150

Nunn, Dorsey, Exec. Dir.
Legal Services for Prisoners with
Children [5287]
1540 Market St., Ste. 490
San Francisco, CA 94102
Ph: (415)255-7036
Fax: (415)552-3150

Nunn, Douglas, Officer
Association of Trust Companies
[1276]
2313 N Broadway
Ada, OK 74820
Ph: (405)680-7869
Fax: (580)332-4714

Nunn, Michelle, President, CEO
CARE USA [12633]
151 Ellis St. NE
Atlanta, GA 30303-2440
Ph: (404)681-2552
(202)595-2800
Toll Free: 800-422-7385

Nunn, Steve, CEO, President
Open Group [1805]
44 Montgomery St., Ste. 960
San Francisco, CA 94104-4704
Ph: (415)374-8280
Fax: (415)374-8293

Nunnally, Philip, Chairman
Partners and Peers for Diabetes
Care [14542]
PO Box 5128
Chattanooga, TN 37406
Ph: (423)505-0558

Nuñez, Abel, Exec. Dir.
Central American Resource Center
[19016]
1460 Columbia Rd. NW, Ste. C-1
Washington, DC 20009
Ph: (202)328-9799
Fax: (202)328-7894

Nurisio, Robert, President
Parents Active for Vision Education
[17736]
4135 54th Pl.
San Diego, CA 92105

Nuseir, Rami, Director, Founder
American MidEast Leadership
Network [18513]
PO Box 2156
Astoria, NY 11102
Ph: (347)924-9674
Fax: (917)591-2177

Nuss, Daryl, Exec. Dir., CEO
National Network of Youth Ministries
[20660]
PO Box 501748
San Diego, CA 92150-1748
Ph: (858)451-1111
Fax: (858)451-6900

Nuss, Laura L., President
National Association of State Direc-
tors of Developmental Disabilities
Services [12329]
301 N Fairfax St., Ste. 101
Alexandria, VA 22314-2633
Ph: (703)683-4202

Nussbaum, Debra, Mgr.
Laurent Clerc National Deaf Educa-
tion Center [11933]
800 Florida Ave. NE
Washington, DC 20002-3695
Ph: (202)651-5051

Nussbaum, Jeffrey, President,
Founder
Historic Brass Society [9918]
148 W 23rd St., No. 5F
New York, NY 10011
Ph: (212)627-3820
Fax: (212)627-3820

Nussman, Mike, CEO, President
American Sportfishing Association
[22839]
1001 N Fairfax St., Ste. 501
Alexandria, VA 22314
Ph: (703)519-9691
Fax: (703)519-1872

Nutt, Charlie, Exec. Dir.
National Academic Advising Associa-
tion [7689]
Kansas State University
2323 Anderson Ave., Ste. 225
Manhattan, KS 66502-2912
Ph: (785)532-5717
Fax: (785)532-7732

Nutter, Franklin W., President
Reinsurance Association of America
[1922]
1445 New York Ave., 7th Fl.
Washington, DC 20005
Ph: (202)638-3690
Fax: (202)638-0936

Nutter, Kathleen Banks, PhD,
Treasurer
Coordinating Council for Women in
History [18205]

Nutter, Robin, Dir. of Dev.
Pilgrim Society [21083]
Pilgrim Hall Museum
75 Court St.
Plymouth, MA 02360-3823
Ph: (508)746-1620

Nuzzi, Joseph F., President
NOVA Hope for Haiti, Inc. [12294]
176 Palisade Ave.
Emerson, NJ 07630
Ph: (201)675-9413

Nwabukwu, Ify Anne, Founder, Exec.
Dir.
African Women's Cancer Awareness
Association [13873]
8701 Georgia Ave., Ste. 600
Silver Spring, MD 20910
Ph: (301)565-0420

Nwokah, Eva, President
The Association for the Study of
Play [10147]
1 Manhattan Sq.
Rochester, NY 14607
Ph: (585)263-2700

Nwosu, John, President
National Black Graduate Student
Association [19294]
MSC 590507
Washington, DC 20059
Toll Free: 800-471-4102

Nyatika, Zachary, Managing Dir.
Ambassadors for Sustained Health
[14974]
3 Petrel St.
West Roxbury, MA 02132-4110
Ph: (646)481-0844

Nyblad, Mary Jo, Trustee
APA: The Engineered Wood As-
sociation [1429]
7011 S 19th St.
Tacoma, WA 98466
Ph: (253)565-6600
(253)620-7400
Fax: (253)565-7265

Nye, Bill, CEO
The Planetary Society [5871]
60 S Los Robles Ave.
Pasadena, CA 91101
Ph: (626)793-5100
Fax: (626)793-5528

Nye, Mr. David E., President
Christopher Columbus Philatelic
Society [22318]

c/o Leslie Seff, Secretary
3750 Hudson Manor Ter. E
Bronx, NY 10463-1126

Nye, Jane Meader, Secretary
The Meader Family Association, Inc.
[20899]
158 Ashdown Rd.
Ballston Lake, NY 12019
Ph: (518)399-5013

Nye, Joseph S., Jr., Chairman
Trilateral Commission [18530]
1156 15th St. NW
Washington, DC 20005
Ph: (202)467-5410
Fax: (202)467-5415

Nyei, Mr. Abraham Habib, Founder,
President
From Hunger to Harvest [12096]
Charlotte, NC

Nygren, Margaret A., Exec. Dir.,
CEO
American Association on Intellectual
and Developmental Disabilities
[15812]
501 3rd St. NW, Ste. 200
Washington, DC 20001
Ph: (202)387-1968
Fax: (202)387-2193

Nyktas, George, President
BMW Riders Association
International [22216]
PO Box 570
Mukwonago, WI 53149-0570
Ph: (262)409-2899
Toll Free: 866-924-7102
Fax: (262)409-2899

Nyman, Karen, Membership Chp.,
Treasurer
Miniature Book Society [9131]
c/o Karen Nyman, Membership
Chair
702 Rosecrans St.
San Diego, CA 92106-3013
Ph: (619)226-4441

Nystuen, John D., Chairman
Community Systems Foundation
[16214]
219 S Main St., Ste. 206
Ann Arbor, MI 48104-2105
Ph: (734)761-1357
Fax: (734)761-1356

Nyx, Tim, President
Working Riesenschnauzer Federation [21995]
c/o Tim Nyx, President
2303 Pete Smith Rd.
Louisburg, NC 27549

O

O Connell, Wanda, Coord.
National Center for Children in
Poverty [11255]
215 W 125th St., 3rd Fl.
New York, NY 10027
Ph: (646)284-9600
Fax: (646)284-9623

Oakes, Graham, Chairman
Digital Watermarking Alliance [6697]
9405 SW Gemini Dr.
Beaverton, OR 97008-7192
Ph: (818)444-4777
(503)469-4771
Fax: (503)469-4686

Oakes, Wendy Peia, President
Council for Children with Behavior
Disorders [8579]

Council for Exceptional Children
2900 Crystal Dr., Ste. 1000
Arlington, VA 22202-3557

Oates, Brian, Founder, Chairman
Golf Fights Cancer [13978]
300 Arnold Palmer Blvd.
Norton, MA 02766
Ph: (774)430-9060
Fax: (774)430-9031

Obalil, Deborah, Exec. Dir.
Association of Independent Colleges
of Art and Design [7626]
236 Hope St.
Providence, RI 02906
Ph: (401)270-5991
Fax: (401)270-5993

Obama, Michelle, Chairman
Wolf Trap Foundation for the
Performing Arts [9007]
1645 Trap Rd.
Vienna, VA 22182
Ph: (703)255-1900
Toll Free: 877-WOLFTRAP

Obando, Carlos, Mem.
International Gay and Lesbian
Aquatics [23284]

O'Bannon, Michael J., President
Statue of Liberty - Ellis Island
Foundation [9438]
History Ctr.
17 Battery Pl., No. 210
New York, NY 10004-3507
Ph: (212)561-4588

Obasi, Onyeka, President
Friends of Africa International
[18401]
619 W 140th St., Ste. 2H
New York, NY 10031
Ph: (917)261-4472
Fax: (212)590-6164

Oberbeck, Tamara, President
National Association of Vision
Professionals [16395]
1775 Church St. NW
Washington, DC 20036
Ph: (202)234-1010
Fax: (202)234-1020

Oberhelman, David, Administrator
Mythopoeic Society [9762]
PO Box 6707
Altadena, CA 91003-6707

Oberkfell, Larry, CEO, President
International Foodservice
Manufacturers Association [1344]
2 Prudential Plz.
180 N Stetson Ave., Ste. 850
Chicago, IL 60601
Ph: (312)540-4400

Oberkircher, Jim, Exec. Dir.
International Association of
Directional Drilling [7001]
525 North Sam Houston Pky. E, No.
525
Houston, TX 77060
Ph: (281)931-8811

Oberlander, Lynn, Chairman
Media Law Resource Center [5433]
266 W 37th St., 20th Fl.
New York, NY 10018
Ph: (212)337-0200
Fax: (212)337-9893

Obie-Barrett, Christy, Exec. Dir.
A Family for Every Child [10968]
880 Beltline Rd.
Springfield, OR 97477
Ph: (541)343-2856
Toll Free: 877-343-2856
Fax: (541)343-2866

O'Block, Dr. Robert, Founder,
Publisher
American Association of Integrative
Medicine [15703]
2750 E Sunshine St.
Springfield, MO 65804-2047
Ph: (417)881-9995
Toll Free: 877-718-3053
Fax: (417)823-9959

O'Block, Robert L., PhD, CEO,
Founder
American College of Forensic
Examiners International [5235]
2750 E Sunshine St.
Springfield, MO 65804
Ph: (417)881-3818
Toll Free: 800-423-9737
Fax: (417)881-4702

O'Boyle, Mr. Jamie, Treasurer
American Creativity Association
[9530]
School of Education
Drexel University
3141 Chestnut St.
Philadelphia, PA 19104
Ph: (215)895-6771

O'Brasky-Britland, Roxanne,
Founder, Chairperson
International Society of Six Sigma
Professionals [2742]
7301 RR 620 N, Ste. 155 O362
Austin, TX 78726-4537
Ph: (512)233-2721
Toll Free: 844-477-7746

OBrien, John, Exec. Asst.
National Association of Stationary
Operating Engineers [6728]
212 Elmwood Ave. Ext., Ste. 500
Gloversville, NY 12078
Ph: (518)620-3683

O'Brien, Barbara, Officer
Dairy Management, Inc. [973]
10255 W Higgins Rd., Ste. 900
Rosemont, IL 60018-5616
Toll Free: 800-853-2479
Fax: (847)627-2077

O'Brien, Catherine, Coord.
United States of America
Transactional Analysis Association
[13806]
7881 Church St., Ste. F
Gilroy, CA 95020
Ph: (408)848-2293

O'Brien, Jane, Treasurer
American Association of Handwriting
Analysts [10409]
PO Box 4576
Spanaway, WA 98387
Ph: (360)455-4551
Toll Free: 800-826-7774
Fax: (253)846-6448

O'Brien, Jim, Contact
Historians Against the War [19235]
PO Box 442154
Somerville, MA 02144

O'Brien, Jim, Treasurer
Resist [18873]
PO Box 441155
Somerville, MA 02144
Ph: (617)623-5110

O'Brien, Jon, President
Catholics for Choice [19031]
1436 U St. NW, Ste. 301
Washington, DC 20009-3997
Ph: (202)986-6093
Fax: (202)332-7995

O'Brien, Joseph P., CEO, President
National Scoliosis Foundation
[17184]

5 Cabot Pl.
Stoughton, MA 02072-4624
Ph: (781)341-6333
Toll Free: 800-673-6922
Fax: (781)341-8333

O'Brien, Kathy, Director, President
Real Foundation [13395]
550 Hinesburg Rd.
South Burlington, VT 05403
Ph: (802)846-7871

O'Brien, Kevin, President
Inland Marine Underwriters Associa-
tion [1861]
14 Wall St., 8th Fl.
New York, NY 10005
Ph: (212)233-0550
Fax: (212)227-5102

O'Brien, Kim, MBA, President, CEO
National Association for Fixed Annui-
ties [1891]
1155 F St. NW, Ste. 1050
Washington, DC 20004
Ph: (414)332-9306
Fax: (888)946-3532

O'Brien, Michael, CEO, President
Window and Door Manufacturers
Association [601]
330 N Wabash Ave., Ste. 2000
Chicago, IL 60611
Ph: (312)321-6802
     (202)367-1157

O'Brien, Morgan, Dir. of Dev.
Native American Rights Fund
[18711]
1506 Broadway
Boulder, CO 80302-6296
Ph: (303)447-8760
Fax: (303)443-7776

O'Brien, Patrick, Exec. Dir.
Concrete Sawing and Drilling As-
sociation [786]
100 2nd Ave. S, Ste. 402N
Saint Petersburg, FL 33701
Ph: (727)577-5004
Fax: (727)577-5012

O'Brien, Sheila, Exec. Dir.
Skating Association for the Blind and
Handicapped [23156]
2607 Niagara St.
Buffalo, NY 14207-1029
Ph: (716)362-9600
Fax: (716)362-9601

O'Brien, Prof. Thomas W., PhD,
President
Mitochondria Research and
Medicine Society [14596]
PO Box 55322
Birmingham, AL 35255
Ph: (205)934-2735
Fax: (205)934-2766

Obrow, Norman C., Chairman
Joseph Drown Foundation [11726]
1999 Avenue of the Stars, Ste. 2330
Los Angeles, CA 90067
Ph: (310)277-4488
Fax: (310)277-4573

O'Bryan, Bernard, III, Trustee
Sons of Spanish American War
Veterans [21096]
c/o James McAteer, President
145 Tiverton Ct.
Lebanon, PA 17042
Ph: (803)345-2025

O'Bryon, David S., CAE, President
Association of Chiropractic Colleges
[14256]
4424 Montgomery Ave., Ste. 202

Bethesda, MD 20814
Toll Free: 800-284-1062

Ocampo, Jennifer, Exec. Dir.
American Gynecological and
Obstetrical Society [16273]
230 W Monroe St., Ste. 710
Chicago, IL 60606
Ph: (312)676-3920
Fax: (312)235-4059

Ochal, Frank, President
Chevy Club [21352]
5433 N Ashland Ave.
Chicago, IL 60640
Ph: (773)769-7458
Fax: (773)769-3240

Ochal, Frank J., President
American MGB Association [21321]
PO Box 11401
Chicago, IL 60611
Ph: (773)769-7084
Fax: (773)769-3240

Ochal, Frank, President
Mazda Club [21428]
5433 N Ashland Ave.
Chicago, IL 60640
Ph: (773)769-7396
Fax: (773)769-3240

Ochal, Frank, President
National Firebird and Trans Am Club
[21454]
5433 N Ashland Ave.
Chicago, IL 60640
Ph: (773)769-7166
Fax: (773)769-3240

Oches, Sam, Co-Ch.
International Foodservice Editorial
Council [2686]
7 Point Pl.
Hyde Park, NY 12538
Ph: (845)229-6973
     (845)527-5679
Fax: (845)229-6973

O'Connell, Jack, Secretary,
Treasurer
Baseball Writers Association of
America [2667]
PO Box 610611
Bayside, NY 11361-0611
Ph: (718)767-2582
Fax: (718)767-2583

O'Connell, Mr. Jamie, JD, President
International Professional Partnerships for Sierra Leone [18493]
2042 Swans Neck Way
Reston, VA 20191-4030

O'Conner, Pat, CEO, President
National Association of Professional
Baseball Leagues [22557]
9550 16th St. N
Saint Petersburg, FL 33716
Ph: (727)822-6937
Fax: (727)821-5819

O'Connor, Chris M., VP, CIO
MIB Group, Inc. [15420]
50 Braintree Hill Pk., Ste. 400
Braintree, MA 02184-8734
Ph: (781)751-6000

O'Connor, Jen, VP
North American Torquay Society
[21703]
13607 Maxson Ct.
Spotsylvania, VA 22553

O'Connor, Kevin, Chmn. of the Bd.
American Home Furnishings Alliance
[1473]
1912 Eastchester Dr., Ste. 100

High Point, NC 27265
Ph: (336)884-5000
Fax: (336)884-5303

O'Connor, Mary, Secretary
International Institute of Synthetic
Rubber Producers, Inc. [2985]
207 S Gessner Rd., Ste. 133
Houston, TX 77063
Ph: (713)783-7511
Fax: (713)783-7253

O'Connor, Nuala, President, CEO
Center for Democracy and Technol-
ogy [17940]
1401 K St. NW, Ste. 200
Washington, DC 20005
Ph: (202)637-9800
Fax: (202)637-0968

O'Connor, Rick, Exec. Dir.
RapidIO Trade Association [6260]
8650 Spicewood Springs, No. 145-
515
Austin, TX 78759
Ph: (512)401-2900
     (512)827-7680

O'Connor, Tim, President
Wheat Foods Council [1525]
51 Red Fox Ln., Unit D
Ridgway, CO 81432
Ph: (970)275-4440

Octavien, Nixon, President
A Chance for Kids [10888]
601 W Oakland Park Blvd., No. 14
Oakland Park, FL 33311
Ph: (954)326-0513

O'Day, Mary, Contact
The Havana Silk Dog Association of
America [21892]
35394 Linda Rosea Rd.
Temecula, CA 92592

O'Day, Paul T., President
American Fiber Manufacturers As-
sociation [3252]
3033 Wilson Blvd., Ste. 700
Arlington, VA 22201
Ph: (703)875-0432
Fax: (703)875-0907

O'Dea, Joe, President
United States Team Penning As-
sociation [22934]
PO Box 1359
Weatherford, TX 76086
Ph: (817)599-4455
Fax: (817)599-4461

Odede, Kennedy, CEO, President
Shining Hope for Communities
[11435]
175 Varick St., 6th Fl.
New York, NY 10014
Ph: (860)218-9854

O'Dell, Carla, PhD, CEO
APQC [2148]
123 N Post Oak Ln., 3rd Fl.
Houston, TX 77024
Toll Free: 800-776-9676
Fax: (713)681-8578

O'Dell, John, HCCP, Exec. Dir.
Certified Claims Professional Ac-
creditation Council [3324]
PO Box 550922
Jacksonville, FL 32255-0922

O'Dell, Mollie, VP, Comm.
National Propane Gas Association
[4265]
1899 L St. NW, Ste. 350
Washington, DC 20036-4623
Ph: (202)466-7200
Fax: (202)466-7205

Oden, Jim, President
National Ice Cream Retailers Association **[976]**
1028 W Devon Ave.
Elk Grove Village, IL 60007
Ph: (847)301-7500
Toll Free: 866-303-6960
Fax: (847)301-8402

Odjo, Nadia, President
Bringing Relief Internationally
Through Education **[10876]**
1520 N K St.
Lake Worth, FL 33460
Ph: (561)384-8474

Odland, Peter, Founder
Hunt for a Cure **[15645]**
2687 44th St. SE
Kentwood, MI 49512
Ph: (616)455-9405
Fax: (616)897-0345

Odom, James, President
American Guild of Musical Artists
[23493]
1430 Broadway, 14th Fl.
New York, NY 10018
Ph: (212)265-3687
Toll Free: 800-543-2462
Fax: (212)262-9088

Odom, Linda C., President
ITC Trial Lawyers Association **[5826]**
Benjamin Franklin Sta.
Washington, DC 20044

ODonnell, Frank, Exec. Dir.
Medical Missions for Children
[14202]
600 W Cummings Pk., Ste. 2850
Woburn, MA 01801
Ph: (508)697-5821
Fax: (781)501-5225

O'Donnell, Anne, President
Association for Research of Childhood Cancer **[13894]**
PO Box 251
Buffalo, NY 14225-0251
Ph: (716)681-4433

O'Donnell, Brenda, VP
Highway Loss Data Institute **[1859]**
1005 N Glebe Rd., Ste. 700
Arlington, VA 22201
Ph: (703)247-1600
Fax: (703)247-1595

O'Donnell, Frank, President
Clean Air Watch **[4540]**
1250 Connecticut Ave. NW, Ste. 200
Washington, DC 20036-2643
Ph: (202)558-3527

O'Donnell, Leigh, Exec. Dir.
Handcrafted Soap and Cosmetic
Guild **[21759]**
178 Elm St.
Saratoga Springs, NY 12866-4009
Ph: (518)306-6934
Toll Free: 866-900-7627

O'Donnell, Mary, President
Amyloidosis Foundation **[14559]**
7151 N Main St., Ste. 2
Clarkston, MI 48346-1584
Toll Free: 877-269-5643
Fax: (248)922-9620

O'Donnell, Maureen, Secretary
American Friends of the Hakluyt
Society **[9749]**
c/o The John Carter Brown Library
PO Box 1894
Providence, RI 02912

O'Donnell, Patrick E., Chairman
American Council for Kosovo
[18607]

PO Box 14522
Washington, DC 20044

O'Donnell, Patrick, Comm. Chm.
Outdoor Advertising Association of
America, Inc. **[106]**
1850 M St. NW, Ste. 1040
Washington, DC 20036
Ph: (202)833-5566
Fax: (202)833-1522

O'Donovan, Peter, Exec. Dir.
International Foundation for Ethical
Research **[10647]**
53 W Jackson Blvd., Ste. 1552
Chicago, IL 60604
Ph: (312)427-6025
Fax: (312)427-6524

Odunsi, Kunle, MD, Investigator,
Director
Gilda Radner Familial Ovarian
Cancer Registry **[13967]**
Roswell Park Cancer Institute
Elm and Carlton St.
Buffalo, NY 14263
Ph: (716)845-4503
Toll Free: 800-682-7426

Oduro, Erika, Exec. Dir.
Access to Empowerment
International **[11720]**
12523 Limonite Ave., No. 440-222
Mira Loma, CA 91752
Ph: (951)440-5542
Fax: (951)346-3897

Oechslin, Erwin N., MD, FRCPC,
President
International Society for Adult
Congenital Heart Disease **[14124]**
1500 Sunday Dr., Ste. 102
Raleigh, NC 27607
Ph: (919)861-5578
Fax: (919)787-4916

Oelerich, Vikki, President
American Pomeranian Club Inc.
[21817]
c/o Kelly D. Reimschiissel, 6214 W
10150 N
6214 West 10150 North
Highland, UT 84003
Ph: (801)361-8619

Oelke, Ken, President
Quarter Century Wireless Association **[21273]**
12967 N Normandy Way
West Palm Beach, FL 33410-1412
Ph: (352)425-1097

Oessenich, Kevin, Exec. Dir.
World Team **[20480]**
1431 Stuckert Rd.
Warrington, PA 18976
Ph: (215)491-4900
Toll Free: 800-967-7109

Offenheiser, Raymond C., President
Oxfam America **[12557]**
226 Causeway St., 5th Fl.
Boston, MA 02114
Ph: (617)482-1211
Toll Free: 800-776-9326
Fax: (617)728-2594

Offenheiser, Raymond C., President
Oxfam International Advocacy Office
[12177]
226 Causeway St., 5th Fl.
Boston, MA 02114-2206
Ph: (617)482-1211
Toll Free: 800-776-9326
Fax: (617)728-2594

Offringa, Kate, President
Vinyl Siding Institute, Inc. **[598]**
National Housing Ctr.

1201 15th St. NW, Ste. 220
Washington, DC 20005
Ph: (202)587-5100
Fax: (202)587-5127

Offutt, James, Counsel
Navy League of the United States
[5618]
2300 Wilson Blvd., Ste. 200
Arlington, VA 22201
Ph: (703)528-1775
Toll Free: 800-356-5760
Fax: (703)528-2333

Ofori-Diallo, Jay, President
Pan-African Education **[11733]**
PO Box 16653
Tucson, AZ 85732
Ph: (520)465-0976

Ofwono, Juliet, Consultant
Access Research Network **[8543]**
7668 Dartmoor Ave.
Goleta, CA 93117
Ph: (805)448-9505

Ogbuta, Chidi, RN, Founder,
President
Angels for Premature Babies
[16794]
1112 Scotts Bluff Dr.
Allen, TX 75002
Ph: (469)441-2387
Fax: (214)291-5242

Ogden, Amy, Secretary, Treasurer
Hagiography Society **[20575]**
302 Cabel Hall
Charlottesville, VA 22904

Ogden, Cassandra Sneed, CEO,
Exec. Dir.
Council on Legal Education Opportunity **[8213]**
1101 Mercantile Ln., Ste. 294
Largo, MD 20774
Ph: (240)582-8600
Fax: (240)582-8605

Ogden, John, Sr., Chairman
Christian Motorcyclists Association
[22218]
4278 Highway 71 S
Hatfield, AR 71945-7119
Ph: (870)389-6196

Ogden, Kirk, Exec. Dir.
South America Mission **[20465]**
1021 Maxwell Mill Rd., Ste. B
Fort Mill, SC 29708
Ph: (803)802-8580
Fax: (803)548-7955

Ogden, Tim, President
Laurence-Moon-Bardet-Biedl
Syndrome Network **[14835]**
c/o Robert Haws, Committee Chair
Marshfield Clinic
1000 N Oak Dr.
Marshfield, WI 54449
Ph: (715)387-5240

Ogle, Jan, President
Mothers Against Sexual Predators At
Large **[12928]**
PO Box 606
Bonner, MT 59823

Ogle, Steve, Tech. Dir.
INDA, Association of the Nonwoven
Fabrics Industry **[3259]**
1100 Crescent Green, Ste. 115
Cary, NC 27518
Ph: (919)459-3700
    (919)233-1210
Fax: (919)459-3701

O'Gorman, Ms. Linda J., Secretary,
Treasurer
International Association for Pattern
Recognition **[6995]**

O'Gorman, Michael, Exec. Dir.
Farmer-Veteran Coalition **[21121]**
4614 2nd St., Ste. 4
Davis, CA 95618
Ph: (530)756-1395

O'Grady, Lorraine, Exec. Dir.
The Society for Pediatric Urology
[17562]
500 Cummings Ctr., Ste. 4550
Beverly, MA 01915
Ph: (978)927-8330
Fax: (978)524-0498

Ogrean, Dave, Exec. Dir.
USA Hockey **[22911]**
1775 Bob Johnson Dr.
Colorado Springs, CO 80906-4090
Ph: (719)576-8724
Fax: (719)538-1160

Ogrodzinski, Henry M., President,
CEO
Center for Aviation Research and
Education **[5057]**
Washington National Airport
Hangar 7, Ste. 218
Washington, DC 20001
Ph: (703)417-1883

Ogunyipe, Benro, MPA, Comm.
Chm.
National Black Deaf Advocates
[11623]
PO Box 564
Secane, PA 19018

Ogur, Scott, Treasurer
Independent Diplomat **[18479]**
45 E 20th St., 6th Fl.
New York, NY 10003
Ph: (212)594-8295
Fax: (212)594-8430

Ogwuche, Grace Dama, Secretary
Idoma Association USA **[19596]**
12031 Lackland Rd.
Saint Louis, MO 63146
Ph: (314)878-1400

Ohadi, Pauline, Membership Chp.
National Church Conference of the
Blind **[13277]**
PO Box 276
Edmond, OK 73083-0276
Ph: (405)330-1331

Ohanyan, Kristen Lee, President,
Founder
Vegan Society of People for the
Earth, Animals, Compassion and
Enlightenment **[17585]**
PO Box 6128
Katy, TX 77491-6128
Ph: (832)303-0834

O'Hara, Jim, Officer
Vergilian Society **[9109]**
c/o Keely Lake, Secretary
Wayland Academy
101 N University Ave.
Beaver Dam, WI 53916

O'Hara, Robert J., Jr., Exec. Dir.
National Association of State
Catholic Conference Directors
[19872]
Ph: (717)238-9613
Fax: (717)238-1473

Ohashi, Wataru, Director
Ohashi Institute **[16458]**
PO Box 505
Kinderhook, NY 12106
Ph: (518)758-6879
Toll Free: 800-810-4190
Fax: (518)758-6809

Ohgushi, Sara, ND, President
American Association of Naturopathic Midwives **[15854]**

c/o Jill Edwards
Vibrant Family Medicine & Midwifery
22400 SE Stark St.
Gresham, OR 97030

Ohlensehlen, Bob, Exec. Dir.
Epsilon Sigma Phi [23715]
c/o Bob Ohlensehlen, Executive
Director
450 Falls Ave., Ste. 106
Twin Falls, ID 83301
Ph: (208)736-4495
Fax: (208)736-6081

Ohlerking, Jean, VP, Founder
Children's Cup [12637]
PO Box 400
Prairieville, LA 70769
Ph: (225)673-4505

Ohm, Dr. Jeanne, Exec. Dir.
International Chiropractic Pediatric
Association [14273]
327 N Middletown Rd.
Media, PA 19063
Ph: (610)565-2360
Fax: (610)656-3567

Ohonme, Emmanuel, Founder,
President
Samaritan's Feet [11146]
1836 Center Park Dr.
Charlotte, NC 28217
Ph: (980)939-8150
Toll Free: 866-833-7463
Fax: (704)341-1687

Ohrenberg, Laura, Comm. Chm.
Ninety Nines, Inc. International
Organization of Women Pilots
[153]
4300 Amelia Earhart Dr., Ste. A
Oklahoma City, OK 73159
Ph: (405)685-7969
Toll Free: 800-994-1929
Fax: (405)685-7985

Oines, Dough, President
American Nyckelharpa Association
[9864]
c/o Tim Newcomb
579 Hampshire Hill Rd.
Worcester, VT 05682
Ph: (802)229-4604

Ojala, Dr. Rosalind Skyhawk, Dir. of
Admin., Founder
Pan American Indian Association
[10046]
8355 Sevigny Dr.
North Fort Myers, FL 33917
Ph: (707)725-9627

Ojeda, Martha A., Exec. Dir.
Coalition for Justice in the
Maquiladoras [19103]
3611 Golden Tee Ln.
Missouri City, TX 77459
Ph: (210)732-8957
    (210)210-1084

Okafor, Mary, President
Ogwashi-Uku Association USA
[19597]
PO Box 836
Riverdale, MD 20737

O'Kane, Margaret E., President
National Committee for Quality As-
surance [17031]
1100 13th St., Ste. 1000
Washington, DC 20005
Ph: (202)955-3500
Toll Free: 888-275-7585
Fax: (202)955-3599

Okazaki, Sumie, Officer
Asian American Psychological Association [16898]

5025 N Central Ave.
Phoenix, AZ 85012-1520

O'Keefe, Denis J., Treasurer
International Psychohistorical Association [9491]
c/o Denis O'Keefe, Treasurer
142A Main St.
Highland Falls, NY 10928

O'Keefe, Mike, Bd. Member
Custer Battlefield Historical and
Museum Association [9473]
PO Box 902
Hardin, MT 59034-0902

O'Keefe, Thomas Andrew, President
Uruguayan-American Chamber of
Commerce in the USA [23637]
401 E 88th St., Ste. 12-A
New York, NY 10128
Ph: (212)722-3306
Fax: (212)996-2580

O'Kelly, Walter, Contact
DeSoto Club of America [21370]
403 S Thorton St.
Richmond, MO 64085
Ph: (816)470-3048
    (816)421-6006

Okelo, Rebecca Conte, Exec. Dir.
MED25 International [15032]
PO Box 1459
Mercer Island, WA 98040

Okon, Ted, Exec. Dir.
Community Oncology Alliance
[16341]
1101 Pennsylvania Ave. NW, Ste.
700
Washington, DC 20004
Ph: (202)756-2258

Okounkova, Inna, President
Society of Quantitative Analysts
[1267]
1450 Western Ave., Ste. 101
Albany, NY 12203
Toll Free: 800-918-7930

Okulski, Robert V., President,
Treasurer
The Christophers [19823]
5 Hanover Sq., 22nd Fl.
New York, NY 10004
Ph: (212)759-4050
Toll Free: 888-298-4050
Fax: (212)838-5073

Okun, Andy, President
American Go Association [22045]
PO Box 4668
New York, NY 10163

Okure, Aniedi, Exec. Dir.
Africa Faith and Justice Network
[17771]
3025 4th St. NE, Ste. 122
Washington, DC 20017
Ph: (202)817-3670
Fax: (202)817-3671

Okure, Aniedi, Treasurer
Jubilee U.S.A. Network [18244]
212 E Capitol St. NE
Washington, DC 20003
Ph: (202)783-3566
Fax: (202)546-4468

Olade, Dr. Rosaline, President
African Good Samaritan Mission
[13000]
6700 150th Ave. N, Unit No. 705
Clearwater, FL 33764

Oladele, Dr. Alawode, Bd. Member
Global Initiative for the Advancement
of Nutritional Therapy, Inc. [17442]

4426 Hugh Howell Rd., Ste. B-333
Tucker, GA 30084
Ph: (770)491-8667
Fax: (770)491-8655

O'Laughlin, Michael C., President,
Founder
Irish Genealogical Foundation
[20978]
PO Box 7575
Kansas City, MO 64116
Ph: (816)399-0905

Olberding, David A., Chmn. of the
Bd.
Label Printing Industries of America
[3175]
301 Brush Creek Rd.
Warrendale, PA 15086
Ph: (412)741-6860
Toll Free: 800-910-4283
Fax: (412)741-2311

Olchefske, Joseph, Act. Pres.
Education Industry Association
[8647]
c/o Jim Giovannini, Executive Director
120 Main St., Ste. 202
Park Ridge, IL 60068
Ph: (703)938-2429

Ole Maimai, Kakuta, Managing Dir.
Maasai Association [10490]
PO Box 868
Medina, WA 98039
Ph: (206)697-9826

Olean, Jim, Membership Chp.
Candy Container Collectors of
America [21632]
c/o Jim Olean, Membership
Chairperson
115 Mac Beth Dr.
Lower Burrell, PA 15068-2628

O'Leary, Kim, President
International Glove Association
[1738]
PO Box 146
Brookville, PA 15825
Ph: (814)328-5208
Fax: (814)328-2308

O'Leary, Ray, Administrator
Professional Administrative Co-
Employers [1102]
c/o Ray O'Leary, Administrator
3535 S Woodland Cir.
Quinton, VA 23141
Ph: (804)932-9159
Toll Free: 888-436-6227
Fax: (804)932-9461

Olesiejuk, Michelle, Exec. Dir.
Gaming Standards Association
[22061]
48377 Fremont Blvd., Ste. 117
Fremont, CA 94538
Ph: (510)492-4060

Olewnik, Dr. Maureen C., VP of
Tech. Svcs.
AIB International [365]
1213 Bakers Way
Manhattan, KS 66505-3999
Ph: (785)537-4750
Toll Free: 800-633-5137
Fax: (785)537-1493

Olexy, Tamara Gallo, President
Ukrainian Congress Committee of
America [19206]
203 2nd Ave.
New York, NY 10003
Ph: (212)228-6840
Fax: (212)254-4721

Olig, Alison, Exec. Dir.
Sarcoma Alliance [14059]
775 E Blithedale, No. 334

Mill Valley, CA 94941
Ph: (415)381-7236
Fax: (415)381-7235

Olin, Joseph, Exec. Dir.
International Digital Media and Arts
Association [6836]
c/o Digital Communications
101 N College Ave.
Annville, PA 17003
Ph: (423)794-9996

Olin, Julia, Exec. Dir.
National Council for the Traditional
Arts [9330]
8757 Georgia Ave., Ste. 450
Silver Spring, MD 20910
Ph: (301)565-0654
Fax: (301)565-0472

Oliva, Manolo Garcia, President
Hispanic Organization of Latin Actors
[9357]
107 Suffolk St., Ste. 302
New York, NY 10002
Ph: (212)253-1015
Fax: (212)256-9651

Oliva, Marcie, Exec. Dir.
Association of Zoo Veterinary
Technicians [17641]
c/o Marcie Oliva, CVT, Executive
Director
White Oak Conservation Center
581705 White Oak Rd.
Yulee, FL 32097-2169

Oliveira, Rosângela, Exec. Dir.
World Day of Prayer International
Committee [20650]
475 Riverside Dr., Rm. 729
New York, NY 10115
Ph: (212)870-3049

Oliver, Bill, Publisher
Longwave Club of America [21270]
45 Wildflower Rd.
Levittown, PA 19057-3209

Oliver, Debbie, Exec. Dir.
AmeriFace [14329]
PO Box 751112
Las Vegas, NV 89136
Ph: (702)769-9264
Toll Free: 888-486-1209
Fax: (702)341-5351

Oliver, James H., Chairman
Ruffed Grouse Society [4878]
451 McCormick Rd.
Coraopolis, PA 15108
Ph: (412)262-4044
Toll Free: 888-564-6747

Oliver, Mike, Exec. Dir.
National Operating Committee on
Standards for Athletic Equipment
[3004]
c/o Mike Oliver, Executive Director
11020 King St., Ste. 215
Overland Park, KS 66210-1201

Oliver, Rebecca, Exec. Dir.
School Social Work Association of
America [8574]
PO Box 3068
London, KY 40743
Toll Free: 800-588-4149

Oliver, Samuel, President, Chmn. of
the Bd.
International Association of Baptist
Colleges and Universities [8709]
c/o Samford University
PO Box 293935
Birmingham, AL 35229
Ph: (205)726-2036

Oliver, Stephen, CEO
National Association of Professional
Martial Artists [23005]

14143 Denver West Pky., Ste. 100
Golden, CO 80401
Ph: (727)540-0500
Fax: (727)683-9581

Oliver, Stephen, President
Power Sources Manufacturers Association **[1119]**
PO Box 418
Mendham, NJ 07945-0418
Ph: (973)543-9660
Fax: (973)543-6207

Oliveto, Frank, Officer
Automotive Aftermarket Suppliers Association | Brake Manufacturers Council **[307]**
1030 15th St. NW, Ste. 500 E
Washington, DC 20005
Ph: (919)406-8856
Fax: (919)549-4824

Oliviero, Melanie Beth, Exec. Dir.
Panos Institute **[12178]**
Webster House
1718 P St. NW, Ste. T-6
Washington, DC 20036
Ph: (202)429-0730
    (202)429-0731
Fax: (202)483-3059

Olk, Dr. Dan, Coord.
International Humic Substances Society **[7136]**
1991 Upper Buford Cir., Rm. 439
Saint Paul, MN 55108
Ph: (612)626-1204

Olme, Al, President
United Sidecar Association **[22233]**
c/o Steve Woodward
PO Box 4301
Salem, OR 97302-8301
Ph: (612)759-4666

Olobo, Rev. Leonard, CSC, Director
Holy Cross Mission Center **[19841]**
PO Box 543
Notre Dame, IN 46556
Ph: (574)631-5477

Olsen, Anne D., PhD, President
Academy of Rehabilitative Audiology **[15165]**
PO Box 2323
Albany, NY 12220-0323
Fax: (866)547-3073

Olsen, Brad, Exec. Dir.
World Peace Through Technology Organization **[12447]**
San Francisco, CA 94105

Olsen, Heather, EdD, Exec. Dir.
National Program for Playground Safety **[19080]**
University of Northern Iowa
103 Human Performance Ctr.
Cedar Falls, IA 50614-0618
Toll Free: 800-554-PLAY
Fax: (319)273-7308

Olsen, Janet, Arch.
Woman's Christian Temperance Union **[13188]**
1730 Chicago Ave.
Evanston, IL 60201-4585
Ph: (847)864-1397
Toll Free: 800-755-1321

Olsen, Juliann, President
National Association of Health Unit Coordinators **[14951]**
1947 Madron Rd.
Rockford, IL 61107-1716
Ph: (815)633-4351
Toll Free: 888-226-2482
Fax: (815)633-4438

Olsen, Marilyn, President
Public Safety Writers Association **[3518]**
PO Box 4825
Ventura, CA 93007-0825

Olsen, Tim, Officer
Guitar and Accessories Marketing Association **[2424]**
875 W 181st St., No. 2D
New York, NY 10033
Ph: (212)795-3630

Olsen, Timothy L., President
Guild of American Luthiers **[2423]**
8222 S Park Ave.
Tacoma, WA 98408-5226
Ph: (253)472-7853

Olson, Becky, Founder, CEO
Breast Friends **[13910]**
14050 SW Pacific Hwy., Ste. 201
Tigard, OR 97224
Toll Free: 888-386-8048
Fax: (866)734-3762

Olson, Gary, VP
Lutheran Braille Evangelism Association **[17723]**
1740 Eugene St.
White Bear Lake, MN 55110-3312
Ph: (651)426-0469

Olson, Jerry C., Consultant
Epsilon Pi Tau **[23692]**
Bowling Green State University
Technology Bldg.
Bowling Green, OH 43403
Ph: (419)372-2425
Fax: (419)372-9502

Olson, Joy, Exec. Dir.
Washington Office on Latin America **[18624]**
1666 Connecticut Ave. NW, Ste. 400
Washington, DC 20009
Ph: (202)797-2171
Fax: (202)797-2172

Olson, Kathryn, CEO
Women's Sports Foundation **[23265]**
424 W 33rd St., Ste. 150
New York, NY 10001
Ph: (646)845-0273
Fax: (212)967-2757

Olson, Kristina, Treasurer
American Boccaccio Association **[9034]**
c/o Timothy Kircher, President
5800 W Friendly Ave.
Greensboro, NC 27410-4108

Olson, Steve, President
Wildlands Network **[4108]**
1402 3rd Ave., Ste. 1019
Seattle, WA 98101
Ph: (206)538-5363
Toll Free: 877-554-5234

Olsson, Kristine, President
American Society of Trace Evidence Examiners **[5240]**
c/o Chad Schennum, Treasurer
Virginia Department of Forensic Science
700 N 5th St.
Richmond, VA 23219
Ph: (804)588-4105
Fax: (804)786-6305

Olszewski, Bud, Treasurer
Association of Grace Brethren Ministers **[20358]**
PO Box 394
Winona Lake, IN 46590
Ph: (209)872-4921

Olszewski, Claire, Dir. of Fin.
Women's Leadership Forum **[18119]**
Democratic National Committee

430 S Capitol St. SE
Washington, DC 20003-4024
Ph: (202)863-8000
Toll Free: 877-336-7200

Olszowy, Alex, III, President
International Code Council **[5068]**
500 New Jersey Ave. NW, 6th Fl.
Washington, DC 20001
Ph: (202)370-1800
Toll Free: 888-422-7233
Fax: (202)783-2348

Olubayi, Dr. Olubayi, Trustee
Global Literacy Project **[8242]**
PO Box 1859
New Brunswick, NJ 08903-1859

Olver, Kim, Exec. Dir.
William Glasser Institute **[16991]**
4053 W 183rd St., No. 2666
Country Club Hills, IL 60478
Ph: (708)957-6048

O'Mara, Collin, President, CEO
National Wildlife Federation **[3908]**
11100 Wildlife Center Dr.
Reston, VA 20190
Ph: (703)438-6000
Toll Free: 800-822-9919

O'Martin, Yvonne, Exec. Dir.
Bradley O'Martin Melanoma Foundation **[13907]**
655 Duncan Dr.
Coppell, TX 75019
Ph: (972)462-7326

O'Meara, James, President
International Council on Education for Teaching **[8648]**
1000 Capitol Dr.
Wheeling, IL 60090-7201
Ph: (847)947-5881
Fax: (847)947-5881

O'Meara Moynihan, Mary, Chmn. of the Bd.
Hoo-Hoo International **[1410]**
207 Main St.
Gurdon, AR 71743
Ph: (870)353-4997
Fax: (870)353-4151

O'Meara, Sara, Chairman, Founder, CEO
Childhelp **[10912]**
Bldg. F250
4350 E Camelback Rd.
Phoenix, AZ 85018-2701
Ph: (480)922-8212
Fax: (480)922-7061

Omidyar, Pamela, Chairman, Founder
HopeLab **[15643]**
1991 Broadway St., Ste. 136
Redwood City, CA 94063-1957
Ph: (650)569-5900
Fax: (650)569-5901

Omokha, Emmanuel M.I., Sr., Exec. Dir.
American Pan-African Relief Agencies **[12617]**
PO Box 723
Bronx, NY 10467
Ph: (646)558-6363
    (646)558-6364
Toll Free: 877-368-8241
Fax: (646)853-3393

O'nan, E.M.T., Director
Protect All Children's Environment **[14723]**
396 Sugar Cove Rd.
Marion, NC 28752
Ph: (828)724-4221

Onate, John, Treasurer
Association of Medicine and Psychiatry **[16826]**
4747 N 1st St., Ste. 140
Fresno, CA 93726
Toll Free: 800-544-6283
Fax: (559)227-1463

O'Neal, Mike, President
League of World War I Aviation Historians **[21237]**
c/o Daniel Polglaze, Membership Secretary
16820 25th Ave. N
Plymouth, MN 55447-2228

O'Neal, Terry, President
American Society for the Positive Care of Children **[10852]**
777 E Tahquitz Canyon Way, Ste. 323
Palm Springs, CA 92262
Ph: (760)990-2200
Toll Free: 800-422-4453

O'Neil, Mike, President
North American Security Products Organization **[3066]**
204 E St. NE
Washington, DC 20002
Ph: (202)608-1322
Fax: (202)547-6348

O'Neil, Peter J., FASAE, CAE, Exec. VP, CEO
ASIS International **[1782]**
1625 Prince St.
Alexandria, VA 22314-2882
Ph: (703)519-6200
Fax: (703)519-6299

O'Neill, Colonel (Retired) Jack, Exec. Dir.
Army Engineer Association **[4972]**
PO Box 30260
Alexandria, VA 22310-8260
Ph: (703)428-7084
    (703)428-6049
Fax: (703)428-6043

O'Neill, Dr. Kevin, Director
Experiential Learning International **[7912]**
1557 Ogden St., Ste. 5
Denver, CO 80218
Ph: (303)321-8278

O'Neill, Rachel, Contact
Little Dresses for Africa **[11070]**
24614 Curtis Dr.
Brownstown, MI 48134
Ph: (734)637-9064

O'Neill, Robert, Exec. Dir.
Manufacturers Standardization Society **[1746]**
127 Park St. NE
Vienna, VA 22180-4602
Ph: (703)281-6613
Fax: (703)281-6671

O'Neill, Terry, President
National Organization for Women **[18227]**
1100 H St. NW, Ste 300
Washington, DC 20005-5488
Ph: (202)628-8669

Oni, Dr. Richard, Bd. Member
Angel Eyes Foundation **[13427]**
7710 Brooklyn Blvd., Ste. 206F
Brooklyn Park, MN 55443
Ph: (763)208-8339
Fax: (763)208-8526

Onoday, Heather, BSN, MN, FNP-C, President
Dermatology Nurses' Association **[16130]**

435 N Bennett St.
Southern Pines, NC 28387
Toll Free: 800-454-4362
Fax: (856)439-0525

Onyeuku, Saul, President
Igbere Progressive Association
International [11380]
c/o Chuck Oko, Board Secretary
PO Box 540814
Houston, TX 77254
Ph: (713)773-4887
Fax: (713)779-0233

Onyewuenyi, Nonye, Ph.D,
Secretary
Nigerian Association of Pharmacists
and Pharmaceutical Scientists in
the Americas [2564]
483 Northland Blvd.
Cincinnati, OH 45240
Ph: (513)641-3300
Fax: (513)861-3629

Opong, Senyo, Secretary
International Society of African
Scientists [7137]
c/o Senyo Opong, Secretary
PO Box 9209
Wilmington, DE 19809

Opre, Tom, President
Professional Outdoor Media Associa-
tion [2318]
PO Box 1569
Johnstown, PA 15907
Ph: (814)254-4719
Fax: (206)350-1047

Orazietti, Phil F., President
Appliance Parts Distributors Associa-
tion [211]
3621 N Oakley Ave.
Chicago, IL 60618
Ph: (773)230-9851
Fax: (888)308-1423

Orcutt, Kathy, Founder, President
Hugs for Our Soldiers [10747]
PO Box 532
Vonore, TN 37885

Ordesch, Edward L., Act. Pres.
National Association of Shooting
Sports Athletes [23134]
2103 Wheaton Dr.
Richardson, TX 75081

Orduna, KC, Admin. Asst.
Tiny Hands International [11166]
PO Box 67195
Lincoln, NE 68506
Ph: (402)601-4816

Oreamuno, Ignacio, Exec. Dir.
Art Directors Club [8840]
106 W 29th St.
New York, NY 10001
Ph: (212)643-1440
Fax: (212)643-4266

Oremland, Barry, President
Crowncap Collectors Society
International [21645]
c/o Kevin Kirk, Treasurer
1990 Holland Brook Rd.
Branchburg, NJ 08876

Orenbuch, Dr. Evelyn, President
American Association of Rehabilita-
tion Veterinarians [17599]
1230 Johnson Ferry Rd.
Marietta, GA 30068
Ph: (678)803-2626

Orf, Deborah, Secretary
International Color Consortium [757]
1899 Preston White Dr.

Reston, VA 20191
Ph: (703)264-7200

Orfanedes, Laura
Association of Energy Services
Professionals [6459]
15215 S 48th St., Ste. 170
Phoenix, AZ 85044
Ph: (480)704-5900
Fax: (480)704-5905

Orford, Robert R., MD, President
Airlines Medical Directors Associa-
tion [13507]
c/o Petra A. Illig, MD, Secretary
5011 Spenard Rd., No. 205
Anchorage, AK 99517
Ph: (907)245-4359
Fax: (907)245-2212

Organ, Robin, Exec. Dir., Prog. Dir.
Green Schools [7893]
PO Box 323
Mansfield, MA 02048
Ph: (508)272-9653
(425)663-1757

Orgill, Von, CEO, President
Polynesian Cultural Center [9215]
55-370 Kamehameha Hwy.
Laie, HI 96762
Ph: (808)293-3333
Toll Free: 844-572-2347
Fax: (808)293-3339

Orhun, Efe, Founder
Turkish American Business Connec-
tion [670]
2784 Homestead Rd., No. 118
Santa Clara, CA 95051
Ph: (408)404-5208
Fax: (408)404-5208

Orient, Jane M., MD, President
Doctors for Disaster Preparedness
[14662]
1601 N Tucson Blvd., Ste. 9
Tucson, AZ 85716
Ph: (520)325-2680

Orloff, Keith, Exec. Dir.
Accreditation Review Council on
Education in Surgical Technology
and Surgical Assisting [15670]
6 W Dry Creek Cir., Ste. 110
Littleton, CO 80120
Ph: (303)694-9262
Fax: (303)741-3655

Orloff, Kim, Coord., Founder
Mixed Harmony Barbershop Quartet
Association [9956]
c/o Kim Orloff, Coordinator
PO Box 1209
Aptos, CA 95001

Orlow, Gayle, Contact
Albanian American National
Organization [19296]
c/o Gayle Orlow
31057 Rivers Edge Ct.
Beverly Hills, MI 48025
Ph: (248)761-1184

Orlowski, Jeff, Secretary
Donate Life America [14617]
701 E Byrd St., 16th Fl.
Richmond, VA 23219-3921
Ph: (804)377-3580

Orosz, Matt, Director, President
STG International [7212]
PO Box 426152
Cambridge, MA 02142

O'Rourke, John, VP
International Waterless Printing Association [1539]

5 Southside Dr., Unit 11-328
Clifton Park, NY 12065-3870
Ph: (518)387-9321

Orpilla, Mel, President
Filipino American National Historical
Society [9389]
810 18th Ave., Rm. 100
Seattle, WA 98122
Ph: (206)322-0204
(707)477-1159

Orr, Catherine, Co-Ch.
Roundtable Association of Catholic
Diocesan Social Action Directors
[20566]
415 Michigan Ave. NE, Ste. 210B
Washington, DC 20017
Ph: (202)635-5858
(202)635-5828

Orr, Dan, Chairman
Historical Diving Society U.S.A.
[22811]
c/o Greg Platt, Treasurer
PO Box 453
Fox River Grove, IL 60021-0453
Ph: (805)934-1660

Orr, Stan, President, Chief Sales
Ofc.
Association of Equipment Manage-
ment Professionals [1713]
823 Grand Ave.Ste. 300
Glenwood Springs, CO 81601
Ph: (970)384-0510
Fax: (970)384-0512

Orrison, Linda, President
National Barbecue Association
[1354]
PO Box 9686
Naperville, IL 60567-9686
Ph: (331)444-7347

Orsini, Lynne, Exec. Dir.
American RSDHope [16552]
PO Box 875
Harrison, ME 04040
Ph: (207)583-4589

O'Brien, Dennis, Treasurer
96th Infantry Division Association
[20714]
c/o Don Klimkowicz, President
2817 Townline Rd.
Madison, OH 44057
Ph: (440)259-4212

O'Campo, Patricia, Treasurer
International Society for Urban
Health [15150]
New York Academy of Medicine
1216 5th Ave.
New York, NY 10029

O'Malia, Scott, CEO
International Swaps and Derivatives
Association [2024]
360 Madison Ave., 16th Fl.
New York, NY 10017-7111
Ph: (212)901-6000
Fax: (212)901-6001

O'Neal, Mark, President
Professional Baseball Athletic Trainers Society [22566]
400 Colony Sq., Ste. 1750
1201 Peachtree St.
Atlanta, GA 30361

O'Sullivan, David, Amb.
European Union Delegation to the
United States [18320]
2175 K St. NW
Washington, DC 20037
Ph: (202)862-9500
Fax: (202)429-1766

Orta, Carlos F., Mem.
Hispanic Association on Corporate
Responsibility [18066]
1220 L St. NW, Ste. 701
Washington, DC 20005-6502
Ph: (202)682-4012
Fax: (202)682-0086

Ortega, Leonardo, Contact
Alpha Zeta Omega [23843]
c/o Lou Flacks, Director
2485 Pine Grove Ct.
Yorktown Heights, NY 10598

Ortega, Suzanne, President
Council of Graduate Schools [7959]
1 Dupont Cir. NW, Ste. 230
Washington, DC 20036
Ph: (202)223-3791
Fax: (202)331-7157

Ortiz, Raul, Contact
International Seven-Star Mantis
Style Lee Kam Wing Martial Art
Association USA [22994]
Ortiz Chinese Boxing Academy
148-B Middle Neck Rd.
Great Neck, NY 11021
Ph: (516)972-1670

Ortiz, Suzette, Office Mgr.
EMTA [3042]
360 Madison Ave., 17th Fl.
New York, NY 10017
Ph: (646)289-5410
Fax: (646)289-5429

Ortman, Michael V., Chairman
Arthritis Foundation [17153]
1330 Peachtree St. NE, 6th Fl.
Atlanta, GA 30309
Ph: (404)872-7100

Orujyan, Armen, PhD, CEO,
Founder, President
Athgo International [13428]
13636 Ventura Blvd., Ste. 222
Sherman Oaks, CA 91423
Ph: (818)345-6734
Fax: (818)345-0955

Orvedahl, Leslie, Exec. Dir.
American Society of Neuroimaging
[17047]
5841 Cedar Lake Rd., Ste. 204
Minneapolis, MN 55416
Ph: (952)545-6291
Fax: (952)545-6073

Orwick, Peter, Exec. Dir.
American Sheep Industry Associa-
tion [4663]
9785 Maroon Cir., Ste. 360
Englewood, CO 80112
Ph: (303)771-3500

Osborne, David, Chmn. of the Bd.
NTL Institute [7914]
8380 Colesville Rd., Ste. 560
Silver Spring, MD 20910
Ph: (301)565-3200

Osborne, Frederik R-L., V. Chmn. of
the Bd.
Osborne Association [11542]
809 Westchester Ave.
Bronx, NY 10455
Ph: (718)707-2600
Fax: (718)707-3102

Osborne, Joe, President
Utility Arborist Association [4737]
2009 W Broadway Ave., Ste. 400,
PMB 315
Forest Lake, MN 55025
Ph: (651)464-0380
Fax: (651)409-3819

Osborne, Linda, Mem.
Alden Kindred of America [20776]
105 Alden St.

Duxbury, MA 02332
Ph: (781)934-9092

Osbrink, Rory, President
U.S. Deaf Cycling Association
[22800]
c/o Bobby Skedsmo, Secretary/
Treasurer
247 Jack London Ct.
Pittsburg, CA 94565-3661
Ph: (925)203-1045
(925)203-1262

Osburn, Johanna, Exec. Dir.
Design Industries Foundation Fight-
ing AIDS [10537]
16 W 32nd St., Ste. 402
New York, NY 10001
Ph: (212)727-3100
Fax: (212)727-2574

Osei-Boateng, Marian, MPA, Exec.
Dir.
Ready Hands International [11140]
PO Box 925
New York, NY 10274
Toll Free: 877-732-3942

Osei-Bonsu, Ama, Founder
The Heart Smiles [11017]
PO Box 592798
San Antonio, TX 78259
Ph: (210)771-8157

Osemwenkhae, Steve, Contact
AfriHope International, Inc. [10471]
PO Box 190796
Boston, MA 02119
Ph: (617)957-1613

O'Shaughnessy, Andrew Jackson,
Director
Robert H. Smith International Center
for Jefferson Studies [8446]
PO Box 316
Charlottesville, VA 22902
Ph: (434)984-9800
Toll Free: 800-243-0743

O'Shaughnessy, Lt. Col. Paul, Cmdr.
His Majesty's 10th Regiment of Foot
in America [8794]
40 Spring St.
Wrentham, MA 02093
Ph: (781)862-2586

O'Shea, Lynn, President
Association for Individual Develop-
ment [11562]
309 New Indian Trail Ct.
Aurora, IL 60506
Ph: (630)966-4000
Fax: (630)844-2065

O'Shea, Dr. Patrick, DSPE, Officer
International Society for Philosophi-
cal Enquiry [9343]
Dr. Patrick M. O'Shea, Acting
Comptroller
700 Terrace Heights, No. 60
Winona, MN 55987

Oshman, Michael, CEO, Founder
Green Restaurant Association [2939]
89 South St., Ste. 802
Boston, MA 02111
Ph: (617)737-3344
(617)737-4422

Oshry, Gary, Treasurer
National Association of Trade
Exchanges [3303]
926 Eastern Ave.
Malden, MA 02148
Ph: (781)388-9200
Fax: (781)321-4443

Osinski, E. David, Exec. Dir.
American Baseball Foundation
[22542]

2660 10th Ave. S, Ste. 620
Birmingham, AL 35205
Ph: (205)558-4235
Fax: (205)918-0800

Osipoff, Olga, Exec. Dir.
Russian American Medical Associa-
tion [15745]
36100 Euclid Ave., Ste. 330-B
Willoughby, OH 44094
Ph: (440)953-8055
Fax: (440)953-0242

Oskvig, Cameron, Director
Federal Facilities Council [5195]
National Academy of Sciences
500 5th St. NW, Keck 912
Washington, DC 20001

Osman, Todd, Exec. Dir.
Materials Research Society [6815]
506 Keystone Dr.
Warrendale, PA 15086-7573
Ph: (724)779-3003
Fax: (724)779-8313

Osmus, Carla, Chairman
Junior Billboard Association [100]
PO Box 582096
Elk Grove, CA 95758

Osner, Terry, Coord., Admin.
National Environmental Health As-
sociation [14719]
720 S Colorado Blvd., Ste. 1000-N
Denver, CO 80246
Ph: (303)756-9090
Fax: (303)691-9490

Osselburn, James, President
Allied Finance Adjusters [606]
956 S Bartlett Rd., Ste. 321
Bartlett, IL 60103
Toll Free: 800-843-1232
Fax: (888)949-8520

Ossinger, Joanna, President
Society of American Business Edi-
tors and Writers [2719]
c/o Walter Cronkite School of
Journalism and Mass Communica-
tion
555 N Central Ave., Ste. 406E
Phoenix, AZ 85004-1248
Ph: (602)496-7862
Fax: (602)496-7041

Ostendorf, John, President
American Tax Token Society [22259]
c/o Jim Calvert, Secretary &
Treasurer
1984 B Lyn Rd.
Arroyo Grande, CA 93420

Oster, Susan M., Exec. Dir.
American Orthopedic Foot and Ankle
Society [16466]
9400 W Higgins Rd., Ste. 220
Rosemont, IL 60018-3315
Ph: (847)698-4654
Toll Free: 800-235-4855
Fax: (847)692-3315

Osterhaus, Matthew C., President
APhA Academy of Pharmaceutical
Research and Science [16648]
2215 Constitution Ave. NW
Washington, DC 20037
Ph: (202)628-4410
Toll Free: 800-237-2742
Fax: (202)783-2351

Osterman, Kate, Contact
A Chance to Heal [14635]
PO Box 2342
Jenkintown, PA 19046
Ph: (215)885-2420

Ostman, Heather, President
Kate Chopin International Society
[10385]

c/o Heather Ostman, President
English Dept.
Westchester Community College
75 Grasslands Rd.
Valhalla, NY 10595

Ostrom, John, Contact
Bird Strike Committee U.S.A. [4796]
Metropolitan Airports Commn.
Minneapolis-St. Paul International
Airport
4300 Glumack Dr.
Saint Paul, MN 55111
Ph: (612)726-5780
Fax: (612)726-5074

Ostrowski, Don
Early Slavic Studies Association
[10217]
Eugene, OR

Ostrowski, Jay, President
International Society for Mental
Health Online [15778]
Ph: (608)618-1774

Oswald, Dr. Brian, Comm. Chm.
Association for Fire Ecology [3990]
PO Box 50412
Eugene, OR 97405
Ph: (541)852-7903

Otaño, Lucas, President
International Society for Prenatal
Diagnosis [17427]
154 Hansen Rd., Ste. 201
Charlottesville, VA 22911
Ph: (434)979-4773
Fax: (434)977-1856

Oto-Kent, Debra, Exec. Dir.
Health Education Council [14938]
3950 Industrial Blvd., Ste. 600
West Sacramento, CA 95691
Ph: (916)556-3344
Toll Free: 888-442-2836
Fax: (916)446-0427

O'Toole, Milagros Baez, Contact
Puerto Rican Family Institute, Inc.
[11946]
145 W 15th St.
New York, NY 10011
Ph: (212)924-6320
Fax: (212)691-5635

Ott, Betsy, President
Human Anatomy and Physiology
Society [13689]
251 SL White Blvd.
LaGrange, GA 30241-9417
Ph: (706)845-8204
Toll Free: 800-448-4277
Fax: (706)883-8215

Ott, Denise, Bus. Mgr.
National Guardianship Association,
Inc. [1560]
174 Crestview Dr.
Bellefonte, PA 16823
Toll Free: 877-326-5992
Fax: (814)355-2452

Otter, Samuel, Editor
Melville Society [9078]
c/o Johns Hopkins University Press
PO Box 19966
Baltimore, MD 21211-0966

Otterstrom, Sarah, PhD, Exec. Dir.
Paso Pacifico [3928]
PO Box 1244
Ventura, CA 93002-1244
Ph: (805)643-7044

Otto, Faye Battiste, President
American Forensic Nurses [16105]
255 N El Cielo Rd., Ste. 140-195

Palm Springs, CA 92262
Ph: (760)322-9925
Fax: (760)322-9914

Otto, Linda, Founder
Find the Children [10973]
2656 29th St., Ste. 203
Santa Monica, CA 90405-2984
Ph: (310)314-3213
Toll Free: 888-477-6721
Fax: (310)314-3169

Otto, Linda, Exec. Dir.
International Association of
Counselors and Therapists [15362]
8852 SR 3001
Laceyville, PA 18623
Ph: (570)869-1021
Toll Free: 800-553-6886
Fax: (570)869-1249

Otto, Linda, Exec. Dir.
International Medical and Dental
Hypnotherapy Association [15363]
8852 SR 3001
Laceyville, PA 18623
Ph: (570)869-1021
Toll Free: 800-553-6886
Fax: (570)869-1249

Otto, Martin, Chairman
National Association of Chain Drug
Stores [16674]
1776 Wilson Blvd., Ste. 200
Arlington, VA 22209
Ph: (703)549-3001
Fax: (703)836-4869

Otto, Randy K., PhD, Officer
American Academy of Forensic
Psychology [5230]
c/o Anita L. Boss, President
1200 Prince St.
Alexandria, VA 22314
Ph: (703)299-2422

Otto, Randy K., PhD, President
American Board of Professional
Psychology [16859]
600 Market St., Ste. 201
Chapel Hill, NC 27516
Ph: (919)537-8031
Fax: (919)537-8034

Otto, Robert, CEO
International Alliance of Professional
Hypnotists [15361]
8852 SR 3001
Laceyville, PA 18623
Ph: (570)869-1021
Fax: (570)869-1249

Otto, Tim, Treasurer
American Handwriting Analysis
Foundation [10410]
1011 S Tuxedo Ave.
Stockton, CA 95204-6219
Ph: (209)518-6886
(805)658-0109

Ouellet, Kathi, President
Indian Arts and Crafts Association
[10041]
4010 Carlisle Blvd. NE, Ste. C
Albuquerque, NM 87107
Ph: (505)265-9149
Fax: (505)265-8251

Outlaw, Karen, Exec. Dir.
Norcross Wildlife Foundation [4853]
PO Box 611
New York, NY 10024
Ph: (212)362-4831
Fax: (212)362-4783

Overman, Jennifer, President
Association for Women in Sports
Media [2666]

7742 Spalding Dr., No. 377
Norcross, GA 30092

Overstreet, Gene, CEO, President
Non Commissioned Officers As-
sociation of the United States of
America **[5619]**
9330 Corporate Dr., Ste. 701
Selma, TX 78154
Ph: (210)653-6161
Toll Free: 800-662-2620
Fax: (210)637-3337

Overton, Joe, President
Japan Studies Association **[9625]**
c/o John Paine, Editor
Belmont University
1900 Belmont Blvd.
Nashville, TN 37212
Ph: (615)460-6244

Overton, Willis, Officer
Society for the Study of Human
Development **[9543]**
c/o Monika Ardelt, Executive
Secretary
University of Florida
PO Box 117330
Gainesville, FL 32611-7330

Ovington, Kay, Exec. Dir.
Society of General Internal Medicine
[15431]
1500 King St., Ste. 303
Alexandria, VA 22314
Ph: (202)887-5150
Toll Free: 800-822-3060

Owen, Bruce, Secretary, Treasurer
Institute of Andean Studies **[8808]**
PO Box 9307
Berkeley, CA 94709

Owen, Chad, Chairman
Convenience Distribution Association
[1322]
11311 Sunset Hills Rd.
Reston, VA 20190
Ph: (703)208-3358
Toll Free: 800-482-2962
Fax: (703)573-5738

Owen, Cliff, President
Owen Family Association **[20910]**
4190 Hurricane Shores Dr.
Benton, AR 72019

Owen, Ethel, President
National Organization of Rheumatol-
ogy Managers **[17161]**
1121 Military Cutoff Rd., No. 337
Wilmington, NC 28405
Ph: (910)520-0515
Fax: (910)254-1091

Owen, Richard Sundance, Exec.
Dir., Founder
Environmental Cleanup Coalition
[4544]
10507 E Zayante Rd.
Felton, CA 95018
Ph: (808)563-9963

Owens, Alexandra, Exec. Dir.
American Society of Journalists and
Authors **[10359]**
355 Lexington Ave. 15th Fl.
New York, NY 10017
Ph: (212)997-0947

Owens, Christine L., Exec. Dir.
National Employment Law Project
[11774]
75 Maiden Ln., Ste. 601
New York, NY 10038
Ph: (212)285-3025
Fax: (212)285-3044

Owens, Dean M., Contact
Loss Executives Association **[1884]**
PO Box 37

Tenafly, NJ 07670
Ph: (201)569-3346

Owens, Gary, MD, Co-Chmn. of the
Bd.
Association for Value-Based Cancer
Care **[13895]**
241 Forsgate Dr., Ste. 205B
Monroe Township, NJ 08831
Ph: (732)992-1538

Owens, Jody, Co-Ch.
National Juvenile Justice Network
[5143]
1319 F St. NW, Ste. 402
Washington, DC 20004
Ph: (202)467-0864

Owens, John, Esq., Director
American Veterinary Medical Law
Association **[5416]**
1701 K St. NW, Ste. 650
Washington, DC 20006
Ph: (202)449-3818
Fax: (202)449-8560

Owens, Linda, President
International Nursing Association for
Clinical Simulation and Learning
[16138]
2501 Aerial Center Pky., Ste. 103
Morrisville, NC 27560
Ph: (919)674-4182
Fax: (919)459-2075

Owens, Lorna, Founder, Exec. Dir.
Footprints Foundation **[12274]**
4000 Ponce Deleon Blvd., Ste. 470
Coral Gables, FL 33146
Ph: (305)573-8423
Fax: (305)854-2980

Owens, Richard, Chairman
American Coke and Coal Chemicals
Institute **[736]**
25 Massachusetts Ave. NW, Ste.
800
Washington, DC 20001
Ph: (724)772-1167
Toll Free: 866-422-7794

Owusu, Dr. Samuel Kwapong,
Founder
Ghana Medical Relief **[15600]**
114 Jules Dr.
State College, PA 16801

Oxendine, Jesse, Chairman
325th Glider Infantry Association
[21181]
c/o Jesse Oxendine, Chairman
1812 Woodberry Rd.
Charlotte, NC 28212
Ph: (704)537-4912

Oxendine, Mr. W.H., Jr., Exec. Dir.
American Student Government As-
sociation **[8612]**
412 NW 16th Ave.
Gainesville, FL 32602-4203
Ph: (352)373-8120
Fax: (352)373-8120

Oxendine-Medley, Jill, CHSE, Chmn.
of the Bd.
Association of Meeting Professionals
[1651]
2025 M St. NW, Ste. 800
Washington, DC 20036-2422
Ph: (202)973-8686
Fax: (202)973-8722

Oxler, Thomas, President
GTO Association of America **[21390]**
PO Box 213
Timnath, CO 80547

Oyebog, Relindis A., President,
Founder, CEO
Angel of Mercy **[10534]**
PO Box 28086

Oakdale, MN 55128
Ph: (651)283-3546

Ozar, Sue Horrigan, President,
Founder
Friends of Kenyan Orphans **[10986]**
920 Berkshire Rd.
Grosse Pointe, MI 48230-1822
Ph: (313)815-9900
Fax: (313)822-9380

Ozer, Katherine, Exec. Dir.
National Family Farm Coalition
[17790]
110 Maryland Ave. NE, Ste. 307
Washington, DC 20002
Ph: (202)543-5675
Fax: (202)543-0978

Ozkan, Seyhan, President
International Strabismological As-
sociation **[17288]**
1160 W Michigan St., No. 220
Indianapolis, IN 46202-5209
Fax: (317)328-8864

Ozz, Robin, President
National Association for
Developmental Education **[7713]**
170 Kinnelon Rd., Ste. 33
Kinnelon, NJ 07405
Toll Free: 877-233-9455
Fax: (973)838-7124

P

Pace, Colleen, President
The American Association of Riding
Schools, Inc. **[22936]**
8375 Coldwater Rd.
Davison, MI 48423-8966
Ph: (810)496-0360

Pace, Louise, Founder, President
Cushing's Support and Research
Foundation **[14702]**
60 Robbins Rd., No. 12
Plymouth, MA 02360
Ph: (617)723-3674

Pace, Teresa, President
IEEE - Aerospace and Electronics
Systems Society **[6422]**
445 Hoes Ln.
Piscataway, NJ 08854-4141
Ph: (571)220-9257

Pace, William R., President
Center for U.N. Reform Education
[19208]
PO Box 3195
New York, NY 10163-3195
Ph: (646)465-8520

Pace, William R., Facilitator
Coalition for the International
Criminal Court **[5131]**
c/o WFM
708 3rd Ave., Ste. 1715
New York, NY 10017
Ph: (212)687-2863
Fax: (212)599-1332

Pace, William R., Exec. Dir.
World Federalist Movement **[19215]**
708 3rd Ave., Ste. 1715
New York, NY 10017
Ph: (212)599-1320
Fax: (212)599-1332

Pacelle, Wayne, President, CEO
The Humane Society of the United
States **[10643]**
1255 23rd St., NW, Ste. 450
Washington, DC 20037
Ph: (202)452-1100
Toll Free: 866-720-2676

Packard, Dr. George R., President
United States-Japan Foundation
[9218]
145 E 32nd St., 12th Fl.
New York, NY 10016
Ph: (212)481-8753
Fax: (212)481-8762

Packer, Edward E., VP
American College of Osteopathic
Pediatricians **[16506]**
2209 Dickens Rd.
Richmond, VA 23230-2005
Ph: (804)565-6333
Fax: (804)282-0090

Packer, Joel, Exec. Dir., Secretary
Committee for Education Funding
[7832]
1341 G St. NW, 5th Fl.
Washington, DC 20005
Ph: (202)383-0083
Fax: (202)463-4803

Packer, Sharon, Secretary, Treasurer
The American Civil Defense Associa-
tion **[5074]**
12162 S Business Park Dr., No. 208
Draper, UT 84020
Ph: (801)501-0077
Toll Free: 800-425-5397
Fax: (888)425-5339

Padgett, John B., III, President
Naval Submarine League **[18088]**
5025D Backlick Rd.
Annandale, VA 22003-6044
Ph: (703)256-0891
Toll Free: 877-280-7827
Fax: (703)642-5815

Padilla, Erik, President
American Board of Registration of
EEG and EP Technologists
[14654]
2908 Greenbriar Dr., Ste. A
Springfield, IL 62704
Ph: (217)726-7980
Fax: (217)726-7989

Padilla, Joe, Founder, Exec. Dir.
Mental Health Grace Alliance
[15784]
105 Old Hewitt Dr., Ste. 100A
Waco, TX 76712
Ph: (254)235-0616

Padilla, Luis, VP
Cordage Institute **[911]**
994 Old Eagle School Rd., Ste.
1019
Wayne, PA 19087
Ph: (610)971-4854
Fax: (610)971-4859

Padilla, Veronica, Bd. Member
MANA, A National Latina Organiza-
tion **[18218]**
1140 19th St. NW, Ste. 550
Washington, DC 20036
Ph: (202)525-5113

Padua, Maria Socorro, Chairperson
International Society of Filipinos in
Finance and Accounting **[38]**
801 S Grand Ave., Ste. 400
Los Angeles, CA 90017
Toll Free: 800-375-2689

Paed-Pedrajas, Teresita, President
World Council for Curriculum and
Instruction **[7697]**
Hufstedler School of Education -
HSOE 306
Alliant International University
10455 Pomerado Rd.
San Diego, CA 92131-1717
Ph: (858)635-4718
Fax: (858)635-4714

Paemen, Amb. Hugo, Chmn. of the
Bd.
Trans-Atlantic Business Council
[23622]
919 18th St. NW, Ste. 220
Washington, DC 20006
Ph: (202)828-9104
Fax: (202)828-9106

Page, Bill, Secretary
Accessibility Equipment Manufactur-
ers Association [11566]
PO Box 92255
Nashville, TN 37209
Toll Free: 800-514-1100
Fax: (949)270-7710

Page, Lawrence, Secretary
Natural Science Collections Alliance
[6093]
1313 Dolley Madison Blvd., Ste. 402
McLean, VA 22101
Ph: (202)628-1500

Page, Dr. Ogden C., Founder,
President
Bulgarian-American Chamber of
Commerce [23569]
1427 N Wilcox Ave.
Hollywood, CA 90028-8123
Ph: (323)962-2414
Fax: (323)962-2010

Pagett, Robert J., Founder, CEO
Assist International [12265]
230 Mt. Hermon Rd., Ste. 206
Scotts Valley, CA 95066-4034
Ph: (831)438-4582
Fax: (831)439-9602

Paglia, Todd J., Exec. Dir.
Stand [4219]
1 Haight St.
San Francisco, CA 94102
Ph: (415)863-4563

Pagliocco, Tony, President
Omega Delta Phi Fraternity [23908]
8111 Mainland, Ste. 104-417
San Antonio, TX 78240
Ph: (206)234-6424

Pai-Espinosa, Jeannette, Chmn. of
the Exec. Committee
National Foster Care Coalition
[11094]
1220 L St. NW, Ste. 100-241
Washington, DC 20005-4018

Paige, Leslie, Secretary
National Association of School
Psychologists [16928]
4340 E West Hwy., Ste. 402
Bethesda, MD 20814
Ph: (301)657-0270
Toll Free: 866-331-NASP
Fax: (301)657-0275

Paine, David, Founder, President
My Good Deed [13210]
503 32nd St., Ste. 120
Newport Beach, CA 92663
Ph: (949)233-0050

Painter, Bill, President
American Baptist Homes and Caring
Ministries [19713]
PO Box 239
Southworth, WA 98386

Painter, Ron, CEO
National Association of Workforce
Boards [11769]
1155 15th St. NW, Ste. 350
Washington, DC 20005
Ph: (202)857-7900
Fax: (202)857-7955

Pair, Daron, President
U.S.A. Climbing [21600]
4909 Pearl East Cir., Ste. 102

Boulder, CO 80301-2498
Ph: (303)499-0715
Fax: (561)423-0715

Paisner, Bruce, CEO, President
International Academy of Television
Arts and Sciences [463]
25 W 52nd St.
New York, NY 10019
Ph: (212)489-6969
(212)489-1946
Fax: (212)489-6557

Pajuelo, Dr. Antonio, President
Spanish Neuromodulation Society
[16037]
c/o Tia Sofatzis, Executive Director
2000 Van Ness Ave., Ste. 414
San Francisco, CA 94109
Ph: (415)683-3237
Fax: (415)683-3218

Paksoy, Allison, Mgr., Comm.
Baptist Peace Fellowship of North
America [18771]
300 Hawthorne Ln., Ste. 205
Charlotte, NC 28204-2434
Ph: (704)521-6051
Fax: (704)521-6053

Palacios, Mar González, President
Association of Architecture School
Librarians [9682]
c/o Jennifer Parker, Teasurer
117 Bond Hall
School of Architecture
University of Notre Dame
Notre Dame, IN 46556
Ph: (574)631-9401

Palade, Jadwiga, Exec. Ofc.
Polish Assistance [19607]
15 E 65th St.
New York, NY 10065
Ph: (212)570-5560
Fax: (212)570-5561

Paladino, Ms. Martha, Mgr.
Society of African Missions [19906]
23 Bliss Ave.
Tenafly, NJ 07670-3001
Ph: (201)567-0450
(201)567-9085
Toll Free: 800-670-8328
Fax: (201)541-1280

Palanca, Rod, President
Metal Boat Society [436]
721 Marine Dr.
Bellingham, WA 98225
Ph: (425)485-2100

Palasis, Susan, MD
American Society of Pediatric Neuroradiology [17049]
c/o Kristine Kulpaka, Coordinator
800 Enterprise Dr., Ste. 205
Oak Brook, IL 60523-4216
Ph: (630)574-0220

Palau, Kevin, President
Luis Palau Association [20158]
1500 NW 167th Pl.
Beaverton, OR 97006
Ph: (503)614-1500
Fax: (503)614-1599

Palcanis, Kent G., Assoc. Exec.,
Director
American Board of Periodontology
[14399]
877 Baltimore Annapolis Blvd., Ste.
111
Severna Park, MD 21146
Ph: (410)647-1324
Fax: (410)647-1260

Paleari, Stefano, President
Technology Transfer Society [7297]
2005 Arthur Ln.

Austin, TX 78704

Palla, Tonya, Exec. Dir.
National Coalition for Campus
Children's Centers [10811]
2036 Larkhall Cir.
Folsom, CA 95630
Ph: (916)790-8261

Pallasch, Brian, Co-Ch.
Dam Safety Coalition [13319]
101 Constitution Ave. NW, Ste. 375
E
Washington, DC 20001-2133
Ph: (202)789-7850
Toll Free: 800-548-2723

Pallasch, Brian T., CAE, Co-Ch.
Water Resources Coalition [7380]
c/o American Society of Civil
Engineers
101 Constitution Ave. NW
Washington, DC 20001
Ph: (202)789-7850

Pallat, John, Chairman
Business-Industry Political Action
Committee [18861]
888 16th St. NW, Ste. 305
Washington, DC 20006-4103
Ph: (202)833-1880
Fax: (202)833-2338

Pallis, Dr. Christos, President
Greek National Tourist Organization
[3330]
305 E 47th St., 2nd Fl.
New York, NY 10017
Ph: (212)421-5777
Fax: (212)826-6940

Palm, Bob, President
Association for Refugee Service
Professionals [12123]
PO Box 80692
Austin, TX 78708

Palm, Sherrie, Founder, CEO
Association for Pelvic Organ
Prolapse Support [14984]
8225 State Road 83
Mukwonago, WI 53149-8901
Ph: (262)642-4338

Palmaz, Martin, Exec. Dir.
United States Hang Gliding and
Paragliding Association [22492]
1685 W Uintah St.
Colorado Springs, CO 80904
Ph: (719)632-8300
Toll Free: 800-616-6888
Fax: (719)632-6417

Palmer, Anita, President
American Bunka Embroidery Association [22252]
c/o Cathy Dean, Treasurer
222 Double Springs Rd.
Fall Branch, TN 37656
Ph: (317)882-2851
(423)863-1023

Palmer, Brett, President
Small Business Investor Alliance
[3127]
1100 H St. NW, Ste. 1200
Washington, DC 20005
Ph: (202)628-5055

Palmer, David A., CCP, Officer
American Board of Cardiovascular
Perfusion [14088]
2903 Arlington Loop
Hattiesburg, MS 39401
Ph: (601)268-2221
Fax: (601)268-2229

Palmer, Edward L., Sr., Chairperson
Coalition for Juvenile Justice [5132]
1319 F St. NW, Ste. 402

Washington, DC 20004
Ph: (202)467-0864
Fax: (202)887-0738

Palmer, Glenn, Exec. Dir.
Peace Science Society
(International) [18819]
c/o Glenn Palmer, Executive Director
The Pennsylvania State University
Dept. of Political Science
208 Pond Bldg.
University Park, PA 16802

Palmer, Jeff, Exec. Dir.
Baptist Global Response [12626]
402 BNA Dr., Ste. 411
Nashville, TN 37217-2546
Ph: (615)367-3678
Toll Free: 866-974-5623
Fax: (615)290-5045

Palmer, Jim, CEO
National Association of Wheat Grow-
ers [3765]
415 2nd St. NE, Ste. 300
Washington, DC 20002
Ph: (202)547-7800

Palmer, Kate, MA, CCP, CAS,
President, CEO
Global and Regional Asperger
Syndrome Partnership [15936]
419 Lafayette St.
New York, NY 10003
Toll Free: 888-474-7277

Palmer, Martin, Founder
National Association for the
Advancement of Preborn Children
[12781]
21 Summit Ave.
Hagerstown, MD 21740
Ph: (301)790-0640

Palmer, Nathaniel, Exec. Dir.
Workflow Management Coalition
[2197]
759 CJC Hwy., Ste. 363
Cohasset, MA 02025-2115
Ph: (781)719-9209

Palmer, Paul, VP
Nonprofit Academic Centers Council
[12392]
1717 Euclid Ave.
Cleveland, OH 44115-2214
Ph: (216)687-5233

Palmer, Dr. Stephen, Chmn. of the
Bd.
American Society of Podiatric
Surgeons [16786]
9312 Old Georgetown Rd.
Bethesda, MD 20814
Ph: (301)581-9214
Toll Free: 877-277-7616

Palmer, Prof. Vernon, President
World Society of Mixed Jurisdiction
Jurists [5450]
c/o Vernon Valentine Palmer,
President
Tulane Law School
6329 Freret St.
New Orleans, LA 70118
Ph: (504)865-5978
(504)862-8859

Palmisciano, Bess, Exec. Dir.,
Founder
Rain for the Sahel and Sahara
[12180]
56 Middle St.
Portsmouth, NH 03801
Ph: (603)371-0676
Fax: (603)397-0681

Palochik, Robert, Treasurer
Vietnam Dog Handler Association
[21160]

c/o Robert Palochik, Treasurer
8203 Parting Clouds Ct.
Las Vegas, NV 89117-7614
Ph: (702)255-6265

Paloma, Diane
Asian and Pacific Islander American
Health Forum [14927]
1 Kaiser Plz., Ste. 850
Oakland, CA 94612
Ph: (415)954-9988
Fax: (510)419-0263

Palomarez, Javier, CEO, President
United States Hispanic Chamber of
Commerce [23631]
1424 K St. NW, Ste. 401
Washington, DC 20005
Ph: (202)842-1212
Fax: (202)842-3221

Palomino, Norma, Libn., Access
Svcs.
Inter-American Development Bank
[18151]
1300 New York Ave. NW
Washington, DC 20577
Ph: (202)623-1000
Fax: (202)623-3096

Palos, Ricardo Sandoval, President
Fund for Investigative Journalism
[17946]
529 14th St. NW, 13th Fl.
Washington, DC 20045
Ph: (202)662-7564

Paltrow, Lynn M., JD, Exec. Dir.
National Advocates for Pregnant
Women [18429]
875 6th Ave., Ste. 1807
New York, NY 10001
Ph: (212)255-9252
Fax: (212)255-9253

Paluzzi, Pat, President, CEO
Healthy Teen Network [11842]
1501 St. Paul St., Ste. 124
Baltimore, MD 21202
Ph: (410)685-0410
Fax: (410)685-0481

Palys, Beth W., CAE, Exec. Dir.
Association of Language Companies
[3312]
9707 Key West Ave., Ste. 100
Rockville, MD 20850
Ph: (240)404-6511

Pan, Dr. Hui, Sec. Gen.
Plastic Optical Fiber Trade Organiza-
tion [2459]
c/o Hui Pan, Secretary General
PO Box 35880
Brighton, MA 02135
Ph: (617)782-5033

Pan, Qisheng, Chairperson
International Association for China
Planning [18855]
Texas A&M University
Dept. of Landscape Architecture and
Urban Planning
MS 3137
College Station, TX 77843-3137

Pandey, Sanjay, VP
Brahman Samaj of North America
[20200]
c/o BSNA Treasurer
8418 Bishop Oaks Dr.
Richmond, TX 77406

Pandin, Jolanda M., VP
Council of Teachers of Southeast
Asian Languages [8181]
c/o Sheila Zamar, Secretary
1240 Van Hise Hall

University of Wisconsin-Madison
1220 Linden Dr.
Madison, WI 53706

Pandya, MD, FACP, CMD, Naushira,
President
AMDA - The Society for Post-Acute
and Long-Term Care Medicine
[16195]
11000 Broken Land Pky., Ste. 400
Columbia, MD 21044
Ph: (410)740-9743
Toll Free: 800-876-2632
Fax: (410)740-4572

Pandya Patel, Priti, President
Asian Indian Chamber of Commerce
[23558]
402 Main St., Ste. 214
Metuchen, NJ 08840
Ph: (732)777-4666

Panek, Thomas, CEO, President
Guiding Eyes for the Blind [17710]
611 Granite Springs Rd.
Yorktown Heights, NY 10598-3411
Ph: (914)245-4024
Toll Free: 800-942-0149
Fax: (914)245-1609

Pankaj, Veena, Director
Innovation Network [6759]
1625 K St. NW, Ste. 1050
Washington, DC 20006
Ph: (202)728-0727
Fax: (202)728-0136

Pankiewicz, Ron, President
Tibetan Terrier Club of America
[21970]
c/o Ron Pankiewicz, President
1645 Seaks Run Rd.
Glen Rock, PA 17327-8484

Pankratz, Scott, Exec. Dir., Founder
Ecology Project International [7875]
315 S 4th St. E
Missoula, MT 59801
Ph: (406)721-8784
Fax: (406)721-7060

Pannell, Alan, Web Adm.
National Information Center for
Educational Media [8035]
c/o Access Innovations, Inc.
4725 Indian School Rd. NE, Ste.100
Albuquerque, NM 87110
Toll Free: 800-926-8328
Fax: (505)256-1080

Pannucci, Cynthia, Exec. Dir.
Art and Science Collaborations Inc.
[9015]
130 E End Ave. 1A
New York, NY 10028
Ph: (505)990-0781

Pansky, Scott, VP
Entertainment Publicists Professional
Society [1135]
PO Box 5841
Beverly Hills, CA 90209

Pant, Dinesh, VP
Uttaranchal Association of North
America [9573]
10560 Main St., Ste. L1-1
Fairfax, VA 22030

Panton, Jennifer, President
United Action for Animals [10707]
PO Box 635
New York, NY 10021
Ph: (212)249-9178

Panza, Carol M., CPT, President
International Society for
Performance Improvement -
Europe [7325]

ISPI Europe/EMEA
66 Fanok Rd.
Morristown, NJ 07960-6551
Ph: (973)455-0420

Paolucci, Anne Marie, Founder
Chemo Comfort [10785]
154 Christopher St., Ste 3C
New York, NY 10014
Ph: (212)675-3744
Fax: (212)675-3786

Papadeas, Paul, President
International Auto Sound Challenge
Association [1050]
2200 S Ridgewood Ave.
South Daytona, FL 32119
Ph: (386)322-1551

Papasadero, Otto, Exec. Dir.
North American Retail Dealers As-
sociation [1058]
222 S Riverside Plz., Ste. 2100
Chicago, IL 60606
Ph: (312)648-0649
Toll Free: 800-621-0298
Fax: (312)648-1212

Papazian, Charlie, Founder
Brewers Association [181]
1327 Spruce St.
Boulder, CO 80302-5006
Ph: (303)447-0816
Toll Free: 888-822-6273
Fax: (303)447-2825

Papazian, Gerald S., Esq., Chairman
Armenian Film Foundation [8825]
2219 E Thousand Oaks Blvd., Ste.
292
Thousand Oaks, CA 91362
Ph: (805)495-0717
Fax: (805)379-0667

Pappadopoulos, Polly, Contact
International Log Rolling Association
[23231]
c/o Polly Pappadopoulos
3111 S Pleasant Dr.
Holmen, WI 54636

Pappas, Christina, Exec. Dir.
International Society of Hotel As-
sociation Executives [2106]
374 Marlborough St.
Boston, MA 02115
Ph: (617)536-0590

Pappas, Harry P., CEO, Founder,
President
International RFID Business As-
sociation, Inc. [275]
5 W 37th St. & 5th Ave., 9th Fl.
New York, NY 10018
Ph: (610)357-0990

Pappas, James, Exec. VP
Association for Continuing Higher
Education [7668]
OCCE Admin Bldg.
1700 Asp Ave., Rm. 129C
Norman, OK 73072-6407
Toll Free: 800-807-2243
Fax: (405)325-4888

Pappas, Stephen, President
American Standard Chinchilla Rabbit
Breeders Association [4594]
c/o Patricia Gest, Secretary/
Treasurer
1607 9th St. W
Palmetto, FL 34221
Ph: (941)729-1184

Pappas, Virginia, CAE, CEO
American College of Nuclear
Medicine [16075]
1850 Samuel Morse Dr.

Reston, VA 20190-5316
Ph: (703)326-1190
(703)708-9000
Fax: (703)708-9015

Paque, Mike, Exec. Dir.
Ground Water Protection Council
[3450]
13308 N MacArthur Blvd.
Oklahoma City, OK 73142
Ph: (405)516-4972

Paquette, Rene, President
Patti Page Appreciation Society
[24057]
c/o Rene Paquette, President
4565 S Atlantic Ave., Ste. 5103
Ponce Inlet, FL 32127
Ph: (386)756-6682

Paranzino, Michael, President
Psoriasis Cure Now [14511]
PO Box 2544
Kensington, MD 20891
Ph: (301)571-2393
Fax: (703)997-6528

Pardain, Hannele, Exec. Dir.
Christian Friends of Israel USA
[19956]
c/o Hannele Pardain, Executive
Director
PO Box 470258
Charlotte, NC 28247-0258
Ph: (704)544-9110

Pardello, Renee, President
Association for International
Agricultural and Extension Educa-
tion [7472]
c/o Anita Zavodska, Treasurer
School of Professional and Career
Education
Barry University
4900 S University Dr., Ste. 203-205
Davie, FL 33328

Pardini, Samuele F.S., VP
Italian American Studies Association
[9614]
The Calandra Institute
25 W 43rd St., 17th Fl.
New York, NY 10036

Pardue, Kerry, Exec. Sec.
National Association of Medics and
Corpsmen [4974]
c/o Lloyd Beemer, Treadurer
13915 SW Azalea Ct.
Beaverton, OR 97008

Parell, Shawn, Prog. Dir.
Anahata International [13603]
c/o Anahata International
1450 P St. NW
Washington, DC 20005

Parella, Tony, President, CEO
Sportscar Vintage Racing Associa-
tion [22529]
1598 Hart St., Ste. 100
Southlake, TX 76092
Ph: (817)521-5158
Fax: (817)953-3550

Parent, Michael, Exec. Dir.
National Ataxia Foundation [15963]
2600 Fernbrook Ln., No. 119
Minneapolis, MN 55447
Ph: (763)553-0020
Fax: (763)553-0167

Parfet, Donald R., Chairman
W.E. Upjohn Institute for Employ-
ment Research [11786]
300 S Westnedge Ave.
Kalamazoo, MI 49007-4686
Ph: (269)343-5541
Fax: (269)343-3308

Parikh, Nidhish, Director
Digital Living Network Alliance
[1041]
PO Box 8637
Portland, OR 97286

Parillo, Mark P., Secretary, Editor
World War Two Studies Association
[9529]
141h Old Horticulture
Michigan State University
506 E Circle Dr.
East Lansing, MI 48824
Ph: (517)432-5134
Fax: (517)884-6994

Paris, Benedetto, Director
Bishop Baraga Association [19804]
347 Rock St.
Marquette, MI 49855-4725
Ph: (906)227-9117

Paris, Debbie, Officer
Presbyterian Women [20529]
100 Witherspoon St.
Louisville, KY 40202-1396
Toll Free: 888-728-7228
Fax: (502)569-8600

Paris, Kendis, Director
Truckers Against Trafficking [12017]
PO Box 816
Englewood, CO 80151

Paris, Leroy H., II, Chairman
National Center for Fathering
[12417]
1600 W Sunset Ave., Ste B
Springdale, AR 72762
Toll Free: 800-593-3237

Pariser, David M., Hist.
American Dermatological Association
[14481]
PO Box 551301
Davie, FL 33355
Ph: (954)452-1113
Fax: (954)252-2093

Parish, Jane, Exec. Dir.
Beef Improvement Federation [6642]
10223 Highway 382
Prairie, MS 39756
Ph: (662)369-4426
Fax: (662)369-9547

Parish, Lawrence C., MD, President
History of Dermatology Society
[9483]
c/o Lawrence Charles Parish, MD,
President
1760 Market St., Ste. 301
Philadelphia, PA 19103
Ph: (215)563-8333
Fax: (215)563-3044

Parish, Lawrence Charles, President
International Academy of Cosmetic
Dermatology [14495]
c/o Ms. Anna Gjeci, Executive
Secretary
1508 Creswood Rd.
Philadelphia, PA 19115
Ph: (215)677-3060
Fax: (215)695-2254

Parish, Winifred, President
Liga International [12285]
19671 Lucaya Ct.
Apple Valley, CA 92308
Ph: (714)257-9952
Fax: (714)257-9952

Parisi, Valerie M., MD, Chairperson
American Board of Medical Special-
ties [15661]
353 N Clark St., Ste. 1400
Chicago, IL 60654
Ph: (312)436-2600

Pariyar, Bishnu Maya, Founder
Empower Dalit Women of Nepal
[13413]
PO Box 550076
North Waltham, MA 02455
Ph: (617)864-1224

Park, Kimberly, President, CEO
Federation of International Trade
Associations [1967]
172 5th Ave., No. 118
Brooklyn, NY 11217
Ph: (703)634-3482
Toll Free: 888-491-8833

Park, Paul, Exec. Dir.
First Fruit [20142]
14 Corporate Plz., Ste. 200
Newport Beach, CA 92660

Park, Philip I., Exec. Dir.
National Board of Podiatric Medical
Examiners [16790]
PO Box 510
Bellefonte, PA 16823
Ph: (814)357-0487

Park, Tae Hong, VP
International Computer Music As-
sociation [2425]
1819 Polk St., Ste. 330
San Francisco, CA 94109
Fax: (734)878-3031

Parke, Becky, President
National Association of Collegiate
Marketing Administrators [23238]
24651 Detroit Rd.
Westlake, OH 44145
Ph: (440)892-4000
Fax: (440)892-4007

Parke, Beth, Exec. Dir.
Society of Environmental Journalists
[8161]
PO Box 2492
Jenkintown, PA 19046-8492
Ph: (215)884-8174
Fax: (215)884-8175

Parke, David W., II, CEO
American Academy of Ophthalmol-
ogy [16361]
655 Beach St.
San Francisco, CA 94109
Ph: (415)561-8500
Fax: (415)561-8533

Parke, Margaret Ellen, President
Circumnavigators Club [6624]
50 Vanderbilt Ave.
New York, NY 10017
Ph: (201)612-9100
Fax: (201)786-9133

Parker, Alice, Art Dir.
Melodious Accord [9953]
Park West Sta.
New York, NY 10025-01516
Ph: (413)339-8508
    (212)665-4405

Parker, Amelia, Exec. Dir.
Peace Brigades International -
U.S.A. [18815]
PO Box 75880
Washington, DC 20013
Ph: (202)232-0142
Fax: (202)232-0143

Parker, Bob, President
Southern Connecticut State
University Alumni Association
[19348]
501 Crescent St.
New Haven, CT 06515
Ph: (203)392-6500
    (203)392-8824

Parker, Bruce, CEO, President
National Waste and Recycling As-
sociation [3454]
4301 Connecticut Ave. NW, Ste. 300
Washington, DC 20008-2304
Ph: (202)244-4700
Toll Free: 800-424-2869
Fax: (202)966-4824

Parker, Jim, Publisher
Do It Now Foundation [13136]
PO Box 27921
Tempe, AZ 85285
Ph: (480)736-0599
Fax: (480)736-0771

Parker, John Henry, Founder
Purple Star Veterans and Families
[21137]
5042 Wilshire Blvd., No. 32196
Los Angeles, CA 90036
Ph: (760)576-5649

Parker, John P., Chairperson
Direct Selling Education Foundation
[3011]
1667 K St. NW, Ste. 1100
Washington, DC 20006-1660
Ph: (202)452-8866
Fax: (202)452-9015

Parker, Karen, Exec. Asst.
America's Natural Gas Alliance
[2512]
701 8th St. NW, Ste. 800
Washington, DC 20001
Ph: (202)789-2642

Parker, Karen, Secretary
Society of Ethnobiology [6099]
Dept. of Sociology and Anthropology
University of Puget Sound
1500 N Warner St., CMB 1092
Tacoma, WA 98416

Parker, Lee, Exec. Dir.
White Plate Flat Trackers Association [23042]
18101 Johnson Memorial Dr.
Jordan, MN 55352

Parker, Lysa, MS, Director, Founder
Attachment Parenting International
[12408]
PO Box 4615
Alpharetta, GA 30023
Fax: (800)850-8320

Parker, Marilyn B., Secretary,
Treasurer
North American Colleges and Teach-
ers of Agriculture [7481]
c/o Marilyn Parker, Secretary and
Treasurer
151 West 100 South
Rupert, ID 83350
Ph: (208)957-7001
Fax: (208)436-1384

Parker, Michael L., Sr., Officer
Children of the Dump [10915]
718 Griffin Ave.
Enumclaw, WA 98022
Ph: (360)825-1099
    (322)299-3515
Toll Free: 877-224-2792

Parker, Michelle, Exec. Dir.
Society of Emergency Medicine
Physician Assistants [16727]
4950 W Royal Ln.
Irving, TX 75063
Toll Free: 877-297-7594

Parker, Mitchell, President
International Society of Hospitality
Purchasers [1665]
c/o Mitchell Parker, President

Parker Company
6205 Blue Lagoon Dr., Ste. 300
Miami, FL 33126
Ph: (305)421-6900

Parker, Paul, President
Center for Resource Management
[3827]
1861 E Beaumont Cir.
Salt Lake City, UT 84121-1204
Ph: (801)509-5308

Parker, Ronald C., President, CEO
The Executive Leadership Council
[2393]
1001 N Fairfax St., Ste. 300
Alexandria, VA 22314
Ph: (703)706-5200
Fax: (703)535-6830

Parker, Ms. Sasha S., President
American Academy of Medical
Esthetic Professionals [16084]
2000 S Andrews Ave.
Fort Lauderdale, FL 33316
Ph: (954)463-5594
Fax: (954)653-2499

Parker, Scott D., Exec. Dir.
NORA, An Association of
Responsible Recyclers [4633]
7250 Heritage Village Plz., Ste. 201
Gainesville, VA 20155
Ph: (703)753-4277
Fax: (703)753-2445

Parker, Dr. Tabatha, Exec. Dir.,
Founder
Natural Doctors International [15861]
9240 Alaska St. SE
Salem, OR 97317

Parker, Tony, VP
Lop Rabbit Club of America [4600]
c/o Russ Scott, President
7013 Fairland Rd.
Berrien Springs, MI 49103
Ph: (269)687-8431

Parker-Thornburg, Jan, President
International Society for Transgenic
Technologies [6113]
Roswell Park Cancer Institute
Elm and Carlton St.
Buffalo, NY 14263
Ph: (716)845-5843
Fax: (716)845-5908

Parkin, Ruth, DVM, President
International Veterinarians Dedicated
to Animal Health [17651]
PO Box 20246
Boulder, CO 80308-3246

Parkin, Scott, Contact
Access to Benefits Coalition [18325]
1901 L St. NW, 4th Fl.
Washington, DC 20036
Ph: (202)479-6670
Fax: (202)479-0735

Parkinson, Rev. Caroline Smith,
President
John Marshall Foundation [9409]
1108 E Main St., Ste. 800
Richmond, VA 23219
Ph: (804)775-0861
Fax: (804)775-0862

Parks, Dr. Lawrence M., Exec. Dir.
Foundation for the Advancement of
Monetary Education [7919]
909 3rd Ave., No. 625
New York, NY 10150
Ph: (212)818-1206

Parks, Fr. Michael, Exec. Dir.
Parke Society [20913]
c/o Ronald Neal Parks, Registrar

722 Warm Springs Ave.
Huntingdon, PA 16652-2424
Ph: (814)643-2576

Parlapiano, Joe, Founder, CEO
One Heart for Haiti [11730]
54 Barbara St.
Newark, NJ 07105
Ph: (973)589-6611
Fax: (973)817-8011

Parlow, Dr. A. F., Science Dir.
National Hormone and Pituitary
Program [16770]
Harbor - UCLA Medical Ctr.
1000 W Carson St.
Torrance, CA 90509
Ph: (310)222-3537
    (310)415-2994
Fax: (310)222-3432

Parman, Lynn, President, CEO
American Royal Association [4452]
1701 American Royal Ct.
Kansas City, MO 64102
Ph: (816)221-9800
Fax: (816)221-8189

Parmer, Ida, Contact
International German Coolie Society
and Registry [21899]
c/o Ida Parmer
1139 LCR 454
Groesbeck, TX 76642
Ph: (903)390-0300

Parmlee, Dr. Randy A., President
Xi Psi Phi [23722]
160 S Bellwood Dr., Ste. Z
East Alton, IL 62024
Ph: (618)307-5433
Fax: (618)307-5430

Parnell, Steve, President
Fraternal Order Orioles [19433]
PO Box 530447
Debary, FL 32753

Parr, Ann M., Secretary
Women in Neurosurgery [16072]
5550 Meadowbrook Dr.
Rolling Meadows, IL 60008-3852
Ph: (847)378-0500
Toll Free: 888-566-2267

Parr, Mary, President
Academy of Leisure Sciences [7161]
1807 N Federal Dr.
Urbana, IL 61801
Ph: (217)819-5994
Fax: (217)359-5975

Parr, Tom, Director
North American Trap Collector Association [21704]
c/o Tom Parr, Director
6106 Bausch Rd.
Galloway, OH 43119
Ph: (614)878-6011

Parra, Victor, President, CEO
United Motorcoach Association
[3361]
113 S W St., 4th Fl.
Alexandria, VA 22314-2824
Toll Free: 800-424-8262
Fax: (703)838-2950

Parrino, Mark W., MPA, President
American Association for the Treat-
ment of Opioid Dependence
[17305]
225 Varick St., Ste. 402
New York, NY 10014-4304
Ph: (212)566-5555
Fax: (212)566-4647

Parris, O'Neall E., Chairman
Barbados Cancer Association USA
[13897]

PO Box 3094
Grand Central Sta.
New York, NY 10163-3094
Toll Free: 866-729-1011

Parrish, R.B., Chairman
American Lumber Standard Commit-
tee, Incorporated [1426]
PO Box 210
Germantown, MD 20875-0210
Ph: (301)972-1700
Fax: (301)540-8004

Parrish, Robert B., Director
The Maritime Law Association of the
United States [5576]
c/o Robert Clyne, President
16855 Northchase Dr.
Houston, TX 77060
Ph: (281)877-5989
Fax: (281)877-6646

Parry, Hugh R., CEO, President
Prevent Blindness [17738]
211 W Wacker Dr., Ste. 1700
Chicago, IL 60606
Toll Free: 800-331-2020

Parsa, Kami, MD, President
Surgical Friends [17410]
465 N Roxbury Dr., Ste. 1001
Beverly Hills, CA 90210
Ph: (310)562-3631

Parsi, Dr. Trita, President
National Iranian American Council
[9596]
1411 K St. NW, Ste. 250
Washington, DC 20005
Ph: (202)386-6325

Parsley, Brian S., MD, Bd. Member
American Association of Hip and
Knee Surgeons [17360]
9400 W Higgins Rd.
Rosemont, IL 60018-4976
Ph: (847)698-1200

Parsley, Nancy L., DPM, MHPE,
Chairman
American Association of Colleges of
Podiatric Medicine [16775]
15850 Crabbs Branch Way, Ste. 320
Rockville, MD 20855
Ph: (301)948-9760
Fax: (301)948-1928

Parsons, Doug, Chairman
NAHB Log Homes and Timber
Council [2200]
1201 15th St. NW
Washington, DC 20005
Toll Free: 800-368-5242
Fax: (202)266-8400

Parsons, Jeffrey, Chairman
Council for Accreditation of Counsel-
ing and Related Educational
Programs [7687]
1001 N Fairfax St., Ste. 510
Alexandria, VA 22314
Ph: (703)535-5990
Fax: (703)739-6209

Parsons, Jim, VP
National Aquaculture Association
[3644]
PO Box 12759
Tallahassee, FL 32317
Ph: (850)216-2400
Fax: (850)216-2480

Parsons, Paul L., Dep. Chief
National Association of College and
University Attorneys [5163]
1 Dupont Cir., Ste. 620
Washington, DC 20036
Ph: (202)833-8390
Fax: (202)296-8379

Parsons, Theodore W., III, MD,
FACS, President
Musculoskeletal Tumor Society
[15848]
9400 W Higgins Rd., Ste. 500
Rosemont, IL 60018
Ph: (847)698-1625
Fax: (847)823-0536

Parther, Hal, Secretary
Mosquito Association, Inc. [20684]
2202 County Road 331
Nacogdoches, TX 75961

Partlow, Darlene, President
English Shepherd Club [21873]
2146 380th St.
Grafton, IA 50440

Partlow, Doug, VP
International Footprint Association
[5473]
PO Box 1652
Walnut, CA 91788

Parton, Sue, President
Federation of Indian Service
Employees [8395]
1218 Lomas Blvd. NW
Albuquerque, NM 87102-1856
Ph: (505)243-4088
Toll Free: 888-433-2382
Fax: (505)243-4098

Partovi, Hadi, Founder, CEO
Code.org [7653]
1301 5th Ave., Ste. 1225
Seattle, WA 98101

Parvin, Dr. Mohammad, President
Mission for Establishment of Human
Rights in Iran [18427]
PO Box 2037
Palos Verdes Peninsula, CA 90274
Ph: (310)377-4590
Fax: (310)694-8039

Pasarell, Charlie, Founder
National Junior Tennis and Learning
[23302]
c/o United States Tennis Association
70 W Red Oak Ln.
White Plains, NY 10604-3602

Pasarón, Raquel
American Pediatric Surgical Nurses
Association [16110]
1 Parkview Plz., Ste. 800
Oakbrook Terrace, IL 60181
Ph: (605)376-4742
Toll Free: 855-984-1609

Pascarella, Mark, Chairman
State Debt Management Network
[5788]
National Association of State
Treasurers
201 E Main St., Ste. 540
Lexington, KY 40507
Ph: (859)721-2190

Paschal, Michael, Exec. Dir.
Association for Asian Studies [7522]
825 Victors Way, Ste. 310
Ann Arbor, MI 48108
Ph: (734)665-2490
Fax: (734)665-3801

Pasion, Kimberley, President
Ethiopian Orphan Relief, Inc.
[10965]
3020 SW Christy Ave.
Beaverton, OR 97005

Paskach, Christopher H., Chairman
Constitutional Rights Foundation
[18035]
601 S Kingsley Dr.

Los Angeles, CA 90005
Ph: (213)487-5590
Fax: (213)386-0459

Paskey, Amanda, President
Society for Anthropology in Com-
munity Colleges [7495]
2200 Wilson Blvd., Ste. 600
Arlington, VA 22201-3357
Ph: (703)528-1902

Pasquale, Andrea, Program Mgr.
International Association of Audio
Information Services [17714]
c/o Lori Kesinger
PO Box 847
Lawrence, KS 66044
Toll Free: 800-280-5325
Fax: (785)864-5278

Passanisi, Robert, Chairman
Merrill's Marauders Association
[21197]
c/o Robert Passanisi, Chairman
111 Kramer Dr.
Lindenhurst, NY 11757-5407

Past, Elena, Treasurer
American Association for Italian
Studies [9612]
c/o Dana Renga, Executive
Secretary
200 Hagerty Hall
Dept. of French and Italian
Ohio State University
1775 College Rd.
Columbus, OH 43210-1340
Ph: (573)882-2030

Paster, Howard, President
Little League Foundation [22551]
539 US Route 15 Hwy.
Williamsport, PA 17701-0485
Ph: (570)326-1921
Fax: (570)326-1074

Pasternak, Anne, Art Dir., President
Creative Time [8972]
59 E 4th St., 6th Fl.
New York, NY 10003
Ph: (212)206-6674
Fax: (212)255-8467

Pasternak, Marc, VP, Exec. Dir.
Valve Manufacturers Association of
America [1579]
1050 17th St. NW, Ste. 280
Washington, DC 20036-5521
Ph: (202)331-8105
Fax: (202)296-0378

Pasternak, Marc, Exec. Dir., VP
Valve Repair Council [1580]
1050 17th St. NW, Ste. 280
Washington, DC 20036
Ph: (202)331-8105
Fax: (202)296-0378

Pastrano, Ramon A., President,
CEO
ImpactLives [9173]
6985 Oxford St.
Saint Louis Park, MN 55426
Ph: (612)817-0791

Pate, Gary, Mem.
United States Quad Rugby Associa-
tion [23114]
302 S Main St., Ste. 201
Royal Oak, MI 48067
Ph: (248)850-8973

Patel, Alkesh R., Contact
Asian American Hotel Owners As-
sociation [1649]
1100 Abernathy Rd., Ste. 1100
Atlanta, GA 30328-6707
Ph: (404)816-5759
Toll Free: 888-692-2462
Fax: (404)816-6260

Patel, Harshad, President
Leuva Patidar Samaj of USA **[9567]**
9005 Overlook Blvd.
Brentwood, TN 37027
Toll Free: 866-201-2353
Fax: (866)201-5183

Patel, Neilesh, Co-CEO
HealthCare Tourism International
[15017]
809B Cuesta Dr., Ste. 141
Mountain View, CA 94040
Ph: (310)928-3611

Patel, Neilesh, Founder
HealthCare Volunteer **[15018]**
595 Loyola Dr.
Los Altos, CA 94024-5944

Patel, Mr. Nilkanth, President
BAPS Charities, Inc. **[13033]**
81 Suttons Ln., Ste. 103
Piscataway, NJ 08854-5723
Toll Free: 888-227-3881

Patel, Rina, Founder
Cents of Relief **[12635]**
109 Church St., No. 202
New Haven, CT 06510
Ph: (860)251-9004

Patel, Sheevum, President
Beta Chi Theta National Fraternity,
Inc. **[23889]**
5868 E 71st St., Ste. E-120
Indianapolis, IN 46220-4081
Ph: (847)238-2244

Patel, Shirish, Director
Polio Children **[16793]**
155 Dunrovin Ln.
Rochester, NY 14618
Ph: (585)442-2505

Patel, Vijay, President
Association of College and
University Auditors **[7422]**
18000 W 105th St.
Olathe, KS 66061
Ph: (913)895-4620
Fax: (913)895-4652

Paterno, Mia, President
American Association of Eye and
Ear Centers of Excellence **[15302]**
1655 Noth Fort Myer Dr., Ste. 700
Arlington, VA 22209
Ph: (703)243-8848
Fax: (703)351-5298

Paternoster, Vincent, Secretary,
Treasurer
Coronado 15 National Association
[22609]
30025 Torrepines Pl.
Agoura Hills, CA 91301-4070
Ph: (916)832-8015

Paterson, Eva, President
Equal Justice Society **[5728]**
1999 Harrison St., Ste. 800
Oakland, CA 94612
Ph: (415)288-8700
Fax: (510)338-3030

Paterson, Jim, President
National Drowning Prevention Alliance **[12831]**
1 Hall of Fame Dr.
Fort Lauderdale, FL 33316
Ph: (951)659-8600
(209)323-5438

Patil, Raj, President, Trustee
Association of Kannada Kootas of
America **[19472]**
3174 Bourgogne Ct.
San Jose, CA 95135

Patlin, Mike, Director
Motion Picture Pilots Association
[364]
7641 Densmore Ave.
Van Nuys, CA 91406
Ph: (818)947-5454

Patric, Will, Exec. Dir.
Rivers Without Borders **[3936]**
c/o Terry Portillo, Finance and
Outreach Director
PO Box 154
Clinton, WA 98236
Ph: (360)341-1976

Patrick, Brint, Chmn. of the Bd.
Shelter for Life International **[12727]**
10201 Wayzata Blvd., Ste. 230
Minnetonka, MN 55305-1505
Ph: (763)253-4082
Fax: (763)253-4085

Patrick, Burton, President
American Marinelife Dealers As-
sociation **[4463]**
PO Box 1052
Madison, FL 32341
Ph: (850)973-3488

Patrick, Ray, Chairman
National Rural Education Advocacy
Coalition **[8509]**
1615 Duke St.
Alexandria, VA 22314
Ph: (703)528-0700
Fax: (703)841-1543

Patrick, Susan, President
International Association for K-12
Online Learning **[7486]**
1934 Old Gallows Rd., Ste. 350
Vienna, VA 22182-4040
Ph: (703)752-6216
Toll Free: 888-956-2265
Fax: (703)752-6201

Patrick, Tandy, Director
American Saddlebred Horse As-
sociation **[4324]**
4083 Iron Works Pky.
Lexington, KY 40511
Ph: (859)259-2742
Fax: (859)259-1628

Patrick, Tandy, President
Half Saddlebred Registry of America
[4358]
c/o American Saddlebred Horse Association
4083 Iron Works Pky.
Lexington, KY 40511
Ph: (859)259-2742
Fax: (859)259-1628

Patrick-Goudreau, Colleen, Founder
Compassionate Cooks **[17584]**
PO Box 16104
Oakland, CA 94610
Ph: (510)550-5374

Patrikis, Peter C., Exec. Dir.
Winston Churchill Foundation of the
United States **[7924]**
600 Madison Ave., Ste. 1601
New York, NY 10022-1737
Ph: (212)752-3200
Fax: (212)246-8330

Patten, Ezekiel, Chairman
National Council of Minorities in
Energy **[1116]**
1725 I St. NW, Ste. 300
Washington, DC 20006
Toll Free: 866-663-9045
Fax: (866)663-8007

Patterson, Bob, President
American Assembly for Men in Nursing **[16086]**

c/o Karen Mota, Account Executive
PO Box 7867
Philadelphia, PA 19101-7867
Ph: (215)243-5813
Fax: (215)387-7497

Patterson, Bob, Co-Ch.
Giraffe Heroes Project **[9547]**
PO Box 759
Langley, WA 98260
Ph: (360)221-7989
Fax: (360)221-7817

Patterson, Brian, President
United South and Eastern Tribes,
Inc. **[12385]**
711 Stewarts Ferry Pke.
Nashville, TN 37214
Ph: (615)872-7900
Fax: (615)872-7417

Patterson, Carrie, Chairperson
Camp To Belong **[10880]**
PO Box 1147
Victor, ID 83455
Ph: (520)413-1395
(208)390-0950
Toll Free: 855-500-RIDE

Patterson, Don, Chairman
Good News Jail and Prison Ministry
[11528]
PO Box 9760
Henrico, VA 23228-0760
Ph: (804)553-4090
Toll Free: 800-220-2202
Fax: (804)553-4144

Patterson, James G., President
Sam Davis Memorial Association
[10323]
1399 Sam Davis Rd.
Smyrna, TN 37167
Ph: (615)459-2341

Patterson, Judy, President
Vacuum and Sewing Dealers Trade
Association **[213]**
2724 2nd Ave.
Des Moines, IA 50313-4933
Ph: (515)282-9101
Toll Free: 800-367-5651
Fax: (515)282-4483

Patterson, Koni, President
Minorities in Agriculture, Natural
Resources and Related Sciences
[3572]
1720 Peachtree Rd. NW, Ste. 776 S
Atlanta, GA 30309-2449
Ph: (404)347-2975
Fax: (404)892-9405

Patterson, Matt, Exec. Dir.
Center for Worker Freedom **[23537]**
722 12th St. NW, Ste. 400
Washington, DC 20005
Ph: (202)785-0266
Fax: (202)785-0261

Patterson, Michael, President
International Executive Housekeep-
ers Association **[2130]**
1001 Eastwind Dr., Ste. 301
Westerville, OH 43081-3361
Ph: (614)895-7166
Toll Free: 800-200-6342
Fax: (614)895-1248

Patterson, Dr. Ron, Exec. Dir.
Christian Disaster Response
International **[11653]**
209 Bridgers Ave.
Auburndale, FL 33823
Ph: (863)967-4357

Patterson, Rusty, Chairman, CEO
National Council for Advanced
Manufacturing **[2229]**

2025 M St. NW, Ste. 800
Washington, DC 20036
Ph: (202)367-1178

Patterson, Sue, Founder
WINGS **[17121]**
1043 Grand Ave., No. 299
Saint Paul, MN 55105
Ph: (415)230-0441

Patton, David, President
National Council for Eurasian and
East European Research **[10218]**
1828 L St. NW, Ste. 1200
Washington, DC 20036
Ph: (202)572-9095
(202)572-9125
Fax: (866)937-9872

Patton, Guy L., Chmn. of the Bd.
Jobs for the Future **[11767]**
505 14th St., Ste. 900
Oakland, CA 94612
Ph: (617)728-4446
Fax: (617)728-4857

Patton, Leah, Office Mgr.
American Donkey and Mule Society
[3592]
PO Box 1210
Lewisville, TX 75067
Ph: (972)219-0781

Patureau, Gary, President
National Alliance of Medicare Set-
Aside Professionals **[18334]**
275 N York St., Ste. 401
Elmhurst, IL 60126
Ph: (630)617-5047

Paul, Elena M., Esq., Exec. Dir.
Volunteer Lawyers for the Arts
[5554]
1 E 53rd St., 6th Fl.
New York, NY 10022-4200
Ph: (212)319-2787

Paul, Judith, Founder
LENA Research Foundation **[17242]**
5525 Central Ave., Ste. 100
Boulder, CO 80301
Toll Free: 866-503-9918
Fax: (305)545-2166

Paul, Linda, President, CEO
USA Diving **[22814]**
1060 N Capitol Ave., Ste. E-310
Indianapolis, IN 46204
Ph: (317)237-5252
Fax: (317)237-5257

Paul, Mike, CEO
National Junior Swine Association
[4712]
2639 Yeager Rd.
West Lafayette, IN 47906
Ph: (765)463-3594
Fax: (765)497-2959

Paul, Randy, President
North American Association of Inven-
tory Services **[660]**
PO Box 120145
Saint Paul, MN 55112
Ph: (651)402-9032

Paul, Congressman Ron, Founder,
Chairman
Foundation for Rational Economics
and Education **[18036]**
PO Box 1776
Lake Jackson, TX 77566

Paul, Scott, President
Alliance for American Manufacturing
[2210]
711 D St. NW, 3rd Fl.
Washington, DC 20004
Ph: (202)393-3430

Paul, Suresh, Exec. Dir.
International Counselor Exchange
Program [8080]
38 W 88th St.
New York, NY 10024
Ph: (212)787-7706

Paul, T. V., President
International Studies Association
[8115]
337 Mansfield Rd., Unit 1013
Storrs, CT 06269-1013
Ph: (860)486-5850

Pauley, Gayle, Rep.
National Title I Association [7441]
532 N Franklin St.
Fort Bragg, CA 95437
Toll Free: 800-256-6452
Fax: (800)915-3291

Paulishak, Amy, VP of Bus. Dev.
Brides Against Breast Cancer
[13911]
6279 Lake Osprey Dr.
Sarasota, FL 34240
Ph: (941)907-9350
Toll Free: 877-721-4673
Fax: (877)471-8353

Paull, Dalene, Exec. Dir.
International Conference of Funeral
Service Examining Boards of the
United States [2398]
1885 Shelby Ln.
Fayetteville, AR 72704
Ph: (479)442-7076
Fax: (479)442-7090

Pauls, Toni, Contact
Christian Adult Higher Education As-
sociation [7608]
c/o Renee Hyatt, Coordinator
2100 Westway Ave.
Garland, TX 75042
Ph: (972)864-2010
Fax: (972)278-8486

Paulson, Erik, President
Society of Computed Body
Tomography and Magnetic
Resonance [17066]
1891 Preston White Dr.
Reston, VA 20191
Ph: (703)476-1117
Fax: (703)716-4487

Paulson, Hank, Founder
New Hope International [20445]
5550 Tech Center Dr., Ste. 307
Colorado Springs, CO 80919
Ph: (719)577-4450
Toll Free: 877-874-3264

Paulus, Byron, Exec. Dir.
Life Action Revival Ministries [20150]
2727 Niles-Buchanan Rd.
Buchanan, MI 49107
Ph: (269)697-8600
Fax: (269)695-2474

Pauna, Zamfira, President, Founder
Heart of Romania's Children
Foundation [11016]
399 Fairfield Dr.
Sanford, FL 32771
Ph: (407)392-6817
Fax: (407)964-1693

Pavely, Melissa, Chairperson
American Mock Trial Association
[5824]
c/o Paige Blankenship, Department
of Political Science3300 Poinsett
Hwy.
Dept. of Political Science
3300 Poinsett Hwy.
Greenville, SC 29613
Ph: (515)259-6625
Fax: (864)294-3513

Pavina, Linda J., Exec. Dir.
American Osteopathic Association of
Prolotherapy Regenerative
Medicine [16510]
303 S Ingram Ct.
Middletown, DE 19709
Ph: (302)530-2489
Toll Free: 800-889-9898

Pavlak, Jeannine, Secretary
APSE: The Network on Employment
[11572]
416 Hungerford Dr., Ste. 418
Rockville, MD 20850
Ph: (301)279-0060
Fax: (301)279-0075

Pavlick, Rev. John A., Exec. Dir.
Conference of Major Superiors of
Men [19825]
8808 Cameron St.
Silver Spring, MD 20910
Ph: (301)588-4030
Fax: (301)587-4575

Pavulaan, Harry, Bd. Member
The International Lepidoptera Survey
[6613]
PO Box 1124
Herndon, VA 20172

Pawlak, Kim, Dir. of Operations
Text and Academic Authors Associa-
tion [10404]
PO Box 367
Fountain City, WI 54629
Ph: (727)563-0020

Pawloski, Jim, President
Association of State Dam Safety Of-
ficials [5745]
239 S Limestone
Lexington, KY 40508-2501
Ph: (859)550-2788

Pawlowski, Andrzej, President
Polish-American Engineers Association [6582]
1 Watergate Dr.
South Barrington, IL 60010

Pawlowski, Steve, Agent
Eastern Coast Breweriana Associa-
tion [21261]
PO Box 826
South Windsor, CT 06074-0826

Paxton, John, Chmn. of the Bd.
Material Handling Industry [1748]
8720 Red Oak Blvd., Ste. 201
Charlotte, NC 28217-3996
Ph: (704)676-1190
Toll Free: 800-345-1815
Fax: (704)676-1199

Paxton, John, Chairman
Material Handling Industry of
America - Order Fulfillment Solu-
tions [3439]
8720 Red Oak Blvd., Ste. 201
Charlotte, NC 28217-3996
Ph: (704)676-1190
Fax: (704)676-1199

Paxton, John, Chairman
Materials Handling Institute [6814]
8720 Red Oak Blvd., Ste. 201
Charlotte, NC 28217
Ph: (704)676-1190
Fax: (704)676-1199

Paxton, John, Exec. Dir.
United States Marine Corps Combat
Correspondents Association [2730]
110 Fox Ct.
Wildwood, FL 34785

Paxton, Matt, President
Shipbuilders Council of America
[2257]

20 F St. NW, Ste. 500
Washington, DC 20001
Ph: (202)737-3234
Fax: (202)737-0264

Payne, Andrea Herz, Chairperson,
Founder
Aid Still Required [11650]
PO Box 7353
Santa Monica, CA 90406
Ph: (310)454-4646
Toll Free: 888-363-GIVE

Payne, Dr. Buryl, Founder, President
Academy for Peace Research
[18767]
600 Park Ave., Apt. 4D
Capitola, CA 95010
Ph: (831)475-4250

Payne, Gary C., President
Circus Fans Association of America
[9161]
3660 Morningside Way, No. 105
Lorain, OH 44053

Payne, Jerry, Founder, President
United States Entertainment Force
[10763]
6504 N 7th St.
Fresno, CA 93710
Ph: (559)981-5132

Payne, Dr. John C., MD, President
Medical Ambassadors International
[20372]
5012 Salida Blvd.
Salida, CA 95368
Ph: (209)543-7500
Toll Free: 888-403-0600
Fax: (209)543-7550

Payne, John, Chairperson
Motor Control and Motion Associa-
tion [1027]
900 Victors Way, Ste. 140
Ann Arbor, MI 48108
Ph: (734)994-6088

Payne, Dr. Keith B., CEO, President
National Institute for Public Policy
[18992]
9302 Lee Hwy., Ste. 750
Fairfax, VA 22031-1214
Ph: (703)293-9181
Fax: (703)293-9198

Payne, Kevin, Exec. Dir., CEO
U.S. Club Soccer [23193]
192 E Bay St., Ste. 301
Charleston, SC 29401
Ph: (843)614-4140
Fax: (843)614-4146

Payne, Michael, Treasurer
AMC Institute [253]
700 N Fairfax St., Ste. 510
Alexandria, VA 22314
Ph: (571)527-3108
Fax: (571)527-3105

Payne, Pamela, Secretary, Treasurer
National Council on Family Relations
- Religion and Family Life Section
[11827]
1201 W River Pky., Ste. 200
Minneapolis, MN 55454

Payne, Thomas, President
Association for the Treatment of
Tobacco Use and Dependence
[17308]
c/o Thomas Payne, President
University of Mississippi Medical Ctr.
Jackson Medical Mall, Ste. 61
350 W Woodrow Wilson Dr.
Jackson, MS 39213

Paz, Daniel, President
Long Way Home [10725]
c/o Mike Smith

227 W Hersey St.
Ashland, OR 97520

Paz, Oded, Contact
Unrecognised States Numismatic
Society [22290]
PO Box 0534
Castaic, CA 91310-0534

Pazo, Edward W, President
Croatian Fraternal Union of America
[9192]
100 Delaney Dr.
Pittsburgh, PA 15235
Ph: (412)843-0380
Fax: (412)823-1594

Peace, Derryle, Director
Texas A&M University - Commerce
Alumni Association [19351]
1706 Stonewall
Commerce, TX 75429
Ph: (903)886-5765
Toll Free: 866-268-4844
Fax: (903)886-5768

Pérez, Norma A., MD, VP
Hispanic-Serving Health Professions
Schools [8324]
2639 Connecticut Ave. NW, Ste. 203
Washington, DC 20008
Ph: (202)290-1186
Fax: (202)290-1339

Pearce, Dorcas, Managing Dir.
Financial Markets Association [1235]
333 2nd St. NE, No. 104
Washington, DC 20002
Ph: (202)544-6327

Pearce, Jeni, President
Professionals in Nutrition for
Exercise and Sport [16238]
358 South 700 East (B-247)
Salt Lake City, UT 84102

Pearce, Larry, Exec. Dir.
Governors' Wind Energy Coalition
[7388]
2200 Wilson Blvd., Ste. 102-22
Arlington, VA 22201
Ph: (402)651-2948

Pearce, Michael, President
Loyal Escorts of the Green Garter
[21011]
c/o Michael Pearce, President
1645 E Madge Ave.
Hazel Park, MI 48030

Pearce, Paul, Director
Unbound [13092]
1 Elmwood Ave.
Kansas City, KS 66103-2118
Ph: (913)384-6500
Toll Free: 800-875-6564
Fax: (913)384-2211

Pearce, Sue, Administrator
Society of Military Otolaryngologists
- Head and Neck Surgeons
[15842]
PO Box 923
Converse, TX 78109-0923
Ph: (210)945-9006
Fax: (210)867-5495

Pearl, Amy, Chairperson
Emerge America [19243]
44 Montgomery St., Ste. 2310
San Francisco, CA 94104-4711
Ph: (415)344-0323
Fax: (415)500-4065

Pearl, Marc, President, CEO
Homeland Security and Defense
Business Council [3055]
1990 M St., Ste. 760

Washington, DC 20036
Ph: (202)470-6440

Pearlman, Dena, Exec. Dir.
Contemporary Ceramic Studios Association **[694]**
217 N Seacrest Blvd., No. 295
Boynton Beach, FL 33425-0295
Toll Free: 888-291-2272

Pearlman, Nancy, Exec. Dir.
Educational Communications **[7876]**
PO Box 351419
Los Angeles, CA 90035-9119
Ph: (310)559-9160

Pearlman, Nancy, VP
Universal Pantheist Society **[20616]**
PO Box 3499
Visalia, CA 93278

Pearman, Robert C., Jr.,
Chairperson
National Housing Law Project **[5283]**
703 Market St., Ste. 2000
San Francisco, CA 94103
Ph: (415)546-7000
Fax: (415)546-7007

Pearson, Ann Lisa, President
International Society for British
Genealogy and Family History
[20975]
PO Box 3345
Centennial, CO 80161

Pearson, Barbro, Chairman
Independent Order of Svithiod
[10200]
5518 W Lawrence Ave.
Chicago, IL 60630
Ph: (773)736-1191

Pearson, Cathy, President
National Oil and Acrylic Painters'
Society **[8875]**
PO Box 5567
Bella Vista, AR 72714
Ph: (479)899-4961

Pearson, Christina, Founder
The TLC Foundation for Body-
Focused Repetitive Behaviors
[15809]
716 Soquel Ave., Ste. A
Santa Cruz, CA 95062
Ph: (831)457-1004
Fax: (831)427-5541

Pearson, Cynthia, Exec. Dir.
National Women's Health Network
[17763]
1413 K St. NW, 4th Fl.
Washington, DC 20005
Ph: (202)682-2640
   (202)682-2646
Fax: (202)682-2648

Pearson, Cynthia, Officer
Wendt Center for Loss and Healing
[13218]
4201 Connecticut Ave. NW, Ste. 300
Washington, DC 20008
Ph: (202)624-0010
Fax: (202)624-0062

Pearson, Elisabeth, Exec. Dir.
Democratic Governors Association
[5775]
1401 K St. NW, Ste. 200
Washington, DC 20005-3497
Ph: (202)772-5600
Fax: (202)772-5602

Pearson, Greg, Chairman
National Pasta Association **[1361]**
750 National Press Bldg.
529 14th St. NW

Washington, DC 20045
Ph: (202)591-2459
Fax: (202)591-2445

Pearson, Keith, Gen. Sec.
World Packaging Organisation
[2486]
1833 Centre Point Cir., Ste. 123
Naperville, IL 60563
Ph: (630)596-9007
Fax: (630)544-5055

Pearson, Kim, Director
Trans Youth Family Allies **[18728]**
PO Box 1471
Holland, MI 49422-1471
Toll Free: 888-462-8932

Pearson, Lauren B., President
Brent Schoening Strike Out
Leukemia Foundation **[15533]**
2525 Auburn Ave.
Columbus, GA 31906
Ph: (706)536-1933

Pearson, Maria, Mgr.
LAM Foundation **[14590]**
4520 Cooper Rd., Ste. 300
Cincinnati, OH 45242
Ph: (513)777-6889
Toll Free: 877-287-3526

Pearson, Robert W., CEO, Founder
Horizon International **[11040]**
350 JH Walker Dr.
Pendleton, IN 46064-0180
Ph: (765)778-1016
Toll Free: 866-778-7020
Fax: (765)778-9490

Pearson, Dr. Roger, Editor
Council for Social and Economic
Studies **[18972]**
1133 13th St. NW
Washington, DC 20005
Ph: (202)371-2700
Fax: (202)371-1523

Pease, Rita Chaudhuri, President
Cultural Integration Fellowship
[9026]
2650 Fulton St.
San Francisco, CA 94118
Ph: (415)668-1559

Peaton, Diana, President
Pony of the Americas Club **[4402]**
3828 S Emerson Ave.
Indianapolis, IN 46203
Ph: (317)788-0107
Fax: (317)788-8974

Peays, Ben, PhD, Exec. Dir.
The Gospel Coalition **[19983]**
2065 Half Day Rd.
Deerfield, IL 60015

Peck, Catherine, Bd. Member
Engineering World Health **[15448]**
The Prizery, Ste. 200
302 E Pettigrew St.
Durham, NC 27701
Ph: (919)682-7788

Peck, Eric, President
Z Series Car Club of America
[21526]

Peck, Hoddy, Chairman
Specialty Graphic Imaging Association **[1550]**
10015 Main St.
Fairfax, VA 22031
Toll Free: 888-385-3588

Peck, James M., President
International Insolvency Institute
[1812]

10332 Main St.
PMB 112
Fairfax, VA 22030-2410
Ph: (703)591-6336
Fax: (703)802-0207

Peck, Magda G., ScD, Advisor,
Founder
CityMatch **[14185]**
982170 Nebraska Medical Ctr.
University of Nebraska Medical
Center
Omaha, NE 68198-2170
Ph: (402)552-9500
Fax: (402)552-9593

Peck, Mike, Founder, President
Outreach Asia **[11124]**
5608 Benton Ave.
Edina, MN 55436
Ph: (952)922-8536
Fax: (952)920-2377

Peck, Ronald C., MBA, Founder
Blind Judo Foundation **[22778]**
24145 NE 122nd St.
Redmond, WA 98053
Ph: (425)444-8256

Peddicord, Douglas, PhD, Exec. Dir.
Association of Clinical Research
Organizations **[14289]**
915 15th St. NW, 2nd Fl.
Washington, DC 20005
Ph: (202)464-9340

Pede, Lt. Col. Wallace H., CEO
Senior Conformation Judges Association **[21960]**
c/o Lt. Col. Wallace H. Pede, Chief
Executive Officer
7200 Tanager St.
Springfield, VA 22150
Ph: (703)451-5656
Fax: (703)451-5979

Pedersen, Kim, Founder, President
The Monorail Society **[22461]**
36193 Carnation Way
Fremont, CA 94536-2641

Pedersen, Neil, Exec. Dir.
National Academy of Sciences
National Research Council I
Transportation Research Board
[7350]
The National Academies, 500 Fifth
St. NW
500 5th St. NW
Washington, DC 20001-2736
Ph: (202)334-2934
   (202)334-2000

Pedersen, Noa, President
International Window Cleaning Association **[2134]**
1100-H Brandywine Blvd.
Zanesville, OH 43701-7303
Toll Free: 800-875-4922
Fax: (740)452-2552

Pederson, Dr. William D., Exec. Dir.
Association of Third World Studies
[18485]
PO Box 1232
Americus, GA 31709
Ph: (318)797-5349
   (318)797-5158
Fax: (318)795-4203

Pedigo, Rev. Thomas L., Exec. Dir.,
Founder
National Alliance Against Christian
Discrimination, Inc. **[19995]**
c/o Rev. Thomas L. Pedigo, Founder
and Executive Director
PO Box 62685
Colorado Springs, CO 80962

Pedraza, Linda, Founder
Autism Answers **[13744]**
PO Box 2632
Oakland, CA 94619
Ph: (510)749-7072
Fax: (510)749-0269

Pedulla, Tom, President
National Turf Writers and Broadcasters **[2708]**
PO Box 541
Prospect, KY 40059
Ph: (646)337-6955

Peek, Warren, President
Southern Baptist Foundation **[19741]**
901 Commerce St., Ste. 600
Nashville, TN 37203
Ph: (615)254-8823
Toll Free: 800-245-8183
Fax: (615)255-1832

Peeper, Jeannie, Founder, President
International Fibrodysplasia Ossificans Progressiva Association
[14831]
101 Sunnytown Rd., Ste. 208
Casselberry, FL 32707
Ph: (407)365-4194
Fax: (407)365-3213

Peeples, Mark, President
Sigma Xi, The Scientific Research
Society **[23861]**
3106 E NC Highway 54, Ste. 300
Research Triangle Park, NC 27709
Ph: (919)549-4691
Toll Free: 800-243-6534
Fax: (919)549-0090

Peer, Marion D., Contact
National Guild of Decoupeurs
[21774]
1017 Pucker St.
Stowe, VT 05672-4496
Fax: (802)253-9552

Pe'er, Jacob, MD, President
International Society of Ocular
Oncology **[16346]**
Wills Eye Hospital
Ocular Oncology Service
840 Walnut St.
Philadelphia, PA 19107
Fax: (215)928-1140

Pegram, Steve, President
International Society for Fire Service
Instructors **[5210]**
14001C St. Germain Dr., Ste. 128
Centreville, VA 20121
Toll Free: 800-435-0005
Fax: (800)235-9153

Pegues, Mrs. Princess A., President
Christian Methodist Episcopal
Church Women's Missionary
Council **[20341]**
c/o Dr. Princess Pegues, President
2309 Bonnie Ave.
Bastrop, LA 71220-4171
Ph: (318)281-3044

Pei, Zhonghua, PhD, President
Chinese American Biopharmaceutical Society **[16655]**
268 Bush St., Ste. 1888
San Francisco, CA 94104

Peifer, Kathryn J., Co-Pres.
National Client Protection Organization **[5439]**
c/o Michael J. Knight, President
New York Lawyers' Fund for Client
Protection
119 Washington Ave.
Albany, NY 12210
Ph: (518)434-1935
Toll Free: 800-442-3863
Fax: (518)434-5614

Peiffer, Tim, President
Creative Play Project [13440]
3849 E Broadway Blvd., No. 293
Tucson, AZ 85716

Peiser, Judy, Exec. Producer, Director
Center for Southern Folklore [8797]
119 S Main St.
Memphis, TN 38101
Ph: (901)525-3655

Pelech, Jim, President
Association for Constructivist Teaching [8642]
23900 Greening Dr.
Novi, MI 48375

Pelham, Fiona, Chairman
Meeting Professionals International [2334]
3030 Lyndon B. Johnson Fwy., Ste. 600
Dallas, TX 75234-7349
Ph: (972)702-3000
Fax: (972)702-3070

Pelland, Roland, President
Finnish Spitz Club of America [21878]
c/o Mary Ellis, Membership Chairperson
317 Manzanita Dr.
Los Osos, CA 93402
Ph: (805)528-3419

Pellegrino, Joan, President, Treasurer
Biomass Energy Research Association [6461]
901 D St. SW, Ste. 100
Washington, DC 20024
Ph: (410)953-6202
Fax: (410)290-0377

Pelletier, William, President
Affordable Housing Investors Council [485]
PO Box 986
Irmo, SC 29063
Ph: (347)392-9983
Toll Free: 800-246-7277
Fax: (803)732-0135

Peloquin, Tracy, Chmn. of the Bd.
Law Enforcement and Emergency Services Video Association, Inc. [5480]
84 Briar Creek Rd.
Whitesboro, TX 76273-4603
Ph: (469)285-9435
Fax: (469)533-3659

Pelosi, Dr. Marco A., II, Founder, President
International Society of Cosmetogynecology [14317]
350 Kennedy Blvd.
Bayonne, NJ 07002
Ph: (201)436-8025
Fax: (201)339-5030

Pelosi, Rep. Nancy, Leader
Democratic Congressional Campaign Committee [18110]
430 S Capitol St. SE
Washington, DC 20003-4024
Ph: (202)863-1500

Pels, Laurence, Exec. Dir.
Theodore Roosevelt Association [10349]
PO Box 719
Oyster Bay, NY 11771
Ph: (516)921-6319
Fax: (516)921-6481

Pelton, Rebecca, Exec. Dir., President
Montessori Accreditation Council for Teacher Education [7781]

420 Park St.
Charlottesville, VA 22902
Ph: (434)202-7793
Toll Free: 888-525-8838

Peluso, Dr. Paul, President
International Association for Marriage and Family Counselors [11491]
c/o Dr. Paul Peluso, President
Bldg. 47, Rm. 270
Dept. of Counselor Education
Florida Atlantic University
777 Glades Rd.
Boca Raton, FL 33431-0991
Ph: (561)297-3625

Pembroke, John, President, CEO
Credit Union Executives Society [948]
5510 Research Park Dr.
Madison, WI 53711-5377
Ph: (608)271-2664
Toll Free: 800-252-2664
Fax: (608)271-2303

Pena, Alex, Chmn. of the Bd.
National Latina/Latino Law Student Association [18622]
900 19th Ave. S, Apt. 509
Nashville, TN 37212-2172

Pena, David, Jr., CEO, Exec. Dir.
Hispanic Dental Association [14439]
3910 South IH 35., Ste. 245
Austin, TX 78704-7441
Ph: (512)904-0252

Penalosa, Carmen, President
America Developing Smiles [13026]
8300 NW 53rd St., Ste. 350
Doral, FL 33166
Ph: (305)742-2136
Fax: (305)742-2161

Pence, Caroline, Exec. Dir.
Postpartum Education and Support [16625]
PO Box 33751
Raleigh, NC 27636
Ph: (919)889-3221

Pence, George, President
Pantera International [21474]
PO Box 920
Ventura, CA 93002
Ph: (805)648-6464
Fax: (805)648-8074

Pendergast, Christopher, Founder, President
Ride for Life [13686]
Stony Brook University
Health Sciences Center, Level 2, Rm. 106
Stony Brook, NY 11794-8231
Ph: (631)444-1292

Pendergast, Lori, President
National Shiba Club of America [21924]
c/o Lisa Sakashita, Corresponding Secretary
15508 Janine Dr.
Whittier, CA 90603

Pendergraft, Mary, Chairperson
National Committee for Latin and Greek [9165]
Hodges 316
Dept. of Foreign Languages and Literatures
Louisiana State University
Baton Rouge, LA 70803
Ph: (225)578-6616

Pendergraft, Rachel, Coord.
Knights of the Ku Klux Klan [19239]
PO Box 2222

Harrison, AR 72601
Ph: (870)427-3414

Pendergrass, Bill, Exec. VP
Beefmaster Breeders United [3719]
6800 Park 10 Blvd., Ste. 290 W
San Antonio, TX 78213
Ph: (210)732-3132
Fax: (210)732-7711

Peng, Cheng, Chairman
North America Chinese Clean-tech & Semiconductor Association [1057]
809-B Cuesta Dr., Ste. 208
Mountain View, CA 94040-3666

Peng, Dr. Ding Lun, President
Traditional Chinese Medicine Association and Alumni [13661]
108-A E 38th St.
New York, NY 10016
Ph: (212)889-4802
Fax: (646)309-7633

Peng, Sharon, President
IEEE - Consumer Electronics Society [6425]
c/o Bill Orner, Secretary
1513 Meadow Ln.
Mountain View, CA 94040

Penn, Laura, Exec. Dir.
Stage Directors and Choreographers Foundation [10273]
321 W 44th St.
New York, NY 10036-5653
Ph: (646)524-2226
Fax: (212)302-6195

Penn, Su, Treasurer
Friends for Lesbian, Gay, Bisexual, Transgender, and Queer Concerns [20180]
2206 Iroquois Rd.
Okemos, MI 48864

Pennaz, Steve, Exec. Dir.
North American Fishing Club [22851]
12301 Whitewater Dr.
Minnetonka, MN 55343
Toll Free: 800-843-6232

Penner, Rob, Chairman
North American Transportation Management Institute [7725]
2460 W 26th Ave., Ste. 245-C
Denver, CO 80211
Ph: (303)952-4013
Fax: (775)370-4055

Pennington, Deneen, Exec. Dir.
National Career Development Association [11772]
305 N Beech Cir.
Broken Arrow, OK 74012
Ph: (918)663-7060
Toll Free: 866-367-6232
Fax: (918)663-7058

Pennington, Joyce Eaton, Owner, President, CEO
Dance/Drill Team Directors of America [9251]
339 Van Bibber Rd.
Salado, TX 76571
Ph: (254)947-0613
Toll Free: 800-462-5719
Fax: (254)947-3040

Pennoyer, Russell, Chairman
William T. Grant Foundation [10819]
570 Lexington Ave., 18th Fl.
New York, NY 10022-6837
Ph: (212)752-0071
Fax: (212)752-1398

Penny, Dale, President, CEO
Up With People [7804]
6800 Broadway, Unit 106

Denver, CO 80221-2848
Ph: (303)460-7100
Fax: (303)225-4649

Pennybacker, Susan, President
North American Conference on British Studies [9140]
c/o Paul Deslandes, Executive Secretary
University of Vermont
133 S Prospect St.
Burlington, VT 05405
Ph: (802)656-3535

Pensinger, Kim, President
Dominican Advance, Inc. [19421]
PO Box 6354
Phoenix, AZ 85005
Ph: (520)908-7324

Penta, Dr. Gerard C., President
American Dog Show Judges [21808]
c/o Carl Liepmann, Secretary
9144 W Mt. Morris Rd.
Flushing, MI 48433
Ph: (480)991-0216
Fax: (480)991-0217

Pentz, Ed, Exec. Dir.
CrossRef [2780]
50 Salem St.
Lynnfield, MA 01940
Ph: (781)295-0072
Fax: (781)295-0077

Peoples, Daryl J., President
International Boxing Federation [22711]
899 Mountain Ave., Ste. 2C
Springfield, NJ 07081
Ph: (973)564-8046
Fax: (973)564-8751

Peppel, Alan, President
American Knife Manufacturers Association [2065]
30200 Detroit Rd.
Westlake, OH 44145
Ph: (440)899-0010
Fax: (440)892-1404

Pepper, Christine, CEO
National Funeral Directors Association [2412]
13625 Bishop's Dr.
Brookfield, WI 53005
Ph: (262)789-1880
Toll Free: 800-228-6332
Fax: (262)789-6977

Pepper, La Rhea, Managing Dir.
Textile Exchange [4518]
511 S 1st St.
Lamesa, TX 79331
Ph: (806)428-3411

Pepperman, Scott E., Exec. Dir.
National Association State Agencies for Surplus Property [5687]
c/o Steve Ekin, President
200 Piedmont Ave. SE, Ste. 1802 W
Atlanta, GA 30334-9030
Ph: (405)657-8544

Perch, Elizabeth, CFO, COO
Center for the Study of the Presidency and Congress [17852]
601 13th St., NW Ste. 1050N
Washington, DC 20005
Ph: (202)872-9800
Fax: (202)872-9811

Perch, Liz, Receptionist
Smocking Arts Guild of America [21783]
PO Box 5828
Savannah, GA 31414-5828
Ph: (817)350-4883
Toll Free: 855-350-7242
Fax: (817)886-0393

Percy, Dr. Livius T., President
Romanian Missionary Society
[20457]
PO Box 527
Wheaton, IL 60187
Ph: (630)665-6503
Fax: (630)665-6538

Perdue, Randy, Bd. Member
International Association of Cor-
rectional Training Personnel
[11531]
PO Box 274
Walsenburg, CO 81089
Ph: (719)738-9969
Fax: (719)744-9561

Perez, Daniel Paul, President, CEO
FSH Society [15934]
450 Bedford St.
Lexington, MA 02420
Ph: (781)301-6060
(781)301-6650
Fax: (781)862-1116

Perez, Hector, Dir. of Info. Technol-
ogy
Cancer Care [13917]
275 7th Ave., 22nd Fl.
New York, NY 10001-6708
Ph: (212)712-8400
Toll Free: 800-813-4673
Fax: (212)712-8495

Perez, Marc Houston, CEO
Society for the Promotion of
Japanese Animation [8891]
1522 Brookhollow Dr., No. 1
Santa Ana, CA 92705
Ph: (714)937-2994

Perez, Penny, CEO, Founder
Williams Syndrome Changing Lives
Foundation [14867]
PO Box 76021
Saint Petersburg, FL 33734
Ph: (727)557-7177

Perez, Salvador, President
Costume Designers Guild [23407]
11969 Ventura Blvd., 1st Fl.
Studio City, CA 91604-2630
Ph: (818)752-2400
Fax: (818)752-2402

Perez, Sonia, Founder
Angel's Pediatric Heart House
[14096]
151 N Nob Hill Rd., Ste. 139
Plantation, FL 33324
Ph: (954)318-2020

Perez, Victoria, Bd. Member
ColombiaCare [10944]
PO Box 254
Lincroft, NJ 07738-0254

Perez, Wendi, Administrator
American Rhinologic Society [16537]
PO Box 495
Warwick, NY 10990
Ph: (845)988-1631
Fax: (845)986-1527

Perez, Yamileth, Director
Esperanza en Accion [13047]
PO Box 1011
Okemos, MI 48805

Periago, Dr. Mirta Roses, Director
PALTEX-Expanded Textbook and
Instructional Materials Program
[8694]
525 23rd St. NW
Washington, DC 20037
Ph: (202)974-3000
Fax: (202)974-3663

Perkins, Bob, Chairman, Founder
American Association of Inside Sales
Professionals [3009]

1593 112th Ct. W
Inver Grove Heights, MN 55077
Toll Free: 800-604-7085

Perkins, Clara Whaley, PhD, Chair-
man
The Life After Trauma Organization
[13235]
PO Box 56243
Philadelphia, PA 19130

Perkins, MD, PhD, Sherrie L.,
President
Society for Hematopathology
[16592]
33 W Monroe, Ste. 1600
Chicago, IL 60603-5617
Ph: (312)541-4853
(312)541-4944
Fax: (312)541-4998

Perkins, Ron, Exec. Dir.
Ag Container Recycling Council
[4623]
223 S Main St.
Lexington, VA 24450
Toll Free: 877-952-2272

Perkins, Tommy, PhD, Exec. VP
International Brangus Breeders As-
sociation [3729]
5750 Epsilon
San Antonio, TX 78249
Ph: (210)696-8231
Fax: (210)696-8718

Perkins, Tony, President
Family Research Council [11818]
801 G St. NW
Washington, DC 20001
Toll Free: 800-225-4008

Perkowitz, Bob, Founder, President
ecoAmerica [3850]
1730 Rhode Island Ave. NW, Ste.
200
Washington, DC 20036-3120
Ph: (202)457-1900
Fax: (509)351-1900

Perlin, MD, PhD, Jonathan B., Chair-
man
American Hospital Association Sec-
tion for Psychiatric and Substance
Abuse Services [16819]
155 N Wacker Dr.
Chicago, IL 60606
Ph: (312)422-3000
Toll Free: 800-424-4301
Fax: (312)422-4796

Perlman, Lee, Chairman
Healthcare Supply Chain Association
[15078]
1341 G Street NW, 6th Fl.
Washington, DC 20005
Ph: (202)629-5833
Fax: (202)466-9666

Perlman, Michael, President
Western Cover Society [22380]
430 Ponderosa Ct.
Lafayette, CA 94549

Perlman, Sharon, President
Colon Cancer Alliance for Research
and Education for Lynch Syndrome
[14818]
127 W Oak St., Unit C
Chicago, IL 60610
Ph: (312)725-9769
Fax: (847)267-0746

Perlmutter, Stacey, President
Women in Philanthropy [18854]
PO Box 224
Northampton, MA 01061

Perone, Michael, Officer
Association for Behavior Analysis
[6029]

550 W Centre Ave.
Portage, MI 49024
Ph: (269)492-9310

Perotto, Michael, President
Preferred Funeral Directors
International [2414]
PO Box 335
Indian Rocks Beach, FL 33785
Toll Free: 888-655-1566

Perrie, Brian, VP
International Society for Concrete
Pavements [539]
c/o Neeraj Buch, President
3556 Engineering Bldg.
Department of Civil and
Environmental Engineering
Michigan State University
East Lansing, MI 48824
Ph: (517)432-0012
Fax: (517)432-1827

Perrin, James M., MD, President
American Academy of Pediatrics
[16598]
141 NW Point Blvd.
Elk Grove Village, IL 60007-1098
Ph: (847)434-4000
Toll Free: 800-433-9016
Fax: (847)434-8000

Perron, Brandon A., Director
Criminal Defense Investigation Train-
ing Council [5147]
416 SE Balboa Ave., Ste. 2
Stuart, FL 34994
Toll Free: 800-465-5233

Perrone, David, President
National Association of General
Merchandise Representatives
[2208]
16 Journey, Ste. 200
Aliso Viejo, CA 92656-3317
Ph: (847)380-7489

Perrone, Mike, President
Professional Aviation Safety Special-
ists [23390]
1150 17th St. NW, Ste. 702
Washington, DC 20036
Ph: (202)293-7277
Fax: (202)293-7727

Perry, Candace, Secretary
Women's International League for
Peace and Freedom U.S. Section
[18843]
11 Arlington St.
Boston, MA 02116
Ph: (617)266-0999
Fax: (617)266-1688

Perry, Dave, CNMT, PET, Exec. Dir.
Nuclear Medicine Technology
Certification Board [16076]
Bldg. I
3558 Habersham at Northlake
Tucker, GA 30084-4009
Ph: (404)315-1739
Toll Free: 800-659-3953
Fax: (404)315-6502

Perry, Dick, President
Navy Carrier Society [22203]
c/o Ted Kraver, Secretary/Treasurer
225 W Orchid Ln.
Phoenix, AZ 85021

Perry, George, PhD, Chairman
National Organization of Portuguese
Americans [19618]
PO Box 2652
Falls Church, VA 22042
Ph: (703)389-3512

Perry, Glenn, PhD, Director
Association for Psychological Astrology [5989]

133 Injun Hollow Rd.
Haddam Neck, CT 06424
Ph: (860)467-6919

Perry, Glenn, Director
International Society for Astrological
Research [5993]
PO Box 358945
Gainesville, FL 32635-8945
Ph: (805)525-0461
Toll Free: 800-731-9456

Perry, Jennifer, President, Founder
Li-Fraumeni Syndrome Association
[14836]
PO Box 6458
Holliston, MA 01746
Toll Free: 855-239-5372

Perry, Joy, CEO
Prison Pen Pals [21739]
PO Box 120997
Fort Lauderdale, FL 33312
Ph: (954)583-6958
(828)765-2461

Perry, Dr. Kim B., VP
National Dental Association [14460]
3517 16th St. NW
Washington, DC 20010
Ph: (202)588-1697
Fax: (202)588-1244

Perry, Lynne, Contact
National Human Resources Associa-
tion [2500]
PO Box 36
House Springs, MO 63051
Toll Free: 866-523-4417

Perry, Mathew, Officer
American Deer and Wildlife Alliance
[4782]
PO Box 10
Liberty Hill, TX 78642

Perry, Paul, Officer
COLAGE [11878]
3815 S Othello St., Ste. 100, No.
310
Seattle, WA 98118
Ph: (504)313-0555
Toll Free: 855-426-5243

Perry, Ravi K., President, Comm.
Chm.
National Association for Ethnic Stud-
ies [9291]
Founders Hall
Virginia Commonwealth University
827 W Franklin St., 3rd Fl.
Richmond, VA 23284
Ph: (804)828-2706
(804)828-8051

Perry, Sean, Partner, Dept. Head
Junior Hollywood Radio and Televi-
sion Society [465]
16530 Ventura Blvd., Ste. 411
Encino, CA 91436
Ph: (818)789-1182

Perry, Thomas, Secretary
107th Engineer Association [4971]
900 Palms Ave.
Ishpeming, MI 49849-1064

Persse, David, MD, Chairman
National Registry of Emergency
Medical Technicians [14689]
6610 Busch Blvd.
Columbus, OH 43229
Ph: (614)888-4484
Fax: (614)888-8920

Persun, Hal, President
509th Parachute Infantry Association
[21185]

47 Washington Ave.
Wheeling, WV 26003

Perucca, Kirk P., VP
Road Map Collectors Association
[21720]
PO Box 478
Rowlett, TX 75030

Perugini, Rocco, President
Gonstead Clinical Studies Society
[14271]
1280 17th Ave., Ste. 101
Santa Cruz, CA 95062
Ph: (831)476-1873
Toll Free: 888-556-4277

Pesner, Jonah, Rabbi, Director
Religious Action Center of Reform
Judaism [18594]
2027 Massachusetts Ave. NW
Washington, DC 20036
Ph: (202)387-2800
Fax: (202)667-9070

Pestino, Joe, Hist.
College English Association [7866]
Johns Hopkins University Press
Journal Publishing Division
PO Box 19966
Baltimore, MD 21211-0966

Peter, Mike, Secretary, Treasurer
Germany Philatelic Society [22330]
PO Box 6547
Chesterfield, MO 63006-6547

Peterka, Sara, President
United States Lakeland Terrier Club
[21983]
c/o Mark Brandsema
PO Box 7292
Philadelphia, PA 19101
Ph: (215)266-6059

Petermann, Mr. Nils, Project Mgr.
Efficient Windows Collaborative
[3476]
c/o Kerry Haglund
21629 Zodiac St. NE
Wyoming, MN 55092
Ph: (202)530-2254
Fax: (202)331-9588

Peters, Brock, President
International Erosion Control Association [3887]
3401 Quebec St., Ste. 3500
Denver, CO 80207
Ph: (303)640-7554
Toll Free: 800-455-4322

Peters, Christine, Exec. Dir.
Roycrofters-at-Large Association
[21782]
1054 Olean Rd.
East Aurora, NY 14052
Ph: (716)655-7252

Peters, Don, Director
Canary and Finch Society [3659]
c/o Helen Jones, Treasurer
348 Magnolia Dr.
Huffman, TX 77336
Ph: (281)259-7951

Peters, Ellen, Treasurer
508th Parachute Infantry Regiment
Association [21184]
3630 Townsend Dr.
Dallas, TX 75229
Ph: (214)632-1360

Peters, Mr. Geoffrey, Esq., Gen.
Counsel, Secretary
American Charities for Reasonable
Fundraising Regulation [11854]
333 Church Ave. SW

Roanoke, VA 24016
Ph: (301)675-7741
Fax: (831)603-3462

Peters, Gerhard, Chairman
Rotary on Stamps Fellowship
[22359]
c/o Gerald FitzSimmons, Secretary
105 Calle Ricardo
Victoria, TX 77904-1203

Peters, Jim, President
Responsible Hospitality Institute
[11635]
4200 Scotts Valley Dr., Ste. B
Scotts Valley, CA 95066
Ph: (831)469-3396
(831)438-1404

Peters, John, Exec. Dir.
Undersea and Hyperbaric Medical
Society [17542]
631 US Highway 1, Ste. 307
North Palm Beach, FL 33408
Ph: (919)490-5140
Toll Free: 877-533-8467
Fax: (919)490-5149

Peters, Dr. Kenneth S., Exec.
American Equilibration Society
[14410]
207 E Ohio St., Ste. 399
Chicago, IL 60611
Ph: (847)965-2888
Fax: (609)573-5064

Peters, Matt, VP
Association for Glycogen Storage
Disease [15818]
PO Box 896
Durant, IA 52747
Ph: (563)514-4022

Peters, Ms. Susan, President, COO
Arab Bankers Association of North
America [380]
150 W 28th St., Ste. 801
New York, NY 10001
Ph: (212)599-3030
Fax: (212)599-3131

Peters, Tia Oros, Exec. Dir.
Seventh Generation Fund for
Indigenous Peoples [18713]
425 I St.
Arcata, CA 95518
Ph: (707)825-7640
Fax: (707)825-7639

Peters, Tracy Wilson, CEO
Childbirth and Postpartum Professional Association [14224]
PO Box 547
Flowery Branch, GA 30542
Ph: (770)965-9777
Toll Free: 888-688-5241

Peters-Campbell, Rebecca,
President
Borzoi Club of America [21845]
c/o Joy Windle, Recording Secretary
2255 Strasburg Rd.
Coatesville, PA 19320-4437
Ph: (610)380-0850
(678)957-9544

Petersen, Bob, Officer
American Association of Grain
Inspection and Weighing Agencies
[1516]
PO Box 26426
Kansas City, MO 64196
Ph: (816)912-2993
(816)912-2084

Petersen, Chris, Exec. Dir.
Schedules Direct [6333]
8613 42nd Ave. S

Seattle, WA 98118

Petersen, Dorene, Chairperson
Aromatherapy Registration Council
[13604]
1350 Broadway, 17th Fl.
New York, NY 10018-0903
Ph: (503)244-0726

Petersen, Kathy, President
American KuneKune Pig Society
[4707]
c/o Matt Burton, Webmaster
321 Hurricane Creek Rd.
Sandy Hook, MS 39478

Petersen, Matt, Bd. Member
Global Green U.S.A. [4063]
2218 Main St., 2nd Fl.
Santa Monica, CA 90405
Ph: (310)581-2700
Fax: (310)581-2702

Petersen, Patricia, Exec. Dir.
Air Medical Physician Association
[16731]
951 E Montana Vista Ln.
Salt Lake City, UT 84124-2467
Ph: (801)263-2672
Fax: (801)534-0434

Petersen, Paul, Founder
A Minor Consideration [11494]
15003 S Denker Ave.
Gardena, CA 90247-3113

Petersen, Robert R., President
Transportation, Elevator and Grain
Merchants Association [1522]
PO Box 26426
Kansas City, MO 64196
Ph: (816)569-4020
(816)912-2084
Fax: (816)221-8189

Petersen, Rev. Rodney L., Exec. Dir.
Lord's Day Alliance of the United
States [20593]
2715 Peachtree Rd. NE
Atlanta, GA 30305
Ph: (404)693-5530

Peterson, Arianne, Officer
Nukewatch [18735]
740-A Round Lake Rd.
Luck, WI 54853
Ph: (715)472-4185
Fax: (715)472-4184

Peterson, Boyd M., D.C., F.A.C.O.,
President
American College of Chiropractic
Orthopedists [14254]
c/o Boyd M. Peterson, President
1155 N Mayfair Rd.
Wauwatosa, WI 53226
Ph: (414)955-7999
Fax: (414)955-0110

Peterson, Carla, President
Association of Donor Recruitment
Professionals [13838]
PO Box 150790
Austin, TX 78715
Ph: (512)658-9414
Fax: (866)219-7008

Peterson, Don, Contact
Stampe Club International [21249]
2940 Falcon Way
Midlothian, TX 76065
Ph: (214)723-1504

Peterson, Douglas B., Chairman,
Founder
The Alliance for Safe Children
[14166]
213 Adahi Rd.

Vienna, VA 22180-5937
Ph: (703)652-3873

Peterson, Frank, Founder, President
Partner for Surgery [17397]
PO Box 388
McLean, VA 22101
Ph: (703)893-4335

Peterson, Mr. Ivan, President
Association for Historical Fencing
[22830]
PO Box 2013
Secaucus, NJ 07096-2013

Peterson, Jeff, Mgr.
Connected International Meeting
Professionals Association [2323]
8803 Queen Elizabeth Blvd.
Annandale, VA 22003
Ph: (512)684-0889
Fax: (267)390-5193

Peterson, Jeff, Exec. Dir.
Foil and Specialty Effects Association [2347]
2150 SW Westport Dr., Ste. 101
Topeka, KS 66614
Ph: (785)271-5816
Fax: (785)271-6404

Peterson, John A., Editor
Les Amis de Panhard and Deutsch-
Bonnet USA [21418]
c/o John A. Peterson, Editor
7992 Oak Creek Dr.
Reno, NV 89511-1065
Ph: (775)853-8452

Peterson, John, AIA, President,
Founder
Public Architecture [235]
1211 Folsom St., 4th Fl.
San Francisco, CA 94103
Ph: (415)861-8200
Fax: (415)431-9695

Peterson, Ken, President
National Association of
Governmental Labor Officials
[5399]
c/o Ken Peterson, President
443 Lafayette Rd. N
Saint Paul, MN 55155
Ph: (651)284-5010
Fax: (651)284-5721

Peterson, Kristine, Chairperson
Associated Koi Clubs of America
[22030]
PO Box 10879
Costa Mesa, CA 92627
Ph: (949)548-3690

Peterson, Mr. Larry, Treasurer
Rose Hybridizers Association
[22121]
c/o Mr. Larry Peterson, Treasurer
21 S Wheaton Rd.
Horseheads, NY 14845-1077

Peterson, Laura, MA, Exec. Dir.,
Founder
Hands to Hearts International
[11013]
1611 Telegraph Ave., Ste. 1420
Oakland, CA 94612
Ph: (510)763-7045
Fax: (510)763-6545

Peterson, Lowell, VP
American Society of
Cinematographers [1186]
1782 N Orange Dr.
Los Angeles, CA 90078
Ph: (323)969-4333
Toll Free: 800-448-0145

Peterson, Maggie, MBA, Exec. Dir.
Society of Biological Psychiatry
[16836]

Mayo Clinic of Jacksonville
Research-Birdsall 310
4500 San Pablo Rd.
Jacksonville, FL 32224
Ph: (904)953-2842
Fax: (904)953-7117

Peterson, Mark A., President
Clan Douglas Society of North
America [20807]
4115 Bent Oak Ct.
Douglasville, GA 30135-3658

Peterson, Mical Anne, President
Association of Administrators of the
Interstate Compact on the Place-
ment of Children [10858]
American Public Human Services
Association
1133 19th St. NW, Ste. 400
Washington, DC 20036
Ph: (202)682-0100
Fax: (202)289-6555

Peterson, Nancy, Secretary
International Society for Business
Education [7553]
c/o Ruth DiPieri, President
1301 Avenida Cesar Chavez
Monterey Park, CA 91754
Ph: (619)469-5067

Peterson, Randy, Act. Pres., VP
Advanced Laboratory Physics As-
sociation [8436]
c/o Dr. Steven K. Wonnell, Treasurer
Bloomberg Ctr., Rm. 366
Physics and Astronomy Dept.
Johns Hopkins University
3400 N Charles St.
Baltimore, MD 21218

Peterson, Ruth, President
American Society of Criminology
[5152]
1314 Kinnear Rd., Ste. 212
Columbus, OH 43212-1156
Ph: (614)292-9207
Fax: (614)292-6767

Peterson, Scott, Contact
Hearing Instrument Manufacturers'
Software Association [15194]
2600 Eagan Woods Dr., Ste. 460
Eagan, MN 55121
Ph: (651)644-2921
Toll Free: 800-435-9246
Fax: (651)644-3046

Peterzell, Marc, JD, Chairman
American Sudden Infant Death
Syndrome Institute [17331]
528 Raven Way
Naples, FL 34110
Ph: (239)431-5425
Fax: (239)431-5536

Petit, Anne, President
Association of Appraiser Regulatory
Officials [220]
13200 Strickland Rd., Ste. 114-264
Raleigh, NC 27613
Ph: (919)235-4544
Fax: (919)870-5392

Petrarca, Justin, President
North American Association of
Educational Negotiators [23412]
PO Box 1068
Salem, OR 97308
Ph: (519)503-0098

Petravich, Alan, Director, President
North American Clivia Society [4438]
PO Box 1098
Kennett Square, PA 19348

Petree, Sheree, Exec. Dir.
Mission Cataract USA [17727]
1233 E Brandywine Ln., PMB 211

Fresno, CA 93720
Ph: (559)797-1629

Petrella, Vincent J., Exec. Dir.
Yacht Brokers Association of
America [2261]
105 Eastern Ave., Ste. 104
Annapolis, MD 21403
Ph: (410)940-6345
Fax: (410)263-1659

Petrescu, Dr. Corina L., Secretary,
Treasurer
The Romanian Studies Association
of America [9590]
Mount Holyoke College
50 College St.
South Hadley, MA 01075
Ph: (662)915-7716

Petrie, Scott, CEO
Delta Waterfowl [4806]
PO Box 3128
Bismarck, ND 58502
Toll Free: 888-987-3695

Petrilli, Mark, Chairman
America's Small Business Develop-
ment Center [3114]
8990 Burke Lake Rd., 2nd Fl.
Burke, VA 22015
Ph: (703)764-9850
Fax: (703)764-1234

Petrilli, Michael J., President
Thomas B. Fordham Institute
[11727]
1016 16th St. NW, 8th Fl.
Washington, DC 20036
Ph: (202)223-5452
Fax: (202)223-9226

Petrosino, Linda, PhD, President
Association of Schools of Allied
Health Professions [8313]
122 C St. NW, Ste. 650
Washington, DC 20001
Ph: (202)237-6481

Petrossian, Vahik, President
Armenian Educational Foundation
[7829]
600 W Broadway, Ste. 130
Glendale, CA 91204
Ph: (818)242-4154
Fax: (818)242-4913

Petrotta, George I., Director,
Founder
International Sungja-Do Association
[22996]
2009 Butterfly Lake Dr.
Florence, SC 29505-3343
Ph: (843)676-5280

Petrou, Karen, Director
Foundation Fighting Blindness
[17700]
7168 Columbia Gateway Dr., Ste.
100
Columbia, MD 21046-3256
Ph: (410)423-0600
Toll Free: 800-683-5555

Petry, Dr. Don D., Exec. Dir.
National Council for Private School
Accreditation [7415]
PO Box 13686
Seattle, WA 98198-1010
Fax: (253)874-3409

Pettet, David J., Exec. Dir.
National Gay Pilot's Association
[152]
PO Box 11313
Norfolk, VA 23517
Ph: (757)626-1848

Pettett, Alex, Exec. Dir.
World Witness, The Board of
Foreign Missions of the Associate
Reformed Presbyterian Church
[20482]
1 Cleveland St., Ste. 220
Greenville, SC 29601
Ph: (864)233-5226
Fax: (864)233-5326

Pettit, Cindi, Exec. Asst.
Federation of Analytical Chemistry
and Spectroscopy Societies [6200]
Bldg. I
2019 Gallisteo St.
Santa Fe, NM 87505-2143
Ph: (505)820-1648
Fax: (505)989-1073

Pettit, Clark, CEO, President
Association of Business Information
& Media Companies [2768]
675 3rd Ave., 7th Fl.
New York, NY 10017-5704
Ph: (212)661-6360
Fax: (212)370-0736

Pettit, Ms. Kim, Exec. Dir.
ChristianTrade Association
International [19968]
9240 Explorer Dr., No. 200
Colorado Springs, CO 80920
Ph: (719)265-9895

Petty, CMRP, Brent, Chairman
Association for Healthcare Resource
and Materials Management
[15315]
155 N Wacker Dr., Ste. 400
Chicago, IL 60606
Ph: (312)422-3840
Fax: (312)422-4573

Petty, Sean Michael, President,
Exec. Dir.
American Society of Cosmetic Physi-
cians [14310]
8040 S Kolb Rd.
Tucson, AZ 85756
Ph: (520)574-1050
Fax: (520)545-1254

Pevsner, Diane, President
Council for Exceptional Children-
Division on Visual Impairments
[8581]
c/o Diane Pevsner, President
University of Alabama at Birmingham
School of Education
901 S 13th St. S
Birmingham, AL 35294
Ph: (205)975-5351

Pexton, Larry, Exec. Ofc.
Custom Electronic Design Installa-
tion Association [987]
7150 Winton Dr., Ste. 300
Indianapolis, IN 46268
Ph: (317)328-4336
Toll Free: 800-669-5329

Peyton, Margo, Founder
Ocean Wishes [4131]
PO Box 291030
Columbia, SC 29229
Ph: (803)419-2838
Fax: (843)353-2537

Pezold, George Carl, Exec. Dir.
Transportation and Logistics Council,
Inc. [3109]
120 Main St.
Huntington, NY 11743-8001
Ph: (631)549-8988
Fax: (631)549-8962

Pfaffl, Nasima, President, Sec.
(Actg.)
Citizens for Midwifery [14226]
PO Box 82227

Athens, GA 30608-2227
Toll Free: 888-CFM-4880

Pfafflin, Goetz E., President
BMW Vintage and Classic Car Club
of America [21339]
4862 Silver Sage Ct.
Boulder, CO 80301
Ph: (303)300-9946
(303)808-9135
Fax: (303)575-3234

Pfaltzgraff, Dr. Robert L., Jr.,
President
Institute for Foreign Policy Analysis
[18269]
Central Plz. Bldg.
675 Massachusetts Ave., 10th Fl.
Cambridge, MA 02139-3309
Ph: (617)492-2116
Fax: (617)492-8242

Pfautz, Leanne, Director
American Bar Association - Section
of International Law [5346]
321 N Clark St.
Chicago, IL 60654
Ph: (312)988-5000

Pfeffer, Linda D., RN, President
Aerobics and Fitness Association of
America [16691]
1750 E Northrop Blvd., Ste. 200
Chandler, AZ 85286-1744
Toll Free: 800-446-2322

Pfeifer, Jessica, Exec. Dir.
Philosophy of Science Association
[10114]
c/o Jessica Pfeifer, Executive Direc-
tor
Dept. of Philosophy
University of Maryland, Baltimore
County
1000 Hilltop Cir.
Baltimore, MD 21250
Ph: (410)455-2014

Pfeifer, Joseph, President
Liederkranz Foundation, Inc. [9949]
6 E 87th St.
New York, NY 10128
Ph: (212)534-0880
Fax: (212)828-5372

Pfeifer, Mark, Director
International Coalition of Apostolic
Leaders [20370]
PO Box 164217
Fort Worth, TX 76161
Ph: (817)232-5815
Fax: (817)232-1290

Pfeiffer, Bill, Director, President,
Facilitator
Sacred Earth Network [4100]
93A Glasheen Rd.
Petersham, MA 01366
Ph: (978)724-0120

Pfeiffer, Bruce, President
International Association of Plumbing
and Mechanical Officials [5067]
4755 E Philadelphia St.
Ontario, CA 91761
Ph: (909)472-4100
Fax: (909)472-4150

Pfeiffer, Jeanine, Exec. Dir.
Ethnobotanical Conservation
Organization for South East Asia
[3860]
PO Box 77
Fort Bragg, CA 95437
Fax: (815)331-0850

Pfeiffer, Linda, PhD, CEO, President
INMED Partnerships for Children
[15478]

21630 Ridgetop Cir., Ste. 130
Sterling, VA 20166-6564
Ph: (703)729-4951
Fax: (703)858-7253

Pfeiffer, Richard, PhD, President
National Anger Management Association [15786]
100 Orchard Park Dr., No. 26629
Greenville, SC 29616-9998
Ph: (646)485-5116
Fax: (646)390-1571

Pfifferling, John-Henry, PhD, Director, Founder
Center for Professional Well-Being [15115]
21 W Colony Pl., Ste. 150
Durham, NC 27705
Ph: (919)489-9167
Fax: (919)419-0011

Phalan, Fr. James H., Officer
Mariological Society of America [19859]
The Marian Library
University of Dayton
300 College Pk.
Dayton, OH 45469-1390
Ph: (937)229-4294
    (313)883-8515
Fax: (937)229-4258

Phalen, Rev. John, CSC, President
Family Rosary [19832]
518 Washington St.
North Easton, MA 02356-1200
Ph: (508)238-4095
Toll Free: 800-299-7729

Pham, Trieu, Dir. of Operations
Vietnam Village Health [12063]
PO Box 32973
San Jose, CA 95152
Ph: (408)661-6751
    (408)923-7262

Phang, Polin, Exec. Dir.
Sustainable Cambodia [11447]
101 SE 2nd Pl., Ste. 201-B
Gainesville, FL 32601
Ph: (352)371-2075

Phelan, Jacquie, Founder
Women's Mountain Bike and Tea Society [22761]
PO Box 757
Fairfax, CA 94978
Ph: (415)459-7093

Phelan, Patrick, CFO
National Safety Council [12835]
1121 Spring Lake Dr.
Itasca, IL 60143-3201
Ph: (630)285-1121
Toll Free: 800-621-7615

Phelps, Michael, Treasurer
Order of Americans of Armorial Ancestry [20759]
c/o David Carline Smith, Registrar/ Genealogist General
PO Box 339
Pembroke, KY 42266
Ph: (270)475-4572

Phifer, Russ, Exec. Dir.
National Registry of Certified Chemists [6208]
c/o Russ Phifer, Executive Director
125 Rose Ann Ln.
West Grove, PA 19390-8946
Ph: (610)322-0657
Fax: (800)858-6273

Philbin, Jack, Bd. Member
National Runaway Safeline [12794]
3141B N Lincoln

Chicago, IL 60657
Ph: (773)880-9860
Toll Free: 800-344-2785
Fax: (773)929-5150

Philbrook, Bud, Founder, Chairman, Trustee
Global Volunteers [18546]
375 E Little Canada Rd.
Saint Paul, MN 55117-1628
Toll Free: 800-487-1074
Fax: (651)482-0915

Philips, Corley, Chairman
Friends of the River [3871]
1418 20th St., Ste. 100
Sacramento, CA 95811
Ph: (916)442-3155
Toll Free: 888-464-2477
Fax: (916)442-3396

Philipson, Katherine, Office Mgr.
Women's Ordination Conference [19922]
PO Box 15057
Washington, DC 20003
Ph: (202)675-1006
Fax: (202)675-1008

Phillips, Allie, Director
National Center for Prosecution of Child Abuse [11089]
1400 Crystal Dr., Ste. 330
Arlington, VA 22202
Ph: (703)549-9222
Fax: (703)836-3195

Phillips, Brian, President
Utility Communicators International [778]
150 Mark Trl.
Sandy Springs, GA 30328
Ph: (970)368-2021

Phillips, David L., Chmn. of the Bd.
Bilateral US-Arab Chamber of Commerce [23565]
PO Box 571870
Houston, TX 77257-1870
Ph: (713)880-8168

Phillips, David, Exec. Dir.
National Clogging Organization Inc. [9267]
2986 Mill Park Ct.
Dacula, GA 30019
Ph: (678)889-4355
Fax: (603)925-0967

Phillips, Doyle T., President
American Society of Professional Estimators [7663]
2525 Perimeter Place Dr., Ste. 103
Nashville, TN 37214
Ph: (615)316-9200
Fax: (615)316-9800

Phillips, Frank, VP
United Schutzhund Clubs of America [21977]
4407 Meramec Bottom Rd., Ste. J
Saint Louis, MO 63129
Ph: (314)638-9686
Fax: (314)638-0609

Phillips, Ginger, Exec. Dir.
American Council on Consumer Interests [18039]
PO Box 2528
Tarpon Springs, FL 34688-2528
Ph: (727)940-2658

Phillips, Harry, V. Ch.
Network of International Christian Schools [7612]
3790 Goodman Rd. E
Southaven, MS 38672
Ph: (662)892-4300
Toll Free: 800-887-6427
Fax: (662)892-4310

Phillips, Helen, SNS, Officer
School Nutrition Association [8609]
120 Waterfront St., Ste. 300
National Harbor
Oxon Hill, MD 20745-1142
Ph: (301)686-3100
Toll Free: 800-877-8822
Fax: (301)686-3115

Phillips, Howard, Founder
Americans for Constitutional Liberty [18020]
92 Main St., Ste. 202-8
Warrenton, VA 20186
Ph: (540)219-4536

Phillips, Howard, President
Conservative Caucus Research Analysis and Education Foundation [18022]
92 Main St., Ste. 202-8
Warrenton, VA 20186
Ph: (703)281-6782

Phillips, James D., Bd. Member
Iowa Wesleyan College Alumni Association [19328]
601 N Main St.
Mount Pleasant, IA 52641
Ph: (319)385-6215
Toll Free: 800-582-2383

Phillips, Jason, President
American Society of Furniture Designers [1474]
4136 Coachmans Ct.
High Point, NC 27262-5445
Ph: (336)307-0999

Phillips, Jim, President
Canadian/American Border Trade Alliance [3299]
PO Box 929
Lewiston, NY 14092
Ph: (716)754-8824
Fax: (716)754-8824

Phillips, Ken, Treasurer
American Childhood Cancer Organization [13884]
10920 Connecticut Ave., Ste. A
Kensington, MD 20895
Ph: (301)962-3520
Toll Free: 855-858-2226
Fax: (301)962-3521

Phillips, Ken, Secretary
Feeding Hungry Children International [12088]
300 E State St., Ste. 531
Redlands, CA 92373
Ph: (909)793-2009
Fax: (909)793-6880

Phillips, Kimberley, PhD, President
American Society of Primatologists [5903]
c/o Dr. Corinna Ross, Treasurer
Dept. of Arts and Sciences
Texas A&M University
1 University Way
San Antonio, TX 78224
Ph: (210)784-2227
Fax: (210)784-2299

Phillips, Libba, CEO, Founder
Outpost for Hope [12364]
3438 E Lake Rd., Ste. 14
Palm Harbor, FL 34685

Phillips, Maxine, Editor
Foundation for the Study of Independent Social Ideas [18637]
120 Wall St., 31st Fl.
New York, NY 10005

Phillips, Mil, President
USS Coral Sea CVA-43 Association [21066]

52 Woodland Pl.
Fort Thomas, KY 41075-1605

Phillips, Pat, Admin. Asst.
Grottoes of North America [19559]
430 Beecher Rd.
Gahanna, OH 43230
Ph: (614)933-9193
Fax: (614)933-9098

Phillips, Patti, CEO
National Association of Collegiate Women Athletics Administrators [8430]
2024 Main St., No. 1W
Kansas City, MO 64108
Ph: (816)389-8200

Phillips, Peter, VP
North American Power Sweeping Association [2138]
136 S Keowee St.
Dayton, OH 45402
Ph: (937)424-3344
Toll Free: 888-757-0130
Fax: (937)222-5794

Phillips, Philip Edward, President
Poe Studies Association [9092]
c/o Carole Shaffer-Koros, Secretary-Treasurer
58 Normandy Dr.
Westfield, NJ 07090-3432

Phillips, Rhonda, President
International Society for Quality-of-Life Studies [6042]
c/o Rhonda Phillips, President
Windsor Halls, Duhme Rm. 134
205 N Russell St. W
Lafayette, IN 47906-4238
Ph: (765)496-3021

Phillips, Scott, President
Association for Technology in Music Instruction [8362]
312 E Pine St.
Missoula, MT 59802

Phillips, William C., Founder
Patience T'ai Chi Association [23011]
845 65th St., 2nd Fl.
Brooklyn, NY 11220
Ph: (718)332-3477

Phillips, Zack, Founder, President
RollerSoccer International Federation [23253]
PO Box 423318
San Francisco, CA 94142-3318
Ph: (415)864-6879

Phippen, Winthrop, Treasurer
Association for the Advancement of Industrial Crops [3558]
c/o Winthrop Phippen, Treasurer
Western Illinois University
1 University Cir.
Macomb, IL 61455

Phipps, Willetta, Secretary
American Bridge Association [21557]
c/o Willetta Phipps, Secretary
2828 Lakewood Ave. SW
Atlanta, GA 30315-5804
Ph: (404)768-5517

Phoenix, Kelly Leonhardt, Exec. Dir.
Nourish International [10728]
723 Mt. Carmel Church Rd.
Chapel Hill, NC 27517
Ph: (919)338-2599

Phreaner, Linda, Treasurer
HomeAID for Africa [10477]
1191 Shady Grove Way
West Chester, PA 19382
Ph: (610)399-0823

Piacentino, Bonnie, Comm. Chm.
Workers Compensation Insurance
Organizations **[1936]**
30 S 17th St., Ste. 1500
Philadelphia, PA 19103-4007
Ph: (215)320-4456

Piaget, Gerry, President
Institute for the Advancement of Hu-
man Behavior **[13796]**
PO Box 5527
Santa Rosa, CA 95402
Ph: (650)851-8411
Toll Free: 800-258-8411
Fax: (707)755-3133

Piasecki, Jeremy, Exec. Dir.
Afghanistan Water Polo **[23359]**
PO Box 438
Bonsall, CA 92003
Ph: (760)451-1783

Picard, Dan, President
Builders Hardware Manufacturers
Association **[1566]**
355 Lexington Ave., 15th Fl.
New York, NY 10017
Ph: (212)297-2122
Fax: (212)370-9047

Picchi, Tina, MA, Exec. Dir.
Supportive Care Coalition **[15283]**
18530 NW Cornell Rd., Ste. 101
Hillsboro, OR 97124
Ph: (503)216-5376

Piccigallo, Philip R., PhD, Exec. Dir.,
CEO
Commission for Social Justice
[17888]
219 E St. NE
Washington, DC 20002-4922
Ph: (202)547-2900
Fax: (202)546-8168

Pichot, Delphine S., President
Saving Animals Via Education
[10694]
PO Box 2961
Ponte Vedra Beach, FL 32004
Ph: (904)476-7532

Pickard, Elizabeth, President
International Museum Theatre Alliance **[9833]**
c/o New England Museum Association
22 Mill St., Ste. 409
Arlington, MA 02476

Pickard, Lee A., Counsel
Alliance in Support of Independent
Research **[2016]**
1990 M St. NW, Ste. 660
Washington, DC 20036-3417
Ph: (202)223-4418

Pickens, Jeremy, President
Northern Michigan University Alumni
Association **[19338]**
1401 Presque Isle Ave.
Marquette, MI 49855
Ph: (906)227-2610
   (906)227-1000
Toll Free: 877-GRA-DNMU

Pickering, Thomas, Chmn. of the Bd.
Givat Haviva Educational Foundation
[18682]
424 W 33rd St., Ste. 150
New York, NY 10001
Ph: (212)989-9272

Pickhardt, D. Mark, Exec. Dir.
Sigma Alpha Lambda **[23792]**
501 Village Green Pky., Ste. 1
Bradenton, FL 34209
Ph: (941)866-5614
Fax: (941)827-2924

Pieber, Rev. Carl L., PhD, Exec. Dir.
Central Association of the
Miraculous Medal **[19821]**
475 E Chelten Ave.
Philadelphia, PA 19144
Ph: (215)848-1010
Toll Free: 800-523-3674*
Fax: (215)848-1014

Piechowski, Lisa Drago, President
American Board of Forensic
Psychology **[16857]**
c/o Lisa Drago Piechowski,
President
5425 Wisconsin Ave., Ste. 600
Chevy Chase, MD 20815-3588
Ph: (870)740-4452

Pier, Gwen, Exec. Dir.
National Sculpture Society **[10210]**
75 Varick St., 11th Fl.
New York, NY 10013
Ph: (212)764-5645
Fax: (212)764-5651

Pierangelo, Dr. Roger, Exec. Dir.
National Association of Special
Education Teachers **[8588]**
1250 Connecticut Ave. NW, Ste. 200
Washington, DC 20036
Toll Free: 800-754-4421

Pierce, Mr. David, Secretary,
Treasurer
Phi Theta Pi **[23699]**
6552 Bradford Dr.
West Des Moines, IA 50266-2308
Ph: (515)440-2045
   (515)271-1540

Pierce, Dennis R., President
Brotherhood of Locomotive
Engineers and Trainmen **[23514]**
7061 E Pleasnt Valley Rd.
Independence, OH 44131
Ph: (216)241-2630
Fax: (216)241-6516

Pierce, Laurie, President
Society to Advance Opticianry
[16417]
14901 N State Ave.
Middlefield, OH 44062

Pierce, Sam, PT, Contact
Physical Therapy Pro Bono National
Honor Society **[23849]**
c/o Widener University, One
University Pl.
Institute for Physical Therapy Educa-
tion
One University Pl.
Chester, PA 19013

Pierce-Boggs, Kimberly, Exec. Dir.
Alliance of Independent Academic
Medical Centers **[15619]**
401 N Michigan Ave., Ste. 1200
Chicago, IL 60611-4264
Ph: (312)836-3712

Piereson, James, President
William E. Simon Foundation
[18168]
140 E 45th St., Ste. 14D
New York, NY 10017
Ph: (212)661-8366
Fax: (212)661-9450

Pieretti, Lisa J., Exec. Dir., Founder
International Hyperhidrosis Society
[14707]
1260 Smythe St.
Charleston, SC 29492

Pierre, Colleen, President
To Love a Child, Inc. **[11167]**
PO Box 165

Clifton Park, NY 12065-0165
Ph: (518)859-4424

Pierre, Pete St., Comm. Chm.
The American Judo and Jujitsu
Federation **[22965]**
c/o Central Office Administrator
PO Box 596
Penryn, CA 95663-0596
Toll Free: 800-850-AJJF
Fax: (415)457-9730

Piervincenzi, Ronald T., PhD, CEO
United States Pharmacopeial
Convention **[16689]**
12601 Twinbrook Pky.
Rockville, MD 20852-1790
Ph: (301)881-0666
Toll Free: 800-227-8772

Pietranton, Arlene A., CEO
American Speech-Language-Hearing
Association **[17237]**
2200 Research Blvd.
Rockville, MD 20850-3289
Ph: (301)296-5700
   (301)296-5650
Toll Free: 800-638-8255
Fax: (301)296-8580

Pietrantoni, Nadine, VP
International Academy of Aquatic Art
[23283]
803 E Washington Blvd.
Lombard, IL 60148

Pietrolungo, Al, President
United States Braille Chess Association **[21592]**
c/o Alan Schlank, Treasurer
1881 N Nash St., Unit 702
Arlington, VA 22209
Ph: (516)223-8685

Pietruszka, Ray, President
Rossica Society of Russian Philately
[22358]
c/o Ray Pietruszka, President
211 Evalyn St.
Madison, AL 35758-2203

Pietrzak, Jeanne, Mem.
National Abandoned Infants As-
sistance Resource Center **[11252]**
University of California - Berkeley
1918 University Ave., Ste. 3D
Berkeley, CA 94704-7402
Ph: (510)643-8390
Fax: (510)643-7019

Pigazzi, Alessio, President
Clinical Robotic Surgery Association
[17385]
2 Prudential Plz.
180 N Stetson Ave., Ste. 3500
Chicago, IL 60601
Ph: (312)268-5754
   (312)355-2494
Fax: (312)355-1987

Pigozzi, Maria, President
HALTER, Inc. **[17443]**
17410 Clay Rd.
Houston, TX 77084
Ph: (281)861-9138
   (281)508-6501

Pike, Diane K., Director
Teleos Institute **[12016]**
7439 E Beryl Ave.
Scottsdale, AZ 85258
Ph: (480)948-1800
Fax: (480)948-1870

Pike, John E., Director
GlobalSecurity.org **[18792]**
300 N Washington St., Ste. B-100
Alexandria, VA 22314
Ph: (703)548-2700
Fax: (703)548-2424

Pike, Sarah, President
International Society for the Study of
Religion, Nature and Culture
[8044]
107 Anderson Hall
Gainesville, FL 32611-7410
Ph: (352)392-1625

Pilarski, Michael, Director, Founder
Friends of the Trees Society **[3872]**
PO Box 1133
Port Hadlock, WA 98339
Ph: (360)643-9178

Pilavin, Rabbi Robert, Chairman
Union for Traditional Judaism
[20286]
82 Nassau St., No. 313
New York, NY 10038
Ph: (201)801-0707
Fax: (201)801-0449

Pilger, John, Treasurer
American Microscopical Society
[6865]
Dept. of Biological Sciences
CSU, Long Beach
1250 Bellflower Blvd.
Long Beach, CA 90840
Ph: (562)985-5378
Fax: (562)985-8878

Pilger, LeAnn, Coord.
American Birding Association **[6952]**
PO Box 744
Delaware City, DE 19706
Ph: (302)838-3660
Toll Free: 800-850-2473
Fax: (302)838-3651

Pilgrim, Mike, Chairman
Loading Dock Equipment
Manufacturers **[1742]**
c/o MHI
8720 Red Oak Blvd., Ste. 201
Charlotte, NC 28217-3996
Ph: (704)676-1190
Fax: (704)676-1199

Pillack, Penny, President
National Kindergarten Alliance
[8450]
c/o Penny Pillack, President
PO Box 309
Agua Dulce, TX 78330
Fax: (361)998-2333

Pillis, Lisette de, Treasurer
Society for Mathematical Biology
[6103]
c/o Lisette de Pillis, Treasurer
Department of Mathematics
Harvey Mudd College
Claremont, CA 91711

Pillitteri, Paul, Sr. VP of Comm. &
Planning
National Academy of Television Arts
and Sciences **[468]**
1697 Broadway, Ste. 404
New York, NY 10019
Ph: (212)586-8424
Fax: (212)246-8129

Pillow, Gary, President
Educational Audiology Association
[15189]
700 McKnight Park Dr., Ste. 708
Pittsburgh, PA 15237
Toll Free: 800-460-7322
Fax: (888)729-3489

Pillsbury, Charlie, Exec. Dir.
Mediators Beyond Borders
International **[4964]**
1901 N Fort Myer Dr., Ste. 405
Arlington, VA 22209
Ph: (703)528-6552
Fax: (703)528-5776

Pillsbury, David, President
American Institute of Building Design
[5954]
7059 Blair Rd. NW, Ste. 400
Washington, DC 20012
Ph: (202)750-4900
Toll Free: 800-366-2423
Fax: (866)204-0293

Pimm, William G., Jr., President
The National Crossbowmen of the
USA, Inc. [22504]
38 B Ave.
Richwood, WV 26261
Ph: (304)846-6420

Pincus, David, Comm. Chm.
Society for Chaos Theory in
Psychology and Life Sciences
[7070]
c/o Society for Chaos Theory in
Psychology & Life Sciences
PO Box 484
Pewaukee, WI 53072

Pine, Dee, Exec. Dir.
World Organization of China Paint-
ers [21789]
2700 N Portland
Oklahoma City, OK 73107-5400
Ph: (405)521-1234
Fax: (405)521-1265

Pine, Jeryl, Dir. of Member Svcs.
Society of Trust and Estate
Practitioners USA [1168]
40 E 84th St., Ste. 5D
New York, NY 10028
Ph: (212)737-3690
Fax: (917)206-4306

Pine, Pamela, PhD, Founder
Stop the Silence [10800]
PO Box 127
Glenn Dale, MD 20769
Ph: (301)464-4791

Pineiro, Judith, Exec. Dir.
Association of Art Museum Curators
[9821]
174 E 80th St.
New York, NY 10075
Ph: (646)405-8057
Fax: (212)537-5571

Pinizzotto, Nick, President
U.S. Sportsmen's Alliance [22964]
801 Kingsmill Pky.
Columbus, OH 43229
Ph: (614)888-4868
Fax: (614)888-0326

Pinkett, Preston, III, Chairman, CEO
National Bankers Association [412]
1513 P St. NW
Washington, DC 20005
Ph: (202)588-5432
Fax: (202)588-5443

Pinkham, Douglas G., President
Foundation for Public Affairs [18978]
2121 K St. NW, Ste. 900
Washington, DC 20037
Ph: (202)787-5970
Fax: (202)787-5942

Pinkowitz, Jackie, MPH, Chairperson
CCAL - Advancing Person-Centered
Living [10501]
2342 Oak St.
Falls Church, VA 22046
Ph: (732)212-9036

Pinkson, Kimberly Danek, Founder,
President
EcoMom Alliance [13376]
PO Box 2121
San Anselmo, CA 94979
Toll Free: 866-506-9012

Pinney, Molly Ola, CEO, Founder
Global Autism Project [13767]
252 3rd Ave.
Brooklyn, NY 11215
Ph: (718)764-8225

Pino, Joseph Algazi, President
Cuban Numismatic Association
[22267]
c/o Joseph A. Crespo, Treasurer
PO Box 47304
Tampa, FL 33646

Pino, Manuel, President
Southwest Research and Information
Center [18060]
105 Stanford SE
Albuquerque, NM 87196
Ph: (505)262-1862
Fax: (505)262-1864

Pinsky, Mark, President, CEO
Opportunity Finance Network
[17991]
Public Ledger Bldg., Ste. 572
620 Chestnut St.
Philadelphia, PA 19106
Ph: (215)923-4754
Fax: (215)923-4755

Pintar, Frank A., PhD, President
Association for the Advancement of
Automotive Medicine [12815]
35 E Wacker Dr., Ste. 850
Chicago, IL 60601
Ph: (847)844-3880
Fax: (312)644-8557

Pintar, Karen A, Secretary
Slovene National Benefit Society
[19653]
247 W Allegheny Rd.
Imperial, PA 15126-9774
Ph: (724)695-1100
Toll Free: 800-843-7675
Fax: (724)695-1555

Pio, Anthony, Treasurer
Luso-American Education Founda-
tion [10170]
7080 Donlon Way, Ste. 200
Dublin, CA 94568
Ph: (925)828-4884
Toll Free: 877-525-5876
Fax: (925)828-4554

Pioli, Giampaolo, President
United Nations Correspondents As-
sociation [2727]
United Nations Secretariat Bldg.,
Rm. S-308
405 E 42nd St.
New York, NY 10017
Ph: (212)963-7137

Piper, Kevin, President
Institutional Locksmiths' Association
[994]
PO Box 9560
Naperville, IL 60567-9560

Piper, Ti, Secretary
Aquatic Resources Education Association [4768]
c/o Barb Gigar, President
Iowa Dept. of Natural Resources
57744 Lewis Rd.
Lewis, IA 51544
Ph: (641)747-2200
(515)494-3891

Pipes, Jesse, Exec. Dir.
Access Health Africa [10828]
PO Box 57
Boone, NC 28607
Ph: (828)263-6877

Pipes, Sally C., President, CEO
Pacific Research Institute for Public
Policy [18997]

101 Montgomery St., Ste. 1300
San Francisco, CA 94111
Ph: (415)989-0833
Fax: (415)989-2411

Piro, Bev, President
North American Association for the
Catechumenate [19893]
c/o Elise Eslinger
1843 Ruskin Rd.
Dayton, OH 45406
Ph: (623)444-6963

Pirrong, Cary, Director
Oklahoma City University Alumni
Office [19341]
2501 N Blackwelder Ave.
Oklahoma City, OK 73106-1493
Ph: (405)208-5463
(405)208-5077

Pirtle, Bridgette, President
Musical Dog Sport Association
[22816]
PO Box 148
Chandler, AZ 85244-0148

Pisano, Robert A., Chairman
Motion Picture and Television Fund
[11795]
23388 Mulholland Dr.
Woodland Hills, CA 91364-2733
Ph: (818)876-1977
(818)876-1900
Toll Free: 855-760-6783

Pisciotta, Frank, Liaison
Jesse Cause Foundation [15388]
567 W Channel Islands Blvd., No.
235
Port Hueneme, CA 93041
Ph: (805)228-2222

Pister, Phil, Exec. Sec.
Desert Fishes Council [3845]
c/o Phil Pister, Executive Secretary
437 E South St.
Bishop, CA 93514

Pitcher, Larry, Secretary, President
Christian Record Services for the
Blind [13275]
4444 S 52nd St.
Lincoln, NE 68516-1302
Ph: (402)488-0981
Fax: (402)488-7582

Pitman, Brian, President
International Carnival Glass Associa-
tion [21671]
17186 Old State Road 37
Leopold, IN 47551
Ph: (812)843-4611

Pitre, Menta, Director
Organic Acidemia Association
[14849]
c/o Kathy Stagni, Executive Director
9040 Duluth St.
Golden Valley, MN 55427
Ph: (763)559-1797
Toll Free: 866-539-4060
Fax: (866)539-4060

Pitt, Dan, Exec. Dir.
Open Networking Foundation [6911]
2275 E Bayshore Rd., Ste. 103
Palo Alto, CA 94303
Ph: (510)492-4070

Pittenger, Michele Marini, President,
CEO
Travel Goods Association [3399]
301 N Harrison St., No. 412
Princeton, NJ 08540-3512
Toll Free: 877-842-1938
Fax: (877)842-1938

Pittman, Joe, President
Society for Research on Identity
Formation [8412]

College of Arts and Science
Florida International University
University Pk., DM 269-F
11200 SW 8th St.
Miami, FL 33199
Ph: (305)348-3941

Pitzer, Carole, President
Coalition for Animal Rescue and
Education [10601]
PO Box 2203
Hillsboro, MO 63050
Ph: (636)535-3253
(314)280-5428

Piwko, Paul, Bus. Mgr.
Dollars and Sense [6388]
95 Berkeley St., Ste. 305
Boston, MA 02116
Ph: (617)447-2177
Fax: (617)447-2179

Pixley, Stuart, President
National Association of Attorneys
with Disabilities [5026]
1491 Polaris Pky., PMB 295
Columbus, OH 43240
Ph: (347)455-1521

Plachter, Natalie, RN, Chairperson
Pediatric Urology Nurse Specialists
[16179]
500 Cummings Ctr., Ste. 4550
Beverly, MA 01915
Ph: (978)927-8330
Fax: (978)524-0498

Plansker, Stephanie, Rec. Sec.
Cecchetti Council of America [7699]
23393 Meadows Ave.
Flat Rock, MI 48134
Ph: (734)379-6710
Fax: (734)379-3886

Plant, Mike, President
U.S. Speedskating [23158]
5662 South Cougar Ln.
Kearns, UT 84118
Ph: (801)417-5360
Fax: (801)417-5361

Plaster, Amy, Chairman
Women's Policy, Inc. [19251]
409 12th St. SW, Ste. 310
Washington, DC 20024
Ph: (202)554-2323

Plaster, Dan, President
Cowboy Mounted Shooting Associa-
tion [23128]
PO Box 157
Roswell, NM 88202
Ph: (719)426-2774
Toll Free: 888-960-0003

Plath, Robert W., Exec. Dir.,
Founder
Worldwide Forgiveness Alliance
[12449]
20 Sunnyside Ave., Ste. A-268
Mill Valley, CA 94941
Ph: (415)342-2650

Plati, Crystal, Exec. Dir.
21st Century Democrats [18107]
2120 L St. NW, Ste. 305
Washington, DC 20037
Ph: (202)768-9222

Plati, Crystal, Chmn. of the Bd.
Management Assistance Group
[12403]
1155 F St. NW, Ste. 1050
Washington, DC 20004
Ph: (202)659-1963
Fax: (866)403-6080

Platt, Jeff, President
Horseplayers Association of North
America [22153]

93 Campbell Rd.
Keswick, VA 22947

Platt, Teresa, Exec. Dir.
Fur Commission USA [10626]
PO Box 1532
Medford, OR 97501
Ph: (541)595-8568
Fax: (541)566-7489

Plaus, Karen, CEO
National Board on Certification and
  Recertification for Nurse
  Anesthetists [16157]
8725 W Higgins Rd., Ste. 525
Chicago, IL 60631
Toll Free: 855-285-4658
Fax: (708)669-7636

Player, Roger W., Chairman
Western Catholic Union [19411]
510 Maine St.
Quincy, IL 62301
Ph: (217)223-9721
Toll Free: 800-223-4928
Fax: (217)223-9726

Plaza, Sandra, Exec. Dir.
Rebuild Global [5975]
241 14th Ave.
San Diego, CA 92101
Ph: (619)796-4796

Pledger, Rev. Phil, President
Lutheran Braille Workers [17724]
13471 California St.
Yucaipa, CA 92399
Ph: (909)795-8977
Toll Free: 800-925-6092
Fax: (909)795-8970

Plentl, Selena, Bd. Member
National Energy Services Associa-
  tion [6498]
17515 Spring-Cypress Rd., Ste.
  C-327
Cypress, TX 77429
Ph: (713)856-6525
Fax: (713)856-6199

Pless, Albert W., President
American Muslim Health Professionals [15438]
2118 Plum Grove Rd., No. 201
Rolling Meadows, IL 60008

Pletcher, Stan, MD, President
Christian Ophthalmology Society
  [16381]
333 Whitesport Ctr., Ste. 101
Huntsville, AL 35801
Ph: (616)439-4267

Pletcher, Valerie Mullen, Chief Dev.
  Ofc.
Million Mom March [18252]
c/o The Brady Campaign to Prevent
  Gun Violence, 840 First St. NE,
  Ste. 400
840 1st St. NE, Ste. 400
Washington, DC 20002
Ph: (202)370-8100

Plitt, Kay, Dir. of Fin.
Friends of Tent of Nations North
  America [12436]
c/o Kay Plitt, Finance Director
5621 N 9th Rd.
Arlington, VA 22205
Ph: (703)524-5657

Plizka, Laura, Asst. Sec., Treasurer
Delta Nu Alpha Transportation
  Fraternity [23981]
1720 Manistique Ave.
South Milwaukee, WI 53172
Ph: (414)764-3063
Fax: (630)499-8505

Plonski, Patrick, Exec. Dir.
Books For Africa [9123]
26 E Exchange St., Ste. 411
Saint Paul, MN 55101
Ph: (651)602-9844
Fax: (651)602-9848

Plotkin, Andrew, President
Edna Hibel Society [9829]
c/o Hibel Museum of Art
5353 Parkside Dr.
Jupiter, FL 33458
Ph: (561)622-5560

Plotz, Mark, Program Mgr.
National Center for Bicycling and
  Walking [22751]
1612 K St. NW, Ste. 802
Washington, DC 20006
Ph: (202)223-3621

Plowman, Jeff, V. Chmn. of the Bd.
Sustainable Biodiesel Alliance [4268]
PO Box 1677
Kahului, HI 96732
Ph: (512)410-7841
Fax: (512)410-7841

Ployhar, Matt, Bd. Member
Open Gaming Alliance [6328]
9450 SW Gemini Dr., No. 67608
Beaverton, OR 97008

Pluimer, Mark, President
One Child Matters [12555]
15475 Gleneagle Dr.
Colorado Springs, CO 80921
Toll Free: 800-864-0200
Fax: (719)481-4649

Plumb, Susan, President
Cherokee National Historical Society
  [10036]
PO Box 515
Tahlequah, OK 74465-0515
Ph: (918)456-6007
Toll Free: 888-999-6007

Plumlee, Mary Ann, Founder
Workroom Resource Group [1964]
802 N Robinson Dr.
Waco, TX 76706
Ph: (254)662-4021
Toll Free: 888-395-1959

Plummer, Beth, Rec. Sec.
Society for Reformation Research
  [20204]
c/o Victoria and Robert Christman,
  Treasurer and Membership
  Secretary
Dept. of History
Luther College
700 College Dr.
Decorah, IA 52101-1045

Plummer, David B., Chairperson
The Coalition of Spirit-filled
  Churches, Inc. [20020]
PO Box 6606
Newport News, VA 23606
Toll Free: 877-208-8189
Fax: (425)977-1360

Plummer, Shari Sant, Director
International League of Conservation
  Photographers [10139]
1003 K St. NW, Ste. 404
Washington, DC 20001
Ph: (202)347-5695

Plutte, Chris, Exec. Dir.
Global Nomads Group [8768]
132 Nassau St., Ste. 822
New York, NY 10038
Ph: (212)529-0377

Poage, Wendy L., President
Prostate Conditions Education
  Council [17555]

7009 S Potomac St., Ste. 125
Centennial, CO 80112
Ph: (303)316-4685
Toll Free: 866-477-6788
Fax: (303)320-3835

Pochatko, Beverly, Secretary
German-American National
  Congress [19444]
4740 N Western Ave., Ste. 206
Chicago, IL 60625-2013
Ph: (773)275-1100
Toll Free: 888-872-3265
Fax: (773)275-4010

Podber, Michael, President
NYPD Shomrim Society [12229]
c/o Murray Ellman, Financial
  Secretary
PO Box 598
New York, NY 10002

Podeschi, David, President
American Recorder Society [9866]
PO Box 480054
Charlotte, NC 28269-5300
Ph: (704)509-1422
Toll Free: 844-509-1422

Podgurski, Walt, CLU, Publisher
Workplace Benefits Association
  [1078]
1770 Breckenridge Pky., Ste. 500
Duluth, GA 30096
Ph: (770)381-2511
Toll Free: 800-221-1809
Fax: (770)935-9484

Podjasek, Mary, President
Diabetes Scholars Foundation
  [14530]
2118 Plum Grove Rd., No. 356
Rolling Meadows, IL 60008
Ph: (312)215-9861
Fax: (847)991-8739

Podlesni, Michelle DeLizio,
  President, CEO
National Nurses in Business As-
  sociation [657]
8941 Atlanta Ave., Ste. 202
Huntington Beach, CA 92646
Toll Free: 877-353-8888

Poe, Melissa, Founder
Kids for a Clean Environment [4079]
PO Box 158254
Nashville, TN 37215
Ph: (615)331-7381

Poe, Shelly, Director
College Sports Information Directors
  of America [23223]
PO Box 7818
Greenwood, IN 46142-6427
Ph: (785)691-7708

Poffenberger, Mark, PhD, Exec. Dir.
Community Forestry International
  [4197]
1356 Mokelumne Dr.
Antioch, CA 94531
Ph: (925)706-2906
Fax: (925)706-2906

Pogacar, Timothy, Treasurer
Society for Slovene Studies [19655]
c/o Raymond Miller, President
381 Cathance Rd.
Topsham, ME 04086

Pohlman, Lindsay, President
Embrace It Africa [11350]
PO Box 25
Saint Bonaventure, NY 14778

Pohlman, Tina, President, Founder,
  Exec. Dir.
APS Foundation of America [13784]
PO Box 801

La Crosse, WI 54602-0801
Ph: (608)782-2626
Fax: (608)782-6569

Pointer, Mary, CFO
Council of International Neonatal
  Nurses [16129]
c/o Carole Kenner, Chief Executive
  Officer
2110 Yardley Rd.
Yardley, PA 19067
Ph: (405)684-1476
Fax: (267)392-5637

Poisant, Molly, Exec. Dir.
International Microwave Power
  Institute [6870]
PO Box 1140
Mechanicsville, VA 23111
Ph: (804)559-6667

Pola, Caryn, President, Chmn. of the
  Bd.
English Springer Rescue America,
  Inc. [10616]
19518 Nashville St.
Northridge, CA 91326-2240

Polapink, Tom, Secretary, Treasurer
World War 1 Aeroplanes [21258]
PO Box 730
Red Hook, NY 12571-0730

Polastre, Shevonne, President
Stop Alcohol Deaths [13185]
12103 Green Leaf Ct., Ste. 202
Fairfax, VA 22033
Fax: (202)670-1448

Polastri, Gonzalo Nicolás Ríos,
  Chairman
Junta Interamericana de Defensa
  [18086]
2600 NW 16th St.
Washington, DC 20441
Ph: (202)939-6041
Fax: (202)319-2791

Poler, Omar, VP
American Indian Library Association
  [9667]
c/o Heather Devine-Hardy, Membership Coordinator
PO Box 41296
San Jose, CA 95160

Poliakoff, Michael B., President
American Council of Trustees and
  Alumni [7405]
1730 M St. NW, Ste. 600
Washington, DC 20036-4525
Ph: (202)467-6787
Fax: (202)467-6784

Policastro, Cosimo, Director
Fragrance Foundation [1451]
621 2nd Ave., 2nd Fl.
New York, NY 10016
Ph: (212)725-2755
Fax: (646)786-3260

Polito, Lisa, Exec. Dir.
Lutheran Deaconess Association
  [20305]
1304 LaPorte Ave.
Valparaiso, IN 46383
Ph: (219)464-6925

Polito, Lisa, Exec. Dir.
Lutheran Deaconess Conference
  [20306]
1304 LaPorte Ave.
Valparaiso, IN 46383
Ph: (219)464-6925
Fax: (219)464-6928

Polito, Robert, President
The Poetry Foundation [10156]
61 W Superior St.

Chicago, IL 60654
Ph: (312)787-7070
Fax: (312)787-6650

Polka, Matthew M., Treasurer
American Cable Association [690]
7 Parkway Ctr., Ste. 755
Pittsburgh, PA 15220
Ph: (412)922-8300
Fax: (412)922-2110

Pollack, Ron, Exec. Dir.
Families U.S.A. Foundation [10506]
1201 New York Ave. NW, Ste. 1100
Washington, DC 20005
Ph: (202)628-3030
Fax: (202)347-2417

Pollack, Ron, Exec. Dir.
Families USA [15001]
1201 New York Ave. NW, Ste. 1100
Washington, DC 20005
Ph: (202)628-3030
Fax: (202)347-2417

Pollack, Susan, Exec. Dir.
Friends of Ethiopian Jews [17977]
PO Box 960059
Boston, MA 02196
Ph: (202)262-5390

Pollak, Thomas H., Prog. Dir.
National Center for Charitable
  Statistics [12489]
Urban Institute
2100 M St. NW, 5th Fl.
Washington, DC 20037
Toll Free: 866-518-3874
Fax: (202)833-6231

Pollard, Eli, Chairman
Global Children [11001]
37 W 28th St., 3rd Fl.
New York, NY 10001
Ph: (917)359-7085

Pollard, Elizabeth, Exec. Dir.
World Parkinson Coalition [16000]
1359 Broadway, Ste. 1509
New York, NY 10018
Ph: (212)923-4700
Fax: (212)923-4778

Pollard, Margie, Exec. Asst.
Thoroughbred Racing Associations
  [22931]
420 Fair Hill Dr., Ste. 1
Elkton, MD 21921-2573
Ph: (410)392-9200
Fax: (410)398-1366

Pollard, Paige, Exec. Dir.
National Alliance of Preservation
  Commissions [9412]
208 E Plume St., Ste. 327
Norfolk, VA 23510
Ph: (757)802-4141

Pollet, Gerry, Exec. Dir.
Heart of America Northwest [18944]
444 NE Ravenna Blvd., Ste. 406
Seattle, WA 98115
Ph: (206)382-1014

Pollin, Irene, PhD, Chairperson
Sister to Sister: The Women's Heart
  Health Foundation [14156]
4701 Willard Ave., Ste. 221
Chevy Chase, MD 20815
Ph: (301)718-8033
Toll Free: 888-718-8033

Pollock, A.D., Jr., President
Clan Pollock International [20837]
PO Box 404
Greenville, KY 42345
Ph: (615)456-1699
Fax: (208)362-5460

Pollock, Alex J., Director
Great Books Foundation [9127]
35 E Wacker Dr., Ste. 400
Chicago, IL 60601-2105
Ph: (312)332-5870
Toll Free: 800-222-5870
Fax: (312)407-0224

Polnick, Barbara, Chairperson
Women Educators [8758]
c/o Paula Lane, Treasurer
School of Education
Sonoma State University
1801 E Cotati
Rohnert Park, CA 94928
Ph: (231)869-5939

Polt, Richard, Editor
Harry Stephen Keeler Society [9069]
4745 Winton Rd.
Cincinnati, OH 45232-1522
Ph: (513)591-1226

Poltrack, David, Chairman
Advertising Research Foundation
  [81]
432 Park Ave. S, 6th Fl.
New York, NY 10016-8013
Ph: (212)751-5656
Fax: (212)319-5265

Pomilia, Joe, Exec. Dir.
Insurance Accounting and Systems
  Association [1862]
3511 Shannon Rd., Ste. 160
Durham, NC 27707
Ph: (919)489-0991
Fax: (919)489-1994

Pomo, Dick, President
United States Blind Golf Association
  [22799]
125 Gilberts Hill Rd.
Lehighton, PA 18235

Ponak, Allen, President
National Academy of Arbitrators
  [4966]
NAA Operations Ctr.
1 N Main St., Ste. 412
Cortland, NY 13045
Ph: (607)756-8363
Toll Free: 888-317-1729

Ponce De Leon, Rusty, Chairman
Association for Advancing Automa-
  tion [6016]
900 Victors Way, Ste. 140
Ann Arbor, MI 48108
Ph: (734)994-6088
Fax: (734)994-3338

Poncher, Dennis, Founder
Because I Love You: The Parent
  Support Group [13201]
PO Box 2062
Winnetka, CA 91396-2062
Ph: (818)884-8242

Ponder, Steve, Exec. Dir.
Geothermal Resources Council
  [6690]
630 Pena Dr., Ste. 400
Davis, CA 95618
Ph: (530)758-2360
Fax: (530)758-2839

Ponsky, Todd A., MD, Secretary
International Pediatric Endosurgery
  Group [16609]
11300 W Olympic Blvd., Ste. 600
Los Angeles, CA 90064
Ph: (310)437-0553
Fax: (310)437-0585

Ponts, Jeff, President
Technology Channel Association
  [7658]

191 Clarksville Rd.
Princeton Junction, NJ 08550-5391
Ph: (609)799-4900
Fax: (609)799-7032

Pool, Jeannie, Secretary
American Society of Music Arrangers
  and Composers [9869]
5903 Noble Ave.
Van Nuys, CA 91411
Ph: (818)994-4661

Poole, Kathy, Exec. Dir.
AHA International [8051]
1585 E 13th Ave., No. 333
Eugene, OR 97403
Ph: (541)346-5888
Toll Free: 800-654-2051
Fax: (541)346-9100

Poole, Dr. Kenneth E., Exec. Dir.
Council for Community and
  Economic Research [23577]
1700 N Moore St., Ste. 2225
Arlington, VA 22209
Ph: (703)522-4980
Fax: (480)393-5098

Poole, Tony, President
Document Security Alliance [5302]
204 E St. NE
Washington, DC 20002
Ph: (202)543-5552
Fax: (202)547-6348

Pooley, Mr. Albert M., Founder,
  President
Native American Fatherhood and
  Families Association [12420]
1215 E Brown Rd.
Mesa, AZ 85203
Ph: (480)833-5007

Poore, Mr. Paul, Exec. Dir.
Association of American Schools in
  South America [8101]
1911 NW 150 Ave., Ste. 101
Pembroke Pines, FL 33028
Ph: (954)436-4034
Fax: (954)436-4092

Popal, Heela, President
Unclaimed Property Professionals
  Organization [5689]
8441 Wayzata Blvd., Ste. 270
Minneapolis, MN 55426
Ph: (763)253-4340

Pope, Gene, President
Junior Shag Association [9265]
c/o Gene Pope, President
3753 E Geer St.
Durham, NC 27704
Ph: (919)682-4266

Pope, Michael, Dir. Ed.
Electrical Generating Systems As-
  sociation [1019]
1650 S Dixie Hwy., Ste. 400
Boca Raton, FL 33432
Ph: (561)750-5575
Fax: (561)395-8557

Pope-Levison, Priscilla, President
Historical Society of the United
  Methodist Church [9482]
c/o Priscilla Pope-Levison, President
Seattle Pacific University
3307 3rd Ave. W
Seattle, WA 98119

Popenoe, Dr. Hugh, Founder
American Water Buffalo Association
  [4453]
2415 N Mosley Rd.
Texarkana, AR 71854

Popow, Dre, Exec. Ofc.
Veterans Rebuilding Life [13253]
PO Box 327

Glen Cove, NY 11542
Ph: (212)560-2235

Popper, Eric, President
Organized Flying Adjusters [1916]
1380 W Hume Rd.
Lima, OH 45806-1860
Ph: (567)712-2097
Fax: (800)207-9324

Poprac, John, President
Christian Family Movement [11815]
PO Box 540550
Omaha, NE 68154
Toll Free: 800-581-9824
Fax: (888)354-1094

Porcino, Antony, Secretary
International Society for
  Complementary Medicine
  Research [13637]

Porr, Susannah F., Exec. Dir.
National Association of Steel Pipe
  Distributors [2607]
1501 E Mockingbird Ln., Ste. 307
Victoria, TX 77904
Ph: (361)574-7878
Fax: (832)201-9479

Porr, Valerie, MA, Founder,
  President
Treatment and Research Advance-
  ments Association for Personality
  Disorder [15810]
23 Greene St.
New York, NY 10013
Ph: (212)966-6514

Porrata, Trinka, President
Project GHB [13176]
2753 E Broadway Rd., Ste. 101
PMB 434
Mesa, AZ 85204
Ph: (480)219-1180

Porte, Phillip, Exec. Dir.
National Association for Medical
  Direction of Respiratory Care
  [15587]
8618 Westwood Center Dr., Ste. 210
Vienna, VA 22182-2222
Ph: (703)752-4359
Fax: (703)752-4360

Porter, Christine, President
National C Scow Sailing Association
  [22650]
N30 W29273A Hillcrest Dr.
Pewaukee, WI 53072

Porter, Dr. John, Exec. Dir.
American Grant Writers' Association
  [12459]
13801 Walsingham Rd., No. A-410
Largo, FL 33774
Ph: (727)596-5150
Fax: (727)596-5192

Porter, Johnny W., Exec. Dir.
Kappa Psi Pharmaceutical Fraternity,
  Inc. [23844]
2060 N Collins Blvd., Ste. 128
Richardson, TX 75080-2657
Ph: (972)479-1879
Fax: (972)231-5171

Porter, Lana G., President
Leadership Women [8749]
25 Highland Park Village, No. 100-
  371
Dallas, TX 75205
Ph: (214)421-5566

Porter, Martin, Exec. Dir.
Content Delivery and Storage Association [1189]
39 N Bayles Ave.

Port Washington, NY 11050
Ph: (516)767-6720
Fax: (516)883-5793

Porter, Matt, Contact
Young Democratic Socialists [19147]
75 Maiden Ln., Ste. 702
New York, NY 10038
Ph: (212)727-8610
Fax: (212)608-6955

Porter, Pamela, MA, President
National Association of Psychometrists [16927]
275 Century Circle, Ste 203
275 Century Cir., Ste. 203
Louisville, CO 80027

Porter, Rod
Children's Organ Transplant As-
sociation [14183]
2501 W COTA Dr.
Bloomington, IN 47403
Toll Free: 800-366-2682
Fax: (812)336-8885

Porter, Ron, President
Showmen's League of America
[1159]
1023 W Fulton Market
Chicago, IL 60607
Ph: (312)733-9533
Fax: (312)733-9534

Porter, York, President
Immortalist Society [6356]
24355 Sorrentino Ct.
Clinton Township, MI 48035-3229
Ph: (586)791-5961

Porterfield, Naomi, Chmn. of the Bd.,
Founder
Pink Isn't Always Pretty [14046]
PO Box 697
Fresno, TX 77545-0697
Toll Free: 877-495-7427

Porterfield, Robert, President
Naval Intelligence Professionals
[5614]
PO Box 11579
Burke, VA 22009-1579

Portier, William, President
College Theology Society [8707]
c/o Brian Flanagan, Treasurer
Marymount University
Butler Hall
2807 N Glebe Rd.
Arlington, VA 22207
Ph: (937)229-4435
      (703)284-6516

Portillo, Tom, President
Academy of Veterinary Consultants
[17586]
PO Box 24305
Overland Park, KS 66283
Ph: (913)766-4373
Fax: (913)766-0474

Portnow, Neil, President, CEO
GRAMMY Foundation [9912]
3030 Olympic Blvd.
Santa Monica, CA 90404
Ph: (310)392-3777
Fax: (310)392-2188

Portnoy, Elliott I., President
Kids Enjoy Exercise Now [14552]
1301 K St. NW, Ste. 600
Washington, DC 20005
Toll Free: 866-903-5336
Fax: (866)597-5336

Portnoy, Steven, President
Men of Reform Judaism [20265]
633 3rd Ave.

New York, NY 10017
Ph: (212)650-4100

Porto, Ed, President
Federation of Petanque U.S.A.
[23058]
PO Box 180
Kenwood, CA 95452

Posner, Louis, Esq., Director,
Founder
Voter Rights March [18187]
PO Box 3275
New York, NY 10163

Possiel, Bill, President
National Forest Foundation [3904]
Bldg. 27, Ste. 3
Fort Missoula Rd.
Missoula, MT 59804-7212
Ph: (406)542-2805
Fax: (406)542-2810

Post, Carol, President
The Protein Society [6060]
PO Box 9397
Glendale, CA 91226
Fax: (844)377-6834

Post, Mary E., MBA, Exec. Dir.
American Board of Anesthesiology
[13691]
4208 Six Forks Rd., Ste. 1500
Raleigh, NC 27609-5765
Toll Free: 866-999-7501
Fax: (866)999-7503

Post, Whitney, Treasurer
Eating for Life Alliance [14638]
396 Washington St., Ste. 392
Wellesley, MA 02481

Postlethwait, David, President
U.S.A. Ploughing Organization
[4169]
c/o Roger Neate, Secretary/
Treasurer
14837 Greenville Rd.
Van Wert, OH 45891

Postma, Kathlene, Chairwoman
Fuling Kids International [10990]
6110 Kestrel Park Dr.
Lithia, FL 33547

Potakis, Mr. Evangelos, Trustee
Pan Arcadian Federation of America
[19456]
880 N York Rd.
Elmhurst, IL 60126
Ph: (630)833-1900

Potegal, Mike, President
International Society for Research
on Aggression [6043]
c/o Eric F. Dubow, PhD, Treasurer
Dept. of Psychology
Bowling Green State University
Bowling Green, OH 43403-0232
Fax: (419)372-6013

Potente, Daniel, President
United Peafowl Association [3673]
c/o Loretta Smith, Vice President/
Membership
5156A US Highway 52
Stout, OH 45684
Ph: (740)935-6556

Poterba, James, CEO, President
National Bureau of Economic
Research [6397]
1050 Massachusetts Ave.
Cambridge, MA 02138-5398
Ph: (617)868-3900
Fax: (617)868-2742

Pothier, Diane, Editor, Dir. Ed.
American Society of Abdominal
Surgeons [17370]

824 Main St., 2nd Fl., Ste. 1
Melrose, MA 02176
Ph: (781)665-6102
Fax: (781)665-4127

Potrzebowski, Patricia, PhD, Exec.
Dir.
National Association for Public
Health Statistics and Information
Systems [5718]
962 Wayne Ave., Ste. 701
Silver Spring, MD 20910
Ph: (301)563-6001
Fax: (301)563-6012

Potter, Adam, Exec. Dir.
Claims and Litigation Management
Alliance [5528]
4100 S Hospital Dr., Ste. 209
Plantation, FL 33317
Ph: (954)587-2488

Potter, Barry, VP of Personnel
OMF International U.S. [20450]
10 W Dry Creek Cir.
Littleton, CO 80120-4413
Ph: (303)730-4165
Toll Free: 800-422-5330

Potter, Bob, Chairman
Joint Labor Management Committee
of the Retail Food Industry [23418]
2153 Wealthy St. SE
Grand Rapids, MI 49506
Toll Free: 800-304-5540
Fax: (248)274-1036

Potter, Bruce, President
Island Resources Foundation [4495]
1718 P St. NW, Ste. T-4
Washington, DC 20036
Ph: (202)265-9712
Fax: (202)232-0748

Potter, Donna, President, Genealo-
gist, Editor
Crandall Family Association [20850]
PO Box 1472
Westerly, RI 02891-0907

Potter, Mr. Edward, CAE, Director
International Cooperative and Mutual
Insurance Federation/Regional As-
sociation for The Americas [1878]
1775 Eye St., NW 8th Fl.
Washington, DC 20006-2402
Ph: (202)442-2305
Fax: (202)318-0753

Potter, Nancy Nyquist, PhD, Exec.
Association for the Advancement of
Philosophy and Psychiatry [8419]
c/o Claire Pouncey, President
Eudaimonia Associates, LLC
210 W Rittenhouse Sq., Ste. 404
Philadelphia, PA 19103
Ph: (215)545-9700

Potter, Sandra, CEO, Founder
Dreamcatchers for Abused Children
[10794]
c/o Sandra Potter, Chief Executive
Officer/Founder
PO Box 142
Peck, MI 48466
Ph: (810)275-0755

Potter, Shelley Eubanks, President
Chi Omega [23949]
3395 Players Club Pky.
Memphis, TN 38125
Ph: (901)748-8600
Fax: (901)748-8686

Potter, Sheri, Project Mgr.
Coalition on the Public Understanding of Science [7127]
American Institute of Biological Sciences

1900 Campus Commons Dr., Ste.
200
Reston, VA 20191
Ph: (571)748-4415
Fax: (703)674-2509

Potts, Kyle, President
Chihuahua Club of America [21854]
c/o Craig Eugene, Membership
Chairman
24515 Anthony Rd.
Marengo, IL 60152
Ph: (815)568-6450

Potts, Liza, Chairperson
Association for Computing
Machinery - Special Interest Group
on Design of Communication
[6308]
2 Penn Plz., Ste. 701
New York, NY 10121-0701
Ph: (212)626-0500
Toll Free: 800-342-6626
Fax: (212)944-1318

Potts, Tricia, Exec. Dir.
Antique Caterpillar Machinery Own-
ers Club [21619]
7501 N University St., Ste. 117
Peoria, IL 61614
Ph: (309)691-5002
Fax: (309)296-4518

Potvin, Gary, President
Commercial Food Equipment
Service Association [1381]
3605 Centre Cir.
Fort Mill, SC 29715
Ph: (336)346-4700
Fax: (336)346-4745

Poulin, Brian, President
Institute for Responsible Housing
Preservation [5278]
799 9th St., NW Ste. 500
Washington, DC 20001
Ph: (202)737-0019
Fax: (202)737-0021

Poulin, Lucy, Exec. Dir.
Homeworkers Organized for More
Employment [11765]
90 School House Rd.
Orland, ME 04472
Ph: (207)469-7961
Fax: (207)469-1023

Poulos, Harry, Treasurer
Pickard Collectors Club [21714]
PO Box 317
Glencoe, IL 60022

Pound, William T., Exec. Dir.
National Council of State
Legislatures [18330]
7700 E 1st Pl.
Denver, CO 80230
Ph: (303)364-7700
Fax: (303)364-7800

Pourier, Cholena, Exec. Dir.
Native American Coalition for
Healthy Alternatives [12382]
1038 E Tallent St.
Rapid City, SD 57701
Ph: (605)891-9413
Fax: (605)791-5225

Pover, Peter, President
U.S.A. Dance [9272]
PO Box 152988
Cape Coral, FL 33915-2988
Toll Free: 800-447-9047
Fax: (239)573-0946

Powell, Abby, Secretary
Cooper Ornithological Society [6956]
c/o Martin Raphael, President

3625 93rd Ave. SW
Olympia, WA 98512
Ph: (360)753-7662

Powell, Allen C., Exec. Dir.
National Technical Honor Society
[23985]
PO Box 1336
Flat Rock, NC 28731
Ph: (828)698-8011
Fax: (828)698-8564

Powell, Claudia, Exec. Dir.
Women's International Network of
Utility Professionals [1035]
PO Box 64
Grove City, OH 43123-0064

Powell, Don R., PhD, CEO,
President
American Institute for Preventive
Medicine [16799]
30445 Northwestern Hwy., Ste. 350
Farmington Hills, MI 48334
Ph: (248)539-1800
Toll Free: 800-345-2476
Fax: (248)539-1808

Powell, Doug, President,
Chairperson
Professional Electrical Apparatus
Recyclers League [1033]
10200 W 44th Ave., Ste. 304
Wheat Ridge, CO 80033
Ph: (720)881-6043
Fax: (720)881-6101

Powell, Geoffrey, President
National Customs Brokers and
Forwarders Association of America,
Inc. [1989]
1200 18th St. NW, No. 901
Washington, DC 20036
Ph: (202)466-0222
Fax: (202)466-0226

Powell, Jeff, Mem.
Unlimited Scale Racing Association
[22207]
PO Box 819
Brea, CA 92822
Ph: (214)649-8342
      (714)255-7488

Powell, Kimberly T., President
Association of Professional Genealo-
gists [20957]
PO Box 535
Wheat Ridge, CO 80034-0535
Ph: (303)465-6980

Powell, Linda, Secretary
DeLorean Owners Association
[21369]
879 Randolph Rd.
Santa Barbara, CA 93111
Ph: (805)964-5296

Powell, Lynne, Exec. Dir.
Institute of Certified Professional
Managers [2170]
c/o James Madison University
800 S Main St.
Harrisonburg, VA 22807
Ph: (540)568-3247

Powell, Michael, President, CEO
National Cable and Telecommunica-
tions Association [475]
25 Massachusetts Ave. NW, Ste.
100
Washington, DC 20001
Ph: (202)222-2300
Fax: (202)222-2514

Powell, Norman S., Chairman
Caucus for Producers, Writers &
Directors [17938]

PO Box 11236
Burbank, CA 91510-1236
Ph: (818)843-7572
Fax: (818)221-0347

Powell, Robert, Chairman
ManKind Project [12874]
PO Box 383
Kaysville, UT 84037
Toll Free: 800-870-4611
Fax: (800)405-7840

Powell, R.Todd, VP
Association for Non-Traditional
Students in Higher Education
[7453]
19134 Olde Waterford Rd.
Hagerstown, MD 21742
Ph: (301)992-2901
Fax: (301)766-9162

Powell, Shirley, President
Chihuahuan Desert Research
Institute [3828]
43869 State Hwy. 19
Fort Davis, TX 79734
Ph: (432)364-2499
Fax: (432)364-2686

Powell, Suzanne, Contact
Utility Technology Association [7358]
PO Box 695
Clermont, GA 30527
Ph: (770)519-1676

Powell, Thomas, Exec. Dir.
American Meat Science Association
[6639]
1 E Main St., Ste. 200
Champaign, IL 61820
Ph: (217)356-5370
Toll Free: 800-517-AMSA
Fax: (217)356-5370

Powell, Victoria, RN, President
American Association of Nurse Life
Care Planners [16095]
3267 East 3300 South, No. 309
Salt Lake City, UT 84109
Ph: (801)274-1184
Fax: (801)274-1535

Power, Jane Routt, President
Hereditary Order of the Families of
the Presidents and First Ladies of
America [21080]
1716 Bigley Ave.
Charleston, WV 25302-3938

Power, Kristin, Contact
Automotive Specialty Products Alli-
ance [285]
1667 K St. NW, Ste. 300
Washington, DC 20006
Ph: (202)833-7308
Fax: (202)223-2636

Power, Mary E., CAE, President,
CEO
U.S. Council of Better Business
Bureaus [671]
3033 Wilson Blvd., Ste. 600
Arlington, VA 22201
Ph: (703)276-0100

Powers, D. J., President
Association for Neurologically
Impaired Children [15906]
2109 Eva St.
Austin, TX 78704
Ph: (972)264-7983

Powers, Daryle, President
Saab Club of North America [21487]
30 Puritan Dr.
Port Chester, NY 10573-2504

Powers, Jeremy, Founder
Rural Education and Community
Health for Ghana [11932]

PO Box 889
Richmond, VA 23218
Ph: (804)925-8548

Powers, Mary Beth, CEO
SeriousFun Children's Network
[11149]
228 Saugatuck Ave.
Westport, CT 06880
Ph: (203)562-1203
Fax: (203)341-8707

Powsner, Laurie, President
Funeral Consumers Alliance [2404]
33 Patchen Rd.
South Burlington, VT 05403
Ph: (802)865-8300
Fax: (802)865-2626

Poynor, Phil, VP of Government
Rel., VP of Indl. Rel.
National Association of Flight
Instructors [150]
3101 E Milham Ave.
Portage, MI 49002
Toll Free: 866-806-6156

Poynter, R. Kinney, Exec. Dir.
National Association of State Audi-
tors, Comptrollers, and Treasurers
[5708]
449 Lewis Hargett Cir., Ste. 290
Lexington, KY 40503-3669
Ph: (859)276-1147
Fax: (859)278-0507

Pozzi, Ambra, Secretary, Treasurer
American Society for Matrix Biology
[6070]
c/o Kendra LaDuca, Executive Director
9650 Rockville Pke.
Bethesda, MD 20814
Ph: (301)634-7456
Fax: (301)634-7455

Prabasi, Sarina, CEO
WaterAid America, Inc. [13348]
315 Madison Ave., Rm. 2301
New York, NY 10017
Ph: (212)683-0430
      (202)833-1341
Fax: (212)683-0293

Prado, Eileen, Exec. Dir.
Solar Rating and Certification
Corporation [7211]
500 New Jersey Ave., 6th Fl. NW
Washington, DC 20001
Ph: (321)213-6037
Toll Free: 888-422-7233
Fax: (321)821-0910

Prager, Dr. Martin, President
Materials Properties Council [6848]
c/o Welding Research Council
PO Box 201547
Shaker Heights, OH 44120-8109
Ph: (216)658-3847
Fax: (216)658-3854

Prager, Dr. Martin, Contact
Pressure Vessel Research Council
[2615]
c/o Welding Research Council
PO Box 201547
Shaker Heights, OH 44122
Ph: (216)658-3847
Fax: (216)658-3854

Prager, Peter, President
Sweet and Fortified Wine Associa-
tion [3481]
PO Box 193
Applegate, CA 95703
Ph: (916)258-7115

Prahlad, Mr. K.C., President
NRN National Coordination Council
of U.S. [19593]

48 Garden St.
Cambridge, MA 02138
Ph: (617)640-1390
Fax: (617)267-1617

Prakash, Suresh, President
U.S.A. Sanatan Sports and Cultural
Association [23198]
PO Box 5050
Elk Grove, CA 95758

Prall, Richard D., Editor
Prall Family Association [20916]
14104 Piedras Rd. NE
14104 Piedras Rd. NE
Albuquerque, NM 87123

Prasad, Kailash, MD, Chmn. of the
Bd.
International College of Angiology
[17574]
161 Morin Dr.
Jay, VT 05859-9283
Ph: (802)988-4065
Fax: (802)988-4066

Prasad, Kathleen, President
Shelter Animal Reiki Association
[17103]
369B 3rd St., No. 156
San Rafael, CA 94901

Prasun, Marilyn A., President
American Association of Heart
Failure Nurses [16089]
1120 Route 73, Ste. 200
Mount Laurel, NJ 08054
Toll Free: 888-452-2436
Fax: (856)439-0525

Prater, Marcus, Exec. Dir.
Association of Gaming Equipment
Manufacturers [22060]
c/o Marcus Prater, Executive Direc-
tor
PO Box 50049
Henderson, NV 89016-0049
Ph: (702)812-6932

Prato, Bonnie, President
American Shih Tzu Club, Inc.
[21822]

Pratt, Anthony P., President
American Shore & Beach Preserva-
tion Association [3805]
5460 Beaujolais Ln.
Fort Myers, FL 33919
Ph: (239)489-2616
Fax: (239)362-9771

Pratt, Anthony, Officer
Society of Automotive Analysts [302]
1729 Southfield Rd.
Birmingham, MI 48009
Ph: (248)804-6433

Pratt, Elieen, Contact
Dachshund Rescue of North
America [10610]
c/o Elieen Pratt
1197 Allaire Loop
The Villages, FL 32163

Pratt, James W., Exec. Sec.
American Forensic Association
[8592]
PO Box 256
River Falls, WI 54022
Ph: (715)425-3198
Toll Free: 800-228-5424
Fax: (715)425-9533

Pratt, Larry, Exec. Dir.
Gun Owners of America [5217]
8001 Forbes Pl., Ste. 102
Springfield, VA 22151
Ph: (703)321-8585
Fax: (703)321-8408

Pratt, Michael, Chairman
International Christian Accrediting
Association **[20083]**
2448 E 81st St., Ste. 600
Tulsa, OK 74137
Ph: (918)493-8880
Fax: (918)493-8041

Pratt, Mike, President
The Scherman Foundation **[13088]**
16 E 52nd St., Ste. 601
New York, NY 10022
Ph: (212)832-3086
Fax: (212)838-0154

Pratt, Robert L., Chmn. of the Bd.
International Institute for Energy
Conservation **[6493]**
1850 Centennial Park Dr., Ste. 105
Reston, VA 20191
Ph: (443)934-2279

Preble, Christopher, PhD, Exec. Dir.,
Founder
Coalition for a Realistic Foreign
Policy **[18264]**
1220 L St. NW, Ste. 100-221
Washington, DC 20005-4018

Precop, Jessica, Officer
American Romanian Orthodox Youth
[20590]
c/o Stephen Maxim, President
832 Indian Lake Rd.
Lake Orion, MI 48362
Ph: (586)260-3342

Preidis, Geoff, Founder, President
Health Empowering Humanity
[15011]
PO Box 300618
Houston, TX 77230

Preiss, Paul, CEO, Founder
International Association of Software
Architects **[6277]**
12325 Hymeadow Dr., Ste. 2-200
Austin, TX 78750-1847
Ph: (512)637-4272
Toll Free: 866-399-4272
Fax: (512)382-5327

Preisser, Bernhard, President
Catholic Kolping Society of America
[19812]
c/o Bernhard Preisser, President
19 Revere Rd.
Ardsley, NY 10502-1219
Ph: (914)693-5537
   (516)364-0800
Fax: (516)364-0802

Prelozni, Sue, MA, Founder, Exec.
Dir.
Sustainable Surplus Exchange
[3953]
2647 Gateway Rd., Ste. 105-404
Carlsbad, CA 92009
Ph: (760)736-4416

Prendergast, John, Director
Enough Project **[18304]**
1333 H St. NW, 10th Fl.
Washington, DC 20005
Ph: (202)682-1611
Fax: (202)682-6140

Prendergast, John, Treasurer
North American Manx Association
[19545]
1751 Olde Towne Rd.
Alexandria, VA 22307-1457
Ph: (703)718-0172
   (410)531-6685

Prentice, E. Miles, III, Chmn. of the
Bd.
Center for Security Policy **[7152]**

1901 Pennsylvania Ave. NW, Ste.
201
Washington, DC 20006
Ph: (202)835-9077

Prentice, Elisabeth, President
Educate the Children International
[11227]
PO Box 414
Ithaca, NY 14851-0414
Ph: (607)272-1176

Prescott, Carol, Exec.
Behavior Genetics Association
[14878]
Dept. of Psychology and Neurosci-
ence
University of Colorado
Boulder, CO 80309

Presley, Sharon, Exec. Dir.
Association of Libertarian Feminists
[18639]
1155C Arnold Dr., No. 418
Martinez, CA 94553
Ph: (925)228-0565

Presley, Sharon, PhD, Exec. Dir.
Resources for Independent Thinking
[10116]
39 California St., No. 153
Valley Springs, CA 95252-8777
Ph: (209)772-2721
Fax: (925)391-3515

Press, Dr. Stephen J., DC, Chairman
International Academy of Olympic
Chiropractic Officers **[14272]**
546 Broad Ave.
Englewood, NJ 07631
Ph: (201)569-1444

Presson, Greg, CEO, President
American Alliance of Ethical Movers
[824]
118A Gerloff Rd.
Schwenksville, PA 19473
Toll Free: 888-764-2936

Preston, Drew, DDS, President
Society of American Indian Dentists
[14469]
3940 Laurel Canyon Blvd., No. 1068
Studio City, CA 91604

Preston, Jim, Gen. Sec.
Red River Valley Fighter Pilots As-
sociation **[21138]**
PO Box 1553
Front Royal, VA 22630-0033
Ph: (540)636-9798
Fax: (540)636-9776

Preston, Joanne C., Editor
International Society for Organization
Development and Change **[2462]**
PO Box 50827
Colorado Springs, CO 80949

Preston, Kenneth O., Director
Homes for Our Troops **[21124]**
6 Main St.
Taunton, MA 02780
Toll Free: 866-787-6677

Preston, Stephen W., Gen. Counsel
Military Reporters and Editors **[5683]**
Medill School of Journalism
1325 G St. NW, Ste. 730
Washington, DC 20005

Preus, Anthony, Secretary
Society for Ancient Greek
Philosophy **[10120]**
Binghamton University
Binghamton, NY 13902-6000
Ph: (607)777-2886
   (607)777-2646
Fax: (607)777-6255

Prevratil, Deborah, Exec. Dir.
International Veterinary Acupuncture
Society **[17652]**
1730 S College Ave., Ste. 301
Fort Collins, CO 80525
Ph: (970)266-0666
Fax: (970)266-0777

Prewitt, Jean M., President, CEO
Independent Film & Television Alli-
ance **[1192]**
10850 Wilshire Blvd., 9th Fl.
Los Angeles, CA 90024-4321
Ph: (310)446-1000
Fax: (310)446-1600

Prewitt, Orvalene, President
National Chronic Fatigue Syndrome
and Fibromyalgia Association
[14600]
PO Box 18426
Kansas City, MO 64133-8426
Ph: (816)737-1343
Fax: (816)524-6782

Prewitt, Stephen R., Mem.
Grand Lodge Order of the Sons of
Hermann in Texas **[19485]**
515 S Saint Mary St.
San Antonio, TX 78205
Ph: (210)226-9261
Toll Free: 800-234-4124
Fax: (210)892-0299

Prewitt, Steve, President
Mustang Club of America **[21446]**
4051 Barrancas Ave.
Pensacola, FL 32507
Ph: (850)438-0626

Prey, Dr. John H., Secretary
Delta Sigma Delta **[23718]**
c/o Dr. John Prey, Supreme Scribe
296 15th Ave.
Nekoosa, WI 54457
Ph: (715)325-6320
Toll Free: 800-335-8744
Fax: (715)325-3057

Pribe, Bill, President
Inter-Lake Yachting Association
[22622]
18705 Mt. Pleasant Dr.
Chagrin Falls, OH 44023-6061
Ph: (440)543-5008

Price, Barbara, Secretary
Epsilon Sigma Alpha **[23872]**
363 W Drake Rd.
Fort Collins, CO 80526
Ph: (970)223-2824
Fax: (970)223-4456

Price, Dr. Francis, Jr., President,
Founder
Cornea Research Foundation of
America **[15642]**
9002 N Meridian St., Ste. 212
Indianapolis, IN 46260
Ph: (317)814-2993
Fax: (317)814-2806

Price, Jane, President
American Singles Golf Association
[22874]
1122 Industrial Dr., Ste. 170
Matthews, NC 28105
Ph: (980)833-6450
Toll Free: 888-465-3628
Fax: (704)889-4607

Price, Kevin, Exec. Dir.
United States Hunter Jumper As-
sociation **[22951]**
3870 Cigar Ln.
Lexington, KY 40511-8931
Ph: (859)225-6700
Fax: (859)258-9033

Price, Marilyn, Director
Trips for Kids **[7899]**
138 Sunnyside Ave.
Mill Valley, CA 94941
Ph: (415)458-2986

Price, Michele, VMD, Contact
American Association of Housecall
and Mobile Veterinarians **[17597]**
c/o Around Town Mobile Veterinary
Clinic
9030 Sainsbury Ct.
Bristow, VA 20136
Ph: (703)753-7988

Price, Rusty, President
International Slurry Surfacing As-
sociation **[538]**
3 Church Cir., PMB 250
Annapolis, MD 21401
Ph: (410)267-0023
Fax: (410)267-7546

Price, Thomas M., M.D., VP
Society for Reproductive Endocrinol-
ogy and Infertility **[17128]**
1209 Montgomery Hwy.
Birmingham, AL 35216
Ph: (205)978-5000
Fax: (205)978-5005

Price, Tom, Curator
James K. Polk Memorial Association
[10334]
301-305 W 7th St.
Columbia, TN 38401
Ph: (931)388-2354

Price, Winston, MD, President,
Chairman
National African American Drug
Policy Coalition **[13158]**
2900 Van Ness St. NW
Washington, DC 20008
Ph: (202)577-8365

Price, Yolanda
National Association of Volunteer
Programs in Local Government
[13303]
c/o Kay Sibetta, President
75 Langley Dr.
Lawrenceville, GA 30046

Prichard, Rev. Robert W., President
Historical Society of the Episcopal
Church **[20109]**
82 Cherry Ct.
Appleton, WI 54915
Ph: (920)383-1910

Pride, Eric, Treasurer
Association for Astrological Network-
ing **[5988]**
8306 Wilshire Blvd., PMB 537
Beverly Hills, CA 90211
Ph: (404)477-4121

Pridgen, Cindi, Exec. Dir.
Zero Balancing Health Association
[15273]
8640 Guilford Rd., Ste. 241
Columbia, MD 21046-2667
Ph: (410)381-8956
Fax: (410)381-9634

Priebus, Reince, Chairman
Republican National Committee
[19049]
310 1st St. SE
Washington, DC 20003
Ph: (202)863-8500

Priest, Dannis, President
National Association of Independent
Labor **[23433]**
One City Ctr., Ste. 300
11815 Fountain Way

Newport News, VA 23606
Ph: (757)926-5216
Fax: (757)926-5204

Priest, Doug, PhD, Exec. Dir.
Christian Missionary Fellowship
[20400]
5525 E 82nd St.
Indianapolis, IN 46250
Ph: (317)578-2700
Fax: (317)578-2827

Priestas, Matt, President
Association of Public Pension Fund
Auditors [23490]
PO Box 16064
Columbus, OH 43216-6064

Priester, Andy, Chairman
National Air Transportation Associa-
tion [147]
818 Connecticut Ave. NW, Ste. 900
Washington, DC 20006
Ph: (202)774-1535
Toll Free: 800-808-6282
Fax: (202)452-0837

Priestley, Raymond, President
Colorado School of Mines Alumni
Association [23675]
PO Box 1410
Golden, CO 80402
Ph: (303)273-3295
Toll Free: 800-446-9488
Fax: (303)273-3583

Prince, Janice, Operations Mgr.
Spotted Saddle Horse Breeders' and
Exhibitors Association [4413]
PO Box 1046
Shelbyville, TN 37162
Ph: (931)684-7496
Fax: (931)684-7215

Prince, Nancy, VP
The International Bengal Cat Society
[3679]
7915 S Emerson Ave., Ste. B 142
Indianapolis, IN 46237

Prince, Vicky, Secretary
Society for Developmental Biology
[6098]
9650 Rockville Pke.
Bethesda, MD 20814-3998
Ph: (301)634-7815
Fax: (301)634-7825

Princing, Chris, Comm. Chm.
International J/22 Class Association
[22633]
12900 Lake Ave., No. 2001
Lakewood, OH 44107
Ph: (216)226-4411

Principato, Greg, President
Airports Council International - North
America [126]
1615 L St. NW, Ste. 300
Washington, DC 20036
Ph: (202)293-8500
Toll Free: 888-424-7767
Fax: (202)331-1362

Principato, Greg, President, CEO
National Association of State Avia-
tion Officials [5060]
8400 Westpark Dr., 2nd Fl.
McLean, VA 22102
Ph: (703)417-1880
Fax: (703)417-1885

Prinz, Mechthild, VP
International Society for Forensic
Genetics [14774]
c/o Mechthild Prinz, President
Dept. of Sciences
John Jay College of Criminal Justice

524 W 59th St.
New York, NY 10019

Prior, E. J., Treasurer
National Council on International
Trade Development [1970]
1901 Pennsylvania Ave. NW, Ste.
804
Washington, DC 20006-3438
Ph: (202)872-9280
Fax: (202)293-0495

Priore, Anthony, VP of Mktg., VP,
Comm.
Council of Residential Specialists
[2855]
430 N Michigan Ave., 3rd Fl.
Chicago, IL 60611
Ph: (312)321-4400
Toll Free: 800-462-8841
Fax: (312)329-8551

Priser, Michael, VP, Secretary,
Treasurer
Federal Education Association
[23409]
1201 16th St. NW, Ste. 117
Washington, DC 20036-3201
Ph: (202)822-7850
Fax: (202)822-7867

Pritchard, J. Russ, Jr., President
ASCEND Foundation [13889]
PO Box 80925
Charleston, SC 29416
Ph: (843)225-4055

Pritchard, Jack, Contact
National Welsh-American Founda-
tion [19688]
c/o Jack Pritchard, NWAF
24 Carverton Rd.
Shavertown, PA 18708-1711
Ph: (717)696-1525
Fax: (717)696-1808

Pritchard, Dr. Robert Starling, II,
Chairman, Founder
Panamerican/Panafrican Association
[18078]
3986 Melting Snow Pl.
Dumfries, VA 22025
Ph: (202)487-4143
Fax: (703)373-2347

Pritchard-Kerr, Mrs. Jory, Exec. Dir.
Association for Healthcare
Philanthropy [15314]
313 Park Ave., Ste. 400
Falls Church, VA 22046
Ph: (703)532-6243
Fax: (703)532-7170

Pritchartt, Day Smith, Exec. Dir.
Evangelical Education Society of the
Episcopal Church [20105]
PO Box 7297
Arlington, VA 22207
Ph: (703)807-1862

Pritcher, Mark, President
Chet Atkins Appreciation Society
[24025]
c/o Mark Pritcher, President
3716 Timberlake Rd.
Knoxville, TN 37920
Ph: (865)577-2828

Pritchett, Tony, Contact
Southwest Bluegrass Association
[10014]
PO Box 720974
Pinon Hills, CA 92372-0974

Pritts, Marvin, VP
American Pomological Society
[4227]
102 Tyson Bldg.

University Park, PA 16802
Ph: (814)863-6163
Fax: (814)863-6139

Probst, Lawrence F., III, Chmn. of
the Bd.
United States Olympic Committee
[23049]
1 Olympic Plz.
Colorado Springs, CO 80909
Ph: (719)632-5551
    (719)866-4618
Toll Free: 888-222-2313

Probst, Maralyn R., Exec. Sec.
Veterinary Orthopedic Society
[17674]
PO Box 665
Parker, CO 80134
Ph: (720)335-6051

Prochazka, Scott, Chairman
GridWise Alliance, Inc. [6487]
1800 M St. NW, Ste. 400S
Washington, DC 20036
Ph: (202)530-5910
Fax: (202)530-0659

Proctor, Bill, Founder
Proving Innocence [11545]
535 Griswold St., Ste. 111-254
Detroit, MI 48226
Ph: (313)718-2890

Proctor, Ray, Reg. Dir.
Military Impacted Schools Associa-
tion [8345]
6327 S 196th St.
Omaha, NE 68135
Ph: (402)305-6468
Toll Free: 800-291-6472

Proevska, Pavlina, Exec. Dir.,
Founder
Macedonian Arts Council [8984]
380 Rector Pl., Apt. 21E
New York, NY 10280-1449
Ph: (212)799-0009
Fax: (815)301-3893

Profit, Richard H., Jr., CEO,
President
Prostate Advocates Aiding Choices
in Treatments [14051]
11555 Jadon Ct. NE
Sparta, MI 49345
Ph: (616)453-1477
Fax: (616)453-1846

Promis, Fr. Christopher P., Director
Archconfraternity of the Holy Ghost
[19794]
6230 Brush Run Rd.
Bethel Park, PA 15102-2214
Ph: (412)831-0302

Proost, Jay, Exec. Dir.
American Society of Agricultural Ap-
praisers [214]
1126 Eastland Dr. N, Ste. 100
Twin Falls, ID 83303-0186
Toll Free: 800-704-7020
Fax: (208)733-2326

Proost, Jay, Exec. Dir.
American Society of Farm Equip-
ment Appraisers [216]
1126 Eastland Dr. N, Ste. 100
Twin Falls, ID 83303-0186
Ph: (208)733-2323
Toll Free: 800-488-7570
Fax: (208)733-2326

Prophet, Elizabeth Claire, Founder
Church Universal and Triumphant
[20535]
63 Summit Way
Gardiner, MT 59030-9314
Ph: (406)848-9500
Toll Free: 800-245-5445
Fax: (406)848-9555

Protopapas, Deacon John, Director,
Founder
Orthodox Christians for Life [20587]
c/o Hierodeacon Herman
575 Scarsdale Rd.
Yonkers, NY 10707
Ph: (914)961-8313

Proudfit, Richard, CEO, Founder
Kids Against Hunger [12099]
13702 B St.
Omaha, NE 68144
Ph: (952)542-5600
Toll Free: 866-654-0202

Province, Charles M., Founder,
President
Patton Society [10344]
17010 S Potter Rd.
Oregon City, OR 97045

Provost, Jeff, Exec. Dir.
Exhibit Designers and Producers
Association [1171]
19 Compo Rd. S
Westport, CT 06880
Ph: (203)557-6321
Fax: (203)557-6324

Provost, Dr. Robert W., President
Slavic Gospel Association [20462]
6151 Commonwealth Dr.
Loves Park, IL 61111
Ph: (815)282-8900
Toll Free: 800-242-5350
Fax: (815)282-8901

Prud'homme, Kimberly, Exec. Dir.,
Founder
Two Hearts for Hope [11174]
PO Box 1928
Lebanon, MO 65536-1928

Prudon, Theo, President
DOCOMOMO US [9388]
PO Box 230977
New York, NY 10023-0017

Pruett, Patrick, Exec. Dir.
Auto Dealers CPAs [17]
1801 West End Ave., Ste. 800
Nashville, TN 37203
Ph: (615)373-9880
Toll Free: 800-231-2524
Fax: (615)377-7092

Pruett, Patrick, Exec. Dir.
Community Banking Advisory
Network [20]
111 E Wacker Dr.
Chicago, IL 60601
Ph: (312)729-9900

Pruett, Sarah, MOT, Contact
Universal Design Partners [990]
PO Box 570
Harrisonburg, VA 22803
Ph: (540)908-3473

Pruitt, Matthew, Contact
Elberton Granite Association [3183]
1 Granite Plz.
Elberton, GA 30635
Ph: (706)283-2551
Fax: (706)283-6380

Pruitt, Tom, President
Health Industry Representatives As-
sociation [2281]
8 The Meadows
Newnan, GA 30265
Ph: (303)756-8115
Fax: (770)683-4648

Pruthi, Sandhya, President
American Society of Breast Disease
[13849]
2591 Dallas Pky., Ste. 300

Frisco, TX 75034-8563
Ph: (214)368-6836

Prutzman, Priscilla, Officer
Children's Creative Response to
    Conflict [11222]
521 N Broadway
Nyack, NY 10960
Ph: (845)353-1796
Fax: (845)358-4924

Pryke, Douglas C., Exec. Dir.
Alliance for Environmental Technol-
    ogy [1424]
1250 24th St. NW, Ste. 300
Washington, DC 20037-1186
Ph: (519)217-5162

Przypyszny, Michele, President
Metastatic Breast Cancer Network
    [14014]
PO Box 1449
New York, NY 10159
Toll Free: 888-500-0370

Psarouthakis, Peter, Exec. Dir.
International Intelligence Network
    [3060]
PO Box 350
Gladwyne, PA 19035-0350
Ph: (610)520-9222
Toll Free: 800-784-2020

Psihoyos, Louie, Founder, CEO
Oceanic Preservation Society [3924]
336 Bon Air Ctr., No. 384
Greenbrae, CA 94904
Ph: (303)444-2454
Fax: (303)545-9938

Pucci, Aldo R., DCBT, President
National Association of Cognitive-
    Behavioral Therapists [16951]
102 Gilson Ave.
Weirton, WV 26062-3912
Ph: (304)224-2534
Toll Free: 800-253-0167

Puchalski, Dr. Robert, Chairman
American Medical Political Action
    Committee [18857]
25 Massachusetts Ave. NW, Ste.
600
Washington, DC 20001-7400
Ph: (202)789-7400

Puchovsky, Milosh, PE, President
Society of Fire Protection Engineers
    [6634]
9711 Washingtonian Blvd., Ste. 380
Gaithersburg, MD 20878
Ph: (301)718-2910
Fax: (240)328-6225

Pucker, Lee, CEO
Wireless Innovation Forum [6290]
12100 Sunset Hills Rd., Ste. 130
Reston, VA 20190
Ph: (602)843-1634
Fax: (604)608-9593

Puckett, Gary, Exec. Dir., President
Council on Occupational Education
    [7757]
Bldg. 300, Ste. 325
7840 Roswell Rd.
Atlanta, GA 30350
Ph: (770)396-3898
Toll Free: 800-917-2081
Fax: (770)396-3790

Pudaite, Dr. Lalrimawii, Founder,
    President
Bibles For The World [20388]
1105 Garden of the Gods Rd.
Colorado Springs, CO 80949-9759
Ph: (719)630-7733
Toll Free: 888-382-4253

Puechner, Ron, President
American Political Items Collectors
    [21614]
PO Box 55
Avon, NY 14414-0055
Ph: (585)226-8620

Puettmann, Maureen, President
Forest Products Society [4201]
15 Technology Pky. S, Ste. 115
Peachtree Corners, GA 30092
Toll Free: 855-475-0291

Puffer, James C., MD, President,
    CEO
American Board of Family Medicine
    [14747]
1648 McGrathiana Pky., Ste. 550
Lexington, KY 40511-1247
Ph: (859)269-5626
Fax: (859)335-7501

Pugliaresi, Lucian (Lou), President
Energy Policy Research Foundation,
    Inc. [7000]
1031 31st St. NW
Washington, DC 20007-4401
Ph: (202)944-3339
Fax: (202)944-9830

Pugliese, Joe
Hemophilia Alliance [15230]
1758 Allentown Rd., Ste. 183
Lansdale, PA 19446
Ph: (215)279-9236
Fax: (215)279-8679

Pugrud, Jessica H., Secretary
Association of Administrative Law
    Judges [5377]
c/o Jessica H. Pugrud, Secretary
3024 Mactavish Cir.
Billings, MT 59101-9451
Fax: (406)247-7555

Puhlmann, Greg, President
Rainbow Alliance of the Deaf
    [11943]
c/o Barbara Hathaway, Treasurer
PO Box 1616
Langley, WA 98260

Pujol, Andrew, Chairman, President,
    Founder
Building Homes for Heroes [10738]
65 Roosevelt Ave., Ste. 105
Valley Stream, NY 11581-1106
Ph: (516)684-9220
Fax: (516)206-0181

Pulham, Mr. Elliot Holokauahi, CEO
Space Foundation [7460]
4425 Arrowswest Dr.
Colorado Springs, CO 80907
Ph: (719)576-8000
Toll Free: 800-691-4000

Pulin, Dr. Carol, Director
American Print Alliance [8954]
302 Larkspur Turn
Peachtree City, GA 30269-2210

Pullen, Karen, Contact
Sisters in Crime [3519]
PO Box 442124
Lawrence, KS 66044
Ph: (785)842-1325
Fax: (785)856-6314

Pulley, Debbie, Secretary
North American Registry of Midwives
    [14239]
5257 Rosestone Dr.
Lilburn, GA 30047
Ph: (770)381-9051
Toll Free: 888-842-4784

Pulliam, Lynn, Bd. Member
International Society of NeuroVirol-
    ogy [16026]

Dept. of Neuroscience, Rm. 740
Temple University School of
    Medicine
3500 N Broad St.
Philadelphia, PA 19140
Ph: (215)707-9788
Fax: (215)707-9838

Pullinger, Amanda, CEO
100 Women in Hedge Funds [1214]
888C 8th Ave., No. 453
New York, NY 10019

Pullinger, Amanda, Chairperson
HALO Trust [18001]
1730 Rhode Island Ave. NW, Ste.
403
Washington, DC 20036
Ph: (202)331-1266
Fax: (202)331-1277

Puls, Chris, President
Dog Scouts of America [11689]
PO Box 158
Harrison, OH 45030
Ph: (989)389-2000

Pulsifer, Henry, Founder
Brothers and Sisters in Christ
    [19947]
PO Box 633
Grapevine, TX 76099
Ph: (228)255-9251

Pumariega, Andres, President
American Association for Social
    Psychiatry [16815]
c/o Carol Coffman, Office
    Administrator
250 Crawford Ave.
Lansdowne, PA 19050
Ph: (610)626-5133

Pumphrey, Linda, President
International Quilt Association
    [21764]
7660 Woodway, Ste. 550
Houston, TX 77063-1528
Ph: (713)781-6882
Fax: (713)781-8182

Purcell, Candace, Dir. of Fin., Dir. of
    Operations
American Volkssport Association
    [23214]
1001 Pat Booker Rd., Ste. 101
Universal City, TX 78148-4147
Ph: (210)659-2112
Fax: (210)659-1212

Purcell, Douglas Clare, President
Purcell Family of America [20917]
9101 Mace Arch
Norfolk, VA 23503-4503
Ph: (334)687-9787

Purcell, Dyanne, CEO
National Domestic Violence Hotline
    [11708]
PO Box 161810
Austin, TX 78716
Ph: (512)794-1133
Toll Free: 800-799-7233

Purcell, Jennifer, Director
Unwanted Horse Coalition [10711]
1616 H St. NW, 7th Fl.
Washington, DC 20006
Ph: (202)296-4031
Fax: (202)296-1970

Purcell, Kevin, Founder, President
Arthritis Introspective [17154]
5217 E 26th St.
Tucson, AZ 85711
Ph: (520)440-0771

Purcell, Dr. Luann L., Exec. Dir.
Council of Administrators of Special
    Education [8578]

Osigian Office Ctre.
101 Katelyn Cir., Ste. E
Warner Robins, GA 31088
Ph: (478)333-6892
Fax: (478)333-2453

Purciello, Maria Anne, Treasurer
Society for Seventeenth-Century
    Music [10011]
c/o Maria Anne Purciello, Treasurer
University of Delaware
Department of Music
317 Amy E. du Pont Music Bldg.
Newark, DE 19716
Ph: (319)335-1622

Purdy, Lisa L., CEO, President
Council of International Programs
    USA [13108]
100 N Main St., Ste. 309
Chagrin Falls, OH 44022
Ph: (440)247-1088
Fax: (440)247-1490

Purser, Craig A., Ph.D., President
National Beer Wholesalers Associa-
    tion [188]
1101 King St., Ste. 600
Alexandria, VA 22314-2944
Ph: (703)683-4300
Toll Free: 800-300-6417
Fax: (703)683-8965

Purse-Wiedenhoeft, Jane, Coord.
Institute for Theatre Journalism and
    Advocacy [10255]
c/o Jane Purse-Wiedenhoeft,
    Coordinator
University of Wisconsin Oshkosh
Arts and Communication Theatre
    Dept.
800 Algoma Blvd.
Oshkosh, WI 54901-8657
Ph: (920)424-4425

Purtill, Yvette, Ed.-in-Chief
Naval Enlisted Reserve Association
    [5613]
6703 Farragut Ave.
Falls Church, VA 22042-2189
Toll Free: 800-776-9020

Purvin, Robert L., Jr., Chairman,
    CEO
American Association of Franchisees
    and Dealers [1455]
PO Box 10158
Palm Desert, CA 92255-0158
Ph: (619)209-3775
Toll Free: 800-733-9858

Pusey, Leigh Ann, CEO, President
American Insurance Association
    [1831]
2101 L St. NW, Ste. 400
Washington, DC 20037
Ph: (202)828-7100
Fax: (202)293-1219

Pyle, Lesley Spencer, Founder,
    President
Home-Based Working Moms [634]
PO Box 1628
Spring, TX 77383-1628
Ph: (281)757-2207

Pyle, Thomas J., President
American Energy Alliance [18189]
1155 15th St. NW, Ste. 900
Washington, DC 20005-2706
Ph: (202)621-2940
Fax: (202)741-9170

Pynoos, Robert S., Director
National Child Traumatic Stress
    Network [17528]
11150 W Olympic Blvd., Ste. 650
Los Angeles, CA 90064
Ph: (310)235-2633
Fax: (310)235-2612

Pyrtek-Blond, Stella, Secretary
Packard Club [21472]
c/o Cornerstone Registration
PO Box 1715
Maple Grove, MN 55311-6715
Ph: (763)420-7829
Toll Free: 866-427-7583
Fax: (763)420-7849

Pyzik, Dr. Larry, Exec. Dir.
American Chiropractic Registry of
  Radiologic Technologists [17040]
52 W Colfax St.
Palatine, IL 60067
Ph: (847)705-1178
Fax: (847)705-1178

Q

Qamruddin, Jumana, President
Friends of Mali [18786]
PO Box 27417
Washington, DC 20038-7417

Qi, Xiaoning, Chairman, President
Chinese American Semiconductor
  Professional Association [1038]
1159 Sonora Ct., Ste. 105
Sunnyvale, CA 94086
Ph: (408)940-4600

Quach, Hoa, President
Rolling Readers [12249]
2515 Camino del Rio S, Ste. 330
San Diego, CA 92108
Ph: (619)516-4095
Fax: (619)516-4096

Quackenbush, Debbie, Founder,
  CEO
American Military Family [21038]
PO Box 1101
Brighton, CO 80601
Ph: (303)746-8195

Quackenbush, Margery, Exec. Dir.
National Association for the
  Advancement of Psychoanalysis
  [16848]
80 8th Ave., Ste. 1501
New York, NY 10011-7158
Ph: (212)741-0515
Fax: (212)366-4347

Quackenbush, Margery, Exec. Dir.
World Organization and Public
  Education Corp. of the National
  Association for the Advancement
  of Psychoanalysis [16853]
80 8th Ave., Ste. 1501
New York, NY 10011
Ph: (212)741-0515
Fax: (212)366-4347

Quaid, Barbara, President
Western Fairs Association [1162]
1776 Tribute Rd., Ste. 210
Sacramento, CA 95815
Ph: (916)927-3100
Fax: (916)927-6397

Quancard, Bernard, CEO, President
Strategic Account Management As-
  sociation [2304]
10 N Dearborn St., 2nd Fl.
Chicago, IL 60602
Ph: (312)251-3131
Fax: (312)251-3132

Quarles, Sherri, Exec. Dir.
American Academy of Osteopathy
  [16501]
3500 DePauw Blvd., Ste. 1100
Indianapolis, IN 46268-1138
Ph: (317)879-1881
Fax: (317)879-0563

Quarles, Tom, President
The Cairn Terrier Club of America
  [21849]

c/o Pauli Christy
226 Kilmer Ln.
Winter Haven, FL 33884-2314

Quarles, William, Managing Ed.
Bio-Integral Resource Center [4527]
PO Box 7414
Berkeley, CA 94707
Ph: (510)524-2567
Fax: (510)524-1758

Quatrale, Andrea, President
Latin America Parents Association
  [10458]
PO Box 339-340
Brooklyn, NY 11234
Ph: (718)236-8689

Quattlebaum, Jay L., Exec. Dir.,
  Founder
Primero Agua [13333]
2675 Stonecrest Dr.
Washington, MO 63090
Ph: (636)239-1573

Que, Lawrence, Ed.-in-Chief
Society of Biological Inorganic
  Chemistry [6214]
9650 Rockville Pke.
Bethesda, MD 20814-3998
Ph: (301)634-7194
Fax: (301)634-7099

Queen, Dr. Carol, Founder, Exec.
  Dir.
Center for Sex and Culture [12942]
1349 Mission St.
San Francisco, CA 94103
Ph: (415)902-2071

Querner, Mike, Bd. Member
American Cowboy Culture Associa-
  tion [8800]
PO Box 6638
Lubbock, TX 79493
Ph: (806)798-7825

Quick, Charity A., MBA, Exec. Dir.
AACE International [6354]
1265 Suncrest Towne Centre Dr.
Morgantown, WV 26505-1876
Ph: (304)296-8444
Fax: (304)291-5728

Quick-Andrews, Beth, CAE, Exec.
  Dir.
Institute for Challenging Disorganiza-
  tion [9538]
1693 S Hanley Rd.
Saint Louis, MO 63144
Ph: (314)416-2236

Quiggins, Amy, Mgr.
National Blood Foundation [13841]
8101 Glenbrook Rd.
Bethesda, MD 20814-2749
Ph: (301)215-6552
Fax: (301)215-5751

Quigley, Ann, President
Komondor Club of America [21909]
c/o Anna Quigley, President
159 Beville Rd.
Chehalis, WA 98532-9115
Ph: (360)245-3464

Quigley, Prof. Eamonn, Comm.
  Chm.
World Gastroenterology Organisation
  [14799]
555 E Wells St., Ste. 1100
Milwaukee, WI 53202-3823
Ph: (414)918-9798
Fax: (414)276-3349

Quillen, Ellen, PhD, Secretary,
  Treasurer
American Association of
  Anthropological Genetics [6663]

c/o Ellen Quillen, Secretary/
  Treasurer
Texas Biomedical Research Institute
Dept. of Genetics
San Antonio, TX 78245

Quilty, Tom, 1st VP
High Technology Crime Investigation
  Association [5360]
140 Bogart Ct.
Roseville, CA 95747
Ph: (916)408-1751
Fax: (916)384-2232

Quinby, Roger, President
Scandinavian Collectors Club
  [22361]
PO Box 16213
Saint Paul, MN 55116-0213

Quinlan, Terence, Director
I.T. Financial Management Associa-
  tion [1247]
PO Box 30188
Santa Barbara, CA 93130
Ph: (805)687-7390
Fax: (805)687-7382

Quinn, Dan, Contact
North American Truck Camper Own-
  ers Association [22475]
PO Box 30408
Bellingham, WA 98228

Quinn, Dion, Founder
God's Kids [11006]
11700 Industry Ave.
Fontana, CA 92337
Toll Free: 877-246-3754

Quinn, Howard, Advisor
Council of Ethical Organizations
  [11798]
214 S Payne St.
Alexandria, VA 22314
Ph: (703)683-7916

Quinn, James, Treasurer
Association of Productivity Specialists [2155]
521 5th Ave., Ste. 1700
New York, NY 10175

Quinn, Jim, V. Ch.
National Summer Learning Associa-
  tion [8633]
575 S Charles St., Ste. 310
Baltimore, MD 21201
Ph: (410)856-1370
Fax: (410)856-1146

Quinn, Katherine, MBA, Exec. Dir.
Support Connection [14070]
40 Triangle Ctr., Ste. 100
Yorktown Heights, NY 10598
Ph: (914)962-6402
Toll Free: 800-532-4290
Fax: (914)962-1926

Quinn, Victoria, Sr. VP
Helen Keller International [17712]
352 Park Ave. S, 12th Fl.
New York, NY 10010-1723
Ph: (212)532-0544

Quirk, Lisa, Dir. of MIS
National Association for Law Place-
  ment [8217]
1220 19th St. NW, Ste. 401
Washington, DC 20036-2405
Ph: (202)835-1001
Fax: (202)835-1112

Quirt, Brian, Chmn. of the Bd.
Literary Managers and Dramaturgs
  of the Americas [10259]
PO Box 36
New York, NY 10129
Toll Free: 800-680-2148

Quiver, Robert, Contact
Lakota Student Alliance [19581]
PO Box 225
Kyle, SD 57752
Ph: (605)867-1507

Qureshi, M. Nasar, President
Association of Physicians of
  Pakistani Descent of North
  America [16743]
6414 S Cass Ave.
Westmont, IL 60559-3209
Ph: (630)968-8585
Fax: (630)968-8677

R

Raab, Tanya, President
United Kennel Club [21975]
100 E Kilgore Rd.
Kalamazoo, MI 49002-5584
Ph: (269)343-9020
Fax: (269)343-7037

Raad, Issam, President
American Lebanese Medical As-
  sociation [15707]
Pacifica Orthopedics
18800 Delaware St., Ste. 1100
Huntington Beach, CA 92648

Raasch, Jona, CEO
The Governance Institute [2168]
9685 Via Excelencia, Ste. 100
San Diego, CA 92126
Toll Free: 877-712-8778
Fax: (858)909-0813

Rabac, Ken, Director
American Association for Higher
  Education and Accreditation [7737]
2020 Pennsylvania Ave. NW 975
Washington, DC 20006
Ph: (202)293-6440
Fax: (855)252-7622

Rabadi, Dina, Exec. Dir., Founder,
  President
Global Alliance of Artists [8921]
2405 N Sheffield Ave., No. 14199
Chicago, IL 60614

Rabalais, Nancy, President
National Association of Marine
  Laboratories [6805]
1313 Dolley Madison Blvd., Ste. 402
McLean, VA 22101
Ph: (703)790-1745
Toll Free: 800-955-1236
Fax: (703)790-2672

Rabb, Diana, Treasurer
Continental Mi-Ki Association
  [21861]
c/o Bonnie Campbell, President
6290 East 850 South
Saint Paul, IN 47272
Ph: (317)512-7119

Rabens, Capt. Mike, President
F-14 Tomcat Association [21527]
PO Box 1347
Somis, CA 93066

Rabiah, Janan, Exec. Dir.
Association for Contract Textiles
  [3255]
PO Box 101981
Fort Worth, TX 76185
Ph: (817)924-8048
Fax: (817)924-8050

Raborn, Charles W., Jr., Exec. Dir.
Association of Certified Fraud
  Specialists [1784]
4600 Northgate Blvd., Ste. 105
Sacramento, CA 95834-8777
Ph: (916)419-6319
Toll Free: 866-HEY-ACFS
Fax: (916)419-6318

Raby, Dedrick J., President
Kappa Psi Kappa Fraternity, Inc.
[23757]
PO Box 733
Philadelphia, PA 19105
Ph: (516)841-5865

Rachlin, Joan, JD, Chairperson
Our Bodies, Ourselves [17765]
PO Box 400135
Cambridge, MA 02140-0002
Ph: (617)245-0200

Rachuig, Brenda, Exec. Dir.
Association of Attorney-Mediators
[4993]
PO Box 741955
Dallas, TX 75374-1955
Ph: (972)669-8101
Toll Free: 800-280-1368
Fax: (972)669-8180

Rachwitz, Dr. Erich, Treasurer
Foundation for Veterinary Dentistry
[14435]
3905 Twin Creek Dr., No. 103
Bellevue, NE 68123
Ph: (402)505-9033

Rackauskas, Jonas, PhD, President
Institute of Lithuanian Studies
[19539]
5600 S Claremont Ave.
Chicago, IL 60636-1039
Ph: (773)434-4545
Fax: (773)434-9363

Radcliff, Kris, MD, President
Association for Collaborative Spine
Research [15640]
PO Box 420942
San Diego, CA 92142-0942
Ph: (951)553-3556
Fax: (951)302-8629

Rader, Jim, Founder
Rader Association [20918]
2633 Gilbert Way
Rancho Cordova, CA 95670-3513

Radford, Katie, Office Mgr.
Do Something [17974]
19 W 21st St., 8th Fl.
New York, NY 10010
Ph: (212)254-2390

Radics-Johnson, Jennifer, Exec. Dir.
Alisa Ann Ruch Burn Foundation
[13866]
50 N Hill Ave., Ste. 305
Pasadena, CA 91106
Ph: (818)848-0223
Toll Free: 800-242-BURN
Fax: (818)848-0296

Radke, Laura, Director
National Association for Justice
Information Systems [5141]
c/o Thomas Welch, President
984 Keynote Cr.
Cleveland, OH 44131
Ph: (216)739-6254
Fax: (216)739-3520

Radoszewski, Tony, President
Plastics Pipe Institute [2614]
105 Decker Ct., Ste. 825
Irving, TX 75062
Ph: (469)499-1044
Fax: (469)499-1063

Radsliff, Peter, President
Aging Technology Alliance [7256]
3701 Sacramento St., No. 496
San Francisco, CA 94118

Radtke, Robert W., President
Episcopal Relief and Development
[12659]

815 2nd Ave.
New York, NY 10017
Toll Free: 855-312-4325
Fax: (212)687-5302

Rae, Dawn, President
National Association of Exclusive
Buyer Agents [2868]
1481 N Eliseo C. Felix Jr. Way, Ste.
110
Avondale, AZ 85323
Ph: (623)932-0098
Toll Free: 888-623-2299
Fax: (623)932-0212

Raehl, Chris, Coord.
American Paintball Players Associa-
tion [23054]
530 E South Ave.
Chippewa Falls, WI 54729
Ph: (715)720-9131

Raehl, Chris, President
National Collegiate Paintball As-
sociation [23055]
530 E South Ave.
Chippewa Falls, WI 54729
Ph: (612)605-8323
Fax: (612)605-9255

Raezer, Joyce Wessel, Exec. Dir.
National Military Family Association
[21042]
3601 Eisenhower Ave., Ste. 425
Alexandria, VA 22304
Ph: (703)931-6632
Fax: (703)931-4600

Rafaty, Hoss, President
International Association of Ice
Cream Distributors and Vendors
[3430]
3601 E Joppa Rd.
Baltimore, MD 21234
Ph: (410)931-8100
Fax: (410)931-8111

Rafeld, Blake, President
National Christmas Tree Association
[4733]
16020 Swingley Ridge Rd., Ste. 300
Chesterfield, MO 63017
Ph: (636)449-5070
Fax: (636)449-5051

Raffio, Cindy, President
Sealant, Waterproofing and Restora-
tion Institute [62]
400 Admiral Blvd.
Kansas City, MO 64106
Ph: (816)472-7974
Fax: (816)472-7765

Rafkin, John M., Chmn. of the Bd.
Frank Lloyd Wright Trust [9445]
209 S LaSalle St., Ste. 118
Chicago, IL 60604
Ph: (312)994-4000

Rafn, Jeffrey, President, Chmn. of
the Bd.
Community Colleges for International
Development [8063]
c/o Lone Star College
Bldg. 11, Rm. 11296
20515 State Highway 249
Houston, TX 77070
Ph: (281)401-5389

Rager, John, President
American Red Poll Association
[3709]
PO Box 847
Frankton, IN 46044
Ph: (765)425-4515

Ragosta, Dr. Summer, Founder
Surfing Medicine International
[13659]

PO Box 548
Waialua, HI 96791
Ph: (518)635-0899

Raguz, Stan, President
Croatian American Association
[18521]
6607 W Archer Ave.
Chicago, IL 60638-2407

Raheb, Mitri, CEO, President,
Founder
Bright Stars of Bethlehem [20514]
PO Box 185
Mount Morris, IL 61054
Ph: (815)315-0682

Rahimian, Saeid, Chairman
Petroleum Equipment Suppliers As-
sociation [2534]
2500 Citywest Blvd., Ste. 1110
Houston, TX 77055
Ph: (713)932-0168

Rahkonen, Ossi, President
Finlandia Foundation National [9320]
470 W Walnut St.
Pasadena, CA 91103
Ph: (626)795-2081
Fax: (626)795-6533

Rahman, Dr. Babu S., Bd. Member
Agami [7579]
PO Box 3178
Fremont, CA 94539

Rahmani, M. Kajal, President,
Founder
Kurdistan Justice and Peace
Academy [19526]
955 Massachusetts Ave., Ste. 252
Cambridge, MA 02139
Ph: (617)209-4331

Rahrig, Philip G., BS, Exec. Dir.
American Galvanizers Association
[743]
6881 S Holy Cir., Ste. 108
Centennial, CO 80112
Ph: (720)554-0900
Fax: (720)554-0909

Rainey, Allen, Founder, Dir. of
Programs
SonLight Power Inc. [11442]
7100 Dixie Hwy.
Fairfield, OH 45014
Ph: (513)285-9960

Rainey, Brad, Exec. Dir.
Golden Key International Honour
Society [23781]
1040 Crown Pointe Pky., Ste. 900
Atlanta, GA 30338
Ph: (678)689-2200
Toll Free: 800-377-2401
Fax: (678)689-2297

Rainey, Eddie, President
Artist-Blacksmith's Association of
North America [434]
259 Muddy Fork Rd.
Jonesborough, TN 37659
Ph: (423)913-1022
Fax: (423)913-1023

Rainley, Paul, President
National Alliance of General Agents
[1887]
Concorde General Agency, Inc.
720 28th St. SW
Fargo, ND 58103
Fax: (701)239-9941

Rainone, Michael, President
American Reflexology Certification
Board [13599]
2586 Knightsbridge Rd. SE

Grand Rapids, MI 49546
Ph: (303)933-6921
Fax: (303)904-0460

Rajagopalan, Dr. Sampath,
President
Child Vikaas International [10816]
6674 E Bonita Ct.
Orange, CA 92867

Rajbhandari, Sarju, Director
NepalAama [7593]
PO Box 1565
Simi Valley, CA 93062-1565

Rajec, Andrew M., President
First Catholic Slovak Union of the
U.S.A. and Canada [19645]
6611 Rockside Rd., Ste. 300
Independence, OH 44131
Ph: (216)642-9406
Toll Free: 800-533-6682
Fax: (216)642-4310

Rajec, Elizabeth, President
Kafka Society of America [9067]
c/o Marie Luise Caputo-Mayr, Direc-
tor
160 E 65th St., No. 2C
New York, NY 10065
Ph: (212)744-0821
Fax: (212)744-0821

Rakow, Dr. Tom C., Founder,
President
Christian Deer Hunters Association
[19955]
PO Box 432
Silver Lake, MN 55381
Ph: (320)327-2266
(320)587-7127

Rallapalli, Emelia, Secretary
Political Research Associates
[18919]
1310 Broadway, Ste. 201
Somerville, MA 02144-1837
Ph: (617)666-5300
Fax: (617)666-6622

Rallo, Joseph S., PhD, Director
Association of State and Provincial
Psychology Boards [16909]
215 Market Rd.
Tyrone, GA 30290
Ph: (678)216-1175
Toll Free: 800-513-6910
Fax: (678)216-1176

Ralls, Dr. Stephen A., Exec. Dir.
American College of Dentists
[14401]
839J Quince Orchard Blvd.
Gaithersburg, MD 20878-1614
Ph: (301)977-3223
Fax: (301)977-3330

Ralston, Richard E., Exec. Dir.
Americans for Free Choice in
Medicine [15713]
1525 Superior Ave., Ste. 101
Newport Beach, CA 92663

Ramakrishna, Revathy, VP
Vision-Aid [17748]
8 Vine Brook Rd.
Lexington, MA 02421
Ph: (781)333-5252

Ramarui, Jennifer, Exec. Dir.
The Oceanography Society [6943]
PO Box 1931
Rockville, MD 20849-1931
Ph: (301)251-7708
Fax: (301)251-7709

Ramaswamy, Izzy, Comm. Chm.
Association of Vascular and Interventional Radiographers [17572]

2201 Cooperative Way, Ste. 600
Herndon, VA 20171-3005
Ph: (571)252-7174

Rambacher, Penny, Chairperson,
President
Miracles in Action [12553]
241 Countryside Dr.
Naples, FL 34104
Ph: (239)348-0815

Rambo, Cat, President
Science Fiction and Fantasy Writers
of America [10397]
PO Box 3238
Enfield, CT 06083-3238

Ramesh, S.K., President
IEEE-Eta Kappa Nu [23737]
445 Hoes Ln.
Piscataway, NJ 08854
Ph: (732)465-5846
Toll Free: 800-406-2590
Fax: (732)465-5808

Ramey, Angie, President
International Society of Glass Bead-
makers [8981]
118 Graceland Blvd., Ste. 316
Columbus, OH 43214
Ph: (614)222-2243
Fax: (614)983-0389

Ramirez, Robert D., CCE, Director
CUES Financial Suppliers Forum
[2277]
5510 Research Park Dr.
Madison, WI 53711-5377
Ph: (608)271-2664
Toll Free: 800-252-2664
Fax: (608)271-2303

Ramirez, Saul N., Jr., CEO
National Association of Housing and
Redevelopment Officials [5280]
630 Eye St. NW
Washington, DC 20001-3736
Ph: (202)289-3500
Toll Free: 877-866-2476
Fax: (202)289-8181

Ramirez, Stacey, Exec. Dir.
Global Pediatric Alliance [16607]
PO Box 640046
San Francisco, CA 94164
Ph: (415)567-3698

Ramos, Eileen, President
Association of Practicing Certified
Public Accountants [16]
932 Hungerford Dr., No. 17A
Rockville, MD 20850
Ph: (301)340-3340

Ramprasad, Gayathri, MBA,
Founder, President
ASHA International [15761]
PO Box 91232
Portland, OR 97291-0004
Ph: (971)340-7190

Ramsay, John, Jr., President
Clan Ramsay Association of North
America [20838]
434 Skinner Blvd., Ste. 105
Dunedin, FL 34698
Ph: (727)409-4639
Fax: (775)781-3812

Ramsbottom, Claire, President
Association for Collaborative Leader-
ship [7953]
101 S Mills Ave.
Claremont, CA 91711
Ph: (909)607-9870
Fax: (909)607-9837

Ramsby, Mike, Researcher
Pacific Northwest Christmas Tree
Association [4734]

PO Box 3366
Salem, OR 97302
Ph: (503)364-2942
Fax: (503)581-6819

Ramsey, Christopher, CEO
United States Water Polo [23352]
2124 Main St., Ste. 240
Huntington Beach, CA 92648-7456
Ph: (714)500-5445
Fax: (714)960-2431

Ramsey, Christopher, CEO
USA Water Polo [23353]
2124 Main St., Ste. 240
Huntington Beach, CA 92648-7456
Ph: (714)500-5445
Fax: (714)960-2431

Ramsey, Karen, Chairperson
VHL Alliance [14865]
2001 Beacon St., Ste. 208
Boston, MA 02135-7787
Ph: (617)277-5667
Toll Free: 800-767-4845
Fax: (858)712-8712

Ramsey, Virginia, Exec. Producer
INFORM Inc. [19133]
PO Box 320403
Brooklyn, NY 11232
Ph: (212)361-2400
Fax: (212)361-2412

Ramus, Dr. Robert L., DDS, Exec.
Dir.
Academy of Dentistry International
[14364]
3813 Gordon Creek Dr.
Hicksville, OH 43526
Ph: (419)542-0101
Fax: (419)542-6883

Rana, Sarosh, MD, MPH, Secretary,
Treasurer
North American Society for the
Study of Hypertension in
Pregnancy [17114]
c/o Sara Gauthier
6905 N Wickham Rd., Ste. 302
Melbourne, FL 32940
Ph: (321)421-6699
Fax: (321)821-0450

Ranavaya, Prof. Mohammed, MD,
President, Director
American Board of Independent
Medical Examiners [15627]
6470A Merritts Creek Rd.
Huntington, WV 25702-9739
Ph: (304)733-0095
    (304)733-0096
Toll Free: 877-523-1415
Fax: (304)733-5243

Ranck, Rob, President
HomePlug Powerline Alliance, Inc.
[1049]
10260 SW Greenburg Rd., Ste. 400
Portland, OR 97223
Ph: (503)766-2516
Fax: (503)766-2516

Rand, Ilene, Asst. Treas.
United Yorkie Rescue [10710]
c/o Carl Sullenberger, Treasurer
3924 Miami Ave.
Lorain, OH 44053

Rand, William Lee, Founder,
President
International Center for Reiki Train-
ing [17101]
21421 Hilltop St., Unit No. 28
Southfield, MI 48033
Ph: (248)948-8112
Toll Free: 800-332-8112
Fax: (248)948-9534

Randall, Diane, Exec. Sec.
Friends Committee on National
Legislation [20168]
245 2nd St. NE
Washington, DC 20002-5761
Ph: (202)547-6000
Toll Free: 800-630-1330
Fax: (202)547-6019

Randall, Harriet L., CEO, President
North American Alliance for the
Advancement of Native Peoples
[18712]
29780 Highway UU
Keytesville, MO 65261-2455

Randall, Martha L., Chairperson
American Academy of Teachers of
Singing [8356]
c/o Jeannette LoVetri, Secretary/
Director
317 W 93rd St., Apt. 3B
New York, NY 10025
Ph: (301)649-5260

Randall, Nana-Fosu, Founder,
President
Voices of African Mothers, Inc.
[12445]
777 United Nations Plz., Ste. 6G
New York, NY 10017
Ph: (212)661-5860
Fax: (212)661-5861

Randecker, Harvey, President
National Association of Alternative
Benefits Consultants [1608]
435 Pennsylvania Ave.
Glen Ellyn, IL 60137
Toll Free: 800-627-0552

Randel, Don M., Chmn. of the Bd.
American Academy of Arts and Sciences [9013]
136 Irving St.
Cambridge, MA 02138

Randell, Gil, Secretary
Hawk Migration Association of North
America [6960]
PO Box 721
Plymouth, NH 03264

Randle, Josh, COO
Miss America Organization [21735]
PO Box 1919
Atlantic City, NJ 08404-1919
Ph: (609)344-1800

Rando, John, Exec. VP
Stage Directors and Choreographers
Society [23500]
321 W 44th St., Ste. 804
New York, NY 10036
Ph: (212)391-1070
Toll Free: 800-541-5204
Fax: (212)302-6195

Randolph, Mary, Treasurer
Partners for Rural America [19077]
c/o Mary Randolph, Treasurer
214 W 15th St.
Cheyenne, WY 82002
Ph: (307)777-6430
Fax: (307)777-2935

Rangel, Rose, Chairperson
National Association of Credit Union
Chairmen [952]
PO Box 160
Del Mar, CA 92014
Ph: (858)792-3883
Toll Free: 888-987-4247
Fax: (858)792-3884

Rangel-Posada, Juliana, President
American Association of Professional
Apiculturists [3631]

c/o Dr. Juliana Rangel-Posada,
President
Texas A&M University
401 Joe Routt Blvd.
College Station, TX 77843-2475
Ph: (979)845-3211
    (517)353-8136
Fax: (517)353-4354

Ranieri, William, Exec. Dir.
KampGround Owners Association
[2911]
3416 Primm Ln.
Birmingham, AL 35216
Ph: (205)824-0022
Toll Free: 800-678-9976
Fax: (205)823-2760

Rankin, Catharine, President
International Society for Neuroethol-
ogy [5897]
PO Box 1897
Lawrence, KS 66044
Ph: (785)865-9401
Toll Free: 800-627-0629

Rankin, Natasha, Exec. Dir.
Employers Council on Flexible
Compensation [1069]
1444 I St. NW, Ste. 700
Washington, DC 20005-2210
Ph: (202)659-4300
Fax: (202)216-9646

Rankin, Natasha, Exec. Dir.
Greeting Card Association [3173]
1444 I St. NW, Ste. 700
Washington, DC 20005
Ph: (202)216-9627
Fax: (202)216-9646

Rankin, Robert, President
American Brittany Club [21800]
Ph: (618)985-2336

Rankin, Scott, President
Federation of Animal Science Societ-
ies [3616]
1800 S Oak St., Ste. 100
Champaign, IL 61820-6974
Ph: (217)356-3182
Fax: (217)398-4119

Rankin, William, PhD, Founder
Global AIDS Interfaith Alliance
[13541]
2171 Francisco Blvd. E, Ste. 1
San Rafael, CA 94901
Ph: (415)461-7196
Fax: (415)785-7389

Rankl, David, Contact
American Lock Collectors Association [21612]
c/o David Rankl
13115 Millersburg Rd. SW
Massillon, OH 44647-9773

Ranney, Rachael, Founder,
President
All Our Children International
Outreach [10846]
PO Box 1807
Claremont, CA 91711
Ph: (909)450-1177

Ranzino, David, Founder, President
The Love Alliance [17985]

Raola, Orlando, President
Esperanto-USA [9288]
1500 Park Ave., Ste. 134
Emeryville, CA 94608
Ph: (510)653-0998
Toll Free: 800-377-3726

Rapaport, Mark, MD, President
American Society of Clinical Psy-
chopharmacology [16643]

5034 Thoroughbred Ln., Ste. A
Brentwood, TN 37027-4231
Ph: (615)649-3085
Fax: (888)417-3311

Rapaport, Peter, Chairman
Anne Frank Center U.S.A. [18344]
44 Park Pl.
New York, NY 10007-2500
Ph: (212)431-7993
Fax: (212)431-8375

Raphael, Carol, Chairperson
AARP [12752]
601 E St. NW
Washington, DC 20049-0001
Ph: (202)434-3525
Toll Free: 888-687-2277

Raphaelson, Katherine, President
Society for International Develop-
ment - USA [18499]
1101 15th St. NW, 3rd Fl.
Washington, DC 20005
Ph: (202)331-1317

Rapoport, Miles, President
Common Cause [18863]
805 15th St. NW, 11th Fl.
Washington, DC 20005
Ph: (202)833-1200

Rapp, Barbara, Exec. Dir.
Connective Tissue Oncology Society
[16342]
PO Box 320574
Alexandria, VA 22320
Ph: (301)502-7371
Fax: (703)548-4882

Rapp, Janet, Exec. Dir.
Association of Professional
Researchers for Advancement
[11857]
330 N Wabash Ave., Ste. 2000
Chicago, IL 60611
Ph: (312)321-5196
Fax: (312)673-6966

Rappaport, Charley, Founder
Balalaika and Domra Association of
America [9879]
2801 Warner St.
Madison, WI 53713-2160

Rappaport, Joanne, President
Latin American Studies Association
[9662]
315 S Bellefield Ave.
Pittsburgh, PA 15260
Ph: (412)648-7929
Fax: (412)624-7145

Rapson, Rip, CEO, President
The Kresge Foundation [12979]
3215 W Big Beaver Rd.
Troy, MI 48084
Ph: (248)643-9630

Raqib, Mariam, Founder, Director
Afghanistan Samsortya [12022]
200 Swanton St., Ste. 418
Winchester, MA 01890
Ph: (617)319-3717

Rasco, Carol H., CEO, President
Reading Is Fundamental [8490]
1730 Rhode Island Ave. NW, 11th
Fl.
Washington, DC 20036
Ph: (202)536-3400
Toll Free: 877-743-7323

Rasher, Bruce, Chairman, Treasurer
Association for Redevelopment
Initiatives [4577]
2200 E Devon Ave., Ste. 354
Des Plaines, IL 60018
Ph: (312)987-1050

Rashid, Abbas, Exec. Dir.
Society for the Advancement of
Education [7799]
766 Bermuda Rd., Ste. 2
West Babylon, NY 11704
Ph: (516)729-4618

Rasmussen, Anne K., President
Society for Ethnomusicology [10007]
Indiana University
800 E 3rd St.
Bloomington, IN 47405-3700
Ph: (812)855-6672
Fax: (812)855-6673

Rasmussen, Dick, Exec. Sec.
University Athletic Association
[23263]
115 Sully's Trl., Ste. 14
Pittsford, NY 14534-4571
Ph: (585)419-0575
Fax: (585)218-0951

Rasmussen, Judy, Exec. VP, CFO
Boys Town [12791]
14100 Crawford St.
Boys Town, NE 68010-7520
Ph: (402)498-1300
Toll Free: 800-488-3000
Fax: (402)498-1348

Rasmussen, Judy, Exec. Dir.
Tibetan Aid Project [12599]
2210 Harold Way
Berkeley, CA 94704-1425
Ph: (510)848-4238
Toll Free: 800-338-4238

Rasmussen, Teresa J., President
Association of Life Insurance
Counsel [5312]
14350 Mundy Dr., Ste. 800, No. 258
Noblesville, IN 46060
Ph: (317)774-7500
Fax: (317)614-7147

Raspotnik, Ken, President
Dales Pony Society of America
[4347]
4161 Leon Dr.
Clayton, CA 94517
Ph: (925)788-0655

Ratje, Randall J., Chairman
Steuben Society of America [19448]
1 S Ocean Ave.
Patchogue, NY 11772-3738
Ph: (631)730-5111

Ratley, James D., President
Association of Certified Fraud
Examiners [1783]
The Gregor Bldg.
716 West Ave.
Austin, TX 78701-2727
Ph: (512)478-9000
Toll Free: 800-245-3321
Fax: (512)478-9297

Ratner, Charles Horowitz, Chmn. of
the Bd.
Israel Aliyah Center [20253]
633 3rd Ave.
New York, NY 10017-6706
Ph: (212)339-6000

Ratner, Gary, Exec. Dir., Founder
Citizens for Effective Schools [8474]
c/o Gary Ratner, Executive Director
8209 Hamilton Spring Ct.
Bethesda, MD 20817
Ph: (301)469-8000

Ratynski, Deborah, RN, Founder,
President, CEO
Pediatric Angel Network [11261]
PO Box 213
Mendham, NJ 07945
Toll Free: 800-620-3620
Fax: (866)546-7493

Rauner, Robert, President
United Leukodystrophy Foundation
[15998]
224 N 2nd St., Ste. 2
DeKalb, IL 60115
Ph: (815)748-3211
Toll Free: 800-728-5483
Fax: (815)748-0844

Rausch, Fr. John, Director
Catholic Committee of Appalachia
[20392]
885 Orchard Run Rd.
Spencer, WV 25276
Ph: (304)927-5798

Raven, Leanne, Chairperson
International Society for the Study
and Prevention of Perinatal and
Infant Death [16621]
1314 Bedford Ave., Ste. 210
Baltimore, MD 21208

Ravencraft, Jeff, President, COO
USB Implementers Forum [6338]
3855 SW 153rd Dr.
Beaverton, OR 97006
Ph: (503)619-0426
Fax: (503)644-6708

Ravicher, Daniel B., President, Exec.
Dir.
Public Patent Foundation [5676]
55 5th Ave.
New York, NY 10003
Ph: (212)545-5337
Fax: (212)591-6038

Rawal, Sucheta, Founder, Exec. Dir.
Go Eat Give [9210]
2366 Oberon Walk SE
Smyrna, GA 30080
Ph: (678)744-8306

Rawlings, Hunter R., President
Association of American Universities
[7622]
1200 New York Ave. NW, Ste. 550
Washington, DC 20005-6122
Ph: (202)408-7500
Fax: (202)408-8184

Rawls, Mr. S. Waite, III, CEO
Museum of the Confederacy [9495]
1201 E Clay St.
Richmond, VA 23219
Ph: (804)649-1861
Toll Free: 855-649-1861

Rawson, Cheryl, Contact
Life Resources Institute [15268]
c/o Kristin Abbott, Financial Director
61 Morse Ave.
Ashland, OR 97520
Ph: (541)482-1289

Ray, Brian D., PhD, Founder
National Home Education Research
Institute [7999]
PO Box 13939
Salem, OR 97309
Ph: (503)364-1490
Fax: (503)364-2827

Ray, Charles, III, CEO, Founder,
President
CR3 Diabetes Association, Inc.
[14521]
PO Box 792
Apex, NC 27502-0792
Ph: (919)303-6949
Fax: (919)267-9629

Ray, David, President
National Cambridge Collectors, Inc.
[22137]
136 S 9th St.
Cambridge, OH 43725-2453
Ph: (740)432-4245

Ray, G. Mark, President
Association of Tourist Railroads and
Railway Museums [2836]
PO Box 1189
Covington, GA 30015
Ph: (770)278-0088

Ray, Greg, Secretary
Society for Exact Philosophy [10123]
Dept. of Philosophy
University of Florida
330 Griffin-Floyd Hall
Gainesville, FL 32611-8545
Ph: (352)392-2084
Fax: (352)392-5577

Ray, Krishnendu, President
Association for the Study of Food
and Society [6641]
c/o Amy Bentley, Editor
NYU Steinhardt
Dept. of Nutrition, Food Studies, and
Public Health
411 Lafayette St., 5th Fl.
New York, NY 10003

Ray, Melinda Mercer, Exec. Dir.
National Association of Clinical
Nurse Specialists [16146]
100 N 20th St., 4th Fl.
Philadelphia, PA 19103-1462
Ph: (215)320-3881
Fax: (215)564-2175

Ray, Meredith K., President
Society for the Study of Early
Modern Women [8756]
c/o Deborah Uman, Treasurer
3690 E Ave.
Rochester, NY 14618
Ph: (585)385-5258

Ray, Michelle, VP
Association of Black Women in
Higher Education [8746]
University of Pennsylvania
3537 Locust Walk, Ste. 200
Philadelphia, PA 19104-6225

Ray, Rachael, Founder
Yum-O Organization [12121]
132 E 43rd St., No. 223
New York, NY 10017

Rayburn, Mr. Eric, Info. Technology
Mgr.
United Producers, Inc. [3578]
8351 N High St., Ste. 250
Columbus, OH 43235
Toll Free: 800-456-3276

Raylman, Rob, Exec. Dir., CEO
Gift of Life International [12276]
22 Clovebrook Rd.
Valhalla, NY 10595
Ph: (845)546-2104
Toll Free: 855-734-3278

Raymer, Dr. Roger, Chairman
Camino Global [20391]
8625 La Prada Dr.
Dallas, TX 75228
Ph: (214)327-8206
Toll Free: 800-366-2264
Fax: (214)327-8201

Raymond, David A., CEO, President
American Council of Engineering
Companies [6528]
1015 15th St. NW, 8th Fl.
Washington, DC 20005-2605
Ph: (202)347-7474
Fax: (202)898-0068

Raymond, Matt, Contact
Alliance to Feed the Future [3557]
1100 Connecticut Ave. NW
Washington, DC 20036

Raymond, Sandra C., CEO, President
Lupus Foundation of America [15541]
2000 L St. NW, Ste. 410
Washington, DC 20036-4952
Fax: (202)349-1156

Raynard, Tricia, Exec. Dir.
Empower Peace [18782]
240 Commercial St., 2nd Fl.
Boston, MA 02109
Ph: (617)912-3800

Rayner, Wendy, President
Galapagos Conservancy [3874]
11150 Fairfax Blvd., Ste. 408
Fairfax, VA 22030
Ph: (703)383-0077
Fax: (703)383-1177

Raynes, Linda J., CEO, President
Electrical Apparatus Service Association [1017]
1331 Baur Blvd.
Saint Louis, MO 63132
Ph: (314)993-2220
Fax: (314)993-1269

Raysbrook, Julie, Contact
Disability Advocates for Cystic Fibrosis [11585]
C/O Julie Pereira 513 203rd PL SW
Mukilteo, WA 98275
Ph: (425)280-7310
Fax: (425)672-5133

Razani, Rezwan, Exec. Dir.
Focus Fusion Society [6485]
128 Lincoln Blvd.
Middlesex, NJ 08846
Ph: (732)356-5900
Fax: (732)377-0381

Razaq, Janice Larzon, VP
American Matthay Association [8359]
c/o Mary Pendleton-Hoffer, President
405 E Hermosa Cir.
Tempe, AZ 85282

Rea, Glen, Director
The American Chestnut Foundation [6129]
50 N Merrimon Ave., Ste. 115
Asheville, NC 28804
Ph: (828)281-0047
Fax: (828)253-5373

Rea, William J., MD, Founder
American Environmental Health Foundation [14712]
8345 Walnut Hill Ln., Ste. 225
Dallas, TX 75231
Ph: (214)361-9515
Toll Free: 800-428-2343
Fax: (214)361-2534

Read, Dale, President
Specialty Sleep Association [1488]
c/o Tambra Jones, Executive Director
46639 Jones Ranch Rd.
Friant, CA 93626
Ph: (559)868-4187
Toll Free: 888-220-6173

Read, David, Bd. Member
Association of Food and Drug Officials [5221]
2550 Kingston Rd., Ste. 311
York, PA 17402
Ph: (717)757-2888
Fax: (717)650-3650

Reade, Amanda, Dir. of Comm.
Monterey County Vintners and Growers Association [4929]

PO Box 1793
Monterey, CA 93942
Ph: (831)375-9400

Reading, Michael, Chmn. of the Bd.
CONTACT USA [20040]
165 Nedobity Rd.
Higganum, CT 06441
Toll Free: 800-273-8255

Ream, Rob, Chairman
Energy Security Council [1787]
9720 Cypresswood Dr., Ste. 206
Houston, TX 77070
Ph: (281)587-2700
Fax: (281)807-6000

Ream, Roger, Chairman
Foundation for Economic Education [18955]
1718 Peachtree Rd. NE, Ste. 300
Atlanta, GA 30309
Ph: (404)554-9980
Toll Free: 800-960-4333
Fax: (404)393-3142

Ream, Roger, President
Foundation for Teaching Economics [7730]
260 Russell Blvd., Ste. B
Davis, CA 95616-3839
Ph: (530)757-4630
Fax: (530)757-4636

Ream, Roger R., President
Fund for American Studies [8194]
1706 New Hampshire Ave. NW
Washington, DC 20009
Ph: (202)986-0384
Fax: (202)986-0390

Reardon, David C., PhD, Director
Elliot Institute [10428]
PO Box 7348
Springfield, IL 62791-7348
Ph: (217)525-8202
Toll Free: 888-412-2676
Fax: (217)525-8212

Reardon, Roberta, Bd. Member
Screen Actors Guild - American Federation of Television and Radio Artists [23499]
5757 Wilshire Blvd., 7th Fl.
Los Angeles, CA 90036
Ph: (323)954-1600
Toll Free: 855-724-2387

Reardon, Susan K., CEO
Military Operations Research Society [5604]
2111 Wilson Blvd., Ste. 700
Arlington, VA 22201
Ph: (703)933-9070
Fax: (703)933-9066

Reasoner, Mark, President
American Stamp Dealers Association [1640]
PO Box 692
Leesport, PA 19533
Toll Free: 800-369-8207

Reaves, Charles, Exec. Dir.
Children Awaiting Parents [10448]
274 N Goodman St., Ste. D103
Rochester, NY 14607
Ph: (585)232-5110
Toll Free: 888-835-8802
Fax: (585)232-2634

Reavis, Mr. Charlie, President
National Spasmodic Dysphonia Association [15971]
300 Park Blvd., Ste. 335
Itasca, IL 60143
Toll Free: 800-795-6732
Fax: (630)250-4505

Rebuck, Patricia, Contact
Palomino Horse Association [4399]
c/o Patricia Rebuck
10171 Nectar Ave.
Nelson, MO 65347
Ph: (660)859-2064
(660)859-2058

Rechler, Evelyn, President
Ladies Kennel Association of America [21911]
c/o Patricia Cruz, Secreatary
15 Shiloh Ct.
Coram, NY 11727
Ph: (631)928-1517

Rechler, Scott, CEO, Director
LearnServe International [8538]
PO Box 6203
Washington, DC 20015
Ph: (202)370-1865
Fax: (202)355-0993

Recht, Michael, MD, PhD, Chairman
American Thrombosis and Hemostasis Network [15222]
72 Treasure Ln.
Deerfield, IL 60015
Toll Free: 800-360-2846
Fax: (847)572-0967

Reckford, Jonathan, CEO
Habitat for Humanity International [11971]
121 Habitat St.
Americus, GA 31709-3498
Ph: (229)924-6935
Toll Free: 800-422-4828

Reckmeyer, Dr. Richard, Exec. Dir., Team Ldr.
Rural Rwanda Dental [15088]
14109 N 69th Dr.
Peoria, AZ 85381
Ph: (623)258-5084

Rectenwald, Michael, PhD, Chairman, Founder
Citizens for Legitimate Government [18311]
PO Box 1142
Bristol, CT 06011-1142

Redd, Margaret, Exec. Dir.
National African-American Insurance Association [1886]
1718 M St. NW
Washington, DC 20036-4504
Toll Free: 866-56-NAAIA
Fax: (513)563-9743

Reddell, Jeff, President
National Windshield Repair Association [352]
PO Box 569
Garrisonville, VA 22463
Ph: (540)720-7484
Fax: (540)720-5687

Redden, Clif, President
Ameraucana Breeders Club [3654]
c/o Susan Mouw, Secretary-Treasurer
156 Titanic Rd.
Aiken, SC 29805

Redding, Charles, President, CEO
MedShare International [12292]
3240 Clifton Springs Rd.
Decatur, GA 30034-4608
Ph: (770)323-5858
Fax: (770)323-4301

Reddington, John, President, CEO
Morris Animal Foundation [10661]
720 S Colorado Blvd., Ste. 174A
Denver, CO 80246
Ph: (303)790-2345
Toll Free: 800-243-2345
Fax: (303)790-4066

Reddy, Ms. Diane, President
World War II War Brides Association [21047]
c/o Erin Craig
PO BOX 1812
El Centro, CA 92244-1812
Ph: (928)237-1581

Reddy, Karra, Mgr.
Maryknoll Sisters of Saint Dominic [20433]
PO Box 311
Maryknoll, NY 10545-0311
Ph: (914)941-7575
Toll Free: 866-662-9900
Fax: (914)923-0733

Reddy, Leo, Chmn. of the Bd., President, CEO
Manufacturing Skill Standards Council [7232]
901 N Washington St., Ste. 600
Alexandria, VA 22314
Ph: (703)739-9000
(703)739-9000

Reddy, Narend, President
American Hindu Association [20199]
PO Box 628243
Middleton, WI 53562
Ph: (608)234-8634

Reddy, Vanita, President
Indo-American Eyecare Organization [16386]
2975 Leslie Park Cir.
Ann Arbor, MI 48105
Ph: (734)996-2866
Fax: (734)996-1638

Redford, Katie, Chmn. of the Bd.
Bank Information Center [386]
1023 15th St. NW, 10th Fl.
Washington, DC 20005
Ph: (202)737-7752
Fax: (202)737-1155

Redford, Katie, Director, Founder
EarthRights International [18394]
1612 K St. NW, Ste. 401
Washington, DC 20006
Ph: (202)466-5188

Redford, Robert, President, Founder
Sundance Institute [9314]
1825 Three Kings Dr.
Park City, UT 84060
Ph: (435)658-3456
Fax: (435)658-3457

Redinger, Sally, President
Daughters of Union Veterans of the Civil War, 1861-1865 [20740]
503 S Walnut St.
Springfield, IL 62705
Ph: (217)544-0616

Redlener, Irwin, MD, Founder, President
Children's Health Fund [14179]
215 W 125th St., Ste. 301
New York, NY 10027
Ph: (212)535-9400

Redman-Gress, Warren, Exec. Dir.
Alliance for Full Acceptance [11871]
29 Leinbach Dr.
Charleston, SC 29407
Ph: (843)883-0343
Fax: (843)723-3859

Redmond, Brooke G., Dir. of Comm., Dir. of Dev.
Farm-Based Education Network [7475]
c/o Shelburne Farms
1611 Harbor Rd.
Shelburne, VT 05482
Ph: (802)985-0382

Redmond, Katherine, Founder
National Coalition Against Violent
Athletes **[22511]**
PO Box 620453
Littleton, CO 80162
Ph: (303)524-9853

Redner, Michele
Circum-Pacific Council for Energy
and Mineral Resources **[6872]**
c/o Michele Redner, Secretariat
12201 Sunrise Valley Dr.
MS-917
Reston, VA 20192
Ph: (703)648-5042
Fax: (703)648-4227

Redstone, Leanne H., Exec. Dir.,
Secretary
Small Business Council of America
[18063]
1523 Concord Pke., Ste. 300
Brandywine E
Wilmington, DE 19803
Ph: (302)691-7222

Reed, Ms. Cindy, Mgr.
Wally Byam Caravan Club
International **[22420]**
PO Box 612
Jackson Center, OH 45334
Ph: (937)596-5211
Fax: (937)596-5542

Reed, Debbie, Exec. Dir.
Coalition on Agricultural Greenhouse
Gases **[6660]**
c/o New Venture Fund
1201 Connecticut Ave. NW, Ste. 300
Washington, DC 20036
Ph: (202)701-4298

Reed, Debbie, Exec. Dir.
International Biochar Initiative **[5885]**
640 Brook Run Dr.
Westerville, OH 43081
Ph: (802)257-5359

Reed, Dirk, President
Riva Club USA **[22664]**
2528 Ptarmigan Dr., No. 4
Walnut Creek, CA 94595-3254
Ph: (530)277-7507
   (954)609-6485

Reed, Florence, Founder, President
Sustainable Harvest International
[3577]
104 Main St.
Ellsworth, ME 04605
Ph: (207)669-8254
Fax: (207)591-4742

Reed, Glenn, President
Pacific Seafood Processors Associa-
tion **[3036]**
1900 W Emerson Pl., Ste. 205
Seattle, WA 98119
Ph: (206)281-1667

Reed, Kathy Trexel, VP
Guild of American Papercutters
[21758]
214 S Harrison Ave.
Somerset, PA 15501
Ph: (456)867-2365

Reed, Kimberly, JD, CAE, President
International Food Information
Council **[1343]**
1100 Connecticut Ave. NW, Ste. 430
Washington, DC 20036
Ph: (202)296-6540

Reed, Lea Ann, Dir. of Operations
Association of Diesel Specialists
[1125]
400 Admiral Blvd.

Kansas City, MO 64106
Ph: (816)285-0810
Fax: (847)770-4952

Reed, Linda Soley, VP
American Accordionists' Association
[9850]
c/o Mary J. Tokarski, President
15 Maplewood Ln.
Northford, CT 06472
Ph: (203)484-5095
Fax: (203)484-5095

Reed, Lyle, Chairman, Exec. Dir.
Recreation Vehicle Industry Associa-
tion **[2920]**
1896 Preston White Dr.
Reston, VA 20191
Ph: (703)620-6003
Fax: (703)620-5071

Reed, Susan, President
Association of Official Seed Analysts
[4945]
653 Consitution Ave. NE
Washington, DC 20002
Ph: (202)870-2412

Reed, Tamela A., Founder, CEO
Rock Cancer C.A.R.E **[14058]**
5402 Ruffin Rd., Ste. 205
San Diego, CA 92123
Toll Free: 888-251-0620

Reed, Thomas M., Chairman
Forest Resources Association, Inc.
[1409]
1901 Pennsylvania Ave. NW, Ste.
303
Washington, DC 20006
Ph: (202)296-3937
Fax: (202)296-0562

Reed, William, Chairman
Professional Convention Manage-
ment Association **[2336]**
35 E Wacker Dr., Ste. 500
Chicago, IL 60601-2105
Ph: (312)423-7262
Toll Free: 877-827-7262
Fax: (312)423-7222

Reed, Mr. Worley Lee, Chairperson
American Society for the Support of
Injured Survivors of Terrorism
[13256]
c/o Mr. Worley Lee Reed,
Chairperson
4371 Dinner Lake Blvd.
Lake Wales, FL 33859-2135
Ph: (863)223-1818
Fax: (863)582-9318

Reede, Deborah L., President
Association of Program Coordinators
in Radiology **[17053]**
820 Jorie Blvd.
Oak Brook, IL 60523
Ph: (630)368-3737
Fax: (630)571-2198

Reede, Deborah L., President
Association of Program Directors in
Radiology **[15622]**
820 Jorie Blvd.
Oak Brook, IL 60523
Ph: (630)368-3737

Reedenauer, Mark, President, Exec.
Dir.
National Marine Electronics Associa-
tion **[2253]**
692 Ritchie Hwy., Ste. 104
Severna Park, MD 21146-3919
Ph: (410)975-9425
Fax: (410)975-9450

Reeder, Deborah B., Exec. Dir.
American Association of Equine
Veterinary Technicians and As-
sistants **[17594]**

c/o Deborah B. Reeder, Executive
Director
539 Wild Horse Ln.
San Marcos, CA 92078
Fax: (760)301-0349

Reeder, Michele M., Exec. Dir.
American Academy of Oral Medicine
[14383]
2150 N 107th St., Ste. 205
Seattle, WA 98133
Ph: (206)209-5279

Reedy, Gary, CEO
American Cancer Society **[13882]**
250 Williams St. NW
Atlanta, GA 30303-1002
Toll Free: 800-227-2345

Reedy, Keith, Director
Bibles for the Blind and Visually
Handicapped International **[19754]**
3228 E Rosehill Ave.
Terre Haute, IN 47805-1297
Ph: (812)466-4899

Rees, Mary ', Membership Chp.
Gottscheer Heritage and Genealogy
Association **[19447]**
PO Box 725
Louisville, CO 80027-0725

Rees, Michael, CEO, Medical Dir.
Alliance for Paired Donation **[15867]**
PO Box 965
Perrysburg, OH 43552
Ph: (419)866-5505
Toll Free: 877-273-4255
Fax: (419)383-5579

Rees, Nina, President, CEO
National Alliance for Public Charter
Schools **[8477]**
1101 15th St. NW, Ste. 1010
Washington, DC 20005
Ph: (202)289-2700

Rees, Susan, Director
Society for Psychophysiological
Research **[16943]**
2424 American Ln.
Madison, WI 53704
Ph: (608)443-2472
Fax: (608)443-2474

Reese, Benjamin D., Jr., President
National Association of Diversity Of-
ficers in Higher Education **[7963]**
4440 PGA Blvd., Ste. 600
Palm Beach Gardens, FL 33410
Ph: (561)472-8479
Fax: (561)472-8401

Reese, Marily, Exec. Dir.
National Forest Recreation Associa-
tion **[2913]**
PO Box 488
Woodlake, CA 93286
Ph: (559)564-2365
Fax: (559)564-2048

Reese, William S., CEO, President
International Youth Foundation
[13453]
32 South St.
Baltimore, MD 21202-3214
Ph: (410)951-1500
Fax: (410)347-1188

Reeves, Christy, CEO
SingleStop USA **[12565]**
123 William St., Ste. 901
New York, NY 10038
Ph: (212)480-2870

Reeves, Claire R., CCDC, Founder
Mothers Against Sexual Abuse
[12927]

404 Wilson St.
Union, SC 29379

Reeves, Mark, President
Alumni Association, School of
Medicine of Loma Linda University
[7492]
11245 Anderson St., Ste. 200
Loma Linda, CA 92354
Ph: (909)558-4633
Fax: (909)558-4638

Reeves, Mr. Norman, Secretary,
Treasurer, Membership Chp.
International Association of
Bloodstain Pattern Analysts **[5154]**
12139 E Makohoh Trl.
Tucson, AZ 85749-8179
Ph: (520)760-6620
Fax: (520)760-5590

Reeves, Scott, Contact
Society of Cardiovascular
Anesthesiologists **[13709]**
8735 W Higgins Rd., Ste. 300
Chicago, IL 60631
Toll Free: 855-658-2828
Fax: (847)375-6323

Reeves-Pepin, Jaclyn, Exec. Dir.
National Association of Biology
Teachers **[8650]**
PO Box 3363
Warrenton, VA 20188
Ph: (703)264-9696
Toll Free: 888-501-NABT
Fax: (202)962-3939

Reff, Michael J., RPh, Founder,
President
National Community Oncology
Dispensing Association, Inc.
[16350]
PO Box 308
East Syracuse, NY 13057
Ph: (315)256-4935

Refo, Carter B., Exec. Dir.
Robert E. Lee Memorial Association
[10348]
Stratford Hall Plantation
483 Great House Rd.
Stratford, VA 22558-0001
Ph: (804)493-8038

Regan, Carol, Assoc. Dir.
Religious Formation Conference
[19901]
3025 4th St. NE, Ste. 124
Washington, DC 20017-1101
Ph: (202)827-4562
Fax: (202)827-4564

Regan, Elizabeth, President
Organizational Systems Research
Association **[8664]**
Morehead State University
150 University Blvd.
Morehead, KY 40351-1689
Ph: (606)783-2718
Fax: (606)783-5025

Regan, Jerry, President
Hawk Mountain Sanctuary **[4825]**
1700 Hawk Mountain Rd.
Kempton, PA 19529
Ph: (610)756-6961
Fax: (610)756-4468

Regan, Margaret, President, CEO
International MultiCultural Institute
[11492]
595 6th St.
Brooklyn, NY 11215
Ph: (718)832-8625

Regan, Ron, Exec. Dir.
Association of Fish and Wildlife
Agencies **[3813]**

444 N Capitol St. NW, Ste. 725
Washington, DC 20001
Ph: (202)624-7890
Fax: (202)624-7891

Regan, Tom, Founder, President
Culture and Animals Foundation
[10609]
3509 Eden Croft Dr.
Raleigh, NC 27612
Ph: (919)782-3739

Regelbrugge, Craig J., VP
AmericanHort [4501]
525 9th St. NW, Ste. 800
Washington, DC 20004
Ph: (202)789-2900
Fax: (202)789-1893

Reger, Jason, President
National Wildlife Control Operators
Association [4847]
PO Box 655
Fredericksburg, VA 22404
Ph: (540)374-5600
Toll Free: 855-GON-WCOA

Regis, Nicolette, Administrator
THIS for Diplomats [18559]
1630 Crescent Pl. NW
Washington, DC 20009
Ph: (202)232-3002

Regmi, Ashok, Mem.
Youth Action Network [18508]
32 South St.
Baltimore, MD 21202
Ph: (410)951-1500
Fax: (410)347-1188

Rehberg, Sarah, President
National Association of Agriculture
Employees [4947]
9080 Torrey Rd.
Willis, MI 48191
Fax: (734)229-1654

Rehder, Jens, 1st VP
American/Schleswig-Holstein
Heritage Society [20955]
PO Box 506
Walcott, IA 52773-0506
Ph: (563)284-4184
Fax: (563)284-4184

Rehkop, T.G., Secretary
Precancel Stamp Society [22357]
c/o T.G. Rehkop, Secretary
PO Box 1013
Fenton, MO 63026-1013

Reichardt, Mark, CEO, President
Open Geospatial Consortium [6329]
35 Main St., Ste. 5
Wayland, MA 01778-5037
Ph: (508)655-5858
Fax: (508)655-2237

Reichen, Ron, Officer
Society of Collision Repair Special-
ists [354]
PO Box 909
Prosser, WA 99350
Ph: (302)423-3537
Toll Free: 877-841-0660
Fax: (877)851-0660

Reichenberg, Neil, Exec. Dir.
International Public Management
Association for Human Resources
[1094]
1617 Duke St.
Alexandria, VA 22314
Ph: (703)549-7100
Fax: (703)684-0948

Reichert, Janice M., PhD, President
Antibody Society [15373]
PO Box 162

Waban, MA 02468

Reichert, Kelli, Secretary
Toy Australian Shepherd Association
of America [21971]
c/o Kelli Reichert, Championship
Secretary
495 Robinson Rd.
Woodland, WA 98674

Reichle, Janice, President
United Silver and Golden Fanciers
[21575]
c/o Sally Daniels, Treasurer
5242 Vista Grande Dr.
Santa Rosa, CA 95403
Ph: (707)545-8927

Reid, Eustace
International Lead Zinc Research
Organization [6845]
1822 NC Hwy. 54 E, Ste. 120
Durham, NC 27713-3210
Ph: (919)361-4647
Fax: (919)361-1957

Reid, Frances, Director, Producer
Iris Films [10304]
2443 Fillmore St., No. 380-3013
San Francisco, CA 94115

Reid, Fritz, President
Boreal Songbird Initiative [4800]
1904 3rd Ave., Ste. 305
Seattle, WA 98101
Ph: (206)956-9040
Fax: (206)447-4824

Reid, Gloria, Treasurer
Graham Owners Club International
[21389]
c/o Gloria Reid, Treasurer, 4028
Empire Creek Cir.
4028 Empire Creek Cir.
Georgetown, CA 95634
Ph: (530)333-4105

Reid, James R., Secretary,
Treasurer
90th Division Association [21098]
c/o James R. Reid, Executive
Secretary/Treasurer
17 Lake Shore Dr.
Willowbrook, IL 60527-2221
Ph: (630)789-0204
Fax: (630)789-0499

Reid, Kenneth D., CAE, Exec. VP
American Water Resources Associa-
tion [7364]
PO Box 1626
Middleburg, VA 20118
Ph: (540)687-8390
Fax: (540)687-8395

Reid, Laura, Chairperson
Pet Industry Joint Advisory Council
[2549]
1146 19th St. NW, Ste. 350
Washington, DC 20036-3746
Ph: (202)452-1525

Reid, Louann, Chairperson
Conference on English Education
[7868]
National Council of Teachers of
English
1111 W Kenyon Rd.
Urbana, IL 61801-1010
Ph: (217)328-3870
Toll Free: 877-369-6283

Reid, Michelle M., Dir. of Mtgs.,
Exec. Asst.
The Real Estate Roundtable [2891]
801 Pennsylvania Ave. NW, Ste. 720
Washington, DC 20004
Ph: (202)639-8400
Fax: (202)639-8442

Reid, Mike, Director
Pellet Fuels Institute [4267]
2150 N 107th St., Ste. 205
Seattle, WA 98133
Ph: (206)209-5277
Fax: (206)367-8777

Reidy, Christine, Exec. Dir.
Commission on Dietetic Registration
[16213]
120 S Riverside Plz., Ste. 2000
Chicago, IL 60606-6995
Ph: (312)899-0040
Toll Free: 800-877-1600
Fax: (312)899-4772

Reiff, Linda, President, CEO
Napa Valley Vintners [4931]
1475 Library Ln.
Saint Helena, CA 94574
Ph: (707)963-3388
Fax: (707)963-3488

Reiling, David, Director
Community Development Bankers
Association [390]
1444 Eye St., Ste. 201
Washington, DC 20005
Ph: (202)689-8935

Reilly, Beth, President
Abyssinian Cat Club of America
[21563]
23700 Stagecoach Rd.
Volcano, CA 95689-9663
Ph: (716)839-5919

Reilly, Carol, Exec. Dir.
Pharmaceutical Business Intel-
ligence and Research Group
[2567]
114 Madison Way
Lansdale, PA 19446
Ph: (215)855-5255
Fax: (215)855-5622

Reilly, Jane, Exec. Dir.
Overseas Press Club Foundation
[8159]
40 W 45 St.
New York, NY 10036
Ph: (201)493-9087
Fax: (201)612-9915

Reilly, Mark, President
APA Division 25: Behavioral Analysis
[16877]
750 1st St. NE
Washington, DC 20002-4242
Ph: (202)336-5500

Reilly, Patrick J., President
Cardinal Newman Society [7578]
9720 Capital Ct., Ste. 201
Manassas, VA 20110
Ph: (703)367-0333
Fax: (703)396-8668

Reilly, Mgr. Phillip, Founder
Helpers of God's Precious Infants
[19059]
Monastery of the Precious Blood
5300 Fort Hamilton Pky.
Brooklyn, NY 11219
Fax: (718)853-0599

Reilly, William K., Co-Ch.
Global Water Challenge [4757]
2900 S Quincy St., Ste. 375
Arlington, VA 22206
Ph: (703)379-2713

Reim, Jason, Mgr.
HRO Today Services and Technol-
ogy Association [1695]
SharedXpertise Media, LLC
123 S Broad St., Ste. 1930
Philadelphia, PA 19109
Ph: (215)606-9520

Reiman, Rose, Gov.
Pilgrim Edward Doty Society [20751]
c/o Judy Wilson
PO Box 247
Manzanita, OR 97130

Reimanis, Cathy, DNP, MS, CNS,
ANP-BC, CWOCN, President
Wound, Ostomy and Continence
Nursing Certification Board [16193]
555 E Wells St., Ste. 1100
Milwaukee, WI 53202-3823
Toll Free: 888-496-2622
Fax: (414)276-2146

Reimann, Martin
Association for NeuroPsychoEconomics [6382]
c/o Catherine Wattenberg
750 1st St. NE
Washington, DC 20002

Reimer, Gen. Dennis J., President
Army Emergency Relief [19380]
200 Stovall St., Rm. 5S33
Alexandria, VA 22332-4005
Ph: (703)428-0000
Toll Free: 866-878-6378
Fax: (703)325-7183

Reimer, Henry, Chairman
Lamp for Haiti [11928]
PO Box 39703
Philadelphia, PA 19106
Ph: (267)295-2822

Reimnitz, Arlen, Exec. Dir.
American Society of Electroneurodi-
agnostic Technologists [14656]
402 E Bannister Rd., Ste. A
Kansas City, MO 64131-3019
Ph: (816)931-1120
Fax: (816)931-1145

Reindollar, Richard H., MD, CEO
American Society for Reproductive
Medicine [14753]
1209 Montgomery Hwy.
Birmingham, AL 35216-2809
Ph: (205)978-5000
Fax: (205)978-5005

Reiner, Frank, President
Chlorine Institute [714]
1300 Wilson Blvd., Ste 525
Arlington, VA 22209
Ph: (703)894-4140
Fax: (703)894-4130

Reiner, Nancy, Founder
Green Pro Bono [5531]
727 Massachusetts Ave.
Cambridge, MA 02139
Ph: (617)603-3537

Reiner, Rob, Founder
Parents' Action For Children [12421]
4117 Hillsboro Pike, Ste. 103-130
Nashville, TN 37215
Toll Free: 888-447-3400
Fax: (954)745-1133

Reinfeld, Jennifer, Exec. Dir.,
Founder
Children of the Earth United [4113]
PO Box 258035
Madison, WI 53725
Ph: (608)237-6577

Reinhard, Johnny, Director, Founder
American Festival of Microtonal
Music [9857]
c/o Johnny Reinhard, Director
318 E 70th St., Ste. 5FW
New York, NY 10021

Reinhard, Stephen, President
Young Stamp Collectors of America
[22382]

100 Match Factory Pl.
Bellefonte, PA 16823-1367
Ph: (814)933-3803
Fax: (814)933-6128

Reinhardt, Christy, Chmn. of the Bd.
Crew's Voice [13762]
14 Maple Ln.
Pawling, NY 12564
Ph: (914)804-4740

Reinhardt, Mary Jane, Director
North American Association of Utility
    Distributors [3422]
c/o Mary Jane Reinhardt, Director
3105 Corporate Exchange Ct.
Bridgeton, MO 63044
Ph: (314)506-0724
Fax: (314)506-0790

Reinhardt, Susan, Chairman
National Academy for State Health
    Policy [15038]
10 Free St., 2nd Fl.
Portland, ME 04101
Ph: (207)874-6524
Fax: (207)874-6527

Reinhold, Susan D., Chmn. of the
    Bd.
Worldwide Pollution Control Associa-
    tion [4558]
12190 Hubbard St.
Livonia, MI 48150
Ph: (734)525-0300
Fax: (734)525-0303

Reinke, Denise, President, CEO
Sarcoma Alliance for Research
    through Collaboration [14060]
24 Frank Lloyd Wright Dr., Lobby A,
    Ste. 3100
Ann Arbor, MI 48105
Ph: (734)930-7600
Fax: (734)930-7557

Reinsch, William A., President
National Foreign Trade Council
    [1971]
1625 K St. NW, Ste. 200
Washington, DC 20006
Ph: (202)887-0278
Fax: (202)452-8160

Reinsdorf, Andrew, V. Chmn. of the
    Bd.
Satellite Broadcasting and Com-
    munications Association [3238]
1100 17th St. NW, Ste. 1150
Washington, DC 20036
Ph: (202)349-3620
Toll Free: 800-541-5981
Fax: (202)318-2618

Reinwald, Charles, Jr., President
Cancer Cure Coalition [13920]
325 Beach Rd., Ste. 204
Tequesta, FL 33469
Ph: (561)747-2174
Fax: (561)747-2174

Reip, David O., Treasurer
Patent Office Professional Associa-
    tion [5338]
PO Box 25287
Alexandria, VA 22313
Ph: (571)272-7161

Reis, Jennifer, VP
Surface Design Association [3271]
PO Box 360
Sebastopol, CA 95473-0360
Ph: (707)829-3110
Fax: (707)829-3285

Reisch, Jennifer, Dir. of Legal Svcs.
Equal Rights Advocates [5722]
1170 Market St., Ste. 700

San Francisco, CA 94102
Ph: (415)621-0672
Toll Free: 800-839-4372
Fax: (415)621-6744

Reisdorff, Earl J., MD, Exec. Dir.
American Board of Emergency
    Medicine [14672]
3000 Coolidge Rd.
East Lansing, MI 48823-6319
Ph: (517)332-4800
Fax: (517)332-2234

Reisen, Matthias, President, Trustee
International Herb Association [4294]
PO Box 5667
Jacksonville, FL 32247-5667

Reisenauer, Kevin, Officer
DECA Inc. [8270]
1908 Association Dr.
Reston, VA 20191-1502
Ph: (703)860-5000

Reiser, Thomas, Exec. Dir.
International Society on Thrombosis
    and Haemostasis [15239]
610 Jones Ferry Rd., Ste. 205
Carrboro, NC 27510-6113
Ph: (919)929-3807
Fax: (919)929-3935

Reisfeld, Joanie, Founder
Better BedRest [16278]
PO Box 212
Savage, MD 20763
Ph: (410)740-7662

Reising, Steven C., Chairman
International Union of Radio
    Science-United States National
    Committee [7315]
Colorado State University
Electrical and Computer Engineering
    Dept.
1373 Campus Delivery
Fort Collins, CO 80523-1373
Ph: (970)491-2228
Fax: (970)491-2249

Reisinger, Brenda, Exec. Dir.
National Association of Independent
    Insurance Adjusters [1894]
1880 Radcliff Ct.
Tracy, CA 95376-2330
Ph: (209)832-6962
Fax: (209)832-6964

Reisinger, Rev. Franz, Founder
Secular Institute of Saint Francis de
    Sales [19904]
c/o DeSales Secular Institute
104 W Main St.
Middletown, PA 17057-1215

Reiss, Ellen, Chairperson, Chmn. of
    the Bd.
Aesthetic Realism Foundation
    [10074]
141 Greene St.
New York, NY 10012
Ph: (212)777-4490

Reiss, Gail, CEO, President
American Friends of Tel Aviv
    University [8131]
39 Broadway, Ste. 1510
New York, NY 10006
Ph: (212)742-9070
Toll Free: 800-989-1198
Fax: (212)742-9071

Reister, Christian, President
International Livestock Identification
    Association [4455]
c/o Tammy Bridges, Secretary/
    Treasurer
6335 Mt. Vista

Helena, MT 59602
Ph: (406)457-0087

Reiter, Ed, Exec. Dir.
Numismatic Literary Guild [22279]
c/o Ed Reiter, Executive Director
1517 Stewart Dr.
Nanticoke, PA 18634
Ph: (570)740-2181
Fax: (570)740-2723

Reiter, Dr. Kimberly, Chairperson
Interdisciplinary Environmental As-
    sociation [4117]
Assumption College
Dept. of Economics & Global Stud-
    ies
500 Salisbury St.
Worcester, MA 01609
Ph: (508)767-7296
Fax: (508)767-7382

Reiter, Scott, President
National Association of Business
    Political Action Committees
    [18872]
101 Constitution Ave. NW, Ste.
    L-110
Washington, DC 20001-2115
Ph: (202)341-3780
Fax: (202)478-0342

Reiter-Palmon, Dr. Roni, Secretary
APA Division 10: Society for the
    Psychology of Aesthetics, Creativ-
    ity and the Arts [16869]
750 1st St. NE
Washington, DC 20002-4241
Ph: (202)336-6013
Fax: (202)218-3599

Reither, Eric, Secretary
Association of Population Centers
    [6366]
c/o Lisa Berkman, President
Massachusetts Hall
Harvard University
Cambridge, MA 02138

Reitmeier, Glenn, Bd. Member
Advanced Television Systems Com-
    mittee [451]
1776 K St. NW, 8th Fl.
Washington, DC 20006-2304
Ph: (202)872-9160
Fax: (202)872-9161

Relave, Nanette, Director
Center for Workers with Disabilities
    [11579]
1133 19th St. NW, Ste. 400
Washington, DC 20036
Ph: (202)682-0100
Fax: (202)204-0071

Remak, Bill, BSc, Chairman
National Association of Hepatitis
    Task Forces [15257]
Miller Depot
Miller, NE 68858
Ph: (308)457-2641
Fax: (308)457-2641

Rembiesa, Barbara, Founder,
    President, CEO
International Association of Informa-
    tion Technology Asset Managers
    Inc. [1790]
4848 Munson St. NW
Canton, OH 44718
Ph: (330)628-3012
Toll Free: 877-942-4826
Fax: (330)628-3289

Remer, Randa, Treasurer
APA Division 51: Society for the
    Psychological Study of Men and
    Masculinity [16894]

750 1st St. NE
Washington, DC 20002-4241
Toll Free: 800-336-6013

Remick, Gloria, CEO
American Darters Association
    [22765]
PO Box 627
Wentzville, MO 63385-0627
Ph: (636)614-4380
Fax: (636)673-1092

Remington, Cheryl, President
National Association of County Col-
    lectors, Treasurers and Finance
    Officers [5707]
c/o Cheryl Remington, President
PO Box 127
Gove, KS 67736
Ph: (785)938-2275
Fax: (785)938-2222

Remirez, Felix, Treasurer
Republican National Hispanic As-
    sembly [19050]
247 Boca Ciega Rd.
Mascotte, FL 34753-9275
Ph: (202)800-8334

Remple, Melanie, Secretary
Rainbow Division Veterans Memorial
    Foundation [21209]
1400 Knolls Dr.
Newton, NC 28658
Ph: (828)464-1466

Rems-Smario, Julie, Director,
    Founder
DeafHope [11939]
470 27th St.
Oakland, CA 94612
Ph: (510)267-8800
    (510)735-8553
Fax: (510)740-0946

Ren, Justin, Mem.
Chinese Entrepreneur Association
    [622]
PO Box 2752
Acton, MA 01720
Ph: (978)266-1254

Ren, Dr. William, President
Association of Chinese Finance
    Professionals [1222]
240 Hazelwood Ave.
San Francisco, CA 94127

Renaud, Margaret, Administrator
Woman Within International Ltd.
    [13404]
269 Walker St., Ste. 204
Detroit, MI 48207-4258
Toll Free: 800-732-0890
Fax: (519)732-0890

Rencher, Jen, President
National Multicultural Greek Council,
    Inc. [23760]
PO Box 250430
New York, NY 10025

Renchie, Don, President
American Association of Pesticide
    Safety Educators [4123]
PO Box 580
Delphi, IN 46923
Ph: (765)494-4567
Fax: (765)496-1556

Renee, Terra, President
African American Women in Cinema
    [9293]
Manhattan, NY
Ph: (212)769-7949
Fax: (212)871-2074

Renfroe, Rev. Rob, President
Good News, A Forum for Scriptural
    Christianity [20344]

PO Box 132076
The Woodlands, TX 77393-2076
Ph: (832)813-8327
Fax: (832)813-5327

Renich, Jonathan, CEO, Founder
Edurelief [12658]
85334 Lorane Hwy.
Eugene, OR 97405
Ph: (541)554-2992
Fax: (541)343-0568

Renner, Judy, Dir. of HR
National Eating Disorders Associa-
tion [14648]
165 W 46th St., Ste. 402
New York, NY 10036
Ph: (212)575-6200
Toll Free: 800-931-2237
Fax: (212)575-1650

Renner, Megan, Exec. Dir.
United States Breastfeeding Com-
mittee [13858]
4044 N Lincoln Ave., No. 288
Chicago, IL 60618
Ph: (773)359-1549
Fax: (773)313-3498

Renner, Ron, President, Founder
Certified Interior Decorators
International [1942]
649 SE Central Pky.
Stuart, FL 34994
Ph: (772)287-1855
Toll Free: 800-624-0093
Fax: (772)287-0398

Renner, Sylvester, Founder,
President
Develop Africa [10487]
1906 Knob Creek Rd., Ste. 3
Johnson City, TN 37604
Ph: (423)282-0006

Rennert, James R., Director
Auxiliaries of Our Lady of the Ce-
nacle [19802]
513 W Fullerton Pky.
Chicago, IL 60614-6428
Ph: (773)528-6300
Fax: (773)549-0554

Rennie, Ms. Renate, President
Tinker Foundation [9664]
55 E 59th St.
New York, NY 10022-1112
Ph: (212)421-6858

Rennolds, Edmund, Exec. Dir.,
Founder
Citizens to Stop Nuclear Terrorism
[19178]
612 S Laurel St.
Richmond, VA 23220
Ph: (214)478-8314

Repchuk, Tracy Lynn, Founder,
President
Canadian Federation of Poets
[10149]
1248 E Elmwood Ave.
Burbank, CA 91501-1616

Resch, Rhone, President, CEO
Solar Energy Industries Association
[7207]
600 14th St. NW, Ste. 400
Washington, DC 20005
Ph: (202)682-0556

Reshetniak, Mr. Peter, President
Raptor Education Foundation [4875]
PO Box 200400
Denver, CO 80220
Ph: (303)680-8500
     (720)685-8100
Fax: (720)685-9988

Restrepo, Marcela Tovar,
Chairperson
Women's Environment and Develop-
ment Organization [18238]
355 Lexington Ave., 3rd Fl.
New York, NY 10017
Ph: (212)973-0325
Fax: (212)973-0335

Restuccia, Robert, Exec. Dir.
Community Catalyst [14991]
1 Federal St.
Boston, MA 02110
Ph: (617)338-6035
Fax: (617)451-5838

Rethwisch, Gus, Chairman,
President
World Association of Benchers and
Dead Lifters [23369]
PO Box 515
Willard, UT 84340
Ph: (503)901-1622
Fax: (435)723-0308

Reuben, Carolyn, Bd. Member,
Founder
Alliance for Addiction Solutions
[15892]
PO Box 13375
Fort Pierce, FL 34979-3375
Ph: (424)256-8227

Revelle, Rhonda, President
National Fastpitch Coaches Associa-
tion [23243]
2641 Grinstead Dr.
Louisville, KY 40206-2840
Ph: (502)409-4600
Fax: (502)409-4622

Rey, Ana Silva, President
Latin American Women's Association
[13381]
3440 Toringdon Way, Ste. 205
Charlotte, NC 28277
Ph: (704)552-1003

Reyes, Darlene, Exec. Dir.
Phi Mu Fraternity [23960]
400 Westpark Dr.
Peachtree City, GA 30269
Ph: (770)632-2090
Fax: (770)632-2136

Reyes, Gene F, III, DTM, President
National Federation of Tourist Guide
Associations USA [23663]
c/o Gene Reyes, President
3 Boimare Ave.
Kenner, LA 70065-3103

Reyes, Zoila, Exec. Dir.
Hermandad, Inc. [17840]
PO Box 286269
New York, NY 10128
Ph: (347)709-0190

Reyna, Michael, President
Military Benefit Association [19381]
14605 Avion Pky.
Chantilly, VA 20151-1104
Ph: (703)968-6200
Toll Free: 800-336-0100
Fax: (703)968-6423

Reynell, John, Contact
Nocturnal Adoration Society [19892]
184 E 76th St.
New York, NY 10021
Ph: (212)266-5679

Reynes-Delobel, Anne, President
Kay Boyle Society [10365]
Dept. of English
Columbia College
1301 Columbia College Dr.
Columbia, SC 29203

Reynolds, Audrey, Founder
Saving Horses, Inc. [4407]
3224 Wildflower Valley Dr.
Encinitas, CA 92024
Ph: (619)247-7237

Reynolds, Bob, Dir. of Advertising
National Street Rod Association
[21459]
4030 Park Ave.
Memphis, TN 38111-7406
Ph: (901)452-4030

Reynolds, Daniel, Chmn. of the Bd.
Mount Diablo Peace and Justice
Center [18805]
55 Eckley Ln.
Walnut Creek, CA 94596
Ph: (925)933-7850

Reynolds, Frank, Director
Friends of the Sea Otter [4820]
PO Box 223260
Carmel, CA 93922
Ph: (831)915-3275

Reynolds, Geoffrey D., Secretary
Association for the Advancement of
Dutch-American Studies [9280]
c/o Joint Archives of Holland
Hope College
PO Box 9000
Holland, MI 49422-9000

Reynolds, Jeff, CMCA, AMS, Comm.
Chm.
National Franchisee Association
[1463]
1701 Barrett Lakes Blvd. NW, Ste.
180
Kennesaw, GA 30144
Ph: (678)797-5160
Fax: (678)797-5170

Reynolds, John, Exec. Dir., Founder
Veterans2Work [21153]
95 Shelley Dr.
Mill Valley, CA 94941
Ph: (415)925-1515

Reynolds, Karen, Treasurer
PACER Center [14557]
8161 Normandale Blvd.
Bloomington, MN 55437
Ph: (952)838-9000
Toll Free: 800-537-2237
Fax: (952)838-0199

Reynolds, Karla, Chairman
Hands4Uganda [11014]
2900 Summit Dr.
Pocatello, ID 83201

Reynolds, Mark, Director
Ford Galaxie Club of America
[21383]
PO Box 429
Valley Springs, AR 72682-0429
Ph: (870)743-9757

Reynolds, Mark, Secretary
International Star Class Yacht Rac-
ing Association [22639]
914 Bay Ridge Rd., Ste. 220
Annapolis, MD 21403
Ph: (443)458-5733
Fax: (443)458-5735

Reynolds, Mary- Clare, Exec. Dir.
Learning Disabilities Association of
America [12237]
4156 Library Rd.
Pittsburgh, PA 15234-1349
Ph: (412)341-1515
Toll Free: 888-300-6710
Fax: (412)344-0224

Reynolds, Michael C., President
Airlift/Tanker Association [5056]
655 Julian Rd.

Chattanooga, TN 37421
Ph: (423)902-2297

Reynolds, Shelley Hendrix, Founder,
President
Unlocking Autism [13782]
Byron, GA
Toll Free: 866-366-3361

Reynolds-Hogland, Melissa, PhD,
Exec. Dir.
Bear Trust International [4792]
PO Box 4006
Missoula, MT 59806-4006
Ph: (406)523-7779

Reznicek, Larry, President
American Association of School
Personnel Administrators [7417]
11863 W 112th St., Ste. 100
Overland Park, KS 66210-1375
Ph: (913)327-1222
Fax: (913)327-1223

Rhadigan, Floyd, Mem.
Caricature Carvers of America
[21751]
c/o Donald K. Mertz, Secretary
729 Prairie Rd.
Wilmington, OH 45177-9683

Rhea, Bob, Exec. Dir.
National Association of Farm Busi-
ness Analysis Specialists [3526]
c/o Bob Rhea, Executive Director
PO Box 467
Camp Point, IL 62320

Rhea, Dr. Timothy, President
American Bandmasters Association
[9851]
c/o Thomas V. Fraschillo, Secretary-
Treasurer
11738 Big Canoe
209 Cherokee Trl.
Jasper, GA 30143

Rheaume, Sr. Claire, Contact
Missionary Sisters of the Society of
Mary [20441]
349 Grove St.
Waltham, MA 02453
Ph: (781)893-0149
Fax: (781)899-6838

Rhees, Carol A., President
Hope for Children-United States
[11036]
5801 Searl Terr.
Bethesda, MD 20816

Rhoad, Julie, Exec. Dir.
Names Project Foundation I AIDS
Memorial Quilt [13554]
204 14th St. NW
Atlanta, GA 30318
Ph: (404)688-5500
Fax: (404)688-5552

Rhoades, Rev. Kevin C., Rep.
National Catholic Office for the Deaf
[19879]
c/o Arrow Bookkeeping
8737 Colesville Rd., Ste. 501
Silver Spring, MD 20910
Ph: (301)577-1684

Rhoads, CJ, Managing Dir.
Taijiquan Enthusiasts Organization
[17424]
PO Box 564
Douglassville, PA 19518
Ph: (484)332-3331

Rhoads, Linda, Exec. Dir.
Alliance for Childhood [10814]
Park W PO
New York, NY 10025
Ph: (202)643-8242

Rhoads, Loren, Contact
Broad Universe **[22483]**
4725 S 172nd Pl.
Seatac, WA 98188

Rhodes, Allen, Chairman
Save Humanity Initiative **[12725]**
PO Box 647
Bronx, NY 10469
Ph: (914)219-3355
   (914)219-3344
Toll Free: 877-657-3121
Fax: (914)412-7676

Rhodes, Katrina, President
American Association of Public
  Health Physicians **[16992]**
1605 Pebble Beach Blvd.
Green Cove Springs, FL 32043-8077
Toll Free: 888-447-7281
Fax: (202)333-5016

Rhodes, Mr. Kingston, Chairman
International Civil Service Commis-
  sion **[23486]**
2 United Nations Plz., 10th Fl.
New York, NY 10017
Ph: (212)963-5465
Fax: (212)963-0159

Rhodes, Marcia, Contact
Telework Advisory Group of Worldat-
  Work **[3243]**
1100 13th Street, NW
Suite 800
Washington, DC 20005

Rhyne, Rhonda F., President, CEO
Association for Innovative
  Cardiovascular Advancements
  [14098]
13661 62nd Ave. NE
Kirkland, WA 98034
Ph: (858)204-4116
Fax: (425)823-0669

Riad, Mrs. Nermien, Founder
Coptic Orphans Support Association
  [10950]
PO Box 2881
Merrifield, VA 22116
Ph: (703)641-8910
Fax: (703)641-8787

Riak, Jordan, Exec. Dir., Founder
Parents and Teachers Against
  Violence in Education **[7721]**
PO Box 1033
Alamo, CA 94507-7033
Ph: (925)831-1661

Ribble, Anne, Secretary, Treasurer
Bibliographical Society of the
  University of Virginia **[9121]**
PO Box 400152
Charlottesville, VA 22904-4152
Ph: (434)924-7013
Fax: (434)924-1431

Ribeiro, Brian, President
Federal Physicians Association
  [16749]
5868 Mapledale Plz., Ste. 104
Woodbridge, VA 22193
Toll Free: 877-FED-PHYS

Riben, Mike, President
Association for Pathology Informatics
  [16580]
c/o Nova Smith, Executive Director
Dept. of Biomedical Informatics
University of Pittsburgh
5607 Baum Blvd., Rm. 518A
Pittsburgh, PA 15206
Ph: (412)648-9552
Fax: (412)624-5100

Ricard, Rev. John, President
National Black Catholic Congress
  [19874]

320 Cathedral St., 3rd Fl.
Baltimore, MD 21201
Ph: (410)547-8496
Fax: (410)752-3958

Ricard, Marc, President
Numismatic Bibliomania Society
  [22278]
c/o Terry White, Treasurer
PO Box 39
Hilliard, OH 43026

Riccardi, Todd, Chairman
United States Formula 18 Association **[22680]**

Ricci, Joseph, President, CEO
Textile Rental Services Association
  of America **[2933]**
1800 Diagonal Rd., Ste. 200
Alexandria, VA 22314
Ph: (703)519-0029
Toll Free: 877-770-9274
Fax: (703)519-0026

Ricciardi, Peter F., Secretary
Bond Club of New York **[389]**
c/o Peter F. Ricciardi
Dresver Securities
75 Wall St.
New York, NY 10005
Ph: (212)363-5191

Rice, Alan, President
Professional Association of Social
  Workers in HIV and AIDS **[13558]**
1000 10th Ave., Ste. 2T
New York, NY 10019
Ph: (212)523-6683

Rice, Catherine S., Exec. Dir.
International Essential Tremor
  Foundation **[15945]**
11111 W 95th St., Ste. 260
Overland Park, KS 66214-1846
Ph: (913)341-3880
Toll Free: 888-387-3667
Fax: (913)341-1296

Rice, Charles E., Chairman,
  President
Bellarmine Forum **[19803]**
PO Box 542
Hudson, WI 54016-0542
Ph: (651)276-1429

Rice, David, President
Deaf in Government **[5276]**
PO Box 76087
Washington, DC 20013
Ph: (202)618-3009

Rice, David H., Chairman, Founder
Organization of Black Designers
  [9279]
300 M St. SW, Ste. N110
Washington, DC 20024
Ph: (202)489-4822

Rice, Mr. Douglas, Contact
Hotel Technology Next Generation
  [1661]
650 E Algonquin Rd., Ste. 207
Schaumburg, IL 60173
Ph: (847)303-5560

Rice, Frances, Chairperson
National Black Republican Association **[19040]**
4594 Chase Oaks Dr.
Sarasota, FL 34241-9183

Rice, George, Director
National Association for Search and
  Rescue **[12745]**
PO Box 232020
Centreville, VA 20120-2020
Toll Free: 877-893-0702

Rice, Rev. John, Chap.
International Order of Saint Luke the
  Physician **[20544]**
PO Box 780909
San Antonio, TX 78278-0909
Ph: (210)492-5222
Toll Free: 877-992-5222

Rice, John, Treasurer
International Society of Psychiatric
  Genetics **[14881]**
5034 Thoroughbred Ln., Ste. A
Brentwood, TN 37027-4231
Ph: (615)649-3086
Toll Free: 888-417-3311

Rice, Keren, VP
Society for the Study of Indigenous
  Languages of the Americas **[9658]**
PO Box 1295
Denton, TX 76202-1295

Rice, Michelle L., Chairman
National Association for Multi-
  Ethnicity in Communications **[773]**
50 Broad St., Ste. 1801
New York, NY 10004
Ph: (212)594-5985
Fax: (212)594-8391

Rice, Paul, President, CEO
Fair Trade USA **[3301]**
1500 Broadway, Ste. 400
Oakland, CA 94612-2079
Ph: (510)663-5260
Fax: (510)663-5264

Rice, Dr. Robert F., Owner
Literacy and Evangelism
  International **[8246]**
1800 S Jackson Ave.
Tulsa, OK 74107-1857
Ph: (918)585-3826
Fax: (918)585-3224

Rich, Andrew, Exec. Sec.
Harry S. Truman Scholarship
  Foundation **[7928]**
712 Jackson Pl. NW
Washington, DC 20006
Ph: (202)395-4831

Rich, Craig R., President
Rich Family Association **[20920]**
PO Box 142
Wellfleet, MA 02667

Rich, Vanessa, Chairperson
National Head Start Association
  [8449]
1651 Prince St.
Alexandria, VA 22314
Ph: (703)739-0875
Toll Free: 866-677-8724

Richard, Celeste, Exec. Dir.
American Camellia Society **[22068]**
Massee Lane Gardens
100 Massee Ln.
Fort Valley, GA 31030
Ph: (478)967-2358
Toll Free: 877-422-6355
Fax: (478)967-2083

Richard, Denis, President
Water Planet USA **[4475]**
203 Greenwood Dr.
Panama City Beach, FL 32407
Ph: (850)230-6030
Toll Free: 866-449-5591

Richard, Kevin, President
Information Systems Security As-
  sociation **[1788]**
9220 SW Barbur Blvd., Ste. 119-333
Portland, OR 97219
Ph: (206)388-4584
Toll Free: 866-349-5818
Fax: (206)299-3366

Richard, Leslie, Exec. Dir.
Marine Machinery Association **[2262]**
8665 Sudley Rd., Ste. 270
Manassas, VA 20110-4588
Ph: (703)791-4800
Fax: (703)791-4808

Richard, Paul S., RFC, Exec. Dir.
Institute of Consumer Financial
  Education **[7920]**
PO Box 34070
San Diego, CA 92163-4070
Ph: (619)239-1401
Fax: (619)923-3284

Richards, Brenda, President
Public Lands Council **[4581]**
1301 Pennsylvania Ave. NW, Ste.
  300
Washington, DC 20004
Ph: (202)347-0228

Richards, Cecile, President
Planned Parenthood Federation of
  America **[11847]**
New York, NY
Ph: (212)541-7800
Fax: (212)245-1845

Richards, Gerald, CEO
826 National **[8762]**
44 Gough St., Ste. 206
San Francisco, CA 94103
Ph: (415)864-2098
Fax: (415)864-2388

Richards, Glenn S., Exec. Dir.
VON Coalition **[2008]**
c/o Pillsbury Winthrop Shaw Pittman
  LLP
1200 17th St. NW
Washington, DC 20036-3006
Ph: (202)663-8215
Fax: (202)513-8006

Richards, Jennifer, Dir. of Mtgs.
Anxiety and Depression Association
  of America **[12503]**
8701 Georgia Ave., Ste. 412
Silver Spring, MD 20910
Ph: (240)485-1001
   (240)485-1030
Fax: (240)485-1035

Richards, Jennifer, President
National Association of Shell Market-
  ers **[2530]**
PO Box 658
Garrisonville, VA 22463-0658
Ph: (703)582-8478
Fax: (540)356-0029

Richards, Liz, CEO
Material Handling Equipment
  Distributors Association **[1747]**
201 US Highway 45
Vernon Hills, IL 60061
Ph: (847)680-3500
Fax: (847)362-6989

Richards Mooney, Heidi, MS, CEO,
  Founder
WECAI Network **[1001]**
PO Box 550856
Fort Lauderdale, FL 33355-0856
Ph: (954)625-6606
Toll Free: 877-947-3337

Richards, Terry, President
National Democratic Club **[18114]**
30 Ivy St. SE
Washington, DC 20003-4006
Ph: (202)543-2035
Fax: (202)479-4273

Richards, Thomas, President
Social Anxiety Association **[13723]**
2058 E Topeka Dr.

Phoenix, AZ 85024-2404
Ph: (602)230-7316

Richardson, Alan, President
HOPOS, The International Society
for the History of Philosophy of
Science **[8546]**
c/o The University of Chicago Press
Journals Division
PO Box 37005
Chicago, IL 60637

Richardson, Blair, President, CEO
United States Potato Board **[4257]**
4949 S Syracuse St., Ste. 400
Denver, CO 80237
Ph: (303)369-7783
Fax: (303)369-7718

Richardson, Dennis, President
North American Family Campers As-
sociation **[22721]**
PO Box 345
Billerica, MA 01821
Ph: (781)584-6443

Richardson, Ed, President
United States Magnetic Materials
Association **[6877]**
c/o Ed Richardson, President
1120 E 23rd St.
Indianapolis, IN 46206
Ph: (317)418-0137

Richardson, Henry, President
Human Development and Capability
Association **[12002]**
PO Box 1051
Brewster, MA 02631

Richardson, Jackie, Registrar
International Curly Horse Organiza-
tion **[4364]**
322 Tulie Gate Rd.
Tularosa, NM 88352
Ph: (575)740-4159

Richardson, John, Exec. Dir.
Physician Hospitals of America
[15744]
2025 M St. NW, Ste. 800
Washington, DC 20036
Ph: (202)367-1113
Fax: (202)367-2113

Richardson, Jonathan, Secretary
National Bar Association **[5032]**
1225 11th St. NW
Washington, DC 20001
Ph: (202)842-3900
Fax: (202)289-6170

Richardson, Mary S., MD, President
North American Society of Head and
Neck Pathology **[16589]**
Medical University of South Carolina
Dept. of Pathology and Laboratory
Medicine
Division of Anatomic Pathology
PO Box 250908
Charleston, SC 29425-0686
Ph: (843)792-1994
Fax: (843)792-8974

Richardson, Rob, President
Aquatic Plant Management Society,
Inc. **[6137]**
7922 NW 71st St.
Gainesville, FL 32653
Ph: (662)617-4571
Fax: (352)392-3462

Richardson, Robert, Secretary,
Treasurer
United States Society for Ecological
Economics **[4018]**
c/o Valerie Luzadis, President
106 Marshall Hall

1 Forestry Dr.
Syracuse, NY 13210-2712
Ph: (315)470-6636
   (315)470-6695

Richardson, Sharon, Chairperson
CCSVI Alliance **[15912]**
5019 Gladiola Way
Golden, CO 80403

Richardson, Steve, Exec. Dir.
Football Writers Association of
America **[22857]**
18652 Vista Del Sol Dr.
Dallas, TX 75287-4021
Ph: (972)713-6198

Richardson, Wayne, Master
Modern Free and Accepted Masons
of the World **[19564]**
627 5th Ave.
Columbus, GA 31901
Ph: (706)322-3326
Fax: (706)322-3805

Richardson-Atubeh, Carolyn, Exec.
Dir., Founder
Asperger Spirit **[15904]**
PO Box 360207
Decatur, GA 30036
Ph: (404)626-2403

Richaud, PT, Yvonne Garcia,
President
InterAmerican Heart Foundation
[14119]
7272 Greenville Ave.
Dallas, TX 75231-4596

Rich-Bonn, Michelle, Exec. Dir.
NGA - Needlework Guild of America
[12902]
822 Veterans Way
Warminster, PA 18974-3500
Ph: (215)682-9183
Toll Free: 866-295-9974
Fax: (215)682-9185

Richerson, Peter, President
American Anthropological Associa-
tion - Evolutionary Anthropology
Society **[5898]**
2200 Wilson Blvd., Ste. 600
Arlington, VA 22201-3357
Ph: (703)528-1902

Richey, Daniel, President
Diabetes National Research Group
[14527]
11350 SW Vilage Pkwy.
Port Saint Lucie, FL 34987
Ph: (858)597-3816
Toll Free: 800-877-3457
Fax: (858)597-3804

Richie, Robert, Exec. Dir.
FairVote **[18909]**
6930 Carroll Ave., Ste. 240
Takoma Park, MD 20912
Ph: (301)270-4616

Richmond, Ann, Officer
Society for Leukocyte Biology
[17150]
9650 Rockville Pke.
Bethesda, MD 20814
Ph: (301)634-7814
Fax: (301)634-7455

Richmond, Fia, Founder, President
Pediatric Brain Foundation **[15985]**
1223 Wilshire Blvd., No. 937
Santa Monica, CA 90403
Ph: (310)889-8611
Fax: (866)267-5580

Richmond, Greg, CEO, President
National Association of Charter
School Authorizers **[7784]**

105 W Adams St., Ste. 1900
Chicago, IL 60603-6253
Ph: (312)376-2300
Fax: (312)376-2400

Richmond, Jack, Chairman
Amputee Coalition of America
[14545]
9303 Center St., Ste. 100
Manassas, VA 20110
Toll Free: 888-267-5669

Richmond, John C., MD, President
Arthroscopy Association of North
America **[16469]**
9400 W Higgins Rd., Ste. 200
Rosemont, IL 60018
Ph: (847)292-2262
Fax: (847)292-2268

Richmond, Susan, Exec. Dir.
Neighborhood Cats **[3630]**
2576 Broadway, No. 555
New York, NY 10025
Ph: (212)662-5761

Richmond, Mr. Todd, Director,
President
Topaz Arts **[9004]**
55-03 39th Ave.
Woodside, NY 11377
Ph: (718)505-0440

Richstone, David, Chairman
Association of Healthcare Internal
Auditors **[15580]**
10200 W 44th Ave., Ste. 304
Wheat Ridge, CO 80033
Ph: (303)327-7546
Toll Free: 888-ASK-AHIA
Fax: (720)881-6101

Richter, Joseph E., Exec. Dir.
FARMS International **[12153]**
PO Box 270
Knife River, MN 55609-0270
Ph: (218)834-2676

Richter, Robert D., President
Toy Train Collectors Society **[22191]**
c/o Robert D Richter, President
2015 Bay Rd.
Remsen, NY 13438-4286
Ph: (315)831-8302

Richtman, Max, Chairman
Leadership Council of Aging
Organizations **[10513]**
10 G St. NE
Washington, DC 20002
Ph: (202)216-8387
Fax: (202)787-3726

Richtman, Mr. Max, JD, CEO,
President
National Committee to Preserve
Social Security and Medicare
[19138]
10 G St. NE, Ste. 600
Washington, DC 20002
Ph: (202)216-0420
Toll Free: 800-966-1935
Fax: (202)216-0446

Richwine, Linda, President
National Walking Horse Association
[4390]
4059 Iron Works Pky., Ste. 4
Lexington, KY 40511
Ph: (859)252-6942
Fax: (859)252-0640

Richy, Brad, Treasurer
National Emergency Management
Association **[14667]**
1776 Avenue of the States
Lexington, KY 40511
Ph: (859)244-8000
Fax: (859)244-8239

Rickenbach, Fran, CAE, Exec. Dir.
National Association of Nephrology
Technicians/Technologists **[15881]**
11 W Monument Ave., Ste. 510
Dayton, OH 45402
Ph: (937)586-3705
Toll Free: 877-607-NANT
Fax: (937)586-3699

Rickenberger, Kathy, Exec. Dir.
Association of Former Agents of the
U.S. Secret Service **[5356]**
6919 Vista Dr.
West Des Moines, IA 50266
Ph: (515)282-8192
Fax: (515)282-9117

Ricketts, Glenn, Dir. Pub. Aff.
National Association of Scholars
[7964]
8 W 38th St., Ste. 503
New York, NY 10018
Ph: (917)551-6770

Rickman, Bryant, Chairman
Southwest Spanish Mustang As-
sociation **[4409]**
PO Box 329
Hugo, OK 74743
Ph: (580)579-3467

Rickman, Ray, President, Founder
Adopt a Doctor **[16730]**
101 Dyer St.
Providence, RI 02903
Ph: (401)421-0606

Riddell, M. Gatz, Exec. VP
American Association of Bovine
Practitioners **[17592]**
3320 Skyway Dr., Ste. 802
Opelika, AL 36801
Ph: (334)821-0442
Fax: (334)821-9532

Riddick, Eric W., PhD, Officer
Black Entomologists **[6608]**
c/o Dept. of Entomology & Plant
Pathology
301 Funchess Hall
Auburn, AL 36849
Ph: (662)686-3646
   (334)844-5098
Fax: (662)686-5281

Riddiough, Timothy, Bd. Member
American Real Estate and Urban
Economics Association **[2847]**
The Center for Real State Education
and Research
821 Academic Way, 223 RBB
Tallahassee, FL 32306-1110
Ph: (850)644-7898
Toll Free: 866-273-8321
Fax: (850)644-4077

Riddle, Duncan, Exec. Dir.
United States Adult Soccer Associa-
tion **[23192]**
7000 S Harlem Ave.
Bridgeview, IL 60455-1160
Ph: (708)496-6870
Fax: (708)496-6879

Riddle, Kelly, President
Association of Christian Investigators
[5355]
2553 Jackson Keller Rd., Ste. 200
San Antonio, TX 78230
Ph: (210)342-0509
Fax: (210)342-0731

Riddle, Lawrence, President
Guang Ping Yang T'ai Chi Association **[23295]**
268 Kinderkamack Rd.
Emerson, NJ 07630

Ridenour, Amy Moritz, Chairman
National Center for Public Policy
Research **[18991]**

20 F St. NW, Ste. 700
Washington, DC 20001
Ph: (202)507-6398

Rider, Brenda M., President
A Way With Words Foundation
[10793]
PO Box 2334
Youngstown, OH 44509
Ph: (330)538-7000
(330)360-3300

Rider, Rev. David M., Exec. Dir.,
President
Seamen's Church Institute of New
York and New Jersey [20114]
50 Broadway, Fl. 26
New York, NY 10004-3802
Ph: (212)349-9090

Rider, William, CEO, President
American Combat Veterans of War
[21105]
3508 Seagate Way, Ste. 160
Oceanside, CA 92056-2686
Ph: (706)696-0460

Ridgeway, Roslyn, Chmn. of the Bd.
Business and Professional Women's
Foundation [3489]
1030 15th St., NW, Ste. B1, No. 148
Washington, DC 20005
Ph: (202)293-1100
Fax: (202)861-0298

Riebel, Karen Hanson, Treasurer
National Association of Shareholder
and Consumer Attorneys [5088]
c/o Samuel H. Rudman, President
58 S Service Rd., Ste. 200
Melville, NY 11747
Ph: (631)367-7100
Fax: (631)367-1173

Rieber, Edith Finton, Director,
President
Scriabin Society of America [10002]
353 Lindsey Dr.
Berwyn, PA 19312

Rieck, Donald, Exec. Dir.
George Mason University I Center
for Media and Public Affairs
[17947]
2338 S Queen St.
Arlington, VA 22202
Ph: (202)302-5523

Rieckhoff, Paul, CEO, Founder
Iraq and Afghanistan Veterans of
America [21126]
114 W 41st St., 19th Fl.
New York, NY 10036
Ph: (212)982-9699
Fax: (917)591-0387

Riedel, Col. Jay E., President
80th Fighter Squadron Headhunters'
Association [20676]
2830 S Hulen, PMB 174
Fort Worth, TX 76109

Rieder, James L., Chairman
Us TOO International [14078]
2720 S River Rd., Ste. 112
Des Plaines, IL 60018
Ph: (630)795-1002
Fax: (630)795-1602

Riederer, Anne, Treasurer
International Society of Exposure
Science [6620]
c/o Infinity Conference Group Inc.
1035 Sterling Rd., Ste. 202
Herndon, VA 20170-3838
Ph: (703)925-9620
Toll Free: 800-869-1551
Fax: (703)925-9453

Rieg, Dietmar, President, CEO
Deutsch-Amerikanische Handel-
skammern [23581]
80 Pine St., 24th Fl.
New York, NY 10005
Ph: (212)974-8830
Fax: (212)974-8867

Riehle, Gregory, President, CEO
Resort Hotel Association [1677]
2100 E Cary St., Ste. 3
Richmond, VA 23223
Ph: (804)525-2020
Fax: (804)525-2021

Riemann, Bradley C., PhD,
President
Anxiety Disorders Foundation
[13721]
PO Box 560
Oconomowoc, WI 53066
Ph: (262)567-6600
Fax: (262)567-7600

Riemer, Brenda, Treasurer
North American Society for the
Sociology of Sport [7187]
c/o Brenda Riemer, Treasurer
School of HPHP
319 N Porter Bldg.
Eastern Michigan University
Ypsilanti, MI 48197

Riepe, Don, Director
American Littoral Society - Northeast
Region [6800]
18 Hartshorne Dr., Ste. 1
Highlands, NJ 07732
Ph: (732)291-0055

Ries, Shauna, President, Founder
Mediators Without Borders [4965]
885 Arapahoe Ave.
Boulder, CO 80302
Ph: (720)565-4055
Toll Free: 877-268-5337

Riesenberg, Thomas, President
Association of Securities and
Exchange Commission Alumni
[3039]
PO Box 5767
Washington, DC 20016
Ph: (202)462-1211

Rietema, Marcus, President
International Gravity Sports Association [23230]

Rieth, Pastor Bob, Exec. Dir.,
Founder, President
Media Fellowship International
[20154]
PO Box 82685
Kenmore, WA 98028
Ph: (425)488-3965
Fax: (425)488-8531

Rietmeijer, Cornelis A., MD,
President
American Sexually Transmitted
Diseases Association [17193]
1005 Slater Rd., Ste. 330
Durham, NC 27703
Ph: (919)861-9399
Fax: (919)361-8425

Rifka, Safa, MD, Chairman
American-Arab Anti-Discrimination
Committee [17864]
1990 M St. NW, Ste. 610
Washington, DC 20036
Ph: (202)244-2990
Fax: (202)333-3980

Rifkin, Adam J., President
Brandeis University Alumni Association [19309]

415 South St.
Waltham, MA 02453-2728
Ph: (781)736-4100
Toll Free: 800-333-1948
Fax: (781)736-4101

Rifkin, Bathsheva, President
Friends of Bezalel Academy of Arts
[9610]
370 Lexington Ave., Ste. 1612
New York, NY 10017
Ph: (212)687-0542
Fax: (212)687-1140

Rifkin, Jeremy R., President
Foundation on Economic Trends
[19108]
4520 East West Hwy., Ste. 600
Bethesda, MD 20814
Ph: (301)656-6272
Fax: (301)654-0208

Rigaud, Marie-Claude, MPH, Exec.
Chmn. of the Bd.
Rebati Sante Mentale [15803]
18503 Pines Blvd., Ste. 214
Pembroke Pines, FL 33029
Ph: (954)432-3800

Rigby, Dick, Director
The Waterfront Center [11460]
PO Box 53351
Washington, DC 20009-5351
Ph: (202)337-0356

Rigel, Vicki, Secretary, Treasurer
American Cotswold Record Associa-
tion [4651]
18 Elm St.
Plympton, MA 02367
Ph: (781)585-2026
Fax: (781)585-2026

Rigg, Darren, Founder, President
Greyhound Adoption Center [10630]
PO Box 2433
La Mesa, CA 91943-2433
Toll Free: 877-478-8364

Riggle, Doug, Founder
Orphan World Relief [11117]
700 Morse Rd., Ste. 100
Columbus, OH 43214
Toll Free: 855-677-4265

Riggs, Andy, Director
Chris Craft Antique Boat Club
[22607]
PO Box 787
Oxford, OH 45056

Riggs, Marion J., Founder, Exec. Dir.
Student Society for Stem Cell
Research [15658]
Ph: (813)368-8937

Riggs, Robert, Exec. VP
Phi Kappa Theta National Fraternity
[23914]
3901 W 86th St., Ste. 360
Indianapolis, IN 46268
Ph: (317)872-9934
(317)536-4747

Riggs, Robert, CEO
Scleroderma Foundation [17181]
300 Rosewood Dr., Ste. 105
Danvers, MA 01923
Ph: (978)463-5843
Toll Free: 800-722-4673
Fax: (978)463-5809

Righter, Elisabeth, President
Phi Rho Sigma Medical Society
[23820]
PO Box 90264
Indianapolis, IN 46290

Rigmaiden, Kenneth E., President
International Union of Painters and
Allied Trades [23489]

7234 Parkway Dr.
Hanover, MD 21076
Ph: (410)564-5900
Toll Free: 800-554-2479

Rigney, Anne M., Gen. Counsel
Society of Financial Service Profes-
sionals [1929]
3803 W Chester Pke., Ste. 225
Newtown Square, PA 19073
Ph: (610)526-2500
Toll Free: 800-392-6900
Fax: (610)359-8115

Riley, Dorothy, President
White Ironstone China Association
[21587]
c/o Mary Ann and Chuck Ulmann
1320 Ashbridge Rd.
West Chester, PA 19380

Riley, Joyce, RN, Spokesperson
American Gulf War Veterans As-
sociation [21106]
PO Box 85
Versailles, MO 65084
Ph: (573)378-6049
Toll Free: 877-817-9829

Riley, Michael, President
Illinois Physical Therapy Association
[17444]
905 N Main St.
Naperville, IL 60563
Ph: (630)904-0101
Fax: (630)904-0102

Riley, Michael, Secretary, Treasurer
The International Society of Motor
Control [6917]
c/o Michael A. Riley, Secretary/
Treasurer
Psychology Dept., ML 0376
University of Cincinnati
Cincinnati, OH 45221-0376

Riley, Mike, Secretary, Treasurer
Association of Communication
Engineers [6544]
c/o Mike Riley, Secretaty/Treasurer
1475 North 200 West
Nephi, UT 84648-0311
Ph: (435)623-8601

Riley, Patrick F., President
The Inter-American Conductive
Education Association, Inc. [8584]
PO Box 3169
Toms River, NJ 08756-3169
Ph: (732)797-2566
Toll Free: 800-824-2232
Fax: (732)797-2599

Riley, Tim, President
National Conservation District
Employees Association [23535]
c/o Rich Duesterhaus, Executive
Director
509 Capitol Ct. NE
Washington, DC 20002-4937
Ph: (202)547-6223
Fax: (202)547-6450

Rill, Bryan, President
Society for the Anthropology of
Consciousness [7496]
American Anthropological Associa-
tion
2300 Clarendon Blvd., Ste. 1301
Arlington, VA 22201
Ph: (703)528-1902
Fax: (703)528-3546

Rillera, Marri J., Registrar
International Soundex Reunion
Registry, Inc. [10454]
PO Box 371179
Las Vegas, NV 89137
Toll Free: 888-886-4777

Rilling, Ms. Juanita, Director
Center for International Disaster
Information [11652]
529 14th St. NW, Ste. 700W
Washington, DC 20045-1000
Ph: (202)821-1999
    (202)821-4040

Rimel, Rebecca W., CEO, President
Pew Charitable Trusts [12986]
1 Commerce Sq., Ste. 2800
2005 Market St.
Philadelphia, PA 19103-7077
Ph: (215)575-9050
Fax: (215)575-4939

Rimpoche, Gelek, President,
Founder
Jewel Heart [19779]
1129 Oak Valley Dr.
Ann Arbor, MI 48108
Ph: (734)994-3387

Rinaldi, Kara Saul, Exec. Dir.
Home Performance Coalition [3883]
1620 Eye St. NW, Ste. 501
Washington, DC 20006
Ph: (202)463-2005

Rinaldi, Paul, President
National Air Traffic Controllers As-
sociation [23389]
1325 Massachusetts Ave. NW
Washington, DC 20005
Ph: (202)628-5451
Toll Free: 800-266-0895
Fax: (202)628-5767

Rinaldi, Dr. Robert, Exec. Dir.
American Association of Oral and
Maxillofacial Surgeons [16441]
9700 W Bryn Mawr Ave.
Rosemont, IL 60018-5701
Ph: (847)678-6200
Toll Free: 800-822-6637
Fax: (847)678-6286

Rindelaub, Jim, Exec. Dir.
Choristers Guild [20487]
12404 Park Central Dr., Ste. 100
Dallas, TX 75251-1802
Ph: (469)398-3606
Toll Free: 800-246-7478
Fax: (469)398-3611

Rinehart, Kathy, Exec. Dir.
Positive Discipline Association
[7067]
PO Box 9595
San Diego, CA 92169
Toll Free: 866-767-3472
Fax: (855)415-2477

Rinehart, Michelle A., President
Architectural Research Centers
Consortium [5959]
c/o Saif Haq, Treasurer
College of Architecture, Rm. 604B
Texas Tech University
1800 Flint Ave.
Lubbock, TX 79409-2091
Ph: (806)834-6317

Rinella, Anthony S., MD, President
Global Spine Outreach [17255]
12701 W 143rd St., Ste. 110
Homer Glen, IL 60491
Toll Free: 866-GSO-0880

Ring, Rusty, Chairman
Public Affairs Council [18068]
2121 K St. NW, Ste. 900
Washington, DC 20037
Ph: (202)787-5950
Fax: (202)787-5942

Ringer-Ross, Doreen, V. Ch.
The Mr. Holland's Opus Foundation
[8374]

4370 Tujunga Ave., Ste. 330
Studio City, CA 91604
Ph: (818)762-4328
Fax: (818)643-2463

Ringler, Whitney, Contact
Chase After a Cure [13937]
89B Old Trolley Rd., Ste. 201
Summerville, SC 29483

Ringo, Robin S., Exec. Dir.
Public Investors Arbitration Bar As-
sociation [5374]
2415 A Wilcox Dr.
Norman, OK 73069
Ph: (405)360-8776
Toll Free: 888-621-7484
Fax: (405)360-2063

Ringo, Stefanie, Treasurer
International Society of Beverage
Technologists [426]
14070 Proton Rd., Ste. 100, LB 9
Dallas, TX 75244-3601
Ph: (972)233-9107
Fax: (972)490-4219

Rinholm, Murney, President
Chromosome 22 Central [14814]
c/o Murney Rinholm, President
7108 Partinwood Dr.
Fuquay Varina, NC 27526
Ph: (919)567-8167

Riniker, Paul, VP
National Farmers Organization
[4161]
528 Billy Sunday Rd., Ste. 100
Ames, IA 50010
Toll Free: 800-247-2110

Rink-Abel, Marju, President
Estonian American National Council
[19427]
c/o Linda Rink, Executive Director
1420 Locust St., Ste. 31N
Philadelphia, PA 19102
Ph: (215)546-5863

Rink-Abel, Marju, Treasurer
Joint Baltic American National Com-
mittee [17823]
400 Hurley Ave.
Rockville, MD 20850-3121
Ph: (301)340-1954
Fax: (301)309-1405

Rintamaki, Michelle, BA, President,
Treasurer
Kids With Heart National Association
for Children's Heart Disorders, Inc.
[14132]
1578 Careful Dr.
Green Bay, WI 54304-2941

Rinvelt, Patricia, MBA, Exec. Dir.
National Network of Depression
Centers [15799]
2350 Green Rd., Ste. 191
Ann Arbor, MI 48105
Ph: (734)332-3914
Fax: (734)332-3939

Rio, Carlos del, MD, Chairman
HIV Medicine Association [13545]
1300 Wilson Blvd., Ste. 300
Arlington, VA 22209
Ph: (703)299-1215
Fax: (703)299-8766

Rios, Elena, MD, CEO, President
National Hispanic Medical Associa-
tion [15739]
1920 L St. NW, Ste. 725
Washington, DC 20036-5050
Ph: (202)628-5895
Fax: (202)628-5898

Riotto, Charles M., President
International Licensing Industry
Merchandisers' Association [5332]

350 5th Ave., Ste. 6410
New York, NY 10118
Ph: (212)244-1944

Ripley, Kate, Exec. Dir.
University of Alaska Fairbanks
Alumni Association [19354]
201 Constitution Hall
Fairbanks, AK 99775
Ph: (907)474-7081
Toll Free: 800-770-2586
Fax: (907)474-6712

Ripley, Mary, Founder, President
International Association for
Volunteer Effort [13299]
c/o Civil Society Consulting Group
LLC
805 15th St. NW, Ste. 100
Washington, DC 20005
Ph: (202)628-4360
Fax: (202)330-4597

Riplinger, Andrew, Exec. Dir.
Rafiki Collaborative [13560]
PO Box 14825
Chicago, IL 60614

Risher, David, Founder, President
Worldreader [8256]
120 Hickory St.
San Francisco, CA 94102
Ph: (206)588-6057
Fax: (831)299-5366

Riskey, Curtis, President
CBA: The Association for Christian
Retail [2950]
1365 Garden of the Gods Rd., Ste.
105
Colorado Springs, CO 80907
Ph: (719)265-9895
Toll Free: 800-252-1950
Fax: (719)272-3510

Riskin, Rabbi Shlomo, Chancellor
Ohr Torah Institutions of Israel
[8133]
49 W 45th St., Ste. 701
New York, NY 10036
Ph: (212)935-8672
Fax: (212)935-8683

Risley, Clark, Secretary, Treasurer
Risley Family Association [20993]
29 Dana Point Ave.
Ventura, CA 93004-1656

Risley, Dr. Rod A., Exec. Dir.
Phi Theta Kappa, International
Honor Society [23733]
1625 Eastover Dr.
Jackson, MS 39211
Ph: (601)984-3518
    (601)984-3504
Toll Free: 800-946-9995
Fax: (601)984-3544

Rislov, Ken, President
American and Foreign Christian
Union [19942]
2885 Sanford Ave. SW, No. 29934
Grandville, MI 49418-1342

Risman, Barbara, VP
American Sociological Association
[7176]
1430 K St. NW, Ste. 600
Washington, DC 20005
Ph: (202)383-9005
Fax: (202)638-0882

Risman, Barbara, President
Council on Contemporary Families
[11816]
305 E 23rd St., G1800
Austin, TX 78712
Ph: (512)471-8339

Risser, Robert J., Jr., CEO,
President
Concrete Reinforcing Steel Institute
[513]
933 N Plum Grove Rd.
Schaumburg, IL 60173-4758
Ph: (847)517-1200
Fax: (847)517-1206

Risser, Robert, President
Precast/Prestressed Concrete
Institute [795]
200 W Adams St., No. 2100
Chicago, IL 60606
Ph: (312)786-0300

Ritch, Jerry, OD
Association of Regulatory Boards of
Optometry [16426]
200 S College St., Ste. 2030
Charlotte, NC 28202
Ph: (704)970-2710
Toll Free: 866-869-6852
Fax: (704)970-2720

Ritchie, Chelsea, Coord.
Roof Coatings Manufacturers As-
sociation [748]
750 National Press Bldg.
529 14th St. NW
Washington, DC 20045
Ph: (202)591-2452
Fax: (202)591-2445

Ritt, Stefan, VP
IEEE - Nuclear and Plasma Sciences Society [6927]
3 Park Ave.
New York, NY 10016-5902

Ritter, Chris, Librarian
Antique Automobile Club of America
[21327]
501 W Governor Rd.
Hershey, PA 17033
Ph: (717)534-1910
    (717)534-2082
Fax: (717)534-9101

Ritter, Cindy, Rep., Media Spec.
National Barley Foods Council
[1520]
2702 W Sunset Blvd.
Spokane, WA 99224
Ph: (509)456-2481

Ritter, Hon. Donald, CEO, President
Afghan-American Chamber of Com-
merce [23550]
8201 Greensboro Dr., Ste. 103
McLean, VA 22102
Ph: (703)442-5005
Fax: (703)442-5008

Ritter, Mr. Michael, CEO
Deep Springs International [4756]
PO Box 694
Grove City, PA 16127

Ritter, Michele, President
Bearded Collie Club of America
[21837]

Ritter, Wayne, CFO
Affiliated Warehouse Companies
[3435]
PO Box 295
Hazlet, NJ 07730-0295
Ph: (732)739-2323

Ritterbusch, Chad, Exec. Dir.
American Society of Golf Course
Architects [5955]
125 N Executive Dr., Ste. 302
Brookfield, WI 53005
Ph: (262)786-5960
Fax: (262)786-5919

Rittner, Toby, CEO, President
Council of Development Finance
Agencies [18149]

100 E Broad St., Ste. 1200
Columbus, OH 43215
Ph: (614)705-1300
　　(614)705-1317

Ritz, Eric, Exec. Dir.
Global Inheritance [19272]
1855 Industrial St., Ste. 613
Los Angeles, CA 90021
Ph: (213)626-0061

Riutta, Shelley, MSE, Founder,
　President
Global Association of Holistic
　Psychotherapy [16973]
2221 S Webster Ave.
PMB 122
Green Bay, WI 54301
Toll Free: 877-346-1167

Riutzel, Kevin, President
Asian Pacific American Medical
　Student Association [8306]
c/o Calvin Sheng; Chief Financial
　Officer
5 Winchester St., Apt. 202
Brookline, MA 02446

Riva, Maria T., PhD, Mem.
APA Division 49: Society of Group
　Psychology and Group
　Psychotherapy [16892]
750 1st St. NE
Washington, DC 20002-4242
Ph: (202)336-6013
Fax: (202)218-3599

Rivard, James, President
American Academy of Orthopaedic
　Manual Physical Therapists
　[17430]
8550 United Plaza Blvd., Ste. 1001
Baton Rouge, LA 70809
Ph: (225)360-3124
Fax: (225)408-4422

Rivard, Nancy, Founder, President
Airline Ambassadors International
　[13024]
1500 Massachusetts Ave., No. 648
Washington, DC 20005
Ph: (415)359-8006
Toll Free: 866-264-3586

Rivenbark, Rev. Rosalie F.,
　Chairperson
The Way International [20475]
PO Box 328
New Knoxville, OH 45871-0328
Ph: (419)753-2523

Rivera, Doris, Admin. Asst.
Agricultural Missions, Inc. [20380]
475 Riverside Dr., Ste. 700
New York, NY 10115
Ph: (212)870-2553

Rivera, Freddie, President
American Racing Pigeon Union
　[22385]
PO Box 18465
Oklahoma City, OK 73154
Ph: (405)848-5801
Fax: (405)848-5888

Rivera, Jose, CEO
Control Systems Integrators Associa-
　tion [3192]
22 N Carroll St., Ste. 300
Madison, WI 53703
Ph: (608)310-7851
Toll Free: 800-661-4914
Fax: (888)581-3666

Rivera, Lisa, Chairperson
Association for Feminist Ethics and
　Social Theory [10078]
c/o Margaret A. Crouch, Treasurer

Dept. of History and Philosophy
Eastern Michigan University
701 Pray Harold
Ypsilanti, MI 48197

Rivera, Ramon, Chairman
American Society of Baking [369]
7809 N Chestnut Ave.
Kansas City, MO 64119
Toll Free: 800-713-0462
Fax: (888)315-2612

Rivera, Veronica, Exec. Dir.
Association of Latino Administrators
　and Superintendents [7426]
PO Box 65204
Washington, DC 20035
Ph: (202)466-0808

Riverkamp, Don, Secretary
Hof Reunion Association [20704]
232 Green View Dr.
Dover, DE 19901-5748

Rivers, Mr. C. Joseph, Bd. Member
National Father's Day/Mother's Day
　Council [19149]
37 W 39th St., Ste. 1102
New York, NY 10018-0580
Ph: (212)594-5977
　　(212)594-6421
Fax: (212)594-9349

Rivers, Dr. William P., Exec. Dir.
Joint National Committee for
　Languages and the National
　Council for Languages and
　International Studies [9655]
4646 40th St. NW, No. 310
Washington, DC 20016
Ph: (202)580-8684

Rives, Jack L.
American Bar Association Center on
　Children and the Law [10849]
1050 Connecticut Ave. NW, Ste. 400
Washington, DC 20036
Ph: (202)662-1720
Toll Free: 800-285-2221
Fax: (202)662-1755

Rivo, Sharon Pucker, Exec. Dir.
National Center for Jewish Film
　[9308]
Brandeis University
Lown 102 MS053
Waltham, MA 02454
Ph: (781)736-8600
Fax: (781)736-2070

Rizzo, Peter, CEO
United States Polo Association
　[23070]
9011 Lake Worth Rd.
Lake Worth, FL 33467
Toll Free: 800-232-8772

Roach, Daniel R., Gen. Counsel
Society of Corporate Compliance
　and Ethics [1169]
6500 Barrie Rd., Ste. 250
Minneapolis, MN 55435
Ph: (952)933-4977
Toll Free: 888-277-4977
Fax: (952)988-0146

Roach, Nancy, Chairperson,
　Founder
Fight Colorectal Cancer [13968]
1414 Prince St., Ste. 204
Alexandria, VA 22314
Ph: (703)548-1225
Toll Free: 877-427-2111

Roadman, Larry, Exec. Dir.
endPoverty.org [12536]
PO Box 3380
Oakton, VA 22124
Ph: (240)396-1146
Fax: (240)235-3550

Roba, William H., Officer
Society for German-American Stud-
　ies [9340]
c/o Karyl Rommelfanger, Member-
　ship Chair
4824 Morgan Dr.
Manitowoc, WI 54220

Robanske, Carl, Chairman
Embracing Orphans [10959]
PO Box 2615
Walla Walla, WA 99362
Ph: (509)540-9408

Robb, Brian D., Chairman
The Travel Institute [3400]
945 Concord St.
Framingham, MA 01701
Ph: (781)237-0280
Toll Free: 800-542-4282
Fax: (781)237-3860

Robb, James A., President
National Training and Simulation As-
　sociation [6257]
2111 Wilson Blvd., Ste. 400
Arlington, VA 22201-3061
Ph: (703)247-9471
　　(703)247-2567
Fax: (703)243-1659

Robb, Lisa, Exec. Dir.
Alliance for the Arts [8950]
330 W 42nd St.
New York, NY 10036
Ph: (212)947-6340

Robbin, Jerry, President
International Mercury Owners As-
　sociation [21404]
PO Box 1245
Northbrook, IL 60065-1245
Ph: (847)997-8624
Fax: (847)272-1850

Robbins, David L., Coord.
InterFuture [8120]
PO Box 51294
Boston, MA 02205

Robbins, Jill, COO
Soccer in the Streets [11439]
236 Auburn Ave., Ste. 207
Atlanta, GA 30303
Toll Free: 888-436-5833

Robbins, Karen, Founder
American Fancy Rat and Mouse As-
　sociation [22241]
9230 64th St.
Riverside, CA 92509-5924
Ph: (626)626-0829

Robbins, Mark, President, CEO
American Academy in Rome [9611]
7 E 60 St.
New York, NY 10022-1001
Ph: (212)751-7200
Fax: (212)751-7220

Robbins, Dr. Robert, Founder
African Wild Dog Conservancy
　[4778]
208 N California Ave.
Silver City, NM 88061

Roberson, Nancy, President
National Association of Bar Execu-
　tives [5436]
321 N Clark St.
Chicago, IL 60654
Ph: (312)988-6008

Roberson, Will, Jr., Chmn. of the Bd.
Swift Museum Foundation [21251]
223 County Road 552
Athens, TN 37303
Ph: (423)745-9547
Fax: (423)745-9869

Robert, James, MD, MPH,
　Chairperson
Children's Environmental Health
　Network [14713]
110 Maryland Ave. NE, Ste. 402
Washington, DC 20002
Ph: (202)543-4033
Fax: (202)543-8797

Robert, Maryse, Director
Organization of American States
　[17798]
17th St. & Constitution Ave. NW
Washington, DC 20006
Ph: (202)370-5000
Fax: (202)458-3967

Roberts, Alpha, Founder, President
National Association of Minority
　Government Contractors [879]
PO Box 44609
Washington, DC 20026

Roberts, Amy, Exec. Dir.
Outdoor Industry Association [2469]
4909 Pearl E Cir., Ste. 300
Boulder, CO 80301
Ph: (303)444-3353
Fax: (303)444-3284

Roberts, Annie, Chmn. of the Bd.
National Qigong Chi Kung Associa-
　tion [13643]
PO Box 270065
Saint Paul, MN 55127
Toll Free: 888-815-1893
Fax: (888)359-9526

Roberts, Dr. Arturo, President
Welsh-American Genealogical
　Society [21000]
60 Norton Ave.
Poultney, VT 05764-1029

Roberts, Bob, Jr., Founder, Chair-
　man
Glocal Ventures, Inc. [12156]
1870 Rufe Snow Dr.
Keller, TX 76248-5629
Ph: (817)656-5136
Fax: (817)656-4671

Roberts, Brian C., Exec. Dir.
National Association of County
　Engineers [6573]
25 Massachusetts Ave. NW, Ste.
　580
Washington, DC 20001
Ph: (202)393-5041
Fax: (202)393-2630

Roberts, Mr. Carter S., President,
　CEO
World Wildlife Fund [3975]
1250 24th St. NW
Washington, DC 20037
Ph: (202)293-4800
Toll Free: 800-960-0993

Roberts, Cecil E., President
United Mine Workers of America
　[23484]
18354 Quantico Gateway Dr., Ste.
　200
Triangle, VA 22172
Ph: (703)291-2400

Roberts, Cheryl L., Exec. Dir.
African American Alliance for Home-
　ownership [1687]
825 NE 20th Ave.
Portland, OR 97232
Ph: (503)595-3517
Fax: (503)595-3519

Roberts, Clara, Mgr., Dir. of Admin.
National Center for Higher Education
　Management Systems [7438]

3035 Center Green Dr., Ste. 150
Boulder, CO 80301-2205
Ph: (303)497-0301
Fax: (303)497-0338

Roberts, Corina, Founder
Redbird [19589]
PO Box 702
Simi Valley, CA 93062-0702
Ph: (805)217-0364

Roberts, David A., Chairman
American Coalition for Fathers and
Children [12407]
1718 M St. NW, No. 1187
Washington, DC 20036
Ph: (202)330-3248
Toll Free: 800-978-3237

Roberts, David, President
American Casting Association
[22838]
c/o Patrick McFadden, Secretary
1719 Versailles Rd.
Lexington, KY 40504

Roberts, David, Chairperson
Jewish Reconstructionist Movement
[20260]
1299 Church Rd.
Wyncote, PA 19095-1824
Ph: (215)576-0800
Fax: (215)576-6143

Roberts, Don, Chairman
Professional Paddlesports Associa-
tion [3145]
PO Box 10847
Knoxville, TN 37939
Ph: (865)558-3595

Roberts, Dwight, CEO, President
US Rice Producers Association
[1524]
2825 Wilcrest Dr., Ste. 218
Houston, TX 77042-6041
Ph: (713)974-7423
Fax: (713)974-7696

Roberts, Eugene Bowie, Jr., Gov.
Society of the Ark and the Dove
[20761]
PO Box 401
Riderwood, MD 21139-0401

Roberts, Jennifer, CFO, Sr. VP
National Safe Skies Alliance, Inc.
[19198]
110 McGhee Tyson Blvd., Ste. 201
Alcoa, TN 37701
Ph: (865)970-0515
Toll Free: 888-609-4957

Roberts, Jennifer, Admin. Asst.
Tall Timbers Land Conservancy
[3955]
Tall Timbers Research Sta.
13093 Henry Beadel Dr.
Tallahassee, FL 32312-0918
Ph: (850)893-4153
Fax: (850)668-7781

Roberts, John C., President
Leadership Enterprise for a Diverse
America [8619]
501 7th Ave., 7th Fl.
New York, NY 10018
Ph: (212)672-9750
Fax: (212)986-1857

Roberts, John, Exec. Dir.
International Grooving & Grinding
Association [790]
12573 Route 9W
West Coxsackie, NY 12192
Ph: (518)731-7450
Fax: (518)731-7490

Roberts, Julian, Exec. Dir.
National Association of Specialty
Health Organizations [15043]

222 S 1st St., Ste. 303
Louisville, KY 40202
Ph: (502)403-1122
Fax: (502)403-1129

Roberts, Julian, Exec. Dir.
National Association of Vision Care
Plans [15104]
974 Breckenridge Ln. No. 162
Louisville, KY 40202
Ph: (502)403-1122
Fax: (502)403-1129

Roberts, Lady Carol Sue, Mem.
Grand Council of the Ladies Oriental
Shrine of North America [19557]

Roberts, Mark, President
International Society of Arboriculture
[4731]
2101 W Park Ct.
Champaign, IL 61821
Ph: (217)355-9411
Toll Free: 888-472-8733
Fax: (217)355-9516

Roberts, Matt, Exec. Dir.
Energy Storage Association [3416]
1800 M St. NW, No. 400S
Washington, DC 20036
Ph: (202)293-0537

Roberts, Michael, President
First Nations Development Institute
[12375]
2432 Main St., 2nd Fl.
Longmont, CO 80501
Ph: (303)774-7836
Fax: (303)774-7841

Roberts, Michael, Chairman
National Association of Black Hotel
Owners, Operators and Develop-
ers [1667]
3520 W Broward Blvd., Ste. 119
Fort Lauderdale, FL 33312
Ph: (954)797-7102
Fax: (954)337-2877

Roberts, Michele, Exec. Dir.
National Basketball Players Associa-
tion [23523]
1133 Avenue of Americas
New York, NY 10036
Ph: (212)655-0880
Toll Free: 800-955-6272
Fax: (212)655-0881

Roberts, Richard, Chairman
Global Kids [7811]
137 E 25th St., 2nd Fl.
New York, NY 10010
Ph: (212)226-0130
Fax: (212)226-0137

Roberts, Roy, CEO
Alliance of Professionals and
Consultants, Inc. [814]
8200 Brownleigh Dr.
Raleigh, NC 27617-7411
Ph: (919)510-9696

Roberts, Suellen, President, Founder
Christian Women in Media Associa-
tion [2314]
PO Box 571566
Dallas, TX 75357

Roberts, Terri, Exec. Dir.
American Holistic Nurses Associa-
tion [15264]
2900 SW Plass Ct.
Topeka, KS 66612-1213
Ph: (785)234-1712
Toll Free: 800-278-2462
Fax: (785)234-1713

Roberts, Dr. Terry, Director
National Paideia Center [7845]
29 1/2 Page Ave.

Asheville, NC 28801
Ph: (828)575-5592

Roberts, Tom, President
AFCOM [6291]
9100 W Chester Towne Centre Rd.
West Chester, OH 45069
Ph: (513)322-1550

Roberts, Tom, Secretary
International Mobjack Association
[22636]
1313 Cambridge Way
Chesapeake, VA 23320-8247
Ph: (757)312-0768

Roberts, Tom, Partner
Telecommunications Risk Manage-
ment Association [3242]
4 Becker Farm Rd.
Roseland, NJ 07068
Ph: (973)871-4080
Fax: (973)871-4075

Roberts-Frenzel, Caren, Contact
The Rita Hayworth Fan Club [23998]
c/o Caren Roberts-Frenzel
3943 York Ave. S
Minneapolis, MN 55410

Robertson, Charles, Comm. Chm.
Victorian Society in America [10301]
1636 Sansom St.
Philadelphia, PA 19103
Ph: (215)636-9872
    (202)265-6669
Fax: (215)636-9873

Robertson, David N., Exec. Dir.
Association of Finance and Insur-
ance Professionals [1836]
4104 Felps Dr., Ste. H
Colleyville, TX 76034
Ph: (817)428-2434
Fax: (817)428-2534

Robertson, Mr. H. V. Ross, President
Parliamentarians for Global Action
[18131]
132 Nassau St., Ste. 1419
New York, NY 10038
Ph: (212)687-7755
Fax: (212)687-8409

Robertson, John
Corning Cinderella Softball League,
Inc. [23200]
Baker St.
Corning, NY 14830
Ph: (607)346-5838

Robertson, Kevin, Exec. Dir.
Miracle Babies [14237]
8745 Aero Dr., Ste. 111
San Diego, CA 92123
Ph: (858)633-8540

Robertson, Mike, Membership Chp.
Capri Club North America [21348]
PO Box 701
Johnstown, OH 43031

Robertson, Mr. Patrick J., President
CityTeam Ministries [12645]
2304 Zanker Rd.
San Jose, CA 95131
Ph: (408)232-5600
Fax: (408)428-9505

Robertson, Robb, President
Society of the Fifth Division [21031]
c/o Wayne Cumer, President
150 Cumer Ln.
Burgettstown, PA 15021
Ph: (724)947-3859

Robertson, Sammi, President
Bailey's Team for Autism [13759]
164 Westside Ave.

North Attleboro, MA 02760
Ph: (508)699-4483

Robertson, Sara, Treasurer
Association for Accounting Marketing
[2265]
9 Newport Dr., Ste. 200
Forest Hill, MD 21050
Ph: (443)640-1061

Robertson, Scott, President
Professional Sporting Clays Associa-
tion [23142]
9219 Katy Fwy., Ste. 291
Houston, TX 77024
Ph: (614)660-6174

Robertson, Stuart, GG, President
Accredited Gemologists Association
[2038]
3315 Juanita St.
San Diego, CA 92105
Toll Free: 844-288-4367

Robertson, Terry, President
Association of Seventh-Day
Adventist Librarians [9690]
c/o Sarah Kimakwa, Treasurer
James White Library, Rm. 271
4910 Administration Dr.
Berrien Springs, MI 49104

Robey, Jerry, President
United Square Dancers of America
[9271]
c/o Jerry Robey, President
2702 Aldersgate Dr.
Rockford, IL 61103
Ph: (815)977-5763

Robins, Perry, MD, President,
Founder
Skin Cancer Foundation [14063]
149 Madison Ave., Ste. 901
New York, NY 10016
Ph: (212)725-5176

Robinson, Bean, PhD, Exec. Dir.
World Professional Association for
Transgender Health [12953]
2575 Northwest Pky.
Elgin, IL 60124
Ph: (612)624-9397
Fax: (612)624-9541

Robinson, Blades, Exec. Dir.
International Association of Dive
Rescue Specialists [2097]
8103 E US Highway 36
Avon, IN 46123
Ph: (317)464-9787
Fax: (317)641-0730

Robinson, Brady, Exec. Dir.
Access Fund [23208]
207 Canyon, Ste. 201
Boulder, CO 80302
Ph: (303)545-6772
Fax: (303)545-6774

Robinson, Brooks, President
Major League Baseball Players
Alumni Association [22553]
Copper Bldg., Ste. D
1631 Mesa Ave.
Colorado Springs, CO 80906
Ph: (719)477-1870
Fax: (727)898-8911

Robinson, Deborah, Exec. Dir.,
Founder
International Possibilities Unlimited
[19127]
Metro Plz. II
8403 Colesville Rd., Ste. 865
Silver Spring, MD 20910
Ph: (301)562-0883
Fax: (301)562-8084

Robinson DelBusso, Ms. Sharon,
Administrator
American Board of Medical Genetics
and Genomics [14873]
9650 Rockville Pke.
Bethesda, MD 20814-3998
Ph: (301)634-7315
Fax: (301)634-7320

Robinson, Donzell, President
Association for Conflict Resolution
[4957]
c/o Cheryl L. Jamison, J.D., Executive Director
1639 Bradley Park Dr., Ste. 500-142
Columbus, GA 31904
Ph: (202)780-5999
Fax: (703)435-4390

Robinson, Edward H., Exec. Dir.,
Secretary
Bill Raskob Foundation [18171]
PO Box 507
Crownsville, MD 21032-0507
Ph: (410)923-9123
Fax: (410)923-9124

Robinson, Erin, Exec. Dir.
Federation of Earth Science Informa-
tion Partners [6374]
6300 Creedmoor Rd., Ste. 170-315
Raleigh, NC 27612
Ph: (314)369-9954

Robinson, Frank, Exec. VP of Dev.
Major League Baseball [22552]
75 9th Ave., 5th Fl.
New York, NY 10167-3000
Fax: (212)949-5654

Robinson Haden, Laurie, CEO,
Founder
Corporate Counsel Women of Color
[5000]
Radio City Sta.
New York, NY 10101-2095
Ph: (646)483-8041

Robinson, Rabbi Harold, Director
JWB Jewish Chaplains Council
[19931]
520 8th Ave.
New York, NY 10018-6507
Ph: (212)532-4949
Fax: (212)481-4174

Robinson, Ian, Secretary
Global Federation of Animal
Sanctuaries [10628]
PO Box 32294
Washington, DC 20007
Ph: (928)472-1173
    (623)252-5122

Robinson, Jenice, Dir. of Comm.
Citizens for Tax Justice [5721]
1616 P St. NW, Ste. 200
Washington, DC 20036
Ph: (202)299-1066
Fax: (202)299-1065

Robinson, John, President
American Taxation Association
[5790]
c/o John Robinson, President
Dept. of Accounting
College of Business Administration
Texas A&M University
College Station, TX 77843-4353
Ph: (979)845-3457

Robinson, John F., CEO, President,
Publisher
National Minority Business Council
[2395]
100 Church St., Ste. 800
New York, NY 10007
Ph: (347)289-7620
    (212)245-2652

Robinson, John, VP
International Union for Conservation
of Nature [3888]
1630 Connecticut Ave. NW, 3rd Fl.
Washington, DC 20009
Ph: (202)387-4826
Fax: (202)387-4823

Robinson, Larry, Treasurer
North American Packgoat Associa-
tion [4281]
PO Box 170166
Boise, ID 83717
Ph: (208)331-0772
Fax: (208)331-0772

Robinson, Madeline, President
Wheelchairs 4 Kids [11646]
1406 Stonehaven Way
Tarpon Springs, FL 34689
Ph: (727)946-0963

Robinson, Mikel, Exec. Dir.
International Association of Wildland
Fire [4205]
1418 Washburn St.
Missoula, MT 59801
Ph: (406)531-8264
Toll Free: 888-440-4293

Robinson, Monica, Exec. Dir.
National Coalition of Black Meeting
Planners [2335]
700 N Fairfax St., Ste. 510
Alexandria, VA 22314
Ph: (571)527-3110

Robinson, Peggy, President
Diagnostic Marketing Association
[2278]
10293 N Meridian St., Ste. 175
Indianapolis, IN 46290
Ph: (201)653-2420
Fax: (201)653-5705

Robinson, Peter M., CEO, President
International Chamber of Commerce
- USA [23593]
US Council for International Busi-
ness
1212 Avenue of the Americas
New York, NY 10036-1689
Ph: (212)354-4480
Fax: (212)575-0327

Robinson, Richard, Chairman
Metals Service Center Institute
[2359]
4201 Euclid Ave.
Rolling Meadows, IL 60008-2025
Ph: (847)485-3000
Fax: (847)485-3001

Robinson, Ron, Director
Citizens United [18312]
1006 Pennsylvania Ave. SE
Washington, DC 20003
Ph: (202)547-5420
Fax: (202)547-5421

Robinson, Rev. Ron, Exec. Dir.
Unitarian Universalist Christian Fel-
lowship [20627]
PO Box 6702
Tulsa, OK 74156
Ph: (918)794-4637

Robinson, Russ, President
International Songwriters Guild
[2426]
5108 Louvre Ave.
Orlando, FL 32812-1028
Ph: (407)760-2153

Robinson, Sandra, President
National Garden Clubs [22111]
4401 Magnolia Ave.
Saint Louis, MO 63110-3406
Ph: (314)776-7574
Fax: (314)776-5108

Robinson, Scottie, Treasurer
National Women's Sailing Association [22655]
c/o Scottie Robinson
4 Turtle Back Rd.
Essex, MA 01929
Ph: (401)682-2064

Robinson, Shane, Exec. Dir.
Ehlers Danlos National Foundation
[17483]
7918 Jones Branch Dr., Ste. 300
McLean, VA 22102
Ph: (703)506-2892
Fax: (703)506-3266

Robison, Geoff L., President
EAA Vintage Aircraft Association
[21222]
3000 Poberezny Rd.
Oshkosh, WI 54902
Ph: (920)426-6110
Toll Free: 800-843-3612
Fax: (920)426-6579

Robison, James, Founder, President,
Chairman
Life Outreach International [20152]
PO Box 982000
Fort Worth, TX 76182-8000
Toll Free: 800-947-5433

Robison, Richard J., Exec. Dir.
Federation for Children with Special
Needs [12323]
529 Main St., Ste. 1M3
Boston, MA 02129
Ph: (617)236-7210
Toll Free: 800-331-0688
Fax: (617)241-0330

Robitscher, John W., CEO
National Association of Chronic
Disease Directors [14597]
2200 Century Pky., Ste. 250
Atlanta, GA 30345
Ph: (770)458-7400

Robledo Montecel, Maria, PhD,
CEO, President
Intercultural Development Research
Association [7533]
5815 Callaghan Rd., Ste. 101
San Antonio, TX 78228-1102
Ph: (210)444-1710
Fax: (210)444-1714

Rocco, Heather, Chairman
Conference on English Leadership
[7848]
National Council of Teachers of
English
1111 W Kenyon Rd.
Urbana, IL 61801-1096
Ph: (217)328-3870
Toll Free: 877-369-6283
Fax: (217)328-9645

Rocha, Robert, President
National Marine Educators Associa-
tion [8263]
4321 Hartwick Rd., Ste. 300
College Park, MD 20740
Ph: (844)687-6632

Roche, Celine, Account Exec.
Women in Flavor and Fragrance
Commerce, Inc. [3507]
55 Harristown Rd., Ste. 106
Glen Rock, NJ 07452
Ph: (732)922-0500
    (201)857-8955
Fax: (732)922-0560

Roche, David, Managing Dir.
Jewelers Shipping Association
[2053]
125 Carlsbad St.

Cranston, RI 02920
Ph: (401)943-6020
Toll Free: 800-688-4572

Roche, Douglas, Advisor
Middle Powers Initiative [18129]
866 United Nations Plz., Ste. 4050
New York, NY 10017
Ph: (646)289-5170
Fax: (646)289-5171

Rochman, Julie, CEO, President
Insurance Institute for Business &
Home Safety [1867]
4775 E Fowler Ave.
Tampa, FL 33617
Ph: (813)286-3400
Fax: (813)286-9960

Rock, Anthony, CEO, President
Association of Science-Technology
Centers [9826]
818 Connecticut Ave. NW, 7th Fl.
Washington, DC 20006
Ph: (202)783-7200
Fax: (202)783-7207

Rock, Brian, Fac. Adv.
Phi Alpha Epsilon [23739]
c/o Civil, Environmental, and
Architectural Engineering Dept.
University of Kansas
2150 Learned Hall
1530 W 15th St.
Lawrence, KS 66045-7618

Rock, Elizabeth, Treasurer
Ladies of the Grand Army of the
Republic [20742]
c/o Madeline Rock, Editor
68 W Marion St.
Doylestown, OH 44230

Rock, Linda, Chairperson
National Hospice and Palliative Care
Organization [15297]
1731 King St., Ste. 100
Alexandria, VA 22314
Ph: (703)837-1500

Rockefeller, David, Jr., Chairman
Sailors for the Sea [3937]
449 Thames St., 300D
Newport, RI 02840
Ph: (401)846-8900
Fax: (401)846-7200

Rockefeller, Stuart, Director
North American Congress on Latin
America [17797]
c/o NYU CLACS
53 Washington Sq. S, Fl. 4W
New York, NY 10012
Ph: (646)535-9085
    (646)613-1440

Rockne, Jennifer, Chmn. of the Bd.,
Founder
American Independent Business Alli-
ance [3111]
222 S Black Ave.
Bozeman, MT 59715-4716
Ph: (406)582-1255

Rockoff, Maxine L., PhD, Officer
Union Settlement Association
[12567]
237 E 104th St.
New York, NY 10029-5404
Ph: (212)828-6000
Fax: (212)828-6022

Rockwell, Blake, Exec. Dir.
Special Spectators [13209]
333 E 79th St., No. 1W
New York, NY 10075

Rocourt, Gladys Doebeli, Founder
Rebuilding Haiti Now [12716]
2314 Alamance Dr.

West Chicago, IL 60185-6447

Rodd, Jim, President
Automatic Transmission Rebuilders
Association [306]
2400 Latigo Ave.
Oxnard, CA 93030
Ph: (805)604-2000
Toll Free: 866-464-2872
Fax: (805)604-2003

Rode, Prof. Heinz, Gen. Sec.
European Club for Paediatric Burns
[16605]
c/o Matthias B. Donelan, MD,
Membership Chairperson
Shriners Hospitals for Children -
Boston
51 Blossom St.
Boston, MA 02114

Rodeghier, Mark, Science Dir.
J. Allen Hynek Center for UFO Stud-
ies [7012]
PO Box 31335
Chicago, IL 60631
Ph: (773)271-3611

Rodell, Pat, President
Transparent Watercolor Society of
America [8894]
249 E US Route 6, No. 209
Morris, IL 60450

Rodenburg, John R., President
Federated Funeral Directors of
America [2403]
1622 S MacArthur Blvd.
Springfield, IL 62794
Toll Free: 800-877-3332
Fax: (217)525-2104

Rodewald, Dr. Mike, Exec. Dir.
Lutheran Bible Translators [19761]
PO Box 789
Concordia, MO 64020
Ph: (660)255-0810
Toll Free: 800-532-4253
Fax: (660)225-0810

Rodewald, Paul, President
Association of Field Ornithologists
[3657]
c/o Paul Rodewald, President
Cornell Lab of Ornithology
159 Sapsucker Woods Rd.
Ithaca, NY 14850
Ph: (607)254-6276

Rodger, Susan H., Chairperson
Association for Computing
Machinery - Special Interest Group
on Computer Science Education
[7651]
2 Penn Plz., Rm. 701
New York, NY 10121-0799

Rodgers, Griffin P., Director
National Diabetes Information
Clearinghouse [14541]
1 Information Way
Bethesda, MD 20892-3560
Toll Free: 800-860-8747
Fax: (301)634-0716

Rodgers, Jonathan H., Secretary,
Treasurer
American Oriental Society [9021]
Hatcher Graduate Library
University of Michigan
Ann Arbor, MI 48109-1190
Ph: (734)764-7555
Fax: (734)647-4760

Rodgers, Kevin, MD, FAAEM,
President
American Academy of Emergency
Medicine [14670]

555 E Wells St., Ste. 1100
Milwaukee, WI 53202-3823
Toll Free: 800-884-2236
Fax: (414)276-3349

Rodgers, Loren, Exec. Dir.
National Center for Employee
Ownership [1082]
1629 Telegraph Ave., Ste. 200
Oakland, CA 94612
Ph: (510)208-1300
Fax: (510)272-9510

Rodgers, Novella M., MS, Exec. Dir.
American Society for Mohs Surgery
[16336]
6475 E Pacific Coast Hwy.
Long Beach, CA 90803-4201
Ph: (714)379-6262
Toll Free: 800-616-2767
Fax: (714)379-6272

Rodgers, Nyla, Director, Founder
Mama Hope [11401]
582 Market St., Ste. 611
San Francisco, CA 94104-5307
Ph: (415)986-3310

Rodgers, Randy, Exec. Dir.
Bretton Woods Committee [18144]
1701 K St. NW, Ste. 950
Washington, DC 20006
Ph: (202)331-1616

Rodgers-Fox, De, Exec. Dir.
American Academy of Environmental
Medicine [14711]
6505 E Central Ave., No. 296
Wichita, KS 67206
Ph: (316)684-5500
Fax: (316)684-5709

Rodgers-Rose, Dr. La Francis,
Founder
International Black Women's
Congress [18215]
645 Church St., Ste. 200
Norfolk, VA 23510-1772
Ph: (757)625-0500
Fax: (757)625-1905

Rodin, Robert, Bd. Member
CommerceNet [7262]
955A Alma St.
Palo Alto, CA 94301
Ph: (650)289-4040
Fax: (650)289-4041

Rodman, Karen E., Founder,
President
Families of Adults Affected by
Asperger's Syndrome [17337]
PO Box 514
Centerville, MA 02632-0514
Ph: (508)790-1930

Rodrigues, Emily Neilan, Exec. Dir.
Association for Contextual
Behavioral Science [6033]
1880 Pinegrove Dr.
Jenison, MI 49428

Rodriguez, Arturo S., President
United Farm Workers of America
[23379]
29700 Woodford-Tehachapi Rd.
Keene, CA 93531
Ph: (661)823-6151

Rodriguez, Gilbert, Exec.
National Republican Club of Capitol
Hill [19042]
300 1st St. SE
Washington, DC 20003
Ph: (202)484-4590
Fax: (202)479-9110

Rodriguez, Jennifer, Exec. Dir.
Youth Law Center [13488]
200 Pine St., Ste. 300

San Francisco, CA 94104
Ph: (415)543-3379
Fax: (415)956-9022

Rodriguez, Juan, Founder
Stop Calling It Autism! [13777]
PO Box 155728
Fort Worth, TX 76155
Toll Free: 888-724-2123

Rodriguez, Manon, Administrator
Society of American Magicians
[22179]
c/o Manon Rodriguez, Administrator
4927 S Oak Ct.
Littleton, CO 80127
Ph: (303)362-0575

Rodriguez, Mary, COO, Dep. Dir.
Society of Diagnostic Medical
Sonography [17233]
2745 Dallas Pky., Ste. 350
Plano, TX 75093-8730
Ph: (214)473-8057
Toll Free: 800-229-9506
Fax: (214)473-8563

Rodriguez, Melanie, President
Kappa Delta Chi Sorority [23799]
PO Box 4317
Lubbock, TX 79409

Rodriguez, Monica, President, CEO
Sexuality Information and Education
Council of the U.S. [17203]
1012 14th St. NW, Ste. 1108
Washington, DC 20005-3424
Ph: (202)265-2405
Fax: (202)462-2340

Rodriguez, Richard, Exec. Dir.
National Hispanic Foundation for the
Arts [19463]
1010 Wisconsin Ave. NW, Ste. 650
Washington, DC 20007
Ph: (202)293-8330
Fax: (202)772-3101

Rodriguez, Samuel, Contact
Alliance for Marriage [12253]
PO Box 2490
Merrifield, VA 22116-2490
Ph: (703)934-1212
Fax: (703)934-1211

Roe, Bill, Director
BeachFront USA [10056]
PO Box 328
Moreno Valley, CA 92556

Roeder, Jennifer, Exec. Asst., Office
Mgr.
American Association of Veterinary
State Boards [17606]
380 W 22nd St., Ste. 101
Kansas City, MO 64108
Ph: (816)931-1504
Toll Free: 877-698-8482
Fax: (816)931-1604

Roehrig, Steven A., Managing Dir.
Steel Deck Institute [581]
PO Box 426
Glenshaw, PA 15116
Ph: (412)487-3325
Fax: (412)487-3326

Roerich, Helena, Director
Agni Yoga Society [20652]
319 W 107th St.
New York, NY 10025-2799
Ph: (212)864-7752
Fax: (212)864-7704

Roesler, Grant, Founder, Prog. Dir.
Oncology Youth Connection [14036]
205 SE Spokane St., Ste. 300-64
Portland, OR 97202
Ph: (503)869-7632

Roetert, E. Paul, CEO
Society of Health and Physical
Educators [16715]
1900 Association Dr.
Reston, VA 20191-1598
Toll Free: 800-213-7193
Fax: (703)476-9527

Roets, Margaret, Corr. Sec.
Genealogical Society of Flemish
Americans [20969]
18740 13 Mile Rd.
Roseville, MI 48066
Ph: (586)777-2770

Roff, Derek, Director
Builders Without Borders [11965]
119 Main St.
Hillsboro, NM 88042
Ph: (510)525-0525

Rogala, Joan E., CAE, Exec. Dir.
Lambda Kappa Sigma [23845]
PO Box 570
Muskego, WI 53150-0570
Toll Free: 800-557-1913
Fax: (262)679-4558

Rogan, Michael, President
Music Library Association [9718]
1600 Aspen Commons, Ste. 100
Middleton, WI 53562
Ph: (608)836-5825
Fax: (608)831-8200

Rogen, Alex, Chairman
National Junior Angus Association
[3740]
3201 Frederick Ave.
Saint Joseph, MO 64506
Ph: (816)383-5100
Fax: (816)233-9703

Roger, John, Founder, President
Institute for Individual and World
Peace [12005]
3500 W Adams Blvd.
Los Angeles, CA 90018
Ph: (323)328-1905

Rogers, Barbara, President, CEO
National Emphysema/COPD As-
sociation [17144]
850 Amsterdam Ave., Ste. 9A
New York, NY 10025
Ph: (212)666-2210
Fax: (212)666-0642

Rogers, Bert, President
Tall Ships America [22673]
Bldg. 2, Ste. 101
221 3rd St.
Newport, RI 02840-1088
Ph: (401)846-1775
Fax: (401)849-5400

Rogers, Brian, Director
American Academy of Urgent Care
Medicine [13675]
2813 S Hiawassee Rd., Ste. 206
Orlando, FL 32835
Ph: (407)521-5789
Fax: (407)521-5790

Rogers, Cheryl, President
Aquatic Gardeners Association
[4269]
PO Box 51536
Denton, TX 76206

Rogers, George E., EdD, President
Association for sTEm Teacher
Education [8016]
1489 County Road 23
Lafayette, AL 36862
Ph: (309)438-3502

Rogers, Gregory T., V. Chmn. of the
Bd.
Ackerman Institute for the Family
[11808]

936 Broadway, 2nd Fl.
New York, NY 10010
Ph: (212)879-4900
Fax: (212)744-0206

Rogers, Jeff, President
The Pesticide Stewardship Alliance
  [14721]
11327 Gravois Rd., No. 201
Saint Louis, MO 63126-3657
Ph: (314)849-9137
Fax: (314)849-0988

Rogers, Joseph, Exec. Dir.
National Mental Health Consumers'
  Self-Help Clearinghouse [12310]
1211 Chestnut St., Ste. 1100
Philadelphia, PA 19107
Ph: (215)751-1810
Toll Free: 800-553-4539
Fax: (215)636-6312

Rogers, Judy, Contact
International Food Additives Council
  [1341]
1100 Johnson Ferry Rd., Ste. 300
Atlanta, GA 30342-1733
Ph: (404)252-3663

Rogers, Kathleen, President
Earth Day Network [4049]
1616 P St. NW, Ste. 340
Washington, DC 20036
Ph: (202)518-0044
Fax: (202)518-8794

Rogers, Kit, Office Mgr.
National Storytelling Network
  [10225]
PO Box 795
Jonesborough, TN 37659
Ph: (423)913-8201
Toll Free: 800-525-4514
Fax: (423)753-9331

Rogers, Lynn, Chairperson
North American Bear Center [4854]
1926 Highway 169
Ely, MN 55731
Ph: (218)365-7879
Toll Free: 877-365-7879

Rogers, Maureen, Director
Herb Growing and Marketing
  Network [4293]
PO Box 245
Silver Spring, PA 17575-0245
Ph: (717)393-3295
Fax: (717)393-9261

Rogers, Mike, Chairman
Americans for Peace Prosperity and
  Security [18263]
707 8th St. SE, Ste. 100
Washington, DC 20003

Rogers, Mike, Founder
Grind for Life [10788]
81 N Atlantic Ave.
Cocoa Beach, FL 32931
Ph: (561)252-3839

Rogers, Mike, Chief Dev. Ofc.
Keep America Beautiful [4078]
1010 Washington Blvd.
Stamford, CT 06901
Ph: (203)659-3000

Rogers, Nancy, President
Washington Capitals Fan Club
  [24080]
PO Box 2802
Springfield, VA 22152

Rogers, Patricia, Founder
The Equine Rescue League, Inc.
  [10618]
PO Box 4366

Leesburg, VA 20177
Ph: (540)822-4577

Rogers, Dr. Phillip, Exec. Dir.
National Association of State Direc-
  tors of Teacher Education and
  Certification [8663]
1629 K St. NW, Ste. 300
Washington, DC 20006
Ph: (202)204-2208
Fax: (202)204-2210

Rogers, Ralph, MD, Chairman
Commission on Accreditation of
  Medical Transport Systems
  [14692]
117 Chestnut Ln.
Anderson, SC 29625
Ph: (864)287-4177
Fax: (864)287-4251

Rogers, Rebecca, Founder,
  President
International Spotted Horse Registry
  Association [4372]
2120 Scotch Hollow Rd.
Noel, MO 64854
Ph: (417)475-6273
Toll Free: 866-201-3098

Rogers, Ruth, Contact
Parrotlet Alliance [3668]
3405 Camden Rd.
Marshville, NC 28103

Rogers, Tamre, Contact
Women's Professional Billiard As-
  sociation [22590]
2710 Alpine Blvd., Ste. O-332
Alpine, CA 91901
Toll Free: 855-367-9722

Rogowski, Leneia R., Corr. Sec.
Alaskan Malamute Club of America
  [21794]

Rohde, Fritz, President
North American Native Fishes As-
  sociation [6717]
PO Box 1596
Milton, WA 98354-1596
Ph: (256)824-6992

Rohde, Michael, Director
American Tapestry Alliance [8835]
PO Box 28600
San Jose, CA 95159-8600
Ph: (360)438-5386

Rohde, Stephen, Chairman
Bend the Arc [12528]
330 7th Ave., 19th Fl.
New York, NY 10001
Ph: (212)213-2113

Rohde, Steve, President
Child Care Aware of America
  [10805]
1515 N Courthouse Rd., 2nd Fl.
Arlington, VA 22201
Toll Free: 800-424-2246
Fax: (703)341-4101

Rohe, Dr. William M., Director
Center for Urban and Regional Stud-
  ies [8723]
University of North Carolina at
  Chapel Hill
108 Battle Ln.
Chapel Hill, NC 27599-3410
Ph: (919)962-3074
Fax: (919)962-2518

Rohila, Pritam, PhD, Exec. Dir.
Association for Communal Harmony
  in Asia [12433]
4410 Verda Ln. NE
Keizer, OR 97303

Rohner, Ronald P., Exec. Dir.
International Society for
  Interpersonal Acceptance-Rejection
  [9550]
348 Mansfield Rd., U-1058
Storrs, CT 06269-1058
Ph: (860)486-0073

Rohnke, Angie, President
Souvenir Wholesale Distributors As-
  sociation [2978]
32770 Arapahoe Rd., No. 132-155
Lafayette, CO 80026
Toll Free: 888-599-4474
Fax: (888)589-7610

Rohrer, Susan, Chairperson
Children of Tanzania [10719]
3 Little Cove Pl.
Old Greenwich, CT 06870-2137
Ph: (203)570-0337

Rohrs, Alvin, President, CEO
Enactus [18283]
1959 E Kerr St.
Springfield, MO 65803-4775
Ph: (417)831-9505

Roig, Julia, President
Partners for Democratic Change
  [18496]
1800 Massachusetts Ave. NW, Ste.
  401
Washington, DC 20036-2131
Ph: (202)942-2166
Fax: (202)939-0606

Rojahn, Christopher, Director
Applied Technology Council [6540]
201 Redwood Shores Pky., Ste. 240
Redwood City, CA 94065
Ph: (650)595-1542
Fax: (650)593-2320

Rokeby-Mayeux, Jennifer, Mem.
DONA International [16282]
35 E Wacker Dr., Ste. 850
Chicago, IL 60601-2106
Ph: (312)224-2595
Toll Free: 888-788-3662
Fax: (312)644-8557

Rolack, William T., Sr., CEO
National Association of African
  Americans in Human Resources
  [1696]
PO Box 311395
Atlanta, GA 31131
Ph: (404)346-1542
Fax: (866)571-0533

Roland, Jon, Founder, President,
  Web Adm.
Constitution Society [5101]
11447 Woollcott St.
San Antonio, TX 78251
Ph: (512)299-5001

Rolando, Fredric V., President
National Association of Letter Carri-
  ers [23506]
100 Indiana Ave. NW
Washington, DC 20001-2144
Ph: (202)393-4695

Rolando, Fredric V., President
U.S. Letter Carriers Mutual Benefit
  Association [19497]
100 Indiana Ave. NW, Ste. 510
Washington, DC 20001-2144
Ph: (202)638-4318
Toll Free: 800-424-5184

Rolens, Vicki, Managing Dir.
Federation of American Consumers
  and Travelers [13236]
318 Hillsboro Ave.
Edwardsville, IL 62025
Toll Free: 800-872-3228
Fax: (618)656-5369

Rolfe, James G., President, Founder
Afghanistan Dental Relief Project
  [14369]
PO Box 734
Santa Barbara, CA 93102
Ph: (805)963-2329
  (805)448-2812

Rolfs, Alma, President
National Association for Poetry
  Therapy [16983]
c/o Dottie Joslyn
1403 E Dunkirk St.
Springfield, MO 65804

Roll, Fr. Jason, Director
Greek Orthodox Young Adult League
  [20194]
8 E, 79 th St.
New York, NY 10024
Ph: (646)519-6780
Fax: (646)478-9358

Roll, Richard J., Founder, President
American Homeowners Association
  [2123]
3001 Summer St.
Stamford, CT 06905
Ph: (203)323-7715
Toll Free: 800-470-2242

Rolland, Jannick, PhD, Contact
Medical Image Perception Society
  [15691]
c/o Elizabeth Krupinski, PhD
Dept. of Radiology
University of Arizona
Tucson, AZ 85724
Ph: (520)626-4498

Rolling, Chris, Exec. Dir.
Clean Water for Haiti [4754]
PO Box 871181
Vancouver, WA 98687
Ph: (360)450-2929

Rollins, James, President
Religion Communicators Council
  [20032]
475 Riverside Dr., Rm. 1505
New York, NY 10115
Ph: (212)870-2402

Rollins, James, Dir. of Mktg., Dir. of
  Comm.
United Methodist Committee on
  Relief [20349]
475 Riverside Dr., Rm. 1520
New York, NY 10115
Ph: (212)870-3951
Toll Free: 800-554-8583

Rollins, Wendy E., Dir. of Fin.
American Lighting Association
  [2098]
2050 N Stemmons Fwy., Unit 100
Dallas, TX 75207-3206
Ph: (214)698-9898
Toll Free: 800-605-4448

Rolls, Linda, President
Disneyana Fan Club [24003]
PO Box 19212
Irvine, CA 92623-9212
Ph: (714)731-4705

Romain, James, Dir. of Member
  Svcs.
North American Saxophone Alliance
  [9988]
Dept. of Music
Drake University
2507 University Ave.
Des Moines, IA 50311-4505
Ph: (515)271-3104

Roman, Alpa, President
Chemical Sources Association
  [1450]

Bldg. C, Ste. 205
3301 Route 66
Neptune, NJ 07753
Ph: (732)922-3008
Fax: (732)922-3590

Roman, Nan, CEO, President
National Alliance to End Homeless-
ness [11955]
1518 K St. NW, 2nd Fl.
Washington, DC 20005
Ph: (202)638-1526
Fax: (202)638-4664

Romanisky, Andy, President
146th Alumni Association [19297]
1534 N Moorpark Rd., No. 365
Thousand Oaks, CA 91360

Romano, Pat, President
Stunts Unlimited [19662]
15233 Ventura Blvd., Ste. 425
Sherman Oaks, CA 91403
Ph: (818)501-1970

Romanowski, Andrew, President
Lamborghini Club America [21417]
PO Box 701963
Plymouth, MI 48170
Ph: (734)216-4455

Rome, Ellen, MD, President
North American Society for Pediatric
and Adolescent Gynecology
[16301]
19 Mantua Rd.
Mount Royal, NJ 08061
Ph: (856)423-3064
Fax: (856)423-3420

Rome, Dr. Ellen S., President
Federation Internationale de Gyne-
cologie Infantile et Juvenile
[16284]
9500 Euclid Ave., No. A120
Cleveland, OH 44195-0001
Ph: (216)444-3566
Fax: (216)445-3523

Rome, Gerald, Treasurer
North American Securities
Administrators Association [3049]
750 1st St. NE, Ste. 1140
Washington, DC 20002
Ph: (202)737-0900
Fax: (202)783-3571

Romeo, Bob, CEO
Academy of Country Music [9845]
5500 Balboa Blvd.
Encino, CA 91316
Ph: (818)788-8000
Fax: (818)788-0999

Romeo, Joan, President
International Bowling Media Association [2683]
c/o Joan Romero, President
6544 Gloria Ave.
Van Nuys, CA 91406
Ph: (818)787-2310

Romero, Anthony D., Exec. Dir.
ACLU Foundation [17862]
125 Broad St., 18th Fl.
New York, NY 10004
Ph: (212)549-2500

Romero, Anthony D., Exec. Dir.
American Civil Liberties Union
[17867]
125 Broad St., 18th Fl.
New York, NY 10004
Ph: (212)549-2500

Romero, Carlos, Exec. Dir.
Mennonite Education Agency
[20330]

3145 Benham Ave., Ste. 2
Elkhart, IN 46517
Ph: (574)642-3164
Toll Free: 866-866-2872

Romig, Alton D., Jr., Exec. Ofc.
National Academy of Engineering
[6572]
500 5th St. NW
Washington, DC 20001
Ph: (202)334-3200
Fax: (202)334-2290

Romita, Mauro C., Chmn. of the Bd.
Boys' and Girls' Towns of Italy
[13431]
250 E 63rd St., Ste. 204
New York, NY 10065
Ph: (212)980-8770
Fax: (212)409-8740

Ronca, April, President
American Society for Gravitational
and Space Research [7217]
12209 Wheat Mill Loop
Bristow, VA 20136
Ph: (703)392-0272

Roncevic, Janina, Officer
American News Women's Club
[2652]
1607 22nd St. NW
Washington, DC 20008
Ph: (202)332-6770
Fax: (202)265-6092

Rondberg, Dr. Terry A., President,
Founder
World Chiropractic Alliance [14285]
2683 Via de La Valle, Ste. G629
Del Mar, CA 92014-1911
Toll Free: 800-347-1011
Fax: (866)789-8073

Rone, Robin, Director
American Bar Association - Young
Lawyers Division [4983]
321 N Clark St., 18th Fl.
Chicago, IL 60654-7598
Ph: (312)988-5611
Toll Free: 800-285-2221
Fax: (312)988-6231

Ronnei, Todd, Chairman
American First Day Cover Society
[22298]
PO Box 16277
Tucson, AZ 85732-6277
Ph: (520)321-0880

Ronsheim, Douglas M., Exec. Dir.
American Association of Pastoral
Counselors [20037]
9504A Lee Hwy.
Fairfax, VA 22031-2303
Ph: (703)385-6967
Fax: (703)352-7725

Rooker, LeRoy, Exec. Dir.
American Association of Collegiate
Registrars and Admissions Officers
[7443]
1 Dupont Cir. NW, Ste. 520
Washington, DC 20036
Ph: (202)293-9161
    (301)490-7651
Fax: (202)872-8857

Rooney, Rev. Don, President
Catholic Association of Diocesan
Ecumenical and Interreligious Of-
ficers [20056]
1009 Stafford Ave.
Fredericksburg, VA 22401
Ph: (540)373-6491
Fax: (540)371-0251

Rooney, Patrick, Managing Dir.
Association of Executive Search and
Leadership Consultants [1086]

425 5th Ave., 4th Fl.
New York, NY 10016
Ph: (212)398-9556

Rooney, Patrick, Dir. of Dev.
Brotherhood Organization of a New
Destiny [19102]
6146 W Pico Blvd.
Los Angeles, CA 90035-0090
Ph: (323)782-1980

Rooney, Patrick, Bd. Member
Emerson College Alumni Association
[19322]
99 Summer St., 9th Fl.
Boston, MA 02110
Ph: (617)824-8535
    (617)824-8275

Rooney, Patrick, PhD, Assoc. Dean
Women's Philanthropy Institute
[12501]
c/o Lilly Family School of
Philanthropy, Indiana University
University Hall, Ste. 3000
301 N University Blvd.
Indianapolis, IN
Ph: (317)274-4200
    (317)278-8990
Fax: (317)684-8900

Rooney, Robert, Exec. Dir.
National Association of Independent
Publishers Representatives [2804]
111 E 14th St.
New York, NY 10003-4103
Ph: (267)546-6561
Toll Free: 888-624-7779

Roop, Rick, Chairman
Automation Federation [6017]
67 Alexander Dr.
Research Triangle Park, NC 27709-
0185
Ph: (919)314-3920
Fax: (919)314-3921

Roos, Pieter N., Exec. Dir.
Newport Restoration Foundation
[9423]
51 Touro St.
Newport, RI 02840
Ph: (401)849-7300
Fax: (401)849-0125

Roose, David, Founder
Christian Bowhunters of America
[22500]
2423 Oak Orchard River Rd.
Erie, PA 16504
Ph: (716)402-5650
Toll Free: 877-912-5724

Roosenberg, Dick, Exec. Dir.
Tillers International [12191]
10515 E OP Ave.
Scotts, MI 49088
Ph: (269)626-0223
Toll Free: 800-498-2700

Roosendaal, Denise, Exec. Dir.
American Evaluation Association
[6622]
2025 M St. NW, Ste. 800
Washington, DC 20036
Ph: (202)367-1166
Fax: (202)367-2166

Roosevelt, Eleanor, Founder
National Committee for an Effective
Congress [18014]
218 D St. SE, 3rd Fl.
Washington, DC 20003
Ph: (202)639-8300

Root, Kathy, President
International Motor Contest Association [22525]

1800 W D St.
Vinton, IA 52349-2500
Ph: (319)472-2201
Fax: (319)472-2218

Root, Rick, President
World Waterpark Association [1163]
8826 Santa Fe Dr., Ste. 310
Overland Park, KS 66212
Ph: (913)599-0300
Fax: (913)599-0520

Root, Steven, CCM, President, CEO
American Weather and Climate
Industry Association [6855]
c/o Steven Root, 1015 Waterwood
Pky., Ste. J
Weatherbank Inc.
1015 Waterwood Pky., Ste. J
Edmond, OK 73034

Roper, Jimmy, President
Barrel Futurities of America [22914]
c/o Cindy Arnold, Secretary
Box 120 K, Route 2
Vian, OK 74962

Ropiequet, John L., Chairman
Conference on Consumer Finance
Law [5104]
PO Box 17981
Clearwater, FL 33762
Ph: (405)208-5198

Roppolo, Dr. Kimberly G., Act. Pres.
Wordcraft Circle of Native Writers'
and Storytellers [10051]
230 Armstrong Hall
English Dept.
Minnesota State University
Mankato, MN 56001
Ph: (505)948-4517

Rosa, Dinelia, PhD, President
APA Division 31: State, Provincial
and Territorial Affairs [16881]
750 1st St. NE
Washington, DC 20002-4241
Ph: (202)336-5500

Rosa, Mr. Fernando G., Chairman,
CEO
Portuguese American Leadership
Council of the United States
[19619]
9255 Center St., Ste. 404
Manassas, VA 20110
Ph: (202)466-4664
Fax: (202)466-4661

Rosa, Kathy, Director
American Library Association Office
for Research and Statistics [9673]
50 E Huron St.
Chicago, IL 60611
Ph: (312)280-4283
Toll Free: 800-545-2433

Rosa-Casanova, Sylvia, President
National Association of State
Administrators and Supervisor of
Private Schools [8463]
403 Marquis Ave., Ste. 200
Lexington, KY 40502

Rosado, Milton, President
Labor Council for Latin American
Advancement [23459]
815 16th St. NW, 4th Fl.
Washington, DC 20006
Ph: (202)508-6919
Fax: (202)508-6922

Rosales, Henry, Dir. of Operations
Geospatial Information and Technol-
ogy Association [6314]
1360 University Ave. W, Ste. 455
Saint Paul, MN 55104-4086
Ph: (303)337-0513
Toll Free: 844-447-4482
Fax: (303)337-1001

Rosard, Steve, President
Big Picture Alliance [17280]
Stenton Artists Guild
4732 Stenton Ave.
Philadelphia, PA 19144
Ph: (215)381-2588
Fax: (215)381-2593

Rosario, Tristian, COO
Latino America Unida, Lambda
  Alpha Upsilon Fraternity [23802]
244 5th Ave., Ste. C-140
New York, NY 10001
Ph: (203)392-5792

Rosati, Kelly, VP
Focus on the Family [11820]
8605 Explorer Dr.
Colorado Springs, CO 80920
Toll Free: 800-232-6459
Fax: (719)548-5947

Rosbeck, Kari Luther, President,
  CEO
Tuberous Sclerosis Alliance [15997]
801 Roeder Rd., Ste. 750
Silver Spring, MD 20910
Ph: (301)562-9890
Toll Free: 800-225-6872
Fax: (301)562-9870

Rosch, Dr. Paul J., Chairman
American Institute of Stress [17289]
6387B Camp Bowie Blvd., No. 334
Fort Worth, TX 76116
Ph: (682)239-6823
Fax: (817)394-0593

Roscher, Marc B., MD, President
Dermatologic and Aesthetic Surgery
  International League [14491]
453 Williamsburg Ln.
Prospect Heights, IL 60070
Ph: (847)577-6543
Fax: (847)577-6583

Rose, Barbara Alison, Exec. Dir.
Aid for Africa [12609]
6909 Ridgewood Ave.
Chevy Chase, MD 20815
Ph: (202)531-2000
Fax: (301)986-7902

Rose, Carol, President
Underwater Society of America
  [23347]
PO Box 628
Daly City, CA 94017
Ph: (707)343-7132

Rose, Clifford, CFO
American Humane Association
  [13028]
1400 16th St. NW, Ste. 360
Washington, DC 20036
Ph: (818)501-0123
Toll Free: 800-227-4645

Rose, Daniel, Chairman
Urban Design Forum [5980]
45-50 30th St., Ste. 10
Long Island City, NY 11101
Ph: (718)663-8478
Fax: (718)663-8390

Rose, Gary R., Bd. Member
ADAP Advocacy Association [13516]
PO Box 15275
Washington, DC 20003

Rose, Greg, President
Clan Rose Society of America
  [20839]
c/o Patrice A. May, Membership
  Director
1188 Cragmont Ave.
Berkeley, CA 94708-1613
Ph: (510)848-1188

Rose, Jeff, Officer
International Marina Institute [2246]
50 Water St.
Warren, RI 02885
Toll Free: 866-367-6622
Fax: (401)247-0074

Rose, Lee, Director
Scripps Howard Foundation [8160]
PO Box 5380
Cincinnati, OH 45201
Ph: (513)977-3035
Toll Free: 800-888-3000
Fax: (513)977-3800

Rose, Lila, Founder, President
Live Action [19060]
2200 Wilson Blvd., Ste. 102
Arlington, VA 22201-3324
Ph: (323)454-3304

Rose, Marshall, President
American Association for Access,
  Equity and Diversity [11751]
1701 Pennsylvania Ave. NW, Ste.
  206
Washington, DC 20006
Ph: (202)349-9855
Fax: (202)355-1399

Rose, Morgan, MS, Exec. Dir.,
  Founder
America's Angel [11813]
PO Box 3124
San Diego, CA 92103

Rose, Patrick, Exec. Dir.
Save the Manatee Club [4880]
500 N Maitland Ave.
Maitland, FL 32751
Ph: (407)539-0990
Toll Free: 800-432-JOIN
Fax: (407)539-0871

Rose, Rebecca, President
National Association of Veterinary
  Technicians in America [17655]
PO Box 1227
Albert Lea, MN 56007
Toll Free: 888-996-2882
Fax: (507)489-4518

Rose, Seymour T., Owner
Rose Family Association [20921]
761 Villa Teresa Way
San Jose, CA 95123

Rose, Tifanie, President
Association for the Education of
  Children with Medical Needs
  [7582]
c/o Scott Menner, Treasurer
580 Chapelacres Ct.
Cincinnati, OH 45233

Roseboro, Paulette, Exec. Dir.
African-American Life Alliance
  [10493]
PO Box 3722
Capitol Heights, MD 20791

Roselli, Mike, Exec. Dir.
Collegiate Association of Table Top
  Gamers [22049]
Campus Box 7306
North Carolina State University
Raleigh, NC 27695
Ph: (919)809-9456

Rosellini, Taale Laafi, MFA, Exec.
  Dir., Founder
African Family Film Foundation
  [8775]
PO Box 630
Santa Cruz, CA 95061-0630

Roseman, Will, Exec. Dir.
The Explorers Club [6625]
46 E 70th St.

New York, NY 10021
Ph: (212)628-8383
Fax: (212)288-4449

Rosen, Charles, MD, Founder, Bd.
  Member
Association for Medical Ethics
  [17252]
14 Monarch Bay Plz., Ste. 405
Dana Point, CA 92629-3424
Ph: (215)322-6654
Toll Free: 800-497-0641

Rosen, Jack, President
American Jewish Congress [20227]
260 Madison Ave., 2nd Fl.
New York, NY 10016
Ph: (212)879-4500
Fax: (212)758-1633

Rosen, Jeffrey A., President
International Center of Photography
  [8424]
1114 Avenue of the Americas
New York, NY 10036
Ph: (212)857-0000
     (212)857-0004

Rosen, Jesse, CEO, President
League of American Orchestras
  [9946]
33 W 60th St.
New York, NY 10023
Ph: (212)262-5161
Fax: (212)262-5198

Rosen, Jim, President
Colonial Coin Collectors Club
  [22265]
c/o Charlie Rohrer, Treasurer
PO Box 25
Mountville, PA 17554

Rosen, Jo, President, Founder
Parkinson's Resource Organization
  [15983]
74-090 El Paseo, Ste. 104
Palm Desert, CA 92260
Ph: (760)773-5628
Toll Free: 877-775-4111

Rosen, Norm, President
Orangutan Conservancy [4860]
5001 Wilshire Blvd., No. 112
Los Angeles, CA 90036

Rosen, Penny, Comm. Chm.
American Association for
  Psychoanalysis in Clinical Social
  Work [13100]
10302 Bristow Center Dr.
Bristow, VA 20136
Ph: (703)369-1268

Rosen, Sigita Simkuviene, President
Lithuanian-American Community Inc.
  [19541]
43 Anthony St.
New Haven, CT 06515
Ph: (203)415-7776
Fax: (703)773-1257

Rosenbaum, Erin, President, Direc-
  tor
Clothes for the World [12646]
294 Chestnut Ave., No. 2
Jamaica Plain, MA 02130
Ph: (857)492-3494

Rosenbaum, Greg, Chairman
National Jewish Democratic Council
  [18916]
PO Box 65683
Washington, DC 20035

Rosenberg, David, Bd. Member
Joseph and Edna Josephson
  Institute of Ethics [11802]

9841 Airport Blvd., Ste. 300
Los Angeles, CA 90045
Ph: (310)846-4800
Toll Free: 800-711-2670
Fax: (310)846-4858

Rosenberg, Donald, Editor
Early Music America [8366]
801 Vinial St., Ste. 300
Pittsburgh, PA 15212
Ph: (412)642-2778
Fax: (412)642-2779

Rosenberg, Donald P., Founder
National Traditionalist Caucus
  [18028]
PO Box 971
New York, NY 10116
Ph: (212)685-4689

Rosenberg, Ernie, President, CEO
American Cleaning Institute [710]
1331 L St. NW, Ste. 650
Washington, DC 20005
Ph: (202)347-2900
Fax: (202)347-4110

Rosenberg, Leonard C., AIA, Exec.
  Dir.
Ministry Architecture, Inc. [5971]
1904 S Union Pl.
Lakewood, CO 80228-5704
Ph: (303)989-4870
Fax: (303)989-0884

Rosenberg, Ms. Linda, MSW, CEO,
  President
National Council for Behavioral
  Health [15795]
1400 K St. NW, Ste. 400
Washington, DC 20005
Ph: (202)684-7457

Rosenberg, Mark L., MD, CEO,
  President
Task Force for Global Health
  [12302]
325 Swanton Way
Decatur, GA 30030
Ph: (404)371-0466
Toll Free: 800-765-7173
Fax: (404)371-1087

Rosenberg, Mark, M.D., President
Society of Medical Friends of Wine
  [22477]
511 Jones Pl.
Walnut Creek, CA 94597
Ph: (925)933-9691
Fax: (925)933-9691

Rosenberg, Tracy, Exec. Dir.
Media Alliance [17949]
2830 20th St., Ste. 102
San Francisco, CA 94110
Ph: (415)746-9475
Fax: (510)238-8557

Rosenberg, Zeda F., CEO, Founder
International Partnership for Microbi-
  cides [13550]
8401 Colesville Rd., Ste. 200
Silver Spring, MD 20910
Ph: (301)608-2221
Fax: (301)608-2241

Rosenberger, Jeanne, President
Jesuit Association of Student
  Personnel Administrators [7429]
1 Dupont Cir. NW, Ste. 405
Washington, DC 20036

Rosenblatt, William H., MD,
  President
Recovered Medical Equipment for
  the Developing World [15613]
333 Cedar St.
New Haven, CT 06520-8051
Ph: (203)737-5356
     (203)785-6750
Fax: (203)785-5241

Rosenbleeth, Herb, Exec. Dir.
Jewish War Veterans of the United
    States of America [21128]
1811 R St. NW
Washington, DC 20009
Ph: (202)265-6280
Fax: (202)234-5662

Rosenbloom, Alan, President
Alliance for Quality Nursing Home
Care [16082]
1350 Connecticut Ave. NW, Ste. 900
Washington, DC 20036
Ph: (202)459-6313
Fax: (202)459-6308

Rosenbloom, Eric, President
National Wind Watch [7389]
63 W Hill Rd.
Charlemont, MA 01339

Rosenblum, Bruce, Chairman, CEO
Academy of Television Arts and Sci-
    ences [450]
5220 Lankershim Blvd.
North Hollywood, CA 91601
Ph: (818)754-2800

Rosenblum, Howard A., CEO
National Association of the Deaf
[15200]
8630 Fenton St., Ste. 820
Silver Spring, MD 20910
Ph: (301)587-1788
Fax: (301)587-1791

Rosenbursch, Walt, COO, Exec. VP
International Association of
    Geophysical Contractors [2526]
1225 North Loop W, Ste. 220
Houston, TX 77008-1761
Ph: (713)957-8080
Toll Free: 866-558-1756
Fax: (713)957-0008

Rosener, James, President
European-American Chamber of
    Commerce [23584]
The New York Times Bldg.
620 8th Ave., 37th Fl.
New York, NY 10018
Ph: (212)808-2730
    (212)808-2707

Rosengard, Paul, Co-Ch.
YMA Fashion Scholarship Fund
[210]
1501 Broadway, Ste. 1810
New York, NY 10036
Ph: (212)278-0008

Rosenheim, David, Exec. Dir.
The Climate Registry [4542]
601 W 5th St., Ste. 220
Los Angeles, CA 90071
Toll Free: 866-523-0764

Rosenkrans, Wayne, Editor
Flight Safety Foundation [135]
701 N Fairfax St., Ste. 250
Alexandria, VA 22314-1754
Ph: (703)739-6700
Fax: (703)739-6708

Rosenkranz, Stephan, PhD,
    President
Neutron Scattering Society of
    America [7030]
c/o Stephan Rosenkranz, President,
    Materials Science Division, Ar-
    gonne National Laboratory
Argonne National Laboratory
Materials Science Div.
9700 S Cass Ave.
Lemont, IL 60439
Ph: (630)252-5475

Rosenshein, Norman, President
National Museum of American Jew-
    ish Military History [21134]

1811 R St. NW
Washington, DC 20009
Ph: (202)265-6280
Fax: (202)462-3192

Rosenstein, Hans, President
Vintage BMW Motorcycle Owners
[22236]
PO Box 341
Clarksville, OH 45113-0341
Ph: (414)333-6987
Fax: (414)456-9790

Rosenstiel, Blanka A., Contact
American Institute of Polish Culture
[10163]
1440 79th St. Causeway, Ste. 117
Miami, FL 33141
Ph: (305)864-2349
Fax: (305)865-5150

Rosenstiel, Stephen F., Secretary
American Academy of Fixed Prost-
    hodontics [14376]
Office of the Secretary
6661 Merwin Rd.
Columbus, OH 43235
Ph: (614)761-1927
Fax: (614)292-0941

Rosenstiel, Tom, Exec. Dir.
American Press Institute [8147]
4401 Wilson Blvd., Ste. 900
Arlington, VA 22203-4195
Ph: (571)366-1200
    (571)366-1035

Rosenthal, Donald A., MD, Exec. Dir.
American Alternative Medical As-
    sociation [13587]
2200 Market St., Ste. 803
Galveston, TX 77550-1530
Ph: (409)621-2600
Toll Free: 888-764-2237
Fax: (775)703-5334

Rosenthal, Eric, Exec. Dir., Founder
Disability Rights International
[12322]
1666 Connecticut Ave. NW, Ste. 325
Washington, DC 20009
Ph: (202)296-0800
Fax: (202)697-5422

Rosenthal, Joel H., President
Carnegie Council for Ethics in
    International Affairs [18476]
Merrill House
170 E 64th St.
New York, NY 10065-7478
Ph: (212)838-4120
Fax: (212)752-2432

Rosenthal, Philip, Ed.-in-Chief
American Society of Tropical
    Medicine and Hygiene [17534]
1 Parkview Plz., Ste. 800
Oakbrook Terrace, IL 60181
Ph: (847)480-9592
    (847)686-2238
Fax: (847)480-9282

Rosenthal, Steven C., Exec. Dir.
Cross-Cultural Solutions [9228]
2 Clinton Pl.
New Rochelle, NY 10801
Ph: (914)632-0022
Toll Free: 800-380-4777
Fax: (914)632-8494

Rosentrater, Kurt, Exec. Dir., CEO
Distillers Grains Technology Council
[1518]
Iowa State University
3327 Elings Hall
Ames, IA 50011
Ph: (515)294-4019
Toll Free: 800-759-3448

Roseth, Lisa, Exec. Dir.
College of St. Scholastica Alumni
    Association [19317]
Tower Hall 1410
1200 Kenwood Ave.
Duluth, MN 55811-4199
Ph: (218)723-6071
    (218)723-6016
Toll Free: 866-935-3731

Roshkowski, Greg, Exec. VP
Associated Cooperage Industries of
    America [827]
10001 Taylorsville Rd., Ste. 201
Louisville, KY 40299-3116
Ph: (502)261-2242
Fax: (502)261-9425

Rosier, Ronald C., Director
Conference Board of the Mathemati-
    cal Sciences [6819]
1529 18th St. NW
Washington, DC 20036
Ph: (202)293-1170
Fax: (202)293-3412

Rosin, Nancy, President
National Valentine Collectors' As-
    sociation [21701]
c/o Nancy Rosin, President
PO Box 647
Franklin Lakes, NJ 07417
Ph: (201)337-5834
Fax: (201)337-3356

Roskey, Dana, Exec. Dir.
Ethiopia Reads [8240]
PO Box 581302
Minneapolis, MN 55458
Ph: (612)354-2184

Rosman, Lori, Rec. Sec.
APLIC [9678]
c/o Yan Fu, Vice President
University of Michigan
426 Thompson St.
Ann Arbor, MI 48104-2321
Ph: (734)763-2152

Rosner, David, President
International Society for the
    Comparative Study of Civilizations
[7168]
c/o David Hahn, Treasurer
School for Management
Metropolitan College of New York
431 Canal St.
New York, NY 10013
Ph: (212)343-1234
Fax: (212)343-8476

Rosnik, Phil, Chmn. of the Bd.
World Association for Children and
    Parents [11188]
315 S 2nd St.
Renton, WA 98057
Ph: (206)575-4550
Toll Free: 800-732-1887
Fax: (206)575-4148

Rosoff, Lyn, Dir. of Comm.
SmartPower [4030]
1120 Connecticut Ave. NW, Ste.
    1040
Washington, DC 20036
Ph: (202)775-2040
Fax: (202)775-2045

Rosquist, Elaine, Director
Destination Marketing Association
International [2325]
2025 M St. NW, Ste. 500
Washington, DC 20036
Ph: (202)296-7888
Fax: (202)296-7889

Ross, Carl, Director, Founder
Save America's Forests [3938]
4 Library Ct. SE

Washington, DC 20003
Ph: (202)544-9219

Ross, David, Bd. Member
National Association of Air Medical
    Communication Specialists [13510]
2311 Yellow Mountain Rd.
Roanoke, VA 24014
Ph: (262)409-8884
Toll Free: 877-396-2227
Fax: (866)827-2296

Ross, Frank, VP
Plasticville Collectors Association
[21715]
601 SE 2nd St.
Ankeny, IA 50021-3207
Ph: (515)964-0562

Ross, Dr. Hugh, Founder, President
Reasons to Believe [20598]
818 S Oak Park Rd.
Covina, CA 91724
Ph: (626)335-1480
Toll Free: 855-732-7667
Fax: (626)852-0178

Ross, Jane B., Exec. Dir., Founder
Smart Kids with Learning Disabilities
[12241]
38 Kings Hwy. N
Westport, CT 06880
Ph: (203)226-6831
Fax: (203)226-6708

Ross, Jay, President
Association of Zoological Horticulture
[4430]

Ross, Jerry, VP
North American Performing Arts
    Managers and Agents [164]
459 Columbus Ave., No. 133
New York, NY 10024
Ph: (212)769-1000

Ross, Liz, President
Clan Ross America [20840]
PO Box 6341
River Forest, IL 60305

Ross, Marc, Chmn. of the Bd.
National Apartment Association
[2867]
4300 Wilson Blvd., Ste. 400
Arlington, VA 22203
Ph: (703)518-6141
Fax: (703)248-9440

Ross, Marc, Exec. Dir.
Rock the Earth [4099]
1536 Wynkoop St., Ste. B200
Denver, CO 80202
Ph: (303)454-3304
Fax: (303)454-3306

Ross, Patti, President
Lutheran Women's Missionary
    League [20314]
3558 S Jefferson Ave.
Saint Louis, MO 63118
Toll Free: 800-252-5965
Fax: (314)268-1532

Ross, Stephen, President
Modernist Studies Association
[8048]
Journals Publishing Div.
The Johns Hopkins University Press
PO Box 19966
Baltimore, MD 21211-0966
Toll Free: 800-548-1784
Fax: (410)516-3866

Ross, Steven, Dir. of Corp. Comm.
Scripture Union-USA [19764]
PO Box 215
Valley Forge, PA 19481
Ph: (610)935-2807
Toll Free: 800-621-5267
Fax: (610)935-2809

Rossel, Eugene D., Contact
Air Commando Association [21101]
PO Box 7
Mary Esther, FL 32569
Ph: (850)581-0099
Fax: (850)581-8988

Rossetto, Lynn, President, Exec. Dir.
March Forth Kenya Kids [11075]
PO Box 69A92
West Hollywood, CA 90069

Rossi, Mark, Exec. Dir.
Clean Production Action [4136]
1310 Broadway, Ste. 101
Somerville, MA 02144-1837
Ph: (781)391-6743
Fax: (781)285-3091

Rossi, Mark, Mem.
Sustainable Biomaterials Collabora-
tive [5890]
Ph: (202)898-1610

Rosskamp, Alison, Mem.
Gordon Setter Club of America
[21888]
c/o Sharon Hultquist, Membership
Chairperson
13332 Redding Dr.
Fort Wayne, IN 46814-9773
Ph: (260)672-3338

Rossman, Susan, President
America's Blood Centers [13837]
725 15th St. NW, Ste. 700
Washington, DC 20005
Ph: (202)393-5725
Fax: (202)393-1282

Rost, Burkhard, PhD, President
International Society for
Computational Biology [1791]
9500 Gilman Dr.
MC 0505
La Jolla, CA 92093-0505
Ph: (858)534-0852
(858)822-0852
Fax: (619)374-2894

Rosta, Sara, Coord.
ITEM Coalition [15099]
1501 M St., NW, 7th Fl.
Washington, DC 20005-1700
Ph: (202)446-6550
Fax: (202)785-1756

Rotenberg, Marc, President, Exec.
Dir.
Electronic Privacy Information
Center [6742]
1718 Connecticut Ave. NW, Ste. 200
Washington, DC 20009
Ph: (202)483-1140

Roth, Bruce, Exec. Dir., Founder
Daisy Alliance [18780]
990 Hammond Dr., Ste. 830
Atlanta, GA 30328
Ph: (770)261-4274
Fax: (770)804-5631

Roth, Carol, Bd. Member
Mennonite Women U.S.A. [20333]
718 N Main St.
Newton, KS 67114-1819
Ph: (316)281-4396
Toll Free: 866-866-2872
Fax: (316)283-0454

Roth, Christina, President, Founder
College Diabetes Network [14520]
350 Lincoln St., Ste. 2400
Hingham, MA 02043

Roth, Daniel J., President, CEO
National Futures Association [1494]
300 S Riverside Plz., Ste. 1800

Chicago, IL 60606-6615
Ph: (312)781-1300
Toll Free: 800-621-3570
Fax: (312)781-1467

Roth, Debra, Chmn. of the Bd.
Exotic Dancers League of America
[9255]
Burlesque Hall of Fame
520 Fremont St., No. 120
Las Vegas, NV 89101
Toll Free: 888-661-6465

Roth, Mr. Eric, Exec. Dir.
Visual Effects Society [1209]
5805 Sepulveda Blvd., Ste. 620
Sherman Oaks, CA 91411
Ph: (818)981-7861
Fax: (818)981-0179

Roth, Gil, President
Pharma & Biopharma Outsourcing
Association [2566]
10 Alta Vista Dr.
Ringwood, NJ 07456
Ph: (201)788-7994

Roth, Kenneth, Exec. Dir.
Human Rights Watch [18407]
350 5th Ave., 34th Fl.
New York, NY 10118-3299
Ph: (212)290-4700
Fax: (212)736-1300

Roth, Kenneth, Exec. Dir.
Human Rights Watch - Asia [18408]
350 5th Ave., 34th Fl.
New York, NY 10118-3299
Ph: (212)290-4700

Roth, Kenneth, Exec. Dir.
Human Rights Watch - Children's
Rights [18409]
350 5th Ave., 34th Fl.
New York, NY 10118-3299
Ph: (212)290-4700
Fax: (212)736-1300

Roth, Lisa, Dep. Dir.
University of Iowa Injury Prevention
Research Center [7109]
2190 Westlawn
University of Iowa
Iowa City, IA 52242
Ph: (319)467-4504

Roth, Scott, Exec. Dir.
Art Directors Guild [9296]
11969 Ventura Blvd., 2nd Fl.
Studio City, CA 91604-2630
Ph: (818)762-9995
Fax: (818)762-9997

Rothenberg, David, Founder
Fortune Society [11526]
29-76 Northern Blvd.
Long Island City, NY 11101
Ph: (212)691-7554

Rothenberg, David, Secretary
North American Association of
Synagogue Executives [20565]
Rapaport House
120 Broadway, No. 1540
New York, NY 10271
Ph: (631)732-9461
Fax: (631)732-9461

Rothenberg, Randall, CEO,
President
Interactive Advertising Bureau [97]
116 E 27th St., 7th Fl.
New York, NY 10016
Ph: (212)380-4700

Rothenberg, Russell, MD, Chairman
National Fibromyalgia Partnership
Inc. [14770]

140 Zinn Way
Linden, VA 22642-5609
Toll Free: 866-725-4404

Rothenberger, Lisa, Chairman
IMA World Health [15476]
1730 M St. NW, Ste. 1100
Washington, DC 20036
Ph: (202)888-6200
Fax: (202)470-3370

Rother, Franklyn, President
National Organization for Human
Services [13075]
1600 Sarno Rd., Ste. 16
Melbourne, FL 32935-4993
Toll Free: 800-597-2306

Rother, John C., President, CEO
National Coalition on Health Care
[18335]
1825 K St. NW, Ste. 411
Washington, DC 20006
Ph: (202)638-7151

Rothfuss, Bill, Contact
Association of Applied IPM Ecolo-
gists [4524]
PO Box 1119
Coarsegold, CA 93614
Ph: (559)761-1064

Rothman, Brian, President
Society for Technology in Anesthesia
[13714]
6737 W Washington St., Ste. 4210
Milwaukee, WI 53214-5636
Ph: (414)389-8600
Fax: (414)275-7704

Rothman, Heathcliff, Co-Ch.,
Founder
Global Vision for Peace [18791]
5419 Hollywood Blvd., Ste. C208
Los Angeles, CA 90027

Rothman, Joel, Chairman
Juvenile Arthritis Association [17160]
8549 Wilshire Blvd., Ste. 103
Beverly Hills, CA 90211

Rothschild, Richard, President
American Book Producers Associa-
tion [2761]
31 W 8th St., 2nd Fl.
New York, NY 10011-4116
Ph: (212)944-6600

Rothstein, Roz, CEO
StandWithUs [18588]
PO Box 341069
Los Angeles, CA 90034-1069
Ph: (310)836-6140
Fax: (310)836-6145

Rotoloni, Robert J., Editor, Publisher
Nikon Historical Society [10143]
RJR Publishing Inc.
PO Box 3213
Munster, IN 46321

Roton, Francis M., Dir. of Admin.
American Association of Community
Psychiatrists [16810]
c/o Francis Roton Bell, Administra-
tive Director
PO Box 570218
Dallas, TX 75357-0218
Ph: (972)613-0985
(972)613-3997
Fax: (972)613-5532

Rotondaro, Alfred M., Chairman
Catholics in Alliance for the Common
Good [19819]
1612 K St., Ste. 400
Washington, DC 20006
Ph: (202)499-4968

Rotterdam, Howard, Comm. Chm.
Society of Israel Philatelists [22367]
25250 Rockside Rd.
Bedford Heights, OH 44146

Rottman, Colonel (Retired) Ray,
Exec. Dir.
Association of Military Colleges and
Schools of the United States
[8342]
12332 Washington Brice Rd.
Fairfax, VA 22033-2428
Ph: (703)272-8406

Roumain, Regine M., Exec. Dir.
Haiti Cultural Exchange [9211]
c/o FiveMyles Gallery
558 St. John Pl.
Brooklyn, NY 11238
Ph: (347)565-4429

Rödlach, Alexander, Treasurer
Society for Medical Anthropology
[5925]
American Anthropological Associa-
tion
Box 353100
Seattle, WA 98195

Rountree, John
Popular Rotorcraft Association
[21244]
12296 West 600 South
Mentone, IN 46539
Ph: (574)353-7227
Fax: (574)353-7021

Rouse, James, Chairman
American Institute of Musical Studies
[8358]
28 E 69th St.
Kansas City, MO 64113-2512
Ph: (816)268-3657

Rouse, Michael J., Director
Accreditation Council for Pharmacy
Education [16630]
135 S LaSalle St., Ste. 4100
Chicago, IL 60603-4810
Ph: (312)664-3575
Fax: (312)664-4652

Roush, Gary, President
Saluki Club of America [21955]
c/o Sharon Walls
100 Wrangler Rd.
Reno, NV 89510-9303

Roush, Gary, Officer
Vietnam Helicopter Pilots Associa-
tion [21172]
2100 N Highway 360, Ste. 907
Grand Prairie, TX 75050-1030
Toll Free: 800-505-8472
Fax: (817)200-7309

Roush, James L., Editor
Foundation for P.E.A.C.E. [18785]
PO Box 9151
Asheville, NC 28815-0151
Ph: (828)296-0194

Roush, Kathy W., Secretary,
Treasurer
Beta Beta Beta [23683]
University of North Alabama
Math Bldg. M1 - A
1 Harrison Plz.
Florence, AL 35632
Ph: (256)765-6220
Fax: (256)765-6221

Roush, Mark, President
Illuminating Engineering Society of
North America [6784]
120 Wall St., 17th Fl.
New York, NY 10005
Ph: (212)248-5000
Fax: (212)248-5018

Rovero, April, CEO, Founder
National Coalition Against Prescrip-
    tion Drug Abuse [11717]
PO Box 87
San Ramon, CA 94583
Ph: (925)480-7723
Fax: (925)901-1250

Rovner, Eric Scott, MD, President
Society of Urodynamics, Female
    Pelvic Medicine and Urogenital
    Reconstruction [17564]
1100 E Woodfield Rd., Ste. 350
Schaumburg, IL 60173
Ph: (847)517-7225
Fax: (847)517-7229

Rowan, Mr. John, President
Vietnam Veterans of America
    [19227]
8719 Colesville Rd., Ste. 100
Silver Spring, MD 20910
Ph: (301)585-4000
Toll Free: 800-882-1316
Fax: (301)585-0519

Rowan, Matthew, President, CEO
Health Industry Distributors Associa-
    tion [1601]
310 Montgomery St.
Alexandria, VA 22314-1516
Ph: (703)549-4432
    (703)838-6118
Fax: (703)549-6495

Rowe, Amanda, Exec. Dir.
International Society for Heart &
    Lung Transplantation [17512]
14673 Midway Rd., Ste. 200
Addison, TX 75001
Ph: (972)490-9495
Fax: (972)490-9499

Rowe, Carol, President
Contemporary Art Pottery Collectors
    Association [21579]
PO Box 175
Lake Geneva, WI 53147

Rowe, Kaye, Treasurer
National Christ Child Society [19881]
6110 Executive Blvd., Ste. 504
Rockville, MD 20852
Ph: (301)881-2490
Toll Free: 800-814-2149
Fax: (301)881-2493

Rowe, Marieli, Editor
National Telemedia Council [9146]
1922 University Ave.
Madison, WI 53726
Ph: (608)218-1182
Fax: (608)218-1183

Rowe, Sandra Mims, Chairman
Committee to Protect Journalists
    [17942]
330 7th Ave., 11th Fl.
New York, NY 10001
Ph: (212)465-1004
Fax: (212)465-9568

Rowe, Rev. Sean, Chmn. of the Bd.
Episcopal Church Building Fund
    [20099]
563A Southlake Blvd.,
Richmond, VA 23236
Ph: (804)893-3436
Fax: (804)893-3439

Rowland, Virginia, President
French Bull Dog Club of America
    [21881]
c/o Adrienne Soler
206 Smedley Rd.
South Royalton, VT 05068

Rowlett, Prof. Roger S., President
National Conferences on
    Undergraduate Research [8503]

734 15th St. NW, Ste. 550
Washington, DC 20005
Ph: (202)783-4810
Fax: (202)783-4811

Rowley, Craig, Exec. Dir.
National Procurement Institute
    [2819]
PO Box 370192
Las Vegas, NV 89137
Ph: (702)989-8095
Toll Free: 866-877-7641
Fax: (702)967-0744

Rowsom, Christopher, Exec. Dir.
Historic Ships in Baltimore [9774]
301 E Pratt St.
Baltimore, MD 21202
Ph: (410)539-1797
Fax: (410)539-6238

Roy, Kaushik, Exec. Dir.
The Shanti Project Inc. [11498]
730 Polk St.
San Francisco, CA 94109
Ph: (415)674-4700
    (415)674-4722
Fax: (415)674-0373

Roy, Stephanie, Exec. Dir.
Hospitality Asset Managers Associa-
    tion [1657]
c/o Stephanie Roy, Executive Direc-
    tor
PO Box 381
North Scituate, MA 02060-0381
Ph: (781)544-7330

Roy, Sylvain, President, CEO
Cultivating New Frontiers in
    Agriculture [18522]
1828 L St. NW, Ste. 710
Washington, DC 20036
Ph: (202)296-3920
Fax: (202)296-3948

Royal, Angel, Chief of Staff
American Association of Community
    Colleges [7640]
1 Dupont Cir. NW, Ste. 410
Washington, DC 20036-1145
Ph: (202)728-0200
Fax: (202)833-2467

Royall, Penelope, Director
U.S. Department of Health and Hu-
    man Services | Office of Disease
    Prevention and Health Promotion |
    National Health Information Center
    [14967]
1101 Wootton Pky., Ste. LL100
Rockville, MD 20852
Ph: (301)565-4167
Toll Free: 800-336-4797
Fax: (301)984-4256

Roybal, Richard, Exec. Dir.
LULAC National Educational Service
    Centers [7779]
1133 19th St. NW, Ste. 1000
Washington, DC 20036
Ph: (202)835-9646
Fax: (202)835-9685

Royce, Michael, Founder
Green Empowerment [3781]
140 SW Yamhill St.
Portland, OR 97204
Ph: (503)284-5774
Fax: (503)460-0450

Roye, Dr. David P., Jr., CEO,
    President
International Healthcare Leadership
    [15122]
Columbia University Medical Ctr.
3959 Broadway, 8 N
New York, NY 10032

Royse, Alvin J., JD, Chairman
American Stroke Association [17294]
7272 Greenville Ave.
Dallas, TX 75231
Toll Free: 888-478-7653

Ru, Ji, Chairman
Mid-America Buddhist Association
    [19781]
299 Heger Ln.
Augusta, MO 63332-1445
Ph: (636)482-4037
Fax: (636)482-4078

Ruane, Pete, President, CEO
American Road & Transportation
    Builders Association [5809]
1219 28th St. NW
Washington, DC 20007
Ph: (202)289-4434

Ruark, Joel K., Exec. Dir.
New Dramatists [10266]
424 W 44th St.
New York, NY 10036
Ph: (212)757-6960
Fax: (646)390-8705

Rubash, Harry E., MD, President
Hip Society [16476]
9400 W Higgins Rd., Ste. 500
Rosemont, IL 60018-4976
Ph: (847)698-1638
Fax: (847)823-0536

Rubel, Adam, Founder, Director
Saq' Be': Organization for Mayan
    and Indigenous Spiritual Bodies
    [9578]
PO Box 31111
Santa Fe, NM 87594

Rubens, Craig E., PhD, Exec. Dir.
Global Alliance to Prevent
    Prematurity and Stillbirth [14231]
1100 Olive Way, Ste. 1000
Seattle, WA 98101
Ph: (206)884-2777
Fax: (206)884-1040

Rubens, Deborah, President
American Society for Healthcare Hu-
    man Resources Administration
    [15309]
155 N Wacker Dr., Ste. 400
Chicago, IL 60606
Ph: (312)422-3720
Fax: (312)422-4577

Rubenstein, David M., Chairman
Friends of the Kennedy Center
    [8974]
2700 F St. NW
Washington, DC 20566
Ph: (202)467-4600
Toll Free: 800-444-1324

Rubick, Jade, Founder
Stop Abuse for Everyone [11713]
4939 Calloway Dr., Ste. 104
Bakersfield, CA 93312
Ph: (661)829-6848

Rubik-Rothstein, Trish, Director
Alliance of the American Dental As-
    sociation [14370]
211 E Chicago Ave., Ste. 730
Chicago, IL 60611-2616
Toll Free: 800-621-8099
Fax: (312)440-2587

Rubin, Barry, President
Independent Time & Labor Manage-
    ment Association [3278]
2049 Stout Dr., Ste. A-1
Warminster, PA 18974
Ph: (215)443-8720
Fax: (215)443-8709

Rubin, Jon, Founder, President
KISS Rocks Fan Club [24052]
c/o Jon Rubin, Founder
15 Maple Rd.
Briarcliff Manor, NY 10510

Rubin, Jon, Chairman
Rock the Vote [17839]
1875 Connecticut Ave. NW, 10th Fl.
Washington, DC 20009
Ph: (202)719-9910

Rubin, Lance, President
William Dean Howells Society [9112]
English Dept.
Middle Tennessee State University
1301 E Main St.
Murfreesboro, TN 37132

Rubinger, Michael, President, CEO
Local Initiatives Support Corporation
    [17984]
501 7th Ave.
New York, NY 10018
Ph: (212)455-9800
Fax: (212)682-5929

Rubingisa, Providence, President,
    Exec. Dir.
Stuff for the Poor [11445]
PO Box 6477
Villa Park, IL 60181
Ph: (630)401-4719
Toll Free: 877-579-7387

Rubio, Barbara, VP
American Women for International
    Understanding [12203]
2100 S Wolf Rd.
Des Plaines, IL 60018-1932
Ph: (847)298-0442

Ruby, Byron, President
Harvard Environmental Law Society
    [5182]
Wasserstein Hall
Harvard Law School
1563 Massachusetts Ave.
Cambridge, MA 02138

Rucker, Craig, Exec. Dir., Founder
Committee for a Constructive Tomor-
    row [18044]
PO Box 65722
Washington, DC 20035-5722
Ph: (202)429-2737

Rucker, Doug, President
United Association of Mobile
    Contract Cleaners [2144]
PO Box 1914
Gilbert, AZ 85299
Toll Free: 800-816-3240

Rucker, Kenneth, Dir. of Admin.,
    President
National Capital Trolley Museum
    [9497]
1313 Bonifant Rd.
Colesville, MD 20905-5955
Ph: (301)384-6088

Rucker, Tumiko, Advisor
Association of Public Treasurers of
    the United States and Canada
    [5705]
7044 S 13th St.
Oak Creek, WI 53154
Ph: (414)908-4947
Fax: (414)768-8001

Ruckman, Dave, Bd. Member
Adopt-a-Village International [11305]
PO Box 26599
Colorado Springs, CO 80936
Ph: (719)492-8736

Ruddy, Kathleen T., Founder
Breast Health and Healing Founda-
    tion [13850]

36 Newark Ave., Ste. 130
Belleville, NJ 07109
Ph: (973)450-9955
Fax: (973)450-2552

Rudek, Sylvia, Director
National Association to Stop Guard-
ian Abuse [11749]
PO Box 886
Mount Prospect, IL 60056

Rudel, Tom, President
Rural Sociological Society [7188]
Western Illinois University
1 University Cir.
Macomb, IL 61455-1367
Ph: (309)298-3518

Rudelius-Palmer, Ms. Kristi, Director
Human Rights Resource Center
[18406]
University of Minnesota Law School
229 19th Ave. S, Ste. N-120
Minneapolis, MN 55455
Ph: (612)626-0041
Toll Free: 888-HRE-DUC8
Fax: (612)625-2011

Rudman, Lisa, Exec. Dir.
National Radio Project [18660]
1904 Franklin St., Ste. 405
Oakland, CA 94612
Ph: (510)251-1332
    (510)459-8558

Rudmann, Jerry, PhD, Exec. Dir.
Psi Beta [23854]
c/o Kathleen Hughes, President
Pasco-Hernando State College
10230 Ridge Rd.
New Port Richey, FL 34654
Ph: (727)816-3330

Rudnyk, Rebecca, Exec. Dir.
National Dental EDI Council [14461]
9240 E Raintree Dr.
Scottsdale, AZ 85260-7518
Ph: (480)734-2890
Fax: (480)734-2895

Rudolph, Janet A., Director, Editor
Mystery Readers International
[24017]
PO Box 8116
Berkeley, CA 94707-8116

Rudolph, Walter, President
Jussi Bjorling Society U.S.A. [8927]
c/o Dan Shea, Director
3337 Conservancy Ln.
Middleton, WI 53562
Ph: (608)836-6911

Rudolphi, Linda, Registrar
Hungarian Horse Association of
America [4360]
281 Ruby Rd.
Noble, IL 62868
Ph: (618)752-7181

Rudrapatna, Ashok, President
North American Sankethi Association
[9174]
34 Longwood Dr.
Clifton Park, NY 12065

Rudzinski, Laura J., Exec. Dir.
National Institute of Pension
Administrators [1076]
330 N Wabash Ave., Ste. 2000
Chicago, IL 60611-7621
Toll Free: 800-999-6472
Fax: (312)673-6609

Ruestow, Brian, President
Society of Manufacturing Engineers
Education Foundation [7863]
1 SME Dr.

Dearborn, MI 48128-2408

Rueter, Mr. Ted, Contact
Noise Free America [6924]
PO Box 2754
Chapel Hill, NC 27515
Toll Free: 877-664-7366

Ruff, Dianne, Comm. Chm.
National Association of Wheat
Weavers [21771]
c/o Kate Farris, Treasurer
9360 Warnick Rd.
Frankenmuth, MI 48734
Ph: (989)928-0477

Ruffing, Victoria, RN, CCRP,
Founder
Rheumatology Nurses Society
[16183]
8437 Tuttle Ave., Ste. 404
Sarasota, FL 34243
Toll Free: 800-380-7081
Fax: (410)384-4222

Ruhland, Polly, CEO
Cattlemen's Beef Promotion and
Research Board [3725]
9000 E Nichols Ave., Ste. 215
Centennial, CO 80112
Ph: (303)220-9890
Fax: (303)220-9280

Ruhlman, Robert, VP
International Lightning Class As-
sociation [22635]
1528 Big Bass Dr.
Tarpon Springs, FL 34689-5604
Ph: (727)942-7969
Fax: (727)942-0173

Rui, Bai, Bd. Member
Chinese American Educational
Research and Development As-
sociation [7599]
PO Box 355
Bloomington, IL 61702

Ruiter, Rene, President
Association of Natural Biocontrol
Producers [4525]
PO Box 1609
Clovis, CA 93613-1609
Ph: (559)360-7111

Ruiz, Luz Marina, President
California Society of Printmakers
[1531]
PO Box 194202
San Francisco, CA 94119-4202

Ruiz, Xavier, Director
Spain-United States Chamber of
Commerce [23618]
80 Broad St., Ste. 2103
New York, NY 10004
Ph: (212)967-2170

Ruiz-Sanchez, Eduardo, Exec. Dir.
Bamboo of the Americas [3818]
c/o Sue Turtle, Treasurer
30 Myers Rd.
Summertown, TN 38483-7323

Rukavina, Phillip, President
Lute Society of America, Inc. [9951]
PO Box 6499
Concord, CA 94524
Ph: (925)686-5800

Rulli, Angelo, President
Carousel Organ Association of
America [22247]
c/o Marc Dannecker, Treasurer
1900 E Cora Ave.
Saint Francis, WI 53235

Rumberg, Steve, President
National Organization for Disorders
of the Corpus Callosum [15969]

18032-C Lemon Dr., PMB 363
Yorba Linda, CA 92886
Ph: (714)747-0063
Fax: (714)693-0808

Rummel, Chad, Exec. Dir.
Society for Personality and Social
Psychology [7075]
1660 L St. NW, No. 1000
Washington, DC 20036
Ph: (202)524-6545

Rumsey, David C., President
American Translators Association
[3311]
225 Reinekers Ln., Ste. 590
Alexandria, VA 22314
Ph: (703)683-6100
Fax: (703)683-6122

Rumsey, Jim, Exec. Dir., COO
Society for Investigative Dermatol-
ogy [14513]
526 Superior Ave. E, Ste. 540
Cleveland, OH 44114-1999
Ph: (216)579-9300
Fax: (216)579-9333

Rundle, Pamela M., CEO, President
Children's Cross Connection
International [14178]
2192 Greencliff Dr.
Atlanta, GA 30345
Ph: (404)358-7960
Fax: (770)234-4147

Runkle, Nathan, President, Founder
Mercy For Animals [10659]
8033 Sunset Blvd., Ste. 864
Los Angeles, CA 90046
Toll Free: 866-632-6446

Runnels, Joel, Exec. Dir.
Global Deaf Connection [15190]
1301 E American Blvd., Ste. 109
Minneapolis, MN 55425
Ph: (612)724-8565
Fax: (612)729-3839

Runyan, Nikki, President
Flat-Coated Retriever Society of
America [21879]
c/o Mary Ann Abbott, Membership
Secretaury
19275 Whispering Trl.
Traverse City, MI 49686-9771
Ph: (231)223-4473

Ruppal, Michael, Exec. Dir.
AIDS Alliance for Children, Youth
and Families [13520]
1705 DeSales St. NW, Ste. 700
Washington, DC 20036
Ph: (202)754-1858

Ruppel, Brent, VP
Guide Dogs for the Blind [17709]
350 Los Ranchitos Rd.
San Rafael, CA 94903
Ph: (415)499-4000
Toll Free: 800-295-4050
Fax: (415)499-4035

Ruppel, Jan, President
Big Thicket Association [3819]
PO Box 198
Saratoga, TX 77585
Ph: (936)274-1181

Ruppel, Jan, President
Big Thicket Natural Heritage Trust
[3820]
Box 1049
Kountze, TX 77625

Ruppel, Col. John L., Jr., President
129th Alumni and Heritage Association [21099]

c/o Col. John L. Ruppel, Jr.,
President
6718 Zerillo Dr.
Riverbank, CA 95367-2122
Ph: (209)869-2879

Rurka, Steve, Founder, Exec. Dir.
Appendiceal Cancer Advocacy
Network [13888]
2825 McKinley Pl. NW
Washington, DC 20015
Ph: (301)512-0708
Fax: (301)654-8508

Ruscetta, Rusty, CEO
Inventors Assistance League [6770]
PO Box 55
La Canada, CA 91011
Ph: (818)246-6542
Toll Free: 877-433-2246
Fax: (818)246-6546

Rusche, Sue, CEO, President
National Families in Action [13169]
PO Box 133136
Atlanta, GA 30333-3136
Ph: (404)248-9676

Ruschival, Adam, Treasurer
American Council of Blind Lions
[17682]
148 Vernon Ave.
Louisville, KY 40206
Ph: (502)897-1472

Rusczyk, Bob, Exec., Administrator
Associated Pipe Organ Builders of
America [2418]
PO Box 8268
Erie, PA 16505
Toll Free: 800-473-5270

Rush, Grahame, Exec. Dir.
CTSNet: Cardiothoracic Surgery
Network [17472]
633 N St. Clair St., 23rd Fl.
Chicago, IL 60611-3658
Ph: (312)202-5848
Fax: (312)202-5801

Rush, Iris M., Exec. Dir.
Association for Research in Vision
and Ophthalmology [16374]
1801 Rockville Pke., Ste. 400
Rockville, MD 20852-5622
Ph: (240)221-2900
Fax: (240)221-0370

Rush, Peter, Exec. Dir.
Window Covering Safety Council
[3477]
355 Lexington Ave., Ste. 1500
New York, NY 10017
Ph: (212)297-2100
Fax: (212)370-9047

Rush, Sharron, Exec. Dir.
Knowbility [11613]
1033 La Posada Dr., Ste. 372
Austin, TX 78752
Ph: (512)527-3138
Toll Free: 800-735-2989

Rushdoony, Rev. Mark R., President
Chalcedon Foundation [20583]
3900 Highway 4
Vallecito, CA 95251
Ph: (209)736-4365
Fax: (209)736-0536

Rushford, Michael D., CEO,
President
Criminal Justice Legal Foundation
[5134]
2131 L St.
Sacramento, CA 95816
Ph: (916)446-0345
Fax: (916)446-1194

Rushing, Hugh J., Exec. Ofc.
Society of Classified Advertising
  Managers Association [110]
PO Box 531335
Mountain Brook, AL 35253
Ph: (205)592-0389
Fax: (205)599-5598

Russell, Rev. Allen, Director
Conservative Baptist Association of
  America [19727]
3686 Stagecoach Rd., Ste. F
Longmont, CO 80504
Ph: (720)283-3030

Russell, Barry, President, CEO
Independent Petroleum Association
  of America [2524]
1201 15th St. NW, Ste. 300
Washington, DC 20005
Ph: (202)857-4722
Fax: (202)857-4799

Russell, Dianne J., President
Institute for Conservation Leadership
  [4069]
6930 Carroll Ave., Ste. 1050
Takoma Park, MD 20912
Ph: (301)270-2900
Fax: (301)270-0610

Russell, Jeff, Exec. Dir.
International Association for Physicians in Aesthetic Medicine
  [14315]
848 N Rainbow Blvd., No. 713
Las Vegas, NV 89107
Toll Free: 800-485-5759

Russell, Jerry, President
National Concrete Burial Vault As-
  sociation [2411]
136 S Keowee St.
Dayton, OH 45402
Toll Free: 888-88N-CBVA
Fax: (937)222-5794

Russell, John K., PhD, President
Academy of Managed Care Provid-
  ers [15092]
1945 Palo Verde Ave., Ste. 202
Long Beach, CA 90815-3445
Ph: (562)682-3559
Toll Free: 800-297-2627
Fax: (562)799-3355

Russell, Dr. Robert, Exec. Dir.
Cartoonists Rights Network
  International [18381]
PO Box 7272
Fairfax Station, VA 22039

Russell, Thomas A., Comm. Chm.
Maritime Arbitration Association of
  the United States [4963]
PO Box 11466
Newport Beach, CA 92658
Toll Free: 800-717-5750

Russell, William B., III, Director
International Society for the Social
  Studies [8565]
PO Box 161250
Orlando, FL 32816-1250

Russo, Daniella, Exec. Dir.
Plastic Pollution Coalition [4556]
2150 Allston Way, Ste. 460
Berkeley, CA 94704
Ph: (323)936-3010

Russo, Domenico, Chairman
Office Furniture Distribution Associa-
  tion [3475]
PO Box 2548
Secaucus, NJ 07096

Russo, Dominic, President
United States Power Soccer Association [23195]

Russo, Jamie, Exec. Dir.
Global Workspace Association [70]
1900 S Norfolk St., Ste. 350
San Mateo, CA 94403
Ph: (650)931-2588

Russo, Kimberly, Director
America's Great Loop Cruisers' As-
  sociation [21552]
500 Oakbrook Ln.
Summerville, SC 29485
Toll Free: 877-478-5667

Russo, Nolan, Jr., Chairman
American Institute for Stuttering
  [17235]
27 W 20th St., Ste. 1203
New York, NY 10011
Ph: (212)633-6400
Toll Free: 877-378-8883
Fax: (212)220-3922

Russo, Richard, VP
Authors Guild [10362]
31 E 32nd St., 7th Fl.
New York, NY 10016
Ph: (212)563-5904
Fax: (212)564-5363

Russo, Robert, President
National Federation of Opticianry
  Schools [16415]
c/o Randall L. Smith, Executive
  Manager
4500 Enterprise Dr.
Allen Park, MI 48101
Ph: (313)425-3815

Russomagno, Vince, CEO, Founder
American Hearing Aid Associates
  [15171]
225 Wilmington W Chester Pike,
  Ste. 300
Chadds Ford, PA 19317-9011
Toll Free: 800-984-3272

Rust-Tierney, Diann, Exec. Dir.
National Coalition to Abolish the
  Death Penalty [17831]
1620 L St., NW, Ste. 250
Washington, DC 20036-5698
Ph: (202)331-4090

Ruthen, Russell, President
Day Before Birth [14228]
101 Great Rd., Ste. 201
Bedford, MA 01730
Toll Free: 866-213-1140
Fax: (781)313-8188

Rutherford, Laura Boyajian, Director,
  President
Kate's Voice [16982]
PO Box 365
Sudbury, MA 01776-0365
Ph: (978)440-9913

Rutherford, Nancy, Exec. Dir.
International Textile and Apparel As-
  sociation [3261]
PO Box 70687
Knoxville, TN 37938-0687
Ph: (865)992-1535

Rutherfurd, Winthrop, Jr., Chmn. of
  the Bd.
Metropolitan Opera Guild [9955]
70 Lincoln Center Plz., 6th Fl.
New York, NY 10023-6593
Ph: (212)769-7000

Rutkauskas, John S., CEO
American Academy of Pediatric
  Dentistry [14386]
211 E Chicago Ave., Ste. 1600
Chicago, IL 60611-2637
Ph: (312)337-2169
Fax: (312)337-6329

Rutkowski, Anne, Chairwoman
Cure CMD [15920]
PO Box 701
Olathe, KS 66051
Toll Free: 866-400-3626

Rutkowski, John, President
Hovawart Club of North America
  [21893]
PO Box 455
Montgomery, NY 12549-0455

Rutledge, Andrea S., CAE, Exec.
  Dir.
National Architectural Accrediting
  Board [7500]
1101 Connecticut Ave. NW, Ste. 410
Washington, DC 20036
Ph: (202)783-2007
Fax: (202)783-2822

Rutter, Deborah F., President
John F. Kennedy Center for the
  Performing Arts - Department of
  VSA and Accessibility [11610]
2700 F St. NW
Washington, DC 20566-0002
Ph: (202)467-4600
Toll Free: 800-444-1324

Rutzen, Douglas, President
International Center for Not-for-Profit
  Law [5429]
1126 16th St. NW, Ste. 400
Washington, DC 20036-4837
Ph: (202)452-8600
Fax: (202)452-8555

Ruud, Susan, Secretary
American Homebrewers Association
  [177]
1327 Spruce St.
Boulder, CO 80302
Ph: (303)447-0816
Toll Free: 888-822-6273

Ruvalcaba, Jovan, President
National Association of Law
  Students With Disabilities [8218]
Washington, DC

Ruzin, Francesca, VP
Society of Young Philanthropists
  [12496]
8322 Beverly Blvd., Ste. 301
Los Angeles, CA 90048

Ryan, Cynthia, MBA, Exec. Dir.
Vestibular Disorders Association
  [16543]
5018 NE 15th Ave.
Portland, OR 97211
Toll Free: 800-837-8428
Fax: (503)229-8064

Ryan, Emilie, CFO
LightHawk [3896]
PO Box 2710
Telluride, CO 81435
Ph: (970)797-9355

Ryan, Erik, President
Steamship Historical Society of
  America [22440]
2500 Post Rd.
Warwick, RI 02886
Ph: (401)463-3570
Fax: (401)463-3572

Ryan, Gary, Secretary
American Wheelchair Bowling Association [22775]
c/o Wayne Webber
1533 Pelican Pl.
Palm Harbor, FL 34683
Ph: (727)728-1342

Ryan, Mr. John, President, CEO
Conference of State Bank Supervisors [391]

1129 20th St. NW, 9th Fl.
Washington, DC 20036
Ph: (202)296-2840
Fax: (202)296-1928

Ryan, John R., Chairman
United States Naval Academy
  Alumni Association [19590]
247 King George St.
Annapolis, MD 21402-1306
Ph: (410)295-4000

Ryan, Mr. Kevin, President, CEO
Covenant House [13439]
461 8th Ave.
New York, NY 10001
Toll Free: 800-388-3888

Ryan, Lauren, Founder
Angiosarcoma Awareness [14562]
PO Box 570442
Whitestone, NY 11357

Ryan, V. Adm. (Ret.) Norbert R., Jr.,
  President
Military Officers Association of
  America [21076]
201 N Washington St.
Alexandria, VA 22314-2537
Ph: (703)549-2311
Toll Free: 800-234-6622

Ryan, Norma, Chairperson
Dandie Dinmont Terrier Club of
  America [21866]

Ryan, Dr. Pamela, Bd. Member,
  Founder
Psychology Beyond Borders [11676]
1000 Rio Grande St.
Austin, TX 78701
Ph: (512)900-8898

Ryan, Patrick P., Exec. Dir.
IEEE - Power Engineering Society
  [6410]
445 Hoes Ln.
Piscataway, NJ 08854-1331
Ph: (732)562-3883
Fax: (732)562-3881

Ryan, Sean, President
Service Specialists Association [353]
c/o Sean Ryan, President
7307 Grand Ave.
Pittsburgh, PA 15225
Ph: (847)760-0067

Ryberg, Paul, President
Mauritius-U.S. Business Association,
  Inc. [1986]
401 9th St. NW, Ste. 640
Washington, DC 20004
Ph: (202)531-4028

Ryder, Beverly P., Bd. Member
National Women's Hall of Fame
  [20738]
76 Fall St.
Seneca Falls, NY 13148
Ph: (315)568-8060

Ryder, E. Roberta, President, CEO
National Center for Farmworker
  Health [15045]
1770 FM 967
Buda, TX 78610
Ph: (512)312-2700
Toll Free: 800-531-5120
Fax: (512)312-2600

Rydfors, Jan, Chief Med. Ofc.
American Pregnancy Association
  [16274]
1425 Greenway Dr., Ste. 440
Irving, TX 75038
Ph: (972)550-0140
Toll Free: 800-672-2296

Ryerson, William, Chmn. of the Bd.,
CEO
Population Institute [12517]
107 2nd St. NE
Washington, DC 20002
Ph: (202)544-3300
Fax: (202)544-0068

Ryerson, William, President
Population Media Center [12518]
PO Box 547
Shelburne, VT 05482-0547
Ph: (802)985-8156
Fax: (802)985-8119

Ryland, Kenneth, VP
Bible Sabbath Association [20592]
802 NW 21st Ave.
Battle Ground, WA 98604
Ph: (253)447-7913
Toll Free: 888-687-5191

Rylko, Theresa E., President
Mystic Valley Railway Society
[10185]
PO Box 365486
Hyde Park, MA 02136-0009
Ph: (617)361-4445
Fax: (617)361-4451

Rynd, Chase W., Exec. Dir.
National Building Museum [5972]
401 F St. NW
Washington, DC 20001
Ph: (202)272-2448
Fax: (202)272-2564

Rynearson, Edward K., MD, Director
Violent Death Bereavement Society
[10777]
Lavin-Bernick Ctr.
31 McAlister Dr.
New Orleans, LA 70118
Ph: (206)223-6398

Rynerson, Diane, Exec. Dir.
National Conference of Women's
Bar Associations [5036]
PO Box 82366
Portland, OR 97282
Ph: (503)775-4396
    (816)360-4116

Rynerson, Jan Stone, Contact
Society of the Descendants of
Washington's Army at Valley Forge
[20697]
908 Washington St.
Columbus, IN 47201
Ph: (432)393-5790

Rypins, Amy, President
Center for Community Solutions
[18202]
4508 Mission Bay Dr.
San Diego, CA 92109-4919
Ph: (858)272-5777

Ryser, Rudolph C., Chairman
Fourth World Documentation Project
[18472]
1001 Cooper Point Rd. SW, No.
104, PMB 214
Olympia, WA 98502-1107
Ph: (360)529-4896

Ryun, Jim, Chairman
Madison Project [19039]
PO Box 655
Aledo, TX 76008

Rzepka, Jennifer, Exec. Dir.
National Industrial Belting Associa-
tion [1755]
6737 W Washington St., Ste. 1300
Milwaukee, WI 53214
Ph: (414)389-8606
Fax: (414)276-7704

Rzeszutko, Rick, President
International Polka Association
[9930]
4608 S Archer Ave.
Chicago, IL 60632
Toll Free: 800-867-6552

S

S., Mike, Founder
Heroin Anonymous [13143]
5025 N Central Ave., No. 587
Phoenix, AZ 85012

Sánchez-Flores, Héctor, Exec. Dir.
National Compadres Network
[18669]
1550 The Alameda, Ste. 303
San Jose, CA 95126-2304
Ph: (408)676-8215

Saah, Andrea Imredy, Treasurer
Al-Bustan Seeds of Culture [8811]
526 S 46th St.
Philadelphia, PA 19143
Ph: (267)303-0070
    (267)809-3668

Sabath, F, President
IEEE - Electromagnetic Compatibility
Society [6426]
445 Hoes Ln.
Piscataway, NJ 08855-6802
Ph: (732)562-5539
Fax: (732)981-0225

Sabatino, Charles P., Director
American Bar Association Commis-
sion on Law and Aging [5405]
1050 Connecticut Ave. NW, Ste. 400
Washington, DC 20036
Ph: (202)662-8690
Fax: (202)662-8698

Sabelnik, Natalie, President
Congress of Russian Americans
[19630]
2460 Sutter St.
San Francisco, CA 94115
Ph: (415)928-5841
Fax: (415)928-5831

Sabharwal, Dr. Nilima, Chairperson
Home of Hope [11033]
190 Tobin Clark Dr.
Hillsborough, CA 94010
Ph: (650)520-3204

Sabin, Scott C., Exec. Dir.
Plant With Purpose [18497]
4747 Morena Blvd., Ste. 100
San Diego, CA 92117-3466
Toll Free: 800-633-5319
Fax: (858)274-3728

Sabitoni, Armand, Treasurer, Tax
Ofc.
Laborers' International Union of
North America [23399]
905 16th St. NW
Washington, DC 20006
Ph: (202)737-8320

Sable, Dr. Craig, President
Heart Healers International [14114]
9601 Hall Rd.
Potomac, MD 20854

Saborio, Rigoberto, Chairman
Health Outreach Partners [12339]
405 14th St., Ste. 909
Oakland, CA 94612
Ph: (510)268-0091
Fax: (510)268-0093

Sabri, Mazin, President
Iraqi Medical Sciences Association
[15481]

PO Box 1154
Libertyville, IL 60048-1154

Saccardi, Kathleen, Office Mgr.
National Coalition of Mental Health
Professionals and Consumers
[15793]
PO Box 438
Commack, NY 11725
Ph: (631)979-5307
Toll Free: 866-826-2548
Fax: (631)979-5293

Sacco, Michael, President
AFL-CIO-Maritime Trades Depart-
ment [23472]
815 16th St. NW
Washington, DC 20006-4101
Ph: (202)628-6300

Sacco, Michael, President
Seafarers International Union
[23478]
5201 Auth Way
Camp Springs, MD 20746
Ph: (301)899-0675
Fax: (301)899-7355

Sachs, Adam, Contact
Coalition for Patients' Rights [14988]
c/o Adam Sachs, Public Relations
Writer
American Nurses Association
8515 Georgia Ave., Ste. 400
Silver Spring, MD 20910-3492
Ph: (301)628-5034
Fax: (301)628-5340

Sachs, Samuel, II, President
Pollock-Krasner Foundation [8938]
863 Park Ave.
New York, NY 10075-0342
Ph: (212)517-5400
Fax: (212)288-2836

Sackler, Elizabeth A., PhD, Founder,
President
American Indian Ritual Object
Repatriation Foundation [18706]
463 E 57th St.
New York, NY 10022-3003
Ph: (212)980-9441
Fax: (212)421-2746

Sackman, Bruce, President
Society of Professional Investigators
[5371]
PO Box 1087
Bellmore, NY 11710
Ph: (718)490-7288

Sacks, Steven E., CPA, Exec. Dir.
Moore Stephens North America, Inc.
[42]
Plaza II, Ste. 200
250 Pehle Ave., Park 80 W
Saddle Brook, NJ 07663
Ph: (201)291-2660
Fax: (201)368-1944

Sadigova, Susan, Exec. Dir.
United States - Azerbaijan Chamber
of Commerce [18532]
1212 Potomac St. NW
Washington, DC 20007
Ph: (202)333-8702
Fax: (202)333-8703

Sadik, Wunmi, President, Founder
Sustainable Nanotechnology
Organization [7296]
2020 Pennsylvania Ave. NW, Ste.
200
Washington, DC 20006

Sadler, Pastor Paul M., President
Berean Bible Society [19751]
PO Box 756

Germantown, WI 53022-0756
Ph: (262)255-4750
Fax: (262)255-4195

Sadovsky, Yoel, President
Society for Reproductive Investiga-
tion [16307]
555 E Wells St., Ste. 1100
Milwaukee, WI 53202-3823
Ph: (414)918-9888
Fax: (414)276-3349

Saeed, Dr. Agha, Chairman
American Muslim Alliance [18701]
39675 Cedar Blvd., Ste. 220 E
Newark, CA 94560
Ph: (510)252-9858
Fax: (510)252-9863

Saeger, Chris, Exec. Dir.
North American Simulation and
Gaming Association [22063]
4023 Kennett Pke., No. 530
Wilmington, DE 19807
Ph: (980)224-2637

Saenz, Thomas, President, Gen.
Counsel
Mexican American Legal Defense
and Educational Fund [17911]
634 S Spring St.
Los Angeles, CA 90014

Safer, Ms. Ricky, President
PSC Partners Seeking a Cure
[13790]
5237 S Kenton Way
Englewood, CO 80111
Ph: (303)771-5227

Sagall, Rich, MD, President
NeedyMeds [15609]
PO Box 219
Gloucester, MA 01931
Ph: (978)221-6666
Toll Free: 800-503-6897
Fax: (206)260-8850

Sagan, Andrew, II, Exec. Dir.
Phi Alpha Delta [23804]
606 Baltimore Ave., Ste. 303
Towson, MD 21204
Ph: (410)347-3118

Sagoff, Prof. Mark, PhD, Founder
Institute for Philosophy and Public
Policy [18984]
4400 University Dr., 3F1
Fairfax, VA 22030-4422
Ph: (703)993-1290

Sahin, Funda, President
Decision Sciences Institute [7550]
C.T. Bauer College of Business
334 Melchor Hall
4750 Calhoun Rd., Ste. 325
Houston, TX 77204-6021
Ph: (713)743-4815
Fax: (713)743-8984

Saia, Tony, VP
Afghan Hound Club of America, Inc.
[21791]
PO Box 1838
Cedar Park, TX 78630

Saidah, George, Founder
Heart of Sailing [22619]
PO Box 4776
Laguna Beach, CA 92652
Ph: (949)236-7245
Fax: (866)609-0807

Saif, Taher, President
Society of Engineering Science
[6591]
c/o Pradeep Sharma, Vice-President
Dept. of Mechanical Engineering

Cullen College of Engineering
University of Houston
Houston, TX 77204-4006

Saigh, Phil, Exec. Dir.
American Academy of Pain Medicine
Foundation [16548]
8735 W Higgins Rd., Ste. 300
Chicago, IL 60631
Ph: (847)375-4731

Saine, KB, President
Black Theatre Network [10244]
2609 Douglas Rd. SE, Ste. 102
Washington, DC 20020
Ph: (202)274-5667
Fax: (202)806-6708

Saint, Rod, CEO
American Hot Rod Association
[22521]
c/o Rod Saint, Chief Executive
Offcer
PO Box 10278
Panama City, FL 32404
Ph: (850)215-1019

Saint-Pierre, Pamela, Treasurer
National Basketry Organization
[21772]
PO Box 1524
Gloucester, MA 01930-1524
Ph: (617)863-0366

Sakamoto, Pauline, MS, President
Human Milk Banking Association of
North America [14195]
4455 Camp Bowie Blvd., Ste. 114-88
Fort Worth, TX 76107
Ph: (817)810-9984
Fax: (817)810-0087

Sak-Humphry, Dr. Chhany, President
National Association for the Educa-
tion and Advancement of
Cambodian, Laotian, and
Vietnamese Americans [19684]
c/o Dr. Chhany Sak-Humphry,
President
University of Hawaii
Dept. of Indo-Pacific Languages and
Literatures
Spalding Hall 255
2540 Maile Way
Honolulu, HI 96822
Ph: (808)956-8070
Fax: (808)956-5978

Sakurai, Motoatsu, President
Japan Society [9624]
333 E 47th St.
New York, NY 10017
Ph: (212)832-1155
    (212)715-1270

Salam, Sarwar B., CPA, Chairman
The Optimists [11112]
25-78 31st St.
Astoria, NY 11102
Ph: (718)278-4953
    (718)577-1048

Salamone, Lee, Director
Center for the Polyurethanes
Industry of the American Chemistry
Council [2621]
700 2nd St. NE
Washington, DC 20002
Ph: (202)249-7000

Salamone, Liz, Secretary
Mothers & More [11768]
PO Box 8091
Prairie Village, KS 66208-0091
Toll Free: 855-373-MORE
Fax: (845)463-0537

Salas-Uruena, Pollyanna, President,
Founder
KiteChild [11064]
8252 1/2 Santa Monica Blvd., Ste. A

West Hollywood, CA 90046

Salau, Dr. Ibrahim, President
Zumunta Association USA [19598]
10411 Motor City Dr., Ste. 750
Bethesda, MD 20817

Salazar, Christian, Web Adm.
National Art Exhibitions of the
Mentally Ill [8987]
PO Box 350891
Miami, FL 33135
Ph: (954)922-8692

Salazar, Gabby, Bd. Member
North American Nature Photography
Association [2588]
6382 Charleston Rd.
Alma, IL 62807-2026
Ph: (618)547-7616
Fax: (618)547-7438

Salberg, Lisa, CEO, Founder
Hypertrophic Cardiomyopathy As-
sociation [14118]
18 E Main St., Ste. 202
Denville, NJ 07834
Ph: (973)983-7429
Fax: (973)983-7870

Salbi, Zainab, Founder
Women for Women International
[13407]
2000 M St. NW, Ste. 200
Washington, DC 20036
Ph: (202)737-7705
    (202)521-0016
Fax: (202)737-7709

Sale, David M., JD, Exec. Dir.
Council of Colleges of Acupuncture
and Oriental Medicine [16454]
PO Box 65120
Baltimore, MD 21209
Ph: (410)464-6040
Fax: (410)464-6042

Saleeby, Eli Leonard, President
Saleeby-Saliba Association of
Families [20923]
PO Box 87094
Fayetteville, NC 28304

Salem, Michael, MD, FACS, CEO,
President
National Jewish Health [17145]
1400 Jackson St.
Denver, CO 80206
Ph: (303)388-4461
Toll Free: 877-225-5654

Salem, Richard J., CEO, Founder
Enable America, Inc. [11595]
101 E Kennedy Blvd.
Tampa, FL 33602-5179
Toll Free: 877-362-2533
Fax: (813)221-8811

Salerno, Judith A., President, CEO
Susan G. Komen for the Cure
[13999]
5005 LBJ Freeway, Ste. 250
Dallas, TX 75244
Toll Free: 877-465-6636

Sales, Brian, Chairman
Association of Average Adjusters of
the United States and Canada
[1835]
126 Midwood Ave.
Farmingdale, NY 11735

Saliga, Pauline, Exec. Dir.
Society of Architectural Historians
[9511]
1365 N Astor St.
Chicago, IL 60610-2144
Ph: (312)573-1365

Salisbury, Dallas L., President, CEO
Employee Benefit Research Institute
[1067]
1100 13th St. NW, Ste. 878
Washington, DC 20005-4051
Ph: (202)659-0670
Fax: (202)775-6312

Salisbury, Darryl A., Chairman
American Motors Owners Associa-
tion [21323]
892 N Jackson Ave.
Jefferson, WI 53549
Ph: (920)674-4482

Salisbury, Franklin C., Jr., CEO
National Foundation for Cancer
Research [16351]
4600 E West Hwy., Ste. 525
Bethesda, MD 20814
Ph: (301)654-1250
Toll Free: 800-321-2873
Fax: (301)654-5824

Salisbury, Tom, President
Navy Nuclear Weapons Association
[21058]
c/o Frank Kelly, Treasurer
1087 Frank Kelly Rd.
Society Hill, SC 29593
Ph: (843)378-4026

Salit, Jacqueline, President
Committee for a Unified Independent
Party [18886]
225 Broadway, Ste. 2010
New York, NY 10007
Ph: (212)609-2800

Salke, Taraneh R., Founder,
President
Family Health Alliance [17105]
6520 Platt Ave., Ste. 433
West Hills, CA 91307-3218
Ph: (818)610-7278

Sallee, Brian, President
International Association of
Undercover Officers [5472]
142 Banks Dr.
Brunswick, GA 31523
Toll Free: 800-876-5943
Fax: (800)876-5912

Salley, Mike, Founder, Exec. Dir.,
Dir. of Operations
Show Mercy International [11270]
PO Box 1003
Port Gibson, MS 39150
Ph: (541)981-1469

Sallot, John, Dir. of Mktg.
Desert Botanical Garden [6139]
1201 N Galvin Pkwy.
Phoenix, AZ 85008
Ph: (480)941-1225
    (480)481-8133
Toll Free: 888-314-9480
Fax: (480)481-8124

Salmon, Adam, Founder, President
Child Empowerment International,
Inc. [10894]
225 Crossroads Blvd., No. 123
Carmel, CA 93923-8674
Ph: (821)622-9094
Toll Free: 800-725-8098

Salmon, Jo, President
International Society for Behavioral
Nutrition and Physical Activity
[13797]
University of Texas
313 E 12th St., Ste. 220
Minneapolis, MN 55455

Salmon, Scott, President
Mulch and Soil Council [1442]
7809 FM 179

Shallowater, TX 79363
Ph: (806)832-1810
Fax: (806)832-5244

Salmon, William C., PE, Secretary,
Treasurer
International Council of Academies
of Engineering and Technological
Sciences [8547]
3004 The Mall
Williamsburg, VA 23185
Ph: (703)527-5782

Salmond, Jeff, President
Sports Turf Managers Association
[2073]
805 New Hampshire St., Ste. E
Lawrence, KS 66044
Ph: (785)843-2549
Toll Free: 800-323-3875
Fax: (785)843-2977

Salo, Matt, Exec. Dir.
National Association of Medicaid
Directors [15102]
444 N Capitol St. NW, Ste. 524
Washington, DC 20001
Ph: (202)403-8620

Salo, Sheila, Treasurer
Gypsy Lore Society [9589]
5607 Greenleaf Rd.
Cheverly, MD 20785
Ph: (301)341-1261
    (212)229-5308
Fax: (810)592-1768

Salser, Cathy, Founder
A Window Between Worlds [11715]
710 4th Ave., Ste. 5
Venice, CA 90291
Ph: (310)396-0317
Fax: (310)396-9698

Saltas, Joanne, Mem.
Daughters of Penelope [19452]
1909 Q St. NW, Ste. 500
Washington, DC 20009
Ph: (202)234-9741
Fax: (202)483-6983

Saltzberg, Matt, Secretary
Association of Theatre Movement
Educators [8697]
977 Seminole Trl., No. 228
Charlottesville, VA 22901-2824

Saltzman, Charles L., MD, President
International Federation of Foot and
Ankle Societies [16789]
6300 N River Rd., Ste. 510
Rosemont, IL 60018-4235
Ph: (847)698-4654
Fax: (847)692-3315

Saltzman, Gary P., President
B'nai B'rith International [20237]
1120 20th St. NW, Ste. 300 N
Washington, DC 20036
Ph: (202)857-6600
Toll Free: 888-388-4224

Saltzman, Simon, President
Outer Critics Circle [10268]

Salvani, Jon, President
Pi Sigma Epsilon [23811]
5217 S 51st St.
Greenfield, WI 53220
Ph: (414)328-1952
Fax: (414)235-3425

Salwen, Dr. Barry D., Exec. Dir.
Roger Sessions Society [9184]
Dept. of Music
University of North Carolina Wilming-
ton
601 S College Rd.

Wilmington, NC 28403-3201
Ph: (910)962-3890
Fax: (910)962-7106

Salyer, Kenneth E., MD, Chairman,
    Founder
World Craniofacial Foundation
    [14348]
7777 Forest Ln., Ste. C-616
Dallas, TX 75230
Ph: (972)566-6669
Toll Free: 800-533-3315
Fax: (972)566-3850

Salyer, Stephen, President, CEO
Salzburg Global Seminar [9582]
1250 H St., NW, Ste. 1150
Washington, DC 20005
Ph: (202)637-7683
Fax: (202)637-7699

Salzman, Sarna, Exec. Dir.
Seeking Ecology Education and
    Design Solutions [4011]
PO Box 2454
Traverse City, MI 49685
Ph: (231)947-0312

Sam, Dr. Peter A., Chairman
African Environmental Research and
    Consulting Group [4034]
14912 Walmer St.
Overland Park, KS 66223
Ph: (913)897-6132
Fax: (913)891-6132

Samad, Djamillah, Exec. Dir.
Church Women United [20640]
475 Riverside Dr., Ste. 243
New York, NY 10115
Ph: (212)870-2347
Toll Free: 800-298-5551
Fax: (212)870-2338

Samadder, Gautam, MD, VP
American Association of Physicians
    of Indian Origin [16734]
600 Enterprise Dr., Ste. 108
Oak Brook, IL 60523
Ph: (630)990-2277
Fax: (630)990-2281

Samargian, Ani, Founder
Arthrogryposis Multiplex Congenita
    Support Inc. [15903]
PO Box 1883
Salyersville, KY 41465

Samarotto, Alexa, President
Australian Terrier Club of America
    [21834]
c/o Marilyn Harban, Corresponding
    Secretary
6675 Sawtooth Dr.
Ooltewah, TN 37363-5865

Samblanet, Phillip J., Exec. Dir.
The Masonry Society [6812]
105 S Sunset St., Ste. Q
Longmont, CO 80501-6172
Ph: (303)939-9700
Fax: (303)541-9215

Sammons, Morgan T., PhD, ABPP,
    Exec. Ofc.
Council for the National Register of
    Health Service Providers in
    Psychology, Inc. [16913]
1200 New York Ave. NW, Ste. 800
Washington, DC 20005
Ph: (202)783-7663
Fax: (202)347-0550

Samper, Cristian, PhD, President,
    CEO
Wildlife Conservation Society [4910]
2300 Southern Blvd.
Bronx, NY 10460
Ph: (718)220-5100

Sample, Kate, President
Sunshine Foundation [11276]
1041 Mill Creek Dr.
Feasterville, PA 19053
Ph: (215)396-4770
Fax: (215)396-4774

Sampson, David A., President, CEO
Property Casualty Insurers Associa-
    tion of America [1920]
8700 W Bryn Mawr Ave., Ste. 1200S
Chicago, IL 60631-3512
Ph: (847)297-7800
Fax: (847)297-5064

Sampson, John B., MD, Founder,
    President
Doctors for United Medical Missions
    [15446]
313 Tidewater Dr.
Havre de Grace, MD 21078-4144
Ph: (410)688-0691
Fax: (240)331-2417

Samson, George V., CEO, President
World Medical Relief [12304]
21725 Melrose Ave.
Southfield, MI 48075
Ph: (313)866-5333
Fax: (313)866-5588

Samson, Jon, Secretary
Agricultural and Food Transporters
    Conference [3316]
c/o Jon Samson, Secretary
950 N Glebe Rd., Ste. 210
Arlington, VA 22203-4181
Ph: (703)838-1700
Fax: (703)838-1781

Samuel, Mr. Bill, President
Consistent Life [18779]
PO Box 9295
Silver Spring, MD 20916-9295
Toll Free: 866-444-7245
Fax: (413)485-2881

Samuel, Deborah, MBA, Bd.
    Member
Society for Academic Continuing
    Medical Education [8336]
3416 Primm Ln.
Birmingham, AL 35216-5602
Ph: (205)978-7990
Fax: (205)823-2760

Samuels, Craig, Exec. Dir.
American College of Psychiatrists
    [16818]
122 S Michigan Ave., Ste. 1360
Chicago, IL 60603
Ph: (312)662-1020
Fax: (312)662-1025

Samuels, Peter, Chairman
Wildcat Service Corporation [11789]
2 Washington St. 3rd Fl.
New York, NY 10004-3415
Ph: (212)209-6000

Samuelson, Dana, President
Professional Numismatists Guild
    [22283]
28441 Rancho California Rd., Ste.
    106
Temecula, CA 92590-3618
Ph: (951)587-8300

Samuelson, Mr. Peter, Founder,
    President, Chairman
First Star [10976]
901 K St. NW, Ste. 700
Washington, DC 20001
Ph: (202)293-3703

San Martin, Tessie, CEO
Plan International U.S.A. [11262]
155 Plan Way

Warwick, RI 02886
Ph: (401)562-8400
Toll Free: 800-556-7918

San, Dr. Myat, Chairman
The Myanmar American Medical
    Education Society, Inc. [8327]
PO Box 740576
Rego Park, NY 11374-0576

San Rafael, Jerry South, President
United States Bocce Federation
    [22695]
c/o Julie Belfi, Treasurer
10013 Shapfield Ln.
Saint Louis, MO 63123
Ph: (630)257-2854

San Roman, Tina, Treasurer
International Association of Service
    Evaluators [2823]
c/o Matt Corrow, President
1988 E Rd.
Shaftsbury, VT 05262-9778
Ph: (802)681-7940

Sanabria, Salvador, Exec. Dir.
El Rescate [12588]
1501 W 8th St., Ste. 100
Los Angeles, CA 90017
Ph: (213)387-3284
Fax: (213)387-9189

San-Blas, Dr. Ernesto, VP
International Federation of Nematol-
    ogy Societies [6908]
c/o Larry Duncan, President
Citrus Research and Education Ctr.
University of Florida, IFAS
700 Experiment Station Rd.
Lake Alfred, FL 33850
Ph: (863)956-8821
Fax: (863)956-4631

Sanbrailo, John, Exec. Dir.
Pan American Development Founda-
    tion [17799]
1889 F St. NW, 2nd Fl.
Washington, DC 20006
Ph: (202)458-3969
Toll Free: 877-572-4484
Fax: (202)458-6316

Sanbrano, Angela, President
Alianza Americas [11312]
1638 S Blue Island Ave.
Chicago, IL 60608
Toll Free: 877-683-2908

Sancheti, Ashok, President
Indian Diamond and Colorstone As-
    sociation [2049]
56 W 45th St., Ste. 705
New York, NY 10036
Ph: (212)921-4488
Fax: (212)769-7935

Sanchez, Frank E., Exec. Dir.,
    Founder
World Head of Family Sokeship
    Council [23027]
6035 Ft. Caroline Rd., Ste. 22
Jacksonville, FL 32277-1883
Ph: (904)361-9218
Fax: (904)744-4625

Sanchez, Frank, Exec. Dir.
The Needmor Fund [12984]
539 E Front St.
Perrysburg, OH 43551
Ph: (419)872-1490

Sandbakken, John, Exec. Dir.
National Sunflower Association
    [3768]
2401 46th Ave. SE, Ste. 206
Mandan, ND 58554-4829
Ph: (701)328-5100
Toll Free: 888-718-7033

Sandberg, Mark, President
Ibsen Society of America [9056]
c/o Gergana May, Treasurer
Germanic Studies Dept.
Indiana University
Bloomington, IN 47405

Sandeen, Peg, Exec. Dir.
Death with Dignity National Center
    [17889]
520 SW 6th Ave., Ste. 1220
Portland, OR 97204-1510
Ph: (503)228-4415

Sander, David, Chairman
National Civic League [5643]
6000 E Evans Ave., Ste. 3-012
Denver, CO 80222
Ph: (303)571-4343

Sander, David, Chairman
New England M.G. "T" Register
    Limited [21460]
PO Box 1028
Ridgefield, CT 06877-9028
Ph: (802)434-8418
Fax: (203)261-9131

Sanders, Bruce A., Exec. Dir.
American College of Phlebology
    [17569]
101 Callan Ave., Ste. 210
San Leandro, CA 94577-4558
Ph: (510)346-6800
    (510)834-6500
Fax: (510)346-6808

Sanders, Christine, President
Christmas Philatelic Club [22317]
PO Box 744
Geneva, OH 44041-0744

Sanders, Dr. David, Director
National Music Council [9974]
c/o Dr. David Sanders, Director
425 Park St.
Montclair, NJ 07043
Ph: (973)655-7974

Sanders, James, President
Hypoparathyroidism Association, Inc.
    [14706]
PO Box 2258
Idaho Falls, ID 83403
Ph: (208)524-3857
Toll Free: 866-213-0394

Sanders, Jim, VP
National Association of Christian
    Financial Consultants [1281]
1055 Maitland Center Commons
    Blvd.
Maitland, FL 32751-7205
Toll Free: 877-966-2232
Fax: (716)204-0904

Sanders, Judith, Secretary
On the Lighter Side, International
    Lighter Collectors [21707]
PO Box 1733
Quitman, TX 75783

Sanders, Keith, Contact
American MGC Register [21322]
c/o Fran Lewis, Treasury Director
1053 Forest Bay Dr.
Waterford, MI 48328

Sanders, Dr. Keith P., Exec. Dir.
Kappa Tau Alpha [23794]
University of Missouri
School of Journalism
76 Gannett Hall
Columbia, MO 65211-1200
Ph: (573)882-7685
Fax: (573)884-1720

Sanders, Lucinda R., FASLA, VP
Landscape Architecture Foundation
    [5970]

1129 20th St. NW, Ste. 202
Washington, DC 20036
Ph: (202)331-7070
Fax: (202)331-7079

Sanders, Lynn, Founder, President
Ehlers-Danlos Syndrome Network
CARES [14821]
PO Box 66
Muskego, WI 53150
Ph: (262)514-2851
Fax: (262)514-2851

Sanders, Mary Ellen, PhD, Exec.
Ofc.
International Scientific Association
for Probiotics and Prebiotics
[16225]
3230 Arena Blvd., No. 245-172
Sacramento, CA 95834
Ph: (303)793-9974

Sanders, Patrick, President
American Shetland Pony Club l
American Miniature Horse Registry
[4327]
81 B Queenwood Rd.
Morton, IL 61550
Ph: (309)263-4044
Fax: (309)263-5113

Sanders, Scott, Treasurer
International Guards Union of
America [23520]
c/o Scott Sanders, Treasurer
PO Box 4098
Oak Ridge, TN 37831
Ph: (865)456-9110

Sanderson, Brenda, Exec. Dir.
Interaction Design Association
[6370]
PO Box 2833
Westport, CT 06880

Sanderson, Emily, Contact
Student Global AIDS Campaign
[13562]
540 President Street, 3rd Floor
540 President St., 3rd Fl.
Brooklyn, NY 11215

Sanderson, Sandy, President,
Treasurer
National Club Baseball Association
[22560]
850 Ridge Ave., Ste. 301
Pittsburgh, PA 15212
Ph: (412)321-8440
Fax: (412)321-4088

Sandford, Byron, Exec. Dir.
William Penn House [18275]
515 E Capitol St. SE
Washington, DC 20003
Ph: (202)543-5560
Fax: (202)543-3814

Sandgren, Hudi, President
American Gourd Society [22072]
PO Box 2186
Kokomo, IN 46904-2186

Sandherr, Stephen E., CEO
Associated General Contractors of
America [854]
2300 Wilson Blvd., Ste. 300
Arlington, VA 22201
Ph: (703)548-3118
Toll Free: 800-242-1767
Fax: (703)548-3119

Sandlin, Jack, Officer
ION Inc. [2011]
5235 Decatur Blvd.
Indianapolis, IN 46241
Toll Free: 800-338-3463

Sandone, Cory, President
Association of Medical Illustrators
[15632]

201 E Main St., Ste. 1405
Lexington, KY 40507
Toll Free: 866-393-4264

Sandoval, Daniel, Exec. Dir.
Spanish World Ministries [20466]
PO Box 542
Winona Lake, IN 46590-0542
Ph: (574)267-8821

Sandri, Joseph M., Sr. VP
Wireless Communications Associa-
tion International [3247]
1333 H St. NW, Ste. 700 W
Washington, DC 20005
Ph: (202)452-7823
Fax: (202)452-0041

Sands, Danny, Chmn. of the Bd.
Society for Participatory Medicine
[15064]
PO Box 1183
Newburyport, MA 01950-1183

Sands, Janice, Exec. Dir.
Pen and Brush [8937]
29 E 22nd St.
New York, NY 10010
Ph: (212)475-3669

Sandt, Lorren, Exec. Dir., Founder
Caring Ambassadors Hepatitis C
Program [15252]
PO Box 1748
Oregon City, OR 97045
Ph: (503)632-9032
Fax: (503)632-9038

Sandu, Terri Burgess, President
Hard Hatted Women [3491]
41957 N Ridge, Unit 2
Elyria, OH 44035
Ph: (216)861-6500

Sandusky, Dale, President
Clan Forsyth Society U.S.A. [20811]
4336 South 3150 West
West Valley City, UT 84119-5856

Sandusky, Vincent R., CEO
Sheet Metal and Air Conditioning
Contractors' National Association
[1637]
4201 Lafayette Center Dr.
Chantilly, VA 20151-1209
Ph: (703)803-2980
Fax: (703)803-3732

Sane, Alassin, President
Women's Flat Track Derby Associa-
tion [23160]
PO Box 14100
Austin, TX 78761
Ph: (512)587-1859

Sanford, Ms. Beverly, Secretary, VP,
Comm.
Woodrow Wilson National Fellowship
Foundation [7930]
5 Vaughn Dr., Ste. 300
Princeton, NJ 08540-6313
Ph: (609)452-7007
Fax: (609)452-0066

Sanford, Maizie, Secretary
Gorilla Foundation [5894]
1733 Woodside Rd., Ste. 330
Redwood City, CA 94061
Toll Free: 800-634-6273

Sanicola, Doug, V. Chmn. of the
Exec. Committee
International Casual Furnishings As-
sociation [1484]
1912 Eastchester Dr., Ste. 100
High Point, NC 27265
Ph: (336)881-1016
Fax: (336)884-5303

SanInocencio, Christina, President,
Founder
Lennox-Gastaut Syndrome Founda-
tion [14742]
192 Lexington Ave., Ste. 216
New York, NY 10016
Ph: (718)374-3800

Sanow, Gil, II, Editor
Association of American Military
Uniform Collectors [22181]
PO Box 1876
Elyria, OH 44036
Ph: (440)365-5321

Sanson, Marilyn, Treasurer
American Austin/Bantam Club
[21316]
c/o Marilyn Sanson, Treasurer
PO Box 63
Kirkville, NY 13082-0063
Ph: (315)656-7568

Sansone, Torry Mark, Exec. Dir.
American Society of Hypertension
[15346]
244 Madison Ave., Ste. 136
New York, NY 10016
Ph: (212)696-9099
Fax: (347)916-0267

Sant, Bradley M., Director
Safety Equipment Institute [3005]
1307 Dolley Madison Blvd., Ste. 3A
McLean, VA 22101-3913
Ph: (703)442-5732
Fax: (703)442-5756

Santamaria, Thomas, Rec. Sec.
Societe Culinaire Philanthropique
[19494]
305 E 47th St., Ste. 11B
New York, NY 10017-2323
Ph: (212)308-0628
Fax: (212)308-0588

Santana, Luz, Director
Right Question Institute [13085]
2464 Massachusetts Ave., Ste. 314
Cambridge, MA 02140
Ph: (617)492-1900

Santana, Michelle, President
Doberman Pinscher Club of America
[21869]
c/o Lesley Reeves-Hunt, Membership Secretary
6400 Tripp Rd.
China, MI 48054-2518

Santee, Jimmie, Exec. Dir.
Professional Skaters Association
[23151]
3006 Allegro Park SW
Rochester, MN 55902
Ph: (507)281-5122

Santelices, Armando, Treasurer
Cuban American Veterans Associa-
tion [21120]
PO Box 140305
Coral Gables, FL 33114-0305

Santelli, Maria, Exec. Dir.
Center on Conscience and War
[18135]
1830 Connecticut Ave. NW
Washington, DC 20009-5732
Toll Free: 800-379-2679
Fax: (202)483-1246

Santi, Pat, Secretary
Dog Writers Association of America
[2677]
c/o Susan Ewing, Secretary
66 Adams St.
Jamestown, NY 14701

Santiago, Juan, President
Venezuelan-American Chamber of
Commerce [23639]

1600 Ponce de Leon Blvd., 10th Fl.,
Ste. 1033
Coral Gables, FL 33134
Ph: (786)350-1190
Fax: (786)350-1191

Santiago, Rolando, Exec. Dir.
Lancaster Mennonite Historical
Society [20983]
2215 Millstream Rd.
Lancaster, PA 17602-1499
Ph: (717)393-9745
Fax: (717)393-8751

Santilli, Nicholas, Chairman
Society for College and University
Planning [8442]
1330 Eisenhower Pl.
Ann Arbor, MI 48108
Ph: (734)669-3270

Santistevan, Jamie, Contact
American Association of Women
Emergency Physicians [14671]
c/o American College of Emergency
Physicians
1125 Executive Cir.
Irving, TX 75038-2522
Ph: (972)550-0911
Toll Free: 800-798-1822
Fax: (972)580-2816

Santoli, Albert, Founder, Director
Asia America Initiative [11314]
1523 16th St. NW
Washington, DC 20036
Ph: (202)232-7020
Fax: (202)232-7023

Santore, Beth, Trustee
Association for Gravestone Studies
[9376]
101 Munson St., Ste. 108
Greenfield, MA 01301
Ph: (413)772-0836

Santoro, Jack, Founder
The Old Appliance Club [21294]
PO Box 65
Ventura, CA 93002-0065
Ph: (805)643-3532

Santos, Antonio, Contact
Manufacturers of Emission Controls
Association [2642]
2200 Wilson Blvd., Ste. 310
Arlington, VA 22201
Ph: (202)296-4797

Santos, Victoria, Director
Sister Island Project [11437]
PO Box 1413
Langley, WA 98260
Ph: (360)321-4012

Sanville, Tom, Contact
International Coalition of Library
Consortia [9710]
1438 W Peachtree St. NW, Ste. 200
Atlanta, GA 30309
Ph: (404)892-0943

Sanzio, RN, MPA, JD, Teressa M.,
President
American Association of Nurse At-
torneys [15526]
3416 Primm Ln.
Birmingham, AL 35216
Ph: (205)824-7615
Toll Free: 877-538-2262
Fax: (205)823-2760

Sapiel, Gail, Bus. Mgr., Bus. Dev.
Mgr.
National Poetry Foundation [10154]
61 W Superior St.
Chicago, IL 60654
Ph: (312)787-7070
Fax: (312)787-6650

Sapienza, Michael, Exec. Dir.
Chris4Life Colon Cancer Foundation
[13944]
8330 Boone Blvd., Ste. 450
Vienna, VA 22182
Toll Free: 855-610-1733

Saporta, Vicki, CEO, President
National Abortion Federation [10431]
1660 L St. NW, Ste. 450
Washington, DC 20036
Ph: (202)667-5881
Toll Free: 800-772-9100
Fax: (202)667-5890

Sapp, Peggy B., CEO, President
National Family Partnership [13170]
2490 Coral Way
Miami, FL 33145-3430
Toll Free: 888-474-0008

Sappier, Brian, V. Chmn. of the Bd.
Society of American Indian Govern-
ment Employees [23438]
PO Box 7715
Washington, DC 20044
Ph: (202)564-0375
Fax: (202)564-7899

Saputelli, Ms. Linda, President
Association of Former International
Civil Servants - New York [5077]
1 United Nations Plz., Rm. DC1-580
New York, NY 10017
Ph: (212)963-2943
Fax: (212)963-5702

Sarabandi, Prof. Kamal, President
IEEE - Geoscience and Remote
Sensing Society [6691]
c/o Dr. Kamal Sarabandi, President
Dept. of Electrical Eng. and
Computer Science
Ann Arbor, MI 48109-2122
Ph: (734)936-1575
Fax: (734)647-2106

Saragovitz, Ms. Martha, Asst.
Radio Amateur Satellite Corporation
[7319]
10605 Concord St., No. 304
Kensington, MD 20895-2526
Ph: (301)822-4376
Toll Free: 888-322-6728
Fax: (301)822-4371

Sarano, Maurice, MD, Officer
Heart Valve Society [15217]
500 Cummings Ctr., Ste. 4550
Beverly, MA 01915-6534
Ph: (978)927-8330
Fax: (978)524-8890

Sarasin, Hon. Ronald A., President
U.S. Capitol Historical Society
[9525]
200 Maryland Ave. NE
Washington, DC 20002
Toll Free: 800-887-9318
Fax: (202)544-8244

Sarath, Ed, President
International Society for Improvised
Music [9934]
PO Box 1603
Ann Arbor, MI 48106

Sargent, Jim, President
Vintage Radio and Phonograph
Society [22406]
PO Box 165345
Irving, TX 75016-5345
Ph: (972)742-8085

Sågänger, Jonny, President
Servas International [18557]
1125 16th St., Ste. 201
Arcata, CA 95521-5585
Ph: (707)825-1714
Fax: (707)825-1762

Sarkar, Dilip, MD, President
International Association of Yoga
Therapists [10421]
PO Box 251563
Little Rock, AR 72225
Ph: (928)541-0004

Sarkar, Kajal, Chairman
Cultural Association of Bengal
[9229]
35 Windfall Ln.
Marlboro, NJ 07746

Sarles, Harry E., Jr., MD, FACG,
Trustee
American College of Gastroenterol-
ogy [14776]
6400 Goldsboro Rd., Ste. 200
Bethesda, MD 20817
Ph: (301)263-9000
Fax: (301)263-9025

Sarno, Amy L, MBA, Exec. Dir.
American Society of Dentist
Anesthesiologists [14415]
4411 Bee Ridge Rd., No. 172
Sarasota, FL 34233
Ph: (312)624-9591
Fax: (773)304-9894

Sarraf, Ramin, President
American Association of Teachers of
Persian [8639]
c/o Ramin Sarraf, President
3824 Creststone Pl.
San Diego, CA 92130
Ph: (858)642-8580

Sarrat, Christi, Exec. VP
International Oil Scouts Association
[2527]
PO Box 940310
Houston, TX 77094-7310

Sarrouf, Camille, Jr., V. Chmn. of the
Bd.
St. Jude Children's Research
Hospital [14212]
262 Danny Thomas Pl.
Memphis, TN 38105-3678
Ph: (901)595-2305
(901)535-3300
Toll Free: 800-822-6344

Sarvey, Sharon Isenhour, PhD
National Association of Bariatric
Nurses Inc. [16259]
110 E Arlington Blvd.
East Carolina University, Mail Stop
162
Greenville, NC 27858
Ph: (252)744-6440

Sasena, Camille, Coord.
National Advertising Review Board
[104]
c/o Camille Sasena, Coordinator
112 Madison Ave., 3rd Fl.
New York, NY 10016
Ph: (212)705-0115
Fax: (212)705-0134

Sashi, Claire, Gen. Mgr.
Econometric Society [7241]
Dept. of Economics
19 W 4th St., 6th Fl.
New York, NY 10012
Ph: (212)998-3820
Fax: (212)995-4487

Sasser, Scott, President, Founder
One Hundred Days [14958]
PO Box 29715
Atlanta, GA 30359

Sassower, Doris L., JD, Administra-
tor, Founder
Center for Judicial Accountability,
Inc. [18596]

PO Box 8101
White Plains, NY 10602-8101
Ph: (914)421-1200
Fax: (914)684-6554

Sataloff, Robert Thayer, Chmn. of
the Bd.
Voice Foundation [17249]
219 N Broad St., 10th Fl.
Philadelphia, PA 19107
Ph: (215)735-7999
Fax: (215)762-5572

Sater, Gregory, Chmn. of the Bd.
Electronic Retailing Association
[2280]
607 14th St. NW, Ste. 530
Washington, DC 20005
Ph: (703)841-1751
Toll Free: 800-987-6462
Fax: (425)977-1036

Satkowiak, Larry, President
Institute of Nuclear Materials
Management [6928]
1 Parkview Plz., Ste. 800
Oakbrook Terrace, IL 60181
Ph: (847)686-2236
Fax: (847)686-2253

Satz, Debra, Rresident
American Society for Political and
Legal Philosophy [10077]
c/o Andrew Valls, Secretary-
Treasurer, 7749 SE 17th Ave.
7749 SE 17th Ave.
Portland, OR 97202

Sauer, Paul R., Exec. Dir.
American Lutheran Publicity Bureau
[20301]
PO Box 327
Delhi, NY 13753-0327
Ph: (607)746-7511

Sauers, Philip E., Founder, Chair-
man
World Water Rescue Foundation
[4776]
Airport Park Plz., Ste. 306
Palm Springs, CA 92262

Sauerwein, Andrew, President
Christian Fellowship of Art Music
Composers [9180]
c/o Andrew Sauerwein, President
Belhaven University
1500 Peachtree St., No. 286
Jackson, MS 39202
Ph: (585)567-9424

Saujani, Reshma, Founder, CEO
Girls Who Code [11479]
28 W 23rd St., 4th Fl.
New York, NY 10010
Ph: (646)629-9735

Saul, Bradley, Founder, President
OrganicAthlete [22513]
19 S Circle Dr.
Chapel Hill, NC 27516-3104
Ph: (707)861-0004

Saules, Karen, Secretary
Association of Psychology Training
Clinics [16908]
c/o Karen Saules, Secretary
Eastern Michigan University
611 W Cross St.
Ypsilanti, MI 48197

Saunders, David A., Exec. Dir.
International Oxygen Manufacturers
Association [1498]
1025 Thomas Jefferson St. NW, Ste.
500 E
Washington, DC 20007
Ph: (202)521-9300
Fax: (202)833-3636

Saunders, David A., Exec. Dir.
National Pressure Ulcer Advisory
Panel [15050]
1000 Potomac St. NW, Ste. 108
Washington, DC 20007
Ph: (202)521-6789
Fax: (202)833-3636

Saunders, Dorothy, Co-Pres.
Well Spouse Association [17353]
63 W Main St., Ste. H
Freehold, NJ 07728
Toll Free: 800-838-0879
Fax: (732)577-8644

Saunders, Gene, CEO, Founder
Project Lifesaver International
[12748]
201 SW Port St. Lucie Blvd. S
Port Saint Lucie, FL 34984
Ph: (772)446-1271

Saunders, Lee, President
American Federation of State,
County and Municipal Employees
[23425]
1625 L St. NW
Washington, DC 20036-5687
Ph: (202)429-1000
Fax: (202)429-1293

Saunders, Michael, Exec. Ofc.
HandsNet Inc. [12390]
PO Box 90477
San Jose, CA 95109
Ph: (408)291-5111
(408)829-3342
Fax: (408)904-4874

Saunders, Pam, President
Newfoundland Club of America
[21926]
1155 Raymond Rd.
Ballston Spa, NY 12020-3719
Toll Free: 866-622-6393

Saunders, Steve, President
North America-Mongolia Business
Council, Inc. [1991]
1015 Duke St.
Alexandria, VA 22314
Ph: (703)549-8444
Fax: (703)549-6526

Saunders, William L., Esq.,
President
The Fellowship of Catholic Scholars
[19834]
c/o William L. Saunders, Esq.,
President
655 15th St., Ste. 410
Washington, DC 20005-5709
Ph: (202)289-1478

Saundry, Peter, Exec. Dir.
National Council for Science and the
Environment [4085]
1101 17th St. NW, Ste. 250
Washington, DC 20036
Ph: (202)530-5810
Fax: (202)628-4311

Sauter, Ed, Exec. Dir.
Tilt-Up Concrete Association [902]
113 1st St. W
Mount Vernon, IA 52314
Ph: (319)895-6911
Fax: (320)213-5555

Sauter, J. Edward, Exec. Dir.
Concrete Foundations Association
[861]
113 W 1st St.
Mount Vernon, IA 52314
Ph: (319)895-6940
Fax: (320)213-5556

Sautner, Barbara, President
Society for Siberian Irises [22126]
c/o Barbara Sautner

106th St., No. 2100
Bloomington, MN 55431

Savage, Brian, Dir. of Logistics
Council for a Parliament of the
    World's Religions [20536]
70 E Lake St., Ste. 205
Chicago, IL 60601
Ph: (312)629-2990
Fax: (312)629-2991

Savage, Brian, President
GI Joe Collectors' Club [22448]
225 Cattle Baron Parc
Fort Worth, TX 76108
Ph: (817)448-9863

Savage, Brigitte, VP of Dev.
James Renwick Alliance [8885]
4405 East West Hwy., Ste. 510
Bethesda, MD 20814
Ph: (301)907-3888

Savage, Diane, V. Ch.
Association of Administrators of the
    Interstate Compact on Adoption
    and Medical Assistance [10445]
1133 19th St. NW
Washington, DC 20036
Ph: (202)682-0100
Fax: (202)289-6555

Savage, Hallie, Exec. Dir.
National Collegiate Honors Council
    [7791]
University of Nebraska-Lincoln
1100 Neihardt Residence Ctr.
540 N 16th St.
Lincoln, NE 68588-0627
Ph: (402)472-9150
Fax: (402)472-9152

Savage, John, Registrar
American Romeldale/CVM Associa-
    tion, Inc. [4661]
c/o John Savage, Register
1039 State Route 168
Darlington, PA 16115
Ph: (724)843-2084
Fax: (724)891-1440

Savage, Kelly, Founder
Soles for Kidz [11151]
5821 Imes Ln.
Fort Worth, TX 76179
Toll Free: 866-905-5439

Savage, Laurie, Exec. Dir.
Spondylitis Association of America
    [17164]
16360 Roscoe Blvd., Ste. 100
Van Nuys, CA 91406
Ph: (818)892-1616
Toll Free: 800-777-8189
Fax: (818)892-1611

Savage, Ronald C., Chairman
North American Brain Injury Society
    [14914]
PO Box 1804
Alexandria, VA 22313
Ph: (703)960-6500
Fax: (703)960-6603

Savanick, George, PhD, Treasurer
WaterJet Technology Association
    and Industrial and Municipal
    Cleaning Association [6637]
906 Olive St., Ste. 1200
Saint Louis, MO 63101-1448
Ph: (314)241-1445
Fax: (314)241-1449

Savarese, John F., Chairman
Vera Institute of Justice [11549]
233 Broadway, 12th Fl.
New York, NY 10279
Ph: (212)334-1300
Fax: (212)941-9407

Savenije, Hubert H.G., President
International Association of
    Hydrological Sciences [7366]
c/o Chuck Onstad, Treasurer
18241 County Rd. 1
Morris, MN 56267

Savesky, Kathleen, Chairperson
International Fund for Animal
    Welfare [10648]
290 Summer St.
Yarmouth Port, MA 02675-0193
Ph: (508)744-2000
Toll Free: 800-932-4329
Fax: (508)744-2009

Saviano, Kimberly, President
Androgen Insensitivity Syndrome-
    Disorders of Sex Development
    Support Group [14808]
PO Box 2148
Duncan, OK 73534-2148

Saville, Anthony, President
American Game Fowl Society [3655]
PO Box 800
Belton, SC 29627-0800
Ph: (864)237-5280

Savine, Steffanie, President
Automotive Communications Council
    [282]
28203 Woodhaven Rd.
Edwards, MO 65326
Ph: (240)333-1089

Savoie, Brent, Founder, VP of
    Strategic Planning
Inter-American Health Alliance
    [15022]
PO Box 5518
Washington, DC 20016

Sawaya, Richard, Director
USA Engage [18163]
1625 K St. NW, Ste. 200
Washington, DC 20006
Ph: (202)887-0278
    (202)822-9491
Fax: (202)452-8160

Sawchuk, Alexander, Chairman
Optical Society of America Founda-
    tion [6949]
2010 Massachusetts Ave. NW
Washington, DC 20036
Ph: (202)416-1985
Fax: (202)416-6130

Sawerthal, Inge, President
American International Chamber of
    Commerce [23553]
355 S Grand Ave., Ste. 2450
Los Angeles, CA 90071-1504
Ph: (213)255-2066
Fax: (213)255-2077

Sawhney, Nitin, PhD, Contact
Voices Beyond Walls [13487]
20 Ames St., E15-223
Cambridge, MA 02139
Ph: (617)324-0031
Fax: (617)253-3977

Sawicki, Dr. Dorothea L., Secretary,
    Treasurer
American Society for Virology [6051]
c/o Dr. Dorothea L. Sawicki,
    Secretary-Treasurer
3000 Arlington Ave., Mail Stop 1021
Department of Medical Microbiology
    and Immunology
University of Toledo College of
    Medicine
Toledo, OH 43614-2598
Ph: (419)383-5173
Fax: (419)383-2881

Sawma, Mr. Martin J., Exec. Dir.
Emergency Committee to Defend
    Constitutional Welfare Rights USA
    [18974]

c/o Mr. Martin J. Sawma, Executive
    Director
3501 Westwood Dr., Rm. 4
Niagara Falls, NY 14305-3416
Ph: (716)297-7273
Fax: (630)929-3839

Sawyer, Deborah, Membership Chp.
Whirly-Girls International Women
    Helicopter Pilots [21256]
c/o Deb Sawyer, Membership
    Coordinator
4617 Gilronan Ct.
Palm Harbor, FL 34685-2655

Sawyer, Donald C., DVM, President
International Association of Fly Fish-
    ing Veterinarians [22041]
c/o Pantano Animal Clinic
8333 E 22nd St.
Tucson, AZ 85710
Ph: (517)349-0454
    (520)572-6790

Sawyer, Frederick W., III, Editor,
    President
North American Sundial Society
    [8712]
27 Ninas Way - Humpton Run
Manchester, CT 06040-6388

Sawyer, Laura, Exec. Dir.
International Communication As-
    sociation [3230]
1500 21st St. NW
Washington, DC 20036
Ph: (202)955-1444
Fax: (202)955-1448

Sawyer, Ron, Administrator
National Coalition for Electronics
    Education [6438]
71 Columbia St.
Cohoes, NY 12047-2939
Toll Free: 888-777-8851

Sawyer, Mr. Sean E., PhD, Exec.
    Dir.
Royal Oak Foundation [9432]
20 W 44th St., Ste. 606
New York, NY 10036-6603
Ph: (212)480-2889
Toll Free: 800-913-6565
Fax: (212)785-7234

Sax, Dr. Leonard, Founder
National Association for Choice in
    Education [8478]
64 E Uwchlan Ave., No. 259
Exton, PA 19341-1203
Ph: (610)296-2821
Fax: (610)993-3139

Saxon, Susan, Founder, Exec. Dir.
Kazakh Aul of the United States
    [9584]
PO Box 6185
Providence, RI 02940
Ph: (401)486-4023

Saya, Wayne P., Sr., Exec. Dir.
Association for Facilities Engineering
    [6545]
8200 Greensboro Dr., Ste. 400
Herndon, VA 20170
Ph: (571)203-7171
Fax: (571)766-2142

Saye, Matu, President, Founder
Technology for Liberia [11746]
PO Box 40882
Philadelphia, PA 19107

Sayles, Wayne G., Exec. Dir.
Ancient Coin Collectors Guild
    [22260]
PO Box 911
Gainesville, MO 65655
Ph: (417)499-9831

Saylor, Bonnie, Exec. Dir.
Society for Applied Spectroscopy
    [7225]
168 W Main St., No. 300
New Market, MD 21774
Ph: (301)694-8122
Fax: (301)694-6860

Saylor, Eric, President
North American British Music Stud-
    ies Association [9986]
c/o Nathaniel Lew, Secretary
St. Michael's College
1 Winooski Pk.
Colchester, VT 05439-1000

Saylor, Scott, VP
Parents of Galactosemic Children
    [15833]
PO Box 1512
Deerfield Beach, FL 33443
Toll Free: 866-900-7421

Sbeiti, Adam, Director
Association of Genetic Technologists
    [6075]
PO Box 19193
Lenexa, KS 66285
Ph: (913)895-4605
Fax: (913)895-4652

Scaburri, Adriano, Chairman
RF Energy Alliance [6509]
3855 SW 153rd Dr.
Beaverton, OR 97003
Ph: (503)619-0692
Fax: (503)644-6708

Scafati, Laura, Treasurer
House Rabbit Network [10639]
PO Box 2602
Woburn, MA 01888-1102
Ph: (781)431-1211

Scaglione, Mr. Anthony, Chairman
Association for Financial Profession-
    als [1223]
4520 E West Hwy., Ste. 750
Bethesda, MD 20814
Ph: (301)907-2862
Fax: (301)907-2864

Scales, Aileen, Exec. Dir.
Consortium of College and
    University Media Centers [8026]
Indiana University
306 N Union St.
Bloomington, IN 47405-3888
Ph: (812)855-6049

Scalzo, Michael, President
National Lighting Contractors As-
    sociation of America [6786]
3301 E Hill St., Ste. 406-408
Signal Hill, CA 90755
Ph: (310)890-0878
Fax: (562)976-7648

Scanlan, Kristy, Co-Pres.
Women in Animation [1211]
c/o Marine Hekimian
11400 W Olympic Blvd., No. 590
Los Angeles, CA 90064

Scanlan, Susan, President
Women's Research and Education
    Institute [18241]
714 G St. SE, Ste. 200
Washington, DC 20003
Ph: (202)506-9804
    (703)837-1977

Scanlon, Karen A., Exec. Dir.
Conservation Technology Information
    Center [3841]
3495 Kent Ave., Ste. L100
West Lafayette, IN 47906
Ph: (765)494-9555
Fax: (765)463-4106

Scanniello, Stephen, President
Heritage Rose Foundation [22099]
PO Box 831414
Richardson, TX 75083

Scantland, Leah, President
National Greenhouse Manufacturers
  Association [170]
2207 Forest Hill Dr.
Harrisburg, PA 17112
Ph: (717)238-4530
Toll Free: 800-792-6462
Fax: (717)238-9985

Scarano, Mario, President
Awards and Personalization Associa-
  tion [20730]
8735 W Higgins Rd., Ste. 300
Chicago, IL 60631
Ph: (847)375-4800
Fax: (847)375-6480

Scardelletti, Robert A., President
Transportation Communications
  International Union [23516]
3 Research Pl.
Rockville, MD 20850
Ph: (301)948-4910

Scardelletti, Robert A., President
Transportation Communications
  Union - Brotherhood Railway Car-
  men Division [23517]
3 Research Pl.
Rockville, MD 20850
Ph: (301)840-8730

Scardigli, Ms. Maria Teresa, Exec.
  Dir.
International Stevia Council [1347]
750 National Press Bldg.
529 14th St. NW
Washington, DC 20045-1000
Ph: (202)591-2467

Scarlata, Suzanne, President
Biophysical Society [6117]
11400 Rockville Pke., Ste. 800
Rockville, MD 20852
Ph: (240)290-5600
Fax: (240)290-5555

Scarlatoiu, Greg, Exec. Dir.
Committee for Human Rights in
  North Korea [18388]
1001 Connecticut Ave. NW, Ste. 435
Washington, DC 20036
Ph: (202)499-7970
Fax: (202)758-2348

Scarola, Susan, Chairman
Students Against Destructive Deci-
  sions [12845]
255 Main St.
Marlborough, MA 01752-5505
Toll Free: 877-SADD-INC
Fax: (508)481-5759

Scarpace, Sarah, President
Hematology/Oncology Pharmacy
  Association [16663]
8735 W Higgins Rd., Ste.300
Chicago, IL 60631
Toll Free: 877-467-2791

Schaal, John, President
United States of America Snowboard
  and Freeski Association [23177]
PO Box 15500
South Lake Tahoe, CA 96151
Toll Free: 800-404-9213

Schacher, Laurence, VP
The Fiber Society [6631]
c/o Janice R. Gerde, Secretary
PO Box 564
Fort Meade, MD 20755-0564

Schacht, Prof. Richard, Exec. Dir.
North American Nietzsche Society
  [10107]

105 Gregory Hall
Dept. of Philosophy
University of Illinois
810 S Wright St.
Urbana, IL 61801
Ph: (217)333-1939

Schader, Kevin, Exec. Dir.
EMerge Alliance [523]
2400 Camino Ramon, Ste. 375
San Ramon, CA 94583-4373
Ph: (925)275-6617
Fax: (925)884-8668

Schaefer, Aaron, Treasurer
Amana Heritage Society [9366]
PO Box 81
Amana, IA 52203
Ph: (319)622-3567

Schaefer, Kevin, Assoc. Dir.
National Association of Qualified
  Developmental Disability Profes-
  sionals [15815]
301 Veterans Pky.
New Lenox, IL 60451
Ph: (815)320-7301
  (815)485-4781
Fax: (815)320-7357

Schaefer, Michael R., Officer
Education Through Music [8367]
122 E 42nd St., Ste. 1501
New York, NY 10168
Ph: (212)972-4788
Fax: (212)972-4864

Schaefer, Susannah, CEO
Smile Train USA [14346]
41 Madison Ave., 28th Fl.
New York, NY 10010
Toll Free: 800-932-9541

Schaeffer, Jack, President
Ocular Surface Society of Optometry
  [16433]
1 Prospect Park SW, Ste. 4B
Brooklyn, NY 11215

Schaeffer, Janis I., MD, Founder
Breathe Easy Play Hard Foundation
  [16696]
3003 New Hyde Park Rd., Ste. 204
New Hyde Park, NY 11042
Ph: (516)355-2374

Schaeffer, Jim, Dir. Gen.
Center for Contemporary Opera
  [9885]
236 E 31st St.
New York, NY 10016
Ph: (646)481-8110

Schaeffer, Sabrina L., Exec. Dir.
Independent Women's Forum
  [18879]
1875 I St. NW, Ste. 500
Washington, DC 20006
Ph: (202)857-3293
Fax: (202)429-9574

Schafer, Charlie, President
Agricultural Drainage Management
  Coalition [4767]
c/o Charlie Schafer, President
PO Box 458
Adair, IA 50002
Toll Free: 800-232-4742
Fax: (800)282-3353

Schafer, Donna, PhD, Exec. Dir.
National Association for Professional
  Gerontologists [14896]
PO Box 1209
Los Altos, CA 94023
Ph: (650)947-9132

Schafer, Fred, Cmdr.
National Association of Atomic
  Veterans, Inc. [13244]

130 Cleveland St.
Lebanon, OR 97355-4505
Ph: (541)258-7453

Schafer, Heather, CEO
National Volunteer Fire Council
  [5214]
7852 Walker Dr., Ste. 375
Greenbelt, MD 20770
Ph: (202)887-5700
Toll Free: 888-275-6832
Fax: (202)887-5291

Schafer, Shawn, Exec. Dir.
North American Deer Farmers As-
  sociation [4166]
4501 Hills and Dales Rd. NW, Ste. C
Canton, OH 44708-1572
Ph: (330)454-3944
Fax: (330)454-3950

Schaffer, Amy, Exec. Dir.
Recycled Paperboard Technical As-
  sociation [842]
PO Box 5774
Elgin, IL 60121-5774
Ph: (847)622-2544

Schaffer, Kirsten, Exec. Dir.
Women in Film [1212]
6100 Wilshire Blvd., Ste. 710
Los Angeles, CA 90048
Ph: (323)935-2211
Fax: (323)935-2212

Schaffer, Michael J., Chairman
First Candle [17333]
9 Newport Dr., Ste. 200
Forest Hill, MD 21050
Ph: (443)640-1049
Toll Free: 800-221-7437

Schaffer, Suzane, President
Professional Fraternity Association
  [23764]
5217 S 51st St.
Greenfield, WI 53220
Ph: (512)789-9530

Schaffer, Suzanne, Editor, Exec. Dir.
Phi Sigma Pi National Honor
  Fraternity [23807]
2119 Ambassador Cir.
Lancaster, PA 17603
Ph: (717)299-4710
Fax: (717)390-3054

Schaffner, Melissa A., Officer
International Military Community
  Executives Association [21026]
14080 Nacogdoches Rd.
San Antonio, TX 78247-1944
Ph: (940)463-5145
Fax: (866)369-2435

Schafnitz-Hogg, Jan, President
Operation Quiet Comfort [10754]
c/o Jan Hogg, President
307 Palmer Ln.
McCormick, SC 29835
Ph: (864)614-1894

Schaitberger, Harold A., President
International Association of Fire
  Fighters [23416]
1750 New York Ave. NW, Ste. 300
Washington, DC 20006-5395
Ph: (202)737-8484
Fax: (202)737-8418

Schaller, Mary, President
Q Place [19763]
25W560 Geneva Rd.
Carol Stream, IL 60188
Ph: (630)668-4399
Toll Free: 800-369-0307
Fax: (630)668-4363

Schallheim, James, Exec. Sec.,
  Treasurer
American Finance Association
  [1218]

c/o James Schallheim, Executive
  Secretary/Treasurer
1655 E Campus Center Dr.
Salt Lake City, UT 84112
Ph: (781)388-8599
Toll Free: 800-835-6770

Schallip, Robert, President
International Shipmasters Associa-
  tion [2247]
c/o Robert Schallip, President
17592 Simonsen Rd.
Neebish Island
Barbeau, MI 49710-9416
Ph: (906)635-0941

Schaly, John, Director
American Baseball Coaches As-
  sociation [22541]
4101 Piedmont Pky., Ste. C
Greensboro, NC 27410
Ph: (336)821-3140

Schamiloglu, Dr. Uli, President
American Association of Teachers of
  Turkic Languages [10283]
c/o Dr. Feride Hatiboglu, Treasurer
Dept. of Near Eastern languages
  and Civilizations
Williams Hall, Rm. 847
255 S 36th St.
Philadelphia, PA 19104-6305

Schantag, Mary, Chairperson
P.O.W. Network [21092]
PO Box 68
Skidmore, MO 64487-0068
Ph: (660)928-3304

Schantz, John, President
Concrete Pump Manufacturers As-
  sociation [6343]
2310 S Green Bay Rd., Ste. C
Racine, WI 53406
Fax: (262)284-7878

Schanze, Stet, Chairman
Automotive Lift Institute [312]
80 Wheeler Ave.
Cortland, NY 13045
Ph: (607)756-7775
Fax: (607)756-0888

Schanzenbach, Janet, VP
Families Affected by Fetal Alcohol
  Spectrum Disorder [17310]
PO Box 427
Pittsboro, NC 27312
Ph: (919)360-7073

Schardt, Sue, Mem.
Association of Independents in
  Radio [454]
1452 Dorchester Ave., 2nd Fl.
Dorchester, MA 02122
Ph: (617)825-4400
Fax: (617)825-4422

Scharf, Brian K., President
Christian Chiropractors Association
  Inc. [19953]
2550 Stover B-102
Fort Collins, CO 80525
Ph: (970)482-1404
Toll Free: 800-999-1970
Fax: (970)482-1538

Scharfenberg, Christa, Officer
Center for Investigative Reporting
  [17941]
1400 65th St., Ste. 200
Emeryville, CA 94608
Ph: (510)809-3160
Fax: (510)849-6141

Scharko, Patty B., President
American Association of Small
  Ruminant Practitioners [17600]

765 Tiger Oak Dr.
Pike Road, AL 36064-3060
Ph: (334)517-1233
Fax: (334)270-3399

Schatz, Sharon, Mgr. of Fin. &
Admin.
International Housewares Associa-
tion [1683]
6400 Shafer Ct., Ste. 650
Rosemont, IL 60018
Ph: (847)292-4200
Fax: (847)292-4211

Schatzman, Leigha, Exec. Dir.
Association for High Technology
Distribution [1037]
N19 W24400 Riverwood Dr.
Waukesha, WI 53188

Schaub, Laird, Exec. Sec., Coord.
Fellowship for Intentional Community
[9171]
PO Box 156
Rutledge, MO 63563-9720
Toll Free: 800-462-8240

Schaub, Laird, Exec. Sec., Coord.
Fellowship for Intentional Community
[17975]
PO Box 156
Rutledge, MO 63563-9720
Toll Free: 800-462-8240

Schaublin, Patrice, President
American Syringomyelia & Chiari
Alliance Project [15901]
PO Box 1586
Longview, TX 75606-1586
Ph: (903)236-7079
Toll Free: 800-ASAP-282
Fax: (903)757-7456

Schaudel, Stephanie, Chairman
Community United Against Violence
[11879]
427 S Van Ness Ave.
San Francisco, CA 94103
Ph: (415)777-5500
Fax: (415)777-5565

Schauer, David A., Exec. Sec.
International Commission on Radia-
tion Units and Measurements
[7082]
7910 Woodmont Ave., Ste. 400
Bethesda, MD 20814-3076
Ph: (301)657-2652
Fax: (301)907-8768

Schauer, Kirk, Founder
Seeds of Hope International Partner-
ships [11428]
1023 Nipomo St., Ste. 110
San Luis Obispo, CA 93401
Ph: (805)439-1489

Schauffele, Roy, Chairman
Air Barrier Association of America
[487]
1600 Boston-Providence Hwy.
Walpole, MA 02081
Toll Free: 866-956-5888
Fax: (866)956-5819

Schebaum, Bill, Bd. Member
International Water Levels Coalition
[4770]
PO Box 316
Clayton, NY 13624

Schechter, Danny, Editor
MediaChannel.org [18659]
PO Box 677
New York, NY 10035

Schechter, Jennifer, Exec. Dir.,
Founder
Hope Through Health [12202]
PO Box 605

Medway, MA 02053
Ph: (631)721-5917

Schechter-Shaffin, Shoshanna,
Exec. Dir.
ALEPH: Alliance for Jewish Renewal
[18739]
7000 Lincoln Dr., No. B2
Philadelphia, PA 19119-3046
Ph: (215)247-9700
Fax: (215)247-9703

Scheck, Barry C., Director, Founder
Innocence Project [5135]
40 Worth St., Ste. 701
New York, NY 10013
Ph: (212)364-5340

Schecter, Kate, President, CEO
World Neighbors [18566]
PO Box 270058
Oklahoma City, OK 73137-0058
Ph: (405)752-9700
Toll Free: 800-242-6387

Schedler, Tom, President
National Association of Secretaries
of State [5777]
444 N Capitol St. NW, Ste. 401
Washington, DC 20001
Ph: (202)624-3525

Scheer, David W., Mem.
Heavy Duty Distribution Association
[320]
Auto Care Association
7101 Wisconsin Ave., Ste. 1300
Bethesda, MD 20814-3415
Ph: (301)654-6664
Fax: (301)654-3299

Scheffer, Sherri, CPA, Treasurer
Women Contractors Association
[3503]
PO Box 70966
Houston, TX 77270
Ph: (713)807-9977
Fax: (713)807-9917

Scheffy, Karl, Contact
American Camaro Association
[21318]
1116 Laurelee Ave.
Reading, PA 19605

Scheibel, Mary, Contact
Iprex [2753]
735 N Water St., No. 200
Milwaukee, WI 53202
Ph: (414)272-6898

Scheiber, Prof. Harry N., PhD, Prog.
Dir.
Law of the Sea Institute [5575]
University of California, Berkeley
381 Boalt Hall
Berkeley, CA 94720-7200
Ph: (510)643-5699
    (510)643-9788

Scheidler, Joseph M., Exec.
Pro-Life Action League [19069]
6160 N Cicero Ave., Ste. 600
Chicago, IL 60646
Ph: (773)777-2900
    (773)777-2525
Fax: (773)777-3061

Scheidler, Peter, President
Society of Flight Test Engineers
[5874]
44814 N Elm Ave.
Lancaster, CA 93534
Ph: (817)320-1587
Fax: (817)320-1587

Schenck, Eric, President, Director
Multiple Sclerosis Foundation
[15957]

6520 N Andrews Ave.
Fort Lauderdale, FL 33309-2130
Ph: (954)776-6805
Toll Free: 800-225-6495
Fax: (954)938-8708

Schenck, Frank, Director
Von Braun Astronomical Society
[6012]
PO Box 1142
Huntsville, AL 35807
Ph: (256)539-0316

Schendel, Kaye, President
Sigma Sigma Sigma [23965]
Mabel Lee Walton House
225 N Muhlenberg St.
Woodstock, VA 22664-1424
Ph: (540)459-4212
Fax: (540)459-2361

Schenk, Pamela W., Dir. of Admin.
Gravure Association of the Americas,
Inc. [1536]
8281 Pine Lake Rd.
Denver, NC 28037
Ph: (201)523-6042
Fax: (201)523-6048

Scherer, Alice, Secretary, Treasurer
Society of Bead Researchers [5948]
PO Box 13719
Portland, OR 97213
Ph: (503)655-3078

Scherer, Chriss, President, Div. Dir.
Society of Broadcast Engineers
[482]
9102 N Meridian St., Ste. 150
Indianapolis, IN 46260
Ph: (317)846-9000
Fax: (317)846-9120

Scherr, Sara J., PhD, CEO,
President
Ecoagriculture Partners [4696]
1100 17th St. NW, Ste. 600
Washington, DC 20036
Ph: (202)393-5315
Fax: (202)393-2424

Scherr, Ted, Chairman
Healthcare Distribution Management
Association [16662]
901 N Glebe Rd., Ste. 1000
Arlington, VA 22203
Ph: (703)787-0000
Fax: (703)812-5282

Scherry, Rev. Jenny, Treasurer
International New Thought Alliance
[10094]
5003 E Broadway Rd.
Mesa, AZ 85206
Ph: (480)830-2461

Scherzer, Norman, Exec. Dir.
Life Raft Group [14002]
155 Route 46 W, Ste. 202
Wayne, NJ 07470
Ph: (973)837-9092
Fax: (973)837-9095

Schexnayder, Jerry, Treasurer
Serama Council of North America
[3671]
PO Box 159
Vacherie, LA 70090
Ph: (225)265-2238

Schiappacasse, Rick, President
International Propeller Club of the
United States [3090]
3927 Old Lee Hwy., Ste. 101A
Fairfax, VA 22030
Ph: (703)691-2777

Schick, Tom, Chairman
International Professional Rodeo Association [23096]

1412 S Agnew
Oklahoma City, OK 73108
Ph: (405)235-6540
Fax: (405)235-6577

Schieber, Doug, President
Process Equipment Manufacturers
Association [1763]
201 Park Washington Ct.
Falls Church, VA 22046
Ph: (703)538-1796

Schiefenhovel, Wulf, Trustee
International Society for Human
Ethology [6040]
c/o Thomas Alley, President
312J Brackett Hall
Clemson, SC 29634
Ph: (864)656-4974

Schieffer, Jerry, President
United Chainsaw Carvers Guild
[21786]
PO Box 255
Ridgway, PA 15853-0255

Schieron, Laureen, Asst. Dir.
Hoover Institution on War, Revolu-
tion and Peace [19262]
434 Galvez Mall
Stanford University
Stanford, CA 94305
Ph: (650)723-1754

Schiffer, Howard, Founder, President
Vitamin Angel Alliance, Inc. [16241]
111 W Micheltorena St., Ste. 300
Santa Barbara, CA 93101
Ph: (805)564-8400
Fax: (805)564-8400

Schilder, Steffanie, President
APA Division 30: Society of
Psychological Hypnosis [16880]
750 1st St. NE
Washington, DC 20002-4242
Ph: (202)336-5500

Schiller, Matthew, President
Catholic Press Association [2775]
205 W Monroe St., Ste. 470
Chicago, IL 60606
Ph: (312)380-6789
Fax: (312)361-0256

Schilling, Dave, Chmn. of the Bd.
National Plasterers Council, Inc.
[2618]
1000 N Rand Rd., Ste. 214
Wauconda, IL 60084
Ph: (847)416-7272
Fax: (847)526-3993

Schimelman, Ellie, Clerk, President
Cross Cultural Collaborative [9207]
45 Auburn St.
Brookline, MA 02446
Ph: (857)261-0474

Schiminger, Paul, Exec. Dir.
International Bluegrass Music As-
sociation [9924]
608 W Iris Dr.
Nashville, TN 37204
Ph: (615)256-3222
Toll Free: 888-438-4262
Fax: (615)256-0450

Schimmels, Karyn Corpron,
President
National Staff Development and
Training Association [3132]
2115 Wardrobe Ave.
Merced, CA 95341
Ph: (209)385-3000
Fax: (209)354-2501

Schimmels, Karyn Corpron,
President
National Staff Development and
Training Association [13076]

2115 Wardrobe Ave.
Merced, CA 95341
Ph: (209)385-3000
Fax: (209)354-2501

Schipper, Katherine, President
International Association for Account-
ing Education & Research [35]
c/o Katherine Schipper, President
Duke University
The Fuqua School of Business
100 Fuqua Dr.
Durham, NC 27708

Schippers, Nicolle, President
Group Legal Services Association
[5532]
321 N Clark St., 19th Fl.
Chicago, IL 60610
Ph: (312)988-5751
Fax: (312)932-6436

Schira, Dottie, Founder
Out of Love Sugar Glider Rescue
[10676]
PO Box 183
Medina, OH 44258
Ph: (330)722-1627

Schlabach, Andrew, Founder,
President
Acupuncture Relief Project [13500]
3712 NE 40th Ave.
Vancouver, WA 98661
Ph: (360)695-9591

Schlaefer, Erica Walther, President,
Founder
Parenthood for Me [11846]
PO Box 67750
Rochester, NY 14617

Schlafly, Eleanor, President
Cardinal Mindszenty Foundation
[17801]
7800 Bonhomme Ave.
Saint Louis, MO 63105
Ph: (314)727-6279
Fax: (314)727-5897

Schlansky, Mark, CEO, Founder
Uplift International [15504]
PO Box 27696
Seattle, WA 98165-2696
Ph: (206)455-0916

Schleicher, Dr. Antonia, Exec. Dir.
African Language Teachers Associa-
tion [8637]
708 Eigenmann Hall
Indiana University
1900 E 10th St.
Bloomington, IN 47406
Ph: (812)856-4185
Fax: (812)856-4189

Schleicher, Antonia Folarin, PhD,
Exec. Dir.
National Council of Less Commonly
Taught Languages [8189]
Eigenmann Hall, Rm. 708
1900 E 10th St.
Bloomington, IN 47406
Ph: (812)856-4185
Fax: (812)856-4189

Schleiden, Roy, Chmn. of the Exec.
Committee
CAUCUS - The Association of
Technology Acquisition Profession-
als [7261]
PO Box 2970
Winter Park, FL 32790-2970
Ph: (407)740-5600

Schlenk, Elizabeth A., President
American College of Rheumatology
[17152]

2200 Lake Blvd. NE
Atlanta, GA 30319
Ph: (404)633-3777
Fax: (404)633-1870

Schlesinger, Elaine, Secretary
Fire Mark Circle of the Americas
[21654]
c/o Elaine Schlesinger, Secretary
PO Box 6738
Metairie, LA 70009-6738

Schlesinger, Kenneth, President
Independent Media Arts Preservation
[9784]
c/o Lehman College
Lief Library 201
250 Bedford Park Blvd. W
Bronx, NY 10468

Schlessinger, Daniel, President
American Friends of the Hebrew
University [8130]
1 Battery Park Plz., 25th Fl.
New York, NY 10004
Ph: (212)607-8500
Toll Free: 800-567-AFHU
Fax: (212)809-4430

Schlitt, John, President
School-Based Health Alliance
[15063]
1010 Vermont Ave. NW, Ste. 600
Washington, DC 20005
Ph: (202)638-5872
Fax: (202)638-5879

Schloff, Anna, COO, President
WCFO, Inc. [22823]
4547 Bedford Ave.
Brooklyn, NY 11235-2525
Ph: (718)332-8336

Schloss, Lawrence Mark, MA, Prog.
Dir.
American Guild of Judaic Art [8833]
135 Shaker Hollow
Alpharetta, GA 30022
Ph: (404)981-2308

Schlossberg, Bert, Director
International Committee for the
Rescue of KAL 007 Survivors
[12743]
34 Blackbird St.
Edwards, CA 93523
Ph: (661)475-4079

Schlote, Olaf, President
International Unicycling Federation
[22749]
4100 Redwood Rd., No. 257
Oakland, CA 94619

Schluckebier, Mary A., Exec. Dir.
Celiac Support Association United
States of America [14785]
413 Ash St.
Seward, NE 68434
Ph: (402)643-4101
Toll Free: 877-272-4272
Fax: (402)643-4108

Schmader, Mr. Steven Wood, CEO,
President
International Festivals & Events As-
sociation [1142]
2603 W Eastover Ter.
Boise, ID 83706
Ph: (208)433-0950
Fax: (208)433-9812

Schmahmann, Jeremy, MD, FANPA,
President
American Neuropsychiatric Associa-
tion [16820]
The Menninger Clinic
12301 Main St.

Houston, TX 77035
Ph: (713)275-5777

Schmal, John P., Mem.
FAMILIA Ancestral Research As-
sociation [20966]
PO Box 10425
Westminster, CA 92685
Ph: (714)687-0390

Schmedake, Robert, Exec. VP
System Safety Society [3006]
PO Box 70
Unionville, VA 22567-0070
Ph: (540)854-8630

Schmelz, Brenda, CCR, CVR-M,
President
National Verbatim Reporters As-
sociation [3515]
629 N Main St.
Hattiesburg, MS 39401
Ph: (601)582-4345

Schmelz, Kim, Director
University of Wisconsin-Platteville
Alumni Association [19369]
1500 Ullsvik Hall
1 University Plz.
Platteville, WI 53818-3099
Ph: (608)342-1181
Toll Free: 800-897-2586
Fax: (608)342-1196

Schmelzer, Heidi, Director
Cliff Richard Fan Club of America
[24030]
c/o Heidi Schmelzer
3 Kelley Rd.
Acton, MA 01720-3614

Schmelzer, Peter L., CAE, Exec. Dir.
American College of Osteopathic
Family Physicians [16504]
330 E Algonquin Rd., Ste. 1
Arlington Heights, IL 60005
Ph: (847)952-5100
     (847)952-5108
Toll Free: 800-323-0794
Fax: (847)228-9755

Schmider, Mary Ellen Heian,
Secretary
Fulbright Association [8073]
1900 L St. NW, Ste. 302
Washington, DC 20036-5016
Ph: (202)775-0725
Fax: (202)775-0727

Schmidt, Barbara A., Treasurer
American Veterinary Medical As-
sociation [17630]
1931 N Meacham Rd., Ste. 100
Schaumburg, IL 60173-4360
Toll Free: 800-248-2862
Fax: (847)925-1329

Schmidt, Brian, President
Game Audio Network Guild [22051]

Schmidt, Cliff, Founder, President
Literacy Bridge [8244]
1904 3rd Ave., Ste. 733
Seattle, WA 98101
Ph: (425)780-5669
Fax: (425)780-5669

Schmidt, Dave, President
TPG International Health Academy
[15594]
160 Oak St.
Glastonbury, CT 06033

Schmidt, Dwight, Contact
Corrugated Packaging Alliance
[2475]
500 Park Blvd., Ste. 985
Itasca, IL 60143
Ph: (847)364-9600
Fax: (847)364-9739

Schmidt, Harry, President, CEO
Religious Conference Management
Association [2337]
7702 Woodland Dr., Ste. 120
Indianapolis, IN 46278
Ph: (317)632-1888
Fax: (317)632-7909

Schmidt, Jan, President
Paws for Friendship [13305]
PO Box 341378
Tampa, FL 33694
Ph: (813)969-1954
     (913)957-6829
Fax: (813)968-2848

Schmidt, Jim, Director
Avenues, National Support Group for
Arthrogryposis Multiplex Congenita
[15908]
c/o Cathy Graubert
Seattle Children's Hospital
4800 Sand Point Way NE
Seattle, WA 98105
Ph: (206)987-2113

Schmidt, Jim, Bd. Member
National Watermelon Association
[4245]
190 Fitzgerald Rd., Ste. 3
Lakeland, FL 33813
Ph: (813)619-7575
Fax: (813)619-7577

Schmidt, Jon, President
American Embryo Transfer Associa-
tion [3613]
1800 S Oak St., Ste. 100
Champaign, IL 61820-6974
Ph: (217)398-2217
Fax: (217)398-4119

Schmidt, Master Jurgen R.,
President
International Disabled Self-Defense
Association [12864]
22-C New Leicester Hwy., No. 259
Asheville, NC 28806

Schmidt, Kay, VP
Colored Pencil Society of America
[8851]
c/o Ruth Arthur, Membership Direc-
tor
PO Box 8638
Long Beach, CA 90808-0638
Ph: (562)425-1609

Schmidt, Maria, Secretary
Epiphyllum Society of America
[22093]
c/o Geneva Coats, Treasurer
13674 Geranium St.
Chino, CA 91710-5080

Schmidt, Megan, Officer
International Coalition for the
Responsibility to Protect [19013]
c/o World Federalist Movement
Institute for Global Policy
708 3rd Ave., Ste. 1715
New York, NY 10017
Ph: (212)599-1320
Fax: (212)599-1332

Schmidt, Ms. Pamela J., Exec. Dir.
Instructional Systems Association
[8032]
5868 Mapledale Plz., No. 120
Dale City, VA 22193
Ph: (703)730-2838
Fax: (703)730-2857

Schmidt, Peter, Sr. VP
National Parkinson Foundation
[15970]
200 SE 1st St., Ste. 800
Miami, FL 33131
Toll Free: 800-473-4636
Fax: (305)537-9901

Schmidt, Rick, President
Technology Student Association
[8019]
1914 Association Dr.
Reston, VA 20191-1538
Ph: (703)860-9000
Toll Free: 888-860-9010
Fax: (703)758-4852

Schmidt, Ronald, Director
3-A Sanitary Standards, Inc. [965]
6888 Elm St., Ste. 2D
McLean, VA 22101
Ph: (703)790-0295
Fax: (703)761-6284

Schmidt, Shirley, Mgr., Member
Svcs.
International Society of Antique
Scale Collectors [21679]
c/o Shirley Schmidt, Membership
Chairman
5790 N Lakeshore Rd.
Palms, MI 48465-9626
Ph: (612)925-1386

Schmidt, Susan, Exec. Dir.
American Association of Teachers of
Japanese [8173]
366 University of Colorado
1424 Broadway
Boulder, CO 80309-0366
Ph: (303)492-5487
Fax: (303)492-5856

Schmitt, Joe, President
Foodservice Equipment Distributors
Association [1383]
2250 Point Blvd., Ste. 200
Elgin, IL 60123
Ph: (224)293-6500
Fax: (224)293-6505

Schmitt, Margaret, President
National Catholic Society of Forest-
ers [19410]
320 S School St.
Mount Prospect, IL 60056
Ph: (847)342-4500
Toll Free: 800-344-6273
Fax: (847)342-4556

Schmitz, Michael, PsyD, President
Society of Behavioral Sleep
Medicine [17222]
1522 Player Dr.
Lexington, KY 40511
Ph: (859)312-8880
Fax: (859)303-6055

Schmitz, Peter E., President
Professional Lacrosse Players Association [23524]
52 Haynes Rd.
Sudbury, MA 01776

Schnabel, J., Chairman
International Christian Concern
[19985]
2020 Pennsylvania Ave. NW, No.
941
Washington, DC 20006-1846
Ph: (301)585-5915
Toll Free: 800-ICC-5441
Fax: (301)585-5918

Schnarrenberger, William, President
Japanese Chin Club of America, Inc.
[21907]
PO Box 74
Versailles, KY 40383-0074

Schnatzmeyer, Todd, Exec. Dir.
Indiana Limestone Institute of
America, Inc. [3184]
1502 I St., Ste. 400
Bedford, IN 47421
Ph: (812)275-4426

Schneck, Joy S., Exec. Dir.
Certification Board for Music
Therapists [16968]
506 E Lancaster Ave., Ste. 102
Downingtown, PA 19335
Ph: (610)269-8900
Toll Free: 800-765-2268
Fax: (610)269-9232

Schneebaum, Steven, Chairman
International Law Students Associa-
tion [5351]
701 13th St. NW, 6th Fl.
Washington, DC 20005
Ph: (202)729-2470
Fax: (202)639-9355

Schneegas-Nevills, Lee A., President
North American Lionhead Rabbit
Club [4610]
c/o Theresa Mueller
PO Box 43
Ravensdale, WA 98051
Ph: (425)413-5995

Schneider, André, President
International Sustainable Campus
Network [7634]
c/o Sustainserv
31 State St., 10th Fl.
Boston, MA 02109
Ph: (617)330-5001

Schneider, Dan, Exec. Dir.
American Conservative Union
[18019]
1331 H St. NW, Ste. 500
Washington, DC 20005
Ph: (202)347-9388
Fax: (202)347-9389

Schneider, Frank, President
Society for Organizational Learning
[2466]
PO Box 425005
Cambridge, MA 02142
Ph: (617)300-9500

Schneider, Jim, Founder
Homosexual Information Center
[11891]
8721 Santa Monica Blvd., Ste. 37
West Hollywood, CA 90069
Ph: (818)527-5442

Schneider, Jim, President
National Association of Executive
Recruiters [1095]
1 E Wacker Dr., Ste. 2600
Chicago, IL 60601
Ph: (618)398-6027

Schneider, John, VP
Epilepsy Foundation [14740]
8301 Professional Pl. E, Ste. 200
Landover, MD 20785-2353
Toll Free: 866-332-1000
Fax: (301)459-1569

Schneider, John k., President
Council of Professional Surveyors
[7250]
American Council of Engineering
Companies
1015 15th St. NW, 8th Fl.
Washington, DC 20005-2605
Ph: (202)347-7474
Fax: (202)898-0068

Schneider, Luana, Founder, Exec.
Dir.
Tempered Steel [13249]
16039 274th Rd.
Atchison, KS 66002
Ph: (913)370-0238
Fax: (866)377-3343

Schneider, Mark, President
Austin Healey Club USA [21333]
c/o Mark Schneider, President

12465 NW McDaniel Rd.
Portland, OR 97229
Ph: (503)643-7208

Schneider, Mark, Sr. VP
International Crisis Group -
Washington Office [18002]
1629 K St. NW, Ste. 450
Washington, DC 20006
Ph: (202)785-1601
Fax: (202)785-1630

Schneider, Martin, Chairman
Peer Health Exchange [8769]
70 Gold St.
San Francisco, CA 94133
Ph: (415)684-1234
Fax: (415)684-1222

Schneider, Richard, Exec. Dir.
Operation Appreciation [20771]
Non-Commissioned Officers As-
sociation of the USA
9330 Corporate Dr., Ste. 701
Selma, TX 78154
Ph: (210)653-6161
Toll Free: 800-662-2620
Fax: (210)637-3337

Schneider, Scarlett, VP
National Association of Athletic
Development Directors [23236]
24651 Detroit Rd.
Westlake, OH 44145-2524
Ph: (440)892-4000
Fax: (440)892-4007

Schneier, Rabbi Arthur, Founder,
President
Appeal of Conscience Foundation
[19024]
119 W 57th St.
New York, NY 10019-2401
Ph: (212)535-5800
Fax: (212)628-2513

Schniderman, Saul, Director, Chair-
man, Founder
Labor Heritage Foundation [8983]
815 16th St. NW
Washington, DC 20006
Ph: (202)639-6204
Fax: (202)639-6204

Schnipke, Rita J., Bd. Member
Agricultural Development Initiatives,
Inc. [3534]
PO Box 50006
Nashville, TN 37205
Ph: (540)278-4596

Schnitzer, Dan, Exec. Dir., Founder
EarthSpark International [4024]
1616 H St. NW, Ste. 900
Washington, DC 20006

Schnorr, Jim, Dir. of Comm.
Coated Abrasives Fabricators Association [2217]
c/o Jim Schnorr, Director, Communications
259 Chicago St.
Buffalo, NY 14204
Ph: (636)272-7432
(716)972-0333
Fax: (716)972-0334

Schnur, Jonathan, Founder
New Leaders [8201]
30 W 26th St.
New York, NY 10010-2011
Ph: (646)792-1070

Schoch, William, CEO, President
Western Payments Alliance [1270]
300 Montgomery St., Ste.400
San Francisco, CA 94104
Ph: (415)433-1230
Toll Free: 800-977-0018
Fax: (415)433-1370

Schoelkopf, Robert C., Director,
Founder
Marine Mammal Stranding Center
[4842]
3625 Brigantine Blvd.
Brigantine, NJ 08203
Ph: (609)266-0538

Schoenbach, Gail R., Secretary
Eating Disorders Coalition for
Research, Policy and Action
[14637]
PO Box 96503-98807
Washington, DC 20090
Ph: (202)543-9570

Schoenberg, Linda, Rec. Sec.
Na'amat U.S.A. [20267]
21515 Vanowen St., Ste. 102
Canoga Park, CA 91303
Ph: (818)431-2200
Toll Free: 844-777-5222
Fax: (818)937-6883

Schoenbrun, Lois, CAE, FAAO,
Exec. Dir.
American Academy of Optometry
[16419]
2909 Fairgreen St.
Orlando, FL 32803
Ph: (321)710-3937
Toll Free: 800-969-4226
Fax: (407)893-9890

Schoendorfer, Don, PhD, Founder,
President
Free Wheelchair Mission [11598]
15279 Alton Pky., Ste. 300
Irvine, CA 92618
Ph: (949)273-8470
Toll Free: 800-733-0858
Fax: (949)453-0085

Schoenhals, Jonathan, President
Viva Bolivia [11458]
PO Box 1505
Edmonds, WA
Ph: (206)347-7054
Fax: (206)400-1586

Schoening, Palmer, Chairman
Family Business Coalition [17826]
PO Box 722
Washington, DC 20044
Ph: (202)393-8959

Schoep, Comdr. Jeff, Director
National Socialist Movement [19240]
PO Box 13768
Detroit, MI 48213
Ph: (651)659-6307

Schoetz, David J., Jr., Exec. Dir.
American Board of Colon and Rectal
Surgery [16803]
20600 Eureka Rd., Ste. 600
Taylor, MI 48180
Ph: (734)282-9400
Fax: (734)282-9402

Schofield, Lee, President
Associated Locksmiths of America
[1565]
3500 Easy St.
Dallas, TX 75247
Ph: (214)819-9733
Toll Free: 800-532-2562

Schoka, Andy, Chairman
National Fatherhood Initiative
[18198]
12410 Milestone Center Dr., Ste.600
Germantown, MD 20876
Ph: (301)948-0599
(301)948-4325
Fax: (301)948-6776

Scholte, Dr. Suzanne, President
Defense Forum Foundation [18083]
6312 Seven Corners Ctr., No. 167

Falls Church, VA 22044
Ph: (703)534-4313

Scholte, Dr. Suzanne, Chairman
North Korea Freedom Coalition
[18606]
c/o Jubilee Campaign USA
9689 Main St., Ste. C
Fairfax, VA 22031

Scholz, K.W., President
Applied Voice Input/Output Society
[6235]
PO Box 20817
San Jose, CA 95160
Ph: (408)323-1783
Fax: (408)323-1782

Scholz, Sally J., President
North American Society for Social
Philosophy [10109]
PO Box 7147
Charlottesville, VA 22906-7147
Ph: (434)220-3300
Toll Free: 800-444-2419
Fax: (434)220-3301

Schomaker, Kath, Exec. Dir.
Gray is Green: The National Senior
Conservation Corps [3879]
PO Box 6055
Hamden, CT 06517

Schonemann, Peter, President
World Detector Dog Organization
[5523]
55 Kennel Dr.
Vincent, AL 35178
Ph: (252)227-9227

Schonfeld, Rabbi Julie, Exec. VP
Rabbinical Assembly [20275]
3080 Broadway
New York, NY 10027
Ph: (212)280-6000
Fax: (212)749-9166

Schonfeld, Victoria, COO
American Jewish Committee [20226]
165 E 56th St.
New York, NY 10022
Ph: (212)891-1314
(212)751-4000
Fax: (212)891-1460

Schonholtz, Cindy, Mem.
Animal Welfare Council [3621]
PO Box 85
Eastwood, KY 40018-0085
Ph: (719)440-7255

Schoolland, Ken, President
International Society for Individual
Liberty [18640]
237 Kearny St., No. 120
San Francisco, CA 94108-4502
Ph: (415)859-5174

Schools, Randy, Chairman
Employee Morale and Recreation
Association [12576]
PO Box 10517
Rockville, MD 20849

Schoonen, Tony, Chief of Staff
Boone and Crockett Club [4799]
250 Station Dr.
Missoula, MT 59801
Ph: (406)542-1888
Toll Free: 888-840-4868
Fax: (406)542-0784

Schoonmaker, L. Craig, Chairman
Expansionist Party of the United
States [18889]
295 Smith St.
Newark, NJ 07106-2517
Ph: (973)416-6151

Schoonover, Jim, Chairman
H2O for Life [13326]
1310 Highway 96 E, No. 235
White Bear Lake, MN 55110
Ph: (651)756-7577
Toll Free: 866-427-7183

Schor, Nina F., MD, PhD, President
Child Neurology Society [16013]
1000 W County Road E, Ste. 290
Saint Paul, MN 55126
Ph: (651)486-9447
Fax: (651)486-9436

Schor, Robert H., President, Chair-
man
Stroke Help Association [17299]
65 Circle Dr.
Hastings on Hudson, NY 10706
Ph: (914)478-3687

Schorr, Jim, President, CEO
Social Enterprise Alliance [19118]
41 Peabody St.
Nashville, TN 37210
Ph: (202)758-0194
(615)727-8551

Schorsch, Prof. Ismar, President
Memorial Foundation for Jewish
Culture [9640]
50 Broadway, 34th Fl.
New York, NY 10004
Ph: (212)425-6606
Fax: (212)425-6602

Schott, Tina M., Exec. Dir.
Vesalius Trust [7949]
491 Carlisle Dr., Ste. A
Herndon, VA 20170
Ph: (703)437-9555
Fax: (703)437-0727

Schouton, Arnold, President
International Wild Waterfowl As-
sociation [4832]
500 Sylvan Heights Pkwy.
Scotland Neck, NC 27874
Ph: (252)826-3186

Schoville, Charles, President
National Alliance of Gang Investiga-
tors Associations [5127]
c/o Charles Schoville, President
PO Box 574
Queen Creek, AZ 85142
Ph: (602)223-2569

Schrader, Dr. Bruce, Exec. Dir.
American Society of Forensic Odontology [14416]
4414 82nd St., Ste. 212
Lubbock, TX 79424

Schrader, David, Chairman
International Federation of
Philosophical Societies [10093]
Purdue University
Dept. of Philosophy
100 N University St.
West Lafayette, IN 47907-2098
Ph: (765)494-4285
Fax: (765)496-1616

Schrader, Julie A., Director
Betsy-Tacy Society [9043]
PO Box 94
Mankato, MN 56002-0094
Ph: (507)345-9777

Schrader, Steven, Treasurer
Teachers and Writers Collaborative
[8766]
520 8th Ave., Ste. 2020
New York, NY 10018
Ph: (212)691-6590
Fax: (212)675-0171

Schrager, Marla, Exec. Dir.
Society of American Travel Writers
[2720]

1 Parkview Plz.
Oakbrook Terrace, IL 60181

Schramm, J. B., CEO, Founder
College Summit [7958]
1763 Columbia Rd. NW, 2nd Fl.
Washington, DC 20009-2834
Ph: (202)319-1763
Fax: (202)319-1233

Schramm, Melinda, Chairperson,
Founder
National Introducing Brokers As-
sociation [1495]
55 W Monroe St., Ste. 3600
Chicago, IL 60603
Ph: (312)977-0598
Fax: (312)977-0733

Schramm, Susan, Director
Telecommunications Industry As-
sociation [3241]
1320 N Courthouse Rd., Ste. 200
Arlington, VA 22201
Ph: (703)907-7700
Fax: (703)907-7727

Schreck, Harley, Co-Ch.
Anabaptist Sociology and Anthropol-
ogy Association [7178]
Bethel University
Dept. of Anthropology and Sociology
3900 Bethel Dr.
Saint Paul, MN 55112
Ph: (651)638-6104
(651)635-8611

Schreiber, Brian, President
National Residential Appraisers
Institute [2885]
2001 Cooper Foster Park Rd.
Amherst, OH 44001
Ph: (440)935-1698
Fax: (888)254-5314

Schreibman, Ron, Exec. Dir.
Institute for Distribution Excellence
[3471]
1325 G St. NW, Ste. 1000
Washington, DC 20005-3100
Ph: (202)872-0885
Fax: (202)785-0586

Schreier, David P., President
National Tractor Pullers Association
[23316]
6155-B Huntley Rd.
Columbus, OH 43229
Ph: (614)436-1761
Fax: (614)436-0964

Schreiner, Ellyn T., MPH, President
American Society for Pain Manage-
ment Nursing [16113]
18000 W 105th St.
Olathe, KS 66061
Ph: (913)895-4606
Toll Free: 888-34-ASPMN
Fax: (913)895-4652

Schreiner, Erin, Secretary
American Printing History Associa-
tion [9347]
PO Box 4519
Grand Central Sta.
New York, NY 10163

Schretzmann, Charles, Treasurer
American Cryptogram Association
[21790]
56 Sanders Ranch Rd.
Moraga, CA 94556-2806

Schroedel, Brig. Gen. Joseph, PE,
Exec. Dir.
Society of American Military
Engineers [6588]
607 Prince St.

Alexandria, VA 22314-3117
Ph: (703)549-3800
Fax: (703)684-0231

Schroeder, Amy, Exec. Sec.
American Delaine and Merino
Record Association [4652]
305 Lincoln St.
Wamego, KS 66547
Ph: (785)456-8500
Fax: (785)456-8599

Schroeder, Brian, Exec. Dir.
Society for Phenomenology and
Existential Philosophy [10124]
c/o Christopher P. Long, Webmaster
119 Sparks Bldg.
Pennsylvania State University
University Park, PA 16802

Schroeder, Dr. Fredric K., Exec. Dir.
National Rehabilitation Association
[17094]
PO Box 150235
Alexandria, VA 22315
Ph: (703)836-0850
Toll Free: 888-258-4295
Fax: (703)836-0848

Schroeder, Kellie A., CEO, Exec. VP
Moulding and Millwork Producers
Association [548]
507 1st St.
Woodland, CA 95695
Ph: (530)661-9591
Toll Free: 800-550-7889
Fax: (530)661-9586

Schromm, Andra, Secretary
International Endotoxin and Innate
Immunity Society [7341]
c/o Amy Hise, Treasurer
Dept. of Pathology
Case Western Reserve University
2109 Adelbert Rd.
Cleveland, OH 44106

Schryver, Dave, Exec. VP
American Public Gas Association
[3411]
201 Massachusetts Ave. NE, Ste.
C-4
Washington, DC 20002
Ph: (202)464-2742
Toll Free: 800-927-4204
Fax: (202)464-0246

Schubart, Jane, President
Norwich Terrier Club of America
[21936]
c/o Patty Warrender, Membership
Chairperson
PO Box 1431
Middleburg, VA 20118
Ph: (540)364-4901

Schubert, Lynn M., President
Surety & Fidelity Association of
America [1934]
1101 Connecticut Ave. NW, Ste. 800
Washington, DC 20036
Ph: (202)463-0600
Fax: (202)463-0606

Schubert, Matthew B., President
Little City Foundation [12327]
1760 W Algonquin Rd.
Palatine, IL 60067-4799
Ph: (847)358-5510
Fax: (847)358-3291

Schuermeyer, Isabel, President
American Psychosocial Oncology
Society [16333]
154 Hansen Rd., Ste. 201
Charlottesville, VA 22911-8839
Ph: (434)293-5350
Toll Free: 866-276-7443
Fax: (434)977-1856

Schuessler, John, Director
Mutual UFO Network [7015]
3822 Campus Dr., Ste. 201
Newport Beach, CA 92660
Ph: (949)476-8366

Schuhle, Betsey, President
National School Development
Council [7792]
28 Lord Rd.
Marlborough, MA 01752
Ph: (508)481-9444
Fax: (508)481-5655

Schulberg, Fran, Exec. Dir.
China-U.S. Energy Efficiency Alliance [6465]
555 Mission St., Ste. 3300
San Francisco, CA 94105
Ph: (415)951-8975

Schulhof, Annie, President
National Board of Review of Motion
Pictures [9307]
40 W 37th St., Ste. 501
New York, NY 10018
Ph: (212)465-9166
Fax: (212)465-9168

Schulhof, Sam, Chairperson
Myasthenia Gravis Foundation of
America, Inc. [15960]
355 Lexington Ave., 15th Fl.
New York, NY 10017
Toll Free: 800-541-5454
Fax: (212)370-9047

Schulte, John D., Mgr.
National Mail Order Association
[2295]
2807 Polk St. NE
Minneapolis, MN 55418-2954
Ph: (612)788-1673

Schulte, Travis, VP
Bluetick Breeders of America
[21843]
c/o Darren Batterson, President
17821 60th St.
Ottumwa, IA 52501
Ph: (641)680-0117

Schultz, Allison, Comm. Chm.
National Association of Catering and
Events [1668]
10440 Little Patuxent Pky., Ste. 300
Columbia, MD 21044
Ph: (410)290-5410
Fax: (410)630-5768

Schultz, David, V. Chmn. of the Bd.
Network of Trial Law Firms [5045]
303 S Broadway, Ste. 222
Tarrytown, NY 10591
Ph: (914)332-4400
Fax: (914)332-1671

Schultz, Debbie Wasserman,
Chairperson
Democratic National Committee
[18111]
430 S Capitol St. SE
Washington, DC 20003-4024
Ph: (202)863-8000
Toll Free: 877-336-7200

Schultz, Gary, DC, President
American Chiropractic College of
Radiology [14252]
PO Box 986
Plainfield, IL 60544

Schultz, Jim E., President
National Antique Oldsmobile Club
[21448]
121 N Railroad St.
Myerstown, PA 17067

Schultz, John, Web Adm.
Veteran's Association of the USS
Iowa [21074]

24307 Magic Mountain Pky., No. 342
Valencia, CA 91355

Schultz, Lorraine H., CEO, Founder
Women's Automotive Association
International [304]
PO Box 2535
Birmingham, MI 48012
Ph: (248)390-4952

Schultz, Peggy L., Exec. Dir.
Association of Defense Trial Attorneys [5310]
4135 Topsail Trail
New Port Richey, FL 34652
Ph: (727)859-0350

Schultz, Rob, President
North American Invasive Species
Management Association [3553]
Bldg. 4, Ste. 5
205 W Boutz Rd.
Las Cruces, NM 88005
Ph: (575)649-7157

Schulz, Monika, Exec. Dir., CEO
American String Teachers Association [8361]
4155 Chain Bridge Rd.
Fairfax, VA 22030
Ph: (703)279-2113
Fax: (703)279-2114

Schulz, Roger, Secretary, Treasurer
Old Reel Collectors Association
[21706]
160 Shoreline Walk
Alpharetta, GA 30022

Schulz, T.J., President
Airport Consultants Council [813]
908 King St., Ste. 100
Alexandria, VA 22314
Ph: (703)683-5900
Fax: (703)683-2564

Schulz, Rev. William F., CEO,
President, Act. Pres.
Unitarian Universalist Service Committee [20630]
689 Massachusetts Ave.
Cambridge, MA 02139-3302
Ph: (617)868-6600
Toll Free: 800-388-3920
Fax: (617)868-7102

Schulz-Menger, Jeanette, President
Society for Cardiovascular Magnetic
Resonance [15699]
19 Mantua Rd.
Mount Royal, NJ 08061
Ph: (856)423-8955
Fax: (856)423-3420

Schumacher, Don, Exec. Dir.
National Association of Sports Commissions [23269]
9916 Carver Rd., Ste. 100
Cincinnati, OH 45242
Ph: (513)281-3888
Fax: (513)281-1765

Schumacher, Jesse, President
Rocky Mountain Cichlid Association
[22036]
PO Box 172403
Denver, CO 80217-2403
Ph: (303)915-4992

Schuman, Hans, Exec. Dir.
JazzReach, Inc. [9942]
45 Main St., Ste. 728
Brooklyn, NY 11201
Ph: (718)625-5188
Fax: (718)625-4979

Schumann, Bryce, CEO
American Angus Association [3682]
3201 Frederick Ave.

Saint Joseph, MO 64506
Ph: (816)383-5100
Fax: (816)233-9703

Schumann, Ralf R., VP
Scholars for Peace in the Middle
East [18693]
PO Box 2241
Bala Cynwyd, PA 19004

Schunemann, Peter, Officer
American Association for Crystal
Growth [6358]
10922 Main Range Trl.
Littleton, CO 801287
Ph: (303)539-6907
Fax: (303)600-5144

Schuss, Russell E., President
Mariner Class Association [22646]
PO Box 273
Ship Bottom, NJ 08008
Toll Free: 866-457-2582

Schuster, Jane, Exec. Dir.
American Society of Breast
Surgeons [17371]
10330 Old Columbia Rd., Ste. 100
Columbia, MD 21046
Ph: (410)381-9500
Toll Free: 877-992-5470
Fax: (410)381-9512

Schuster, Mark, President
Academic Pediatric Association
[16597]
6728 Old McLean Village Dr.
McLean, VA 22101
Ph: (703)556-9222
Fax: (703)556-8729

Schutes, Paul J., Exec. Dir.
100% Recycled Paperboard Alliance
[2490]
1601 K St. NW
Washington, DC 20006
Ph: (202)347-8000
Toll Free: 877-772-6200

Schutte, Edgar, President
American Hanoverian Society [4310]
4067 Iron Works Pkwy., Ste. 1
Lexington, KY 40511
Ph: (859)255-4141
Fax: (859)255-8467

Schutzer, Dan, Exec. Dir.
Financial Services Technology
Consortium [7267]
600 13th St., NW, Ste. 400
Washington, DC 20005

Schutzman, Dr. Bart, Editor
The Cycad Society [3844]
c/o Larry Kraus, Membership Director
3355 Blanchette Trl.
Lake Worth, FL 33467-1130

Schuyler, Chuck, President
National Shoe Retailers Association
[1401]
7386 N La Cholla Blvd.
Tucson, AZ 85741-2305
Ph: (520)209-1710
Toll Free: 800-673-8446

Schwab, Richard, President
American Loggers Council [1407]
c/o Daniel J. Dructor, Executive Vice
President
PO Box 966
Hemphill, TX 75948
Ph: (409)625-0206
Fax: (409)625-0207

Schwab, Ruth, Managing Dir.
American Haflinger Registry [4308]
1064 Northview Ave.

Barberton, OH 44203
Ph: (330)784-0000
Fax: (330)784-9843

Schwaitzberg, Steven D., M.D.,
President
Society of American Gastrointestinal
and Endoscopic Surgeons [14797]
11300 W Olympic Blvd., Ste. 600
Los Angeles, CA 90064
Ph: (310)437-0544

Schwalbach, Pamela, Founder
Simple Hope [12729]
PO Box 4
Menomonee Falls, WI 53052-0004

Schwaller, Dr. John F., Mgr.
Academy of American Franciscan
History [19786]
4050 Mission Ave.
Oceanside, CA 92057
Ph: (510)548-1755

Schwallier, Phil, President
International Fruit Tree Association
[4729]
16020 Swingley Ridge Rd., Ste. 300
Chesterfield, MO 63017
Ph: (636)449-5083
Fax: (636)449-5051

Schwalm, Hal, Contact
Johannes Schwalm Historical Association [20995]
PO Box 127
Scotland, PA 17254

Schwarting, Brad, President
Griswold and Cast Iron Cookware
Association [22157]
210 Kralltown Rd.
Dillsburg, PA 17019-9683
Ph: (315)376-6328
    (717)432-3370

Schwartz, Rabbi Barry L., CEO
Jewish Publication Society [9639]
2100 Arch St., 2nd Fl.
Philadelphia, PA 19103
Ph: (215)832-0600
Toll Free: 800-234-3151
Fax: (215)568-2017

Schwartz, Benedict, Founder
All Kids Can Learn International
[11211]
224 N Washington St.
Havre de Grace, MD 21078
Toll Free: 800-785-1015

Schwartz, Bob, Exec. Dir.
Disarm Education Fund [18126]
113 University Pl., 8th Fl.
New York, NY 10003
Ph: (212)353-9800
Fax: (212)353-9676

Schwartz, Bob, Exec. Dir., Founder
Global Health Partners [15006]
113 University Pl., 8th Fl.
New York, NY 10003
Ph: (212)353-9800
Fax: (212)353-9676

Schwartz, Bob, Co-Ch.
Good360 [12478]
675 N Washington St. Ste. 330
Alexandria, VA 22314

Schwartz, Eileen A., Founder,
President
Flags Across the Nation [20946]
PO Box 78995
Charlotte, NC 28271-7045
Ph: (704)962-1868

Schwartz, Jeanne, Exec. Dir.
Society of School Librarians
International [9727]

c/o Jeanne Schwartz, Executive
Director
19 Savage St.
Charleston, SC 29401
Ph: (843)577-5351

Schwartz, Karl, Founder, President
Patients Against Lymphoma [15548]
3774 Buckwampum Rd.
Riegelsville, PA 18077
Ph: (610)346-8419
Fax: (801)409-5736

Schwartz, Katie, President
Corporate Speech Pathology
Network [765]
Ph: (901)907-6699

Schwartz, Kevin, Director
The Child is Innocent [10899]
139 E Berkeley St., Ste. 501
Boston, MA 02118
Ph: (603)781-8346

Schwartz, Louis, CFO
International AIDS Vaccine Initiative
[13548]
125 Broad St., 9th Fl.
New York, NY 10004
Ph: (212)847-1111
Fax: (212)847-1112

Schwartz, Matthew, Chairman
Association of Insolvency and
Restructuring Advisors [14]
221 W Stewart Ave., Ste. 207
Medford, OR 97501
Ph: (541)858-1665
Fax: (541)858-9187

Schwartz, Maureen, Exec. Dir.
BKR International [18]
19 Fulton St., Rm. 401
New York, NY 10038
Ph: (212)964-2115
Toll Free: 800-BKR-INTL
Fax: (212)964-2133

Schwartz, Richard, President
Jewish Vegetarians of North America
[10292]
9 Hawthorne Rd.
Pittsburgh, PA 15221
Ph: (412)965-9210

Schwartz, Rita C., President
National Association of Catholic
School Teachers [7576]
1700 Sansom St., Ste. 303
Philadelphia, PA 19103
Toll Free: 800-99N-ACST

Schwartz, Ron, President, Chmn. of
the Bd.
Tile Contractors Association of
America [901]
10434 Indiana Ave.
Kansas City, MO 64137
Toll Free: 800-655-8453
Fax: (816)767-0194

Schwartz, Ms. Sandra, Exec. Dir.
Society of Otorhinolaryngology and
Head-Neck Nurses [16184]
207 Downing St.
New Smyrna Beach, FL 32168
Ph: (386)428-1695
Fax: (386)423-7566

Schwartz, Scott, President
Society of Federal Labor and
Employee Relations Professionals
[5401]
PO Box 25112
Arlington, VA 22202
Ph: (703)403-3039
Fax: (703)852-4461

Schwartz, Tamara, Treasurer
National Association of Portable
X-ray Providers [15694]

1065 Executive Pkwy., No. 220
Saint Louis, MO 63141
Ph: (314)227-2700
Fax: (800)533-9729

Schwartzenburg, Randy, Exec. Dir.
Trucker Buddy International [7596]
3200 Rice Mine Rd.
Tuscaloosa, AL 35406
Ph: (205)248-1261
Toll Free: 800-692-8339
Fax: (205)345-0958

Schwartzman, Neil, Exec. Dir.
Coalition Against Unsolicited Com-
mercial Email [6442]
PO Box 727
Trumansburg, NY 14886
Ph: (303)800-6345

Schwarz, Barb, CEO, Founder
International Association of Home
Staging Professionals [1947]
2420 Sand Creek Rd. C-1, No. 263
Brentwood, CA 94513
Toll Free: 800-392-7161

Schwarzbach, Daniel B., Exec. Dir.,
CEO
Airborne Law Enforcement Associa-
tion [5451]
50 Carroll Creek Way, Ste. 260
Frederick, MD 21701
Ph: (301)631-2406
Fax: (301)631-2466

Schwarzlander, Pat, Contact
New Environment Association [4091]
c/o Charlotte Haas Quirk
1200 Euclid Ave.
Syracuse, NY 13210-2610

Schwebel, David, Exec.
Rack Manufacturers Institute [1764]
8720 Red Oak Blvd., Ste. 201
Charlotte, NC 28217-3996
Ph: (704)676-1190
Fax: (704)676-1199

Schwebel, David, Exec.
Storage Manufacturers Association
[1771]
c/o Material Handling Institute
8720 Red Oak Blvd., Ste. 201
Charlotte, NC 28217
Ph: (704)676-1190
Fax: (704)676-1199

Schweidenback, Dave, Founder,
CEO
Pedals for Progress [12710]
PO Box 312
High Bridge, NJ 08829
Ph: (908)638-4811

Schweiger, Ron, President
Brooklyn College Alumni Association
[19310]
2900 Bedford Ave.
Brooklyn, NY 11210
Ph: (718)951-5065

Schweinzger, Jacky, Mgr.
American Association for Public
Opinion Research [18922]
1 Parkview Plz., Ste. 800
Oakbrook Terrace, IL 60181
Ph: (847)686-2230
Fax: (847)686-2251

Schweitz, David T., Exec. Dir.
Farm Safety For Just Kids [12820]
11304 Aurora Ave.
Urbandale, IA 50322
Ph: (515)331-6506
Toll Free: 800-423-5437

Schweitz, Michael, MD, President
Coalition of State Rheumatology
Organizations [17157]

1100 E Woodfield Rd., Ste. 350
Schaumburg, IL 60173
Ph: (847)517-7225

Schweitzer, Mary, Treasurer
August Derleth Society [9038]
PO Box 481
Sauk City, WI 53583

Schweitzer, Peter, Exec. Dir.
Plenty International [12713]
PO Box 394
Summertown, TN 38483-0394
Ph: (931)964-4323

Schweizer, Bernard, Secretary,
Treasurer
International Rebecca West Society
[10380]
100 St. Anselm Dr.
Manchester, NH 03102-1308
Ph: (718)488-1098

Sciarrotta, Tony, Exec. Dir.
Reverse Logistics Association [685]
2300 Lakeview Pky., Ste. 700
Alpharetta, GA 30009
Ph: (801)331-8949
Fax: (801)206-0090

Scioscia, Mrs. Clarita, Exec. Dir.
American Board of Oral and Maxillo-
facial Pathology [16571]
One Urban Ctr., Ste. 690
4830 W Kennedy Blvd.
Tampa, FL 33609-2571
Ph: (813)286-2444
Fax: (813)289-5279

Scislaw, Ken, President
Shirley Family Association [20927]
10256 Glencoe Dr.
Cupertino, CA 95014

Sclar, Dr. Casey, Exec. Dir.
American Public Gardens Associa-
tion [4429]
351 Longwood Rd.
Kennett Square, PA 19348
Ph: (610)708-3010
Fax: (610)444-3594

Scoggin, Gary, Contact
Myotubular Myopathy Resource
Group [17345]
2602 Quaker Dr.
Texas City, TX 77590
Ph: (409)945-8569
Fax: (409)945-2162

Scorca, Marc A., CEO, President
OPERA America [9989]
330 7th Ave.
New York, NY 10001-5010
Ph: (212)796-8620
Fax: (212)796-8621

Scotese-Wojtila, Lynette, Founder
S.U.C.C.E.S.S. for Autism [13779]
28700 Euclid Ave., No. 120
Wickliffe, OH 44092
Ph: (440)943-7607

Scothorn, Mr. Marvin, Director
71 429 Mustang Registry [21308]
c/o Marvin Scothorn, Dir.
6250 Germantown Pke.
Dayton, OH 45439-6634

Scotland, Lynton, VP
Opportunities Industrialization
Centers International [13080]
1875 Connecticut Ave. NW, 10th Fl.
Washington, DC 20009
Ph: (202)499-2380
Fax: (202)499-2382

Scott, Bob, Comm. Chm.
National Association of Abandoned
Mine Land Programs [18700]

c/o Chuck Williams, President
Alabama Dept. of Labor
11 W Oxmoor Rd., Ste. 100
Birmingham, AL 35209

Scott, Brad, President
United States Hydrofoil Association
[23356]
320 Starlight Pl.
Lutherville, MD 21093
Toll Free: 800-533-2972

Scott, Dana, President
National Association for the Educa-
tion of Homeless Children and
Youth [7812]
PO Box 26274
Minneapolis, MN 55426
Toll Free: 866-862-2562
Fax: (763)545-9499

Scott, David, Chairman
Canine Assistants [11576]
3160 Francis Rd.
Milton, GA 30004
Ph: (770)664-7178
Toll Free: 800-771-7221
Fax: (770)664-7820

Scott, Mr. David, Secretary
Clan Scott Society [20841]
PO Box 13021
Austin, TX 78711-3021

Scott, Douglas R., Founder,
President
Life Decisions International [12778]
PO Box 439
Front Royal, VA 22630-0009
Ph: (540)631-0380

Scott, E. Michael D., Director
National Organization for Rare
Disorders [14605]
55 Kenosia Ave.
Danbury, CT 06810
Ph: (203)744-0100
Fax: (203)798-2291

Scott, Elijah, Treasurer
Online Imperial Club [21467]
c/o Elijah Scott, Treasurer
70 Boyd Rd. SW
Rome, GA 30161

Scott, Dr. Franklyn, Jr., President
American Tennis Association [23298]
9701 Apollo Dr., Ste. 301
Largo, MD 20774
Ph: (240)487-5953

Scott, Howard, Founder, Chief
Engineer
Technocracy Inc. [19120]
2475 Harksell Rd.
Ferndale, WA 98248-9764
Ph: (360)366-1012
Toll Free: 855-277-3748
Fax: (360)547-7664

Scott, Ida, President
Business Retention and Expansion
International [1003]
PO Box 15011
Hattiesburg, MS 39404
Toll Free: 800-677-9930

Scott, Jack, Founder
National Fibromyalgia Research As-
sociation [15967]
PO Box 500
Salem, OR 97308
Ph: (503)315-7257
Fax: (503)315-7205

Scott, Jennifer, President
North American Students of
Cooperation [8627]

330 S Wells St., Ste. 618-F
Chicago, IL 60606
Ph: (773)404-2667
Fax: (331)223-9727

Scott, John, VP
Fire Safe North America [1289]
200 NE 2nd Ave., Unit 309
Delray Beach, FL 33444
Ph: (561)278-8776
Fax: (561)771-1701

Scott, Julie, Master, Director
Ancient Mystical Order Rosae Crucis
[19625]
1342 Naglee Ave.
San Jose, CA 95191
Ph: (408)947-3600
Toll Free: 800-882-6672
Fax: (408)947-3677

Scott, J.W., PhD, Managing Ed.
Tomato Genetics Cooperative [4252]
Gulf Coast Research and Education
Center
University of Florida
14625 County Road 672
Wimauma, FL 33598
Ph: (813)633-4135

Scott, Polly, President
National Association of Government
Defined Contribution Administra-
tors, Inc. [2030]
201 E Main St., Ste. 1405
Lexington, KY 40507
Ph: (859)514-9161

Scott, Rebecca J., President
American Society for Legal History
[9457]
c/o Patricia Minter, Membership
Committee
Western Kentucky University
1906 College Heights Blvd., No.
21086
Bowling Green, KY 42101-1000
Fax: (270)793-0040

Scott, Robert L., Chairman
National Shooting Sports Foundation
[1294]
Flintlock Ridge Office Ctr.
11 Mile Hill Rd.
Newtown, CT 06470
Ph: (203)462-1320
Fax: (203)426-1087

Scramlin, L.C., Comm. Chm.
American Southdown Breeders' As-
sociation [4665]
100 Cornerstone Rd.
Fredonia, TX 76842
Ph: (325)429-6226
Fax: (325)429-6225

Scribner, Julie, CFO, Director
American Law Institute Continuing
Legal Education [8208]
4025 Chestnut St.
Philadelphia, PA 19104
Toll Free: 800-CLE-NEWS
Fax: (215)243-1664

Scripture, Burt, VP
North American Gladiolus Council
[22115]
c/o Karen Otto, Secretary
302 Sandpiper Ct.
Delano, MN 55328-9783

Scriven, Dr. Charles, President
Association of Adventist Forums
[20601]
AF 518 Riverside Ave.
Roseville, CA 95678-3126
Ph: (916)774-1080
Fax: (916)791-4938

Scruggs, Dr. Julius R., Mem.
National Baptist Convention U.S.A.
Inc. [19735]
1700 Baptist World Center Dr.
Nashville, TN 37207
Ph: (615)228-6292
Toll Free: 866-531-3054
Fax: (615)262-3917

Scruggs, Kevin, Director
American Bar Association Criminal
Justice Section [5407]
1050 Connecticut Ave. NW, Ste. 400
Washington, DC 20036
Ph: (202)662-1500
Fax: (202)662-1501

Scruggs, Sid L., III, Contact
Lions Clubs International [12897]
300 W 22nd St.
Oak Brook, IL 60523-8842
Ph: (630)571-5466

Scudieri, Alfred W., Comm. Chm.
Society of Former Special Agents of
the Federal Bureau of Investigation
[19538]
3717 Fettler Park Dr.
Dumfries, VA 22025
Ph: (703)445-0026
Fax: (703)445-0039

Scudner, Peter D., Director
U.S.A. Table Tennis [23294]
4065 Sinton Rd., Ste 120
Colorado Springs, CO 80907-5093
Ph: (719)866-4583
Fax: (719)632-6071

Sculco, Thomas P., MD, Exec. Dir.
International Society of Orthopaedic
Centers [16481]
c/o Hospital for Special Surgery
535 E 70th St.
New York, NY 10021
Ph: (212)774-2315
Fax: (212)734-3833

Scurlock, Cindy, Exec. Dir.
Turner Syndrome Society of the U.S.
[14862]
11250 West Rd., Ste. G
Houston, TX 77065
Ph: (832)912-6006
Toll Free: 800-365-9944
Fax: (832)912-6446

Sea, Nexus U., President
Nigerian Lawyers Association [5046]
305 Broadway, 14th Fl.
New York, NY 10007-1134
Ph: (212)323-7408
Fax: (212)323-7409

Seaberry, Nettie, Director
National Minority Supplier Develop-
ment Council [2396]
1359 Broadway, 10th Fl., Ste. 1000
New York, NY 10018
Ph: (212)944-2430

Seahorn, Lin, President
Children Without a Voice, USA
[10925]
PO Box 4351
Alpharetta, GA 30023
Toll Free: 800-799-7233

Seale, Charly, Exec. Dir.
Exotic Wildlife Association [4816]
105 Henderson Branch Rd. W
Ingram, TX 78025-5078
Ph: (830)367-7761
Fax: (830)367-7762

Seale, Charly, President
North American Elk Breeders Association [4857]

9086 Keats Ave. SW
Howard Lake, MN 55349-5500
Ph: (320)543-3665
Fax: (320)543-2983

Seale, Judy G., CEO, President
Stars for Stripes [21034]
109 Rivers Edge Ct.
Nashville, TN 37214
Ph: (615)872-2122

Seale, Ronald A., Cmdr.
Ancient and Accepted Scottish Rite
of Free Masonry - Southern
Jurisdiction [19550]
1733 16th St. NW
Washington, DC 20009-3103
Ph: (202)232-3579
Fax: (202)464-0487

Seaman, Barrett, President
Choose Responsibility [13129]
PO Box 284
Ardsley on Hudson, NY 10503-0284
Ph: (202)543-8760

Seaman, Jane, President
Association of Image Consultants
International [817]
1000 Westgate Dr., Ste. 252
Saint Paul, MN 55114
Ph: (615)290-7468
Fax: (615)290-2266

Seaman, William E., MD, Dir. of
Res.
American Asthma Foundation
[17133]
4 Koret Way, LR-216
San Francisco, CA 94143-2218
Ph: (415)514-0730
Fax: (415)514-0734

Sears, Donald A., President
Apert International [13823]
PO Box 2571
Columbia, SC 29202
Ph: (803)732-2372

Sears, Matt, President
Sharps Collector Association [22023]
PO Box 81566
Billings, MT 59108

Sears, Stephanie, Exec. Dir.
Indoor Air Quality Association [4550]
1791 Tullie Cir. NE
Atlanta, GA 30329
Toll Free: 844-802-4103

Sears, Stephen, COO
Brick Industry Association [503]
1850 Centennial Park Dr., Ste. 301
Reston, VA 20191
Ph: (703)620-0010
Fax: (703)620-3928

Searson, Michael, Officer
Society for Information Technology
and Teacher Education [8675]
PO Box 719
Waynesville, NC 28786
Fax: (828)246-9557

Seats, Lee, President
International King Midget Car Club,
Inc. [21402]
c/o Brenda Arnold, Secretary
20280 State Route 676
Marietta, OH 45750-6552

Seats, Nancy, President
Homeowners Against Deficient
Dwellings [11972]
c/o Paula Schulman, National
Treasurer
22393 N 76th Pl.
Scottsdale, AZ 85255
Ph: (816)560-0030

Seatvet, Daniel, President
Colorado Christian University Alumni
Association [19318]
8787 W Alameda Ave.
Lakewood, CO 80226
Ph: (303)963-3330
Toll Free: 800-44F-AITH

Seavey, William L., Director
Greener Pastures Institute [11970]
PO Box 2916
Orcutt, CA 93457
Toll Free: 800-688-6352
Fax: (805)938-1396

Sebastian, Irene, Trustee
American Institute of Homeopathy
[15286]
c/o Sandra M. Chase, MD, Trustee
10418 Whitehead St.
Fairfax, VA 22030
Toll Free: 888-445-9988

Sebenick, Lisa, President
National Knife Collectors Association
[22176]
PO Box 21070
Chattanooga, TN 37424-0070
Ph: (423)667-8199

Sebes, Amy L., Director, Founder
Association of Albanian Girls and
Women [12919]
6240 Mumbai Pl.
Dulles, VA 20189-6240

Sebright, Danny E., President
U.S.-U.A.E. Business Council [2006]
505 9th St. NW, Ste. 6010
Washington, DC 20004
Ph: (202)863-7285

Sebunya, Kaddu, President
African Wildlife Foundation [4779]
1400 16th St. NW, Ste. 120
Washington, DC 20036
Ph: (202)939-3333
Toll Free: 888-494-5354
Fax: (202)939-3332

Sechrest, Wes, PhD, CEO
Global Wildlife Conservation [4821]
PO Box 129
Austin, TX 78767
Ph: (512)593-1883

Secilmis, Mr. Celal, VP
Turkish American Chamber of Com-
merce & Industry [23623]
2 W 45th St., Ste. 1709
New York, NY 10036
Ph: (212)354-5470
Fax: (212)354-8050

Seckman, David, President, CEO
Food Processing Suppliers Associa-
tion [974]
1451 Dolley Madison Blvd., Ste. 101
McLean, VA 22101
Ph: (703)663-1200
Fax: (703)761-4334

Sectish, Theodore C., MD, Exec. Dir.
Federation of Pediatric Organiza-
tions [16606]
c/o Theodore C. Sectish, MD,
Executive Director
Boston's Children Hospital
300 Longwood Ave.
Boston, MA 02115

Seddon, Brian, President
International Molyneux Family As-
sociation [20887]
PO Box 10306
Bainbridge Island, WA 98110

Sedler, Tommy, Chairman
International Packaged Ice Association [1629]

238 E Davis Blvd., Ste. 213
Tampa, FL 33606
Ph: (813)258-1690

Sedory Holzer, Susan E., Exec. Dir.
Society of Interventional Radiology
[17068]
3975 Fair Ridge Dr., Ste. 400 N
Fairfax, VA 22033
Ph: (703)691-1805
Toll Free: 800-488-7284
Fax: (703)691-1855

Sedransk, Nell, Director
National Institute of Statistical Sci-
ences [7244]
19 TW Alexander Dr.
Research Triangle Park, NC 27709
Ph: (919)685-9300
Fax: (919)685-9310

See, Julie, President, Dir. Ed.
Aquatic Exercise Association
[23061]
201 Tamiami Trl. S, Ste. 3
Nokomis, FL 34275-3198
Ph: (941)486-8600
Toll Free: 888-232-9283
Fax: (941)486-8820

See, Karen J., Coord., Member
Svcs.
Coalition of Labor Union Women
[23531]
815 16th St. NW
Washington, DC 20006
Ph: (313)926-5415

Seebeck, Doug, President
Partners Worldwide [20004]
6139 Tahoe Dr.
Grand Rapids, MI 49546
Ph: (616)818-4900
Toll Free: 800-919-7307

Seelbach, Ryan, Secretary
Save the Waves Coalition [4773]
3500 Highway 1
Davenport, CA 95017
Ph: (831)426-6169
Fax: (831)460-1256

Seele, Pernessa C., CEO, Founder
Balm in Gilead [13531]
620 Moorefield Park Dr., Ste. 150
Midlothian, VA 23236
Ph: (804)644-2256

Seeley, Scott, Chairman
American Traffic Safety Services As-
sociation [2989]
15 Riverside Pkwy., Ste. 100
Fredericksburg, VA 22406-1077
Ph: (540)368-1701
Toll Free: 800-272-8772
Fax: (540)368-1717

Seeley, Valerie, President
Great Pyrenees Club of America
[21890]
c/o Ilene Agosto, Membership Committee Chairman
11604 NW 27th Ave.
Vancouver, WA 98685-4418
Ph: (360)576-6857

Seely, Bruce, President
Society for the History of Technology
[9521]
Dept. of History
310 Thach Hall
Auburn University, AL 36849-5207
Ph: (334)844-6770
Fax: (334)844-6673

Seemes, Sam, CEO
United States Track and Field and
Cross Country Coaches Associa-
tion [23122]

1100 Poydras St., Ste. 1750
New Orleans, LA 70163
Ph: (504)599-8900
Fax: (504)599-8909

Seep, Sue, Exec. Sec.
British White Cattle Association of
America [3598]
6656 45th Ave. SW
Pequot Lakes, MN 56472
Ph: (218)568-7003

Seffrin, John R., PhD, CEO
American Cancer Society Cancer
Action Network [13883]
555 11th St. NW, Ste. 300
Washington, DC 20004
Ph: (202)661-5700

Segal, Donald J., President
Conference of Consulting Actuaries
[1850]
3880 Salem Lake Dr., Ste. H
Long Grove, IL 60047-5292
Ph: (847)719-6500

Segal, Dr. Jerome M., President
The Jewish Peace Lobby [18270]
PO Box 7778
Silver Spring, MD 20907
Ph: (301)589-8764
Fax: (301)589-2722

Segal, Lauren, Founder, Exec. Dir.
NextAid [11099]
357 S Fairfax Ave., Ste. 267
Los Angeles, CA 90036
Ph: (213)663-8638
Fax: (213)663-8638

Segal, Susan L., CEO, President
Council of the Americas [23649]
680 Park Ave.
New York, NY 10065
Ph: (212)249-8950
Fax: (212)249-5868

Seger, Lindsey, President
International Cesarean Awareness
Network [16287]
PO Box 573
Glen Alpine, NC 28628
Toll Free: 800-686-4226

Segermark, Mr. David O., President
Leif Ericson Viking Ship [10335]
PO Box 779
West Chester, PA 19381-0779
Ph: (410)275-8516

Segero, Rosemary, Chairperson
Hope for Tomorrow [11378]
901 New Jersey Ave. NW, Ste. 101
Washington, DC 20001
Ph: (202)705-8547

Segura-Aguilar, Juan, Secretary
Neurotoxicity Society [17499]
PO Box 370
Mountain Home, TN 37684

Sehnert, Carl, Contact
Promotional Glass Collectors As-
sociation [21717]
4595 Limestone Ln.
Memphis, TN 38141
Ph: (901)794-8723

Seibert, Andrew, Chairman
The Content Council [2779]
355 Lexington Ave., 15th Fl.
New York, NY 10017
Ph: (212)297-2191
Fax: (212)297-2149

Seidelman, Carole-Anne, Chairman
International Association of Tour
Managers-North American Region
[3380]

345 W 58th St.
New York, NY 10019

Seiden, Stephen, Chairman
JCC Association [12223]
520 8th Ave.
New York, NY 10018
Ph: (212)532-4949
Fax: (212)481-4174

Seidenberg, Channa A., VP
Lyre Association of North America
[22250]
13 Morgan St.
Phoenixville, PA 19460
Ph: (610)608-9281

Seidler, Dr. Todd, Exec. Dir.
Sport and Recreation Law Association [5768]
c/o Mary Myers
1621 N Melrose Dr.
Wichita, KS 67212

Seif, Prof. Farouk Y., Exec. Dir.
Semiotic Society of America [7160]
204 Raven Ln.
Olga, WA 98279
Ph: (206)268-4910

Seifer, Sarena, Founder, Exec. Dir.
Community-Campus Partnerships
For Health [11336]
PO Box 12124
Raleigh, NC 27605
Ph: (206)666-3406
Fax: (206)666-3406

Seify, Hisham, MD, President
Egypt Cancer Network [13963]
20301 SW Birch St., No. 101
Newport Beach, CA 92660
Ph: (617)242-7970
Toll Free: 866-987-2869

Seikaly, Fadi, Dir. of Programs
Foundation for Advancing Alcohol
Responsibility [17312]
2345 Crystal Dr., Ste. 710
Arlington, VA 22202
Ph: (202)637-0077
Fax: (202)637-0079

Seiler, Paul, Exec. Dir., CEO
U.S.A. Baseball [22568]
1030 Swarbia Crt., Ste. 201
Durham, NC 27701
Ph: (919)474-8721
Fax: (919)474-8822

Seip, Norman R., General, Chmn. of
the Bd.
Council for a Strong America
[19269]
1212 New York Ave. NW, Ste. 300
Washington, DC 20005
Ph: (202)464-7005

Seipler, Shawn, Chairman, Founder
Clean the World [4628]
28 W Central Blvd., Ste. 280
Orlando, FL 32801-1408
Ph: (407)574-8353
Fax: (732)847-5446

Seiter, Doug, Advisor
Association of Energy and
Environmental Real Estate Profes-
sionals [7884]
PO Box 1985
Evergreen, CO 80437
Ph: (303)674-7770
Fax: (303)674-6599

Seits, Mark, Chairman
Floodplain Management Association
[4486]
PO Box 712080

Santee, CA 92072
Ph: (760)936-3676

Seitter, Keith L., Exec. Dir.
American Meteorological Society
[6854]
45 Beacon St.
Boston, MA 02108-3693
Ph: (617)227-2425
Fax: (617)742-8718

Seki, Hoshin, Coord., President
American Buddhist Study Center
[19770]
331 Riverside Dr.
New York, NY 10025
Ph: (212)864-7424

Sekulow, Jay Alan, Chief Counsel
American Center for Law and
Justice [12759]
PO Box 90555
Washington, DC 20090-0555
Ph: (757)226-2489
Toll Free: 800-342-2255
Fax: (757)226-2836

Seldman, Neil, President
Institute for Local Self-Reliance
[11384]
1710 Connecticut Ave. NW, 4th Fl.
Washington, DC 20009
Ph: (202)898-1610

Selendy, Jennifer, Chairwoman
National Center for Law and
Economic Justice [19014]
275 7th Ave., Ste. 1506
New York, NY 10001-6660
Ph: (212)633-6967
Fax: (212)633-6371

Self, Desi, Admin. Asst.
Campus Pride [11875]
PO Box 240473
Charlotte, NC 28224
Ph: (704)277-6710

Selig, Wendy K.D., President, CEO
Melanoma Research Alliance
[14011]
1101 New York Ave. NW, Ste. 620
Washington, DC 20005

Seligmann, Peter A., Chairman,
CEO
Conservation International -
Headquarters [3838]
2011 Crystal Dr., Ste. 500
Arlington, VA 22202
Ph: (703)341-2400
Toll Free: 800-429-5660

Sell, Rebecca, President
Associated Press Photo Managers
[2576]
450 W 33rd St.
New York, NY 10001-2603

Sellers, Marchelle L., MBA, Exec.
Dir.
Mending Kids [14204]
2307 W Olive Ave., Ste. B
Burbank, CA 91506
Ph: (818)843-6363
Fax: (818)843-6365

Sellers, Rochelle, Exec. Dir., Bd.
Member
Hope Arising [11376]
3604 E Leah Ct.
Gilbert, AZ 85234
Ph: (480)313-6116
Fax: (480)654-1449

Sellers-Earl, Laura, President
Associated Press Media Editors
[2657]

450 W 33rd St.
New York, NY 10001
Ph: (212)621-7007

Selnow, Gary, PhD, Exec. Dir.
Wired International [15507]
PO Box 371132
Montara, CA 94037-1132

Selsdon, Helen, Arch.
American Foundation for the Blind
[17684]
2 Penn Plz., Ste. 1102
New York, NY 10121-1100
Ph: (212)502-7600

Seltzer, Steven E., MD, Chairman
Coalition for Imaging and
Bioengineering Research [13819]
1001 Connecticut Ave. NW, Ste. 601
Washington, DC 20036
Ph: (202)347-5872
Fax: (202)347-5876

Seman, Liz, Chairman
Meals on Wheels America [12102]
1550 Crystal Dr., Ste. 1004
Arlington, VA 22202
Toll Free: 888-998-6325
Fax: (703)548-5274

Semler, Jean, Founder, President
ChangeALife Uganda [10890]
46 Oakmont Ln.
Jackson, NJ 08527

Semmel, Andrew K., Exec. Dir.
Partnership for a Secure America
[5758]
2000 P St. NW, Ste. 505
Washington, DC 20036
Ph: (202)293-8580

Sena, Mike, President
National Fusion Center Association
[5345]
1609 N Edgewood St.
Arlington, VA 22201

Senator, Ted, Secretary, Treasurer
Association for the Advancement of
Artificial Intelligence [5983]
2275 E Bayshore Rd., Ste. 160
Palo Alto, CA 94303
Ph: (650)328-3123
Fax: (650)321-4457

Sencenbaugh, Bob, President
Samoyed Club of America [21956]
c/o Darlene Rautio, Membership
Chairperson
1759 E Garwood Rd.
Hayden, ID 83835-5129

Sender, Leonard S., MD, President
Society for Adolescent and Young
Adult Oncology [16354]
140 Huguenot St., 3rd Fl.
New Rochelle, NY 10801
Ph: (914)740-2242

Senecal, Michele, Exec. Dir.
International Fine Print Dealers As-
sociation [250]
250 W 26th St., Ste. 405
New York, NY 10001-6737
Ph: (212)674-6095
Fax: (212)674-6783

Seng, Daniel, Chairman
National Association of Lutheran
Interim Pastors [20316]
PO Box 5235
Midlothian, VA 23112
Ph: (804)564-5389

Sengstack, Patricia, Bd. Member
American Nursing Informatics Association [16108]

200 E Holly Ave.
Sewell, NJ 08080
Toll Free: 866-552-6404

SenGupta, Ira, MA, Exec. Dir.
Cross Cultural Health Care Program
[14995]
1200 12th Ave. S, Ste. 1001
Seattle, WA 98144-2712
Ph: (206)860-0329

Senjem, Rosemary, Exec. Dir.
Commission for the Accreditation of
Birth Centers [14227]
c/o Rosemary Senjem, Executive
Director
2269 5th St.
White Bear Lake, MN 55110
Ph: (305)420-5198
Toll Free: 877-241-0262

Senkovich, Dr. Vlado Z., President
World Safety Organization [12849]
PO Box 518
Warrensburg, MO 64093
Ph: (660)747-3132
Fax: (660)747-2647

Senn, William, President
Excelsior College Alumni Association
[19324]
7 Columbia Cir.
Albany, NY 12203-5159
Ph: (518)464-8500
Toll Free: 888-647-2388
Fax: (518)464-8777

Sensabaugh, Cindy, VP
Sigma Phi Alpha [23721]
c/o Cindy Sensabaug, Vice
President
2208 Edmonton St.
Winter Haven, FL 33881
Ph: (919)537-3464

Sensei, Bill Sosa, Founder
International Aikido Association
[22497]
726 W Jefferson Blvd.
Dallas, TX 75208
Ph: (214)331-6696

Sepp, Cecilia, CAE, President, CEO
American College of Health Care
Administrators [16196]
1101 Connecticut Ave. NW, Ste. 450
Washington, DC 20036
Ph: (202)536-5120
Fax: (866)874-1585

Sepp, Pete, President
National Taxpayers Union [19173]
25 Massachusetts Ave. NW, Ste.
140
Washington, DC 20001
Ph: (703)683-5700
Fax: (703)683-5722

Septembre, Djumy, Director
Christian Action and Relief for Haiti
[12639]
PO Box 880145
Port Saint Lucie, FL 34988-0145
Ph: (901)412-1829
(772)882-1125

Sepulveda, Patricio, President
Chile-U.S. Chamber of Commerce
[23572]
8600 NW 17th St., Ste. 110
Doral, FL 33126-1034
Ph: (786)400-1748
Fax: (305)599-2992

Serafin, Glenn, President
National Association of Media
Brokers [2873]
c/o Glenn Serafin, President

Serafin Bros.
PO Box 262888
Tampa, FL 33685

Seraphin, Barbara G., MS, Exec. Dir.
Haitian American Professionals
Coalition [11373]
PO Box 693118
Miami, FL 33269
Ph: (305)771-3585
Fax: (954)728-8660

Serfass, Jeff, Exec. Dir.
Biomass Thermal Energy Council
[6462]
1211 Connecticut Ave. NW, Ste. 650
Washington, DC 20036-2701
Ph: (202)596-3974
Fax: (202)223-5537

Serfass, Jeff, Gen. Mgr.
Partnership for Advancing the
Transition to Hydrogen [6506]
1211 Connecticut Ave. NW, Ste. 650
Washington, DC 20036-2701
Ph: (202)457-0076
Fax: (202)223-5537

Serfass, Patrick, Exec. Dir.
American Biogas Council [5881]
1211 Connecticut Ave. NW, Ste. 650
Washington, DC 20036-2701
Ph: (202)640-6595
(202)904-0220

Sergeant, Paul, President
Corvair Society of America [21362]
PO Box 607
Lemont, IL 60439-0607
Ph: (630)257-6530

Sergey, Shannon, Founder,
President, CEO
Forever Found [10979]
2321 Tapo St., Ste. C
Simi Valley, CA 93063
Ph: (805)306-8018

Serlin, Omri, Founder
Transaction Processing Performance
Council [6266]
572B Ruger St.
San Francisco, CA 94129-1770
Ph: (415)561-6272
Fax: (415)561-6120

Serota, Scott P., CEO, President
Blue Cross and Blue Shield Associa-
tion [15419]
225 N Michigan Ave.
Chicago, IL 60601
Toll Free: 888-630-2583

Serr, Jim, President
American Jeepster Club [21320]
PO Box 653
Lincoln, CA 95648
Ph: (916)645-8761

Serrano, Lisa, Specialist
NiUG International [6752]
300 Community Dr., Ste. B2
Tobyhanna, PA 18466
Ph: (570)243-8700
Toll Free: 866-301-6484
Fax: (775)257-1661

Serratelli, Bishop Arthur, Comm.
Chm.
United States Conference of
Catholic Bishops - Committee on
Divine Worship [19918]
3211 4th St. NE
Washington, DC 20017-1104
Ph: (202)541-3000

Serrato, Marylouise, Exec. Dir.
American Citizens Abroad [19376]
11140 Rockville Pke., Ste. 100-162

Rockville, MD 20852
Ph: (540)628-2426

Serure, Pamela, Exec. Dir.
Events of the Heart [15215]
350 Central Park W, Ste. 12G
New York, NY 10025
Ph: (212)662-7887

Sessa, Michael, CEO, President
Postsecondary Electronic Standards
Council [7235]
1250 Connecticut Ave. NW, Ste. 200
Washington, DC 20036
Ph: (202)261-6514
(202)261-6516
Fax: (202)261-6517

Sessions, Jean Arnold, Exec. Dir.
Sonoma County Vintners [4933]
400 Aviation Blvd., Ste. 500
Santa Rosa, CA 95403
Ph: (707)522-5840
Fax: (707)573-3942

Sessions, Kathy, Director
Health & Environmental Funders
Network [14716]
817 Silver Spring Ave.
Silver Spring, MD 20910
Ph: (301)565-0500

Setford, David, Exec. Dir.
Spanish Colonial Arts Society [9361]
750 Camino Lejo
Santa Fe, NM 87505
Ph: (505)982-2226
Fax: (505)982-4585

Setrakian, Berge, President
Armenian General Benevolent Union
[19385]
55 E 59th St.
New York, NY 10022-1112
Ph: (212)319-6383

Setzer, Chip, VP
Pacific Lumber Exporters Associa-
tion [1416]
720 NE Flanders St., Ste. 207
Portland, OR 97232
Ph: (503)701-6510
Fax: (503)238-2653

Sevcenko, Nancy Patterson,
President
International Center of Medieval Art
[9786]
The Cloisters, Fort Tryon Pk.
99 Margaret Corbin Dr.
New York, NY 10040
Ph: (212)928-1146
Fax: (212)928-9946

Sevelle, Taja, Exec. Dir., Founder
Urban Farming [4171]
19785 W 12 Mile Rd., No. 537
Southfield, MI 48076
Ph: (313)664-0615
Toll Free: 877-679-8300
Fax: (313)664-0625

Severe, Jodi, Founder, Director
GDE Haiti [10992]
5119 Butler Ridge Dr.
Windermere, FL 34786
Ph: (407)929-7205

Severe, Stephen, VP
Farm Financial Standards Council
[3562]
c/o Carroll Merry
N78 W14573 Appleton Ave., No. 287
Menomonee Falls, WI 53051
Ph: (262)253-6902
Fax: (262)253-6903

Sevier, Greg, Treasurer
National Baseball Congress [22558]
110 S Main, Ste. 600

Wichita, KS 67202
Ph: (316)977-9400
Fax: (316)462-4506

Sevilla, Francisco T., Exec. Dir.,
President
Forest Bird Society [3864]
10969 SW 47th Ter.
Miami, FL 33165
Ph: (305)223-2680

Sevush, Ralph, Exec. Dir.
Dramatists Guild of America [10248]
1501 Broadway, Ste. 701
New York, NY 10036
Ph: (212)398-9366
Fax: (212)944-0420

Sewall, Gilbert T., Director
American Textbook Council [8693]
1150 Park Ave., 12th Fl.
New York, NY 10128
Ph: (212)289-5177

Sexton, Dale, President
Avanti Owners Association
International [21336]
P.O. Box 1715
Maple Grove, MN 55311-6743
Ph: (763)420-7829
Fax: (763)420-7849

Seydel, Jennifer, PhD, Exec. Dir.
Green Schools National Network
[7895]
PO Box 14744
Madison, WI 53708-0744

Seyfer, Donny, Chairman
Automotive Service Association
[341]
8209 Mid Cities Blvd.
North Richland Hills, TX 76182-4712
Ph: (817)514-2900
    (817)514-2900
Fax: (817)514-0770

Seymour, Christopher, MBA, Liaison
National Lipid Association [13814]
6816 Southpoint Pky., Ste. 1000
Jacksonville, FL 32216
Ph: (904)998-0854
Fax: (904)998-0855

Seymour, Mike, President, Director
Heritage Institute [19578]
PO Box 1273
Freeland, WA 98249
Ph: (360)341-3020
Toll Free: 800-445-1305
Fax: (360)341-3070

Seymour, Mike, Chmn. of the Bd.
Retail Solutions Providers Associa-
tion [6332]
9920 Couloak Dr., Unit 120
Charlotte, NC 28216
Toll Free: 800-782-2693
Fax: (704)357-3127

Sganga, Fred, Officer
National Association of State
Veterans Homes [13245]
D.J. Jacobetti Home For Veterans
425 Fisher St.
Marquette, MI 49855-4521
Ph: (906)226-3576

Sgueo, James M., President, CEO
National Alcohol Beverage Control
Association [4953]
4401 Ford Ave., Ste. 700
Alexandria, VA 22302-1433
Ph: (703)578-4200
Fax: (703)820-3551

Shabbas, Audrey, Exec. Dir.,
President
Arab World and Islamic Resources
and School Services [8814]

PO Box 174
Abiquiu, NM 87510
Ph: (505)685-4533
    (510)704-0517
Fax: (505)685-4533

Shabout, Nada, PhD, President
Association for Modern and
Contemporary Art of the Arab
World, Iran, and Turkey [8966]
PO Box 305100
Denton, TX 76203

Shaer, Susan, Exec. Dir.
WAND Education Fund [18763]
691 Massachusetts Ave.
Arlington, MA 02476
Ph: (781)643-6740
Fax: (781)643-6744

Shaer, Susan, Exec. Dir.
Women's Action for New Directions
[18764]
691 Massachusetts Ave.
Arlington, MA 02476
Ph: (781)643-6740
Fax: (781)643-6744

Shafer, CandiAnne, President
National Leather Association -
International [12949]
PO Box 470395
Aurora, CO 80047
Ph: (780)454-1992

Shafer, Patricia, Contact
Mothering Across Continents [11081]
310 Arlington Ave., Ste. 303
Charlotte, NC 28203
Ph: (704)607-1333

Shafer, Terry, Exec. VP
North Central Wholesalers Associa-
tion [2637]
7107 Crossroads Blvd., Ste. 106
Brentwood, TN 37027-7972
Ph: (615)371-5004
Fax: (615)371-5444

Shafer, Wade, PhD, Exec. VP
American Simmental Association
[3713]
1 Genetics Way
Bozeman, MT 59718
Ph: (406)587-4531
Fax: (406)587-9301

Shaffer, Diane Christie, Secretary
American Academy of
Psychotherapists [16955]
1450 Western Ave., Ste. 101
Albany, NY 12203
Ph: (518)694-5360
    (202)328-2035
Fax: (518)463-8656

Shaffer, Franklin A., EdD, CEO
CGFNS International [16127]
3600 Market St., Ste. 400
Philadelphia, PA 19104-2651
Ph: (215)222-8454

Shaffer, Dr. Fred, PhD, Chairman
Biofeedback Certification
International Alliance [13817]
5310 Ward Rd., Ste. 201
Arvada, CO 80002
Ph: (720)502-5829
    (303)420-2902
Fax: (303)422-8894

Shaffer, Susan, President, Exec. Dir.
Mid-Atlantic Equity Consortium
[7780]
5272 River Rd., Ste. 340
Bethesda, MD 20816
Ph: (301)657-7741
Toll Free: 877-637-2736
Fax: (301)657-8782

Shah, Dhirendra A., Dr., Treasurer
World Association for Vedic Studies
[9222]
c/o Dhirenda A. Shah, Treasurer
780 Ullswater Cove
Alpharetta, GA 30022-6661
Ph: (770)664-8779
Fax: (770)664-8780

Shah, Ketan M., President
International Alumni Association of
Shri Mahavir Jain Vidyalaya
[19634]
24 River Rd., Unit 1
Clifton, NJ 07014
Ph: (919)661-3904

Shah, Parag, Treasurer
Diamond Manufacturers & Importers
Association of America [2044]
580 5th Ave. No.2000
New York, NY 10036
Ph: (212)382-2200
    (212)944-2066
Fax: (212)202-7525

Shah, Raj, Chmn. of the Exec. Com-
mittee
American Flock Association [3253]
PO Box 1090
Cherryville, NC 28021
Ph: (617)303-6288
Fax: (617)671-2366

Shahani, Ravinder, Chairman
Asian Pacific American Chamber of
Commerce [23559]
3155 W Big Beaver Rd., Ste. 106A
Troy, MI 48084
Ph: (248)430-5855

Shahani, Shanti, Dir. of Comm.
Globe Aware [13294]
6500 E Mockingbird Ln., Ste. 104
Dallas, TX 75214-2497
Ph: (214)824-4562
Toll Free: 877-588-4562
Fax: (214)824-4563

Shaikh, Munir A., Exec. Dir.
Institute on Religion and Civic
Values [8124]
PO Box 20186
Fountain Valley, CA 92728-0186
Ph: (714)839-2929
Fax: (714)839-2714

Shailer, Matthew, Exec. Dir.
World Energy Cities Partnership
[1124]
c/o Matthew Shailer, Executive
Director
901 Bagby St., 4th Fl.
Houston, TX 77002

Shakarian, Richard, President
Full Gospel Business Men's Fellow-
ship International [19982]
18101 Von Karman Ave., No. 330
Irvine, CA 92612
Ph: (949)529-4688

Shamel, Roger, Founder
Global Warming Education Network
[4064]
8 Northbrook Park
Lexington, MA 02420
Ph: (781)863-1400
Fax: (781)863-1441

Shamim, Tasneem, MD, Exec. Dir.
Muslim Women's Coalition [20501]
1283 Highway 27
Somerset, NJ 08873
Ph: (732)545-8833
    (732)745-4844
Fax: (732)545-3423

Shamley, Mark, CEO, President
Association of Corporate Contributions Professionals [912]

1150 Hungryneck Blvd., Ste. C344
Mount Pleasant, SC 29464
Ph: (734)655-3221
    (843)216-3442

Shanahan, Brendan, President
United States Optimist Dinghy As-
sociation [22682]
PO Box 506
Saint Petersburg, FL 33731
Ph: (609)510-0798
Toll Free: 866-410-7456

Shanahan, Bishop Joseph, Founder
Missionary Sisters of the Holy
Rosary [19864]
Holy Rosary Convent
741 Polo Rd.
Bryn Mawr, PA 19010
Ph: (610)520-1974

Shanahan-Haas, Bernadette, Dir. of
Operations
Retail Bakers of America [376]
15941 Harlem Ave., No. 347
Tinley Park, IL 60477
Toll Free: 800-638-0924

Shanda, Mark, President
United States Institute for Theatre
Technology [10279]
315 S Crouse Ave., Ste. 200
Syracuse, NY 13210-1844
Ph: (315)463-6463
Toll Free: 800-938-7488
Fax: (315)463-6525

Shane, Allen, President
American Association of Medical
Audit Specialists [15571]
7044 S 13th St.
Oak Creek, WI 53154
Ph: (414)908-4941
Fax: (414)768-8001

Shane, Jeffrey R., Chairman
Committee on Research Materials
on Southeast Asia [9700]
c/o Jeffrey R. Shane, Chairperson
Ohio University
Alden Library
Athens, OH 45701-2978
Ph: (740)593-2657
Fax: (740)597-1879

Shanfield, Jon, Chairman
Caregiver Action Network [15276]
1130 Connecticut Ave. NW, Ste. 300
Washington, DC 20036-3981
Ph: (202)454-3970

Shank, Barbara W., Chmn. of the
Bd.
Council on Social Work Education
[8571]
1701 Duke St., Ste. 200
Alexandria, VA 22314
Ph: (703)683-8080
Fax: (703)683-8099

Shankar, Sri Sri Ravi, Founder
International Association for Human
Values [12007]
2401 15th St. NW
Washington, DC 20009

Shanks, Gabriel J., Exec. Dir.
The Drama League [10247]
32 Avenue of the Americas, 1st Fl.
New York, NY 10013
Ph: (212)244-9494
Fax: (212)244-9191

Shanmuga, Santosh, President
Carp Anglers Group [22039]
PO Box 1502
Bartlesville, OK 74005-1502

Shannon, Dan, Founder, President
Operation Homelink [10751]
25 E Washington St., Ste. 1501

Chicago, IL 60602
Ph: (312)863-6336
Fax: (312)863-6206

Shannon, Denise, Exec. Dir.
Funders Network on Population,
  Reproductive Health and Rights
  [17106]
PO Box 750
Rockville, MD 20851
Ph: (301)294-4157

Shannon, Don, Coord.
P.T. Boats Inc. [21200]
PO Box 38070
Germantown, TN 38183-0070
Ph: (901)755-8440
Fax: (901)751-0522

Shannon, James M., President, CEO
Coalition for Fire-Safe Cigarettes
  [5202]
National Fire Protection Association
1 Batterymarch Pk.
Quincy, MA 02169-7471
Ph: (617)770-3000
Fax: (617)770-0700

Shannon, Sarah, Exec. Dir.
Hesperian Health Guides [15470]
1919 Addison St., Ste. 304
Berkeley, CA 94704-1143
Ph: (510)845-1447
Toll Free: 888-729-1796
Fax: (510)845-9141

Shannon, Susan, Mgr.
Association of Children's Prosthetic-
  Orthotic Clinics [16494]
9400 W Higgins Rd., Ste. 500
Rosemont, IL 60018-4976
Ph: (847)698-1637
Fax: (847)268-9560

Shapero, Donald L., Founder,
  President
United States Indoor Sports Associa-
  tion [23194]
1340 N Great Neck Rd., Ste. 1272-
  142
Virginia Beach, VA 23454-2268
Fax: (509)357-7096

Shapiro, Gary, CEO, President
Consumer Technology Association
  [1040]
1919 S Eads St.
Arlington, VA 22202-3028
Ph: (703)907-7600
  (703)907-7650
Fax: (703)907-7690

Shapiro, Harold M., President
Partners for Progressive Israel
  [18813]
424 W 33rd St., Ste. 150
New York, NY 10001
Ph: (212)242-4500
Fax: (212)242-5718

Shapiro, Mark, President
Society of General Physiologists
  [7035]
555 8th Ave., Ste. 1902
New York, NY 10018
Ph: (646)595-1800
Fax: (646)417-6378

Shapiro, Marty, President
Antiques Council [196]
PO Box 1508
Warren, MA 01083
Ph: (413)436-7064
Fax: (413)436-7066

Shapiro, Rebecca, PhD, Exec. Sec.
Dictionary Society of North America
  [9126]

c/o Rebecca Shapiro, Executive
  Secretary
Dept. of English
New York City College of Technology
300 Jay St.
Brooklyn, NY 11201

Shapiro, Rita, Exec. Dir.
National Symphony Orchestra
  [9979]
John F. Kennedy Center for the
  Performing Arts
2700 F St. NW
Washington, DC 20566
Ph: (202)416-8100
Fax: (202)416-8105

Shapiro, Shelly Zima, Director
Holocaust Survivors and Friends
  Education Center [18349]
184 Washington Ave.
Albany, NY 12203-5347
Ph: (518)694-9984
  (518)694-9965
Fax: (518)783-1557

Sharadin, Daniel, Commissioner
Collegiate Water Polo Association
  [23351]
129 W 4th St.
Bridgeport, PA 19405
Ph: (610)277-6787
Fax: (610)277-7382

Sharangpani, Mukta, President
Maitri [13382]
PO Box 697
Santa Clara, CA 95052
Ph: (408)436-8393
Toll Free: 888-862-4874
Fax: (408)503-0887

Sharav, Vera, President
Alliance for Human Research
  Protection [18368]
142 W End Ave., Ste. 28P
New York, NY 10023

Share, Allan, President
Day Spa Association [15140]
1551 Sandbar Cir.
Waconia, MN 55387
Ph: (952)767-2202
Toll Free: 877-851-8998
Fax: (844)344-8990

Sharfstein, Steven, President
Group for the Advancement of
  Psychiatry [16829]
PO Box 570218
Dallas, TX 75357-0218
Ph: (972)613-0985
Fax: (972)613-5532

Sharifzadeh, Khalil, DVM, President
Iranian American Medical Associa-
  tion [15732]
PO Box 8218
Haledon, NJ 07538
Ph: (973)595-8888
Fax: (973)790-7755

Sharma, Micky M., President
Association for University and College Counseling Center Directors
  [7686]
1101 N Delaware St., Ste. 200
Indianapolis, IN 46202
Ph: (317)635-4755

Sharma, Mr. Narinder, President,
  CEO
AMD Alliance International [17680]
10519 Old Court Rd.
Woodstock, MD 21163

Sharma, Suresh, President
Milan Cultural Association [9568]
75 Ruff Cir.

Glastonbury, CT 06033
Ph: (860)657-4271

Sharon, Deke, Founder
Contemporary A Cappella Society
  [9893]
1354 W Hedding St.
San Jose, CA 95126
Ph: (415)358-8067

Sharp, Chris, President
National Hockey League Booster
  Clubs [24076]
PO Box 805
Saint Louis, MO 63188

Sharp, Chuck, President
American Small Business Travelers
  Alliance [3368]
3112 Bent Oak Cir.
Flower Mound, TX 75022
Ph: (972)836-8064

Sharp, Claudia, President
Bull Terrier Club of America [21848]
c/o Naomi Waynee, Executive
  Secretary
19135 W Taylor St.
Buckeye, AZ 85326-8506

Sharp, Duer, Commissioner
Southwestern Athletic Conference
  [23255]
2101 6th Ave. N, Ste. 700
Birmingham, AL 35203-2761
Fax: (205)297-9820

Sharp, Fawn, President
Affiliated Tribes of Northwest Indians
  [19575]
6636 NE Sandy Blvd.
Portland, OR 97213
Ph: (503)249-5770
Fax: (503)249-5773

Sharp, Hasana, Sec. Gen.
Society for Social and Political
  Philosophy [10130]
PO Box 7147
Charlottesville, VA 22906-7147
Toll Free: 800-444-2419

Sharp, Dr. Tim, Exec. Dir.
American Choral Directors Associa-
  tion [9854]
545 Couch Dr.
Oklahoma City, OK 73102-2207
Ph: (405)232-8161
Fax: (405)232-8162

Sharp, Victoria L., MD, President
HealthRight International [12283]
240 Greene St., 2nd Fl.
New York, NY 10003
Ph: (212)226-9890
Fax: (212)226-7026

Sharpe, Joan, President
Civilian Conservation Corps Legacy
  [23430]
PO Box 341
Edinburg, VA 22824
Ph: (540)984-8735

Sharples, Fran, PhD, Dir. (Actg.)
The National Academies of Sci-
  ences, Engineering, Medicine |
  Division on Earth and Life Studies
  | Institute for Laboratory Animal
  Research [13719]
500 5th St. NW
Washington, DC 20001
Ph: (202)334-2590
Fax: (202)334-1687

Sharpless, Andrew, CEO
Oceana [4772]
1350 Connecticut Ave. NW, 5th Fl.

Washington, DC 20036
Ph: (202)833-3900
Toll Free: 877-7-OCEANA
Fax: (202)833-2070

Sharpton, Rev. Al, Founder,
  President
National Action Network [17913]
106 W 145th St.
New York, NY 10039-4138
Ph: (212)690-3070
Toll Free: 877-626-4651

Sharry, Craig, Exec. Dir.
International Barbeque Cookers As-
  sociation [22147]
202 Walton Way, Ste. 192-200
Cedar Park, TX 78613
Ph: (682)232-7972

Shatrau, Mike, Director
Richardson Boat Owners Association
  [22663]
c/o Bill Beall, 2nd Vice-President
3623 Melvin Rd. S
Baldwinsville, NY 13027-9229
Ph: (315)635-1356

Shattock, Joanne, President
Research Society for Victorian
  Periodicals [10300]
PO Box 19966
Baltimore, MD 21211-0966
Toll Free: 800-548-1784
Fax: (410)516-3866

Shaughnessy, Roxane, President
Textile Society of America [3273]
PO Box 5617
Berkeley, CA 94705-0617
Ph: (510)363-4541

Shaver, Jeff, Liaison
American Rottweiler Club [21819]
c/o Nancy Griego, President
PO Box 1004
Belen, NM 87002-1004
Ph: (505)681-8020

Shaver, Joe, Coord.
Delta Sigma Pi [23897]
330 S Campus Ave.
Oxford, OH 45056-2405
Ph: (513)523-1907
Fax: (513)523-7292

Shaver, Theresa, Founder, President
White Ribbon Alliance [11198]
1120 20th St. NW, 500 N
Washington, DC 20036
Ph: (202)742-1214

Shaw, Beth Portnoi, President
Professional Women Photographers
  [2593]
119 W 72nd St., No. 223
New York, NY 10023

Shaw, Donald, Exec. Dir.
National Society, Sons of the
  American Revolution [20695]
809 W Main St.
Louisville, KY 40202
Ph: (502)589-1776
Fax: (502)589-1671

Shaw, Dr. Douglas, CEO, President
International Students Inc. [20148]
PO Box C
Colorado Springs, CO 80901
Ph: (719)576-2700
Fax: (719)576-5363

Shaw, Jarrine, Chmn. of the Bd.
Exotic Bird Rescue [10620]
PO Box 14863
Portland, OR 97293
Ph: (541)461-4333

Shaw, Mr. Meredith L., President
Clan Shaw Society [20842]
c/o Meredith L. Shaw, President
3031 Appomattox Ave., No. 102
Olney, MD 20832-1498

Shaw, Robert G., VP
Society of Maritime Arbitrators
[4968]
1 Penn Plz., 36th Fl.
New York, NY 10119
Ph: (212)786-7404
Fax: (212)786-7317

Shaw, Sam, President
American Hereford Association
[3694]
PO Box 014059
Kansas City, MO 64101
Ph: (816)842-3757
Fax: (816)842-6931

Shaw, Susanne, Exec. Dir.
Accrediting Council on Education in
Journalism and Mass Communica-
tions [8146]
Stauffer-Flint Hall
1435 Jayhawk Blvd.
Lawrence, KS 66045-7575
Ph: (785)864-3973
(785)864-3986
Fax: (785)864-5225

Shaw, Tate, Director
Visual Studies Workshop [9318]
31 Prince St.
Rochester, NY 14607
Ph: (585)442-8676
Fax: (585)442-1992

Shaw, Tiger, President, CEO
United States Ski and Snowboard
Association [23171]
1 Victory Ln.
Park City, UT 84060
Ph: (435)649-9090
Fax: (435)649-3613

Shaw, Todd, PhD, President
National Conference of Black Politi-
cal Scientists [7048]
14000 Highway 82 W, MVSU 5098
Itta Bena, MS 38941-1400
Ph: (601)750-7318
Fax: (662)254-3130

Shay, Reese, President
Fellowship of Christian Cowboys
[19976]
PO Box 1210
Canon City, CO 81215
Ph: (719)275-7636

Shay, Steven, President
American Tax Policy Institute
[19164]
c/o Ms. Charmaine Wright, Director
National Tax Association
725 15th St. NW, Ste. 600
Washington, DC 20005-2109
Ph: (202)737-3325
Fax: (202)737-7308

Shea, Brian, Chairman
European American Musical Alliance
[9906]
1160 5th Ave., Ste. 201
New York, NY 10029
Ph: (212)831-7424

Shea, George, Contact
Major League Eating [23234]
18 E 41st St., 15th Fl.
New York, NY 10017
Ph: (212)352-8651
Fax: (212)627-5430

Shea, Robert M., Chmn. of the Bd.
Marine Toys for Tots Foundation
[11251]

The Cooper Ctr.
18251 Quantico Gateway Dr.
Triangle, VA 22172
Fax: (703)649-2054

Sheahen, Dr. Thomas P., Director
Institute for Theological Encounter
with Science and Technology
[12006]
20 Archbishop May Dr., Ste. 3400A
Saint Louis, MO 63119
Ph: (314)792-7220
Fax: (314)977-7211

Shear, Gin, Exec. Dir.
Women's Motorcyclist Foundation
[22239]
7 Lent Ave.
Le Roy, NY 14482-1009
Ph: (585)768-6054
(585)415-8230
Fax: (585)502-0418

Shearburn, Web, MD, Officer
American Society of General
Surgeons [17372]
4582 S Ulster St., Ste 201
Denver, CO 80237-2633
Ph: (303)771-5948
Toll Free: 800-998-8322
Fax: (303)771-2550

Shearer, David, Exec. Dir.
International Information Systems
Security Certification Consortium
[6318]
311 Park Place Blvd., Ste. 400
Clearwater, FL 33759
Ph: (727)785-0189

Shearer, David, President
International Society of Veterinary
Dermatopathology [17650]
c/o Jennifer Ward, DVM
14810 15th Ave. NE
Shoreline, WA 98155
Fax: (206)453-3309

Shearer, David, Chairman
SkyTruth [4145]
PO Box 3283
Shepherdstown, WV 25443-3283
Ph: (304)885-4581

Shearer, Rev. Marian P., President
International Association of Women
Ministers [20642]
579 Main St.
Stroudsburg, PA 18360
Ph: (412)734-2263

Shearer, Mika R., Founder, CEO
United Rheumor Arthritis Society
[17170]
PO Box 6874
North Port, FL 34290
Ph: (941)564-9443
Toll Free: 855-355-8727

Shearer-McMahon, Jas, VP
Akhal-Teke Association of America
[4295]
c/o Catrina Quantrell, President
Gods Cavalry Ranch
1010 Randall Rd.
Centerville, WA 98613
Ph: (509)823-0877

Shearn, Regina, Exec. Dir.
Alpha Phi Sigma [23751]
3301 College Ave.
Fort Lauderdale, FL 33314
Ph: (954)262-7004
Fax: (954)262-3646

Sheckels, Tom, Treasurer
International Association of
Panoramic Photographers [2582]

Sheehan, Fr. John R., Chairman,
CEO
Xavier Society for the Blind [17750]
2 Penn Plz., Ste. 1102
New York, NY 10121
Ph: (212)473-7800
Toll Free: 800-637-9193
Fax: (212)473-7801

Sheehan, Maureen, President
Association of Child Neurology
Nurses [16118]
Child Neurology Society
1000 W County Road E, Ste. 290
Saint Paul, MN 55126
Ph: (651)486-9447
Fax: (651)486-9436

Sheehan, Tara, Exec. Dir.
Association for Public Policy
Analysis and Management [18962]
1100 Vermont Ave. NW, Ste. 650
Washington, DC 20005
Ph: (202)496-0134
Fax: (202)496-0134

Sheehy, John, President
National Star Route Mail Contractors
Association [2120]
324 E Capitol St.
Washington, DC 20003-3897
Ph: (202)543-1661
Fax: (202)543-8863

Sheehy, Julie R., President
Council on Employee Benefits
[1066]
1501 M St. NW, Ste. 620
Washington, DC 20005
Ph: (202)861-6025
Fax: (202)861-6027

Sheeran, James, Chmn. of the Bd.
National Association of Worksite
Health Centers [16326]
125 S Wacker Dr., Ste. 1350
Chicago, IL 60606
Ph: (312)372-9090
Fax: (312)372-9091

Sheeran, Josette, President
Asia Society [9023]
725 Park Ave.
New York, NY 10021
Ph: (212)288-6400
Fax: (212)517-8315

Sheeran, Kristen A., PhD, Exec. Dir.,
Founder
Economics for Equity and the
Environment Network [4114]
Ecotrust
721 NW 9th Ave., Ste. 200
Portland, OR 97209
Ph: (503)467-0811

Sheeran, Rev. Michael J., SJ,
President
Association of Jesuit Colleges and
Universities [7574]
1 Dupont Cir., Ste. 405
Washington, DC 20036
Ph: (202)862-9893

Sheeran, Patricia Marcucci,
President
Mike's Angels [11077]
2090 Dunwoody Club Dr., Ste. 106-
120
Atlanta, GA 30350-5424
Ph: (770)396-7858

Sheets, Kyle, MD, Founder, Chairman
Physicians Aiding Physicians Abroad
[15057]
3004 50th St, Ste. D
Lubbock, TX 79413
Ph: (806)729-9061

Sheets, Marty, Exec. Dir.
Association for People with Dogs
Named Marty [21831]
22201 King Rd.
Woodhaven, MI 48183

Shefchik, Leroy, President
International Silo Association [168]
E106 Church Rd.
Luxemburg, WI 54217
Ph: (920)655-3301

Sheffel, Ashley, Contact
Community Development Corporation of the Americas [11337]
8110 Haddington Ct.
Fairfax Station, VA 22039

Sheffield, Jill, President
Women Deliver [17123]
584 Broadway, Ste. 306
New York, NY 10012
Ph: (646)695-9100
Fax: (646)695-9145

Sheffield, Mike, Officer
Heinlein Society [9054]
3553 Atlantic Ave., No. 341
Long Beach, CA 90807-5606

Sheffield, Victoria M., CEO,
President
International Eye Foundation
[16388]
10801 Connecticut Ave.
Kensington, MD 20895
Ph: (240)290-0263
Fax: (240)290-0269

Sheffield, Victoria M., President,
CEO
Society of Eye Surgeons [16408]
International Eye Foundation
10801 Connecticut Ave.
Kensington, MD 20895
Ph: (240)290-0263
Fax: (240)290-0269

Shefte, Whitney, President
White House News Photographers
Association [2597]
7119 Ben Franklin Sta.
Washington, DC 20044-7119

Shehane, Miriam, Mgr.
Victims of Crime and Leniency
[13267]
422 S Court St.
Montgomery, AL 36104-4102
Ph: (334)262-7197
Toll Free: 800-239-3219
Fax: (334)834-5645

Sheidy, Ricky, Founder, President
Another Chance 4 Horses [10587]
166 Station Rd.
Bernville, PA 19506
Ph: (610)488-5647
Fax: (610)488-5648

Shelby, Debra, PhD, President,
Founder
National Academy of Dermatology
Nurse Practitioners [14503]
17427-B Bridge Hill Ct., Ste. J
Tampa, FL 33647

Shelk, John E., CEO, President
Electric Power Supply Association
[6475]
1401 New York Ave. NW, Ste. 1230
Washington, DC 20005-2110
Ph: (202)628-8200
Fax: (202)628-8260

Shell, Jeffrey, Chmn. of the Bd.
Radio Free Europe/Radio Liberty
[17954]

1201 Connecticut Ave. NW
Washington, DC 20036
Ph: (202)457-6900
Fax: (202)457-6962

Shelnutt, Thad, Treasurer, Secretary
Funk Aircraft Owners Association
[21228]
2836 California Ave.
Carmichael, CA 95608
Ph: (916)971-3452

Shelton, Allan, President, Exec. Dir.
Vre Lavi Ayiti **[11459]**
10422 37th St. SE
Lake Stevens, WA 98258

Shelton, Chris, President
Communications Workers of America
[23405]
501 3rd St. NW
Washington, DC 20001-2797
Ph: (202)434-1100

Shelton, Jodi, President
Global Semiconductor Alliance
[1048]
12400 Coit Rd., Ste. 650
Dallas, TX 75251
Ph: (972)866-7579
Toll Free: 888-322-5195
Fax: (972)239-2292

Shelton, Laura, Exec. Dir.
Drug & Alcohol Testing Industry As-
sociation **[13137]**
1325 G St. NW, Ste. 500, No. 5001
Washington, DC 20005
Toll Free: 800-355-1257
Fax: (202)315-3579

Shelton, Norris, Founder, President
Descendants of American Slaves
[17890]
2100 W Muhammad Ali Blvd.
Louisville, KY 40212
Ph: (502)939-6688

Shelton, Vanessa, Exec. Dir.
Quill and Scroll International Honor-
ary Society **[23795]**
University of Iowa
100 Adler Journalism Bldg.
Iowa City, IA 52242
Ph: (319)335-3457
Fax: (319)335-3989

Shely, Lynda C., President
Association of Professional
Responsibility Lawyers **[4998]**
2 1st National Plz.
20 S Clark St., Ste. 1050
Chicago, IL 60603
Ph: (312)782-4396
Fax: (312)782-4725

Shen, Eveline, Exec. Dir.
Forward Together **[12960]**
1440 Broadway, Ste. 301
Oakland, CA 94612
Ph: (510)663-8300
Fax: (510)663-8301

Shen, Dr. Sinyan, Director
Global Warming International Center
[4065]
22W381, 75th St.
Naperville, IL 60565-9245
Ph: (630)910-1551
Fax: (630)910-1561

Shenoy, Dinesh, CFO
National Eczema Association
[14505]
4460 Redwood Hwy., Ste. 16-D
San Rafael, CA 94903-1953
Ph: (415)499-3474
Toll Free: 800-818-7546

Shepard, Brian, CEO
United Network for Organ Sharing
[17521]
700 N 4th St.
Richmond, VA 23219
Ph: (804)782-4800
(804)782-4862
Toll Free: 888-894-6361
Fax: (804)782-4817

Sheperis, Carl, President
Association for Assessment and
Research in Counseling **[8681]**
c/o American Counseling Association
6101 Stevenson Ave., Ste. 600
Alexandria, VA 22304-3540
Toll Free: 800-347-6647
Fax: (800)473-2329

Shephard, Susan, Act. Pres.
Pekingese Club of America **[21942]**
c/o Elizabeth Tilley-Poole, Treasurer
9455 SW 140th Ave.
Dunnellon, FL 34432-3973
Ph: (352)465-1628

Shepherd, Barbara, Director
Kennedy Center Alliance for Arts
Education Network **[7513]**
John F. Kennedy Center for the
Performing Arts
2700 F St. NW
Washington, DC 20566
Ph: (202)416-8843
Toll Free: 800-444-1324
Fax: (202)416-4844

Shepherd, Barry, CEO
American Federation of Police and
Concerned Citizens **[5454]**
6350 Horizon Dr.
Titusville, FL 32780
Ph: (321)264-0911

Shepherd, Brent, COO
National Association of Chiefs of
Police **[5488]**
6350 Horizon Dr.
Titusville, FL 32780
Ph: (321)264-0911

Shepherd, Dave, President
International Association for
Structural Mechanics in Reactor
Technology **[7276]**
Campus Box 7908
North Carolina State University
Raleigh, NC 27695-7908
Ph: (919)515-5277

Shepherd, Judith G., Founder
Native American Recreation and
Sport Institute **[23044]**
116 W Osage St.
Greenfield, IN 46140-2429
Ph: (317)604-1649
Fax: (317)462-4245

Shepherd, Renee, President
Home Garden Seed Association
[4642]
PO Box 93
Maxwell, CA 95955
Ph: (530)438-2126

Shepherd, Robert, President
The Izaak Walton League of
America Endowment **[3890]**
George M. Guyant, 10598 Hotvedt
Rd.
10598 Hotvedt Rd.
Amherst Junction, WI 54407-9073
Ph: (715)824-2405

Shepherd, Ron, Dir. of Member
Svcs.
FCIB **[1966]**
8840 Columbia 100 Pky.

Columbia, MD 21045-2158
Ph: (410)423-1840
Toll Free: 888-256-3242
Fax: (410)740-5574

Sheppard, Beth, President
National Society for HistoTechnology
[15697]
8850 Stanford Blvd., Ste. 2900
Columbia, MD 21045
Ph: (443)535-4060
Fax: (443)535-4055

Sheppard, Craig, Exec. Dir.
Association of International Mettaliz-
ers, Coaters and Laminators **[744]**
201 Springs St.
Fort Mill, SC 29715
Ph: (803)948-9470
Fax: (803)948-9471

Sheppard, Mr. Craig, Exec. Dir.
Converting Equipment Manufactur-
ers Association **[1722]**
201 Springs St.
Fort Mill, SC 29715
Ph: (803)802-7820
Fax: (803)802-7821

Sheppard, Mr. Michael T., CPA,
Exec. Dir.
American Urological Association
[17549]
1000 Corporate Blvd.
Linthicum, MD 21090
Ph: (410)689-3700
Toll Free: 866-746-4282
Fax: (410)689-3800

Shepps, Averill, VP
Enamelist Society **[21756]**
PO Box 920220
Norcross, GA 30010
Ph: (770)807-0142
Fax: (770)409-7280

Sher, Dr. Kenneth, VP
Research Society on Alcoholism
[17326]
7801 N Lamar Blvd., Ste. D-89
Austin, TX 78752-1038
Ph: (512)454-0022
Fax: (512)454-0812

Sher, Prof. Richard B., Exec. Sec.
Eighteenth-Century Scottish Studies
Society **[7983]**
New Jersey Institute of Technology
University Heights
Newark, NJ 07102-1982

Sheramy, Rona, PhD, Exec. Dir.
Association for Jewish Studies
[8135]
15 W 16th St.
New York, NY 10011-6301
Ph: (917)606-8249
Fax: (917)606-8222

Sheren, Kevin, VP
International Model Power Boat Association **[22198]**
c/o Chris Rupley, President
4630 Stengel Ave.
Toledo, OH 43614
Ph: (419)360-3230
(517)321-6230

Sherer, Steph, Exec. Dir.
Americans for Safe Access **[18645]**
1806 Vernon St. NW
Washington, DC 20009
Ph: (202)857-4272

Sheridan, Abigail, Dep. Dir.
Congress for the New Urbanism
[19217]
PO Box A3104

Chicago, IL 60690
Ph: (312)551-7300
Fax: (312)346-3323

Sheridan, M. Kathleen, CAE, Exec.
Sec.
American Society of
Temporomandibular Joint
Surgeons **[16445]**
4407 Wilshire Blvd., No. 302
Mound, MN 55364
Ph: (952)472-4762
Fax: (952)472-1638

Sheriff, Wayne S., President
Train Collectors Association **[22193]**
PO Box 248
Strasburg, PA 17579-0248
Ph: (717)687-8623
Fax: (717)687-0742

Sherlock, Rick, Contact
Association of Air Medical Services
[14660]
909 N Washington St., Ste. 410
Alexandria, VA 22314-3143
Ph: (703)836-8732
Fax: (703)836-8920

Sherman, Betty, Treasurer
National Air-Racing Group **[22489]**
1932 Mahan
Richland, WA 99352-2121
Ph: (509)946-5690

Sherman, Cary, Chairman, CEO
Alliance of Artists and Recording
Companies **[2899]**
700 N Fairfax St., Ste. 601
Alexandria, VA 22314
Ph: (703)535-8101
Fax: (703)535-8105

Sherman, Cary, Chairman, CEO
Recording Industry Association of
America **[2904]**
1025 F St. NW, 10th Fl.
Washington, DC 20004
Ph: (202)775-0101

Sherman, David, President
International Society for Self and
Identity **[7066]**
c/o Camille Johnson, Secretary/
Treasurer
San Jose State University
1 Washington Sq.
San Jose, CA 95192
Ph: (520)621-7434
Fax: (520)621-9306

Sherman, Debbie, Exec. Dir.
Save the Turtles **[4881]**
5114 Parkhurst Dr.
Santa Rosa, CA 95409
Ph: (707)538-8084

Sherman, Ed, Director
American Boat & Yacht Council
[2234]
613 3rd St., Ste. 10
Annapolis, MD 21403
Ph: (410)990-4460
Fax: (410)990-4466

Sherman, Jack, MD, President
National Cancer Center **[16348]**
88 Sunnyside Blvd., Ste. 307
Plainview, NY 11803-1518
Ph: (516)349-0610
Fax: (516)349-1755

Sherman, John J., Chairman
Truman Library Institute **[10353]**
500 W US Highway 24
Independence, MO 64050
Ph: (816)268-8200
Toll Free: 800-833-1225

Sherman, Julie, Exec. Dir.
Pan African Sanctuary Alliance
[4866]
1405 NE 52nd Ave.
Portland, OR 97213
Ph: (971)712-8360

Sherman, Lee, President, CEO
Association of Jewish Family and
Children's Agencies [12219]
5750 Park Heights Ave.
Baltimore, MD 21215
Toll Free: 800-634-7346
Fax: (410)664-0551

Sherman, Lisa, President, CEO
Advertising Council [79]
815 2nd Ave., 9th Fl.
New York, NY 10017
Ph: (212)922-1500

Sherman, Michelle B., Director
Associate Missionaries of the As-
sumption [20383]
16 Vineyard St.
Worcester, MA 01603
Ph: (508)767-1356

Sherman, Ronald A., MD, Chmn. of
the Bd.
Biotherapeutics, Education and
Research Foundation [13611]
36 Urey Ct.
Irvine, CA 92617
Ph: (949)246-1156
Fax: (949)679-3001

Sherman, Tanya, President
Insurance Regulatory Examiners
Society [1870]
1821 University Ave. W, Ste. S256
Saint Paul, MN 55104
Ph: (651)917-6250
Fax: (651)917-1835

Sherman, Terry, Treasurer
Environic Foundation International
[7877]
12035 Stonewick Pl.
Glen Allen, VA 23059-7152
Ph: (804)360-9130

Sherman-Warne, Jill, Exec. Dir.
Native American Environmental
Protection Coalition [3909]
EDGE-SCI Bldg.
27368 Via Industria, Ste. 105
Temecula, CA 92590
Ph: (951)296-5595
Toll Free: 877-739-9243
Fax: (951)926-5109

Shermer, Dr. Michael, Exec. Dir.,
Ed.-in-Chief
The Skeptics Society [7144]
PO Box 338
Altadena, CA 91001
Ph: (626)794-3119
Fax: (626)794-1301

Shermer, Richard C., Sr., CEO,
Founder
Today's Children, Africa's Future
[11168]
PO Box 28548
Fresno, CA 93729
Ph: (559)433-6926

Shern, David, PhD, CEO, President
Mental Health America [15783]
2000 N Beauregard St., 6th Fl.
Alexandria, VA 22311
Ph: (703)684-7722
Toll Free: 800-969-6642
Fax: (703)684-5968

Sherrer, Ron, President
International Physical Fitness Association [3159]

3407 Southgate Dr.
Flint, MI 48507
Toll Free: 877-520-4732
Fax: (810)239-3320

Sherrod, Lonnie, PhD, Exec. Dir.
Society for Research in Child
Development [10823]
2950 S State St., Ste. 401
Ann Arbor, MI 48104
Ph: (734)926-0600
Fax: (734)926-0601

Shever, Amy, Director, Founder
2nd Chance 4 Pets [10557]
1484 Pollard Rd., No. 444
Los Gatos, CA 95032
Ph: (408)871-1133
Toll Free: 888-843-4040
Fax: (408)866-6659

Shewokis, Robin, President
International Association of Avian
Trainers and Educators [21540]
301 E Hollywood St.
Tampa, FL 33604

Shi, Tommy, President
Asian American Legal Defense and
Education Fund [17876]
99 Hudson St., 12th Fl.
New York, NY 10013
Ph: (212)966-5932
Fax: (212)966-4303

Shiao, Jerry, President
Chinese Consolidated Benevolent
Association [19414]
62 Mott St.
New York, NY 10013
Ph: (212)226-6280
Fax: (212)431-5883

Shields, Donald, MD, President
Child Neurology Foundation [15914]
201 Chicago Ave., No. 200
Minneapolis, MN 55415
Ph: (877)263-5430

Shields, Jeffrey N., President, CEO
National Business Officers Associa-
tion [7564]
1400 I St. NW, Ste. 850
Washington, DC 20005
Ph: (202)407-7140
Fax: (202)354-4944

Shields, Tim, President
Christian Media Association [20363]
6310 Wendover Ct.
Fredericksburg, VA 22407

Shields, Tim, President
League of Resident Theatres
[10258]
1501 Broadway, Ste. 2401
New York, NY 10036
Ph: (212)944-1501
Fax: (212)768-0785

Shields, Wayne C., President, CEO
Association of Reproductive Health
Professionals [11836]
1300 19th St. NW, Ste. 200
Washington, DC 20036
Ph: (202)466-3825
Fax: (202)466-3826

Shiff, Blair, President
Zeta Phi Eta, Inc. [23713]
c/o Tyler Wilson, Executive Director
85 Victoria St. N, Apt. 2
Saint Paul, MN 55104

Shifflet, Drew, Exec. Dir.
Society for Basic Urologic Research
[17558]
1000 Corporate Blvd.

Linthicum, MD 21090
Ph: (410)689-3950
Fax: (410)689-3825

Shiffman, Roger, Director
Starlight Children's Foundation
[11274]
2049 Century Pk. E, Ste. 4320
Los Angeles, CA 90067
Ph: (310)479-1212

Shifrin, Debra, Mem.
National Organization of Social
Security Claimants' Representa-
tives [19139]
560 Sylvan Ave., Ste. 2200
Englewood Cliffs, NJ 07632
Ph: (201)567-4228
Fax: (201)567-1542

Shifrin, Joan, Founder, Co-Pres.
Global Goods Partners [12155]
115 W 30th St., Ste. 400
New York, NY 10001
Ph: (212)461-3647
Toll Free: 800-463-3802

Shih, Francoise, VP
Institute of Chinese Culture [9155]
10550 Westoffice Dr.
Houston, TX 77042
Ph: (713)781-2888
(713)339-1992

Shilad, Selena, Exec. Dir.
Alliance for Aviation Across America
[6025]
1025 Connecticut Ave. NW, Ste.
1000
Washington, DC 20036
Ph: (202)223-9523

Shiley, Dawn M., Exec. Dir.
Association of Vacuum Equipment
Manufacturers [1716]
201 Park Washington Ct.
Falls Church, VA 22046
Ph: (703)538-3543
(703)538-3542
Fax: (703)241-5603

Shiller, Robert J., President
American Economic Association
[6377]
2014 Broadway, Ste. 305
Nashville, TN 37203
Ph: (615)322-2595
Fax: (615)343-7590

Shima, Terry, Chairman
Japanese American Veterans As-
sociation [21127]
PO Box 341398
Bethesda, MD 20827
Ph: (703)503-3431

Shimada, Alexis, President
National Asian Pacific American Law
Student Association [5435]
c/o Lianne Baldridge, Treasurer
8910 Southwestern Blvd., No. 1226
Dallas, TX 75214

Shimmens, Mike, Exec. Dir.
National Rural Recruitment and
Retention Network [15128]
228 Little Creek Ln.
Jefferson City, MO 65109
Toll Free: 800-787-2512

Shimoda, Dori, Founder, President
Give Children a Choice [8448]
PO Box 2298
Matthews, NC 28106

Shimoda, Risa, Exec. Dir.
River Management Society [3934]
PO Box 5750

Takoma Park, MD 20913-5750
Ph: (301)585-4677

Shin, Richard T., VP
International Council on Korean
Studies [8164]
5508 Chestermill Dr.
Fairfax, VA 22030-7248
Ph: (703)803-7088
Fax: (703)803-7088

Shine, Judith Kullas, President
American Council for School Social
Work [8567]
5011 W Fairy Chasm Ct.
Milwaukee, WI 53223
Fax: (224)649-4408

Shing, Angela, Exec. Dir.
The Aneurysm and AVM Foundation
[14561]
3636 Castro Valley Blvd., Ste. 3
Castro Valley, CA 94546
Ph: (510)464-4540
Fax: (510)464-4540

Shingler, John, CEO, President
Association of Starwood Franchisees
and Owners North America [1652]
c/o John Shingler, President
420A Lovett Blvd.
Houston, TX 77006
Ph: (713)523-1352
Fax: (713)524-3319

Shinn, Alan, Officer
National Asian Pacific American
Families Against Substance Abuse
[13160]
340 E 2nd St., Ste. 409
Los Angeles, CA 90012
Ph: (213)625-5795
(231)625-5796

Shinn, Jerri, Founder
International Smile Power [14453]
704 228th Ave. NE, No. 204
Sammamish, WA 98074-7222
Ph: (206)715-6322

Shipe, Matthew, President
Philip Roth Society [10393]
c/o Christopher Gonzalez, Treasurer
Dept. of Literature and Languages
Texas A&M University-Commerce
PO Box 3011
Commerce, TX 75429

Shipley, Fernando, Treasurer
National Association of Latino
Elected and Appointed Officials
[18339]
1122 W Washington Blvd., 3rd Fl.
Los Angeles, CA 90015
Ph: (213)747-7606
Fax: (213)747-7664

Shipp, Daniel K, President
International Safety Equipment As-
sociation [2998]
1901 N Moore St.
Arlington, VA 22209-1762
Ph: (703)525-1695
Fax: (703)528-2148

Shireman, Bill, President, CEO
The Future 500 [18006]
230 California St., Ste. 301
San Francisco, CA 94111
Toll Free: 800-655-2020
Fax: (415)520-0830

Shirinian, Sanan, Chairperson
United Human Rights Council
[18447]
104 N Belmont St., Ste. 313
Glendale, CA 91206
Ph: (818)507-1933

Shirley, Janet, Contact
Neighbors Without Borders [12172]
223 Mirada Ave.
San Rafael, CA 94903
Ph: (415)497-8465

Shivaram, Indu, Contact
Forum for Religious Freedom
[20572]
PO Box 60425
Staten Island, NY 10306-0425
Ph: (240)506-0396

Shivdasani, Aroon, Exec. Dir.,
President
Indo-American Arts Council, Inc.
[8976]
351 E 74th St., 3rd Fl.
New York, NY 10021
Ph: (212)594-3685
Fax: (212)594-8476

Shnider, Sara, Exec. Dir.
Prize4Life [15988]
2081 Center St.
Berkeley, CA 94704
Ph: (617)545-4882

Shoaf, Holt, Chmn. of the Bd.
Southern Cotton Ginners Association
[939]
874 Cotton Gin Pl.
Memphis, TN 38106
Ph: (901)947-3104
Fax: (901)947-3103

Shober, Megan, Secretary
Organization of Agreement States
[5741]
201 Monroe St.
Montgomery, AL 36130-3017
Ph: (334)396-9444

Shockley, Floyd W., President
The Entomological Collections
Network [6611]
c/o Floyd W. Shockley, President
PO Box 37012, MRC 165
Washington, DC 20013-7012
Ph: (202)633-0982
Fax: (202)786-2894

Shockley, Linda, Managing Dir.
Dow Jones News Fund, Inc. [8154]
Bldg. 5
4300 Route 1 N
Monmouth Junction, NJ 08852
Ph: (609)452-2820
Fax: (609)520-5804

Shockney, Bethany, Secretary
Association for Skilled and Technical
Sciences [8015]
c/o Ed Sullivan, Executive Director
176 Rappahannock Beach Dr.
Tappahannock, VA 22560

Shoemake, Jim, Chairman
American Horse Council [4312]
1616 H St. NW, 7th Fl.
Washington, DC 20006
Ph: (202)296-4031

Shoemaker, Calise A., President
Federation for the American
Staffordshire Terrier [21282]
619 W 35th St.
Long Beach, CA 90806

Sholer, Michael, Asst. Sec.
Children's Relief Mission [10933]
PO Box 597
Owensville, MO 65066-0597
Ph: (818)502-1989
Fax: (818)502-9040

Sholts, Erwin A., Chairman
North American Industrial Hemp
Council [6632]

PO Box 232
Oregon, WI 53575

Sholtys, Elizabeth, Founder
Ashraya Initiative for Children
[10857]
5804 Renee Dr.
Durham, NC 27705
Ph: (607)301-1242

Shomaker, Lynn, President
La Sertoma International [12895]
PO Box 14521
Des Moines, IA 50306-4521
Toll Free: 800-503-9227

Shonce, Emmala Ryan, RN,
President
Association of Pediatric
Gastroenterology and Nutrition
Nurses [16121]
c/o Emmala Ryan Shonce, RN,
President
Levine Children's Hospital
1001 Blythe Blvd., MCP Ste. 200F
Charlotte, NC 28203
Ph: (704)381-8898
Fax: (704)381-6851

Shonkoff, Jack, MD, Chairperson
National Scientific Council on the
Developing Child [14161]
Harvard University
50 Church St., 4th Fl.
Cambridge, MA 02138
Ph: (617)496-0578

Shoop, Dr. Sally, Deputy
International Society for Terrain-
Vehicle Systems [6727]
72 Lyme Rd.
Hanover, NH 03755
Ph: (603)646-4405
Fax: (603)646-4280

Shoor, Dr. Daniel, President
American Society of Aerospace
Medicine Specialists [13508]
c/o Aerospace Medical Association
320 S Henry St.
Alexandria, VA 22314

Shoppe, Allen E., President
82nd Airborne Division Association
[21097]
PO Box 87482
Fayetteville, NC 28304-7482
Ph: (910)223-1182
Toll Free: 844-272-0047

Shopper, Cresco, President
Midwest Free Community Papers
[2801]
PO Box 5720
Coralville, IA 52241-5720
Ph: (319)341-4352
Toll Free: 800-248-4061
Fax: (319)343-1112

Shor, Cynthia, Exec. Dir.
Walt Whitman Birthplace Association
[9111]
246 Old Walt Whitman Rd.
Huntington Station, NY 11746-4148
Ph: (631)427-5240
Fax: (631)427-5247

Shore, Bill, CEO, Founder
Share Our Strength [12114]
1030 15th St. NW, Ste. 1100 W
Washington, DC 20005
Ph: (202)393-2925
Toll Free: 800-969-4767
Fax: (202)347-5868

Shore, Elliott, Exec. Dir.
Association of Research Libraries
[9689]

21 Dupont Cir. NW, Ste. 800
Washington, DC 20036-1543
Ph: (202)296-2296
Fax: (202)872-0884

Shore, Nicole, Exec. Dir.
Society of Invasive Cardiovascular
Professionals [14147]
1500 Sunday Dr., Ste. 102
Raleigh, NC 27607-5151
Ph: (919)861-4546
Fax: (919)787-4916

Shoretz, Rochelle, Exec. Dir.,
Founder
Sharsheret [14061]
1086 Teaneck Rd., Ste. 2G
Teaneck, NJ 07666
Ph: (201)833-2341
Toll Free: 866-474-2774
Fax: (201)837-5025

Shorney, John, President
Church Music Publishers Association
[20489]
PO Box 158992
Nashville, TN 37215-8992
Ph: (615)791-0273
Fax: (615)790-8847

Short, Barb, Managing Dir.
Committee Encouraging Corporate
Philanthropy [12469]
5 Hanover Sq., Ste. 2102
New York, NY 10004
Ph: (212)825-1000

Short, James, President
Vintage Sailplane Association
[22493]
31757 Honey Locust Rd.
Jonesburg, MO 63351-3195

Short, Marsha, President
North American Kai Association
[21929]
3410 Galbraith Line Rd.
Yale, MI 48097

Short, Ron, Chairman
Marines Helping Marines [12252]
512 Thorton Ct.
Myrtle Beach, SC 29579
Ph: (443)465-1406

Shortt, Elizabeth, Arch.
Woodrow Wilson Presidential Library
and Museum [10355]
20 N Coalter St.
Staunton, VA 24401
Ph: (540)885-0897

Shoss, Brenda, President, Founder
Kinship Circle [10655]
7380 Kingsbury Blvd.
Saint Louis, MO 63130
Ph: (314)795-2646

Shovak, Jim, President
United States Billiard Association
[22587]
58 Hawthorne Ave.
East Islip, NY 11730-1926
Ph: (516)238-6193

Show, Brad, President
Vintage Base Ball Association
[22569]
2445 Londin Ln. E, Unit 410
Maplewood, MN 55119
Ph: (651)739-6986

Showalter, Jeanette, President
Association of Disciple Musicians
[9876]
c/o Brenda Tyler
Disciples Home Missions
PO Box 1986

Indianapolis, IN 46206
Ph: (317)713-2652

Showalter, Joe, President
Rosedale Mennonite Missions
[20334]
2120 E 5th Ave.
Columbus, OH 43219
Ph: (614)429-3211
Toll Free: 866-883-1367

Showers, Jim, Exec. Dir.
Friends of Israel Gospel Ministry
[20143]
PO Box 908
Bellmawr, NJ 08099
Ph: (856)853-5590
Toll Free: 800-257-7843
Fax: (856)384-8522

Showler, Whitney, Exec. Dir.
Music for Relief [12702]
8820 Wilshire Blvd., Ste. 300
Beverly Hills, CA 90211
Ph: (310)358-0260

Shperling, Andrey, Exec. VP
Russian-American Chamber of Com-
merce [23615]
30 Wall St., 8th Fl.
New York, NY 10005-3817
Ph: (212)844-9455
Fax: (678)559-0418

Shreffler, Karina M., Chairperson
National Council on Family Relations
Family and Health Section [14750]
1201 W River Pky., Ste. 200
Minneapolis, MN 55454
Ph: (763)781-9331
Toll Free: 888-781-9331
Fax: (763)781-9348

Shrestha, Rajendra, PhD, President
American Society of Nepalese
Engineers [6537]
PO Box 39524
Baltimore, MD 21212

Shrestha, Roman, Director
Nepal Public Health Network
[17014]
872 Vernon St.
Manchester, CT 06042
Ph: (903)407-0387

Shrestha, Mr. Season, Advisor
Newah Organization of America
[11413]
7425 Morrison Dr.
Greenbelt, MD 20770
Ph: (240)581-0078
Fax: (301)769-6264

Shrivastava, Anusha, Contact
South Asian Journalists Association
[2725]
Columbia University Graduate
School of Journalism
New York, NY 10020
Ph: (212)854-5979

Shriver, Ann L., Exec. Dir.
International Institute of Fisheries
Economics and Trade [1299]
Dept. of Agricultural and Resource
Economics
Oregon State University
Corvallis, OR 97331-3601
Ph: (541)737-1439
(541)737-1416
Fax: (541)737-2563

Shriver, Anthony K., Chairman,
Founder
Best Buddies International [12318]
100 SE 2nd St., Ste. 2200
Miami, FL 33131-2151
Ph: (305)374-2233
Toll Free: 800-892-8339
Fax: (305)374-5305

Shriver, Timothy P., PhD, Chairman, CEO
Special Olympics [22797]
1133 19th St. NW
Washington, DC 20036-3604
Ph: (202)628-3630
Toll Free: 800-700-8585
Fax: (202)824-0200

Shriver, W. Gregory, Treasurer
Association of Field Ornithologists [6954]
c/o Gregory Shriver, Treasurer
257 Townsend Hall
University of Delaware
Newark, DE 19717-2160
Ph: (302)831-1300

Shrout, Patrick E., PhD, Treasurer
American Psychopathological Association [16950]
39 Marion Rd.
Montclair, NJ 07043

Shrum, Dr. Wesley, Officer
Society for Social Studies of Science [7148]
Dept. of Sociology, Anthropology and Criminal Justice
University of Wisconsin
River Falls, WI 54022

Shubow, Justin, President
National Civic Art Society [8873]
300 New Jersey Ave. NW, Ste. 900
Washington, DC 20001
Ph: (202)670-1776
Fax: (202)543-3311

Shuff, Ruthie, President
National Derby Rallies [23182]
c/o Terry Henry, Executive Director
6644 Switzer Ln.
Shawnee, KS 66203
Ph: (913)962-6360

Shuler, Tonya, V. Chmn. of the Bd.
Council of Engineers and Scientists Organizations [23532]
15205 52nd Ave. S
Seattle, WA 98188
Ph: (205)433-0991

Shulman, Dr. William L., President
Association of Holocaust Organizations [18345]
PO Box 230317
Hollis, NY 11423
Ph: (516)582-4571

Shults, Bob, President
National Federation of Pachyderm Clubs [18915]
PO Box 1295
Cape Girardeau, MO 63702-1295
Toll Free: 888-467-2249

Shultz, Scott M., President
Patriotic Order Sons of America [21081]
240 S Centre Ave., Rte. 61
Leesport, PA 19533
Ph: (610)926-3324
Fax: (610)926-3340

Shumway, Robert A., President
American Academy of Cosmetic Surgery [14300]
225 W Wacker Dr., Ste. 650
Chicago, IL 60606
Ph: (312)981-6760
Fax: (312)265-2908

Shundi, Siena, Coord.
Musicians' Assistance Program [12371]
322 W 48th St., 6th Fl.
New York, NY 10036
Ph: (212)397-4802

Shungu, Dr. Daniel L., Exec. Dir., Chairman
United Front Against Riverblindness [17536]
PO Box 218
Princeton Junction, NJ 08550
Ph: (609)771-3674

Shupper, Steve, Chmn. of the Bd.
Art Glass Association [1501]
PO Box 2537
Zanesville, OH 43702-2537
Ph: (740)450-6547
Toll Free: 866-301-2421
Fax: (740)454-1194

Shur, Stephen, President
Travel Technology Association [3401]
c/o Stephen Shur, President
3033 Wilson Blvd., Ste. 700
Arlington, VA 22201
Ph: (202)503-1422
     (703)842-3745

Shurna, David, Exec. Dir., Founder
No Barriers Youth [8718]
224 Canyon Ave., Unit 207
Fort Collins, CO 80521
Ph: (970)484-3633

Shusterman, Jack, Contact
Contemporary Record Society [9894]
724 Winchester Rd.
Broomall, PA 19008
Ph: (610)205-9897
Fax: (707)549-5920

Shuttleworth, Mary, Founder
Shuttleworth Leadership Society International [8204]
PO Box 27306
Los Angeles, CA 90027
Ph: (323)663-5797

Shuttleworth, Dr. Mary, Founder, President
Youth for Human Rights International [12067]
1920 Hillhurst Ave., No. 416
Los Angeles, CA 90027-2712
Ph: (323)663-5799

Shymanski, Michael, President
Historic Pullman Foundation [9399]
614 E 113th St.
Chicago, IL 60628
Ph: (773)785-8181
Fax: (773)785-8182

Siansky, Cory, VP of Operations
Equal Employment Advisory Council [11763]
1501 M St. NW, Ste. 400
Washington, DC 20005
Ph: (202)629-5650
Fax: (202)629-5651

Sibia, Sirtaz Singh, DO, President
American Osteopathic Colleges of Ophthalmology and Otolaryngology - Head and Neck Surgery [16517]
4764 Fishburg Rd., Ste. F
Huber Heights, OH 45424
Toll Free: 800-455-9404
Fax: (937)233-5673

Sibio, Mike, Director
Community Managers International Association [2163]
PO Box 848
Dana Point, CA 92629-0848
Ph: (949)940-9263

Sibley, Ludwell, President, Editor
Tube Collectors Association [21728]
PO Box 636

Ashland, OR 97520
Ph: (541)855-5207

Siciliano, Deborah, Co-Pres.
Lyme Research Alliance [15408]
2001 W Main St., Ste. 280
Stamford, CT 06902
Ph: (203)969-1333

Sickbert, Bryan W., Consultant
Council for Health and Human Service Ministries of the United Church of Christ [13040]
700 Prospect Ave.
Cleveland, OH 44115
Ph: (216)736-2260
Toll Free: 866-822-8224

Sickler, Roger, Chairman
Professional Aviation Maintenance Association [156]
400 N Washington St., Ste. 300
Alexandria, VA 22314
Toll Free: 866-610-5549
Fax: (817)769-2674

Sickmund, Melissa, PhD, Director
National Center for Juvenile Justice [11538]
3700 S Water St., Ste. 200
Pittsburgh, PA 15203
Ph: (412)227-6950
Fax: (412)227-6955

Sidana, Anna, Founder, CEO, Bd. Member
One Million Lights [11298]
PO Box 444
Palo Alto, CA 94302
Ph: (650)387-3150
Fax: (801)788-1420

Siddiqi, Dr. Muzammil, Chairman
Fiqh Council of North America [20217]
PO Box 38
Plainfield, IN 46168
Ph: (317)839-8157
Fax: (317)839-1840

Siddiqi, Dr. Muzammil, Bd. Member
North American Islamic Trust [9608]
721 Enterprise Dr.
Oak Brook, IL 60523
Ph: (630)789-9191
Fax: (630)789-9455

Siddiqi, Nadeem, Chairman
Muslim American Society [20500]
1206 Apollo Rd., No. 851255
Richardson, TX 75085
Ph: (913)888-5555

Siddiqui, Ellen, Contact
Cure Mommy's Breast Cancer [13954]
PO Box 434
Long Beach, NY 11561
Ph: (516)967-1148
Toll Free: 888-519-9185

Siddiqui, Shariq, Exec. Dir.
Association for Research on Nonprofit Organizations and Voluntary Action [13285]
550 W North St., Ste. 301
Indianapolis, IN 46202
Ph: (317)684-2120
Fax: (317)684-2128

Sideman, Richard, President
Jacob Blaustein Institute for the Advancement of Human Rights [18378]
165 E 56th St.
New York, NY 10022
Ph: (212)891-1315
Fax: (212)891-1460

Sidenstecker, Maris, Exec. Dir.
Save the Whales [4882]
1192 Waring St.
Seaside, CA 93955
Ph: (831)899-9957
Fax: (831)394-5555

Sidibe, Kadiatou Fatima, CEO, Founder
A Child For All, Inc. [10897]
21 Arbor Ln.
Stafford, VA 22554
Ph: (540)659-6497

Sidibeh, Dr. Ingrid Feder, CEO, President
Healing Hands of Gambia [15601]
PO Box 638
East Lyme, CT 06333

Sidle, Aubryn Allyn, Exec. Dir.
Advancing Girls' Education in Africa [7944]
PO Box 15298
Washington, DC 20003
Ph: (202)760-4299

Sidwell, Casey, Director
Continental Dorset Club [4669]
c/o Debra Hopkins, Executive Secretary/Treasurer
PO Box 506
North Scituate, RI 02857-0506
Ph: (401)647-4676
Fax: (401)647-4679

Sieber-Laughlin, Kassi, President
Mini Lop Rabbit Club of America [4601]
c/o Kassi Sieber-Laughlin, President
9684 Warnerville Rd.
Oakdale, CA 95361
Ph: (209)480-1216

Siebold, Michael, Chmn. of the Bd.
Interlaw [5109]
1900 Avenue of the Stars, 7th Fl.
Los Angeles, CA 90067

Siegel, Bernard, JD, Exec. Dir., Founder
Regenerative Medicine Foundation [14885]
9314 Forest Hill Blvd., Ste. 2
2875 S Ocean Blvd.
Wellington, FL 33411
Toll Free: 888-238-1423
Fax: (561)791-3889

Siegel, Mo, President
Urantia Foundation [20617]
533 Diversey Pky.
Chicago, IL 60614
Ph: (773)525-3319
Fax: (773)525-7739

Siegel, Patricia, President
American Society of Professional Graphologists [6701]
23 South Dr.
Great Neck, NY 11021
Ph: (516)487-5287

Siegel, Sanford J., Officer
Transverse Myelitis Association [15995]
1787 Sutter Pky.
Powell, OH 43065-8806
Ph: (614)317-4884
Toll Free: 855-380-3330

Sieger, Carol E., JD, COO
Center to Advance Palliative Care [15318]
55 W 125th St., 13th Fl.
New York, NY 10027
Ph: (212)201-2670

Sielman, Martha, Exec. Dir.
Studio Art Quilt Associates [9002]
PO Box 572

Storrs, CT 06268-0572
Ph: (860)487-4199

Siemon, George, Chairman
Global Animal Partnership [3625]
7421 Burnet Rd., No. 237
Austin, TX 78757
Toll Free: 877-427-5783

Sienkewicz, Thomas J., Exec. Sec.
Eta Sigma Phi, National Classics
  Honorary Society [23711]
c/o David H. Sick, Executive
  Secretary
Greek and Roman Studies
Rhodes College
2000 N Pkwy.
Memphis, TN 38112
Ph: (901)843-3907
Fax: (901)843-3363

Sieverdes, Dr. Christopher M., Exec.
  Dir.
Blue Key Honor Society [23777]
7501 Whitehill Ln.
Whitehill Farm
Millersburg, OH 44654-9270
Ph: (330)674-2570

Sievers, Leah, Secretary
Council of American Jewish
  Museums [9827]
PO Box 12025
Jackson, MS 39236-2025

Siff, Barry, President
U.S.A. Triathlon [23339]
5825 Delmonico Dr., Ste. 200
Colorado Springs, CO 80919
Ph: (719)597-9090
  (719)955-2807
Fax: (719)597-2121

Sigal, Janet, President
International Council of Psychologists [16917]
c/o Janet Sigel, President
Pace University 888, 8th Ave., Apt
  1p
New York, NY 10019

Sigler, Rachel, President
National Osteopathic Women
  Physician's Association [23841]
ATSU - Kirksville College of Osteo-
  phatic Medicine
800 W Jefferson St.
Kirksville, MO 63501

Sigmund, Deborah, Founder
Innocents at Risk [12043]
1101 30th St. NW, Ste. 500
Washington, DC 20007
Ph: (202)625-4338
Fax: (202)625-4363

Signer, Mona M., MPH, President,
  CEO
National Resident Matching Program
  [8334]
2121 K St. NW, Ste. 1000
Washington, DC 20037
Ph: (202)400-2233
Toll Free: 866-653-6767

Sikes, Rev. Robert Bruce, Contact
Christian Fencers Association
  [22831]
c/o Bruce Sikes
912 S Rock Hill
Saint Louis, MO 63119

Silas, Pamala M., Exec. Dir.
National American Indian Housing
  Council [5279]
900 2nd St. NE, Ste. 107
Washington, DC 20002
Ph: (202)789-1754
Toll Free: 800-284-9165
Fax: (202)789-1758

Silberg, Joyanna, PhD, Act. Pres.
Leadership Council on Child Abuse
  & Interpersonal Violence [11705]
c/o Joyanna Silberg, Acting
  President
6501 N Charles St.
Baltimore, MD 21285-6815

Silberstein, Shari, Exec. Dir.
Equal Justice USA [18072]
81 Prospect St.
Brooklyn, NY 11201
Ph: (718)801-8940
Fax: (718)801-8947

Silbert Aumiller, Mira, Exec. Dir.
Beta Sigma Kappa [23840]
PO Box 1765
Voorhees, NJ 08043

Silbert, Mimi Halper, PhD, CEO,
  President
Delancey Street Foundation [12872]
600 Embarcadero
San Francisco, CA 94107
Ph: (415)957-9800
  (415)512-5104
Fax: (415)512-5141

Siler, Micala, Exec. Dir.
Family for Every Orphan [10969]
PO Box 34628
Seattle, WA 98124
Ph: (360)358-3293

Silkes, Elizabeth, Exec. Dir.
International Coalition of Sites of
  Conscience [9403]
10 W 37th St., 6th Fl.
New York, NY 10018
Ph: (646)397-4272

Silva, Brian D., Chairperson
Society for Human Resource
  Management [2502]
1800 Duke St.
Alexandria, VA 22314
Ph: (703)548-3440
Toll Free: 800-253-7476
Fax: (703)535-6490

Silva, Brian, Exec. Dir.
Marriage Equality USA, Inc. [12255]
PO Box 121, Old Chelsea Sta.
New York, NY 10113
Ph: (347)913-6369
Fax: (347)479-1700

Silva, Kishani De, President
Association for Women in
  Architecture + Design [233]
1315 Storm Pky.
Torrance, CA 90501
Ph: (310)534-8466
Fax: (310)257-1942

Silvano, Vicky, Chairperson
Asian Real Estate Association of
  America [2850]
3990 Old Town Ave., C304
San Diego, CA 92110
Ph: (619)795-7873

Silver, Abby, Director
Potters for Peace [21778]
c/o Abby Silver, Director
PO Box 2214
Boulder, CO 80306
Ph: (303)442-1253

Silver, Bruce S., CEO, President
National Housing Endowment [558]
1201 15th St. NW
Washington, DC 20005
Toll Free: 800-368-5242

Silver, David F., President
International Photographic Historical
  Organization [10140]

PO Box 16074
San Francisco, CA 94116
Ph: (415)681-4356

Silver, Roxane Cohen, President
Society of Experimental Social
  Psychology [7072]
c/o Nilanjana Dasgupta, Membership
  Chair
Tobin Hall
Dept. of Psychology
University of Massachusetts at Am-
  herst
135 Hicks Way
Amherst, MA 01003
Ph: (413)545-0049
  (413)545-0996

Silver-Isenstadt, Dr. Jean, Exec. Dir.
National Physicians Alliance [16760]
1001 G St. NW, Ste. 800
Washington, DC 20001
Ph: (202)420-7896
  (202)753-0428
Fax: (202)747-2969

Silverman, Frank, Exec. Dir.
Martial Arts Industry Association
  [23001]
Toll Free: 866-626-6226

Silverman, Herb, President
Secular Coalition for America
  [20599]
1012 14th St. NW, Ste. 205
Washington, DC 20005-3429
Ph: (202)299-1091
Fax: (202)293-0922

Silverman, Prof. Hugh J., Exec. Dir.
International Association for
  Philosophy and Literature [10090]
310 Administration Bldg.
Philosophy Dept.
Stony Brook University
Stony Brook, NY 11794
Ph: (631)331-4598

Silverman, Jerry, CEO, President
The Jewish Federations of North
  America [12225]
25 Broadway, 17th Fl.
New York, NY 10004
Ph: (212)284-6500
  (212)284-6903
Toll Free: 866-844-0070

Silverman, Jill K., MSPH, CEO,
  President
Institute for Medical Quality [17029]
180 Howard St., Ste. 210
San Francisco, CA 94105
Ph: (415)882-5151
Fax: (415)882-5149

Silverman, Kali, Director
Habonim Dror North America
  [20247]
1000 Dean St., No. 353
Brooklyn, NY 11238
Ph: (718)789-1796
Fax: (718)789-1799

Silverman, Pamela, Dir. of Opera-
  tions
National Association of Television
  Program Executives [474]
5757 Wilshire Blvd., Penthouse 10
Los Angeles, CA 90036-3681
Ph: (310)857-1621
Fax: (310)453-5258

Silverman, Silvia, President
Altrusa International, Inc. [12882]
1 N LaSalle St., Ste. 1955
Chicago, IL 60602-4006
Ph: (312)427-4410

Silverman, Steve, Exec. Dir.
Flex Your Rights [18398]
PO Box 21497

Washington, DC 20009

Silverstein, Duane, Exec. Dir.
Seacology [3943]
1623 Solano Ave.
Berkeley, CA 94707
Ph: (510)559-3505
Fax: (510)559-3506

Silverstein, Ken, Exec. Dir.
American Society of Podiatric
  Dermatology [14488]
c/o Ken Silverstein, Executive Direc-
  tor
Ken Silverstein and Associates
17825 Sandcastle Ct.
Olney, MD 20832
Ph: (301)570-6664

Simek, James A., Secretary
Professional Currency Dealers As-
  sociation [22282]
c/o James A. Simek, Secretary
PO Box 7157
Westchester, IL 60154
Ph: (414)807-0116
Fax: (414)423-0343

Simes, Dimitri K., CEO, President
Nixon Center [18273]
1025 NW Connecticut Ave., Ste.
  1200
Washington, DC 20036
Ph: (202)887-1000
Fax: (202)887-5222

Simeus, Kimberly, President
Sove Lavi [11444]
401 N Carroll Ave., Ste. 124
Southlake, TX 76092
Ph: (817)239-7298

Siminovsky, Gail S., Officer
Academy of Laser Dentistry [14366]
9900 W Sample Rd., Ste. 400
Coral Springs, FL 33065-4079
Ph: (954)346-3776
Toll Free: 877-527-3776
Fax: (954)757-2598

Simman, Richard, MD, President,
  Chairman
American Board of Wound Medicine
  and Surgery [15705]
PO Box 133
Aspers, PA 17304
Ph: (717)677-0165
Fax: (717)398-0396

Simmons, Bill, Officer
Country Music Association [9895]
1 Music Cir. S
Nashville, TN 37203-4312
Ph: (615)244-2840

Simmons, Bobby, President
Racking Horse Breeders' Association
  of America [4405]
67 Horse Center Rd., Ste. B
Decatur, AL 35603
Ph: (256)353-7225
Fax: (256)353-7266

Simmons, David, President
Association of Black Anthropologists
  [5906]
AAA Member Services
2300 Clarendon Blvd., Ste. 1301
Arlington, VA 22201
Ph: (703)528-1902

Simmons, Glenda, Chairman
Arizona Archaeological Society
  [5932]
PO Box 9665
Phoenix, AZ 85068
Ph: (928)684-3251
  (928)284-9357

Simmons, Ira, CEO, President
Oneworld Works **[12176]**
2138 Penmar Ave., Ste. 3
Venice, CA 90291
Ph: (310)572-1090

Simmons, James W., MD, President
American Back Society **[16463]**
2648 International Blvd., Ste. 502
Oakland, CA 94601
Ph: (510)536-9929
Fax: (510)536-1812

Simmons, Monica Martinez,
President
International Institute of Municipal
Clerks **[5639]**
8331 Utica Ave., Ste. 200
Rancho Cucamonga, CA 91730
Ph: (909)944-4162
Toll Free: 800-251-1639
Fax: (909)944-8545

Simmons, Dr. Patricia, President
National Science Teachers Associa-
tion **[8555]**
1840 Wilson Blvd.
Arlington, VA 22201-3000
Ph: (703)243-7100
Fax: (703)243-7177

Simmons, Tammy, President
Cooperative Communicators As-
sociation **[763]**
174 Crestview Dr.
Bellefonte, PA 16823-8516
Toll Free: 877-326-5994
Fax: (814)355-2452

Simmons, Vaughn, Treasurer
Mid-West Tool Collectors Association
[22170]
c/o Vaughn Simmons, Treasurer
3315 Clement Dr.
Harrisonburg, VA 22801

Simmons, Virginia, President
National Community Education As-
sociation **[7648]**
3929 Old Lee Hwy., No. 91-A
Fairfax, VA 22030-2401
Ph: (703)359-8973
Fax: (703)359-0972

Simms, Ann, CFO, COO
American Planning Association
[5095]
205 N Michigan Ave., Ste. 1200
Chicago, IL 60601
Ph: (312)431-9100
Fax: (312)786-6700

Simms, Vance, CEO, Founder
Father Matters **[18765]**
PO Box 13575
Tempe, AZ 85284-3575
Ph: (602)774-3298

Simon, David, President
North American Collectors Inc.
[22277]
10605 Balboa Blvd., No. 260
Granada Hills, CA 91344
Toll Free: 800-370-4720
Fax: (818)488-8787

Simon, Ellen, Exec. Dir.
HEAR Center **[15192]**
301 E Del Mar Blvd.
Pasadena, CA 91101-2714
Ph: (626)796-2016
Fax: (626)796-2320

Simon, James H., Gen. Mgr.
American Sugar Cane League of the
U.S.A. **[4693]**
206 E Bayou Rd.
Thibodaux, LA 70301
Ph: (985)448-3707
Fax: (985)448-3722

Simon, Janeen, Exec. Dir.
WINGS Guatemala **[17122]**
1043 Grand Ave., No. 299
Saint Paul, MN 55105
Ph: (415)230-0441

Simon, Jerrold, President
Council of Chiropractic Physiological
Therapeutics and Rehabilitation
[14266]
11600 Wilshire Blvd., Ste. 412
Los Angeles, CA 90025
Ph: (310)339-0442

Simon, Jonathan, Director, Founder
Election Defense Alliance **[18180]**
82 Hutchinson Rd.
Arlington, MA 02474-1920
Ph: (617)538-6012

Simon, Marlin, Act. Pres.
Christian Boaters Association
[20135]
c/o Earlene Nelson, Membership
Coordinator
193 Plantation Dr.
Tavernier, FL 33070
Ph: (305)852-4799

Simon, Pauline Jean, President,
CEO
Association of Haitians Living
Abroad for Development **[12140]**
10 S Dixie Hwy.
Lake Worth, FL 33460
Ph: (561)935-4545

Simon, Rabbi Charles E., Exec. Dir.
Federation of Jewish Men's Clubs
[20246]
475 Riverside Dr., Ste. 832
New York, NY 10115-0022
Ph: (212)749-8100

Simon, Richard, Editor
Psychotherapy Networker **[16988]**
5135 MacArthur Blvd. NW
Washington, DC 20016
Ph: (202)537-8950
Toll Free: 888-851-9498
Fax: (202)537-6869

Simon, Robert, VP
Art and Antique Dealers League of
America, Inc. **[237]**
Lennox Hill Sta.
New York, NY 10021
Ph: (212)879-7558
Fax: (212)772-7197

Simon, Robert J., VP
American Chemistry Council-
Chlorine Chemistry Division **[6181]**
700 2nd St. NE
Washington, DC 20002
Ph: (202)249-7000
Fax: (202)249-6100

Simon, Robert, President
Private Art Dealers Association **[248]**
Lenox Hill Sta.
New York, NY 10021
Ph: (917)302-3087

Simon, Sue, President
Hepatitis C Association, Inc. **[15255]**
1351 Cooper Rd.
Scotch Plains, NJ 07076-2844
Ph: (908)769-8479

Simonds, Paul, Mgr., Comm.
Western Growers Association **[4260]**
15525 Sand Canyon
Irvine, CA 92618-3114
Ph: (949)863-1000
Toll Free: 800-333-4942
Fax: (949)863-9028

Simone, Karen, PharmD, President
American Academy of Clinical
Toxicology **[17490]**

6728 Old McLean Village Dr.
McLean, VA 22101
Ph: (703)556-9222
Fax: (703)556-8729

Simone, Michael, President
REG - The International Roger
Waters Fan Club **[24060]**
c/o Michael Simone, President, 128
onyx dr.
128 Onyx Dr.
Watsonville, CA 95076

Simonian, Yasmin, MLS, CM,
FASAPH, President
National Accrediting Agency for Clini-
cal Laboratory Sciences **[15692]**
5600 N River Rd., Ste. 720
Rosemont, IL 60018-5119
Ph: (773)714-8880
    (847)939-3597
Fax: (773)714-8886

Simons, Barbie, President
World Health Services **[15509]**
PO Box 186
Keene, TX 76059
Ph: (817)933-2088

Simons, Daryn, President
Talent Managers Association **[1160]**
10061 Riverside Dr., Ste. 582
Toluca Lake, CA 91602-2560
Ph: (818)487-5556

Simons, Kurt, Director
The Swedenborg Project **[20613]**
c/o Washington New Church
11914 Chantilly Ln.
Mitchellville, MD 20721

Simons, Suzanne, Exec. Dir.
American Academy of Home Care
Medicine **[15275]**
8735 W Higgins Rd., Ste. 300
Chicago, IL 60631
Ph: (847)375-4719
Fax: (847)375-6395

Simons, Virgil, Founder, President
The Prostate Net **[14053]**
PO Box 2192
Secaucus, NJ 07096-2192
Toll Free: 888-477-6763
Fax: (270)294-1565

Simonton, Ann, Director, Founder,
Coord.
Media Watch **[17951]**
PO Box 618
Santa Cruz, CA 95061-0618
Ph: (831)423-6355

Simpler, Jana, Chairman
Governors Highway Safety Associa-
tion **[5812]**
444 N Capitol St. NW, Ste. 722
Washington, DC 20001
Ph: (202)789-0942
Fax: (202)789-0946

Simpson, Freddie N., President
Brotherhood of Maintenance of Way
Employees Division of the
International Brotherhood of
Teamsters **[23512]**
41475 Gardenbrook Rd.
Novi, MI 48375-1328
Ph: (248)662-2660
Fax: (248)662-2659

Simpson, Jeff, President
International Association for
Relationship Research **[7094]**
Purdue University
Dept. of Psychological Sciences
703 3rd St.
West Lafayette, IN 47907-2081

Simpson, Laurence, DDS, Gen. Sec.
General Society, Sons of the
Revolution **[20692]**
412 W Francis St.
Williamsburg, VA 23185
Ph: (757)345-0757
Toll Free: 800-593-1776
Fax: (757)345-0780

Simpson, Shawn, President
Maverick/Comet Club International
[21427]
c/o Don Comfort, Treasurer
4952 Black Run Rd.
Chillicothe, OH 45601

Simpson, Stan, Chairman
American Motorcyclist Association
[23036]
13515 Yarmouth Dr.
Pickerington, OH 43147
Ph: (614)856-1900
Toll Free: 800-262-5646
Fax: (614)856-1924

Simpson, Thomas D., President
Railway Supply Institute **[2841]**
425 3rd St. SW, Ste. 920
Washington, DC 20024
Ph: (202)347-4664
Fax: (202)347-0047

Simrany, Joseph P., President
Tea Association of the U.S.A. **[431]**
362 5th Ave., Ste. 801
New York, NY 10001
Ph: (212)986-9415
Fax: (212)697-8658

Simrany, Joseph P., President
Tea Council of the United States of
America **[432]**
362 5th Ave., Ste. 801
New York, NY 10001
Ph: (212)986-9415
Fax: (212)697-8658

Sims, Eris T., Exec. Dir.
Links Foundation, Incorporated
[12896]
1200 Massachusetts Ave. NW
Washington, DC 20005-4501
Ph: (202)842-8686
Fax: (202)842-4020

Sims, J. Robert, President
American Society of Mechanical
Engineers Auxiliary **[6830]**
2 Park Ave.
New York, NY 10016-5990
Ph: (973)882-1170
Toll Free: 800-843-2763

Sims, Jeff, President
Truck Trailer Manufacturers Associa-
tion **[334]**
7001 Heritage Village Plz., Ste. 220
Gainesville, VA 20155
Ph: (703)549-3010

Sims, Karen L., President
Colonial Rottweiler Club **[21860]**
c/o Sue Chodorov
61 Sea View Ave.
Niantic, CT 06357

Sims, Pat, President
Association of Labor Relations Agen-
cies **[23465]**
National Labor Relations Board
1099 14th St. NW
Washington, DC 20570-0001
Ph: (202)273-1067
Fax: (202)273-4270

Sims, Robert, President
Association of American Schools in
Central America, Colombia, Carib-
bean and Mexico **[8528]**

c/o Sonia Keller, Executive Director
2812 Cypress Bend Rd.
Florence, SC 29506-8353
Ph: (843)799-5754

Sinclair, David G., Director
Watch Tower Bible and Tract Society
of Pennsylvania [20222]
25 Columbia Hts.
Brooklyn, NY 11201-2483
Ph: (718)560-5000

Sinclair, Jim, Contact
Autism Network International
[13749]
PO Box 35448
Syracuse, NY 13235-5448
Ph: (315)476-2462

Sinclair, Mel, President
Clan Sinclair USA [20843]
c/o Mel Sinclair, President Emeritus
224 Bransfield Rd.
Greenville, SC 29615
Ph: (919)542-2795

Singer, Alison Tepper, Founder,
President
Autism Science Foundation [13753]
10 W 32nd St., Ste. 182
New York, NY 10001
Ph: (914)810-9100

Singer, Dale, Exec. Dir.
Renal Physicians Association
[15886]
1700 Rockville Pke., Ste. 220
Rockville, MD 20852-1631
Ph: (301)468-3515
Fax: (301)468-3511

Singer, Dave, VP
International Fortean Organization
[7014]
PO Box 50088
Baltimore, MD 21211

Singer, Diana, President
American Society of Jewelry
Historians [9629]
1333A North Ave., No. 103
New Rochelle, NY 10804
Ph: (914)235-0983
Fax: (914)235-0983

Singer, Linda R., Founder, President
Center for Dispute Settlement [4958]
1666 Connecticut Ave. NW, Ste. 525
Washington, DC 20009-1039
Ph: (202)265-9572
Fax: (202)332-3951

Singer, Paul E., Chairman
Manhattan Institute for Policy
Research [18956]
52 Vanderbilt Ave.
New York, NY 10017
Ph: (212)599-7000
Fax: (212)599-3494

Singer, Rebecca, Exec. Dir.
Coffee Kids [11333]
1 Penn Plz., Ste. 2225
New York, NY 10119

Singer, Robert H., Contact
Harvey Society [15726]
c/o M. Elizabeth Ross, PhD,
Treasurer
Weill Cornell Medical College
1300 York Ave.
New York, NY 10065
Ph: (718)270-1370
(212)746-5550

Singer, Suzanne F., Editor
Biblical Archaeology Society [5934]
4710 41st St. NW

Washington, DC 20016
Ph: (202)364-3300
Toll Free: 800-221-4644

Singh, Inder, Chairman
Global Organization of People of
Indian Origin [19474]
PO Box 560117
New York, NY 11356
Ph: (818)708-3885

Singh, Jasjit, Exec. Dir.
Sikh American Legal Defense and
Education Fund [19098]
1012 14th St. NW, Ste. 450
Washington, DC 20005
Ph: (202)393-2700
Fax: (202)318-4433

Singh, Meenakshi, Dr., Liaison
Association of Indian Pathologists in
North America [16577]
1812 Kings Isle Dr.
Plano, TX 75093-2422

Singh, Dr. Rajwant, Chairman
Sikh Council on Religion and Education [20603]
2621 University Blvd. W
Silver Spring, MD 20902
Ph: (202)460-0630
(301)946-2800

Singler, Laura, CAE, Exec. Dir.
American Academy on Communica-
tion in Healthcare [16732]
201 E Main St., Ste. 1405
Lexington, KY 40507-2004
Ph: (859)514-9211
Fax: (859)514-9207

Singleton, Knox, President
Community Coalition for Haiti
[11920]
PO Box 1222
Vienna, VA 22183
Ph: (703)880-4160

Singleton, Mark, Exec. Dir.
American Whitewater [23092]
629 W Main St.
Sylva, NC 28779
Ph: (828)586-1930
Toll Free: 866-262-8429
Fax: (828)586-2840

Sinha, Amit, Founder, Bd. Member,
President
Prana International [12562]
PO Box 362
Flourtown, PA 19031-9998
Ph: (267)270-5551

Sinha, Ashish, Prog. Dir.
Alliance for Nuclear Accountability
[18740]
c/o Nuclear Watch of New Mexico
903 W Alameda St., No. 505
Santa Fe, NM 87505-1681
Ph: (505)989-7342

Sinha, Sanjay, Director
International Alliance for the Preven-
tion of AIDS [13549]
1955 W Baseline Rd., Ste. 113-624
Mesa, AZ 85202
Ph: (480)274-3561

Sink, Kevin, President
Kiger Mesteno Association [4374]
11124 NE Halsey St., Ste. 591
Portland, OR 97220

Sinkinson, Craig A., MD, President
Mayan Medical Aid [12288]
6988 Pinehaven Rd.
Oakland, CA 94611-1018

Sinnett, William, Director
Financial Executives Research
Foundation [2166]

Financial Executives International
West Twr., 7th Fl.
1250 Headquarters Plz.
Morristown, NJ 07960
Ph: (973)765-1000
(973)765-1004
Fax: (973)765-1018

Sioui, Georges, Investigator
Community Information and
Epidemiological Technologies
[14728]
511 Avenue of the Americas, No.
132
New York, NY 10011
Ph: (212)242-3428
Fax: (212)504-0848

Sipe, Vicki L., Secretary
Association for Library Collections &
Technical Services [9686]
50 E Huron St.
Chicago, IL 60611-2795
Ph: (312)280-5037
Toll Free: 800-545-2433
Fax: (312)280-5033

Sipior, Janice C., Chairperson
Association for Computing
Machinery - Special Interest Group
on Management Information
Systems [6309]
c/o Janice C. Sipior, Chairperson
800 Lancaster Ave.
Villanova, PA 19085
Ph: (610)519-4347

Sipma, Stuart, President
National Horseshoe Pitchers Association of America [22957]
c/o Stuart Sipma, President
2826 Domino Dr.
Bismarck, ND 58503-0831
Ph: (701)258-5686

Sippl, Dan, President
Randolph-Sheppard Vendors of
America [3433]
940 Parc Helene Dr.
Marrero, LA 70072-2421
Ph: (504)328-6373
Toll Free: 800-467-5299
Fax: (504)328-6372

Siracusa, Mimi, President
Gulf Coast GTOs [21391]
429 Apache Run
Wallisville, TX 77597
Ph: (281)452-0855
Toll Free: 800-935-7663

Sirangelo, Jennifer, President, CEO
National 4-H Council [13460]
7100 Connecticut Ave.
Chevy Chase, MD 20815
Ph: (301)961-2800

Sircy, Otice, Curator, Librarian
Percussive Arts Society [9995]
110 W Washington St., Ste. A
Indianapolis, IN 46204
Ph: (317)974-4488
Fax: (317)974-4499

Sirey, Aileen Riotto, PhD,
Chairperson, Founder
National Organization of Italian-
American Women [19507]
25 W 43rd St. Ste. 1005
New York, NY 10036-7406
Ph: (212)642-2003
Fax: (212)642-2006

Sirianni, Jim, Director
American Council on Education
[7738]
1 Dupont Cir. NW
Washington, DC 20036
Ph: (202)939-9300

Siriwardana, Mrs. Kaushalya,
Founder
Helping Hands, Inc. [11023]
2918 Churchill Way
Garland, TX 75044-4626
Ph: (972)635-3903
Toll Free: 877-623-5200
Fax: (214)703-3283

Sirman, Eva, Mgr.
National Association of Disability
Representatives [19137]
PO Box 96503
Washington, DC 20090-6503
Ph: (202)822-2155
Fax: (972)245-6701

Sirois, David A., PhD, Director
International Pemphigus and Pem-
phigoid Foundation [14588]
1331 Garden Hwy., Ste. 100
Sacramento, CA 95833-9773
Ph: (916)922-1298
Toll Free: 855-473-6744

Siskel, Suzanne E., Exec. VP, COO
Asia Foundation [18936]
465 California St., 9th Fl.
San Francisco, CA 94104
Ph: (415)982-4640
Fax: (415)392-8863

Siskowski, Connie, PhD, President
American Association of Caregiving
Youth [13423]
1515 N Federal Hwy., No. 218
Boca Raton, FL 33432
Ph: (561)391-7401
Toll Free: 800-725-2512

Sisson, Rob, President
ConservAmerica [3835]
971 S Centerville Rd., PMB 139
Sturgis, MI 49091-2502
Ph: (269)651-1808

Sites, Carianne, Exec. Dir.
Therapet Animal Assisted Therapy
Foundation [17465]
PO Box 130118
Tyler, TX 75713
Ph: (903)535-2125

Sitler, Ms. Penny, Exec. Dir.
The Knitting Guild Association
[21768]
1100-H Brandywine Blvd.
Zanesville, OH 43701-7303
Ph: (740)452-4541

Siuciak, Judith A., Exec. Ofc.
American Society for Pharmacology
and Experimental Therapeutics
[16647]
9650 Rockville Pke.
Bethesda, MD 20814-3995
Ph: (301)634-7060
Fax: (301)634-7061

Sivak, Maryann, President
Carpatho-Rusyn Society [19629]
915 Dickson St.
Munhall, PA 15120-1929
Ph: (412)567-3077

Sivard, Jim, Contact
World Priorities [19011]
38664 Mt. Gilead Rd.
Leesburg, VA 20175
Ph: (703)777-4352

Sixel, Dave, President
U.S.A. Federation of Pankration Ath-
lima [22518]
11301 W 88th St.
Overland Park, KS 66214-1701
Ph: (816)728-7360
Fax: (816)222-0447

Sizemore, Don, President
Independent Medical Specialty Dealers Association **[1603]**
113 Space Pk. N
Goodlettsville, TN 37072
Toll Free: 866-463-2937
Fax: (614)467-2071

Sjeklocha, Dave, Treasurer
Professional Animal Auditor Certification Organization **[3620]**
PO Box 31
Redfield, IA 50233-0031
Ph: (402)403-0104
Fax: (402)920-6396

Skala, Suzanne, Exec. Dir.
SuperSibs! **[11277]**
660 N 1st Bank Dr.
Palatine, IL 60067
Ph: (847)462-4742
Fax: (847)984-9292

Skedsvold, Paula, Exec. Dir.
Federation of Associations in Behavioral and Brain Sciences **[6037]**
1001 Connecticut Ave. NW, Ste. 1100
Washington, DC 20036
Ph: (202)888-3949

Skeel, Mr. Joe, Exec. Dir.
Sigma Delta Chi Foundation **[23796]**
3909 N Meridian St.
Indianapolis, IN 46208
Ph: (317)927-8000
Fax: (317)920-4789

Skeel, Joe, Exec. Dir.
Society of Professional Journalists **[2723]**
Eugene Pulliam National Journalism Ctr.
3909 N Meridian St.
Indianapolis, IN 46208
Ph: (317)927-8000
Fax: (317)920-4789

Skellie, Brian, President
Association of Professional Piercers **[3198]**
PO Box 1287
Lawrence, KS 66044
Ph: (785)841-6060
Toll Free: 888-888-1277
Fax: (267)482-5650

Skelton, Shaun, PhD, Director, Founder
Africa Development Corps **[12134]**
2710 Ontario Rd. NW
Washington, DC 20009
Ph: (301)944-3370

Skiba, Thomas M., CEO
Community Associations Institute **[17972]**
6402 Arlington Blvd., Ste. 500
Falls Church, VA 22042
Ph: (703)970-9220
Toll Free: 888-224-4321
Fax: (703)970-9558

Skiba, Tom, CEO
Community Association Managers International Certification Board **[2162]**
6402 Arlington Blvd., Ste. 510
Falls Church, VA 22042
Ph: (703)970-9300
Toll Free: 866-779-2622

Skidmore, Kyle, Director
American Beefalo Association **[3588]**
9824 E YZ Ave.
Vicksburg, MI 49097
Ph: (660)347-5448
Toll Free: 800-BEEFALO

Skinner, Alexis, Exec. Sec.
National Association of Dramatic and Speech Arts, Inc. **[10261]**
c/o Dr. King Godwin, President
Grambling State University
PO Box 4276
Grambling, LA 71245
Ph: (318)274-3225

Skinner, Anna, Exec. Sec., Treasurer
Iota Lambda Sigma **[23984]**
c/o Anna Skinner, Executive Secretary-Treasurer
607 Park Way W
Oregon, OH 43616
Ph: (419)693-6860
Fax: (419)693-6859

Skinner, Cecily, President
Soft Coated Wheaten Terrier Club of America, Inc. **[21964]**
c/o Mary Ann Curtis, Treasurer
6206 Sheffield Ln. E
Fife, WA 98424-2268

Skinner, Jim, Bd. Member
National Entomology Scent Detection Canine Association **[2503]**
PO Box 121
Pleasant Mount, PA 18453

Skinner, John H., PhD, Officer
Solid Waste Association of North America **[5846]**
1100 Wayne Ave., Ste. 650
Silver Spring, MD 20910
Toll Free: 800-467-9262
Fax: (301)589-7068

Skinner, Kathy, President
Pacific Dragon Boat Association **[22660]**
c/o Diane McCabe, Treasurer
607 30th St.
Hermosa Beach, CA 90254

Skinner, Dr. Leane, President
Association for Career and Technical Education Research **[8734]**
c/o Dr. Leane Skinner, President
Dept. of Curriculum and Teaching
Auburn University
5040 Haley
Auburn, AL 36849-5212
Ph: (334)844-3823

Skivolocke, Daniel, VP
Professional Car Society **[21481]**
64 Mudcut Rd.
Lafayette, NJ 07848-4607

Skoff, Ilana Hoffer, MA, Exec. Dir.
Milestones Autism Resources **[13772]**
23880 Commerce Pk., Ste. 2
Beachwood, OH 44122
Ph: (216)464-7600
Fax: (216)464-7602

Skog, Judith, Secretary
American Institute of Biological Sciences **[6067]**
1313 Dolley Madison Blvd., Ste. 402
McLean, VA 22101
Ph: (703)790-1745
(202)628-1500
Toll Free: 800-992-2427
Fax: (703)790-2672

Skold, Lee, Chairman
Outward Bound **[13206]**
910 Jackson St., Ste. 150
Golden, CO 80401-1977
Toll Free: 866-467-7651

Skor, Emily, CEO
Growth Energy **[6488]**
777 N Capitol St. NE, Ste. 805

Washington, DC 20002
Ph: (202)545-4000
Fax: (202)545-4001

Skrdla, Lt. Wayne, Mem.
International Association of Marine Investigators **[2245]**
711 Medford Ctr., No. 419
Medford, OR 97504
Ph: (573)691-9569

Skrebes, Robyn, Founder
Child Protection International **[10902]**
267 19th Ave. S
Minneapolis, MN 55455-0499
Ph: (612)624-8384

Skutnik, Lisa, President
Multiple Sclerosis Coalition **[15956]**
706 Haddonfield Rd.
Cherry Hill, NJ 08002
Toll Free: 800-532-7667
Fax: (856)661-9797

Skvoretz, John, President
International Network for Social Network Analysis **[7167]**
c/o JulNet Solutions, LLC
1404 1/2 Adams Ave.
Huntington, WV 25704
Ph: (304)208-8001
Fax: (304)523-9701

Skye, Elysia, Founder
Elysia Skye Breast Cancer Organization **[13964]**
5805 Whitsett Ave., No. 211
Valley Village, CA 91607
Ph: (310)255-0460

Slack, David, Chmn. of the Bd.
Canadian-American Business Council **[619]**
1900 K St. NW, Ste. 100
Washington, DC 20006
Ph: (202)496-7255

Slafsky, Ted, President, CEO
Safety Net Hospitals for Pharmaceutical Access **[16684]**
1101 15th St. NW, Ste. 910
Washington, DC 20005
Ph: (202)552-5850
Fax: (202)552-5868

Slate, Stephen, Exec. Dir.
Institute for Mediation and Conflict Resolution **[4959]**
384 E 149th St., Ste. 330
Bronx, NY 10455-3908
Ph: (718)585-1190

Slate, William K., II, CEO, President
American Arbitration Association **[4955]**
1633 Broadway, 10th Fl.
New York, NY 10019
Ph: (212)716-5800
Toll Free: 800-778-7879

Slate, William K., III, Director
Inter-American Commercial Arbitration Commission **[4960]**
c/o American Arbitration Association, 140 West 51st St.
140 W 51st St.
New York, NY 10020-1203
Ph: (212)484-4000
Fax: (212)765-4874

Slater, Dennis, Secretary
Association of Equipment Manufacturers **[166]**
6737 W Washington St., Ste. 2400
Milwaukee, WI 53214-5647
Ph: (414)272-0943
Toll Free: 866-AEM-0442
Fax: (414)272-1170

Slater, Joe, Secretary
Association of American Plant Food Control Officials **[4943]**
c/o April Hunt, President
PO Box 30017
Lansing, MI 48909
Ph: (517)284-5644
Fax: (517)335-4540

Slater, Michael, President, Exec. Dir.
Project Vote! **[18920]**
1420 K St., Ste. 700
Washington, DC 20005
Ph: (202)546-4173
Fax: (202)733-4762

Slaughter, Chris, President, CEO
Thanks-Giving Square **[20615]**
1627 Pacific Ave.
Dallas, TX 75201
Ph: (214)969-1977

Slauterbeck, Julie, Treasurer
National Toy Fox Terrier Association **[21925]**
c/o Julie Slauterbeck, Treasurer
22481 Bohn Rd.
Belleville, MI 48111
Ph: (734)652-5184

Slay, Joe, Chmn. of the Bd.
FightSMA **[17270]**
8016 Staples Mill Rd.
Richmond, VA 23228-2713
Ph: (703)299-1144

Slayter, Doreen, President
Automotive Content Professionals Network **[309]**
7101 Wisconsin Ave., Ste. 1300
Bethesda, MD 20814-3415
Ph: (301)654-6664

Slazer, Frank A., Director
American Astronautical Society **[5856]**
6352 Rolling Mill Pl., Ste. 102
Springfield, VA 22152-2370
Ph: (703)866-0020
Fax: (703)866-3526

Slee, Valerie, RN, Chairperson
The Mastocytosis Society **[14593]**
PO Box 129
Hastings, NE 68902-0129
Ph: (508)842-3080
Fax: (508)842-2051

Sleeper, Steve, Exec. Dir.
Professional Beauty Association **[928]**
15825 N 71st St., No. 100
Scottsdale, AZ 85254
Ph: (480)281-0424
Toll Free: 800-468-2274
Fax: (480)905-0708

Sleeter, John, President
Wolf Haven International **[3968]**
3111 Offut Lake Rd. SE
Tenino, WA 98589
Ph: (360)264-4695
Toll Free: 800-448-9653
Fax: (360)264-4639

Slepian, Prof. Marvin, President
International Society for Rotary Blood Pumps **[14130]**
Baylor College of Medicine
1 Baylor Plz., BMC M390
Houston, TX 77030
Ph: (713)798-6309
Fax: (713)798-8439

Sligar, James S., Secretary
Family Care International **[17196]**
45 Broadway, Ste. 320
New York, NY 10006
Ph: (212)941-5300
Fax: (212)941-5563

Sligh, Charles
International Lawrence Durrell
 Society [9057]
c/o Paul H. Lorenz, Secretary/
 Treasurer
5601 W Barraque St.
White Hall, AR 71602
Ph: (870)575-8618
Fax: (870)575-8040

Slikkers, Randall G., Exec. Dir.
Consortia of Administrators for Na-
 tive American Rehabilitation
 [19577]
1775 Eye Street NW, Ste. 1150
Washington, DC 20006
Ph: (202)587-2741
Toll Free: 877-260-8098

Slingerland, Dixon, VP
Youth Policy Institute [19012]
634 S Spring St., 10th Fl.
Los Angeles, CA 90014
Ph: (213)688-2802
Toll Free: 800-999-6877

Slive, Mike, Commissioner
Southeastern Conference [23254]
2201 Richard Arrington Jr. Blvd. N
Birmingham, AL 35203-1103
Ph: (205)458-3000

Slivinski, Jeremy, Secretary
Alpha Kappa Lambda [23884]
354 Gradle Dr.
Carmel, IN 46032
Ph: (317)564-8003
Toll Free: 866-556-8719

Slivinski, Krystal Geyer, Exec. Dir.
Alpha Sigma Alpha [23946]
9002 Vincennes Cir.
Indianapolis, IN 46268-3018
Ph: (317)871-2920
Fax: (317)871-2924

Sliwa, Curtis, President, Founder
Alliance of Guardian Angels [11499]
982 E 89th St.
Brooklyn, NY 11236
Ph: (718)649-2607

Sloan, Debra, President
National Association of State
 Aquaculture Coordinators [3645]
c/o Joe Myers, Secretary-Treasurer
PO Box 330
Trenton, NJ 08625
Ph: (609)984-2502
Fax: (609)633-7229

Sloan, Katie Smith, Exec. Dir.
International Association of Homes
 and Services for the Ageing
 [10510]
2519 Connecticut Ave. NW
Washington, DC 20008-1520
Ph: (202)508-9468
 (202)508-9472

Sloan, Kenneth Edwin, Exec. Dir.
Stanislav & Christina Grof Founda-
 tion [13626]
PO Box 400267
Cambridge, MA 02140
Ph: (617)674-2474
Fax: (617)674-2474

Sloan, Melanie, Exec. Dir.
Citizens for Responsibility and Ethics
 in Washington [18195]
1400 Eye St. NW, Ste. 450
Washington, DC 20005
Ph: (202)408-5565

Sloane, William M., PhD, President
Council on Chiropractic Practice
 [14267]

2950 N Dobson Rd., Ste. 1
Chandler, AZ 85224-1819

Slocomb, Mark, Chairman
National Children's Cancer Society
 [14023]
500 N Broadway, Ste. 800
Saint Louis, MO 63102
Ph: (314)241-1600
Fax: (314)241-1996

Slocumb, Bill, Treasurer
Episcopal Communicators [20100]
PO Box 6885
San Antonio, TX 78209

Slome, Jesse, Contact
American Association for Long-Term
 Care Insurance [1826]
3835 E Thousand Oaks Blvd., Ste.
 336
Westlake Village, CA 91362-3637
Ph: (818)597-3227
 (818)597-3205
Fax: (818)597-3206

Slome, Jesse, Exec. Dir.
American Association for Medicare
 Supplement Insurance [15418]
3835 E Thousand Oaks Blvd., Ste.
 336
Westlake Village, CA 91362
Ph: (818)597-3205

Slonager, Kathleen, President
Homeopathic Nurses Association
 [15287]
c/o Margo Cohen, Membership
 Secretary
3737 Moraga Ave., No. A-207
San Diego, CA 92117

Slotnick, Howard, Treasurer
National Maritime Historical Society
 [9783]
5 John Walsh Blvd.
Peekskill, NY 10566
Ph: (914)737-7878
Toll Free: 800-221-6647
Fax: (914)737-7816

Sluijter, Jaap, Exec. Dir.
Krishnamurti Foundation of America
 [12008]
1130 Mc Andrew Rd.
Ojai, CA 93023
Ph: (805)646-2726

Slupski, Charles, Chairman
American Polygraph Association
 [5237]
PO Box 8037
Chattanooga, TN 37414-0037
Ph: (423)892-3992
Toll Free: 800-272-8037
Fax: (423)894-5435

Slusar, John, Editor, Contact
Chrysler Town and Country Owners
 Registry [21354]
3006 S 40th St.
Milwaukee, WI 53215
Ph: (414)384-1843
Fax: (414)384-1843

Small, Aaron, President
National Coil Coating Association
 [746]
1300 Sumner Ave.
Cleveland, OH 44115
Ph: (216)241-7333
Fax: (216)241-0105

Small, Rev. Andrew, OMI, Director
Missionary Childhood Association
 [19863]
70 W 36th St., 8th Fl.
New York, NY 10018
Ph: (212)563-8700
Fax: (212)563-8725

Small, Rev. Andrew, OMI, Director
Pontifical Mission Societies in the
 United States [19897]
70 W 36th St., 8th Fl.
New York, NY 10018
Ph: (212)563-8700
Fax: (212)563-8725

Small, Rev. Andrew, OMI, Director
Society for the Propagation of the
 Faith [19910]
70 W 36th St., 8th Fl.
New York, NY 10018-8007
Ph: (212)563-8700
Fax: (212)563-8725

Small, Arnie, President
American Art Pottery Association
 [8829]
c/o Marie Latta, Trustee
2115 W Fulliam Ave.
Muscatine, IA 52761

Small, David, Exec. Dir.
Variety - The Children's Charity
 International [11178]
4601 Wilshire Blvd., Ste. 260
Los Angeles, CA 90010
Ph: (323)934-4688
Fax: (323)658-8789

Small, Rhonda, President
Esophageal Cancer Awareness As-
 sociation [13965]
PO Box 55071
Boston, MA 02205-5071
Toll Free: 800-601-0613

Small, Theodore W., Jr., Chairman
American Bar Association Commis-
 sion on Homelessness and
 Poverty [11947]
1050 Connecticut Ave. NW, Ste. 400
Washington, DC 20036
Ph: (202)662-1693
Fax: (202)638-3844

Smalling, Tom, PhD, Exec. Dir.
Committee on Accreditation for
 Respiratory Care [17440]
1248 Harwood Rd.
Bedford, TX 76021-4244
Ph: (817)283-2835
Fax: (817)354-8519

Smart, Audrey D.F., Exec. Dir.,
 Founder
National Association of Blessed Bil-
 lionaires [7556]
199 N Columbus Ave.
Mount Vernon, NY 10553
Ph: (914)559-8765

Smart, Mary Ann, President
Italian Greyhound Club of America
 [21905]

Smart, Tom, President
Emerald Society of the Federal Law
 Enforcement Agencies [19534]
PO Box 16413
Rochester, NY 14616-0413

Smeal, Eleanor, President
Feminist Majority Foundation
 [18207]
1600 Wilson Blvd., Ste. 801
Arlington, VA 22209
Ph: (703)522-2214
Fax: (703)522-2219

Smeallie, Peter H., Exec. Dir.
American Rock Mechanics Associa-
 tion [3181]
600 Woodland Ter.
Alexandria, VA 22302-3319
Ph: (703)683-1808
Fax: (703)997-6112

Smeallie, Shawn, Exec. Dir.
Coalition for Anabolic Steroid Precur-
 sor and Ephedra Regulation
 [17281]
2099 Pennsylvania Ave. NW, Ste.
 850
Washington, DC 20006
Ph: (202)419-2521

Smedley, Gloria, Treasurer,
 Secretary
National Society for the Preservation
 of Covered Bridges [9421]
c/o Jennifer Caswell, Membership
 Chair
535 2nd NH Tpke.
Hillsborough, NH 03244-4601

Smets, Eva, Exec. Dir.
Watchlist on Children and Armed
 Conflict [11182]
122 E 42nd St., 16th Fl., Ste. 1620
New York, NY 10168-1289
Ph: (212)972-0695
Fax: (212)972-0701

Smidt, Nina, President
American Friends of Bucerius
 [19442]
10 Rockefeller Plz., 16th Fl.
New York, NY 10020
Ph: (212)713-7651

Smigel, Irwin, DDS, President,
 Founder
American Society for Dental Aesthet-
 ics [14414]
635 Madison Ave.
New York, NY 10022-1009
Ph: (212)371-4575
Toll Free: 888-988-ASDA
Fax: (212)308-5182

Smigel, Libby, PhD, Advisor
Dance Heritage Coalition [9252]
1111 16th St. NW, Ste. 300
Washington, DC 20036
Ph: (202)223-8392
Fax: (202)833-2686

Smiley, Stephen, Mem.
University of Virginia Alumni As-
 sociation [19367]
211 Emmet St.
Charlottesville 22904
Ph: (434)243-9000

Smiley, Wynn R., CEO
Alpha Tau Omega [23888]
1 N Pennsylvania St., 12th Fl.
Indianapolis, IN 46204
Ph: (317)684-1865
Fax: (317)684-1862

Smiley, Wynn R., President
Fraternity Executives Association
 [23756]
3201 E 56th St.
Indianapolis, IN 46220
Ph: (317)490-1924

Sminkey, Patrice V., CEO
Commission for Case Manager
 Certification [15117]
1120 Route 73, Ste. 200
Mount Laurel, NJ 08054
Ph: (856)380-6836
Fax: (856)439-0525

Smirnow, John P., Sec. Gen.
Global Solar Council [7201]
1717 K St. NW, Ste. 1120
Washington, DC 20006

Smith, Alex, Chairman
College Republican National Committee [19037]
1500 K St. NW, Ste. 325

Washington, DC 20005-1265
Ph: (202)608-1411
Fax: (202)608-1429

Smith, Alex, President
Student Osteopathic Medical As-
sociation [16526]
142 E Ontario St.
Chicago, IL 60611-2864
Ph: (312)202-8193
Toll Free: 800-621-1773
Fax: (312)202-8200

Smith, Alison, President
American Quaternary Association
[6892]
c/o Colin Long, Secretary
800 Algoma Blvd.
Oshkosh, WI 54901-8642
Ph: (920)424-2182

Smith, Alison, Advisor
C-Change [13913]
2445 L St., NW, Ste. 601
Washington, DC 20037
Ph: (202)753-9791
Fax: (708)430-1191

Smith, Amy, CEO
American Berkshire Association
[4705]
2637 Yeager Rd.
West Lafayette, IN 47906
Ph: (765)497-3618
Fax: (765)497-2959

Smith, Amy, President
HandsOn Network [13296]
600 Means St., Ste. 210
Atlanta, GA 30318
Ph: (404)979-2900
Fax: (404)979-2901

Smith, Amy, Contact
INCOMPAS [3417]
1200 G St. NW, Ste. 350
Washington, DC 20005
Ph: (202)296-6650
Fax: (202)296-7585

Smith, Amy, Secretary
International Corporate Chefs As-
sociation [700]
PO Box 2005
Winter Park, FL 32790-2005
Ph: (407)539-1459
Fax: (407)985-4538

Smith, Amy, Secretary
Sustainable Furnishings Council
[1489]
100 E King St., Ste. 1
Edenton, NC 27932
Ph: (252)368-1098

Smith, Anita M., President
Children's AIDS Fund International
[10536]
PO Box 16433
Washington, DC 20041
Ph: (703)433-1560
Fax: (703)433-1561

Smith, Arlene, President
International Association of Duncan
Certified Ceramic Teachers
[21581]
3434 W Earll Dr., Ste. 101
Phoenix, AZ 85017
Ph: (480)264-6982

Smith, Arthur, Chairman
National Council for Public-Private
Partnerships [18287]
2020 K St. NW, Ste. 650
Washington, DC 20006
Ph: (202)962-0555
Fax: (202)289-7499

Smith, Barbara R., CAE, Exec. Dir.
American Thyroid Association
[17480]
6066 Leesburg Pke., Ste. 550
Falls Church, VA 22041
Ph: (703)998-8890
Fax: (703)998-8893

Smith, Barbie, Secretary
United Professional Horsemen's As-
sociation [4416]
4059 Iron Works Pky., Ste. 2
Lexington, KY 40511
Ph: (859)231-5070
Fax: (859)255-2774

Smith, Bernadine, Founder
Friends of Patrick Henry [10326]
PO Box 1776
Hanford, CA 93232
Ph: (559)584-5209
Fax: (559)584-4084

Smith, Bernadine, Founder
Second Amendment Committee
[5220]
PO Box 1776
Hanford, CA 93232
Ph: (559)584-5209
Fax: (559)584-4084

Smith, Betsy, President
Lesbian and Gay Band Association
[9947]
1718 M St. NW, No. 500
Washington, DC 20036-4504
Ph: (202)656-5422

Smith, Bill, Exec. Dir.
Industrial Foundation of America
[1092]
179 Enterprise Pky., Ste. 102
Boerne, TX 78006
Ph: (830)249-7899
Toll Free: 800-592-1433
Fax: (800)628-2397

Smith, Bob, President
National Association of Field Training
Officers [5491]
7942 W Bell Rd., Ste. C5, No. 463
Glendale, AZ 85308

Smith, Bob, VP
Society of Wood Science and
Technology [4218]
PO Box 6155
Monona, WI 53716-6155
Ph: (608)577-1342
Fax: (608)254-2769

Smith, Brad, Chairman
Kids in Need of Defense [5535]
1300 L St. NW, Ste. 1100
Washington, DC 20005
Ph: (202)824-8680

Smith, Brad, Exec. Dir.
Percussion Marketing Council [2435]
PO Box 33252
Cleveland, OH 44133
Ph: (440)582-7006
Fax: (440)230-1346

Smith, Bradley A., Founder, Chair-
man
Center for Competitive Politics
[17880]
124 S West St., Ste. 201
Alexandria, VA 22314
Ph: (703)894-6800
Fax: (703)894-6811

Smith, Bram, Exec. Dir.
Loan Syndications and Trading As-
sociation [404]
366 Madison Ave., 15th Fl.
New York, NY 10017
Ph: (212)880-3000
Fax: (212)880-3040

Smith, Brian, President
Editorial Photographers [2578]
PO Box 51192
Seattle, WA 98115

Smith, Brian, Founder, President
Helping Assist Nepal's Disabled
[11602]
315 Laurelwood Dr.
Jacksonville, OR 97530

Smith, Brian K., Founder
Educators Serving the Community
[7808]
9701 Apollo Dr., Ste. 301
Largo, MD 20774-4783
Ph: (301)498-2899
    (301)584-3179

Smith, Bruce, President
Glass Molders, Pottery, Plastics, and
Allied Workers International Union
[23422]
608 E Baltimore Pke.
Media, PA 19063-0607
Ph: (610)565-5051
Fax: (610)565-0983

Smith, Carole, Editor
Scotch-Irish Society of the United
States of America [20997]
PO Box 53
Media, PA 19063

Smith, Cary, Treasurer
International Ground Source Heat
Pump Association [1627]
1201 S Innovation Way Dr., Ste. 400
Stillwater, OK 74074-1583
Ph: (405)744-5175
Toll Free: 800-626-4747
Fax: (405)744-5283

Smith, Cate K., Exec. Dir.
Education Law Association [5525]
2121 Euclid Ave. LL 212
Cleveland, OH 44115-2214
Ph: (216)523-7377
    (937)229-3589
Fax: (216)687-5284

Smith, Charlie, VP, Treasurer
Brewery Collectibles Club of America
[21628]
747 Merus Ct.
Fenton, MO 63026-2092
Ph: (636)343-6486

Smith, Christie, President
Retail Print Music Dealers Associa-
tion [2438]
14070 Proton Rd., Ste. 100
Dallas, TX 75244-3601
Ph: (972)233-9107
Fax: (972)490-4219

Smith, Chuck, President
National Cutting Horse Association
[4381]
260 Bailey Ave.
Fort Worth, TX 76107
Ph: (817)244-6188
Fax: (817)244-2015

Smith, D. L., Chairman
Associated Specialty Contractors
[855]
3 Bethesda Metro Ctr., Ste. 1100
Bethesda, MD 20814

Smith, Dan, 1st VP
Council of Citizens With Low Vision
International [11583]
1703 N Beauregard St., Ste. 420
Alexandria, VA 22311-1764
Toll Free: 800-733-2258

Smith, Dr. Darrell, Exec. Dir.
Global Environmental Relief [11661]
PO Box 81628

Conyers, GA 30013
Ph: (770)679-0942

Smith, Darrell L., Exec. Dir.
International Window Film Associa-
tion [540]
PO Box 3871
Martinsville, VA 24115
Ph: (276)666-4932

Smith, Dave, Exec. Dir.
International Federation of Leather
Guilds [2082]
c/o David Smith, Executive Director
10 Park Pl.
Mansfield, TX 76063
Ph: (817)453-2386

Smith, Dave, Secretary
Phi Kappa Sigma [23912]
2 Timber Dr.
Chester Springs, PA 19425
Ph: (610)469-3282
Fax: (610)469-3286

Smith, Dave, Liaison
Society for a Science of Clinical
Psychology [16944]
PO Box 1082
Niwot, CO 80544
Ph: (303)652-3126
Fax: (303)652-2723

Smith, David, V. Chmn. of the Bd.
Pine Creek Railroad [22410]
New Jersey Museum of Transporta-
tion, Inc.
PO Box 622
Farmingdale, NJ 07727-0622
Ph: (732)938-5524

Smith, David, President
Portuguese Water Dog Club of
America [21947]
20217 NE 163rd St.
Woodinville, WA 98077-9446

Smith, Dennis, President
Coalition of Jamaican Organizations
[12213]
351 Massachusetts Ave.
Boston, MA 02115
Ph: (617)266-8604
Fax: (617)266-0185

Smith, Dennis, President
Scholastic Rowing Association of
America [23112]

Smith, Diane, Office Mgr.
University of Colorado at Boulder |
Natural Hazards Center [6890]
1440 15th St.
Boulder, CO 80309
Ph: (303)492-6818
Fax: (303)492-2151

Smith, Domenic, President
AIESEC United States [7540]
11 Hanover Sq., Ste. 1700
New York, NY 10005
Ph: (212)757-3774

Smith, Don, Founder, Director
Village Empowerment [11457]
PO Box 720004
Atlanta, GA 30358
Ph: (404)290-1354

Smith, Brig. Gen. (Ret.) Donald B.,
Chairman
American Security Council Founda-
tion [19086]
1250 24th St. NW, Ste. 300
Washington, DC 20037
Ph: (202)263-3661
Fax: (202)263-3662

Smith, Donna, President
Keeshond Club of America [21908]
c/o Donna Smith, President

652 Grafton Hills Dr.
Grafton, IL 62037

Smith, Donna, Exec. Asst.
Society for Imaging Science and
Technology **[7294]**
7003 Kilworth Ln.
Springfield, VA 22151
Ph: (703)642-9090
Fax: (703)642-9094

Smith, Douglas, Director
PRBA - The Rechargeable Battery
Association **[1059]**
1776 K St., 4th Fl.
Washington, DC 20006
Ph: (202)719-4978

Smith, Drew, Exec. Dir.
Friends Council on Education **[8483]**
1507 Cherry St.
Philadelphia, PA 19102
Ph: (215)241-7245
(215)241-7289
Fax: (215)241-7299

Smith, Edwin, VP
Vietnam Security Police Association
[21162]
c/o Paul Shave, Membership
Chairperson
2909 Sol De Vida NW
Albuquerque, NM 87120
Ph: (501)831-9401

Smith, Elton, President
Worldwide Friendship International
[21743]
3607 Briarstone Rd.
Randallstown, MD 21133-4232
Ph: (410)922-2795

Smith, Emily, Exec. Dir. (Actg.)
Labor and Employment Relations
Association **[23467]**
c/o Emily Smith, Interim Executive
Director
121 Labor & Employment Relations
Bldg.
School of Labor & Employment
Relations
University of Illinois at Urbana-
Champaign
504 E Armory Ave.
Champaign, IL 61820
Ph: (217)333-0072
Fax: (217)265-5130

Smith, F. Aaron, Exec. Dir.
National Cannabis Industry Associa-
tion **[18648]**
PO Box 78062
Washington, DC 20013
Toll Free: 888-683-5650
Fax: (888)683-5670

Smith, Frank, President
American Orchid Society **[6132]**
10901 Old Cutler Rd.
Coral Gables, FL 33156
Ph: (305)740-2010
Fax: (305)740-2011

Smith, Frederick Madison, President
National Society of Madison Family
Descendants **[20987]**
c/o Frederick Madison Smith,
President
1180 Peachtree St., Ste. 1700
Atlanta, GA 30309-7525
Ph: (404)572-4714

Smith, Mr. Gar, Editor
Environmentalists Against War
[19234]
PO Box 27
Berkeley, CA 94701
Ph: (650)223-3306

Smith, Gary A., Exec. Dir.
National Board for Respiratory Care
[17455]
18000 W 105th St.
Olathe, KS 66061-7543
Ph: (913)895-4900
Toll Free: 888-341-4811
Fax: (913)895-4650

Smith, Mr. Gary C., CEO, President
National Association for the
Exchange of Industrial Resources
[7826]
560 McClure St.
Galesburg, IL 61401
Toll Free: 800-562-0955

Smith, Gary M., President
Genealogical Speakers Guild
[10174]
PO Box 152987
Cape Coral, FL 33915

Smith, Gary, President
Metal Building Contractors and Erec-
tors Association **[2199]**
PO Box 499
Shawnee Mission, KS 66201
Ph: (913)432-3800
Toll Free: 800-866-6722
Fax: (913)432-3803

Smith, Gary, President
Metal Buildings Institute **[545]**
PO Box 4308
Bethlehem, PA 18018
Ph: (484)239-3337

Smith, Gary, Treasurer
World Piano Competition **[10026]**
1241 Elm St.
Cincinnati, OH 45202-7531
Ph: (513)744-3501
Fax: (513)744-3504

Smith, Gene A., Treasurer
Society for Historians of the Early
American Republic **[9516]**
3355 Woodland Walk
Philadelphia, PA 19104-4531
Ph: (215)746-5393

Smith, Gene, President
North American Society for Oceanic
History **[9776]**
Dept. of History
Texas Christian University
Box 297260
Fort Worth, TX 76129

Smith, Geoffrey, VP
North American Ski Joring Associa-
tion **[23248]**
PO Box 1602
Whitefish, MT 59937
Ph: (406)261-7464

Smith, George, Contact
Cherry Marketing Institute **[4231]**
12800 Escanaba Dr., Ste. A
Dewitt, MI 48820

Smith, Georggina, President
Association of Public-Safety Com-
munications Officials International
[5744]
351 N Williamson Blvd.
Daytona Beach, FL 32114-1112
Ph: (386)322-2500
Toll Free: 888-272-6911
Fax: (386)322-2501

Smith, Gladys, Admin. Asst.
Catholic News Service **[2670]**
3211 4th St. NE
Washington, DC 20017
Ph: (202)541-3250
Fax: (202)541-3255

Smith, Glenn, Fac. Memb.
International Association of Applied
Control Theory **[6039]**
643 Barrocliff Rd.
Clemmons, NC 27012-8543
Ph: (336)813-8484

Smith, Gordon H., President, CEO
National Association of Broadcasters
[470]
1771 N St. NW
Washington, DC 20036
Ph: (202)429-5300
(202)429-5490

Smith, Gordon, Exec. Dir., COO
United States Tennis Association
[23309]
70 W Red Oak Ln., 4th Fl.
White Plains, NY 10604
Ph: (914)697-2300
Fax: (914)694-2402

Smith, Greg, V. Chmn. of the Bd.
Common Ground Alliance **[12818]**
2300 Wilson Blvd., Ste. 310
Arlington, VA 22201
Ph: (703)836-1709

Smith, Gregory A., Chairman,
President
Apollo Society **[20667]**
PO Box 61206
Honolulu, HI 96839-61206

Smith, Gregory, PhD, President
Baltimore and Ohio Railroad Histori-
cal Society **[10179]**
5620 Southwestern Blvd.
Baltimore, MD 21227-0725
Ph: (410)247-8165

Smith, Gregory V., President
Association of Programs for Female
Offenders **[11520]**
c/o Judy Anderson, Treasurer
PO Box 5293
Columbia, SC 29250-5293

Smith, Heather, President
Optical Women's Association **[6950]**
14070 Proton Rd., Ste. 100, LB9
Dallas, TX 75244
Ph: (972)233-9107

Smith, J. Michael, President
Home School Legal Defense As-
sociation **[7828]**
PO Box 3000
Purcellville, VA 20134
Ph: (540)338-5600
Fax: (540)338-2733

Smith, J. W., Director
American Fox Terrier Club **[21810]**
6838 Lake Shore Rd.
Derby, NY 14047-9749

Smith, Jacquelyn, RN, President
American Association of Managed
Care Nurses **[16091]**
4435 Waterfront Dr., Ste. 101
Glen Allen, VA 23060
Ph: (804)747-9698
Fax: (804)747-5316

Smith, James Allen, Chairman
Robert Sterling Clark Foundation
[9227]
135 E 64th St.
New York, NY 10065
Ph: (212)288-8900
Fax: (212)288-1033

Smith, James, Secretary
American Association for Aerosol
Research **[6177]**
12100 Sunset Hills Rd., Ste. 130

Reston, VA 20190
Ph: (703)437-4377
Toll Free: 800-485-3106

Smith, James, DO, Treasurer
American Board of Clinical Metal
Toxicology **[17492]**
c/o James Smith, Treasurer
367 Hennepin Dr.
Maineville, OH 45039
Ph: (513)942-3226
Fax: (513)942-3934

Smith, James, President
International Coleman Collectors
Club **[21672]**
c/o Leonard Johnson, Treasurer
PO Box 122
Okemah, OK 74859

Smith, James P., MA, Exec. Dir.
American International Health Alli-
ance **[15134]**
1225 Eye St. NW, Ste. 205
Washington, DC 20005
Ph: (202)789-1136
Fax: (202)789-1277

Smith, James, President
United States Association for Energy
Economics **[6514]**
28790 Chagrin Blvd., Ste. 350
Cleveland, OH 44122-4642
Ph: (216)464-2785
Fax: (216)464-2768

Smith, James Wayne, President
Jim Smith Society **[19658]**
c/o Jim Smith, Membership Chairman
256 Lake Meade Dr.
East Berlin, PA 17316-9374

Smith, Janeen, President
National Black Women's Society
[13388]
PO Box 240907
Dorchester, MA 02124

Smith, Janellen, President
Pacific Dermatologic Association
[14510]
575 Market St., Ste. 2125
San Francisco, CA 94105
Toll Free: 888-388-8815
Fax: (415)764-4915

Smith, Janita, President
International Andalusian and Lus-
itano Horse Association **[4361]**
101 Carnoustie N, No. 200
Birmingham, AL 35242
Ph: (205)995-8900
Fax: (205)995-8966

Smith, Jeanne, President
National Criminal Justice Association
[11540]
720 7th St. NW, 3rd Fl.
Washington, DC 20001
Ph: (202)628-8550
Fax: (202)448-1723

Smith, Jeff, Chairman
United Indians of All Tribes Founda-
tion **[18714]**
5011 Bernie Whitebear Way
Seattle, WA 98199
Ph: (206)285-4425

Smith, Jenean, Director
Grid Alternatives' International
Program **[7202]**
1171 Ocean Ave., Ste. 200
Oakland, CA 94608
Ph: (510)731-1310
Fax: (510)225-2585

Smith, Jennifer, Exec. Dir.
International Legal Foundation
[5534]

111 John St., Ste. 1040
New York, NY 10038
Ph: (212)608-1188

Smith, Jim, Director
United Braford Breeders [3758]
Box 358
5380 Old Bullard Rd. Ste. 600
Tyler, TX 75703
Ph: (904)563-1816

Smith, John, Accountant
Institute for Resource and Security
   Studies [18987]
27 Ellsworth Ave.
Cambridge, MA 02139
Ph: (617)491-5177
Fax: (617)491-6904

Smith, John K., President, CEO
Association of Retired Americans
   [12755]
6505 E 82nd St., No. 130
Indianapolis, IN 46250
Toll Free: 800-806-6160
Fax: (317)915-2510

Smith, Joyce E., CEO
National Association for College
   Admission Counseling [7449]
1050 N Highland St., Ste. 400
Arlington, VA 22201-2197
Ph: (703)836-2222
Toll Free: 800-822-6285
Fax: (703)243-9375

Smith, Judi, VP
Association of Medical Diagnostics
   Manufacturers [3025]
c/o Leif Olsen, Director
Columbia Sq.
555 13th St. NW
Washington, DC 20004

Smith, Mrs. Julia Ann, Founder
Families with Autism Spectrum
   Disorders [13764]
PO Box 269
Milford, OH 45150
Ph: (513)444-4979

Smith, Karen, Exec. Asst.
Judge David L. Bazelon Center for
   Mental Health Law [17878]
1101 15th St. NW, Ste. 1212
Washington, DC 20005
Ph: (202)467-5730
Fax: (202)223-0409

Smith, Karen, Exec. Dir.
International Morab Registry [4368]
S 101 W 34628 Highway LO
Eagle, WI 53119
Ph: (262)594-3667

Smith, Kathy, President
National Blood Clot Alliance [14134]
8321 Old Courthouse Rd., Ste. 255
Vienna, VA 22182
Ph: (703)935-8845
Toll Free: 877-4NO-CLOT

Smith, Ms. Kay Johnson, CEO,
   President
Animal Agriculture Alliance [1316]
2101 Wilson Blvd., Ste. 916-B
Arlington, VA 22201
Ph: (703)562-5160

Smith, Kevin, President, CEO
Council of Supply Chain Manage-
   ment Professionals [3468]
333 E Butterfield Rd., Ste. 140
Lombard, IL 60148
Ph: (630)574-0985
Fax: (630)574-0989

Smith, Kevin P., Exec. Dir.
Academy of Osseointegration
   [14368]

85 W Algonquin Rd., Ste. 550
Arlington Heights, IL 60005
Ph: (847)439-1919
Toll Free: 800-656-7736
Fax: (847)427-9656

Smith, Kris, President
Scottish Deerhound Club of America
   [21958]
c/o Wendy Fast, Membership
   Secretary
8406 Green Rd.
Dansville, NY 14437

Smith, Larry, Dir. of Indl. Rel.
American Mosquito Control Associa-
   tion [4522]
1120 Route 73, Ste. 200
Mount Laurel, NJ 08054
Ph: (856)439-9222
Fax: (856)439-0525

Smith, Leslie M., Chmn. of the Bd.
SeniorNet [8674]
5237 Summerlin Commons Blvd.,
   Ste. 314
Fort Myers, FL 33907
Ph: (239)275-2202
Fax: (239)275-2501

Smith, Linda, Founder, President
Shared Hope International [13416]
PO Box 65337
Vancouver, WA 98665
Ph: (360)693-8100
   (703)351-8062
Toll Free: 866-437-5433

Smith, Lois, Mgr.
Public Works Historical Society
   [9507]
2345 Grand Blvd., Ste. 700
Kansas City, MO 64108-2625
Ph: (816)472-6100
Toll Free: 800-848-APWA
Fax: (816)472-1610

Smith, Loukie, President
Model A Ford Foundation [21436]
PO Box 95151
Nonantum, MA 02495-0151

Smith, Luther E., Jr., PhD, VP
L'Arche USA [11561]
1130 SW Morrison St., Ste. 230
Portland, OR 97205
Ph: (503)282-6231
Fax: (503)249-9264

Smith, Marc, VP
American Black Hereford Association
   [3683]
1704 S Cannon Blvd.
Shelbyville, TN 37160
Ph: (913)677-1111

Smith, Marcie, Exec. Dir.
Responsible Endowments Coalition
   [8771]
33 Flatbush Ave., 5th Fl.
Brooklyn, NY 11217
Ph: (718)989-3949

Smith, Marcus Lovell, CEO
Diagnostics for All [14996]
840 Memorial Dr.
Cambridge, MA 02139
Ph: (617)494-0700

Smith, Marcy, Bd. Member
Crochet Guild of America [22254]
1100-H Brandywine Blvd.
Zanesville, OH 43701-7303
Ph: (740)452-4541
Fax: (740)452-2552

Smith, Maria, Director
Alliance for Higher Education [7951]
2602 Rutford Ave.

Richardson, TX 75080
Ph: (972)234-8373

Smith, Marie, Director
Prescott College Alumni Association
   [19345]
c/o Prescott College
220 Grove Ave.
Prescott, AZ 86301
Toll Free: 877-350-2100

Smith, Mark, Bd. Member
Kempe Center for the Prevention
   and Treatment of Child Abuse and
   Neglect [11055]
13123 E 16th Ave., Ste. B390
Aurora, CO 80045-7106
Ph: (303)864-5300

Smith, Mark, Chairman
Taxpayers for Common Sense
   [19163]
651 Pennsylvania Ave. SE
Washington, DC 20003
Ph: (202)546-8500

Smith, Martha Nell, President
Emily Dickinson International Society
   [10150]
133 Lackawanna Rd.
Lexington, KY 40503

Smith, Mary, Secretary
Benign Essential Blepharospasm
   Research Foundation [15910]
637 N 7th St., Ste. 102
Beaumont, TX 77702
Ph: (409)832-0788
Fax: (409)832-0890

Smith, Mary Lou, President, Founder
Research Advocacy Network
   [14055]
6505 W Park Blvd., Ste. 305
Plano, TX 75093
Toll Free: 877-276-2187

Smith, Maureen, Chief Dev. Ofc.
National Alopecia Areata Foundation
   [17177]
65 Mitchell Blvd., Ste. 200-B
San Rafael, CA 94903
Ph: (415)472-3780
Fax: (415)480-1800

Smith, Maurine P., President
International Society Daughters of
   Utah Pioneers [21084]
300 N Main St.
Salt Lake City, UT 84103-1699
Ph: (801)532-6479
Fax: (801)532-4436

Smith, Michael, Treasurer
Benton Foundation [11318]
1560 Sherman Ave., Ste. 440
Evanston, IL 60201
Ph: (847)328-3049
Fax: (847)328-3046

Smith, Michael, Director, Founder
From Us With Love [12035]
2000 Corporate Square Blvd., Ste.
   101
Jacksonville, FL 32216
Toll Free: 800-392-8717

Smith, Michael M., Exec. Dir.
Association for Children with Down
   Syndrome [12316]
4 Fern Pl.
Plainview, NY 11803
Ph: (516)933-4700
Fax: (516)933-9524

Smith, Michael, Exec.
National Roadside Vegetation
   Management Association [4288]

c/o, John Reynolds, Executive Direc-
   tor
5616 Lynchburg Cir.
Hueytown, AL 35023
Ph: (205)491-7574
Fax: (205)491-2725

Smith, Michael W., President
American College of Trial Lawyers
   [5823]
19900 MacArthur Blvd., Ste. 530
Irvine, CA 92612
Ph: (949)752-1801
Fax: (949)752-1674

Smith, Mignon, RN, Founder,
   President
Global Associates for Health
   Development, Inc. [15450]
PO Box 790
Freeport, NY 11520
Ph: (516)771-1220
Fax: (516)771-1210

Smith, Mike, Exec. Dir.
Interstate Oil and Gas Compact
   Commission [5170]
900 NE 23rd St.
Oklahoma City, OK 73105
Ph: (405)525-3556
Fax: (405)525-3592

Smith, Mitchell, VP
American Junior Shorthorn Associa-
   tion [3700]
7607 NW Prairie View Rd.
Kansas City, MO 64151
Ph: (816)599-7777
Fax: (816)599-7782

Smith, Molly, Director
A is for Africa [11052]
14344 Harrisville Rd.
Mount Airy, MD 21771

Smith, Monica, Exec. Dir.
Bladder Cancer Advocacy Network
   [13904]
4915 St. Elmo Ave., Ste. 202
Bethesda, MD 20814
Ph: (301)215-9099
Toll Free: 888-901-BCAN

Smith, Nathan, Chairman
Manufactured Housing Institute
   [2198]
1655 N Fort Myer Dr., Ste. 104
Arlington, VA 22209-3108
Ph: (703)558-0400
Fax: (703)558-0401

Smith, Neal, CEO
American Jersey Cattle Association
   [3697]
6486 E Main St.
Reynoldsburg, OH 43068-2362
Ph: (614)861-3636
Fax: (614)861-8040

Smith, Nina, Exec. Dir.
GoodWeave International [11008]
1111 14th St. NW, Ste. 820
Washington, DC 20005
Ph: (202)234-9050
Fax: (202)234-9056

Smith, Pamela, Founder
Psychiatrists Global Training
   Network [15802]
PO Box 480482
Los Angeles, CA 90048
Ph: (310)954-1986

Smith, Patricia V., BA, President
Lyme Disease Association [14591]
PO Box 1438
Jackson, NJ 08527
Toll Free: 888-366-6611
Fax: (732)938-7215

Smith, Patsy, Secretary
Association of Black Nursing Faculty
[8308]
c/o Dr. Sallie Tucker Allen, Founder
PO Box 580
Lisle, IL 60532
Ph: (630)969-0221
Fax: (630)969-3895

Smith, Paul H., Ph.D., President
International Remote Viewing As-
sociation [6227]
PO Box 1471
South Windsor, CT 06074
Ph: (860)882-1210
Toll Free: 866-374-4782
Fax: (860)648-4005

Smith, Paul J., Mem.
International Society for Advance-
ment of Cytometry [6085]
9650 Rockville Pke.
Bethesda, MD 20814
Ph: (301)634-7435
Fax: (301)634-7429

Smith, Peggy, SCRP, CEO,
President
Worldwide ERC [1104]
4401 Wilson Blvd., Ste. 510
Arlington, VA 22203
Ph: (703)842-3400
Fax: (703)527-1552

Smith, Pete, Chairman
American Sports Builders Associa-
tion [851]
9 Newport Dr., Ste. 200
Forest Hill, MD 21050
Ph: (410)730-9595
Toll Free: 866-501-2722
Fax: (410)730-8833

Smith, Randy, Chmn. of the Bd.
Global Teams [20108]
3821 Mt. Vernon Ave.
Bakersfield, CA 93306
Ph: (661)323-1214
Fax: (661)323-1252

Smith, Reid K., MD, Dir. of Dev.
Students for Concealed Carry
[18257]
2885 Sanford Ave. SW, No. 24704
Grandville, MI 49418

Smith, Richard G., III, Exec. Dir.
National InterCollegiate Flying As-
sociation [21242]
2160 W Case Rd.
Columbus, OH 43235
Ph: (614)247-5444

Smith, Richard, President
International Federation of American
Homing Pigeon Fanciers [22386]
c/o Richard Smith, President
289 W Valley Stream Blvd.
Valley Stream, NY 11580-5340
Ph: (516)794-3612

Smith, Richard, Exec. Dir.
Masonry Heater Association of North
America [1630]
2180 S Flying Q Ln.
Tucson, AZ 85713-6793
Ph: (520)883-0191
Fax: (480)371-1139

Smith, Richard, President
North American Horticultural Supply
Association [4439]
100 N 20th St., 4th Fl.
Philadelphia, PA 19103-1443
Ph: (215)564-3484
Fax: (215)963-9784

Smith, Rick, President
BueLingo Beef Cattle Society [3723]
15904 W Warren Rd.

Warren, IL 61087-9601
Ph: (815)745-2147

Smith, Rick, Exec. Dir.
International Dyslexia Association
[14630]
40 York Rd., 4th Fl.
Baltimore, MD 21204-5243
Ph: (410)296-0232
Fax: (410)321-5069

Smith, Rick, VP
National Association of Amusement
Ride Safety Officials [1147]
PO Box 638
Brandon, FL 33509-0638
Ph: (813)661-2779
Toll Free: 800-669-9053
Fax: (813)685-5117

Smith, Robert A., III, President
Carrie Estelle Doheny Foundation
[13045]
707 Wilshire Blvd., Ste. 4960
Los Angeles, CA 90017
Ph: (213)488-1122
Fax: (213)488-1544

Smith, Robert, Exec. Dir.
Electronic System Design Alliance
[6419]
3081 Zanker Rd.
San Jose, CA 95134
Ph: (408)287-3322

Smith, Robert J., Secretary
American College of Construction
Lawyers [4986]
PO Box 4646
Austin, TX 78765-4646
Ph: (512)343-1808

Smith, Robert Michael, Comm. Chm.
Sculptors Guild [10211]
55 Washington St., Ste. 256
Brooklyn, NY 11201
Ph: (718)422-0555

Smith, Ron, Director
Competitive Carriers Association
[3222]
805 15th St. NW, Ste. 401
Washington, DC 20005
Toll Free: 800-722-1872
Fax: (866)436-1080

Smith, Rosalyn-Sue, CEO
Operation Stars and Stripes [10756]
483 Old Canton Rd., Ste. 100
Marietta, GA 30068
Ph: (770)509-1156

Smith, Dr. Roy, Treasurer
American Association of Feline
Practitioners [17595]
390 Amwell Rd., Ste. 402
Hillsborough, NJ 08844-1247
Toll Free: 800-874-0498
Fax: (908)292-1188

Smith, Sharon, Chairperson
Institute of Business Appraisers
[226]
5217 S State St., Ste. 400
Salt Lake City, UT 84107
Toll Free: 800-299-4130
Fax: (866)353-5406

Smith, Shirley F., CEO, Founder
Grooming Future World Leaders Inc.
[13449]
2701 Del Paso Rd., No. 130-191
Sacramento, CA 95835
Ph: (916)889-8195

Smith, Stacey, Exec. Dir.
Association of Freestanding Radiation Oncology Centers [17034]

12100 Sunset Hills Rd., Ste. 130
Reston, VA 20190
Ph: (202)442-3762
Fax: (202)638-0604

Smith, Standish, Founder
Heirs, Inc. [18051]
PO Box 292
Villanova, PA 19085
Ph: (610)527-6260

Smith, Stephan J., Exec. Dir.
Association on Higher Education and
Disability [7714]
107 Commerce Centre Dr., Ste. 204
Huntersville, NC 28078
Ph: (704)947-7779
Fax: (704)948-7779

Smith, Stephen, President
Tennessee Walking Horse Breeders'
and Exhibitors' Association [4415]
250 N Ellington Pky.
Lewisburg, TN 37091
Ph: (931)359-1574
Fax: (931)359-7530

Smith, Steve R., CAE, CEO, Exec.
Dir.
American Academy of Hospice and
Palliative Medicine [16733]
8735 W Higgins Rd., Ste. 300
Chicago, IL 60631
Ph: (847)375-4712
Fax: (847)375-6475

Smith, Susan, Secretary, Treasurer
American Netherland Dwarf Rabbit
Club [4591]
c/o Susan Smith, Secretary and
Treasurer
864 Barkers Creek Rd.
Whittier, NC 28789

Smith, Terry, Secretary
American Pheasant and Waterfowl
Society [4783]
7153 Piney Island Rd.
Chincoteague Island, VA 23336
Ph: (757)824-5828

Smith, Tom, Manager
American Association of Petroleum
Geologists [6675]
1444 S Boulder Ave.
Tulsa, OK 74119
Ph: (918)584-2555
Toll Free: 800-364-2274
Fax: (918)560-2665

Smith, Tommy, Exec. Dir.
School Science and Mathematics
Association [8556]
School of Education, EB 246B
University of Alabama Birmingham
Birmingham, AL 35233
Ph: (205)934-5067

Smith, Trevor, President
Ecological Landscape Alliance
[4445]
PO Box 3
Sandown, NH 03873
Ph: (617)436-5838

Smith, Trevor, President
Ecological Landscaping Association
[4446]
PO Box 3
Sandown, NH 03873
Ph: (617)436-5838

Smith, Victor, VP
Dogue de Bordeaux Society of
America [21870]
679 W Market St.
Akron, OH 44303-1407

Smith, Wade, Exec. Dir.
Air Movement and Control Association International, Inc. [1614]

30 W University Dr.
Arlington Heights, IL 60004
Ph: (847)394-0150
Fax: (847)253-0088

Smith, William A., Exec. Dir.
National Coalition of STD Directors
[17200]
1029 Vermont Ave. NW, Ste. 500
Washington, DC 20005
Ph: (202)842-4660
Fax: (202)842-4542

Smith, William S., Exec. Ofc.
World Phenomenology Institute
[10134]
1 Ivy Pointe Way
Hanover, NH 03755
Ph: (802)295-3487
Fax: (802)295-5963

Smith, Dr. William T., CEO,
President
Aging in America [10496]
2975 Westchester Ave., Ste. 301
Purchase, NY 10577
Ph: (914)205-5030

Smith, William, VP
U.S. Aquatic Sports [23287]
Ph: (636)675-1230

Smithhisler, Peter, President
Gamma Sigma Alpha [19434]
PO Box 3948
Parker, CO 80134
Toll Free: 866-793-5406

Smith-LeGore, Sharon, President
MOMSTELL [13153]
PO Box 450
Mechanicsburg, PA 17055
Ph: (717)384-6066

Smith-Nilson, Marla, Exec. Dir.,
Founder
Water 1st International [13340]
1904 3rd Ave., Ste. 1012
Seattle, WA 98101
Ph: (206)297-3024

Smith-Pliner, Dawn, Director,
Founder
Friends in Adoption [10453]
212 Main St.
Poultney, VT 05764
Toll Free: 800-982-3678

Smith-Vaughan, Reuben, Exec. Dir.
Association of American Chambers
of Commerce in Latin America and
the Caribbean [23560]
1615 H St. NW
Washington, DC 20062-0001
Ph: (202)463-5485

Smith-Vaughan, Reuben, Contact
Latin America Trade Coalition [1985]
1615 H St. NW
Washington, DC 20062-2000
Ph: (202)463-5485
Fax: (202)463-3126

Smitley, Vicky, President
Contract Packaging Association
[2474]
1 Parkview Plz., Ste. 800
Oakbrook Terrace, IL 60181
Ph: (630)544-5053
Fax: (630)544-5055

Smock, Jill, Director
Youth to Youth International [13491]
1420 Fields Ave.
Columbus, OH 43211
Ph: (614)224-4506
Fax: (614)675-3318

Smoke, Kathryn, Chairperson
Arabian Jockey Club [22913]
10805 E Bethany Dr.

Aurora, CO 80014
Ph: (303)696-4523
Fax: (303)696-4599

Smolich, Fr. Thomas H., SJ;
  President
Jesuit Conference [19847]
1016 16th St. NW, Ste. 400
Washington, DC 20036
Ph: (202)462-0400

Smuck, Matthew, MD, Secretary
Spine Intervention Society [17265]
161 Mitchell Blvd., Ste. 103
San Rafael, CA 94903
Ph: (415)457-4747
Toll Free: 888-255-0005
Fax: (415)457-3495

Smyth, Susan M., PhD, FSME,
  Secretary
Society of Manufacturing Engineers -
  Composites Manufacturing Tech
  Group [2231]
1 SME Dr.
Dearborn, MI 48128
Ph: (313)425-3000
Toll Free: 800-733-4763
Fax: (313)425-3400

Snead, Rebecca P., CEO, Exec. VP
National Alliance of State Pharmacy
  Associations [16672]
2530 Professional Rd., Ste. 202
Richmond, VA 23235
Ph: (804)285-4431
Fax: (804)612-6555

Snee, Thomas J., Exec. Dir.
Fleet Reserve Association [21053]
125 N West St.
Alexandria, VA 22314-2709
Ph: (703)683-1400
Toll Free: 800-FRA-1924

Snider, Katherine, President
Lupus Clinical Trials Consortium
  [15540]
221 E 48th St., 2nd Fl.
New York, NY 10017
Ph: (212)593-7227

Snider, Pamela, ND, Secretary
CodeBlueNow! [17000]
705 2nd Ave., Ste. 901
Seattle, WA 98104
Ph: (206)217-9430

Snodgress, Faye, Exec. Dir.
Kappa Delta Pi [23730]
3707 Woodview Trace
Indianapolis, IN 46268
Ph: (317)871-4900
Toll Free: 800-284-3167
Fax: (317)704-2323

Snook, Jeremi, President, CEO
Friendship Force International
  [18542]
127 Peachtree St., Ste. 501
Atlanta, GA 30303
Ph: (404)522-9490

Snow, Deborah, Contact
National Service-Learning
  Clearinghouse [8541]
4 Carbonero Way
Scotts Valley, CA 95066
Ph: (831)461-0205
Toll Free: 866-245-7378
Fax: (831)430-9471

Snow, Dr. Matthew, President
Miami Rare Fruit Council
  International [4239]
14735 SW 48 Ter.
Miami, FL 33185-4066
Ph: (305)554-1333

Snow, Michael, Exec. Dir.
American Hardwood Export Council
  [1406]
1825 Michael Faraday Dr.
Reston, VA 20190
Ph: (703)435-2900
Fax: (703)435-2537

Snow, Richard, CEO, President
International SeaKeepers Society
  [4468]
355 Alhambra Cir., Ste. 1100
Coral Gables, FL 33134
Ph: (305)448-7089

Snow, Tom, V. Chmn. of the Exec.
  Committee
Resistance Welding Manufacturing
  Alliance [1765]
c/o Adrian Bustillo
8669 Doral Blvd., Ste. 130
Doral, FL 33166
Ph: (305)443-9353

Snow, William, Director
Global HIV Vaccine Enterprise
  [13542]
64 Beaver St., No. 352
New York, NY 10004
Ph: (212)461-3692
Fax: (866)966-4483

Snowman, Stanwood, Officer
Fiber Economics Bureau [6630]
3033 Wilson Blvd., Ste. 700
Arlington, VA 22201
Ph: (703)875-0676
Fax: (703)875-0675

Snyder, April, Contact
American Board of Managed Care
  Nursing [16099]
4435 Waterfront Dr., Ste. 101
Glen Allen, VA 23060
Ph: (804)527-1905
Fax: (804)747-5316

Snyder, Claire, Ph.D., President
International Society for Quality of
  Life Research [6041]
555 E Wells St., Ste. 1100
Milwaukee, WI 53202
Ph: (414)918-9797
Fax: (414)276-3349

Snyder, Dale, Exec. Dir.
Haiti Outreach [10721]
50 9th Ave. S, Ste. 203
Hopkins, MN 55343
Ph: (612)929-1122
Fax: (612)216-3777

Snyder, Dan, Mgr.
Short Span Steel Bridge Alliance
  [6159]
25 Massachusetts Ave. NW, Ste.
  800
Washington, DC 20001
Ph: (301)367-6179

Snyder, Dr. Elise, President
China American Psychoanalytic Alliance [16911]
76-26 113th St., 5G
Forest Hills, NY 11375

Snyder, Ivan D., Secretary,
  Treasurer
American Amateur Press Association
  [22390]
1327 NE 73rd Ave.
1327 NE 73rd Ave.
Portland, OR 97213-6112

Snyder, Jack, Exec. Dir.
Styrene Information and Research
  Center [729]
910 17th St. NW, 5th Fl.

Washington, DC 20006
Ph: (202)787-5996

Snyder, John M., Founder, Chairman
St. Gabriel Possenti Society, Inc.
  [18254]
PO Box 183
Cabin John, MD 20818
Ph: (202)239-8005

Snyder, Judy, Admin. Asst.
Federation of Fly Fishers [22843]
5237 US Highway 89 S, Ste. 11
Livingston, MT 59047
Ph: (406)222-9369

Snyder, Kent, Treasurer
American Leadership Forum [18627]
738 Broadway, Ste. 301
Tacoma, WA 98402-3777
Ph: (713)807-1253
Fax: (713)807-1064

Snyder, Dr. O. Peter, Jr., Founder,
  President
Hospitality Institute of Technology
  and Management [1658]
PO Box 13734
Saint Paul, MN 55113-0734
Ph: (651)646-7077

Snyder, Patrick, Exec. Dir.
United States Association for Small
  Business and Entrepreneurship
  [3130]
c/o Patrick Snyder, Executive Direc-
  tor
1214 Hyland Hall
University of Wisconsin, Whitewater
Whitewater, WI 53190
Ph: (262)472-1449

Snyder, Terry, President, CEO
Allinial Global [7]
1745 N Brown Rd., Ste. 350
Lawrenceville, GA 30043
Ph: (770)279-4560
Fax: (770)279-4566

Snyder, Val, Director
Pipeline Association for Public
  Awareness [2612]
16361 Table Mountain Pky.
Golden, CO 80403-1826
Ph: (719)375-3873
  (248)205-7604

So, Brandi, Exec. Dir.
Charlotte Perkins Gilman Society
  [10373]
c/o Peter Betjemann, President
Dept. of English
Oregon State University
Moreland Hall
Corvallis, OR 97331

Sobel, Chloe, Exec. Dir.
Jewish Student Press Service [8140]
125 Maiden Ln., 8th Fl.
New York, NY 10038

Sobel, Mark E., PhD, Exec. Ofc.
American Society for Investigative
  Pathology [16575]
9650 Rockville Pke., Ste. E133
Bethesda, MD 20814
Ph: (301)634-7130
Fax: (301)634-7990

Sobel, Robert, President
Pedorthic Footcare Association
  [1402]
PO Box 72184
Albany, GA 31708-2184
Ph: (229)389-3440
Fax: (888)563-0954

Sobel, Rochelle, Founder, President
Association for Safe International
  Road Travel [13230]

12320 Parklawn Dr.
Rockville, MD 20852-1726
Ph: (240)249-0100
Fax: (301)230-0411

Sobel, Ronald, President
Leo Baeck Institute [9633]
15 W 16th St.
New York, NY 10011-6301
Ph: (212)744-6400
  (212)294-8340

Sobell, Mark, PhD, Rep.
APA Division 12: Society of Clinical
  Psychology [16870]
PO Box 1082
Niwot, CO 80544-1082
Ph: (303)652-3126
Fax: (303)652-2723

Sobien, Daniel A., President
National Weather Service
  Employees Organization [6858]
601 Pennsylvania Ave. NW, Ste. 900
Washington, DC 20004
Ph: (202)907-3036

Sobieraj, Jim, President
Licensing Executives Society [5336]
1800 Diagonal Rd., Ste. 280
Alexandria, VA 22314-2840
Ph: (703)836-0026
Fax: (703)836-3107

Sobotka-Soles, Robbin, President,
  Exec. Dir.
A Hope for Autism Foundation
  [13769]
2900 SW Peaceful Ln.
Portland, OR 97239
Ph: (503)516-9085

Soby, Dr. Lynn, Exec. Dir.
International Union of Pure and Ap-
  plied Chemistry [6205]
Bldg. 4201, Ste. 260
79 TW Alexander Dr.
Research Triangle Park, NC 27709
Ph: (919)485-8700
Fax: (919)485-8706

Sochacki, Stacy, MS, Exec. Dir.
Certification of Disability Manage-
  ment Specialists Commission
  [13495]
8735 W Higgins Rd., Ste. 300
Chicago, IL 60631
Ph: (847)375-6380
Fax: (847)375-6379

Sochet, Mary, Chairperson
Perhaps Kids Meeting Kids Can
  Make a Difference [18555]
380 Riverside Dr.
New York, NY 10025-1858
Ph: (212)662-2327

Soden, Jack, President, CEO
Elvis Presley Fan Club [24013]

Soderlund, Kurt, CEO
Safe Water Network [13335]
122 E 42nd St., Ste. 2600
New York, NY 10168
Ph: (212)355-7233

Sofatzis, Tia, Exec. Dir.
International Neuromodulation
  Society [16021]
c/o Tia Sofatzis, Executive Director
2000 Van Ness Ave., Ste. 414
San Francisco, CA 94109-3019
Ph: (415)683-3237
Fax: (415)683-3218

Sohn, Raymond G., DO, Bd.
  Member
American Osteopathic College of
  Anesthesiologists [13692]

3085 Stevenson Dr., Ste. 200
Springfield, IL 62703
Ph: (217)529-6503
Toll Free: 800-842-2622
Fax: (217)529-9120

Sohnen-Moe, Cherie, President
Alliance for Massage Therapy
Education [8274]
1232 Bonefish Ct.
Fort Pierce, FL 34949-2901
Toll Free: 855-236-8331
Fax: (786)522-2440

Sokol, David L., Chairman
Horatio Alger Association of
Distinguished Americans [20734]
99 Canal Center Plz., Ste. 320
Alexandria, VA 22314-1588
Ph: (703)684-9444
Toll Free: 844-422-4200

Solano, Alberto, Exec. Dir.
Agros International [11310]
2225 4th Ave., 2nd Fl.
Seattle, WA 98121
Ph: (206)528-1066

Solem, Marshall, Chairman
Sigma Phi Society [23931]
PO Box 57417
Tucson, AZ 85711-7417
Ph: (520)777-3055

Soler, Esta, Founder, President
Futures Without Violence [11703]
The Presidio
100 Montgomery St.
San Francisco, CA 94129
Ph: (415)678-5500
Fax: (415)529-2930

Soletski, Rick, Exec. Dir.
International Association of Lemon
Law Administrators [5055]
c/o Pauline Liese, President
New Motor Vehicle Arbitration Board
14 Baldwin St., Rm. 103
Montpelier, VT 05602-2109
Ph: (802)828-2943
Fax: (802)828-5809

Solis, Dan J., President
National Organization for Mexican
American Rights, Inc. [18341]
c/o Dan J. Solis, President
PO Box 681205
San Antonio, TX 78268-1205
Ph: (210)520-1831
Fax: (210)520-1831

Solley, Steve, President
Denison Homestead [20853]
120 Pequotsepos Rd.
Mystic, CT 06355-3043
Ph: (860)536-9248

Sollins, Susan, Founder
Art21 [8842]
133 W 25th St., No. 3E
New York, NY 10001
Ph: (212)741-7133
Fax: (212)741-5709

Solo, Nancy, Founder
Chronic Syndrome Support Association [14571]
801 Riverside Dr.
Lumberton, NC 28358-4625

Solo-Gabriele, Dr. Helena, Contact
Asociacion de Ingenieros Cubano-
Americanos [6542]
PO Box 941436
Miami, FL 33194-1436

Solomon, Brett, Exec. Dir.
Access Now [17861]
PO Box 115

New York, NY 10113
Toll Free: 888-414-0100

Solomon, Dan, Coord.
Institute on Religion in an Age of
Science [20597]
c/o Dan Solomon, Membership
Coordinator
6434 N Mozart St.
Chicago, IL 60645

Solomon, Ms. Marianne, Exec. Dir.
Future Problem Solving Program
International [7678]
2015 Grant Pl.
Melbourne, FL 32901
Ph: (321)768-0074

Solomon, Norman, Exec. Dir.
Institute for Public Accuracy [18986]
1714 Franklin St., No. 100-133
Oakland, CA 94612-3409
Ph: (510)788-4541

Solomon, Saige W., Director
Centenary College of Louisiana
Alumni Association [19314]
PO Box 41188
Shreveport, LA 71134
Ph: (318)869-5115
Toll Free: 800-259-6447
Fax: (318)841-7266

Solon, Kathryn, Chairperson
Democrats Abroad [18113]
PO Box 15130
Washington, DC 20003
Ph: (202)621-2085

Solorzano, Rev. Miguel, Secretary
Asociación National de Sacerdotes
Hispanos en Estados Unidos
[19795]
1120 52nd St.
Lubbock, TX 79411
Ph: (806)781-7832

Soltani, Atossa, Founder
Amazon Watch [3797]
2201 Broadway, Ste. 508
Oakland, CA 94612
Ph: (510)281-9020
Fax: (510)281-9021

Soltero, Ernesto, MD, President
Michael E. DeBakey International
Surgical Society [14111]
c/o Kenneth L. Mattox, MD,
Secretary-Treasurer
1 Baylor Plz.
Houston, TX 77030
Ph: (713)798-4557

Somerman, Martha J., PhD, Director
National Institute of Health | National
Institute of Dental and Craniofacial
Reaserch | National Oral Health
Information Clearinghouse [14465]
1 NOHIC Way
Bethesda, MD 20892-3500

Somerman, Martha J., PhD, Director
National Institutes of Health |
National Institute of Dental and
Craniofacial Research [14466]
Bldg. 31, Rm. 5B55
31 Center Dr., MSC 2190
Bethesda, MD 20892-2190
Ph: (301)496-4261
   (301)496-3571
Fax: (301)496-9988

Somers, Frederick P., Exec. Dir.
The American Occupational Therapy
Association, Inc. [17434]
4720 Montgomery Ln., Ste. 200
Bethesda, MD 20814-3449
Ph: (301)652-6611
Toll Free: 800-729-2682
Fax: (301)652-7711

Somers, Keith, President
Association of Alternate Postal
Systems [2115]
1725 Oaks Way
Oklahoma City, OK 73131
Ph: (405)478-0006

Somerville, Nancy C., Exec. VP
American Society of Landscape
Architects [5956]
636 Eye St. NW
Washington, DC 20001-3736
Ph: (202)898-2444
Toll Free: 888-999-2752
Fax: (202)898-1185

Sommariva, Dr. Corrado, President
International Desalination Associa-
tion [7367]
94 Central St., Ste. 200
Topsfield, MA 01983-1838
Ph: (978)887-0410
Fax: (978)887-0411

Sommer, Josh, Exec. Dir.
Chordoma Foundation [13943]
PO Box 2127
Durham, NC 27702
Ph: (919)809-6779
Fax: (866)367-3910

Sommer, Marni, Exec. Dir.
Grow and Know [11202]
35 W 64th St., Ste. 6B
New York, NY 10023

Song, David H., MD, President
American Society of Plastic
Surgeons [14312]
444 E Algonquin Rd.
Arlington Heights, IL 60005
Ph: (847)228-9900
Toll Free: 800-514-5058

Song, Hannah, President, CEO
Liberty in North Korea [18605]
1751 Torrance Blvd., Ste. L
Torrance, CA 90501
Ph: (310)212-7190
Fax: (202)315-3748

Songer, Marquis, President
Hovercraft Club of America [22159]
PO Box 389
Goshen, IN 46527

Sonik, Susanne, Director
American Hospital Association - Sec-
tion for Long-Term Care and
Rehabilitation [15306]
155 N Wacker Dr., Ste. 400
Chicago, IL 60606
Ph: (312)422-3000

Sonin, Andrew, MD, President
Society of Skeletal Radiology
[17073]
2575 Northwest Pky.
Elgin, IL 60124
Ph: (847)752-6249
Fax: (847)960-3861

Sonnefeld, Ralf, Chairman
Manufacturing Enterprise Solutions
Association International [2225]
107 S Southgate Dr.
Chandler, AZ 85226
Ph: (480)893-6883
   (952)548-5664
Fax: (480)893-7775

Sonnenstrahl, Mr. Sam, Exec. Dir.
Gallaudet University Alumni Associa-
tion [19325]
c/o Gallaudet University
800 Florida Ave. NE
Washington, DC 20002
Ph: (202)651-5060
Fax: (202)651-5062

Sonntag, Tim, President
National Seasoning Manufacturers
Association [1304]
228 Phelps Ave.
Cresskill, NJ 07626
Ph: (201)657-1989

Soon-taek, Mrs. Ban, Chairwoman
Hospitality Committee for United Na-
tions Delegations [18547]
United Nations General Assembly
Bldg. Rm. GA-0142
New York, NY 10017
Ph: (212)963-8753
Fax: (212)963-1320

Soos, Jennifer, Coord.
MISS Foundation [11919]
77 E Thomas Rd., No. 221
Phoenix, AZ 85012-3109
Ph: (602)279-6477
Toll Free: 888-455-6477

Sopoci-Belknap, Kaitlin, Director
Move to Amend [5072]
PO Box 610
Eureka, CA 95502
Ph: (707)269-0984

Sorensen, Jay, President
Kids First Fund [10796]
1916 E Kensington Blvd.
Shorewood, WI 53211
Ph: (414)961-1939

Sorenson, Melissa, Exec. Dir.
National Association of Professional
Background Screeners [1697]
2501 Aerial Center Pky., Ste. 130
Morrisville, NC 27560-7655
Ph: (919)459-2082
Fax: (919)459-2075

Sorg, Linda, President
Chromosome Disorder Outreach
[14815]
PO Box 724
Boca Raton, FL 33429-0724
Ph: (561)395-4252

Sorhondo, Nicole, Secretary
Basque Educational Organization
[9648]
PO Box 31861
San Francisco, CA 94131-0861

Sorkin, Donna L., MA, Exec. Dir.
American Cochlear Implant Alliance
[15169]
PO Box 103
McLean, VA 22101-0103
Ph: (703)536-6146

Sorrells, Keira, President
Preemie Parent Alliance [12426]
201 Cotton Wood Dr.
Madison, MS 39110
Ph: (601)345-1772

Sosa, Eileen, Founder, Director
OutreachPARAGUAY [11290]
761 Chickies Dr.
Columbia, PA 17512
Ph: (717)684-6062

Sosa, Rev. Juan J., President
National Hispanic Institute of Liturgy
[19888]
620 Michigan Ave. NE
Washington, DC 20064
Ph: (305)274-6333
Fax: (305)274-6337

Sothmann, Stephen, President
U.S. Hide, Skin and Leather As-
sociation [2088]
1150 Connecticut Ave. NW, 12th Fl.
Washington, DC 20036
Ph: (202)587-4250

Soti, Praveen, Chairman
Microsoft Health Users Group
[15154]
1 Microsoft Way
Redmond, WA 98052-6399
Ph: (425)870-4880

Soto, Renata, Chairman
National Council of La Raza [17919]
1126 16th St. NW, Ste. 600
Washington, DC 20036-4845
Ph: (202)785-1670
Fax: (202)776-1792

Sotonyi, Dr. Peter, VP
World Association of Veterinary
  Anatomists [17677]
Dept. of Anatomy and Physiology
College of Veterinary Medicine
Kansas State University
Manhattan, KS 66506-5601
Ph: (785)532-4530
Fax: (785)532-4557

Soucie, Urszula M., Dir. of Opera-
  tions
Railway Engineering-Maintenance
  Suppliers Association [2840]
500 New Jersey Ave. NW, Ste. 400
Washington, DC 20001
Ph: (202)715-2921
Fax: (202)204-5753

Soules, Montie D., CEO, Exec. Sec.
American Shorthorn Association
[3712]
7607 NW Prairie View Rd.
Kansas City, MO 64151
Ph: (816)599-7777
Fax: (816)599-7782

Southey, Sean, CEO
PCI-Media Impact [12511]
777 United Nations Plz., 5th Fl.
New York, NY 10017
Ph: (212)687-3366
Fax: (212)661-4188

Southwell, Gil, Comm. Chm.
National Federation of Municipal
  Analysts [51]
PO Box 14893
Pittsburgh, PA 15234

Southworth, Don, Treasurer
Religion News Service [2717]
National Press Bldg.
529 14th St. NW
Washington, DC 20045
Ph: (202)463-8777
Toll Free: 888-707-3755
Fax: (202)662-7154

Sow, Dr. Christine, Exec. Dir.,
  President
Global Health Council [15455]
1199 N Fairfax St., Ste. 300
Alexandria, VA 22314
Ph: (703)717-5200
Fax: (703)717-5215

Sowell, Urmilla, Tech. Dir.
Glass Association of North America
[1503]
800 SW Jackson St., Ste. 1500
Topeka, KS 66612-1200
Ph: (785)271-0208

Sowels-Jenkins, Holly, President
VOICES in Action [12940]
8041 Hosbrook Rd., Ste. 236
Cincinnati, OH 45236
Toll Free: 800-786-4238
Fax: (773)327-4590

Sowers, Marsha D., Chairman
Daughters of the Nile, Supreme
  Temple [19554]

c/o Eleanor Green, Recorder
112 Skyridge St.
Ludlow, MA 01056

Sowle, Michael, Dir. of Fin.
Astronomical Society of the Pacific
[6002]
390 Ashton Ave.
San Francisco, CA 94112
Ph: (415)337-1100
Toll Free: 800-335-2624
Fax: (415)337-5205

Spadaro, Paul, President, Comm.
  Chm.
United States Association of
  Independent Gymnastic Clubs
[3165]
450 N End Ave., Apt. 20F
New York, NY 10282

Spade, Dean, Founder
Sylvia Rivera Law Project [13228]
147 W 24th St., 5th Fl.
New York, NY 10011
Ph: (212)337-8550
Fax: (212)337-1972

Spagnolli, Richard, President
Antique Motorcycle Club of America
[22212]
Cornerstone Registration Ltd.
PO Box 1715
Maple Grove, MN 55311-6715
Ph: (763)420-7829
Toll Free: 866-427-7583
Fax: (763)420-7849

Spagnolo, Samuel V., MD, President
National Association of Veterans Af-
  fairs Physicians and Dentists
[16758]
PO Box 15418
Arlington, VA 22215-0418
Toll Free: 866-836-3520
Fax: (540)972-1728

Spahr, Charles, Exec. Dir.
American Ceramic Society [6169]
600 N Cleveland Ave., Ste. 210
Westerville, OH 43082
Ph: (240)646-7054
Toll Free: 866-721-3322
Fax: (204)396-5637

Spaid, Susan, President
National Brittany Rescue and Adop-
  tion Network [10665]
PO Box 5046
Greensburg, PA 15601-5058

Spalding, Carol, Treasurer
Instructional Technology Council
[8033]
426 C St. NE
Washington, DC 20002-5839
Ph: (202)293-3110
    (202)293-3132

Spangenberg, Ted, Jr., President
Association of Baptists for Scouting
[12850]
PO Box 152079
Irving, TX 75015-2079
Ph: (706)366-4998

Spangler, Kathi, VP, Director
Complex Weavers [243]
PO Box 1237
Laporte, CO 80535-1237

Spaniola, Dan, Chairman
International Association of Pipe
  Smokers Clubs [22387]
647 S Saginaw St.
Flint, MI 48502

Spann, Christine, Dir. of Comm.
Electric Drive Transportation Association [6019]

1250 Eye St. NW, Ste. 902
Washington, DC 20005
Ph: (202)408-0774

Spannuth, John R., CEO, President
United States Water Fitness As-
  sociation [23067]
PO Box 243279
Boynton Beach, FL 33424-3279
Ph: (561)732-9908
Fax: (561)732-0950

Sparks, Ben, VP
Western Saddle Clubs Association
[4428]
c/o Leslie Mason, Secretary
15128 240th St.
Scandia, MN 55073
Ph: (651)724-3421

Sparks, Darron, President
Dogs Against Drugs/Dogs Against
  Crime [11690]
3320 Main St., Ste. G
Anderson, IN 46013
Ph: (765)642-9447
Toll Free: 888-323-3227
Fax: (765)642-4899

Sparks, George, Chairman
National Catholic Committee on
  Scouting [12855]
1325 W Walnut Hill Ln.
Irving, TX 75038-3008
Ph: (972)580-2114
Fax: (972)580-2535

Sparks, John D., Dir. of Comm.
Millenium Water Alliance [13330]
1001 Connecticut Ave. NW, Ste. 710
Washington, DC 20036
Ph: (202)296-1832
Fax: (202)296-1786

Sparks, Les, President
Affordable Housing Association of
  Certified Public Accountants [1686]
459 North 300 West, Ste. 11
Kaysville, UT 84037
Ph: (801)547-0809
Toll Free: 800-532-0809

Sparks, Mike, Chairman
Electrification and Controls
  Manufacturers Association [1726]
c/o MHI
8720 Red Oak Blvd., Ste. 201
Charlotte, NC 28217-3996
Ph: (704)676-1190
Fax: (704)676-1199

Sparks, Ronda, Registrar
American Dorper Sheep Breeders'
  Society [4653]
PO Box 259
Hallsville, MO 65255-0259
Ph: (573)696-2550
Fax: (573)696-2030

Sparrey, Andrea, President
Association of International Graduate
  Admissions Consultants [7446]
3121 Park Ave., Ste. C
Soquel, CA 95073
Ph: (831)464-4892

Sparrow, G. Scott, Ed.D., Chmn. of
  the Bd.
International Association for the
  Study of Dreams [17217]
1672 University Ave.
Berkeley, CA 94703
Ph: (209)724-0889
Fax: (209)724-0889

Sparrow, Lisa A., Bd. Member
National Association of Water
  Companies [3459]

2001 L St. NW, Ste. 850
Washington, DC 20036
Ph: (202)833-8383
Fax: (202)331-7442

Spatola, Mark, Chairman
ThinkFirst National Injury Prevention
  Foundation [17267]
1801 N Mill St., Ste. F
Naperville, IL 60563-4869
Ph: (630)961-1400
Toll Free: 800-844-6556
Fax: (630)961-1401

Spaugy, Phil, Cmdr.
North-South Skirmish Association
[23140]
480 Chalybeate Springs Rd.
Winchester, VA 22603-2364
Ph: (540)888-4334

Spaulding, Wallace H., President
Fellowship of Concerned Churchmen
[19703]
1215 Independence Ave. SE
Washington, DC 20003-1445
Ph: (202)621-6729

Spavone, Sandy, Exec. Dir.
Family, Career and Community
  Leaders of America [7916]
1910 Association Dr.
Reston, VA 20191-1584
Ph: (703)476-4900
Fax: (703)439-2662

Speakman, David, Chairperson,
  Treasurer
National Fantasy Fan Federation
[10204]
PO Box 1925
Mountain View, CA 94042

Spear, DNP, ACNP-BC, CWS,
  CPSN, Marcia, President
American Society of Plastic Surgical
  Nurses [16115]
500 Cummings Ctr., Ste. 4550
Beverly, MA 01915
Toll Free: 877-337-9315
Fax: (978)524-0498

Spear, Jeffrey W., President
Sons and Daughters of Pioneer Riv-
  ermen [21089]
PO Box 352
Marietta, OH 45750

Speare, Ed, Chairman
Sharing of Ministries Abroad U.S.A.
[20461]
2501 Ridgmar Plz., No. 99
Fort Worth, TX 76116
Ph: (817)737-7662

Spears, Tony, President
Ranching Heritage Association
[9509]
3121 4th St.
Lubbock, TX 79409

Spears, Vanessa, President
Society of Urologic Nurses and As-
  sociates [16187]
Box 56
E Holly Ave.
Pitman, NJ 08071-0056
Ph: (856)256-2335
Toll Free: 888-827-7862
Fax: (856)589-7463

Speckhard, Daniel, CEO, President
Lutheran World Relief [20315]
700 Light St.
Baltimore, MD 21230
Ph: (410)230-2800
Toll Free: 800-597-5972
Fax: (410)230-2882

Speckhardt, Mr. Roy, Exec. Dir.
American Humanist Association
[20208]
1777 T St. NW
Washington, DC 20009-7102
Ph: (202)238-9088
Toll Free: 800-837-3792
Fax: (202)238-9003

Spector, Jennifer, Secretary
American Association for Women
Podiatrists [16776]
c/o Karen A. Langone, DMP,
Treasurer
365 Country Road 39A, Ste. 9
Benton Plz.
Southampton, NY 11968

Spector, Seth, MD, President
Association of VA Surgeons [17380]
2610 164th St. SW, No. A524
Lynnwood, WA 98087
Ph: (206)794-9124
Fax: (206)319-4601

Speer, Dr. J. Alexander, Exec. Dir.
Mineralogical Society of America
[6875]
3635 Concorde Pky., Ste. 500
Chantilly, VA 20151-1110
Ph: (703)652-9950
Fax: (703)652-9951

Speil, Steven, Sr. VP
Federation of American Hospitals
[15325]
750 9th St. NW, Ste. 600
Washington, DC 20001-4524
Ph: (202)624-1500
Fax: (202)737-6462

Speilberger, Don, Director
Scale Ship Modelers Association of
North America [22205]
7325, 176th St. SW
7325 176th St. SW
Edmonds, WA 98026

Spellman, Tom, President
Citrus Label Society [21637]
c/o Noel Gilbert, Secretary
131 Miramonte Dr.
Fullerton, CA 92835-3607

Spelman, Justin, Exec. Dir.
Village Science [11471]
10707 W Center Ave.
Lakewood, CO 80226

Spelman, Niyanta, Exec. Dir.
Rainforest Partnership [4615]
800 W 34th St., Ste. 105
Austin, TX 78705
Ph: (512)420-0101

Spelts, Tanya, Administrator
Organization Design Forum [2188]
5016 E Mulberry Dr.
Phoenix, AZ 85018-6525
Ph: (602)510-9105

Speltz, Ann, PhD, President,
Founder
Kid Support [10790]
The Wellness Community
919 18th St. NW
Washington, DC 20006
Ph: (202)659-9709
Fax: (202)659-9703

Spence, Dr. Betty, President
National Association for Female
Executives [649]
2 Park Ave.
New York, NY 10016

Spencer, Angelina, Exec. Dir.
Association of Club Executives
[1650]

601 Pennsylvania Ave. NW, Ste. 900
S
Washington, DC 20004-3647
Ph: (202)220-3019

Spencer, Gene L., President
Kappa Delta Rho [23905]
331 S Main St.
Greensburg, PA 15601
Ph: (724)838-7100
Toll Free: 800-536-5371
Fax: (724)838-7101

Spencer, Karen, Founder, CEO
Whole Child International [11187]
610 Santa Monica Blvd., No. 215
Santa Monica, CA 90401
Ph: (310)394-1000

Spencer, Patrick, Exec. Dir.
Cork Forest Conservation Alliance
[3843]
565 Oxford St. SE
Salem, OR 97302-3001
Ph: (503)931-9690

Sperling, Emily, President
ShelterBox USA [11679]
8374 Market St., No. 203
Lakewood Ranch, FL 34202
Ph: (941)907-6036
Fax: (941)907-6970

Sperling, Laurence S., MD,
President
American Society for Preventive
Cardiology [14095]
6816 Southpoint Pky., Ste. 1000
Jacksonville, FL 32216
Ph: (904)309-6235
Fax: (904)998-0855

Sperry, Raphael, President
Architects/Designers/Planners for
Social Responsibility [18741]
PO Box 9126
Berkeley, CA 94709
Ph: (510)845-1000

Spertus, John, Director
Cardiovascular Outcomes [14153]
18 W 52nd St.
Kansas City, MO 64112
Ph: (816)932-8270
Fax: (816)932-5613

Spice, Amanda, Director
Key Club International [12893]
3636 Woodview Trace
Indianapolis, IN 46268-3196
Ph: (317)875-8755
Toll Free: 800-KIW-ANIS
Fax: (317)879-0204

Spicer, Robert, Rep.
Council of Pediatric Subspecialties
[16604]
6728 Old McLean Village Dr.
McLean, VA 22101
Ph: (703)556-9222
Fax: (703)556-8729

Spiegel, Dr. Allan, Founder
Healing Heroes Network [21123]
31640 US Hwy. 19 N, Ste. 2
Palm Harbor, FL 34684
Ph: (727)781-4376
Toll Free: 877-470-4376

Spielman, Victoria E., Exec. Dir.
Affordable Housing Tax Credit Coali-
tion [486]
1909 K St. NW, 12th Fl.
Washington, DC 20006
Ph: (202)661-7698
Fax: (202)661-2299

Spielvogel, Steven, Esq., President
International Network of Boutique
Law Firms [5013]

c/o Spiegel Liao & Kagay, PC
388 Market St., Ste. 900
San Francisco, CA 94111
Ph: (415)956-6062

Spier, Kathryn, President
American Law and Economics As-
sociation [5413]
127 Wall St.
New Haven, CT 06511-8918
Ph: (203)432-7801
Fax: (203)432-7225

Spier, Zeke, President
Resource Generation [12997]
18 W 27th St., 2nd Fl.
New York, NY 10001
Ph: (646)634-7727
Fax: (646)417-7950

Spies, Jeff, Secretary
North American Board of Certified
Energy Practitioners [6503]
56 Clifton Country Rd., Ste. 202
Clifton Park, NY 12065
Toll Free: 800-654-0021
Fax: (518)899-1092

Spies, Rhaelee, Secretary
American Junior Brahman Associa-
tion [3698]
PO Box 14100
Kansas City, MO 64101-4100
Ph: (816)595-2442
Fax: (816)842-6931

Spiezle, Craig, Exec. Dir., President
Online Trust Alliance [6327]
11011 NE 9th St., Ste. 420
Bellevue, WA 98004
Ph: (425)455-7400

Spigner, Carol Wilson, Chairperson
Center for the Study of Social Policy
[18968]
1575 Eye St. NW, Ste. 500
Washington, DC 20005
Ph: (202)371-1565
Fax: (202)371-1472

Spikes, Bonnita, Director
National Alliance for Prisoners'
Rights [18430]
Penal Reform International
2100 M St. NW, Ste. 170-350
Washington, DC 20037

Spilhaus, Karl H., President
Cashmere and Camel Hair
Manufacturers Institute [3256]
3 Post Office Sq., 8th Fl.
Boston, MA 02109-3905
Ph: (617)542-7481

Spindler, Bob, Assoc. Dir.
National Association of Credit Union
Supervisory and Auditing Commit-
tees [954]
PO Box 160
Del Mar, CA 92014
Toll Free: 800-287-5949
Fax: (858)792-3884

Spinelli, Emily, Exec. Dir., Director
American Association of Teachers of
Spanish and Portuguese [8175]
900 Ladd Rd.
Walled Lake, MI 48390
Ph: (248)960-2180
Fax: (248)960-9570

Spinelli, Emily, Exec. Dir.
Sociedad Honoraria Hispánica
[7976]
900 Ladd Rd.
Walled Lake, MI 48390
Ph: (248)960-2180
Fax: (248)960-9570

Spinks, Jonathan, CEO, President
OSU Tour [11796]
120 E FM 544, Ste. 72, No. 108
Murphy, TX 75094

Spinola, Fran, Coord.
Association for Computing
Machinery - Special Interest Group
on Mobility Systems Users, Data
and Computing [6310]
2 Penn Plz., Ste. 701
New York, NY 10121-0701
Ph: (212)626-0603
Fax: (212)302-5826

Spinola, Fran, Program Mgr.
Association for Computing
Machinery - Special Interest Group
on MultiMedia [6311]
2 Penn Plz., Ste. 701
New York, NY 10121-0701
Ph: (212)869-7440
Toll Free: 800-342-6626
Fax: (212)944-1318

Spisak, Diane, Bd. Member
North American Babydoll Southdown
Sheep Association and Registry
[4678]
305 Lincoln St.
Wamego, KS 66547-1629
Ph: (785)456-8500
Fax: (785)456-8599

Spiteri, Louise, President
Association for Library and Informa-
tion Science Education [8229]
2150 N 107th St., Ste. 205
Seattle, WA 98133
Ph: (206)209-5267
Fax: (206)367-8777

Spitzer, Fr. Robert J., PhD, Chair-
man, Founder
Healing the Culture [12768]
605 2nd St., Ste. 218
Snohomish, WA 98290
Ph: (360)243-3811

Spivey, Angela, Exec. Asst.
Elephant Sanctuary in Tennessee
[10615]
27 E Main St.
Hohenwald, TN 38462
Ph: (931)796-6500
Fax: (931)796-1360

Spoerl, Bob, Contact
New England Trails Conference
[23329]
c/o Bob Spoerl
242 Island Pond Rd.
Derry, NH 03038
Ph: (603)473-0541

Spoerl, Wendy, President
Adopt America Network [10435]
3100 W Central Ave., Ste. 225
Toledo, OH 43606
Ph: (419)726-5100
Toll Free: 800-246-1731
Fax: (419)726-5089

Sponar, Ralph, President
Windmill Class Association [22692]
1200 14th St. NW, Apt. 1104
Washington, DC 20005
Ph: (336)414-2327

Spong, Catherine Y., MD, Dir. (Actg.)
U.S. Department of Health and Hu-
man Services | National Institutes
of Health | Eunice Kennedy Shriver
National Institute of Child Health
and Human Development [14216]
Bldg. 31, Rm. 2A32
31 Center Dr.
Bethesda, MD 20892-2425
Toll Free: 800-370-2943

Spradlin, Rev. Byron, CEO, President
Artists in Christian Testimony **[20126]**
7003 Chadwick Dr., Ste. 354
Brentwood, TN 37027
Ph: (615)376-7861
Toll Free: 888-376-7861
Fax: (615)376-7863

Sprague, Daniel, President
International Book Project **[8079]**
Van Meter Bldg.
1440 Delaware Ave.
Lexington, KY 40505
Ph: (859)254-6771

Spretnjak, Christine, President
Interfaith Church of Metaphysics **[20607]**
163 Moon Valley Rd.
Windyville, MO 65783
Ph: (417)345-8411

Springer, Bryan, MD, President
MusculoSkeletal Infection Society **[15409]**
PO Box 422
Rochester, MN 55903-0422

Springman, Anthony, Founder
Touch the Life of a Child Organization **[11171]**
31811 Pacific Hwy. S, Ste. B-220
Federal Way, WA 98003
Ph: (253)838-2038

Sprouse, Jandy, President
International Yak Association **[4457]**
c/o Stephanie David, Secretary-Treasurer
1676 Y Rd.
Lenora, KS 67645

Spruill, Vikki N., President, CEO
Council on Foundations **[12401]**
2121 Crystal Dr., Ste. 700
Arlington, VA 22202-3706
Ph: (703)879-0600
Toll Free: 800-673-9036

Sprung, Dennis B., CEO, President
American Kennel Club **[21811]**
8051 Arco Corporate Dr., Ste. 100
Raleigh, NC 27617-3390
Ph: (919)233-9767

Spula, Frank J., President
Polish American Congress **[19605]**
1612 K St. NW, Ste. 1200
Washington, DC 20006
Ph: (202)296-6955
Fax: (202)835-1565

Spungen, Elizabeth F., Exec. Dir.
The Print Center **[8939]**
1614 Latimer St.
Philadelphia, PA 19103-6308
Ph: (215)735-6090
Fax: (215)735-5511

Spurling, Richard, Founder, President
ACEing Autism **[13736]**
9064 Nemo St.
Los Angeles, CA 90069
Ph: (617)901-7153

Spurlock, Norm, President
Police Car Owners of America **[21478]**
1106 Lafayette Ave.
Story City, IA 50248-1434
Ph: (515)778-5618

Squire, Rev. Bill, President
Children's Medical Mission of Haiti **[10930]**

925 Hertzler Rd.
Mechanicsburg, PA 17055-6128
Ph: (717)796-1852

Squires, Cindy L., Exec. Dir.
International Wood Products Association **[1412]**
4214 King St.
Alexandria, VA 22302
Ph: (703)820-6696
Fax: (703)820-8550

Sredanovic, Blazo, President
Montenegrin Association of America **[9213]**
805 Magnolia St.
Menlo Park, CA 94025

Srinivasan, Dr. Erica, Director
Center for Grief & Death Education **[13216]**
University of Wisconsin - La Crosse
Center for Grief & Death Education
302G Graff Main Hall
La Crosse, WI 54601-3742
Ph: (608)785-8440

Srodon, Jan, VP
Clay Minerals Society **[6873]**
3635 Concorde Pky., Ste. 500
Chantilly, VA 20151-1110
Ph: (703)652-9960
Fax: (703)652-9951

Srour, George, Exec. Dir., Founder
Building Tomorrow **[12464]**
407 Fulton St.
Indianapolis, IN 46202
Ph: (317)632-3545

St. Amour, Lynn, Trustee
Internet Society **[6767]**
1775 Wiehle Ave., Ste. 201
Reston, VA 20190-5108
Ph: (703)439-2120
Fax: (703)326-9881

St. Clair, Larry, President
American Bryological and Lichenological Society **[6128]**
c/o Susan Wolf, Secretary
430 Lincoln Dr.
Madison, WI 53706-1381
Ph: (608)262-2754

St. George, Joyce, Director
Pact Training **[11497]**
c/o Steven R. Hitt, Team Leader
LaGuardia Community College
31-10 Thomson Ave., Ste. E-241
Long Island City, NY 11101
Ph: (718)482-5154

St. Hilaire, Dr. Rolston, Exec. Dir.
Metropolitan Tree Improvement Alliance **[4732]**
c/o Bert Cregg, Secretary/Treasurer
Michigan State University
Dept. of Horticulture
East Lansing, MI 48824-1325

St. James, Melanie, MPA, Exec. Dir., Founder
Empowerment Works **[11352]**
1793 Northwood Ct.
Oakland, CA 94611-1167
Ph: (415)967-1711

St. John, William, CAE, Exec. Dir.
Healthcare Caterers International **[1335]**
c/o William St. John, Executive Director
3045 Meadow Dr.
Saint Charles, IL 60175
Ph: (630)878-0724

St. Martin, Charlotte, President
Broadway League **[10245]**
729 7th Ave., 5th Fl.

New York, NY 10019
Ph: (212)764-1122
Fax: (212)944-2136

Staab, Richard A., President
Tyler's Hope for a Dystonia Cure **[16038]**
13351 Progress Blvd.
Alachua, FL 32615
Ph: (386)462-5220

Staatz, Rod, Chairman
Credit Union National Association **[949]**
5710 Mineral Point Rd.
Madison, WI 53705
Ph: (202)638-5777
Toll Free: 800-356-9655
Fax: (202)638-7734

Stack, Michael J., Treasurer
International OCD Foundation **[15776]**
18 Tremont St., Ste. 903
Boston, MA 02108
Ph: (617)973-5801
Fax: (617)973-5803

Stack, Robert, Founder, President, CEO
Community Options, Inc. **[11563]**
16 Farber Rd.
Princeton, NJ 08540
Ph: (609)951-9900
Fax: (609)951-9112

Stacy, Carole, Exec. Dir.
National Consortium for Health Science Education **[15085]**
2123 University Park Dr., Ste.100
Okemos, MI 48864
Ph: (517)253-8044
(517)331-8668

Staebell, Dan, Director
Asphalt Pavement Alliance **[495]**
5100 Forbes Blvd.
Lanham, MD 20706
Ph: (301)918-8391
Toll Free: 877-APA-0077
Fax: (301)731-4621

Staehle, Bob, Director
National Marine Distributors Association **[2252]**
37 Pratt St.
Essex, CT 06426
Ph: (860)767-7898
Fax: (860)767-7932

Stafford, Dr. Mark L., Founder, President
Parrot International **[3667]**
15332 Antioch Ave., No. 417
Pacific Palisades, CA 90272
Fax: (310)454-9915

Stafford, Michael, Exec. Dir.
Institute of Clean Air Companies **[2641]**
3033 Wilson Blvd., Ste. 700
Arlington, VA 22201
Ph: (571)858-3707
Fax: (703)243-8696

Stafford, Mimi, Secretary, Treasurer
Reef Relief **[4471]**
631 Greene St.
Key West, FL 33040
Ph: (305)294-3100
Fax: (305)294-9515

Stafford, Pete, Exec. Dir.
Center for Construction Research and Training **[23455]**
8484 Georgia Ave., Ste. 1000
Silver Spring, MD 20910
Ph: (301)578-8500
Fax: (301)578-8572

Stafford, Rod, Secretary
International Amateur Radio Union **[21268]**
PO Box 310905
Newington, CT 06131

Stager, Chad, Rep.
International Titanium Association **[2352]**
11674 Huron St., Ste. 100
Northglenn, CO 80234
Ph: (303)404-2221
Fax: (303)404-9111

Staheli, Kimberlie, Chairperson
North American Society for Trenchless Technology **[7356]**
14500 Lorain Ave., No. 110063
Cleveland, OH 44111
Ph: (216)570-8711

Stahl, Andy, Exec. Dir.
Forest Service Employees for Environmental Ethics **[4578]**
PO Box 11615
Eugene, OR 97440
Ph: (541)484-2692
Fax: (541)484-3004

Stahl, Jim, Jr., President
International FireStop Council **[6633]**
2660 S Utica Ave.
Tulsa, OK 74114
Ph: (918)200-3757

Stahl, Sheri, President
Cremation Association of North America **[2402]**
499 Northgate Pky.
Wheeling, IL 60090-2646
Ph: (312)245-1077
Fax: (312)321-4098

Stahl, Ms. Stanlee Joyce, Exec. VP
Jewish Foundation for the Righteous **[18350]**
305 7th Ave., 19th Fl.
New York, NY 10001-6008
Ph: (212)727-9955
Fax: (212)727-9956

Stahl, William L., Exec. Dir.
Histochemical Society **[6201]**
9650 Rockville Pke.
Bethesda, MD 20814
Ph: (301)634-7026
Fax: (301)634-7099

Stahr, Patricia D., Exec. Dir.
Society for Maternal-Fetal Medicine **[16627]**
409 12th St. SW
Washington, DC 20024
Ph: (202)863-2476
Fax: (202)554-1132

Stainkamp, Cristina, President
Protect Allergic Kids **[13581]**
PO Box 227
Holtsville, NY 11742
Ph: (631)207-1681

Staley, Bryan F., PhD, CEO, President
Environmental Research and Education Foundation **[4139]**
3301 Benson Dr., Ste. 101
Raleigh, NC 27609
Ph: (919)861-6876
Fax: (919)861-6878

Staley, Chris, President
National Council on Education for the Ceramic Arts **[21773]**
4845 Pearl East Cir., Ste. 101
Boulder, CO 80301
Ph: (303)828-2811
Toll Free: 866-266-2322
Fax: (303)828-0911

Stalknecht, Paul T., CEO, President
Air Conditioning Contractors of
America Association, Inc. [1610]
2800 S Shirlington Rd., Ste. 300
Arlington, VA 22206
Ph: (703)575-4477
Toll Free: 888-290-2220

Stallings, Margaret K., Exec. Dir.
North American Society for Pediatric
Gastroenterology, Hepatology and
Nutrition [14795]
PO Box 6
Flourtown, PA 19031
Ph: (215)233-0808
Fax: (215)233-3918

Stallman, Bob, President
American Farm Bureau Federation
[4149]
600 Maryland Ave. SW, Ste. 1000W
Washington, DC 20024
Ph: (202)406-3600
   (202)406-3614

Stallman, Richard M., President,
Founder
Free Software Foundation [6275]
51 Franklin St., 5th Fl.
Boston, MA 02110-1301
Ph: (617)542-5942
Fax: (617)542-2652

Stallmer, Eric W., President
Commercial Spaceflight Federation
[133]
500 New Jersey Ave. NW, Ste. 400
Washington, DC 20001
Ph: (202)715-2928

Stallworthy, Guy, President, CEO
Grounds for Health [13979]
600 Blair Park, Ste. 330
Williston, VT 05495
Ph: (802)876-7835
Fax: (802)876-7795

Stalters, Linda, Founder
Schizophrenia and Related
Disorders Alliance of America
[15805]
PO Box 941222
Houston, TX 77094-8222
Ph: (240)423-9432
Toll Free: 866-800-5199

Stamas, Stephen, Chairman
American Assembly [18959]
475 Riverside Dr., Ste. 456
New York, NY 10115-0084
Ph: (212)870-3500

Stamboulian, Dr. Daniel, Founder,
President
Fighting Infectious Diseases in
Emerging Countries [15398]
2050 Coral Way, Ste. 407
Miami, FL 33145
Ph: (305)854-0075
Fax: (305)856-7847

Stamper, Robert Dale, President
Blinded Veterans Association
[17692]
477 H St. NW
Washington, DC 20001-2694
Ph: (202)371-8880
Toll Free: 800-669-7079
Fax: (202)371-8258

Stanard, Esther, Founder
Miscarriage Matters Inc. [12353]
PO Box 9614
Naperville, IL 60567
Toll Free: 888-520-7743

Stanchek, Jeffrey, VP
National Mine Rescue Association
[6882]

c/o Chris Melvin, President
132 Forest Glen Dr.
Imperial, PA 15126

Stanco, Sr. Mary, Prog. Dir.
Humility of Mary Volunteer Service
[19844]
PO Box 534
Villa Maria, PA 16155
Ph: (724)964-8920

Standiford, Cathy, Contact
Soroptimist International of the
Americas [12909]
1709 Spruce St.
Philadelphia, PA 19103-6103
Ph: (215)893-9000
Fax: (215)893-5200

Staneviius, Vytas, President
Lithuanian Catholic Press Society
[19543]
4545 W 63rd St.
Chicago, IL 60629-5532
Ph: (773)585-9500
Fax: (773)585-8284

Stanfield, Cindy, PhD, President
Alpha Epsilon Delta [23815]
Texas Christian University, Box
298810
Fort Worth, TX 76129
Ph: (817)257-4550
Fax: (817)257-0201

Stanford, Howard, Chairman
Black Culinarian Alliance [961]
244 Madison Ave., Ste. 305
New York, NY 10016-2817
Ph: (212)643-6570
Fax: (212)967-4184

Stanga, Pete, Exec. Dir.
Grantmakers Without Borders
[12483]
Global Fund for Women
222 Sutter St., Ste. 500
San Francisco, CA 94129
Ph: (415)248-4800
Fax: (415)248-4801

Stange, Judy, Ph.D., Exec. Dir.
National Association of Mental
Health Planning and Advisory
Councils [15788]
2000 N Beauregard St., 6th Fl.
Alexandria, VA 22311
Ph: (703)797-2595
Fax: (703)684-5968

Stanhope, Marcia, Ph.D, VP
Association of Community Health
Nursing Educators [16119]
10200 W 44th Ave., Ste. 304
Wheat Ridge, CO 80033
Ph: (303)422-0769
   (720)881-6044
Fax: (303)422-8894

Stanitski, Debbie, MD, President
Equestrian Medical Safety Associa-
tion [17283]
PO Box 100236
Gainesville, FL 32610-0236

Stanley, Debra, President
American Society of Victimology
[13257]
c/o Thomas Underwood, Treasurer
Washburn University
1700 SW College Ave.
Topeka, KS 66621
Ph: (785)670-1242

Stanley, John, Contact
Just for Openers [21681]
c/o John Stanley
PO Box 51008

Durham, NC 27717

Stanley, Michael, President
Kappa Pi International Art Honor
Society [23679]
307 S 5th Ave.
Cleveland, MS 38732
Ph: (662)846-4729

Stanley, Sarah, Bd. Member
Committee for Children [10946]
2815 2nd Ave., Ste. 400
Seattle, WA 98121-3207
Ph: (206)343-1223
Toll Free: 800-634-4449
Fax: (206)438-6765

Stansberry, Tammy, Coord.
Amerind Foundation and Museum
[5904]
2100 N Amerind Rd.
Dragoon, AZ 85609
Ph: (520)586-3666

Stanton, Dr. Gregory H., President
Genocide Watch [18306]
PO Box 809
Washington, DC 20044
Ph: (703)448-0222

Stanton, Kim, Exec. Dir.
Council for Accreditation in Oc-
cupational Hearing Conservation
[16320]
555 E Wells St., Ste. 1100
Milwaukee, WI 53202-3823
Ph: (414)276-5338
Fax: (414)276-2146

Stanton, Sam, Exec. Dir.
Maryknoll Lay Missioners [20432]
PO Box 307
Maryknoll, NY 10545-0307
Ph: (914)762-6364
Toll Free: 800-867-2980

Stants, Heather, President
American Brussels Griffon Associa-
tion [21801]
c/o Linda G. Vance, Secretary
PO Box 11
Shirley, IL 61772-0011
Ph: (309)453-1674

Staple-Clark, Jennifer, CEO,
Founder
Unite for Sight [13279]
234 Church St., 15th Fl.
New Haven, CT 06510
Ph: (203)404-4900

Stargot, Ilene, President
National Infertility Network Exchange
[12419]
PO Box 204
East Meadow, NY 11554
Ph: (516)794-5772
Fax: (516)794-0008

Stark, Kathy, CRP, President
Recognition Professionals
International [11782]
1000 Westgate Dr., Ste. 252
Saint Paul, MN 55114
Ph: (651)290-7490
Fax: (651)290-2266

Stark, Michelle, Founder, President
Matanya's Hope [12551]
PO Box 562
Homewood, IL 60430
Ph: (708)822-4673

Stark, Robert, Treasurer
Congregation of the Blessed Sacra-
ment [19827]
5384 Wilson Mills Rd.
Cleveland, OH 44143-3023
Ph: (440)442-6311

Stark, Sonia, Director
National Association of Women Art-
ists [8930]
80 5th Ave., Ste. 1405
New York, NY 10011
Ph: (212)675-1616

Starkey, Gary, President
United Postal Stationery Society
[22375]
1659 Branham Ln., Ste. F-307
San Jose, CA 95118-2291

Starkey, Jennifer, Exec. Dir.
National Council for Continuing
Education and Training [7672]
PO Box 2916
Columbus, OH 43216
Toll Free: 888-771-0179
Fax: (877)835-5798

Starkey, John, President
U.S. Poultry and Egg Association
[4574]
1530 Cooledge Rd.
Tucker, GA 30084-7303
Ph: (770)493-9401
Fax: (770)493-9257

Starks, Shirley, President
Set Decorators Society of America
[1959]
7100 Tujunga Ave., Ste. A
North Hollywood, CA 91605-6216
Ph: (818)255-2425
Fax: (818)982-8597

Starnes, Stephen, President
Alpha Delta Phi [23881]
21 Byron Pl.
New Haven, CT 06515
Ph: (508)226-1832
Fax: (508)226-4456

Starns, Gary, President
Treeing Walker Breeders and Fanciers Association [21972]
c/o Danielle Champ, Secretary
293 Paddy Rd.
Duck, WV 25063
Ph: (304)651-9028

Starowicz, Sharon, President
Orthopedic Surgical Manufacturers
Association [1605]
c/o Valerie Frank
7302 Texas Heights Ave.
Germantown, TN 38183-0805
Ph: (901)758-0806

Starr, Amelia, V. Chmn. of the Bd.
Fund for Modern Courts [5384]
205 E 42nd St., 6th Fl.
New York, NY 10017
Ph: (212)541-6741
Fax: (212)541-7301

Starr, Gordon, Chairman
Pachamama Alliance [4614]
Presidio Bldg., No. 1009
San Francisco, CA 94129
Ph: (415)561-4522

Starr, Joan, CEO
Kids Ecology Corps [4118]
3299 SW 4th Ave.
Fort Lauderdale, FL 33315
Ph: (954)524-0366

Starr, Joshua P., CEO
Phi Delta Kappa [23853]
320 W 8th St., Ste. 216
Bloomington, IN 47404
Ph: (812)339-1156
Toll Free: 800-766-1156
Fax: (812)339-0018

Starr, Prof. Martha A., Contact
International Confederation of Associations for Pluralism in Economics [6394]

Dept. of Economics
Bucknell University
1 Dent Dr.
Lewisburg, PA 17837
Ph: (570)577-1666

Starrett, Ben, Exec. Dir., Founder
Funders' Network for Smart Growth
and Livable Communities [11361]
1500 San Remo Ave., Ste. 249
Coral Gables, FL 33146
Ph: (305)667-6350
Fax: (305)667-6355

Stassen, Ms. Corrie, Exec. Dir.
It's My Heart [14131]
1304 Langham Creek, No. 235
Houston, TX 77084
Ph: (713)334-4244
    (713)334-4243
Toll Free: 888-HEART-07
Fax: (866)222-0334

Stasz, Meghan, Contact
Food Waste Reduction Alliance
    [4191]
1350 Eye I St. NW, Ste. 300
Washington, DC 20005

Staudt, Danielle, Exec. Dir.
Population Association of America
    [6368]
8630 Fenton St., Ste. 722
Silver Spring, MD 20910
Ph: (301)565-6710
Fax: (301)565-7850

Stauffer, Gary, President
Youth Maritime Training Association
    [8266]
PO Box 70425
Seattle, WA 98127-0425
Ph: (206)300-5559

Stautzenbach, Thomas E., Exec.
    Dir., CEO
American Academy of Physical
    Medicine and Rehabilitation
    [17076]
9700 W Bryn Mawr Ave., Ste. 200
Rosemont, IL 60018-5706
Ph: (847)737-6000
Toll Free: 877-227-6799
Fax: (847)737-6001

Stavanja, Rick, President
CAD Society [6273]
Strategic Reach PR
7100 N Broadway, Bldg. 2, Ste.
    2LPH
Denver, CO 80221
Ph: (303)487-7406
Toll Free: 888-750-0839

Stavig, Kyle R., Chairman
Industrial Steel Drum Institute [835]
120 Hatton Dr.
Severna Park, MD 21146-4400
Ph: (410)544-0385

Stavros, Gina, Founder
Peruvian Partners [13081]
PO Box 735
Delano, MN 55328

Stayton, Scott, VP
Sump and Sewage Pump
    Manufacturers Association [589]
c/o Blake Jeffery, Managing Director
PO Box 44071
Indianapolis, IN 46244
Ph: (317)636-0278

Steaban, Robin, President
American College of Cardiovascular
    Administrators [15573]
American Academy of Medical
    Administrators

330 N Wabash Ave., Ste. 200
Chicago, IL 60611
Ph: (312)321-6815
Fax: (312)673-6705

Stead, Mark, VP
Cast Iron Seat Collectors Associa-
    tion [22169]
c/o Olan Bentley, President
1168 Jamison Rd.
Washington Court House, OH
    43160-8479
Ph: (740)335-0964

Stearns, David, Founder
Imagine World Health [14940]
105 E Dolphin Blvd.
Ponte Vedra Beach, FL 32082-1714
Ph: (904)285-0240

Stearns, Richard, President
World Vision [12739]
PO Box 9716
Federal Way, WA 98063-9716
Toll Free: 888-511-6548

Stebbins, Chad, Exec. Dir.
International Society of Weekly
    Newspaper Editors [2690]
Missouri Southern State University
3950 E Newman Rd.
Joplin, MO 64801-1595

Stebner, Dr. Aaron, President
International Organization on Shape
    Memory and Superelastic
    Technologies [6846]
9639 Kinsman Rd.
Novelty, OH 44073-0001
Ph: (440)338-5151
Fax: (440)338-4634

Stec, Marc, President
Society of Government Travel
    Professionals [3393]
PO Box 158
Glyndon, MD 21071-0158
Ph: (202)241-7487
Fax: (202)379-1775

Steckel, Les, President, CEO
Fellowship of Christian Athletes
    [20141]
8701 Leeds Rd.
Kansas City, MO 64129
Ph: (816)921-0909
Toll Free: 800-289-0909
Fax: (816)921-8755

Steckel, Marie-Monique, President
French Institute Alliance Francaise
    [9335]
22 E 60th St.
New York, NY 10022
Ph: (212)355-6100

Stedman, Brooke, Dep. Dir.
Women in International Security
    [19097]
1779 Massachusetts Ave. NW, Ste.
    510
Washington, DC 20036

Steele, Andrew, Exec. Dir., Founder,
    Chmn. of the Bd.
BLOOM Africa [10870]
PO Box 4646
Chicago, IL 60680-4646
Ph: (856)905-8779

Steele, Charles, Jr., President, CEO
Southern Christian Leadership
    Conference [17931]
320 Auburn Ave. NE
Atlanta, GA 30303
Ph: (404)522-1420

Steele, Darrin, CEO
U.S. Bobsled and Skeleton Federa-
    tion [23178]

196 Old Military Rd.
Lake Placid, NY 12946
Ph: (518)523-1842
Fax: (518)523-9491

Steele, Dave, Exec. Dir.
International Sled Dog Racing As-
    sociation [22826]
22702 Rebel Rd.
Merrifield, MN 56465
Ph: (218)765-4297

Steele, Julie Friedman, Chairperson
World Future Society [6658]
333 N Lasalle St.
Chicago, IL 60654
Toll Free: 800-989-8274

Steele, Ruth, Arch.
Center for Pacific Northwest Studies
    [7163]
Western Washington University
808 25th St.
Bellingham, WA 98225-9103
Ph: (360)650-7534
Fax: (360)650-3323

Steele, Scott L., Exec. Dir.
University Resident Theatre Associa-
    tion [8702]
1560 Broadway, Ste. 1103
New York, NY 10036
Ph: (212)221-1130
Fax: (212)869-2752

Steele, Shari, Director
Electronic Frontier Foundation
    [7265]
815 Eddy St.
San Francisco, CA 94109-7701
Ph: (415)436-9333
Fax: (415)436-9993

Steele, Tammy, Exec. Dir.
National Women in Agriculture As-
    sociation [3574]
1701 N Martin Luther King Ave.
Oklahoma City, OK 73111
Ph: (405)424-4623
Fax: (405)424-4624

Steen, Carol, Founder
American Synesthesia Association,
    Inc. [16009]
75 E 4th St., Ste. 573
New York, NY 10003

Steen, Scott, CEO
American Forests [3799]
1220 L St. NW, Ste. 750
Washington, DC 20005
Ph: (202)737-1944

Steenbeek, Gerben, Director
Friesian Horse Association of North
    America [4351]
4037 Iron Works Pky., Ste. 160
Lexington, KY 40511-8483
Ph: (859)455-7430
Fax: (859)455-7457

Steenstra, Eric, Exec. Dir.
Hemp Industries Association [3258]
PO Box 575
Summerland, CA 93067
Ph: (707)874-3648

Steenstra, Eric, President
Vote Hemp [18649]
PO Box 1571
Brattleboro, VT 05302-1571
Ph: (202)318-8999
Fax: (202)318-8999

Stefanak, Matthew, Secretary,
    Treasurer
Public Health Foundation [17017]
1300 L St. NW, Ste. 800

Washington, DC 20005
Ph: (202)218-4400
    (202)218-4420
Fax: (202)218-4409

Stefanak, Matthew, Chairman
Public Health Leadership Society
    [17018]
1515 Poydras St., Ste. 1200
New Orleans, LA 70112-4536
Ph: (504)301-9821
Fax: (504)301-9820

Stefandel, Roland, President
Chemists' Club [19656]
30 W 44th St.
New York, NY 10036
Ph: (212)626-9300

Stefani, Jeff, Secretary, Treasurer
Wood I-Joist Manufacturers Associa-
    tion [1447]
c/o Dave Anderson, Member
Roseburg Forest Products
PO Box 1088
Roseburg, OR 97470

Stefaniak, Thomas L., MBA, Exec.
    Dir.
Society for Vascular Ultrasound
    [17582]
4601 Presidents Dr., Ste. 260
Lanham, MD 20706-4831
Ph: (301)459-7550
Toll Free: 800-788-8346
Fax: (301)459-5651

Stefanson, Valdi, President
Antique Snowmobile Club of
    America [22417]
c/o Valdi Stefanson, President
8660 Fawn Lake Dr. NE
Stacy, MN 55079-9306
Ph: (651)462-4497

Steffen, Leah, President
Music EdVentures [8375]
c/o Leah Steffen, President
26276 Redwing Ave.
Shafer, MN 55074
Ph: (651)257-1698

Steffen, Richie, President
Hardy Fern Foundation [4431]
PO Box 3797
Federal Way, WA 98063-3797
Ph: (253)838-4646
Fax: (253)838-4686

Steffen, Tony, Owner
Anheuser-Busch Collectors Club
    [21617]
1070 Dundee Ave., Ste. A
East Dundee, IL 60118
Ph: (847)428-3150
Toll Free: 800-498-3215
Fax: (847)428-3170

Steffler, Ann, Bd. Member
South African Boerboel Breeders
    Association - U.S.A. and Canada
    [22820]
PO Box 353
Arivaca, AZ 85601
Ph: (480)650-4406

Stegman, Judith M., President
United States Association of
    Consecrated Virgins [19915]
300 W Ottawa St.
Lansing, MI 48933-1577
Fax: (253)270-5507

Stehle, Jon, Director
American Association for Budget and
    Program Analysis [5703]
PO Box 1157
Falls Church, VA 22041
Ph: (703)941-4300

Steil, Peter, CEO
National Council of Real Estate
Investment Fiduciaries **[2031]**
Aon Ctr.
200 E Randolph St., Ste. 5135
Chicago, IL 60601
Ph: (312)819-5890
Fax: (312)819-5891

Steimer-King, Ashley, Prog. Dir.
Girls Learn International, Inc. **[7945]**
433 S Beverly Dr.
Beverly Hills, CA 90212
Ph: (310)556-2500
Fax: (310)556-2509

Stein, Daniel, President
Federation for American Immigration
Reform **[18464]**
25 Massachusetts Ave. NW, Ste.
330
Washington, DC 20001
Ph: (202)328-7004
Toll Free: 877-627-3247
Fax: (202)387-3447

Stein, Dean K., Exec. Dir.
American Psychoanalytic Association
[16841]
309 E 49th St.
New York, NY 10017-1601
Ph: (212)752-0450

Stein, Eileen Pollock, Chairperson
Cosmic Baseball Association
[22548]
907 6th St. SW, Ste. 214
Washington, DC 20024

Stein, Judith A., JD, Exec. Dir.
Center for Medicare Advocacy
[15096]
PO Box 350
Willimantic, CT 06226
Ph: (860)456-7790
Fax: (860)456-2614

Stein, Ken, Exec. Dir.
League of Historic American
Theatres **[10257]**
9 Newport Dr., Ste. 200
Forest Hill, MD 21050
Ph: (443)640-1058
Fax: (443)640-1031

Stein, Ken Shubin, Founder, Chair-
man
Crutches 4 Kids, Inc. **[10951]**
459 Columbus Ave., Ste. 381
New York, NY 10024
Ph: (646)535-4629

Stein, Robert, President, CEO
American Society on Aging **[10498]**
575 Market St., Ste. 2100
San Francisco, CA 94105-2938
Ph: (415)974-9600
Toll Free: 800-537-9728
Fax: (415)974-0300

Stein, Terry L., President, CEO
Autism 4 Parents **[13740]**
209 Lawton Blvd.
Knoxville, TN 37934
Toll Free: 855-273-5437

Steinbacher, Ann, Director
Border Terrier Club of America
[21844]
c/o Susan Friedenberg, Membership
Chairperson
55 Marble St.
Staten Island, NY 10314-2131
Ph: (718)761-2439

Steinberg, Arthur, President
Psi Omega Fraternity **[23720]**
1040 Savannah Hwy.

Charleston, SC 29407-7804
Ph: (843)556-0573
Fax: (843)556-6311

Steinberg, Edward L., MSc, Chair-
man
Keren Or **[17720]**
350 7th Ave., Ste. 701
New York, NY 10001-1942
Ph: (212)279-4070
Fax: (212)279-4043

Steineck, Raji, President
International Society for the Study of
Time **[10282]**
c/o Jo Alyson Parker
St. Joseph's University
English Dept.
5600 City Ave.
Philadelphia, PA 19131-1395

Steiner, Betsy, Exec. Dir.
EPS Industry Alliance **[4741]**
1298 Cronson Blvd., Ste. 201
Crofton, MD 21114-2035
Toll Free: 800-607-3772
Fax: (410)451-8343

Steiner, Dale, Chairman
National Council for History Educa-
tion **[7987]**
13940 Cedar Rd., No. 393
University Heights, OH 44118
Ph: (240)696-6600
Fax: (240)523-0245

Steiner, Todd, Exec. Dir.
Turtle Island Restoration Network
[3961]
9255 Sir Francis Drake Blvd.
Olema, CA 94950
Ph: (415)663-8590
Toll Free: 800-859-7283
Fax: (415)663-9534

Steiner, Tom, President
Space Topic Study Unit **[22369]**
PO Box 780241
Maspeth, NY 11378-0241

Steinke, Greg A., Ph.D, President,
Chairman, Coord., Member Svcs.
National Association of Composers
U.S.A. **[9967]**
PO Box 49256, Barrington Sta.
Los Angeles, CA 90049
Ph: (541)765-2406

Steinman, A., Chmn. of the Bd.
National Center for Manufacturing
Sciences **[2228]**
3025 Boardwalk St.
Ann Arbor, MI 48108
Toll Free: 800-222-6267
Fax: (734)995-0380

Steinmann, David P., Chairman
Jewish Institute for National Security
Affairs **[18085]**
1101 14th St. NW, Ste. 1110
Washington, DC 20005
Ph: (202)667-3900
Fax: (202)667-0601

Steinmann, Sean, President
Security Hardware Distributors As-
sociation **[1576]**
105 Eastern Ave., Ste. 104
Annapolis, MD 21403
Ph: (410)940-6346
Fax: (410)263-1659

Steinmetz, Fr. Thomas P., Director
National Association of Melkite Youth
[19997]
c/o Fr. Thomas P. Steinmetz, Director
140 Mitchell St.

Manchester, NH 03103
Ph: (603)623-8944

Steinmiller, Sharon, Director
New Wineskins Missionary Network
[20447]
PO Box 278
Ambridge, PA 15003
Ph: (724)266-2810

Stelpstra, Rev. William, Founder,
Director
World for Christ Crusade **[20476]**
1005 Union Valley Rd.
West Milford, NJ 07480-1220
Ph: (973)728-3267

Stelton, Susan, President
World Council of Enterostomal
Therapists **[16529]**
1000 Potomac St. NW, Ste. 108
Washington, DC 20007
Ph: (202)567-3030
Fax: (202)833-3636

Stemley, Wendell, President
National Association of Minority
Contractors **[878]**
The Barr Bldg.
910 17th St. NW, Ste. 413
Washington, DC 20006
Ph: (202)296-1600
Fax: (202)296-1644

Stemm, Laurie Defrain, VP
Homeopaths Without Borders
[15289]
20 Brookside Ln.
Hebron, NH 03241

Stencel, Mark, Chairperson
International Institute of Ammonia
Refrigeration **[1628]**
1001 N Fairfax St., Ste. 503
Alexandria, VA 22314
Ph: (703)312-4200
Fax: (703)312-0065

Stenersen, Steve, CEO, President
U.S. Lacrosse **[22976]**
113 W University Pkwy.
Baltimore, MD 21210
Ph: (410)235-6882
Fax: (410)366-6735

Stenersen, Steve, CEO, President
United States Lacrosse Association-
Women's Div. **[22977]**
113 W University Pkwy.
Baltimore, MD 21210
Ph: (410)235-6882
Fax: (410)366-6735

Stenstrom, Steve, President
Pro Athletes Outreach **[20160]**
640 Plaza Dr., Ste. 110
Highlands Ranch, CO 80129
Fax: (408)674-6161

Stephen, Timothy, President
Communication Institute for Online
Scholarship **[7484]**
PO Box 57
Rotterdam Junction, NY 12150-0057
Ph: (518)887-2443
Fax: (518)887-5186

Stephens, Anthony T., Chairman
Hope for Grieving Children Africa
[11038]
1011 Lake St., Ste. 404
Oak Park, IL 60301
Ph: (708)445-8678

Stephens, Elaine D., Director
Home Healthcare Nurses Association **[16134]**
228 7th St. SE

Washington, DC 20003
Ph: (202)547-7424
Fax: (202)547-3540

Stephens, Greg, Exec. Dir.
National CML Society **[15537]**
130 Inverness Plz., Ste. 307
Birmingham, AL 35242
Toll Free: 877-431-2573

Stephens, John F., Exec. Dir.
American Studies Association **[8788]**
1120 19th St. NW, Ste. 301
Washington, DC 20036
Ph: (202)467-4783
Fax: (202)467-4786

Stephens, Larry D., Exec. VP
U.S. Committee on Irrigation and
Drainage **[7376]**
1616 17th St., No. 483
Denver, CO 80202
Ph: (303)628-5430
Fax: (303)628-5431

Stephens, Larry D., Exec. Dir.
United States Society on Dams
[7377]
1616 17th St., Ste. 483
Denver, CO 80202-1277
Ph: (303)628-5430
Fax: (303)628-5431

Stephens, Oscar, VP
North American-Chilean Chamber of
Commerce **[23609]**
866 United Nations Plz., Rm. 4019
New York, NY 10017
Ph: (212)317-1959
Fax: (212)758-8598

Stephens, Pat, Chmn. of the Bd.
International Academy of
Compounding Pharmacists **[16664]**
4638 Riverstone Blvd.
Missouri City, TX 77459-6157
Ph: (281)933-8400
Toll Free: 800-927-4227
Fax: (281)495-0602

Stephens, Dr. Ronald D., Exec. Dir.
National School Safety Center
[8525]
141 Duesenberg Dr., Ste. 7B
Westlake Village, CA 91362-3472
Ph: (805)373-9977

Stephenson, Chris, Exec. Dir.
Association for Computing
Machinery **[6292]**
2 Penn Plz., Ste. 701
New York, NY 10121-0701
Ph: (212)869-7440
Toll Free: 800-342-6626

Stephenson, David, Exec. Dir.
Engineers in Action **[11353]**
10759 E Admiral Pl.
Tulsa, OK 74116
Ph: (918)770-9840
(918)481-9009

Stephenson, Rebecca, ACAP, Co-
Pres.
Alliance of Claims Assistance
Professionals **[1821]**
c/o Rebecca Stephenson, Co-
President
9600 Escarpment, Ste. 745-65
Austin, TX 78749-1982
Toll Free: 888-394-5163

Stephey, Wendy, Secretary,
Treasurer
National Quarter Pony Association
[4385]
PO Box 171
Melrose, OH 45861
Ph: (419)594-2968

Sterling, Mr. Eric E., President
Criminal Justice Policy Foundation
[18597]
8730 Georgia Ave., Ste. 400
Silver Spring, MD 20910
Ph: (301)589-6020
Fax: (301)589-5056

Sterling, Eric E., Coord.
National Drug Strategy Network
[17920]
Criminal Justice Policy Foundation
8730 Georgia Ave., Ste. 400
Silver Spring, MD 20910
Ph: (301)589-6020
Fax: (301)589-5056

Stern, Andrew, Treasurer
International Partners **[12168]**
15437 Tindlay St.
Silver Spring, MD 20905
Ph: (301)318-2545
Fax: (301)587-3299

Stern, David, Exec. Dir.
Equal Justice Works **[5381]**
1730 M St. NW, Ste. 1010
Washington, DC 20036-4511
Ph: (202)466-3686

Stern, David J., Commissioner
National Basketball Association
[22574]
Olympic Tower
645 5th Ave.
New York, NY 10022
Ph: (212)407-8000
Fax: (212)832-3861

Stern, Diana, Liaison
National Women Law Students'
Organization **[8222]**
PO Box 77546
San Francisco, CA 94107

Stern, Diann, Exec. Dir.
International Liver Transplantation
Society **[17511]**
1120 Route 73, Ste. 200
Mount Laurel, NJ 08054-5113
Fax: (856)439-0525

Stern, Diann, MS, Exec. Dir.
OsteoArthritis Research Society
International **[17163]**
1120 Route 73, Ste. 200
Mount Laurel, NJ 08054
Ph: (856)642-4215
   (856)439-1385
Fax: (856)439-0525

Stern, Geoffrey, President
PEF Israel Endowment Funds Inc.
[12211]
630 3rd Ave., 15th Fl.
New York, NY 10017
Ph: (212)599-1260
Fax: (212)599-5981

Stern, Kalika, Exec. Dir.
Society for Folk Arts Preservation
Inc. **[9332]**
308 E 79th St.
New York, NY 10075-0906
Ph: (845)436-7314

Stern, Mark S., MD, Founder
Friends of Neurosurgery
International **[16064]**
705 E Ohio Ave.
Escondido, CA 92025
Ph: (760)489-9490
Fax: (760)489-7638

Sternbach, Melissa, Exec. Dir.
National Board of Trial Advocacy
[5827]
200 Stonewall Blvd., Ste. 1

Wrentham, MA 02093
Ph: (508)384-6565
Fax: (508)384-8223

Sternberg, Dana Von, President
Active 20-30 U.S. & Canada **[12881]**
2800 W Higgins Rd., Ste. 440
Hoffman Estates, IL 60169-7286
Ph: (847)852-5206
Fax: (847)885-8393

Sternberg, Sue, Editor
Latham Foundation **[10658]**
1320 Harbor Bay Pky., Ste. 200
Alameda, CA 94502
Ph: (510)521-0920
Fax: (510)521-9861

Sterne, Jeff, Exec. Dir.
All Star Association **[966]**
1050 Monarch St., Ste. 101
Lexington, KY 40513
Toll Free: 800-930-3644
Fax: (859)255-3647

Sterne, Jim, Chmn. of the Bd.
Digital Analytics Association **[6766]**
401 Edgewater Pl., Ste. 600
Wakefield, MA 01880-6200
Ph: (781)876-8933
Fax: (781)224-1239

Sternicki, Vicki, Founder, President
Heroes Forever **[13981]**
PO Box 1872
Arvada, CO 80001
Ph: (303)428-6171

Stertzer, David, FLMI, CEO
Association for Advanced Life
Underwriting **[1834]**
11921 Freedom Dr., Ste. 1100
Reston, VA 20190
Ph: (703)641-9400
Toll Free: 888-275-0092
Fax: (703)641-9885

Stertzer, Jennifer E., President
Association for Documentary Editing
[9461]
c/o Constance B. Schulz, Secretary
Department of History
University of South Carolina
Columbia, SC 29208

Stessin-Cohn, Susan, Dir. Ed.
Huguenot Historical Society **[21002]**
88 Huguenot St.
New Paltz, NY 12561-1403
Ph: (845)255-1660
   (845)255-0180
Fax: (845)255-0376

Stetter, Tim, Officer
National Alliance of Concurrent
Enrollment Partnerships **[7636]**
PO Box 578
Chapel Hill, NC 27514
Ph: (919)593-5205
Toll Free: 877-572-8693

Stetter, Trudy, President
Devils Fan Club **[24073]**
Prudential Ctr.
25 Lafayette St.
Newark, NJ 07102-3611
Ph: (201)768-9680

Stevens, Constance, MBA, President
Short Wing Piper Club **[21246]**
PO Box 10822
Springfield, MO 65808-0822
Ph: (417)883-1457
Toll Free: 855-797-2411

Stevens, Dr. David, Exec. Dir.
American Academy of Medical Ethics **[14743]**

PO Box 7500
Bristol, TN 37621
Ph: (423)844-1095

Stevens, Dr. David, CEO
Christian Medical and Dental As-
sociations **[20323]**
2604 Highway 421
Bristol, TN 37620
Ph: (423)844-1000
Toll Free: 888-231-2637
Fax: (423)844-1005

Stevens, Ernest L., Chairman
National Indian Gaming Association
[5257]
224 2nd St. SE
Washington, DC 20003-1943
Ph: (202)546-7711

Stevens, John, Chairman
Friends of Honduran Children
[10985]
PO Box 501213
Indianapolis, IN 46250

Stevens, John, VP
National Association of Mortgage
Brokers **[408]**
2701 W 15th St., Ste. 536
Plano, TX 75075
Ph: (972)758-1151
Fax: (530)484-2906

Stevens, John, Bd. Member
PE4life **[8434]**
127 W 10th St., Ste. 208
Kansas City, MO 64105
Ph: (816)472-7345

Stevens, Laura M., President
Society of Early Americanists **[8792]**
c/o Kristina Bross, Advisory Officer
Dept. of English
Purdue University
500 Oval Dr.
West Lafayette, IN 47907

Stevens, Rachel, Director
National Center for Policy Analysis
[18990]
14180 Dallas Pky., Ste. 350
Dallas, TX 75254
Ph: (972)386-6272

Stevens, Robert, President
Southwest Case Research Associa-
tion **[7570]**
c/o Robert Stevens, President
John Massey School of Business
Southern Oklahoma State University
1405 N 4th Ave.
Durant, OK 74701
Ph: (580)745-3181
   (580)745-3190

Stevens, Wally, Exec. Dir.
Global Aquaculture Alliance **[3640]**
4111 Telegraph Rd., Ste. 302
Saint Louis, MO 63129
Ph: (314)293-5500

Stevenson, Bryan, Exec. Dir.
Equal Justice Initiative **[18071]**
122 Commerce St.
Montgomery, AL 36104
Ph: (334)269-1803
Fax: (334)269-1806

Stevenson, Douglas B., Director
Center for Seafarers' Rights **[5574]**
118 Export St.
Newark, NJ 07114
Ph: (973)589-5828
Fax: (973)817-8565

Stevenson, Jennifer, Treasurer
National Women's Martial Arts
Federation **[23008]**

9450 SW Gemini Dr.
Beaverton, OR 97005-2343
Ph: (206)339-5251
Fax: (206)339-5251

Stevenson, Mark, COO
Air Force Sergeants Association
[5586]
5211 Auth Rd.
Suitland, MD 20746
Ph: (301)899-3500
Toll Free: 800-638-0594
Fax: (301)899-8136

Stevenson, Mary, Exec. Dir.
COAR Peace Mission **[18174]**
28700 Euclid Ave.
Wickliffe, OH 44092-2585
Ph: (440)943-7615
Fax: (440)943-7618

Stevenson, Richard, Secretary
Academy of Operative Dentistry
[14367]
PO Box 25637
Los Angeles, CA 90025
Ph: (310)794-4387
Fax: (310)825-2536

Stevenson, Richard, Officer
American Academy for Cerebral
Palsy and Developmental Medicine
[15893]
555 E Wells St., Ste. 1100
Milwaukee, WI 53202-3800
Ph: (414)918-3014
Fax: (414)276-2146

Stevers, Paul H., Founder, Chmn. of
the Bd., President
CharityHelp International **[10891]**
PO Box 1904
Annapolis, MD 21404
Ph: (443)283-0677

Steward, David, Secretary
Association of Personal Computer
User Groups **[6294]**
PO Box 1384
Pine, AZ 85544-1384

Steward, Kaki, President
Silk Painters International **[8940]**
PO Box 1074
Eastpoint, FL 32328

Stewart, Ann, Admin. Asst.
Historical Society of Early American
Decoration **[8902]**
PO Box 30
Cooperstown, NY 13326-0030
Ph: (607)547-5667
Toll Free: 866-304-7323

Stewart, Bill, President
National Association for Rights
Protection and Advocacy **[17918]**
c/o Ann Marshall, Administrator
PO Box 855
Huntsville, AL 35804
Ph: (256)650-6311

Stewart, Bob, CEO
UniPro Foodservice **[1377]**
2500 Cumberland Pky. SE, Ste. 600
Atlanta, GA 30339
Ph: (770)952-0871

Stewart, Cate, President
Chinese Shar-Pei Club of America
[21855]
c/o Bob Callthorp, Membership
Chairman
44 Mt. Parnasus Rd.
East Haddam, CT 06423
Ph: (860)873-2572

Stewart, Cheri, President
Neurofibromatosis Network **[14847]**
213 S Wheaton Ave.

Wheaton, IL 60187
Ph: (630)510-1115
Toll Free: 800-942-6825
Fax: (630)510-8508

Stewart, Dawn C., MPA, Founder,
CEO
Caribbean People International Col-
lective [19395]
4710 Church Ave., 3rd Fl.
Brooklyn, NY 11203
Ph: (718)576-1839

Stewart, Ed, Founder, President
Performing Animal Welfare Society
[10678]
PO Box 849
Galt, CA 95632
Ph: (209)745-2606
Fax: (209)745-1809

Stewart, Eric, President
American-Lithuanian Business
Council [609]
701 8th St. NW, Ste. 500
Washington, DC 20001
Ph: (202)973-5975
Fax: (202)659-5249

Stewart, Eric, Exec. Dir.
American Rabbit Breeders Associa-
tion [4592]
PO Box 5667
Bloomington, IL 61702
Ph: (309)664-7500
Fax: (309)664-0941

Stewart, Faye, Chairperson
National Organization of Blacks in
Government [5080]
3005 Georgia Ave. NW
Washington, DC 20001-3807
Ph: (202)667-3280
Fax: (202)667-3705

Stewart, Frank, Exec. Dir.
Forest Landowners Tax Council
[5792]
1602 Belle View Blvd. No. 245
Alexandria, VA 22307-6531
Ph: (703)549-0347

Stewart, Heather, President
Bowls USA [22702]
c/o Heather Stewart, President
Laguna Beach LBC
455 Cliff Dr.
Laguna Beach, CA 92651

Stewart, Jason, President
Circle K International [12886]
3636 Woodview Trace
Indianapolis, IN 46268
Ph: (317)875-8755
    (317)879-0204
Toll Free: 800-KIWANIS
Fax: (317)879-0204

Stewart, Joe, Exec. Dir.
Narcotic Educational Foundation of
America [13156]
28245 Avenue Crocker, Ste. 230
Valencia, CA 91355-1201
Ph: (661)775-6960

Stewart, Julie, Founder, President
Families Against Mandatory
Minimums Foundation [11524]
1100 H St. NW, Ste. 1000
Washington, DC 20005
Ph: (202)822-6700
Fax: (202)822-6704

Stewart, Leland P., Founder, Coord.
Unity-and-Diversity World Council
[18561]
PO Box 661401
Los Angeles, CA 90066-9201
Ph: (424)228-2087
Fax: (310)827-9187

Stewart, Mark, President
American Youth Soccer Organization
[23185]
19750 S Vermont Ave., Ste. 200
Torrance, CA 90502
Toll Free: 800-USA-AYSO
Fax: (310)525-1155

Stewart, Mizell, President
American Society of News Editors
[2655]
209 Reynolds Journalism Institute
Missouri School of Journalism
Columbia, MO 65211
Ph: (573)882-2430
Fax: (573)884-3824

Stewart, Patricia, President
Society of State Leaders of Health
and Physical Education [8435]
1432 K St. NW, Ste. 400
Washington, DC 20005

Stewart, Robert, Exec. Dir.
Rural Community Assistance
Partnership [7375]
1701 K St. NW, Ste. 700
Washington, DC 20006
Ph: (202)408-1273
Toll Free: 800-321-7227
Fax: (202)408-8165

Stewart, Ronia, President
Nubian United Benevolent
International Association [12594]
149 Roxbury St.
Roxbury, MA 02119
Ph: (617)669-2642

Stewart, Susan K., Exec. Dir.
Blood and Marrow Transplant
Information Network [17508]
1548 Old Skokie Rd., Ste. 1
Highland Park, IL 60035
Ph: (847)433-3313
Toll Free: 888-597-7674
Fax: (847)433-4599

Stewart, Walter, Chmn. of the Bd.
Program of Academic Exchange
[8088]
14 Willett Ave.
Port Chester, NY 10573
Toll Free: 800-555-6211
Fax: (914)690-0350

Stieger, Carolyn, Mgr.
National Association of Senior Move
Managers [2184]
PO Box 209
Hinsdale, IL 60522
Toll Free: 877-606-2766
Fax: (630)230-3594

Stieger, Jan, Exec. Dir.
DBA International [983]
1050 Fulton Ave., Ste. 120
Sacramento, CA 95825
Ph: (916)482-2462
Fax: (916)482-2760

Stiehler, Debbie, Contact
National Academy of Needlearts
[21770]
c/o Debbie Stiehler
1 Riverbanks Ct.
Greer, SC 29651

Stier, Max, CEO, President
Partnership for Public Service
[18947]
Office Bldg.
1100 New York Ave. NW
Washington, DC 20005
Ph: (202)775-9111
Fax: (202)775-8885

Stiles, William B., PhD, President
APA Division 29: The Society for the
Advancement of Psychology
[16879]

c/o Tracey Martin
6557 E Riverdale St.
Mesa, AZ 85215
Ph: (602)363-9211
Fax: (480)854-8966

Stillwaggon, James, Exec. Dir.
Philosophy of Education Society
[8422]
c/o James Stillwaggon, Executive
Director
Iona College
715 North Ave.
New Rochelle, NY 10801

Stillwagon, Gary B., MD, CEO,
President
Struggling Kids [13117]
227 Sandy Springs Pl., Ste.
G-28416
Atlanta, GA 30358
Ph: (770)953-0437

Stime, Amber, MSW, Exec. Dir.,
Founder
African Cradle, Inc. [11210]
2672 Bayshore Pky., Ste. 1000
Mountain View, CA 94043-1010
Ph: (650)461-9192
Fax: (650)215-9897

Stimpert, Ryan, Chairman, Founder
SafeChildrenUSA [12936]
1935 S Tamiami Trail
Sarasota, FL 34239
Ph: (941)600-3262
Fax: (941)375-0506

Stimpson, Catharine R., Chairman
Scholars at Risk Network [7407]
c/o New York University
194 Mercer St., Rm. 410
New York, NY 10012
Ph: (212)998-2179
Fax: (212)995-4402

Stimson, Sandra, CALA, CEO
National Council of Certified
Dementia Practitioners [15965]
1 A Main St., Ste. 8
Sparta, NJ 07871-1909
Ph: (973)729-6601
Toll Free: 877-729-5191
Fax: (973)860-2244

Stinebert, Chris, President, CEO
American Financial Services Association [2089]
919 18th St. NW, Ste. 300
Washington, DC 20006

Stipeche, Juliet, Program Mgr.
Empowering Leadership Alliance
[7960]
6100 Main St., MS 134
Houston, TX 77005-1827
Ph: (713)348-6122
Fax: (713)348-3679

Stirling, Steve, President, CEO
MAP International [15151]
4700 Glynco Pky.
Brunswick, GA 31525-6800
Toll Free: 800-225-8550

Stites, Charles H., Exec. Dir.
Able Flight [11565]
91 Oak Leaf Ln.
Chapel Hill, NC 27516
Ph: (919)942-4699

Stith, Jennifer, MAT, MA, Exec. Dir.
WINGS Foundation [12941]
7550 W Yale Ave., Ste. B-201
Denver, CO 80227
Ph: (303)238-8660
Fax: (303)238-4739

Stitt, Malcolm, Dir. of Info. Technology
International Schools Services
[8105]

15 Roszel Rd.
Princeton, NJ 08543-5910
Ph: (609)452-0990
Fax: (609)452-2690

Stivers, Donna, Administrator,
Managing Ed.
Intersociety Council for Pathology
Information, Inc. [16588]
9650 Rockville Pke., Rm. E123
Bethesda, MD 20814-3993
Ph: (301)634-7200
Fax: (301)634-7990

Stock, Elisabeth, CEO, Founder
PowerMyLearning [7659]
520 8th Ave., 10th Fl.
New York, NY 10018
Ph: (212)563-7300
Fax: (212)563-1215

Stock, Fuzzy, VP
North American Gamebird Association [3608]
c/o Brian Beavers, Treasurer
01406 E Highway 50
Pierceville, KS 67868
Ph: (620)335-5405

Stockard, Jennifer, President, CEO
One Warm Coat [12556]
2443 Fillmore St., No. 380-5363
San Francisco, CA 94115

Stockdale, Dan, Founder, CEO
World Nature Coalition [4920]
601 Pennsylvania Ave. NW, South
Bldg., Ste. 900
Washington, DC 20004
Ph: (865)300-3232

Stocker, Michael, Exec. Dir.
Ocean Conservation Research
[3920]
PO Box 559
Lagunitas, CA 94938-0559
Ph: (415)488-0553

Stockman, Brian, Exec. VP, CEO
American Society of Farm Managers
and Rural Appraisers [217]
950 S Cherry St., Ste. 508
Denver, CO 80246-2664
Ph: (303)758-3513
Fax: (303)758-0190

Stockord, Michael, Chairman
Consortium for Energy Efficiency,
Inc. [1109]
98 N Washington St., Ste. 101
Boston, MA 02114-1918
Ph: (617)589-3949

Stocks, John C., Exec. Dir.
National Education Association
[23411]
1201 16th St. NW
Washington, DC 20036-3290
Ph: (202)833-4000
Fax: (202)822-7974

Stockton, Susan, VP
Kappa Delta [23957]
3205 Players Ln.
Memphis, TN 38125
Toll Free: 888-668-4293

Stockwell, Bob, President
Cobra Owners Club of America
[21360]
4676 Lakeview Ave., Ste. 109G
Yorba Linda, CA 92886
Ph: (714)546-5670

Stoddard, Bob, Founder
Pepsi-Cola Collectors Club [21712]
c/o Diane Gabriel, Secretary
335 Mathews Way

New Castle, PA 16101
Ph: (724)658-6310
(804)748-5769

Stoddard, Teri, Prog. Dir.
Stop Abusive and Violent Environments [11714]
PO Box 1221
Rockville, MD 20849
Ph: (301)801-0608

Stoeckel, Jim, Secretary
International Association of Astacology [6716]
c/o Jim Stoeckel, Secretary
203 Swingle Hall
Dept. of Fisheries and Allied
Aquaculture
Auburn University
Auburn, AL 36849-5419
Ph: (334)844-9249
Fax: (334)844-9208

Stoeolting, Robert K., MD, President
Anesthesia Patient Safety Foundation [13697]
Bldg. 1, Ste. 2
8007 S Meridian St.
Indianapolis, IN 46217-2922
Fax: (317)888-1482

Stoicovy, Donnan, Officer
National Association for Professional
Development Schools [8539]
1 Bear Pl., No. 97477
Waco, TX 76798-7477
Toll Free: 855-936-2737

Stoik, Brian M., Chairman
Building Enclosure Council -
National [6162]
c/o Philip J. Schneider, Program
Director
1090 Vermont Ave. NW, Ste. 700
Washington, DC 20005
Ph: (202)289-7800
Fax: (202)289-1092

Stoinski, Tara, PhD, President, CEO
Dian Fossey Gorilla Fund
International [4807]
800 Cherokee Ave. SE
Atlanta, GA 30315
Ph: (404)624-5881
Toll Free: 800-851-0203

Stokebrand, Jeanne, President
The Questers [21291]
210 S Quince St.
Philadelphia, PA 19107-5534
Ph: (215)923-5183

Stokely, Fran, President, Treasurer
Christian Alliance For Humanitarian
Aid, Inc. [12640]
1525 Mmain St., L-3
Pearland, TX 77581
Ph: (281)412-2285
(713)644-2010

Stokes, Carla, PhD, CEO, Founder
Helping Our Teen Girls in Real Life
Situations [11028]
3645 Marketplace Blvd., Ste. 130-190
Atlanta, GA 30344

Stokes, Janet, Chairperson, CEO
Film Advisory Board, Inc. [9305]
263 W Olive Ave., No. 377
Burbank, CA 91502
Ph: (323)461-6541
Fax: (323)469-8541

Stokes, Lisa, Advisor
Executive Women International [69]
3860 South 2300 East, Ste. 211
Salt Lake City, UT 84109
Ph: (801)355-2800
Fax: (801)355-2852

Stokes, Sydney N., Jr., Chairman
Jefferson Legacy Foundation [8445]
PO Box 76
Ripton, VT 05766
Ph: (802)388-7676
Fax: (802)388-1776

Stokes, Tom, Prog. Dir.
Climate Crisis Coalition [3831]
c/o Tom Strokes, Project Director
PO Box 125
South Lee, MA 01260
Ph: (413)243-5665

Stokey, Steve, President
United States Cutting Tool Institute
[1776]
1300 Sumner Ave.
Cleveland, OH 44115-2851
Ph: (216)241-7333
Fax: (216)241-0105

Stoklosa, Raymond J., Exec. Dir.
National Association of Real Estate
Buyer Brokers [2875]
2704 Wemberly Dr.
Belmont, CA 94002
Ph: (512)827-8323

Stolarski, Bob, Chmn. of the Bd.
Northwest Energy Efficiency Alliance
[4028]
421 SW 6th Ave., Ste. 600
Portland, OR 97204
Ph: (503)688-5400
Toll Free: 800-411-0834
Fax: (503)688-5447

Stolberg, Adam, Exec. Dir.
Submersible Wastewater Pump Association [588]
1866 Sheridan Rd., Ste. 212
Highland Park, IL 60035
Ph: (847)681-1868
Fax: (847)681-1869

Stolfi, Leonie, President
Yorkshire Terrier Club of America
[21999]

Stoll, Becky, LCSW, Officer
International Critical Incident Stress
Foundation [17291]
3290 Pine Orchard Ln., Ste. 106
Ellicott City, MD 21042
Ph: (410)750-9600
Fax: (410)750-9601

Stoller, David, President
Coalition of Organic Landscape
Professionals [2068]
1125 NE 152nd St.
Shoreline, WA 98155
Ph: (206)362-8947

Stolpe, Birgitta, PhD, President
Irish Wolfhound Club of America
[21904]
c/o Kathy Welling, Secretary
180 W 3rd St.
Campbellsburg, IN 47108
Ph: (317)727-4954

Stomberg, Eric, 1st VP
International Double Reed Society
[9927]
2423 Lawndale Rd.
Finksburg, MD 21048-1401
Ph: (410)871-0658
Fax: (410)871-0659

Stonacek, Mark, Chairman
National Oilseed Processors Association [2454]
1300 L St. NW, Ste. 1020
Washington, DC 20005
Ph: (202)842-0463
Fax: (202)842-9126

Stone, Ann, Chairperson
Republicans for Choice [19036]
3213 Duke St., No. 808
Alexandria, VA 22314
Ph: (703)447-1404

Stone, Ashley, President
United Dance Merchants of America
[979]
PO Box 57086
Chicago, IL 60657
Toll Free: 800-304-8362
Fax: (800)517-6070

Stone, Beverly G., Exec. Dir.,
President
Expanding Opportunities [10967]
84 Payson Rd.
Brooks, ME 04921-3701
Ph: (207)722-3708
Fax: (207)930-8012

Stone, Dr. Jessie, Director, Founder
Soft Power Health [15498]
2887 Purchase St.
Purchase, NY 10577-2214
Ph: (914)282-7354

Stone, Jim, Exec. Dir.
Intertribal Buffalo Council [3627]
2497 W Chicago St.
Rapid City, SD 57702
Ph: (605)394-9730
Fax: (605)394-7742

Stone, Katherine, Founder, Exec.
Dir.
Postpartum Progress Inc. [16626]
4920 Atlanta Hwy., No. 316
Alpharetta, GA 30004
Toll Free: 877-470-4877

Stone, Kendall, Treasurer, Secretary
Poverty Awareness Coalition for
Equality [12560]
210 Burrus Hall
Blacksburg, VA 24061

Stone, Margaret, Chairman,
President
Veterans Healing Initiative [13252]
108 Veronese Dr.
Greenville, SC 29609
Ph: (917)509-7873
Toll Free: 855-247-8500

Stone, Stephen, President
Renew America [3782]
PO Box 50502
Provo, UT 84605-0502

Stone, Mr. Terry, Exec. Dir.
CenterLink [11476]
PO Box 24490
Fort Lauderdale, FL 33307-4490
Ph: (954)765-6024
Fax: (954)206-0469

Stoneback, Harry R., President
Hemingway Foundation and Society
[9055]
c/o Gail Sinclair
Rollins College
1000 Holt Ave. 2770
Winter Park, FL 32789

Stonehill, Harriett, Co-Pres.
Clearinghouse on Women's Issues
[18203]
700 7th St. SW, Ste. 3
Washington, DC 20024-2469
Ph: (202)232-8173

Stoneman, Dorothy, Founder, CEO
YouthBuild USA [13492]
58 Day St.
Somerville, MA 02144-2827
Ph: (617)623-9900
Fax: (617)623-4331

Stoner, Nadine, President
Common Ground - U.S.A. [19167]
PO Box 57
Evanston, IL 60204
Ph: (847)475-0391

Stonesifer, Susan, President
National Episcopal Historians and
Archivists [9418]
c/o Cathedral Church of St. Mark
231 East 100 South
Salt Lake City, UT 84111
Ph: (920)543-6342

Stoney, Ronald J., Founder
Vascular Cures [17583]
555 Price Ave., Ste. 180
Redwood City, CA 94063
Ph: (650)358-6022

Storek, Ms. Karen, CEO, Exec. Dir.
New Parents Network [8404]
3760 N Bay Horse Loop, Ste. 210
Tucson, AZ 85719
Ph: (520)461-6806

Storen, Stephen J., Chairman
Federation of Protestant Welfare
Agencies [20530]
40 Broad St.
New York, NY 10004
Ph: (212)777-4800
Fax: (212)533-8792

Storer, Shawn T., Director
Catholic Peace Fellowship [18774]
PO Box 4232
South Bend, IN 46634
Ph: (574)232-2811

Storey, Linda, President
Case for MS [15911]
4588 S Acoma St.
Englewood, CO 80110
Ph: (303)781-0475

Storey, Maureen, PhD, President,
CEO
Alliance for Potato Research and
Education [4559]
2000 Corporate Ridge, Ste. 1000
McLean, VA 22102
Ph: (703)245-7694

Storkey, Mike, DTM, President
Toastmasters International [10177]
23182 Arroyo Vista
Rancho Santa Margarita, CA 92688-2620
Ph: (949)858-8255
(949)835-1300
Fax: (949)858-1207

Storm, Christina M., Esq., Exec. Dir.,
Founder
Lawyers Without Borders, Inc.
[5539]
59 Elm St.
New Haven, CT 06510
Ph: (203)823-9397
Fax: (203)823-9438

Stormes, Keith E., Exec. Dir.
Lifespan Resources [10515]
33 State St., 3rd Fl.
New Albany, IN 47151-0995
Ph: (812)948-8330
Toll Free: 888-948-8330
Fax: (812)948-0147

Storozynski, Alex, Chmn. of the Bd.
Kosciuszko Foundation [10164]
15 E 65th St.
New York, NY 10065
Ph: (212)734-2130
Fax: (212)628-4552

Storto, Pamela, President
Canine Cancer Awareness, Inc.
[17642]

44 Devoe St.
Brooklyn, NY 11211

Stothers, William G., Chairperson,
President
Post-Polio Health International
[11632]
4207 Lindell Blvd., No. 110
Saint Louis, MO 63108-2930
Ph: (314)534-0475
Fax: (314)534-5070

Stott, Chris, Director
Society of Satellite Professionals
International [3239]
The New York Information Technol-
ogy Ctr.
250 Park Ave., 7th Fl.
New York, NY 10177-0799
Ph: (212)809-5199
Fax: (212)825-0075

Stott, Colin, Exec. Dir.
Gospel Recordings Network [20421]
41823 Enterprise Cir. N, Ste. 200
Temecula, CA 92590-5682
Ph: (951)719-1650
Toll Free: 888-444-7872
Fax: (951)719-1651

Stottlemyer, Christine, Contact
American Association of Healthcare
Administrative Management
[15569]
11240 Waples Mill Rd., Ste. 200
Fairfax, VA 22030
Ph: (703)281-4043
Fax: (703)359-7562

Stotz, Keysto, Chairman
National Junior Hereford Association
[3741]
PO Box 014059
Kansas City, MO 64101
Ph: (816)842-3757
Fax: (816)842-6931

Stoumbelis, Alexis, Coord.
Committee in Solidarity With the
People of El Salvador [18175]
1525 Newton St. NW
Washington, DC 20010
Ph: (202)521-2510
Fax: (202)332-3339

Stout, Bill, President
Textile Bag and Packaging Associa-
tion [847]
3000 Royal Marco Way PH-N
Marco Island, FL 34145
Ph: (616)481-4739

Stout, Claude, Exec. Dir.
Telecommunications for the Deaf &
Hard of Hearing, Inc. [15211]
8630 Fenton St., Ste. 121
Silver Spring, MD 20910-3803

Stout, Hugh, President
Tall Bearded Iris Society [22129]
4728 Jade St., NE
Salem, OR 97305-3138
Ph: (806)792-1878

Stoutnar, Helen, Corr. Sec.
The Strong Family Association of
America, Inc. [20933]
c/o Helen M. Stoutnar, Corresponding Secretary
10667 South Ave. 10 E-71
Yuma, AZ 85365–7008

Stovall, Tom, Treasurer
Stovall Family Association [20931]
c/o Tom Stovall, Treasurer
3345 Tibey Ct.
Dubuque, IA 52002-2849
Ph: (563)581-7220

Stover, Jean, Exec. Dir.
American Society of Crime Labora-
tory Directors [5238]
139A Technology Dr.
Garner, NC 27529
Ph: (919)773-2044
Fax: (919)861-9930

Stover Wright, Michelle, Dir. of Res.
Child and Family Policy Center
[10895]
505 5th Ave., Ste. 404
Des Moines, IA 50309
Ph: (515)280-9027

Stowe, Eric, Director, Founder
Splash [13337]
1115 E Pike St.
Seattle, WA 98122
Ph: (206)535-7375

Stowell, Mr. Shannon, President
Adventure Travel Trade Association
[3365]
601 Union St., 42nd Fl.
Seattle, WA 98101
Ph: (360)805-3131
(206)290-4410
Fax: (360)805-0649

Strader, Theresa, RN, Founder,
Exec. Dir.
National Mill Dog Rescue [10672]
5335 JD Johnson Rd.
Peyton, CO 80831
Ph: (719)445-6787
Toll Free: 888-495-DOGS
Fax: (866)718-1185

Strain, Gary, Officer
National Society of Accountants for
Cooperatives [53]
136 S Keowee St.
Dayton, OH 45402
Ph: (937)222-6707
Fax: (937)222-5794

Strait, Kimberly, President
American Pre-Veterinary Medical
Association [17625]
c/o Alexa Brandsetter
2183 Wyandotte Ave.
Alva, FL 33920

Stranathan, Ike E., Founder
Netting Nations [14607]
7119 W Sunset Blvd., Ste. 317
Los Angeles, CA 90046

Strange, David, Director
Thomas Wolfe Society [9115]
PO Box 1146
Bloomington, IN 47402-1146

Strange, Steve, Contact
Boss 429 Mustang World Registry
[21342]
PO Box 8035
Spokane, WA 99203
Ph: (509)448-0252

Stranges, Julie, Director
National Investigations Committee
on Unidentified Flying Objects
[7016]
PO Box 3847
Chatsworth, CA 91313-9998
Ph: (818)882-0039
Fax: (818)998-6712

Stranges, Peggy, Founder
Clinica Esperanza [15138]
PO Box 44510
Indianapolis, IN 46244

Strassberg, Valerie, PE, Exec. Dir.
Nature's Voice Our Choice [4761]
1940 Duke St., Ste. 200

Alexandria, VA 22314
Ph: (202)341-9180
(202)360-8373

Strasser, Don, CEO, Exec. Dir.
A Midwinter Night's Dream [13685]
155 Main St., Ste. 4
Northport, NY 11768
Ph: (631)262-7428
(516)680-6658

Strasser, Mary, Director
AmeriCorps VISTA [13280]
250 E St. SW
Washington, DC 20005
Ph: (202)606-5000
Toll Free: 800-942-2677

Stratakis, John C., Advisor
Hellenic-American Chamber of Com-
merce [23589]
370 Lexington Ave., 27th Fl.
New York, NY 10017
Ph: (212)629-6380
Fax: (212)564-9281

Strate, Lance, Advisor
Media Ecology Association [8289]
Communication Dept.
Santa Clara University
500 El Camino Real
Santa Clara, CA 95053-0277
Ph: (408)554-4022
Fax: (408)554-4913

Stratton, Steve, President
Bricklin International Owners Club
[21343]
George Malaska, VP Membership
BI, 38083 Princeton Dr.
38083 Princeton Dr.
North Ridgeville, OH 44039

Stratton, Torie, Office Mgr.
Early Childhood Music and Move-
ment Association [12369]
805 Mill Ave.
Snohomish, WA 98290
Ph: (360)568-5635
Fax: (360)568-5635

Stratton, William, Chairman
University of Illinois Alumni Associa-
tion [19356]
Alice Campbell Alumni Ctr.
601 S Lincoln Ave.
Urbana, IL 61801
Ph: (217)333-1471
Toll Free: 800-355-2586

Straub, Ed, President
Pilot Dogs [17737]
625 W Town St.
Columbus, OH 43215-4444
Ph: (614)221-6367
Fax: (614)221-1577

Straus, David, Exec. Dir.
Association for Commuter
Transportation [13229]
1 Chestnut Sq., 2nd Fl.
Sharon, MA 02067
Ph: (202)792-8501

Straus, Phil, Chairman
Foundation for National Progress
[18977]
c/o Mother Jones
222 Sutter St., Ste. 600
San Francisco, CA 94108
Ph: (415)321-1700
Fax: (415)321-1701

Strausbaugh, Linda, PhD, Director
National Professional Science
Master's Association [7967]
PO Box 3455
Riverview, FL 33568-3455
Ph: (508)471-4487

Strauss, Marshall, President
Human and Civil Rights Organiza-
tions of America [17900]
125 Washington St., Ste. 201
Salem, MA 01970
Ph: (978)744-2608
Fax: (978)236-7272

Strauss, Monty J., Officer
Mathematical Study Unit [22342]
c/o Monty Strauss
4209 88th St.
Lubbock, TX 79423

Straw, John, Exec. Dir.
Concern America [12650]
2015 N Broadway Ave.
Santa Ana, CA 92706
Ph: (714)953-8575
Toll Free: 800-266-2376
Fax: (714)953-1242

Strawman, Dr. Tom, Dept. Chm.
International Boethius Society
[10092]
c/o Noel Harold Kaylor Jr., Executive
Director
Smith Hall 274
Dept. of English
Troy University
Troy, AL 36082
Ph: (334)670-3519

Streeper, Martha J., Exec. Dir.
Federation of Defense and
Corporate Counsel [5313]
11812 N 56th St.
Tampa, FL 33617
Ph: (813)983-0022
Fax: (813)988-5837

Streeter, Patricia A., President
Lithuanian-American Bar Association
[5021]
PO Box 871578
Canton, MI 48187
Ph: (734)222-0088
Fax: (734)667-3357

Streeter, Perry, President
Streeter Family Association [20932]
3273 State Route 248
Canisteo, NY 14823

Streett, J.D., President
Alliance of Special Effects and
Pyrotechnic Operators [2820]
12522 Moorpark St.
Studio City, CA 91604-1355
Ph: (818)506-8173
Fax: (818)769-9438

Strege, Roger, President, Treasurer
Autism Allies [13742]
2400 Prairie View Ln.
Buffalo, MN 55313-2450
Ph: (612)384-4265

Strehlow, Ammon, VP
Council on Diagnostic Imaging
[17056]
c/o Doctor Brian Batenchuk,
President
PO Box 5092
Pasadena, TX 77508
Ph: (281)881-4578
Fax: (281)954-6800

Streichert, Laura, PhD, Exec. Dir.
International Society for Disease
Surveillance [14589]
26 Lincoln St., Ste. 3
Brighton, MA 02135
Ph: (617)779-0880

Streltzer, Jon M., Founder
World Association of Cultural
Psychiatry [16839]

Stressman, Karl, Commissioner
Professional Rodeo Cowboys Association [23103]
101 Pro Rodeo Dr.
Colorado Springs, CO 80919
Ph: (719)593-8840
Fax: (719)548-4876

Streufert, Duane, Jr., Contact
National Flag Foundation [10297]
PO Box 435
Riderwood, MD 21139
Toll Free: 800-615-1776

Stribling, Elizabeth F., Chmn. of the Bd.
French Heritage Society [9390]
14 E 60th St., No. 605
New York, NY 10022-7131
Ph: (212)759-6846
Fax: (212)759-9632

Strickland, David, Chmn. of the Bd.
Mothers Against Drunk Driving [12827]
511 E John Carpenter Fwy., Ste. 700
Irving, TX 75062-3983
Toll Free: 877-275-6233
Fax: (972)869-2206

Strickland, James, Jr., Founder
Creative Global Relief [12654]
749 Boush St.
Norfolk, VA 23510
Ph: (757)627-7672

Strickland, Patty, President, COO
Communicating for America [3524]
112 E Lincoln Ave.
Fergus Falls, MN 56537
Ph: (218)739-3241
Toll Free: 800-432-3276
Fax: (218)739-3832

Strickland, Sue C., Exec. Dir.
Americas Apparel Producers' Network [199]
PO Box 720693
Atlanta, GA 30358
Ph: (404)843-3171
Fax: (404)671-9456

Strickland, Vernon L., III, Founder
Delta Lambda Phi National Social Fraternity [23895]
2020 Pennsylvania Ave. NW, No. 355
Washington, DC 20006-1811
Ph: (202)558-2801
Fax: (202)318-2277

Striitmatter, Aimee, Exec. Dir.
Association for Library Service to Children [9687]
50 E Huron St.
Chicago, IL 60611-2795
Toll Free: 800-545-2433
Fax: (312)280-5271

String, Richard F., Exec. Dir.
Etruscan Foundation [5937]
PO Box 26
Fremont, MI 49412-0026
Ph: (231)519-0675
Fax: (231)924-0777

Stringer, Daniel, Chmn. of the Bd.
Child Care Law Center [10806]
445 Church St.
San Francisco, CA 94114
Ph: (415)558-8005

Stringer, Daniel, President
Let Hope Rise [12981]
4808 N 24th St., Ste. 902
Phoenix, AZ 85016
Ph: (480)779-0530
Fax: (866)298-3607

Stringham, Edward, President
Society for the Development of Austrian Economics [6401]
c/o Tony Carilli, Treasurer
Hampden-Sydney College
Hampden Sydney, VA 23943

Stritmatter, Claude, President
National Association of Waterfront Employers [2263]
1200 19th St., Flr. 3
Washington, DC 20036
Ph: (202)587-4800
Fax: (202)587-4888

Stroia, John, V. Chmn. of the Exec. Committee
Security Industry Association [3069]
8405 Colesville Rd., Ste. 500
Silver Spring, MD 20910
Ph: (301)804-4700
Fax: (301)804-4701

Strom, Margot Stern, Exec. Dir.
Facing History and Ourselves National Foundation [9476]
16 Hurd Rd.
Brookline, MA 02445
Ph: (617)232-1595
Toll Free: 800-856-9039
Fax: (617)232-0281

Strong, Lester, CEO, VP
Experience Corps [7850]
601 E St. NW
Washington, DC 20049-0001
Toll Free: 800-687-2277
Fax: (202)434-6480

Strong, Mark W., Bd. Member
National League of Postmasters of the United States [23508]
1 Beltway Ctr.
5904 Richmond Hwy., Ste. 500
Alexandria, VA 22303-1864
Ph: (703)329-4550
Fax: (703)329-0466

Strong, Renee, Secretary
National American Eskimo Dog Association [21917]
c/o Diana Allen, President
8767 S Edinburgh Rd.
Edinburgh, IN 46124
Ph: (812)526-6682

Strong, Shirley, Exec. Dir.
Institute for Global Communications [7310]
PO Box 29047
San Francisco, CA 94129-0047

Stroock, Lucy, Contact
Peace Educators Allied for Children Everywhere [18759]
c/o Lucy Stroock
55 Frost St.
Cambridge, MA 02140

Strother, Jay, VP
International Warehouse Logistics Association [3438]
2800 S River Rd., Ste. 260
Des Plaines, IL 60018
Ph: (847)813-4699
Fax: (847)813-0115

Strother, Ms. Sandi, Exec. Dir.
Veterinary Cancer Society [17668]
PO Box 30855
Columbia, MO 65205
Ph: (573)823-8497
Fax: (573)445-0353

Strothman, Nicole, President
International Aesthetic and Laser Association [15523]
4830 W Kennedy Blvd., Ste. 440

Tampa, FL 33609
Ph: (813)676-7704

Stroud, Dr. Elaine C., Asst. Dir.
American Institute of the History of Pharmacy [16640]
777 Highland Ave.
Madison, WI 53705-2222
Ph: (608)262-5378

Stroud, Ms. Pamela, Dir. of Bus. Dev.
International Institute of Forecasters [6657]
53 Tesla Ave.
Medford, MA 02155
Ph: (781)234-4077

Stroud, Robert E., Bd. Member
Information Systems Audit and Control Association [71]
3701 Algonquin Rd., Ste. 1010
Rolling Meadows, IL 60008
Ph: (847)253-1545
Fax: (847)253-1443

Stroud, Susan, Exec. Dir., Founder
Innovations in Civic Participation [17859]
PO Box 39222
Washington, DC 20016
Ph: (202)775-0290

Struble, Robert, Jr., Founder
Twelve Lights League [5557]
PO Box 1415
Bremerton, WA 98337
Ph: (360)373-9999

Strumpf, Herk, President
International Stinson Club [21234]
3005 6th St.
Sacramento, CA 95818
Ph: (916)421-8942

Strumpf, Peter, Treasurer
Cosmopolitan Soccer League [23186]
115 River Rd., Ste. 1029
Edgewater, NJ 07020
Ph: (201)943-3390
Fax: (201)943-3394

Strutz, Kathy, Treasurer
Rhythmical Massage Therapy Association of North America [15562]
c/o Kathy Strutz, Treasurer
3302 Parks Ln.
Carmichael, CA 95608
Ph: (916)486-6127

Struwe, Sara, President
Spina Bifida Association of America [17250]
1600 Wilson Blvd., Ste. 800
Arlington, VA 22209
Ph: (202)944-3285
Fax: (202)944-3295

Stryker, Jon, Founder, President
Arcus Foundation [18851]
44 W 28th St., 17th Fl.
New York, NY 10001
Ph: (212)488-3000
Fax: (212)488-3010

Stuart, Betty, CFO, Dir. of Dev.
Water is Life International [13343]
PO Box 540318
Orlando, FL 32854-0318
Ph: (407)716-4214

Stuart, Gail W., Ph.D., President
Annapolis Coalition on the Behavioral Health Workforce [15759]
3665 Erie Ave.
Cincinnati, OH 45208-1982
Ph: (203)494-7491
   (513)404-3232

Stuart, Greg Stuart, CEO
Mobile Marketing Association [102]
41 E 11 St., 11th Fl.
New York, NY 10003
Ph: (646)257-4515

Stuart, Jay, Treasurer
Albert Ellis Institute [16969]
145 E 32nd St., 9 Fl.
New York, NY 10016
Ph: (212)535-0822
Toll Free: 800-323-4738
Fax: (212)249-3582

Stuart, Jennifer, President
Sigmund Freud Archives, Inc. [16852]
c/o Louis Rose, Executive Director
Dept. of History
Otterbein University
Westerville, OH 43081

Stuart, Karen, Exec. Dir.
Association of Talent Agents [162]
9255 Sunset Blvd., Ste. 930
Los Angeles, CA 90069
Ph: (310)274-0628
Fax: (310)274-5063

Stuart, Rev. Marianne, President
Episcopal Conference of the Deaf [20101]
1804 Hollow Branch Way
The Villages, FL 32162-2350
Ph: (352)350-5357

Stuart, R. Scott, CEO
National Institute for Animal Agriculture [4460]
13570 Meadowgrass Dr., Ste. 201
Colorado Springs, CO 80921
Ph: (719)538-8843
Fax: (719)538-8847

Stuart, Scott, Exec. Ofc.
International Society for Interpersonal Psychotherapy [16981]
University of Iowa
Department of Psychiatry
1-293 Medical Education Bldg.
Iowa City, IA 52242
Ph: (319)353-4230
Fax: (319)353-3003

Stuart, Scott, President
National Livestock Producers Association [4480]
13570 Meadowgrass Dr., Ste. 201
Colorado Springs, CO 80921
Ph: (719)538-8843
Toll Free: 800-237-7193
Fax: (719)538-8847

Stuart, Susan A., CEO, President
Center for Organ Recovery and Education [17509]
RIDC Pk.
204 Sigma Dr.
Pittsburgh, PA 15238
Ph: (412)963-3550
Toll Free: 800-366-6777

Stubbs, Tracy, President
Hunting Retriever Club [21895]
c/o Tracy Stubbs, President
850 Hennecy Ln.
Saint Cloud, FL 34773-9119
Ph: (407)744-2797

Stubstad, Martin, President
Archery Range and Retailers Organization [3150]
156 N Main St., Ste. D
Oregon, WI 53575
Ph: (608)835-9060
Toll Free: 800-234-7499
Fax: (608)835-9360

Stuchlik, Terry, Contact
NSU Enthusiasts U.S.A. [21463]
2909 Utah Pl.
Alton, IL 62002
Ph: (618)462-9195

Stuckey, Rick, Secretary
National Lesbian and Gay Journal-
ists Association [2701]
2120 L St. NW, Ste. 850
Washington, DC 20037
Ph: (202)588-9888

Studebaker, Charles, Trustee
Studebaker Family National Associa-
tion [20934]
6555 S State Rte. 202
Tipp City, OH 45371
Ph: (937)405-6539

Student, Michael, Director
Finnish American Chamber of Com-
merce [23586]
54 W 40th St.
New York, NY 10018
Ph: (917)414-1603

Studney, Peter, Exec. Dir.
American Dairy Science Association
[3979]
1880 S Oak St., Ste. 100
Champaign, IL 61820-6974
Ph: (217)356-5146
Fax: (217)398-4119

Stueber, Dr. Ross, Administrator
Association of Lutheran Secondary
Schools [8257]
c/o Ross Stueber, Head Administra-
tor
12800 N Lake Shore Dr.
Mequon, WI 53097
Ph: (262)243-4210

Stulack, Nancy, Librarian
United States Golf Association
[22895]
PO Box 708
Far Hills, NJ 07931
Ph: (908)234-2300
Fax: (908)234-1883

Stull, John, Chairman
Portland Cement Association [794]
5420 Old Orchard Rd.
Skokie, IL 60077-1083
Ph: (847)966-6200
Fax: (847)966-8389

Stull, Todd, MD, Treasurer
International Society for Sports
Psychiatry [16831]
c/o Todd Stull, MD, Treasurer
Inside Performance Mindroom
16262 L St.
Omaha, NE 68135
Ph: (402)917-7132
Fax: (402)595-1874

Stumpf, Robert M., II, President
Leopold Stokowski Club [9187]
3900 SE 33 Ave.
Ocala, FL 34480

Stumph, David, Exec. Dir.
Association for Applied Psychophysi-
ology and Biofeedback [13816]
10200 W 44th Ave., Ste. 304
Wheat Ridge, CO 80033-2840
Ph: (303)422-8436
Toll Free: 800-477-8892

Stupski, Karen, Exec. Dir.
School of Living [9542]
215 Julian Woods Ln.
Julian, PA 16844-8617
Ph: (814)353-0130

Sturdevant, Patricia, President
Consumer Action [18045]
11901 Santa Monica Blvd., PMB 563

Los Angeles, CA 90025
Ph: (213)624-4631
Fax: (213)624-0574

Sturgeon, Jodi, President
PHI [1594]
400 E Fordham Rd., 11th Fl.
Bronx, NY 10458
Ph: (718)402-7766
Fax: (718)585-6852

Sturm, Brad, Chmn. of the Bd.
Bereavement Services [10772]
1900 South Ave., AVS-003
La Crosse, WI 54601
Ph: (608)782-7300
Toll Free: 800-362-9567

Sturm, James, Director
National Association of Comics Art
Educators [7516]
94 South Main St.
The Center for Cartoon Studies
PO Box 125
White River Junction, VT 05001
Ph: (802)295-3319
Fax: (802)295-3399

Sturm, Mike, President
National Guard Executive Directors
Association [5610]
Bldg. 8
2002 S Holt Rd.
indianapolis, IN 46241
Ph: (317)247-3301

Sturzl, Bart, President
National Association of Residential
Property Managers [2748]
638 Independence Pky., Ste. 100
Chesapeake, VA 23320
Toll Free: 800-782-3452
Fax: (866)466-2776

Stusser, Michael, Bd. Member
Green Spa Network [2907]
PO Box 15428
Atlanta, GA 30333
Toll Free: 800-275-3045

Stutte, Gary, Exec. Dir.
American Council for Medicinally
Active Plants [13593]
18110 NE 189th St.
Brush Prairie, WA 98606
Fax: (360)882-2089

Stutz, Ward, Director
CHA - Certified Horsemanship As-
sociation [22942]
1795 Alysheba Way, Ste. 7102
Lexington, KY 40509
Ph: (859)259-3399
Fax: (859)255-0726

Stuyt, Elizabeth, MD, President
National Acupuncture Detoxification
Association [17318]
PO Box 1066
Laramie, WY 82073
Ph: (307)460-2771
Toll Free: 888-765-6232
Fax: (573)777-9956

Suafoa-Dinino, Susan, Founder,
President
SpeakingOut Against Child Sexual
Abuse [12937]
PO Box 5826
Oak Ridge, TN 37831
Ph: (865)230-8600

Suarez, MA, RN, Dan, President
National Association of Hispanic
Nurses [16148]
6301 Ranch Dr.
Little Rock, AR 72223
Ph: (501)367-8616
Fax: (501)227-5444

Suarez, Ramon, MD, Founder,
President
No-Scalpel Vasectomy International
[17113]
3579 Midas Pl.
Naples, FL 34105
Ph: (813)787-6809

Suba, Eric, MD, President, Exec. Dir.
Viet/American Cervical Cancer
Prevention Project [14079]
c/o Eric Suba, MD, President/Execu-
tive Director
350 S. Josephs Ave.
San Francisco, CA 94115
Ph: (415)833-3870

Suber, Elke, Chairman
Black Entertainment and Sports
Lawyers Association [5174]
PO Box 230794
New York, NY 10023-0014

Suber, Tom, President
United States Dairy Export Council
[3983]
2101 Wilson Blvd., Ste. 400
Arlington, VA 22201-3061
Ph: (703)528-3049
Fax: (703)528-3705

Suberville, Sophie, Exec. Dir.
Mental Research Institute [13799]
555 Middlefield Rd.
Palo Alto, CA 94301
Ph: (650)321-3055
     (650)322-2252
Fax: (650)321-3785

Sublett, James, MD, Director
Joint Council of Allergy, Asthma and
Immunology [13578]
50 N Brockway
Palatine, IL 60067
Ph: (847)934-1918

Subramanian, Prem S., Secretary
North American Neuro-
Ophthalmology Society [16398]
5841 Cedar Lake Rd., Ste. 204
Minneapolis, MN 55416
Ph: (952)646-2037
Fax: (952)545-6073

Suchocki, Andrew, Founder
Ride for World Health [22753]
PO Box 8234
Columbus, OH 43201

Suddaby, Steve, President
The World War One Historical Association [9811]
2625 Alcatraz Ave. No. 237
Berkeley, CA 94705-2702

Suddarth, Jim, President
Gaited Morgan Horse Organization
[4354]
c/o Janet Hunter, Secretary
337 Hess Ln.
Cobden, IL 62920
Ph: (618)833-3728

Sudduth, Ken, Dr., President
International Society of Precision
Agriculture [3571]
107 S State St., Ste. 300
Monticello, IL 61856-1968
Ph: (217)762-7955

Sudges, John, President
Powder Coating Institute [747]
PO Box 2112
Montgomery, TX 77356
Ph: (936)597-5060
Toll Free: 800-988-2628
Fax: (936)597-5059

Sudman, Philip D., President
Southwestern Association of Naturalists [6900]

c/o Philip D. Sudman, President
Box T-0620
Department of Biological Sciences
Tarleton State University
Stephenville, TX 76402

Sufka, Kenneth M., Exec. Dir.
Associated Air Balance Council
[498]
1518 K St. NW, Ste. 503
Washington, DC 20005
Ph: (202)737-0202
Fax: (202)638-4833

Sufrin, Gerald, President
American Association of
Genitourinary Surgeons [17544]
Fahey Bldg. 54, Rm. 267
2160 S 1st Ave.
Maywood, IL 60153
Ph: (708)216-5100
Fax: (708)216-8991

Sugar, Meredith K., Director
Alexander Graham Bell Association
for the Deaf and Hard of Hearing
[15166]
3417 Volta Pl. NW
Washington, DC 20007
Ph: (202)337-5220

Sugarbaker, David J., MD,
Counselor
American Association for Thoracic
Surgery [17469]
500 Cummings Ctr., Ste. 4550
Beverly, MA 01915-6183
Ph: (978)927-8330
Fax: (978)524-0498

Sugarmann, Josh, Exec. Dir.
Violence Policy Center [19231]
1730 Rhode Island Ave. NW, Ste.
1014
Washington, DC 20036
Ph: (202)822-8200
     (202)822-8200

Sugerman-Brozan, Jodi, Exec. Dir.
Bikes Not Bombs [18772]
284 Amory St.
Jamaica Plain, MA 02130
Ph: (617)522-0222
Fax: (617)522-0922

Sugulle, Bile, Chmn. of the Bd.
Read Horn of Africa USA [12181]
2955 Chicago Ave. S
Minneapolis, MN 55407

Suilebhan, Gwydion, Director
National New Play Network [10263]
641 D St. NW
Washington, DC 20004
Ph: (202)312-5270
Fax: (202)289-2446

Suino, Mr. Nicklaus, Director
Shudokan Martial Arts Association
[23013]
PO Box 6022
Ann Arbor, MI 48106-6022
Ph: (734)645-6441

Suk, Gabriel, Founder
Prevention Through Education
[13557]
1007 Church St., Ste. 302
Evanston, IL 60201

Suk, Michael, MD, President
International Geriatric Fracture
Society [16478]
1215 E Robinson St.
Orlando, FL 32801
Ph: (813)909-0450
Fax: (813)949-8994

Sukup, Alicia, Assoc. Dir.
American Society of Gene and Cell
Therapy [14875]

555 E Wells St., Ste. 1100
Milwaukee, WI 53202-3800
Ph: (414)278-1341
Fax: (414)276-3349

Sule, Abraham O., Exec. Dir., CEO
African Children's HIV/AIDS Relief
Global Alliance [13518]
PO Box 3115
Berkeley, CA 94703
Ph: (510)520-1097
Fax: (510)530-8055

Sulkala, Chuck, Exec. Dir.
National Auto Body Council [300]
7044 S 13th St.
Oak Creek, WI 53154-1429
Ph: (414)908-4957
Fax: (414)768-8001

Sulkes, Destry J., MD, MBA, Mem.
Alliance for Continuing Education in
the Health Professions [8300]
2025 M St. NW, Ste. 800
Washington, DC 20036
Ph: (202)367-1151
Fax: (202)367-2151

Sullins, John, Secretary, Treasurer
Society for Philosophy and Technology [10128]
c/o Shannon Vallor, President
500 El Vamino Real
Santa Clara, CA 95053
Ph: (408)554-5190

Sullivan, Rev. Angel L, President
American Baptist Women's
Ministries [19715]
PO Box 851
Valley Forge, PA 19482-0851
Ph: (610)768-2288
Fax: (610)768-2286

Sullivan, Brian, Director
Maria Mitchell Association [6008]
4 Vestal St.
Nantucket, MA 02554
Ph: (508)228-9198
(508)228-2896

Sullivan, Mr. Charles, Founder
Citizens United for Rehabilitation of
Errants [11522]
PO Box 2310
Washington, DC 20013-2310
Ph: (202)789-2126

Sullivan, Cheryl G., MSES, CEO
American Academy of Nursing
[16085]
1000 Vermont Ave. NW, Ste. 910
Washington, DC 20005-4903
Ph: (202)777-1170

Sullivan, David, VP
American Copy Editors Society
[2649]
c/o Teresa Schmedding, President
155 E Algonquin Rd.
Arlington Heights, IL 60005-4617

Sullivan, David, Office Mgr.
International Naval Research
Organization [9803]
PO Box 48
Holden, MA 01520-0048
Ph: (508)799-9229

Sullivan, Diane, Chairperson
Two Ten Footwear Foundation
[1404]
1466 Main St.
Waltham, MA 02451
Toll Free: 800-346-3210
Fax: (781)736-1554

Sullivan, Edmund J., Exec. Dir.
Columbia Scholastic Press Association [8454]

Columbia University
90 Morningside Dr., Ste. B01
New York, NY 10027
Ph: (212)854-9400

Sullivan, Frank, Commissioner
National Junior Baseball League
[22562]
4 White Spruce Ln.
Hauppauge, NY 11788
Ph: (631)582-5191

Sullivan, Gordon R., President, CEO
Association of the United States
Army [5593]
2425 Wilson Blvd.
Arlington, VA 22201
Ph: (703)841-4300
Toll Free: 800-336-4570

Sullivan, Janet, Membership Chp.
Institute for Expressive Analysis
[16974]
303 5th Ave., Ste. 1103
New York, NY 10016
Ph: (646)494-4324

Sullivan, Jay, Treasurer
Marketing Executives Networking
Group [2290]
3 Anchorage Ln.
Old Saybrook, CT 06475
Ph: (860)984-6186
Fax: (860)510-0249

Sullivan, Joanne, President
National Federation of Democratic
Women [18115]
c/o Joanne Sullivan, President
4 Gorman Pl.
East Hartford, CT 06108

Sullivan, Kristie, Secretary
American Society for Cellular and
Computational Toxicology [7336]
4094 Majestic Ln., Ste. 286
Fairfax, VA 22033
Ph: (202)527-7335
Fax: (202)527-7435

Sullivan, Laura, Exec. Dir., Secretary
United States Collegiate Ski and
Snowboard Association [23169]
320 Stage Rd.
Cummington, MA 01026-9646
Ph: (413)634-0110
Fax: (413)634-0110

Sullivan, Lauren, Director, Founder
Reverb [3932]
386 Fore St., No. 202
Portland, ME 04101
Ph: (207)221-6553

Sullivan, Michael, President
Council on Governmental Ethics
Laws [5772]
PO Box 81237
Athens, GA 30608
Ph: (706)548-7758
Fax: (706)548-7079

Sullivan, Michael, Treasurer
Global Grassroots [13415]
Box 1
1950 Lafayette Rd., Ste. 200
Portsmouth, NH 03801
Ph: (603)643-0400
Fax: (603)619-0076

Sullivan, Robert, Exec. Dir.
American Institute of Organbuilders
[2417]
PO Box 35306
Canton, OH 44735
Ph: (330)806-9011

Sullivan, Rose, Operations Mgr.
Tear Film and Ocular Surface
Society [16439]

PO Box 130146
Boston, MA 02113

Sullivan, Ruth C., PhD, Founder
Autism Services Center [13755]
929 4th Ave.
Huntington, WV 25710-0507
Ph: (304)525-8014
Fax: (304)525-8026

Sullivan, Sean, JD, CEO, President,
Founder
Institute for Health and Productivity
Management [2171]
17470 N Pacesetter Way
Scottsdale, AZ 85255-5445
Ph: (480)305-2100
Fax: (480)305-2189

Sullivan, Steve, President
Twirly Birds [21253]
c/o Steve Sullivan, President
PO Box 70158
Sunnyvale, CA 94086-0158

Sullivan, Ms. Veronica, Bus. Mgr.
Graymoor Ecumenical and Inter-
religious Institute [20062]
c/o Elizabeth Matos, Secretary
475 Riverside Dr., Rm. 1960
New York, NY 10115
Ph: (212)870-2330
Fax: (212)870-2001

Sulmasy, Lois Snyder, Director
American College of Physicians -
Ethics, Professionalism and Hu-
man Rights Committee [14744]
190 N Independence Mall W
Philadelphia, PA 19106-1572
Ph: (215)351-2400
(215)351-2835
Toll Free: 800-523-1546

Sultan, Alexander T., President
Alpha Kappa Psi [23687]
7801 E 88th St.
Indianapolis, IN 46256-1233
Ph: (317)872-1553
Fax: (317)872-1567

Sumerford Jr., Harold, Chmn. of the
Bd.
National Tank Truck Carriers [3097]
950 N Glebe Rd., Ste. 520
Arlington, VA 22203
Ph: (703)838-1960

Summerour, Neil, Chairman
Society of Typographic Aficionados
[1549]
PO Box 457
Jefferson, GA 30549

Summers, Allison, Exec. Dir.
Zonta International [12913]
1211 W 22nd St., Ste. 900
Oak Brook, IL 60523-3384
Ph: (630)928-1400
Fax: (630)928-1559

Summers, Annette, Exec. Dir.
Cheese Importers Association of
America [972]
204 E St. NE
Washington, DC 20002
Ph: (202)547-0899
Fax: (202)547-6348

Summers, Deborah, President
National Hook-Up of Black Women
[18226]
1809 E 71st St., Ste. 205
Chicago, IL 60649-2000
Ph: (773)667-7061
Fax: (773)667-7064

Summers, Kent, Asst. Dir.
NFHS Music Association [8388]

c/o National Federation of State
High School Associations
PO Box 690
Indianapolis, IN 46206-0690
Ph: (317)972-6900
Fax: (317)822-5700

Summers, Marcy, Director
Alliance for Tompotika Conservation
[3794]
c/o Marcy Summers, Director
21416 86th Ave. SW
Vashon, WA 98070
Ph: (206)463-7720
Fax: (206)463-7720

Summers, Nancy, President
New Horizons International Music
Association [9981]
c/o William Gates, Treasurer
PO Box 127
Philomath, OR 97370

Summers, Rick, CEO, Chairman
Golf Range Association of America
[3158]
PO Box 240
Georgetown, CT 06829-0240
Ph: (610)745-0862
Toll Free: 800-541-1123

Summers, Stephanie, CEO
Center for Public Justice [18967]
1115 Massachusetts Ave. NW
Washington, DC 20005
Ph: (202)695-2667
Toll Free: 866-275-8784

Summerville, Sarah, Director
Unexpected Wildlife Refuge [10706]
PO Box 765
Newfield, NJ 08344-0765
Ph: (856)697-3541

Sumner, Mr. Charles Hanson, Director
Sumner Family Association [20935]
c/o Charles H. Sumner, Director
7540 Rolling River Pky.
Nashville, TN 37221-3322
Ph: (615)646-9946

Sumner, Diane, Founder
Children's Liver Association for Sup-
port Services [15253]
25379 Wayne Mills Pl., Ste. 143
Valencia, CA 91355
Ph: (661)263-9099
Toll Free: 877-679-8256
Fax: (661)263-9099

Sumner, James H., President
U.S.A. Poultry and Egg Export
Council [4575]
2300 W Park Place Blvd., Ste. 100
Stone Mountain, GA 30087
Ph: (770)413-0006
Fax: (770)413-0007

Sumner, Lucy, President, Director
The Magic Penny, Inc. [12803]
c/o Lucy Sumner, President and
International Director
24 Eldorado Dr.
East Northport, NY 11731
Ph: (631)486-3822

Sumners, Mr. Bill, Director
Southern Baptist Historical Library
and Archives [19742]
901 Commerce St., Ste. 400
Nashville, TN 37203-3630
Ph: (615)244-0344
Fax: (615)782-4821

Sun, Lei, Exec.
Federation Des Grandes Tours Du
Monde [7499]

PO Box 11278
Chicago, IL 60611
Ph: (312)363-7093

Sun, Robert, President
American-Chinese CEO Society
[3296]
World Trade Ctr., Ste. 425, 350 S
Figueroa St.
350 S Figueroa St.
Los Angeles, CA 90071

Sun, Prof. Ron, Bd. Member
International Neural Network Society
[16020]
1123 Comanche Path
Bandera, TX 78003-4212
Ph: (830)796-9393
Fax: (830)796-9394

Sun, Weijing, President
Chinese American Hematologist and
Oncologist Network [15227]
PO Box 1308
Scarsdale, NY 10583

Sunderlal, Shefali, President
Child Rights and You America
[10904]
PO Box 850948
Braintree, MA 02185-0948
Ph: (339)235-0792
(617)959-1273

Sundt, Jon, Founder
Natural High [13470]
6310 Greenwich Dr., Ste. 145
San Diego, CA 92122
Ph: (858)551-7006
Fax: (858)551-1855

Sung, Vivian, MD, President
Society of Gynecologic Surgeons
[16305]
7800 Wolf Trail Cove
Germantown, TN 38138
Ph: (901)682-2079
Fax: (901)682-9505

Sung-Gon, Kim, Secretary
International Society for Biomedical
Research on Alcoholism [17314]
PO Box 202332
Denver, CO 80220-8332
Ph: (303)355-6420
Fax: (303)355-1207

Sun-Saenz, Mariesa, Director,
Founder
US Cuba Artist Exchange [9219]
3359 36th Ave. S
Minneapolis, MN 55406
Ph: (612)267-8363

Sunshine, Robert H., Exec. Dir.
International Cinema Technology
Association [1196]
c/o Robert H. Sunshine, Executive
Director
825 8th Ave. 29th Fl.
New York, NY 10019
Ph: (212)493-4097
(212)493-4058
Fax: (212)257-6428

Sunwoo, Sophia, CEO, Founder
Water Collective [13358]
209 Quincy St. Ste., 2R
Brooklyn, NY 11216

Suomi, Marvin J., Chmn. of the Bd.
Education Development Center
[7764]
43 Foundry Ave.
Waltham, MA 02453-8313
Ph: (617)969-7100
Fax: (617)969-5979

Supera, India, Founder
Feathered Pipe Foundation [11998]
2409 Bear Creek Rd.

Helena, MT 59601
Ph: (406)442-8196
Fax: (406)442-8110

Supper, Bill, Exec. Dir.
Billiard and Bowling Institute of
America [3137]
PO Box 6573
Arlington, TX 76005-6573
Ph: (817)649-5105
Fax: (817)385-8268

Supper, Bill, Exec. Dir.
International Bowling Pro Shop and
Instructors Association [22703]
c/o Russ Wilson, President
355 N Iowa St.
Lawrence, KS 66044
Ph: (513)705-6497
Toll Free: 800-255-6436

Surch, Randell, VP
International Test and Evaluation
Association [7326]
4400 Fair Lakes Ct., Ste. 104
Fairfax, VA 22033-3801
Ph: (703)631-6220
Fax: (703)631-6221

Surdej, Jeff, Chairman
National Collegiate Water Ski As-
sociation [23355]
1251 Holy Cow Rd.
Polk City, FL 33868
Ph: (863)324-4341
Fax: (863)325-8259

Suro, Roberto, Director
Tomás Rivera Policy Institute
[19531]
Lewis Hall
Sol Price School of Public Policy
University of Southern California
650 Childs Way, Ste. 102
Los Angeles, CA 90089-0626
Ph: (213)821-5615
Fax: (213)821-1976

Suro, Thomas P., Secretary
American Institute of Hydrology
[7360]
Southern Illinois University Carbon-
dale
1230 Lincoln Dr.
Carbondale, IL 62901
Ph: (618)453-7809
(651)484-8169
Fax: (651)484-8357

Susalka, Stephen J., Exec. Dir.
Association of University Technology
Managers [5323]
1 Parkview Plz., Ste. 800
Oakbrook Terrace, IL 60181
Ph: (847)686-2244
Fax: (847)686-2253

Susi, Paul, President
Gesneriad Society [22097]
1122 E Pike St.
Seattle, WA 98122-3916

Sussex, Mary K., MBA, Secretary,
Treasurer
American Association of Legal Nurse
Consultants [15525]
330 N Wabash Ste. 2000
Chicago, IL 60611-4267
Toll Free: 877-402-2562
Fax: (312)673-6655

Susskind, Yifat, Exec. Dir.
MADRE [12287]
121 W 27th St., No. 301
New York, NY 10001
Ph: (212)627-0444
Fax: (212)675-3704

Sussman, Bob, President
Society for Pacific Coast Native Iris
[22125]

c/o Kathleen Sayce, Secretary
PO Box 91
Nahcotta, WA 98637-0091

Sussman, Karen A., President
International Society for the Protec-
tion of Mustangs and Burros
[4831]
PO Box 55
Lantry, SD 57636-0055
Ph: (605)964-6866
(605)430-2088

Suter, Debbie, Exec. Dir.
Society of Petroleum Evaluation
Engineers [7003]
c/o Debbie Suter, Executive
Secretary
20333 State Highway 249, Ste. 200
Houston, TX 77070
Ph: (832)972-7733

Sutherland, George W., Commissioner
Clan Sutherland Society of North
America, Inc. [20844]
c/o Robert F. Sutherland, President
188 Simpson Rd.
Marlboro, MA 01752

Sutherland, Tracey, Exec. Dir.
American Accounting Association [9]
5717 Bessie Dr.
Sarasota, FL 34233-2399
Ph: (941)921-7747
Fax: (941)923-4093

Sutton, Bob L., Chmn. of the Bd.
International Wildfowl Carvers As-
sociation [21766]
PO Box 115
Hanover, VA 23069-0115
Ph: (804)537-5033

Sutton, David J., CAE, Exec. Dir.,
Gen. Counsel
Scientific Equipment and Furniture
Association [3031]
65 Hilton Ave.
Garden City, NY 11530
Ph: (516)294-5424
Toll Free: 877-294-5424
Fax: (516)294-2758

Sutton, Dennis L., Exec. Dir.
Crude Oil Quality Association [2518]
2324 N Dickerson St.
Arlington, VA 22207-2641
Ph: (703)282-2461

Sutton, Dr. Joi, Founder
Veterinary Ventures [10712]
c/o Amber Holland, Treasurer
PO Box 10553
Portland, OR 97296

Sutton, Mark, President, CEO
Gas Processors Association [2521]
6060 American Plz., Ste. 700
Tulsa, OK 74135
Ph: (918)493-3872

Sutton, Prof. R. Anderson, President
Association for Korean Music
Research [9877]
455 North Park St.,
University of Wisconsin-Madison
455 N Park St.
Madison, WI 53706
Ph: (608)263-1900

Sutton, Susan, President
National Orphan Train Complex
[20986]
300 Washington St.
Concordia, KS 66901
Ph: (785)243-4471

Sutula, Martha, Secretary
Coastal and Estuarine Research
Federation [6801]

2150 N 107th St., Ste. 205
Seattle, WA 98133-9009
Ph: (206)209-5262
Fax: (206)367-8777

Suzara, Aileen, Director
Filipino/American Coalition for
Environmental Solidarity [4140]
PO Box 566
Berkeley, CA 94701-0566

Suzuki, Brian J., JD, MPP, Exec. Dir.
Omicron Kappa Upsilon [23719]
c/o Hai Zhang, President
Box 357456
School of Dentistry
University of Washington
1959 NE Pacific St.
Seattle, WA 98195-7456
Ph: (206)543-5948
Fax: (206)543-7783

Svart, Maria, Director
Democratic Socialists of America
[19140]
75 Maiden Ln., Ste. 702
New York, NY 10038
Ph: (212)727-8610
Fax: (212)608-6955

Svazas, Ms. Janet, Exec. Dir.
American Academy of Oral and Max-
illofacial Pathology [16568]
214 N Hale St.
Wheaton, IL 60187
Ph: (630)510-4552
Toll Free: 888-552-2667
Fax: (630)510-4501

Svazas, Janet, Exec. Dir.
National Retail Hobby Stores As-
sociation [658]
214 N Hale St.
Wheaton, IL 60187
Ph: (630)510-4596
Fax: (630)510-4501

Svinicki, Jane, CAE, Exec. Dir.
International Society for Anaesthetic
Pharmacology [13703]
6737 W Washington St., Ste. 4210
Milwaukee, WI 53214
Ph: (414)755-6296
Fax: (414)276-7704

Svinicki, Jane, CAE, Exec. Dir.
Society of Anesthesia and Sleep
Medicine [13708]
6737 W Washington St., Ste. 1300
Milwaukee, WI 53214
Ph: (414)389-8608
Fax: (414)276-7704

Svinicki, Jane, CAE, Exec. Dir.
Society for Obstetric Anesthesia and
Perinatology [16628]
6737 W Washington St., Ste. 4210
Milwaukee, WI 53214
Ph: (414)389-8611
Fax: (414)276-7704

Svochak, Jan, President
Contact Lens Manufacturers As-
sociation, Inc. [1598]
PO Box 29398
Lincoln, NE 68529-0398
Ph: (402)465-4122
Toll Free: 800-344-9060
Fax: (402)465-4187

Swafford, Katy, PhD, Mem.
United States Association for Body
Psychotherapy [16947]
8639 B 16th St., Ste. 119
Silver Spring, MD 20910
Ph: (202)466-1619

Swaim-Staley, Beverly, Chairperson
Women's Transportation Seminar
[3363]

1701 K St. NW, Ste. 800
Washington, DC 20006
Ph: (202)955-5085
Fax: (202)955-5088

Swallow, Judith A., Treasurer
American Board of Examiners of
  Psychodrama, Sociometry, and
  Group Psychotherapy [16958]
PO Box 15572
Washington, DC 20003
Ph: (202)483-0514

Swami, Nishwant, Founder
Vishwam [12581]
3 Eastmans Rd.
Parsippany, NJ 07054-3702
Ph: (973)886-8170

Swan, Bonnie, President
National Association of Test Directors [8688]
c/o Dr. Dale Whittington, Director -
  Research, Evaluation and Assessment
15600 Parkland Dr.
Shaker Heights, OH 44120
Ph: (216)295-4363

Swan, Rita, PhD, Founder, President
Children's Healthcare is a Legal
  Duty [15530]
136 Blue Heron Pl.
Lexington, KY 40511
Ph: (859)255-2200
     (208)985-0414

Swan, Sharon J., CAE, CEO
American Society for Clinical
  Pharmacology and Therapeutics
  [16642]
528 N Washington St.
Alexandria, VA 22314-2314
Ph: (703)836-6981
Fax: (703)836-5223

Swank, Edgar, President
American Cryonics Society [14355]
510 S Mathilda Ave., Ste. 8
Sunnyvale, CA 94086
Ph: (408)530-9001
Toll Free: 800-523-2001

Swank, Larry, Secretary
Council on Chiropractic Orthopedics
  [16474]
4409 Sterling Ave.
Kansas City, MO 64133-1854
Ph: (816)358-5100
Fax: (816)358-6565

Swankin, David A., CEO, President
Citizen Advocacy Center [18331]
1400 16th St. NW, Ste. 101
Washington, DC 20036
Ph: (202)462-1174
Fax: (202)354-5372

Swann, Crystal D., Asst. Dir.
United States Conference of City
  Human Services Officials [5764]
United States Conference of Mayors
1620 Eye St. NW, 4th Fl.
Washington, DC 20006
Ph: (202)861-6707
Fax: (202)293-2352

Swanson, Diane, Exec. Dir.
American Women Artists [8914]
PO Box 4125
Queensbury, NY 12804

Swanson, Mr. Erik, Founder, Exec.
  Dir.
Roots and Wings International
  [12183]
5018 N Allen Pl.
Spokane, WA 99205
Ph: (503)564-8831

Swanson, Gregg, Exec. Dir., Chmn.
  of the Bd.
HumaniNet [12676]
4068 Ridge Ct.
West Linn, OR 97068-8285
Ph: (503)957-2960

Swanson, Heather, Exec. Dir.
Society for the Study of Male
  Reproduction, Inc. [17119]
1100 E Woodfield Rd., Ste. 350
Schaumburg, IL 60173
Ph: (847)517-7225
Fax: (847)517-7229

Swanson, LeAnn N., Exec. Dir.
Organ Donation and Transplantation
  Alliance [17518]
PO Box 140027
Coral Gables, FL 33114
Ph: (757)818-1205

Swanson, Mary, Chairman
Clery Center for Security on Campus
  [11502]
110 Gallagher Rd.
Wayne, PA 19087-2959
Ph: (484)580-8754
Fax: (484)580-8759

Swanson, Michele S., Chairperson
American Academy of Microbiology
  [6066]
1752 N St. NW
Washington, DC 20036
Ph: (202)737-3600

Swanson, Robert, Chairman
Airlines Electronic Engineering Com-
  mittee [6525]
ARINC Inc.
2551 Riva Rd.
Annapolis, MD 21401-7435
Ph: (240)334-2579

Sward, Robert, President
Post-Tensioning Institute [572]
38800 Country Club Dr.
Farmington Hills, MI 48331
Ph: (248)848-3180
Fax: (248)848-3181

Swarmer, Sean, Bd. Member
CancerClimber Association [13933]
Boulder, CO

Swaroop, Prem, President
Two Cents of Hope [11173]
423 Westfalen Dr.
Cary, NC 27519-9751

Swartz, Ann, DVM, Secretary
American Holistic Veterinary Medical
  Association [17624]
33 Kensington Pky.
Abingdon, MD 21009
Ph: (410)569-0795
Fax: (410)569-2346

Swartz, Barry, VP
Conexx: America Israel Business
  Connector [23576]
400 Northridge Rd., No. 250
Sandy Springs, GA 30350
Ph: (404)843-9426
Fax: (404)843-1416

Swartz, Brecken Chinn, PhD, Exec.
  Dir.
HandReach [13058]
28 Robinwood Ave.
Jamaica Plain, MA 02130
Ph: (202)213-9267

Swartz, F. Randolph, Art Dir., Bd.
  Member
Dance Affiliates [9249]
Bldg. 46B

4701 Bath St.
Philadelphia, PA 19137-2235
Ph: (215)636-9000
Fax: (267)672-2912

Swartz, John, Founder, Chairman
Food Aid International [12090]
PO Box 853
Apex, NC 27502
Toll Free: 888-407-5125

Swartz, Melissa, President
Society of Telecommunications
  Consultants [3240]
PO Box 70
Old Station, CA 96071
Ph: (530)335-7313
Toll Free: 800-782-7670
Fax: (800)859-3205

Swatos, William H., Ph.D., Exec.
  Ofc.
Religious Research Association
  [20586]
c/o Kevin D. Dougherty
1 Bear Pl., No. 97326
Waco, TX 76798
Ph: (254)710-6232
Fax: (254)710-1175

Swayze, Carroll, Chairperson
National Association of Independent
  Artists [8929]
1125 US Highway 1
Sebastian, FL 32958

Sweanor, Linda, Officer
Wild Felid Research and Manage-
  ment Association [4903]
PO Box 3335
Montrose, CO 81402-3335
Ph: (970)252-1928

Sweat, Herbert, Director
Black Veterans for Social Justice
  [21112]
665 Willoughby Ave.
Brooklyn, NY 11206
Ph: (718)852-6004
Fax: (718)852-4805

Sweeney, Ariane E., VP, Comm.
Citizens Against Government Waste
  [18316]
1301 Pensylvania Ave. NW, Ste.
  1075
Washington, DC 20004
Ph: (202)467-5300
Fax: (202)467-4253

Sweeney, Bill, President, CEO
International Foundation for Election
  Systems [18183]
2011 Crystal Dr., 10th Fl.
Arlington, VA 22202
Ph: (202)350-6700
Fax: (202)350-6701

Sweeney, Chuck, President, CEO
The Distinguished Flying Cross
  Society [20732]
PO Box 502408
San Diego, CA 92150
Toll Free: 866-332-6332

Sweeney, Col. James R., President
Reserve Officers Association of the
  United States [5622]
1 Constitution Ave. NE
Washington, DC 20002
Ph: (202)479-2200
Toll Free: 800-809-9448
Fax: (202)547-1641

Sweeney, Jerry L., Officer
National Chief Petty Officers' Association [21056]
c/o Richard A. Oubre, Treasurer

5730 Misty Glen
San Antonio, TX 78247-1373
Ph: (210)637-6304

Sweeney, Jill, President
Association for Women in Comput-
  ing [6295]
PO Box 2768
Oakland, CA 94602

Sweeney, Matt, Chairman
National Judicial College [5398]
Judicial College Bldg., MS 358
Reno, NV 89557
Ph: (775)784-6747
Toll Free: 800-255-8343
Fax: (775)784-1253

Sweeney, Ric, Chairperson
American Marketing Association
  [2264]
311 S Wacker Dr., Ste. 5800
Chicago, IL 60606
Ph: (312)542-9000
Toll Free: 800-AMA-1150
Fax: (312)542-9001

Sweet, Debby, Founder
Rescue Alliance of Hairless and
  Other Breeds [10687]
PO Box 1135
Atascadero, CA 93423-1135
Ph: (805)544-2480

Sweet, Lisa, Chief Clin. Ofc.,
  Founder
National Association of Health Care
  Assistants [14895]
501 E 15th St.
Joplin, MO 64804
Ph: (417)623-6049
     (417)623-2230

Sweet, Mr. Robert, Jr., President,
  Founder
National Right to Read Foundation
  [8487]
PO Box 560
Strasburg, VA 22657
Ph: (913)788-6773

Sweet, Sher, Bd. Member
Traprock Center for Peace and
  Justice [18831]
PO Box 1201
Greenfield, MA 01302
Ph: (413)522-8892

Sweetman, Prof. Brendan, PhD,
  President
Gabriel Marcel Society [10087]
c/o Brendan Sweetman, PhD,
  President
Rockhurst University
Dept. of Philosophy
1100 Rockhurst Rd.
Kansas City, MO 64110-2561
Ph: (816)501-4681

Sweets, Henry, Exec. Dir.
Mark Twain Boyhood Home Associ-
  ates [9075]
120 N Main St.
Hannibal, MO 63401-3537
Ph: (573)221-9010
Fax: (573)221-7975

Sweets, Henry, Exec. Dir.
Mark Twain Home Foundation
  [9106]
120 N Main St.
Hannibal, MO 63401
Ph: (573)221-9010
Fax: (573)221-7975

Swendson, Ted, Officer
Carriage Association of America
  [21633]

4075 Iron Works Pky.
Lexington, KY 40511
Ph: (859)231-0971
Fax: (859)231-0973

Swensen, Pam, CEO
Executive Women's Golf Association
[22879]
8895 N Military Trl., Ste. 102e
Palm Beach Gardens, FL 33410
Ph: (561)691-0096

Swenson, Dean
Association of Credit Union Internal
Auditors **[946]**
1727 King St., Ste. 300
Alexandria, VA 22314
Ph: (703)688-2284
Fax: (703)348-7602

Swetland, Paul, President
Roving Volunteers in Christ's Service
[22469]
1800 SE 4th St.
Smithville, TX 78957-2906
Toll Free: 800-727-8914

Swick, Herbert M., President
American Osler Society **[15710]**
c/o Renee Ziemer, Administrator
141 County Road 132 SE
Dover, MN 55929
Ph: (507)259-5125

Swift, Byron, President
Nature and Culture International
[3915]
1400 Maiden Ln.
Del Mar, CA 92014
Ph: (858)259-0374

Swift, Byron, Founder
Rainforest Trust **[4098]**
7078 Airlie Rd.
Warrenton, VA 20187
Toll Free: 800-456-4930

Swift, Diane S., Chmn. of the Bd.
Research to Prevent Blindness
[17739]
360 Lexington Ave., 22nd Fl.
New York, NY 10017
Ph: (212)752-4333
Toll Free: 800-621-0026
Fax: (212)688-6231

Swift, Gerry, Bd. Member
Floor Covering Installation Contrac-
tors Association **[865]**
7439 Millwood Dr.
West Bloomfield, MI 48322
Ph: (248)661-5015
Fax: (248)661-5018

Swift, Ginger, President
Association of Premier Nanny Agen-
cies **[10804]**
2125 N Josey Ln., No. 100
Carrollton, TX 75006
Ph: (301)654-1242

Swift, Pari, President
National Association of Government
Archives and Records Administra-
tors **[5305]**
444 N Capitol St. NW, Ste. 237
Washington, DC 20001
Ph: (202)508-3800
Fax: (202)508-3801

Swift, Sally, Founder
Centered Riding, Inc. **[22941]**
PO Box 429
Millstone Township, NJ 08510
Ph: (609)208-1100
Fax: (609)208-1101

Swift, Mr. Vince, President
Statue of Liberty Club **[21723]**
c/o Lebo Newman, Treasurer

3705 Barron Way
Reno, NV 89511

Swifth, Ed, LM, Chairman
Coast Guard Combat Veterans As-
sociation **[21118]**
c/o Gary Sherman, Secretary/
Treasurer
3245 Ridge Pke.
Eagleville, PA 19403
Ph: (610)539-1000

Swiggart, Brad, President
Metropolitan Owners Club of North
America **[21430]**
2308 Co. Hwy. V
2308 County Hwy. V
Sun Prairie, WI 53590
Ph: (608)825-1903

Swing, Rev. William E., President,
Founder
United Religions Initiative **[20567]**
1009 General Kennedy Ave.
San Francisco, CA 94129-1706
Ph: (415)561-2300
Fax: (415)561-2313

Swinnen, Prof. Johan, President
International Association of
Agricultural Economists **[6390]**
555 E Wells St., Ste. 1100
Milwaukee, WI 53202-3800
Ph: (414)918-3199
Fax: (414)276-3349

Swinney, Dan, Exec. Dir.
Manufacturing Renaissance **[18611]**
3411 W Diversey Ave., Ste. 10
Chicago, IL 60647
Ph: (773)278-5418
Fax: (773)278-5918

Swinson, Mary Ann, Exec.
Arthur Rackham Society **[8843]**
20705 Wood Ave.
Torrance, CA 90503-2755

Swintosky, John A., President
Holly Society of America **[4728]**
309 Buck St.
Millville, NJ 08332-0803
Ph: (856)825-4300
Fax: (856)825-5283

Swiontek, Lisa Fedler, Exec. Dir.
Sigma Kappa Foundation **[23963]**
695 Pro Med Ln., Ste. 300
Carmel, IN 46032
Ph: (317)381-5531
Fax: (317)872-0716

Swistel, Daniel, President
Ukrainian Institute of America
[10289]
2 E 79th St.
New York, NY 10075
Ph: (212)288-8660
Fax: (212)288-2918

Switalski, Erin, Exec. Dir.
Women's Voices for the Earth **[4109]**
114 W Pine St.
Missoula, MT 59807
Ph: (406)543-3747
Fax: (406)543-2557

Swofford, John D., Commissioner
Atlantic Coast Conference **[23216]**
4512 Weybridge Ln.
Greensboro, NC 27407
Ph: (336)854-8787
Fax: (336)854-8797

Sybert, Tom, Chairman
Elevator Escalator Safety Foundation **[1064]**
356 Morgan Ave.

Mobile, AL 36606-1737
Ph: (251)479-2199
Toll Free: 800-949-6442
Fax: (251)479-7099

Sychak, Les, Chmn. of the Bd.
Aviation Crime Prevention Institute
[359]
PO Box 730118
Ormond Beach, FL 32173
Ph: (386)843-2274
Toll Free: 800-969-5473

Sygall, Susan, CEO, Founder
Mobility International USA **[11618]**
132 E Broadway, Ste. 343
Eugene, OR 97401-3155
Ph: (541)343-1284
Fax: (541)343-6812

Sylla, Dr. Sekou M., President
Guinea Development Foundation,
Inc. **[17777]**
140 W End Ave., Ste. 17G
New York, NY 10023
Ph: (212)874-2911

Sylte, Matt, Secretary, Treasurer
American Association of Veterinary
Immunologists **[17603]**
c/o Dr. Glenn Zhang, Secretary-
Treasurer
212 Animal Science
Animal Molecular Biology
Oklahoma State University
Stillwater, OK 74074

Sylvan, Ms. Linda L., Exec. Dir.
Rice Design Alliance **[5976]**
M.D. Anderson Hall, Rm. 149
Rice University
6100 Main St.
Houston, TX 77005-1827
Ph: (713)348-4876
Fax: (713)348-5924

Sylvester, Glenn, President
Filipino-American Law Enforcement
Officers Association **[5463]**
PO Box 77086
San Francisco, CA 94107

Sylvia, Dr. Gilbert, President
North American Association of
Fisheries Economists **[1302]**
213 Ballard Hall
Oregon State University
Corvallis, OR 97330-3601
Ph: (541)737-1439
Fax: (541)737-2563

Syme, Don, Secretary, Treasurer,
Director
National Association for Cave Diving
[23342]
PO Box 14492
Gainesville, FL 32604

Symons, Sarah, Founder, Exec. Dir.
Made By Survivors **[12070]**
PO Box 3403
Saint Augustine, FL 32085
Toll Free: 800-831-6089

Synder, Fred, Consultant, Director
Native American Indian Information
and Trade Center **[23652]**
PO Box 27626
Tucson, AZ 85726-7626
Ph: (520)622-4900

Synder, Fred, Consultant, Director
North America Native American
Information and Trade Center
[10045]
PO Box 27626
Tucson, AZ 85726-7626
Ph: (520)622-4900

Synesiou, Karen, CEO
Center for Surrogate Parenting, Inc.
[13203]
West Coast Office
15821 Ventura Blvd., Ste. 625
Encino, CA 91436
Ph: (818)788-8288
Fax: (818)981-8287

Sypolt, Arika, President
United Hellenic Voters of America
[19459]
861 W Lake St.
Addison, IL 60101
Ph: (630)628-1721

Szasz, Margaret Connell, Officer
Western History Association **[8806]**
University of Alaska Fairbanks
Dept. of History
605 Gruening Bldg.
Fairbanks, AK 99775-6460
Ph: (907)474-6509
    (907)474-6508
Fax: (435)797-3899

Szasz, Patricia, President
American Association of Intensive
English Programs **[7864]**
PO Box 170128
Atlanta, GA 30317
Ph: (415)926-1975

Sze, S., President
Community Partners International
[11341]
225 Bush St., No. 590
San Francisco, CA 94104
Ph: (415)217-7015

Szego, Robert, President
Bellanca-Champion Club **[21216]**
PO Box 100
Coxsackie, NY 12051

Szeto, Dr. Paul C.C., Director,
President
Evangelize China Fellowship
[20415]
PO Box 418
Pasadena, CA 91102-9969

Szorad, Gabor, Gen. Sec.
Hungarian Scouts Association
[12853]
c/o Gabor Szorad
2850 Route 23 N
Newfoundland, NJ 07435-1443
Ph: (973)874-0384

Szymani, Dr. Ryszard, Director,
Founder
Wood Machining Institute **[3512]**
PO Box 476
Berkeley, CA 94701
Ph: (925)943-5240
Fax: (925)945-0947

Szymaszek, Stacy, Director
Poetry Project **[10157]**
St. Marks Church
131 E 10th St.
New York, NY 10003
Ph: (212)674-0910

T

Ta, Hoai, Act. Chm.
International Children Assistance
Network **[11047]**
532 Valley Way
Milpitas, CA 95035-4106
Ph: (408)509-8788
    (408)509-1958
Fax: (408)935-9657

Tabart, Deborah, CEO
Friends of the Australian Koala
Foundation **[4819]**

c/o The Nolan Lehr Group, Inc.
214 W 29th St., Ste. 1002
New York, NY 10001
Ph: (212)967-8200
Fax: (212)967-7292

Tabatabai, Mr. M.R., President
Iran Freedom Foundation [18575]
PO Box 34422
Bethesda, MD 20827
Ph: (301)215-6677
    (301)335-7717
Fax: (301)907-8877

Taber, Andrew, Exec. Dir.
Mountain Institute [9329]
3000 Connecticut Ave. NW, Ste. 101
Washington, DC 20008
Ph: (202)234-4050
Fax: (202)234-4054

Tabor, Kristin, Founder, President
Colon Cancer Coalition [13947]
5666 Lincoln Dr., Ste. 270
Edina, MN 55436
Ph: (952)426-6521
Fax: (952)674-1179

Tacci, James A., Officer
American College of Occupational
    and Environmental Medicine
    [16312]
25 NW Point Blvd., Ste. 700
Elk Grove Village, IL 60007-1030
Ph: (847)818-1800
Fax: (847)818-9266

Tackett, Chief Daniel G., Director
International Police and Fire
    Chaplain's Association [19930]
9393 Pardee Rd.
Taylor, MI 48180
Ph: (313)291-2571

Tackett, Julian, Chairman
Council on Standards for
    International Educational Travel
    [8066]
212 S Henry St.
Alexandria, VA 22314
Ph: (703)739-9050

Tactaquin, Catherine, Exec. Dir.
National Network for Immigrant and
    Refugee Rights [18467]
310 8th St., Ste. 310
Oakland, CA 94607
Ph: (510)465-1984
Fax: (510)465-1885

Tada, Joni Eareckson, CEO,
    Founder
Joni and Friends [11611]
30009 Ladyface Ct.
Agoura Hills, CA 91301
Ph: (818)707-5664
Toll Free: 800-736-4177
Fax: (818)707-2391

Tada, Joni Eareckson, CEO,
    Founder
Wheels for the World [11647]
PO Box 3333
Agoura Hills, CA 91376-3333
Ph: (818)707-5664
Toll Free: 800-736-4177
Fax: (818)707-2391

Tadesse, Demissie, MD, Contact
Sight For Souls [17745]
3300 Tyson Ave.
Philadelphia, PA 19149
Ph: (215)222-1933

Tadjiki, Brian, President
Education for Chinese Orphans
    [7762]
PO Box 8630

Bend, OR 97708
Ph: (541)610-6967

Tadros, Nadia, President
Egyptians Relief Association [11349]
6121 Winnepeg Dr.
Burke, VA 22015-3847
Ph: (703)503-8816

Tafazzoli, Mrs. Negin, President,
    Director
International Society for Children
    with Cancer [13994]
17155 Gillette Ave., Unit B
Irvine, CA 92614
Ph: (949)679-9911
Fax: (949)679-3399

Taft, Barrett, Secretary
National DeSoto Club [21453]
c/o Dennis Pitchford, Treasurer
14947 Leigh Ave.
San Jose, CA 95124-4524

Taft, Jim, Exec. Dir.
Association of State Drinking Water
    Administrators [5713]
1401 Wilson Blvd., Ste. 1225
Arlington, VA 22209
Ph: (703)812-9505
Fax: (703)812-9506

Tafur, Angela M., President, Founder
Give To Colombia [12476]
6705 Red Rd., Ste. 502
Coral Gables, FL 33143
Ph: (305)669-4630
Fax: (305)675-2946

Tagawa, Koichi, Chairman
NFC Forum [6230]
401 Edgewater Pl., Ste. 600
Wakefield, MA 01880
Ph: (781)876-8955
Fax: (781)610-9864

Tagg, Barbara, Contact
Chorus America [9889]
1156 15th St. NW, Ste. 310
Washington, DC 20005-1747
Ph: (202)331-7577
Fax: (202)331-7599

Taggie, Benjamin F., Exec. Dir.
Mediterranean Studies Association
    [9794]
PO Box 79351
North Dartmouth, MA 02747-0984
Ph: (508)979-8687

Taglienti, John, President
National Fireproofing Contractors
    Association [1291]
4415 W Harrison St., No. 436
Hillside, IL 60162
Ph: (708)236-3411
Fax: (708)449-0837

Taglione, Rosemarie, Exec. Dir.
Ellis Island Medal of Honor Society
    [19428]
National Ethnic Coalition of
    Organizations
12 East 33rd St., 12th Fl.
New York, NY 10016
Ph: (212)755-1492
Fax: (212)755-3762

Taguchi, Mr. Shin, President
American Supplier Institute [7259]
30200 Telegraph Rd., Ste. 100
Bingham Farms, MI 48025-4503
Ph: (612)293-7337

Tai, Dr. Dwan, Founder, Chairperson
Allies Building Community [9019]
PO Box 57250
Washington, DC 20037-0250
Ph: (202)496-1555

Taie, JoAnn, Exec. Dir.
Organization for Human Brain Map-
    ping [6920]
5841 Cedar Lake Rd., Ste. 204
Minneapolis, MN 55416
Ph: (952)646-2029
Fax: (952)545-6073

Taimoorazy, Juliana, Founder,
    President
Iraqi Christian Relief Council [12688]
PO Box 3021
Glenview, IL 60025
Ph: (847)401-8846

Tait, Kelly, Comm. Chm.
National Association of State Judicial
    Educators [8219]
c/o Kelly Tait, Committee Chairman
KT Consulting
362 Hillcrest Dr.
Reno, NV 89509

Takahashi, Motomu, President, CEO
Nippon Club [19512]
145 W 57th St.
New York, NY 10019-2220
Ph: (212)581-2223
Fax: (212)581-3332

Takaragawa, Stephanie, President
Society for Visual Anthropology
    [5927]
c/o American Anthropological Asso-
    ciatoin
2300 Clarendon Blvd., Ste. 1301
Arlington, VA 22201.

Takashima, Dr. Gregg, President
American Association of Human-
    Animal Bond Veterinarians [10566]
618 Church St., Ste. 220
Nashville, TN 37219
Ph: (766)621-0830

Takata, Yuriko, Contact
Women's Caucus for Art [8947]
PO Box 1498, Canal Street Sta.
New York, NY 10013
Ph: (212)634-0007

Takayanagi, Susumu, MD, President
International Society of Aesthetic
    Plastic Surgery [14316]
45 Lyme Rd., Ste. 304
Hanover, NH 03755
Ph: (603)643-2325
Fax: (603)643-1444

Talanian, Nancy, Director
No More Guantanamos [17923]
PO Box 618
Whately, MA 01093
Ph: (413)665-1150

Talbert, Megan, Exec. Dir.
Helping Hands: Monkey Helpers for
    the Disabled Inc. [11603]
541 Cambridge St.
Boston, MA 02134
Ph: (617)787-4419

Talbot, Tammy, COO
Sweet Adelines International [10016]
9110 S Toledo Ave.
Tulsa, OK 74137
Ph: (918)622-1444
Toll Free: 800-992-7464
Fax: (918)665-0894

Talbott, Jay, Dir. of Member Svcs.
Shelby American Automobile Club
    [21489]
PO Box 788
Sharon, CT 06069

Talbott, Joel, President
International Internet Leather Craft-
    ers' Guild [2083]

c/o Pat Hay, Treasurer
PO Box 98
Cary, MS 39054

Talbott, Strobe, Chairman
American Ditchley Foundation
    [18510]
275 Madison Ave., 6th Fl.
New York, NY 10016
Ph: (212)878-8854

Taliaferro-Bazile, Denise, President
American Educational Studies As-
    sociation [7741]
c/o Pamela J. Konkol, Secretary
Concordia University Chicago
7400 Augusta St.
River Forest, IL 60305

Tally, P.J., President
National Church Goods Association
    [20582]
Bldg. C, Ste. 312
800 Roosevelt Rd.
Glen Ellyn, IL 60137
Ph: (630)942-6599
Fax: (630)790-3095

Tamajong, Peter, President
Nkwen Cultural and Development
    Association USA [19289]
7381 La Tijera Blvd.
Los Angeles, CA 90045
Ph: (909)528-4904

Tamarkin, Tanya A., Dir. of Accred.
Commission on Accreditation for
    Marriage and Family Therapy
    Education [8273]
112 S Alfred St.
Alexandria, VA 22314-3061
Ph: (703)253-0473
Fax: (703)253-0508

Tamminen, Terry, President, Founder
Seventh Generation Advisors [4103]
3435 Ocean Park Blvd., Ste. 203
Santa Monica, CA 90405
Ph: (310)664-0300
Fax: (310)664-0305

Tamvakis, Stefanos, President
World Council of Hellenes Abroad
    [19460]
801 W Adams St., Ste. 235
Chicago, IL 60607
Ph: (312)627-1821
Fax: (312)627-1943

Tan, Chek, CEO
Singapore America Business As-
    sociation [668]
3 Twin Dolphin Dr., Ste. 150
Redwood City, CA 94065
Ph: (650)260-3388
Fax: (650)593-3276

Tan, Noel EK, Chairman
International Association of Facilita-
    tors [2740]
15050 Cedar Ave. S, No. 116-353
Apple Valley, MN 55124
Ph: (952)891-3541
Toll Free: 800-281-9948

Tan, Song, MD, President
Cambodian Health Professionals
    Association of America [14985]
1025 Atlantic Ave.
Long Beach, CA 90813
Ph: (562)491-9292
Fax: (562)495-1878

Tanaka, Aaron, Co-Chmn. of the Bd.
New Economy Coalition [17809]
89 S St., Ste. 406
Boston, MA 02111
Ph: (617)946-3200

Tanaka, Kenneth, President
Japanese American Bar Association
[5017]
PO Box 71961
Los Angeles, CA 90071

Tanaka, Stefan, Chairman
American Historical Association -
Conference on Asian History
[9020]
H&SS 4062
University of California San Diego
9500 Gilman Dr.
La Jolla, CA 92093
Ph: (858)534-3401

Tang, Carol, Exec. Dir.
National AfterSchool Association
[10809]
2961A Hunter Mill Rd., No. 626
Oakton, VA 22124
Ph: (703)610-9002

Tang, Lei, Officer
Sino-American Pharmaceutical
Professionals Association [16686]
PO Box 282
Nanuet, NY 10954

Tang, Sheldon, President
Society of Asian Federal Officers
[5519]
PO Box 1021
New York, NY 10002

Tang, Simon F.T., MD, President
International Society for Restorative
Neurology [16027]
2020 Peachtree Rd. NW
Atlanta, GA 30309

Taniguchi, Tadatsugu, President
International Cytokine and Interferon
Society [15648]
c/o Federation of American Societies
for Experimental Biology
9650 Rockville Pke.
Bethesda, MD 20814
Ph: (301)634-7250
Fax: (301)634-7455

Tannahill, Mrs. Sharon K., Exec. Dir.
Flag Manufacturers Association of
America [20945]
994 Old Eagle School Rd., Ste.
1019
Wayne, PA 19087
Ph: (610)971-4850
Fax: (610)971-4859

Tannahill, Sharon K., Exec. Dir.
NCMS Inc. - The Society of
Industrial Security Professionals
[1789]
994 Old Eagle School Rd., Ste.
1019
Wayne, PA 19087-1802
Ph: (610)971-4856
Fax: (610)971-4859

Tanne, Emanuel, MD, Founder,
Chairman
Intracranial Hypertension Research
Foundation [15949]
6517 Buena Vista Dr.
Vancouver, WA 98661
Ph: (360)693-4473
Fax: (360)694-7062

Tanne, Frederick, Chairman
American Society for the Prevention
of Cruelty to Animals [10571]
424 E 92nd St.
New York, NY 10128-6804
Ph: (212)876-7700
Toll Free: 800-582-5979

Tannehill, Doss K., President
American Society of Ocularists
[15662]

PO Box 5275
Herndon, VA 20172
Ph: (661)633-1746
Toll Free: 888-973-4066
Fax: (661)458-1660

Tannen, Michael F., CESP, Exec. Dir.
International Association of
Corporate Entertainment Produc-
ers [1139]
PO Box 9826
Wilmington, DE 19809-9826
Ph: (312)285-0227

Tannenbaum, Saul, Director
Society for Industrial Archeology
[5950]
Social Sciences Dept.
Michigan Technological University
1400 Townsend Dr.
Houghton, MI 49931-1295
Ph: (906)487-1889

Tanner, Elizabeth, Ph.D, Secretary
National Gerontological Nursing As-
sociation [14897]
446 E High St., Ste. 10
Lexington, KY 40507
Ph: (859)977-7453
Toll Free: 800-723-0560
Fax: (859)271-0607

Tanner, Maynard, Director
Romagnola and RomAngus Cattle
Association [3754]
14305 W 379th St.
La Cygne, KS 66040
Ph: (913)594-1080

Tanner, Randy, Contact
International Rescue and Emergency
Care Association [14664]
PO Box 431000
Minneapolis, MN 55443

Tanter, Prof. Raymond, Founder,
President
Iran Policy Committee [18576]
Alban Towers
3700 Massachusetts Ave. NW, Ste.
L34
Washington, DC 20016-5807
Ph: (202)333-7346

Tantillo, Auggie, President
National Council of Textile Organiza-
tions [3265]
1701 K St. NW, Ste. 625
Washington, DC 20006
Ph: (202)822-8028
Fax: (202)822-8029

Tanz, Jayne M., Exec. Dir.
International Electrical Testing As-
sociation [1024]
3050 Old Centre Ave., Ste. 102
Portage, MI 49024
Ph: (269)488-6382
Fax: (269)488-6383

Tanzella, John, President
International Gay and Lesbian Travel
Association [3381]
1201 NE 26th St., Ste. 103
Fort Lauderdale, FL 33305
Ph: (954)630-1637
Fax: (954)630-1652

Tanzer, Sharon, VP
Nuclear Control Institute [18753]
1000 Connecticut Ave. NW, Ste. 400
Washington, DC 20036-5302
Ph: (202)822-8444
Fax: (202)452-0892

Taormina, Latifah, Director
Subud International Cultural Association U.S.A. [9003]

9509 Ketona Cove
Austin, TX 78759
Ph: (512)560-3397

Tapanian, Aza, Principal
American Society for Management
[2147]
2505 Anthem Village Dr., Ste. E-222
Henderson, NV 89052
Ph: (702)293-7389
    (818)974-4004
Fax: (702)293-5260

Tapia, Mario E., CEO, President
Latino Center on Aging [10512]
576 5th Ave., Ste. 903
New York, NY 10036
Ph: (212)330-8120

Tappe, Mary, Chairman
Sudden Cardiac Arrest Association
[14148]
910 17th St. NW, Ste. 800
Washington, DC 20006
Ph: (202)441-5982

Tarantino, Lisa M., President
International Behavioural and Neural
Genetics Society [16049]
1123 Comache Path
Bandera, TX 78003-4212
Ph: (919)843-7292

Tarasi, Megan, Administrator
Federation of Schools of Ac-
countancy [7408]
c/o Megan Tarasi, Administrator
Pailadian I
220 Leigh Farm Rd.
Durham, NC 27707-8110
Ph: (919)402-4825

Tardrew, Karen, President
International Visual Literacy Associa-
tion [7777]
c/o Dr. Carolyn Berenato, Treasurer
Merion Hall 212
St. Joseph's University
5600 City Ave.
Philadelphia, PA 19131

Tarica, Marcelo, Chairman
International Mystery Shopping Alli-
ance [2958]
210 Crossways Park Dr.
Woodbury, NY 11797
Ph: (516)576-1188

Tariche, Reynaldo, President
Federal Bureau of Investigation
Agents Association [5462]
PO Box 320215
Alexandria, VA 22320
Ph: (703)247-2173
Fax: (703)247-2175

Tarker, Lisa, Asst.
Catholic Biblical Association of
America [8706]
Catholic University of America
433 Caldwell Hall
Washington, DC 20064
Ph: (202)319-5519
Fax: (202)319-4799

Tarker, Lisa, Exec. Dir.
Federation of Diocesan Liturgical
Commissions [19833]
415 Michigan Ave. NE
Washington, DC 20017-4503
Ph: (202)635-6990
Fax: (202)529-2452

Tarne, Gene, Contact
Americans to Ban Cloning [17871]
1100 H St. NW, Ste. 700
Washington, DC 20005
Ph: (202)347-6840
Fax: (202)347-6849

Tarosky, Dennis, VP
National Utility Locating Contractors
Association [894]
1501 Shirkey Ave.
Richmond, MO 64085
Toll Free: 888-685-2246
Fax: (504)889-9898

Tarsitano, Dr. Frank, CEO, President
NACEL Open Door [8085]
380 Jackson St., Ste. 200
Saint Paul, MN 55101-4810
Ph: (651)686-0080
Toll Free: 800-622-3553
Fax: (651)686-9601

Tartaglia, Benjamin W., Exec. Dir.
International Disaster Recovery As-
sociation [7312]
PO Box 4515
Shrewsbury, MA 01545
Ph: (508)845-6000
Fax: (508)842-9003

Tarulis, Jennifer, Contact
Gold and Silver Plate Society
[20733]
c/o Jenniefer Tarulis
180 N Stetson Ave., Ste. 850
Chicago, IL 60601
Ph: (312)540-4400

Tarzi, Nadia, Exec. Dir., Founder
Association for the Protection of
Afghan Archaeology [5933]
PO Box 6798
San Rafael, CA 94903-0798

Tasch, Woody, Founder, Chairman
Slow Money Alliance [4701]
PO Box 2231
Boulder, CO 80306
Ph: (303)443-1154

Tasende, Ms. Betina, President
Fine Art Dealers Association [244]
9663 Santa Monica Blvd., Ste. 316
Beverly Hills, CA 90210
Ph: (310)659-9888

Tasher, Raychelle A., President
Ms. JD [5023]
PO Box 77546
San Francisco, CA 94107

Tasini, Oren, Officer
National Association of Dealer
Counsel [299]
1800 M St. NW, Ste. 400 S
Washington, DC 20036
Ph: (202)293-1454
Fax: (202)530-0659

Tasker, Wayne E., Chairman
American Psychotherapy Association
[16962]
2750 E Sunshine St.
Springfield, MO 65804
Ph: (417)823-0173
Toll Free: 800-205-9165

Tassa, Krista Altok, Founder,
President
Estonian American Chamber of
Commerce & Industry [23583]
111 John St., Ste. 1910
New York, NY 10038
Ph: (917)744-2765

Tate, Florence, Exec. Dir.
Accrediting Bureau of Health Educa-
tion Schools [15671]
7777 Leesburg Pke., Ste. 314 N
Falls Church, VA 22043
Ph: (703)917-9503
Fax: (703)917-4109

Tatroe, Randy, President
American Penstemon Society
[22080]

c/o Dale Lindgren, Membership
Secretary
9202 Maloney Dr.
North Platte, NE 69101

Tatsch, Kenneth, President
United States Dog Agility Association
[22821]
PO Box 850955
Richardson, TX 75085
Ph: (972)487-2200
Fax: (972)231-9700

Tatum, Janet, President
Sandplay Therapists of America
[17462]
PO Box 4847
Walnut Creek, CA 94596
Ph: (925)820-2109

Taupy, Jean-Alain, Officer
International DME Association
[5886]
1425 K St. NW, Ste. 350
Washington, DC 20005
Ph: (202)587-5760

Tavera, Gloria, President
Universities Allied for Essential
Medicines [15503]
641 S St. NW
Washington, DC 20001
Ph: (510)868-1159

Tavoletti, Rich, Exec. Dir.
Canned Food Alliance [1320]
Foster Plaza Plz. 10
680 Andersen Dr.
Pittsburgh, PA 15220
Ph: (412)922-2772

Tavora-Jainchill, Barbara, President
United Nations Staff Union [23488]
866 United Nations Plz., 2nd Fl.,
Rm. A-0248
48th St.
New York, NY 10017
Ph: (212)963-7075
Fax: (212)963-3367

Tavoussi, Mohsen, MD, President
American Society of Cosmetic
Breast Surgery [14308]
1419 Superior Ave., Ste. 2
Newport Beach, CA 92663
Ph: (949)645-6665
Fax: (949)645-6784

Tawwater, Larry A., President
American Association for Justice
[5821]
777 6th St. NW, Ste. 200
Washington, DC 20001
Ph: (202)965-3500
Toll Free: 800-424-2725

Tax, Richard F., President
American Engineering Association
[6530]
c/o Harold Ruchelman
533 Waterside Blvd.
Monroe Township, NJ 08831

Tayeb, Lorraine, President
United Poodle Breeds Association
[21976]
c/o Andrea Hungerford, Treasurer
1175 Peckerwood Rd.
Hayesville, NC 28904

Taylor, Alex, Chairman
American Rivers [3804]
1101 14th St. NW, Ste. 1400
Washington, DC 20005
Ph: (202)347-7550
Toll Free: 877-347-7550
Fax: (202)347-9240

Taylor, Brent, Contact
Interstate Club [21236]
c/o Brent Taylor

PO Box 127
Blakesburg, IA 52536-0127

Taylor, Connie, Registrar
Navajo-Churro Sheep Association
[4677]
1029 Zelinski Rd.
Goldendale, WA 98620
Ph: (509)773-3671

Taylor, Dr. Crispin, Exec. Dir.
American Society of Plant Biologists
[6135]
15501 Monona Dr.
Rockville, MD 20855-2768
Ph: (301)251-0560
Fax: (301)279-2996

Taylor, Sir Cyril, Founder, Chairman
American Institute for Foreign Study
[8108]
1 High Ridge Pk.
Stamford, CT 06905
Ph: (203)399-5000
Toll Free: 866-906-2437
Fax: (203)399-5590

Taylor, David, Founder, President
Colombia ChildCare International
[10943]
Calvary Assembly
1199 Clay St.
Winter Park, FL 32789
Ph: (407)644-1199

Taylor, Diana, Chairman
ACCION International [17964]
10 Fawcett St., Ste. 204
Cambridge, MA 02138
Ph: (617)625-7080
Toll Free: 800-931-9951
Fax: (617)625-7020

Taylor, Mr. Dick, Founder
Foundation of Compassionate
American Samaritans [20418]
64 E McMicken Ave.
Cincinnati, OH 45202-8510
Ph: (513)621-5300

Taylor, Dora, President
Parents Across America [8479]
c/o Siegel and Assoc.
53 W Jackson Blvd., Ste. 405
Chicago, IL 60604

Taylor, Elizabeth, V. Ch.
Good Bears of the World [12889]
PO Box 13097
Toledo, OH 43613
Ph: (419)531-5365
Toll Free: 877-429-2327

Taylor, Elizabeth, VP
International Franchise Association
[1461]
1900 K St., NW Ste. 700
Washington, DC 20006
Ph: (202)628-8000
Fax: (202)628-0812

Taylor, Elizabeth, Exec. Dir.
National Health Law Program [5275]
3701 Wilshire Blvd., Ste. 750
Los Angeles, CA 90034
Ph: (310)204-6010
Fax: (213)368-0774

Taylor, Ellie, Chairman
Food Industry Association Executives [2953]
c/o Bev Lynch, President
664 Sandipiper Bay Dr. SW
Sunset Beach, NC 28468
Ph: (910)575-3423

Taylor, Fred, Treasurer
77th Artillery Association [21164]
PO Box 8621

Jacksonville, FL 32239-8621
Ph: (904)236-4856
Toll Free: 877-220-0393

Taylor, Gay LeCleire, President
National American Glass Club
[22136]
PO Box 24
Elkland, PA 16920

Taylor, Gray, Exec. Dir.
Conexxus [2516]
1600 Duke St.
Alexandria, VA 22314
Ph: (703)518-7960

Taylor, H. Art, Chairman
OIC of America [11779]
Leon H. Sullivan Human Services
Ctr.
1415 N Broad St., Ste. 227
Philadelphia, PA 19122-3323
Ph: (215)236-4500
Fax: (215)236-7480

Taylor, Humphrey, Chairman
National Council on Public Polls
[18924]
1425 Broad St., Ste. 7
Clifton, NJ 07013
Ph: (202)293-4710
Fax: (202)293-4757

Taylor, James, Exec. Ofc., COO
American Physical Society [7023]
1 Physics Ellipse
College Park, MD 20740-3844
Ph: (301)209-3200
Fax: (301)209-0865

Taylor, James D., President
The National Humane Education
Society [10671]
PO Box 340
Charles Town, WV 25414-0340
Ph: (304)725-0506
Fax: (304)725-1523

Taylor, Jeffrey, PhD, Director
Hitchcock Institute for Studies in
American Music [8371]
Brooklyn College, CUNY
2900 Bedford Ave.
Brooklyn, NY 11210-2889
Ph: (718)951-5655
(718)951-5000

Taylor, Dr. Jim, President
International Federation of Postcard
Dealers [21673]
PO Box 749
Alamo, TX 78516
Ph: (956)787-1717

Taylor, John, Founder
The Coalition for Hemophilia B
[15228]
835 3rd Ave., Ste. 226
New York, NY 10022
Ph: (212)520-8272
Fax: (212)520-8501

Taylor, John, Chairman, Founder,
CEO
Wildlife Media [4915]
1208 Bay St., Ste. 202
Bellingham, WA 98225
Ph: (360)734-6060

Taylor, Johnny C., Jr., CEO,
President
Thurgood Marshall College Fund
[7469]
901 F St. NW, Ste. 300
Washington, DC 20004
Ph: (202)507-4851
Fax: (202)652-2934

Taylor, Joshua, President
Federation of Genealogical Societies
[20967]

PO Box 200940
Austin, TX 78720-0940
Toll Free: 888-347-1350

Taylor, Julie, Exec. Dir.
National Farm Worker Ministry
[12343]
112 Cox Ave., Ste. 208
Raleigh, NC 27605-1817
Ph: (919)807-8707
Fax: (919)807-8708

Taylor, Ms. Karla, MS, CEO,
President
National Association of Forensic
Counselors [5140]
PO Box 8827
Fort Wayne, IN 46898
Ph: (260)426-7234
Fax: (260)426-7431

Taylor, Kay, Founder, Exec. Dir.
Prevention International: No Cervical
Cancer [14050]
PO Box 13081
Oakland, CA 94661
Ph: (510)452-2542

Taylor, Ken, Exec. Dir.
Power of Pain Foundation [16563]
213 Nottingham Dr.
Colonial Heights, VA 23834
Ph: (804)657-7246

Taylor, L. Roy, Bd. Member
National Association of Evangelicals
[20156]
PO Box 23269
Washington, DC 20026
Ph: (202)479-0815

Taylor, Laura K., Officer
Women's Business Enterprise
National Council [3508]
1120 Connecticut Ave. NW, Ste.
1000
Washington, DC 20036
Ph: (202)872-5515
Fax: (202)872-5505

Taylor, Lauren, Founder, President
End Slavery Now [17893]
PO Box 65007
Washington, DC 20035

Taylor, Lon R., President
Feed My Hungry Children [10972]
PO Box 83775
Phoenix, AZ 85071-3775
Ph: (602)241-2873

Taylor, Loris Ann, CEO, President
Native Public Media [18661]
PO Box 3955
Flagstaff, AZ 86003
Ph: (602)820-4907

Taylor, Meg North, Founder
Lending Promise [11396]
479 Tovar Dr.
San Jose, CA 95123

Taylor, Michael A., Exec. Dir.
National Committee for a Human
Life Amendment Inc. [19062]
PO Box 34116
Washington, DC 20043
Ph: (202)393-0703

Taylor, Nancy, Dir. of Programs
Presbyterian Historical Society
[20525]
425 Lombard St.
Philadelphia, PA 19147
Ph: (215)627-1852
Fax: (215)627-0115

Taylor, Mr. Pat D., Exec. Dir.
Council of Educators in Landscape
Architecture [4444]

PO Box 1915
Keller, TX 76244
Ph: (817)741-9730
Fax: (817)741-9731

Taylor, Paul, VP
Clan Keith Society [20816]
c/o Dorothy G. Keith, Treasurer
1256 Tinderbox Ln. NW
Kennesaw, GA 30144-3038
Ph: (404)539-5222

Taylor, Paul, VP
Seeley Genealogical Society [20926]
c/o Lynda Simmons,
125 Parkview Dr.
Park City, UT 84098
Ph: (453)649-9878

Taylor, Priscilla, Founder
Autism Service Dogs of America
[13754]
20340 SW Boones Ferry Rd.
Tualatin, OR 97062
Ph: (503)488-5983

Taylor, Rich, VP
Corvette Club of America [21363]
Gaithersburg, MD 20885

Taylor, Richard, Chairman
Delta Upsilon [23898]
8705 Founders Rd.
Indianapolis, IN 46268
Ph: (317)875-8900
Fax: (317)876-1629

Taylor, Dr. R.L., President
World's Poultry Science Association,
U.S.A. Branch [4576]
PO Box 1705
Clemson, SC 29633-7105
Ph: (864)633-8633
(864)654-0809

Taylor, Robert, Secretary, Treasurer
Association of Professors of Cardiol-
ogy [14101]
2400 N St. NW
Washington, DC 20037
Ph: (202)375-6191

Taylor, Robert, President
Corben Club [21221]
PO Box 127
Blakesburg, IA 52536
Ph: (515)938-2773
Fax: (515)938-2773

Taylor, Robert L., President
Antique Airplane Association [21215]
22001 Bluegrass Rd.
Ottumwa, IA 52501
Ph: (641)938-2773
Fax: (641)938-2093

Taylor, Ron, Chairman
Utilities Telecom Council [3245]
1129 20th St. NW, Ste. 350
Washington, DC 20036
Ph: (202)872-0030
Fax: (202)872-1331

Taylor, Ronnie, President
American Association for Geodetic
Surveying [7249]
c/o Ronnie Taylor
2905 Carnaby Ct.
Tallahassee, FL 32309-2537
Ph: (850)933-9155

Taylor, Sarah, President
Parenting Media Association [2808]
287 Richards Ave.
Norwalk, CT 06850
Ph: (310)364-0193
Fax: (310)364-0196

Taylor, Stephanie, Account Exec.
Association of University Radiologists [17055]

820 Jorie Blvd.
Oak Brook, IL 60523
Ph: (630)368-3730
Fax: (630)571-7837

Taylor, Ms. Stephanie, Account
Exec.
Society of Chairs of Academic
Radiology Departments [17065]
820 Jorie Blvd.
Oak Brook, IL 60523
Ph: (630)368-3731
Fax: (630)590-7709

Taylor, Steve, CEO
Appaloosa Horse Club [4335]
2720 W Pullman Rd.
Moscow, ID 83843
Ph: (208)882-5578
Fax: (208)882-8150

Taylor, Steve, President
National Pedigreed Livestock
Council [3605]
177 Palermo Pl.
177 Palermo Pl.
The Villages, FL 32159-0094
Ph: (352)259-6005

Taylor, Steve, President
Western Music Association [10023]
PO Box 648
Coppell, TX 75019
Ph: (505)563-0673

Taylor, Steven, CEO
Sjogren's Syndrome Foundation
[17166]
6707 Democracy Blvd., Ste. 325
Bethesda, MD 20817
Ph: (301)530-4420
Toll Free: 800-475-6473
Fax: (301)530-4415

Taylor, Susan, Exec. Dir.
Actors and Others for Animals
[10559]
11523 Burbank Blvd.
North Hollywood, CA 91601
Ph: (818)755-6045
(818)755-6323
Fax: (818)755-6048

Taylor, Terence, Chairman, President
International Council for the Life Sci-
ences [7134]
1713 Gosnell Rd., Ste. 203
Vienna, VA 22182
Ph: (202)659-8058
Fax: (202)659-8074

Taylor, Terri, Exec. Sec.
Forty and Eight [20688]
250 E 38th St.
Indianapolis, IN 46205
Ph: (317)639-1879
(317)634-1804
Fax: (317)632-9365

Taylor, Tess, President
National Association of Record
Industry Professionals [2898]
PO Box 2446
Los Angeles, CA 90078-2446
Ph: (818)769-7007

Taylor, Dr. Thomas D., Exec. Dir.
American Board of Prosthodontics
[14400]
PO Box 271894
West Hartford, CT 06127-1894
Fax: (860)206-1169

Taylor, Troy, President, Founder
American Ghost Society [6980]
Toll Free: 888-446-7859

Taylor, Troy, Secretary
Callmakers and Collectors Association of America [21630]

2925 Ethel Ave.
Alton, IL 62002
Ph: (216)978-8589

Taylor-Hopkins, Linda W., CPA,
Contact
Global Accounting Aid Society [31]
19785 W 12 Mile Rd., Ste. 394
Southfield, MI 48076
Ph: (765)206-6654
Fax: (765)662-3216

Tayman, William P., Jr., CFO,
Treasurer
Corporation for Public Broadcasting
[9142]
401 9th St. NW
Washington, DC 20004-2129
Ph: (202)879-9600
Toll Free: 800-272-2190

Tebbett, Ian, President
American Distance Education
Consortium [7740]
PO Box 830952
Lincoln, NE 68583-0952
Ph: (402)472-7000
Fax: (402)472-9060

Tebrinke, Kevin, PE, President
International Society of Lyophiliza-
tion - Freeze Drying, Inc. [6122]
917 Lexington Way
Waunakee, WI 53597
Ph: (608)577-6790

Ted, Foster, Exec. Dir., Secretary
Ford/Fordson Collectors Association
[22453]
2435 Hansen Ave.
Racine, WI 53405-2518

Tedeschi, George, President
Graphic Communications Conference of the International Brotherhood of Teamsters [23440]
25 Louisiana Ave. NW
Washington, DC 20001
Ph: (202)624-6800

Tedesco, Daniel, Chairman
Global China Connection [8099]
116 E 55th St.
New York, NY 10022

Tedhams, Gale, Bd. Member
Assistance Dogs of America, Inc.
[11573]
5605 Monroe St.
Sylvania, OH 43560
Ph: (419)885-5733
Fax: (419)882-4813

Teegarden, Heather, CSEP, Exec.
Dir.
Association of Green Property Own-
ers and Managers [2746]
3400 Capitol Blvd. SE, Ste. 101
Tumwater, WA 98501
Ph: (425)233-6481

Teegarden, Karen, President, CEO
UniteWomen.org [13417]
1221 Bowers St., No. 2225
Birmingham, MI 48012

Teeguarden, Iona Marsaa, Exec. Dir.
Jin Shin Do Foundation for
Bodymind Acupressure [16455]
PO Box 416
Idyllwild, CA 92549
Ph: (951)767-3393
Fax: (951)767-2200

Teems, Kim, Prog. Dir., Dir. of
Comm.
FACES: The National Craniofacial
Association [14334]

PO Box 11082
Chattanooga, TN 37401
Ph: (423)266-1632
Toll Free: 800-322-2373

Teeples, Bonnie, Chairperson
National Association for Family and
Community Education [7992]
73 Cavalier Blvd., Ste. 106
Florence, KY 41042
Toll Free: 877-712-4477
Fax: (859)525-6496

Teferra, Tsehaye, PhD, President
Ethiopian Community Development
Council [12589]
901 S Highland St.
Arlington, VA 22204
Ph: (703)685-0510
Fax: (703)685-0529

Teghtmeyer, Suzi, Mgr., Member
Svcs.
Council on Botanical and
Horticultural Libraries [9701]
c/o Esther Jackson, Secretary
LuEsther T. Mertz Library
New York Botanical Garden
2900 Southern Blvd.
Bronx, NY 10458-5126

Tehako-Esser, Dana, President,
CEO
Noah's Never Ending Rainbow
[14848]
7737 6th Ave.
Kenosha, WI 53143
Ph: (262)605-3690

Teicher, Oren, CEO
American Booksellers Association
[2944]
333 Westchester Ave., Ste. S202
White Plains, NY 10604
Ph: (914)406-7500
Toll Free: 800-637-0037
Fax: (914)417-4013

Teien, Martha, President
Montessori Educational Programs
International [8353]
PO Box 6
Smithville, IN 47458
Ph: (812)824-6366
Toll Free: 888-708-2470

Tekancic, Lisa Ann, President,
Chmn. of the Bd., CEO
WildCat Conservation Legal Aid
Society [4907]
1725 I St. NW, Ste. 300
Washington, DC 20006
Ph: (202)349-3760

Tekippe, Rita, Editor
International Society for the Study of
Pilgrimage Art [8868]
324 Humanities Hall
Art Dept.
University of West Georgia
Carrollton, GA 30118
Ph: (770)836-4532
(740)427-5347
Fax: (770)836-4392

Teleki, Mr. Maximilian, President
Hungarian American Coalition
[18524]
2400 N St. NW, Ste. 603
Washington, DC 20037
Ph: (202)296-9505
Fax: (202)775-5175

Telfer, Ian, Chairman
World Gold Council [2384]
444 Madison Ave.
New York, NY 10022
Ph: (212)317-3800
Fax: (212)688-0410

Telford, Dustin, President
Medical Equipment & Technology
    Association **[15689]**
c/o Dustin Telford, President
McKay-Dee Hospital
4401 Harrison Blvd.
Ogden, UT 84403-3195
Ph: (801)879-5433

Tellefsen, Mr. Steven, CEO,
    President
Babe Ruth Baseball/Softball **[22546]**
1770 Brunswick Ave.
Trenton, NJ 08648-4632
Ph: (609)695-1434
Toll Free: 800-880-3142
Fax: (609)695-2505

Tellem, Ms. Susan, Founder
American Tortoise Rescue **[4784]**
30745 Pacific Coast Hwy., Ste. 243
Malibu, CA 90265

Teller, Ellen, Chairwoman
Coalition on Human Needs **[13038]**
1120 Connecticut Ave. NW, Ste. 312
Washington, DC 20036
Ph: (202)223-2532
Fax: (202)223-2538

Tellie, Mary, Chairperson
Roasters Guild **[751]**
117 W 4th St., Ste. 300
Santa Ana, CA 92701
Ph: (562)624-4100

Telliho, Nancy, President
Publishers Information Bureau **[117]**
c/o John Ciotoli, Director
Kantar Media
11 Madison Ave., 12th Fl.
New York, NY 10010

Tellin, William, Mem.
American College of Chiropractic
    Consultants **[14253]**
c/o David Cox, Secretary/Treasurer
8219 Kennedy Ave.
Highland, IN 46322
Ph: (219)838-3141
Fax: (708)895-2268

Temeemi, Sean, CFE, CICA, Comp.
    Ofc.
FHI 360 **[8469]**
359 Blackwell St., Ste. 200
Durham, NC 27701
Ph: (919)544-7040
    (212)367-4573
Fax: (919)544-7261

Temko, Wendy, Admin. Ofc.
Fetal Alcohol Syndrome Consulta-
    tion, Education and Training
    Services **[17311]**
PO Box 69242
Portland, OR 97239
Ph: (503)621-1271
Fax: (503)621-1271

Tempchin, Robert, Chairman
Everybody Solar **[7198]**
3129 Branciforte Dr.
Santa Cruz, CA 95065
Ph: (978)310-1042

Tempich, Louanne, VP
International EECP Therapists As-
    sociation **[17449]**
PO Box 315
Westbury, NY 11590
Ph: (513)777-0964

Templet, Shannon, Officer
National Association of State
    Personnel Executives **[5780]**
2760 Research Park Dr.
Lexington, KY 40511
Ph: (859)244-8182
Fax: (859)244-8001

Templeton Dill, Heather, President
John Templeton Foundation **[20555]**
300 Conshohocken State Rd., Ste.
    500
West Conshohocken, PA 19428
Ph: (610)941-2828
Fax: (610)825-1730

Templeton, Ed, Chairman
National Association of Federal
    Credit Unions **[955]**
3138 10th St. N
Arlington, VA 22201-2149
Toll Free: 800-336-4644

Templeton, Kimberly, MD, President
American Medical Women's Associa-
    tion **[15110]**
12100 Sunset Hills Rd., Ste. 130
Reston, VA 20190
Ph: (703)234-4069
Toll Free: 866-564-2483
Fax: (703)435-4390

Templeton, Robert, President
National Association of Arms Shows
    [22020]
PO Box 290
Kaysville, UT 84037-0290
Ph: (801)544-9125

Tenconi, Francesca, Founder
Children's Skin Disease Foundation
    [14490]
1600 S Main St., Ste. 192B
Walnut Creek, CA 94596
Ph: (925)947-3825
Fax: (866)236-6474

Teng, Mabel, Exec. Dir.
Chinese Culture Foundation of San
    Francisco **[9153]**
750 Kearny St., 3rd Fl.
San Francisco, CA 94108-1861
Ph: (415)986-1822
Fax: (415)986-2825

Tenn, Jolyn, Treasurer
FORCES International **[18399]**
PO Box 4267
Kaneohe, HI 96744
Ph: (808)721-8384

Tenner, Andrea Joan, President
International Complement Society
    [15381]
c/o Dr. Wenchao Song, Treasurer
1254 BRBII/III
University of Pennsylvania
421 Curie Blvd.
Philadelphia, PA 19104
Ph: (215)573-6641
Fax: (215)746-8941

Tennille, Carl, Treasurer
Canine Freestyle Federation **[22815]**
14430 Overlook Ridge Ln.
Beaverdam, VA 23015-1787
Ph: (804)883-1174

Teo, Thomas, President
APA Division 24: Society for
    Theoretical and Philosophical
    Psychology **[16876]**
c/o Mary Beth Morrissey, Treasurer
7 Ellis Dr.
White Plains, NY 10605

Tepper, Alan M., Exec. Dir.,
    Treasurer
Tau Epsilon Rho Law Society
    [23805]
133 Paisley Pl.
133 Paisley Pl.
Hainesport, NJ 08036
Ph: (609)864-1838
    (609)284-4584

Tepper, Paul, Exec. Dir.
Western Center on Law and Poverty
    [5555]

3701 Wilshire Blvd., Ste. 208
Los Angeles, CA 90010-2826
Ph: (213)487-7211
Fax: (213)487-0242

Terbo, William H., Exec. Sec.
Tesla Memorial Society **[10352]**
21 Maddaket
Scotch Plains, NJ 07076-3136

Terpstra, Nicholas, Editor
Renaissance Society of America
    [10196]
CUNY Graduate Ctr.
365 5th Ave., Rm. 5400
New York, NY 10016-4309
Ph: (212)817-2130
Fax: (212)817-1544

Terrazas, Tarianne, President
Silky Terrier Club of America **[21962]**
c/o Suzanne Detwiler
1 Clipper Rd., Unit A
Rancho Palos Verdes, CA 90275-
    5956

Terrell, Daphne, Exec. Dir.,
    Secretary
Infrared Data Association **[6363]**
PO Box 3883
Walnut Creek, CA 94598

Terrell-Brooks, Tabatha, Exec. Dir.
Jackson State University National
    Alumni Association, Inc. **[19329]**
PO Box 17820
Jackson, MS 39217
Ph: (601)979-2281
Toll Free: 800-578-6622
Fax: (601)979-3701

Terrill, Marc B., Bd. Member
JPRO Network **[12226]**
25 Broadway, Ste. 1700
New York, NY 10004
Ph: (212)284-6945
Fax: (212)284-6566

Terris, Bruce, President
IEEE - Magnetics Society **[6429]**
445 Hoes Ln.
Piscataway, NJ 08855-0459
Ph: (908)981-0060
Fax: (908)981-0225

Terry, Jack, PhD, CEO
National Board of Examiners in
    Optometry **[16430]**
200 S College St., No. 2010
Charlotte, NC 28202
Ph: (704)332-9565
Toll Free: 800-969-EXAM
Fax: (704)332-9568

Terry, Lisa, President
Viola da Gamba Society of America
    [10020]
PO Box 582628
Minneapolis, MN 55458-2628
Toll Free: 855-846-5415

Terry, Lonnie, President, CEO
North American Steel Alliance **[2365]**
30448 Rancho Viejo Rd., Ste. 250
San Juan Capistrano, CA 92675
Ph: (949)240-0100
Fax: (949)240-0106

Terry, Pamela H., President
American Organ Transplant Associa-
    tion **[17502]**
PO Box 418
Stilwell, KS 66085
Ph: (713)344-2402
Fax: (281)617-4274

Terry, Patrick F., President
PXE International **[14855]**
4301 Connecticut Ave. NW, Ste. 404

Washington, DC 20008-2369
Ph: (202)362-9599
Fax: (202)966-8553

Terry, Sharon F., Chairperson
Coalition for Genetic Fairness
    [17887]
4301 Connecticut Ave. NW, No. 404
Washington, DC 20008-2369
Ph: (202)966-5557
Fax: (202)966-8553

Terry, Sharon, CEO, President
Genetic Alliance **[17342]**
4301 Connecticut Ave. NW, Ste. 404
Washington, DC 20008-2369
Ph: (202)966-5557
Fax: (202)966-8553

Terry, Simeon, Secretary
Airport Minority Advisory Council
    [2391]
2001 Jefferson Davis Hwy., Ste. 500
Arlington, VA 22202
Ph: (703)414-2622
Fax: (703)414-2686

Teske, Donn, VP
National Farmers Union **[4162]**
20 F St. NW, Ste. 300
Washington, DC 20001
Ph: (202)554-1600
Fax: (202)554-1654

Teske, Todd J., Chairman
Outdoor Power Equipment Institute
    [1128]
341 S Patrick St.
Alexandria, VA 22314
Ph: (703)549-7600

Teter, Beverly, PhD, MACN, CNS,
    President
American College of Nutrition
    [16203]
300 S Duncan Ave., Ste. 225
Clearwater, FL 33755
Ph: (727)446-6086
Fax: (727)446-6202

Tetrault, Dr. Michel, Exec. Dir.
Chiropractic Diplomatic Corps
    [14260]
17602 17th St., Ste. 102
Tustin, CA 92780

Tetreault, Paul R., Director
Ford's Theatre Society **[10251]**
511 10th St. NW
Washington, DC 20004
Ph: (202)638-2941
    (202)434-9545
Fax: (202)347-6269

Tetschner, Stacy, CAE, FASAE, CEO
National Speakers Association
    [10176]
1500 S Priest Dr.
Tempe, AZ 85281
Ph: (480)968-2552

Thacker, John R., President
National Conference of Firemen and
    Oilers **[23417]**
1212 Bath Ave., Fl. F and O
Ashland, KY 41101
Ph: (606)324-3445
Fax: (606)326-7039

Thacker, Lloyd, Exec. Dir.
The Education Conservancy **[7447]**
c/o Lloyd Thacker, Executive Direc-
    tor
805 SW Broadway, Ste. 1600
Portland, OR 97205
Ph: (503)290-0083
Fax: (503)973-5252

Thacker, Randall, President
Affirmation/Gay and Lesbian
    Mormons **[20173]**

PO Box 898
Anoka, MN 55303
Ph: (661)367-2421

Thacker, Tim, Secretary
National Taxidermists Association
[3203]
PO Box 549
Green Forest, AR 72638
Ph: (855)772-8543
Fax: (870)438-4218

Thaler, Rudolf, Commissioner
Austrian Trade Commissions in the
United States [23563]
11601 Wilshire Blvd., Ste. 2420
Los Angeles, CA 90025
Ph: (310)477-9988
Fax: (310)477-1643

Thanas, Susan C., Chairperson
Sino-American Bridge for Education
and Health [9585]
c/o Anne Watt, Development Committee Director
15R Sargent St.
Cambridge, MA 02140
Ph: (617)497-1357

Thanhouser, Ned, President
Thanhouser Company Film
Preservation Inc. [9315]
2335 NE 41st Ave.
Portland, OR 97212

Tharp, Mr. David W., CAE, Exec. Dir.
International Association for Food
Protection [5224]
6200 Aurora Ave., Ste. 200W
Des Moines, IA 50322-2864
Ph: (515)276-3344
Toll Free: 800-369-6337
Fax: (515)276-8655

Thatcher, Michelle, CEO
U.S. Green Chamber of Commerce
[23630]
249 S Highway 101, No. 420
Solana Beach, CA 92075

Thau, Larry, Chairperson
National Fire Sprinkler Association
[3002]
40 Jon Barrett Rd.
Patterson, NY 12563-2164
Ph: (845)878-4200
Fax: (845)878-4215

Thayne, Tamira Ci, Founder
Dogs Deserve Better [11691]
1915 Moonlight Rd.
Smithfield, VA 23430
Ph: (757)357-9292

Theil, Carey M., Exec. Dir.
GREY2K USA [4287]
7 Central St.
Arlington, MA 02476
Ph: (781)488-3526
Fax: (617)666-3568

Theis, George I., Treasurer
National World War II Glider Pilots
Association [20671]
c/o Charles L. Day
PO Box 439
Lambertville, MI 48144-0439

Theisen, Nick, Exec. Dir.
Instrument Contracting and
Engineering Association [867]
c/o Nick Theisen, Executive Director
4312 Rochard Ln.
Fort Mill, SC 29707-5851
Ph: (704)905-0319
Fax: (803)547-7697

Thelen, David C., CEO, Founder
Committee for Missing Children
[12356]

934 Stone Mill Run
Lawrenceville, GA 30046
Ph: (678)376-6265
Toll Free: 800-525-8204
Fax: (678)376-6268

Themba, Makani, Exec. Dir.
Praxis Project [11299]
7731 Alaska Ave. NW
Washington, DC 20012
Ph: (202)234-5921
Fax: (202)234-2689

Thenstedt, Paul, Director
Business Golf Association of
America [22875]
c/o David Pitkin, Executive Director
PO Box 157
Cary, NC 27512-0157
Ph: (919)906-2076

Theragood, Renée, Exec. Dir.
Trucking Industry Defense Associa-
tion [3358]
3601 E Joppa Rd.
Baltimore, MD 21234
Ph: (410)931-8100
Fax: (410)931-8111

Theros, Amb. Patrick N., President
US-Qatar Business Council [23638]
1341 Connecticut Ave. NW, Ste. 4A
Washington, DC 20036
Ph: (202)457-8555
Fax: (202)457-1919

Theventhiran, Rajam, MD, VP
International Medical Health
Organization [15026]
400 W Wilson Bridge Rd., Ste. 230
Worthington, OH 43085-2259
Ph: (614)659-9922
Fax: (614)659-9933

Thiadens, Saskia R.J., RN, Exec.
Dir.
National Lymphedema Network
[15546]
2288 Fulton St., Ste. 307
Berkeley, CA 94704
Ph: (510)809-1660
Toll Free: 800-541-3259
Fax: (510)809-1699

Thibadeau, Richard, Founder,
President
Medical Aid to Haiti [12289]
80 S Main St.
West Hartford, CT 06107
Ph: (860)760-7009

Thiboldeaux, Kim, CEO
Cancer Support Community [13931]
1050 17th St. NW, Ste. 500
Washington, DC 20036
Ph: (202)659-9709
Toll Free: 888-793-9355
Fax: (202)974-7999

Thiboutot, Diane, MD, President
American Acne and Rosacea
Society [14478]
201 Claremont Ave.
Montclair, NJ 07042
Ph: (973)783-4575
Toll Free: 888-744-3376
Fax: (973)783-4576

Thiebauth, Bruce, Treasurer
Bridal Show Producers International
[444]
1510 SE 17th St., Ste. 200
Fort Lauderdale, FL 33316
Toll Free: 800-573-6070

Thien, William A., Cmdr.
Veterans of Foreign Wars of the
United States [21149]

406 W 34th St.
Kansas City, MO 64111
Ph: (816)756-3390
Fax: (816)968-1169

Thimons, J. James, Chairman
National Glaucoma Society [16397]
PO Box 4092
Andover, MA 01810
Ph: (978)470-2555
Toll Free: 800-661-6471
Fax: (978)470-4520

Thiringer, Lotta, Mem.
VisitSweden [3408]
PO Box 4649, Grand Central Sta.
New York, NY 10163-4649
Ph: (212)885-9700
Fax: (212)885-9710

Thissen, Richard G., President
National Active and Retired Federal
Employees Association [5197]
606 N Washington St.
Alexandria, VA 22314
Ph: (703)838-7760
Fax: (703)838-7785

Thoma, Carol A., MBA, Exec. Dir.
American Osteopathic Board of
Family Physicians [16511]
330 E Algonquin Rd., Ste. 6
Arlington Heights, IL 60005
Ph: (847)640-8477

Thomas, Alan M., II, Chairman
Committee for the Advancement of
Role-Playing Games [22050]
1127 Cedar St.
Bonham, TX 75418-2913

Thomas, Alfredia, President
Women Alive Coalition [13565]
1524 W 95th St.
Los Angeles, CA 90047-3914
Ph: (323)965-1564

Thomas, Alvin B., Founder,
President
International Orthopedic Rehabilita-
tion Organization [16479]
14254 43rd Ave. N, Unit C
Plymouth, MN 55446
Ph: (763)291-7088
Fax: (763)432-3059

Thomas, Anne, President
National Organization of Nurse
Practitioners Faculties [16164]
1615 M St. NW, Ste. 270
Washington, DC 20036
Ph: (202)289-8044
Fax: (202)289-8046

Thomas, Ashley, Mem.
Aerospace Physiology Society
[7032]
c/o The Aerospace Medical Association
320 S Henry St.
Alexandria, VA 22314-3579

Thomas, Bob, CEO
Rainbows for All Children [11264]
1007 Church St., Ste. 408
Evanston, IL 60201
Ph: (847)952-1770
Fax: (847)952-1774

Thomas, Dalene, Contact
Lighthouse Stamp Society [22383]
c/o Dalene Thomas
1805 S Balsam St., Apt. 106
Lakewood, CO 80232

Thomas, David, CEO
American Dairy Products Institute
[971]

126 N Addison Ave.
Elmhurst, IL 60126
Ph: (630)530-8700
Fax: (630)530-8707

Thomas, Dennis, President
Groove Phi Groove Social Fellow-
ship, Inc. [23900]
PO Box 8337
Silver Spring, MD 20907

Thomas, G. William, Jr., President
James Monroe Memorial Foundation
[10339]
113 N Foushee St.
Richmond, VA 23220
Ph: (804)231-1827

Thomas, George, Exec. Dir.
Center for Environmental Information
[4037]
700 W Metro Pk.
Rochester, NY 14623
Ph: (585)233-6086
    (585)262-2870
Fax: (585)262-4156

Thomas, Gloria, Secretary
Re:Gender [18234]
11 Hanover Sq.
New York, NY 10005-2843
Ph: (212)785-7335

Thomas, Greg, Founder, CEO
Efficiency First [3854]
55 New Montgomery St., Ste. 802
San Francisco, CA 94105
Ph: (415)449-0551
Fax: (415)449-0559

Thomas, James, Asst. VP of Mktg. &
Sales
ASTM International [7323]
100 Barr Harbor Dr.
West Conshohocken, PA 19428-
2959
Ph: (610)832-9585
    (610)832-9598
Toll Free: 877-909-2786

Thomas, James, President
International Association of
Workforce Professionals [5165]
1801 Louisville Rd.
Frankfort, KY 40601
Ph: (502)223-4459
Toll Free: 888-898-9960

Thomas, Jay, Chmn. of the Bd.
Green Building Initiative [533]
PO Box 80010
Portland, OR 97280
Ph: (503)274-0448
Toll Free: 877-424-4241

Thomas, Jeanine, Founder
MRSA Survivors Network [17007]
PO Box 241
Hinsdale, IL 60522
Ph: (630)325-4354

Thomas, John, Treasurer
International Coalition of Art Deco
Societies [8864]
c/o John Thomas, Treasurer
280 Molino Ave., No. 101
Long Beach, CA 90803

Thomas, Joshua, President, Chair-
man
Sigma Phi Beta Fraternity [23929]
PO Box 937
Tempe, AZ 85280-0937
Toll Free: 888-744-2382

Thomas, Karluss, Contact
Silicones Environmental, Health and
Safety Council [726]

700 2nd St. NE
Washington, DC 20002
Ph: (703)249-7000
Fax: (703)249-6100

Thomas, Larry, Editor, Secretary,
Treasurer
Terminal Railroad Association of St.
Louis Historical and Technical
Society, Inc. [10193]
PO Box 1688
Saint Louis, MO 63188-1688
Ph: (314)535-3101
(636)326-3026

Thomas, Lynn, Exec. Dir.
Equine Assisted Growth and Learn-
ing Association [16971]
PO Box 993
Santaquin, UT 84655
Ph: (801)754-0400
Toll Free: 877-858-4600
Fax: (801)754-0401

Thomas, Lynn, VP of Fin. Admin.
Unitarian Universalist Women's
Federation [20631]
258 Harvard St., No. 322
Brookline, MA 02446-2904
Ph: (414)750-4404

Thomas, Marcia, Exec. Dir.
U.S.A. for Africa [12734]
5670 Wilshire Blvd., Ste. 1740
Los Angeles, CA 90036
Ph: (323)954-3124

Thomas, Marilyn, Coord.
Professionals in Workers'
Compensation [23540]
PO Box 65893
Tacoma, WA 98464
Ph: (206)249-7922
Fax: (206)888-4697

Thomas, Mark, Founder
FORE Cancer Research [13970]
PO Box 30827
Gahanna, OH 43230
Ph: (614)975-8319

Thomas, Mary K., Exec. Dir.
Appalachian Studies Association
[8809]
1 John Marshall Dr.
Huntington, WV 25755-0002
Ph: (304)696-2904
Fax: (304)696-6221

Thomas, Melinda, Chairperson
Save the Redwoods League [3941]
111 Sutter St., 11th Fl.
San Francisco, CA 94104
Ph: (415)362-2352
Toll Free: 888-836-0005

Thomas, Norman R., Chancellor
International College of Cranio-
Mandibular Orthopedics [16477]
PO Box 1491
Cannon Beach, OR 97110
Ph: (503)436-0703
Toll Free: 866-379-3656
Fax: (503)436-0612

Thomas, Pat, Chairman
American Trucking Associations
[3322]
950 N Glebe Rd., Ste. 210
Arlington, VA 22203-4181
Ph: (703)838-1700

Thomas, Ralph D., President, Direc-
tor
National Association of Investigative
Specialists [2012]
PO Box 82148
Austin, TX 78708-2148
Ph: (512)719-3595
Fax: (512)719-3594

Thomas, R.B., Jr., Exec. Dir.
International Senior Softball Associa-
tion [23201]
9114 I-Beam Ln.
Manassas, VA 20110
Ph: (571)436-9704
Fax: (703)361-0344

Thomas, Robert, Sec. (Actg.),
Treasurer
Academy of Legal Studies in Busi-
ness [8205]
c/o Dan Cahoy, President
Dept. of Risk Management
Smeal College of Business
Penn State University
310 Business Bldg.
University Park, PA 16802
Ph: (814)865-6205

Thomas, Robert D., President
National Concrete Masonry Associa-
tion [791]
13750 Sunrise Valley Dr.
Herndon, VA 20171
Ph: (703)713-1900
Fax: (703)713-1910

Thomas, Rose, Exec. Dir.
Society of Air Force Clinical
Surgeons [17400]
1511 Paddington Way
Plumas Lake, CA 95961-9129
Ph: (530)741-0680
Fax: (530)741-0680

Thomas, Rusty, Director
Operation Save America [19067]
PO Box 740066
Dallas, TX 75374
Ph: (254)304-0016

Thomas, Sandra, Founder, President
American Hemochromatosis Society
[14926]
PO Box 950871
Lake Mary, FL 32795-0871
Ph: (407)829-4488
Toll Free: 888-655-4766
Fax: (407)333-1284

Thomas, Tina, Exec. Dir.
Association for the Advancement of
Wound Care [14929]
70 E Swedesford Rd., Ste. 100
Malvern, PA 19355
Ph: (610)560-0484
Toll Free: 866-AAWC-999
Fax: (610)560-0502

Thomas, Tracie L., Mgr.
Association of American Law
Schools [8209]
1614 20th St. NW
Washington, DC 20009-1001
Ph: (202)296-8851
Fax: (202)296-8869

Thomas, Wayne E.A., Founder
Firehawk Association of America
[21382]
6446 Bonneville Dr.
Indianapolis, IN 46237

Thomas, Dr. Wayt, Exec. Dir.
Organization for Flora Neotropica
[6151]
c/o Dr. Wm. Wayt Thomas, Execu-
tive Director
Institute of Systematic Botany
New York Botanical Garden
Bronx, NY 10458-5126
Ph: (718)817-8625
Fax: (718)817-8648

Thomashauer, Robin J., Exec. Dir.
Council for Affordable Quality
Healthcare [14994]

1900 K St. NW, Ste. 650
Washington, DC 20006-1110
Ph: (202)517-0400

Thomashower, James E., Exec. Dir.
American Guild of Organists [9859]
475 Riverside Dr., Ste. 1260
New York, NY 10115
Ph: (212)870-2310
Fax: (212)870-2163

Thomason, Carl, President
Studebaker Driver's Club Inc.
[21496]
43306 Running Deer Dr.
Coarsegold, CA 93614-9662

Thomason, Dr. Daniel, Director,
Founder
International Viola d'Amore Society
e.V [9939]
c/o Dr. Daniel Thomason, Co-
Director/Co-Founder
10917 Pickford Way
Culver City, CA 90230
Ph: (310)838-5509

Thomason, Metty, President
American Collectors of Infant Feeders [21608]
c/o Charna Sansbury, Treasurer
30 White Birch Ct.
Gibsonville, NC 27249

Thomasson, Catherine, MD, Exec.
Dir.
Physicians for Social Responsibility
[18822]
1111 14th St. NW, Ste. 700
Washington, DC 20005-5603
Ph: (202)667-4260
Fax: (202)667-4201

Thomforde, Michael, Founder,
President
Serving Our World [11150]
30025 Alicia Pky., No. 179
Laguna Niguel, CA 92677

Thomley, Dr. Rebecca Hage, CEO
Headwaters Relief Organization
[11666]
9400 Golden Valley Rd.
Golden Valley, MN 55427
Ph: (612)251-2853

Thompkins, Nathaniel, Exec. Dir.
Twenty-First Century Foundation
[12499]
c/o Nathaniel Thompkins, Executive
Director
55 Exchange Pl. No. 402
New York, NY 10005-3304
Ph: (212)662-3700
Fax: (212)662-3700

Thompson, Allen, VP
International Society for
Environmental Ethics [4072]
c/o Ben Hale, Vice President
University of Colorado, Boulder
1333 Grandview, UCB 0488
Boulder, CO 80309
Ph: (303)735-3624
(970)491-2061
Fax: (303)735-1576

Thompson, Arthur R., CEO
The John Birch Society [18027]
770 N Westhill Blvd.
Appleton, WI 54914
Ph: (920)749-3780
Toll Free: 800-527-8721
Fax: (920)749-5062

Thompson, Ben, President
US Oil & Gas Association - Missis-
sipi/Alabama Divison [2539]

513 N State St., Ste. 202
Jackson, MS 39201
Ph: (601)948-8903
Fax: (601)948-8919

Thompson, Carole J., President,
Treasurer
Friends of Robert Frost [10151]
121 Historic Route 7A
Shaftsbury, VT 05262

Thompson, Mr. Chant, Exec. Dir.
North American Coalition for
Christian Admissions Professionals
[7451]
PO Box 5211
Huntington, IN 46750-5211
Toll Free: 888-423-2477

Thompson, Christine, President,
Chmn. of the Bd.
Humanity Road [13064]
230 Washington St.
Boydton, VA 23917

Thompson, Christy, Administrator
Carpenters' Company of the City
and County of Philadelphia [9380]
320 Chestnut St., Carpenters Hall
Philadelphia, PA 19106
Ph: (215)925-0167

Thompson, Chuck, Exec. Dir., Gen.
Counsel
International Municipal Lawyers As-
sociation [5012]
7910 Woodmont Ave., Ste. 1440
Bethesda, MD 20814
Ph: (202)466-5424
Fax: (202)785-0152

Thompson, Dean, President
Resilient Floor Covering Institute
[574]
115 Broad St., Ste. 201
LaGrange, GA 30240-2757
Ph: (706)882-3833
Fax: (706)882-3880

Thompson, Rev. Donald
Association of Episcopal Colleges
[7625]
Colleges and Universities of the
Anglican Communion
815 2nd Ave.
New York, NY 10017-4559
Ph: (212)716-6149
Fax: (212)986-5039

Thompson, Elizabeth, Exec. Dir.
Buckminster Fuller Institute [10315]
181 N 11th St., Ste. 402
Brooklyn, NY 11211
Ph: (718)290-9280
(718)290-9283
Fax: (718)290-9281

Thompson, Elizabeth, Mgr. Dir.
Conference on Asian Pacific
American Leadership [19391]
PO Box 65073
Washington, DC 20035
Toll Free: 877-892-5427

Thompson, Elizabeth, President
International Biometric Society
[7243]
1444 I St. NW, Ste. 700
Washington, DC 20005
Ph: (202)712-9049
Fax: (202)216-9646

Thompson, Evan, Chairman
Alzheimer's Impact Movement
[13671]
225 N Michigan Ave., 17th Fl.
Chicago, IL 60601-7633

Thompson, Fred, Exec. VP
International Buckskin Horse Association [4362]

PO Box 268
Shelby, IN 46377
Ph: (219)552-1013
Fax: (219)552-1013

Thompson, Gordon, PhD, Treasurer
Langston Hughes Society [9070]
English Dept.
City College of New York/CUNY
160 Convent Ave.
New York, NY 10031

Thompson, Gregory E, Hist.,
Membership Chp.
Elder William Brewster Society
[20789]
17 David Dr.
East Haven, CT 06512

Thompson, Helen, Secretary
F-4 Phantom II Society [21225]
PO Box 2680
Alamogordo, NM 88310

Thompson, Jim, President
Broadcasters' Foundation of America
[457]
125 W 55th St., 4th Fl.
New York, NY 10019-5366
Ph: (212)373-8250
Fax: (212)373-8254

Thompson, Jim, President
National Aeronca Association
[21240]
10563 Milton Carlisle Rd.
New Carlisle, OH 45344

Thompson, Jim, CEO, Founder
Positive Coaching Alliance [22738]
1001 N Rengstorff Ave., Ste. 100
Mountain View, CA 94043-1766
Toll Free: 866-725-0024
Fax: (650)969-1650

Thompson, John david, President
Caribbean Desalination Association
[7365]
2409 SE Dixie Hwy.
Stuart, FL 34996
Ph: (772)781-8507
Fax: (772)463-0860

Thompson, Jonathan, Exec. Dir.
National Association of Triads
[12829]
1450 Duke St.
Alexandria, VA 22314
Ph: (703)836-7827
Fax: (703)519-8567

Thompson, Mr. Kevin, Exec. Dir.
Cross World Africa [13043]
14 Redwood Ln., B-101
Ithaca, NY 14850
Ph: (607)227-1594

Thompson, Linda, Director
Council of State Community
Development Agencies [5774]
1825 K St. NW, Ste. 515
Washington, DC 20006
Ph: (202)293-5820
Fax: (202)293-2820

Thompson, Michael, Director
Council of State Governments
Justice Center [5133]
100 Wall St., 20th Fl.
New York, NY 10005
Ph: (212)482-2320

Thompson, Michael, President, CEO
National Business Coalition on
Health [14953]
1015 18th St. NW, Ste. 730
Washington, DC 20036-5207
Ph: (202)775-9300
Fax: (202)775-1569

Thompson, Michael, Comm. Chm.
Refrigeration Service Engineers
Society [1636]
1911 Rohlwing Rd., Ste. A
Rolling Meadows, IL 60008-1397
Ph: (847)297-6464
Toll Free: 800-297-5660
Fax: (547)297-5038

Thompson, Michelle, Director
Real Estate Business Institute
[2888]
430 N Michigan Ave.
Chicago, IL 60611
Ph: (312)321-4414
Toll Free: 800-621-8738
Fax: (312)329-8882

Thompson, Dr. Mike, President
Society for Theriogenology [17660]
PO Box 3007
Montgomery, AL 36109-3007
Ph: (334)395-4666
Fax: (334)270-3399

Thompson, Nainoa, President
Polynesian Voyaging Society [5945]
10 Sand Island Pky.
Honolulu, HI 96819-4355
Ph: (808)842-1101

Thompson, Nara, Founder
Care 4 Kids Worldwide [10883]
PO Box 630704
Littleton, CO 80163

Thompson, Pam, Officer
Society for Social Work Leadership
in Health Care [13116]
100 N 20th St., Ste. 400
Philadelphia, PA 19103-1462
Toll Free: 866-237-9542

Thompson, Pamela A., RN, CEO
American Organization of Nurse
Executives [16109]
Two City Ctr., Ste. 400
800 10th St. NW
Washington, DC 20001
Ph: (202)626-2240
Fax: (202)638-5499

Thompson, Patricia E., RN, CEO
Sigma Theta Tau International
[23839]
550 W North St.
Indianapolis, IN 46202
Ph: (317)634-8171
Toll Free: 888-634-7575

Thompson, Randi, CEO, Founder
Kidsave International [10457]
100 Corporate Pointe, Ste. 380
Culver City, CA 90230
Ph: (310)642-7283
Fax: (310)641-7283

Thompson, Renate, Managing Dir.
Cover Collectors Circuit Club
[22324]
PO Box 266
Lake Clear, NY 12945-0266

Thompson, Richard, President
Association of Professional Reserve
Analysts [2739]
W175 N11117 Stonewood Dr., Ste.
204
Germantown, WI 53022
Toll Free: 877-858-5047
Fax: (262)532-2430

Thompson, Richard, President
Sharing Resources Worldwide
[15495]
2405 Industrial Dr.
Madison, WI 53713
Ph: (608)445-8503

Thompson, Rev. Sam, Founder,
President
Clearer Vision Ministries [13276]
251B San Marco Ave.
Saint Augustine, FL 32084
Ph: (904)201-1358

Thompson, Sarah, Exec. Dir.
Christian Peacemaker Teams
[12435]
PO Box 6508
Chicago, IL 60680-6508
Ph: (773)376-0550
Fax: (773)376-0549

Thompson, Shannon Pfarr, Exec.
Dir.
Qualitative Research Consultants
Association [7096]
1000 Westgate Dr., Ste. 252
Saint Paul, MN 55114
Ph: (651)290-7491
Toll Free: 888-674-7722
Fax: (651)290-2266

Thompson, Shanti, Director, VP
Legacy International [8121]
1020 Legacy Dr.
Bedford, VA 24523
Ph: (540)297-5982
Fax: (540)297-1860

Thompson, Steve, Editor
Pogo Fan Club and Walt Kelly
Society [24006]
Spring Hollow Books
6908 Wentworth Ave.
Richfield, MN 55423

Thompson, Ted, JD, President, CEO
Parkinson's Action Network [14610]
1025 Vermont Ave. NW, Ste. 1120
Washington, DC 20005
Ph: (202)638-4101
Toll Free: 800-850-4726

Thompson, Terri, President
Chris Young Fan Club [24071]

Thompson, Terry L., Chmn. of the
Bd.
The Macedonian Outreach [20431]
PO Box 398
Danville, CA 94526-0398
Ph: (925)820-4107

Thompson, Ms. Therese, Dir. of Dev.
Girls Education International [8748]
PO Box 537
Boulder, CO 80306-0537

Thompson, Tim, Regional VP
International Union of Bricklayers
and Allied Craftworkers [23397]
620 F St. NW
Washington, DC 20004
Ph: (202)783-3788
Toll Free: 888-880-8222

Thompson, Tom, Exec. Dir.
United States Marine Safety As-
sociation [5567]
5050 Industrial Rd., Ste. 2
Wall Township, NJ 07727
Ph: (732)751-0102
Fax: (732)751-0508

Thompson, V. Bruce, President
American Exploration & Production
Council [2508]
101 Constitution Ave. NW, Ste. 700
Washington, DC 20001
Ph: (202)742-4540

Thompson, William T., CEO,
President
Association of Graduates of the
United States Air Force Academy
[19305]

3116 Academy Dr.
USAF Academy, CO 80840-4475
Ph: (719)472-0300
Fax: (719)333-4194

Thomson, Angie, Founder, President
Children's Relief Network [10934]
PO Box 668
Deerfield Beach, FL 33443
Ph: (561)620-2970
Toll Free: 800-326-6500
Fax: (561)393-3151

Thomson, Jeffrey C., President,
CEO
Institute of Management Ac-
countants, Cost Management
Group [2172]
10 Paragon Dr., Ste. 1
Montvale, NJ 07645-1760
Ph: (201)573-9000
Toll Free: 800-638-4427
Fax: (201)474-1600

Thomson, John, Trustee
Antiquarian Booksellers Association
of America [9119]
20 W 44th St., Ste. 507
New York, NY 10036-6604
Ph: (212)944-8291
Fax: (212)944-8293

Thomson, John D., President
Spring Research Institute [330]
422 Kings Way
Naples, FL 34104
Ph: (239)643-7769

Thomson, Keith Stewart, Exec. Ofc.
American Philosophical Society
[7118]
104 S 5th St.
Philadelphia, PA 19106-3387
Ph: (215)440-3400
Fax: (215)440-3423

Thomson, Tom, Exec. Dir.
Coalition for Intellectual Property
Rights [5326]
c/o Tom Thompson
607 14th St. NW, Ste. 500
Washington, DC 20036
Ph: (202)466-6210

Thorenson, Dale, Contact
National Barley Growers Association
[4177]
c/o Dale Thorenson
600 Pennsylvania Ave. SE, Ste. 320
Washington, DC 20003
Ph: (202)548-0734
Fax: (202)969-7036

Thorn, Amy Z., Ed. Dir.
Distribution Business Management
Association [3469]
2938 Columbia Ave., Ste. 1102
Lancaster, PA 17603
Ph: (717)295-0033
Fax: (717)299-2154

Thorn, Matt, Exec. Dir. (Actg.)
OutServe-SLDN [5620]
PO Box 65301
Washington, DC 20035-5301
Toll Free: 800-538-7418

Thorn, Pete, Contact
Tanzer 16 Class Association [22674]
7111 Crescent Ridge Dr.
Chapel Hill, NC 27516
Ph: (919)933-8208

Thornberry, Jeannie, Founder
Melanoma Hope Network [14009]
101 W Argonne Dr., No. 220
Saint Louis, MO 63122

Thornburg, John, CFO
National Governors' Association
[5784]

Hall of the States
444 N Capitol St. NW, Ste. 267
Washington, DC 20001-1512
Ph: (202)624-5300
Fax: (202)624-5313

Thornburgh, Dick, Chairman
Washington Legal Foundation [5727]
2009 Massachusetts Ave. NW
Washington, DC 20036
Ph: (202)588-0302

Thorndal, Mary, Founder
Gay and Lesbian Association of
  Retiring Persons [10507]
10940 Wilshire Blvd., Ste. 1600
Los Angeles, CA 90024
Ph: (310)722-1807
Fax: (310)477-0707

Thorne, Deborah L., VP, Comm.
American Bankruptcy Institute [5083]
66 Canal Center Plz., Ste. 600
Alexandria, VA 22314
Ph: (703)739-0800
Fax: (703)739-1060

Thorne, Deborah L., V. Chmn. of the
  Bd.
Women Employed [11790]
65 E Wacker Pl., Ste. 1500
Chicago, IL 60601
Ph: (312)782-3902
Fax: (312)782-5249

Thorngate, Rev. Dale, President
Seventh Day Baptist World Federa-
  tion [19740]
2612 Arcadia Dr.
Miramar, FL 33023
Ph: (954)684-4961

Thornton, Gray, CEO, President
Wild Sheep Foundation [4683]
720 Allen Ave.
Cody, WY 82414
Ph: (307)527-6261
Fax: (307)527-7117

Thornton, Jennifer, Exec. Dir.
Ataxia Telangiectasia Children's
  Project [14565]
5300 W Hillsboro Blvd., Ste. 105
Coconut Creek, FL 33073-4395
Ph: (954)481-6611
Toll Free: 800-543-5728
Fax: (954)725-1153

Thornton, Jennifer, Mktg. Mgr.
National Association of School
  Resource Officers [8523]
2020 Valleydale Rd., Ste. 207A
Hoover, AL 35244-4803
Ph: (205)739-6060
Toll Free: 888-316-2776
Fax: (205)536-9255

Thornton, Jim, MS, President
National Athletic Trainers' Associa-
  tion [23334]
1620 Valwood Pkwy., Ste. 115
Carrollton, TX 75006
Ph: (214)637-6282
Fax: (214)637-2206

Thornton, Kymberly, Mgr.
American Psychological Association
  Science Directorate [16865]
750 1st St. NE
Washington, DC 20002-4242
Ph: (202)336-6000
Fax: (202)336-5953

Thornton, Robert P., President, CEO
International District Energy Associa-
  tion [1626]
24 Lyman St., Ste. 230
Westborough, MA 01581-2841
Ph: (508)366-9339
Fax: (508)366-0019

Thornton, Tara, Contact
Military Toxics Project [4551]
PO Box 558
Lewiston, ME 04243

Thornton, Verena, Exec. Dir.
American Friends Musee d'Orsay
  [8832]
c/o PJSC
1345 Ave. of the Americas, 31st Fl.
New York, NY 10105
Ph: (212)508-1614

Thorp, Ellen, Exec. Dir.
EPDM Roofing Association [526]
529 14th St. NW, Ste. 750
Washington, DC 20045
Ph: (202)591-2474
Fax: (202)591-2474

Thorpe, Grace, President
National Environmental Coalition of
  Native Americans [4086]
PO Box 988
Claremore, OK 74018
Ph: (405)567-4297
Fax: (405)567-4297

Thorpe, Kenneth, President
National Business and Economics
  Society [7562]
PO Box 65657
Tucson, AZ 85728
Ph: (520)395-2622
Fax: (520)395-2622

Thorsby, Mark, Exec. Dir.
Metal Framing Manufacturers As-
  sociation [547]
330 N Wabash Ave.
Chicago, IL 60611
Ph: (312)644-6610

Thorson, Kristin, President
American Fibromyalgia Syndrome
  Association [14765]
7371 E Tanque Verde Rd.
Tucson, AZ 85715-3475
Ph: (520)733-1570
Fax: (520)290-5550

Thorwarth, William T., CEO
American College of Radiology
  [17041]
1891 Preston White Dr.
Reston, VA 20191
Ph: (703)648-8900

Thrall, Laura, President, CEO
CureSearch for Children's Cancer
  [13956]
4600 EW Hwy., Ste. 600
Bethesda, MD 20814
Toll Free: 800-458-6223
Fax: (301)718-0047

Thrasher, J. Brantley, MD, VP
American Board of Urology [17546]
c/o Gerald H. Jordan MD, Executive
  Secretary
600 Peter Jefferson Pky., Ste. 150
Charlottesville, VA 22911
Ph: (434)979-0059
Fax: (434)979-0266

Thrasher, J. Brantley, MD, President
Society of Urology Chairpersons and
  Program Directors [17565]
Two Woodfield Lake
1100 E Woodfield Rd., Ste. 350
Schaumburg, IL 60173
Ph: (847)517-7225
Fax: (847)517-7229

Thrasher, Julianne, Contact
The International Educator [8103]
PO Box 513
Cummaquid, MA 02637
Ph: (508)790-1990
Toll Free: 877-375-6668
Fax: (508)790-1922

Thumann, Albert, PE, Exec. Dir.
Association of Energy Engineers
  [6458]
3168 Mercer University Dr.
Atlanta, GA 30341
Ph: (770)447-5083

Thundup, Paljor, Administrator
Project Tibet [19191]
403 Canyon Rd.
Santa Fe, NM 87501
Ph: (505)982-3002
Fax: (505)988-4142

Thurman, Lindsey, Secretary
Society for Northwestern Vertebrate
  Biology [6899]
2103 Harrison Ave. NW, No. 2132
Olympia, WA 98502

Thurner, Donald, Dir. of Fin. &
  Admin.
American Society of Plumbing
  Engineers [6538]
6400 Shafer Ct., Ste. 350
Rosemont, IL 60018-4914
Ph: (847)296-0002
Fax: (847)296-2963

Thurrott, Jay, President
Bromeliad Society International
  [22089]
c/o Jay Thurrott, President
713 Breckenridge Dr.
Port Orange, FL 32127

Tiandem-Adamou, Yvonne, Founder
A Place of Hope [11735]
PO Box 3341
Huntersville, NC 28070
Ph: (980)230-6511

Tibbetts, Mark, President
Tag and Label Manufacturers
  Institute [3178]
1 Blackburn Ctr.
Gloucester, MA 01930
Ph: (978)282-1400
Fax: (978)282-3238

Tice, David, President
Grand Aerie, Fraternal Order of
  Eagles [19423]
1623 Gateway Cir. S
Grove City, OH 43123-9309
Ph: (614)883-2200
    (614)883-2177
Fax: (614)883-2201

Tichansky, Peter J., CEO, President
Business Council for International
  Understanding [18518]
1501 Broadway, Ste. 2300
New York, NY 10018
Ph: (212)490-0460
Fax: (212)697-8526

Tickell, Joshua, Founder
I'll Be the One Organization [4631]
659A Sunset Ave.
Venice, CA 90291
Ph: (310)392-1370

Tickman, Marsha, Exec. Dir.
IEEE - Components, Packaging, and
  Manufacturing Technology Society
  [6424]
445 Hoes Ln.
Piscataway, NJ 08854
Ph: (732)562-5529
Fax: (732)465-6435

Tiechner, Renee, President
American Canine Foundation
  [21803]
23969 NE State Rte. 3, Ste. G101
Belfair, WA 98528
Ph: (703)451-5656
Fax: (703)451-5979

Tiede, Jim, President
National Potato Council [4244]
1300 L St. NW, Ste. 910
Washington, DC 20005
Ph: (202)682-9456
Fax: (202)682-0333

Tielborg, J. Patrick, Gen. Counsel,
  Managing Dir.
Pipe Line Contractors Association
  [2536]
1700 Pacific Ave., Ste. 4100
Dallas, TX 75201-4675
Ph: (214)969-2700

Tierney, Bryn, President
World Care [11741]
Sam Levitz Warehouse
3430 E 36th St.
Tucson, AZ 85713
Ph: (520)514-1588
Fax: (520)514-1589

Tierney, Jessica Peterson, Exec. Dir.
American Women's Self Defense
  Association [12863]
PO Box 1533
Mason City, IA 50402
Toll Free: 888-STOP RAPE
Fax: (641)424-3496

Tierney, Terry, Chairman, Exec. Dir.
National Christian Choir [20493]
17B Firstfield Rd., Ste. 108
Gaithersburg, MD 20878
Ph: (301)670-6331
Toll Free: 800-599-4710

Tighe, Monica, Chairman
Association of Veterinary Technician
  Educators [17640]
206 S 6th St.
Springfield, IL 62701
Ph: (701)231-7531

Tigunait, Pandit Rajmani, Chairman
Himalayan Institute [12000]
952 Bethany Tpke.
Honesdale, PA 18431-4194
Ph: (570)253-5551
Toll Free: 800-822-4547

Tikkanen, Mike, Founder, President
Kids at Risk Action [13067]
PO Box 4091
Hopkins, MN 55343
Ph: (612)508-7272
Fax: (952)400-8457

Tilburt, Bryan, Exec. Dir.
Highway Melodies Inc. [20367]
PO Box 8451
Grand Rapids, MI 49518-8451
Ph: (616)455-5760
Toll Free: 800-452-0951

Tillapaugh, Mr. Tom, Founder,
  President
StreetSchool Network [8772]
1380 Ammons St.
Lakewood, CO 80214
Ph: (720)299-3420
    (720)425-1642

Tillar, Tressie, Mgr. of Admin.
United Fresh Produce Association
  [4253]
1901 Pennsylvania Ave. NW, Ste.
  1100
Washington, DC 20006
Ph: (202)303-3400
Fax: (202)303-3433

Tiller, Michael, President, CEO
Compressed Gas Association [1496]
14501 George Carter Way, Ste. 103
Chantilly, VA 20151
Ph: (703)788-2700
Fax: (703)961-1831

Tillery, Loretta, VP
Conference of Minority Public
  Administrators [5694]
1120 G St. NW, Ste. 700
Washington, DC 20005

Tillet, Salamishah, PhD, President
A Long Walk Home [13731]
1658 N Milwaukee, Ste. 104
Chicago, IL 60647
Toll Free: 877-571-1751
Fax: (877)571-1751

Tilley, Scott, President
Space Coast Writers' Guild [10402]
7900 Greenboro Dr.
Melbourne, FL 32902-0262
Ph: (321)723-7345

Tillipman, Harvey, COO
American Association of Colleges of
  Osteopathic Medicine [16502]
5550 Friendship Blvd., Ste. 310
Chevy Chase, MD 20815-7231
Ph: (301)968-4100
Fax: (301)968-4101

Tillman, Mark S., President
Alpha Phi Alpha Fraternity [23864]
2313 St. Paul St.
Baltimore, MD 21218-5211
Toll Free: 800-373-3089
Fax: (301)206-9789

Tilstone, Mr. Dave, President
International Special Tooling and
  Machining Association [1739]
c/o Dave Tilstone, President
1357 Rockside Rd.
Cleveland, OH 44134
Ph: (301)248-6862

Tilstone, Mr. Dave, President
National Tooling and Machining As-
  sociation [2109]
1357 Rockside Rd.
Cleveland, OH 44134
Toll Free: 800-248-6862
Fax: (216)264-2840

Tilton, Terry L., Exec. Sec.
Philalethes Society [19566]
PO Box 379
Penryn, CA 95663-0379

Timberlake, Margaret H., President
American Small Business Coalition
  [3112]
PO Box 2786
Columbia, MD 21045
Ph: (410)381-7378

Timmermans, Steven, Exec. Dir.
Christian Reformed Church-Spanish
  and World Literature Committee
  [19964]
1700 28th St. SE
Grand Rapids, MI 49508
Ph: (616)241-1691
Toll Free: 877-279-9994
Fax: (616)224-0834

Timmes, Mr. Mark E., CEO
Pi Kappa Phi [23921]
2015 Ayrsley Town Blvd., Ste. 200
Charlotte, NC 28273
Ph: (704)504-0888
Fax: (980)318-5295

Timmons, James, President
USS Nitro AE-2/AE-23 Association
  [4976]
PO BOX 1254
PO Box 1254
Mishawaka, IN 46546-1254

Timmons, Ms. Sandra E., President
A Better Chance [7816]
253 W 35th St., 6th Fl.

New York, NY 10001-1907
Ph: (646)346-1310
Toll Free: 800-562-7865
Fax: (646)346-1311

Timmons, Vianne, President
International Association for the
  Scientific Study of Intellectual Dis-
  abilities [15647]
School of Medicine and Dentistry
University of Rochester
10 Ellis Ct.
Hilton Head Island, SC 29926-2701

Timony, Margaret M., Exec. Dir.
Drug, Chemical & Associated
  Technologies Association [2557]
1 Union St., Ste. 208
Robbinsville, NJ 08691
Ph: (609)208-1888
Toll Free: 800-640-3228
Fax: (609)208-0599

Tinberg, Christine, Founder,
  President
U.S. Blind Tandem Cycling Connec-
  tion [22757]
21063 Winfield Rd.
Topanga, CA 90290
Ph: (310)455-1954

Tindell, Kip, Chmn. of the Bd.
National Retail Federation [2970]
1101 New York Ave. NW
Washington, DC 20005
Ph: (202)783-7971
    (202)347-1932
Toll Free: 800-673-4692
Fax: (202)737-2849

Tinker, William, Exec. Dir.
National Conference of Law Enforcement Emerald Societies [19537]
2121 New York Ave.
Brooklyn, NY 11210-5423

Tinkleman, Alan R., MPA, Director
Council on Podiatric Medical Educa-
  tion [16787]
9312 Old Georgetown Rd.
Bethesda, MD 20814-1621
Ph: (301)581-9200
Fax: (301)571-4903

Tinning, Matt, Exec. Dir.
Marine Fish Conservation Network
  [3898]
Washington, DC

Tipley, Roger, President, Chmn. of
  the Bd.
The Green Grid [3211]
3855 SW 153rd Dr.
Beaverton, OR 97006
Ph: (503)619-0653
Fax: (503)644-6708

Tippens, Darryl, President
Conference on Christianity and
  Literature [9756]
Wheaton College
501 College Ave.
Wheaton, IL 60187

Tippett, Terry, President
United Ford Owners [21509]
PO Box 32419
Columbus, OH 43232

Tippie, Jim, President
Southwestern Donkey and Mule
  Society [21284]
PO Box 1633
Johnson City, TX 78636
Ph: (830)868-4645

Tips, Scott, President
National Health Federation [14956]
PO Box 688

Monrovia, CA 91017
Ph: (626)357-2181

Tipton, David, Treasurer
Association of Christian Therapists
  [19944]
PO Box 4961
Louisville, KY 40204
Ph: (502)632-3036

Tirado, Martin, CAE, CEO
Snow & Ice Management Associa-
  tion, Inc. [5819]
7670 N Port Washington Rd., Ste.
  105
Milwaukee, WI 53217-3174
Ph: (414)375-1940
Fax: (414)375-1945

Tirfe, Abyssinia, Asst.
The Andrew W. Mellon Foundation
  [12487]
140 E 62nd St.
New York, NY 10065-8124
Ph: (212)838-8400
Fax: (212)888-4172

Tirpak, Jon D., PE, FASM, President
ASM International [6841]
9639 Kinsman Rd.
Materials Park, OH 44073
Ph: (440)338-5151

Tiscione, Kristen, Secretary
Association of Legal Writing Directors [5527]
c/o Catherine Wasson, Treasurer
Elon University School of Law
201 N Greene St.
Greensboro, NC 27401

Tisdale, Betty, Founder, President
Helping and Loving Orphans [11025]
2416 2nd Ave. N
Seattle, WA 98109
Ph: (206)282-7337

Tisdale, Cathy, President, CEO
Camp Fire [13436]
1801 Main, Ste. 200
Kansas City, MO 64108
Ph: (816)285-2010

Tisdale, Cathy, Secretary
Nonprofit Leadership Alliance [8202]
1801 Main St., Ste. 200
Kansas City, MO 64108
Ph: (816)561-6415
Fax: (816)531-3527

Tiseo, Mary, Exec. Dir.
South Africa Partners [18500]
89 South St., Ste. 701
Boston, MA 02111
Ph: (617)443-1072
Fax: (617)443-1076

Tishman, Daniel R., Chairman
Natural Resources Defense Council
  [4496]
40 W 20th St.
New York, NY 10011
Ph: (212)727-2700
Fax: (212)727-1773

Titchener, Dr. Frances B., Editor
International Plutarch Society
  [10095]
Utah State University
Dept. of History
0710 Old Main Hill
Logan, UT 84322-0710
Ph: (435)797-1290
Fax: (435)797-3899

Titkemeier, Pat, Secretary
Currier and Ives Dinnerware Collectors [21646]

c/o Carol Hasse, Treasurer
922 East 1st Ave.
Monmouth, IL 61462

Titon, Emily, President
Autism National Committee [18377]
3 Bedford Green
South Burlington, VT 05403
Ph: (802)658-3374
Fax: (802)658-8061

Titus, Bethany, Exec. Dir.
Alpha Kappa Delta [7175]
2507 James St., Ste. 210
Syracuse, NY 13206
Ph: (315)883-0528
Fax: (315)410-5408

Titze, Ingo R., PhD, Exec. Dir.
National Center for Voice and
  Speech [17244]
136 S Main St., Ste. 320
Salt Lake City, UT 84101-1623
Ph: (801)596-2012
Fax: (801)596-2013

Tiven, Rachel B., V. Ch.
The Children's Tumor Foundation
  [15916]
120 Wall St., 16th Fl.
New York, NY 10005-3904
Ph: (212)344-6633
Toll Free: 800-323-7938
Fax: (212)747-0004

Tjelmeland, Michelle, Founder,
  Chairman
Cochlear Implant Awareness
  Foundation [15182]
130 S John St.
Rochester, IL 62563
Ph: (202)895-2781
Fax: (202)895-2782

Tjian, Robert, PhD, President
Howard Hughes Medical Institute
  [15644]
4000 Jones Bridge Rd.
Chevy Chase, MD 20815-6720
Ph: (301)215-8500

Toalson, Tammy, Coord.
Country Coach International [22465]
1574 Coburg Rd., No. 530
Eugene, OR 97401-4802
Ph: (515)708-3391

Tobal, Jane, President, Founder
Visionary Alternatives, Inc. [13666]
7725 Kenway Pl. E
Boca Raton, FL 33433-3323
Ph: (561)750-4551
Toll Free: 866-750-4551
Fax: (561)750-4541

Tobias, Carol, President
National Right to Life Committee
  [12784]
512 10th St. NW
Washington, DC 20004-1401
Ph: (202)626-8800

Tobias, Carol, President
National Right to Life Educational
  Trust Fund [19065]
512 10th St. NW
Washington, DC 20004
Ph: (202)626-8829

Tobias, Janalee, Founder, President
Women Against Gun Control [18259]
PO Box 95357
South Jordan, UT 84095
Ph: (801)328-9660

Tobias, Ms. Patricia Eliot, President
Damfinos: The International Buster
  Keaton Society [24008]

2222 S Mesa St., No. 27
San Pedro, CA 90731
Ph: (310)547-2207

Tobias, Peter S., PhD, President,
Director
Orchid Conservation Alliance **[3925]**
564 Arden Dr.
Encinitas, CA 92024
Ph: (720)518-5120

Tobin, Chuck, President
Association of Threat Assessment
Professionals **[3053]**
700 R St., Ste. 200
Sacramento, CA 95811
Ph: (916)231-2146
Fax: (916)231-2141

Tobin, Jack, President
Special Forces Association **[21032]**
4990 Doc Bennett Rd.
Fayetteville, NC 28306
Ph: (910)485-5433
Fax: (910)485-1041

Tobin, Janet, President
MERCAZ USA **[20266]**
475 Riverside Dr., Ste. 820
New York, NY 10115
Ph: (212)533-2061
Fax: (212)870-3897

Tobin, Jonathan N., PhD, CEO,
President
Clinical Directors Network **[15139]**
5 W 37th St., 10th Fl.
New York, NY 10018
Ph: (212)382-0699

Tobin, Walter, CEO
Electronics Representatives Associa-
tion **[1045]**
309 W Washington St., Ste. 500
Chicago, IL 60606
Ph: (312)419-1432
Fax: (312)419-1660

Tobyne, Claire, Regional VP
Clan MacKenzie Society in the
United States **[20823]**
c/o Barbara Mackenzie, Treasurer
PO Box 20454
Cheyenne, WY 82003-7011
Ph: (307)214-4817

Tocker, Joel E., President
Inflammation Research Association
[14582]
c/o Joel E. Tocker, President
145 King of Prussia Rd.
Radnor, PA 19087
Ph: (610)651-6107

Todaro, John, President
National Association of EMS Educa-
tors **[8329]**
250 Mt. Lebanon Blvd., Ste. 209
Pittsburgh, PA 15234-1248
Ph: (412)343-4775
Fax: (412)343-4770

Todd, Brian, President, CEO
Food Institute **[1327]**
10 Mountainview Rd., Ste. S125
Upper Saddle River, NJ 07458
Ph: (201)791-5570
Fax: (201)791-5222

Todd, Brian, Exec. Dir.
Gay and Lesbian Rowing Federation
[23109]
10153 Riverside Dr., Ste. 698
Toluca Lake, CA 91602
Ph: (323)774-1903
Fax: (208)977-2045

Todd, Dale, President
Jamaica Impact, Inc. **[12214]**
PO Box 3794

New York, NY 10163
Ph: (212)459-4390

Todd, Kathryn, President
National Association of Unemployment Insurance Appeals Professionals **[5317]**
c/o Kathryn Todd, President
4020 E 5th Ave.
Columbus, OH 43219-1811
Fax: (405)208-4552

Todd, Tracy, PhD, Exec. Dir.
American Association for Marriage
and Family Therapy **[16957]**
112 S Alfred St.
Alexandria, VA 22314-3061
Ph: (703)838-9808
Fax: (703)838-9805

Todt, Annie Elble, PhD, Founder,
Exec. Dir.
Give Hope, Fight Poverty **[10997]**
2436 N Alabama St.
Indianapolis, IN 46205

Toensing, Chris, Exec. Dir.
Middle East Research and Informa-
tion Project **[18689]**
1344 T St. NW, No. 1
Washington, DC 20009
Ph: (202)223-3677
Fax: (202)223-3604

Tolbert, David, President
International Center for Transitional
Justice **[18413]**
5 Hanover Sq., 24th Fl.
New York, NY 10004
Ph: (917)637-3800
Fax: (917)637-3900

Tolbert, Marilyn, President
National Down Syndrome Congress
[12330]
30 Mansell Ct., Ste. 108
Roswell, GA 30076-4858
Ph: (770)604-9500
Toll Free: 800-232-6372
Fax: (770)604-9898

Tolentino, Felipe L., MD, President
Restoring Sight International **[17740]**
PO Box 692457
Quincy, MA 02269
Ph: (617)327-6002

Toll, Rev. Richard K., Trustee,
Secretary
Friends of Sabeel - North America
[18787]
PO Box 9186
Portland, OR 97207
Ph: (503)653-6625

Tolle, John, President
North American Society of Pipe Col-
lectors **[21702]**
PO Box 9642
Columbus, OH 43209

Tollefson, Marc D., Secretary
American Academy of Gold Foil
Operators **[14378]**
c/o Marc D. Tollefson, Secretary
701 Regents Blvd.
Tacoma, WA 98466
Ph: (253)565-5414

Tollman, Victoria, Secretary,
Treasurer
Fell Pony Society and Conservancy
of the Americas **[4349]**
775 Flippin Rd.
Lowgap, NC 27024
Ph: (336)352-5520

Tolonen, Andrea, President
Finnish-American Historical Society
of the West **[9322]**

PO Box 5522
Portland, OR 97228-5522

Tolson, Pamela J., CAE, Contact
American Association of Public
Health Dentistry **[14393]**
3085 Stevenson Dr., Ste. 200
Springfield, IL 62703
Ph: (217)529-6941
Fax: (217)529-9120

Toma, Robin S., VP
International Association of Official
Human Rights Agencies **[12045]**
444 N Capitol St. NW, Ste. 536
Washington, DC 20001
Ph: (202)624-5410

Tomar, Jon, President
Deaf-REACH **[15186]**
3521 12th St. NE
Washington, DC 20017
Ph: (202)832-6681

Tomaselli, Valerie, Bd. Member
Women's National Book Association
[2733]
PO Box 237
New York, NY 10150
Ph: (212)208-4629
Fax: (212)208-4629

Tomasi, Corinne, Secretary
National Economists Club **[6399]**
PO Box 33511
Washington, DC 20033-3511
Ph: (703)493-8824

Tombrello, Pat, Secretary, Treasurer
Equipment Service Association
[3073]
c/o Curt Williams, President
5225 Womack Rd.
Sanford, NC 27330
Ph: (443)640-1053
Toll Free: 866-372-3155
Fax: (443)640-1031

Tombrello, Stephanie M., Exec. Dir.
SafetyBeltSafe U.S.A. **[19083]**
L A BioMed
Bldg. B-1 W
1124 W Carson St.
Torrance, CA 90502
Ph: (310)222-6860
Toll Free: 800-745-SAFE
Fax: (310)222-6862

Tomczykowska, Caria, President
Polish Arts and Culture Foundation
[19606]
4077 Waterhouse Rd.
Oakland, CA 94602
Ph: (510)599-2244

Tomedi, Angelo, MD, President
Global Health Partnerships **[15459]**
PO Box 4385
Albuquerque, NM 87196

Tomes, Charles, President
North American Voyageur Council
[9426]
4449 Xerxes Ave. S
Minneapolis, MN 55410
Ph: (612)929-1087

Tomlinson, Jeannie, President
American Association of Oc-
cupational Health Nurses **[16097]**
330 N Wabash Ave., Ste. 2000
Chicago, IL 60611
Ph: (312)321-5173
Fax: (312)673-6719

Tomson, Tracy, Exec. Dir.
Restaurant Facility Management Association **[2941]**

5600 Tennyson Pky., Ste. 265
Plano, TX 75024
Ph: (972)805-0905
Fax: (972)805-0906

Tonai, Rosalyn, Exec. Dir.
National Japanese American Histori-
cal Society **[9627]**
1684 Post St.
San Francisco, CA 94115-3604
Ph: (415)921-5007
Fax: (415)921-5087

Tong, Alex, President
American Amateur Karate Federa-
tion **[22980]**
1801 Century Park, 24th Fl.
Los Angeles, CA 90067
Toll Free: 888-939-8882
Fax: (888)939-8555

Tongco, Diann, President
Curly-Coated Retriever Club of
America **[21863]**

Tonkin, Leo M., Founder
Salt Therapy Association **[13655]**
120 NW 11th St.
Boca Raton, FL 33432
Toll Free: 844-STA-INFO

Tonova, Nadia, Director
National Network for Arab American
Communities **[10734]**
c/o ACCESS
2651 Saulino Ct.
Dearborn, MI 48120
Ph: (313)842-1933
Fax: (313)554-2801

Toohey, Mike, President, CEO
Waterways Council **[19201]**
499 S Capitol St. SW, Ste. 401
Washington, DC 20003
Ph: (202)765-2166
Fax: (202)765-2167

Toohig, Michael, President
Association of United States Night
Vision Manufacturers **[2376]**
7040 Highfields Farm Dr.
Roanoke, VA 24018
Ph: (540)774-1783
Fax: (540)774-1802

Tooley, Jim, CEO, Exec. Dir.
U.S.A. Basketball **[22578]**
5465 Mark Dabling Blvd.
Colorado Springs, CO 80918-3842
Ph: (719)590-4800
Fax: (719)590-4811

Tooley, Dr. Mark, President
Institute on Religion and Democracy
[18099]
1023 15th St. NW, Ste. 601
Washington, DC 20005-2601
Ph: (202)682-4131
(202)413-5639
Fax: (202)682-4136

Topakian, Karen, Chairperson
Greenpeace U.S.A. **[4068]**
702 H St. NW, Ste. 300
Washington, DC 20001
Ph: (202)462-1177
Toll Free: 800-722-6995
Fax: (202)462-4507

Topping, John C., Jr., CEO,
President
Climate Institute **[4043]**
1400 16th St. NW, Ste. 430
Washington, DC 20036
Ph: (202)552-0163

Torano, Jimmy, VP
National Hunter Jumper Association,
Inc. **[22945]**

PO Box 11635
Lexington, KY 40576
Ph: (610)644-3283
    (772)201-9340

Torbert, Michelle, Chairperson
Prader-Willi Syndrome Association
  USA [14852]
8588 Potter Park Dr., Ste. 500
Sarasota, FL 34238
Ph: (941)312-0400
Toll Free: 800-926-4797
Fax: (941)312-0142

Tordillo, Señor Myrna, MSCS, Direc-
  tor
Apostleship of the Sea in the United
  States of America [19793]
1500 Jefferson Dr.
Port Arthur, TX 77642-0646
Ph: (409)985-4545
Fax: (409)985-5945

Toren, Jim, Contact
FootPrints for Peace [18784]
1225 N Bend Rd.
Cincinnati, OH 45224
Ph: (513)843-1205

Torgerson, Randy, President
United States Association of Profes-
  sional Investigators [5372]
175 Hutton Ranch Rd., Ste. 103-165
Kalispell, MT 59901
Ph: (406)545-2177
Toll Free: 877-894-0615

Torres, Mr. Alejandro, CEO,
  President
Christ for the Poor [12638]
PO Box 601181
North Miami Beach, FL 33160
Ph: (305)891-2242

Torres, Helen Iris, Exec. Dir., CEO
Hispanas Organized for Political
  Equality [18337]
634 S Spring St., Ste. 920
Los Angeles, CA 90014-3903
Ph: (213)622-0606
Fax: (213)622-0007

Torres, Juan, President
National Hispanic Landscape Alli-
  ance [2071]
c/o Jose Arroyo, Secretary
PO Box 309
Lyman, SC 29365
Toll Free: 877-260-7995

Torres, Richard, Secretary
German Shepherd Dog Club of
  America-Working Dog Association
  [21883]
PO Box 5021
Woodland Hills, CA 91365
Ph: (747)900-6805
Fax: (747)200-2560

Torrey, Lisa, Contact
National Tick-Borne Disease
  Advocates [15412]
PO Box 866096
Plano, TX 75086
Ph: (972)832-6703

Torrey, Mike, Exec. VP
Crop Insurance and Reinsurance
  Bureau [1855]
440 1st St. NW, Ste. 500
Washington, DC 20002
Ph: (202)544-0067

Torsilieri, Guy J., President
National Steeplechase Association
  [22925]
400 Fair Hill Dr.
Elkton, MD 21921
Ph: (410)392-0700
Fax: (410)392-0706

Toscano, Jose, CEO, Dir. Gen.
International Telecommunications
  Satellite Organization [7314]
4400 Jenifer St. NW, Ste. 332
Washington, DC 20015
Ph: (202)243-5096
Fax: (202)243-5018

Tosch, Debra, Exec. Dir.
National Disaster Search Dog
  Foundation [12746]
501 E Ojai Ave.
Ojai, CA 93023
Toll Free: 888-459-4376
Fax: (805)640-1848

Toth, Delphi, Director
Lipizzan Association of North
  America [4376]
c/o Andrea Iannuzzi, Associate
  Registrar
133 Seabury Dr.
Bar Harbor, ME 04609

Toth, Dimitrie, President
International Watch Fob Association
  [3279]
c/o Louise Harting, Secretary and
  Treasurer
18458 Boston Rd.
Strongsville, OH 44136-8642

Totten, Julie, Founder, President
Families for Depression Awareness
  [15769]
391 Totten Pond Rd., Ste. 101
Waltham, MA 02451
Ph: (781)890-0220
Fax: (781)890-2411

Totten, Norman, President
Epigraphic Society [5936]
97 Village Post Rd.
Danvers, MA 01923
Ph: (978)774-1275

Totushek, John, Exec. Dir.
Association of the United States
  Navy [5594]
1619 King St.
Alexandria, VA 22314
Ph: (703)548-5800
Toll Free: 877-628-9411
Fax: (703)683-3647

Totushek, John, President, CEO
United States Navy Memorial
  Foundation [21064]
701 Pennsylvania Ave. NW
Washington, DC 20004
Ph: (202)380-0710
    (202)380-0714

Touchette, Charlie, Exec. Dir.
North American Farmers' Direct
  Marketing Association [4482]
62 White Loaf Rd.
Southampton, MA 01073
Fax: (413)233-4285

Touchstone, Mike, President
National EMS Management Associa-
  tion [14688]
2901 Williamsburg Terr., Ste. G
Platte City, MO 64079
Toll Free: 888-424-9850

Toughhill, Jeffrey M., CEO, President
Histiocytosis Association [15233]
332 N Broadway
Pitman, NJ 08071
Ph: (856)589-6606
Fax: (856)589-6614

Touma, Leslie, Exec. Dir.
American Task Force for Lebanon
  [18634]
1100 Connecticut Ave. NW, Ste.
  1250

Washington, DC 20036
Ph: (202)223-9333
Fax: (202)223-1399

Toussaint, Cynthia, Founder
For Grace [16555]
PO Box 1724
Studio City, CA 91614
Ph: (818)760-7635
Fax: (818)760-7635

Toussaint, Marcel, President
Haitian Orphans Wish [11010]
PO Box 138
Uniondale, NY 11553

Tovar, Richard M., President
Fight Slavery [12033]
PO Box 358531
Gainesville, FL 32635-8531

Towers, Mr. Frank W., Hist.,
  President
30th Infantry Division Veterans of
  WWII [20698]
2915 W State Rd. 235
Brooker, FL 32622-5167
Ph: (352)485-1173
Fax: (352)485-2763

Towery, Justin, Chairman
U.S.A. Rice Council [3775]
2101 Wilson Blvd., Ste. 610
Arlington, VA 22201
Ph: (703)236-2300
Fax: (703)236-2301

Townsend, Homer S., Jr., Exec. Dir.
Paralyzed Veterans of America
  [20772]
801 18th St. NW
Washington, DC 20006-3517
Toll Free: 800-424-8200

Townsend, Robert, VP
Society for the Advancement of
  Economic Theory [6400]
108 John Pappajohn Business Bldg.,
  W288
Dept. of Economics
University of Iowa
Iowa City, IA 52242

Toyoda, Fumio, Founder
Aikido Association of America
  [22494]
1016 W Belmont Ave.
Chicago, IL 60657
Ph: (773)525-3141

Traa, Claudia, Director
Chromosome 18 Registry and
  Research Society [14813]
7155 Oakridge Dr.
San Antonio, TX 78229-3640
Ph: (210)657-4968

Trabb, Bruce, President
Morgan Car Club of Washington DC
  [21442]
c/o Marline Riehle, Membership/
  Registrar
PO Box 539
Nokesville, VA 20182
Ph: (703)594-2054

Trabilsy, Steve, President
Petroleum Equipment Institute
  [2533]
PO Box 2380
Tulsa, OK 74101
Ph: (918)494-9696
Fax: (918)491-9595

Tracey, Jack, CAE, Exec. Dir.
National Automotive Finance Association [348]
7037 Ridge Rd., Ste. 300

Hanover, MD 21076-1343
Ph: (410)712-4036
Toll Free: 800-463-8955
Fax: (410)712-4038

Trachtenberg, Matthew J., Chair-
  man, CEO, President
National Orchestral Association
  [9977]
PO Box 7016
New York, NY 10150-7016
Ph: (212)208-4691
Fax: (212)208-4691

Tracy, Eldon L., President
Feeding Children Worldwide [12087]
PO Box 883
Mount Prospect, IL 60056

Tracy, John, Secretary, Treasurer
The National Institutes for Water
  Resources [7371]
c/o Dr. John C. Tracy, Secretary-
  Treasurer
Idaho Water Resources Institute
322 E Front St.
Boise, ID 83702

Tracy, Mary, President
Scenic America [4102]
1307 New Hampshire Ave. NW
Washington, DC 20036-1351
Ph: (202)463-1294
Fax: (202)463-1299

Trader, Barbara, Exec. Dir.
TASH [11642]
2013 H St. NW
Washington, DC 20006
Ph: (202)540-9020
Fax: (202)540-9019

Traggis, Hannah, Director
National Green Schools Society
  [7897]
PO Box 323
Mansfield, MA 02048

Traill, Stacie, President
Online Audiovisual Catalogers
  [9720]
c/o Autumn Faulkner, Treasurer
366 W Circle Dr.
East Lansing, MI 48824

Trainer, Chad, Chmn. of the Bd.
Bertrand Russell Society [9095]
c/o Michael Berumen, Treasurer
37155 Dickerson Run
Windsor, CO 80550
Ph: (802)295-9058

Tran, Diana Phuong My, Chmn. of
  the Bd.
Hope for Children in Vietnam
  [11037]
3900A Watson Pl. NW, Apt. 2B
Washington, DC 20016

Tran, Ho Luong, President, CEO
National Council of Asian Pacific
  Islander Physicians [16759]
445 Grant Ave., Ste. 202
San Francisco, CA 94108
Ph: (415)399-6565

Tran, Hoang, Administrator
National Cursillo Movement [19883]
PO Box 799
Jarrell, TX 76537
Ph: (512)746-2020
Fax: (512)746-2030

Tran, Lloyd, President
International Association of
  Nanotechnology [7275]
NASA Ames Research Ctr.
PO Box 151

Moffett Field, CA 94035
Ph: (408)280-6222
Toll Free: 877-676-6266

Tran, Lucy, VP
Union of North American
 Vietnamese Student Associations
 [19686]
340 S Lemon Ave., No. 8246
Walnut, CA 91789

Tran, Nhan H., Contact
Vietnamese Professionals Society
 [19687]
5150 Fair Oaks Blvd., Ste. 101-128
Carmichael, CA 95608-5758

Tran, VietThuy, President
Group of Universities for the
 Advancement of Vietnamese in
 America [10302]
Rockefeller Hall
Department of Asia Studies
Cornell University
Ithaca, NY 14853

Trapp, Norm, Contact
Quality Bakers of America Coopera-
 tive [375]
1275 Glenlivet Dr., Ste. 100
Allentown, PA 18106-3107
Ph: (203)531-7100
Fax: (203)531-1406

Trasatti, Terry, President
Kaiser-Darrin Owners Roster
 [21412]
c/o Terry Trasatti
3500 Collins Rd.
Oakland, MI 48363
Ph: (248)656-1882

Trask, Robyn, Exec. Dir.
Loving More [12946]
PO Box 1658
Loveland, CO 80539
Ph: (970)667-5683

Tratner, Alan A., President
Inventors Workshop International
 [5334]
PO Box 285
Santa Barbara, CA 93102-0285
Ph: (805)735-7261

Tratt, Noah, Secretary
U.S. Travel Association [3405]
1100 New York Ave. NW, Ste. 450
Washington, DC 20005-3934
Ph: (202)408-8422
Fax: (202)408-1255

Trauernicht, Ms. Liz, President, Dir.
 of Comm.
Macular Degeneration Foundation
 [17726]
PO Box 531313
Henderson, NV 89053
Ph: (702)450-2908
Toll Free: 888-633-3937
Fax: (702)450-3396

Traum, Richard, PhD, Founder,
 President
Achilles International [22768]
42 W 38th St., 4th Fl.
New York, NY 10018-6242
Ph: (212)354-0300
Fax: (212)354-3978

Trautman, Deborah, CEO
American Association of Colleges of
 Nursing [8301]
1 Dupont Cir. NW, Ste. 530
Washington, DC 20036
Ph: (202)463-6930
Fax: (202)785-8320

Trautmann, M., President
American Oil Chemists' Society
 [6185]

2710 S Boulder Dr.
Urbana, IL 61802-6996
Ph: (217)359-2344
Fax: (217)351-8091

Trautwein, Janet, CEO, Exec. VP
National Association of Health
 Underwriters [1893]
1212 New York Ave. NW, Ste. 1100
Washington, DC 20005
Ph: (202)552-5060
Fax: (202)747-6820

Travers, David, President
International Society for
 Experimental Hematology [15237]
330 N Wabash Ave., Ste. 2000
Chicago, IL 60611
Ph: (312)321-5114
Fax: (312)673-6923

Travers, Susan, President
Association for Chemoreception Sci-
 ences [6188]
5841 Cedar Lake Rd.
Minneapolis, MN 55416
Ph: (952)646-2035
Fax: (952)545-6073

Travers, Will, Secretary
Born Free USA [10595]
PO Box 32160
Washington, DC 20007
Ph: (202)450-3168

Traylor, Clayton, Officer
Leading Builders of America [541]
1455 Pennsylvania Ave. NW, Ste.
 400
Washington, DC 20004
Ph: (202)621-1815

Treas, Emily
Building Bridges: Middle East-US
 [8097]
PO Box 101958
Denver, CO 80250
Ph: (303)691-2393
Fax: (303)691-2394

Trebbin, Wayne, MD, President
World Organization of Renal
 Therapies [15889]
21 Bradlee Ave.
Swampscott, MA 01907
Ph: (781)586-8830

Trefz, Marilyn, Exec. Dir.
American Association for Agricultural
 Education [7471]
Columbus, OH

Treija, Linda, President
American Latvian Artists Association
 [8834]
639 Kerper St.
Philadelphia, PA 19111
Ph: (215)904-7265

Treinish, Gregg, Founder, Exec. Dir.
Adventurers and Scientists for
 Conservation [3788]
PO Box 1834
Bozeman, MT 59771
Ph: (406)624-3320

Trejo, Gilbert, Secretary
WateReuse Association [4766]
1199 N Fairfax St., Ste. 410
Alexandria, VA 22314
Ph: (703)548-0880
Fax: (703)548-5085

Tremel, Frank, President
American Cream Draft Horse Association [4303]
193 Crossover Rd.
Bennington, VT 05201

Trese, Michael T., MD, Chmn. of the
 Bd.
Retina Global [17741]
2 Windflower
Aliso Viejo, CA 92656
Ph: (626)737-1232

Tretheway, Dana, President
American Peony Society [22081]
713 White Oak Ln.
Kansas City, MO 64116-4607

Trethewey, Claire, Corr. Sec.
Belgian Sheepdog Club of America
 [21838]
c/o Julie Fiechter, Corresponding
 Secretary
7805 Sherve Rd.
Falls Church, VA 22043-3313

Trettin, Kenneth, Secretary,
 Treasurer
APS Writers Unit No. 30 [22308]
c/o Kenneth Trettin, Secretary-
 Treasurer
PO Box 56
Rockford, IA 50468-0056

Trevino, Amy, President
Theta Chi Omega National
 Multicultural Sorority [23978]
University of Texas at Arlington
701 S Nedderman Dr.
Arlington, TX 76019

Trewin, Shari, Chairman
Association for Computing
 Machinery - Special Interest Group
 on Accessible Computing [6293]
2 Penn Plz., Ste. 701
New York, NY 10121-0701
Ph: (212)626-0500
Toll Free: 800-342-6626
Fax: (212)944-1318

Trezza, Roseann, Exec. Dir.
Associated Humane Societies
 [10590]
124 Evergreen Ave.
Newark, NJ 07114-2133
Ph: (973)824-7080
Fax: (973)824-2720

Triantafilou, Constantine M., CEO,
 Exec. Dir.
International Orthodox Christian
 Charities [19992]
110 West Rd., Ste. 360
Baltimore, MD 21204
Ph: (410)243-9820
Toll Free: 877-803-4622
Fax: (410)243-9824

Tribble, Linda, Advisor
National Association of Educational
 Office Professionals [7433]
1841 S Eisenhower Ct.
Wichita, KS 67209
Ph: (316)942-4822
Fax: (316)942-7100

Tribble, Romie, Jr., Secretary
National Economic Association
 [6398]

Trick, Michael, President
International Federation of
 Operational Research Societies
 [6946]
7240 Pky. Dr., Ste. 310
Hanover, MD 21076
Ph: (443)757-3534
Fax: (443)757-3535

Trieber, Jerry, Contact
Hospitality Financial and Technology
 Professionals [1239]
11709 Boulder Ln., Ste. 110

Austin, TX 78726
Ph: (512)249-5333
Toll Free: 800-646-4387
Fax: (512)249-1533

Trillin, Abigail, Exec. Dir.
Legal Services for Children [5541]
1254 Market St., 3rd Fl.
San Francisco, CA 94102-4816
Ph: (415)863-3762
Fax: (415)863-7708

Trim, Donna, President
International Rose O'Neill Club
 Foundation [22003]
PO Box 668
Branson, MO 65615

Trimble, Preston, Rep.
Amateur Field Trial Clubs of America
 [21795]
c/o Piper Huffman, Secretary
2873 Whippoorwill Rd.
Michigan City, MS 38647
Ph: (662)223-0126
Fax: (662)223-0126

Trimble, William, Chairman
Aircrafts Owners and Pilots Associa-
 tion [6024]
421 Aviation Way
Frederick, MD 21701
Ph: (301)695-2000
Toll Free: 800-872-2672

Tringali, Glenn R., Exec. Dir.
Adult Congenital Heart Association
 [14085]
3300 Henry Ave., Ste. 112
Philadelphia, PA 19129
Ph: (215)849-1260
Toll Free: 888-921-2242
Fax: (215)849-1261

Trippe, Steve, President, Exec. Dir.
New Ways to Work [11777]
555 S Main St., No. 1
Sebastopol, CA 95472
Ph: (707)824-4000

Trippi, Peter, President
Association of Historians of
 Nineteenth-Century Art [8846]
PO Box 5730
Austin, TX 78763-5730

Trister, Jon, MD, Fac. Memb.
American Association of Orthopedic
 Medicine [16462]
555 Waterview Ln.
Ridgway, CO 81432
Toll Free: 888-687-1920
Fax: (970)626-5033

Tritton, Tom, CEO, President
Chemical Heritage Foundation
 [9472]
315 Chestnut St.
Philadelphia, PA 19106
Ph: (215)925-2222

Trog, Ronda, Dir. of Member Svcs.
International Association of Reserva-
 tion Executives [3291]
c/o Denise Pullen
9805 Q St.
Omaha, NE 68127
Ph: (402)915-1905

Troiani, Sheryl, President
National Association of Real Estate
 Companies [2876]
6348 N Milwaukee Ave., No. 103
Chicago, IL 60646
Ph: (773)283-6362

Trojan, Robert, CEO
Commercial Finance Association
 [2090]

370 7th Ave., Ste. 1801
New York, NY 10001
Ph: (212)792-9390
Fax: (212)564-6053

Trombino, C. James, Exec. Dir.,
CEO
APMI International **[6840]**
105 College Rd. E
Princeton, NJ 08540-6992
Ph: (609)452-7700
Fax: (609)987-8523

Trombino, C. James, Exec. Dir.
Metal Injection Molding Association
[2354]
105 College Rd. E
Princeton, NJ 08540-6992
Ph: (609)452-7700
Fax: (609)987-8523

Tromp, Marlene, President
North American Victorian Studies
Association **[10299]**
Dept. of English
Purdue University
500 Oval Dr.
West Lafayette, IN 47907
Fax: (765)494-3780

Troost, Dr. Kathy, Treasurer
Association of Environmental &
Engineering Geologists **[6679]**
1100-H Brandywine Blvd.
Zanesville, OH 43701
Toll Free: 844-331-7867
Fax: (740)452-2552

Trossbach, Liza Fleeson, President
Association of Structural Pest
Control Regulatory Officials **[4526]**
663 Lacy Oak Dr.
Chesapeake, VA 23320
Ph: (757)753-8162

Trost, Robb, Secretary
Corporate Event Marketing Associa-
tion **[2275]**
5098 Foothills Blvd., Ste. 3-386
Roseville, CA 95747
Ph: (916)740-3623

Trotter, David, President
American Guernsey Association
[3693]
1224 Alton Darby Creek Rd., Ste. G
Columbus, OH 43228
Ph: (614)864-2409
Fax: (614)864-5614

Troutman, Matthew, Comm. Chm.
Patent and Trademark Office Society
[5339]
PO Box 2089
Arlington, VA 22202
Ph: (571)270-1805

Troutman, Tracy, Asst.
National Frozen and Refrigerated
Foods Association **[1358]**
4755 Linglestown Rd., Ste. 300
Harrisburg, PA 17112
Ph: (717)657-8601
Fax: (717)657-9862

Trowbridge, Terry O., Director,
Founder
Center for Reduction of Religious-
Based Conflict **[19026]**
649 5th Ave. S, Ste. 201
Naples, FL 34102-6601
Ph: (239)821-4850
Fax: (239)263-2824

Troxel, Tom, Exec. Dir.
Intermountain Forest Association
[1411]
2218 Jackson Blvd., No. 10

Rapid City, SD 57702-3452
Ph: (605)341-0875
Fax: (605)341-8651

Troxell, Mickey Kay, President,
Founder
National Association of Certified
Professionals of Equine Therapy
[13639]
711 W 17th St., No. A8
Costa Mesa, CA 92627
Ph: (949)646-8010

Troy, Bill, CEO
American Society for Quality **[7079]**
600 N Plankinton Ave.
Milwaukee, WI 53201
Ph: (414)272-8575
Toll Free: 800-248-1946
Fax: (414)272-1734

Troy, Bill, President
Thompson Collectors Association
[22025]
PO Box 66
Hartland, MI 48353

Troy, Karen, Ph.D, Treasurer
American Society of Biomechanics
[6068]
c/o Stacie Ringleb, Secretary/
Membership Chairman
Old Dominion University
Norfolk, VA 23529
Ph: (757)683-5934

Troy, Richard, Founder, President
Karmann Ghia Club of North
America **[21414]**
4200 Park Blvd., No. 151
Oakland, CA 94602-1361
Ph: (510)717-6942

Troyk, Diana, President
Mounted Archery Association of the
Americas **[22501]**
c/o Joey Ogburn, Membership Of-
ficer
31711 N 164th St.
Scottsdale, AZ 85262
Ph: (602)400-0826

Truax, Don, President
National Barn Alliance **[9414]**
55 S Commonwealth Ave.
Aurora, IL 60506

Truax, Lee, President
Christian Business Men's Connec-
tion **[19952]**
Osborne Ctr., Ste. 602
5746 Marlin Rd.
Chattanooga, TN 37411
Ph: (423)698-4444
Toll Free: 800-566-2262
Fax: (423)629-4434

Trubiano, Franca, President
Building Technology Educators'
Society **[7498]**
c/o Dept. of Architecture and Interior
Design
University of Idaho
207 AAS
Moscow, ID 83844-2451

Truby, Cindy, Director
National Milk Glass Collectors
Society **[22143]**
c/o Helen Engel
32 Brown Dr.
Oswego, NY 13126
Ph: (315)343-9678

Trudeau, Lee, President
West Highland White Terrier Club of
America **[21990]**
c/o Vonda Kuechler, Membership
Chairperson

PO Box 25264
Overland Park, KS 66225-5264
Ph: (913)963-3806

Trueman, Patrick A., CEO, President
National Center on Sexual Exploita-
tion **[18927]**
1100 G St. NW, No. 1030
Washington, DC 20005
Ph: (202)393-7245

Truett, Beth, CEO, President
Oral Health America **[7710]**
180 N Michigan Ave., Ste. 1150
Chicago, IL 60601
Ph: (312)836-9900
Fax: (312)836-9986

Trugman, Linda B., President
American Society of Appraisers
[215]
11107 Sunset Hills Rd., Ste. 310
Reston, VA 20190
Ph: (703)478-2228
Toll Free: 800-272-8258
Fax: (703)742-8471

Truitt, April D., Founder
Primate Rescue Center **[10685]**
2515 Bethel Rd.
Nicholasville, KY 40356-8199
Ph: (859)858-4866
Fax: (859)858-0044

Trujillo, Tom, President
American Waterslager Society
[21539]
556 S Cactus Wren St.
556 S Cactus Wren St.
Gilbert, AZ 85296
Ph: (480)892-5464

Trull, Ms. Frankie L., President,
Founder
Foundation for BioMedical Research
[13717]
1100 Vermont Ave. NW, Ste. 1100
Washington, DC 20005
Ph: (202)457-0654
Fax: (202)457-0659

Trull, R. Scott, Chmn. of the Bd.
Trull Foundation **[12498]**
404 4th St.
Palacios, TX 77465
Ph: (361)972-5241
Fax: (361)972-1109

Trulson, Reid, Exec. Dir.
American Baptist International
Ministries **[19714]**
PO Box 851
Valley Forge, PA 19482
Toll Free: 800-222-3872

Truluck, Phillip N., Chairman
The Heritage Foundation **[18285]**
214 Massachusetts Ave. NE
Washington, DC 20002-4999
Ph: (202)546-4400
    (202)675-1761
Toll Free: 800-544-4843

Trumble, Steven R., CEO, President
American Consumer Credit Counsel-
ing **[940]**
130 Rumford Ave., Ste. 202
Newton, MA 02466
Ph: (617)559-5700
Toll Free: 800-769-3571
Fax: (617)244-1116

Trumka, Richard L., President
AFL-CIO **[23450]**
815 16th St. NW
Washington, DC 20006
Ph: (202)637-5010
    (202)637-5000

Trusdale, Pam, Exec. Dir.
National Association of Trailer
Manufacturers **[327]**
2420 SW 17th St.
Topeka, KS 66604-2627
Ph: (785)272-4433
Fax: (785)272-4455

Trusko, Brett, President, CEO
International Association of Innova-
tion Professionals **[1811]**
4422 Castle Wood St., Ste. 200
Sugar Land, TX 77479
Toll Free: 800-276-1180

Trusten, Paul, Editor
U.S. Metric Association **[7239]**
PO Box 471
Windsor, CO 80550-0471
Ph: (310)832-3763

Tsagaris, George S., President
National Juvenile Court Services As-
sociation **[5192]**
c/o George S. Tsagaris, President
Cleveland State University
2121 Euclid Ohio
Cleveland, OH 44115
Ph: (216)523-7474

Tschirhart, Mary, President
Pi Alpha Alpha **[23856]**
1029 Vermont Ave. NW, Ste. 1100
Washington, DC 20005
Ph: (202)628-8965
Fax: (202)626-4978

Tsereteli, Mamuka, President
America-Georgia Business Council
[1975]
2200 Pennsylvania Ave. NW, 4th Fl.
E
Washington, DC 20037
Ph: (202)416-1606

Tsereteli, Mamuka, President
Georgian Association in the United
States of America **[19439]**
2200 Pennsylvania Ave. NW, 4th Fl.
East Washington, DC 20037
Ph: (202)234-2441

Tshimanga, Felix, MD, President,
Chairman
Africa Hope, Inc. **[10836]**
PO Box 127
Dacula, GA 30019
Ph: (770)573-0676
Fax: (678)528-3025

Tsiagbe, Vincent K., PhD, President
Association of African Biomedical
Scientists **[7121]**
c/o Rutgers School of Dental
Medicine
185 S Orange Ave., MSB C-636
Newark, NJ 07103

Tsiatis, George M., Exec. Dir.
Resolution Project **[12999]**
1120 Avenue of the Americas, 4th Fl.
New York, NY 10036
Ph: (212)626-6504

Tsigas, Eleni Z., Exec. Dir.
Preeclampsia Foundation **[14241]**
6767 N Wickham Rd., Ste. 400
Melbourne, FL 32940-2025
Ph: (321)421-6957
Toll Free: 800-665-9341
Fax: (321)821-0450

Tsokos, Chris P., President
International Federation of Nonlinear
Analysts **[7153]**
c/o Dr. Rebecca Wooten, Vice
President/Treasurer
University of South Florida, CMC
319

4202 E Fowler Ave.
Tampa, FL 33620

Tsuchida, John N., President
National Association for Asian and
Pacific American Education [8621]
PO Box 3471
Palos Verdes Peninsula, CA 90274
Ph: (416)393-9400

Tsuji, Kazuto, Chairman
Consultative Group to Assist the
Poor [18487]
1825 I Street, NW 7th Fl.
Washington, DC 20006
Ph: (202)473-9594

Tublin, Mitchell E.
Society of Radiologists in Ultrasound
[17072]
1891 Preston White Dr.
Reston, VA 20191
Ph: (703)858-9210
Fax: (703)880-0295

Tucci, Keith, Founder
Life Coalition International [12777]
PO Box 360221
Melbourne, FL 32936-0221
Ph: (321)726-0444

Tucker, Brian E., President
GeoHazards International [4487]
687 Bay Rd.
Menlo Park, CA 94025
Ph: (650)614-9050
Fax: (650)614-9051

Tucker, Debra, CMP, Exec. Dir.
International Association for
Women's Mental Health [15774]
c/o Debra Tucker Associates LLC
8213 Lakenheath Way
Potomac, MD 20854
Ph: (301)983-6282
Fax: (301)983-6288

Tucker, John, Treasurer
National Association of Appellate
Court Attorneys [5024]
c/o Mary Ellen Donaghy, Executive
Director
University of Richmond Law School
Richmond, VA 23173
Ph: (804)289-8204
Fax: (804)289-8992

Tucker, John, Founder, Advisor
New Hope for Cambodian Children
[11097]
PO Box 690597
Killeen, TX 76549

Tucker, Judy, CAE, Exec. Dir.
The Coastal Society [6939]
55 Winster Fax
Williamsburg, VA 23185
Ph: (757)565-0999
Fax: (757)565-0922

Tucker, Karen, Exec. Dir.
Adler Aphasia Center [13725]
60 W Hunter Ave.
Maywood, NJ 07607
Ph: (201)368-8585
Fax: (201)587-1909

Tucker, Marc S., CEO, President
National Center on Education and
the Economy [7786]
2121 K St. NW, Ste. 700
Washington, DC 20037
Ph: (202)379-1800
Fax: (202)293-1560

Tucker, Mary, Secretary
Finnsheep Breeders Association
[4670]

c/o Mary Tucker, Secretary
PO Box 85
West Clarksville, NY 14786
Ph: (585)928-1721

Tucker, Pat, Chairman
Society of Parrot Breeders and
Exhibitors [21550]
c/o Ray Schwartz, Membership
Director
19 Olde Common Dr.
Atkinson, NH 03811-2177

Tucker, Patty, President
American Bridge Teachers' Associa-
tion [21558]
PO Box 232
Greenwood, MO 64034-0232
Ph: (816)237-0519

Tucker, Randolph W., Chairman
International Fire Marshals Associa-
tion [5209]
1 Batterymarch Pk.
Quincy, MA 02169-7471
Ph: (617)770-3000
Toll Free: 800-344-3555
Fax: (617)770-0700

Tucker, Tanya, Sr. VP
America's Promise - The Alliance for
Youth [13426]
1110 Vermont Ave. NW, Ste. 900
Washington, DC 20005
Ph: (202)657-0600
Fax: (202)657-0601

Tucker, Tim, President
American Beekeeping Federation
[3632]
3525 Piedmont Rd., Bldg. 5, Ste.
300
Atlanta, GA 30305
Ph: (404)760-2875
Fax: (404)240-0998

Tudor, Lou, President
Kennedy's Disease Association
[15950]
PO Box 1105
Coarsegold, CA 93614-1105
Toll Free: 855-532-7762

Tudryn, Joyce M., President, CEO
International Radio and Television
Society Foundation [464]
1697 Broadway, 10th Fl.
New York, NY 10019
Ph: (212)867-6650

Tuerack, Gary, Founder
National Society of Leadership and
Success [8626]
50 Harrison St., Ste. 308
Hoboken, NJ 07030
Ph: (201)222-6544
Toll Free: 800-601-6248
Fax: (201)839-4604

Tuggle, Peter, President
Air Distribution Institute [1613]
4415 Harrison St., Ste. 426
Hillside, IL 60162

Tuk Su, Koo, Rev., CEO, Gen. Sec.
Food for the Hungry International
Federation [12092]
2937 Strathmeade St.
Falls Church, VA 22042
Ph: (703)966-1901

Tulipane, Barbara, CEO, President
National Recreation and Park As-
sociation [5667]
22377 Belmont Ridge Rd.
Ashburn, VA 20148-4501
Ph: (703)858-0784
Toll Free: 800-262-6772

Tummons, Emily, Founder
Wuqu' Kawoq [15511]
PO Box 91
Bethel, VT 05032-0091
Ph: (513)393-9878

Tun, Dr. Sovan, President
Cambodian Buddhist Society
[19774]
13800 New Hampshire Ave.
Silver Spring, MD 20904
Ph: (301)622-6544
    (301)602-6612

Tung, Dr. Nguyen Ba, DPA,
President
Vietnam Human Rights Network
[12062]
8971 Colchester Ave.
Westminster, CA 92683-5416
Ph: (714)657-9488

Tunick, Susan, President
Friends of Terra Cotta [9392]
771 W End Ave., No. 10E
New York, NY 10025

Tunney, Greg, Director
Footwear Distributors and Retailers
of America [1400]
1319 F St. NW, Ste. 700
Washington, DC 20004
Ph: (202)737-5660
Fax: (202)645-0789

Tunstall, Graydon A., Jr., Exec. Dir.
Phi Alpha Theta [23770]
University of South Florida
4202 E Fowler Ave., SOC107
Tampa, FL 33620-8100
Toll Free: 800-394-8195
Fax: (813)974-8215

Tunstall, Larry, President
United Council of Corvette Clubs
[21508]
PO Box 532605
Indianapolis, IN 46253

Turgeon, Kitty, Exec. Dir.
Foundation for the Study of the Arts
and Crafts Movement at Roycroft
[21289]
46 Walnut St.
East Aurora, NY 14052-2330
Ph: (716)653-4477

Turk, Tonya, President
East Coast Timing Association
[22398]
c/o Tonya Turk, President
206 Sylvan Dr.
Enterprise, AL 36330
Ph: (334)806-5749

Turley, William, Exec. Dir.
Construction and Demolition
Recycling Association [514]
1585 Beverly Ct., Ste. 112
Aurora, IL 60502-8725
Ph: (630)585-7530

Turnage, Andy, Secretary
Association of Space Explorers
U.S.A. [5860]
141 Bay Area Blvd.
Webster, TX 77598
Ph: (281)280-8172

Turnbeaugh, Treasa M., Ph.D.,
CEO, Secretary
Board of Certified Safety Profession-
als [7107]
2301 W Bradley Ave.
Champaign, IL 61821
Ph: (217)359-9263
Fax: (217)359-0055

Turnbull, Brian P., Treasurer, VP
Turnbull Clan Association [20938]
c/o Wally Turnbull, President

5216 Tahoe Dr.
Durham, NC 27713
Ph: (919)361-5041
Fax: (866)585-4635

Turnbull, Karen, President
Skye Terrier Club of America
[21963]

Turner, Alan, President
Automatic Musical Instrument Col-
lectors' Association [9878]
416 Colfax Dr.
San Jose, CA 95123-3403
Ph: (408)508-6019

Turner, Ann Tourigny, Exec. Dir.
American Association for Laboratory
Animal Science [13715]
9190 Crestwyn Hills Dr.
Memphis, TN 38125-8538
Ph: (901)754-8620
Fax: (901)753-0046

Turner, Carol A., Exec. Dir.
E3 Kids International [10957]
PO Box 8111
Fredericksburg, VA 22404
Ph: (540)538-3437

Turner, Charlene, Exec. Dir.
Solar Light for Africa [11441]
PO Box 361752
Melbourne, FL 32936

Turner, Chevese, CEO, Founder
Binge Eating Disorder Association
[14634]
637 Emerson Pl.
Severna Park, MD 21146-3409
Toll Free: 855-855-2332
Fax: (410)741-3037

Turner, George, CEO, President
American Nuclear Insurers [1833]
95 Glastonbury Blvd., Ste. 300
Glastonbury, CT 06033-4412

Turner, Helen Lee, Secretary
National Association of Baptist
Professors of Religion [8710]
900 College St.
UMHB Box 8374
Belton, TX 76513

Turner, Ivy A., V. Chmn. of the Bd.
ACMP - The Chamber Music
Network [9846]
1133 Broadway, Rm. 810
New York, NY 10010
Ph: (212)645-7424
Fax: (212)741-2678

Turner, James S., Founder, Principal
National Institute for Science, Law
and Public Policy [3552]
1400 16th St. NW, Ste. 101
Washington, DC 20036
Ph: (202)462-8800
Fax: (202)265-6564

Turner, Jane, Editor
Master Drawings Association [8871]
225 Madison Ave.
New York, NY 10016
Ph: (212)590-0369
Fax: (212)685-4740

Turner, Dr. Jon D., Exec. Dir.
Association for Tropical Lepidoptera
[6607]
PO Box 141210
Gainesville, FL 32614-1210
Fax: (352)373-3249

Turner, Marsha L., CEO
International Association of Lighting
Designers [1948]

440 N Wells St., Ste. 210
Chicago, IL 60654
Ph: (312)527-3677
Fax: (312)527-3680

Turner, Nicholas, President, Director
Family Justice Program [11525]
233 Broadway, 12th Fl.
New York, NY 10279-1299
Ph: (212)334-1300
Fax: (212)941-9407

Turner, Pamela, Chairperson
Society for Animation Studies [7493]
c/o Pamela Turner, Chairperson
2615 Fendall Ave.
Richmond, VA 23222
Ph: (804)937-2942

Turner, Paul Rodney, President
Food for Life Global [12662]
10310 Oaklyn Dr.
Potomac, MD 20854
Ph: (202)407-9090

Turner, Raechelle, Exec. Dir.
Healing Minds [15771]
PO Box 45836
Seattle, WA 98145
Ph: (206)718-2022
     (253)632-1547

Turner, Rhonda F., PhD, Founder,
   President
American Association of Breast Care
   Professionals [13848]
3375 Westpark Dr., No. 573
Houston, TX 77005
Fax: (888)892-1684

Turner, Samantha, Chairman
Industrial Asset Management
   Council [2863]
6625 The Corners Pky., Ste. 200
Peachtree Corners, GA 30092
Ph: (770)325-3461
Fax: (770)263-8825

Turner, Starla, Co-Pres.
Gemological Institute of America
   Alumni Association [19513]
The Robert Mouawad Campus
5345 Armada Dr.
Carlsbad, CA 92008
Ph: (760)603-4000
     (760)603-4145
Toll Free: 800-421-7250
Fax: (760)603-4080

Turner, Walter, President
Global Exchange [18098]
2017 Mission St., 2nd Fl.
San Francisco, CA 94110
Ph: (415)255-7296
Toll Free: 800-497-1994
Fax: (415)255-7498

Turner, Willis, President
Sales and Marketing Executives
   International [3019]
PO Box 1390
Sumas, WA 98295-1390
Ph: (312)893-0751

Turner-Harris, Myrtle I., President
National Environmental, Safety and
   Health Training Association [4553]
584 Main St.
South Portland, ME 04106
Ph: (602)956-6099
Fax: (602)956-6399

Turnham, Tim, PhD, Exec. Dir.
Melanoma Research Foundation
   [14012]
1411 K St. NW, Ste. 800
Washington, DC 20005
Ph: (202)347-9675
Toll Free: 800-673-1290
Fax: (202)347-9678

Turnquist, Jan, Exec. Dir.
Louisa May Alcott Memorial Associa-
   tion [9032]
399 Lexington Rd.
Concord, MA 01742-0343
Ph: (978)369-4118

Turpin, Diane, Exec. Dir.
Association of Dermatology
   Administrators and Managers
   [14489]
1120 G St. NW, Ste. 1000
Washington, DC 20005
Toll Free: 866-480-3573
Fax: (800)671-3763

Turpin, Paul, Treasurer
International DB2 Users Group
   [6364]
330 N Wabash, Ste. 2000
Chicago, IL 60611-4267
Ph: (312)321-6881
Fax: (312)673-6688

Turpin, Tim, Director
National American Semi-Professional
   Baseball Association [22556]
4609 Saybrook Dr.
Evansville, IN 47711-7771
Ph: (812)430-2725

Turrentine, Deacon Bill, Chairman
Couple to Couple League [11838]
4290 Delhi Ave.
Cincinnati, OH 45238-5829
Ph: (513)471-2000
Toll Free: 800-745-8252
Fax: (513)557-2449

Turrill, Rev. Robert, President, CEO
Evangelical Church Alliance [20119]
205 W Broadway St.
Bradley, IL 60915
Ph: (815)937-0720
Toll Free: 888-855-6060
Fax: (815)937-0001

Tuschen, Bryan, Mgr.
Signal Corps Regimental Association
   [20724]
4570 Dewey Dr.
Martinez, GA 30907

Tutle, Gene, President
Angelo State University Alumni As-
   sociation [19304]
ASU Station No. 11049
San Angelo, TX 76909

Tutt, Lou, Contact
Association for Education and
   Rehabilitation of the Blind and
   Visually Impaired [17689]
1703 N Beauregard St., Ste. 440
Alexandria, VA 22311
Ph: (703)671-4500

Tuttle, Christopher A., PhD, Exec.
   Dir.
Council of American Overseas
   Research Centers [7089]
PO Box 37012
Washington, DC 20013-7012
Ph: (202)633-1599
Fax: (202)633-3141

Tuttle, Dave, Treasurer
Hudson-Essex-Terraplane Club
   [21395]
7115 Franklin Ave.
Windsor Heights, IA 50324

Tuttle, Doug, CEO, President
Loyal Christian Benefit Association
   [19488]
8811 Peach St.
Erie, PA 16509-4738
Ph: (888)382-2716
Toll Free: 800-234-5222

Tuttle, John D., President
National School Boards Association
   [8522]
1680 Duke St., FL2
Alexandria, VA 22314-3493
Ph: (703)838-6722
Fax: (703)683-7590

Tuttle, Warren, President
United Inventors Association of the
   United States of America [6772]
1025 Connecticut Ave., Ste. 1000
Washington, DC 20036-5417

Twarog, Daniel L., President
North American Die Casting Associa-
   tion [1757]
3250 N Arlington Heights Rd., Ste.
   101
Arlington Heights, IL 60004
Ph: (847)279-0001
Fax: (847)279-0002

Tweedy, Jim, Exec. Dir.
Board of Certified Hazard Control
   Management [2992]
173 Tucker Rd., Ste 202
Helena, AL 35080
Ph: (205)664-8412
Fax: (205)663-9541

Tweedy, Jim, Exec. Dir.
International Board for Certification
   of Safety Managers [2996]
173 Tucker Rd., Ste. 202
Helena, AL 35080
Ph: (205)664-8412

Twiss, Julie, RN, Officer
National Association of Orthopaedic
   Nurses [16152]
330 N Wabash Ave., Ste.2000
Chicago, IL 60611
Toll Free: 800-289-6266
Fax: (312)673-6941

Two Feathers, Morwen, Contact
Earth Drum Council [9231]
PO Box 1284
Concord, MA 01742
Ph: (978)985-7421

Twombly, A.J., V. Chmn. of the Bd.
America Scores [23183]
2nd Fl., Ste. 201C
520 8th Ave.
New York, NY 10018
Ph: (212)868-9510
Fax: (212)868-9533

Twombly, Sean, Exec. Dir.
Pi Sigma Alpha [23851]
1527 New Hampshire Ave. NW
Washington, DC 20036
Ph: (202)349-9285

Tyagi, Amelia Warren, Chairman
Demos [18095]
220 5th Ave., 2nd Fl.
New York, NY 10001
Ph: (212)633-1405

Tykulsker, David, Chairman
Clean Water Action [4750]
1444 Eye St. NW, Ste. 400
Washington, DC 20005-6538
Ph: (202)895-0420
Fax: (202)895-0438

Tylenda, Ed, Chairman
American Credit Card Collectors
   Society [21609]
c/o Scott Nimmo
3563 B Long Hollow Pk.
Goodlettsville, TN 37072

Tyner, Rob, Chairman
Box Project [12629]
315 Losher St., Ste. 100

Hernando, MS 38632-2124
Ph: (662)449-5002
Toll Free: 800-268-9928
Fax: (662)449-5006

Tynes, Bayard, Chairman
NPTA Alliance [2493]
330 N Wabash Ave., Ste. 2000
Chicago, IL 60611
Ph: (312)321-4092
Fax: (312)673-6736

Tyo, J. Scott, Secretary, Treasurer
IEEE - Antennas and Propagation
   Society [6423]
c/o J. Scott Tyo, Secretary/Treasurer
University of Arizona
Meinel Bldg., Rm. 623
Tucson, AZ 85745
Ph: (520)626-8183
Fax: (520)621-4358

Tyson, Brian, Exec. Dir.
American Board of Trial Advocates
   [5822]
2001 Bryan St., Ste. 3000
Dallas, TX 75201
Ph: (214)871-7523
Toll Free: 800-932-2682
Fax: (214)871-6025

Tyson, Brian, Exec. Dir.
American Board of Trial Advocates
   Foundation [4985]
2001 Bryan St., Ste. 3000
Dallas, TX 75201
Ph: (214)871-7523
Toll Free: 800-932-2682
Fax: (214)871-6025

Tyson, Jesse J., President, CEO
National Black MBA Association
   [7561]
1 E Wacker Dr., Ste. 3500
Chicago, IL 60601

Tyson, Priscilla, President
National Black Caucus of Local
   Elected Officials [5642]
National League of Cities
1301 Pennsylvania Ave. NW, Ste.
   550
Washington, DC 20004
Toll Free: 877-827-2385

Tzap, Steve, 1st VP
Gas Processors Suppliers Associa-
   tion [2522]
6060 American Plz., Ste. 700
Tulsa, OK 74135
Ph: (918)493-3872
Fax: (918)493-3875

Tzvi Friedman, Howard, Chairman
Orthodox Union [20274]
11 Broadway
New York, NY 10004
Ph: (212)563-4000

U

Ubl, Steve, President, CEO
Pharmaceutical Research and
   Manufacturers of America [2570]
950 F St. NW, Ste. 300
Washington, DC 20004
Ph: (202)835-3400

Uchefuna, Rev. Gloria Obioma,
   Exec. Dir.
Health and Life International [15013]
PO Box 7822
Fredericksburg, VA 22404
Ph: (540)295-2374

Uddin, M. Nasim, PhD, President
Global Automotive Management
   Council [293]

5340 Plymouth Rd., Ste. 205
Ann Arbor, MI 48105
Ph: (734)997-9249
Fax: (734)786-2242

Ude, Christina, Founder
Reading Hamlets [12248]
PO Box 575
New York, NY 10116
Ph: (347)856-8357

Udoff, Amanda B., Coord.
Star-Spangled Banner Flag House
Association [20949]
844 E Pratt St.
Baltimore, MD 21202-4403
Ph: (410)837-1793

Uebel, Kathleen S., Exec. Dir.
American Academy of Dental
Practice Administration [14374]
c/o Kathleen Uebel, Executive Director
1063 Whippoorwill Ln.
Palatine, IL 60067
Ph: (847)934-4404

Uffer-Marcolongo, M. Assunta,
President
Foundation for the Support of
International Medical Training
[15449]
c/o International Association for
Medical Assistance to Travellers
1623 Military Rd., No. 279
Niagara Falls, NY 14304-1745
Ph: (716)754-4883

Ufford-Chase, Rick, Director
Presbyterian Peace Fellowship
[18823]
17 Cricketown Rd.
Stony Point, NY 10980
Ph: (845)786-6743

Ugorji, Julia, RN, President
National Association of Nigerian
Nurses in North America [16150]
2195 Hoffman Ave.
Elmont, NY 11003
Ph: (516)528-1644

Uhl, Steve, President
Rhodes 19 Class Association
[22662]
c/o Jeff Shoreman, Secretary
34 Ticehurst Ln.
Marblehead, MA 01945-2837

Uhler, Lewis K., Founder, President
National Tax-Limitation Committee
[19172]
1700 Eureka Rd., Ste. 150A
Roseville, CA 95661-7777

Ujereh, Sebastine, Director, Founder
Anti-Poverty Initiative [17803]
10444 Kensington Way
Indianapolis, IN 46234
Ph: (317)504-4528

Ulferts, Dr. Gregory W., Exec. Dir.
Alpha Iota Delta [23686]
c/o Gregory Ulferts, Executive Director
University of Detroit Mercy
4001 W McNichols Rd.
Detroit, MI 48221
Ph: (313)993-1219
Fax: (313)993-1052

Ulferts, Dr. Gregory W., Exec. Dir.,
Secretary
International Association of Jesuit
Business Schools [7552]
4001 W McNichols Rd.
Detroit, MI 48221
Ph: (313)993-1219
Fax: (313)993-1052

Ulfik, Rick, Chmn. of the Bd.,
Founder
We, The World [12964]
PO Box 750651
Forest Hills, NY 11375-0651
Ph: (212)867-0846

Ullman, Chana, President
International Association for
Relational Psychoanalysis and
Psychotherapy [16846]
799 Broadway, Ste. 305
New York, NY 10003-6811

Ullman, John, President
OurEarth.org [3927]
PO Box 62133
Durham, NC 27715
Ph: (410)878-6485

Ullman, Michael D., President
American Custom Gunmakers Guild
[1292]
445 Harness Way
Monument, CO 80132

Ullman, Myron E., III, Chairman
Mercy Ships International Operations
Center [15606]
PO Box 2020
Garden Valley, TX 75771-2020
Ph: (903)939-7000
Toll Free: 800-772-7447

Ulman, Doug, President, CEO
LIVESTRONG Foundation [14003]
2201 E 6th St.
Austin, TX 78702
Toll Free: 877-236-8820

Ulman, Douglas, Founder
4K for Cancer [13867]
1215 E Fort Ave., Ste. 104
Baltimore, MD 21230
Ph: (410)964-0202

Ulman, Josh, Exec. Dir.
National Armored Car Association
[3093]
11911 Fawn Ridge Ln.
Reston, VA 20194
Ph: (202)642-1970

Ulman, Mike, Secretary
Alaskan Malamute Assistance
League [10562]
PO Box 7161
Golden, CO 80403

Umayam, Christine, Founder
Child United [10905]
500 Yale Ave. N, 1st Fl.
Seattle, WA 98109
Ph: (425)954-5288

Unal, Haluk, President, Chmn. of the
Bd.
Turkish American Scientists and
Scholars Association [7149]
1526 18th St. NW
Washington, DC 20036
Toll Free: 855-827-7204

Underhill, Randall, Exec. Sec.
101st Airborne Division Association
[5580]
PO Box 929
Fort Campbell, KY 42223-0929
Ph: (931)431-0199
Fax: (931)431-0195

Underwood, Brett, Comm. Chm.
Cotton Warehouse Association of
America [935]
316 Pennsylvania Ave. SE, Ste. 401
Washington, DC 20003
Ph: (202)544-5875
Fax: (202)544-5874

Underwood, Joanna D.,
Chairperson, Founder
Energy Vision [6484]
138 E 13th St.
New York, NY 10003
Ph: (212)228-0225

Underwood, Katherine, President
National Council of Urban Education
Associations [8728]
1201 16th St. NW, Ste. 410
Washington, DC 20036
Ph: (202)822-7155

Underwood, Tom, Exec. Ofc.
American Horticultural Society
[22075]
7931 E Boulevard Dr.
Alexandria, VA 22308-1300
Ph: (703)768-5700
Fax: (703)768-8700

Ungar, Mr. Irvin, Curator
Arthur Szyk Society [8945]
1200 Edgehill Dr.
Burlingame, CA 94010
Ph: (650)343-9588

Ungaro, Maria, Exec. Dir.
GWA: The Association for Garden
Communicators [22098]
355 Lexington Ave., 5th Fl.
New York, NY 10017
Ph: (212)297-2198
Fax: (212)297-2149

Ungaro, Maria, Exec. Dir.
New York Women in Communica-
tions Foundation [774]
355 Lexington Ave., 15th Fl.
New York, NY 10017-6603
Ph: (212)297-2133
Fax: (212)370-9047

Ungaro, Susan, President
James Beard Foundation [10313]
167 W 12th St.
New York, NY 10011
Ph: (212)675-4984

Unger, Geri, Exec. Dir.
Society for Conservation Biology
[6097]
1133 15th St. NW, Ste. 300
Washington, DC 20001
Ph: (202)234-4133
Fax: (703)995-4633

Unger, Joe, President
Sacro Occipital Research Society
International [14281]
2184 Channing Way, No. 460
Idaho Falls, ID 83404
Ph: (913)239-0228
Fax: (913)239-0305

Ungerer, Richard A., Exec. Dir.
American Montessori Society [8349]
116 E 16th St.
New York, NY 10003-2163
Ph: (212)358-1250
Fax: (212)358-1256

Unruh, Leslee J., Founder, President
Abstinence Clearinghouse [17188]
801 E 41st St.
Sioux Falls, SD 57105
Ph: (605)335-3643
Toll Free: 888-577-2966

Unver, Bircan, Founder, President
Light Millennium [17909]
87-82 115th St.
Richmond Hill, NY 11418
Ph: (718)846-5776

Updegrove, Lynne, VP
Cotswold Breeders Association
[3599]

PO Box 441
Manchester, MD 21102
Ph: (410)374-4383
Fax: (410)374-2294

Upham, Mark, President
United States Yngling Association
[22689]
c/o Mark Upham, President
7171 US Highway 23 S
Ossineke, MI 49766
Ph: (989)471-3545

Upham, Peter, Exec. Dir.
The Association of Boarding Schools
[8460]
1 N Pack Sq., Ste. 301
Asheville, NC 28801
Ph: (828)258-5354
Fax: (828)258-6428

Upledger, John E., President
American CranioSacral Therapy As-
sociation [15261]
c/o The Upledger Institute
International, Inc.
11211 Prosperity Farms Rd., Ste.
D-325
Palm Beach Gardens, FL 33410
Ph: (561)622-4334
Toll Free: 800-233-5880
Fax: (561)622-4771

Upledger, John Matthew, President
Upledger Institute [13665]
11211 Prosperity Farms Rd., Ste.
D-325
Palm Beach Gardens, FL 33410
Ph: (561)622-4334
Toll Free: 800-233-5880
Fax: (561)622-4771

Upperman, Jaclyn, Director, Editor
American Junior Chianina Associa-
tion [3699]
1708 N Prairie View Rd.
Platte City, MO 64079
Ph: (816)431-2808
Fax: (816)431-5381

Upright, Rob, President
Scale Manufacturers Association
[3467]
PO Box 26972
Columbus, OH 43226-0972
Toll Free: 866-372-4627

Upson, Lisa, Exec. Dir.
Keystone Conservation [4838]
104 E Main St., Ste. 307
Bozeman, MT 59715
Ph: (406)587-3389
Fax: (406)587-3178

Upton, Devin, President
Medical Mission Group [15485]
134 Grove St.
Pearl River, NY 10965
Ph: (845)920-9001

Upton, Roy, RH, President, CEO
American Herbal Pharmacopoeia
[13594]
PO Box 66809
Scotts Valley, CA 95067
Ph: (831)461-6318
Fax: (831)438-2196

Ural, Prof. Oktay, President, Founder
International Association for Housing
Science [11974]
PO Box 340254
Coral Gables, FL 33134

Urbanowicz, Nancy, Exec. Dir.
Academy of Management [8260]
PO Box 3020
Briarcliff Manor, NY 10510-8020
Ph: (914)923-2607
Fax: (914)923-2615

Urbashich, Mary Ann
Alzheimer's Association **[13669]**
225 N Michigan Ave., 17th Fl.
Chicago, IL 60601-7633
Ph: (312)335-8700
   (312)335-5886
Toll Free: 866-699-1246

Urbiztondo, Mario B., President
CarCanMadCarLan Association
U.S.A. **[12631]**
25564 Wedmore Dr.
Moreno Valley, CA 92553
Ph: (951)880-5614
   (951)247-8522

Urdang, Stephanie, Coord.
Rwanda Gift for Life **[12935]**
PO Box 840
Montclair, NJ 07042
Ph: (973)783-4057

Urhausen, Diane, Exec. Dir.
National Association for Down
Syndrome **[14627]**
1460 Renaissance Dr., Ste. 405
Park Ridge, IL 60068
Ph: (630)325-9112
Fax: (847)376-8908

Uricchio, Joesph, Jr., MD, Treasurer
American Academy of Thermology
[15674]
500 Duvall Dr.
Greenville, SC 29607
Ph: (864)236-1073
Fax: (864)236-5918

Urlage, Brian, President
NSX Club of America **[21464]**
333 Mamaroneck Ave., PMB No.
399
White Plains, NY 10605
Toll Free: 877-679-2582
Fax: (844)329-6790

Usher, Maj. Gen. Edward, CEO,
President
Marine Corps Association **[5568]**
PO Box 1775
Quantico, VA 22134
Toll Free: 866-622-1775

Utada, Yukio, President
Aikido Association of North America
[22495]
5836 Henry Ave., No. 38
Philadelphia, PA 19128-1703
Ph: (215)483-3000

Utberg, Debra, President
Association of Sewing and Design
Professionals **[200]**
2885 Sanford Ave. SW, No. 19588
Grandville, MI 49418
Toll Free: 877-755-0303

Utian, Wulf H., PhD, Medical Dir.
North American Menopause Society
[16299]
5900 Landerbrook Dr., Ste. 390
Mayfield Heights, OH 44124
Ph: (440)442-7550
Fax: (440)442-2660

Uttal, David, President
Cognitive Development Society
[13811]
c/o Amanda Woodward, President
5801 S Ellis Ave.
Chicago, IL 60637
Toll Free: 800-354-1420
Fax: (215)625-8914

Uyemura, Ray, COO
Japanese American Living Legacy
[9626]
PO Box 10179

Torrance, CA 905050
Ph: (424)230-7723

V

Vaccaro, Nick, Administrator
Foodservice Consultants Society
International **[820]**
PO Box 4961
Louisville, KY 40204-0961
Ph: (502)379-4122

Vaccaro, Tony, Act. Pres.
Lotus Ltd. **[21422]**
PO Box L
College Park, MD 20741
Ph: (301)982-4054
Fax: (301)982-4054

Vadgama, Ashok, President
Consortium for Advanced Manage-
ment International **[2218]**
6836 Bee Cave Rd., Ste. 256
Austin, TX 78746
Ph: (512)296-6872

Vaghar, Sam, Exec. Dir.
Millennium Campus Network **[17806]**
101 Huntington Ave., Ste. 2205
Boston, MA 02199-7603
Ph: (617)492-9099

Vaid, Dr. Jyotsna, Editor
Committee on South Asian Women
[18204]
Texas A&M University
Dept. of Psychology
College Station, TX 77843-4235
Ph: (979)845-2576
Fax: (979)845-4727

Vaidya, Shilpa, Secretary
Earth Council Alliance **[18717]**
1250 24th St. NW, Ste. 300
Washington, DC 20037
Ph: (202)467-2786

Vaidyanathan, Rajiv, Exec. Dir.
Association for Consumer Research
[18040]
11 E Superior St., Ste. 210
Duluth, MN 55802
Ph: (218)726-7853
Fax: (218)726-8016

Vail, Walter, President
Gravure Education Foundation
[7947]
PO Box 25617
Rochester, NY 14625-0617
Ph: (201)523-6042
Fax: (201)523-6048

Vair, Scott, President
World Orphans **[11190]**
PO Box 1840
Castle Rock, CO 80104
Toll Free: 888-677-4267

Valachovic, Richard, President, CEO
American Dental Education Associa-
tion **[7707]**
655 K St. NW, Ste. 800
Washington, DC 20001
Ph: (202)289-7201
Fax: (202)289-7204

Valdes, Roland, Jr., PhD, Officer
Association of Clinical Scientists
[14290]
33 W Monroe St., Ste. 1600
Chicago, IL 60603
Toll Free: 800-267-2727
Fax: (312)541-4998

Valen, Terry, President
National Alliance for Filipino
Concerns **[17814]**

4681 Mission St.
San Francisco, CA 94112
Ph: (415)333-6267

Valencia, Jorge, CEO, Exec. Dir.
Point Foundation **[4010]**
5055 Wilshire Blvd., Ste. 501
Los Angeles, CA 90036
Ph: (323)933-1234
Toll Free: 866-337-6468

Valencic, Joe, President
American-Slovenian Polka Founda-
tion **[9867]**
605 E 222nd St.
Euclid, OH 44123
Ph: (216)261-3263
Fax: (216)261-4134

Valente, Carmine M., PhD, CEO
American Institute of Ultrasound in
Medicine **[17230]**
14750 Sweitzer Ln., Ste. 100
Laurel, MD 20707-5906
Ph: (301)498-4100
Toll Free: 800-638-5352
Fax: (301)498-4450

Valente, Dominic S., Bd. Member
National Association of Flour
Distributors **[1353]**
c/o G. Timothy Dove
5350 Woodland Pl.
Canfield, OH 44406
Ph: (330)718-6563
Fax: (877)573-1230

Valenti, Thomas, President
Allied Artists of America **[8906]**
15 Gramercy Pk. S
New York, NY 10003

Valentina, Elizabeth, VP
Croatian American Bar Association
[5001]
6 Papette Cir.
Ladera Ranch, CA 92694-1090
Ph: (949)274-5360

Valentine, Linda, President
Presbyterian Health Education and
Welfare Association **[13082]**
100 Witherspoon St.
Louisville, KY 40202-1396
Toll Free: 800-728-7228

Valentine, R. James, MD, President
Western Surgical Association
[17418]
14005 Nicklaus Dr.
Overland Park, KS 66204
Ph: (913)402-7102
Fax: (913)273-1116

Valentino, Joanne, Dir. of Comm.,
Dir. of Mktg.
The Medical Letter, Inc. **[16670]**
145 Huguenot St., Ste. 312
New Rochelle, NY 10801-7537
Ph: (914)235-0500
Toll Free: 800-211-2769
Fax: (914)632-1733

Valenzuela, Pamela, Exec. Dir.
Association for Women in Com-
munications **[761]**
3337 Duke St.
Alexandria, VA 22314
Ph: (703)370-7436
Fax: (703)342-4311

Valenzuela, Pamela, Exec. Dir.
National Multifamily Resident
Information Council **[2884]**
3337 Duke St.
Alexandria, VA 22314
Ph: (703)370-7436
Fax: (703)342-4311

Valera, Milton G., President
National Notary Association **[5656]**
9350 De Soto Ave.
Chatsworth, CA 91313-2402
Toll Free: 800-876-6827

Valero, Caterina, Prog. Dir.
Disaster Management Alliance
[11657]
Pan American Development Founda-
tion
1889 F St. NW, 2nd Fl.
Washington, DC 20006
Ph: (202)458-3969
Toll Free: 877-572-4484

Valero, Noel, Founder, President
American Dystonia Society **[15899]**
17 Suffolk Ln.
Princeton Junction, NJ 08550
Ph: (310)237-5478
Fax: (609)275-5663

Valery, Rukhledev, President
International Committee of Sports for
the Deaf **[22782]**
PO Box 91267
Washington, DC 20090
Fax: (499)255-0436

Valiente, Ernesto O., Chmn. of the
Bd.
Christians for Peace in El Salvador
[20403]
808 Brookhill Rd.
Louisville, KY 40223
Ph: (502)592-5295

Valk, Anne M., President
Oral History Association **[9502]**
c/o Gayle Knight, Program Associate
Dept. of History
Georgia State University
Atlanta, GA 30302-4117
Ph: (404)413-5751
Fax: (404)413-6384

Vallarino, Barbara, Exec. Dir.
EcoLogic Development Fund **[3999]**
186 Alewife Brook Pky., Ste. 214
Cambridge, MA 02138
Ph: (617)441-6300

Valle, David, CEO
Esperanza International **[11356]**
PO Box 140807
Dallas, TX 75214
Ph: (425)451-4359
Fax: (425)451-4360

Van, Albert T., Contact
Van Voorhees Association **[20939]**
c/o Albert T. Van
9 Purdy Ave.
East Northport, NY 11731-4501

Van Alstyne, John S., President,
CEO
Inter-Industry Conference on Auto
Collision Repair **[344]**
5125 Trillium Blvd.
Hoffman Estates, IL 60192
Ph: (847)590-1198
Toll Free: 800-590-1215

Van Alstyne, Stacy, Mgr.
International Foundation of
Employee Benefit Plans **[1072]**
18700 W Bluemound Rd.
Brookfield, WI 53045
Ph: (262)786-6700
   (262)786-6710
Toll Free: 888-334-3327

Van Andel, David L., Chairman, CEO
Van Andel Education Institute **[7805]**
333 Bostwick Ave. NE
Grand Rapids, MI 49503
Ph: (616)234-5000
Fax: (616)234-5001

Van Belkom, Tony, President
Retail Packaging Association [2483]
105 Eastern Ave., Ste. 104
Annapolis, MD 21403-3366
Ph: (410)940-6459
Fax: (410)263-1659

Van den Brink, Paul, President
Society of Environmental Toxicology
   and Chemistry [14724]
229 S Baylen St., 2nd Fl.
Pensacola, FL 32502
Ph: (850)469-1500
Fax: (888)296-4136

van de Broek, Marcel, President
International Carnivorous Plant
   Society [22105]
2121 N California Blvd., Ste. 290
Walnut Creek, CA 94596-7351

Van Bylevett, Lloyd, President
Peace Education Foundation
   [18009]
1900 Biscayne Blvd.
Miami, FL 33132
Ph: (305)576-5075
Toll Free: 800-749-8838
Fax: (305)576-3106

Van Cleef, Scott, Chmn. of the Bd.
Air Force Association [5584]
1501 Lee Hwy.
Arlington, VA 22209-1198
Ph: (703)247-5800
Toll Free: 800-727-3337
Fax: (703)247-5853

van der Colff, Marius, Exec. Dir.,
   Founder
Cargo of Dreams [12634]
17320 Red Hill Ave., Ste. 320
Irvine, CA 92614
Ph: (949)340-6825

Van Coverden, Tom, CEO, President
National Association of Community
   Health Centers [14948]
7501 Wisconsin Ave., Ste. 1100W
Bethesda, MD 20814
Ph: (301)347-0400

Van Dahlen, Barbara, PhD,
   President, Founder
Give an Hour [10742]
PO Box 5918
Bethesda, MD 20824-5918

Van Deman, Bruce, President
English Toy Spaniel Club of America
   [21875]
c/o Susan Plance, Secretary
505 Whitehill Rd.
Georgetown, PA 15043-9634
Ph: (714)893-0053
Fax: (714)893-5085

Van Dusen, Dr. Ann, Chairwoman
Centre for Development and Popula-
   tion Activities [12145]
1255 23rd St. NW, Ste. 300
Washington, DC 20037
Ph: (202)617-2300
Fax: (202)332-4496

Van Dyk, Alison, Chairperson
Temple of Understanding [20614]
777 United Nations Plz., Office 3E
New York, NY 10017
Ph: (914)610-5146

Van Dyke, Christina, Exec. Dir.
Society of Christian Philosophers
   [10122]
Dept. of Philosophy
Calvin College
1845 Knollcrest Cir. SE
Grand Rapids, MI 49546-4402

Van Dyke, Craig, President
Western Fraternal Life Association
   [19420]
1900 1st Ave. NE
Cedar Rapids, IA 52402-5321
Ph: (319)363-2653
Toll Free: 877-935-2467
Fax: (319)363-8806

van Es, Harold M., President
Soil Science Society of America
   [7194]
5585 Guilford Rd.
Madison, WI 53711
Ph: (608)273-8080
Fax: (608)273-2021

Van Gorder, Dana, Exec. Dir.
Project Inform [13559]
273 9th St.
San Francisco, CA 94103
Ph: (415)558-8669
Toll Free: 877-435-7443
Fax: (415)558-0684

Van Greuning, Martmari
International Society for Mushroom
   Science [4236]
c/o Christine Smith, Secretary
1507 Valley Rd.
Coatesville, PA 19320
Ph: (610)384-5031
Fax: (610)384-0390

van Heyningen, Zoltan, Exec. Dir.
U.S. Lumber Coalition [1445]
1750 K St. NW, Ste. 800
Washington, DC 20006
Ph: (703)597-8651

van Holsbeeck, Marnix, MD, Director
Musculoskeletal Ultrasound Society
   [17540]

Van Kerckhove, Michael, Exec. Dir.
Theatre for Young Audiences USA
   [10278]
c/o Theatre School at DePaul
   University
2350 N Racine Ave.
Chicago, IL 60614
Ph: (773)325-7981
Fax: (773)325-7920

van der Leer, David, Exec. Dir.
Van Alen Institute: Projects in Public
   Architecture [7501]
30 W 22nd St.
New York, NY 10010
Ph: (212)924-7000

van Matre, Steve, Chmn. of the Bd.
Institute for Earth Education [7878]
Cedar Cove
Greenville, WV 24945
Ph: (304)832-6404

Van Ness, Brundene, President
Allied Stone Industries [3180]
c/o Brundene Van Ness, President
10500 Kinsman Rd.
Newbury, OH 44065

Van Petten, Aleeta, Inst.
Feminist Karate Union [22991]
1426 S Jackson St., 3rd Fl.
Seattle, WA 98144
Ph: (206)325-3878

Van Petten, Vance, Exec. Dir.
Producers Guild of America [1203]
8530 Wilshire Blvd., Ste. 400
Beverly Hills, CA 90211
Ph: (310)358-9020
Fax: (310)358-9520

Van Quill, DeDe, Exec. Dir.
Foundation for Nager and Miller
   Syndromes [14824]

13210 SE 342nd St.
Auburn, WA 98092
Ph: (253)333-1483
Toll Free: 800-507-3667
Fax: (253)288-7679

van Rens, Ger, Mem.
International Society for Low Vision
   Research and Rehabilitation
   [16391]
243 Charles St.
Boston, MA 02114
Ph: (617)573-4177
Fax: (617)573-4178

van Rooijen, Dr. Maurits, Co-Chmn.
   of the Bd.
World Association for Cooperative
   Education [7680]
Wannalancit Business Ctr., Ste. 125
600 Suffolk St.
Lowell, MA 01854
Ph: (978)934-1867
Fax: (978)934-4084

Van Sambeek, Jerry, President
Walnut Council [4515]
Wright Forestry Ctr.
1007 N 725 W
West Lafayette, IN 47906-9431
Ph: (765)583-3501
Fax: (765)583-3512

Van Sant, Ms. Jules, Exec. Dir.
Pacific Printing Industries Associa-
   tion [1545]
6825 SW Sandburg St.
Portland, OR 97223
Ph: (503)221-3944
Toll Free: 877-762-7742
Fax: (503)221-5691

Van Sickle, Mary, Chairman
Alliance for Community Media
   [17936]
4248 Park Glen Rd.
Minneapolis, MN 55416
Ph: (952)928-4643

Van Slyke, Melinda, President
Network in Solidarity with the People
   of Guatemala [18272]
PO Box 70494
Oakland, CA 94612-2728
Ph: (510)763-1403

Van der Swaagh, Rev. Kirk, VP
National Pro-Life Religious Council
   [19064]
PO Box 61838
Staten Island, NY 10306
Ph: (718)980-4400
Fax: (718)980-6515

Van Tiggelen, Conrad, Dir. of Mktg.
Netherlands Board of Tourism and
   Conventions [23653]
Netherlands Board of Tourism and
   Conventions
215 Park Ave. S
New York, NY 10003

van der Veer, Gerrit, President
Association for Computing
   Machinery - Special Interest Group
   on Computer and Human Interac-
   tion [6032]
1515 Broadway
New York, NY 10036
Ph: (212)626-0500
Toll Free: 800-342-6626
Fax: (212)944-1318

van Voorst, Mark, CEO, President
Lifespire [12326]
1 Whitehall St., 9th Fl.
New York, NY 10004-2141
Ph: (212)741-0100
Fax: (212)463-9814

Van Wagner, Marianne, Coord.
International Behavioral Neurosci-
   ence Society [16048]
1123 Comanche Path
Bandera, TX 78003-4212
Ph: (830)796-9393
Toll Free: 866-377-4416
Fax: (830)796-9394

Van Wagner, Marianne, Web Adm.
International Society for
   Developmental Psychobiology
   [16920]
1123 Comanche Path
Bandera, TX 78003-4212
Ph: (830)796-9393
Toll Free: 866-377-4416
Fax: (830)796-9394

Van Yperen, Jim, Founder, President
Metanoia Ministries [20043]
PO Box 448
Washington, NH 03280
Ph: (603)495-0035

van der Zande, Irene, Exec. Dir.,
   Founder
Kidpower Teenpower Fullpower
   International [12825]
PO Box 1212
Santa Cruz, CA 95061
Toll Free: 800-467-6997

Van Zwieten, Robert W., President,
   CEO
Emerging Markets Private Equity
   Association [1232]
1077 30th St. NW, Ste. 100
Washington, DC 20007
Ph: (202)333-8171

Vance, Josh, Director, President
Travel China Roads [7604]
1719 E Feemster Ct.
Visalia, CA 93292
Ph: (559)636-6026

Vance, Rev. Suzanne, Exec. Dir.
Association of Full Gospel Women
   Clergy [20357]
PO Box 1504
Annandale, VA 22003
Ph: (301)879-6958

Vance, V. Ellis, Exec. Dir.
U.S. Board on Books for Young
   People [9137]
c/o V. Ellis Vance, Executive Director
5503 N El Adobe Dr.
Fresno, CA 93711-2373
Ph: (559)351-6119

Vandagriff, Cris, President
Historic Motor Sports Association
   [21393]
2029 Verdugo Blvd., No. 1010
Montrose, CA 91020
Ph: (818)249-3515
Fax: (818)249-4917

VanDe Hei, Diane, CEO
Association of Metropolitan Water
   Agencies [5650]
1620 I St. NW, Ste. 500
Washington, DC 20006
Ph: (202)331-2820
Fax: (202)785-1845

VandeKopple, Julius J., Chairman
CAS Forum of the Violin Society of
   America [9884]
14070 Proton Rd., Ste. 100, LB 9
Dallas, TX 75244-3601
Ph: (972)233-9107

Vanden Berghe, 1st Lt. Raymond J,
   Sr., Cmdr.
Heroes of '76 [19560]
National Sojourners, Inc.

7942R Cluny Ct.
Springfield, VA 22153-2810
Ph: (703)765-5000
Fax: (703)765-8390

vanden Wyngaard, Julianne, VP
Guild of Carillonneurs in North
America [9913]
2255 S 133rd Ave.
Omaha, NE 68144-2506

Vandenberg, Kelle, VP of Dev.
International Women's Coffee Alliance [11388]
Ph: (217)529-6601

Vandenberg, Kristine, Exec. Dir.
Vegan Action [10294]
PO Box 7313
Richmond, VA 23221-0313
Ph: (804)502-8341
Fax: (804)254-8346

VanDenzen, Liz, Director
Alaska Coalition [3791]
122 C St. NW, Ste. 240
Washington, DC 20001
Ph: (505)438-4245

Vander Linden, Merry, Mgr.
Ultra Marathon Cycling Association
[22755]
c/o Paul Carpenter, President
7982 Hillmont Dr., Apt. B
Oakland, CA 94605
Ph: (303)545-9566
Fax: (303)545-9619

Vander Veer, Greg, VP
Dance Films Association [7701]
252 Java St., Ste. 333
Brooklyn, NY 11222
Ph: (347)505-8649

Vanderbilt, Henry, Founder
Space Access Society [7221]
PO Box 16034
Phoenix, AZ 85011

Vanderhoff, Mike, Director
New Hope in Africa [13356]
PO Box 3092
Cumming, GA 30028
Ph: (770)888-9269

Vanderhoof, Randy, Exec. Dir.
Smart Card Alliance [7293]
191 Clarksville Rd.
Princeton Junction, NJ 08550
Toll Free: 800-556-6828
Fax: (609)799-7032

Vanderlaan, Mary, Director, Founder
CCHS Family Network [14568]
PO Box 230087
Encinitas, CA 92023-0087

Vanderlei, Russ, RJF, President
Guild of Professional Farriers [1180]
PO Box 4541
Midway, KY 40347
Ph: (630)707-7877

Vanderpool, David, MD, Founder,
CEO
LiveBeyond [12286]
1508 Delmar Ave., Ste. 122
Nashville, TN 37212
Ph: (615)460-8296

Vandervoort, Robert, Exec. Dir.
ProEnglish [9284]
20 F St. NW, 7th Fl.
Washington, DC 20001
Ph: (202)507-6203
Fax: (571)527-2813

Vandervort, Michael, Exec. Dir.
CUE: An Organization for Positive
Employee Relations [23533]

900 NE Loop 410, Ste. D-103
San Antonio, TX 78209
Ph: (210)545-3499
Toll Free: 866-409-4283
Fax: (210)545-4284

VanderZanden, Karla, Exec. Dir.
Canyonlands Field Institute [3993]
1320 S Highway 191
Moab, UT 84532
Ph: (435)259-7750
Toll Free: 800-860-5262
Fax: (435)259-2335

Vandine, Jane, Administrator
Protected Harvest [4700]
2901 Park Ave., Ste. A2
Soquel, CA 95073
Ph: (831)477-7797
     (530)601-0740

vanDuyvenbode, Carla, President
North American Working Bouvier
Association [21933]
1677 Dexter St.
Broomfield, CO 80020
Toll Free: 866-457-2582

Vandyke, Gary, President
Food for Orphans [12093]
PO Box 26123
Colorado Springs, CO 80936
Ph: (719)591-7777

VanDyke, JoAnne, President
International Topical Steroid Addiction Network [14500]
11380 Prosperity Farms Rd., No.
221E
Palm Beach Gardens, FL 33410

Vanek, Joann, Director
Women in Informal Employment:
Globalizing and Organizing
[13406]
Harvard University
79 John F. Kennedy St.
Cambridge, MA 02138
Ph: (617)496-7037

Vang, Bao, President, CEO
Hmong National Development
[18473]
1628 16th St. NW
Washington, DC 20009
Ph: (202)588-1661

VanHerreweghe, Barb, President
Support Organization for Trisomy 18,
13, and Related Disorders [14861]
2982 S Union St.
Rochester, NY 14624
Toll Free: 800-716-7638

VanHorn, Edward, Exec. Dir.
Southern Newspaper Publishers Association [2814]
3680 N Peachtree Rd., Ste. 300
Atlanta, GA 30341
Ph: (404)256-0444
Fax: (404)252-9135

VanMeerhaeghe, Ms. Dana, Exec.
Dir.
American College of Healthcare
Architects [14976]
18000 W 105th St.
Olathe, KS 66061-7543
Ph: (913)895-4604
Fax: (913)895-4652

Vann, Rev. Kevin W., Chairman
Catholic Legal Immigration Network
Inc. [5290]
8757 Georgia Ave., Ste. 850
Silver Spring, MD 20910-3742
Ph: (301)565-4800
Fax: (301)565-4824

Vannuccini, Robert, President
American Salvage Pool Association
[277]
2900 Delk Rd., Ste. 700
Marietta, GA 30067
Ph: (678)560-6678
Fax: (678)229-2777

Vanoceur, Andrew, Chairman
American Computer Scientists Association [6233]
General Delivery Box ACSA
Los Alamos, NM 87544-9999
Toll Free: 888-532-5540

VanReepinghen, Sharyn, VP
Association for the Help of Retarded
Children [15813]
83 Maiden Ln.
New York, NY 10038
Ph: (212)780-2500
     (212)780-4491

Vansagi, Tom, PhD, Exec. Dir.
North American Primary Care
Research Group [13678]
11400 Tomahawk Creek Pky., Ste.
240
Leawood, KS 66211
Ph: (913)906-6000
Toll Free: 888-371-6397

VanStralen, Dave, President
The National Needle Arts Association [3266]
1100-H Brandywine Blvd.
Zanesville, OH 43701-7303
Ph: (740)455-6773
Toll Free: 800-889-8662

Vanterpool, Brenda, VP
World Federation of Methodist and
Uniting Church Women North
America Area [20350]
c/o Dr. Sylvia Faulk
623 San Fernanco Ave.
Berkeley, CA 94707

Vantiger, D., Secretary
International Guild of Lamp
Researchers [21290]
Lamplighters Farm
10111 Lincoln Way W
Saint Thomas, PA 17252-9513

VanVactor, Darrell, Operations Mgr.
American Crappie Association
[22038]
220 Mohawk Ave.
Louisville, KY 40209
Ph: (502)384-5924
     (270)748-5703
Fax: (502)384-4232

VanWyk, Jason, Officer
William Penn University Alumni Association [19373]
201 Trueblood Ave.
Oskaloosa, IA 52577-1799
Ph: (641)673-1046
Toll Free: 800-779-7366

Vapiwala, Neha, MD, President
Association for Directors of Radiation Oncology Programs [17033]
8280 Willow Oaks Corporate Dr.,
Ste. 500
Fairfax, VA 22031
Ph: (703)502-1550
Toll Free: 800-962-7876
Fax: (703)502-7852

Vaquerano, Carlos Antonio H., Exec.
Dir.
Salvadoran American Leadership
and Educational Fund [18176]
1625 W Olympic Blvd., Ste. 718
Los Angeles, CA 90015
Ph: (213)480-1052
Fax: (213)487-2530

Varanauski, Daniel E, DN, President
American Naprapathic Association
[15851]
2731 N Lincoln Ave.
Chicago, IL 60614
Ph: (312)698-9855
Fax: (312)380-4637

Varble, Dana M., DVM, Exec. Dir.
Association of Reptilian and Amphibian Veterinarians [17636]
810 E 10th St.
Lawrence, KS 66044
Ph: (480)703-4941

Vargas, Fidel A., President, CEO
Hispanic Scholarship Fund [7926]
1411 W 190th St., Ste. 700
Gardena, CA 90248
Ph: (310)975-3700
Fax: (310)349-3328

Vargas, Hector, Exec. Dir.
Gay and Lesbian Medical Association [14800]
1326 18th St., Ste. 22
Washington, DC 20036
Ph: (202)600-8037
Fax: (202)478-1500

Vargas, Yolanda, President
Professional Dancers Federation
[22764]
6830 N Broadway, Ste. D
Denver, CO 80221
Ph: (858)560-4372

Vargo, Trina, President, Founder
US-Ireland Alliance [689]
2800 Clarendon Blvd., Ste. 502W
Arlington, VA 22201

Varley, Judy, Exec. Dir.
Society of Singers [12372]
26500 W Agoura Rd., No. 102-554
Calabasas, CA 91302
Ph: (818)995-7100
Fax: (818)995-7466

Varvel, Dr. Doyle E., Cmdr.
National Chaplains Association
[20028]
c/o Dr. Doyle E. Varvel, National
Commander
PO Box 6418
Kingsport, TN 37663-1437
Ph: (276)466-0599

Vasami, Ralph, Esq., Exec. Dir.
PET Resin Association [2627]
355 Lexington Ave., Ste. 1500
New York, NY 10017
Ph: (212)297-2108
Fax: (212)370-9047

Vasey, Meg, Exec. Dir.
Tradeswomen, Inc. [11784]
337 17th St., Ste. 204
Oakland, CA 94612-3356
Ph: (510)891-8773
Fax: (510)891-8775

Vasina, Ute, VP
Original Doll Artists Council of
America [22007]
c/o Donna Sims, Treasurer
105 Cedar Ln.
Channelview, TX 77530

Vasquez, Mario, Contact
Stanford Chicano/Latino Alumni Association [19350]
c/o Frances C. Arrillaga Alumni
Center
326 Galvez St.
Stanford, CA 94305-6105
Ph: (650)723-2021
Toll Free: 800-786-2586

Vasquez, Tino, President
National Citizens Police Academy
  Association [5498]
PO Box 241
South Bend, IN 46624-0241

Vassar, Murray, President
Insurance Advertising Compliance
  Association [1863]
PO Box 26364
Tampa, FL 33623
Ph: (813)288-7492

Vaudt, David A., Chairman
Governmental Accounting Standards
  Board [4939]
401 Merritt 7
Norwalk, CT 06856-5116
Ph: (203)847-0700
Fax: (203)849-9714

Vaughan, Alex, Treasurer
Christian Association of World
  Languages [8179]
c/o Jennifer Good
Dept. of Modern Foreign Languages
1 Bear Pl., No. 97390
Waco, TX 76798-7390

Vaughn, Ben, CEO
American Association of adapted-
  SPORTS Programs [22770]
PO Box 451047
Atlanta, GA 31145
Ph: (404)294-0070

Vaughn, Eric, Exec. Dir.
National Structured Settlements
  Trade Association [5548]
1100 New York Ave. NW, Ste. 750W
Washington, DC 20005
Ph: (202)289-4004
Fax: (202)289-4002

Vaughn, Rob, Founder
Christian Wrestling Federation
  [23370]
331 County Line Rd.
Rockwall, TX 75032
Ph: (214)460-0477

Vaughn-Wiles, Gayle, President
American Overseas Schools Histori-
  cal Society [9373]
704 W Douglas Ave.
Wichita, KS 67203-6401
Ph: (316)265-6837

Vaught, Sir Knight Duane L, Officer
Grand Encampment of Knights Tem-
  plar [19558]
5909 West Loop South, Ste. 495
Bellaire, TX 77401-2402
Ph: (713)349-8700
Fax: (713)349-8710

Vaught, Russel S., Director
Association for Computing
  Machinery - Special Interest Group
  on University and College Comput-
  ing Services [7423]
c/o ACM
PO Box 3077
New York, NY 10087-0777
Ph: (814)863-0421
Fax: (814)863-7049

Vaught, Brig. Gen. (Ret.) Wilma L.,
  President
Women in Military Service for
  America Memorial Foundation
  [5850]
Dept. 560
Washington, DC 20042-0560
Ph: (703)533-1155
Toll Free: 800-222-2294
Fax: (703)931-4208

VavRosky, Linda, Director, President
Curly Sporthorse International [4346]
17829 Hubbard Gulch

Juliaetta, ID 83535
Ph: (208)276-7540

Vawter, Bruce, President
Vawter - Vauter - Vaughter Family
  Association [20940]
c/o Patricia Vawter Renton
2372 Bear Creek Rd.
Pipe Creek, TX 78063
Ph: (903)624-9632

Vazquez, Maj. Gen. Joseph R.,
  Cmdr.
Civil Air Patrol [5058]
105 S Hansell St., Bldg. 714
Maxwell AFB, AL 36112-6332
Toll Free: 877-227-9142

Veach, Damon, VP
American Hibiscus Society [22074]
PO Box 1580
Venice, FL 34284-1580
Ph: (941)627-1332

Veasley, Ms. Christin, Mem.
National Vulvodynia Association
  [17762]
PO Box 4491
Silver Spring, MD 20914-4491
Ph: (301)299-0775
Fax: (301)299-3999

Vecchia, Tracy Della, Exec. Dir.
MarineParents.com [12251]
3208 LeMone Industrial Blvd.
Columbia, MO 65205
Ph: (573)449-2003
Fax: (573)303-5502

Vecchione, Bob, Mem.
College Athletic Business Manage-
  ment Association [23222]
PO Box 24044
PO Box 24044
Los Angeles, CA 90024-0044
Ph: (310)825-2343
Fax: (310)267-2334

Vega, Elizabeth Sanchez, Founder,
  President
International Solidarity for Human
  Rights [18419]
12555 Biscayne Blvd., No. 915
North Miami, FL 33181

Vega, Ivan Martinez, Director
Mexico Tourism Board [23651]
152 Madison Ave., Ste. 1800
New York, NY 10016
Ph: (212)308-2110
Fax: (212)308-9060

Vehrs, Kris, JD, Exec. Dir.
Association of Zoos and Aquariums
  [7399]
8403 Colesville Rd., Ste. 710
Silver Spring, MD 20910-3314
Ph: (301)562-0777
Fax: (301)562-0888

Veit, Chuck, President
Navy & Marine Living History Association Inc. [9805]
41 Kelley Blvd.
North Attleboro, MA 02760-4734

Vela, Diana Richardson, President,
  CEO
Catholic Association of Latino Lead-
  ers [19808]
3424 Wilshire Blvd., 4th Fl.
Los Angeles, CA 90010
Ph: (213)637-7400

Vela, Henry, Treasurer
National Colorbred Association
  [21543]
c/o Henry Vela, Treasurer

620 Arawe Cir. E
Irving, TX 75060

Velasquez, Baldemar, President
Farm Labor Organizing Committee
  [23378]
1221 Broadway St.
Toledo, OH 43609
Ph: (419)243-3456
Fax: (419)243-5655

Velasquez, John, Chairman
Jockeys' Guild [22921]
448 Lewis Hargett Cir., Ste. 220
Lexington, KY 40503
Ph: (859)523-5625
Toll Free: 866-465-6257
Fax: (859)219-9892

Velazquez, Marianna, Coord.
Student Organization of North
  America [8630]
University Services Annex Bldg.
  300A, Rm. 108
University of Arizona
220 W 6th St.
Tucson, AZ 85701
Ph: (520)621-7761
Fax: (520)626-2675

Velazquez, Pauline, MSW, Founder
National Association of Puerto Rican
  Hispanic Social Workers [13112]
PO Box 651
Brentwood, NY 11717
Ph: (631)864-1536
Fax: (631)864-1536

Veldkamp, Steve, Exec. Dir.
Center for the Study of the College
  Fraternity [23755]
900 E 7th St., Ste. 371
Bloomington, IN 47405
Ph: (812)855-1235

Velebir, Ms. Arlys K., President
Bicuspid Aortic Foundation [15214]
30100 Town Center Dr., Ste. O-299
Laguna Niguel, CA 92677
Ph: (949)371-9223

Velhuizen, Laurie, Exec. Dir.
Gamma Phi Beta [23955]
12737 E Euclid Dr.
Centennial, CO 80111
Ph: (303)799-1874
Fax: (303)799-1876

Venator-Santiago, Charles, Mem.
Puerto Rican Studies Association
  [19621]
Dept. of Africana, Puerto Rican/
  Latino Studies
Hunter College, City University of
  New York
695 Park Ave., HW 1711
New York, NY 10065
Ph: (860)486-9052
Fax: (860)486-3794

Vendley, Dr. William F., Sec. Gen.
Religions for Peace International
  [18825]
777 United Nations Plz., 9th Fl.
New York, NY 10017
Ph: (212)687-2163

Veneman, Jim, Mem.
Baptist Communicators Association
  [19721]
c/o Margaret Colson, Executive
  Director
4519 Lashley Ct.
Marietta, GA 30068
Ph: (678)641-4457

Venneri, Joanna E., Director
National Braille Association [17730]

95 Allens Creek Rd., Bldg. 1, Ste.
  202
Rochester, NY 14618
Ph: (585)427-8260
Fax: (585)427-0263

Ventrell, Marvin, JD, Exec. Dir.
National Association of Addiction
  Treatment Providers [13161]
PO Box 6693
Denver, CO 80206
Toll Free: 888-574-1008
Fax: (888)574-1008

Ventura, Bernadette, President
Society for Hospitality and Foodser-
  vice Management [1397]
328 E Main St.
Louisville, KY 40202-2554
Ph: (502)574-9931
Fax: (502)589-3602

Veppert, Chuck, President
National Association of Professional
  Accident Reconstruction Special-
  ists [5749]
PO Box 866
Farmington, NH 03835
Ph: (603)332-3267

Vera Rocha, Ya'anna, Founder
Spirit of the Sage Council [3948]
439 Westwood SC, No. 144
Fayetteville, NC 28314-1532

Vera-Yu, Ayesha, CEO, Founder
Advancement for Rural Kids [10832]
10 E 85th St.
New York, NY 10028-0412

Verbruggen, Sandra, President
Shoe Service Institute of America
  [1403]
305 Huntsman Ct.
Bel Air, MD 21015
Ph: (410)569-3425
Fax: (410)569-8333

Verdugo-Peralta, Cynthia, CEO,
  President
Strategic Energy, Environmental and
  Transportation Alternatives [7898]
c/o Cynthia Verdugo-Peralta,
  President/Chief Executive Officer
18340 Yorba Linda Blvd., Ste. 107-
  509
Yorba Linda, CA 92886
Ph: (714)777-7729
Fax: (714)777-7728

Verespy, Nancy, Exec. Dir.
Veterans of the Vietnam War
  [21169]
805 S Township Blvd.
Pittston, PA 18640-3327
Ph: (570)603-9740
Toll Free: 800-843-8626
Fax: (570)603-9741

Verge, Laurie, Director
Surratt Society [9439]
Surratt House Museum
9118 Brandywine Rd.
Clinton, MD 20735
Ph: (301)868-1121
Fax: (301)868-8177

Verhagen, Dr. Frans C., President
Citizens Aviation Watch Association
  [361]
97-37 63rd Rd. 15 E
Rego Park, NY 11374-1600
Ph: (718)275-3932
Fax: (718)275-3932

Verma, Anil, Secretary
Burmese American Democratic Alliance [17824]

1952 Mcnair St.
Palo Alto, CA 94303
Ph: (415)895-2232

Vermeer, Dr. Maarten H., Ph.D.,
President
International Society for Cutaneous
Lymphomas [14498]
303 W State St.
Geneva, IL 60134
Ph: (630)578-3991
Fax: (630)262-1520

Vermeersch, B.C., Exec. Dir.
Musicians Foundation, Inc. [9961]
875 6th Ave., Ste. 2303
New York, NY 10001
Ph: (212)239-9137
Fax: (212)239-9138

Vermillion, Steve, Contact
Vietnam Dustoff Association [21171]
3103 31st Ave. SE
Puyallup, WA 98374
Ph: (253)906-2938

Vernikoff, Steven, Exec. Dir.
The Center for Family Support
[12320]
2811 Zulette Ave.
Bronx, NY 10461
Ph: (718)518-1500
Fax: (718)518-8200

Vernon, Simon, Chairman
Institute of International Container
Lessors [836]
1120 Connecticut Ave. NW, Ste. 440
Washington, DC 20036-3946
Ph: (202)223-9800
Fax: (202)223-9810

Verny, Thomas R., Founder
Association for Prenatal and Perinatal Psychology and Health [16905]
420 N Twin Oaks Valley Rd., Ste.
412
San Marcos, CA 92069
Ph: (760)492-9048

Verrier, Thomas, Exec. Sec.
College Band Directors National As-
sociation [8363]
c/o Thomas Verrier, Executive
Secretary
Blair School of Music
Vanderbilt University
2400 Blakemore Ave.
Nashville, TN 37212
Ph: (615)322-7651
Fax: (615)343-0324

Verrill, Mr. John H., Exec. Dir.
Early American Industries Associa-
tion [8901]
PO Box 524
Hebron, MD 21830-0524
Ph: (508)993-9578

Versteegh, Dr. Pien, Exec. Dir.
Polish American Historical Associa-
tion [10166]
Central Connecticut State University
1615 Stanley St.
New Britain, CT 06050
Ph: (860)832-3010
Fax: (248)738-6736

Vervliet, Jeroen, President
International Association of Law
Libraries [5563]
c/o Barbara Garavaglia, Secretary
University of Michigan Law Library
801 Monroe St.
Ann Arbor, MI 48109
Ph: (734)764-9338
Fax: (734)764-5863

Vessels, Lisa, President
National Federation of Paralegal Associations [5660]

1 Parkview Plz., Ste. 800
Oakbrook Terrace, IL 60181
Ph: (847)686-2247
Fax: (847)686-2251

Vessey, Mrs. Judy, Exec. Dir.
Klippel-Trenaunay Support Group
[13830]
1471 Greystone Ln.
Milford, OH 45150
Ph: (513)722-7724

Vest, Terri, President
American White Shepherd Association [21828]
c/o Shelley Caldwell, Chair
48 Aber Rd.
Finleyville, PA 15332
Ph: (412)384-5537

Vetter, Louise, CEO, President
Huntington's Disease Society of
America [15942]
505 8th Ave., Ste. 902
New York, NY 10018
Ph: (212)242-1968
Toll Free: 800-345-4372

Vetter, Stephen G., President, CEO
Partners of the Americas [17800]
1424 K St. NW, Ste. 700
Washington, DC 20005
Ph: (202)628-3300

Vial, Vanessa, Mgr.
Biscuit & Cracker Manufacturers As-
sociation [372]
6325 Woodside Ct., Ste. 125
Columbia, MD 21046
Ph: (443)545-1645
Fax: (410)290-8585

Viale, Pamela Hallquist, RN,
President
Advanced Practitioner Society for
Hematology and Oncology [16328]
Bldg. 1, Ste. 205
3131 Princeton Pke.
Lawrenceville, NJ 08648
Ph: (609)832-3000

Vibert, Joseph, Exec. Dir.
Association of Specialized and
Professional Accreditors [1012]
3304 N Broadway St., No. 214
Chicago, IL 60657
Ph: (773)857-7900
Fax: (888)859-4932

Vicente, Joana, Exec. Dir.
Independent Filmmaker Project
[1193]
30 John St.
Brooklyn, NY 11201
Ph: (212)465-8200
Fax: (212)465-8525

Vickers, Nancy, Treasurer
Dante Society of America [9049]
PO Box 600616
Newtonville, MA 02460
Ph: (617)831-9288

Vickers, Stephanie, President
Friends of Liberia [12961]
c/o Nimu Sidhu, Treasurer
648 E Johnson St., No. 3
Madison, WI 53703

Victor, Douglas R., Founder
International Association for Creative
Dance [9257]
PO Box 64213
Tucson, AZ 85728-4213

Victor, J. Scott, Chairman
Turnaround Management Association [2195]

150 N Wacker Dr., Ste. 1900
Chicago, IL 60606
Ph: (312)578-6900
Fax: (312)578-8336

Victor, Richard S., Exec. Dir.,
Founder
Grandparents Rights Organization
[11918]
1760 S Telegraph Rd.
Bloomfield Hills, MI 48302

Victor, Ron, President
Vibha [11179]
1030 E El Camino Real, No. 424
Sunnyvale, CA 94087
Ph: (408)997-9992
Fax: (775)593-1061

Vidales, Divina, Chairperson
Alpha Pi Sigma [23752]
PO Box 15374
San Diego, CA 92175-0374

Vidaver, Regina, PhD, Exec. Dir.
Free to Breathe [13973]
1 Point Pl., Ste. 200
Madison, WI 53719
Ph: (608)833-7905
Fax: (608)833-7906

Vidmer, Nina Albano, Exec. Dir.
American Osteopathic Academy of
Addiction Medicine [17306]
PO Box 3278
Oak Brook, IL 60522
Ph: (708)338-0760
Fax: (708)401-0360

Vidu, Prof. Ruxandra, President
American Romanian Academy of
Arts and Sciences [9014]
University of California Davis
1 Shields Ave.
Davis, CA 95616

Viebranz, Curtis G., President, CEO
Mount Vernon Ladies' Association
[10341]
3600 Mt. Vernon Memorial Hwy.
Mount Vernon, VA 22121
Ph: (703)780-2000

Viehland, Mr. Douglas, CAE, Mem.
Accreditation Council for Business
Schools and Programs [7618]
11520 W 119th St.
Overland Park, KS 66213-2002
Ph: (913)339-9356
Fax: (913)339-6226

Vieira, Carlos Alberto, President,
Chmn. of the Bd.
Brazilian-American Chamber of
Commerce [23567]
509 Madison Ave., Ste. 304
New York, NY 10022
Ph: (212)751-4691
Fax: (212)751-7692

Vieira, Guiga, President
People for Haiti [12711]
12157 W Linebaugh Ave., No. 357
Tampa, FL 33626
Ph: (813)750-7346

Vieira, Joseph B., Director
Luso-American Life Insurance
Society [19490]
7080 Donlon Way, Ste. 200
Dublin, CA 94568-2787
Ph: (925)828-4884
Toll Free: 877-525-5876
Fax: (925)828-4554

Viera, Rev. Manuel, President
Canon Law Society of America
[19806]

The Hecker Ctr., Ste. 111
415 Michigan Ave. NE
Washington, DC 20017-1102
Ph: (202)832-2350
Fax: (202)832-2331

Vieten, Cassandra, President, CEO
Institute of Noetic Sciences [20606]
101 San Antonio Rd.
Petaluma, CA 94952
Ph: (707)775-3500
Fax: (707)781-7420

Vieth, Mr. Victor, Director
Jacob Wetterling Resource Center
[11186]
2021 E Hennepin Ave., Ste.360
Minneapolis, MN 55413
Ph: (651)714-4673
Toll Free: 800-325-HOPE
Fax: (612)767-8585

Vietor, Carolynn, President
Women's Professional Rodeo As-
sociation [23105]
431 S Cascade Ave.
Colorado Springs, CO 80903
Ph: (719)447-4627
Fax: (719)447-4631

Vigil, Daryl A., Exec. Dir.
National Major Gang Task Force
[5144]
PO Box 3689
Pueblo, CO 81005
Ph: (719)226-4915

Vignola, Chad, Exec. Dir.
Literacy Design Collaborative [8245]
48 Wall St., 11th Fl.
New York, NY 10005

Viken, Pat, President
Norwegian Elkhound Association of
America [21934]
c/o Karen V. Freudendorf, Corresponding Secretary
4 Jerusalem Hollow Rd.
Manorville, NY 11949

Vikner, David W., President
Japan International Christian
University Foundation [20084]
475 Riverside Dr., Ste. 439
New York, NY 10115-0090
Ph: (212)870-3386

Vilkomerson, Rebecca, Exec. Dir.
Jewish Voice for Peace [19520]
1611 Telegraph Ave., Ste. 1020
Oakland, CA 94612
Ph: (510)465-1777
Fax: (510)465-1616

Villaflor, Marcel, Treasurer
International Society of Bassists
[9931]
14070 Proton Rd., Ste. 100
Dallas, TX 75244
Ph: (972)233-9107
Fax: (972)490-4219

Villafranca, Nancy, Director
Inter-University Program for Latino
Research [19429]
College of Liberal Arts and Sciences
University of Illinois at Chicago
412 S Peoria St., 3rd Fl.
Chicago, IL 60607
Ph: (312)413-7871

Villarreal, Lisa, Chairperson
Coalition for Community Schools
[8535]
c/o Institute for Educational Leadership
4301 Connecticut Ave. NW, Ste. 100
Washington, DC 20008-2304
Ph: (202)822-8405
Fax: (202)872-4050

Villata, Mark, Exec. Dir.
North American Blueberry Council
   [4246]
80 Iron Point Cir., Ste. 114
Folsom, CA 95630
Ph: (616)399-2052

Villers, Jim, President
International 190SL Group [21399]
c/o Jim Villers, President
3133 Inlet Rd.
Virginia Beach, VA 23454
Ph: (757)481-6398

Vincent, Howard K., CEO, President
Pheasants Forever [4870]
1783 Buerkle Cir.
Saint Paul, MN 55110
Ph: (651)773-2000
Toll Free: 877-773-2070
Fax: (651)773-5500

Vincent, John, President
United Drive-In Theatre Owners As-
   sociation [1207]
PO Box 24771
Middle River, MD 21220
Ph: (443)490-1250

Vincent, Mark, President
Federal Bar Association [5005]
1220 N Fillmore St., Ste. 444
Arlington, VA 22201
Ph: (571)481-9100
Fax: (571)481-9090

Vincent, Paul, MSW, Director,
   Founder
Child Welfare and Policy and
   Practice Group [10909]
428 E Jefferson St.
Montgomery, AL 36104
Ph: (334)264-8300
Fax: (334)264-8310

Vincent-Brunacini, Kelly, Exec. Dir.
Feminists For Nonviolent Choices
   [18208]
1255 University Ave., Ste. 146
Rochester, NY 14607
Ph: (585)319-4565

Vines, Eric, Exec. Dir.
World Forest Institute [4224]
World Forestry Ctr.
4033 SW Canyon Rd.
Portland, OR 97221
Ph: (503)228-1367
      (503)488-2130

Vinson, Christine, Chmn. of the Bd.
World Association of Detectives
   [2014]
7501 Sparrows Point Blvd.
Baltimore, MD 21219
Ph: (443)982-4586
Fax: (410)388-9746

Vinson, John, President
American Immigration Control
   Foundation [18461]
PO Box 525
Monterey, VA 24465
Ph: (540)468-2023
Fax: (540)468-2026

Vinson, Rev. Richard, Director,
   President
Recovered Alcoholic Clergy Associa-
   tion [13178]
PO Box 377
Solebury, PA 18963-0377
Ph: (215)297-5135

Vinson, Mr. Stephen L., CEO,
   President
United Methodist Association of
   Health and Welfare Ministries
   [14966]

218 S Thomas St., Ste. 212
Tupelo, MS 38801-3027
Ph: (662)269-2955
Fax: (662)269-2956

Vinyard, Roland, Exec. Sec.
IOCALUM [23326]
c/o Roland Vinyard, Executive
   Secretary, 597 State Highway 162
597 State Highway 162
Sprakers, NY 12166
Ph: (518)673-3212
Fax: (518)673-3219

Viola, Giulio, Rep.
Italy-America Chamber of Com-
   merce [23597]
730 5th Ave., Ste. 502
New York, NY 10019
Ph: (212)459-0044
Fax: (212)459-0090

Viola, Dr. Michael V., Director
Medicine for Peace [17006]
2732 Unicorn Ln. NW
Washington, DC 20015
Ph: (202)441-4545
Fax: (301)571-0769

Viola, Tom, Exec. Dir.
Broadway Cares/Equity Fights AIDS
   [10535]
165 W 46th St., Ste. 1300
New York, NY 10036
Ph: (212)840-0770
Fax: (212)840-0551

Virgo, Mr. Jeffery J., OTC, Chairman
National Board for Certification of
   Orthopaedic Technologists, Inc.
   [16484]
4736 Onondaga Blvd., No. 166
Syracuse, NY 13219
Toll Free: 866-466-2268
Fax: (866)466-7067

Virnig, Annie, Consultant
Equator Initiative [11355]
Bureau for Policy and Programme
   Support
304 E 45th St., Rm. 614
New York, NY 10017
Ph: (646)781-4023

Virtanen, Beth L., PhD, President
Finnish North American Literature
   Association [9323]
c/o Beth L. Virtanen, President
PO Box 212
L'Anse, MI 49946

Virtue, Ryan, Asst. Treas., Asst. Sec.
International Collegiate Licensing
   Association [2286]
c/o Robin Cooper, President
400 E. 7th St., Poplars Rm. No. 410
Bloomington, IN 47405
Ph: (440)892-4000
      (440)788-7466
Fax: (440)892-4007

Visco, Frances M., President
National Breast Cancer Coalition
   [14020]
1010 Vermont Ave. NW, Ste. 900
Washington, DC 20005
Ph: (202)296-7477
Toll Free: 800-622-2838
Fax: (202)265-6854

Visconti, Charles G., Chairman,
   President
International Cargo Gear Bureau
   [5566]
321 W 44th St.
New York, NY 10036
Ph: (212)757-2011
Fax: (212)757-2650

Viso, Mark, CEO, President
Private Agencies Collaborating
   Together [5445]
1828 L St. NW, Ste. 300
Washington, DC 20036-5104
Ph: (202)466-5666
Fax: (202)466-5665

Visotzky, Rabbi Burton L., PhD,
   Director
Louis Finkelstein Institute for
   Religious and Social Studies
   [20080]
c/o Jewish Theological Seminary
3080 Broadway
New York, NY 10027-4650
Ph: (212)678-8989

Vispo, Carol, VP of Admin.
Assistance League [12884]
3100 W Burbank Blvd., Ste. 100
Burbank, CA 91505-2348
Ph: (818)846-3777
Fax: (818)846-3535

Vissicaro, Pegge, President
Cross-Cultural Dance Resources
   [9248]
PO Box 872002
Tempe, AZ 85287-2002
Ph: (480)727-9532
Fax: (480)965-2247

Vissichelli, Mike, Officer
FireFlag/EMS [14695]
208 W 13th St.
New York, NY 10011
Ph: (917)885-0127

Vitas, Robert A., Exec. Dir.,
   Treasurer
Inter-University Seminar on Armed
   Forces and Society [5600]
Dept. of Political Science
Loyola University Chicago
1032 W Sheridan Rd.
Chicago, IL 60660
Ph: (773)508-2930
Fax: (773)508-2929

Vitek, Jan, Chairman
Special Interest Group on Program-
   ming Languages of ACM [7060]
c/o Jan Vitek, Chairman
Northeastern University
College of Computer & Information
   Science
440 Huntington Ave.
Boston, MA 02115
Fax: (765)494-0739

Vitelli, Francesca, Secretary
International Cellular Medicine
   Society [14879]
PO Box 371034
Las Vegas, NV 89137
Ph: (702)664-0017
Toll Free: 866-878-7717

Vivian, Mr. Robert Pond, Contact
Baronial Order of Magna Charta
   [9465]
c/o Robert Pond Vivian, Marshall
1285 Branch Rd.
Wells, ME 04090-6057

Vladeck, Bruce C., Chairperson
Medicare Rights Center [18328]
266 W 37th St., 3rd Fl.
New York, NY 10018
Ph: (212)869-3850
Toll Free: 800-333-4114
Fax: (212)869-3532

Vladich, Edward, Office Mgr.
Physicians' Research Network
   [16761]
39 W 19th St., Ste. 605

New York, NY 10011
Ph: (212)924-0857
Fax: (212)924-0759

Vliet, Marty Van, President
American Maine-Anjou Association
   [3701]
204 Marshall Rd.
Platte City, MO 64079-1100
Ph: (816)431-9950
Fax: (816)431-9951

Voce, Maria, President
Focolare Movement [19835]

Voeck, Julie, President
Professional Association of Volleyball
   Officials [23272]
c/o Julie Voeck, President
6905 Wellauer Dr.
Wauwatosa, WI 53213
Ph: (414)607-9918
Toll Free: 888-791-2074

Voegele, Robert, President
National Muzzle Loading Rifle As-
   sociation [23136]
State Road 62 Maxine Moss Dr.
Friendship, IN 47021
Ph: (812)667-5131
Toll Free: 800-745-1493
Fax: (812)667-5136

Vogel, Heidi, Exec. Sec.
International Horn Society [9929]
c/o Heidi Vogel, Executive Secretary
PO Box 630158
Lanai City, HI 96763-0158
Ph: (808)565-7273
Fax: (808)565-7273

Vogel, Michelle, MPA, Founder,
   Exec. Dir.
Alliance for Patient Advocacy
   [14973]
1747 Pennsylvania Ave. NW, Ste.
   470
Washington, DC 20006
Ph: (202)775-9110
Toll Free: 877-775-9110
Fax: (202)775-2074

Vogelzang, Jeanne M., Exec. Dir.
National Council of Structural
   Engineers Associations [6575]
645 N Michigan Ave., Ste. 540
Chicago, IL 60611
Ph: (312)649-4600
Fax: (312)649-5840

Vogt, Dr. Brent A., Founder
Cingulum NeuroSciences Institute
   [16044]
4435 Stephanie Dr.
Manlius, NY 13104

Voie, Ellen, CEO, President
Women in Trucking [3362]
PO Box 400
Plover, WI 54467-0400
Toll Free: 888-464-9482

Voisine, Don, Asst. Sec.
American Abstract Artists [8907]
PO Box 1076
New York, NY 10013

Voit, Walter E., President
Council on Ionizing Radiation
   Measurements and Standards
   [7081]
PO Box 851391
Richardson, TX 75085-1391
Ph: (301)591-8776
Fax: (972)883-5725

Volberding, Paul A., MD, Chairman
International AIDS Society USA
   [13547]

425 California St., Ste. 1450
San Francisco, CA 94104-2120
Ph: (415)544-9400
Fax: (415)544-9401

Volcy, Dr. Julio, Exec. Dir.
Haiti Teen Challenge [11745]
1619 Portland Ave. S
Minneapolis, MN 55404
Ph: (651)592-8774

Volk, Ben, Bd. Member
Ride and Tie Association [23252]
2709 Road 64
Pasco, WA 99301
Ph: (509)521-6249

Volk, Christine, VP
Independent Online Booksellers As-
sociation [2790]
c/o Chris Korczak, Vice-President
PO Box 311
Easthampton, MA 01027

Volk, Jason, Officer
International SalonSpa Business
Network [922]
4712 E 2nd St.
Belmont Shore, CA 90803
Ph: (562)453-3995
Toll Free: 866-444-4272

Volk, Tom, VP
Mycological Society of America
[6887]
PO Box 1897
Lawrence, KS 66044-8897
Toll Free: 800-627-0326
Fax: (785)843-6153

Volkman, Marian, President
Traumatic Incident Reduction As-
sociation [17533]
5145 Pontiac Trl.
Ann Arbor, MI 48105
Ph: (734)761-6268
Toll Free: 800-499-2751
Fax: (734)663-6861

Volkow, Dr. Nora D., Director
National Institutes of Health |
National Institute on Drug Abuse
[17323]
6001 Executive Blvd., Rm. 5213,
MSC 9561
Bethesda, MD 20892-9561
Ph: (301)443-1124

Volland, Len, Assoc. Dir.
Steamboaters [3949]
PO Box 41266
Eugene, OR 97404

Vollen, Lola, MD, Exec. Dir.,
Founder
The Life After Exoneration Program
[18073]
760 Wildcat Canyon
Berkeley, CA 94708
Ph: (510)292-6010

Vollman, David, Treasurer
Association of Veterans Affairs
Ophthalmologists [16377]
655 Beach St.
San Francisco, CA 94109
Ph: (415)561-8523
Fax: (415)561-8531

Vollmer, Amy Cheng, President
Waksman Foundation for Microbiol-
ogy [6107]
Swarthmore College
Dept. of Biology
500 College Ave.
Swarthmore, PA 19081-1390
Ph: (610)328-8044
Fax: (610)328-8663

Vollweiler, Cheryl, President
Association of Professional Insurance Women [1840]
c/o Susan Barros
The Beaumont Group, Inc.
990 Cedar Bridge Ave., Ste. B, PMB
210
Brick, NJ 08723-4157
Ph: (973)941-6024

Voltmann, Robert A., President, CEO
Transportation Intermediaries As-
sociation [3108]
1625 Prince St., Ste. 200
Alexandria, VA 22314
Ph: (703)299-5700
Fax: (703)836-0123

Von Ellefson, Randi, President
National Collegiate Choral Organiza-
tion [9159]
c/o Randi Von Ellefson, President
Wanda L. Bass School of Music
Oklahoma City University
2501 N Blackwelder Ave.
Oklahoma City, OK 73106

Von Fange, Michelle, Exec. Dir.
Smile for a Lifetime Foundation
[15160]
4565 Hilton Pkwy., Ste. 203
Colorado Springs, CO 80907

von Friedeburg, Arnim, Managing
Dir.
German Foods North America
[4476]
719 6th St. NW
Washington, DC 20001
Toll Free: 800-881-6419

von Gruber, Pamela, Exec. Dir.,
Publisher
International Strategic Studies As-
sociation [18084]
PO Box 320608
Alexandria, VA 22320
Ph: (703)548-1070
Fax: (703)684-7476

von Mogel, Karl Haro, Chairman
Biology Fortified, Inc. [6078]
6907 University Ave., No. 354
Middleton, WI 53562
Ph: (608)284-8842

von Stroebel, James-Michael,
President
Delta Phi Epsilon, Professional
Foreign Service Fraternity [23748]
3401 Prospect St. NW
Washington, DC 20007
Ph: (202)337-9702

Vonumu, Rena, Founder
Uplift a Child International [11280]
8705 Kodiak Dr.
Silver Spring, MD 20903-3500
Ph: (301)768-3020
(240)832-9234

Voorhees, Bob, President
Building Africa [11322]
5901 Warner Ave., Ste. 171
Huntington Beach, CA 92649
Ph: (714)625-8172

Vorp, David A., PhD, President
International Society for Applied
Cardiovascular Biology [14125]
c/o Steven P. Schmidt, PhD
1023 Rambling Way
Akron, OH 44333
Ph: (330)730-3331

Vos, Nelvin, Exec. Dir.
Society for the Arts, Religion and
Contemporary Culture [9001]

15811 Kutztown Rd., Box 15
Maxatawny, PA 19538
Ph: (610)683-7581
Fax: (610)683-7581

Vosburgh, Kris, Exec. Dir.
Howard Jarvis Taxpayers Association [19160]
621 S Westmoreland Ave., Ste. 202
Los Angeles, CA 90005-3903
Ph: (213)384-9656
(916)444-9950

Vosburgh, Richard, Chairman
HR People and Strategy [2169]
1800 Duke St.
Alexandria, VA 22314
Toll Free: 888-602-3270
Fax: (703)535-6490

Voss, Katherine, President, Exec.
Dir.
Open DeviceNet Vendor Association
[6281]
4220 Varsity Dr., Ste. A
Ann Arbor, MI 48108-5006
Ph: (734)975-8840
Fax: (734)922-0027

Voss, Tom, Treasurer
Ariel Motorcycle Club North America
[22213]
c/o Tom Voss, Treasurer
PO Box 77737
Stockton, CA 95267-1037

Voth, Eric, Chairman
Institute on Global Drug Policy
[13145]
Journal of Global Drug Policy and
Practice
2600 9th St. N, Ste. 200
Saint Petersburg, FL 33704-2744
Ph: (727)828-0211
Fax: (727)828-0210

Vough, Kelly, Program Mgr., Coord.
Pacific Whale Foundation [4865]
300 Ma'alaea Rd.
Wailuku, HI 96793
Ph: (808)249-8811
Toll Free: 800-942-5311
Fax: (808)243-9021

Voyatzis, Lisette, Cmte. Mgmt. Ofc.
National Endowment for the Humani-
ties [8006]
400 7th St. SW
Washington, DC 20506
Ph: (202)606-8400
(202)606-8244
Toll Free: 800-634-1121

Vrac, James, Exec. Dir.
Academy of Psychosomatic
Medicine [16953]
5272 River Rd., Ste. 630
Bethesda, MD 20816-1453
Ph: (301)718-6520
Fax: (301)656-0989

Vrana Cunningham, Jodene,
President
D'Youville College Alumni Associa-
tion [19321]
631 Niagara St.
Buffalo, NY 14201
Ph: (716)829-7805
Fax: (716)829-7821

Vranas, Chris, Exec. Dir.
American Association of
Orthodontists [14392]
401 N Lindbergh Blvd.
Saint Louis, MO 63141-7816
Ph: (314)993-1700
Toll Free: 800-424-2841
Fax: (314)997-1745

Vredenburg, Elliot, Prog. Dir.
PEN Center USA [10392]
PO Box 6037
Beverly Hills, CA 90212
Ph: (323)424-4939
Fax: (323)424-4944

Vredenburg, Seth, President
Omega Tau Sigma [23982]
PO Box 876
Ithaca, NY 14851-0876

Vredenburgh, Judy, CEO, President
Girls Inc. [13447]
120 Wall St.
New York, NY 10005-3902
Ph: (212)509-2000

Vroom, Jay J., CEO, President
CropLife America [717]
1156 15th St. NW
Washington, DC 20005
Ph: (202)296-1585
Fax: (202)463-0474

Vukelich, Daniel J., Esq., President,
CEO
Association of Medical Device Re-
processors [15715]
429 R St. NW
Washington, DC 20001
Ph: (202)747-6566

W

W., Tom, Office Mgr.
Marijuana Anonymous World
Services [12875]
340 S Lemon Ave., No. 9420
Walnut, CA 91789-2706
Toll Free: 800-766-6779

Wacht, Peter G., CAE, Exec. Dir.
National Academy of Elder Law At-
torneys [5546]
1577 Spring Hill Rd., Ste. 310
Vienna, VA 22182
Ph: (703)942-5711
Fax: (703)563-9504

Wachter, Donna, Exec. Dir.
Association of Professors of
Gynecology and Obstetrics
[16277]
2130 Priest Bridge Dr., Ste. 7
Crofton, MD 21114-2457
Ph: (410)451-9560
Fax: (410)451-9568

Wachtler, Janice, Exec. Dir.
American College of Osteopathic
Emergency Physicians [14674]
142 E Ontario St., Ste. 1500
Chicago, IL 60611-5277
Ph: (312)587-3709
Toll Free: 800-521-3709
Fax: (312)587-9951

Wackernagel, Mathis, President
Global Footprint Network [4003]
312 Clay St., Ste. 300
Oakland, CA 94607-3510
Ph: (510)839-8879
Fax: (510)251-2410

Wacks, Mr. Mel, President
American-Israel Numismatic As-
sociation [22255]
PO Box 20255
Fountain Hills, AZ 85269-0255
Ph: (818)225-1348

Wada, Yoshihiro, Dep. Dir.
Japan Foundation [9623]
152 W 57th St., 17th Fl.
New York, NY 10019
Ph: (212)489-0299
Fax: (212)489-0409

Wadas, Alicia A., Founder, President
Mothers Arms [12865]
4757 E Greenway Rd., No. 124
Phoenix, AZ 85032
Toll Free: 800-464-4840

Waddell, Kristen Myers, President
Commission on Missing and
 Exploited Children [10945]
616 Adams Ave., Ste. 102
Memphis, TN 38105
Ph: (901)405-8441

Waddick, Jim, Chairman
Species Iris Group of North America
 [22127]
8871 NW Brostrom Rd.
Kansas City, MO 64152-2711

Wade, Alvin, Treasurer
The Elisa Project [14639]
10300 N Central Expy., Ste. 330
Dallas, TX 75231
Ph: (214)369-5222
Toll Free: 866-837-1999
Fax: (214)987-4518

Wade, Drew, Exec. Dir.
International Christian Cycling Club
 [22747]
6834 S University, No. 232
Centennial, CO 80122
Ph: (720)870-3707

Wade, Jeanie, HT, President
American Society for Mohs Histo-
 technology [15679]
555 E Wells St., Ste. 1100
Milwaukee, WI 53202-3800
Ph: (414)918-9813
Fax: (414)276-3349

Wade, Julian, President
Association of Information Technol-
 ogy Professionals [7652]
1120 Route 73, Ste. 200
Mount Laurel, NJ 08054-5113
Ph: (856)380-6910
Toll Free: 800-224-9371
Fax: (856)439-0525

Wade, Kara Jenelle, Founder
Delta Chi Xi Honorary Dance
 Fraternity [23716]
3218 Hiddenwood Ln.
Burlington, NC 27215
Ph: (336)437-4479

Wade, Lisa, President
ImpactAVillage [11382]
5859 Wedgewood Dr.
Granite Bay, CA 95746
Ph: (916)214-0579

Wade, Melissa, Mgr.
Special Military Active Recreational
 Travelers [21033]
600 University Office Blvd., Ste. 1A
Pensacola, FL 32504-6238
Ph: (850)478-1986
Toll Free: 800-354-7681

Wade, Sam, CEO
National Rural Water Association
 [12805]
2915 S 13th St.
Duncan, OK 73533
Ph: (580)252-0629
Fax: (580)255-4476

Wadeborn, Ulf, President
Swedish Warmblood Association of
 North America [4414]
24875 SW Middleton Rd.
Sherwood, OR 97140
Ph: (575)835-1318
Fax: (575)835-1321

Wadler, Julie, President, Exec. Dir.
AHOPE for Children [10840]
104 Hume Ave.

Alexandria, VA 22301-1015
Ph: (703)683-7500
Fax: (703)683-4482

Wadley, Bill, President
College Swimming Coaches As-
 sociation of America [23282]
1585 Wesleyan Dr., Unit A
Norfolk, VA 23502
Ph: (540)460-6563

Wadsworth, Harrison M., Exec. Dir.
Coalition of Higher Education As-
 sistance Organizations [7831]
1101 Vermont Ave. NW, Ste. 400
Washington, DC 20005-3521
Ph: (202)289-3910
Fax: (202)371-0197

Wadsworth, Jonathan, Sec. Gen.,
 Exec. Sec.
Consultative Group on International
 Agricultural Research [12148]
900 19th St. NW, 6th Fl.
Washington, DC 20433
Ph: (202)473-8951
Fax: (202)473-8110

Wadsworth, Sophie, Exec. Dir.
The Nature Connection [10675]
PO Box 155
Concord, MA 01742
Ph: (978)369-2585

Wadsworth, Susan, Director,
 Founder
Young Concert Artists [10027]
250 W 57th St., Ste. 1222
New York, NY 10107
Ph: (212)307-6655
Fax: (212)581-8894

Waeger, Daniel, Founder
National Collegiate Cancer Founda-
 tion [14025]
4858 Battery Ln., No. 216
Bethesda, MD 20814
Ph: (240)515-6262

Wafer, Joani, Founder
Kids Korps USA [13302]
11526 Sorrento Valley Rd.
San Diego, CA 92121
Ph: (858)500-8136
Fax: (858)847-9161

Wager, Jody, President
American Dance Therapy Associa-
 tion [16959]
10632 Little Patuxent Pky., Ste. 108
Columbia, MD 21044
Ph: (410)997-4040
Fax: (410)997-4048

Wager, Joe, VP
New York State Turf and Landscape
 Association [2072]
1 Prospect Ave.
White Plains, NY 10607
Ph: (914)993-9455
Fax: (914)993-9051

Waggoner, Darrel, MD, President
Association of Professors of Human
 and Medical Genetics [14877]
c/o Darrel Waggoner, President
5841 S Maryland Ave., Rm. L161
Chicago, IL 60637
Ph: (773)834-0555
Fax: (773)834-0556

Waggoner, Martha, Chairperson
The Newspaper Guild [23485]
501 3rd St. NW
Washington, DC 20001-2797
Ph: (202)434-7177
Fax: (202)434-1472

Wagner, Charles P., President
Browning Collectors Association
 [22018]

c/o Charles P. Wagner, President
711 Scott St.
Covington, KY 41011
Ph: (859)431-1712

Wagner, Derik, President
International Superyacht Society
 [435]
757 SE 17th St., No. 744
Fort Lauderdale, FL 33316
Ph: (954)525-6625
Fax: (954)525-5325

Wagner, Dick, Founder, Curator
Center for Wooden Boats [22606]
1010 Valley St.
Seattle, WA 98109-4468
Ph: (206)382-2628
Fax: (206)382-2699

Wagner, Emily, Secretary
National Association of Royalty Own-
 ers [2529]
15 W 6th St., Ste. 2626
Tulsa, OK 74119
Ph: (918)794-1660
Toll Free: 800-558-0557
Fax: (918)794-1662

Wagner, J. Richard, Chairman
National Standard Plumbing Code
 Committee [5069]
180 S Washington St.
Falls Church, VA 22046
Ph: (703)237-8100
Toll Free: 800-533-7694
Fax: (703)237-7442

Wagner, Bro. Jolleen, Director
Lasallian Volunteers [20429]
415 Michigan Ave. NE, 3rd Fl.
Washington, DC 20017
Ph: (202)529-0047
Fax: (202)529-0775

Wagner, Judith
World Organization for Early Child-
 hood Education - U.S. National
 Committee [7597]
c/o Bronwyn Fees, Ph.D., Member-
 ship Chairperson
Family Studies & Human Services
College of Human Ecology
Kansas State University
303 Justin Hall
Manhattan, KS 66506

Wagner, Leslie, Exec. Dir.
Southern Peanut Growers [4514]
1025 Sugar Pike Way
Canton, GA 30115
Ph: (770)751-6615

Wagner, Paul, Chairman
American Registry for Diagnostic
 Medical Sonography [17231]
1401 Rockville Pke., Ste. 600
Rockville, MD 20852-1402
Ph: (301)738-8401
Toll Free: 800-541-9754
Fax: (301)738-0312

Wagner, Steve, Director
Society for the Eradication of Televi-
 sion [17957]
PO Box 10491
Oakland, CA 94610-0491

Wagner, Susan, Founder, President
Equine Advocates [10617]
PO Box 354
Chatham, NY 12037-0354
Ph: (518)245-1599

Wagner, Susan, Exec. Dir.
International Society for Computer-
 ized Electrocardiology [14127]
6 Boston Rd., Ste. 202

Chelmsford, MA 01824
Ph: (978)250-9847
Fax: (978)250-1117

Wagoner, James, President
Advocates for Youth [11834]
2000 M St. NW, Ste. 750
Washington, DC 20036
Ph: (202)419-3420
Fax: (202)419-1448

Wagoner, James, Director
Pro-Choice Public Education Project
 [10433]
PO Box 3952
New York, NY 10163
Ph: (212)977-4266

Wah, Marcel, Exec. Dir., Founder
Haitian Art Education and Appraisal
 Society [8975]
11 S Main St., Ste. 1
Boonsboro, MD 21713
Ph: (301)637-4934
Fax: (240)715-6416

Wahlers, Larry, Exec. Dir.
Moderation Management [17315]
2795 E Bidwell St., Ste. 100-244
Folsom, CA 95630-6480

Wahlquist, Mr. Richard, CEO,
 President
American Staffing Association [1085]
277 S Washington St., Ste. 200
Alexandria, VA 22314
Ph: (703)253-2020
Fax: (703)253-2053

Wahmann, Robert, President
Neuroendocrine Cancer Awareness
 Network [14033]
2480 Hull Ave.
North Bellmore, NY 11710
Ph: (516)781-7814
Toll Free: 866-850-9555

Waidelich, William D., EdD, Exec.
 Dir.
Association for Middle Level Educa-
 tion [8341]
4151 Executive Pky., Ste. 300
Westerville, OH 43081-3871
Ph: (614)895-4730
Toll Free: 800-528-6672
Fax: (614)895-4750

Waites, Dick, Secretary
Professional Knifemakers Associa-
 tion, Inc. [21779]
2905 N Montana Ave., Ste. 30027
Helena, MT 59601
Ph: (618)753-2147

Wakefield, Nathan, Chairman,
 Coord.
International Jugglers' Association
 [22968]
PO Box 580005
Kissimmee, FL 34758
Ph: (714)584-4533

Walborn, Rachel, President
Everyone Needs a Hero [11357]
27596 Sweetbrier Ln.
Mission Viejo, CA 92691
Ph: (619)807-0415

Walbrun, Dan, President
Thimble Collectors International
 [21727]
1209 Hill Rd. N, No. 253
Pickerington, OH 43147

Walbrun, Mark, Director
Central Electric Railfans' Association
 [22408]
PO Box 503

Chicago, IL 60690-0503
Ph: (312)987-4391

Walczyk, Teresa, VP
Catholic Alumni Clubs International
[19313]
13517 Teakwood Ln.
Germantown, MD 20874-1034

Wald, Sara, Mem.
North Dakota State University
Foundation and Alumni Association
[19337]
1241 University Dr. N
Fargo, ND 58102-2524
Ph: (701)231-6800
(701)231-6834
Toll Free: 800-279-8971
Fax: (701)231-6801

Walda, John, CEO, President
National Association of College and
University Business Officers **[7432]**
1110 Vermont Ave. NW, Ste. 800
Washington, DC 20005
Ph: (202)861-2500
(202)861-2517
Toll Free: 800-462-4916
Fax: (202)861-2583

Waldbart, Ted, CEO, President
Health and Education Relief
Organization **[12160]**
PO Box 670804
Marietta, GA 30066
Ph: (678)494-5595
Fax: (678)494-5533

Walden, Greg, Chairman
National Republican Congressional
Committee **[19043]**
320 1st St. SE
Washington, DC 20003
Ph: (202)479-7000

Walden, Richard M., CEO, President
Operation U.S.A. **[12296]**
7421 Beverly Blvd.
Los Angeles, CA 90036
Ph: (323)413-2353
Toll Free: 800-678-7255
Fax: (323)931-5400

Walder, Bethanie, Exec. Dir.
Society for Ecological Restoration
International **[4014]**
1133 15th St. NW, Ste. 300
Washington, DC 20005
Ph: (202)299-9518
Fax: (270)626-5485

Waldman, Michael, President
New York University School of Law |
Brennan Center for Justice **[5680]**
161 Avenue of the Americas, 12th
Fl.
New York, NY 10013
Ph: (646)292-8310
Fax: (212)463-7308

Waldron, Roger, President
Coalition for Government Procure-
ment **[1513]**
1990 M St. NW, Ste. 450
Washington, DC 20036
Ph: (202)331-0975
Fax: (202)521-3533

Waldrop, Alex, CEO, President
National Thoroughbred Racing As-
sociation **[22926]**
2525 Harrodsburg Rd., Ste. 510
Lexington, KY 40504
Ph: (859)245-6872
Fax: (859)422-1230

Waldrop, Mark, President
United States Permafrost Association **[7195]**

PO Box 750141
Fairbanks, AK 99775-0141
Ph: (302)831-0852
Fax: (302)831-6654

Walen, Andrew, President
National Association for Males with
Eating Disorders **[14647]**
164 Palm Dr., No. 2
Naples, FL 34112

Walenta, Christian, Advisor
International Association for Information and Data Quality **[6743]**
6920 Brookmill Rd.
Baltimore, MD 21215
Ph: (410)484-0304
(813)343-2163

Wali, Ashutosh, President
Society for Airway Management
[15669]
5753 Tanager St.
Schererville, IN 46375
Ph: (773)834-3171
Fax: (773)834-3166

Walker, Clint, Chairman
Cancer Care Connection **[13918]**
1 Innovation Way, Ste. 400
Newark, DE 19711
Ph: (302)266-8050
Toll Free: 866-266-7008
Fax: (302)266-9687

Walker, David A., Founder, President
National Double Dutch League
[23106]
888 Grand Concourse, Ste. 6i
Bronx, NY 10451
Ph: (212)865-9606

Walker, David W., President, CEO
Coalition to Salute America's Heroes
[21117]
552 Ft. Evans Rd., Ste. 300
Leesburg, VA 20176-3378
Ph: (703)291-4605
Toll Free: 888-447-2588

Walker, Dee Anne, Secretary,
Treasurer
United Furniture Workers Insurance
Fund **[1491]**
1910 Air Lane Dr.
Nashville, TN 37210
Ph: (615)889-8860
Fax: (615)391-0865

Walker, Gail, Exec. Dir.
Interreligious Foundation for Com-
munity Organization **[11472]**
418 W 145th St.
New York, NY 10031
Ph: (212)926-5757
Fax: (212)926-5842

Walker, Jack, VP
Chain Drug Marketing Association
[2555]
43157 W 9 Mile Rd.
Novi, MI 48376
Ph: (248)449-9300
Fax: (248)449-9396

Walker, James, PhD, President
American Board of Sexology **[17191]**
PO Box 1166
Winter Park, FL 32790-1166
Ph: (407)645-1641

Walker, James K., President
Watchman Fellowship **[20051]**
PO Box 13340
Arlington, TX 76094-0340
Ph: (817)277-0023
Fax: (817)277-8098

Walker, Jason, Exec. Dir.
Sigma Pi Fraternity, International
[23932]

106 N Castle Heights Ave.
Lebanon, TN 37087
Ph: (615)921-2300
Toll Free: 800-332-1897
Fax: (615)373-8949

Walker, Jim, CEO
International Certified Floorcovering
Installers Association **[870]**
12201 W 88th St.
Lenexa, KS 66215
Ph: (816)231-4646
Fax: (816)231-4343

Walker, Johnnie, Chairperson,
Founder
National Association of Black
Female Executives in Music and
Entertainment **[1148]**
111 S Highland, Ste. 388
Memphis, TN 38111
Ph: (901)236-8439

Walker, Kevin S., Director, President,
Founder
Project Appleseed: The National
Campaign for Public School
Improvement **[7824]**
520 Melville Ave.
Saint Louis, MO 63130-4506
Ph: (314)292-9760
Fax: (314)725-2319

Walker, Kiera, Associate
Advertising Women of New York **[82]**
25 W 43rd St., Ste. 912
New York, NY 10036
Ph: (212)221-7969
Fax: (212)221-8296

Walker, Leah A., Chairperson
Association of Reporters of Judicial
Decisions **[5378]**
c/o Kevin J. Loftus, Treasurer
157 Pease Rd.
East Longmeadow, MA 01028-3113

Walker, Lisa, President
North American Association of Com-
mencement Officers **[7968]**
191 Clarksville Rd.
Princeton Junction, NJ 08550
Ph: (254)710-8534
Toll Free: 877-622-2606

Walker, Margaret, President
The Benjamin Banneker Association,
Inc. **[8278]**
PO Box 55864
Little Rock, AR 72215

Walker, Marie, Contact
Anguilla Tourist Board **[23656]**
246 Central Ave.
White Plains, NY 10606
Ph: (914)287-2400
Toll Free: 877-4AN-GUILLA
Fax: (914)287-2404

Walker, Mark A., Chmn. of the Bd.
Population Council **[12515]**
1 Dag Hammarskjold Plz.
New York, NY 10017
Ph: (212)339-0500
Toll Free: 877-339-0500
Fax: (212)755-6052

Walker, MD, William B., Contact
America's Essential Hospitals
[15301]
401 9th St. NW, Ste. 900
Washington, DC 20004-1712
Ph: (202)585-0100

Walker, Dr. Michael D., Chairman
Brain Attack Coalition **[17295]**
Bldg. 31, Rm. 8A-16
31 Center Dr., MSC 2540

Bethesda, MD 20892
Ph: (301)496-5751

Walker, Muffy, Chairman
International Bipolar Foundation
[15775]
8895 Town Centre Dr., Ste. 105-360
San Diego, CA 92122
Ph: (858)764-2496
Fax: (858)764-2491

Walker, Patricia, President
American Association of Philatelic
Exhibitors **[21606]**
c/o Mike Ley, Secretary
330 Sonja Dr.
Doniphan, NE 68832-9795
Ph: (248)540-0948
Fax: (248)540-0905

Walker, Patricia, President
Society of Military Widows **[21043]**
5535 Hempstead Way
Springfield, VA 22151-4010
Toll Free: 800-842-3451

Walker, Paul, V. Chmn. of the Bd.
Arms Control Association **[18121]**
1313 L St. NW, Ste. 130
Washington, DC 20005
Ph: (202)463-8270
Fax: (202)463-8273

Walker, Paulette C., President
Delta Sigma Theta Sorority, Inc.
[23871]
1707 New Hampshire Ave. NW
Washington, DC 20009
Ph: (202)986-2400
Fax: (202)986-2513

Walker, Quiteya, President
American Rehabilitation Counseling
Association **[17082]**
c/o Quiteya Walker, President
Albany State University
504 College Dr.
Albany, GA 31705
Ph: (229)430-4783

Walker, Ronnie, Founder, CEO
Alliance of Hope for Suicide Loss
Survivors **[13190]**
PO Box 7005
Evanston, IL 60201
Ph: (847)868-3313

Walker, Rusty, President
International Dodge Ball Federation
[23229]
3451A Washington Ave.
Gulfport, MS 39507
Ph: (228)863-9000

Walker, Sandra, Officer
International Compressor Remanu-
facturers Association **[1625]**
1505 Carthage Rd.
Lumberton, NC 28358
Ph: (910)301-7060
Fax: (910)738-6994

Walker, Shane, Director
International Federation of
Chiropractors and Organizations
[14275]
2276 Wassergass Rd.
Hellertown, PA 18055
Toll Free: 800-521-9856

Walker, Teresa, President
Association of Legal Administrators
[5417]
Presidents Plz.
8700 W Bryn Mawr Ave., Ste. 110S
Chicago, IL 60631-3512
Ph: (847)267-1252
Fax: (847)267-1329

Walker, Valencia, MD, President
Association of Black Women Physicians [16740]
4712 Admiralty Way, Ste. 175
Marina del Rey, CA 90292
Ph: (310)321-8688

Walker, W. Danforth, Officer
American Philatelic Society [22302]
100 Match Factory Pl.
Bellefonte, PA 16823
Ph: (814)933-3803
Fax: (814)933-6128

Walker, Wendy, Coord.
Association for Slavic, East European, and Eurasian Studies [10215]
University of Pittsburgh
203C Bellefield Hall
Pittsburgh, PA 15260-6424
Ph: (412)648-9911
Fax: (412)648-9815

Walker, Wren, Founder
The Witches' Voice [20638]
PO Box 341018
Tampa, FL 33694-1018

Walker-Daniels, Kim, Secretary
American Water Spaniel Club [21826]
c/o Sue Liemohn, President
18515 Lake George Blvd. NW
Anoka, MN 55303-8439
Ph: (651)748-2830
(920)435-3558

Walkinshaw, Charlie, Director
Experience International [3861]
PO Box 680
Everson, WA 98247
Ph: (360)966-3876
Fax: (360)966-4131

Walkup, Kenny, Exec. Dir.
Phi Delta Chi [23846]
PO Box 320
Pinckney, MI 48169
Toll Free: 800-732-1883
Fax: (248)446-6065

Wall, Bruce, Treasurer
International Society of Crime Prevention Practitioners [11507]
PO Box 15584
Scottsdale, AZ 85267
Ph: (657)888-4277

Wall, Rev. John J., President, CEO
Catholic Church Extension Society of the U.S.A. [19810]
150 S Wacker Dr., Ste. 2000
Chicago, IL 60606
Ph: (312)795-5109
Toll Free: 800-842-7804
Fax: (312)236-5276

Wall, Lori, Corr. Sec.
Mid Atlantic Fiber Association [246]
c/o David Banks, Membership Chairman
215 Charter House Ln.
Williamsburg, VA 23188-7808
Ph: (757)258-8632

Wall, Mark, VP
Lewy Body Dementia Association, Inc. [15951]
912 Killian Hill Rd. SW
Lilburn, GA 30047-3110
Ph: (404)935-6444
Toll Free: 800-539-9767
Fax: (480)422-5434

Walla, Joseph, Chmn. of the Bd.
The Society of Marine Port Engineers of New York [3102]

111 Broad St.
Eatontown, NJ 07724
Ph: (732)389-2009
Fax: (732)389-2264

Wallace, Brian, CEO, President
Coin Laundry Association [2076]
1 S 660 Midwest Rd., Ste. 205
Oakbrook Terrace, IL 60181
Toll Free: 800-570-5629
Fax: (630)953-7925

Wallace, Candy, Exec. Dir., Founder
American Personal and Private Chef Association [698]
4572 Delaware St.
San Diego, CA 92116-1005
Ph: (619)294-2436
Toll Free: 800-644-8389

Wallace, Carol, Chairman
Childhood Arthritis and Rheumatology Research Alliance [17156]
2608 Erwin Rd., Ste. 148-191
Durham, NC 27705
Ph: (919)668-7531
Toll Free: 800-377-5731

Wallace, Darrell, Exec. Dir., Secretary, Treasurer
Society of the First Infantry Division [20725]
c/o Jen Sanford
PO Box 607
Ambler, PA 19002
Ph: (215)654-1969
Fax: (215)654-0392

Wallace, David, Exec. Sec.
Brown Swiss Association [3722]
800 Pleasant St.
Beloit, WI 53511-5456
Ph: (608)365-4474
Fax: (608)365-5577

Wallace, Deanna, Founder, Exec. Dir.
All As One - USA [10844]
PO Box 4903
Spanaway, WA 98387
Ph: (253)846-0815
Fax: (253)846-0815

Wallace, Don, Chairman
International Council for Middle East Studies [18684]
The Old Foundry Bldg., Ste. M100
1055 Thomas Jefferson St. NW
Washington, DC 20007-5219
Ph: (212)758-3817

Wallace, Prof. Don, Jr., Chairman
International Law Institute [5350]
1055 Thomas Jefferson St. NW, Ste. M-100
Washington, DC 20007
Ph: (202)247-6006
Fax: (202)247-6010

Wallace, Don, Comm. Chm.
National Auto Auction Association [262]
5320 Spectrum Dr., Ste. D
Frederick, MD 21703
Ph: (301)696-0400
Fax: (301)631-1359

Wallace, Elizabeth, Exec. Dir.
Mobile Health Clinics Association [15036]
2275 Schuetz Rd.
Saint Louis, MO 63146
Ph: (314)764-2288
Fax: (314)569-0721

Wallace, James, Exec. Dir., President
Society for the Preservation of English Language and Literature [7870]

PO Box 321
Braselton, GA 30517
Ph: (770)586-0184

Wallace, Jo-Ann, CEO, President
National Legal Aid and Defender Association [5547]
1901 Pennsylvania Ave. NW, Ste. 500
Washington, DC 20006
Ph: (202)452-0620
Fax: (202)872-1031

Wallace, Jon, Founder
Personal Submersibles Organization [6905]
PO Box 53
Weare, NH 03281
Ph: (603)232-9157

Wallace, Mr. J.W. George, Editor
American Defenders of Bataan and Corregidor [21189]
945 Main St.
Wellsburg, WV 26070

Wallace, Kacie, President
International Junior Brangus Breeders Association [3730]
5750 Epsilon
San Antonio, TX 78249
Ph: (405)867-1421

Wallace, Mark, CEO
United Against Nuclear Iran [18762]
PO Box 1028
New York, NY 10185-1028
Ph: (212)554-3296
Fax: (212)682-1238

Wallace, Marsha, Founder
Dining for Women [13374]
PO Box 25633
Greenville, SC 29616-0633
Ph: (864)335-8401

Wallace, Paul, CEO
AcademyHealth [14921]
1666 K St. NW, Ste. 1100
Washington, DC 20036
Ph: (202)292-6700
Fax: (202)292-6800

Wallace, Richard, Treasurer
Society for Economic Anthropology [5922]
c/o Dolores Koenig, President
Hamilton - 202A
College of Arts and Sciences - Anthropology
American University
Washington, DC 20016

Wallace, Richard, VP, Comm.
Southern Pine Council [3511]
c/o Southern Forest Product Association
6660 Riverside Dr., Ste. 212
Metairie, LA 70003-3200
Ph: (504)443-4464
Fax: (504)443-6612

Wallace, Ronald A., President
Creative Musicians Coalition [2422]
PO Box 6205
Peoria, IL 61601-6205
Ph: (309)685-4843
Toll Free: 800-882-4262
Fax: (309)685-4879

Wallace, Twyla, President, Editor
Federation for Accessible Nursing Education and Licensure [16132]
PO Box 1418
Lewisburg, WV 24901-4418
Ph: (304)645-4357

Wallace-Padgett, Bishop Debra, President
General Commission on the Status and Role of Women [18209]

77 W Washington St., Ste. 1500
Chicago, IL 60602
Ph: (312)346-4900
Toll Free: 800-523-8390
Fax: (312)346-3986

Waller, Irvin, President
International Organization for Victim Assistance [13260]
32465 NE Old Parrett Mountain Rd.
Newberg, OR 97132
Ph: (503)554-1552
Fax: (503)554-1532

Wallis, Hilary, Exec. Dir., Founder
Artfully AWARE [8959]
201 E 17th St., 27D
New York, NY 10003

Wallis, Jim, President, Founder
Sojourners [20008]
3333 14th St. NW, Ste. 200
Washington, DC 20010
Ph: (202)328-8842
(917)288-9529
Toll Free: 800-714-7474
Fax: (202)328-8757

Wallis, Norman, PhD, Exec. Dir.
The American College of Foot and Ankle Orthopedics and Medicine [16781]
5272 River Rd., Ste. 630
Bethesda, MD 20816
Ph: (301)718-6505
Toll Free: 800-265-8263
Fax: (301)656-0989

Wallis, Norman, PhD, Exec. Dir.
American College of Radiation Oncology [17032]
5272 River Rd., Ste. 630
Bethesda, MD 20816
Ph: (301)718-6515
Fax: (301)656-0989

Wallmeyer, Henry, President, CEO
National Club Association [733]
1201 15th St. NW, Ste. 450
Washington, DC 20005
Ph: (202)822-9822
Toll Free: 800-625-6221
Fax: (202)822-9808

Walls, Rick, Officer
International Sports Heritage Association [23232]
PO Box 2384
Florence, OR 97439
Ph: (541)991-7315
Fax: (541)997-3871

Waln, Donna, Conferences Coord.
Evangelical Church Library Association [9705]
PO Box 353
Glen Ellyn, IL 60138
Ph: (630)474-1080

Walsemann, Gary, DC, Chmn. of the Bd.
International Chiropractors Association [14274]
6400 Arlington Blvd., Ste. 800
Falls Church, VA 22042
Ph: (703)528-5000
Toll Free: 800-423-4690
Fax: (703)528-5023

Walsh, Anne, President
Federation of Naturopathic Medicine Regulatory Authorities [15860]
9220 SW Barbur Blvd., Ste.119, No. 321
Portland, OR 97219
Ph: (503)244-7189

Walsh, Bill, Founder, Exec. Dir.
Healthy Building Network [4129]
1710 Connecticut Ave.

Washington, DC 20009
Ph: (202)741-5717
Toll Free: 877-974-2767

Walsh, Chelsea M., President
Mothers Against Pedophiles [11082]
PO Box 3426
Running Springs, CA 92382

Walsh, Christina, Director
Castle Coalition [18930]
901 N Glebe Rd., Ste. 900
Arlington, VA 22203-1854
Ph: (703)682-9320
Fax: (703)682-9321

Walsh, Christopher, President
Cajal Club [16012]
c/o Charles E. Ribak, Secretary/
Treasurer
Dept. of Anatomy & Neurobiology
School of Medicine
University Of California
Irvine, CA 92697-1275

Walsh, Denise, President
Women's Caucus for Political Sci-
ence [7050]
c/o Michelle Wade, Treasurer
West Chester University Graduate
Ctr., Ste. 101
Dept. of Public Policy and
Administration
1160 McDermott Dr.
West Chester, PA 19383

Walsh, Dr. Donald, President,
Founder
Animal Health Foundation [17632]
3615 Bassett Rd.
Pacific, MO 63069

Walsh, Elaine Baugh, Comm. Chm.
Communications Marketing Associa-
tion [3221]
PO Box 5680
Lago Vista, TX 78645
Ph: (512)267-7747

Walsh, Jean T., Treasurer
OPP Concerned Sheep Breeders
Society [17657]
228 Main St.
Jordanville, NY 13361
Ph: (315)858-6042
(952)955-2596

Walsh, Kate, President
National Council on Teacher Quality
[8655]
1120 G St. NW, Ste. 800
Washington, DC 20005
Ph: (202)393-0020
Fax: (202)393-0095

Walsh, Fr. Martin de Porres, OP,
Director
Dominican Mission Foundation
[20409]
2506 Pine St.
San Francisco, CA 94115
Ph: (415)931-2183
Fax: (415)931-1772

Walsh, Mike, Chairman
Chess in the Schools [21590]
520 8th Ave., 2nd Fl.
New York, NY 10018
Ph: (212)643-0225
Fax: (212)564-3524

Walsh, Shaun, Director
Nets for Life Africa [13077]
Episcopal Relief and Development
815 2nd Ave.
New York, NY 10017
Toll Free: 855-312-4325

Walsh, Sue, Founder, President
Little By Little [15031]
PO Box 934

Glenview, IL 60025-0934

Walsh, Susi, Exec. Dir.
Center for Independent
Documentary [9300]
1600 Providence Hwy.
Walpole, MA 02081
Ph: (888)220-0918

Walsh, Dr. Thomas G., President
Universal Peace Federation [18836]
200 White Plains Rd., 1st Fl.
Tarrytown, NY 10591
Ph: (914)631-1331
Fax: (914)332-1582

Walske, Steven C., Author
Philatelic Foundation [22353]
341 W 38th St., 5th Fl.
New York, NY 10018-9692
Ph: (212)221-6555
Fax: (212)221-6208

Walter, Mr. Jerry, President, CEO
National Fabry Disease Foundation
[15966]
4301 Connecticut Ave. NW, Ste. 404
Washington, DC 20008
Toll Free: 800-651-9131
Fax: (919)932-7786

Walter, Olga, President
National Association of Resource
Conservation and Development
Councils [3902]
444 N Capitol St. NW, Ste. 618
Washington, DC 20001
Ph: (202)434-4780
Fax: (202)434-4783

Walter, Ms. Suzan, President
American Holistic Health Association
[15263]
PO Box 17400
Anaheim, CA 92817-7400
Ph: (714)779-6152

Walter, Will, President
National Farm and Ranch Business
Management Education Associa-
tion, Inc. [4160]
6540 65th St. NE
Rochester, MN 55906-1911
Ph: (507)951-3610
Toll Free: 888-255-9735

Walters, Carol A., Chmn. of the Bd.
National Association for Lay Ministry
[20295]
5401 S Cornell, Rm. 210
Chicago, IL 60615
Ph: (773)595-4042
Fax: (773)595-4020

Walters, Caroline, Asst. Dir.
American Bar Association Section of
Civil Rights and Social Justice
[17865]
1050 Connecticut Ave. NW, Ste. 400
Washington, DC 20036
Ph: (202)662-1030
Toll Free: 800-285-2221
Fax: (202)662-1031

Walters, Ms. Davie, Founder
Medical Relief Alliance [12696]
244 5th Ave., Ste. B293
New York, NY 10001
Ph: (917)292-4866

Walters, Dustin, President
Thoracic Surgery Residents Associa-
tion [17478]
633 N St. Clair St., 23rd Fl.
Chicago, IL 60611-3234
Ph: (312)202-5854
Fax: (773)289-0871

Walters, Honey, President
Solar Cookers International [4104]
2400 22nd St., Ste. 210

Sacramento, CA 95818
Ph: (916)455-4499
Fax: (916)455-4497

Walters, James, Secretary, Treasurer
Sigma Gamma Epsilon [23768]
c/o Aaron Johnson, President
Dept. of Natural Sciences
Northwest Missouri State University
1335 Garret-Strong
800 College Park Dr.
Maryville, MO 64468
Ph: (660)562-1569
Fax: (660)562-1055

Walters, John, VP, Prog. Dir.
Journey Forward [17258]
755 Dedham St.
Canton, MA 02021
Ph: (781)828-3233
Toll Free: 866-680-5636
Fax: (781)828-4777

Walters, Dr. Margaret, Exec. Dir.
Georgia Writers Association [10372]
440 Bartow Ave.
Kennesaw, GA 30144

Walters, Roger, Commissioner
National InterCollegiate Rodeo As-
sociation [23100]
2033 Walla Walla Ave.
Walla Walla, WA 99362
Ph: (509)529-4402
Fax: (509)525-1090

Walters, Sean, CAE, CEO, Exec.
Dir.
Investment Management
Consultants Association [2025]
5619 DTC Pky., Ste. 500
Greenwood Village, CO 80111
Ph: (303)770-3377
Fax: (303)770-1812

Walters, Tali K., PhD, Mem.
Society for Terrorism Research
[13213]
PO Box 590094
Newton, MA 02459-0001

Waltmunson, Kymber, President
Association of Local Government
Auditors [5268]
449 Lewis Hargett Cir., Ste. 290
Lexington, KY 40503-3669
Ph: (859)276-0686
Fax: (859)278-0507

Waltner, Aileen, Bd. Member
Alpha Tau Delta [23837]
1904 Poinsettia Ave.
Manhattan Beach, CA 90266

Walton, Bobby, Chairman
American Cotton Shippers Associa-
tion [931]
88 Union Ave., Ste. 1204
Memphis, TN 38103
Ph: (901)525-5352
Fax: (901)527-8303

Walton, Carol J., CEO
The Parkinson Alliance [15982]
PO Box 308
Kingston, NJ 08528-0308
Ph: (609)688-0870
Toll Free: 800-579-8440
Fax: (609)688-0875

Walton, Jeanne, President
American Belgian Hare Club [4584]
c/o Jeanne Walton, President
15330 Sharp Rd.
Rockton, IL 61072
Ph: (815)629-2465

Walton, Sue, Administrator
Council of Georgist Organizations
[19168]

c/o Sue Walton, Administrator
PO Box 57
Evanston, IL 60204
Ph: (847)209-0047

Wambold, Rev. Roger L., Director
Hebrew Christian Fellowship [20145]
PO Box 245
Harleysville, PA 19438
Ph: (215)256-4500

Wamsley, Kevin, President
North American Society for Sport
History [9500]
c/o Jaime Schultz, Secretary
Pennsylvania State University
268M Recreation Bldg.
University Park, PA 16802

Wamsley, Lisa, President
American Pinzgauer Association
[3707]
W5702 Grouse Dr.
Endeavor, WI 53930
Ph: (608)697-5968
(936)443-9205

Wan, Enoch, Editor
Evangelical Missiological Society
[20413]

Wan, Tracy, Bd. Member
Asian Financial Society [1220]
PO Box 357, Church St. Sta.
New York, NY 10008
Ph: (646)580-5066

Wandel, Eric, President
Association of Federal Communica-
tions Consulting Engineers [7305]
PO Box 19333
Washington, DC 20036-0333

Wang, Danyun, President
Chinese-American Environmental
Professionals Association [4040]
5237 Heavenly Ridge Ln.
El Sobrante, CA 94803

Wang, Dong, President
Historical Society for Twentieth-
Century China [9481]
c/o Xiaoping Cong, Secretary-
Treasurer
Department of History
University of Houston
Houston, TX 77204

Wang, Francis S.L., President
International Association of Law
Schools [8215]
c/o Barbara Holden-Smith,
Secretary-Treasurer
Cornell Law School
124 Myron Taylor Hall
Ithaca, NY 14853
Fax: (607)255-7033

Wang, Dr. George, President
U.S.-China Exchange Association
[18533]
52 Bridge St.
Metuchen, NJ 08840
Ph: (732)771-5083
Fax: (732)494-5802

Wang, Huali, Secretary
International Psychogeriatric As-
sociation [14893]
555 E Wells St., Ste. 1100
Milwaukee, WI 53202
Ph: (414)918-9889
Fax: (414)276-3349

Wang, Michelle, Treasurer
World Congress of Poets [10161]
4423 Pitch Pine Ct.
San Jose, CA 95136

Wang, Robin R., President
Society for Asian and Comparative
Philosophy [10121]
c/o Geoffrey Ashton, Treasurer
University of Colorado
1800 Grant St., Ste. 800
Denver, CO 80203

Wang, Sean, Sec. Gen.
Monte Jade Science and Technology
Association [7283]
2870 Zanker Rd., Ste. 140
San Jose, CA 95134
Ph: (408)428-0388
Fax: (408)428-0378

Wang, Yanan, Prof., Coord.
Air Transport Research Society
[6023]
c/o Prof. Yanan Wang, Coordinator
3433 Van Munching Hall
Robert H. Smith School of Business
University of Maryland
College Park, MD 20742
Ph: (301)405-2204
Fax: (301)314-1023

Wangdu, Sonam, Chairman
U.S. Tibet Committee [19193]
241 E 32nd St.
New York, NY 10016
Ph: (212)481-3569
    (212)481-3569

Wangman, Carl, CAE, Exec. Dir.
International Association of
Rehabilitation Professionals
[17088]
1926 Waukegan Rd., Ste. 1
Glenview, IL 60025-1770
Ph: (847)657-6964
Toll Free: 888-427-7722
Fax: (847)657-6963

Wangpo, Jigme Losel, Contact
Shenpen America [13089]
PO Box 12
Mendham, NJ 07945

Wanko, John, President
Russian Brotherhood Organization of
the U.S.A. [19631]
301 Oxford Valley Rd., Ste. 1602B
Yardley, PA 19067
Ph: (215)563-2537
Fax: (215)563-8106

Wannabe, Ms. Katie, Chairperson
Renaissance Transgender Associa-
tion [12951]
987 Old Eagle School Rd., Ste. 719
Wayne, PA 19087
Ph: (610)636-1990

Wantland, Clydette L., Exec. Dir.
Society for the Advancement of
Scandinavian Study [10201]
Brigham Young University
3168 JFSB
Provo, UT 84602-6702

Wapnick, Kenneth, PhD, President
Foundation for a Course in Miracles
[20605]
41397 Buecking Dr.
Temecula, CA 92590-5668
Ph: (951)296-6261
Fax: (951)296-9117

Warbington, Joseph, Chairperson
Sarvodaya U.S.A. [11427]
1127 University Ave.
Madison, WI 53715
Ph: (608)567-4421
Fax: (608)310-5865

Ward, Rev. Alida, Contact
Friends of Christ in India [19981]
1045 Old Academy Rd.

Fairfield, CT 06824
Ph: (203)259-1790

Ward, Calvin, President
American Spaniel Club [21824]
c/o Kevin Carter, Assistant Treasurer
6973 Davis-Bonne Rd.
Boones Mill, VA 24065
Ph: (540)772-1272

Ward, Mr. Charles, Exec. Dir.
Vets With a Mission [17817]
1307 Caldwell St., 3rd Fl.
Newberry, SC 29108-2799
Ph: (803)405-9926
Fax: (803)405-9926

Ward, Curt, President
North American Council of Automo-
tive Teachers [7525]
1820 Shiloh Rd., Ste. 1403
Tyler, TX 75703
Ph: (682)465-4662

Ward, Darrell, Bd. Member
Better Healthcare for Africa [15080]
PO Box 361132
Columbus, OH 43236
Ph: (614)475-6038

Ward, Earl, Chairman
Housing Works [13546]
57 Willoughby St., 2nd Fl.
Brooklyn, NY 11201
Ph: (347)473-7400

Ward, Ernie, DVM, Founder
Association for Pet Obesity Preven-
tion [16248]
51 Newport St.
Ocean Isle Beach, NC 28469
Ph: (910)579-5550

Ward, Dr. Jeff, Administrator
Mega Society [9345]
c/o Jeff Ward, Administrator
13155 Wimberly Sq., No. 284
San Diego, CA 92128

Ward, Jennifer, President
Trauma Center Association of
America [17531]
108 Gateway Blvd., Ste. 103
Mooresville, NC 28117
Ph: (704)360-4665
Fax: (704)677-7052

Ward, John, Coord.
American Coal Ash Association
[3443]
38800 Country Club Dr.
Farmington Hills, MI 48331
Ph: (720)870-7897
Fax: (720)870-7889

Ward, John, Exec. Dir.
Game Manufacturers Association
[1136]
240 N 5th St., Ste. 340
Columbus, OH 43215
Ph: (614)255-4500
Fax: (614)255-4499

Ward, Jonathan, Consultant
ICA Group [1081]
1330 Beacon St., Ste. 355
Brookline, MA 02446
Ph: (617)232-8765

Ward, Kerry, Exec. Dir.
Library Leadership and Management
Association [9714]
50 E Huron St.
Chicago, IL 60611-2729
Toll Free: 800-545-2433
Fax: (312)280-2169

Ward, LaTerrie, Treasurer
National Association of Human
Rights Workers [12051]

c/o LaTerrie Ward, Treasurer
PO Box 283
Goldsboro, NC 27533
Ph: (919)580-4359

Ward, Malcolm, CEO
AGN International [5]
2851 S Parker Rd., Ste. 850
Aurora, CO 80014
Ph: (303)743-7880
Fax: (303)743-7660

Ward, Marc W., President
Sea Turtles Forever [4886]
PO Box 845
Seaside, OR 97138
Ph: (503)739-1446

Ward, Maryanne, President,
Treasurer
Ghana Together [11468]
808 Addison Pl.
Mount Vernon, WA 98273
Ph: (360)848-6568
    (360)708-5735

Ward, Peter, Rec. Sec.
Unite Here [23463]
275 7th Ave., 16th Fl.
New York, NY 10001-6708
Ph: (212)265-7000

Ward, Susanna, President
Clinical Social Work Association
[13107]
PO Box 10
Garrisonville, VA 22463
Ph: (202)203-9350

Ward, William W., Sr., Chairman
Tall Cedars of Lebanon of North
America [19571]
4309 Linglestown Rd.Ste 116
Harrisburg, PA 17112
Ph: (717)232-5991
Fax: (717)232-5997

Ward-Cook, Dr. Kory, CEO
National Certification Commission for
Acupuncture and Oriental Medicine
[16457]
76 S Laura St., Ste. 1290
Jacksonville, FL 32202
Ph: (904)598-1005
Fax: (904)598-5001

Ware, Jeff, Exec. Dir.
American Rose Society [22084]
8877 Jefferson Paige Rd.
Shreveport, LA 71119-8817
Ph: (318)938-5402
Toll Free: 800-637-6534
Fax: (318)938-5405

Warfield, Susanne S., Exec. Dir.
National Coalition of Estheticians,
Manufacturers/Distributors and As-
sociations [925]
484 Spring Ave.
Ridgewood, NJ 07450-4624
Ph: (201)670-4100
Fax: (201)670-4265

Warfield, Thomas, Founder, Art Dir.
PeaceArt International [8995]
PO Box 40028
Rochester, NY 14604-0028
Ph: (585)482-0778
Fax: (585)288-2572

Wargo, Lorraine, Exec. Dir.
National Association of State Head
Injury Administrators [14913]
PO Box 878
Waitsfield, VT 05673
Ph: (802)498-3349
Fax: (205)823-4544

Wark, Tom, Exec. Dir.
National Association of Wine Retailers [3480]

621 Capitol Mall, Ste. 2500
Sacramento, CA 95814
Ph: (707)266-1449
Fax: (916)442-0382

Warne, Myra, Exec. Dir.
Society of Glass and Ceramic
Decorated Products [1510]
PO Box 2489
Zanesville, OH 43702
Ph: (740)588-9882
Fax: (740)588-0245

Warnecke, Tonia, President
Association for Institutional Thought
[6381]
Dept. of Economics
Raj Soin College of Business
Wright State University
3640 Colonel Glenn Hwy.
Dayton, OH 45435-0001

Warner, Bill, Mem.
Gleaner Life Insurance Society
[19484]
5200 W US Highway 223
Adrian, MI 49221-9461
Toll Free: 800-992-1894
Fax: (517)265-7745

Warner, Brig. Gen. (Ret.) David B.,
Exec. Dir.
Officers' Christian Fellowship of the
U.S.A. [20002]
3784 S Inca St.
Englewood, CO 80110-3405
Ph: (303)761-1984
Toll Free: 800-424-1984

Warner, Jeanne L., Bd. Member
International Center for Research on
Women [18216]
1120 20th St. NW, Ste. 500 N
Washington, DC 20036-3491
Ph: (202)797-0007
Fax: (202)797-0020

Warner, Keith R.P., CEO
Carcinoid Cancer Foundation
[13935]
333 Mamaroneck Ave., No. 492
White Plains, NY 10605
Ph: (914)683-1001
Toll Free: 888-722-3132
Fax: (914)683-0183

Warner, Mary Jane, President
World Dance Alliance Americas
[9273]
c/o Scott Martin, Vice President
816 N Bell Ave., No. 14
Denton, TX 76209
Ph: (214)460-6844

Warner, Rick, President
World History Association [9528]
Northeastern University
Meserve Hall
360 Huntington Ave.
Boston, MA 02130
Ph: (617)373-6818
Fax: (617)373-2661

Warner, Solange, Founder, Co-
Chmn. of the Bd.
World Chamber of Commerce
[23641]
2870 Peachtree Rd., No. 435
Atlanta, GA 30305
Toll Free: 800-590-9227

Warner, Teemus, Mktg. Coord.
National Career Pathways Network
[7843]
PO Box 21689
Waco, TX 76702-1689
Ph: (254)772-5095
Toll Free: 800-518-1410
Fax: (254)776-2306

Warner, Vessela, President
Bulgarian Studies Association [9148]
51 Davis Ave.
West Newton, MA 02465-1925

Warren, Alan, Secretary
American Society of Polar
Philatelists [22305]
c/o John Young, President
146 N Lincoln St.
Pearl River, NY 10965

Warren, Anne, Exec. Dir.
American Academy of Forensic Sciences [5231]
c/o Susan Ballou, Secretary
100 Bureau Dr.
Gaithersburg, MD 20899-8102
Ph: (301)975-8750

Warren, Bill, Exec. Dir.
Fellowship of Associates of Medical
Evangelism [20324]
4545 Southeastern Ave.
Indianapolis, IN 46203
Ph: (317)358-2480

Warren, Brian, Exec. Dir.
Sigma Phi Epsilon [23930]
310 S Blvd.
Richmond, VA 23220
Ph: (804)353-1901
Toll Free: 800-767-1901
Fax: (804)359-8160

Warren, Dan, Founder
One Village Planet [11418]
1440 Coral Ridge Dr., Ste. 104
Coral Springs, FL 33071
Ph: (954)290-9147

Warren, Dr. David L., President
National Association of Independent
Colleges and Universities [8012]
1025 Connecticut Ave. NW, Ste. 700
Washington, DC 20036
Ph: (202)785-8866
Fax: (202)835-0003

Warren, Eddie, VP
Burley Tobacco Growers Cooperative Association [4720]
620 S Broadway
Lexington, KY 40508
Ph: (859)252-3561

Warren, Jim, Exec. Dir.
Association of Steel Distributors
[2344]
833 Featherstone Rd.
Rockford, IL 61107
Ph: (312)673-5793
    (815)227-8227
Fax: (312)527-6705

Warren, Joan, President
Association for Nursing Professional
Development [16120]
330 N Wabash Ave., Ste. 2000
Chicago, IL 60611
Ph: (312)673-5135
Fax: (312)673-6835

Warren, Joe, President
Amalgamated Printers' Association
[1553]
c/o Cindy Iverson
12236 S Tonalea Dr.
Phoenix, AZ 85044

Warren, John, Secretary
The India Study Circle for Philately
[22333]
PO Box 7326
Washington, DC 20044-7326
Ph: (202)564-6876
Fax: (202)565-2441

Warren, Dr. John, Director
Research Partnership to Secure
Energy for America [6508]

1650 Highway 6, Ste. 325
Sugar Land, TX 77478
Ph: (281)313-9555
Fax: (281)313-9560

Warren, Mr. Roland, President, CEO
Care Net [18033]
44180 Riverside Pky., Ste. 200
Lansdowne, VA 20176
Ph: (703)554-8734
Toll Free: 800-518-7909
Fax: (703)554-8735

Warren, Vincent, Exec. Dir.
Center for Constitutional Rights
[17881]
666 Broadway, 7th Fl.
New York, NY 10012
Ph: (212)614-6464
Fax: (212)614-6499

Warshaw, Larry, President
International Bridal Manufacturers
Association [445]
118 W 20th St., 3rd Fl.
New York, NY 10011-3627

Warshenbrot, Amalia
Association of Jewish Libraries
[9685]
PO Box 1118
Teaneck, NJ 07666
Ph: (201)371-3255

Wartell, Sarah Rosen, President
Urban Institute [19220]
2100 M St. NW
Washington, DC 20037
Ph: (202)833-7200

Wartman, Mr. Steven, MD, CEO,
President
Association of Academic Health
Centers [14928]
1400 16th St. NW, Ste. 720
Washington, DC 20036
Ph: (202)265-9600
Fax: (202)265-7514

Wasch, Ken, President
Software and Information Industry
Association [5341]
1090 Vermont Ave. NW, 6th Fl.
Washington, DC 20005-4095
Ph: (202)289-7442
Fax: (202)289-7097

Washburn, Connie, VP
Friends of the Everglades [3870]
11767 S Dixie Hwy., No. 232
Miami, FL 33156
Ph: (305)669-0858
Fax: (305)479-2893

Washburn, John L., Facilitator
American Non-Governmental
Organizations Coalition for the
International Criminal Court
[18069]
Columbia University Institute for the
Study of Human Rights
MC 3365
New York, NY 10027
Ph: (212)851-2106

Washburn, Mary K., Officer
Degree of Pocahontas, Improved
Order of Red Men [19622]
4521 Speight Ave.
Waco, TX 76711
Ph: (254)756-1221
Fax: (254)756-4828

Washburn, Roger, Contact
World Sport Stacking Association
[23267]
11 Inverness Way S
Englewood, CO 80112
Ph: (303)962-5667

Washburn, Sarah, Exec. Dir.
Interior Design Educators Council
[8050]
1 Parkview Plz., Ste. 800
Oakbrook Terrace, IL 60181
Ph: (630)544-5057

Washburn, Scott, CFRE, Treasurer
North American YMCA Development
Organization [13419]
21 Chateau Trianon Dr.
Kenner, LA 70065
Ph: (504)464-7845

Washburne, Mark, President
United States Running Streak Association, Inc. [23121]
c/o Mark Washburne, President
31 Galway Dr.
Mendham, NJ 07945

Washbush, Charles E., Chairman
National Counter Intelligence Corps
Association [21029]
1185 Bastion Cir.
Mount Juliet, TN 37122-6148
Ph: (615)758-6092

Washington, Barry, Contact
Challenger T/A Registry [21349]
c/o Barry Washington
4511 Spring Rd.
Shermans Dale, PA 17090-9403

Washington, Carla D., Exec. Dir.
Direct Care Alliance [15118]
4 W 43rd St., Unit 610
New York, NY 10036
Ph: (212)730-0741
Fax: (212)302-4345

Washington, Kadeem, Chairperson
National Society of Minorities in
Hospitality [1675]
6933 Commons Plz., Ste. 537
Chesterfield, VA 23832
Ph: (703)549-9899
Fax: (703)539-1049

Washington, Knitasha, Exec. Dir.
Consumers Advancing Patient
Safety [17172]
405 N Wabash Ave., Ste. P2W
Chicago, IL 60611
Ph: (312)464-0602
Fax: (312)277-3307

Washington, Lisa, Exec. Dir., CEO
Design-Build Institute of America
[520]
1331 Pennsylvania Ave. NW, 4th Fl.
Washington, DC 20004-1721
Ph: (202)682-0110
Fax: (202)682-5877

Washington, Dr. Raleigh, President
Promise Keepers [20006]
PO Box 11798
Denver, CO 80211-0798
Toll Free: 866-776-6473
Fax: (303)433-1036

Washington, Ressheda N, Exec. Dir.
Communities First Association
[11334]
PO Box 6104
Chicago, IL 60680

Washington, Valora, President, CEO
Council for Professional Recognition
[10807]
2460 16th St. NW
Washington, DC 20009-3547
Ph: (202)265-9090
Toll Free: 800-424-4310
Fax: (202)265-9161

Washum, Duane, Director
Ex-Masons for Jesus [19975]
PO Box 28702

Las Vegas, NV 89126

Waskul, Dennis, President
Society for the Study of Symbolic
Interaction [7189]
c/o Patrick McGinty, Vice President
Morgan Hall 404
1 University Cir.
Macomb, IL 61455

Wassall, Donald B., Exec. Dir.
American Freedom Union [18885]
PO Box 218
Wildwood, PA 15091

Wasser, Dan, President
Communications Workers of America
- Printing, Publishing and Media
Workers Sector [23439]
219 Fort Pitt Blvd., 3rd Fl.
Pittsburgh, PA 15222
Ph: (412)281-7268
Fax: (412)281-7815

Wasserman, Becky, Chairperson
USSA Foundation [8632]
United States Student Association
1211 Connecticut Ave. NW, Ste. 406
Washington, DC 20036
Ph: (202)640-6570
Fax: (202)223-4005

Wasserman, Lee, Secretary
Rockefeller Family Fund [12495]
475 Riverside Dr., Ste. 900
New York, NY 10115
Ph: (212)812-4252
Fax: (212)812-4299

Wasserman, Stephen I., MD,
President
American Board of Allergy and Immunology [13571]
1835 Market St., Ste. 1210
Philadelphia, PA 19106-2512
Toll Free: 866-264-5568
Fax: (215)592-9411

Wasserstein, Ronald, Exec. Dir.
American Statistical Association
[7240]
732 N Washington St.
Alexandria, VA 22314-1943
Ph: (703)684-1221
Toll Free: 888-231-3473
Fax: (703)684-2037

Wasson, Fr. William B., Founder
Nuestros Pequenos Hermanos
International [20449]
134 N La Salle St., Ste. 500
Chicago, IL 60602-1036
Ph: (312)386-7499
Toll Free: 888-201-8880
Fax: (312)658-0040

Waters, Al, Exec. Sec.
North American Model Boating Association [22204]
c/o Al Waters
162 Avenida Chapala
San Marcos, CA 92069
Ph: (760)746-2408
Fax: (760)539-9009

Waters, Jerry W., Sr., President
National Conference of State Liquor
Administrators [4954]
543 Long Hill Rd.
Gurnee, IL 60031
Ph: (847)721-6410

Waters, Susan, Contact
Sponge and Chamois Institute
[2087]
10024 Office Center Ave., Ste. 203
Saint Louis, MO 63128
Ph: (314)842-2230
Fax: (314)842-3999

Watkins, Jeff, Director
Shakespeare Theatre Association
[10272]
c/o Lisa Tromovitch, President
PO Box 2616
Livermore, CA 94551-2616

Watner, Carl, Editor
The Voluntaryists [18644]
PO Box 275-D
Gramling, SC 29348

Watral, Bohdan, President, CEO
Selfreliance Association of American
Ukrainians [19677]
2332 W Chicago Ave.
Chicago, IL 60622
Ph: (773)328-7500
Toll Free: 888-222-8571
Fax: (773)328-7501

Watson, David, President
Steel Tank Institute and Steel Plate
Fabricators Association [845]
944 Donata Ct.
Lake Zurich, IL 60047
Ph: (847)438-8265
Fax: (847)438-8766

Watson, Prof. James R., President
Society for the Philosophical Study
of Genocide and the Holocaust
[10125]
c/o Prof. James R. Watson,
President
Dept. of Philosophy
Loyola University
6363 St. Charles Ave.
New Orleans, LA 70118
Ph: (501)922-3382

Watson, Jim, Secretary
North American Police Work Dog
Association [5513]
4222 Manchester Rd.
Perry, OH 44081
Ph: (502)523-4452
Toll Free: 888-4-CANINE
Fax: (866)236-0753

Watson, Linda, President
Emphysema Foundation for Our
Right to Survive [17140]
PO Box 20241
Kansas City, MO 64195
Toll Free: 866-END-COPD

Watson, Lynn, Dir. of Comm.
Ductile Iron Pipe Research Associa-
tion [2604]
PO Box 19206
Golden, CO 80402-6053
Ph: (205)402-8700

Watson, Margaret Howard, Founder,
President
Green Schools Alliance [7894]
1875 Connecticut Ave. NW, 10th Fl.
Washington, DC 20009
Ph: (860)468-5289

Watson, Melyssa, Chairperson
American Wilderness Coalition
[4785]
PO Box 2622
Durango, CO 81302-2622
Ph: (202)266-0455

Watson, Michael R., President
American Pilots' Association [128]
Fairchild Bldg.
499 S Capitol St. SW, Ste. 409
Washington, DC 20003
Ph: (202)484-0700
Fax: (202)484-9320

Watson, Michael S., PhD, Exec. Dir.
American College of Medical Genetics and Genomics [14874]

7220 Wisconsin Ave., Ste. 300
Bethesda, MD 20814-4854
Ph: (301)718-9603
Fax: (301)718-9604

Watson, Nina, CMA (AAMA), CPC,
President
American Association of Medical As-
sistants [15615]
20 N Wacker Dr., Ste. 1575
Chicago, IL 60606
Ph: (312)899-1500
Toll Free: 800-228-2262
Fax: (312)899-1259

Watson, Capt. Paul, Founder
Sea Shepherd Conservation Society
[4884]
PO Box 2616
Friday Harbor, WA 98250
Ph: (360)370-5650
Fax: (360)370-5651

Watson, Robert, Exec. Dir.
DateAble, Inc. [11584]
15520 Bald Eagle School Rd.
Brandywine, MD 20613-8545
Ph: (301)888-1177
     (301)657-3283

Watson, Sara, Director
ReadyNation [18173]
1212 New York Ave. NW, Ste. 300
Washington, DC 20005-3988
Ph: (202)408-9282
Fax: (202)776-0110

Watson, Sharon D., Contact
Medical Association of Billers
[15635]
2620 Regatta Dr., Ste. 102
Las Vegas, NV 89128
Ph: (702)240-8519
Fax: (702)243-0359

Watson, Stuart, Chairman
National Wildlife Refuge Association
[4848]
1001 Connecticut Ave. NW, Ste. 905
Washington, DC 20036
Ph: (202)417-3803

Watson, Vicki, Exec. Dir.
National Community Development
Association [17989]
1825 K St. NW, Ste. 515
Washington, DC 20006
Ph: (202)587-2772
Fax: (202)887-5546

Watson, William, Contact
Space Frontier Foundation [7222]
42354 Blacow Rd.
Fremont, CA 94538
Toll Free: 800-787-7223

Watt, Andrew, President, CEO
Association of Fundraising Profes-
sionals [11856]
4300 Wilson Blvd., Ste. 300
Arlington, VA 22203
Ph: (703)684-0410
Toll Free: 800-666-3863
Fax: (703)684-0540

Watt, David, Bd. Member
American Running Association
[23060]
4405 E West Hwy., Ste. 405
Bethesda, MD 20814-4535
Toll Free: 800-776-2732
Fax: (301)913-9520

Watt, Lynda, Admin. Asst.
American College of Surgeons Com-
mission on Cancer [13885]
633 N St. Clair St.
Chicago, IL 60611-3211
Ph: (312)202-5085
Fax: (312)202-5009

Watt, Robin, Secretary, Treasurer
National Association of Independent
Lighting Distributors [2102]
191 Clarksville Rd.
Princeton Junction, NJ 08550
Ph: (609)297-2216
Fax: (609)799-7032

Wattenbarger, Randy, Chairman
Marine Retailers Association of
Americas [2249]
8401 73rd Ave. N, Ste. 71
Minneapolis, MN 55428
Ph: (763)315-8043

Watter, Daniel N., EdD, President
Society for Sex Therapy and
Research [17205]
6311 W Gross Point Rd.
Niles, IL 60714
Ph: (847)647-8832
Fax: (847)647-8940

Watters, Ms. Kate, Exec. Dir.
Crude Accountability [4046]
PO Box 2345
Alexandria, VA 22301
Ph: (703)299-0854
Fax: (703)299-0854

Watters, Lisa, Founder
Benny's World [13898]
PO Box 372
Lake Forest, IL 60045
Ph: (847)612-5567
Fax: (847)810-7400

Watters, Randall, President, Founder
Free Minds, Inc. [20047]
c/o Randall Watters, President
PO Box 3818
Manhattan Beach, CA 90266
Ph: (310)545-7831

Watterson-Diorio, Nancy, Exec. Dir.
National Association of Veterans'
Research and Education Founda-
tions [5840]
5480 Wisconsin Ave., Ste. 214
Chevy Chase, MD 20815-3529
Ph: (301)656-5005
Fax: (301)656-5008

Watts, Alan, President
Society for the Study of Ingestive
Behavior [13805]
2111 Chestnut Ave., Ste. 145
Glenview, IL 60025
Ph: (847)807-4924
Fax: (312)896-5614

Watts, Brenda, President
National Agricultural Aviation As-
sociation [3652]
1440 Duke St.
Alexandria, VA 22314
Ph: (202)546-5722
Fax: (202)546-5726

Watts, Geoff, Chairman
Alliance for Coffee Excellence [420]
2250 NW 22nd Ave., Ste. 612
Portland, OR 97210
Ph: (503)208-2872

Watts, J.C, Jr., President, CEO
Feed the Children [12661]
333 N Meridian
Oklahoma City, OK 73107
Toll Free: 800-627-4556

Watts, John, Chairman
World Policy Institute [18277]
108 W 39th St., Ste. 1000
New York, NY 10018
Ph: (212)481-5005
Fax: (212)481-5009

Watts, Jonathan K., Secretary
Oligonucleotide Therapeutics Society
[17458]

4377 Newport Ave.
San Diego, CA 92107
Ph: (619)795-9458
Fax: (619)923-3230

Watts, Kenn, Chmn. of the Bd.
American Friends of Guinea [15436]
PO Box 940505
Houston, TX 77079
Ph: (832)456-8100
Fax: (832)300-2516

Watts, Russ, President
Association of Outdoor Recreation
and Education [8399]
1100 N Main St., Ste. 101
Ann Arbor, MI 48104
Ph: (810)299-2782
Fax: (810)299-3436

Watts, Dr. Stuart, Treasurer
National Certification Board for
Therapeutic Massage & Bodywork
[15561]
1333 Burr Ridge Pky., Ste. 200
Burr Ridge, IL 60527
Ph: (630)627-8000
Toll Free: 800-296-0664

Waugh, Don, VP
Clan Montgomery Society
International [20834]
9 Poplar Springs Ct.
Columbia, SC 29223

Waugh, Scott, Chairman
Center for Research Libraries [9697]
6050 S Kenwood Ave.
Chicago, IL 60637-2804
Ph: (773)955-4545
Toll Free: 800-621-6044
Fax: (773)955-4339

Wawrzewski, Michael J., CEO,
Founder
Hospitals of Hope [15475]
3545 N Santa Fe St.
Wichita, KS 67219
Ph: (316)262-0964
Fax: (316)262-0953

Wax, Paul M., MD, Exec. Dir.
American College of Medical Toxicol-
ogy [17493]
10645 N Tatum Blvd., Ste. 200-111
Phoenix, AZ 85028
Ph: (623)533-6340
Fax: (623)533-6520

Waxter, Dorsey, Officer
Art Dealers Association of America
[238]
205 Lexington Ave., Rm. 901
New York, NY 10016
Ph: (212)488-5550
Fax: (646)688-6809

Waycott, Richard, CEO
Almond Board of California [4505]
1150 9th St., Ste. 1500
Modesto, CA 95354
Ph: (209)549-8262
Fax: (209)549-8267

Wayman, Ronald, President
Energy Kinesiology Association
[13620]
7862 Mayfair Cir.
Ellicott City, MD 21043
Toll Free: 866-365-4336

Wayne, Euwayne Denise, President
Professional Football Players Moth-
ers' Association [22865]
c/o Chris Johnson, Treasurer
340 Glengarry Ln.
State College, PA 16801
Ph: (504)392-7781
Fax: (740)879-4454

Wayne, Kirk, President
Tobacco Associates [3286]
8452 Holly Leaf Dr.
McLean, VA 22102
Ph: (703)821-1255
Fax: (703)821-1511

Wear, John, President
USMC Vietnam Tankers Association
[21159]
5537 Lower Mountain Rd.
New Hope, PA 18938

Weatherford, Dani, Exec. Dir.
National Panhellenic Conference
[23762]
3901 W 86th St., Ste. 398
Indianapolis, IN 46268
Ph: (317)872-3185
Fax: (317)872-3192

Weathers, K. Russell, Chairman,
CEO
Agriculture Future of America [3540]
PO Box 414838
Kansas City, MO 64141-4838
Ph: (816)472-4232
Toll Free: 888-472-4232
Fax: (816)472-4239

Weaver, Benjamin W., DPM,
President
American Academy of Podiatric
Practice Management [16774]
1000 W St. Joseph Hwy., Ste. 200
Lansing, MI 48915
Ph: (517)484-1930
Fax: (517)485-9408

Weaver, Celia, President
MSPAlliance [6324]
1380 E Ave., Ste. 124-376
Chico, CA 95926-7349
Ph: (530)891-1340
Fax: (530)433-5707

Weaver, Doug, VP
Baptist History and Heritage Society
[19722]
c/o Jackie Riley, Office Manager
151 Broadleaf Dr.
Macon, GA 31210
Ph: (406)600-7433

Weaver, Pastor Mel, VP
Association of Christian Truckers
[20355]
1366 US Highway 40
Brownstown, IL 62418
Ph: (618)427-3737

Weaver, Robin, President
Women's National Republican Club
[19052]
3 W 51st St.
New York, NY 10019
Ph: (212)582-5454
Fax: (212)265-5633

Weaver, Stan, Founder
CHAP International [12636]
1390 Columbia Ave., No. 251
Lancaster, PA 17603
Ph: (717)553-2427

Weaver, Tracy, Director
Martina McBride Fan Club [24054]
PO Box 291627
Nashville, TN
Ph: (512)371-6924

Webb, Bob, President
National Association of Video
Distributors [1202]
16530 Ventura Blvd., Ste. 400
Encino, CA 91436
Ph: (818)385-1500
Fax: (818)933-0911

Webb, Howard, Exec. Dir.
American Council on Criminal
Justice Training [5128]
PO Box 7053
Helena, MT 59604
Ph: (406)241-6150

Webb, Kelvin, Treasurer
International Hajji Baba Society
[8867]
1105 D St. SE
Washington, DC 20003-2231

Webb, Dr. Molly, President
North American Sturgeon and
Paddlefish Society [3918]
c/o Dr. Molly Webb, President
USFWS, Bozeman Fish Technology
Center
4050 Bridger Canyon Rd.
Bozeman, MT 59715
Ph: (406)994-9907
Fax: (406)586-5942

Webb, Sam, Chairman
Communist Party USA [18887]
235 W 23rd St., 7th Fl.
New York, NY 10011-2302
Ph: (212)989-4994
Fax: (212)229-1713

Weber, Brad, CEO, President
Gray Line Sightseeing Association
[3329]
1835 Gaylord St.
Denver, CO 80206
Ph: (303)539-8502
Toll Free: 800-472-9546
Fax: (303)484-2185

Weber, C.T., Officer
Peace and Freedom Party [18893]
PO Box 24764
Oakland, CA 94623
Ph: (510)465-9414

Weber, Danielle, President
National MedPeds Residents' As-
sociation [15430]
School of Medicine
Tulane University
1430 Tulane Ave., SL-37
New Orleans, LA 70112
Ph: (504)988-1332
Fax: (504)988-3971

Weber, Heidi, Exec. Dir.
Alpha Omega International Dental
Fraternity [23717]
50 W Edmonston Dr., No. 206
Rockville, MD 20852
Ph: (301)738-6400
Toll Free: 877-368-6326
Fax: (301)738-6403

Weber, Judy Stokes, Treasurer
Association for Conservation
Information [3811]
c/o Judy Stokes Weber, Treasurer
854 Quincy Rd.
Rumney, NH 03266

Weber, Lynne, Exec. Dir.
Dance Notation Bureau [9253]
111 John St., Ste. 704
New York, NY 10038
Ph: (212)571-7011
Fax: (212)571-7012

Weber, Mark, Director
Institute for Historical Review [9446]
PO Box 2739
Newport Beach, CA 92659-1339
Ph: (714)593-9725
Fax: (714)465-3176

Weber, MD, Kristy, President
Ruth Jackson Orthopaedic Society
[16482]

9400 W Higgins Rd., Ste. 500
Rosemont, IL 60018
Ph: (847)698-1626
Fax: (847)268-9461

Weber, Peter, Exec. Dir.
Cork Quality Council [1436]
Forestville, CA
Ph: (707)887-0141

Weber, Tim, Chairman
American Association of Crop Insur-
ers [1823]
1 Massachusetts Ave. NW, Ste. 800
Washington, DC 20001
Ph: (202)789-4100
Fax: (202)408-7763

Webermann, Michael A., Exec. Dir.
Farm Animal Rights Movement
[10621]
10101 Ashburton Ln.
Bethesda, MD 20817
Toll Free: 888-327-6872

Webre, Craig, VP
Commission on Accreditation for
Law Enforcement Agencies [5460]
13575 Heathcote Blvd., Ste. 320
Gainesville, VA 20155
Ph: (703)352-4225
Fax: (703)890-3126

Webster, Brooke, President
Reserve Police Officers Association
[5518]
c/o Brooke Webster, President
89 Rockland Ave.
Yonkers, NY 10705
Toll Free: 800-326-9416

Webster, Kathy, Chairman
WomenHeart: National Coalition for
Women with Heart Disease
[14150]
1100 17th St. NW, Ste. 500
Washington, DC 20036
Ph: (202)728-7199
Fax: (202)728-7238

Webster, Patty, President
Amazon Promise [12263]
PO Box 1304
Newburyport, MA 01950

Webster, Ross, President
Memphis Cotton Exchange [3778]
65 Union Ave.
Memphis, TN 38103
Ph: (901)531-7826
Fax: (901)531-7827

Webster, Steve, Director
Pakistan American Business Association [663]
9302 Old Keene Mill Rd., Ste. B
Burke, VA 22015-4278

Wechsler, Dr. Howell, CEO
Alliance for a Healthier Generation
[14165]
606 SE 9th Ave.
Portland, OR 97214
Toll Free: 888-KID-HLTH

Weckstein, Paul, Director
Center for Law and Education
[5161]
1875 Connecticut Ave. NW, Ste. 510
Washington, DC 20009
Ph: (202)986-3000

Weddle Irons, Kendra, Coord.
Christian Feminism Today [20118]
PO Box 78171
Indianapolis, IN 46278

Weddle, Peter, Exec. Dir.
International Association of Employment Web Sites [1093]

2052 Shippan Ave.
Stamford, CT 06902

Weed, Geoff, President
International Home Furnishings
Representatives Association [1486]
209 S Main St.
High Point, NC 27260
Ph: (336)889-3920

Weeg, Judith, President
Lyme Disease United Coalition
[15407]
PO Box 86
Story City, IA 50248
Toll Free: 800-311-7518
Fax: (888)746-3810

Weeks, Brenda, President
Blair Society for Genealogical
Research [20961]
c/o Brenda Weeks, President
4430 Berrymore Ct.
Terre Haute, IN 47803-2085

Weeks, Grier, Exec. Dir.
National Association to Protect
Children [11086]
PO Box 2187
Knoxville, TN 37901
Ph: (865)525-0901

Weeks, Kimmie, Exec. Dir., Founder
Youth Action International [11193]
125 Park St., Ste. 450
Traverse City, MI 49684
Ph: (231)946-6283
Fax: (880)866-5437

Wegmann, M.K., CEO, President
National Performance Network
[10264]
1024 Elysian Fields Ave.
New Orleans, LA 70117
Ph: (504)595-8008
Fax: (504)595-8006

Wegner, Lyn, President
Bromeliad Society International
[22088]
c/o Annette Dominguez, Membership
Chairpersom
8117 Shenandoah Dr.
Austin, TX 78753
Ph: (512)619-2750

Wegner, Dr. Phillip E., Membership
Chp.
Society for Utopian Studies [10132]
c/o Dr. Phillip E. Wegner, Member-
ship Chairman
Dept. of English
University of Florida
Gainesville, FL 32611-7310
Ph: (352)392-6650

Wehrle, Joseph H., Jr., CEO,
President
National Insurance Crime Bureau
[1908]
1111 E Touhy Ave., Ste. 400
Des Plaines, IL 60018
Ph: (847)544-7000
Toll Free: 800-447-6282
Fax: (847)544-7100

Wehrman, Christine, CEO
American Rental Association [2925]
1900 19th St.
Moline, IL 61265-4179
Ph: (309)764-2475
Toll Free: 800-334-2177
Fax: (309)764-1533

Wehrwein, Chuck, CEO, Act. Pres.
Neighborhood Reinvestment Corp.
[11988]
999 N Capitol St. NE, Ste. 900

Washington, DC 20002
Ph: (202)760-4000
Fax: (202)376-2600

Wei, Steven, President
Association of Physician Assistants
in Oncology [16338]
30658 USF Holly Dr.
Tampa, FL 33620-3065
Ph: (813)988-7795
Fax: (813)988-7796

Weichel, Kimberly, CEO
Peace X Peace [18820]
1776 I St. NW, 9th Fl.
Washington, DC 20006
Toll Free: 877-684-3770

Weidenfeller, Tara, Exec. Dir.
Coalition for a Healthy and Active
America [16256]
301 W Platt St.
Tampa, FL 33606
Toll Free: 866-881-7666
Fax: (561)746-4023

Weidner, Jim, Founder
Amateur Radio Lighthouse Society
[9367]
114 Woodbine Ave.
Merchantville, NJ 08109
Ph: (856)486-1755

Weidner, Mr. Scott A., CEO,
President
Transport for Christ, International
[20470]
1525 River Rd.
Marietta, PA 17547-9403
Ph: (717)426-9977
Toll Free: 877-797-7729
Fax: (717)426-9980

Weidner, Stephen, Founder
American Association of Paranormal
Investigators [6979]
13973 E Utah Cir.
Aurora, CO 80012
Ph: (720)432-2746

Weigand, Kathy, Comm. Chm.
Dietetics in Health Care Communi-
ties [16217]
c/o Academy of Nutrition and Dietet-
ics
PO Box 4489
Carol Stream, IL 60197-4489
Ph: (319)235-0991
Toll Free: 800-877-1600
Fax: (319)235-7224

Weigel, Ronald J., MD, President
Society of Surgical Oncology
[16358]
9525 W Bryn Mawr Ave., Ste. 870
Rosemont, IL 60018
Ph: (847)427-1400
Fax: (847)427-1411

Weil, Patrick, Chairman
Libraries Without Borders [9712]
1875 Connecticut Ave. NW
Washington, DC 20009

Weiland, Cindy, Exec. Dir.
Joint Review Committee on Educa-
tion in Diagnostic Medical Sonog-
raphy [8297]
6021 University Blvd., Ste. 500
Ellicott City, MD 21043
Ph: (443)973-3251
Toll Free: 866-738-3444

Weiland, Eric, Treasurer
National Association of State Boards
of Geology [6681]
PO Box 5219
Douglasville, GA 30154
Ph: (678)713-1251
Fax: (678)839-4071

Weild, David, IV, Chairman
Tuesday's Children [11680]
10 Rockefeller Plz., Ste. 1007
New York, NY 11020
Ph: (516)562-9000
    (516)332-2980

Weilerstein, Philip J., President
VentureWell [6760]
100 Venture Way, 3rd Fl.
Hadley, MA 01035
Ph: (413)587-2172
Fax: (413)587-2175

Weilgus, Suzanne, Founder
American Communities Helping
Israel [12206]
PO Box 556
Monsey, NY 10952-0550
Fax: (845)426-5392

Weil-Kazzaz, Susan, President
Association of Biomedical Com-
munications Directors [14294]
c/o Susan Weil-Kazzaz, President
Memorial Sloan-Kettering Cancer
Ctr.
1275 York Ave.
New York, NY 10065
Ph: (646)888-2040
Fax: (646)422-0161

Weill, James D. (Jim), President
Food Research and Action Center
[12094]
1200 18th St. NW, Ste. 400
Washington, DC 20036
Ph: (202)986-2200
Fax: (202)986-2525

Weill, Michael A., Chmn. of the Bd.
Medical Bridges [15604]
2706 Magnet St.
Houston, TX 77054
Ph: (713)748-8131
Fax: (713)748-0118

Wein, Lawrence, President
National Conference of Shomrim
Societies [12228]
PO Box 598
Knickerbocker Sta.
New York, NY 10002

Weinberg, Allan D., Exec. Dir.
Children's Leukemia Research As-
sociation [13941]
585 Stewart Ave., Ste. 18
Garden City, NY 11530
Ph: (516)222-1944
Fax: (516)222-0457

Weinberg, Carl, V. Chmn. of the Bd.
Regulatory Assistance Project [5835]
50 State St., Ste. 3
Montpelier, VT 05602
Ph: (802)223-8199
Fax: (802)223-8172

Weinberg, Karen Fisher, QDE,
President
Coalition of Handwriting Analysts
International [6702]
c/o Jerry Fishow
19025 Jamieson Dr.
Germantown, MD 20874

Weinberger, Steve, Administrator
American Federation of Mineralogi-
cal Societies [6871]
c/o Steve Weinberger
PO Box 302
Glyndon, MD 21071-0302
Ph: (410)833-7926

Weindruch, Larry, President
National Ski and Snowboard Retailers Association [3143]

1601 Feehanville Dr., Ste. 300
Mount Prospect, IL 60056
Ph: (847)391-9825
Toll Free: 888-257-1168
Fax: (847)391-9827

Weinel, Jennifer, President
Society for International Affairs Inc.
[1994]
PO Box 9466
Arlington, VA 22219
Ph: (703)946-5683

Weiner, Susan L., PhD, Founder
Children's Cause for Cancer
Advocacy [13940]
122 C St. NW, Ste. 240
Washington, DC 20001-2109
Ph: (202)304-1850

Weingarten, Randi, President
AFT Nurses and Health Profession-
als [23442]
555 New Jersey Ave. NW
Washington, DC 20001
Ph: (202)879-4400

Weingarten, Randi, President
American Federation of Teachers
[23408]
555 New Jersey Ave. NW
Washington, DC 20001
Ph: (202)879-4400

Weinholtz, Donn, Clerk
Friends Association for Higher
Education [7961]
1501 Cherry St.
Philadelphia, PA 19102
Ph: (215)241-7116
Fax: (215)241-7078

Weinig, Cynthia, Secretary
Society for the Study of Evolution
[6623]
4475 Castleman Ave.
Saint Louis, MO 63110-3201
Ph: (314)577-9554

Weinman, Janice, CEO
Hadassah, The Women's Zionist
Organization of America [20248]
40 Wall St.
New York, NY 10005
Ph: (212)355-7900
Toll Free: 888-303-3640
Fax: (212)303-8282

Weinshank, John, President
Association of Trade and Forfaiting
in the Americas [1224]

Weinstein, Amy, Contact
National Scholarship Providers As-
sociation [8517]
2222 14th St.
Boulder, CO 80302
Fax: (303)443-5098

Weinstein, Barbara, Assoc. Dir.
Reform Judaism [20279]
2027 Massachusetts Ave. NW
Washington, DC 20036
Ph: (202)387-2800

Weinstein, Howard, President
United States Bridge Federation
[21561]
c/o Stan Subeck
106 Penn Ct.
Glenview, IL 60026

Weinstein, Lauren, Founder
People for Internet Responsibility
[18571]
SRI International EL-243
333 Ravenswood Ave.
Menlo Park, CA 94025-3453
Ph: (818)225-2800
    (650)859-2375

Weinstein, Loribeth, Exec. Dir.
Jewish Women International [20261]
1129 20th St. NW, Ste. 801
Washington, DC 20036
Ph: (202)857-1300
Toll Free: 800-343-2823
Fax: (202)857-1380

Weinstein, Marc A., Exec. Dir.
National Association of Forensic
Economics [5561]
PO Box 394
Mount Union, PA 17066
Ph: (814)542-3253
Toll Free: 866-370-6233
Fax: (814)542-3253

Weinstein, Mark H., MD, Director,
Founder
Changing Children's Lives [15442]
136 Sherman Ave., Ste. 407
New Haven, CT 06511
Ph: (203)907-0040
Fax: (203)907-4593

Weinstein, Michael, President
AIDS Healthcare Foundation [13523]
6255 W Sunset Blvd., Ste. 2100
Los Angeles, CA 90028
Ph: (323)860-5200
    (323)860-0173
Toll Free: 877-274-2548
Fax: (323)962-8513

Weinzweig, Dr. Jeffrey, Founder,
Exec. Dir.
Komedyplast [14340]
222 N Columbus Dr., Ste. 4702
Chicago, IL 60601
Ph: (617)530-0250
Fax: (312)276-4452

Weisend, John, II, Chairman
Cryogenic Society of America [6355]
c/o Laurie Huget, Executive Director
218 Lake St.
Oak Park, IL 60302-2609
Ph: (708)383-6220
Fax: (708)383-9337

Weisenfeld, Dr. Michael D.,
President
American Association of Dental
Consultants [1824]
10032 Wind Hill Dr.
Greenville, IN 47124
Ph: (812)923-2600
Toll Free: 800-896-0707
Fax: (812)923-2900

Weiser, Michael, Chairman
National Conference on Citizenship
[17857]
1100 17th St. NW, 12th Fl.
Washington, DC 20036
Ph: (202)601-7096

Weiser, Nora, Exec. Dir.
American Cheese Society [969]
2696 S Colorado Blvd., Ste. 570
Denver, CO 80222-5954
Ph: (720)328-2788
Fax: (720)328-2786

Weiser, Wendy J., Exec. Dir.
Society for Behavioral Neuroendocri-
nology [13804]
1100 E Woodfield Rd., Ste. 350
Schaumburg, IL 60173-5121
Ph: (847)517-7225
Fax: (847)517-7229

Weislogel, Carolyn, Contact
Angel Harps [16965]
c/o Carolyn Weislogel
6813 Windsor Rd.
Hudson, OH 44236-3253
Ph: (330)655-2185

Weisman, Serena, Exec. Dir.
Society of Vertebrate Paleontology
[6975]
9650 Rockville Pke.
Bethesda, MD 20814
Ph: (301)634-7024
Fax: (301)634-7455

Weismantle, Peter, President
Safety Glazing Certification Council
[577]
205 W Main St.
Sackets Harbor, NY 13685
Ph: (315)646-2234
Fax: (315)646-2297

Weiss, Allison, President
Latin American Art Song Alliance
[9945]
3333 S 900 E, No. 110
Salt Lake City, UT 84106-3167

Weiss, Rabbi Avi, Chairman
Israel Service Organization [12210]
151 Oxford Rd.
New Rochelle, NY 10804

Weiss, Danny L., Director, CEO
Hollow Earth Research Society
[12001]
c/o Danny Weiss
1529 Kenard St. NW
Salem, OR 97304
Ph: (503)990-6969

Weiss, David A., CEO, President
Global Communities [11969]
8601 Georgia Ave., Ste. 300
Silver Spring, MD 20910
Ph: (301)587-4700
Fax: (301)587-7315

Weiss, Ellen, President
VOSH International [12303]
12660 Q St.
Omaha, NE 68137

Weiss, Farley, President
National Council of Young Israel
[20271]
50 Eisenhower Dr., Ste. 102
Paramus, NJ 07652
Ph: (212)929-1525
Toll Free: 800-617-NCYI
Fax: (212)727-9526

Weiss, Prof. Gail, Gen. Sec.
Merleau-Ponty Circle [10101]
University of Rhode Island
Kingston, RI 02881
Ph: (401)874-1000

Weiss, Dr. Gary B., VP
Ryukyu Philatelic Specialist Society
[22360]
PO Box 240177
Charlotte, NC 28224-0177

Weiss, Harvey, Exec. Dir.
National Inhalant Prevention Coali-
tion [17322]
318 Lindsay St.
Chattanooga, TN 37403
Ph: (423)265-4662
Toll Free: 855-704-4400
Fax: (423)265-4889

Weiss, Johnny, Advisor, Founder
Solar Energy International [7208]
520 S 3rd St., Rm. 16
Carbondale, CO 81623
Ph: (970)963-8855
Fax: (970)963-8866

Weiss, Kay, Exec. Dir.
Mu Alpha Theta [23813]
c/o Kay Weiss, Executive Director
University of Oklahoma

3200 Marshall Ave., Ste. 190
Norman, OK 73019
Ph: (405)325-4489
Fax: (405)325-7184

Weiss, Mr. Kyle, Founder, Exec. Dir.
FUNDaFIELD [10991]
20 Alamo Springs Ct.
Danville, CA 94526

Weiss, Larry, Director
Copier Dealers Association [2443]
c/o John Lowery, President
5282 E Paris Ave. SE
Grand Rapids, MI 49512-9634

Weiss, Marc, Chairman, CEO
Global Urban Development [11368]
PO Box 1510
Rehoboth Beach, DE 19971

Weiss, Mark, Dir. Ed.
Operation Respect [7905]
199 New Rd., Ste. 61, No. 397
New York, NY 10121
Ph: (866)546-9291

Weiss, Randy, Chairperson
Partnership for Quality Medical
Donations [12298]
326 1st St., Ste. 32
Annapolis, MD 21403
Ph: (410)848-7036
Fax: (410)871-9031

Weiss, Robert, Treasurer
International Technology Law As-
sociation [5091]
7918 Jones Branch Dr., Ste. 300
McLean, VA 22102
Ph: (703)506-2895
Fax: (703)579-4366

Weiss, Steven P., President
National Association of Marine
Surveyors [6806]
3105 American Legion Rd., Ste. E
Chesapeake, VA 23321-5654
Ph: (757)638-9638
Toll Free: 800-822-6267
Fax: (757)638-9639

Weiss, Susan, President
The Educational Foundation for
Women in Accounting [8747]
136 S Keowee St.
Dayton, OH 45402
Ph: (937)424-3391
Fax: (937)222-5794

Weissberg, Ted, CEO
Association of Certified Anti-Money
Laundering Specialists [381]
Brickell City Twr.
80 SW 8th St., Ste. 2350
Miami, FL 33130
Ph: (305)373-0020
Fax: (305)373-7788

Weisslinger, Eileen M., Founder,
Chairman
Mir Pace International [12700]
137 Hampton Cir.
Hull, MA 02045
Ph: (781)925-0950

Weissman, Jane, President, CEO
Interstate Renewable Energy
Council [6495]
PO Box 1156
Latham, NY 12110-1156
Ph: (518)621-7379

Weissman, Peter, President
RadTech International North America
[7084]
7720 Wisconsin Ave., Ste. 208
Bethesda, MD 20814
Ph: (240)497-1242

Weissman, Robert, Managing Ed.
Commercial Alert [18940]
1600 20th St. NW
Washington, DC 20009-1001
Ph: (202)588-7741

Weissman, Robert, President
Public Citizen [18057]
1600 20th St. NW
Washington, DC 20009-1001
Ph: (202)588-1000
Toll Free: 800-289-3787
Fax: (202)588-7798

Weissman, Robert, President
Public Citizen Litigation Group
[18058]
1600 20th St. NW
Washington, DC 20009-1001
Ph: (202)588-1000

Weissmann, Rabbi Shlomo, Director
Beth Din of America [20236]
305 7th Ave., 12th Fl.
New York, NY 10001-6008
Ph: (212)807-9042
    (212)807-9072
Fax: (212)807-9183

Weisz, Jesse, Exec. Dir.
Global Exploration for Educators
Organization [8636]
2945 Morris Rd.
Ardmore, PA 19003
Toll Free: 877-600-0105

Weitzen, Gary, Exec. Dir.
Parents Of Autistic Children [13776]
1989 Route 88
Brick, NJ 08724
Ph: (732)785-1099
Fax: (732)785-1003

Wel, Jok Kuol, Founder, President
HELPSudan [11205]
5255 N Ashland Ave.
Chicago, IL 60640-2001
Ph: (773)353-1919

Welber, Chris, Exec. Dir.
North American Neuromodulation
Society [16562]
8735 W Higgins Rd., Ste. 300
Chicago, IL 60631
Ph: (847)375-4714
Fax: (847)375-6424

Welch, Michael, Contact
Redwood Alliance [18193]
PO Box 293
Arcata, CA 95518
Ph: (707)822-7884

Welch, Mike, President
American Football Coaches Associa-
tion [22854]
100 Legends Ln.
Waco, TX 76706
Ph: (254)754-9900
Fax: (254)754-7373

Welch, Peter, President
National Automobile Dealers As-
sociation [347]
8400 Westpark Dr.
Tysons, VA 22102
Ph: (703)821-7000
Toll Free: 800-252-6232
Fax: (703)821-7234

Welch, Stephen J., Sr. VP, Publisher
American College of Chest Physi-
cians [14090]
2595 Patriot Blvd.
Glenview, IL 60026
Ph: (224)521-9800
Toll Free: 800-343-2227
Fax: (224)521-9801

Welch, Theodor J., 1st VP
32nd Red Arrow Veteran Association
[20699]
c/o Theodor J. Welch, 1st Vice
President
1113 N 8th St.
Manitowoc, WI 54220-2817
Ph: (608)271-3075

Welcome, Jerry, President, CEO
Reusable Packaging Association
[4636]
PO Box 25078
Tampa, FL 33622
Ph: (813)358-5327

Weld, Yvonne, President
International Virtual Assistants As-
sociation [74]
2360 Corporate Cir., Ste. 400
Henderson, NV 89074-7739
Ph: (702)583-4970
Toll Free: 877-440-2750

Weldon, James R., Secretary
HealthCare Chaplaincy Network
[20561]
65 Broadway, 12th Fl.
New York, NY 10006
Ph: (212)644-1111
Fax: (212)486-1440

Weldon, Susan, Founder, President
Unite for HER [14077]
PO Box 351
Pocopson, PA 19366
Ph: (610)322-9552
    (484)431-6776

Welf, Kelley A., Dir. of Comm.
Charles A. and Anne Morrow Lind-
bergh Foundation [4080]
PO Box 861
Berkeley Springs, WV 25411
Ph: (703)623-1944

Welle, Kenneth, President
Association of Avian Veterinarians
[17634]
PO Box 9
Teaneck, NJ 07666
Ph: (720)458-4111
Fax: (720)398-3496

Weller, Paul S., Jr., President
Apple Processors Association [4228]
1701 K St. NW, Ste. 650
Washington, DC 20006
Ph: (202)785-6715
Fax: (202)331-4212

Weller, Tom, President
National Association of Milk Bottle
Collectors [21690]
18 Pond Pl.
Cos Cob, CT 06807-2220

Wellikson, Laurence, MD, CEO
Society of Hospital Medicine [15336]
1500 Spring Garden St., Ste. 501
Philadelphia, PA 19130
Ph: (267)702-2601
Toll Free: 800-843-3360
Fax: (267)702-2690

Welling, Bradley, Officer
American Otological Society [16536]
c/o Kristen Bordignon, Administrator
4960 Dover St. NE
Saint Petersburg, FL 33703
Ph: (217)638-0801
Fax: (727)800-9428

Wellman, Rikki, Exec. Dir.
Pacific Logging Congress [1415]
PO Box 1281
Maple Valley, WA 98038
Ph: (425)413-2808

Wellman, Susan, Founder
Ophelia Project [13472]
718 Nevada Dr.
Erie, PA 16505
Ph: (814)456-5437
Fax: (814)455-2090

Wells, Barby, Director
National Teen Age Republicans
[19045]
10610-A Crestwood Professional Ctr.
Manassas, VA 20108
Ph: (703)368-4220

Wells, Bruce, Exec. Dir., Founder
American Oil and Gas Historical
Society [2510]
c/o Bruce A. Wells, Executive Direc-
tor
1201 15th St. NW, Ste. 300
Washington, DC 20005
Ph: (202)387-6996
Fax: (202)857-4799

Wells, Carol A., Exec. Dir., Founder
Center for the Study of Political
Graphics [8849]
3916 Sepulveda Blvd., Ste. 103
Culver City, CA 90230
Ph: (310)397-3100
Fax: (310)397-9305

Wells, Carolyn, Exec. Dir.
Kansas City Barbeque Society
[22149]
11514 Hickman Mills Dr.
Kansas City, MO 64134
Ph: (816)765-5891
Toll Free: 800-963-5227

Wells, Dr. Christopher, Bd. Member
American Friends of the Anglican
Centre in Rome [19701]

Wells, Dr. Christopher, Exec. Dir.,
Editor
Living Church Foundation [20111]
816 E Juneau Ave.
Milwaukee, WI 53202-2793
Ph: (414)276-5420
        (414)292-1240
Toll Free: 800-211-2771
Fax: (414)276-7483

Wells, Elizabeth, VP
SNAC International [1372]
1600 Wilson Blvd., Ste. 650
Arlington, VA 22209
Ph: (703)836-4500
Toll Free: 800-628-1334

Wells, G. Brian, President
Energy and Mineral Law Foundation
[5651]
340 S Broadway, Ste. 101
Lexington, KY 40508
Ph: (859)231-0271
Fax: (859)226-0485

Wells, Orin R., President
Wells Family Research Association
[20942]
PO Box 5427
Kent, WA 98064-5427
Ph: (253)630-5296
Fax: (253)639-2701

Wells, Richard, VP
Offshore Marine Service Association
[2255]
935 Graver St., Ste. 2040
New Orleans, LA 70112-1657
Ph: (504)528-9411
Fax: (504)528-9415

Wells, Rocky, Gen. Mgr.
The Doe Network [12361]
420 Airport Rd.

Livingston, TN 38570-1268
Ph: (931)397-3893

Welna, Christopher, President
Associated Colleges of the Midwest
[7620]
11 E Adams St., Ste. 800
Chicago, IL 60603
Ph: (312)263-5000
Fax: (312)263-5879

Welsh, Cheryl, Director
Mind Justice [18425]
c/o Cheryl Welsh, Director
915 Zaragoza St.
Davis, CA 95618

Welsh, Richard, Exec. Dir.
National Association of Reversionary
Property Owners [18932]
227 Bellevue Way NE, Ste. 719
Bellevue, WA 98004
Ph: (425)646-8812

Welsh, Rev. Robert K., President
Council on Christian Unity [20059]
PO Box 1986
Indianapolis, IN 46206
Ph: (317)635-3100
        (317)713-2585

Welsh, Dr. Robert K., Gen. Sec.
Disciples Ecumenical Consultative
Council [20023]
c/o Council on Christian Unity
PO Box 1986
Indianapolis, IN 46206
Ph: (317)713-2585

Welsher, Terry, President
Electrical Overstress/Electrostatic
Discharge Association [6418]
Bldg. 3
7900 Turin Rd.
Rome, NY 13440-2069
Ph: (315)339-6937
Fax: (315)339-6793

Wempe, Evelyn P., President
Association for Radiologic and Imag-
ing Nursing [17054]
2201 Cooperative Way, Ste. 600
Herndon, VA 20171
Ph: (703)884-2229
Toll Free: 866-486-2762

Wendel, Jeffrey, Chairman
Association for the Accreditation of
Human Research Protection
Programs [7085]
2301 M St. NW, Ste. 500
Washington, DC 20037-1427
Ph: (202)783-1112
Toll Free: 888-601-1112
Fax: (202)783-1113

Wendell, Daren, Exec. Dir., Founder
ActiveWater [13312]
PO Box 3131
San Luis Obispo, CA 93403
Toll Free: 888-543-3426

Wender, Dr. Richard, Chairman
National Colorectal Cancer
Roundtable [14026]
901 E St. NW, Ste. 500
Washington, DC 20004
Ph: (202)661-5729
Fax: (202)661-5750

Wendorf, Richard, Director
Friends of the American Museum in
Britain/Halcyon Foundation [8791]
555 5th Ave., 17th Fl.
New York, NY 10017
Ph: (212)370-0198

Wendt, Alan, President
Boating Writers International [2668]
108 9th St.

Wilmette, IL 60091
Ph: (847)736-4142

Wenger, Laura, RN, Contact
Practice Greenhealth [14722]
12355 Sunrise Valley Dr., Ste. 680
Reston, VA 20191
Toll Free: 888-688-3332
Fax: (866)379-8705

Wenk, Janet, President, Founder
Friends of Namibian Children
[10987]
PO Box 5572
Phoenix, AZ 85010
Ph: (623)444-8171
Fax: (623)466-0688

Wenmark, William H., President
National Association for Ambulatory
Care [13676]
5396 Ashcroft Rd.
Minnetonka, MN 55345
Ph: (952)544-6199
Toll Free: 866-793-1396
Fax: (952)544-0979

Wensel, Kevin, President
Stucco Manufacturers Association
[587]
5753 E Santa Ana Cyn Rd.
Anaheim, CA 92807
Ph: (949)387-7611
Fax: (949)701-4476

Wenskunas, Patricia, CEO, Founder
Crime Survivors [11504]
PO Box 54552
Irvine, CA 92619-4552
Ph: (949)872-7895
Toll Free: 844-853-4673
Fax: (775)245-4798

Wentz, Darrin, Sales Mgr.
Waterfowl U.S.A. [3963]
Waterfowl Bldg.
Edgefield, SC 29824
Ph: (803)637-5767

Wenzel, Frank, President
Antique Studebaker Club [21328]
PO Box 1715
Maple Grove, MN 55311-6715
Ph: (763)420-7829

Werden, Jeffrey, President
National Psychological Association
for Psychoanalysis [16849]
40 W 13th St.
New York, NY 10011
Ph: (212)924-7440
Fax: (212)989-7543

Werneke, Mike, Contact
National Institute of Packaging,
Handling and Logistics Engineers
[6969]
5903 Ridgeway Dr.
Grand Prairie, TX 75052
Ph: (817)466-7490

Werner, Bret, VP
Great War Association [9802]
c/o Chris Garcia, Treasurer
418 Chinaberry Ct.
Virginia Beach, VA 23454-3331
Ph: (757)631-0661

Werner, Carol, Exec. Dir.
Environmental and Energy Study
Institute [4001]
1112 16th St. NW, Ste. 300
Washington, DC 20036
Ph: (202)628-1400
Fax: (202)204-5244

Werner, David, Director
Health Wrights [17004]
PO Box 1344

Palo Alto, CA 94302
Ph: (650)325-7500
Fax: (650)325-1080

Werner, Lois, Founder
People for Guatemala Inc. [12807]
400 5th Ave. S, Ste. 304
Naples, FL 34102
Ph: (941)244-8692

Werner, Michael, Exec. VP
Lymphoma Research Foundation
[14006]
115 Broadway, Ste. 1301
New York, NY 10006-1623
Ph: (212)349-2910
Toll Free: 800-500-9976
Fax: (212)349-2886

Werner, Richard, Exec.
Steel Tube Institute of North America
[846]
2516 Waukegan Rd., Ste. 172
Glenview, IL 60025
Ph: (847)461-1701
Fax: (847)660-7981

Wernick, Rabbi Steven C., CEO
United Synagogue of Conservative
Judaism [20287]
120 Broadway, Ste. 1540
New York, NY 10271-0016
Ph: (212)533-7800
Fax: (212)353-9439

Werse, Steven, Secretary, Treasurer
International Organization of
Masters, Mates and Pilots [23475]
700 Maritime Blvd., Ste. B
Linthicum, MD 21090-1953
Ph: (410)850-8700
Toll Free: 877-667-5522

Werstler, Ronnie, Founder
Caring Now for Kids with Cystic
Fibrosis [17136]
PO Box 851777
Mobile, AL 36685
Ph: (251)623-3684

Wertz, Ryan, President
National Council of State Supervi-
sors for Languages [8190]
25 S Front St.
Ohio Dept. of Education
25 S Front St.
Mail Stop No. 509
Columbus, OH 43215-4183
Ph: (614)728-4630

Wescott, George, President
National Intercollegiate Soccer Officials Association [23188]
c/o NISOA Foundation Fund
1030 Ohio Ave.
Cape May, NJ 08204

Wesloh, Karen, Exec. Dir.
Incentive Manufacturers and
Representatives Alliance [2205]
4248 Park Glen Rd.
Minneapolis, MN 55416
Ph: (952)928-4661

Wesloh, Karen, Exec. Dir.
Incentive Marketing Association
[2283]
4248 Park Glen Rd.
Minneapolis, MN 55416
Ph: (952)928-4649

Wesolowski, Paul G., Director
Marx Brotherhood [24010]
335 Fieldstone Dr.
New Hope, PA 18938-1012
Ph: (215)862-9734

Wessel, Paul, Exec. Dir.
Green Parking Council [4519]
55 Church St., 7th Fl.

New Haven, CT 06510
Ph: (203)672-5892

Wessel, Rusty, V. Chmn. of the Bd.
American Cichlid Association
[22027]
c/o Dr. Tim Hovanec, Tresurer
530 Los Angeles Ave., Ste. 115-243
Moorpark, CA 93021
Ph: (631)668-5125

Wessels, Dione, President, CEO
North American Strongman [22699]
PO Box 1973
Maryland Heights, MO 63043
Ph: (314)565-5970

Wessels, Sally, Chmn. of the Bd.
Committee on US/Latin American
Relations [19529]
316 Anabel Taylor Hall
Cornell University
Ithaca, NY 14853
Ph: (607)255-7293
Fax: (607)255-9550

Wessen, Doug, Comm. Chm.
Mountain Rescue Association
[12744]
PO Box 880868
San Diego, CA 92168-0868

Wessman, Ann, President
National Student Employment As-
sociation [8439]
9600 Escarpment Blvd., Ste. 745,
PMB 11
Austin, TX 78749
Ph: (512)423-1417
Fax: (972)767-5131

West, John, Chairman
Society of International Business
Fellows [1972]
Peachtree Ctr., Ste. 1410
South Twr.
225 Peachtree St. NE
Atlanta, GA 30303
Ph: (404)525-7423
Fax: (404)525-5331

West, Melanie F., CEO, Exec. Dir.
American Tinnitus Association
[17238]
522 SW 5th Ave., Ste. 825
Portland, OR 97204
Ph: (503)248-9985
Toll Free: 800-634-8978
Fax: (503)248-0024

West, Robert, Exec. Dir., Founder
Working Films [9319]
624 1/2 S 7th St
Wilmington, NC 28401
Ph: (910)342-9000
Fax: (910)342-9003

West, Scot, President
Sail America [438]
50 Water St.
Warren, RI 02885-3034
Ph: (401)289-2540
Fax: (401)247-0074

West, Terry, Secretary, Treasurer
National Association of State Credit
Union Supervisor [5124]
1655 N Ft. Myer Dr., Ste. 650
Arlington, VA 22209
Ph: (703)528-8351
Fax: (703)528-3248

West, Todd, Dir. of Dev.
Committee for Economic Develop-
ment [18146]
1530 Wilson Blvd., Ste. 400
Arlington, VA 22209
Ph: (202)296-5860
Toll Free: 800-676-7353
Fax: (202)223-0776

West, Travis, President
U.S. Army Ranger Association
[20727]
PO Box 52126
Fort Benning, GA 31995-2126
Ph: (608)561-1779

Westaway, Maxine, Exec. Dir.
The International Alliance for Women
[637]
1101 Pennsylvania Ave. NW, 6th Fl.
Washington, DC 20004-2544
Toll Free: 888-712-5200

Westbrook, Ray, Chairperson
Columbia Scholastic Press Advisers
Association [8453]
Columbia Scholastic Press Associa-
tion
Columbia University
90 Morningside Dr., Ste. B01, MC
5711
New York, NY 10027-6902
Ph: (212)854-9400

West-Conforti, Linda, CEO, Founder
Angels In Waiting [10855]
PO Box 1221
Blue Jay, CA 92317
Toll Free: 800-974-4274

Westenhofer, Cindy, President
Credit Professionals International
[1229]
10726 Manchester Rd., Ste. 210
Saint Louis, MO 63122
Ph: (314)821-9393
Fax: (314)821-7171

Wester, Thomas, Chairman
National Board for Certification in
Dental Laboratory Technology
[14459]
325 John Knox Rd., No. L103
Tallahassee, FL 32303
Ph: (850)205-5627
Toll Free: 800-684-5310
Fax: (850)222-0053

Westerfield, Allen D., President
Imaging Supplies Coalition [5329]
MBN 249
1435 E Venice Ave., No. 104
Venice, FL 34292-3074
Ph: (941)961-7897

Westerfield, William, President
Park Law Enforcement Association
[5668]
4397 McCullough St.
Port Charlotte, FL 33948
Ph: (941)286-7410

Westermann, Dwayne, President
Godparents for Tanzania [11004]
PO Box 20221
Roanoke, VA 24018

Westgate, Chris, President
The Eugene O'Neill Society [9087]
700 Hawthorn Ct.
San Ramon, CA 94582

Westhaver, Susan, Admin. Ofc.,
Memb. Ofc.
World Wide Web Consortium [6268]
Massachusetts Institute of Technol-
ogy
32 Vassar St., Rm. 32-G515
Cambridge, MA 02139
Ph: (617)253-2613
Fax: (617)258-5999

Westin, Monica, Founder, President
World of Hope International [12199]
Dag Hammarskjold Ctre., No. 20149
884 2nd Ave., UN Plz.
New York, NY 10017
Ph: (347)323-9333
Fax: (347)323-9333

Westine, Lezlee, President, CEO
Personal Care Product Council
[1587]
1620 L St. NW, Ste. 1200
Washington, DC 20036
Ph: (202)331-1770
Fax: (202)331-1969

Westley, Elizabeth, Coord.
International Consortium for
Emergency Contraception [11843]
Family Care International
45 Broadway, Ste. 320
New York, NY 10006
Ph: (212)941-5300

Westmoreland, Andrew, President
American Association of Presidents
of Independent Colleges and
Universities [8008]
c/o Steven M. Sandberg, Executive
Director
PO Box 7070
Provo, UT 84602-7070
Ph: (801)422-2235
Fax: (801)422-0265

Weston, Frank, Chairman, President
International Multiracial Shared
Cultural Organization [18548]
4 Park Ave.
New York, NY 10016-5339
Ph: (212)532-5449

Weston, Greg, President
College Broadcasters, Inc. [458]
UPS - Hershey Square Ctr.
1152 Mae St.
Hummelstown, PA 17036
Toll Free: 855-275-4224

Weston, Ian, Exec. Dir.
American Trauma Society [17526]
201 Park Washington Ct.
Falls Church, VA 22046
Ph: (703)538-3544
Toll Free: 800-556-7890
Fax: (703)241-5603

Westrich, Tiffany, CEO, Founder
International Autoimmune Arthritis
Movement [17158]
646 S Barrington Ave.
Los Angeles, CA 90049
Toll Free: 877-609-4226

Wethington, Susan, Exec. Dir.,
Founder
Hummingbird Monitoring Network
[3663]
PO Box 115
Patagonia, AZ 85624

Wetstone, Gregory, President, CEO
American Council on Renewable
Energy [6453]
1600 K St. NW, Ste. 650
Washington, DC 20006
Ph: (202)393-0001
Fax: (202)393-0606

Wettemann, Robert P., President
American Registry of Professional
Animal Scientists [3614]
1800 S Oak St., Ste. 100
Champaign, IL 61820-6974
Ph: (217)356-5390
Fax: (217)398-4119

Wetter, Paul Alan, MD, Chairman
Society of Laparoendoscopic
Surgeons [17403]
7330 SW 62nd Pl., Ste. 410
Miami, FL 33143-4825
Ph: (305)665-9959

Wexler, Chuck, Exec. Dir.
Police Executive Research Forum
[5514]

1120 Connecticut Ave. NW, Ste. 930
Washington, DC 20036
Ph: (202)466-7820

Wexler, Deborah L., MD, Exec. Dir.
Immunization Action Coalition
[15380]
2550 University Ave. W, Ste. 415 N
Saint Paul, MN 55114
Ph: (651)647-9009
Fax: (651)647-9131

Wexler, Nancy S., PhD, President
Hereditary Disease Foundation
[15939]
3960 Broadway, 6th Fl.
New York, NY 10032
Ph: (212)928-2121
Fax: (212)928-2172

Wexler, Richard, Exec. Dir.
National Coalition for Child Protec-
tion Reform [11091]
53 Skyhill Rd., Ste. 202
Alexandria, VA 22314-4997
Ph: (703)212-2006

Wexner, Steven D., MD,PhD,
President
American Society of Colon and
Rectal Surgeons [16804]
85 W Algonquin Rd., Ste. 550
Arlington Heights, IL 60005
Ph: (847)290-9184
Fax: (847)290-9203

Weyhmuller, Gary J., MBA, Exec.
VP, COO
National Comprehensive Cancer
Network [14027]
275 Commerce Dr., Ste. 300
Fort Washington, PA 19034
Ph: (215)690-0300
Fax: (215)690-0280

Weyrich, Dr. James, CEO
EyeCare WeCare Foundation
[17698]
304 N Talbot
Montesano, WA 98563
Ph: (360)593-2353
Fax: (360)249-3024

Wezeman, Phyllis, President
Malawi Matters [13552]
PO Box 11694
South Bend, IN 46634
Ph: (574)255-3570

Whalen, Douglas H., Founder, Chair-
man
Endangered Language Fund [9650]
300 George St., Ste. 900
New Haven, CT 06511-6660
Ph: (203)865-6163
Fax: (203)865-8963

Whalen, Edward, Chairman
American Railway Car Institute
[2832]
c/o Railway Supply Institute, Inc.,
425 Third St., SW, Ste. 920
425 3rd St. SW, Ste. 920
Washington, DC 20024
Ph: (202)347-4664
(202)347-0047

Whan, Michael, Commissioner
Ladies Professional Golf Association
[22885]
100 International Golf Dr.
Daytona Beach, FL 32124-1092
Ph: (386)274-6200
Fax: (386)274-1099

Whan, Dr. Norm, Chairman,
President, Founder
Canning Hunger [12079]
407 W Imperial Hwy., Ste. H-313

Brea, CA 92821
Ph: (714)990-9234
Fax: (714)582-2452

Wheat, J. Marc, President
Memorial Foundation of the Ger-
manna Colonies in Virginia [9410]
PO Box 279
Locust Grove, VA 22508-0279
Ph: (540)423-1700
Fax: (540)423-1747

Wheat, Tim, Exec. Dir.
Phi Delta Phi International Legal
Fraternity [23806]
PO Box 11570
Fort Lauderdale, FL 33339
Ph: (202)223-6801
Fax: (202)223-6808

Wheeler, Bill, President
Thunderbird and Cougar Club of
America [21501]
422 Cooper St.
Mountain Home, AR 72653

Wheeler, Darrell P., PhD, MPH,
President
National Association of Social Work-
ers I National Committee on
Lesbian, Gay and Bisexual Issues
[11897]
750 1st St. NE, Ste. 700
Washington, DC 20002
Ph: (202)408-8600
Toll Free: 800-742-4089

Wheeler, Ernest, President
Metropolitan Air Post Society
[22344]
c/o Ernest Wheeler, President
7 Evelyn Ter.
Wayne, NJ 07470-3446

Wheeler, Geoff, President
International Association of Jazz
Record Collectors [22249]
c/o Ian Tiele, Treasurer
PO Box 524
Brookfield, IL 60513-0524

Wheeler, Gordon, President
Esalen Institute [9535]
55000 Highway 1
Big Sur, CA 93920-9546
Ph: (831)667-3000
Toll Free: 888-837-2536

Wheeler, Judy, Chmn. of the Bd.
The Global Child [11000]
5 Short Bluff Rd.
Newport, VT 05855
Ph: (518)423-8780

Wheeler, Kelly, President
Animal Transportation Association
[10581]
12100 Sunset Hills Rd., Ste. 130
Reston, VA 20190-3221
Ph: (703)437-4377
Fax: (703)435-4390

Wheeler, Mark, President
American Power Boat Association
[22594]
17640 E 9 Mile Rd.
Eastpointe, MI 48021-2563
Ph: (586)773-9700
Fax: (586)773-6490

Wheeler, Sarah Kay, President
Health Care Compliance Association
[15008]
6500 Barrie Rd., Ste. 250
Minneapolis, MN 55435-2358
Ph: (952)405-7900
    (952)988-0141
Toll Free: 888-580-8373
Fax: (952)988-0146

Wheeler, Terry, President
Natural History Network [6898]
PO Box 533
Bar Harbor, ME 04609

Whelan, Elizabeth M., Founder
American Council on Science and
Health [14923]
1995 Broadway, Ste. 202
New York, NY 10023-5882
Toll Free: 866-905-2694
Fax: (212)362-4919

Whelan, Jean, President
American Association for the History
of Nursing [9450]
10200 W 44th Ave., Ste. 304
Wheat Ridge, CO 80033
Ph: (303)422-2685
Fax: (720)881-6101

Whelchel, Sandy, Editor
National Writers Association [2709]
10940 S Parker Rd., No. 508
Parker, CO 80134
Ph: (303)841-0246
Fax: (303)841-2607

Whetter, Kevin, VP
International Arthurian Society -
North American Branch [9758]
c/o Evelyn Meyer, Secretary/
Treasurer
6637A San Bonita Ave.
Clayton, MO 63105-3121

Whidden, Richard R., Jr., Counsel,
Exec. Dir.
National Law Center for Children
and Families [5193]
501 W Broadway, Ste. 1310
San Diego, CA 92101
Ph: (703)548-5522

Whinston, James P., Contact
Kids Need Both Parents [18197]
PO Box 6481
Portland, OR 97228-6481
Ph: (503)727-3686
    (516)942-2020

Whipple, Jack, Secretary
International Edsel Club [21401]
PO Box 312
Muskego, WI 53150

Whipple, Krista, VP
Alpha Omicron Pi [23944]
5390 Virginia Way
Brentwood, TN 37027
Ph: (615)370-0920
Toll Free: 855-230-1183
Fax: (615)371-9736

Whipple, Michael, Chmn. of the Bd.
International Orphan Care [11050]
23201 Mill Creek Dr., Ste. 130
Laguna Hills, CA 92653-1692
Ph: (949)939-1712

Whipple, Randy, Treasurer
Working Ranch Cowboys Associa-
tion [4621]
408 SW 7th Ave.
Amarillo, TX 79101
Ph: (806)374-9722

Whipple, Robert, President
Death Valley '49ers Inc. [9386]
24601 Glen Ivy Rd., No. 39
Corona, CA 92883

Whisenand, Tymothy, Cmdr.
National Society of Pershing Rifles
[23823]
2 Spring Meadow Ln.
Hockessin, DE 19707
Ph: (605)390-3001

Whistler, Donald M., Treasurer
High Twelve International Inc.
[19561]
11404 W Olive Dr.
Avondale, AZ 85392-4210
Fax: (623)239-6170

Whiston, Julia, Exec. Dir.
White House Correspondents' As-
sociation [2732]
600 New Hampshire Ave., Ste. 800
Washington, DC 20037
Ph: (202)266-7453
Fax: (202)266-7454

Whitacre, Bruce E., Exec. Dir.
Theatre Forward [10276]
505 8th Ave., Ste. 2303
New York, NY 10018
Ph: (212)750-6895
Fax: (212)750-6977

Whitaker, Angie, Exec. Dir.
National Association of State
Contractors Licensing Agencies
[884]
Bldg. 1, Unit 110
23309 N 17th Dr.
Phoenix, AZ 85027
Ph: (623)587-9354
Toll Free: 866-948-3363
Fax: (623)587-9625

Whitaker, Jeff, VP
Passenger Vessel Association
[2256]
103 Oronoco St., Ste. 200
Alexandria, VA 22314
Ph: (703)518-5005
Toll Free: 800-807-8360
Fax: (703)518-5151

Whitaker, Kathryn, Secretary
Legal Marketing Association [2288]
330 N Wabash Ave., Ste. 2000
Chicago, IL 60611
Ph: (312)321-6898
Fax: (312)673-6894

Whitcraft, Paul, Chmn. of the Bd.
Materials Technology Institute [721]
1215 Fern Ridge Pky., Ste. 206
Saint Louis, MO 63141-4405
Ph: (314)576-7712
Fax: (314)576-6078

White, Alan, President
Florence Ballard Fan Club [24036]
PO Box 360502
Los Angeles, CA 90036

White, Andy, Coord.
Rights and Resources Initiative
[4215]
1238 Wisconsin Ave. NW, Ste. 300
Washington, DC 20007
Ph: (202)470-3900
    (202)470-3890
Fax: (202)944-3315

White, Bailey, President
United States A-Class Catamaran
Association [22678]
33 Broadcommon Rd.
Bristol, RI 02809-2721

White, Bill, Treasurer
Association for the Rhetoric of Science and Technology [10197]
c/o William J. White, Treasurer
3000 Ivyside Pk.
Altoona, PA 16601

White, Bryan, Exec. Dir.
Automotive Oil Change Association
[339]
330 N Wabash Ave., Ste. 2000
Chicago, IL 60611
Ph: (312)321-5132
Toll Free: 800-230-0702
Fax: (312)673-6832

White, Camille, Contact
Association of Otolaryngology
Administrators [15582]
2400 Ardmore Blvd., Ste. 302
Pittsburgh, PA 15221
Ph: (412)243-5156
Fax: (412)243-5160

White, Claire, Director
Evidence Photographers
International Council [5244]
229 Peachtree St. NE, No. 2200
Atlanta, GA 30303
Toll Free: 866-868-3742
Fax: (404)614-6406

White, Claire, VP
National Lawyers Guild [5042]
132 Nassau St., Rm. 922
New York, NY 10038
Ph: (212)679-5100
Fax: (212)679-2811

White, Cora E., President, CEO
Foster Care Children & Family Fund
[12413]
PO Box 2534
Madison, WI 53701-2534
Ph: (608)274-9111
Fax: (608)274-4838

White, Debbie, Director
Christian Overcomers [11581]
PO Box 2007
Garfield, NJ 07026
Ph: (973)253-2343

White, Deborah, Exec. VP
Retail Industry Leaders Association
[2976]
1700 N Moore St., Ste. 2250
Arlington, VA 22209
Ph: (703)841-2300
Fax: (703)841-1184

White, Debra, Dir. of Accred.
Commission on Opticianry Accredita-
tion [16413]
c/o Debra White, Director of Ac-
creditation
PO Box 592
Canton, NY 13617
Ph: (703)468-0566

White, Deirdre, CEO, President
PYXERA Global [18498]
1030 15th St. NW, Ste. 730 E
Washington, DC 20005
Ph: (202)872-0900
Fax: (202)872-0923

White, Diana, Director
National Association of Math Circles
[8282]
c/o Mathematical Sciences Research
Institute
17 Gauss Way
Berkeley, CA 94720-5070
Ph: (510)642-0143

White, DJ, CEO, President, Founder
Earthtrust [4809]
1118 Maunawili Rd.
Kailua, HI 96734
Ph: (415)662-3264
Fax: (206)202-3893

White, Donald, President
United States Air Consolidator As-
sociation [3403]
C and H International
4751 Wilshire Blvd., Ste. 201
New York, NY 10036
Toll Free: 800-833-8888

White, Dr. Gary, Director
Society of Physics Students [7031]
1 Physics Ellipse

College Park, MD 20740
Ph: (301)209-3007

White, Mr. Gary, CEO, Founder
Water.org [13349]
920 Main St., Ste. 1800
Kansas City, MO 64105
Ph: (816)877-8400

White, Greg, Exec. Dir.
National Association of Regulatory
  Utility Commissioners [5833]
1101 Vermont Ave. NW, Ste. 200
Washington, DC 20005
Ph: (202)898-2200
Fax: (202)898-2213

White, Gregory, Exec. Dir.
National Academy of Education
  [7783]
500 5th St. NW
Washington, DC 20001

White, Jack, Secretary
Restoration Industry Association
  [2140]
2025 M St. NW, Ste. 800
Washington, DC 20036
Ph: (202)367-1180
Fax: (202)367-2180

White, James, President
National CPA Health Care Advisors
  Association [50]
1801 W End Ave., Ste. 800
Nashville, TN 37203
Ph: (615)373-9880
Toll Free: 800-231-2524
Fax: (615)377-7092

White, Jeff, Secretary, Treasurer
National Association of Shortwave
  Broadcasters [473]
175 Fontainebleau Blvd., Ste. 1N4
Miami, FL 33172
Ph: (305)559-9764
Fax: (305)559-8186

White, Jerry, Director
Christian Leadership Alliance
  [20560]
635 Camino de los Mares, Ste. 216
San Clemente, CA 92673
Ph: (949)487-0900
Fax: (949)487-0927

White, Joel, President
Council for Affordable Health Cover-
  age [15097]
1101 14th St. NW, Ste. 700
Washington, DC 20005
Ph: (202)559-0205

White, John, Treasurer
Air Forces Escape and Evasion
  Society [20682]
c/o Richard Shandor, Membership
  and Corresponding Secretary
PO Box 254
Cresson, PA 16630-2129
Ph: (814)886-2735
  (978)869-3035

White, John, Secretary, Treasurer
National Association of Naval
  Photography [5678]
1435 Lake Baldwin Ln.
Orlando, FL 32814

White, John, Director
National Senior Games Association
  [23065]
PO Box 82059
Baton Rouge, LA 70884-2059
Ph: (225)766-6800
Fax: (225)766-9115

White, Judith, Contact
Support Our Shelters [10700]
100 Walsh Rd.

Lansdowne, PA 19050-2117
Ph: (610)626-6647

White, Kevin, Founder, Exec. Dir.
Global Vision 2020 [17704]
102 E Dover St.
Easton, MD 21601-3332
Ph: (410)253-1543

White, Lawrence M., Secretary
International Skeletal Society
  [17057]
1100 E Woodfield Rd., Ste. 350
Schaumburg, IL 60173
Ph: (847)517-7225
Fax: (847)517-7229

White, Lee, VP
American Photographic Artists
  [2572]
5042 Wilshire Blvd., No. 321
Los Angeles, CA 90036
Toll Free: 888-272-6264

White, Lee, Exec. Dir.
National Coalition for History [9498]
400 A St. SE
Washington, DC 20003
Ph: (202)544-2422

White, Lisa L., PhD, Founder, Exec.
  Dir.
Rock Against Cancer [14057]
4711 Hope Valley Rd.
Durham, NC 27707
Toll Free: 877-246-0976

White, Megan, Coord.
Lama Foundation [9540]
PO Box 240
San Cristobal, NM 87564-0240
Ph: (575)586-1269
Fax: (206)984-0916

White, Melanie, Chairperson
Light Truck Accessory Alliance [325]
1575 Valley Vista Dr.
Diamond Bar, CA 91765

White, Michael, President
Screen Manufacturers Association
  [1575]
c/o Kathryn R. Fitzgerald
10526 S Ave. J
Chicago, IL 60617
Fax: (801)469-9727

White, Penny L., JD, President
National Contract Management As-
  sociation [1514]
21740 Beaumeade Cir., Ste. 125
Ashburn, VA 20147
Ph: (571)382-0082
Toll Free: 800-344-8096
Fax: (703)448-0939

White, Regina Lee, President
American Academy of Physician Assistants in Occupational Medicine
  [16310]
174 Monticello Pl.
Elizabethtown, KY 42701

White, Rich, Exec. Dir.
Car Care Council [289]
7101 Wisconsin Ave., Ste. 1300
Bethesda, MD 20814
Ph: (240)333-1088

White, Rich, President
Lutheran Men in Mission [20311]
8765 W Higgins Rd.
Chicago, IL 60631
Toll Free: 800-638-3522
Fax: (773)380-2632

White, Richard A., Act. Pres., Acting
  CEO
American Public Transportation As-
  sociation [3321]

1300 I St. NW, Ste. 1200 E
Washington, DC 20005
Ph: (202)496-4800
Fax: (202)496-4324

White, Robert, President
Society of Saint Gianna Beretta
  Molla [11830]
PO Box 2946
Warminster, PA 18974-0095
Ph: (215)657-3101

White, Signe, President
National Lutheran Outdoors Ministry
  Association [20317]
PO Box 1965
Hailey, ID 83333
Ph: (208)720-4371

White, Stephen C., President
International Congress of Maritime
  Museums [9831]
c/o Stephen C. White, President
Mystic Seaport
75 Greenmanville Ave.
Mystic, CT 06355-1946

White, Stephen C., President
Mystic Seaport [9775]
75 Greenmanville Ave.
Mystic, CT 06355-0990
Ph: (860)572-0711
  (860)572-5367
Toll Free: 888-973-2767
Fax: (860)572-5395

White, Stephen L., Chairman
Pulmonary Hypertension Association
  [15350]
801 Roeder Rd., Ste. 1000
Silver Spring, MD 20910
Ph: (301)565-3004
Toll Free: 800-748-7274
Fax: (301)565-3994

White, Tacey, President
Teratology Society [6105]
1821 Michael Faraday Dr., Ste. 300
Reston, VA 20190
Ph: (703)438-3104
Fax: (703)438-3113

White, Terri, VP
Portuguese Historical and Cultural
  Society [19620]
PO Box 161990
Sacramento, CA 95816
Ph: (916)391-7356
  (530)662-8246
Fax: (916)427-3903

White, Timothy P., Chairman
Second Nature [7971]
18 Tremont St., Ste. 930
Boston, MA 02108
Ph: (617)722-0036
Fax: (320)451-1612

White, V. John, Exec. Dir.
Center for Energy Efficiency and
  Renewable Technologies [4022]
1100 11th St., Ste. 311
Sacramento, CA 95814
Ph: (916)442-7785

White, Ward, President
Eddy Family Association [20860]
c/o Elaine Darrah, Treasurer
3151 Erie Ave.
Merced, CA 95340-1408

White, Wayne, President
National Mitigation Banking Associa-
  tion [3905]
107 SW St., No. 573
Alexandria, VA 22314
Ph: (202)457-8409

White, William S., Chairman, CEO
Charles Stewart Mott Foundation
  [12982]

Mott Foundation Bldg.
503 S Saginaw St., Ste. 1200
Flint, MI 48502-1851
Ph: (810)238-5651

Whitefoot, Patricia, President
National Indian Education Associa-
  tion [8397]
1514 P St. NW, Ste. B
Washington, DC 20005
Ph: (202)544-7290
Fax: (202)544-7293

Whitehead, Bruce, Director
East West Ministries International
  [12472]
2001 W Plano Pky., Ste. 3000
Plano, TX 75075-8644
Ph: (972)941-4500
Fax: (469)440-7633

Whitehead, Bruce, CMAA, Exec. Dir.
National Interscholastic Athletic
  Administrators Association [8432]
9100 Keystone Xing, Ste. 650
Indianapolis, IN 46240
Ph: (317)587-1450
Fax: (317)587-1451

Whitehead, James, Exec. Ofc.
Joint Commission on Sports
  Medicine & Science [17284]
1620 Valwood Pky., No. 115
Carrollton, TX 75006
Ph: (972)532-8854

Whitehead, John W., Chairman
The Rutherford Institute [19030]
PO Box 7482
Charlottesville, VA 22906-7482
Ph: (434)978-3888
Toll Free: 800-225-1791
Fax: (434)978-1789

Whitehead, Kathryn, Founder, Exec.
  Dir.
Community Alliance for the Ethical
  Treatment of Youth [10948]
450 Lexington Ave., No. 1319
New York, NY 10163
Ph: (202)681-8499

Whitehead, Robert, Chairman
American Association for Laboratory
  Accreditation [6773]
5202 President's Ct., Ste. 220
Frederick, MD 21703
Ph: (301)644-3248
Fax: (240)454-9449

Whitehead-Stotland, Tara, President
Mozambique Development in Motion
  [11405]
3634 Long Prairie Rd., Ste. 108-128
Flower Mound, TX 75022

Whitehouse, Jo, CEO
United States Eventing Association
  [22950]
525 Old Waterford Rd. NW
Leesburg, VA 20176
Ph: (703)779-0440
Fax: (703)779-0550

Whiteside, Jane, Adj. Gen.,
  Secretary
Northwest Territory Alliance [8796]
c/o Jane Whiteside, Adjutant
  General
8417 Adbeth Ave.
Woodridge, IL 60517
Ph: (630)985-1124

Whiteside, Terry, Chairman
Alliance for Rail Competition [2829]
412 1st St. SE, Ste. 1
Washington, DC 20003
Ph: (202)484-7133
Fax: (202)484-0770

Whiteway, Preston, Exec. Dir.
Eugene O'Neill Theater Center
[10250]
305 Great Neck Rd.
Waterford, CT 06385
Ph: (860)443-5378
Fax: (860)443-9653

Whiteway, Preston, Exec. Dir.
National Theater Institute at the
Eugene O'Neill Theater Center
[8700]
Eugene O'Neill Theater Ctr.
305 Great Neck Rd.
Waterford, CT 06385
Ph: (860)443-7139
Fax: (860)444-1212

Whitfield, Christina, Assoc. VP
State Higher Education Executive
Officers **[8443]**
3035 Center Green Dr., Ste. 100
Boulder, CO 80301-2205
Ph: (303)541-1600
Fax: (303)541-1639

Whitfield, Jim, VP
Materials & Methods Standards Association **[543]**
4000 Pinemont Dr.
Houston, TX 77018

Whitling, Laurie, President
International Quarter Pony Associa-
tion **[4369]**
PO Box 230
Lyles, TN 37098
Ph: (931)996-3987
     (931)996-8242

Whitman, Christine Todd, Co-Ch.
Clean and Safe Energy Coalition
[6470]
607 14th St. NW, Ste. 300
Washington, DC 20005
Ph: (202)338-2273

Whitman, Martha, Treasurer
Cooperative Grocer Network **[906]**
2600 E Franklin Ave., Ste. 3
Minneapolis, MN 55406-1172
Ph: (612)436-9177
     (612)436-9166
Fax: (612)692-8563

Whitman, Torrey L., Exec. Dir.
Institute of Judicial Administration
[5385]
Wilf Hall, Rm. 116
New York University School of Law
139 MacDougal St.
New York, NY 10012
Ph: (212)998-6149
Fax: (212)995-4769

Whitmer, Mariana, Exec. Dir.
Society for American Music **[10003]**
PO Box 99534
Pittsburgh, PA 15233
Ph: (412)624-3031

Whitney, Brian Austin, Founder
Just Plain Folks Music Organization
[2427]
5327 Kit Dr.
Indianapolis, IN 46237

Whitney, Ron D., Exec. Dir.
International Reciprocal Trade As-
sociation **[3302]**
524 Middle St.
Portsmouth, VA 23704
Ph: (757)393-2292
Fax: (757)257-4014

Whittaker, Jamie, President
American Federation of Aviculture
[21537]

PO Box 91717
Austin, TX 78709-1717
Ph: (512)585-9800
Fax: (512)858-7029

Whittaker, Jamie, President
Lineolated Parakeet Society **[3666]**
c/o June DiCiocco, Treasurer
606 Cherokee Dr.
North Augusta, SC 29841

Whittenhall, John, President
Petroleum Packaging Council **[2481]**
c/o ATD Management Inc.
1519 via Tulipan
San Clemente, CA 92673-3715
Ph: (949)369-7102
Fax: (949)366-1057

Whittington, Erik, Exec. Dir.
Rock For Life **[19071]**
9900 Courthouse Rd.
Spotsylvania, VA 22553
Ph: (540)834-4600

Whittington, Ms. Jenny, Exec. Dir.
University Risk Management and
Insurance Association **[8040]**
PO Box 1027
Bloomington, IN 47402-1027
Ph: (812)727-7130
Fax: (812)727-7129

Whitus, Tony, Dep. Dir.
American Design Drafting Associa-
tion **[6696]**
105 E Main St.
Newbern, TN 38059
Ph: (731)627-0802
Fax: (731)627-9321

Whitworth, Tom, President
WebWhispers, Inc. **[17416]**
PO Box 1275
Powder Springs, GA 30127

Whysong, Christan, President
Alpha Epsilon **[23735]**
University of Kentucky
Biosystems and Agricultural
Engineering
202 CE Barnhart Bldg.
Lexington, KY 40546
Ph: (859)257-3000
Fax: (859)257-5671

Whyte, Don, President, CEO
National Center for Construction
Education and Research **[18286]**
13614 Progress Blvd.
Alachua, FL 32615-9407
Ph: (386)518-6500
Toll Free: 888-622-3720
Fax: (386)518-6303

Whyte, Dr. Tonye, Gen. Sec.
Ijaw National Alliance of the
Americas **[11381]**
PO Box 24435
Brooklyn, NY 11202-4435

Wibbenmeyer, Lucy, MD, President
North American Burn Society
[13864]
c/o Holly Schnetzler, Treasurer
1290 Hammond Rd.
Saint Paul, MN 55110-5959

Wible, Robert C., Secretary
Alliance for Building Regulatory
Reform in the Digital Age **[6160]**
10702 Midsummer Dr.
Reston, VA 20191
Ph: (703)568-2323
Fax: (703)620-0015

Wichert, Paul, President
Red Wing Collectors Society **[21719]**
240 Harrison St., Unit No. 3

Red Wing, MN 55066-0050
Ph: (651)388-4004
Toll Free: 800-977-7927
Fax: (651)388-4042

Wicker, Jim, President
National Pop Can Collectors **[21696]**
1082 S 46th St.
West Des Moines, IA 50265-5239

Wicker, Roger F., Senator, Chairman
National Republican Senatorial Com-
mittee **[19044]**
425 2nd St. NE
Washington, DC 20002
Ph: (202)675-6000

Wicker, Stewart, Director, President
Society of Anglican Missionaries and
Senders **[20464]**
PO Box 399
Ambridge, PA 15003
Ph: (724)266-0669
Fax: (724)266-5681

Wickre, Wade, President
International Association of Special
Investigation Units **[1876]**
N83 W13410 Leon Rd.
Menomonee Falls, WI 53051
Ph: (414)375-2992
Fax: (414)359-1671

Wickström, Håkan, Treasurer
International Federation for Choral
Music **[9928]**
c/o Dr. Michael J. Anderson,
President
1040 W Harrison St., Rm. L216
Chicago, IL 60607-7130

Widder, Edie, PhD, CEO
Ocean Research & Conservation
Association, Inc. **[3923]**
Duerr Laboratory for Marine
Conservation
1420 Seaway Dr.
Fort Pierce, FL 34949
Ph: (772)467-1600
Fax: (772)467-1602

Wiebe, Dr. Keith, President
American Association of Christian
Schools **[7605]**
602 Belvoir Ave.
East Ridge, TN 37412-2602
Ph: (423)629-4280
Fax: (423)622-7461

Wiebe, Mickey, Exec. Dir.
Supplier Excellence Alliance **[1772]**
6789 Quail Hill Pky., No. 733
Irvine, CA 92603
Ph: (949)476-1144

Wiegerink, Robin L., MNPL, CEO
American Society of Echocardiogra-
phy **[14093]**
2100 Gateway Centre Blvd., Ste.
310
Morrisville, NC 27560
Ph: (919)861-5574

Wiehe, Ms. Nancy, Associate
Interstate Migrant Education Council
[12340]
1 Massachusetts Ave., Ste. 700
Washington, DC 20001
Ph: (202)336-7078
Fax: (202)336-7078

Wieland, Lynn, Secretary
American Association of Candy
Technologists **[6638]**
711 W Water St.
Princeton, WI 54968
Ph: (920)295-6969
Fax: (920)295-6843

Wielgus, Chuck, Exec. Dir.
U.S.A. Swimming **[23290]**
1 Olympic Plz.
Colorado Springs, CO 80909
Ph: (719)866-4578

Wiener, Robin K., Liaison
Institute of Scrap Recycling
Industries **[4632]**
1615 L St. NW, Ste. 600
Washington, DC 20036-5610
Ph: (202)662-8500
Fax: (202)626-0900

Wiese, Mr. Larry, Exec. Dir.
Kappa Alpha Order **[23901]**
115 Liberty Hall Rd.
Lexington, VA 24450
Ph: (540)463-1865
Fax: (540)463-2140

Wiesenmaier, Hubert, Exec. Dir.
American Import Shippers Associa-
tion **[3080]**
662 Main St.
New Rochelle, NY 10801
Ph: (914)633-3770
Fax: (914)633-4041

Wieser, Andy, Chairman
National Precast Concrete Associa-
tion **[792]**
1320 City Center Dr., Ste. 200
Carmel, IN 46032
Ph: (317)571-0041
Toll Free: 800-366-7731
Fax: (317)571-0041

Wieser, Jeffrey N., President
Alumni Association of Princeton
University **[19301]**
PO Box 291
Princeton, NJ 08542-0291
Ph: (609)258-1900

Wiesner, Ms. Ulrike, Managing Dir.
American-Austrian Cultural Society
[9030]
c/o Ulli Wiesner, Managing Director
5618 Dover Ct.
Alexandria, VA 22312

Wietecha, Mark, President, CEO
Children's Hospital Association
[15319]
600 13th St. NW, Ste. 500
Washington, DC 20005
Ph: (202)753-5500
Fax: (202)347-5147

Wiewel, Frank D., Editor, Founder
People Against Cancer **[14044]**
604 East St.
Otho, IA 50569
Ph: (515)972-4444
Toll Free: 800-662-2623
Fax: (515)972-4415

Wigger, John H., President
Conference on Faith and History
[20203]
c/o Glenn Sanders
Dept. of History
Oklahoma Baptist University
PO Box 61232
Shawnee, OK 74804
Ph: (405)585-4157

Wiggin, Kendall, President
Chief Officers of State Library Agen-
cies **[9698]**
201 E Main St., Ste. 1405
Lexington, KY 40507
Ph: (859)514-9151
Fax: (859)514-9166

Wiggins, Dena, President
Natural Gas Supply Association
[4266]

1620 Eye St. NW, Ste. 700
Washington, DC 20006
Ph: (202)326-9300

Wiggins, Rebecca, Exec. Dir.
Association for Financial Counseling
and Planning Education [1275]
1940 Duke St., Ste. 200
Alexandria, VA 22314-3452
Ph: (703)684-4484
Fax: (703)684-4485

Wigginton, Phyliss, Chairman
American Association of Exporters
and Importers [1976]
1717 K St. NW, Ste. 1120
Washington, DC 20006
Ph: (202)857-8009
Fax: (202)857-7843

Wiginton, Norm, President
Basset Hound Club of America, Inc.
[21836]
c/o Anne Testoni, Corresponding
Secretary
8 Mount Wachusett Ln.
Bolton, MA 01740-2014

Wigo, Bruce, CEO, President
International Swimming Hall of Fame
[23285]
1 Hall of Fame Dr.
Fort Lauderdale, FL 33316
Ph: (954)462-6536
Fax: (954)525-4031

Wikoff, Naj, President, Chairman
Wyckoff House and Association
[9843]
5816 Clarendon Rd.
Brooklyn, NY 11203
Ph: (718)629-5400

Wilbert, Duffy J., Exec. Dir.
Professional Audio Manufacturers
Alliance [1060]
11242 Waples Mill Rd., Ste. 200
Fairfax, VA 22030
Ph: (703)279-9938

Wilcox, Donna, VP, Chmn. of the Bd.
Alley Cat Allies [10563]
7920 Norfolk Ave., Ste. 600
Bethesda, MD 20814-2525
Ph: (240)482-1980
Fax: (240)482-1990

Wilcox, John E., Jr., Exec. Dir.
29th Infantry Division Association
[20709]
PO Box 1546
Frederick, MD 21702-1546
Ph: (410)242-1820

Wilcox, Todd, President
American College of Correctional
Physicians [16735]
1145 W Diversey Pky.
Chicago, IL 60614-1318·
Toll Free: 800-229-7380
Fax: (773)880-2424

Wilcox, William E., Chmn. of the Bd.
Call For Action [11475]
11820 Parklawn Dr., Ste. 340
Rockville, MD 20852
Ph: (240)747-0229

Wilder, Margaret, Exec. Dir.
Urban Affairs Association [8725]
University of Wisconsin-Milwaukee
Urban Studies Program
3210 N Maryland Ave.
Bolton 702
Milwaukee, WI 53211
Ph: (414)229-3025

Wilder, Ruthie, Director
National Association of Housing
Cooperatives [11977]

1444 I St. NW, Ste. 700
Washington, DC 20005-6542
Ph: (202)737-0797
Fax: (202)216-9646

Wilderman, Wayne, President
International Flying Farmers [4156]
PO Box 309
Mansfield, IL 61854
Ph: (217)489-9300
Fax: (217)489-9280

Wilderotter, Peter T., President, CEO
Christopher and Dana Reeve
Foundation [17260]
636 Morris Tpke., Ste. 3A
Short Hills, NJ 07078
Ph: (973)379-2690
    (973)467-8270
Toll Free: 800-225-0292

Wilder-Smith, Annelies, President
International Society of Travel
Medicine [15731]
1200 Ashwood Pky., Ste. 310
Dunwoody, GA 30338-4767
Ph: (404)373-8282
Fax: (404)373-8283

Wildmon, Donald E., Chairman,
Founder
American Family Association
[17937]
PO Box 2440
Tupelo, MS 38803
Ph: (662)844-5036

Wiles, Charlie
American Council for Accredited
Certification [4536]
PO Box 1000
Yarnell, AZ 85362
Toll Free: 888-808-8381
Fax: (888)894-3590

Wiley, Angela R., Chairperson
International Section of the National
Council on Family Relations
[11822]
1201 W River Pky., Ste. 200
Minneapolis, MN 55454
Toll Free: 888-781-9331
Fax: (763)781-9348

Wiley, Birne D., Founder
Missionary TECH Team [20442]
25 FRJ Dr.
Longview, TX 75602-4703
Ph: (903)757-4530
Toll Free: 800-871-7795

Wiley, Chap. Craig, Exec. Dir.
Race Track Chaplaincy of America
[19938]
2365 Harrodsburg Rd., Ste. A120
Lexington, KY 40504
Ph: (859)410-7822
Fax: (859)219-1424

Wiley, J.I., President
O.J. Noer Research Foundation
[4284]
PO Box 94
Juneau, WI 53039-0094

Wiley, Ladd, JD, Exec. Dir.
Alliance for a Stronger FDA [18260]
PO Box 7508
Silver Spring, MD 20907-7508
Ph: (202)887-4211
    (301)539-9660
Fax: (301)576-5416

Wiley, Michael, Sr., Secretary,
Treasurer
American English Spot Rabbit Club
[4587]
c/o Michael Wiley Sr., Secretary-
Treasurer

5772 Owenton Rd.
Stamping Ground, KY 40379
Ph: (502)535-7051
    (651)674-7614

Wilfrid, Thomas N., Exec. Dir.
The Charlotte W. Newcombe
Foundation [11580]
35 Park Pl.
Princeton, NJ 08542-6918
Ph: (609)924-7022

Wilhelm, Carl, Chmn. of the Bd.
Mission Training International
[20439]
421 Highway 105
Palmer Lake, CO 80133
Ph: (719)487-0111
Toll Free: 800-896-3710
Fax: (719)487-9350

Wilhelm, Karen L., Ph.D., President
American Board of Professional
Neuropsychology [16858]
c/o Geoffrey Kanter, Executive
Director
1090 S Tamiami Trl.
Sarasota, FL 34239
Ph: (941)363-0878

Wilhelm, Robert M., Editor
American Spoon Collectors [21616]
PO Box 243
Rhinecliff, NY 12574
Ph: (845)876-0303
Fax: (845)876-0303

Wilkerson, Dean, Exec. Dir.
American College of Emergency
Physicians [14673]
1125 Executive Cir.
Irving, TX 75038-2522
Ph: (972)550-0911
Toll Free: 800-798-1822
Fax: (972)580-2816

Wilkerson, Katie, Exec. Dir.
Surfaces in Biomaterials Foundation
[6124]
1000 Westgate Dr., Ste. 252
Saint Paul, MN 55114
Ph: (651)290-6267

Wilkerson, Thomas L., President,
CEO
National Association for Uniformed
Services [5606]
5535 Hempstead Way
Springfield, VA 22151
Toll Free: 800-842-3451

Wilkes, Brent A., Exec. Dir.
League of United Latin American
Citizens [19461]
1133 19th St. NW, Ste. 1000
Washington, DC 20036
Ph: (202)833-6130
Fax: (202)833-6135

Wilkewitz, Precilla Landry, President
Disabled Veterans National Founda-
tion [20768]
1020 19th St. NW, Ste. 475
Washington, DC 20036
Ph: (202)737-0522

Wilkie, Nancy C., President
U.S. Committee of the Blue Shield
[9237]
1025 Thomas Jefferson St. NW, Ste.
500 E
Washington, DC 20007
Ph: (507)222-4231

Wilkins, Donele, Co-Ch.
National Black Environmental Justice
Network [4084]
PO Box 15845

Washington, DC 20003
Ph: (202)265-4919
Fax: (202)326-3357

Wilkins, Jeanie Guthans,
Chairperson
Autism Avenue [13745]
164 St. Francis St., Ste. 210
Mobile, AL 36602
Ph: (251)432-0757
Toll Free: 866-953-8644
Fax: (251)432-3999

Wilkins, Max, President, CEO
The Mission Society [20346]
6234 Crooked Creek Rd.
Norcross, GA 30092-3106
Ph: (770)446-1381
Toll Free: 800-478-8963
Fax: (770)446-3044

Wilkins, Richard, President
American Soybean Association
[4691]
12125 Woodcrest Executive Dr., Ste.
100
Saint Louis, MO 63141-5009
Ph: (314)576-1770
Toll Free: 800-688-7692
Fax: (314)576-2786

Wilkins, Ronnie D., EdD, Exec. Dir.
American College of Neuropsychop-
harmacology [16638]
5034-A Thoroughbred Ln.
Brentwood, TN 37027
Ph: (615)324-2360
Fax: (615)523-1715

Wilkins, William M., Exec. Dir.
The Road Information Program
[3356]
3000 Connecticut Ave. NW, Ste. 208
Washington, DC 20008
Ph: (202)466-6706

Wilkinson, Anne, PhD, Director
Palliative Care Policy Center [11557]
2000 M St. NW, Ste. 400
Washington, DC 20036

Wilkinson, Anthony R., CEO,
President
National Association of Government
Guaranteed Lenders [2093]
215 E 9th Ave.
Stillwater, OK 74074
Ph: (405)377-4022

Wilkinson, Barb, Exec. Dir.
National Cattlemen's Foundation
[3737]
9110 E Nichols Ave., Ste. 300
Centennial, CO 80112
Ph: (303)694-0305

Wilkinson, Bert Andrew, Chairman,
President
Hand in Hand in Africa [13544]
7653 Bridge Water Cir.
Frisco, TX 75034
Toll Free: 866-908-3518

Wilkinson, Bill, Exec. Dir.
Surface Transportation Policy
Partnership [19199]
750 1st St. NE, Ste. 901
Washington, DC 20002
Ph: (202)466-6251

Wilkinson, Bob, President
Hotot Rabbit Breeders International
[4599]
5988 S Mohawk Ave.
Ypsilanti, MI 48197

Wilkinson, Bruce, President, CEO
Catholic Medical Mission Board
[12267]

100 Wall St., 9th Fl.
New York, NY 10005
Ph: (212)242-7757
Toll Free: 800-678-5659

Wilkinson, Dr. Georgalyn, President
Gospel Literature International
[20420]
2940 Inland Empire Blvd., Ste. 101
Ontario, CA 91764-4898
Ph: (909)481-5222
Fax: (909)481-5216

Wilkowske, Doug, Founder
E-quip Africa [11348]
PO Box 3178
Willmar, MN 56201-8178

Will, Emily J., President
Association of Forensic Document
Examiners [5242]
c/o Emily J. Will, President
PO Box 58552
Raleigh, NC 27658
Ph: (919)556-7414

Willard, Marsha, Exec. Dir.,
Secretary
International Society of Sustainability
Professionals [4143]
1429 Park St., Ste. 114
Hartford, CT 06106
Ph: (860)231-9197

Willburn, Gerry, Membership Chp.
Morgan Plus Four Club [21443]
5073 Melbourne Dr.
Cypress, CA 90630
Ph: (714)828-3127

Willeman, Juli, Exec. Dir.
Pi Beta Phi [23919]
1154 Town and Country Commons
Dr.
Town and Country, MO 63017
Ph: (636)256-0680
Fax: (636)256-8095

Williams, Akinyi, Founder, Exec. Dir.
Hope for the Child [11035]
8315 Emerald Ln.
Woodbury, MN 55125
Ph: (651)246-0552

Williams, Mr. Alfred W., President,
Chmn. of the Bd.
San Francisco African American
Historical and Cultural Society
[8787]
762 Fulton St.
San Francisco, CA 94102
Ph: (415)292-6172

Williams, Amber, Exec. Dir.
Safe States Alliance [19082]
2200 Century Pkwy., Ste. 700
Atlanta, GA 30345
Ph: (770)690-9000
Fax: (770)690-8996

Williams, Andre, Exec. Dir.
Healthcare Billing and Management
Association [15727]
2025 M St. NW, Ste. 800
Washington, DC 20036
Toll Free: 877-640-4262
Fax: (202)367-2177

Williams, Arlanda J., Treasurer
National Association of Black County
Officials [5112]
25 Massachusetts Ave. NW, Ste.
500
Washington, DC 20001
Ph: (202)350-6696

Williams, Dr. Betty Smith, RN,
President
National Coalition of Ethnic Minority
Nurse Associations [16158]

c/o Betty Smith Williams, President
6101 W Centinela Ave., Ste. 378
Culver City, CA 90230
Ph: (310)258-9515
Fax: (310)258-9513

Williams, Bill, MD, President,
Founder
American Association of Working
People [11752]
4435 Waterfront Dr., Ste. 101
Glen Allen, VA 23058
Ph: (804)527-1905
Fax: (804)747-5316

Williams, Brendan E., Exec. VP
American Fuel and Petrochemical
Manufacturers [2509]
1667 K St. NW, Ste. 700
Washington, DC 20006
Ph: (202)457-0480
Fax: (202)457-0486

Williams, Carol, Program Mgr.
Genetic Metabolic Dietitians
International [15824]
c/o Carol Williams, Program
Coordinator
PO Box 33985
Fort Worth, TX 76162

Williams, Cheryl, Exec. Dir.
Learning First Alliance [7778]
1615 Duke St.
Alexandria, VA 22314
Ph: (703)518-6290
Fax: (703)548-6021

Williams, Coke, Exec. Sec.,
Treasurer
Aluminum Foil Container
Manufacturers Association [826]
10 Vecilla Ln.
Hot Springs Village, AR 71909
Ph: (440)781-5819
Fax: (440)247-9053

Williams, Craig, Comm. Chm.
American Association of Airport
Executives [127]
The Barclay Bldg. I
601 Madison St., Ste. 400
Alexandria, VA 22314
Ph: (703)824-0500
    (703)824-0504
Fax: (703)820-1395

Williams, Craig, Contact
Heritage of Pride [11889]
154 Christopher St., Ste. 1D
New York, NY 10014-2840
Ph: (212)807-7433
Fax: (212)807-7436

Williams, Dale, VP
McDonald's Collectors Club [21686]
c/o Jim Gegorski, Treasurer
424 White Rd.
Fremont, OH 43420-1539

Williams, David A., CEO, President
Make-A-Wish Foundation of America
[11250]
4742 N 24th St., Ste. 400
Phoenix, AZ 85016
Ph: (602)279-9474
Toll Free: 800-722-9474
Fax: (602)279-0855

Williams, David E., Chief Med. Ofc.
Pet Partners [17460]
875 124th Ave. NE, No. 101
Bellevue, WA 98005
Ph: (425)679-5500
    (425)679-5530

Williams, David, Comm. Chm.
Tissue Engineering International and
Regenerative Medicine Society
[6115]

223 Park Pl.
San Ramon, CA 94583
Ph: (925)362-0998
Fax: (925)362-0808

Williams, Dennis, President
UAW Community Action Program
[18876]
Solidarity House
8000 E Jefferson Ave.
Detroit, MI 48214
Ph: (313)926-5000

Williams, Dennis, President
United Auto Workers [23380]
Solidarity House
8000 E Jefferson Ave.
Detroit, MI 48214
Ph: (313)926-5000
Toll Free: 800-243-8829

Williams, Dick, VP
Rocky Mountain Llama and Alpaca
Association [3612]
c/o Lougene Baird, President
PO Box 385403
Waikoloa, HI 96738
Ph: (808)747-5023

Williams, Dusty, President
National Association of Flood and
Stormwater Management Agencies
[5654]
PO Box 56764
Washington, DC 20040
Ph: (202)289-8625
Fax: (202)530-3389

Williams, Dr. E. Faye, President,
CEO
National Congress of Black Women
[18914]
1250 4th St. SW, Ste. WG-1
Washington, DC 20024
Ph: (202)678-6788

Williams, Edward, Sr., President
International Allied Printing Trades
Association [23441]
6210 N Capitol St. NW
Washington, DC 20011
Ph: (202)882-3000
Fax: (202)291-8951

Williams, Elizabeth Anne, MD,
President
Society of Women in Urology
[17566]
1100 E Woodfield Rd., Ste. 520
Schaumburg, IL 60173
Ph: (847)517-7225
Fax: (847)517-7229

Williams, Frank J., President
Ulysses S. Grant Association
[10328]
395 Hardy Rd.
Mississippi State, MS 39762-5408
Ph: (662)325-4552

Williams, Gee Gee, Founder
Project Baobab [13476]
c/o Philanthropic Ventures Foundation
1222 Preservation Pky.
Oakland, CA 94612

Williams, George, Chairman
American Association of Blacks in
Energy [6451]
1625 K St. NW, Ste. 405
Washington, DC 20006
Ph: (202)371-9530
Fax: (202)371-9218

Williams, George, Dir. of Operations
Foundation for the Preservation of
the Mahayana Tradition [19778]

1632 SE 11th Ave.
Portland, OR 97214-4702
Ph: (503)808-1588
Toll Free: 866-241-9886
Fax: (503)232-0557

Williams, Gerald R., Jr., MD,
President
Board of Specialty Societies [15846]
9400 W Higgins Rd.
Rosemont, IL 60018
Ph: (847)823-7186
Fax: (847)823-8125

Williams, Gordon, President
National Silver Fox Rabbit Club
[4608]
c/o Kimberly R. Esquilla, Secretary
648 Forestbrook Rd.
Myrtle Beach, SC 29579
Ph: (843)450-9019

Williams, J. Robert, Chairman
National Black United Fund [12404]
17 Academy St.
Newark, NJ 07102
Ph: (973)643-5122
Toll Free: 800-223-0866

Williams, Jack, Exec. Dir.
Mass Finishing Job Shops Associa-
tion [1287]
808 13th St.
East Moline, IL 61244
Ph: (309)755-1101
Fax: (309)755-1121

Williams, Jackie, Administrator
Alliance for Aging Research [10497]
1700 K St. NW, Ste. 740
Washington, DC 20006
Ph: (202)293-2856
Fax: (202)955-8394

Williams, Jackie, CPA, Exec. Dir.
National Council of Acoustical
Consultants [556]
9100 Purdue Rd., Ste. 200
Indianapolis, IN 46268
Ph: (317)328-0642
Fax: (317)328-4629

Williams, Jackie, CPA, Exec. Dir.
Society for Nutrition Education and
Behavior [16239]
9100 Purdue Rd., Ste. 200
Indianapolis, IN 46268
Ph: (317)328-4627
Toll Free: 800-235-6690
Fax: (317)280-8527

Williams, James A., CEO
National Military Intelligence As-
sociation [5369]
PO Box 354
Charlotte Court House, VA 23923
Fax: (703)738-7487

Williams, James Herbert, President
Society for Social Work and
Research [8575]
11240 Waples Mill Rd., Ste. 200
Fairfax, VA 22030-6078
Ph: (703)352-7797
Fax: (703)359-7562

Williams, Jamie, President
The Wilderness Society [3966]
1615 M St. NW
Washington, DC 20036
Ph: (202)833-2300
Toll Free: 800-843-9453

Williams, Jane, Exec. Dir.
Mercury Policy Project [17488]
1420 North St.
Montpelier, VT 05602-9592
Ph: (802)223-9000

Williams, Jennifer, Officer
Institute for Tribal Environmental
Professionals [19580]
PO Box 15004
Flagstaff, AZ 86011-5004
Ph: (928)523-9555
Fax: (928)523-1266

Williams, Jeremy, Contact
National Association of Managed
Care Physicians [16756]
4435 Waterfront Dr., Ste. 101
Glen Allen, VA 23060
Ph: (804)527-1905
Fax: (804)747-5316

Williams, Jill, Director
Polish Tatra Sheepdog Club of
America [21944]
c/o Donna Gnuechtel, Secretary
110 Jack Dylan Dr.
Hampshire, IL 60140
Ph: (414)329-1373

Williams, Jody, President
American Society of Botanical Artists
[8911]
The New York Botanical Garden
2900 Southern Blvd.
Bronx, NY 10458-5126
Ph: (718)817-8814
Toll Free: 866-691-9080

Williams, Joe, Exec. Dir.
Democrats for Education Reform
[18172]
840 1st St. NE, 3rd Fl.
Washington, DC 20002
Ph: (212)614-3213

Williams, John G., President
Potomac Antique Tools and
Industries Association [22172]
c/o David Murphy
9121 Bramble Pl.
Annandale, VA 22003-4015
Ph: (301)253-4892

Williams, Dr. John P., Jr., Reg. Dir.
Evangelical Friends International -
North American Region [20167]
18639 Yorba Linda Blvd.
Yorba Linda, CA 92886
Ph: (714)779-7662
Toll Free: 888-704-9393
Fax: (714)779-7740

Williams, Kurt, President
National EMS Pilots Association
[14669]
PO Box 2128
Layton, UT 84041-9128
Ph: (801)436-7505

Williams, Lawrence, Chairman, CEO
United States Healthful Food Council
[15091]
1200 18th St. NW, Ste. 700
Washington, DC 20036
Ph: (202)503-9122

Williams, Lloyd B., Chairman
HelpMercy International [15019]
Salt Lake City, UT

Williams, Marcus, Exec. Dir.
National Association for Regulatory
Administration [15042]
403 Marquis Ave., Ste. 200
Lexington, KY 40502
Ph: (859)687-0262

Williams, Mark, Chairman
Association of Independent Cor-
rugated Converters [828]
PO Box 25708
Alexandria, VA 22313
Ph: (703)836-2422
Toll Free: 877-836-2422
Fax: (703)836-2795

Williams, Mark, CEO
Starfleet Command [24082]
PO Box 348
Anderson, IN 46015

Williams, Dr. Megan, Exec. Sec.
Welsh North American Association
[19689]
PO Box 1054
Trumansburg, NY 14886
Ph: (607)279-7402
Fax: (877)448-6633

Williams, Melanie, Bd. Member
African American Breast Cancer Alli-
ance [13872]
PO Box 8981
Minneapolis, MN 55408-0981
Ph: (612)825-3675
Fax: (612)827-2977

Williams, Meredith, Exec. Dir.
National Council on Teacher Retire-
ment [23410]
9370 Studio Ct., Ste. 100E
Elk Grove, CA 95758
Ph: (916)897-9139
Fax: (916)897-9315

Williams, Michael, Director
e-Learning for Kids [7586]
c/o Marlene Zimmerman
953 Cloud Ln.
West Chester, PA 19382

Williams, Michael, Director
National Utility Training and Safety
Education Association [3421]
PO Box 1163
Youngsville, NC 27596
Ph: (919)671-4496

Williams, Michael, VP of Operations
North American Equipment Dealers
Association [171]
1195 Smizer Mill Rd.
Fenton, MO 63026-3480
Ph: (636)349-5000
Fax: (636)349-5443

Williams, Mr. Morgan, CEO,
President, Chairman
U.S.-Ukraine Business Council [688]
1030 15th St. NW, Ste. 555 W
Washington, DC 20005
Ph: (202)216-0995
    (202)437-4707
Fax: (202)216-0997

Williams, Nikki, Exec. Dir.
Collegiate Women's Lacrosse Of-
ficiating Association [22972]
2310 N Centennial St., Ste. 102
High Point, NC 27265

Williams, Pam, President
Fine Chocolate Industry Association
[1324]
2265 Georgia Pine Ct.
Las Vegas, NV 89134
Ph: (206)577-9983

Williams, Pamela V., Exec. Dir.
Cable and Telecommunications Hu-
man Resources Association [1694]
1717 N Naper Blvd., Ste. 102
Naperville, IL 60563
Ph: (630)416-1166
Fax: (630)416-9798

Williams, Patricia, Director
Trinity Health International [15162]
34605 12 Mile Rd.
Farmington Hills, MI 48331-3221
Ph: (248)489-6100

Williams, Paul, President, Chmn. of
the Bd.
American Society of Composers,
Authors and Publishers [5322]

1900 Broadway
New York, NY 10023
Ph: (212)621-6000
Fax: (212)621-8453

Williams, Peter, Founder, Exec. Dir.
Architecture for Health in Vulnerable
Environments [11962]
894 6th Ave., 5th Fl.
New York, NY 10001
Ph: (917)793-5901

Williams, Rachel M., PhD,
Chairperson
National Black Association for
Speech-Language and Hearing
[17243]
700 McKnight Park Dr., Ste. 708
Pittsburgh, PA 15237
Toll Free: 855-727-2836

Williams, Rebecca, Treasurer
National Association of Foreign-
Trade Zones [1988]
National Press Bldg.
529 14th St. NW, Ste. 1071
Washington, DC 20045
Ph: (202)331-1950
Fax: (202)331-1994

Williams, Rob, President
Action Coalition for Media Education
[18650]
PO Box 1121
Waitsfield, VT 05673

Williams, Rob, Treasurer
United States Lifesaving Association
[12750]
PO Box 366
Huntington Beach, CA 92648
Toll Free: 866-367-8752

Williams, Robert, PhD, Editor
World Methodist Historical Society
[20352]
PO Box 127
Madison, NJ 07940
Ph: (973)408-3189
Fax: (973)408-3909

Williams, Robin, Commissioner
North American Football League
[22863]
5775 Glenridge Dr. NE
Atlanta, GA 30328

Williams, Roger J.
Accrediting Council for Continuing
Education and Training [7665]
1722 N St. NW
Washington, DC 20036
Ph: (202)955-1113
Fax: (202)955-1118

Williams, Ron, Exec. Dir.
Free Speech TV [19109]
PO Box 44099
Denver, CO 80201
Ph: (303)442-8445

Williams, Ron, President
National Association of Local Hous-
ing Finance Agencies [5281]
2025 M St. NW, Ste. 800
Washington, DC 20036
Ph: (202)367-1197

Williams, Roxanne J., President
Urban Ed, Inc. [8730]
2041 Martin Luther King, Jr. Ave.
SE, Ste. M-2
Washington, DC 20020
Ph: (202)610-2344
Fax: (202)610-2355

Williams, Sarah, President
United States Agricultural Information Network [3579]

c/o Chris Long & Associates
PO Box 117
West Milton, OH 45383
Ph: (937)698-4188
Fax: (937)698-6153

Williams Skinner, Dr. Barbara,
Founder, President
Skinner Leadership Institute [20162]
PO Box 190
Tracys Landing, MD 20779
Ph: (301)261-9800
Fax: (443)498-4935

Williams, Steve, Secretary
Society of Cable Telecommunica-
tions Engineers [6590]
14 Philips Rd.
Exton, PA 19341-1318
Ph: (610)363-6888
Toll Free: 800-542-5040
Fax: (610)363-5898

Williams, Storm, Founder
Books For Soldiers [10737]
116 Lowes Food Dr., No. 123
Lewisville, NC 27023

Williams, Susan Michelle, President
Phi Zeta [23983]
c/o Cheryl A. Blaze, Secretary-
Treasurer
Tufts Cummings School of
Veterinary Medicine
200 Westboro Rd.
North Grafton, MA 01536
Ph: (508)887-4249
Fax: (508)839-7922

Williams, Tessa, President
Jeanette MacDonald International
Fan Club [23995]
PO Box 180172
Chicago, IL 60618-0172

Williams, Dr. William C., President
Anglican Fellowship of Prayer
[19702]
1106 Mansfield Ave.
Indiana, PA 15701
Ph: (724)463-6436
    (814)725-4484

Williams-Gates, Regina V.K., Exec.
Dir. (Actg.)
National Forum for Black Public
Administrators [5698]
777 N Capitol St. NE, Ste. 550
Washington, DC 20002
Ph: (202)408-9300
Fax: (202)408-8558

Williamson, Corrie, Officer
Alternative Energy Resources
Organization [6450]
PO Box 1558
Helena, MT 59624
Ph: (406)443-7272
Fax: (406)442-9120

Williamson, Darlene S., President
National Aphasia Association
[13726]
PO Box 87
Scarsdale, NY 10583
Toll Free: 800-922-4622

Williamson, Dawn, Founder,
President
CHERUBS - Association of
Congenital Diaphragmatic Hernia
Research, Awareness and Support
[13827]
152 S White St., Upstairs Ste.
Wake Forest, NC 27587
Ph: (919)610-0129
Toll Free: 855-CDH-BABY
Fax: (815)425-9155

Williamson, Gail, Assoc. Exec.
American Academy of Oral and Maxillofacial Radiology [14382]
3085 Stevenson Dr., Ste. 200
Springfield, IL 62703

Williamson, Jennifer, VP
Girls for a Change [10995]
PO Box 1436
San Jose, CA 95109
Ph: (866)738-4422

Williamson, Shelli, Exec. Dir.
Scottsdale Institute [15131]
7767 Elm Creek Blvd. N, Ste. 208
Maple Grove, MN 55369
Ph: (763)710-7089
Fax: (763)432-5635

Williamson, Spike, VP
Icelandic Sheepdog Association of
America [21896]
24417 E Rosewood
Newman Lake, WA 99025

Williard, Karl, Exec. Dir.
Universities Council on Water
Resources [7378]
Southern Illinois University Carbon-
dale
1231 Lincoln Dr.
Carbondale, IL 62901
Ph: (618)536-7571
Fax: (618)453-2671

Willing, Laurie, Exec. Dir.
Honduras Outreach, Inc. [17979]
1990 Lakeside Pky., Ste. 140
Tucker, GA 30084
Ph: (404)327-5770

Willingham, Elaine, Founder
Beyond the Rainbow [23986]
956 Briar Green Ct.
Kirkwood, MO 63122-5149
Ph: (314)799-1724
Fax: (314)596-4549

Willingham, Gayle, President
National Deaf Women's Bowling Association [22788]
3314 64th St.
Urbandale, IA 50322

Willingham, John, President
Hearts for Kenya [10723]
1514 Norris Pl.
Louisville, KY 40205
Ph: (502)459-4582

Willingham-Hinton, Shelley, CEO,
Founder
The National Organization for
Diversity in Sales and Marketing,
Inc. [2296]
PO Box 99640
Raleigh, NC 27624-9640
Toll Free: 800-691-6380
Fax: (888)260-0836

Willinghan, Eric, Exec. VP
American Association of Food
Hygiene Veterinarians [17596]
1730 S Federal Highway 205
Delray Beach, FL 33483

Willis, Mike, Exec. Dir.
United States Deputy Sheriffs' As-
sociation [5520]
319 S Hydraulic St., Ste. B
Wichita, KS 67211-1908
Ph: (316)263-2583

Willis, Robert, President
Electronic Components Industry As-
sociation [1043]
1111 Alderman Dr., Ste. 400
Alpharetta, GA 30005
Ph: (678)393-9990
Fax: (678)393-9998

Willis, Steve, Exec. Sec.
United States Society for Education
Through the Arts [7520]
SUNY New Paltz, Department of Art,
Art Education
SUNY New Paltz
Dept. of Art
New Paltz, NY 12561
Ph: (845)257-3850
(845)257-3837

Willis, Will, President
Inliners International [21398]
c/o Linda Henry, Membership Chair
6558 Red Hill Rd.
Boulder, CO 80302-3400
Ph: (303)443-8185
Fax: (303)449-7937

Willner, Alan, President
Optical Society of America [6948]
2010 Massachusetts Ave. NW
Washington, DC 20036
Ph: (202)223-8130
Fax: (202)223-1096

Willott, Dorothy, President
Dwarf Iris Society of America
[22092]
c/o Dorothy Willott, President
26231 Shaker Blvd.
Beachwood, OH 44122

Willoughby, Ann, Liaison
EYH Network [8280]
5000 MacArthur Blvd., PMB 9968
Oakland, CA 94613-1301
Ph: (510)277-0190

Willoughby, Dr. Jim, Trustee
International Convention of Faith
Ministries [19987]
5500 Woodland Park Blvd.
Arlington, TX 76013
Ph: (817)451-9620
Toll Free: 877-348-4236
Fax: (817)451-9621

Willoughby, Rev. William, III, Gen.
Sec.
Confraternity of the Blessed Sacra-
ment [20098]
224 E 34th St.
Savannah, GA 31401

Wills, Betty, Founder, Exec. Dir.
EarthWave Society [4055]
16151 S Highway 377
Fort Worth, TX 76126
Ph: (817)443-3780
Toll Free: 800-668-WAVE
Fax: (817)443-3858

Willsey, Judy, Founder
World Class Ghana [12065]
PO Box 325
Lagrangeville, NY 12540

Willuhn, Mark, Exec. Dir.
Mesoamerican Ecotourism Alliance
[3383]
c/o Mark Willuhn, Director
4076 Crystal Ct.
Boulder, CO 80304
Ph: (303)440-3362
Toll Free: 800-682-0584
Fax: (303)447-0815

Willumsen, Sue, President
National Labrador Retriever Club
[21923]
c/o Sandra Underhill, Secretary
12515 Woodside Ave., No. 1905
Lakeside, CA 92040

Wilsker, Chuck, CEO, President,
Founder
Telework Coalition [3244]
204 E St. NE

Washington, DC 20002

Wilson, Amy, Exec. Dir.
National Postdoctoral Association
[8505]
1200 New York Ave. NW, Ste. 610
Washington, DC 20005
Ph: (202)326-6424
Fax: (202)371-9489

Wilson, Andrea J., President, Exec.
Dir.
Blue Faery: The Adrienne Wilson
Liver Cancer Association [13905]
1135 N Valley St.
Burbank, CA 91505
Ph: (818)636-5624

Wilson, Bascombe J., Exec. Dir.
International Association for Disaster
Preparedness and Response
[14663]
PO Box 797
Longmont, CO 80502-0797

Wilson, Mr. Benjamin C., Founder,
President
Children of Vietnam [10924]
4361 Federal Dr., Ste. 160
Greensboro, NC 27410-8147
Ph: (336)235-0981
Fax: (336)294-9566

Wilson, Betty P., Secretary
National Coalition for Aviation and
Space Education [7527]
c/o Virginia Dept. of Aviation
5702 Gulfstream Rd.
Richmond, VA 23250-2422
Ph: (505)362-8232

Wilson, Bill, President
International Defensive Pistol As-
sociation [23131]
2232 County Rd. 719
Berryville, AR 72616
Ph: (870)545-3886
Fax: (870)545-3894

Wilson, Bill, VP of Bus. Dev.
Music Business Association [2902]
1 Eves Dr., Ste. 138
Marlton, NJ 08053
Ph: (856)596-2221
Fax: (856)596-7299

Wilson, Bob, Director
Cougar Network [4804]
c/o Michelle LaRue, Executive Direc-
tor
Dept. of Earth Sciences
University of Minnesota
310 Pillsbury Dr. SE
Minneapolis, MN 55455-0231
Ph: (612)625-6358

Wilson, Bob, Chairman
Cranberry Institute [4233]
PO Box 497
Carver, MA 02330
Ph: (508)866-1118
Fax: (508)866-1199

Wilson, Mr. Bob, Consultant
National Amputee Golf Association
[22886]
701 Orkney Ct.
Smyrna, TN 37167-6395
Ph: (615)967-4555

Wilson, Brian, Bd. Member
Beach Boys Fan Club [24026]
50 S Emery St., No. 4E
Pahrump, NV 89048

Wilson, Charles P., Chairman
National Association of Black Law
Enforcement Officers [5487]

PO Box 1182
Newark, NJ 07102
Ph: (401)465-9152

Wilson, Chuck, Exec. Dir.
Agency for Instructional Technology
[8020]
8111 Lee Paul Rd.
Bloomington, IN 47404-7916
Ph: (812)339-2203
Toll Free: 800-457-4509
Fax: (812)333-4218

Wilson, Chuck, Exec. Dir.
National Systems Contractors As-
sociation [1056]
3950 River Ridge Dr. NE
Cedar Rapids, IA 52402
Ph: (319)366-6722
Toll Free: 800-446-6722

Wilson, Chuck, President
North American Llewellin Breeders
Association, Inc. [21930]
3413 Forrester Ln.
Waco, TX 76708-1719
Ph: (254)752-1526

Wilson, Chuck, VP
United States Rottweiler Club
[21985]
c/o Lucy Ang
Bay Area Rottweiler Klub
14724 W Sunset
Livingston, CA 95334-9627
Ph: (608)825-9509
(209)394-8000

Wilson, Cindy
Playworks [12507]
380 Washington St.
Oakland, CA 94607
Ph: (510)893-4180
Fax: (510)893-4378

Wilson, Constance, Administrator
Episcopal Partnership for Global
Mission [20102]
815 2nd Ave.
New York, NY 10017-4503
Ph: (212)716-6000
Toll Free: 800-334-7626

Wilson, Cynthia, Exec. Dir., Founder
Chemical Injury Information Network
[17487]
PO Box 301
White Sulphur Springs, MT 59645
Ph: (406)547-2255

Wilson, Cynthia, VP
League for Innovation in the Com-
munity College [7643]
1333 S Spectrum Blvd., Ste. 210
Chandler, AZ 85286
Ph: (480)705-8200
Fax: (480)705-8201

Wilson, Darryl L., Jr., Exec. Dir.
Delta Phi Upsilon Fraternity, Inc.
[23705]
PO Box 573013
Houston, TX 77257

Wilson, David, VP
American Cutting Horse Association
[22937]
PO Box 2443
Brenham, TX 77834
Ph: (979)836-3370
Fax: (979)251-9971

Wilson, David, Officer
Great Council of U.S. Improved
Order of Red Men [19623]
4521 Speight Ave.
Waco, TX 76711
Ph: (254)756-1221
Fax: (254)756-4828

Wilson, Dawn K., PhD, Exec.
Society of Behavioral Medicine
[13803]
555 E Wells St., Ste. 1100
Milwaukee, WI 53202-3800
Ph: (414)918-3156
Fax: (414)276-3349

Wilson, Del, Mem.
Fellowship of Christian Magician
International [19977]

Wilson, Diane, Librarian
American Historical Society of
Germans From Russia [19443]
631 D St.
Lincoln, NE 68502-1199
Ph: (402)474-3363
Fax: (402)474-7229

Wilson, Donna, President
International Association of Insur-
ance Receivers [1875]
610 Freedom Business Ctr., Ste. 110
King of Prussia, PA 19406
Ph: (610)992-0017
Fax: (610)992-0021

Wilson, Duane, Secretary, CFO
American Society of Theatre
Consultants [816]
PO Box 22
La Luz, NM 88337
Toll Free: 855-800-2782

Wilson, Edward
Earthwatch Institute [7090]
114 Western Ave.
Boston, MA 02134
Ph: (978)461-0081
Toll Free: 800-776-0188
Fax: (978)461-2332

Wilson, Elizabeth M., President,
CEO
American Brain Tumor Association
[13880]
8550 W Bryn Mawr Ave., Ste. 550
Chicago, IL 60631
Ph: (773)577-8750
Toll Free: 800-886-2282
Fax: (773)577-8738

Wilson, Jerry, President
American Recovery Association
[982]
5525 N MacArthur Blvd., No. 135
Irving, TX 75038
Ph: (972)755-4755

Wilson, Jerry, President
Oldsmobile Club of America [21466]
PO Box 80318
Lansing, MI 48908-0318
Ph: (314)878-5651

Wilson, Mr. Jim, Exec. Dir.
National Broadcasting Society -
Alpha Epsilon Rho [23685]
PO Box 4206
Chesterfield, MO 63006
Ph: (636)536-1943
Fax: (636)898-6920

Wilson, John, Founder
Golden Raspberry Award Foundation
[24018]
PO Box 835
Artesia, CA 90701-0835
Fax: (562)860-4136

Wilson, Josh, Exec. Dir.
Farmers and Hunters Feeding the
Hungry [12084]
PO Box 323
Williamsport, MD 21795
Ph: (301)739-3000
Toll Free: 866-438-3434
Fax: (301)745-6337

Wilson, Kathabela, Secretary
Tanka Society of America [10160]
c/o Kathabela Wilson, Secretary
439 S Catalina Ave., No. 306
Pasadena, CA 91106

Wilson, Dr. Katie, Exec. Dir.
University of Mississippi School of
Applied Sciences I Institute of
Child Nutrition [1398]
6 Jeanette Phillips Dr.
University, MS 38677
Ph: (662)915-7658
Toll Free: 800-321-3054
Fax: (800)321-3061

Wilson, Kelli, Chairman
Asthma and Allergy Foundation of
America [13574]
8201 Corporate Dr., Ste. 1000
Landover, MD 20785-2266
Toll Free: 800-727-8462

Wilson, Kelly L., Coord.
Coalition of National Health Educa-
tion Organizations [8316]
Illinois Station University
Campus Mail 5220
Normal, IL 61790-5220
Ph: (309)438-2324
Fax: (309)438-2450

Wilson, Lee, President
National Poultry and Food Distribu-
tors Association [1362]
2014 Osborne Rd.
Saint Marys, GA 31558
Ph: (678)850-9311
    (770)535-9901
Fax: (770)535-7385

Wilson, Lynn C., Exec. Dir.
Association of Consulting Foresters
of America [4194]
312 Montgomery St., Ste. 208
Alexandria, VA 22314
Ph: (703)548-0990

Wilson, Margaret C., President
Institute for Professionals in Taxation
[5793]
600 Northpark Town Ctr.
1200 Abernathy Rd., Ste. L-2
Atlanta, GA 30328-1040
Ph: (404)240-2300
Fax: (404)240-2315

Wilson, Martha, Director
Franklin Furnace Archive [8855]
c/o Pratt Institute
ISC Bldg., Rm. 209-211
200 Willoughby Ave.
Brooklyn, NY 11205
Ph: (718)687-5800
Fax: (718)687-5830

Wilson, Mary Ann, RN, Founder,
Exec. Dir.
Sit and Be Fit [16714]
PO Box 8033
Spokane, WA 99203-0033
Ph: (509)448-9438
Toll Free: 888-678-9438
Fax: (509)448-5078

Wilson, Mercedes Arzú, Founder,
President
Family of the Americas Foundation
[11840]
5929 Talbot Rd.
Lothian, MD 20711
Ph: (301)627-3346
Toll Free: 800-443-3395

Wilson, Michael E., CEO
Automotive Recyclers Association
[3446]
9113 Church St.

Manassas, VA 20110
Ph: (571)208-0428
Toll Free: 888-385-1005
Fax: (571)208-0430

Wilson, Mike, Officer
National Imperial Glass Collectors
Society [22142]
PO Box 534
Bellaire, OH 43906

Wilson, Mitchell B., Exec. Dir.
Kappa Sigma Fraternity [23906]
1610 Scottsville Rd.
Charlottesville, VA 22902
Ph: (434)295-3193
Fax: (434)296-9557

Wilson, Nancy, CEO, President
Relief International [12719]
1101 14th St. NW, Ste. 1100
Washington, DC 20006
Ph: (202)639-8660
Fax: (202)639-8664

Wilson, Dr. Nancy, Contact
Sparrow Clubs U.S.A. [11272]
906 NE Greenwood Ave., Ste. 2
Bend, OR 97701
Ph: (541)312-8630

Wilson, Patti, President
Professional Women Controllers,
Inc. [1263]
PO Box 23924
Washington, DC 20024

Wilson, Phill, President, CEO
Black AIDS Institute [13533]
1833 W 8th St., No. 200
Los Angeles, CA 90057-4920
Ph: (213)353-3610
Fax: (213)989-0181

Wilson, Quentin, Chairman
National Council of Higher Education
Resources [7837]
1100 Connecticut Ave. NW, Ste.
1200
Washington, DC 20036-4110
Ph: (202)822-2106
Fax: (202)822-2143

Wilson, Ryan, MS III, Mem.
Association of Native American
Medical Students [15621]
1225 Sovereign Row, Ste. 103
Oklahoma City, OK 73108-1854
Ph: (405)946-7072
Fax: (405)946-7651

Wilson, Stephanie, Exec. Dir.
American Osteopathic College of
Physical Medicine and Rehabilita-
tion [16516]
210 Lantwyn Ln.
Narberth, PA 19072
Ph: (908)387-1750
    (610)664-4466
Fax: (866)925-8568

Wilson, Stephanie, Exec. Dir.
Association of Military Osteopathic
Physicians and Surgeons [16519]
PO Box 4
Phillipsburg, NJ 08865-0004
Ph: (908)387-1750
Fax: (866)925-8568

Wilson, Steve, Secretary
Children's HopeChest [10928]
PO Box 63842
Colorado Springs, CO 80962-3842
Ph: (719)487-7800
Fax: (719)487-7799

Wilson, Steve, Chairperson
National Society for American Indian
Elderly [19585]

PO Box 50070
Phoenix, AZ 85076
Ph: (602)424-0542

Wilson, Stew, Secretary, Treasurer
American Yankee Association
[21214]
PO Box 1531
Cameron Park, CA 95682-1531

Wilson, Susanne, Exec. Dir.
Water to Thrive [13346]
PO Box 26747
Austin, TX 78755
Ph: (512)206-4495

Wilson, Thomas, President
National Rehabilitation Counseling
Association [17095]
PO Box 4480
Manassas, VA 20108
Ph: (703)361-2077
Fax: (703)361-2489

Wilson, Timothy, Chairman
Amref Health Africa, USA [16994]
4 W 43rd St., 2nd Fl.
New York, NY 10036
Ph: (212)768-2440
Fax: (212)768-4230

Wilson, Tom, Director
Davis Registry [21368]
6487 Munger Rd.
Ypsilanti, MI 48197
Ph: (734)434-5581

Wilson, Tyler J., President, CEO
National Home Infusion Association
[15740]
100 Daingerfield Rd.
Alexandria, VA 22314
Ph: (703)549-3740
Fax: (703)683-1484

Wilson, Wanda, Exec. Dir.
American Association of Nurse
Anesthetists [16094]
222 S Prospect Ave.
Park Ridge, IL 60068-4001
Ph: (847)692-7050
    (847)655-1106
Toll Free: 855-526-2262
Fax: (847)692-6968

Wilson, Weldon, Chairman
Associated Male Choruses of
America [9874]
5143 S 40th St.
Saint Cloud, MN 56301
Ph: (320)260-1081

Wilson, Wesley, President
Let Me Live [12775]
130 Amberwood Rd.
Pickens, SC 29671

Wilt, David, Director
Transported Asset Protection As-
sociation [7154]
140 Island Way, Ste. 316
Clearwater Beach, FL 33767
Ph: (561)206-0344

Wilt, Donna, Chairperson
Society of Aviation and Flight Educa-
tors [7528]
PO Box 4283
Ventura, CA 93007
Ph: (901)687-5217

Wilt, Mr. Steve, Dir. Gen.
Fellowship International Mission
[20416]
555 S 24th St.
Allentown, PA 18104-6666
Ph: (610)435-9099
Toll Free: 888-346-9099
Fax: (610)435-2641

Wilt-Hild, Bonnie, Contact
National Association of Mortgage
   Processors **[409]**
1250 Connecticut Ave. NW, Ste. 200
Washington, DC 20036
Ph: (202)261-6505
Toll Free: 800-977-1197
Fax: (202)318-0655

Wiltraut, Douglas, Membership Chp.
National Society of Painters in
   Casein and Acrylic **[8934]**
c/o Douglas Wiltraut, Membership
   Chairperson
969 Catasauqua Rd.
Whitehall, PA 18052

Wiltz, Bernadette, Exec. Dir.
Southern United States Trade As-
   sociation **[3531]**
701 Poydras St., Ste. 3845
New Orleans, LA 70139
Ph: (504)568-5986
Fax: (504)568-6010

Wimer, Ross, President
Graham Foundation **[234]**
Madlener House
4 W Burton Pl.
Chicago, IL 60610-1416
Ph: (312)787-4071

Wimmer, Lindsay, Exec. Dir.
Star Legacy Foundation **[15389]**
11305 Hawk High Ct.
Eden Prairie, MN 55347
Ph: (952)715-7731

Winbush, Rev. Robina M., President
Churches Uniting in Christ **[20058]**
PO Box 6496
Louisville, KY 40206

Winchester, David P., MD, Exec. Dir.
American Joint Committee on
   Cancer **[16332]**
633 N St. Clair St.
Chicago, IL 60611-3211
Ph: (312)202-5205
Fax: (312)202-5009

Windham, Robert E., President
35th Infantry Division Association
   [20701]
PO Box 5004
Topeka, KS 66605

Windle, Karen, Chmn. of the Bd.
Nurse Practitioner Associates for
   Continuing Education **[16167]**
209 W Central St., Ste. 228
Natick, MA 01760
Ph: (508)907-6424
Fax: (508)907-6425

Windle, Rev. Martin, President
BCM International **[19750]**
201 Granite Run Dr., Ste. 260
Lancaster, PA 17601
Ph: (717)560-9601
Toll Free: 888-226-4685
Fax: (717)560-9607

Wines, James, Creative Dir.,
   Founder, President
Sculpture in the Environment
   [17995]
25 Maiden Ln.
New York, NY 10038
Ph: (212)285-0120

Winfield, Ryan, Coord.
American Institute for Conservation
   of Historic & Artistic Works **[9371]**
1156 15th St. NW, Ste. 320
Washington, DC 20005
Ph: (202)452-9545
Fax: (202)452-9328

Wingate, Martha, DrPH, Chairperson
Association of Teachers of Maternal
   and Child Health **[14168]**
c/o Julie McDougal, Coordinator
1720 2nd Ave. S, Ryals 310G
Birmingham, AL 35294-0022
Ph: (205)975-0531
Fax: (205)934-3347

Winger, Amanda Burton, Exec. Dir.
Conductors Guild Inc. **[9892]**
719 Twinridge Ln.
Richmond, VA 23235-5270
Ph: (804)553-1378
Fax: (804)553-1876

Wingfield, John D., President
Wingfield Family Society **[20943]**
c/o John D. Wingfield
5300 Zebulon Rd., Unit 32
Macon, GA 31210
Ph: (478)957-5974

Wingfield, Laura Ross, Div. Dir.
Beta Sigma Phi **[23870]**
1800 W 91st Pl.
Kansas City, MO 64114
Ph: (816)444-6800
Toll Free: 888-238-2221
Fax: (816)333-6206

Wingo, Ajume, Founder
Developing Opportunities for
   Orphans and Residents of
   Cameroon **[11346]**
PO Box 1439
Boulder, CO 80306

Wingren, Ann
Kidney Transplant/Dialysis Associa-
   tion, Inc. **[17513]**
PO Box 51362
Boston, MA 02205-1362
Ph: (781)641-4000

Wingrove, Brian, President
Society for Physician Assistants in
   Pediatrics **[16728]**
PO Box 90434
San Antonio, TX 78209
Ph: (614)824-2102
   (210)722-7622
Fax: (614)824-2103

Wink, Judy, Exec. Dir.
Chesapeake Bay Environmental
   Center **[4803]**
600 Discovery Ln.
Grasonville, MD 21638
Ph: (410)827-6694
Fax: (410)827-6713

Winkelman, Ms. Eli, Founder
Challah for Hunger **[12080]**
201 S Camac St., 2nd Fl.
Philadelphia, PA 19107

Winkelman, Nancy, President
American Academy of Appellate
   Lawyers **[4979]**
9707 Key W Ave., Ste. 100
Rockville, MD 20850
Ph: (240)404-6498
Fax: (301)990-9771

Winkle, C. Christian, Chairman
Association for Quality Imaging
   [15681]
1629 K St. NW, Ste. 300
Washington, DC 20006
Ph: (202)355-6406
Fax: (202)355-6407

Winkler, Carol, Reg. Dir.,
   Chairperson
Federation of Chiropractic Licensing
   Boards **[14269]**
5401 W 10th St., Ste. 101

Greeley, CO 80634-4468
Ph: (970)356-3500
Fax: (970)356-3599

Winkler, Jim, President, Gen. Sec.
National Council of the Churches of
   Christ in the USA **[20069]**
110 Maryland Ave. NE, Ste. 108
Washington, DC 20002-5603
Ph: (202)544-2350
Toll Free: 800-379-7729
Fax: (212)543-1297

Winn, Robert, Chairman
Global Action Project **[19271]**
130 W 25th St., Fl. 2C
New York, NY 10001-7406
Ph: (212)594-9577

Winnegrad, Mark H., President
Graphics Philately Association
   [22331]
1030 E El Camino Real, Ste. 107
Sunnyvale, CA 94087-3759

Winnekins, Brian, President
National Association of Farm
   Broadcasters **[471]**
1100 Platte Falls Rd.
Platte City, MO 64079
Ph: (816)431-4032
Fax: (816)431-4087

Winship, Ms. Joan, Exec. Dir.
International Association of Women
   Judges **[5387]**
1901 L St. NW, Ste. 640
Washington, DC 20036
Ph: (202)223-4455
Fax: (202)223-4480

Winslow, Hon. Cleta, Director
National Association of Neighbor-
   hoods **[11295]**
1300 Pennsylvania Ave. NW, Ste.
   700
Washington, DC 20004
Ph: (202)332-7766

Winsor, Rebecca D., President
The William H. Donner Foundation,
   Inc. **[13961]**
520 White Plains Rd., Ste. 500
Tarrytown, NY 10591
Ph: (914)524-0404
Fax: (914)524-0407

Winstead, Mr. Tom, Sr., President
Christian Golfers' Association
   [22877]
1285 Clara Louise Kellogg Dr.
Sumter, SC 29153
Toll Free: 800-784-2171

Winstein, Carolee, PhD, PT, FAPTA,
   VP
American Society of Neurorehabilita-
   tion **[16008]**
5841 Cedar Lake Rd., Ste. 204
Minneapolis, MN 55416
Ph: (952)545-6324
Fax: (952)545-6073

Winstel, Thomas, President
Carriage Travel Club **[22464]**
514 Americans Way, No. 3384
Box Elder, SD 57719-7600
Ph: (931)707-0299

Winston, Barbara, President
UN Women for Peace Association
   [12444]
410 Park Ave., Ste. 1500
New York, NY 10022

Winston, Carol, Asst. to the Pres.
Black Women's Health Imperative
   [17753]

55 M St. SE, Ste. 940
Washington, DC 20003
Ph: (202)548-4000

Winter, Leslie F., RT, CEO
Joint Review Committee on Educa-
   tion in Radiologic Technology
   [8298]
20 N Wacker Dr., Ste. 2850
Chicago, IL 60606-3182
Ph: (312)704-5300
Fax: (312)704-5304

Winter, Rymann, President
Aviation for Humanity **[12624]**
269 S Beverly Dr., No. 674
Beverly Hills, CA 90212
Ph: (310)968-3503
Fax: (310)861-9041

Winter, Simon, Sr. VP
TechnoServe Inc. **[18501]**
1120 19th St. NW, 8th Fl.
Washington, DC 20036
Ph: (202)785-4515
Toll Free: 800-999-6757
Fax: (202)785-4544

Winters, Abe, Contact
Tree Climbing USA **[21599]**
PO Box 142062
Fayetteville, GA 30214
Ph: (770)487-6929

Wintroub, Bruce U., Chairman
Dermatology Foundation **[14492]**
1560 Sherman Ave., Ste. 870
Evanston, IL 60201-4808
Ph: (847)328-2256
Fax: (847)328-0509

Wipperman, Sarah, Mgr.
Penn Center for Bioethics **[6064]**
3420 Walnut St.
Philadelphia, PA 19104-3318
Ph: (215)898-7555

Wirtanen, Tracy, Founder
Littlest Tumor Foundation **[14837]**
PO Box 7051
Appleton, WI 54912
Ph: (920)475-6599

Wirth, Fritz, Exec. Dir.
Society of Inkwell Collectors **[21721]**
c/o Jeffrey Pisetzner
2203 39th St. SE
Puyallup, WA 98372-5223

Wirth, Laurie, Exec. Dir.
American Board of Facial Plastic
   and Reconstructive Surgery
   [17363]
115C S St. Asaph St.
Alexandria, VA 22314
Ph: (703)549-3223
Fax: (703)549-3357

Wirth, Teri, VP
International Perfume Bottle Associa-
   tion **[21676]**
PO Box 7644
Northridge, CA 91327

Wirtzfeld, Carey, President
Pioneers **[11861]**
1801 California St., Ste. 225
Denver, CO 80202
Ph: (303)571-1200
Toll Free: 800-872-5995
Fax: (303)572-0520

Wisbauer, Stefan, Bd. Member
Center for Nonviolent Communica-
   tion **[18716]**
9301 Indian School Rd. NE, Ste.
   204
Albuquerque, NM 87112-2861
Ph: (505)244-4041
Toll Free: 800-255-7696
Fax: (505)547-0414

Wiscombe, Allan, Director
Nims Family Association [20908]
c/o Jane D. Nimbs, Treasurer
1103 Peachtree Blvd.
Richmond, VA 23226-1137

Wise, Bob, President
Alliance for Excellent Education
  [8558]
1201 Connecticut Ave. NW, Ste. 901
Washington, DC 20036
Ph: (202)828-0828
Fax: (202)828-0821

Wise, Carol, Exec. Dir.
Brethren/Mennonite Council for
  Lesbian, Gay, Bisexual and Trans-
  gender Interest [20175]
PO Box 6300
Minneapolis, MN 55406
Ph: (612)343-2060

Wise, David, Chmn. of the Bd.
Pulp & Paperworkers' Resource
  Council [23420]
USW Local 9-1877
Florence, SC 29505

Wise, John, Coord.
Hank Williams International Fan
  Club [24069]
c/o Ed Kirby, President
103 Summit Cir.
Daphne, AL 36526
Ph: (251)626-1645

Wise, Marcia, Secretary
American Behcet's Disease Associa-
  tion [13812]
PO Box 80576
Rochester, MI 48308
Ph: (631)656-0537
Toll Free: 800-723-4238
Fax: (480)247-5377

Wise, Marsha A., Exec. Dir.
American Osteopathic College of
  Dermatology [14483]
2902 N Baltimore St.
Kirksville, MO 63501
Ph: (660)665-2184
Toll Free: 800-449-2623
Fax: (660)627-2623

Wiseman, Brooke, CEO
Blessings in a Backpack [10868]
4121 Shelbyville Rd.
Louisville, KY 40207
Toll Free: 800-872-4366

Wiseman, Dr. David, PhD, Founder
International Adhesions Society
  [16556]
Synechion, Inc.
18208 Preston Rd., Ste. D9
Dallas, TX 75252-6011
Ph: (972)931-5596
Fax: (972)931-5476

Wiseman, Nancy D., Founder,
  President
First Signs [14160]
PO Box 358
Merrimac, MA 01860
Ph: (978)346-4380
Fax: (978)346-4638

Wish, David, CEO, Founder
Little Kids Rock [8373]
Bldg. E2
271 Grove Ave.
Verona, NJ 07044
Ph: (973)746-8248
Fax: (973)746-8240

Wisneski, Gerald D., Chairman
InFaith [20424]
145 John Robert Thomas Dr.

Exton, PA 19341
Ph: (610)527-4439

Wisniewski, Carolyn, Director
Writers Workshop [10407]
208 English Bldg.
608 S Wright St.
Urbana, IL 61801
Ph: (217)333-8796

Wisotsky, Arielle, Founder, VP
Help Darfur Now [18307]
51 Schweinberg Dr.
Roseland, NJ 07068

Wispelwey, June C., Exec. Dir.
Society for Biological Engineering
  [6096]
100 Mill Plain Rd., 3rd Fl.
Danbury, CT 06811
Toll Free: 800-242-4363
Fax: (203)775-5177

Withers, Jan, Secretary
National Association of State Agencies of the Deaf and Hard of Hearing [11942]
c/o Delaware Office for the Deaf and
  Hard of Hearing
4425 N Market St.
Wilmington, DE 19802-1307

Withrow, Paul, Exec. Dir.
Deliver the Dream, Inc. [12873]
3223 NW 10th Terr., Ste. 602
Fort Lauderdale, FL 33309-5940
Ph: (954)564-3512
Toll Free: 888-687-3732
Fax: (954)564-4385

Witschi, Nicolas, Exec. Sec.
Western Literature Association
  [9771]
PO Box 6815
Logan, UT 84341

Witt, Hal J., VP
American Friends of the Paris Opera
  and Ballet [8953]
972 5th Ave.
New York, NY 10075
Ph: (212)439-1426
Fax: (212)439-1455

Witte, M.H., MD, Sec. Gen.
International Society of Lymphology
  [15542]
PO Box 245200
Tucson, AZ 85724
Ph: (520)626-6118
Fax: (520)626-0822

Wittek, Michael R., Chmn. of the Bd.
Worldwide Fistula Fund [14244]
1100 E Woodfield Rd., Ste. 350
Schaumburg, IL 60173
Ph: (847)592-2438

Wittenberg, Jan, Membership Chp.
Fluorescent Mineral Society [6874]
PO Box 572694
Tarzana, CA 91357-2694
Ph: (862)259-2367

Wittenborn, John, Gen. Counsel
Steel Manufacturers Association
  [2373]
1150 Connecticut Ave. NW, Ste. 715
Washington, DC 20036-4131
Ph: (202)296-1515
Fax: (202)296-2506

Witter, Ray, Chairman
Association for Enterprise Informa-
  tion [613]
2111 Wilson Blvd., Ste. 400
Arlington, VA 22201
Ph: (703)247-2597
Fax: (703)522-3192

Wittingham, Kaylin L., President
Association of Black Women At-
  torneys [4994]
1001 Avenue of the Americas, 11th
  Fl.
New York, NY 10017

Wittkamp, Nancy, Dir. of Fin.
American Youth Foundation [20657]
6357 Clayton Rd.
Saint Louis, MO 63117
Ph: (314)719-4343

Wittkuhn, Klaus, President
International Society for
  Performance Improvement [8687]
PO Box 13035
Silver Spring, MD 20910
Ph: (301)587-8570
Fax: (301)587-8573

Wittling, Michele, Exec. Dir.
North American Society for
  Cardiovascular Imaging [14137]
1891 Preston White Dr.
Reston, VA 20191
Ph: (703)476-1350
   (703)476-1121
Fax: (703)716-4487

Witty, Nancy, CEO
International Society for Stem Cell
  Research [14882]
5215 Old Orchard Rd., Ste. 270
Skokie, IL 60077
Ph: (224)592-5700
Fax: (224)365-0004

Witzel, Michael, President
International Association for
  Comparative Mythology [10031]
c/o Dept. of South Asian Studies
Harvard University
1 Bow St., 3rd Fl.
Cambridge, MA 02138
Ph: (617)496-2990

Wnek, Warren E., Bd. Member
Anglers for Conservation [3808]
PO Box 372423
Satellite Beach, FL 32937

Woeckner, Elizabeth, President
Citizens for Responsible Care and
  Research, Inc. [6063]
1024 N 5th St.
Philadelphia, PA 19123-1404
Ph: (215)627-5335
Fax: (267)639-4950

Woesner, Clint, Founder
Betty's Foundation for the Elimina-
  tion of Alzheimer's Disease
  [13672]
PO Box 451477
Los Angeles, CA 90045

Woffington, Julie, Exec. Dir.
Educational Theatre Association
  [8698]
2343 Auburn Ave.
Cincinnati, OH 45219-2815
Ph: (513)421-3900
Fax: (513)421-7077

Wofford, Robin, Chmn. of the Bd.
National Association of Minority and
  Women Owned Law Firms [5029]
150 N Michigan Ave., Ste. 800
Chicago, IL 60601
Ph: (312)733-7780

Wohlberg, Seth, Contact
Rasmussen's Encephalitis Children's
  Project [15989]
79 Christie Hill Rd.
Darien, CT 06820

Wohlsen, Victoria, Exec. Dir.
Tolstoy Foundation Inc. [19632]
104 Lake Rd.

Valley Cottage, NY 10989
Ph: (845)268-6722
Fax: (845)268-6937

Wohlstein, Julie, CSFS, President
Health Care Administrators Associa-
  tion [15584]
5353 Wayzata Blvd., Ste. 350
Minneapolis, MN 55416
Toll Free: 888-637-1605
Fax: (952)252-8096

Woika, Lucy, President
Dwarf Athletic Association of
  America [22515]
1095 Hilltop Dr., No. 361
Redding, CA 96003
Toll Free: 888-598-3222

Wojcik, Nancy, MS, Dir. of Comm.
National Hearing Conservation As-
  sociation [15205]
12011 Tejon St., Ste. 700
Westminster, CO 80234
Ph: (303)224-9022
Fax: (303)458-0002

Wojtan, Katherine, Coord.
Women-Church Convergence
  [20647]
PO Box 806
Mill Valley, CA 94942
Ph: (708)974-4220

Wolanyk, Betty, Chairperson
Project Food, Land and People
  [3575]
7023 Alhambra Dr.
Tallahassee, FL 32317
Ph: (850)219-1175

Wolden, Bill, Bd. Member
International Marine Animal Trainers
  Association [3617]
1880 Harbor Island Dr.
San Diego, CA 92101
Ph: (312)692-3193
Fax: (312)939-2216

Wolden, Colin, Editor
AVS Science and Technology
  Society [7359]
125 Maiden Ln., 15th Fl.
New York, NY 10038
Ph: (212)248-0200
Fax: (212)248-0245

Wolf, Andrew, Exec. Dir., Founder
Children's Future International
  [10926]
1031 33rd St., Ste. 174
Denver, CO 80205
Ph: (720)295-3312

Wolf, Dr. Bruce, Founder
Hope Beyond Hope [15472]
4230 Harding Rd., Ste. 307
Nashville, TN 37205
Ph: (615)292-8299

Wolf, Dr. Catherine, Exec. Dir.
Friends for Health in Haiti [15003]
PO Box 122
Pewaukee, WI 53072
Ph: (262)227-9581

Wolf, Craig, CEO, President
Wine and Spirits Wholesalers of
  America [194]
805 15th St. NW, Ste. 430
Washington, DC 20005
Ph: (202)371-9792
Fax: (202)789-2405

Wolf, David G., Director
National Greyhound Adoption
  Program [10670]
10901 Dutton Rd.

Philadelphia, PA 19154-3203
Ph: (215)331-7918
Fax: (215)331-1947

Wolf, Erik, Founder, Exec. Dir.
World Food Travel Association **[704]**
4110 SE Hawthorne Blvd., Ste. 440
Portland, OR 97214
Ph: (503)213-3700

Wolf, James R., Director
Continental Divide Trail Society
[23323]
3704 N Charles St., No. 601
Baltimore, MD 21218
Ph: (410)235-9610

Wolf, Mr. Jay, Contact
Elgin Motorcar Owners Registry
[21376]
2226 E Apache Ln.
Vincennes, IN 47591
Ph: (812)888-4172
Fax: (812)888-5471

Wolf, Kay, Chairman
Women in Government **[5648]**
1319 F St. NW, Ste. 710
Washington, DC 20004
Ph: (202)333-0825
Fax: (202)333-0875

Wolf, Laura J., Exec. Dir.
IEEE - Engineering in Medicine and
Biology Society **[6112]**
445 Hoes Ln.
Piscataway, NJ 08854
Ph: (732)981-3433
Fax: (732)465-6435

Wolf, Lois, Director
Edison Birthplace Association
[10324]
c/o Edison Birthplace Museum
9 N Edison Dr.
Milan, OH 44846
Ph: (419)499-2135

Wolf, Rachel, CEO
American Committee for Shaare
Zedek Medical Center in
Jerusalem **[12205]**
55 W 39th St., 4th Fl.
New York, NY 10018
Ph: (212)354-8801
Fax: (212)391-2674

Wolf, Steve, Chmn. of the Bd.
United States Harness Writers' As-
sociation **[2729]**
PO Box 1314
Mechanicsburg, PA 17055
Ph: (717)651-5889

Wolfe, Bill, II, VP
Epicor Users Group **[6300]**
PO Box 10368
Lancaster, PA 17605
Ph: (717)209-7177
Fax: (717)209-7189

Wolfe, Dr. Charles, President
Plymouth Rock Foundation **[7797]**
1120 Long Pond Rd.
Plymouth, MA 02360
Toll Free: 800-210-1620

Wolfe, Hy, Director
Central Yiddish Culture Organization
[9634]
CYCO Publishing
51-02 21st St., 7th Fl. A-2
Long Island City, NY 11101-5357
Ph: (718)392-0002

Wolfe, Mark, VP
National Conference of State
Historic Preservation Officers
[9417]

Hall of States
444 N Capitol St. NW, Ste. 342
Washington, DC 20001
Ph: (202)624-5465
Fax: (202)624-5419

Wolfe, Mark, Exec. Dir.
National Energy Assistance Directors' Association **[1702]**
c/o Mark Wolfe, Executive Director
1350 Connecticut Ave. NW, No.
1100
Washington, DC 20007
Ph: (202)237-5199

Wolfe, Maxine, Coord.
Lesbian Herstory Archives **[10306]**
484 14th St.
Brooklyn, NY 11215
Ph: (718)768-3953
Fax: (718)768-4663

Wolfe, Michael, Secretary
Society for Text and Discourse
[8232]
c/o Catherine Bohn-Gettler,
Treasurer, 125 HAB, 37 S College
Ave.
College of Saint Benedict
Education Department, 125 HAB
37 S College Ave.
Saint Joseph, MN 56374

Wolfe, Nathan, Founder
Global Viral **[15401]**
1 Sutter St., Ste. 600
San Francisco, CA 94104
Ph: (415)398-4712
Fax: (415)398-4716

Wolfe, Norman S., Chairman
Web Wise Kids **[11185]**
PO Box 27203
Santa Ana, CA 92799
Ph: (714)435-2885
Toll Free: 866-WEB-WISE
Fax: (714)435-0523

Wolfe, Richard, Treasurer, Exec.
Sec.
International Sprout Growers As-
sociation **[3539]**
685 Bald Hill Rd., Box No. 8
Warwick, RI 02886
Ph: (508)657-4742

Wolfe, Sidney M., MD, Founder,
Advisor
Public Citizen Health Research
Group **[17016]**
1600 20th St. NW
Washington, DC 20009
Ph: (202)588-1000

Wolfersberger, Jon Rhan, President
Wolfensberger Family Association
[20944]
c/o Barbara Snavely, Treasurer
218 Belaire Dr.
Mount Laurel, NJ 08054-2702

Wolff, Nancy E., VP
Copyright Society of the U.S.A.
[5328]
1 E 53rd St., 8th Fl.
New York, NY 10022
Ph: (212)354-6401

Wolff, Patricia B., MD, Exec. Dir.,
Founder
Meds & Food for Kids **[11076]**
4488 Forest Park Ave., Ste. 230
Saint Louis, MO 63108-2215
Ph: (314)420-1634

Wolford, Harry, Mem.
Society for Louisiana Irises **[22124]**
c/o Ron Killingsworth, Treasurer

10329 Caddo Lake Rd.
Mooringsport, LA 71060-9057

Wolfowitz, Paul D., Chairman
U.S.-Taiwan Business Council
[2005]
1700 N Moore St., Ste. 1703
Arlington, VA 22209
Ph: (703)465-2930
Fax: (703)465-2937

Wolfsdorf, Bernard, Mem.
Alliance of Business Immigration
Lawyers **[5071]**
11 Dupont Cir. NW, Ste. 775
Washington, DC 20036
Ph: (404)949-8150
Fax: (404)816-8615

Wolfson, Elaine M., PhD, Founder,
President
Global Alliance for Women's Health
[17756]
777 United Nation Plz., 7th Fl.
New York, NY 10017
Ph: (212)286-0424
Fax: (212)286-9561

Wolk, Andrew, CEO, Founder
Root Cause **[19117]**
11 Ave. de Lafayette
Boston, MA 02111
Ph: (617)492-2300

Wolke, Howie, President, Founder
Big Wild Advocates **[4793]**
222 Tom Miner Creek Rd.
Emigrant, MT 59027-6010
Ph: (406)848-7000

Woll, Lisa, CEO
US SIF: The Forum for Sustainable
and Responsible Investment
[19135]
1660 L St. NW, Ste. 306
Washington, DC 20036
Ph: (202)872-5361
Fax: (202)775-8686

Woloschak, Dr. Gayle E., President
Orthodox Theological Society in
America **[20055]**

Wolosewicz, Andrzej, Treasurer
Gift from the Heart Foundation
[14191]
3860 25th Ave.
Schiller Park, IL 60176
Ph: (847)671-2711
Fax: (847)671-2713

Wolters, Kevin, President
Equipment Marketing and Distribu-
tion Association **[2204]**
PO Box 1347
Iowa City, IA 52244
Ph: (319)354-5156
Fax: (319)354-5157

Womack, Virginia Booth, President,
Exec. Dir.
National Association of Multicultural
Engineering Program Advocates
[7861]
701 W Stadium Ave.
West Lafayette, IN 47907
Ph: (765)400-0637

Wondrak, Georg, President
American Society for Photobiology
[6072]
1313 Dolley Madison Blvd., Ste. 402
McLean, VA 22101
Ph: (703)790-1745

Wong, Catherine, Exec. Dir.
Phi Sigma **[23684]**
Dept. of Arts and Sciences

Endicott College
376 Hale St.
Beverly, MA 01915-2096

Wong, Fanny, Exec. Dir.
South-East Asia Center **[19021]**
5120 N Broadway St.
Chicago, IL 60640
Ph: (773)989-6927
Fax: (888)831-5471

Wong, Felicia, President, CEO
Roosevelt Institute **[10350]**
570 Lexington Ave., 5th Fl.
New York, NY 10022
Ph: (212)444-9130

Wong, Germaine Q., Chairman
Chinese for Affirmative Action
[17884]
17 Walter U. Lum Pl.
San Francisco, CA 94108
Ph: (415)274-6750
Fax: (415)397-8770

Wong, Hee Kit, President
International Society for the
Advancement of Spine Surgery
[16065]
2397 Waterbury Cir., Ste. 1
Aurora, IL 60504
Ph: (630)375-1432

Wong, Master Jimmy K., Founder,
President
North America Wu (Hao) Taiji
Federation **[23009]**
PO Box 742703
Dallas, TX 75374
Ph: (214)878-4598

Wong, Ms. Melanie G., Exec. Dir.
National Adrenal Diseases Founda-
tion **[14708]**
505 Northern Blvd.
Great Neck, NY 11021 .
Ph: (516)487-4992

Wong, Nancy, OD, President
National Association of Veterans Affairs Optometrists **[16429]**
c/o Dr. Makesha Sink, Treasurer
111 Harbor Dr.
Hampton, VA 23661

Wong, Prof. Richard, Exec. Dir.
American School Counselor Associa-
tion **[7683]**
1101 King St., Ste. 310
Alexandria, VA 22314
Ph: (703)683-2722
Toll Free: 800-306-4722
Fax: (703)997-7572

Wong, Steven H., PhD, President
American Association for Clinical
Chemistry **[6178]**
900 7th St., NW, Ste. 400
Washington, DC 20006
Toll Free: 800-892-5093
Fax: (202)887-0717

Wong, Tony, Chairman, President
National Neigong Research Society
[9793]
3060 El Cerrito Plz., No. 237
El Cerrito, CA 94530
Ph: (510)854-6374

Woo, Carolyn, President, CEO
Catholic Relief Services **[12586]**
228 W Lexington St.
Baltimore, MD 21201-3443
Toll Free: 888-277-7575

Woo, John C., Exec. Dir.
Asian CineVision **[9297]**
30 John St.

Brooklyn, NY 11201
Ph: (212)989-1422
Fax: (212)727-3584

Woo, Lillian, Chairman
Asian Americans/Pacific Islanders in
   Philanthropy [12460]
2201 Broadway, Ste. 720
Oakland, CA 94612
Ph: (510)463-3155

Woo, Savio L-Y., PhD, Founder,
   Chairperson
World Association for Chinese
   Biomedical Engineers [6116]
210 Lothrop St., E1641 BST
Pittsburgh, PA 15213-2536
Ph: (412)648-1494
Fax: (412)648-8548

Wood, Anthony C., Exec. Dir.,
   Secretary
Ittleson Foundation [12978]
c/o Anthony C. Wood, Executive
   Director
15 E 67th St.
New York, NY 10065
Ph: (212)794-2008

Wood, Antony, Exec. Dir.
Council on Tall Buildings and Urban
   Habitat [5966]
c/o Patti Thurmond, Manager of
   Operations
SR Crown Hall
Illinois Institute of Technology
3360 S State St.
Chicago, IL 60616
Ph: (312)567-3487
Fax: (312)567-3820

Wood, April, Chairman
National Voluntary Organizations
   Active in Disaster [12704]
615 Slaters Ln.
Alexandria, VA 22314
Ph: (703)778-5088
Fax: (703)778-5091

Wood, Barry C., Contact
Gaylord Family Organization [20869]
1910 S Church St.
Lodi, CA 95240
Ph: (209)366-2773

Wood, Dan, Exec. Dir.
National Christian College Athletic
   Association [23240]
302 W Washington St.
Greenville, SC 29601-1919
Ph: (864)250-1199
Fax: (864)250-1141

Wood, Diane W., President
National Environmental Education
   Foundation [7896]
4301 Connecticut Ave. NW, Ste. 160
Washington, DC 20008
Ph: (202)833-2933

Wood, Don, Founder
Child Watch of North America
   [10906]
PO Box 691782
Orlando, FL 32869-1782
Ph: (407)290-5100
Toll Free: 888-CHILDWATCH

Wood, Doris, Chairperson, Founder
Multi-Level Marketing International
   Association [2293]
119 Stanford Ct.
Irvine, CA 92612
Ph: (949)257-0931

Wood, Doug, Exec. Dir.
Soccer Association for Youth [23190]
Enterprise Business Park

2812 E Kemper Rd.
Cincinnati, OH 45241
Ph: (513)769-3800
Toll Free: 800-233-7291
Fax: (513)769-0500

Wood, Funlayo E., Director
African and Diasporic Religious
   Studies Association [20574]
12 Quincy St.
Barker Ctr.
Department of African and African
   American Studies
Harvard University
Cambridge, MA 02138

Wood, Geoff, Treasurer
Angel Flight West [12264]
3161 Donald Douglas Loop S
Santa Monica, CA 90405
Ph: (310)390-2958
Toll Free: 888-426-2643
Fax: (310)397-9636

Wood, George, Chairman
Coalition on Essential Schools [7695]
482 Congress St., Ste. 500A
Portland, ME 04101
Ph: (401)426-9638

Wood, George, Exec. Dir.
Forum for Education and Democracy
   [7821]
PO Box 15
Stewart, OH 45778
Ph: (740)590-1579

Wood, Hilary, President
Front Range Equine Rescue [4352]
PO Box 458
Ocala, FL 34478
Ph: (352)209-7510

Wood, J.B., CEO, President
Technology Services Industry As-
   sociation [3214]
17065 Camino San Bernadino, Ste.
   200
San Diego, CA 92127-5737
Ph: (858)674-5491
Fax: (858)946-0005

Wood, Jennie, Exec. Dir.
TECH, Technical Exchange for
   Christian Healthcare [20326]
PO Box 912
Lawrenceburg, TN 38464
Ph: (989)600-6536
Fax: (989)600-6536

Wood, John, Founder
Room to Read [11736]
465 California St., Ste. 1000
San Francisco, CA 94104
Ph: (415)839-4400
Fax: (415)591-0580

Wood, Michael, Exec. Dir.
Association of Architecture Organiza-
   tions [5962]
224 S Michigan Ave., Ste. 116
Chicago, IL 60604
Ph: (312)561-2159
Fax: (312)922-2607

Wood, Michael, Secretary
The Society of United States Air
   Force Flight Surgeons [13511]
PO Box 1776
Fairborn, OH 45324-7776

Wood, Nancy, Founder, Director
Hope for Children of Africa [10478]
PO Box 399
Alma, CO 80420
Ph: (303)902-9276

Wood, Patricia J., Exec. Dir.
Grassroots Environmental Education
   [7892]

52 Main St.
Port Washington, NY 11050
Ph: (516)883-0887

Wood, Patricia V., Founder,
   President
NBIA Disorders Association [15974]
2082 Monaco Ct.
El Cajon, CA 92019-4235
Ph: (619)588-2315
Fax: (619)588-4093

Wood, Rev. Raymond B., President
Kate Smith Commemorative Society
   [24063]
PO Box 242
Syracuse, NY 13214-0242

Wood, Richard E., Exec. Dir.
Theta Delta Chi [23937]
214 Lewis Wharf
Boston, MA 02110
Toll Free: 800-999-1847

Wood, Scott, Treasurer
International Association of Certified
   Thermographers [7331]
38 Raft Island Dr. NW
Gig Harbor, WA 98335
Ph: (253)509-3742

Wood, Terri, Officer
International Society for IGF
   Research [6057]

Wood, Thomas J., Editor
James Jones Literary Society
   [10384]
PO Box 68
Robinson, IL 62454-0068

Wood, Warren, President
United Flying Octogenarians [21254]
24 Arboleda Ln.
Carmel Valley, CA 93924-9633
Ph: (831)659-7523

Woodard, Amy, Chairperson
United States Equine Rescue
   League, Inc. [4418]
1851 W Erhinghaus St., Ste. 146
Elizabeth City, NC 27909
Toll Free: 800-650-8549

Woodard, Diann, President
American Federation of School
   Administrators [7420]
1101 17th St. NW, Ste. 408
Washington, DC 20036
Ph: (202)986-4209
Fax: (202)986-4211

Woodard, Richard N., Chairman
National Campaign for a Peace Tax
   Fund [19171]
2121 Decatur Pl. NW
Washington, DC 20008
Ph: (202)483-3751

Woodcock, Sarah K., Founder
The Abolitionist Vegan Society
   [10290]
PO Box 44875
Eden Prairie, MN 55344

Wooderson, Stephen A., CEO
Council of State Administrators of
   Vocational Rehabilitation [17087]
1 Research Ct., Ste. 450
Rockville, MD 20850
Ph: (301)519-8023

Woodin, Mr. Dale, Exec. Dir.
American Society for Healthcare
   Engineering [15308]
155 N Wacker Dr., Ste. 400
Chicago, IL 60606-1719
Ph: (312)422-3800
Fax: (312)422-4571

Woodin, Mary Beth, President
Menopause Alliance [16293]
350 Broadway, Ste. 307
New York, NY 10013
Ph: (212)625-3311
Fax: (917)591-5606

Woodland, Paula, VP
American Ferret Association [21279]
PO Box 554
Frederick, MD 21705-0554
Toll Free: 888-FERRET-1
Fax: (240)358-0673

Woodlief, Dr. Ann, Librarian
Huguenot Society of the Founders of
   Manakin in the Colony of Virginia
   [21003]
981 Huguenot Trail
Midlothian, VA 23113

Woodman, Mark, President
Color Marketing Group [753]
1908 Mt. Vernon Ave.
Alexandria, VA 22301
Ph: (703)329-8500
Fax: (703)329-0155

Woodman, Nick, CEO, Founder
Professional Association of Small
   Business Accountants [57]
6405 Metcalf Ave., Ste. 503
Shawnee Mission, KS 66202
Toll Free: 866-296-0001
Fax: (913)384-5112

Woodmansee, Denni J., Chairman
National Commission on Certification
   of Physician Assistants [16723]
12000 Findley Rd., Ste. 100
Johns Creek, GA 30097
Ph: (678)417-8100
Fax: (678)417-8135

Woodruff, Cynthia, Exec. Dir.
American Art Therapy Association
   [16956]
4875 Eisenhower Ave., Ste. 240
Alexandria, VA 22304
Ph: (703)548-5860
Toll Free: 888-290-0878
Fax: (703)783-8468

Woodruff, Frank, Exec. Dir.
National Alliance of Community
   Economic Development Associa-
   tions [18154]
1660 L St. NW, Ste. 306
Washington, DC 20036
Ph: (202)518-2660

Woodruff, Phil, President
First Flight Society [21227]
PO Box 1903
Kitty Hawk, NC 27949
Ph: (252)441-1903

Woods, Ellen, MSC, Exec. Dir.
American Osteopathic Board of
   Pediatrics [16512]
142 E Ontario St., 4th Fl.
Chicago, IL 60611
Toll Free: 800-621-1773
Fax: (312)202-8441

Woods, Ellen, MSC, Contact
American Osteopathic Board of
   Preventive Medicine [16513]
142 E Ontario St., 4th Fl.
Chicago, IL 60611
Toll Free: 800-621-1773
Fax: (312)202-8319

Woods, James, Dir. of Public Rel.
Steel Recycling Institute [3455]
680 Andersen Dr.
Pittsburgh, PA 15220-2700
Ph: (412)922-2772

Woods, Mark H., CEO, Founder
Operation Troop Aid **[10758]**
2441-Q Old Fort Pky., No. 317
Murfreesboro, TN 37128
Ph: (921)355-8844
Toll Free: 877-435-7682

Woods, Tom, Chmn. of the Bd.
National Association of Home Build-
ers **[554]**
1201 15th St. NW
Washington, DC 20005
Toll Free: 800-268-5242

Woodsmall, Wyatt L., PhD, Director,
Founder
International Neuro-Linguistic
Programming Trainers Association
[16980]
1201 Delta Glen Ct.
Vienna, VA 22182

Woodson, Sarah, President
RNA Society **[6061]**
9650 Rockville Pke.
Bethesda, MD 20814-3998
Ph: (301)634-7166

Woodward, David, President, CEO
Associates in Cultural Exchange
[9204]
200 W Mercer St., Ste. 108
Seattle, WA 98119-3958
Ph: (206)217-9644
Fax: (206)217-9643

Woodward, John W., Mem.
Serra International **[19905]**
333 W Wacker Dr., Ste. 500
Chicago, IL 60606-2218
Ph: (312)419-7411

Woody, Gavin, Director
Mountaineers **[23327]**
7700 Sand Point Way NE
Seattle, WA 98115
Ph: (206)521-6000
Toll Free: 800-573-8484
Fax: (206)523-6763

Woody, Kirstin, President
Nuevas Esperanzas US **[11416]**
3517 Laurel View Rd.
Birmingham, AL 35216
Ph: (507)205-7150

Woolard, Jennifer, President
American Psychology-Law Society
[16866]
750 1st St. NE
Washington, DC 20002-4242
Ph: (202)336-5500

Woolcock, Kylie, Exec. Sec.
Councils on Chiropractic Education
International **[14268]**
PO Box 4943
Pocatello, ID 83205
Ph: (208)241-4855

Woolley, Linda A., President, CEO
Catalog and Multichannel Marketing
Council **[1532]**
1333 Broadway, Ste. 301
New York, NY 10018
Ph: (212)768-7277

Woolley, Linda A., President, CEO
Direct Marketing Association **[2279]**
1333 Broadway, Ste. No. 301
New York, NY 10018
Ph: (212)768-7277

Woolley, Mary, President
Research! America **[15655]**
1101 King St., Ste. 520
Alexandria, VA 22314-2960
Ph: (703)739-2577
Fax: (703)739-2372

Woolridge, Berto, President
American Federation of Motorcyclists
[22209]
395 Taylor Blvd., No. 130
Pleasant Hill, CA 94523
Ph: (510)833-7223

Woolsey, Lynn, President
Americans for Democratic Action
[18636]
1629 K St. NW, Ste. 300
Washington, DC 20006
Ph: (202)600-7762
Fax: (202)204-8637

Worel, Nann, President
National Association of Free and
Charitable Clinics **[15155]**
1800 Diagonal Rd., Ste. 600
Alexandria, VA 22314
Ph: (703)647-7427
Toll Free: 866-875-3827

Workman, James, Exec. Dir.
Environmental Outreach and
Stewardship Alliance **[4059]**
1445 NW Mall St., Ste. 4
Issaquah, WA 98027
Ph: (425)270-3274

Workman, Jim, Managing Dir.
Technical Association of the Graphic
Arts **[6699]**
301 Brush Creek Rd.
Warrendale, PA 15086
Ph: (412)259-1706
Fax: (412)741-2311

Works, Raphael K., PhD, Chairman,
CEO
Veterans Association of America,
Inc. **[21146]**
Audubon Sta.
New York, NY 10032
Toll Free: 800-590-2173
Fax: (888)859-8131

Worley, Ms. Bette, President
National Student Exchange **[8608]**
4656 W Jefferson Blvd., Ste. 140
Fort Wayne, IN 46804
Ph: (260)436-2634
Fax: (260)436-5676

Worlton, Tom, President
American Lhasa Apso Club **[21812]**
c/o Joyce Johanson, Membership
Chair, 126 W Kurlene Dr.
126 W Kurlene Dr.
Macomb, IL 61455
Ph: (309)837-1665

Worms, William M., Exec. Dir.
SSPC: The Society for Protective
Coatings **[2489]**
800 Trumbull Dr.
Pittsburgh, PA 15222
Ph: (412)281-2331
Toll Free: 877-281-7772
Fax: (412)281-9992

Worrall, Linda, RN, Exec. Dir.
Oncology Nursing Society Founda-
tion **[16175]**
125 Enterprise Dr.
Pittsburgh, PA 15275-1214
Ph: (412)859-6228
Toll Free: 866-257-4667
Fax: (412)859-6163

Worsham, Tara, Coord.
Hurst/Olds Club of America **[21397]**
304 S Clippert St.
Lansing, MI 48912

Worth, Dan, Exec. Dir.
National Association of
Environmental Law Societies
[5184]

6408 Western Ave.
Glen Arbor, MI 49636
Ph: (617)610-7399

Worthman, Carol, President
Human Biology Association **[6082]**
c/o Ellen W. Demerath, Ph.D.
Division of Epidemiology and Com-
munity Health, School of Public
Health
University of Minnesota
1300 S 2nd St., Ste. 300
Minneapolis, MN 55454

Wosinski, Marek, Facilitator, Exec.
Ofc.
University-Community Partnership
for Social Action Research **[11454]**
PO Box 875402
Tempe, AZ 85287-5402

Woytovich, Betsy, Exec. Dir.
Children's Alopecia Project **[13785]**
PO Box 6036
Wyomissing, PA 19610
Ph: (610)468-1011

Wozney, John, Chairman
Pierce-Arrow Society **[21475]**
PO Box 402
Catharpin, VA 20143-0402

Wrage, Alexandra, President
TRACE International **[5111]**
151 West St., Ste. 300
Annapolis, MD 21401
Ph: (410)990-0076
Fax: (410)990-0707

Wrangham, Theresa, Exec. Dir.
National Vaccine Information Center
[14207]
21525 Ridgetop Cir., Ste. 100
Sterling, VA 20166
Ph: (703)938-0342
Fax: (571)313-1268

Wray, Ms. Carleen, Exec. Dir.
Students Against Violence
Everywhere **[18727]**
322 Chapanoke Rd., No. 110
Raleigh, NC 27603
Ph: (919)661-7800
Toll Free: 866-343-SAVE
Fax: (919)661-7777

Wright, Angus, Chairman
The Land Institute **[4157]**
2440 E Water Well Rd.
Salina, KS 67401
Ph: (785)823-5376
Fax: (785)823-8728

Wright, Anita, President
Papillon Club of America **[21939]**
c/o Lori Landis, Secretary
8697 134th St.
Seminole, FL 33776

Wright, Anne, Events Coord.
Aston Martin Owners Club **[21329]**
120 E 75th St.
New York, NY 10021
Ph: (212)628-7448

Wright, Rev. Christina, Co-Pres.
Methodist Federation for Social Ac-
tion **[20345]**
212 E Capitol St. NE
Washington, DC 20003
Ph: (202)546-8806
Fax: (202)546-6811

Wright, Christopher J., President
Federal Communications Bar As-
sociation **[5090]**
1020 19th St. NW, Ste. 325
Washington, DC 20036-6101
Ph: (202)293-4000
Fax: (202)293-4317

Wright, Esther, Secretary
American Academy of Counseling
Psychology **[16855]**
c/o James Deegear, PhD, President
Texas A&M University
1263 TAMU
College Station, TX 77843
Ph: (979)845-4427
Fax: (979)862-4383

Wright, Evelyn L., President
National Association of University
Women **[8750]**
1001 E St. SE
Washington, DC 20003
Ph: (202)547-3967
Fax: (202)547-5226

Wright, Mrs. Frances, CEO,
President
Black on Black Love Campaign
[11501]
1000 E 87th St.
Chicago, IL 60619-6397
Ph: (773)978-0868
Fax: (773)978-7345

Wright, Fred, Chairman
International Food Service Execu-
tives Association **[1390]**
4955 Miller St., Ste. 107
Wheat Ridge, CO 80033
Toll Free: 800-893-5499

Wright, Gary, CEO
National Bridal Service **[447]**
2225 Grove Ave.
Richmond, VA 23220
Ph: (804)342-0055
Fax: (804)342-6062

Wright, Graham, President
American Boat Builders & Repairers
Association **[2233]**
1075 SE 17th St.
Fort Lauderdale, FL 33316
Ph: (954)654-7821
Fax: (954)239-2600

Wright, Rev. J. Robert, President
Anglican Society **[20091]**
c/o Linda Bridges, 215 Lexington
Ave., 11th Fl.
215 Lexington Ave., 11th Fl.
New York, NY 10016

Wright, Janet E.H., APR, Asst. Sec.,
Asst. Treas.
Professional Insurance Communica-
tors of America Inc. **[775]**
PO Box 68700
Indianapolis, IN 46268-0700
Ph: (317)446-9367

Wright, Jeff, President
Council of Petroleum Accountants
Societies **[22]**
445 Union Blvd., Ste. 207
Lakewood, CO 80228
Ph: (303)300-1131
Toll Free: 877-992-6727
Fax: (303)300-3733

Wright, Jimmy, President
Pastel Society of America **[8880]**
15 Gramercy Pk. S
New York, NY 10003
Ph: (212)533-6931
Fax: (212)353-8140

Wright, Krista, Exec. Dir.
Polar Bears International **[4871]**
PO Box 3008
Bozeman, MT 59772

Wright, Larry, Membership Chp.
Bullwhip Squadron Association
[21113]

c/o Joe Bowen, President
5566 County Road 18
Ozark, AL 36360-5927

Wright, Merry Ann T., President
National Society, Daughters of the
American Revolution [20694]
1776 D St. NW
Washington, DC 20006
Ph: (202)628-1776

Wright, Mia, President
National Basketball Wives Associa-
tion [12488]
555 Madison Ave., 5th Fl.
New York, NY 10022
Ph: (917)472-0539
Fax: (917)472-0501

Wright, Nathan, Contact
ThinkTwice Global Vaccine Institute
[15387]
PO Box 9638
Santa Fe, NM 87504
Ph: (505)983-1856
Fax: (505)983-1856

Wright, Raymond, Exec. Dir.
Independent Professional
Representatives Organization
[266]
c/o Ray Wright, Executive Director
34157 W 9 Mile Rd.
Farmington Hills, MI 48335
Ph: (248)474-0522
Toll Free: 800-420-4268

Wright, Sandra, VP
The National Jersey Wooly Rabbit
Club [4604]
c/o Angel LeSage, President
PO Box 663
Sutter Creek, CA 95685

Wright, Sean, Exec. Dir.
Performing Arts Foundation [8997]
401 N 4th St.
Wausau, WI 54403-5420
Ph: (715)842-0988

Wright, Sigrid, CEO, Exec. Dir.
Community Environmental Council
[4739]
26 W Anapamu St., 2nd Fl.
Santa Barbara, CA 93101
Ph: (805)963-0583

Wright, Steven, Director
National Alliance for Medicaid in
Education, Inc. [15101]
c/o Mary Hall
12055 Meriturn Pl.
Ashland, VA 23005
Ph: (614)752-1493

Wright, Wyatt, President
Society of Ethical Attorneys at Law
[5049]
PO Box 5993
San Antonio, TX 78201-0993
Ph: (210)785-0935
Fax: (210)785-9254

Wrinn, Marie, CEO, Founder
No Child Dies Alone [11556]
7014 E Golf Links Rd.
PMB 126
Tucson, AZ 85730

Wrobel, Bruce, Chairman, Exec. Dir.
All for Africa [10472]
277 Park Ave., 40th Fl.
New York, NY 10172
Ph: (212)351-0055
Fax: (212)351-0001

Wrobel, Leo A., President, Director
NaSPA [6303]
7044 S 13th St.

Oak Creek, WI 53154
Ph: (414)908-4945
Fax: (414)768-8001

Wrone, David, PhD, Secretary
Assassination Archives and
Research Center [19228]
962 Wayne Ave., Ste. 910
Silver Spring, MD 20910
Ph: (301)565-0249

Wu, Harry, Exec. Dir., Founder
Laogai Research Foundation
[18422]
1734 20th St. NW
Washington, DC 20009

Wu, Jacqui, President
Taiwanese American Citizens
League [19670]
3001 Walnut Grove Ave., No. 7
Rosemead, CA 91770
Ph: (626)551-0227

Wu, Ming-chi, Sec. Gen.
North America Taiwanese Engineers'
Association [6579]
PO Box 2772
Sunnyvale, CA 94087-0772

Wu, Robert S., Chairman, CEO
US-China Green Energy Council
[6516]
1964 Deodara Dr.
Los Altos, CA 94024-7054

Wu, Tangchun, President
Cell Stress Society International
[17290]
91 N Eagleville Rd.
Storrs, CT 06269-3125
Ph: (860)486-6304
Fax: (860)486-5709

Wu, Vivian, President
Chinese American Food Society
[6644]
c/o Zachary Zheng, Treasurer
2390 Chambound Dr.
Buffalo Grove, IL 60089

Wu, Wanchu, Chairperson
Overseas Chinese - American
Entrepreneurs Association [3304]
219 Quincy Ave.
Quincy, MA 02169

Wu, Xiaojin, VP
Japan Art History Forum [8900]
Santa Clara University
Dept. of Art and Art History
500 El Camino Real
Santa Clara, CA 95053

Wuellner, Cindy Frewen,
Chairperson
Association of Professional Futurists
[6654]

Wuestenberg, Jason, Exec. Dir.
National Law Enforcement Firearms
Instructors Association [5501]
6635 W Happy Valley Rd., Ste.
A104-108
Glendale, AZ 85310
Toll Free: 800-930-2953
Fax: (623)225-7793

Wulf, Eric, CEO
International Carwash Association
[345]
230 E Ohio St.
Chicago, IL 60611
Toll Free: 888-422-8422

Wulff, Ella May, Membership Chp.
North American Heather Society
[22116]

c/o Ella May Wulff, Membership
Chairperson
2299 Wooded Knolls Dr.
Philomath, OR 97370

Wulkow, Rick, President
National Federation of State High
School Associations [23244]
PO Box 690
Indianapolis, IN 46206-0690
Ph: (317)972-6900
Fax: (317)822-5700

Wunn, J. Scott, Exec. Dir.
National Speech & Debate Associa-
tion [8600]
125 Watson St.
Ripon, WI 54971
Ph: (920)748-6206
Fax: (920)748-9478

Wunsch, Bonnie, Exec. Dir.
Alpha Epsilon Phi [23942]
11 Lake Avenue Ext., Ste. 1A
Danbury, CT 06811
Ph: (203)748-0029
Fax: (203)748-0039

Wunstell, Erik, Director, Founder
Earth Ecology Foundation [3996]
4175 S Decatur 205
Las Vegas, NV 89103
Ph: (702)778-9930

Wurm, Jim, Exec. Dir.
Exhibit and Event Marketers As-
sociation [1172]
2214 NW 5th St.
Bend, OR 97701
Ph: (541)317-8768
Fax: (541)317-8749

Wustrack, Paul, Mgr., Web Adm.
Arctic Cat Club of America [22418]
c/o Paul Wustrack
PO Box 528
Rosendale, WI 54974-0528

Wyant, Tim, Exec. Dir.
National Urban Squash and Educa-
tion Association [23273]
555 8th Ave., Ste. 1102
New York, NY 10018-4311
Ph: (646)218-0456

Wyatt, Jeremy, President
American Society of Anesthesia
Technologists and Technicians
[15617]
7044 S 13th St.
Oak Creek, WI 53154-1429
Ph: (414)908-4942
    (808)547-9872
Fax: (414)768-8001

Wyatt, John, Chairperson
Association of Technology, Management and Applied Engineering
[8017]
275 N York St., Ste. 401
Elmhurst, IL 60126
Ph: (630)433-4514

Wydra, Nancilee, Founder
Feng Shui Institute of America
[9277]
7547 Bruns Ct.
Canal Winchester, OH 43110
Ph: (614)837-8370

Wyerman, Barry, President
American Boxer Club [21799]
c/o Jeri Poller, Membership
Chairperson
6013 SW 23rd Ave.
Boca Raton, FL 33496-3504
Ph: (561)350-0889

Wylie, Christopher, President
International Society of Differentia-
tion [6090]

PO Box 55
Higganum, CT 06441
Fax: (860)838-4242

Wyner, Susan, Consultant
Schechter Day School Network
[8145]
85 Broad St., 18th Fl.
New York, NY 10004
Ph: (646)655-7730

Wynn, Alexander C., III, President
National Funeral Directors and Morti-
cians Association [2413]
6290 Shannon Pky.
Union City, GA 30291
Ph: (770)969-0064
Toll Free: 800-434-0958
Fax: (770)969-0505

Wynne, Anne S., Founder
Atticus Circle [18300]
Bldg. 6, Ste. 450
2901 Via Fortuna
Austin, TX 78746
Ph: (512)275-7880
    (512)450-5188

Wynne, Carol, Exec. Dir.
National Society of Certified Health-
care Business Consultants [15129]
12100 Sunset Hills Rd., Ste. 130
Reston, VA 20190
Ph: (703)234-4099
Fax: (703)435-4390

Wypych, Leah, Chmn. of the Bd.
Alliance for Eating Disorders Aware-
ness [14632]
1649 Forum Pl., No. 2
West Palm Beach, FL 33401
Ph: (561)841-0900
Toll Free: 866-662-1235

Wyrick, Claudia, M.D., President
International Midwife Assistance
[16289]
PO Box 916
Boulder, CO 80306
Ph: (303)241-1355
    (303)588-1663

Wysockey-Johnson, Doug, Exec. Dir.
Lumunos [20067]
38 S Winooski Ave.
Burlington, VT 05401
Ph: (802)860-1936

Wysocki, Joe, VP
Hartford Whalers Booster Club
[24074]
PO Box 273
Hartford, CT 06141
Ph: (860)956-3839

Wysocki, Susan, Treasurer
American Sexual Health Association
[17192]
PO Box 13827
Research Triangle Park, NC 27709-
3827
Ph: (919)361-8400

Wysocki, Susan, Treasurer
National Cervical Cancer Coalition
[14022]
PO Box 13827
Research Triangle Park, NC 27709
Toll Free: 800-685-5531
Fax: (919)361-8425

Wysocki, Tim, President
APA Division 54: Society of Pediatric
Psychology [16896]
PO Box 3968
Lawrence, KS 66046
Ph: (785)856-0713
Fax: (785)856-0759

X

Xiaoping, Cong, PhD, President
Chinese Historians in the United
States [7980]
c/o Xiaoping Cong, President
University of Houston
Dept. of History
524 Agnes Arnold Hall
Houston, TX 77204
Ph: (713)743-3096

Xing, Fan, President
The Chinese Finance Association
[1226]
PO Box 4058, Grand Central Sta.
New York, NY 10163

Xiqiu, Bob Fu, Founder, President
China Aid Association [20569]
PO Box 8513
Midland, TX 79708
Ph: (432)689-6985
Toll Free: 888-889-7757
Fax: (432)686-8355

Xu, Haoliang, Director
United Nations Development
Programme in Asia and the Pacific
[18504]
Regional Bureau for Asia and the
Pacific
1 United Nations Plz.
New York, NY 10017
Ph: (212)906-5000
Fax: (212)906-5898

Xu, Nu, VP
International Organization of
Chinese Physicist and
Astronomers [7025]
c/o Albert M. Chang, President-elect
PO Box 90305
Durham, NC 27708
Ph: (919)660-2569
Fax: (919)660-2525

Xue, Jun, President
Chinese American Cooperation
Council [12147]
PO Box 12028
Pleasanton, CA 94588

Xulam, Kani, Director
American Kurdish Information
Network [19525]
2722 Connecticut Ave. NW, No. 42
Washington, DC 20008
Ph: (202)483-6444

Y

Yaasky, Rachel, Treasurer
Solidarity and Action Against the HIV
Infection in India [10553]
c/o Rachel Yaasky, Treasurer
20 Plaza St. E, Apt. C11
Brooklyn, NY 11238

Yablonski, Cindy A., PhD, Exec. Dir.
International Society for Neurofeed-
back and Research [6912]
c/o Cindy A. Yablonski, Exeutive
Director
1350 Beverly Rd., Ste. 115, PMB
114
McLean, VA 22101-3633
Ph: (415)485-1344
Fax: (703)738-7341

Yablonski, Cindy A., PhD, Exec. Dir.
International Society for Neurofeedback and Research [16024]
c/o Cindy A. Yablonski, Executive
Director
1350 Beverly Rd., Ste. 115, PMB
114

McLean, VA 22101-3633
Ph: (415)485-1344
Fax: (703)738-7341

Yacino, Brian, President
AMC Rambler Club [21315]
77 County Rd.
Simsbury, CT 06070
Ph: (860)923-0485
     (860)658-0027

Yacobucci, Margaret, Secretary
Paleontological Society [6973]
PO Box 9044
Boulder, CO 80301
Toll Free: 855-357-1032
Fax: (303)357-1070

Yacoubian, George S., Chairman
Society for Orphaned Armenian
Relief [12730]
c/o George Yacoubian Jr., Chairman
150 N Radnor Chester Rd., Ste.
F-200
Radnor, PA 19087
Ph: (267)515-1944
Fax: (610)229-5168

Yadao, Alex, MD, Chairman,
President
American College of International
Physicians [15435]
9323 Old Mt. Vernon Rd.
Alexandria, VA 22309
Ph: (703)221-1500

Yagyu, Kuniyoshi, MD, President
International Society of Hair Restora-
tion Surgery [14902]
303 W State St.
Geneva, IL 60134
Ph: (630)262-5399
Toll Free: 800-444-2737
Fax: (630)262-1520

Yale, Carolyn, President
Peace Corps Iran Association
[18849]
4101 SW Hillsdale Ave.
Portland, OR 97239

Yam, Siva, President
United States of America-China
Chamber of Commerce [23624]
55 W Monroe St., Ste. 630
Chicago, IL 60603
Ph: (312)368-9911
Fax: (312)368-9922

Yamada, Akari, President
PPSEAWA International United
States of America [18556]

Yamamoto, Keith R., Chmn. of the
Bd.
Coalition for the Life Sciences
[7126]
8120 Woodmont Ave., Ste. 750
Bethesda, MD 20814-2762
Ph: (301)347-9309
Fax: (301)347-9310

Yamani, Ummul Banin, Founder
SURGE [13338]
1254 W Jackson Blvd., No. 4W
Chicago, IL 60607

Yan, Ruqiang, VP
IEEE - Instrumentation and
Measurement Society [6761]
c/o Robert M. Goldberg
1360 Clifton Ave., PMB 336
Clifton, NJ 07012
Ph: (785)532-6224

Yancey, Mr. Eben, Exec. Dir.
International College of Prosthodontists [14451]

McLean, VA 22101-3633
Ph: (415)485-1344
Fax: (703)738-7341

4425 Cass St., Ste. A
San Diego, CA 92109-4015
Ph: (858)270-1814
Fax: (858)272-7687

Yancey, Kenneth W., Jr., CEO
SCORE [3125]
1175 Herndon Pky., Ste. 900
Herndon, VA 20170
Toll Free: 800-634-0245

Yandle, Abbie G., President
Emergency Response Massage
International [15555]
227 S Peak St.
Columbus, NC 28722-9493
Ph: (704)763-6099

Yanek, Bill, Exec. VP
Protective Glazing Council [1508]
800 SW Jackson St., Ste. 1500
Topeka, KS 66612-1200
Ph: (785)271-0208
Fax: (785)271-0166

Yang, Chi-Hui, President
The Flaherty [9306]
6 E 39th St., 12th Fl.
New York, NY 10016
Ph: (212)448-0457
Fax: (212)448-0458

Yang, Fenggang, President
Society for the Scientific Study of
Religion [20553]
Indiana University - Purdue
University Indianapolis
Cavanaugh Hall 417
425 University Blvd.
Indianapolis, IN 46202-5148
Ph: (317)278-6491

Yang, Jenny R., Chairman
U.S. Equal Employment Opportunity
Commission [5168]
131 M St. NE, 4th Fl., Ste. 4NWO2F
Washington, DC 20507
Toll Free: 800-669-4000
Fax: (202)419-0739

Yang, Jihui, President
International Thermoelectric Society
[7332]
c/o Jihui Yang, President
Materials Science and Engineering
Dept.
University of Washington
302 Roberts Hall
Seattle, WA 98195

Yang, Mira, Director
Asian American Music Society
[9873]
39 Eton Overlook
Rockville, MD 20850
Ph: (301)424-3379

Yang, Mr. Vincent C.S., President
International Association for Teach-
ers of Chinese to Speakers of
Other Languages [7602]
9 E Loockerman St., Ste. 3A
Dover, DE 19901-7316

Yankellow, Jeff, Chmn. of the Bd.
Bread Bakers Guild of America [373]
670 W Napa St., Ste. B
Sonoma, CA 95476
Ph: (707)935-1468
Fax: (707)935-1672

Yankelovich, Daniel, Chairman,
Founder
Public Agenda [19002]
6 E 39th St., 9th Fl.
New York, NY 10016-0112
Ph: (212)686-6610
Fax: (212)889-3461

Yao, Zhijun, Exec. Dir.
International Association for Chinese
Management Research [2175]
c/o Xiaomeng Zhang, Executive
Secretary
8636 Waterside Ct.
Laurel, MD 20723
Ph: (316)978-6788
Fax: (316)978-3349

Yarbro, Dr. Jody, Treasurer
Christian Dental Society [14423]
PO Box 296
Sumner, IA 50674
Ph: (563)578-8887

Yarbrough, Trisha, Exec. Dir.
Alpha Chi [23773]
Alpha Chi National College Honor
Scholarship Society
915 E Market Ave.
Searcy, AR 72149
Ph: (501)279-4443
Toll Free: 800-477-4225
Fax: (501)279-4589

Yarbrough, Trisha, Secretary
Association of College Honor Societ-
ies [23776]
1749 Hamilton Rd., Ste. 106
Okemos, MI 48864
Ph: (517)351-8335
Fax: (517)351-8336

Yard, Sharon, President
American Sealyham Terrier Club
[21820]
c/o Sharon Yard, President
14111 Rehoboth Church Rd.
Lovettsville, VA 20180-3217
Ph: (540)882-3492

Yardley, Dr. Lee, VP, Co-Ch.
National Upper Cervical Chiropractic
Association [14279]
5353 Wayzata Blvd., Ste. 350
Minneapolis, MN 55416-1300
Ph: (952)564-3056
Toll Free: 800-541-5799
Fax: (877)558-0410

Yarnold, David, President, COO
National Audubon Society [3903]
225 Varick St.
New York, NY 10014
Toll Free: 800-274-4201

Yassine, Farouk N., Exec. Dir.
Insurance Data Management As-
sociation [1865]
545 Washington Blvd., 17th Fl.
Jersey City, NJ 07310
Ph: (201)469-3069
Fax: (201)748-1690

Yates, Martha, Chairperson
Patent Information Users Group, Inc.
[5337]
40 E Main St., No. 1438
Newark, DE 19711
Ph: (302)660-3275
Fax: (302)660-3276

Yates, Rita J., Exec. Dir.
American Academy of Podiatric
Sports Medicine [17273]
3121 NE 26th St.
Ocala, FL 34470
Ph: (352)620-8562
Fax: (352)620-8765

Yates, Scott, Chmn. of the Bd.
National Lumber and Building Mate-
rial Dealers Association [1444]
2025 M St. NW, Ste. 800
Washington, DC 20036-3309
Ph: (202)367-1169
Fax: (202)367-2169

Yates, Tom, President
American Dairy Products Association
  [970]
2501 Aerial Center Pky.
Morrisville, NC 27560-7655
Ph: (919)459-2076
Fax: (919)459-2075

Yatskievych, Dr. George, Curator
American Fern Society **[6130]**
c/o Dr. Blanca Leon, Membership
  Secretary
1 University Sta.
Austin, TX 78712-0471

Yavalar, Hudai, Chairman, Founder
Atatürk Society of America **[18905]**
4731 Massachusetts Ave. NW
Washington, DC 20016
Ph: (202)362-7173

Yayehyirad, Mulusew, Exec. Dir.,
  Founder
Clinic at a Time **[15444]**
PO Box 14457
Madison, WI 53708-0457
Ph: (608)239-3091

Yazdani, Dr. Ramin, Ph.D., President
Sahaya International **[12184]**
c/o Koen Van Rompay
1504 Portola St.
Davis, CA 95616-7306
Ph: (530)756-9074

Yazzie, Lynnann, Coord.
United National Indian Tribal Youth
  [10049]
1 N MacDonald Dr., Ste. 212
Mesa, AZ 85201
Ph: (480)718-9793
Fax: (480)773-6369

Ye, Pov, President
Light of Cambodian Children **[11069]**
Mogan Cultural Ctr., 3rd Fl.
40 French St.
Lowell, MA 01852
Ph: (978)275-1822
Fax: (978)275-1824

Yeager, Alice, President, Founder
American Healing Arts Alliance, Inc.
  [15262]
3157 Rolling Rd.
Edgewater, MD 21037
Ph: (410)956-0055

Yeago, Sharon, Treasurer
Farmers Market Coalition **[3538]**
PO Box 499
Kimberton, PA 19442

Yebri, Sam, President
30 Years After **[18573]**

Yedlin, Barry, Editor
Novelty Salt & Pepper Shakers Club
  [21705]
16468 W Juniper Ct.
Surprise, AZ 85387
Ph: (623)975-6870

Yeghiayan, Raffi P., Chairman
National Association for Armenian
  Studies and Research **[8826]**
395 Concord Ave.
Belmont, MA 02478
Ph: (617)489-1610
Fax: (617)484-1759

Yehuda, Rachel, PhD, Officer
International Society of Psychoneu-
  roendocrinology **[15649]**
c/o Nicolas Rohleder, PhD,
  Secretary General
Dept. of Psychology
Brandeis University

415 South St.
Waltham, MA 02453

Yelich, Joel V., VP
National Block and Bridle Club
  [3619]
c/o Janeal Yancey, PhD, Editor
University of Arkansas
1120 W Maple St.
Fayetteville, AR 72701
Ph: (479)575-4115
Fax: (479)575-7294

Yellen, Dr. John, President
Paleoanthropology Society **[6971]**
810 E St. SE
Washington, DC 20003

Yellon, Lawrence, VP
National Association of Professional
  Process Servers **[5685]**
PO Box 4547
Portland, OR 97208-4547
Ph: (503)222-4180
Toll Free: 800-477-8211
Fax: (503)222-3950

Yen, Master Sheng, President
Dharma Drum Mountain Buddhist
  Association **[19775]**
90-56 Corona Ave.
Elmhurst, NY 11373
Ph: (718)592-6593

Yep, Richard, Exec. Dir.
American Counseling Association
  [11482]
6101 Stevenson Ave.
Alexandria, VA 22304
Ph: (703)823-9800
Toll Free: 800-347-6647
Fax: (703)823-0252

Yerich, Kathy, VP
North American Mycological Association **[6888]**
2019 Ashmore Dr.
Ames, IA 50014

Yeske, Charles, President
Society for the Preservation of Old
  Mills **[9437]**
PO Box 422
Great Falls, VA 22066
Ph: (860)423-2033

Yetman, Bert, President
Professional Pilots Association
  [23391]

Yett, Gerri, Chairman
Association of Immunization Manag-
  ers **[15374]**
620 Hungerford Dr., Ste. 29
Rockville, MD 20850
Ph: (301)424-6080
Fax: (301)424-6081

Yevzlin, Alexander S., MD, Officer
American Society of Diagnostic and
  Interventional Nephrology **[15872]**
134 Fairmont St., Ste. B
Clinton, MS 39056
Ph: (601)924-2220
Fax: (601)924-6249

Yewcic, Patricia Hile, Officer
John More Association **[20902]**
c/o Mike Williams, Treasurer
295 Williams Rd.
Oxford, NY 13830

Yineman, Kimberlie, President
Association of State and Territorial
  Dental Directors **[14421]**
3858 Cashill Blvd.
Reno, NV 89509
Ph: (775)626-5008
Fax: (775)626-9268

Yingst, Deb, Deputy, Gov.
The Fuller Society **[20868]**
42 Sugar Maple Ln.
Tinton Falls, NJ 07724

Yingst, Dick, CEO, President
Financial Managers Society **[2167]**
1 N La Salle St., Ste. 3100
Chicago, IL 60602-4003
Ph: (312)578-1300
Toll Free: 800-275-4367
Fax: (312)578-1308

Yiu, Edmund, President
United States Othello Association
  [22057]
c/o Othello Quarterly
7 Peter Cooper Rd., No. 10G
New York, NY 10010

Yoak, Dr. Stuart, Exec. Dir.
Association for Practical and Profes-
  sional Ethics **[8420]**
Indiana University
618 E 3rd St.
Bloomington, IN 47405-3602
Ph: (812)855-6450
Fax: (812)856-4969

Yoder, Aaron, President
International Society for Agricultural
  Safety and Health **[12823]**
Ph: (304)728-0011

Yoder, Anne, President
Society of Systematic Biologists
  [7404]
c/o Anne Yoder, President
Dept. of Biology
Duke University
315 Science Dr.
Durham, NC 27708

Yoder, Linda, Trustee, VP
Early American Pattern Glass
  Society **[21650]**
c/o Fred Phelps, Membership
  Coordinator
PO Box 266
Colesburg, IA 52035-0266

Yoke, Beth, Exec. Dir.
American Library Association Young
  Adult Library Services Association
  [9675]
50 E Huron St.
Chicago, IL 60611
Ph: (312)280-4390
Toll Free: 800-545-2433
Fax: (312)280-5276

Yokoyama, Hiroshi, PhD, President
International Liquid Crystal Society
  [6360]
c/o Hiroshi Yokoyama, President
Liquid Crystal Institute
Kent State University
1425 Lefton Esplanade
Kent, OH 44242

Yonan, Michael, President
Historians of Eighteenth-Century Art
  and Architecture **[8898]**
Ithaca College, 953 Danby Rd.
113 Gannett Ctr.
Ithaca, NY 14850

Yoo, Jo-Ann, Exec. Dir.
Asian American Federation **[19390]**
120 Wall St., 9th Fl.
New York, NY 10005-3904
Ph: (212)344-5878
Fax: (212)344-5636

Yoon, Euna, Mgr. of Admin.
Korean-American Scientists and
  Engineers Association **[6568]**
1952 Gallows Rd., Ste. 300

Vienna, VA 22182
Ph: (703)748-1221
Fax: (703)748-1331

Yoosefi, Nooshin, President
Iranian American Society of
  Engineers and Architects **[6567]**
15333 Culver Dr., Ste. 340-402
Irvine, CA 92604

Yorgey, James M., Chairman
National Lighting Bureau **[2104]**
180 Reachcliff Dr.
Shepherdstown, WV 25443
Ph: (301)587-9572
   (304)870-4249

Yorio, Dr. Thomas, President
Association for Ocular Pharmacology
  and Therapeutics **[16373]**
c/o Thomas Yorio, President
University of North Texas Health Science Ctr.
3500 Camp Bowie Blvd.
Fort Worth, TX 76107
Ph: (817)765-0268

York, Donna, President
Hark **[13684]**
PO Box 6627
Hillsborough, NJ 08844
Ph: (908)285-9202

York, Scott, Treasurer
American Airgun Field Target As-
  sociation **[23125]**
c/o Scott York, Treasurer
PO Box 245
Somerville, TX 77879
Ph: (979)255-8324

Yorksmith, Bryan, Managing Ed.
Self-Guided Hunting Association
  [22168]
PO Box 2771
Pinetop, AZ 85935
Fax: (928)521-2063

Yoshida, Kyoko, Exec. Dir.
U.S./Japan Cultural Trade Network
  [9217]
1471 Guerrero St., Ste. 3
San Francisco, CA 94110-4371
Ph: (415)867-7080

Yosie, Dr. Terry F., President, CEO
World Environment Center **[3970]**
734 15th St. NW, Ste. 720
Washington, DC 20005
Ph: (202)312-1370
Fax: (202)637-2411

Yost, Sandra L., MBA, Director
American Academy of Disability
  Evaluating Physicians **[14297]**
2575 Northwest Pky.
Elgin, IL 60124
Ph: (312)663-1171
Toll Free: 800-456-6095
Fax: (312)663-1175

Young, Autumn, Exec. Dir.
People-Animals-Love **[17459]**
731 8th St. SE, Ste. 202
Washington, DC 20003
Ph: (202)966-2171
Fax: (202)966-2172

Young, Blake, President, CEO
Sacramento Food Bank & Family
  Services **[12112]**
3333 3rd Ave.
Sacramento, CA 95817
Ph: (916)456-1980
Fax: (916)451-5920

Young, Brian C., Contact
Del Shannon Appreciation Society
  [24032]

PO Box 44201
Tacoma, WA 98448

Young, Carl, Secretary, Treasurer,
Coord.
American Radio Association **[23395]**
1755 E Plumb Ln., Ste. 111
Reno, NV 89502-3545
Ph: (510)281-0706

Young, Carl, Pres. of Indl. Cos.
Numismatics International **[22280]**
PO Box 570842
Dallas, TX 75357-0842

Young, Cris, President
National Association of Small Busi-
ness Contractors **[883]**
700 12th St. NW, Ste. 700
Washington, DC 20005
Toll Free: 888-861-9290

Young, Don, VP, Director
Early Day Gas Engine and Tractor
Association **[22011]**
c/o Carrie Jo Parmley, Secretary
15246 Seven League Rd.
Tyler, TX 75703
Ph: (903)360-0396

Young, Gerald, PhD, President
Association for Scientific Advance-
ment in Psychological Injury and
Law **[13809]**
University at Buffalo
School of Medicine, Ste. 203
5820 Main St.
Williamsville, NY 14221
Ph: (716)866-8517
Fax: (716)565-1511

Young, Gretchen, Sr. VP
ERISA Industry Committee **[1070]**
1400 L St. NW, Ste. 350
Washington, DC 20005
Ph: (202)789-1400
Fax: (202)789-1120

Young, Helen Faraday, Founder
Bee Native **[3635]**
Mantis Farm
68 Fingar Rd.
Hudson, NY 12534-7208
Ph: (917)679-0567

Young, Holly, Exec. Dir.
Association for Communication
Excellence in Agriculture, Natural
Resources, and Life and Human
Sciences **[3546]**
Taylor Hall
59 College Rd.
Durham, NH 03824
Ph: (603)862-1564
Toll Free: 855-657-9544
Fax: (603)862-1585

Young, Jeanette, President
American Association of Professional
Technical Analysts **[3206]**
c/o Larry McMillan, Treasurer
39 Meadowbrook Rd.
Randolph, NJ 07869

Young, Jeanne P., President, Bd.
Member
Childhood Brain Tumor Foundation
[14569]
20312 Watkins Meadow Dr.
Germantown, MD 20876
Ph: (301)515-2900
Toll Free: 877-217-4166

Young, Prof. John, Exec. Dir.
Society for Textual Scholarship
[9769]
c/o Gabrielle Dean, Treasurer
The Sheridan Libraries

Johns Hopkins University
3400 N Charles St.
Baltimore, MD 21218

Young, Ms. Kathleen T., CEO
Alliance for the Prudent Use of
Antibiotics **[16631]**
M & V, Ste. 811
136 Harrison Ave.
Boston, MA 02111
Ph: (617)636-0966

Young, Kendall, Director
Asian American Architects and
Engineers **[5961]**
1167 Mission St., 4th Fl.
San Francisco, CA 94103
Ph: (415)392-9688
    (415)777-2166

Young, Kimberly H., VP of Bus. Dev.
America's Charities **[11855]**
14150 Newbrook Dr., Ste. 110
Chantilly, VA 20151-2274
Toll Free: 800-458-9505
Fax: (703)222-3867

Young, Kirsten, VP
National Investor Relations Institute
[2033]
225 Reinekers Ln., Ste. 560
Alexandria, VA 22314
Ph: (703)562-7700
Fax: (703)562-7701

Young, Kristi Ridd, VP
Midwifery Education Accreditation
Council **[14236]**
850 Mt. Pleasant Ave.
Ann Arbor, MI 48103
Ph: (360)466-2080

Young, Kyle, Director
Country Music Foundation **[9896]**
222 5th Ave. S
Nashville, TN 37203
Ph: (615)416-2001
Toll Free: 800-852-6437

Young, Larry, President
Society for Social Neuroscience
[16056]
c/o TM Events, Inc.
2100 Valley View Pky., Ste. 1526
El Dorado Hills, CA 95762

Young, Lynn Forney, President
Junior American Citizens **[8795]**
1776 D St. NW
Washington, DC 20006-5303
Ph: (202)628-1776

Young, Marci P., Director
Center for the Child Care Workforce
[11758]
American Federation of Teachers,
AFL-CIO
555 New Jersey Ave. NW
Washington, DC 20001
Ph: (202)879-4400

Young, Dr. Mark A., President
National Institute of Electromedical
Information **[15696]**
PO Box 43058
Nottingham, MD 21236
Ph: (410)808-9700

Young, Mark, President
Willys-Overland-Knight Registry
[21521]
c/o Duanne Perrin
4177 Spring Hill Rd.
Staunton, VA 24401-6320

Young, Michael, President
Southeastern Composers League
[10013]

Young, Michelle D., Exec. Dir.
University Council for Educational
Administration **[7442]**
Ruffner Hall
Curry School of Education
University of Virginia
405 Emmet St., Rm. 141
Charlottesville, VA 22903
Ph: (434)243-1041

Young, Patricia, Coord.
U.S. National Committee for World
Food Day **[12119]**
2121 K St. NW, Ste. 800-B
Washington, DC 20037-1896

Young, Peggy, President
Association of Scottish Games and
Festivals **[19637]**
c/o Deb Anderson, Treasurer
1836 Boothsville Rd.
Bridgeport, WV 26330
Ph: (719)630-0923

Young, Peter, Chairman
Société de Chimie Industrielle -
American Section **[6213]**
10 Winton Farm Rd.
Newtown, CT 06470
Ph: (212)725-9539

Young du Pont, Jenny, President
Garden Conservancy **[3875]**
20 Nazareth Way
Garrison, NY 10524
Ph: (845)424-6500
Fax: (845)424-6501

Young, Richard A., PhD, Exec. Dir.
National Registry of Environmental
Professionals **[4087]**
PO Box 2099
Glenview, IL 60025-6099
Ph: (847)724-6631
Fax: (847)724-4223

Young, Stan, President
Advanced Transit Association **[7346]**
c/o Tony Newkirk, Treasurer
44027 Florence Terr.
Ashburn, VA 20147

Young, Steve, V. Chmn. of the Bd.
Energy Communities Alliance **[4025]**
1101 Connecticut Ave. NW, Ste.
1000
Washington, DC 20036-4374
Ph: (202)828-2317
Fax: (202)828-2488

Youngberg, Bob, Contact
The Henry Nyberg Society **[21465]**
17822 Chicago Ave.
Lansing, IL 60438
Ph: (708)474-3416
Fax: (708)474-3416

Youngblood, James, CEO
Heart Rhythm Society **[14115]**
1325 G St. NW, Ste. 400
Washington, DC 20005
Ph: (202)464-3400
Fax: (202)464-3401

Youngson, Dr. Jeanne Keyes,
Founder, President
The International Society for the
Study of Ghosts and Apparitions
[6987]
29 Washington Sq. W
Penthouse N
New York, NY 10011-9180

Yount, Joanne, Exec. Dir.
Vulvar Pain Foundation **[16308]**
Graham Office Bldg., Ste. 203
203 1/2 N Main St.
Graham, NC 27253-2836
Ph: (336)226-0704
Fax: (336)226-8518

Yourofsky, Gary, Founder
Animals Deserve Absolute Protection
Today and Tomorrow **[10584]**
PO Box 725
Royal Oak, MI 48068-0725

Yousip, Joe, VP
Bet-Nahrain **[10768]**
3119 S Central Ave.
Ceres, CA 95307-3632
Ph: (209)538-4130
    (209)538-9801

Youssoufian, Annie, Secretary
Armenian Women's Welfare Association, Inc. **[19388]**
435 Pond St.
Jamaica Plain, MA 02130

Youtz, David, Exec. Dir.
Yale-China Association **[8095]**
442 Temple St.
New Haven, CT 06520
Ph: (203)432-0884
Fax: (203)432-7246

Yrastorza, Jaime, DMD, Founder
Uplift Internationale **[16448]**
PO Box 181658
Denver, CO 80218
Ph: (303)707-1361

Yu, Lawrence, PhD, Chmn. of the
Bd.
American Chinese Pharmaceutical
Association **[16634]**
PO Box 10193
Rockville, MD 20849-0193

Yu, Pauline, President
American Council of Learned Societ-
ies **[9552]**
633 3rd Ave., 8th Fl.
New York, NY 10017-6795
Ph: (212)697-1505
Fax: (212)949-8058

Yu, Pauline, Secretary
National Humanities Alliance **[9555]**
21 Dupont Cir. NW, Ste. 800
Washington, DC 20036
Ph: (202)296-4994
Fax: (202)872-0884

Yu, Robert, President
Chinese Chamber of Commerce of
Hawaii **[23574]**
8 S King St., Ste. 201
Honolulu, HI 96813
Ph: (808)533-3181
Fax: (808)537-6767

Yu, Tony, Dir. of Info. Technology
American Network of Community
Options and Resources **[12314]**
1101 King St., Ste. 380
Alexandria, VA 22314-2962
Ph: (703)535-7850
Fax: (703)535-7860

Yuan, Dr. Chun-Su, Director
Tang Center for Herbal Medicine
Research **[15500]**
Pritzker School of Medicine
University of Chicago
5841 S Maryland Ave., MC 4028
Chicago, IL 60637
Ph: (773)834-2399
    (773)702-4055
Fax: (773)834-0601

Yudice, Santiago, President
Asociacion Filatelica Salvadorena
[22310]
c/o Pierre Cahen
PO Box 02-5364
Miami, FL 33102

Yudis, Carol, Chairperson
Affiliated Woodcarvers **[8949]**
1212 E Quarry St.

Maquoketa, IA 52060
Ph: (563)505-2700
    (563)676-8264

Yue, Lisa, President, Exec. Dir.
Children's Cardiomyopathy Foundation [14107]
PO Box 547
Tenafly, NJ 07670
Toll Free: 866-808-2873
Fax: (201)227-7016

Yuhasz, Louis H., Founder
Louie's Kids [16258]
PO Box 21291
Charleston, SC 29413
Ph: (843)883-5026
Fax: (800)457-7497

Yuktatmananda, Swami, Min., Founder
Ramakrishna - Vivekananda Center of New York [20634]
17 E 94th St.
New York, NY 10128-0611
Ph: (212)534-9445
Fax: (212)828-1618

Yun Won, Cho, Exec. Dir.
Cambridge in America [9138]
1120 Avenue of the Americas, 17th Fl.
New York, NY 10036
Ph: (212)984-0960
Fax: (212)984-0970

Yung, Larry A., Jr., President
American Carnival Glass Association [22130]
PO Box 10022
Lancaster, PA 17605-0022

Yunker, Claire, Exec. Dir.
PeaceTrees Vietnam [18132]
509 Olive Way, Ste. 1226
Seattle, WA 98101
Ph: (206)441-6136

Yurek, Stephen, President, CEO, Contact
Air-Conditioning, Heating, and Refrigeration Institute [1611]
2111 Wilson Blvd., Ste. 500
Arlington, VA 22201
Ph: (703)524-8800
Fax: (703)562-1942

Yurek, Stephen, Officer
North American Technician Excellence [1634]
2111 Wilson Blvd., Ste. 510
Arlington, VA 22201-3051
Ph: (703)276-7247
Toll Free: 877-420-6283
Fax: (703)527-2316

Yuschak, Sherrie, RVT, Director
Society of Veterinary Behavior Technicians [17662]
c/o Donna Dyer
7400 Kirkwall Dr.
Richmond, VA 23235

Yusin, Joseph S., MD, President, Founder
Asthma Athletics [14169]
1928 E Highland, Ste. F-104
Phoenix, AZ 85016
Ph: (602)999-3325

Yusuf, Dr. Nurun N., M.D, President
MAAWS for Global Welfare [12169]
64-17 Broadway, 2nd Fl.
Woodside, NY 11377
Ph: (718)478-1045
Fax: (718)565-6941

Z

Zabel, Richard A., Exec. Dir.
Western Forestry and Conservation Association [4223]
4033 SW Canyon Rd.
Portland, OR 97221
Ph: (503)226-4562

Zaborowski, Shelley, Exec. Dir.
Alumni Association of the University of Nebraska [19303]
1520 R St.
Lincoln, NE 68508
Ph: (402)472-2841
Toll Free: 888-353-1874

Zacharias, Claudia, MBA, CAE, President, CEO
Board for Orthotist/Prosthetist Certification [16495]
10451 Mill Run Cir., Ste. 200
Owings Mills, MD 21117-5575
Ph: (410)581-6222
Toll Free: 877-776-2200
Fax: (410)581-6228

Zacharias, Claudia, MBA, CAE, Chairperson
Institute for Credentialing Excellence [14941]
2025 M St. NW, Ste. 800
Washington, DC 20036
Ph: (202)367-1165
Fax: (202)367-2165

Zacharias, Roy, President
Association of Surgical Technologists [15682]
6 W Dry Creek Cir., Ste. 200
Littleton, CO 80120-8031
Ph: (303)694-9130
Toll Free: 800-637-7433
Fax: (303)694-9169

Zachary, Matthew, Founder
Stupid Cancer [14068]
40 Worth St., Ste. 808
New York, NY 10013
Toll Free: 877-735-4673

Zadrozny, Kathy, Founder
Letter Writers Alliance [21738]
PO Box 221168
Chicago, IL 60622

Zagieboylo, Cyndi, President, CEO
National Multiple Sclerosis Society [15968]
733 3rd Ave., 3rd Fl.
New York, NY 10017
Ph: (212)463-7787
Toll Free: 800-344-4867
Fax: (212)986-7981

Zaher, Richard, Chairman
Air Charter Association of North America [172]
2 Main St.
Salem, NH 03079
Toll Free: 888-359-2226

Zahir, Homaira, Founder, President
American Support for Afghanistan [10467]
3905 State St., Ste. 7-177
Santa Barbara, CA 93105
Ph: (805)455-4066

Zahir, Khalique, MD, Chairman
Islamic Medical Association of North America [16754]
101 W 22nd St., Ste. 104
Lombard, IL 60148
Ph: (630)932-0000
Fax: (630)932-0005

Zahn, Mr. Jay, President
Muskies Inc. [3643]
1509 Stahl Rd.

Sheboygan, WI 53081-8894
Toll Free: 888-710-8286

Zahn, Peter, Commodore, Assoc. Ed., Web Adm.
International Catalina 27/270 Association [22627]
c/o Peter Zahn, Commodore
106 Riggs Ave.
Severna Park, MD 21146

Zahringer, Dwight, Founder
Recycling for Charities [4635]
5541 Central Ave., Ste. 125
Boulder, CO 80301
Toll Free: 866-630-7557
Fax: (248)543-7677

Zain, Thomas, Officer
Fellowship of St. John the Divine [20054]
PO Box 5238
Englewood, NJ 07631
Ph: (201)871-1355
Fax: (201)871-7954

Zajac, Marianna, President
Ukrainian National Women's League of America Inc. [19681]
203 2nd Ave.
New York, NY 10003-5706
Ph: (212)533-4646
Fax: (212)533-5237

Zajicek, Paul W., Dir. of Dev.
Striped Bass Growers Association [4187]
PO Box 12759
Tallahassee, FL 32317
Ph: (850)216-2400
Fax: (850)216-2480

Zak, Colleen B., President, Founder
ARPKD/CHF Alliance [15875]
PO Box 70
Kirkwood, PA 17536
Ph: (717)529-5555
Toll Free: 800-708-8892
Fax: (800)807-9110

Zakaria, Anam, Director
Association for the Development of Pakistan [11317]
PO Box 2492
San Francisco, CA 94126

Zakeri, Dr. Zahra, President
International Cell Death Society [14359]
c/o Dr. Zahra Zakeri, President
Dept. of Biology
Queens College and Graduate Center of CUNY
65-30 Kissena Blvd.
Flushing, NY 11367-1575
Ph: (718)997-3450
Fax: (718)997-3429

Zaki, Abdel Fattah, CEO, President
American Egyptian Cooperation Foundation [18511]
235 E 40th St.
New York, NY 10016
Ph: (212)867-2323
    (347)470-4622
Fax: (212)697-0465

Zaky, Mrs. Dwitra, President
Indonesia Relief - USA [11671]
20 Bluehosta Way
Rockville, MD 20850-2871

Zaleski, Jeff, Ed.-in-Chief
Society for the Study of Myth and Tradition [10032]
Parabola
20 W 20th St., 2nd Fl.
New York, NY 10011
Ph: (212)822-8806
Toll Free: 877-593-2521

Zaleski, Jennifer, Exec. Dir.
Children's Cancer and Blood Foundation [15226]
333 E 38th St., Ste. 830
New York, NY 10016-2772
Ph: (212)297-4336
Fax: (212)297-4340

Zama, Alec, President
Wings of Hope International [13097]
902 SE 5th St.
Ankeny, IA 50021
Ph: (515)964-4164

Zaman, Mariam, Founder
Afghan Association for Women and Children [13021]
20033 Blythe St.
Winnetka, CA 91306
Ph: (818)709-6359

Zamora, Cecilia, President
National Association of Commissions for Women [18220]
1732 1st Ave., No. 27315
New York, NY 10128-5177
Ph: (415)492-4420
    (317)232-6720
Toll Free: 855-703-6229

Zamora, Diomy, President
Association for Temperate Agroforestry [4195]
University of Missouri
Center for Agroforestry
203 ABNR Bldg.
Columbia, MO 65211
Ph: (573)882-3234
Fax: (573)882-1977

Zane, Mike, Chairperson
PKS Kids [14851]
PO Box 12211
Green Bay, WI 54307

Zaniolo, Fr. Michael G., President
National Conference of Catholic Airport Chaplains [19935]
PO Box 66353
Chicago, IL 60666-0353
Ph: (773)686-2636
Fax: (773)686-0130

Zapanta, Al, CEO, President
United States-Mexico Chamber of Commerce [23633]
PO Box 14414
Washington, DC 20044
Ph: (703)752-4751
Fax: (703)642-1088

Zapletal, Peter, Trustee
Puppeteers of America [22394]
336 Chestnut Hill Rd.
Stevenson, CT 06491
Ph: (860)462-8072

Zarate, Laura, Exec. Dir., Founder
Arte Sana [10765]
PO Box 1334
Dripping Springs, TX 78620
Toll Free: 800-656-4673

Zarate, Roberto, Chairman
Association of Community College Trustees [7641]
1101 17th St. NW, Ste. 300
Washington, DC 20036
Ph: (202)775-4667
Fax: (202)223-1297

Zarelli, Steve, President
Comic Book Collecting Association [21734]
PO Box 655
Valley Center, CA 92082

Zarnikow, Barbara, Co-Ch.
Interstitial Cystitis Association [17551]

7918 Jones Branch Dr., Ste. 300
McLean, VA 22102
Ph: (703)442-2070
Fax: (703)506-3266

Zarnowski, Dr. Frank, Founder
DECA The Decathlon Association
[23312]
c/o Frank Zarnowski, Founder
58 2nd Ave.
Emmitsburg, MD 21727
Ph: (301)447-6122

Zarr, Robert, President
Physicians for a National Health
Program [18881]
29 E Madison St., Ste. 1412
Chicago, IL 60602-4406
Ph: (312)782-6006
Fax: (312)782-6007

Zasler, Nathan, V. Ch.
International Brain Injury Association
[14912]
c/o MCC Association Management
5909 Ashby Manor Pl.
Alexandria, VA 22310-2267
Ph: (703)960-0027
Fax: (703)960-6603

Zaslow, Molly, Mgr.
Students for the Exploration and
Development of Space [7461]
3840 E Robinson Rd.
PMB 176
Amherst, NY 14228

Zaterman, Sunia, Exec. Dir.
Council of Large Public Housing
Authorities [5277]
455 Massachusetts Ave. NW, Ste.
425
Washington, DC 20001
Ph: (202)638-1300
Fax: (202)638-2364

Zavin, Joshua, PhD, President
International Integrative
Psychotherapy Association [16978]
c/o Wayne Carpenter, Trustee
5900 Greenwalt Ln.
Fort Collins, CO 80524-9508

ZayZay, Edman, President
Association of Liberian Engineers
USA, Inc. [6546]
PO Box 2960
Germantown, MD 20874
Ph: (240)343-5971

Zdatny, Steven, Exec. Dir.
Society for French Historical Studies
[9514]
905 W Main St., Ste. 18B
Durham, NC 27701

Zea, Philip, President
Historic Deerfield [9396]
84B Old Main St.
Deerfield, MA 01342
Ph: (413)774-5581
(413)775-7125

Zeb, Shazad, PA-C, MPAS,
President
Association of Physician Assistants
in Cardiology [14099]
2415 Westwood Ave., Ste. B
Richmond, VA 23230
Toll Free: 800-863-1207
Fax: (804)288-3551

Zeese, Kevin B., President
Common Sense for Drug Policy
[18970]
1377-C Spencer Ave.
Lancaster, PA 17603

Zeh, Katey, Chairman
Religious Coalition for Reproductive
Choice [19035]

1413 K St. NW, 14th Fl.
Washington, DC 20005
Ph: (202)628-7700
Fax: (202)628-7716

Zehme, Richard, President
Federal Criminal Investigators As-
sociation [5148]
5868 Mapledale Plz., Ste. 104
Woodbridge, VA 22193
Toll Free: 800-403-3374

Zehnder, James L., President
North American Specialized
Coagulation Laboratory Association
[15520]
c/o James L. Zehnder, President
Dept. of Pathology
Stanford University
Stanford, CA 94305
Ph: (650)723-9232
Fax: (650)736-1476

Zeichner, Wendy, President, CEO
Origami USA [22292]
15 W 77th St.
New York, NY 10024-5192
Ph: (212)769-5635
Fax: (212)769-5668

Zeidler, D. Zeke, President
International Association of Lesbian,
Gay, Bisexual and Transgender
Judges [5386]
PO Box 122724
San Diego, CA 92112-2724

Zeig, Jeffrey K., PhD, Founder, CEO
The Milton H. Erickson Foundation
[16972]
2632 E Thomas Rd., Ste. 200
Phoenix, AZ 85016
Ph: (602)956-6196
Toll Free: 877-212-6678
Fax: (602)956-0519

Zeimetz, Greta P., Exec. Dir.
National Association of Legal As-
sistants [5659]
7666 E 61st St., Ste. 315
Tulsa, OK 74133
Ph: (918)587-6828
Fax: (918)582-6772

Zeiss, Judy, President
International Organization of Lace
Inc. [21763]
PO Box 132
Paola, KS 66071

Zekanis, Loretta, President
Polish Beneficial Association [19608]
2595 Orthodox St.
Philadelphia, PA 19137
Ph: (215)535-2626
Fax: (215)535-0169

Zelazo, Phil, President
Jean Piaget Society: Society for the
Study of Knowledge and Develop-
ment [16923]
c/o Phil Zelazo, President
University of Minnesota
Institute of Child Development
170 ChDev 51 E River Pky.
Minneapolis, MN 55455
Ph: (612)625-5957

Zelina, Chele, President
MHE Coalition [14843]
c/o Chele Zelina, President
6783 York Rd., No. 104
Cleveland, OH 44130-4596
Ph: (440)842-8817

Zelinsky, Rob, Director
United Suffolk Sheep Association
[4682]

PO Box 872000
Canton, MI 48187
Ph: (641)684-5291
Fax: (734)335-7646

Zelkin, Carol, Exec. Dir.
Interactive Multimedia and Col-
laborative Communications Alli-
ance [769]
PO Box 756
Syosset, NY 11791
Ph: (516)818-8184

Zellner, Gary, President
National Retriever Club [22818]
c/o Gary Zellner, President
39300 Montgomery Dr.
Scio, OR 97374
Ph: (503)394-2139

Zellner, Michael, President
International Shuffleboard Associa-
tion, Inc. [23147]
Ph: (419)581-7103

Zelnar, Lynelle Chauncey, Exec. Dir.,
Founder
Forgotten Soldiers Outreach [10741]
3550 23rd Ave. S, Ste. 7
Lake Worth, FL 33461
Ph: (561)369-2933
Fax: (561)493-9819

Zelt, Al, Chairman
Fabricators and Manufacturers As-
sociation, International [1727]
833 Featherstone Rd.
Rockford, IL 61107
Ph: (815)399-8700
Toll Free: 888-394-4362

Zelt, Al, Chairman
Tube and Pipe Association,
International [2616]
833 Featherstone Rd.
Rockford, IL 61107-6301
Ph: (815)399-8700
Toll Free: 888-394-4362

Zemler, Jessica, President
American Society of Business
Publication Editors [2653]
214 N Hale St.
Wheaton, IL 60187
Ph: (630)510-4588
Fax: (630)510-4501

Zeno, Mark, Act. Pres.
Marlin Auto Club [21423]
5 Howards Grove
Derry, NH 03038

Zentner, Gerard, Chairman
International Truck Parts Association
[323]
1720 10th Ave. S, Ste. 4
Great Falls, MT 59405
Toll Free: 866-346-5692
Fax: (800)895-4654

Zepeda, Julie, President, CEO
National Latino Cosmetology As-
sociation [927]
7925 W Russell Rd., Unit 401285
Las Vegas, NV 89140
Ph: (702)448-5020
Toll Free: 877-658-3801
Fax: (702)448-8993

Zeppenfeldt-Cestero, George A.,
President
Association of Hispanic Healthcare
Executives [15113]
153 W 78th St., Ste. 1
New York, NY 10024
Ph: (212)877-1615
Fax: (212)877-2406

Zern, Kristin, Exec. Dir.
The Association of Travel Marketing
Executives [3373]

c/o Kristin Zern, Executive Director
PO Box 3176
West Tisbury, MA 02575

Zervantonakis, Ioannis, Treasurer
Hellenic Bioscientific Association in
the USA [7132]
PO Box 1998
Brookline, MA 02446

Zhang, Dou Alvin, MD, President
Chinese American Doctors Associa-
tion [16747]
PO Box 6627
Ellicott City, MD 21042-0627
Ph: (713)201-7928

Zhang, George, President
Society for Molecular Biology and
Evolution [6104]
810 E 10th St.
Lawrence, KS 66044
Ph: (785)865-9405
Toll Free: 800-627-0326
Fax: (785)843-6153

Zhang, Huichun, President
Chinese-American Professors in
Environmental Engineering and
Science [6550]
c/o Baoxia Mi, Secretary
623 Davis Hall
Dept. of Civil and Environmental
Engineering
University of California, Berkeley
Atlanta, GA 30332
Ph: (510)664-7446

Zhang, Dr. Yan, President
North American Chinese Clinical
Chemists Association [6210]
c/o Yusheng Zhu, PhD, Advisor
Medical University of South Carolina
165 Ashley Ave., Ste. 309
Charleston, SC 29425-8905

Zhen, Weining, President
Sino-American Network for
Therapeutic Radiology and Oncol-
ogy [17463]

Zhenduo, Yang, Chairman
International Yang Family Tai Chi
Chuan Association [22998]
PO Box 786
Bothell, WA 98041
Ph: (425)869-1185

Zheng, Lu, President
Overseas Young Chinese Forum
[7603]
11423 Potomac Oaks Dr.
Rockville, MD 20850-3576

Zherka, Ilir, Exec. Dir.
Alliance for International Educational
and Cultural Exchange [8052]
1828 L St. NW, Ste. 1150
Washington, DC 20036
Ph: (202)293-6141
Fax: (202)293-6144

Zhou, Henry Haifeng, President
Chinese American Society of
Anesthesiology [13700]
4 Hickory Ln.
Warren, NJ 07059

Zia, Maimoona, Chairperson
Council for American Students in
International Negotiations [8098]
PO Box 2243
New York, NY 10101-2240

Ziai, Abdi, President
Society of Iranian Architects and
Planners [5979]
PO Box 643066

Los Angeles, CA 90064

Ziefle, William, President, CEO
Divers Alert Network **[22810]**
6 W Colony Pl.
Durham, NC 27705
Ph: (919)684-2948
Toll Free: 800-446-2671
Fax: (919)490-6630

Ziegler, Cynthia R., Exec. Dir.,
 Secretary, Treasurer
Casualty Actuarial Society **[1844]**
4350 N Fairfax Dr., Ste. 250
Arlington, VA 22203
Ph: (703)276-3100
Fax: (703)276-3108

Ziegler, Laurie, Secretary, Treasurer
National Association of Enrolled
 Agents **[5798]**
1730 Rhode Island Ave., NW, Ste.
 400
Washington, DC 20036-3953
Ph: (202)822-6232
Toll Free: 855-880-6232
Fax: (202)822-6270

Ziegler, Mrs. Melissa, Exec. Dir.
American Kinesiotherapy Association
 [17080]
118 College Dr., No. 5142
Hattiesburg, MS 39406
Toll Free: 800-296-2582

Zielke, Dr. Thomas, President
Representative of German Industry
 and Trade **[667]**
1130 Connecticut Ave. NW, Ste.
 1200
Washington, DC 20006
Ph: (202)659-4777
Fax: (202)659-4779

Ziemba, Elizabeth A., President
SHARED Inc. **[15494]**
1018 Beacon St., Ste. 201
Brookline, MA 02446-4058
Ph: (617)277-7800
Fax: (617)739-5929

Ziemian, Ronald, Treasurer
Structural Stability Research Council
 [7248]
c/o Janet T. Cummins, Coordinator
1 E Wacker Dr., Ste. 700
Chicago, IL 60601

Ziemkiewicz, Matt, President
National Air Disaster Alliance
 [17821]
2020 Pennsylvania Ave., No. 315
Washington, DC 20006-1846
Toll Free: 888-444-6232
Fax: (336)643-1394

Zigler, Christina, Exec. Asst.
Council for Christian Colleges and
 Universities **[7610]**
321 8th St. NE
Washington, DC 20002
Ph: (202)546-8713
Fax: (202)546-8913

Zilke, Tim, Secretary
Automotive Training Managers
 Council **[287]**
101 Blue Seal Dr. SE
Leesburg, VA 20175
Ph: (703)669-6670

Zilke, Tim, CEO, President
National Institute for Automotive
 Service Excellence **[351]**
101 Blue Seal Dr. SE, Ste. 101
Leesburg, VA 20175
Ph: (703)669-6600
Toll Free: 877-346-9327
Fax: (703)669-6127

Zilonis, Stephen A., Chairman
World Alliance for Decentralized
 Energy **[6520]**
1513 16th St. NW
Washington, DC 20036
Ph: (202)667-5600
Fax: (202)315-3719

Zimbelman, Melissa, PMN, Chair-
 man, President
Women's Council of Realtors **[2897]**
430 N Michigan Ave.
Chicago, IL 60611
Toll Free: 800-245-8512
Fax: (312)329-3290

Zimbler, Richard, Act. Pres.
World Trade Center Survivors'
 Network **[13214]**
511 Avenue of the Americas, Ste.
 302 G
New York, NY 10011-8436

Zimmer, Kyle, CEO, President
First Book **[8241]**
1319 F St. NW, Ste. 1000
Washington, DC 20004
Ph: (202)393-1222
Toll Free: 866-732-3669

Zimmer, Steve, Exec. Dir.
United States Council for Automotive
 Research **[6022]**
1000 Town Center Dr., Ste. 300
Southfield, MI 48075-1219
Ph: (248)223-9000

Zimmerman, David W., President
Caring for Orphans - Mozambique
 [10886]
45895 Piute St.
Temecula, CA 92592
Ph: (714)632-9972

Zimmerman, Ms. Dawnmarie, Exec.
 Dir.
Society of American Mosaic Artists
 [8941]
PO Box 624
Ligonier, PA 15658-0624
Ph: (724)238-3087
Fax: (724)238-3973

Zimmerman, Debra, Exec. Dir.
Women Make Movies **[10311]**
115 W 29th St., Ste. 1200
New York, NY 10001
Ph: (212)925-0606
Fax: (212)925-2052

Zimmerman, Ms. Heidi, Exec. Dir.
Association of Water Technologies
 [3458]
9707 Key West Ave., Ste. 100
Rockville, MD 20850
Ph: (301)740-1421
Fax: (301)990-9771

Zimmerman, Joanne, Chmn. of the
 Bd.
Dolphin Research Center **[6792]**
58901 Overseas Hwy.
Marathon, FL 33050-6019
Ph: (305)289-1121
Fax: (305)743-7627

Zimmerman, Tanya, Secretary,
 Treasurer
Havana Rabbit Breeders Association
 [4597]
c/o Tanya Zimmerman, Secretary/
 Treasurer
N-9487 Walnut Rd.
Clintonville, WI 54929
Ph: (715)823-5020

Zimmerman, Tim, Chmn. of the Bd.
Research and Development Associates for Military Food and Packaging Systems **[6649]**

16607 Blanco Rd., Ste. 501
San Antonio, TX 78232
Ph: (210)493-8024
Fax: (210)493-8036

Zimmermann, Eric, Reg.
Triple Nine Society **[9346]**
c/o Dr. Ina Bendis, Membership Officer
3129 Barkley Ave.
Santa Clara, CA 95051

Zimmermann, Kristin, Exec. Dir.,
 Secretary
Society for Experimental Mechanics
 [7247]
7 School St.
Bethel, CT 06801-1405
Ph: (203)790-6373
Fax: (203)790-4472

Zimmermann, Laurel, Exec. Dir.
British American Educational
 Foundation **[8061]**
c/o Laurel Zimmermann, Executive
 Director
520 Summit Ave.
Oradell, NJ 07649
Ph: (201)261-4438

Zimmermann, Sabrina, Sr. VP of
 Operations, Founder
Aguayuda, Inc. **[13314]**
PO Box 2056
Easton, MD 21601
Ph: (410)989-2134

Zinaich, Samuel, President,
 Secretary, Treasurer
National Philosophical Counseling
 Association **[16985]**
c/o Samuel Zinaich, President
Purdue University Calumet
2200 169th St.
Hammond, IN 46323-2094

Zingaro, Susan, Membership Chp.
REO Club of America **[21483]**
203 Crestwood Dr
203 Crestwood Dr.
Sarver, PA 16055

Zinia, Quamrun, Editor
Akashleena Literary and Cultural
 Organization **[7529]**
c/o Quamrun Zinia, Editor
18055 Ira Babin Rd.
Prairieville, LA 70769
Ph: (225)673-3277
Fax: (225)673-3277

Zinnert, Michelle, Exec. Dir.
American Urogynecologic Society
 [17548]
2025 M St. NW, Ste. 800
Washington, DC 20036-2422
Ph: (301)273-0570
Fax: (301)273-0778

Zinone, Greg, Founder, President
Joint Forces Initiative **[22062]**
4 Montage
Irvine, CA 92614
Ph: (818)371-1283

Zinone, Stephen, President
National Court Reporters Association
 [5121]
12030 Sunrise Valley Dr., Ste. 400
Reston, VA 20191
Ph: (703)556-6272
Toll Free: 800-272-6272
Fax: (703)391-0629

Zinsstag, Jakob, President
International Association for Ecology
 and Health **[4004]**
c/o Ecohealth Alliance

460 W 34th St., 17th Fl.
New York, NY 10001
Ph: (212)380-4460

Zinszer, Kathya, DPM, MAPWCA,
 Secretary
American Professional Wound Care
 Association **[17525]**
3639 Ambassador Caffery Pky., Ste.
 605
Lafayette, LA 70503
Ph: (215)942-6095
 (337)541-2223
Fax: (215)993-7922

Ziolkowski, Jim, CEO
buildOn **[11325]**
PO Box 16741
Stamford, CT 06905

Ziomek, Kim, Secretary
Automotive Women's Alliance
 Foundation **[288]**
PO Box 4305
Troy, MI 48099
Toll Free: 877-393-2923
Fax: (248)239-0291

Ziozios, Dave, Treasurer
Performance Warehouse Association
 [3440]
79405 Highway 111, Ste. 9
La Quinta, CA 92253
Ph: (760)346-5647

Zippert, John, Chmn. of the Bd.
Rural Coalition **[19078]**
1029 Vermont Ave. NW, Ste. 601
Washington, DC 20005
Ph: (202)628-7160
Fax: (202)393-1816

Zirkle, Lewis J., MD, Founder
SIGN Fracture Care International
 [17398]
451 Hills St., Ste. B
Richland, WA 99354
Ph: (509)371-1107
Fax: (509)371-1316

Zitman, Matt, President
International Society of Caricature
 Artists **[1144]**

Zlokovich, Dr. Martha S., Exec. Dir.
Psi Chi, The International Honor
 Society in Psychology **[23855]**
825 Vine St.
Chattanooga, TN 37403
Ph: (423)756-2044
Toll Free: 877-774-2443

Zmyslowski, Allan, Treasurer
Storage Networking Industry As-
 sociation **[6265]**
4360 ArrowsWest Dr.
Colorado Springs, CO 80907-3444
Ph: (719)694-1380
 (415)402-0006
Fax: (719)694-1389

Zniewski, Mike, Exec. Dir.
American Monument Association
 [9372]
c/o Mike Zniewski, Executive Director
414 Lincoln Ave. NE
Saint Cloud, MN 56304-0244
Ph: (614)248-5866

Zodhiates, Philip, Chairman
Advancing Native Missions **[19939]**
PO Box 5303
Charlottesville, VA 22905
Ph: (540)456-7111
Fax: (540)456-7222

Zoephel, Denise, Asst. CEO
Selected Independent Funeral
 Homes **[2415]**

500 Lake Cook Rd., Ste. 205
Deerfield, IL 60015
Toll Free: 800-323-4219
Fax: (847)236-9968

Zogby, Dr. James J., Treasurer
Arab American Leadership Council
[18628]
1600 K St. NW, Ste. 601
Washington, DC 20006
Ph: (202)429-9210
Fax: (202)429-9214

Zoidis, Ann, Exec. Dir.
Cetos Research Organization [3995]
11 Des Isle Ave.
Bar Harbor, ME 04609
Ph: (207)266-6252

Zokaites, Carol, Coord.
Project Underground [6883]
c/o Carol Zokaites, Coordinator
8 Radford St., Ste. 201
Christiansburg, VA 24073
Ph: (540)381-7132

Zola, Gary P., PhD, Exec. Dir.
American Jewish Archives [9631]
3101 Clifton Ave.
Cincinnati, OH 45220-2404
Ph: (513)221-1875
Fax: (513)221-7812

Zollar, Carolyn C., VP of Govern-
ment Rel.
American Medical Rehabilitation
Providers Association [17081]
c/o Carolyn C. Zollar, Vice President
of Government Relations
1710 N St. NW
Washington, DC 20036
Ph: (202)223-1920
Toll Free: 888-346-4624
Fax: (202)223-1925

Zollo, Bob, Chairman
Optical Storage Technology Associa-
tion [2457]
65 Washington St.
Santa Clara, CA 95050
Ph: (650)938-6945

Zornberg, Jorge G., Mem.
International Geosynthetics Society
[6223]
1934 Commerce Ln., Ste. 4
Jupiter, FL 33458
Ph: (561)768-9489
Fax: (561)828-7618

Zubkoff, Dr. Michael, President
Medical Outcomes Trust [15033]
c/o Dr. Michael Zubkoff, President
Dept. of Community and Family
Medicine
Darmouth Medical School, HB 7250
Hanover, NH 03755

Zubrin, Dr. Robert, Founder,
President
Mars Society [7218]
11111 W 8th Ave., Unit A
Lakewood, CO 80215-5516
Ph: (303)980-0890

Zuck, Jonathan, President
Association for Competitive Technol-
ogy [3207]
1401 K St. NW, Ste. 501
Washington, DC 20005
Ph: (202)331-2130
Fax: (202)331-2139

Zucker, Dr. Sheva, Exec. Dir.
League for Yiddish, Inc. [20263]
64 Fulton St., Ste. 1101
New York, NY 10038
Ph: (212)889-0380
Fax: (212)889-0380

Zuckerberg, Elizabeth Ring, COO
Sargent Shriver National Center on
Poverty Law [5551]
50 E Washington St., Ste. 500
Chicago, IL 60602
Ph: (312)263-3830
Fax: (312)263-3846

Zuckermandel, Mike, Officer
Direct Gardening Association [2952]
PO Box 429
Lagrange, GA 30241-0008
Ph: (706)298-0022
Toll Free: 888-820-6646
Fax: (706)883-8215

Zuelow, Jim, President
Alaska Collectors' Club [22296]
c/o Eric Knapp, Secretary and
Treasurer
4201 Folker St., Unit C102
Anchorage, AK 99508-5377

Zugger, Fr. Christopher L., Chap.,
Editor
Mission Society of the Mother of
God of Boronyavo [20547]
1838 Palomas Dr. NE
Albuquerque, NM 87110
Fax: (505)256-1278

Zuidema, Dr. Jason, Exec. Dir.
North American Maritime Ministry
Association [12861]
PO Box 460158
Fort Lauderdale, FL 33346-0158
Ph: (514)993-6528

Zuidema, Roy, President
World Renew [12200]
1700 28th St. SE
Grand Rapids, MI 49508
Ph: (616)241-1691
    (616)224-0740
Toll Free: 800-552-7972

Zulauf, Dawn, President
American Board of Medicolegal
Death Investigators [15628]
900 W Baltimore St.
Baltimore, MD 21223
Ph: (410)807-3007
Fax: (410)807-3006

Zuniga, Jose M., Ph.D,MPH, CEO,
President
International Association of Providers
of AIDS Care [16752]
2200 Pennsylvania Ave., NW, 4th Fl.
E
Washington, DC 20037
Ph: (202)507-5899
Fax: (202)315-3651

Zupan, Marty, President, CEO
Institute for Humane Studies [12044]
George Mason University
3434 Washington Blvd., MS 1C5
Arlington, VA 22201
Ph: (703)993-4880
Toll Free: 800-697-8799
Fax: (703)993-4890

Zur, Jonathan, V. Chmn. of Admin.
National Federation for Just Com-
munities [11289]
525 New Ctr. One
3031 W Grand Blvd.
Detroit, MI 48202-3025
Ph: (804)515-7950
Fax: (804)515-7177

Zurek, Melanie, Director
Provide [10434]
PO Box 410164
Cambridge, MA 02141
Ph: (617)661-1161
Fax: (617)252-6878

Zweigenhaft, Burt, President
National Association of Specialty
Pharmacy [16675]

1800 Diagonal Rd., Ste. 600
Alexandria, VA 22314
Ph: (703)842-0122

Zwerling, Charles S., MD, Chmn. of
the Bd.
American Academy of Micropigmentation [14302]
c/o Charles S. Zwerling, Chairman of
the Board
2709 Medical Office Pl.
Goldsboro, NC 27534
Ph: (919)736-3937
Toll Free: 888-302-3482
Fax: (919)735-3701

Zwieg, Steve, Chairman
Parcel Shippers Association [2121]
PO Box 450
Oxon Hill, MD 20750
Ph: (571)257-7617
Fax: (301)749-8684

Zwisler, Eric V., Director
International Federation of
Pharmaceutical Wholesalers, Inc.
[2559]
10569 Crestwood Dr.
Manassas, VA 20109-3406
Ph: (703)331-3714
Fax: (703)331-3715

Zyglis, Adam, President
The Association of American Edito-
rial Cartoonists [2659]
PO Box 460673
Fort Lauderdale, FL 33346

Zylstra, Steve, Chairman
Technology Councils of North
America [6755]
3500 Lacey Rd., Ste. 100
Downers Grove, IL 60515-5439

Zynda, Christopher M., President
Shotcrete Concrete Contractors As-
sociation [796]
23565 Morrill Rd.
Los Gatos, CA 95033-9322
Ph: (408)640-6219

Zyne, Richard G., Mem.
Foundation for PSP/CBD and
Related Brain Diseases [14577]
30 E Padonia Rd., Ste. 201
Timonium, MD 21093-2308
Ph: (410)785-7004
Toll Free: 800-457-4777
Fax: (410)785-7009